INTERNATIONAL HANDBOOK OF UNIVERSITIES

2013

twenty-fourth edition

Volume 1

INTERNATIONAL
ASSOCIATION OF
UNIVERSITIES

INTERNATIONAL UNIVERSITIES BUREAU

palgrave
macmillan

Edited by the IAU/UNESCO Information Centre on Higher Education, International Association of Universities
Director: Isabelle Turmaine
Manager, Reference Publications: Geneviève Rabreau

IAU ISBN 978-92-9002-195-7

First published 2012 by
PALGRAVE MACMILLAN

Palgrave Macmillan in the UK is an imprint of Macmillan Publishers Limited, registered in England, company number 785998, of Houndmills, Basingstoke, Hampshire RG21 6XS.

Palgrave Macmillan in the US is a division of St Martin's Press LLC, 175 Fifth Avenue, New York, NY 10010.

Palgrave Macmillan is the global academic imprint of the above companies and has companies and representatives throughout the world.

Palgrave® and Macmillan® are registered trademarks in the United States, the United Kingdom, Europe and other countries.

ISBN 978-0-230-22348-6
ISSN 0074-6215

This book is printed on paper suitable for recycling and made from fully managed and sustained forest sources. Logging, pulping and manufacturing processes are expected to conform to the environmental regulations of the country of origin.

A catalogue record for this book is available from the British Library.

A catalog record for this book is available from the Library of Congress.

10   9   8   7   6   5   4   3   2   1
21 20 19 18 17 16 15 14 13 12

Printed in China

CONTENTS

PREFACE

The International Association of Universities and its IAU/UNESCO Information Centre on Higher Education are pleased to present the Twenty-fourth edition of the *International Handbook of Universities*, which offers updated, comprehensive information on universities and university-level institutions worldwide.

The *Handbook* was first published by the International Association of Universities in 1959 in response to the growing demand for authoritative information about higher education institutions worldwide. It has grown considerably over the years in both the quantity and the quality of its entries. Today, it includes over 17,000 institutions extracted from the lists provided by the competent authorities or academic bodies in over 180 countries and territories, their websites or official documents. The *Handbook* also comprises basic information on the education system of all countries, two indexes (institutions and fields of study), and a list of specialized regional/international organizations. The differentiation between university/university-level and other higher education institutions is based on the degrees/diplomas delivered by the institution, a university/university-level institution being an institution offering at least a postgraduate degree or a professional diploma in four years or more.

The compilation of the *Handbook* involves working on documents in many languages, covering a wide range of continuously evolving systems of higher education. Every effort has been made to ensure that the entries are as comprehensive as possible and that the information is accurate. The IAU/UNESCO Information Centre on Higher Education is indebted to those many universities/university-level institutions, governmental agencies and academic bodies which have provided material for this edition in order to make it a unique and authoritative source of information. Where information was not available in time for inclusion, entries have remained the same as in the previous edition. The date of the last update is indicated at the bottom of each entry. Comments and corrections to help to improve the next edition of the *Handbook* are most welcome at: centre@iau-aiu.net

The full wealth of data held by the IAU/UNESCO Information Centre - including the information in the *Handbook*, as well as more comprehensive data on higher education systems and credentials offered in over 180 countries - is available at www.whedonline.com, the World Higher Education Database (WHED) Online. Free single-user access is available to all purchasers of the Handbook for 12 months following the publication date, and offers users the opportunity to search and browse the information with ease and convenience. For multiple user access please contact onlinesales@palgrave.com. WHED is also available as a CD-Rom[1].

The production of the *Handbook* and of WHED is part of the drive by the International Association of Universities to provide access to information on higher education worldwide. The quarterly scholarly Journal Higher Education Policy[2] provides a deeper and more analytical understanding of higher education policy worldwide.

---

[1] World Higher Education Database CD-Rom, IAU, Palgrave Macmillan (see p. xvii).
[2] Higher Education Policy, Palgrave Macmillan (see p. xvii).

GUIDE TO THE ENTRIES

This edition of the *International Handbook of Universities* comprises entries for over 17,000 universities and university-level institutions in over 180 countries and territories.

COUNTRY CHAPTERS

A short presentation of the education system based upon the information provided by the appropriate higher education authorities in the countries concerned or found on their official website or documentation is provided for each country. It comprises a short description of the overall structure of the higher education system; the different stages of study; the admission requirements (including for foreign students); the quality assurance/recognition system; and information on national bodies responsible for higher education. The designations employed for countries and territories are those in use in the United Nations system and do not imply any expression of opinion with regard to their status or the delimitations of their frontiers.

INSTITUTIONAL ENTRIES

Entries are selected on the basis of the information contained in the listings provided by the appropriate higher education authorities in the countries concerned or found on their official websites. Questionnaires are then sent to those degree-granting institutions which offer at least a post-graduate degree and/or a professional diploma in four years or more to obtain more detailed information. The inclusion or omission of an institution, therefore, does not imply any judgement on the part of the IAU/UNESCO Information Centre on Higher Education as to the status or quality of that institution.

Membership of a higher education institution in the International Association of Universities is indicated by ⎮⚏ preceding its name. Higher education institutions wishing to become members should contact: iau@iau-aiu.net.

The institutional entries within each country are generally listed within Public and Private Sections, where relevant, with their postal address and telecommunication, email and website information. The name of each institution is given first in English, followed by the name in the national language(s), where appropriate. Where available, the names and full contact details of the Academic Head, the Chief Administrative Officer, and the Director of International Relations are given.

The lists of faculties, colleges, departments, schools, institutes, etc., are intended primarily as a general guide to the academic structure of the institution of which they form a part. They normally include the various fields of study offered (standardized list). The names of their heads are provided where available. This information is followed by a brief description of the history and structure of the institution and, where available, by information on co-operation programmes with institutions in other countries.

Admission requirements are usually listed for courses leading to a first degree or similar qualification. Special requirements for admission to studies leading to higher degrees and specialized diplomas are indicated where appropriate.

The names of degrees, diplomas and professional qualifications are generally given in the language of the country concerned. Fields and duration of studies are indicated when available. Tuition fees, library holdings, special facilities and student services available in each university are also indicated when provided.

Overall Academic Staff (including Staff with Doctorates) and Student Enrolment statistics complete the entry and include a breakdown of number of foreign students and part-time, evening and distance education students, if available. A breakdown by Men and Women for both Academic Staff and Students is also given where available.

Four regional and international universities are listed after country chapters.

LIST OF REGIONAL/INTERNATIONAL ORGANIZATIONS

A comprehensive list of higher education regional and international organisations is provided on the following pages. Entries are entered in alphabetical order. Membership of an organization in the International Association of Universities is indicated by ⬛ preceding its name. Organizations wishing to become members should contact: iau@iau-aiu.net.

LIST OF FIELDS OF STUDY

The complete list of fields of study used in the *Handbook* is provided to help users in their search of the field of study index.

INDEXES

An index to higher education institutions which comprises the name of each institution in English, in the national language (when available) and the alternative name (when appropriate) is provided at the end of the *Handbook*.

An index to fields of study is also provided to allow for searches of institutions providing courses in a specific specialty.

IAU - THE INTERNATIONAL ASSOCIATION OF UNIVERSITIES

The International Association of Universities (IAU), founded in 1950, is a worldwide organization with Member Institutions and Organizations in over 130 countries. It cooperates with a vast network of international, regional and national bodies. Its permanent Secretariat, the International Universities Bureau, is located at UNESCO, Paris, and provides a wide variety of services to Member Institutions and Organizations and to the international higher education community at large. Institutions/organizations interested in becoming members should contact iau@iau-aiu.net.

MEETINGS

IAU provides a forum for higher education leaders to discuss major current trends and issues in higher education and higher education policy. Heads of all Member Institutions and Organizations or their representatives are invited to the IAU quadrennial General Conferences as well as to annual international events, such as Colloquia, Seminars and Round Tables. These events are organized by the Association, either alone or in co-operation with other academic bodies, and provide unique opportunities for the exchange of experience and ideas on issues of international interest and importance. The 13th General Conference was held in Utrecht, The Netherlands in July 2008, and discussed the theme "Higher Education and Research Addressing Local and Global Needs". The 14th IAU General Conference will take place in San Juan, Puerto Rico in November 2012. It will discuss the theme "Higher Education and the Global Agenda: Alternative Paths to the Future".

PUBLICATIONS

Services traditionally offered to Member Institutions and Organizations include the right to receive the Association's publications either on a complimentary basis or at considerably reduced rates. As from 2008, these include two major reference works the *International Handbook of Universities* and the *World Higher Education Database (WHED)* CD-Rom (both published annually), the quarterly journal *Higher Education Policy*, a quarterly Newsletter *IAU Horizons* and a monthly *E-Bulletin*. The first reference work is a long-established, invaluable tool for all those concerned with international cooperation in higher education, providing detailed information on thousands of higher education institutions worldwide. The CD-Rom, more recent, provides, in addition, more comprehensive data on higher education systems and credentials, and many search facilities. A series of regional guides has also been launched with the *Guide to Higher Education in Africa*. All three reference tools are prepared from IAU's database. The academic publication *Higher Education Policy* focuses on policy issues and the role of higher education in society today, offering a platform for the exchange and sharing of information and debate within the world community of higher education.

INFORMATION SERVICES

Also available to Member Institutions and Organizations is the vast body of information housed in the specialized IAU/UNESCO Information Centre on Higher Education. The Centre, managed by the IAU, contains over 50,000 volumes on higher education worldwide and operates two major databases (WHED, mentioned above, and HEDBIB, the Higher Education Bibliographical Database) from which directories and CD-Roms are produced. Different types of information services (topical bibliographies, institutional data, and address labels) are also provided. The IAU website (http://www.iau-aiu.net) is another important source of information and links.

COOPERATION

The IAU, through its unique networking capacity, provides an important clearing house function to Members for academic exchange and cooperation, implying active involvement and participation of Member universities in the important mission of bringing a real international perspective to the life of universities. Among the major areas retained for cooperation are Sustainable Development; Intercultural Dialogue; Internationalization; Access; and Education For All (EFA) and Higher Education.

HEADQUARTERS

International Association of Universities
1, rue Miollis
75732 Paris Cedex 15, France
Telephone: + 33 1-45-68-48-00
Fax: + 33 1-47-34-76-05
E-Mail: iau@iau-aiu.net
Website: http://www.iau-aiu.net

PRESIDENT

Juan Ramon de la Fuente, Former Rector,
National Autonomous University of Mexico

SECRETARY-GENERAL

Eva Egron-Polak, Executive Director
International Association of Universities

OFFICERS OF THE INTERNATIONAL ASSOCIATION OF UNIVERSITIES

Administrative Board 2008-2012

President
Juan Ramón de la Fuente   Former Rector, National Autonomous University of Mexico

Vice-Presidents

Abdul Razak Dzulkifli	Vice-Chancellor, Albukhary International University, Malaysia
Pier Ugo Calzolari	Former Rector, University of Bologna, Italy
Molly Corbett Broad	President, American Council on Education (ACE), USA
Olive Mugenda	Vice-Chancellor, Kenyatta University, Kenya

Immediate Past President
Goolam Mohammedbhai   Former Secretary-General, Association of African Universities (AAU)

Honorary Presidents

Guillermo Soberón	President 1980-1985, Former Rector, National University of Mexico
Blagovest Sendov	Acting President 1984, Former Rector, University of Sofia, Bulgaria
Justin Thorens	President 1985-1990, Former Rector, Université de Genève, Switzerland
Wataru Mori	President 1995-2000, Former President, University of Tokyo, Japan
Hans Van Ginkel	President 2000-2004, Former Rector, United Nations University (UNU)

Members of the Administrative Board

AFRICA

Piyushi Kotecha	CEO, Southern African Regional Universities Association (SARUA), South Africa
Clifford Nii Boi Tagoe	Former Vice-Chancellor, University of Ghana

AMERICAS

Stephen Freedman	Provost, Fordham University, USA
Manual J. Fernos	President, Interamerican University of Puerto Rico
Janyne Hodder	Former President, The College of The Bahamas, The Bahamas
Juan Tobias	Rector, University of Salvador, Argentina

ASIA & PACIFIC

Makoto Asashima	Former Managing Director & Executive Vice-President, University of Tokyo, Japan
Pornchai Mongkhonvanit	President, Siam University, Thailand
Walid Moussa	President, Notre Dame University Louaize, Lebanon
Mohammad Huss Sorouraddin	Former Chancellor, Tabriz University, Iran
Jun Zhu	Vice-President, Zhejiang University, China

EUROPE

Agneta Bladh	Former Rector, University of Kalmar, Sweden
Norbert Kis	Former Vice-Rector, Corvinus University of Budapest, Hungary
Antonio Marques	Vice-Rector, University of Porto, Portugal
Patricia Pol	Vice-President, Université Paris-Est Créteil Val de Marne, France
Alvyda Pumputis	Rector, Mykolas Romeris University, Lithuania

Deputy Board Members

AFRICA

Is-Haq Oloyede	Vice-Chancellor, University of Ilorin, Nigeria

AMERICAS

Roberto Escalante Semerena	Secretary-General, Union of Universities of Latin America and the Caribbean (UDUAL)

ASIA & PACIFIC

Arun Diwakar Nath Bajpai	Secretary-General, Association of Indian Universities (AIU), India
Carmen Lamagna	Vice-Chancellor, American International University, Bangladesh

Secretary-General

Eva Egron-Polak	Executive Director, International Universities Bureau

xvi

IAU – INTERNATIONAL ASSOCIATION OF UNIVERSITIES
LIST OF PUBLICATIONS

For a worldwide Association, sharing information, expertise and experience amongst leaders and decision-makers on the central issues facing higher education, is key. IAU has made - and continues to make - a very substantial input to informed debate on public policy. It maintains databases and produces reference works on higher education systems, institutions and credentials and brings out state of the art research on vital issues that concern higher education. By doing so, it serves the academic community and its leadership, stimulating discussion and advancing action. Major publications resulting from this commitment are:

REFERENCE WORKS

- *International Handbook of Universities.* 24th Edition, Palgrave Macmillan, 2012.
- *World Higher Education Database 2012.* CD-ROM, Palgrave Macmillan,
Also available at www.whed-online.com. Please contact onlinesales@palgrave.com for details.
- *Guide to Higher Education in Africa.* 5th ed. Palgrave Macmillan, 2010.

PUBLISHED BY: Palgrave Macmillan, Houndmills, Basingstoke, Hampshire RG21 6XS and 175 Fifth Avenue, New York, N.Y. 10010. www.palgrave.com

HIGHER EDUCATION POLICY
IAU Quarterly Journal

Editor: Professor Jeroen Huisman, Director International Centre for Higher Education Management, UK

- Untitled   vol. 25, no. 1, 2012
- Sustainability in Higher Education   vol. 24, no. 4, 2011
- Untitled   vol. 24, no. 3, 2011
- Untitled   vol. 24, no. 2, 2011
- Untitled   vol. 24, no. 1, 2011
- Untitled   vol. 23, no. 4, 2010
- Untitled   vol. 23, no. 3, 2010
- Two great European ideas: Comparing Humboldt and   vol. 23, no. 2, 2010
  Bologna
- Untitled   vol. 23, no. 1, 2010
- Untitled   vol. 22, no. 4, 2009
- African Universities and Internationalisation   vol. 22, no. 3, 2009
- Untitled   vol. 22, no. 2, 2009
- Celebrations and Challenges: Gender in Higher   vol. 22, no. 1, 2009
  Education
- Realizing the Global University: Comparative   vol. 21, no. 4, 2008
  Perspectives and Critical Reflexions
- Academic Vigour in Changing Contexts   vol. 21, no. 3, 2008
- Diversity of Missions   vol. 21, no. 2, 2008
- World-Class Universities   vol. 21, no. 1, 2008
- Sustaining Diversity: Differentiating Higher Education   vol. 20, no. 4, 2007
  Systems in a Knowledge Society

Editor: Professor Guy Neave, International Association of Universities

SUBSCRIPTIONS AT: Palgrave Macmillan, Houndmills, Basingstoke, Hampshire, RG21 6XS and 175, Fifth Avenue, suite 203, New York, N.Y. 10010. www.palgrave-journals.com/hep/subscribe.html

OTHER PUBLICATIONS

- *Internationalization of Higher Education: Global Trends, Regional Perspectives*, Paris IAU, 2010
- *IAU Horizons/AIU Horizons* - A quarterly newsletter mostly for IAU Members.

AVAILABLE FROM: International Association of Universities, UNESCO House, 1, rue Miollis, 75732 Paris Cedex 15, France. Tel: +33-1-45 68 48-00 - Fax: +33-1-47 34 76 05 iau@iau-aiu.net and on IAU website.

- *IAU E-Bulletin/Bulletin électronique de l'AIU* – A monthly electronic publication for all publics.

FREE SUBSCRIPTION AT: http://www.iau-aiu.net/iau_e_bulletin.html

- IAU Website/Site Web de l'AIU: http://www.iau-aiu.net

LIST OF REGIONAL/INTERNATIONAL ORGANIZATIONS

Academic Cooperation Association - ACA

President: Rolf Tarrach
Director: Bernd Wächter
Egmontstraat 15
Brussels 1000
BELGIUM
Tel: +32 2 513 2241
Fax: +32 2 513 1776
EMail: info@aca-secretariat.be
WWW: http://www.aca-secretariat.be

African Council for Distance Education - ACDE

President: Tolly S. A. Mbwette
Executive Director: Fred Simiyu Barasa
P.O. Box 8023
Nairobi 00100
KENYA
Tel: +254(20) 271 1278
Fax: +254(20) 271 1350
EMail: director@acde-africa.org
WWW: http://www.acde-africa.org/index.html
The African Council for Distance Education (ACDE)
is a continental educational organization comprising
African universities and other higher education
institutions, which are committed to expanding
access to quality education and training through
open and distance learning.

African Network for the Internationalisation of Education - ANIE

Chairperson: Chacha Nyaigotti Chacha
Secretary / Executive Director: James Otieno Jowi
c/o Margaret Thatcher Library
Moi University
PO Box 3900
Eldoret 30100
KENYA
Tel: +254 721 917 461 (Mob)
Fax: +254(53) 43047
EMail: sec@anienetwork.org
WWW: http://www.anienetwork.org/
ANIE is an independent, non-profit,
non-governmental membership organisation whose
aim is to develop research capacity and constitute
an expert network in advancing the understanding
of internationalisation of higher education to meet
the professional needs of individuals, institutions
and organisations.

African Network of Scientific and Technological Institutions - ANSTI

Réseau africain d'Institutions scientifiques et
technologiques
*Vice-Chairman of ANSTI Governing
Council*: Eric Edroma
Coordinator: Joseph G.M. Massaquoi
PO Box 30592
Nairobi
KENYA
Tel: +254(2) 762 2619/20
Fax: +254(2) 762 2750
EMail: info@ansti.org
WWW: http://www.ansti.org/
The aim of ANSTI is to develop active collaboration
among African scientific institutions so as to promote
research and development in areas of relevance to
the development of the region.

African Quality Assurance Network - AfriQAN

President: Mayunga Nkunya
African Universities House
P.O. Box AN 5744
Accra North
GHANA
Tel: +233(302) 774 495
Fax: +233(302) 774 821
EMail: asey@aau.org
WWW: http://afriqan.aau.org/
To provide assistance to institutions concerned with
quality assurance in higher education in Africa.

Agence universitaire de la Francophonie - AUF

President: Yvon Fontaine
Rector: Bernard Cerquiglini
3034, Boul. Edouard-Montpetit
Case postale du Musée
C.P. 49714
Montréal
Québec H3T 2A5
CANADA
Tel: +1(514) 343 6630
Fax: +1(514) 343 2107
EMail: rectorat@auf.org
WWW: http://www.auf.org

All-Africa Students Union - AASU
Secretary-General: Oludare Ogunlana
P.O Box M274
Accra
GHANA
Tel: +233(244) 233092
EMail: aasusecgen@yahoo.com
WWW: http://www.aasuonline.org/
Continental representative organization of
democratic student unions founded in 1972 with 54
member unions from Francophone and Anglophone
Africa.

ASEAN University Network - AUN
Executive Director: Nantana Gajaseni
Room 210 Jamjuree 1 Building
Chulalongkorn University
Phyathai Road
Bangkok 10330
THAILAND
Tel: +66 2215 3640
Fax: +66 2216 8808
EMail: secretariat@aun-sec.org
WWW: http://www.aun-sec.org/

**Asia-Pacific Association for International
Association - APAIE**
President: Doo-Hee Lee
Executive Director: Grace Kim
Room 203 Dongwon Global Leadership Hall
Korea University
Anam-Dong, Seongbuk-Gu
Seoul 136-701
KOREA (REPUBLIC OF)
Tel: +82(2) 3290 2935
Fax: +82(2) 921 0684
EMail: apaie@apaie.org
WWW: http://www.apaie.org/
The aim of APAIE is to achieve greater
cooperation among those responsible for
international activities in Asia Pacific institutions of
higher learning, and to promote the quality of
international programs, activities, and exchanges for
the harmony and advancement of the Asia Pacific
region worldwide.

**Asociación de Universidades e Institutos
de Investigación del Caribe - UNICA (Association
of Caribbean Universities and Research
Institutes)**
c/o Office of Administration & Special Initiatives
University of the West Indies
Kingston 7
JAMAICA

Tel: +1 (876) 977 6065
Fax: +1 (876) 977 7525
EMail: unica@uwimona.edu.jm
The Association was founded in 1967 to foment
co-operation among centres for higher learning in
the Caribbean region.

Asociación de Universidades Grupo Montevideo
President: Targino de Araújo Filho
Executive Secretary: Alvaro Maglia
Guayabo 1729 Ap. 502
Montevideo 11.200
URUGUAY
Tel: +598(2) 400 5411
Fax: +598(2) 400 5401
WWW: http://www.grupomontevideo.edu.uy

**Asociación Iberoamericana de Educación
Superíor a Distancia - AIESAD (Ibero-American
Association for Open University Education)**
Secretaría Permanente
Calle Bravo Murillo, 38 4 planta
Madrid 28015
SPAIN
Fax: + 34(91) 398 6587
EMail: aiesad@adm.uned.es
WWW: http://info.uned.es/aiesad

**Associação das Universidades de Língua
Portuguesa - AULP (Association of Portuguese
Language Universities - APLU)**
President: Clélio Campolina Diniz
Avenida Santos Dumont, 67, 2°
Lisboa 1050-203
PORTUGAL
Tel: +351 217 816 360
Fax: +351 217 816 369
EMail: aulp@aulp.org
WWW: http://aulp.org
The aim of this international association is the
development of cooperation between universities
and higher research institutions by means of
promoting the interchange of researchers and
students and the development of joint projects of
scientific and technological research as well as the
exchange of information.

**Associação de Universidades
Amazônicas - UNAMAZ (Association of
Amazonian Universities)**
Secretário Geral: Luis Eduardo Aragón Vaca
Trav. 3 de Maio 1573 - São Braz

Belém
Para 66063-390
BRAZIL
Tel: +55(91) 3229 4478
Fax: +55(91) 3229 4478
EMail: unamaz@ufpa.br
WWW: http://www.ufpa.br/unamaz/

Association for Tertiary Education Management - ATEM
President: Stephen Weller
Executive Director: Paul Abela
Head Office Building M University of Sydney
Cumberland College 75 East Street (PO Box 170)
Lidcombe NSW2141
AUSTRALIA
Fax: +61 2 6125 5262
WWW: http://www.atem.org.au/
The Association for Tertiary Education Management Inc (ATEM Inc) is a professional body for tertiary education administrators and managers in Australasia.

Association of African Universities - AAU (Association des Universités africaines - AUA)
President: Is-Haq Oloyede
Secretary-General: Olugbemiro Jegede
PO Box 5744
Accra North
GHANA
Tel: +233(21) 774 495/ 761 588
Fax: +233(21) 774 821
EMail: info@aau.org
WWW: http://www.aau.org
International non-governmental organization founded in Rabat, Morocco in November 1967 having its headquarters in Accra, Ghana. Designated the lead implementing agency for the higher education component of the Action Plan for the Second Decade (2006-2015) of Education of the African Union.

Association of Arab Universities - AArU
Secretary-General: Sultan Abu Orabi
PO Box 401Jubeyha
Amman
Jordan
JORDAN
Tel: +962(6) 534 5131
Fax: +962(6) 533 2994
EMail: secgen@aaru.edu.jo
WWW: http://www.aaru.edu.jo

Association of Christian Universities and Colleges in Asia - ACUCA
President: Norihiko Suzuki
Secretary-General: Johannes Unsok Ro
International Christian University 3-10-2 Osawa, Mitaka-shi
Tokyo
JAPAN
WWW: http://www.acuca.net/

Association of Commonwealth Universities - ACU
Chairperson: Theuns Eloff
Secretary-General: John Wood
Woburn House 20-24
Tavistock Square
London
England WC1H 9HF
UNITED KINGDOM OF GREAT BRITAIN AND NORTHERN IRELAND
Tel: +44(20) 7380 6700
Fax: +44(20) 7387 2655
EMail: info@acu.ac.uk
WWW: http://www.acu.ac.uk

Association of Pacific Rim Universities - APRU
Chair, Steering Committee: Henry T. Yang
Secretary General: Christopher Tremewan
NUS Shaw Foundation Alumni House
11 Kent Ridge Drive
Singapore 119244
SINGAPORE
Tel: +65 6516 3140
Fax: +65 6778 2285
EMail: apru@apru.org
WWW: http://www.apru.org/

Association of Southeast Asian Institutions of Higher Learning - ASAIHL
President: Mai Trong Nhuan
Secretary-General: Ninnat Olanvoravuth
THAILAND
WWW: http://www.seameo.org/asaihl/
Assisting member institutions in their development through cooperation.

Association of the Carpathian Region Universities - ACRU
President: Paul-Serban Agachi
Secretary-General: Jana Mojžišová
University of Veterinary Medicine and Pharmacy in Košice
Komenského 73

Košice 041 20
SLOVAK REPUBLIC
Tel: +421 55 602 2114
Fax: +421 55 633 4960
EMail: erna.beres@tuke.sk
WWW: http://acru.uvlf.sk/
Groups university institutions from the Carpathian region in the Slovak Republic, Ukraine, Poland and Hungary.

Association of Universities of Asia and the Pacific - AUAP
President: Prasart Suebka
Secretary-General: Ruben C. Umaly
c/o Centre for International Affairs
Suranaree University of Technology
111 University Avenue, Muang
Nakhon Ratchasima 30000
THAILAND
Tel: +66 4422 4143
Fax: +66 4422 4140
EMail: auap@sut.ac.th
WWW: http://www.sut.ac.th/auap/

Centre européen pour la Gestion stratégique des Universités (European Centre for Strategic Management of Universities - ESMU)
Chairman: Frans van Vught
Secretary-General: Nadine Burquel
rue Montoyer 31 Box 2
Brussels 1000
BELGIUM
Tel: +32 2 513 8622
Fax: +32 2 289 2467
EMail: administration@esmu.be
WWW: http://www.esmu.be/

Caribbean Area Network for Quality Assurance in Tertiary Education - CANQATE
President: Valda Alleyne
C/o Barbados Accreditation Council 123A & B
"Plaza Centrale" Roebuck Street
Bridgetown 11080
BARBADOS
Tel: +246 429 8760
Fax: +246 429 9233
EMail: info@canqate.org
WWW: http://www.canqate.org/
The Caribbean Area Network for Quality Assurance in Tertiary Education was established as a sub-network of the International Network for Quality Assurance Agencies in Higher Education (INQAAHE). The aims and objectives of CANQATE

are compatible with those of INQAAHE whose principal purpose is to "enable members to share information about the maintenance, evaluation, accreditation and improvement of higher education and to disseminate good practices in the field of Quality Assurance".

Commonwealth of Learning - COL
President and Chief Executive Officer: John Daniel
1055 West Hastings Street, Suite 1200
Vancouver
BC V6E 2E9
CANADA
Tel: +1(604) 775 8200
Fax: +1(604) 775 8210
EMail: info@col.org
WWW: http://www.col.org
The Commonwealth of Learning (COL) is an intergovernmental organisation created by Commonwealth Heads of Government to encourage the development and sharing of open learning/distance education knowledge, resources and technologies.

Conseil africain et malgache pour l'Enseignement supérieur - CAMES (African and Malagasy Council for Higher Education)
Secretary General: Bertrand Mbatchi
01 BP 134
Ouagadougou
BURKINA FASO
Tel: +226 5036 8146
Fax: +226 5036 8573
EMail: cames@bf.refer.org
WWW: http://www.lecames.org/
Regional body aiming at research dissemination in Africa and in the long-term at accreditation provision within the region.

Consejo Centroamericano de Acreditación de la Educación Superior - CCA (Central American Council for the Accreditation of Higher Education)
President: Gabriel Macaya Trejos
Chief Executive: Marianela Aguilar Arce
100 m. norte y 75 m. este de Office Depot, Avenida Central, San Pedro, Montes de Oca
San José
COSTA RICA
Tel: +506 2511 6133
Fax: +506 2224 6903
EMail: cca@ucr.ac.cr
WWW: http://www.cca.ucr.ac.cr/

Consejo Superior Universitario Centroamericano - CSUCA (Central-American University Higher Council)
Secretary-General: Juan Alfonso Fuentes Soria
Avenida Las Américas 1-03, zona 14 Club Los Arcos
Guatemala 01014
GUATEMALA
Tel: +502 2367 1833
Fax: +502 2367 4517
EMail: sg@csuca.org
WWW: http://www.csuca.org/
Regional organization that promotes the integration and strengthening of higher education in Central America.

Consortium of North American Higher Education Collaboration - CONAHEC
Executive Director: Francesco J. Marmolejo
University of Arizona
PO Box 210300
Tucson
Arizona 85721-0300
UNITED STATES OF AMERICA
Tel: +520 621 7761
Fax: +520 626 2675
WWW: http://www.conahec.org/

Danube Rectors' Conference
President: Hristo Beloev
University of Maribor
International Relations Office
Slomskov Trg 15
Maribor 2000
SLOVENIA
Tel: +386(2) 235 5380
Fax: +386(2) 235 5438
EMail: drc@uni-mb.si
WWW: http://www.d-r-c.org/

Euro-Asian Association of Universities
President: Viktor Sadovnitchy
Secretary-General: Nikolai Semin
Officer: Tatiana Kozlova
Moscow State University, Leninskie Gory
Moscow 19992
RUSSIAN FEDERATION
Tel: +7(495) 939 2769
Fax: +7(495) 939 2769
EMail: eau_msu@rector.msu.ru;eau_msu@mail.ru
WWW: http://www.eau.msu.ru/

European Association for International Education - EAIE
President: Gudrun Paulsdottir
Director: Leonard Engel
PO Box 11189
Amsterdam 1001 GD
NETHERLANDS
Tel: +31(20) 344 5100
Fax: +31(20) 344 5119
EMail: eaie@eaie.nl
WWW: http://www.eaie.org

European Association for Quality Assurance in Higher Education - ENQA
President: Achim Hopbach
Director: Maria Kelo
Rue Abbé Cuypers, 3
Brussels 1040
BELGIUM
Tel: +32 2 741 2445
Fax: +32 2 734 7910
WWW: http://www.enqa.eu/

European Association for University Lifelong Learning - EUCEN
Executive Secretary: Carme Royo
Balmes, 132
Barcelona
SPAIN
Tel: +34(93) 542 1825
Fax: +34(93) 542 2975
EMail: executive.office@eucen.org
WWW: http://www.eucen.org/

European Association of Distance Teaching Universities - EADTU
President: Carlos Reis
Secretary-General: Piet Henderikx
PO Box 2960
Heerlen 6401
NETHERLANDS
Tel: +31(45) 576 2214
Fax: +31(45) 574 1473
EMail: secretariat@eadtu.eu
WWW: http://www.eadtu.eu/

European Association of Institutions in Higher Education - EURASHE
President: Lars Lynge Nielsen
Secretary General: Stefan Delplace
Ravensteingalerij 27/3
Brussels 1000

BELGIUM
Tel: +32 2 211 4197
Fax: +32 2 211 4199
EMail: eurashe@eurashe.eu
WWW: http://www.eurashe.eu
EURASHE is the association of European Higher
Education Institutions - Polytechnics, Colleges,
University Colleges, etc. - devoted to Professional
Higher Education and related research within the
Bachelor-Masters structure.

**European Council of Doctoral Candidates and
Junior Researchers - EURODOC**
President: Ludovic Garattini
Rue d'Egmont 11
Brussels 1000
BELGIUM
EMail: board@eurodoc.net
WWW: http://www.eurodoc.net/
International federation of 34 national organizations
of PhD candidates, and more generally of young
researchers from 33 countries of the European
Union and the Council of Europe.

European Physics Education Network
Chair: Hendrik Ferdinande
Universiteit Gent, Department of Subatomic and
Radiation Physics, Proeftuinstraat 86
Gent 9000
BELGIUM
Tel: +32 9 264 6539
Fax: +32 9 264 66 97
EMail: Sophie.Butt@UGent.be
WWW: http://www.eupen.ugent.be

European University Association - EUA
President: Jean-Marc Rapp
Secretary-General: Lesley Wilson
Avenue de l'Yser, 24
Brussels 1040
BELGIUM
Tel: +32 2 230 5544
Fax: +32 2 230 5751
WWW: http://www.eua.be/

**Federation of the Universities of the Islamic
World - FUIW**
Secretary-General: Abdulaziz Bin Othman Altwaijri
c/o ISESCO, BP 2275
Rabat 10104
MOROCCO

Tel: +212(537) 715 298
Fax: +212(537) 777 459
EMail: fumi@isesco.org.ma
WWW: http://www.fuiw.org/

**Fundación Universidad.es
(Public Foundation for the Promotion
of Spanish Universities)**
President: Ángel Gabilondo Pujol
Director: José Manuel Martínez Sierra
C/Albacete, 5. 1♀ planta, ala este
Madrid 28027
SPAIN
Tel: +34 (91) 603 8277
Fax: +34 (91) 603 8823
EMail: universidad.es@educacion.es
WWW: http://www.universidad.es/
Spanish agency for the internationalization of
the Spanish university system abroad, and the
promotion of the Spanish higher education
system abroad. Its principal objectives are: to
enhance the international visibility of Spanish
universities; to improve the attractiveness of Spain
in the field of higher education; to attract the "best"
international students, faculty and researchers to
Spain; to increase the level of mobility within the
university sector; and to contribute to the
internationalization of the Spanish higher
education sector.

Global University Network for Innovation - GUNI
President: Antoni Giró Roca
Executive Director: Cristina Escrigas
Universitat Politècnica de Catalunya (UPC)
C. Jordi Girona 31 Edifici TG (S-1)
Barcelona 08034
SPAIN
Tel: +34(93) 401 7009
Fax: +34(93) 401 0855
EMail: info@guni-rmies.net
WWW: http://www.guni-rmies.net/

**Groupement International des Secrétaires
Généraux des Universités
Francophones - GISGUF**
President: Stéphane Berthet
c/o Université de Geneve, 24, rue du Général-Dufour
Geneve 1211
SWITZERLAND
Tel: +41(22) 379 7518/19
Fax: +41(22) 379 1135
WWW: http://www.gisguf.org

Grupo Compostela de Universidades (Compostela Group of Universities)
President: Maurits van Rooijen
Executive Secretary: Beatriz Iglesias Seoane
Ed. Jimena y Elisa Fernández de la Vega
Casas Reales, 8
Santiago de Compostela 15782
SPAIN
Tel: +34(98) 152 8052
Fax: +34(98) 152 8053
EMail: secretaria@gcompostela.org
WWW: http://www.gcompostela.org/
The Compostela Group of Universities is a non-profit association aimed at fostering cooperation and promoting dialogue in all fields related to higher education.

Inter-American Organisation for Higher Education - IOHE (Organisation universitaire inter-américaine - OUI)
President: Raúl Arias Lovillo
Executive Director: Patricia Gudiño
Université de Montréal, 3744, Jean-Brillant
bureau 592
Montreal Québec H3T 1P1
CANADA
Tel: +1(514) 343 6111 ext. 3775
Fax: +1(514) 343 6454
EMail: fbrown@oui-iohe.org
WWW: http://www.oui-iohe.qc.ca

Inter-University Council for East Africa - IUCEA
Executive Secretary: Mayunga H.H. Nkunya
Plot 4 Nile Avenue 3rd Floor, EADB Building
P.O. Box 7110
Kampala
UGANDA
Tel: +256(41) 256 251-2
Fax: +256(41) 342 007
EMail: info@iucea.org;exsec@iucea.org
WWW: http://www.iucea.org
The mission of the IUC is to encourage and develop mutually beneficial collaboration between its member Universities, and between them and Governments and other organisations, both public and private. Its aim is to help its members to contribute to meeting national and regional development needs, to the resolution of problems in every appropriate sector of activity in the region, and to the development of human resource capacity particularly in the disciplines of Science, Technology and Business Studies.

International Association of Universities - IAU (Association internationale des Universités - AIU)
President: Juan Ramón de la Fuente
Secretary-General: Eva Egron-Polak
UNESCO House1
Rue Miollis
Paris Cedex 15 75732
FRANCE
Tel: +33 1 4568 4800
Fax: +33 1 4734 7605
EMail: iau@iau-aiu.net
WWW: http://www.iau-aiu.net
IAU, founded in 1950, is the UNESCO-based worldwide association of higher education institutions. It brings together institutions and organisations from some 150 countries for reflection and action on common concerns and collaborates with various international, regional and national bodies active in higher education.

International Association of University Presidents - IAUP
President: J. Michael Adams
Secretary-General: Neal King
809 United Nations Plaza
New York
NY10017-3580
UNITED STATES OF AMERICA
WWW: http://www.iaup.org

International Council for Open and Distance Education - ICDE
President: Frits Pannekoek
Secretary-General: Gard Titlestad
Lilleakerveien 23
Oslo 0283
NORWAY
Tel: +47 2206 2630
Fax: +47 2206 2631
EMail: icde@icde.org
WWW: http://www.icde.org/
ICDE is the global organization for flexible learning and teaching. An important aim of ICDE is to promote intercultural co-operation and understanding through flexible learning and teaching throughout the world.

International Federation of Catholic Universities - IFCU (Fédération internationale des Universités catholiques - FIUC)
President: Anthony J. Cernera
Secretary-General: Guy-Réal Thivierge
21, rue d'Assas

Paris 75270
FRANCE
Tel: +33 1 4439 5226
Fax: +33 1 4439 5228
EMail: sgfiuc@bureau.fiuc.org
WWW: http://www.fiuc.org
Created by a Decree of the Holy See in 1948, it was recognized by Pope Pius XII in 1949 and became the International Federation of Catholic Universities (IFCU) in 1965.

International Federation of University Women - IFUW
President: Marianne Haslegrave
Secretary General: Leigh Bradford Ratteree
10 rue du Lac
Geneva 1207
SWITZERLAND
Tel: +41(22) 731 2380
Fax: +41(22) 738 0440
EMail: info@ifuw.org
WWW: http://www.ifuw.org/

International Network for Quality Assurance Agencies in Higher Education - INQAAHE
President: María José Lemaitre
Secretary: Guido Langouche
P.O. Box 85498
The Hague 2508 CD
NETHERLANDS
Tel: +31(70) 312 2300
Fax: +31(70) 312 2301
EMail: secretariat@inqaahe.org
WWW: http://www.inqaahe.org/
The main purpose of the Network is to collect and disseminate information on current and developing theory and practice in the assessment, improvement and maintenance of quality in higher education.

Islamic Educational, Scientific and Cultural Organization - ISESCO
Director General: Abdelhaziz Othman Altwaijri
Avenue des F.A.R , Hay Ryad
PO Box 2275
Rabat 10104
MOROCCO
Tel: +212(53) 756 6052/3
Fax: +212(53) 756 6012/3
EMail: education@isesco.org.ma
WWW: http://www.isesco.org.ma

Magna Charta Observatory
Council President: Üstün Ergüder
Secretary-General: Anna Glass
Via Zamboni 25
Bologna 40126
ITALY
Tel: +39(051) 209 8709
Fax: +39(051) 209 8710
EMail: magnacharta@unibo.it
WWW: http://www.magna-charta.org/
The Magna Charta Observatory aims to gather information, express opinions and prepare documents relating to the respect for, and protection of, the fundamental university values and rights laid down in the Magna Charta Universitatum signed in Bologna in 1988 by 388 Rectors of worldwide main universities.

Network for Education and Academic Rights - NEAR
Executive Director: John Akker
London South Bank University
90 London Road
London SE1 9LN
UNITED KINGDOM OF GREAT BRITAIN AND NORTHERN IRELAND
Tel: +44(207) 902 7700
Fax: +44(207) 021 0881
EMail: contact@nearinternational.org
WWW: http://www.nearinternational.org/

Network of Universities from the Capitals of Europe - UNICA
President: Stavros A. Zenios
Secretary-General: Kris Dejonckheere
C/o University Foundationrue
d'Egmont n°11
Brussels 1000
BELGIUM
Tel: +32 2 514 7800
Fax: +32 2 514 7900
EMail: office@unica-network.eu
WWW: http://www.unica-network.eu/
UNICA is a network of 40 universities from the capital cities of Europe. Its role is to promote academic excellence, integration and co-operation between member universities throughout Europe.

Nederlands-Vlaams Accreditatie Orgaan - NVAO (Accreditation Organisation of the Netherlands and Flanders)
Postbus 85498
Den Haag 2508

BELGIUM
Tel: +31 (0) 70 312 2300
Fax: +31 (0) 70 312 2301
EMail: info@nvao.net
WWW: http://www.nvao.net/
The organisation was established by international
treaty and it ensures the quality of higher education
in the Netherlands and Flanders.

**Observatory on Borderless Higher
Education - OBHE**
Chairperson: Drummond Bone
Chief Executive: Don Olcott
International Graduate Insight Group,
Redhill Chambers, 2d High Street
Redhill Surrey RH1 1RJ
UNITED KINGDOM OF GREAT BRITAIN AND
NORTHERN IRELAND
Tel: +44 (20) 7222 7890
Fax: +44 (20) 7182 7152
EMail: info@obhe.ac.uk
WWW: http://www.obhe.ac.uk/

**Programme on Institutional Management in
Higher Education - IMHE (Programme sur la
Gestion des Etablissements d'Enseignement
supérieur)**
Chair of the Board: Peter Coaldrake
Head: Richard Yelland
OECD 2, rue André Pascal
Paris 75775 Cedex 16
FRANCE
Tel: +33 1 4524 9260
Fax: +33 1 4430 6176
EMail: imhe@oecd.org
WWW: http://www.oecd.org/department/
0,3355,en_2649_35961291_1_1_1_1_1,00.html

**Red de Macrouniversidades de América
Latina y del Caribe (Network of of
Macrouniversities of Latin America and the
Caribbean)**
President: Suely Vilela
Regional Coordinator: Rosaura Ruiz Gutiérrez
Edificio UDUAL, costado poniente del Estadio
Olimpico
Ciudad Universitaria
UNAM
Mexico D.F. 04510
MEXICO

Tel: +52(55) 5550 1350
Fax: +52(55) 5550 7168
EMail: mcruzm@servidor.unam.mx
WWW: http://www.redmacro.unam.mx/

**Santander Group - European Universities
Network**
President: John Tuppen
Executive Secretary: Wioletta Węgorowska
Rue Stassart 119
Brussels 1050
BELGIUM
Tel: +32 2 511 6620
Fax: +32 2 502 9611
EMail: sgroup@sgroup.be
WWW: http://www.sgroup.be/

**SEAMEO Regional Centre for Higher Education
and Development - RIHED**
Director: Sauwakon Ratanawijitrasin
5th Floor, Commission on Higher Education Building,
328 Sri Ayuthaya Road, Rajthewee
Bangkok 10400
THAILAND
Tel: +66(2) 644 9856-62
Fax: +66(2) 644 5421
WWW: http://www.rihed.seameo.org/

**Southern African Regional Universities
Association - SARUA**
CEO: Piyushi Kotecha
P O Box 662
Wits 2050
SOUTH AFRICA
Tel: +27(11) 717 3951/2
Fax: +27(11) 717 3950
EMail: info@sarua.org
WWW: http://www.sarua.org

**UNESCO - Instituto Internacional para la
Educación Superior en América Latina y el
Caribe - IESALC (International UNESCO Institute
for Higher Education in Latin America and the
Caribbean)**
Acting Director: Pedro Henríquez Guajardo
Edificio Asovincar, Av Los Chorros c/c Calle
Acueducto, Altos de Sebucán

Caracas
VENEZUELA (BOLIVARIAN REPUBLIC OF)
Tel: +58(212) 286 0555
WWW: http://www.iesalc.unesco.org.ve/

**Unión de Universidades de América Latina
y el Caribe - UDUAL (Union of Universities of
Latin America and the Caribbean)**
President: Gustavo García de Paredes
Secretario General: Roberto Escalante Semerena
Apartado postal 70232 Cuidad Universitaria
México D.F., Mexico 04510
MEXICO
Tel: +52(55) 5622 0091/ 5616 2383
Fax: +52(55) 5622 0092
EMail: contacto@udual.org;udual@servidor.unal.mx
WWW: http://www.unam.mx/udual

**University Network of the European Capitals of
Culture - UNeECC**
President: Flora Carrijn
Secretary General: Pozsgai Gyöngyi

University of Pécs
Pécs
HUNGARY
WWW: http://www.uneecc.org

WC2 University Network
International Development City University London
Northampton Square
Londoc EC1V 0HB
UNITED KINGDOM OF GREAT BRITAIN AND
NORTHERN IRELAND
Tel: +44 (0)20 7040 0113
EMail: internationalpartnerships@city.ac.uk
WWW: http://www.city.ac.uk/international/
international-partnerships/wc2-university-network
The WC2 University Network has been developed
with the goal of bringing together top universities
located in the heart of major world cities in order to
address cultural, environmental and political issues
of common interest to world cities and their
universities.

INTERNATIONAL HANDBOOK OF UNIVERSITIES

2013

twenty-fourth edition

Volume 1

Afghanistan

STRUCTURE OF HIGHER EDUCATION SYSTEM

Description:

Higher education institutions reopened in 2002. The higher education system is centralized under the responsibility of the Ministry of Higher Education. Students are accepted by the Ministry. Higher education is evolving rapidly and reforms are underway.

Stages of studies:

University level first stage: Bachelor's degree
The first stage of higher education leads in Arts, Education, Social Science, Engineering, Veterinary Medicine, Science and Agriculture, to the award of the Bachelor's degree after four years. Studies in Medicine last for seven years (including one year pre-medical and one year internship).

ADMISSION TO HIGHER EDUCATION

Admission to university-level studies:

Name of secondary school credential required: Baccaluria

Entrance exam requirements: According to Article 21 of the Law on Universities, admission to the University is done through competitive examinations, with the exceptions provided for in Article 56.

NATIONAL BODIES

Ministry of Higher Education
Minister: Mohammad Sarwar Danesh
Kabul
WWW: http://mohe.gov.af/

Ministry of Education
Minister: Farooq Wardak
Kabul
WWW: http://moe.gov.af/

Data for academic year: 2006-2007
Source: IAU from the United Nations Development Programme, Kabul, 2003, updated from documentation, 2007. Bodies updated in 2011

INSTITUTIONS

PUBLIC INSTITUTIONS

ALBERONI UNIVERSITY
Gulbahar, Kapisa
Website: http://www.parwan-in.edu.af/

President: Abdul Rashid

Vice-Chancellor: Moh. Naeem Shareef (2005-)
Tel: +799 181-883

International Relations: Abdul Malik Hamwar Tel: +799 302-429

Faculties
Agriculture (Agriculture; Botany; Zoology); **Engineering** (Civil Engineering; Engineering); **Languages and Literature** (English; Journalism; Literature; Modern Languages; Native Language); **Law and Political Science** (Administrative Law; International Law; International Relations; Law; Political Sciences); **Medical and Health Sciences** (Health Sciences; Medicine); **Shari'a** (Islamic Law; Islamic Studies)

History: Founded 1999. Acquired present status 2005.

Governing Bodies: Academic Council; Administrative Council

Academic Year: March to December

Fees: None

Main Language(s) of Instruction: Dari

Accrediting Agencies: Ministry of Higher Education

Degrees and Diplomas: *Bachelor's Degree*: Agriculture (BSc); Laws; Islamic Knowledge; Languages (BA), 4 yrs; *Bachelor's*

Degree: Engineering (BSc), 5 yrs; *Bachelor's Degree*: Medical Sciences (MD), 6 yrs

Student Services: Academic counselling, Canteen, Cultural centre, Health services, Language programs, Nursery care, Social counselling, Sports facilities

Student Residential Facilities: Student hostels; Guest house

Libraries: Yes

Academic Staff *2008-2009*	MEN	WOMEN	TOTAL
FULL-TIME	–	–	61
Student Numbers *2008-2009*			
All (Foreign Included)	1,581	62	1,643

BADAKHSHAN INSTITUTE OF HIGHER EDUCATION

Faizabad, Badakhshan

President: Qudratullah

Faculties
Pedagogy (Pedagogy)

History: Founded 1961 as a Teacher Training Center. Succesively renamed Institution of Teacher Training 1987 and Nasir Khusraw Pedagogical College 1988. Acquired present status 2003.

Degrees and Diplomas: *Bachelor's Degree*

Academic Staff *2008-2009*	MEN	WOMEN	TOTAL
FULL-TIME	14	4	18
Student Numbers *2008-2009*			
All (Foreign Included)	235	134	369
Last Updated: 04/10/10			

BALKH UNIVERSITY

Mazar-e-Sharif, Balkh
Tel: +93 50-3487 +93 50-3554
EMail: balkh_university@yahoo.com
Website: http://www.balkh-un.edu.af/

President: Habibullah Habib

Faculties
Agriculture (Agriculture; Animal Husbandry; Botany; Forest Products); **Economics** (Economics; Finance); **Education** (Education; Foreign Languages Education; Mathematics Education; Native Language Education; Science Education); **Engineering** (Chemical Engineering; Electrical Engineering; Geology; Industrial Engineering; Mathematics; Mining Engineering; Physics); **Law and Political Sciences** (Criminal Law; International Law; Political Sciences; Public Law); **Literature** (Education; English; History; Journalism; Oriental Languages); **Medicine** (Anaesthesiology; Anatomy; Biochemistry; Biology; Chemistry; Dermatology; Epidemiology; Gynaecology and Obstetrics; Mathematics; Medicine; Neurology; Ophthalmology; Otorhinolaryngology; Paediatrics; Pathology; Pharmacology; Physics; Physiology; Social and Preventive Medicine; Surgery); **Shari'a (Theology)** (Islamic Law; Islamic Theology)

History: Founded 1988.

Admission Requirements: Secondary school certificate (baccalaureate) or equivalent

Main Language(s) of Instruction: Dari, Pashtu, English

Degrees and Diplomas: *Bachelor's Degree (BA/BSc)*: 4 yrs; *Bachelor's Degree*: Medicine, 6 yrs

Student Services: Academic counselling, Canteen, Cultural centre, Employment services, Health services, Language programs, Nursery care, Social counselling, Sports facilities

Academic Staff *2008-2009*	MEN	WOMEN	TOTAL
FULL-TIME	181	51	232
Student Numbers *2008-2009*			
All (Foreign Included)	3,718	1,835	5,553
Last Updated: 04/10/10			

HERAT UNIVERSITY

Herat
Tel: +93 40 226-770 +93 40 223-570
EMail: nazir@heratuniversity.org
Website: http://www.hu.edu.af/

Chancellor: Mir Ghulam Osman Bariz Hossanini
Tel: +93 79554-0570 EMail: barizhossaini@yahoo.com

Faculties
Agriculture (Agriculture; Agronomy; Animal Husbandry); **Computer Science** (Computer Networks; Computer Science); **Economics** (Economics; Management); **Education** (Education; English; History; Mathematics; Physics); **Engineering** (Civil Engineering; Engineering); **Fine Art** (Fine Arts; Painting and Drawing; Writing); **Law and Political Sciences** (Law; Political Sciences); **Literature** (Arabic; Asian Studies; English; German; International Relations; Journalism; Literature; Modern Languages); **Science**; **Theology and Islamic Law** (Islamic Law; Islamic Theology; Theology)

History: Founded 1987.

Admission Requirements: Secondary school certificate (baccalaureate) or equivalent

Libraries: 2,000 vols

Academic Staff *2009-2010*: Total 284
Student Numbers *2009-2010*: Total 5,107
Last Updated: 04/10/10

KABUL EDUCATION UNIVERSITY (KEU)

Near to the Kabul police Academy, Afshar-Silo, Kabul
Tel: +93 75 201-4369
EMail: yasserhoseini2008@yahoo.com
Website: http://www.keu.edu.af/

Chancellor: Amanullah Hamidzai

Faculties
Language (Arabic; English; Literature; Modern Languages; Native Language; Russian); **Natural Sciences** (Biology; Chemistry; Computer Science; Mathematics; Natural Sciences; Physics); **Physical Education** (Physical Education; Sports); **Social Sciences** (Geography; History; Islamic Studies; Social Sciences; Sociology); **Special Education** (Education of the Handicapped; Special Education); **Vocational Education** (Education; Psychology)

History: Founded 1913 as Teachers Training Centre. Changed name to Darul Malimeen (DM). Became a Teacher Training Academy (TTA) 1946. Transformed into Kabul Institute of Pedagogy (KIP) 1984. Acquried present status and title 2003.

Admission Requirements: High school leaving certificate; entrance examination

Fees: None

Main Language(s) of Instruction: Pashtu and Dari; English (for candidates of scholarship or upon organisational request)

Student Services: Language programs, Sports facilities

Student Residential Facilities: Yes (1118 dormitory students)

Libraries: Yes

Publications: Payam-e-Maarifat, Seasonal magazine published since 1383, that contains scientific and researched articles from university teachers *(annually)*

Academic Staff *2008-2009*	MEN	WOMEN	TOTAL
FULL-TIME	122	42	164
STAFF WITH DOCTORATE FULL-TIME	6	–	6
Student Numbers *2008-2009*			
All (Foreign Included)	2,537	1,602	4,139
Last Updated: 04/10/10			

KABUL MEDICAL UNIVERSITY

Karte Sakhi, Kabul
Tel: +93 20 250-0326 +93 70 278-115 (mobile)
Fax: +93 20 250-0326
Website: http://www.kmu.edu.af

Chancellor: Obaidullah Obaid

Faculties

Curative Medicine (Medicine); **Nursing** (Nursing); **Paediatrics** (Paediatrics); **Stomatology** (Stomatology)

History: Founded 1932 as Kabul Medical Faculty (KMF). Initially maintained by collaboration with the Turkish and French government, it acquired a status of single self-autonomous University in 2005.

Admission Requirements: Secondary school certificate (baccalaureate) or equivalent

Main Language(s) of Instruction: Dari

Degrees and Diplomas: *Bachelor's Degree*

Academic Staff 2008-2009	MEN	WOMEN	TOTAL
FULL-TIME	190	23	213
Student Numbers 2009-2010			
All (Foreign Included)	1,647	1,098	2,745

Last Updated: 04/10/10

KABUL POLYTECHNIC UNIVERSITY (KPU)

Kabul
Tel: +93 20 220-1114
EMail: chancellor@kpu.edu.af
Website: http://www.polytechnic-kabul.org

Chancellor: Ezatullah Amed
Tel: +93(0) 75200-1933 EMail: amed@kpu.ac.af

Vice-Rector, Administrative Affairs: Amanulla Faqiri
Tel: +93 70 275-621 (mobile)
EMail: zhgorandoi@polytechnic-kabul.org

International Relations: Abdulbaqi Rahmani
Tel: +93 75 201 5034 (mobile)
EMail: rahmani@polytechnic-kabul.org

Courses

Computer Science (Computer Engineering; Computer Science; Information Technology)

Faculties

Construction and Civil Engineering (Architecture; Civil Engineering; Construction Engineering; Environmental Engineering; Road Engineering; Water Management); **Electromechanical Engineering** (Automotive Engineering; Mathematics; Mechanics; Modern Languages; Physics; Power Engineering); **Geology and Mining** (Chemical Engineering; Geology; Mining Engineering; Petroleum and Gas Engineering)

History: Founded 1963. Acquired present status 1979.

Governing Bodies: Academic Council

Academic Year: March to December (March-July; September-December)

Admission Requirements: Secondary school certificate (baccalaureate) or equivalent

Fees: None

Main Language(s) of Instruction: Dari, Pashtu

Accrediting Agencies: Ministry of Higher Education

Degrees and Diplomas: *Bachelor's Degree*: Industrial and Civil Construction; Hydraulic and Hydro-technical Construction; Road and Bridge Construction; Architecture; Mining Engineering; Geological Engineering; Petroleum and Gas Engineering; Chemical Technology; Geodesy; Automobile and Tractor (BSc), 5 yrs; *Master's Degree*: Industrial and Civil Construction; Hydraulic and Hydro-technical Construction; Road and Bridge Construction; Architecture; Mining Engineering; Geological Engineering; Petroleum and Gas Engineering; Chemical Technology; Geodesy; Automobile and Tractor (MSc)

Student Services: Academic counselling, Canteen, Cultural centre, Foreign Studies Centre, Health services, Language programs, Nursery care, Social counselling, Sports facilities

Student Residential Facilities: Yes

Libraries: 3,000 vols

Publications: Kabul Polytechnic Institute Academic Journal *(biennially)*; Science and Technology *(biennially)*

Academic Staff 2008-2009: Total 150
STAFF WITH DOCTORATE: Total 39
Student Numbers 2008-2009: Total 4,000
Last Updated: 05/10/10

KABUL UNIVERSITY

Pohantoon Kabul
Karte Sakhi, Kabul
Tel: +93 20 250-0326 +93 70 276-174 (mobile)
Fax: +93 20 250-0326
EMail: info@ku.edu.af
Website: http://www.ku.edu.af/

Chancellor: Hamidullah Amin EMail: hamedullahamin@ku.edu.af

Faculties

Agriculture (Agriculture; Animal Husbandry; Forestry) *Dean*: Mohd. Yaseen Mohsini; **Computer Science** (Computer Science); **Economics** (Economics) *Dean*: Mohd. Ashraf Yadgari; **Engineering** (Architecture; Engineering) *Dean*: Abdul Wahid Zia; **Fine Arts** (Fine Arts) *Dean*: Sayd Farooq Faryad; **Geosciences** (Geology) *Dean*: Mohd. Hussain Gerziwani; **Islamic Studies** (Islamic Studies) *Dean*: Abdul Aziz; **Journalism** (Journalism) *Dean*: Mohd. Kazim Ahang; **Language and Literatures** (Literature; Modern Languages) *Dean*: Mohd. Sabir Khuishkai; **Law** (Law) *Dean*: Abdul Iqrar Wasil; **Pharmacy** (Pharmacy) *Dean*: Mohd. Osman Baburi; **Psychology** (Psychology); **Science** (Mathematics and Computer Science; Natural Sciences); **Social Sciences** (Social Sciences) *Dean*: Abdul Baqi Hisari; **Veterinary Science** (Veterinary Science) *Dean*: Noor Ahmad Ahmad

History: Founded 1932 as a Faculty of Medicine. Became University by State Decree 1945. Co-educational since 1958. Faculty of Medicine detached 1979. A State institution under the jurisdiction of the Ministry of Higher Education.

Academic Year: March to January (March-July; September-January)

Admission Requirements: Secondary school certificate (baccalaureate) or equivalent

Fees: None

Main Language(s) of Instruction: Dari (Persian), Pashtu, English

Degrees and Diplomas: *Bachelor's Degree*; *Master's Degree*; *Doctor's Degree*

Student Services: Canteen, Cultural centre, Health services, Language programs, Nursery care, Sports facilities

Student Residential Facilities: Yes

Libraries: Central Library, c. 200,000 vols

Publications: Journal of Da Kabul Pohantoon *(quarterly)*
Last Updated: 05/10/10

KANDAHAR UNIVERSITY

loya wiyala new Eid gah Kandahar Afghansitan, District 9, Kandahar 25000
Tel: +93 79 930-5478
EMail: tawab@kandahar-university.af
Website: http://kan.edu.af/

Vice-Chancellor: Abdul Tawab Balakarzai

Faculties

Agriculture (Agriculture); **Economics** (Economics); **Education** (Education); **Engineering** (Engineering); **Medicine** (Medicine); **Sharia Law** (Islamic Law)

History: Founded 1988.

Admission Requirements: Secondary school certificate (baccalaureate) or equivalent

Academic Staff 2008-2009	MEN	WOMEN	TOTAL
FULL-TIME	82	1	83
Student Numbers 2008-2009			
All (Foreign Included)	1,509	78	1,587

Last Updated: 20/03/12

NANGARHAR UNIVERSITY

Jalalabad, Nangarhr
Tel: +93(0) 2076-5423
EMail: info@nu.edu.af; chancellor@nu.edu.af
Website: http://www.nu.edu.af/

Vice-Chancellor: Del Aqa Waqar EMail: vice.chancellor@nu.edu.af

Faculties

Agriculture (Agriculture); **Civil Law and Political Sciences** (Civil Law; Political Sciences); **Economics** (Economics); **Education** (Education); **Engineering** (Engineering); **Literature and Language** (Literature; Modern Languages); **Medicine** (Medicine); **Shariah** (Theology); **Veterinary Science** (Veterinary Science)

History: Founded 1962 from Medical Faculty of Kabul University. Reorganized in 1978. A State institution responsible to the Ministry of Education.

Academic Year: September to June

Main Language(s) of Instruction: Pashtu

International Co-operation: With San Diego State University (USA); partnerships funded by the World Bank and Streghthening Higher Education Program (SHEP)

Student Residential Facilities: Dormitories for 3,750 students

Academic Staff *2008-2009*: Total 335

Student Numbers *2008-2009*: Total 8,000

Last Updated: 05/10/10

SHEIKH ZAYED UNIVERSITY (KHOST)

Khust

Tel: +93 88-216 +93 52 001-649

Chancellor: Gul Hassan Walizei

Faculties

Agriculture (Agriculture); **Education** (Education); **Engineering** (Engineering); **Medicine** (Medicine); **Political Sciences** (Political Sciences); **Sharia** (Islamic Law; Theology)

Academic Staff *2008-2009*: Total 118

Student Numbers *2008-2009*: Total 2,545

TAKHAR UNIVERSITY

Taloqan, Takhar

Tel: +93 70-071-2462

President: Kashifi Barmaki

Faculties

Agriculture (Agriculture); **Education** (Education); **Engineering** (Engineering); **Languages and Literature** (Literature; Modern Languages); **Medicine** (Medicine); **Theology** (Theology)

History: Founded as Abdullah Bin Masoud University and registered with the MoHE 1995.

Academic Staff *2008-2009*	MEN	WOMEN	TOTAL
FULL-TIME	42	5	47
Student Numbers *2008-2009*			
All (Foreign Included)	1,406	166	1,572

Last Updated: 20/03/12

Albania

STRUCTURE OF HIGHER EDUCATION SYSTEM

Description:

Higher education is offered by public and private institutions. All higher education (HE) institutions are governed by the Law on Higher Education (2007). Universities offer up to third cycle study programmes; higher schools and professional colleges offer mainly first cycle and sometimes second cycle programmes. Research is carried out mainly in universities, but higher education schools and professional colleges may carry out research in arts, sports, etc., depending on their statutes. Study programmes are offered full-time and part-time, distance learning is also available.

Admission. The National Exam Agency, under the Ministry of Education and Science, governs admission procedures. Admission to all public and private HE institutions requires successful completion of secondary education and the 4 State Matura Exams. In certain study programmes requiring specific skills like Arts, Sports, Architecture, and some foreign languages, there is an admission/entrance examination at the HE institution level. The number of admissions to public HE institutions is determined each year by the Government in a special Act, based on proposals made by the HE institutions.

Study Programmes. Pre-Bologna Programmes: The first cycle usually consisted of 4 years' study (for primary teachers and a few others, 3 years'), followed by the Postgraduate School (1-2 years) and the PhD, consisting of a doctoral thesis only. Within the 2007 HE Law, these 4-year programmes were recognized at the level of Integrated Second Cycle (Bologna's 3 + 2). The Postgraduate School has been recognized at Post Master's level (and can also cover the 60 ECTS of the first doctoral year). Post Bologna Programmes: There are non-university HE study programmes of 120 ECTS, basically in applied fields. The first cycle programmes are no less than 180 ECTS with 60 ECTS per year. The completion of the first cycle leads to the second cycle of (i) 120 ECTS, of 2 years' length for the Master of Science or the Master of Fine Arts or (ii) 60-90 ECTS, of 1,5 years for Professional Masters. In field such as Medicine, Stomatology, Pharmacy, Veterinary Science and Architecture, HE institutions offer integrated second cycle programmes with a minimum of 300 ECTS and of 5 years' length. To receive their second cycle diploma, students are required to provide evidence of an internationally recognized English language test in accordance with the Common European Framework of Reference for Languages. Only the completion of the second cycle programme, leading to a Master of Science or Master of Fine Arts, gives access to the third cycle. The third cycle includes: a) Long term specialization studies, basically in Medicine, Stomatology, Pharmacy, Veterinary Science, Engineering and Law, lasting for 2 years as stipulated by the law on regulated professions; and b) Doctoral programmes, lasting for at least 3 academic years with 60 ECTS for taught subjects leading to the award of the Doctor diploma. Doctoral students have to prepare and defend a thesis and submit evidence of English language command in accordance with the Common European Framework of Reference for Languages. The holders of the former Master of the Second Level or the Post University School, may have such credits transferred and have the 60 ECTS completed, passing directly to the doctoral thesis. After 2007, research is mainly carried out at universities. The former Research Institutes have been integrated into universities and academies. Some units at the department or faculty levels are mainly focused on research but can also teach. The other departments focus on teaching, but may carry out a little research. The Inter-University Center of Albanological Studies mostly focuses on research.

Accreditation. Accreditation falls under the responsibility of the National Accreditation Council. There is accreditation at the institution and study programme levels for all three cycles. A new HE institution has to be recognized by a Government Act, based on a proposal from the Ministry of Education and Science. Prior to the Act, the National Agency of Accreditation carries out a pre-accreditation. Following recognition, the new HE institution will have to undergo accreditation, and only after that, it will be allowed to award degrees. Accreditation usually takes place once every 6 years.

Stages of studies:

University level first stage: Bachelor – First Cycle Degree
Studies last for a minimum of 3 years. Undergraduate study programmes include at least 180 credits and are offered at universities and professional colleges. If the profession is not regulated, the degree can give access to

the labour market. Academically, it can give access to the second cycle of higher education or to the Master of Science or to the Professional Master. A thesis is not a standard requirement. The study programme must be accredited.

University level second stage: *Master of Science, Master of Fine Arts, Professional Master - Second Cycle Degree*
The second cycle degree of Master of Science or Master of Fine Arts confers 120 ECTS and studies last for 2 years. Students must prepare a thesis. It is the required standard for a number of professions. In certain fields like Medicine, Pharmacy, Dentistry, Veterinary Medicine, Architecture, universities offer only integrated first and second cycle study programmes of a length of no less than 5 years of study. The study programme must be accredited. It provides for entry to the third cycle study programme – a) long term specialization; and/or b) PhD study programmes.
The Professional Master is open to those with at least a first cycle degree. It is mainly professional. Teachers, in particular, need this Master in their field. It comprises no less than 60 ECTS. It includes taught subjects and training. It does not give access to the third cycle. It cannot lead directly to third cycle programmes, but holders may have access to a Master of Science or Master of Fine Arts programme, with credits being transferred.

University level third stage: *Long term specialization studies; Doktor i Shkencave (Doctor of Sciences)*
With studies lasting for at least 2 years and comprising a minimum of 120 ECTS, the long-term specialization studies advance theoretical and professional knowledge and skills in Medicine, Pharmacy, Stomatology, Veterinary science, Engineering, Law, etc. These studies comprise both taught subjects and research. Holders of this diploma may enter a doctoral programme and may not have to take the 60 ECTS of taught subjects which are normally compulsory for doctoral programmes. Students have to take the English Language Test in accordance with the Common European Framework of Refence for Languages.
The Doktor i Shkencave (Doctor of Sciences) studies last at least for 3 years. They comprise 60 ECTS of taught subjects and a doctoral thesis after individual study and research (while working). The title of Doktor i Shkencave is conferred. The candidate, under the supervision of a scientific researcher, must prepare and defend a thesis. He/she needs to fulfill the requirement of the English language test and other criteria set out by HEIs.

Distance higher education:
Part-time distance learning and correspondence courses are offered but they need special approval. Online study programmes are also provided.

ADMISSION TO HIGHER EDUCATION

Admission to university-level studies:

Name of secondary school credential required: Diplomë e Maturës Shtetërore

Minimum score/requirement: Minimum score of 25 out of 100

For entry to: all HE programmes.

Alternatives to credentials: "A" level equivalents such as the International Baccalaureate (IB) or a pass in year 1 or an undergraduate programme from a recognized university abroad. IB points of certain points.

Entrance exam requirements: Certain undergraduate programmes require candidates to pass an interview, a written test conducted by the university.

Foreign students admission:

Quotas: Set by special decree of the Council of Ministers.

Entrance exam requirements: The same as for Albanian nationals.

Language requirements: Albanian language test at scores set by HEIs.

RECOGNITION OF STUDIES

Quality assurance system:

The first part of QA is the licensing procedure. Within the framework of the Government's Act for the opening of a new higher education institution or a new study programme, the Accreditation Council checks the fulfillment of standards and requirements. Only a positive evaluation from the Accreditation Council can lead to the Government's license. Until the award of the first diplomas, the new HE institution will have to undergo institutional and study programme accreditation. The new HE Law provides for internal QA which is under the responsibility of each HE institution. The external QA leads then to the final procedures for accreditation. The National Agency of Accreditation is responsible for the implementation of these procedures. The Accreditation Council may decide to approve, reject or grant conditional accreditation based on internal and external evaluation reports. Relying on recommendations from the Accreditation Council, the Minister of Education and Science, or the Minister in charge in case of specific HE institutions, then issues the accreditation decree.

Bodies dealing with recognition:

Agjencia Publike e Akreditimit të Arsimit të Lartë - APAAL (Public Agency for Accreditation of Higher Education)

Director: Avni Meshi
Bulevardi "Zhan D'Ark", Pallatet e Lanës, Nr 2
Tiranë
Tel: +355 42 266302
Fax: +355 42 266302
EMail: infoaaal@gmail.com
WWW: http://www.aaal.edu.al/
Services provided and students dealt with: The Public Agency for Accreditation of Higher Education is responsible for managing external evaluation procedures. It serves as the technical arm for the National Accreditation Council.

Drejtoria e Arsimit të Lartë dhe Kërkimit Shkencor (Directorate for Higher Education and Research)

Ministry of Education and Science
Rruga e Durrësit, 23
Tiranë

Special provisions for recognition:

Recognition for university level studies: According to the Law on Higher Education, HE institutions are responsible for recognition when the purpose of recognition is enrolment in higher levels of education. (Article 38 of Law No. 9741 on HE). Recognition of post secondary qualifications is done by the Ministry of Education and Science, through its Diploma Recognition Unit (Article 37 of the same Law). Albania has ratified the Lisbon Convention on Recognition.Further provisions on recognition requirements and procedures, should be found in the HE institutions' charters. For details on the recognition procedures and requirements by the Ministry of Education and Science, see www.mash.gov.al (Arsimi i Lartë (Higher Education), Njohja e Diplomave (Diploma Recognition).

The Division for Diploma Recognition (serving also as the Albanian ENIC-NARIC) is responsible for assuring the authenticity and comparability of foreign higher education qualifications with the levels of higher education

For access to advanced studies and research: In accordance with Law no. 9741, dated 21.05.2007, with amendments, Article 38, academic recognition is vested with the universities. Therefore, in the case of advanced studies and research, universities have the power to recognize qualifications from foreign HE institutions.

For exercising a profession: The Law no. 10171, dated 22.10.2009 "On regulated professions in the Republic of Albania" with amendments, provides for the exercise of several regulated professions such as: Medicine, Pharmacy, Stomatology, Nursing, Midwifery, Physiotherapy, Veterinary Medicine, Law, Urban Planning, Architecture, Construction, Teaching etc. In the case of unregulated professions, recognition is at the discretion of employers.

Continuous efforts are being made to introduce standards such as those under the 2005/36 EU Directive.

NATIONAL BODIES

Ministria e Arsimit dhe Shkencës (Ministry of Education and Science)

Minister: Myqerem Tafaj
Rruga e Durrësit, 23

Tiranë
Tel: +355 42 226307
Fax: +355 42 226307
EMail: ministri@mash.gov.al
WWW: http://mash.gov.al/
Role of national body: The Ministry of Education and Science carries periodically, at least once every 3 years, the supervision for the compliance with the law provisions in the public or private Higher Education Institutions, and at least once a year it performs a financial assessment of public HEIs.

Drejtoria e Arsimit të Lartë dhe Kërkimit Shkencor (Directorate for Higher Education and Research)

Director: Linda Pustina
Head, Diploma Recognition Section: Mimoza Gjika
Ministry of Education and Science
Rruga e Durrësit, 23
Tiranë
Role of national body: Oversees the implementation of the law and relevant by-laws on higher education by HEIs. Supervises national quality standards in higher education. Proposes student quotas for admission in public HEIs. Reviews requests for opening, re-organisation and closure of study programmes by public HEIs.

Data for academic year: 2011-2012
Source: IAU from the Albanian ENIC-NARIC, 2011

INSTITUTIONS

PUBLIC INSTITUTIONS

ACADEMY OF FINE ARTS

Akademia e Arteve
Bulevardi "Dëshmoret e Kombit", Sheshi "Nënë Tereza", Tiranë
Tel: +355(42) 25488
Fax: +355(42) 25488
EMail: petritmalaj@hotmail.com
Website: http://www.artacademy.al

Rector: Petrit Malaj

Vice-Rector: Artan Peqini EMail: artpeqini@yahoo.com

Faculties
Dramatic Arts (Acting; Dance; Theatre); **Music** (Conducting; Music; Music Theory and Composition; Musicology); **Visual Arts** (Fine Arts; Multimedia; Painting and Drawing; Sculpture)

History: Founded 1966 as High Institute of Arts, incorporating the Conservatory, the High School of Figurative Arts and the High School of Actors. Acquired present status and title 1991.

Governing Bodies: Senate; Council

Admission Requirements: Secondary school certificate

Fees: (Leks): 120,000

Main Language(s) of Instruction: Albanian

Accrediting Agencies: Ministria e Arsimit dhe Shkences (MASH) (Ministry of Education and Science)

Degrees and Diplomas: *Bachelor – Diplomë e Ciklit të Parë*: Musicology; Composition; Conducting, 4 yrs; *Master Profesional*; *Master i Shkencave/Master i Arteve të Bukura*

Student Services: Academic counselling

Special Facilities: Art Gallery; Concert Hall

Academic Staff *2007-2008*	TOTAL
FULL-TIME	110
PART-TIME	250
STAFF WITH DOCTORATE	
FULL-TIME	c. 60

Student Numbers *2007-2008*	
All (Foreign Included)	c. 860

Last Updated: 17/09/10

AGRICULTURAL UNIVERSITY OF TIRANA

Universiteti Bujqësor i Tiranës (AUT/UBT)
Kamez, Tiranë
Tel: +355(47) 200-893
Fax: +355(47) 353-893
EMail: iroaut@yahoo.com
Website: http://www.ubt.edu.al

Rector: Fatos Harizaj (2008-)
Tel: +355(47) 200-869, Fax: +355(47) 200-874
EMail: harizajf@yahoo.it

Faculties
Agriculture and Environment (Agricultural Business; Agricultural Economics; Agronomy; Animal Husbandry; Aquaculture; Food Technology; Horticulture; Plant and Crop Protection); **Biotechnology and Food Technology** (Biotechnology; Food Technology); **Economy and Agribusiness** (Agricultural Business; Agricultural Economics; Economics); **Forestry** (Forestry; Harvest Technology; Wood Technology); **Veterinary Science** (Veterinary Science)

History: Founded 1951 as the Higher Agricultural Institute. Acquired present status 1991.

Governing Bodies: Senate

Academic Year: October to July

Admission Requirements: High school certificate and entrance examination

Main Language(s) of Instruction: Albanian

International Co-operation: With universities in Italy; Greece; Germany; France; USA. Also participates in Tempus and INTER-REG

Accrediting Agencies: Ministria e Arsimit dhe Shkences (MASH) (Ministry of Education and Science)

Degrees and Diplomas: *Bachelor – Diplomë e Ciklit të Parë*; *Master i Shkencave/Master i Arteve të Bukura*. Also postgraduate diplomas

Student Services: Canteen, Cultural centre, Health services, Sports facilities

Student Residential Facilities: Yes

Libraries: Scientific Library, 126,000 vols

Publications: Revista Shqiptare e Shkencave Bujqesore (*quarterly*)
Last Updated: 20/09/10

ALEKSANDËR MOISIU UNIVERSITY OF DURRES

Universiteti Aleksandër Moisiu i Durrësit
Lagja 1, Rr. Currilave, Durrës
Tel: +355(5) 239-161
Fax: +355(5) 239-162
EMail: contacts@uamd.edu.al
Website: http://www.uamd.edu.al

Rector: Agim Kukeli

Faculties
Business (Administration; Banking; Economics; Finance; Management; Public Administration); **Education** (Computer Education; Education; Foreign Languages Education; Mathematics Education; Primary Education; Science Education; Teacher Training)

History: Founded 2006.

Degrees and Diplomas: *Bachelor – Diplomë e Ciklit të Parë*; *Master Profesional*; *Master i Shkencave/Master i Arteve të Bukura*; *Doktor*: Economic Sciences
Last Updated: 20/09/10

ALEKSANDËR XHUVANI UNIVERSITY OF ELBASAN

Universiteti Aleksandër Xhuvani
Elbasan
Tel: +355(545) 7747
Fax: +355(545) 2593
EMail: info@uniel.edu.al
Website: http://www.uniel.edu.al

Rector: Liman Varoshi

International Relations: Fatbardha Kazazi, Head, International Relations Office
Tel: +355(545) 7728, Fax: +355(545) 7728
EMail: int_rel_office@yahoo.com

Faculties
Economics (Accountancy; Business Administration; Economics; Finance); **Education** (Education; Teacher Training); **Humanities** (Albanian; Geography; History; Journalism; Literature; Modern Languages); **Natural Sciences** (Biology; Chemistry; Mathematics; Nursing; Physics)

History: Founded 1909, acquired present status 1991.

Governing Bodies: Senate; University Council

Academic Year: October to July (October-February; March-July)

Admission Requirements: Secondary school certificate and entrance examination

Fees: (US Dollars): 120 per annum

Main Language(s) of Instruction: Albanian

International Co-operation: Participates in the Tempus and Erasmus Programmes

Accrediting Agencies: Ministria e Arsimit dhe Shkences (MASH) (Ministry of Education and Science)

Degrees and Diplomas: *Bachelor – Diplomë e Ciklit të Parë*; *Master i Shkencave/Master i Arteve të Bukura*; *Doktor*. Also teaching qualifications.

Student Services: Academic counselling, Canteen, Cultural centre, Employment services, Foreign student adviser, Foreign Studies Centre, Handicapped facilities, Health services, Language programs, Nursery care, Social counselling, Sports facilities

Special Facilities: Laboratories of Natural and Social Sciences

Libraries: University Library, c. 100,000 vols

Publications: Scientific Bulletin, Publication on scientific research works, seminars, conferences, symposiums
Last Updated: 20/09/10

🔲 EQREM ÇABEJ UNIVERSITY OF GJIROKSTRA

Universiteti 'Eqrem Çabej' Gjirokastër (UGJ)
Lagja "18 Shtatori", Gjirokstër
Tel: +355(842) 63408
Fax: +355(842) 63776
EMail: rektori@uogj.edu.al
Website: http://www.uogj.edu.al/

Rector: Gëzim Sala (2008-)
Tel: +355(842) 66146 EMail: gezimsala@yahoo.com

Chancellor: Sotira Goçi
Tel: +355(842) 67571 EMail: sotiragoci@yahoo.com

International Relations: Liljana Reçka, Vice-Rector, Science and International Relations
Tel: +355(842) 68024 EMail: liljanarecka@yahoo.com

Faculties
Education and Social Sciences (Albanian; Economics; Education; Educational Sciences; Geography; Greek; Greek (Classical); History; Modern Languages; Social Sciences; Teacher Training); **Natural Sciences** (Biology; Chemistry; Information Technology; Mathematics; Mathematics and Computer Science; Nursing)

History: Founded 1971. Acquired current status in 1991.

Governing Bodies: Rectorate; Senate; Administrative Council; Deanery

Academic Year: October to September

Admission Requirements: Secondary school certificate.

Fees: (Leks): 12,000 per annum

Main Language(s) of Instruction: Albanian; Greek; English; Italian

International Co-operation: With institutions in Cyprus, Greece, Italy, USA, Romania

Accrediting Agencies: Ministria e Arsimit dhe Shkences (MASH) (Ministry of Education and Science); Member of the Balkan Universities Network and the Community of Mediterranean Universities; Participates in Tempus Phare

Degrees and Diplomas: *Bachelor – Diplomë e Ciklit të Parë*: Accounting and Finance; Public Administration; Tourism Management; History; Geography; Language and Literature (Albanian; English; Italian; Greek); Mathematics; Computer Science; Physics; Biology; Chemistry; Nursing, 3-4 yrs; *Master Profesional*

Student Services: Academic counselling, Canteen, Cultural centre, Employment services, Foreign student adviser, Foreign Studies Centre, Health services, Language programs, Nursery care, Social counselling, Sports facilities

Libraries: Yes

Publications: Journal of Mathematics and Natural Sciences *(biannually)*; Journal of Social, Economics and Educational Sciences *(biannually)*

Academic Staff 2008-2009	MEN	WOMEN	TOTAL
FULL-TIME	57	70	127
STAFF WITH DOCTORATE			
FULL-TIME	21	8	29
PART-TIME	5	–	5
Student Numbers 2008-2009			
All (Foreign Included)	1,364	1,619	2,983

Part-time students, 1,355.
Last Updated: 20/09/10

FAN S. NOLI UNIVERSITY KORÇË

Universiteti 'Fan S. Noli' Korçë
Rr. Gjergj Kastrioti, Korçë
Tel: +355(824) 2580
Fax: +355(824) 2230
EMail: iro@unkorce.edu.al
Website: http://www.unkorce.edu.al

Rector: Gjergji Mero

Faculties
Agriculture (Agriculture; Farm Management; Food Science; Horticulture); **Economics** (Economics; Finance; Management; Marketing; Tourism); **Education** (Education)

Units
Nursing (Nursing)

History: Founded 1971 as Higher Agricultural Institute. Acquired present status and title 1992.

Governing Bodies: Senate

Academic Year: October to July

Admission Requirements: Secondary school certificate and entrance examination

Main Language(s) of Instruction: Albanian

International Co-operation: With universities in Italy; Greece; Sweden; Bulgaria. Also participates in Tempus and INTEREG-3 programmes

Accrediting Agencies: Ministria e Arsimit dhe Shkences (MASH) (Ministry of Education and Science)

Degrees and Diplomas: *Bachelor – Diplomë e Ciklit të Parë*: Agriculture; Education; Economics, 4 yrs; *Bachelor – Diplomë e Ciklit të Parë*: Nursing, 3 1/2 yrs. Also teaching qualifications.

Student Services: Canteen, Cultural centre, Health services, Nursery care, Social counselling, Sports facilities

Student Residential Facilities: Yes

Libraries: Central Library, 28,000 vols

Publications: Bulletin *(quarterly)*
Last Updated: 15/12/08

LUIGJ GURAKUQI UNIVERSITY OF SHKODRA

Universiteti i Shkodrës 'Luigj Gurakuqi' (USH)
Sheshi 2 Prilli, Shkodër
Tel: +355 (2) 242-235
Fax: +355 (2) 243-747
EMail: rektori@unishk.tirana.al
Website: http://www.unishk.edu.al

Rector: Artan Haxhi EMail: ahaxhi@unishk.edu.al

Faculties
Economics (Accountancy; Business Administration; Finance; Tourism); **Education Sciences** (Art Education; Humanities and Social Science Education; Pedagogy; Physical Education; Pre-school Education; Primary Education; Psychology; Science Education; Secondary Education; Social Work; Teacher Training); **Foreign Languages** (English; French; German; Italian; Modern Languages); **Law** (Law); **Natural Sciences** (Biology; Chemistry; Mathematics; Nursing; Physics); **Social Sciences** (Geography; History; Linguistics; Literature)

History: Founded 1957 as Higher Pedagogical Institute. Acquired present status and title 1991.

Governing Bodies: Senate

Academic Year: October to July (October-January; February-July)

Admission Requirements: Secondary school certificate and entrance examination

Fees: Registration fee for first year students

Main Language(s) of Instruction: Albanian

International Co-operation: With universities in Austria; Italy; Serbia and Montenegro; USA. Also participates in Tempus, INTERREG II,III and CMU programmes

Accrediting Agencies: Ministria e Arsimit dhe Shkences (MASH) (Ministry of Education and Science)

Degrees and Diplomas: *Bachelor – Diplomë e Ciklit të Parë*; *Master Profesional*; *Master i Shkencave/Master i Arteve të Bukura*

Student Services: Academic counselling, Canteen, Cultural centre, Health services, Nursery care, Sports facilities

Student Residential Facilities: Yes

Special Facilities: Exhibition Hall

Libraries: Central Library, 250,000 vols. Department libraries

Publications: Didactics Bulletin *(biannually)*; Natural Sciences Bulletin *(biannually)*; Social Sciences Bulletin *(biannually)*
Last Updated: 20/09/10

POLYTECHNIC UNIVERSITY OF TIRANA

Universiteti Politeknik i Tiranës
Sheshi "Nene Tereza", Nr.4, Tiranë
Tel: +355(42) 27914
Fax: +355(42) 27914
EMail: axhuvani@yahoo.com
Website: http://www.upt.al

Rector: Jorgaq Kacani Fax: +355(42) 27996
EMail: jorkacani@yahoo.com

Vice-Rector: Akli Fundo
Tel: +355(42) 23793 EMail: aklifundo@yahoo.com

Faculties
Construction Engineering (Architecture; Construction Engineering; Environmental Engineering; Geological Engineering; Structural Architecture; Town Planning; Urban Studies); **Electrical Engineering** (Electrical Engineering); **Geology and Mining** (Earth Sciences; Geology; Mining Engineering); **Information Technology** (Electronic Engineering; Information Technology; Telecommunications Engineering); **Mathematical Engineering and Physical Engineering** (Chemistry; Mathematics; Physical Engineering; Physics); **Mechanical Engineering** (Energy Engineering; Mechanical Engineering; Production Engineering; Textile Technology)

Institutes
Energy, Water and Environment (Energy Engineering; Environmental Management; Water Management); **Geo-Sciences** (Geological Engineering; Seismology; Surveying and Mapping)

History: Founded 1957 incorporating former institutes of Engineering, Medicine, Economics, Law and Sciences. Acquired present status 1991.

Governing Bodies: University Council

Academic Year: October to July (October-January; February-July)

Admission Requirements: Secondary school certificate and entrance examination

Fees: None

Main Language(s) of Instruction: Albanian

Accrediting Agencies: Ministria e Arsimit dhe Shkences (MASH) (Ministry of Education and Science)

Degrees and Diplomas: *Bachelor – Diplomë e Ciklit të Parë*; *Bachelor – Diplomë e Ciklit të Parë*: 5 yrs

Student Services: Academic counselling, Cultural centre, Health services, Sports facilities

Special Facilities: Geological Museum

Libraries: Central Library: c. 250,000 vols

Publications: Bulteni i Shkencave Teknike *(bimonthly)*
Last Updated: 21/09/10

SPORTS UNIVERSITY OF TIRANA

Universiteti i Sporteve të Tiranës
Rr. Muhamet Gjollesha, Tiranë
Tel: +355(42) 25354
Fax: +355(42) 26652
EMail: contact@ust.edu.al
Website: http://www.aefs.edu.al

Rector: Vesel Rizvanolli
Tel: +355(42) 26652, Fax: +355(42) 26652
EMail: vrizvanolli@ust.edu.al

Departments
Individual Sports (Sports); **Professional Education and Sciences** (Arts and Humanities; Natural Sciences); **Sports Medicine** (Sports Medicine); **Team Sports** (Sports)

History: Founded 1948. Previously known as Akademia e Edukimit Fizik dhe Sporteve Vojo Kushi (Vojo Kushi Academy of Physical Education). Acquired present title 2010.

Governing Bodies: Senate

Main Language(s) of Instruction: English; Italian; French; German

International Co-operation: Participates in the Tempus programme

Accrediting Agencies: Ministria e Arsimit dhe Shkences (MASH) (Ministry of Education and Science)

Degrees and Diplomas: *Bachelor – Diplomë e Ciklit të Parë*; *Master Profesional*; *Master i Shkencave/Master i Arteve të Bukura*; *Doktor*

Student Residential Facilities: None

Libraries: No

Press or Publishing House: SHBLU

Academic Staff 2007-2008	TOTAL
FULL-TIME	50
PART-TIME	50
STAFF WITH DOCTORATE	
FULL-TIME	15
PART-TIME	c. 5

Student Numbers 2007-2008

All (Foreign Included)	c. 550
FOREIGN ONLY	5

Last Updated: 20/09/10

UNIVERSITY OF TIRANA

Universiteti i Tiranës

Sheshi "Nënë Tereza", Kutia Postare Nr 183, Tiranë
Tel: +355(4) 222-840
Fax: +355(4) 222-3981
EMail: info@unitir.edu.al
Website: http://www.unitir.edu.al

Rector: Dhori Kule EMail: dhorikule@unitir.edu.al

Faculties

Economics (Accountancy; Business Administration; Economics; Finance; Management; Marketing; Tourism); **Foreign Languages** (English; French; German; Italian; Modern Languages); **History and Philology** (Albanian; Geography; History; Journalism; Linguistics; Literature; Philology); **Law** (Civil Law; Criminal Law; Law; Public Law); **Medicine** (Medicine; Pharmacy; Stomatology); **Natural Sciences** (Biology; Biotechnology; Chemistry; Computer Science; Industrial Chemistry; Mathematics; Natural Sciences; Pharmacy; Physics); **Nursing** (Nursing); **Social Sciences** (Pedagogy; Philosophy; Political Sciences; Psychology; Social Work; Sociology)

Further Information: Branches in: Bérat, Durrës, Elbasan, Korça, Shkodër, Vlorë

History: Founded 1957 incorporating former institutes of Engineering, Medicine, Economics, Law and Science.

Governing Bodies: University Senate, Faculty Council

Academic Year: October to July (October-December; January-July).

Admission Requirements: Secondary school certificate and admission exam

Fees: (Leks): 12,500 per annum

Main Language(s) of Instruction: Albanian

International Co-operation: With universities in Italy, Greece, Germany, Macedonia FYROM, USA

Accrediting Agencies: Ministria e Arsimit dhe Shkences (MASH) (Ministry of Education and Science)

Degrees and Diplomas: *Bachelor – Diplomë e Ciklit të Parë:* Law; Social Sciences; Economics; History; Geography; Journalism; Modern Languages, 4 yrs; *Bachelor – Diplomë e Ciklit të Parë:* Medicine, 6 yrs; *Bachelor – Diplomë e Ciklit të Parë:* Stomatology; Physics; Biology, 5 yrs; *Master Profesional; Master i Shkencave/ Master i Arteve të Bukura; Doktor (PhD):* 2 yrs

Student Services: Canteen, Cultural centre, Health services, Sports facilities

Student Residential Facilities: Yes

Special Facilities: Museum of Natural Sciences

Libraries: Central Library, 493,014 vols

Publications: Buletini i shkencave mjeksore; Buletini i shkencave te Natyres; Buletini i shkencave Ekonomike
Last Updated: 20/09/10

UNIVERSITY OF VLORA 'ISMAIL QEMALI'

Universiteti i Vlorës 'Ismail Qemali' (UV)

L. Pavarësia, Vlorë 9400
Tel: +355(33) 222-288
Fax: +355(33) 224-952
EMail: rektor@univlora.edu.al
Website: http://univlora.edu.al/

Rector: Albert Qarri (2012-) EMail: berti.qarri@univlora.edu.al

Executive Assistant: Dorjan Tozaj EMail: dtozaj@univlora.edu.al
International Relations: Erald Pelari
Tel: +355(69) 426-6110 EMail: epelari@univlora.edu.al

Colleges

Economics (Accountancy; Administration; Finance; Hotel and Restaurant; Management; Marketing; Public Administration; Real Estate; Tourism); **Humanities** (Albanian; Educational Sciences; English; Italian; Law; Preschool Education; Special Education; Teacher Training); **Public Health** (Midwifery; Nursing; Public Health); **Technical Sciences and Engineering** (Actuarial Science; Biology; Chemistry; Computer Education; Computer Science; Electrical Engineering; Fishery; Information Technology; Marine Engineering; Marine Science and Oceanography; Mathematics; Mathematics Education; Mechanical Engineering; Physics)

History: Founded 1994 as a Technological University.

Governing Bodies: Academic Senate; Administration Committee; Ethics Committee; Rector; Vice-Rectors; Chancellor

Academic Year: October-January; February-May; July-September

Admission Requirements: Secondary school certificate and entrance examination

Fees: None

Main Language(s) of Instruction: Albanian

Accrediting Agencies: Ministria e Arsimit dhe Shkences (MASH) (Ministry of Education and Science)

Degrees and Diplomas: *Bachelor – Diplomë e Ciklit të Parë:* Business Administration; Engineering; Public Health; Information Sciences; Mathematics and Computer Science; Natural Sciences, 3 yrs; *Master Profesional:* Mechanical Engineering; Information Technology, 1 yr; *Master i Shkencave/Master i Arteve të Bukura:* Mathematics; Mathematics and Physics; Foreign Langauges; Information Technology; Education; Industrial Operations; Naval Engineering, a further 2 yrs; *Doktor:* Mathematics, 5 yrs

Student Services: Academic counselling, Canteen, Employment services, Foreign student adviser, Foreign Studies Centre, Handicapped facilities, Health services, Language programs, Sports facilities

Student Residential Facilities: Yes

Special Facilities: Mathematics laboratories, computer science centre, environment monitoring centre, food and beverage testing centre, amphitheatre.

Libraries: Three libraries

Publications: Albanian Journal of Mathematics, 163 *(quarterly)*; Bulletini Shkencor, Science bulletin *(quarterly)*

Academic Staff 2008-2009	MEN	WOMEN	TOTAL
FULL-TIME	163	182	345
PART-TIME	27	43	70
STAFF WITH DOCTORATE			
FULL-TIME	64	35	99
PART-TIME	9	–	9

Student Numbers 2008-2009

	MEN	WOMEN	TOTAL
All (Foreign Included)	6,270	8,017	14,287
FOREIGN ONLY	2	–	2

Part-time students, 1,246.
Last Updated: 20/09/10

PRIVATE INSTITUTIONS

ALDENT UNIVERSITY

Universiteti Aldent

Rruga e Dibrës, nr.235, Tiranë
Tel: +355(4) 2231-835
EMail: shkollaaldent@hotmail.com
Website: http://www.universitetialdent.com/

President: Adem Alushi

Programmes

Dental Technician (Dental Technology); **Nursing** (Nursing); **Pharmacy** (Pharmacy); **Physical Therapy** (Physical Therapy); **Stomatology** (Stomatology)

History: Created 2009.

Degrees and Diplomas: *Bachelor – Diplomë e Ciklit të Parë:* Nursing; Denetal Technology; *Master i Shkencave/Master i Arteve të Bukura:* Stomatology
Last Updated: 26/03/12

EUROPEAN UNIVERSITY IN TIRANA
Universiteti Europian i Tiranës
Bulevardi "Gjergj Fishta", Nr.2, Tiranë
Tel: +355(4) 2421-806
EMail: info@uet.edu.al/
Website: http://www.uet.edu.al/

Rector: Adrian Civici

Faculties
Economics (Administration; Banking; Business Administration; Economics; Finance; Management); **Law** (Commercial Law; Constitutional Law; European Union Law; International Law; Law; Public Law); **Social Sciences** (International Relations; Political Sciences)

History: Created 2006.

Degrees and Diplomas: *Bachelor – Diplomë e Ciklit të Parë;* *Master Profesional; Master i Shkencave/Master i Arteve të Bukura; Doktor*
Last Updated: 21/09/10

JUSTINIANI I UNIVERSITY
Universiteti Justiniani I
Bulevardi "Zogu I", Tiranë
Tel: +355(4) 2225-280
EMail: info@justinianiipare.com
Website: http://justinianiipare.com/

Rector: Ismet Elezaj

Faculties
Diplomacy (International Relations); **Law** (Civil Law; Criminal Law; Justice Administration; Law; Public Law)

History: Created 2006.

Degrees and Diplomas: *Bachelor – Diplomë e Ciklit të Parë;* *Master Profesional; Master i Shkencave/Master i Arteve të Bukura*
Last Updated: 21/09/10

LUARASI UNIVERSITY
Universiteti Luarasi
Rruga Avdi Kazan, nr.1, Tiranë
Tel: +355(04) 267-200
Fax: +355(04) 267-200
EMail: info@luarasi-univ.edu.al
Website: http://www.luarasi-univ.edu.al

Rector: Aleks Luarasi **EMail:** rector@luarasi-univ.edu.al

Programmes
Law (Civil Law; Criminal Law; Law; Private Law; Public Law); **Public Administration** (Administration; Public Administration)

History: Founded 2003.

Main Language(s) of Instruction: Albanian

Accrediting Agencies: Ministria e Arsimit dhe Shkences (MASH) (Ministry of Education and Science)

Degrees and Diplomas: *Bachelor – Diplomë e Ciklit të Parë;* *Master Profesional; Master i Shkencave/Master i Arteve të Bukura*
Last Updated: 20/09/10

MARIN BARLETI UNIVERSITY
Universiteti 'Marin Barleti'
Rr. "Sami Frashëri", nr. 41, Tiranë
Tel: +355(4) 2240-706
Fax: +355(4) 2250-911
EMail: info@umb.edu.al
Website: http://www.umb.edu.al/

Rector: Nikolla Dhamo **EMail:** rektori@umb.edu.al

Faculties
Economics and Business (Accountancy; Applied Mathematics; Business Administration; Economics; Finance; Management);

Humanities (English; French; German; Law; Modern Languages; Philology; Political Sciences; Psychology; Sociology)

History: Created 2005.

Degrees and Diplomas: *Bachelor – Diplomë e Ciklit të Parë;* *Master Profesional*
Last Updated: 21/09/10

OUR LADY OF GOOD COUNSEL UNIVERSITY
Zoja e Këshillit të Mirë
Rruga r Durresit, Kompleksi Spitalor, Tiranë
Tel: +355(4) 2273-290
Fax: +355(4) 2273-291
EMail: info@unizkm.edu.al
Website: http://www.unizkm.edu.al

Rector: Paolo Ruatti
Vice-Rector: Tritan Shehu

Faculties
Economics and Political Science (Economics; Political Sciences); **Medicine** (Dentistry; Medicine; Nursing; Physical Therapy; Stomatology; Surgery); **Pharmacy** (Pharmacy)

History: Founded 2004.

Accrediting Agencies: Ministria e Arsimit dhe Shkences (MASH) (Ministry of Education and Science)

Degrees and Diplomas: *Bachelor – Diplomë e Ciklit të Parë:* 3-6 yrs; *Master Profesional; Master i Shkencave/Master i Arteve të Bukura*
Last Updated: 21/09/10

POLIS UNIVERSITY INTERNATIONAL SCHOOL OF ARCHITECTURE AND URBAN DEVELOPMENT POLICIES
Universiteti POLIS - Shkolla nderkombetare e Arkitektures dhe politikave te zhvillimit urban (U-POLIS)
Rr. "Vaso Pasha", Nr. 20, Tiranë KP 2995
Tel: +355(4) 22-3922 +355(4) 23-7236
Fax: +355(4) 22-0517
EMail: contact@universitetipolis.edu.al
Website: http://www.universitetipolis.edu.al/

Rector: Besnik Aliaj
Tel: + 355(69) 20-34126
EMail: besnik_aliaj@universitetipolis.edu.al

General Administrator: Sotir Dhamo
Tel: + 355(69) 20-81881
EMail: sotir_dhamo@universitetipolis.edu.al

International Relations: Elona Karafili
Tel: +355(69) 29-38625
EMail: elona_karafili@universitetipolis.edu.al

Departments
Planning and Environment (Environmental Management; Town Planning)

Faculties
Architecture and Design Art (Architectural and Environmental Design; Architecture; Design)

History: Created 2006.

Governing Bodies: Founding Board

Admission Requirements: Diploma e shkolles se mesme (High school Diploma); Entrance exam; English proficiency

Fees: (Euros): Architecture, 4,400 per annum; Urban Planning, 3,900 per annum

Main Language(s) of Instruction: Albanian

International Co-operation: With institutions in Germany and Italy. Also participates in Erasmus

Accrediting Agencies: Agjensia e akreditimit per arsimin e larte (AAAL) (Higher Education Accreditation Agency); Ministria e Arsimit dhe Shkences (MASH) (Ministry of Education and Science)

Degrees and Diplomas: *Bachelor – Diplomë e Ciklit të Parë:* Architecture; Urban Planning; *Master Profesional:* Design; Urban Management; *Master i Shkencave/Master i Arteve të Bukura:* Architecture; Urban Planning

Student Services: Academic counselling, Canteen, Handicapped facilities, Language programs, Social counselling

Student Residential Facilities: None

Special Facilities: Exhibition facilities; Conference suite.

Libraries: The only specialised library in Albania in Habitat Development.

Publications: Forum A + P, Information on research findings of the University and it's partners. *(quarterly)*; U-POLIS Newsletter *(monthly)*

Academic Staff *2007-2008*	MEN	WOMEN	TOTAL
FULL-TIME	8	3	**11**
PART-TIME	26	10	**36**
STAFF WITH DOCTORATE			
FULL-TIME	3	1	**4**
PART-TIME	12	3	**15**
Student Numbers *2007-2008*			
All (Foreign Included)	82	56	**138**
FOREIGN ONLY	–	–	**2**

Last Updated: 21/09/10

UFO UNIVERSITY

Rruga "Kajo Karafili", Nr. 22, Tiranë
Tel: +355(4) 266-374 +355(4) 223-562
Fax: +355(4) 266-374
Website: http://www.ufouniversity.al

Rector: Pavli Kongo

Faculties

Applied Science (Architecture; Finance); **Dentistry** (Dentistry; Pharmacy); **Social Sciences** (Communication Studies; Law; Political Sciences; Psychology)

History: Founded 2004.

Accrediting Agencies: Ministria e Arsimit dhe Shkences (MASH) (Ministry of Education and Science)

Degrees and Diplomas: *Bachelor – Diplomë e Ciklit të Parë*; *Master Profesional*; *Master i Shkencave/Master i Arteve të Bukura*

Last Updated: 20/09/10

UNIVERSITY OF NEW YORK AT TIRANA

Rruga "Komuna e Parisit", PO Box 2301, Tiranë
Tel: +355(4) 273-056 +355(4) 273-057 +355(4) 273-058
Fax: +355(4) 273-059
EMail: admissions@unyt.edu.al; info@unyt.edu.al
Website: http://www.unyt.edu.al

President: Elias Foutsis

Programmes

Administrative Sciences (Business Administration; Economics; Finance; Management; Marketing); **Computing** (Computer Networks; Computer Science; Information Management); **Humanities and Social Studies** (Communication Studies; English; International Relations; Journalism; Law; Political Sciences; Psychology)

History: Founded 2002. Acquired present status 2004.

Accrediting Agencies: Ministria e Arsimit dhe Shkences (MASH) (Ministry of Education and Science)

Degrees and Diplomas: *Bachelor – Diplomë e Ciklit të Parë*; *Master i Shkencave/Master i Arteve të Bukura*. MBA (in collaboration with the Institut Universitaire Kurt Bösch in Sion, Switzerland and the University of Sunderland)

Last Updated: 21/09/10

Algeria

STRUCTURE OF HIGHER EDUCATION SYSTEM

Description:

Higher education is provided by universities, university centres, national schools and institutes, and higher teacher training institutes (Ecoles normales supérieures), which fall under the responsibility of the Ministry of Higher Education and Scientific Research, as well as by institutes run by other Ministries. A National Conference of Universities was created in 2000. It is a coordinating and evaluation body. The higher education system of Algeria started introducing the LMD reform in the 2004/2005 academic year and is now considering opening private institutions.

Stages of studies:

University level first stage:
At undergraduate level, higher education is divided into a short (three-year) cycle, leading to a Diplôme d'Etudes universitaires appliquées (DEUA), and a long (four- to seven-year) cycle, leading to the Licence, the Diplôme d'Etudes supérieures, the Diplôme d'Ingénieur or the Diplôme de Docteur. Courses for the Diplôme in Engineering, Dental Surgery, Pharmacy, Architecture and Veterinary Medicine last for five years while the title of Doctor in Medicine is awarded after seven years' study. In 2004/2005 a new undergraduate level consisting of a Licence awarded three years after the Baccalauréat was introduced as part of the three-tier system reform which is in the process of being implemented.

University level second stage:
The Master is awarded after two years' study after the new Licence in three years.

University level third stage:
The last stage leads to the Doctorat. Lasting three years, studies involve individual research work and submission of a thesis.

ADMISSION TO HIGHER EDUCATION

Admission to university-level studies:

Name of secondary school credential required: Baccalauréat

Alternatives to credentials: Specific competitive examinations give access to certain streams (filières) to candidates having attended third-year classes without obtaining the Baccalauréat. Postsecondary programmes in sports, fine arts, music and youth affairs admit students on the basis of an aptitude test rather than Baccalauréat results.

Foreign students admission:

Entrance exam requirements: Students must hold the Baccalauréat or an equivalent qualification.

Entry regulations: Foreign students must hold a visa or copy of the agreement between their country and Algeria (e.g. proof of an equivalence agreement).

Language requirements: Students must have good knowledge of Arabic. Arabic language courses are compulsory for specialized studies.

NATIONAL BODIES

Ministère de l'Enseignement supérieur et de la Recherche scientifique (Ministry of Higher Education and Scientific Research)
Minister: Rachid Haraoubia
Secretary-General: Mohamed Gherras
Director: Arezki Saidani
11 Chemin Doudou Mokhtar
Ben Aknoun
Alger

Tel: +213 2191 2323
Fax: +213 2191 1717
EMail: info@mesrs.dz
WWW: http://www.mesrs.dz/
Role of national body: Coordinates higher education.

Agence nationale pour le Développement de la Recherche universitaire - ANDRU (National Agency for the Development of Academic Research)
Head: L. Ghazi
Av. Pasteur Hacène Badi (INA)
BP 62
El Hanach 16200
Tel: +213 2152 6801/2
Fax: 0213 2152 6240
EMail: contacts@andru.gov.dz
WWW: http://www.andru.gov.dz

Data for academic year: 2009-2010
Source: IAU from the website of the Ministry of Higher Education and documentation, 2009, Bodies updated in 2011

INSTITUTIONS

08 MAY 45 UNIVERSITY OF GUELMA
Université 08 mai 45 de Guelma
BP 401, Avenue du 19 mai 1956, 24000 Guelma
Tel: +213(37) 20-62-95
Fax: +213(37) 20-87-58
EMail: recteur@univ-guelma.dz
Website: http://www.univ-guelma.dz

Recteur: Mohamed Nemamcha
Tel: +213(37) 20-62-95, Fax: +213(37) 20-87-58
EMail: nemamcha@yahoo.fr

Faculties
Economics and Management (Accountancy; Economics; Management; Taxation); **Humanities and Social Sciences** (Arts and Humanities; Communication Studies; Information Sciences; Psychology; Social Sciences; Sociology); **Languages and Letters** (Arabic; English; French; Literature); **Law and Political Science** (Law; Political Sciences); **Matter Sciences and Mathematics in Computing Science** (Computer Science; Materials Engineering; Mathematics; Physics); **Natural Sciences** (Agronomy; Biology; Ecology; Natural Sciences); **Science and Engineering** (Civil Engineering; Computer Engineering; Electrical and Electronic Engineering; Industrial Engineering; Mechanical Engineering)

History: Founded 1992 as Centre universitaire de Guelma. Acquired present status 2001, modified 2004 and 2010.

Degrees and Diplomas: *Licence (LMD)*; *Master*; *Doctorat*

Libraries: 186.68,400 vols.
Last Updated: 05/03/12

20 AUGUST 1955 UNIVERSITY OF SKIKDA
Université 20 août 1955 de Skikda
BP 26, 26 Route El Hadaiek, 21000 Skikda
Tel: +213(38) 70-10-24
EMail: rectorat@univ-skikda.dz
Website: http://www.univ-skikda.dz

Recteur: Ali Kouadria Tel: +213(38) 70-10-00

Vice-Recteur: Mouloud Belachia EMail: belachia@yahoo.fr

International Relations: Amara Otmani
EMail: amara_otmani@yahoo.fr

Faculties
Engineering (Civil Engineering; Computer Engineering; Electrical Engineering; Mechanical Engineering); **Law** (Administration; Law); **Management and Economics**; **Science** (Agriculture; Biological and Life Sciences; Biology; Mathematics and Computer Science; Natural Sciences; Physics); **Social Sciences and Human Sciences** (Arabic; English; French; Literature; Psychology; Social Sciences; Sociology)

History: Founded 1986. Acquired present status 2001.

Academic Year: September to June

Fees: (Algerian Dinars): 200 per annum

Main Language(s) of Instruction: Arabic and French

Degrees and Diplomas: *Diplôme d'Etudes universitaires appliquées*; *Licence (LMD)*; *Diplôme d'Etudes supérieures*; *Diplôme d'Ingénieur*

Student Residential Facilities: Yes

Libraries: One central library and one library in each faculty

Academic Staff 2008-2009	MEN	WOMEN	TOTAL
FULL-TIME	208	222	430
PART-TIME	222	74	296
STAFF WITH DOCTORATE			
FULL-TIME	313	263	576
PART-TIME	–	–	433
Student Numbers 2008-2009			
All (Foreign Included)	6,956	13,072	20,028
FOREIGN ONLY	36	29	65

Last Updated: 29/05/09

ABBÈS LAGHROUR UNIVERSITY CENTRE OF KHENCHELA
Centre Universitaire Abbès Laghrour Khenchela
BP 1252, Route de Constantine, El Houria, 4004 Khenchela
Tel: +213(32) 33-19-66
Fax: +213(32) 33-19-63
EMail: cuniv_khenchela@cuniv-khenchela.edu.dz
Website: http://www.cuniv-khenchela.edu.dz

Directeur: Azzeddine Haftari

Institutes

Economics, Commerce and Management (Business and Commerce; Economics; Management); **Law and Administration** (Administration; Law); **Literature and Languages** (Literature; Modern Languages); **Natural and Life Sciences** (Biochemistry; Biology; Ecology; Genetics); **Science and Technology** (Computer Science; Technology)

History: Founded 2001.

Degrees and Diplomas: *Diplôme d'Etudes universitaires appliquées; Licence (LMD); Diplôme d'Ingénieur; Master*
Last Updated: 16/02/09

ABDELHAK BENHAMOUDA UNIVERSITY OF JIJEL

Université Abdelhak Benhamouda de Jijel
BP 98, Ouled Aissa, 18000 Jijel
Tel: +213(34) 49-80-16
Fax: +213(34) 49-55-78
Website: http://www.univ-jijel.dz

Recteur: Abdelmalek Zenir

Faculties

Engineering; **Law and Political Sciences** (Law; Political Sciences); **Management** (Business and Commerce; Economics; Management); **Modern Languages and Social Sciences** (Arabic; English; French; Sociology); **Science** (Biochemistry; Biology; Chemistry; Ecology; Geology; Mathematics; Microbiology; Physics)

History: Founded 2003

Degrees and Diplomas: *Diplôme d'Etudes universitaires appliquées*: Computer Science; Biology; International Trade, 6 semesters; *Licence (LMD)*: Mathematics; Physics; Chemistry; Management; Law, 4 yrs; *Diplôme d'Ingénieur*: Biology; Electrical and Electronic Engineering; Civil Engineering; Chemical Engineering; Automation; Computer Science; Agronomy; Geology; Regional Planning, 5 yrs; *Master*

Libraries: 80,000 vols
Last Updated: 03/09/09

ABDELHAMID IBN BADIS UNIVERSITY OF MOSTAGANEM

Université Abdelhamid Ibn Badis de Mostaganem (UNIV MOSTA)
BP 227, 27000 Mostaganem
Tel: +213(45) 26-54-55 +213(45) 30-10-18/19
Fax: +213(45) 26-54-52 +213(45) 30-10-16
EMail: recteur@univ-mosta.dz
Website: http://www.univ-mosta.dz

Rector: Mohammed Salah Eddine Seddiki

Secretary General: Ouinassa Abid Charef
Tel: +213(45) 30-10-20, Fax: +213(45) 30-10-20

International Relations: Ahmed Chaalal
Tel: Vice-Rector, International Relations, Fax: +213(45) 30-10-43

Faculties

Arts and Humanities *Dean*: Farid Benramdane; **Engineering** (Architecture; Civil Engineering; Computer Science; Electronic Engineering; Engineering; Industrial Chemistry; Mathematics; Measurement and Precision Engineering; Mechanical Engineering) *Dean*: Fodil Hamzaoui; **Law and Commerce** *Dean*: Nourreddine Cherif Touil; **Natural Sciences** (Agronomy; Biology; Chemistry; Civil Engineering; Computer Science; Electronic Engineering; Mathematics; Measurement and Precision Engineering; Mechanical Engineering; Natural Sciences; Physics) *Dean*: Abdallah Berkani; **Social Sciences** (Communication Studies; Psychology; Social Sciences; Sociology) *Dean*: Djillali Hadj Smaha

Institutes

Physical Training and Sports *Dean*: Khelifa Said Aissa

History: Founded 1978 as Centre universitaire de Mostaganem. Acquired present status and title 1998, modified in 2004.

Academic Year: September-June

Admission Requirements: Baccalaureat

Fees: (Algerian Dinars): 200

Main Language(s) of Instruction: Arabic, French, English
International Co-operation: Participates in Erasmus Mundus; Tempus

Degrees and Diplomas: *Diplôme d'Etudes universitaires appliquées (DEAU)*: 3 yrs; *Licence (LMD)*: Fine Arts; Arabic; French; English; Spanish; Arts and Humanity; Social Sciences; Law; Physical Training and Sports; Mathematics; Computer Science; Civil Engineering; Electric Engineering; Mechanical Engineering, 3 yrs; *Diplôme d'Ingénieur*: Computer Science; Civil Engineering; Electric Engineering; Mechanical Engineering; Architecture; Electronic Engineering, 5 yrs; *Licence*: Fine Arts; Arabic; French; English; Spanish; Communication Studies; Psychology; Sociology; Mathematics; Physical Training; Sports; Computer Science; Civil Engineering; Electric Engineering; Mechanical Engineering, 4 yrs; *Master*: Fine Arts; Civil Engineering; Mechanical Engineering; Law; Social Sciences; Communication Studies; Training Science; Psychology, 5 yrs; *Doctorat*: French; English; Arabic; Chemistry; Physics; Mathematics; Physical Training and Sports, 8-10 yrs. Also Magistère (6 yrs): Mathematics; Engineering; Arts and Humanities; Social Sciences; Physical Training and Sports; Arabic; English; Law; Business and Commerce; Psychology; Sociology; Agronomy; Biology; Physics; Natural Sciences; Architecture

Student Services: Academic counselling, Canteen, Cultural centre, Employment services, Foreign student adviser, Handicapped facilities, Health services, Nursery care, Social counselling, Sports facilities

Libraries: Central Library, c. 109.080 vols
Publications: Revue des Sciences de l'Ingénieur

Academic Staff 2008-2009	MEN	WOMEN	TOTAL
FULL-TIME	352	262	**614**
STAFF WITH DOCTORATE FULL-TIME	154	23	**177**
Student Numbers 2008-2009			
All (Foreign Included)	–	–	**27,668**
FOREIGN ONLY	–	–	**170**

Last Updated: 16/09/09

ABDELLAH ARBAOUI NATIONAL SCHOOL OF HYDRAULIC ENGINEERING OF BLIDA

Ecole nationale supérieure d'Hydraulique Abdellah Arbaoui de Blida (ENSH)
BP 31, 09000 Blida
Tel: +213(25) 39-94-47
Fax: +213(25) 39-94-46
EMail: miah@ensh.edu.dz
Website: http://www.ensh.dz

Directeur: M.S. Benhafid EMail: mbenhafid@ensh.dz

Programmes

Hydraulic Engineering and Environment (Environmental Engineering; Hydraulic Engineering); **Irrigation and Draining** (Irrigation); **Non-conventional Water Re-use** (Water Management; Water Science); **Urban Hydraulics** (Hydraulic Engineering); **Urban Techniques** (Urban Studies)

History: Founded 1972. Acquired present status 1998.

Degrees and Diplomas: *Diplôme d'Ingénieur; Master*
Last Updated: 16/02/09

ABDERAHMANE MIRA UNIVERSITY OF BÉJAÏA

Université Abderrahmane Mira de Béjaïa
Route de Terga Ouzemour, 06000 Béjaïa
Tel: +213(34) 21-43-33
Fax: +213(34) 21-43-32
EMail: rectorat@univ-bejaia.dz
Website: http://www.univ-bejaia.dz

Recteur: Djoudi Merabet EMail: Dmerabet@univ_bejaia.dz

Secrétaire général: Brahim Mira

Faculties

Arts and Humanities (Arabic; Arts and Humanities; English; French; Literature; Modern Languages; Oriental Languages); **Economics, Commerce and Management**; **Exact Sciences** (Chemistry; Computer Science; Mathematics; Operations Research;

Physics); **Law** (Business and Commerce; Economics; Law; Management); **Medicine** (Medicine); **Natural and Life Sciences**; **Technology** (Civil Engineering; Earth Sciences; Electronic Engineering; Hydraulic Engineering; Mechanical Engineering)

History: Founded 1983 as Centre universitaire de Béjaia. Acquired present status 1998, modified in 2004.

Degrees and Diplomas: *Diplôme d'Etudes universitaires appliquées*; *Licence (LMD)*; *Diplôme d'Etudes supérieures*; *Diplôme d'Ingénieur*; *Doctorat*

Last Updated: 16/02/09

ADVANCED SCHOOL OF COMMERCE

Ecole supérieure de Commerce (ESC)
1 Rampe Salah Gharbi, Alger
Tel: +213(21) 42-32-31
Fax: +213(21) 42-37-32
EMail: contact@esc-alger.com
Website: http://www.esc-alger.com

Departments
Accountancy (Accountancy); **Finance** (Finance); **Management** (Management); **Marketing** (Marketing)

Degrees and Diplomas: *Licence (LMD)*; *Master*; *Doctorat*
Last Updated: 17/02/09

AKLI MOHAND OULHAD UNIVERSITY CENTRE OF BOUIRA

Centre Universitaire Akli Mohand Oulhadj de Bouira
Bouira
EMail: info@cu-bouira.dz
Website: http://www.cu-bouira.dz

Directeur: Ahmed Hidouch

Institutes
Economics (Economics); **Languages and Arabic Literature** (Arabic; Literature; Modern Languages); **Law** (Law)

History: Founded 2005.

Main Language(s) of Instruction: Arabic
Last Updated: 25/06/09

ALGERIAN BUSINESS SCHOOL

Ecole supérieure algérienne des Affaires
BP 63F, Les Pins Maritimes, Mohammadia, 16130 Alger
Tel: +213(21) 21 90 09
Fax: +213(21) 21 00 89
EMail: contact@esaa.dz
Website: http://www.esaa.dz

Directeur: Bruno Ponson **EMail:** bponson@esaa.dz

Programmes
Business Administration (Business Administration); **Management** (Management)

History: Founded 2005.

Main Language(s) of Instruction: French

Degrees and Diplomas: *Master*. Also MBA
Last Updated: 16/02/09

ALGERIAN PETROLEUM INSTITUTE

Institut algérien du Pétrole
Avenue 1er Novembre, 35000 Boumerdès
Tel: +213(24) 81 90 56
EMail: iap@iap.dz
Website: http://www.iap.dz

President: Salah Khebri

Departments
Petroleum Economics & Management (Economics; Management)

Units
Drilling, Production & Reservoir Engineering; Gas Engineering and Refining; Geosciences and Mines (Geological Engineering; Geology; Geophysics; Mining Engineering); **Industrial Main-** tenance (Industrial Maintenance); **Instrumentation & Electrical Engineering; Languages and Communication** (English); **Polymers, Petrochemicals & Plastics** (Petrology; Polymer and Plastics Technology)

Further Information: Also branches in Oran and Skikda

History: Founded 1965.

Degrees and Diplomas: *Master*
Last Updated: 26/06/09

AMAR TELIDJI UNIVERSITY OF LAGHOUAT

Université Amar Telidji de Laghouat (UATL)
BP 37 G, route de Ghardaia, 03000 Laghouat
Tel: +213(29) 93-17-91
Fax: +213(29) 93-26- 98
EMail: dep.inf@mail.lagh-univ.dz
Website: http://web.lagh-univ.dz/web/fr/index.php

Recteur: Azib Makhlouf
Tel: +213(29) 93-10-24, Fax: +213(29) 93-26-98

Faculties
Economics and Management (Economics; Management); **Engineering** (Architecture; Biology; Civil Engineering; Computer Engineering; Electrical Engineering; Engineering; Hydraulic Engineering; Industrial Chemistry; Mechanical Engineering; Technology); **Law and Humanities** (Arabic; English; Law; Psychology; Social Sciences; Sociology)

History: Founded 1986 as a high school for technical teaching. Became university centre 1997. Acquired present status 2001, modified in 2004.

Governing Bodies: Conseil d'orientation

Admission Requirements: Secondary school certificate (baccalauréat)

Fees: None

Main Language(s) of Instruction: Arabic and French

Degrees and Diplomas: *Diplôme d'Etudes universitaires appliquées*: 3 yrs; *Licence (LMD)*: 4 yrs; *Diplôme d'Ingénieur*: Engineering, 5 yrs

Student Services: Health services, Sports facilities

Libraries: Yes
Last Updated: 16/02/09

AMINE ELOKKAL EL HADJ MOUSSA EGAKHAMOUK UNIVERSITY CENTRE OF TAMANRASSET

Centre Universitaire Amine Elokkal El Hadj Moussa Egakhamouk de Tamanrasset
Tamanrasset

Institutes
Humanities (Arts and Humanities); **Law** (Law)

History: Founded 2005.
Last Updated: 26/04/07

BADJI MOKHTAR UNIVERSITY OF ANNABA

Université Badji Mokhtar Annaba
BP 12 Sidi Ammar, 23000 Annaba
Tel: +213(38) 87-24-10
Fax: +213(38) 87-24-36
EMail: abdelkrim.kadi@univ-annaba.org
Website: http://www.univ-annaba.org

Recteur: Abdelkrim Kadi
Tel: +213(38) 87-15-19 **EMail:** laskri@univ-annaba.org

Secrétaire général: Saïd Arabi
Tel: +213(38) 87-15-19 **EMail:** sg@univ-annaba.org

International Relations: L'hadi Atoui **EMail:** atouilhadi@yahoo.fr

Faculties
Arts and Humanities and Social Sciences (Arabic; Arts and Humanities; Modern Languages; Psychology; Sociology; Translation and Interpretation); **Earth Sciences** *(Sidi-Amar)* (Agronomy; Earth Sciences; Geology; Mining Engineering; Regional Planning); **Economics and Management** *(Sidi-Achour)* (Communication

Studies; Economics; Finance; Management); **Engineering** *(Sidi Amar)* (Civil Engineering; Computer Science; Electronic Engineering; Hydraulic Engineering; Materials Engineering; Mechanical Engineering; Production Engineering); **Law** *(Annaba)* (Law; Political Sciences; Private Law; Public Law); **Medicine** D:/ Pagination/33-PALGRAV/IHU24-3980993/DZ*(Annaba)* (Medicine; Pharmacy; Stomatology); **Science** (Biochemistry; Biology; Chemistry; Marine Science and Oceanography; Mathematics; Physics)

Research Centres
Entrepreneurial Training (Management); **Environment** (Environmental Studies; Sanitary Engineering); **Industrial Health** (Occupational Health); **Materials Science** (Materials Engineering)

History: Founded 1975 as Institute of Mining and Metallurgy, acquired present status 1988.

Governing Bodies: Conseil d'Université; Conseil scientifique

Academic Year: September to July (September-February; March-July)

Admission Requirements: Secondary school certificate (baccalauréat) or foreign equivalent

Main Language(s) of Instruction: Arabic, French

Accrediting Agencies: Ministry of Higher Education and Scientific Research

Degrees and Diplomas: *Licence (LMD)*: 4 yrs; *Diplôme d'Etudes supérieures*: 4 yrs; *Diplôme d'Ingénieur*: 5 yrs; *Master*: 2 yrs; *Doctorat*: a further 4 yrs

Student Services: Canteen, Cultural centre, Handicapped facilities, Health services, Sports facilities

Libraries: Central Library, c. 400,000 vols; libraries of the faculties and departments

Publications: El - Tawassol *(biannually)*; Synthèse *(biannually)*
Last Updated: 03/06/09

BÉCHAR UNIVERSITY
Université de Béchar
BP 417 Route Kenadsa-Béchar, 08000 Béchar
Tel: +213(7) 81-55-81
Fax: +213(7) 81-52-44
EMail: a.slimani@mesrs.dz
Website: http://www.univ-bechar.dz/

Recteur: Slimani Abd Al-Kader

Faculties
Economics, Management and Commerce (Business and Commerce; Economics; Management); **Law and Political Science** (Administration; Law; Political Sciences); **Literature, Languages, and Human and Social Sciences** (Arabic; Arts and Humanities; English; French; History; Literature; Social Sciences; Translation and Interpretation); **Science and Technology** (Architecture; Biology; Computer Science; Materials Engineering; Technology)

Institutes
Electrical Engineering (Electrical Engineering)
History: Founded 1986. Acquired present status 2009.

Degrees and Diplomas: *Diplôme d'Etudes universitaires appliquées*; *Licence (LMD)*; *Diplôme d'Ingénieur*; *Master*; *Doctorat*
Last Updated: 25/06/09

COLONEL AHMED DRAYA UNIVERSITY - ADRAR
Université Colonel Ahmed Draïa - Adrar
Rue 11 décembre, 1960 Adrar
Tel: +213(49) 96-85-32
Fax: +213(49) 96-75-71
EMail: recteur@univadrar.org
Website: http://www.univadrar.org/francais/Francais.html

Recteur: A. Abassi

Faculties
Arts and Humanities (Arabic; Business and Commerce; English; Law; Literature; Management; Political Sciences); **Science and Engineering**; **Social Sciences and Islamic Studies**
History: Founded 2001. Acquired present status 2004.

Degrees and Diplomas: *Licence (LMD)*; *Master*
Last Updated: 16/02/09

DJILLALI LIABES UNIVERSITY OF SIDI BEL ABBÈS
Université Djillali Liabes de Sidi Bel Abbès
BP 89, 22000 Sidi-Bel-Abbès
Tel: +213(48) 54-30-18
Fax: +213(48) 54-11-52
EMail: rectorat@univ-sba.dz
Website: http://www.univ-sba.dz

Recteur: Abdel Nacer Tou

Faculties
Economics *Dean*: M. Dani Elkbir; **Engineering** *Dean*: A. Khalfi; **Humanities** (Arts and Humanities; Literature) *Dean*: N. Sebbar; **Law** *Dean*: B. Mekelkel; **Medicine** (Medicine) *Dean*: A. Djadel; **Science** (Biology; Chemistry; Mathematics; Natural Sciences; Physics) *Dean*: M. Benyahya

History: Founded 1978. Acquired present status 1989, modified 2004.

Degrees and Diplomas: *Diplôme d'Etudes universitaires appliquées*; *Licence (LMD)*; *Diplôme d'Etudes supérieures*; *Diplôme d'Ingénieur*; *Master*; *Doctorat*
Last Updated: 10/09/09

DR YAHIA FARÈS UNIVERSITY OF MEDEA
Université Dr Yahia Farès de Médéa
Quartier Ain D'heb, 26000 Médéa
Tel: +213(25) 58-16-87
Fax: +213(25) 58-28-09
EMail: sg@univ-medea.dz
Website: http://www.univ-medea.dz/fr

Recteur: Saadane Chebaiki (2005-)
EMail: rectorat@univ-medea.dz

Faculties
Economic, Trading and Management (Business and Commerce; Economics; Management); **Law** (Law); **Sciences and Technology** (Civil Engineering; Electrical and Electronic Engineering; Industrial Chemistry; Mechanical Engineering); **Social Sciences, Arts and Humanities, Communication Studies**

History: Founded 2000. Acquired present status 2004.

Academic Year: September to June (September-December; January-March; April-June)

Admission Requirements: Baccalaureat (A-Level)

Fees: (Algerian Dinars): 200 per annum

Main Language(s) of Instruction: Arabic, French

Accrediting Agencies: Ministry of Higher Education and Scientific Research

Degrees and Diplomas: *Diplôme d'Etudes universitaires appliquées*: Management (Business Computing), 3 yrs; *Licence (LMD)*: Law; Economic; Management; Trading; Literature; Arabic; French; Communication Studies, 4 yrs; *Diplôme d'Ingénieur*: Electrical and Electronic Engineering; Civil Engineering; Industrial Chemistry; Mechanical Engineering, 5 yrs; *Master*: Civil Engineering; Electrical and Electronic Engineering; Industrial Chemistry; Economic; Management; Trading; Arabic Literature; French, 2 yrs

Student Services: Canteen, Cultural centre, Health services, Nursery care, Sports facilities

Student Residential Facilities: Yes

Libraries: Central Library
Last Updated: 21/04/09

EMIR ABDELKADER UNIVERSITY OF ISLAMIC SCIENCES, CONSTANTINE
Université des Sciences Islamiques Emir Abdelkader
BP 137, 25000 Constantine
Tel: +213(31) 93-92-92
Fax: +213(31) 93-80-73
Website: http://www.univ-emir.dz

Faculties

Humanities (Administration; Arabic; Arts and Humanities; Economics; Koran; Literature); **Oussoul Eddine, Shariah and Islamic Civilization** (Islamic Law; Islamic Studies; Islamic Theology)

History: Founded 1984. Acquired present status 2004.

Academic Year: September to June (September-February; February-June)

Admission Requirements: Secondary school certificate (baccalauréat)

Fees: None

Main Language(s) of Instruction: Arabic

Degrees and Diplomas: *Licence (LMD)*: 4 yrs; *Doctorat*: a further 2 yrs

Student Residential Facilities: Yes

Libraries: University library, c. 10 000 vols

Publications: Revue de l'Université *(biannually)*

Press or Publishing House: Emir Abdelkader University Press
Last Updated: 30/04/07

FERHAT ABBAS UNIVERSITY OF SÉTIF

Université Ferhat Abbas de Sétif
Cité Mabouda, 19000 Sétif
Tel: +213(36) 90-00-80
Fax: +213(36) 90-38-79
EMail: sg@univ-setif.dz
Website: http://www.univ-setif.dz

Recteur: Chekib-Arslane Baki
Tel: +213(36) 92-51-20, Fax: +213(36) 92-51-27
EMail: recteur@univ-setif.dz

Faculties

Arts and Social Sciences (Arabic; Arts and Humanities; Modern Languages; Psychology; Social Sciences; Sociology); **Economics and Management**; **Engineering** (Architecture; Civil Engineering; Computer Science; Electronic Engineering; Engineering; Industrial Chemistry; Measurement and Precision Engineering); **Law** (Law; Private Law; Public Law); **Medicine** (Medicine; Pharmacy); **Science** (Biology; Chemistry; Mathematics; Physics)

History: Founded 1978 as Centre universitaire, acquired present status and title 1989, modified 2004.

Academic Year: September to June (September-January; March-June)

Admission Requirements: Secondary school certificate (baccalauréat)

Main Language(s) of Instruction: Arabic, French

Accrediting Agencies: Ministry of Higher Education and Scientific Research

Degrees and Diplomas: *Licence (LMD)*: 4 yrs; *Diplôme d'Etudes supérieures*: 4 yrs; *Diplôme d'Ingénieur*. 5 yrs; *Master*

Student Residential Facilities: Yes

Libraries: c. 100,000 vols
Last Updated: 17/02/09

HADJ LAKHDAR UNIVERSITY OF BATNA

Université Hadj Lakhdar de Batna
1, rue Chahid Boukhlouf Mohamed El Hadi, 05000 Batna
Tel: +213(33) 81-47-07
Fax: +213(33) 81-24-80
EMail: recteur@univ-batna.dz
Website: http://www.univ-batna.dz

Recteur: Moussa Zereg Tel: +213(33) 81-24-80

Secrétaire général: Rachid Fourtas

Faculties

Economics and Management (Economics; Management) *Dean*: Aissa Merazga; **Engineering** (Architecture; Civil Engineering; Computer Engineering; Electronic Engineering; Engineering; Hydraulic Engineering; Hygiene; Industrial Engineering; Mechanical Engineering; Safety Engineering) *Dean*: Noureddine Bouguechal; **Humanities** (Arts and Humanities) *Dean*: Abdelmadjid Amrani; **Law** (Law) *Dean*: Hocine Kadri; **Medicine** (Health Sciences; Medicine;

Pharmacy) *Dean*: Hachemi Makhloufi; **Science** (Agronomy; Biology; Chemistry; Earth Sciences; Mathematics; Natural Sciences; Physics; Veterinary Science) *Dean*: Tahar Bendaikha; **Social Sciences and Islamic Sciences** (Islamic Studies; Social Sciences) *Dean*: Saïd Fekra

Institutes

Hygiene and Industrial Security (Industrial Maintenance)

History: Founded 1977 as Centre universitaire. Acquired present status 2001, modified 2004.

Degrees and Diplomas: *Diplôme d'Etudes universitaires appliquées*; *Licence (LMD)*; *Diplôme de Docteur*. Medicine, 6 yrs; *Diplôme de Docteur*. Veterinary Medicine, 5 yrs; *Diplôme d'Ingénieur*; *Master*

Libraries: Central University Library

Press or Publishing House: University of Batna Press
Last Updated: 17/02/09

HASSIBA BEN BOUALI UNIVERSITY OF CHLEF

Université Hassiba Ben Bouali de Chlef
Hay Salem, route nationale N° 19, 02000 Chlef
Tel: +213(27) 72-28-77
Fax: +213(27) 72-17-88
EMail: info@univ-chlef.dz; univ-chlef@wissal.dz
Website: http://www.univ-chlef.dz/

Recteur: Abdellah Ouagued EMail: recunivchlef02@yahoo.fr

Faculties

Agronomy and Biological Sciences (Agronomy; Earth Sciences); **Economics and Management** (Economics; Management); **Humanities and Languages** (Arabic; Arts and Humanities; Literature; Social Sciences); **Law and Administration** (Administration; Law); **Science and Engineering** (Engineering)

Institutes

Physical Education (Physical Education)

History: Founded 1983. Acquired present status 2001, modified 2006.

Degrees and Diplomas: *Licence (LMD)*; *Master*
Last Updated: 30/04/07

HIGHER TEACHER TRAINING SCHOOL OF KOUBA

Ecole normale supérieure de Kouba (ENS-KOUBA)
BP 92, 16050 Kouba, Alger
Tel: +213(21) 29-75-11
Fax: +213(21) 28-20-67
EMail: info@ens-kouba.dz
Website: http://www.ens-kouba.dz

Directeur: Abdelhamid Meraghni (2000-)
EMail: meraghni@ens-kouba.dz

Sous-Directeur: Omar Guenane

International Relations: Abdelmalek Bouzari, Chef de Service des Relations extérieures
EMail: malek_bouzari@yahoo.fr; bouzari@ens-kouba.dz

Departments

Chemistry (Chemistry); **Computer Science** (Computer Science); **Distance Education**; **Educational Sciences** (Education; Educational Sciences); **Mathematics** (Mathematics); **Music** (Music); **Natural Sciences** (Natural Sciences); **Physics** (Physics); **Postgraduate Studies and Scientific Research**

History: Founded 1964.

Academic Year: September to June

Admission Requirements: Baccalaureat; Licence for Post Graduate Studies

Main Language(s) of Instruction: Arabic, French, English

International Co-operation: With universities in France, Italy and Spain

Degrees and Diplomas: *Licence (LMD)*; *Master*; *Doctorat*

Student Services: Cultural centre, Health services, Language programs, Nursery care, Social counselling, Sports facilities

Special Facilities: Movie and audiovisual room; Internet

Libraries: Central and Department Library

Publications: Cahier d'Ibn al-Haytham, Information Bullettin related to Mathematics *(quarterly)*; Revue Maghrébine de Mathématiques, Scientific review *(annually)*

Academic Staff *2008-2009*	TOTAL
FULL-TIME	221
PART-TIME	182
STAFF WITH DOCTORATE	
FULL-TIME	42
PART-TIME	19

Student Numbers *2008-2009*
All (Foreign Included) **6,170**

Distance students, 1,913. Evening students, 4,257.
Last Updated: 12/05/09

HIGHER TECHNICAL TEACHER TRAINING SCHOOL OF ORAN

Ecole normale supérieure d'Enseignement technique d'Oran (ENSET)
BP 1523, El-M'naouer, 31000 Oran
Tel: +213(41) 41-98-05
Fax: +213(41) 41-98-06
Website: http://www.enset-oran.dz

Directeur: Abdelbaki Benziane EMail: benziane_baki@yahoo.fr

Departments

Chemistry (Chemistry); **Civil Engineering** (Civil Engineering); **Electrical Engineering** (Electrical Engineering); **Mathematics** (Mathematics); **Mechanical Engineering** (Mechanical Engineering); **Physics** (Physics)

History: Founded 1970 as Ecole Normale Supérieure d'Enseignement polytechnique, became Ecole normale supérieure d'Enseignement technique 1984.

Degrees and Diplomas: Diplôme de Professeur de l'Enseignement Secondaire Technique; Postgraduation
Last Updated: 03/09/09

HOUARI BOUMEDIÈNE UNIVERSITY OF SCIENCE AND TECHNOLOGY

Université des Sciences et de la Technologie Houari Boumediène (USTHB)
BP 32, El Alia, Bab-Ezzouar, 16123 Alger
Tel: +213(21) 24-79-50
Fax: +213(21) 24-79-92
EMail: recteur@usthb.dz
Website: http://www.usthb.dz

Recteur: Benali Benzaghou

Faculties

Biological Sciences (Biological and Life Sciences); **Chemistry** (Chemistry); **Civil Engineering** (Civil Engineering); **Earth Sciences and Regional Planning** (Earth Sciences; Geography; Geology; Geophysics; Regional Planning) *Dean:* H. Benhallou; **Electronic and Computer Science** *Dean:* A. Aissani; **Mathematics**; **Mechanical and Process Engineering** (Mechanical Engineering; Systems Analysis); **Physics** (Physics)

History: Founded 1974, acquired present status 1984, modified 2004.

Governing Bodies: Scientific Council

Academic Year: September to June (September-December; January-April; April-June)

Admission Requirements: Secondary school certificate (baccalauréat)

Main Language(s) of Instruction: Arabic, French

Accrediting Agencies: Ministry of Higher Education and Scientific Research

Degrees and Diplomas: *Diplôme d'Etudes universitaires appliquées:* 3 yrs; *Licence (LMD)*; *Diplôme d'Etudes supérieures:* 3-4 yrs; *Diplôme d'Ingénieur.* 5 yrs; *Master*, Doctorat

Student Services: Academic counselling, Canteen, Cultural centre, Employment services, Health services, Social counselling, Sports facilities

Special Facilities: Earth Sciences Museum. Biological Garden. Experimental Station (In Sahara, Beni Abbes)

Libraries: Central Library, c. 30,000 vols; Faculty libraries
Last Updated: 17/02/09

IBN KHALDOUN UNIVERSITY OF TIARET

Université Ibn Khaldoun de Tiaret (UIKT)
BP 78, Zaaroura, 14000 Tiaret
Tel: +213(46) 42-42-13
Fax: +213(46) 42-47-10
EMail: rectorat@mail.univ-tiaret.dz
Website: http://www.univ-tiaret.dz

Recteur: Nasreddine Hadj-Zoubir (1997-)
Tel: +213(46) 45-22-14 EMail: hadj_zoubir@univ-tiaret.dz

Faculties

Agronomy and Veterinary Science (Agronomy; Biology; Veterinary Science); **Humanities and Social Sciences** (Accountancy; Arabic; Business Administration; Business and Commerce; Fiscal Law; French; Law; Literature; Management); **Science and Engineering** (Chemistry; Civil Engineering; Computer Science; Electrical Engineering; Hydraulic Engineering; Mechanical Engineering; Organic Chemistry; Physics)

History: Founded 1980 as Centre Universitaire de Tiaret, acquired present status and title by decree n° 01-261 of 2001, modified by decree n° 04-261 of 2004.

Admission Requirements: Baccalauréat

Main Language(s) of Instruction: Arabic, French

International Co-operation: With universities in France, United Kingdom, Jordan and South Korea.

Accrediting Agencies: Agence nationale du Développement de la Recherche universitaire (ANDRU), Agence nationale du Développement de la Recherche en Santé (ANDRS)

Degrees and Diplomas: *Diplôme d'Etudes universitaires appliquées:* Computer Science; Mechanics; Electrical Engineering; Hydraulics; Veterinary Science; Biology; Accountancy; Fiscal Law, 3 yrs; *Licence (LMD):* Law and Administration; Management; Commerce and Management; French Literature and Language; Arabic Language and Literature, 4 yrs; *Diplôme de Docteur.* Veterinary Medicine, 5 yrs; *Diplôme d'Etudes supérieures:* Physics; Chemistry; Biology, 4 yrs; *Diplôme d'Ingénieur.* Agronomy; Mechanics; Electrical Engineering; Rural Engineering; Nutrition (DIE), 5 yrs; *Master.* Physical Engineering; Chemistry and Environment; Mechanics; Reproduction; Arabic Language and Literature; Commerce and Management, 2

Student Services: Academic counselling, Canteen, Cultural centre, Foreign Studies Centre, Health services, Nursery care, Social counselling, Sports facilities

Student Residential Facilities: Yes

Special Facilities: Veterinary hospital; Experimental Farm

Libraries: 8 libraries

Publications: Bulletin de l'Université Ibn Khaldoun *(monthly)*; Revue "Al-Khaldunia" *(biennially)*; Revue d'Ecologie et d'Environnement *(biennially)*
Last Updated: 17/02/09

KASDI MERBAH UNIVERSITY OF OUARGLA

Université Kasdi Merbah Ouargla
Route Ghardaia, Ouargla
Tel: +213(29) 71-24-68
Fax: +213(29) 71-51-61
EMail: info@ouarla-univ.dz; univ.ouargla@gmail.com
Website: http://www.ouargla-univ.dz

Directeur: Ahmed Boutarfaia EMail: univ.ouargla@gmail.com

Faculties

Arab Literature and Modern Languages (Arabic; English; French; Literature; Translation and Interpretation); **Economics, Management and Commerce** (Business and Commerce; Economics; Management); **Humanities and Social Sciences** (Educational

Sciences; Psychology; Sociology; Sports); **Law and Political Science** (Economics; Law; Management; Political Sciences); **Natural and Life Sciences and Earth and Universe Sciences** (Agronomy; Biological and Life Sciences; Earth Sciences; Natural Sciences); **Science and Technology and Science of Matter** (Chemical Engineering; Civil Engineering; Engineering; Hydraulic Engineering; Materials Engineering; Mathematics and Computer Science; Mechanical Engineering; Natural Sciences)

History: Founded 1987 as Ecole Nationale Supérieure. Became University Centre 1997. Acquired present status 2001, modified 2004.

Academic Year: September to June

Admission Requirements: Baccalauréat

Fees: (Algerian Dinars): 200 per annum

Main Language(s) of Instruction: Arabic and French

International Co-operation: With universities in France, Iraq and USA. Also participates in the Cisco and Oracle Programmes

Degrees and Diplomas: *Licence (LMD)*: 4 yrs; *Diplôme d'Ingénieur*: 5 yrs; *Doctorat*

Student Services: Canteen, Cultural centre, Health services, Social counselling, Sports facilities

Student Residential Facilities: Yes

Publications: El-Athar, Literature division *(biennially)*; El-Bahith, Economics division
Last Updated: 03/09/09

LARBI BEN M'HIDI UNIVERSITY -OUM-EL BOUAGHI

Université Larbi Ben M'hidi de Oum-El Bouaghi
BP 358, Route de Constantine, 04000 Oum-El Bouaghi
Tel: +213(32) 42-10-36
Fax: +213(32) 42-10-36
EMail: a.bouras@univ-oeb.dz
Website: http://www.univ-oeb.dz

Recteur: Ahmed Bouras (2005-)
Tel: +213(32) 42-73-17, Fax: +213(32) 42-73-17

Secrétaire général: Boudjamaâ Belefreikh

Vice-Recteur: Abderahmane Dib

Faculties
Arts and Humanities, Languages and Literature (Arabic; Arts and Humanities; Communication Studies; English; French; Psychology; Sociology); **Economics and Management** (Business and Commerce; Economics; Management); **Law and Administration and Political Sciences**; **Sciences and Exact Sciences** (Biology; Mathematics; Natural Sciences; Physics); **Technological Sciences** (Computer Engineering; Electronic Engineering; Mechanical Engineering; Technology)

Institutes
Urban Technical Management (Urban Studies)

History: Founded 1983. Acquired present status 1997.

Admission Requirements: Baccalaureat

Fees: (Algerian Dinars): 200

Main Language(s) of Instruction: Arabic; French

International Co-operation: With universities in France; Egypt; Tunisia; Italy; Syria and Jordan

Degrees and Diplomas: *Licence (LMD)*; *Master*; *Doctorat*

Student Services: Academic counselling, Canteen, Cultural centre, Handicapped facilities, Health services, Language programs, Nursery care, Social counselling, Sports facilities

Student Residential Facilities: Yes

Academic Staff *2008-2009*	MEN	WOMEN	TOTAL
FULL-TIME	195	233	**428**
PART-TIME	50	180	**230**
STAFF WITH DOCTORATE			
FULL-TIME	87	10	**97**

Student Numbers *2008-2009*			
All (Foreign Included)	6,300	11,300	**17,600**

Last Updated: 23/04/09

LARBI TEBESSI UNIVERSITY OF TEBESSA

Université Larbi Tebessi de Tebessa
Route de Constantine, 12002 Tebessa
Tel: +213(37) 49-03-02
Fax: +231(37) 49-03-02
EMail: cutebessa@ist.cerist.dz
Website: http://www.univ-tebessa.dz

Recteur: Abdelkrim Gouasmia

Faculties
Economics, Commerce and Business Administration (Business Administration; Business and Commerce; Economics; International Business; Management); **Exact Sciences and Natural and Life Sciences** (Biological and Life Sciences; Biology; Chemistry; Earth Sciences; Geography; Geology; Mathematics; Natural Sciences; Physics; Regional Planning); **Law and Political Science** (Law; Political Sciences; Private Law); **Literature, Humanities and Social Sciences** (Anthropology; Arabic; Arts and Humanities; Communication Studies; History; Literature; Modern Languages; Social Sciences; Sociology); **Science and Technology**

History: Founded 1992. Acquired present status 2009.

Governing Bodies: Ministry of Higher Education and Scientific Research

Academic Year: September to June

Admission Requirements: Baccalauréat

Fees: None

Main Language(s) of Instruction: French and Arabic

Degrees and Diplomas: *Licence (LMD)*: 3 yrs; *Diplôme d'Etudes supérieures*: 4 yrs; *Diplôme d'Ingénieur*: 5 yrs; *Master*: 5 yrs; *Doctorat*

Student Services: Academic counselling, Canteen, Cultural centre, Foreign student adviser, Foreign Studies Centre, Handicapped facilities, Health services, Language programs, Nursery care, Social counselling, Sports facilities

Academic Staff *2008-2009*	MEN	WOMEN	TOTAL
FULL-TIME	554	327	**881**
STAFF WITH DOCTORATE			
FULL-TIME	289	136	**425**

Student Numbers *2008-2009*			
All (Foreign Included)	4,778	7,883	**12,661**
FOREIGN ONLY	70	10	**80**

Last Updated: 29/05/09

M'HAMED BOUGARA UNIVERSITY OF BOUMERDÈS

Université M'Hamed Bougara de Boumerdès
Avenue de l'Indépendance, 35000 Boumerdès
Tel: +213(24) 81-64-20
Fax: +213(24) 81-63-73
EMail: rectorat@umbb.dz
Website: http://www.umbb.dz

Recteur: Rafika Kesri (2000-)

Secrétaire général: Ahmed Boufellah
Tel: +213(24) 81-69-29, Fax: +213(24) 81-69-29
EMail: secr-gener@umbb.dz

International Relations: Abdelaziz Tairi, Vice-Recteur
Tel: +213(24) 81-99-87, Fax: +213(24) 81-99-87
EMail: vrpgr@umbb.dz

Faculties
Economics, Management and Commerce (Business and Commerce; Economics; Management); **Engineering** (Energy Engineering; Engineering; Environmental Engineering; Industrial Engineering; Materials Engineering; Mechanical Engineering); **Hydrocarburates and Chemistry** (Automation and Control Engineering; Chemical Engineering; Engineering Management; Industrial Management; Marketing; Mining Engineering; Petroleum and Gas Engineering); **Law** (Law; Private Law; Public Law); **Science**

History: Founded 1998 following merger of six former national institutes, modified 2004.

Governing Bodies: Rectorate, Vice-Rectorate, General-Secretary and Deans of faculties

Admission Requirements: Baccalauréat

Fees: (Algerian Dinars): 200

Main Language(s) of Instruction: Arabic, French, English

International Co-operation: With universities in France, Belgium, Spain, Russian Federation, Czech Republic and Ukraine.

Accrediting Agencies: Ministry of Higher Education and Scientific Research

Degrees and Diplomas: *Diplôme d'Etudes universitaires appliquées:* Business Computing; International Commerce; Mechanical Engineering; Food Technology; Computer Science; Hydrocarbons and Chemistry; Civil Engineering; Materials Engineering; Industrial Technology; Biology; Electrical Engineering, 3 yrs; *Licence (LMD):* Commerce; Management; Administration and Law; Social Sciences, 4 yrs; *Diplôme d'Ingénieur:* Mechanical Engineering; Food Technology; Computer Science; Hydrocarbons and Chemistry; Civil Engineering; Materials Engineering; Industrial Technology; Water Science; Biology; Statistics; Electrical Engineering (IE), 5 yrs; *Master:* Electrical Engineering; Computer Science, a further 2 yrs; *Doctorat*

Student Services: Canteen, Cultural centre, Health services, Language programs, Nursery care, Social counselling, Sports facilities

Student Residential Facilities: Five residences

Libraries: University library; Faculty libraries; department libraries

Publications: Lettre de la Faculté des Sciences *(monthly)*

Academic Staff *2008-2009*	MEN	WOMEN	TOTAL
FULL-TIME	595	443	1,038
PART-TIME	509	228	737
STAFF WITH DOCTORATE			
FULL-TIME	197	27	224
Student Numbers *2008-2009*			
All (Foreign Included)	11,618	12,477	24,095
FOREIGN ONLY	167	26	193

Last Updated: 30/07/09

MENTOURI UNIVERSITY OF CONSTANTINE
Université Mentouri de Constantine
BP 325, Route de Aïn-El-Bey, 25017 Constantine
Tel: +213(31) 61-43-48
Fax: +213(31) 61-43-49
EMail: Université-mentouri@umc.edu.dz
Website: http://www.umc.edu.dz

Recteur: Abdelhamid Djekoun
Tel: +231(31) 81-88-92, Fax: +213(31) 81-87-11
EMail: rectorat@umc.edu.dz

Secrétaire général: Foudil Belaouira
Tel: +213(31) 92-57-79, Fax: +213(31) 81-85-01
EMail: secretariat-g@umc.edu.dz

International Relations: Farida Hobar, Vice-Recteur des Relations extérieures
Tel: +213(31) 81-86-83 EMail: vicerect-relex@umc.edu.dz

Faculties
Biological and Life Sciences; **Earth Sciences, Geography and Regional Planning** (Architecture; Earth Sciences; Regional Planning; Town Planning) *Dean:* Salaheddine Cherad; **Economics and Management** (Economics; Management); **Engineering** (Civil Engineering; Computer Engineering; Electronic Engineering; Industrial Chemistry; Mechanical Engineering; Meteorology) *Dean:* Abdelmadjid Benghalia; **Humanities and Social Sciences** (Arts and Humanities; History; Library Science; Philosophy; Psychology; Social Sciences; Sociology; Sports) *Dean:* Abdelhamid Khrouf; **Languages and Literature** (Arabic; French; Literature; Modern Languages; Translation and Interpretation) *Dean:* Youssef Ghioua; **Law** (Law; Political Sciences; Private Law; Public Law) *Dean:* Abdelmadjid Guemouh; **Medicine** (Medicine; Pharmacy; Stomatology); **Science** (Chemistry; Mathematics; Natural Sciences; Nutrition; Physics; Veterinary Science) *Dean:* Djamel Hamana

Institutes
Nutrition and Food Technology (Food Technology; Nutrition)
Further Information: Also Audiovisual Centre

History: Founded 1969 as University Centre, acquired present status 1984, modified 2006.

Governing Bodies: Conseil universitaire

Academic Year: September to June (September-January; February-June)

Admission Requirements: Secondary school certificate (baccalauréat)

Main Language(s) of Instruction: Arabic, French, English

Accrediting Agencies: Ministry of Higher Education and Scientific Research

Degrees and Diplomas: *Diplôme d'Etudes universitaires appliquées:* 3 yrs; *Licence (LMD); Diplôme de Docteur:* Veterinary Medicine, 5 yrs; *Diplôme d'Etudes supérieures:* 4 yrs; *Diplôme d'Ingénieur:* Architecture; *Master; Doctorat:* 4 yrs

Student Residential Facilities: Yes

Libraries: Central Library, 260,000 vols

Last Updated: 17/02/09

MOHAMED BOUDIAF UNIVERSITY OF SCIENCE AND TECHNOLOGY OF ORAN
Université des Sciences et de la Technologie d'Oran Mohamed Boudiaf (USTOMB)
BP 1505, M'Naouer, 31000 Oran
Tel: +213(41) 56-03-33
Fax: +213(41) 56-03-22
EMail: mekdam@univ-usto.dz
Website: http://www.univ-usto.dz

Recteur: Mohamed Bensafi (2006-)

Faculties
Architecture and Civil Engineering (Architecture; Civil Engineering; Hydraulic Engineering); **Electrical Engineering** (Electrical Engineering; Electronic Engineering); **Mechanical Engineering** (Marine Engineering; Mechanical Engineering; Metallurgical Engineering; Mining Engineering); **Science** (Biotechnology; Chemistry; Computer Science; Mathematics; Natural Sciences; Physics)

Institutes
Physical Education (Physical Education)

History: Founded 1975. Acquired present status 1984, modified 2004.

Academic Year: September to June

Admission Requirements: Secondary school certificate (baccalauréat) or equivalent

Main Language(s) of Instruction: French

Accrediting Agencies: Ministry of Higher Education and Scientific Research

Degrees and Diplomas: *Diplôme d'Etudes universitaires appliquées; Diplôme d'Ingénieur; Master*

Student Residential Facilities: Yes
Last Updated: 17/02/09

MOHAMED KHIDER UNIVERSITY OF BISKRA
Université Mohamed Khider de Biskra
BP 145, 07000 Biskra
Tel: +213(33) 73-32-06
Fax: +213(33) 73-32-07
EMail: info@umkbiskra.net
Website: http://www.umkbiskra.net

Recteur: Belkacem Selatnia EMail: recteur@univ-biskra.dz

Secrétaire général: Nacer Ghamri
Tel: +213(33) 74-61-63, Fax: +213(33) 73-86-88
EMail: sg@univ-biskra.dz

Faculties
Economics, Commerce and Management; **Exact, Natural and Life Sciences** (Agronomy; Biological and Life Sciences; Chemistry; Computer Science; Mathematics; Physics); **Humanities and Sociology** (Arabic; Arts and Humanities; Demography and Population; English; Literature; Social Sciences; Sociology); **Law and Political Science** (Law; Political Sciences); **Literature and Languages** (Literature; Modern Languages); **Science and Tech-**

nology (Architecture; Automation and Control Engineering; Civil Engineering; Electronic Engineering; Hydraulic Engineering; Industrial Chemistry; Mechanical Engineering; Metallurgical Engineering)

History: Founded 1998, acquired present status 2004.

Degrees and Diplomas: *Licence (LMD)*; *Master*
Last Updated: 17/02/09

MOULOUD MAMMERI UNIVERSITY OF TIZI-OUZOU

Université Mouloud Mammeri de Tizi-Ouzou (UMMTO)
BP 17, 15000 Tizi-Ouzou
Tel: +213(26) 21-53-14
Fax: +213(26) 21-29-68
EMail: univ_tizi@mail.ummto.dz
Website: http://www.ummto.dz/

Recteur: Rabah Kahlouche
Tel: +213(26) 21-89-95, Fax: +213(26) 21-29-68

Faculties
Arts and Humanities (Arabic; Arts and Humanities; English; French; Psychology; Translation and Interpretation); **Biology and Agronomy** (Agronomy; Biology); **Construction Engineering** (Construction Engineering; Engineering); **Economics and Management** (Economics; Management); **Electrical and Computer Engineering** (Computer Engineering; Electrical Engineering); **Law** (Law); **Medicine** (Medicine); **Science** (Mathematics; Natural Sciences)

History: Founded 1977 as University Centre of Tizi-Ouzou. Became university 1989, modified 2004.

Academic Year: September to June (September-January; February-June)

Admission Requirements: Secondary school certificate (baccalauréat) and entrance examination

Main Language(s) of Instruction: Arabic, French

Accrediting Agencies: Ministry of Higher Education and Scientific Research

Degrees and Diplomas: *Licence (LMD)*; *Diplôme d'Etudes supérieures*; *Diplôme d'Ingénieur*; *Doctorat*: Medicine

Libraries: Central Library; libraries of the institutes
Last Updated: 16/02/09

MUSTAPHA STOMBOULI UNIVERSITY OF MASCARA

Université Mustapha Stombouli de Mascara
BP 305, Route de Mamounia, 29000 Mascara
Tel: +231(45) 80-41-69
Fax: +231(45) 80-41-69
EMail: cum@univ-mascara.dz
Website: http://www.univ-mascara.dz/

Directeur: Abdelkader Khaldi

Faculties
Economics, Commerce and Management (Business and Commerce; Economics; Management); **Law and Political Science** (Administration; Law; Political Sciences); **Literature, Languages, Humanities and Social Sciences**; **Natural and Life Sciences** (Biological and Life Sciences; Natural Sciences); **Science and Technology** (Natural Sciences; Technology)

History: Founded 1986. Acquired present status 1992.

Degrees and Diplomas: *Diplôme d'Etudes universitaires appliquées*: Computer Science; Biology; Business Computing, 6 sems; *Licence (LMD)*: Economics; Management; Law, 4 yrs; *Diplôme d'Ingénieur*: Biology; Hydraulics; Mechanical Engineering; Computer Science; Agronomy, 5 yrs; *Master*
Last Updated: 16/02/09

NATIONAL INSTITUTE OF COMMERCE

Institut National de Commerce (INC)
11, Chemin Doudou Mokhtar, Ben Aknoun, Alger
Tel: +213(21) 91-11-76
Fax: +213(21) 91-12-02
EMail: info@incdz.org
Website: http://www.incdz.org/inc/

Directeur: Abdesselam Saadi

Programmes
Accounting and Audit; **Business Management** (Management); **Enterprise Management** (Management); **Human Resources and Communication** (Communication Studies; Human Resources); **International Business** (International Business); **Management** (Management); **Marketing** (Marketing)

History: Created in 1970.

Admission Requirements: Baccalauréat

Main Language(s) of Instruction: French

Degrees and Diplomas: *Licence (LMD)*: Business Sciences, 4 yrs; *Master*: Business Management; Marketing; *Doctorat*: Business Sciences
Last Updated: 17/02/09

NATIONAL INSTITUTE OF PLANNING AND STATISTICS

Institut national de la Planification et de la Statistique (INPS)
11 chemin Doudou Mokhtar, Ben Aknoun, Alger
Tel: +213(21) 91-21-33
Fax: +213(21) 91-21-39
EMail: inps-dz@wissal.dz
Website: http://www.inps-alger.dz/

Directeur général: Ahmed Zakane
Tel: +213(21) 91-21-33, Fax: +213(21) 91-21-39
EMail: zakane-dg@inps-alger.dz

Departments
Planning and Statistics (Statistics)

History: Founded 1970 as institut des techniques de planification. Acquired present title 1983.

Degrees and Diplomas: *Diplôme d'Ingénieur*; *Doctorat*
Last Updated: 17/02/09

NATIONAL INSTITUTE OF POST, INFORMATION AND COMMUNICATION TECHNOLOGIES

Institut national de la Poste et des Technologies de l'Information et de la Communication
BP 156 Route de l'arbaa, Eucalyptus, 16220 Alger
Tel: + 213(21) 50- 01-51
Fax: + 213(21) 50-00-98
EMail: inptic@inptic.edu.dz
Website: http://www.inptic.edu.dz

Programmes
Communication (Information Technology); **Telecommunications and Computer Networks** (Computer Networks; Telecommunications Engineering)

Degrees and Diplomas: *Licence (LMD)*; *Master*
Last Updated: 10/09/09

NATIONAL INSTITUTE OF TELECOMMUNICATIONS AND INFORMATION AND COMMUNICATION TECHNOLOGIES

Institut National des Télécommunications et des Technologies de l'Information et de la Communication
BP 1518, Route de Senia, 31000 Oran
Tel: +213(41) 59-44-21
Fax: +213(41) 59-44-18
Website: http://www.ito.dz

Directeur: Lahouari Mekaliche

Programmes
Information and Communications Technology (Information Technology); **Telecommunications Engineering** (Telecommunications Engineering)

History: Founded 1964 as École Nationale des Télécommunications in Algiers. Became Institut des Télécommunications à Oran 1971. Acquired present title 2008.

Degrees and Diplomas: *Diplôme d'Etudes universitaires appliquées; Diplôme d'Ingénieur; Master; Doctorat*
Last Updated: 17/02/09

NATIONAL MARINE SCIENCE AND COASTAL MANAGEMENT SCHOOL

Ecole nationale supérieure des Sciences de la Mer et de l'Aménagement du Littoral (ISMAL)
BP 19, Campus universitaire de Delly Brahim, Alger
Tel: +213(21) 91-77-87
Fax: +213(21) 91-77-87
EMail: dg_enssmal@enssmal.dz
Website: http://www.enssmal.dz

Directeur: Chekib-Arslane Baki
Tel: +213(21) 91-77-91, Fax: +213(21) 91-77-91
EMail: ismal@ismal.net

Programmes
Aquaculture (Aquaculture); **Coast Planning** (Coastal Studies); **Environment** (Environmental Studies); **Fishery** (Fishery)

History: Founded 1964 as Institut d'Océanographie d'Alger. Became Institut national des Sciences de la Mer et de l'Aménagement du Littoral 1983. Acquired present title 2008.

Admission Requirements: Baccalauréat

Degrees and Diplomas: *Diplôme d'Etudes universitaires appliquées; Licence (LMD); Diplôme d'Ingénieur; Master*
Last Updated: 05/06/09

NATIONAL SCHOOL OF ADMINISTRATION

Ecole nationale d'Administration (ENA)
13 Chemin Abdelkader Gadouche, Hydra, Alger
Tel: +213(21) 60-13-50
Fax: +213(21) 60-49-41
EMail: ena@wissal.dz
Website: http://www.ena.dz/

Directeur: Hocine Cherhabil

Programmes
Economics and Finance (Economics; Finance); **International Institutions** (International Relations); **Law** (Private Law; Public Law); **Public Administration** (Public Administration)

History: Founded 1964. Acquired present status 1987.
Last Updated: 26/04/07

NATIONAL SCHOOL OF AGRONOMY

Ecole nationale supérieure Agronomique (INA)
10, avenue Hassen Badi, El-Harrach, Alger
Tel: +213(21) 52-50-84
Fax: +213(21) 82-27-29
EMail: ina@ina.dz
Website: http://www.ina.dz/index.php3

Directeur: Mohand Mouloud Bellal

Departments
Agricultural Engineering (Agricultural Engineering; Agricultural Equipment); **Animal Production** (Animal Husbandry; Cattle Breeding; Zoology); **Botany**; **Food Technology**; **Forestry** (Forestry); **Rural Economics** (Agricultural Economics); **Soil Science**; **Zoology**

History: Founded 1905, acquired present title 2008.

Degrees and Diplomas: *Diplôme d'Ingénieur; Master; Doctorat*
Last Updated: 17/02/09

NATIONAL SCHOOL OF CIVIL ENGINEERING

Ecole nationale supérieure des Travaux publics (ENSTP)
BP 32, Rue Sidi Garidi, 16051 Alger
Tel: +213(21) 28-68-38
Fax: +213(21) 28-14-07
EMail: entp@entp.edu.dz
Website: http://www.entp.edu.dz

Programmes
Civil Engineering (Civil Engineering); **Computer Science** (Computer Science); **Economics and Management** (Economics; Management); **Hydraulics** (Hydraulic Engineering); **Transport** (Transport and Communications)

History: Founded 1966. Acquired present status 1998.

Degrees and Diplomas: *Diplôme d'Ingénieur; Master*
Last Updated: 17/02/09

NATIONAL SCHOOL OF COMPUTER SCIENCE

Ecole nationale supérieure d'Informatique (INI)
BP 68 M Oued Smar, El Harrach, 16309 Alger
Tel: +213(21) 51-60-77
Fax: +213(21) 51-61-56
EMail: de@ini.dz
Website: http://www.ini.dz

Directeur général: Mouloud Koudil EMail: m_koudil@ esi.dz

Programmes
Computer Science (Computer Science)

History: Founded 1969 as Institut national de Formation en Informatique.

Degrees and Diplomas: *Diplôme d'Ingénieur; Master; Doctorat*
Last Updated: 03/09/09

NATIONAL SCHOOL OF TECHNOLOGY

Ecole nationale supérieure de Technologie
Alger
EMail: enst@wissal.dz
Website: http://www.enst.dz

Programmes
Technology (Technology)

History: Founded 2009.

Degrees and Diplomas: *Licence; Master; Doctorat*
Last Updated: 29/06/09

NATIONAL SCHOOL OF VETERINARY SCIENCE

Ecole nationale supérieure vétérinaire d'Alger (ENSV)
10 Avenue Hassen Badi, El Harrach, 16000 Alger
Tel: +213(21) 52-51-32
Fax: +213(21) 82-44-81
EMail: de@env.dz
Website: http://www.ensv.dz

Directeur: L. Guezlane

Librarian: Chouarfia Wassila EMail: wass.ch@gmail.com

Programmes
Veterinary Science (Health Sciences; Veterinary Science)

History: Founded 1970.

Academic Year: September to December (September-December; January-March; April-June)

Admission Requirements: Baccalaureate in Natural Sciences

Main Language(s) of Instruction: French

Degrees and Diplomas: *Diplôme de Docteur*: Veterinary Science, 5 yrs; *Doctorat*: Veterinary Science. Also Postgraduation spécialisée (PGS) 1 yr

Student Services: Academic counselling, Health services, Language programs

Student Residential Facilities: Yes

Special Facilities: Internet access

Libraries: Print, Periodical, Electronic and Online resources

Academic Staff 2008-2009	MEN	WOMEN	TOTAL
FULL-TIME	20	49	69
PART-TIME	2	3	5
STAFF WITH DOCTORATE			
FULL-TIME	5	7	12
PART-TIME	–	–	1
Student Numbers 2008-2009			
All (Foreign Included)	645	398	1,043
FOREIGN ONLY	2	4	6

Last Updated: 21/04/09

SAAD DAHLAB UNIVERSITY OF BLIDA

Université Saad Dahlab de Blida (USDB)
BP 270, Route de Soumma, 09000 Blida
Tel: +213(25) 43-36-25
Fax: +213(25) 43-38-64
EMail: contact@univ-blida.dz
Website: http://www.univ-blida.dz

Rector: Abdellatif Baba Ahmed
Tel: +213(25) 43-81-38, Fax: +213(25) 43-81-38
EMail: rectorat@mail.univ-blida.dz

Secretary -General: Bouhzam Abdelmadjid

International Relations: Oukid-Khouas Saliha, Vice-Rector
Tel: +213(25) 43-04-66, Fax: +231(25) 43-81-46
EMail: osalyha@yahoo.com

Faculties
Agro-Veterinary and Biological Science (Agronomy; Biology; Veterinary Science); **Arts and Social Sciences** (Arabic; Demography and Population; English; French; Modern Languages; Psychology; Social Sciences; Sociology; Speech Therapy and Audiology); **Economics and Management** (Economics; Finance; Management); **Engineering** (Aeronautical and Aerospace Engineering; Architecture; Civil Engineering; Electronic Engineering; Engineering; Industrial Chemistry; Mechanical Engineering); **Law** (Law); **Medicine** (Dentistry; Medicine; Pharmacy); **Science** (Chemistry; Computer Science; Mathematics; Physics)

History: Founded 1981. Acquired present status 1989, modified 2004.

Academic Year: (Algerian Dinars): 200 per annum

Admission Requirements: Baccalaureat

Main Language(s) of Instruction: Arabic; French

International Co-operation: Participates in Tempus (France, Belgium, Switzerland); AUF; FP6; CMEP (France)

Accrediting Agencies: Ministry of Higher Education and Scientific Research

Degrees and Diplomas: Licence (LMD): Mathematics, Computer Science; Science and Technology; Natural Science; Biological Life Sciences, 3 yrs; Licence (LMD): Modern Languages; Human Science; Law; Economics; Management, 4 yrs; Diplôme d'Etudes supérieures; Diplôme d'Ingénieur: Science and Technology; Biology; Agronomy, 5 yrs; Master: Mathematics, Computer Science; Science and Technology; Natural Science; Biological Life Sciences, 2 yrs; Doctorat: Medicine; Pharmacy; Dentistry; Veterinary Sciences, 5-7 yrs

Student Services: Canteen, Foreign student adviser, Health services, Nursery care, Sports facilities

Special Facilities: Visio-Conference, E-Learning

Libraries: c. 94.000 vols; 33,148 titles (scientifc reviews; Encyclopedy; on-line data base. Also 7 faculty libraries with 20,642 tittles, 84,822 vols.

Academic Staff 2008-2009	MEN	WOMEN	TOTAL
FULL-TIME	842	590	1,432
PART-TIME	74	12	86
STAFF WITH DOCTORATE			
FULL-TIME	231	50	281
PART-TIME	77	11	88
Student Numbers 2008-2009			
All (Foreign Included)	17,933	29,594	47,527
FOREIGN ONLY	207	99	306

Last Updated: 19/06/09

SCHOOL OF ARCHITECTURE AND TOWN PLANNING

Ecole polytechnique d'Architecture et d'Urbanisme (EPAU)
BP 177, route de beaulieu, El Harrache, 16200 Alger
Tel: +213(21) 52-47-26/27
Fax: +213(21) 82-17-57
Website: http://www.epau.edu.dz/

Directeur: Mohamed Salah Zerouala
EMail: zerouala54@yahoo.com

Programmes
Architecture and Town Planning (Architecture; Town Planning)

History: Founded 1970.

Degrees and Diplomas: Diplôme d'Ingénieur: Architecture; Doctorat

Last Updated: 17/02/09

SCHOOL OF BANKING

Ecole supérieure de Banque (ESB)
BP 156, Route de Baïnem Bouzaréah, 16340 Alger
Tel: +213(21) 90-29-29
Fax: +213(21) 90-43-16
Website: http://www.esb.edu.dz

General Manager: Mahmoud Hemidet
Tel: +213(21) 90-38-15, Fax: +213(21) 90-43-16

Manager: Djamel Elksouri
Tel: +213(21) 90-44-50, Fax: +213(21) 90-44-50
EMail: ekdjkouba@yahoo.fr

Programmes
Banking I (Accountancy; Banking; Economics; Finance; Law) Manager: Fouad Metalta; **Banking II** (Formation qualifiante) (Accountancy; Banking; Economics; Finance; Law) Manager: Abdelhamid Belouadnine; **Computer Science and Audiovisual Studies** (Cinema and Television; Computer Science) Manager: Saad Abdi

History: Founded 1995.

Governing Bodies: Bank of Algeria

Admission Requirements: Secondary School certificate (baccalauréat), Licence

Fees: (Algerian Dinars): 300 per annum (including accommodation)

Main Language(s) of Instruction: French

Degrees and Diplomas: Master: Brevet Supérieur de la Banque (BSB, 30 months), Diplôme Supérieur des Études Bancaires; Postgraduate diplomas (Master in collaboration with the Ecole supérieure de Commerce d'Amiens, France)

Student Services: Canteen, Cultural centre, Employment services, Health services, Nursery care, Social counselling, Sports facilities

Student Residential Facilities: Yes

Libraries: Yes
Last Updated: 17/02/09

SCHOOL OF ENGINEERING OF ALGIERS

Ecole nationale polytechnique d'Alger (ENP)
BP 162, 10, Avenue Hassen Badi, El Harrach, 16200 Alger
Tel: +213(21) 52-53-01/03
Fax: +213(21) 52-29-73
EMail: enp@enp.edu.dz
Website: http://www.enp.edu.dz

Directrice: Ghania Nezzal

Departments
Basic Sciences (Mathematics; Physics) Head: M. Ouadjaout; **Chemical Engineering** (Chemical Engineering) Head: Toudert Ahmed Zaïd; **Civil Engineering** (Civil Engineering) Head: Saadi Lakhal; **Electrical Engineering** (Electrical Engineering) Head: Abdelouahab Mekhaldi; **Electronics** (Electronic Engineering; Information Management; Microwaves; Telecommunications Engineering) Head: Mohamed Trabelsi; **Environmental Engineering** (Environmental Engineering) Head: Djazia Arar; **Hydraulics** (Hydraulic Engineering) Head: Saadia Benmamar; **Industrial Engineering** (Industrial Engineering) Head: Nacéra Aboun;

Languages (English; Modern Languages) *Head*: C. Larbes; **Mechanical Engineering** (Mechanical Engineering); **Metallurgical Engineering** (Metallurgical Engineering) *Head*: Med Lamine Djeghlal; **Mining Engineering** (Mining Engineering) *Head*: Salima Chabou

History: Founded 1925 as Institut Industriel d'Algérie. Acquired present status 1966.

Degrees and Diplomas: *Diplôme d'Ingénieur; Master; Doctorat*
Last Updated: 16/02/09

SCHOOL OF HEALTH MANAGEMENT AND ADMINISTRATION
Ecole nationale supérieure de Management et de l'Administration de la Santé
Alger
EMail: enmas@sante.dz
Website: http://www.sante.dz/ensp/lasante.htm

Programmes
Health Administration (Health Administration)

History: Founded 1989. Acquired present title and status 2009.
Last Updated: 29/06/09

SCHOOL OF MAGISTRACY
Ecole supérieure de la Magistrature (ESM)
Boulevard du 11 décembre 1960, El Biar, Alger
Tel: +213(21) 91-51-92/93
Fax: +213(21) 91-52-01
EMail: webmaster@esm.dz
Website: http://www.esm.dz

Directeur: Hocine Mabrouk
Tel: +213(21) 91-51-99, Fax: +213(21) 91-52-02
EMail: hocinemabrouk@inm-dz.org

Secrétaire général: Hocine Trifa
Tel: +213(21) 91-51-95, Fax: +213(21) 91-52-01
EMail: hocinetrifa@esm-dz.org

Programmes
Law (Administrative Law; Commercial Law; Criminal Law; Law; Maritime Law)

History: Founded 1990.

Admission Requirements: Licence en droit (eight semesters) or equivalent
Last Updated: 09/06/09

TAHAR MOULAY UNIVERSITY OF SAÏDA
Université Tahar Moulay de Saïda
BP 138, Cité ENNASR, Saïda
Tel: +213(48) 47-11-24
Fax: +213(48) 47-76-85
EMail: derkaoui@univ-saida.dz
Website: http://www.univ-saida.dz/

Directeur: Berrezouge Belgoumen

Faculties
Economics, Commerce and Management (Business and Commerce; Economics; Management); **Law and Administration** (Administration; Law); **Literature and Languages** (Literature; Modern Languages); **Science and Technology** (Natural Sciences; Technology)

History: Founded 1986. Acquired present title and status 2009.

Degrees and Diplomas: *Diplôme d'Etudes universitaires appliquées*: Computer Science; Electronic Engineering; Electrical Technology; Hydraulics; Business Computing, 6 sems; *Licence (LMD)*: Mathematics; Physics and Chemistry; Law; Arab Literature, 4 yrs; *Diplôme d'Etudes supérieures*; *Diplôme d'Ingénieur*: Electrical Technology; Electronic Engineering; Hydraulics, 5 yrs; *Master*; *Doctorat*
Last Updated: 16/02/09

TEACHER TRAINING SCHOOL OF CONSTANTINE
Ecole normale supérieure de Constantine (ENSC)
Plateau du Mansourah, Constantine
Tel: +213(31) 61-21-53
Fax: +213(31) 63-00-75
EMail: directeur@ens-constantine.dz
Website: http://www.ens-constantine.dz/

Director: Mohamed Reghioua

Head of Administration: Cherif Touami

International Relations: Soulef Boulmerka, Head of Cooperation and Exchanges Tel: +213(31) 62-48-60, Fax: +213(31) 62-48-60

Departments
Arabic Language and Literature *Head*: Dris Hamrouche; **English** *Head*: Amina Haddad; **French** (French) *Head*: Sakina Benmoussa; **Philosophy, History and Geography** (Geography; History; Philosophy) *Head*: Tahar Amri

History: Founded 1984.

Fees: None

Main Language(s) of Instruction: Arabic, French, English

International Co-operation: With universities in France

Degrees and Diplomas: *Licence*; *Master*

Student Services: Academic counselling

Student Residential Facilities: None

Libraries: 9,568 catalogues; 33,771 vols

Publications: Forum de l'Enseignement, Specialised Journal in Pedagogy and Didactics *(biannually)*

Academic Staff *2008-2009*	MEN	WOMEN	TOTAL
FULL-TIME	46	85	**131**
PART-TIME	46	25	**71**
STAFF WITH DOCTORATE			
FULL-TIME	16	6	**22**
PART-TIME	19	1	**20**
Student Numbers *2008-2009*			
All (Foreign Included)	350	2,665	**3,015**

Last Updated: 21/04/09

UNIVERSITY CENTRE OF AIN TÉMOUCHENT
Centre Universitaire d'Ain Témouchent
Route de Sidi Bellabes - BP 284, 46000 Aïn Témouchent
Website: http://www.cuniv-aintemouchent.dz/planification.html

Institutes
Economics, Commerce and Management (Business and Commerce; Economics; Management); **Literature and Languages** (Literature; Modern Languages); **Science and Technology** (Natural Sciences; Technology)

History: Founded 2005.

Main Language(s) of Instruction: Arabic

Degrees and Diplomas: *Licence*
Last Updated: 29/06/09

UNIVERSITY CENTRE OF BORDJ BOU ARRERIDJ
Centre Universitaire de Bordj Bou Arreridj
Bordj Bou Arreridj
Tel: +213(35) 66-65-17
Fax: +231(35) 66-65-21
EMail: direction_cubba@wissal.dz
Website: http://www.univ-bba.dz

Institutes
Economics and Management (Business and Commerce; Economics; Management); **Letters, Languages, Humanities and Social Sciences** (Arabic; Arts and Humanities; Literature; Modern Languages; Sociology); **Mathematics and Computer Science** (Computer Science; Mathematics); **Science and Technology** (Biological and Life Sciences; Civil Engineering; Electronic Engineering; Environmental Engineering; Mechanical Engineering; Natural Sciences; Technology)

History: Founded 2001.

Degrees and Diplomas: *Licence (LMD)*; *Master*, *Doctorat*
Last Updated: 10/09/09

UNIVERSITY CENTRE OF EL OUED

Centre Universitaire d'El Oued
BP 789, El Oued
Tel: +213(32) 24-41-81
Fax: +213(32) 24-47-67
EMail: admin@mail.univ-eloued.dz
Website: http://www.univ-eloued.dz

Directeur: Azzedine Haftari (2007-)

Institutes
Commerce (Business and Commerce); **Law** (Law); **Literature and Languages** (Literature; Modern Languages)
History: Founded 2001.
Last Updated: 14/06/07

UNIVERSITY CENTRE OF EL TARF

Centre Universitaire d'El Tarf
BP 73, Route de Matroha, 36000 El Tarf
Tel: +213(38) 60-15-33
Fax: +213(38) 60-14-17
EMail: sgcuet@cuniv-eltaref.edu.dz
Website: http://www.cuniv-eltaref.edu.dz

Directeur: Rachid Siab
Tel: +213(38) 60-18-93 EMail: r.siab@mesrs.dz

Institutes
Agronomy (Agronomy) *Director:* Saddek Abdelmadjid; **Arabic and Arab Literature** (Arabic; Literature); **Biology** (Biology; Biotechnology; Plant and Crop Protection); **Veterinary Science** (Veterinary Science) *Director:* Ryad Bouzid
History: Founded as Agro-veterinary Institute of Annaba University 1992. Acquired present status 2001.

Academic Year: September to June

Admission Requirements: Secondary school certificate (baccalauréat)

Fees: None

Main Language(s) of Instruction: Arabic; French

Degrees and Diplomas: *Licence (LMD)*; *Diplôme de Docteur:* Veterinary Science, 5 yrs; *Diplôme d'Etudes supérieures:* 4 yrs; *Diplôme d'Ingénieur:* 5 yrs; *Master*

Student Services: Academic counselling, Canteen, Health services, Sports facilities
Last Updated: 25/06/09

UNIVERSITY CENTRE OF GHARDAIA

Centre Universitaire de Ghardaia
Ghardaia
Website: http://www.cu-ghardaia.edu.dz
Directeur: Mohamed Rajraj

Institutes
Commerce (Business and Commerce); **Social Sciences** (Social Sciences)
History: Founded 2005.
Last Updated: 14/06/07

UNIVERSITY CENTRE OF KHEMIS MILIANA

Centre Universitaire de Khemis Miliana
Route de theniet el-had khemis Miliana, 44225 Khemis Miliana
Tel: +213(27) 66-42-32
Fax: +213(27) 66-48-63
EMail: cukm@cukm.org
Website: http://www.cukm.org

Directeur: Tayeb Ferhat Benabbad

International Relations: El Hadj Ailam, Directeur Adjoint de la Post Graduation et de la Recherche Scientifique
Tel: +213(27) 669-442, Fax: +213(27) 664-863
EMail: ailam_elhadj@yahoo.fr

Departments
Human Sciences (Arts and Humanities; Social Sciences); **Political Sciences** (Political Sciences)

Institutes
Economics and Management (Economics; Management); **Law and Administration** (Administration; Law); **Natural and Earth Sciences** (Earth Sciences; Natural Sciences); **Science and Technology** (Automation and Control Engineering; Civil Engineering; Computer Science; Electrical Engineering; Energy Engineering; Mathematics; Mechanical Engineering; Physical Chemistry; Thermal Engineering)

History: Founded 2001.

Degrees and Diplomas: *Diplôme d'Etudes universitaires appliquées:* 3 yrs; *Licence (LMD):* 3 yrs; *Diplôme d'Ingénieur:* 5 yrs; *Licence:* 4 yrs; *Master:* 5 yrs

Publications: Economics *(biannually)*

Academic Staff *2008-2009*	MEN	WOMEN	TOTAL
FULL-TIME	157	80	**237**
Student Numbers *2008-2009*			
All (Foreign Included)	3,797	5,254	**9,051**

Last Updated: 20/05/09

UNIVERSITY CENTRE OF MILA

Centre Universitaire de Mila
Mila
EMail: directeur@centre-univ-mila.dz
Website: http://www.centre-univ-mila.dz/
Directeur: Ali Boukaroura

Institutes
Economics, Commerce and Management (Business and Commerce; Economics; Management); **Literature and Languages** (Literature; Modern Languages); **Science and Technology** (Natural Sciences; Technology)

History: Founded 2008.

Main Language(s) of Instruction: Arabic

Degrees and Diplomas: *Licence*
Last Updated: 29/06/09

UNIVERSITY CENTRE OF RÉLIZANE

Centre universitaire de Rélizane
BP: 48000, Bormadia
EMail: cur48@cu-relizane.dz
Website: http://www.cu-relizane.dz

Directeur: Benaissa Bekouche

Institutes
Economics, Commerce and Management (Business and Commerce; Economics; Management); **Humanities and Social Sciences** (Arts and Humanities; Social Sciences); **Law and Administration** (Administration; Law); **Literature and Languages** (Arabic; Literature)

History: Founded 2008.

Main Language(s) of Instruction: Arabic

Degrees and Diplomas: *Licence*

Libraries: Yes
Last Updated: 26/06/09

UNIVERSITY CENTRE OF SOUK-AHRAS

Centre Universitaire de Souk-Ahras
Souk-Ahras
Tel: +213(37) 32-62-62
Fax: +213(37) 32-65-65
Website: http://www.cu-soukahras.dz

Institutes
Law (Law); **Science and Engineering** (Engineering)
History: Founded 2001.
Degrees and Diplomas: *Licence (LMD)*; *Master*

UNIVERSITY CENTRE OF TISSEMSILT
Centre Universitaire de Tissemsilt
Tissemsilt

Institutes
Economics, Commerce and Management (Business and Commerce; Economics; Management); **Law and Administration** (Administration; Law); **Literature and Languages** (Literature; Modern Languages); **Science and Technology** (Technology)

History: Founded 2005.
Last Updated: 29/06/09

UNIVERSITY OF ALGIERS 1
Université d'Alger Benyoucef Benkhedda
2, rue Didouche Mourad, 16000 Alger
Tel: +213(21) 64-69-70
Fax: +213(21) 63-53-03
EMail: rectorat@mail.univ-alger.dz; Contact@univ-alger.dz
Website: http://www.univ-alger.dz

Recteur: Tahar Hadjar

Faculties
Islamic Studies (Arabic; Islamic Law; Islamic Studies; Law; Religious Studies); **Law** (Civil Law; Constitutional Law; Criminal Law; Islamic Law; Labour Law; Law; Notary Studies; Private Law; Public Administration; Public Law); **Medicine** (Biochemistry; Biology; Dentistry; Mathematics; Medicine; Pharmacy; Physiology)

History: Founded 1859 as a School of Medicine and Pharmacy, followed in 1879 by schools of Law, Science, and Letters. Formally established as University 1909. Acquired present status 1984, modified in 2004. Foremerly known as Université d'Alger Benyoucef Benkhedda. Acquired present title 2010.

Academic Year: October to June (October-December; January-April; April-June)

Admission Requirements: Secondary school certificate (baccalauréat) or recognized equivalent or entrance examination

Main Language(s) of Instruction: Arabic, French

Accrediting Agencies: Ministry of Higher Education and Scientific Research

Degrees and Diplomas: *Diplôme d'Etudes universitaires appliquées*: Midwifery, 3 yrs; *Licence (LMD)*: 4 yrs; *Diplôme de Docteur*: Dentistry, 4 yrs; *Diplôme de Docteur*: Medicine, 6 yrs; *Diplôme de Docteur*: Pharmacy, 5 yrs; *Master*, *Doctorat*: by thesis

Student Residential Facilities: Yes

Special Facilities: Musée du Bardo; Musée national des Beaux-Arts; Musée Savorgnan de Brazza; Musée Stéphane Csell; Musée Franchet d'Esperey

Publications: Bulletin d'Information historique; Errihla el Maghribia; Majalatou Koulyat el Adab; Revue africaine; Revue Lybica; Sciences médicales de Constantine
Last Updated: 09/11/11

UNIVERSITY OF ALGIERS 2
Université d'Alger 2
Boulevard Djamel Eddine, El Afghani Bouzareah, Alger
Tel: +213(21) 90-95-78
Fax: +213(21) 90-89-92
EMail: contact@univ-alger2.dz
Website: http://www.univ-alger2.dz

Recteur: Abdelkader Henni

Faculties
Human and Social Sciences (History; Library Science; Philosophy; Psychology; Sociology); **Letters and Languages** (Arabic; English; French; Literature)

Institutes
Archaeology (Archaeology)

History: Founded 1984 as Ecole normale supérieure des Lettres et Sciences humaines de Bouzareah. Acquired present status and title 2010.

Admission Requirements: Baccalauréat

Degrees and Diplomas: *Licence (LMD)*; *Master*
Last Updated: 09/11/11

UNIVERSITY OF M'SILA
Université de M'sila
BP 166, Ichbilia, 28000 M'sila
Tel: +231(35) 55-09-06
Fax: +231(35) 55-04-04
EMail: sgunivmsila@yahoo.fr
Website: http://www.univ-msila.dz

Recteur: Slimane Barhoumi

Secrétaire général: Abdelhamid Alia Tel: +213(35) 55-64-68

International Relations: Lahcène Mezrag
EMail: lmezrag@yahoo.fryes

Faculties
Arts and Social Sciences; **Economics, Management and Commerce**; **Law**; **Science and Engineering** (Agronomy; Biology; Civil Engineering; Computer Science; Electronic Engineering; Hydraulic Engineering; Mathematics; Mechanical Engineering; Physics)

Institutes
Town Planning (Town Planning)

History: Founded 1985 as Centre Universitaire de M'sila. Acquired present status 2001.

Academic Year: September to July

Admission Requirements: Baccalauréat

Fees: (Algerian Dinars): 200 per annum

Main Language(s) of Instruction: Arabic, French, English

International Co-operation: With universities in Arab countries and Europe

Degrees and Diplomas: *Licence (LMD)*: 3 yrs; *Master*: 5 yrs; *Doctorat*: 8 yrs

Student Services: Academic counselling, Canteen, Cultural centre, Foreign student adviser, Handicapped facilities, Health services, Language programs, Social counselling, Sports facilities

Academic Staff 2008-2009	MEN	WOMEN	TOTAL
FULL-TIME	543	183	**726**
STAFF WITH DOCTORATE FULL-TIME	88	30	**118**

Student Numbers 2008-2009			
All (Foreign Included)	12,978	17,922	**30,900**

Last Updated: 15/06/09

UNIVERSITY OF ORAN
Université d'Oran
BP 1524, El-M'nouar, 31000 Oran
Tel: +213(41) 41-61-55
Fax: +213(41) 41-60-21
EMail: contact@univ-oran.dz
Website: http://www.univ-oran.dz

Recteur: Larbi Chahed

Faculties
Earth Sciences, Geography and Regional Planning (Earth Sciences; Geography; Regional Planning); **Economics, Management and Commerce** (Business and Commerce; Economics; Management); **Humanities and Islamic Civilization** (Arts and Humanities; History; Islamic Studies; Library Science); **Law and Political Science** (Law; Political Sciences; Private Law; Public Law); **Literature, Languages and Arts** (Arabic; English; French; German; Literature; Russian; Spanish; Theatre; Translation and Interpretation); **Medicine** (Medicine; Pharmacy; Stomatology); **Science** (Biology; Biotechnology; Chemistry; Computer Science; Mathematics; Physics); **Social Sciences** (Demography and Population; Philosophy; Psychology; Social Sciences; Sociology)

Institutes
Industrial Maintenance

History: Founded 1961 as Centre universitaire d'Oran attached to the University of Algiers. Became University 1966.

Academic Year: October to July (October-February; March-July)

Admission Requirements: Secondary school certificate (baccalauréat)

Main Language(s) of Instruction: Arabic, French

Degrees and Diplomas: *Licence (LMD)*: 4 yrs; *Diplôme de Docteur*. Medicine, 6 yrs; *Diplôme de Docteur*. Pharmacy, 5 yrs; *Diplôme d'Ingénieur*; *Master*; *Doctorat*
Last Updated: 16/02/09

UNIVERSITY OF TLEMCEN
Université Abou Bekr Belkaid de Tlemcen
BP 119, 22 rue Abi Ayed Abdelkrim, Faubourg Pasteur,
13000 Tlemcen
Tel: +213(43) 20-23-36
Fax: +213(43) 20-41-89
EMail: cri@univ-tlemcen.dz
Website: http://www.univ-tlemcen.dz

Recteur: Noureddine Ghouali

Faculties
Arts, Humanities and Social Sciences (Arabic; Archaeology; Arts and Humanities; English; French; History; Literature; Modern Languages; Sociology); **Economics and Management** (Accountancy; Business and Commerce; Economics; Management); **Engineering** (Civil Engineering; Computer Engineering; Electronic Engineering; Engineering; Hydraulic Engineering); **Law** (Law); **Medicine** (Medicine; Pharmacy; Stomatology); **Science**

History: Founded as Centre universitaire de Tlemcen 1974, acquired present status and title 1998, modified in 2004.

Governing Bodies: Scientific Council

Academic Year: September to July (September-December; January-March; April-July)

Admission Requirements: Secondary school certificate (baccalauréat) or equivalent

Main Language(s) of Instruction: Arabic, French

Accrediting Agencies: Ministry of Higher Education and Scientific Research

Degrees and Diplomas: *Diplôme d'Etudes universitaires appliquées*: 3 yrs; *Licence (LMD)*: 4 yrs; *Diplôme de Docteur*. Medicine, 6 yrs; *Diplôme d'Etudes supérieures*: 4 yrs; *Diplôme d'Ingénieur*: 5 yrs; *Master*; *Doctorat*: by thesis
Student Services: Canteen, Health services, Sports facilities
Student Residential Facilities: For c. 5 300 students
Libraries: Libraries of the Institutes
Publications: Arabic Literature Magazine *(biannually)*; Popular Culture Magazine
Last Updated: 17/02/09

ZIANE ACHOUR UNIVERSITY OF DJELFA
Université Ziane Achour de Djelfa
BP 3117cudjelfa, 17000 Djelfa
Tel: +213(27) 90-02-03/04
Fax: +213(27) 90-02-01
EMail: Dg_cud@yahoo.fr
Website: http://www.univ-djelfa.dz/web/

Faculties
Economics, Commerce and Management (Business and Commerce; Economics; Management); **Law and Political Science** (Law; Political Sciences); **Literature and Languages and Social Sciences and Humanities** (Arts and Humanities; Literature; Modern Languages; Social Sciences); **Natural and Life Sciences** (Biological and Life Sciences; Natural Sciences); **Science and Technology** (Natural Sciences; Technology)

Degrees and Diplomas: *Diplôme d'Etudes universitaires appliquées*: Computer Science; Electronic Engineering, 6 sem.; *Licence (LMD)*: 4 yrs; *Diplôme d'Ingénieur*: Electronic Engineering, 5 yrs
Last Updated: 24/06/09

Andorra

STRUCTURE OF HIGHER EDUCATION SYSTEM

Description:

Higher education is provided by one public institution (Universitat d'Andorra) offering courses in Nursing, Computer Science, Business and Administration, Educational Studies, in on-campus and distance modes; and two private institutions, one specialized in the field of Dentistry, the other in online Business and Computering studies. For other higher education degrees, students enter the French or the Spanish higher education systems.

Stages of studies:

University level first stage: *Estudis universitaris*
Bàtxelor - 180 ECTS.

University level second stage: *Estudis universitaris*
Bàtxelor d'especialització - 120 ECTS; Màster - 300 ECTS.

University level third stage: *Estudis universitaris*
Doctorat (3 years)
Distance higher education:
Distance higher education is provided at both the Universitat d'Andorra and at the Universitat Oberta la Salle.

ADMISSION TO HIGHER EDUCATION

Admission to university-level studies:

Name of secondary school credential required: Batxillerat

For entry to: 1st year university studies.

Alternatives to credentials: Diplomas enabling access to higher education issued by Member Countries of the Bologna Process are accepted as Títol de Batxillerat.

Entrance exam requirements: When too many people wish to study a specific field of study, the University organises an entrance exam.

Foreign students admission:

Definition of foreign student: All those non Andorran or not living in Andorra.

Entrance exam requirements: Diplomas enabling access to higher education issued by Member countries of the Bologna Process are accepted as Títol de Batxillerat.

Entry regulations: Foreign students must fulfill the immigration requirements.

Language requirements: The main teaching language is Catalan.

RECOGNITION OF STUDIES

Quality assurance system:

The Agència per a la Qualitat de l'Ensenyament Superior d'Andorra (AQUA) was created by decree in 2006 to supervise the quality of the degrees offered by the University of Andorra and other higher education institutions.

Special provisions for recognition:

Recognition for university level studies: The Department for the Recognition of Diplomas of the Govern d'Andorra is in charge of the recognition of these diplomas.

For access to advanced studies and research: Universitat d'Andorra

For exercising a profession: The Department for the Recognition of Diplomas of the Govern d'Andorra and the Labor Ministry are in charge of the recognition of these diplomas.

NATIONAL BODIES

Ministeri d'Educació, Joventut i Esports (Ministry of Education, Youth and Sport)
Minister: Roser Suñé Pascuet
Av. Rocafort, 21-23
Edifici El Molí
Sant Julià de Lòria 600
Tel: +376 743 300
Fax: +376 743 313
WWW: http://www.educacio.ad/

Departament d'Ensenyament Superior i Recerca
Ministeri d'Educació i Joventut
Av. Rocafort, 21-23,
Ed. El Molí, 5a planta
Sant Julià de Lòria 600
Tel: +376 743 300
Fax: + 376 743 313
EMail: esuperior.gov@andorra.ad
WWW: http://www.ensenyamentsuperior.ad/

Agència de Qualitat de l'Ensenyament Superior d'Andorra - AQUA (Andorran Agency for Quality Assurance)
Director: Eric Jover
Av. Rocafort, 21-23
Sant Julià de Lòria 600
EMail: info@aqua.ad
WWW: http://www.ensenyamentsuperior.ad/index.php?option = com_content&view = article&id = 39&Itemid = 37

Data for academic year: 2012-2013
Source: IAU from the website of the Department of Higher Education of the Government of Andorra, 2012

INSTITUTIONS

PUBLIC INSTITUTIONS

UNIVERSITY OF ANDORRA
Universitat d'Andorra
Plaça de la Germandat 7, AD 600 Sant Julià de Lòria
Tel: +376 743-000
Fax: +376 743-043
EMail: uda@uda.ad
Website: http://www.uda.ad

Rector: Daniel Bastida Obiols (2005-)
Tel: +376 743-000, Fax: +376 743-043 EMail: dbastida@uda.ad

Manager: Joan Obiols

International Relations: Miquel Nicolau i Vila, Rectorate Coordinator EMail: mnicolau@uda.ad; eia@uda.ad

Centres
Virtual Studies and Continuing Education

Schools
Computer Science and Administration (Accountancy; Business Administration; Computer Science; Finance; Information Technology; Management; Marketing); **Nursing** (Anatomy; Child Care and Development; Community Health; Demography and Population; Dietetics; Environmental Studies; Epidemiology; Ethics; Family Studies; Gerontology; Health Administration; Health Education; Microbiology; Nursing; Nutrition; Parasitology; Pharmacology; Physiology; Psychiatry and Mental Health; Psychology; Public Health; Statistics)

History: Higher education in Andorra started in 1988 with two faculties : the School of Nursing and the School of Computer Systems. The University of Andorra was formally created by law In July 1997. Now, the University of Andorra is constituted by public centres devoted to higher education.

Governing Bodies: Consell Universitari; Junta Academica

Admission Requirements: Established by the government depending on the degree

Fees: (Euros): 600 per semester

Main Language(s) of Instruction: Catalan

International Co-operation: With universities in Spain; France and USA

Accrediting Agencies: Comissio per a la qualitat del sistema universitari d'Andorra

Degrees and Diplomas: *Bàtxelor; Màster; Doctorat*

Libraries: 5,100 vols; 36 subscriptions to periodicals

Last Updated: 16/09/11

PRIVATE INSTITUTIONS

OPEN UNIVERSITY OF LA SALLE

Universitat Oberta La Salle
Ordino
EMail: info@uols.org
Website: http://www.uols.org/

President: Pierre-Oliver Davasse

Programmes

Business Administration (Business Administration); **Computer Science** (Computer Science)

History: Created 2010.

Degrees and Diplomas: *Bàtxelor; Màster*

Last Updated: 20/12/11

UNIVERSITY OF THE VALLEYS

Universitat de les Valls
Av. Meritxell, 28, 500 Andorra la Vella
Tel: +376 813-781
Fax: +376 813-981
EMail: info@udv.ad
Website: http://www.udv.ad

Vice-Chancellor: Philip Garcia Ricart EMail: rector@udv.ad

Programmes

Dentistry (Biochemistry; Cell Biology; Chemistry; Dental Hygiene; Dental Technology; Dentistry; Gerontology; Medicine; Molecular Biology; Nursing; Nutrition; Orthodontics; Pharmacology; Radiology)

History: Created 2011.

Degrees and Diplomas: *Màster*

Last Updated: 20/12/11

Angola

STRUCTURE OF HIGHER EDUCATION SYSTEM

Description:

Since 2008, Angola has been restructuring its educational system to include both government and private educational institutions.

Stages of studies:

University level first stage: Graduação
The Bacharelato is obtained after three years' study. It is a terminal degree. The title of Licenciado is obtained after four to six years' study.

University level second stage: Pos-Graduação
There are two types of post-graduate degrees in Angola. The first is the pos-graduação academico which leads to the Mestrado in two to three years and to the Doutoramento after four to five years following the Licenciatura. The second, the pos-graduação profissional, offers Especializadas of various durations after the Licenciatura.

Distance higher education:
Teachers can follow distance education courses to upgrade their professional training.

ADMISSION TO HIGHER EDUCATION

Admission to university-level studies:

Name of secondary school credential required: Habilitações Literárias

Entrance exam requirements: Entrance examination

Foreign students admission:

Entrance exam requirements: Secondary-school-leaving certificate equivalent to the Habilitações Literárias and success in the entrance examination.

Language requirements: Good knowledge of Portuguese.

NATIONAL BODIES

Ministério do Ensino Superior e Ciência e Tecnologia (Ministry for Higher Education, Science and Technology)
   Minister: Maria Candida Teixeira
   Secretary of State, Higher Education: Adão Gaspar Pereira do Nascimento
   Luanda
   WWW: http://www.mesct.gov.ao/

Data for academic year: 2010-2011
Source: IAU from the website of the Ministry of Higher Education, Angola, 2010. Bodies updated in 2011

INSTITUTIONS

AGOSTINHO NETO UNIVERSITY

Universidade Agostinho Neto

Caixa postal 815, Avenida 4 de Fevereiro 7, 2°andar, Luanda
Tel: +244(222) 332-089 +244(222) 311-125
Fax: +244(222) 330-520 +244(222) 310-283
EMail: info@uan.ao
Website: http://www.uan.ao

Reitor: João Sebastião Teta (2006-)

Executive Director: Joaquim Rescova
Tel: +244(222) 310-296, Fax: +244(222) 310-283

International Relations: Aida Pegado, Director, Cooperation and International Affairs
Tel: +244(222) 310-296, Fax: +244(222) 310-283

Faculties
Agrarian Sciences *(Huambo)* (Agricultural Engineering; Agriculture; Agronomy; Veterinary Science) *Dean:* António Alicerces Chicinda Eduardo; **Economics** *(Luanda) Dean:* Sebastião Luvumbo; **Engineering** *(Luanda) Dean:* Albano Kanga; **Law** *(Luanda)* (Law) *Dean:* José Ocxtavio Serra Van-Dunen; **Letters** (History; Modern Languages; Political Sciences; Psychology; Public Administration; Social Sciences; Sociology) *Dean:* Joao Fernandes; **Medicine** *(Luanda)* (Medicine; Surgery) *Dean:* Cristovão Simoes; **Science** (Biology; Chemistry; Engineering; Geophysics; Mathematics; Physics) *Dean:* Orlando da Mata

Higher Institutes
Educational Sciences *(Benguela) Dean:* José Calelessa; **Educational Sciences** *(Luanda) Dean:* Daniel Mingas; **Educational Sciences** *(Lubango) Dean:* Matondo Tomalela; **Nursing** (Nursing) *Dean:* Helena Luzizila

History: Founded 1962 as Estudos Gerais Universitários, became University of Luanda 1968, University of Angola 1976 and acquired present title 1985. An autonomous State institution.

Governing Bodies: Conselho Universitário

Academic Year: October to June (October-February; March-June)

Admission Requirements: Secondary school certificate and entrance examination

Fees: None

Main Language(s) of Instruction: Portuguese

International Co-operation: With universities in USA; Europe; Brazil; South Africa and Japan

Degrees and Diplomas: *Licenciatura; Licenciatura:* Medicine, 6 yrs; *Mestrado; Doutoramento*

Student Services: Canteen, Cultural centre, Social counselling, Sports facilities

Student Residential Facilities: Yes

Special Facilities: Geology Museum; Archaeology Museum

Libraries: Central Library, c. 8,000 vols; libraries of the faculties

Last Updated: 26/04/07

AGRARIAN HIGH SCHOOL OF KUANZA-SUL

Escola Superior Agrária do Kuanza-Sul (ESAKS)

Sumbe, Kuanza-Sul
Tel: +244 923-379-361

Programmes
Agronomy (Agronomy)
History: Founded 2007.

Main Language(s) of Instruction: Portuguese

Degrees and Diplomas: *Licenciatura*
Last Updated: 31/05/07

BELAS UNIVERSITY

Universidade de Belas (UNIBELAS)

Luanda
Tel: +244(222) 40-16-79
EMail: unibelas@hotmail.com

Rector: Agatângelo Estêvão Zua

Programmes
Accountancy and Management (Accountancy; Management); **Administration and Marketing** (Administration; Marketing); **Computer Science** (Computer Science); **Health Services** (Health Administration); **International Relations** (International Relations); **Law** (Law); **Nursing** (Nursing); **Petroleum Engineering** (Petroleum and Gas Engineering); **Physiotherapy** (Physical Therapy)

History: Founded 2007.
Last Updated: 07/08/09

CATHOLIC UNIVERSITY OF ANGOLA

Universidade Católica de Angola (UCAN)

Caixa postal 2064, Rua Nossa Sennhora da Muxima 29, Luanda
Tel: +244(222) 331-973
Fax: +244(222) 398-759
EMail: info@ucan.edu
Website: http://www.ucan.edu

Reitor: Damião António Franklin
EMail: damiaofranklin@ucan.edu; damiaof@ucan.edu

Vice-Reitor: Antonio Martins da Torre

Faculties
Economics (Economics); **Engineering** (Engineering); **Law** (Law); **Social Sciences** (English; Portuguese; Psychology; Social Sciences; Translation and Interpretation)

History: Founded 1997.

Degrees and Diplomas: *Licenciatura*
Last Updated: 06/08/09

GREGÓRIO SEMEDO UNIVERSITY

Universidade Gregório Semedo

Rua Kwamme N'Krumah, 16-18, Ingombotas, Luanda
Tel: +244(222) 239-4668
Fax: +244 923 690-274
EMail: ugs@snet.co.ao.
Website: http://www.ugs.ed.ao/

Reitor: José António Lopes Semedo

Faculties
Economics and Business Studies *Dean:* Luis F.E. Rocha; **Engineering and New Technologies** (Computer Engineering; Technology) *Dean:* José Luis Ferreira; **Law and Political Science** *Dean:* José Antonio Lopes Semedo; **Social Sciences and Human Development** (Human Resources; Social Sciences) *Dean:* Julian M. Francisco

History: Founded 2003.

Main Language(s) of Instruction: Portuguese

Degrees and Diplomas: *Licenciatura:* Law; Computer Engineering; Marketing; Human Resource; Business Adminstration; Business Computing
Last Updated: 06/08/09

HIGHER INSTITUTE OF SOCIAL SCIENCES AND INTERNATIONAL RELATIONS

Instituto superior de Ciencias Sociais e Relações Internacionais (ISCRI)

Largo António Jacinto, Edificio do Mirex 7° andar, Luanda
Tel: +222 33-16-18 +222 912-501-091
EMail: geral@cis-edu.org
Website: http://www.cis-edu.org/

Presidente Conselho Directivo: Emmanuel Moeira Carneiro

Programmes

Economics (Economics); **International Relations** (International Relations); **Political Science** (Political Sciences); **Public Administration** (Public Administration); **Sociology** (Sociology)

History: Founded 2007.

Degrees and Diplomas: *Licenciatura*
Last Updated: 06/08/09

HIGHER TECHNICAL INSTITUTE OF ANGOLA

Instituto Superior Técnico de Angola (ISTA)
Quilómetro Nove, Viana, Luanda
Tel: +244 924-88-96-36 +244 923-39-97-77

Director: Manuel Brito Neto

Programmes

Accounting and Administration (Accountancy; Administration); **Engineering** (Computer Engineering; Electronic Engineering; Telecommunications Engineering)

History: Founded 2007.

Degrees and Diplomas: *Licenciatura*
Last Updated: 01/06/07

INDEPENDENT UNIVERSITY OF ANGOLA

Universidade Independente de Angola (UNIA)
Rua da Missão, Barrio Morro Bento II Corimba, Luanda
Tel: +224(222) 33-89-70
Fax: +244(222) 33-89-68
EMail: unia@unia.ao
Website: http://www.unia.ao

Reitor: Carlos Alberto Burity da Silva **EMail:** reitor@unia.ao

Vice-Rector: Filipe Silvino de Pina Zau

Departments

Civil Engineering (Civil Engineering); **Communication Sciences** (Journalism; Radio and Television Broadcasting); **Computer Engineering** (Computer Engineering); **Electronic Engineering and Telecommunications** (Electronic Engineering; Telecommunications Engineering); **Law** (Law); **Management and Marketing** (Management; Marketing); **Natural Resources and Environmental Engineering** (Environmental Engineering; Natural Resources); **Social Sciences** (Social Sciences)

History: Founded 2004.

Degrees and Diplomas: *Licenciatura*
Last Updated: 06/08/09

JEAN PIAGET UNIVERSITY OF ANGOLA

**Universidade Jean Piaget de Angola
(UNIPIAGET DE ANGOLA)**
Caixa postal 81, Bairro Capalanca, Viana, Luanda
Tel: +244(222) 29-04-48
Fax: +244(222) 29-02-59
EMail: info@angola.ipiaget.org
Website: http://www.angola.ipiaget.org

Reitor: Pedro Domingos Peterson

Vice-Rector: José Eduardo do Carmo Nelumba

Courses

Clinical Psychology (Clinical Psychology); **Computer Engineering** (Computer Engineering); **Construction Engineering and Territorial Planning** (Construction Engineering); **Dentistry** (Dentistry); **Economics and Management**; **Electrical and Mechanical Engineering** (Electrical Engineering; Mechanical Engineering); **Human Motricity and Rehabilitation**; **Law** (Criminal Law; Law); **Medicine**; **Nursing** (Nursing); **Petroleum Engineering** (Petroleum and Gas Engineering); **Pharmacy** (Pharmacy); **Physiotherapy** (Physical Therapy); **Portuguese** (Native Language; Portuguese); **Sociology** (Sociology)

History: Founded 2000.

Main Language(s) of Instruction: Portuguese

Degrees and Diplomas: *Licenciatura*
Last Updated: 07/08/09

METHODIST UNIVERSITY OF ANGOLA

Universidade Metodista de Angola (UMA)
Rua Nossa Senhora da Muxima, 10, Kinaxixi, Luanda
Tel: +224(222) 338-984
Fax: +224(222) 330-572
EMail: geral@uma.co.ao
Website: http://www.uma.co.ao/UMA

Reitora: Teresa José Adelina da Silva Neto
EMail: tjasn@uma.co.ao

Administrative Officer: Armindo da Costa Gameiro

Courses

Architecture and Town Planning (Architecture; Art History; Design; Town Planning); **Civil Engineering** (Civil Engineering); **Electrical, Mechanical and Computer Engineering** (Computer Engineering; Electrical and Electronic Engineering; Mechanical Engineering); **Industrial Engineering and Electrical Systems** (Electrical Engineering; Industrial Engineering); **Law** (Administrative Law; Constitutional Law; International Law; Law); **Management and Business Administration** (Accountancy; Banking; Business Administration; Finance; Management)

History: Founded 2007.

Main Language(s) of Instruction: Portuguese

Degrees and Diplomas: *Licenciatura*; *Mestrado*
Last Updated: 07/08/09

NATIONAL INSTITUTE OF PUBLIC ADMINISTRATION

Institut national d'Administration publique (INAP)
BP 6852, Estrago do Futungo, Luanda
Tel: +244(222) 351-160
Fax: +244(222) 354-555

Direitor: José Joào Lourenço

Programmes

Economics (Economics); **Law** (Law); **Political Science** (Political Sciences); **Public Administration** (Public Administration); **Social Sciences** (Social Sciences)
Last Updated: 30/07/09

OSCAR RIBAS UNIVERSITY

Universidade Óscar Ribas (UOR)
Av. Centro de Convenções Talatona s/n, Luanda
Tel: +244 927-007-765 +244(4) 222-401-513
Fax: +244(4) 222-397-591
EMail: admin@uor-angola.org
Website: http://www.uor-ao.com

Rector: Alberto Chocolate
Tel: +244 923-608-652,
Fax: +244 912-678-066; +244 925-065-882
EMail: amabach@hotmail.com; amabach@yahoo.com

Secretary-General: Madaleno De Andrade
Tel: +244 923-307-902; +244 912-688-514
EMail: lenoandrade@hotmail.com

International Relations: Maria Fatima, Vice Rector
Tel: +244 925-482-765 EMail: fatyma66@yahoo.com

Departments

Civil Engineering; **Engineering** (Computer Science; Electrical Engineering; Engineering; Mechanical Engineering; Telecommunications Engineering); **International Relations** (International Relations); **Law** (Law); **Management** (Management); **Psychology**

History: Founded 2007.

Admission Requirements: Certificate of Secondary Studies

Fees: (US Dollars): 250 per month for Social Science course; 280 per month for Engineering course

Main Language(s) of Instruction: Portuguese

International Co-operation: With institutions in Portugal, Spain and Brazil

Degrees and Diplomas: *Licenciatura*: Law, 4 yrs; *Mestrado (M.Sc.) (Master/MBA)*: 2 yrs; *Doutoramento (Ph.D.)*: 3-4 yrs

Student Services: Academic counselling, Canteen, Language programs, Nursery care

Student Residential Facilities: None

Special Facilities: None

Libraries: Yes

Academic Staff 2008-2009	MEN	WOMEN	TOTAL
FULL-TIME	9	6	**15**
PART-TIME	122	27	**149**
STAFF WITH DOCTORATE			
FULL-TIME	8	2	**10**
PART-TIME	9	3	**12**
Student Numbers 2008-2009			
All (Foreign Included)	1,747	1,535	**3,282**

Evening students, 1,378.
Last Updated: 05/05/09

PRIVATE UNIVERSITY OF ANGOLA
Universidade Privada de Angola (UPRA)
Estrada de Catete- Edificio da Filda, Luanda
Tel: +244(222) 265-645
EMail: upra@upra.lubango.org

Reitor: Carlos Alberto Pinto de Sousa

International Relations: Helena Coelho
Tel: +244(925) 184-047 EMail: helena@upra.ao

Departments
Accountancy and Business Administration (Accountancy; Business Administration); **Architecture** (Architecture); **Civil Engineering** (Civil Engineering); **Computer Science** (Computer Science); **Dentistry** (Dentistry); **International Relations** (International Relations); **Nursing** (Nursing); **Pharmacy** (Pharmacy); **Physiotherapy** (Physical Therapy); **Psychology** (Psychology); **Social Communication** (Communication Studies); **Tourism and Hotel Management** (Hotel Management; Tourism)

History: Founded 2000 as Instituto Superior Privado de Angola. Acquired present status and title 2007.

Main Language(s) of Instruction: Portuguese

Degrees and Diplomas: *Licenciatura*; *Mestrado*: Health Management

Last Updated: 06/07/09

TECHNICAL UNIVERSITY OF ANGOLA
Universidade Técnica de Angola (UTANGA)
Bairro Capolo II, Rua A4 N°. 14, Kilamba Kiaxi, Luanda
Tel: +244(222) 912-08-85-50 +244(222) 912-07-11-46
EMail: info@utanga.co.ao
Website: http://www.utanga.co.ao

Reitor: Paulo Victorino dos Reis Afonso

Secretario-General: Felipe Zeferino

Courses
Accountancy and Administration (Accountancy; Administration); **Architecture and Town Planning** (Architecture; Town Planning); **Computer Engineering** (Business Computing; Computer Engineering); **Environmental Engineering** (Environmental Engineering); **Human Resources** (Human Resources); **Marketing**; **Mining Engineering** (Mining Engineering); **Modern Languages** (English); **Political Sciences and International Relations** (International Relations; Political Sciences)

History: Founded 2007.

Degrees and Diplomas: *Licenciatura*
Last Updated: 07/08/09

Argentina

STRUCTURE OF HIGHER EDUCATION SYSTEM

Description:

Higher education is provided by public and private universities, university institutes and institutes devoted to higher studies in the Fine Arts or to technical and professional studies, as well as teacher-training institutes. The Consejo Interuniversitario Nacional (CIN) coordinates policies of the State-run universities and their relationship with public and private, national and foreign bodies; draws up proposals for the national recognition of complete and partial studies and degrees and diplomas; and the national validation of foreign qualifications. Private universities are autonomous but must be recognized by the State, and their statutes, courses and programmes must be approved by it. They are grouped under the Consejo de Rectores de Universidades Privadas (CRUP). Through their Steering Committees, CIN and CRUP make up the Universities Council, to which the Ministry turns to in order to address some affairs regarding university policies. The Consejo Nacional de Evaluación y Acreditación Universitaria (CONEAU) oversees the external evaluations of all universities and provides authorization for the establishment of new universities. It also accredits graduate programmes and some undergraduate programmes where the public interest needs to be protected (e.g. Medicine and Engineering). State-run higher education institutions do not generally charge any fees but private universities do.

Stages of studies:

University level first stage: Licenciatura, Professional Title
The first stage of university level education lasts between four and six years. It leads to the award of the Licenciatura or a professional qualification. The first stage corresponds to the study of basic subjects and practical experience in a given subject. In fields such as Architecture, Law and Medicine, first professional degrees are awarded after 5-6 years of study. The title of Profesor en ... is awarded after three to four-and-a-half years' study. The number of 4-year Licenciatura programmes is increasing.
Intermediate professional titles of Técnico or Técnico Universitario, Bachillerato Universitario, Perito, Analista, Profesor de Nivel Inicial o Primario, Profesor de Nivel Secundario o Polimodal are also offered and are conferred after studies that last for a minimum of two to three years.

University level second stage: Especialización, Maestría
The Especialización consists in further training in a profession. It leads to the title of Especialista in a given field after a minimum of one year or 360 hours.
The Maestría offers further training in a discipline or in an interdisciplinary field and is conferred after two years of further study or 540 hours. Training includes carrying out a research project or defending a thesis under the guidance of a supervisor which is evaluated by a jury which comprises at least one member that is external to the University. It leads to a Título Académico de Magister and the specification of the field of study.

University level third stage: Doctorado
The Doctorado is the highest degree. Candidates must submit a thesis. Since it is not a prerequisite for the practice of a profession, no time limit is imposed.

ADMISSION TO HIGHER EDUCATION

Admission to university-level studies:

Name of secondary school credential required: Bachillerato

Entrance exam requirements: There is an entrance examination in some cases.

Foreign students admission:

Entrance exam requirements: Students must hold the Bachillerato or its equivalent and sit for an entrance examination for the faculty or institution. To be admitted to post-graduate studies and research, candidates must have completed a degree course in a foreign university and have obtained the approval of the academic unit offering the post-graduate course.

Entry regulations: Foreign students non residing in Argentina and wanting to study in a national higher education institution, must go to the Argentine Consulate in their home countries and apply for a vacancy under the scope of the 1523/90 Ministerial Resolution. Such a formality is not required to study at a private higher education institution.

Health requirements: At the time of enrollment, students are required by universities to submit a copy of the international health insurance policy. This insurance plan should cover the entire length of the student's stay in Argentina.

Language requirements: Students must be proficient in Spanish.

RECOGNITION OF STUDIES

Quality assurance system:

Higher education institutions and courses are assessed and accredited by the National Commission for University Evaluation and Accreditation (Comisión Nacional de Evaluación y Acreditación Universitaria - CONEAU).

Bodies dealing with recognition:

Comisión Nacional de Evaluación y Acreditación Universitaria - CONEAU (National Commission for University Evaluation and Accreditation)
Av. Santa Fe 1385, Piso 4
Buenos Aires C1059ABH
Tel: +54(11) 4819 9050
Fax: +54(11) 4815 0744
EMail: consulta@coneau.gob.ar
WWW: http://www.coneau.edu.ar

NATIONAL BODIES

Ministerio de Educación (Ministry of Education)
Minister: Alberto Estanislao Sileoni
Director, University Policies: Alberto Dibbern
Pizzurno 935
Buenos Aires 1020
Tel: +54(11) 4129 1000
WWW: http://portal.educacion.gov.ar/

Ministerio de Ciencia, Tecnología e Innovación Productiva (Ministry of Science, Technology and Productive Innovation)
Minister: José Lino Barañao
Avda. Córdoba 831
Buenos Aires
Tel: +54(11) 4891 8300
EMail: info@mincyt.gob.ar
WWW: http://www.mincyt.gov.ar/

Comisión Nacional de Evaluación y Acreditación Universitaria - CONEAU (National Commission for University Evaluation and Accreditation)
Av. Santa Fe 1385, Piso 4
Buenos Aires C1059ABH
Tel: +54(11) 4819 9050
Fax: +54(11) 4815 0744
EMail: consulta@coneau.gob.ar
WWW: http://www.coneau.edu.ar
Role of national body: Oversees the external evaluations of all universities and the authorization process for the establishment of new universities. It also accredits graduate programmes and some undergraduate programmes where the public interest needs to be protected.

Consejo Interuniversitario Nacional - CIN (National Interuniversity Council)

President: Flavio Fama
Executive Secretary: Norma Beatriz Costoya
Pacheco de Melo 2084
Buenos Aires C1126AAF
Tel: +54(11) 4806 2269
Fax: +54(11) 4806 2269
WWW: http://www.cin.edu.ar
Role of national body: Coordinates State-run university activities, recommends the creation of academic units, participates in university policy planning and makes recommendations to the Ministry.

Consejo de Rectores de Universidades Privadas - CRUP (Council of Rectors of Private Universities)

President: Héctor César Sauret
Montevideo 1910 PB
Buenos Aires C1021AAH
WWW: http://www.crup.org.ar
Role of national body: Coordinates the activities of private universities.

Data for academic year: 2010-2011
Source: IAU from the website of the Ministry of Education, Argentina, 2010. Bodies updated in 2011

INSTITUTIONS

PUBLIC INSTITUTIONS

AUTONOMOUS UNIVERSITY OF ENTRE RÍOS

Universidad Autónoma de Entre Ríos
Avenida F. Ramirez 1143, 3100 Paraná, Entre Ríos
Tel: +54(343) 420-7880
EMail: rectorado@uader.edu.ar
Website: http://www.uader.edu.ar

Rector: Mario Mathieu Tel: +54(343) 420-7908

Secretario Académico: Roberto Fariña
EMail: academica@uader.edu.ar

Faculties
Business Administration *Dean*: Graciela Mingo Bevilacqua; **Humanities, Arts and Social Sciences** (Arts and Humanities; Education; English; Fine Arts; French; Geography; Gerontology; History; Italian; Literature; Modern Languages; Music; Philosophy; Portuguese; Psychology; Social Sciences; Special Education; Visual Arts); **Life and Health Sciences** (Biological and Life Sciences; Health Sciences; Nursing; Physical Education) *Dean*: Inés Patricia Riobó; **Science and Technology** *Dean*: Marino Schneerberger

History: Founded 2000.

Degrees and Diplomas: *Profesorado*; *Licenciatura*; *Maestría*
Last Updated: 26/02/09

GENERAL SARMIENTO NATIONAL UNIVERSITY

Universidad Nacional de General Sarmiento (UNGS)
José M. Gutiérrez 1150, 1613 Los Polvorines, Buenos Aires
Tel: +54(11) 4469-7500
EMail: rectorado@ungs.edu.ar
Website: http://www.ungs.edu.ar

Rector: Silvio Israel Feldman (2002-)
EMail: sfeldman@ungs.edu.ar

Secretaria Académica: Maria Fernanda Musso
Tel: +54(11) 4469-7592 EMail: mfmusso@ungs.edu.ar

International Relations: Alicia Goldman
Tel: +54(11) 4469-7595 EMail: agoldman@ungs.edu.ar

Institutes
Human Development *(IDH) Director*: Eduardo Rinesi; **Industry** *(IDEL)* (Business Administration; Industrial and Production Economics; Industrial Engineering; Industrial Management; Social Sciences) *Director*: Néstor Braidot; **Science** *(ICI)* (Arts and Humanities; Mathematics and Computer Science; Natural Sciences; Social Sciences) *Directora*: Rosa Belvedresi; **Urban Studies** *(Conurbano, ICO)* (Ecology; Public Administration; Social Policy; Urban Studies) *Directora*: Magdalena Chiara

History: Founded 1993.

Governing Bodies: Consejo de Institutos; Consejo Superior; Asamblea Universitaria

Academic Year: March to December

Admission Requirements: Secondary school certificate or equivalent

Main Language(s) of Instruction: Spanish

Degrees and Diplomas: *Licenciatura*: Communication; Education; Industrial Economics; Public Administration; Social Policy; Urban Ecology; Urbanism; Political Science, 5 yrs; *Professional Title*: Industrial Engineering, 5 yrs; *Professional Title*: Teacher Training (Economics, History, Mathematics, Philosophy, Physics), 4 yrs; *Especialización*: Management of Science, Technology and Innovation; Local Development; Urban Studies, a further 1 yr; *Maestría*: Economics and Industrial Development; Economics and Social Studies; Engineering Management; Technology; Small Business, a further 2 yrs; *Doctorado*: Social Sciences; Science and Technology, a further 4 yrs. Also Diploma Universitario de Estudios Generales in Exact Sciences, Social Sciences, Humanities, Technology and Administration, 2 1/2 yrs

Student Services: Academic counselling, Canteen, Handicapped facilities

Libraries: Biblioteca 'Pucciarelli'. Historical collection 'Eduardo Monzón

Evening students, 1,845.
Last Updated: 27/02/09

NATIONAL TECHNICAL UNIVERSITY
Universidad Tecnológica Nacional (UTN)
Sarmiento 440, Piso 3, 5, 6, 7, 8, 1347 Buenos Aires,
Capital Federal
Tel: +54(11) 5371-5600
Fax: +54(11) 5371-5697
EMail: postmaster@rec.utn.edu.ar
Website: http://www.utn.edu.ar

Rector: Héctor Carlos Brotto
Tel: +54(11) 5371-5702 EMail: privada@utn.edu.ar

Vicerrector: Carlos E. Fantini

International Relations: Alfredo Lobeira Lazzari
Tel: +54(11) 4394-8428, Fax: +54(11) 4394-8428
EMail: internacionales@rec.utn.edu.ar

Faculties
Aeronautical Engineering *(Haedo)* (Aeronautical and Aerospace Engineering) *Dean:* Elio Biagini; **Civil Engineering** *(Avellaneda)* (Civil Engineering; Construction Engineering) *Dean:* José Maria Virgili; **Civil Engineering** *(Bahía Blanca) Dean:* Liberto Ercoli; **Civil Engineering** *(Buenos Aires) Dean:* Luis Ángel De Marco; **Civil Engineering** *(Concepción del Uruguay) Dean:* Juan Carlos Piter; **Civil Engineering** *(Córdoba) Dean:* Benito César Possetto; **Civil Engineering** *(General Pacheco) Dean:* Eugenio Bruno Ricciolini; **Civil Engineering** *(La Plata) Dean:* Carlos Eduardo Fantini; **Civil Engineering** *(Mendoza) Dean:* Julio César Cleto Cobos; **Civil Engineering** *(Paraná) Dean:* Raúl E. Arroyo; **Civil Engineering** *(Rafaela) Dean:* Raul Antonio Ricotti; **Civil Engineering** *(Rosario) Dean:* Ruben Fernando Ciccarelli; **Civil Engineering** *(San Rafael) Dean:* Horacío Paulino Pessano; **Civil Engineering** *(Santa Fé) Dean:* Ricárdo Omar Scholtus; **Civil Engineering** *(Tucumán) Dean:* Hector Nosetti; **Electrical Engineering** *(Delta)* (Electrical Engineering) *Dean:* Gustavo Bauer; **Electronic and Mechanical Engineering** *(Resistencia)* (Electronic Engineering; Mechanical Engineering) *Dean:* Sebastián Vicente Martín; **Electronic and Mechanical Engineering** *(San Francisco) Dean:* Daniel Eduardo Ferradas; **Electronic Engineering** *(Villa María) Dean:* Juan Carlos Peretti; **Electronic Engineering** *(Río Grande)* (Electronic Engineering) *Dean:* Mario Félix Ferreyra; **Metallurgical Engineering** *(San Nicolás)* (Metallurgical Engineering) *Dean:* Neorén Pedro Franco

Units
Chemical and Electronic Engineering *(Confluencia)* (Chemical Engineering; Electronic Engineering) *Dean:* Enrique Ariel Sierra; **Civil, Electrical and Mechanical Engineering** *(Venardo Tuerto) Director:* Alfredo A. Guillaumet; **Civil, Electronic and Mechanical Engineering** *(La Rioja) Director:* Diego Osvaldo Di Lorenzo; **Electrical and Mechanical Engineering** *(Reconquista) Director:* Osvaldo Héctor del Valle Fatala; **Electrical and Mechanical Engineering** *(Río Gallegos) Director:* Luis A. Maraschin; **Industrial Management** *(Chubut)* (Fishery; Industrial Management) *Director:* Norberto A. Cantalejos; **Rural Studies** *(Concordia)* (Rural Studies) *Director:* Oscar Amado Gerard; **Rural Studies and Industrial Management** *(Trenque Lauquen) Director:* Guillermo A. Gil

History: Founded 1948 as Universidad Obrera Nacional. Acquired present status and title 1959.

Governing Bodies: Consejo Superior

Academic Year: February to November (February -July; August-November)

Admission Requirements: Secondary school certificate (bachillerato)

Main Language(s) of Instruction: Spanish

Degrees and Diplomas: *Professional Title:* Engineering (Ingeniero), 5 yrs; *Especialización; Maestría; Doctorado:* Engineering

Student Services: Academic counselling, Canteen, Cultural centre, Employment services, Foreign student adviser, Handicapped facilities, Health services, Nursery care, Social counselling, Sports facilities

Libraries: Buenos Aires Faculty Library, c. 11,520 vols. Libraries of the faculties

Publications: Revista de la Universidad Tecnológica Nacional *(monthly)*
Last Updated: 05/07/07

NATIONAL UNIVERSITY INSTITUTE OF ART
Instituto Universitario Nacional del Arte (IUNA)
Paraguay 786, C1057AAJ Buenos Aires, Capital Federal
Tel: +54(11) 4516-0992
EMail: secretariaprivada@iuna.edu.ar
Website: http://www.iuna.edu.ar

Rectora: Liliana Demaio EMail: rectora@iuna.edu.ar

Secretaria General: Silvia César
EMail: secretaria.general@iuna.edu.ar

International Relations: Marcelo González Magnasco
EMail: udi@iuna.edu.ar

Areas
Art Criticism *Director:* Oscar Traversa; **Folklore** (Dance; Folklore) *Director:* Susana Gomez; **Multimedia** (Multimedia) *Director:* Carmelo Saitta; **Teacher Training** *Director:* Susana Vega

Departments
Audiovisual (Cinema and Television) *Director:* Jose Luis Castiñeira de Dios; **Dance** *(María Ruanova)* (Dance; Folklore) *Director:* Diana Leila Piazza; **Drama** *(Antonio Cunill Cabanellas) Director:* Sandra Torlucci; **Music and Sound** *(Carlos López Buchardo)* (Music; Music Education; Music Theory and Composition; Musical Instruments; Singing) *Director:* Julio García Canepa; **Visual Arts** *(Prilidiano Pueyrredón)* (Ceramic Art; Design; Painting and Drawing; Sculpture; Visual Arts) *Director:* Rodolfo Agüero

History: Founded 1996.

Governing Bodies: Consejo Consultivo Institucional

Admission Requirements: Secondary school certificate and other minimum requirements

Main Language(s) of Instruction: Spanish

Accrediting Agencies: Ministerio de Educación, Ciencia y Tecnología

Degrees and Diplomas: *Licenciatura:* 4 yrs; *Professional Title:* 4 yrs; *Especialización:* 2-4 yrs; *Maestría:* 4 yrs; *Doctorado*

Student Services: Canteen

Special Facilities: Sculpture Museum. Art Gallery

Libraries: Yes
Last Updated: 26/02/09

NATIONAL UNIVERSITY OF CATAMARCA
Universidad Nacional de Catamarca (UNCA)
Esquiú 612, 4700 San Fernando del Valle de Catamarca,
Catamarca
Tel: +54(3833) 424-099 +54(3833) 435-177
Fax: +54(3833) 424-099
EMail: sef@tecno.unca.edu.ar; privadaunca@arnet.com.ar
Website: http://www.unca.edu.ar

Rector: Flavio Sergio Fama
Tel: +54(3833) 424-099 EMail: ffama@tecno.unca.edu.ar

Secretaria Académica y de Posgrado: María del Valle Coronel
Tel: +54(3833) 430-373 EMail: academicaunca@arnet.com.ar

Faculties
Agriculture (Agricultural Engineering; Agriculture; Landscape Architecture) *Dean:* Oscar Alfonso Arellano; **Economics and Administration** (Administration; Economics) *Dean:* Beatriz Maza; **Exact and Natural Sciences** (Mathematics; Natural Sciences) *Dean:* Elina Silvera de Buenader; **Health Sciences** (Health Sciences) *Dean:* Omar T. Barrionuevo; **Humanities** (Arts and Humanities; Educational Sciences; English; French; Geography; History; Literature; Philosophy; Social Work; Teacher Training) *Dean:* Luis Eduardo Segura; **Law** (Law) *Dean:* Claudia Patricia Pacheco; **Technology and Applied Sciences** (Electrical Engineering; Geology; Mining Engineering; Natural Sciences; Technology) *Dean:* Carlos Savio

Schools
Archaeology (Archaeology) *Director:* Graciela Neyra

History: Founded 1972. An autonomous State institution.

Academic Year: March to November

Admission Requirements: Secondary school certificate (bachillerato) or equivalent

Main Language(s) of Instruction: Spanish

Degrees and Diplomas: *Título Menor*: Administration; Haemotherapy; Nursing; Technical Studies, 2-3 yrs; *Licenciatura*: Biology; Chemistry; Education; English; French; Geography; Geology; History; Letters; Mathematics; Nursing; Philosophy; Physics, 5 yrs; *Professional Title*: Accountancy; Agriculture; Mining; Surveying, 5-6 yrs; *Professional Title*: Teacher Training (secondary level); *Especialización*; *Maestría*; *Doctorado*
Last Updated: 27/02/09

NATIONAL UNIVERSITY OF CHILECITO

Universidad Nacional de Chilecito
9 de Julio 22, 5333 Chilecito, La Rioja
Tel: +54(3825) 42-2631
EMail: info@undec.edu.ar
Website: http://www.undec.edu.ar

Rector: Norberto Raúl Caminoa
Tel: +54(3825) 42-6291 EMail: rector@undec.edu.ar

Vicerrector: José Tomás Yoma

Departments
Exact, Physical and Natural Sciences (Agricultural Engineering; Agronomy; Biology; Systems Analysis); **Social, Legal and Economic Sciences**

History: Founded 2003.

Main Language(s) of Instruction: Spanish

Degrees and Diplomas: *Licenciatura*: 5 yrs; *Professional Title*: 5 yrs. Also posgrado in social communication
Last Updated: 27/02/09

NATIONAL UNIVERSITY OF COMAHUE

Universidad Nacional del Comahue (UNCOMA)
Buenos Aires 1400, 8300 Neuquén, Neuquén
Tel: +54(299) 449-0363
Fax: +54(299) 449-0351
EMail: sprector@uncoma.edu.ar
Website: http://www.uncoma.edu.ar

Rectora: Teresa Vega Tel: +54(299) 449-0300

Secretario Académico: Luis Bertani
Tel: +54(299) 449-0356 EMail: saunc@uncoma.edu.ar

Faculties
Agriculture *(Cinco Saltos)* (Agriculture) *Dean*: Jorge Luis Girardin; **Economics and Administration** (Administration; Economics) *Dean*: Susana G. Landriscini; **Educational Sciences** *(Cipoletti)* (Education) *Dean*: Guillermo Villanueva; **Engineering** (Engineering) *Dean*: Daniel Rodolfo Boccanera; **Humanities** (Arts and Humanities) *Dean*: Pedro A. Barreiro; **Law and Social Sciences** *(General Roca)* (Law; Social and Community Services; Social Sciences; Sociology) *Dean*: Omar Jurgeit; **Tourism** (Leisure Studies; Tourism) *Dean*: Julia Gerlero

Higher Schools
Languages *(General Roca)* (Modern Languages) *Director*: Juan Gauna

Institutes
Health Sciences (Health Sciences) *Director*: Juan Gauna; **Marine Biology and Fisheries** *(San Antonio Oeste)* (Fishery; Marine Biology) *Director*: Raúl González

Schools
Medicine *(Cipolletti)* (Medical Technology) *Director*: Horacio Panisse

History: Founded 1965 as Universidad Provincial del Neuquén, acquired present status 1972.

Governing Bodies: Asamblea Universitaria; Consejo Superior

Academic Year: March to December (March-July; August-December)

Admission Requirements: Secondary school certificate (bachillerato)

Fees: None for undergraduate studies

Main Language(s) of Instruction: Spanish

Accrediting Agencies: CONEAU

Degrees and Diplomas: *Licenciatura*: Geography; History; Tourism, 5 yrs; *Professional Title*: Accountancy; Engineering; Social Work, 5-6 yrs; *Professional Title*: Teacher Teaching (secondary level), 4 yrs

Student Services: Academic counselling, Canteen, Cultural centre, Employment services, Handicapped facilities, Health services, Language programs, Social counselling, Sports facilities

Student Residential Facilities: Yes

Special Facilities: Palaeontology Museum

Libraries: Central Library. Branch Libraries
Last Updated: 27/06/07

ATLANTIC ZONE REGIONAL CENTRE
CENTRO UNIVERSITARIO REGIONAL 'ZONA ATLÁNTICA' (CURZA)

Monseñor Esandi y Ayacucho, 8500 Viedma, Río Negro
Tel: +54(2920) 42-2921
Fax: +54(2920) 42-3198
EMail: curza@uncoma.edu.ar
Website: http://curza.uncoma.edu.ar

Decano: Miguel A. Silva EMail: masilva@uncoma.edu.ar

Secretaria Académica: Adriana Goycochea

Programmes
Agricultural Management (Agricultural Management); **Agricultural Production Technology** (Agricultural Engineering); **Language and Communication** (Communication Studies; Modern Languages); **Political Science** (Political Sciences); **Postgraduate Studies**; **Psychopedagogy** (Educational Psychology); **Public Administration** (Public Administration)

BARILOCHE REGIONAL CENTRE
CENTRO UNIVERSITARIO REGIONAL 'BARILOCHE' (CURB)

Quintral s/n 1250, Barrio Jardín Botánico, 8400 San Carlos de Bariloche, Río Negro
Tel: +54(2944) 42-3374
Fax: +54(2944) 42-2111
EMail: ingreso@crub.uncoma.edu.ar
Website: http://crub1.uncoma.edu.ar

Decano: Juan Daniel Nataine
EMail: dnataine@crub.uncoma.edu.ar

Secretaria Académica: María Inés Sánchez
EMail: academica@crub.uncoma.edu.ar

Programmes
Agricultural Technology; **Biological and Life Sciences** (Biological and Life Sciences); **Biological Sciences**; **Postgraduate Studies**

SAN MARTÍN DE LOS ANDES BRANCH
ASENTAMIENTO UNIVERSITARIO 'SAN MARTÍN DE LOS ANDES' (AUSMA)

Pasaje de la Paz 235, 8370 San Martín de Los Andes, Neuquén
Tel: +54(2972) 42-7618
Fax: +54(2972) 42-7164
EMail: ausma@uncoma.edu.ar
Website: http://ausma.uncoma.edu.ar

Director: Uriel Mele

Programmes
Forestry Engineering (Forestry); **Tourism** (Tourism)

VILLA REGINA BRANCH
ASENTAMIENTO UNIVERSITARIO 'VILLA REGINA' (AUVR)

25 de Mayo y Reconquista, 8336 Villa Regina, Río Negro
Tel: +54(2941) 46-3200
Fax: +54(2941) 46-2593
EMail: auvrunc@uncoma.edu.ar
Website: http://auvr.uncoma.edu.ar

Directora: Adriana Caballero EMail: director@auvr.com.ar

Programmes

Food Conservation Technology; **Food Science** (Food Science); **Food Technology**; **Postgraduate Studies**

ZAPALA BRANCH

ASENTAMIENTIO UNIVERSITARIO 'ZAPALA' (AUZA)

Avenida 12 de Julio y Rahue, 8340 Zapala, Neuquén
Tel: +54(2942) 42-1574
Fax: +54(2942) 42-1847
EMail: uncadmin@zapala.com.ar
Website: http://auza.uncoma.edu.ar

Director: Juan F. Caro
Tel: +54(2942) 421-847 EMail: jfcaro_44@yahoo.com.ar

Programmes

Agricultural Management; **Agricultural Production Technology**; **Language and Communication**; **Political Science**; **Postgraduate Studies**; **Psychopedagogy**; **Public Administration**

NATIONAL UNIVERSITY OF CÓRDOBA

Universidad Nacional de Córdoba (UNCOR)
Haya de la Torre s/n, Ciudad Unversitaria, Pabellón Argentina,
5000 Córdoba, Córdoba
Tel: +54(351) 433-4157
Fax: +54(351) 433-4157
EMail: protocolo@sri.trejo.unc.edu.ar
Website: http://www.unc.edu.ar

Rectora: Silvia Carolina Scotto (2001-)
Tel: +54(351) 433-4072 EMail: rector@unc.edu.ar

Vicerrector: Gerardo Fidelio

Secretaria Académica: Hebe Goldenhersch
Tel: +54(351) 433-3049 EMail: secadad@saa.unc.edu.ar

Centres

Microscope Electronics (Microelectronics)

Faculties

Agriculture (Agriculture) *Dean*: Daniel Esteban di Giusto; **Architecture, Town Planning, and Design** (Architecture; Design; Town Planning) *Dean*: Carlos Feretti; **Chemistry** (Chemistry) *Dean*: Gerardo Fidelio; **Dentistry** (Dentistry) *Dean*: Nazario Kuyumllián; **Economics** (Economics) *Dean*: Ana Karl de Vega; **Exact, Physical and Natural Sciences** (Natural Sciences; Physics) *Dean*: Hector Gabriel Tavella; **Languages** (Modern Languages) *Director*: Cristina Elgue de Martini; **Law and Social Sciences** (Information Sciences; Law; Social Welfare) *Dean*: Ramón Pedro Yanzi Ferreira; **Mathematics, Astronomy, and Physics** (Astronomy and Space Science; Mathematics; Physics) *Dean*: Daniel E. Barraco Díaz; **Medical Sciences** (Ergotherapy; Medical Technology; Medicine; Nursing; Nutrition; Physical Therapy; Speech Therapy and Audiology) *Dean*: José María Willington; **Philosophy and Humanities** (Archiving; Arts and Humanities; Education; History; Library Science; Philosophy; Psychology) *Dean*: Liliana Aguiar de Zapiola; **Psychology** (Psychology) *Dean*: Ana M. Alderete

Schools

Archives (Archiving); **Arts** (Fine Arts); **Audiology** (Speech Therapy and Audiology); **Educational Sciences** (Educational Sciences); **History** (History); **Information Sciences** (Information Sciences); **Kinesiology and Physical Therapy** (Physical Therapy); **Letters** (Arts and Humanities); **Library Science** (Library Science); **Medical Technology** (Medical Technology); **Nursing** (Nursing); **Nutrition** (Nutrition); **Philosophy** (Philosophy); **Public Health** (Public Health); **Social Work** (Social Work)

Further Information: Also University Hospital

History: Founded 1613 as El Nuevo Colegio Máximo under the direction of the Society of Jesus; became university 1621. Recognized by Royal Decree 1680. In 1767 the Jesuits were expelled and the university was then directed by the Franciscans. Received the title of Royal University of San Carlos y Nuestra Señora de Monserrat in 1800 and became an autonomous State University by law in 1854.

Governing Bodies: Asamblea Universitaria; Consejo Superior

Academic Year: February to December (February-July; August-December)

Admission Requirements: Secondary school certificate (bachillerato) or equivalent

Main Language(s) of Instruction: Spanish

Degrees and Diplomas: *Título Menor*: Audiotherapy; Laboratory Sciences; Library Science; Physical Therapy; Radiology, 3 yrs; *Licenciatura*: Accountancy; Business Administration, 6 yrs; *Licenciatura*: Administration; Astronomy; Economics; Education; History; Letters; Mathematics; Philosophy; Physics; Psychology, 5 yrs; *Licenciatura*: Cinematography; Dramatic Art, 4 yrs; *Licenciatura*: Pharmacy, 4 1/2 yrs; *Professional Title*: Accountancy; Dentistry; Dietetics; Geology; Law (Prosecutor); Pedagogy; Social Work; Translation, 5 yrs; *Professional Title*: Actuarial Sciences; Architecture; Biochemistry; Engineering; Law (Lawyer); Notarial Studies, 6 yrs; *Professional Title*: Teacher Training (secondary level); *Maestría*; *Doctorado*: by thesis

Special Facilities: Museum of Natural Sciences. Astronomic Observatory

Libraries: Central Library, c. 200,000 vols; libraries of the various faculties, institutes and schools, c. 170,000 vols

Publications: Revista de la Universidad Nacional de Córdoba; Revista y Boletines de las Facultades e Institutos
Last Updated: 27/02/09

NATIONAL UNIVERSITY OF CUYO

Universidad Nacional de Cuyo (UNCU)
Centro Universitario, Parque 'General San Martín',
M5500JMA Mendoza, Mendoza
Tel: +54(261) 449-4000
Fax: +54(261) 449-4022
EMail: cicun@uncu.edu.ar
Website: http://www.uncu.edu.ar

Rector: Arturo Somoza
Tel: +54(261) 449-4018 EMail: rector@uccuyo.edu.ar

Faculties

Agriculture (Chacras de Coria) (Agricultural Engineering; Agriculture; Oenology) *Dean*: José Guillermo Rodríguez; **Art and Design** (Ceramic Art; Design; Fine Arts; Music; Theatre; Visual Arts) *Dean*: Silvia Persio; **Dentistry** (Dentistry) *Dean*: Alberto Abramovitch; **Economics** (Accountancy; Administration; Economics; Statistics) *Dean*: Roberto Varo; **Elementary and Special Education** (Curriculum; Educational Administration; Physical Education; Primary Education; Special Education; Speech Therapy and Audiology) *Dean*: María Luisa Porcar de Yelós; **Engineering** (Mendoza) (Civil Engineering; Engineering; Industrial Engineering; Petroleum and Gas Engineering) *Dean*: Eduardo Fortunato Manfredi; **Law** (Law) *Dean*: Luis Enrique Abbiati; **Medical Sciences** (Cardiology; Community Health; Medical Auxiliaries; Medicine; Nursing; Pneumology; Psychiatry and Mental Health; Public Health) *Dean*: Norma Circé Magnelli; **Philosophy and Literature** (English; French; Geography; History; Philosophy; Science Education) *Dean*: Adolfo Omar Cueto; **Political and Social Sciences** (Political Sciences; Public Administration; Social Sciences; Social Work; Sociology) *Dean*: Juan Carlos Aguiló; **Science Applied to Industry** (San Rafael) (Industrial Engineering) *Dean*: Fabio Tarantola

Institutes

Basic Sciences *Director*: Manuel Tovar; **Physics and Nuclear Engineering** (Balseiro, Bariloche) (Nuclear Engineering; Physics) *Director*: José Lolich; **Technological** (University) *Director*: Guillermo Cruz

Further Information: Also Nuclear Medicine School Foundation

History: Founded 1939 as a State institution to serve the three provinces of Cuyo.

Governing Bodies: Asamblea Universitaria; Consejo Superior; Consejo Académico

Academic Year: April to November (April-July; August-November)

Admission Requirements: Secondary school certificate (bachillerato) and entrance examination

Main Language(s) of Instruction: Spanish

Degrees and Diplomas: *Licenciatura*: Administration; Chemistry; Economics, 6 yrs; *Licenciatura*: Education; French and English

Literature; Geography; History; Letters; Mathematics; Music; Philosophy; Physics; Plastic Arts; Political and Social Sciences and Public Administration; Psychology; Sociology, 5 yrs; *Professional Title*: Accountancy; Chemistry; Pharmacy, 4 yrs; *Professional Title*: Agriculture; Design, 5 yrs; *Professional Title*: Architecture; Engineering, 6 yrs; *Professional Title*: Dentistry, 5 yrs with 1 yr internship; *Professional Title*: Fine arts, 4-6 yrs; *Professional Title*: Medicine, 6 yrs with 1 yr internship; *Professional Title*: Teacher Training (Secondary Education); *Especialización*; *Maestría*: Biological Sciences; Drainage and Irrigation; International Business; Rural Technology; Territorial Organization, a further 2 yrs; *Doctorado*

Student Residential Facilities: Some

Special Facilities: Museum of Archaeology and Ethnology; Museum of Natural Sciences

Libraries: Central Library, c. 80,000 vols; libraries of various faculties and schools, c. 180,000

Publications: Acta Cuyana de Ingeniería; Anales, Foreign Languages and Literature; Anales de Arqueología y Etnología; Anales del Instituto de Investigaciones Psicopedagógicas; Anales del Instituto de Lingüística; Anuario Estadístico; Artes Plásticas; Boletín Bibliográfico; Boletín Bibliográfico; Boletín de Estudios Geográficos: Serie I, Fuentes Documentales; Serie III Ensayos (History); Boletín de Estudios Germánicos; Boletín de Estudios Políticos y Sociales; Cuadernos de Filosofía; Cuadernos de Historia del Arte; Cuadernos de la Escuela de Pedagogía; Cuadernos de Psiquiatría; Cuadernos del Instituto de Investigaciones Políticas y Sociales; Filosofía; Guía del Estudiante; Noticias de Ingeniería de Petróleos; Nuestro Mundo, Medicine; Publicación (Extension Department); Revista de Estudios Clásicos; Revista de Historia Americana y Argentina; Revista de la Facultad de Ciencias Agrarias; Revista de la Facultad de Ciencias Económicas; Revista de Literaturas Modernas; Serie de Cuadernos
Last Updated: 06/07/07

NATIONAL UNIVERSITY OF ENTRE RÍOS
Universidad Nacional de Entre Ríos (UNER)
Eva Perón 24, 3260 Concepción del Uruguay, Entre Ríos
Tel: +54(3442) 42-1500
Fax: +54(3442) 42-1563
EMail: sprivada@rect.uner.edu.ar
Website: http://www.uner.edu.ar

Rector: Eduardo Francisco José Asueta
Tel: +54(3442) 42-1530, Fax: +54(3442) 42-1530
EMail: rector@rect.uner.edu.ar

Secretaria Académica: Susana Celman
EMail: scelman@rect.uner.edu.ar

Vicerrectora: Eloisa De Jong

Faculties
Administration *(Concordia)* (Accountancy; Administration) *Dean*: Miguel Antonio Fernandez; **Agriculture** *(Oro Verde)* (Agriculture) *Dean*: Gabriel Villanova; **Bromatology** *(Gualeguaychú)* (Chemistry; Food Science) *Dean*: María Clara Melchiori; **Economics** *(Paraná)* (Economics) *Dean*: Eduardo Ramon Muani; **Educational Sciences** *(Paraná)* (Education) *Dean*: Maria Laura Méndez; **Engineering** *(Oro Verde) Dean*: César Osella; **Food Science** *(Concordia)* (Food Technology) *Dean*: Hugo Cives; **Health Sciences** (Health Sciences; Nursing) *Dean*: Jorge Pepe; **Social Work** *(Paraná)* (Social Work) *Dean*: Sandra Arito

Further Information: Also branches in Paraná, Concordia and Gualeguaychú

History: Founded 1973. An autonomous State institution.

Governing Bodies: Consejo Superior

Academic Year: April to November (April-July; August-November)

Admission Requirements: Secondary school certificate (bachillerato) or equivalent

Main Language(s) of Instruction: Spanish

Degrees and Diplomas: *Licenciatura*: Administration; Bromatology; Education; Information Sciences; Social Service, 5 yrs; *Professional Title*: Accountancy, 5 yrs; *Professional Title*: Agriculture; Bioengineering; Food Technology, 6 yrs; *Professional Title*: Nursing, 3 yrs; *Professional Title*: Social Work, 4 yrs; *Especialización*: 1 yr following first degree; *Maestría*

Student Services: Health services, Sports facilities

Libraries: Total, c. 27,000 vols
Last Updated: 27/02/09

NATIONAL UNIVERSITY OF FORMOSA
Universidad Nacional de Formosa (UNAF)
Don Bosco 1082, 3600 Formosa, Formosa
Tel: +54(3717) 43-0485
Fax: +54(3717) 43-0485
EMail: rector@unf.edu.ar
Website: http://www.unf.edu.ar

Rector: Martín René Romano EMail: rectorado@unf.edu.ar

Vicerrector: Roque Silguero
Tel: +54(3717) 42-3930 EMail: rsilguero@arnet.com.ar

Faculties
Business, Administration and Economics (Business Administration; Business and Commerce; Economics) *Dean*: Oscar Ramón Montenegro; **Health Sciences** (Health Sciences; Laboratory Techniques; Nursing; Nutrition; Radiology) *Dean*: Rafael Portocarrero; **Humanities** (Arts and Humanities) *Dean*: Maria de la Cruz Colombera; **Natural Resources** (Agricultural Business; Civil Engineering; Forestry; Natural Resources; Zoology) *Dean*: Julio César Gomez

History: An autonomous State institution since 1988.

Academic Year: February to December

Admission Requirements: Secondary school certificate (Bachillerato)

Fees: None

Main Language(s) of Instruction: Spanish

International Co-operation: None

Degrees and Diplomas: *Profesorado*: Arts and Humanities, 4 yrs; *Licenciatura*: Nutrition; Food Science; Nursing; Natural Sciences; Obstetrics; Exterior Commerce, 5 yrs; *Professional Title*: Accountancy (Contador Público), 5 yrs; *Professional Title*: Civil Engineering; Forest Engineering; Zootechnic Engineering; *Especialización*: Curriculum; Pedagogy, 2 yrs; *Maestría*: Forestry; Medical Education, 2 yrs

Student Services: Academic counselling, Canteen, Health services, Social counselling, Sports facilities

Student Residential Facilities: None

Special Facilities: None

Libraries: Central Library

Publications: Revista de Ciencia y Tecnología de la Universidad Nacional De Formosa, Research Publication on Sciences and Technology *(annually)*; Revista de Geografía, Research Publication on Geography *(biennially)*; Revista de la Facultad de Ciencias de la Salud, Research Publication on Health Sciences *(annually)*; Revista de la Facultad de Recursos Naturales - Serie Forestal, Research Publication on Natural Resources and Forestry *(annually)*

Academic Staff *2007-2008*: Total 626
STAFF WITH DOCTORATE: Total 15
Student Numbers *2007-2008*: Total 12,300
Last Updated: 27/02/09

NATIONAL UNIVERSITY OF JUJUY
Universidad Nacional de Jujuy (UNJU)
Avenida Bolivia N° 1239, 4600 San Salvador de Jujuy, Jujuy
Tel: +54(388) 422-1502
Fax: +54(388) 422-1507
EMail: seu@unju.edu.ar
Website: http://www.unju.edu.ar

Rector: Enrique Mateo Arnau
Tel: +54-(388) 422-1506 EMail: rector@unju.edu.ar

Vicerrector: Carlos Gregorio Torres
Tel: +54(388) 422-1501 EMail: vicerrector@unju.edu.ar

International Relations: Jaquelina Sanchez
Tel: +54(388) 422-1506 EMail: jsanchez@unju.edu.ar

Faculties
Agriculture (Agronomy) *Dean*: Carlos Gregorio Torres; **Economics** (Accountancy; Administration; Economics) *Dean*: Humberto

Leopoldo Quintana; **Engineering** (Engineering) *Dean*: Jose Lucas Sanchez Mera; **Humanities and Social Sciences** (Anthropology; Arts and Humanities; Communication Studies; Education; Health Education; History; Social Sciences; Social Work) *Dean*: Ernesto Francisco Max Aguero

Research Institutes
Geology and Mining (Geology; Mining Engineering) *Director*: Waldo Chayle; **Mountain Biology** (Biology; Mountain Studies) *Director*: Susana Ocampo

Schools
Mining *(Horacío Carillo)* (Mining Engineering) *Director*: P. Puca
History: Founded 1972 as provincial University, acquired present status and title 1974. An autonomous State institution.
Governing Bodies: Asamblea Universitaria; Consejo Superior Universitario
Academic Year: February to December (February-June; August-December)
Admission Requirements: Secondary school certificate (bachillerato) or equivalent
Main Language(s) of Instruction: Spanish
Degrees and Diplomas: *Título Menor*: Technical Studies, 3 yrs; *Licenciatura*: Anthropology; Chemistry; Educational Sciences; Letters; Social Communication, 4-5 yrs; *Professional Title*: Accountancy; Engineering, 5 yrs; *Professional Title*: Teaching, 4-5 yrs
Special Facilities: Museum of Palaeontology and Minerals. Estación de Fauna Silvestre 'Dr. Vucetin'
Libraries: Total, 40,394 vols
Publications: Didactic Notes of the School of Agriculture *(monthly)*; Geological Sciences Review *(quarterly)*; Revista XUXUY
Press or Publishing House: Secretaría de Extensión Universitaria - Editorial UNJU
Last Updated: 26/06/07

NATIONAL UNIVERSITY OF LA MATANZA
Universidad Nacional de La Matanza (UNLAM)
Florencio Varela 1903, B 1754 JEC San Justo, Buenos Aires
Tel: +54(11) 4480-8900
Fax: +54(11) 4680-8962
EMail: webmaster@unlam.edu.ar
Website: http://www.unlam.edu.ar
Rector: Daniel Eduardo Martínez (1999-)
Tel: +54(11) 4480-8992, Fax: +54(11) 4480-8862
EMail: rector@unlam.edu.ar
Vicerrector: Víctor René Nicoletti
Tel: +54(11) 4480-8915, Fax: +54(11) 4480-8915
EMail: vicerectorado@unlam.edu.ar
International Relations: Andres Miguel Fontana
Tel: +54(11) 4480-8923, Fax: +54(11) 4480-8960
EMail: ici@unlam.edu.ar

Departments
Economics (Accountancy; Administration; Economics; International Business) *Dean*: Alberto Longo; **Engineering and Technological Research** (Computer Engineering; Electronic Engineering; Engineering; Industrial Engineering; Technology) *Dean*: Alfredo Vázquez; **Humanities and Social Sciences** (Arts and Humanities; Labour and Industrial Relations; Physical Education; Social Sciences; Social Work) *Dean*: Fernando Lujan Acosta; **Law and Political Science** (Law; Political Sciences; Private Law; Public Law) *Dean*: Alejandro Finocchiaro

Programmes
Postgraduate Studies *Secretary*: Mario Enrique Burkún

Schools
Continuing Education (Insurance; International Business; Literature; Modern Languages; Physical Education) *Director*: Alejandro Martínez
History: An autonomous State institution since 1989.
Governing Bodies: Consejo Superior; Asamblea General
Academic Year: February to December

Admission Requirements: Secondary school certificate (bachillerato) or equivalent and admission examination
Fees: None
Main Language(s) of Instruction: Spanish
International Co-operation: With universities in USA; Canada; Cuba; Dominican Republic; Colombia; Chile; Venezuela; Brazil; Spain; Italy; France; Hungary; Russia. Also participates in international cooperation networks
Degrees and Diplomas: *Licenciatura*: Accountancy; Administration; Electronic Engineering; Industrial Engineering; International Commerce; Social Communication; Social Work; Systems Engineering, 4 1/2 yrs; *Licenciatura*: Labour Relations; Physical Education, 4 1/2 yrs; *Especialización*; *Maestría*: Computer Science; Environmental Management; Psychoanalysis; Public Finance; Social Sciences, a further 2 yrs; *Doctorado*: Economics
Student Services: Academic counselling, Canteen, Cultural centre, Employment services, Foreign student adviser, Handicapped facilities, Health services, Language programs, Social counselling, Sports facilities
Special Facilities: Language laboratories; Radio and TV laboratories; Radio
Publications: Periodico Uno *(weekly)*; Propuestas
Last Updated: 27/02/09

NATIONAL UNIVERSITY OF LA PAMPA
Universidad Nacional de La Pampa (UNLPAM)
Coronel Gil 353 3°, 6300 Santa Rosa, La Pampa
Tel: +54(2954) 451600
Fax: +54(2954) 433408
EMail: info@unlpam.edu.ar
Website: http://www.unlpam.edu.ar
Rector: Sergio Daniel Maluendres (2002-)
Tel: +54(2954) 423191 EMail: rector@unlpam.edu.ar
Secretaria Académica: Alicia Saenz
EMail: secacademica@unlpam.edu.ar
International Relations: Verónica Suárez Lorences
Tel: +54(2954) 451614

Faculties
Agronomy (Agricultural Engineering; Agricultural Management; Agriculture; Agronomy; Dairy) *Dean*: Héctor Daniel Estelrich; **Economics and Law** (Accountancy; Law) *Dean*: Roberto Vassia; **Engineering** *Dean*: Carlos Norberto d'Amico; **Exact and Natural Sciences** (Biological and Life Sciences; Chemistry; Computer Science; Geology; Mathematics; Natural Resources; Physics) *Dean*: María Cristina Martín; **Human Sciences** (Education; English; Geography; History; Humanities and Social Science Education; Physical Education; Social Work) *Dean*: Jorge Saab; **Veterinary Science** *(General Pico)* (Veterinary Science) *Dean*: Hugo Roberto Alvarez

Institutes
Labour Studies (Labour and Industrial Relations; Labour Law)
Further Information: Branch in General Pico
History: Founded 1958 as a provincial University, became National University 1973.
Academic Year: March to November (March-July; August-November)
Admission Requirements: Secondary school certificate (bachillerato) or equivalent
Main Language(s) of Instruction: Spanish
Degrees and Diplomas: *Licenciatura*: History; Geography; Literature; English; Education Sciences; Modern Languages, 5 yrs; *Professional Title*: Accountancy, Economics; Agronomy; Engineering; Law; Veterinary Medicine, 5 yrs; *Maestría*: Criminal Law; Business Administration; Water Science, 2 yrs
Student Services: Academic counselling, Canteen, Foreign student adviser, Health services, Language programs, Sports facilities
Student Residential Facilities: for 48 students in Santa Rosa and for 48 in General Pico
Libraries: c. 64,650 vols; 34,421 tittles

Publications: Contexto Universitario, Information and articles about the University. Interviews *(monthly)*
Last Updated: 27/02/09

NATIONAL UNIVERSITY OF LA PLATA
Universidad Nacional de La Plata (UNLP)
Calle 7 N° 776, 1900 La Plata, Buenos Aires
Tel: +54(221) 423-6804
Fax: +54(221) 425-6967
EMail: privada@presi.unlp.edu.ar
Website: http://www.unlp.edu.ar

Presidente: Gustavo Adolfo Azpiazu

Secretario General: Fernando Alfredo Tauber
Tel: +54(221) 422-6967
EMail: secretaria.general@presi.unlp.edu.ar

Faculties
Agriculture and Forestry (Agricultural Engineering; Agriculture; Forestry) *Dean*: Guillermo Hang; **Architecture and Town Planning** (Architecture; Town Planning) *Dean*: Nestor Bono; **Astronomy and Geophysics** (Astronomy and Space Science; Geophysics) *Dean*: Pablo Miguel Cincotta; **Computer Science** (Computer Networks; Computer Science; Software Engineering) *Dean*: Armando de Giusti; **Dentistry** (Dentistry) *Dean*: Isaac Meschiany; **Economics** (Accountancy; Administration; Economics; Tourism) *Dean*: Luis Scuriatti; **Engineering** (Aeronautical and Aerospace Engineering; Chemical Engineering; Civil Engineering; Electrical and Electronic Engineering; Hydraulic Engineering; Metallurgical Engineering; Telecommunications Engineering) *Dean*: Pablo Antonio C. Massa; **Exact Sciences** (Biotechnology; Chemistry; Mathematics; Molecular Biology; Optics; Optometry; Physics) *Dean*: Carlos della Védova; **Fine Arts** (Conducting; Fine Arts; Industrial Design; Music Theory and Composition; Musical Instruments; Theatre; Visual Arts) *Dean*: Daniel Horacio Belinche; **Humanities and Education** (Arts and Humanities; Biology; Education; Educational Sciences; English; Geography; History; Library Science; Literature; Philosophy; Physical Education; Psychology; Sociology) *Dean*: Ana María Barletta; **Journalism and Social Communication** (Communication Studies; Journalism) *Dean*: Alejandro Raúl Verano; **Law and Social Sciences** (Law; Social Sciences) *Dean*: Hernán Rodolfo Gomez; **Medical Sciences** (Gynaecology and Obstetrics; Medicine; Nursing; Speech Therapy and Audiology) *Dean*: Jorge Guillermo Martinez; **Natural Sciences** (Anthropology; Biology; Ecology; Geology; Natural Sciences; Paleontology) *Dean*: Evelia Oyhenart; **Social Work** (Social Work) *Directora*: Margarita Rosas Pagaza; **Veterinary Science** (Veterinary Science) *Dean*: Edgardo O. Nosetto

Further Information: Also 43 research laboratories, institutes and regional university centres of Junín, San Carlos de Bariloche, Viedma and Río Gallegos

History: Founded 1897 by law as a provincial University with faculties of Law, Chemistry, Medicine, and Physical and Mathematical Sciences. Reorganized 1906 and became a National University.

Governing Bodies: Asamblea Universitaria; Consejo Superior

Academic Year: March to November (March-June; June-September; September-November)

Admission Requirements: Secondary school certificate (bachillerato) or equivalent. Foreign qualifications are recognized if covered by formal international agreements

Main Language(s) of Instruction: Spanish

Degrees and Diplomas: *Licenciatura*: Administration; Astronomy; Biochemistry; Biology; Chemistry; Economics; Education; Geography; Geology; Geophysics; History; Letters; Library Science; Mathematics; Music; Pharmacy; Philosophy; Physics; Plastic Arts; Social Service; Zoology, 5 yrs; *Professional Title*: Accountancy; Dentistry; Engineering; Geophysics; Industrial Design; Journalism; Law; Pharmacy; Psychology; Translation; Veterinary Medicine, 5 yrs; *Professional Title*: Medicine, 6 yrs; *Professional Title*: Teacher Training, 4 yrs; *Especialización*; *Maestría*; *Doctorado*: Astronomy and Geophysics; Biochemistry; Chemistry; Dentistry; Economics; Education; Geology; History; Law and Social Sciences; Letters; Mathematics; Medicine; Natural Sciences; Pharmacy; Philosophy; Physics; Veterinary Science, by thesis

Student Services: Canteen, Cultural centre, Employment services, Health services, Nursery care, Sports facilities

Special Facilities: Natural History Museum; 'Dr Emilio Azzarini' Collection (Musical Instruments). Observatory

Libraries: Biblioteca Pública de la Universidad, c. 500,000 vols

Publications: Revista de la Universidad

Press or Publishing House: Imprenta de la Universidad
Last Updated: 02/03/09

NATIONAL UNIVERSITY OF LA RIOJA
Universidad Nacional de La Rioja (UNLAR)
Av. Dr. René Favaloro S/N, 5300 La Rioja, La Rioja
Tel: +54(3822) 457-000
Fax: +54(3822) 457-000
EMail: unlar@unlar.edu.ar
Website: http://www.unlar.edu.ar

Rector: Enrique Daniel Tello Roldán
Tel: +54(3822) 457-003 EMail: rector@unlar.edu.ar

Vicerrector: Claudia del Carmen Santander
Tel: +54(3822) 457-042 EMail: csantander@unlar.edu.ar

International Relations: Francisco Antonio Asis Filonzi
Tel: +54(3822) 457-044

Centres
Graduate Studies *(Main Campus) Director*: Patricio Tello Roldan

Departments
Applied Sciences (Agricultural Engineering; Applied Chemistry; Applied Physics; Engineering; Mining Engineering; Natural Sciences) *Dean*: Peña Pollastri Carolina; **Basic Sciences** (Mathematics; Natural Sciences) *Dean*: Marcelo Camargo; **Health and Educational Sciences** (Educational Sciences; Medicine) *Dean*: Antonino C. Casida; **Humanities** (Educational and Student Counselling; Psychology) *Dean*: Rosa Beatriz Morales; **Social Sciences, Law and Economics** (Economics; Social Sciences) *Dean*: José Nicolas Chumbita

Institutes
Arid Zone Research (Arid Land Studies; Natural Resources) *Director*: Omar Vera; **Natural Sciences** (Natural Sciences) *Director*: Sergio Martin; **Provincial Studies** (Regional Studies) *Director*: Lorenza Herrera

Schools
Business (Business and Commerce; Business Computing; English; Hotel Management; Marketing) *Director*: Lorena Romero

Further Information: Branches in Chamical, Chepes, Aimogasta, Villa Unión and Catuna

History: Founded 1960 as school, and became provincial University 1972.

Governing Bodies: Asamblea; Consejo Superior; Consejos Académicos

Academic Year: March to November (March-July; August-November)

Admission Requirements: Secondary school certificate (bachillerato) and entrance examination

Fees: None

Main Language(s) of Instruction: Spanish, French, English

Accrediting Agencies: Organización Universitaria Interamericana (OUI); International Association of University Presidents (IAUP)

Degrees and Diplomas: *Licenciatura*: Administration, 5 yrs; *Licenciatura*: Nursing, 4 yrs; *Professional Title*: Accountancy; Law, 5 yrs; *Professional Title*: Engineering, 5-6 yrs; *Professional Title*: Medicine, 6 yrs; *Professional Title*: Occupational Therapy; Teacher Training (secondary level), 4 yrs; *Especialización*; *Doctorado*

Student Services: Academic counselling, Canteen, Cultural centre, Foreign student adviser, Health services, Language programs, Nursery care, Sports facilities

Student Residential Facilities: Yes

Special Facilities: Yes

Libraries: Central Library, c. 45,000 vols

Publications: UNLaR Ciencia *(quarterly)*
Last Updated: 02/03/09

NATIONAL UNIVERSITY OF LANÚS
Universidad Nacional de Lanús (UNLA)
29 de Septiembre 3901, Remedios de Escalada, 1826 Lanús,
Buenos Aires
Tel: +54(11) 6322-9200
Fax: +54(11) 6322-9200
EMail: info@unla.edu.ar
Website: http://www.unla.edu.ar

Rectora: Ana María Jaramillo
Tel: +54(11) 4202-4778 EMail: acercate@unla.edu.ar

Vicerrector: Juan Carlos Geneyro EMail: geneyro@unla.edu.ar

International Relations: Daniel Toribio, Secretario Académico
Tel: +54(11) 4228-5359 EMail: dtoribio@unla.edu.ar

Departments
Arts and Humanities (Arts and Humanities; Design; Educational Administration; Industrial Design; Music; Translation and Interpretation) *Director*: Héctor Muzzopappa; **Community Health** (Community Health; Epidemiology; Nursing; Physical Education; Psychiatry and Mental Health) *Director*: Daniel Rodríguez; **Planning and Public Policy** (Government; Public Administration; Social Work; Town Planning) *Director*: Mirta Fabris; **Production and Labour Development** (Business Administration; Environmental Management; Food Technology; Labour and Industrial Relations; Labour Law; Tourism; Urban Studies) *Director*: Oscar Tangelson

History: Founded 1995.

Governing Bodies: Asamblea Universitaria; Consejo Superior; Consejo Académico

Academic Year: April to November (April-July; August-November)

Admission Requirements: Secondary school certificate (bachillerato) and entrance examination

Main Language(s) of Instruction: Spanish

Degrees and Diplomas: *Licenciatura*: Audiovisual Studies; Painting and Drawing; Visual Communication; Industrial Design; Arts; Music; Educational Technology; Physical Education; Social Work; Nursing; Educational Administration; Political Science and Government; Civil Security; Business Economics; Town Planning; Food Science and Technology; Tourism; *Especialización*: Health Administration; Community Boarding; Cultural Tourism Management; Sustainable Development; Educational Research; *Maestría*: Applied Ethics; Scientific Research Methodology; Business Administration; Food Technology; Sustainable Development; Public Policy and Government; Energy Management; Epidemiology, Health Management and Policy; *Doctorado*: Philosophy; Community Mental Health
Last Updated: 02/03/09

NATIONAL UNIVERSITY OF LOMAS DE ZAMORA
Universidad Nacional de Lomas de Zamora (UNLZ)
Ruta provincial 4 Km. 2, 1836 Llavallol, Capital Federal
Tel: +54(11) 4282-7818
Fax: +54(11) 4282-8043
EMail: sae@unlz.edu.ar
Website: http://www.unlz.edu.ar

Rector: Horacio A. Gegunde
Tel: +54(11) 4282-4245
EMail: rector@unlz.edu.ar; secpriv@unlz.edu.ar

Secretario Académico: Diego Saiovici
Tel: +54(11) 4282-8046 EMail: academic@unlz.edu.ar

Faculties
Agriculture (Agriculture; Animal Husbandry; Crop Production; Genetics) *Dean*: Fernando José Luis Rumiano; **Economics** *(Lomas de Zamora)* (Accountancy; Economics) *Dean*: Alejandro Daniel Kuruc; **Engineering** *(Lomas de Zamora)* (Industrial Engineering; Mechanical Engineering) *Dean*: Oscar Manuel Pascal; **Law** *(Lomas de Zamora)* (Law) *Dean*: Lucas Liendro Kapustik; **Social Sciences** *(Lomas de Zamora)* (Advertising and Publicity; Education; Educational Sciences; Journalism; Labour and Industrial Relations; Literature; Public Relations; Social Sciences; Social Work) *Dean*: Gabriel Mariotto

History: Founded 1972. An autonomous State institution.

Governing Bodies: Asamblea Universitaria; Consejo Superior

Academic Year: March to December (March-July; August-December)

Admission Requirements: Secondary school certificate (bachillerato) or equivalent

Main Language(s) of Instruction: Spanish

Degrees and Diplomas: *Licenciatura*: Administration; Education; International Letters; Journalism; Labour Relations; Public Relations, 5 yrs; *Professional Title*: Agriculture; Animal Husbandry, 5 yrs; *Professional Title*: Law, 6 yrs; *Professional Title*: Teacher Training (secondary level), 4 yrs; *Especialización*; *Maestría*

Special Facilities: Museo Pío Collivadino

Libraries: Central Library, c. 10,000 vols; libraries of the faculties
Last Updated: 02/03/09

NATIONAL UNIVERSITY OF LUJÁN
Universidad Nacional de Luján (UNLU)
Int. Ruta 5 y 7, 6700 Luján, Buenos Aires
Tel: +54(2323) 42-0380
Fax: +54(2323) 42-5795
EMail: informes@unlu.edu.ar
Website: http://www.unlu.edu.ar

Rector: Osvaldo Arizio
Tel: +54(2323) 42-7701 EMail: rector@mail.unlu.edu.ar

Secretaria Académica: María Cristina Serafini
Tel: +54(2323) 42-0380, Ext 208/209
EMail: seacad@mail.unlu.edu.ar

Departments
Basic Sciences (Biology; Chemistry; Mathematics and Computer Science; Natural Sciences; Physics; Statistics) *Director*: Mario Guillermo Oloriz; **Education** (Adult Education; Distance Education; Education; Modern Languages; Pedagogy; Psychology) *Director*: Susana Muraro; **Social Sciences** (Administration; Business Administration; Economics; Geography; History; Law; Social Studies; Sociology) *Director*: Alicia Rey; **Technology** (Agronomy; Food Technology; Natural Sciences; Technology) *Director*: Susana Vidales

Institutes
Physical Education (Physical Education)

Further Information: Regional Centres in Campana, Chivilcoy, General Sarmiento

History: Founded 1972. Acquired present status 1984. An autonomous State institution.

Governing Bodies: University Assembly, Superior Council

Academic Year: March to November

Admission Requirements: Secondary school certificate (bachillerato) or equivalent

Fees: None

Main Language(s) of Instruction: Spanish

International Co-operation: With universities in Spain; France; Chile; Brazil; Canada; USA; Uruguay. Also participates in Mobility Programme International Cooperation Agency, Spain; Mobility and Academic Exchange Programme (PIMA); ALFA Programme - European Union

Degrees and Diplomas: *Licenciatura*: Administration; Biology; Computer Systems; Educational Sciences; Geography; History; Information Environment; International Trade; Social Services, 5 yrs; *Professional Title*: Agricultural Engineering; Industrial Engineering, 5 yrs; *Professional Title*: Food Production, 6 yrs; *Especialización*; *Maestría*: Educational Management; Social Demography; Social Sciences, 3-4 yrs; *Doctorado*. Also technical qualifications, 3-4 yrs

Student Services: Academic counselling, Canteen, Employment services, Health services, Sports facilities

Student Residential Facilities: None

Special Facilities: Art Gallery. University Radio Station

Libraries: Yes

Publications: UNlu Ciencia *(annually)*
Last Updated: 02/03/09

NATIONAL UNIVERSITY OF MAR DEL PLATA
Universidad Nacional de Mar del Plata (UNMDP)
Diagonal Juan Bautista Alberdi 2659, B 7600 GYI Mar del Plata,
Buenos Aires
Tel: +54(223) 492-1705
Fax: +54(223) 492-1711
Website: http://www.mdp.edu.ar

Rector: Francisco Morea
Tel: +54(223) 491-6646 EMail: rector@mdp.edu.ar

Secretario Académico: Rubén Buceta
EMail: secadem@mdp.edu.ar

Faculties
Agriculture *(Balcarce)* (Agricultural Economics; Agricultural Engineering; Agriculture; Animal Husbandry; Food Technology; Plant and Crop Protection; Soil Science; Vegetable Production) *Dean*: José A. Capurro; **Architecture, Town Planning and Design** (Architecture; Industrial Design; Town Planning) *Dean*: Juan José Garamendy; **Economics and Social Sciences** (Accountancy; Administration; Economics; Social Sciences; Tourism) *Dean*: Francisco Morea; **Engineering** (Chemical Engineering; Electrical Engineering; Electronic Engineering; Engineering; Materials Engineering; Mathematics; Mechanical Engineering) *Dean*: Jorge Domingo Petrillo; **Exact and Natural Sciences** (Biology; Chemistry; Mathematics; Natural Sciences; Physics) *Dean*: Gustavo Daleo; **Health Sciences and Social Work** (Health Sciences; Nursing; Occupational Therapy; Social and Community Services; Social Work); **Humanities** (Arts and Humanities; English; Geography; History; Library Science; Literature; Pedagogy; Philosophy) *Dean*: María Luz González Mesquita; **Law** (Civil Law; Criminal Law; Law; Public Law) *Dean*: Miguel Ángel Acosta; **Psychology** (Psychoanalysis; Psychology) *Dean*: Alicia Marta Zanghellini

Further Information: Also 26 Regional Distance and Lifelong Centres

History: Founded 1961 as provincial University, acquired present status and title 1975. An autonomous State institution.

Governing Bodies: Consejo Superior

Academic Year: April to March

Admission Requirements: Secondary school certificate (bachillerato) or equivalent

Fees: For postgraduate studies

Main Language(s) of Instruction: Spanish

International Co-operation: With universities in Bolivia; Brazil; Canada; Colombia; Costa Rica; Cuba; Chile; USA; Ecuador; Mexico; Peru; El Salvador; Uruguay; Venezuela; China; Japan; Israel; Vietnam; Germany; Spain; France; Hungary; Italy; Netherlands and United Kingdom. Also participates in the CINTERFOR programme

Degrees and Diplomas: *Título Menor*: Cultural Management, 3 yrs; *Título Menor*: Library Science, 2 yrs; *Licenciatura*: Biology; Economics; Geography; Letters; Mathematics; Psychology, 5 yrs; *Professional Title*: Accountancy; Administration; Architecture; Engineering, 6 yrs; *Professional Title*: Agriculture; Biology; Mathematics; Physics; Chemistry; Economics; Tourism; English; Geography; History; Literature; Philosophy; Library Science; Heath Sciences; Social Services; Industrial Design; Law; Psychology, 5 yrs; *Professional Title*: Teacher Teaching (secondary and university levels), 4-5 yrs; *Especialización*: Administrative Law; Animal Husbandry; Business Administration; Fisheries; Higher Education; Work Studies, 1 yr following Professionnal Title; *Especialización*: Bioethics, 2 yrs following Professionnal Title; *Especialización*: Occupational Health, 1 yr following Professional Title; *Maestría*: Town Planning; Agriculture; Economics; Political Science; Humanities; Engineering, 2 yrs following Professionnal Title; *Doctorado*: Agricultural Sciences; Materials Science, 2 yrs; *Doctorado*: Biology; Chemistry; Mathematics; Physics, at least 2 yrs

Student Services: Academic counselling, Employment services, Health services, Language programs, Nursery care, Social counselling, Sports facilities

Student Residential Facilities: None

Libraries: Central Library, c. 100,000 vols

Publications: Revista 'Nexos' *(biennially)*
Last Updated: 02/03/09

NATIONAL UNIVERSITY OF MISIONES
Universidad Nacional de Misiones (UNAM)
Campus Universitario, Ruta Nacional 12, Km. 7 1/2, Estafeta postal "Miguel Lanús", 3304 Posadas, Misiones
Tel: +54(3752) 48-0916
Fax: +54(3752) 48-0500
EMail: info@unam.edu.ar
Website: http://www.unam.edu.ar

Rector: Aldo Luis Caballero
Tel: +54(3752) 48-0916, Fax: +54(3752) 48-0500
EMail: rector@unam.edu.ar

Secretario Académico: José Miguel Ramos
Tel: +54(3752) 48-0490 EMail: jmramos@campus.unam.edu.ar

International Relations: Aldo Montini, Vicerrector
EMail: vicerector@unam.edu.ar

Faculties
Arts *(Oberá)* (Ceramic Art; Fine Arts; Graphic Design; Painting and Drawing) *Dean*: Rubén Arturo Gastaldo; **Economics** (Accountancy; Administration; Economics; Finance; Law) *Dean*: Rogelio Cesar Krause; **Engineering** *(Oberá)* (Civil Engineering; Electronic Engineering; Engineering; Industrial Engineering; Mathematics; Mechanical Engineering) *Dean*: Sergio Alberto Garassino; **Exact, Natural and Chemical Sciences** *(Posadas)* (Biochemistry; Biology; Chemical Engineering; Chemistry; Food Science; Food Technology; Genetics; Mathematics; Microbiology; Natural Sciences; Nursing; Pharmacy; Physics) *Dean*: Andrés Ramón Linares; **Forestry** *(Eldorado)* (Forestry; Wood Technology) *Dean*: Oscar Arturo Gauto; **Humanities and Social Sciences** *(Posadas)* (Arts and Humanities; Social Sciences) *Dean*: Javier Gortari

Schools
Nursing *(Posadas)* (Nursing)

History: Founded 1973. An autonomous State institution.

Governing Bodies: Asamblea Universitaria; Consejo Superior Provisorio

Academic Year: February to December (February-July; August-December)

Admission Requirements: Secondary school certificate (bachillerato) or equivalent

Main Language(s) of Instruction: Spanish

Degrees and Diplomas: *Título Menor*: Library Science; Nursing; Secretarial Studies; Tourism, 3 yrs; *Título Menor*: Technical Studies, 3-4 yrs; *Licenciatura*: Business Administration; Genetics; History; Literature; Social Anthropology; Social Work; Tourism, 5 yrs; *Professional Title*: Accountancy, 5 yrs; *Professional Title*: Engineering, 6 yrs; *Professional Title*: Journalism, 3-4 yrs; *Professional Title*: Pharmacy, 3 yrs; *Professional Title*: Teacher Training; *Especialización*; *Maestría*; *Doctorado*

Libraries: Total, c. 16,400 vols
Last Updated: 02/03/09

NATIONAL UNIVERSITY OF PATAGONIA SAN JUAN BOSCO
Universidad Nacional de la Patagonia San Juan Bosco (UNPSJB)
Ciudad Universitaria Km 4, 9005 Comodoro Rivadavia, Chubut
Tel: +54(297) 455-7856
Fax: +54(297) 455-7453
EMail: rector@unp.edu.ar
Website: http://www.unp.edu.ar

Rector: Jorge Manuel Gil Tel: +54(297) 455-7453

Vicerrectora: Elsa Bonini
Tel: +54(297) 455-7856 EMail: virector@unp.edu.ar

Faculties
Economics *(Esquel)* (Economics); **Economics** *(Ushuaia)* (Economics); **Economics** (Economics); **Engineering** *(Esquel)* (Engineering); **Engineering** *(Puerto Madryn)* (Engineering); **Engineering** *(Trelew)* (Engineering); **Engineering** *(Ushuaia)* (Engineering); **Engineering** (Chemical Engineering; Engineering); **Humanities and Social Sciences** (Communication Studies; Educational Sciences; Geography; History; Literature; Social Work); **Humanities and Social Sciences** *(Trelew)* (Humanities and Social

Science Education; Social Sciences); **Humanities and Social Sciences** *(Ushuaia)* (Humanities and Social Science Education; Social Sciences); **Law** (Law); **Natural Sciences** (Biochemistry; Biology; Forestry; Geology; Marine Biology; Microbiology; Nursing; Pharmacy); **Natural Sciences** *(Esquel)* (Natural Sciences); **Natural Sciences** *(Puerto Madryn)* (Natural Sciences); **Natural Sciences** *(Trelew)* (Natural Sciences)

History: Founded 1980, incorporating Universidad Nacional de la Patagonia, founded 1973, and Universidad de la Patagonia 'San Juan Bosco' (1963). Acquired present status 1996. An autonomous State institution.

Governing Bodies: Asamblea Universitaria; Consejo Superior; Consejo Académico; Consejo Consultivo

Academic Year: March to November

Admission Requirements: Secondary school certificate (bachillerato) or equivalent

Main Language(s) of Instruction: Spanish

Degrees and Diplomas: *Licenciatura*: 5-6 yrs; *Professional Title*: 5-6 yrs; *Professional Title*: Teacher Training; *Especialización*; *Maestría*: Biochemistry; Biology; Geology; Pharmacy; Political Science; *Doctorado*: Biochemistry; Biology; Geology; Pharmacy

Special Facilities: Museum of Petroleum (Comodoro Rivadavia)

Libraries: Central Library, c. 130,000 vols

Publications: Naturalia Patagónica *(quarterly)*

Press or Publishing House: Editorial Universitaria de la Patagonia
Last Updated: 27/02/09

NATIONAL UNIVERSITY OF QUILMES

Universidad Nacional de Quilmes (UNQ)
Roque Sáenz Peña 352, B1876BXD Bernal, Buenos Aires
Tel: +54(11) 4365-7100
Fax: +54(11) 4365-7101
EMail: info@unq.edu.ar
Website: http://www.unq.edu.ar

Rector: Gustavo Lugones
Tel: +54(11) 4365-7124 EMail: rectorado@unq.edu.ar

Secretaria Académica: Sara Pérez
EMail: secretaria_academica@unq.edu.ar

International Relations: Juan Luis Mérega
EMail: jlmerega@unq.edu.ar

Centres
Studies and Research *Director*: Carlos Altamirano

Departments
Science and Technology (Automation and Control Engineering; Bioengineering; Food Technology; Naval Architecture; Technology) *Director*: Mario Lozano; **Social Sciences** (Communication Studies; Education; Hotel Management; International Business; Music; Music Theory and Composition; Occupational Therapy; Social Sciences) *Director*: Sabina Frederic

History: Founded 1989. An autonomous State institution.

Governing Bodies: Asamblea Universitaria; Consejo Superior; Consejos Departamentales

Admission Requirements: Secondary school certificate (bachillerato) or equivalent and approval of the admission course

Degrees and Diplomas: *Licenciatura*; *Especialización*; *Maestría*; *Doctorado*
Last Updated: 02/03/09

NATIONAL UNIVERSITY OF RÍO CUARTO

Universidad Nacional de Río Cuarto (UNRC)
Ruta Nacional 36 Km. 601, 5800 Río Cuarto, Córdoba
Tel: +54(358) 467-6200
Fax: +54(358) 468-0280
EMail: secpriv@rec.unrc.edu.ar
Website: http://www.unrc.edu.ar

Rector: Oscar Federico Spada (2005-) Tel: +54(358) 467-6200

Secretaria Académica: Silvia Nicoletti
Tel: +54(358) 467-6310, Fax: +54(358) 467-6142
EMail: secacad@rec.unrc.edu.ar

Faculties
Agronomy and Veterinary Science (Agricultural Engineering; Agronomy; Veterinary Science) *Dean*: Roberto Luis Rovere; **Economics** (Accountancy; Administration; Economics; Finance; Marketing) *Dean*: Roberto Tafani; **Engineering** (Chemical Engineering; Electrical Engineering; Engineering; Mechanical Engineering; Telecommunications Engineering) *Dean*: Pedro Enrique Ducanto; **Exact, Natural Sciences and Physical Chemistry** (Biology; Chemistry; Computer Networks; Geology; Mathematics; Microbiology; Natural Sciences; Physical Chemistry; Physics) *Dean*: Gladys B. Mori; **Human Sciences** (Arts and Humanities; Communication Studies; English; French; Geography; History; Linguistics; Literature; Nursing; Pedagogy; Philosophy; Physical Education; Political Sciences) *Dean*: Enrique Arturo Grote

Schools
Graduate Studies *Director*: Norma Martínez de Pérez

History: Founded 1971. An autonomous State institution.

Governing Bodies: University Council

Academic Year: March to November (March-July; August-November)

Admission Requirements: Secondary school certificate (bachillerato) or equivalent

Main Language(s) of Instruction: Spanish

International Co-operation: With universities in Spain; Cuba; Brazil; Germany; Italy; Belgium; USA and Mexico

Accrediting Agencies: CONEAU

Degrees and Diplomas: *Título Menor*: Nursing, 2 1/2 yrs; *Título Menor*: Technical Studies, 2-3 yrs; *Licenciatura*: Biology; Business Administration; Chemistry; Communication; Computer Studies; Initial Education; Mathematics; Physical Education; Political Science; Psychopedagogy, 5 yrs; *Licenciatura*: Economics, 5 1/2 yrs; *Professional Title*: Accountancy; Chemical Engineering; Electrical Engineering; Law; Mechanical Engineering; Microbiology; Telecommunications Engineering, 5 yrs; *Professional Title*: Agriculture; Geology; Veterinary Medicine, 5 1/2 yrs; *Professional Title*: Computer Science, 3 yrs; *Professional Title*: History; Languages and Literatures; Teacher Training (secondary level), 4 yrs; *Especialización*: Clinical Sciences; Human Resources; Education; Environmental Geology; Health and Animal Husbandry; Statistics, 1 yr; *Maestría*: Animal Husbandry; Mathematics Education; Applied Mathematics; Industrial Chemistry; Biotechnology; Animal Reproduction; Chemical Engineering; Mechanical Engineering; Electrical Engineering; Agriculture; Veterinary Medicine, 2 yrs; *Doctorado*: Chemistry; Biology; Geology; Educational Sciences; Communication Studies; Physics; Economics; Animal Husbandry, 4 yrs

Student Services: Cultural centre, Health services, Nursery care, Social counselling, Sports facilities

Libraries: Yes

Publications: Revista *(biennially)*

Press or Publishing House: Departamento de Imprenta y Publicaciones
Last Updated: 02/03/09

NATIONAL UNIVERSITY OF ROSARIO

Universidad Nacional de Rosario (UNR)
Córdoba 1814, S2000AXD Rosario, Santa Fé
Tel: +54(341) 480-2621
Fax: +54(341) 480-2621
EMail: vicerrectoria@unr.edu.ar; gladystlechini@yahoo.com.ar
Website: http://www.unr.edu.ar

Rector: Darío Maiorana (2007-)
Tel: +54(341) 480-2626, Fax: +54(341) 480-2626
EMail: rector@unr.edu.ar

International Relations: Mariano Gárate, Secretary of International Relations
Tel: +54(341) 447-2173, Fax: +54(341) 447-2173
EMail: rrii@unr.edu.ar

Centres
Interdisciplinary Studies (International Studies; Public Health) *Director*: Hugo Quiroga

Faculties

Agriculture *(Zavalla)* (Agricultural Engineering; Agriculture; Harvest Technology; Natural Resources; Plant and Crop Protection) *Dean*: Liliana Ramirez; **Architecture, Planning and Design** (Architectural and Environmental Design; Architecture; Architecture and Planning; Design) *Dean*: Héctor Floriani; **Biochemistry and Pharmacy** (Analytical Chemistry; Biochemistry; Microbiology; Organic Chemistry; Pharmacy; Physical Chemistry; Physiology) *Dean*: Claudia Balague; **Dentistry** (Dentistry) *Dean*: Guillermo J. Francella; **Economics and Statistics** (Accountancy; Business Administration; Economics; Statistics) *Dean*: Javier Eduardo Ganem; **Exact Sciences, Engineering and Land Surveying** (Civil Engineering; Electrical Engineering; Industrial Engineering; Mathematics; Mechanical Engineering; Physics; Rural Planning; Surveying and Mapping) *Dean*: David Esteban Asteggiano; **Humanities and Arts** (Anthropology; Arts and Humanities; Educational Sciences; Fine Arts; History; Literature; Music; Philosophy) *Dean*: Daniel Musitano; **Law** (Law) *Dean*: Ricardo Silberstein; **Medical Sciences** (Health Sciences; Medicine; Nursing; Speech Therapy and Audiology) *Dean*: Carlos D. Crisci; **Political Science and International Relations** (Communication Studies; International Relations; Political Sciences; Social Work) *Dean*: Fabián Bicciré; **Psychology** (Psychology) *Dean*: Ovide Menin; **Veterinary Science** *(Casilda)* (Veterinary Science) *Dean*: Gustavo A. Sanmiguel

Higher Institutes

Business *(Libertador General San Martín)* (Accountancy; Business and Commerce; Communication Arts; Economics; English; French; Law; Mathematics; Music; Physical Education; Social Sciences; Theatre) *Director*: Gabriela Zamboni; **Polytechnic** *(General San Martín)* (Chemistry; Computer Science; Electrical Engineering; Food Technology; Industrial Management; Mathematics; Mechanical Engineering; Optics; Physical Education; Physics; Polymer and Plastics Technology; Technology) *Director*: Oscar E. Peire

Schools

Agricultural Technology *(Libertador San Martín)* (Agricultural Equipment)

History: Founded 1968. A State Institution.

Governing Bodies: Asamblea Universitaria; Consejo Superior

Academic Year: March to November (March-June; August-November)

Admission Requirements: Secondary school certificate (bachillerato)

Main Language(s) of Instruction: Spanish

Degrees and Diplomas: *Licenciatura*: Economics; History; Industrial and Public Relations; International Relations; Journalism; Letters; Mathematics; Midwifery; Nursing; Philosophy; Physics; Political Science; Visual Arts, 4-5 yrs; *Professional Title*: Accountancy; Agriculture; Architecture; Biochemistry; Civil Engineering; Dentistry; Electrical Engineering; Geography; Law; Mechanical Engineering; Medicine; Pharmacy; Psychology; Statistics; Veterinary Medicine, 4-6 yrs; *Professional Title*: Library Science; Phonoaudiology; Radiology, 3 yrs; *Professional Title*: Medical Law; Orthopaedics, 2 yrs; *Professional Title*: Nursing, 2 1/2 yrs; *Professional Title*: Teacher Training, 5 yrs; *Especialización*; *Maestría*; *Doctorado*: by thesis, 2 yrs following Licenciatura

Student Services: Academic counselling, Cultural centre, Foreign student adviser, Health services, Social counselling, Sports facilities

Student Residential Facilities: For medical students

Libraries: Faculty of Medicine, c. 32,170 vols; Faculty of Economics, c. 95,580 vols; Faculty of Philosophy, c. 49,760 vols; Faculty of Exact Sciences and Engineering, c. 40,830 vols; Faculty of Dentistry, c. 3,900 vols; Faculty of Biochemistry, c. 2,500 vols; Faculty of Law, c. 3,650 vols; Faculty of Agriculture, c. 5,070 vols; Institute of Music, c. 1,370 vols

Publications: Revista de la Universidad

Academic Staff *2009-2010*	TOTAL
FULL-TIME	806
PART-TIME	1,728
STAFF WITH DOCTORATE	
FULL-TIME	514

Student Numbers *2009-2010*	
All (Foreign Included)	77,180

Last Updated: 02/03/09

NATIONAL UNIVERSITY OF SALTA
Universidad Nacional de Salta (UNSA)
Buenos Aires 177, 4400 Salta, Salta
Tel: +54(387) 432-5703
Fax: +54(387) 432-5704
EMail: info@unsa.edu.ar
Website: http://www.unsa.edu.ar

Rectora: Stella Maris Pérez de Bianchi
Tel: +54(387) 425-5427 EMail: rectora@unsa.edu.ar

Secretaria Académica: Maria Celia Ilvento
Tel: +54(387) 425-5574 EMail: secadem@unsa.edu.ar

Centres

History and Anthropology Research *(CEPIHA)* (Anthropology; History); **Interdisciplinary Research** *(CICIO, Oran)*; **Public Health** *(CESAP)* (Public Health); **Tropical Cultivation** *(CE.CU.TRO)* (Tropical Agriculture)

Faculties

Economics, Law, and Social Sciences (Accountancy; Administration; Business Administration; Economics; Law; Social Sciences) *Dean*: Víctor Hugo Claros; **Engineering** (Chemical Engineering; Civil Engineering; Engineering; Food Technology; Industrial Engineering) *Dean*: Jorge Feliz Almazan; **Exact Sciences** (Chemistry; Computer Science; Electronic Engineering; Mathematics; Natural Sciences; Physics; Systems Analysis) *Dean*: Norberto Alejandro Bonini; **Health Sciences** (Health Sciences; Nursing; Nutrition) *Dean*: Niever Chavez; **Humanities** (Anthropology; Arts and Humanities; Communication Studies; Educational Sciences; History; Philosophy) *Dean*: Flor De Maria Del Valle Rionda; **Natural Sciences** (Agricultural Engineering; Biology; Environmental Studies; Geology; Natural Sciences) *Dean*: Guillermo Andres Baudino

Groups

Demography Studies (Demography and Population)

Institutes

Accountancy (Accountancy); **Administration** (Administration); **Chemical Research** *(INIQUI)* (Chemistry); **Distance Education**; **Ecology and Human Environment** (Ecology; Environmental Studies); **Economic Research** (Economics); **Folklore and Regional Literature** *(Augusto Raúl Cortazár)* (Folklore; Literature); **Food Research** *(IIASA)* (Food Science); **Geology** *(GEONORTE)* (Geology); **Human Nutrition Evaluation** *(IIEMPO)* (Food Science); **Industrial Chemistry Research** *(INIQUI)* (Industrial Chemistry); **Mathematics** (Mathematics); **Natural Resources and Ecological Development** *(IRNED)* (Ecology); **Non-conventional Energy Research** *(INENCO)* (Ecology); **Rural Development** (Development Studies); **Social Studies** (Social Studies)

Laboratories

Experimental Pathology (Pathology)

Further Information: Also Regional Centres in Orán and Tartagal

History: Founded 1973, incorporating the Faculty of Natural Sciences, Department of Economics, and Institute of Endocrinology of the National University of Tucumán. An autonomous State institution.

Governing Bodies: Asamblea Universitaria; Consejo Superior

Academic Year: March to November (March-June; August-November)

Admission Requirements: Secondary school certificate (bachillerato) or equivalent

Main Language(s) of Instruction: Spanish

Degrees and Diplomas: *Licenciatura*: 4-5 yrs; *Licenciatura*: Social Work, 1 yr (Postítulo); *Professional Title*: 4 yrs; *Professional Title*: Accountancy; Agriculture; Civil Engineering; Construction; Geology; Hydrology; Industrial Engineering, 5 yrs; *Professional Title*: Chemical Analysis; Natural Resources, 4 yrs; *Professional Title*: Chemical Engineering; Communications, 6 yrs; *Professional Title*: Computing; Drilling; Nursing; Stockraising Administration, 3 yrs; *Professional Title*: Electronics, 2 1/2 yrs; *Professional Title*: Social Communication, 3 1/2 yrs; *Especialización*: Accountancy; Business Administration; Public Administration, a further 2 yrs; *Especialización*: Economics; Law, 1 yr (Postítulo); *Especialización*: Ethics and Citizenship; Public Health; Social Politics, a further $1\frac{1}{2}$ yrs; *Especialización*: Renewable Energy, a further 2 yrs and by thesis; *Maestría*: a further 2 yrs; *Doctorado*: Biology; Civil Engineering; Industrial Engineering, a further 5 yrs; *Doctorado*: Chemistry; Humanities;

Research and Innovation in Education, a further 2-5 yrs; *Doctorado*: Renewable Energy, a further 2-5 ys

Student Services: Canteen, Cultural centre, Foreign student adviser, Health services, Sports facilities

Student Residential Facilities: Yes

Special Facilities: Museum of Natural Sciences. Observatory. Radio Studio. Osvalde Juane Art Gallery

Libraries: Branch libraries

Publications: Andes, Anthropology-History *(annually)*; Castañares, Economics *(annually)*; Literatura de Salta, Social/cultural History *(annually)*

Press or Publishing House: Dirección de Publicaciones e Impresiones

Last Updated: 09/07/07

NATIONAL UNIVERSITY OF SAN JUAN

Universidad Nacional de San Juan (UNSJ)
Avenida 25 de Mayo 1921(O), J5400AIM San Juan, San Juan
Tel: +54(264) 426-4000
Fax: +54(264) 423-7943
Website: http://www.unsj.edu.ar

Rector: Benjamin Rafael Kuchen (2001-)
EMail: rector@unsj.edu.ar

Secretaria Académica: Ana Cristina Deiana
Tel: +54(264) 426-3187 Ext.156-157
EMail: academica@unsj.edu.ar

Faculties

Architecture, Town Planning and Design *(Rivadavia)* (Architecture; Graphic Design; Industrial Design; Town Planning) *Dean*: José Guillermo Rodriguez; **Engineering** (Bioengineering; Chemical Engineering; Civil Engineering; Electrical and Electronic Engineering; Food Technology; Mechanical Engineering; Mining Engineering; Surveying and Mapping) *Dean*: Oscar Herminio Nasisi; **Exact, Physical and Natural Sciences** *(Rivadavia)* (Astronomy and Space Science; Biology; Geology; Geophysics; Information Sciences) *Dean*: Rodolfo Herman Bloch; **Philosophy, Humanities and Arts** (Arts and Humanities; Fine Arts; Literature; Music; Pedagogy; Philosophy; Visual Arts) *Dean*: Paolo V.P. Landini; **Social Sciences** *(Rivadavia)* (Business Administration; Economics; Journalism; Law; Political Sciences; Public Administration; Social Sciences; Social Work; Sociology) *Dean*: Marcelo Ricardo Coca

Further Information: Also 26 institutes

History: Founded 1973, incorporating faculties and schools of the National University of Cuyo. An autonomous State institution.

Governing Bodies: Consejo Superior

Academic Year: April to November (April-July; August-November)

Admission Requirements: Secondary school certificate (bachillerato) or equivalent

Main Language(s) of Instruction: Spanish

Degrees and Diplomas: *Licenciatura*: Business Administration; Communication; Geology; Geophysics; Political Science; School Administration; Social Service; Sociology, 5 yrs; *Professional Title*: Architecture, 6 yrs; *Professional Title*: Engineering, 5-6 yrs; *Professional Title*: Social Work, 4 yrs; *Professional Title*: Teacher Training; *Especialización*; *Maestría*; *Doctorado*: by thesis

Last Updated: 02/03/09

NATIONAL UNIVERSITY OF SAN LUIS

Universidad Nacional de San Luis (UNSL)
Avenida Ejército de los Andes 950, D5700HHW San Luis, San Luis
Tel: +54(2652) 42-4027
Fax: +54(2652) 43-0224
EMail: rector@unsl.edu.ar
Website: http://www.unsl.edu.ar

Rector: José Luis Riccardo Tel: +54(2652) 42-0822

Secretaria Académica: Ana Lía Cometta
EMail: sacade@unsl.edu.ar

Faculties

Chemistry, Biochemistry, and Pharmacy (Biochemistry; Chemistry; Pharmacy) *Dean*: Maria Isabel Sanz; **Engineering and**

Socio-Economics *(Villa Mercedes)* (Chemical Engineering; Economics; Electrical and Electronic Engineering) *Dean*: Sergio Ribotta; **Human Sciences** (Education; Human Rights; Psychology) *Dean*: Martha María Pereyra González; **Physics, Mathematics, and Natural Sciences** (Geology; Information Sciences; Mathematics; Mining Engineering; Physics) *Dean*: Félix Daniel Nieto Quintas

Higher Schools

Teacher Training *(ENJPP)* (Educational Sciences; Teacher Trainers Education; Teacher Training) *Head*: Juan Enrique Gallardo

Research Institutes

Chemical Technology *(INTEQUI)* (Chemical Engineering)

History: Founded 1973. An autonomous State institution.

Governing Bodies: Consejo Superior; Consejos Directivos de las Facultades

Academic Year: March to November

Admission Requirements: Secondary school certificate (bachillerato) or equivalent

Main Language(s) of Instruction: Spanish

Degrees and Diplomas: *Título Menor*: Phonoaudiology; Statistics; Technical Studies, 3 yrs; *Licenciatura*: Administration; Biochemistry; Chemistry; Education; Geology; Mathematics; Physics; Psychology, 5 yrs; *Professional Title*: Agriculture; Engineering, 5-6 yrs; *Professional Title*: Pharmacy, 4 yrs; *Professional Title*: Teacher Training; *Especialización*; *Maestría*; *Doctorado*: Education; Psychology, by thesis

Student Residential Facilities: Yes

Special Facilities: Museo Regional 'German Ave Lallement' (Archaeological and Anthropological Museum)

Libraries: Total, c. 184,000 vols
Last Updated: 02/03/09

NATIONAL UNIVERSITY OF SAN MARTÍN

Universidad Nacional de San Martín (UNSAM)
Martín de Irigoyen 3100, 1650 San Martín, Buenos Aires
Tel: +54(11) 4006-1500 +54(11) 4724-1500
Fax: +54(11) 4006-1500 +54(11) 4724-1500
EMail: rectorado@unsam.edu.ar
Website: http://www.unsam.edu.ar

Rector: Carlos Rafael Ruta (2006-)

Secretario General: Guillermo Schweinheim
EMail: secretaria.general@unsam.edu.ar

International Relations: Valeria Pattachini, Coordinator
Tel: +54(11) 4580-7500 51/59, Fax: +54(11) 4580-7500 51/59
EMail: internacionales@unsam.edu.ar

Institutes

Biotechnological Research *(Migueletes)* *Director*: Alberto Carlos Frasch; **Higher Social Studies** *(Buenos Aires)* (Social Sciences) *Director*: Alejandro Grimson; **Industrial Quality** *(INCALIN)* (Safety Engineering) *Director*: Joaquin Valdés; **Nuclear Technology** *(Dan Beninson, Ezeiza)* (Nuclear Engineering) *Dean*: Carla Notari; **Rehabilitation and Movement Sciences** *(Belgrano, Buenos Aires)* (Rehabilitation and Therapy) *Director*: Hugo Rodríguez Isarn; **Technology** *(Sabato)* (Materials Engineering) *Director*: José Rodolfo Galvele

Schools

Economics and Business *(San Martín)* (Business and Commerce; Economics) *Director*: Horacio Val; **Graduate Studies** *(San Martín)* (Educational Administration; Environmental Studies; Family Studies; Justice Administration; Molecular Biology) *Director*: Alberto Pochettino; **Humanities** *(San Martín)* (Arts and Humanities; Education; Museum Studies; Performing Arts; Social Sciences) *Director*: José Villella; **Political Science and Government** *(Buenos Aires)* (Government; Political Sciences) *Director*: Marcelo Cavarozzi; **Science and Technology** *(Villa Ballester)* (Biomedical Engineering; Computer Networks; Computer Science; Natural Sciences; Radiology; Technology) *Director*: Daniel Di Gregorio

History: Founded 1992, acquired present status 1994. Previously known as National University General de San Martín (Universidad Nacional de General San Martín)

Governing Bodies: Consejo Superior; Asamblea Universitaria

Academic Year: March to December

Admission Requirements: Secondary school certificate (bachillerato)

Main Language(s) of Instruction: Spanish

International Co-operation: With universities in Spain and USA

Accrediting Agencies: Consejo Nacional de Evaluación y Acreditación Universitaria (CONEAU)

Degrees and Diplomas: *Licenciatura*: Social Science; Health Sciences; Business Administration; Economics; Arts and Humanities; Education; Technology, 4 yrs; *Professional Title*: Health Sciences; Edcuation; Business Administration, 2 yrs; *Especialización*: Education; Family Studies; Environmental Studies; Latin American Studies; International Cooperation, 1 yr; *Maestría*: Education; Family Studies; Environmental Studies; Latin American Studies; International Cooperation; Technology; Biotechnology (MA), a further 2 yrs; *Doctorado*: Microbiology; Technology (PhD), a further 4 yrs

Student Services: Academic counselling, Cultural centre, Employment services, Foreign student adviser, Language programs, Social counselling, Sports facilities

Libraries: Central Library

Publications: Nómada
Last Updated: 02/03/09

NATIONAL UNIVERSITY OF SANTIAGO DEL ESTERO

Universidad Nacional de Santiago del Estero (UNSE)
Avenida Belgrano Sur 1912, 4200 Santiago del Estero,
Santiago del Estero
Tel: +54(385) 450-9500
Fax: +54(385) 450-9544
EMail: info@unse.edu.ar
Website: http://www.unse.edu.ar

Rector: Arnaldo Sergio Tenchini
Tel: +54(385) 450-9510 EMail: rector@unse.edu.ar

Secretaria Académica: Maria de las Mercedes Arce de Vera
Tel: +54(385) 450-9501 EMail: academica@unse.edu.ar

Centres
Rural Education *(Secondary level)* (Rural Studies; Secondary Education)

Faculties
Agronomy and Food Industry (Agronomy; Food Science; Food Technology; Landscape Architecture) *Dean*: José Ramón Kobylañski; **Exact Sciences and Technology** (Civil Engineering; Electrical Engineering; Electronic Engineering; Hydraulic Engineering; Mathematics; Natural Sciences; Technology) *Dean*: Carlos Alberto Bonetti; **Forestry** (Ecology; Forestry; Wood Technology) *Dean*: Juan Carlos Medina; **Humanities, Social Sciences and Health** (Arts and Humanities; Communication Studies; Education; Health Sciences; Law; Modern Languages; Philosophy; Psychology; Social Sciences) *Dean*: Natividad Nassif

Schools
Educational Innovation (Education) *Director*: Mariana Hernández Úbeda de Gómez

History: Founded 1973. An autonomous State institution.

Governing Bodies: Asamblea; Consejo Superior; Consejos Académicos

Academic Year: February to December (March-July; August-December)

Admission Requirements: Secondary school certificate (bachillerato) or equivalent

Main Language(s) of Instruction: Spanish

Degrees and Diplomas: *Licenciatura*: 4-5 yrs; *Professional Title*: 4-5 yrs; *Professional Title*: Engineering, 5-6 yrs; *Professional Title*: Health Education; Nursing, 3 yrs; *Professional Title*: Technical Studies, 2-3 yrs; *Especialización*; *Maestría*: a further 2 yrs; *Doctorado*: a further 3 yrs

Special Facilities: University Radio

Libraries: Central Library, c. 25,000 vols

Publications: Quebracho, Forestry *(annually)*; Revista de Ciencia y Técnica *(annually)*
Last Updated: 02/03/09

NATIONAL UNIVERSITY OF SOUTHERN PATAGONIA

Universidad Nacional de la Patagonia Austral (UNPA)
Lisandro de la Torre 860, 9400 Río Gallegos, Santa Cruz
Tel: +54(2966) 44-2376
Fax: +54(2966) 44-2376
EMail: info@unpa.edu.ar
Website: http://www.unpa.edu.ar

Rector: Eugenia Márquez (2007-)
Tel: +54(2966) 44-2370, Fax: +54(2966) 44-2377
EMail: rector@unpa.edu.ar

Vicerrector: Hugo Santos Rojas

Units
Caleta Olivia *Dean*: Héctor Daniel Lorenzetti; **Río Gallegos** *Dean*: Alejandro Súnico; **Río Turbio** *Dean*: Virginia Barbieri; **San Julían** *Dean*: Claudia Malik De Tchara

History: Founded 1962, acquired present status and title 1994.

Governing Bodies: Asemblea Universitaria; Consejo Superior; Consejo de Unidades

Main Language(s) of Instruction: Spanish

Degrees and Diplomas: *Título Menor*: 3 yrs; *Licenciatura*: 5 yrs; *Professional Title*: 4 yrs; *Professional Title*: Engineering, 4 yrs
Last Updated: 27/02/09

NATIONAL UNIVERSITY OF THE CENTRE OF THE PROVINCE OF BUENOS AIRES

Universidad Nacional del Centro de la Provincia de Buenos Aires (UNCPBA)
General Pinto 399, B7000GHG Tandil, Buenos Aires
Tel: +54(2293) 42-2000
Fax: +54(2293) 42-1608
EMail: sprivada@rec.unicen.edu.ar
Website: http://www.unicen.edu.ar

Rector: Roberto Tassara
Tel: +54(2293) 42-2063 EMail: rector@rec.unicen.edu.ar

Secretaria Académica: Mabel Pacheco
Tel: +54(2293) 42-1876, Fax: +54(2293) 42-1892
EMail: academica@rec.unicen.edu.ar

Faculties
Agronomy *(Azul)* (Agricultural Business; Agricultural Management; Agronomy; Biology; Water Science); **Art**; **Economics**; **Engineering** *(Olavarría)*; **Exact Sciences**; **Human Sciences** (Arts and Humanities; Education; Educational Sciences; Environmental Management; Geography; History; International Relations; Primary Education; Social Studies; Social Work; Surveying and Mapping); **Social Sciences** *(Olavarría)* (Anthropology; Archaeology; Communication Studies; Cultural Studies; Media Studies; Social Policy; Social Sciences; Social Studies); **Veterinary Science** (Animal Husbandry; Apiculture; Biology; Dairy; Epidemiology; Veterinary Science; Zoology)

Higher Schools
Health Sciences (Nursing); **Law** (Law)

Further Information: Branches in Azul and Olavarría

History: Founded 1964 as University of Tandil, a private institution. Acquired present status and title 1974, incorporating previously existing institutions in Olavarría and Azul. An autonomous State institution.

Governing Bodies: Asamblea Universitaria

Academic Year: March to December (March-July; August-December)

Admission Requirements: Secondary school certificate (bachillerato) or equivalent

Fees: None

Main Language(s) of Instruction: Spanish

Degrees and Diplomas: *Licenciatura*: 3-5 yrs; *Professional Title*: 4-6 yrs; *Especialización*; *Maestría*: 2 yrs; *Doctorado*: 4 yrs

Student Services: Academic counselling, Canteen, Cultural centre, Employment services, Health services, Language programs, Nursery care, Social counselling, Sports facilities

Student Residential Facilities: Yes

Libraries: Central and branches libraries

Publications: Anuario del Instituto de Estudios Históricos y Sociales *(annually)*; Espacios en Blanco *(annually)*; Estudios Socioterritoriales *(annually)*; Intersecciones en Antropología *(annually)*; Intersecciones en Comunicación *(annually)*; Revista Alternativas *(annually)*; Revista de la Escuela de Perfeccionamiento en Investigación Operativa *(biennially)*; Revista El Peldaño-Cuaderno de Teatrología *(biennially)*; Revista La Escalera *(annually)*

Press or Publishing House: Departamento de Impresiones
Last Updated: 02/03/09

NATIONAL UNIVERSITY OF THE LITTORAL
Universidad Nacional del Litoral (UNL)
Bulevar Pellegrini 2750, S3000ADQ Santa Fé, Santa Fé
Tel: +54(342) 457-1110
Fax: +54(342) 457-1110
EMail: informes@unl.edu.ar
Website: http://www.unl.edu.ar

Rector: Albor Cantard (2000-)
Tel: +54(342) 457-1125, Fax: +54(342) 457-1125
EMail: rector@unl.edu.ar

Faculties
Agronomy (Agricultural Engineering; Apiculture; Dairy) *Dean*: Luis Rista; **Architecture, Design and Town Planning** *Dean*: Miguel Irigoyen; **Biochemistry and Biological Sciences** (Biochemistry; Environmental Studies; Epidemiology) *Dean*: Amadeo Ángel Cellino; **Chemical Engineering** (Chemical Engineering; Chemistry; Food Technology; Industrial Engineering; Mathematics) *Dean*: Alberto Castro; **Economics** (Accountancy; Administration; Economics) *Dean*: Hugo Rodriguez Jauregui; **Humanities and Sciences** *Dean*: Liliana Paiz de Izaguire; **Hydraulic Resources Sciences** (Computer Engineering; Environmental Engineering; Hydraulic Engineering; Measurement and Precision Engineering; Surveying and Mapping) *Dean*: Mario Schreider; **Law and Social Sciences** (Law; Library Science; Social Sciences; Social Studies) *Dean*: Albor Cantard; **Veterinary Science** *Dean*: José Luis Peralta

Higher Institutes
Music (Music) *Director*: Hugo Druetta

Higher Schools
Food Analysis (Food Technology) *Director*: Mónica De Santis; **Food Studies** (Food Science; Food Technology) *Director*: Luis Nickisch; **Health Services** *(Ramon Carrillo)* (Environmental Studies; Public Health) *Director*: María del Carmen Rossler; **Industrial Engineering** *Director*: Héctor Aymerich; **Medicine** *(School) Dean*: José Hadad

Schools
Agriculture and Farming *Director*: Mercedes Romanos

History: Founded 1889 as provincial University, became National University by law in 1919. An autonomous State institution.

Governing Bodies: Asamblea Universitaria; Consejo Superior

Academic Year: March to November

Admission Requirements: Secondary school certificate (bachillerato)

Main Language(s) of Instruction: Spanish

International Co-operation: Participates in PROINMES (International programme of students mobility). Member of the AUGM, and ESCALA-AUGM programmes

Degrees and Diplomas: *Licenciatura*: 3 yrs; *Professional Title*: 2 yrs; *Especialización*: a further 2 yrs; *Maestría*: a further 3 yrs; *Doctorado*: a further 4 yrs

Student Services: Academic counselling, Canteen, Cultural centre, Employment services, Foreign student adviser, Foreign Studies

Centre, Handicapped facilities, Health services, Language programs, Nursery care, Social counselling, Sports facilities

Student Residential Facilities: For c. 350 students

Special Facilities: Museum of Contemporary Arts

Libraries: c. 14,000 vols

Publications: Conciencia, Scientific Publication *(biennially)*
Last Updated: 02/03/09

NATIONAL UNIVERSITY OF THE NORTH-EAST
Universidad Nacional del Nordeste (UNNE)
Calle 25 de Mayo 868, 3400 Corrientes, Corrientes
Tel: +54(3783) 42-5064
Fax: +54(3783) 42-4678
EMail: rector@unne.edu.ar
Website: http://www.unne.edu.ar

Rector: Oscar Vicente Valdés Tel: +54(3722) 42-4678

Secretario General Académico: Orlando Maccio
EMail: secacad@unne.edu.ar

Faculties
Agricultural Sciences (Agricultural Engineering; Agriculture) *Dean*: Abel R. Ferrero; **Agroindustry** *(Saenz Peña)* (Agricultural Engineering; Chemical Engineering; Food Technology; Forestry; Pharmacy) *Dean*: Omar Vicente Judis; **Architecture and Town Planning** *(Resistencia)* (Architecture; Town Planning) *Dean*: José Luis Solé; **Dentistry** (Dentistry) *Dean*: Adolfo D. Torres; **Economics** *(Resistencia)* (Accountancy; Economics; Public Administration) *Dean*: Beatriz del C. Monfardini de Franchini; **Engineering** *(Resistencia)* (Civil Engineering; Computer Engineering; Electrical Engineering; Engineering; Hydraulic Engineering; Mechanical Engineering; Thermal Engineering) *Dean*: Jorge Victor Pilar; **Exact Natural Sciences and Surveying** (Biology; Chemistry; Engineering; Mathematics; Natural Sciences; Physics; Surveying and Mapping) *Dean*: Eduardo Enrique del Valle; **Humanities** *(Resistencia)* (Arts and Humanities; Educational Sciences; Geography; History; Literature; Philosophy) *Dean*: Maria Delfina Veiravé; **Law, Social Sciences and Political Science** (Law; Political Sciences; Social Sciences) *Dean*: Verónica Torres de Breard; **Medicine** (Medicine; Nursing; Physical Therapy) *Dean*: Samuel Bluvstein; **Veterinary Science** (Veterinary Science) *Dean*: Hugo A. Domitrovic

Institutes
Agricultural Economics; **Criminology and Criminal Science**; **Management of Agricultural Enterprises**

History: Founded 1956, incorporating various schools attached to the National University of the Littoral. The institution, which enjoys academic and administrative autonomy, is responsible to the Ministry of Education and Culture.

Governing Bodies: Asamblea Universitaria; Consejo Superior; Consejos Directivos

Academic Year: March to November (March-July; July-November)

Admission Requirements: Secondary school certificate (bachillerato) or equivalent

Main Language(s) of Instruction: Spanish

Degrees and Diplomas: *Licenciatura*: Botany; Chemistry; Economics; Education; Geography; History; Literature; Mathematics; Philosophy; Physics; Zoology, 5-6 yrs; *Professional Title*: Accountancy; Nursing; Teacher Teaching (secondary level), 4 yrs; *Professional Title*: Agriculture; Dentistry; Physical Therapy; Veterinary Medicine, 4-5 yrs; *Professional Title*: Architecture; Civil Engineering; Law; Surgery, 6-7 yrs; *Maestría*; *Doctorado*: Economics; Economics and Administration, 6 yrs; *Doctorado*: Education; Geography; History; Law; Philosophy, by thesis

Student Residential Facilities: Yes

Special Facilities: Museum of Anthropology; Museum of Archaeology

Libraries: Central Library (Resistencia), c. 56,700 vols; Corrientes, c. 32,000 vols

Publications: Anales del Instituto de Patología Regional; Bomplandia; Nordeste; Revista de la Facultad de Derecho; Revista Veterinaria
Last Updated: 02/03/09

NATIONAL UNIVERSITY OF THE NORTH-WEST OF THE PROVINCE OF BUENOS AIRES

Universidad Nacional del Noroeste de la Provincia de Buenos Aires

Roque Sáenz Peña 456, 6000 Junín, Buenos Aires
Tel: +54(2362) 44-5479 +54(2362) 42-8781
Fax: +54(2362) 44-5479 +54(2362) 42-8781
EMail: secretariaprivada@unnoba.edu.ar
Website: http://www.unnoba.edu.ar

Rector: Guillermo Ricardo Tamarit (2007-)
EMail: rectorado@unnoba.edu.ar

Secretaria Académica: Lilián J. Lértora
EMail: academica@unnoba.edu.ar

International Relations: Gabriela Messing
Tel: +54(2477) 42-9614 +54(2477) 42-9569,
Fax: +54(2477) 42-9614 +54(2477) 42-9569
EMail: rrii@unnoba.edu.ar

Schools

Agrarian, Natural and Environmental Sciences (Agronomy; Biological and Life Sciences; Food Science; Genetics; Natural Sciences); **Economics and Law** (Accountancy; Administration; Economics; Law; Public Administration); **Social and Human Sciences**; **Technology** (Computer Science; Design; Industrial Engineering; Industrial Maintenance; Mechanical Engineering)

Further Information: Also branches in Pergamino and Junín

History: Founded 2002.

Admission Requirements: High School Certificate

Fees: None

Main Language(s) of Instruction: Spanish

International Co-operation: With universities in Chile; Cuba; Spain. Member of the 'Red de responsables de Cooperación Internacional de las Universidades Nacionales' (REDCIUN)

Degrees and Diplomas: *Título Menor:* Agronomy; Food Sciences; Nursing; Industrial Maintenance; Mechanics, 3 yrs; *Título Menor:* Computer Science, 2 yrs; *Título Menor:* Public Administration; Animal Husbandry, 2 1/2 yrs; *Licenciatura:* Administration; Clothes and Textile Design; Graphic Design, 4 yrs; *Licenciatura:* Agronomy; Nursing; Computer Science, 4 1/2 yrs; *Licenciatura:* Journalism; Genetics; Food Science, 5 yrs; *Professional Title:* Accountancy; Law;, 4 1/2 yrs; *Professional Title:* Industrial Engineering; Mechanical Engineering; Computer Signals Processing; Software Engineering; Food Technology, 5 yrs; *Professional Title:* System Analysis, 3 yrs

Student Services: Language programs, Sports facilities

Student Residential Facilities: None

Libraries: Two libraries (on Junin and Pergamino Campuses); also virtual library part of the Proyecto de Enlaces de Bibliotecas (PREBI)

Academic Staff 2007-2008	MEN	WOMEN	TOTAL
PART-TIME	267	175	442
PART-TIME	27	19	46
Student Numbers 2007-2008			
All (Foreign Included)	2,596	2,276	4,872
FOREIGN ONLY	5	9	14

Last Updated: 02/03/09

NATIONAL UNIVERSITY OF THE SOUTH

Universidad Nacional del Sur (UNS)

Avenida Colón 80, B8000FTN Bahía Blanca, Buenos Aires
Tel: +54(291) 459-5015
Fax: +54(291) 459-5016
EMail: rectorado@uns.edu.ar
Website: http://www.uns.edu.ar

Rector: Guillermo Héctor Crapiste (2000-)
Tel: +54(291) 459-5017 EMail: rector@uns.edu.ar

Secretario General Académico: Marcelo Armando Villar
Tel: +54(291) 459-5027, Fax: +54(291) 459-5028
EMail: secac@uns.edu.ar

International Relations: Susana Rodríguez
Tel: +54(291) 459-5039, Fax: +54(291) 459-5040
EMail: secext@uns.edu.ar

Centres

Renewable Resources in the Semi-Arid Region *(CERZOS)* (Arid Land Studies; Natural Resources) *Director:* Néstor Curvetto

Departments

Administration (Accountancy; Administration; Business Administration) *Director:* Regina del Carmen Durán; **Agronomy** (Agriculture; Agronomy; Animal Husbandry; Apiculture; Horticulture; Soil Science) *Director:* Mario Ricardo Sabbatini; **Biology, Biochemistry and Pharmacy** (Biochemistry; Biological and Life Sciences; Biology; Pharmacy) *Directora:* Marta Aveldaño; **Chemical Engineering** (Chemical Engineering; Food Science) *Directora:* Verónica Bucalá; **Chemistry** (Chemistry) *Director:* María Susana Rodriguez; **Computer Science and Engineering** (Computer Engineering; Computer Science) *Director:* Rafael García; **Economics** (Economics) *Director:* Andrea Barbero; **Electrical Engineering** (Electrical Engineering; Electronic Engineering) *Director:* Pedro Doñate; **Engineering** (Civil Engineering; Engineering; Industrial Engineering; Mechanical Engineering) *Director:* Carlos Rossit; **Geography and Tourism** (Geography; Tourism) *Director:* Silvia Grippo; **Geology** (Geology) *Director:* Graciela Raquel Mas; **Humanities** (Arts and Humanities; History; Literature; Modern Languages; Philosophy) *Director:* Adriana Claudia Rodriguez; **Law** *(Bahia Bianca) Director:* Andrés Bouzat; **Mathematics** (Mathematics) *Directora:* Liliana Castro; **Medical Sciences** *Director:* Miguel Hugo Lliteras; **Physics** (Physics) *Director:* Walter Rubén Cravero

Institutes

Applied Mechanics *(IMA)* (Mechanical Engineering) *Director:* Mario J. Mauziri; **Electrical Engineering** *(Alfredo Desages) Director:* Osvaldo Agamennoni; **Mathematics** *(Bahía Bianca)* (Mathematics) *Director:* María Inés Platzeck; **Oceanography** *(Argentina (IADO))* (Marine Science and Oceanography) *Director:* María Cintia Píccolo; **Pilot Chemical Engineering Plant** *(PLAPIQUI)* (Food Technology; Polymer and Plastics Technology; Production Engineering) *Director:* Daniel Damiani

Research Institutes

Biochemical *(Bahía Blanca (INIBIBB))* (Biochemistry; Biophysics; Biotechnology) *Director:* Francisco Barrante

History: Founded 1948 as Instituto Tecnológico del Sur, became National University 1956. An autonomous State institution.

Governing Bodies: Asamblea Universitaria; Consejo Universitario

Academic Year: February to December

Admission Requirements: Secondary school certificate (bachillerato) or equivalent and entrance examination

Main Language(s) of Instruction: Spanish

International Co-operation: With universities in Europe; USA; Latin America. Also participates in Ecos; Alfa; Cyted; Orion; Columbus; V Framework Programme; Aeci; Fulbright; Laspau; DAAD; Saint-Exupery and JICA programmes

Accrediting Agencies: National Commission of University Accreditation (CONEAU) - Ministerio de Educación, Ciencia y Tecnología

Degrees and Diplomas: *Licenciatura:* Administration; Biology; Chemistry; Computer Science; Economics; Geography; Geology; Mathematics; Physics; Tourism, 5 yrs; *Licenciatura:* History; Letters; Philosophy, 4-5 yrs; *Professional Title:* Accountancy; Biochemistry; Law; Pharmacy, 5 yrs; *Professional Title:* Agrarian Food Business; Audiovisual Studies; Land and Water Sciences; Management and Commercialization of Grains; Municipal Affairs; Small and Medium Business Creation and Administration; Tourism, 3 yrs; *Professional Title:* Engineering; Teacher Training, 4-5 yrs; *Professional Title:* Land Surveying, 4 yrs; *Especialización:* Accountancy; Agrarian Sciences; Biology; Economics; Electrical and Electronic Engineering, a further 1-2 yrs following upon Licenciatura or Ingeniero; *Maestría:* 2-3 yrs with thesis; *Doctorado:* Agronomy; Administration; Biology-Biochemistry; Computer Sciences-Economy; Geography-Geology; Letters-History-Philosophy; Engineering-Systems Control-Chemistry Mathematics; Chemical Engineering; Materials Science and Technology-Food Science and Technology

Student Services: Academic counselling, Cultural centre, Health services, Language programs, Social counselling, Sports facilities

Student Residential Facilities: For 120 students

Special Facilities: Art Gallery

Libraries: Central Library, 99,000 vols; libraries of the institutes, 65,000 vols; c. 600 journals

Publications: Cuadernos del Sur, History, Spanish language and Philosophy *(annually)*; Escritos Contables (Ciencias de la Administración) *(biannually)*; Latin American Applied Research (PLAPIQUI) *(quarterly)*; Revista Estudios Económicos *(annually)*; Revista Universitaria de Geografía *(annually)*

Last Updated: 02/03/09

NATIONAL UNIVERSITY OF THE THIRD OF FEBRUARY

Universidad Nacional de Tres de Febrero (UNTREF)
Avenida San Martín 2921, 1678 Caseros, Buenos Aires
Tel: +54(11) 4759-9810
Fax: +54(11) 4759-9686
EMail: sprivada@untref.edu.ar
Website: http://www.untref.edu.ar

Rector: Aníbal Y. Jozami EMail: ajozami@untref.edu.ar

Vicerrector: Martín Kaufmann EMail: mkaufmann@untref.edu.ar

International Relations: Marta Pini, Directora
EMail: mpini@untref.edu.ar

Departments
Administration and Economics (Administration; Economics) *Director*: Martín Gras; **Art and Culture** (Arts and Humanities; Cultural Studies) *Director*: Norberto Griffa; **Engineering** (Engineering) *Director*: Pablo Fontdevilla; **Health and Social Security** (Health Sciences; Social and Preventive Medicine; Social Welfare) *Director*: Carlos Torres; **Methodology, Statistics and Mathematics** (Mathematics; Statistics) *Director*: Ernesto Rosa; **Social Sciences** (Social Sciences) *Director*: César Lorenzano

History: Founded 1995.

Governing Bodies: Rector, Vice-Rector, Superior Council of Representatives

Academic Year: March to December

Admission Requirements: Secondary school certificate and admission course

Fees: (US Dollars): 200-250 per month

Main Language(s) of Instruction: Spanish

International Co-operation: With universities in France; Spain; Chile. Participates in Columbus and Alfa programmes

Accrediting Agencies: CONEAU

Degrees and Diplomas: *Licenciatura*: 4 yrs; *Especialización*; *Maestría*; *Doctorado*

Student Services: Academic counselling, Canteen, Cultural centre, Employment services, Foreign student adviser, Handicapped facilities, Language programs, Social counselling

Special Facilities: Art Gallery

Libraries: c. 11,000 vols.

Publications: Cibertronic, Electronic Magazine
Last Updated: 02/03/09

NATIONAL UNIVERSITY OF TUCUMÁN

Universidad Nacional de Tucumán (UNT)
Ayacucho 491, 4000 San Miguel de Tucumán, Tucumán
Tel: +54(381) 424-7752
Fax: +54(381) 424-8025
EMail: webmaster@unt.edu.ar
Website: http://www.unt.edu.ar

Rector: Juan Alberto Cerisola (2006-)
Tel: +54(381) 424-7762, Fax: +54(381) 424-8654
EMail: rector@unt.edu.ar

Secretaria Académica: Marta Azucena Pesa
EMail: mpesa@rectorado.unt.edu.ar

International Relations: Albarracin Ramiro
Tel: +54(381) 424-7036 EMail: direint@rectorado.unt.edu.ar

Faculties
Agronomy and Animal Husbandry (Agriculture; Agronomy; Animal Husbandry) *Dean*: Alberto Bruno Andrada; **Architecture and Town Planning** (Architecture; Town Planning) *Dean*: Pablo Francisco Holgado; **Arts** (Arts and Humanities) *Dean*: Mirtha Chambeaud; **Biochemistry, Chemistry and Pharmacy** (Biochemistry; Biological and Life Sciences; Chemistry; Pharmacy) *Dean*: Alicia Bardon De Jimenez; **Dentistry** (Dentistry) *Dean*: María Isabel Ferrari De Hernández; **Economics** (Economics) *Dean*: Santiago di Lullo; **Exact Sciences and Technology** (Natural Sciences; Technology) *Dean*: Mario Arnaldo Donzelli; **Law and Social Sciences** (Law; Social Sciences) *Dean*: José Luis Vásquez; **Medicine** (Medicine) *Dean*: Horacio Deza; **Natural Sciences** *(Instituto 'Miguel Lillo')* (Natural Sciences) *Dean*: Ricardo Mon; **Philosophy and Letters** (Arts and Humanities; Philosophy) *Dean*: Elena de Rojas Mayer; **Physical Education** (Physical Education) *Dean*: Mario Alfredo Abaca; **Psychology** (Psychology) *Dean*: Adela Estofán de Terraf

Higher Institutes
Music (Music) *Director*: Josefina Nieva De Bossi

Institutes
Technology (Technology) *Director*: José Ángel Mordini

Schools
Agriculture and Agricultural Technology (Agricultural Engineering; Agricultural Equipment; Agriculture); **Fine Arts, Decorative Arts and Industrial Arts** (Design; Fine Arts; Industrial Arts Education; Industrial Design; Painting and Drawing; Sculpture); **Nursing** *(Agüilares)* (Nursing) *Director*: Norma Yolanda Salto De Dupuy

History: Founded 1912, and inaugurated 1914 as a provincial University. Became a National University 1921.

Governing Bodies: Consejo Superior; Consejos Directivos

Academic Year: February to December

Admission Requirements: Secondary school certificate (bachillerato). Foreign qualifications are recognized if covered by formal international agreements

Main Language(s) of Instruction: Spanish

Degrees and Diplomas: *Licenciatura*: Biology; Chemistry; Economics; Education; English; French; Geography; History; Letters; Mathematics; Music; Nursing; Philosophy; Physics; Plastic Arts; Psychology, 4-6 yrs; *Professional Title*: Accountancy; Architecture; Biochemistry; Chemistry; Dentistry; Engineering; Geology; Law; Nursing; Pharmacy; Surveying, 3-6 yrs; *Professional Title*: Medicine, 7 yrs; *Professional Title*: Teacher Training (secondary level); *Especialización*; *Maestría*; *Doctorado*: by thesis

Student Services: Foreign student adviser, Language programs

Special Facilities: Museum of Archaeology; Museum of Natural Sciences

Libraries: Central Library, 70,935 vols; libraries of faculties, 424,124 vols

Publications: Acta Zoológica Lilloana; Archivos de Bioquímica; Boletín de Jurisprudencia; Eventos del Paleozoico Inferior América Latina; Geología de América del Sur; Humanitas; Lilloa; Química y Farmacia; Revista Agronómica del Nordeste Argentino; Revista de Medicina; Revista Desarollo Rural; Revista Entomológica Argentina; Revista Jurídica; Revista Matemáticas y Física Teórica
Last Updated: 02/03/09

NATIONAL UNIVERSITY OF VILLA MARÍA

Universidad Nacional de Villa María (UNVM)
Lisandro de la Torre 252, 5900 Villa María, Córdoba
Tel: +54(353) 453-9100/5
Fax: +54(353) 453-9117
EMail: rectorado@unvm.edu.ar
Website: http://www.unvm.edu.ar/

Rector: Martín Rodrigo Gill (2007-) Tel: +54(353) 453-9100/55

Secretaria Académica: Rita Margarita Schweitzer
EMail: secacad@rec.unvm.edu.ar

International Relations: Marta Susana Ancarani
Tel: +54(353) 453-9100, Fax: +54(353) 453-9100

Centres
Antonio Sobral *Director*: Silvia Maria Paredes; **Mediterranean Studies** *Director*: José Luis Ferrero

Institutes
Basic and Applied Sciences (Agricultural Engineering; Food Technology; Mathematics and Computer Science; Natural

Sciences; Ophthalmology; Veterinary Science) *Director*: Hugo Emilio Traverso; **Human Sciences** (Arts and Humanities; Computer Graphics; Design; Education; Educational Administration; Educational Psychology; Educational Sciences; English; Mathematics; Mathematics Education; Music; Nursing; Occupational Therapy; Pedagogy; Physical Education; Spanish) *Director*: Carlos Daniel Lasa; **Social Sciences** (Accountancy; Administration; Business Administration; Communication Studies; Development Studies; Economics; Political Sciences; Social Sciences; Social Work; Sociology) *Director*: Aldo Paredes

History: Founded 1995.

Governing Bodies: Asemblea Universitaria; Consejo Superior

Academic Year: March to November (March-June; August-November)

Admission Requirements: Secondary school certificate. Adults over 25 years of age not holding a secondary school certificate may register after complying with specific requirements

Main Language(s) of Instruction: Spanish

Degrees and Diplomas: *Profesorado*: English, Spanish, Mathematics, 4 yrs; *Licenciatura*: Business Administration; Economy; Music; Occupational Therapy, 5 yrs; *Licenciatura*: Communications Studies; Computer Sciences; Educational Management; Educational Psychology; Educational Sciences; Nursing; Ophthalmic Optometry, 2 yrs (after complying with special enrolment requirements); *Licenciatura*: Development Studies; Political Science; Sociology, 4 1/2 yrs; *Licenciatura*: Educational Psychology, 4-5 yrs; *Licenciatura*: Image Production and Design, 5 yrs; *Licenciatura*: Physical Education, 2 yrs (after complying with special enrolment requirements); *Licenciatura*: Protective Services, 2 yrs; *Licenciatura*: Social Work, 1 1/2 yrs (after complying with special enrolment requirements); *Professional Title*: Accountancy, 5 yrs; *Professional Title*: Agricultural Engineering, 2 yrs (after complying with special enrolment requirement); *Professional Title*: Food Technology, 1 1/2 yrs (after complying with special enrolment requirements); *Professional Title*: Veterinary Science, 5 yrs and a semester; *Maestría*: Development Studies; Arts and Humanities, 2 yrs and by thesis. Also Associate Degrees in University Administration and Management (3 yrs)

Student Services: Academic counselling, Canteen, Employment services, Health services, Language programs, Social counselling, Sports facilities

Special Facilities: Film Recording Studio. TV and Audio Studio. Laboratory for Computer Assisted Language Learning. Video room. Theatre.

Libraries: Central Library
Last Updated: 02/03/09

NAVAL UNIVERSITY INSTITUTE
Instituto Universitario Naval (INUN)
Avenida Comodoro Py 2055, Piso 10, 1104 Buenos Aires, Capital Federal
Tel: +54(11) 4317-2000
Fax: +54(11) 4317-2399
EMail: administra@inun.edu.ar
Website: http://www.inun.edu.ar

Rector: César Carlos Moujan EMail: rector@inun.edu.ar

Secretaria Académica: Liliana Laco
EMail: secretacad@inun.edu.ar

Colleges
Naval War

Schools
Marine Sciences; **Military Naval Studies**; **Nautical Science**; **Navy Officers Studies**

Further Information: Academic Units in Río Santiago and Puerto Belgrano

History: Founded 1978 as Instituto Universitario de Estudios Navales y Maritimes, acquired present title 1991. University Institute responsible to the Armada Argentina (Argentine Navy).

Academic Year: March to December

Admission Requirements: High School Certificate

Main Language(s) of Instruction: Spanish

Accrediting Agencies: Comisión Nacional de Evaluación y Acreditación Universitaria

Degrees and Diplomas: *Licenciatura*: Marine Sciences; Naval Techniques; Maritime Transport, 4 yrs; *Maestría*

Student Services: Academic counselling, Canteen, Health services, Language programs, Sports facilities

Student Residential Facilities: None

Libraries: Yes
Last Updated: 05/07/07

UNIVERSITY INSTITUTE OF AERONAUTICS
Instituto Universitario Aeronáutico (IUA)
Avenida Fuerza Aérea 6500, X5010JMX Guarnición Aérea, Córdoba
Tel: +54(351) 568-8800
Fax: +54(351) 568-8800
EMail: informes@iua.edu.ar
Website: http://www.iua.edu.ar

Rector: Alvaro Luis Jesús Pérez (2007-) EMail: rector@iua.edu.ar

Secretario General: Pedro Emilio Murillo
EMail: sgeneral@iua.edu.ar

International Relations: José María Zarate, Head, Institutional Relations Tel: +54(351) 568-8837 EMail: rrii@iua.edu.ar

Centres
Applied Research (Aeronautical and Aerospace Engineering) *Director*: Héctor Eduardo Ré

Faculties
Administration (Accountancy; Administration; Business Administration; Human Resources; Management; Transport Management) *Dean*: Jorge Adolfo Ortiz Valverde; **Engineering** *Dean*: Fernando Aníbal Alvarez

Further Information: Distance Learning Programmes offered.

History: Founded 1947 as School of Aeronautical Engineering (Escuela de Ingeniería Aeronáutica), acquired present status and title 1971.

Academic Year: February to December (February-June; July-December)

Admission Requirements: Certificate of Completion of secondary education. Admission exam required for some study tracks.

Fees: (Pesos): Administration programme, 270 per month; Engineering programme, 380 per month

Main Language(s) of Instruction: Spanish

International Co-operation: With universities in Chile, France and Spain

Accrediting Agencies: Ministerio de Educación, Ciencia y Tecnología; CONEAU

Degrees and Diplomas: *Profesorado*: Accountancy, 4 1/2 yrs; *Licenciatura*: Administration; Human Resources, 5 yrs; *Licenciatura*: Transports Management, 4 1/2 yrs; *Professional Title*: Mechanical and Aeronautical Engineering; Electronic Engineering; Telecommunications Engineering; Software Engineering; Systems Engineering, 5 yrs; *Especialización*: Engineering; *Maestría*: Aeronautic and Spatial Law; Analysis of Strategic Intelligence

Student Services: Academic counselling, Canteen, Cultural centre, Employment services, Foreign student adviser, Handicapped facilities, Health services, Language programs, Nursery care, Sports facilities

Student Residential Facilities: None

Special Facilities: Aerospace Museum

Libraries: c. 6,500 vols

Publications: Noticias de Nuestra Universidad *(monthly)*

Academic Staff *2007-2008*	MEN	WOMEN	TOTAL
PART-TIME	320	348	668
PART-TIME	13	2	15
Student Numbers *2007-2008*			
All (Foreign Included)	3,250	2,517	5,767
FOREIGN ONLY	35	5	40

Part-time students, 756. **Distance students**, 5,011.
Last Updated: 26/02/09

UNIVERSITY INSTITUTE OF POLICE STUDIES

Instituto Universitario de la Policía Federal Argentina (IUPFA)
Rosario 532, 2° Piso, 1424 Buenos Aires, Capital Federal
Tel: +54(11) 4902-4201
Fax: +54(11) 4901-9783
EMail: academica@universidad-policial.edu.ar
Website: http://www.universidad-policial.edu.ar

Rector: Luis María Desimoni
EMail: rectoria@universidad-policial.edu.ar

Secretario Académico: Hugo Alberto Méndez
Tel: +54(11) 4901-0364, Fax: +54(11) 4902-1685

Faculties

Biomedical Sciences; **Criminology** (Criminology; Police Studies); **Law and Social Sciences** (International Relations; Law; Social Sciences; Social Work); **Security Sciences** (Civil Security; Fire Science; Welfare and Protective Services)

History: Founded 1974 as Academia Federal de Estudios Policiales, acquired present status and title 1995.

Governing Bodies: Consejo Académico Superior

Academic Year: March to December (March-July; July-December)

Admission Requirements: Secondary school certificate (bachillerato)

Fees: (US Dollars): Registration, 50; tuition, 20-40

Main Language(s) of Instruction: Spanish

Accrediting Agencies: Ministerio de Educación, Ciencia y Tecnología

Degrees and Diplomas: *Licenciatura*: Criminal and Social Sciences; Criminology; International Relations; Losses Protection System; Telecommunications Security Systems; Welfare and Protective Services, 4 yrs; *Licenciatura*: Nursing, 5 yrs; *Professional Title*: Ballistic Studies; Documentation; Fingerprints Studies, 2 yrs; *Professional Title*: Law, 5 yrs; *Professional Title*: Nursing, 3 yrs; *Maestría*. Also Postgraduate Diplomas, 1-2-3 yrs

Student Services: Canteen, Health services, Language programs, Social counselling

Libraries: Biblioteca de la Policia Federal Argentina, 20,000 vols

Press or Publishing House: Editorial Policial
Last Updated: 26/02/09

UNIVERSITY OF BUENOS AIRES

Universidad de Buenos Aires (UBA)
Calle Viamonte 430/444, C1053ABH Buenos Aires, Capital Federal
Tel: +54(11) 4511-8120
Fax: +54(11) 4511-8155
EMail: academico@rec.uba.ar
Website: http://www.uba.ar

Rector: Rubén E. Hallú (2002-) Tel: +54(11) 4510-1100 Ext: 1,204

Vicerrectora: Beatriz Guglielmotti
Tel: +54(11) 4511-8120 Ext: 1,201, Fax: +54(11) 4511-8139

Faculties

Agronomy (Agricultural Business; Agricultural Economics; Agronomy; Environmental Studies; Floriculture; Food Science; Food Technology; Horticulture; Landscape Architecture) *Dean*: Lorenzo Ricardo Basso; **Architecture, Design and Town Planning** (Architecture; Design; Graphic Design; Industrial Design; Landscape Architecture; Town Planning) *Dean*: Jaime Sorin; **Dentistry** *Dean*: Máximo Giglio; **Economics** (Accountancy; Actuarial Science; Administration; Economics; Information Management) *Dean*: Alberto Edgardo Barbieri; **Engineering** (Agricultural Engineering; Chemical Engineering; Civil Engineering; Computer Engineering; Electrical Engineering; Engineering; Food Technology; Industrial Engineering; Mechanical Engineering; Systems Analysis) *Dean*: Carlos Alberto Rosito; **Exact and Natural Sciences** (Biology; Chemistry; Computer Science; Food Technology; Geology; Marine Science and Oceanography; Mathematics; Meteorology; Natural Sciences; Paleontology; Physics; Science Education) *Dean*: Jorge Aliaga; **Law** (Law; Translation and Interpretation) *Dean*: Atilio Alterini; **Medicine** (Gynaecology and Obstetrics; Medicine; Nursing; Nutrition; Physical Therapy; Radiology; Speech Therapy and

Audiology; Surgery) *Dean*: Alfredo Buzzi; **Pharmacy and Biochemistry** (Biochemistry; Food Science; Food Technology; Pharmacy) *Dean*: Alberto Boveris; **Philosophy and Literature** (Anthropology; Archaeology; Art History; Arts and Humanities; Communication Studies; Economics; Educational Sciences; Fine Arts; History; Information Sciences; Library Science; Linguistics; Literature; Music; Painting and Drawing; Philosophy; Sculpture; Sociology) *Dean*: Héctor Hugo Trinchero; **Psychology** (Occupational Therapy; Psychology; Rehabilitation and Therapy) *Dean*: Sara Slapak; **Social Sciences** (Communication Studies; Labour and Industrial Relations; Political Sciences; Social Sciences; Social Work; Sociology) *Dean*: Federico Schuster; **Veterinary Science** (Veterinary Science) *Dean*: Marcelo Sergio Míguez

Further Information: Also 75 Research institutes, and regional university centres. SISBI, integrating 19 university libraries, 10 museums, 6 university health centres and hospitals

History: Founded 1821. Acquired present status 1881. An autonomous State institution.

Governing Bodies: Asamblea Universitaria; Consejo Superior; Consejos Directivos

Academic Year: March to December (March- July; August-December)

Admission Requirements: Secondary school certificate (bachillerato) and entrance examination

Fees: None

Main Language(s) of Instruction: Spanish

International Co-operation: Participates in European Union Programmes (ALFA and ALBAN); DAAD; UNICAMP (Programa de la Cátedra de Estudiantes Argentinos en la Universidad Estadual de Campinhas, y brasileños en la Universidad de Buenos Aires); PCI (Programa de Cooperación Iberoamericana de la Agencia de Cooperación Española); FOAR (Programa de Asistencia Técnica a Terceros Paises); AUGM (Programa Asociación de Universidades del Grupo Montevideo)

Accrediting Agencies: No accrediting agency for undergraduate programmes; National Commission for University Evaluation and Accreditation (CONEAU) for Graduate programmes

Degrees and Diplomas: *Licenciatura*: 4-6 yrs; *Professional Title*: Accountancy; Actuarial Sciences; Agriculture; Architecture; Atmosphere Sciences; Biochemistry; Biology; Chemical Engineering; Chemistry; Civil Engineering; Computer Engineering; Dentistry; Electrical Engineering; Electronic Engineering; Engineering; Food Science (Ing.); Geology; Industrial Engineering (Ing.); Marine and Mechanical Engineering (Ing); Mathematics (Lic.); Mechanical Engineering (Ing.); Oceanography (Lic); Physical Therapy (Lic); Physics (Lic), 6 yrs; *Professional Title*: Administration; Anthropology; Arts; Business Computing; Communication Studies; Economics; Educational Sciences; Geography; Health Sciences; History; Industrial Design; Labour/Industrial Relations; Landscape Design and Planning; Lawyer Studies; Library Science/Information Sciences; Literature; Nutrition (Lic.); Obstetrics (Lic); Paleontology (Lic); Pharmacy (Farm); Philosophy (Lic); Political Science (Lic); Psychology (Lic); Sociology (Lic), 5 yrs; *Professional Title*: Agronomy Business; Agronomy Engineering; Prosecutor Studies, 4 1/2 yrs; *Professional Title*: Computer Science, 4 1/2 yrs-6 yrs; *Professional Title*: Food Science (Lic.); Food Management; Food Science and Technology (Faculty of Pharmacy and Biochemistry) (Lic.), 2 1/2 yrs; *Professional Title*: Food Engineering, 3 yrs; *Professional Title*: Food Science and Technology (Faculty of Exact and Natural Sciences) (Lic.), 6 1/2 yrs; *Professional Title*: Graphic Design; Image and Sound Design; Law/Information Studies; Midwifery; Occupational Therapy (Lic); Social Work (Lic); Surveying and Mapping (Ing); Textile Design, 4 yrs; *Professional Title*: Medicine (Med.), 6-7 yrs; *Professional Title*: Nursing (Lic), 3-4 yrs; *Professional Title*: Technical Studies, 2 yrs; *Professional Title*: Translation, 2-5 yrs; *Professional Title*: Veterinary Science (Vet), 6-6 1/2 yrs; *Especialización*; *Maestría*; *Doctorado*: by thesis

Student Services: Academic counselling, Canteen, Cultural centre, Employment services, Health services, Language programs, Nursery care, Social counselling, Sports facilities

Student Residential Facilities: none

Special Facilities: 10 Museums. Ricardo Rojas Cultural Centre

Libraries: Central Library, c. 12,400 vols; faculty libraries connected on line through RedUBA

Publications: Cien por Cien, Ciencia y Técnica, Electronic Journal *(monthly)*
Press or Publishing House: Editorial Universitaria De Buenos Aires-EUDEBA
Last Updated: 27/02/09

PRIVATE INSTITUTIONS

ARGENTINE BUSINESS UNIVERSITY
Universidad Argentina de la Empresa (UADE)
Lima 717 Edificio Lima 1, 5° Piso, C1073AAO Buenos Aires, Capital Federal
Tel: +54(11) 4000-7600
Fax: +54(11) 4381-2807
EMail: informe@uade.edu.ar
Website: http://www.uade.edu.ar

Rector: Jorge del Águila Tel: +54(11) 4000-7601
Secretaria Académica: Ana María Mass
Tel: +54(11) 4000-7636 EMail: secretariaacademica@uade.edu.ar
International Relations: Eduardo Andrés Ossoinak
Tel: +54(11) 4000-7317 EMail: relinter@uade.edu.ar

Faculties
Communication and Design (Advertising and Publicity; Communication Arts; Communication Studies; Design; Public Relations; Tourism) *Dean:* Claudia Cortez; **Economics** (Accountancy; Business Administration; Economics; Finance; Human Resources; Labour and Industrial Relations; Marketing) *Dean:* Ricardo Felipe Smurra; **Engineering and Applied Sciences** (Computer Engineering; Food Technology; Industrial Engineering; Information Technology; Mathematics and Computer Science; Production Engineering) *Dean:* Ricardo F. Orosco; **Law and Social Sciences** (English; Government; International Relations; Law; Modern Languages; Psychology; Social Sciences; Translation and Interpretation) *Dean:* Mario Serrafero

Schools
Business (Business Administration) *Director:* Juan Segura
History: Founded 1957 as a private Foundation, and officially recognized by the government 1963 as a private University. Acquired present status 1982.
Governing Bodies: Consejo Académico; Consejo de Administración
Academic Year: March to December (March-July; August-December)
Admission Requirements: Secondary school certificate (bachillerato) or recognized equivalent
Fees: (Pesos): Tuition, 700 per annum
Main Language(s) of Instruction: Spanish
Degrees and Diplomas: *Licenciatura:* Agricultural Management; Biotechnology; Business Administration; Business and Commerce; Communication Studies; Communication Technology; Computer Science; Economics; Electronic and Mechanical Engineering; English; Finance; Food Technology; Hotel and Restaurant; Government and International Relations; Graphic Design; Textile Design; Human Resources; International Commerce; Marketing; Organization of Production; Psychology; Public and Institutional Relations; Publicity; Tourism and Hotel Management; *Professional Title:* Accountancy; Computer Engineering; Electronic and Mechanical Engineering; Food Engineering; Industrial Engineering; Law; Translation; *Maestría:* Business Administration; Business and Commerce; Communication Studies; Information Science; Finance; Human Resource
Student Services: Academic counselling, Canteen, Cultural centre, Employment services, Health services, Sports facilities
Student Residential Facilities: Yes
Libraries: Central Library, 47,342 vols
Publications: Base de datos del Sector Construcción; Construcción y Mercado Inmobiliario; Indice de Producción Industrial; Información de AFJP; Panorama Industrial; Principales Indicadores de la Economía Argentina
Last Updated: 20/03/08

ARGENTINE UNIVERSITY JOHN F. KENNEDY
Universidad Argentina John F. Kennedy (UK)
Calle Bartolomé Mitre 1411, 1° Piso, 1037 Buenos Aires, Capital Federal
Tel: +54(11) 4116-1000
Fax: +54(11) 4116-1000
EMail: info@kennedy.edu.ar
Website: http://www.kennedy.edu.ar

Rectora: María Elisa Herren de David
Tel: +54(11) 4116-1151 EMail: rectorado@kennedy.edu.ar
Secretario del Consejo Académico: Mario Alberto Coscio

Departments
Anthropology (Anthropology) *Dean:* Pedro Neiff; **Architecture** *Dean:* Enrique Lombardi; **Art** (Fine Arts) *Dean:* María del Valle Romanelli; **Biology** (Biology) *Dean:* Marta Carballo; **Biopsychology** (Psychology) *Dean:* Eduardo Mascolombo; **Business** (Business and Commerce) *Dean:* Claudio Sapetnitzky; **Chemistry** (Chemistry; Inorganic Chemistry; Organic Chemistry) *Dean:* Irenej Lypynskyj; **Clinical Psychology** (Clinical Psychology) *Dean:* Héctor Fischer; **Communications** (Communication Studies; Journalism) *Dean:* Damián Sánchez Rival; **Computer Science** *Dean:* Rodolfo Naveiro; **Computer Technologies** (Computer Engineering) *Dean (Acting):* Alberto Foti; **Construction and Structural Architecture** (Construction Engineering; Structural Architecture) *Dean:* Carmen Montes de Barani; **Criminal Law** *Dean:* Carlos Mahiqués; **Demography and Tourism** (Demography and Population; Tourism) *Dean:* Maria Prina de Vandam; **Design** *Dean:* Mercedes Filpe; **Economics** (Economics) *Dean:* Olver Benvenuto; **History** (History) *Dean:* César García Belsunce; **Human Resources** (Human Resources) *Dean:* Emilio Petrarca; **Law** (Law; Private Law; Public Law) *Dean:* Rodolfo Capón Filas; **Literature** (Literature) *Dean:* Alicia Genovese; **Marketing** (Marketing) *Dean:* Aldo Gelso; **Mathematics and Physics** (Mathematics; Physics) *Dean:* Elisabet Borrino; **Modern Languages** *Dean:* Marta Jeannot; **Odontology** *(Clinic)* (Dentistry) *Dean:* Carlos Peña; **Pedagogy** (Education) *Dean:* Mario Coscio; **Philosophy** (Philosophy) *Dean:* Francisco García Bazán; **Planning and Development** (Architecture and Planning; Development Studies) *Dean:* Aldo Gelso; **Political Science** (Political Sciences) *Dean:* Alberto Castells; **Psychoanalysis** (Psychoanalysis) *Dean:* Amelia Imbriano; **Psychology** (Psychology) *Dean:* Eleonora Zenequelli; **Public Relations** (Public Relations) *Dean:* Graciela Ferreira; **Social Services** (Social and Community Services; Social Work) *Dean:* Ingrid de Rivera; **Sociology** (Sociology) *Dean:* Estela Tófalo de Vivern; **Stomatology** (Dentistry) *Dean:* Mabel Raguso; **Systems Design** (Computer Engineering; Systems Analysis) *Dean:* Rosa Rojas

Schools
Accountancy *Dean:* Roberto Vázquez; **Administration** *Dean:* Juan Carlos Alonso; **Architecture** *Dean:* Roberto Capelli; **Biochemistry** (Biochemistry) *Dean:* Emilio Labal; **Chemistry** *Dean:* Liliana Valiente; **Computer Education** *Dean:* Rosa Rojas; **Demography and Tourism** (Demography and Population; Tourism) *Dean:* Olga Villalba; **Educational Sciences** *Dean:* Raquel Burman; **Graphic Design** *Dean:* Mercedes Filpe; **Hotel Management** *Dean:* María P. de Vandam; **International Business** (International Business) *Dean:* Aldo Pera; **International Relations** *Dean:* Raúl Romero; **Journalism and Communication** *Dean:* Edgar Zavala; **Labour Relations** (Labour and Industrial Relations) *Dean:* Pedro Núñez; **Law** (Law) *Dean:* Felipe Ferrer Lavalle; **Marketing** *Dean:* Walter Coscio; **Odontology** *Dean:* Carlos Peña; **Pharmacy** (Pharmacy) *Dean:* María del C. Magariños; **Political Science** (Political Sciences) *Dean:* Ramiro Caro Figueroa; **Psychology** (Psychology) *Dean:* Mario Coscio; **Psychopedagogy** (Educational Psychology) *Dean:* María T. Fernández Lagos; **Public Relations** *Dean:* Carlos Méndez; **Publicity** *Dean:* Ada Forni; **Social Services** (Social and Community Services) *Dean:* Ingrid de Rivera; **Sociology** (Sociology) *Dean:* Roberto Pérez; **Systems Analysis** *Dean:* Alberto Foti; **Theatre** (Theatre) *Dean:* Mónica D'Amato

History: Founded 1964 as college, became University 1981. A private institution authorized by governmental decree and responsible to the Ministry of Education and Justice.
Governing Bodies: Consejo Asesor; Consejo Consultivo; Consejo Honorario
Academic Year: March to November; December to March

Admission Requirements: Secondary school certificate (bachillerato)

Main Language(s) of Instruction: Spanish

Degrees and Diplomas: *Licenciatura*: 4-5 yrs; *Professional Title*: 4-5 yrs; *Especialización*: 2-3 yrs; *Maestría*: 2 yrs; *Doctorado*: 2 yrs, by thesis. Also Profesorado Universitario, 2 yrs

Libraries: c. 40,000 vols
Last Updated: 26/02/09

ATLÁNTIDA ARGENTINA UNIVERSITY
Universidad Atlántida Argentina
Diagonal Rivadavia 515, 7109 Mar de Ajó, Buenos Aires
Tel: +54(2257) 42-0388
EMail: atlantida@atlantida.edu.ar
Website: http://www.atlantida.edu.ar

Rector: Osvaldo Juan De Carli
Tel: +54(2257) 42-9300 EMail: uaarector@atlantida.edu.ar

Secretaria Académica: Alicia Gil

Faculties
Economics (Accountancy; Administration; Economics); **Engineering** (Engineering; Systems Analysis); **Humanities** (Arts and Humanities; Tourism); **Law and Social Sciences** (Law; Social Sciences); **Psychology** (Psychology)

Further Information: Also Branch in Mar del Plata and Dolores

History: Founded 1994.

Main Language(s) of Instruction: Spanish

Degrees and Diplomas: *Licenciatura*; *Professional Title*
Last Updated: 26/02/09

BLAS PASCAL UNIVERSITY
Universidad Blas Pascal (UBP)
Avenida Donato Álvarez 380, 5147 Córdoba, Córdoba
Tel: +54(3543) 414-4444
Fax: +54(3543) 414-4400
EMail: secrectorado@ubp.edu.ar
Website: http://www.ubp.edu.ar

Rector: Eduardo Sánchez Martínez
EMail: esanchezmartinez@ubp.edu.ar

Secretario General: Rafael Cecconello
EMail: rcecconello@ubp.edu.ar

International Relations: Alberto Ferral, Secretario de Extensión y Relaciones Institucionales EMail: aferral@ubp.edu.ar

Departments
Administration (Accountancy; Business Administration; Environmental Management) *Head*: Alejandra Garbino; **Architecture** (Architecture) *Head*: Diego Schmukler; **Communication Sciences** (Communication Studies) *Head*: Mercedes Outumuro; **Computer Science** (Computer Science) *Head*: Waldo Geremía; **Graphic Design** (Graphic Design) *Head*: Victoria Solis; **Information Technologies and Telecommunications** (Information Technology; Telecommunications Engineering) *Head*: Raúl Echegaray; **Law** (Law) *Head*: Guillermo Ford; **Physical Education** (Education; Physical Education) *Head*: Silvia Berdakin; **Psychopedagogy** *Head*: Maria Teresa Aglietto; **Research and Development** *Head*: Néstor Pisciotta; **Tourism** (Social Sciences) *Head*: Marta Botti

Institutes
Environmental Studies *Dean*: Alberto Ferral

History: Founded 1990.

Governing Bodies: Consejo Superior

Academic Year: March to December (March-July; August-December)

Admission Requirements: Secondary school certificate (bachillerato) and entrance examination

Fees: (Pesos): c. 2,090 per semester

Main Language(s) of Instruction: Spanish, English

Degrees and Diplomas: *Título Menor*: Technology, 2 yrs; *Licenciatura*: 4-5 yrs; *Maestría*: a further 1-2 yrs

Student Services: Canteen, Employment services, Foreign student adviser, Foreign Studies Centre, Language programs, Sports facilities

Student Residential Facilities: Yes

Special Facilities: Exhibition room; Internet

Libraries: Biblioteca Universidad Blas Pascal; Biblioteca Argentum

Publications: Revista Tendencia, Scientific Divulgation *(biennially)*
Last Updated: 26/02/09

BUENOS AIRES TECHNOLOGY INSTITUTE
Instituto Tecnológico de Buenos Aires (ITBA)
Avenida Eduardo Madero 399, C1106ACD Buenos Aires, Capital Federal
Tel: +54(11) 4314-7778
Fax: +54(11) 4314-3433
EMail: informes@itba.edu.ar
Website: http://www.itba.edu.ar

Rector: Enrique Molina Pico
Tel: +54(11) 4314-0270 EMail: rector@itba.edu.ar

Secretario Académico: Benito Alvarez Ovide
EMail: aoviede@itba.edu.ar

Departments
Mathematics, Physics and Chemistry (Chemistry; Mathematics; Physics); **Professional Development**

Schools
Administration and Technology (Marine Science and Oceanography); **Engineering**

History: Founded 1960 as a private institution, recognized by the federal government and operating under its supervision. Financed from private sources.

Governing Bodies: Consejo de Regencia; Consejo Académico

Academic Year: March to November (March-July; August-November)

Admission Requirements: Secondary school certificate and entrance examination

Main Language(s) of Instruction: Spanish

Degrees and Diplomas: *Licenciatura*: Computer Science; Oceanography, 5 yrs; *Professional Title*: Engineering, 6 yrs; *Especialización*: Environmental Management; Telecommunications; Gas and Petrol Engineering; Data Network; *Maestría*: 2 yrs; *Doctorado*: Engineering; Geophysics, 3 yrs

Libraries: c. 1,320 vols

Publications: Revista *(quarterly)*
Last Updated: 26/02/09

BUSINESS UNIVERSITY OF THE TWENTY-FIRST CENTURY
Universidad Empresarial Siglo 21 (UE21)
Ituzaingó 484, 5000 Nueva Córdoba, Córdoba
Tel: +54(351) 420-4003
EMail: informes@uesiglo21.edu.ar
Website: http://www.uesiglo21.edu.ar

Rector: Juan Carlos Rabbat
Tel: +54(351) 475-7572, Fax: +54(351) 475-7522
EMail: jcrabbat@uesiglo21.edu.ar

Secretaria de Organización Académica: Isabel Carrizo
Tel: +54(351) 414-0350 EMail: icarrizo@uesiglo21.edu.ar

Departments
Communication Studies (Communication Studies); **Economics** (Administration; Business Administration; Business and Commerce); **Exact Sciences** (Chemistry; Mathematics; Natural Sciences; Physics); **Languages** (Modern Languages); **Law** (Law); **Physics and Natural Sciences** (Natural Sciences; Physics); **Professional Practice**; **Psychology** (Psychology); **Social Sciences** (Social Sciences); **Systems**

History: Founded 1995.

Governing Bodies: Consejo de Administración

Academic Year: March to November (March-July; August-November)

Admission Requirements: Secondary school certificate (bachillerato)

Main Language(s) of Instruction: Spanish, English, Portuguese

Degrees and Diplomas: *Título Menor*: Agricultural Administration; Graphic Design; Human Resources; International Trade; Technology, 3 yrs; *Licenciatura*: Advertising; Agricultural Administration; Business Administration; Clinical Psychology; Computer Science; Graphic Design; Human Resources; International Trade; Marketing; Organizational Psychology; Organizational Sociology; Public and Institutional Relations, 4 1/2 yrs; *Maestría*. Also Diplomaturas

Student Services: Academic counselling, Canteen, Cultural centre, Employment services, Foreign student adviser, Handicapped facilities, Health services, Social counselling, Sports facilities

Libraries: c. 1,200 vols

Last Updated: 27/02/09

CAECE UNIVERSITY
Universidad CAECE (CAECE)
Tte. Gral. J.D.Perón 2933, 1198 Buenos Aires, Capital Federal
Tel: +54(11) 5217-7888
Fax: +54(11) 4878-7898
EMail: info@caece.edu.ar
Website: http://www.caece.edu.ar

Rector: Jorge Eduardo Bosch EMail: rectorado@caece.edu.ar

Vicerrector Académico: Carlos Lac Prugent

Centres
Biomedical Sciences

Departments
Administration (Accountancy; Administration; Business Administration; Human Resources; Marketing) *Director*: Claudia Aguilar; **Biological Sciences** (Biological and Life Sciences; Environmental Management) *Director*: Silvia Copelli; **Humanities** (Arts and Humanities; Biology; Chemistry; Communication Studies; Computer Science; English; Geography; History; Hotel Management; Journalism; Music Education; Philosophy; Physical Education; Physics; Tourism) *Director*: Henri Bosch; **Mathematics** (Mathematics; Mathematics and Computer Science) *Director*: Daniel Prelat; **Philosophy** *Director*: Nilda Robles; **Psychology and Pedagogical Sciences** (Pedagogy; Psychology) *Director*: Gerardo N. Bettinotti; **Systems** (Computer Networks; Systems Analysis) *Director*: Fernando López Gil

History: Founded 1967.

Academic Year: April to November (April-June; August-November)

Admission Requirements: Secondary school certificate (bachillerato)

Degrees and Diplomas: *Licenciatura*: Biological Sciences; Mathematics Education; Psychopedagogy; Systems, 5 yrs; *Licenciatura*: Marketing; Social Communications, 4 yrs; *Professional Title*: 3-5 yrs; *Especialización*; *Maestría*

Special Facilities: Visual Aids Centre

Libraries: Central Library 'Marisel Montoto Rodríguez', c. 10,000 vols. Specialized libraries

Publications: Mathematical Elements (Scientific publication) *(quarterly)*

Press or Publishing House: Editorial CAECE

Last Updated: 26/02/09

CATHOLIC UNIVERSITY OF ARGENTINA
Pontificia Universidad Católica Argentina Santa María de los Buenos Aires (UCA)
Edificio Santa María de los Buenos Aires, Avenida Alicia Moreau de Justo 1300 2° Piso, C1107AAZ Buenos Aires, Capital Federal
Tel: +54(11) 4349-0200
Fax: +54(11) 4349-0273
EMail: info@uca.edu.ar
Website: http://www.uca.edu.ar

Rector: Víctor Manuel Fernández
Tel: +54(11) 4349-0251, Fax: +54(11) 4349-0273
EMail: rector@uca.edu.ar

Secretario Académico: Santiago Bellomo
Tel: +54(11) 4349-0200, Fax: +54(11) 4349-0230
EMail: secacad@uca.edu.ar

International Relations: Soledad Zapiola, Coordinator, International Relations
Tel: +54(11) 4338-0606, Fax: +54(11) 4338-0862
EMail: uca_internacional@uca.edu.ar

Faculties
Agriculture *(Buenos Aires Campus)* (Agriculture; Animal Husbandry; Food Technology); **Arts and Music** *(Buenos Aires Campus)* (Conducting; Music; Music Theory and Composition; Musicology); **Canon Law** *(Graduate School; Buenos Aires Campus)* (Canon Law); **Chemistry and Engineering** *(Fray R. Bacon, Rosario Campus)*; **Economics** *(Rosario Campus)* (Accountancy; Business Administration; Economics); **Economics** *(Mendoza Campus)* (Accountancy; Business Administration; Safety Engineering; Systems Analysis); **Humanities** *(Teresa de Ávila, Paraná Campus)* (Arts and Humanities; History; Library Science; Philosophy; Psychology) *Dean*: Miguel Angel Nesa; **Humanities and Education** *(Mendoza Campus)* (Arts and Humanities; Education); **Law** *(Buenos Aires and Paraná Campus)* (Law); **Law and Social Sciences** *(Rosario Campus)* (Arts and Humanities; Education; History; Law; Social Sciences); **Medical Sciences** *(Buenos Aires Campus)* (Health Sciences; Medicine); **Philosophy and Letters** (English; History; Literature; Philosophy; Translation and Interpretation); **Physics, Mathematical Sciences and Engineering** *(Buenos Aires Campus)* (Civil Engineering; Computer Engineering; Electronic Engineering; Engineering; Environmental Engineering; Environmental Studies; Industrial Engineering); **Psychology and Educational Sciences** (Education; Educational Psychology; Psychology); **Social Sciences and Economics** *(Buenos Aires Campus)* (Accountancy; Business Administration; Economics; Social Sciences; Sociology); **Theology** *(Buenos Aires Campus)* (Theology)

Institutes
Bioethics *(Graduate; Buenos Aires Campus) Director*: Alberto Bochatey; **Marriage and Family Studies** (Family Studies); **Political Science and International Relations** *(Buenos Aires and Paraná Campus)* (International Relations; Political Sciences) *Director*: Enrique Aguilar; **Social Communication, Journalism and Advertising; Social Communication, Journalism and Publicity** *(Buenos Aires Campus)* (Advertising and Publicity; Communication Studies; Journalism) *Director*: Alicia Casermeiro de Pereson; **Spirituality and Pastoral Activities** (Pastoral Studies)

Further Information: Also regional centre in Pergamino

History: Founded 1958 as a private University based on former Institute of Catholic Culture created in 1922. Accorded status of Pontifical University by the Holy See 1960. The University and the degrees it awards are formally recognized by the National Government. Financed by student fees and gifts. The Archbishop of Buenos Aires is Grand Chancellor.

Governing Bodies: Consejo Superior; Consejo de Administración

Academic Year: March to December

Admission Requirements: Secondary school certificate (bachillerato) or equivalent and competitive entrance examination

Main Language(s) of Instruction: Spanish

International Co-operation: With universities in South America; USA; Europe; Oceania, Canada and Asia

Accrediting Agencies: CONEAU, AMBA

Degrees and Diplomas: *Bachiller Universitario*: Theology, 6 yrs; *Licenciatura*: Agriculture (Animal Husbandry); Canon Law; Choral Direction; Composition; Industrial Chemistry; Music and Musicology; Orchestral Direction; Philosophy; Psychology; Public Administration, 5 yrs; *Licenciatura*: Business Administration; Economics; Education; English; Environmental Sciences; History; International Relations; Journalism; Letters; Political Science; Psychopedagogy; Publicity and Institutional Communication; Security and Laboral Hygiene; Systems and Computing, 4 yrs; *Licenciatura*: Educational Direction and Supervision, 2 yrs; *Professional Title*: Accountancy; English Translation; Food Technology, 4 yrs; *Professional Title*: Attorney-at-Law; Civil Engineering; Industrial Engineering; Environmental Engineering; Computer Science; Food Engineering; Agricultural Production; Electronic Engineering, 5 yrs; *Professional Title*: English Teaching; Literature Teacher; Philosophy Teaching; *Professional Title*: Higher Education, 2 yrs; *Especialización*: Clinical Microbiology; Nutrition; Maxilar Orthodontics; Otorhinolaringology; Phlebology; Gastroenterology; Plastic and Restorative Surgery; Paediatric Ophtalmology; Endodoncy; Bucomaxilofacial Surgery and Traumatology; Criminal Law; Business Economic Law; Environmental Law; High Technology Law; Labour Law; Legal Information and Legislative Techniques; Constitutional Law; Security, Hygiene and Environmental Protection; Software Engineering; Logistics; Restoration of Historic Buildings; Transport Engineering; Alternative Energy; Cardiology; Critical Care Medicine; Oncology; Infectious Deseases; Psychiatry; Legal Medicine; Geriatrics; Nephrology; Paediatric Care; Oral Implantology; Cardiorespiratory Kinesiology; Paediatric Plastic Surgery; Stomatology; Neurosurgery; Periodontics; Agrofood Industry Management; Social Doctrine of the Church; Tax Law; Damages Law; Judiciary law; Security and Labour Hygiene; *Maestría*: Environmental Engineering and Sustainable Development; Food Technology; Tax Law; Business Economic Law; Business Administration; Applied Economics; Sociology; Biomedical Ethics; Agrofood Industry Management; Audiovisual Communication; *Doctorado*: Business Administration; Economics; Philosophy; Political Science; Sociology, a further 2 yrs, by thesis; *Doctorado*: Legal and Social Sciences; Canon Law; Education; Theology; Psychology; Psychopedagogy; History; Literature; Medicine; Legal Sciences

Student Services: Academic counselling, Canteen, Cultural centre, Employment services, Sports facilities

Student Residential Facilities: Casa Universitaria Santísima Trinidad (for teachers only)

Special Facilities: Radio and TV studio

Libraries: Central Library, c. 150,000 vols and multimedia material; faculty libraries

Publications: Antiguo Oriente; Anuario Argentino de Derecho Canónico; Colección; Consonancias; Creciendo en Familia; Cultura Económica; El Derecho; Estudios de Historia de Espana; Lecturas Sociales y Económicas; Prudentia Juris; Res Gesta; Revista de Psicologia; Revista Teología; Sapientia; Stylos; Temas de Historia Argentina y Americana; Universitas; Vida e Ética

Press or Publishing House: EDUCA - Editorial de la Universidad Católica Argentina
Last Updated: 30/03/11

CATHOLIC UNIVERSITY OF CÓRDOBA

Universidad Católica de Córdoba (UCC)
Obispo Trejo 323, X5000IG Córdoba, Córdoba
Tel: +54(351) 493-8000
Fax: +54(351) 493-8002
EMail: secrec@uccor.edu.ar
Website: http://www.ucc.edu.ar

Rector: Luis Rafaél Velasco (2006-)
Tel: +54(351) 493-8001, Fax: +54(351) 493-8002
EMail: rector@uccor.edu.ar

Secretario Académico: Juan Carlos Boggio
EMail: sac@uccor.edu.ar

International Relations: Nelso-Gustavo Specchia, Secretario de Desarrollo y Asuntos Internacionales
Tel: +54(351) 493-8003, Fax: +54(351) 493-8002
EMail: sedeai@uccor.edu.ar

Faculties
Agriculture (Agriculture; Animal Husbandry; Food Technology; Vegetable Production; Veterinary Science) *Dean*: Marcelo Raul Rosmini; **Architecture** (Architecture; Landscape Architecture; Structural Architecture) *Dean*: Esteban Tristán Bonodone; **Chemistry** (Biochemistry; Food Technology; Pharmacy) *Dean*: Paula María Cooke; **Economics and Administration** (Accountancy; Administration) *Dean*: María Teresa Galfione; **Education** (Educational Psychology; Educational Sciences; Higher Education Teacher Training; Special Education) *Dean*: Aída Manitta; **Engineering** (Civil Engineering; Computer Engineering; Electrical and Electronic Engineering; Electronic Engineering; Engineering; Industrial Engineering; Mechanical Engineering; Systems Analysis) *Dean*: Raúl Juan Vaca Narvaja; **Law and Social Sciences** (Law; Notary Studies) *Dean*: Luis Maximiliano Zarazaga; **Medicine** (Dentistry; Medicine; Nursing; Nutrition; Occupational Therapy) *Dean*: Rubén Horacio Sambuelli; **Philosophy and Humanities** (Arts and Humanities; History; Philosophy; Psychology; Religious Studies) *Dean*: Miguel Koleff; **Political Science and International Relations** (Government; International Relations; Political Sciences; Public Administration) *Dean*: Mario Germán Riorda

Institutes
Administration (Administration; Management; Public Administration) *Director*: Guillermo Martínez Ferrer

History: Founded 1956 as Institute, became University and received government recognition 1959, authorized to award degrees and professional qualifications. A private institution under the direction of the Society of Jesus within the Archbishopric of Córdoba.

Governing Bodies: Consejo Directivo; Consejo Académico

Academic Year: February to December (February-July; July-December)

Admission Requirements: High school Diploma (bachillerato) or recognized equivalent and entrance examination

Fees: (Pesos): Registration, 425; tuition, 420,535 or 585 per month depending on the faculty

Main Language(s) of Instruction: Spanish

International Co-operation: Exchange programmes with c. 100 universities in USA through the International Students Exchange Programme

Degrees and Diplomas: *Título Menor*: Management; Social Sciences, 2 yrs; *Licenciatura*: Business Administration; Educational Sciences, 5 yrs; *Licenciatura*: Food Technology; International Relations; Political Science, 4 yrs; *Licenciatura*: History; Literature; Philosophy; Religious Studies, 2 yrs; *Professional Title*: Accountancy; Agriculture; Architecture; Biochemistry; Engineering; Law; Notarial Studies; Veterinary Medicine, 5 yrs; *Professional Title*: Medicine, 6 yrs; *Professional Title*: Pharmacy, 4 yrs; *Especialización*: Management; Stockraising, 2 yrs; *Maestría*: Architectural and Environmental Design; Business Administration; Food Technology; Health Services; Political Management, a further 2 yrs; *Doctorado*: Medicine; Political Science and Government; Government and Public Administration

Student Services: Canteen, Foreign student adviser, Foreign Studies Centre, Handicapped facilities, Health services, Language programs, Sports facilities

Libraries: c. 60,000 vols

Publications: Dialogos Pedagógicos; Noticias UGC; Studia Politicae
Last Updated: 20/03/08

CATHOLIC UNIVERSITY OF CUYO

Universidad Católica de Cuyo (UCCUYO)
Avenida Jose Ignacio la Roza 1516, 5400 Rivadavia, San Juan
Tel: +54(264) 429-2300
Fax: +54(264) 429-2310
EMail: rectorado@uccuyo.edu.ar
Website: http://www.uccuyo.edu.ar

Rectora: María Isabel Larrauri Tel: +54(264) 429-2317

Secretario Académico: Cecilia Trincado de Murúa
Tel: +54(264) 429-2313 EMail: s.academica@uccuyo.edu.ar

International Relations: Susana Lahoz de Astorga, Secretaria de Extensión y Relaciones Institucionales
Tel: +54(264) 429-2314 EMail: extension@uccuyo.edu.ar

Faculties
Economics and Business Science *(San Luis)* (Accountancy; Business Administration; Economics; Hotel Management; International Business; Marketing; Tourism) *Dean*: Alejandro Largacha; **Education** *Dean*: Lucía Ghilardi; **Food Science, Biochemistry and Pharmacy** (Biochemistry; Food Science; Food Technology; Oenology; Pharmacy) *Dean*: Claudio Larrea; **Law and Social Sciences** *(Cervantes Institute-Rio Cuarto Córdoba)* (Law; Social Sciences) *Dean*: Miryam Andújar; **Medicine** *(Immaculate Conception Institute- Mendoza- Cervantes Institute- Río Cuarto- Córdoba)* (Medicine; Nursing; Nutrition; Physical Therapy) *Dean*: Mercedes Gómez de Herrera; **Philosophy and Humanities** *(Immaculate Conception Institute- Mendoza- Cervantes Institute- Río Cuarto-Córdoba)* (Arts and Humanities; Philosophy) *Dean*: Lucía Ghilardi

History: Founded 1959.

Governing Bodies: Consejo Superior

Academic Year: March to November

Admission Requirements: Secondary school certificate (bachillerato); Egresado del Nivel Polimodal

Fees: (US Dollars): c. 600 per trimester

Main Language(s) of Instruction: Spanish

International Co-operation: International cooperation programme with Spain

Accrediting Agencies: CONEAU; DGU; Ministry of Education, Science and Technology

Degrees and Diplomas: *Licenciatura*: Economics; Education; Food Technology, 4 yrs; *Licenciatura*: Law; Medicine; Nursing; Psychology: Humanities, 5 yrs; *Especialización*; *Maestría*

Student Services: Academic counselling, Canteen, Cultural centre, Language programs, Nursery care, Sports facilities

Special Facilities: Museum

Libraries: Yes

Last Updated: 26/02/09

CATHOLIC UNIVERSITY OF LA PLATA
Universidad Católica de La Plata (UCALP)
Calle 13 N° 1227, 1900 La Plata, Buenos Aires
Tel: +54(221) 422-2886
Fax: +54(221) 422-2886
EMail: rectorado@ucalp.edu.ar
Website: http://www.ucalp.edu.ar

Rector: Rafael Breide Obeid

Secretario General Académico: Miguel Ángel Sarni

Faculties
Architecture and Design (Architecture; Graphic Design; Interior Design) *Dean*: Raúl Horacio Meda; **Dentistry** (Dentistry) *Dean*: Carlos Conesa Alegre; **Economics** (Accountancy; Business Administration; Economics) *Dean*: Carlos A. Iglesias Monica; **Exact Sciences and Technology** (Hygiene; Information Sciences; Technology) *Dean*: Luis Padín; **Health Sciences** *Dean*: Leopoldo Enrique Acuña; **Humanities** *Dean*: Alfredo Raúl Oller; **Law** (Law) *Dean*: Hernán Mathieu; **Political and Social Sciences** (International Relations; Political Sciences; Social Sciences; Sociology) *Dean*: Miguel A. Iribarne

Institutes
Bioethics (Ethics; Family Studies) *Director*: Juan Carlos Caprile

Further Information: Also Branch in Bernal

History: Founded 1964 as a private institution. Recognized by the government and authorized to award degrees.

Governing Bodies: Consejo Superior

Academic Year: March to November

Main Language(s) of Instruction: Spanish

Degrees and Diplomas: *Licenciatura*: Administration; Economics; Sociology, 5 yrs; *Licenciatura*: Applied Mathematics; Statistics; Systems Analysis, 4 yrs; *Licenciatura*: Education, 2 yrs; *Professional Title*: Accountancy; Law, 5 yrs; *Professional Title*: Architecture, 6 yrs; *Professional Title*: Teacher Training (secondary level), 4 yrs; *Especialización*: 2 yrs; *Maestría*

Publications: Revista
Last Updated: 26/02/09

CATHOLIC UNIVERSITY OF SALTA
Universidad Católica de Salta (UCS)
Casilla 18, Ciudad Universitaria, 4400 Campo Castañares, Salta
Tel: +54(387) 426-8924
EMail: informes@ucasal.net
Website: http://www.ucasal.net/

Rector: Gustavo Alfredo Puig **EMail:** rectorado@ucasal.net

Secretaria General: Lilian Constanza Diedrich de Duba
EMail: secretariageneral@ucasal.net

Faculties
Agriculture and Veterinary Science *Dean*: Carlos Tabeada Candiotti; **Architecture and Town Planning** (Architecture; Interior Design; Town Planning) *Dean*: Pedro Colombo Speroni; **Arts and Science** (Arts and Humanities; Communication Studies; English; History; Natural Sciences; Philosophy; Psychology; Radio and Television Broadcasting; Translation and Interpretation) *Dean*: Gustavo Iovino, **Economics and Administration** (Accountancy; Administration; Agricultural Management; Business Administration; Eco-

nomics; Human Resources; Public Relations; Secretarial Studies) *Dean*: Roberto Cadar; **Engineering and Computer Science** (Building Technologies; Business and Commerce; Civil Engineering; Computer Science; Engineering) *Dean*: Claudio Mondada; **Law** (Criminal Law; International Relations; Law) *Dean*: Victor René Martínez

Programmes
Distance Education (Accountancy; Business Administration; International Relations; Law) *Head*: Omar Carranza

Schools
Commerce *Director*: Nora Nieva; **Music** *Director*: Jorge Lhez; **Physical Education** *Director*: Carlos Zuccotti; **Social Work** (Social Welfare; Social Work) *Director*: Sonia Zamora; **Tourism** *Director*: Carlos Francisco Sánchez

Further Information: Also Academic Centres in Metan and Buenos Aires

History: Founded 1963 and began regular courses 1967. Recognized by the government 1968 and authorized to award degrees and professional qualifications. A private institution operated with the co-operation of the Society of Jesus.

Governing Bodies: Directorio; Consejo Académico; Consejo Administrativo; Consejo Estudiantil

Academic Year: March to December (March-July; August-December)

Admission Requirements: Secondary school certificate (bachillerato) and entrance examination

Main Language(s) of Instruction: Spanish

Degrees and Diplomas: *Licenciatura*: Business Administration; Economics; International Relations; Criminal Law; Public Relations; Human Resources; Agricultural Business; Tourism; Business; Safety Engineering, 4 yrs; *Licenciatura*: History; Literature; Modern Languages; Philosophy; Psychology; Social Work; Social Communications; Physical Education; Music, 5 yrs; *Professional Title*; *Especialización*; *Maestría*

Libraries: 30,000 vols
Last Updated: 26/02/09

CATHOLIC UNIVERSITY OF SANTA FÉ
Universidad Católica de Santa Fé (UCSF)
Echagüe 7151, 3000 Santa Fé, Santa Fé
Tel: +54(342) 460-3030
Fax: +54(342) 460-3030
EMail: rector@ucsf.edu.ar
Website: http://www.ucsf.edu.ar

Rector: Gerardo Nélson Galetto (2007-)
Tel: +54(342) 460-3030, Ext. 116 EMail: ggaletto@ucsf.edu.ar

Secretario General: Eduardo Nicolás Kinen
EMail: sgeneral@ucsf.edu.ar; ekinen@ucsf.edu.ar

Departments
Pastoral *Director*: Carlos Hugo Scatizza; **Philosophy and Theology** (Philosophy; Theology) *Director*: Fabián Antonio Jerkovich; **Postgraduate Studies** *Director*: Juan Carlos Ballesteros

Faculties
Architecture (Architecture) *Dean*: Ricardo Mario Rocchetti; **Communication Studies** *Dean*: Rodolfo Julio Acebal; **Economics** (Accountancy; Administration; Economics) *Dean*: Néstor Héctor Dona; **Engineering, Geo-ecology and Environmental Studies** (Engineering; Environmental Engineering; Environmental Studies; Geology) *Dean*: Susana Alicia Tardivo; **Humanities** (Arts and Humanities; Education; Gerontology) *Dean*: María Luisa Russo; **Law** (Law; Political Sciences) *Dean*: Zully María Degano; **Philosophy** (Philosophy; Theology) *Secretaria Academica*: Carmen Gnozáles; **Psychology** *Dean*: Silvia Tornimbeni

Further Information: Also Branch in Posadas

History: Founded 1957, became University 1960.

Governing Bodies: Administrative Council; Academic Council

Academic Year: March to December

Admission Requirements: Secondary school certificate (bachillerato) or equivalent

Main Language(s) of Instruction: Spanish

Degrees and Diplomas: *Licenciatura*: Administration; Economics; Education; Educational Psychology; Philosophy; Soil Science, 5 yrs;

Licenciatura: Communication Sciences; Co-operative Studies, 4 yrs; *Professional Title*: Accountancy; Architecture; Environmental Studies; Law (Lawyer Studies), 5 yrs; *Professional Title*: Educational Psychology; Law (Prosecutor Studies); Teacher Training (secondary and university), 4 yrs; *Professional Title*: Technical Studies, Display and Stage Design, Communication Studies, 3 yrs; *Especialización*: International Relations; *Maestría*: Environmental Management; *Doctorado*: Law, Education, Philosophy

Libraries: c. 25,500 vols

Press or Publishing House: Editorial Universidad Católica de Santa Fé

Last Updated: 14/01/08

CATHOLIC UNIVERSITY OF SANTIAGO DEL ESTERO

Universidad Católica de Santiago del Estero (UCSE)
Campus Universitario, Avenida Alsina y Dalmacio Vélez Sársfield,
4200 Santiago del Estero, Santiago del Estero
Tel: +54(385) 421-1777
Fax: +54(385) 421-1777
EMail: ucserec@ucse.edu.ar
Website: http://www.ucse.edu.ar

Rector: Aníbal Vicente Aguirre

Vicerrector: Luis Alberto Rezola
Tel: +54(385) 421-2955 EMail: ariel.avaldes@ucse.edu.ar

Faculties
Applied Mathematics (Applied Mathematics; Computer Engineering; Computer Science; Electronic Engineering) *Dean*: Carlos Vega Ugozzoli; **Economics** (Accountancy; Business Administration; Economics; International Business; Tourism) *Dean*: Eduardo F. Barragán; **Education** (Communication Studies; Education; Educational Administration; Geography; Psychology; Special Education) *Dean*: Graciela Mühn; **Law and Political and Social Sciences** (Criminology; Human Rights; International Law; Labour Law; Law; Political Sciences; Social Sciences) *Dean*: Eva Valev de Jensen

History: Founded 1960 as University institute attached to the Universidad Católica de Santa Fé. Recognized by the national government as an independent autonomous University 1969.

Governing Bodies: Consejo Superior; Consejo Académico

Academic Year: April to November (April-June; August-November)

Admission Requirements: Secondary school certificate (bachillerato) or foreign equivalent and entrance examination

Fees: (US Dollars): Registration, 150; tuition, 150 per month

Main Language(s) of Instruction: Spanish

International Co-operation: Participates in the Programa de Movilidad Estudiantil del Consejo de Rectores para la Integración de la Subregión Centro Oeste de Sudamérica (PME-CRISCOS); Programa de Cooperación Interuniversitaria AL.E-E.AL de la Agencia Española de Cooperación Iberoamericana

Degrees and Diplomas: *Licenciatura*: Business Administration; Commerce; International Relations; Political Science; Social Communication; Sociology, 4 yrs; *Licenciatura*: Educational Administration; Educational Sciences; Mathematics Education; Special Education, 2 yrs; *Licenciatura*: Educational Psychology; Psychology; Psychopedagogy; Theology, 5 yrs; *Licenciatura*: Geography, 1 yr; *Professional Title*: Accountancy (Conta), 4 1/2 yrs; *Professional Title*: Audiovisual Production; Computer Engineering; Graphic Design; Journalism, 3 yrs; *Professional Title*: Educational Sciences; Legal Procedure; Social Communication; Systems Analysis, 4 yrs; *Professional Title*: Electronic Engineering; Law; Notary Studies; Theology, 5 yrs; *Professional Title*: Tourism, 2-4 yrs; *Especialización*: Human Resources Development, 1 yr; *Maestría*: Business Administration, 2 yrs. Also Diplomaturas Universitarias

Student Services: Academic counselling, Canteen, Employment services, Foreign student adviser, Handicapped facilities, Health services, Sports facilities

Libraries: Central Library 'Dr. Orestes Di Lullo', c. 16,600 vols

Publications: Revista de la Secretaria de Ciencia y Técnica *(3 per annum)*; Revista 'Nuevas Propuestas' *(biennially)*; Señales *(3 per annum)*

Last Updated: 26/02/09

OLIVOS UNIT
SEDE BUENOS AIRES
SEDE OLIVOS
Avenida Corrientes 180, 1636 Olivos, Buenos Aires
Tel: +54(11) 4790-4110/8327
Fax: +54(11) 4790-4110
EMail: info.daba@ucse.edu.ar
Website: http://www.ucse.edu.ar/web/olivos/sede_olivos.htm

Director: Guillermo Jensen

Programmes
Administration (Administration); **Education** (Educational Sciences); **Educational Institutions Administration** (Educational Administration; Public Administration); **Law** (Law); **Marketing** (Marketing); **Public Administration** (Public Administration)

History: Founded 1994.

Main Language(s) of Instruction: Spanish

Degrees and Diplomas: *Licenciatura*: Administration; Business and Commerce, 4 yrs; *Licenciatura*: Educational Administration, 2 yrs; *Professional Title*: Accountancy, 4 1/2 yrs; *Professional Title*: Law, 5 yrs

RAFAELA UNIT
SEDE RAFAELA
Boulevard Hipólito Irigoyen 1502, 2300 Rafaela, Santa Fé
Tel: +54(3492) 43-2832
Fax: +54(3492) 43-3408
EMail: ucsedar@ucse.edu.ar
Website: http://www.ucse.edu.ar/web/rafaela/sede_rafaela.htm

Director: Edgardo Agustín Allochis

Secretario Administrativo: Jorge Alberto

Programmes
Accountancy; **Administration** (Administration); **Computer Engineering**; **Education**; **Law** (Law); **Management** (Management); **Public Administration** (Public Administration)

History: Founded 1995.

Main Language(s) of Instruction: Spanish

Degrees and Diplomas: *Licenciatura*: Administration, 5 yrs; *Licenciatura*: Educational Administration, 2 yrs; *Professional Title*: Accountancy (Contador Público); Law (Lawyer Studies), 5 yrs; *Professional Title*: Law (Prosecutor Studies), 4 yrs; *Professional Title*: Work Relations, 1 yr; *Especialización*; *Maestría*

SAN SALVADOR DE JUJUY UNIT
SEDE SAN SALVADOR DE JUJUY
Lavalle 333, 4600 San Salvador de Jujuy, Jujuy
Tel: +54(388) 423-6139
Fax: +54(388) 423-6139
EMail: postmaster@dass.ucse.edu.ar
Website: http://www.ucse.edu.ar

Directora: Delly Brunelli de Antoraz
EMail: dantoraz@dass.ucse.edu.ar

Programmes
Business Administration (Business Administration); **Computer Engineering**; **Computer Science** (Computer Science); **Educational Administration**; **Educational Sciences**; **Geography**; **Graphic Design**; **Journalism** (Journalism); **Law** (Law); **Notary Studies** (Notary Studies); **Political Science** (Political Sciences); **Psychology** (Psychology); **Psychopedagogy**; **Special Education**; **Systems Analysis**

History: Founded 1993.

Main Language(s) of Instruction: Spanish

Degrees and Diplomas: *Licenciatura*: Educational Administration; Political Science; Special Education, 2 yrs; *Licenciatura*: Geography, 1 yr; *Professional Title*: Computer Engineering; Law; Notary Studies, 5 yrs; *Maestría*: Business Management, 2 yrs

CEMA UNIVERSITY
Universidad del CEMA (CEMA)
Avenida Córdoba 374, C1054AAP Buenos Aires, Capital Federal
Tel: +54(11) 6314-3000
Fax: +54(11) 4314-1654
EMail: info@ucema.edu.ar
Website: http://www.ucema.edu.ar

Rector: Carlos Alfredo Rodríguez
Tel: +54(11) 4314-2269 EMail: car@ucema.edu.ar

Secretario Académico: Marcos Gallacher
EMail: gmg@ucema.edu.ar

International Relations: Ariela Vinitzky, Director, Department for Professional Development EMail: av@ucema.edu.ar

Departments
Accountancy (Accountancy) *Director:* Antonio Marín; **Business Administration** (Business Administration) *Director:* Luisa Monstuschi; **Economics** (Economics) *Director:* Mariana Conte Grand; **Engineering** (Computer Science; Engineering) *Director:* Ricardo Pantazis; **Finance** (Finance) *Director:* Edgardo Zablotsky; **Mathematics** (Mathematics) *Director:* Gabriel Pérez Lance; **Political Science** *Director:* Alejandro Corbacho; **Research** *Director:* Jorge Streb

History: Founded 1978 as Centro de Estudios Macroeconómicos de Argentina (CEMA), acquired present status and title 1995.

Governing Bodies: Consejo Académico

Academic Year: March to December

Admission Requirements: Secondary school certificate (bachillerato) or recognized equivalent and entrance examination

Main Language(s) of Instruction: Spanish

International Co-operation: With Universities in Brazil; Canada; France; Italy; Mexico; Peru; Spain; Netherlands; United Kingdom and USA

Accrediting Agencies: Association of MBAs (AMBA); Association to Advanced Collegiate Schools of Business (AACSB); National Commission for University Evaluation and Accreditation (CONEAU); Ministerio de Educación, Ciencia y Tecnología

Degrees and Diplomas: *Licenciatura:* Business Administration; Economics; Political Science, 4 yrs; *Professional Title:* Computer Engineering, 5 yrs; *Professional Title:* Public Accountancy, 4 yrs; *Maestría:* Bank Management; Business Administration; Agribusiness; Public Policy; Project Evaluation; Economics, 2 yrs; *Maestría:* Finance, 1 yr; *Doctorado:* Economics; Business Administration; Finance, 5 yrs

Student Services: Academic counselling, Canteen, Cultural centre, Employment services, Foreign student adviser, Foreign Studies Centre, Handicapped facilities, Sports facilities

Student Residential Facilities: None

Special Facilities: Auditorium; Art Gallery

Libraries: Yes

Publications: Journal of Applied Economics, Original contributions on applied issues in micro and macroeconomics *(biennially)*; Revista Análisis *(biennially)*; Revista Temas de Management *(3 per annum)*

Press or Publishing House: Departamento Editorial de la Universidad del CEMA
Last Updated: 27/02/09

CEMIC UNIVERSITY INSTITUTE
Instituto Universitario CEMIC (IUC)
Avenida Galván 4102, 1431 Buenos Aires, Capital Federal
Tel: +54(11) 4546-8290
Fax: +54(11) 4546-8274
EMail: iuc@cemic.edu.ar
Website: http://www.cemic.edu.ar

Rector: Mario D. Turin (1998-) EMail: mturin@cemic.edu.ar

Secretario Académico: Sergio Solmesky
EMail: iuc_rectorado@cemic.edu.ar

Institutes
Research *Director:* Enrique Gadow

Schools
Medicine *Dean:* Julio Ravioli

Further Information: Also 2 Teaching Hospitals and 6 ambulatory care centres

History: Founded 1958 as Centro de Educación Médica e Investigaciones Clínicas (CEMIC) 'Norberto Quirno'. CEMIC University Institute was founded by CEMIC 1997.

Governing Bodies: Consejo Superior

Academic Year: March to December (undergraduate); June to May (postgraduate)

Main Language(s) of Instruction: Spanish

International Co-operation: With universities within the Marca-Mercosur programmes

Accrediting Agencies: Comisión Nacional de Evaluación y Acreditación Universitaria (CONEAU)

Degrees and Diplomas: *Professional Title:* Biochemistry; Medicine; Gynaecology and Obstetrics; Radiology; Internal Medicine; Orthodedics; Pathology; Pediatrics; Surgery, 4 yrs; *Professional Title:* Medicine, 6 yrs; *Especialización:* Dermatology; Infectology; Genetics; Nephrology; Urology, 3 yrs; *Maestría:* Medical Education, 2 yrs. Also Diploma in Cytotechnology (2 yrs)

Student Services: Academic counselling, Canteen, Foreign student adviser, Handicapped facilities, Health services

Student Residential Facilities: None

Libraries: Yes

Publications: Revista, Research activities *(biannually)*

Press or Publishing House: Main University Press
Last Updated: 26/02/09

CHAMPAGNAT UNIVERSITY
Universidad Champagnat
Belgrano 721, 5501 Godoy Cruz
Tel: +54(261) 424-8443
Fax: +54(261) 424-2253
EMail: informes@uch.edu.ar
Website: http://www.uch.edu.ar

Vice Rector Financiero: Francisco Lucena Prospero
EMail: lucenafrancisco@uch.edu.ar

Secretario Académico: Ulrico Ortega Beeckmann
EMail: orbeeck@uch.edu.ar

Faculties
Computer Science (Computer Science) *Dean:* Eduardo Pedro Santamaria; **Economics** (Accountancy; Business Administration; Economics; International Business) *Coordinator:* Gustavo de Luca; **Law**; **Social Sciences** (Human Resources; Public Relations; Social Sciences; Tourism) *Dean:* Alicia Anzorena

History: Founded 1983.

Main Language(s) of Instruction: Spanish

Degrees and Diplomas: *Licenciatura; Professional Title; Maestría*
Last Updated: 26/02/09

DEL PLATA ADVENTIST UNIVERSITY
Universidad Adventista del Plata (UAP)
25 de Mayo 99, 3103 Libertador San Martín, Entre Ríos
Tel: +54(343) 491-8000
Fax: +54(343) 491-8001
EMail: informes@uap.edu.ar
Website: http://www.uapar.edu

Rector: Oscar Anibal Ramos EMail: rectorado@uapar.edu

International Relations: Juan Francisco Darrichón, Vicerrector
EMail: direlins@uapar.edu

Faculties
Economics and Administration (Accountancy; Administration; Business Administration; Computer Science; Secretarial Studies) *Dean:* Horacio Casali; **Health Sciences** (Health Sciences; Medicine; Nursing) *Dean:* Abraham Acosta Bustillo; **Humanities, Education and Social Sciences** (Arts and Humanities; Communication Studies; Education; Educational Psychology; English; Modern Languages; Physical Education; Preschool Education; Primary Education; Psychology; Social Sciences; Translation and Interpretation)

Dean: Raúl Nikolaus; **Theology** (Pastoral Studies; Religion; Religious Education; Theology) *Dean*: Roberto Pinto

History: Founded as College 1898, acquired present status and title 1990.

Governing Bodies: Board of Trustees, Academic University Board

Academic Year: March to November (March-June; August-November)

Admission Requirements: Secondary school certificate (bachillerato); admission approval by the University; entrance examination

Fees: (US Dollars): 2,400-3,900 per annum

Main Language(s) of Instruction: Spanish

International Co-operation: With universities in USA, Brazil and Peru

Accrediting Agencies: National Board of University Accreditation and Assesment; Accrediting Association of Seventh-Day Adventist Schools, Colleges and Universities

Degrees and Diplomas: *Licenciatura*: Psychology; Computer Science; Theology; Nutrition; Nursing; Administration; Physical Therapy; Educational Psychology, 5 yrs; *Professional Title*: Accountancy, 5 yrs; *Professional Title*: Communication Studies; Physical Education, 4 yrs; *Professional Title*: Medicine, 7 yrs; *Maestría*: Theology; Ministry, 3 yrs; *Doctorado*: Theology, 4 yrs. Also Diploma in Secretarial Studies, 2 yrs; Associate Degree in Secretarial Studies, Systems Analysis, Primary Education, Preschool Education, 3 yrs

Student Services: Academic counselling, Cultural centre, Foreign student adviser, Foreign Studies Centre, Health services, Language programs, Nursery care, Social counselling, Sports facilities

Student Residential Facilities: Yes

Special Facilities: Museum. Multimedia studio. Radio station. Computer Laboratories

Libraries: Biblioteca 'E.I. Mohr', c. 61,000 vols

Publications: Davarlogos *(biannually)*; Enfoques *(biannually)*; Sumando *(annually)*
Last Updated: 26/02/09

FAVALORO UNIVERSITY
Universidad Favaloro
Solís 453, C1078AAI Buenos Aires, Capital Federal
Tel: +54(11) 4378-1100
EMail: info@favaloro.edu.ar
Website: http://www.favaloro.edu.ar

Rector: Ricardo Horacio Pichel
Tel: +54(11) 4378-1169 EMail: pichel@favaloro.edu.ar

Secretaria General: Silvana Simonovich
Tel: +54(11) 4378-1161 EMail: ssimonovich@favaloro.edu.ar

International Relations: Edmundo Cabiera Fischer
Tel: +54(11) 4378-1160, Fax: +54(11) 4384-8458
EMail: fischer@favaloro.edu.ar

Faculties
Engineering, Exact and Natural Sciences (Biomedical Engineering; Computer Engineering; Mathematics; Natural Sciences) *Dean*: Ricardo Luis Armentano Feijoo; **Medicine** (Medicine; Nursing; Physical Therapy; Psychology) *Dean*: Branco Mautner; **Postgraduate** *Secretary*: Jaime Alberto Moguilevsky

Research Centres
Science, Research and Development (Biology; Electronic Engineering; Mathematics; Medicine; Physics) *Secretary*: Mario Parisi

History: Founded 1992. Acquired present status 1998. A private Institution named after René Gerónimo Favaloro.

Governing Bodies: Consejo de Administración; Consejo Superior

Academic Year: March to December

Admission Requirements: Secondary school certificate

Fees: (Pesos): Medicine, 12,100 per annum; Engineering, 6,050; Kinesiology, 4,950; Nursery, 2,200; Psychology, 4,290

Main Language(s) of Instruction: Spanish

Accrediting Agencies: Comisión Nacional de Evaluación y Acreditación Universitaria (CONEAU)

Degrees and Diplomas: *Bachiller Universitario*: Engineering, 3 yrs; *Professional Title*: Biomedical Engineering; Medical Physics Engineering; Computer Engineering; Kinesiology and Physical Therapy, 5 yrs; *Professional Title*: Medicine, 6 yrs; *Professional Title*: Nursery; Psychology, 4 yrs; *Especialización*: Heart Electrophysiology; Cardiology; Gynecology and Reproduction Endocrinology; Sport Kinesiology; Occupational Health, 2 yrs; *Maestría*: Endocrinology; Biomedical Engineering; Clinical Engineering; Arterial Hypertension; Molecular Biology and Genetics; Health Administration, 2 yrs; *Maestría*: Psychoneuropharmacology, 4 yrs

Student Services: Academic counselling, Language programs, Sports facilities

Libraries: Biblioteca Ezequiel Martínez Estrada
Last Updated: 27/02/09

GASTÓN DACHARY UNIVERSITY
Universidad Gastón Dachary (IUGD)
Salta y Colón Piso 2, 3300 Posadas, Misiones
Tel: +54(3752) 43-8677
Fax: +54(3752) 43-8677
EMail: secretaria_rectorado@dachary.edu.ar
Website: http://www.dachary.edu.ar

Rector: Luis Enrique Lichowski EMail: lichowski@dachary.edu.ar

Secretario Académico: Fernando Arias
EMail: academica@dachary.edu.ar

Departments
Administration and Commerce; **Computer Science**

History: Founded 1990 as Instituto Privado de Estudios Superiores de Misiones (IPESMI), acquired present status and title 2009.

Governing Bodies: Consejo de Administracíon

Main Language(s) of Instruction: Spanish

Accrediting Agencies: Comisión Nacional de Evaluación y Acreditación Universitaria

Degrees and Diplomas: *Licenciatura*; *Especialización*; *Maestría*
Last Updated: 26/02/09

INTERAMERICAN OPEN UNIVERSITY
Universidad Abierta Interamericana (UAI)
Chacabuco 90, 1° Piso, 1069 Buenos Aires, Capital Federal
Tel: +54(11) 4342-7788
Fax: +54(11) 4342-7654
EMail: uai@vaneduc.edu.ar
Website: http://www.vaneduc.edu.ar/uai

Rector: Edgardo Néstor De Vincenzi (1995-)
EMail: edgardo.devincenzi@vaneduc.edu.ar

Vice President for Management and Evaluation: Marcelo De Vincenzi EMail: marcelo.devincenzi@vaneduc.edu.ar

International Relations: Luis Franchi, Extension Vice President
EMail: luis.franchi@vaneduc.edu.ar

Faculties
Architecture (Architecture) *Dean*: Jorge Fucaracce; **Business Administration** (Accountancy; Administration; Business Administration; Business and Commerce; Management; Marketing) *Dean*: Fernando Leilo Grosso; **Communication Sciences** (Advertising and Publicity; Cinema and Television; Communication Studies; Graphic Design; Journalism; Mass Communication; Performing Arts) *Dean*: Román Tambini; **Computer Technology** (Computer Engineering; Computer Science; Mathematics; Software Engineering; Systems Analysis) *Dean*: Marcelo De Vincenzi; **Educational Development and Research** (Educational Sciences; Pedagogy; Preschool Education; Teacher Trainers Education; Teacher Training) *Dean*: Perpetuo Lentijo; **Human Development and Sport** (Education of the Handicapped; Physical Therapy; Sports) *Dean*: Hugo Lizza; **Law and Political Sciences** (International Relations; Law; Political Sciences) *Dean*: Carlos María Cloppet; **Medicine and Health Sciences** (Dentistry; Health Administration; Medicine; Nursing; Nutrition; Rehabilitation and Therapy) *Dean*: Roberto Cherjovsky; **Psychology and Human Relations** (Occupational Therapy; Psychology) *Dean*: Fernando Adrover; **Tourism and Hotel Management** (Hotel Management; Tourism) *Dean*: Elisa Beltritti

History: Founded 1995.

Governing Bodies: Consejo Superior

Academic Year: February to December

Admission Requirements: Secondary school certificate (bachillerato)

Fees: (Pesos): 148-937 per month

Main Language(s) of Instruction: Spanish

International Co-operation: With universities in France, USA, China, Spain and Germany

Accrediting Agencies: Ministerio de Educación, Ciencia y Tecnología. Comisión de Evaluación y Acreditación Universitaria (CONEAU)

Degrees and Diplomas: *Título Menor*: Business Administration (Técnico); Events Organisation and Management; Nursing, 2 yrs; *Título Menor*: Dental Prosthetics; Surgery Assistant, 3 yrs; *Título Menor*: Tourism, 2 1/2 yrs; *Profesorado*: Educational Psychology, 5 yrs; *Profesorado*: Educational Sciences; Mathematics and Computer Sciences; Physical Education and Sports, 4 yrs; *Profesorado*: Polymodal Education, 2 yrs; *Licenciatura*: Advertising and Publicity; Audiovisual Production and Realisation; Bioimages Production; Fine Arts; Graphic Design; Health Administration; Hotel Management; Information Sciences; Mass Communication; Journalism; International Relations; Mathematics and Computer Sciences; Nursing; Nutrition; Occupational Therapy; Physical Education and Sports (High Performance and Sports Technology); Physical Education and Sports (Sports Education Management); Political Science; Tourism, 4 yrs; *Licenciatura*: Basic Education; Education; Preschool Education; Educational Administration, 2 yrs; *Licenciatura*: Business and Commerce; Business Administration; Marketing; Business Engineering; Educational Sciences; International Business; Music Therapy; Physical Therapy; Psychology, 5 yrs; *Licenciatura*: Educational Psychology, 5 yrs; *Professional Title*: Accountancy, 4 1/2 yrs; *Professional Title*: Architecture and Planning; Architecture; Computer Engineering; Law; Odontology, 5 yrs; *Professional Title*: Medicine, 6 yrs; *Especialización*: 2 yrs following first degree; *Especialización*: Architecture; Business Administration, 2 yrs; *Especialización*: Computer Networks, 1 1/2 yrs; *Maestría*: Clinical Research in Parmacology; Computer Engineering; Educational Technology; International Management; Organisational Psychology, 2 yrs

Student Services: Academic counselling, Canteen, Cultural centre, Employment services, Health services, Language programs, Nursery care, Social counselling, Sports facilities

Libraries: Yes

Publications: Conexión Abierta, Scientific Research Magazine *(monthly)*

Academic Staff *2007-2008*	MEN	WOMEN	TOTAL
FULL-TIME	226	150	376
PART-TIME	641	491	1,132
STAFF WITH DOCTORATE			
FULL-TIME	15	7	22
PART-TIME	38	11	49
Student Numbers *2007-2008*			
All (Foreign Included)	8,989	8,601	17,590
FOREIGN ONLY	258	355	613

Part-time students, 3,408. **Evening students**, 8,320.
Last Updated: 20/03/08

ISALUD UNIVERSITY
Universidad ISALUD
Venezuela 925/31, C1095AAS Buenos Aires, Capital Federal
Tel: +54(11) 5239-4000
Fax: +54(11) 5239-4003
EMail: informes@isalud.edu.ar
Website: http://www.isalud.org

Rector: Carlos Garavelli

Secretaria Académica: Silvia Zambonini
EMail: academica@isalud.org

International Relations: Claudio Mate Rothgerber
EMail: mate@isalud.com

Departments
Economics (Economics; Health Administration; Public Health); **Epidemiology** (Epidemiology; Health Education; Information Management; Social and Preventive Medicine; Social Policy); **Organization and Management** (Health Administration; Human Resources; Management); **Political Science** (Comparative Sociology; Political Sciences; Public Administration; Social and Community Services; Social Policy; Social Welfare)

History: Founded 1991.

Governing Bodies: Comité de Gestión

Main Language(s) of Instruction: Spanish

Accrediting Agencies: Comisión Nacional de Evaluación y Acreditación Universitaria (CONEAU)

Degrees and Diplomas: *Licenciatura*; *Especialización*; *Maestría*
Last Updated: 26/02/09

ITALIAN UNIVERSITY INSTITUTE OF ROSARIO
Instituto Universitario Italiano de Rosario
Virasoso 1249, S2001ODA Rosario, Santa Fé
Tel: +54(341) 485-8893
Fax: +54(341) 482-5065
EMail: iunir@iunir.edu.ar
Website: http://www.iunir.edu.ar/escmedicina/emedi.asp

Rector: Emilio A. Navarini

Secretario Académico: Eugenio José Lerro
EMail: secretariaacademica@iunir.edu.ar

Schools
Medicine (Cardiology; Child Care and Development; Gynaecology and Obstetrics; Haematology; Immunology; Surgery; Urology) *Director*: Mario Secchi; **Nursing** (Biology; Computer Science; Nursing; Social Sciences) *Director*: Maria del Carmen Ruiz; **Psychology**

Further Information: Also Teaching Hospital

History: Founded 1999.

Governing Bodies: Consejo de Administración

Main Language(s) of Instruction: Spanish

Accrediting Agencies: Comisión Nacional de Evaluación y Acreditación Universitaria (CONEAU)

Degrees and Diplomas: *Licenciatura*; *Especialización*: Medicine; Surgery; *Maestría*: Medical Education; *Doctorado*: Biomedicine
Last Updated: 26/02/09

JUAN AGUSTÍN MAZA UNIVERSITY
Universidad Juan Agustín Maza (UMAZA)
Avenida de Acceso Este Lateral Sur N° 2245, 5519 Guaymallén, Mendoza
Tel: +54(261) 405-6200
Fax: +54(261) 405-6209
EMail: umaza@umaza.edu.ar
Website: http://www.umaza.edu.ar

Rector: Carlos Eduardo Villarreal (1999-)
EMail: cvillarreal@umaza.edu.ar

Vicerrectora Académica: María Amalia Salafia
EMail: asalafia@umaza.edu.ar

International Relations: Eduardo José Salvarini, Vicerrector de Extensión Universitaria EMail: esalvarini@umaza.edu.ar

Faculties
Business Administration *Dean*: Enrique Osvaldo Guilhou; **Engineering** (Engineering) *Dean*: Vicente Gonzalo Cremades; **Environmental and Veterinary Sciences** *Dean*: Alberto Duarte; **Journalism** (Advertising and Publicity; Journalism) *Dean*: Ángel Puente Guerra; **Kinesiology and Physiotherapy** *Dean*: Edgardo Longo; **Nutrition** (Nutrition) *Dean*: Cecilia Llaver; **Oenology and Agricultural Industries** (Fruit Production; Horticulture; Oenology) *Dean*: Aurelio Sesto; **Pharmacy and Biochemistry** (Biochemistry; Pharmacy) *Dean*: Gabriela Giornelli; **Physical Education** *Dean*: Guillermo Sosa Tallei

History: Founded 1960. Acquired present status 1980.

Governing Bodies: Asemblea de Asociados; Consejo Superior

Academic Year: April to March

Admission Requirements: Completed intermediary, secondary or polymodal studies

Main Language(s) of Instruction: Spanish

Degrees and Diplomas: *Profesorado*: Chemistry; Physical Education, 4 yrs; *Licenciatura*: Advertising and Publicity; Computer Science; Human Resources; Kinesiology and Physiotherapy; Oenology; Physical Education; Social Communication, 4 yrs; *Licenciatura*: Nutrition, 5 yrs; *Professional Title*: Accountancy; Agrimensure; Chemistry; Nutrition; Pharmacy, 4 yrs; *Professional Title*: Biochemistry; Veterinary Science, 5 yrs; *Especialización*: Geomatics Applied to Environmental Processes; Higher Education; Sterilisation and Biomedial Equipement; Clinical Study of Domestic Dogs and Cats; Kinesiology and Physiotherapy Management and Audit; *Maestría*: Corporate and Institutional Communication; Viticulture Strategic Management; *Doctorado*

Student Services: Academic counselling, Canteen, Handicapped facilities, Language programs, Sports facilities

Special Facilities: Television and Radio stations; Physics and Chemistry Laboratories; Kynesiology Cabinet

Libraries: Library with free access for alumni and faculty; free internet access; newspaper library

Publications: UJAM News, Academic Publication *(biennially)*

Academic Staff 2007-2008	MEN	WOMEN	TOTAL
FULL-TIME	225	285	**510**
Student Numbers 2007-2008			
All (Foreign Included)	1,523	1,934	**3,457**

Last Updated: 20/03/08

MAIMÓNIDES UNIVERSITY
Universidad Maimónides (UM)
Hidalgo 775, 1013 Buenos Aires, Capital Federal
Tel: +54(11) 4905-1101
Fax: +54(11) 4982-8181
Website: http://www.maimonides.edu.ar

Chairman of Board of Governors: Ernesto Goberman
Tel: +54(11) 4382-4526, Fax: +54(11) 4382-7127
EMail: rectorado@maimonides.edu

Secretario Académico: Eduardo Criado
Tel: +54(11) 4905-1116 EMail: sectecnica@maimonides.edu.ar

Faculties
Health Sciences (Biochemistry; Biology; Dentistry; Dermatology; Medicine; Nursing; Nutrition; Physical Therapy) *Dean*: Abraam Sonis; **Humanities, Social and Managerial Sciences** (Administration; Arts and Humanities; Business and Commerce; Education; Educational Sciences; Gerontology; Human Resources; Law; Music; Psychology; Social Sciences; Tourism) *Dean*: Regina Steiner

Schools
Multimedia (Information Technology; Multimedia) *Director*: Alejandra Marinaro

Further Information: Distance learning courses in Contemporary Strategy; Geopolitics; International Relations; Political Science; Strategy

History: Founded 1990.

Governing Bodies: Board of Governors

Academic Year: March to December (March-June; August-December)

Admission Requirements: Secondary school certificate (bachillerato) or equivalent

Fees: (US Dollars): 1,200-9,000 per annum

Main Language(s) of Instruction: Spanish

International Co-operation: With universities in Spain; Switzerland; France; Italy; Israel; USA; Canada; Paraguay; Venezuela; Peru; Brazil

Accrediting Agencies: CONEAU

Degrees and Diplomas: *Licenciatura*: Health Administration; Social Gerontology; Family Psychotherapy; Mediation, 4 yrs; *Professional Title*: Accountancy, 4 yrs; *Professional Title*: Law, 5 yrs; *Professional Title*: Medicine, 6 yrs; *Especialización*: Dental Assistant; Dental Protheses; Nuclear Medicine; Skin Cosmetics, 2 yrs; *Especialización*: Paramedical Therapy; Family Medicine; Forensic Medicine; Psycho Gerontology; Rhumatology; Paediatrics; Intensive Care; Psychotherapy; Diagnosis through Images; Ecography and

Echo Doppler, 2 yrs following first degree; *Maestría*: Administration; International Relations; Geopolitics; General Management of Nursery Services; Research and Management of Clinical Tests; Dentistry; Ecology Management, 2 yrs (Postgraduate); *Doctorado*: Dentistry; Medicine; Administration

Student Services: Academic counselling, Cultural centre, Handicapped facilities, Language programs, Sports facilities

Libraries: Yes

Last Updated: 27/02/09

PALERMO UNIVERSITY
Universidad de Palermo (UP)
Av. Córdoba 3501, esq. Mario Bravo, 1175ABT Buenos Aires, Capital Federal
Tel: +54(11) 4964-4610
Fax: +54(11) 4963-1560
EMail: informes@palermo.edu; rectorado@palermo.edu
Website: http://www.palermo.edu

Rector: Ricardo H. Popovsky (1990-)
EMail: rectorado@palermo.edu

Secretario Administrativo Académico: Fernando Díaz

International Relations: Matías Popovsky, Head, International Relations EMail: mpopov@palermo.edu

Faculties
Architecture (Architecture; Town Planning); **Business and Economics** (Accountancy; Administration; Business Administration; Finance; Human Resources; International Business; Management; Marketing); **Design and Communication** (Advertising and Publicity; Cinema and Television; Design; Film; Fine Arts; Public Relations); **Engineering** (Computer Engineering; Computer Networks; Computer Science; Electronic Engineering; Engineering; Industrial Engineering; Information Technology; Telecommunications Engineering); **Law** (Administrative Law; Civil Law; Commercial Law; Constitutional Law; Criminal Law; Labour Law; Law); **Psychology** (Psychology); **Social Sciences** (Arts and Humanities; Education; Fine Arts; Health Sciences; Social Sciences)

Graduate Schools
Business (Business Administration; Business and Commerce)

Further Information: Branch in Catalinas

History: Founded 1986 as Community College, acquired present status and title 1990.

Governing Bodies: Consejo Superior Universitario; Consejo Académico

Academic Year: March to June; August to December

Admission Requirements: Secondary school certificate (bachillerato)

Fees: (US Dollars): 4,900 per annum, undergraduate; 5,000-9,000 per annum, postgraduate.

Main Language(s) of Instruction: Spanish

International Co-operation: with institutions in Switzerland and US.

Accrediting Agencies: CONEAU (Comisión Nacional de Evaluación y Acreditación Universitaria); RIBA (Royal Institute of British Architects).

Degrees and Diplomas: *Licenciatura*: 4 yrs; *Professional Title*: Accountancy, 4 yrs; *Professional Title*: Architecture; Law, 5 yrs; *Especialización*; *Maestría*: a further 2-2 1/2 yrs; *Doctorado (PhD)*: 2 yrs following Maestría

Student Services: Academic counselling, Canteen, Cultural centre, Employment services, Foreign student adviser, Foreign Studies Centre, Handicapped facilities, Language programs, Social counselling, Sports facilities

Libraries: 86,325 vols; 6,118 periodical subscriptions.

Publications: Creación y Producción en Diseño y Comunicación, Articels by students and graduates of the Production Centre of the Design and Communication Faculty. *(other/irregular)*; Cuadermos del Centro de Estudios, Design and communication journal. *(biannually)*; Palermo Business Review *(biannually)*; Revista de Ciencia y Tecnología, Engineering journal. *(biannually)*; Revista Escritos en la Facultad - Diseño y Comunicación, Collection of articles written by students and teachers. *(other/irregular)*; Revista JurídicaRevista Juridica, Law review. *(biannually)*

Press or Publishing House: Editorial Universidad de Palermo

Academic Staff 2010-2011	MEN	WOMEN	TOTAL
FULL-TIME	93	106	199
PART-TIME	703	818	1,521
STAFF WITH DOCTORATE			
FULL-TIME	87	96	183
PART-TIME	–	–	0
Student Numbers 2010-2011			
All (Foreign Included)	5,553	7,161	12,714
FOREIGN ONLY	1,206	1,487	2,693

Last Updated: 07/12/10

SAINT THOMAS AQUINUS UNIVERSITY OF THE NORTH

Universidad del Norte Santo Tomás de Aquino (UNSTA)
9 de Julio 165, 4000 San Miguel de Tucumán, Tucumán
Tel: +54(381) 422-8805
EMail: info@unsta.edu.ar
Website: http://www.unsta.edu.ar

Rector: Juan Carlos Veiga
Tel: +54(381) 421-8659 EMail: jcveiga@unsta.edu.ar

Secretario Académico: Bernardo Pedro Carlino
EMail: bcarlino@unsta.edu.ar

Centres
Institutional Studies (Public Administration) *Dean*: Jorge Alejandro Scampini

Faculties
Economics and Administration (Accountancy; Administration; Business Administration; Economics; Social Sciences; Tourism) *Dean*: Guillermo Di Lella; **Engineering** (Computer Engineering; Industrial Engineering; Multimedia) *Dean*: Luis Raúl Alcaide; **Health Sciences** (Health Sciences; Psychology; Social Sciences) *Dean*: Fernando Koch; **Humanities** (Educational Administration; Educational Sciences; Graphic Design; Humanities and Social Science Education; Information Sciences; Journalism; Philosophy; Social Studies; Technology) *Dean*: Juan José Herrera; **Law and Political Science** (Law; Notary Studies; Political Sciences) *Dean*: María Gilda Pedicone de Valls

Further Information: Also University Centre in Concepción

History: Founded 1956 as institute, acquired present status and title 1965. A private institution.

Governing Bodies: Junta de Gobierno; Consejo Superior

Academic Year: March to November

Admission Requirements: Secondary school certificate (bachillerato)

Main Language(s) of Instruction: Spanish

Degrees and Diplomas: *Bachiller Universitario*: Philosophy, 3 yrs; *Licenciatura*: Business Administration; Philosophy; Psychology; Social Communication; Tourism, 5 yrs; *Licenciatura*: Educational Administration, 2 yrs following Teacher's Diploma; *Licenciatura*: Educational Sciences; Graphic Design; Nutrition, 4 yrs; *Professional Title*: Accountancy; Computer Engineering; Industrial Engineering; Law, 5 yrs; *Professional Title*: Notarial Studies, 1 yr following Lawyer's Diploma; *Maestría*. Also postgraduate diplomas of specialization

Student Services: Academic counselling, Foreign student adviser, Health services, Language programs, Sports facilities

Libraries: c. 10,000 vols

Publications: Propuestas, Economics and Business Administration Topics; Sto. Tomás Moro, Juridical articles; STUDIUM Filosofía y Teología, Philosophical and Theological Topics
Last Updated: 27/02/09

SAN ANDRÉS UNIVERSITY

Universidad de San Andrés (UDESA)
Vito Dumas 284, B1644BID Victoria, Buenos Aires
Tel: +54(11) 4725-7000
EMail: admision@udesa.edu.ar
Website: http://www.udesa.edu.ar

Rector: Eduardo Zimmermann (2001-)
EMail: zimmer@udesa.edu.ar

Director Ejecutivo: Luis La Rosa
Tel: +54(11) 4799-7055 EMail: llarosa@udesa.edu.ar

Chairs
Entrepreneurship *(Karl Steur)* (Business Administration; Finance; Management) *Director*: Eduardo Zimmermann

Departments
Administration (Administration; Business Administration; Human Resources; Management; Marketing) *Director*: Ernesto Gore; **Economics** (Economics; Finance) *Director*: Mariano Tommasi; **Humanities** (Arts and Humanities; Communication Studies; International Relations; Political Sciences) *Director*: Roberto Barros; **Mathematics and Science** (Mathematics; Natural Sciences; Statistics) *Coordinator*: Ricardo Fraiman Maus

Schools
Education (Education) *Director*: Silvina Gvirtz

History: Founded 1989 by members of 'St. Andrew's Scots' School, an educational institution established in Buenos Aires 1838 by the Presbiterian Church of the River Plata. A private institution.

Governing Bodies: Consejo Superior

Academic Year: March to December (March-July; August-December)

Admission Requirements: Secondary school certificate (bachillerato) and entrance examination

Fees: (Pesos): 1,460 per course

Main Language(s) of Instruction: Spanish, English

International Co-operation: With universities in USA; United Kingdom; France; Spain; Canada; Belgium and Sweden

Degrees and Diplomas: *Licenciatura*: 4 yrs; *Especialización*; *Maestría*; *Doctorado*

Student Services: Academic counselling, Canteen, Cultural centre, Employment services, Foreign student adviser, Foreign Studies Centre, Handicapped facilities, Language programs, Sports facilities

Student Residential Facilities: None

Libraries: 47,142 vols; 956 periodical subscriptions; 497 videos; 103 CD Roms

Publications: Documentos de Trabajo; Investigaciones; Trabajos Docentes
Last Updated: 27/02/09

SOUTHERN UNIVERSITY

Universidad Austral
Avenida Juan de Garay 125, 6° Piso, C1063ABB Buenos Aires, Capital Federal
Tel: +54(11) 5921-8000
Fax: +54(11) 5921-8013
EMail: admisiones@austral.edu.ar
Website: http://www.austral.edu.ar

Rector: Marcelo J. Villar EMail: rectorado@rec.austral.edu.ar

Administrador: Fernando Macario

International Relations: Julio C. Durand
Tel: +54(11) 5921-8016 EMail: internacional@rec.austral.edu.ar

Faculties
Biomedical Sciences *(Derqui, Pilar)* (Biomedicine); **Business Studies** (Accountancy; Business Administration) *Dean*: Alcira Attala de Boggione; **Communication** (Communication Studies; Journalism); **Engineering** (Automation and Control Engineering; Computer Engineering; Engineering; Systems Analysis) *Dean*: Ariel Gulisano; **Law** (Law) *Dean*: Juan Cianciardo

Institutes
Family Studies (Family Studies) *Director*: Carlos Camean Ariza; **Philosophy**

Schools
Business *(IAE, Derqui, Pilar)* (Business Administration; Business and Commerce; Management) *Director*: Fernando Fragueiro; **Education** (Education; Educational Administration; Higher Education) *Director*: Julio C. Durand

Further Information: Also University Hospital

History: Founded as Graduate School of Business (IAE), acquired present status and title 1991. A private institution promoted by the Asociación Civil de Estudios Superiores.

Governing Bodies: Consejo Superior

Academic Year: March to November (March-July; August-November)

Admission Requirements: Secondary school certificate (bachillerato) or equivalent and competitive entrance examination

Fees: (US Dollars): 3,000 per annum; graduate, 5,000-17,000

Main Language(s) of Instruction: Spanish

Degrees and Diplomas: *Licenciatura*: 4-5 yrs; *Maestría*: a further 2 yrs; *Doctorado*

Student Services: Canteen, Employment services, Foreign student adviser, Handicapped facilities, Language programs, Sports facilities

Libraries: Central Library, 55,000 vols

Last Updated: 26/02/09

UNIVERSITY INSTITUTE - ARGENTINA SCHOOL OF BUSINESS

Instituto Universitario Escuela Argentina de Negocios (IUEAN)
Av. Córdoba 1690, C1055AAT Buenos Aires, Capital Federal
Tel: +54(11) 5032-3900
EMail: informes@ean.edu.ar
Website: http://www.iuean.edu.ar

President: Alberto Kañevsky EMail: albertok@ean.edu.ar

Rector: Guilermo Ondarts
EMail: rectorado@ean.edu.ar; investigacion@ean.edu.ar

Areas
E-Learning and Distance Education *Coordination*: Analía Rymberg

Departments
Corporate Education *((Educacion Empresarial)) Director*: Alejandro Stofenmacher

Programmes
Business Administration *Coordinator*: Emilio Cisilino; **Computer Engineering** *Coordinator*: Fernanda Miccoli; **Hotel Management** *Coordinator*: Carolina Pairola; **Human Resources** (Human Resources) *Coordinator*: Viviana Oller; **International Business** (International Business) *Coordinator*: Daniel Iglesias; **Marketing** (Marketing) *Coordinator*: Daniel Tristezza Coloma

Further Information: Also another site in Martinez

History: Founded 1993. Acquired present status 2004.

Governing Bodies: Consejo de Administración de la Fundación; Rectorado; Consejo Superior Academico

Academic Year: March to December

Admission Requirements: Secondary school certificate; Basic knowledge of spanish

Fees: (Pesos): 5,820 per annum

Main Language(s) of Instruction: Spanish

Accrediting Agencies: Comisión Nacional de Evaluation y Acreditacíon Universitaria (CONEAU)

Degrees and Diplomas: *Licenciatura*: Marketing; Human Resources; International Business; Computer Engineering; Hotel Management, 4 yrs. Also Diplomado (6-9 months), Analista Universitario 3 yrs

Student Services: Academic counselling, Employment services, Foreign student adviser, Language programs

Special Facilities: 4 Computer laboratories

Libraries: Yes

Publications: Carrera & Negocios *(biennially)*; Innova *(biennially)*
Last Updated: 26/02/09

UNIVERSITY INSTITUTE - GRADUATE SCHOOL OF ECONOMICS AND BUSINESS ADMINISTRATION

Instituto Universitario 'Escuela Superior de Economía y Administración de Empresas' (ESEADE)
Uriarte 2472, 1425 Buenos Aires, Capital Federal
Tel: +54(11) 4773-5825
Fax: +54(11) 4772-7243
EMail: patriciaaragon@eseade.edu.ar
Website: http://www.eseade.edu.ar

Rector: Carlos Newland
Tel: +54(11) 4773-3735 EMail: newland@eseade.edu.ar

Secretario Académico: Martín Sisto EMail: sisto@eseade.edu.ar

Departments
Administration and Business Studies; Economics and Social Sciences

History: Founded 1978. Acquired present status 1999. A private Graduate School.

Governing Bodies: Consejo Directivo; Consejo Consultivo

Main Language(s) of Instruction: Spanish

Degrees and Diplomas: *Licenciatura*; *Especialización*; *Maestría*: 2 yrs

Student Services: Academic counselling

Special Facilities: Computing Laboratory

Libraries: 7,000 vols

Publications: Libertas *(biannually)*
Last Updated: 26/02/09

UNIVERSITY INSTITUTE OF HEALTH SCIENCES - HÉCTOR A. BARCELÓ FOUNDATION

Instituto Universitario de Ciencias de la Salud - Fundación 'Héctor A. Barceló'
Avenida Las Heras 2191, 1127 Buenos Aires, Capital Federal
Tel: +54(11) 4800-0200
Fax: +54(11) 4800-0239
EMail: rectorado@barcelo.edu.ar
Website: http://www.barcelo.edu.ar

Rector: Héctor Alejandro Barceló (2006-) Tel: +54(11) 4800-0219

Secretario Académico: Ricardo Znaidak
EMail: secretariaacademica@barcelo.edu.ar

International Relations: Carlos Álvarez Bermúdez
Tel: +54(11) 4800-0200, ext 236
EMail: cbermudez@barcelo.edu.ar

Departments
Health Sciences *(La Rioja)* (Dietetics; Health Administration; Health Sciences; Medical Technology; Medicine; Physical Therapy)

Faculties
Medicine (Health Sciences; Medical Technology; Medicine; Neurology; Nursing; Pharmacology; Physical Therapy; Psychology; Surgery) *Dean*: Felix Etchegoyen

Further Information: Branches in La Rioja and Santo Tomé. Also 3 Teaching Hospitals

History: Founded 1968 as Biological Foundation and Research Institute. Acquired present status and title 1992.

Governing Bodies: Consejo Superior

Academic Year: February to December

Admission Requirements: Secondary school certificate (bachillerato)

Fees: (US Dollars): c. 4,200 per annum; Medicine, c. 6,600; Postgraduate, c. 2,400

Main Language(s) of Instruction: Spanish

Accrediting Agencies: Comisión Nacional de Evaluación y Acreditación Universitaria (CONEAU)

Degrees and Diplomas: *Professional Title*: Dietetics, 5 yrs; *Professional Title*: Medicine, 7 yrs; *Especialización*; *Maestría*; *Doctorado (PhD)*: a further 2 yrs

Student Services: Academic counselling, Canteen, Cultural centre, Employment services, Health services, Social counselling, Sports facilities

Libraries: c. 10,000 vols; 193 periodical subscriptions
Last Updated: 02/12/08

UNIVERSITY INSTITUTE OF MENTAL HEALTH OF THE BUENOS AIRES PSYCHOANALYTICAL ASSOCIATION (APDEBA)

Instituto Universitario de Salud Mental de la Asociación Psicoanalítica de Buenos Aires (APdeBA) (IUSAM)
Maure 1850, C1426CUH Buenos Aires, Capital Federal
Tel: +54(11) 4775-7867/7985
Fax: +54(11) 4775-7867/7985 Ext.16
EMail: info@iusam.edu.ar
Website: http://www.iusam.edu.ar

Rector: Héctor Ferrari (2005-)
Tel: +54(11) 4775-7867/7985, Ext.19

General Secretary: Clelia Manfredi de Poderoso

Areas
Culture *Director.* Félix Schuster; **Psychoanalysis** *Director.* Pedro Boscan; **Psychopatology** *Director.* Carlos Alberto Bucahi

Departments
Extention *Director.* Raquel Berezovsky de Chemes; **Research on Psychoanalysis and Mental Health** *Director.* Graciela Grivot de Benito Silva

History: Founded 2005. Part of the International Psychoanalytical Association (IPA)

Governing Bodies: University Council, Rector, Vice-Rectors, Secretary-General

Academic Year: March to December

Admission Requirements: A Degree in Medicine or Psychology; University Degree or equivalent for Masters

Fees: (Pesos): 1,640-4,990 per annum depending on subjects

Main Language(s) of Instruction: Spanish

International Co-operation: With Agora Institute in Uruguay, and with universities in Chile; USA; France and Italy

Accrediting Agencies: Comisión Nacional de Evaluación y Acreditación Universitaria (CONEAU)

Degrees and Diplomas: *Especialización:* Children and Teenagers Psychoanalysis; Psychopathology and Mental Health, 2 yrs; *Especialización:* Psychoanalysis, 4 yrs; *Maestría:* Culture and Mental Health, 2 yrs; *Maestría:* Family Studies, 2 yrs; *Maestría:* Psychopathology and Mental Health, 3 yrs

Student Services: Academic counselling, Foreign student adviser, Handicapped facilities

Student Residential Facilities: None

Special Facilities: Auditorium

Libraries: Yes

Publications: Revista Psicoanálisis, Scientific Activities of APdeBA *(3 per annum)*
Last Updated: 26/02/09

UNIVERSITY INSTITUTE OF THE ITALIAN HOSPITAL

Instituto Universitario del Hospital Italiano
Potosí 4240, 1119 Buenos Aires, Capital Federal
Tel: +54(11) 4983-2624
Fax: +54(11) 4983-2624
EMail: escuelademedicina@hospitaliano.org.ar
Website: http://www.hospitalitaliano.org.ar/escuela/index.php

Rector: Osvaldo A. Blanco

Secretaria Académica: Elsa Mercedes Nucifora
EMail: enucifora@hitalba.edu.ar

Departments
Diagnostics and Medical Treatment (Health Sciences; Medicine); **Health Professions and Research** (Health Sciences); **Medical Computer Science** (Computer Science); **Medicine** (Medicine); **Paediatrics** (Paediatrics); **Surgery** (Surgery)

History: Founded 1854.

Governing Bodies: Consejo Académico

Fees: (US Dollars): Tuition, 300

Main Language(s) of Instruction: Spanish

Accrediting Agencies: Comisión Nacional de Evaluación y Acreditación Universitaria (CONEAU)

Degrees and Diplomas: *Licenciatura:* Nursing, 5 yrs; *Professional Title:* Medicine, 6 yrs; *Especialización; Maestría*
Last Updated: 26/02/09

UNIVERSITY OF ARGENTINIAN SOCIAL STUDIES

Universidad del Museo Social Argentino (UMSA)
Avenida Corrientes 1723, 1042 Buenos Aires, Capital Federal
Tel: +54(11) 4375-4601
Fax: +54(11) 4375-4600
EMail: informes@umsa.edu.ar
Website: http://www.umsa.edu.ar

Rector: Guillermo E. Garbarini Islas
Tel: +54(11) 4375-4602 EMail: rectorado@umsa.edu.ar

Secretario General: Patricio M. Asensio Vives
EMail: rectorado@umsa.edu.ar

Faculties
Arts and Heritage Preservation *Dean:* Enrique Vaccaro; **Economics, Administration and Trade** (Accountancy; Business Administration; Business and Commerce; Economics; International Business) *Dean:* Carlos Giménez; **Human Sciences** (Educational Sciences; Pedagogy; Psychology; Speech Therapy and Audiology) *Dean:* Camilo Bruzzoni; **Law and Social Sciences** (Labour and Industrial Relations; Law; Social Studies) *Dean:* Federico Polak; **Modern Languages** (English; French; Italian; Translation and Interpretation) *Director.* María Cristina De Ortúzar; **Rehabilitation and Therapy** (Speech Therapy and Audiology) *Dean:* Estela Salazar; **Social Interactions Sciences** (Communication Studies; Journalism; Library Science; Radio and Television Broadcasting; Social Work) *Dean:* Lydia Rodríguez

History: Founded 1956, acquired present status 2001.

Governing Bodies: Board of Directors and University Council

Academic Year: March to November (March-June; July-November)

Admission Requirements: Secondary school certificate, and other minimum requirements

Main Language(s) of Instruction: Spanish

Accrediting Agencies: Comisión Nacional de Evaluación y Acreditación Universitaria (CONEAU) and National Evaluation and Accreditation Commission

Degrees and Diplomas: *Licenciatura:* Art History and Heritage Preservation; Arts and Heritage Preservation; Business Administration; Commerce; Communication Studies; Education; International Business; Journalism and Communication; Labour Relations; Library Science and Documentation; Museology; Pedagogy; Psychology; Radio and TV; Visual Arts, 4 yrs; *Licenciatura:* Speech Therapy and Audiology, 5 yrs; *Professional Title:* Accountancy; Law; Social Work, 5 yrs; *Professional Title:* Foreign Languages Teaching (English, French, Italian); Interpretation (English, French, Italian); Translation (English, French, Italian), 4 yrs; *Especialización; Maestría:* Information Sciences, 2 yrs; *Doctorado:* Business Administration; Law and Social Sciences, 2 yrs; *Doctorado:* Speech Therapy and Audiology, 1 yr

Student Services: Academic counselling, Canteen, Cultural centre, Employment services, Language programs, Sports facilities

Special Facilities: Languages Lab; Computing Laboratory; Voice and Speech Laboratory; Audiometer cabinet; Camara Gessel (Gessel Box)

Publications: Conceptos, Magazine with scientific and literature articles *(quarterly)*; Foro Politico/ Foro Economico, Magazine of Political Science *(quarterly)*
Last Updated: 27/02/09

UNIVERSITY OF BELGRANO

Universidad de Belgrano (UB)
Zabala 1837/51 2° Piso, 1426 Buenos Aires, Capital Federal
Tel: +54(11) 4788-5400
Fax: +54(11) 4788-5400 Ext. 2557
EMail: comunica@ub.edu.ar; ingresos@ub.edu.ar
Website: http://www.ub.edu.ar

Presidente: Avelino Jose Porto (1964-)
Tel: +54(11) 4576-3928, Fax: +54(11) 4576-3923
EMail: porto@ub.edu.ar

Vicepresidente de Gestión Técnica y Administrativa: Eustaquio
Castro EMail: castro@ub.edu.ar

Departments

Postgraduate Studies and Continuing Education (Business
Administration; Communication Studies; Economics; Finance;
Human Resources; Management; Marketing) *Director*: Carlos
Steiger

Faculties

Agriculture (Agricultural Business; Agriculture) *Dean*: Carlos
Manuel Méndez Acosta; **Architecture and Town Planning**
(Advertising and Publicity; Architecture; Graphic Design; Interior
Design; Town Planning) *Dean*: Mónica Fernández; **Computer
Technology** *Dean*: Juan Ramón Lestani; **Distance Learning
Education** *(2-yr programmes)* (Farm Management; International
Business; Sales Techniques; Small Business; Tourism) *Dean*:
Clara Bonfill; **Economics** (Accountancy; Business Administration;
Economics; Hotel Management; Human Resources; International
Business; Marketing; Sales Techniques) *Dean*: Guillermo Vinitzky;
Engineering (Civil Engineering; Electrical and Electronic Engi-
neering; Engineering; Industrial Engineering; Mechanical Engi-
neering; Telecommunications Engineering) *Dean*: Luis Raul Vaca
Arenaza; **Exact and Natural Sciences** (Biological and Life Sci-
ences; Biology; Chemistry; Food Science; Food Technology;
Natural Sciences; Pharmacy) *Dean*: Marcelo Jorge Vernengo;
Graduate Studies (International Economics; International Relations; Political Sciences; Sociology) *Dean*: Andrés Fontana;
Health Sciences (Health Sciences; Nutrition) *Dean*: Marcelo
Jorge Vernengo; **Humanities** *(Undergraduate)* (Cinema and Tel-
evision; Clinical Psychology; Industrial and Organizational Psychology; Psychology; Public Relations; Radio and Television
Broadcasting; Tourism) *Dean*: Susana Seidmann; **Languages
and Foreign Studies** *(Undergraduate)* (English; Modern Languages; Translation and Interpretation) *Dean*: Raquel Albornoz;
Law and Social Sciences *(Undergraduate)* (International Relations; Journalism; Law; Political Sciences) *Dean*: Juan Ángel
Confalonieri

Schools

Economics and International Business *(Graduate)* (Agricultural
Business; Banking; Business Administration; Economics; Finance;
Human Resources; International Business; Management; Market-
ing) *Dean*: Carlos Steiger

Further Information: Also Study Abroad programmes. Courses for
foreign students

History: Founded 1964. A private institution under the jurisdiction of
the Federal Government.

Governing Bodies: Administrative Board

Academic Year: March to December (March-July; August-
December)

Admission Requirements: Secondary school certificate (bachillerato) or equivalent

Main Language(s) of Instruction: Spanish

Degrees and Diplomas: *Licenciatura*: 4 yrs; *Professional Title*:
Accountancy; Law; Psychology; Teacher Training (secondary level);
Translation, 4 yrs; *Professional Title*: Architecture; Engineering, 5
yrs; *Especialización*; *Maestría*: a further 1-2 yrs and thesis; *Doc-
torado*: Engineering; Political Science; Sociology, 2 yrs following
Mastría or equivalent and thesis. Also Diplomado Internacional en
Management Estratégico

Student Services: Academic counselling, Canteen, Cultural centre,
Employment services, Foreign student adviser, Health services,
Language programs, Social counselling, Sports facilities

Special Facilities: Art Gallery. Agriculture and Livestock
Research Centre. Computer Laboratory. Television Department.
Auditoriums

Libraries: Total, 73,248 vols

Press or Publishing House: Editorial de Belgrano
Last Updated: 26/03/12

UNIVERSITY OF BUSINESS AND SOCIAL SCIENCES
**Universidad de Ciencias Empresariales y Sociales
(UCES)**
Paraguay 1338, 7° Piso, C1057AAV Buenos Aires, Capital Federal
Tel: +54(11) 4815-3290
Fax: +54(11) 4813-5635
EMail: informes@uces.edu.ar
Website: http://www.uces.edu.ar

Rector: Juan Carlos Gómez Barinaga

Secretaria Académica: María Laura Persico
Tel: +54(11) 4815-3290, Ext. 122, Fax: +54(11) 4813-2915
EMail: lpersico@uces.edu.ar

Faculties

Business Administration *Dean*: Juan Carlos Gómez Barinaga;
Economics *Dean*: Jose A. Basso; **Health Sciences** *Dean*: Luis N.
Ferreira; **Law and Political Sciences** *Dean*: Gastón Alejandro
O'Donnell; **Psychology and Social Sciences** *Dean*: Eduardo Said;
Social Communication *Dean*: Enrique Costa Lieste

Further Information: Also Regional Centre in Rafaela

History: Founded 1988.

Governing Bodies: Consejo Superior Académico; Consejo de
Administración

Main Language(s) of Instruction: Spanish

Degrees and Diplomas: *Licenciatura*; *Especialización*; *Maestría*;
Doctorado
Last Updated: 27/02/09

UNIVERSITY OF CONCEPCIÓN DEL URUGUAY
Universidad de Concepción del Uruguay (UCU)
8 de Junio 522, 3260 Concepción del Uruguay, Entre Ríos
Tel: +54(3442) 42-5606
Fax: +54(3422) 42-7721
EMail: info@ucu.edu.ar
Website: http://www.ucu.edu.ar

Rector: Héctor César Sauret
EMail: rectorado@ucu.universia.com.ar

Secretaria Académica: Carolina Thompson
EMail: academica@ucu.edu.ar

Faculties

Agricultural Sciences *Dean*: María del Carmen Blázquez; **Archi-
tecture and Town Planning** (Architecture; Interior Design; Town
Planning) *Dean*: Cristina Bonus; **Communication and Education**
Dean: Luis A. Cerrudo; **Economics** (Accountancy; Administration;
Business and Commerce; Economics; International Business;
Marketing) *Dean*: Marcelo Granillo; **Law and Social Sciences**
Dean: Federico Lacava

Further Information: Also Regional Centres in Gualeguaychú,
Federación, Paraná and Rosario

History: Founded 1969.

Academic Year: February to December

Degrees and Diplomas: *Profesorado*; *Licenciatura*: 5 yrs; *Professional Title*: 6 yrs; *Especialización*; *Maestría*

Libraries: 4,300 vols
Last Updated: 27/02/09

UNIVERSITY OF CONGRESO
Universidad de Congreso
Avenida Colón 90, M5500GEN Mendoza, Mendoza
Tel: +54(261) 423-0630
Fax: +54(261) 423-0630
EMail: ucongreso@ucongreso.edu.ar
Website: http://www.ucongreso.edu.ar

Rector: Daniel Sebastían Pereyra (1999-)
Tel: +54(261) 423-0960 EMail: pereyrad@ucongreso.edu.ar

Vicerrectora de Gestión Académica: Luz Arrigoni de Allamand
EMail: arrigonilm@ucongreso.edu.ar

International Relations: María Landa
EMail: landama@ucongreso.edu.ar

Departments
Business *Director:* Jorge Hermida; **Communication Studies** *Director:* Luz Arrigoni; **Computer Science** *Director:* Fernando Pincirolly; **Environmental Sciences** *Director:* Aldo Rodríguez Salas; **Law**

History: Founded 1989, acquired present status 1994.

Governing Bodies: Consejo Académico Universitario

Academic Year: March to February

Admission Requirements: Secondary school certificate (bachillerato) and competitive entrance examination

Fees: (Pesos): 250 per annum

Main Language(s) of Instruction: Spanish, English and Portuguese

Degrees and Diplomas: *Licenciatura:* Accountancy; Business Administration; Communication; Information Systems; International Relations; Law; Marketing, 4 yrs

Student Services: Academic counselling, Canteen, Cultural centre, Foreign student adviser, Language programs, Sports facilities

Libraries: Yes

Publications: Magazine of Trasandinian Studies *(biennially)*
Last Updated: 27/02/09

UNIVERSITY OF FLORES
Universidad de Flores (UFLO)
Av. Nazca 274, 1406 Buenos Aires, Capital Federal
Tel: +54(11) 4611-4800
Fax: +54(11) 4613-3636
EMail: informes@uflo.edu.ar
Website: http://www.uflo.edu.ar

Rector: Roberto Kertész (1994-)
Tel: +54(11) 4631-4208, Fax: +54(11) 4631-4208
EMail: rkertesz@uflo.edu.ar; rectorado@unflo.edu.ar

Secretaria Académica: Ruth Fische
EMail: Sacademica@uflo.edu.ar

Faculties
Administration (Accountancy; Administration) *Dean:* Haydée Kravetz; **Engineering** (Environmental Engineering; Safety Engineering) *Dean:* Roberto Castro; **Law** (Law) *Dean:* Cecilia Garau; **Physical Education and Sports** (Physical Education; Sports) *Dean:* Jorge Gómez; **Psychology and Social Sciences** (Communication Studies; Psychology) *Dean:* Beatriz Labrit; **Socio-environmental Design** (Architectural and Environmental Design; Architecture and Planning; Graphic Design; Town Planning) *Dean:* Alejandro César Delucchi

Further Information: Also Teaching Hospitals. Branch in Comahue

History: Founded 1994.

Governing Bodies: Consejo Superior

Academic Year: March to December (March-July; August-December)

Admission Requirements: Secondary school certificate (bachillerato); entrance examination for students over 25 without secondary title

Main Language(s) of Instruction: Spanish

Degrees and Diplomas: *Profesorado*; *Licenciatura:* 4 yrs; *Licenciatura:* Administration; Psychology, Psychopedagogy; Sports, 4 yrs; *Professional Title:* Architecture, 6 yrs; *Professional Title:* Environmental Engineering; Law (Lawyer), 5 yrs; *Professional Title:* Graphic Design; Law (Prosecutor), 3 yrs; *Professional Title:* Toxicology, 2 yrs; *Doctorado:* Psychology (PhD), a further 2 yrs and thesis

Student Services: Academic counselling, Canteen, Cultural centre, Handicapped facilities, Health services, Social counselling, Sports facilities

Libraries: Central Library, c. 7,500 vols. Library of ISEDET (adjoining institute), c. 110,000 vols

Press or Publishing House: Editorial UFLO. Editorial IPPEM
Last Updated: 27/02/09

UNIVERSITY OF MENDOZA
Universidad de Mendoza (UM)
Boulogne sur Mer 683, 5500 Mendoza, Mendoza
Tel: +54(261) 420-2017
Fax: +54(261) 420-1100
EMail: rectorado@um.edu.ar
Website: http://www.um.edu.ar

Rector: Juan Carlos Menghini (1993-) Tel: +54(261) 420-0740

Secretario Académico: Carlos Massini Correas
EMail: carlos.massini@um.edu.ar

Faculties
Architecture, Town Planning and Design (Architecture; Design; Interior Design; Textile Design; Town Planning) *Dean:* Ricardo Bekerman; **Engineering** (Bioengineering; Computer Engineering; Electrical and Electronic Engineering; Industrial Engineering; Systems Analysis; Telecommunications Engineering) *Dean:* Salvador B. Navarria; **Health Sciences** *Dean:* Juan Carlos Behler; **Law and Social Sciences** (Law; Social Sciences) *Dean:* Emilio Vazquez Viera

Institutes
Environmental Studies (Environmental Studies)

Further Information: Also branch in San Rafael

History: Founded 1959. A private institution officially recognized by the government.

Governing Bodies: Asamblea Universitaria; Consejo Superior; Consejo Académico

Academic Year: March to November (March-June; August-November)

Admission Requirements: Secondary school certificate (bachillerato) and entrance examination

Main Language(s) of Instruction: Spanish

Degrees and Diplomas: *Licenciatura:* Systems Analysis; *Professional Title:* Architecture; Computer Science; Electronic Engineering; Electrical Engineering, 6 yrs; *Professional Title:* Law, 5 yrs; *Especialización*; *Maestría*; *Doctorado:* Law; Social Sciences, a further 2 yrs by thesis. Also Diplomados

Libraries: Faculty libraries: Law and Social Sciences, c. 14,820 vols; Architecture and Town Planning, c. 5,920 vols; Engineering, c. 4,120 vols

Publications: Revista Idearium (Law and Social Sciences)

Press or Publishing House: Editorial 'Idearium'
Last Updated: 27/02/09

UNIVERSITY OF MORÓN
Universidad de Morón (UM)
Cabildo 134, B1708JPD Morón, Buenos Aires
Tel: +54(11) 5627-2000
Fax: +54(11) 5627-2002
EMail: webmaster@unimoron.edu.ar
Website: http://www.unimoron.edu.ar

Rector: Hector Norberto Porto Lemma (2005-)
Fax: +54(11) 5627-4598
EMail: rectorado@unimoron.edu.ar; coopint@unimoron.edu.ar

Secretario General: José María Baños

International Relations: Alejandro Gavric, Director de la Oficina de Comunicaciones y Relaciones Institucionales
Tel: +54(11) 5627-2000 Ext. 334 EMail: coopint@unimoron.edu.ar

Faculties
Agronomy and Food Science (Agricultural Economics; Agriculture; Agronomy; Farm Management; Food Science) *Dean:* Antonio Angrisani; **Architecture, Design, Art and Town Planning** (Architecture; Design; Interior Design; Theatre; Town Planning; Visual Arts) *Dean:* Oscar Anibal Borracchia; **Computer Science and Communication** (Communication Studies; Computer Science; Technology; Translation and Interpretation) *Dean:* Hugo René Padovani; **Economics and Business** (Business Administration; Business and Commerce; Economics; Human Resources; International Business; Public Relations) *Dean:* Jorge Raúl Lemos; **Engineering** (Civil Engineering; Electrical and Electronic Engineering; Engineering; Industrial Engineering; Surveying and Mapping; Telecommunications Engineering) *Dean:* Oscar Nuñez; **Exact and**

Natural Sciences and Chemistry (Biochemistry; Biology; Biotechnology; Chemistry; Cosmetology; Ecology; Genetics; Natural Sciences; Optics; Pharmacy) *Dean*: Aquiles Carlos Ferranti; **Law, Political and Social Sciences** (International Relations; Law; Notary Studies; Political Sciences; Social Sciences) *Dean*: Bruno Oscar Corbo; **Medicine** (Medicine; Nursing; Nutrition; Physical Therapy; Surgery) *Dean*: Domingo Liotta; **Philosophy, Education and Humanities** (Arts and Humanities; Education; History; Latin American Studies; Literature; Philosophy; Teacher Training) *Dean*: Roberto Mario Paterno; **Sciences Applied to Tourism and Population Studies** (Anthropology; Demography and Population; Food Science; Geography; Hotel Management; Leisure Studies; Physical Education; Sociology; Tourism) *Dean*: Alejandro Fabián Gavric

History: Founded 1960.

Governing Bodies: Consejo Superior

Academic Year: April to November (April-July; August-November)

Admission Requirements: Secondary school certificate (bachillerato)

Main Language(s) of Instruction: Spanish

International Co-operation: With universities in France; Brazil; Mexico; Chile; Germany and Colombia.

Degrees and Diplomas: *Licenciatura*: Advertising; Business Administration; Chemistry; Computer Science; Human Resources; Marketing; Psychology; Public Relations; Taxation; Work Hygiene and Security, 4 yrs; *Licenciatura*: Economics; Education; History; Letters; Philosophy, 4-6 yrs; *Licenciatura*: Pharmacy; Tourism, 5 yrs; *Professional Title*: Accountancy; Business Studies; Law; Social Services, 4 yrs; *Professional Title*: Agronomy; Architecture; Biochemistry; Civil Engineering; Computer Engineering; Electronic Engineering, 5 yrs; *Professional Title*: Graphic Design; Translation, 3 yrs; *Professional Title*: Medicine, 6 yrs; *Professional Title*: Notarial Studies, 2 yrs; *Professional Title*: Surveying; *Especialización*: 1-3 yrs; *Maestría*: 2 yrs; *Doctorado*: Philosophy, by thesis. Also Técnico Universitario in Hotel Management and Tourism, 3 yrs

Student Services: Cultural centre, Employment services, Foreign student adviser, Language programs, Sports facilities

Special Facilities: Scientific and Technical Laboratories. TV and Radio Studio. Engineering laboratories

Libraries: University Library

Publications: UM - Labor *(monthly)*; UM - Saber *(quarterly)*
Last Updated: 27/02/09

UNIVERSITY OF NOTARIAL STUDIES
Universidad Notarial Argentina (UNA)
Avenida 51, N° 435, B1900AVI La Plata, Buenos Aires
Tel: +54(221) 421-9283
Fax: +54(221) 421-0552
EMail: uninotlp@universidadnotarial.edu.ar
Website: http://www.universidadnotarial.edu.ar

Rector: Néstor O. Pérez Lozano
EMail: rector@universidadnotarial.edu.ar

Vicerrectora: Cristina N. Armella

Institutes
Administrative Law (Administrative Law); **Civil Law** (Civil Law); **Commercial Law** (Commercial Law); **Comparative and Integrative Law** (Comparative Law); **Constitutional Law** (Constitutional Law); **Consumer Law** (Consumer Studies); **Copyright** (Law); **Customary Law** (Taxation); **Environmental Law** (Environmental Studies); **International Private Law** (International Law; Private Law); **Justice Studies** (Law); **Law** (Law); **Law and Mass Communication** (Law; Mass Communication); **Minorities Rights** (Demography and Population; Law); **Notarial Computer Systems** (Notary Studies; Software Engineering); **Notarial Further Training** (Notary Studies); **Notarial History** (Notary Studies); **Notarial Law** (Law; Notary Studies); **Notarial Management** (Notary Studies); **Notarial Studies** (Notary Studies); **Public, Provincial, Municipal Law and Town Planning** (Public Law; Regional Planning; Town Planning)

Further Information: Branches in Morón; Corrientes; Paraná; Rosario and Santa Fé

History: Founded 1962 and recognized by the federal government as a private postgraduate institution 1968.

Governing Bodies: Consejo Superior

Academic Year: March to December (March-July; August-December)

Admission Requirements: A University degree (in Law and Social Sciences, Philosophy, Economics)

Main Language(s) of Instruction: Spanish

International Co-operation: With universities in Guatemala, Paraguay and Puerto Rico

Degrees and Diplomas: *Especialización*; *Maestría*; *Doctorado*: by thesis

Student Residential Facilities: Yes

Special Facilities: Museo y Archivo 'Roberto Mario Arata'

Libraries: c. 10,000 vols

Publications: Cuadernos Notariales
Last Updated: 02/03/09

UNIVERSITY OF SALVADOR
Universidad del Salvador (USAL)
Viamonte 1856, C1056ABB Buenos Aires, Capital Federal
Tel: +54(11) 4813-9630
Fax: +54(11) 4812-4625
EMail: uds-rect@salvador.edu.ar
Website: http://www.salvador.edu.ar

Rector: Juan Alejandro Tobías (1985-)
EMail: rect@salvador.edu.ar

Secretario General: Pablo Gabriel Varela
Tel: +54(11) 4813-9630 EMail: uds-secr@salvador.edu.ar

International Relations: Fernando Lucero Schmidt, Vicerrector de Investigación y Desarollo
Tel: +54(11) 4813-1408, Fax: +54(11) 4813-0631
EMail: fernando.lucero.schmidt@salvador.edu.ar

Centres
Technological Applications (Technology) *Director*: Miguel Guerrero

Colleges
Agronomy *(Graduate)* (Agronomy) *Director a/c*: Sebastian Felgueras; **Food Technology** *(Graduate)* *Director a/c*: Sebastian Felgueras; **Veterinary Science** *(Graduate)* (Veterinary Science) *Director*: Liliana Pagliere

Faculties
Administration (Administration; Business and Commerce; Human Resources; Information Technology) *Dean*: Aquilino López Díez; **Economics** (Accountancy; Actuarial Science; Banking; Economics; Finance; International Business; Management; Taxation) *Dean*: Sergio García; **Education and Social Communication** (Advertising and Publicity; Communication Studies; Education) *Dean*: Gustavo Martinez Pandiani; **History, Geography and Tourism** (Arts and Humanities; Environmental Studies; Geography; History; Tourism) *Dean*: Juan Carlos Lucero Schmidt; **Law** (Law) *Dean*: Práxedes Mateo Sagasta; **Medicine** (Medicine) *Dean*: Eduardo Albanese; **Philosophy** *Dean*: Juan Carlos Scannone; **Philosophy and Literature** (English; French; Literature; Philosophy) *Dean*: Ana Zagari; **Psychology and Psychopedagogy** (Educational Psychology; Psychology) *Dean*: Gabriela María Renault; **Science and Technology** (Chemistry; Industrial Engineering; Mathematics; Natural Sciences; Physics; Technology) *Dean*: Miguel Guerrero; **Social Sciences** (International Relations; Political Sciences; Social Sciences; Social Work; Sociology) *Dean*: Eduardo Suárez; **Theology** *(San Miguel)* (Theology) *Dean*: Gonzalo Javier Zarazaga

Institutes
Continuous Training *Director*: Pablo Narvaja; **International Complex Thought** *Director*: Raúl Motta

Research Institutes
Administration (Administration) *Director*: Orlando Farao; **Applied Geomatics** (Surveying and Mapping) *Director a/c*: Horacio Avila; **Drug Dependency** (Toxicology) *Director*: Guillermo Fernández; **East/West Comparative Studies** (Comparative Politics) *Director*: Luisa Rosel; **Economics** (Economics) *Director*: Juan Massot; **Education and Social Communication** (Education; Social Studies) *Director*: Pedro Naón Argerich; **Environment and Ecology**

(Ecology; Environmental Studies) *Director*: Geneviève De Mahieu; **Geopolitics, Defense and Security** (International Relations) *Direction*: José Gabriel Paz; **History and Geography** (Geography; History) *Director*: Abelardo Levalle; **Law** (Law) *Director*: Silvia Tosti; **Linguistics** (Linguistics) *Director*: María Elena Chinunegui; **Medicine** *Director*: Alfonso Albanese; **Philosophy** *Director a/c*: Ana Zagari; **Psychology** (Psychology) *Director*: Alfredo López Alonso; **Psychopedagogic Counselling** (Educational Psychology) *Director*: Gabriela Renault; **Remote Sensors** (Surveying and Mapping) *Director*: Juan Carlos Lucero Schmidt; **Social Sciences** (Social Sciences) *Director*: Pablo Forli; **Tourism** (Tourism) *Director*: Alejandro Torchiaro

Schools

Arts and Architecture (Architecture; Theatre) *Director*: Pablo Beitía; **Oriental Studies** (Asian Studies; Middle Eastern Studies; Oriental Languages) *Director*: Luisa Rosa Rosell

Further Information: Also Hospital. Branch in Pilar

History: Founded 1944 as Instituto Superior de Filosofía, reorganized as faculty 1954 and officially recognized as University 1956. Under the authority of the Society of Jesus, which designates the Rector.

Governing Bodies: Consejo Superior

Academic Year: January to December

Admission Requirements: Secondary school certificate (bachillerato) or equivalent

Fees: (Pesos): 3,600 per annum

Main Language(s) of Instruction: Spanish

International Co-operation: Member of the International Students Exchange Programme (ISEP)

Degrees and Diplomas: *Título Menor*: Teacher Training, 2 yrs; *Licenciatura*: Administration; Economics; English Language; Environmental Sciences; Geography; Human Resources; Information Systems; Music Therapy; Physical Education; Psychopedagogy; Tourism; International Commerce; Dramatic Art, 4 yrs; *Licenciatura*: History; International Relations; Journalism; Letters; Nutrition; Physical Therapy; Political Science; Publicity; Social Service; Sociology; Oriental Studies; Theatre Arts; Commercialization; Speech Therapy and Audiology, 5 yrs; *Professional Title*: Medicine, 6 yrs; *Professional Title*: Odontology; Law; Industrial Engineering; Agricultural Engineering; Veterinary Medicine; Architecture; Psychology; Computer Engineering, 5 yrs; *Professional Title*: Public Accountancy; Actuarial Sciences, 4 yrs; *Especialización*: Legal Medicine; Plastic Surgery; Gastroenterology; Cardiology; Cardiovascular Surgery; Oncology; Radiology; Ophthalmology; Procedural Law; Penal Law; Family Law; Public Management; Environmental Law; Public Services Law; Periodontal Diseases; Psychiatry; Intensive Care; Orthodontics, a further 2 yrs; *Maestría*: Banking Law; International Commerce; Finance; Business; Economy; Taxation; International Relations; Diabetes; Osteopathy; Ocular Diseases; Education; Toxicology; Family Medicine; Office Management; Human Resources; Information; Public Service; Psychiatry; Marketing; Public Administration; Public Security Administration, a further 2 yrs; *Doctorado*: Medicine; Odontology; Political Science; International Relations; Philosophy; Psychology; History; Geography; Letters; English; Penal Law; Social Communication, 2 yrs

Student Services: Academic counselling, Canteen, Cultural centre, Employment services, Foreign student adviser, Foreign Studies Centre, Handicapped facilities, Health services, Language programs, Social counselling, Sports facilities

Special Facilities: Art Gallery. Observatory. Botanical Garden

Libraries: Central Library, c. 400,000 vols

Publications: Ecosignos *(annually)*; Evalu-Acción *(quarterly)*; Oriente y Occidente *(annually)*; Signos Universitarios *(quarterly)*

Academic Staff *2008-2009*	MEN	WOMEN	TOTAL
FULL-TIME	1,162	1,139	**2,301**
PART-TIME	141	148	**289**
STAFF WITH DOCTORATE			
FULL-TIME	53	72	**125**
PART-TIME	91	96	**187**
Student Numbers *2008-2009*			
All (Foreign Included)	7,005	13,300	**20,305**
FOREIGN ONLY	345	518	**863**

Last Updated: 12/12/08

UNIVERSITY OF THE ACONCAGUA
Universidad del Aconcagua (UDA)
Catamarca 129, 5500 Mendoza, Mendoza
Tel: +54(261) 520-1629
Fax: +54(261) 520-1650
EMail: sec-general@uda.edu.ar
Website: http://www.uda.edu.ar

Rector: Osvaldo S. Caballero EMail: rectorado@uda.edu.ar

Secretaria Académica: María Ester Gibbs
EMail: megibbs@uda.edu.ar

Faculties
Economics and Law (Accountancy; Business and Commerce; Economics; Law; Marketing) *Dean*: Rolando Galli Rey; **Medical Sciences** (Gynaecology and Obstetrics; Hygiene; Medicine; Speech Therapy and Audiology) *Dean*: Gustavo Mauricio; **Psychology** (Criminology; Psychoanalysis; Psychology) *Dean*: Hugo Alberto Lupiañez; **Social Sciences and Administration** (Administration; Advertising and Publicity; Computer Science; International Business; Software Engineering; Telecommunications Engineering) *Dean*: Juan Farrés Cavagnaro

Higher Schools
Foreign Languages (English; Modern Languages; Translation and Interpretation) *Director*: Gloria Ginevra

History: Founded 1965.

Main Language(s) of Instruction: Spanish

Degrees and Diplomas: *Licenciatura*: Accountancy; Commerce, 6 yrs; *Licenciatura*: Business Administration, 4 yrs; *Licenciatura*: Psychology, 5 yrs; *Professional Title*: Accountancy, 5 yrs; *Especialización*; *Maestría*

Last Updated: 27/02/09

UNIVERSITY OF THE CINEMA
Universidad del Cine (UCINE)
Pasaje J. M. Giuffra 330, San Telmo, C1064ADD Buenos Aires, Capital Federal
Tel: +54(11) 4300-1413
Fax: +54(11) 4300-0674
EMail: ucine@ucine.edu.ar
Website: http://www.ucine.edu.ar

Rector: Manuel Antín (1991-)
Tel: +54(11) 4300-1581 EMail: m-antin@ucine.edu.ar

Secretaria Académica: Graciela B. Fernández Toledo
EMail: academic@ucine.edu.ar

International Relations: María Marta Antín
EMail: mmantin@ucine.edu.ar

Faculties
Cinema (Cinema and Television; Display and Stage Design; Film) *Dean*: Manuel Antin; **Communication Sciences** (Communication Studies; Distance Education; Graphic Design; Visual Arts) *Dean*: Manuel Antín

History: Founded 1991, acquired present status and title 1993.

Governing Bodies: Consejo Académico

Academic Year: March to December

Admission Requirements: Secondary school certificate (bachillerato)

Fees: (US Dollars): 3,850-5,500 per annum

Main Language(s) of Instruction: Spanish

Degrees and Diplomas: *Licenciatura*: Cinema; Directing; Script Writing; Editing; Production; Design; Educational Process, 5 yrs; *Maestría*

Student Services: Academic counselling, Canteen, Cultural centre, Employment services, Foreign student adviser, Language programs, Social counselling

Special Facilities: Movie Studio

Libraries: Yes (Books, Videos)
Last Updated: 27/02/09

UNIVERSITY OF THE LATIN AMERICAN EDUCATIONAL CENTRE

Universidad del Centro Educativo Latinoamericano (UCEL)

Avenida Pellegrini 1332, S2000BUN Rosario, Santa Fé
Tel: +54(341) 449-9292
Fax: +54(341) 449-1241
EMail: relacionesinternacionales@ucel.edu.ar
Website: http://www.ucel.edu.ar

Rector: Ovidio Torres (2001-) EMail: presidencia@ucel.edu.ar

Secretaria Académica: Stella Maris Requena
EMail: Secacademica@ucel.edu.ar

International Relations: Fanny Godfrid Tel: +54(341) 449-9292

Faculties
Chemistry (Chemistry; Food Technology; Nutrition) *Director*: Armando Hugo Gelai; **Economics and Business Administration** (Business Administration; Business and Commerce; Economics; Hotel Management; Labour and Industrial Relations; Marketing) *Dean*: Rogelio Pontón; **Social Sciences and Law** (English; Law; Social Sciences) *Dean*: Waldo Villalpando

History: Founded 1875. Acquired present status 1993.

Academic Year: March to November

Main Language(s) of Instruction: Spanish

Degrees and Diplomas: *Licenciatura*: Business Administration; Economics and Business; Public Accountancy; Work Relations, 5 yrs; *Licenciatura*: English Language and Literature; Food Technology; *Professional Title*: Chemistry; Food Technology, 5 yrs; *Maestría*
Last Updated: 27/02/09

UNIVERSITY OF THE MERCHANT NAVY

Universidad de la Marina Mercante (UDEMM)

Avenida Rivadavia 2258, 1034 Buenos Aires, Capital Federal
Tel: +54(11) 4953-9000
Fax: +54(11) 4953-9000
EMail: info@udemm.edu.ar
Website: http://www.udemm.edu.ar

Rector: Norberto Fraga
Tel: +54(11) 4953-4952 EMail: udemm@udemm.edu.ar

Secretario General: Mirko E. Mayer

Faculties
Administration and Economics (Accountancy; Administration; Human Resources; International Business; Marine Transport; Marketing; Tourism; Transport and Communications) *Dean*: Silvia Isabel Gómez Meana; **Engineering** (Computer Science; Electrical and Electronic Engineering; Engineering; Hygiene; Mechanical Engineering; Naval Architecture; Systems Analysis) *Dean*: Vicente Giménez; **Humanities and Social Sciences** *Directora (interina)*: Claudia Etkin; **Law, Social Sciences and Communication** (Communication Studies; Human Resources; Law; Management; Public Relations; Tourism)

History: Founded 1968 as private University.

Governing Bodies: Consejo Superior

Main Language(s) of Instruction: Spanish

Degrees and Diplomas: *Licenciatura*: 4 yrs; *Professional Title*: 5 yrs; *Maestría*; *Doctorado*: Marine Administration, by thesis
Last Updated: 27/02/09

UNIVERSITY OF THE SANTO TOMÁS DE AQUINO FRATERNITY

Universidad de las Fraternidades de Agrupaciones 'Santo Tomás de Aquino' (FASTA)

Gascón 3145, 7600 Mar del Plata, Buenos Aires
Tel: +54(223) 491-6418
Fax: +54(223) 493-7460
EMail: informes@ufasta.edu.ar
Website: http://www.ufasta.edu.ar

Rector: Juan Carlos Mena EMail: jcmena@ufasta.edu.ar

Secretario Académico: Jorge Héctor Razul
Tel: +54(223) 493-7425

International Relations: José Miguel Ravasi
EMail: oai@ufasta.edu.ar

Faculties
Economics (Accountancy; Administration; Business and Commerce; Economics) *Dean*: Agustín Enrique Cordero Mujica; **Engineering** (Computer Science; Engineering; Environmental Engineering; Hygiene; Industrial Engineering; Safety Engineering) *Dean*: Roberto Giordano Lerena; **Health Sciences** (Health Sciences; Nutrition; Physical Therapy; Speech Therapy and Audiology) *Dean*: Julia Susana Elbaba; **Law and Social Sciences** (Law; Social Sciences) *Dean*: Silvano Abelardo Penna

Schools
Communication (Communication Studies) *Director*: Daniel Bertagno; **Educational Sciences** *Directora*: Mónica Prieto de Stantien

Further Information: Also Branch in Bariloche

History: Founded 1992.

Main Language(s) of Instruction: Spanish

Degrees and Diplomas: *Licenciatura*: 4-5 yrs; *Professional Title*: Accountancy; Engineering; Law; Teacher Training, 5 yrs
Last Updated: 27/02/09

UNIVERSITY OF THE VALLEY OF THE PLATA

Universidad de la Cuenca del Plata (UCP)

Lavalle 50, 3400 Corrientes, Corrientes
Tel: +54(3783) 43-6236
EMail: informaciones@ucp.edu.ar
Website: http://www.ucp.edu.ar

Rector: Ángel Enrique Rodríguez (1994-)
Tel: +54(3683) 43-6235 EMail: rector@ucp.edu.ar

Vicerrectora Académica: Ana María Petrone de Maló
EMail: viceacademica@ucp.edu.ar

International Relations: Norma Benitez Boulock
EMail: cooperacion@ucp.edu.ar

Faculties
Economics (Accountancy; Administration; International Business) *Dean*: Nelly Ormaechea; **Engineering** (Engineering; Food Technology) *Dean*: María Teresa Sánchez; **Social Sciences** (Advertising and Publicity; Educational Sciences; Journalism; Law; Psychology; Social Sciences) *Dean*: Pedro Pablo Perrotti

Further Information: Also branches in Goya, Posadas and Paso de los Libres

History: Founded 1993.

Governing Bodies: Jean Piaget Foundation Council of Administration; University Council

Academic Year: February to December

Fees: (Pesos): Tuition, 3,420 per annum

Main Language(s) of Instruction: Spanish

Degrees and Diplomas: *Título Menor*: Accountancy; Administration; Advertising and Publicity; Food Technology; International Business; Journalism, 3-4 yrs; *Licenciatura*: Administration; Advertising and Publicity; Educational Sciences; International Business; Journalism; Psychology, 4-5 yrs; *Professional Title*: Accountancy, 4 yrs; *Professional Title*: Food Science; Law, 5 yrs; *Especialización*; *Maestría*

Student Services: Academic counselling, Canteen, Foreign student adviser, Language programs, Social counselling, Sports facilities

Student Residential Facilities: No

Libraries: Two Libraries
Last Updated: 27/02/09

UNIVERSITY OF TORCUATO DI TELLA

Universidad Torcuato di Tella (UTDT)

Miñones 2177, C1428ATG Buenos Aires, Capital Federal
Tel: +54(11) 5169-7000
EMail: rectorado@utdt.edu
Website: http://www.utdt.edu

Rector: Juan Pablo Nicolini (2001-)
Tel: +54(11) 5169-7177 EMail: jnicolini@utdt.edu

Secretaria Académica: Mónica Fiorini
Tel: +54(11) 5169-7196
EMail: mfiorini@utdt.edu; Sacademica@utdt.edu
International Relations: Emily Stern EMail: estern@utdt.edu

Departments
Economics (Economics; Social Sciences) *Director*: Martín Solá;
History (Arts and Humanities; Contemporary History; History;
Modern History) *Director*: Klaus Gallo; **Mathematics and Statistics**
Director: Pablo Azcue; **Philosophy** (Philosophy) *Director*: Gonzalo
Rodriguez-Pereyra; **Political Science and International Studies**
(Government; International Studies; Political Sciences; Social Sci-
ences) *Directora*: Catalina Smulovitz

Schools
Architecture and Urban Studies *Director*: Jorge Francisco Liernur;
Business (Banking; Business Administration; Business and Com-
merce; Economics; Finance; Management; Marketing) *Director*:
Ernesto Schargrodsky; **Government** *Director*: Pablo Guidotti; **Law**
Director: Horacio Spector

Further Information: Also another site in Saenz Valiente

History: Founded jointly by the Foundation and the Instituto Torcuato Di Tella 1991.

Governing Bodies: Board of Trustees

Academic Year: March to December

Admission Requirements: Secondary school certificate and
entrance examination

Fees: (Pesos): 14,400 per annum for Economics; Business; History;
Political Science; International Studies. 11,520 per annum for Law
and Architecture

Main Language(s) of Instruction: Spanish

Accrediting Agencies: CONEAU (Ministerio de Educación, Ciencia y Tecnología)

Degrees and Diplomas: *Licenciatura*: Business; Economics; His-
tory; International Relations; Political Science, 4 yrs; *Professional
Title*: Law; Architecture, 5 yrs; *Especialización*; *Maestría*: Business
Administration; Economics; Educational Administration; Finance;
History; International Studies; Journalism; Law and Economics;
Non-profit Organizations; Public Policy; Urban Economics; History
and Culture of Architecture and Town; *Doctorado*: Economics;
History; Political Science (PhD)

Student Services: Academic counselling, Canteen, Employment
services, Foreign student adviser, Handicapped facilities, Health
services, Sports facilities

Special Facilities: Art Gallery

Libraries: c. 85,000 vols; 1 500 journal titles in traditional format
(paper) and 6,000 titles digital format

Publications: Block - Revista de Arquitectura; Revista Argentina de
Teoría Jurídica; Working Papers CIF

Press or Publishing House: Press Department
Last Updated: 02/03/09

Armenia

STRUCTURE OF HIGHER EDUCATION SYSTEM

Description:

The aim of higher professional education is to provide high quality education and training that meets the needs of the economy. There are state and private HEIs. The two-level (Bachelor-Master) educational system was introduced in 2007. The third level (Aspirantura) is in the process of being reformed.

Stages of studies:

University level first stage: *Bachelor's degree; Medical Doctor*
The Bachelor's degree is awarded to those having completed secondary education and four years of higher education. For medical studies, the Bachelor's degree (Medical Doctor) is awarded after a minimum of 5 years, depending on the specialization.

University level second stage: *Master's degree*
The Master's degree is conferred on those who hold a Bachelor's degree and have completed two further years of higher education. Clinical Ordinate and Pharmaceutics's degrees are granted to those having studied Medicine and completed at least one year of postgraduate study. The Specialist diploma is conferred on those having completed secondary education and five years of higher education. The academic year 2010/2011 saw the award of the last Specialist diplomas.

University level third stage: *Postgraduate Education*
A Researcher's or Candidate of Science (PhD) degree is granted to those who hold a Master's or Specialist Diploma degree upon completion of three years of postgraduate studies. For the Candidate of Science degree, it is necessary to defend a thesis.

Distance higher education:
Distance training is mostly provided by TNE institutions. Applicants must hold a Secondary Education Certificate.

ADMISSION TO HIGHER EDUCATION

Admission to university-level studies:

Name of secondary school credential required: Mijnakarg Yndhanur Krtoutian Attestat

For entry to: Higher education institutions

Alternatives to credentials: Diploma of Vocational Education (Mijin masnagitakan diplom)

Entrance exam requirements: Entrance Examination

Foreign students admission:

Definition of foreign student: A citizen who holds foreign ID and who studies at an Armenian higher education institution.

Quotas: According to international agreements

Entrance exam requirements: Foreign students must hold a secondary school leaving certificate and sit for an entrance examination.

Entry regulations: All foreign candidates must have a residence visa and be recommended by a competent body of their country.

Health requirements: Medical certificate

Language requirements: Armenian and/or Russian language tests.

RECOGNITION OF STUDIES

Bodies dealing with recognition:

National Center for Professional Education Quality Assurance
Executive Director: Ruben Topchyan
22, Orbeli str.
Yerevan
Tel: +374(10) 229 145
Fax: +374(10) 229 148
EMail: info@anqa.am
WWW: http://www.anqa.am/
Services provided and students dealt with: ANQA organizes and implements quality assurance provisions at Armenian tertiary level institutions.

National Information Centre of Academic Recognition and Mobility
Executive Director: Gayane Harutyunyan
27 Amiryan Street
Yerevan
Tel: +374(10) 530 904
Fax: +374(10) 530 904
EMail: armENIC@cornet.am
WWW: http://www.armenic.am/
Deals with credential recognition for entry to institution: Yes
Services provided and students dealt with: NICARM is responsible for academic recognition as well as for provision of information regarding the national and foreign education systems.

Special provisions for recognition:

Recognition for university level studies: The National Information Centre for Academic Recognition and Mobility is responsible for academic and professional recognition. For further information please visit: http://www.armenic.am.

For access to advanced studies and research: The National Information Centre for Academic Recognition and Mobility is responsible for academic and professional recognition. For further information please visit: http://www.armenic.am.

NATIONAL BODIES

Ministry of Education and Science
Minister: Armen Ashotian
Government Building
3, Republic Square
Yerevan
Tel: +374(10) 526 602
Fax: +374(10) 526 484
EMail: edu@edu.am
WWW: http://www.edu.am
Role of national body: Republican body of executive authority, which elaborates and implements the policies of the government of the Republic of Armenia in the education and science sectors.

Council of Rectors of Higher Educational Establishments in Armenia
President: Aram Simonyan
c/o Yerevan State University, Alex Manoogian Street 1
Yerevan 375049
Tel: +374(10) 554 629
Fax: +374(10) 554 641
EMail: rector@ysu.am

Data for academic year: 2011-2012
Source: IAU from National Information Center for Academic Recognition and Mobility, Armenia, 2011

INSTITUTIONS

PUBLIC INSTITUTIONS

ARMENIAN STATE AGRARIAN UNIVERSITY

Hayastani Petakan Agrarayin Hamalsaran (ASAU)
Teryan Street 74, 0009 Yerevan
Tel: +374(10) 524-541
Fax: +374(10) 522-361
EMail: info@armagrar-uni.am
Website: http://www.armagrar-uni.am

Rector: Arshaluys Tarverdyan (1998-) Tel: +374(10) 524-541

Administrative Officer: Yuri Marmaryan
Tel: +374(1) 521-565, Fax: +374(1) 521-565

International Relations: Hovik Sayadyan

Faculties
Agrarian Studies (Agricultural Management; Agriculture; Agrobiology; Forestry; Fruit Production; Plant and Crop Protection; Soil Management; Vegetable Production) *Dean*: G. Sanstrosyan; **Agricultural Mechanization and Transportation** (Agricultural Engineering; Agricultural Equipment) *Dean*: N. Bazikyan; **Economics** (Agricultural Business; Agricultural Economics) *Dean*: L. Margaryan; **Food Stuffs Technology** (Dairy; Fishery; Food Technology; Leather Techniques; Meat and Poultry; Oenology; Packaging Technology) *Dean*: A. Aghababyan; **Land-reclamation, Land Tenure and Land Cadastre** (Soil Conservation; Water Management) *Dean*: S. Ghazaryan; **Veterinary Medicine and Livestock Breeding** (Animal Husbandry; Epidemiology; Parasitology; Veterinary Science; Zoology) *Dean*: A. Vardanyan

Further Information: Also a branch in Vanadzor and Sisian.

History: Founded 1930 as Armenian Agricultural Academy. Acquired present status 1994 and title 2005.

Fees: (US Dollars): foreign students, 1,000-1,200 per annum

Main Language(s) of Instruction: Armenian

International Co-operation: With universities in Russian Federation, Georgia, China, Greece, Israel, USA

Accrediting Agencies: Ministry of Education and Science of Armenia

Degrees and Diplomas: *Bakalavri Vorakavorum*; *Magistrosi Vorakavorum*; *Candidate/Doctor of Science*

Student Services: Academic counselling, Canteen, Employment services, Foreign student adviser, Language programs, Nursery care, Sports facilities

Student Residential Facilities: Yes

Libraries: Yes

ARMENIAN STATE INSTITUTE OF PHYSICAL CULTURE

Phizikakan Culturayi Haykakan Petakan Institut (AIPC)
Alex Manougian Street 11, 375070 Yerevan
Tel: +374(10) 552-431
Fax: +374(10) 554-104
EMail: info@asipc.am
Website: http://www.asipc.am

Rector: Vahram Arakelyan (1998-) Tel: +374(10) 556-281

International Relations: Haroutun Babayan
Tel: +374(10) 554-406

Faculties
Education (Education); **Sports** (Sports)

History: Founded 1945.

Main Language(s) of Instruction: Armenian

Accrediting Agencies: Ministry of Education and Science of Armenia

Degrees and Diplomas: *Bakalavri Vorakavorum*: 4 yrs; *Magistrosi Vorakavorum*: 1 yr. Postgraduate studies, 3 yrs

Student Services: Academic counselling, Canteen, Foreign student adviser, Health services, Sports facilities

Academic Staff *2008*	MEN	WOMEN	TOTAL
FULL-TIME	119	91	210
PART-TIME	11	12	23
Student Numbers *2008*			
All (Foreign Included)	1,752	256	2,008
FOREIGN ONLY	50	1	51

Part-time students, 1,301. **Distance students**, 707.
Last Updated: 09/11/11

ARMENIAN STATE PEDAGOGICAL UNIVERSITY NAMED AFTER KH. ABOVIAN

Kh. Abovyani Anvan Petakan Manakavarzhakan Hamalsaran (ASPU)
Tigran Mets 17, 010 Yerevan
Tel: +374(10) 522-563
Fax: +374(10) 522-563
EMail: info@aspu.am

Rector: Artush Ghukasyan (2003-)
Tel: +374(10) 526-401, Fax: +374(10) 529-747

Rector's Consultant: Nazik Martirosyan
Tel: +374(10) 529-747, Fax: +374(10) 529-747

International Relations: Naira Hakobyan
Tel: +374(10) 522-563, Fax: +374(10) 522-563
EMail: meghu@mail.ru

Centres
Education (Education; Teacher Training); **Logopedics** (Speech Therapy and Audiology) *Dean*: Kim Sarukhanyan

Colleges
Basic Studies *(ASPU Yerevan Basic College SNGO)* (Biology; Mathematics; Physics)

Faculties
Art (Art History; Fine Arts; Painting and Drawing); **Biology, Chemistry and Geography** (Biology; Chemistry; Ecology; Geography); **Culture** (Cultural Studies; Dance; Journalism; Library Science; Museum Studies; Music; Music Education; Musical Instruments; Photography); **Elementary and Special Education** (Educational Psychology; Ergotherapy; Pedagogy; Primary Education; Special Education; Speech Therapy and Audiology); **Foreign Languages** (English; French; German; Modern Languages; Spanish); **History and Law** (History; Law); **Mathematics and Informatics** (Computer Science; Mathematics); **Philology** (Armenian; Literature; Philology; Russian); **Physics and Technology**; **Psychology and Social Pedagogy** (Pedagogy; Psychology; Social Studies)

History: Founded 1922, acquired present status 2008.

Governing Bodies: University Council; Scientific Council of the University; The rectorate of the University; The rector of the University

Academic Year: September to July

Admission Requirements: Secondary school certificate

Fees: (US Dollars): 450-1,000 per annum

Main Language(s) of Instruction: Armenian

Accrediting Agencies: Ministry of Education and Science of Armenia

Degrees and Diplomas: *Bakalavri Vorakavorum*: 4 yrs; *Magistrosi Vorakavorum*: 2 yrs

Student Services: Academic counselling, Canteen, Cultural centre, Employment services, Foreign student adviser, Foreign Studies Centre, Handicapped facilities, Health services, Language programs, Social counselling, Sports facilities

Student Residential Facilities: Yes

Special Facilities: Observatory; Movie Studio; Museum; Art Gallery; Psychological Centre

Libraries: Yes

Publications: Scientific Periodical of Interuniversity Consortium, Related to Pedagogy and Social Psychology

Press or Publishing House: Mankavarzh

Academic Staff 2007-2008	MEN	WOMEN	TOTAL
FULL-TIME	488	494	982
STAFF WITH DOCTORATE			
FULL-TIME	51	8	59
Student Numbers 2007-2008			
All (Foreign Included)	1,662	6,723	8,385
FOREIGN ONLY	–	–	36

Part-time students, 4,400.
Last Updated: 09/11/11

ARMENIAN STATE UNIVERSITY OF ECONOMICS

Hayastani Petakan Tntesagitakan Hamalsaran (ASUE)
Nalbandyan Street 128, 375025 Yerevan
Tel: +374(10) 585-566
Fax: +374(10) 528-864
EMail: rector@asue.am
Website: http://www.asue.am/

Rector: Koryun Atoyan (2011-) Tel: +374(10) 521-720

Faculties
Business and Marketing (Marketing); **Finance** (Accountancy; Finance); **General Economics** (Economics); **Informatics and Statistics** (Economics; Engineering); **Management** (Management); **Traineeship**

History: Founded 1975 as Yerevani Petakan Tntesagitakan Institut (Yerevan State Institute of Economics). Acquired present status and title 2006.

Academic Year: September to July

Fees: (Drams): 400,000 - 450,000 per annum

Main Language(s) of Instruction: Armenian

International Co-operation: With universities in France; Spain; USA; Japan; United Kingdom

Accrediting Agencies: Ministry of Education and Science of Armenia

Degrees and Diplomas: *Bakalavri Vorakavorum*; *Magistrosi Vorakavorum*: Economics; Finance and Credit; Accountancy and Audit; Management; Commerce; Marketing; Statistics; Insurance; Business Administration; Information Systems

Student Services: Academic counselling, Canteen, Health services, Language programs, Social counselling, Sports facilities

Student Residential Facilities: None

Libraries: 197,300 vols

Publications: Economist *(monthly)*

Academic Staff 2007-2008	TOTAL
FULL-TIME	630
PART-TIME	50
STAFF WITH DOCTORATE	
FULL-TIME	310
PART-TIME	c. 50
Student Numbers 2007-2008	
All (Foreign Included)	c. 4,100
FOREIGN ONLY	60

Last Updated: 20/10/11

GYUMRI BRANCH
GYUMRII MASNACHUOH

32 Leningradyan Street, 377526 Gyumri
Tel: +374(312) 370-08

Rector: Samson Davoyan

EUROPEAN REGIONAL EDUCATION ACADEMY

Evropakan Krtakan Taratsashrjanain Akademia (EREA)
10 Davit Anhaght, Zeitun district, 375037 Yerevan
Tel: +374(10) 246-371
Fax: +374(10) 241-891
EMail: info@eriicta.am
Website: http://www.eriicta.am/

Rector: Andranik Avetisyan
Tel: +374(10) 242-746 EMail: rector@eriicta.am

International Relations: Gurgen Vahanyan, Vice-Rector, International Relations
Tel: +374(10) 241-405 EMail: vahanyan@eriicta.am

Departments
Business Management *(Armenian-American joint project)* (Business Administration; Management); **Education Administration** *(Armenian-American joint project with University of Nebraska-Lincoln)* (Educational Administration); **European Law** (European Union Law); **Information Technology** (Information Technology); **International Economics** (International Economics); **International Relations and European Cooperation** (European Languages; International Relations); **Media and Computing** (Computer Science; Media Studies); **Software Engineering** (Software Engineering); **Tourism and Services** (Tourism); **Vocational Linguistics** (Linguistics)

History: Created 2001. Offers both academic and vocational training using both traditional Armenian and European curricula.

Academic Year: September to May

Admission Requirements: Mijnakarg Yndhanur Krtoutian Attestat or equivalent secondary school certificate.

Fees: (US Dollars): 1,300 for home students; 1,850 for overseas students. Some students exempt from fees depending on academic achievement.

Main Language(s) of Instruction: Armenian, English

International Co-operation: With institutions in France, Germany, UK, USA

Accrediting Agencies: Ministry of Education and Science of Armenia; Armenian National Academy of Science

Degrees and Diplomas: *Bakalavri Vorakavorum*: IT Engineering; Software Engineering; Media & Computer Engineering; European Community & Public Law; Tourism; Economics; International Relations; Linguistics, 4 yrs; *Magistrosi Vorakavorum*: Business Administration; Education Administration, 3 yrs; *Magistrosi Vorakavorum*: IT Engineering; Software Engineering; Media & Computer Engineering; European Community & Public Law; Tourism; Economics; International Relations; Linguistics, 2 yrs

Student Services: Academic counselling, Canteen, Cultural centre, Employment services, Foreign student adviser, Foreign Studies Centre, Health services, Language programs, Social counselling, Sports facilities

Academic Staff 2010-2011	TOTAL
FULL-TIME	100
PART-TIME	c. 75
Student Numbers 2010-2011	
All (Foreign Included)	c. 2,000
FOREIGN ONLY	85

Last Updated: 21/10/11

FRENCH UNIVERSITY OF ARMENIA

Hayastani Fransiakan Hamalsaran
David Anhaght Street 10, 375069 Yerevan
Tel: +374(10) 249-661
Fax: +374(10) 249-645
EMail: info@ufar.am
Website: http://www.ufar.am

Rector: Joëlle Le Morzellec
Tel: +374(10) 249-644 EMail: recteur@ufar.am

Faculties
Economics (Economics); **Law** (Law); **Management** (Management)
History: Founded 2000.

Accrediting Agencies: Ministry of Education and Science of Armenia

Degrees and Diplomas: *Bakalavri Vorakavorum*; *Magistrosi Vorakavorum*

Last Updated: 07/06/11

GAVAR STATE UNIVERSITY
Gavari Petakan Hamalsaran (GSU)
Azatutian Avenue 1, 378630 Gavar, Gegharkunik Region
Tel: +374(10) 282-075
Fax: +374(10) 282-075
EMail: info@gsu.am
Website: http://gsu.am/

Rector: Ruzanna Hakobyan (2006-)
Tel: +374(10) 282-075 +374(10) 557-056
EMail: Rusakob@yahoo.com

Vice-Rector: Varazdat KarapetyanFax: +374(264) 22-466

Faculties
Economics (Accountancy; Economics; Finance; Management) *Dean*: Samvel Amirkhanyan; **Education** *(Part-time) Dean*: Nelli Kutuzyan; **Humanities** (Arts and Humanities; History; Law; Pedagogy) *Dean*: Hamlet Ghajoyan; **Natural Sciences** (Biology; Computer Science; Ecology; Geography) *Dean*: Martin Avagyan; **Philology** (English; German; Native Language; Philology; Russian) *Dean*: Viktor Katvalyan

History: Founded 1993.

Academic Year: September to June

Admission Requirements: Secondary school certificate and state entrance examination

Main Language(s) of Instruction: Armenian

Accrediting Agencies: Ministry of Education and Science

Degrees and Diplomas: *Bakalavri Vorakavorum*: 4 yrs. Also Diplomavorvats Masnaget, 5 yrs

Student Services: Academic counselling, Canteen, Health services, Sports facilities

Student Residential Facilities: None

Special Facilities: Language laboratory; Movie facilities

Libraries: Library and reading room, c. 21,800 vols, magazines, encyclopedias in Armenian, Russian and English

Publications: Collection of Scientific Papers, in Armenian and Russian *(annually)*

Last Updated: 21/10/11

GORIS STATE UNIVERSITY
Gorisi Petakan Hamalsaran
Avangard Street, House 4, 3204 Goris, Syunik Region
Tel: +374(284) 22-767
Fax: +374(284) 23-603
EMail: karapetyandiana@rambler.ru
Website: http://www.spyur.am/gorissu.htm

Rector: Yuri Safaryan

Departments
Arts and Humanities (Arts and Humanities); **Education** (Education; Pedagogy; Primary Education; Secondary Education; Teacher Training); **Engineering** (Economics; Electronic Engineering; Engineering; Industrial Engineering; Mathematics)

History: Founded 1967 acquired present status 1984.
Last Updated: 26/03/08

GYUMRI STATE PEDAGOGICAL INSTITUTE NAMED AFTER M. NALBANDIAN
Gyumrii M. Nalbandiani Anvan Petakan Mankavaržhakan Institut (GSPI)
Paruir Sevak Street 4, 377526 Gyumri, Shirak Region
Tel: +374(312) 37-732
Fax: +374(312) 32-199
EMail: pedinst@gspi.am
Website: http://www.gspi.am

Rector: Vardevan Grigoryan Tel: +374(312) 32-199

First Vice-Rector: Razmik Matevosian EMail: gspi@gspi.am

International Relations: Sergey Hairapetyan

Faculties
Foreign Languages (Modern Languages); **History and Philology** (History; Philology); **Natural Sciences and Geography** (Geography; Natural Sciences); **Pedagogy** (Pedagogy); **Physical Education** (Physical Education); **Physics and Mathematics** (Mathematics; Physics)

History: Founded 1934.

Accrediting Agencies: Ministry of Education and Science of Armenia

Academic Staff *2010-2011*: Total: c. 250
Student Numbers *2010-2011*: Total: c. 2,400
Distance students, 700.
Last Updated: 20/10/11

RUSSIAN-ARMENIAN (SLAVONIC) STATE UNIVERSITY
Rus-Haikakan (Slavonakan) Hamalsaran (RAU)
Hovsep Emina Street 123, 375051 Yerevan
Tel: +374(10) 277-052
Fax: +374(10) 289-701
EMail: rectorat@rau.am
Website: http://www.rau.am

Rector: Armen Darbinyan (2001-)
Tel: +374(10) 229-254 +374(10) 289-700, Fax: +374(10) 221-463
EMail: laghajanyan@rambler.ru

Vice- Rector: Gagik Sargsyan
Tel: +374(10) 269-701, Fax: +374(10) 269-701
EMail: gzsarg@rau.am

International Relations: Emma Yeghiazaryan
Tel: +374(10) 270-523, Fax: +374(10) 289-701

Faculties
Applied Mathematics and Information Technologies (Applied Mathematics; Information Technology) *Dean*: Vladimir Yeghiazaryan; **Biological Medicine** (Biology; Medicine) *Dean*: Hrachik; **Economics** (Economics) *Dean*: Albert Vardanyan; **Foreign Languages** (Foreign Languages Education) *Dean*: Armine Simoyan; **Journalism** (Journalism) *Dean*: Rafael Grigoryan; **Law** (Law) *Dean*: Karen Sardaryan; **Philology** (Philology) *Dean*: Ahaida Khachikyan; **Physics and Engineering** (Engineering; Physics) *Dean*: Stepan Petrosyan; **Political Science** (Political Sciences) *Dean*: Ashot Engoyan; **Psychology** (Psychology) *Dean*: Asya Berberyan; **Tourism and Advertising** (Advertising and Publicity; Tourism) *Dean*: Nina Kevorkova

History: Founded 1998 following the agreement between the Governments of Russian Federation and Armenia. Acquired present status 2000.

Academic Year: September to June

Admission Requirements: Secondary school certificate

Fees: (US Dollars): 900-2,500

Main Language(s) of Instruction: Russian

International Co-operation: With universities in Russian Federation, Armenia and Europe

Accrediting Agencies: Ministry of Education and Science of the Republic of Armenia and the Russian Federation

Degrees and Diplomas: *Bakalavri Vorakavorum*: Law; Physics; Mathematics; Economics; Journalism; Political Sciences; Phillology; Psychology, 4 yrs; *Bakalavri Vorakavorum*: Tourism; International Relations; Medical Biotechnology; Bioengineering; Advertising; *Magistrosi Vorakavorum*: Ecomomics; Political Science; Journalism; Electronics and Microelectronics; Law, 2 yrs; *Candidate/Doctor of Science*: Economics; Law; Applied Mathematics and Information Technologies; Political Sciences; Journalism; Biochemistry; Organic Chemistry; Semiconductor Physics, 3 yrs

Student Services: Canteen, Cultural centre, Employment services, Health services, Language programs, Sports facilities

Student Residential Facilities: none

Special Facilities: Concert hall; Museum; Park

Libraries: c. 65,000 vols; Electronic library; Net services

Publications: Vestnik, Scientific Magazine *(biennially)*

Academic Staff *2008-2009*	MEN	WOMEN	TOTAL
FULL-TIME	89	114	203
PART-TIME	206	182	388
STAFF WITH DOCTORATE			
FULL-TIME	72	44	116
PART-TIME	140	59	199
Student Numbers *2008-2009*			
All (Foreign Included)	1,076	1,510	2,586
FOREIGN ONLY	244	329	573

Last Updated: 21/10/11

STATE ENGINEERING UNIVERSITY OF ARMENIA

Hayastani Petakan Tchartaragitakan Hamalsaran (SEUA)

Teryan Street 105, 0009 Yerevan
Tel: +374(10) 524-629
Fax: +374(10) 545-843
EMail: rector@seua.am
Website: http://www.seua.am

Rector: Vostanik Marukhyan

Academic Secretary: Henry Balabanyan
Tel: +374(1) 525-997 EMail: hbalabanyan@seua.am

International Relations: Maria Mangasarova, Head of International Office Tel: +374(1) 567-968 EMail: intof@seua.am

Departments

Chemical Technology and Environmental Engineering *Dean*: Artashes Tadevosyan; **Computer Systems and Informatics** (Computer Science) *Dean*: Samvel Soghomonyan; **Cybernetics** *Dean*: Gurgen Bareghamyan; **Electrical Engineering** *Dean*: Souren Hovsepyan; **Engineering Graphics** *Dean*: Kolya Soghomonyan; **Machine Building** (Machine Building) *Dean*: Armen Arshakyan; **Mathematics** *Dean*: Vanik Zakaryan; **Mechanics and Machine Study** *Dean*: Karen Arzumanyan; **Mining and Metallurgy** (Metallurgical Engineering; Mining Engineering) *Dean*: Spartak Mamyan; **Physics** *Dean*: Ashot Khachatryan; **Power Engineering** (Environmental Engineering; Power Engineering) *Dean*: Hambardzum Hovsepyan; **Radio Engineering and Communication Systems** (Telecommunications Engineering) *Dean*: Haikaz Stepanyan; **Social Sciences and Languages** *Dean*: Edik Kyureghyan; **Transportation Systems** *Dean*: Gagik Moussaelyan

History: Founded 1933, acquired present status 1991.

Governing Bodies: Council; Academic Council; Rectorate; Student Council

Academic Year: September to June (September-January; February-June)

Admission Requirements: Secondary school certificate and entrance examination

Fees: (US Dollars): Tuition for local students per annum, Undergraduate, 800-1,050, graduate (Master) 1,050-1,200, Postgraduate 700. Tuition for foreign students per annum: Preparatory programme 1,300, Undergraduate 1,300-2,100, Graduate (Master or Doctoral Level) 2,900

Main Language(s) of Instruction: Armenian, English or Russian for foreigners

International Co-operation: With universities in the USA, United Kingdom, Italy, Sweden, Germany, France, Greece, Russian Federation, Czech Republic, etc.

Accrediting Agencies: Ministry of Education and Science of Armenia

Degrees and Diplomas: *Bakalavri Vorakavorum*: Biological and Life Sciences; Engineering (Electricical Engineering, Electronics, Power Engineering; Environment, Automation and Control, Materials, Information Technologies, Biomedicine, Mining, Metallurgy, Mechanics); Engineering Management and Economics; Transport and Communications; Applied Mathematics, 4 yrs; *Magistrosi Vorakavorum*: Biological and Life Sciences, Engineering (Electrical Engineering, Electronics, Power Engineering, Environment, Automation and Control, Materials, Information Technologies, Biomedicine, Mining, Metallurgy, Mechanics), 2 yrs; *Magistrosi Vorakavorum*: Engineering

Management and Economics; Transport and Communications; Applied Mathematics; Sociology; *Candidate/Doctor of Science*: Engineering (Chemistry, Biotechnology, Environment, Electric al Engineering, Electronics, Power Engineering, Information Technologies, Automation and Control, Mechanics, Mining, Metallurgy) (PhD); Mathematics; Engineering Management; Economics; Transport and Communications (PhD), 3 yrs. Also Junior Engineer Degree, 3 yrs

Student Services: Academic counselling, Canteen, Cultural centre, Foreign student adviser, Foreign Studies Centre, Health services, Nursery care, Sports facilities

Student Residential Facilities: Under construction

Libraries: c. 1,200,000 vols and periodicals

Publications: Bulletin of State Engineering University of Armenia *(annually)*; Bulletin of the National Academy of Sciences and the State Engineering University of Armenia *(quarterly)*; Mathematics in Higher School *(quarterly)*; Modeling, Optimization and Control, Selected scientific articles *(biennially)*

Academic Staff *2008*	MEN	WOMEN	TOTAL
FULL-TIME	360	540	900
Student Numbers *2008*			
All (Foreign Included)	7,850	2,900	10,750
FOREIGN ONLY	350	65	415

Last Updated: 20/10/11

GYUMRI CAMPUS

GYUMRII MASNACHUGH (SEUAGC)

Mkrtchyan Street 2, 377526 Gyumri
Tel: +374(312) 31-528
Fax: +374(312) 31-528
EMail: seuagec@shirak.am

Director: Vahagn Shahbazyan (2000-)

Departments

General Engineering (Chemistry; Mathematics; Mechanics; Modern Languages; Physics) *Dean*: Hovhannes Engoyan, **Specialized Engineering** (Automation and Control Engineering; Clothing and Sewing; Economics; Electrical Engineering; Engineering; Leather Techniques; Management; Textile Technology; Transport Engineering) *Dean*: Alexan Arzoumanyan

KAPAN CAMPUS

KAPANI MASNACHUGH (SEUAKC)

Arzumanyan Street 11, 377810 Kapan
Tel: +374(285) 66-761
Fax: +374(285) 67-923
EMail: seua@syunik.am

Director: Seyran Balasanyan (1998-)

Departments

General Education *Dean*: Vachagan Yepremyan; **Specialized Engineering** *Dean*: Anik Yeghiazaryan

History: Founded 1995.

VANADZOR CAMPUS

VANADZORI MASNACHUGH (SEUAVC)

116, Mashtots Street, 375200 Vanadzor
Tel: +374(322) 56-704
EMail: seuavan@freenet.am

Rector: Mikael Simonyan

Departments

General Engineering (Arts and Humanities; Graphic Arts; Mathematics; Mechanics; Physics; Sports) *Dean*: Armen Kharatyan; **Specialized Engineering** (Automation and Control Engineering; Chemical Engineering; Civil Engineering; Machine Building; Textile Technology) *Dean*: Misha Symonyan

VANADZOR STATE PEDAGOGICAL INSTITUTE NAMED AFTER HOVHANNES TOUMANYAN

Vanadzori Hovhannes Toumanyani anvan Petakan Mankavaržakan Institut (VSPI)
Tigran Mets Street 36, 377200 Vanadzor, Lori Region
Tel: +374(322) 46-387
Fax: +374(322) 41-856
EMail: rector@vspi.am
Website: http://www.vspi.am

Rector: Gurgen Khachatryan (2006-)
EMail: gxchatryan@yahoo.com

Vice-Rector: Susanna Toumanyan
Tel: +374(322) 43-114 EMail: stoumanyan@vspi.am

International Relations: Sirapi Arustamyan, Department Manager
Tel: +374(322) 41-853 EMail: foreign@vspi.am

Faculties

Biology and Chemistry (Biology; Chemistry; Ecology; Natural Sciences; Pharmacology; Physical Education; Physics; Sports) *Dean*: Zaruhi Vardanyan; **History and Geography** (Cultural Studies; Geography; History; Management; Social Work) *Dean*: Samvel Jhamharyan; **Pedagogy** (Educational Psychology; Fine Arts; Music Education; Painting and Drawing; Pedagogy; Preschool Education; Primary Education) *Dean*: Tereza Shahverdyan; **Philology** (Armenian; English; Journalism; Philology; Russian; Translation and Interpretation) *Dean*: Albert Poghosyan; **Physics and Mathematics** (Applied Mathematics; Computer Science; Mathematics; Physics; Technology) *Dean*: Sergei Kharatyan

History: Founded 1969.

Governing Bodies: Academic Council; Academic Board

Admission Requirements: Secondary school certificate and entrance examination

Fees: (US Dollars): 500-900 per annum

Main Language(s) of Instruction: Armenian

Accrediting Agencies: Ministry of Education and Science of Armenia

Degrees and Diplomas: *Bakalavri Vorakavorum (BA)*: 4 yrs; *Magistrosi Vorakavorum (MA)*: 2 yrs. Also Dotori Astichan, 3 yrs

Student Services: Canteen, Language programs, Nursery care, Sports facilities

Libraries: Yes

Publications: Apaga Mankavarjh, Institute Newspaper *(monthly)*

Press or Publishing House: Yes

Academic Staff 2010-2011	MEN	WOMEN	TOTAL
FULL-TIME	136	177	313
PART-TIME	1	5	6
Student Numbers 2010-2011			
All (Foreign Included)	–	–	2,197
FOREIGN ONLY	–	–	25

Distance students, 1,882.
Last Updated: 22/06/11

YEREVAN KOMITAS STATE CONSERVATORY

Yerevani Komitasi Anvan Petakan Conservatoria (YKSC)
1A, Sajat-Nova Street, 0001 Yerevan
Tel: +374(10) 581-164
Fax: +374(10) 563-540
EMail: yksc@conservatory.am
Website: http://www.conservatory.am/

Rector: Sergey Sarajyan

Assistant to Rector: Shushanik Mehrabyan
Tel: +374(10) 581-290

International Relations: Arkadi Avanesov, Vice-Rector

Faculties

Orchestra (Musical Instruments) *Dean*: Eduard Tatevosyan; **Piano** (Musical Instruments) *Dean*: Igor Yavryan; **Vocal Theory** (Conducting; Music Theory and Composition; Singing) *Dean*: David Ghazaryan

History: Founded 1921.

Academic Year: September to June

Admission Requirements: Secondary school certificate

Fees: (Drams): Local students, c. 600,000 per annum; Foreign students, c. 900,000 per annum

Main Language(s) of Instruction: Armenian

Accrediting Agencies: Ministry of Education and Science of Armenia

Degrees and Diplomas: *Bakalavri Vorakavorum*: 4 yrs; *Magistrosi Vorakavorum*: 2 yrs. Also Certificate of Postgraduate Studies in Musicology, a further 3 yrs

Student Services: Academic counselling, Canteen, Foreign student adviser, Foreign Studies Centre, Language programs, Social counselling, Sports facilities

Libraries: Yes

Publications: Yeražshtakan Hayastan *(quarterly)*

Academic Staff 2010-2011	TOTAL
FULL-TIME	490
PART-TIME	33
Student Numbers 2010-2011	
All (Foreign Included)	1,180
FOREIGN ONLY	151

Last Updated: 14/09/11

GYUMRI CAMPUS

GYUMRII MASNACHUOH (YSCGC)

Ankakhutyan Square 1, 377526 Gyumri
Tel: +374(312) 36-937

Rector: Karine Avdalyan

History: Founded 1997.

YEREVAN STATE ACADEMY OF FINE ARTS

Yerevani Gegharvesti Petakan Academia (YSAFA)
Isahakyan Street 36, 375009 Yerevan
Tel: +374(10) 560-726
Fax: +374(10) 542-706
EMail: ysifa@edu.am
Website: http://www.iatp.am/yafa

Rector: Aram Issabekyan (1994-) Tel: +374(10) 560-726

International Relations: Marianna Nalbandyan
Tel: +374(1) 567-981 EMail: n_manan@yahoo.com

Faculties

Applied Arts and Design (Computer Graphics; Design; Fashion Design; Fine Arts; Graphic Arts; Handicrafts; Sculpture) *Dean*: Avertik Avetsyan; **Fine Arts** (Art History; Fine Arts; Graphic Arts; Painting and Drawing; Sculpture) *Dean*: Edvard Vardanyan

History: Founded 1945 as Yerevan State Institute of Fine Arts, acquired present status and title 1999.

Accrediting Agencies: Ministry of Education and Science of Armenia

Degrees and Diplomas: *Bakalavri Vorakavorum*; *Magistrosi Vorakavorum*

Last Updated: 20/10/11

DILIJAN MASNACHUOH

Getapnya Street 18, Dilijan
Tel: 374 (680) 61-84

Dean: Ghazar Ghazaryan

Divisions

Applied Arts and Handicrafts (Fine Arts; Handicrafts)

History: Founded 1999.

Degrees and Diplomas: *Bakalavri Vorakavorum*; *Magistrosi Vorakavorum*

GYUMRII MASNACHUOH

Ankakhutyan Street 1, Gyumri
Tel: +374(312) 22-355
EMail: gcca@shirak.am

Dean: Hambarcum Ghukasyan (1997-) Tel: +374(322) 22-355

Divisions
Fine Arts (Fashion Design; Graphic Arts; Handicrafts; Metal Techniques; Painting and Drawing; Sculpture)

History: Founded 1997.

International Co-operation: With universities in Bulgaria, Italy, Russian Federation

Degrees and Diplomas: *Bakalavri Vorakavorum*; *Magistrosi Vorakavorum*

YEREVAN STATE INSTITUTE OF THEATRE AND CINEMA

Yerevani Tatroni ev Kinoi Petakan Institut (YSITC)
Amiryan Street 26, 375002 Yerevan
Tel: +374(10) 536-221
Fax: +374(10) 536-233
EMail: bccp@arminco.com

Rector: Armen Mazmanyan Tel: +374(10) 536-221

International Relations: Artur Ghukasyan

Departments
Arts and Humanities *Head:* Laura Muradyan; **Cinematography** *Head:* Rudolf Vatinyan; **Stage Speech, Vocal, Dance and Movement** (Dance; Speech Studies) *Head:* Alexander Kocharyan; **Theatre Acting and Directing** (Acting; Display and Stage Design; Theatre) *Head:* Nikolay Tsaturyan; **Theatre Criticism and Art History** (Art Criticism; Cinema and Television; Theatre) *Head:* Suren Hasmikyan

Further Information: Also branches in Gyumri and Goris

History: Founded 1944, acquired present status and title 1997.

Governing Bodies: Rector; Vice-Rectors of Educational-Scientific Affairs and Financial Affairs; Deans of Departments

Academic Year: September to June

Admission Requirements: Secondary school certificate; College graduation or diploma of other institution

Fees: (US Dollars): Residents, 500-750 per annum; Non-residents, 1,000-1,400

Main Language(s) of Instruction: Armenian

Accrediting Agencies: Ministry of Education and Science of Armenia

Degrees and Diplomas: *Bakalavri Vorakavorum*: Acting (Theatre and Cinema, Musical Theatre, Puppet Theatre, Marionette Theatre, Mime); Directing (Theatre, Documental Film, Film, Mass Events, TV, Photography, Dance); Arts Management; Theatre and Cinema Criticism; Stage Design (BA), 4 yrs; *Magistrosi Vorakavorum*: Cinema Criticism; Theatre Criticism; Arts Management; Directing (MA), a further 2 yrs; *Candidate/Doctor of Science*: Theatre; Arts Criticism (PhD), 2 yrs

Student Services: Academic counselling, Canteen, Cultural centre, Foreign student adviser, Foreign Studies Centre, Handicapped facilities, Health services, Language programs, Nursery care, Social counselling, Sports facilities

Student Residential Facilities: None

Special Facilities: Gallery Hall; Student Theatre; Cinema Hall

Libraries: Movie, Photo, Phonogram and Book Libraries

Publications: Arvest, Scientific and Art Criticism articles *(monthly)*; Handes, Scientific articles *(annually)*

Academic Staff *2007-2008*	TOTAL
FULL-TIME	150
PART-TIME	50
STAFF WITH DOCTORATE	
FULL-TIME	c. 20

Student Numbers *2007-2008*	
All (Foreign Included)	c. 540
FOREIGN ONLY	20

Last Updated: 16/12/08

VANADZOR BRANCH
VANADZOR MASNACHUOH (YSITCVB)

Taterakan Square 3a, Vanadzor
Tel: +374(322) 44-773

Director: Hakob Azizyan (2003-)

Departments
Acting (Acting)

History: Founded 2003.

YEREVAN STATE LINGUISTIC UNIVERSITY 'V. BRUSOV'

Yerevani V. Brusovi Anvan Petakan Lezerabanakan Hamalsaran (YSLU)
42 Toumanyan Street, 375002 Yerevan
Tel: +374(10) 530-552
Fax: +374(10) 530-552
EMail: yslu@brusov.am
Website: http://www.brusov.am

Rector: Suren Zolyan (1997-)
Tel: +374(10) 530-552 EMail: zolyan@brusov.am

Vice-Rector for Legal, Administrative and Economic Affairs: Gabriel Kimi Balayan
Tel: +374(10) 534-172, Fax: +374(10) 585-554
EMail: gabrbal@brusov.am

International Relations: L. Fljyan, Vice Rector for Science and International Relations
Tel: +374(10) 533-331 EMail: vicerector_si@brusov.am

Faculties
Foreign Languages (Arabic; Dutch; English; Foreign Languages Education; French; German; Greek; Hindi; Italian; Japanese; Korean; Linguistics; Modern Languages; Pedagogy; Persian; Portuguese; Slavic Languages; Spanish); **Linguistics and Intercultural Communication** (Chinese; Communication Studies; English; French; German; Italian; Journalism; Linguistics; Persian; Political Sciences; Psychology; Spanish; Tourism; Translation and Interpretation; Turkish); **Russian Language, Literature and Foreign Languages** (Communication Studies; Literature; Russian; Translation and Interpretation)

History: Founded 1935. Acquired present status and title 2000.

Governing Bodies: Council; Scientific Council

Academic Year: September to June

Admission Requirements: Secondary school certificate

Fees: (Drams): c. 350,000 per annum

Main Language(s) of Instruction: Armenian, Russian

Accrediting Agencies: Ministry of Education and Science of Armenia

Degrees and Diplomas: *Bakalavri Vorakavorum*; *Magistrosi Vorakavorum*; *Doctor of Science*

Student Services: Academic counselling, Canteen, Cultural centre, Health services, Language programs, Social counselling, Sports facilities

Special Facilities: Laboratory

Libraries: Yes

Publications: Newspapers; Research Papers

Academic Staff *2010-2011*	TOTAL
FULL-TIME	350
PART-TIME	70
STAFF WITH DOCTORATE	
FULL-TIME	110
PART-TIME	c. 40

Student Numbers *2010-2011*	
All (Foreign Included)	c. 3,180
FOREIGN ONLY	40

Last Updated: 20/10/11

YEREVAN STATE MEDICAL UNIVERSITY M. HERATSI

Yerevani M. Heratsu Anvan Petakan Bjshkakan Hamalsaran (YSMU)
2 Koryun Street, 0025 Yerevan
Tel: +374(10) 582-532
Fax: +374(10) 582-532
EMail: info@ysmu.am
Website: http://www.ysmu.am

Rector: Derenik H. Dumayan (2011-)
Tel: +374(10) 581-802, Fax: +374(10) 581-802
EMail: rector@ysmu.am

Vice-Rector for Academic Affairs: Samvel A. Avetisyan

International Relations: Yervand S. Sahakyan, Vice-Rector for International Relations
Tel: +374(10) 560-594, Fax: +374(10) 529-605
EMail: international@ysmu.am

Faculties
General Medicine (Medicine) Dean: Samvel A. Avetisyan; **Military Medicine** (Medicine) Dean: Samvel G. Galstyan; **Pharmacy** (Pharmacy) Dean: Hasmik Hasratyan; **Public Health** (Public Health); **Stomatology** (Stomatology) Dean: Karine Baroyan

History: Founded 1920, acquired present status and title 1995.

Governing Bodies: University Council; Rector

Academic Year: September to June (September-January; February-June)

Admission Requirements: Secondary school certificate

Main Language(s) of Instruction: Armenian, Russian, English

Accrediting Agencies: Ministry of Education and Science of Armenia

Degrees and Diplomas: Bakalavri Vorakavorum: General Medicine; Magistrosi Vorakavorum: Pharmacy, 6 yrs; Candidate/Doctor of Science: Stomatology (PhD). Also Post-Doctoral degrees of 'Professor'

Student Services: Academic counselling, Canteen, Cultural centre, Foreign student adviser, Health services, Language programs, Nursery care, Social counselling, Sports facilities

Student Residential Facilities: Yes

Special Facilities: Scientific Laboratory; University Museum

Libraries: Yes

Publications: Apaga Bjisk-Future Doctor (monthly); Hajastani Bjshkagitutjun-Medical Science of Armenia (quarterly); Medicus (monthly); The New Armenian Medical Journal (quarterly)

Academic Staff 2010-2011	MEN	WOMEN	TOTAL
FULL-TIME	–	–	344
PART-TIME	–	–	524
STAFF WITH DOCTORATE			
FULL-TIME	–	–	217
PART-TIME	–	–	213
Student Numbers 2010-2011			
All (Foreign Included)	1,959	2,455	4,414
FOREIGN ONLY	435	382	817

Last Updated: 21/10/11

YEREVAN STATE UNIVERSITY

Yerevani Petakan Hamalsaran (YSU)
Alex Manoogian Street 1, 0025 Yerevan
Tel: +374(10) 554-629
Fax: +374(10) 554-641
EMail: pr-int@ysu.am; international@ysu.am
Website: http://www.ysu.am

Rector: Aram Simonyan (2006-)
Tel: +374(10) 554-629, Fax: +374(10) 554-641
EMail: rector@ysu.am

International Relations: Gegham G. Gevorgyan, Vice-Rector for Scientific Policy and Int Cooperation (2008-)
Tel: +374(10) 554-702, Fax: +374(10) 554-641
EMail: ggg@ysu.am

Faculties
Armenian Philology (Armenian; Literature; Pedagogy; Philology) Dean: Artsrun Avagyan; **Biology** (Biochemistry; Biology; Biophysics; Botany; Ecology; Genetics; Microbiology; Physiology; Plant and Crop Protection; Zoology) Dean: Emil Gevorgian; **Chemistry** (Analytical Chemistry; Chemistry; Inorganic Chemistry; Organic Chemistry; Pharmacology) Dean: Aida Avetisyan; **Computer Science and Applied Mathematics** (Applied Mathematics; Computer Science; Software Engineering; Systems Analysis) Dean: Vahram Dumanyan; **Economics** (Business and Commerce; Economics; Finance; International Economics; Management; Mathematics) Dean: Haik Sarkissian; **Geography and Geology** (Ecology; Environmental Studies; Geochemistry; Geography; Geology; Geophysics; Mineralogy; Petrology; Surveying and Mapping) Dean: Marat Grigiryan; **History** (Archaeology; Art History; Cultural Studies; Ethnology; History) Dean: Hayk Avetisyan; **International Relations** Dean: Gegham Petrosyan; **Journalism** (Journalism; Radio and Television Broadcasting) Dean: Naghash Martirosyan; **Law** (Civil Law; Constitutional Law; Criminal Law; European Union Law; International Law; Law) Dean: Gagik Ghazinyan; **Mathematics and Mechanics** (Mathematics; Mechanics) Dean: Artush Sahakyan; **Oriental Studies** (Arabic; Cultural Studies; Middle Eastern Studies; Oriental Languages; Turkish) Dean: Gurgen Melikyan; **Philosophy and Psychology** (Ethics; Logic; Philosophy; Psychology) Dean: Hrachik Mirzoyan; **Physics** (Applied Mathematics; Applied Physics; Astrophysics; Nuclear Physics; Optics; Physics; Solid State Physics) Dean: Roland Avagyan; **Radiophysics** (Applied Mathematics; Astrophysics; Microelectronics; Microwaves; Radiophysics) Dean: Yuri Vardanyan; **Romance and Germanic Philology** (English; Germanic Languages; Literature; Philology; Romance Languages; Translation and Interpretation) Dean: Karapet Karapetyan; **Russian Philology** (Comparative Literature; Grammar; Journalism; Linguistics; Literature; Russian; Translation and Interpretation) Dean: Pavel Balayan; **Sociology** (Social Work; Sociology) Dean: Arthur Mkrtchyan; **Theology** (History of Religion; Theology) Dean: Ter Anushavan Bishop Jamkochyan

History: Founded 1919.

Governing Bodies: Academic Council

Academic Year: September to June (September-January; February-June)

Admission Requirements: Competitive entrance examination following general or special secondary school certificate

Fees: (US Dollars): None for 70% of students; for others: c. 600 per annum

Main Language(s) of Instruction: Armenian

Accrediting Agencies: Ministry of Education and Science of Armenia

Degrees and Diplomas: Bakalavri Vorakavorum: 4 yrs; Magistrosi Vorakavorum: a further 2 yrs; Candidate/Doctor of Science: a further 3 yrs

Student Services: Health services, Sports facilities

Student Residential Facilities: For 900 students

Special Facilities: History Museum; Geology Museum

Libraries: University Library, c. 2m. vols

Publications: Transactions (quarterly)

Academic Staff 2008-2009: Total 1,500
Student Numbers 2010-2011: Total 19,289
Last Updated: 20/10/11

IJEVAN BRANCH

IJEVAN MASNACHUOGH

Usanoghakan Street 3, 377260 Ijevan
Tel: +374(63) 32-202

Director: Samvel Arakelyan (2000-)

Faculties
Applied Arts Dean: Spartak Sargsyan; **Economics** (Economics) Dean: Artak Djagaryan; **Humanities** (Arts and Humanities) Dean: Vardan Alexanyan; **Natural Sciences** (Natural Sciences) Dean: Artak Tsutsulyan

History: Founded 1994.

Governing Bodies: Council; Academic Council

Academic Year: September to June (September-January; February-June)

YEREVAN STATE UNIVERSITY OF ARCHITECTURE AND CONSTRUCTION

Yerevani Tchartarapetutyan ev Shinararutyan Institut (YSUAC)
Terian Street 105, 375009 Yerevan
Tel: +374(10) 547-425
Fax: +374(10) 587-284
EMail: manager@ysuac.am
Website: http://www.ysuac.am

Rector: Hovhannes Vache Tokmajyan Tel: +374(10) 583-773

Vice Rector Academic Affairs: Arkadi Barkhudaryan

Faculties
Architecture (Architecture) *Dean:* Tigran Barseghyan; **Construction Technology** (Construction Engineering); **Hydrotechnical Construction and Municipal Services** (Building Technologies; Hydraulic Engineering; Urban Studies); **Industrial and Civil Construction** (Construction Engineering) *Dean:* Hrant Tsolak Poghosyan; **Transport Construction** (Transport Engineering)

History: Founded 1921, acquired present status and title 1989.

Governing Bodies: Board of Trustees

Academic Year: September to August

Admission Requirements: Secondary school certificate or university diploma and entrance examination

Fees: (US Dollars): Tuition for foreign students only: Preparatory Group, 600 per annum; Faculty of Architecture, 900 per annum; other faculties, 800 per annum; Postgraduate Course, 1,000 per annum

Main Language(s) of Instruction: Armenian, Russian, French

Accrediting Agencies: Ministry of Education and Science of Armenia

Degrees and Diplomas: *Magistrosi Vorakavorum:* Architecture, 6 yrs; *Magistrosi Vorakavorum:* Construction Technology; Hydrotechnical Construction and Urban Economy; Industrial and Civil Construction; Transport Construction, 5 yrs

Student Services: Canteen, Cultural centre, Health services, Language programs, Social counselling, Sports facilities

Student Residential Facilities: Yes

Libraries: 1,373,300 vols

Publications: Proceedings of the Institute Scientific Workers and Professor Staff *(annually)*; Proceedings of the Institute Young Scientific Workers and Post-graduates *(annually)*

Last Updated: 20/10/11

PRIVATE INSTITUTIONS

AMERICAN UNIVERSITY OF ARMENIA

Hayastani Amerikyan Hamalsaran (AUA)
40 Marshal Baghramyan Avenue, 0019 Yerevan
Tel: +374(10) 512-525
Fax: +374(10) 512-512
EMail: info@aua.am
Website: http://www.aua.am

President: Bruce M. Boghosian EMail: president@aua.am

Provost (Acting): Armen Der Kiureghian Tel: +374(10) 512-526

International Relations: Rebecca Carter, Registrar/Director of Student Affairs Tel: +374(10) 512-794

Centres
Business Research and Development (Business Administration; Management) *Director:* Rubina Ohanian; **Engineering Research** (Engineering) *Director:* Kenell Touryan; **Environmental Con**servation and Research *Director:* Jennifer Lyman; **Health Services Research and Development** (Health Sciences) *Director:* Varduhi Petrosyan; **Legal Research** (Law) *Director:* Tom Samuelian; **Policy Analysis** *(Turpanjian)* (Political Sciences) *Director:* Lucig Danielian; **Research and Development in Applied Linguistics and Language Teaching** (English; Linguistics) *Director:* Sivakumar Sivasubramaniam

Colleges
Engineering (Engineering) *Assistant Dean:* Aram Hajian; **Health Sciences** (Health Sciences) *Dean:* Robert Bagramian

Departments
English (English) *Dean:* Antony Kunnan; **Law** (Law) *Dean:* Tom Samuelian

Schools
Business and Management *Dean:* Rubina Hanian; **Political Science and International Affairs** (International Relations; Political Sciences; Public Administration) *Dean:* Lucig H. Danielian

Further Information: Branch in Oakland, California (USA)

History: Founded 1991. An Institution of Graduate Studies.

Governing Bodies: Board of Trustees

Academic Year: February to November (February-May; June-August; September-November)

Admission Requirements: Undergraduate degree. English language proficiency (TOEFL = 550), GRE or GMAT

Fees: (US Dollars): Tuition, 10,800 per annum

Main Language(s) of Instruction: English

Accrediting Agencies: Western Association of Schools and Colleges 5WASC)

Degrees and Diplomas: *Magistrosi Vorakavorum:* Business Administration; Computer and Information Science; Engineering and Systems Management; Law; Political Science and International Affairs; Public Health, 2 yrs. Also Certificates in Teaching English as a Foreign Language , 1 yr; Certificate in Public Health, 1 yr

Student Services: Academic counselling, Canteen, Employment services, Handicapped facilities, Health services, Language programs

Special Facilities: Computer Laboratories. Videoconference Room

Libraries: Papazian Library, c. 38,490 vols; subscription to 25 databases and electronic journals

Academic Staff 2011	TOTAL
FULL-TIME	30
PART-TIME	60
STAFF WITH DOCTORATE	
FULL-TIME	20
PART-TIME	c. 40

Student Numbers 2011	
All (Foreign Included)	c. 260
FOREIGN ONLY	30

Last Updated: 07/06/11

AMIRDOVLAT AMASIATSI MEDICAL INSTITUTE

Amirdovlat Amasiatsi Bgskakan Institute
Tigran Mets Street 30a, Vanadzor, Lori Region
Tel: +374(10) 74-70-40
Fax: +374(10) 74-70-35

Rector: Vatchik Brutyan

Programmes
Dental Technology (Dental Technology); **Medicine and Stomatology** (Medicine; Stomatology); **Nursing** (Nursing)

History: Founded 1996 by Mkhitar Gosh Armenian-Russian International University.

Last Updated: 09/11/11

ARMENIAN INSTITUTE OF ECOLOGY, ECONOMICS AND LAW,

Yerevani Ecologuiayi, Tntesagitutyan ev Iravunqi Haykakan Institut
Hakob Hokobyan 3, 0028 Yerevan
Tel: +374(10) 27-19-05

Rector: Hamlet Zakaryan

Programmes

Ecology (Ecology); **Economics** (Economics); **Law** (Law)

History: Founded 1992. Acquired present status 2002.

Accrediting Agencies: Ministry of Education and Science of Armenia

Degrees and Diplomas: Diploma Specialst in Ecology and Journalism

Last Updated: 09/11/11

ARMENIAN MEDICAL INSTITUTE

Haikakan Bžhshkakan Hamalsaran (AMI)
Titogradyan 14, 375087 Yerevan
Tel: +374(10) 451-923; +374(10) 470-844
Fax: +374(10) 451-923
EMail: info@armedin.com; ami@web.am
Website: http://www.armedin.com/

Rector: Mushegh Astabacyan

Programmes

Medicine (Medicine); **Stomatology** (Stomatology)

History: Founded 1990. Acquired present status 2001.

Fees: (US Dollars): 800 per annum

Main Language(s) of Instruction: Armenian, Russian

Accrediting Agencies: Ministry of Education and Science of Armenia

Degrees and Diplomas: Degrees in Medicine (6 yrs) and Stomatology (5 yrs)

Student Services: Academic counselling, Canteen, Employment services, Sports facilities

Last Updated: 09/11/11

ARTASHAT 'ARTASHAT' UNIVERSITY

Artashati 'Artashat' Hamalsaran
Isakov 47a, Artashat, Ararat Region
Tel: +374(235) 2-38-28

Rector: Artak Yeghikyan

Programmes

Education (Education; Pedagogy; Primary Education); **Finance and Credit** (Finance); **Journalism** (Journalism); **Law** (Law)

History: Founded 1996.

Degrees and Diplomas: *Bakalavri Vorakavorum*

Last Updated: 18/12/08

EURASIA INTERNATIONAL UNIVERSITY

Yevrasia Mijazgain Hamalsaran (EIU)
Azatutyan Ave. 24/2, 0014 Yerevan
Tel: +374(10) 299-088 +374(10) 249-438
Fax: +374(10) 249-438
EMail: info@eiu.am
Website: http://www.eiu.am/

Rector: Souren Hekim Ohanyan (1996-)
Tel: +374(10) 249-438 EMail: president@eiu.am

Vice Rector for Academic Affairs: A. Aghabekyan
EMail: vp@eiu.am

Faculties

Foreign Languages (English; French; German; Modern Languages; Spanish); **Law** (Law); **Management** (Finance; Management)

History: Founded 1996 as Mkhitar Gosh Migazgain Hamalsaran - Yerevan. Acquired present status 2001 and title 2004.

Governing Bodies: University Council

Academic Year: September to May (September-December; February-May)

Admission Requirements: Secondary school certificate and entrance examination

Fees: (Drams): 250,000

Main Language(s) of Instruction: Armenian; English

International Co-operation: With universities in Bulgaria and Ukraine

Accrediting Agencies: Ministry of Education and Science of Armenia

Degrees and Diplomas: *Bakalavri Vorakavorum*; *Magistrosi Vorakavorum*

Student Services: Academic counselling, Canteen, Health services, Sports facilities

Student Residential Facilities: University hostel

Special Facilities: University Museum

Libraries: Library and electronic library

Publications: Periodical of Conference Articles, Scientific articles *(biennially)*

Last Updated: 09/11/11

FINANCIAL ACADEMY

Finansakan Akademia
Pushkin Street 25/3, 375010 Yerevan
Tel: +374(10) 538-607
Fax: +374(10) 539-148
EMail: ges@finacademy.am
Website: http://www.finacademy.am

Rector: Eduard Gasparyan
Tel: +374(10) 539-148 EMail: rector@finacademy.am

Director: Karen Gasparyan

Programmes

Accounting (Accountancy); **Finance** (Finance)

History: Founded 1999 as Banking Economical Institute. Acquired present title and state status 2001.

Governing Bodies: President of the Academy

Admission Requirements: Atestat

Main Language(s) of Instruction: Armenian, Russian

International Co-operation: Participates in the Erasmus programme

Accrediting Agencies: Ministry of Education and Science of Armenia

Degrees and Diplomas: *Bakalavri Vorakavorum*: Finance; Accounting, 4 yrs; *Magistrosi Vorakavorum*: Finance; Accounting, 2 yrs; *Candidate/Doctor of Science*: Accounting

Student Services: Cultural centre, Health services, Language programs, Sports facilities

Student Residential Facilities: Yes

Libraries: Yes

Publications: Finansist Magazine

Academic Staff *2008*	MEN	WOMEN	TOTAL
FULL-TIME	2	10	**12**
STAFF WITH DOCTORATE			
FULL-TIME	14	28	**42**
Student Numbers *2008*			
All (Foreign Included)	165	320	**485**
FOREIGN ONLY	–	–	**1**

Part-time students, 62.
Last Updated: 09/11/11

GORIS SYUNIQ INSTITUTE

2, Kapan highway, Goris
Tel: +374(284) 229- 97

Rector: Gravik Babayan

Programmes

Finance (Banking; Finance); **Law**
Last Updated: 09/11/11

GRIGOR LUSAVORICH UNIVERSITY OF EDZMIATSIN

Spandayryan 1b, Edzmiatsin
Tel: +374(321) 432-58
EMail: sarineht@mail.ru

Head: Khachatur Harutyunyan

Programmes
Accounting

Degrees and Diplomas: Diploma Specialist: Accounting and Auditing
Last Updated: 09/11/11

GYUMRI IMASTASER ANANIA SHIRAKATSI UNIVERSITY

Gyumrii Imastaser Anania Shirakatsi Hamalsaran
Sayat-Nova Street 1, 377500 Gyumri, Shirak Region
Tel: +374(312) 39-394
Fax: +374(312) 33-015
EMail: roman@gyumri.am
Website: http://www.iasu.am

Rector: Robert Manvelyan

Pro-Rector: Levon Manandyan

International Relations: Gayane Grigoryan, Lecturer
Tel: +374(312) 4-06-75 EMail: gayaneg73@yahoo.com

Faculties
Economics (Economics; Management; Marketing) *Head*: Laura Nazaryan; **Languages** (Armenian; English; French; Modern Languages) *Dean*: Lyord Mkhoyan; **Law** (Civil Law; Law) *Head*: Lena Hovhannisyan; **Philology** (Armenian; English; French; Literature; Philology) *Head*: Marietta Khachatryan

History: Founded 1991. Acquired present status 2001.

Main Language(s) of Instruction: Armenian

Accrediting Agencies: Ministry of Education and Science of Armenia

Degrees and Diplomas: *Bakalavri Vorakavorum*: Philology, Law, Economics, Computer Science, 4 yrs

Student Services: Academic counselling, Canteen, Cultural centre, Language programs, Nursery care

Libraries: 17.000 vols. (of which 13.000 concern Modern Literature)

Publications: Anania Shirakatsi, Newspaper *(monthly)*
Last Updated: 09/11/11

GYUMRI PROGRESS UNIVERSITY

Gyumrii Progres Hamalsaran
Tigran Mets Street 1, 3101 Gyumri, Shirak Region
Tel: +374 (312) 25-180 +374 (312) 35-735
Fax: +374 (312) 30-222
EMail: Progress_am@rambler.ru

Rector: Rafik Khachatryan

Vice-Rector: Karen Tonoyan

Colleges
Medical (Dentistry; Nursing; Pharmacy)

Departments
Design (Design); **Pedagogy** (Pedagogy; Teacher Trainers Education)

Schools
Biochemistry (Biochemistry); **Dentistry** (Dentistry; Oral Pathology); **Economics** (Accountancy; Economics; Finance); **Journalism** (Journalism); **Law** (Law); **Pedagogy** (Pedagogy); **Philology** (Armenian; English; Philology); **Psychology** (Psychology)

History: Founded 1990. Acquired present status 2001.

Governing Bodies: Rector; Scientific Council

Admission Requirements: Armenian Secondary school certificate

Fees: (Drams): 150,000-225,000 per annum

Main Language(s) of Instruction: Armenian

Accrediting Agencies: Ministry of Education and Science of Armenia

Degrees and Diplomas: *Bakalavri Vorakavorum*: 4-5 yrs

Student Services: Academic counselling, Canteen, Cultural centre, Foreign student adviser, Health services, Language programs, Nursery care, Social counselling, Sports facilities

Student Residential Facilities: Free residence for students and staff

Libraries: Library and reading hall for students and staff

Academic Staff 2007-2008	TOTAL
FULL-TIME	70
PART-TIME	10
STAFF WITH DOCTORATE	
FULL-TIME	50
PART-TIME	5

Last Updated: 15/12/08

HRAZDAN INSTITUTE OF HUMANITIES

Hrazdani Humanitar Institut (HIH)
Hrazdan Centre, Kotayk Region, 2301 Hrazdan
Tel: +374(223) 255-18
Fax: +374(223) 255-18
EMail: hrhumanitar@mail.ru
Website: http://www.hinstitute.am/

Rector: Liparit Arakelyan (1996-)
Tel: +374(223) 2-55-18 EMail: liparitar@mail.ru

Executive Director: Gohar Danielyan EMail: gohardaniel@mail.ru

International Relations: Christine Ghazaryan
EMail: kristarm@mail.ru

Programmes
Economics (Economics; Finance) *Dean*: Karlen Ghulyan; **Jurisprudence** (Law) *Dean*: Henrik Harutyunyan; **Pedagogy** (Education; Educational Sciences; Pedagogy) *Dean*: Vilem Sahakyan

History: Founded 1996. Acquired present status 2002.

Governing Bodies: Administrative Board

Academic Year: September to June

Admission Requirements: Secondary school certificate and entrance examination

Main Language(s) of Instruction: Armenian

International Co-operation: With universities in Russian Federation and USA

Accrediting Agencies: Ministry of Education and Science of Armenia

Degrees and Diplomas: *Bakalavri Vorakavorum (BA; BS)*: 4 yrs; *Magistrosi Vorakavorum (MA; MS)*: 2 yrs following Bakalavri Kochum

Student Services: Academic counselling, Canteen, Cultural centre, Foreign student adviser, Language programs, Social counselling, Sports facilities

Student Residential Facilities: None

Libraries: c. 32,600 vols

Publications: Newspaper *(quarterly)*

Academic Staff 2010-2011	MEN	WOMEN	TOTAL
FULL-TIME	45	27	72
STAFF WITH DOCTORATE			
FULL-TIME	35	16	51
Student Numbers 2010-2011			
All (Foreign Included)	248	356	604

Distance students, 128.
Last Updated: 23/05/11

HUMANITY UNIVERSITY OF YEREVAN

Amiryan 26, Yerevan
Tel: +374(10) 530-973
Fax: +374(10) 530-973

Rector: Michael Amirxanyan

Programmes
Translation Studies (Translation and Interpretation)
Degrees and Diplomas: *Bakalavri Vorakavorum*
Last Updated: 10/11/11

INSTITUTE OF FORENSIC EXPERTISE AND PSYCHOLOGY

Azpat-Veteran Datakan Porcagitutyan ev Hogebanutyan Institut
Hanrapetutyan Street 2-19, 0010 Yerevan
Tel: +374(10) 525-787
EMail: tadevosyangroup@mail.ru

Head: Azat Tadevosyan

Executive Director: Jevon Tadevosyan

Programmes
Forensic Expertise and Psychology (Forensic Medicine and Dentistry; Psychology)

History: Acquired present status 2002.

Accrediting Agencies: Ministry of Education and Science of Armenia

Student Services: Academic counselling, Canteen, Employment services, Health services, Language programs, Nursery care, Sports facilities
Last Updated: 15/12/08

INTERLINGUA LINGUISTIC UNIVERSITY OF YEREVAN

Yerevani Interlingva Lezvagitakan Hamalsaran
Pushkin Street, 21, 0010 Yerevan
Tel: +374(10) 526-307
Fax: +374(10) 586-072
EMail: inlingua@arminco.com

Rector: Iveta Arakelyan

Programmes
Foreign Language (English; Modern Languages; Philology); **Translation** (English; French; Spanish; Translation and Interpretation)

History: Founded 1996. Acquired present status 2002.

Main Language(s) of Instruction: Armenian

Accrediting Agencies: Ministry of Education and Science of Armenia

Degrees and Diplomas: *Bakalavri Vorakavorum*; *Magistrosi Vorakavorum*
Last Updated: 09/11/11

INTERNATIONAL ACCOUNTANCY TRAINING CENTER (IATC)

Charenci 1, 0025 Yerevan
Tel: +374(10) 575-940 +374(10) 575-238
Fax: +374(10) 574-579
EMail: info@iatc.am
Website: http://www.iatc.am/

Executive Director: Hasmik Sahakyan

Head, Administration: Knarik Mkrtchyan **EMail:** admin@iatc.am

Courses
English (English)

Programmes
Accountancy, Audit and Financial Management (Accountancy; Finance)

History: Founded 1998.

Degrees and Diplomas: *Magistrosi Vorakavorum*

Student Numbers *2010-2011*: Total: c. 300
Last Updated: 10/11/11

LORIS KALASHYANI ARMENIAN OPEN UNIVERSITY

Loris Kalashyani Anvan Haykakan Bats Hamalsaran
Griboedov 15, 0051 Yerevan
Tel: +374(10) 576-036
Fax: +374(10) 576-036
EMail: openuni@academedu.org
Website: http://www.academedu.org

Rector: Artush Harutyunyan

Faculties
Applied Arts (Applied Mathematics; Design; Interior Design; Textile Technology); **Humanities** (English; Fashion Design; Fine Arts; Foreign Languages Education; French; German; International Relations; Pedagogy; Philology; Psychology; Spanish); **Law and Economics** (Accountancy; Business Administration; Computer Engineering; Economics; Law; Management)

History: Founded 1991. Acquired present status 2001. Joined with Yerevan Haybusak University, International Relations Institute after H. Lazaryan, and Yerevan Haybusak University base College into a structure called International Academy of Education (IAE) 2006.

Main Language(s) of Instruction: Armenian

Accrediting Agencies: Ministry of Education and Science of Armenia
Last Updated: 15/12/08

MKHITAR GOSH ARMENIAN-RUSSIAN INTERNATIONAL UNIVERSITY

Vanadzori Mkhitar Gosh hay-rusakan Midjazgayn Hamalsaran
Tigran Mets Street 30A, Vanadzor, Lori Region
Tel: +374(10) 74-7040
EMail: mguniv@mail.com
Website: http://www.mkhitargosh.com

Rector: Vatchik Brutyan

Programmes
Education (Education; Pedagogy; Primary Education); **Foreign Languages** (English; French; German; Modern Languages); **Law** (Law); **Management** (Management)

History: Founded 1996. Acquired present status 2002.

Accrediting Agencies: Ministry of Education and Science of Armenia

Degrees and Diplomas: *Bakalavri Vorakavorum*; *Magistrosi Vorakavorum*
Last Updated: 09/11/11

NATIONAL ACADEMY OF FINE ARTS

Gegecik Arvestneri Azgain Academia
Komitas Street 37, Yerevan
Tel: +374(10) 230-089
EMail: geghecik_arvestner@yahoo.com

Rector: Edward Setrakyan (1996-)

Programmes
Design (Design; Fine Arts)

History: Founded 1996. Acquired present status 2002.

Fees: (Dram): 130,000 (College)-230,000 (Academy) per semester

Main Language(s) of Instruction: Armenian; Italian; Russian

International Co-operation: With universities in Italy and Russian Federation

Accrediting Agencies: Ministry of Education and Science of Armenia

Degrees and Diplomas: *Bakalavri Vorakavorum*

Student Services: Academic counselling, Cultural centre
Last Updated: 09/11/11

NORTH UNIVERSITY
Hyusisain Hamalsaran
Alek Manougyan Street 15/9, 0070 Yerevan
Tel: +374(10) 573-317
EMail: hyusisayin@gmail.com
Website: http://www.northern.am/en/

Rector: Boris Makichyan

Programmes
Economics and Management (Business Administration; Economics; Management); **Accounting** (Accountancy); **Computer Science** (Computer Science; Software Engineering); **Education** (Education; Pedagogy; Primary Education); **Foreign Languages** (English; French; Modern Languages); **Journalism** (Journalism); **Law** (Law)

History: Founded 1996. Acquired present status 2002.

Accrediting Agencies: Ministry of Education and Science of Armenia

Degrees and Diplomas: *Bakalavri Vorakavorum*
Last Updated: 09/11/11

PEDAGOGICAL INSTITUTE OF VARDENIS NAMED AFTER V. HAMBARDZUMYAN
Azgaldyan 7, +374(269) 249-05 Vardenis

Programmes
Armenian Language and Literature (Armenian; Literature); **History** (History); **Teacher's Training** (Pedagogy; Primary Education; Teacher Training)

Degrees and Diplomas: *Bakalavri Vorakavorum*
Last Updated: 10/11/11

ROSLIN ART INSTITUTE
Yerevani Roslin Arvesti Institut
Malkhasyan 25, Yerevan
Tel: +374(2) 236-220 +374(10) 237-386
Fax: +374(10) 235-895
EMail: roslin@freenet.am

Rector: Khachik Khachiki Samvelyan

Programmes
Design (Advertising and Publicity; Design; Fine Arts; Graphic Design; Industrial Design; Interior Design; Packaging Technology; Textile Design)

History: Founded 1992.

Fees: (Drams): c. 200,000 per

Main Language(s) of Instruction: Armenian

Degrees and Diplomas: *Bakalavri Vorakavorum*; *Magistrosi Vorakavorum*
Last Updated: 09/11/11

UNIVERSITY OF CULTURE
Sebastia 3A, Yerevan
Tel: +374(10) 741-848

Rector: Knarik Bleyan

Programmes
Cultural Studies (Dance; Folklore; Music; Musical Instruments; Singing); **Design** (Design; Industrial Design; Interior Design)

History: Founded 1996.

Degrees and Diplomas: *Bakalavri Vorakavorum*
Last Updated: 10/11/11

UNIVERSITY OF ECONOMY AND LAW AFTER AVETIK MKRTCHYAN
Avetik Mkrtchyan Tntesairavagitakan Hamalsaran
Khorhrdarani Street 32/1, 0015 Yerevan
Tel: +374(10) 569-161 +374(10) 569-163
Fax: +374(10) 569-162
EMail: info-mtih@mail.ru; l.mkrtchyan@edu.mtih.am
Website: http://mtih.croncms.com

President: Laura Mkrtchyan EMail: laura.mkrtchyan@mtih.am

Departments
Finance (Finance); **Foreign Languages and Language Teaching Methods** (English; Foreign Languages Education; Modern Languages); **International Relations** (International Relations); **Law** (Law); **Mathematics, Natural Science and Technology** (Mathematics; Natural Sciences; Technology); **Pedagogy** (Education; Pedagogy; Primary Education; Teacher Training); **Psychology** (Psychology)

History: Founded 1990 as Yerevani Tntesairavagitakan Hamalsaran (Yerevan University of Economics and Law). Acquired present status 2001. Acquired present title 2008.

Accrediting Agencies: Ministry of Education and Science of Armenia

Degrees and Diplomas: *Bakalavri Vorakavorum*; *Magistrosi Vorakavorum*
Last Updated: 09/11/11

UNIVERSITY OF TRADITIONAL MEDICINE
Avandakan Bžhshkutyan Hamalsaran
Avan, Babajanyan Street 38A, 375040 Yerevan
Tel: +374(10) 616-470
EMail: tradmeduni@mail.ru
Website: http://www.tradmed-uni.am/

Rector: Norik Kh. Saribekyan
Tel: +374(10) 616-290 EMail: saribekyan@tradmed-uni.am

Vice-Chacellor for Training: Vahagn P. Kirakosyan

Vice-Chancellor for Scientific activity: Inna G. Persoyan
EMail: inna_persyan@list.ru

Departments
Traditional Medecine (Acupuncture; Homeopathy; Physical Therapy; Traditional Eastern Medicine)

Programmes
Clinical Medicine (Dermatology; Epidemiology; Forensic Medicine and Dentistry; Gynaecology and Obstetrics; Medicine; Ophthalmology; Otorhinolaryngology; Paediatrics; Psychiatry and Mental Health; Psychology; Rehabilitation and Therapy; Stomatology; Surgery) *Dean*: Sahakanush Arustamyan; **Humanities and Socioeconomic Sciences** (Armenian; Arts and Humanities; Economics; English; History; Latin; Law; Modern Languages; Philosophy; Social Studies; Terminology) *Dean*: Amalya Grigoryan; **Medical and Biological Sciences** (Anatomy; Biological and Life Sciences; Biology; Embryology and Reproduction Biology; Epidemiology; Histology; Hygiene; Immunology; Medicine; Pharmacology; Physics; Physiology; Social and Preventive Medicine; Virology) *Dean*: Susanna Sargsyan; **Natural and Scientific Studies** (Biochemistry; Chemistry; Mathematics; Medicine; Natural Sciences; Pharmacology) *Dean*: Razmik Mkhitaryan; **Stomatology N1** (Orthodontics; Stomatology) *Head*: Vahagan Kirakosyan; **Stomatology N2** (Orthopaedics; Stomatology) *Head*: Gohar Gevorgyan; **Surgery** (Oncology; Orthopaedics; Surgery; Urology) *Head*: Gagik Mkrtchyan; **Therapeutic Studies** (Endocrinology; Nursing; Pharmacology) *Dean*: Hasmik Matevosyan

History: Founded 1991. Acquired present status 2001.

Academic Year: From September to June (Sep-Jan; Apr-June)

Main Language(s) of Instruction: Armenian

Accrediting Agencies: Ministry of Education and Science of Armenia

Degrees and Diplomas: *Bakalavri Vorakavorum*: Medicine; Stomatology; *Magistrosi Vorakavorum*: Medicine; Stomatology

Student Services: Academic counselling, Canteen, Foreign student adviser, Language programs, Nursery care

Libraries: Yes

Academic Staff *2010-2011*: Total: c. 80
Student Numbers *2010-2011*: Total: c. 300
Last Updated: 08/11/11

USEL UNIVERSITY
Usel Hamalsaran
Koryuni Street, House 23, 0009 Yerevan
Tel: +374(10) 529-397
EMail: info@usel.am
Website: http://www.usel.am/

Rector: Dayana Moskovyan

Programmes
Economics (Economics); **Foreign Languages** (Modern Languages); **Journalism** (Journalism); **Law** (Law)

History: Founded 1991 as Grigor Zohrab University. Acquired present status and title 2006.

Degrees and Diplomas: *Bakalavri Vorakavorum*; *Magistrosi Vorakavorum*
Last Updated: 09/11/11

YEREVAN AGRICULTURAL UNIVERSITY / YEREVAN INSTITUTE OF APPLIED BIOTECHNOLOGY
Yerevani Gyughatntesakan Hamalsaran / Yerevani Kirarakan Biotechnologaji Institut
Futchiki 27/5, 0048 Yerevan
Tel: +374(10) 351-469 +374(10) 351-301
Fax: +374(10) 341-300
Website: http://www.spyur.am/agriculuniv.htm

Rector: Norayr Gasarjyan

Programmes
Bread, Confectionary and Makaroni Food Technology (Food Technology); **Finances and Credit** (Banking; Finance); **Law** (Law); **Veterinary Medicine** (Veterinary Science)

History: Founded 1992.

Degrees and Diplomas: *Bakalavri Vorakavorum*. Also specialist diploma.
Last Updated: 09/11/11

YEREVAN ANANIA SHIRAKATSI UNIVERSITY OF INTERNATIONAL RELATIONS
Yerevani Anania Shirakatsi Mijazgain Haraberutyunneri Hamalsaran
Tigran Mets Street 65A, 0005 Yerevan
Tel: +374(10) 573-171
EMail: info@shirakatsi.com
Website: http://www.shirakatsi.com/

Rector: Seyran Afyan

Programmes
Foreign Languages (English; German; Modern Languages); **International Relations** (International Relations); **Journalism** (Journalism); **Law** (Law)

History: Founded 1990. Acquired present status 2002.

Accrediting Agencies: Ministry of Education and Science of Armenia

Degrees and Diplomas: *Bakalavri Vorakavorum*
Last Updated: 09/11/11

YEREVAN FINANCIAL BANKING AND STOCK EXCHANGE UNIVERSITY
Yerevani Finansabankayin ev Borsayakan Hamalsaran
P. Byuzand Street 1/3, Yerevan
Tel: +374(10) 522-720

Rector: Yuri Alaverdyan **Tel:** +374(91) 417-138

Programmes
Finance and Credit (Banking; Finance); **Law** (Law)

History: Founded 1996.

Degrees and Diplomas: Diploma Specialist : Law; Finance and Credit
Last Updated: 09/11/11

YEREVAN GALIK UNIVERSITY
Yerevani Galik Hamalsaran
Teryan Street 105a, 0009 Yerevan
Tel: +374(10) 589-698
Fax: +374(10) 525-651
EMail: galik@hi-teck.com

Rector: Frunzeh Kharatyan

Departments
Foreign Languages (Modern Languages); **Journalism** (Journalism); **Law** (Law); **Management** (Management)

History: Founded 1989.

Accrediting Agencies: Ministry of Education and Science of Armenia
Last Updated: 09/11/11

YEREVAN GLADZOR UNIVERSITY
Gladzor Karavarman Hamalsaran
G. Lousavorchi Street 7/1, 375015 Yerevan
Tel: +374(10) 545-987
Fax: +374(10) 545982
EMail: gladzor_um@xter.net
Website: http://www.gladzor.am

Rector: Zhora Jhangiryan

Departments
Economics (Economics); **Foreign Languages** (English; French; German; Spanish); **Information Technologies** (Information Technology); **International Journalism** (Journalism); **International Relations** (International Relations); **Law** (Law)

History: Founded 1990. Acquired present status 2001.

Main Language(s) of Instruction: Armenian

Accrediting Agencies: Ministry of Education and Science of Armenia
Last Updated: 09/11/11

YEREVAN HRACHYA ACHARYAN UNIVERSITY
Yerevani Hrachya Acharyan Hamalsaran
Moskovan Street 3, 0001 Yerevan
Tel: +374(10) 561-777
Fax: +374(10) 561-551
EMail: hau@info.am
Website: http://www.hau.info.am

Rector: Avagi Khachatryan (2010-)

Programmes
Applied Mathematics (Applied Mathematics); **Architecture** (Architecture); **Economics** (Economics); **Geography** (Geography); **History** (History); **International Relations** (International Relations); **Journalism** (Journalism); **Law** (Law); **Oriental Studies** (Oriental Studies); **Philology** (Philology); **Psychology** (Psychology); **Speech Therapy** (Speech Therapy and Audiology)

History: Founded 1991. Acquired present status 2001.

Accrediting Agencies: Ministry of Education and Science of Armenia

Degrees and Diplomas: *Bakalavri Vorakavorum*; *Magistrosi Vorakavorum*; *Doctor of Science*
Last Updated: 09/11/11

YEREVAN 'MANTS' UNIVERSITY
Yerevani Mants Hamalsaran
Sosei 13, 0019 Yerevan
Tel: +374(10) 279-751 +374(10) 279-754
EMail: manc@cornet.am
Website: http://manc.cornet.am/

Rector: Ruben Avagyan

Departments
Economics (Economics; Finance; Management); **Foreign Languages** (Modern Languages; Translation and Interpretation); **Informatics and Applied Mathematics** (Applied Mathematics; Computer Science); **Law** (Civil Law; Criminal Law; International Law; Law)

History: Created 2002. Acquired status 2007.

Fees: (Dram): 180-000-250,000 per annum

Main Language(s) of Instruction: Armenian

Degrees and Diplomas: *Bakalavri Vorakavorum*; *Magistrosi Vorakavorum*

Last Updated: 09/11/11

YEREVAN 'MARTIG' UNIVERSITY OF INTERNATIONAL ECONOMIC RELATIONS

Yerevani Martig Artakin Tntesakan Kaperi Hamalsaran (MARTIG UIER)

Myasnikyan Ave 5, 0025 Yerevan
Tel: +374(10) 589-198 +374(10) 561-646
EMail: martig@arminco.com
Website: http://martig-edu.com/

Rector: Marianna Voskanyan

Schools

Accountancy (Accountancy; Behavioural Sciences; Economics; Finance; Marketing; Statistics; Taxation); **Computer Sciences** (Computer Engineering; Computer Graphics; Computer Networks; Computer Science; Data Processing; Software Engineering; Statistics); **Economics** (Agricultural Economics; Banking; Econometrics; Economics; Environmental Studies; Finance; International Business; International Economics; Mathematics; Statistics); **Finance** (Business Administration; Commercial Law; Economics; Finance; Government; International Business; Management; Real Estate); **Law** (Civil Law; Constitutional Law; Criminal Law; Environmental Studies; Ethics; European Union Law; History of Law; Insurance; International Law; Labour Law; Law; Taxation); **Management** (Accountancy; Business Computing; Commercial Law; Communication Studies; Management; Marketing)

History: Founded 1991. Acquired present status 2002.

Accrediting Agencies: Ministry of Education and Science of Armenia

Degrees and Diplomas: *Bakalavri Vorakavorum*

Last Updated: 09/11/11

YEREVAN MEDICAL UNIVERSITY NAMED AFTER SAINT TERESA

Yerevani Surb Terezayi Anvan Gutyan Qureri Bghshkakan Institut

Mashtaots Street 54A, 375033 Yerevan
Tel: +374(10) 587-418 +374(10) 563-370
Fax: +374(10) 587-418
EMail: charity-sisters@hotmail.com

Rector: Larisa L. HambardzumyanFax: +374(10) 587-411
EMail: charity_sisters@hotmail.com

Pro-Rector: Arpik Hartosnyian Tel: +374(10) 531-648

International Relations: Younis Mir, Foreign Students Advisor
EMail: miryounis@hotmail.com

Programmes

Computer Science and Software Engineering (Computer Science; Software Engineering); **Management** (Management); **Medicine** (Medicine); **Pharmacy** (Pharmacy); **Stomatology** (Stomatology)

History: Founded 1992, acquired present status 2002.

Governing Bodies: Council

Admission Requirements: Secondary school certificate

Fees: (Drams): 400,000

Main Language(s) of Instruction: Armenian, Russian, English

International Co-operation: With universities in Finland and Thailand

Accrediting Agencies: Ministry of Education and Science of Armenia

Degrees and Diplomas: *Bakalavri Vorakavorum*; *Magistrosi Vorakavorum*

Student Services: Academic counselling, Canteen, Cultural centre, Foreign student adviser, Foreign Studies Centre, Health services, Language programs, Social counselling, Sports facilities

Student Residential Facilities: Yes

Libraries: Yes

Publications: Yerevan Educational Directory, Magazine *(weekly)*

Academic Staff 2010-2011	TOTAL
FULL-TIME	c. 70

Student Numbers 2010-2011	
All (Foreign Included)	c. 500
FOREIGN ONLY	80

Last Updated: 09/11/11

YEREVAN MESROP MASHTOS PEDAGOGICAL UNIVERSITY

Yerevani Mesrop Mashtoci Anvan Mankavargakan Hamalsaran

Heratsu 2/1, 025 Yerevan
Tel: +374(10) 575-012

Rector: Zaven V. Sargsyan

Programmes

Accounting and Audit (Accountancy; Business Administration; Economics); **Armenian Language and Literature** (Armenian; Literature); **Design** (Design; Fashion Design; Industrial Design); **Education**; **Foreign Languages** (French; Modern Languages); **Law** (Civil Law; International Law; Law); **Socio-cultural Service and Tourism** (Social and Community Services; Tourism); **Teacher Training and Psychology** (Psychology; Teacher Training)

History: Founded 1990. Acquired present status 2002.

Accrediting Agencies: Ministry of Education and Science of Armenia

Degrees and Diplomas: *Bakalavri Vorakavorum*

Last Updated: 09/11/11

YEREVAN UNIVERSITY NAMED AFTER MOVSES KHORENATSI

Yerevani Movses Khorenatsu Anvan Hamalsaran

Teryan Street 105, 0009 Yerevan
Tel: +374(10) 520-541
Website: http://www.mkhu.am/

Rector: Arthur Aghababyan

Faculties

Armenian Language and Literature (Armenian; Linguistics; Literature; Philology); **Economics** (Accountancy; Banking; Computer Science; Economics; Finance; International Economics; Management; Marketing); **Informatics and Mathematics** (Applied Mathematics; Automation and Control Engineering; Computer Science; Foreign Languages Education; Mathematics Education); **Law** (International Law; Law; Notary Studies); **Modern Languages** (English; French; German; Romance Languages); **School Education** (Education; Pedagogy; Primary Education; Teacher Training)

History: Founded 1996. Acquired present status 2002.

Fees: (Dram): 125,000-180,000 per annum

Accrediting Agencies: Ministry of Education and Science of Armenia

Degrees and Diplomas: *Bakalavri Vorakavorum*; *Magistrosi Vorakavorum*

Last Updated: 09/11/11

YEREVAN UNIVERSITY OF HYABUSAK

Yerevani Haybusak Hamalsaran

Abelian Street 6, Yerevan
Tel: +374(10) 390-698
Fax: +374(10) 399-015
EMail: info@haybusak.com
Website: http://www.academedu.org/en/faculties/
haybusak-univercity

Rector: Anahit L. Harutyunyan

Faculties

Economics (Accountancy; Computer Science; Economics; Finance; Management); **Humanities** (Arts and Humanities; English;

French; German; Germanic Languages; Pedagogy; Philology; Primary Education; Psychology; Romance Languages; Spanish); **Medicine** (Dentistry; Medicine; Pharmacology; Stomatology)

History: Founded 1990. Acquired present status 2001. Joined with Armenian Open University after L. Kalashyan, International Relations Institute after H. Lazaryan, and Yerevan Haybusak University base College into a structure called International Academy of Education (IAE) 2006.

Main Language(s) of Instruction: Armenian

Accrediting Agencies: Ministry of Education and Science of Armenia

Degrees and Diplomas: *Bakalavri Vorakavorum*; *Magistrosi Vorakavorum*; *Doctor of Science*. Also Post-graduate courses in Medicine

Academic Staff *2010-2011*: Total 300

STAFF WITH DOCTORATE: Total 64

Student Numbers *2010-2011*: Total: c. 5,400
Last Updated: 09/11/11

YEREVAN UNIVERSITY OF MANAGEMENT
Yerevani Menegmenti Hamalsaran
Teryan Street 105, 375009 Yerevan
Tel: +374(10) 583-518
EMail: yum@seua.am

Rector: Ruben Arushanyan

Programmes
Banking (Banking); **Business Administration**; **Dentistry** (Dentistry); **Government** (Government); **Information Technology**; **Journalism** (Journalism); **Law** (Civil Law; Commercial Law; Criminal Law; Labour Law; Law); **Organizational Economics and Management** (Business Administration; Economics; Management); **Public Administration** (Public Administration); **Stomatology** (Dentistry; Stomatology); **Tourism** (Tourism); **Translation** (Translation and Interpretation)

Further Information: Also branch in Gyumri and Stepanakert

History: Founded 1996. Acquired present status 2001.

Main Language(s) of Instruction: Armenian

Accrediting Agencies: Ministry of Education and Science of Armenia

Degrees and Diplomas: *Bakalavri Vorakavorum*; *Magistrosi Vorakavorum*
Last Updated: 16/12/08

YEREVAN UNIVERSITY OF MANAGEMENT AND INFORMATION TECHNOLOGY
Yerevani Karavarman ev Informacion Tecnologianeri Hamalsaran
Kievyan 16, 375028 Yerevan
Tel: +374(10) 266-780
EMail: info@yumit.am

Rector: Vitaly Aleksandryan
Pro-Rector: Edward Gharslyan

Programmes
Information Sciences (Information Management; Information Sciences; Information Technology)

History: Founded 1991. Acquired present status 2002.

Main Language(s) of Instruction: Armenian

Accrediting Agencies: Ministry of Education and Science of Armenia

Degrees and Diplomas: *Bakalavri Vorakavorum*
Last Updated: 09/11/11

YEREVAN URARTU UNIVERSITY OF PRACTICAL PSYCHOLOGY AND SOCIOLOGY
Yerevani Gorcnakan Hogebanutyan ev Sociologiai Urartu Hamalsaran
Koryun Street 19A, Yerevan
Tel: +374(10) 528-242
Fax: +374(10) 566-463
EMail: info@urartuuniversity.com
Website: http://www.urartuuniversity.com

Rector: Sedrak Sedrakyan (1991-)
Tel: +374(10) 586-961 EMail: sedraks@urartuuniversity.com

Vice-Rector: Anahit Nersisyan
EMail: anahitn@urartuuniversity.com

International Relations: Naira Sargsyan, Chairperson of the Department of Foreign Languages
EMail: nairas@urartuuniversity.com

Departments
Foreign Languages (Foreign Languages Education; Modern Languages); **Humanities** (Arts and Humanities; Social Work); **Natural Sciences** (Natural Sciences); **Psychology** (Clinical Psychology; Physical Therapy; Psychology; Psychotherapy)

History: Founded 1991. Acquired present status 2002.

Academic Year: September to June

Admission Requirements: High school diploma

Fees: (Drams): 250,000 per annum

Main Language(s) of Instruction: Armenian, English

International Co-operation: With universities in USA, France and Greece

Accrediting Agencies: Ministry of Education and Science of Armenia

Degrees and Diplomas: *Bakalavri Vorakavorum*: Psychology, Social Work, 4 yrs; *Magistrosi Vorakavorum*: Psychology, Social Work, a further 2-3 yrs; *Candidate/Doctor of Science*: Psychology (PhD), a further 3-4 yrs

Student Services: Academic counselling, Canteen, Cultural centre, Employment services, Foreign student adviser, Foreign Studies Centre, Handicapped facilities, Health services, Language programs, Social counselling, Sports facilities

Libraries: c. 17,000 vols

Publications: University Newspaper *(monthly)*

Press or Publishing House: 'Zangak-97' publishing house
Last Updated: 09/11/11

Australia

STRUCTURE OF HIGHER EDUCATION SYSTEM

Description:

Higher education in Australia refers to university and non-university higher education institutions which award degree or sub-degree qualifications based on the Australian Qualifications Framework. Australia has self-accrediting public and private universities, self-accrediting higher education institutions, and accredited higher education institutions. Universities and other self-accrediting higher education institutions are established or recognised under state and territory or Commonwealth legislation. Non-self-accrediting higher education institutions and their programmes are accredited by state and territory government authorities. The Australian Qualifications Framework register lists self-accrediting institutions and links to lists of non-self-accrediting institutions in each state and territory (http://www.aqf.edu.au/RegisterAccreditation/AQFRegister/tabid/174/Default.aspx). Universities are autonomous multidisciplinary institutions that are responsible for their own management structure, budgets, resource allocation, staff, student enrolments, accreditation of qualifications, quality assurance and curriculum. Australia also has around 170 higher education institutions accredited by state and territory authorities to offer higher education courses. Non-university higher education institutions tend to offer programmes in only one or two fields of study. The Australian Government is responsible for higher education policy and finance through the Department of Education, Employment and Workplace Relations. State and territory governments have legislative responsibility. Consultation between the Australian Government and the states and territories occurs at Ministerial level through the Ministerial Council on for Tertiary Education and Employment (MCTEE), and at an official level through the Joint Committee on Higher Education (JCHE), which advises MCTEE on higher education matters. Higher education students in Australia are subject to a range of fees. There are several financial support options available to students. Australian students can undertake higher education studies at an approved Australian higher education provider as a Commonwealth supported student. Students pay a subsidised student contribution for their education, but the Government pays for the majority of costs.

Stages of studies:

University level first stage: Undergraduate
Undergraduate studies include several qualifications, both sub-degree and degree level. The Diploma and Advanced Diploma on the Australian Qualifications Framework are dual sector qualifications. The other sub-degree qualification is the Associate degree, which is at the same AQF level as the Advanced Diploma. Associate degrees and Advanced Diplomas can provide advanced standing into a Bachelor degree programme in a similar field. This is usually 1.5 years for an Advanced Diploma or 2 years for an Associate degree. The other qualification offered at the undergraduate level is the Bachelor degree. Australian Bachelor degrees are diverse and range from 3 to 6 years of study. There are several types of Bachelor degrees including 3-year degrees, 4-year degrees, professional degrees, combined degrees and Bachelor Honours degrees.

University level second stage: Postgraduate
Postgraduate qualifications on the AQF include the Graduate Certificate, Graduate Diploma and Master degree. Length of study varies between one semester and four years. Admission is normally based on a Bachelor degree. Graduate Certificate and Graduate Diploma programmes are specialised and can be professionally-oriented. There are three types of Master degree programmes: coursework, research and extended.

University level third stage: Doctoral
The final stage of higher education is Doctoral degree studies. There are three types of Doctoral degree - research, professional and higher. A typical Doctoral degree programme requires 3 to 4 years of full-time study and research. Students are expected to make a substantial original contribution to knowledge in the form of new knowledge or significant and original adaptation, application and interpretation of existing knowledge. Admission is based on a Master degree, or a Bachelor Honours degree.

Distance higher education:

Distance education is a major feature of higher education in Australia. The geographic size of Australia and the relatively few large population centres means that distance education is popular. Traditionally, distance education was text-based, but new technologies such as internet-based learning, email, telephone, video conferencing, web, TV, radio and television are now common. Students who complete their studies via distance education receive the same qualifications as the on-campus students. Qualifications obtained through distance education receive the same level of recognition as qualifications obtained through full-time or part-time study for both employment purposes and admission to further studies.

A major provider of distance education is Open Universities Australia, which offers higher education and vocational education and training courses. It is owned and operated by a consortium of universities. It offers bridging courses, vocational education and training programmes and higher education programmes leading to formal qualifications on the Australian Qualifications Framework.

ADMISSION TO HIGHER EDUCATION

Admission to university-level studies:

Name of secondary school credential required: Senior Secondary Certificate of Education

Minimum score/requirement: Varies according to course and institution, student's age, whether student has disabilities or special needs

For entry to: For Diploma and Advanced Diploma, Associate degree and Bachelor degree courses

Alternatives to credentials: Entry may be based on prior experience or other learning.

Numerus clausus/restrictions: Entry to a higher education course is normally determined by the student's tertiary entrance score, rank or index. This is calculated on the basis of results in the Senior Secondary Certificate of Education. Tertiary Admissions Centres in New South Wales, Queensland, South Australia, Victoria and Western Australia coordinate admissions.

Other admission requirements: A portfolio, interview, audition or exam may also be taken into account in conjunction with the tertiary entrance score for certain courses. There are also alternative schemes for mature age students, students with disabilities and students with special needs.

Foreign students admission:

Definition of foreign student: A student who is not an Australian citizen, but is enrolled in (or will enrol in) a course of study with an Australian education provider.

Entrance exam requirements: Individual institutions determine the acceptability of overseas qualifications for the purposes of admission or credit transfer.

Entry regulations: Students require confirmation of enrolment, a student visa and sufficient funds to support themselves.

Health requirements: Students must undergo a medical examination as part of their visa application and must have Overseas Students Health Cover for the period covered by their visa.

Language requirements: Students should have a good command of the English language and may be required to pass an English test.

RECOGNITION OF STUDIES

Quality assurance system:

Quality assurance in Australia's higher education system is based on a strong partnership between the Australian Government, state and territory governments and the higher education sector. In 2011, the Australian Government is establishing a new national regulatory and quality agency for higher education, the Tertiary Education Quality and Standards Agency (TEQSA). TEQSA will be an independent regulatory body. It will monitor quality and establish standards for university and non-university higher education providers. TEQSA will register providers, evaluate standards and performance, quality assure international education and consolidate current regulatory arrangements. TEQSA will work with state and territory regulatory bodies and will assume quality assurance responsibilities currently undertaken by the Australian Universities Quality Agency (AUQA).

Bodies dealing with recognition:

Department of Education, Employment and Workplace Relations
GPO Box 9880
Canberra, ACT 2601
Tel: +61 354 545 245
WWW: http://www.deewr.gov.au/

Tertiary Education Quality and Standards Agency - TEQSA
GPO Box 1672
Melbourne, VIC 3001
EMail: enquires@teqsa.gov.au
WWW: http://www.teqsa.gov.au/

Australian Education International - AEI
Groupe Manager: Colin Walters
GPO Box 9880
Canberra, ACT 2601
Tel: +61 3 9938 2543
EMail: aei@deewr.gov.au
WWW: http://www.aei.gov.au/
Services provided and students dealt with: AEI provides official information and advice on the comparability of overseas qualifications with Australian qualifications. This aims to help overseas qualified people work and study in Australia.

AEI-NOOSR
Director: Margaret Proctor
GPO Box 9880
Canberra 2601
Tel: +61 3 9938 2543
EMail: educational.noosr@deewr.gov.au
WWW: http://www.aei.gov.au/SERVICES-AND-RESOURCES/Pages/AEINOOSR.aspx

Special provisions for recognition:

Recognition for university level studies: Individual institutions determine the acceptability of qualifications and studies for the purpose of admission.

For access to advanced studies and research: Individual institutions determine the acceptability of qualifications and studies for the purpose of admission.

For exercising a profession: Professional recognition is undertaken by the relevant professional body. The Australian Skills Recognition Information website, http://www.immi.gov.au/asri, lists assessing authorities, registration/licensing authorities and industry bodies for professional occupations within Australia and provides full contact details.

NATIONAL BODIES

Department of Education, Employment and Workplace Relations
Secretary: Lisa Paul
GPO Box 9880
Canberra, ACT 2601
Tel: +61 354 545 245
WWW: http://www.deewr.gov.au/
Role of national body: Supports the Australian Government's objectives in education, employment and workplace relations by providing national leadership and working in partnership with the state and territory governments, industry, other agencies and the general community. The Department is responsible for the Australian Government's contribution to: school education; vocational education and training; higher education; indigenous education; international education; employment and workplace relations policy.

Tertiary Education Quality and Standards Agency - TEQSA

Chief Commissioner: Carol Nicoll
GPO Box 1672
Melbourne, VIC 3001
EMail: enquires@teqsa.gov.au
WWW: http://www.teqsa.gov.au/
Role of national body: Independent body with powers to regulate university and non-university higher education providers, monitor quality and set standards.

Australian Qualifications Framework Council - AQFC

Chairperson: John Dawkins
Executive Director: Ann Doolette
GPO Box 320
Adelaide, SA 5001
Tel: +61 8 8226 2775
Fax: +61 8 8226 3071
EMail: aqfc@sa.gov.au
WWW: http://www.aqf.edu.au
Role of national body: Develops the AQF qualifications guidelines, and promotes and monitors national implementation of the AQF.

Universities Australia

Chairperson: Glyn Davis
Chief Executive Officer: Belinda Robinson
Director, Communication and Government Relations: Michael Hartmann
GPO Box 1142
Canberra, ACT 2601
Tel: +61 2 6285 8100
Fax: +61 2 6285 8101
EMail: contact@universitiesaustralia.edu.au
WWW: http://www.universitiesaustralia.edu.au
Role of national body: Represents higher education Institutions nationally and internationally and advances higher education through voluntary, cooperative and coordinated action.

International Education Association of Australia - IEAA

President: Stephen Connelly
Executive Director: Dennis Murray
P.O. Box 12917
Melbourne, VIC 8006
Tel: +61 3 9925 4579
Fax: +61 3 9925 2023
EMail: admin@ieaa.org.au
WWW: http://www.ieaa.org.au/
Role of national body: The International Education Association of Australia is an association of international education professionals. The Association has been established to serve the needs and interests of the large number of individuals working in international education across all education sectors, to encourage informed and ethical professional practice among members, and to promote international education to governments, education organisations and within the community.

IDP Education Pty Ltd - IDP

Chairperson: Peter Polson
CEO: Andrew Thompson
Level 8,
535 Bourke Street
Melbourne, VIC 3000
Tel: +61 3 9612 4400
EMail: info@idp.com
WWW: http://www.idp.com/

Role of national body: IDP Education Pty Ltd (IDP) is a company offering student placement and English language testing services. It places students into all sectors of the Australian education system, including higher education, vocational education and training (VET), English language intensive courses for overseas students (ELICOS) and schools.

International Education Association - ISANA

President: Danielle Hartridge
Head, Secretariat: Tracy Noble
228 Liverpool Street
Hobart, TAS 7000
Tel: +61 3 6231 0253
Fax: +61 3 6231 1522
EMail: isana@cdesign.com.au
WWW: http://www.isana.org.au/

Role of national body: ISANA, a body for international education professionals in Australia and New Zealand, works in student services, advocacy, teaching, and policy development in Australia and New Zealand.

Association for Tertiary Education Management - ATEM

President: Stephen Weller
Executive Director: Paul Abela
Head Office
Building M
University of Sydney
Cumberland College
75 East Street
(PO Box 170)
Lidcombe, NSW 2141
Fax: +61 2 6125 5262
WWW: http://www.atem.org.au/

Role of national body: The Association for Tertiary Education Management Inc (ATEM Inc) is a professional body for tertiary education administrators and managers in Australasia.

Data for academic year: 2011-2012
Source: IAU from the Educational and Professional Recognition Unit (AEI-NOOSR) - International Cooperation Branch, Australian Government Department of Education, Employment and Workplace Relations, 2011

INSTITUTIONS

PUBLIC INSTITUTIONS

AUSTRALIAN CATHOLIC UNIVERSITY (ACU NATIONAL)

PO Box 968, North Sydney, New South Wales 2059
Tel: +61(2) 9739-2437
Fax: +61(2) 9739-2001
EMail: international@acu.edu.au
Website: http://www.acu.edu.au

Vice-Chancellor: Greg Craven (2008-)
Tel: +61(2) 9739-2910, Fax: +61(2) 9739-2955
EMail: vc@acu.edu.au

Deputy, Vice-Chancellor, Administration and Resources: John Cameron
Tel: +61(2) 9739-2912, Fax: +61(2) 9739-2905
EMail: john.cameron@acu.edu.au

International Relations: Chris Riley, Executive Director
Tel: +61(2) 9739-2327, Fax: +61(2) 9739-2001
EMail: chris.riley@acu.edu.au

Faculties
Arts and Sciences (Arts and Humanities; Chemistry; History; Information Technology; Literature; Modern Languages; Music; Physics; Psychology; Social Sciences; Social Work; Theology; Visual Arts) *Dean*: Gail Crossley; **Business** (Accountancy; Business Administration; Commercial Law; Finance; Management; Marketing); **Education** (Adult Education; Continuing Education; Education; Primary Education; Religious Education; Secondary Education; Special Education) *Dean*: Marie Emmitt; **Health Sciences** (Health Sciences; Midwifery; Nursing; Physical Therapy) *Dean*: Michelle Campbell; **Theology and Philosophy** (Philosophy; Theology) *Dean*: Anne Hunt

Further Information: International Offices, Elicos Units (Brisbane, Melbourne, Sydney)

History: Founded 1991 by amalgamation of institutions of higher education in Australian Capital Territory, New South Wales, Queensland, and Victoria.

Governing Bodies: Senate

Academic Year: February to November (February-June; July-November)

Admission Requirements: Secondary school certificate with matriculation or Australian Year 12 Equivalent.

Fees: (Aus Dollars): Foreign students, c. 17,000-27,000 per annum

Main Language(s) of Instruction: English

International Co-operation: With universities in China, Hong Kong, Pakistan, New Zealand, Philippines and Singapore

Degrees and Diplomas: *Diploma*: Arts and Humanities; Business Administration; Education (Dip), 2 yrs; *Bachelor Degree*: Arts and Humanities; Business Administration; Commerce; Education; Media and Communication; Health Sciences; Physiotherapy; Religion; Social Sciences; Welfare and Protective Services; Visual Arts (B), 3-4 yrs; *Bachelor Honours Degree*: Arts and Humanities; Business Administration; Education; Information Sciences; Health Sciences; Media and Communication; Theology; Social Sciences; Welfare and Proctective Services; Visual Arts (B (Hons)), 4 yrs; *Graduate Certificate/Diploma*: Arts and Humanities; Business Administration; Education; Information Sciences; Health Sciences; Religion; Social Sciences; Welfare and Proctective Services; Visual Arts, a further 6 mths; *Graduate Certificate/Diploma*: Arts and Humanities; Business Administration; Education; Information Sciences; Health Sciences; Religion; Social Sciences; Welfare and Proctective Services; Visual Arts, a further yr; *Master Degree*: Accounting; Arts and Humanities; Business Administration; Health Sciences; Social Sciences; Welfare and Protective Services; Education; Theology (M), a further 1-2 yrs; *Doctoral Degree*: Arts and Humanities; Business; Health Sciences; Education; Social Sciences; Theology (PhD), at least 2-4 yrs following Master; *Doctoral Degree*: Education (EdD), a further 2-4 yrs

Student Services: Academic counselling, Canteen, Employment services, Foreign student adviser, Handicapped facilities, Social counselling, Sports facilities

Libraries: 450,000 vols, 650 paper serial titles and over 50,000 online databases, ejournals and ebooks
Last Updated: 07/10/11

BALLARAT CAMPUS (AQUINAS)

PO Box 650, Ballarat, Victoria 3353
Tel: +61(3) 5336-5360
Fax: +61(3) 5336-5408
EMail: international@acu.edu.au

Campus Head: Joe Flemming
Tel: +61(3) 5336-5342, Fax: +61(3) 5336-5303
EMail: joe.flemming@acu.edu.au

Faculties
Arts and Sciences (Accountancy; Arts and Humanities; Business Administration; Business and Commerce; Chemistry; History; Information Technology; Literature; Modern Languages; Music; Natural Sciences; Philosophy; Physics; Psychology; Social Sciences; Social Work; Theology; Visual Arts) *Dean*: Gail Crossley; **Business** (Business Administration) *Dean*: Elizabeth More; **Education** (Education; Educational Sciences; Primary Education; Religious Education; Secondary Education; Teacher Training) *Dean*: Marie Emmitt; **Health Sciences** (Health Sciences; Midwifery; Nursing; Physical Education) *Dean (Acting)*: Michelle Campbell; **Theology and Philosophy** (Philosophy; Theology) *Dean*: Anne Hunt

History: Founded 1991 by amalgamation of higher education institutions in Australian Capital Territory, New South Wales, Queensland and Victoria.

Governing Bodies: Senate

Academic Year: February to November (February-June; July-November)

Admission Requirements: Secondary school certificate with matriculation or Australian Year 12 equivalent

Degrees and Diplomas: *Diploma*: Arts and Humanities; Business Administration; Education, 1 yr; *Bachelor Degree*: Arts and Humanities; Business Administration; Education; Information Sciences; Health Sciences; Religion; Social Sciences; Welfare and Protective Services; Visual Arts, 3-4 yrs; *Bachelor Honours Degree*: Arts and Humanities; Business Administration; Education; Information Sciences; Health Sciences; Religion; Social Sciences; Welfare and Protective Services; Visual Arts; *Graduate Certificate/Diploma*: Arts and Humanities; Business Administration; Education; Information Sciences; Health Sciences; Social Sciences; Welfare and Protective

Services, a further 6 mths; *Master Degree*: Arts and Humanities; Business Administration; Education; Information Sciences; Health Sciences; Social Sciences; Welfare and Protective Services, a further 1-2 yrs; *Doctoral Degree*: Arts and Humanities; Education; Social Sciences, at least 2 yrs following Master

Student Services: Academic counselling, Canteen, Employment services, Foreign student adviser, Handicapped facilities, Social counselling, Sports facilities

Libraries: 450,000 items, 650 paper serial titles and over 50,000 online databases, eJournals and E Books

BRISBANE CAMPUS (MCAULEY AT BANYO)

PO Box 456, Virginia, Queensland QLD 4014
Tel: +61(7) 3623-7340
Fax: +61(7) 3623-7161
EMail: international@acu.edu.au

Associate Vice-Chancellor: Lindsay Farrell
Tel: +61(7) 3623-7191, Fax: +61(7) 3623-7245
EMail: lindasay.farrell@acu.edu.au

Faculties
Arts and Sciences (Accountancy; Arts and Humanities; Chemistry; History; Information Technology; Literature; Modern Languages; Music; Natural Sciences; Philosophy; Physics; Psychology; Social Sciences; Social Work; Theology; Visual Arts) *Dean*: Gail Crossley; **Business**; **Education** (Adult Education; Continuing Education; Education; Primary Education; Religious Education; Secondary Education; Teacher Training) *Dean*: Marie Emmitt; **Health Sciences** (Health Sciences; Midwifery; Nursing) *Dean*: Michelle Campbell; **Theology and Philosophy** (Philosophy; Theology) *Dean*: Anne Hunt

History: Founded 1991by amalgamation of higher education institutions in Australian Capital Territory, New South Wales, Queensland and Victoria.

Governing Bodies: Senate

Academic Year: February to November (February-June; July-November)

Admission Requirements: Secondary school certificate with matriculation or Australian Year 12 equivalent

Fees: (Aus Dollars) Foreign students: 13,000-17,000 per annum

Main Language(s) of Instruction: English

International Co-operation: With universities in Hong Kong, Pakistan, New Zealand, Philippines, China and Singapore

Degrees and Diplomas: *Diploma*: Arts and Humanities; Business Administration; Education, 1 yr; *Bachelor Degree*: Arts and Humanities; Business Administration; Education; Information Sciences; Health Sciences; Religion; Social Sciences; Welfare and Protective Services; Visual Arts, 3-4 yrs; *Bachelor Honours Degree*: Arts and Humanities; Business Administration; Education; Information Sciences; Health Sciences; Religion; Social Sciences; Welfare and Protective Services; Visual Arts, 4 yrs; *Graduate Certificate/Diploma*: Arts and Humanities; Business Administration; Education; Information Sciences; Health Sciences; Social Sciences; Welfare and Protective Services, a further 6 mths; *Master Degree*: Education; Information Sciences; Health Sciences; Social Sciences; Welfare and Protective Services, a further 1-2 yrs; *Doctoral Degree*: Arts and Humanities; Education; Social Sciences, at least 2 yrs following Master's

Student Services: Academic counselling, Employment services, Foreign student adviser, Handicapped facilities, Social counselling, Sports facilities

Libraries: 450,000 items, 650 paper serial titles and over 50,000 online databases, eJournals and E Books

CANBERRA CAMPUS (SIGNADOU)

Victoria 3800
Tel: +61(3) 9902-6000
Fax: +61(3) 9905-4007
EMail: international@acu.edu.au

Campus Dean: Patrick McArdle
Tel: +61(2) 6209-1110, Fax: +61(2) 6209-1160
EMail: patrick.mcardle@.acu.edu.au

Faculties

Business (Business Administration) *Head*: Elisabeth More; **Education** (Administration; Primary Education; Teacher Training) *Head*: Marie Emmitt; **Health Sciences** (Health Sciences) *Dean (Acting)*: Michelle Campbell; **Theology and Philosophy** (Philosophy; Theology) *Head*: Kerrie Hide

History: Founded by amalgamation of higher educations in Australian Capital Territory, New South Wales, Queensland and Victoria

Governing Bodies: Senate

Academic Year: February to November (February-June; July-November)

MELBOURNE CAMPUS (SAINT PATRICK'S)

Locked Bag 4115 MDC, Fitzroy, Victoria 3065
Tel: +61(3) 9953-3062
Fax: +61(3) 9953-3115
EMail: international@acu.edu.au

Assistant Vice-Chancellor: Chris Sheargold (2001-)
Tel: +61(3) 9953-3308, Fax: +61(3) 9953-3615
EMail: chris.sheargold@acu.edu.au

Faculties

Arts and Sciences (Arts and Humanities; Environmental Studies; Ethics; History; Literature; Modern Languages; Music; Natural Sciences; Philosophy; Social Sciences; Visual Arts) *Dean*: Gail Crossley; **Business** (Business Administration); **Education** (Education; Leadership; Primary Education; Secondary Education; Special Education; Teacher Training) *Dean*: Marie Emmitt; **Health Sciences** (Health Sciences; Midwifery; Nursing; Sports) *Dean*: Michelle Campbell; **Theology and Philosophy** (Philosophy; Theology)

History: Founded 1991 by amalgamation of higher education institutions in Australian Capital Territory, New South Wales, Queensland and Victoria.

Governing Bodies: Senate

Academic Year: February to November

Admission Requirements: Secondary school certificate with matriculation or Australian Year 12 equivalent

Fees: (Aus Dollars) Foreign students: c. 13,000-17,000 per annum

Main Language(s) of Instruction: English

International Co-operation: With universities in Hong Kong, Pakistan, New Zealand, Philippines, China and Singapore

Degrees and Diplomas: *Diploma*: 1 yr; *Bachelor Degree*: 3/4 yrs; *Graduate Certificate/Diploma*: a further 6 mths; *Master Degree*: a further 1-2 yrs; *Doctoral Degree*: a further 2-4 yrs

NORTH SYDNEY CAMPUS (MACKILLOP)

PO Box 968, North Sydney, New South Wales 2059
Tel: +61(2) 9739-2305
Fax: +61(2) 9739-2310
EMail: international@acu.edu.au

Associate Vice-Chancellor: Marea Nicholson
Tel: +61(2) 9701-4322, Fax: +61(2) 9701-4034
EMail: marea.nicholson@acu.edu.au

Faculties

Arts and Sciences (Biology; Chemistry; Environmental Management; Natural Sciences; Physics; Visual Arts; Welfare and Protective Services) *Dean*: Gail Crossley; **Business** (Accountancy; Administration; Business and Commerce; Computer Science; Human Resources; Information Technology; Mathematics and Computer Science; Systems Analysis) *Dean*: Elisabeth More; **Education** (Education) *Dean*: Marie Emmitt; **Health Sciences** (Health Sciences; Nursing) *Dean (Acting)*: Michelle Campbell; **Theology and Philosophy** (Philosophy; Theology) *Dean*: Anne Hunt

History: Founded 1991.

Governing Bodies: Senate

Academic Year: February to November (February-June; July-November)

STRATHFIELD (MOUNT SAINT MARY)

Locked Bag 2002, Strathfield, New South Wales 2135
Tel: +61(2) 9701-4012
Fax: +61(2) 9701-4284
EMail: international@acu.edu.au

Associate Vice-Chancello: Marea Nicholson
Tel: +61(2) 9701-4322, Fax: +61(2) 9701-4034
EMail: marea.nicholson@acu.edu.au

Faculties

Arts and Sciences (Arts and Humanities; Social Sciences; Visual Arts) *Dean*: Gail Crossley; **Business** (Business Administration) *Dean*: Elisabeth More; **Education** (Primary Education; Secondary Education; Teacher Training) *Dean*: Marie Emmitt; **Health Sciences** (Health Sciences) *Dean*: Michelle Campbell; **Theology and Philosophy** (Philosophy; Theology) *Dean*: Anne Hunt

History: Founded 1991 by amalgamation of higher education institutions in Australian Capital Territory, New South Wales, Queensland and Victoria.

Governing Bodies: Senate

Academic Year: February to November (February-June; July-November)

AUSTRALIAN MARITIME COLLEGE (AMC)

Locked Bag 1399, Launceston, Tasmania 7250
Tel: +61(3) 6324-3775
Fax: +61(3) 6326-6493
EMail: amcinfo@amc.edu.au
Website: http://www.amc.edu.au

Pro-Vice Chancellor: Malek Pourzanjani Tel: +61(3) 6335-4700

Courses

Postgraduate Courses (Marine Engineering; Marine Science and Oceanography; Marine Transport; Naval Architecture); **Undergraduate** (Aquaculture; Fishery; Marine Engineering; Marine Science and Oceanography; Marine Transport)

History: Founded 1978.

Main Language(s) of Instruction: English

Degrees and Diplomas: *Bachelor Degree*; *Master Degree*; *Doctoral Degree*
Last Updated: 23/11/11

BATCHELOR INSTITUTE OF INDIGENOUS TERTIARY EDUCATION

Post Office Batchelor, Batchelor, Northern Territory 0845
Tel: +61(8) 8939-7111
Fax: +61(8) 8939-7334
EMail: enquiries@batchelor.edu.au
Website: http://www.batchelor.edu.au/

Director: Adrian Mitchell
Tel: +61(8) 8939-7345, Fax: +61(8) 8939-7130

Academic Registrar: Karl Ashton

Schools

Business, Health and Sciencesand Sciences (Administration; Botany; Communication Studies; Dietetics; Ecology; Econometrics; Economics; Health Sciences; Law; Management; Marketing; Natives Education; Natural Resources; Nursing; Nutrition; Occupational Health; Soil Science; Wildlife); **Education, Arts and Social Sciences** (Curriculum; Education; Educational Sciences; Indigenous Studies; Linguistics; Media Studies; Natives Education; Philosophy; Political Sciences; Social Sciences; Social Work; Sociology; Teacher Training; Writing)

History: Founded 1965, acquired present status and title 1999.

Degrees and Diplomas: *Bachelor Degree*; *Graduate Certificate/Diploma*; *Master Degree*
Last Updated: 23/11/11

CENTRAL QUEENSLAND UNIVERSITY (CQU)

Building 5 Bruce Highway, Rockhampton, Queensland 4702
Tel: +61(7) 4930-9000
Fax: +61(7) 4923-2100
EMail: international-enquiries@cqu.edu.au
Website: http://www.cqu.edu.au

Vice-Chancellor and President: Scott Bowman
Tel: +61(7) 4930-9752, Fax: +61(7) 4930-9018
EMail: vc@cqu.edu.au

Faculties
Arts, Business, Informatics and Education (Arts and Humanities; Business and Commerce; Computer Science; Education; Information Sciences; Information Technology; Management; Marketing); **Sciences, Engineering and Health** (Biological and Life Sciences; Biology; Biomedicine; Building Technologies; Chemistry; Engineering; Environmental Studies; Health Sciences; Industrial Engineering; Nursing; Psychology; Social Work; Technology; Welfare and Protective Services)

Further Information: Also Bundaberg, Emerald, Gladstone, Sydney, Melbourne, Mackay, Brisbane, Noosa, Gold Coast, New Zealand, Shanghai, and Singapore international campuses

History: Founded 1967 as Queensland Institute of Technology (Capricornia), acquired university status 1992 and title 1994.

Governing Bodies: University Council

Academic Year: Queensland Regional and Head Campus in Rockhampton, three terms year from March to November (March-June; July-November; November-February)

Admission Requirements: Secondary school certificate with matriculation or recognized foreign equivalent. English Language proficiency: IELTS of 6.0 or TOEFL score of 550 or equivalent for undergraduate and postgraduate programmes; IETLS of 6.5 or equivalent for research programmes

Fees: (Aus Dollars): 1,350-2,298 per course. Students are to study 4 undergraduate courses per term and 3 postgraduate courses per term

Main Language(s) of Instruction: English

International Co-operation: With universities in USA; Germany; Japan; Republic of Korea; Hong Kong; Sweden

Degrees and Diplomas: *Advanced Diploma*: Business and Information Technology, 2 yrs; *Diploma*; *Bachelor Degree*: Business and Informatics; Science; Engineering and Health, 3-4 yrs; *Graduate Certificate/Diploma*: Business and Informatics; Arts, Humanities and Education; Sciences; Health and Engineering, 6 months; *Master Degree*: Business and Informatics; Arts, Humanities and Education; Sciences; Health and Engineering, a further 1-2 yrs; *Doctoral Degree*: Business and Informatics; Arts, Humanities and Education; Health and Engineering (PhD), a further 2-5 yrs. Also undergraduate Diplomas

Student Services: Academic counselling, Canteen, Cultural centre, Employment services, Foreign student adviser, Foreign Studies Centre, Handicapped facilities, Health services, Language programs, Nursery care, Social counselling, Sports facilities

Student Residential Facilities: Yes (On campus accommodation at Brisbane, Mackay, Rockhampton and New Zealand Campuses)

Libraries: On-line and physical library
Last Updated: 23/11/11

CHARLES DARWIN UNIVERSITY (CDU)

Casuarina Campus, Ellengowan Drive, Darwin, Northern Territory 0909
Tel: +61(8) 8946-6666 +61(8) 8946-7215
Fax: +61(8) 8927-0612
EMail: international@cdu.edu.au
Website: http://www.cdu.edu.au

Vice-Chancellor: Barney Glover (2009-)
Tel: +61(8) 8946-6040, Fax: +61(8) 8927-3480
EMail: vc@cdu.edu.au

Executive Director, Corporate Services: Scott Snyder
Tel: +61(8) 8946-6439 EMail: kirsty.mawer@cdu.edu.au

International Relations: Monica Turvey, Director, International Office

Tel: +61(8) 8946-7215, Fax: +61(8) 8946-6644
EMail: monica.turvey@cdu.edu.au

Centres
Access and English as Second Language (Part of Faculty of Education, Science and Health) (English) *Director:* Peter Wignall

Divisions
Vocational Education and Training ((VET))

Faculties
Engineering, Health, Science and the Environment (Engineering; Environmental Engineering; Health Sciences; Natural Sciences); **Law, Education, Business and Arts** (Arts and Humanities; Business Administration; Education; Law)

Research Centres
Aboriginal Health *(Cooperative)*; **Desert Knowledge** *(Cooperative)* (Arid Land Studies); **Remote Health**; **Remote Telecommunications Solutions**; **Sustainable Tourism** *(Cooperative)* (Social Studies; Tourism); **Tropical Plant Protection** *(Cooperative)*; **Tropical Savannas Management** *(Cooperative)*; **Tropical Wetland Studies** *(National)*; **Tropical Wildlife Management** *(Arc Key Centre)* (Wildlife)

Schools
Academic Language and Learning; **Creative Arts and Humanities** (Anthropology; Archaeology; Arts and Humanities; Greek; Indonesian; Music; Visual Arts) *Head:* Bill Wade; **Education** (Education) *Director:* Peter Kell; **Engineering and Information Technology** (Biomedical Engineering; Computer Engineering; Engineering; Information Technology; Telecommunications Engineering; Water Science) *Director:* Friso de Boer; **Health Sciences** (Health Sciences; Midwifery; Nursing; Occupational Health; Psychology; Social Welfare; Social Work); **Law and Business** (Business Administration; Business and Commerce; Law); **School of Environmental and Life Sciences** (Biological and Life Sciences; Chemistry; Earth Sciences; Environmental Studies; Geography; Health Sciences; Horticulture; Natural Resources; Natural Sciences; Physical Education; Physics; Sports) *Head:* Chris Austin

Further Information: Campuses at Casuarina, Palmerson and Alice Springs, Jabiru, Katherine, Nhulunbuy and Tennant Creek. A Study Abroad Programme is also available

History: Founded 1989 as Northern Territory University, amalgamating the University College of the Northern Territory and Darwin Institute of Technology. Acquired present title 2003 after merger with Centralian College in Alice Springs.

Governing Bodies: University Council; Academic Board; Technical and Further Education (TAFE) Board

Academic Year: February to October (February-June; July-October); Vocational Education and Training (VET) courses, February to December (February-June; July-December)

Admission Requirements: Secondary school certificate or recognized foreign equivalent, or previous tertiary study. Direct entrance to second year on successful completion of studies in another tertiary institution

Fees: (Aus Dollars): VET courses, c. 4,250-17,000; Undergraduate Courses, c. 5,900-74,500; Postgraduate, c. 6,650-69,200

Main Language(s) of Instruction: English

Degrees and Diplomas: *Certificate IV*; *Advanced Diploma*; *Associate Degree*; *Diploma*; *Bachelor Degree*: Aboriginal and Torres Strait Islander Studies; Arts; Business; Information Technology; Library and Information Management; Music; Tourism and Hospitality; Visual Arts, 3 yrs; *Bachelor Degree*: Education; Nursing, 2-4 yrs; *Bachelor Degree*: Engineering; Laws, 4 yrs; *Bachelor Honours Degree*: Arts; Information Technology, 4 yrs; *Graduate Certificate/Diploma*: 6 months; *Master Degree*: Accounting, 1 1/2 yrs; *Master Degree*: Applied Linguistics, 1-2 yrs; *Master Degree*: Arts; Business; Business Administration; Fine Arts; Laws; Science, 2 yrs; *Master Degree*: Education; Engineering, 1 yr; *Master Degree*: Public Governance; Tropical Environmental Management, 11/2 yrs; *Doctoral Degree (PhD)*: 4 yrs

Student Services: Academic counselling, Canteen, Foreign student adviser, Handicapped facilities, Health services, Nursery care, Social counselling, Sports facilities

Student Residential Facilities: North Flinders International House with more than 250 rooms available

Special Facilities: Art Gallery. Theatre. Aboriginal Traditional Medicine Garden

Libraries: University Library, 330,000 vols

Publications: Northern Perspective *(biannually)*; Origins; Research Report *(annually)*

Press or Publishing House: NTU Press
Last Updated: 23/11/11

CHARLES STURT UNIVERSITY (CSU)

Panorama Avenue, Bathurst, New South Wales 2795
Tel: +61(2) 6338-6077
Fax: +61(2) 6338-6001
EMail: inquiry@csu.edu.au
Website: http://www.csu.edu.au

Vice-Chancellor: Ian Goulter
Tel: +61(2) 6338-4209 EMail: vc@csu.edu.au

Deputy Vice-Chancellor (Administration): Mark Burdack
EMail: mburdack@csu.edu.au

Campuses Abroad
Canada

Centres
Inland Health *Division Head*: A. Kolbe; **Water and Food Society** *(International) Director*: M. Finlayson

Faculties
Agriculture and Veterinary Sciences (Agricultural Business; Animal Husbandry; Horticulture; Oenology; Veterinary Science; Viticulture); **Arts** (Advertising and Publicity; Anthropology; Arts and Humanities; Communication Studies; Cultural Studies; English; Fine Arts; Graphic Design; History; Journalism; Justice Administration; Law; Literature; Media Studies; Philosophy; Photography; Police Studies; Political Sciences; Psychology; Public Relations; Radio and Television Broadcasting; Social Policy; Social Sciences; Sociology; Theatre; Theology; Visual Arts) *Dean*: A. Calahan; **Business** (Accountancy; Banking; Business Administration; Business and Commerce; E-Business/Commerce; Economics; Finance; Human Resources; International Business; Labour and Industrial Relations; Management; Marketing; Public Administration; Tourism) *Dean*: L. White; **Education** (Archiving; Education; Foreign Languages Education; Library Science; Physical Education; Preschool Education; Primary Education; Secondary Education; Sports) *Dean*: T. Downes; **Environmental Sciences** (Ecology; Environmental Studies; Geography; Heritage Preservation; Natural Resources; Surveying and Mapping; Tourism; Viticulture; Water Management; Wildlife); **Health Science and Allied Health** (Dental Hygiene; Dentistry; Dietetics; Health Administration; Medicine; Midwifery; Nursing; Nutrition; Occupational Therapy; Oral Pathology; Paramedical Sciences; Pathology; Physical Therapy; Podiatry; Psychology; Rehabilitation and Therapy; Respiratory Therapy; Speech Therapy and Audiology); **Science** (Biology; Biotechnology; Chemistry; Microbiology) *Dean*: N. Klomp

Institutes
Land, Water and Society (Social Studies; Soil Management; Soil Science; Water Management; Water Science) *Director*: M. Finlayson

Research Centres
Applied Philosophy and Public Ethics *(CAPPE) Director*: T. Campbell; **Complex System** *Director*: T. Bossomaier; **EH Graham Centre for Agricultural Innovation** (Agriculture; Farm Management); **Management of Dryland Salinity** (Bioengineering; Farm Management; Plant and Crop Protection; Soil Science; Water Management) *Director*: D. Lemerle; **National Wine and Grape Industry** (Oenology; Viticulture) *Director*: J. Hardie; **Public and Contextual Theology** (Theology) *Director*: J. Haire; **Rural Social Research** (Gender Studies; Rural Studies; Social Policy) *Director*: M. Alston

Research Institutes
Professional Practice, Learning and Education *(RIPPLE)* (Educational Research) *Director*: T. Lowrie

Further Information: Also Charles Sturt University in Ontario (Canada)

History: Founded 1989. A federated network Institution incorporating the former Mitchell College of Advanced Education at Bathurst and Riverina-Murray Institute of Higher Education at Wagga Wagga and Albury-Wodonga. Campuses are located in Bathurst, Wagga Wagga, Albury-Wodonga and Dubbo.

Governing Bodies: Council

Academic Year: February to November (February-June; July-November)

Admission Requirements: New South Wales higher school certificate, or equivalent. Also previous tertiary or postsecondary studies

Main Language(s) of Instruction: English

Degrees and Diplomas: *Bachelor Degree*: Applied Sciences (Agriculture, Ecotourism, Environmental Science, Equine Studies, Food Science, Horticulture, Irrigation, Parks Recreation and Horticulture, Viticulture, Wine Science); Arts (Fine Arts, Graphic Design, Photography, Multimedia, Television Production); Business (Accountancy, Banking, Business Management, Economics, E-Commerce, Finance, Human Resources Management, Industrial Relations, Insurance, International Business, Management, Marketing, Public Administration, Tourism Management); Communication (Advertising, Commercial Radio, Journalism, Media and Cultural Studies, Online Media Production, Public Relations, Organisational Communication, Theatre and Media); Health Sciences (Community Health, Complementary Medicine, Gerontology, Leisure and Health, Mental Health, Nursing, Nutrition, Occupational Therapy, Podiatry, Speech Pathology, Pre-Hospital Care) (BHealthSc); Information Technology; Social Sciences (Criminal Justice, Psychology, Social Welfare), 3 yrs (6 yrs part-time); *Bachelor Degree*: Arts (Library and Information Science), 3 yrs; *Bachelor Degree*: Dentistry, 5 yrs; *Bachelor Degree*: Education (Early Childhood, Primary, Secondary, Technology and Applied Studies, Vocational) (BEd); Psychology, 4 yrs (8 yrs part-time); *Bachelor Degree*: Pharmacy; Physiotherapy, 4 yrs; *Bachelor Degree*: Social Work, 4 yrs (part-time); *Bachelor Honours Degree*: Applied Science (BAppSc); Arts; Social Science (Bsoc (Hons)), 1-8 yrs (full and part-time); *Master Degree*: Accountancy (MAcc); Health Sciences (MHlthSc); Information Studies, 3 yrs (part-time); *Master Degree*: Applied Science (MAppSc); Business; Education (Contemporary Literacies, Educational Leadership; Educational Research; Information Technologies, 2 yrs (4 yrs part-time); *Master Degree*: Arts (Communication-Cultural Performance) (MACom), 4 yrs; *Master Degree*: Education (Inclusive Education); Teaching English to Speakers of Other Languages; Exercise Science (Rehabilitation); Social Sciences (Criminology and Welfare/Social Policy), 2 yrs (part-time); *Doctoral Degree (PhD)*: a further 3 yrs (6 yrs part-time); *Doctoral Degree*: Public Policy, Psychology, Business Administration, Education, Health Sciences, Public Health, Communication, Ministry, Information Technology, a further 2-4 yrs. Also undergraduate and postgraduate Diplomas and Certificates

Student Services: Academic counselling, Canteen, Employment services, Foreign student adviser, Handicapped facilities, Health services, Language programs, Nursery care, Social counselling, Sports facilities

Special Facilities: Public Radio Station at Bathurst. Conservatoires at Bathurst, Wagga Wagga and Albury. TV Studio, Winery, Farm, University Art Collection; allied health clinics at Albury-Wodinga. Allied health clinics at Albury-Wodonga. Veterinary clinics at Wagga Wagga.

Libraries: Truskett Library at CSU Bathurst, 268,600 vols; William Merrylees Library, CSU-Wagga Wagaa, 236,600 vols; CSU Albury-Wodonga, 76,200 vols; CSU at Orange 20,000 vols; CSU at Ontario 6,500 vols; and CSU at Dubbo 6,700 vols; Electronic books 12,500; Electronic serial titles 77,000
Last Updated: 12/10/11

CURTIN UNIVERSITY OF TECHNOLOGY

GPO Box U1987, Perth, Western Australia 6845
Tel: +61(8) 9266-9266
Fax: +61(8) 9266-2255
EMail: internationaloffice@curtin.edu.au
Website: http://www.curtin.edu.au

Vice-Chancellor: Jeanette Hacket
Tel: +61(8) 9266-7001, Fax: +61(8) 9266-2779
EMail: vcsec@vc.curtin.edu.au

University Secretary: Gem Cheong
Tel: +61(8) 9266-3552, Fax: +61(8) 9266-3551
EMail: g.cheong@curtin.edu.au

International Relations: Kevin McKenna, Deputy Vice-Chancellor,
International Tel: +61(8) 9266-3064, Fax: +61(8) 9266-3960

Divisions

Business Administration *(Curtin Sarawak)* (Business Administration; Business and Commerce; Chemical Engineering; Civil Engineering; Computer Engineering; Computer Science; Electrical Engineering; Engineering; Mechanical Engineering; Petroleum and Gas Engineering) *Executive Dean*: John Evans; **Engineering, Science and Computing** (Applied Chemistry; Astronomy and Space Science; Chemical Engineering; Civil Engineering; Computer Engineering; Computer Science; Electrical Engineering; Engineering; Geology; Mathematics; Mechanical Engineering; Natural Sciences; Statistics); **Health Sciences** (Biomedicine; Dental Hygiene; Health Sciences; Nursing; Occupational Therapy; Pharmacy; Physical Therapy; Psychology; Public Health; Speech Therapy and Audiology); **Humanities** (Architecture; Arts and Humanities; Cultural Studies; Design; Education; Fine Arts; Indigenous Studies; Information Sciences; Leisure Studies; Library Science; Modern Languages; Performing Arts; Publishing and Book Trade; Social Sciences; Social Work; Technology; Town Planning; Welfare and Protective Services); **Resources and Environment** (Agriculture; Aquaculture; Arid Land Studies; Environmental Studies; Geological Engineering; Geophysics; Horticulture; Hydraulic Engineering; Petroleum and Gas Engineering)

Schools

Business *(Curtin Business School)* (Accountancy; Advertising and Publicity; Banking; Business Administration; Business Computing; Commercial Law; Economics; Finance; Human Resources; International Business; Leadership; Management; Management Systems; Marketing; Public Relations; Real Estate; Small Business; Taxation; Tourism) *Pro Vice-Chancellor*: Duncan Bentley

Further Information: Also campuses in Bentley, Geraldton, Kalgoorlie, Margaret River,Northam, Shenton Park, Sydney. Overseas Campus: Miri, Sarawak, Malaysia

History: Founded 1967 as Western Australian Institute of Technology, acquired present status and title 1986.

Governing Bodies: Council

Academic Year: 2 semesters, commencing February and July (12 weeks each)

Admission Requirements: Secondary graduation and demonstrated competence in English, plus attainment of a sufficiently high Tertiary Entrance Rank (TER) or recognized international equivalent. Some courses require specific subjects to have been satisfactorily completed prior to entry

Main Language(s) of Instruction: English

International Co-operation: With universities in China, Hong Kong, Indonesia, Iran, Malaysia, Mauritius, Singapore, Vietnam

Degrees and Diplomas: *Advanced Diploma*: 2 yrs; *Bachelor Degree*: 3-5 yrs; *Bachelor Honours Degree*: included in Bachelor Degree; *Graduate Certificate/Diploma*: 6 months; *Master Degree*: 1 further yr; *Doctoral Degree (PhD)*: 2-3 yrs

Student Services: Academic counselling, Canteen, Cultural centre, Employment services, Foreign student adviser, Foreign Studies Centre, Handicapped facilities, Health services, Language programs, Nursery care, Social counselling, Sports facilities

Student Residential Facilities: Yes

Special Facilities: Art Collection of 2,000 items covering all areas of the visual arts. John Curtin Gallery

Libraries: Robertson Library, 599,436 vols. 45,690 current serial titles

Publications: Annual Report to Parliament, Overview of University's Annual Activities and Expenditure *(annually)*
Last Updated: 30/03/11

DEAKIN UNIVERSITY

1 Gheringhap St, Geelong, Victoria 3220
Tel: +61(3) 5227-1100
Fax: +61(3) 5227-2001
EMail: deakin-international@deakin.edu.au
Website: http://www.deakin.edu.au

Vice-Chancellor: Jane den Hollander
Tel: +61(3) 5227-8503, Fax: +61(3) 5227-8500
EMail: vcoffice@deakin.edu.au

Vice-Chancellor (Academic): John Catford
Tel: +61(3) 5227-8507 EMail: dvca@deakin.edu.au

International Relations: Robin Buckham, Deputy Vice-Chancellor (International and Development)
Tel: +61(3) 9246-8017 EMail: dvcid@deakin.edu.au

Faculties

Arts and Education (Asian Studies; Communication Arts; Education; Fine Arts; Heritage Preservation; History; International Studies; Pacific Area Studies; Political Sciences; Social Sciences) *Dean*: Jennifer Radbourne; **Business and Law** (Accountancy; Business Administration; Economics; Finance; Information Technology; Law; Management; Marketing; Social Sciences) *Dean*: Gael Mc Donald; **Health** (Health Sciences; Medicine; Midwifery; Nursing; Nutrition; Physical Education; Psychology; Social and Preventive Medicine); **Science and Technology** (Architecture and Planning; Biological and Life Sciences; Engineering; Environmental Engineering; Environmental Studies; Information Sciences; Information Technology; Mathematics and Computer Science; Natural Sciences; Technology) *Dean*: Chris Gray

Institutes

Research *(Alfred Deakin) Director*: David Lowe; **Koorie Education** (Education) *Director*: Wendy Brabham; **Teaching and Learning** *Director*: Colin Mason; **Technology Research and Innovation** *Director*: Peter Hodgson

Further Information: Also Melbourne campus at Burwood; Geelong Waterfront campus; Geelong campus at Waurn Ponds; Warrnambool campus

History: Founded 1974. It was Victoria's only regionally based University. Following the mergers with Warrnambool Institute of Advanced Education, 1990 and Victoria College 1991, Deakin is a multi-campus institution. A second Geelong campus was established at the Geelong Waterfront in 1996.

Governing Bodies: University Council

Academic Year: March to November (March-June; July-October; November-February)

Admission Requirements: Victorian Certificate of Education (VCE) or equivalent qualification, or tertiary or TAFE study.

Fees: (Aus Dollars): International, 17,500-52,290 (undergraduate); 18,500-26,580 (postgraduate) per annum

Main Language(s) of Instruction: English

Degrees and Diplomas: *Bachelor Degree*; *Graduate Certificate/ Diploma*: 6 mths; *Master Degree*: 11/2-2 yrs; *Doctoral Degree (PhD)*: a further 2-3 yrs. Also combined Bachelors Degree 4/5 yrs

Student Services: Academic counselling, Canteen, Cultural centre, Employment services, Foreign student adviser, Handicapped facilities, Health services, Nursery care, Social counselling, Sports facilities

Student Residential Facilities: For 893 students

Libraries: Total, 1,47Million vols, 127,000 e-books, 86,419 e-journals, 435 online databases, over 81,300 items in special collections.

Press or Publishing House: Deakin University Press

Academic Staff 2010	MEN	WOMEN	TOTAL
FULL-TIME	577	611	1,188
Student Numbers 2010			
All (Foreign Included)	16,076	23,530	39,606
FOREIGN ONLY	4,164	4,343	8,507

Part-time students, 13,557.
Last Updated: 22/06/11

EDITH COWAN UNIVERSITY (ECU)

270 Joondalup Drive, Joondalup, Western Australia 6027
Tel: +61(8) 6304-0000 +61(8) 6304-2205
Fax: +61(8) 9300-1257 +61(8) 6304-2666
EMail: enquiries@ecu.edu.au
Website: http://www.ecu.edu.au

Vice-Chancellor: Kerry O. Cox (2006-)
Tel: +61(8) 6304-2205, Fax: +61(8) 6304-2666
EMail: k.cox@ecu.edu.au; vc@ecu.edu.au

Deputy Vice-Chancellor (Academic) and Vice President: Arshad Omari Tel: +61(8) 6304-2600 EMail: j.bovington@ecu.edu.au

International Relations: Tony Watson, Deputy Vice Chancellor (International)
Tel: +61(8) 6304-5377, Fax: +61(8) 6304-2116
EMail: international@ecu.edu.au

Faculties

Business and Law (Accountancy; Business Administration; Economics; Finance; Justice Administration; Law; Leisure Studies; Management; Marketing; Public Administration; Service Trades; Tourism); **Computing, Health and Science** (Biomedicine; Engineering; Health Sciences; Information Sciences; Mathematics and Computer Science; Medicine; Midwifery; Natural Sciences; Nursing; Public Health; Sports); **Education and Arts** (Arts and Humanities; Communication Arts; Education; Performing Arts); **Regional Professional Studies** *(ECU South West Campus, Bunbury)* (Business Administration; Communication Studies; Computer Science; Education; Health Sciences; Nursing; Social Work; Visual Arts; Welfare and Protective Services)

Further Information: Also Mount Lawley and South West campuses.

History: Founded 1991 with four campuses: Bunbury, Churchlands, Joondalup, and Mount Lawley. Formerly the Western Australia College of Advanced Education. Roots extend back to 1902 when first tertiary institution was established in Western Australia.

Governing Bodies: University Council

Academic Year: February to November (February-June; July-November). Summer Session: December-January.

Admission Requirements: Secondary school certificate with matriculation or recognized foreign equivalent

Fees: Vary per course. Details on request at www.ecu.edu.au/iso/content/fees/index.php for international students

Main Language(s) of Instruction: English

International Co-operation: Member of the Commonwealth Universities Study Abroad Consortium and UMAP. The University has more than 80 active agreements with educational organizations across 30 countries.

Degrees and Diplomas: *Bachelor Degree*: Arts (BA); Business (BBus); Communications (BComms); Education (BEd); Health Sciences (BHSc); Nursing (BNurs); Sciences (Human Biology; Sports Science; Biological Sciences; Environmental Management; Computer Science; Communication and Information Technology; Internet Computing; Software Engineering; Library Technology; Security; Aviation) (BSc), 3 yrs; *Bachelor Degree*: Engineering (Computer Systems Engineering; Communication Systems Engineering; Electronic Systems Engineering) (BEng); Music (BMusic), 4 yrs; *Bachelor Honours Degree (BHon)*: 1 further yr; *Graduate Certificate/Diploma (Gdip)*: 1 yr following Bachelor Degree; *Master Degree (MA)*: a further 1-2 yrs beyond Bachelor Degree; *Doctoral Degree (PhD)*: a further 3 yrs beyond Honours or Master's Degree

Student Services: Academic counselling, Canteen, Cultural centre, Employment services, Foreign student adviser, Foreign Studies Centre, Handicapped facilities, Health services, Language programs, Nursery care, Social counselling, Sports facilities

Student Residential Facilities: Mount Lawley campus, 165; Joondalup campus, 148; Bunbury campus, 52

Special Facilities: Museum of Childhood; University Art Collection

Libraries: Each campus has a library and access to electronic journal titles
Last Updated: 05/12/11

FLINDERS UNIVERSITY (FLINDERS)

GPO Box 2100, Adelaide, South Australia 5001
Tel: +61(8) 8201-3911
Fax: +61(8) 8201-3000
EMail: central.records@flinders.edu.au
Website: http://www.flinders.edu.au

Vice-Chancellor and President: Michael N. Barber (2008-)
Tel: +61(8) 8201-2101, Fax: +61(2) 8277-2534

Vice-President Strategic Finance and Resources: Shane McGregor
Tel: +61(8) 8201-2701, Fax: +61(8) 8201-3934
EMail: shane.mcgregor@Flinders.edu.au

Vice-President Strategy & Planning: Brownwyn Simondson
Tel: +61(8) 8201-3532, Fax: +61(8) 8201-3934
EMail: bronwyn.simondson@flinders.edu.au

International Relations: Dean Forbes, Deputy-Vice-Chancellor (International and Communities)
Tel: +61(8) 8201-5462, Fax: +62(8) 8201-3980
EMail: Dean.Forbes@Flinders.edu.au

Centres

Cancer Prevention and Control (Oncology); **Climate Adaptation and Animal Behaviour**; **Epidemiology and Biostatistics** (Epidemiology; Statistics); **Gambling Research**; **Marine Bioprocessing and Bioproducts** (Marine Biology); **Marine Science** *(Lincoln (LMSC))* (Marine Science and Oceanography; Natural Sciences); **Mental Health and Violence Prevention in Educational Settings** (Psychiatry and Mental Health); **Nanoscale Sciences and Technology** (Nanotechnology); **Neurosciences** (Neurosciences); **Ophthalmology, Eye and Vision Research** (Ophthalmology); **Point-of-Care Testing**; **Remote Health** (Health Sciences)

Faculties

Education, Humanities, Law (Archaeology; Arts and Humanities; Cinema and Television; Cultural Studies; Education; English; Law; Theatre; Tourism) *Executive Dean*: Richard Maltby; **Health Sciences** (Health Sciences; Medicine; Midwifery; Nursing) *Executive Dean*: Michael Kidd; **Science and Engineering** (Biological and Life Sciences; Biotechnology; Chemistry; Computer Science; Earth Sciences; Engineering; Environmental Management; Geography; Mathematics; Physics; Statistics) *Executive Dean*: Warren Lawrence; **Social Sciences** (American Studies; Asian Studies; Business and Commerce; Economics; History; International Studies; Political Sciences; Psychology; Social Sciences; Social Work; Sociology; Women's Studies) *Executive Dean*: John Phyllis Tharenou

Institutes

Health, Society and Equity; **Palliative and Supportive Studies** *(International Institute)* (Health Sciences); **Public Policy and Management** *(FIPPM)* (Management; Social and Community Services); **Research in the Humanities** (Humanities and Social Science Education)

Research Centres

Aboriginal Health *(Flinders) Director*: Inge Kowanko; **Ageing Studies** *(CAS)* (Gerontology) *Director*: Mary Luszcz; **Airborne** *((ARA))* (Natural Sciences); **Australian Seafood**; **Clinical Change and Health Care** (Health Sciences; Meteorology); **Community Services** *(ACCSR)* (Service Trades); **Disaster Resilience and Health** (Psychiatry and Mental Health); **Economic Studies** *(Jointly with University of Adelaide South Australian Centre for Economic Studies)* (Economics; Social Sciences); **Education and Training on Addiction** *(National (NCETA))* (Health Sciences; Toxicology) *Director*: Ann Roche; **Injury Studies** (Health Sciences); **Molecular Technologies** (Chemistry); **Water and Environment** *(Jointly with other institutions)* (Environmental Studies; Water Science)

Research Institutes

Australian Housing and Urban Studies *(AHURI)*; **Educational Futures Studies** (Science Education); **Labour Studies** *(National Institute)* (Labour and Industrial Relations; Social Sciences) *Director*: Sue Richardson; **Primary Health Care Research and Information Service** (Health Sciences; Medicine) *Director*: Libby Kalucy

History: Flinders University of South Australia founded 1966 by proclamation of Act of South Australian Parliament. The Sturt Campus of the South Australian College of Advanced Education was amalgamated with the University 1991.

Governing Bodies: Council

Academic Year: March to November (March-June; July-November)

Admission Requirements: South Australian Certificate of Education or recognized equivalent. Credit for work done at other recognized institutions may be counted towards a Flinders award. Applicants from countries where English is not the first language are required to demonstrate a minimum standard of English language competence (TOEFL score of 550, IELTS score of 6, or 213 in the computer-based TOEFL)

Fees: (Aus Dollars): 15,200-19,300 per annum; postgraduate, 17,900-27,700; Medicine, 40,000

Main Language(s) of Instruction: English

International Co-operation: With universities in Austria, Argentina, Brazil, Canada, Chile, China, Cyprus, Denmark, France, Germany, Hong Kong, Hungary, Iceland, India, Indonesia, Iran, Italy, Japan, Korea, Malaysia, Mexico, Northern Ireland, Norway, Philippines; Singapore, Slovenia, Sweden, Spain, The Netherlands, Taiwan, Thailand, United Kingdom, USA, Vietnam

Degrees and Diplomas: *Bachelor Degree*: Accountancy (Bacc); Social Work (BSocWk), 2 yrs (graduate entry); *Bachelor Degree*: Applied Geospatial and Information Technology (BAppGeoInfo Tech); Applied Sciences (Disability Studies) (BAppSc (DisSt)); Archaeology (BArchaeol); Arts (BA); Banking and International Finance (BBgIntFin); Behavioural Science (BBehavSc); Biodiversity and Conservation (BSc(BiodivCon)); Business and Economics (BBusEc); Commerce (BCom); Creative Arts (BCreatArts); Cultural Tourism (BCulT); Environmental Health (BEnvHlth); Environmental Management (BEnvMgmt); Environmental Science (BScEnvSc); Forensic and Analytical Chemistry (BTech); Government and Public Management; Health Sciences (BHlthSc); Information Technology (BInfoTech); International Business (BIntBus); International Studies (BIntSt); Justice and Society (BJus&Soc); Marine Biology (BScMarBiol); Medical Science (BMedSc); Medicinal Chemistry (BSc(MedChem)); Midwifery (Bmid); Nursing (BNg); Paramedic; Science (BSc); Technology (Aquaculture) (BTech(Aqua)); Technology (Ecotourism) (BTech(Ecot)), 3 yrs; *Bachelor Degree*: Biotechnology (BBiotech); Computer Engineering (Beng(CompEng)); Education; Junior Primary/Primary Education; Middle School Education; Secondary Education (BEd); Electrical and Electronic Engineering (BEng(Elec)); Nutrition and Dietetics (BNuDiet); Social Work and Planning (BSocWk,BSocPg); Software Engineering (Beng(SoftEng)); Theology (BTh), 4 yrs; *Bachelor Degree*: Computer Science (BCompSc), 1 1/2-2 yrs (graduate entry); *Bachelor Degree*: Education (Special Education) (Bed(SpecEd)), 2 yrs; *Bachelor Degree*: Engineering (Biomedical) (BEng (Biomed)); Laws and Legal Practice (LLB/LP), 5 yrs; *Bachelor Degree*: Innovation and Enterprise (Science and Technology) (BIE(S&T)), 1 yr (with another degree); *Bachelor Degree*: Medicine and Surgery (BMBS), 4 yrs (plus 1 yr teaching internship); *Bachelor Degree*: Special Education (BSpecEd), 1 yr (graduate entry); *Bachelor Degree*: Speech Pathology (BSpPath), 3 1/2 yrs; *Bachelor Honours Degree*: Nanotechnology (BScNano(Hons)); Psychology (BPsych(Hons)), 4 yrs; *Graduate Certificate/Diploma*; *Master Degree*: Applied Social and Market Research (MA(AppSocMktRes)); Asian Economics (MA(AsianEc)); Asian Studies (MA(AsianSt)); Biodiversity (Mbiod); Biotechnology (Mbiotech); Biotechnology Studies (MBiotechSt); Clinical Rehabilitation (MClinRehab); Disability Studies (MDisSt); Education (Med); Educational Management (MEdMgmt); Gifted Education (MGiftEd); Health Sciences (Pre-Hospital and Emergency Care) (MHlthSc(Pre-HospEmergC)); International Development (MA(IntDev)); International Relations (MA(IntRel)); Maritime Archaeology (MMarArchaeol); Mental Health Sciences (MMenHlthSc); Midwifery (Mmid); Nursing (MNg); Nursing (Nurse Practitioner) (MNg(NgPrac)); Palliative Care (MPallC); Policy and Administration (MPolAdmin); Population and Human Resources (MPopHumRes); Psychology (Clinical) (Mpsych(Clin)); Remote Health Management (MRemoteHlthMgmt); Science (Groundwater Hydrology) (MSc(GwHyd)); Science (Health Service Management) (MSc(HlthServMgmt)); Science (Palliative Care) (MSc(PallC)); Science (Primary Health Care) (MSc(PHC)); Social Work (MA(SocWk)); Sociology (MA(Soc)); Surgery (Msurg); Women's Studies (MA(WomSt)), a further 1-2 yrs; *Master Degree*: Arts (MA), a further 1-2 yrs (by coursework or by research); *Master Degree*: Audiology (MAud); Clinical Nursing (MClinNg); Environmental Management (MEnvMgmt); Health Service Management (MHlthSerMgmt); Information Technology (Computing) (MInfoTech(Comp)); International Business (MBA(IntBus)); Nutrition and

Dietetics (MNutDiet); Primary Health Care (MPHC); Public Management (MPubMgmt); Public Policy (MPubPol); Remote Health Practice (MRemoteHlthPrac); Social Work (MSocWk); Special Education (MSpecEd); *Master Degree*: Commerce (MCom); Economics (MEc); Engineering (Meng); Science (MSc); Theology (MTh), by research; *Master Degree*: Creative Arts (MCreatArts), by course work and research; *Master Degree*: Laws (LLM), a further 1-2 yrs (by course work or research); *Master Degree*: Theological Studies (MTheolSt), a further 2 yrs; *Doctoral Degree*: Clinical Psychology (PhD(ClinPsych)), 4 yrs; *Doctoral Degree*: Education (EdD); Public Health (DrPH), 3 yrs, coursework and research; *Doctoral Degree*: Law (LLD); Science (DSc); Theology (DTh), by published work; *Doctoral Degree*: Literature (DLitt), by published work; *Doctoral Degree*: Medicine (MD), 3 yrs, by thesis; *Doctoral Degree*: Philosophy (PhD), 2-4 yrs; *Doctoral Degree*: Policy and Administration (DPA), 2-4 yrs, by course work and research. See also http://www. flinders. edu .au/ calendar lvol2lhome.html

Student Services: Academic counselling, Canteen, Employment services, Foreign student adviser, Handicapped facilities, Health services, Language programs, Nursery care, Social counselling, Sports facilities

Student Residential Facilities: Yes

Special Facilities: Art Museum; Pathology Museum; Anatomical Museum. Rare Book Room. Fossil Collection

Libraries: Central Library, Gus Fraenkel Medical Library, Law Library, and Sturt Library, total, c. 950,000 vols

Publications: Australian Economic Papers *(3 per annum)*; C.R.N.L.E. Reviews Journal *(biannually)*; Research Report, Only electronically *(annually)*; The Australian Bulletin of Labour *(quarterly)*

Press or Publishing House: Flinders Press

Academic Staff 2010	MEN	WOMEN	TOTAL
FULL-TIME	412	446	858
Student Numbers 2010			
All (Foreign Included)	6,688	12,147	18,835
FOREIGN ONLY	1,571	1,969	3,540

Part-time students, 9,383. **Distance students**, 2,675.
Last Updated: 03/08/11

GRIFFITH UNIVERSITY

170 Kessels Road, Nathan, Brisbane, Queensland 4111
Tel: +61(7) 3735-7111
Fax: +61(7) 3735-7507
EMail: griffith.university@griffith.edu.au
Website: http://www.griffith.edu.au

Vice-Chancellor and President: Ian O'Connor (2005-)
Tel: +61(7) 5552-8178, Fax: +61(7) 3735-7320
EMail: vc@griffith.edu.au; i.oconnor@griffith.edu.au

Director, External Relations: Meredith Jackson (2011-)
Tel: +61(7) 5552-7845, Fax: +61(7) 5552-8517
EMail: meredith.jackson@griffith.edu.au

International Relations: Christopher Madden, Pro-Vice Chancellor (International)
Tel: +61(7) 5552-9101, Fax: +61(7) 5552-9096
EMail: c.madden@griffith.edu.au

Colleges
Arts *(Queensland) Director*: Paul Cleveland

Conservatories
Conservatorium *(Queensland)*

Departments
Accountancy, Finance and Economics (Accountancy; Economics; Finance); **Employment Relations and Human Resources** (Human Resources; Industrial Management); **International Business and Asian Studies** (Accountancy; Asian Studies; Business and Commerce; Finance; Hotel Management; Human Resources; International Business; Leisure Studies; Management; Marketing; Political Sciences; Sports Management; Tourism) *Head*: Leong Liew; **Marketing** (Marketing); **Politics and Public Policy** (Political Sciences; Public Administration); **Tourism, Leisure, Hotel and Sport Management** (Hotel Management; Leisure Studies; Sports Management; Tourism)

Schools

Applied Psychology (Psychology); **Arts, Education and Law** (Arts and Humanities; Education; Law); **Biomolecular and Physical Sciences** (Biomedical Engineering; Molecular Biology); **Business** (Asian Studies; International Business); **Criminology and Criminal Justice** (Criminal Law; Criminology); **Dentistry and Oral Health** (Dentistry; Oral Pathology); **Education and Professional Studies** (Art Education; Curriculum; Education; Foreign Languages Education; Pedagogy; Special Education; Technology; Technology Education; Vocational Education); **Engineering** (Electronic Engineering; Engineering; Environmental Engineering; Microelectronics); **Environment** (Environmental Management; Environmental Studies); **Human Services and Social Work** (Social and Community Services; Social Welfare); **Humanities** (Arts and Humanities); **Information and Communication Technology** (Computer Engineering; Computer Science; Information Technology; Telecommunications Engineering); **Languages and Linguistics** (Linguistics; Modern Languages); **Law** (Law); **Management** (Management); **Medical Science** (Biomedical Engineering; Biomedicine; Molecular Biology; Natural Sciences); **Medicine** (Medicine); **Nursing and Midwifery** (Midwifery; Nursing); **Pharmacy** (Pharmacy); **Physiotherapy and Exercise Science** (Physical Therapy; Physiology; Rehabilitation and Therapy); **Public Health** (Anatomy; Dentistry; Health Sciences; Medicine; Nursing; Oral Pathology; Pharmacy; Physical Therapy; Psychology; Public Health); **Science, Environment, Engineering and Technology** (Computer Engineering; Engineering; Environmental Engineering; Information Technology; Microelectronics); **Vocational, Technology and Arts Education** (Art Education; Technology Education)

Further Information: Also Campuses at Nathan, Mount Gravatt, Gold Coast, Logan and South Bank. the Gold Coast in south-east Queensland. Over 30 Reseach centres. Several independent academic centres, institutes and colleges

History: Founded 1971 and officially opened 1975. The University has adopted a 'School' Structure as its academic unit.

Governing Bodies: Council

Academic Year: January to December (February-June; July-November; November-February)

Admission Requirements: Secondary school certificate or recognized foreign equivalent, or previous tertiary study. Candidates who have completed relevant studies from another institution may apply for exemption from some studies

Fees: (Aus Dollars): 14,720-61,520 per annum

Main Language(s) of Instruction: English

International Co-operation: With universities in Europe; USA and Asia

Degrees and Diplomas: *Bachelor Degree*: 3-5 yrs; *Graduate Certificate/Diploma*; *Master Degree*: a further 1-4 yrs; *Doctoral Degree*

Student Services: Academic counselling, Canteen, Cultural centre, Employment services, Foreign student adviser, Foreign Studies Centre, Handicapped facilities, Health services, Language programs, Nursery care, Social counselling, Sports facilities

Student Residential Facilities: For over 950 students

Special Facilities: Griffith Artworks; Dell gallery

Libraries: 875,325 vols; 75,947 serial titles

Academic Staff *2010-2011*	TOTAL
FULL-TIME	c. 3,600

Student Numbers *2010-2011*	
All (Foreign Included)	c. 36,000
FOREIGN ONLY	8,400

Last Updated: 29/11/11

JAMES COOK UNIVERSITY (JCU)

Townsville Campus, Angus Smith Drive, Townsville, Queensland 4811
Tel: +61(7) 4781-4111 +61(7) 4781-4942
Fax: +61(7) 4779-6371 +61(7) 4781-6116
EMail: registrar@jcu.edu.au
Website: http://www.jcu.edu.au

Vice-Chancellor: Sandra Harding (2007-)
Tel: +61(7) 4781-4165, Fax: +61(7) 4781-4050
EMail: vc@jcu.edu.au; sandra.harding@jcu.edu.au

Deputy Vice-Chancellor: Chris Cocklin
Tel: +61(7) 4781-6884 EMail: sdvc@jcu.edu.au

International Relations: Scott Bowman
Tel: +61(7) 4781-5601, Fax: +61(7) 4781-5988
EMail: international@jcu.edu.au; scott.bowman@jcu.edu.au

Centres

Advanced Analytical; **Astronomy** *(Co-operative Research)* (Astronomy and Space Science); **Australian Tropical Freshwater Research** (Water Science); **Biotechnology Applications Research** (Biotechnology; Medical Technology); **Coastal Zone Estuary and Waterway Management** (Coastal Studies; Water Management); **Comparative Genomics**; **Coral Reef Biodiversity**; **Disaster Studies**; **English Language** (English); **Great Barrier Reef World Heritage Area** *(Co-operative Research)* (Ecology; Marine Biology); **Interactive Multimedia** (Multimedia); **Melanesian Studies** (Pacific Area Studies); **North Queensland Magnetic Resonance**; **Remote Sensing** (Surveying and Mapping); **Rural Education Research and Development** (Agricultural Education; Educational Sciences); **Study of Teaching and Teacher Development** (Staff Development); **Sustainable Development of Tropical Savannas** (Forest Biology); **Sustainable Sugar Production** (Food Technology); **Sustainable Tourism** (Tourism); **Tropical Freshwater Research** (Water Science); **Tropical Health and Medicine** *(Anton Breinl)* (Tropical Medicine); **Tropical Marine Studies** *(Sir George)* (Marine Science and Oceanography); **Tropical Rainforest Ecology and Management** *(Co-operative Research)* (Forest Biology; Forest Management); **Tropical Urban and Regional Planning** (Regional Planning; Urban Studies); **Women's Studies** (Women's Studies)

Faculties

Arts, Education and Social Sciences (Arts and Humanities; Education; Social Sciences) *Pro-Vice-Chancellor*: Janet Greeley; **Law, Business and Creative Arts** (Arts and Humanities; Business and Commerce; Economics; Fine Arts; Law) *Pro-Vice-Chancellor*: Robini Woellner; **Medicine, Health and Molecular Sciences** (Health Sciences; Medicine; Molecular Biology) *Pro-Vice-Chancellor*: Ian Wronski; **Science and Engineering** (Engineering; Natural Sciences) *Pro-Vice-Chancellor (Acting)*: Michael Kingsford

Institutes

Gas Research *(Coalseam)* (Petroleum and Gas Engineering); **Interdisciplinary Studies**; **Northern Australia Social Research** (Social Sciences); **Sports and Exercise Science** (Sports); **Tropical Medical Laboratory Science** (Medical Technology)

Programmes

Arts and Social Sciences (Arts and Humanities; Psychology; Social Sciences; Social Work)

Schools

Anthropology, Archaeology and Sociology (Anthropology; Archaeology; Sociology); **Business and Information Technology** (Accountancy; Business and Commerce; Computer Engineering; Economics; Information Technology; International Business; Management; Marketing; Tourism); **Creative Arts** (Music; Theatre; Visual Arts); **Earth and Environmental Sciences** (Earth Sciences; Environmental Studies; Forestry; Geography; Tropical Agriculture); **Education** (Education); **Engineering** (Engineering); **Humanities** (Arts and Humanities); **Indigenous Australian Studies** (Indigenous Studies); **Law** (Law); **Marine and Tropical Biology** (Aquaculture; Biological and Life Sciences; Marine Biology); **Mathematics, Physics and Information Technology** (Information Technology; Mathematics; Physics); **Medicine** (Medicine); **Nursing Sciences** (Nursing); **Psychology** (Psychology); **Public Health and Tropical Medicine** (Public Health; Tropical Medicine); **Social Work and Community Welfare** (Social Welfare; Social Work); **Veterinary and Biomedical Sciences**

Units

Economic Geology Research (Metal Techniques); **JCU Sugar-Advanced Technology** (Food Technology); **Marine and Aquaculture Research Facilities** (Aquaculture); **Optical Microscope** (Optical Technology)

Further Information: Also campuses at Mackay, Cairns, Mount Isa, Brisbane, Singapour and Thursday Island. Most university courses available to overseas students on a fee-paying basis

History: Founded 1961 as University College of Townsville, acquired present status and title 1970. Townsville College of Advanced Education amalgamated with the University 1982.

Governing Bodies: Council

Academic Year: February to November (February-June; July-November)

Admission Requirements: Secondary school certificate or recognized foreign equivalent, or previous tertiary study. Credit may be granted for studies in another tertiary institution. Students whose language is not English must show proficiency in English (6.0 IELTS, with non-component lower than 5.5 or 550 TOEFL minimum, with a test of written English-minimum score of 19) (iscadmissions@jcu.edu.au)

Fees: (Aus Dollars): 18,000-23,500 per annum for Bachelor studies

Main Language(s) of Instruction: English

Degrees and Diplomas: *Bachelor Degree*: 3-4 yrs; *Bachelor Honours Degree*: 4 yrs, or 1 further yr; *Master Degree*: a further 1-2 yrs; *Doctoral Degree (PhD)*: at least a further 2 yrs full-time

Student Residential Facilities: For c. 1,470 students

Special Facilities: Teaching and Reference Museums: Biological Sciences; Collection of Minerals, Ores, Rocks and Fossils; Material Cultural of North Queensland; Radio Research Stations; Experimental Animal Unit. Medical; Marine Research Stations; Cyclone Structural Testing Station

Libraries: c. 500,000 vols

Publications: Bibliographic Record

Academic Staff : Total: c. 650
Last Updated: 05/12/11

LA TROBE UNIVERSITY

Bundoora, Victoria 3086
Tel: +61(3) 9479-1111
Website: http://www.latrobe.edu.au

Vice-Chancellor: Paul Johnson (2007-)
Tel: +61(3) 9479-2000 EMail: vc@latrobe.edu.au

Vice-President (Operation), Chief Operating Officer: David Ensor
Tel: +61(3) 9479-3397, Fax: +61(3) 9479-3353
EMail: d.ensor@latrobe.edu.au

International Relations: John Rosenberg, Senior Deputy Vice-Chancellor and Vice-President
Tel: +61(3) 9479-6598, Fax: +61(3) 9479-1910
EMail: j.molony@latrobe.edu.au

Centres
Advanced Materials Manufacturing *(Victorian)*; **Australian Centre for Evidence Based Aged Care; Centre for China Studies; Centre for Dialogue; Centre for Ergonomics and Human Factors; Centre for Professional Development; Centre for Public Health Law; Centre for Sustainable Regional Communities; Centre for the Study of Professions; Philippines Australian Study Centre; Prosthétics and Orthodontics** *(National)*; **The Bouverie Centre; Thesis Eleven Centre for Critical Theory**

Faculties
Education (Education) *Dean*: Lorraine Ling; **Health Sciences** (Health Sciences) *Dean (Acting)*: Hal Swerissen; **Humanities and Social Sciences** (Communication Disorders; European Studies; Social Sciences; Visual Arts) *Dean*: Tim Murray; **Law and Management** *Dean*: Leigh Drake; **Science, Technology and Engineering** (Engineering; Natural Sciences; Technology) *Dean*: Brian McGaw

Graduate Schools
Management *Head*: Geoff Durden

Institutes
Australian Institute for Primary Care; Australian Institute of Archaeology; Human Security; Institute of Latin American Studies; Italian Australian Institute; La Trobe Institute of Indian

and South Asian Studies; **Michael J Osborne Institute for Advanced Study** *(Research activity in any discipline by distinguished visiting scholars)*; **Molecular Sciences; National Institute for Deaf Studies and Sign Language Research; Social and Environmental Sustainability; Social Participation**

Research Centres
A D Trendall Research Centre; Agribioscience (Agrobiology); **Australian Research Centre in Sex, Health and Society; Centre for Excellence for Mathematics and Statistics of Complex Systems** *(ARC)*; **Computer, Communication and Social Innovation; Conflict Resolution; Excellence for Coherent X-Ray Science** *(Australian Research Council (ARC))*; **Greek Studies** (Greek); **Innovative Universities European Research Centre; Linguistic Typology; Materials and Surface Science; Mother and Child Health; Murray Darling Frenswater Reasearch Centre; Musculoskeletal; Olga Tennison Austim; Public Sector Governance and Accountability Research Centre; Technology Infusion** (Technology)

Research Units
Refugee Health Research Unit

Schools
Accounting (Accountancy) *Head*: Paul Mather; **Business** *(Regional)* (Business Administration) *Head*: Malcom Rimmer; **Clinical Vision Sciences** *Head*: Zoran Georgievski; **Communication, Arts and Critical Enquiry** (Cinema and Television; English; Gender Studies; Linguistics; Logic; Media Studies; Philosophy; Religious Studies; Theatre; Visual Arts) *Head*: Geoff Mayer; **Dentistry and Oral Health** (Dentistry; Oral Pathology) *Head*: Peter Wilson; **Economics and Finance** (Economics; Finance) *Head*: Jae (Paul) Kim; **Education** (Art Education; Cultural Studies; Education; English; Foreign Languages Education; Health Education; Natural Resources; Physical Education; Preschool Education; Primary Education; Secondary Education; Special Education; Tourism); **Engineering and Mathematical Sciences** (Civil Engineering; Computer Engineering; Computer Science; Electronic Engineering; Mathematics; Physics; Statistics) *Head*: Philip Broadbridge; **Historical and European Studies** (American Studies; Archaeology; Art History; Catalan; Cultural Studies; European Studies; French; German; Greek; History; Italian; Latin American Studies; Portuguese; Religion; Religious Studies; Spanish) *Head*: Chris Mackie; **Human Biosciences** *Head*: John Schuijers; **Human Communication Sciences** (Speech Therapy and Audiology) *Head*: Jenni Oates; **Law** (Commercial Law; Law; Public Law) *Head*: Paula Baron; **Life Sciences** (Agriculture; Botany; Ecology; Environmental Management; Environmental Studies; Microbiology; Zoology) *Head*: Roger Parish; **Management** (Human Resources; Information Sciences; Management; Marketing; Sports Management; Tourism) *Head*: Terri Joiner; **Molecular Sciences** (Biochemistry; Chemistry; Genetics; Pharmacy) *Head*: Nick Hoogenraad; **Nursing and Midwifery** (Midwifery; Nursing) *Head*: Bill McGuiness; **Occupational Therapy** (Occupational Therapy) *Head*: Mary Kennedy-Jones; **Physiotherapy** (Physical Therapy) *Head*: Karen Dodd; **Podiatry** *Head (Acting)*: Adam Bird; **Psychology** *Head*: Stephen Kent; **Public Health** *Head*: Sandra Leggart; **Social Sciences** (Anthropology; Asian Studies; Development Studies; Indigenous Studies; International Relations; Law; Pacific Area Studies; Peace and Disarmament; Political Sciences; Social Sciences; Sociology) *Head*: Judith Brett; **Social Work and Social Policy** *Head*: Margarita Frederico; **Sport, Tourism and Hospitality Management** (Hotel Management; Leisure Studies; Sports; Tourism) *Head*: Sue Beeton; **Visual Arts and Design** *Head*: James McArdle

Units
Palliative Care Unit

Further Information: Foundation Studies and Diploma Programmes for overseas students. Off-shore teaching in China, Hong Kong, Japan, Malaysia, Mongolia, Singapore and Vietnam. Study Abroad / Student Exchange programmes

History: Founded 1964, admitted first students 1967.

Governing Bodies: Council; Academic Board

Academic Year: March to October (March-June; July-October)

Admission Requirements: Secondary school certificate or recognized international equivalent, or previous tertiary study

Fees: Information on fees for overseas students is available at www.latrobe.edu.au/international/fees

Main Language(s) of Instruction: English

International Co-operation: Over 80 international collaborative agreements which include staff and student exchanges, joint research and collaborative teaching programmes. Major links are in the Asian region and there are strong links with partner institutions in Europe, and North and South America.

Degrees and Diplomas: *Bachelor Degree*: 3-4 yrs; *Bachelor Honours Degree*: 1 further yr; *Graduate Certificate/Diploma*: 1-2 yrs; *Master Degree*: a further 1-2 yrs; *Doctoral Degree (PhD)*: 4 yrs following Master Degree. Also postgraduate Diploma, 1-2 yrs

Student Services: Academic counselling, Canteen, Foreign Studies Centre, Handicapped facilities, Language programs, Sports facilities

Student Residential Facilities: Colleges Halls and apartments

Special Facilities: University Art Gallery. Wildlife Reserve. Media Centre. Research and Development Park, including Technology Enterprise Centre, Innovation and Knowledge Transfer Division and the Victorian AgriBiosciences Centre.

Libraries: c. 1,870,000 vols; 30,833 subscriptions to periodicals; 150,000 audiovisual items

Publications: Research Report, Account of research activities, grants and publications *(annually)*

Press or Publishing House: La Trobe University Press

Academic Staff *2010*	MEN	WOMEN	TOTAL
FULL-TIME	1,154	1,703	**2,857**
Student Numbers *2010*			
All (Foreign Included)	12,047	18,811	**30,858**
FOREIGN ONLY	–	–	**7,630**

Last Updated: 05/10/11

ALBURY-WODONGA CAMPUS

PO Box 821, University Drive, Wodonga, Victoria 3689
Tel: +61(2) 6024-9700
Fax: +61(2) 6024-9797
EMail: oed.awd@latrobe.edu.au
Website: http://www.latrobe.edu.au

Campus Director: Lin Crase
Tel: +61(2) 6024-9834, Fax: +61(2) 6024-9777

Faculties

Education (Education); **Health Sciences** (Health Sciences; Midwifery; Nursing; Occupational Health; Paramedical Sciences; Podiatry; Social Policy; Social Work; Speech Therapy and Audiology); **Humanities and Social Sciences** (Arts and Humanities; Social Sciences); **Law and Management** (Accountancy; Business Administration; Economics; Law; Management); **Science, Technology and Engineering** (Agriculture; Biology; Ecology; Educational Sciences; Engineering; Environmental Management; Natural Sciences; Psychology; Technology)

History: Founded 1990.

BENDIGO CAMPUS

PO Box 199, Edwards Road, Flora Hill, Bendigo, Victoria 3550
Tel: +61(3) 5444-7222
Fax: +61(3) 5447-7777
EMail: director.bendigo@latrobe.edu.au
Website: http://www.latrobe.edu.au/bendigo

Director: Andrew Skewes
Tel: +61(3) 5444-7881, Fax: +61(3) 5444-7880

Centres
Information and Communication Technology; **Professional Development**

Faculties
Education (Education; Environmental Studies; Natural Resources; Physical Education; Tourism); **Health Sciences** (Dentistry; Health Sciences; Midwifery; Nursing; Occupational Therapy; Oral Pathology; Physical Therapy; Podiatry; Public Health; Social Work; Speech Therapy and Audiology); **Humanities and Social Sciences**

(Arts and Humanities; Communication Studies; Design; Development Studies; Environmental Studies; European Studies; Graphic Design; Rural Planning; Social Policy; Social Sciences; Social Work; Town Planning; Visual Arts); **Law and Management** (Accountancy; Business Administration; Business and Commerce; Law); **Science, Technology and Engineering** (Computer Engineering; Engineering; Information Technology; Multimedia; Natural Sciences); **Sport, Tourism and Hospitality Management** (Sports; Tourism)

Research Centres
Biotechnology

FRANKLIN ST CAMPUS

215 Franklin Street, Melbourne, Victoria 3000
Tel: +61(3) 9285-5100
Fax: +61(3) 9285-5111
EMail: CityCampus@latrobe.edu.au
Website: http://www.latrobe.edu.au/city/

Campus Management Facilities Officer: Wayne Hannah
EMail: w.hannah@latrobe.edu.au

Courses
Postgraduate Studies (Health Sciences; Law; Management)

MILDURA CAMPUS

PO Box 4095, 471 Benetook Ave, Mildura, Victoria 3502
Tel: +61(3) 5051-4000
Fax: +61(3) 5022-0043
EMail: mildura@latrobe.edu.au
Website: http://www.latrobe.edu.au/mildura

Executive Director: Neil Feetling
Tel: +61(3) 5051-4004 EMail: n.fettling@latrobe.edu.au

Departments
Business (Accountancy; Business Administration); **Education**; **Graphic Design** (Graphic Design); **Health Sciences** (Nursing; Social Work); **Humanities and Social Sciences** (Arts and Humanities; Fine Arts; Social Sciences; Visual Arts)

Further Information: Deakin Ave Campus: 29 Deakin Avr, Mildura

SHEPPARTON CAMPUS

PO Box 6044, 210 Fryers St, Shepparton, Victoria 3632
Tel: +61(3) 5820-8600
Fax: +61(3) 5820-8699
Website: http://www.shepparton.latrobe.edu.au

Campus Director: Elizabeth Lavender
Tel: +61(3) 5820-8606 EMail: e.lavender@latrobe.edu.au

Faculties
Education (Education; Vocational Education); **Health Sciences** (Health Sciences; Nursing; Occupational Therapy; Paramedical Sciences; Podiatry; Speech Therapy and Audiology); **Humanities and Social Sciences** (Arts and Humanities; Social Sciences); **Law and Management** (Accountancy; Business Administration; Business and Commerce; Law)

Degrees and Diplomas: *Bachelor Degree*; *Graduate Certificate/Diploma*

MACQUARIE UNIVERSITY

Balaclava Road, North Ryde, Sydney, New South Wales 2109
Tel: +61(2) 9850-7111
Fax: +61(2) 9850-7433
EMail: mqinfo@mq.edu.au
Website: http://www.mq.edu.au

Vice-Chancellor: Steven Schwartz (2006-)
Tel: +61(2) 9850-7440, Fax: +61(2) 9850-9950
EMail: vc@vc.mq.edu.au

Registrar and Vice-Principal: Brian J. Spencer
Tel: +61(2) 9850-7300, Fax: +61(2) 9850-9476
EMail: bspencer@remus.reg.mq.edu.au

International Relations: Tony Adams
Tel: +61(2) 9850-7963, Fax: +61(2) 9850-9198
EMail: iso@mq.edu.au

Divisions
Economic and Financial Studies (Accountancy; Actuarial Science; Business and Commerce; Demography and Population; Economics; Finance; Statistics); **Environmental and Life Sciences** (Astronomy and Space Science; Biological and Life Sciences; Chemistry; Chiropractic; Demography and Population; Earth Sciences; Environmental Studies; Geophysics); **Humanities** (Ancient Civilizations; Asian Studies; English; European Languages; International Relations; Justice Administration; Modern History; Political Sciences); **Information and Communication Sciences** (Computer Science; Electronic Engineering; Information Sciences; Laser Engineering; Mathematics); **Law** (Commercial Law; Criminal Law; Environmental Studies; Law); **Linguistics and Psychology** (Cognitive Sciences; Linguistics; Psychology); **Society, Culture, Media and Philosophy** (Anthropology; Communication Studies; Cultural Studies; Indigenous Studies; Media Studies; Philosophy; Sociology; Women's Studies)

Schools
Education (Primary Education; Secondary Education; Teacher Trainers Education)

History: Founded 1964 by an Act of the N.S.W. State Parliament. First postgraduate students accepted 1966 and undergraduate teaching began 1967. Institute of Early Childhood at Waverley became a school of the University 1990. In order to break down divisions between Humanities, Sciences and Social Sciences and to allow students as much freedom as possible in choice of studies, the University is organized as a single integrated body composed of 9 Divisions, with Departments and Academic Units, and 3 Academic Colleges.

Governing Bodies: Council; Academic Senate

Academic Year: March to December (March-July; July-December)

Admission Requirements: Secondary New South Wales higher school certificate or interstate recognized foreign equivalent, or previous tertiary study. Advanced standing for studies in recognized tertiary institution

Main Language(s) of Instruction: English

International Co-operation: Links with North America, Europe, Asia/Pacific and the Middle East

Degrees and Diplomas: *Bachelor Degree*: Arts (BA); Business Administration (BBA); Business, Hospitality and Tourism (BBHT); Commerce (BCom); Economics (BEc); Education (BEd); Environmental Science (BEnvSc); Media (BM); Medical Sciences (BMedScs); Science (BSc); Science/Laws (BScLLB); Social Sciences (BSocSc); Speech and Hearing Sciences (BSp&HSc); Technology (Btech); *Bachelor Honours Degree*: Psychology (BPsych(Hons)); *Graduate Certificate/Diploma*; *Master Degree*: 1-2 further yrs; *Doctoral Degree*: 1-4 yrs

Student Services: Academic counselling, Canteen, Employment services, Foreign student adviser, Foreign Studies Centre, Handicapped facilities, Health services, Language programs, Nursery care, Social counselling, Sports facilities

Student Residential Facilities: Yes

Special Facilities: Australian History Museum; Biological Sciences Museum; Earth Sciences Museum. Institute of Early Childhood Art Collection. Museum of Ancient Cultures. Sculpture Park. Lachlan Macquarie Room

Libraries: 1m. vols, including 11,000 current serials

Publications: Research Report *(annually)*

Vice-Chancellor and President: Edward Byrne (2009-)
Tel: +61(3) 9905-2046, Fax: +61(3) 9905-2096

International Relations: Stephanie Fahey, Vice-President, International
Tel: +61(3) 9902-0075, Fax: +61(3) 9902-0055
EMail: Stephanie.Fahey@adm.monash.edu

Colleges
Pharmacy *(Victorian)* (Pharmacy) *Dean*: C. Chapman

Faculties
Art and Design (Architecture; Design; Fine Arts; Multimedia) *Dean*: John Redmond; **Arts** (Ancient Civilizations; Anthropology; Arts and Humanities; Communication Studies; Comparative Literature; Cultural Studies; Eastern European Studies; English; Environmental Studies; Geography; Germanic Studies; Greek; History; Indigenous Studies; International Studies; Japanese; Journalism; Linguistics; Music; Oriental Languages; Oriental Studies; Philosophy; Political Sciences; Religion; Romance Languages; Social Sciences; Social Work; Theology; Visual Arts) *Dean*: Raelene Frances; **Business and Economics** (Accountancy; Banking; Business and Commerce; Economics; Finance; Management; Marketing; Taxation) *Dean*: Stephen King; **Education** (Education; Preschool Education; Primary Education; Secondary Education; Sports) *Dean*: John Loughran; **Engineering** (Aeronautical and Aerospace Engineering; Bioengineering; Chemical Engineering; Civil Engineering; Computer Engineering; Electrical Engineering; Engineering; Materials Engineering; Mechanical Engineering) *Dean*: Tam Sridhar; **Information Technology** (Archiving; Computer Engineering; Computer Science; Information Management; Information Technology; Library Science; Software Engineering) *Dean*: Ron Weber; **Law** (Law) *Dean*: Arie Freiberg; **Medicine, Nursing and Health Sciences** (Anatomy; Biochemistry; Biomedicine; Clinical Psychology; Community Health; Epidemiology; Gynaecology and Obstetrics; Haematology; Immunology; Medicine; Midwifery; Molecular Biology; Nursing; Nutrition; Occupational Therapy; Paediatrics; Pharmacology; Physiology; Psychiatry and Mental Health; Psychology; Surgery) *Dean*: Steve Wesselingh; **Science** (Biological and Life Sciences; Chemistry; Earth Sciences; Ecology; Genetics; Mathematics; Natural Sciences; Physics; Psychology) *Dean*: Robert K. Norris

Further Information: Also 188 Centres for research and teaching. Also Campuses outside Australia in Italy (Prato Centres), in Malaysia (Monash University Sunway Campus), and South Africa (Monash University South Africa).

History: Founded 1958.

Governing Bodies: University Council; Academic Board

Academic Year: February to November (February-June; July-November)

Admission Requirements: Victorian Certificate of Education or national or international equivalent

Fees: Vary according to courses

Main Language(s) of Instruction: English

Degrees and Diplomas: *Bachelor Degree*: All fields; *Master Degree*; *Doctoral Degree (PhD)*

Student Services: Academic counselling, Canteen, Cultural centre, Employment services, Foreign student adviser, Handicapped facilities, Health services, Nursery care, Social counselling, Sports facilities

Student Residential Facilities: Yes

Special Facilities: Monash University Museum of Modern Art; Australian Synchrontron; Art and Design studio

Libraries: c. 3,2 million items in the library's collection, 2.1 million book, over 100,000 print and electronic journals, 341.825; 298,888 electronic books and 1,118 netwoeked electronic databases

Press or Publishing House: Office of Marketing and Communications

Last Updated: 11/10/11

MONASH UNIVERSITY

PO Box 3A, University Administration, Melbourne, Victoria 3800
Tel: +61(3) 9902-6000 +61(3) 9903-4788
Fax: +61(3) 9905-4007
EMail: study@monash.edu.au
Website: http://www.monash.edu.au

BERWICK CAMPUS

100 Clyde Road, Berwick, Victoria 3806
Tel: +61(3) 9904-7000 +61 3 9903 4788
EMail: study@monash.edu.au
Website: http://www.berwick.monash.edu.au

Faculties

Arts (Behavioural Sciences; Indonesian; International Studies; Journalism; Psychology; Tourism; Visual Arts); **Business and Economics** (Accountancy; Commercial Law; Economics; Finance; Management; Marketing; Taxation); **Education** (Education); **Medicine, Nursing and Health Sciences** (Health Sciences; Medicine; Nursing)

CAULFIELD CAMPUS

900 Dandenong Road, Caulfield East, Victoria 3145
Tel: +61(3) 9903-2000
Fax: +61(3) 9903-2400
Website: http://www.monash.edu.au/campuses/caulfield

Faculties

Art and Design (Design; Fine Arts); **Arts** (Arts and Humanities); **Business and Economics**; **Information Technology** (Information Technology); **Medecine, Nursing and Health Sciences** (Engineering); **Medicine, Nursing and Health Sciences**

CLAYTON CAMPUS

Wellington Road, Clayton, Victoria 3800
Tel: +61(3) 9905-4000
Fax: +61(3) 9905-4007
Website: http://www.monash.edu.au/campuses/clayton

Faculties

Arts (Arts and Humanities); **Business and Economics** (Business Administration; Economics); **Education**; **Engineering** (Engineering); **Information Technology**; **Law** (Law); **Medicine, Nursing and health Sciences** (Health Sciences; Medicine; Nursing); **Science** (Natural Sciences)

History: Founded 1958.

GIPPSLAND CAMPUS

Northways Road, Churchill, Victoria 3842
Tel: +61(3) 9902-6200 +61(3) 9903 4788
EMail: gippsland.campus@monash.edu.au
Website: http://www.gippsland.monash.edu.au

Faculties

Art and Design (Design; Fine Arts); **Arts** (Arts and Humanities); **Business and Economics** (Business Administration; Economics); **Education** (Education); **Engineering** (Engineering); **Information Technology** (Information Technology); **Medicine, Nursing and Heath Sciences** (Health Sciences; Medicine; Nursing)

MONASH SOUTH AFRICA

144 Peter Road, Ruimsig
Tel: +27(11) 950 4000
Fax: +27(11) 950 4004
EMail: inquiries@monash.ac.za
Website: http://www.monash.ac.za

Schools

Arts (Arts and Humanities); **Business and Economics** (Business Administration; Economics); **Health Sciences** (Health Sciences); **Information Technology** (Information Technology)

MONASH SUNWAY MALAYSIA

Jalan Lagoon Selatan, 46150, Bandar Sunway, Petaling Jaya, Selangor
Tel: +603 5514 6000
Fax: +603 5514 6001
EMail: info@monash.edu.my
Website: http://www.monash.edu.my

Schools

Arts and Social Sciences (Arts and Humanities; Social Sciences); **Business** (Business Administration); **Engineering** (Engineering); **Information Technology** (Information Technology); **Medicine and Health Sciences** (Health Sciences; Medicine); **Science** (Natural Sciences)

PARKVILLE CAMPUS

381 Royal Parade, Parkville, Victoria 3052
Tel: +61(3) 9903-9635
Fax: +61(3) 9903-9581
EMail: pharmacy.info@monash.edu
Website: http://www.pharm.monash.edu.au

Faculties

Pharmacy and Pharmaceutical Sciences (Pharmacy) *Dean*: William Charman

PENINSULA CAMPUS

McMahons Road, Frankston, Victoria 3199
Tel: +61(3) 9904-4000
Fax: +61(3) 9904-4190
EMail: peninsula.campus@monash.edu.au
Website: http://www.monash.edu.au/campuses/peninsula

Faculties

Business and Economics (Business Administration; Economics); **Education** (Education); **Medicine, Nursing and Health Sciences** (Health Sciences; Medicine; Nursing)

MURDOCH UNIVERSITY

South Street, Murdoch, Western Australia 6150
Tel: +61(8) 9360-6000
Fax: +61(8) 9360-6847
EMail: internat@murdoch.edu.au
Website: http://www.murdoch.edu.au

Vice-Chancellor: Richard Higgott (2011-)

Deputy-Vice-Chancellor (Corporate): Ian Callahan
Tel: +61(8) 9360-2571, Fax: +61(8) 9360-2931
EMail: I.callahan@murdoch.edu.au

International Relations: Gary Martin
Tel: +61(8) 9360-2114, Fax: +61(8) 9360-2931
EMail: g.martin@murdoch.edu.au

Academies

Screen and Sound *(National)* (Communication Studies; Cultural Studies; Media Studies) *Director*: Josko Petkovic

Centres

Asia Research (Asian Studies) *Director*: Gary Rodan; **Atomic, Molecular and Surface Physics** (Atomic and Molecular Physics) *Director*: Andreis Stelbovics; **Australian Sheep Industry** (Animal Husbandry) *Contact*: David Pethick; **Beef Genetic Technologies Solutions** (Animal Husbandry) *Contact*: David Pethick; **Bioinformatics and Biological Computing** (Biotechnology; Computer Science) *Director*: Matthew Bellgard; **Biomolecular Control of Disease** (Biomedicine; Molecular Biology) *Director*: R.C. Andrew Thompson; **Clinical Immunology and Biomedical Statistics** (Biomedicine; Biotechnology; Statistics) *Director*: Simon Mallal; **Companion Animal Research** *(Australasian)* (Veterinary Science) *Director*: Peter Irwin; **Co-operative Research for Sustainable Tourism** (Tourism); **Enterprise Collaboration in Innovative Systems** (Information Technology) *Director*: Lance Fung; **Environmental Biotechnology Cooperative Research** *Contact*: Steven Halls; **Environmental Technology** *Director*: Martin Anda; **Everyday Life** *Director*: Geoffrey Craig; **Fish and Fisheries Research** (Aquaculture; Fishery) *Director*: Neil Loneragan; **Irish Studies** (Irish) *Director*: Robert Reece; **Labour Market Research** (Labour and Industrial Relations) *Contact*: Paul Flatau; **Learning, Change and Development** (Education) *Director*: Judith MacCallum; **Legumes in Mediterranean Agriculture** (Agronomy; Vegetable Production) *Director*: Kadambot Siddique; **Microscopy** *(Western Australian)* *Contact*: Stephen Thurgate; **Necrotrophic Fungal Pathogens** *(Australian)* (Biomedical Engineering) *Director*: Richard Oliver; **Organic Waste Management** (Waste Management) *Direc-

tor: Arthur McComb; **Phytrophtora Science and Management** (Biological and Life Sciences; Biotechnology) *Director*: Giles Hardy; **Production Animal Research** (Animal Husbandry) *Director*: David Pethick; **Rhizobium Studies** (Biological and Life Sciences; Biotechnology; Crop Production) *Director*: John Howieson; **Social and Community Research** (Sociology) *Director*: Patricia Harris; **Sustainable Mine Lakes** *Director*: Alan Lymbery; **Western Australian State Agricultural Biotechnology** *Director*: Michael Jones

Institutes

Asia Pacific Intellectual Property Law (Law) *Director*: Michael Pendleton; **Clinical Research** (Biomedicine; Mathematics; Statistics) *Executive Director*: Simon Mallal; **Energy Research** *(Murdoch University)* *Director*: Philip Jennings; **Housing and Urban Research** *(Western Australia)* (Social Policy; Urban Studies) *Director*: Fiona Haslam McKenzie; **Interactive Television Research** (Media Studies) *Director*: Duane Varan; **Sustainable Energy** (Energy Engineering) *Director*: David Harries

Research Centres

Biomedical Science (Biomedicine) *Contact*: John Edwards; **Desert Knowledge** (Arid Land Studies); **Integrated Hydrometallurgy Solutions** *(A.J. Paker Cooperative)* (Metallurgical Engineering) *Chief Executive Officer*: Mark Woffenden; **Interaction Design** *(Australasian Cooperative)* *Contact*: Duane Varan; **Internationally Competitive Pork Industry** *Contact*: John Pluske; **Medical Engineering** *(Australian)* *Director*: Yianni Attikiouzel; **Molecular Plant Breeding** *(Cooperative)* (Molecular Biology) *Chief Executive Officer*: Bryan Whan; **Planning and Transport** (Transport and Communications) *Director*: Fred Affleck; **Plant Biosecurity** *(National)* (Biotechnology) *Chief Executive Officer*: Simon McKirdy; **Sustainable Forest Landscapes** *(Cooperative)* (Biotechnology; Forestry) *Contact*: Giles Hardy; **Women** (Gender Studies; Women's Studies) *Contact*: Beverley Thiele

Schools

Biological Sciences and Biotechnology *Head*: Max Cake; **Business** *(Murdoch)* (Accountancy; Banking; Business Administration; Commercial Law; E-Business/Commerce; Economics; Finance; Hotel Management; Human Resources; International Business; Management; Marketing; Tourism); **Chemical and Mathematical Sciences** (Chemistry; Mathematics; Metallurgical Engineering; Statistics) *Head*: Peter May; **Chiropractic** *Head*: Stefan Pallister; **Education** (Adult Education; Higher Education; Mathematics Education; Preschool Education; Primary Education; Secondary Education; Special Education; Theatre) *Dean*: Barry Kissane; **Electrical, Energy and Process** (Electrical Engineering; Energy Engineering); **Engineering** (Automation and Control Engineering; Computer Engineering; Energy Engineering; Engineering; Nanotechnology; Physics) *Head*: Keith Godfrey; **Environmental Science** (Ecology; Environmental Studies; Marine Science and Oceanography; Natural Resources) *Head*: Nick Costa; **Information Technology** (Business Computing; Computer Networks; Computer Science; Information Sciences; Information Technology; Multimedia) *Head*: Peter Cole; **Law** (Criminology; Law) *Dean*: Gabriel Moens; **Mathematical and Physical Sciences** (Chemistry; Earth Sciences; Mathematics; Physics; Statistics) *Head*: Graeme Hocking; **Media, Communication and Culture** (Cultural Studies; Gender Studies; Indigenous Studies; Journalism; Media Studies; Multimedia; Public Relations; Women's Studies) *Head*: Alec McHoul; **Nursing** (Health Administration; Nursing) *Head*: Rhonda Marriott; **Pharmacy** (Pharmacy) *Head*: Robert Coltrona; **Psychology** (Psychology) *Dean*: Iain Walker; **Social Sciences and Humanities** (Asian Studies; Community Health; English; History; Peace and Disarmament; Philosophy; Political Sciences; Religion; Sociology; Tourism) *Head*: Brian De Garis; **Veterinary Biology and Biomedical Sciences** (Biological and Life Sciences; Biomedicine; Veterinary Science) *Dean*: John Edwards

Further Information: Also Co-operative Multimedia Centre; Office of Continuing Veterinary Education

History: First admitted students to the Murdoch campus in 1975 and in 1996 opened a regional campus at Rockingham. Peel campus at Mandurah opened 2005.

Governing Bodies: Senate

Academic Year: February to November (Semesters: February-July; July-November. Trimesters: January-April; May-August; August-November)

Admission Requirements: Demonstrated merit and evidence of suitability for a university education. Western Australian school leavers must demonstrate competence in English or English literature and obtain a sufficiently high Tertiary Entrance Rank (TER) score.

Fees: Please refer to http:// www.oss.murdoch.edu.au/fees

Main Language(s) of Instruction: English

International Co-operation: Member of the Council on International Education Exchange (CIEE)

Degrees and Diplomas: *Bachelor Degree*: Animal Science; Arts; Business Informatics; Commerce; Economics; Engineering Technology; International Business; Legal Studies; Marketing and the Media; Mass Communication; Media Studies; Multimedia; Nursing; Science; Tourism, 3 yrs; *Bachelor Degree*: Applied Science in Energy Studies; Applied Science in Environmental Science; Engineering Science; Journalism (BJour), 1 yr following 1st Degree; *Bachelor Degree*: Asian Studies (Specialist); Education-Primary; Education-Secondary; Engineering in Power Engineering; Environmental Science; Extractive Metallurgy; Industrial Engineering and Computer System Engineering; Instrumentation and Control Engieering; Laws; Psychology; Renewable Energy Engineering; Theology, 4 yrs; *Bachelor Degree*: Chiropractic; Education - Primary (Graduate); Education - Secondary (Graduate); Veterinary Medicine and Surgery, 2 yrs following 1st degree; *Bachelor Degree*: Laws (Graduate), 3 yrs following 1st degree; *Graduate Certificate/Diploma*; *Master Degree*; *Doctoral Degree*

Student Services: Academic counselling, Canteen, Cultural centre, Employment services, Foreign student adviser, Foreign Studies Centre, Handicapped facilities, Health services, Nursery care, Social counselling, Sports facilities

Student Residential Facilities: Yes

Special Facilities: Anatomy Museum (Veterinary and Biomedical Sciences)

Libraries: Main Library, c. 570,000 items (monographs, serials vols, items of non-book materials, including films, maps, video cassettes, audio records, slides) Law Library; Veterinary Studies Library

Publications: Synergy *(quarterly)*

Press or Publishing House: Murdoch Design; Murdoch Print
Last Updated: 03/11/11

PEEL CAMPUS

15-17 Carleton Place, Mandurah, Western Australia 6210
Tel: +61(8) 9582-5501
Fax: +61(8) 9582-5515
EMail: v.reicheld@murdoch.edu.au
Website: http://www.murdoch.edu.au/peel

Schools

Business (Business Administration); **Nursing** (Nursing)

History: In 2003, Murdoch was awarded funding for a University Learning Centre in the Peel region. Completed in 2005, the building is co-located with Mandurah Senior College and Challenger TAFE at the Peel Education and TAFE Campus in the city of Mandurah.

ROCKINGHAM CAMPUS

Dixon Road, Rockingham, Western Australia 6168
Tel: +61(8) 9360-7070
Fax: +61(8) 9360-7077
Website: http://www.murdoch.edu.au/rocko/rocko.html

Schools

Business *(Murdoch)* (Business Administration; Human Resources; Management); **Education** (Education; Primary Education; Special Education); **Engineering** (Engineering); **Information Technology** (Business Computing; Computer Science; Information Technology); **Social Sciences and Humanities** (Arts and Humanities; Community Health; History; Social Sciences)

History: Founded 1996. First intake of students 1997. Officially opened 1998.

QUEENSLAND UNIVERSITY OF TECHNOLOGY (QUT)

GPO Box 2434, George Street, Brisbane, Queensland 4001
Tel: +61(7) 3183-2111
EMail: qut.international@qut.edu.au
Website: http://www.qut.edu.au

Vice-Chancellor: Peter Coaldrake (2003-)
Tel: +61(7) 3138-2365, Fax: +61(7) 3138-4061
EMail: p.coaldrake@qut.edu.au

International Relations: Scott Sheppard, Deputy Vice Chancellor (International and Development)
Tel: +6(7) 3138-2147, Fax: +6(7) 3138-9064
EMail: scott.sheppard@qut.edu.au

Faculties
Built Environment and Engineering (Aeronautical and Aerospace Engineering; Architecture; Civil Engineering; Computer Engineering; Construction Engineering; Electrical and Electronic Engineering; Industrial Design; Interior Design; Landscape Architecture; Mechanical Engineering; Medical Technology; Production Engineering; Real Estate; Regional Planning; Software Engineering; Surveying and Mapping; Town Planning; Urban Studies) *Executive Dean*: Martin Betts; **Business** (Accountancy; Advertising and Publicity; Banking; Business and Commerce; E-Business/Commerce; Economics; Finance; Human Resources; International Business; Management; Marketing; Public Relations) *Executive Dean*: Peter Little; **Creative Industries** (Acting; Cinema and Television; Communication Studies; Dance; Fashion Design; Film; Information Sciences; Journalism; Leisure Studies; Literature; Mass Communication; Media Studies; Music; Sound Engineering (Acoustics); Theatre; Visual Arts; Writing) *Executive Dean*: Rod Wissler; **Education** (Cultural Studies; Mathematics Education; Modern Languages; Preschool Education; Science Education; Technology) *Executive Dean*: Wendy Patton; **Health** (Human Rights; Midwifery; Nursing; Optometry; Psychology; Public Health; Social and Community Services; Social Welfare) *Dean*: Andrew Wilson; **Law and Justice** (Justice Administration; Law) *Dean*: Michael Lavarch; **Science and Technology** (Biochemistry; Biomedical Engineering; Chemistry; Computer Science; Forensic Medicine and Dentistry; Information Sciences; Mathematics; Molecular Biology; Natural Sciences; Pharmacy; Radiology) *Dean*: Margaret Britz

Institutes
Creative Industries and Innovation; **Health and Biomedical Innovation**; **Information Security**; **Sustainable Resources**

Further Information: Also International College-English Language Programmes, Foundation Programmes, University Diploma for International Students. Oodergroo Unit - recruitement and subsequent academic and counselling support of Aboriginal and Torres Strait Islander students enrolled in degree programmes

History: Founded 1965 as Queensland Institute of Technology, acquired present status and title 1989. Brisbane College of Advanced Education incorporated 1990.

Governing Bodies: Council

Academic Year: February to December (February-June; July-November). Summer programme, November to February

Admission Requirements: Secondary school certificate or recognized foreign equivalent, or previous tertiary study

Main Language(s) of Instruction: English

Degrees and Diplomas: *Bachelor Degree*: 3-5 yrs; *Bachelor Honours Degree*: 1 further yr; *Master Degree*: a further 1-2 yrs; *Doctoral Degree (PhD)*: 3 yrs. Also undergraduate and postgraduate Certificates and Diplomas

Student Services: Academic counselling, Canteen, Cultural centre, Employment services, Foreign student adviser, Foreign Studies Centre, Handicapped facilities, Health services, Nursery care, Social counselling, Sports facilities

Student Residential Facilities: Forc. 120 students

Special Facilities: The Gardens Cultural Precinct (including the QUT Art Museum with over 1600 items and the QUT Theatre). Creative Industries Precinct

Libraries: Total, 780,000 vols
Last Updated: 30/11/11

CABOOLTURE CAMPUS

PO Box 1376, Manley & Tallon Streets, Caboolture, Queensland 4510
Tel: +61(7) 5433-7400
Fax: +61(7) 5433-7421
EMail: caboolture@qut.edu.au
Website: http://www.qut.edu.au/about/campuses-and-precincts/caboolture

Programmes
Business Administration (Business Administration); **Creative Industries** (Communication Studies; Fashion Design; Media Studies; Performing Arts; Visual Arts); **Education** (Education; Primary Education); **Nursing** (Nursing)

GARDENS POINT CAMPUS

GPO Box 2434, 2 George Street, Brisbane, Queensland 4001
Tel: +61(7) 3864-2111
EMail: qutinformation@qut.edu.au

Areas
Creative Industries; **Education** (Education); **Health** (Health Sciences)

KELVIN GROVE CAMPUS

Victoria Park Road, Kelvin Grove, Queensland 4059
Tel: +61(7) 3864-2111
Fax: +61(7) 3864-1510
EMail: askqut@qut.edu.au
Website: http://www.qut.edu.au

Faculties
Creative Industries (Cinema and Television; Communication Arts; Dance; Film; Music; Sound Engineering (Acoustics); Theatre; Visual Arts); **Education** (Adult Education; Education; Preschool Education; Primary Education; Secondary Education); **Health** (Health Sciences; Nursing; Optometry; Podiatry; Public Health)

Schools
Justice Studies (Law)

History: Founded 1965.

ROYAL MELBOURNE INSTITUTE OF TECHNOLOGY (RMIT UNIVERSITY)

PO Box 2476V, Melbourne, Victoria 3001
Tel: +61(3) 9925-2000 +61(3) 9925-1078
Fax: +61(3) 9663-2764 +61(3) 9925-3185
EMail: study@rmit.edu.au
Website: http://www.rmit.edu.au

Vice-Chancellor and President: Margaret Gardner AO (2005-)
Tel: +61(3) 9925-1999, Fax: +61(3) 9925-3185
EMail: vc@rmit.edu.au

Academic Registrar: Maddy McMaster
Tel: +61(3) 9925-8609, Fax: +61(3) 9925-8805
EMail: academic.registrar@rmit.edu.au

International Relations: Stephen Connelly, Deputy Vice-Chancellor, International, Enterprise and Community Development
Tel: +61(3) 9925-3790, Fax: +61(3) 9925-5029
EMail: stephen.connelly@rmit.edu.au

Faculties
Business (Accountancy; Business Computing; Economics; Finance; Information Technology; Law; Management; Marketing); **Design and Social Context** (Architectural and Environmental Design; Architecture; Architecture and Planning; Communication Studies; Design; Development Studies; Education; Fashion Design; Fine Arts; Graphic Arts; Media Studies; Social Sciences; Textile Design); **Science, Engineering and Technology** (Aeronautical and Aerospace Engineering; Applied Chemistry; Applied Mathematics; Applied Physics; Biological and Life Sciences; Building Technologies; Chemical Engineering; Chiropractic; Civil Engineering; Computer Engineering; Computer Science; Construction Engineering; Electrical Engineering; Engineering; Environmental

Engineering; Health Sciences; Information Technology; Laboratory Techniques; Mathematics; Mechanical Engineering; Nursing; Pharmacy; Production Engineering; Psychology)

Research Centres

Advanced Composite Structures; **Aerospace Studies** (*Sir Lawrence Wackett*) (Aeronautical and Aerospace Engineering); **Bushfires**; **Construction Innovation**; **Globalism**; **Governance, Work and Technologies** (Government; Technology); **Intelligent Manufacturing Systems and Technologies** (Production Engineering); **Interaction Design**; **Management Quality Research** (Management); **Polymers** (Polymer and Plastics Technology); **Satellite Positioning for Atmosphère, Climate and Environment Studies** (*(SPACE)*); **SMART Internet Technology**; **Water Quality and Treatment** (Water Science)

Research Institutes

Australian Housing and Urban Studies (House Arts and Environment; Urban Studies); **Design** (*RMIT*) (Design); **Global Cities** (*RMIT*) (Urban Studies); **Health Innovations** (*RMIT*) (Health Sciences); **Platform Technologies** (*RMIT*) (Technology)

Further Information: RMIT has moved from a Faculty structure to a College structure (Design and Social Context; Science, Engineering and Technology; Business)

History: Founded 1887 as Melbourne Working Men's College, renamed Melbourne Technical College 1934, and acquired present title of Royal Melbourne Institute of Technology (RMIT) 1960. Established as University of Technology by Act of State Parliament of Victoria 1992, amalgamating with Phillip Institute of Technology. RMIT is one of Australia's largest multi-level universities offering a fully-integrated programme of courses at Diploma, Degree and Postgraduate levels. The University emphasizes education for employment and for research which uses technology to solve real world problems.

Governing Bodies: Council

Academic Year: March to November (March-July; July-November)

Admission Requirements: For Bachelor degree programme, satisfactory completion of interstate secondary schooling or Victorian Certificate of Education (VCE), or recognized foreign equivalent

Fees: (Aus Dollars): Australian Government Higher Education Contribution Scheme (HECS), 4,355-9,080; International, 15,000 - 18,750 per annum.

Main Language(s) of Instruction: English

Degrees and Diplomas: *Bachelor Degree*: 3 yrs; *Master Degree*; *Doctoral Degree*. Also Advanced Diplomas; Double Degrees; Associate Degrees; Professional Doctorates

Student Services: Academic counselling, Canteen, Cultural centre, Employment services, Foreign student adviser, Handicapped facilities, Health services, Nursery care, Social counselling, Sports facilities

Libraries: Brunswick, Bundoora, Business, Carlton and Swanston Libraries: total print serial titles 1,799; electronic serial titles 60,000; book and AV items 691,000; Pcs available for public access 450

Press or Publishing House: University Marketing

Academic Staff 2010	MEN	WOMEN	TOTAL
FULL-TIME	1,779	1,869	3,648
Student Numbers 2010			
All (Foreign Included)	37,144	36,760	73,904
Last Updated: 08/08/11			

RMIT INTENATIONAL UNIVERSITY VIETNAM

Saigon South Campus, 702 Nguyen Van Lihn Boulevard, Tan Phong Ward, District 7, Ho Chi Minh City
Tel: +848 3776-1300
Fax: +848 3776-1399
EMail: enquiries@rmit.edu.vn
Website: http://www.rmit.edu.vn

President, General Director: Merilyn Liddell AM (2009-)
Tel: +848 3776-1305 EMail: president@rmit.edu.vn

Director Marketing: Robyn McCutchan
Tel: +848 3776-1407, Fax: +848 3776-1399
EMail: robyn.mccutchan@rmit.edu.vn

Centres

Commerce and Management (Accountancy; Business Administration; Business and Commerce; Economics; Finance; Information Technology; Management; Marketing); **Design and Communication** (Communication Studies; Design; Management); **English** (English; English Studies); **Technology** (Engineering; Information Technology)

Further Information: Also a campus in Hanoi: Handi Resco Building, 521 Kim Ma, Ba Dinh District

History: Founded 2001. RMIT Vietnam is the Asian hub of RMIT University (Melbourne).

Governing Bodies: Board of Management

Academic Year: February to January (February-June; June-October; October-January)

Admission Requirements: Successful completion of year 12 (or equivalent). In addition students must satisfy one of the following English requirements: Successful completion of RMIT Vietnam English Advanced Level 7; IELTS 6.5+; TOEFEL Paper based 580+; TOEFEL Computer based 233+; TOEFEL Internet based 92+

Fees: (US Dollars): 22,000 for a Bachelor program

Main Language(s) of Instruction: English

International Co-operation: DOET (Department of Education and Training) Vietnam

Student Services: Academic counselling, Canteen, Employment services, Handicapped facilities, Health services, Language programs, Social counselling, Sports facilities

Student Residential Facilities: Yes for 100 students

Libraries: Yes

SOUTHERN CROSS UNIVERSITY

PO Box 157, Lismore, New South Wales 2480
Tel: +61(2) 6620-3000
Fax: +61(2) 6622-3700
Website: http://www.scu.edu.au

Vice-Chancellor: Peter Lee (2009-)
Tel: +61(2) 6620-3703, Fax: +61(2) 6622-1789
EMail: vc@scu.edu.au

Executive Director Corporate Services: Malcolm Marshall
Tel: +61(2) 6620-3730, Fax: +61(2) 6620-3692
EMail: mmarshal@scu.edu.au

International Relations: Ulirike Baker
Tel: +61(2) 6620-3876, Fax: +61(2) 6620-3227
EMail: directorinternational@scu.edu.au

Faculties

Arts and Sciences (Aquaculture; Behavioural Sciences; Coastal Studies; Cultural Studies; Education; Educational Technology; Environmental Management; Environmental Studies; Fishery; Forestry; Health Sciences; Indigenous Studies; Marine Science and Oceanography; Media Studies; Music; Nursing; Nutrition; Occupational Therapy; Preschool Education; Primary Education; Psychology; Secondary Education; Social Sciences; Sports; Sports Management; Visual Arts; Writing); **Business and Law** (Accountancy; Business Administration; Business and Commerce; Computer Science; Finance; Human Resources; Information Technology; International Business; Law; Management; Marketing; Tourism)

Research Centres

Animal Conservation Genetics (Genetics); **Graduate Research College**; **Phytochemistry and Pharmacology** (Biochemistry; Pharmacology; Plant Pathology) *Director*: Michael Heinrich; **Plant Conservation Genetics** (Genetics; Plant Pathology) *Head*: Robert Henry; **Regional Tourism** (Tourism); **Sustainable Production Forestry** (*Cooperative*) (Forest Products); **Sustainable Tourism** (*Cooperative*) (Tourism)

Schools

Arts and Social Sciences (Cultural Studies; Fine Arts; Media Studies; Music; Social Sciences; Sociology; Visual Arts; Writing) *Head*: Rebecca Coyle; **Business** (Accountancy; Business Administration; Business and Commerce; Information Technology; Law; Management) *Head*: Stephen Kelly; **Commerce and Management** (Accountancy; Arts and Humanities; Business and Commerce; Information Technology; Law; Management) *Head*: Keith Sloan; **Education** (Education; Educational Technology; Primary Education) *Head*: Martin Hayden; **Environmental Science and Management** (Applied Chemistry; Applied Physics; Aquaculture; Coastal Studies; Environmental Studies; Fishery; Forestry; Geochemistry) *Head*: Jerry Vanclay; **Exercise Science and Sports Management** (Nutrition; Physical Education; Sports Management) *Head*: Iain Graham; **Law and Justice** (Justice Administration; Law) *Head*: Jennifer Nielsen; **Multimedia and Information Technology** *(Coffs Harbour)* (Business Computing; Computer Science; Information Technology; Multimedia; Software Engineering) *Head*: Stephen Kelly; **Natural and Complementary Medicine** (Alternative Medicine; Occupational Therapy; Osteopathy) *Head*: Iain Graham; **Nursing and Health Care Practices** (Health Sciences; Midwifery; Nursing) *Head*: Iain Graham; **Psychology** *Head*: Iain Graham; **Tourism and Hospitality Management** (Cooking and Catering; Hotel Management; Management; Tourism) *Director*: Kevin Markwell

Further Information: Campuses in Coffs Harbour and Tweed Gold Coast. Also one-semester Study Abroad programmes

History: Founded 1971. Began operations under current title 1994.

Governing Bodies: University Council

Academic Year: February to November (February-June; June-October; November-February)

Admission Requirements: Qualifications deemed equivalent to completion of secondary school in Australia. Specific information available on request. Recognition of prior learning (RPL) applies to specific awards

Fees: (Aus Dollars): 15,000-20,000 per annum; graduate,16,000-22,500

Main Language(s) of Instruction: English

Degrees and Diplomas: *Associate Degree*; *Diploma*: 1-2 yrs; *Bachelor Degree*: 3-4 yrs; *Graduate Certificate/Diploma*: 1-2 yrs; *Master Degree*: 1-2 yrs; *Doctoral Degree (PhD)*: 3 yrs

Student Services: Academic counselling, Canteen, Cultural centre, Employment services, Foreign student adviser, Foreign Studies Centre, Handicapped facilities, Health services, Language programs, Nursery care, Social counselling, Sports facilities

Student Residential Facilities: Yes

Special Facilities: Art Gallery. Media Production Centre. North Coast Academy of Sport. Naturopathy Teaching Clinic

Libraries: Information Services

Publications: Research Report *(annually)*

Academic Staff *2010*	TOTAL
FULL-TIME	240
PART-TIME	60
STAFF WITH DOCTORATE	
FULL-TIME	c. 150

Student Numbers *2010*	
All (Foreign Included)	c. 15,200
FOREIGN ONLY	3,530

Distance students, 4,700.
Last Updated: 10/08/11

SWINBURNE UNIVERSITY OF TECHNOLOGY (SUT)

PO Box 218, Hawthorn, Victoria 3122
Tel: +61(3) 9214-8000
Fax: +61(3) 9819-5454
EMail: international@swin.edu.au
Website: http://www.swin.edu.au

Vice-Chancellor: Linda Kristjanson (2011-)
Tel: +61(3) 9214-8131, Fax: +61(3) 9818-3649
EMail: vc@swin.edu.au

Registrar: T. Kilsby
Tel: +61(3) 9214-5278 EMail: tkilsby@swin.edu.au

International Relations: Zena Burgess, Director, International Student Unit
Tel: +61(3) 9214-8718, Fax: +61(3) 9818-3647
EMail: zburgess@swin.edu.au

Centres

Advanced Internet Architectures (Computer Networks) *Director*: Greenville Armitage; **Astrophysics and Superconducting** (Astrophysics) *Director*: Matthew Bailes; **Atom Optics and Ultrafast Laser Spectroscopy** *Director*: Peter Hannaford; **Business and Management Research** *(CBMR)* (Business Administration; Business and Commerce; Management) *Director*: Miles Nicholls; **E-Business and Communication** *(Lilydale)* (Business Computing; Information Technology; Telecommunications Engineering) *Director*: Bruce Calway; **Emerging Technologies and Society** *(Australian Centre)* (Social Studies; Technology) *Manager*: Janet Wheeler; **Environment and Biotechnology** (Applied Chemistry; Biochemistry; Biomedicine; Biotechnology; Environmental Studies; Microbiology; Molecular Biology; Nanotechnology; Packaging Technology; Paper Technology) *Director*: Russell Crawford; **Gender and Cultural Diversity** *(National Centre)* (Cultural Studies; Gender Studies) *Director*: Sue Lewis; **Imaging and Applied Optics** (Applied Physics; Laser Engineering; Optical Technology; Optics) *Director*: Alex Mazzolini; **Intelligent Systems and Complex Processes** *(CISCP)* (Artificial Intelligence; Computer Science) *Director*: Tim Hendtlass; **International Agents and Multi Agent Systems** (Software Engineering) *Director*: Ryszard Kowalczyk; **Internet Computing and E-Business** (Computer Networks; E-Business/Commerce) *Director*: Yun Yang; **Mathematical Modelling** (Mathematics and Computer Science) *Director*: Manmohan Singh; **Microphotonics** (Optical Technology) *Director*: Min Gu; **Molecular Stimulation** *Director*: Richard Sadus; **Neuropsychology** (Industrial and Organizational Psychology; Psychology) *Director*: Con Stough; **Psychological Services** (Psychology) *Director*: Roger Cook; **Software Engineering** (Software Engineering) *Director*: Chen Tsong

Divisions

Higher Education *(Hawthorn, Prahran)* (Applied Chemistry; Applied Mathematics; Applied Physics; Arts and Humanities; Business and Commerce; Computer Science; Design; Engineering; Health Sciences; Information Technology; Management; Multimedia; Social Sciences; Technology) *Divisional Deputy Vice-Chancellor*: Dale Murphy; **Technical and Further Education** *(TAFE; Hawthorn, Lilydale, Prahran, Healesville, Wantirna, Croydon)* (Applied Chemistry; Business Administration; Child Care and Development; Computer Science; Design; Engineering; Environmental Studies; Fine Arts; Fire Science; Horticulture; Industrial Management; Information Technology; Occupational Health; Performing Arts; Social and Community Services; Social Sciences; Social Welfare; Technology; Tourism; Visual Arts; Writing) *Divisional Deputy-Vice-Chancellor*: Alistair Crozier; **Technology** *(Lilydale-University)* (Accountancy; Business Administration; Economics; Information Technology; Management; Marketing; Mathematics and Computer Science; Media Studies; Psychology; Social Sciences; Sociology; Statistics; Tourism) *Divisional Deputy-Vice-Chancellor*: Barbara van Ernst

Graduate Schools

Entrepreneurship *(AGSE)* (Business Administration; Management) *Director*: Adolph Hanich; **Integrative Medicine** *(GSIM)* *Director*: Avni Sali

Institutes

Australian Foresight (Development Studies) *Director*: Richard Slaughter; **Brain Sciences** *(BSI)* (Biological and Life Sciences; Natural Sciences; Neurology; Neurosciences; Treatment Techniques) *Director*: David Crewther; **Design** *(National Institute)* (Communication Arts; Design; Film; Industrial Design; Interior Design; Multimedia; Production Engineering; Radio and Television Broadcasting) *Head*: Helmut Lueckenhausen; **Industrial Research** *(IRIS; Hawthorn)* (Aeronautical and Aerospace Engineering; Automation and Control Engineering; Bioengineering; Biomedical Engineering; Computer Engineering; Engineering; Industrial Engineering; Management; Materials Engineering; Measurement and Precision Engineering; Mechanical Engineering; Production Engineering; Software Engineering; Systems Analysis) *Chair*: Jean Austin; **Social Research** *(ISR)* (Behavioural Sciences; Communication

Studies; Information Sciences; Social Policy; Social Sciences; Urban Studies) *Director*: Terry Burke

Schools

Arts, Hospitality and Sciences *(TAFE)* (Arts and Humanities; Natural Sciences; Tourism) *Director*: Howard Coats; **Biophysical Sciences and Electrical Engineering** (Astronomy and Space Science; Biomedicine; Biophysics; Electrical Engineering; Multimedia; Optics; Physiology; Social Sciences) *Head*: David Booth; **Business** (Accountancy; Business Administration; Business and Commerce; Human Resources; International Business; Italian; Japanese; Management; Marketing) *Head*: Barbara Cargill; **Business and e-Commerce** *(TAFE)* *Director*: Ingrid Wittman; **Engineering** *(TAFE)* (Aeronautical and Aerospace Engineering; Automotive Engineering; Building Technologies; Computer Engineering; Construction Engineering; Information Technology; Natural Resources) *Director*: Carlo Demartinis; **Engineering and Science** (Air Transport; Biotechnology; Civil Engineering; Electronic Engineering; Mechanical Engineering; Production Engineering; Robotics; Transport Management) *Head*: Ian Jones; **Information Technology** (Computer Science; Information Technology; Software Engineering) *Head*: Doug Grant; **Mathematical Sciences** (Mathematics; Statistics) *Head*: Peter Jones; **Social and Behavioural Sciences** (Arts and Humanities; Behavioural Sciences; Social Sciences) *Head*: Julie Mulvany; **Social Sciences** *(TAFE)* (Child Care and Development; Family Studies; Health Sciences; Parks and Recreation; Social Sciences) *Director*: Robyn Jackson

Further Information: Also International Office and International Student Unit. Division in Sarawak, Malaysia

History: Founded 1908. Affiliated with Victorian Institute of Colleges 1965. Acquired university status 1992 by Act of Parliament. It has two divisions - Higher Education and Technical and Further Education (TAFE). It comprises six campuses at Hawthorn, Prahan, Lilydale, Wantima, Croydon and Healesville. Responsible to Commonwealth and State Ministries of Education and Training.

Governing Bodies: University Council

Academic Year: Higher Education Division: February to November (February-May; July-November). Summer School: December-February. Technical and Further Education Division: February to December (February-April; April-June; July-September; October-December)

Admission Requirements: Victorian Certificate of Education (VCE) or recognized foreign equivalent

Fees: (Aus Dollars): Foreign students, 8,500-15,000 per annum; 29,400 for MBA

Main Language(s) of Instruction: English

International Co-operation: With universities in Canada, Denmark, Finland, France, Germany, Hong Kong, Hungary, Ireland, Italy, Japan, Korea, Malaysia, Netherlands, Poland, Sweden, Thailand, United Kingdom, USA, Vietnam. Also participates in Erasmus and University Mobility in Asia and the Pacific (UMAP) programmes

Degrees and Diplomas: *Bachelor Degree*: 3-4 yrs; *Graduate Certificate/Diploma*: 1 yr; *Master Degree*: 2-4 yrs following Bachelor; *Doctoral Degree (PhD)*: $3\frac{1}{2}$ yrs

Student Services: Academic counselling, Canteen, Employment services, Foreign student adviser, Foreign Studies Centre, Handicapped facilities, Health services, Language programs, Nursery care, Social counselling, Sports facilities

Student Residential Facilities: Yes

Special Facilities: Virtual Reality Theatre. David Williamson Theatre. Gallery 369. Gallery PB

Libraries: Bernard Hames Library; 150,000 vols; Collection strengths: Applied Science, Business, Computer Science, Engineering, Environmental Health, Film and Television, Graphic Design, Humanities, Social Studies, Japanese and Korean Languages, Mathematics

Press or Publishing House: Swinburne Press
Last Updated: 14/04/11

THE AUSTRALIAN NATIONAL UNIVERSITY (ANU)

Canberra, ACT 0200
Tel: +61(2) 6125-5111 +61(2) 6125-3354
Fax: +61(2) 6125-5931 +61(2) 6125-5550
Website: http://www.anu.edu.au

Vice-Chancellor: Ian Young (2011-)
Tel: +61(2) 6125-2510, Fax: +61(2) 6125-5550
EMail: vc@anu.edu.au

International Relations: Tim Beckett
Tel: +61(2) 6125-3682 EMail: Tim.Beckett@anu.edu.au

Centres

Aboriginal and Economic Policy Research *Director*: J.C. Altman; **Aboriginal Economic Policy Research** (Economic and Finance Policy; Economics) *Director*: J. Altman; **Arab and Islamic Studies** (Arabic; Islamic Studies; Middle Eastern Studies) *Director*: A. Saikal; **Archaeological Research** (Archaeology) *Director*: A. Anderson; **Arts and Technology** (Fine Arts; Technology) *Director*: E. Gates-Stuart; **Contemporary Pacific** (Pacific Area Studies) *Director*: L. Brij; **Continuing Education** (Education) *Director*: J. Dash; **Cross-Cultural Research** (Anthropology; Cultural Studies) *Director*: H. Morphy; **Democratic Institutions** (Institutional Administration; Political Sciences) *Director*: R. Rich; **Educational Development and Academic Methods** *Director*: L. Hort; **Epidemiology and Population Health** (Community Health; Epidemiology) *Director*: A. McMichael; **Financial Mathematics** (Finance; Mathematics) *Director*: C.C. Heyde; **Humanities Research** (Arts and Humanities) *Director*: I.D. McCalman; **Immigration and Multicultural Studies** (Cultural Studies; Demography and Population) *Director*: J. Jupp; **International and Public Law** (International Law; Public Law) *Director*: H. Charlesworth; **Mathematics and its Applications** (Applied Mathematics) *Director*: A. McIntosh; **Mental Health Research** (Health Sciences) *Director*: A. Jorm; **Mind** (Psychology) *Director*: A. Snyder; **Public Awareness of Science** (Administration; Natural Sciences) *Director*: S. Stocklmayer; **Resource and Environmental Studies** (Environmental Studies; Leisure Studies; Welfare and Protective Services) *Director*: R. Wasson; **Science and Engineering Materials** (Materials Engineering; Natural Sciences) *Director*: Z. Stachurski; **Study of the Chinese Southern Diaspora** (Demography and Population) *Director*: C. Reynolds; **Sustainable Energy Systems** (Energy Engineering) *Director*: A. Blakers; **Theoretical Physics** (Physics) *Coordinator*: R. Dewar; **Visual Sciences** (Natural Sciences) *Director*: M. Srinivasan; **Women's Studies** (Women's Studies) *Director*: J.J. Pettman

Faculties

Arts (Arts and Humanities; Social Sciences) *Dean*: A. Shoemaker; **Asian Studies** (Asian Studies; Cultural Studies; Social Sciences) *Dean*: A.C. Milner; **Economics and Commerce** (Business Administration; Business and Commerce; Economics; Social Sciences) *Dean*: T.J. Brailsford; **Engineering and Information Technology** (Engineering; Information Sciences; Mathematics and Computer Science) *Dean*: J. Baird; **Law** (Law) *Dean*: M.D. Coper; **Science** (Mathematics and Computer Science; Natural Sciences) *Dean*: T. Brown

Institutes

Advanced Studies *Director*: F.C. Jackson; **Arts** *(National)* (Art Education; Ceramics and Glass Technology; Jewelry Art; Painting and Drawing; Sculpture; Textile Design; Wood Technology) *Director*: P.H. Karmel

Research Schools

Astronomy and Astrophysics *Director*: J. Norris; **Biological Sciences** (Biological and Life Sciences) *Director*: J. Gibson; **Chemistry** (Chemistry) *Director*: D.J. Evans; **Earth Sciences** (Earth Sciences) *Director*: M. Harrison; **Information Sciences and Engineering** (Engineering; Information Sciences) *Director*: B. Anderson; **Pacific and Asian Studies** (Asian Studies; Pacific Area Studies; Social Sciences) *Director*: J. Fox; **Physical Sciences and Engineering** (Engineering; Mathematics and Computer Science; Natural Sciences) *Director*: E. Weigold; **Social Sciences** (Social Sciences) *Director*: I. McAllister

Schools

Archaeology and Anthropology (Anthropology; Archaeology); **Art** *(Canberra)* (Fine Arts; Graphic Arts) *Director*: D. Williams; **Economics and Management** *(Asia Pacific)* *Director*: R. Garnaut; **Humanities** (Arts and Humanities); **Language Studies** (Modern Languages); **Mathematical Sciences** (Mathematics; Mathematics and Computer Science) *Director*: N.S. Trudinger; **Medical Research** *(John Curtin)* (Health Sciences; Medicine) *Director*: J.A. Whitworth; **Music** *(Canberra)* (Fine Arts; Graphic Arts; Music) *Director*: N. Fraillon; **Resources Management and Environmental**

Science (Ecology; Environmental Management; Natural Resources); **Social Sciences** (Social Sciences; Sociology)

History: Founded 1946 by Act of Parliament of the Commonwealth of Australia. The original function of the University, research and research training, now carried out by the Institute of Advanced Studies. The Faculties provide teaching and undertake research training at all levels. Merged with Canberra University College 1960 and with the Institute of the Arts in 1992.

Governing Bodies: Council

Academic Year: March to November

Admission Requirements: Secondary school certificate with matriculation or recognized foreign equivalent. Direct entrance to second year on completion of studies in another tertiary institution

Main Language(s) of Instruction: English

Degrees and Diplomas: *Bachelor Degree*: 3-4 yrs; *Master Degree*: a further 1-2 yrs; *Doctoral Degree (PhD)*: 2-3 yrs. Also postgraduate Diploma, 1 yr

Student Residential Facilities: Yes

Special Facilities: Museum of Archaeology; Museum of Anthropology; Museum of Classics. Art Gallery (paintings, ceramics, sculpture and woven materials). Mount Sromlo and Siding Springs Observatories

Libraries: c. 2,000,000 vols and 11,000 serial titles. Licensed databases: 150; Electronic Journals: 1,140; Other electronic resources (indexes, gateways): 70; Audiovisual material: 7,300 items; Special collections: Asian languages; The kapper of Australiana; The Mortlake of 19th century literature; Political economy donated by J.A. La Nauze

Press or Publishing House: University Press (Pergamon Press Aust. Ltd)

Last Updated: 14/04/11

THE UNIVERSITY OF ADELAIDE

Adelaide, South Australia 5005
Tel: +61(8) 8303-4455
Fax: +61(8) 8303-4401
EMail: student.centre@adelaide.edu.au
Website: http://www.adelaide.edu.au

Vice-Chancellor: James McWha (2002-)
Tel: +61(8) 8303-5780, Fax: +61(8) 8303-4343
EMail: vice-chancellor@adelaide.edu.au

International Relations: John Taplin, Pro Vice-Chancellor
Tel: +61(8) 8303-5229, Fax: +61(8) 8303-8333
EMail: john.taplin@adelaide.edu.au

Faculties
Engineering, Computer and Mathematical Sciences (Chemical Engineering; Civil Engineering; Computer Science; Electrical and Electronic Engineering; Engineering; Environmental Engineering; Mathematics; Mechanical Engineering; Petroleum and Gas Engineering) *Executive Dean*: Peter Dowd; **Health Sciences** (Anatomy; Dentistry; Forensic Medicine and Dentistry; Gynaecology and Obstetrics; Health Sciences; Medicine; Nursing; Paediatrics; Pathology; Pharmacology; Psychology; Public Health; Surgery) *Executive Dean*: Justin Beilby; **Humanities and Social Sciences** (Ancient Civilizations; Anthropology; Arts and Humanities; Asian Studies; Austronesian and Oceanic Languages; Chinese; Classical Languages; Environmental Studies; French; Geography; German; Greek (Classical); History; Indigenous Studies; International Studies; Japanese; Latin; Linguistics; Literature; Modern Languages; Philosophy; Political Sciences; Psychology; Social Sciences; Sociology; Women's Studies; Writing) *Executive Dean*: Nick Harvey; **Professions** (Architecture; Business Administration; Business and Commerce; Economics; Education; Landscape Architecture; Law; Town Planning) *Executive Dean*: Christopher Findlay; **Science** (Agriculture; Biochemistry; Botany; Earth Sciences; Food Science; Genetics; Geology; Geophysics; Immunology; Microbiology; Molecular Biology; Natural Resources; Natural Sciences; Oenology; Pharmacology; Physiology; Zoology) *Executive Dean*: Robert Hill

Further Information: Member of the Group of Eight (Australia's leading research universities). Cooperative Research Centres; national research centres and research cooperation with publicly-funded research agencies (http://www.adelaide.edu.au/research/centre). Affiliated with 5 Teaching Hospitals, the South Australian Dental Service, the Institute of Medical and Veterinary Science and the Spencer Gulf Rural Health School.

History: Founded 1874 by Act of provincial legislature. Became autonomous under Act of Parliament.

Governing Bodies: Council

Academic Year: March to November (1st semester: March-April; April-June; 2nd semester: July-September; October-November). Summer Semester (January-February); Winter Semester (June-July).

Admission Requirements: South Australian Certificate of Education (SACE), International Baccalaureate or recognized foreign equivalent. Special Entry Schemes for mature students, Aboriginal and Torres Strait Islander students, and non-award students in the Faculty of Humanities and Social Sciences

Fees: (Aus Dollars): Foreign students, c. 20,000-44,000 per annum; postgraduate, 22,000-43,000. Australian students are eligible for Commonwealth Supported places where students make a contribution towards the cost of their education.

Main Language(s) of Instruction: English

Degrees and Diplomas: *Bachelor Degree*: 3-4 yrs; *Bachelor Degree*: Dental Surgery, 5 yrs; *Bachelor Degree*: Medicine and Surgery, 6 yrs; *Bachelor Honours Degree*: An honours yr following Bachelor Degree; *Master Degree*: a further 1-2 yrs following Bachelor Degree with Honours; *Doctoral Degree (PhD)*: a further 3-4 yrs. Also combined degrees, 5 yrs; Postgraduate Diplomas, 1-2 years following Bachelor Degree; Professional Certificates 1-2 sems, Associate Diploma, Diploma

Student Services: Academic counselling, Canteen, Cultural centre, Employment services, Foreign student adviser, Handicapped facilities, Health services, Language programs, Nursery care, Social counselling, Sports facilities

Student Residential Facilities: Yes

Special Facilities: Australian Centre for Plant Functional Genomics; Australia Plant Phenomics Facility; Confucius Institute; Institute for International Trade; Radio Adelaide; Wine Industry Cluster

Libraries: Bar Smith Library, c. 2m vols. Separate collections include: Law Library; Elder Music Library; Roseworthy Library; and Waite Campus Library

Press or Publishing House: Barr Smith Press

Academic Staff *2009*	MEN	WOMEN	TOTAL
FULL-TIME	857	496	**1,353**
Student Numbers *2009*			
All (Foreign Included)	11,518	10,953	**22,471**
FOREIGN ONLY	–	–	**6,290**

Last Updated: 06/09/11

THE UNIVERSITY OF NEWCASTLE

University Drive, Callaghan, New South Wales 2308
Tel: +61(2) 4921-5000
Fax: +61(2) 4921-4200
EMail: EnquiryCentre@newcastle.edu.au
Website: http://www.newcastle.edu.au

Vice-Chancellor and President: Nicholas Saunders
Tel: +61(2) 4921-5101, Fax: +61(2) 4921-5115
EMail: Nicholas.Saunders@newcastle.edu.au

International Relations: Kevin McConkey, Deputy
Tel: +61(2) 4921-5114, Fax: +61(2) 4921-7060
EMail: Kevin.McConkey@newcastle.edu.au

Centres
English Language and Foundation Studies (English) *Director*: Seamus Fagan

Faculties
Business and Law (Accountancy; Business and Commerce; E-Business/Commerce; Economics; Finance; Human Resources; International Business; Labour and Industrial Relations; Law; Management; Marketing; Political Sciences) *Dean*: Stephan Nicholas; **Education and Arts** (Anthropology; Arts and Humanities; Chinese; Cinema and Television; Classical Languages; Cultural Studies; Education; Fine Arts; French; Gender Studies; German; History; Indigenous Studies; Japanese; Leisure Studies; Linguistics; Modern Languages; Music; Performing Arts; Philosophy; Political Sciences;

Religion; Religious Studies; Social Sciences; Social Welfare; Social Work; Sociology; Speech Studies; Theatre; Theology; Welfare and Protective Services; Writing) *Dean*: John Germov; **Engineering and Built Environment** (Architecture; Chemical Engineering; Civil Engineering; Computer Engineering; Computer Science; Construction Engineering; Electrical and Electronic Engineering; Engineering; Engineering Drawing and Design; Environmental Engineering; Industrial Design; Materials Engineering; Mechanical Engineering; Mining Engineering; Software Engineering; Surveying and Mapping; Telecommunications Engineering) *Dean*: John Carter; **Health** (Anaesthesiology; Anatomy; Behavioural Sciences; Biochemistry; Biology; Cell Biology; Child Care and Development; Community Health; Dermatology; Dietetics; Epidemiology; Genetics; Health Sciences; Immunology; Indigenous Studies; Medicine; Microbiology; Midwifery; Neurological Therapy; Neurosciences; Nursing; Nutrition; Occupational Health; Occupational Therapy; Oral Pathology; Paediatrics; Pathology; Pharmacology; Pharmacy; Physical Therapy; Physiology; Podiatry; Psychiatry and Mental Health; Public Health; Radiology; Surgery; Toxicology) *Dean*: Nick Talley; **Science and Information Technology** (Biological and Life Sciences; Biology; Chemistry; Communication Studies; Design; Development Studies; Earth Sciences; Environmental Management; Environmental Studies; Geography; Geology; Graphic Design; Information Sciences; Information Technology; Journalism; Mass Communication; Mathematics; Mathematics and Computer Science; Media Studies; Multimedia; Natural Resources; Natural Sciences; Physics; Psychology; Radio and Television Broadcasting; Statistics) *Dean*: Bill Hogarth

Institutes

Newcastle Bone and Joint Institute (Anatomy) *Director*: Nik Bogduk; **Wollotuka** (Indigenous Studies)

Research Centres

Advanced Particle Processing *Director*: Kevin Galvin; **Asthma and Respiratory Diseases** (Respiratory Therapy) *Director*: Pablo Moscato; **Bioinformatics, Biomarker Discovery and Information-Based Medicine**; **Cancer**; **Chemical Biology** (Biology); **Complex Dynamic Systems and Control**; **Computer Assisted Research Mathematics and itsApplication** *Director*: Graham C. Goodwin; **Energy** (Energy Engineering) *Director*: Bogdan Dlugogrski; **Gender, Health and Ageing** (Gender Studies) *Director*: Julie Byles; **Geothechnical and Materials Modelling**; **Health Behaviour**; **Organic Electronics**; **Physical Activity and Nutrition**; **Reproductive Science**

Further Information: Also Commonwealth Funded Centres and Industry Funded Institutes in partnership with External Organizations. Online postgraduate education. Research Institutes. An offshore campus in Singapore, and Sidney, two domestic campuses at Ourimbah and Port Macquarie.

History: Founded 1951 as College of New South Wales University of Technology. Became an autonomous Institution 1965 and amalgamated with the Hunter Institute of Higher Education 1989.

Governing Bodies: University Council; Academic Senate

Academic Year: March to November (March-June; July-November)

Admission Requirements: Higher School Certificate (HSC) or recognized foreign equivalent, or previous tertiary study. Admission to some undergraduate courses requires additional testing, audition or portfolio. Prior tertiary studies may be recognized for course credit

Fees: Full details available from International Admissions: http://www.newcastle.edu.au/students/international/our-programs/tuition-fees.html

Main Language(s) of Instruction: English

International Co-operation: With universities in Austria, Belgium, Canada, Czech Republic, Denmark, Finland, France, Germany, Iceland, Japan, Korea, Norway, Singapore, Sweden, Netherlands, United Kingdom, USA.

Degrees and Diplomas: *Bachelor Degree*: 3-4 yrs full-time/ 4-8 years part-time; *Bachelor Honours Degree*: 1 further yr full-time/ 2 yrs part-time; *Master Degree*: 1-2 years full-time, a further 1-2 yrs; *Doctoral Degree (PhD)*: a further 3-3,5 yrs full-time / 6-7 years part-time. Also postgraduate certificates and diplomas, and research higher degrees

Student Services: Academic counselling, Canteen, Cultural centre, Employment services, Foreign student adviser, Foreign Studies Centre, Handicapped facilities, Health services, Language programs, Nursery care, Social counselling, Sports facilities

Student Residential Facilities: Yes

Special Facilities: University Gallery. Watt Space Student Art Gallery. Griffith Duncan Theatre. Conservatorium. FM Radio Station

Libraries: 4 principal libraries. Books, Journals (online and print), Videos/DVDs, Music Scores, CDs, Online catalogue and resources, Computing facilities, Disability services, Assistance and training, Microforms, Rare books, Information and IT support, Information literacy training

Publications: Research Report, All university publications including annual and research reports are avalaible at the website : http://www.newcastle.edu.au/

Last Updated: 07/10/11

THE UNIVERSITY OF QUEENSLAND (UQ)

St Lucia, Queensland 4072
Tel: +61(7) 3365-1111
Fax: +61(7) 3365-1266
EMail: study@uq.edu.au
Website: http://www.uq.edu.au

Vice-Chancellor and President: Paul Greenfield (2008-)
Tel: +61(7) 3365-1300, Fax: +61(7) 3365-1266
EMail: vc@uq.edu.au

AO Executive Director (Operations) and University Secretary: Maurie Mcnarn
Tel: +61(7) 3365-1310, Fax: +61(7) 3365-2680
EMail: m.mcnarn@uq.edu.au

International Relations: Anna Ciccarelli, Deputy Vice-Chancellor and Vice-President (International) (2010-)
Tel: +61(7) 3365-7366, Fax: +61(7) 3365-1314
EMail: a.ciccarelli@uq.edu.au

Faculties

Arts (Art History; Classical Languages; Cultural Studies; English; History; Media Studies; Modern Languages; Music; Philosophy; Religion) *Executive Dean*: Nancy Wright; **Business Economics and Law** (Business Administration; Economics; Law; Leisure Studies; Tourism) *Executive Dean*: Tim Brailsford; **Engineering, Architecture and Information Technology** (Architecture and Planning; Chemical Engineering; Civil Engineering; Electrical Engineering; Engineering; Information Technology; Mechanical Engineering; Mining Engineering; Water Management) *Executive Dean*: Graham Schaffer; **Health Sciences** (Community Health; Dentistry; Health Sciences; Medicine; Midwifery; Nursing; Pharmacy; Public Health; Rehabilitation and Therapy; Toxicology; Tropical Medicine) *Executive Dean*: Nick Fisk; **Science** (Agriculture; Animal Husbandry; Biological and Life Sciences; Biomedical Engineering; Biomedicine; Earth Sciences; Ecology; Environmental Engineering; Environmental Management; Environmental Studies; Food Science; Food Technology; Geography; Marine Science and Oceanography; Mathematics; Microbiology; Molecular Biology; Nanotechnology; Nutrition; Physics; Regional Planning; Toxicology; Veterinary Science; Zoology) *Executive Dean*: Stephen Walker; **Social and Behavioural Sciences** (Archaeology; Communication Studies; Education; International Studies; Journalism; Political Sciences; Psychology; Social Sciences; Social Work) *Executive Dean*: David De Vaus

Further Information: Also Teaching Hospitals, University Mine, Veterinary Science facilities and Agricultural Farms, Marine Research Stations and Study Abroad, Study Exchange and Twinning Programmes, Institute for Continuing and TESOL Education (ICTE), and 8 research institutes

History: Established by Act of the Queensland Parliament 1909. Officially founded 1910, it began teaching in 1911. In 1990, it merged with the Queensland Agricultural College (now UQ Gatton) as part of a unified national system abolishing the binary system of universities and colleges of advanced education. In 1999, opened UQ Ipswich.

Governing Bodies: The University of Queensland Senate

Academic Year: February to December (February-July; July-December). Summer session (November-February) for some courses

Admission Requirements: Senior secondary school certificate or recognized foreign equivalent with appropriate grades and prerequisites. English language proficiency is required either via IELTS-test, overall band score of at least 6.5, with a writing band score of at least 6; or TOEFL test score of 550, with a writing band of 5. Higher English language proficiency is required for some programs of study

Fees: (Aus Dollars): 8,800-27,500 per semester

Main Language(s) of Instruction: English

Degrees and Diplomas: *Diploma*; *Bachelor Degree*: 3 yrs; *Bachelor Honours Degree*: 4 yrs; *Graduate Certificate/Diploma*: 1 further semester; *Master Degree*: a further 1- 2 yrs; *Doctoral Degree (PhD)*: a further 3-4 yrs. Also undergraduate Diploma (2 yrs part time only). For full details on UQ's 400 programmes and 4,500 courses, visit www.uq.edu.au

Student Services: Academic counselling, Canteen, Employment services, Foreign student adviser, Handicapped facilities, Health services, Language programs, Nursery care, Social counselling, Sports facilities

Student Residential Facilities: For 2,600 students. On-campus accommodation at St. Lucia (10 residential colleges) and UQ Gatton. Off-campus college-style accommodation near UQ Ipswich. Family and Homestay accommodation near St. Lucia Campus.

Special Facilities: Museums and collections: Anatomy; Anthropology; Medical History; Antiquities; Entomology; Zoology. University Art Museum (c. 3,000 works of Australian art and Nat Yuen Collection of Chinese Antiquities)

Libraries: Total, c. 2m. vols, 30,000 electronic journals, videos, microforms, videos, manuscripts, pictorial collections, 864 networked databases, 358,000 e-books. Fryer Memorial Library

Publications: German-Australian Studies; Law Journal; Queensland Archaeological Research; Queensland Studies in German Language and Literature; The Australian Journal of Educational Studies, Publications of the Faculties and Departments

Press or Publishing House: The University of Queensland Press

Academic Staff 2010-2011	MEN	WOMEN	TOTAL
FULL-TIME	1,774	1,219	**2,993**
Student Numbers 2010-2011			
All (Foreign Included)	19,481	24,350	**43,831**
FOREIGN ONLY	–	–	**10,522**

Last Updated: 03/08/11

THE UNIVERSITY OF WESTERN AUSTRALIA

35 Stirling Highway, Crawley, Western Australia 6009
Tel: +61(8) 6488-6000
Fax: +61(8) 6488-1580
EMail: general.enquiries@uwa.edu.au
Website: http://www.uwa.edu.au

Vice-Chancellor: Paul Johnson
Tel: +61(8) 6488-2809, Fax: +61(8) 6488-1013
EMail: vc@uwa.edu.au

Academic Services and Registrar: Peter Curtis
Tel: +61(8) 9380-3001, Fax: +61(8) 9380-1075
EMail: Peter.Curtis@uwa.edu.au

International Relations: Kelly Smith
Tel: +61(3) 9380-1853, Fax: +61(3) 9380-1129
EMail: Kelly.g.smith@uwa.edu.au

Centres
Aboriginal Medical and Dental Health; **Advanced Consumer Research**; **Atomic, Molecular and Surface Physics**; **Callaway**; **Child and Adolescent Related Disorders** (Behavioural Sciences); **Child Study** (Child Care and Development); **Crime Research**; **Ear Sciences** (Otorhinolaryngology); **Ecohydrology**; **Electro-Optic Propagation and Sensing** (Optical Technology); **Energy Systems** (Energy Engineering); **Engineering Design and Consultancy** (Engineering Drawing and Design); **Evolutionary Biology**; **Excellence in Natural Resource Management**; **Forensic Science** (Forensic Medicine and Dentistry); **Geomechanics** *(Australian)* (Geological Engineering; Mechanical Engineering); **Health Services Research** (Health Administration); **Indigenous History and the Arts**; **Industrial Solid Mechanics**; **Infectious Diseases Research** *(Marshall)*; **Integrated Human Sciences**; **Intelligent Information Processing Systems**; **Labour Market Research** (Social Studies); **Land Rehabilitation**; **Legumes in Mediterranean Agriculture** (Agriculture; Vegetable Production); **Micro-**

scopy, **Characterisation and Analysis**; **Mining, Energy and Natural Resources Law**; **Mobile Health Care Solutions** *(e-Med)*; **Musculoskeletal Studies** (Anatomy); **Music** (Music); **Muslim States and Societies**; **Neuromuscular and Neurological Disorders**; **Offshore Foundation Systems**; **Ophthalmology and Visual Science**; **Organisational Research** (Management; Psychology); **Plant Energy Biology**; **Plant Metabolomics** (Plant and Crop Protection); **Remote and Rural Oral Health** (Oral Pathology); **Rural Health** *(Combined Universities)* (Health Sciences); **Software Practice** (Software Engineering); **Strategic Nano-Fabrication** (Nanotechnology); **Sustainable Mine Lakes**; **Timber Technology** (Wood Technology); **Western Australian History** (History)

Faculties
Architecture, Landscape and Visual Arts (Architecture; Landscape Architecture; Visual Arts) *Dean*: Simon Anderson; **Arts, Humanities and Social Sciences** (Arts and Humanities; Cultural Studies; Music; Social Sciences) *Dean*: Krishna Sen; **Business** (Business and Commerce; Economics) *Dean*: Tracey Horton; **Education** (Education) *Dean*: Bill Louden; **Engineering, Computing and Mathematics** (Civil Engineering; Computer Engineering; Computer Science; Electrical and Electronic Engineering; Engineering; Environmental Engineering; Mathematics; Mechanical Engineering; Software Engineering; Statistics) *Dean*: John Dell; **Law** (Law) *Dean*: Kaye Stuart; **Medicine, Dentistry and Health Sciences** (Dentistry; Health Education; Medicine; Neurosciences; Paediatrics; Pathology; Pharmacology; Psychiatry and Mental Health; Surgery) *Dean*: Ian Puddey; **Natural and Agricultural Sciences** (Agriculture; Biology; Earth Sciences; Geography; Natural Sciences; Plant and Crop Protection) *Dean*: Lynette Abbott; **Sciences** (Anatomy; Biological and Life Sciences; Biomedicine; Chemistry; Molecular Biology; Physics; Psychology; Sports) *Dean*: Tony O'Donnell

Institutes
Advanced Studies; **Agriculture** (Agriculture); **Confucius** (Chinese); **Energy and Minerals** (Energy Engineering; Mineralogy); **Oceans** (Marine Science and Oceanography); **Regional Development** (Regional Studies)

Research Centres
Advanced Mineral and Materials Processing; **Anthropological**; **Applied Cancer Studies**; **Applied Dynamics and Optimization**; **Archaeological** *(Eureka)* (Archaeology); **Asthma, Allergy and Respiratory**; **Clinical Research in Neuropsychiatry** (Neurology; Psychiatry and Mental Health); **Consumer** *(Advanced)*; **Crystallography**; **Energy Systems**; **Future Farm Industries** *(Cooperative)*; **Global Studies** *(Australian)*; **Gravitational** *(Australian International)*; **Medical Engineering** *(Australian)*; **Molecular Immunology and Instrumentation**; **Oil and Gas Engineering**; **Urban Research**; **Water Research**

Further Information: Also 30 Teaching Hospitals

History: Founded 1911, endowed by an Act of the State legislature with Royal Assent.

Governing Bodies: Senate

Academic Year: February to November (February-June; July-November)

Admission Requirements: Western Australia Tertiary Entrance Examination following secondary school certificate or recognized foreign equivalent, or previous tertiary study. Direct entrance to second year on satisfactory completion of studies in another recognized tertiary institution

Fees: (Aus Dollars): 22,000-46,000

Main Language(s) of Instruction: English

International Co-operation: Inter-university cooperation through the International Centre located within the University campus

Degrees and Diplomas: *Bachelor Degree*: Arts (BA), 3 yrs; *Bachelor Degree*: Commerce (Bcom); Design (Bdes); Philosophy (Bphil); Science (BSc); *Graduate Certificate/Diploma*; *Master Degree*: Accountancy; Agriculture; Clinical Audiology; Cognitive Science; Dentistry; Economics; Fine Arts; Forensic Science; Horticulture; Laboratory Medicine; Medical Science; Oil and Gas Engineering; Physical and Health Education; Primary Health Care; Psychology; Public Health, a further 2 yrs; *Master Degree*: Architecture; Building Science; Commerce; Engineering; Environmental Design; Landscape Architecture; Law; Music; Music Education; Natural Resource Management; Philosophy; Science, a further

1-2 yrs; *Master Degree*: Arts; Banking and Finance Law; Criminal Justice; Education; Education in Applied Lingusitics; Educational Management; E-Marketing and Information Management; Human Resources and Management; Industrial Relations; Information Management; Japanese Studies; Marketing; Science Education; Social Work, 1 further yr; *Master Degree*: Business Administration, a further 1 1/2 yrs; *Master Degree*: Dental Science, a further 3 yrs; *Master Degree*: Finance; *Master Degree*: Teachers Training, 1-2 further yrs; *Doctoral Degree*: Business Administration (DBA); Dental Science, 3-4 yrs; *Doctoral Degree*: Education (EdD); Educational Psychology; Juridical Science, 3 yrs; *Doctoral Degree*: Engineering in Information and Communications technology; Medicine; Musical Arts; Philosophy; Physiotherapy; Psychology; Social Work. Additional information at http://courses.handbooks.uwa.edu.au/courses

Student Services: Academic counselling, Canteen, Cultural centre, Employment services, Foreign student adviser, Handicapped facilities, Health services, Nursery care, Social counselling, Sports facilities

Student Residential Facilities: For 1,093 students

Special Facilities: Museums of Agriculture; Anatomy; Anthropology; Archaeology; Botany; Geology; Pathology; Zoology. Lawrence Wilson Art Gallery. Octagon Theatre; New Fortune Theatre (Elizabethan replica, open-air); Callaway Auditorium; Dolphin Theatre

Libraries: Business, Humanities and Social Sciences, Scholar's Centre, Biological Sciences, Chemistry, Education, Fine Arts and Architecture, Medicine, Dentistry, Geology, Law, Mathematics and Physical Sciences, Music, total, 1,113,343 vols

Press or Publishing House: The University of Western Australia Press

Academic Staff 2010	MEN	WOMEN	TOTAL
FULL-TIME	830	414	1,244
STAFF WITH DOCTORATE			
FULL-TIME	697	317	1,014
PART-TIME	84	103	187
Student Numbers 2011			
All (Foreign Included)	11,811	11,812	23,623
FOREIGN ONLY	2,611	2,637	5,248

Last Updated: 12/07/11

UNIVERSITY OF BALLARAT

P.O. Box 663, Ballarat, Victoria 3353
Tel: +61(3) 5327-8510
Fax: +61(3) 5327-8001
EMail: international@ballarat.edu.au
Website: http://www.ballarat.edu.au

Vice-Chancellor and President: David Battersby
Tel: +61(3) 5327-9000, Fax: +61(3) 5327-9704
EMail: vc@ballarat.edu.au

Public Relations Manager: Le-Anne O'Brien
Tel: +61(3) 5327-9637 EMail: l.obrien@ballarat.edu.au

International Relations: Rowena Coutts, Secretary to Council
Tel: +61(3) 5327-9506 EMail: r.coutts@ballarat.edu.au

Schools

Business (Accountancy; Business Administration; Business and Commerce; Information Technology; Leadership; Public Administration); **Education and Arts** (Art Education; Arts and Humanities; Ceramic Art; Curriculum; Education; Educational Administration; Fine Arts; Graphic Design; Music; Painting and Drawing; Pedagogy; Performing Arts; Preschool Education; Primary Education; Secondary Education; Social Sciences; Theatre); **Food, Land and Service Industries** (Cooking and Catering; Food Science; Horticulture; Rural Studies; Tourism; Transport Engineering; Transport Management); **Health Sciences** (Biomedicine; Food Science; Health Sciences; Nursing; Nutrition; Occupational Health; Psychology; Sports); **Human Services** (Adult Education; English; Social and Community Services; Social Sciences; Welfare and Protective Services); **Manufacturing Services** (Automotive Engineering; Building Technologies; Engineering; Technology); **Science, Information Technology and Engineering** (Civil Engineering; Computer Education; Engineering; Engineering Management; Environmental Engineering; Geology; Information Technology;

Mathematics; Mechanical Engineering; Metallurgical Engineering; Mining Engineering; Natural Sciences; Software Engineering)

Further Information: Six campuses in Ararat, Ballarat, Horsham and Stawell

History: Founded 1870 as School of Mines and Industries Ballarat. Became University 1994. Merged with the Horsham-based Wimmera Institute of TAFE 1998, to become a dual sector University incorporating both higher education and technical and further education.

Governing Bodies: Council

Academic Year: February to November (February-June; July-November)

Admission Requirements: Successful completion of an approved year 12 course of study

Main Language(s) of Instruction: English

Degrees and Diplomas: *Certificate I*: 6-12 months; *Advanced Diploma*: 1 yr; *Diploma*: 1 yr; *Bachelor Degree*: 3-4 yrs; *Graduate Certificate/Diploma*: 6 months; *Master Degree*: a further 18 months; *Doctoral Degree*: 3 yrs

Student Residential Facilities: For 787 students

Libraries: 4 Libraries, 250,000 vols; 21,000 serial titles - print and electronic

Student Numbers *2010-2011*: Total: c. 25,810
Last Updated: 05/12/11

UNIVERSITY OF CANBERRA (UC)

Canberra, ACT 2601
Tel: +61(2) 6201-5111
Fax: +61(2) 6201-5999
EMail: international@canberra.edu.au
Website: http://www.canberra.edu.au

Vice-Chancellor: Stephen Parker (2007-)
Tel: +61(2) 6201-5000, Fax: +61(2) 6201-5036
EMail: ovc@canberra.edu.au

Registrar: Bruce Lines EMail: Registrar@canberra.edu.au

International Relations: Jules Wills, Director, International and Marketing Tel: +61(2) 6201-5029

Centres

Customs and Excise Studies (International Law; Law) *Director*: David Widdowson; **Learning and Teaching** (Educational Research) *Director*: Helen Carter

Faculties

Applied Science (Biology; Biomedical Engineering; Environmental Studies; Forensic Medicine and Dentistry; Natural Sciences) *Dean*: Arthur Georges; **Arts and Design** (Advertising and Publicity; Architecture; Communication Studies; Foreign Languages Education; Graphic Design; Industrial Design; Interior Design; International Studies; Journalism; Landscape Architecture; Marketing; Media Studies; Modern Languages; Writing) *Dean*: Lyndon Anderson; **Business and Government** (Administration; Banking; Economics; Finance; Government; Management; Marketing; Regional Planning; Tourism; Urban Studies) *Dean*: Lawrence Pratchett; **Education** *Dean*: Cathryn Mc Conaghy; **Health** (Nursing; Pharmacy; Physical Therapy; Psychology; Sports) *Dean (Acting)*: Judith Anson; **Information Sciences and Engineering** (Computer Engineering; Information Technology; Mathematics; Software Engineering; Statistics) *Dean*: Dharmendra Sharma; **Law** (Law) *Dean*: Murray Raffe

Further Information: Also research centres

History: Founded as Canberra College of Advanced Education. Acquired present title and status 1989.

Governing Bodies: University Council

Academic Year: February to November (February-June; July-November)

Admission Requirements: Higher school certificate (HSC) or national or international equivalent. Advanced standing may be granted on satisfactory completion of studies in another recognized higher education institution

Fees: (Aus Dollars): International students, c. 15,000 per annum

Main Language(s) of Instruction: English

International Co-operation: With universities in China; Indonesia; Japan; Malaysia; Taiwan; Thailand; Finland; Germany; Italy; Norway; Spain; Sweden; Canada; Mexico; USA

Degrees and Diplomas: *Diploma*: Chinese; Japanese; Spanish (can only be taken in conjunction with a UC undergraduate degree); *Bachelor Degree*: Architecture; Laws (when combined with another degree), 5 yrs; *Bachelor Degree*: Commerce in Accounting; Communication; Arts; Commerce in Banking and Finance; Business Administration; Coaching Science; Community Education; Applied Economics; Forensic Studies; Hotel Management; Applied Sciences; Human Nutrition; Information Technology; Journalism; Management; Management Sciences; Media/Multimedia Production; Medical Sciences; Creative Writing; Applied Psychology; Public Relations; Resources and Environmental Science; Science; Social Sciences; Software Engineering; Sports Management; Sports Media; Tourism Management, 3 yrs; *Bachelor Degree*: Computer Engineering; Early Childhood Teaching; Electronics and Communications Engineering; Graphic Design; Industrial Design; Landscape Architecture; Laws; New Media Production; Primary Teaching; Secondary Teaching; Software Engineering, 4 yrs; *Bachelor Degree*: Nursing, $3\frac{1}{2}$ yrs; *Master Degree*: Accounting; Business and Finance; Communication; Community Development; Counselling; Creative Writing; Cultural Heritage Management; Customs Administration; Design; Education; Facilities Management; Health Sciences; Information Management; Information Technology; Landscape Architecture; Languages; Law; Management; Marketing; Media; Nursing; Nutrition; Pharmacy; Physiotherapy; Psychology; Resource Management & Environmental Science; Science; Sports Studies; Tourism; Urban & Regional Planning, 2 yrs; by coursework; *Master Degree*: Architecture; Communication; Community Development; Counselling; Cultural Heritage Management; Design; Education; Engineering; Information Management; Information Technology; Landscape Architecture; Law; Management; Nursing; Resource Management and Environmental Science; Science; Sports Studies; Tourism; Urban and Regional Planning, 2 yrs; by research; *Doctoral Degree*: Applied Science; Commerce; Communication; Corporate Law; Economics; Education; Environmental Design; Information Sciences and Engineering; Public Sector Management (PhD), 3 yrs

Student Services: Academic counselling, Canteen, Cultural centre, Employment services, Foreign student adviser, Foreign Studies Centre, Handicapped facilities, Health services, Language programs, Nursery care, Social counselling, Sports facilities

Student Residential Facilities: For c. 1,200 students

Libraries: c. 480,000 vols; 5,000 current serials

Publications: Research publications *(other/irregular)*

Academic Staff *2011*	TOTAL
FULL-TIME	310
PART-TIME	3,050
STAFF WITH DOCTORATE	
FULL-TIME	c. 170
Student Numbers *2011*	
All (Foreign Included)	c. 7,200

Part-time students, 1,260.
Last Updated: 05/12/11

UNIVERSITY OF MELBOURNE

Melbourne, Victoria 3010
Tel: +61(3) 8344-4000
Website: http://www.unimelb.edu.au

Vice-Chancellor: Glyn Conrad Davis, AC
Tel: +61(3) 8344-6134, Fax: +61(3) 9347-7253
EMail: vc@unimelb.edu.au

Senior Vice-Principal: R. Ian Marshman
Tel: +61(3) 8344-6121, Fax: +61(3) 9347-0071
EMail: i.marshman@unimelb.edu.au

International Relations: Sue Elliott, Deputy Vice-Chancellor (Global Engagement)
Tel: +61(3) 8344-9666, Fax: +61(3) 8344-9999
EMail: s.elliott@unimelb.edu.au

Colleges
Arts *(Victorian College of the Arts)* (Dance; Film; Fine Arts; Music; Radio and Television Broadcasting; Theatre)

Faculties
Architecture, Building and Planning (Architectural and Environmental Design; Building Technologies; Heritage Preservation; Landscape Architecture; Real Estate; Regional Planning; Regional Studies; Rural Planning; Rural Studies; Structural Architecture; Town Planning; Transport Management; Urban Studies) *Dean*: K. Kvan; **Arts** (American Studies; Ancient Languages; Anthropology; Arabic; Archaeology; Art Criticism; Art History; Asian Studies; Behavioural Sciences; Catalan; Chinese; Cinema and Television; Classical Languages; Cognitive Sciences; Communication Arts; Comparative Literature; Comparative Religion; Cultural Studies; Development Studies; Earth Sciences; East Asian Studies; Environmental Studies; Eurasian and North Asian Languages; European Languages; European Studies; French; French Studies; Gender Studies; Geography; German; Germanic Studies; Greek; Hebrew; Hispanic American Studies; History; History of Religion; Holy Writings; Indigenous Studies; Indonesian; International Studies; Islamic Studies; Italian; Japanese; Jewish Studies; Korean; Latin; Linguistics; Literature; Mass Communication; Media Studies; Middle Eastern Studies; Modern Languages; Museum Studies; Natural Sciences; Philosophy; Political Sciences; Portuguese; Psychology; Russian; Sociology; South and Southeast Asian Languages; South Asian Studies; Southeast Asian Studies; Spanish; Swedish; Thai Languages; Theatre; Translation and Interpretation; Urban Studies; Vietnamese; Visual Arts; Women's Studies; Writing) *Dean*: M. Considine; **Arts** *(VCA and Music)* (Acting; Art Management; Cinema and Television; Dance; Film; Music; Music Theory and Composition; Opera; Painting and Drawing; Photography; Printing and Printmaking; Sculpture; Theatre) *Dean*: B. Conyngham; **Business and Economics** (Accountancy; Actuarial Science; Administration; Business and Commerce; Economics; Finance; Management) *Dean*: M. Abernethy; **Education** (Adult Education; Art Education; Arts and Humanities; Child Care and Development; Computer Education; Continuing Education; Curriculum; Distance Education; Education of the Handicapped; Education of the Socially Disadvantaged; Educational Administration; Educational and Student Counselling; Educational Sciences; Educational Testing and Evaluation; Health Education; Higher Education; Literacy Education; Mathematics Education; Music Education; Philosophy of Education; Physical Education; Preschool Education; Primary Education; Science Education; Secondary Education; Social Sciences; Special Education; Teacher Training; Vocational Education) *Dean*: F. Rickards; **Engineering** (Bioengineering; Chemical Engineering; Civil Engineering; Computer Engineering; Computer Science; Electrical and Electronic Engineering; Environmental Engineering; Materials Engineering; Mechanical Engineering; Production Engineering; Surveying and Mapping) *Dean*: J. Van Deventer; **Land and Environment** (Environmental Studies) *Dean*: R. Roush; **Law** (Law) *Dean*: C. Evans; **Medicine, Dentistry and Health Sciences** (Anatomy; Behavioural Sciences; Biochemistry; Biological and Life Sciences; Biomedicine; Biotechnology; Cardiology; Cell Biology; Dentistry; Dermatology; Diabetology; Embryology and Reproduction Biology; Endocrinology; Epidemiology; Forensic Medicine and Dentistry; Gastroenterology; Genetics; Gerontology; Gynaecology and Obstetrics; Haematology; Hepatology; Histology; Immunology; Medical Parasitology; Medical Technology; Medicine; Microbiology; Molecular Biology; Nephrology; Neurology; Neurosciences; Nursing; Oncology; Ophthalmology; Optical Technology; Orthopaedics; Otorhinolaryngology; Paediatrics; Parasitology; Pathology; Pharmacology; Physiology; Plastic Surgery; Pneumology; Psychiatry and Mental Health; Psychology; Public Health; Rehabilitation and Therapy; Rheumatology; Social Work; Surgery; Toxicology; Treatment Techniques; Tropical Medicine; Urology; Venereology; Virology) *Dean*: J. Angus; **Science** (Actuarial Science; Anatomy; Astronomy and Space Science; Biochemistry; Biological and Life Sciences; Biology; Biomedicine; Biophysics; Biotechnology; Botany; Cell Biology; Chemistry; Computer Science; Earth Sciences; Embryology and Reproduction Biology; Genetics; Geochemistry; Geography; Geology; Geophysics; Immunology; Information Management; Information Technology; Marine Biology; Marine Science and Oceanography; Mathematics; Meteorology; Microbiology; Mineralogy; Molecular Biology; Neurosciences; Optometry; Paleontology; Parasitology; Petrology; Pharmacology; Physics; Physiology; Plant Pathology; Seismology; Statistics; Surgery; Toxicology; Zoology) *Dean*: R. Saint; **Veterinary Science** (Veterinary Science) *Dean*: K. Hinchcliff

Institutes
Bio21 Molecular Science and Biotechnology *(Bio21 Institute) Director*: T. Bacic; **Global Health** *(Nossal) Director*: G. Brown

Schools

Business *(Melbourne)* (Business Administration) *Dean and Director:* J. George

Further Information: Campuses: Burnley Campus, Richmond, Victoria; Creswick Campus, Creswick, Victoria; Dookie Campus, Dookie College, Victoria; Hawthorn Campus, Victoria; Parkville Campus, Parkville, Victoria; Shepparton Campus and Administration Centre, Shepparton, Victoria; Werribee Campus, Werribee, Victoria. Also Teaching Hospitals; Veterinary Clinic

History: Founded 1853 by an Act of the Victorian State Parliament, Melbourne was Victoria's first University and Australia's second. Funding is through the Australian Government and non-governmental sources. The University amalgamated with the Melbourne College of Advanced Education in 1989, with the Hawthorn Institute of Education in 1996 and with the Victorian College of Agriculture and Horticulture in 1997. Victorian College of the Arts became a full faculty in 2007.

Governing Bodies: University Council

Academic Year: March to December (March-June; July-December)

Admission Requirements: Satisfactory completion of an approved final year of high school equivalent to the Victorian Certificate of Education (VCE) or, in countries without a recognised high school qualification, completion of a foundation programme in Australia or first year standing from a recognised overseas tertiary institution, and satisfactory completion of any special course requirements; admission quotas apply and completion of entrance qualifications does not guarantee right of entry.

Fees: (Aus Dollars): Up to 64,000 per annum depending on course of study. Information on fees for overseas students available from the International Centre

Main Language(s) of Instruction: English

Degrees and Diplomas: *Bachelor Degree:* 3-4 yrs; *Bachelor Degree:* Medicine, 6 yrs; *Bachelor Honours Degree:* 4 yrs; *Graduate Certificate/Diploma:* 1 sem; *Master Degree:* a further 1-2 yrs; *Doctoral Degree:* a further 3-4 yrs

Student Services: Academic counselling, Canteen, Cultural centre, Employment services, Foreign student adviser, Handicapped facilities, Health services, Nursery care, Social counselling, Sports facilities

Student Residential Facilities: Yes

Special Facilities: Ian Potter Museum of Art; Art Conservation Center; Melbourne Theatre Company; Sidney Myer Asia Centre

Libraries: Baillieu Library; 20 specialist branch libraries, total, 3.5m. vols and 63,000 periodical subscriptions

Publications: Publications on the History of Melbourne University; Research and Research Training Plan 2006 *(annually)*; Research Annual Review

Press or Publishing House: Melbourne University Publishing
Last Updated: 13/10/11

UNIVERSITY OF NEW ENGLAND (UNE)

Armidale, New South Wales 2351
Tel: +61(2) 6773-3333
Fax: +61(2) 6773-3122 +61(2) 6773-3100
Website: http://www.une.edu.au

Vice-Chancellor and Chief Executive Officer: James Barber (2010-)
Tel: +61(2) 6773-3367, Fax: +61(2) 6773-3509
EMail: vc@une.edu.au

Executive Officer to the Vice-Chancellor: Katherine Gash
Tel: +61(2) 6773-2144 EMail: vcadministration@une.edu.au

Centres

Agriculture and Law (Agriculture; Law) *Director:* Julian Prior; **Applied Research in Social Sciences** (Educational Administration; Educational Sciences; Higher Education) *Director:* Tony Sorenson; **Beef Industry** *Director:* Bill McKiernan; **Oorala Aboriginal Studies** (Cultural Studies; Indigenous Studies) *Director:* Debra Bennell; **Primary Industries Innovation** *Director:* Bob Martin; **Rural Greenhouse Gas Research** *(National) Director:* Annette Cowie; **Science, Information and Communication Technology** *(National)* (Information Sciences; Information Technology; Telecommunications Engineering) *Director:* John Pegg

Conservatories

New England Conservatorium of Music (Music) *Director:* Julie Croft

Institutes

Genetics and Bioinformatics (Animal Husbandry; Genetics) *Director:* John Gibson; **Rural Futures** (Management; Natural Resources) *Director:* David J. Brunckhorst

Research Institutes

Agricultural Business (Agricultural Business; Information Technology; Software Engineering) *Director:* Philip Arthur Rickards

Schools

Arts (Asian Studies; Chinese; Communication Studies; English; European Studies; French; German; Indonesian; Italian; Japanese; Media Studies; Music; Theatre; Writing); **Behavioural Cognitive and Social Sciences** (Criminology; Geography; Linguistics; Psychology; Sociology) *Head:* Patrick Nunn; **Business, Economics, and Public Policy** (Accountancy; Agricultural Economics; Econometrics; Economic History; Economics; Finance; Management) *Dean:* Alison Sheridan; **Education** (Art Education; Education; Educational Sciences; English; Health Education; Higher Education; Information Technology; Literacy Education; Mathematics Education; Physical Education; Preschool Education; Science Education; Social Sciences; Special Education; Sports) *Dean:* Len Unsworth; **Environmental and Rural Science** (Agriculture; Environmental Engineering; Environmental Studies; Natural Resources; Natural Sciences; Rural Studies) *Head:* Iain Young; **Health** (Community Health; Gerontology; Health Administration; Health Sciences; Nursing; Social Work) *Head:* Steven Campbell; **Humanities** (Ancient Civilizations; Archaeology; Asian Studies; Classical Languages; Family Studies; History; Indigenous Studies; International Studies; Islamic Studies; Paleontology; Peace and Disarmament; Philosophy; Political Sciences; Religion) *Head:* Lynda Garland; **Law** (Law) *Head:* Jurgen Brohmer; **Rural Medicine** (Medicine) *Head:* Rafat Hussein; **Sciences and Technology** (Biology; Biomedical Engineering; Cell Biology; Chemistry; Computer Science; Electronic Engineering; Mathematics; Molecular Biology; Natural Sciences; Pharmacy; Physics; Physiology; Sports; Statistics) *Dean:* John Scott (Acting)

Further Information: Also Clinical Schools, International Office, and Off-shore Programmes

History: Founded 1938 as New England University College, acquired present status and title 1954.

Governing Bodies: Council; Academic Board

Academic Year: February to November (February-June; July-November).

Admission Requirements: Secondary school certificate or recognized foreign equivalent, or previous tertiary study. Overseas applicants must provide evidence of proficiency in English

Fees: (Aus Dollars): International students, 14,175 (Undergraduate) - 24,100 (PhD) per annum

Main Language(s) of Instruction: English

International Co-operation: With universities in Austria, Canada, China, Denmark, England, France, Germany, Hong Kong, Italy, Japan, USA, Vietma, Bhutan

Degrees and Diplomas: *Bachelor Honours Degree*; *Master Degree:* 1-4 yrs; *Doctoral Degree (PhD):* 4-6 yrs

Student Services: Academic counselling, Canteen, Employment services, Foreign student adviser, Foreign Studies Centre, Handicapped facilities, Health services, Language programs, Nursery care, Social counselling, Sports facilities

Student Residential Facilities: 7 fully catered Colleges; Self-catering apartments

Special Facilities: Zoology Museum; Museum of Antiquities (Artefacts from Greece, Rome, and other Mediterranean and Middle Eastern cultures). Drama Studio

Libraries: Dixson Library, Law Library, UNE Heritage Centre

Press or Publishing House: University of New England Press (commercial publications); Publications Unit (official publications)
Last Updated: 08/07/11

UNIVERSITY OF NEW SOUTH WALES (UNSW)

Sydney, New South Wales 2052
Tel: +61(2) 9385-1000
EMail: internationaloffice@unsw.edu.au
Website: http://www.unsw.edu.au

Vice-Chancellor and President: Fred Hilmer (2006-)
Tel: +61(2) 9385-2884, Fax: +61(2) 9385-1949
EMail: f.hilmer@unsw.edu.au

Pro Vice-Chancellor and Registrar: Joan Cooper
Tel: +61(2) 9385-1067, Fax: +61(2) 9385-1385
EMail: j.cooper@unsw.edu.au

International Relations: Jennie Lang, Executive Director, UNSW International
Tel: +61(2) 9385-6983, Fax: +61(2) 9313-7382
EMail: jennie.lang@unsw.edu.au

Academies
Australian Defence Force (Aeronautical and Aerospace Engineering; Arts and Humanities; Business Education; Chemistry; Civil Engineering; Computer Science; Economics; Electrical Engineering; Environmental Studies; Geography; Information Technology; Marine Science and Oceanography; Mathematics; Physics; Political Sciences; Social Sciences; Statistics) *Rector*: Michael Frater

Colleges
Fine Arts (Art Education; Art History; Art Management; Design; Fine Arts) *Dean*: Ian Howard

Faculties
Arts and Social Sciences (Anthropology; Arts and Humanities; Asian Studies; Chinese; Cognitive Sciences; Criminology; Cultural Studies; Dance; Education; English; Environmental Studies; European Studies; Film; French; Gender Studies; Greek; History; Indonesian; International Studies; Irish; Italian; Japanese; Jewish Studies; Journalism; Korean; Latin; Latin American Studies; Linguistics; Media Studies; Natural Sciences; Performing Arts; Philosophy; Political Sciences; Portuguese; Russian; Social Sciences; Social Work; Sociology; Spanish; Technology; Theatre; Women's Studies) *Dean*: James Donald; **Built Environment** (Architecture; Building Technologies; Construction Engineering; Development Studies; Industrial Design; Interior Design; Landscape Architecture; Real Estate; Town Planning) *Dean*: Alec Tzannes; **Engineering** (Aeronautical and Aerospace Engineering; Artificial Intelligence; Biomedical Engineering; Chemical Engineering; Civil Engineering; Coastal Studies; Communication Studies; Computer Engineering; Computer Science; Electrical Engineering; Engineering; Environmental Engineering; Industrial Chemistry; Industrial Engineering; Mechanical Engineering; Mining Engineering; Naval Architecture; Petroleum and Gas Engineering; Production Engineering; Software Engineering; Surveying and Mapping; Telecommunications Engineering; Transport Engineering; Waste Management; Water Management; Water Science) *Dean*: Graham Davies; **Law** (Law; Taxation) *Dean*: David Dixon; **Medicine** (Anatomy; Community Health; Health Education; Medicine; Paediatrics; Pathology; Pharmacology; Physiology; Psychiatry and Mental Health; Public Health; Sports Medicine; Surgery) *Dean*: Peter Smith; **Science** (Aeronautical and Aerospace Engineering; Anatomy; Applied Mathematics; Astronomy and Space Science; Astrophysics; Biochemistry; Biological and Life Sciences; Biophysics; Biotechnology; Chemistry; Coastal Studies; Earth Sciences; Ecology; Environmental Studies; Food Science; Food Technology; Genetics; Geography; Geography (Human); Geology; Immunology; Marine Science and Oceanography; Materials Engineering; Mathematics; Media Studies; Microbiology; Molecular Biology; Neurosciences; Nutrition; Optometry; Philosophy; Physics; Physiology; Psychology; Safety Engineering; Statistics; Technology; Toxicology) *Dean*: Merlin Crossley

Schools
Business *(The Australian)* (Accountancy; Actuarial Science; Banking; Economics; Finance; Human Resources; International Business; Law; Management; Marketing; Real Estate; Taxation) *Dean*: Alec Cameron

Further Information: Also Research Centres (http://www.gmo.unsw.edu.au/Centres-Secretariat/List OfUNSWCentres.html)

History: Founded 1949 as the New South Wales University of Technology, acquired present status and title 1958.

Governing Bodies: Council

Academic Year: February to November (March-June; July-November)

Admission Requirements: Higher School Certificate or recognized national or foreign equivalent, or previous post-secondary study.

Fees: (Aus Dollars): Undergraduate, 54,000-200,000 for full programme (Bachelor); Postgraduate coursework, 16,300-33,600

Main Language(s) of Instruction: English

Degrees and Diplomas: *Bachelor Degree*: Architecture (Barch), 51/2 yrs; *Bachelor Degree*: Art Education (BArtEd); Arts/Education (BA/ BEd); Bioinformatics (BE); Building Construction Management (BBCM); Business Information Technology (BSc); Dance Education (BA(Dance)); Design (BDes); Engineering (BEng); Environmental Science (BEnvSc); Food Science and Technology (BSc); Industrial Chemistry (BE); Industrial Design (BIndDes); Interior Architecture (BIA); International Studies (BInSt); Landscape Architecture (BLArch); Music Education (BMusEd); Nanotechnology (BSc); Optometry (Boptom); Planning (BTP); Psychology (Bpsychol); Science (Advanced) (BSc); Surveying and Spatial Information Systems (BE), 4 yrs; *Bachelor Degree*: Art Theory (BArtTh); Arts (BA); Aviation (Bav); Commerce (Bcom); Digital Media (BDM); Economics (Bec); Fine Arts (BFA); Law (Graduate) (LLB); Media and Communications (BA(Media), BSc (Media)); Medical Science (BMedSc); Music (Bmus); Science (BSc); Science - Architecture (BSc(Arch)); Social Sciences (BSocSc), 3 yrs; *Bachelor Degree*: Arts/Law (BA/ LLB), 5-7 yrs; *Bachelor Degree*: Commerce/Law (BCom/LLB); Science/Education (BSc/Bed), 5 yrs; *Bachelor Degree*: Health and Exercise Science (BSc), 4 yrs; *Master Degree*: Architecture; Built Environment; Business Administration; Commerce; Computing and Information Technology; Couple and Family Therapy; Psychology, 2 yrs; *Master Degree*: Arts; Social Development, 1yr; *Master Degree*: Building; *Master Degree*: Clinical Education; Design; Environmental Management; Sports Medicine; Sustainable Development, 11/2 yrs; *Master Degree*: Conservation Biology; Digital Media; Education; Educational Administration; Engineering; Environmental Engineering; Health Administration; Health Informatics; Industrial Design; International Social Development; Law; Legal Studies; Music; Optometry; Policy Studies; Professional Ethics; Public Health; Real Estate; Science; Science and Technology; Statistics; Taxation; Technology Management, 1 yr; *Master Degree*: Drug Development, 3 yrs; *Master Degree*: Law and Management, 21/2 yrs; *Doctoral Degree (PhD)*: 3 yrs. Also Combined Bachelors and postgraduate Certificates and Diplomas

Student Services: Academic counselling, Canteen, Cultural centre, Employment services, Foreign student adviser, Handicapped facilities, Health services, Nursery care, Social counselling, Sports facilities

Student Residential Facilities: Yes

Special Facilities: Ivan Dougherty Art Gallery

Libraries: Total, 2.7m. Items

Press or Publishing House: The New South Wales University Press

Academic Staff *2010-2011*	TOTAL
FULL-TIME	4,911

Student Numbers *2010-2011*	
All (Foreign Included)	52,582
FOREIGN ONLY	14,607

Last Updated: 21/11/11

UNIVERSITY OF SOUTH AUSTRALIA (UNISA)

PO Box 2471, Adelaide, South Australia 5001
Tel: +61(8) 8302-6611
Fax: +61(8) 8302-2466
EMail: international.office@unisa.edu.au
Website: http://www.unisa.edu.au

Vice-Chancellor: Peter Høj (2007-)
Tel: +61(8) 8302-0502, Fax: +61(8) 8302-0501
EMail: peter.hoj@unisa.edu.au

Executive Officer to the Vice-Chancellor and President: David Cox
Tel: +61(8) 8302-0650, Fax: +61(8) 8302-0501
EMail: david.cox@unisa.edu.au

International Relations: Nigel Relph, Pro-Vice-Chancellor (International and Development)
Tel: +61(8) 8302-0038, Fax: +61(8) 8302-0225

Centres
Centre for Regional Engagement (Business Administration; Management; Midwifery; Nursing; Social Policy; Social Work) *Director*: Guy Robinson

Divisions
Business (Accountancy; Administration; Banking; Business Administration; Business and Commerce; Criminal Law; Economics; Finance; Hotel Management; Human Resources; Labour and Industrial Relations; Labour Law; Law; Leadership; Leisure Studies; Marketing; Private Law; Public Law; Real Estate; Sports Management; Taxation; Tourism) *Pro Vice-Chancellor*: Gerry Griffin; **Education, Arts and Social Sciences** (Architecture; Art History; Art Management; Behavioural Sciences; Cinema and Television; Cognitive Sciences; Communication Studies; Cultural Studies; Dance; Design; Education; Educational Sciences; Fine Arts; Gender Studies; Handicrafts; Indigenous Studies; Industrial Design; Interior Design; International Studies; Journalism; Linguistics; Mass Communication; Media Studies; Modern Languages; Multimedia; Performing Arts; Political Sciences; Psychology; Radio and Television Broadcasting; Social and Community Services; Social Policy; Social Welfare; Social Work; Sociology; Special Education; Teacher Training; Theatre; Visual Arts) *Pro Vice-Chancellor*: Pal Ahluwalia; **Health Sciences** (Health Sciences) *Pro Vice-Chancellor*: Allan Evans; **Information Technology, Engineering and the Environment** (Civil Engineering; Computer Engineering; Electrical and Electronic Engineering; Energy Engineering; Environmental Studies; Industrial Engineering; Information Management; Information Technology; Materials Engineering; Mathematics; Mechanical Engineering; Parks and Recreation; Production Engineering; Statistics; Surveying and Mapping; Water Science) *Pro Vice-Chancellor*: Andrew Parfitt

Research Centres
Accounting, Governance and Sustainability *Contact*: Roger Burritt; **Advanced Computing** *Contact*: Markus Stumptner; **Applied Psychological Research** *Contact*: Maureen Dollard; **Comparative Water Policies and Law** (Law; Water Management) *Contact*: Jennifer McKay; **Defence and Systems Institute** *Contact*: Stephen Cook; **Environmental Risk Assessment and Remediation** *Contact*: Megh Mallavarapu; **Human Resource Management** (Human Resources) *Contact*: Carol Kulik; **Industrial and Applied Mathematics** (Applied Mathematics; Mathematics and Computer Science) *Contact*: Vladimir Ejov; **Languages and Culture** *Contact*: Angela Scarino; **Nutritional Physiology Research** *Contact*: Jon Buckley; **Regulation and Market Analysis** *Contact*: David Round; **Rural Health and Community Development** *Contact*: Guy Robinson; **Sleep Research** *Contact*: Kurt Lushington; **Sustainable Design and Behaviour** *(Zero Waste SA) Contact*: Steffen Lehmann; **Water Management and Reuse** (Water Management) *Contact*: Christopher Saint; **Work and Life** *Contact*: Barbara Pocock

Research Groups
Tourism and Leisure Management (Leisure Studies; Tourism) *Contact*: Gary Howat

Research Institutes
Bartbara Handy *Contact*: Chris Daniels; **Ian Wark** (Polymer and Plastics Technology) *Contact*: John Ralston; **Marketing Science** *(Ehrenberg-Bass) Contact*: Byron Sharp; **Mawson Institute** *Contact*: Rob Short; **Sansom Institute** (Medicine; Pharmacy) *Contact*: Kerin O'Dea; **Sustainable Societies** *(Hawke) Contact*: Pal Ahluwalia; **Sustainable Systems and Technologies** *Contact*: Mike Taylor; **Telecommunications Research** (Telecommunications Engineering) *Contact*: Alex Grant

Further Information: In 2008 the University of South Australia and the University of Adelaide have joined forces to establish a new defence research and education centre that aims to combat one of the greatest challenges facing the defence industry globally. Under the leadership of Chief Executive Officer, defence industry identity Mr Lloyd Groves, the new Defence Systems Innovation Centre (DSIC) will focus on the major challenge of systems integration for defence

History: Founded 1991 through the amalgamation of the South Australian Institute of Technology and several campuses of the South Australian College of Advanced Education.

Governing Bodies: University Council; Academic Board; Divisional Boards

Academic Year: February to November (February - June; July - November); Summer programme, December - February

Admission Requirements: Undergraduate entrants require senior secondary school (year 12) certificate or recognised foreign equivalent with appropriate grades and prerequisites. Postgraduate entrants shall normally hold a recognised University undergraduate degree or equivalent professional experience. The minimum English language entry requirements for international students who speak English as a foreign language are: International English Language Testing System (IELTS) Academic - overall 6.0 obtained within the last two years or corresponding results from an equivalent test. Note that many programs have a higher IELTS (Academic) requirement, some of which include specific subscore requirements.

Main Language(s) of Instruction: English, Chinese

International Co-operation: Student exchange agreements with institutions in 23 countries and formal agreements with institutions in 35 countries.

Degrees and Diplomas: *Associate Degree*: Accounting, Business Administration, Engineering, Information Technology, Built Environment, Cultural Studies, Modern Languages, 1-2 yrs; *Bachelor Degree*: Architecture and Planning, Arts and Humanities, Business Administration, Commerce, Human Resource Management, Marketing, Education ,Engineering, Fine Arts, Health Sciences, Nursing (Bachelor's Degree (with or without Honours)); Rehabilitation Therapies, Pharmacy, Information Sciences, Law, Mathematics and Computer Science, Performing Arts, Social Sciences, Environmental Studies, Sport and Leisure Studies (Bachelor's Degree (with or without Honours)); *Graduate Certificate/Diploma*: see Bachelor's degree list, 1 yr; *Master Degree*: see Bachelor's degree list, 1-2 yrs (by coursework or by research); *Doctoral Degree*: Business Administration, Pharmacy, Counselling, Psychology, Project Management, Education (Professional Doctorate); see Bachelor's Degree list (PhD), 3-4 yrs

Student Services: Academic counselling, Canteen, Cultural centre, Employment services, Foreign student adviser, Foreign Studies Centre, Handicapped facilities, Health services, Language programs, Nursery care, Social counselling, Sports facilities

Student Residential Facilities: Only at Whyalla Campus

Special Facilities: Museums, art galleries, theatre, observatory, fitness hub.

Libraries: Research collection with over 700,000 monographs and print journals together with a rapidly expanding collection of electronic resource holdings, including over 32,000 electronic journal titles, 24,000 ebooks, 16,000 ereadings and 350 databases as well as print resources including manuscripts and pictorial materials and AV materials.

Publications: Students@UniSA *(quarterly)*; The Graduate *(other/irregular)*; UniSA News *(other/irregular)*; UniSA Researcher *(other/irregular)*

Academic Staff 2007-2008	MEN	WOMEN	TOTAL
FULL-TIME	525	430	**955**
PART-TIME	53	100	**153**
STAFF WITH DOCTORATE			
FULL-TIME	354	266	**620**
PART-TIME	22	31	**53**
Student Numbers 2007-2008			
All (Foreign Included)	8,758	11,942	**20,700**

Last Updated: 21/11/11

UNIVERSITY OF SOUTHERN QUEENSLAND (USQ)

West Street, Toowoomba, Queensland 4350
Tel: +61(7) 4631-2100 +61(7) 4631-2168
Fax: +61(7) 4636-1762 +61(7) 4631-2893
EMail: international@usq.edu.au
Website: http://www.usq.edu.au

Vice-Chancellor and President: William Lovegrove (2003-)
Tel: +61(7) 4631-2168, Fax: +61(7) 4631-2782
EMail: vc@usq.edu.au

Faculties

Arts (Arts and Humanities; International Studies; Mass Communication; Multimedia; Music; Social Sciences; Theatre; Visual Arts) *Dean*: Peter Goodall; **Business and Law** (Business and Commerce; Economics; Human Resources; Information Technology; International Business; Labour and Industrial Relations; Law; Marketing; Transport Management) *Dean*: Allan Layton; **Education** (Child Care and Development; Distance Education; Education; Educational Administration; Primary Education; Secondary Education; Special Education) *Dean*: Nita Temmerman; **Engineering and Surveying** (Agricultural Engineering; Civil Engineering; Electrical and Electronic Engineering; Engineering; Mechanical Engineering; Surveying and Mapping) *Dean*: Frank Bullen; **Science** (Astronomy and Space Science; Biology; Biomedicine; Information Technology; Mathematics and Computer Science; Midwifery; Natural Sciences; Nursing; Oenology; Psychology) *Dean*: Janet Verbyla

Research Centres

Computational Engineering and Science (Computer Engineering; Computer Science); **Public Memory**; **Rural and Remote Area Health** (Health Sciences); **Sustainable Catchments** *(Australian)*; **Systems Biology** (Biology); **Transformative Pedagogies**

Sections

Distance and E-Education; **Kumbari/Ngurpai Lage Higher Education** *(academic and personal support for Aboriginal and Torres Strait Islander students)* (Higher Education); **Learning and Teaching Support Unit**; **Preparatory and Academy Support**

Further Information: Also two other campuses: Fraser Coast and Springfield. A number of Centres throughout the University which cover a range of research fields.

History: Founded 1992 by Act of the Queensland Parliament; previously University College of Southern Queensland (1990), Institute of Technology, Darling Downs (1967).

Governing Bodies: University Council

Academic Year: February to November (February-July; July-November). (Summer Term, November to February)

Admission Requirements: Completion of 12 years of schooling or equivalent with passes at required levels

Fees: Full details obtainable from the Academic Registrar

Main Language(s) of Instruction: English

International Co-operation: With universities in USA, China and Germany

Degrees and Diplomas: *Certificate I*: Arts; Commerce, 1-2 yrs; *Diploma*: Arts; Business, 1 yr; *Bachelor Degree*: Arts; Business; Commerce; Education; Engineering; Information Technology; Technology (Engineering, Surveying), 3-6 yrs; *Bachelor Degree*: Nursing; Teaching (primary level, and further education and training), 3-4 yrs; *Bachelor Honours Degree*: Arts; Business; Commerce; Creative Arts; Engineering; Information Technology; Nursing; Science, 3-6 yrs; *Graduate Certificate/Diploma*: Business Law; Commerce; Education Technology; Engineering; Management; Sciences; Surveying and Geographic Systems; Teaching Second Languages, 1-2 yrs; *Master Degree*: Applied Linguistics; Arts; Business; Commerce; Education; Engineering; Information Technology; Sciences; Surveying and Geographic Systems, 1-3 yrs; *Master Degree*: Business Administration; Business Administration (International Tourism Management); Philosophy; Psychology; *Doctoral Degree*: Arts; Business; Commerce; Education; Engineering and Surveying; Sciences, 3-5 yrs

Student Services: Academic counselling, Canteen, Cultural centre, Employment services, Foreign student adviser, Foreign Studies Centre, Handicapped facilities, Health services, Language programs, Nursery care, Social counselling, Sports facilities

Student Residential Facilities: Yes

Special Facilities: Art Gallery. Performance Centre. Japanese Gardens. Observatory. Concert Hall. Theatre. Recreation Centre

Libraries: c. 320,000 vols; Electronic books, c. 20,000; Print journals, c. 1,600; Electronic titles, c. 23,000

Publications: Annual and Research Report *(annually)*; Copper Tails, Poetry and Literature *(annually)*; E-JIST, Electronic Journal of Instructional Science and Technology

Press or Publishing House: USQ Press

Last Updated: 21/11/11

UNIVERSITY OF SYDNEY (USYD)
Building A14, Sydney, New South Wales 2006
Tel: +61(2) 9351-2222
Fax: +61(2) 9351-4596
EMail: info.centre@sydney.edu.au
Website: http://www.usyd.edu.au

Vice-Chancellor and Principal: Michael Spence (2008-)
Tel: +61(2) 9351-5051, Fax: +61(2) 9351-4596
EMail: vice.chancellor@sydney.edu.au

Provost and Deputy Vice-Chancellor: Stephen Garton
EMail: dvc.provost@sydney.edu.au

International Relations: John Hearn, Deputy Vice-Chancellor, International
Tel: +61(2) 9351-4461, Fax: +61(2) 9351-4462
EMail: dvc.international@sydney.edu.au

Centres

Advanced Materials Technology (Polymer and Plastics Technology) *Director*: Yiu-Wing Mai; **Advanced Structural Engineering** (Civil Engineering) *Director*: S. Reid; **Advanced Technologies in Animal Genetics** *(Reprogen)* *Director*: Herman Reaadsma; **Animal Immunology Research** (Immunology; Zoology) *Director*: Alan Husband; **Australian Mekong Resource Centre** *(AMRC)* *Director*: Phil Hirsch; **Australian National Genomic Information Service** (Biology; Genetics) *Director*: Chris Moran; **Biological Information and Technology** *(SUBIT)* (Biotechnology) *Director*: Lars Jermiin; **Celtic Studies** (Celtic Languages and Studies) *Director*: Helen Fulton; **Classical Civilizations** (Ancient Civilizations; Classical Languages) *Director*: Suzanne MacAllister; **Clinical Trials** *(National Health and Medical Council Centre of)* (Clinical Psychology) *Director*: John Simes; **Design Computing and Cognition** *(Key Centre)* (Computer Graphics; Design) *Director*: Mary Lou Maher; **English Teaching** (English) *Director*: Janet Conroy; **Environmental Law** *(Australian Centre)* *Director*: Bernhard Boer; **European Studies** *Director*: Kathryn Welch; **Finite Element Analysis** (Aeronautical and Aerospace Engineering) *Director*: L. Tong; **Geotechnical Research** (Civil Engineering) *Director*: J. Carter; **Health Economics Research and Evaluation** *(CHERE)* *Director*: Jane Hall; **Health Promotion** *(Australian Centre)* (Health Education) *Director*: Marilyn Wise; **Heavy Metals Research** (Chemistry) *Director*: Len Lindoy; **Human Aspects of Science and Technology** *Director*: Michael Thomas; **Industrial Relations Research and Teaching** *(ACIRRT)* (Industrial Management; Labour and Industrial Relations) *Director*: Ron Callus; **Innovation and International Competitiveness** (International Business; Marketing) *Director*: Ron Johnston; **Mathematics Learning** (Mathematics) *Director*: Jacqueline Nicholas; **Medieval Studies** *Director*: Margaret Clunies Ross; **Molonglo Observatory** (Astronomy and Space Science) *Director*: Anne Green; **Nitrogen Fixation** *(SUNfix; Syndey University Nitrogen Fixation Centre)* *Director*: Ivan Kennedy; **Optical Fibre Technology** (Information Technology; Optical Technology) *Director*: Simon Fleming; **Organic Synthesis** (Organic Chemistry) *Director*: Les Field; **Peace and Conflict Studies** (Peace and Disarmament) *Director*: Stuart Rees; **Polymer Colloids** *(Key Centre)* (Polymer and Plastics Technology) *Director*: Bob Gilbert; **Precision Agriculture** *(Australian Centre)* (Agricultural Management; Agriculture; Crop Production) *Director*: Alex McBartney; **Risk, Envrionment, Systems Technology and Analysis** (Chemical Engineering) *Director*: Jim Petrie; **Rural Sustainability** *Director*: David Kemp; **Salinity Assessment and Management** (Soil Science; Water Science) *Director*: Les Copeland; **Visualisation Lab** *(VISLAB)* (Computer Graphics; Computer Networks; Data Processing) *Director*: Masahiro Takatsuko

Colleges

Health Sciences (Dentistry; Health Administration; Health Sciences; Medicine; Nursing; Pharmacy; Public Health; Rehabilitation and Therapy; Surgery; Treatment Techniques) *Head*: Don Hutbeam; **Humanities and Social Sciences** (Arts and Humanities; Business Administration; Economics; Education; Fine Arts; Information Sciences; Law; Music; Social Sciences; Social Work;

Vocational Counselling) *Head*: June Sinclaie; **Sciences and Technology** (Agriculture; Architecture; Engineering; Natural Sciences; Rural Planning; Science Education; Technology; Veterinary Science) *Head*: Beryl Hesketh

Faculties

Agriculture, Food and Natural Resources (Agricultural Economics; Agricultural Engineering; Agriculture; Agrobiology; Agronomy; Animal Husbandry; Crop Production; Food Science; Plant and Crop Protection; Soil Science; Water Science) *Dean (Acting)*: Peter McCallum; **Architecture** (Architectural Restoration; Architecture; Landscape Architecture; Regional Planning; Structural Architecture; Town Planning) *Dean*: Gary T. Moore; **Arts** (Ancient Civilizations; Anthropology; Applied Linguistics; Archaeology; Art History; Arts and Humanities; Asian Studies; Celtic Languages and Studies; Chinese; Classical Languages; Contemporary History; English; Fine Arts; French; German; Grammar; Greek; Hebrew; History; Indic Languages; Italian; Japanese; Korean; Latin; Linguistics; Literature; Mathematics; Medieval Studies; Modern History; Modern Languages; Music; Philology; Philosophy; Phonetics; Prehistory; Russian; South and Southeast Asian Languages; Spanish; Speech Studies; Statistics; Terminology; Thai Languages; Translation and Interpretation; Writing) *Dean*: Stephen Garton; **Dentistry** (Dental Hygiene; Dental Technology; Dentistry; Oral Pathology; Orthodontics; Periodontics; Radiology) *Dean*: Ivan J. Klineberg; **Economics and Business** (Accountancy; Administration; Banking; Business Administration; Business and Commerce; Econometrics; Economic History; Economics; Finance; Human Resources; Industrial Management; Institutional Administration; International Business; Labour and Industrial Relations; Law; Management; Management Systems; Marketing; Public Administration; Transport Economics) *Dean*: Peter Wolnizer; **Education and Social Work** (Curriculum; Education; Educational Psychology; Educational Sciences; Higher Education Teacher Training; Literacy Education; Primary Education; Secondary Education; Social Policy; Special Education) *Dean (Acting)*: Gerard Sullivan; **Engineering** (Aeronautical and Aerospace Engineering; Chemical Engineering; Civil Engineering; Electrical Engineering; Engineering; Environmental Engineering; Information Technology; Mechanical Engineering) *Dean*: Gregory Hancock; **Health Sciences** (Community Health; Dietetics; Health Sciences; Hygiene; Occupational Health; Public Health; Social and Preventive Medicine; Sports Medicine) *Dean*: Hal Kendig; **Law** (Administrative Law; Civil Law; Commercial Law; Comparative Law; Constitutional Law; Criminal Law; Human Rights; International Law; Labour Law; Law; Public Law) *Dean*: Ron McCallum; **Medicine** (Anaesthesiology; Cardiology; Community Health; Dermatology; Endocrinology; Epidemiology; Gastroenterology; Gerontology; Gynaecology and Obstetrics; Haematology; Medicine; Nephrology; Neurology; Oncology; Ophthalmology; Paediatrics; Parasitology; Pathology; Psychiatry and Mental Health; Radiology; Urology; Venereology; Virology) *Dean*: Andrew J.S. Coates; **Nursing** (Anatomy; Chemistry; Community Health; Dietetics; Hygiene; Microbiology; Nursing; Pharmacology; Physics; Physiology; Psychology; Public Health; Sociology) *Dean*: Jocalyn Lawler; **Pharmacy** *(Orange Campus)* (Pharmacology; Pharmacy) *Dean*: Charlie Benrimoj; **Rural Management** *(Orange College)* (Agricultural Business; Agricultural Economics; Agriculture; Farm Management; Horticulture; Management; Rural Planning) *Dean*: Kevin Parton; **Science** (Applied Physics; Astronomy and Space Science; Astrophysics; Biochemistry; Biological and Life Sciences; Biophysics; Chemistry; Computer Science; Entomology; Geography; Geology; Geophysics; Immunology; Marine Science and Oceanography; Mathematics; Microbiology; Natural Sciences; Neurosciences; Nuclear Physics; Nutrition; Optics; Pharmacy; Physics; Psychology; Soil Science; Solid State Physics; Statistics; Thermal Physics; Zoology) *Dean*: Merlin Crossley; **Sydney College of Arts** *Dean*: Ron Newman; **Sydney Conservatorium of Music** (Conducting; Music; Music Education; Music Theory and Composition; Musical Instruments; Musicology; Performing Arts; Singing) *Dean*: Kim Walker; **Veterinary Science** (Animal Husbandry; Cell Biology; Chemistry; Genetics; Veterinary Science) *Dean (Acting)*: Paul J. Canfield

Foundations

Chemical Engineering (Chemical Engineering) *Director*: Jim Petrie; **Chemistry** *(Cornforth)* (Chemistry) *Director*: Maxwell Crossley; **Civil Engineering** *Director*: Rob Wheen; **Dairy Research** *Director*: Bill Fulkerson; **Earth Resources** (Natural Resources) *Director*: Peter Davies; **Electrical Engineering** *Director*: Robert Minasian;

Information Technology *(Research Foundation)* (Information Technology) *Director*: Peter Eades; **Inorganic Chemistry** *Director*: Leonard Lindoy; **Nutrition Research** *Director*: Ian Caterson; **Physics** *(Science Foundation)* (Physics) *Director*: Robert Hewitt; **Planning Research** (Public Administration; Urban Studies) *Director*: Ed Blakely; **Poultry Research** (Food Science; Meat and Poultry); **Save Sight Institute** (Ophthalmology) *Director*: Francis Billson; **Veterinary Science** (Veterinary Science) *Director*: Paul Canfield; **Veterinary Science** *(Postgraduate)* (Veterinary Science) *Director*: Michele Cotton; **Warren Centre of Advanced Engineering** (Engineering) *Director*: Michael Dureau

Graduate Schools

Government *(Run jointly with the University of New South Wales)* (Administration; Government) *Dean*: Robert McLean; **Government** *Director*: David Richmond

Institutes

Astronomy (Astronomy and Space Science) *Director*: Richard Hunstead; **Marine Science** (Marine Science and Oceanography) *Director*: Dietmar Muller; **Medical Physics** *Director*: Clive Baldock; **Plant Breeding** (Plant and Crop Protection) *Director*: Peter Sharp; **Teaching and Learning** *Director*: Michael Prosser; **Transport Studies** (Transport and Communications; Transport Management) *Director*: David Hensher; **Wildlife Research** (Wildlife) *Director*: Christopher Dickson

Research Centres

Accountancy Foundation (Accountancy; Business and Commerce) *Director*: Terry Walter; **Advanced Composite Structures** *(Australian Cooperative)* (Materials Engineering) *Director*: Lin Ye; **Asian Agribusiness** (Agricultural Business) *Director*: Zhangyue Zhou; **Australian Marine Mammal** (Marine Biology) *Director*: Tracey Rogers; **Autonomous** *(Australian Research Council Centre of Excellence) Director*: N. Price; **Biological Control of Pest Animals** *(Australian Cooperative Research Centre)* (Pest Management) *Director*: Richard Whittington; **Biosecurity, Emerging Infectious Diseases** *(Australian Cooperative Research Centre)* (Immunology) *Director*: Stephen Prowse; **Ecological Impacts of Coastal Cities** (Coastal Studies; Ecology; Environmental Studies) *Director*: Tony Underwood; **Field Robotics** *(Australian Key Research Centre(ACFR)) Director*: Hugh Durrant-Whyte; **Fruit Fly** (Fruit Production; Pest Management) *Director*: Chris Gilles; **Herbal Medicines** *(Research and Education Centre)* (Alternative Medicine) *Director*: Basil Roufogalis; **IA Watson Grains** (Crop Production; Food Science) *Director*: Peter Sharp; **Ian Buchan Fell Housing** *Director*: Col James; **Innovation Dairy Products** *(Australian Cooperative Research Centre)* (Crop Production; Food Science) *Director*: Paul Donnelly; **Innovative Grain Food Products** *(Australian Cooperative Research Centre)* (Crop Production; Food Science) *Director*: Gordon MacAulay; **Mining** *(Australian Cooperative Research Centre)* (Mining Engineering) *Director*: EM Nebot; **Nursing** *(Sydney Nursing Research Centre)* (Midwifery; Nursing) *Director*: Sue Armitage; **One Tree Island** (Biology; Marine Biology) *Director*: Maria Byrne; **Photonics** *(Australian Cooperative Research Center)* (Optical Technology) *Director*: Mark Sceats; **Polymers** *(Australian Cooperative Research Centre)* (Polymer and Plastics Technology) *Director*: RI Tanner; **Quaternary Dating** (Archaeology; Prehistory) *Director*: Mike Barbetti; **Rehabilitation** (Rehabilitation and Therapy) *Director*: Glen Davis; **Structural Biology and Structural Chemistry** (Biology; Chemistry) *Director*: Trevor Hambley; **Stuttering Research** (Speech Therapy and Audiology) *Director*: Mark Onslow; **Sustainable Cotton Production** *(Australian Cooperative Research Centre)* (Crop Production) *Director*: Les Copeland; **Sustainable Resource Processing** *(Australian Cooperative Research Centre)* (Chemical Engineering) *Director*: Mary Stewart; **Sustainable Rice Production** *(Australian Cooperative Research Centre)* (Crop Production; Food Science) *Director*: Beryl Hesketh and Bruce Sutton; **Technology Enabled Capital Markets** *(Australian Cooperative Research Centre)* (Electrical and Electronic Engineering) *Director*: Richards Coggins; **Theoretical Astrophysics** (Astrophysics) *Director*: Donald Melrose; **Ultrahigh-Bandwidth Devices for Optical Systems** *(Australian Cooperative Research Centre(CUDOS))* (Optical Technology) *Director*: Ben Eggleton; **Value-added Wheat Cooperative** (Crop Production; Food Science) *Director*: Les Copeland; **Wave Physics** *Director*: Peter Robinson

Research Institutes

Asia and Pacific (Asian Studies; Pacific Area Studies) *Director*: Stephanie Fahey; **Asian and Pacific Law** (Comparative Law; Law) *Director*: Alex Ziegert; **Criminology** (Criminology) *Director*: Christopher Cunneen; **Humanities and Social Sciences** *(RIHSS)* *Director*: Margaret Harris; **Rural Management** (Agricultural Management) *Director*: Geoff Curr

Units

Electron Microscope (Atomic and Molecular Physics; Optical Technology) *Director*: Simon Ringer; **Spatial Science Innovation Unit** *Director*: Eleanor Bruce

Further Information: Also Teaching Hospitals and Study Abroad Programme

History: Founded 1850. The oldest University in Australia. Cumberland College of Health Sciences, Sydney College of the Arts, N.S.W. State Conservatorium of Music and two parts of Sydney College of Advanced Education, Institute of Nursing Studies, and Sydney Institute of Education (formerly Sydney Teachers' College) amalgamated with the University 1990.

Governing Bodies: Senate; Academic Board

Academic Year: February to December (February-June; July-December)

Admission Requirements: Secondary higher school certificate or recognized foreign equivalent, or previous tertiary study. Direct entrance to second year on completion of studies in another tertiary institution. Overseas students must show proficiency in English (6.5 IELTS or 577 TOEFL minimum with a test of written English minimum of 4.5)

Main Language(s) of Instruction: English

International Co-operation: With universities in Asia-Pacific; Canada; Europe; Scandinavia; United Kingdom; USA

Degrees and Diplomas: *Bachelor Degree*: 3-6 yrs; *Bachelor Honours Degree*: 1 further yr; *Master Degree*: a further 1-2 yrs; *Doctoral Degree (PhD)*: a further 3-6 yrs. Also postgraduate certificates and undergraduate and postgraduate diplomas

Student Services: Academic counselling, Canteen, Employment services, Foreign student adviser, Foreign Studies Centre, Handicapped facilities, Health services, Language programs, Nursery care, Social counselling, Sports facilities

Student Residential Facilities: Yes

Special Facilities: Nicholson Museums (Egyptian, Near Eastern, Cypriot, Greek, Roman and European Antiquities); Macleay Museum (Zoology, Anthropology, Historic Photographs, Scientific Instruments); University of Sydney Art Collection and War Memorial Gallery; Museum of Pathology; Tin Sheds Gallery; Raymond Bullock Veterinary Anatomy Museum; Sir Hermann Gallery and Sculpture Terrace

Libraries: Fisher Library, total, c. 5,185,528 vols

Publications: Report of University Research *(annually)*

Note: Australian Graduate School of Management (joint school with University): 3,221 students
Last Updated: 21/11/11

UNIVERSITY OF TASMANIA (UTAS)

Private Bag 51, Hobart, Tasmania 7001
Tel: +61(3) 6226-2999
Fax: +61(3) 6226-2001 +61(3) 6226-2018
EMail: admissions@utas.edu.au
Website: http://www.utas.edu.au

Vice-Chancellor: Peter Rathjen
Tel: +61(3) 6226-2003, Fax: +61(3) 6226-2001
EMail: vice.chancellor@utas.edu.au

International Relations: Paul Rigby, Director, International Services
Tel: +61(3) 6226-7492, Fax: +61(3) 6226-7862
EMail: paul.rigby@utas.edu.au

Faculties

Arts (Asian Studies; Classical Languages; English; European Languages; European Studies; Fine Arts; Government; History; Indigenous Studies; Music; Performing Arts; Philosophy; Social Work; Sociology; Visual Arts) *Dean*: Jan Pakulski; **Business** (Accountancy; Business and Commerce; Economics; Finance; Information Sciences; Management) *Dean*: Gary O'Donovan; **Education**

(Education; Educational Research; Preschool Education; Primary Education; Secondary Education) *Dean*: Ian Hay; **Health Sciences** (Anatomy; Biochemistry; Biomedical Engineering; Child Care and Development; Community Health; Epidemiology; Gynaecology and Obstetrics; Medicine; Nursing; Paediatrics; Pathology; Pharmacy; Physiology; Psychiatry and Mental Health; Surgery) *Dean*: Allan Carmichael; **Law** (Law) *Dean*: Don Chalmers; **Science, Engineering and Technology** (Agricultural Engineering; Aquaculture; Architecture; Arctic Studies; Botany; Chemistry; Computer Science; Earth Sciences; Engineering; Environmental Studies; Geography; Geology; Marine Science and Oceanography; Mathematics; Physics; Psychology; Technology; Zoology) *Dean*: Jim Reid

Further Information: Also Schools, Centres and Institutes corresponding to the fields of study, 3 Affiliated Colleges and Teaching Hospitals. Also Sandy Bay campus, Cradle Coast campus and Newnham campus

History: Founded 1890 as University of Tasmania in Hobart, amalgamated with Tasmanian State Institute of Technology in Launceston to form new University 1991.

Governing Bodies: Academic Council

Academic Year: February to November (February-June; July-November)

Admission Requirements: Secondary school certificate or recognized foreign equivalent, or previous tertiary studies in another tertiary institution

Main Language(s) of Instruction: English

Degrees and Diplomas: *Bachelor Degree*: 3-6 yrs; *Master Degree*: a further 1-3 yrs; *Doctoral Degree (PhD)*: 3 yrs following Master. Also undergraduate and postgraduate Diplomas

Student Services: Academic counselling, Canteen, Cultural centre, Employment services, Foreign student adviser, Foreign Studies Centre, Handicapped facilities, Language programs, Nursery care, Social counselling

Student Residential Facilities: Yes

Special Facilities: Art gallery. Observatory

Libraries: c. 609,000 vols; c. 361,000 serial vols in microform

Publications: Research Report *(annually)*
Last Updated: 16/01/09

UNIVERSITY OF TECHNOLOGY, SYDNEY (UTS)

PO Box 123, Broadway, New South Wales 2007
Tel: +61(2) 9514-2000
Fax: +61(2) 9514-1551 +61(2) 9514-1300
EMail: international@uts.edu.au
Website: http://www.uts.edu.au

Vice-Chancellor and President: Ross Milbourne (2002-)
Tel: +61(2) 9514-1330, Fax: +61(2) 9514-1300
EMail: ross.milbourne@uts.edu.au; vc@uts.edu.au

International Relations: Tze Ay Chuan, Director
Tel: +61(2) 9514-8076, Fax: +61(2) 9514-1272
EMail: DirectorUTSInternational@uts.edu.au

Centres

Anti-Slavery Australia *Director*: Jennifer Burn; **Australasian Legal Information** *Co-Director*: Andrew Mowbray; **Cardiovascular and Chronic Care** *Director*: Patricia Davidson; **Child and Youth Culture and Wellbeing** *Director*: Rosemary Johnston; **China Research** *Director*: Maurizio Marinelli; **Communitcation Law Centre** *Director*: Michael Fraser; **Community Organizations and Management** *Director*: Jenny Onyx; **Cooperative Research and Development** *Director*: Mark Lyons; **E-Business and Knowledge Management** *Director*: Robert Lal; **Ecotoxicology** *Director*: Richard Lim; **Electrical Machines and Power Electronics** *Director*: Jianguo Zhu; **Event Management** *Director*: John Allen; **Forensic Science** *Director*: Claude Roux; **Health Services Management** *Director*: Christine Duffield; **Independent Journalism** *Director*: Tom Morton; **Information and Knowledge Management** *Director*: Gobinda Chowdhury; **Local Government** *Director*: Graham Sansom; **Media Arts Innovation** *Director*: Megan Heyward; **Midwifery, Child and Family Health** *Director*: Caroline Homer; **New Writing** *Director*: John Dale; **Nursing, Midwifery and Health Development** *(WHO Collaborating)* (Health Sciences; Midwifery; Nursing) *Director*: John Daly; **Object Technology Applications and Research** *Director*: Brian Henderson-Sellers; **Popular Education** *Director*: Rick Flowers; **Public Communication**

Director: Ellen Blunden; **Public History** *Co-Directors*: Hamilton; Ashton; **Research and Education in the Arts** *Director*: Rosemary Johnston; **Training and Development Services** *Director*: Gary Bennett; **Vocational Education and Training** *Director*: Clive Chappel

Departments

Communication (Communication Studies; Cultural Studies; History of Societies; Humanities and Social Science Education; Information Sciences; Journalism; Media Studies; Music; Social Sciences; Social Studies; Sound Engineering (Acoustics); Writing); **Education** (Adult Education; Applied Linguistics; Education; English; Indigenous Studies; Literacy Education; Primary Education; Secondary Education; Special Education; Staff Development; Teacher Training; Vocational Education); **International Studies** (Cultural Studies; Modern Languages)

Faculties

Arts and Social Sciences (Communication Studies; Education; International Studies) *Dean*: Theo van Leeuwen; **Business** (Accountancy; Administration; Art Management; Business Administration; Business and Commerce; Economics; Finance; Management; Marketing; Sports Management; Tourism) *Dean*: Roy Green; **Design, Architecture and Building** (Architecture; Building Technologies; Communication Studies; Construction Engineering; Design; Fashion Design; Industrial Design; Interior Design; Management; Photography; Town Planning; Visual Arts) *Dean*: Desley Luscombe; **Engineering and Information Technology** (Civil Engineering; Computer Engineering; Construction Engineering; Electrical Engineering; Engineering; Environmental Engineering; Information Technology; Mechanical Engineering; Software Engineering; Telecommunications Engineering) *Dean*: Hung Nguyen; **Law** (Law) *Dean*: jill McKeough; **Nursing, Midwifery and Health** (Health Administration; Health Sciences; Midwifery; Nursing) *Dean*: Bruce Milthorpe; **Science** (Applied Physics; Biological and Life Sciences; Biomedicine; Biotechnology; Cell Biology; Chemistry; Clinical Psychology; Earth Sciences; Environmental Studies; Forensic Medicine and Dentistry; Horticulture; Mathematics; Mathematics and Computer Science; Medicine; Molecular Biology; Natural Sciences; Technology) *Dean*: Bruce Milthorpe

Institutes

Interactive Multimedia and Learning (Media Studies; Multimedia) *Director*: Shirley Alexander; **International Studies** (International Studies) *Director*: David Goodman; **Sustainable Futures** (Development Studies) *Director*: Stuart White

Research Centres

Built Infrastructure *Director*: Bijan Samali; **Corporate Governance** *Director*: Thomas Clarke; **Cosmopolitan Civil Societies** *Director*: Jenny Onyx; **Creative Practices and Cultural Economy** *Co-Directors*: Hamilton, Ashton, Dale; **Entreprise Distributed Systems Technology** *(Cooperative) Director*: Tim Mansfield; **Health Communication** (Health Sciences) *Director*: Rick Iedema; **Health Economics Research and Evaluation** *Director*: Jane Hall; **Health Technologies** *Directors*: Simpson; Nguyen; **Human Centred Technology Design** *Director*: Toni Robertson; **Innovation in IT Services and Applications** *Director*: Doan Hoang; **Intelligent Mechatronic Systems** *Director*: Gamini Dissanayake; **Learning and Change** *Director*: Alison Lee; **Organizational Researchers on Collaborations and Alliances** *Director*: Stewart Clegg; **Quantitative Finance Research** *Director*: Erik Schlogl; **Quantum Computation and Intelligent Systems** *Director*: Chengqi Zhang; **Real-time Information Networks** *Director*: David Lowe; **Renewable Energy** *(Cooperative) Director*: Jianguo Zhu; **Satellite Systems** *(Cooperative) Director*: Sam Riesenfeld; **Sustainable Aquaculture of Finfish** *(Cooperative) Director*: Peter Montague; **Technology Enabled Capital Markets** *(Cooperative) Director*: Donald Stokes; **Technology in Water and Waste Water** *(Cooperative) Director*: Saravanamuh Vigneswaran; **Transforming Cultures** *Director (Acting)*: Katrina Schlunke

Research Institutes

Infection, Immunity and Innovation (Immunology; Medicine; Parasitology; Virology) *Division Head*: Ian Charles; **Nanoscale Technology** *Director*: Michael Cortie; **Plant Functional Biology and Climate Change Cluster (C3)** (Earth Sciences; Environmental Studies) *Director*: Peter Ralph

Schools

Accountancy (Accountancy) *Head*: Peter Wells; **Business** *(Graduate)* (Business and Commerce) *Head*: Ben Hunt; **Economics**

(Economics) *Head (Acting)*: Peter Docherty; **Finance** (Finance) *Head*: Tony Hall; **Leisure, Sports and Tourism** (Leisure Studies; Sports; Tourism) *Head*: Bruce Hayllar; **Management** (Management) *Head*: Stephen Fox; **Marketing** (Marketing) *Head*: Sandra Burke

Further Information: Also campuses in Kuring-Gai. Study Abroad Programme. Most of the University's extensive range of undergraduate and postgraduate courses are available to international students. Detailed course information may be obtained at the following Web site: http://www.uts.edu.au/international

History: Founded 1965 as New South Wales Institute of Technology, acquired present status and title 1988. Kuring-gai College of Advanced Education and the Institute of Technology and Adult Teacher Education of Sydney College of Advanced Education amalgamated with the University 1990.

Governing Bodies: Council

Academic Year: March to November (March-June; August-November). Summer session November-February

Admission Requirements: New South Wales higher school Certificate (NSW HSC) with matriculation, or recognized equivalent

Fees: (Aus Dollars): None for local undergraduate students; Local postgraduates 5,000-18,000 per annum; Foreign students: undergraduates, 19,000-22,000; postgraduates, 20,000-24,000

Main Language(s) of Instruction: English

International Co-operation: Co-operation with a large number of universities around the world. Contact UTS International Programmes for further information by e-mail: international@uts.edu.au or view the website at http://www.uts.edu.au/international

Degrees and Diplomas: *Bachelor Degree*: 3-6 yrs; *Bachelor Honours Degree*: 1 further yr; *Master Degree*: a further 1-2 yrs; *Doctoral Degree*: 3-5 yrs. Also postgraduate Certificates (one semester) and Diplomas (one year)

Student Services: Academic counselling, Canteen, Employment services, Foreign student adviser, Handicapped facilities, Health services, Language programs, Nursery care, Social counselling, Sports facilities

Student Residential Facilities: Yes

Special Facilities: UTS Gallery. Radio Station 2 SER-FM; Media Centre; Microbial Imaging Facility; Electroscopy Mass Spectrometry Facility; Microstructural Analysis Unit and Electron Microscope Unit; Facilities for Toxicological Testing and Chemical Analysis; Biomolecular Imaging Facility

Libraries: University Library: Two campus libraries: City, Kuring-gai. Total non-serial collection, 595,192 vols; total print serial collection, 1,355 titles; total electronic serial collection 100,650 titles

Last Updated: 14/10/11

CITY CAMPUS

15 Broadway, Ultimo, New South Wales 2007
Tel: +61(2) 9514-2000
Fax: +61(2) 9514-1551
Website: http://www.uts.edu.au

KURING-GAI CAMPUS

PO Box 222, Eton Road, Lindfield, New South Wales 2070
Tel: +61(2) 9514-2000
Fax: +61(2) 9514-1551

Vice-Chancellor and President: Ross Milbourne

Faculties

Arts and Social Sciences *Dean*: Theo van Leuven; **Business** (Business and Commerce); **Nursing, Midwifery and Health** (Health Sciences; Midwifery; Nursing) *Dean*: John Daly

UNIVERSITY OF THE SUNSHINE COAST (USC)

Maroochydore DC, Queensland 4558
Tel: +61(7) 5430-1234
Fax: +61(7) 5430-1111
EMail: information@usc.edu.au
Website: http://www.usc.edu.au

Vice-Chancellor and President: Greg Hill (2010-)
Tel: +61(7) 5430-1101, Fax: +61(7) 5430-1105
EMail: ghill@usc.edu.au; vcoffice@usc.edu.au

Deputy Vice-Chancellor: Birgit Lohmann
Tel: +61(7) 5459-4465, Fax: +61(7) 5459-4467
EMail: dvcoffice@usc.edu.au

International Relations: Robert Elliot, Pro-Vice-Chancellor, International and Quality
Tel: +61(7) 5459-4884, Fax: +61(7) 5459-4885
EMail: relliot@usc.edu.au

Faculties

Arts and Social Sciences (Arts and Humanities; Communication Arts; Communication Studies; Environmental Studies; Fine Arts; Graphic Design; Indonesian; Information Sciences; International Studies; Italian; Japanese; Journalism; Mass Communication; Media Studies; Modern Languages; Multimedia; Pacific Area Studies; Political Sciences; Social Sciences; Social Studies; Social Work) *Dean:* Joanne Scott; **Business** (Accountancy; Business Administration; Business and Commerce; Business Computing; Human Resources; Information Management; Information Technology; International Business; Management; Marketing; Small Business; Tourism) *Dean:* Evan J. Douglas; **Science, Health and Education** (Biological and Life Sciences; Biotechnology; Community Health; Ecology; Environmental Studies; Leisure Studies; Marine Science and Oceanography; Microbiology; Natural Sciences; Physiology; Public Health; Sports; Water Science) *Dean (Acting):* Brendan Burkett

History: Founded as Sunshine Coast University College 1994. Acquired present status and title 1998.

Governing Bodies: University Council

Academic Year: Undergraduate and postgraduate : February to November (February-June; July-November). Postgraduate Business: Business Administration and International Business coursework programs run on a session basis.

Admission Requirements: Senior secondary school certificate comparable to Australian Year 12. Entry is competitive and admission dependent on standard of results

Fees: (Aus Dollars): Undergraduate,17,200-23,000 per annum; Postgraduate, 17,200-23,000 per annum (fees are suject to annual review)

Main Language(s) of Instruction: English

Degrees and Diplomas: *Bachelor Degree:* 3 yrs; *Bachelor Honours Degree:* 1 yr following Bachelor; *Master Degree:* Arts and Social Sciences, Business, Science, Health and Education, a further 1-1 1/2 yrs by course work; *Master Degree:* Arts; Business; Science, by research, a further 2 yrs; *Master Degree:* Creative Arts, a further 1 yr; *Doctoral Degree:* Arts and Social Sciences; Business; Science, Health and Education (PhD), 3 yrs; *Doctoral Degree:* Business Administration, 1 1/2-2 yrs; *Doctoral Degree:* Creative Arts, 2 yrs. Also Combined Degree, 4 yrs

Student Services: Academic counselling, Canteen, Employment services, Foreign student adviser, Foreign Studies Centre, Handicapped facilities, Language programs, Social counselling, Sports facilities

Student Residential Facilities: Yes

Special Facilities: Art Gallery. Innovation Centre and Business Incubator. National Seniors Productive Aging Centre. Fraser Island Research and Learning Centre. Psychology Clinic

Libraries: Main Library

Academic Staff *2010*	MEN	WOMEN	TOTAL
FULL-TIME	89	97	**186**
PART-TIME	10	14	**24**
STAFF WITH DOCTORATE			
FULL-TIME	66	52	**118**
PART-TIME	4	6	**10**
Student Numbers *2010*			
All (Foreign Included)	2,512	4,764	**7,276**
FOREIGN ONLY	329	541	**870**

Part-time students, 1,788. **Distance students**, 128.
Last Updated: 02/08/11

UNIVERSITY OF WESTERN SYDNEY (UWS)

Locked Bag 1797, Penrith, New South Wales 2751
Tel: +61(2) 9852-5222
Fax: +61(2) 9678-7525
EMail: study@uws.edu.au
Website: http://www.uws.edu.au

Vice-Chancellor: Janice C. Reid (1998-)
Tel: +61(2) 9678-7801, Fax: +61(2) 9678-7809
EMail: vc@uws.edu.au

Deputy Vice-Chanellor (Corporate Strategy and Services):
Rhonda Hawkins
Tel: +61(2) 9678-7819, Fax: +61(2) 9678-7880
EMail: r.hawkins@uws.edu.au

International Relations: John Ingleson, Deputy Vice-Chancellor (International Development)
Tel: +61(2) 9678-7051, Fax: +61(2) 9678-7694
EMail: dvcid@uws.edu.au

Colleges

Arts *(Bankstown);* **Business** *(Parramatta);* **Health and Science** *(Campbelltown);* **UWS** *(Nirimba; Blacktown)*

Further Information: Also branches in Campbeltown; Penrith; Nirimba; Parramata; Bankstown; Hawkesbury

History: Founded 1989 as a federated network of three members (UWS Hawkesbury, UWS Macarthur, and UWS Nepean) under the banner of the University of Western Sydney. In 2000 the federated network became a unified entity with six campuses.

Governing Bodies: Board of Trustees

Academic Year: Autumn (March to June); Spring (July to November)

Admission Requirements: Secondary School diploma or equivalent .

Fees: See website

Main Language(s) of Instruction: English

International Co-operation: With institutions in Canada, UK, USA, Europe, Latin American, Scandinavia, Asia

Degrees and Diplomas: *Bachelor Degree:* Arts; Law (Graduate entry); Business and Commerce; Communication; Information and Communication Technology; Health Science; Natural Science; Nursing; Policing; Social Science, 3-4 yrs; *Bachelor Honours Degree:* Engineering; Psychology;Social Work, 4 yrs; *Bachelor Honours Degree:* Medicine; Surgery;Law, 5 yrs; *Graduate Certificate/Diploma:* Accountancy, Applied Finance, Arts (TESOL); Bushfire Protection; Business Administration; Convergent Media; Counselling; Education (Social Ecology); Engineering; Health Informatics; Health Science; HRIMR; Information and Communication Technologies; International Business; International Hospitality and Hotel Management; Interpreting and Translation; Marketing; Public Health; Research Studies; Science; Social Science; Spécial Education; Urban Management and Planning; Public Health; Psychological Studies; Social Science; TESOL, Translation, Urban Management and Planning; *Master Degree:* Accountancy, Applied Finance, Arts (TESOL); Art Therapy; Building Surveying, Business Administration (MBA); Commerce; Convergent Media; Creative Music Therapy; Education; Engineering; Finance; Fire Safety Engineering; Health Science; Information and Communication Technologies; International Business; International Hospitality and Hotel Management; International Trade and Finance; Mental Health Nursing; Nursing; Physiotherapy; Podiatric Medecine; Primary Health Care; Professional Accounting; Professional Communication; Public Health; Psychology; (Clinical Psychology; Urban Management and Planning; Science; Social Science; Special Education; Teaching; Traditional Chinese Medecine; Translation and Interpreting; *Doctoral Degree (PhD)*

Student Services: Academic counselling, Canteen, Cultural centre, Employment services, Foreign student adviser, Foreign Studies Centre, Handicapped facilities, Health services, Language programs, Nursery care, Social counselling, Sports facilities

Libraries: UWS Library; Ward Library (Penrith); Parramatta Library; Bankstown Library; Campbelltown; Hawkesbury Library. Blacktown Campus (Nirimba Education Precinct). Access to Library catalogue; e-versions, research resources, Whitlam Prime Ministerial e-collection

Academic Staff 2009-2010	MEN	WOMEN	TOTAL
FULL-TIME	425	399	**824**
PART-TIME	143	236	**379**
STAFF WITH DOCTORATE			
FULL-TIME	296	232	**528**
PART-TIME	9	18	**27**
Student Numbers 2009-2010			
All (Foreign Included)	17,577	22,203	**39,780**
FOREIGN ONLY	2,138	2,700	**4,838**

Part-time students, 9,915.
Last Updated: 01/07/11

BANKSTOWN CAMPUS

Bullecourt Avenue, Milperra, New South Wales 2214
Tel: +61(2) 9852-5222
Fax: +61(2) 4628-1492
EMail: study@uws.edu.au

Provost: Gary Smith

Programmes
Arts and Languages (Arts and Humanities; Modern Languages); **Business and Commerce** (Business and Commerce); **Community Welfare** (Social Welfare); **Education** (Education); **Engineering** (Engineering); **International Studies** (International Studies); **Police Studies** (Police Studies); **Psychology** (Psychology); **Social Sciences** (Social Sciences); **Social Work** (Social Work); **Teacher Training** (Teacher Training)

CAMPBELLTOWN CAMPUS

Narellan Road, Campbelltown, New South Wales 2560
Tel: +61(2) 9852-5222
Fax: +61(2) 4628-1492
EMail: study@uws.edu.au

Provost: Anne Cusick

Programmes
Business and Commerce (Business and Commerce); **Communication Studies** (Communication Studies); **Design** (Design); **Engineering** (Engineering); **Health Sciences** (Health Sciences); **Information and Communication Technology**; **Law** (Law); **Medical Science** (Medicine); **Nursing** (Nursing); **Science** (Applied Chemistry; Applied Mathematics; Applied Physics; Computer Science); **Surgery** (Surgery)

HAWKESBURY CAMPUS

Bourke Street, Richmond, New South Wales 2753
Tel: +61(2) 9852-5222
Fax: +61(2) 4750-1553
EMail: study@uws.edu.au

Provost: Shelley Burgin

Programmes
Forensic Science (Forensic Medicine and Dentistry); **Natural Sciences** (Applied Chemistry; Applied Physics; Natural Sciences); **Nursing** (Nursing); **Science**

NIRIMBA (BLACKTOWN) CAMPUS

Nirimba Education Centre, Eastern Road, Quakers Hill, New South Wales 2763
Tel: +61(2) 9852-4488
Fax: +61(2) 9852-4480
EMail: pathwaystouni@uws.edu.au

Provost: Kerry Hudson

Programmes
Business and Commerce (Business and Commerce); **Construction Management** (Building Technologies; Construction Engineering); **Engineering** (Engineering); **Environmental Studies**; **Health Sciences** (Health Sciences); **Information and Communication Technology** (Information Technology; Telecommunications Engineering); **Science** (Natural Sciences); **Social Sciences** (Social Sciences)

PARRAMATTA CAMPUS

Corner James Ruse Drive and Victoria Road, Rydalmere, Parramatta, New South Wales
Tel: +61(2) 9852-5222
EMail: study@uws.edu.au

Provost: Eric Sidoti

Programmes
Arts and Languages (Arts and Humanities; Modern Languages); **Business and Commerce** (Business and Commerce); **Computer Science** (Computer Science); **Economics** (Economics); **Financial Advising** (Finance); **Health Sciences** (Health Sciences; Nursing); **Information and Communications Technology** (Computer Science; Information Technology; Telecommunications Engineering); **International Studies** (International Studies); **Law** (Law); **Nursing** (Nursing); **Science** (Natural Sciences); **Social Sciences** (Social Sciences)

PENRITH CAMPUS

Second Avenue, Kingswood, Penrith, New South Wales 2797
Tel: +61(2) 9852-5222
Fax: +61(2) 9852-5960
EMail: study@uws.edu.au

Provost: Geoff Scott

Programmes
Arts and Languages (Arts and Humanities; Modern Languages); **Communication Arts**; **Computer Forensics** (Computer Science); **Computer Science** (Computer Science); **Construction Management** (Construction Engineering); **Contemporary Atrs** (Design; Fine Arts); **Design (Visual Communication)**; **Design and Technology** (Design; Technology); **Education** (Education); **Engineering**; **Health Sciences** (Health Sciences; Physical Education); **Housing** (House Arts and Environment; Household Management); **Industrial Design** (Industrial Design); **Information and Communication Technology**; **Music** (Music); **Policing** (Police Studies)

UNIVERSITY OF WOLLONGONG (UOW)

Administrative Building, Northfields Avenue, Wollongong, New South Wales 2522
Tel: +61(2) 4221-3218
Fax: +61(2) 4221-3233
EMail: uniadvice@uow.edu.au
Website: http://www.uow.edu.au

Vice-Chancellor and Principal: Paul Wellings (2012-)
Tel: +61(2) 4221-3932, Fax: +61(2) 4227-1771
EMail: paul_wellings@uow.edu.au

Vice-Principal (Administration): Chris Grange
Tel: +61(2) 4221-3960, Fax: +61(2) 4227-1771

International Relations: Joe Chicharo, Deputy Vice-Chancellor(-International) and Managing Director (ITC)
Tel: +61(2) 4221-5190, Fax: +61(2) 4221-1771
EMail: chicharo@uow.edu.au

Campuses
Shoalhaven Campus *Head*: Robbie Collins

Centres
Asia-Pacific Social Transformation (Asian Studies; Pacific Area Studies; Social Studies) *Director*: Christopher Antons; **Canadian-Australian Studies** (Canadian Studies; Pacific Area Studies) *Director*: Gerry Turcotte; **Equity Research in Education** (Education; Ethics) *Director*: Jan Wright; **Health Services Development** (Health Administration; Health Sciences) *Director*: K. Eagar; **Landscape Change** (Environmental Management; Landscape Architecture) *Director*: Lesley Head; **Medical Radiation Physics** (Radiology) *Director*: Anatoly Rozenfeld; **Smart Foods** *(Key Centre)* (Food Science) *Director*: Peter Howe

Faculties

Arts (Arts and Humanities; Social Sciences) *Dean*: Andrew Wells; **Commerce** (Business and Commerce; Economics; Finance; Management; Marketing) *Dean*: John Glynn; **Creative Arts** (Fine Arts; Music; Theatre) *Dean*: Andrew Schultz; **Educational Sciences** (Educational Sciences; Physical Education; Special Education; Teacher Trainers Education) *Dean*: Barry Harper; **Engineering** (Civil Engineering; Computer Engineering; Electrical Engineering; Engineering; Environmental Engineering; Management; Materials Engineering; Mechanical Engineering; Physics; Telecommunications Engineering) *Dean*: Chris Cook; **Health and Behavioural Sciences** (Behavioural Sciences; Biomedical Engineering; Dietetics; Health Sciences; Midwifery; Nursing; Psychology; Public Health) *Dean*: Don Iverson; **Informatics** (Information Management; Information Technology; Mass Communication; Mathematics and Computer Science) *Dean*: Philip Ogunbona; **Law** (Administrative Law; Civil Law; Commercial Law; Comparative Law; Constitutional Law; Criminal Law; Human Rights; International Law; Labour Law; Law; Maritime Law) *Dean*: Stuart Kaye; **Science** (Biological and Life Sciences; Chemistry; Earth Sciences; Marine Science and Oceanography; Natural Sciences; Physics) *Dean*: Rob Whelan

Institutes

Biomolecular Science (Molecular Biology) *Director*: John Bremnel; **Conservation Biology and Law** (Biological and Life Sciences; Ethics; Law) *Director*: David Ayre; **Social Change and Critical Enquiry** (Social Sciences; Social Studies) *Director*: Sue Dodds

Research Centres

Advanced Materials Processing (Materials Engineering) *Director*: Druce Dunne; **Bulk Solids and Particulate Technologies** *(Key Centre)* (Solid State Physics) *Director*: Peter Wypyeh; **Digital Media Initiative** (Electronic Engineering) *Director*: Barry Harper; **Engineering Mechanics** (Mechanical Engineering) *Director*: A.K. Tieu; **Image, Performance and Text** (Film; Graphic Arts; Performing Arts; Photography; Writing) *Director*: Diana Wood-Conroy; **Industrial Automation** (Automation and Control Engineering) *Director*: Chris Cook; **Intelligent Manufacturing Systems** *(CRC)* (Production Engineering) *Director*: Chris Cook; **Legal Intersection** (Ethics; Law) *Director*: Rick Mohr; **Metabolic Research** (Biological and Life Sciences) *Director*: Julie Steele; **Ocean and Coastal Research** (Coastal Studies; Marine Science and Oceanography) *Director*: John Morrison; **Railway Engineering and Technologies** *(CRC)* (Railway Engineering) *Director*: Buddhima Indraratna; **Smart Internet Technology** *(CRC)* (Computer Networks) *Director*: Darell Williamson; **Sustainable Earth Research** (Earth Sciences) *Director*: Muffucumaru Sivakumar; **Welded Structures** *(CRC)* (Metal Techniques) *Director*: Colin Chipperfield

Research Groups

Atmospheric Chemistry (Chemistry; Meteorology) *Director*: David Griffith

Research Institutes

Brain and Behaviour (Behavioural Sciences; Neurosciences; Psychology) *Director*: Robert Barry; **Intelligent Polymer** (Polymer and Plastics Technology) *Director*: Gordon Wallace; **Mathematical Modelling and Computational Systems** (Mathematics and Computer Science) *Director*: John Rayner; **Steel Processing and Products** *(BHP)* (Metal Techniques; Metallurgical Engineering) *Director*: Rian Dippenaar; **Superconducting and Electronic Materials** (Conducting; Electronic Engineering; Materials Engineering) *Director*: S.X. Dou; **Telecommunications and Information Technology** (Information Technology; Telecommunications Engineering) *Director*: Farzad Safaei

Further Information: A campus in Dubai

History: Founded 1951 as Division of New South Wales University of Technology. Became later College of University of New South Wales. In 1975 University of Wollongong was established as an autonomous institution.

Governing Bodies: Council; Academic Senate

Academic Year: February to December (February-July; July-December). Also optional Summer Session (December-January)

Admission Requirements: Candidates must achieve the required mark in an Australian Yr 12, Senior secondary school certificate or recognized foreign equivalent. Any tertiary studies completed prior to enrolment may lead to advanced standing or credit

Main Language(s) of Instruction: English

International Co-operation: With universities in Asia; Europe; North America and South America

Degrees and Diplomas: *Bachelor Degree*: Arts; Commerce; Creative Arts; Education; Engineering; Informatics; Law; Science; Health and Behavioural Science, 3-4 yrs; *Graduate Certificate/Diploma*: Arts; Commerce; Creative Arts; Education; Engineering; Informatics; Law; Science; Health and Behavioural Science, 6 months; *Master Degree*: a further 1-2 yrs; *Doctoral Degree (PhD)*: 3 yrs following Master Degree

Student Services: Academic counselling, Canteen, Cultural centre, Employment services, Foreign student adviser, Foreign Studies Centre, Handicapped facilities, Health services, Language programs, Nursery care, Social counselling, Sports facilities

Student Residential Facilities: For 1,150 students

Libraries: c. 500,000 items

Publications: Research Report *(annually)*
Last Updated: 23/03/12

VICTORIA UNIVERSITY (VU)

PO Box 14428, Melbourne, Victoria 8001
Tel: +61(3) 9688-4000
Fax: +61(3) 9688-4069
EMail: vice-chancellor@vu.edu.au
Website: http://www.vu.edu.au

Vice-Chancellor and President: Peter Dawkins
Tel: +61(3) 9919-4011

Senior Administrative Officer: Angela Hickey
Tel: +61(3) 9919-4531 EMail: angela.hickey@vu.edu.au

Faculties

Arts, Education and Human Development (Arts and Humanities; Clinical Psychology; Communication Studies; Criminal Law; Development Studies; Education; English; Indigenous Studies; International Studies; Law; Leadership; Multimedia; Physical Education; Preschool Education; Primary Education; Psychology; Public Relations; Secondary Education; Social Work; Sports; Sports Management; Vocational Education); **Business and Law** (Accountancy; Banking; Business and Commerce; Commercial Law; Computer Science; Econometrics; Economics; Finance; Hotel Management; Human Resources; Information Sciences; Information Technology; International Business; International Economics; Labour and Industrial Relations; Law; Management; Marketing; Music; Notary Studies; Retailing and Wholesaling; Small Business; Tourism; Transport Management) *Dean*: David Lamond; **Health, Engineering and Science** (Architecture; Biomedicine; Biotechnology; Building Technologies; Chemistry; Civil Engineering; Computer Engineering; Computer Networks; Computer Science; Dietetics; Electrical and Electronic Engineering; Fire Science; Mathematics; Mechanical Engineering; Midwifery; Nanotechnology; Natural Sciences; Nursing; Nutrition; Osteopathy; Paediatrics; Paramedical Sciences; Physics) *Dean*: Michelle Towstoless; **Workforce Development; Technical and Trades Innovation and VU College** *(TAFE)* (Accountancy; Adult Education; Advertising and Publicity; Aesthetics; Animal Husbandry; Building Technologies; Business Administration; Construction Engineering; Electrical Engineering; Energy Engineering; Engineering; English; Food Science; Government; Graphic Design; Health Sciences; Horticulture; Human Resources; Indigenous Studies; Information Technology; International Business; International Economics; Laboratory Techniques; Law; Library Science; Management; Marine Engineering; Marketing; Media Studies; Museum Studies; Music; Natural Sciences; Nursing; Occupational Health; Painting and Drawing; Paramedical Sciences; Public Relations; Railway Transport; Real Estate; Retailing and Wholesaling; Road Transport; Sales Techniques; Small Business; Social and Community Services; Sound Engineering (Acoustics); Sports; Theatre; Tourism; Toxicology; Transport Management; Veterinary Science; Visual Arts; Vocational Education; Writing; Zoology)

Research Institutes

Diversity, Educational Access and Success; **Sports, Exercice and Active Living**; **Supply Chain and Logistics**; **Sustainability and Innovation**

Further Information: Also nine(9) campuses and one site in Melbourne's CBD and western region

History: Founded 1916 as Footscray Technical College. Established as Victoria University of Technology in 1990. Acquired present status and title 2005. Federally funded.

Governing Bodies: Council; Academic Board; Vocational Education Board ; Faculty Boards of Studies

Academic Year: February to November

Admission Requirements: Victorian Certificate of Education or equivalent

Fees: Local Higher Education students pay a fee partly governement subsidised - based on units/course studied, and make payments after graduating via the Federal Government 's Higher Education Contribution Scheme. International students are full-fee paying students

Main Language(s) of Instruction: English

Degrees and Diplomas: *Diploma*: Accountancy; Creative Industry; Education; Information Technology; Vocational Education and Training Practice, 1 yr; *Diploma*: Applied Sciences; Arts; Building; Community Services; Liberal Arts; Dermal Therapy, 2 yrs; *Diploma*: Beauty Therapy; Hospitality, 11/2 yrs; *Bachelor Degree*: Arts; Applied Science; Business; Communication; Creative Arts Industries; Exercise Science and Human Movement; Health Sciences; Nursing; Midwifery; Science; Interactive Media; International Studies; Psychology; Social Work; Sport and Recreation Management; Sport Coaching; Youth Work, 3 yrs; *Bachelor Degree*: Education; Engineering, 4 yrs; *Graduate Certificate/Diploma*: Business; Arts; Communication Studies; Educational Learning and Leadership; Engineering; Human Development; International Community Development; Multimedia; Professional English Communication; Science; TESOL; Youth Service Management; Neonatal and Infant Pediatric Manual Therapy, 1semester; *Graduate Certificate/Diploma*: Engineering; Exercice for Rehabilitation; Exercice Science; Human Development; International Community Development; Multimedia; Primary Teaching; Psychological Studies; Psychology; Science; Secondary Teaching; TESOL; Youth Services Management; Neonatal and Infant Pediatric Manual Therapy; Performance-Based Building and Fire Codes; Arts; Business; Clinical Exercice Practice; Communication; Counselling; Early Childhood Teaching; Educational Learning and Leadership, 1yr; *Graduate Certificate/ Diploma*: Pediatric Manual Therapy, 2 yrs; *Master Degree*: Applied Science; Arts; Health Sciences; Nursing; Psychology (Clinical Psychology); Science, 2 yrs, by coursework; *Master Degree*: Arts; Education; Engineering; Science, 2 yrs, by research; *Master Degree*: Business; Education; Health Sciences (Aged Services); Multimedia; TESOL; Youth Services Management, 18 months, by coursework; *Master Degree*: Business, 18 months, by research; *Master Degree*: Engineering Science, 1 yr, by coursework; *Master Degree*: Human Movement, 3 yrs, by research; *Master Degree*: International Community Development, 18 months by coursework; *Doctoral Degree (PhD)*: 3 yrs; *Doctoral Degree*: Education, 3 yrs (1 yr coursework; 2&3 yrs research); *Doctoral Degree*: Psychology (Clinical Psychology), 3 yrs, by coursework. Also postgraduate Diplomas and Certificates

Student Services: Academic counselling, Canteen, Employment services, Foreign student adviser, Handicapped facilities, Health services, Nursery care, Social counselling, Sports facilities

Student Residential Facilities: Yes

Libraries: 10 campus libraries; 12,169 serial titles; 516,454 monographs

Publications: Bulletin of sport and culture; JIPAM, Journal of Inequalities in Pure and Applied Mathematics; Journal of business systems, governance and ethics; RGMIA Research Report Collection, Research Group in Mathematical Inequalities and Applications; Working Paper Series, Department of Applied Economics, School of Management, School of Information Systems

Last Updated: 07/10/11

PRIVATE INSTITUTIONS

AUSTRALIAN INSTITUTE OF BUSINESS (AIB)

82 Flinders Street, Adelaide, South Australia 5000
Tel: +61(8) 8212-8111
Fax: +61(8) 8212-0032
EMail: enquiries@aib.edu.au
Website: http://www.aib.edu.au

Chief Executive: Param Abraham (2006-)
EMail: param.abraham@aib.edu.au

Director Operations and Corporate Affairs: Sanjay Abraham
EMail: sanjay.abraham@aib.edu.au

International Relations: Olga Carroll, International Marketing Manager EMail: olga.carroll@aib.edu.au

Departments
Business Administration (Business Administration)

History: Created 1984. Acquired status 1994. AIB was formerly known as Gibaran Graduate School of Business. The other members of the Gibaran Learning Group, namely, Australian Institute of Business Administration, Entrepreneurship Institute Australia and Tourism Institute Australia, have now merged with AIB as part of a corporate restructuring exercise

Governing Bodies: Academic Board.

Academic Year: Student intake in March, June and November.

Admission Requirements: Undergraduate: a qualification deemed equivalent to year 12 under the Australian Qualifications Framework; Postgraduate: relevant undergraduate degree, and / or work experience in some cases; Doctorates: relevant Master's degree and relevant work experience. All candidates whose native language is not English must show proof of English proficiency (undergraduate applicants: TOEFL 550, or 6.0 IELTS, or a credit or better in English in the GCE 'O' or 'A' levels or equivalent; postgraduate and doctoral applicants: TOEFL 575, or 6.5 IELTS). More detailed information available from the institution.

Fees: (Aus Dollars): 17,000 – 48,000. Total fees per course and vary according to whether domestic or overseas students, and distance learning students. Contact institution for more details.

Main Language(s) of Instruction: English

Accrediting Agencies: Department of Further Education, Employment, Science and Technology, South Australia

Degrees and Diplomas: *Bachelor Honours Degree*: Business Administration, 2 - 3 yrs; *Master Degree*: Management (Research); Management (Professional); Business Administration (MMgt/MBA), 1 - 1 1/2 yrs; *Doctoral Degree*: Business and Management (PhD; DBA), 3 yrs full time. Also Advanced MBA. All degrees offered full time as well as intensive mode.

Student Services: Academic counselling, Foreign student adviser, Foreign Studies Centre, Handicapped facilities, Social counselling

Publications: Gibaran Journal of Applied Management, Case studies and original articles on management *(biannually)*

Last Updated: 23/08/11

AVONDALE COLLEGE OF HIGHER EDUCATION

PO Box 19, Freemans Drive, Cooranbong, New South Wales 2265
Tel: +61(2) 4980-2222
Fax: +61(2) 4980-2118
EMail: enquiries@avondale.edu.au
Website: http://www.avondale.edu.au

President: Ray Roennfeldt
Tel: +61(2) 4980-2101, Fax: +61(2) 4980-2119
EMail: ray.roennfeldt@avondale.edu.au

Academic Registrar: Gwen Wilkinson
EMail: gwen.wilkinson@avondale.edu.au

Faculties
Arts and Theology (Arts and Humanities; Theology); **Business and Information Technology** (Business and Commerce; Information Technology); **Education and Science** (Education; Mathematics; Natural Sciences); **Nursing and Health** (Health Sciences; Nursing)

History: Founded 1897 by the Seventh-Day Adventist Church.

Degrees and Diplomas: *Bachelor Degree*: Arts and Humanities; Business Administration; Ministry and Theology; Nursing, Education; *Graduate Certificate/Diploma*: Ministry and Theology; Education; Nursing; Business Administration; *Master Degree*: Arts and Humanities; Business Administration; Ministry and Theology; Nursing; Education (by coursework and research); *Doctoral Degree*: Arts and Humanities; Ministry and Theology; Education (PhD)

Last Updated: 27/05/11

WAHROONGA CAMPUS

Wahroonga, New South Wales 2076
Tel: +61(2) 9487-9630
Fax: +61(2) 9487-9625
EMail: enquiries@avondale.edu.au
Website: http://www.avondale.edu.au

BOND UNIVERSITY

University Drive (Off Cottesloe Drive), Robina, Gold Coast,
Queensland 4229
Tel: +61(7) 5595-1024
Fax: +61(7) 5595-1140
EMail: international@bond.edu.au
Website: http://www.bond.edu.au

Vice-Chancellor: Robert Stable
Tel: +61(7) 5595-1048, Fax: +61(7) 5595-1026
EMail: vc@bond.edu.au

Pro-Vice Chancellor, Student and Academic Support: Alan
Finch
Tel: +61(7) 5595-1117, Fax: +61(7) 5595-1025
EMail: afinch@bond.edu.au

Centres
**Applied Research in Learning, Engagement, Andragogy and
Pedagogy** (LEAP) (Educational Sciences; Pedagogy); **Autism
Spectrum Disorder** (CASD) Director: Vicki Bitsika; **Commercial
Law** Director: Jim Corkery; **Dispute Resolution** (Family Studies;
Peace and Disarmament) Director: John Wade; **Family Business**
(Business and Commerce; Family Studies) Director: Ken Moores;
Film, Television and Screen-Based Media Director: Michael
Sergi; **Global Trade and Finance** Director: Noel Gaston; **Health
Informatics** (Computer Science; Health Sciences) Director: Iain
Morrison; **Health, Exercise and Sports Sciences** (Health Sci-
ences; Sports) Director: Bon Gray; **Law, Gouvernance and Public
Policy** Director: Patrick Keyzer; **Leadership Studies** (Leadership)
Director: Ken Parry; **Owen Dixon Society**; **Population Health and
Neuroimmunology** (PHANU) (Media Studies) Director: Sonya
Marshall-Gradisnik; **Primary Health Care Research, Evaluation
and Development (PHCRED) Collaboration** Division Head: Mieke
van Driel; **Psychology Clinic** Director: Betty Headley; **Technology
Innovation** (Technology) Director: Iain Morrison

Colleges
Bond Director: Rowan Hinton; **Bond University English Language School** (BUELI) (English) Director: Paulo Vieira

Faculties
Business (Business Administration; Finance; Multimedia); **Health
Sciences and Medicine** (Biomedical Engineering; Forensic Medi-
cine and Dentistry; Health Sciences; Medicine; Physical Therapy;
Sports; Sports Management; Surgery) Dean: Richard Hays;
Humanities and Social Sciences (Advertising and Publicity;
Applied Linguistics; Arts and Humanities; Austronesian and Oceanic
Languages; Behavioural Sciences; Communication Studies; Com-
puter Science; Criminology; Film; International Relations; Journal-
ism; Media Studies; Modern Languages; Multimedia; Philosophy;
Psychology; Public Relations; Radio and Television Broadcasting;
Social Sciences) Dean: Raoul Mortley; **Law** (Commercial Law;
Criminal Law; E-Business/Commerce; International Law; Law;
Public Law) Dean: Geraldine Mackenzie

Institutes
Sustainable Development and Architecture (Architecture; Build-
ing Technologies; Constitutional Law; Environmental Management;
Environmental Studies; Management; Real Estate; Surveying and
Mapping; Town Planning; Urban Studies) Director: George Earl

Research Centres
Health, Exercises and Sports Science (BURCHESS) (Health
Sciences; Sports); **Research in Evidence Based Practice**
(CREBP) Director: Paul Glasziou; **Software Assurance** (Software
Engineering) Director: Padmanabhan Krishnan; **Sustainable
Healthy Communities** Director: Bhishna Bajacharya

Further Information: Also 1 affiliated Institution

History: Founded 1987 by Act of the Queensland Parliament. The
first non-profit, privately funded, and independent university to be
established in Australia. Classes started May 1989.

Governing Bodies: Council

Academic Year: January to December (January-April; May-August;
September-December)

Admission Requirements: Selection on the basis of a combination
of academic merit, work experience and references, as well as other
factors considered important indicators for success at Bond University. In some cases an interview may be required.

Fees: (Aus Dollars): Basic undergraduate fees 3,605 per subject

Main Language(s) of Instruction: English

Degrees and Diplomas: Bachelor Degree: 2 yrs (minimum 6 sem);
Bachelor Degree: Law, 2.6 yrs (minimum 8 sem); Master Degree: 1
yr (minimum 3 sem); Doctoral Degree (PhD): minimum 2-4 yrs. Also
postgraduate Certificates and Diplomas

Student Services: Canteen, Employment services, Foreign student
adviser, Handicapped facilities, Health services, Social counselling,
Sports facilities

Student Residential Facilities: For 631 students

Special Facilities: Macquarie Trading Room; Multimedia center;
Wireless; Blackboard for mobile technologies

Libraries: 2,009 Non-Serial Items 124.084, E-books current 57,523

Academic Staff 2010	MEN	WOMEN	TOTAL
FULL-TIME	131	104	**235**
PART-TIME	12	18	**30**
Student Numbers 2010			
All (Foreign Included)	3,241	3,110	**6,351**
FOREIGN ONLY	–	–	**2,404**

Last Updated: 13/10/11

JOHN PAUL II INSTITUTE FOR MARRIAGE AND FAMILY (JPII INST)

PO Box 146, East Melbourne, Victoria 8002
Tel: +61(3) 9412 3378
Fax: +61(3) 9417 2107
EMail: info@jp2institute.org
Website: http://www.jp2institute.org/

Director: Peter Elliott (2004-)

Registrar: Toby Hunter
Tel: +61(3) 3 9412 3386 EMail: thunter@jp2institute.org

Programmes
Ethics (Ethics); **Philosophy** (Philosophy); **Religion** (Catholic
Theology)

History: Created 2001 under the auspices of the Melbourne Archdiocese.

Governing Bodies: Council

Academic Year: February to November

Admission Requirements: Bachelor's degree

Fees: (Aus Dollars): 875 per subject unit

Main Language(s) of Instruction: English

Accrediting Agencies: Victorian Registration and Qualifications
Authority

Degrees and Diplomas: Graduate Certificate/Diploma: Bioethics
and Theology, 1 yr; Master Degree: Bioethics and Theology, 2 yrs;
Doctoral Degree: Bioethics and Theology, 3 yrs

Student Services: Academic counselling, Foreign student adviser,
Social counselling

Student Residential Facilities: None

Academic Staff 2007-2008	MEN	WOMEN	TOTAL
FULL-TIME	3	2	**5**
PART-TIME	11	2	**13**
STAFF WITH DOCTORATE			
FULL-TIME	3	2	**5**
PART-TIME	11	2	**13**
Student Numbers 2010-2011			
All (Foreign Included)	63	34	**97**
FOREIGN ONLY	12	10	**22**

Part-time students, 75.
Last Updated: 30/06/11

UNIVERSITY OF NOTRE DAME AUSTRALIA

PO Box 1225, 19 Mouat Street, Fremantle, Perth WA 6959
Tel: +61(8) 9433-0555
Fax: +61(8) 9433-0544
EMail: international@nd.edu.au
Website: http://www.nd.edu.au

Vice-Chancellor: Celia Hammond
Tel: +61(8) 9433-0850 EMail: VC@nd.edu.au

Registrar: Murray Alessandrini
EMail: Murray.Alessandrini@nd.edu.au

Deputy Vice-Chancellor: Jan Thomas

Schools

Arts and Science (Archaeology; Arts and Humanities; Behavioural Sciences; Communication Disorders; English; Greek; International Relations; Italian; Law; Mathematics; Media Studies; Natural Sciences; Political Sciences; Sociology; Theatre) *Dean*: Dylan Korczynskyj; **Business** (Accountancy; Finance; Management; Marketing; Public Relations) *Dean*: Chris Doepel; **Education** (Education; Religious Education; Teacher Training) *Dean*: Michael O'Neil; **Health Sciences** (Behavioural Sciences; Biomedicine; Health Sciences; Nursing; Physical Education; Physical Therapy; Sports; Sports Management) *Dean*: Helen Parker; **Law** (Law) *Executive Dean*: Jane Power; **Medicine** (Medicine) *Dean*: Gavin Frost; **Nursing** (Nursing) *Dean*: Selma Alliex; **Philosophy and Theology** (Ethics; Philosophy; Theology) *Dean*: Matthew C. Ogilvie; **Physiotherapy** (Physical Therapy) *Dean*: Peter Hamer

History: Founded 1990. A private institution established under its own Act of Parliament. In the process of development, as a Catholic university.

Academic Year: February to November

Admission Requirements: Secondary school certificate with matriculation or recognized foreign equivalent. Direct entrance to second year on completion of studies in another tertiary institution

Fees: (Aus Dollar): 18,000 per annum

Main Language(s) of Instruction: English

International Co-operation: With universities in: Argentina, Brazil, China, Colombia, Indonesia, Phillipines, Taiwan, Thailand, USA

Degrees and Diplomas: *Bachelor Degree*: Applied Science (Health and Physical Education) (BApplSc); Arts (Aboriginal Studies, Behavioural Science, Communications, English Literature, Environmental Studies, Geography, Greek Language and Culture, History, Italian Language and Culture, Performing Arts, Politics, Philosophy, Theology) (BArts); Behavioural Sciences (BBehSc); Business (BComm); Commerce (BE-Com); Communications (BComms); Counselling (BCouns); Environmental Management (BEnvMgt); Environmental Studes (BEnvStudies); History and Law (BHist&Law); Human Resources Management (BHRM); Information and Communication Technology (BICT); Marketing and Public Relations; Nursing (BNurse); Performing Arts (BPerfArts); Politics and Law (BPoli&Law); Social Sciences (Aboriginal Studies, Behavioural Science, Communications, English Literature, Environmental Studies, Geography, Greek Language and Culture, History, Italian Language and Culture, Performing Arts, Politics, Philosophy, Theology) (BSocSc); Sports and Recreation Management (BSport&RecMgt), 3 yrs; *Bachelor Degree*: Education (BEd); Health and Physical Education (BHealth&PhysEd); Laws (BLaws), 4 yrs; *Graduate Certificate/Diploma*: Aboriginal Studies (GCert AborSt); Counselling (GDipCouns); Environmental Management (GDip(EnvMgt)); Exercise Medicine (GCert ExMed); Nursing (GCN), 1 yr; *Graduate Certificate/Diploma*: Business (GCertBus); E-Commerce (GCert(E-Com)); Human Resources Management (GCHRM); Information Systems (GCertInfSys); Marketing (GCMktg); Research Methods (GCResMeth), 1 sem; *Graduate Certificate/Diploma*: Education (GDEd), 2 yrs; *Master Degree*: Aboriginal Studies (MAborSt), 1 yr; *Master Degree*: Business (MBus); Counselling (MCouns); Electronic (ME-Com); Environmental Management (MEnvMgt); Information Systems (MInfoSys), 3 sem; *Master Degree*: Business Administration (MBA); Nursing (MN); Professional Accounting (MPA); Teaching (MTch), 2 yrs; *Master Degree*: Education (MEd); Education Leadership (MEdL); Leadership (MLdrs); Religious Education (MREd), 2-3 sem; *Master Degree*: Philosophy (MPhil), 1 1/2 yrs; *Doctoral Degree*: Business Administration (DBA); Education (DEdD); Natural Resources Management (DNRM), 2-5 yrs; *Doctoral Degree*: Law; Nursing (DN), 3 yrs

Student Services: Academic counselling, Canteen, Cultural centre, Employment services, Foreign student adviser, Foreign Studies Centre, Handicapped facilities, Health services, Language programs, Social counselling, Sports facilities

Student Residential Facilities: For American exchange students

Libraries: General Library and Law Library

Publications: In Principio *(3 per annum)*
Last Updated: 21/11/11

BROOME CAMPUS

PO Box 2287, Broome, Western Australia 6725
Tel: +61(8) 9192-0600
Fax: +61(8) 9192-1247
EMail: broome@nd.edu.au
Website: http://www.broome.nd.edu.au

Deputy Vice-Chancellor: Lynette Henderson-Yates
EMail: Lynette.Henderson-Yates@nd.edu.au

Courses
Aboriginal Studies (Indigenous Studies; Social Sciences); **Education** (Education); **Law**; **Nursing** (Nursing)

History: Founded 1989.

Main Language(s) of Instruction: English

SYDNEY CAMPUS

PO Box 944, Broadway, New South Wales 2007
Tel: +61(2) 8204-4400
Fax: +61(2) 8904-4422
EMail: sydney@nd.edu.au
Website: http://www.sydney.nd.edu.au

Deputy Vice-Chancellor: Hayden Ramsay
EMail: dvc.syd@nd.edu.au

Provost: Margot Kearns EMail: Margot.Kearns@nd.edu.au

Schools
Arts and Science (Behavioural Sciences; Communication Studies; English; History; Journalism; Literature; Philosophy; Political Sciences; Theatre); **Business** (Business Administration); **Education** (Education; Preschool Education; Primary Education; Secondary Education); **Law** (Law); **Nursing** (Nursing); **Philosophy and Theology** (Philosophy; Theology)

History: Founded 1989.

Main Language(s) of Instruction: English

Degrees and Diplomas: *Bachelor Degree*; *Graduate Certificate/Diploma*; *Master Degree*; *Doctoral Degree*

Austria

STRUCTURE OF HIGHER EDUCATION SYSTEM

Description:

Higher education: Various different educational paths are open to pupils after completion of their secondary education, that is, after passing the Reifeprüfung (upper secondary school leaving examination); or after passing the Studienberechtigungsprüfung (the university entrance examination); or the Berufsreifeprüfung (external upper secondary school leaving examination). Higher education is provided by public universities, universities of applied sciences (Fachhochschulen, introduced in 1994), private universities (introduced in 2000), university colleges of education (Pädagogische Hochschulen), and Schools of Theology under the auspices of the Catholic Church. There are also Academies (e.g. Medical-Technical Colleges). Study programmes lead to the following degrees: Degree programmes: - Diploma (after 8-12 semesters), or, respectively Diploma (FH) (after 8-10 semesters); - Bachelor (6-8 semesters); - Master (2-4 semesters after the bachelor); - Doctor (6 semesters after the master or diploma degree), only at public and private universities.

Further education programmes: Certificate ("Akademische/r ..."); Master.

The 2002 University Reform redefined the relationship between the universities and the State. The universities remain State institutions, and the State continues to finance them. Universities are, however, fully autonomous in terms of their statutes, their internal affairs and the curricula. The law provides for the establishment of a university board (Universitätsrat) at each institution which comprises leading figures from public life and the private sector. It is also responsible for providing the Federal Minister of Science and Research with expert opinion on issues of the given university and launching evaluation measures. The University Assembly elects the rector. The Ministry assumes a supervisory function only in legal affairs and continues to be responsible for strategic planning and research. The law establishes which groups of degree programmes may be introduced at universities and lays general rules concerning admissions and the award of academic degrees. In 1999, the University Accreditation Act was enacted which allows private institutions to obtain accreditation as a private university by the Accreditation Council which works under the supervision of the Ministry. At private universities, study programmes can be offered either in accordance with state programmes and degrees, or without reference to them.

Stages of studies:

University level first stage: Bachelor
Bachelor programmes are offered by public universities, universities of applied sciences, private universities and university colleges of education. Access to Bachelor programmes is normally based on the Reifeprüfung Certificate. Bachelor programmes last for 3-4 years and end with a Bachelor examination (Bachelorprüfung). They lead to the academic degree of Bachelor.

The former diploma programmes, however, can be continued instead of Bachelor and Master programmes.

University level second stage: Master
Master programmes are offered by public universities, universities of applied sciences and private universities. Access to Master programmes is based on completion of a relevant Bachelor programme. Master programmes last for 1-2 years and require a master thesis and end with a Master examination (Masterprüfung). They lead to the academic degree of Master, in Engineering to the Diplom Ingenieur/Diplom Ingenieurin.

University level third stage: Doktorat
Doctoral studies, which are offered only by universities, generally require a minimum of 6 semesters. Access is based on completion of a relevant Master programme at a university, university of applied sciences or private university. Doctoral programmes demand greater independence of students in their scientific work. Doctoral candidates are required to present a thesis approved by at least two professors and an examining Commission, and pass the final oral examination (Rigorosum). They can be Doctor or PhD programmes; the latter are subdivided into a more study-oriented and a purely scientific stages.

University level fourth stage: Habilitation
The Habilitation is acquired within the university system and is based on special research achievements after the Doctorate and production of a research monograph. It is awarded with the title Universitätsdozent/in or Privatdozent/in, respectively. This is not an academic degree, but a special university qualification. It is often, but not necessarily, a prerequisite to be appointed professor at a university.

Distance higher education:

Distance education (Fernstudien) has been provided since 1979 by the Interuniversitäres Forschungsinstitut für Fernstudien. This Institute has links with all major Austrian universities and offers special courses for adults seeking employment. Students may also study at the Fernuniversität Hagen (Germany), which offers normal degree courses in Economics, Law, Social Sciences, Education and Management. Students at the Fernuniversität Hagen living in Austria may turn to the centres in Linz, Bregenz and Vienna for technical and social advice. There is a similar study centre at the Open University London located in Vienna. Under the Universities Act, Austrian universities may set up distance study courses. One should mention in particular the study programme in Law, offered by the University of Linz in cooperation with some distance learning centers in Austria. Furthermore there are special regulations as far as the admission, the documentation and the examination for distance studies are concerned.

ADMISSION TO HIGHER EDUCATION

Admission to university-level studies:

Name of secondary school credential required: Reifeprüfung / Reife- und Diplomprüfung

Minimum score/requirement: 4

For entry to: All higher education institutions (public universities, universities of applied sciences, private universities, university colleges of teacher education).

Alternatives to credentials: Studienberechtigungsprüfung: examination giving access to higher education to Austrian nationals who are over 22 years of age and do not possess a Reifezeugnis, but who have a professional or non-professional experience. It is valid only for those fields of study for which it has been taken. Relevant professional qualification in combination with certain additional examinations in subjects of general education.

Numerus clausus/restrictions: At universities in some fields of study (e.g. Medicine, artistic programmes); at universities of applied sciences, most private universities and all university colleges of education.

Other admission requirements: Besondere Universitätsreife (special university entrance qualification) additional qualifications specific to the requirements of a given study programme in addition to Reifeprüfung in the country of its origin (this does not apply to EU citizens).

Foreign students admission:

Definition of foreign student: A person who does not have Austrian citizenship. Foreign nationals who enjoy equal status with Austrian nationals are: EU citizens. children of diplomats, refugees and some other groups.

Quotas: The prerequisite is that there are sufficient places available for foreign students. EU and EEA citizens are admitted regardless of the number of places available.

Entrance exam requirements: Foreign students are admitted to study courses at university if their qualifications are equivalent to the "Matura" (Reifezeugnis) and qualify them for entry to a university in their own country. They also must give evidence that a higher education institution in the awarding country would accept them immediately for university studies in the respective field. This does not apply to EC citizens.

Language requirements: Good knowledge of German is essential. In case of doubt, students must pass the compulsory German language examination (both written and oral) at the university before registering as full-time students. German language study facilities are available in all university towns and at a number of language schools. For students from the Near East, special courses are also conducted by the Hammer-Purgstall Society.

RECOGNITION OF STUDIES

Quality assurance system:

Since 1 January 2002, action has been taken to create a unified national system for accrediting higher education institutions. The Accreditation Council, which is responsible for the accreditation of Private Universities, has been established along the lines of the Universities of Applied Sciences Council already in existence. The new Council has already started to monitor the level of education in several institutions. The Universities' Conference ("Universities Austria"), the Ministry of Science and Research, the Universities of Applied Sciences sector, and the Austrian National Union of Students have established an Austrian Agency for Quality Assurance from December 2003.

Bodies dealing with recognition:

Österreichischer Akkreditierungsrat – ÖAR (Austrian Accreditation Council)
Palais Harrach
Freyung 3
Wien 1010
EMail: elisabeth.fiorioli@bmwf.gv.at
WWW: http://www.akkreditierungsrat.at

ENIC NARIC AUSTRIA. BMWF
Director: Heinz Kasparovsky
Organisational Officer: Elizabeth Tschokert
International Officer: Christoph Demand
Teinfaltstraße 8
Vienna 1014
Tel: +43 1 53120 5921
Fax: +43 1 53120 7890
EMail: naric@bmwf.gv.at
WWW: http://www.bmwf.gv.at
Services provided and students dealt with: Austrian National Recognition Information Center.

Fachhochschulrat - FHR (FH Council)
Liechtensteinstraße 22A
Vienna 1090
Tel: +43 1 319 5034-0
Fax: +43 1 319 5034-30
EMail: office@fhr.ac.at
WWW: http://www.fhr.ac.at

Österreichische Qualitätssicherungsagentur - AQA (Austrian Agency for Quality Assurance)
Wickenburggasse 26
Vienna 1080
Tel: +43 1 319 4450-0
Fax: +43 1 319 4450-20
EMail: office@aqa.ac.at
WWW: http://www.aqa.ac.at

Special provisions for recognition:

Recognition for university level studies: Higher education entrance qualifications are declared equivalent according to international agreements, such as the Lisbon Recognition Convention or bilateral agreements with certain European countries.

For access to advanced studies and research: This is decided by the receiving higher education institution; in some cases multilateral or bilateral agreements will apply.

For exercising a profession: Regulated professions: either professional recognition on the basis of the Directive on the recognition of professional qualifications, 2005/36/EC, or, if this is not applicable, nostrification by a higher education institution.

Non-regulated professions: no formal recognition; decision lies with the employer. In any case, the Federal Ministry for Science and Research (ENIC NARIC AUSTRIA) provides advice to employers or public authorities as well as assessments of diplomas in single cases.

NATIONAL BODIES

Bundesministerium für Wissenschaft und Forschung – BMWF (Federal Ministry of Science and Research)

Minister: Karlheinz Töchterle
Protocol Officer: Ingrid Friedrich
Minoritenplatz 5
Wien 1014
Tel: +43 1 53120-0
EMail: ministerium@bmwf.gv.at
WWW: hhttp://www.bmwf.gv.at/
Role of national body: Central authority which is politically responsible for higher education and research.

Österreichische Universitätenkonferenz - UNIKO (Universities Austria)

President: Hans Sünkel
Secretary General: Heribert Wulz
Floragasse 7 / 7
Vienna 1040
Tel: +43 1 310 5656-0
Fax: +43 1 310 5656-22
EMail: office@uniko.ac.at
WWW: http://www.uniko.ac.at/
Role of national body: Umbrella organization for public universities at national level.

Österreichischer Akkreditierungsrat – ÖAR (Austrian Accreditation Council)

President: Hans-Uwe Erichsen
Managing Director: Elisabeth Fiorioli
Palais Harrach
Freyung 3
Wien 1010
EMail: elisabeth.fiorioli@bmwf.gv.at
WWW: http://www.akkreditierungsrat.at
Role of national body: Body responsible for accreditation of private universities.

Fachhochschulrat - FHR (FH Council)

President: Leopold März
Managing Director: Kurt Sohm
Liechtensteinstraße 22A
Vienna 1090
Tel: +43 1 319 5034-0
Fax: +43 1 319 5034-30
EMail: office@fhr.ac.at
WWW: http://www.fhr.ac.at
Role of national body: Body responsible for accreditation of universities of applied sciences.

Österreichische Fachhochschul-Konferenz - FHK (Association of Universities of Applied Sciences)

President: Helmut Holzinger
Secretary-General: Kurt Koleznik
Bösendorferstraße 4/11
Vienna 1010
WWW: http://www.fhk.ac.at
Role of national body: Umbrella organization for universities of applied sciences at national level.

Österreichische Qualitätssicherungsagentur - AQA (Austrian Agency for Quality Assurance)

Chairperson: Heinrich Schmidinger
Managing Director: Alexander Kohler
Wickenburggasse 26
Vienna 1080
Tel: +43 1 319 4450-0

Fax: +43 1 319 4450-20
EMail: office@aqa.ac.at
WWW: http://www.aqa.ac.at
Role of national body: Central agency for quality assurance.

Data for academic year: 2011-2012
Source: IAU from ENIC NARIC AUTRIA, BMWF, 2011

INSTITUTIONS

PUBLIC INSTITUTIONS

ACADEMY OF FINE ARTS VIENNA
Akademie der bildenden Künste Wien (BIKU)
Schillerplatz 3, 1010 Wien, Vienna
Tel: +43(1) 588-160
Fax: +43(1) 587-7977
EMail: info@akbild.ac.at
Website: http://www.akbild.ac.at

Rector: Eva Blimlinger (2011-)
Tel: +43(1) 588-16-1001, Fax: +43(1) 587-16-1099
EMail: rektor@akbild.ac.at

International Relations: Gabriele Reinharter-Schrammel
Tel: +43(1) 588-16-2100, Fax: +43(1) 588-16-2199
EMail: international@akbild.ac.at

Institutes
Art and Architecture (Architecture; Arts and Humanities); **Art Theory and Cultural Studies** (Arts and Humanities; Cultural Studies); **Conservation and Restoration** (Restoration of Works of Art); **Education in the Arts** (Art Education); **Fine Arts** (Fine Arts); **Natural Sciences and Technologies in Art** (Natural Sciences; Technology)

History: Founded 1696, acquired present status 2004.
Academic Year: October to June (October-February; March-June)
Admission Requirements: Entrance examination
Fees: (Euros): non EU residents, 364
Main Language(s) of Instruction: German
International Co-operation: Erasmus, Bilateral exchange programmes
Degrees and Diplomas: *Bachelor's Degree*: Architecture; *Master's Degree*: Architecture; *Doctor of Philosophy*: Natural Sciences and Technologies in Art ans Art Therory ans Cultural Studies
Student Services: Canteen, Nursery care
Special Facilities: Paintings Gallery; Graphic Collection
Libraries: c. 160,000 vols
Last Updated: 08/06/11

DANUBE UNIVERSITY KREMS
Donau-Universität Krems (DUK)
Dr.-Karl-Dorrek-Strasse 30, 3500 Krems, Lower Austria
Tel: +43(2732) 893-2000
Fax: +43(2732) 893-4000
EMail: info@donau-uni.ac.at
Website: http://www.donau-uni.ac.at

President: Jürgen Willer
Tel: +43(2732) 893-2210, Fax: +43(2732) 893-4210

International Relations: Viviana Mungia Monterroso
Tel: 43(2732) 893-2287, Fax: 43(2732) 893-4280
EMail: viviana.mungia@donau-uni.ac.at

Faculties
Arts, Culture and Building (Architecture; Engineering; Film; Music; Real Estate; Safety Engineering) *Dean*: Renate Hammer; **Business and Law** (Banking; Commercial Law; Economics; Eur-opean Union Law; Finance; Law; Management; Media Studies; Public Administration) *Dean*: Walter Seböck; **Communication and Globalization** (Communication Studies; Information Sciences; Information Technology; Journalism; Political Sciences); **Education and Media** (Adult Education; Cultural Studies; Educational Administration; Educational Technology; Media Studies) *Head*: Peter Baumgartner; **Health and Medicine** (Biomedicine; Biotechnology; Clinical Psychology; Dentistry; Epidemiology; Health Sciences; Medicine; Neurosciences; Psychotherapy; Social and Preventive Medicine)

History: Founded 1995. The first University in Austria offering only postgraduate and continuing education programmes. A special cost-splitting model reinforces the autonomous character of the University. The Austrian Federal Government assumes the basic costs of personnel, investments and running operations. Province of Lower Austria has planned facilities at its disposal and is responsible for maintaining them. The University is run along the guidelines of a private enterprise.
Governing Bodies: University Council; Senate
Academic Year: October to July (October-February; February-July)
Admission Requirements: University degree and professional experience, and/or equivalent professional experience
Fees: (Euros): 5,000-29,000
Main Language(s) of Instruction: German, English (knowledge of both languages is compulsory)
International Co-operation: With universities in Canada; Czech Republic; Cyprus; Finland; Germany; Greece; Italy; Japan; Liechtenstein; Lithuania; Poland; Portugal; Russia; Slovak Republic; Sweden; Switzerland; United Kingdom; USA
Accrediting Agencies: Foundation for International Business Administration Accreditation
Degrees and Diplomas: *Master's Degree*: Arts (MA); Banking and Finance (MBF); Business Administration (MBA); Corporate Finance (MCF); European Studies (MES); Financial Planning (MFP); Fine Arts (MFA); Laws (LLM); Legal Studies (MLS); Public Administration (MPA); Science (MSc)
Student Services: Academic counselling, Canteen, Cultural centre, Foreign student adviser, Handicapped facilities, Nursery care, Social counselling, Sports facilities
Libraries: Library (including European Documentation Centre - EDZ), 40,000 vols; 450 periodical subscriptions
Last Updated: 03/11/11

GRAZ UNIVERSITY OF TECHNOLOGY
Technische Universität Graz (TU GRAZ)
Rechbauerstrasse 12, 8010 Graz, Styria
Tel: +43(316) 873-6000
Fax: +43(316) 873-6009
EMail: info@tugraz.at
Website: http://www.tugraz.at/

Rektor: Harald Kainz (2011-2015)
Tel: +43(316) 873-6000, Fax: +43(316) 873-6009
EMail: rektor@tugraz.at

Head of Rectorate's Office: Ursula Tomantschger-Stessl
Tel: +43(316) 873-6416, Fax: +43(316) 827-6421
EMail: Ursula.tomantschger-stessl@tugraz.at

International Relations: Sabine Prem
Tel: +43(316) 873-6061, Fax: +43(316) 827-6009
EMail: Sabine.prem@tugraz.at

Faculties

Architecture (Architecture) *Dean*: Urs Hirschberg; **Civil Engineering** (Civil Engineering; Economics; Geophysics) *Dean*: Martin Fellendorf; **Computer Science** (Computer Graphics; Computer Science) *Dean*: Franz Wotawa; **Electrical Engineering and Information Technology** (Electrical Engineering; Information Technology) *Dean*: Heinrich Stiegler; **Mechanical Engineering** (Chemical Engineering; Economics; Mechanical Engineering) *Dean*: Franz Heitmeir; **Technical Chemistry, Chemical and Process Engineering and Biotechnology** (Biotechnology; Chemical Engineering; Chemistry; Engineering Management) *Dean*: Frank Dieter Uhlig; **Technical Mathematics and Technical Physics** (Mathematics; Physical Engineering) *Dean*: Robert Tichy

Laboratories

Electron Microscopy and Fine Structure Research *(FELMI, Research Institute) Head*: Ferdinand Hofer; **Medical Engineering** (Medical Technology) *Head*: Norbert Leitgeb

Further Information: Also 104 Institutes; Interuniversity Centre; Women Studies Co-ordination Centre

History: Founded 1811, acquired University rank and new status 1865/66 and right to award doctorate 1901. Reorganized 1955 with limited autonomy. Latest University Organization Act passed 2002.

Academic Year: October to June (October-February; March-June)

Admission Requirements: Secondary school certificate (Reifezeugnis) or recognized equivalent

Fees: (Euros): 363 per semester for EU and EEA students; 727 for other foreign students

Main Language(s) of Instruction: German

International Co-operation: With universities in all EU and associated countries; Australia; Canada; Venezuela and Asia

Degrees and Diplomas: *Bachelor's Degree*; *Diplom-Ingenieur*: Engineering (Dipl.-Ing.), 5 yrs; *Master's Degree*; *Doctor of Philosophy*: Natural Sciences; Technical Sciences; *Doctor of Philosophy*: Philosophy; Science (DrPhil), a further 2 yrs

Student Services: Academic counselling, Canteen, Foreign student adviser, Foreign Studies Centre, Handicapped facilities, Language programs, Social counselling, Sports facilities

Student Residential Facilities: Yes

Libraries: University Library, c. 400,000 vols. Special Libraries for Geodesy/Mathematics and for Chemistry

Publications: Research Journal *(biannually)*
Last Updated: 20/05/11

JOHANNES KEPLER UNIVERSITY LINZ

Johannes Kepler Universität Linz
Altenberger Strasse 69, 4040 Linz, Upper Austria
Tel: +43(732) 2468-0
Fax: +43(732) 2468-8822
EMail: bdr@jku.at
Website: http://www.jku.at

Rektor: Richard Hagelauer
Tel: +43(732) 2468-3366, Fax: +43(732) 2468-3365
EMail: rektor@jku.at

Vice-Rector of Academic Affairs: Herbert Kalb
EMail: herbert.kalb@jku.at

International Relations: Christine Hinterleitner
Tel: +43(732) 2468-3290, Fax: +43(732) 2468-3294
EMail: christine.hinterleitner@jku.at

Faculties

Law (Law) *Dean*: Heribert F. Köck; **Social Sciences** (Business Administration; Business Education; Economics; Social Sciences; Sociology; Statistics) *Dean*: Johann Brunner; **Technology and Natural Sciences** (Chemistry; Computer Science; Electronic Engineering; Mathematics; Mechanical Engineering; Physics) *Dean*: Richard Hagelauer

Further Information: Also 58 institutes

History: Founded 1966 as Hochschule für Sozial-und Wirtschaftswissenschaften. Acquired present status and title 1975. A State

institution under the jurisdiction of the Federal Ministry of Education, Science and Culture.

Governing Bodies: Universitätsrat; Universitätsleitung; Senat

Academic Year: October to July (October-February; March-July)

Admission Requirements: Completed secondary or commercial education or foreign equivalent

Fees: (Euros): EU students, 363 per semester ; non EU students, 727

Main Language(s) of Instruction: German

Degrees and Diplomas: *Bachelor's Degree*: Computer Science; Statistics; Technical Mathematics, 3 yrs; *Diplom-Ingenieur*: Computer Mathematics (Dipl.-Ing); Computer Science (Dipl.-Ing); Industrial Mathematics (Dipl.-Ing); Mathematics for Natural Sciences (Dipl.-Ing), a further 2 yrs; *Diplom-Ingenieur*: Economics-Technical Chemistry (Dipl.-Ing.); Mechatronics (Dipl.-Ing); Technical Chemistry (Dipl.-Ing); Technical Physics (Dipl.-Ing), 5 yrs; *Master's Degree*: Business and Economics (Mag.rer.soc.oec.); Business and Vocational Education and Training; Business Informatics; Law; Socio-Economics; Sociology; Statistics; Teacher Training Programmes in Mathematics; Physics; Chemistry; Computer Science and Computer Management; *Doctor of Philosophy*: Engineering Sciences; Law; Natural Sciences; Social and Economic Sciences

Student Services: Academic counselling, Canteen, Cultural centre, Employment services, Foreign student adviser, Handicapped facilities, Health services, Language programs, Nursery care, Social counselling, Sports facilities

Student Residential Facilities: Yes

Libraries: Universitätsbibliothek, c. 500,000 vols

Press or Publishing House: Stabsstelle für Public Relations
Last Updated: 04/11/11

KLAGENFURT UNIVERSITY

Alpen-Adria-Universität Klagenfurt
Universitätsstrasse 65-67, 9020 Klagenfurt, Carinthia
Tel: +43(463) 2700-0
Fax: +43(463) 2700-101
EMail: uni@uni-klu.ac.at
Website: http://www.uni-klu.ac.at

Rektor: Heinrich C. Mayr
Tel: +43(463) 2700-9201, Fax: +43(463) 2700-9299
EMail: rektor@uni-klu.ac.at

Administrative Officer: Astrid Wedenig
Tel: +43(463) 2700-9208 EMail: astrid.wedenig@uni-klu.ac.at

International Relations: Nesen Ertugrul
Tel: +43(463) 2700-9214
EMail: nesen.ertugrul@uni-klu.ac.at; internationales@uni-klu.ac.at

Faculties

Cultural Sciences (Cultural Studies; Human Rights; Peace and Disarmament; Political Sciences; Psychotherapy); **Economics and Computer Science** (Computer Science; Economics; Finance; Health Administration; International Economics; Management; Public Administration; Sports Management; Tourism); **Interdisciplinary Studies**; **Management and Economics** (Economics; Management); **Technical Sciences** (Technology)

Programmes

Applied Business Administration (Business Administration); **Applied Cultural Studies**; **Economics and Law** (Economics); **Educational Sciences** (Educational Research; Educational Sciences); **English and American Studies** (American Studies; English); **Geography and Regional Research** (Geography); **German Studies** (Germanic Studies); **History** (History); **Informatics** (Computer Science); **Information Technology** (Information Technology); **Media and Communication Sciences** (Communication Studies; Educational Technology; Media Studies); **Philosophy** (Philosophy); **Psychology** (Psychology); **Romance Studies** (Literature; Romance Languages); **Secondary Teacher Accrediation** (Civics; Computer Science; Economics; English; French; Geography; German; History; Information Technology; Italian; Mathematics; Slavic Languages; Social Sciences); **Slavonic Studies** (Literature; Slavic Languages); **Social Human Ecology**; **Technical Mathematics** (Mathematics)

Further Information: Summer courses in German/English/Italian/Slovenian

History: Founded 1970 as college, acquired present status and title 1975. A State institution under the jurisdiction of the Federal Ministry of Education, Science and Culture.

Governing Bodies: Senate

Academic Year: October to June (October-January; March-June)

Admission Requirements: Secondary school certificate (Reifezeugnis)

Main Language(s) of Instruction: German, English

International Co-operation: With 180 universities around the world

Degrees and Diplomas: *Bachelor's Degree*; *Master's Degree*; *Doctor of Philosophy (Dr. phil; Dr. rer. Nat.; Dr. techn; PhD)*; *Doctor of Philosophy*: Natural Sciences (DrRerNat), a further 1-2 yrs

Student Services: Academic counselling, Canteen, Cultural centre, Employment services, Foreign student adviser, Handicapped facilities, Nursery care, Social counselling, Sports facilities

Student Residential Facilities: Yes

Libraries: c. 700,000 vols

Publications: UNISONO *(quarterly)*

Last Updated: 13/09/11

MEDICAL UNIVERSITY OF GRAZ
Medizinische Universität Graz
Auenbruggerplatz 2, A-8036 Graz
Tel: +43(316) 385-72011
Fax: +43(316) 385-72030
EMail: rektor@medunigraz.at
Website: http://www.meduni-graz.at

Rektor: Josef Smolle

Departments
Dentistry (Dentistry); **Human Medicine** (Medicine); **Nursing** (Nursing)

History: Founded 2004 from the Medical Faculty of the University of Graz.

Governing Bodies: University Council; Senate; Rectorate

Academic Year: October to June

Main Language(s) of Instruction: German

Degrees and Diplomas: *Bachelor's Degree*: Nursing Science (BNSc); *Doktor der gesamten Heilkunde / Doktor der Zahnheilkunde*: Dentistry (DentD); Medicine (MD); Medicine and Medical Science (MDMedScD); *Master's Degree*; *Doctor of Philosophy*: Molecular Medicine (PhD)

Last Updated: 26/03/12

MEDICAL UNIVERSITY OF INNSBRUCK
Medizinische Universität Innsbruck
Christoph-Probst-Platz, 6020 Innsbruck, Tyrol
Tel: +43(512) 507-3001
Fax: +43(512) 507-2995
EMail: rektorat@i-med.ac.at
Website: http://www.i-med.ac.at

Rektor: Herbert Lochs
Tel: +43(512) 9003-70001, Fax: +43(512) 9003-73001

Centres
Medical Studies (Anaesthesiology; Dentistry; Dermatology; Gynaecology and Obstetrics; Medical Technology; Medicine; Neurology; Ophthalmology; Oral Pathology; Orthopaedics; Otorhinolaryngology; Paediatrics; Plastic Surgery; Psychiatry and Mental Health; Psychology; Psychotherapy; Radiology; Surgery; Toxicology; Urology; Venereology)

Departments
Theoretical Studies

Institutes
Neurosciences (Neurosciences)

Laboratories
Animal Facilities (Veterinary Science)

History: Founded 2004 from the Medical Faculty of the University of Innsbruck.

Governing Bodies: Senat, Universitätsrat

Academic Year: October to June

Degrees and Diplomas: *Doktor der gesamten Heilkunde / Doktor der Zahnheilkunde*; *Doctor of Philosophy*

Last Updated: 31/05/11

MEDICAL UNIVERSITY OF VIENNA
Medizinische Universität Wien
Spitalgasse 23, 1090 Wien, Vienna
Tel: +43(1) 40160-0
Fax: +43(1) 40160-910000
EMail: Infopoint-Meduni@meduniwien.ac.at
Website: http://www.meduniwien.ac.at/

Rektor: Wolfgang Schütz
Tel: +43(1) 40160-10001 EMail: buero-rektor@meduniwien.ac.at

Programmes
Applied Medical Science; **Dentistry** (Dentistry); **Human Medicine**; **Medical Informatics**; **Medical Science** (Medicine)

History: Founded 2004.

Governing Bodies: Senat; Universitätsrat

Academic Year: October to June

Main Language(s) of Instruction: German

Degrees and Diplomas: *Doktor der gesamten Heilkunde / Doktor der Zahnheilkunde (MedScD)*; *Doctor of Philosophy*: Dentistry; Medicine

Last Updated: 26/12/08

UNIVERSITY MOZARTEUM SALZBURG
Universität Mozarteum Salzburg
Schrannengasse 10a, 5020 Salzburg, Salzburg
Tel: +43(662) 6198-0
Fax: +43(662) 6198-3033
Website: http://www.moz.ac.at

Rektor: Reinhart von Gutzeit (2006-)
Tel: +43(662) 6198-2000, Fax: +43(662) 6198-2009
EMail: rektor@moz.ac.at

International Relations: Ilse Kainz
Tel: +43(662) 6198-2230, Fax: +43(662) 6198-2219
EMail: ilse.kainz@moz.ac.at

Institutes
Art Education (Art Education; Fine Arts; Handicrafts) *Director*: Dieter Kleinpeter; **Brass, Wind and Percussion Instruments** (Musical Instruments) *Chairman*: Hansjörg Angerer; **Church Music** (Religious Music) *Director*: Albert Anglberger; **Composition, Music Theory and Conducting** (Conducting; Music Theory and Composition) *Chairman*: Ernst Ludwig Leitner; **Dramatic Arts and Directing** (Theatre) *Chairwoman*: Sabine Andreas; **Fine Arts, Art and Craft Education** (Art Education; Fine Arts; Handicrafts) *Chairman*: Franz Billmayer; **Keyboard Studies** (Musical Instruments) *Chairman*: Klaus Kaufman; **Music and Dance Education** (Orff) (Music) *Chairwoman*: Manuela Widmer; **Music Education (Innsbruck)** (Music Education) *Chairman*: Armin Langer; **Music Education** (Music Education) *Director*: Monika Oebelsberger; **Music Theatre** (Music; Opera; Singing) *Chairman*: Josef Wallnig; **Musicology and Interdisciplinary Studies** (Musicology) *Chairman*: Peter-Maria Krakauer; **Stage Design** (Art Education; Fine Arts) *Chairman*: Herbert Kapplmüller; **String and Plucking Instruments** (Musical Instruments) *Chairman*: Harald Herzl; **Vocal Studies** (Music; Opera; Singing) *Chairman*: Michael Hornig

Further Information: Also Abteilung Musikerziehung in Innsbruck

History: Founded 1841, transferred to the Mozarteum Foundation 1881, became Conservatory 1914, a State institution 1921 and Akademie 1953 and University institution with title of Hochschule 1970. Acquired present title 1998.

Academic Year: October to June (October-January; March-June)

Admission Requirements: Entrance examination

Fees: (Euros): Foreign students 363 - 727 per semester (except countries of the EU and some other countries with bilateral agreements)

Main Language(s) of Instruction: German

International Co-operation: With universities in Estonia, France, Germany, Lithuania, Spain, Netherlands, United Kingdom

Degrees and Diplomas: *Bachelor's Degree*: Art; *Master's Degree*; *Doctor of Philosophy*: Philosophy, Arts and Humanities

Student Services: Academic counselling, Canteen, Social counselling

Student Residential Facilities: Yes

Libraries: 238,807 vols
Last Updated: 26/12/08

UNIVERSITY OF APPLIED ARTS VIENNA

Universität für angewandte Kunst Wien
Oskar Kokoschka Platz 2, 1010 Wien, Vienna
Tel: +43(1) 71133
Fax: +43(1) 71133-2089
EMail: pr@uni-ak.ac.at
Website: http://www.dieangewandte.at/

Rector: Gerald Bast (2003-)
Tel: +43(1) 71133-2000, Fax: +43(1) 71133-2009
EMail: gerald.bast@uni-ak.ac.at

Vice-Rector: Josef Kaiser

International Relations: Brigitte Christoph
Tel: +43(1) 71133-2170, Fax: +43(1) 71133-2179
EMail: brigitte.christoph@uni-ak.ac.at

Institutes
Architecture (Architecture; Structural Architecture) *Head*: Wolf D. Prix; **Artistic Sciences, Art Education and Communication** (Art Education; Art History; Cultural Studies; Philosophy; Textile Design) *Head*: Barbara Putz-Plecko; **Design** (Design; Fashion Design; Graphic Design; Industrial Design; Landscape Architecture) *Head*: Paolo Piva; **Fine and Media Arts** (Ceramic Art; Fine Arts; Graphic Arts; Painting and Drawing; Photography); **Restoration and Conservation** (Heritage Preservation; Restoration of Works of Art) *Dean*: Alfred Vendl; **Visual Communications** (Film; Media Studies; Visual Arts) *Head*: Bernhard Leitner

History: Founded 1867 as School, reorganized 1940 and 1945, and became Academy 1948 and University institution with title of Hochschule 1970. Acquired present status 1998. A State institution.

Governing Bodies: Universitätsrat, Senat, Rektorat

Academic Year: October to June (October-February; March-June)

Admission Requirements: Secondary school certificate (Reifezeugnis) or equivalent and entrance examination

Fees: (Euros): 363; foreign students 727 per semester

Main Language(s) of Instruction: German

International Co-operation: Participates in the Socrates programme

Degrees and Diplomas: *Bachelor's Degree*; *Master's Degree*: Art and Economy; Exhibition and Culture Communication Management (MAS); *Doctor of Philosophy*

Student Services: Academic counselling, Canteen, Foreign student adviser

Special Facilities: Archives; Art Gallery

Libraries: University Library, c. 75,000 vols; Museums, c. 180,000 vols
Last Updated: 04/11/11

UNIVERSITY OF ART AND INDUSTRIAL DESIGN LINZ

Universität für künstlerische und industrielle Gestaltung Linz
Hauptplatz 8, 4010 Linz, Upper Austria
Tel: +43(732) 7898
Fax: +43(732) 783-508
EMail: international.office@ufg.ac.at
Website: http://www.ufg.ac.at

Rektor: Reinhard Kannonier
Tel: +43(732) 7898-222 EMail: reinhard.kannonier@ufg.ac.at

Universitätsdirektorin: Christine Windsteiger
Tel: +43(732) 7898-221 EMail: christine.windsteiger@ufg.ac.at

International Relations: Robert Klug Tel: +43(732) 7898-252

Institutes
Architecture and Design (Architecture; Industrial Design) *Head*: Roland Geigner; **Art and Design** (Ceramic Art; Design; Fashion Design; Fine Arts; Textile Design) *Head*: Margareta Petrascheck-Persson; **Fine Arts and Cultural Studies** (Cultural Studies; Fine Arts); **Media Studies** (Communication Arts) *Head*: Karin Bruns

History: Founded as School of Art 1947, acquired present status 1998. A State institution under the jurisdiction of the Federal Ministry of Education, Science and Culture. Financed by the Federal Government, the Land Oberösterreich and the City of Linz.

Academic Year: October to July (October-February; March-July)

Admission Requirements: Secondary school certificate (Reifezeugnis) for secondary Art teacher's education and/or entrance examination for Art study programmes

Main Language(s) of Instruction: German

International Co-operation: Participates in the Socrates-Erasmus programmes

Degrees and Diplomas: *Bachelor's Degree*; *Master's Degree*; *Doctor of Philosophy*

Student Services: Canteen, Cultural centre, Foreign student adviser, Social counselling, Sports facilities

Libraries: c. 35,000 vols
Last Updated: 26/12/08

UNIVERSITY OF GRAZ

Karl-Franzens-Universität Graz
Universitätsplatz 3, 8010 Graz, Styria
Tel: +43(316) 380-0
Fax: +43(316) 380-9140
EMail: rektor@uni-graz.at
Website: http://www.uni-graz.at

Rektor: Christa Neuper
Tel: +43(316) 380-2201, Fax: +43(316) 380-9001
EMail: christa.neuper@uni-graz.at

Universitätsdirektorin: Maria Edlinger
Tel: +43(316) 380-2101, Fax: +43(316) 380-9029
EMail: bud.zv@uni-graz.at

International Relations: Sabine Pendl
Tel: +43(316) 380-2211, Fax: +43(316) 380-9156
EMail: sabine.pendl@uni-graz.at

Faculties
Catholic Theology (Catholic Theology; Theology) *Dean*: Rainer Maria Bucher; **Human Sciences** (American Studies; Archaeology; Art History; Arts and Humanities; English Studies; Ethnology; German; History; Modern Languages; Musicology; Pedagogy; Philology; Romance Languages; Slavic Languages; Sports; Translation and Interpretation) *Dean*: Bernhard Hurch; **Law** (Law) *Dean*: Willibald Posch; **Natural Sciences** (Botany; Chemistry; Computer Science; Earth Sciences; Mathematics; Molecular Biology; Pharmacy; Physics; Psychology; Regional Studies; Zoology) *Dean*: Georg Hoinkes; **Social Sciences and Economics** (Business Administration; Business Education; Economics; Environmental Management; Social Sciences; Sociology) *Dean*: Ursula Schneider

Further Information: Also 74 sub-units and institutes and language preparatory courses for foreign students

History: Founded 1585 by the Society of Jesus. Following reforms of the Society, University status withdrawn in 1782. Re-established as Karl-Franzens Universität 1827. Moved into present campus 1895. Karl-Franzens Universität is an autonomous university under the jurisdiction of the Federal Ministry of Education, Science and Culture.

Governing Bodies: Rector; Vice-Rectors; Senate; Supervisory Board

Academic Year: October to June (October-January; March-June)

Admission Requirements: Secondary school certificate (Reifezeugnis) or recognized equivalent

Fees: (Euros): 363 per semester for students from Austria, EU, EEC; 727 per semester for students of other nationalities

Main Language(s) of Instruction: German

International Co-operation: Erasmus; Utrecht Network; Coimbra Group; Ceepus; Tempus; Isep; Isep Multilateral; Maui; Aen; Asea Uninet; Eurasia-Pacific Uninet; Arge; Alpen Adria

Degrees and Diplomas: *Bachelor's Degree*; *Master's Degree*; *Doctor of Philosophy*

Student Services: Academic counselling, Canteen, Foreign student adviser, Foreign Studies Centre, Handicapped facilities, Language programs, Nursery care, Social counselling, Sports facilities

Student Residential Facilities: Yes

Special Facilities: Archaeological Museum; Museum of Crime of the University of Graz. Solar Observatory Kanzelhöhe; Observatory Lustbühel Graz. Media Resource Centre. Franz Nabel Institute; Alexius Meinong Institute. WegCenter. Centre of Social Competence. Akademie Neue Medien. Vestigia Manuscript Research Centre; Gender Studies; Language Centre of the University of Graz

Libraries: Central Library/Institute and faculty libraries

Publications: UNIZEIT, Scientific Research at Graz University *(quarterly)*

Last Updated: 03/11/11

UNIVERSITY OF INNSBRUCK
Leopold-Franzens Universität Innsbruck
Christof-Probst Platz Innrain 52, 6020 Innsbruck, Tyrol
Tel: +43(512) 507-2061
Fax: +43(512) 507-2804
EMail: international-relations@uibk.ac.at
Website: http://www.uibk.ac.at

Rektor (Acting): Tilmann Märk
Tel: +43(512) 507-2000 EMail: rektor@uibk.ac.at

Public Relations: Jürgen Steinberger
Tel: +43(512) 507-2007 EMail: juergen.steinberger@uibk.ac.at

International Relations: Mathias Schennach
Tel: +43(512) 507-2040

Faculties
Architecture (Architecture); **Biology** (Biology); **Catholic Theology** (Bible; Christian Religious Studies; Religious Practice; Theology); **Chemistry and Pharmacy** (Chemistry; Pharmacy); **Civil Engineering** (Applied Mathematics; Civil Engineering; Construction Engineering; Environmental Engineering; Hydraulic Engineering; Materials Engineering; Mechanics; Structural Architecture; Surveying and Mapping; Transport Engineering); **Economics and Statistics** (Economic History; Economics; Finance; Political Sciences; Statistics); **Education** (Education; Educational Research; Teacher Training); **Geo- and Atmospheric Sciences** (Geography; Geology; Geophysics; Meteorology; Mineralogy; Paleontology; Petrology); **Humanities I (Philosophy and History)** (Arts and Humanities; History; Philosophy); **Humanities II ((Language and Literature)** (Literature; Modern Languages); **Law** (Civil Law; Commercial Law; Criminal Law; European Union Law; International Law; Labour Law; Law; Private Law; Public Law); **Mathematics, Computer Science and Physics** (Computer Science; Mathematics; Physics); **Psychology and Sport Science** (Psychology; Sports)

Schools
Management (Accountancy; Banking; Finance; Information Technology; Management; Marketing; Modern Languages; Taxation; Tourism; Transport Management); **Political Science and Sociology** (Political Sciences; Sociology)

Further Information: Also 73 Institutes of the Faculties

History: Founded 1669, acquired present status 1862. A State institution under the jurisdiction of the Federal Ministry of Education, Science and Culture.

Governing Bodies: University Board, Senate

Academic Year: October to July (October-February; March-July)

Admission Requirements: Secondary school certificate (Reifezeugnis) or foreign equivalent

Fees: (Euros): 377-740 per semester

Main Language(s) of Instruction: German

International Co-operation: With more than 300 universities (c. 260 in Europe; c. 40 outside Europe). Also participates in Erasmus, ASEA-UNINET programmes

Degrees and Diplomas: *Bachelor's Degree*; *Master's Degree*; *Doctor of Philosophy*: Economics; Law; Natural Sciences; Philosophy, Arts and Humanities; Political Science; Theology

Student Services: Language programs, Sports facilities

Libraries: c. 875,000 vols

Student Numbers *2010*: Total: c. 27,000
Last Updated: 03/11/11

UNIVERSITY OF LEOBEN
Montanuniversität Leoben (MUL)
Franz-Josef-Strasse 18, 8700 Leoben, Styria
Tel: +43(3842) 402-0
Fax: +43(3842) 402-308 +43(3842) 402-7702
EMail: office@unileoben.ac.at
Website: http://www.unileoben.ac.at

Rektor: Wilfried Eichlseder
Tel: +43(3842) 402-7000, Fax: +43(3842) 402-7012
EMail: rektor@unileoben.ac.at

Departments
Applied Geological Sciences and Geophysics (Environmental Engineering; Geology; Geophysics; Mineralogy; Petroleum and Gas Engineering; Soil Science; Systems Analysis); **Economics and Business Management** (Business Administration; Economics; Industrial Management); **General, Analytical and Physical Chemistry**; **Mathematics and Information Technology**; **Metallurgy** (Heating and Refrigeration; Metallurgical Engineering); **Mining Engineering and Tunnelling** (Construction Engineering; Geological Engineering; Mining Engineering); **Petroleum Engineering** (Petroleum and Gas Engineering; Production Engineering); **Physical Metallurgy and Materials Testing** (Metal Techniques; Metallurgical Engineering; Physical Engineering); **Product Engineering** (Automation and Control Engineering; Mechanical Engineering; Polymer and Plastics Technology; Production Engineering; Technology); **Structural and Functional Ceramics** (Ceramics and Glass Technology; Engineering)

Institutes
Ceramics (Engineering); **Chemistry of Polymeric Materials** (Chemistry; Polymer and Plastics Technology); **Electrical Engineering**; **Materials Sciences and Testing of Plastics**; **Mechanics**; **Metal Physics**; **Mineral Processing** (Mineralogy); **Physics**; **Plastics and Composite Material Design**; **Plastics Processing**; **Process Technology and Industrial Environmental Protection** (Environmental Management; Technology); **Sustainable Waste Management and Technology** (Technology; Waste Management)

History: Founded 1840 as a Mining Institute, acquired University status 1904, and present title by law 1975. A State institution under the jurisdiction of the Federal Ministry of Education, Science and Culture.

Governing Bodies: University Council, Senate

Academic Year: October to June (October-February; February-June)

Admission Requirements: Secondary school certificate (Reifezeugnis) or recognized foreign equivalent (Matura/Abitur)

Fees: (Euros): EU residents, 363; international students, 726

Main Language(s) of Instruction: German, English

International Co-operation: With over 30 universities in all continents

Degrees and Diplomas: *Diplom-Ingenieur*: Engineering (Dipl.-Ing.), 10 sem; *Master's Degree*: Engineering, 10 sem; *Doctor of Philosophy*: Engineering

Student Services: Academic counselling, Canteen, Cultural centre, Employment services, Foreign student adviser, Social counselling, Sports facilities

Student Residential Facilities: Yes

Libraries: Universitätsbibliothek, 223,000 vols

Press or Publishing House: Springer-Verlag, Wien

Last Updated: 03/11/11

UNIVERSITY OF MUSIC AND PERFORMING ARTS GRAZ
Universität für Musik und darstellende Kunst Graz (KUG)
Leonhardstrasse 15, 8010 Graz, Styria
Tel: +43(316) 389-0
Fax: +43(316) 389-1101
EMail: info@kug.ac.at
Website: http://www.kug.ac.at

Rektor: Georg Schulz EMail: georg.schulz@kug.ac.at

University Director: Astrid Wedenig
Tel: +43(316) 389-1112 EMail: astrid.wedenig@kug.ac.at

Institutes

Aesthetics of Music (Aesthetics; Art Criticism) *Chairman*: Andreas Dorschel; **Composition, Music Theory, Music History and Conducting** (Conducting; Music Theory and Composition; Musicology) *Chairman*: Peters Revers; **Dramatic Arts** (Acting; Literature; Speech Studies; Theatre) *Chairperson*: Evelyn Deutsch-Schreiner; **Early Music and Performance Practice** *Chairman*: Klaus Hubmann; **Electronic Music and Acoustics** (Music; Music Theory and Composition) *Chairman*: Alois Sontacchi; **Ethnomusicology** (Musicology) *Chairman*: Gerd Grupe; **Jazz** *Chairman*: Antony Partyka; **Jazz Research** (Jazz and Popular Music) *Chairman*: Franz Kerschbaumer; **Music Education** (Music Education) *Chairman*: Gerhard Wanker; **Musical Instruments and Singing** *(Institut Oberschützen)* (Musical Instruments) *Chairman*: Klaus Aringer; **Opera** (Music; Theatre) *Chairman*: Barbara Beyer; **Piano** (Musical Instruments) *Chairman*: Eugen Jakab; **Stage Design** (Display and Stage Design) *Chairman*: Hans Schavernoch; **String Instruments** (Musical Instruments) *Chairman*: Kerstin Feltz; **Voice, Lied and Oratorio** (Singing) *Chairman*: Martin Klietmann; **Wind and Percussion Instruments** (Musical Instruments) *Chairman*: Thomas Eibinger

History: Founded as provincial School of Music 1816, became Conservatory 1920, Akademie 1963, and University Institution with title of Hochschule 1970. Acquired title of University of Music and Dramatic Arts Graz in 1998, became University of Music and Performing Arts Graz in 2009. A State institution.

Governing Bodies: Rector and three Vice-Rectors, Senate and University Council

Academic Year: October to June (October-January; March-June)

Admission Requirements: Secondary school certificate (Reifezeugnis) and entrance examination

Fees: (Euros): EU citizens, 0-363.63 dependant on progress; non EU citizens, 363.63

Main Language(s) of Instruction: German

International Co-operation: With institutions in Europe, Australia, Canada, Mexico, USA, Vietnam. Also participates in LLL/Erasmus programmes.

Accrediting Agencies: Federal Ministry of Science and Research

Degrees and Diplomas: *Bachelor's Degree (BA; BSc)*: 3-4 yrs; *Master's Degree (MA; MSc)*: a further 2 yrs; *Doctor of Philosophy*

Student Services: Canteen, Cultural centre, Employment services, Foreign student adviser, Social counselling, Sports facilities

Libraries: c. 210,000 vols. (books, journals, sheets, records, tapes and other media)

Publications: Research publications

Academic Staff 2010-2011	MEN	WOMEN	TOTAL
FULL-TIME	131	58	**189**
PART-TIME	141	94	**235**
Student Numbers 2010-2011			
All (Foreign Included)	1,207	1,137	**2,344**
FOREIGN ONLY	515	523	**1,038**

Last Updated: 05/07/11

tory of Music (Musicology) *Head*: Cornelia Szabo-Knotik; **Chamber Music** *(Joseph Haydn)* *Head*: Avedis Kouyoumdjian; **Composition and Electro-acoustics** (Music Theory and Composition) *Head*: Reihard Karger; **Conducting and Accompaniment** (Conducting; Music Theory and Composition; Musical Instruments) *Head*: Thomas Kreuzberger; **Cultural Management and Culture Studies** *(IKM)* (Cultural Studies; Management) *Head*: Franz-Otto Hofecker; **Film and Television** *(Film Academy Vienna)* (Cinema and Television; Film; Photography) *Head*: Peter Patzak; **Folk Music and Ethno-musicology** (Folklore; Music; Musicology) *Head*: Ursula Hemetek; **Keyboard Instruments** (Musical Instruments) *Head*: Martin Hugues; **Keyboard Instruments in Music Education** *(Ludwig van Beethoven)* (Music Education; Musical Instruments; Teacher Training) *Head*: Ursula Kneihs; **Music Acoustics** *(Viennese Style)* (Music; Sound Engineering (Acoustics)) *Head*: Wilfried Kausel; **Music Education** (Music Education) *Head*: Franz Niermann; **Music Education, Rhythmic and Musical Therapy** (Music Education) *Head*: Angelika Hauser; **Music Sociology** *Head*: Alfred Smudits; **Music Theory, Aural Training, Ensemble Conducting** *(Anton Bruckner)* (Conducting; Music; Music Theory and Composition) *Head*: Alois Glassner; **Musical Style Research** (Music; Musicology) *Head*: Hartmut Krones; **Organ, Organ Research and Church Music** (Musical Instruments; Religious Music) *Head*: Erwin Ortner; **Popular Music** (Jazz and Popular Music; Music) *Head*: Wolfgang Puschnig; **Singing in Music Education** *(Antonio Salieri)* (Music Education; Opera) *Head*: Maria Bayer; **String Instruments** (Musical Instruments) *Head*: Stefan Kropfitsch; **String Instruments in Music Education** *(Hellmesberger)* (Music Education; Musical Instruments; Teacher Training) *Head*: Wolfgang Aichinger; **Voice and Music Theatre** (Music; Theatre) *Head*: Karlheinz Hansler; **Wind and Percussion Instruments** *(Leonard Bernstein)* (Musical Instruments) *Head*: Barbara Gisler; **Wind and Percussion Instruments in Music Education** *(Franz Schubert)* (Music Education; Musical Instruments; Teacher Training) *Head*: Walter Wretschitsch

History: Founded 1817 as Konservatorium der Gesellschaft der Musikfreunde in Wien, became Academy and State Institution 1909 and University 1998.

Governing Bodies: Rectorate, Senate, University Council

Academic Year: October to June (October-February; March-June)

Admission Requirements: Secondary school certificate (Reifezeugnis) and entrance examination (depends on branch of study)

Fees: (Euros): no fees for EU citizens studying within the statuory minimum period; non EU citizens, 363 per semester

Main Language(s) of Instruction: German

International Co-operation: With 159 universities in Europe, Asia, Northern ans Southern America. Also participates in the Erasmus/Socrates programmes

Degrees and Diplomas: *Bachelor's Degree*; *Master's Degree*: Art; *Doctor of Philosophy (PhD)*: 2 yrs

Student Services: Academic counselling, Canteen, Employment services, Foreign student adviser, Language programs, Social counselling

Libraries: Central Library, department libraries, total c. 220,000 vols; c. 20,000 records and tapes

Last Updated: 12/07/11

UNIVERSITY OF MUSIC AND PERFORMING ARTS VIENNA

Universität für Musik und darstellende Kunst Wien
Anton-von-Webern-Platz 1, 1030 Wien, Vienna
Tel: +43(1) 71155-0
Fax: +43(1) 71155-6099
EMail: rektorsbuero@mdw.ac.at
Website: http://www.mdw.ac.at

Rektor: Werner Hasitschka Tel: +43(1) 71155-6000

Leiter des Bûros der Universitâtsleitung: Karl-Gerhard Strassl

International Relations: Sabine Roth
Tel: +43(1) 71155-7420, Fax: +43(1) 71155-7429
EMail: roth@mdw.ac.at

Institutes

Acting, Production and Directing *(Max-Reinhart-Seminar)* (Acting; Theatre) *Head*: Hubertus Petroll; **Analysis, Theory and His-**

UNIVERSITY OF NATURAL RESOURCES AND APPLIED LIFE SCIENCES, VIENNA

Universität für Bodenkultur Wien (BOKU)
Gregor-Mendel-Strasse 33, 1180 Wien, Vienna
Tel: +43(1) 47-654-0
Fax: +43(1) 47-654-1055
EMail: bdr@boku.ac.at
Website: http://www.boku.ac.at

Rektor: Martin Gerzabek
Tel: +43(1) 47-654-1001, Fax: +43(1) 47-654-1005
EMail: rektorat@boku.ac.at

Research Suport Service: Horst Mayr
Tel: +43(1) 47-654-2609, Fax: +43(1) 47-654-2603
EMail: forschungsservice@boku.ac.at; horst.mayr@boku.ac.at

International Relations: Margarita Calderón-Peter
Tel: +43(1) 47-654-2601, Fax: +43(1) 47-654-2606
EMail: margarita.calderon-peter@boku.ac.at

Centres
Agricultural Sciences; **BOKU Network for Bioconversion of Renewables**; **Development Research**; **Global Change and Sustainability** *(ZGWN)*; **INNOFORCE**; **Natural Hazards and Riskmanagement** *(ZENAR)*; **Scientific Initiatives**; **Vienna Institute of BioTechnology** *(VIBT Muthgasse)*

Departments
Agrobiotechnology (IFA-Tulln) (Agriculture; Biotechnology); **Applied Genetics and Cell Biology** (Cell Biology; Genetics); **Applied Plant Sciences and Plant Biotechnology** (Biotechnology; Horticulture; Plant and Crop Protection); **Biotechnology** (Biotechnology); **Chemistry**; **Civil Engineering and Natural Hazards** (Civil Engineering); **Economics and Social Sciences** (Economics; Social Sciences); **Food Science and Technology** (Biotechnology; Food Science; Food Technology); **Forest and Soil Sciences** (Forest Products; Forestry; Natural Resources; Water Management; Wildlife; Wood Technology); **Integrative Biology and Biodiversity Research**; **Landscape, Spatial and Infrastructure Science** (Bioengineering; Design; Landscape Architecture; Regional Planning); **Material Sciences and Process Engineering** (Materials Engineering); **Nanobiotechnology** (Biotechnology; Nanotechnology); **Sustainable Agricultural Systems** (Agriculture; Botany; Plant and Crop Protection; Soil Science; Zoology); **Water, Atmosphere and Environment** (Civil Engineering; Transport Management; Waste Management; Water Management)

History: Founded 1872 as Hochschule. Acquired present title 1975. A State institution.

Governing Bodies: Rectorat

Academic Year: October to June (October-February; February-June)

Admission Requirements: Secondary school certificate (Reifezeugnis)

Fees: (Euros): 363 per semester for non-EU/non-EEA citizens

Main Language(s) of Instruction: German; 10 Master's programmes offered in English

International Co-operation: Erasmus, Ceepus, Tempus, Erasmus Mundus, EU-US, EU-Australia, Alfa programmes, FR7

Degrees and Diplomas: *Bachelor's Degree (Bakk.techn.)*; *Master's Degree (Dipl.-Ing; DI; MSc)*; *Doctor of Philosophy*

Student Services: Academic counselling, Canteen, Employment services, Foreign student adviser, Language programs

Student Residential Facilities: Yes

Libraries: Central Library, c. 520,000 vols

Publications: Blick Ins Land; BOKU INSIGHT; Die Bodenkultur; Ökoenergie

Academic Staff *2009*	MEN	WOMEN	TOTAL
FULL-TIME	653	464	1,117
Student Numbers *2010-2011*			
All (Foreign Included)	5,627	4,891	10,518
FOREIGN ONLY	–	–	1,781

Last Updated: 30/06/11

UNIVERSITY OF SALZBURG

Universität Salzburg
Kapitelgasse 4-6, 5020 Salzburg, Salzburg
Tel: +43(662) 8044-0
Fax: +43(662) 8044-214
EMail: international@sbg.ac.at
Website: http://www.uni-salzburg.at

Rektor: Heinrich Schmidinger (2001-)
Tel: +43(662) 8044-2000, Fax: +43(662) 8044-145
EMail: heinrich.schmidinger@sbg.ac.at

Vice-Rector for International Relations and Communication: Sonja Puntscher-Riekmann
Tel: +43(662) 8044-2001
EMail: Sonja.Puntscher-Riekmann@sbg.ac.at

International Relations: Markus Bayer
Tel: +43(662) 8044-2040, Fax: +43(662) 8044-154
EMail: markus.bayer@sbg.ac.at

Centres
GeoInformatics; **Interdisciplinary Research on Medieval Studies** (History; Medieval Studies); **Interdisciplinary Research on Metamorphic Changes in the Arts** (Aesthetics; Cultural Studies; Social Studies); **Jewish Culture History** (Jewish Studies); **Neurocognitive Linguistics**; **Poverty Research**

Faculties
Arts and Humanities (Communication Studies; Cultural Studies; Dance; English; Fine Arts; German; History; Linguistics; Music; Philosophy; Political Sciences; Romance Languages; Slavic Languages; Social Sciences; Sociology) *Dean*: Gerhard Petersmann; **Catholic Theology** (Bible; Catholic Theology; History of Religion; Philosophy; Theology) *Dean*: Hans Joachim Sander; **Law** (European Union Law; Labour Law; Law; Private Law; Public Law) *Dean*: Kurt Schmoller; **Natural Sciences** (Cell Biology; Computer Science; Geography; Geology; Mathematics; Molecular Biology; Natural Sciences; Physics; Psychology) *Dean*: Urs Baumann

Research Centres
BioScience and Health (Biological and Life Sciences; Health Sciences); **Education and Art**; **Information and Communication Technologies and Society** *(ICT&S)* (Communication Studies; Information Technology); **Law, Economics and Employment** (Economics; Law)

Further Information: Also 51 Institutes

History: Founded 1617 as School by Archbishop Paris Lodron, became University 1622, dissolved 1810. Re-established 1962. A State institution financed by the Federal Ministry of Education, Science and Culture.

Governing Bodies: Senate

Academic Year: October to June (October-January; March-June)

Admission Requirements: Secondary school certificate (Reifezeugnis), or recognized foreign equivalent

Fees: (Euros): EU citizens, 360 per semester; non EU citizens, 730.

Main Language(s) of Instruction: German

Degrees and Diplomas: *Bachelor's Degree*; *Diplom-Ingenieur*; *Master's Degree*: Law (Mag.iur); Natural Sciences; Philosophy from the Theology Faculty; Philosophy, Arts and Humanities; Theology; *Doctor of Philosophy*

Student Services: Academic counselling, Canteen, Foreign student adviser, Handicapped facilities, Nursery care, Social counselling, Sports facilities

Student Residential Facilities: For c. 1,700 students

Libraries: University Library, c. 720,000 vols; libraries of the institutes, c. 1m.

Press or Publishing House: Universitätsdirektion
Last Updated: 04/04/08

UNIVERSITY OF VETERINARY MEDICINE, VIENNA

Veterinärmedizinische Universität Wien (VMU)
Veterinärplatz 1, A1210 Wien, Vienna
Tel: +43(1) 250-77-0
Fax: +43(1) 250-77-1090
EMail: ursula.schober@vetmeduni.ac.at
Website: http://www.vetmeduni.ac.at

Rektor: Sonja Hammerschmid
Tel: +43(1) 250-77-1000, Fax: +43(1) 250-77-1090

International Relations: Ursula Schober

Departments
Biomedical Sciences (Animal Husbandry; Biochemistry; Biotechnology; Genetics; Histology; Pharmacology; Physics; Physiology; Toxicology); **Companion Animals and Horses** *(Clinical)* (Anaesthesiology; Animal Husbandry; Epidemiology; Gynaecology and Obstetrics; Ophthalmology; Surgery); **Farm Animals and Veterinary Public Health** (Animal Husbandry; Botany; Epidemiology; Food Science; Hygiene; Nutrition; Pharmacology; Public Health); **Integrative Biology and Evolution** (Biology; Environmental Studies; Wildlife); **Pathobiology** (Anatomy; Embryology and Reproduction Biology; Forensic Medicine and Dentistry; Histology; Hygiene; Parasitology; Pathology; Virology; Zoology)

Further Information: Also Veterinary Teaching Hospital

History: Founded 1765 as a school, achieved University status 1908 and was granted the same rights and privileges as other Austrian Universities 1920. Acquired present title 1975.

Governing Bodies: Rectorate;University Council; Senate

Academic Year: October to June (October-January; March-June)

Admission Requirements: Secondary school leaving certificate (Reifezeugnis) or equivalent

Fees: (Euros): 727 per annum

Main Language(s) of Instruction: German

International Co-operation: Member of VetNEST (Ceepus framework) and Socrates programmes (Socrates/Erasmus Intensive programmes)

Degrees and Diplomas: *Bachelor's Degree*: Equine Sciences; Biomedicine and Biotechnology; *Master's Degree*: Biomedecine and Biotechnology; *Doctor of Philosophy (PhD)*. Also Doktor: Veterinary Medicine

Student Services: Academic counselling, Canteen, Cultural centre, Foreign student adviser, Foreign Studies Centre, Handicapped facilities, Nursery care, Sports facilities

Student Residential Facilities: Yes

Special Facilities: Anatomy Museum; Parasitology Museum; Pathology Museum

Libraries: 190,041 vols

Publications: VetmedMagazin *(quarterly)*; Wiener Tierärztliche Monastsschrift *(monthly)*
Last Updated: 11/10/11

UNIVERSITY OF VIENNA

Universität Wien
Dr.-Karl-Lueger-Ring 1, 1010 Wien, Vienna
Tel: +43(1) 4277-0
Fax: +43(1) 4277-9100
EMail: buero.rektorat@univie.ac.at
Website: http://www.univie.ac.at

Rektor: Heinz W. Engl
Tel: +43(1) 4277-10010
EMail: heinz.engl@univie.ac.at; rektor@univie.ac.at

Vice Rector for Human Resources Development and International Relations: Heinz Fassmann

Centres
Molecular Biology; **Sports Sciences and University Sports** (Sports); **Transportation Studies**

Faculties
Business, Economics and Statistics (Business Administration; Business and Commerce; Commercial Law; Economics; Finance; Modern Languages; Statistics); **Catholic Theology** (Theology); **Chemistry**; **Computer Science** (Computer Science); **Earth Sciences, Geography and Astronomy** (Astronomy and Space Science; Earth Sciences; Geography); **Historical-Cultural Sciences** (Ancient Civilizations; Cultural Studies; Ethnology; History); **Law**; **Life Sciences** (Biological and Life Sciences; Biology; Molecular Biology; Pharmacy); **Mathematics** (Mathematics; Mathematics Education); **Philological-Cultural Sciences** (Cultural Studies; Philology); **Philosophy and Educational Sciences** (Educational Sciences; Pedagogy; Philosophy); **Physics** (Physics); **Protestant Theology** (Protestant Theology; Religion; Religious Education; Theology); **Psychology**; **Social Sciences** (Political Sciences; Social Sciences; Sociology)

History: Founded 1365, reorganized 1377, 1384 and 1850 and 2004. A State institution under the jurisdiction of the Federal Ministry of Education, Science and Culture.

Governing Bodies: University Board, Rectorate, Senate

Academic Year: October to June (October-January; March-June)

Admission Requirements: Secondary school certificate (Reifezeugnis) or recognized foreign equivalent

Fees: (Euros): 363 per semester for EU citizens, 726 for non-EU citizens; tuition waivers for some countries

Main Language(s) of Instruction: German

International Co-operation: With 44 international universities. Also Erasmus bilateral agreements with 327 universities as well as Leonardo da Vinci placements and scholarship for research, studies for students and graduates. Participates in the following international research networks: European University Association (EUA); International Network of Universities from the Capitals of Europe (UNICA); Danube Rectors Conference (DRC); Eurasia-Pacific UNINET and ASIA-UNINET.

Degrees and Diplomas: *Bachelor's Degree (Bakk.)*: 3 yrs; *Master's Degree*: 2 yrs; *Doctor of Philosophy (PhD)*: 3-4 yrs. For further information on degrees awarded, please consult http://studieren.univie.ac.at. The University of Vienna also offers continuing education courses (http://www.univie.ac.at/weiterbildung)

Student Services: Academic counselling, Canteen, Employment services, Foreign student adviser, Language programs, Sports facilities

Libraries: Total 6,495,871 vols
Last Updated: 03/11/11

VIENNA UNIVERSITY OF ECONOMICS AND BUSINESS

Wirtschaftsuniversität Wien (WU)
Augasse 2-6, 1090 Wien, Vienna
Tel: +43(1) 31-336-0
Fax: +43(1) 31-336-777
EMail: rektorat@wu.ac.at
Website: http://www.wu.ac.at

Rektor: Christoph Badelt (2003-2015)
Tel: +43(1) 31-336-4700, Fax: +43(1) 31-336-90-4700
EMail: christoph.badelt@wu.ac.at

Manager: Cornelia Moll
Tel: +43(1) 31336-4977, Fax: +43(1) 31 336 90 4977
EMail: cornelia.moll@wu.ac.at

International Relations: Barbara Sporn, Vice-Rector, Research, International Affairs and External Relations (2003-)
Tel: +43(1) 31-336-5522, Fax: +43(1) 31-336-90-5522
EMail: barbara.sporn@wu.ac.at

Departments
Business, Employment and Social Security Law (Business Administration; Civil Law; European Union Law; Labour Law) *Chair*: Susanne Kalss; **Economics** (Economics; Finance; International Economics; Social Policy) *Chair*: Gabriel Obermann; **Family Businesses** *Head*: Hermann Franck; **Finance, Accounting and Statistics** (Accountancy; Banking; Finance; Insurance; Mathematics; Statistics; Taxation) *Chair*: Stefan Bogner; **Foreign Language Business Communication** (English; Romance Languages; Slavic Languages) *Chair*: Wolfgang Obenaus; **Global Business and Trade** (Business Administration; International Business; Small Business; Transport Management) *Chair*: Reinhard Moher; **Information Systems and Operations** (Industrial and Production Economics; Information Management; Information Technology; Media Studies; Production Engineering) *Chair*: Alfred Taudes; **Management** (Management) *Chair*: Helmut Kasper; **Marketing** (Advertising and Publicity; International Business; Leisure Studies; Marketing; Retailing and Wholesaling; Tourism) *Chair*: Fritz Scheuch; **Public Law and Tax Law** (Criminal Law; European Union Law; International Law; Public Law) *Chair*: Josef Schuch; **Socioeconomics** (Economic History; Economics; Environmental Management; Geography; Geography (Human); Regional Studies; Social Policy; Social Sciences; Sociology; Technology) *Chair*: Ulrike Schneider; **Strategic Management and Innovation** (Industrial Management; Management; Public Administration) *Chair*: Gerhard Speckbacher

Research Institutes
Capital Markets *Head*: Engelbert Dockner; **Computational Methods** (Computer Science) *Head*: Kurt Hornik; **Co-Operation and Co-Operatives** *Head*: Dietmar Roessl; **Economics of Ageing** *Head*: Ulrike Schneider; **European Affairs** (European Studies; Management; Marketing) *Head*: Stefan Griller; **Gender and Diversity in Organizations** (Gender Studies) *Head*: Edeltraud Hanappi-Egger; **Health Care Management and Economics** (Health Administration) *Head*: Johaness Steyrer; **Human Capital and Development** *Head*: Wolfgang Lutz; **Independent Professions** *Head*: Leo W. Chini; **International Taxation** (International Business; Taxation) *Head*: Eva Eberhartinger; **Legal Studies** (Law) *Head*: Martin Winner; **Managing Sustainability** *Head*: André Martinuzzi; **Regulatory Economics** *Head*: Stephan Bogner; **Spatial and Real Estate**

Economics (Real Estate) *Head*: Gunther Maier; **Supply Chain Management** *Head*: Sebastian Kummer; **Urban Management and Governance** (Government; Urban Studies) *Head*: Verana Madner

Further Information: International Studies Centre; Career Planning and Placement Centre

History: Founded 1898 as Imperial Export Academy, soon took on the characteristics of a university, received the right to confer doctorates in 1930. Became Vienna University of Economics and Business Administration 1975. It gained full institutional autonomy 2004 through the University Act of 2002. Renamed WU (Vienna University of Economics and Business in 2009.

Governing Bodies: University Board Rector's Council; Senate

Academic Year: October to June (October-January; March-June)

Admission Requirements: Secondary school certificate (Reifepruefungszeugnis) or foreign equivalent at Bachelor level. Bachelor degree or equivalent requirements at Master level (language skills, program-specific knowledge, GPA, GMAT etc.) Master degree or equivalent at Doctoral and PhD level.

Fees: (Euros): 363 per semester. Tuition fees are waived for EU-citizens, EEA-citizens and refugees under the provisions of the Geneva Convention for the length of the standard duration of their degree program, plus two extra semesters

Main Language(s) of Instruction: German or English (depending on program)

Degrees and Diplomas: *Bachelor's Degree*: Business; Economics and Social Sciences; Business Law, 3 yrs; *Master's Degree*: Business Education; Business Law; Economics; Finance and Accounting; Information Systems; Management; Socioeconomics; Taxation and Accounting; International Management; Strategy, Innovation and Management Control, Supply Chain Management; *Doctor of Philosophy*: Finance; International Business Taxation (PhD); Social and Economics Sciences; Business Law

Student Services: Academic counselling, Canteen, Employment services, Foreign student adviser, Foreign Studies Centre, Language programs, Nursery care, Social counselling

Special Facilities: Kindergarten; Multi-faith prayer room

Libraries: Universitätsbibliothek, c. 800,000 vols; 10,000 e-book; 2,250 printed journals, over 9,000e-journal, 95 database

Publications: Journal für Betriebswirtschaft, Journal on Business Administration *(biennially)*

Student Numbers 2010-2011	MEN	WOMEN	TOTAL
All (Foreign Included)	14,076	13,408	**27,484**

Last Updated: 08/07/11

VIENNA UNIVERSITY OF TECHNOLOGY
Technische Universität Wien (TU WIEN)
Karlsplatz 13, 1040 Wien, Vienna
Tel: +43(1) 58801-0
Fax: +43(1) 58801-41099
EMail: webmaster@tuwien.ac.at
Website: http://www.tuwien.ac.at

Rektor: Sabine Seidler
Tel: +43(1) 58801-40110, Fax: +43(1) 58801-40199
EMail: sseidler@mail.zserv.tuwien.ac.at

Vice Rector for Academic Affairs: Adalbert Prechtl

International Relations: Franz Reichl
Tel: +43(1) 58801-4961, Fax: +43(1) 58801-41599

Faculties
Architecture and Regional Planning (Architecture and Planning; Regional Planning) *Dean*: Klaus Semsroth; **Civil Engineering** (Civil Engineering) *Dean*: Johann Litzka; **Computer Science** (Computer Science) *Dean*: Gerald Steinhard; **Electrical Engineering and Information Technology** (Electrical Engineering; Electronic Engineering; Information Technology) *Dean*: Siegried Selberherr; **Mathematics and Geoinformation** (Computer Science; Geophysics; Mathematics; Statistics); **Mechanical Engineering** (Engineering Management; Mechanical Engineering) *Dean*: Bruno Groesel; **Physics** (Physics) *Dean*: Gerald Badurek; **Technical Chemistry** (Chemistry) *Dean*: Johannes Fröhlich; **Technical-Natural and Computer Sciences** (Computer Science; Information

Sciences; Natural Sciences; Technology) *Dean*: Herbert Stachelberger

Further Information: Also 87 institutes of the faculties

History: Founded 1815 as institute of technology, acquired University status 1872 and right to award doctorates 1901. Reorganized 1955, acquired present status and title 1975. A State institution.

Governing Bodies: Senat

Academic Year: October to June (October-January; March-June)

Admission Requirements: Secondary school certificate (Reifezeugnis) or recognized foreign equivalent

Fees: (Euros): 363 per semester for EU residents; 727 for non EU residents

Main Language(s) of Instruction: German, English

International Co-operation: Erasmus and 5th Framework programmes

Degrees and Diplomas: *Bachelor's Degree*; *Master's Degree*; *Doctor of Philosophy*: Natural Sciences; Technical Sciences

Student Services: Academic counselling, Canteen, Cultural centre, Foreign student adviser, Foreign Studies Centre, Handicapped facilities, Language programs, Social counselling, Sports facilities

Libraries: University Library, c. 1m. vols
Last Updated: 03/11/11

PRIVATE INSTITUTIONS

ANTON BRUCKNER UNIVERSITY
Anton Bruckner Privatuniversität
Wildergstrasse 18, 4040 Linz, Upper Austria
Tel: +43(732) 701000-0
Fax: +43(732) 701000-30
EMail: information@bruckneruni.at
Website: http://www.bruckneruni.at

Rektorin: Marianne Betz
Tel: +43(732) 701000-70 EMail: rektorin@bruckneruni.at

Vizerektor: Josef Eidenberger
EMail: j.Eidenberger@bruckneruni.at

Programmes
Classical Music (Music); **Dance**; **Elementary Music Education**; **Jazz and Improvization** (Jazz and Popular Music); **Theatre** (Theatre)

Admission Requirements: Entrance examination

Fees: (Euros): 100 per semester

Degrees and Diplomas: *Bachelor's Degree*; *Master's Degree*
Last Updated: 26/12/08

CAMPUS 02 UNIVERSITY OF APPLIED SCIENCES
Campus 02 - Fachhochschule der Wirtschaft GmbH
Körblergasse 126, 8021 Graz, Styria
Tel: +43(316) 6002-0
Fax: +43(316) 6002-700
EMail: info@campus02.at
Website: http://www.campus02.at

Geschäftsführer / CEO: Peter Hochegger
EMail: peter.hochegger@campus02.at

International Relations: Erich Brugger
Tel: +43(316) 6002-311, Fax: +43(316) 6002-1230
EMail: erich.brugger@campus02.at

Programmes
Accountancy and Auditing *Director*: Siegfried Klopf; **Automation Technology** (Engineering) *Director*: Udo Traussnigg; **Information Technology and IT Marketing** (Information Sciences; Information Technology) *Director*: Ernst Kreuzer; **Innovation Management** *Director*: Hans Lercher; **Marketing and Sales** *Director*: Karin Madenberger

History: Founded 1996.

Governing Bodies: Fachhochschulrat

Academic Year: October to June

Admission Requirements: Graduation from high school (Matura)

Fees: (Euros): 363 per semester

Main Language(s) of Instruction: German

Degrees and Diplomas: *Bachelor's Degree*: Automation Technology; Information Technology; Innovation Management (BSc); Business; Marketing and Sales (BA); *Diplom-Ingenieur*: Information Technology; Automation Technology; *Master's Degree*: International Marketing; Sales Management; Innovation Technology (MA); Marketing; Accounting and Controlling;

Student Services: Canteen, Foreign student adviser, Handicapped facilities, Language programs

Student Residential Facilities: None

Special Facilities: None

Libraries: Yes
Last Updated: 16/01/09

CARINTHIA UNIVERSITY OF APPLIED SCIENCES

Fachhochschule Kärnten

Villacher Strasse 1, 9800 Spittal an der Drau, Carinthia
Tel: +43(5) 90500-0
Fax: +43(5) 90500-1110
EMail: international@fh-kaernten.at
Website: http://www.fh-kaernten.at/

Rektor: Dietmar Brodel
Tel: +43(5) 90500-1200, Fax: +43(5) 90500-1210
EMail: d.brodel@fh-kaernten.at

Executive Director: Siegried Spanz
EMail: siegfried.spanz@fh-kaernten.at

International Relations: Aleksandra Jama
EMail: a.jama@fh-kaernten.at

Schools

Civil Engineering and Architecture *(Spittal)* (Architecture; Civil Engineering); **Geoinformation** *(Villach)* (Geography; Geophysics; Surveying and Mapping); **Health and Care** *(Feldkirchen)* (Health Administration); **Management** *(Villach)* (International Business; Management; Public Administration); **Medical Information Technology** *(Klagenfurt)* (Health Administration; Information Technology; Medical Technology); **Social Work** *(Feldkirchen)*; **Systems Engineering** (Electronic Engineering; Engineering Management; Mechanical Engineering); **Telematics and Network Engineering** (Computer Networks; Telecommunications Engineering)

Further Information: Campuses in Spittal, Villach, Klagenfurt and Feldkirchen.

History: Founded 1995. Previously known as Fachhochschule Technikum Kärnten.

Governing Bodies: Supervisory Board

Academic Year: October to September.

Main Language(s) of Instruction: German, English

Accrediting Agencies: Fachhochschule Council

Degrees and Diplomas: *Bachelor's Degree*: Architecture; Civil Engineering; Geoinformation; Healthcare Management; Management; Medical Information Technology; Social Work; Systems Engineering; Mechanical Engineering; Telematics/Network Engineering; *Diplom-Ingenieur*; *Master's Degree*: Architecture; Civil Engineering; Spatial Information Management; Health Management; International Business Management; Public Management; Health Care IT; Social Work; Systems Design; Integrated Systems and Circuits Design; Communications Engineering

Student Services: Academic counselling, Canteen, Foreign student adviser, Handicapped facilities, Language programs, Sports facilities

Student Residential Facilities: On Spittal and Villach campuses.

Special Facilities: Art galleries; laboratories.

Libraries: Yes.

Academic Staff 2009-2010	MEN	WOMEN	TOTAL
FULL-TIME	102	42	**144**
PART-TIME	180	94	**274**
STAFF WITH DOCTORATE			
FULL-TIME	42	21	**63**
PART-TIME	97	29	**126**
Student Numbers 2009-2010			
All (Foreign Included)	784	734	**1,518**
FOREIGN ONLY	118	53	**171**

Part-time students, 473. **Evening students**, 473.
Note: All parttime study takes place in the evening.
Last Updated: 03/11/11

CATHOLIC THEOLOGICAL PRIVATE UNIVERSITY LINZ

Katholisch-Theologische PrivatUniversität Linz

Bethlehemstrasse 20, 4020 Linz, Upper Austria
Tel: +43(732) 7842-93
Fax: +43(732) 7842-934-155
EMail: rektorat@ktu-linz.ac.at
Website: http://www.ktu-linz.ac.at

Rektor: Ewald Volgger
Tel: +43(732) 7842-934-140 EMail: e.volgger@ktu-linz.ac.at

Prorekto: Michael Rosenberger
Tel: +43(732) 7842-934-139 EMail: m.rosenberger@ktu-linz.ac.at

International Relations: Peter Vondrak

Faculties

Arts and Humanities (Arts and Humanities); **Philosophy** (Philosophy); **Theology** (Bible; Canon Law; History of Religion; Pastoral Studies; Philosophy; Religion; Religious Education; Theology)

Further Information: Also 12 Institutes

History: Founded 1672. Acquired present status 2001.

Degrees and Diplomas: *Bachelor's Degree*: Philosophy; Arts and Humanities; *Lizentiat*: Catholic Theology, 4 sem.; *Master's Degree*: Catholic Theology; Religious Education; Philosophy; Arts and Humanities; *Doctor of Philosophy*: Catholic Theology; *Doctor of Philosophy*: Philosophy; Arts and Humanities (Dr.phil.), 4 sem.
Last Updated: 04/11/11

FACHHOCHSCHULE CAMPUS VIENNA - UNIVERSITY OF APPLIED SCIENCES

Fachhochschule Campus Wien

Favoritenstraße 226, 1100 Wien, Vienna
Tel: +43(1) 606-6877-6600
Fax: +43(1) 606-6877-109
EMail: office@fh-campuswien.ac.at
Website: http://www.fh-campuswien.ac.at

Rektor: Arthur Mettinger
Tel: +43(1) 606-6877-1501
EMail: arthur.mettinger@fh-campuswien.ac.at

International Relations: Wolfgang Sünder
EMail: wolfgang.suender@fh-campuswien.ac.at

Programmes

Civil Engineering and Management (Civil Engineering; Management); **Health Science** (Biomedicine; Dietetics; Health Sciences; Midwifery; Nursing; Occupational Health; Physical Therapy; Radiology); **Information Technology and Telecommunications** (Information Technology; Telecommunications Engineering); **Social Work**; **Technical Project and Process Management** (Management)

History: Founded 1999.

Academic Year: October to June

Main Language(s) of Instruction: German

Accrediting Agencies: Fachhochschule Council

Degrees and Diplomas: *Bachelor's Degree*; *Master's Degree*
Last Updated: 26/03/12

FACHHOCHSCHULE KUFSTEIN TIROL - UNIVERSITY OF APPLIED SCIENCES
Fachhochschule Kufstein Tirol
Andreas Hofer Strasse 7, 6330 Kufstein, Tyrol
Tel: +43(5372) 71819
Fax: +43(5372) 71819-104
EMail: info@fh-kufstein.ac.at
Website: http://www.fh-kufstein.ac.at

Rector: Johannes Lüthi

International Relations: Noureddine Rafili
EMail: Noureddine.Rafili@fh-kufstein.ac.at

Programmes
Business Engineer Sciences (Business Administration); **Business Management** (Business Administration); **Corporate Restructuring**; **ERP-Systems and Business Process Management**; **European Energy Business** (Business Administration); **Facility and Real Estate Management** (Real Estate); **International Business Studies** (International Business; Management) *Director:* Sibylle Jakubowicz; **Marketing and Communication Management** (Communication Studies; Management; Marketing); **Real Estate and Facility Management** (Architecture; Building Technologies; Business Administration; Real Estate) *Director:* Julia Jedelhauser; **Sports, Culture and Event Management** (Cultural Studies; Sports Management); **Web-Business and Technology** (Computer Networks; E-Business/Commerce)

History: Founded 1997.

Academic Year: October to June (October-January; February-June)

Admission Requirements: Secondary school certificate (Reifeprüfung)

Fees: (Euros): 363 per semester

Main Language(s) of Instruction: German. English for foreign students

International Co-operation: Also participates in Erasmus student mobolity and teaching staff mobility

Degrees and Diplomas: *Bachelor's Degree*; *Master's Degree*

Student Services: Academic counselling, Employment services, Foreign student adviser, Language programs, Social counselling, Sports facilities

Student Residential Facilities: 125 students

Libraries: c. 7,000 vols, 80 periodical subscriptions
Last Updated: 13/09/11

FACHHOCHSCHULE PROGRAMMES BURGENLAND
Fachhochschul-Studiengänge Burgenland
Campus 1, 7000 Eisenstadt, Burgenland
Tel: +43(5) 9010609-0
Fax: +43(5) 9010609-15
EMail: office@fh-burgenland.at
Website: http://www.fh-burgenland.at

Geschäftsführerin: Ingrid Schwab-Matkovits (2002-)
Tel: +43(5) 9010609-24 EMail: schwab@fh-burgenland.at

Administrative Officer: Dieter Jauschovetz
Tel: +43(2682) 62600-53 EMail: jauschow@fh-eisenstadt.ac.at

International Relations: Lenka Kovarik
Tel: +43(5) 9010601-21 EMail: lenka.kovarik@fh-burgenland.at

Departments
Building Technology and Management *(Pinkafeld)* (Building Technologies; Engineering; Management); **Energy and Environment Management** *(Pinkafeld)* (Economics; Energy Engineering; Engineering; Environmental Management)

Programmes
Information Management (Information Management; Library Science); **International Business Relations**

History: Founded 1994.

Admission Requirements: Secondary school leaving certificate (Matura) and entrance examination

Fees: None

Main Language(s) of Instruction: German, English
International Co-operation: Erasmus, Ceepus, Leonardo

Degrees and Diplomas: *Bachelor's Degree*; *Diplom-Ingenieur:* Building Technology and Management; *Diplom-Ingenieur:* Energy and Environmental Management, 4 yrs; *Master's Degree*; *Master's Degree*: Information Management; International Business Relations

Student Services: Academic counselling, Canteen, Cultural centre, Employment services, Foreign student adviser, Foreign Studies Centre, Handicapped facilities, Language programs, Social counselling, Sports facilities

Student Residential Facilities: Yes

Special Facilities: Laboratories, computer-facilities

Libraries: Main Library
Last Updated: 04/11/11

FH JOANNEUM - UNIVERSITY OF APPLIED SCIENCES
FH Joanneum
Alte Poststrasse 149, 8020 Graz, Styria
Tel: +43(316) 5453-0
Fax: +43(316) 5453-8801
EMail: international@fh-joanneum.at
Website: http://www.fh-joanneum.at

Rektor: Karl P. Pfeiffer
Tel: +43(316) 5453-8860 EMail: karl-peter.pfeiffer@fh-joanneum.at

International Relations: Ingrid Gehrke
EMail: ingrid.gehrke@fh-joanneum.at

Areas
Health Sciences *(Bad Gleichenberg)* (Biomedical Engineering; Business and Commerce; Dietetics; English; Health Administration; Leisure Studies; Midwifery; Nutrition; Occupational Health; Physical Therapy; Radiology; Tourism); **Information, Design and Technologies** (Air Transport; Architectural and Environmental Design; Automotive Engineering; Communication Arts; Computer Engineering; Design; Electronic Engineering; Graphic Design; Industrial Design; Information Management; Information Technology; Production Engineering; Software Engineering; Technology); **International Business** (Banking; Insurance; International Business; Journalism; Public Relations); **Life, Building, Environment** (Architecture; Building Technologies; Construction Engineering; Economics; Energy Engineering; Environmental Engineering; Environmental Studies; Social Welfare)

History: Founded 1995. Formerly known as Fachhochschul-Studiengänge Technikum Joanneum.

Governing Bodies: Board of Trustees, Executive Directors

Academic Year: September to July

Admission Requirements: Secondary school certificate (Reifezeugniss) or foreign equivalent and entrance examination

Fees: (Euros): 363 per semester

Main Language(s) of Instruction: German

International Co-operation: Socrates/Erasmus; Leonardo programmes (Europe, USA, Australia, Asia)

Degrees and Diplomas: *Bachelor's Degree*; *Master's Degree*

Student Services: Academic counselling, Canteen, Foreign student adviser, Handicapped facilities, Language programs

Libraries: Main Library
Last Updated: 04/11/11

FHWIEN UNIVERSITY OF APPLIED SCIENCES
FHWien-Studiengänge der Wirtschaftskammer Wien
Währinger Gürtel 97, 1180 Wien, Vienna
Tel: +43(1) 47677-5744
Fax: +43(1) 47677-5745
EMail: studienzentrum@fh-wien.ac.at
Website: http://www.fh-wien.ac.at

Geschäftsführer: Michael Heritsch
Tel: +43(1) 47677-5705 EMail: michael.heritsch@fh-wien.ac.at

Administrative Officer: Christian Kreuzer
Tel: +43(1) 6066877-0 EMail: christian.kreuzer@fh-first.ac.at

International Relations: Elena Domaschkina
Tel: +43(1) 47677-5751 EMail: elena.domaschkina@fh-wien.ac.at

Programmes
Business Management (Business Administration); **Communications Management** (Communication Studies); **Coorporate Communication** (Communication Studies); **Entrepreneurship - Executive Management** (Business Administration; Management); **Finance, Accounting and Taxation** (Accountancy; Finance); **Financial Management** (Finance); **Financial Management and Controlling** (Finance); **Hospitality and Tourism Management** (Tourism); **Human Resources and Knowledge Management** (Human Resources); **Journalism and Media Management** (Journalism; Media Studies); **Knowledge Management** (Communication Studies; Information Technology); **Marketing and Sales** (Marketing; Sales Techniques); **Real Estate Management** (Real Estate); **Tourism Management** (Tourism)

History: Founded 1996.

Academic Year: September to June

Main Language(s) of Instruction: German

Accrediting Agencies: Fachhochschule Council

Degrees and Diplomas: *Bachelor's Degree*; *Master's Degree*
Last Updated: 14/09/11

IMC UNIVERSITY OF APPLIED SCIENCES KREMS

IMC Fachhochschule Krems (IMC)
Piaristengasse 1, 3500 Krems, Lower Austria
Tel: +43(2732) 802
Fax: +43(2732) 802-4
EMail: office@fh-krems.ac.at
Website: http://www.fh-krems.ac.at/

Rector: Eva Werner EMail: rektorat@fh-krems.ac.at

Administrative Officer: Dagmar Halm Tel: +43(2732) 802-130

International Relations: Maxililian Schachner
Tel: +43(2732) 802-150

Schools
Business (Business Administration; Health Administration; International Business; Management; Marketing; Tourism); **Health** (Health Sciences; Midwifery; Nursing; Physical Therapy); **Life Sciences** (Biological and Life Sciences; Biotechnology; Pharmacology)

History: Founded 1994.

Governing Bodies: Fachhochschulkollegium

Academic Year: September to June

Admission Requirements: Secondary school leaving certificate or equivalent and entrance examination

Fees: (Euros): 365 per semester;

Main Language(s) of Instruction: German and English

Accrediting Agencies: Fachhochschule Council

Degrees and Diplomas: *Bachelor's Degree*; *Master's Degree*

Student Services: Academic counselling, Canteen

Student Residential Facilities: Independent student Residence; Private Accommodation

Libraries: yes
Last Updated: 27/06/11

LAUDER BUSINESS SCHOOL, UNIVERSITY OF APPLIED SCIENCES (LBS-VIC)

Hofzeile 18-20, 1190 Wien, Vienna
Tel: +43(1) 3691818
Fax: +43(1) 3691817
EMail: office@lbs.ac.at
Website: http://www.lbs.ac.at

President: Ronald S. Lauder

Dean: Silvia Kucera Tel: +43(1) 369-1818-777

Programmes
Intercultural Business Administration (Business Administration); **International Marketing and Management** (International Business; Management; Marketing)

Further Information: LBS is an EU-accredited institution of higher learning offering a four-year Master's degree programme in International Marketing and Management in English as the language of instruction. Foreign languages, German as a second language, and Jewish Studies are also offered, as well as electives in various fields (Philosophy, Psychology, Social and Political Sciences, International Relations,Legal Studies, InformationTechnology.). Students take courses in core subjects of Accountancy,Finance, Management and Marketing in the first 4 semesters, and select specialized courses according to interests in the fifth and sixth semester. A semester of practical training (internship) takes place during the 7th semester, and the writing of a Master's thesis in the 8th and final semester.

History: Founded 2003 by former US ambassador to Austria Ronald S. Lauder with the support of the city of Vienna, the Ronald S. Lauder Foundation and other private donors.

Governing Bodies: Managing Board

Academic Year: October to June

Admission Requirements: High school diploma with university entrance; TOEFL test, placement test and interview, ability to contribute to and benefit from programme (Bachelor's degree not required although advanced standing of up to 2 years may be granted).

Fees: (Euros): 15,000 per annum (tuition and board)

Main Language(s) of Instruction: English

International Co-operation: With universities in Israel, EU, USA.

Accrediting Agencies: Ministry of Education, Science and Culture; Fachhochschulrat

Degrees and Diplomas: *Bachelor's Degree*; *Master's Degree*: International Marketing and Management (MA, MS, Mag (FH)), 4 yrs (8 semesters)

Student Services: Academic counselling, Canteen, Employment services, Foreign student adviser, Language programs, Social counselling

Student Residential Facilities: On-campus dormitory

Libraries: Department library of International Marketing and Management, special holdings in Jewish Studies.
Last Updated: 04/11/11

MANAGEMENT CENTER INNSBRUCK (MCI)

Universitätsstrasse 15, 6020 Innsbruck, Tyrol
Tel: +43(512) 2070-0
Fax: +43(512) 2070-1099
EMail: office@mci.edu
Website: http://www.mci.edu

Geschäftsführer: Andreas Altmann (1996-)
Tel: +43(512) 2070-1050, Fax: +43(512) 2070-1099
EMail: andreas.altmann@mci.edu

Leiter Organisation and Infrastruktur: Tommy Mayr
EMail: tommy.mayr@mci.edu

International Relations: Susanne Lichtmannegger
Tel: +43(512) 2070-1610, Fax: +43(512) 2070-1699
EMail: international@mci.edu; susanne.lichtmannegger@mci.edu

Programmes
Biotechnology *(Full-Time)* (Biotechnology) *Head*: Gerard Hillmer; **Business and Management** *(Part-time)* (Business Administration; Economics; Management) *Head*: Bernd Kirschner; **Engineering and Environmental Management** *(Part-time and Full-time)* (Electronic Engineering; Mechanical Engineering) *Head*: Andreas Mehle; **Engineering and Environmental Management** *(Part-time and Full-time)* (Chemical Engineering; Chemistry; Electrical and Electronic Engineering; Engineering; Engineering Management; Environmental Management; Mathematics; Physics) *Head*: Max Mühlhäuser; **General Management Executive MBA** (Business Administration; Business and Commerce; Economics; Finance; Human Resources; International Studies; Management; Marketing) *Head*: Susanne Herzog; **Management and Applied Informatics** *(Full-time)* (Artificial Intelligence; Business Administration; Computer Science; Information Sciences; Management) *Head*: Peter Mirski; **Management and Law** *(Full-time)* (Business Administration; European Union Law; International Business; International Law; Labour Law; Law; Management; Private Law; Public Law) *Head*: Ralf Geymayer; **Non Profit, Social and Health Care Management**

(Full-time) (Business Administration; Economics; Health Administration; Law; Political Sciences; Social Studies) *Head*: Siegfried Walch; **Social Work** *(Full-time)* (Social Work) *Head*: Michael Klassen; **Tourism and Leisure** *(Full-time)* (Business Administration; Hotel and Restaurant; Leadership; Leisure Studies; Management; Tourism) *Head*: Hubert Siller

Further Information: Also Summer Schools and non degree programmes

History: Founded 1996 by the Business Faculty of the University of Innsbruck and other partners, acquired present status 1997.

Governing Bodies: General Assembly, Administrative Board, Academic Board

Academic Year: September to July

Admission Requirements: High school certificate or equivalent and/or relevant professional qualification; Selection process (written exam, interview)

Fees: (Euros): 363 per semester

Main Language(s) of Instruction: German, English

International Co-operation: With 80 universities in Europe; USA; Canada; Asia and Australia

Accrediting Agencies: Austrian Ministry of Education, Science and Culture; Austrian Accrediting Board for University of Applied Sciences

Degrees and Diplomas: *Bachelor's Degree*: 3 yrs; *Master's Degree (MAS)*

Student Services: Academic counselling, Canteen, Foreign student adviser, Foreign Studies Centre, Language programs, Social counselling, Sports facilities

Student Residential Facilities: Yes

Special Facilities: Computer facilities. Engineering laboratories

Libraries: Library of the Social Sciences Faculty

Last Updated: 23/05/11

MODUL UNIVERSITY

Am Kahlenberg 1, Josefsdorf 2, 1190 Wien, Vienna
Tel: +43(1) 3203555-101 +43(1) 47670-257
Fax: +43(1) 3203555-901 +43(1) 47670-258
EMail: office@modul.ac.at
Website: http://www.modul.ac.at/

President: Karl Wöber
Tel: +43(1) 3203555-300, Fax: +43(1) 3203555-903
EMail: karl.woeber@modul.ac.at

Managing Director: Michael Heritsch
EMail: michael.heritsch@modul.ac.at

Vice-President: Arno Scharl
Tel: +43(1) 3203555-500, Fax: +43(1) 3203555-903
EMail: arno.scharl@modul.ac.at

Departments
New Media Technology (Mass Communication; Media Studies); **Public Governance** (Government; Management); **Tourism and Hospitality Management** (Tourism)

History: Founded 2007.

Degrees and Diplomas: *Bachelor's Degree*: Tourism and Hospitality Management (BBA); *Master's Degree*
Last Updated: 04/11/11

NEW DESIGN UNIVERSITY

Privatuniversität der Kreativwirtschaft (NDU)
Mariazeller Strasse 97, 3100 St. Pölten, Lower Austria
Tel: +43(2742) 890-2412
Fax: +43(2742) 890-2413
EMail: office@ndu.ac.at
Website: http://www.ndu.ac.at

Rektor: Stephan Schmidt-Wulffen EMail: rektor@ndu.ac.at

Prorektor: Johannes Zederbauer
EMail: johannes.zederbauer@ndu.ac.at

Programmes
Architecture (Architecture); **Design** (Design); **Events Engineering**; **Graphic Arts** (Graphic Arts)

Degrees and Diplomas: *Bachelor's Degree*; *Master's Degree*
Last Updated: 04/11/11

PARACELSUS PRIVATE MEDICAL UNIVERSITY

Paracelsus Medizinische Privatuniversität
Strubergasse 21, 5020 Salzburg, Salzburg
Tel: +43(662) 442002-0
Fax: +43(662) 442002-1209
EMail: pmu@pmu.ac.at
Website: http://www.pmu.ac.at

Rektor: Herbert Resch

Dean of Student Affairs: Rosemarie Forstner
EMail: rosemarie.forstner@pmu.ac.at

Vizerektor: Felix Sedlmayer

Programmes
Medicine (Medicine)

History: Founded 2002. Formerly known as Private Medizinische Universität Salzburg.

Governing Bodies: Stiftungsrat

Academic Year: October to June

Main Language(s) of Instruction: German

Degrees and Diplomas: *Doctor of Philosophy*: Medicine; *Doctor of Philosophy*: Molecular Medicine (Ph.D.), 6 sem.
Last Updated: 04/11/11

PEF PRIVATE UNIVERSITY FOR MANAGEMENT VIENNA

PEF Privatuniversität für Management Wien (PEF)
Brahmsplatz 3, 1040 Wien, Vienna
Tel: +43(1) 534 39-0
Fax: +43(1) 534 39-80
EMail: pef@pef.co.at
Website: http://www.pef.at

Academic Director: Karl Zehetner (2004-)

Chief Executive Officer: Stefan Mackowski

Departments
Business Administration (Accountancy; Business Administration; Finance); **Coaching**; **Construction Management** (Building Technologies); **Leadership, Human Resources and International Management** (Human Resources; Leadership; Management); **Organization** (Management); **Strategy**

History: Founded 2002.

Governing Bodies: Kollegium

Academic Year: October to June

Main Language(s) of Instruction: German, English

Degrees and Diplomas: *Master's Degree*: Human Resources Management and Organizational Development; Business Administration Intra- and Entrepreneurship; Construction Management, 3 sem.

PRIVATE UNIVERSITY FOR HEALTH SCIENCES, MEDICAL INFORMATICS AND TECHNIQUES

Private Universität für Gesundheitswissenschaften, Medizinische Informatik und Technik (UMIT)
Eduard Wallnöfer-Zentrum I, 6060 Hall, Tyrol
Tel: +43(50) 8648-0
Fax: +43(50) 8648-3850
EMail: service@umit.at
Website: http://www.umit.at

Rektor: Christa Them

Administrative Officer: Markus Schwab

Institutes
Behavioural Medicine and Prevention (Medicine; Social and Preventive Medicine); **Biomedical Engineering** (Biomedical Engineering); **Biomedical Image Engineering** (Biomedical Engineering); **Computer Systems and Networks**; **Health Information Systems**; **Information Systems**; **Leisure, Travel and Alpine**

Medicine (Leisure Studies); **Management and Health Economics** (Health Administration; Management); **Medical Law, Human Resources and Health Politics** (Forensic Medicine and Dentistry; Health Administration; Health Sciences; Human Resources); **Nursing** (Nursing); **Public Health, Medical Decision Making and HTA** (Medicine; Public Health)

Units

Communication and Behavioural Sciences; **Information and Software Engineering** (Information Technology; Software Engineering); **Medical Basics and Nutrition** (Medicine; Nutrition); **Quality Science, Medical Planning and Medical Information** (Health Sciences; Medicine)

History: Founded 2001. Formerly known as Private Universität für Medizinische Informatik und Technik Tirol.

Governing Bodies: Hochschulrat, Senat

Academic Year: October to June

Main Language(s) of Instruction: German

Degrees and Diplomas: *Bachelor's Degree*; *Master's Degree*; *Doctor of Philosophy*: Public Health; Health Care Management; Biomedical Informatics; Medical Informatics; Nursing
Last Updated: 31/05/11

SALZBURG UNIVERSITY OF APPLIED SCIENCES AND TECHNOLOGIES

Fachhochschule Salzburg
Urstein Süd 1, 5020 Puch, Salzburg
Tel: +43(50) 2211-0
Fax: +43(50) 2211-1099
EMail: office@fh-sbg.ac.at
Website: http://www.fh-salzburg.ac.at

Rektor: Erhard Busek
Tel: +43(50) 2211-1011, Fax: +43(50) 2211-1019
EMail: rektorat@fh-salzburg.ac.at

Vizerektor: Gerhard Jöchtl

International Relations: Laura Streitbürger
EMail: laura.streitbuerger@fh-salzburg.ac.at

Programmes

Business and Information Management (Business Administration; Information Management); **Business Development in Tourism** (Management; Tourism); **Construction and Design with Wood** (Construction Engineering; Design; Wood Technology); **Design and Product Management** (Industrial Design; Industrial Management); **Digital Television** (Radio and Television Broadcasting; Telecommunications Engineering); **Forest Products Technology and Management** (Wood Technology); **Information Technology and Systems Management** (Information Management; Information Technology); **Multimedia Art-Creation and Production** (Multimedia); **Social Work** (Social Work)

History: Founded 1996. Incorporated Holztechnikum Kuchl as a branch 2003.

Academic Year: October to June

Fees: (Euros): 363 per semester

Main Language(s) of Instruction: German

International Co-operation: With universities in Belgium, Germany, Finland, France, Ireland, Italy, Norway, Portugal, Sweden, Switzerland, Spain, United Kingdom, Czech Republic, USA, Brazil.

Degrees and Diplomas: *Bachelor's Degree*; *Master's Degree*

Student Services: Academic counselling, Canteen, Employment services, Foreign student adviser, Foreign Studies Centre, Health services, Language programs, Social counselling, Sports facilities
Last Updated: 04/11/11

KUCHL POLYTECHNIC

HOLZTECHNIKUM KUCHL

Markt 136a, 5431 Kuchl, Salzburg
Tel: +43(6244) 5372
Fax: +43(6244) 5372- 2
EMail: office@holztechnikum.at
Website: http://www.holztechnikum.at/

Geschäftsführer: Erhard Bojanovsky
EMail: erhard.bojanovsky@holztechnikum.at

Programmes

Design and Product Management (Design; Management) *Director*: Günther Grall; **Forest Products Technology and Management** *Director*: Reinhard Lackner; **Wood Constructions and Design** (Architectural Restoration; Structural Architecture) *Director*: Gudrun Matzpora

History: Founded 1995. Became a branch of FH Salzburg Fachhochschulgesellschaft GmbH 2003.

Academic Year: October to June

Main Language(s) of Instruction: German

International Co-operation: With universities in Sweden

Accrediting Agencies: Austrian Ministry of Education and Science

Degrees and Diplomas: *Diplom-Ingenieur*; *Master's Degree*

Student Services: Academic counselling, Canteen, Employment services, Foreign student adviser, Foreign Studies Centre, Handicapped facilities, Language programs, Social counselling

SCHOOL OF PHILOSOPHY AND THEOLOGY OF THE DIOCESE OF ST. PÖLTEN

Philosophisch-Theologische Hochschule der Diözese St. Pölten
Wiener Strasse 38, 3100 St. Pölten, Lower Austria
Tel: +43(2742) 3527-9221
Fax: +43(2742) 3527-9228
EMail: sekretariat@pth-stpoelten.at
Website: http://www.pth-stpoelten.at/

Rektor: Josef Kreiml
Tel: +43(2742) 3527-9222 EMail: rektorat@pth-stpoelten.at

Prorektor: Reinhard Knittel
Tel: +43(2742) 3527-9221 EMail: r.knittel@kirche.at

Programmes
Philosophy (Philosophy); **Theology** (Theology)
History: Founded 1791.
Academic Year: October to June
Main Language(s) of Instruction: German
Degrees and Diplomas: *Bachelor's Degree*; *Master's Degree*
Last Updated: 04/11/11

SIGMUND FREUD PRIVATE UNIVERSITY VIENNA

Sigmund Freud Privatuniversität Wien
Schnirchgasse 9a, 1030 Wien, Vienna
Tel: +43(1) 798-4098
Fax: +43(1) 798-4098/20
EMail: office@sfu.ac.at
Website: http://sfu.ac.at/

Rektor: Alfred Pritz EMail: alfred.pritz@sfu.ac.at
Vizerektorin: Jutta Fiegl EMail: jutta.fiegl@sfu.ac.at

Departments
Child and Adolescent Psychotherapy (Psychotherapy); **Comparative Asset Psychology** (Psychology); **Neuroscientific Principles of Psychotherapy** (Neurosciences; Psychotherapy); **Psychotherapy in the Health Care System** (Health Sciences; Psychotherapy); **Schools of Psychotherapy** (Psychotherapy); **Transcultural and Historical Research in Psychotherapy**

Further Information: Also University Outpatient Clinic

History: Acquired present status 2005.

Degrees and Diplomas: *Bachelor's Degree*; *Master's Degree*
Last Updated: 04/11/11

ST. PÖLTEN UNIVERSITY OF APPLIED SCIENCES
Fachhochschule St Pölten
Matthias Corvinus-Strasse 15, 3100 St. Pölten, Lower Austria
Tel: +43(2742) 313-228
Fax: +43(2742) 313-229
EMail: international@fhstp.ac.at
Website: http://www.fhstp.ac.at/index

Rector: Barbara Schmid

Executive Director: Gabriela Fernandes

Executive Director: Gernot Kohl

International Relations: Barbara Zimmer
Tel: +43(2742) 313-228-261 EMail: barbara.zimmer@fhstp.ac.at

Programmes
Business (Management; Media Studies); **Health and Social Sciences** (Dietetics; Physical Therapy; Social Work); **Technology** (Media Studies; Railway Engineering; Telecommunications Engineering)

History: Founded 1996.

Academic Year: September to June (September-February; February-June)

Admission Requirements: Secondary school certificate (Matura or Studienberechtingungsprüfung)

Main Language(s) of Instruction: German

International Co-operation: With universities in 12 European countries. Also articipates in Socrates/Erasmus

Degrees and Diplomas: *Bachelor's Degree*; *Master's Degree*

Student Services: Academic counselling, Foreign student adviser, Handicapped facilities, Language programs

Special Facilities: Computer Rooms, Audio Laboratory, Video Laboratory, Radio Studio, Network Laboratory

Libraries: Yes
Last Updated: 04/11/11

TCM PRIVATE UNIVERSITY
TCM Privatuniversität
Halirschgasse 16, 1170 Wien, Vienna
Tel: +43(1) 6416738
Fax: +43(1) 6416728

Rektor: Andreas Bayer EMail: rektor@tcm-university.edu

Dekan: Liang Zhi EMail: dekan@tcm-university.edu

Programmes
Traditional Chinese Medicine (Acupuncture; Pharmacology; Traditional Eastern Medicine)

Further Information: Campuses in Munich, Berlin (Germany); Amposta, Barcelona, Valencia, Madrid (Spain)

Degrees and Diplomas: *Bachelor's Degree*: Acupuncture; Chinese Pharmacology; Tuina; Chinese Manual Therapy, 6 sem.; *Master's Degree*: Acupuncture; Chinese Pharmacology; Tuina; Chinese Manual Therapy, 8 sem.; *Master's Degree*: Traditional Chinese Medicine, 12 sem.

UNIVERSITY OF APPLIED SCIENCES - BFI VIENNA
Fachhochschule des bfi Wien (FH BFI WIEN)
Wohlmutstrasse 22, 1020 Wien, Vienna
Tel: +43(1) 7201286-0
Fax: +43(1) 7201286-19
EMail: info@fh-vie.ac.at
Website: http://www.fh-vie.ac.at

Managing Director: Helmut Holzinger (1998-)
Tel: +43(1) 7201286 EMail: helmut.holzinger@fh-vie.ac.at

International Relations: Elisabeth Brunnert
Tel: +43(1) 7201286-956 EMail: elisabeth.brunner@fh-vie.ac.at

Graduate Schools
Risk Management (Management)

Programmes
Banking and Finance Studies *(Full time and career-parallel studies)* (Banking; Finance); **European Economy and Business Management Studies** *(career-parallel studies)* (Business Administration; Economics; European Studies; Management); **Film, TV and Media Production** (Film; Media Studies); **Logistics and Transport Management** *(Full time studies)* (Transport Management); **Project Management and Information Technology** *(Full-time and parallel studies)* (Information Technology; Management)

History: Founded 1996, acquired present status 2002.

Governing Bodies: Fachhochschulkollegium

Academic Year: October to June

Admission Requirements: Secondary school leaving certificate or university entrance qualification

Fees: (Euros): 363 per semester

Main Language(s) of Instruction: German, English

International Co-operation: With universities in Belgium, France, Germany, Poland, Romania, Spain; Netherlands; Australia; Finland; United Kingdom; Czech Republic; Hungary; Norway; India

Accrediting Agencies: Fachhochschule Council Vienna (Fachhochschulrat Wien)

Degrees and Diplomas: *Bachelor's Degree*; *Master's Degree*

Student Services: Academic counselling, Canteen, Foreign student adviser, Handicapped facilities, Language programs, Social counselling

Libraries: Free internet access

Publications: Research Magazine *(biennially)*
Last Updated: 03/11/11

UNIVERSITY OF APPLIED SCIENCES TECHNIKUM VIENNA
Fachhochschule Technikum Wien
Höchstädtplatz 5, 1200 Wien, Vienna
Tel: +43(1) 333 4077-0
Fax: +43(1) 58839-49
EMail: info@technikum-wien.at
Website: http://www.technikum-wien.at

Rector: Fritz Schmöllebeck
EMail: nicole.sagmeister@technikum-wien.at

Vice-Rector: Christian Kollmitzer

Departments
Applied Mathematics and Science (Applied Mathematics; Natural Sciences); **Biochemical Engineering** (Biochemistry; Engineering); **Biomedical Engineering** (Biomedical Engineering); **Computer Science** (Computer Science); **Electronic Engineering** (Electronic Engineering); **Embedded Systems**; **Humanities** (Arts and Humanities; Cultural Studies; Modern Languages); **Information Engineering and Security** (Information Technology); **Information Systems Management** (Information Technology); **Management, Business and Law** (Business Administration; Law; Management); **Mechatronics** (Electronic Engineering; Mechanical Engineering; Robotics); **Renewable Energy** (Energy Engineering); **Social Competence and Management Methods** (Management)

History: Founded 1994.

Admission Requirements: Secondary school certificate (Allgemeine Hochschulreife)

Main Language(s) of Instruction: German

International Co-operation: With universities in Denmark, Finland, Sweden, United Kingdom.

Accrediting Agencies: Fachhochschule Council

Degrees and Diplomas: *Bachelor's Degree*; *Master's Degree*

Student Services: Academic counselling, Employment services, Foreign student adviser, Foreign Studies Centre, Handicapped facilities, Language programs, Social counselling

Libraries: Technical Library

Student Numbers *2010-2011*: Total: c. 2,700
Last Updated: 04/11/11

UNIVERSITY OF APPLIED SCIENCES WIENER NEUSTADT

Fachhochschule Wiener Neustadt
Johannes-Gutenberg-Strasse 3, 2700 Wiener Neustadt,
Lower Austria
Tel: +43(2622) 89084-0
Fax: +43(2622) 89084-99
EMail: international@fhwn.ac.at
Website: http://www.fhwn.ac.at

Rektor: Ferry Stocker

CEO: Gerhard Pramhas

CEO: Susanne Scharnhorst

Faculties
Business (Business Administration; Business and Commerce; Marketing); **Engineering** (Biotechnology; Business and Commerce; Electronic Engineering; Engineering; Information Technology; Microelectronics); **Health Studies** (Health Sciences)

History: Founded 1994.

Governing Bodies: Council

Academic Year: September to June (September-January; February- June)

Admission Requirements: Secondary school certificate (Matura)

Fees: (Euros): 363 per semester

Main Language(s) of Instruction: German; English

International Co-operation: With c. 55 universities in Denmark; Finland; France; Hungary; Netherlands; New Zealand; Poland; United Kingdom and USA

Degrees and Diplomas: *Bachelor's Degree*; *Master's Degree*

Student Services: Academic counselling, Canteen, Employment services, Foreign student adviser, Foreign Studies Centre, Handicapped facilities, Language programs, Social counselling

Student Residential Facilities: Yes
Last Updated: 04/11/11

UPPER AUSTRIA UNIVERSITY OF APPLIED SCIENCES

Fachhochschul-Studiengänge Oberösterreich
Franz-Fritsch Strasse 11/3, 4600 Wels, Upper Austria
Tel: +43(7242) 44808-0
Fax: +43(7242) 44808-77
EMail: info@fh-ooe.at
Website: http://www.fh-ooe.at

Geschäftführer: Gerald Reisinger
Tel: +43(7242) 44808-30, Fax: +43(7242) 44808-77

Executive Director of Studies: Regina Aichinger

Programmes
Automation Engineering *(Wels Campus)* (Automation and Control Engineering); **Bio- and Environmental Technology** *(Wels Campus)* (Biotechnology; Environmental Engineering); **Bioinformatics** *(Undergraduate, Hagenberg Campus)* (Biology; Computer Science); **Communication and Knowledge Media** *(Undergraduate, Hagenberg Campus)* (Communication Studies; Computer Science; Engineering; Media Studies); **Computer and Media Security** *(Undergraduate, Hagenberg Campus)* (Computer Science; Media Studies); **Digital Media** *(Graduate, Hagenberg Campus)* (Computer Science; Design; Media Studies); **E-Business** *(Steyr Campus)* (Computer Science; Management); **Eco-Energy Engineering** *(Wels Campus)* (Energy Engineering; Environmental Studies); **Hardware/Software Co-Engineering** *(Undergraduate, Hagenberg Campus)*; **Human Services for Individuals with Special Needs** *(Linz Campus)* (Social and Community Services); **Human Services Management** *(Linz Campus)*; **Information Engineering and Management** *(Graduate, part-time; Hagenberg Campus)* (Computer Science; Software Engineering); **Innovation and Product Management** *(Wels Campus)* (Engineering; Industrial and Production Economics; Management); **Materials and Process Engineering** *(Wels Campus)* (Materials Engineering; Metallurgical Engineering; Polymer and Plastics Technology); **Mechanical Engineering** *(Wels Campus)* (Mechanical Engineering); **Mechatronics and Management** *(Wels Campus)* (Electronic Engineering; Management); **Media Technology and Design** *(Undergraduate, Hagenberg Campus)* (Computer Science; Design; Media Studies); **Medical Device Technology** *(Linz Campus)*; **Mobile Computing** *(Undergraduate, Hagenberg Campus)* (Computer Science); **Mobile Computing** *(Graduate, Hagenberg Campus)*; **Public Administration** *(Linz Campus)* (Public Administration); **Secure Information Systems** *(Graduate, Hagenberg Campus)*; **Social Work** *(Linz Campus)* (Criminal Law; Social Welfare; Social Work; Welfare and Protective Services); **Software Engineering** *(Undergraduate, Hagenberg Campus)* (Software Engineering); **Software Engineering** *(Graduate, Hagenberg Campus)*

Further Information: Also campuses in Hagenberg, Steyr and Lynz

History: Founded 1994.

Academic Year: October to June

Main Language(s) of Instruction: German

Degrees and Diplomas: *Bachelor's Degree*; *Master's Degree*
Last Updated: 03/11/11

VIENNA CONSERVATOIRE PRIVATE UNIVERSITY

Konservatorium Wien Privatuniversität
Johannesgasse 4a, 1010 Wien, Vienna
Tel: +43(1) 5127747-55
Fax: +43(1) 5127747-99
EMail: studieninfo@konswien.at
Website: http://www.konservatorium-wien.ac.at/

Kaufmännischer Leiter: Gottfried Eisl EMail: g.eisl@konswien.at

Künstlerischer Leiter: Ranko Markovic
EMail: r.markovic@konswien.at

International Relations: Peter Königseder
Tel: +43(1) 512 77 47-89364
EMail: p.koenigseder@konswien.ac.at

Programmes
Music (Conducting; Dance; Jazz and Popular Music; Music; Music Education; Musical Instruments; Opera); **Theatre** (Theatre)

Fees: (Euros): 220 per semester; 250 for non-resident students

Degrees and Diplomas: *Bachelor's Degree*; *Master's Degree*
Last Updated: 04/11/11

VORARLBERG UNIVERSITY OF APPLIED SCIENCES

Fachhochschule Vorarlberg
Hochschulstrasse 1, 6850 Dornbirn, Vorarlberg
Tel: +43(5572) 792
Fax: +43(5572) 792-9500
EMail: rektorat@fhv.at
Website: http://www.fhv.at

Rektor: Rudi Feurstein (2005-)
Tel: +43(5572) 792-1001 EMail: rudi.feurstein@fhv.at

Executive Director: Vaheh Khachatouri
Tel: +43(5572) 792-2000 EMail: vaheh.khachatouri@fhv.at

International Relations: Natasha Doshi
Tel: +43(5572) 792-1009 EMail: international@fhv.at

Departments
Computer Science (Computer Science; Information Technology; Mathematics); **Engineering** (Automation and Control Engineering; Electronic Engineering; Mechanical Engineering; Robotics); **Management and Business Administration** (Business Administration; Management); **Mediabased Communication** (Communication Studies; Design; Media Studies; Visual Arts)

Programmes
Social Sciences and Organization Studies (Social Sciences; Social Work)

History: Founded 1994.

Governing Bodies: Fachhochschulkollegium, Studiengangsleiter

Academic Year: October to June

Admission Requirements: Secondary school certificate and entrance examination

Fees: (Euros): 720 per annum

Main Language(s) of Instruction: German, English

International Co-operation: Erasmus and Leonardo programmes with 100 partners in 30 countries

Accrediting Agencies: Fachhochschulrat, Vienna

Degrees and Diplomas: *Bachelor's Degree*; *Master's Degree*. Also degrees in Professional Training courses

Student Services: Academic counselling, Canteen, Employment services, Foreign student adviser, Handicapped facilities, Sports facilities

Student Residential Facilities: Yes. Student Dormitory or private accommodation.

Special Facilities: TV and radio studios. Multimedia laboratory

Libraries: Yes

Last Updated: 04/11/11

WEBSTER UNIVERSITY VIENNA
Webster University Wien
Berchtoldgasse 1, 1220 Wien, Vienna
Tel: +43(1) 269-9293-0
Fax: +43(1) 269-9293-13
EMail: info@webster.ac.at
Website: http://www.webster.ac.at

Director: Arthur Hirsh (2001-)

Administrative Officer: Olivier Schindler

International Relations: Samuel R. Schubert

Areas
Art and Visual Culture (Art History; Visual Arts); **Business and Management** (Business Administration; Management); **International Relations** (International Relations); **Media Communications** (Communication Studies; Media Studies); **Psychology** (Psychology)

History: Founded 1981.

Governing Bodies: Advisory Board

Academic Year: May to May

Main Language(s) of Instruction: English

International Co-operation: With Webster University campuses in China; United Kingdom; Netherlands; Thailand; Switzerland and USA

Accrediting Agencies: Higher Learning Commission (HLC); Commission on Institutions of Higher Education (USA); Austrian Federal Ministry for Education, Science and Culture; FIBAA (Foundation for International Business Administration Accreditation)

Degrees and Diplomas: *Bachelor's Degree*: Fine Arts; International Relations; Management; Media Communications; Psychology; Business Administration; Computer Science (BA; BS), 3-4 yrs; *Master's Degree*: Finance; Human Resources Management; International Business; International Relations; Marketing (MBA); Finance; Human Resources Management; International Business; International Relations; Marketing (MA; MS), 1 1/2-2 1/2 yrs

Student Services: Academic counselling, Canteen, Cultural centre, Employment services, Foreign student adviser, Language programs, Social counselling

Student Residential Facilities: off campus rooms in student dorms

Special Facilities: Art Gallery, 4 computer labs (including media lab)

Libraries: 6,000 vols

Last Updated: 04/11/11

Azerbaijan

STRUCTURE OF HIGHER EDUCATION SYSTEM

Description:

Higher education is governed by the Cabinet of Ministers and the Ministry of Education. The higher education system consists of state or private institutions. Azerbaijan joined to the Bologna process in 2005, and it defined contours of the reforms carried out in the higher education field.

Stages of studies:

University level first stage: Bakalavr
This stage lasts for three to four years and leads to the Bachelor's degree (Bakalavr).

University level second stage: Magistr
During the second stage, which lasts between one-and-a-half and two years and leads to the Master's degree (Magistr), students acquire in-depth knowledge and professional training.

University level third stage: Doktor
The best graduates of the Master stage are admitted to the doctoral stage. After successful completion of their studies (two or three years), they obtain the Doctoral degree (Ph.D).

ADMISSION TO HIGHER EDUCATION

Admission to university-level studies:

Name of secondary school credential required: Certificate of General Education

For entry to: All higher education institutions

Entrance exam requirements: Students must sit for a National Entrance examination

Foreign students admission:

Entrance exam requirements: For admission to higher education institutions, foreign students must submit a document proving they have completed secondary education.

Entry regulations: Visas are not required for students from Turkey and CIS (the Commonwealth of Independent States) countries.

Health requirements: Foreign students must submit a health certificate.

Language requirements: One-year preparatory language courses are organized for those students who have no knowledge of one of the three languages of instruction (Azerbaijani, Russian or English).

NATIONAL BODIES

Ministry of Education
Minister: Misir Mardanov
Khatai av. 49
Baku 370008
Tel: +994(12) 496 3292
EMail: office@edu.gov.az
WWW: http://www.edu.gov.az

Data for academic year: 2011-2012
Source: IAU from the website of the Ministry of Education, 2011

INSTITUTIONS

PUBLIC INSTITUTIONS

AZERBAIJAN MEDICAL UNIVERSITY

Azjarbajžan Tibb Universiteti (ATU)
ul. Bakihanov 23, Baku AZ 1022
Tel: +994(12) 495-35-66
Fax: +994(12) 495-38-70
EMail: rektor@amu.edu.az
Website: http://www.amu.edu.az

Rector: Ahliman Amiraslanov (1992-)
Tel: +994(12) 95-43-13, Fax: +994(12) 95-38-14
EMail: medic@baku-az.net

International Relations: Mamed Nasirov, Vice-Rector
EMail: m_nasirov @rambler.ru

Faculties
Dentistry (Dental Hygiene; Dentistry); **General Medicine I** (Medicine); **General Medicine II** (Medicine); **Military Medicine** (Medicine); **Paediatrics** (Medicine; Paediatrics); **Pharmacy** (Pharmacology; Pharmacy); **Prophylactic Medicine and Biology** (Biology; Hygiene; Social and Preventive Medicine)

History: Founded 1919 as Medical Faculty of Azerbaijan State University. Reorganized 1930 as Azerbaijan Medical Institute, an independent institution. Named after Nariman Narimanov 1957, and acquired present status and title 1991.

Governing Bodies: Scientific Council

Academic Year: September to May (September-January; February-May)

Admission Requirements: General or special secondary school certificate (Attestat) and Competitive entrance examination

Main Language(s) of Instruction: Azeri, Russian

Accrediting Agencies: Ministry of Education

Degrees and Diplomas: *Bakalavr:* Pharmacy, 4 1/2 yrs; *Magistr:* Dentistry; Prophylactic Medicine; Biology, 5 yrs; *Magistr:* Medicine; Paediatrics, 6 yrs

Student Services: Academic counselling, Canteen, Cultural centre, Employment services, Foreign student adviser, Foreign Studies Centre, Handicapped facilities, Health services, Language programs, Social counselling, Sports facilities

Special Facilities: Museum of Anatomy, Topchibashev Biographical Museum, Museum of History of Medicine

Libraries: Central Library. c. 600,000 vols

Publications: Saglamlig, Journal *(quarterly)*

Press or Publishing House: University Press

Academic Staff 2007-2008	TOTAL
FULL-TIME	2,000

Student Numbers 2007-2008	
All (Foreign Included)	6,226
FOREIGN ONLY	502

Last Updated: 07/11/11

AZERBAIJAN STATE ACADEMY FOR PHYSICAL TRAINING AND SPORTS

ul. Fatali Khan Khoyski 98, Baku 370072
Tel: +994(12) 64-09-05 +994(12) 64-08-19
Fax: +994(12) 93-86-17
EMail: agacanbox@mail.ru

President: Agadjan Abiyev Tel: +994(12) 64-11-62
Vice-President: Dilgam Quliyev Tel: +994(12) 64-10-31

Programmes
Physical Education and Sports (Physical Education; Sports)

History: Founded 1930 as Azerbaijan State Institute of Physical Culture, acquired present status and title 2000.

Main Language(s) of Instruction: Azeri, Russian
Last Updated: 07/11/11

AZERBAIJAN STATE AGRICULTURAL UNIVERSITY (ASAU)

Ataturk avenue 262, Gandja AZ2000
Tel: +994(22) 56-57-33
Fax: +994(22) 56-24-08
EMail: info@adau.edu.az

Rector: Mirdamat Sadigov (2008-)

Faculties
Agricultural Economics (Agricultural Economics; Agriculture); **Agricultural Technology** (Agrobiology; Food Technology; Landscape Architecture; Plant and Crop Protection; Soil Science); **Agronomy** (Agronomy); **Engineering** (Automation and Control Engineering; Electrical Engineering); **Veterinary Medicine and Pharmacy** (Pharmacy; Veterinary Science)

History: Founded 1929 as Azerbaijan Agricultural Academy. Acquired present status and title 2009.

Degrees and Diplomas: *Bakalavr, Magistr, Doktor*

Academic Staff *2010-2011*: Total 445
Student Numbers *2010-2011*: Total 3,200
Last Updated: 08/11/11

AZERBAIJAN STATE ECONOMIC UNIVERSITY

Azjarbajžan Dövljat Iqtisad Universiteti (ASEU)
6 Istiglaliyat st., Baku AZ1001
Tel: +994(12) 492-60-43
Fax: +994(12) 492-59-40
EMail: irit@aseu.az
Website: http://www.aseu.az

Rector: Shamsaddin Hajiyev (2004-)
Tel: +994(12) 492-60-43 EMail: rektor@aseu.az

Vice-Rector: Miranvar Mahmudov
Tel: +994(12) 492-97-27, Fax: +994(12) 492-64-28

International Relations: Rufat Kasumov
Tel: +994(12) 492-64-41, Fax: +994(12) 492-64-41
EMail: rufkm@hotmail.com

Departments
International Relations and Information Technologies (Information Technology; International Relations)

Faculties
Accountancy (Accountancy; Statistics); **Business Administration** (Business Administration); **Commerce** (Business and Commerce; International Business; International Economics; International Relations; Marketing); **Credit**; **Finance** (Finance); **Industry and Services Production** (Industrial and Production Economics); **Informatics and Management** (Business Administration; Computer Science; Management); **International Economic Relations** (Economics; International Economics; Marketing); **Merchandising**; **Preliminary Courses**; **Regulation of Economy** (Economics); **Technology and Design** (Design; Technology); **Turkish World** (International Economics; International Relations)

Further Information: Branch in Derbent, Daghestan Republic

History: Founded 1930. Acquired present status and title 2008.

Governing Bodies: Ministry of Education

Academic Year: September to June

Admission Requirements: Secondary school certificate (Attestat); SSAC (State Student Admission Commission) test results

Main Language(s) of Instruction: Azeri, Russian, English, Turkish

International Co-operation: With Universities in EU countries; FUWI States, CIS States

Accrediting Agencies: Ministry of Education

Degrees and Diplomas: *Bakalavr:* Economy, Business and Management, 4 yrs; *Magistr:* 2 yrs; *Doktor (PhD):* 3 yrs

Student Services: Academic counselling, Canteen, Cultural centre, Employment services, Foreign student adviser, Foreign Studies Centre, Health services, Language programs, Social counselling, Sports facilities

Student Residential Facilities: Yes

Special Facilities: Museum

Libraries: Yes

Publications: Economics Theory and Practice, Scientific Magasine *(quarterly)*; Iqtisadci, University Press Newspaper *(weekly)*

Academic Staff *2010-2011*	TOTAL
FULL-TIME	790
PART-TIME	130
STAFF WITH DOCTORATE	
FULL-TIME	460
PART-TIME	c. 70

Student Numbers *2010-2011*	
All (Foreign Included)	c. 15,800
FOREIGN ONLY	720

Part-time students, 16,500. **Distance students,** 500.
Last Updated: 07/11/11

AZERBAIJAN STATE MARINE ACADEMY

prosp. Azerbaijan 18, Baku 1000
Tel: +994(12) 493-09-63
Fax: +994(12) 493-75-21
EMail: agma@azerin.com

President: Sambur Hamdullah (1997-) Tel: +994(12) 93-75-21

Pro-Rector: Asadullah Suleymanov
EMail: A-Suleymanov@yandex.ru

Faculties

Marine Engineering and Shipping (Marine Engineering; Marine Science and Oceanography; Nautical Science)

History: Founded 1881 as a Centre for training seamen, acquired present status and title 1996.

Admission Requirements: Secondary school certificate

Fees: (Manats): 500-600 per annum

Main Language(s) of Instruction: Azeri, Russian

Accrediting Agencies: Azerbaijan State Caspian Shipping Company

Degrees and Diplomas: *Bakalavr.* Marine Sciences, 4 yrs; *Magistr.* Marine Sciences, 2 yrs

Student Services: Academic counselling, Canteen, Cultural centre, Employment services, Health services, Language programs, Nursery care, Social counselling, Sports facilities

Student Residential Facilities: Student's Hostel

Special Facilities: Museum

Libraries: c. 92,000 vols

Publications: Scientific Works

Press or Publishing House: TI-Media
Last Updated: 19/01/07

AZERBAIJAN STATE OIL ACADEMY

20 Azadlig Avenue, Baku 1010
Tel: +994(12) 934-557
Fax: +994(12) 982-941
EMail: ihm@adna.baku.az
Website: http://www.adna.jis.az

Rector: Siyavush Garayev (1997-) EMail: sgaraev@mail.az

International Relations: Ramiz Humbatov
Tel: +994(12) 493-3261

Faculties

Chemical Engineering (Chemical Engineering; Ecology; Environmental Engineering; Polymer and Plastics Technology; Safety Engineering); **Economics, International Economics and Management** (Applied Mathematics; Economics; Engineering Management; International Economics; Management); **Geology and Prospecting** (Earth Sciences; Geological Engineering; Geology; Petroleum and Gas Engineering); **Mechanical Engineering**

(Machine Building; Materials Engineering; Mechanical Engineering; Production Engineering); **Petroleum Production** (Mining Engineering; Petroleum and Gas Engineering); **Power Engineering** (Electrical Engineering; Energy Engineering; Hydraulic Engineering; Power Engineering); **Production Processing Automation** (Automation and Control Engineering; Business Administration; Computer Engineering; Computer Science; Electrical and Electronic Engineering; Electronic Engineering; Information Management; Information Technology; Measurement and Precision Engineering; Software Engineering)

History: Founded 1920, acquired present status 1992.

Governing Bodies: Rector and Vice-Rectors

Academic Year: September to July

Admission Requirements: Competitive entrance examination following general or special secondary school certificate (Attestat)

Main Language(s) of Instruction: Azeri; Russian

International Co-operation: With universities in France; Germany; Italy; Netherlands; Norway; USA; Poland; China

Degrees and Diplomas: *Bakalavr.* 4 yrs; *Magistr.* a further 2 yrs; *Doktor.* 3 yrs following Master

Student Services: Canteen, Foreign student adviser, Foreign Studies Centre, Health services, Language programs, Nursery care, Sports facilities

Special Facilities: Museum

Libraries: c. 861,000 vols

Academic Staff *2007-2008*	MEN	WOMEN	TOTAL
FULL-TIME	373	304	677
PART-TIME	10	16	26
Student Numbers *2007-2008*			
All (Foreign Included)	5,872	1,028	6,900
FOREIGN ONLY	328	69	397

Part-time students, 487.
Last Updated: 04/08/08

AZERBAIJAN STATE PEDAGOGICAL UNIVERSITY

ul. Uzeir Hajibejov 34, Baku 370000
Tel: +994(12) 493-00-32
Fax: +994(12) 498-89-33
EMail: adpu@azeri.com

President: Bahlul Agayev
Tel: +994(12) 493-0026, Fax: +994(12) 493-3628
EMail: adpu@intrans.az

Faculties

Biology (Biology; Hygiene); **Chemistry** (Biology; Chemistry); **Drawing and Imitation Arts** (Painting and Drawing; Performing Arts); **Elementary Military Education and Physical Training and Geography** (Geography; Physical Education); **History** (History); **Mathematics and Computer Science** (Computer Science; Mathematics); **Pedagogy** (Music; Primary Education); **Pedagogy and Psychology (Preschool)** (Child Care and Development; Pedagogy; Preschool Education; Primary Education; Psychology); **Philology** (English; French; Literature; Native Language; Philology); **Physics** (Physics)

History: Founded 1921.

Governing Bodies: Rector; Vice-Rector; Deans

Admission Requirements: Secondary school certificate (Attestat)

Main Language(s) of Instruction: Azeri, Russian

International Co-operation: With Universities in France, Turkey

Degrees and Diplomas: *Bakalavr.* 4 yrs; *Magistr.* 2 yrs

Student Services: Academic counselling, Canteen, Cultural centre, Employment services, Foreign student adviser, Foreign Studies Centre, Health services, Language programs, Social counselling, Sports facilities

Special Facilities: Museum; Photo Gallery

Libraries: Yes

Publications: Young Teacher *(monthly)*
Last Updated: 07/11/11

AZERBAIJAN STATE UNIVERSITY OF CULTURE AND FINE ARTS

pros. Insaatchilar 9, Baku AZ 1065
Tel: +994(12) 438-43-10
Fax: +994(12) 438-93-48
EMail: rector@admiu.edu.az
Website: http://www.admiu.edu.az/english/xarici

Rector: Teymurchin Afandiyev

Vice-Rector: Rafiq Sadiqov Tel: +994(12) 387-606

International Relations: Chingiz Bargirov Tel: +994(12) 38-93-48

Faculties

Cultural Studies (Cultural Studies) *Dean*: Alekper Mammadov; **Fine Arts** (Art Criticism; Art Management; Fine Arts; Industrial Arts Education) *Dean*: Vefa Aliyev; **Management** (Management) *Dean*: Bayram Hadjiyev; **Music** (Music) *Dean*: Vamig Mammedaliyev; **Painting** (Painting and Drawing) *Dean*: Djabbar Hassanov; **Theatre and Cinema** (Cinema and Television; Theatre) *Dean*: Mammedshah Atayev

History: Founded 1945.

Academic Year: September to July

Admission Requirements: Competitive entrance examination following general or special secondary school certificate (Attestat)

Main Language(s) of Instruction: Azeri

International Co-operation: With universities in Turkey, Germany, United Kingdom, Serbia and Montenegro, Ireland.

Degrees and Diplomas: *Magistr*

Student Services: Canteen, Cultural centre, Employment services, Health services, Language programs, Social counselling, Sports facilities

Special Facilities: Art Gallery.

Libraries: Total, 115,000 vols

Publications: Art and Culture

Last Updated: 04/11/11

AZERBAIJAN STATE UNIVERSITY OF LANGUAGES

ul. Rashid Bahbudov 60, Baku AZ 1010
Tel: +994(12) 440-35-05
Fax: +994(12) 441-58-63
EMail: info@adu.edu.az
Website: http://www.adu.edu.az

Rector: Samad Seyidov (2000-)

International Relations: Ilham Mardanov, Vice-Rector
Fax: +994(12) 41-22-98

Faculties

English, Romance and German Philology (Dutch; English; French; German; Germanic Languages; Modern Languages; Romance Languages); **German, French, English and Regional Studies** (English Studies; French Studies; Germanic Studies; Regional Studies); **Translation and Interpretation** (English; French; German; Italian; Korean; Spanish; Translation and Interpretation)

History: Founded 1937 as Azerbaijan State Institute of Foreign Languages, acquired present status and title 2000.

Governing Bodies: University and Faculty Boards

Admission Requirements: School certificate and entrance examination

Main Language(s) of Instruction: Azeri, Russian.

International Co-operation: With universities in Russian Federation, Turkey, Germany, USA, France.

AZERBAIJAN TEACHERS INSTITUTE

Azerbaycan Muellimler Institutu (AMI)

K. Rahimov, Baku
Tel: +99(12) 465-66-93
Fax: +99(12) 564-80-47
Website: http://www.ami.az/

Rector: Agiya Nakhchivanli

International Relations: Nigar Sultanova, Vice-Rector

Faculties

Pedagogy (Computer Science; Education; Mathematics; Pedagogy; Preschool Education; Primary Education); **Phillology** (Literature; Modern Languages; Philology); **Training and retraining** (Curriculum)

Further Information: Also campuses at different regions

Degrees and Diplomas: *Bakalavr*, *Magistr*

Last Updated: 08/11/11

AZERBAIJAN TECHNICAL UNIVERSITY

Azarbaycan Texniki Universiteti (AZTU)

Hussein Javid Ave. 25, Baku Az 1073
Tel: +994(12) 438-33-43
Fax: +994(12) 438-32-80
EMail: aztu@aztu.org
Website: http://www.aztu.az

Rector: Havar Mamedov (2000-) EMail: rector@aztu.org

Vice-Rector for Education: Xaliq Yaqudov
Tel: +994(12) 438-94-76

International Relations: Zahid Sultanzadeh, Vice-Rector
Tel: +994(12) 439-13-32, Fax: +994(12) 439-13-32
EMail: sultanzadehz@mail.ru

Faculties

Automation and Computer Equipment (Automation and Control Engineering; Measurement and Precision Engineering); **Electrical and Power Engineering** (Electrical Engineering; Power Engineering) *Division Head*: Beshirov; **Engineering Business and Management** (Economics; Management); **Foreign Students Education**; **Machine Building** (Machine Building); **Metallurgy** (Metallurgical Engineering); **Radio Engineering and Communication** (Electronic Engineering; Telecommunications Engineering); **Technological and Light Industry Machines** (Electrical Engineering; Mechanical Equipment and Maintenance; Technology); **Transport** (Automotive Engineering; Transport Management)

History: Founded 1920 as Baku Polytechnical University. Reorganized 1950 as Azerbaijan Polytechnical Institute. Acquired present status and title 1991.

Governing Bodies: Scientific Council

Academic Year: September to June (September-January; February-June)

Admission Requirements: Secondary school certificate (Attestat)

Fees: (Manats): c. 800

Main Language(s) of Instruction: Azeri, Russian

International Co-operation: With universities in Germany; Russian Federation, Turkey, United Kingdom and USA. Also participates in Tempus and DAAD programmes.

Degrees and Diplomas: *Bakalavr*: 4 yrs; *Magistr*: 2 yrs. Also Aspirantura (3 yrs) and Dr (3-5 yrs)

Student Services: Academic counselling, Canteen, Cultural centre, Foreign Studies Centre, Health services, Sports facilities

Student Residential Facilities: For 100 students

Special Facilities: Museum of AzTU History

Libraries: 730,000 vols

Publications: Scientific Proceedings *(quarterly)*

Academic Staff *2008-2009*	MEN	WOMEN	TOTAL
FULL-TIME	–	–	583
PART-TIME	–	–	21
STAFF WITH DOCTORATE			
FULL-TIME	–	–	3
Student Numbers *2008-2009*			
All (Foreign Included)	713	4,867	5,580
FOREIGN ONLY	–	–	405

Part-time students, 588.

Last Updated: 07/11/11

AZERBAIJAN TECHNOLOGICAL UNIVERSITY (AZTECHU)

Heydar Aliyev Avenue 103, Gandja, Az 2011 Gandja-Gazakh
Tel: +994(22) 57-56-29
Fax: +994(22) 57-29-62
EMail: info@aztu.ws; info_tel@inbox.ru

Executive Rector: Telman Malikov

Faculties
Consumer Products Technology and Expertise (Consumer Studies; Telecommunications Engineering) *Dean*: Garay Abbasov; **Economics and Management** (Economics; Marketing) *Dean*: Chalida Agayeva; **Food Production and Tourism** (Food Science; Tourism) *Dean*: Arzu Hasanov; **Standardization and Technological Machinery** (Automation and Control Engineering; Food Technology; Industrial Engineering; Measurement and Precision Engineering; Technology) *Dean*: Namik Askarov

History: Founded 1970. Acquired present status 2000.

Admission Requirements: Secondary school certificate

Main Language(s) of Instruction: Azeri, Russian

International Co-operation: With universities in the USA; Russian Federation; Turkey; Georgia

Degrees and Diplomas: *Bakalavr*: 4 yrs; *Magistr*: 2 yrs

Student Services: Academic counselling, Canteen, Cultural centre, Foreign student adviser, Handicapped facilities, Health services, Language programs, Nursery care, Social counselling, Sports facilities

Student Residential Facilities: Yes

Libraries: c. 300,000 vols

Academic Staff *2007-2008*	MEN	WOMEN	TOTAL
FULL-TIME	172	71	243
Student Numbers *2007-2008*			
All (Foreign Included)	1,549	270	1,819

Last Updated: 06/08/08

AZERBAIJAN UNIVERSITY OF ARCHITECTURE AND CONSTRUCTION

Azarbaycan Memarliq va Inşaat Universiteti
ul. A. Sultanova 5, Baku AZ 1073
Tel: +994(12) 430-30-01
Fax: +994(12) 498-78-36
EMail: interreldep@azmiu.edu.az
Website: http://www.azmiu.edu.az

Rector: Gulchohra Mammadova (1976-)
EMail: rector@azmiu.edu.az

Vice-Rector: Farhad Jafarov
Tel: +994(12) 439-07-45 EMail: prorector-ti@azmiu.edu.az

International Relations: Nargiz Abdullayeva, Vice-Rector
Tel: +994(12) 439-05-97 EMail: prorector-ir@azmiu.edu.az

Colleges
Construction (Building Technologies; Construction Engineering) *Principal*: Ismayil Chobanzadeh

Faculties
Architecture (Architecture) *Dean*: Tofig Abdullayev; **Building Technology** (Building Technologies; Construction Engineering) *Dean*: Namig Agabeyli; **Construction Economics** (Economics; Engineering Management) *Dean*: Nazima Mammadova; **Construction** (Construction Engineering) *Dean*: Hikmat Mammadov; **Mechanization and Automation** (Automation and Control Engineering; Power Engineering) *Dean*: Arif Haciyev; **Transport Engineering** (Bridge Engineering; Road Engineering; Surveying and Mapping; Transport Engineering; Transport Management) *Dean*: Yagub Piriyev; **Water Supply and Engineering Systems** (Ecology; Engineering; Hydraulic Engineering; Water Management) *Dean*: Zakir Musayev

History: Azerbaijan University of Architecture and Construction (AUAC) was founded as construction faculty incorporated with the Polytechnic Institute in 1920; from 1930 to 1934 it functioned as an autonomous Construction Institute and since 1934 it functioned as a civil engineering department within Azerbaijan Industrial Institute.

In 1975, Azerbaijan Civil Engineering Institute began life as an autonomous institution of higher education. In 2000, Azerbaijan Civil Engineering Institute was named Azerbaijan University of Architecture and Construction.

Governing Bodies: Rectorate

Academic Year: September - June

Admission Requirements: School leaving certificate

Fees: (AZN): 650-1,000.00, home students; (US Dollars): 1,000-3,000.00, overseas students

Main Language(s) of Instruction: Azeri, Russian, English

International Co-operation: Participates in the Tempus-Tacis programme, 7FP, Erasmus-Mundus etc.

Accrediting Agencies: Ministry of Education

Degrees and Diplomas: *Bakalavr*: 4 yrs; *Magistr*: a further 2 yrs; *Doktor (PhD)*: a further 3-4 yrs

Student Services: Academic counselling, Canteen, Cultural centre, Employment services, Foreign student adviser, Foreign Studies Centre, Handicapped facilities, Health services, Language programs, Nursery care, Social counselling, Sports facilities

Student Residential Facilities: 5 student hostels

Special Facilities: museum; art gallery

Libraries: 460,000 vols.

Publications: Ecology and water economy; Scientific works; Theoretical and applied mechanics; Urbanizm

Press or Publishing House: Inshaatci Kadrlar

Academic Staff *2010-2011*	MEN	WOMEN	TOTAL
FULL-TIME	405	227	632
Student Numbers *2010-2011*			
All (Foreign Included)	4,214	1,806	6,020
FOREIGN ONLY	567	243	810

Last Updated: 10/08/11

BAKU MUSIC ACADEMY 'UZER HAJIBEJOV'

ul. Šamsi Badelbeyli 98, Baku 370014
Tel: +994(12) 493-22-48
Fax: +994(12) 493-19-28
EMail: info@musigi-dunya.az
Website: http://musakademiya.musigi-dunya.az/

Rector: Farhad Badalbeyli

Academic Secretary of Academic Council: Leyla Mamedova

Programmes
Music (Music; Music Theory and Composition; Musical Instruments; Musicology)

History: Founded 1922.

Main Language(s) of Instruction: Azeri, Russian

Degrees and Diplomas: *Bakalavr*, *Magistr*, *Doktor*
Last Updated: 08/11/11

BAKU SLAVIC UNIVERSITY

Baki Slavyan Universiteti
ul. Suleiman Rustam 25, Baku 370601
Tel: +994(12) 441-60-58
Fax: +994(12) 440-27-70
EMail: bsuinterstud@mail.az
Website: http://bsu-edu.org/ANAE.aspx

Rector: Kamal M. Abdullayev

Vice-Rector: Asif A. Hajiev

Faculties
Creative (Aesthetics; Arts and Humanities); **International Relations and Region studies** (European Studies; Foreign Languages Education; International Relations; Political Sciences; Russian); **Pedagogy** (Educational Psychology; Information Technology; Mathematical Physics; Pedagogy; Primary Education; Russian); **Philology** (English; Foreign Languages Education; French; German; Journalism; Native Language; Russian; Translation and Interpretation); **Retraining and Advanced Training** (Educational Psychology; International Relations; Russian; Translation and

Interpretation); **Translation** (Literature; Translation and Interpretation)

History: Founded 1946 as Azerbaijan Pedagogical Institute of Russian Language and Literature 'Mirza Fatali Akhundov'. Acquired present status and title 2000.

Main Language(s) of Instruction: Azeri, Russian

Degrees and Diplomas: *Bakalavr*; *Magistr*

Last Updated: 08/11/11

BAKU STATE UNIVERSITY (BSU)

ul. Zahad Halilov 23, Baku AZ-1148
Tel: +994(12) 439-0858
Fax: +994(12) 598-3376
EMail: rector@bsu.az
Website: http://www.bsu.az

Rector: Abel Mammadali Maharramov (1999-)
Tel: +994(12) 439-0858

Vice-Rector: Nebi Ramazanli

International Relations: Nargiz Pashayeva
Tel: +994(12) 439-0557

Faculties

Applied Mathematics and Cybernetics (Applied Mathematics; Computer Science; Mathematics); **Biology** (Biology); **Chemistry** (Chemistry); **Ecology and Soil Science** (Ecology; Soil Science); **Geography** (Geography; Geology); **Geology** (Geology); **History** (History); **International Law and International Relations** (International Law; International Relations); **Journalism** (Journalism); **Law** (Law); **Library Science and Information Sciences** (Information Sciences; Library Science); **Mechanics and Mathematics** (Mathematics; Mechanics); **Oriental Studies** (Oriental Studies); **Philology** (Philology); **Physics** (Physics); **Social Science and Psychology** (Psychology; Social Sciences; Social Work; Sociology); **Theology** (Islamic Law; Islamic Theology)

History: Founded 1919 on former Baku Transcaucasus University (founded 1918).

Governing Bodies: Academic Council; Faculty Councils

Academic Year: September to July

Admission Requirements: Competitive entrance examination following general or special secondary school certificate (Attestat)

Main Language(s) of Instruction: Azeri; Russian; English

International Co-operation: Participates in Linkage and Tempus/Tacis.

Accrediting Agencies: Ministry of Education

Degrees and Diplomas: *Bakalavr*. 4 yrs; *Magistr*. a further 2 yrs; *Doktor*. Science, a further 3 yrs and thesis

Special Facilities: Biology Museum; Mineralogy Museum

Libraries: c. 1m. vols

Publications: Učĕnye Zapiski, Scientific papers
Last Updated: 07/11/11

GANDJA STATE UNIVERSITY (GDU)

prosp. Khatai 187, Gandja, AZ 2000 Gandja-Gazakh
Tel: +994(22) 567-310
Fax: +994(22) 456-19-63
Website: http://www.gsu.az/

Rector: Elman Memmedov Tel: +994(22) 56-73-10

Faculties

Chemistry and Biology (Biology; Chemistry); **Educational Psychology** (Educational Psychology; Teacher Training); **Engineering Education** (Engineering; Technology Education); **Foreign Languages** (English; French; German); **History** (History); **Mathematics and Computer Science** (Computer Science; Mathematics); **Philology** (Oriental Languages; Philology)

History: Founded 1938 as Gandja State Pedagogical Institute, named after H. Zardabi 2000, acquired present title 2002.

Governing Bodies: Rectorate

Admission Requirements: General or secondary school certificate (Attestat)

Main Language(s) of Instruction: Azeri, Russian

International Co-operation: With universities in United Kingdom.

Degrees and Diplomas: *Bakalavr*. 4 yrs; *Magistr*. a further 2 yrs; *Doktor*. 3 yrs following Diploma of Specialist

Student Services: Canteen, Cultural centre, Employment services, Foreign student adviser, Foreign Studies Centre, Health services, Language programs, Nursery care

Special Facilities: History Museum; Art Museum. Art Gallery. Movie Studio

Libraries: Central Library

Publications: Handbook of Science Labour, Teachers' Scientific Research *(annually)*
Last Updated: 07/11/11

LANKARAN STATE UNIVERSITY

Lankaran Dövlat Universiteti (LSU)
ul. General H. Aslanov 50, Lankaran AZ4200
Tel: +994(171) 5-25-88
Fax: +994(171) 5-27-86
EMail: office@lsu.edu.az
Website: http://www.lsu.aznet.org

Rector: Asaf Iskanderov
Tel: +994(171) 5-25-88, Fax: +994(171) 5-27-86
EMail: rector@lsu.edu.az

Vice-Rector: Baxişov Memmedşah
Tel: +994(171) 5-0340 EMail: prorector_edu@lsu.edu.az

Faculties

Economics (Consumer Studies; Economics; Forest Products; Fruit Production; Management; Plant and Crop Protection; Taxation; Technology; Tropical Agriculture); **Humanities** (History; Modern Languages; Sociology); **Natural Sciences** (Applied Mathematics; Biology; Computer Engineering; Geography; Mathematics and Computer Science; Natural Resources); **Pedagogy** (English; French; Music; Pedagogy; Physical Education; Primary Education; Psychology)

History: Founded 1991 as branch of Baku State University, acquired present independent status and title 1992.

Governing Bodies: Academic Council

Academic Year: September to June (September-January; February-June)

Admission Requirements: Secondary school certificate (orta tehsil haqqinda attestat) and competitive entrance examination or diploma

Main Language(s) of Instruction: Azeri, Russian

International Co-operation: With universities in France, Iran, Russian Federation, Turkey, Germany, Israel

Degrees and Diplomas: *Bakalavr*. 4 yrs; *Magistr*. 2 yrs following Bakalavr

Student Services: Academic counselling, Canteen, Cultural centre, Employment services, Handicapped facilities, Language programs, Social counselling, Sports facilities

Student Residential Facilities: Yes

Special Facilities: History Museum

Libraries: Scientific Library, 32,372 vols

Press or Publishing House: Publishing-Polygraphic Computer Centre
Last Updated: 07/11/11

NAKHCHIVAN STATE UNIVERSITY

Nakhchivan Delvet Universiteti (NSU)
University Campus, Nakhchivan Az7000
Tel: +994(136) 45-72-88
Fax: +994(136) 45-72-88
EMail: ndu@ndu.edu.az
Website: http://www.ndu.edu.az

Rector: Isa Habibbayli (1996-) EMail: rector@ndu.edu.az

Vice-Rector: Veli Guseinov
Tel: +994(136) 5-45-59 EMail: vgusseinov@yahoo.com

International Relations: Marziya Agayeva, Head of International Office

Tel: +994(136) 4-08-62; +994(50) 348-45-74 (mobile),
Fax: +994(136) 4-08-62 EMail: iro@ndu.edu.az

Faculties

Art (Arts and Humanities); Economics (Accountancy; Economics; Taxation); Engineering Education (Technology Education); History and Philology (Arabic; English; History; Literature; Modern Languages; Philology; Russian); Mathematics and Physics (Astronomy and Space Science; Computer Science; Mathematics; Physics); Medical (Paediatrics); Pedagogy (Pedagogy; Physical Education; Preschool Education; Primary Education; Sports); Science (Biology; Chemistry; Geography); Social Management and Law (Law; Public Administration)

History: Founded 1967, acquired present status and title 1990.

Governing Bodies: Rectorate and Administration; Scientific Council

Academic Year: September to July (September-January; February-July)

Admission Requirements: Secondary school certificate

Main Language(s) of Instruction: Azeri

International Co-operation: Participates in the Tempus, UNICEF, Soros, IREX-IATP programmes

Degrees and Diplomas: Bakalavr. 4 yrs; Magistr. a further 2 yrs. Also postgraduate degree, 3 yrs

Student Services: Academic counselling, Canteen, Cultural centre, Employment services, Foreign student adviser, Foreign Studies Centre, Handicapped facilities, Health services, Language programs, Nursery care, Social counselling, Sports facilities

Special Facilities: University Museum; Art Gallery

Publications: Scientific Journal

Press or Publishing House: Geyret (Honour)
Last Updated: 08/11/11

NAKHCHIVAN TEACHERS INSTITUTE

1 Azadlig St., Nakhchivan
Tel: +994(136) 5-37-02

Rector: Hasanli Oruj (2010-)

Faculties

Pedagogy (Educational Psychology; Mathematics and Computer Science; Pedagogy; Preschool Education; Primary Education)

History: Founded 2000, in the base of the Nakhchivan Polytechnic technical school. It was the branch of the Teachers Institute of Azerbaijan in Nakhchivan during 2000-2003. Acquired present title and status 2003.
Last Updated: 08/11/11

THE ACADEMY OF PUBLIC ADMINISTRATION UNDER THE PRESIDENT OF THE REPUBLIC OF AZERBAIJAN

ul. Lermontov 74, Baku AZ1001
Tel: +994(12) 492-6529
Fax: +994(12) 492-6515
EMail: dia@azeurotel.com
Website: http://www.dia.edu.az/

Rector: Heydar Aliyev

Faculties

Political Administration (International Relations; International Studies; Modern Languages; Philosophy; Political Sciences; Public Administration; Social Psychology); Professional Development and Training; State Administration (Administration; Government; Information Technology; Management; Public Administration; Public Law)

History: Created in 1999 to train quality civil servants and to offer further professional training to current civil servants. Previously known as Academy of Management under the President of the Republic of Azerbaijan.

Degrees and Diplomas: Bakalavr. State Administration; Political Administraion; International Relations; Political Science, 4 yrs; Magistr. State and Municipal Administration, a further 2 yrs

Student Services: Canteen

Student Residential Facilities: Yes

Academic Staff 2007-2008: Total: c. 110
Last Updated: 07/11/11

PRIVATE INSTITUTIONS

AZERBAIJAN INTERNATIONAL UNIVERSITY

Azjarbajžan Beynelxalq Universiteti (ABU)
ul. Hariji Daira 179, 7th Microdistrict, Baku 370130
Tel: +994(12) 61-69-50
Fax: +994(12) 62-14-48
EMail: info@abu.az

Rector: Elshad Abdullayev (1997-)

First Vice-Rector: Husseyn Ahmedov

International Relations: Baylar Hajiyev Tel: +994(12) 47-09-79

Faculties

Arts and Humanities (Linguistics; Modern Languages; Translation and Interpretation); Business Administration (Administration; Business Administration; Finance; Management); Education (Education; Primary Education; Teacher Training); Health Sciences (Health Sciences; Medicine); Information Sciences (Information Sciences; Journalism; Mass Communication); International Law (International Law); Law (Law); Paediatrics and Stomatology (Paediatrics; Stomatology); Social Sciences (Economics; International Economics; International Relations; International Studies; Social Sciences); Transport and Communications (Road Transport; Transport and Communications)

History: Founded 1997.

Governing Bodies: Academic Council

Admission Requirements: Secondary school certificate

Main Language(s) of Instruction: Azeri, Russian, English.

International Co-operation: With universities in USA.

Accrediting Agencies: Supreme Expert Commission, Ministry of Education.

Degrees and Diplomas: Bakalavr. 4 yrs; Magistr. a further 2 yrs; Doktor

Student Services: Canteen, Foreign Studies Centre, Health services, Language programs, Nursery care, Sports facilities

Student Residential Facilities: Yes

Special Facilities: Museum. Movie Studio

Libraries: Total, 40,000 vols

Publications: State and Law (monthly)

Press or Publishing House: ABU Press
Last Updated: 20/01/12

AZERBAIJAN UNIVERSITY

Azjarbajžan Universiteti (AZUN)
Nasimi district R. Safarov-17, Baku 1102
Tel: +994(12) 430-51-79
Fax: +994(12) 430-49-29
EMail: rector@au.edu.az
Website: http://www.au.edu.az

Rector: Qahramanov Aslan Qahramanov (2010-)
Tel: +994(12) 430-49-29 EMail: aslan.qehreman@gmail.com

Centres

Azerbaijani Studies; Care; East-West Research; Law Clinic; Reform

Departments

Administrative Management (Administration; English; Management); Civil Defense and Fundamentals of Medicine (Civil Security; Public Health); Economics (Banking; Finance; International Business); International Relations and History (History; International Relations; Political Sciences); Law (Civil Law; Law); Mathematics and Computer Science (Computer Science; Mathematics); Modern Languages (Arabic; English; French; German; Modern Languages; Russian); Philosophy (Philosophy; Political Sciences; Social Sciences)

Faculties
Arts and Humanities (Translation and Interpretation); **Business Administration** (Business Administration; International Relations); **Economics** (Economics); **Law** (Law)

History: Founded 1991, acquired present status 1995.

Academic Year: September to June (September-December; February-June)

Admission Requirements: Competitive entrance examination following general or secondary school certificate (Attestat)

Main Language(s) of Instruction: Azeri, English

Degrees and Diplomas: *Bakalavr.* 4 yrs; *Magistr.* a further 1-2 yrs; *Doktor (PhD):* 4 yrs

Student Services: Canteen, Cultural centre, Foreign Studies Centre, Health services, Language programs, Sports facilities

Student Residential Facilities: Yes

Libraries: Total, c. 406,603 vols

Publications: Felsefe ve social-siyasi elmler (Philosophy and Social-Political Sciences), International journal in Azeri, Russian and English *(quarterly)*; Ipek Yolu (Silk Road), International journal in Azeri, Russian and English *(monthly)*; Newspaper, Azerbaijan

Press or Publishing House: Azerbaijan University Press

Academic Staff 2007-2008	MEN	WOMEN	TOTAL
FULL-TIME	20	19	39
PART-TIME	35	18	53
STAFF WITH DOCTORATE FULL-TIME	–	–	17
Student Numbers 2007-2008 All (Foreign Included)	–	–	881

Last Updated: 07/11/11

BAKU ASIA UNIVERSITY
Baki Asiya Universiteti
A.Salamzade St. 28, Baku 370102
Tel: +994(12) 430-52-40
Fax: +994(12) 431-36-99
Website: http://www.asia.baku.az

Rector: Jalil Nagiyev

Vice-Rector: Senan Mustafaev

International Relations: Senan Mustafaev

Centres
Scientific Methodic Seminar (Natural Sciences)

Faculties
Economics (Economics); **Law and International Relations** (Law); **Philology** (Arabic; English; Japanese; Journalism; Native Language; Philology)

History: Founded 1993 as a private University. Registered 1995 by the decision of the Cabinet of Ministries of the Azerbaijan Republic.

Academic Year: September to June (September-January; February-June)

Fees: (US Dollars): 1,000-2,000 per annum

Main Language(s) of Instruction: Azeri, Russian

International Co-operation: With universities in Turkey, Kazakhstan

Degrees and Diplomas: *Bakalavr.* 4 yrs; *Magistr.* a further 2 yrs

Special Facilities: Azerbaijan History Museum; Art Museum; Literature Museum 'Nizamy Ganjavi'

Libraries: c. 15,000 vols

Press or Publishing House: 'ASIA' Publishing House

BAKU BUSINESS UNIVERSITY
Baki Biznes Universiteti (BBU)
St. H. Zardabi 88a, Baku, 370122 Zarbadi
Tel: +994(12) 431-79-51
Fax: +994(12) 430-07-80
EMail: info@bbu.edu.az
Website: http://www.bbu.edu.az

President: Ibad Abbasov (1993-)

Vice-Rector of Education: Sabir Amirkhanov

International Relations: Alihuseyn Iskenderov
Tel: +994(12) 431-79-51, Fax: +994(12) 430-07-80
EMail: alihuseyn@cer.az; bbu_inter_relation@yahoo.com

Chairs
Accountancy and Auditing; **Customs Organization** (Taxation); **Economics** (Economics; International Economics; International Relations; Management; Marketing); **Finance and Credit** (Banking; Finance); **Higher Mathematics and Technical Subjetcs** (Economics; Mathematics); **Humanities** (Arts and Humanities); **Languages** (Modern Languages); **Law** (Commercial Law; International Law; Law); **Municipal Management and Legal Regulation of Economy** (Economics; Industrial Management; Labour and Industrial Relations)

Faculties
Business Administration and Management (Business Administration; Business and Commerce; Management; Taxation); **Economy and Law** (Accountancy; Finance; Translation and Interpretation)

History: Founded 1993. Acquired present status 1997.

Governing Bodies: Principal body. Administrative body.

Academic Year: September to June

Admission Requirements: Secondary school certificate

Main Language(s) of Instruction: Azeri; Russian; English

Accrediting Agencies: Ministry of Education

Degrees and Diplomas: *Bakalavr.* Economic Policy; Law, 4 yrs; *Magistr.* Economic Policy; Law, 2 yrs. Also Correspondence course, 5 yrs.

Student Services: Canteen, Cultural centre, Employment services, Foreign student adviser, Foreign Studies Centre, Health services, Language programs, Social counselling, Sports facilities

Student Residential Facilities: Yes

Special Facilities: Museum; Training Center; Youth Centre; Gym

Libraries: Yes

Publications: Audit, Economic journal *(quarterly)*

Press or Publishing House: Business University Publishing House
Last Updated: 07/11/11

BAKU ISLAMIC UNIVERSITY
Baki Islam Universiteti
ul. Mirza Fatali 7, Baku
Tel: +994(12) 492-82-23

President: Sabir Hasanli Tel: +994(12) 92-82-23

Programmes
Islamic Studies (Islamic Law; Islamic Studies; Islamic Theology; Koran)

Main Language(s) of Instruction: Azeri, Russian

KHAZAR UNIVERSITY
11 Mehseti Street, Baku AZ 1096
Tel: +994(12) 421-79-27
Fax: +994(12) 498-93-79
EMail: contact@khazar.org
Website: http://www.khazar.org

President: John Ryder EMail: JRyder@khazar.org

Executive Assistant to the Chancellor: Isaxan Isaxanli
Tel: +994(12) 421-10-93 EMail: iisaxanli@khazar.org

International Relations: Ayten Shadlinskaya
EMail: ashadlinskaya@khazar.org

Centres
Carrer Development *Director.* Raziya Isayeva; **Caucasus Research Resource** *(CRRC) Director.* Ulker Isayeva; **Dictionary and Encyclopaedia** (Publishing and Book Trade; Terminology) *Director.* Tofiq Abaskuliyev; **Distance Learning** *Head:* Leyla Muradkhanli; **Economics Policy and Development** *(CEPD)* (Development Studies; Economics) *Director.* Fikret Pashayev; **Environmental Studies** (Education; Information Sciences) *Head:* Rovshan Abasov; **Eurasia Production Industry Knowledge**

Studies *Director*: Ingilab Ahmedov; **Internet and Society** *(Khazar)* (Computer Networks); **Library and Information Sciences** *Head*: Tatyana Zaytseva; **Media** (Media Studies) *Director*: Natella Barkaya; **Psychological Counseling and Psychotherapy Studies** (Psychology; Psychotherapy) *Director*: Ulker Isayeva; **Quality Assurance in Education** (Education); **Science and Art** (Arts and Humanities; Natural Sciences) *Directeur*: Hamlet Isaxanli; **Translation Studies** (Translation and Interpretation) *Director*: Jamal Mustafayev

Departments

Azerbaijani Language and Literature (Native Language; Philology) *Director*: Elsa Samedova; **Chemistry** (Chemistry) *Head*: Ziyafaddin Asadov; **Civil and Environmental Engineering** (Architecture; Civil Engineering; Environmental Engineering); **Computer Science** (Computer Science) *Head*: Leyla Muradkhanli; **Eastern Languages and Religious Studies** (Arabic; Chinese; Islamic Studies; Japanese; Modern Languages; Oriental Studies; Persian) *Head*: Elnura Azizova; **Economics and Management** (Economics; Management) *Head*: Mahammad Nuriyev; **Education** (Education); **Electronics and Communications** (Electrical and Electronic Engineering; Telecommunications Engineering); **English and Litterature** (English) *Chair*: Eldar Shahqaldiyev; **History and Archaeology** (Archaeology; History) *Chair*: Roza Arazova; **Journalism** *Chair*: Jabir Mammadov; **Law** (Law) *Chair*: Jabir Khalilov; **Life Sciences** (Biology; Biomedicine; Ecology); **Mathematics** (Mathematics) *Head*: Hamlet Isaxanli; **Music and Fine Arts** (Cultural Studies; Dance; Fashion Design; Music) *Head*: Zulffiya Sadikova; **Petroleum Engineering** (Petroleum and Gas Engineering) *Chair*: Gasham Zeynalov; **Philosophy and Human Sciences** (Philosophy; Psychology; Social Sciences) *Chair*: Agalar Mammadov; **Physics** (Physics) *Head*: Hikmat Hasanov; **Political Science and International Relations** (International Relations; Political Sciences) *Chair*: Baba Bayramli

Institutes

Education Policy (Education) *Director*: Hamlet Isaxanli; **Political Science** (Political Sciences) *Director*: Baba Bayramli

Schools

Dunya (Preschool Education; Primary Education; Secondary Education) *Director*: Marufa Madatova; **Economics and Management** (Accountancy; Business Administration; Economics; Finance; Information Technology; International Business; International Economics; Management; Marketing) *Dean*: Ingilab Ahmedov; **Education** (Biology; Chemistry; Education; Geography; History; Primary Education) *Dean*: Elsa Samedova; **Engineering and Applied Science** (Civil Engineering; Computer Engineering; Engineering; Environmental Engineering; Management; Mathematics; Mathematics and Computer Science; Petroleum and Gas Engineering) *Dean*: Rafig Ahmadov; **Humanities and Social Sciences** (Arabic; Arts and Humanities; Design; English; International Relations; Journalism; Linguistics; Literature; Persian; Political Sciences; Psychology; Regional Studies; Translation and Interpretation) *Director*: Jabir Khalilov; **Law** (International Law; Law) *Director*: Jabir Khalilov; **Medicine** (Biology; Dentistry; Medicine) *Dean*: Nigar Bagirova; **Project Management** (Management)

Further Information: Also Teaching Hospitals: Sabuncu Hospital; National Centre of Oncology; Institute of Obstetrics and Gynaecology

History: Founded 1991.

Governing Bodies: Advisory Board; University Council

Academic Year: September to August (September-January; February-June; June-August)

Admission Requirements: Secondary school certificate (Attestat)

Fees: (US Dollars): 3,500 per annum

Main Language(s) of Instruction: English

Degrees and Diplomas: *Bakalavr*: 4 yrs; *Magistr*: a further 1 1/2-2 yrs; *Doktor (PhD)*: 3-5 yrs. Also Certificate programme, Diploma, 3-6 months

Student Services: Academic counselling, Canteen, Cultural centre, Employment services, Foreign student adviser, Health services, Language programs, Social counselling, Sports facilities

Special Facilities: National Costume Museum. Carpet Museum. Applied Fine Arts, TV Studio, Computing Facilities

Libraries: More than 100,000 vols

Publications: Journal of Azerbaijan Archaeology, Researches; Interesting Findings; History of Sciences; Archeological Discoveries *(biennially)*; Khazar Journal of Humanities and Social Sciences, Result of research projects in varoius fields (History, Politics,

International Relations, Education, Culture, History, Language and Litterature, Economics and Law *(quarterly)*; Khazar Journal of Mathematics, English *(quarterly)*; Khazar Journal of Science and Technology; Khazar View, Related to science, art, politics, literature, culture and other field of studies *(monthly)*

Press or Publishing House: Khazar University Press

Academic Staff 2010-2011	MEN	WOMEN	TOTAL
FULL-TIME	16	21	37
PART-TIME	74	60	134
STAFF WITH DOCTORATE			
FULL-TIME	18	10	28
PART-TIME	31	15	46
Student Numbers 2010-2011			
All (Foreign Included)	819	995	1,814

Note: Dunya School: Total Students 293
Last Updated: 27/06/11

ODLAR YURDU UNIVERSITY

Odlar Yurdu Universiteti
835 Koroglu Rahimov Street, Baku 1072
Tel: +994(12) 465-82-00
Fax: +994(12) 465-67-05
EMail: mail@oyu.edu.az
Website: http://www.oyu.edu.az

Rector: Ahmad A. Valiyev (1995-)
Tel: +994(12) 90-82-00 EMail: rektor@oyu.edu.az

Vice-Rector: Samir Valiyev Tel: +994(12) 90-82-62

International Relations: Faik Nagiyev, Vice-Rector
Tel: +994(12) 47-49-59 EMail: odlaryurdu@artel.net.az

Faculties

Business and Management (Business Administration; Economics; Finance; International Economics; International Relations; Management); **Law and International Relations** (International Relations; Law); **Mathematics and Information Technology** (Computer Science; Data Processing; Information Technology; Pedagogy; Primary Education); **Medicine** *Dean*: Zakir Garayev; **Translation and Pedagogy** (English; Modern Languages; Translation and Interpretation); **Transport** *Dean*: Hamid Mamedov

Research Centres

Eurasia (Ecology; Information Technology; Management)

History: Founded 1995. Acquired present status 1996.

Academic Year: September to June

Main Language(s) of Instruction: Azeri, Russian, English

International Co-operation: With universities in USA, United Kingdom, Germany, Turkey, Netherlands, Italy, Russian Federation.

Degrees and Diplomas: *Bakalavr*; *Doktor*: Science

Student Services: Canteen

Libraries: c. 16,300 vols

Publications: The Scientific and Pedagogical News of Odlar Yurdu University *(quarterly)*
Last Updated: 08/11/11

QAFQAZ UNIVERSITY

Qafqaz Universiteti (QU)
Baku-Sumgayit Highway 16th km, Khirdalan, Baku AZ0101
Tel: +994(12) 48-28-62 +994(12) 48-28-63
Fax: +994(12) 98-28-61
EMail: info@qu.edu.az
Website: http://www.qu.edu.az

Rector: Ahmet Sanic (2005-)
Tel: +994(12) 44-82-862, Fax: +994(12) 44-82-861
EMail: rector@qu.edu.az

Chancellor: Sahin Durmaz
Tel: +994(12) 48-28-18 EMail: sdurmaz@qu.edu.az

International Relations: Uzeyir Baghirov, Assistant Manager
EMail: ubagirov@qu.edu.az

Faculties

Economic and Administrative Sciences (Administration; Banking; Business Administration; International Economics; Political

Sciences; Public Administration); **Education** (Arabic; Chemistry; Computer Education; English; Literature; Mathematics Education; Physical Education; Primary Education; Translation and Interpretation; Turkish); **Engineering** (Chemical Engineering; Computer Engineering; Engineering; Industrial Engineering; Information Technology; Mechanical Engineering); **Law** (European Studies; International Law; International Relations; Journalism)

History: Founded 1993. Acquired present status 1995.

Governing Bodies: University Senate

Academic Year: September to June (September-December; February-June)

Admission Requirements: Written statement, secondary school certificate (mekteb attestat)

Fees: (Azerbaijan Manat): 2,000-4,000 per annum

Main Language(s) of Instruction: English, Azerbaijani

International Co-operation: With universities in the USA; Turkey; EU; Egypt, Kyrgyzstan

Accrediting Agencies: Ministry of Education

Degrees and Diplomas: *Bakalavr*: Business Administration;Engineering; International Law; Education; Modern Language and Literature, 4 yrs; *Magistr*: Management; Business Administration; Public Administration; Computer Engineering; Industrial Engineering; International Law; Turkish; Arabic; English; International Relations; Banking; International Economic Relations; Azerbaijani Literature, a further 2 yrs. Also Doktorantura (3 yrs): Economics and Management of Agriculture; Turkish Literature; Thermal and Molecular Physics; World Literature; Mathematics

Student Services: Academic counselling, Canteen, Cultural centre, Employment services, Foreign student adviser, Foreign Studies Centre, Handicapped facilities, Health services, Language programs, Nursery care, Social counselling, Sports facilities

Student Residential Facilities: Yes

Special Facilities: Computer Centre. Electronic Laboratory

Libraries: c. 84,276 vols (Books, E-thesis; E-journals; Periodicals)

Publications: Journal of Qafqaz, Scientific journal *(biennially)*

Press or Publishing House: Qafqaz University Press

Academic Staff 2010-2011	MEN	WOMEN	TOTAL
FULL-TIME	208	56	**264**
PART-TIME	9	5	**14**
Student Numbers 2010-2011			
All (Foreign Included)	1,694	819	**2,513**
FOREIGN ONLY	467	163	**630**

Last Updated: 02/08/11

TAFACCUR UNIVERSITY

ul. Tabriz 19, Baku AZ1008
Tel: +994(12) 441-45-35; +99(12) 496-38-26
Fax: +994(12) 441-55-82
EMail: tafaccur@ab.az

President: Musfig Atakishiyev (2002-)
EMail: mushfig_atakishiyev@yahoo.com

Vice-Chancellor: Ragim Guseynov Tel: +994(12) 496-38-25

International Relations: Faik Nagiyev
Tel: +996(12) 440-72-52 EMail: faik_nagiyev@yahoo.com

Faculties
Economics and Management (Business Administration; Economics; Management) *Dekan:* Ilyas Aliyev; **Philology** (Education; English; Journalism; Native Language; Philology) *Dekan:* Ismail Akhmadov

History: Founded 1992, recognized by the State 1995.

Governing Bodies: Scientific Council

Academic Year: September to July

Admission Requirements: Competitive entrance examination following general or special secondary school certificate (Attestat)

Fees: (Manats): 1,000 per annum

Main Language(s) of Instruction: Azeri, Russian

International Co-operation: With Turkey, USA, Netherlands, UK, China, Ukraine

Accrediting Agencies: Ministry of Education

Degrees and Diplomas: *Bakalavr*: all disciplines, 4 yrs; *Magistr*: all disciplines, a further 1-2 yrs

Student Services: Academic counselling, Canteen, Cultural centre, Employment services, Foreign student adviser, Health services, Social counselling, Sports facilities

Libraries: Central Library, c. 5,000 vols

Publications: Journal 'Tafakkur' *(bimonthly)*

Press or Publishing House: Achiq Soz
Last Updated: 18/01/07

SALYAN BRANCH
ul. Samad Vurgun 112, Salyan

President: Seyran Azizov

Faculties
Education (Education; Primary Education); **Juridical Economics** (Commercial Law; Economics); **Law** (Law); **Transport** (Transport and Communications)

History: Founded 1993, Branch of 'Tafaccur' University 1995.

WESTERN UNIVERSITY
Qarb Universiteti (WU)
ul. Istiglalliyyat 27, Baku 370001
Tel: +994(12) 492-61-63
Fax: +994(12) 492-67-01
EMail: administration@wu.edu.az
Website: http://www.wu.edu.az/

Rector: Zenfira Mammadova

Vice-Rector: Duriya Nuriyeva
Tel: +994(12) 492-74-18, Fax: +994(12) 492-77-81

International Relations: Suleymanova Sheyda
Tel: +994(12) 492-68-43, Fax: +994(12) 492-68-43
EMail: ird@wu.edu.org

Faculties
Economics, Marketing and Management (Banking; Business and Commerce; Hotel Management; International Business; Marketing; Tourism); **Humanitarian Programs** (Arts and Humanities; Graphic Arts; Leisure Studies; Painting and Drawing); **Language Training and English Philology** (American Studies; English; French; German; Literature; Modern Languages; Spanish; Translation and Interpretation); **Law** (Law; Public Administration); **Mathematics and Computer Technologies** (Applied Mathematics; Computer Engineering; Computer Science; Data Processing; Design; Fine Arts; Graphic Design; Information Management; Information Technology; Interior Design; Landscape Architecture; Software Engineering); **Political Science and International Relations** (International Relations; Journalism; Oriental Studies; Political Sciences; Social Sciences)

History: Founded 1991, acquired present title 1993.

Academic Year: September to June (September-January; February-June)

Admission Requirements: Competitive entrance examination following general or special secondary school certificate (Attestat)

Fees: Based on contract

Main Language(s) of Instruction: Azeri, English, Russian

International Co-operation: With universities in Ireland, United Kingdom, Netherlands, and USA.

Degrees and Diplomas: *Bakalavr*: Arts; Business Administration; Law; Science, 4 yrs; *Magistr*: Business Administration; Political Science, a further 2 yrs

Student Services: Academic counselling, Cultural centre, Employment services, Foreign student adviser, Foreign Studies Centre, Language programs, Social counselling

Libraries: Scientific-Librarian Centre, 40,000 vols. (including 20,000 in English); 200 periodicals

Publications: Evolution Journal, Scientific popular journal *(quarterly)*; Human Development Problems, Department of Political Science. In Azeri, English, and Russian *(quarterly)*

Press or Publishing House: Publishing-Paleographic Centre
Last Updated: 08/11/11

Bahamas

STRUCTURE OF HIGHER EDUCATION SYSTEM

Description:

In The Bahamas, higher education is provided principally by the College of The Bahamas which offers Associate and Bachelor's degrees in various fields and several Master's degrees in conjunction with overseas Universities. The Bahamas is also affiliated with the University of the West Indies (UWI) which is a regional Institution with campuses in Jamaica, Trinidad and Barbados. The UWI maintains an administrative office and a full-time representative in Nassau, through whom Bahamian students may seek admission to any campus. Furthermore, the UWI Centre for Hotel and Tourism Management is located in Nassau. In addition, some American universities offer degree programmes in The Bahamas. Higher education is under the jurisdiction of the Ministry of Education which is considering the conversion of the College of The Bahamas into a full University. Higher education is also provided by institutions that are privately managed, including religious and overseas-based institutions.

Stages of studies:

University level first stage:
The highest local qualification is the Bachelor's degree. However, some Master's degrees are offered at a distance or in collaboration with overseas institutions.

ADMISSION TO HIGHER EDUCATION

Admission to university-level studies:

Name of secondary school credential required: Bahamas General Certificate of Secondary Education
Entrance exam requirements: An admission test is required in most institutions.

RECOGNITION OF STUDIES

Quality assurance system:

All higher education institutions wanting to operate in The Bahamas have to seek registration with the Quality Assurance Unit of the Ministry of Education. If the evaluation is positive, the registration will then be submitted to the Minister for approval.

NATIONAL BODIES

Ministry of Education
Minister: Desmond Bannister
Director, Higher Education and Lifelong Learning: Leon Higgs
P.O. Box N-3913
Thompson Boulevard
Nassau
Tel: +1(242) 502 2700
Fax: +1(242) 322 8491
EMail: info@bahamaseducation.com
WWW: http://bahamaseducation.com/
Role of national body: Responsible for education policy and development in the country

Data for academic year: 2010-2011
Source: IAU from the website of the Ministry of Education, The Bahamas, 2010. Bodies updated in 2011

INSTITUTIONS

⑂ THE COLLEGE OF THE BAHAMAS (COB)

Oakes Field Campus, Poinciana Drive and Thompson Boulevard, PO Box N4912, Nassau, N.P.
Tel: +1(242) 302-4300
Fax: +1(242) 302-4539
EMail: cob@cob.edu.bs
Website: http://www.cob.edu.bs

President: Betsy Vogel Boze
Tel: +1(242) 302-4338, Fax: +1(242) 322-2054

International Relations: Valdez Russell, Vice-President, Research, Graduate Programmes and International Relations (2010-)
Tel: +1(242) 302-4379, Fax: +1(242) 322-3207
EMail: vkrussell@cob.edu.bs

Centres
Continuing Education and Extension (Continuing Education); **Distance Education** (Distance Education)

Faculties
Liberal and Fine Arts (Arts and Humanities; Communication Arts; English Studies; Fine Arts; Foreign Languages Education) *Dean:* Earla Carey-Baines; **Pure and Applied Sciences** (Business Administration; Health Sciences; Nursing; Technology) *Dean:* Brenda Cleare; **Social and Educational Studies** (Education; Educational Sciences; Social Sciences; Social Studies) *Dean:* Thaddeus McDonald

Institutes
Culinary and Hospitality Management (Hotel Management; Tourism) *Executive Director:* Lincoln Marshall

Schools
Business (Business Administration; Business and Commerce) *Chair:* Remelda Moxey; **Communication and Creative Arts** (Communication Studies; Fine Arts; French; Journalism; Mass Communication; Modern Languages; Music; Spanish) *Chair:* Christine Diment; **Education** (Education; Pedagogy) *Chair:* Gloria Gomez; **English Studies** (Arts and Humanities; English; English Studies) *Chair:* Marjorie Brookes-Jones; **Nursing and Allied Health Professions** (Health Sciences; Nursing) *Chair:* Laura Colebrooke Knowles; **Sciences and Technology** (Agriculture; Architecture; Biology; Chemistry; Engineering; Mathematics; Physics; Technology) *Chair:* Bridget Hogg; **Social Sciences** (Criminal Law; History; Law; Psychology; Public Administration; Religious Studies; Social Sciences; Social Work; Sociology; Theology) *Chair:* Jessica Minnis

Units
Research

Further Information: 3 Campuses: Oakes Field, Grosvenor Close and Northern Campus.

History: Founded 1974.

Degrees and Diplomas: *Associate Degree; Bachelor's Degree.* Various Master's Degrees programmes offered in collaboration with overseas institutions.
Last Updated: 10/01/11

Bahrain

STRUCTURE OF HIGHER EDUCATION SYSTEM

Description:

Higher education is provided by universities, colleges and institutes.

Stages of studies:

University level first stage: *Bachelor's degree*
Four-year courses lead to the Bachelor's degree in Arabic, Biology, Chemistry, Education, English, Mathematics, Physics, Accounting, Business and Management, Computing, Engineering and Office Management. A Bachelor's degree in general nursing takes four years to complete. A BSc in Medical Studies is conferred following a two-year pre-medical course followed by a two-year pre-clinical internship.

University level second stage: *Master's degree, Postgraduate diploma*
The second stage leads, after two to four years' study, to the Master's degree in Education, Biology, Chemistry, Physical Education and Business Administration. An MD is conferred after a three-year clinical internship following upon the BSc in Medical Studies. A three-year part-time MBA is also available. Postgraduate diplomas are conferred after one year's study.

ADMISSION TO HIGHER EDUCATION

Admission to university-level studies:

Name of secondary school credential required: Tawjihiya

Entrance exam requirements: Students must sit for an entrance examination.

Foreign students admission:

Quotas: 5% reservation for non-Bahraini students to the College of Arts, Science and Education and College of Health Sciences.

Entrance exam requirements: Foreign students should have qualifications equivalent to the Bahrain Secondary School Leaving Certificate.

Entry regulations: Only Gulf State nationals do not require visas.

Language requirements: Students should have a good knowledge of Arabic and English.

RECOGNITION OF STUDIES

Quality assurance system:

The Ministry has established a Committee for the evaluation of academic qualifications made up of representatives of specialized bodies or who are related to academic fields. The Ministerial decree no 6/186-1/85, 1986 indicates the basic conditions to evaluate qualifications and the Committee's role, procedure and techniques.

NATIONAL BODIES

Ministry of Education
Minister: Majid bin Ali Al-Naimi
Secretary General, Higher Education Council: Riyadh Yousif Hamzah
PO Box 43
Manama
Tel: +973 1727 8999
Fax: +973 1727 3656
EMail: moe@moe.gov.bh
WWW: http://www.education.gov.bh

Data for academic year: 2007-2008
Source: IAU from Ministry of Education, Manama, 2007. Bodies updated in 2011.

INSTITUTIONS

PUBLIC INSTITUTIONS

ARABIAN GULF UNIVERSITY (AGU)

Building 293, Road 2904, Complex 329, PO Box 26671, Manama
Tel: +973 239-999
Fax: +973 272-555
EMail: info@agu.edu.bh
Website: http://www.agu.edu.bh/

President: Khalid Abdul Rahman Al Ohaly (2001-)
Tel: +973 239-801 EMail: layla@agu.edu.bh

Vice-President: Khaled Tabbara EMail: farzanahj@agu.edu.bh

Colleges
Graduate Studies (Arid Land Studies; Biotechnology; Distance Education; Education; Education of the Gifted; Environmental Management; Special Education; Technology; Water Management); **Medicine and Medical Sciences** (Anaesthesiology; Anatomy; Biochemistry; Community Health; Demography and Population; Gynaecology and Obstetrics; Health Sciences; Immunology; Laboratory Techniques; Medicine; Microbiology; Paediatrics; Pathology; Pharmacology; Physiology; Surgery)

Schools
Management and Finance *(French Arabian)* (Business Administration; Finance; Health Administration)

History: Founded 1979 by the seven Gulf States. A regional autonomous scientific institution with public status, sponsored by the six GCC countries. Jointly managed by the member countries on the basis of equal representation in the General Conference and on the Board of Trustees.

Governing Bodies: General Conference; Board of Trustees

Academic Year: September to June

Admission Requirements: Must be a national of one of the GCC member states that founded the University. Secondary school certificate with cumulative average of 90%.

Main Language(s) of Instruction: English, Arabic

Degrees and Diplomas: *Bachelor's Degree:* Science in Basic Medical Sciences, 4 yrs; *Medical Doctor Degree:* Medicine (MD), 6 yrs; *Postgraduate Diploma in Education; Postgraduate Diploma in Education; Master's Degree:* Biotechnology; Desert Arid Zones; Environmental Management; Technology Management; Water Resource Management, a further 3 yrs; *Master's Degree:* Special Education for the Gifted and Talented; Special Education for the Mentally Retarded and Slow Learners, 3 yrs; *Doctor's Degree (Ph.D):* 4 yrs

Student Residential Facilities: Yes

Libraries: 65,000 vols
Last Updated: 21/11/11

COLLEGE OF HEALTH SCIENCES
PO Box 12, Manama
Tel: +973 1728-5910
Fax: +973 1728-5920
EMail: CHS@health.gov.bh
Website: http://www.chs.edu.bh

Dean: Aneesa Al Sindi

Divisions
Allied Health (Dental Hygiene; Laboratory Techniques; Pharmacy; Public Health; Radiology); **Integrated Sciences** (Behavioural Sciences; Biomedicine; Social Sciences); **Nursing** (Nursing)

History: Founded 1976.
Degrees and Diplomas: *Bachelor's Degree*

Libraries: Ahmed Al-Farsi Library
Last Updated: 21/11/11

GULF COLLEGE OF HOSPITALITY AND TOURISM
PO Box 22088, Muharraq
Tel: +973 320-191
Fax: +973 332-547

Principal: Abdul Raheem Abdulla Al-Khaja (1983-)
Administrator: Haider Hasan Al-Jamea

Programmes
Hospitality (Hotel and Restaurant; Hotel Management); **Tourism** (Tourism)

History: Founded 1975.

Degrees and Diplomas: *Bachelor's Degree; Master's Degree*

GULF UNIVERSITY
Al-Jame'a Al-Khaleejia
P.O. Box 26489, Adliya 26489
Tel: +973 1762-0092
Fax: +973 1762-2230
EMail: info@gulfuniversity.net
Website: http://www.gulfuniversity.edu.bh

President: Mona R. Al-Zayani
Tel: +973 3964-5749 EMail: president@gulfuniversity.net

Vice-President for Academic Affairs: Yehya T. Mohammed Al-Rawi
Tel: +973 3921-3146 EMail: prof.yehya.alrawi@gulfuniversity.net

International Relations: Mohammed Al-Azzawi
Tel: +973 3676-3762
EMail: dr.mohammed.alazzawi@gulfuniversity.net

Centres
English Language Development (English); **Professional Certification and Consultation**

Colleges
Administrative and Financial Sciences (Accountancy; Finance); **Computer Engineering and Science** (Computer Engineering); **Education** (Curriculum; Education; Educational Administration; Educational and Student Counselling; Educational Psychology; Educational Technology; Pedagogy); **Engineering** (Architectural and Environmental Design; Civil Engineering; Electrical Engineering; Electronic Engineering; Mechanical Engineering); **Law** (Administrative Law; Commercial Law; Constitutional Law; Criminal Law)

History: Founded 2001.

Academic Year: September to July

Admission Requirements: Bahrain Secondary School Certificate or equivalent

Fees: (Bahraini Dinars) 1,500 per semester

Main Language(s) of Instruction: Arabic and English

Accrediting Agencies: Ministry of Education

Degrees and Diplomas: *Bachelor's Degree; Master's Degree; Doctor's Degree*

Libraries: Yes.
Last Updated: 21/11/11

UNIVERSITY COLLEGE OF BAHRAIN
P.O. Box 55040, Manama
Tel: +973(17) 790-828
EMail: president@ku.edu.bh
Website: http://www.ucb.edu.bh

President: Khalid Bin Mohammed Al-Khalifa
EMail: President@ucb.edu.bh

Registrar: Isam Ahmed Al-Saraf EMail: al-saraf@ucb.edu.bh

Programmes
Business Administration (Accountancy; Business Administration; Finance; Management; Marketing); **Communication and Media** (Graphic Design; Journalism; Media Studies; Public Relations; Radio and Television Broadcasting); **Information Technology** (Computer Science; Information Technology; Software Engineering)

Academic Year: September to June

Admission Requirements: Bahraini Secondary School Completion Certificate or equivalent

Degrees and Diplomas: *Bachelor's Degree*; *Master's Degree*
Libraries: Yes
Last Updated: 21/11/11

UNIVERSITY OF BAHRAIN (UOB)
PO Box 32038, Manama, Sakhir, Southern Directorate
Tel: +973(17) 438-888
Fax: +973(17) 449-900
EMail: uobpresident@admin.uob.bh
Website: http://www.uob.edu.bh

President: Ebrahim Mohammed Janahi Tel: +973(17) 438-200

Vice-President (Academic Programmes and Research): Khalid Ahmed Abdulla Bugahoos
Tel: +973(17) 438-090, Fax: +973(17) 449-911

International Relations: Hussain Al Ruffai, Director of Information and Public Relations
Tel: +973(17) 438-555, Fax: +973(17) 449-091
EMail: pri@admin.uob.bh

Centres
American Studies (American Studies); **E-Learning** (Distance Education); **English Language** (English); **French Studies** (French; French Studies); **German Studies** (Germanic Studies); **Japanese Studies** (Japanese); **Measurement and Evaluation; Road and Transport Studies** (Road Transport; Transport and Communications)

Colleges
Applied Studies (Business Administration; Chemical Engineering; Civil Engineering; Electrical Engineering; Electronic Engineering; Information Technology; Instrument Making; Mechanical Engineering); **Arts** *(Sukhair)* (Arabic; Arts and Humanities; Communication Studies; English; Fine Arts; Islamic Studies; Literature; Social Sciences; Tourism); **Business Administration** *(Sukhair)* (Accountancy; Administration; Business Administration; Economics; Marketing); **Engineering** *(Isa Town)* (Architecture; Chemical Engineering; Civil Engineering; Electrical Engineering; Engineering; Mechanical Engineering); **Law** *(Sukhair)* (Law; Private Law; Public Law); **Physical Education and Physiotherapy** (Physical Education; Physical Therapy); **Science** *(Sukhair)* (Biology; Chemistry; Mathematics; Natural Sciences; Physics); **Teachers** *(Bahrain)* (Curriculum; Education; Educational Technology; Psychology)

History: Founded 1986, incorporating the University College of Arts, Science and Education, founded 1978 and the Gulf Polytechnic, College of Business and Administration and Engineering, founded 1981.

Governing Bodies: Board of Trustees

Academic Year: September to September (September-January; February-June; June-September)

Admission Requirements: Secondary school certificate (Twajihia) or equivalent

Fees: (Bahraini Dinars): 120 per semester

Main Language(s) of Instruction: Arabic, English

International Co-operation: With universities in United Kingdom; USA; Jordan; Yemen; New Zealand; Lebanon and Australia

Degrees and Diplomas: *Bachelor's Degree*: 4 yrs; *Postgraduate Diploma in Education*: 1 further yr; *Master's Degree*: Arts; Education; Information Technology; Business Science; Engineering, 2 yrs; *Doctor's Degree*: Engineering; Education; Physical Education (PhD), 3 yrs

Student Services: Academic counselling, Canteen, Cultural centre, Employment services, Handicapped facilities, Health services, Language programs, Social counselling, Sports facilities

Student Residential Facilities: For 353 students

Libraries: Total, 186,891 vols; 2,535 Periodical subscriptions; 6,000 full-text e-journals; 23 online databases; 231 computers; accommodates 1,525 students

Publications: Journal of Education and Psychological Sciences *(quarterly)*; Journal of Human Sciences; Journal of Thaqafat; The Arabian Journal of Accounting *(quarterly)*
Last Updated: 20/03/12

PRIVATE INSTITUTIONS

AHLIA UNIVERSITY (AU)
PO Box 10878, GOSI Complex, Manama
Tel: +973 1729-8999
Fax: +973 1729-0083
EMail: info@ahliauniversity.edu.bh
Website: http://www.ahliauniversity.edu.bh/

President: Abdulla Y. Al-Hawaj
EMail: aalhawaj@ahliauniversity.edu.bh

Colleges
Arts, Science and Education (Arabic; Graphic Design; Interior Design; Mass Communication; Mathematics; Modern Languages; Public Relations); **Banking and Finance** (Accountancy; Business Administration; Economics; Finance; Information Management; Management; Marketing); **Engineering** (Computer Engineering; Telecommunications Engineering); **Information Technology** (Information Technology; Multimedia); **Medical and Health Sciences** (Physical Therapy)

History: Founded 2001.

Main Language(s) of Instruction: English and Arabic

Degrees and Diplomas: *Associate Diploma*; *Bachelor's Degree*; *Master's Degree*

Student Residential Facilities: Dormitory facilities for female students from other countries.

Libraries: Ahlia University Library
Last Updated: 21/11/11

AMA INTERNATIONAL UNIVERSITY - BAHRAIN
P.O. Box 18041, Salmabad
Website: http://www.amaiu.edu.bh
President: Amable R. Aguiluz V

Colleges
Administrative and Financial Sciences (Business Administration; Business Computing; International Studies); **Computer Studies** (Computer Science); **Engineering** (Computer Engineering; Electronic Engineering; Mechanical Engineering); **Medicine** (Medicine)

History: Founded 2002. Part of the AMA EducationSystem (AMAES) based in the Philippines.

Accrediting Agencies: Ministry of Education

Degrees and Diplomas: *Bachelor's Degree*; *Master's Degree*
Last Updated: 08/12/11

APPLIED SCIENCE UNIVERSITY
PO Box 5055, Manama
Tel: +973 1772-8777
Fax: +973 1772-8915
EMail: info@asu.edu.bh
Website: http://www.asu.edu.bh/

President: Waheeb Ahmed Alkhaja (2004-)
EMail: president@asu.edu.bh

International Relations: Fahad A. Abdulkarim, International Relations Officer EMail: fahad@asu.edu.bh; fahad_free@yahoo.co.uk

Colleges
Administrative Sciences (Accountancy; Business Administration; Finance; Marketing; Political Sciences); **Arts and Sciences** (Computer Science; Graphic Design; Interior Design); **Law** (Commercial Law; Law; Private Law; Public Law)

History: Founded 2004.

Main Language(s) of Instruction: English and Arabic

Degrees and Diplomas: *Bachelor's Degree:* Accounting; Finance; Business Administration; Computer Information Systems; Computer Science; Graphic Design; Interior Design; Law; Marketing; Political Science; Management Information Systems, 4 yrs; *Master's Degree:* Accounting and Finance; Business Administration; Human Resources Management; Law; Commercial Law; Computer Science; Management Information Systems, 2 yrs

Libraries: 12,840 vols; 37 periodical subscriptions.
Last Updated: 21/11/11

ARAB OPEN UNIVERSITY - BAHRAIN BRANCH

P.O Box: 18211, AL-Haram Plaza, Sahla Street, Manama
Tel: + 973 1740-7077
Fax: + 973 1740-0916
EMail: info@aou.org.bh
Website: http://www.aou.org.bh

Branch director: Samir Qasim Fakhro

Departments
Business (Business Administration; Business and Commerce); **English** (English); **Information Technology** (Information Technology)

History: Founded 2002.

Degrees and Diplomas: *Bachelor's Degree*
Last Updated: 21/11/11

DELMON UNIVERSITY FOR SCIENCE AND TECHNOLOGY

P.O. Box 2469, Exhibition Avenue, Manama
Tel: +973 1729-4400 +973 1729-5500
Fax: +973 1729-2010 +973 1729-3300
EMail: Info@delmon.bh
Website: http://www.delmon.edu.bh

President: Hasan Al-Qadhi EMail: hassan@delmon.bh

Vice President for Academic Affairs: Saad Darwish
EMail: saad@delmon.bh

Faculties
Administrative and Financial Sciences (Business Administration; Economics; Finance; Marketing); **Arts** (Arabic; English; Journalism; Mass Communication; Sociology; Translation and Interpretation); **Education** (Curriculum; Education; Educational Administration; Educational Psychology; Pedagogy); **Fine Arts** (Graphic Design; Interior Design); **Information Technology and Computer Science** (Computer Science; Information Technology); **Law** (Public Law)

History: Founded in 1992. Acquired current title and status 2004.

Academic Year: September to January; February to May

Admission Requirements: Tawjihiya or equivalent secondary shool certificate

Main Language(s) of Instruction: Arabic and English

Accrediting Agencies: Ministry of Education

Degrees and Diplomas: *Bachelor's Degree (BSc):* 4 yrs; *Master's Degree*

Libraries: Yes
Last Updated: 21/11/11

ROYAL COLLEGE OF SURGEONS IN IRELAND - MEDICAL UNIVERSITY OF BAHRAIN

P.O. Box 15503, Adliya, Busaiteen, Manama 228
Tel: + 973 1735-1450
Fax: + 973 1733-0906
EMail: info@rcsi-mub.com
Website: http://www.rcsibahrain.edu.bh/

President: Thomas Collins (2011-)
EMail: president@rcsi-mub.com

Vice President for Administration and Finance: Mary Alexander
EMail: malexander@rcsi-mub.com

International Relations: Fadi Ghosn, Regulatory Affairs Administrator EMail: fghosen@rcsi-mub.com

Schools
Medicine (Health Administration; Medicine); **Midwifery** (Midwifery; Nursing); **Postgraduate Studies and Research** (Health Administration; Nursing)

History: Created 2004.

Governing Bodies: Board of Governors

Academic Year: September to June

Admission Requirements: Recognized secondary school certificate for undergraduate degrees. For Master's courses, a recognized Bachelor's degree is required. Full information available from the institution.

Fees: (US Dollars): Undergrdauate, Medicine, 38,250; Nursing, 11,630; Master's degree, Nursing, 14,550, Ethics and Law, 18,630, all per annum.

Main Language(s) of Instruction: English

International Co-operation: with institutions in Bahrain, Ireland, USA, Canada, UAE, Jordan, Lebanon.

Accrediting Agencies: Gulf Cooperation Council Medical School Dean's Committee; Bahrain Quality Assurance Authority for Education and Training (QAAET)

Degrees and Diplomas: *Bachelor's Degree:* Nursing, 4 1/2 yrs; *Medical Doctor Degree:* Medicine; Surgery; Obstetrics, 5 - 7 yrs; *Master's Degree:* Nursing; Healthcare Ethics and Law; Healthcare Management; Quality and Safety in Healthcare Management, 2 yrs. Also Bridging courses in Nursing, 1 1/2 yrs

Student Services: Academic counselling, Canteen, Foreign student adviser, Handicapped facilities, Health services, Language programs, Social counselling, Sports facilities

Libraries: Frank O'Kane Learning Resource Centre; Library users have access to 8,000 titles; 5 comprehensive databases, 1,600 online journals, clinical digests, 30 print journals, 250 ebooks and access to e-repository which highlights research output by academics. Resources required from outside the collection is supplemented through document delivery services from the British Library and Informa Journals.

Publications: RCSIsmj: Royal College of Surgeons in Ireland Student Medical Journal, Student medical journal aiming to provide a forum for student contributions to the field of medicine in any discipline. *(annually)*; Surgeon: journal of the Royal Colleges of Surgeons of Edinburgh and Ireland, Articles for the worldwide surgical and dental communities. *(annually)*

Academic Staff *2011-2012*	MEN	WOMEN	TOTAL
FULL-TIME	48	53	**101**
PART-TIME	56	36	**92**
STAFF WITH DOCTORATE			
FULL-TIME	19	9	**28**
PART-TIME	38	19	**57**
Student Numbers *2011-2012*			
All (Foreign Included)	342	672	**1,014**
FOREIGN ONLY	203	193	**396**

Last Updated: 20/02/12

ROYAL UNIVERSITY FOR WOMEN (RUW)

PO Box 37400, West Riffa
Tel: +973 1776-4444
Fax: +973 1776-4445
EMail: info@ruw.edu.bh
Website: http://www.ruw.edu.bh/

President: Mazin Mohammed Ali Tel: +973 1776-4429

Vice-President for Academic Affairs: L. Sykes
EMail: rmokha@ruw.edu.bh

Centres
General Studies

Faculties

Art and Design (Fashion Design; Graphic Design; Interior Design); **Business and Financial Sciences** (Banking; Finance; Human Resources; International Business; Management; Marketing); **Education** (Education; English; Preschool Education; Primary Education; Special Education)

History: Founded 2004.

Academic Year: September to January; February to June

Fees: (Bahraini dinars): 160-180 per credit.

International Co-operation: With McGill University, Canada; Middlesex University, UK; West Virginia University , USA

Accrediting Agencies: Ministry of Education

Degrees and Diplomas: *Diploma*: Art and Design, 1 yr; *Bachelor's Degree*: Arts and Design; Education; Business Administration; Science; Computer Science; Information Technology, 4 yrs

Libraries: Yes
Last Updated: 21/11/11

THE KINGDOM UNIVERSITY

PO Box 40434, Manama
Tel: +973(17) 238-899
Fax: +973(17) 271-001
EMail: info@ku.edu.bh
Website: http://www.ku.edu.bh

President: Yousef Abdul Ghaffar Abdulla (2003-2015)

International Relations: Amanulla Mohammed Salih, International Relations Officer EMail: a.salih@ku.edu.bh

Colleges

Arts (Media Studies; Public Relations); **Business Administration** (Banking; Business Administration; Finance; Insurance; International Business; Marketing); **Computing and Information Technology** (Computer Science; Information Technology); **Engineering** (Architecture; Interior Design); **Law** (Law; Private Law)

History: Founded 2002.

Academic Year: September to July

Admission Requirements: High school certificate or equivalent (Tawjeheya)

Fees: (Bahraini Dinars): Bachelor's Degree: 195 per subject

Main Language(s) of Instruction: Arabic, with some courses in English

Degrees and Diplomas: *Bachelor's Degree*: 4 yrs; *Master's Degree*: 2 yrs

Libraries: 3,500 vols; 12 periodical subscriptions

Academic Staff *2009-2010*	TOTAL
FULL-TIME	30
PART-TIME	26
STAFF WITH DOCTORATE	
FULL-TIME	26

Student Numbers *2009-2010*	
All (Foreign Included)	331

Last Updated: 21/11/11

Bangladesh

STRUCTURE OF HIGHER EDUCATION SYSTEM

Description:

Higher education has 3 streams: general, madrasah (2 stages at higher education level with 2-year Fazil following upon Alim followed by 3-year Kamil) and technology education. Higher education institutions include public and private universities, institutes of technology and colleges. The universities are divided into four categories: general, special, open and affiliating. In affiliating systems, teaching is carried out in the colleges while curriculum and examinations are controlled by the universities.

The President of Bangladesh is the Chancellor of the universities and is responsible for the appointment of Vice-Chancellors. The executive body of each institution is the syndicate which approves accounts and reports. Teaching staff elect the deans of the faculties, who, together with professors and affiliated colleges representatives, make up the Academic Council. Government grants constitute nearly 95% of the income of the universities. They are provided by the University Grants Commission. Tuition fees provide the other main source of funding. The Association of Universities of Bangladesh coordinates the activities of the universities in academic and administrative matters. It also liaises with the government and the UGC concerning administrative and financial affairs. Colleges are administratively and financially under government or private control. All medical colleges are under the administrative control of the Ministry of Health and Family Planning.

Stages of studies:

University level first stage: *Bachelor's degree (Pass degree, Honours degree)*
Pass degrees are obtained after three years' study and Honours degrees after four years.

University level second stage: *Master's degree*
Most postgraduate courses leading to a Master's degree are of two years' duration for Pass graduates and one year for Honours graduates.

University level third stage: *Master of Philosophy (MPhil), Doctor's degree (PhD)*
The MPhil course is of one year' duration after the MA or MSc. The MPhil is a research degree offered in specific fields of study. The Doctor of Philosophy (PhD) is the highest university qualification, usually awarded following a minimum of three years' study beyond the Master's degree. It is only offered in specific fields of study. Candidates must submit a thesis following research.

Distance higher education:
The Bangladesh Open University offers both formal programmes leading to Degrees, Diplomas and Certificates and non-formal public awareness programmes for those who have been unable to follow the traditional system.

ADMISSION TO HIGHER EDUCATION

Admission to university-level studies:

Name of secondary school credential required: Higher Secondary Certificate

Entrance exam requirements: There are admission tests for medical colleges, the BITs and university departments.

Foreign students admission:

Entry regulations: Foreign students must hold a visa.

Language requirements: Students should be proficient in English.

NATIONAL BODIES

Ministry of Education
Minister: Nurul Islam Nahid
Building#6, Floor#17th & 18th, Bangladesh Secretariat

Dhaka 1000
Tel: +88 02 716 8711
Fax: +88 02 951 4114
EMail: info@moedu.gov.bd
WWW: http://www.moedu.gov.bd/
Role of national body: The Ministry is concerned with policy formulation, planning, monitoring, evaluation and execution of plans and programmes related to post primary secondary and higher education including technical & madrasah education.

University Grants Commission of Bangladesh - UGC

Chairman: Nurul Islam Nahid
Secretary: Md Khaled
Agargaon
Dhaka 1207
Tel: +88 02 811 2629
Fax: +88 02 812 2948/416
WWW: http://www.ugc.gov.bd/
Role of national body: The University Grants Commission is responsible for supervision of the public and private universities and allocation of government grants to them.

Bangladesh Bureau for Educational Information and Statistics - BANBEIS

1, Sonargaon Road
Dhaka 1205
Tel: +88 02 966 5457
EMail: banbeis@bdcom.com
WWW: http://www.banbeis.gov.bd/
Role of national body: Responsible for collection, compilation and dissemination of educational information and statistics concerning various levels and types of education.

Bangladesh Madrasah Educational Board - BMEB

Chairman: Abdun Noor
2 Orphanage Road,
Baksibazar
Dhaka
Tel: +88 02 862 6138
Fax: +88 02 861 6681
EMail: info@bmeb.gov.bd
WWW: http://www.bmeb.gov.bd/
Role of national body: Responsible for conducting public examinations from Dakhil to Kamil levels. The Board is also responsible for the recognition of the non-government madrasahs.

Association of Universities of Bangladesh - AUB

Chairman: Musleh U. Ahmed
President: Pram Gopal Datta
Executive Secretary: Sheikh M. Saifuddin
University Grants Commission Office Building,
Agargaon,
Shar-e-Bangla Nagar
Dhaka 1207
Tel: +88 02 812 6101
Fax: +88 02 812 6101
EMail: vc@sust.edu;aub@bangla.net
Role of national body: Coordinates the activities of all public universities in Bangladesh and liaises with the Government and the University Grants Commission (UGC) in administrative and financial matters.

Data for academic year: 2006-2007
Source: IAU from the Ministry of Education and Banbeis websites, 2007. Bodies updated in 2011.

INSTITUTIONS

PUBLIC INSTITUTIONS

BANGABANDHU SHEIKH MUJIBUR MEDICAL UNIVERSITY

PO Box 3048, Shahbag, Dhaka 1000
Tel: +880(2) 966-1065
Fax: +880(2) 956-7899
EMail: bsmmu@bangla.net
Website: http://www.bsmmu.org

Vice-Chancellor: Pran Gopal Datta

Registrar: Muhammad A. Gafur Tel: +880(2) 966-1064

Faculties
Medicine (Anaesthesiology; Anatomy; Biochemistry; Cardiology; Dentistry; Dermatology; Gastroenterology; Gynaecology and Obstetrics; Haematology; Hepatology; Medicine; Microbiology; Nephrology; Oncology; Ophthalmology; Orthopaedics; Otorhinolaryngology; Paediatrics; Pathology; Pharmacology; Physical Therapy; Physiology; Psychiatry and Mental Health; Radiology; Statistics; Surgery; Urology; Venereology; Virology)

History: Founded 1965 as Institute of Postgraduate Medicine and Research, acquired present status and title 1998.

Degrees and Diplomas: *Master's Degree*; *Master of Philosophy*
Last Updated: 09/03/11

BANGABANDHU SHEIKH MUJIBUR RAHMAN AGRICULTURAL UNIVERSITY (BSMRAU)

Salna, 1706 Gazipur
Tel: +880(2) 893-1515
Fax: +880(2) 920-5338 +880(2) 920-5333
EMail: info@bsmrau.edu.bd
Website: http://www.bsmrau.edu.bd

Vice-Chancellor: Md. Abdul Mannan Akanda
Tel: +880(2) 920-5336

Registrar: Abul Kalam Azad
Tel: +880(2) 920-5323 +880(2) 920-5322
EMail: registrar@bsmrau.edu.bd

Faculties
Agriculture (Agricultural Economics; Agricultural Engineering; Agriculture; Agronomy; Animal Husbandry; Biochemistry; Biotechnology; Botany; Crop Production; Entomology; Environmental Studies; Farm Management; Fishery; Forestry; Genetics; Horticulture; Plant Pathology; Soil Science); **Animal Science** (Animal Husbandry); **Fisheries** (Aquaculture; Fishery)

History: Founded 1980 as Bangladesh College of Agricultural Sciences. Acquired present title 1998.

Governing Bodies: Syndicate; Academic Committee; Finance Committee; Planning Committee; Selection Committee; Students Disciplinary Committee

Admission Requirements: SSC (Science Group) and HSC (Science Group) examinations or equivalent examinations from a recognized Board or Institution with at least GPA 3 in each of the examinations. Total GPA of both the examinations should be at least 7.(b) must have at least B grade in Physics, Chemistry, Biology, Mathematics and English in HSC or equivalent examinations.

Fees: (Taka): Bachelor, c. 9,000 per annum; Master, c. 8,000; PhD, c. 10,000

Main Language(s) of Instruction: English

Accrediting Agencies: University Grants Commission (UGC)

Degrees and Diplomas: *Bachelor of Science*: Agriculture, 12 terms; *Master's Degree*: Agriculture (M.S.), 5 terms; *Ph. D.*: 9 terms

Student Services: Academic counselling, Canteen, Cultural centre, Health services, Social counselling, Sports facilities

Student Residential Facilities: Yes

Special Facilities: Entomology Museum

Libraries: University Library, 16,900 vols; 240 journal titles

Publications: Annals of Bangladesh Agriculture *(annually)*; Research Abstract *(annually)*
Last Updated: 01/10/10

BANGLADESH AGRICULTURAL UNIVERSITY

Mymensingh 2202
Tel: +880(91) 556-95
Fax: +880(91) 527-80 +880(91) 558-10
EMail: vcbau@bd.drik.net
Website: http://bau.edu.bd

Vice-Chancellor: Md Abdus Sattar Mondal Tel: +880(91) 54333

Centres
Extension

Faculties
Agricultural Economics and Rural Sociology (Agricultural Economics; Finance; Rural Studies; Sociology; Statistics); **Agricultural Engineering and Technology** (Agricultural Engineering; Farm Management; Food Technology; Irrigation; Water Management); **Agriculture** (Agriculture; Agronomy; Biochemistry; Crop Production; Entomology; Forestry; Genetics; Horticulture; Plant Pathology; Soil Science); **Animal Husbandry** (Animal Husbandry; Dairy; Meat and Poultry; Nutrition); **Fishery** (Aquaculture; Fishery); **Veterinary Science** (Anatomy; Histology; Hygiene; Medicine; Microbiology; Parasitology; Pathology; Pharmacology; Physiology; Surgery; Veterinary Science)

Institutes
Advanced Studies and Research; **Graduate Training**; **Research System**

History: Founded 1961 as East Pakistan Agricultural University, acquired present status and title 1972. A teaching, examining and affiliating body, its main purpose is to provide facilities for higher education and research in agriculture and allied fields.

Governing Bodies: Syndicate; Academic Council

Academic Year: July to June

Admission Requirements: Higher secondary certificate (HSC) or foreign equivalent and entrance examination

Fees: (Taka): 150-600

Main Language(s) of Instruction: Bengali, English

Degrees and Diplomas: *Bachelor's Degree (Honours)*: Science (BSc); *Bachelor's Degree (Pass)*: 4 yrs; *Master's Degree*: 1-2 yrs following BSc (Hons) or equivalent; *Ph. D.*: 3-6 yrs

Student Residential Facilities: Halls of Residence

Special Facilities: Research Farms; Botanical Garden

Libraries: 173,519 vols; periodical subscriptions: 197

Publications: Agricultural Economics (professional scientific journal); Agricultural Science (professional scientific journal); Animal Sciences (professional scientific journal); Aquaculture (professional scientific journal); Crop Science (professional scientific journal); Extension Education (professional scientific journal); Fisheries (professional scientific journal); Horticulture (professional scientific journal); Plant Pathology (professional scientific journal); Progressive Agriculture (professional scientific journal); Training and Development (professional scientific journal); Veterinarian, Agricultural Engineering (professional scientific journal); Veterinary Science (professional scientific journal)
Last Updated: 01/10/10

BANGLADESH OPEN UNIVERSITY

Board Bazar, Gazipur 1704
Tel: +880(2) 980-0801
Fax: +880(2) 980-0822 +880(2) 865-750
EMail: info@bou.bangla. net
Website: http://www.bou.edu.bd

Vice-Chancellor: R I M Aminur Rashid (2009-)
Tel: +880(2) 980-0800 EMail: vc@bou.bangla.net

Schools
Agriculture and Rural Development (Agriculture; Crop Production; Fishery; Forestry; Horticulture; Meat and Poultry; Plant and Crop Protection); **Business** (Accountancy; Banking; Business and Commerce; Economics; Management; Marketing); **Education** (Education); **Open** (Banking; Botany; English; Geography; Home Economics; Mathematics; Philosophy; Physics; Political Sciences); **Science and Technology** (Computer Science; Demography and Population; Health Sciences; Nursing; Nutrition); **Social Sciences, Humanities and Language** (Arabic; Arts and Humanities; English; Religion; Women's Studies)

History: Founded 1992.

Academic Year: July to June

Fees: (US Dollars): c. 700

Main Language(s) of Instruction: Bengali, English

Degrees and Diplomas: *Diploma*; *Bachelor's Degree (Pass)*; *Master's Degree.* Also Postgraduate Diploma

Libraries: 17,500 vols; 990 periodical subscriptions
Last Updated: 01/10/10

BANGLADESH UNIVERSITY OF ENGINEERING AND TECHNOLOGY (BUET)
Dhaka 1000
Tel: +880(2) 966-5650
Fax: +880(2) 861-3046
EMail: daers@buet.edu
Website: http://www.buet.ac.bd/

Vice-Chancellor: S. M. Nazrul Islam Tel: +880(2) 861-1666

Registrar: Kamal Ahammad
Tel: +880(2) 966-5616 EMail: regt@regtr.buet.ac.bd

Centres
Biomedical Engineering Research (Biomedical Engineering); **Energy Studies** (Energy Engineering); **Environmental Resources Management** (Environmental Engineering)

Faculties
Architecture and Planning (Architecture and Planning; Regional Planning; Town Planning); **Civil Engineering** (Civil Engineering; Environmental Engineering; Structural Architecture; Transport Engineering; Water Science); **Electrical and Electronic Engineering** (Computer Engineering; Electrical and Electronic Engineering; Industrial Engineering); **Engineering** (Chemical Engineering; Chemistry; Engineering; Materials Engineering; Mathematics; Metallurgical Engineering; Mineralogy; Petroleum and Gas Engineering; Physics); **Mechanical Engineering** (Industrial Engineering; Marine Engineering; Mechanical Engineering; Naval Architecture; Production Engineering)

Institutes
Accident Research; **Appropriate Technology** (Technology); **Information and Communication Technology** (Computer Science; Information Technology); **Water and Flood Management** (Safety Engineering; Water Management; Water Science)

History: Founded 1846 as Dhaka Survey School. Became Ahsanullah Engineering College as a Faculty of Engineering under the University of Dhaka1947. Became East Pakistan Engineering University 1962 and acquired present title and status 1971. A State Institution.

Governing Bodies: Syndicate; Academic Council

Academic Year: January to December

Admission Requirements: Secondary school certificate (SSC) and higher secondary certificate (HSC) or foreign equivalent. Major with Mathematics, Physics, Chemistry and admission test

Fees: (Taka): 1,000 per term

Main Language(s) of Instruction: English

International Co-operation: With universities in Canada, Netherlands and Japan

Degrees and Diplomas: *Bachelor of Science*; *Master's Degree*: Industrial and Production Engineering; Mechanical Engineering; Civil Engineering; Computer Science and Engineering; Water Resources Engineering; Electrical and Electronic Engineering; Materials and Metallurgical Engineering (MScEngg, MEngg, MPhil, MURP); Petroleum and Mineral Resources Engineering; Naval

Architecture and Marine Engineering; Chemical Engineering; Architecture, Urban and Regional Planning; Water and Flood Management (MScEngg, MEngg, MPhil, MURP), 4 yrs; *Master of Philosophy*: Physics; Chemistry; Mathematics; *Ph. D.*: Industrial and Production Engineering; Mechanical Engineering; Civil Engineering; Computer Science and Engineering; Water Resources Engineering; Electrical and Electronic Engineering; Materials and Metallurgical Engineering; Petroleum and Mineral Resources Engineering; Naval Architecture and Marine Engineering; Chemical Engineering; Architecture, Urban and Regional Planning; Water and Flood Management. Also offers post-graduate diplomas in one year in Water Resources Development; Information and Communication Technology.

Student Services: Academic counselling, Canteen, Cultural centre, Foreign student adviser, Health services, Sports facilities

Student Residential Facilities: Yes

Special Facilities: Auditorium

Libraries: Central Library, c. 139,405 vols

Publications: BUET Studies; Research Abstracts *(annually)*; Technical Journal *(annually)*
Last Updated: 01/10/10

BANGLADESH UNIVERSITY OF PROFESSIONALS
Mirpur Cantonment, Dhaka 1216
Tel: +880(2) 803-5997 +880(2) 900-3187
Fax: +880(2) 901-1311 +880(2) 803-5903
EMail: bup.mil@gmail.com
Website: http://www.bup.edu.bd

Vice-Chancellor: Md. Shafiqul Islam

Faculties
Business Studies (Business Computing; Finance; Human Resources; Management Systems; Marketing)

History: Created 2008 out of the Military Institute of Science and Technology (MIST).

Main Language(s) of Instruction: English

Degrees and Diplomas: *Bachelor's Degree (Pass)*: Business Administration; *Master's Degree*: Business Administration. Also Executive Masters.
Last Updated: 30/03/10

BEGUM ROKEYA UNIVERSITY
House# 14, Road# 2, Lalkuthi, Dhap, Rangpur
Tel: +880(521) 66731
Website: http://www.brur.ac.bd

Vice-Chancellor: M.A. Jalil Miah

Faculties
Arts and Social Sciences (Arts and Humanities; Economics; English; History; Native Language Education; Social Sciences); **Business Administration** (Accountancy; Business Administration; Marketing); **Science and Engineering** (Computer Engineering; Computer Science; Engineering; Geography; Mathematics; Natural Sciences; Statistics)

History: Founded 2001 as Rangpur University of Science and Technology. Became Rangpur University. Acquired present title 2008.

Degrees and Diplomas: *Bachelor's Degree (Pass)*; *Master's Degree*

Libraries: Yes
Last Updated: 04/10/10

CHITTAGONG UNIVERSITY OF ENGINEERING AND TECHNOLOGY (CUET)
Chittagong 4349
Tel: +880(31) 71-4951
EMail: admin@cuet.ac.bd
Website: http://www.cuet.ac.bd

Vice-Chancellor: Shyamal Kanti BiswasFax: +880(31) 71-4910
EMail: vc@cuet.ac.bd

Registrar: Md. Shafiqul Islam
Tel: +880(31) 71-4946, Fax: +880(31) 71-4910
EMail: registrar@cuet.ac.bd

Faculties
Architecture and Planning (Architecture; Town Planning); **Electrical and Computer Engineering** (Computer Engineering; Electrical Engineering); **Engineering** (Civil Engineering; Mathematics; Mechanical Engineering; Petroleum and Gas Engineering; Physics)

Institutes
Energy Technology (Energy Engineering)

History: Founded as an Engineering College 1968. Became an Institute of Technology 1986. Acquired present status 2003.

Governing Bodies: Syndicate; Academic Council; Finance Committee

Academic Year: July to June

Admission Requirements: Higher Secondary Certificate

Main Language(s) of Instruction: English

Degrees and Diplomas: *Bachelor's Degree (Pass) (B.Sc.):* 4 yrs; *Master's Degree (M.Sc./ M. Eng.):* a further 1 1/2- 2 yrs

Student Services: Academic counselling, Canteen, Health services, Sports facilities
Last Updated: 04/10/10

CHITTAGONG VETERINARY AND ANIMAL SCIENCES UNIVERSITY

Zakir Hossain Road, Khulshi, Chittagong 4202
Tel: +880(31) 659-093 +880(31) 659-492
Fax: +880(31) 659-620
EMail: vccvasu@yahoo.com
Website: http://www.cvasu.edu.bd/

Vice-Chancellor: Nitish C. Debnath

Faculties
Food Science and Technology (Food Science; Food Technology); **Veterinary Medicine** (Anatomy; Animal Husbandry; Biochemistry; Dairy; Histology; Meat and Poultry; Microbiology; Parasitology; Pathology; Pharmacology; Physiology; Social Sciences; Surgery; Veterinary Science)

Research Centres
Poultry (Meat and Poultry)

History: Created 1996 as Chittagong Government Veterinary College (then part of the University of Chittagong). Acquired current title and status 2006.

Degrees and Diplomas: *Master's Degree (MSc):* 18 months; *Ph. D. (PhD):* 3 yrs. Also Doctor of Veterinary Medicine (DVM) in 5 yrs

Libraries: 10,000 vols.; 10 periodical subscriptions

Academic Staff *2007-2008:* Total 62
STAFF WITH DOCTORATE: Total 6
Student Numbers *2007-2008:* Total 370
Last Updated: 04/10/10

COMILLA UNIVERSITY

House No. 1, Block D Section 1, Housing Estate, Comilla
Tel: +880 81-6681
EMail: info@unicbd.com
Website: http://www.cou.ac.bd

Vice-Chancellor: Amir Hussain Khan

Registrar: Md. A. Rouf Miah

Schools
Arts and Humanities (English; Native Language Education); **Business** (Accountancy; Management; Marketing); **Science** (Computer Engineering; Computer Science; Information Technology; Mathematics); **Social Sciences** (Anthropology; Mathematics; Public Administration)

History: Founded 2000.

Degrees and Diplomas: *Bachelor's Degree (Pass)*; *Master's Degree*
Last Updated: 04/10/10

DHAKA UNIVERSITY OF ENGINEERING AND TECHNOLOGY (DUET GAZIPUR)

Gazipur 1700
Tel: +880(2) 926-4021
Fax: +880(2) 926-1234
EMail: reg_duet@duet.ac.bd
Website: http://www.duet.ac.bd

Vice-Chancellor: Ali Sabder
Tel: +880(2) 925-2365 EMail: msali@duet.ac.bd

Registrar: Md. Alim Dad
Tel: +880(2) 925-6598 EMail: alim@duet.ac.bd

International Relations: Faruk Hossain Syed
EMail: syedfhossain@yahoo.com

Departments
Chemistry (Chemistry); **Humanities** (Arts and Humanities); **Mathematics**; **Physics** (Physics)

Faculties
Civil Engineering (Chemistry; Civil Engineering; Mathematics; Physics); **Electrical and Electronic Engineering**; **Mechanical Engineering** (Mechanical Engineering; Textile Technology)

History: Founded 1980 as Dakha Engineering College, became Bangladesh Institute of Technology, 1986. Acquired present name and status 2003.

Governing Bodies: Syndicate; Academic Council

Admission Requirements: Secondary School Certificate, 3-year Diploma in Engineering from Polytechnic Institute of Bangladesh

Main Language(s) of Instruction: English

Degrees and Diplomas: *Bachelor's Degree (Pass):* 4 yrs; *Master's Degree:* 2 yrs; *Master of Philosophy:* 2 yrs; *Ph. D.:* 3 yrs

Student Services: Academic counselling, Canteen, Cultural centre, Employment services, Health services, Language programs, Nursery care, Social counselling, Sports facilities

Student Residential Facilities: Yes

Libraries: Yes
Last Updated: 04/10/10

HAJEE MOHAMMAD DANESH UNIVERSITY OF SCIENCE AND TECHNOLOGY (HMDSTU)

Dinajpur 5200
Tel: +880(531) 65-429
Fax: +880(531) 61-344
EMail: registrar@hstu.ac.bd
Website: http://www.hstu.ac.bd

Vice-Chancellor: M. Afzal Hossain

Registrar: R.I. Mahmood Tel: +880(531) 61-355

Faculties
Agriculture (Agricultural Economics; Agriculture; Agronomy; Animal Husbandry; Biochemistry; Botany; Chemistry; Entomology; Forestry; Genetics; Horticulture; Plant Pathology; Soil Science; Statistics) *Dean:* Sadrul Amin; **Agro-Industrial and Food Processing Engineering** *Dean:* Md. Ruhul Amin; **Business Studies** *Dean:* Fahima Khanam; **Computer Science and Engineering** (Computer Engineering; Computer Science; Electrical and Electronic Engineering; Electronic Engineering; Information Technology; Mathematics; Physics; Social Sciences; Telecommunications Engineering) *Dean:* Rafiqul Islam Mahmood; **Fisheries**; **Postgraduate Studies** (Agriculture; Agronomy; Biochemistry; Entomology; Horticulture; Plant Pathology; Soil Science)

History: Founded 1976 as Bangladesh Agricultural Research Institute. Acquired present status 2002.

Governing Bodies: Regents' Board

Academic Year: January to December

Fees: (Taka): 2,000 per semester

Main Language(s) of Instruction: English

Degrees and Diplomas: *Bachelor's Degree (Pass):* Agriculture (BScAg (Hons)), 4 yrs; *Master's Degree:* Agriculture (MS), 11/2 yrs; *Ph. D.*

Student Services: Academic counselling, Canteen, Cultural centre, Employment services, Foreign student adviser, Health services,

Language programs, Nursery care, Social counselling, Sports facilities

Student Residential Facilities: Yes

Libraries: 20,000 vols; 500 journals

Publications: Journal of Science and Technology *(annually)*

Last Updated: 19/06/09

ISLAMIC UNIVERSITY

Shantidanga-Dulalpur, Kushtia 7000
Tel: +880(71) 530-29 +880(71) 546-00
Fax: +880(71) 544-00
Website: http://www.iubd.net

Vice-Chancellor: M. Allaudin (2009-) Tel: +880(71) 546-00

International Relations: M.G. Saklayen
Tel: +880(71) 530-29, Ext. 241

Faculties

Applied Sciences and Technology (Applied Chemistry; Applied Physics; Biotechnology; Computer Science; Food Science; Information Sciences; Natural Sciences; Technology); **Business Administration** (Accountancy; Business Administration; Management); **Humanities and Social Sciences** (Arabic; Arts and Humanities; Economics; English; Indic Languages; Political Sciences; Public Administration; Social Sciences); **Law and Sh'ariah** (Islamic Law); **Theology and Islamic Studies** (Islamic Studies; Islamic Theology)

History: Founded 1979 as a unitary teaching and residential University. Acquired present status and title 2000.

Governing Bodies: Syndicate

Academic Year: July to June

Admission Requirements: Higher school certificate or equivalent

Main Language(s) of Instruction: English, Bengali, Arabic

Accrediting Agencies: Government of Bangladesh

Degrees and Diplomas: *Bachelor's Degree (Honours)*: 4 yrs; *Bachelor's Degree (Pass)*: 4 yrs; *Master's Degree*: a further yr; *Master of Philosophy (Mphil)*: 2-5 yrs; *Ph. D. (PhD)*: 2-5 yrs

Student Services: Academic counselling, Sports facilities

Student Residential Facilities: Yes

Libraries: Total, c. 53,345 vols, 7,000 journals

Press or Publishing House: Islamic University Press

Last Updated: 05/10/10

JAGANNATH UNIVERSITY

9-10 Chittaranjan Avenue, Dhaka 1100
Tel: +880(2) 711-9731
Fax: +880(2) 711-3752
Website: http://www.jnuni.net/index1.html

Vice-Chancellor: Mesbahuddin Ahmed
EMail: sikhan119@yahoo.com

Registrar: Farida Rahman

Faculties

Arts; **Business Studies** (Accountancy; Finance; Management; Marketing); **Science**; **Social Science** (Ecology; Political Sciences; Social Work; Sociology)

History: Created in 1858 as Dhaka Brahma School. Offered degree courses from 1949 as Jagannath Intermediate College. Began honours and masters programmes in 1975. Obtained current status and title 2005.

Degrees and Diplomas: *Bachelor's Degree (Honours)*; *Master's Degree*; *Master of Philosophy*; *Ph. D.*

Last Updated: 05/10/10

JAHANGIRNAGAR UNIVERSITY

Savar, Dhaka 1342
Tel: +880(2) 770-8478
Fax: +880(2) 770-8069
EMail: registr@juniv.edu
Website: http://www.juniv.edu

Vice-Chancellor: Shariff Enamul Kabir
Tel: +880(2) 770-8377 EMail: vc@juniv.edu

Registrar: Mohammad Ali

International Relations: Mir Abul Kashem

Faculties

Arts and Humanities (Archaeology; Arts and Humanities; English; International Relations; Philosophy; Theatre); **Biological Sciences** (Biochemistry; Botany; Microbiology; Molecular Biology; Pharmacy; Zoology); **Business Studies** (Banking; Finance; Marketing); **Mathematical and Physical Sciences** (Chemistry; Computer Science; Electronic Engineering; Environmental Studies; Geology; Mathematics; Physics; Statistics); **Social Sciences** (Anthropology; Economics; Environmental Studies; Geography; Government; International Relations; Public Administration; Regional Planning; Social Sciences; Town Planning)

Institutes

Business Administration (Business Administration); **Computer and Information Technology** (Computer Science; Information Technology) *Director:* Md. Nurul Alam Khan; **Remote Sensing** (Surveying and Mapping)

History: Founded 1970, as a unitary teaching and residential University by the Jahangirnagar Muslim University Ordinance promulgated by the then government of E. Pakistan, now Bangladesh. Acquired present title 1972.

Governing Bodies: Syndicate

Academic Year: July to June

Admission Requirements: Secondary school certificate (SSC) and higher secondary certificate (HSC) or foreign equivalent and admission test

Main Language(s) of Instruction: English, Bengali

Degrees and Diplomas: *Bachelor's Degree (Pass)*: 3 yrs; *Master's Degree*: a further yr; *Master of Philosophy*: a further 2-3 yrs; *Ph. D. (PhD)*: 3-5 yrs

Student Residential Facilities: Yes

Libraries: 95,000 vols, 200 periodical subsriptions

Publications: Anthropology Journal *(annually)*; Asian Studies (Department of Government and Policy) *(quarterly)*; Bangla Shahitya Patra (Department of Bengali) *(annually)*; Bhugol Patrika (Department of Geography) *(annually)*; Clio (Department of History) *(annually)*; Copula (Department of Philosophy) *(annually)*; Harvest (Department of English) *(annually)*; Jahangirnagar Economics Review *(annually)*; Jahangirnagar Physical Studies *(annually)*; Jahangirnagar Review *(annually)*; Journal of Life Sciences *(annually)*; Journal of Mathematical and Mathematics Sciences *(annually)*; Journal of Statistical Studies *(annually)*; Rasayan Samikha (Department of Chemistry) *(annually)*

Last Updated: 05/10/10

JESSORE SCIENCE AND TECHNOLOGY UNIVERSITY

Ambot Tala. P.O-Dogachia Jessore Sadar, Jessore
EMail: jessore.university@gmail.com
Website: http://www.jstu.edu.bd

Vice-Chancellor: Abdus Sattar

Faculties

Applied Science and Technology (Applied Chemistry; Chemical Engineering; Environmental Management; Environmental Studies; Food Technology; Nutrition); **Biological Science and Technology** (Aquaculture; Biotechnology; Fishery; Genetics; Microbiology); **Engineering and Technology** (Computer Engineering; Computer Science; Industrial Engineering; Mining Engineering; Petroleum and Gas Engineering)

History: Founded 2008.

Degrees and Diplomas: *Bachelor of Science*; *Bachelor's Degree (Honours)*; *Master's Degree*

Last Updated: 06/10/10

KHULNA UNIVERSITY

Gollamara, Khulna 9208
Tel: +880(41) 721-791 +880(41) 720-171
Fax: +880(41) 731-244
EMail: ku@bdonline.com
Website: http://www.ku.ac.bd

Vice-Chancellor: Md. Saifuddin Shah Tel: +880(41) 721-393

Registrar: Gazi Abdullah-hel Baqui Tel: +880(41) 720-663

Schools

Arts and Humanities (English); **Life Sciences** (Agricultural Engineering; Biological and Life Sciences; Biotechnology; Environmental Studies; Fishery; Forest Management; Natural Resources; Pharmacy; Soil Science; Wood Technology); **Management and Business Administration** (Accountancy; Business Administration; Communication Studies; Computer Science; Economics; English; Finance; Management); **Science, Engineering and Technology** (Architecture; Arts and Humanities; Computer Engineering; Computer Science; Construction Engineering; Electronic Engineering; Engineering; Environmental Studies; Mathematics; Natural Sciences; Physics; Rural Planning; Social Sciences; Software Engineering; Technology; Telecommunications Engineering; Town Planning); **Social Sciences** (Economics; Sociology)

History: Founded 1987, classes formally inaugurated 1991.

Governing Bodies: Syndicate

Academic Year: July to June (July-December; January-June)

Admission Requirements: Higher secondary certificate examination, or Pass in Aleem from any Madrasha in Bangladesh

Fees: (Taka): Registration, 2,500; foreign students, (US Dollars): 1,000

Main Language(s) of Instruction: English, Bengali

Degrees and Diplomas: *Bachelor's Degree (Pass)*: Honours, 4-5 yrs; *Master's Degree*: Agronomy, 1 1/2 yrs

Student Services: Academic counselling, Canteen, Cultural centre, Employment services, Foreign student adviser, Health services, Language programs, Sports facilities

Student Residential Facilities: Yes

Special Facilities: Computer Laboratory; GIS Laboratory

Libraries: c. 22,000 vols

Publications: Khulna University Studies

Last Updated: 20/03/12

KHULNA UNIVERSITY OF ENGINEERING AND TECHNOLOGY

Khulna 9203
Tel: +880(41) 774-584
EMail: vc@kuet.ac.bd
Website: http://www.kuet.ac.bd

Vice-Chancellor: Muhammed Alamgir
EMail: alamgir63dr@yahoo.com

Faculties

Civil Engineering (Arts and Humanities; Chemistry; Civil Engineering; Mathematics; Physics) *Dean*: Md. Monjur Hossain; **Electrical and Electronic Engineering** *Dean*: Md. Abdus Samad; **Mechanical Engineering** *Dean*: Md. Kutub Uddin

History: Founded 1974 as Bangladesh Institute of Technology. Acquired present status 2003.

Main Language(s) of Instruction: English

Degrees and Diplomas: *Bachelor's Degree (Pass)*; *Master's Degree*; *Master of Philosophy*; *Ph. D.*

Last Updated: 09/03/11

MAWLANA BHASANI SCIENCE AND TECHNOLOGY UNIVERSITY

Santosh, Tangail, Dhaka 1902
Tel: +880(921) 55-399
Fax: +880(921) 55-400
EMail: registrar@mbstu.ac.bd
Website: http://mbstu.ac.bd/

Vice-Chancellor: Nurul Islam

Faculties

Computer Science and Engineering (Computer Engineering; Computer Science; Information Technology; Telecommunications Engineering; Textile Technology); **Life Science** (Biotechnology; Criminology; Environmental Studies; Food Technology; Genetics; Natural Resources; Nutrition; Police Studies)

History: Founded 2001.

Degrees and Diplomas: *Bachelor's Degree (Pass)*: 4 yrs; *Master's Degree*

Last Updated: 05/10/10

NATIONAL UNIVERSITY

Jatiya Biswabiddalay
Board Bazar, Gazipur 1704
Tel: +880(2) 980-0655 +880(2) 980-0657
Fax: +880(2) 811-0261
EMail: vc@nu.edu.bd
Website: http://www.nu.edu.bd

Vice-Chancellor: Kazi Shahidullah
Tel: +880(2) 980-0650, Fax: +880(2) 980-0676

Pro-Vice-Chancellor: Abu Saeed Khan

Centres

Curriculum Development and Evaluation (Curriculum); **Postgraduate Education, Training and Research** (Education)

Institutes

Postgraduate Studies

Schools

Undergraduate Studies (Administration; Business Administration; Education; Home Economics; Law)

History: Founded 1992 by act of Bangladesh Government. Composed of numerous affiliated colleges.

Academic Year: July to June

Main Language(s) of Instruction: English, Bengali

Degrees and Diplomas: *Bachelor's Degree (Honours)*: 4 yrs; *Bachelor's Degree (Pass)*: 3 yrs; *Master's Degree*: 1 yr following Bachelor (Honours)

Student Services: Academic counselling, Social counselling
Last Updated: 19/12/08

PATUAKHALI SCIENCE AND TECHNOLOGY UNIVERSITY (PSTU)

Dumki, Patuakali 8602
Tel: +880(442) 756011
Fax: +880(442) 756009
Website: http://pstu.ac.bd/

Vice-Chancellor: Syed Sakhawat Husain

Faculties

Agriculture (Agriculture; Horticulture; Plant Pathology; Soil Science); **Business Administration** (Business Administration; Management); **Computer Science and Engineering** (Computer Science); **Disaster Management** (Management); **Fishery** (Fishery)

History: Founded 2002 in the campus of former Patuakhali Agricultural College.

Degrees and Diplomas: *Bachelor's Degree (Pass)*; *Master's Degree*; *Ph. D.*
Last Updated: 05/10/10

RAJSHAHI UNIVERSITY

Motihar, Rajshahi 6205
Tel: +880(721) 750-041
Fax: +880(721) 750-064
EMail: registrar@ru.ac.bd
Website: http://www.ru.ac.bd

Vice-Chancellor: M. Abdus Sobhan
Tel: +880(721) 750-783 +880(721) 750-320

Registrar: M.A. Salam Tel: +880(721) 750-244

International Relations: Md. Mahbubar Rahman
Tel: +880(721) 750-025

Faculties

Agriculture (Agronomy; Animal Husbandry; Biotechnology; Crop Production; Fishery; Genetics; Veterinary Science); **Arts** (Arabic; Arts and Humanities; Cultural Studies; English; History; Indic Languages; Islamic Studies; Modern Languages; Philosophy); **Business Studies** (Accountancy; Banking; Finance; Management;

Marketing); **Law** (Law); **Life and Earth Sciences** (Botany; Earth Sciences; Geography; Geology; Mining Engineering; Psychology; Zoology); **Medicine**; **Science** (Applied Chemistry; Applied Mathematics; Applied Physics; Biochemistry; Chemistry; Computer Engineering; Computer Science; Demography and Population; Electronic Engineering; Information Technology; Materials Engineering; Mathematics; Molecular Biology; Pharmacy; Physics; Statistics); **Social Sciences** (Economics; Information Sciences; Library Science; Mass Communication; Political Sciences; Public Administration; Social Sciences; Social Work; Sociology)

Institutes
Bangladesh Studies; **Biological Sciences** (Biological and Life Sciences)

History: Founded 1953.

Governing Bodies: Senate; Syndicate; Academic Council

Academic Year: July to June

Admission Requirements: Secondary school certificate (SSC) and/or higher secondary certificate (HSC) or foreign equivalent. The University has its own admission test

Main Language(s) of Instruction: English, Bengali

Degrees and Diplomas: *Bachelor's Degree (Honours)*: 4 yrs; *Master's Degree*: a further 1-2 yrs; *Master of Philosophy*: 2-5 yrs; *Ph. D. (PhD)*: 2-6 yrs

Student Residential Facilities: Yes

Special Facilities: Rajshahi University Varendra Research Museum

Libraries: Central Library, c. 253,580 vols

Publications: Rajshahi University Studies *(annually)*

Press or Publishing House: Rajshahi University Press
Last Updated: 09/03/11

RAJSHAHI UNIVERSITY OF ENGINEERING AND TECHNOLOGY (RUET)
Rajshahi 6204
Tel: +880 721-6254
Fax: +880 721-6254
EMail: registrar@ru.ac.bd'
Website: http://www.ruet.ac.bd

Vice-Chancellor: Sirajul Karim Choudhury (2009-)

Departments
Chemistry; **Civil Engineering**; **Electrical and Electronic Engineering** (Electrical and Electronic Engineering); **Humanities** (Arts and Humanities); **Mathematics** (Mathematics); **Mechanical Engineering** (Mechanical Engineering); **Physics** (Physics)

History: Founded 2003.

Degrees and Diplomas: *Bachelor's Degree (Pass)*; *Master's Degree*
Last Updated: 09/03/11

SHAHJALAL UNIVERSITY OF SCIENCE AND TECHNOLOGY
Sylhet 3114
Tel: +880(821) 714-479
Fax: +880(821) 715-257
EMail: registrar@sust.edu
Website: http://www.sust.edu

Vice-Chancellor: Aminul Islam
Tel: +880(821) 712-706 +880(821) 714-306 EMail: vc@sust.edu

Registrar: Jamil Ahmed Chowdhury Tel: +880(821) 712-784

Schools
Agriculture and Mineral Sciences (Environmental Studies; Forestry); **Applied Sciences and Technology** (Architecture; Chemical Engineering; Civil Engineering; Computer Science; Electronic Engineering; Environmental Engineering; Petroleum and Gas Engineering; Polymer and Plastics Technology; Technology); **Life Sciences** (Biological and Life Sciences; Biotechnology; Genetics; Molecular Biology); **Management and Business Administration** (Business Administration; Management); **Medical Sciences** (Medicine); **Physical Sciences** (Chemistry; Geography; Mathematics;

Physics; Statistics); **Social Sciences** (Anthropology; Economics; Political Sciences; Social Welfare; Sociology)

History: Founded 1987 by Act of Parliament for the purpose of providing facilities for higher education and research, particularly in Science and Technology. Teaching started 1990.

Governing Bodies: Syndicate

Academic Year: July to June

Admission Requirements: Secondary school certificate (SSC) and higher secondary certificate (HSC); both second division or Ordinary ('O') level in 5 subjects and Advanced ('A') level in 3 subjects

Main Language(s) of Instruction: English, Bengali

Degrees and Diplomas: *Bachelor's Degree (Honours)*: 3 yrs; *Master's Degree*: a further 1-2 yrs

Student Residential Facilities: Yes

Libraries: Central Library, 37,700 vols, periodical subscriptions, 45
Last Updated: 06/10/10

SHER-E-BANGLA AGRICULTURAL UNIVERSITY
Sher-e-Banglanagar, Dhaka 1207
Tel: +880(2) 911-0351
Fax: +880(2) 911-2649
EMail: info@sau.edu.bd
Website: http://www.sau.ac.bd

Vice-Chancellor: Md. Shah-E-Alam

Faculties
Agribusiness Management (Agricultural Business; Agricultural Economics); **Agriculture** (Agriculture; Agronomy; Animal Husbandry; Entomology; Harvest Technology; Horticulture; Soil Science)

History: Founded 1938 as Bangladesh Agricultural Institute. Acquired present status and title 2001.

Degrees and Diplomas: *Bachelor's Degree (Pass)*; *Master's Degree*; *Ph. D.*
Last Updated: 06/10/10

SYLHET AGRICULTURAL UNIVERSITY
SIU, Shamimabad, Bagbari Sylhet
Tel: +880(821) 761-980
EMail: siu_syl@yahoo.com
Website: http://www.sylhetagrivarsity.edu.bd

Vice-Chancellor: Md. Abdul Awal

Faculties
Agricultural Business and Economics (Agricultural Business; Rural Planning); **Agriculture** (Agricultural Equipment; Agronomy; Biotechnology; Botany; Chemistry; Crop Production; Entomology; Environmental Studies; Forestry; Horticulture; Plant Pathology; Soil Science); **Fisheries** (Aquaculture; Fishery); **Veterinary and Animal Science** (Anatomy; Animal Husbandry; Biochemistry; Cattle Breeding; Chemistry; Dairy; Epidemiology; Genetics; Histology; Immunology; Meat and Poultry; Medicine; Microbiology; Parasitology; Pathology; Pharmacology; Physiology; Surgery; Toxicology)

History: Founded 2006.

Degrees and Diplomas: *Bachelor's Degree (Pass)*. Also Doctor of Veterinary Medicine

Student Residential Facilities: Yes
Last Updated: 06/10/10

UNIVERSITY OF CHITTAGONG (CU)
Hathazari, Chittagong 4331
Tel: +880(31) 716-552 +880(31) 716-558
Fax: +880(31) 726-311 +880(31) 726-314
EMail: vc_cu66@yahoo.com
Website: http://www.cu.ac.bd

Vice-Chancellor: Anowarul Azim (2011 -)
Tel: +880(31) 714-949, Fax: +880(31) 726-310

Registrar: Idris Miyan Tel: +880(31) 726-311, Ext. 4201

International Relations: Idris Miyan
Tel: +880(31) 726-310, Ext.4201

Faculties

Arts (Arabic; Arts and Humanities; English; Fine Arts; History; Islamic Studies; Journalism; Oriental Languages; Philosophy); **Biological Science** (Biology); **Commerce** (Accountancy; Business and Commerce; Finance; Management; Marketing); **Law** (Law); **Science** (Applied Physics; Biochemistry; Botany; Chemistry; Computer Science; Electronic Engineering; Geography; Mathematics; Microbiology; Natural Sciences; Physics; Soil Science; Statistics; Zoology); **Social Sciences** (Anthropology; Economics; Political Sciences; Public Administration; Social Sciences; Sociology)

Institutes

Community Ophthalmology *Director:* M. Fazlul Hoq; **Forestry and Environmental Science** (Environmental Studies; Forestry) *Director:* M. Kamal Hossain

Research Centres

Mathematical and Physical Science *Director:* A. Mansur Chowdhury; **Nazrul** *Director:* S. Nath Biswas

History: Founded 1964. Acquired present status 1966. A State Institution.

Governing Bodies: Senate; Syndicate; Academic Council; Board of Advanced Studies; Finance Committee; Planning and Development Committee; Selection Boards

Academic Year: July to June

Admission Requirements: Secondary school certificate (SSC) and higher secondary certificate (HSC) or foreign equivalent and admission test

Fees: (Taka): 1,412-1,558

Main Language(s) of Instruction: English (Examination: Bengali or English)

International Co-operation: With universities in Commonwealth countries

Degrees and Diplomas: *Bachelor's Degree (Honours):* 4 yrs; *Master's Degree:* 1 further yr; *Master of Philosophy (M.Phil):* 2 yrs; *Ph. D. (Ph.D)*

Student Services: Academic counselling, Canteen, Employment services, Handicapped facilities, Health services, Language programs, Sports facilities

Student Residential Facilities: Yes

Special Facilities: Museum

Libraries: Central Library, 197,867 vols

Publications: Bangla Sahitya Samity (Department of Bengali); Eco (Department of Economics) *(annually)*; Hisab Bijyan (Department of Accountancy) *(annually)*; Itihas Patrica (Journal in Bengali, Department of History) *(biannually)*; Managire (Department of Management) *(annually)*

Last Updated: 03/11/11

UNIVERSITY OF DHAKA

Dhaka Bishwabidyalaya
Ramna, Dhaka 1000
Tel: +880(2) 966-1900
Fax: +880(2) 861-5583
EMail: duregstr@bangla.net
Website: http://www.univdhaka.edu

Vice-Chancellor: A. M. S. Arefin Siddique (2009-)
Tel: +800(2) 861-8383

Faculties

Biological Sciences (Aquaculture; Biochemistry; Biological and Life Sciences; Biotechnology; Botany; Clinical Psychology; Fishery; Microbiology; Psychology; Soil Science; Zoology); **Business Studies** (Accountancy; Banking; Business and Commerce; Finance; Management; Marketing); **Earth and Environmental Sciences** (Earth Sciences; Environmental Studies; Geography; Geology); **Education**; **Engineering and Technology** (Applied Chemistry; Applied Physics; Computer Engineering; Computer Science; Electronic Engineering); **Fine Arts** (Arabic; Arts and Humanities; Comparative Religion; English; History; Indic Languages; Information Sciences; Islamic Studies; Journalism; Library Science; Linguistics; Mass Communication; Music; Persian; Philosophy; Sanskrit; Theatre; Urdu); **Law** (Law); **Medicine** (Medicine; Nursing); **Pharmacy** (Pharmacy); **Science** (Applied Chemistry; Applied Physics;

Chemistry; Electronic Engineering; Geography; Geology; Mathematics; Natural Sciences; Physics; Statistics) *Dean:* Tajmeri S.A. Islam; **Social Sciences** (Anthropology; Demography and Population; Economics; International Relations; Peace and Disarmament; Political Sciences; Public Administration; Social Sciences; Sociology; Women's Studies)

Institutes

Business Administration (Business Administration) *Director:* Muhammad Ziaulhaq Mamun; **Education and Research** (Education; Educational Research) *Director:* Iqbal Aziz Muttaqi; **Fine Arts** (Architecture; Fine Arts; Graphic Design; Handicrafts; Painting and Drawing) *Director:* Abdus Shakoor Shah; **Health Economics** *Director:* Azizur Rahman; **Information Technology** *Director:* Zerina Begum; **Modern Languages** (Arabic; Chinese; French; German; Indic Languages; Korean; Modern Languages; Persian; Russian; Spanish; Turkish) *Director:* Md. Anwar Hossain; **Nutrition and Food Science** (Food Science; Nutrition) *Director:* M. Nazmul Hasan; **Social Welfare and Research** *Director:* A.S.M. Atiqur Rahman; **Statistical Research and Training** (Statistics) *Director:* Azmeri Khan

Further Information: Also Research Centres

History: Founded 1921 by Act of Parliament. A State Institution.

Governing Bodies: Senate; Syndicate; Academic Council

Academic Year: July to June (July-December; January-June)

Admission Requirements: Secondary school certificate (SSC) and higher secondary certificate (HSC) or foreign equivalent and admission test

Fees: (Taka): Undergraduate c. 3,365 per session (Arts, Business Studies, Law, Social Sciences); c. 3,450 per session (Biological Sciences, Pharmacy, Science); Postgraduate (MPhil), c. 3,230 per session (Arts, Business Studies, Law, Social Sciences), c. 4,580 (Biological Sciences, Pharmacy, Science; c. 3,000-4,400. (US Dollars): Foreign students, 1,200 per annum (SAARC Countries, 500)

Main Language(s) of Instruction: Bengali, English

Degrees and Diplomas: *Bachelor's Degree (Honours):* Biological Sciences; Business Studies; Education; Fine Arts; Law; Pharmacy; Science; Social Sciences, 4 yrs; *Bachelor's Degree (Honours):* Home Economics, 3 yrs; *Bachelor's Degree (Pass):* Dental Surgery; Homeopathic Medicine and Surgery; Leather Technology; Nursing Science; Textile Technology, 4 yrs; *Bachelor's Degree (Pass):* Home Economics; Science; Technical Education, 2 yrs; *Bachelor's Degree (Pass):* Medicine and Surgery; Unani and Ayurvedic, 5 yrs; *Master's Degree:* Arts; Biological Science; Business Studies; Education; Law; Pharmacy, a further 1 yr; *Master's Degree:* Business Administration; Fine Arts; Home Economics, a further 2 yrs; *Master's Degree:* Social Sciences, a further yr; *Master of Philosophy:* Arts (MPhil); Biological Sciences; Business Studies; Education; Law; Pharmacy; Science; Social Sciences, a further 2 yrs; *Ph. D.:* Arts; Biological Sciences; Business Studies; Education; Law; Pharmacy; Science; Social Sciences, 4 yrs

Student Residential Facilities: Yes

Special Facilities: Museum of Commerce. Art Gallery. Botanical Garden

Libraries: Central Library, 608,744 vols including 300 periodicals

Publications: Bangladesh Journal of Nutrition; Dakha University Journal of Psychology *(annually)*; Dhaka Bishwabidyala Patrika *(3 per annum)*; Dhaka University Studies (Part A) *(annually)*; Dhaka University Studies (Part B) *(annually)*; Dhaka University Studies (Part C) *(annually)*; Dhaka University Studies (Part D) *(annually)*; Dhaka University Studies (Part E) *(annually)*; Dhaka University Studies (Part F) *(annually)*; IML Patrika *(annually)*; Journal of Arabic *(annually)*; Journal of Management; Journal of Statistical Research

Press or Publishing House: Dhaka University Grantha Sangstha
Last Updated: 04/10/10

PRIVATE INSTITUTIONS

AHSANULLAH UNIVERSITY OF SCIENCE AND TECHNOLOGY (AUST)

141-142 Love Road, Tejgaon Industrial Area, Dhaka 1208
Tel: +880(2) 986-0907 +880(2) 989-7020
Fax: +880(2) 986-0564
EMail: regr@aust.edu
Website: http://www.aust.edu

Vice-Chancellor: A.M.M. Safiullah (2010-)
Tel: +880(2) 885-4676 EMail: vc@aust.edu

Registrar: Muhammad Abdul Gafur Tel: +880(2) 986-0779

Faculties

Architecture and Planning (Architecture and Planning); **Business and Social Sciences** (Business Administration); **Education** (Education); **Engineering** (Civil Engineering; Computer Engineering; Computer Science; Electrical and Electronic Engineering; Engineering; Industrial Engineering; Mathematics; Textile Technology)

Institutes

Technical and Vocational Education and Training (Architecture; Chemical Engineering; Civil Engineering; Computer Engineering; Electrical Engineering; Electronic Engineering)

History: Founded 1995 under the Private University Act of 1992. Sponsored by Dhaka Ahsania Mission, the largest Bangladeshi Non-Governmental Organization involved in extensive programmes of Education, Health and Socio-Economic sectors in the country. Also known as Ahsanullah Biggyan O Projucti Bishwabiddalaya.

Governing Bodies: Syndicate

Academic Year: April to March

Admission Requirements: Higher secondary certificate (HSC), or 'A' level or equivalent. Only students with high performance in HSC/ 'A' level or equivalent can apply for admission

Main Language(s) of Instruction: English

Degrees and Diplomas: *Diploma*: 4 yrs; *Bachelor's Degree (Pass)*: Architecture, 5 yrs; *Bachelor's Degree (Pass)*: Engineering; Business Administration, 4 yrs; *Master's Degree*: Business Administration, a further 1-2 yrs; *Master's Degree*: Education; Mathematics, 1 further yr

Student Services: Health services, Sports facilities

Student Residential Facilities: Yes (Student Hostel)

Libraries: 13,000 books and journals

Publications: AUST Journal of Science and Technology
Last Updated: 02/03/12

AMERICAN INTERNATIONAL UNIVERSITY-BANGLADESH (AIUB)

83/B, Rd4, Banani, Kemal Ataturk, Dhaka 1213
Tel: +880(2) 881-1749 +880(2) 988-5907
Fax: +880(2) 881-3233
EMail: clamagna@aiub.edu
Website: http://www.aiub.edu

Vice-Chancellor: Carmen Z. Lamagna (1999-)
Tel: +880(2) 989-0415, Fax: +880(2) 881 3233

Director: Hasanul Hasan EMail: habedin@aiub@edu

International Relations: Ishtiaque Abedin, Vice-President, Director, International Affairs
Tel: +880(2) 988-5907 EMail: iabedin@aiub.edu

Departments
Architecture (Architecture)

Faculties
Arts and Social Sciences (Advertising and Publicity; English; Mass Communication; Media Studies); **Business**; **Engineering** (Computer Engineering; Electrical and Electronic Engineering; Engineering; Telecommunications Engineering); **Science**

History: Founded 1994.

Governing Bodies: Academic Council; Board of Trustees

Academic Year: September to August

Admission Requirements: Secondary school certificate (SSC) and higher secondary certificate (HSC), or 5 'O' Levels and 2 'A' levels, or any US high school certificate or equivalent and admission test

Fees: (Taka): 110,000 per annum

Main Language(s) of Instruction: English

International Co-operation: International Assocation of Universities; International Association of University Presidents (IAUP) and Association of Universities of Asia and the Pacific (AUAP) programmes

Accrediting Agencies: Government and University Grants Commission (UGC)

Degrees and Diplomas: *Bachelor's Degree (Pass)*: Business Administration; Accountacy; Finance; Banking; Taxation; Human Resources; Labour and Industrial Relations; Marketing; Commercial Law; Statistics; Economics; International Economics; Computer Science; Computer Engineering; Electronic and Communication Engineering; Electrical and Electronic Engineering; Management; Production and Operation Management; Information Science; Computer Programming Database Management, 4 yrs; *Master's Degree*: Business Administration; Accountancy; Finance; Economics; Human Resource Management; Marketing; Production and Operation Management; Agri-business, a further 2 yrs. Also Executive MBA

Student Services: Academic counselling, Canteen, Cultural centre, Employment services, Foreign student adviser, Foreign Studies Centre, Handicapped facilities, Health services, Language programs, Social counselling, Sports facilities

Student Residential Facilities: Yes

Special Facilities: Language Laboratory. Auditorium.

Libraries: University Library

Publications: AIUB Journal of Business and Economics, Research and Articles on Business and Economics *(biannually)*; AIUB Journal of Science and Technology, Research and Articles on Science and Technology *(biannually)*
Last Updated: 01/10/10

ASA UNIVERSITY

23/3 Khilji Road, Shyamoli, Dhaka 1207
Tel: +880(2) 812-2555
EMail: info@asaub.edu.bd
Website: http://www.asaub.edu.bd

Vice-Chancellor: Md. Muinuddin Khan

Faculties
Arts and Social Sciences (English; Linguistics; Literature); **Business** (Business Administration); **Law** (Law)

History: Founded 2006.

Degrees and Diplomas: *Bachelor's Degree (Pass)*; *Master's Degree*

Student Residential Facilities: For women

Libraries: Yes
Last Updated: 05/10/10

ASIAN UNIVERSITY OF BANGLADESH (AUB)

House No. 9, Road No. 5, Sector 7, Uttara Model Town, Dhaka 1230
Tel: +880(2) 891-6116
Fax: +880(2) 891-6521
EMail: info@asianuniversity.edu
Website: http://www.aub-bd.org

Vice-Chancellor: Abulhasan M. Sadeq (1997-)
Tel: +880(2) 891-2366 EMail: aub@bdonline.com

Registrar: A.K.M. Salahuddin

Schools
Arts (Arts and Humanities; English; Islamic Studies; Native Language Education; Oriental Languages); **Business** (Accountancy; Business Administration; Finance; Human Resources; International Business; Management Systems; Marketing); **Education and Training** (Education); **Science and Engineering** (Computer Engineering; Computer Science); **Social Sciences** (Anthropology; Economics; Government; Information Management; Library Science; Political Sciences; Social Sciences; Sociology)

Further Information: Also Viz and Dhanmondi campuses

History: Founded 1996.

Governing Bodies: Board of Governors

Admission Requirements: Higher secondary certificate, Advanced ('A') level

Fees: (Taka): 3,600-26,950 per semester

Main Language(s) of Instruction: English

International Co-operation: With universities in Australia, Iran, Jordan, Malaysia, USA

Accrediting Agencies: University Grants Commission (UGC); Ministry of Education; Academy for the Promotion of International Culture and Scientific Exchange (APICS), Switzerland

Degrees and Diplomas: *Bachelor's Degree (Honours)*: Bengali Literature; Islamic Studies (BA (Hons)), 4 yrs; *Bachelor's Degree (Pass)*: Business Administration (BBA); Computer Science; Engineering (BSc), 4 yrs; *Bachelor's Degree (Pass)*: Education (BEd); Social Sciences; Government; Political Science (BSS), 2 yrs; *Master's Degree*: Bengali Literature; Islamic Studies (MA); Business Administration; Finance; Accountancy; Marketing; Human Resources; Management Systems; Education (MBA); Social Sciences; Government; Political Science (MSS), a further 2 yrs

Student Services: Academic counselling, Canteen, Cultural centre, Employment services, Foreign student adviser, Language programs, Social counselling, Sports facilities

Student Residential Facilities: Yes

Libraries: Asian University of Bangladesh (AUB) Library
Last Updated: 01/10/10

ATISH DIPANKAR UNIVERSITY OF SCIENCE AND TECHNOLOGY

Faisal Tower, 27 Gulshan North C/A, Circle 2, Dhaka 1212
Tel: +880(2) 989-1904
Fax: +880(2) 885-7107
EMail: info@atishdipankaruniversity.edu.bd
Website: http://www.atishdipankaruniversity.edu.bd

Vice-Chancellor: Anwara Begum

Faculties
Agriculture, Biological Science and Biotechnology; **Arts and Social Sciences** (English); **Business and Economics** (Business Administration; Economics); **Law**; **Science and Technology** (Computer Engineering; Computer Science; Electronic Engineering; Pharmacy; Telecommunications Engineering)

Degrees and Diplomas: *Bachelor's Degree (Pass)*; *Master's Degree*
Last Updated: 09/03/11

BANGLADESH ISLAMI UNIVERSITY

Gazaria Tower, 89/12, R. K. Mission Road (Maniknagar Bishwa Road), Dhaka 1203
Tel: +880(2)7552-495
EMail: biudhaka@yahoo.com
Website: http://bangladeshislamiuniversity.com

Vice-Chancellor: M. Korban Ali

Faculties
Business Studies (Business Administration); **Human Affairs and Social Sciences** (Social Sciences); **Law** (Law)

History: Founded 2005.

Degrees and Diplomas: *Bachelor's Degree (Pass)*; *Master's Degree*
Last Updated: 05/10/10

BANGLADESH UNIVERSITY

15/1, Iqbal Road, Mohammadpur, Dhaka
Tel: +880(2) 913-6061
EMail: bu@citechco.net
Website: http://www.bangladeshuniversity.edu.bd

Vice-Chancellor: Quazi Azher Ali

Faculties
Arts and Social Sciences (Economics; Education; English; Public Administration; Sociology); **Business** (Accountancy; Business Administration; Marketing); **Engineering** (Architecture; Computer Engineering; Computer Science; Electrical and Electronic Engineering; Telecommunications Engineering); **Law** (Law); **Science** (Chemistry; Environmental Studies; Mathematics; Pharmacy)

Degrees and Diplomas: *Bachelor's Degree (Pass)*; *Master's Degree*

Libraries: c. 15,000 vols.
Last Updated: 06/10/10

BANGLADESH UNIVERSITY OF BUSINESS AND TECHNOLOGY (BUBT)

Dhaka Commerce College Road, Mirpur-2, Dhaka 1216
Tel: +880(2) 8057-581 +880(2) 8057-582
Fax: +880(2) 8057-583
EMail: info@bubt.edu.bd
Website: http://www.bubt.edu.bd/

Vice-Chancellor: Md. Abu Saleh (2007-)
Registrar: Enayet Hossain Mia

Faculties
Arts and Humanities (English); **Business** (Banking; Business Administration); **Computer Science and Technology** (Computer Engineering; Computer Science; Information Technology); **Law** (Law); **Mathematical and Physical Science** (Mathematics); **Social Sciences** (Development Studies; Economics)

History: Founded 2003 by Dhaka Commerce College

Governing Bodies: Board of Trustees, Syndicate, Academic Council

Academic Year: Autumn: October-January; Summer: June-September; Spring: February-May

Admission Requirements: Secondary School Certificate (or equivalent) for undergraduate programmes; Relevant undergraduate degree for postgraduate programmes.

Main Language(s) of Instruction: English

Degrees and Diplomas: *Bachelor of Science*; *Bachelor's Degree (Honours)*; *Bachelor's Degree (Pass)*; *Master's Degree*

Student Services: Academic counselling, Canteen, Cultural centre, Employment services, Foreign student adviser, Foreign Studies Centre, Handicapped facilities, Health services, Language programs, Social counselling, Sports facilities

Academic Staff 2009-2010	MEN	WOMEN	TOTAL
FULL-TIME	53	23	76
PART-TIME	45	3	48
STAFF WITH DOCTORATE			
FULL-TIME	1	–	1
PART-TIME	9	1	10
Student Numbers 2009-2010			
All (Foreign Included)	2,898	1,310	4,208

Evening students, 944.
Last Updated: 01/10/10

BGC TRUST UNIVERSITY BANGLADESH

BGC Viddyanagar, Chandanaish, Chittagong
Tel: +880(31) 636-548 +880(31) 627-040
EMail: registrarbgctub@yahoo.com

Vice-Chancellor: Saroj Kanti Singh Hazari
Tel: +1713 124384 (mob.)
Registrar: Farid Ahmed Tel: +1713 120863 (mob.)

Faculties
Business Administration (Business Administration); **Computer Science and Engineering** (Computer Science; Engineering); **English** (English); **Law** (Law); **Pharmacy**

History: Founded 2001.
Governing Bodies: Board of Trustees
Academic Year: Higher secondary certificate
Main Language(s) of Instruction: English
Accrediting Agencies: UGC and Ministry of Education, Bangladesh

Degrees and Diplomas: *Bachelor's Degree (Pass)*: 4 yrs; *Master's Degree*: 1-2 yrs

Student Services: Academic counselling, Canteen, Cultural centre, Health services, Language programs, Social counselling, Sports facilities

Student Residential Facilities: Yes (for male and female students)

Libraries: Yes
Last Updated: 09/03/11

BRAC UNIVERSITY (BU)

66 Mohakhali, Dhaka 1212
Tel: +880(2) 988-1265
Fax: +880(2) 881-0383
EMail: info@bracuniversity.ac.bd
Website: http://www.bracuniversity.ac.bd

Vice-Chancellor: Ainun Nishat EMail: vc@bracuniversity.ac.bd

Registrar: Ishfaq Ilahi Choudhury
EMail: registrar@bracuniversity.ac.bd

Departments
Architecture (Architecture); **Economics and Social Sciences** (Anthropology; Development Studies; Economics; Gender Studies; Social Sciences); **English and Humanities** (Arts and Humanities; English; Linguistics; Literature; Modern Languages); **Mathematics and Natural Sciences** (Applied Physics; Biotechnology; Mathematics; Natural Sciences; Physics); **Pharmacy** (Pharmacy)

Institutes
Development (Development Studies); **Educational Development** (Education); **Governance Studies** (Government)

Schools
Business (BRAC); **Engineering and Computer Science** (Computer Engineering; Computer Science; Electrical and Electronic Engineering); **Law**; **Public Health** (James P. Grant)

History: Founded 2001.

Governing Bodies: Governing Board

Academic Year: September to August

Admission Requirements: Higher Secondary Certificate: 'A' Level and Admission test

Fees: (Taka): 3,000-4,000 per credit

Main Language(s) of Instruction: English

International Co-operation: With universities in USA, Canada, United Kingdom, Australia, Singapore and Thailand.

Accrediting Agencies: University Grants Commission (UGC), Ministry of Education

Degrees and Diplomas: Bachelor of Science: Computer Science; Electronic and Telecommunications Engineering, 124 credits; Bachelor of Science: Physics, 132 credits; Bachelor's Degree (Honours): Law (LLB), 135 credits; Bachelor's Degree (Pass): Architecture (B.ARCH), 199 credits; Bachelor's Degree (Pass): Business Administration (BBA), 130 credits; Bachelor's Degree (Pass): Computer Science and Engineering, 136 credits; Bachelor's Degree (Pass): Economics; Social Sciences (BSS), 120 credits; Bachelor's Degree (Pass): English (BA), 124 credits; Master's Degree: Business Administration (MBA), 60 credits; Master's Degree: Development Studies (MDS), 48 credits; Master's Degree: Governance and Development (MAGD), 36 credits; Master's Degree: Public Health (MPH), 51 credits; Master of Philosophy: Disaster Management (MDM), 45 credits. Also six months' certificate courses and one-year post-graduate diplomas.

Student Services: Academic counselling, Canteen, Cultural centre, Employment services, Foreign student adviser, Handicapped facilities, Health services, Language programs, Social counselling, Sports facilities

Student Residential Facilities: Yes

Special Facilities: Architectural Studios. Laboratories

Libraries: Ayesha Abed Library, c. 12,842 vols

Publications: BRAC University Journal (biannually)
Last Updated: 04/10/10

CENTRAL WOMEN'S UNIVERSITY

6 Hatkhola Road, Dhaka 1203
Tel: +880(2) 717-1141
EMail: info@cwu-bd.net
Website: http://cwu-bd.net

Vice-Chancellor: Perween Hasan Tel: +880(2) 955-9452

Registrar: Firdaus Ali

Departments
English Language and Literature (English); **Sociology** (Environmental Studies; Gender Studies; Geography; Political Sciences; Sociology)

History: Founded 1993.

Admission Requirements: Secondary school certificate (SSC) and Higher secondary school certificate (HSC)

Fees: (US Dollars): 500

Main Language(s) of Instruction: English

Degrees and Diplomas: Bachelor's Degree (Honours) (BA; BSc): 4 yrs; Master's Degree

Student Services: Academic counselling, Cultural centre, Foreign student adviser, Language programs

Student Residential Facilities: None

Libraries: Yes
Last Updated: 04/10/10

CITY UNIVERSITY (CU)

40, Kemal Ataturk Avenue, Banani, Dhaka 1213
Tel: +880(2) 989-3983
Fax: +880(2) 956-4020
EMail: frs1101@yahoo.com
Website: http://www.cityuniversity.edu.bd

Vice-Chancellor: N.R.M. Borhan Uddin

Registrar: R.A.M.Obaidul Muktadir Chowdhury

Faculties
Business Administration; **Computer Science and Engineering**; **English** (Arts and Humanities; English); **Law** (Law); **Social Sciences** (Social Sciences); **Textile Engineering** (Textile Technology)

History: Founded 2002.

Governing Bodies: Board of Governors; Board of Trustees; Executive Committee

Academic Year: September to August

Admission Requirements: Higher secondary school certificate (HSC)/ A-Level/ GED and admission test

Fees: (Taka): Undergraduate, 2,000 per credit; Graduate Programmes, 2,500

Main Language(s) of Instruction: English

International Co-operation: Exchange Programes with Dublin City University (Ireland), Southern University, University of Colorado and Wichita State University (USA)

Accrediting Agencies: University Grants Commission; Ministry of Education

Degrees and Diplomas: Bachelor's Degree (Pass): Accountancy; Finance; Management; E-Commerce; Marketing; Business Administration; Computer Science; Engineering; Economics; English, 4 yrs; Master's Degree: Bank Management (MBM); Business Administration; Finance; Accountancy; Marketing; Management; International Banking, 2 yrs; Master's Degree: Financial Economics (MFE), 1 yr

Student Services: Academic counselling, Canteen, Cultural centre, Employment services, Foreign student adviser, Foreign Studies Centre, Language programs, Social counselling, Sports facilities

Student Residential Facilities: Separate Accommodation for Male and Female Students

Special Facilities: Multimedia Auditorium
Last Updated: 09/03/11

DAFFODIL INTERNATIONAL UNIVERSITY (DIU)

102, Shukrabad, Mirpur Road, Dhaka 1207
Tel: +880(2) 913-8234
Fax: +880(2) 913-1947
EMail: info@daffodilvarsity.edu.bd;
international@daffodilvarsity.edu.bd
Website: http://www.daffodilvarsity.edu.bd

Chairman, President: Md. Sabur Khan
EMail: chairman@daffodilvarsity.edu.bd; sabur.khan@gmail.com

International Relations: Mohammad Nuruzaman, Director, International Affairs
EMail: international@daffodilvarsity.edu.bd; nzamaan@gmail.com

Faculties

Allied Health (Biotechnology; Dietetics; Food Science; Food Technology; Genetics; Medical Technology; Nutrition; Public Health); **Business and Economics** (Accountancy; Business Administration; Business and Commerce; Economics; Finance; Human Resources; Management; Marketing; Real Estate); **Humanities and Social Sciences** (English; Journalism; Law; Mass Communication); **Science and Information Technology** (Computer Engineering; Computer Science; Electronic Engineering; Environmental Studies; Food Technology; Information Management; Information Technology; Software Engineering; Telecommunications Engineering; Textile Technology)

History: Founded 2002.

Governing Bodies: Board of Trustees

Academic Year: Jan-Apr; May-Aug; Sep-Dec

Admission Requirements: Higher Secondary Certificate

Fees: (Taka): 54,000per semester

Main Language(s) of Instruction: English

International Co-operation: With institutions in Australia, USA, UK, Ireland, Sweden, New Zealand, Malaysia, Hungary, Paraguay, China, India

Degrees and Diplomas: *Bachelor of Science*: Computer Science; Computer Science and Engineering; Computing and Information System; Electronics and Telecommunication Engineering; Electrical and Electronic Engineering; Textile Engineering; Environmental Science and Disaster Management; Software Engineering; Multimedia Technology and Creative Arts; Nutrition and Food Engineering; *Bachelor's Degree (Honours)*: English; Law; Journalism and Mass Communication; Pharmacy; Commerce; *Bachelor's Degree (Pass)*: Real Estate; Business Administration; *Master's Degree*: Business Administration; English; Law; Journalism and Mass Communication; Computer Science and Engineering; Management Information System; Electronics and Telecommunication Engineering; Textile Engineering

Student Services: Academic counselling, Canteen, Cultural centre, Employment services, Foreign student adviser, Foreign Studies Centre, Handicapped facilities, Health services, Language programs, Social counselling, Sports facilities

Libraries: 48,700 vols; 2,500 periodical subscriptions.

Publications: Daffodil International University Journal of Business and Economics *(biannually)*; Daffodil International University Journal of Science and Technology *(biannually)*

Academic Staff 2012	MEN	WOMEN	TOTAL
FULL-TIME	136	61	197
PART-TIME	59	4	63
STAFF WITH DOCTORATE			
FULL-TIME	26	1	27
PART-TIME	20	–	20
Student Numbers 2012			
All (Foreign Included)	6,195	1,487	7,682
FOREIGN ONLY	6	8	14

Evening students, 673.
Last Updated: 09/03/12

DARUL IHSAN UNIVERSITY, DHAKA (DIU)

House 21, Road 9/A, Dhanmondi R/A, Dhaka
Tel: +880(2) 912-5190
Fax: +880(2) 811-4746
EMail: info@diu.dc.bd
Website: http://www.diu.ac.bd

Vice-Chancellor: Anwar Islam
Tel: +880(2) 913-6679 EMail: vc@diu.edu

Faculties

Human Sciences (English; Law; Literature); **Natural Sciences** (Computer Engineering; Computer Science; Information Technology; Telecommunications Engineering); **Religious Sciences** (Religious Studies)

Institutes

Business Studies (Business Administration); **Education** (Education); **Higher Islamic Learning** *(Syed Ali Ashraf (SAAIHIL))*

History: Founded 1989.

Governing Bodies: Board of Trustees

Academic Year: January to December (January-June; July-December)

Admission Requirements: Higher secondary certificate (HSC) or equivalent and entrance examination

Fees: (Taka): c. 2,000-33,000 per semester

Main Language(s) of Instruction: Bengali, English, Arabic.

International Co-operation: With universities in Egypt, USA and the United Kingdom

Accrediting Agencies: University Grants Commission (UGC); Ministry of Education

Degrees and Diplomas: *Bachelor's Degree (Honours)*: English; Islamic Studies and Dawah; Quranic Epistemology; Teaching and Educational Research, 4 yrs; *Bachelor's Degree (Pass)*: Computer Science and Engineering; Communication Science; Information Technology; Business Administration, 4 yrs; *Master's Degree*: English; Islamic Studies and Dawah; Business Administration; Quranic Epistemology; Teaching and Educational Research, 1 further yr

Student Services: Academic counselling, Canteen, Cultural centre, Employment services, Health services, Language programs, Social counselling, Sports facilities

Libraries: Main Library

Publications: Journal of the Institute of Business Studies
Last Updated: 04/10/10

DHAKA INTERNATIONAL UNIVERSITY (DIU)

House 15/A, Road 2/A, Zigatola, Dhanmondi, Dhaka 1209
Tel: +880(2) 862-4747
Fax: +880(2) 861-5443
EMail: info@diu-edu.net
Website: http://www.diu.net.bd

Vice-Chancellor: Nurul Momen

Faculties

Arts and Social Sciences (Arts and Humanities; Education; English; Political Sciences; Sociology); **Business Administration** (Business Administration); **Law** (Law) *Dean*: A. N. M. Samsul Haque; **Pharmacy**; **Science and Engineering** (Computer Engineering; Computer Science; Electrical and Electronic Engineering; Telecommunications Engineering)

History: Founded 1995. Acquired present status 2000.

Governing Bodies: Board of Directors

Academic Year: July to June

Admission Requirements: Secondary school certificate

Fees: (Taka): 25,000 per semester

Main Language(s) of Instruction: Bengali and English

Degrees and Diplomas: *Diploma*: Computer Engineering; *Bachelor's Degree (Honours)*: Law; Business Administration; English; Sociology; Computer Science and Engineering, 4 yrs; *Bachelor's Degree (Pass)*; *Master's Degree*: Business Administration, 1-2 yrs; *Master's Degree*: English; Sociology; Law, 1 yr

Student Services: Academic counselling, Canteen, Cultural centre, Employment services, Foreign student adviser, Handicapped facilities, Health services, Language programs, Sports facilities

Student Residential Facilities: None

Libraries: Yes
Last Updated: 04/10/10

EAST DELTA UNIVERSITY

1267/A Goshaildanga, Agrabad, Chittagong
Tel: +880(31) 251-4441
EMail: enquiry@eastdelta.edu.bd
Website: http://www.eastdelta.edu.bd

Vice-Chancellor: Muhammad Sekandar Khan

Schools

Business Administration (Business Administration); **Liberal Arts and Social Sciences** (Economics; English); **Science, Engineering and Technology** (Electrical and Electronic Engineering; Telecommunications Engineering)

History: Founded 2006.

Admission Requirements: Minimum GPA 2.5 in both SSC & HSC separately. Minimum GPA 2.0 in either SSC or HSC. But the combined GPA is not less than 6.0. 5 subjects in 'O' Level and 2 Subjects in 'A' Level.

Main Language(s) of Instruction: English

Degrees and Diplomas: *Bachelor's Degree (Pass)*; *Master's Degree*

Last Updated: 06/10/10

EAST WEST UNIVERSITY (EWU)

43 Mohakhali, Dhaka 1212
Tel: +880(2) 988-2308 +880(2) 881-1381
Fax: +880(2) 881-2336
EMail: info@ewubd.edu
Website: http://www.ewubd.edu

Vice-Chancellor: Mohammad Sharif
Tel: +800(2) 881-1381 Ext. 217, 121 EMail: vc@ewubd.edu

Registrar: Ali Fardaus
Tel: +880(2) 881-1381 Ext. 242, 102 EMail: fali@ewubd.edu

International Relations: Tauhid Alam, Assistant Director
Tel: +880(2) 881-1381 Ext. 124 EMail: tauhid@ewubd.edu

Faculties

Business and Economics (Business Administration; Economics); **Liberal Arts and Social Sciences** (English; Environmental Studies; International Relations; Philosophy; Psychology; Social Sciences; Sociology); **Science and Engineering** (Applied Physics; Computer Engineering; Computer Science; Electrical and Electronic Engineering; Pharmacy; Telecommunications Engineering)

History: Founded 1996, EWU endeavours to synthesize Eastern culture and values with Western thought and innovation.

Governing Bodies: Board of Directors presided over by the president; G. committees

Academic Year: January to December (January-May; June-July; August-December)

Admission Requirements: Second division in secondary school certificate (SSC) and Higher secondary school certificate (HSC). GCE with passes in 5 subjects at ordinary ('O') level

Fees: (Taka): 35,000 per semester

Main Language(s) of Instruction: English

International Co-operation: With universities in Australia, Canada, United Kingdom, USA

Accrediting Agencies: University Grants Commission (UGC)

Degrees and Diplomas: *Bachelor's Degree (Pass)*: Business, Accountancy, Marketing, Finance (BBA); Computer Science (BSc), 4 yrs; *Bachelor's Degree (Pass)*: English, Economics (BA); *Master's Degree*

Student Services: Academic counselling, Canteen, Cultural centre, Employment services, Foreign student adviser, Health services, Language programs, Sports facilities

Special Facilities: Digital Lab, Computer Labs, Language Lab, Art Gallery

Libraries: c. 7,000 vols
Last Updated: 04/10/10

EASTERN UNIVERSITY

House 15, Road 3, Dhanmondi, Dhaka 1205
Tel: +880(2) 967-6031
Fax: +880(2) 967-5981
EMail: info@easternuni.edu.bd
Website: http://www.easternuni.edu.bd/

Vice-Chancellor: A.K.M. Saiful Majid

Faculties

Arts (English); **Business Administration** (Business Administration); **Engineering and Technology** (Computer Engineering; Computer Science; Information Technology); **Law** (Law)

History: Founded 2003.

Governing Bodies: Board of Governors and Academic Council

Degrees and Diplomas: *Bachelor's Degree (Honours)*; *Bachelor's Degree (Pass)*; *Master's Degree*
Last Updated: 04/10/10

GONO UNIVERSITY

Gono Bishwabidyalay
Gonoshasthaya Kendra Complex Nayarhat, Savar, Dhaka 1344
Tel: 880(2) 770-8004
Fax: 880(2) 770-8336
EMail: gbidyala@bdonline.com
Website: http://www.gonouniversity-bd.com

Vice-Chancellor: Mesbahuddin Ahmad Tel: +880(2) 770-8002

Registrar: Delwar Hossain Tel: +880(2) 770-8079

Faculties

Basic and Social Sciences (Applied Physics; Communication Studies; Computer Engineering; Computer Science; Cultural Studies; Environmental Studies; Modern Languages; Physical Therapy; Social Sciences); **Health Sciences** (Anatomy; Applied Physics; Biochemistry; Biomedical Engineering; Community Health; Dentistry; Forensic Medicine and Dentistry; Health Sciences; Medicine; Microbiology; Pharmacy; Physical Therapy; Physiology)

History: Founded 1998.

Admission Requirements: Higher Secondary Certificate/A level and entrance examination

Main Language(s) of Instruction: Bengali, English

International Co-operation: With universities in Germany

Accrediting Agencies: University Grants Commission (UGC)

Degrees and Diplomas: *Bachelor's Degree (Pass)*: 4 yrs; *Bachelor's Degree (Pass)*: Medicine; Surgery (MBBS), 6 yrs including internship; *Master's Degree*: a further 2 yrs. Also Certificate courses in English language/computer science

Student Residential Facilities: Yes

Special Facilities: Museum

Libraries: Yes
Last Updated: 04/10/10

GREEN UNIVERSITY OF BANGLADESH

Malek Tower, 31, Tejkunipara, Farm Gate, Dhaka 1215
Tel: +880(2) 913-9614
Fax: +880(2) 812-4611
EMail: infogub@yahoo.com
Website: http://www.gub.ac.bd

Vice-Chancellor: Anwarullah Chowdury

Schools

Business (Business Administration); **Law** (Law); **Science** (Computer Engineering; Computer Science; Economics; Electrical and Electronic Engineering; Environmental Studies; Information Technology; Textile Technology)

Degrees and Diplomas: *Bachelor's Degree (Pass)*; *Master's Degree*
Last Updated: 04/10/10

INDEPENDENT UNIVERSITY, BANGLADESH (IUB)

Plot 16, Block B, Aftabuddin Ahmed Road Bashundhara R/A, Dhaka 1219
Tel: +880(2) 986-2386-90 +880(2) 988-4498
Fax: +880(2) 882-3959 +880(2) 885-0226
EMail: info@iub.edu.bd
Website: http://www.iub.edu.bd

Vice-Chancellor: M. Omar Rahman (2010-)
EMail: orahman@iub.edu.bd

Registrar: Tanvir A. Khan

Schools

Business (Accountancy; Banking; Business Administration; Economics; Finance; Human Resources; Management; Marketing)
Director: Nadim Jahangir; **Engineering and Computer Science** (Computer Engineering; Computer Networks; Computer Science; Electrical and Electronic Engineering; Telecommunications

Engineering) *Director:* M. Anwer; **Environmental Science and Management** (Ecology; Environmental Studies; Geography; Waste Management) *Director:* Haroun Er Rashid; **Liberal Arts and Science** (Communication Studies; Computer Science; Cultural Studies; Heritage Preservation; Media Studies; Modern Languages; Social Sciences) *Director:* Nazrul Islam

History: Founded 1993.

Governing Bodies: Governing Council

Academic Year: August to July

Admission Requirements: Higher Secondary Education Certificate or equivalent

Fees: (Taka): Admission: 15,000 per annum; 3,300 per credit per semester

Main Language(s) of Instruction: English

International Co-operation: With universities in USA, Nepal, Netherlands, Russian Federation, Thailand, Belgium, United Kingdom

Accrediting Agencies: University Grants Commission (UGC)

Degrees and Diplomas: *Bachelor of Science:* Computer Engineering; Electrical and Electronic Engineering; Electronic and Telecommunications Engineering (BSc Engineering); Computer Science; Computer Information Systems (BSc); Environmental Management; Population Environment; Land and Water Resources Management (BSc Env), 4 yrs; *Bachelor's Degree (Honours):* Media and Communications (BSS), 4 yrs; *Bachelor's Degree (Pass):* Accountancy; Economics; Finance; General Management; Marketing; Management Information Systems (BBA), 4 yrs; *Master's Degree:* Computer Science; Telecommunications Engineering; Social Sciences; Development Studies; Public Health (MBA; MSc; MSS; MPH), 15 to 24 mths

Student Services: Academic counselling, Canteen, Employment services, Foreign Studies Centre, Sports facilities

Libraries: 23,676 books; 12,162 journals; 160 periodical titles; 2,163 audio-visual materials; access to electronic networks-JSTOR, Emerald, Hinari (journal archives)

Last Updated: 28/03/11

INTERNATIONAL BUSINESS ADMINISTRATION AND INFORMATION SYSTEM (IBAIS) UNIVERSITY (IBAIS UNIVERSITY)

House # 57, Road # 12/A, Dhanmondi R/A, Dhaka 1209
Tel: +880(2) 912-4849
Fax: +880(2) 912-1970
EMail: registrar@ibais.edu
Website: http://www.ibais.edu

Vice-Chancellor: Khandkar Rezaur Rahman
Tel: +880(2) 815-2326 EMail: president@ibais.edu

Registrar: Md. Rowshon Kamal Tel: +880(2) 912-4064

Faculties

Arts (Arts and Humanities; English; Hotel Management; Linguistics; Literature; Tourism); **Business and Economics** (Accountancy; Banking; Business Administration; E-Business/Commerce; Finance; Human Resources; Management; Marketing); **Science and Engineering** (Computer Engineering; Computer Science; Electrical and Electronic Engineering)

History: Founded 1997. Acquired present status 2002.

Governing Bodies: IBAIS Limited

Admission Requirements: Higher Secondary Certificate or equivalent

Fees: (Taka): 15,000

Main Language(s) of Instruction: English

International Co-operation: With universities in Canada, Thailand, United Kingdom, USA

Accrediting Agencies: University Grants Commission (UGC)

Degrees and Diplomas: *Bachelor's Degree (Pass):* Business Administration; Computer Science and Engineering; Computer Science and Information Technology; Electrical and Computer Engineering; Electrical and Electronic Engineering; Textile Engineering; Economics; Pharmacy; English; Business English; Tourism and Hotel Management, 4 yrs; *Master's Degree:* Business Administration; Computer Science and Engineering; Computer Science and Information Technology; Electrical and Computer Engineering; Electrical and Electronic Engineering; Textile Engineering; Economics; Pharmacy; English; Business English; Health Economics; Tourism and Hotel Management, 1-2 yrs

Student Services: Academic counselling, Canteen, Cultural centre, Employment services, Foreign student adviser, Language programs, Social counselling, Sports facilities

Special Facilities: Auditorium

Libraries: 18,750 vols

Publications: IBAISU Quarterly
Last Updated: 05/10/10

INTERNATIONAL ISLAMIC UNIVERSITY CHITTAGONG (IIUC)

154/A, College Road, Chittagong 4203
Tel: +880(2) 610-085
Fax: +880(2) 610-307
EMail: info@iiuc.ac.bd
Website: http://www.iiuc.ac.bd

Vice-Chancellor: Muhammad Mahbub Ullah EMail: vc@iiuc.ac.bd

Registrar: Muhammad Nurul Islam

International Relations: Murtaza Ahmed
EMail: acad_iiuc@fnfbd.net

Faculties

Arts and Humanities (Arabic; Arts and Humanities; English; Literature); **Business Studies** (Business Administration); **Law** (Law); **Science and Engineering** (Computer Engineering; Computer Science; Electrical and Electronic Engineering; Pharmacy); **Shariah and Islamic Studies** (Islamic Law; Islamic Studies; Koran)

Institutes

Arabic Language (Arabic)

History: Founded 1995 by the Islamic University Chittagong Trust.

Governing Bodies: Executive Council (Syndicate)

Admission Requirements: A level Certificate with minimum 2nd division/2.5 GPA (average)

Fees: (Taka): 27,000-289,000

Main Language(s) of Instruction: English; Arabic

International Co-operation: With universities in Canada; Malaysia; France; Egypt; United Kingdom

Accrediting Agencies: University Grants Commission (UGC)

Degrees and Diplomas: *Diploma:* Six months to 1 1/2 yrs; *Bachelor's Degree (Pass):* 4 yrs; *Master's Degree:* 1-2 yrs

Student Services: Academic counselling, Canteen, Cultural centre, Employment services, Foreign student adviser, Foreign Studies Centre, Health services, Language programs, Sports facilities

Student Residential Facilities: Yes

Libraries: 50,000 vols

Publications: Shar'iah Faculty Journal
Last Updated: 05/10/10

INTERNATIONAL UNIVERSITY OF BUSINESS, AGRICULTURE AND TECHNOLOGY (IUBAT)

PO Box 11051, 4 Embankment Drive Road, Sector 10, Uttara Model Town, Dhaka 1230
Tel: +880(2) 896-3523-27 +880(2) 892-3469-70
Fax: +880(2) 896-2625
EMail: info@iubat.edu
Website: http://www.iubat.edu

Vice-Chancellor: M. Alimullah Miyan (1993-)
Tel: +880(2) 892-3471 EMail: miyan@iubat.edu

Registrar: M.A. Hannan
Tel: +880(17) 401-4933, Ext. 114 EMail: registrar@iubat.edu

International Relations: Md. Raihanul Islam

Centres

Computer Education and Training *(CETC)* (Computer Science); **English Language** *(ELC)* (English); **Global Environmental Culture** (Environmental Studies); **Health and Population** (Demography and Population; Health Sciences); **Management**

Development *(CMD)* (Management); **Policy Research** *(CPR)*; **South Asian Disaster Management** *(SADMC)* (Regional Studies; Safety Engineering); **Technology Research Training and Consultancy** (Technology)

Colleges

Agricultural Sciences (Agriculture); **Arts and Science** (Arts and Humanities; Economics); **Business Administration** (Accountancy; Business Administration; Business and Commerce; Finance; Human Resources; Labour and Industrial Relations; Management; Marketing); **Engineering and Technology** (Civil Engineering; Computer Engineering; Computer Science; Electrical and Electronic Engineering; Mechanical Engineering); **Nursing** (Nursing); **Tourism and Hospitality Management** (Tourism)

History: Founded 1991, acquired present status 1992.

Governing Bodies: Board of Governors

Academic Year: January to December (January-April; May-August; September-December)

Admission Requirements: Higher secondary certificate (HSC)

Fees: (Taka): 23,000-36,000 per semester

Main Language(s) of Instruction: English

International Co-operation: With 55 universities worldwide

Accrediting Agencies: Government of Bangladesh; University Grants Commission (UGC)

Degrees and Diplomas: *Diploma*: Accountancy; Computer Science and Engineering, 1.75 yrs; *Bachelor's Degree (Pass)*: Business Administration; Computer Science and Engineering; Civil Engineering; Electrical and Electronic Engineering; Mechanical Engineering; Economics; Agriculture; Tourism and Hospitality Management; Nursing, 4 yrs; *Master's Degree*: Business Administration, a further 2 yrs. Also Certificates in Computer Science; English Language; Disaster Management; Environmental Studies; Management; Marketing; Case Development

Student Services: Academic counselling, Canteen, Cultural centre, Employment services, Foreign student adviser, Health services, Language programs, Social counselling, Sports facilities

Student Residential Facilities: None

Libraries: c. 16,000 vols

Publications: Monographs *(annually)*
Last Updated: 05/10/10

ISLAMIC UNIVERSITY OF TECHNOLOGY (IUT)

Board Bazar, Gazipur 1704
Tel: +880(2) 929-1250 +880(2) 929-1252
Fax: +880(2) 929-1260
EMail: vc@iut-dhaka.edu
Website: http://www.iutoic-dhaka.edu

Vice-Chancellor: M. Imtiaz Hossain (2008-)
Tel: +880(2) 929-1251

Deputy Chief of Establishment: Golam Salek
Tel: +880(2) 929-1254-59 Ext. 231 EMail: mgsalek@iut-dhaka.edu

International Relations: Ahsan Habib, Registrar
Tel: +880(2) 929-1252 EMail: regstrar@iut-dhaka.edu

Departments

Civil and Environmental Engineering *(CEE)* (Civil Engineering; Environmental Engineering); **Computer Science and Information Technology** *(CIT)* (Computer Science; Information Technology); **Electrical and Electronic Engineering** (Electrical and Electronic Engineering); **Instructor Training and General Studies** *(ITS)* (Engineering; Teacher Training; Technology); **Mechanical and Chemical Engineering** *(MCE)* (Chemical Engineering; Mechanical Engineering)

History: Founded by OIC 1981, acquired present status 2001.

Governing Bodies: Governing Board comprising representatives from 9 member states elected in its General Assembly and 2 Ex-officio members (Vice-Chancellor and Secretary-General of the OIC or his representative)

Academic Year: December to October

Admission Requirements: Higher/upper secondary school certificate or equivalent in Science with good grades in Mathematics,

Physics, Chemistry and English for undergraduate programmes in Engineering and Technology

Fees: (US Dollars): Bachelor's Degree, 5,000 (for 4 yrs); Postgraduate studies, 5,000 per annum. Higher diploma free

Main Language(s) of Instruction: English

International Co-operation: With universities in Canada; China; Egypt; Gambia; Indonesia; Ireland; Jordan; Malaysia; Niger; North Cyprus; Pakistan; Senegal; Sudan; Thailand; Uganda; USA

Accrediting Agencies: Accrediting agencies of OIC Member States

Degrees and Diplomas: *Diploma*: Technical Education (DTE), 1 yr following Diploma in Engineering; *Bachelor's Degree (Pass)*: Computer Science and Information Technology; Electrical and Electronic Engineering; Mechanical and Chemical Engineering (BSc; BScEngg), 4 yrs; *Master's Degree*: Computer Science and Information Technology; Electrical and Electronic Engineering; Mechanical Engineering; Technical Education (MSc; MScEngg; MEngg; MScTE), 1 1/2 -2 yrs following Bachelor's Degree; *Ph. D.*. Also postgraduate diploma 1 yr following upon Bachelor's Degree

Student Services: Academic counselling, Canteen, Cultural centre, Employment services, Foreign student adviser, Foreign Studies Centre, Health services, Language programs, Social counselling, Sports facilities

Student Residential Facilities: Yes, for c. 1,000 students

Special Facilities: Auditorium. Computer Centre. Research Extension

Libraries: Total 30,359 vols

Publications: Journal of Engineering and Technology, Scholarly / research publications in Engineering and Technology *(biennially)*
Last Updated: 20/03/12

LEADING UNIVERSITY

Modhubon, Sylhet 31000
Tel: +880(821) 720303
EMail: info@lus.ac.bd
Website: http://www.lus.ac.bd

Vice-Chancellor (Acting): Kabir Hossain

Faculties

Arts and Language (English; Law); **Business** (Business Administration); **Modern Science** (Architecture; Civil Engineering; Computer Engineering; Computer Science; Electrical and Electronic Engineering)

History: Founded 2001.

Degrees and Diplomas: *Bachelor's Degree (Pass)*; *Master's Degree*
Last Updated: 05/10/10

MANARAT INTERNATIONAL UNIVERSITY (MIU)

Plot Number 16, Road Number 106, Gulshan, Dhaka 1212
Tel: +880(2) 881-7525
EMail: info@manarat.ac.bd
Website: http://www.manarat.ac.bd

Vice-Chancellor: Mohammad Abdur Rob

Registrar: Abul Basher Khan

Schools

Arts and Humanities (English; Law); **Business and Economics** (Business Administration); **Science and Technology** (Computer Engineering; Computer Science; Electronic Engineering; Pharmacy; Telecommunications Engineering)

History: Founded 2001.

Accrediting Agencies: University Grants Commission (UGC)

Degrees and Diplomas: *Bachelor's Degree (Pass)*; *Master's Degree*
Last Updated: 05/10/10

METROPOLITAN UNIVERSITY

Al-Hamra, Zindabazar, Sylhet
Tel: +880(821) 713-077
EMail: info@metrouni.edu.bd
Website: http://www.metrouni.edu.bd

Vice-Chancellor: Md. Abdul Aziz (2009-)

Schools
Business (Business Administration); Humanities and Social Sciences (Economics; English); Law (Law); Science and Technology (Computer Engineering; Computer Science; Electronic Engineering; Information Technology; Telecommunications Engineering)

History: Founded 2003.

Degrees and Diplomas: *Bachelor's Degree (Pass)*; *Master's Degree*
Last Updated: 05/10/10

NORTH SOUTH UNIVERSITY

Plot 15, Block B, Bashundhara, Dhaka 1229
Tel: +880(2) 885-2000
Fax: +880(2) 885-2016
EMail: registrar@northsouth.edu
Website: http://www.northsouth.edu

Vice-Chancellor: Hafiz G.A. Siddiqi (1998-)
EMail: hgas@northsouth.edu

Registrar: Mohammad Ali EMail: mali@northsouth.edu

Institutes
Modern Languages (Modern Languages)

Schools
Arts and Social Sciences (Continuing Education; Economics; English); Business (Accountancy; Business Administration; Finance; Human Resources; International Business; Marketing); Engineering and Applied Sciences (Architecture; Computer Engineering; Computer Science; Environmental Management; Environmental Studies)

History: Founded 1992. The first private university in Bangladesh. Established by NSU Foundation.

Governing Bodies: Board of Governors of NSU Foundation; Syndicate; Academic Council

Accrediting Agencies: Universities Grants Commission

Degrees and Diplomas: *Bachelor's Degree (Pass)*: Economics; Business Administration; Computer Science; Environmental Studies; English; *Master's Degree*: Economics; Development Studies; Business Administration

Libraries: Yes
Last Updated: 05/10/10

NORTHERN UNIVERSITY BANGLADESH (NUB)

3/8 Iqbal Road, Mohammadpur, Dhaka 1207
Tel: +880(2) 815-3437-39
Fax: +880(2) 913-5562
EMail: info@nub.ac.bd
Website: http://www.nub.ac.bd

Vice-Chancellor: Shamsul Haque Tel: +880(2) 912-8122

Treasurer: Abu Bakar Siddique
Tel: +880(2) 913-4729 EMail: treasurer@nub.ac.bd

International Relations: Md. Lutfor Rahman, Director, Human Resource Development EMail: director@nub.ac.bd

Faculties
Arts and Humanities (English); Business (Accountancy; Banking; Business Administration; Economics; Finance; Management; Marketing); Health Sciences (Health Sciences; Pharmacy; Public Health); Law (Law); Science and Engineering (Civil Engineering; Computer Engineering; Computer Science; Electrical and Electronic Engineering; Engineering; Textile Technology)

History: Founded 2002. A private university approved by Government.

Governing Bodies: Academic Council, Syndicate members

Academic Year: January to December

Main Language(s) of Instruction: English

Degrees and Diplomas: *Bachelor's Degree (Honours)*; *Master's Degree*

Student Services: Academic counselling, Canteen, Employment services, Foreign student adviser, Health services, Language programs, Social counselling, Sports facilities

Special Facilities: Library and Information Division (LID); Laboratories

Libraries: University Library
Last Updated: 05/10/10

PREMIER UNIVERSITY (PUC)

1/A, O.R. Nizam Road, Panchlaish, Chittagong
Tel: +880(31) 656-917
Fax: +880(31) 687-892
EMail: info@puc.ac.bd
Website: http://www.puc.ac.bd

Vice-Chancellor: Anupam Sen (2006-)
EMail: profdrsen@yahoo.com

Registrar: Mohammed Ibrahim

Faculties
Arts and Social Sciences (Economics; English; Literature); Business Studies; Engineering (Computer Engineering; Computer Science; Electrical and Electronic Engineering); Law

History: Founded 2001.

Degrees and Diplomas: *Bachelor's Degree (Honours)*; *Bachelor's Degree (Pass)*; *Master's Degree*
Last Updated: 05/10/10

PRESIDENCY UNIVERSITY

Tower Building 11a, Road No: 92, Gulshan - 2, Dhaka
EMail: info@presidency.edu.bd
Website: http://www.presidency.edu.bd/

Vice-Chancellor: M. Harunur Rashid EMail: vc@presidency.edu.bd

Registrar: Zafrul Karim EMail: zkarim@presidency.edu.bd

Schools
Business *(Moazzam Hossain)* (Business Administration); Engineering *(Azimur Rahman)* (Civil Engineering; Electrical Engineering; Electronic Engineering; Telecommunications Engineering); Liberal Arts and Social Sciences *(Shamsul Alamin)* (English)

History: Founded 2003.

Degrees and Diplomas: *Bachelor's Degree (Pass)*; *Master's Degree*
Last Updated: 05/10/10

PRIME UNIVERSITY (PU)

2A/1 North East of Darus Salam Road, Section-1 Mirpur, Dhaka 1216
Tel: +880(2) 805-5646
Fax: +880(2) 805-5647
EMail: info@primeuniversity.edu.bd
Website: http://primeuniversity.edu.bd/maincontents

Vice-Chancellor: Md. Abdus Samad
EMail: vc@primeuniversity.edu.bd

Registrar: Mohammad Arshad Ali
EMail: registrar@primeuniversity.edu.bd

Faculties
Arts and Social Sciences (Arts and Humanities; Education; English; Law); Business Studies (Business Administration); Engineering (Computer Engineering; Computer Science; Electronic Engineering; Telecommunications Engineering); Information Technology (Applied Mathematics; Artificial Intelligence; Computer Science; Information Technology; Multimedia; Robotics)

History: Founded 2002.

Degrees and Diplomas: *Bachelor's Degree (Pass)*; *Master's Degree*
Last Updated: 05/10/10

PRIMEASIA UNIVERSITY

HBR Tower, 9, Banani C/A, Dhaka 1213
EMail: info@primeasia.edu.bd
Website: http://www.primeasia.edu.bd

Vice-Chancellor: Gias uddin Ahmad

Schools

Business (Business Administration); **Engineering and Technology** (Architecture; Chemistry; Computer Engineering; Computer Science; Electrical and Electronic Engineering; Information Technology; Mathematics; Mechanical Engineering; Physics; Textile Technology); **Law** (Law); **Science** (Biochemistry; Microbiology; Nutrition; Pharmacy)

Degrees and Diplomas: *Bachelor's Degree (Pass)*; *Master's Degree*
Last Updated: 05/10/10

QUEENS UNIVERSITY

Abedin Tower, 35 Kemal Ataturk Avenue, Banani, Dhaka 1213
Tel: +880(2) 882-4687 +880(2) 882-9012
EMail: info@queensuniversity.edu.bd
Website: http://www.queensuniversity.edu.bd/

Vice-Chancellor: Abdul Khaleque

Adviser, International Programmes and Academic Affairs: Mujibur Rahman
Tel: +880(2) 861-3218, Fax: +880(2) 861-3794
EMail: mujib@bangla.net

Schools

Arts and Humanities (Arts and Humanities; English); **Business Administration** (Business Administration); **Law** (Law); **Science and Engineering** (Computer Science; Engineering)

History: Founded 1996, acquired present status 1997.

Governing Bodies: Board of Directors

Academic Year: March to February (March to August; September to February)

Admission Requirements: Secondary school certificate (SSC) and higher secondary certificate (HSC), or O Level in 5 subjects and A Level in at least 2 subjects

Fees: (Taka): 30,000 per semester; 60,000 per annum

Main Language(s) of Instruction: English

International Co-operation: With universities in USA and Australia

Degrees and Diplomas: *Bachelor's Degree (Honours)*: Arts (BA); Business Administration (BBA); Law (LLB); *Bachelor's Degree (Pass)*: Computer Science, Engineering (BSc); *Master's Degree*: Business Administration

Student Services: Cultural centre, Sports facilities

Libraries: Main Library
Last Updated: 06/10/10

ROYAL UNIVERSITY OF DHAKA

Kemal Ataturk Avenue, Banani, Dhaka 1213
Tel: +880(2) 988-6150
Fax: +880(2) 882-6971
EMail: registrar@royal.edu.bd

Vice-Chancellor: Nurul Alam Khan

Faculties

Arts and Social Sciences (Education; English; Library Science); **Business** (Banking; Business Administration); **Science** (Computer Science; Rural Planning; Technology; Town Planning)

History: Founded 2004

Degrees and Diplomas: *Bachelor's Degree (Pass)*; *Master's Degree*
Last Updated: 20/03/12

SHANTO MARIAM UNIVERSITY OF CREATIVE TECHNOLOGY

House No. 01, Road No. 14, sector No. 13, Uttara, Dhaka 1230
Tel: +880(2) 892-3167
Fax: +880(2) 891-5308
EMail: sgc@bdonline.com
Website: http://www.shantomariamedu.com/shantomariam.htm

Vice-Chancellor: Shamsul Haque

Faculties

Architecture; **Fashion** (Fashion Design); **Fine Arts** (Fine Arts); **Graphic Design** (Graphic Design); **Interior Design** (Interior Design); **Manufacturing**

History: Founded 2003.

Degrees and Diplomas: *Bachelor's Degree (Pass)*; *Master's Degree*
Last Updated: 06/10/10

SOUTHEAST UNIVERSITY (SEU)

House -64/B, Road-18, Kemal Ataturk Avenue, Banani, Dhaka 1213
Tel: +880(2) 988-2914
Fax: +880(2) 989-2914
EMail: info@seu.ac.bd
Website: http://www.seu.ac.bd

Vice-Chancellor: M. Shamsher Ali
Tel: +880(2) 862-8280 EMail: msali@seu.ac.bd

Registrar: Md. Aftabuddin Khan Tel: +880(2) 988-0453

International Relations: Saifur Rahman, Director of Public Relations Tel: +880(2) 989-2340

Schools

Arts and Social Sciences (Development Studies; Economics; Education; English; Islamic Studies; Law); **Business Studies** (Business Administration); **Science and Engineering** (Computer Engineering; Computer Science; Pharmacy; Textile Technology)

History: Founded 2002.

Governing Bodies: Board of Governors

Academic Year: January to December (January - April; May - August; September - December)

Admission Requirements: Higher Secondary School Certificate (HSC)

Fees: (Taka): 40,000-325,000 per programme; distance students, 40,000-70,000

Main Language(s) of Instruction: English

Degrees and Diplomas: *Bachelor's Degree (Pass) (BBA; BSc; LLB; BA)*: 4 yrs; *Master's Degree (MBA; MCA; MA; MSc)*: a further 1- 2 yrs

Student Services: Academic counselling, Canteen, Employment services, Health services, Sports facilities

Libraries: Yes
Last Updated: 06/10/10

SOUTHERN UNIVERSITY BANGLADESH

739 A Mehdibag Road, Chittagong 4000
Tel: +880(31) 285-1336-9; +880(31) 626-744
Fax: +880(31) 285-1340
EMail: info@southern-bd.info
Website: http://www.southern-bd.info

Vice-Chancellor: A.J.M. Nuruddin Chowdhury (2006-)
EMail: vice-chancellor@southern-bd.info

Vice-President: Sarwar Jahan
EMail: vice-president@southern-bd.info

International Relations: Ishrat Jahan
EMail: ishratjahan@mail.com

Faculties

Arts and Social Sciences (Economics; English; Law); **Business Administration** (Accountancy; Administration; Banking; Business Administration; Business and Commerce; E-Business/Commerce; Finance; Hotel Management; Human Resources; International Business; Leadership; Management; Marketing; Tourism); **Science and Technology**

Institutes
Ethics and World Religions *(Continental)* (Ethics; Religion); **Management and Information Technology** *(IMIT)* (Information Technology; Management; Political Sciences)

History: Founded 1998 as Institute of Management and Information Technology by Mr Sawar Jahan. Acquired present status 2002.

Governing Bodies: AJ Foundation

Admission Requirements: At least a second division or CGPA 2.00 in the Secondary School Certificate and Higher Secondary School Certificate examination or University of London GCE O level in 5 subjects and A level in two major subjects. At least 550 in TOEFL

Fees: (Taka): Undergraduate, 1,334 per credit hour per semester; Graduate, 1,500 per credit hour per semester; Advanced study, 2,000 per credit hour per semester

Main Language(s) of Instruction: English

International Co-operation: With universities in USA, Canada

Accrediting Agencies: University Grants Commission; Ministry of Education

Degrees and Diplomas: *Bachelor's Degree (Pass)*: 4 yrs; *Master's Degree*: 1-2 yrs. Also one-year post-graduate diplomas.

Student Services: Academic counselling, Cultural centre, Employment services, Foreign student adviser, Language programs, Sports facilities

Libraries: c. 7,000 vols.

Publications: Journal of Business and Society *(annually)*

Last Updated: 06/10/10

STAMFORD UNIVERSITY BANGLADESH
744, Satmosjid Road, Dhanmondi R/A, Dhaka 1209
Tel: +880(2) 815-3168
Fax: +880(2) 811-9956
EMail: admission@stamforduniversity.edu.bd
Website: http://www.stamforduniversity.edu.bd

Vice-Chancellor: M. Majibur Rahman

Registrar: S. M. Ikramul Haque

Departments
Architecture (Architecture); **Business Administration** (Business Administration; Human Resources); **Civil Engineering** (Civil Engineering); **Computer Science** (Computer Engineering; Computer Science; Information Technology); **Economics**; **Electrical and Electronic Engineering**; **English** (English); **Environmental Science** (Environmental Studies); **Film and Media** (Film; Media Studies); **Journalism and Media Studies**; **Law** (Law); **Microbiology** (Microbiology); **Pharmacy** (Pharmacy)

History: Founded 1994 as Stamford College Group. Acquired present status 2001.

Governing Bodies: Board of Directors

Accrediting Agencies: Government

Degrees and Diplomas: *Bachelor's Degree (Pass)*; *Master's Degree*

Libraries: Yes
Last Updated: 06/10/10

STATE UNIVERSITY OF BANGLADESH
77 Satmasjid Road, Dhanmondi, Dhaka 1205
Tel: +880(2) 815-1781
Fax: +880(2) 812-3296
EMail: info@subd.net
Website: http://www.subd.net

Vice-Chancellor: Iftekhar Ghani Chowdhury

Registrar: A.Y.M. Ekram-ud Daulah EMail: registrar@subd.net

International Relations: Dil Afroze
Tel: +880(2) 812-6272 EMail: afroze@subd.net

Schools
Business and Social Studies (Business Administration; English; Law); **Health Sciences** (Food Science; Food Technology; Nutrition; Optometry; Pharmacy; Public Health); **Science and Technology** (Architecture; Computer Engineering; Computer Science; Environmental Studies)

History: Founded 2002.

Governing Bodies: Board of Governors

Admission Requirements: Secondary school certificate

Main Language(s) of Instruction: English

International Co-operation: With universities in Thailand and Kazakhstan

Degrees and Diplomas: *Bachelor's Degree (Pass)*: 4-5 yrs; *Master's Degree*: 1-1 1/2 yrs

Student Services: Academic counselling, Canteen, Employment services, Foreign student adviser, Foreign Studies Centre, Handicapped facilities, Health services, Language programs, Social counselling, Sports facilities

Student Residential Facilities: Yes

Libraries: Yes
Last Updated: 06/10/10

SYLHET INTERNATIONAL UNIVERSITY (SIU)
Shamimabad, Bagbari, Sylhet
Tel: +880(821) 717-193 +880(821) 720-771
Fax: +880(821) 725-644
EMail: siu_syl@yahoo.com
Website: http://www.siu.edu.bd/

Vice-Chancellor (Acting): Syed Akmal Mahmood (2010-)

Departments
Electronics and Communication Engineering

Schools
Business Administration (Business Administration); **Humanities and Social Sciences** (English; Islamic Studies); **Law** (Law); **Science and Engineering** (Engineering)

History: Created 2001.

Accrediting Agencies: University Grants Commission (UGC)

Degrees and Diplomas: *Bachelor's Degree (Honours)*: Computer Science & Informatics; Computer Engineering; Electronics & Communication Engineering; Business Administration; Law; English; *Bachelor's Degree (Pass)*: Computer Science & Informatics; Computer Engineering; Electronics & Communication Engineering; Business Administration; Law; English; *Master's Degree*: Business Administration (MBA)

Student Residential Facilities: Three hostels: one male, two female
Last Updated: 06/10/10

THE MILLENNIUM UNIVERSITY
Momenbagh, Rajarbagh, Dhaka 1217
Tel: +880(2) 936-0836
EMail: khanfoundation@hotmail.com
Website: http://www.themillenniumuniversity.edu.bd

Vice-Chancellor: A. K. M. Baqure

Faculties
Arts and Humanities (Arts and Humanities; Development Studies; English; Government; Law; Mass Communication; Media Studies; Women's Studies); **Biological Sciences**; **Business Studies**; **Computer Science**; **Engineering** (Engineering); **Medical**

Degrees and Diplomas: *Bachelor's Degree (Pass)*; *Master's Degree*
Last Updated: 06/10/10

THE PEOPLE'S UNIVERSITY OF BANGLADESH
3/2, Asad Avenue. Mohammadpur, Dhaka 1207
Tel: +880(2) 812-8676 +880(2) 913-0726
Fax: +880(2) 912-8009
EMail: info@thepub.com
Website: http://www.peoplesuniv.edu.bd

Vice-Chancellor: Mustafizur Rahman EMail: vc@pub.ac.bd

Registrar: Harunor Rashid Bhuiyan EMail: registrar@pub.ac.bd

International Relations: Ummay Kulsum

Schools

Applied Science and Engineering (Computer Engineering; Computer Science; Electronic Engineering; Telecommunications Engineering); **Arts** (English; Islamic Studies); **Business Administration** (Business Administration; Business Computing; Hotel Management; Tourism); **Health Science** (Physical Therapy); **Social Sciences** (Law; Social Sciences; Social Work; Sociology); **Textile Engineering** (Textile Technology)

History: Founded 1992. Opened 1996.

Academic Year: January-December (January-July; August-December)

Admission Requirements: In science subjects, students passing SSC and SSC examination or equivalent with Physics, Chemistry and Mathematics/Biology obtaining at least 2nd Division in both SSC and HSC examinations or their equivalent may apply for admission to BS Hons programmes.

Fees: (US Dollars): undergraduate, c. 3,000-5,000; postgraduate, c. 1,200

Main Language(s) of Instruction: English

Accrediting Agencies: University Grants Commission (UGC)

Degrees and Diplomas: *Bachelor's Degree (Honours)*: 4 yrs; *Master's Degree*: 1 yr. Admission to postgraduate courses leading to MPhil and PhD degrees in related subjects is available.

Student Services: Academic counselling, Canteen, Cultural centre, Foreign student adviser, Health services, Language programs, Sports facilities

Publications: The Journal of the People's University of Bangladesh *(biennially)*

Press or Publishing House: Centre for Multi-disciplinary Studies
Last Updated: 09/03/11

THE UNIVERSITY OF ASIA PACIFIC

House 73, Road 5A, Dhanmondi R/A, Dhaka 1209
Tel: +880(2) 966-1193
Fax: +880(2) 966-4950
EMail: vicechancellor@uap-bd.edu
Website: http://www.uap-bd.edu

Vice-Chancellor: Abdul Matin Patwari **EMail:** uap1@citechco.net

Faculties

Architecture (Architecture); **Business Administration** (Business Administration); **Civil Engineering** (Civil Engineering; Computer Engineering; Computer Science; Environmental Engineering); **Computer Science and Engineering**; **Electrical and Electronic Engineering** (Electrical and Electronic Engineering); **Law and Human Rights** (Human Rights; Law); **Pharmacy**

History: Founded 1996.

Admission Requirements: At least higher second division in the Secondary School Certificate (SSC) and Higher Secondary Certificate (HSC) examinations

Fees: (Taka): c. 40,000 per semester

International Co-operation: With universities in Australia, Canada, USA

Accrediting Agencies: University Grants Commission (UGC)

Degrees and Diplomas: *Bachelor's Degree (Honours)*: Architecture, 5 yrs; *Bachelor's Degree (Honours)*: Business Administration; Computer Science; Engineering; Pharmacy, 4 yrs; *Master's Degree*: Business Administration, a further 2 yrs

Libraries: c. 4,735 vols
Last Updated: 06/10/10

UNITED INTERNATIONAL UNIVERSITY (UIU)

House # 80, Road # 8/A, Satmasjid Road, Dhanmondi, Dhaka 1209
Tel: +880(2) 912-5912
Fax: +880(2) 912-5916
EMail: info@uiu.ac.bd
Website: http://uiu.ac.bd

Vice-Chancellor: Rezwan Khan
Registrar: A. S. M. Salahuddin

Institutes

English Language (English); **Natural Sciences** (Applied Chemistry; Applied Mathematics; Applied Physics; Physics)

Schools

Business (Accountancy; Banking; Finance; Management; Marketing); **Science and Engineering** (Architecture; Chemical Engineering; Civil Engineering; Electronic Engineering; Environmental Engineering; Fashion Design; Industrial Engineering; Interior Design; Landscape Architecture; Leather Techniques; Mechanical Engineering; Petroleum and Gas Engineering; Production Engineering; Regional Planning; Textile Technology; Town Planning)

History: Founded 2003.

Governing Bodies: Board of Governors; Academic Council; Selection Committee; Finance Committee; Executive Committee

Admission Requirements: Higher Secondary Certificate or 5 O level subjects and 2 A level subjects with minimum GPA of 2.0 or American High School Diploma or equivalent

Fees: (Taka): Undergraduate, 1,800 per credit; Graduate, 2,500 per credit

Main Language(s) of Instruction: English

International Co-operation: With universities in United Kingdom; Australia

Accrediting Agencies: Government; University Grants Commission (UGC)

Degrees and Diplomas: *Bachelor's Degree (Pass)*; *Master's Degree*

Libraries: Yes
Last Updated: 06/10/10

UNIVERSITY OF DEVELOPMENT ALTERNATIVE (UODA)

80 Satmasjid Road, Dhanmondi Residential Area, Dhaka 1209
Tel: +880(2) 914-5741
Fax: +880(2) 815-7339
EMail: registrar@uoda.edu.bd
Website: http://www.uoda.edu.bd

Vice-Chancellor: Emajuddin Ahamed
Tel: +880(2) 914-5741, Fax: +880(2) 815-7339
EMail: president@uoda.org

Registrar: Iffat Chowdhury EMail: iffat@uoda.org

International Relations: Md. Haider Faruque
EMail: haider_faruque@yahoo.com

Faculties

Arts and Social Sciences (Development Studies; Human Rights; Law; Media Studies; Music; Native Language Education; Political Sciences); **Business Administration** (Business Administration); **Life Sciences** (Biological and Life Sciences; Biotechnology; Genetics; Molecular Biology; Pharmacy); **Science and Technology** (Computer Engineering; Computer Science; Mathematics; Telecommunications Engineering)

History: Founded 2002.

Governing Bodies: Academic Council

Academic Year: January to December (January-April; May-August; September-December)

Admission Requirements: Secondary school certificate (SSC) and higher secondary certificate (HSC)

Fees: (Taka): 14,000 per semester

Main Language(s) of Instruction: English

Accrediting Agencies: University Grants Commission (UGC)

Degrees and Diplomas: *Bachelor's Degree (Honours) (BSc; BA; BSS; LLB; BBA)*: 4 yrs; *Master's Degree (MSc; MA; MSS; LLM; MBA)*: 1-1 1/2 yrs

Student Services: Academic counselling, Canteen, Cultural centre, Employment services, Health services, Nursery care, Social counselling, Sports facilities

Student Residential Facilities: Yes (6 hostels for men and 6 hostels for women)

Libraries: 8,000 vols; 50 periodical subscriptions

Publications: UODA Studies: A Scientific Journal *(biennially)*
Last Updated: 07/10/10

UNIVERSITY OF INFORMATION TECHNOLOGY AND SCIENCES (UITS)

17 North Gulshan C/A, PBL Tower, Gulshan Circle-2, Dhaka 1212
Tel: +880(2) 989-2755
Fax: +880(2) 989-1094
EMail: info@uits-bd.org
Website: http://www.uits-bd.org

Vice-Chancellor: Mohammed A. Aziz EMail: amkhan@uits-bd.org

Director, Administration: Shamim Choudhury
Tel: +880(2) 885-0010 EMail: admin@uits-bd.org

International Relations: F.M.A. Salam, Deputy assistant Director, University Relations EMail: salam@uits-bd.org

Schools
Business (Accountancy; Banking; Finance; Insurance; Management; Marketing); **Computer Science and Engineering** (Civil Engineering; Computer Engineering; Computer Science; Electrical and Electronic Engineering; Information Technology); **Liberal Arts** (English; Law)

History: Founded 2003.

Academic Year: September to June

Admission Requirements: Secondary school certificate (SSC) and higher secondary certificate (HEC) or foreign equivalent.

Fees: (Taka): 7,500-9,000 per month

Main Language(s) of Instruction: English

International Co-operation: With universities in India and Thailand

Accrediting Agencies: University Grants Commission (UGC)

Degrees and Diplomas: *Bachelor's Degree (Honours)*: Law (LLB), 4 yrs; *Bachelor's Degree (Pass)*: Computer Education (B.Ed.); Computer Science and Engineering (B.Sc.); Electronic and Communication Engineering (B.Sc.); English Language and Literature (B.A); Finance; Banking; Insurance; Economics; Information Technology; Management; Marketing; Accountancy (B.BA); Information Technology; Nursing; Community Health Sciences; Electronic Engineering; Telecommunications Engineering; Computer Science (B.Sc.), 4 yrs; *Bachelor's Degree (Pass)*: Law, 2 yrs; *Master's Degree*: 1 yr; *Master's Degree*: Business Administration (IMBA); Computer Applications (MCA); Law, 2 yrs; *Master's Degree*: Computer Science (M.Sc.); Telecommunications Engineering (M.Sc.), 1 1/2 yr; *Master's Degree*: English (M.A.), 1-2 yrs

Student Services: Academic counselling, Canteen, Language programs, Sports facilities

Special Facilities: Computer, Communications and Digital Electronic Laboratories, Unlimited Internet Access

Libraries: Central Library c. 5,435 vols and periodical subscriptions
Last Updated: 07/10/10

UNIVERSITY OF LIBERAL ARTS BANGLADESH

House 56, Road 4/A @ Satmosjid Road, Dhanmondi, Dhaka
Tel: +880(2) 966-1255
EMail: info@ulabd.edu.bd
Website: http://www.ulab.edu.bd

Vice-Chancellor: Rafiqul Islam

Departments
Business Administration; Computer Science and Engineering (Computer Engineering; Computer Science); **Electronics and Telecommunication Engineering** (Electronic Engineering; Telecommunications Engineering); **English and Humanities** (English); **Media Studies and Journalism** (Journalism; Media Studies; Radio and Television Broadcasting)

History: Founded 2004.

Degrees and Diplomas: *Bachelor's Degree (Pass)*; *Master's Degree*
Last Updated: 07/10/10

UNIVERSITY OF SCIENCE AND TECHNOLOGY, CHITTAGONG

Main Campus, Foy's Lake, Khulshi, Pahartali, Chittagong 4202
Tel: +880(31) 659-070
Fax: +880(31) 659-545
EMail: ustc-cst@spnetctg.com; ustc-ctag@gmail.com
Website: http://www.ustc.ac.bd

Vice-Chancellor: Nurul Islam
Tel: 880(2) 861-4959 EMail: ustcbd@bangla.net

Registrar: Farid Uddin Ahmed

Faculties
Basic Medical and Pharmaceutical Sciences (Biochemistry; Biotechnology; Pharmacy); **Business Administration** (Banking; Business Administration); **Medicine** (Gynaecology and Obstetrics; Medicine; Paediatrics; Surgery); **Science, Engineering and Technology** (Computer Engineering; Computer Science; Electrical and Electronic Engineering; Engineering; Technology; Telecommunications Engineering); **Social Sciences and Humanities** (English)

History: Founded 1992.

Degrees and Diplomas: *Bachelor's Degree (Pass)*: Engineering; Computer Science; Medicine; Pharmacy; Business Administration; *Master's Degree*: Engineering; Business Administration
Last Updated: 07/10/10

UTTARA UNIVERSITY

House-5, Road-15, Sector-6, Uttara, Dhaka
Tel: +880(2) 891-9794
EMail: uumain_edu@yahoo.com

Vice-Chancellor: Azizur Rahman
EMail: dma_rahman@yahoo.com

Schools
Arts and Social Sciences (Education; English; Islamic Studies); **Business** (Business Administration); **Computer Science and Engineering** (Computer Engineering; Computer Science); **Education and Physical Education** (Education; Physical Education)

History: Founded 2004.

Degrees and Diplomas: *Bachelor's Degree (Pass)*; *Master's Degree*
Last Updated: 07/10/10

VICTORIA UNIVERSITY OF BANGLADESH

58/11/A (3rd floor), Panthapath, Dhaka 1205
Tel: +880(2) 862-2634
Fax: +880(2) 862-2635
EMail: info@vub.edu.bd
Website: http://www.vub.edu.bd

Vice-Chancellor (Acting): Curtis Doyle

Pro-Vice-Chancellor (Acting): M.R. Khan
EMail: mrkhan@vub.edu.bd

Departments
Textile Engineering and Fashion Design (Fashion Design; Textile Technology); **Tourism and Hospitality Management** (Hotel Management; Tourism)

Faculties
Law; Science (Computer Science; E-Business/Commerce; Health Education; Information Technology; Multimedia; Pharmacy; Telecommunications Engineering)

Degrees and Diplomas: *Bachelor's Degree (Honours)*; *Bachelor's Degree (Pass)*; *Master's Degree*
Last Updated: 07/10/10

WORLD UNIVERSITY OF BANGLADESH (WUB)

5/5, Block-E, Lalmatia, Dhaka 1207
Tel: +880(2) 815-5308
EMail: info@wub.edu
Website: http://www.wub.edu/

Vice-Chancellor: Mabdul Mannan Choudury
Tel: +880(2) 811-5004

Faculties

Arts (English; Law); **Business** (Administration; Business and Commerce; Finance; Human Resources; Insurance; Labour and Industrial Relations; Management; Marketing; Real Estate); **Engineering** (Architecture; Civil Engineering; Computer Engineering; Computer Science; Electrical and Electronic Engineering; Mechanical Engineering; Textile Technology); **Pharmacy** (Pharmacy)

History: Founded 2001. Acquired present status 2003.

Governing Bodies: Board of Governors; Syndicate; Academic Council

Academic Year: January to December

Admission Requirements: Higher Secondary Certificate or foreign equivalent

Fees: (Taka): local students, 14,400-28,000 per annum

Main Language(s) of Instruction: English

International Co-operation: With universities in United Kingdom, West Indies, Yemen, United Arab Emirates

Accrediting Agencies: University Grants Commission (UGC)

Degrees and Diplomas: *Bachelor's Degree (Pass)*: 4-5 yrs; *Master's Degree*: a further 1-2 yrs

Student Services: Academic counselling, Canteen, Cultural centre, Employment services, Foreign student adviser, Foreign Studies Centre, Handicapped facilities, Health services, Language programs, Social counselling, Sports facilities

Student Residential Facilities: Yes

Libraries: Yes

Last Updated: 07/10/10

Barbados

STRUCTURE OF HIGHER EDUCATION SYSTEM

Description:

Higher education is provided at academic, vocational and technical colleges as well as at the University of the West Indies, a regional institution to which Barbados is affiliated.

Stages of studies:

University level first stage: *Bachelor's degree*
Bachelor's degree courses usually last for three years.

University level second stage: *Master's degree*
Master's degrees usually take one to two years following upon a first degree.

University level third stage: *Doctorate*
The Doctorate takes a further three years, following upon the Master's degree.

Distance higher education:
There is a Distance Education Centre at the UWI, Cave Hill.

ADMISSION TO HIGHER EDUCATION

Admission to university-level studies:

Name of secondary school credential required: Caribbean Advanced Proficiency Certificate

Foreign students admission:

Entrance exam requirements: Foreign students should have qualifications equivalent to the General Certificate of Education with a combination of either four passes at Ordinary ('O') level or two passes at Advanced ('A') level and three at 'O' level for admission to the University of the West Indies, or three passes at 'A' level and one at 'O' level.

Language requirements: Knowledge of English is essential.

RECOGNITION OF STUDIES

Bodies dealing with recognition:

Barbados Accreditation Council
Executive-Director: Valda Alleyne
123 A&B, "Plaza Centrale"
Roebuck Street
St. Michael 11080
Tel: +246 436 9094
Fax: +246 429 9233
EMail: info@bac.gov.bb
WWW: http://www.bac.gov.bb/
Services provided and students dealt with: The Barbados Accreditation Council has two broad roles: firstly, the registration and re-registration of institutions offering post-secondary or tertiary education and programmes of study, the accreditation and re-accreditation of programmes and institutions in Barbados and related functions, such as recognition and equivalency of local and foreign-based qualifications, articulation and conferral of institutional titles; and secondly, the granting of Certificates of Recognition of CARICOM Skills Qualification to applicants who satisfy the requirements for recognition as skilled CARICOM nationals and examining and verifying of Certificates of Recognition of Caribbean Community Skills granted to community nationals by Member States.

NATIONAL BODIES

Ministry of Education and Human Resource Development
Minister: Ronald Jones
Elsie Payne Complex
St. Michael WI
Tel: +1(246) 430 2700
EMail: mined1@caribsurf.com
WWW: http://www.mes.gov.bb
Role of national body: The Ministry is the Government agency responsible for the formulation of educational policies and for the administration and regulation of education programmes.

Caribbean Area Network for Quality Assurance in Tertiary Education - CANQATE
President: Valda Alleyne
Secretary: Dawn Barrett Adams
C/o Barbados Accreditation Council
123A & B, "Plaza Centrale"
Roebuck Street
Bridgetown 11080
Tel: +246 429 8760
Fax: +246 429 9233
EMail: info@canqate.org
WWW: http://www.canqate.org/
Role of national body: The Caribbean Area Network for Quality Assurance in Tertiary Education was established as a sub-network of the International Network for Quality Assurance Agencies in Higher Education (INQAAHE). The aims and objectives of CANQATE are compatible with those of INQAAHE whose principal purpose is to "enable members to share information about the maintenance, evaluation, accreditation and improvement of higher education and to disseminate good practices in the field of Quality Assurance".

Data for academic year: 2006-2007
Source: IAU from Ministry of Education website, 2007. Bodies updated in 2011.

INSTITUTIONS

PUBLIC INSTITUTION

UNIVERSITY OF THE WEST INDIES
Cave Hill Campus, Bridgetown
Tel: +1(246) 417-4000
Fax: +1(246) 425-1327
EMail: officeoftheprincipal@cavehill.uwi.edu
Website: http://www.cavehill.uwi.edu/

Principal and Pro-Vice-Chancellor: Hilary Beckles
Tel: +1(246) 417-4030, Fax: +1(246) 417-0426
EMail: hilary.beckles@cavehill.uwi.edu

Campus Registrar: Jacqueline Wade
Tel: +1(246) 417-4052, Fax: +1(246) 425-1327
EMail: cregoffice@cavehill.uwi.edu

International Relations: Anthony Fisher
Tel: +1 (246) 417- 4542 EMail: internationaloffice@cavehill.uwi.edu

Centres
Caribbean Law *(CLIC)* (Law); **Resource Management and Environmental Studies** *(CERMES)*; **Shridath Ramphal** (International Business) *Director*: Keith Nurse; **Social and Economic Studies** *(Sir Arthur Lewis Institute)* (Economics; Social Studies)

Faculties
Humanities and Education (Education; History; Linguistics; Literature; Modern Languages; Philosophy) *Dean*: Pedro Welch; **Law** (Administrative Law; Commercial Law; Criminal Law; International Law; Law; Private Law; Public Law); **Medical Sciences** (Anaesthesiology; Epidemiology; Medicine; Ophthalmology; Paediatrics; Psychiatry and Mental Health; Surgery); **Pure and Applied Sciences** (Biological and Life Sciences; Chemistry; Electronic Engineering; Mathematics; Mathematics and Computer Science; Natural Sciences; Physics) *Dean*: Sean Carrington; **Social Sciences** (Economics; Government; Management; Social Work; Sociology; Tourism) *Dean*: George Belle

Research Centres
Chronic Disease (Medicine)

Research Units
Gender and Development Studies (Development Studies; Gender Studies)

Schools
Business (Business Administration); **Continuing Studies**

History: Founded 1962 when the University of the West Indies (UWI) was granted its charter. UWI has campuses at Cave Hill in Barbados (1963), St. Augustine in Trinidad and Tobago and Mona in Jamaica.

Academic Year: August to July

Admission Requirements: General Certificate of Education, CXC's, Associate degree or equivalent

Main Language(s) of Instruction: English

International Co-operation: With universities in USA, Canada, and United Kingdom

Degrees and Diplomas: *Bachelor's Degree*: Arts (BA); Education (BEd); Law (LLB); Science (BSc), 3 yrs (4 yrs part-time); *Master's Degree (MA)*; *Master's Degree*: Business Administration (MBA); *Master's Degree*: Education (MEd); Science (MSc), a further 3 yrs (4 yrs part-time); *Master of Philosophy (MPhil)*: a further 3 yrs (4 yrs part-time); *Ph.D. (PhD)*. Also Doctorate in Medecine (DM)

Student Services: Academic counselling, Canteen, Handicapped facilities, Health services, Language programs, Social counselling, Sports facilities

Student Residential Facilities: Yes

Libraries: Main Library, Law Library

Publications: Pelican, Magazine

Student Numbers *2008-2009*: Total: c. 8,600
Last Updated: 26/02/09

Belarus

STRUCTURE OF HIGHER EDUCATION SYSTEM

Description:

The Belarusian system of higher education includes educational, research and governing institutions that use unified official standards and rules in the processes of teaching, management, assessment and research. Higher education is provided by public (State) and private (non State) accredited higher education institutions (HEIs). Education in public HEIs is free of charge for students who passed the entrance competition. In private HEIs, all students pay tuition fees. Higher education is under the supervision of the Ministry of Education, which is responsible for the accreditation and licensing of HEIs and developing and applying the State Educational Standards. The current higher education system includes 2 stages; after completion of the first stage (4-6 years) a diploma of higher education is issued, after completion of the second stage (1 to 2 years following the first degree) the diploma of Master is issued. In 2011, Belarus has 45 state higher education institutions and 10 private higher education institutions.

Stages of studies:

University level first stage:
The first stage of higher education provides specialists with both research and professional proficiency and gives direct access to work. The Diploma of Higher Education (Diplom o Vyshem Obrazovanii) is awarded in all fields (except Medicine) after defending a Diploma project and sitting for a final state exam. The nominal length of study is 4 to 6 years (in Medicine and Architecture). The Diploma of Higher Education gives access to Master studies (Magistratura).

University level second stage: *Magistratura*
The second stage of higher education leads to the Diploma of Magistr (Master's degree) following upon the first stage. Access to these programmes is competitive. The Magistr is awarded after one to two years of study and the presentation and defense of a thesis. The Magistr gives access to postgraduate studies (Aspirantura).

University level third stage: *Aspirantura and Doktorantura*
This stage corresponds to the training of scientific and pedagogical staff. Studies follow a two-step route: 1) the Candidate of Sciences requires at least 3-4 years of study in postgraduate courses, special examinations and the public defense of a thesis. Following this, students are awarded the degree of Kandidat Nauk (Candidate of Sciences); 2) Holders of the Kandidat Nauk can prepare a Doctorate. After following the required research programme and public defense of a doctoral thesis, candidates are awarded the highest scientific degree of Doktor Nauk (Doctor of Sciences). The Dissertation Councils are supervised by the Supreme Attestation Committee (Vishaya Attestatsionnaya Komissiya, VAK) of the Republic of Belarus. It is possible to do doctorate research and sit for a scientific degree without following postgraduate courses. Higher education and research institutions support this type of students and provide them with a supervisor.

Distance higher education:
Distance training is provided by virtual universities (through Internet) such as Hagen Correspondence University which started operating in Belarus in 1996. Students must hold a secondary school leaving certificate. There is no age restriction and no entrance examination. This type of studies is also provided by franchising institutions, branches of foreign higher education institutions operating in Belarus.

ADMISSION TO HIGHER EDUCATION

Admission to university-level studies:

Name of secondary school credential required: Attestat ob Obschem Srednem Obrazovanii

Alternatives to credentials: Diploma of Professional Technical Education, Diploma of Specialized Secondary Education

Entrance exam requirements: Centralized test program (three subjects)

Numerus clausus/restrictions: Higher education institutions are given the academic freedom to establish privileges for entrants having followed advanced training at lyceums or gymnasiums or for entrants having finished school with excellent marks. Special ability requirements are set for artistic studies, physical education and architectural preservation studies. A certain age limit is set for full-time students.

Other admission requirements: There can be an interview in one subject instead of several exams. The applicant can enter a preparatory department and study for one year before trying to enter the higher education institution.

Foreign students admission:

Definition of foreign student: A foreign citizen who trains at a Belorussian higher education institution and does not have Belorussian citizenship.

Entrance exam requirements: Students must hold a secondary school-leaving certificate or an equivalent qualification to that of general secondary school in Belarus. They must submit a valid passport, a notarized copy of their secondary education qualification, a medical certificate and 6 photos. They are then sent an invitation so as to obtain an entry visa. For postgraduate courses, students must hold a Master's degree. The rules of admission and instruction are specified in the Regulations concerning Training Foreign Citizens in the Republic of Belarus approved by the decree of the Council of Ministers of the Republic of Belarus of July 7, 1993. Admission documents must be submitted at least two-and-a-half months before classes begin in Belarusian, Russian, English, French or Spanish. Admission requirements for foreign students are adopted by the higher education institutions if they are not otherwise provided for by inter-state agreements. Foreign students sign a contract with the institution.

Entry regulations: Students must hold a visa and have financial guarantees.

Health requirements: A medical certificate is required.

Language requirements: Foreign students who have no command of the language of instruction can follow a one-year course at a preparatory department of the institution where they study the language of instruction and specialization subjects that are relevant for the chosen course. At the end of the year, they must sit for an examination. Successful students obtain a graduation certificate and are admitted to the basic course of study in the chosen speciality. Those who fail are dismissed from the institution and asked to leave the country.

RECOGNITION OF STUDIES

Quality assurance system:

Higher education institutions that are accredited by the Ministry of Education may issue State Diplomas which are recognized within the country. Non-accredited HEIs have no right to issue State diplomas.

Bodies dealing with recognition:

Otdel Expertiz i Priznanii Dokumentov (Foreign Credentials Assessment Department (Belarusian ENIC))
Head, Department: Ina Mitskevich
Moskovskaja Str. 15 room 219
Minsk 220007
Tel: +375 17 228 1313
Fax: +375 17 222 8315
Services provided and students dealt with: Recognition of foreign studies, diplomas and degrees; evaluation and recognition of partial studies undertaken or experience obtained abroad; development of a normative quality assurance and recognition system; organization of seminars; publication of material and methodological documents on problems of quality assurance and recognition system.

Vishaya attestacionnaya komissiya - VAK (Supreme Attestation Committee)
Independent Avenue, 66
Minsk 220072
Tel: +375 17 284 0855
EMail: mail@vak.org.by
WWW: http://www.vak.org.by/
Services provided and students dealt with: Recognition of doctoral degrees.

Special provisions for recognition:

Recognition for university level studies: Applicants must submit complete official academic documents together with their application form to the institution.

For access to advanced studies and research: Applicants must submit complete official academic documents to the Ministry of Education of the Republic of Belarus.

For exercising a profession: Applicants must submit complete official academic documents to the Ministry of Education of the Republic of Belarus.

NATIONAL BODIES

Ministerstvo obrazovaniya Respubliki Belarus (Ministry of Education of the Republic of Belarus)
Minister: Sergey Maskevich
Director, Higher Education: Yu I. Miksiuk
Ul. Sovetskaja 9
Minsk 220010
Tel: +375 17 227 4736
Fax: +375 17 200 8483
EMail: root@minedu.unibel.by
WWW: http://www.minedu.unibel.by
Role of national body: Provides State education policy, controls the quality of education, finances educational institutions in the limits of budget allocations, licenses new institutions, grants accreditation.

Data for academic year: 2011-2012
Source: IAU from the National Institute for Higher Education, Belarus, 2011

INSTITUTIONS

PUBLIC INSTITUTIONS

ACADEMY OF PUBLIC ADMINISTRATION UNDER THE AEGIS OF THE PRESIDENT OF THE REPUBLIC OF BELARUS
Akademija Kiravannja pry Prezidence Respubliki Belarus
17 Moskovskaya St, 220007 Minsk
Tel: +375(17) 226-37-45
Fax: +375(17) 222-82-64
EMail: post@pac.by
Website: http://www.pac.by/en

Rector: Anatol Marazevich

Vice-Rector for Academic Affairs: Ihar Hancharonak
Tel: +375(17) 222-83-62, Fax: +375(17) 226-27-30

Institutes
Civil Service (Agricultural Management; Business Administration; Marketing; Public Administration); **Managerial Personnel** (Economics; Law; Public Administration; Staff Development); **Public Administration** (Administration; Business Administration; Public Administration)

Research Institutes
Theory and Practice of Public Administration

History: Founded 1991, acquired present status and title 1995.

Admission Requirements: Secondary school certificate (Attestat o srednjem obrazovanii), entrance examination and interview

Main Language(s) of Instruction: Russian, Belarusian

Accrediting Agencies: Ministry of Education

Degrees and Diplomas: *Diplom o Vyshem Obrazovanii*; *Diplom Magistra*; *Doktor Nauk*. Also Specialist Diploma; Certificate in improvement of professional skills and Diploma in retraining at the level of higher education
Last Updated: 21/09/11

ACADEMY OF THE MINISTRY OF INTERNAL AFFAIRS OF THE REPUBLIC OF BELARUS
Akademija Ministerstva Unutrannyh Sprau Respubliki Belarus (AMIA)
6 Masherov Avenue, 220005 Minsk
Tel: +375(17) 284-89-39
Fax: +375(17) 284-89-39
EMail: info@amia.unibel.by
Website: http://www.academy.mia.by

Rector: Jurij Alexandrovich Melekhovets

Faculties
Law (Law); **Militia Training** (Criminology; Protective Services)

History: Founded 1958, acquired present status and title 1995. Trains specialists in the area of law enforcement.

Governing Bodies: Academic Council

Academic Year: September to July

Admission Requirements: Secondary school certificate (Attestat o srednjem obrazovanii) and entrance examination

Fees: None

Main Language(s) of Instruction: Russian, Belarusian

Accrediting Agencies: Ministry of Education

Degrees and Diplomas: *Diplom o Vyshem Obrazovanii*: Law; Criminal Investigation; Law Enforcement, 5 yrs; *Kandidat Nauk*: Law

Student Services: Canteen, Health services, Sports facilities

Student Residential Facilities: For c. 2,500 students

Special Facilities: Museum of Criminalistics; Movie Studio

Libraries: c. 250,000 vols

Publications: Vestnik of the Academy, Law Issue *(quarterly)*

Press or Publishing House: Publishing Department

Last Updated: 20/03/12

BARANOVICHI STATE UNIVERSITY

Baranavickij Dzjaržauny Universitet (BARSU)
vul. Voikava, 21, 225404 Baranoviči
Tel: +375(163) 45-78-60
Fax: +375(163) 45-78-31
EMail: barsu@brest.by
Website: http://www.barsu.by

Rector: Vassily Ivanovich Kochurko
Tel: +375(163) 45-71-09, Fax: +375(163) 45-78-31

Faculties
Continuing Education (Continuing Education); **Distance Education**; **Economy and Law** (Accountancy; Business Administration; Economics; Law; Marketing); **Education** (Art Criticism; Education; History; Mathematics Education; Music Education; Pedagogy; Philology; Philosophy; Physical Education; Preschool Education; Science Education; Technology Education); **Engineering** (Automation and Control Engineering; Engineering; Information Technology; Machine Building; Mechanical Engineering); **Foreign Languages** (English; German; Literature; Modern Languages; Native Language)

History: Founded 2004.

Main Language(s) of Instruction: Russian, Belarusian

Accrediting Agencies: Ministry of Education

Degrees and Diplomas: *Diplom o Vyshem Obrazovanii*

Last Updated: 21/09/11

BELARUS STATE AGRARIAN AND TECHNICAL UNIVERSITY

Belaruskij Dzjaržauny Agrarny Tehničny Universitet (BATU)
99 Nezavisimosti Avenue, 220023 Minsk
Tel: +375(17) 264-47-71
Fax: +375(17) 264-41-16
EMail: rektorat@batu.edu.by
Website: http://www.batu.edu.by

Rector: Nikolai Kazaravets
Tel: +375(17) 264-61-91 EMail: rektor@batu.edu.by

First Vice-Rector: Ivan Nikolaevich Tel: +375(17) 264-47-90

Faculties
Agro-Industrial Technology (Maintenance Technology; Mechanical Engineering; Safety Engineering); **Agro-Mechanical Engineering** (Agricultural Engineering; Agricultural Equipment; Mechanical Engineering); **Agro-Power Engineering** (Agricultural Engineering; Automation and Control Engineering; Electrical and Electronic Engineering; Power Engineering); **Business Administration and Management** (Business Administration; Management); **Ecology** (Ecology); **Preparatory and Professional Training**

History: Founded 1954, acquired present status and title 2000.

Academic Year: September to July

Admission Requirements: General or special secondary school certificate (Attestat o srednjem /specialnom/obrazovanii)

Fees: None for local students

Main Language(s) of Instruction: Russian, Belarusian

Accrediting Agencies: Ministry of Agriculture and Food; Ministry of Education

Degrees and Diplomas: *Diplom o Vyshem Obrazovanii*: 5 yrs; *Diplom Magistra*

Student Services: Academic counselling, Canteen, Cultural centre, Employment services, Foreign student adviser, Handicapped facilities, Health services, Language programs, Social counselling, Sports facilities

Student Residential Facilities: Yes

Special Facilities: Museum of the History of BSATU. Computer Centre

Libraries: c. 415,000 vols

Publications: Agropanorama, Scientific Technical Journal *(quarterly)*; Proceedings of Conferences *(quarterly)*

Last Updated: 20/03/12

BELARUS STATE ECONOMICS UNIVERSITY

Belaruskij Dzjaržauny Ekanamičny Universitet (BSEU)
26, Partizanski Ave, 220070 Minsk
Tel: +375(17) 209-88-32
Fax: +375(17) 249-11-07
EMail: umoms@bseu.by
Website: http://www.bseu.by/

Rector: Vladimir Nikolaievich Shimov

Campuses
Bobruisk (English; German; Mathematics and Computer Science; Romance Languages)

Faculties
Commerce, Economics and Management (Business and Commerce; Economics; Management)

Higher Schools
Business and Management (Banking; Business Administration; Economics; Finance; Management); **Tourism** (Management; Tourism)

Institutes
Social Sciences and Humanities

Schools
Accounting and Economics (Accountancy; Banking; Statistics); **Finance and Banking** (Banking; Finance; Information Technology; Taxation); **International Business Communication** (International Business); **International Economic Relations** (Economic History; International Business; International Economics); **Law** (Civil Law; Commercial Law; Law; Public Law); **Management** (Applied Mathematics; Economics; Management); **Marketing** (Marketing)

History: Founded 1933. Acquired present status and title 1992.

Main Language(s) of Instruction: Russian, Belarusian

Accrediting Agencies: Ministry of Education

Degrees and Diplomas: *Diplom o Vyshem Obrazovanii*; *Diplom Magistra*

Libraries: c. 174,000 vols

Last Updated: 21/09/11

BELARUSIAN NATIONAL TECHNICAL UNIVERSITY

Belaruski Nacyjanal'ny Tehnichny Universitet (BNTU)
Nezavisimosty ave, 65, 220013 Minsk
Tel: +375(17) 292-77-52
Fax: +375(17) 292-91-37
EMail: bntu@bntu.by
Website: http://www.bntu.by

Rector: Boris Mikhailavich Khroustalev (2000-)
Tel: +375(17) 292-40-55, Fax: +375(17) 292-41-42
EMail: rector@bntu.by

First Vice-Rector: Fiodar I. Pantsialeyenka
Tel: +375(17) 292-86-02

Centres
Information Technology (Information Technology)

Divisions
Research

Faculties
Architecture (Architecture); **Automotive and Tractor** (Automotive Engineering; Design; Petroleum and Gas Engineering; Road Transport; Transport and Communications; Transport Engineering; Transport Management); **Civil Engineering** (Civil Engineering; Construction Engineering; Industrial Engineering); **Engineering**

and **Pedagogy** (Engineering; Pedagogy); **Information Technologies and Robotics** (Artificial Intelligence; Automation and Control Engineering; Information Technology; Robotics; Software Engineering); **Instrument Making** (Engineering; Instrument Making; Laser Engineering; Measurement and Precision Engineering; Safety Engineering; Sports); **International Relations** (Slavic Languages); **Management Technology and Humanities** (Administration; Business and Commerce; Energy Engineering; Engineering Management; Management; Packaging Technology; Power Engineering; Taxation; Technology); **Marketing, Management and Entrepreneurship** (Business Administration; Economics; International Economics; Management; Marketing); **Mechanical and Technological Engineering** (Engineering; Materials Engineering; Mechanical Engineering; Metal Techniques; Metallurgical Engineering; Technology); **Mechanical Engineering** (Automation and Control Engineering; Building Technologies; Machine Building; Materials Engineering; Mechanical Engineering; Metal Techniques; Metallurgical Engineering); **Military Engineering** (Automotive Engineering; Building Technologies; Machine Building; Road Engineering); **Power Engineering** (Electrical Engineering; Heating and Refrigeration; Industrial Engineering; Power Engineering); **Power Plant Construction and Engineering Services** (Construction Engineering; Heating and Refrigeration; Hydraulic Engineering; Marine Engineering; Marine Transport; Naval Architecture; Nuclear Engineering; Petroleum and Gas Engineering; Power Engineering); **Sports** (Physical Education; Sports); **Transport Communication** (Road Engineering; Transport and Communications)

Institutes

Distance Education *(International Institute)* (Computer Science; Economics; Information Technology; Management); **Engineering, Technology and Economics** *(Higher Qualification and Re-Training Institute)* (Economics; Engineering; Technology); **Higher Engineering Education** *(Republican Institute)* (Engineering; Technology Education); **Innovation Technologies** *(Republican Institute)*; **Integrated Educational Methods and Monitoring**; **Management and Personnel Development** *(Inter-Branch Institute of Higher Qualification and Re-Training)* (Human Resources; Management); **Optical Materials and Technologies** (Optical Technology; Optics)

Further Information: Also UNESCO Chair "Energy Conservation and Renewable Energies" with Prof. Victor Bashtovoi.

History: Founded 1920 as Belarusian State Polytechnical Institute. In 1991 renamed Belarusian State Polytechnic Academy. Acquired present status and title 2002.

Governing Bodies: University Council

Academic Year: September to June (September-January; February-June)

Admission Requirements: General or special secondary school certificate (Attestat o srednjem /specialnom/obrazovanii) and entrance examination

Fees: (Euros): 1,300-1,600 per annum (for local and foreign students)

Main Language(s) of Instruction: Belarusian, Russian. Also courses in English, French and German

International Co-operation: With universities in Austria; China; Germany; Iran; Latvia; Lithuania; Netherlands; Norway; Russian Federation; SAR; Serbia; Slovakia; Slovenia; South Korea; Poland; Switzerland; Syria; Tajikistan; Turkey; Ukraine; Uzbekistan; Vietnam; Bulgaria; Sweden; Czech Republic. Also participates in Tempus-Tacis, Socrates, Copernicus, Intas, Baltic University programmes and UNESCO programmes

Accrediting Agencies: Ministry of Education

Degrees and Diplomas: *Diplom o Vyshem Obrazovanii (BSc)*; *Diplom Magistra (MSc)*: 1-2 yrs; *Kandidat Nauk (PhD)*: 3 yrs; *Doktor Nauk*

Student Services: Academic counselling, Canteen, Cultural centre, Employment services, Foreign student adviser, Foreign Studies Centre, Health services, Language programs, Social counselling, Sports facilities

Student Residential Facilities: Yes

Special Facilities: Historical Museum, Art Gallery, Exhibition of Scientific and Technological Achievements, Sanatorium, Scientific Library

Libraries: c. 2,060,000 vols

Publications: Energetika/Power Engineering, Journal *(quarterly)*; VESTNIK BNTU, Journal *(quarterly)*

Press or Publishing House: Yes

Academic Staff *2008-2009*	TOTAL
FULL-TIME	2,042
STAFF WITH DOCTORATE	
FULL-TIME	835
PART-TIME	245
Student Numbers *2008-2009*	
All (Foreign Included)	30,100
FOREIGN ONLY	650

Distance students, 1,200.
Last Updated: 21/09/11

BELARUSIAN STATE ACADEMY OF ARTS
Belaruskaja Dzjaržaunaja Akademija Mastastvau (BSAA)
Independence Avenue, 81, 220012 Minsk
Tel: +375(17) 232-15-42
Fax: +375(17) 232-20-41
EMail: international@belam.by.com
Website: http://www.belam.by.com/

Rector: Richard Balyaslavavič Smolskij (1997-)

Faculties
Design and Decorative Arts and Crafts (Crafts and Trades; Design; Graphic Arts); **Fine Arts** (Fine Arts; Graphic Arts; Painting and Drawing; Sculpture); **Theatre** (Cinema and Television; Theatre)

History: Founded 1945, reorganized 1991 as Belarus Academy of Arts, and acquired present status and title 2001.

Main Language(s) of Instruction: Russian, Belarusian

Accrediting Agencies: Ministry of Education

Degrees and Diplomas: *Diplom o Vyshem Obrazovanii*; *Diplom Magistra*; *Kandidat Nauk*; *Doktor Nauk*

Libraries: 81,000 vols
Last Updated: 21/09/11

BELARUSIAN STATE ACADEMY OF MUSIC
Belaruskaja Dzjaržaunaja Akademija Muzyki (BGAM)
vul. Internaciyanalnaja, 30, 220030 Minsk
Tel: +375(17) 227-49-42
Fax: +375(17) 206-55-01
EMail: international@tut.by
Website: http://www.bgam.edu.by

Rector: Ekaterina Nikolaevna Dulova

Departments
Doctoral Studies (Music; Musicology; Pedagogy); **Folk Instruments** (Conducting; Music Education; Musical Instruments; Pedagogy); **Orchestra** (Musical Instruments); **Pedagogy** *(Mogilyov)* (Conducting; Music; Music Education; Musical Instruments; Pedagogy; Singing); **Piano, Musicology and Composition** (Computer Science; Music; Music Education; Music Theory and Composition; Musical Instruments; Musicology; Pedagogy; Philosophy); **Vocal and Choir** (Conducting; Opera; Singing)

Further Information: Branch in Mogiliev

History: Founded 1932, acquired present status and title 1992.

Governing Bodies: Rectorate

Academic Year: September to June (September-January; February-June)

Admission Requirements: General or special secondary school certificate (Attestat o srednjem /specialnom/obrazovanii). Interview for foreign students. Knowledge of Russian language required, except for performance Diploma programmes

Fees: (US Dollars): None for local students. Foreign students, undergraduate, 2,500 per annum; graduate and postgraduate, 4,000

Main Language(s) of Instruction: Russian, Belarusian

International Co-operation: With institutions in China; Russian Federation; Poland; USA

Accrediting Agencies: Ministry of Education

Degrees and Diplomas: *Diplom o Vyshem Obrazovanii*: 5 yrs; *Diplom Magistra*: Pedagogy (MA), 1 further yr; *Kandidat Nauk*: Musicology (PhD), a further 3 yrs by thesis; *Doktor Nauk*: Musicology, a further 3 yrs by thesis

Student Services: Academic counselling, Canteen, Cultural centre, Employment services, Foreign Studies Centre, Handicapped facilities, Health services, Language programs, Social counselling, Sports facilities

Student Residential Facilities: For c. 1,100 students

Special Facilities: Concert Hall; 2 Chamber Halls. Opera Studio; Sound Engineering/Recording Studio. Sound Archive Department for Belarussian Traditional Music; Laboratory for Music Sciences

Libraries: c. 220,000 vols and Audio/Video Library

Publications: Scientific Papers, Annual Scientific Readings Yearbook *(annually)*; Vesti Belaruskaja Akademii Musyki (Belarus Academy of Music News), Yearbook *(annually)*

Press or Publishing House: Belarussian State Academy of Music Press

Last Updated: 21/09/11

BELARUSIAN STATE AGRICULTURAL ACADEMY

Belaruskaja Dzjaržaunaja Sel'skagaspadarčaja Akademija (BSAA)
vul. Michurina, 5, 213410 Gorki
Tel: +375(2233) 5-94-96
Fax: +375(2233) 5-14-20
EMail: kancel@baa.by
Website: http://www.baa.by/

Rector: Alexandr P. Kurdeko

Faculties

Accountancy (Accountancy); **Accountancy** *(Distance Education)* (Accountancy); **Agricultural Engineering and Machinery** (Agricultural Engineering; Agricultural Equipment; Automotive Engineering; Labour and Industrial Relations; Machine Building; Mechanical Equipment and Maintenance); **Agro-Biology** *(Distance Education)* (Agriculture; Agrobiology; Biology); **Agro-Ecology** (Agriculture; Ecology); **Agronomy** (Agronomy; Crop Production); **Animal Husbandry** (Animal Husbandry; Biotechnology; Cattle Breeding; Ecology; Fishery; Genetics; Hygiene; Limnology; Marine Biology; Microbiology; Physiology; Veterinary Science; Zoology); **Business and Law** (Economics; Law; Marketing); **Economics** (Agricultural Business; Agricultural Economics; Agricultural Management; Econometrics; Economic and Finance Policy; Economics; International Economics; International Relations; Law; Marketing); **Economics and Law** *(Distance Education)* (Agricultural Economics; Economics; Law); **Engineering** *(Distance Education)*; **Land Development and Planning** (Rural Planning; Soil Conservation; Surveying and Mapping); **Land Improvement** (Agricultural Engineering; Agricultural Management; Rural Planning; Water Management; Water Science)

Further Information: Also Preparatory Department

History: Founded 1840 as Gory-Gorecky Agricultural School. Reorganized 1928 as Belarusian Agricultural Academy incorporating Belarusian Institute of Agriculture (founded 1922). Acquired present status and title 1997.

Governing Bodies: Academic Board

Academic Year: September to June (September-January; February-June)

Admission Requirements: Secondary school certificate (Attestat o srednjem obrazovanii) and entrance examination

Fees: (US Dollars): Foreign students, tuition, 800 per annum; Preparatory Department, 700; postgraduate studies, 1,000

Main Language(s) of Instruction: Russian, Belarusian

International Co-operation: Participates in the Tempus, Tacis and Intas programmes

Accrediting Agencies: Ministry of Education

Degrees and Diplomas: *Diplom o Vyshem Obrazovanii*: 5 yrs; *Diplom Magistra*; *Doktor Nauk*

Student Services: Canteen, Cultural centre, Employment services, Foreign student adviser, Health services, Language programs, Nursery care, Social counselling, Sports facilities

Student Residential Facilities: Yes

Special Facilities: Museum. Botanical Garden. Dendropark. Experimental Farm (in Čkalov). Palace of Culture. Sport Complex. Biological Centre

Libraries: Central Library, c. 1m. vols

Press or Publishing House: Gorki Printing House

Last Updated: 14/10/09

BELARUSIAN STATE MEDICAL UNIVERSITY

Belaruskij Dzjaržauny Medycynski Universitet (BSMU)
83, Dzerzinski Ave, 220116 Minsk
Tel: +375(17) 272-66-05
Fax: +375(17) 272-61-97
EMail: bsmu@bsmu.by
Website: http://www.bsmu.by/eng/

Rector: Anatol Sikorski
Tel: +375(17) 271-94-24, Fax: +375(17) 272-61-97
EMail: rector@bsmu.by

Faculties

Dentistry (Child Care and Development; Dental Hygiene; Dentistry; Oral Pathology; Periodontics; Plastic Surgery); **General Medicine** (Cardiology; Endocrinology; Gynaecology and Obstetrics; Haematology; Hepatology; Medicine; Nephrology; Orthopaedics; Physical Therapy; Surgery; Venereology); **Military Medicine** (Medicine); **Paediatrics** (Paediatrics); **Preventive Medicine** (Epidemiology; Medicine; Social and Preventive Medicine; Virology)

Further Information: Also courses for foreign students. Preparatory department for postgraduate Medical Training. Postgraduate research courses

History: Founded 1921 as part of Department of Medicine of Belarus State University, reorganized as Minsk State Medical Institute 1930, and acquired present status and title 2002.

Governing Bodies: Academic Council

Academic Year: September to June (September-January; February-June)

Admission Requirements: General or special secondary school certificate (Attestat o srednjem /specialnom/obrazovanii)

Fees: (US Dollars): 2,200-2,700 per annum

Main Language(s) of Instruction: Russian

International Co-operation: With universities in France, Japan, Canada, USA, Germany

Accrediting Agencies: Ministry of Health; Ministry of Education

Degrees and Diplomas: *Diplom o Vyshem Obrazovanii*; *Diplom Magistra*; *Doktor Nauk*

Student Services: Academic counselling, Canteen, Cultural centre, Foreign student adviser, Foreign Studies Centre, Health services, Language programs, Nursery care, Social counselling, Sports facilities

Student Residential Facilities: Yes

Special Facilities: Anatomy Museum; History of Medicine Museum; Students Theatre

Libraries: Central Institute Library, 539,000 vols; Central Medical Library, 801,000 vols

Publications: Belarusian Medical Journal *(monthly)*; Proceedings of Minsk State Medical University, Scientific Bulletin *(annually)*

Last Updated: 21/09/11

BELARUSIAN STATE PEDAGOGICAL UNIVERSITY NAMED AFTER M. TANK

Belaruskij Dzjaržauny Pedagogiskij Universitet imja Maksima Tanka (BSPU)
vul. Saveckaja, 18, 220050 Minsk
Tel: +375(17) 220-94-17
Fax: +375(17) 226-40-24
EMail: bspu@bspu.unibel.by
Website: http://www.bspu.unibel.by

Rector: Petar D. Kukharcik (2003-) Tel: +375(17) 226-40-20

International Relations: Andreev Aleksandr Alekseevic
Tel: +375(17) 226-40-18

Faculties

Belarus Philology and Culture (Cultural Studies; Native Language; Philology); **Folk Culture** (Cultural Studies; Folklore); **History** (History); **Mathematics** (Mathematics); **Music and Pedagogy** (Music Education; Pedagogy); **Natural Sciences** (Natural Sciences); **Physics** (Physics); **Preschool Education** (Preschool Education); **Primary Education** (Primary Education); **Psychology** (Psychology); **Russian Philology and Culture** (Cultural Studies; Russian); **Social Pedagogical Technologies** (Humanities and Social Science Education; Pedagogy); **Special Education**

Research Centres

Pre-University Training (Higher Education; Pedagogy)

History: Founded 1924, acquired present status and title 1994.

Governing Bodies: University Council

Academic Year: September to June

Admission Requirements: General or special secondary school certificate (Attestat o srednjem /specialnom/obrazovanii) and entrance examination

Main Language(s) of Instruction: Russian, Belarusian

Accrediting Agencies: Ministry of Education

Degrees and Diplomas: *Diplom o Vyshem Obrazovanii; Diplom Magistra; Kandidat Nauk (PhD); Doktor Nauk*

Student Services: Academic counselling, Canteen, Cultural centre, Employment services, Health services, Social counselling, Sports facilities

Special Facilities: Natural Science Museum; History Museum

Libraries: Central Library, c. 1.3m. vols

Publications: Nastaunik
Last Updated: 22/09/11

BELARUSIAN STATE TECHNOLOGICAL UNIVERSITY

Belaruskij Dzjaržauny Tehnalagičny Universitet (BSTU)
13a Sverdlov St, 220006 Minsk
Tel: +375(17) 226-14-32
Fax: +375(17) 227-62-17
EMail: root@bstu.unibel.by
Website: http://www.bstu.unibel.by

Rector: Ivan Zharski (1987-)

Faculties

Chemical Technology and Engineering (Chemical Engineering; Chemistry; Technology); **Economic Engineering** (Accountancy; Economics; Management; Marketing); **Forestry** (Forestry; Landscape Architecture); **Forestry Engineering and Wood Technology** (Forestry; Machine Building; Power Engineering; Wood Technology); **Organic Substances Technology** (Biotechnology; Ecology; Organic Chemistry); **Printing and Publishing** (Printing and Printmaking; Publishing and Book Trade)

History: Founded 1930 as Forestry Institute, became Forestry Technical Institute, 1932, Belarusian Institute of Technology, 1961. Acquired present status and title 1993.

Governing Bodies: University Council

Academic Year: September to June

Admission Requirements: General or special secondary school certificate (Attestat o srednjem /specialnom/obrazovanii)

Fees: (US Dollars): Foreign students, 1,600

Main Language(s) of Instruction: Russian, Belarusian

International Co-operation: UNESCO Chair in Energy Conservation and Renewable Energies

Accrediting Agencies: Ministry of Education

Degrees and Diplomas: *Diplom o Vyshem Obrazovanii; Diplom Magistra; Diplom Magistra:* Science, a further yr; *Kandidat Nauk (PhD):* a further 3 yrs by thesis following Master. Also Graduate Engineer in Science, 5 yrs

Student Services: Canteen, Cultural centre, Employment services, Foreign student adviser, Health services, Nursery care, Social counselling, Sports facilities

Student Residential Facilities: For c. 3,000 students
Special Facilities: History of University Museum
Libraries: 1,200,000 vols

Publications: Chemistry and Inorganic Substances Technology; Chemistry and Organic Substances Technology; Economics and Management; Forestry; Physico-Mathematical and Computer Sciences; Political Science, Philosophy, History and Linguistics; Printing and Publishing; Teaching and Teaching Methods; Timber and Wood-Working Industry
Last Updated: 21/09/11

BELARUSIAN STATE UNIVERSITY

Belaruskij Dzjaržauny Universitet (BSU)
4 Nezavisimosti avenue, 220030 Minsk
Tel: +375(17) 209-50-85
Fax: +375(17) 226-59-40
EMail: bsu@bsu.by
Website: http://www.bsu.by

Rector: Sergey V. Ablameyko (2003-) EMail: rector@bsu.by

Faculties

Applied Mathematics and Computer Science (Applied Mathematics; Computer Science); **Biology** (Biochemistry; Biology; Botany; Ecology; Genetics; Microbiology; Molecular Biology; Physiology; Zoology); **Chemistry** (Analytical Chemistry; Chemistry; Inorganic Chemistry; Organic Chemistry); **Economics** (Economics); **Geography** (Earth Sciences; Ecology; Geography; Geology; Soil Science); **History** (Archaeology; Contemporary History; Ethnology; History; Modern History); **International Relations** (European Union Law; International Law; International Relations; Private Law); **Law** (Law); **Liberal Education** (Clinical Psychology; Cultural Studies; Design; Ecology; Health Administration; Information Technology; Translation and Interpretation); **Mechanics and Mathematics** (Mathematics; Mechanics); **Philology** (Applied Linguistics; English; German; Linguistics; Literature; Philology; Romance Languages; Russian; Slavic Languages); **Philosophy and Social Sciences** (Philosophy; Psychology; Social Sciences; Sociology); **Physics** (Physics); **Radiophysics and Computer Technology** (Computer Science; Electronic Engineering; Radiophysics)

Institutes

Journalism (Journalism); **Management and Social Technologies** (Business Administration; Economics; Finance; Law; Management; Real Estate; Rehabilitation and Therapy; Social Work)

History: Founded 1921.

Governing Bodies: Academic Council

Academic Year: September to June

Admission Requirements: Secondary school certificate (Attestat o srednjem /specialnom/obrazovanii)

Fees: (US Dollars): 1,500-3,000 per annum

Main Language(s) of Instruction: Belarusian, Russian

International Co-operation: Participates in the Tempus, I.A.E.S.T.E., Intas and Copernicus programmes

Accrediting Agencies: Ministry of Education

Degrees and Diplomas: *Diplom o Vyshem Obrazovanii:* 5 yrs; *Diplom Magistra; Diplom Magistra; Kandidat Nauk*

Student Services: Academic counselling, Canteen, Cultural centre, Employment services, Foreign student adviser, Foreign Studies Centre, Handicapped facilities, Health services, Language programs, Nursery care, Social counselling, Sports facilities

Special Facilities: Museum of BSU History; Geology Museum; Ethnography Museum. Lyceum of BSU. Republican Institute of Higher Education Establishment. European Documentation and Information Centre; Scientific-Engineering Centre; Computer Centre

Libraries: c. 2,000,000 vols; c. 250,000 periodicals

Publications: Belarusian Historical Magazine *(quarterly)*; International Relations *(quarterly)*; Sociology, Magazine *(monthly)*

Press or Publishing House: Publishing Centre
Last Updated: 21/09/11

BELARUSIAN STATE UNIVERSITY OF CULTURE AND ART

Belaruskij Dzjaržauny Universitet Kul'tury I Mastatstvau (BUK)

17 Rabkorovskaya Street, 220007 Minsk
Tel: +375(17) 222-83-71
Fax: +375(17) 222-24-09
EMail: buk@buk.by
Website: http://www.buk.by/

Rector: Boris Svetlov (2008-) EMail: rector@buk.by

Faculties

Correspondence Studies (Distance Education); **Culturology and Socio-Cultural Activity** (Cultural Studies; Management); **Library and Information Sciences** (Information Sciences; Library Science); **Music** (Music); **Traditional Belarusian Culture and Modern Arts** (Arts and Humanities; Dance; Folklore; Performing Arts; Theatre)

Institutes

Culture (Arts and Humanities; Cultural Studies)

History: Founded 1975 as as Minsk Institute of Culture, acquired present status and title 2004.

Governing Bodies: University Council

Academic Year: September to June

Fees: (US Dollars): 300 per annum

Main Language(s) of Instruction: Russian, Belarusian

Accrediting Agencies: Ministry of Education

Degrees and Diplomas: *Diplom o Vyshem Obrazovanii*; *Diplom Magistra*; *Kandidat Nauk*; *Doktor Nauk*

Student Services: Academic counselling, Canteen, Employment services, Foreign student adviser, Language programs, Nursery care, Social counselling, Sports facilities

Student Residential Facilities: Student's Hostels

Special Facilities: Art Gallery; Museum of Arts and Crafts, Museum of Music Instruments

Libraries: c. 500,000 vols

Publications: Vestnik Belaruskaga Dzarzaunaga Universiteta Kultury i Mastatstvau, Scientific articles in the field of culture and Arts *(biennially)*

Last Updated: 22/09/11

BELARUSIAN STATE UNIVERSITY OF INFORMATICS AND RADIOELECTRONICS

Belaruskij Dzjaržauny Universitet Informatyki i Radyjoelektroniki (BSUIR)

P. Browka Str., 6, 220013 Minsk
Tel: +375(17) 292-32-35
Fax: +375(17) 202-10-33
EMail: oms@bsuir.by
Website: http://www.bsuir.by

Rector: Mikhail Paylavich Batura (2000-) EMail: rector@bsuir.by

First Vice-Rector: Anatoly Osipov
Tel: +375(17) 293-23-51 EMail: osipov@bsuir.by

International Relations: Anna Titovich, Head of Department
Tel: +375(17) 293-85-72, Fax: +375(17) 293-23-33
EMail: international@bsuir.by

Faculties

Computer Systems and Networks (Computer Networks; Software Engineering); **Computer-Aided Design** (Computer Engineering; Computer Graphics; Electrical and Electronic Equipment and Maintenance; Measurement and Precision Engineering; Optics); **Continuous and Distance Training** (Artificial Intelligence; Automation and Control Engineering; Computer Science; Information Technology; Marketing; Software Engineering); **Economics and Engineering** (Business Administration; Economics; Industrial and Production Economics; Marketing; Telecommunications Engineering); **Extra-mural Training** (Business Administration; Computer Networks; Economics; Information Technology; Nanotechnology; Radio and Television Broadcasting; Telecommunications Engineering); **Information Technology and Control** (Artificial Intelligence; Computer Science; Information Technology; Software

Engineering); **Military** (Military Science; Telecommunications Engineering); **Radioengineering and Electronics** (Electrical and Electronic Engineering; Microelectronics; Microwaves; Radiophysics); **Telecommunications** (Computer Networks; Radio and Television Broadcasting; Telecommunications Engineering)

Further Information: Also courses for foreign students. Distance and part time learning also available.

History: Founded 1964 as Minsk Radioengineering Institute, acquired present status and title 1993.

Governing Bodies: Rector; University Council

Academic Year: September to June (September-January; February-June)

Admission Requirements: General or special secondary school certificate (Attestat o srednjem /specialnom/obrazovanii) and entrance examination

Fees: (US Dollars): Foreign students, 2,000-2,300 per annum

Main Language(s) of Instruction: Russian, Belarusian

International Co-operation: With universities in Germany

Accrediting Agencies: Ministry of Education

Degrees and Diplomas: *Diplom o Vyshem Obrazovanii*; *Diplom Magistra*: 1-2 yrs; *Kandidat Nauk (Ph.D.)*: a further 3 yrs by thesis; *Doktor Nauk (Dr. of Sc.)*: a further 3 yrs by thesis following Candidate of Sciences

Student Services: Academic counselling, Canteen, Cultural centre, Employment services, Foreign student adviser, Foreign Studies Centre, Handicapped facilities, Health services, Language programs, Sports facilities

Student Residential Facilities: For 2,400 students

Special Facilities: University Museum; TV Studio

Libraries: Central Library, 1,300,000 vols

Publications: Doklady Belorusskogo gosudartvennogo universiteta informatiki i radioelektroniki, Scientific magazine of Belarusian State University of Informatics and Radioelectronics *(quarterly)*

Press or Publishing House: Publishing Department of University

Academic Staff 2008	MEN	WOMEN	TOTAL
FULL-TIME	484	266	**750**
STAFF WITH DOCTORATE FULL-TIME	258	68	**326**
Student Numbers 2008			
All (Foreign Included)	–	–	**12,448**
FOREIGN ONLY	–	–	**270**

Part-time students, 3,606. **Distance students**, 824. **Evening students**, 421.

Last Updated: 22/09/11

BELARUSIAN STATE UNIVERSITY OF PHYSICAL EDUCATION

Belaruskij Dzjaržauny Universitet Fizičnaj Kul'tury (BSUPC)

Pieramoshcau ave., 105 - 226, 220020 Minsk
Tel: +375(17) 250-80-08 +375(17) 250-30-84
Fax: +375(17) 250-80-08
EMail: mobgufk@mail.ru
Website: http://www.sportedu.by

Rector: Mihail Yafimavich Kobrinsky (1998-)
Tel: +375(17) 250-68-78 EMail: oo@sportedu.by

Vice-Rector: Olga Gusarova

Departments
Fencing and Boxing (Sports)

Faculties
Health (Physical Education; Sports Management); **Sport and Pedagogic - Mass Sports** (Sports); **Sport and Pedagogic - Sport Games and Combative Sport** (Sports)

Higher Schools
Coaches

Institutes
Tourism (Tourism)

History: Founded 1937, acquired present status and title 2003.

Governing Bodies: Rector, Vice-Rector, Deputy-Rectors, Deans and Heads of Departments

Academic Year: September to June (September-January and February-June)

Admission Requirements: Secondary school certificate (Attestat o srednjem obrazovanii) and entrance examination.

Fees: (US Dollars): 1,500 per annum; postal tuition, 800; preparatory faculty, 900 magistracy, c. 1,500; postgraduate courses, c. 1,700

Main Language(s) of Instruction: Russian, Belarusian

International Co-operation: With universities in Russian Federation, Latvia, Lithuania, Ukraine, Poland; Japan; Turkey; Germany; Kyrgystan; Kazakhstan; Iran

Accrediting Agencies: Ministry of Sport and Tourism

Degrees and Diplomas: *Diplom o Vyshem Obrazovanii*; *Diplom Magistra*; *Kandidat Nauk*; *Doktor Nauk*

Student Services: Academic counselling, Canteen, Cultural centre, Foreign student adviser, Foreign Studies Centre, Handicapped facilities, Health services, Language programs, Social counselling, Sports facilities

Student Residential Facilities: student hostel and sport camp

Special Facilities: Museums; Anatomy, History, Folklore, Ethnography, Physical Education and Sports

Libraries: Scientific Library of Physical Culture (merged with Republican Scientific and Methodological Library of Physical Culture), 657,592 vols; 202 periodical subscripts; 19 data bases

Last Updated: 21/09/11

BELARUSIAN STATE UNIVERSITY OF TRANSPORT

Belaruskij Dzjaržauny Universitet Transpartu (BELGUT)
34 Kirov Street, 246653 Gomel
Tel: +375(232) 77-72-15
Fax: +375(232) 77-44-83
EMail: belsut@belsut.gomel.by
Website: http://www.belsut.gomel.by

Rector: Valentin P. Yaroshevich
Tel: +375(232) 55-11-68, Fax: +375(232) 77-44-83
EMail: eco@gut.belpak.gomel.by

First Vice-Rector: Viktor Negrej Tel: +375(23) 277-52-24

International Relations: Nikolai Volkov
Tel: +7(23) 255-11-68, Fax: +7(23) 255-11-68
EMail: npvolkov@belsut.gomel.by

Faculties
Civil Engineering (Architecture; Building Technologies; Civil Engineering; Industrial Engineering; Road Engineering); **Construction** (Construction Engineering; Road Engineering); **Electrical Engineering** (Automation and Control Engineering; Electrical and Electronic Engineering; Electrical Engineering; Telecommunications Engineering); **Humanities and Economics** (Accountancy; Economics; Humanities and Social Science Education; Management); **Mechanical Engineering** (Mechanical Engineering); **Preparatory Training**; **Transport Management** (Transport and Communications; Transport Management)

Institutes
Continuing Education (Continuing Education); **Railway Research** (Railway Transport)

Research Centres
Ecology in Railway Transport (Ecology; Railway Transport); **Integrated Transport Problems** (Railway Engineering)

Research Laboratories
Estimation of Rolling Stock Units (Railway Transport); **Safety and Electromagnetical Compatibility of Technical Means** (Safety Engineering; Technology); **Soil, Base and Foundation Mechanics** (Mechanics); **Surface and Thin Films Physics** (Materials Engineering); **Track Studies** (Materials Engineering)

Further Information: Also Russian language preparatory course for foreign students

History: Founded 1953 as Belarusian Institute of Railway Engineering, acquired present status and title 1993.

Governing Bodies: University Council

Academic Year: September to July (September-January; February-July)

Admission Requirements: General or special secondary school certificate (Attestat o srednjem /specialnom/obrazovanii) and competitive entrance examination

Fees: (US Dollars): Foreign students, 1,000-1,500 per annum

Main Language(s) of Instruction: Russian, Belarusian

International Co-operation: With universities in China, Germany, Poland

Accrediting Agencies: Ministry of Education

Degrees and Diplomas: *Diplom o Vyshem Obrazovanii*: 5 yrs; *Diplom Magistra*

Student Services: Canteen, Cultural centre, Foreign student adviser, Health services, Language programs, Social counselling, Sports facilities

Student Residential Facilities: For c. 3,500 students

Special Facilities: Museum

Libraries: Scientific and Technical Library, c. 700,000 vols

Publications: Science and Transport *(quarterly)*

Last Updated: 22/09/11

BELARUSIAN-RUSSIAN STATE UNIVERSITY

Dzjaržauny Belorussko-Rossijskij Universitet (BRU)
Prospect Mira, 43, 212005 Mogilev
Tel: +375(222) 26-61-00
Fax: +375(222) 22-58-21
EMail: bru@bru.mogilev.by
Website: http://www.bru.mogilev.by

Rector: Igor Sergeevich Sazonov (1998-)

Vice-Rector: Alexander Zholobov
Tel: +375(222) 25-36-71, Fax: +375(222) 25-10-91

International Relations: Alexander Korotkevich
Tel: +375(222) 25-28-30 EMail: interstudy@bru.mogilev.by

Faculties
Automechanical Engineering (Mechanical Engineering); **Construction** (Construction Engineering); **Economics** (Economics); **Electrical Engineering** (Electrical Engineering); **Mechanical Engineering** (Mechanical Engineering)

History: Founded 1961 as Mogilev Mechanical Engineering Institute, acquired present status and title 2003.

Academic Year: September to June (September-January; February-June)

Admission Requirements: General or special secondary school certificate (Attestat o srednjem specialnom obrazovanii) and entrance examination

Fees: (US Dollars): 1,800 per annum

Main Language(s) of Instruction: Russian

International Co-operation: With universities in Bulgaria; Russian Federation; Ukraine

Accrediting Agencies: Ministry of Education; Federal Agency on Education of Ministry of Education and Science of the Russian Federation

Degrees and Diplomas: *Diplom o Vyshem Obrazovanii*: 5 yrs; *Diplom Magistra*

Student Services: Academic counselling, Canteen, Cultural centre, Foreign student adviser, Foreign Studies Centre, Health services, Language programs, Nursery care, Social counselling, Sports facilities

Student Residential Facilities: Yes

Special Facilities: Museum

Libraries: c. 1,500,000 vols

Publications: Conference Works *(biennially)*
Last Updated: 22/09/11

BREST STATE TECHNICAL UNIVERSITY
Brestskij Gosudarstvennyj Tehnicheskij Universitet (BSTU)
267 Moskovskaya str, 224017 Brest
Tel: +375(162) 42-05-48
Fax: +375(162) 42-21-27
EMail: canc@bstu.by
Website: http://www.bstu.by

Rector: Piotr S. Poyta (2002-)
Tel: +375(162) 42-74-56, Fax: +375(162) 42-21-27

Vice-Rector: Vecheslav I. Dragan
Tel: +375(162) 42-03-61 EMail: 1strector@bstu.by

International Relations: Liana I. Kholodar
Tel: +375(162) 40-83-74, Fax: +375(162) 40-83-74
EMail: liholodar@bstu.by

Faculties
Civil Engineering (Civil Engineering; Construction Engineering; Real Estate; Road Engineering; Structural Architecture); **Economics** (Accountancy; Banking; Business and Commerce; Economic and Finance Policy; Economics; Finance; International Economics; Management; Marketing); **Electronics and Information Systems** (Artificial Intelligence; Computer Engineering; Computer Networks; Computer Science; Data Processing; Electronic Engineering; Industrial Engineering); **Mechanical Engineering** (Automation and Control Engineering; Automotive Engineering; Building Technologies; Maintenance Technology; Mechanical Engineering); **Water Supply and Soil Conservation** (Hydraulic Engineering; Soil Conservation; Water Management; Water Science)

Further Information: Also Language Courses for foreign students; Study Abroad programmes in Poland and Germany

History: Founded 1966 as Civil Engineering Institute, reorganized as Polytechnical Institute, and acquired present status and title 2000.

Governing Bodies: University Council

Academic Year: September to July (September-January; February-July)

Admission Requirements: General or special secondary school certificate (Attestat o srednjem/ specialnom/ obrazovanii)

Fees: (Belarusian Rubles): 1,766,600 per annum

Main Language(s) of Instruction: Russian, Belarusian

International Co-operation: With universities in Poland, Germany, France, China and Vietnam

Accrediting Agencies: Ministry of Education

Degrees and Diplomas: *Diplom o Vyshem Obrazovanii; Diplom Magistra; Kandidat Nauk*

Student Services: Canteen, Health services, Language programs, Social counselling, Sports facilities

Student Residential Facilities: For 2,305 students

Special Facilities: Museum

Libraries: Polytechnic Library, 403,000 vols

Publications: Collected Papers *(annually)*
Last Updated: 22/09/11

BREST STATE UNIVERSITY NAMED AFTER A.S. PUSHKIN
Brestskij Dzjarzauny Universitet imja A.S. Puskina (BRSU)
21 Kosmonavtov Boulevard, 224016 Brest
Tel: +375(162) 23-33-40
Fax: +375(162) 23-09-96
EMail: box@brsu.brest.by
Website: http://www.brsu.brest.by

Rector: Mechyslau Edvardavich Chasnouski (2002-)
Tel: +375(162) 23-01-41

Vice-Rector: Stanislav Grigor'evich Rachevky
Tel: +375(162) 23-33-42, Fax: +375(162) 23-09-96

International Relations: Vladimir Stanislavovich Sekerzickij, Vice-Rector Tel: +375(162) 23-33-44

Faculties
Biology (Biology; Botany; Chemistry; Ecology; Genetics; Zoology); **Foreign Languages** (English; German; Modern Languages); **Geography** (Geography; Tourism); **History** (History); **Law** (Law); **Mathematics** (Mathematics); **Philology** (Literature; Native Language; Philology; Russian); **Physical Education** (Physical Education; Rehabilitation and Therapy; Sports); **Physics** (Mathematics; Physics); **Preparatory Education** (Education); **Psychology-Pedagogy** (Educational Psychology; Foreign Languages Education; Native Language Education; Pedagogy; Primary Education; Psychology; Science Education); **Sociology and Pedagogy** (Pedagogy; Sociology)

History: Founded 1945, acquired present status and title 1995.

Main Language(s) of Instruction: Russian, Belarusian

Accrediting Agencies: Ministry of Education

Degrees and Diplomas: *Diplom o Vyshem Obrazovanii; Diplom Magistra*
Last Updated: 22/09/11

COMMAND AND ENGINEERING INSTITUTE OF THE MINISTRY OF EMERGENCY SITUATIONS
Kamandna-Inzynerny Instytut MNS Respubliki Belarus'
Mashinostroiteley str., 25, 220118 Minsk
Tel: +375(17) 340-35-57
Fax: +375(17) 340-35-57
EMail: oic@kii.gov.by
Website: http://kii.gov.by/

Rector: Vladimir G. Moiseenko
Tel: +375(17) 240-35-58, Fax: +375(17) 241-08-66

Faculties
Commanding; Engineering (Arts and Humanities; Engineering; Fire Science; Safety Engineering)

History: Founded 1933, acquired present status and title 1992.

Academic Year: September to July (September-January; February-July)

Admission Requirements: General or special secondary school certificate (Attestat o srednjem /specialnom/obrazovanii)

Fees: (Belarusian Rubles): c. 15m.

Main Language(s) of Instruction: Russian, Belarusian

International Co-operation: With institutions in Russian Federation, Ukraine, Azerbaijan, Latvia, Lithuania

Accrediting Agencies: Ministry of Education; Ministry of Emergencies of Republic of Belarus

Degrees and Diplomas: *Diplom o Vyshem Obrazovanii; Diplom Magistra*

Student Services: Canteen, Cultural centre, Employment services, Health services, Social counselling, Sports facilities

Student Residential Facilities: For c. 515 students

Special Facilities: History of the Fire Service Museum

Libraries: c. 100,000 vols

Publications: Scientific Journal "Bulletin" (Vestnik), Scientific articles on engineering and psychological sciences *(biennially)*

Press or Publishing House: Publishing Centre of the Belarusian State University
Last Updated: 22/09/11

FRANCISK SKORINA GOMEL STATE UNIVERSITY
Gomel'skij Dzjarzauny Universitet imja Franciska Skarany (GSU)
104 Sovetskaya St, 246019 Gomel
Tel: +375(232) 60-73-71 +375(232) 60-31-13
Fax: +375(232) 57-81-11
EMail: mail@gsu.unibel.by
Website: http://www.gsu.by

Rector: A.V. Rogachev (2004-)
Tel: +375(232) 60-31-13, Fax: +375(232) 57-81-11
EMail: rector@gsu.unibel.by

First Vice-Rector: Yuri Kulazhenko
Tel: +375(232) 57-34-40 EMail: vice-rector@gsu.unibel.by

International Relations: Ludmila Protchenko
Tel: +375(232) 60-31-78, Fax: +375(232) 56-16-45
EMail: interaffairs@gsu.unibel.by

Faculties

Biology (Analytical Chemistry; Anatomy; Biochemistry; Biology; Botany; Cell Biology; Chemistry; Forestry; Genetics; Microbiology; Molecular Biology; Organic Chemistry; Physiology; Zoology); **Economics** (Accountancy; Business Administration; Business and Commerce; Economics; Industrial and Production Economics; Industrial Management; International Business; Management; Marketing; Taxation); **Foreign Languages** (English; French; German; Grammar; Italian; Modern Languages; Phonetics; Translation and Interpretation; Writing); **Geology and Geography** (Crystallography; Ecology; Geography; Geology; Geophysics; Mineralogy); **History** (Ancient Civilizations; Contemporary History; History; Medieval Studies; Modern History; Prehistory); **Law** (Administrative Law; Civil Law; Constitutional Law; Criminal Law; History of Law; International Law; Labour Law; Law); **Mathematics** (Mathematics; Mathematics and Computer Science; Statistics; Systems Analysis); **Philology** (Grammar; Latin; Linguistics; Native Language; Philology; Phonetics; Russian; Speech Studies); **Physical Education** (Physical Education; Sports; Sports Medicine); **Physics** (Applied Physics; Atomic and Molecular Physics; Electronic Engineering; Nuclear Physics; Optics; Physics; Radiophysics); **Psychology** (Psychology; Social Psychology)

Institutes

Management (*Institut Franco-Biélorusse de Gestion*) (Management); **Professional Skills Development** (Accountancy; Computer Education; Computer Science; Education; Higher Education; Psychology; Secretarial Studies; Vocational Education)

History: Founded 1930, acquired present status and title 1969.

Governing Bodies: Academic Council

Academic Year: September to July (September-February; February-July)

Admission Requirements: General or special secondary school certificate (Attestat o srednjem /specialnom/obrazovanii) and competitive entrance examination

Fees: (US Dollars): 950-11,295 per annum

Main Language(s) of Instruction: Russian

International Co-operation: With universities in France, China, United Kingdom, Germany, Poland, Czech Republic

Accrediting Agencies: Ministry of Education

Degrees and Diplomas: *Diplom o Vyshem Obrazovanii*: 5 yrs; *Diplom Magistra*; *Kandidat Nauk*: a further 3 yrs and thesis; *Doktor Nauk*: by thesis following Kandidat Nauk

Student Services: Academic counselling, Canteen, Cultural centre, Foreign student adviser, Health services, Language programs, Social counselling, Sports facilities

Student Residential Facilities: Yes

Special Facilities: Francisk Skoryna Museum; Sports Museum; Zoological Museum; Art Gallery; Cinema

Libraries: c. 1m. vols

Last Updated: 22/09/11

GOMEL ENGINEERING INSTITUTE OF THE MINISTRY OF EMERGENCY SITUATIONS

Gomel'skij Inżynerny Instytut MNS Respubliki Belarus'
35-a Rechitskoye shosse, 246023 Gomel
Tel: +375(232) 46-13-13
Fax: +375(232) 46-00-13
EMail: gii@mail.gomel.by
Website: http://www.gvkiu.gomel.by

Rector: Alexander Ukrainets

Departments

Humanities (Cultural Studies; Economics; Educational Psychology; Ethics; History; Modern Languages; Native Language; Philosophy; Political Sciences; Sociology); **Natural Sciences** (Information Sciences; Information Technology; Mathematics; Mechanics; Physics)

Programmes

Fire-fighting (Fire Science)

History: Creating in 2000 as an institution for fire-fighting and fire-prevention. Acquired present status and title 2003.

Accrediting Agencies: Ministry of Education

Degrees and Diplomas: *Diplom o Vyshem Obrazovanii*; *Diplom Magistra*
Last Updated: 22/09/11

GOMEL STATE MEDICAL INSTITUTE

Gomel'skij Dzjarżauny Medycynski Instytut
5 Lange Street, 246000 Gomel
Tel: +375(232) 74-41-21
Fax: +375(232) 74-98-31
EMail: medinst@mail.gomel.by
Website: http://www.medinstitut.gomel.by/

Rector: Anatoliy N. Lizikov (1990-) **Tel:** +375(232) 53-10-62

Vice-Rector: Evgeni Ivanovich Sokolovsky
Tel: +375(232) 53-06-23

International Relations: Vladimir V. Aničkin

Faculties

Dentistry (Dentistry); **Medicine** (Medicine); **Paediatrics** (Paediatrics); **Treatment and Preventive Medicine** (Social and Preventive Medicine; Treatment Techniques)

History: Founded 1990 as Institute, acquired present status and title 2000.

Main Language(s) of Instruction: Russian, Belarusian

Accrediting Agencies: Ministry of Education

Degrees and Diplomas: *Diplom o Vyshem Obrazovanii*: 5-6 yrs
Last Updated: 19/10/09

GOMEL STATE TECHNICAL UNIVERSITY 'P.O.SUHOGA'

Gomel'skij Dzjarżauny Tehničny Universitet imja P.O. Suhogo (GSTU)
48 Oktiabria Ave, 246746 Gomel
Tel: +375(232) 48-16-00
Fax: +375(232) 47-91-65
EMail: rector@gstu.gomel.by
Website: http://www.gstu.gomel.by

Rector: S. I. Timoshin (2001-)
Tel: +375(232) 48-16-00, **Fax:** +375(232) 47-91-65

Vice-Rector: Oleg D. Asenchik
Tel: +375(232) 48-00-20 **EMail:** prorector@gstu.gomel.by

Faculties

Automation and Information Systems (Automation and Control Engineering; Electronic Engineering; Information Technology; Mathematics); **Humanities and Economics** (Commercial Law; Economics; History; Management; Marketing; Philosophy; Political Sciences; Sociology); **Machine Building** (Engineering Drawing and Design; Machine Building; Petroleum and Gas Engineering; Technology); **Mechanics and Technology** (Agricultural Equipment; Mechanical Equipment and Maintenance; Mechanics; Technology); **Power Engineering** (Electrical Engineering; Physics; Power Engineering; Thermal Engineering)

History: Founded 1981, acquired present status and title 1998.

Governing Bodies: Academic Council

Academic Year: September to June

Admission Requirements: General or special secondary school certificate, (Attestat o srednjem /specialnom/obrazovanii) and certificate of centralised testing.

Main Language(s) of Instruction: Belarusian, Russian

International Co-operation: With universities in Italy, Russian Federation, Ukraine, Poland, Lithuania, Latvia, Turkey

Accrediting Agencies: Ministry of Education

Degrees and Diplomas: *Diplom o Vyshem Obrazovanii*: 5 yrs; *Diplom Magistra*. Magistr equivalent to Master

Student Services: Canteen, Cultural centre, Employment services, Health services, Social counselling, Sports facilities

Student Residential Facilities: Yes

Special Facilities: Museum

Libraries: c. 517,200 vols

Publications: Vestnik GSTU (*quarterly*)
Last Updated: 19/10/09

GRODNO STATE AGRARIAN UNIVERSITY
Grodnenskij Dzjarzhauny Agrarny Universitet (GRSAU)
18 Tereshkovoy St., 230008 Grodno
Tel: +375(152) 770-168
Fax: +375(152) 721-365
EMail: ggau@ggau.by
Website: http://www.ggau.by

Rector: Vitold Kazimirovitch Pestis
Tel: +375(152) 47-01-68, Fax: +375(152) 72-10-42

First Vice-Rector: Dmitriy Arkadievich
Tel: +375(152) 72-00-25, Fax: +375(152) 72-13-65
EMail: fpk@ggau.by

Faculties
Accounting (Accountancy; Finance); **Agronomy** (Agricultural Equipment; Agronomy; Botany; Fruit Production; Physical Education; Plant and Crop Protection; Sports; Vegetable Production); **Continuing Education** (for Directors of Agro-industrial Complex, Specialists and Farmers) (Continuing Education); **Distance Education** (Distance Education); **Economics** (Agricultural Economics; Economics); **Engineering Technology** (Agricultural Engineering; Agricultural Equipment; Chemistry; Machine Building; Plant and Crop Protection); **Plant Protection** (Agriculture; Entomology; Meteorology; Physics; Plant and Crop Protection; Plant Pathology; Soil Science); **Veterinary Medicine** (Animal Husbandry; Veterinary Science); **Zootechniques** (Animal Husbandry; Veterinary Science; Zoology)

Higher Schools
Management (Economics; Management)
Further Information: Also preparatory Department
History: Founded 1951 as Grodno Agricultural Institute, acquired present status and title 2000.
Academic Year: September to June (September-November; February-June)
Admission Requirements: General or special secondary school education (Attestat o srednjem /specialnom/obrazovanii) and competitive entrance examination
Fees: (US Dollars): Foreign students, c. 1,800 per annum
Main Language(s) of Instruction: Belarusian, Russian
Accrediting Agencies: Ministry of Agriculture; Ministry of Education
Degrees and Diplomas: *Diplom o Vyshem Obrazovanii*; *Diplom Magistra*
Student Services: Academic counselling, Canteen, Cultural centre, Employment services, Health services, Sports facilities
Student Residential Facilities: For c. 1,500 students
Libraries: c. 300,000 vols
Last Updated: 22/09/11

GRODNO STATE MEDICAL UNIVERSITY
Grodnenskij Dzjaržauny Medycynski Universitet (GRMSU)
80 Gorkogo St., 230009 Grodno
Tel: +375(152) 33-55-61
Fax: +375(152) 33-53-41
EMail: ief@grsmu.by
Website: http://www.grsmu.by/

Rector: Viktor A. Snerzhitskiy
Tel: +375(152) 33-03-65, Fax: +375(152) 33-53-41

International Relations: Zhanna Motylevich
Tel: +375(152) 33-55-61 EMail: grsmuinternational@mail.ru

Centres
Hepatology (Hepatology)

Departments
Nursing (Nursing)

Faculties
Medical-Prophylactic Studies (Health Sciences; Social and Preventive Medicine); **Medical-Psychological Studies** (Medicine; Psychology); **Paediatrics** (Paediatrics); **Pre-university Training**

Laboratories
Central Research (Medicine); **Narcotics** (Toxicology)

Further Information: Also 21 Clinics. Courses for foreign students
History: Founded 1958, acquired present status and title 2000.
Governing Bodies: Council
Academic Year: September to June (September-January; February-June)
Admission Requirements: General or special secondary school certificate (Attestat o srednjem /specialnom/obrazovanii)
Fees: (US Dollars): c. 1,500 per annum
Main Language(s) of Instruction: Russian; English
Accrediting Agencies: Ministry of Education
Degrees and Diplomas: *Diplom o Vyshem Obrazovanii*: 6 yrs; *Diplom Magistra*
Student Services: Canteen, Cultural centre, Foreign student adviser, Health services, Sports facilities
Special Facilities: History of the Institute Museum
Libraries: Central Library, c. 400,000 vols

Academic Staff 2008-2009	MEN	WOMEN	TOTAL
FULL-TIME	170	130	c. 300
Student Numbers 2008-2009			
All (Foreign Included)	602	1,748	c. 2,350

Last Updated: 22/09/11

GRODNO STATE UNIVERSITY NAMED AFTER YANKA KUPALA
Grodnenskij Dzjaržauny Universitet imja Janki Kupaly (YKSUG)
22 Ozheshko St, 230023 Grodno
Tel: +375(152) 44-85-78
Fax: +375(152) 10-85-99
EMail: mail@grsu.by
Website: http://www.grsu.by

Rector: Yauheni Rovba

Departments
Socio-Humanitarian (Cultural Studies; Economics; Philosophy; Political Sciences)

Faculties
Arts and Design (Conducting; Fashion Design; Fine Arts; Music; Musical Instruments; Singing); **Biology and Ecology** (Biochemistry; Biology; Botany; Chemical Engineering; Chemistry; Ecology; Environmental Studies; Physiology; Zoology); **Economics and Management** (Accountancy; Business Administration; Economics; Finance; Management); **Engineering and Construction** (Building Technologies; Materials Engineering); **History and Sociology** (Archaeology; Ethnology; History; Sociology); **Innovative Mechanical Engineering** (Materials Engineering; Mechanical Engineering); **Law** (Commercial Law; Criminal Law; Criminology; International Law; Labour Law; Law; Private Law); **Mathematics and Information Science** (Applied Mathematics; Artificial Intelligence; Economics; Information Technology; Mathematics Education; Software Engineering); **Pedagogy** (Education of the Handicapped; English; Fine Arts; Music; Musical Instruments; Pedagogy; Preschool Education; Primary Education); **Philology** (English; Foreign Languages Education; German; Linguistics; Philology; Slavic Languages; Translation and Interpretation); **Physical Training** (Physical Education; Sports; Sports Medicine); **Physics and Engineering** (Electrical and Electronic Engineering; Industrial Engineering; Materials Engineering; Measurement and Precision Engineering; Physics); **Psychology**

Schools
Tourism and Hospitality (Cooking and Catering; Tourism)
Further Information: Also Russian language foundation programme; Intensive Russian/Belarusian languages courses; Vocational schools
History: Founded 1940 as State Teacher Training Institute. Placed under the authority of the Ministry of Education of the Republic of Belarus. Financed by the State. Acquired present status and title 1978.
Governing Bodies: University Council

Academic Year: September to June (September-January; February-June). Winter and Summer Sessions

Admission Requirements: General or special secondary school certificate (Attestat o srednjem /specialnom/obrazovanii) and competitive entrance examination; For Doctoral programmes, Master's degree is required

Fees: (US Dollars): Russian/Belarusian Language Courses, c. 100 per week; the Russian/Belarusian Foundation Programme, 1,100 per annum; First Degree, 1,000-1,900 per annum; Doctoral Programmes, 1,500 per annum

Main Language(s) of Instruction: Russian, Belarusian; English

International Co-operation: With institutions in Poland; Russian Federation; Lithuania

Accrediting Agencies: Ministry of Education

Degrees and Diplomas: *Diplom o Vyshem Obrazovanii*; *Diplom Magistra*: 1-2 yrs; *Diplom Magistra*: Business Administration (MBA), a further 1 1/2 yr; *Kandidat Nauk (PhD)*: a further 3-4 yrs and thesis; *Doktor Nauk*

Student Services: Academic counselling, Canteen, Cultural centre, Foreign student adviser, Foreign Studies Centre, Health services, Language programs, Social counselling, Sports facilities

Student Residential Facilities: Student Hostel; University Hotel; Family Accommodation; Employment Services

Special Facilities: Museum of the Polish writer Z. Nalkowske; Multimedia Laboratory; Internet Labs; a TV Centre; Computer-Equipped Classrooms; Research Laboratories; Centre for International Education; Grodno Management School; Institute for Continuous Education; Lida State Industrial Vocational School; Grodno Technological Vocational School

Libraries: University Library, 620,000 vols

Publications: Vestnik GRGU, Magazine *(quarterly)*

Press or Publishing House: Editorial and Publishing Department
Last Updated: 22/09/11

HIGHER STATE COLLEGE OF COMMUNICATIONS

Vyšejšy Dzjaržauny Kaledž Suvjazi (HSCC)
8-2 Staroborisovski Trakt, 220114 Minsk
Tel: +375(17) 267-44-14 +375(17) 217-56-06
Fax: +375(17) 264-44-14
EMail: vks@vks.belpak.by
Website: http://vks.belpak.by/

Rector: Andrey O. Zenevih **Tel:** +375(17) 267-44-14

Faculties
Continuing Education; **Distance Education**; **Economics and Mail** (Computer Science; Economics; Information Technology; Management; Postal Services; Telecommunications Services); **Electronic Communication** (Computer Networks; Computer Science; Electrical Engineering; Mathematics; Physics; Radio and Television Broadcasting; Sports; Telecommunications Engineering; Telecommunications Services)

History: Founded 1993, acquired present status and title 2000.

Main Language(s) of Instruction: Russian, Belarusian

Accrediting Agencies: Ministry of Education

Degrees and Diplomas: *Diplom o Vyshem Obrazovanii*
Last Updated: 29/09/11

INTERNATIONAL SAKHAROV ENVIRONMENTAL UNIVERSITY

Mižnarodny Dzjaržauny Ekalagičny Universitet imja A.D. Saharova (ISEU)
23 Dolgobrodskaya St, 220070 Minsk
Tel: +375(17) 230-69-88
Fax: +375(17) 230-68-88
EMail: info@iseu.by
Website: http://www.iseu.by

Rector: Semjon P. Kundas **EMail:** rector@iseu.by

International Relations: Tamara Bulygina
EMail: interdepart@mail.ru

Faculties
Environmental Medicine (Biochemistry; Biology; Biophysics; Epidemiology; Genetics; Immunology; Physical Education; Radiology); **Environmental Monitoring** (Ecology; Economics; Environmental Engineering; Environmental Management; Philosophy; Sociology)

Further Information: Also Field Station in Hoiniky (Gomel Region) and Pilot Station in Volma (Minsk Region)

History: Founded 1992 as International 'Saharov' College by Decree of Council of the Ministers following a resolution passed at the First International Saharov Memorial Congress and with support of the UN. Reorganized 1994 as International Saharov Institute of Radioecology, and acquired present status and title 1999.

Governing Bodies: University Council

Academic Year: September to July (September-December; January-April; May-July)

Admission Requirements: General or special secondary school certificate (Attestat o srednjem /specialnom/obrazovanii), and entrance examination

Fees: (US Dollars): 850 per annum

Main Language(s) of Instruction: Russian, English

International Co-operation: With universities in Germany, France, Czech Republic, Poland, United Kingdom, Greece, Slovak Republic, Israel, USA and Sweden

Accrediting Agencies: Ministry of Education

Degrees and Diplomas: *Diplom o Vyshem Obrazovanii*: 5 yrs; *Diplom Magistra*: 1 yr; *Doktor Nauk*

Student Services: Academic counselling, Cultural centre, Employment services, Health services, Language programs, Sports facilities

Student Residential Facilities: For c. 600 students

Special Facilities: University Museum. Research Training Centre and Regional Educational and Information Centre on Radiation Safety

Libraries: 21,822 vols

Publications: Sakharov Readings, Scientific works *(annually)*
Last Updated: 22/09/11

MINSK STATE HIGHER AVIATION COLLEGE

Minski Dzjaržauny Vyšejšy Avijacyjny Kaledž (MSHAC)
77 Uborevich St., 220096 Minsk
Tel: +375(17) 341-66-32 +375(17) 345-32-81
Fax: +375(17) 341-66-32
EMail: college@avia.mtk.by; aviacollege@ivcavia.com
Website: http://mgvak.by/

Rector: A. Naumenko

Faculties
Civil Aviation (Aeronautical and Aerospace Engineering; Air Transport; Electrical and Electronic Engineering; Electrical and Electronic Equipment and Maintenance; Engineering; Maintenance Technology); **Military Aviation** (Aeronautical and Aerospace Engineering; Air Transport; Electrical and Electronic Engineering; Electrical and Electronic Equipment and Maintenance; Engineering; Maintenance Technology)

History: Founded 1974, acquired present status and title 2001.

Main Language(s) of Instruction: Russian, Belarusian

Accrediting Agencies: Ministry of Education

Degrees and Diplomas: *Diplom o Vyshem Obrazovanii*: Aircraft & Engine Maintenance; Aircraft Equipment Maintenance; Air Traffic Management
Last Updated: 22/09/11

MINSK STATE HIGHER RADIO-ENGINEERING COLLEGE

Minski Dzjaržauny Vyšejšy Radiotehničny Kaledž
62 Nezavisimosty Ave, 220005 Minsk
Tel: +375(17) 292-62-85
Fax: +375(17) 331-89-45
EMail: office@mgvrk.by
Website: http://www.mgvrk.by

Rector: Sergey N. Ankuda **EMail:** rector@mgvrk.by

Departments

Computer Programming (Computer Engineering); **Electronics** (Electrical and Electronic Engineering; Microelectronics); **Radio Engineering** (Engineering)

History: Founded 1960.

Main Language(s) of Instruction: Russian, Belarusian

Accrediting Agencies: Ministry of Education

Degrees and Diplomas: *Diplom o Vyshem Obrazovanii*
Last Updated: 22/09/11

MINSK STATE LINGUISTICS UNIVERSITY

Minski Dzjaržauny Lingvistyčny Universitet (MSLU)
21 Zakharov St, 220034 Minsk
Tel: +375(17) 248-15-44
Fax: +375(17) 236-75-04
EMail: info@mslu.by
Website: http://www.mslu.by

Rector: N. P. Baranova (1995-)
Tel: +375(17) 213-35-44, Fax: +375(17) 213-35-44
EMail: mslu@mslu.by

Vice-Rector: A.M. Gorlatov
Tel: +375(17) 284-45-71, Fax: +375(17) 213-35-44

Schools

English (English; Grammar; Literature; Phonetics); **French** (French; Grammar; Phonetics); **German** (German; Grammar; Phonetics); **Intercultural Communication** (Communication Studies; Modern Languages; Speech Studies; Translation and Interpretation); **Retraining and Teacher Development** (Teacher Training); **Russian as a Foreign Language** *(for foreign students)* (Russian); **Spanish** (Grammar; Phonetics; Spanish); **Translation and Interpreting** (Translation and Interpretation)

Further Information: Also classes in Russian/Belarusian languages and cultures for non-Russian speaking students. Branches in Sloynik and Padručnik

History: Founded 1948 as Pedagogical Institute, acquired present status and title 1993.

Governing Bodies: Academic Council

Academic Year: September to June (September-January; February-June)

Admission Requirements: General or special secondary school certificate (Attestat o srednjem /specialnom/obrazovanii), and competitive entrance examination

Fees: (US Dollars): Foreign students, c. 1,100 per annum

Main Language(s) of Instruction: Russian, Belarusian

Accrediting Agencies: Ministry of Education

Degrees and Diplomas: *Diplom o Vyshem Obrazovanii*: 4-5 yrs; *Diplom Magistra*: Arts, a further 1-2 yrs

Student Services: Academic counselling, Canteen, Cultural centre, Foreign student adviser, Health services, Language programs, Social counselling, Sports facilities

Special Facilities: University History Museum. Movie Studio

Libraries: c. 700,000 vols

Publications: Lingua (Pedagogics); Vestnik (Philology)

Press or Publishing House: Publishing House of Minsk State Linguistic University
Last Updated: 22/09/11

MOGILEV STATE UNIVERSITY NAMED AFTER A.A.KULESHOV

Magiljouski Dzjaržauny Universitet imja A.A. Kuljašova (MSU)
1 Kosmonavtov Ave., 212022 Mogilev
Tel: +375(222) 28-41-11
Fax: +375(222) 28-36-26
EMail: msu@msu.mogilev.by
Website: http://msu.mogilev.by/

Rector: Konstantin Bondarenko EMail: rector@msu.mogilev.by

Departments

Childhood Psychology and Pedagogy (Child Care and Development; Family Studies; Pedagogy; Psychology); **Economics and Law** (Economics; Law; Management; Political Sciences; Sociology); **Elementary Education** (Music; Music Education; Musical Instruments; Native Language; Pedagogy; Primary Education; Russian); **Foreign Languages** (English; French; German; Modern Languages; Philology; Romance Languages); **History** (Archaeology; History; Philosophy); **Natural Sciences** (Biology; Chemistry; Geography); **Physical Education** (Physical Education; Sports); **Physics and Mathematics** (Mathematics; Physics); **Slavonic Philology** (Journalism; Literature; Native Language; Philology; Russian)

Further Information: Also Regional Lyceums in Krichev and Mogilev

History: Founded 1913 as Teacher Training Institute, reorganized 1918 as Pedagogical Institute, and acquired present status and title 1997.

Governing Bodies: University Council

Academic Year: September to June (September-January; February-June)

Admission Requirements: General or special secondary school certificate (Attestat o srednjem /specialnom/obrazovanii)

Fees: (US Dollars): Foreign students, 800-1,100 per annum

Main Language(s) of Instruction: Russian, Belarusian

Accrediting Agencies: Ministry of Education

Degrees and Diplomas: *Diplom o Vyshem Obrazovanii*: 4-5 yrs; *Diplom Magistra*

Student Services: Academic counselling, Canteen, Cultural centre, Employment services, Foreign student adviser, Health services, Language programs, Social counselling, Sports facilities

Student Residential Facilities: For c. 1,300 students

Special Facilities: Museum: History; Archaeology of Belarus; Belarussian Writers; Ethnography. Biological Garden. Movie Studio

Libraries: Central Library, c. 500,000 vols

Publications: Young University Scientists Works *(annually)*

Press or Publishing House: Mogilev University Publishing House
Last Updated: 22/09/11

MOGILEV STATE UNIVERSITY OF FOOD TECHNOLOGY

Magiljouski Dzjaržauny Universitet Harčavannja (MSFU)
3 Smidta Ave., 212027 Mogilev
Tel: +375(222) 44-32-27
Fax: +375(222) 44-00-11
EMail: mgup@mogilev.by
Website: http://www.mgup.mogilev.by/

Rector: Vyacheslav A. Sharshunov

Faculties

Chemical and Food Technology (Dairy; Food Technology; Meat and Poultry; Technology); **Economics** (Economics); **Mechanical Equipment** (Automation and Control Engineering; Food Science; Mechanical Engineering; Mechanical Equipment and Maintenance); **Technology** (Crop Production; Food Technology; Technology)

History: Founded 1973 as Mogilev Technological Institute, acquired present status and title 2002.

Academic Year: September to June (September-January; February-June)

Admission Requirements: General or special secondary school certificate (Attestat o srednjem /specialnom/obrazovanii)

Fees: (US Dollars): Foreign students, 1,000 per annum

Main Language(s) of Instruction: Russian, Belarusian

Accrediting Agencies: Ministry of Education

Degrees and Diplomas: *Diplom o Vyshem Obrazovanii*; *Diplom Magistra*

Student Services: Canteen, Sports facilities

Student Residential Facilities: For c. 500 students

Libraries: c. 500,000 vols

Publications: Mogilev Technological Institute Works
Last Updated: 20/03/12

MOZYR STATE PEDAGOGICAL UNIVERSITY NAMED AFTER I.P. SHAMYAKIN

Mozyrskij Dzjaržauny Pedagogičny Universitet imja I. P. Shamyakin (MDPI)
28. Studencheskaya Street, 247760 Mozyr
Tel: +375(2351) 2-13-93
Fax: +375(2351) 2-54-26
EMail: mgpu@mail.gomel.by
Website: http://www.mgpu.gomel.by/

Rector: Valentin V. Valetoff (1997-) Tel: +375(2351) 2-15-85

First Pro-Rector: V.S. Bolbas Tel: +375(2351) 2-50-61

Faculties

Biology (Biology; Environmental Studies); **Engineering and Pedagogy** (Agricultural Education; Agricultural Engineering; Civil Engineering; Economics; Machine Building; Management; Power Engineering; Technology Education); **Foreign Languages** (English; Foreign Languages Education; German); **Philology** (History; Humanities and Social Science Education; Literature; Native Language; Native Language Education; Russian); **Physical Education** (Physical Education; Teacher Training); **Physics and Mathematics** (Computer Education; Mathematics; Mathematics Education; Physics; Science Education); **Preparatory Studies** (Mathematics; Native Language; Physics; Russian); **Preschool and Primary Education** (Preschool Education; Primary Education; Psychology); **Technology** (Art Education; Design; Graphic Arts; Technology)

History: Founded 1944 as Mozyr Teachers' Institute, acquired present status and title 2006.

Governing Bodies: University Council

Academic Year: September to June (September-January; February-June)

Admission Requirements: General or special secondary school certificate (Attestat o srednjem /specialnom/obrazovanii)

Fees: (Belarusian Rubles): 900,000 per annum

Main Language(s) of Instruction: Russian, Belarusian

Accrediting Agencies: Ministry of Education

Degrees and Diplomas: *Diplom o Vyshem Obrazovanii*: 5 yrs; *Diplom Magistra*

Student Services: Canteen, Cultural centre, Health services, Social counselling, Sports facilities

Special Facilities: History of the Institute Museum; Museum of Technical Culture

Libraries: c. 435,000 vols

Publications: Vesnik Mazyrskaga Dzaržaunaga Pedagogičnaga Universiteta, Magazine *(biennially)*

Press or Publishing House: Mozyr pedinstitut
Last Updated: 22/09/11

POLESSKY STATE UNIVERSITY

Palesskij Dzjaržauny Universitet
Dneprovskoy Flotilii, 23, 225710 Pinsk
Tel: +375(165) 312-160
Fax: +375(165) 312-195
EMail: polessu@nbrb.by
Website: http://www.psunbrb.by

Rector: Konstantin K. Shebeko

Faculties

Banking (Accountancy; Banking; Finance); **Biotechnology** (Biology; Biotechnology; Landscape Architecture); **Continuing Education** (Banking; Business Administration); **Economics** (Economics; Hotel and Restaurant; Management; Marketing; Tourism); **Health Sciences** (Biology; Biotechnology; Medicine; Parks and Recreation; Physical Education; Physical Therapy; Rehabilitation and Therapy; Sports); **Preparatory Studies**

History: Created 1944 as Pinskij Višejšy Bankauski Kaledž (Pinsk Higher Banking College). Acquired current title and status 2006.

Main Language(s) of Instruction: Belarusian, Russian

Accrediting Agencies: Ministry of Education

Degrees and Diplomas: *Diplom o Vyshem Obrazovanii*; *Diplom Magistra*
Last Updated: 20/03/12

POLOTSK STATE UNIVERSITY

Polatskij Dzjaržauny Universitet (PSU)
29 Blokhina St., 211440 Novopolotsk
Tel: +375(214) 53-23-83 +375(214) 53-21-61
+375(214) 51-13-93
Fax: +375(214) 53-42-63
EMail: post@psu.by
Website: http://www.psu.by/

Rector: Dmitry M. Lazovsky (2003-)
Tel: +375(214) 53-23-83, Fax: +375(214) 53-42-63
EMail: d.lazovski@psu.by

Vice-Rector: Alexander Kastruk
Tel: +375(214) 53-28-98, Fax: +375(214) 53-42-63
EMail: a.kastruk@psu.by

Departments

Social Studies and Humanities (Aesthetics; Cultural Studies; Ethics; Philosophy; Political Sciences; Religious Studies; Slavic Languages; Social Sciences)

Faculties

Civil Engineering (Architecture; Civil Engineering; Construction Engineering; Industrial Engineering); **Finance and Economics** (Accountancy; Economics; Finance; Human Resources; Management); **Geodesy** (Geography; Surveying and Mapping); **History and Philology** (English; French; German; History; Modern Languages; Philology); **Information Technology** (Computer Networks; Computer Science; Information Technology; Software Engineering); **Law** (Law); **Machine Building** (Building Technologies; Machine Building; Mechanical Engineering); **Physical Education** (Physical Education; Sports; Teacher Trainers Education); **Radio Engineering** (Electrical and Electronic Engineering; Telecommunications Engineering)

Further Information: Also Russian courses for foreign specialists (3-6 months). Continuing education programmes in Economics and Chemical Engineering

History: Founded 1968 as Novopolock Polytechnical Institute, acquired present status and title 1993.

Governing Bodies: University Council

Academic Year: September to June (September-February; February-June)

Admission Requirements: General or special secondary school certificate (Attestat o srednjem /specialnom/obrazovanii)

Fees: (US Dollars): Foreign students, c. 1,300 per annum

Main Language(s) of Instruction: Russian, Belarusian

International Co-operation: With universities in Sweden, Italy, Germany, France, United Kingdom, USA, Poland

Accrediting Agencies: Ministry of Education

Degrees and Diplomas: *Diplom o Vyshem Obrazovanii*: 5 yrs; *Diplom Magistra*: a further 1-1/2 yrs; *Kandidat Nauk*: a further 3 yrs by thesis

Student Services: Academic counselling, Canteen, Cultural centre, Health services, Language programs, Social counselling, Sports facilities

Student Residential Facilities: For c. 2,000 students

Special Facilities: TV Studio. Art Gallery

Libraries: c. 600,000 vols

Publications: Bulletin of Polock State University (Humanities and Applied Sciences)
Last Updated: 22/09/11

VITEBSK STATE ACADEMY OF VETERINARY MEDICINE

Vitebskaja Dzjaržaunaja Akademija Veterynarnaj Medycyny (VSAVM)
1st Dovatora str. 7/11, 210602 Vitebsk
Tel: +375(212) 37-07-37 375(212) 37-20-37 +375(212) 37-23-22
Fax: +375(212) 37-02-84
EMail: vet.by@mail.ru
Website: http://www.vsavm.com/

Rector: Anton Ivanovič Yatusevich (1998-)

Colleges
Agrarian (Agriculture)

Departments
Preparatory Studies

Faculties
Correspondence Studies (Animal Husbandry; Veterinary Science); **Specialist Upgrading** (Computer Science; Veterinary Science; Zoology); **Veterinary Medicine** (Veterinary Science); **Zooengineering** (Agricultural Management; Animal Husbandry; Zoology)

History: Founded 1924 as Higher Agricultural Technical School, acquired present status and title 1994.

Governing Bodies: Academic Council

Academic Year: September to July (September-January; February-July)

Admission Requirements: General or special secondary school certificate (Attestat o srednjem /specialnom/obrazovanii) and entrance examination

Fees: (US Dollars): Foreign students, 750-800 per annum

Main Language(s) of Instruction: Russian, Belarusian

International Co-operation: Participates in the Tacis, Tempus and Hops programmes

Accrediting Agencies: Ministry of Agriculture and Food; Ministry of Education

Degrees and Diplomas: *Diplom o Vyshem Obrazovanii*: Veterinary Science, 5 yrs; *Diplom Magistra*; *Doktor Nauk*: by thesis. Also postgraduate Courses in Veterinary Medicine, Agriculture and Biological Sciences

Student Services: Academic counselling, Canteen, Cultural centre, Health services, Social counselling, Sports facilities

Student Residential Facilities: Yes

Special Facilities: History of the Institute Museum

Libraries: 892,000 vols

Publications: Jurnal Veterinarnaja Medicina Belarusi *(quarterly)*
Last Updated: 29/09/11

VITEBSK STATE MEDICAL UNIVERSITY
Vitebskij Dzjaržauny Medycynski Universitet (VSMU)
27 Frunze Ave, 210023 Vitebsk
Tel: +375(212) 24-04-33
Fax: +375(212) 37-09-37 +375(212) 37-21-07
EMail: admin@vgmu.vitebsk.by
Website: http://www.vgmu.vitebsk.by

Rector: Valery P. Deykalo (2006-) Tel: +375(212) 24-11-25

Faculties
Continuing Education (Gynaecology and Obstetrics; Paediatrics; Rehabilitation and Therapy; Surgery); **Medicine** (Anaesthesiology; Anatomy; Biochemistry; Biology; Cell Biology; Chemistry; Dermatology; Ecology; Embryology and Reproduction Biology; Epidemiology; Genetics; Gynaecology and Obstetrics; Health Sciences; Histology; Hygiene; Information Technology; Medicine; Microbiology; Neurology; Oncology; Ophthalmology; Organic Chemistry; Orthopaedics; Otorhinolaryngology; Paediatrics; Pathology; Pharmacology; Physics; Physiology; Pneumology; Psychiatry and Mental Health; Psychology; Public Health; Surgery; Toxicology); **Overseas Students Training** (Anatomy; Biochemistry; Biological and Life Sciences; Botany; Epidemiology; Gynaecology and Obstetrics; Medical Technology; Medicine; Neurology; Otorhinolaryngology; Pedagogy; Pharmacology; Pharmacy; Physiology; Psychiatry and Mental Health; Psychology; Rehabilitation and Therapy; Russian; Stomatology; Surgery; Toxicology; Urology); **Pharmacy** (Analytical Chemistry; Biochemistry; Botany; Chemistry; Laboratory Techniques; Microbiology; Organic Chemistry; Pharmacology; Pharmacy; Toxicology); **Professional Orientation and Preparatory Training (FOPT)** (Biology; Chemistry; Native Language; Russian); **Stomatology**

Further Information: University Clinic; Teaching Hospitals; Teaching Educative-Industrial Drugstore "Vitunipharm"; University Dental Clinic; Control-Analytic Laboratory; Republican Centre "Infection in Surgery"; Lipid Centre; Etc.

History: Founded 1934 as Vitebsk State Medical Institute. Acquired present status and title 1998.

Governing Bodies: Rector; University Council; Central Academic Scientific Methodological Council

Academic Year: September to June (September-January; February-June)

Admission Requirements: Secondary school certificate (Attestat o srednjem obrazovanii) with good estimations (not less than 50%) on Biology, Chemistry, Physics and Mathematics.

Fees: (US Dollars): For native students: 2,300-2,500 per annum; For foregin students: 3,200-3,800 annum (depending on the speciality and medium of training)

Main Language(s) of Instruction: Russian, English

Accrediting Agencies: Ministry of Health of the Republic of Belarus; Ministry of Education

Degrees and Diplomas: *Diplom o Vyshem Obrazovanii*: Medicine (MD); Stomatology (MD), 6 yrs; *Diplom o Vyshem Obrazovanii*: Pharmacy (MScPh), 5 yrs

Student Services: Academic counselling, Canteen, Cultural centre, Employment services, Foreign student adviser, Foreign Studies Centre, Health services, Social counselling, Sports facilities

Student Residential Facilities: For 2,100 students

Special Facilities: Museum of Anatomy; Museum of University History Biological Museum. Central Scientific Research Laboratory; Publishing Editing Polygraphic Centre, etc.

Libraries: Total, 1,522,413 vols: 1,275,093 text-books, 156,787 scientific books, 25,854 on foreign languages

Publications: Bulletin of Pharmacy, Scientific Magazine *(quarterly)*; Bulletin of VSMU, Scientific Magazine *(quarterly)*; Immunology, Allergology, Infectology, Scientific Magazine *(quarterly)*; Maternity and Childhood Protection, Scientific Magazine *(quarterly)*; Medvuzovets, University Newspaper *(monthly)*; News of Surgery, Scientific Magazine *(quarterly)*

Academic Staff 2007-2008	MEN	WOMEN	TOTAL
FULL-TIME	218	252	470
STAFF WITH DOCTORATE FULL-TIME	–	–	60
Student Numbers 2007-2008			
All (Foreign Included)	–	–	5,963
FOREIGN ONLY	–	–	561

Part-time students, 893.
Last Updated: 29/09/11

VITEBSK STATE TECHNOLOGICAL UNIVERSITY
Vitebskij Dzjaržauny Tehnalagičny Universitet (VSTU)
72 Moskovskiy Ave, 210035 Vitebsk
Tel: +375(212) 25-50-26
Fax: +375(212) 25-74-01
EMail: vstu@vitebsk.by
Website: http://www.vstu.vitebsk.by/

Rector: Valeriy S. Bashmetov
Tel: +375(212) 27-50-26, Fax: +375(212) 25-74-01

Vice-Rector: Sergeij Ivanovich Malashenkov

Faculties
Design and Technology (Clothing and Sewing; Design; Handicrafts; Technology; Weaving); **Design Engineering and Light Industry** (Clothing and Sewing); **Economics** (Accountancy; Economics; Finance; Management; Marketing); **Mechanics and Technology** (Graphic Design; Machine Building; Mechanical Equipment and Maintenance; Mechanics; Technology)

History: Founded 1965. Acquired present status 1999.

Main Language(s) of Instruction: Russian, Belarusian

Accrediting Agencies: Ministry of Education

Degrees and Diplomas: *Diplom o Vyshem Obrazovanii*; *Diplom Magistra*

Student Residential Facilities: For c. 1,000 students

Libraries: c. 300,000 vols
Last Updated: 29/09/11

VITEBSK STATE UNIVERSITY NAMED AFTER P.M. MAŠEROV

Vitebskij Dzjaržauny Universitet imja P.M. Mašerova (VSU)
33 Moskovskiy Ave, 210038 Vitebsk
Tel: +375(212) 21-49-59
Fax: +375(212) 21-49-59
EMail: vsu@vsu.by
Website: http://www.vsu.by

Rector: Alexandr P. Solodkov
Tel: +375(212) 21-58-66 EMail: rector@vsu.by

International Relations: Oksana Anatolieva Tulinova
Tel: +375(212) 21-99-16, Fax: +375(212) 21-49-59
EMail: szs@vsu.by

Faculties
Belarusian Philology and Culture (Cultural Studies; Educational Psychology; History; Journalism; Native Language; Philology); **Biology** (Biology; Chemistry; Ecology; Geography; Natural Sciences); **Fine Arts** (Art Education; Education; Fine Arts; Handicrafts; Painting and Drawing; Technology; Visual Arts); **History** (History); **Law**; **Mathematics** (Applied Mathematics; Information Technology; Mathematics; Mechanics); **Pedagogy** (Pedagogy); **Philology** (English; German; Literature; Philology; Russian; Slavic Languages); **Physical Education and Sports** (Physical Education; Sports; Sports Medicine); **Physics** (Astronomy and Space Science; Physical Engineering; Physics); **Social Pedagogy and Psychology** (Arts and Humanities; Preschool Education; Psychology; Social Psychology; Social Sciences)

History: Founded 1910 as Teacher Training Institute, acquired present status and title 1995.

Governing Bodies: University Council

Academic Year: September to June (September-January; February-June)

Admission Requirements: General or special secondary school certificate (Attestat o srednjem /specialnom/obrazovanii) and entrance examination

Main Language(s) of Instruction: Belarusian, Russian

International Co-operation: With universities in Lithuania; Russian Federation; Latvia; Poland; Ukraine; China; Moldova; Canada and Germany

Accrediting Agencies: Ministry of Education

Degrees and Diplomas: *Diplom o Vyshem Obrazovanii*; *Diplom Magistra*. Also postgraduate studies

Student Services: Canteen, Cultural centre, Employment services, Health services, Sports facilities

Student Residential Facilities: For c. 3,500 students

Special Facilities: History of the University Museum; Biology Museum; Museum of Graphic Arts. Agrobiological Station. Botanical Gardens

Libraries: c. 500,000 vols

Publications: Vestnik Vitebskogo Gosudarstvennogo Universiteta (Bulletin of the Vitebsk State University) *(quarterly)*

Press or Publishing House: Vitebsk State University Publishing House (Izdatelstvo Vitebskogo Gosudarstvennogo Universiteta)
Last Updated: 20/03/12

PRIVATE INSTITUTIONS

BELARUSIAN INSTITUTE OF LAW

BIP-Instytut Pravaznaustva (BIP)
3 Korolya Street, 220004 Minsk
Tel: +375(17) 211-01-58
Fax: +375(17) 211-01-58
EMail: bnip@user.unibel.by
Website: http://www.bip-ip.info/

Rector: S.A. Samal Tel: +375(17) 211-01-45

Chairman of the Scientific Institute Council: Stepan Sokol
Tel: +375(17) 211-01-52

International Relations: Vasiliy Bonko, Vice-Rector
Tel: +375(17) 211-01-65

Faculties
Economic Law (Accountancy; Commercial Law; Economics; Management); **International Law and Psychology** (International Law; Law; Political Sciences; Psychology); **Law** (Law)

History: Founded 1990, acquired present status and title 2005.

Governing Bodies: Scientific Institute Council

Academic Year: September to June

Admission Requirements: School Certificate

Main Language(s) of Instruction: Russian, Belarusian

International Co-operation: With universities in Russian Federation, Ukraine, Poland, Kazakhstan

Accrediting Agencies: Ministry of Education

Degrees and Diplomas: *Diplom o Vyshem Obrazovanii*

Student Services: Academic counselling, Canteen, Foreign Studies Centre, Health services, Social counselling, Sports facilities

Libraries: Yes.

Publications: Law and Life, with Moldova *(monthly)*; Social, Economic and Law Researches *(quarterly)*

Press or Publishing House: "BIP-S Plus" Publishing House
Last Updated: 20/03/12

BELARUSIAN TRADE AND ECONOMICS UNIVERSITY OF CONSUMER COOPERATIVES

Belaruskij Gandljova-Ekanamičny Universitet Spažyveckaj Kaaperacyi
pr-t Oktyabrya 50, 246029 Gomel
Tel: +375(232) 48-17-07 +375(232) 48-09-83
Fax: +375(232) 47-80-68 +375(232) 48-10-62
EMail: interbteu@mail.ru
Website: http://www.bteu.by

Rector: Alla A. Naumchik (2003-) Tel: +375(232) 48-17-07

Vice-Rector: Ludmila V. Misnikova EMail: lmis@bteu.by

Faculties
Accountancy and Finance (Accountancy; Finance); **Commerce** (Business and Commerce; Marketing); **Commerce and Management** (Business and Commerce; Management); **Economics and Accountancy** (Accountancy; Economics); **Economics and Management** (Economics; Management); **Improving Professional Skills** (Business Education); **Preparatory and Post-University Training**; **Special Studies** (Accountancy; Economics; Finance; Law)

History: Founded 1964 as Gomel Cooperative Institute, acquired present title 2001.

Governing Bodies: Belcoopsoyuz

Academic Year: September to June (September-February; March-June)

Admission Requirements: General or special secondary school certificate (Attestat o srednjem /specialnom/obrazovanii)

Fees: (Belarusian Rubles): 1.36m. per annum

Main Language(s) of Instruction: Russian, Belarusian

Accrediting Agencies: Belarus Republican Union of Consumer Societies; Ministry of Education

Degrees and Diplomas: *Diplom o Vyshem Obrazovanii*: 5 yrs; *Diplom Magistra*

Student Services: Academic counselling, Canteen, Cultural centre, Employment services, Health services, Nursery care, Social counselling, Sports facilities

Student Residential Facilities: For c. 2,500 students

Special Facilities: Museum of Consumer Co-operation

Libraries: c. 500,000 vols

Publications: Potrebitelskaya cooperatsiya, Magazine *(quarterly)*

Press or Publishing House: Polygraphy
Last Updated: 22/09/11

'ENVILA' WOMEN'S INSTITUTE
Žanočy Instytut 'Envila'
ul.Velozavodskaya 3, 220033 Minsk
Tel: +375(17) 298-10-31
Fax: +375(17) 298-10-31
EMail: envila@nvl.sml.by
Website: http://www.envila.by/

Rector: Larisa Čerepanova Tel: +375(17) 206-53-15

Administrative Officer: Anatolii Alad'in

International Relations: Galina Šaton

Centres
Gender Studies (Gender Studies; Women's Studies)

Faculties
Linguistics and Economics (Economics; Linguistics; Modern Languages); **Psychology** (Psychology)

History: Founded 1994.

Main Language(s) of Instruction: Russian, Belarusian

Accrediting Agencies: Ministry of Education

Degrees and Diplomas: *Diplom o Vyshem Obrazovanii*: Modern Langauges; Business Administration; Psychology, 4-5 yrs
Last Updated: 13/10/09

INSTITUTE OF BUSINESS
Instytut Pradprymal'nickaj Dzejnasci
Serafimovicha str 11, 220033 Minsk
Tel: +375(17) 298-43-59
Fax: +375(17) 298-38-10
EMail: uoipd@tut.by
Website: http://www.uoipd.org/

Rector: V. L. Tsybovsky

Departments
Humanities (Administrative Law; Biological and Life Sciences; Civil Law; Cultural Studies; History; Law; Literature; Management; Native Language; Philology; Philosophy; Political Sciences; Psychology; Public Administration; Public Law; Religious Studies; Sociology); **International Tourism** (Tourism); **Marketing and Management** (Management; Marketing); **Physical Education** (Physical Education); **Translation Theory and Practice (English)**; **Translation Theory and Practice (French and German)** (French; German; Translation and Interpretation)

Faculties
Distance Education (Business and Commerce; Economics; Finance; Mathematics and Computer Science)

History: Founded 1992.

Main Language(s) of Instruction: Russian, Belarusian

Accrediting Agencies: Ministry of Education

Degrees and Diplomas: *Diplom o Vyshem Obrazovanii*; *Diplom Magistra*
Last Updated: 22/09/11

INSTITUTE OF MANAGEMENT AND BUSINESS
Častnij Instytut Kiravannja i Pradprymal'nictva
1 Slavinskogo St, 220086 Minsk
Tel: +375(17) 263-79-83
Fax: +375(17) 263-56-33
EMail: imb@imb.by
Website: http://www.imb.by

Rector: Oleg A. Bezludov Tel: +375(17) 263-00-49

Faculties
Accountancy and Auditing (Accountancy; Systems Analysis); **Finance and Credit** (Business and Commerce; Finance; Taxation); **Global Economics and International Economic Relations** (International Economics; International Relations); **Law** (Law); **Management** (Management)

History: Founded 1993. Acquired present status 2001.

Main Language(s) of Instruction: Russian, Belarusian

Accrediting Agencies: Ministry of Education

Degrees and Diplomas: *Diplom o Vyshem Obrazovanii*; *Diplom Magistra*
Last Updated: 21/10/09

INSTITUTE OF MODERN KNOWLEDGE
Instytut Sučasnyh Vedau
69 Filimonova St., 220023 Minsk
Tel: +375(17) 285-70-83
Fax: +375(17) 285-70-83
EMail: zao@isz.minsk.by
Website: http://www.isz.minsk.by

Rector: A.L. Kapilov

Faculties
Art (Design; Fine Arts; Performing Arts); **Humanities** (Arts and Humanities); **Management** (Ecology; Economics; Finance; Management)

History: Created in 1990. Acquired status 2001.

Main Language(s) of Instruction: Russian, Belarusian

Accrediting Agencies: Ministry of Education

Degrees and Diplomas: *Diplom o Vyshem Obrazovanii*
Last Updated: 21/10/09

INSTITUTE OF PARLIAMENTARISM AND ENTREPRENEURSHIP
Instytut Parlamentaryzma i Pradprymal'nictva (IPE)
65-? Timiryazev Street, 220035 Minsk
Tel: +375(17) 209-06-67
Fax: +375(17) 209-06-83
EMail: rector-ipp@by
Website: http://www.ipp.by

Rector: B. Svetlov (1998-)
Tel: +375(17) 232-43-94, Fax: +375(17) 231-39-45

Departments
Economics and Management (Economics; Management); **Finance and Credit** (Banking; Finance); **Foreign Languages** (English; French; German); **Journalism** (Journalism); **Law** (Law); **Political Science** (Political Sciences)

History: Founded 1994, acquired present status and title 2004.

Main Language(s) of Instruction: Russian, Belarusian

Accrediting Agencies: Ministry of Education

Degrees and Diplomas: *Diplom o Vyshem Obrazovanii*
Last Updated: 22/09/11

INTERNATIONAL HUMANITIES AND ECONOMICS INSTITUTE
Mižnarodny Gumanitarna-Ekanamičny Instytut (IHEI)
129a Mayakovskogo St., 220028 Minsk
Tel: +375(17) 223-17-27
Fax: +375(17) 210-58-75
EMail: mgei2006@tyt.by
Website: http://www.mgei.org

Rector: A. Alpeev

Faculties
Accounting (Accountancy); **Economics and Management** (Accountancy; Business Administration; Economics; Finance; Management); **International Economics** (International Economics); **International Relations** (International Relations); **Law** (Commercial Law; International Law; Law); **Political Science** (Political Sciences); **Psychology** (Psychology); **Sociology** (Sociology)

History: Founded 1994.

Main Language(s) of Instruction: Russian, Belarusian

Accrediting Agencies: Ministry of Education

Degrees and Diplomas: *Diplom o Vyshem Obrazovanii*; *Diplom Magistra*
Last Updated: 22/09/11

 **INTERNATIONAL UNIVERSITY "MITSO"**

Mižnarodny Universitet "MITSO"
21/3 Kazintsa St, 220099 Minsk
Tel: +375(17) 207-04-04
Fax: +375(17) 207-04-04
EMail: mitso@mitso.by
Website: http://mitso.by/

Rector: Stanislav Knyazev (2011-) EMail: knyazev@mitso.by

International Relations: Alena A. Rakhmanko, International Relations Officer
Tel: +375(17) 278-60-29, Fax: +375(17) 278-60-29
EMail: international@mitso.by

Faculties
Economics and Law *(Vitebsk)* (Economics; Law); **Economics and Law** *(Gomel)* (Economics; Law); **International Economic Relations and Management** (Banking; Economics; Finance; International Economics; International Relations; Management; Marketing); **Law** (International Law; Law); **Social Partnership and Personnel Retraining** (Business Administration; Economic History; Human Resources; International Economics; Law; Staff Development; Tourism)

Further Information: Branches in Gomel and Vitebsk

History: Founded 1992 as Mižnarodny Instytut Pracounyh i Sacyjal'nyh Adnosin (International Institute of Labour and Social Relations). Acquired present status and title 2011.

Main Language(s) of Instruction: Russian, Belarusian

Accrediting Agencies: Ministry of Education

Degrees and Diplomas: *Diplom o Vyshem Obrazovanii*; *Diplom Magistra*

Libraries: Library Centre

Publications: Labor Trade Union Society *(quarterly)*

Academic Staff *2010-2011*	TOTAL
FULL-TIME	119
PART-TIME	25
STAFF WITH DOCTORATE	
FULL-TIME	15

Student Numbers *2010-2011*	
All (Foreign Included)	8,615

Last Updated: 12/12/11

MINSK INSTITUTE OF MANAGEMENT
Minskij Instytut Kiravannja (MIM)
12 Lazo Street, 220102 Minsk
Tel: +375(17) 285-47-47
Fax: +375(17) 243-67-61
EMail: miu@miu.by
Website: http://www.miu.by/

Rector: Nikolay Susha (1994-)
Tel: +375(17) 273-76-19 EMail: nsusha@tut.by

Vice-Rector for Academic Affairs: Branislau A. Hedranovich

International Relations: Valiantsina V. Hedranovich
Tel: +375(17) 243-54-72

Departments
Accounting and Finance (Accountancy; Banking; Computer Graphics; Computer Science; Finance; Information Technology); **Economics** (Economics; English; German; International Economics; Management; Marketing; Translation and Interpretation); **Law** (Commercial Law; Law)

History: Founded 1991, acquired present status and title 2001.

Main Language(s) of Instruction: Russian, Belarusian

Accrediting Agencies: Ministry of Education

Degrees and Diplomas: *Diplom o Vyshem Obrazovanii*; *Diplom Magistra*
Last Updated: 22/09/11

Belgium - Flemish Community

STRUCTURE OF HIGHER EDUCATION SYSTEM

Description:

Within the Bologna Process, participating countries have committed to elaborating national qualifications frameworks by 2010 and to launch this work by 2007. The aim was to establish a European Higher Education Area by 2010. Countries have been invited to carry out self-certification exercises to verify the compatibility with the overarching framework of qualifications of the European Higher Education Area (EHEA) http://www.ehea.info/. As these self-certification exercises are completed, the self-certification reports will be published at http://www.enic-naric.net/index.aspx?s = n&r = ena&d = qf.

Thanks to the Bologna Process, all higher education programmes in Flanders (Belgium) were transformed into the Three-Tier structure, "Bachelor-Master-Doctor"-structure, by the Law on Higher Education Reform of 4 April 2003. The National Framework of Qualifications in Higher Education in Flanders is compatible with the overarching Framework for Qualifications of the European Higher Education Area. This is stated by NVAO following the conclusion of an independent and international external verification committee. The self-certification report of Flanders is published at http://www.nvao.net/nqf-fl as well as at http://www.enic-naric.net/index.aspx?s = n&r = ena&d = qf.

The learning outcomes of all programmes in Flanders (Belgium) are legally outlined in cycle descriptors. The higher education in Flanders has a binary structure at Bachelor level. Professional Bachelor's programmes have the objective to bring students to a level of general and specific knowledge and competences required to perform a particular profession or group of professions independently. A professional Bachelor's programme can therefore lead directly to a place on the labour market.

The main objective of the academic Bachelor's programmes is that students will go on to a Master's programme. Thus, they are geared towards bringing the students to a certain level of scientific or artistic knowledge and competences, required for scientific or artistic work in general, and towards a specific field of sciences or arts in particular. Preparing students for the labour market is only a secondary objective. Some Bachelor's programmes are a follow-up to another (professional) Bachelor's programme. This follow-up programme is geared towards the broadening of or specializing in competences acquired during the initial Bachelor's programme.

Master's programmes have the objective to bring students to an advanced level of scientific or artistic knowledge and competences required for scientific or artistic work in general, and to a specific domain of sciences and arts in particular, which is required for autonomous scientific or artistic work or to apply this scientific or artistic knowledge independently in one or a group of professions. Some Master's programmes are considered as advanced or further studies.

The qualification of Doctor is granted by a panel of researchers after a public presentation of the Doctor's thesis in which the writer/researcher/student has demonstrated to be able to conceive new scientific knowledge based on independent research. The doctoral thesis should have the potential to lead to publications in scientific journals.

Only people who have been conferred the title of Bachelor, Master or Doctor, pursuant to the Law of 2003, may carry the corresponding title of Bachelor, Master or Doctor and the legally protected abbreviations "dr" and "PhD".

The European Qualifications Framework for Lifelong Learning (EQF for LLL) was approved by the European Parliament and the European Council in 2008. http://ec.europa.eu/education/lifelong-learning-policy/ doc44_en.htm. The EQF for LLL is a translation tool to make qualifications expressed in competences intelligible and comparable at European level. Subsequent to this European development, Flanders introduced by law in 2009 - totally comparable with the European Qualifications Framework for Lifelong learning (EQF for LLL) - the National Qualification Framework (NQF) of Flanders with also eight levels. The level descriptors of Bachelor, Master and Doctor are legally declared equal to the level descriptors of level 6, level 7 and level 8 of the NQF Flanders and EQF for LLL. Since a secondary school leaving certificate of Flanders is at level 4, Flanders introduced at level 5 "Hoger Beroepsonderwijs" leading to the new qualification in higher education, namely "Diploma van gegradueerde", officially translated as "Associate degree".

Stages of studies:

University level first stage: Bachelor - NQF Flanders level 6
Bachelor programmes have a study load of 180 credits. There are Bachelor's programmes with a professional orientation and Bachelor's programmes with an academic orientation. Professional Bachelor's programmes have the objective to bring students to a level of general and specific knowledge and competences required to perform a particular profession or group of professions independently. A professional Bachelor's programme can therefore lead directly to a place on the labour market. Only the university colleges offer professional Bachelor's programmes. The main objective of the academic Bachelor's programmes is that students will go on to a Master's programme. Thus, they are geared towards bringing the students to a certain level of scientific or artistic knowledge and competences, required for scientific or artistic work in general, and towards a specific field of sciences or arts in particular. Preparing students for the labour market is only a secondary objective. University colleges and universities may offer academic Bachelor's programmes. Some Bachelor's programmes are a follow-up to another (professional) Bachelor's programme. This follow-up programme is geared towards the broadening of or specializing in competences acquired during the initial Bachelor's programme. Only the university colleges may offer such advanced Bachelor's programmes. The study load of these programmes is at least 60 credits.

University level second stage: Master - NQF Flanders level 7
All Master programmes have a study load of minimum 60 credits. Master's programmes have the objective to bring students to an advanced level of scientific or artistic knowledge and competences required for scientific or artistic work in general, and to a specific domain of sciences and arts in particular, which is required for autonomous scientific or artistic work or to apply this scientific or artistic knowledge independently in one or a group of professions. Some Master's programmes are advanced or further studies aiming at deepening the knowledge and/or competences in a certain field of study. University colleges and universities may offer Master's programmes.
Postgraduate Certificate programmes have the goal to increase the professional knowledge and skills by broadening and/or enlarging the competences obtained by graduation after a Bachelor's programme or Master's programme.
University colleges and universities may offer such programmes. The study load of Postgraduate Certificate programmes is at least 20 credits.

University level third stage: Doctor - NQF Flanders level 8
The qualification of Doctor is granted by a panel of researchers after a public presentation of the Doctor's thesis in which the writer/researcher/student has demonstrated to be able to conceive new scientific knowledge based on independent research. The doctoral thesis should have the potential to lead to publications in scientific journals. The organisation of doctoral studies is the autonomous decision of the universities. It can include courses or not and there are different approaches to interdisciplinary training. The common practice is as follows: 1) no credits are used for doctoral studies, but a few universities do use credits but only for the course part of the programme; 2) the normal duration is 4 years of full-time study and this is the standard for the doctoral grant system to doctoral students; 3) each university has a set of rules and procedures on the supervision structure. Doctoral students present a study and research plan to their respective Faculty or Department for approval. The student will be guided by a supervisor and an accompanying committee of professors to which the student has to report at regular intervals, usually every 2 years. The committee can impose a course programme to the student, but this is not obligatory. Most universities have doctoral schools with the mission: 1) to advertise and recruit internationally, 2) to optimize the guidance of doctoral students, 3) to help expand and develop the skills of young researchers. In the doctoral schools they offer doctoral education programmes which have to be completed before admission to the doctoral defence. The aim is to train the doctoral student by enlarging the scientific knowledge (truncus communis) and by acquiring diverse competences. The truncus communis is compulsory and has the following elements: publications, doctoral seminars linked with the own research topic and more general relevant topics, presentations on international conferences, attending doctoral seminars and courses and submitting reports regarding the doctoral progress. The qualification of Doctor is only awarded by universities.

Distance higher education:
The Law on Flexible Learning Paths 2004 gives the opportunity to higher education institutions to adapt their programmes to the needs of mature students by offering programmes and/or programme components partially of totally through distance learning. The higher education institutions provide and develop for this goal appropriate study and learning materials and organizes appropriate guidance.

ADMISSION TO HIGHER EDUCATION

Admission to university-level studies:

Name of secondary school credential required: Diploma van Secundair Onderwijs

For entry to: Bachelor's degrees

Alternatives to credentials: The board of the institution may, pursuant to the regulations, facilitate the access to a particular programme on the basis of deviatory admission requirements, solely based on humanitarian grounds; medical, psychological or social grounds; the overall level of the candidate, which is assessed by the board of the institution. A student who has already obtained a Bachelor's degree can enter another Bachelor's programme without having to take up all the credits of that programme.

Entrance exam requirements: Entrance examinations must be sat for in Civil Engineering, Civil Engineering-Architect, Dental Sciences and Medical Sciences.

Other admission requirements: Entrance examinations must be sat for Dental and Medical Sciences.

Foreign students admission:

Definition of foreign student: Holders of a foreign qualification. Nationality is not at all an issue regarding this matter, namely access to higher education.

Entrance exam requirements: Foreign students who can justify having obtained a secondary school leaving certificate giving access to higher education in their country may start higher education in Flanders. Foreign students also have to pass the entrance examinations for Nautical sciences, Fine Arts, Dental and Medical sciences. Foreign students holding a higher education diploma may obtain a reduction of the total study load of a programme.

Language requirements: Students must be proficient in Dutch for undergraduate studies. Candidates may be required to sit for a language test. The universities organize language courses during the summer.

RECOGNITION OF STUDIES

Quality assurance system:

The concept of accreditation has been incorporated into the Higher Education Act 2003. The accreditation system is organised in close cooperation with the Netherlands by an independent Dutch Flemish Accreditation Body (Nederlands Vlaams Accreditatie Orgaan NVAO) which was set up in September 2003. In Flanders, accreditation is a formal decision by the NVAO that a programme meets the predefined quality criteria. These criteria are laid down in NVAO's (initial) accreditation frameworks. Accreditation is however only one part of the whole quality assurance system of higher education in Flanders. This quality assurance system consists of three parts: an internal part, an external part and the part where the formal decision is taken.

(1) Internal Quality Assurance: the self-evaluation. The self-evaluation of the programme is organized by the higher education institution itself and results in the self-evaluation report.

(2) External Quality Assurance: external quality assessment. The self-evaluation report is the starting point of the external quality assessment. The result of the external quality assessment is the assessment report. The external quality assessment is organised by the VLHORA and VLIR.

The VLHORA, the Council of Flemish University Colleges, was established in 1996 and was awarded the statute of public utility institution by law in 1998. The VLHORA gives advice to the Flemish authorities on all policy aspects regarding university college education, applied research, social services and the practice of the arts. Moreover the VLHORA organises and stimulates consultation between the institutions on all issues related to the university colleges.

Cf. http://www.vlhora.be/. In 1976, the Flemish Interuniversity Council (VLIR) was set up as an autonomous public body with its own institutional status. The council consists of members who represent the Flemish universities. It defends the interests of the universities and gives advice to the Flemish government on university matters (consultation, advice and recommendations). In addition, the council organises consultation between the universities. Cf. http://www.vlir.be/. VLHORA and VLIR organise and coordinate external quality assurance through the external reviews of programmes. In 2010 they merged to VLUHR, "Vlaamse Universiteiten en Hogescholen Raad". VLUHR organizes these assessments by setting up an independent assessment panel of experts responsible for assessing all the programmes in a certain field of study.

The assessment panel consists of experts in the field of study, experts in quality assurance, educational/ pedagogical experts and experts in the international development of the field of study. Students are always involved and represented in the assessment panel.

(3) The formal decision: accreditation. The Netherlands and Flanders have set up an independent accreditation organization by international treaty, the Nederlands-Vlaamse Accreditatieorganisatie (NVAO). Cf. http://www.nvao.net. Higher education programmes that have successfully gone through the external quality assessment sent their assessment report to the NVAO. The NVAO then evaluates the thoroughness of the external assessment and accepts or rejects its findings. If the accreditation decision is positive, the programme is accredited. This means that the programme is included in the Higher Education Register. This registration means that the degree awarded by the programme is recognised by the national authority, Flanders. Additionally, accredited programmes can receive public funding and the students enrolled in these programmes can receive student support (e.g. grants). However, public funding and student support are normally not available for programmes offered by private institutions. A positive accreditation decision by the NVAO is kept or listed in the Higher Education Register for 8 years. If the accreditation decision is negative, the programme looses accreditation. This means the programme is deleted from the Higher Education Register and can no longer be offered. However there is a possibility of temporary recognition during a recovery period. After the negative accreditation decision, the institution has the opportunity to submit an application to the Flemish government for a temporary recognition. This has to be done within one month after the notification of the negative decision. A detailed plan for improvement has to be put forward together with the application. Following advice from the Recognition Commission, the Flemish government takes a decision within three months of the application. Temporary recognition may have a validity of one to three years. In the NVAO's accreditation system, learning outcomes are made use of at the three levels. A programme is expected to explicitly define its intended learning outcomes. These are the competences a graduate should acquire during his studies. An assessment panel first judges whether a programme's intended learning outcomes are in line with the required level and the subject of the programme. The level is evaluated by matching the intended learning outcomes to the Framework for Qualifications of the European Higher Education Area. Additionally, the assessment panel assesses whether these intended learning outcomes are in line with what is (inter)nationally expected of a programme in that subject. NVAO secondly judges the potential learning outcomes. These are the competences a student can achieve in the programme as it is offered. This is mainly done by checking the content of the curriculum with the intended learning outcomes. Thirdly, NVAO assesses the achieved learning outcomes. These are the competences a graduate has actually acquired during his or her studies. An assessment panel needs to read students' work such as essays, end of term papers and theses to be able to judge the achieved learning outcomes and then match those with the required learning outcomes. The required learning outcomes are of course the level-specific and intended subject-specific learning outcomes as defined by the programme and (positively) assessed by the panel

Accreditation is a prerequisite for awarding Bachelor's or Master's degrees education funding and study financing for students.

Bodies dealing with recognition:

Ministerie van Onderwijs en Vorming (Ministry of Education and Training)
Hendrik Consciencegebouw
Koning Albert II-laan 15
Brussels, Vlaams-Brabant 1210
Belgium
Tel: +32 2 553 1700
WWW: http://www.ond.vlaanderen.be/

NARIC-Vlaanderen (NARIC-Flanders)
Hendrik Consciencegebouw Toren C 2
Koning Albert II laan 15
Brussels 1210
Belgium
Tel: +32 2 553 8958
EMail: naric@vlaanderen.be
WWW: http://www.ond.vlaanderen.be/naric/

Services provided and students dealt with: NARIC-Flanders, is the recognition and information centre of Flanders (Belgium) within the ENIC and NARIC Networks of the European Commission, the Council of Europe and UNESCO. It is in charge of the academic recognition of foreign (higher education) qualifications and the professional recognition of teachers based upon the applicable European Directive 2005/36/EC. It belongs to the Agency for Quality Assurance in Education and Training. That Agency belongs to the Ministry of Education and Training (of Flanders).

Nederlands-Vlaams Accreditatie Orgaan - NVAO (Accreditation Organisation of the Netherlands and Flanders)

Postbus 85498
Den Haag 2508
Belgium
Tel: +31 (0) 70 312 2300
Fax: +31 (0) 70 312 2301
EMail: info@nvao.net
WWW: http://www.nvao.net/
Services provided and students dealt with: The organisation was established by international treaty and it ensures the quality of higher education in the Netherlands and Flanders.

NATIONAL BODIES

Ministerie van Onderwijs en Vorming (Ministry of Education and Training)

Minister: Pascal Smet
Director, Higher Education Unit: Noël Vercruysse
Head: Natalie Verstraete
Hendrik Consciencegebouw
Koning Albert II-laan 15
Brussels, Vlaams-Brabant 1210
Belgium
Tel: +32 2 553 1700
WWW: http://www.ond.vlaanderen.be/
Role of national body: The Higher Education Policy Unit belongs to the Department of Education and Training of the Flemish Ministry of Education and Training. It is responsible for policy development and evaluation of higher education. In cooperation with the higher education institutions and other organisations the Higher Education Policy Unit improves, develops and stimulates pro-active initiatives regarding higher education and research.

Vlaamse Onderwijsraad - VLOR (Flemish Education Council)

Kunstlaan 6 bus 6
Brussels 1210
Belgium
Tel: +32 2 219 4299
Fax: +32 2 219 8118
EMail: info@vlor.be
WWW: http://www.vlor.be/
Role of national body: The VLOR is the Strategic Advisory Council for the education and training policy of Flanders. It plays a role in the policy-making process. The council operates independent of the Department of Education and Training and of the competent Minister. Representatives of all the different stakeholders in education and training meet in the VLOR. Together they look for ways to further improve education and training in Flanders.

Vlaamse Interuniversitaire Raad - VLIR (Flemish Interuniversity Council)

Ravensteingalerij 27,
Bus 3
Brussels 1000
Belgium
Tel: +32 2 792 5500
Fax: +32 2 211 4199
EMail: administratie@vlir.be
WWW: http://www.vlir.be

Role of national body: In 1976, the Flemish Interuniversity Council (VLIR) was set up as an autonomous public body with its own institutional status. The council consists of members who represent the Flemish universities. It defends the interests of the universities and gives advice to the Flemish government on university matters (consultation, advice and recommendations). In addition, the council organises consultation between the universities.

VLHORA and VLIR organise and coordinate external quality assurance through the external reviews of programmes. In 2010, the VLHORA and VLIR merged to VLUHR, "Vlaamse Universiteiten en Hogescholen Raad".

Vlaamse Hogescholenraad - VLHORA (Flemish Council of University Colleges)

Ravensteingalerij 27 bus 3 - 1e verd
Brussels 1000
Belgium
Tel: +32 2 211 4190
Fax: +32 2 211 4199
EMail: info@vlhora.be
WWW: http://www.vlhora.be

Role of national body: The VLHORA, the Council of Flemish University Colleges, was established in 1996 and was awarded the statute of public utility institution by law in 1998. The VLHORA gives advice to the Flemish authorities on all policy aspects regarding university college education, applied research, social services and the practice of the arts. Moreover the VLHORA organises and stimulates consultation between the institutions on all issues related to the university colleges.

VLHORA and VLIR organise and coordinate external quality assurance through the external reviews of programmes. In 2010, they merged to VLUHR, "Vlaamse Universiteiten en Hogescholen Raad".

European Association for Quality Assurance in Higher Education - ENQA

President: Achim Hopbach
Director: Maria Kelo
Rue Abbé Cuypers, 3
Brussels 1040
Belgium
Tel: +32 2 741 2445
Fax: +32 2 734 7910
WWW: http://www.enqa.eu/

European Centre for Strategic Management of Universities - ESMU

Chairman: Frans van Vught
Secretary-General: Nadine Burquel
rue Montoyer 31
Box 2
Brussels 1000
Belgium
Tel: +32 2 513 8622
Fax: +32 2 289 2467
EMail: administration@esmu.be
WWW: http://www.esmu.be/

European University Association - EUA

President: Jean-Marc Rapp
Secretary-General: Lesley Wilson
Avenue de l'Yser, 24
Brussels 1040
Belgium
Tel: +32 2 230 5544
Fax: +32 2 230 5751
WWW: http://www.eua.be/

Data for academic year: 2011-2012
Source: IAU from the Higher Education Policy Unit, Department of Education and Training, Flemish Ministry of Education and Training, Belgium, 2011

INSTITUTIONS

ANTWERP MARITIME ACADEMY

Hogere Zeevaartschool Antwerpen (HZS)
Noordkasteel Oost 6, Antwerpen 2030
Tel: +32(3) 205-64-30
Fax: +32(3) 225-06-39
EMail: info@hzs.be
Website: http://www.hzs.be

Algemeen Directeur: Patrick Blondé
Tel: +32(3) 205-64-30 EMail: patrick.blonde@hzs.be

Administratief Directeur: Anne Courbois
Tel: +32(3) 205-64-32 EMail: anne.courbois@hzs.be

International Relations: Eddy de Bondt
EMail: eddy.de.bondt@hzs.be

Programmes
Marine Engineering (Marine Engineering); **Nautical Sciences** (Nautical Science)

History: Founded at the end of the 18th century. Acquired present status 1834.

Governing Bodies: Board of Governors

Academic Year: October to July

Admission Requirements: Secondary school certificate

Fees: (Euros): EU students, c. 460 per annum; foreign students, 3,815

Main Language(s) of Instruction: Dutch, French. English on request for special courses

Degrees and Diplomas: *Bachelor*: Nautical Sciences; Marine Engineering, 3 yrs; *Master*: Nautical Sciences, 1 yr following Bachelor

Student Services: Academic counselling, Canteen, Employment services, Foreign student adviser, Health services, Language programs, Social counselling, Sports facilities

Libraries: Library specialized in Maritime and Transport Publications

Last Updated: 31/08/11

ARTESIS UNIVERSITY COLLEGE ANTWERP

Artesis Hogeschool Antwerpen (HA)
Keizerstraat 15, Antwerpen, Antwerpen 2000
Tel: +32(3) 213-93-00
Fax: +32(3) 213-93-41
EMail: info@artesis.be
Website: http://www.artesis.be/

Algemeen Directeur: Pascale De Groote
Tel: +32(3) 213-93-04 EMail: liliane.huyben@artesis.be

Departments
Audiovisual and Fine Arts (Advertising and Publicity; Fashion Design; Fine Arts; Graphic Design; Photography; Restoration of Works of Art; Textile Design) *Head*: Rafaël De Smedt; **Business Studies, Teacher Training and Social Work** *(Antwerp and Lier)* (Business Administration; Business and Commerce; Management; Social Work; Teacher Training) *Head*: Edward Adriaenssens; **Design Sciences** (Architecture; Interior Design; Production Engineering) *Head*: Richard Foqué; **Dramatic Art, Music and Dance** *(Antwerp and Lier)* (Acting; Dance; Music; Theatre) *Head*: Pascale De Groote; **Health Care** *(Antwerp and Mechelen)* (Gynaecology and Obstetrics; Midwifery; Nursing; Occupational Therapy; Physical Therapy) *Head*: Gerebern Laenen; **Industrial Science and Technology** *(Antwerp, Mechelen and Turnhout)* (Building Technologies; Chemistry; Construction Engineering; Electrical Engineering; Electronic Engineering; Graphic Design; Industrial Engineering; Mechanical Engineering; Technology) *Head*: Boudewijn Peeters; **Translation and Interpreting** (Arabic; Chinese; Danish; English; French; German; Greek; Italian; Portuguese; Russian; Spanish; Translation and Interpretation) *Head*: Frank Peeters

History: Founded 1995 as University College Antwerp, incorporating 17 formerly independent institutions. Acquired present title 2008.

Academic Year: September to July

Admission Requirements: Secondary school certificate, or equivalent

Main Language(s) of Instruction: Dutch

Degrees and Diplomas: *Bachelor*; *Master*

Student Services: Canteen, Cultural centre, Employment services, Foreign student adviser, Handicapped facilities, Health services, Language programs, Social counselling, Sports facilities

Libraries: Department Libraries
Last Updated: 23/01/12

ARTEVELDE UNIVERSITY COLLEGE GHENT

Arteveldehogeschool
Hoogpoort 15, Gent, East Flanders 9000
Tel: +32(9) 235-20-00
Fax: +32(9) 235-20-01
EMail: info@arteveldehs.be
Website: http://www.arteveldehogeschool.be

Algemeen Directeur: Johan Veeckman
Tel: +32(9) 235-20-00, Fax: +32(9) 235-20-01
EMail: johan.veeckman@arteveldehs.be

Secretary-General: Mia Van Coninckxloo
Tel: +32(9) 235-20-29, Fax: +32(9) 235-20-01
EMail: mia.vanconinckxloo@arteveldehs.be

International Relations: Eline Sierens, Head of Office
Tel: +32(9) 235-20-78, Fax: +32(9) 235-20-88
EMail: eline.sierens@arteveldehs.be

Departments
Audiology (Speech Therapy and Audiology); **Business Management** (Business Administration); **Communication Management** (Communication Studies; Management); **Graphic and Digital Media** (Media Studies); **Journalism** (Journalism); **Midwifery** (Midwifery); **Nursing** (Nursing); **Occupational Therapy** (Occupational Therapy); **Office Management** (Management); **Physiotherapy** (Physical Therapy); **Podiatry** (Podiatry); **Social Work** (Social Work); **Teacher Training for Nursery School (Preschool) Education** (Teacher Training); **Teacher Training for Primary School Education** (Teacher Training); **Teacher Training for Secondary School Education** (Teacher Training)

Divisions
Early Childhood Education (Preschool Education)

History: Founded 2000 by the merging of four independent university-level institutions: Katholieke Hogeschool voor Lerarenopleiding en Bedrijfsmanagement Oost Vlaanderen (Gent), Katholieke Hogeschool voor Gezondheidszorg Oost-Vlaanderen (Gent), Hogeschool voor Economisch en Grafisch Onderwijs (Gent), Sociale Hogeschool Katholiek Vormigscentrum Maatschappelijk Werk (Gent).

Governing Bodies: Board

Academic Year: September to June

Admission Requirements: Secondary school certificate or equivalent

Fees: (Euros): c. 600 per annum

Main Language(s) of Instruction: Dutch

International Co-operation: Participates in Erasmus, Tempus, Leonardo da Vinci, Comenius and VLIR-UOS programmes

Accrediting Agencies: Nederlands Vlaamse Accreditatie Organisatie (NVAO)

Degrees and Diplomas: *Bachelor*; *Master*. Also Advanced Bachelor (Special education; Education, Creative Therapy)

Student Services: Academic counselling, Canteen, Employment services, Foreign student adviser, Handicapped facilities, Health services, Language programs, Social counselling, Sports facilities

Special Facilities: Recording Studio

Libraries: Specialized Libraries
Last Updated: 21/07/11

CATHOLIC UNIVERSITY COLLEGE OF BRUGES–OSTEND

Katholieke Hogeschool Brugge-Oostende (KHBO)
Xaverianenstraat 10, Brugge, West-Flanders 8200
Tel: +32(50) 30-51-00
Fax: +32(50) 30-51-01
EMail: info@khbo.be
Website: http://www.khbo.be

Algemeen Directeur: Piet De Leersnyder

Departments
Education and Teacher Training *(Bruges)* (Education; Preschool Education; Primary Education; Secondary Education; Teacher Training); **Engineering Technology** *(Ostende)* (Aeronautical and Aerospace Engineering; Chemical Engineering; Construction Engineering; Electrical Engineering; Energy Engineering; Materials Engineering; Mechanical Engineering); **Health Care** *(Bruges)* (Laboratory Techniques; Midwifery; Nursing; Nutrition; Public Health; Rehabilitation and Therapy; Speech Therapy and Audiology); **Management and Business Studies** *(Bruges)* (Accountancy; Finance; Hotel Management; Insurance; Marketing; Secretarial Studies; Tourism; Translation and Interpretation)

History: Founded 1995. A university-level institution.

Academic Year: October to July (October-February; February-July)

Admission Requirements: Secondary school certificate

Main Language(s) of Instruction: Dutch

International Co-operation: Participates in the Socrates, Leonardo Da Vinci, Interreg programmes

Degrees and Diplomas: *Bachelor; Master*

Student Services: Academic counselling, Canteen, Cultural centre, Employment services, Foreign student adviser, Handicapped facilities, Health services, Social counselling, Sports facilities

Student Residential Facilities: Yes

Libraries: c. 15,000 vols
Last Updated: 01/09/11

CATHOLIC UNIVERSITY OF LEUVEN

Katholieke Universiteit Leuven (KULEUVEN)
Naamssestraat 22, Leuven 3000
Tel: +32(16) 32-40-27
Fax: +32(16) 32-40-22
EMail: secr@dir.kuleuven.ac.be
Website: http://www.kuleuven.ac.be

Rector: Mark Waer Tel: +32(16) 32-40-67, Fax: +32(16) 32-41-96

General Administrator: Koenraad De Backere
Tel: +32(16) 32-41-77, Fax: +32(16) 32-41-67
EMail: Koenraad.Debackere@abh.kuleuven.be

International Relations: Bart De Moor, Vice-Rector, International Policy Tel: +32(16) 32-40-30

Centres
Agrarian Bio and Environment Ethics (Agriculture; Environmental Studies; Ethics); **Biomedical Ethics and Law** *(Interfaculty)* (Biomedicine; Ethics; Law); **Ethics** *(European)* (Ethics); **Risk and Insurance Studies** (Insurance)

Faculties
Arts (American Studies; Archaeology; Arts and Humanities; European Studies; Fine Arts; Latin American Studies; Linguistics; Literature; Medieval Studies; Modern Languages; Musicology); **Bioengineering Sciences** (Bioengineering; Food Technology; Management; Molecular Biology; Nanotechnology; Natural Resources; Water Science); **Business and Economics** (Business Administration; Economics); **Canon Law** (Canon Law); **Engineering** (Architecture; Chemical Engineering; Civil Engineering; Computer Engineering; Electronic Engineering; Engineering); **Kinesiology and Rehabilitation Science** (Physical Education; Physical Therapy; Rehabilitation and Therapy); **Law** (Law); **Medicine** (Medicine); **Pharmaceutical Sciences** (Pharmacy); **Psy-**chology and Educational Sciences (Education; Psychology); **Science** (Astronomy and Space Science; Biology; Chemistry; Earth Sciences; Environmental Studies; Mathematics; Natural Sciences; Physics); **Social Sciences** (Anthropology; Communication Studies; Cultural Studies; Political Sciences; Social Sciences; Sociology); **Theology** (Ethics; Religious Studies; Theology)

Higher Institutes
Labour Studies (Labour and Industrial Relations)

Institutes
Energy (Energy Engineering); **Language** *(Leuven)* (Modern Languages); **Philosophy** (Philosophy)

History: Founded 1425 by Bull of Pope Martin V on the initiative of Duke John of Brabant. Collegium Trilingue established by Erasmus 1517. Suppressed 1797 under French occupation and closed during the reigns of Napoleon and William I of Holland. Re-established 1834 as Catholic University by Belgian episcopate. Reorganized 1969 with two divisions, the Katholieke Universiteit te Leuven and the Université catholique de Louvain which became separate legal entities in 1970. The titular head of the University is the Cardinal Archbishop of Malines; it is independent of direct State control but receives a full State subvention.

Governing Bodies: Beheerraad (Board of Directors); Academic Board

Academic Year: September to June (September-January; February-June)

Admission Requirements: Secondary school leaving certificate or foreign equivalent if formally recognized under agreements concluded with the Belgian Government. Other foreign qualifications subject to the approval of the faculty concerned

Fees: (Euros): 505 per annum

Main Language(s) of Instruction: Dutch, English

International Co-operation: With institutions in The Netherlands, Poland, Spain, USA, Japan, China, South Africa. Participates in Erasmus, Tempus, Atlantis, Asia Link

Degrees and Diplomas: *Bachelor:* Philosophy; Theology; Canon Law; Languages; History; Archaeology; Arts Studies. Law; Notarial Law; Criminology; Education; Economics; Political and Social Sciences; Psychology; Medicine: Engineering; Bio-engineering; Physical Education; Pharmacy, 3 yrs; *Master:* Philosophy; Theology; Languages; History; Archaeology; Arts Studies; Law; Notarial Law; Criminology; Education; Master in Economics; Political and Social Sciences; Physical Education; Natural Sciences, 1-2 yrs; *Doctor (PhD)*

Student Services: Academic counselling, Canteen, Cultural centre, Employment services, Foreign student adviser, Handicapped facilities, Health services, Nursery care, Social counselling, Sports facilities

Student Residential Facilities: For c. 3,840 students

Special Facilities: University Museum

Libraries: Central Library and 14 faculty libraries

Publications: Reviews of faculties and institutes

Press or Publishing House: University Press
Last Updated: 02/09/11

CAMPUS KORTRIJK

AFDELING KORTRIJK

Etienne Sabbelaan 53, Kortrijk 8500
Tel: +32(56) 24-61-11
Fax: +32(56) 24-69-95
EMail: info@kulak.be
Website: http://www.kuleuven-kortrijk.be

Campus Rector: Jan Beirlant

Faculties
Applied Economics (Economics); **Arts** (Arts and Humanities); **Law** (Law); **Medicine** (Medical Technology); **Science** (Natural Sciences)

ERASMUS UNIVERSITY COLLEGE, BRUSSELS

Erasmushogeschool Brussel (EHB)
Nijverheidskaai 170, Brussel 1070
Tel: +32(2) 559-15-15
Fax: +32(2) 523-37-57
EMail: info@ehb.be
Website: http://www.ehb.be

Algemeen Directeur: Luc Van de Velde
EMail: luc.van.de.velde@ehb.be

Administratief Directeur: Ann Langenakens
Tel: +32(2) 559-02-67 EMail: ann.langenakens@ehb.be

International Relations: Annelore Schittecatte
EMail: annelore.schittecatte@ehb.be

Conservatories
Music *(Royal)* (Music)

Departments
Applied Languages (Danish; Dutch; English; French; German; Greek; Italian; Portuguese; Russian; Spanish; Swedish; Translation and Interpretation; Turkish); **Architecture** (Landscape Architecture); **Audiovisual Arts and Techniques** (Film; Radio and Television Broadcasting; Theatre); **Communications** (Business and Commerce; Communication Studies; Journalism; Public Relations; Translation and Interpretation); **Health Care** (Dietetics; Midwifery; Nursing; Nutrition; Pharmacy); **Hotel and Tourism** (Hotel Management; Tourism); **Industrial and Technical Sciences** (Computer Science; Industrial Engineering); **Social Sciences** (Human Resources; Social Sciences; Social Work); **Teacher Training** (Teacher Training)

History: Founded 1995 as a merger of several university colleges. A university-level institution, financed by the State and tuition fees, which is responsible to the Ministry of Education.

Governing Bodies: Board

Academic Year: End of September to July (October-February; February-July)

Admission Requirements: Secondary school certificate

Fees: (Euros): c. 600 per annum

Main Language(s) of Instruction: Dutch

International Co-operation: Participates in the European programmes

Degrees and Diplomas: *Bachelor; Master*

Special Facilities: Art Gallery for young Flemish artists

Libraries: Central Library, c. 10,000 vols

Publications: Medium *(quarterly)*
Last Updated: 02/09/11

FLANDERS OPERASTUDIO

Operastudio Vlaanderen
Bijlokekaai 6, Gent, Oost-Vlaanderen 9160
Tel: +32(9) 233-24-30
Fax: +32(9) 233-37-65
EMail: kristien.heirman@operastudio.be
Website: http://www.operastudio.be

Director: Ronny Lauwers (2004-)
EMail: ronny.lauwers@operastudio.be

Financial Assistant: Dirk Cornelius
EMail: dirk.cornelis@operastudio.be

International Relations: Kristien Heirman, Communication and Student Administration

Departments
Piano (Opera; Performing Arts; Singing); **Singing** (Music; Opera; Singing)

History: Created in 1998. Offers one or two-year specialized training to young singers of all nationalities who are either students or at the start of their professional career.

Governing Bodies: Executive Board; General Board of Directors.

Admission Requirements: Admission by audition.

Fees: (Euro): 1,000 per annum

Main Language(s) of Instruction: English

Degrees and Diplomas: One year postgraduate diploma in Singing and Pianist-Repetitor.

Student Services: Canteen, Foreign student adviser

Special Facilities: Concert Hall.

Libraries: Library containing opera scores. Cooperation with libraries of the Vlaamse Opera and Hogeschool Gent.
Last Updated: 02/09/11

FREE UNIVERSITY OF BRUSSELS

Vrije Universiteit Brussel (VUB)
Pleinlaan 2, Brussel 1050
Tel: +32(2) 629-21-11
Fax: +32(2) 629-22-82
EMail: info@vub.ac.be
Website: http://www.vub.ac.be

Rector: Paul De Knop
Tel: +32(2) 629-21-40, Fax: +32(2) 629-36-50
EMail: rector@vub.ac.be

Algemeen Operationeel Directeur: Jim Van Leemput
Tel: +32(2) 629-21-42, Fax: +32(2) 629-38-27
EMail: algemeen.directeur@vub.ac.be

International Relations: Jacqueline Couder
EMail: international.relations@vub.ac.be

Colleges
Vesalius (Business Education; Communication Studies; International Studies)

Faculties
Arts and Philosophy *(Etterbeek)* (Archaeology; Classical Languages; Communication Studies; Ethics; Germanic Languages; History; Library Science; Linguistics; Literature; Modern Languages; Philosophy; Romance Languages); **Economic, Political and Social Sciences** *(with Solvay Business School)* (Business and Commerce; Business Computing; Economics; Management; Political Sciences); **Engineering** *(Etterbeek)* (Architecture; Chemical Engineering; Civil Engineering; Computer Science; Electronic Engineering; Engineering; Materials Engineering; Natural Resources); **Law and Criminology** *(Etterbeek)* (Criminology; Law; Notary Studies); **Medicine and Pharmacy** *(Medical Campus Jette)* (Biomedicine; Medical Technology; Medicine; Nursing; Pharmacy); **Physical Education and Physiotherapy** *(Etterbeek)* (Physical Education; Physical Therapy; Rehabilitation and Therapy); **Psychology and Educational Sciences** *(Etterbeek)* (Educational Sciences; Psychology; Teacher Training); **Science and Bio-Engineering Science** *(Etterbeek)* (Artificial Intelligence; Astrophysics; Biology; Chemistry; Computer Science; Geography; Geology; Mathematics; Physics; Software Engineering)

Institutes
Contemporary Chinese Studies *(Brussels)* (Chinese); **European Studies** (European Studies; European Union Law; International Law)

Further Information: Also University Hospital

History: Founded 1970 when the former Vrije Universiteit Brussels, founded 1834, was replaced by separate Dutch and French-speaking Universities. A private autonomous institution receiving substantial financial support from the State.

Governing Bodies: Raad van Bestuur

Academic Year: September to July

Admission Requirements: Secondary school certificate or recognized foreign equivalent and entrance examination for Bachelor degree in Medicine

Fees: (Euros): 564-7,000 per annum

Main Language(s) of Instruction: Dutch, English

Degrees and Diplomas: *Bachelor:* Applied Sciences and Engineering; Art Science and Archaeology; Biology; Bio-Engineering Sciences; Biomedical Sciences; Business Engineering; Chemistry; Communication Sciences; Computer Sciences; Criminology; Economic Sciences and Applied Economic Sciences; Pharmaceutical Sciences; Physics; Medicine; Geography; History; Applied Sciences and Engineering; Applied Sciences and Engineering (Architecture); Physical Education and Movement Science; Political Sciences; Psychology; Law; Rehabilitation Sciences and Physiotherapy;

Sociology; Linguistics and Literature; Philosophy and Ethics; Mathematics, 3 yrs (180 ECTs); *Master*: International and European Law; Legal Theory; Management; Urban Culture; Economics; European Integration; American Studies; Human Ecology; Nuclear Engineering; Linguistics; *Master*. Science; Engineering; Medicine; Pharmacy; Economics; Politics; Business; Education; Psychology; Physical Education; Physiotherapy; Law; Criminology; Arts; Philosophy, 1-2 yrs (60-120 ECTs); *Doctor*

Student Services: Academic counselling, Canteen, Cultural centre, Employment services, Foreign student adviser, Foreign Studies Centre, Handicapped facilities, Health services, Language programs, Nursery care, Social counselling, Sports facilities

Student Residential Facilities: For 1,250 students

Libraries: Faculty Libraries, total, c. 147,000 vols

Publications: Akademos

Press or Publishing House: VUB University Press

Academic Staff *2010-2011*	MEN	WOMEN	TOTAL
FULL-TIME	1,176	707	**1,883**
Student Numbers *2010-2011*			
All (Foreign Included)	4,385	5,813	**10,198**
FOREIGN ONLY	–	–	**1,406**

Last Updated: 06/09/11

GHENT UNIVERSITY
Universiteit Gent (UGENT)
Sint-Pietersnieuwstraat 25, Gent 9000
Tel: +32(9) 264-31-11
Fax: +32(9) 264-31-31
EMail: GUIDe@Ugent.be
Website: http://www.ugent.be

Rector: Paul Van Cauwenberge (2005-2013)
Tel: 32 9 264 3001, Fax: 32 9 264 3597 EMail: rector@Ugent.be

International Relations: Valère Meus
Tel: +32(9) 264-70-01, Fax: +32(9) 264-31-31
EMail: Valere.Meus@UGent.be

Faculties
Arts and Philosophy (African Languages; African Studies; Archaeology; Cultural Studies; Dutch; Eastern European Studies; English; Fine Arts; French; German; Greek; History; Latin; Medieval Studies; Modern History; Musicology; Nordic Studies; North African Studies; Oriental Studies; Philosophy; Romance Languages; Slavic Languages; Southeast Asian Studies; Theatre); **Bioscience Engineering** (Agricultural Economics; Agricultural Engineering; Agriculture; Animal Husbandry; Applied Chemistry; Applied Mathematics; Biochemistry; Crop Production; Ecology; Environmental Studies; Food Technology; Forest Management; Nutrition; Organic Chemistry; Plant and Crop Protection; Soil Management; Water Management); **Economics and Business Administration** (Accountancy; Business Administration; Business Computing; Economics; Finance; Management; Management Systems; Marketing); **Engineering** (Applied Physics; Architecture; Automation and Control Engineering; Chemical Engineering; Civil Engineering; Electrical and Electronic Engineering; Industrial Management; Information Technology; Mathematics; Mechanics; Telecommunications Engineering; Textile Technology; Thermal Engineering; Town Planning); **Law; Medicine and Health Sciences** (Anaesthesiology; Biochemistry; Chemistry; Dentistry; Dermatology; Forensic Medicine and Dentistry; Genetics; Gynaecology and Obstetrics; Immunology; Medical Technology; Medicine; Microbiology; Ophthalmology; Orthopaedics; Otorhinolaryngology; Paediatrics; Pathology; Pharmacology; Physical Therapy; Psychiatry and Mental Health; Psychology; Public Health; Radiology; Rehabilitation and Therapy; Sports Medicine; Surgery; Urology); **Pharmaceutical Sciences** (Pharmacy); **Political and Social Sciences** (Communication Studies; Development Studies; Political Sciences; Sociology); **Psychology and Educational Sciences** (Education; Educational Sciences; Educational Technology; Experimental Psychology; Industrial and Organizational Psychology; Pedagogy; Psychoanalysis; Psychology; Special Education); **Sciences**; **Veterinary Medicine** (Animal Husbandry; Veterinary Science)

Further Information: Also University Hospital; courses for foreign students; interuniversity courses

History: Founded 1817 by King William I of the Netherlands. The official language of the University was originally Latin; this changed to French 1830 and to Dutch 1930. Ghent University is today one of the most important academic institutions of Belgium and has an important international educational and scientific role. Acquired present status and title 1991.

Governing Bodies: Board of Governors; Executive Board

Academic Year: October to September

Admission Requirements: Secondary school certificate or recognized foreign equivalent and entrance examination for engineering and medicine

Main Language(s) of Instruction: Dutch

International Co-operation: Participates in the Santander Group and the Socrates/Erasmus, Tempus, Alfa, Leonardo da Vinci programmes

Degrees and Diplomas: *Bachelor*. 3 yrs; *Master*; *Doctor*. at least 4 further yrs

Student Services: Academic counselling, Canteen, Cultural centre, Employment services, Foreign student adviser, Handicapped facilities, Health services, Language programs, Nursery care, Social counselling, Sports facilities

Student Residential Facilities: Yes

Special Facilities: History of Science Museum; Zoology Museum; History of Medicine Museum. Observatory. Botanical Garden

Libraries: Central Library; faculty and laboratory libraries
Last Updated: 08/09/11

GROUP T-INTERNATIONAL UNIVERSITY COLLEGE LEUVEN
Groep T - Internationale Hogeschool Leuven'
Campus Versalius, Vesaliusstraat 13, Leuven, Vlaams-Brabant 3000
Tel: +32(16) 30-10-30
Fax: +32(16) 30-10-40
EMail: group-t@group-t.be
Website: http://www.group-t.be

President: Johan De Graeve EMail: johan.de.graeve@group-t.be

Administrator General: Ingrid Ilsbroux

International Relations: Wim Polet
Tel: +32(16) 30-11-23 EMail: bai.weien@groept.be

Colleges
Education (Preschool Education; Primary Education; Secondary Education; Teacher Training); **Engineering** (Biochemistry; Chemical Engineering; Electrical and Electronic Engineering; Engineering; Hydraulic Engineering; Information Technology; Management; Mass Communication; Mechanical Engineering; Media Studies)

History: Founded 1960 as Technical Institute. Granted legal status as a university-level institution 1977. Merged with the Teacher College of the Flemish-Brabant province and acquired present title 2008.

Governing Bodies: Board of Directors

Academic Year: October to July (October-January; February-July)

Admission Requirements: Secondary school certificate or recognized foreign equivalent

Fees: (Euros): EU students, 523 per annum; non-EU students, 5,600

Main Language(s) of Instruction: Dutch, English

Degrees and Diplomas: *Bachelor*. Electromechanical Engineering; Electronics Engineering; Chemical/Biochemical Engineering, 3 yrs; *Master*. Electromechanical Engineering; Electronics Engineering; Chemical Engineering; Biochemical Engineering, 1-2 yrs; *Master*. e-Media, 1 yr. Postgraduate Programme in Enterprising; Professional Bachelor in Education 3 years.

Student Services: Academic counselling, Canteen, Employment services, Foreign student adviser, Foreign Studies Centre, Handicapped facilities, Health services, Language programs, Social counselling, Sports facilities

Student Residential Facilities: Yes
Last Updated: 31/08/11

HASSELT UNIVERSITY
Universiteit Hasselt (UHASSELT)
Campus Diepenbeek, Agoralaan – Gebouw D, Diepenbeek BE 3590
Tel: +32(11) 26-81-11
Fax: +32(11) 26-81-99
EMail: info@uhasselt.be
Website: http://www.uhasselt.be

Rector: Luc De Schepper (2004-)
Tel: +32(11) 26-80-00, Fax: +32(11) 26-80-19
EMail: luc.deschepper@luc.ac.be

Faculties
Applied Economics (Business Administration; Computer Science; Economics; Marketing); **Law** (Law); **Medicine** (Dentistry; Health Sciences); **Science** (Biology; Chemistry; Mathematics; Natural Sciences; Physics)

Institutes
Transport Sciences (Transport and Communications)

History: Founded 1971. Acquired present status 2005.

Governing Bodies: Board of Trustees

Academic Year: October to September

Admission Requirements: Secondary school certificate or recognized equivalent

Main Language(s) of Instruction: Dutch, with some programmes in English

International Co-operation: Arrangements for cooperation in Research and Development with the European Community

Degrees and Diplomas: *Bachelor*: Biology, 2 yrs; *Bachelor*: Biomedical Sciences; Chemistry; Commercial Engineering; Commercial Engineering in Data Processing Policy; Computer Science; Mathematics; Medicine; Physics; Traffic Studies, 3 yrs; *Master*: Applied Economics; Commercial Engineering; Commercial Engineering in Data Processing Policy; Traffic Studies, 2 yrs; *Master*: Biomedical Sciences; Computer Science, 1 yr after Bachelor; *Master*: Biostatistics, 1 yr following Master; *Master*: Business Administration; Information Technology; International Marketing; Management; Management, a further 1 yr; *Master*: Science of Applied Statistics, 1 yr; *Doctor*

Student Services: Academic counselling, Canteen, Employment services, Foreign student adviser, Foreign Studies Centre, Handicapped facilities, Health services, Language programs, Social counselling, Sports facilities

Libraries: c. 40,000 vols
Last Updated: 20/03/12

HOGESCHOOL-UNIVERSITEIT BRUSSEL (HUB)
Warmoesberg 26, Brussel 1000
Tel: +32(2) 210-12-11
Fax: +32(2) 217-64-64
EMail: info@hubrussel.be
Website: http://www.hubrussel.be/

Algemeen Directeur: Dirk De Ceulaer (2002-)
EMail: dirk.deceulaer@hubrussel.be

International Relations: Martine Vanheulenbrouck
EMail: martine.vanheulenbrouck@hubrussel.be

Faculties
Economics and Management (Business Administration; Economics; Environmental Management; International Business; International Relations; Management); **Law** (Law) *Dean:* Luc Wintgens; **Linguistics and Literature** (Applied Linguistics; Arts and Humanities; Dutch; English; Germanic Languages; Journalism; Literature; Translation and Interpretation)

Programmes
Education (Education; Preschool Education; Primary Education; Secondary Education); **Health Care** (Medical Technology; Nursing; Occupational Therapy; Optics; Optometry); **Social and Community Work** (Family Studies; Social Sciences; Social Work)

Research Centres
Financial Participation *President*: Francine Van den Bulcke; **History of Material Culture** *President*: Eddy Van Cauwenberghe; **Intellectual Property Law** *Director*: Frank Gotzen; **Multilingualism** *President*: Peter Nelde; **Pragmatics** *(IUAP-II) Director*: Dominique Markey

Research Institutes
Communication for Social Change (Communication Studies) *President*: Jan Servaes; **Education and Development** (Development Studies; Education) *Director*: Erik Raymaekers; **Small Business** (Business and Commerce) *President*: Jan Degadt

Further Information: Also postgraduate courses in Legal Theory, Company Law, Quantitative Analysis

History: Founded 1925. Officially recognized 1937. Acquired present status 2008 following integration of HONIM and VLEKHO departments of EHSAL. Acquired present status 2008.

Governing Bodies: Raad van Beheer; Algemene Vergadering

Academic Year: September to June

Admission Requirements: Secondary school certificate or recognized equivalent

Fees: (Euros) 578 per annum

Main Language(s) of Instruction: Dutch; some courses in English

Degrees and Diplomas: *Bachelor*; *Master*

Student Services: Academic counselling, Canteen, Cultural centre, Employment services, Foreign student adviser, Handicapped facilities, Language programs, Social counselling, Sports facilities

Student Residential Facilities: Yes

Libraries: Central Library, c. 70,000 vols
Last Updated: 01/09/11

INSTITUTE OF TROPICAL MEDICINE ANTWERP
Prins Leopold Instituut voor Tropische Geneeskunde (ITG - ANTWERPEN)
Nationalestraat 155, Antwerpen 2000
Tel: +32(3) 247-66-66
Fax: +32(3) 216-14-31
EMail: info@itg.be
Website: http://www.itg.be

Director: Bruno Gryseels EMail: bgryseels@itg.be

Departments
Animal Health (Veterinary Science); **Clinical Sciences** (Medicine); **Microbiology** (Microbiology); **Parasitology** (Parasitology); **Public Health** (Public Health)

History: Founded 1906.

Main Language(s) of Instruction: Dutch, English, French

Degrees and Diplomas: *Master*: Public Health, Disease Control; Tropical Animal Health; *Doctor*: Natural and Health Sciences. Also Postgraduate Certificates in Tropical Medicine and International Health
Last Updated: 02/09/11

KAHO SINT LIVEN
Katholieke Hogeschool 'Sint-Lieven', Gent (KAHO)
Gebr. Desmetstraat 1, Gent 9000
Tel: +32(9) 265-86-45
Fax: +32(9) 225-86-46
EMail: info@kahosl.be
Website: http://www.kahosl.be

Algemeen Directeur: Frank Baert (2007-)
EMail: frank.baert@kahosl.be

International Relations: Hilde Lauwereys

Programmes
Biotechnology *(Waas Campus)* (Agricultural Engineering; Agriculture; Animal Husbandry; Biotechnology; Food Science); **Business Studies** *(Dirk Martens Campus)*; **Health Care** *(Gildestraat Campus, Waas Campus, Dirk Martens Campus)*; **Industrial Science and Technology** *(Waas Campus, Rabot Campus, Dirk*

Martens Campus); **Teacher Training** *(Dirk Martens Campus, Waas Campus)* (Education; Preschool Education; Primary Education; Secondary Education; Teacher Training)

History: Founded 1977, incorporating 8 existing colleges of higher Education. A private university-level institution. Acquired present title 1995.

Governing Bodies: Board of Directors

Academic Year: September to June

Admission Requirements: Secondary school certificate

Fees: (Euros): 520

Main Language(s) of Instruction: Dutch

Degrees and Diplomas: *Bachelor, Master*

Student Services: Academic counselling, Canteen, Cultural centre, Employment services, Foreign student adviser, Handicapped facilities, Health services, Language programs, Social counselling, Sports facilities

Academic Staff *2008-2009*: Total: c. 600

Student Numbers *2008-2009*: Total: c. 5,000
Last Updated: 15/01/09

KAREL DE GROTE UNIVERITY COLLEGE, ANTWERP

Karel de Grote-Hogeschool Katholieke Hogeschool Antwerpen (KDG)
Brusselstraat 45, Antwerpen 2018
Tel: +32(3) 613-13-83
Fax: +32(3) 613-13-04
EMail: info@kdg.be
Website: http://www.kdg.be

Algemeen Directeur: Jan Trommelmans Tel: +32(3) 613-13-10

Head of Administration: Rian Van Nyen
Tel: +32(3) 613-13-30 EMail: ria.vannyen@kdg.be

International Relations: Helene Vanbrabant
Tel: +32(3) 613-13-80, Fax: +32(3) 613-13-04
EMail: helene.vanbrabant@kdg.be

Departments
Applied Social Studies *(SAW)* (Social Work; Special Education); **Arts and Design** *(ABK)* (Fine Arts; Graphic Design; Jewelry Art); **Commercial Sciences and Business Administration** (Business Administration; Business and Commerce; Business Computing; Management); **Health Care** *(GEZ)* (Midwifery; Nursing); **Industrial Sciences and Technology** *(IWT)* (Automotive Engineering; Chemistry; Electronic Engineering; Engineering; Mechanical Engineering; Mechanics; Medical Technology; Photography); **Teacher Training** *(DLO)* (Preschool Education; Primary Education; Secondary Education; Teacher Training)

History: Founded 1994 incorporating 13 Catholic institutions of higher education.

Governing Bodies: Algemene Vergadering; Raad van Bestuur; College van Bestuur; Academisch College; Administratief College; Academische Raad

Academic Year: September to July (September-February; February-July)

Admission Requirements: Secondary school certificate (Diploma secundair onderwijs) and entrance examination for Department of Arts

Fees: (Euros): 100-578 per annum; postgraduate courses, 495-1,000

Main Language(s) of Instruction: Dutch (with some study programmes in English)

International Co-operation: Participates in the Socrates, Erasmus, Minerva, Grundtvig, Lingua, Leonardo, Tempus, Adapt Programmes

Degrees and Diplomas: *Bachelor.* 3 yrs; *Master.* 1 further yr

Student Services: Academic counselling, Canteen, Cultural centre, Employment services, Foreign student adviser, Handicapped facilities, Health services, Language programs, Nursery care, Social counselling, Sports facilities

Special Facilities: Art Gallery

Libraries: 6 specialized libraries, total, c. 140,000 vols

Academic Staff *2010-2011*	TOTAL
FULL-TIME	630
PART-TIME	320
STAFF WITH DOCTORATE	
FULL-TIME	20
PART-TIME	c. 5

Student Numbers *2010-2011*	
All (Foreign Included)	c. 8,000
FOREIGN ONLY	310

Last Updated: 23/01/12

KH KEMPEN UNIVERSITY COLLEGE

Katholieke Hogeschool Kempen (KHK)
Kleinhoefstraat 4, Geel 2440
Tel: +32(14) 56-23-10
Fax: +32(14) 58-48-59
EMail: info@khk.be
Website: http://www.khk.be

Algemeen Directeur: Maurice Vaes EMail: maurice.vaes@khk.be

International Relations: Agnes Dillien, International Relations Manager
Tel: +32(14) 56-23-10, Fax: +32(14) 58-48-59
EMail: agnes.dillien@khk.be

Departments
Commercial Sciences and Business Administration (Business Administration; Business and Commerce); **Health Care** *(Turnhout)* (Midwifery; Nursing; Physical Therapy; Public Health); **Health Care** *(Lier)* (Public Health); **Health Care and Chemistry** (Chemistry; Health Sciences); **Industrial Engineering and Biotechnology** (Agriculture; Biotechnology; Food Technology; Horticulture; Industrial Engineering); **Social Work** (Social Work); **Teacher Training** *(Heilig Graf, Turnhout)*; **Teacher Training** *(Vorselaar)* (Teacher Training); **Technical Sciences** (Technology)

History: Founded 1957. A university-level institution.

Academic Year: September to July (September-January; February-July)

Admission Requirements: Secondary school certificate

Main Language(s) of Instruction: Dutch

International Co-operation: With universities in the European Union

Degrees and Diplomas: *Bachelor.* Agriculture and Biotechnology; Applied Computer Science; Business Management; Bio-Medical Laboratory Technology; Chemistry; Electromechanics; Electronics - ICT; Electrotechnology; Logistics; Midwifery; Nursery Education; Nursing; Nutrition and Dietetics; Occupational Therapy; Office Management; Orthopaedics; Primary Education; Secondary Education; Social Work; *Master.* Agriculture; Electromechanics; Electronics - ICT; Electrotechnology; Food Industry; Horticulture

Student Services: Academic counselling, Canteen, Employment services, Foreign student adviser, Health services, Social counselling

Libraries: Specialized libraries

Publications: Agora *(quarterly)*
Last Updated: 01/09/11

LESSIUS UNIVERSITY COLLEGE

Lessius Antwerp and Lessius Mechelen University Colleges
Jozef De Bomstraat 11, Antwerpen 2018
Tel: +32(32) 06-04-80
Fax: +32(32) 06-04-81
EMail: info@lessius.eu
Website: http://www.lessius.eu

Vice-Chancellor: Johan Cloet

Administrative Officer: Magda Leroy
EMail: magda.leroy@mechelen.lessius.eu

International Relations: Isabel Deprez, Head of the International Office EMail: isabel.deprez@mechelen.lessius.eu

Departments
Applied Engineering (Automotive Engineering; Bioengineering; Chemical Engineering; Construction Engineering; Electronic Engineering; Energy Engineering; Engineering); **Applied Language**

Studies (Arabic; Dutch; English; Foreign Languages Education; French; German; Greek; Hungarian; Italian; Japanese; Journalism; Polish; Portuguese; Russian; Spanish; Translation and Interpretation; Turkish); **Business and Communication** (Accountancy; Business Administration; Communication Studies; Finance; Information Management; International Relations; Journalism; Marketing; Tourism); **Business Studies** (Accountancy; Finance; Human Resources; International Relations; Management; Marketing); **Design and Technology** (Automotive Engineering; Design; Electronic Engineering; Furniture Design; Information Technology; Interior Design; Mechanical Engineering; Mechanics; Technology); **Education and Training** (Preschool Education; Primary Education; Secondary Education; Teacher Training); **Health and Well-being** (Industrial and Organizational Psychology; Nursing; Psychology; Speech Therapy and Audiology)

History: Lessius was founded in 2010 as a merger of the former Lessius Hogeschool, Katholieke Hogeschool Mechelen (founded 1995) and Campus de Nayer of the Hogeschool voor Wetenschap en Kunst (founded 1995). Katholieke Hogeschool Mechelen and Campus De Nayer formed Lessius Mechelen, Lessius Hogeschool changed its name to Lessius Antwerp. Together they for Lessius.

Governing Bodies: Executive Board, Board of Management

Academic Year: September to June

Admission Requirements: Secondary school certificate or recognized foreign equivalent and good results in Dutch as a foreign language test

Fees: (Euros): c. 500 per annum

Main Language(s) of Instruction: Dutch

International Co-operation: Participates in the Socrates-Erasmus programme and other European programmes

Degrees and Diplomas: *Bachelor.* Applied Language Studies; Business Studies; Applied Psychology; Speech Therapy; Audiology; *Master.* Translation and Interpretation; Journalism; Multilingual Business Communication; Business Studies. Also Advanced Bachelors

Student Services: Academic counselling, Cultural centre, Employment services, Foreign student adviser, Handicapped facilities, Language programs, Social counselling, Sports facilities

Special Facilities: Study Centre: Digital Research Centre with Language Technology

Libraries: 5 libraries

Academic Staff *2010-2011*: Total 1,100
Student Numbers *2010-2011*: Total 10,000
Last Updated: 02/09/11

LEUVEN UNIVERSITY COLLEGE
Katholieke Hogeschool Leuven (KH LEUVEN)
Abdij van Park 9, Heverlee 3001
Tel: +32(16) 375-700
Fax: +32(16) 375-799
EMail: administratie@khleuven.be
Website: http://www.khleuven.be

Algemeen Directeur: Toon Martens
EMail: toon.martens@khleuven.be

Departments
Business Studies (Accountancy; Business Administration; Business and Commerce; Finance; Insurance; Management; Marketing; Secretarial Studies; Taxation); **Health Care and Technology** *(Rega)* (Biochemistry; Biology; Chemistry; Dietetics; Environmental Studies; Food Technology; Information Technology; Laboratory Techniques; Midwifery; Nursing; Nutrition; Pharmacy; Secretarial Studies; Technology); **Social Work** (Social Studies; Social Work; Welfare and Protective Services); **Teacher Training** *(Leuven and Diest)* (Education; Preschool Education; Primary Education; Secondary Education)

Further Information: Also Dutch language courses

History: Founded 1995, incorporating six existing Colleges of higher education.

Admission Requirements: Secondary school certificate (Flemish Certificate) or equivalent

Degrees and Diplomas: *Bachelor; Master.* Also Advanced Bachelor Degrees and Postgraduaat

Student Residential Facilities: Yes

Libraries: Campus Libraries
Last Updated: 01/09/11

LIMBURG CATHOLIC UNIVERSITY COLLEGE
Katholieke Hogeschool Limburg (KHLIM)
Agoralaan Gebouw B, Bus 1, Diepenbeek, Limburg 3590
Tel: +32(11) 23-07-70
Fax: +32(11) 23-07-89
EMail: informatie@ad.khlim.be
Website: http://www.khlim.be

Algemeen Directeur: Willy Indeherberge (2002-)
EMail: willy.indeherberge@ad.khlim.be

International Relations: Michaël Joris, International Development Manager
Tel: +32(11) 23-07-70, Fax: +32(11) 23-07-89
EMail: michael.joris@mail.khlim.be

Departments
Commercial Sciences and Business Administration *(HB, Diepenbeek)* (Accountancy; Business Administration; Business and Commerce; Marketing; Secretarial Studies; Taxation); **Health Care** *(GEZ, Hasselt)* (Health Sciences; Midwifery; Nursing); **Industrial Sciences and Technology** *(IWT, Diepenbeek)* (Automation and Control Engineering; Biochemistry; Chemical Engineering; Chemistry; Electrical Engineering; Energy Engineering; Industrial Engineering; Laboratory Techniques; Mechanical Engineering); **Media and Design Academy** *(MDa, Genk)* (Advertising and Publicity; Fine Arts; Graphic Design; Media Studies; Photography; Video); **Social Work** *(SAW, Hasselt)* (Social Work; Special Education); **Teacher Training** *(LER, Hasselt)* (Teacher Training)

History: Founded 1995, incorporating other existing institutes of higher education. A private university-level institution recognized by and receiving financial support from the State.

Governing Bodies: Board of Trustees

Academic Year: September to July (September-February; February-July)

Admission Requirements: Secondary school certificate

Fees: (Euros): 523 per annum

Main Language(s) of Instruction: Dutch

International Co-operation: With universities in Austria; Netherlands; Germany; France; United Kingdom; Spain; Portugal; Sweden; Denmark; Finland; Italy; Ireland; South Africa; Czech Republic; Poland; Slovenia. Also participates in Socrates/Tempus and in the Consortium Nord-Est

Accrediting Agencies: Nederlands Vlaamse Accreditering Organisatie (NVAO)

Degrees and Diplomas: *Bachelor; Master*

Student Services: Academic counselling, Canteen, Employment services, Foreign student adviser, Social counselling, Sports facilities

Libraries: Yes
Last Updated: 02/09/11

PLANTIJN UNIVERSITY COLLEGE
Plantijn Hogeschool
Lange Nieuwstraat 101, Antwerpen 52000
Tel: +32(3) 220 57 99
EMail: info@plantijn.be
Website: http://www.plantijn.be

Algemeen Directeur: Erwin Samson
EMail: Erwin.samson@plantijn.be

International Relations: Marleen Matyn, International Relations Manager
Tel: +32(32) 21-07-097, Fax: +32(32) 21-07-01
EMail: marleen.matyn@plantijn.be

Departments
Applied Sciences and Education (Biochemistry; Chemistry; Dietetics; Laboratory Techniques; Nutrition; Secondary Education;

Teacher Training); **Business Management** (Business Administration; Hotel and Restaurant; Hotel Management; Law; Management; Management Systems); **Communication Management** (Communication Studies; Journalism; Public Relations); **Science and Techniques** (Automation and Control Engineering; Electronic Engineering; Energy Engineering; Heating and Refrigeration; Industrial Design; Industrial Maintenance; Mechanical Engineering); **Socio-Educational Care Work** *(SECW)* (Social Studies; Social Welfare)

History: Founded 1995 by incorporating existing institutions.

Main Language(s) of Instruction: Dutch

Accrediting Agencies: Province of Antwerp

Degrees and Diplomas: *Bachelor*

Student Services: Academic counselling, Canteen, Employment services, Foreign student adviser, Handicapped facilities, Social counselling

Libraries: Central Library. Multimedia Centre

Publications: PLANTIJNnews *(monthly)*
Last Updated: 20/03/12

PROVINCIAL COLLEGE LIMBURG
Provinciale Hogeschool Limburg (PHL)
Elfde-Liniestraat 24, Hasselt 3500
Tel: +32(11) 23-88-88
Fax: +32(11) 23-88-89
EMail: phl@phl.be
Website: http://www.phl.be/

Algemeen Directeur: Ben Lambrechts
Tel: +32(11) 23-86-12 EMail: Ben.Lambrechts@phl.be

Departments
Architecture (Architecture; Interior Design); **Biotechnology** (Agricultural Management; Biotechnology); **Commmercial Sciences and Business Administration** (Accountancy; Business and Commerce; Commercial Law; Computer Science; Environmental Management; Finance; Insurance; Law; Marketing; Secretarial Studies; Taxation; Translation and Interpretation); **Health Care** (Midwifery; Nursing; Occupational Therapy; Physical Therapy); **Plastic Arts** (Advertising and Publicity; Ceramics and Glass Technology; Design; Fine Arts; Glass Art; Graphic Arts; Jewelry Art; Multimedia; Painting and Drawing; Sculpture; Visual Arts); **Teacher Training** (Teacher Training)

Further Information: Also programmes in English

History: Founded 1994.

Main Language(s) of Instruction: Dutch, English

International Co-operation: Participates in the Socrates, Leonardo, Tempus and Lingua programmes

Degrees and Diplomas: *Bachelor*; *Master*
Last Updated: 21/03/12

SINT-LUKAS BRUSSELS UNIVERSITY COLLEGE OF ART AND DESIGN
Hogeschool 'Sint-Lukas' Brussel
Paleizenstraat 70, Brussel 1030
Tel: +32(2) 250-11-00
Fax: +32(2) 250-11-11
EMail: info@sintlukas.be
Website: http://www.sintlukas.be

Directeur-generaal: Joannes Van Heddegem
EMail: joannes.vanheddegem@sintlukas.be

Director of Studies: Willem De Greef
EMail: willem.degreef@sintlukasbrussel.be

International Relations: Wim Aerts
EMail: walter.vervliet@sintlukas.be

Departments
Audiovisual Arts (Cinema and Television; Film; Video)

Programmes
Construction (Building Technologies; Construction Engineering); **Fine Arts** (Fine Arts; Graphic Arts; Painting and Drawing; Sculpture); **Graphic Design** (Design; Graphic Arts; Graphic Design);

Interior Design (Architecture; Interior Design); **Photography** (Photography)

History: Founded 1880 on the basis of a Roman Catholic neo-Gothic Art Philosophy. A private university-level institution. Acquired present status 1991.

Governing Bodies: Board of Governors

Admission Requirements: Entrance examination

Fees: (Euros): 513 per annum

Main Language(s) of Instruction: Dutch

International Co-operation: Participates in the Socrates programme

Degrees and Diplomas: *Bachelor*: Education; Commerce; Agriculture; Health and Rehabiliation; Social Work; Informatics (Professional Bachelor's Degree), 4 yrs; *Bachelor*: Visual Arts; Audio-Visual Arts (Academic Bacherlor' Degree), 3 yrs; *Master*: Visual Arts; Audio-Visual Arts, 1 yr. Also Advanced Master's Degree

Student Services: Canteen, Foreign student adviser, Foreign Studies Centre, Handicapped facilities, Social counselling

Special Facilities: Art Gallery

Libraries: Yes
Last Updated: 31/08/11

UNIVERSITY COLLEGE FOR SCIENCES AND ARTS
Hogeschool voor Wetenschap & Kunst (W&K)
Koningsstraat 328, Brussel 1030
Tel: +32(2) 250-15-11
Fax: +32(2) 218-58-39
EMail: info@wenk.be
Website: http://www.wenk.be

Algemeen Directeur: Maria De Smet
Tel: +32(2) 250-15-14, Fax: +32(2) 250-58-39
EMail: mds@directoraat.wenk.be

International Relations: Jan Dierick, Coordinator
Tel: +32(9) 221-12-11, Fax: +32(9) 221-12-68
EMail: jdierick@vlekho.wenk.be

Departments
Applied Linguistics *(Vlekho, Brussel)* (Modern Languages); **Architecture** *(Sint-Lucas Architectuur, Gent , Brussel)* (Architecture); **Business Administration** *(HONIM, Brussel)* (Business Administration; Business and Commerce); **Business Economics** *(Vlekho, Brussel)* (Economics); **Industrial Engineering** *(De Nayer Institut, Mechelen)* (Industrial Engineering); **Music, Performing Arts and Education** *(Lemmensinstituut, Leuven)* (Education; Music; Performing Arts; Theatre); **Technology** *(Narafi, Brussel)* (Cinema and Television; Photography; Technology); **Technology** *(De Nayer Institut, Mechelen)* (Technology); **Visual Arts** *(Sint-Lucas, Beeldende Kunst, Gent)* (Ceramic Art; Fine Arts; Glass Art; Graphic Design; Textile Design)

History: Founded 1995.

Main Language(s) of Instruction: Dutch

International Co-operation: With universities in the European Union, Mexico, Argentina, Brazil, Cuba, Switzerland, Czech Republic, Poland, USA, Japan and South Africa

Degrees and Diplomas: *Bachelor*: 3 yrs; *Master*: 1-2 yrs. Also Postgraduaten

Student Services: Academic counselling, Canteen, Language programs, Social counselling

Libraries: Specialized libraries
Last Updated: 21/03/12

UNIVERSITY COLLEGE GHENT
Hogeschool Gent (HOGENT)
Kortrijksesteenweg 14, Gent 9000
Tel: +32(9) 243-33-00
Fax: +32(9) 243-33-53
EMail: info@hogent.be
Website: http://www.hogent.be

Principal: Robert Hoogewijs (2004-)
Tel: +32(9) 243-33-02, Fax: +32(9) 243-33-53
EMail: bert.hoogewijs@hogent.be

Faculties

Applied Business (Accountancy; Business Administration; Environmental Management; Finance; Insurance; Marketing; Taxation); **Applied Business and ICT** *(Aalst)* (Business Administration; Information Technology); **Applied Engineering Sciences** (Chemical Engineering; Computer Engineering; Computer Science; Construction Engineering; Electronic Engineering; Mechanical Engineering; Textile Technology); **Bioscience and Landscape Architecture** (Agrobiology; Agronomy; Bioengineering; Biotechnology; Landscape Architecture); **Business Administration and Public Administration** (Business Administration; Public Administration); **Business Information and ICT** (Business Administration; Business Computing; Information Management); **Fine Arts** *(Royal Academy)* (Design; Interior Design; Visual Arts); **Health Care** (Biomedicine; Laboratory Techniques; Nursing; Occupational Therapy; Speech Therapy and Audiology); **Music** *(Royal Conservatory)* (Music); **Social Work and Welfare Studies** (Social Work; Welfare and Protective Services); **Teacher Training** (Preschool Education; Primary Education; Secondary Education); **Technology** (Chemistry; Electronic Engineering; Mechanics; Technology; Textile Technology; Wood Technology); **Translation Studies** (Applied Linguistics; Translation and Interpretation)

History: Founded 1995, incorporating 13 Hogescholen. A university-level institution. Merged with Mercator Hogeschool in 2001. Acquired current status and title 2003.

Academic Year: October to July (October-January; February-July)

Admission Requirements: Secondary school certificate (Diploma secundar onderwijs) or equivalent

Fees: (Euros): 540 per annum

Main Language(s) of Instruction: Dutch

International Co-operation: With institutions in all European countries (LLP, Interreg, EU Aid programmes); Russian Federation; China; South Africa; Congo; Vietnam; United States

Accrediting Agencies: Nederlands Vlaamse Accreditatie Organisatie (NVAO)

Degrees and Diplomas: *Bachelor:* Agriculture and Biotechnology; Applied Information Sciences; Bio-Medical Laboratory Technology; Chemistry; Education (Pre-School, Primary, Secondary); Electromechanics; Fashion Technology; Interior Design; Landscape and Garden Design (Professional Bachelor); Applied Language Studies; Audio-Visual Arts; Biotechnical Sciences; Commercial Sciences; Drama; Chemistry; Computer Sciences (Academic Bachelor); Construction; Electromechanics; Electronics/ICT; Textile Technology; Music; Business Administration; Public Administration; Visual Arts (Academic Bachelor); Nursing; Nutrition and Dietetics; Occupational Therapy; Office Management; Real Estate; Remedial Education; Social Work and Welfare Studies; Speech Therapy and Audiology; Textile Technology; Wood Technology (Professional Bachelor), 3 yrs; *Master:* Drama; Music; Art & Design; Audio-Visual Arts; Business Administration; Public Administration; Interpreting; Multilingual Communication; Translation; Agriculture; Horticulture; Food Industry; Biochemistry; Chemistry; Computer Science; Construction; Electromechanics; Electronics/ICT; Electrotechnology; Surveying; Textile Technology; Social Work; Nursing and Midwifery, 1 yr

Student Services: Academic counselling, Canteen, Employment services, Foreign student adviser, Handicapped facilities, Health services, Social counselling, Sports facilities

Student Residential Facilities: For 350 students

Special Facilities: Recording Studios; Art Gallery; Theatre/ Concert Hall(2)

Libraries: 162,000 vols. 500 periodical subscriptions
Last Updated: 31/08/11

UNIVERSITY COLLEGE OF WEST FLANDERS

Hogeschool West-Vlaanderen (HOWEST)
Marksesteenweg 58, Kortrijk 8500
Tel: +32(56) 24-12-90
Fax: +32(56) 24-12-92
EMail: info@howest.be
Website: http://www.howest.be

Algemeen Directeur: Lode De Geyter
EMail: lode.de.geyter@howest.be

International Relations: Frederik D'hulster
EMail: international.office@howest.be

Departments

Architecture; **Business Studies and Management** *(HIEPSO)* (Business Administration; Communication Arts; Computer Science; Journalism; Leisure Studies; Management; Management Systems; Telecommunications Services; Tourism); **Education** *(HPI, Brugge)* (Preschool Education; Primary Education; Secondary Education; Teacher Training); **Engineering and Technology** (Biochemistry; Chemistry; Communication Studies; Electronic Engineering; Environmental Studies; Industrial Design; Mechanical Engineering; Multimedia; Technology); **Medical Sciences** *(Simon Stevin, Sint-Michels)* (Biomedical Engineering; Nursing; Occupational Therapy); **Social Sciences** *(Vesalius-Hiss De Haan, Oostende)* (Psychology; Social Work)

Further Information: Intensive Dutch course for foreigners. International Semester in English: Digital Business Management (30 ECTS-Fall sem.); Multimedia Communication (30 ECTS -Spring sem). Also 5 Branches: Hiespo and PIH in Kortrijk; Simon Stevin and Leranopleiding in Brugge; Vesalius in Oostende.

History: Founded 1879 as technical institute, acquired present status and title 1977. A university-level provincial institution receiving financial support from the State. Merged and acquired present status 1995.

Governing Bodies: Board of Directors

Academic Year: September to September

Admission Requirements: Secondary school certificate

Fees: (Euros): 490 per annum

Main Language(s) of Instruction: Dutch (with some modules in English)

Accrediting Agencies: Ministry of Education and Training

Degrees and Diplomas: *Bachelor:* Architecture Assistant; Applied Computer Science; Business Management; Communication Management; Journalism; Network Economy; Office Management; Tourism and Leisure Management; Teacher Training (Nursery, Primary, Secondary); Biochemistry; Chemistry; Electromechanics; Electronics-ICT; Electrotechnology; Environmental Sciences; Industrial Design; Multimedia and Communication Technology; Biomedical Laboratory Technology; Nursing; Occupational Therapy; Social Work; Applied Psychology; *Master:* Architecture Assistant; Applied Computer Science; Business Management; Communication Management; Journalism; Network Economy; Office Management; Tourism and Leisure Management; Teacher Training (Nursery, Primary, Secondary); Biochemistry; Chemistry; Electromechanics; Electronics-ICT; Electrotechnology; Environmental Sciences; Industrial Design; Multimedia and Communication Technology; Biomedical Laboratory Technology; Nursing; Occupational Therapy; Social Work; Applied Psychology. Two international semesters are offered, taught in English.

Student Services: Academic counselling, Canteen, Employment services, Foreign student adviser, Handicapped facilities, Language programs, Social counselling

Student Residential Facilities: Yes

Libraries: Central Library
Last Updated: 23/01/12

UNIVERSITY OF ANTWERP

Universiteit Antwerpen (UA)
Prinsstraat, 13, Antwerpen BE-2000
Tel: +32(3) 220-41-11
Fax: +32(3) 220-44-20
EMail: stip@ua.ac.be
Website: http://www.ua.ac.be

Rector: Alain Verschoren EMail: alain.verschoren@ua.ac.be

International Relations: Piet Van Hove
Tel: +32(3) 220-46-27, Fax: +32(3) 220-41-42
EMail: international@ua.ac.be

Faculties

Applied Economics (Business Administration; Business and Commerce; Economic and Finance Policy; Information Sciences; Management Systems); **Arts and Philosophy** (History; Linguistics; Literature); **Law** (Commercial Law; European Union Law;

International Law; Law); **Medicine** (Medicine); **Pharmaceutical, Biomedical and Veterinary Sciences** (Biomedicine; Pharmacy; Veterinary Science); **Political and Social Sciences** (Communication Studies; Political Sciences; Sociology; Women's Studies); **Science** (Biochemistry; Biological and Life Sciences; Biology; Biotechnology; Chemistry; Computer Science; Environmental Studies; Mathematics; Physics)

Institutes
Development Policy and Management *(IDPM)* (Development Studies); **Transport and Maritime Management** (Transport and Communications)

Schools
Management *(UAMS)* (Business Administration; Management)

History: Founded 2003, incorporating Universitaire Instelling Antwerpen (UIA), Universitaire Faculteiten St. Ignatius te Antwerpen (UFSIA) and Universitair Centrum Antwerpen (RUCA).

Academic Year: September/October to June/July

Admission Requirements: Secondary school certificate or recognized equivalent

Fees: (Euros): 525 per annum

Main Language(s) of Instruction: Dutch, English

International Co-operation: Participates in the Socrates, Asia-Link, Tempus, Leonardo, Erasmus Mundus, Alfa programmes and exchanges as a member of the Utrecht Network

Degrees and Diplomas: *Bachelor; Master; Doctor.* by thesis

Student Services: Academic counselling, Canteen, Employment services, Foreign student adviser, Foreign Studies Centre, Handicapped facilities, Health services, Language programs, Social counselling, Sports facilities

Student Residential Facilities: Yes

Libraries: yes
Last Updated: 21/03/12

VLERICK LEUVEN-GENT MANAGEMENT SCHOOL

Vlerick Leuven-Gent Management School (VLGMS)
Reep 1, Gent 9000
Tel: +32(9) 210-97-11
Fax: +32(9) 210-97-00
EMail: info@vlerick.be
Website: http://www.vlerick.com

Dean: Philippe Haspeslagh (2008-)
Tel: +32(9) 210-97-34 EMail: philippe.haspeslagh@vlerick.be

Academic Dean: Dirk Buyens
Tel: +32(9) 210-97-22 EMail: dirk.buyens@vlerick.be

Director, Executive Education: Patrick De Greve
Tel: +32(9) 210-97-31 EMail: patrick.degreve@vlerick.be

International Relations: Peter Rafferty, Director, International Business Tel: +32(16) 32-35-87 EMail: peter.rafferty@vlerick.be

Divisions
Accounting and Finance (Accountancy; Finance); **Governance and Ethics** (Ethics; Government); **Human Resource Management** (Human Resources; Management); **Innovation and Entrepreneurship** (Management); **Marketing and Sales** (E-Business/Commerce; Marketing; Sales Techniques); **Organisational Behaviour** (Leadership; Management); **Specific Industries** (Industrial Arts Education); **Strategy**

Further Information: Also campuses in Leuven (Belgium) and St Petersburg (Russia)

History: Founded 1953. Acquired present status 1998. The management school of the Katholieke Universiteit Leuven and Ghent University.

Governing Bodies: General Council, Board of Directors, Alumni Association

Academic Year: September to July

Admission Requirements: University degree; GMAT; TOEFL

Fees: (Euros): Full-time MBA, 24,500 per annum; Masters, 7,500-8,750 per annum

Main Language(s) of Instruction: English

International Co-operation: With universities in United Kingdom, Spain, Russian Federation

Accrediting Agencies: EQUIS, AACSB, AMBA, Flemish Government

Degrees and Diplomas: *Master.* Business Administration (MBA), 1 yr (full time) 2 yrs (part time) following first degree; *Master.* General Management; Marketing Management; Financial Management, 1 yr. Also Executive Masters, and long- and short-education executive training programmes.

Student Services: Academic counselling, Canteen, Employment services, Foreign student adviser, Foreign Studies Centre, Handicapped facilities, Social counselling

Libraries: On-campus library and access to the libraries of the partner universities Ghent University and Katholieke Universiteit Leuven
Last Updated: 21/03/12

XIOS UNIVERSITY COLLEGE LIMBURG

XIOS Hogeschool Limburg (HL)
Universitaire Campus, Gebouw H, Diepenbeek 3590
Tel: +32(11) 26-00-46
Fax: +32(11) 26-00-55
EMail: info@xios.be
Website: http://www.xios.be

Algemeen Directeur: Dirk Franco EMail: dirk.franco@xios.be

International Relations: Kristien Bauwens, International Coordinator EMail: kristien.bauwens@xios.be

Departments
Commercial and Business Management *(Campus Hasselt & Diepenbeek)* (Business Administration; Business and Commerce; Computer Science; Journalism; Leisure Studies; Secretarial Studies; Tourism); **Industrial Science and Technology Engineering** (Computer Graphics; Construction Engineering; Electronic Engineering; Industrial Engineering; Mechanical Engineering; Mechanics; Nuclear Engineering; Packaging Technology); **Social Studies** *(Campus Hasselt)* (Social Work); **Teacher Training** *(Campus Hasselt)* (Physical Education; Preschool Education; Primary Education; Secondary Education; Special Education; Teacher Training)

History: Founded 1995, incorporating four Hogescholen in the Hasselt region.

Academic Year: September to July (September - January; February - July)

Admission Requirements: Recognised certificate of secondary education.

Main Language(s) of Instruction: Dutch, some tutoring in English

International Co-operation: Participates in the Erasmus programme

Degrees and Diplomas: *Bachelor.* Industrial Sciences (Construction Engineering/Electro-Mechanics Engineering/Electronics-ICT Engineering); Nuclear Engineering; Packaging Engineering (Academic Bachelor's Degree); Social Work; Business Management; Tourism & Leisure Management; Communication Management; Journalism; Office Management; Applied Computer Studies; Teacher Training (Nursery/Primary/Secondary); Electronics-ICT; Electro-Mechanics (Professional Bachelor's Degree), 3 yrs (180 ECTs); *Bachelor.* Journalism; Teacher Training (Special Education/Primary Education); *Master.* Project Management; *Master.* Tourism, 1 yr (60 ECTs). Also other postgraduate and training programmes.

Student Services: Academic counselling, Canteen, Employment services, Health services, Social counselling
Last Updated: 02/09/11

Belgium - French Community

STRUCTURE OF HIGHER EDUCATION SYSTEM

Description:

Higher education is established on a binary scheme: university education and non-university education. University education offers long-cycle education only. The non-university higher education institutions are Hautes Ecoles and Ecoles supérieures des Arts. The Hautes Ecoles and Ecoles supérieures des Arts can offer both long and short cycle studies. The short cycle of non-university education offers technical training leading to a professional qualification in a specific field. The long cycle of both non-university and university education provides general, theoretical and scientific studies at the undergraduate level that lead to specialized graduate studies at the end of which students have to present and defend a personal work (a short thesis, for example).

Stages of studies:

University level first stage: *Bachelier*
The first stage of university level studies is offered at Universities, Hautes Ecoles, and Ecoles supérieures des Arts. It leads to the title of Bachelier after three years' study and 180 ECTS credits.

University level second stage: *Master; Médecin; Médecin vétérinaire*
The second stage of university-level studies is offered at Universities, Hautes Ecoles, and Ecoles supérieures des Arts. It leads to the title of Master after one or two years' study and 60 or 120 ECTS credits; of Médecin (Medicine) after four years' study and 240 ECTS credits; and of Médecin vétérinaire (Veterinary Medicine) after three years' study and 180 ECTS credits.

University level third stage: *Doctorat*
The third stage of university-level studies is offered at universities. Doctoral training lasts for 3 years corresponding to 180 ECTS.

ADMISSION TO HIGHER EDUCATION

Admission to university-level studies:

Name of secondary school credential required: Certificat d'Enseignement secondaire supérieur

For entry to: All institutions

Alternatives to credentials: Attestation of success in one of the admissions examinations organised by the higher education institutions or a jury of the French Community - Academic title conferred by a higher education or university institution and in some cases by social promotion institutions.

Numerus clausus/restrictions: Restriction for access to certain second cycle studies in the health sector. Special entrance examination for access to civil engineering studies.

Foreign students admission:

Definition of foreign student: A foreign student is a person enrolled at a higher education institution in Belgium (French-speaking Community) who is not a permanent resident.

Quotas: Certain students from countries that are not members of the European Union cannot be financed and may see their admission refused by the institutions.

Entrance exam requirements: Students must obtain the equivalence of their secondary school leaving certificate with either the Certificat d'enseignement secondaire supérieur (CESS) or, as the case may be, the Diplôme belge d'aptitude permettant d'accéder à l'enseignement supérieur (DAES).

Entry regulations: Students must register with the communal administration of their town of residence, present proof of their enrolment, as well as financial guarantees.

Language requirements: There are language examinations at the institutional level. Courses are organized by the universities during the summer.

RECOGNITION OF STUDIES

Quality assurance system:

The Agency for the Evaluation of the Quality of Higher Education is an independent public sector agency, practising formative evaluation based on a dialogue between all stakeholders within the French Community. The Agency autonomously develops its procedures used for assessing the quality of teaching in bachelor and masters programmes in the institutions authorised by the French Community.

Bodies dealing with recognition:

Centre NARIC
Attaché: Kevin Guillaume
: Nadia Lahlou
Rue Lavallée, 1
Brussels 1080
Belgium
Fax: +32 2 690 8760
WWW: http://www.enseignement.be/index.php?page=24808&navi=2087

Agence pour l'Evaluation de la Qualité de l'Enseignement Supérieur
Rue Adolphe Lavallée, 1
Brussels 1080
Belgium
WWW: http://www.aeqes.be/

NATIONAL BODIES

Administration générale de l'Enseignement et de la Recherche scientifique (Directorate General for Education and Scientific Research)
Minister, Higher Education: Jean-Claude Marcourt
Ministère de la Fédération Wallonie-Bruxelles
Boulevard du Jardin botanique 20-22
Brussels 1000
Belgium
Tel: +32 2 690 8100
Fax: +32 2 690 8239
EMail: info@enseignement.be
WWW: http://www.enseignement.be

Conseil interuniversitaire de la Communauté française - CIUF
President: Bruno Delvaux
Permanent Secretary: Claude Lalout
Rue d'Egmont, 5
Bruxelles 1000
Belgium
Tel: +32 2 504 9291
Fax: +32 2 502 2768
EMail: secretariat@ciuf.be
WWW: http://www.ciuf.be

Conseil général des Hautes Ecoles - CGHE
President: Pierre Lambert
Secretary: Michèle Lhermitte
Rue Lavallée, 1
Bruxelles 1080
Belgium
Tel: +32 2 690 8853
Fax: +32 2 690 8846
EMail: cghe@cfwb.be

WWW: http://www.cghe.cfwb.be/
Role of national body: Consultation on issues relating to the Hautes Ecoles

Agence pour l'Evaluation de la Qualité de l'Enseignement Supérieur
President: Marianne Coessens
Rue Adolphe Lavallée, 1
Brussels 1080
Belgium
WWW: http://www.aeqes.be/

Conseil des Recteurs des Universités francophones de Belgique - CREF (Rectors' Council)
President: Didier Viviers
Rue d'Egmont, 5
Bruxelles 1000
Belgium
Fax: +32 2 504 9343
EMail: elisabeth.kokkelkoren@cref.be
WWW: http://www.cref.be

Data for academic year: 2011-2012
Source: IAU from the website of the Directorate General for Education and Scientific Research, 2011

INSTITUTIONS

ACADÉMIE DES BEAUX-ARTS DE TOURNAI
Rue de l'Hôpital Notre-Dame, 14, Tournai 7500
Tel: +32(69) 84-12-63
Fax: +32(69) 84-32-53
EMail: info@actournai.be
Website: http://www.actournai.be

Directeur: Bernard Bay
International Relations: Patrick Winberg

Programmes
Graphic and Visual Arts *(long cycle)* (Graphic Arts; Visual Arts);
Plastic and Applied Arts *(long cycle)* (Fine Arts; Furniture Design; Painting and Drawing)
History: Founded 1757 as Académie royale des Beaux-Arts et des Arts décoratifs de Tournai.
Admission Requirements: Baccalauréat and entrance examination
Main Language(s) of Instruction: French
International Co-operation: With institutions in Morocco. Also participates in Erasmus
Degrees and Diplomas: *Bachelier*: 3 yrs; *Master*
Student Services: Cultural centre, Foreign student adviser, Social counselling
Student Residential Facilities: Yes
Libraries: Yes
Last Updated: 01/09/11

ACADÉMIE ROYALE DES BEAUX-ARTS DE LA VILLE DE BRUXELLES - ÉCOLE SUPÉRIEURE DES ARTS (ARBA-ESA)
144 Rue du Midi, Bruxelles 1000
Tel: + 32(2) 506 10 10
Fax: +32(2) 506 10 28
EMail: info@arba-esa.be
Website: http://www.arba-esa.be

Directeur: Marc Partouche
Tel: +32(2) 511-04-91 EMail: direction@arba-esa.be

Programmes
Plastic Arts, Visual Arts and Graphic Arts (Architectural and Environmental Design; Communication Arts; Engraving; Fine Arts; Graphic Arts; Interior Design; Painting and Drawing; Photography; Sculpture; Textile Design; Visual Arts; Weaving)
History: Founded 1711, acquired present status 1980.
Governing Bodies: Conseil de Gestion pédagogique
Academic Year: September to June
Admission Requirements: Secondary school certificate or foreign equivalent and entrance examination
Main Language(s) of Instruction: French
International Co-operation: Participates in the Erasmus/Socrates programme
Degrees and Diplomas: Bachelor 3 yrs; Master 1 yr and Master à finalité (3 options: Master approfondi (préparation au doctorat), Master didactique, Master spécialisé)
Student Services: Canteen, Foreign student adviser, Social counselling
Special Facilities: Art Gallery
Libraries: Academy Library
Publications: La Part de l'Oeil *(annually)*
Last Updated: 01/09/11

CATHOLIC UNIVERSITY OF LOUVAIN
Université catholique de Louvain (UCL)
Place de l'Université, 1, Louvain-la-Neuve 1348
Tel: +32(10) 47-81-03
Fax: +32(10) 47-25-31
EMail: accueil-dic@uclouvain.be
Website: http://www.uclouvain.be

Recteur: Bruno Delvaux (2009-)
Tel: +32(10) 47-88-05, Fax: +32(10) 47-38-03
EMail: Rectorat@uclouvain.be

Administrateur général: Dominique Opfergelt
Tel: +32(10) 47-88-25, Fax: +32(10) 47-40-43
EMail: Dominique.Opfergelt@uclouvain.be

International Relations: Christian Duqué (2009-)
Tel: +32(10) 47-30-95, Fax: +32(10) 47-40-75
EMail: Christian.Duque@uclouvain.be

Faculties
Architecture, Architectural Engineering and Urban Planning (Architecture; Regional Planning; Structural Architecture; Town Planning); **Biological, Agricultural and Environmental Engineering** (Agronomy; Biological and Life Sciences; Environmental Engineering); **Economic, Social and Political Sciences and Communication** (Business Administration; Communication Studies; Demography and Population; Development Studies; Economics; Political Sciences; Social Sciences); **Law and Criminology** (Criminal Law; Criminology; Law); **Medicine and Dentistry** *(Brussels)* (Biomedicine; Dentistry; Medicine; Pharmacy; Public Health); **Motor Science** (Physical Education; Physical Therapy; Rehabilitation and Therapy); **Pharmacy and Biomedical Sciences** (Biomedicine; Pharmacy); **Philosophy, Arts and Letters** (Ancient Civilizations; Archaeology; Art History; Arts and Humanities; Chinese; Classical Languages; Communication Studies; Cultural Studies; Dutch; English; French; German; Greek; History; Information Technology; Italian; Latin; Linguistics; Literature; Medieval Studies; Modern Languages; Musicology; Oriental Languages; Performing Arts; Philosophy; Romance Languages); **Psychology and Educational Sciences** (Education; Educational Psychology; Family Studies; Psychology); **Public Health** (Public Health); **Science** (Biology; Chemistry; Geography; Mathematics; Natural Sciences; Physics); **Theology** (Canon Law; Theology)

Schools
Engineering (Architecture; Civil Engineering; Computer Engineering; Electrical Engineering; Environmental Engineering; Materials Engineering; Mechanical Engineering; Town Planning); **Management** *(Louvain)*

Further Information: Also Research Centres and Institutes (http://www.uclouvain.be/secteurs.html)

History: Founded 1425, UCL is one of the oldest universities in the world. Erasmus, Jansenius, Vesalius, Mercator, Georges Lemaître worked or taught at the UCL. In 1970, separation into two distinct universities, the Flemish-speaking one remained on the original site in Leuven. The French-speaking University moved to Wallonia (Louvain-la-Neuve). The faculty of Medicine moved to Brussels.

Governing Bodies: Conseil d'Administration; Conseil académique

Academic Year: September to July (September-February; February-July)

Admission Requirements: Secondary school certificate and entrance examination, or foreign qualifications if recognized under agreement concluded with the Belgian Government. Other foreign qualifications subject to the approval of the faculty concerned

Main Language(s) of Instruction: French

International Co-operation: With universities in Africa, Asia, Latin America and USA. Also more than 50 agreements with European universities

Degrees and Diplomas: *Bachelier*, *Master*. Agricultural Bioengineering; Chemical Bioengineernig; Environmental Bioengineering; Environmental Management; Electrical Engineering; Mechanical Engineering; Computer Engineering; Construction Engineering; Engineering and Applied Mathematics; Chemical and Materials Engineering; European Studies; Statistics; Biostatistics; Actuarial Sciences; History; History of Art and Archaeology; French and Roman Language and Literature: French as a second Language; Ancient and Modern Languages and Literature; Modern Languages and Literature; Ancient Languages and Literature; Information and Communication; Employment Studies; Human Resources Management; Human Population and Development; Sociology; Anthropology; Political Sciences; Public Administration; Economics; Management; Business Engineering; Law; Criminology; Mathematics; Physics; Biochemistry and Molecular and Cell Biology; Biology; Biology of Organisms and Ecology; Chemistry; Geography; Medicine; Biomedicine; Dentistry; Pharmacy; Motor Skills (General and Physical Education); Physiotherapy and Readaptation; Public Health; Multilingual Communication; Information Technology and Communication; Performing Arts; Linguistics; Philosophy; Ethics; Physical Engineering; Electro-Mechanical Engineering; Biomedical Engineering; Architectural Engineering; Computer Sciences; Psychology; Education; Speech Therapy; Family and Sexuality Studies; Theology; Bible Studies; Religious Studies; *Doctorat*

Student Services: Academic counselling, Employment services, Foreign student adviser

Student Residential Facilities: Yes

Special Facilities: Art Museum; Archaeology Museum; History of Medicine Museum

Libraries: Total, c. 2m. Vols, 5,000 current and 15,000 electronic periodicals, 90 databases - UCL's library portal: www.bib.ucl.ac.be

Publications: La Lucarne, http://www.saintluc.be/news/lucarne/lucarne-001.pdf; Louvain medical, http://www.md.ucl.ac.be/loumed/index.125-09.html; Revue Louvain, General Information magazine *(bimonthly)*

Press or Publishing House: Presses universitaires de Louvain
Last Updated: 08/09/11

CATHOLIC UNIVERSITY OF MONS
Université catholique de Mons (UCM)
151 Chaussée de Binche, Mons 7000
Tel: +32(65) 32-32-11
Fax: +32(65) 31-56-91
EMail: secretariat.etudes@fucam.ac.be
Website: http://www.fucam.ac.be

Recteur: Bart Jourquin
Tel: +32(65) 32-33-18, Fax: +32(65) 32-33-05
EMail: rectorat@fucam.ac.be

Vice-Recteur: Dominique Helbois EMail: vicerectorat@fucam.ac.be

Departments
Management (Management); **Political, Social and Communication Sciences** (Arts and Humanities; Communication Studies; Political Sciences; Social Sciences)

History: Founded 1896 and recognized by the State 1899. Granted legal status as higher education institution 1921, institut supérieur 1934, and University 1965. Acquired present title 2011.

Governing Bodies: Board

Academic Year: September to June (September-December; January-May)

Admission Requirements: Secondary school certificate in relevant fields or recognized equivalent and compulsory French as a foreign language test for non-French-speaking students

Main Language(s) of Instruction: French

Degrees and Diplomas: *Bachelier*, *Master*. Management; Business Engineering; Political Science; Public Administration; International Relations (M.Phil), 2 yrs; *Doctorat*. Economics; Management; Social and Political Science

Student Services: Canteen, Employment services, Handicapped facilities, Social counselling

Student Residential Facilities: Yes

Libraries: c. 18,030 vols; 235 magazines

Publications:
Last Updated: 02/09/11

CONSERVATOIRE ROYAL DE BRUXELLES
Rue de la Régence, 30, Bruxelles 1000
Tel: +32(2) 511-04-27
Fax: +32(2) 512-69-79
EMail: info@conservatoire.be
Website: http://www.conservatoire.be
Directeur: Frédéric de Roos

Programmes
Music (Conducting; Music; Music Theory and Composition; Musical Instruments; Singing; Theatre); **Theatre** (Speech Studies; Theatre)

History: Founded 1832 as Conservatoire royal de Musique de Bruxelles.

Main Language(s) of Instruction: French

Degrees and Diplomas: *Bachelier*, *Master*
Last Updated: 01/09/11

CONSERVATOIRE ROYAL DE LIÈGE

Boulevard Piercot, 29, Liège 4000
Tel: +32(4) 222-03-06
Fax: +32(4) 222-03-84
EMail: info@crlg.be
Website: http://www.crlg.be

Directeur: Bernard Dekaise EMail: direction@crlg.be

Programmes
Music (Conducting; Music; Music Theory and Composition; Musical Instruments; Singing; Theatre); **Theatre** (Speech Studies; Theatre)

History: Founded 1826 as Conservatoire royal de Musique de Liège.

Main Language(s) of Instruction: French

Degrees and Diplomas: *Bachelier*, *Master*. Specialised Master

Libraries: Yes
Last Updated: 01/09/11

CONSERVATOIRE ROYAL DE MONS

Rue de Nimy, 7, Mons 7000
Tel: +32(65) 34-73-77
Fax: +32(65) 34-99-06
EMail: info@conservatoire-mons.be
Website: http://www.conservatoire-mons.be/

Directeur: André Foulon

Programmes
Music (Conducting; Music; Music Theory and Composition; Musical Instruments; Singing; Theatre); **Theatre** (Acting; Theatre)

History: Founded as Conservatoire royal de Musique de Mons.

Main Language(s) of Instruction: French

Degrees and Diplomas: *Bachelier*, *Master*
Last Updated: 01/09/11

ÉCOLE NATIONALE SUPÉRIEURE DES ARTS VISUELS DE LA CAMBRE

Abbaye de La Cambre, 21, Bruxelles 1000
Tel: +32(2) 626-17-80
Fax: +32(2) 640-96-93
EMail: lacambre@lacambre.be
Website: http://www.lacambre.be

Directeur: Caroline Mierop

Divisions
Fine Arts *(long cycle)* (Ceramic Art; Display and Stage Design; Engraving; Fashion Design; Film; Furniture Design; Graphic Arts; Graphic Design; Industrial Design; Painting and Drawing; Photography; Printing and Printmaking; Publishing and Book Trade; Restoration of Works of Art; Sculpture; Video; Visual Arts)

History: Founded 1927.

Degrees and Diplomas: *Bachelier*, *Master*

Libraries: Yes
Last Updated: 19/05/11

ÉCOLE SUPÉRIEURE DES ARTS DE LA VILLE DE LIÈGE

Rue des Anglais, 21, Liège 4000
Tel: +32(4) 221-70-70
Fax: +32(4) 221-38-20
EMail: arba.liege@sup.cfwb.be
Website: http://www.acasupliege.be

Directeur: Daniel Sluse

Programmes
Graphic and Visual Arts *(long cycle)* (Advertising and Publicity; Engraving; Graphic Arts; Painting and Drawing; Sculpture; Video; Visual Arts)

History: Founded 1775 as Académie royale des Beaux-Arts de Liège.

Admission Requirements: Secondary school certificate (Baccalauréat)

Main Language(s) of Instruction: French

International Co-operation: Participates in Erasmus

Degrees and Diplomas: *Bachelier*, *Master*

Student Services: Academic counselling, Canteen, Foreign student adviser, Social counselling

Special Facilities: Art Gallery

Libraries: Yes
Last Updated: 21/03/12

ÉCOLE SUPÉRIEURE DES ARTS - ÉCOLE DE RECHERCHE GRAPHIQUE (ERG)

Rue du Page, 87, Bruxelles 1050
Tel: +32(2) 538-98-29
Fax: +32(2) 539-33-93
EMail: kelly.josse@erg.be
Website: http://www.erg.be

Directrice: Corinne Diserens

Divisions
Graphic and Visual Arts *(long cycle)* (Film; Graphic Arts; Painting and Drawing; Performing Arts; Photography; Sculpture; Video; Visual Arts)

History: Founded as Institut supérieur libre des Arts plastiques - Ecole de Recherche graphique. Erg is associated to Instituts Saint-Luc.

Main Language(s) of Instruction: French

Degrees and Diplomas: *Bachelier*. 3 yrs; *Master*. 4 yrs. Also Master a finalité 60 credits (5yrs)
Last Updated: 01/09/11

ÉCOLE SUPÉRIEURE DES ARTS PLASTIQUES ET VISUELS DE LA COMMUNAUTÉ FRANÇAISE (ESAPV)

Rue des Soeurs Noires, 4A, Mons, Hainaut 7000
Tel: +32(65) 39-47-60
Fax: +32(65) 39-47-61
EMail: esapv.mons@esapv.be
Website: http://www.esapv.be

Directeur: Jean-Pierre Benon EMail: jeanpierre.benon@esapv.be

Administrateur-Secrétaire: Christophe Horlin
Tel: +32(65) 39-47-66 EMail: ch.horlin@esapv.be

Divisions
Fine Arts *(long cycle)* (Engraving; Fine Arts; Furniture Design; Interior Design; Multimedia; Painting and Drawing; Sculpture; Visual Arts)

History: Founded 1976.

Admission Requirements: Secondary school certificate and artistic examination

Fees: (Euros): 310-400

Main Language(s) of Instruction: French

International Co-operation: With universities in Portugal, Spain, Finland and Italy. Also participates in the Erasmus and Socrates programmes

Accrediting Agencies: Communauté française de Belgique

Degrees and Diplomas: *Bachelier*, *Master*. Also Agrégation de l'enseignement secondaire supérieur

Student Services: Canteen, Foreign student adviser, Nursery care, Social counselling

Special Facilities: Audiovisual Laboratory

Libraries: c. 5,500 vols
Last Updated: 21/03/12

ÉCOLE SUPÉRIEURE DES ARTS SAINT-LUC DE BRUXELLES (ESA)

Rue d'Irlande, 57, Bruxelles 1060
Tel: +32(2) 537-08-70
Fax: +32(2) 537-00-63
EMail: info@stluc-bruxelles-esa.be
Website: http://www.stluc-bruxelles-esa.be/

Directrice: Françoise Klein EMail: f.klein@brutele.be

Directeur Adjoint: Marc Streker EMail: m.streker@brutele.be

Courses

Advertising and Publicity (Advertising and Publicity); **Architectural and Planning** (Architecture; Architecture and Planning); **Architecture** (Architecture); **Comics** (Painting and Drawing); **Computer Graphics** (Computer Graphics); **Interior Architecture**; **Interior Design** (Interior Design)

History: Founded 1863 as Institut Saint-Luc.

Main Language(s) of Instruction: French

Degrees and Diplomas: *Bachelier.* 3 yrs; *Master*

Last Updated: 01/09/11

ÉCOLE SUPÉRIEURE DES ARTS SAINT-LUC DE LIÈGE

Boulevard de la Constitution, 41, Liège 4020
Tel: +32(4) 341-80-00
Fax: +32(4) 341-80-80
EMail: beaux-arts@stluc.com
Website: http://www.saintluc-liege.be

Directeur: Eric Van den Berg

Programmes

Plastic Arts (Advertising and Publicity; Fine Arts; Graphic Arts; Industrial Design; Interior Design; Painting and Drawing; Photography; Restoration of Works of Art; Sculpture)

History: Founded as Institut supérieur des Beaux-Arts 'Saint-Luc'.

Main Language(s) of Instruction: French

Degrees and Diplomas: *Bachelier, Master*

Libraries: Yes

Last Updated: 21/03/12

HAUTE ECOLE CHARLEMAGNE

Rue des Rivageois, 6, Liège B4000
Tel: +32(4) 254-76-11
Fax: +32(4) 253-39-15
EMail: secr.presidence@hech.be
Website: http://www.hech.be

Directrice-Présidente: Corine Matillard
Tel: +32(4) 254-76-14 EMail: corine.matillard@hecharlemagne.be

International Relations: Jean Chapelle
Tel: +32(4) 254-76-04, Fax: +32(4) 254-76-03
EMail: relinter@hech.be

Departments

Agronomy *(Huy - Gembloux)* (Agricultural Engineering; Agronomy; Horticulture; Landscape Architecture); **Economics** *(Huy)* (Economics; Hotel Management; Real Estate; Tourism; Transport Management); **Paramedical Sciences** *(Liège-Sart Tilman)* (Biomedicine; Chemistry); **Pedagogy** *(Verviers, Liège)* (Biology; Chemistry; Economics; Ethics; French; Geography; Germanic Languages; History; Physical Education; Physics; Social Sciences; Teacher Training); **Technology** *(Gembloux; Sart Tilman)* (Biology; Chemistry; Electronic Engineering; Engineering; Industrial Engineering; Materials Engineering; Mathematics; Packaging Technology; Statistics)

History: Founded 1878. Acquired present status and title 1996.

Governing Bodies: College de Direction; Conseil d'Administration

Academic Year: September to July

Admission Requirements: Secondary school certificate or recognized equivalent for foreigners

Fees: (Euros): 250-2,500 per annum

Main Language(s) of Instruction: French

International Co-operation: With universities in France, Spain, Portugal, Greece, Hungary, Italy, Netherlands, United Kingdom, Finland, Ireland, Turkey, Cyprus, Canada. Participates in Erasmus, Leonardo, Comenius and Tempus programmes

Degrees and Diplomas: *Bachelier.* Agronomy, Business, Paramedical, Education; Preschool education; Primary education, 3 yrs; *Master.* Agronomy; Industrial Engineering; Landscape Architecture, 5 yrs

Student Services: Academic counselling, Canteen, Employment services, Foreign student adviser, Language programs, Social counselling, Sports facilities

Student Residential Facilities: Yes, in Liège and Huy.

Special Facilities: Language Laboratory; Computer Centre

Libraries: Media Center

Publications: Bulletin International Charlemagne *(3 per annum)*

Last Updated: 05/09/11

HAUTE ECOLE DE BRUXELLES (HEB)

Chaussée de Waterloo, 749, Bruxelles 1180
Tel: +32(2) 340-12-95
Fax: +32(2) 347-52-64
EMail: heb@heb.be
Website: http://www.heb.be

Directrice-Présidente: Marianne Coessens
EMail: mcoessens@heb.be

International Relations: Jean Gomez, Head, International Office
Tel: +32(2) 340-12-80, Fax: +32(2) 346-21-34
EMail: jgomez@heb.be

Institutes

Pedagogy *(Institut pédagogique Defré)* (Pedagogy); **Translation and Interpretation** *(Institut supérieur de Traducteurs et Interprètes)* (Translation and Interpretation)

Schools

Computer Science *(Ecole supérieure d'Informatique)* (Business Computing; Computer Networks; Computer Science; Telecommunications Engineering)

History: Founded 1996, incorporating existing institutions.

Admission Requirements: Secondary school certificate

Fees: (Euros): 322 per annum

Main Language(s) of Instruction: French

International Co-operation: Participates in Erasmus

Degrees and Diplomas: *Bachelier, Master, Doctorat*

Student Services: Language programs, Social counselling

Publications: Equivalences, Translation *(annually)*

Last Updated: 05/09/11

HAUTE ECOLE DE LA COMMUNAUTÉ FRANÇAISE DU LUXEMBOURG SCHUMAN (HERS)

Avenue de Luxembourg, 101, Arlon B-6700
Tel: +32(63) 41-00-00
Fax: +32(63) 41-00-13
EMail: cel.adm@hers.be
Website: http://www.hers.be

Directeur-Président: Marc Fourny
Tel: +32(63) 41-00-01 EMail: dp@hers.be

Departments

Economics and Paramedical Sciences *(Libramont)* (Accountancy; Biomedicine; Business Computing; Computer Science; Neurology; Nursing; Pathology; Physical Therapy; Physiology; Secretarial Studies; Speech Therapy and Audiology); **Pedagogy** *(Virton)* (Arts and Humanities; Economics; Ethics; French; Germanic Languages; Mathematics; Natural Sciences; Physical Education; Preschool Education; Primary Education); **Technical** *(Arlon)* (Building Technologies; Chemistry; Construction Engineering; Electronic Engineering; Industrial Engineering; Mechanical Engineering; Wood Technology)

Admission Requirements: Secondary school certificate

Main Language(s) of Instruction: French

Degrees and Diplomas: *Bachelier, Master.* Also Agrégé de l'enseignement secondaire inférieur

Last Updated: 05/09/11

HAUTE ECOLE DE LA COMMUNAUTÉ FRANÇAISE EN HAINAUT (HECFH)

Rue Pierre-Joseph Duménil, 4, Mons 7000
Tel: +32(65) 34-79-83
Fax: +32(65) 39-45-25
EMail: directeur-president@hecfh.be
Website: http://www.hecfh.be

Directeur-Président: Denis Dufrane

Institutes

Economics *(Institut supérieur économique de Tournai)* (Economics; Law; Secretarial Studies; Tourism); **Industrial** *(Institut supérieur industriel à Mons)* (Chemical Engineering; Computer Engineering; Computer Graphics; Construction Engineering; Electronic Engineering; Industrial Engineering)

Programmes

Pedagogy *(Institut supérieur d'Enseignement pédagogique)* (Arts and Humanities; Economics; Education; Educational Technology; Fine Arts; French; Germanic Languages; Mathematics; Natural Sciences; Pedagogy; Preschool Education; Primary Education; Special Education; Teacher Training)

Schools

Social Studies *(Ecole sociale de Mons)* (Social Studies)

Degrees and Diplomas: *Bachelier; Master*

Student Services: Academic counselling, Social counselling

Special Facilities: Computer Lab

Libraries: Yes
Last Updated: 05/09/11

HAUTE ECOLE DE LA COMMUNAUTÉ FRANÇAISE PAUL-HENRI SPAAK (HEPHS)

Rue Royale, 150, Bruxelles 1000
Tel: +32(2) 227-35-01
Fax: +32(2) 227-35-22
EMail: contact@he-spaak.be
Website: http://www.he-spaak.be

Directeur-Président: François Debast **EMail:** debast@isib.be

Institutes

Economics *(Institut supérieur d'Etudes économiques)* (Economics; Law; Secretarial Studies); **Ergotherapy and Physical Therapy** *(Institut d'Enseignement supérieur d'Ergothérapie et de Kinésithérapie)* (Occupational Therapy; Physical Therapy); **Industry** *(Institut Supérieur Industriel de Bruxelles)* (Aeronautical and Aerospace Engineering; Chemistry; Computer Science; Electrical Engineering; Electronic Engineering; Industrial Engineering; Mechanical Engineering; Nuclear Engineering; Physical Engineering); **Pedagogy** *(Institut d'Enseignement supérieur pédagogique)* (Biology; Chemistry; Economics; Geography; History; Literature; Mathematics; Modern Languages; Physical Education; Physics; Social Sciences; Teacher Training); **Social Work, Library and Documentation Sciences** *(Institut d'Enseignement supérieur social des Sciences de l'Information et de la Documentation)* (Documentation Techniques; Library Science; Social Work)

History: Founded 1996.

Governing Bodies: Administrative Board; Council of Directors

Academic Year: September to July (September-February, February-July)

Admission Requirements: Secondary school certificate (Certificat d'Enseignement secondaire supérieur)

Fees: (Euros): c. 150-520 per annum

Main Language(s) of Instruction: French

International Co-operation: Participates in the Socrates, Erasmus, ODL, Leonardo, Tempus and Alfa programmes

Degrees and Diplomas: *Bachelier.* 3 yrs; *Master.* 3+1 yrs. Also Spécialisation 1 yr

Student Services: Academic counselling, Employment services, Language programs, Social counselling
Last Updated: 23/01/12

HAUTE ECOLE DE LA PROVINCE DE LIÈGE

Avenue Montesquieu, 6, Jemeppe-sur-Meuse 4101
Tel: +32(4) 237-96-01
Fax: +32(4) 237-95-51
EMail: epl@provincedeliege.be
Website: http://haute-ecole.provincedeliege.be/

Directeur-Président: Toni Bastianelli
Tel: +32(4) 237-96-05 EMail: Toni.Bastianelli@provincedeliege.be

Departments

Agronomy *(La Reid)* (Agricultural Management; Agronomy; Biotechnology; Environmental Studies; Forestry); **Chemistry, Biochemistry, Biotechnology** *(Liège)* (Biochemistry; Biotechnology; Chemistry); **Communication** *(Jemeppe)* (Communication Studies; Documentation Techniques; Library Science; Multimedia); **Computer Graphics** *(Seraing)* (Computer Graphics); **Computer Science** *(Seraing)* (Computer Networks; Computer Science; Industrial Engineering; Systems Analysis; Telecommunications Engineering); **Construction** *(Verviers)* (Construction Engineering; Industrial Engineering); **Economics** *(Jemeppe)* (Accountancy; E-Business/Commerce; Economics; International Business; Management; Marketing; Transport Management); **Education** *(Jemeppe)* (Education; Educational Psychology; Physical Education); **Electrical and Mechanical Engineering** *(Seraing)* (Electrical Engineering; Industrial Engineering; Mechanical Engineering; Production Engineering); **Law** *(Jemeppe)* (Law); **Paramedical** *(Liège)* (Biotechnology; Community Health; Dietetics; Ergotherapy; Gerontology; Laboratory Techniques; Midwifery; Nursing; Oncology; Paediatrics; Physical Therapy; Psychiatry and Mental Health; Rehabilitation and Therapy); **Social Studies** *(Jemeppe)* (Human Resources; Social Studies; Social Work)

History: Founded 1995, following the merger of three Hautes Ecoles provinciales: Rennequin Sualem, Léon-Eli Troclet and André Vésale.

Academic Year: September to June

Admission Requirements: Secondary school certificate or foreign equivalent

Fees: (Euros): Registration, 160-320 per annum; foreign students, tuition, 1,490-1,985

Main Language(s) of Instruction: French

International Co-operation: With universities in Germany, Finland, France, Portugal, Spain, Slovenia and Canada

Degrees and Diplomas: *Bachelier.* 3 yrs; *Master.* Also Agrégé(e) de l'enseignement secondaire inférieur (AESI)

Student Services: Academic counselling, Canteen, Employment services, Handicapped facilities, Social counselling

Student Residential Facilities: Yes

Libraries: Department librairies
Last Updated: 05/09/11

HAUTE ÉCOLE DE LA VILLE DE LIÈGE

Rue Hazinelle, 2, Liège 4000
Tel: +32(4) 223-28-08
Fax: +32(4) 221-08-42
EMail: info@hel.be
Website: http://www.hel.be/

Directeur-Président: André Nossent **EMail:** anossent@hel.be

Institutes

Technical Studies *(Institut Supérieur d'Enseignement Technologique)* (Automotive Engineering; Chemistry; Computer Science; Electronic Engineering; Publishing and Book Trade)

Schools

Economics *(ECSSAC)* (Economics; Hotel Management; Public Administration; Public Relations; Secretarial Studies); **Pedagogy** *(Ecole Normale Jonfosse)* (Germanic Languages; Mathematics; Natural Sciences; Preschool Education; Primary Education; Secondary Education; Teacher Training); **Physical Therapy** *(Ecole supérieure de Logopédie)* (Speech Therapy and Audiology); **Translation and Interpretation** (Translation and Interpretation)

History: Founded 1995.

Main Language(s) of Instruction: French

Degrees and Diplomas: *Bachelier; Master*
Last Updated: 07/09/11

HAUTE ÉCOLE DE NAMUR-LIÈGE-LUXEMBOURG (HENAM)

Rue Saint-Donat, 130, Namur 5002
Tel: +32(81) 46-85-00
Fax: +32(81) 46-85-25
EMail: info@henam.be
Website: http://www.henallux.be

Directeur-Président: Albert Leroy EMail: direction@henam.be

International Relations: Isabelle Billard EMail: relint@iesn.be

Programmes

Accountancy *(Arlon, Namur)* (Accountancy; Fiscal Law; Management); **Automation** (Automation and Control Engineering); **Business Computing** *(Namur)* (Business Computing); **Computer Technology** *(Namur)* (Software Engineering); **Electrical and Mechanical Engineering** *(Arlon, Seraing)* (Electrical Engineering; Mechanical Engineering); **Engineering and Social Action** *(Louvain-la-Neuve, Namur)* (Social Welfare; Social Work); **Human Resource Management** *(Namur)* (Human Resources; Management); **Industrial Engineering** *(Virton)* (Industrial Engineering); **Law** *(Namur)* (Law); **Librarianship** *(Malonne)* (Documentation Techniques; Library Science); **Marketing** *(Namur)* (Marketing); **Midwifery** *(Namur)* (Midwifery); **Nursing** *(Namur)* (Nursing); **Preschool and Primary Teaching** *(Bastogne, Champion, Malonne)* (Teacher Training); **Secondary Education Teaching** (Teacher Training); **Secretarial Studies** *(Arlon)* (Secretarial Studies); **Social Assistant** *(Namur)* (Social Welfare; Social Work)

History: Founded 2011 following merger of the Haute École de Namur and the Haute École Blaise Pascal.

Admission Requirements: Secondary school certificate

Main Language(s) of Instruction: French

Degrees and Diplomas: *Bachelier.* 3-4 yrs; *Master*

Libraries: Two libraries
Last Updated: 15/02/12

HAUTE ECOLE FRANCISCO FERRER (HEFF)

Rue de la Fontaine, 4, Bruxelles, Brabant 1000
Tel: +32(2) 279-58-10
Fax: +32(2) 279-58-29
EMail: heff.europe@he-ferrer.eu
Website: http://www.brunette.brucity.be/ferrer/plan.cfm

Directeur-Président: Pierre Lambert Tel: +32(2) 279-58-12

Departments

Applied Arts (Advertising and Publicity; Fashion Design; Textile Design); **Economics** *(Cooremans)* (Accountancy; Administration; Business Administration; Insurance; Public Administration; Secretarial Studies; Transport Management); **Paramedical Studies** (Medical Technology; Midwifery; Nursing); **Pedagogy** (Economics; French; Germanic Languages; Mathematics; Natural Sciences; Physical Education; Preschool Education; Primary Education; Secondary Education); **Translation and Interpretation** (Arabic; Chinese; Dutch; English; Spanish; Translation and Interpretation; Turkish)

Units

Applied Mathematics (Applied Mathematics); **Biomedicine** (Biomedicine); **Physical Education** (Physical Education)

History: Founded 1996.

Main Language(s) of Instruction: French

Degrees and Diplomas: *Bachelier, Master*
Last Updated: 06/09/11

HAUTE ECOLE GALILÉE (HEG)

Rue des Grands Carmes, 23, Bruxelles, Brabant 1000
Tel: +32(2) 289-63-30
Fax: +32(2) 289-63-39
EMail: heg@galilee.be
Website: http://www.galilee.be

Directeur-Président: John Van Tiggelen
EMail: directeur.president@galilee.be

Departments

Economics (Hotel Management; Secretarial Studies; Tourism)

Institutes

Nursing *(Institut supérieur Soins infirmiers Galilée Bruxelles)* (Nursing); **Pedagogy** *(Institut supérieur pédagogique Galilée)* (Biology; Chemistry; Dutch; Economics; English; Fine Arts; French; Geography; History; Mathematics; Pedagogy; Physics; Religion; Social Sciences; Teacher Training); **Social Communication** *(Institut des Hautes Etudes des Communications sociales)* (Advertising and Publicity; Communication Studies; Journalism; Media Studies; Modern Languages; Public Relations)

History: Founded 1996, incorporating 5 existing institutes.

Academic Year: September to June

Admission Requirements: Secondary school certificate and entrance examination in french

Fees: (Euros): EU Students, 396-793 per annum. Non-EU Students, 1,388-1,784

Main Language(s) of Instruction: French

International Co-operation: Participates in Erasmus

Degrees and Diplomas: *Bachelier, Master*
Last Updated: 06/02/09

HAUTE ECOLE GROUPE ICHEC - ISC SAINT LOUIS - ISFSC

Boulevard Brand Whitlock, 6, Bruxelles 1150
Tel: +32(2) 739-37-00
Fax: +32(2) 739-38-03
EMail: info@ichec.be
Website: http://www.he-ichec-isfsc.be

Recteur: Brigitte Chanoine
Tel: +32(2) 739-37-11, Fax: +32(2) 739-38-03

Institutes

Social Work and Communication (Communication Studies; Multimedia; Social and Community Services; Social Welfare; Social Work)

Schools

Management *(Brussels (ICHEC))* (Business Administration; Cultural Studies; E-Business/Commerce; Fiscal Law; Management; Taxation)

History: Founded 1996, incoporating existing institutions.

Academic Year: September to June

Admission Requirements: Secondary school certificate or equivalent. TOEFL exam for foreign students

Fees: (Euros): 780-805 per annum; Foreign Students 2,279-2,775 per annum

Main Language(s) of Instruction: French

International Co-operation: With universities in Europe; USA; Canada; Mexico; China

Degrees and Diplomas: *Bachelier.* 3 yrs; *Master.* 2 yrs

Student Services: Academic counselling, Canteen, Employment services, Foreign student adviser, Foreign Studies Centre, Language programs, Social counselling

Student Residential Facilities: Yes

Libraries: Main Library
Last Updated: 09/09/11

HAUTE ECOLE LÉONARD DE VINCI (HELDV)

Place de l'Alma, 2, Bruxelles 1200
Tel: +32(2) 761-06-80
Fax: +32(2) 761-06-89
EMail: info@vinci.be
Website: http://www.vinci.be

Directeur-Président: Paul Anciaux EMail: paul.anciaux@vinci.be

International Relations: Isabelle Henkinbrant
EMail: isabelle.henkinbrant@vinci.be

Institutes

Industrial Engineering *(ECAM, Institut supérieur industriel)* (Automation and Control Engineering; Computer Engineering; Construction Engineering; Electronic Engineering; Industrial Engineering; Mechanical Engineering; Surveying and Mapping); **Libre Marie Haps** (Clinical Psychology; Educational Psychology; Speech

Therapy and Audiology; Translation and Interpretation); **Nursing** *(Institut Supérieur d'Enseignement Infirmier)* (Anaesthesiology; Community Health; Gerontology; Midwifery; Nursing; Oncology; Paediatrics; Psychiatry and Mental Health); **Parnasse Deux Alices** (Ergotherapy; Nursing; Physical Education; Physical Therapy; Podiatry); **Paul Lambin** (Biomedicine; Business Computing; Chemistry; Dietetics; Laboratory Techniques; Medical Technology)

Schools
Pedagogy *(Ecole Normale Catholique du Brabant wallon)* (Pedagogy; Teacher Training)

History: Founded 1994 incorporating existing institutes. A university-level institution financially supported by the State.

Main Language(s) of Instruction: French

Degrees and Diplomas: *Bachelier; Master.* Also Agrégé(e) de l'enseignement secondaire inférieur.
Last Updated: 06/09/11

HAUTE ECOLE LIBRE DE BRUXELLES ILYA PRIGOGINE (HELB-IP)
Avenue Besme 97, Bruxelles 1090
Tel: +32(2) 349-68-11
Fax: +32(2) 349-68-31
EMail: direction.presidence@helb-prigogine.be
Website: http://www.helb-prigogine.be

Directeur-Président: Jean-Marie Meskens

Institutes
Economics and Paramedical Sciences *(Institut Libre d'Enseignement Supérieur Economique et Paramédical de Bruxelles)* (Business Computing; Physical Therapy; Public Relations); **Paramedical Studies** *(ISCAM)* (Community Health; Ergotherapy; Gerontology; Midwifery; Nursing; Oncology; Paediatrics; Physical Therapy; Podiatry); **Radioelectricy and Cinema** *(Institut National de Radioélectricité et de Cinématographie)* (Cinema and Television; Electrical Engineering; Electronic Engineering; Photography)

Schools
Social Welfare *(Ecole Ouvrière Supérieure)* (Social Welfare; Social Work)

History: Founded 1995

Main Language(s) of Instruction: French

Degrees and Diplomas: *Bachelier:* 3 yrs; *Master:* 5 yrs
Last Updated: 07/09/11

HAUTE ECOLE LIBRE MOSANE (HELMO)
Mont Saint-Martin 41, Liège 4000
Tel: +32(4) 222-22-00
EMail: info@helmo.be
Website: http://www.helmo.be/

Directeur-Président: Alexandre Lodez

International Relations: Julie Guiot
Tel: +32(4) 229-86-69, Fax: +32(4) 229-86-65

Centres
HELMo-CFEL *(Centre de Formation Éducationnelle Liégeois (CFEL))* (Teacher Training)

Institutes
HELMo ESAS (Social Welfare; Social Work); **HELMo Huy** (Primary Education; Teacher Training); **HELMo Lancin** (Physical Education); **HELMo Mode** (Fashion Design); **HELMo Saint Laurent** (Automation and Control Engineering; Biomedicine; Business and Commerce; Computer Science); **HELMo Saint Roch** (Primary Education; Teacher Training); **HELMo Sainte Julienne** (Midwifery; Nursing); **HELMo Sainte-Croix** (Preschool Education; Primary Education; Secondary Education; Teacher Training); **HELMo Sainte-Marie** (Accountancy; Insurance; International Business; Marketing); **HELMo Saint-Martin** (Business Administration; Law); **HELMo Verviers** (Modern Languages; Secretarial Studies); **HELMo-Gramm** (Industrial Engineering)

History: Founded 1996. Acquired present title following merger with ISELL.

Academic Year: September to June (September-January; February-June)

Admission Requirements: Secondary school certificate
Main Language(s) of Instruction: French

International Co-operation: With universities in Germany, Italy, Spain, United Kingdom, Poland, Finland, Ireland, Denmark, Estonia, France

Degrees and Diplomas: *Bachelier:* 3 yrs; *Master*
Student Services: Academic counselling, Employment services, Foreign student adviser, Social counselling
Last Updated: 07/09/11

HAUTE ECOLE LOUVAIN EN HAINAUT
159 Chaussée de Binche, Mons, Hainaut 7000
Tel: +32(65) 40-41-42
Fax: +32(65) 34-04-52
EMail: isabelle.graulich@helha.be
Website: http://www.helha.be

Directeur-Président: Jean-Luc Vreux (1998-)

Divisions
Agronomy *(Fleurus)* (Agricultural Business; Biotechnology); **Applied Arts** *(Mons)* (Advertising and Publicity); **Economics** *(Mons, La Louvière, Charleroi, Fleurus, Montignies-sur-Sambre, Mouscron)* (Accountancy; Business Administration; Business Computing; Hotel Management; Marketing; Public Relations; Secretarial Studies; Tourism); **Paramedical Studies** *(Fleurus, Montignies-sur-Sambre, Gilly, La Louvière, Mouscron, Tournai)* (Biomedicine; Ergotherapy; Medical Technology; Midwifery; Nursing; Physical Therapy); **Pedagogy** *(Gosselles, Braine le Comte, Leuze-en-Hainaut, Mons, Loverval)* (Teacher Training); **Social Work** *(Montignies-sur-Sambre, Louvain la Neuve, Mons, Tournai)* (Communication Studies; Social Work); **Technology** *(Mons, Charleroi, Tournai)* (Automotive Engineering; Chemistry; Computer Science; Construction Engineering; Electronic Engineering; Industrial Engineering)

History: Founded 2009 following merger of the Haute École Charleroi Europe, the Haute École Libre du Hainaut Occidental and the Haute École Roi Baudouin

Governing Bodies: Administration Board; Management Council; Pedagogical Council

Academic Year: September to July

Admission Requirements: Secondary school certificate

Fees: (Euros): c. 245-570 per annum

Main Language(s) of Instruction: French

Degrees and Diplomas: *Bachelier:* 3 yrs; *Master*

Student Services: Academic counselling, Canteen, Foreign student adviser, Language programs, Social counselling

Student Residential Facilities: Yes
Last Updated: 08/09/11

HAUTE ECOLE LUCIA DE BROUCKÈRE (HELDB)
Avenue Emile Gryzon, 1, Bruxelles 1070
Tel: +32(2) 526-73-00
Fax: +32(2) 524-30-82
EMail: info@heldb.be
Website: http://www.heldb.be

Directeur-Président: Patrick Dysseler (1995-)
Tel: +32(2) 526-73-05, Fax: +32(2) 524-30-82
EMail: dysseler@meurice.heldb.be

Departments
Site Ferry (Accountancy; Medical Technology; Primary Education; Teacher Training)

Institutes
Economics *(Site d'Ixelles)* (Law; Marketing); **Haulot** (Dietetics; Hotel Management; Landscape Architecture; Public Relations; Tourism; Urban Studies); **Meurice** (Biochemistry; Chemistry; Industrial Engineering); **Pedagogy and Economics** *(Jodoigne)* (Secretarial Studies; Special Education; Teacher Training)

History: Founded 1891 as Institut Meurice. Acquired present title 1995.

Fees: (Euros): 200 per annum

Main Language(s) of Instruction: French

International Co-operation: With Universities in France, Italy, Germany, United Kingdom, Russian Federation, Hungary, Bulgaria. Also participates in the Socrates/Tempus programme

Degrees and Diplomas: *Bachelier.* 3 yrs; *Master*

Student Services: Academic counselling, Canteen, Employment services, Foreign student adviser, Handicapped facilities, Social counselling, Sports facilities

Student Residential Facilities: Yes

Libraries: Yes
Last Updated: 21/03/12

HAUTE ECOLE PROVINCIALE DE HAINAUT CONDORCET (HEPCUT)

17, Chemin du Champ de Mars, Mons 7000
Tel: +32(65) 40 12 20
Website: http://www.condorcet.be

Directeur-Président: Alain Scandolo

Departments

Agronomy *(Ath)* (Agricultural Business; Agricultural Engineering; Agronomy; Forestry; Horticulture; Rural Planning); **Economics** *(Mons, Charleroi, Mouscron, Tournai, Saint-Ghislain)* (Accountancy; Business Computing; E-Business/Commerce; Economics; Hotel Management; Insurance; International Business; Law; Marketing; Real Estate; Retailing and Wholesaling; Secretarial Studies; Tourism); **Fine Arts** *(Saint-Ghislain)* (Graphic Arts); **Paramedical Sciences** *(Charleroi, Tournai, Saint-Ghislain, Mons)* (Dietetics; Ergotherapy; Medical Technology; Midwifery; Nursing; Physical Therapy); **Pedagogy** *(Charleroi, Mons, Morlanwelz)* (Arts and Humanities; French; Germanic Languages; Mathematics; Physical Education; Special Education; Teacher Training); **Social Work** *(Charleroi)* (Communication Studies; Multimedia; Social Work); **Technical Studies** *(Ath, Charleroi, Tournai)* (Aeronautical and Aerospace Engineering; Automation and Control Engineering; Biochemistry; Biotechnology; Chemistry; Electrical Engineering; Industrial Engineering; Mechanical Engineering)

History: Founded 2009 following merger of the Haute École Provinciale Mons-Borinage-Centre (HEPMBC), the Haute École Provinciale du Hainaut Occidental (HEPHO) and the Haute École Provinciale Charleroi-Université du travail (HEPCUT).

Governing Bodies: Board of Administrators; Managing Council

Admission Requirements: Secondary school certificate

Main Language(s) of Instruction: French

International Co-operation: Participates in the Leonardo and Erasmus programmes

Degrees and Diplomas: *Bachelier.* 3 yrs; *Master*

Student Services: Academic counselling, Canteen, Employment services, Handicapped facilities, Health services, Language programs, Social counselling, Sports facilities
Last Updated: 07/09/11

INSTITUT NATIONAL SUPÉRIEUR DES ARTS DU SPECTACLE ET DES TECHNIQUES DE DIFFUSION (INSAS)

Rue Thérésienne, 8, Bruxelles 1000
Tel: +32(2) 511-92-86
Fax: +32(2) 511-02-79
EMail: info@insas.be
Website: http://www.insas.be

Directeur: Laurent Gross

Divisions

Audio-visual Arts (Cinema and Television; Radio and Television Broadcasting; Writing); **Theatre** (Acting; Theatre)

History: Founded 1962.

Main Language(s) of Instruction: French

Degrees and Diplomas: *Bachelier; Master*

Libraries: Yes
Last Updated: 02/09/11

INSTITUT SUPÉRIEUR DE MUSIQUE ET DE PÉDAGOGIE (ISAI)

28 Rue Juppin, Namur 5000
Tel: +32(81) 73-64-37
Fax: +32(81) 73-95-14
EMail: info@imep.be
Website: http://www.imep.be/

Directeur: Guido Jardon EMail: direction@imep.be

Secrétaire générale: Brigitte Darasse

Institutes
Fugue and Composition *Director:* Michel Hallynck

Programmes
Music (Music; Singing); **Musical Instruments**; **Musical Pedagogy**

History: Founded 1970, acquired present title and status 1975.

Governing Bodies: Les Evêques de Belgique

Admission Requirements: Secondary school certificate and entrance examination in solfeggio and instrument playing

Fees: (Euros): c. 800 per annum

Main Language(s) of Instruction: French

Degrees and Diplomas: *Bachelier.* Music education, 3 yrs; *Master.* 2 yrs

Student Services: Canteen

Libraries: Main library

Publications: Les échos de l'IMEP *(quarterly)*
Last Updated: 08/09/11

INSTITUTE OF MEDIA ARTS

Institut des Arts de Diffusion (IAD)
Rue des Wallons, 77, Louvain-la-Neuve B-1348
Tel: +32(10) 47-80-20
Fax: +32(10) 45-11-74
EMail: iad@iad-arts.be
Website: http://www.iad-arts.be

Directeur: Serge Flamé
Tel: +32(10) 47-80-25, Fax: +32(10) 45-11-47
EMail: flame@iad-arts.be

Directeur adjoint: Michel Wouters
Tel: +32(10) 47-80-23, Fax: +32(10) 45-11-74
EMail: wouteks@iad-arts.be

International Relations: Nathalie Degimbe
Tel: +32(10) 47-90-88 EMail: degimbe@iad-arts.be

Divisions
Arts (Cinema and Television; Computer Graphics; Multimedia; Sound Engineering (Acoustics); Theatre)

History: Founded 1959, acquired present status 1962.

Academic Year: September to June

Admission Requirements: Secondary school certificate and entrance examination

Fees: (Euros): 1,017-1,192 per annum

Main Language(s) of Instruction: French

Degrees and Diplomas: *Bachelier; Master*

Student Services: Academic counselling, Employment services, Social counselling

Special Facilities: TV Studio, Cinema Studio, Multimedia rooms
Last Updated: 12/05/11

STATE UNIVERSITY OF LIÈGE

Université de Liège (ULG)
Place du 20 Août, 9, Liège 4000
Tel: +32(4) 366-21-11
Fax: +32(4) 366-57-00
EMail: info.etudes@ulg.ac.be
Website: http://www.ulg.ac.be

Recteur: Bernard Rentier
Tel: +32(4) 366-97-00, Fax: +32(4) 366-97-05
EMail: Recteur@ulg.ac.be

International Relations: Annick Comblain
EMail: A.Comblain@ulg.ac.be

Faculties

Agro-Bio Tech *(Gembloux)* (Agronomy; Bioengineering; Landscape Architecture); **Applied Sciences** (Architecture; Chemical Engineering; Computer Engineering; Construction Engineering; Geological Engineering; Mechanical Engineering; Mining Engineering; Physical Engineering); **Architecture** (Architecture); **Economics, Management** (Economics; Engineering Management; Management; Social Sciences) *Dean*: Yves Crama; **Law and Political Science** (Criminology; Law; Political Sciences); **Medicine** (Biomedicine; Dentistry; Medicine; Pharmacy; Physical Education; Physical Therapy; Public Health); **Philosophy and Letters** (Art History; Classical Languages; Germanic Languages; History; Information Sciences; Modern Languages; Oriental Languages; Philosophy; Romance Languages); **Psychology and Educational Sciences** (Educational Sciences; Psychology; Speech Therapy and Audiology); **Science** (Biochemistry; Biological and Life Sciences; Chemistry; Environmental Management; Geography; Geology; Mathematics; Physics) *Dean*: Jean-Marie Bouquegneau; **Veterinary Science** (Veterinary Science)

Institutes

Humanities and Social Science (Anthropology; Arts and Humanities; Demography and Population; Labour and Industrial Relations; Social Sciences; Sociology)

Further Information: Also French language courses for foreign students. Inter-University study programmes. Teaching hospital. Teaching veterinary hospital

History: Founded 1817 under King William I of the Netherlands. Following the independence of Belgium designated in 1835 as a State University. In 1959 provision was made for the transfer of the University to a new campus. The University enjoys limited autonomy and receives the major share of its income from the Communauté française de Belgique.

Governing Bodies: Conseil d'Administration

Academic Year: September to July (September-January; January-July)

Admission Requirements: Secondary school certificate or recognized foreign equivalent and entrance examination in French for non-native speakers. Entrance examination for engineers

Fees: (Euros): 739 per annum

Main Language(s) of Instruction: French

International Co-operation: With universities in Austria, Canada, Czech Republic, Denmark, Finland, France, Germany, Greece, Hungary, Ireland, Italy, Lithuania, Malta, Netherlands, Norway, Poland, Portugal, Romania, Russian Federation, Spain, Sweden, United Kingdom, USA. Also participates in Erasmus-Socrates programme

Degrees and Diplomas: *Bachelier*: 3 yrs; *Master*: 1-4 yrs; *Doctorat*

Student Services: Academic counselling, Canteen, Cultural centre, Employment services, Foreign student adviser, Handicapped facilities, Health services, Nursery care, Social counselling, Sports facilities

Student Residential Facilities: Yes

Special Facilities: Museum and Aquarium of the Institute of Zoology. Open air museum of Sart Tilman; Science Museum; Pre-history Museum. Plant Observatory

Libraries: Central Library, c. 3m. vols
Last Updated: 08/09/11

UNIVERSITÉ LIBRE DE BRUXELLES (ULB)

50 avenue Roosevelt, Bruxelles 1050
Tel: +32(2) 650-21-11
Fax: +32(2) 650-35-95
EMail: epi@ulb.ac.be
Website: http://www.ulbruxelles.be/

Recteur: Didier Viviers (2010-)
Tel: +32(2) 650-23-17, Fax: +32(2) 650-36-30
EMail: recteur@admin.ulb.ac.be

Responsable des R.P: Isabelle Pollet
Tel: +32(2) 650-23-98, Fax: +32(2) 650-42-57
EMail: isabelle.pollet@ulb.ac.be

International Relations: Pierre Quertenmont
Tel: +32(2) 650-42-59, Fax: +32(2) 650-49-65
EMail: dri@dri.ulb.ac.be

Faculties

Applied Sciences (Biomedical Engineering; Chemical Engineering; Civil Engineering; Computer Engineering; Construction Engineering; Electrical Engineering; Electronic Engineering; Mechanical Engineering; Structural Architecture); **Architecture** *(La Cambre-Horta)* (Architecture; Art History; Construction Engineering; Fine Arts); **Law and Criminology** (Civil Law; Commercial Law; Criminology; Law; Notary Studies; Private Law; Public Law); **Medicine** (Biomedicine; Dentistry; Health Sciences; Medicine); **Pharmacy** (Pharmacy); **Philosophy and Letters** (Archaeology; Arts and Humanities; Communication Studies; History; Linguistics; Literature; Modern Languages; Philosophy); **Psychology and Education** (Educational Sciences; Psychology; Speech Studies); **Public Health** (Public Health); **Science** (Actuarial Science; Agronomy; Biochemistry; Bioengineering; Biology; Cell Biology; Chemistry; Computer Science; Ecology; Environmental Management; Geography; Geology; Mathematics; Molecular Biology; Physics; Tourism); **Social and Political Sciences** (Anthropology; Business Administration; Economics; Political Sciences; Social Sciences; Sociology)

Institutes

Motor Sciences (Osteopathy; Physical Education; Physical Therapy; Rehabilitation and Therapy; Sports Medicine)

Schools

Economics and Management *(Solvay)* (Economics; Management)

Further Information: Campuses at: Solbosch, Plaine, Erasme, Nivelles (province of Brabant), Treignes, Charleroi; also an academic hospital "Erasme".

History: Founded 1834, the Free University of Brussels was transformed under the law of 28 May 1970 into separate Dutch and French-speaking Universities. The Rector is elected for a four-year term (plus 2 further possible) from amongst the titular professors. As a private autonomous institution with 7 campuses the University receives substantial public financial support.

Governing Bodies: Conseil d'Administration; Faculty Councils

Academic Year: September to July

Admission Requirements: Secondary school certificate or recognized foreign equivalent, or entrance examination. Entrance examination obligatory for the Faculty of Applied Sciences

Fees: (Euros): 811 per annum

Main Language(s) of Instruction: French

International Co-operation: With universities in most European Union countries (France; Germany; Spain; Italy; United Kingdom; Netherlands; Portugal; Scandinavian countries); USA; Canada; Japan. Long-time cooperation with universities in Africa and Far-East Asia

Degrees and Diplomas: *Bachelier*: all fields (Bachelor's Degree), 3 yrs; *Master*: all fields (Master's Degree), 2 yrs; *Doctorat*

Student Services: Canteen, Employment services, Health services, Language programs, Nursery care, Social counselling, Sports facilities

Student Residential Facilities: Yes

Special Facilities: Museums, Art Gallery

Libraries: Total, c. 2m. vols

Publications: Esprit Libre *(other/irregular)*

Press or Publishing House: Les Editions de l'Université de Bruxelles
Last Updated: 08/09/11

UNIVERSITY OF MONS

Université de Mons
Place du Parc 20, Mons 7000
Tel: +32(65) 37-30-14
EMail: info.mons@umons.ac.be
Website: http://www.umons.ac.be

Recteur: Calogero Conti (2009-) EMail: recteur@umons.ac.be

Faculties

Architecture and Urban Planning (Architecture; Town Planning); **Engineering** (Architecture; Chemical Engineering; Civil Engineering; Electrical Engineering; Engineering; Mechanical Engineering; Mining Engineering); **Medicine and Pharmacy** (Medicine; Pharmacy); **Psychology and Education** (Education; Educational Sciences; Psychology); **Science** (Biology; Chemistry; Computer Science; Mathematics; Physics); **Translation and Interpretation** *(School of International Interpreters)* (American Studies; Danish; Dutch; English; German; Italian; Linguistics; Russian; Spanish; Translation and Interpretation)

Institutes

Humanities and Social Sciences (Communication Studies; Educational Sciences; Management; Political Sciences; Psychology; Social Sciences); **Language Sciences** (Communication Studies; Linguistics); **Legal Studies** (Criminology; Law)

Schools

Business and Economics *(Warocqué)* (Business Administration; Economics; Management)

History: Created 2009 from the merger of Faculté polytechnique de Mons (Faculty of Engineering, Mons, created 1837) and Université de Mons-Hainaut (University of Mons-Hainaut, created 1899).

Governing Bodies: Conseil d'Administration

Academic Year: September to September (September-December; January-May; June-September

Admission Requirements: Secondary school certificate or recognized equivalent and entrance examination

Fees: (Euros): c. 800 per annum

Main Language(s) of Instruction: French

Degrees and Diplomas: *Bachelier*: 3 yrs (180 credits); *Master*: a further 2 yrs (120 credits); *Doctorat*

Student Services: Academic counselling, Canteen, Cultural centre, Employment services, Foreign student adviser, Handicapped facilities, Health services, Social counselling

Student Residential Facilities: Yes

Libraries: Central Library, 538,164 vols; Science and Medicine Library, 29,293 vols; Economic and Social Sciences Library, 85,491 vols; Psychology and Education Library, 27,733 vols; Linguistics Library, 23,596 vols

Last Updated: 08/09/11

UNIVERSITY OF NAMUR

Facultés universitaires Notre-Dame de la Paix (FUNDP)
Rue de Bruxelles, 61, Namur 5000
Tel: +32(81) 72-41-11
Fax: +32(81) 23-03-91
EMail: vice.recteur@fundp.ac.be
Website: http://www.fundp.ac.be

Recteur: Yves Poullet
Tel: +32(81) 72-40-00, Fax: +32(81) 72-40-03
EMail: yves.poullet@fundp.ac.be

Vice-recteur: Robert Sporken
Tel: +32(81) 72-52-40, Fax: +32(81) 72-52-41

Faculties

Computer Science (Computer Science); **Economics, Social Sciences and Management** (Communication Studies; Economics; Management; Political Sciences; Social Sciences); **Law** (Law); **Medicine** (Biomedicine; Medicine; Pharmacy) *Dean*: Michel Herin; **Philosophy and Letters** (Archaeology; Art History; Arts and Humanities; Classical Languages; Germanic Studies; History; Literature; Philology; Philosophy; Romance Languages); **Science** (Biology; Chemistry; Geography; Geology; Mathematics; Natural Sciences; Physics; Veterinary Science)

Further Information: Campus in Charleroi

History: Founded 1831 as college by the Society of Jesus and reconstituted under present title 1833. Independent but recognized and financially supported by the State. First authorized to award degrees 1929, granted full University status 1971.

Governing Bodies: Assemblée Générale, Conseil d'Administration

Academic Year: September to August (September-January; January-August)

Admission Requirements: Secondary school certificate or recognized foreign equivalent

Fees: (Euros): 63-749 per annum

Main Language(s) of Instruction: French

International Co-operation: With universities in Spain, Germany, Poland

Degrees and Diplomas: *Bachelier*: Philosophy; History; Modern Languages; Archaelogy; Communication Studies; Political Science; Economics; Management; Law; Mathematics; Physics; Chemistry; Biology; Geography; Geology; Pharmacy; Veterinary Science; Computer Science; Medicine; Biomedicine, 3 yrs; *Master*: Computer Science; Economics; Management, 3 yrs; *Doctorat*: Philosophy; History; Modern Languages; Archaelogy; Communication Studies; Political Science; Economics; Management; Law Science; Pharmacy; Veterinary Science; Medicine; Biomedicine

Student Services: Academic counselling, Canteen, Cultural centre, Employment services, Foreign student adviser, Health services, Nursery care, Social counselling, Sports facilities

Student Residential Facilities: For 430 students

Libraries: Moretus Plantin Library, c. 800,000 vols; Centre de Documentation et de Recherche Religieuse, c. 600,000 vols; bibliothèque de la faculté de droit

Publications: Annales de la Société scientifique de Bruxelles *(quarterly)*; Cahier de Recherche de la Faculté de Sciences économiques et sociales *(other/irregular)*; Cahiers de Formation continue de la Faculté des Sciences économiques et sociales *(other/irregular)*; Documents et Points de Vue de la Faculté des Sciences économiques et sociales *(other/irregular)*; Journal de Réflexion sur l'Informatique *(quarterly)*; Les Etudes classiques *(quarterly)*; Revue des Questions scientifiques *(quarterly)*; Revue régionale de Droit *(quarterly)*

Press or Publishing House: Presses Universitaires de Namur
Last Updated: 02/09/11

UNIVERSITY SAINT-LOUIS, BRUSSELS

Facultés universitaires Saint-Louis, Bruxelles (FUSL)
Boulevard du Jardin Botanique, 43, Bruxelles 1000
Tel: +32(2) 211-78-11
Fax: +32(2) 211-79-97
EMail: communication@fusl.ac.be
Website: http://www.fusl.ac.be

Recteur: Jean-Paul Lambert (2003-2013)
Tel: +32(2) 211-78-81, Fax: +32(2) 211-78-73
EMail: lambert@fusl.ac.be

Faculties

Economics, Political Science, Social Sciences (Anthropology; Communication Studies; Economics; Management; Political Sciences; Sociology); **Law** (Law); **Philosophy, Letters and Humanities** (Germanic Studies; History; Literature; Modern Languages; Philosophy; Romance Languages)

Institutes

European Studies (European Studies)

Research Centres

Economics (Economics); **Environmental Law** (Law); **History of Law and Institutions** (History of Law); **Juridical Studies** (Law); **Linguistics** (Linguistics); **Literature** (Literature); **Political Philosophy** (Philosophy); **Political Science** (Political Sciences); **Regional Studies** (Regional Studies); **Religious History** (Religion); **Sociology** (Sociology)

Schools

Philosophical and Religious Studies (Philosophy; Religious Studies)

Further Information: Also Research Networks on Interdisciplinary Approach of Society and on Urban and Regional Issues

History: Founded 1858 as Section de Philosophie. First authorized to award degrees 1890; reorganized 1969 with separate Dutch and French sections which became legally distinct institutions in 1974. A private, state supported institution with full university status.

Governing Bodies: Conseil d'Administration; Conseil de Direction

Academic Year: September to September

Admission Requirements: Secondary school certificate or foreign recognized equivalent

Main Language(s) of Instruction: French

Degrees and Diplomas: *Bachelier*: Economics and Management; German Languages and Literature; History; Information and Communication; Law; Management Engineering; Philosophy; Political Science; Romance Languages and Literature; Sociology, 3 yrs; *Master*; *Doctorat*

Student Services: Academic counselling, Canteen, Cultural centre, Social counselling, Sports facilities

Libraries: c. 200,000 vols

Publications: Cahiers du CRHIDI *(biannually)*; Revue Anthropologique; Revue interdisciplinaire d'Etudes juridiques *(biannually)*

Press or Publishing House: Publications des Facultés universitaires Saint-Louis

Last Updated: 02/09/11

Belize

STRUCTURE OF HIGHER EDUCATION SYSTEM

Description:

In Belize, degree courses are mostly offered by the University of Belize, founded in 2000 by the merger of the University College of Belize (originally created in 1986), Belize School of Nursing, and Belize Teachers College. The University is directly financed by the Ministry of Education and offers its own Bachelor's degree courses under the authority of the Government of Belize. Through an extra-mural Department, Belize is also affiliated to the University of the West Indies, which is a regional institution with campuses in Jamaica, Barbados and Trinidad.

Stages of studies:

University level first stage: *Associate degree; Bachelor's degree*
Associate degrees are awarded after two years of study and Bachelor's degrees after two years following upon the Associate degree.

ADMISSION TO HIGHER EDUCATION

Admission to university-level studies:

Name of secondary school credential required: Caribbean Advanced Proficiency Examination
Name of secondary school credential required: General Certificate of Education Advanced Level
Alternatives to credentials: Caribbean Examinations Council Certificate + a preliminary year's study.

Foreign students admission:

Entrance exam requirements: Foreign students should have a general certificate of education or equivalent.
Language requirements: A good knowledge of English.

RECOGNITION OF STUDIES

Quality assurance system:

The Quality Assurance and Development Services (QADS) of the Ministry of Education and Labour is in charge of ensuring relevant quality education through the development and monitoring of the implementation of national standards.

NATIONAL BODIES

Ministry of Education and Youth
   Minister: Patrick Faber
   West Block
   Belmopan
   Tel: +501 822 2380/3315
   Fax: +501 822 3389
   WWW: http://www.moes.gov.bz

Data for academic year: 2006-2007
Source: IAU from the Ministry of Education and Labour, Belize, 2007. Bodies updated in 2011.

INSTITUTIONS

PUBLIC INSTITUTIONS

UNIVERSITY OF BELIZE (UB)

PO Box 340, University Drive, Belmopan, Cayo District
Tel: +501(822) 3680
Fax: +501(822) 1107
Website: http://www.ub.edu.bz

President: Cary Fraser

Provost: Ismael Hoare

Departments
Adult and Continuing Education

Faculties
Education and Arts (Anthropology; Education; English; History; Spanish); **Management and Social Sciences** (Accountancy; Business Administration; Business and Commerce; Hotel and Restaurant; Law; Marketing; Public Administration; Tourism) *Dean*: Fatai Akinkuolie; **Nursing, Allied Health and Social Work** (Health Sciences; Laboratory Techniques; Pharmacy; Social Work); **Science and Technology** (Agriculture; Architecture; Biology; Chemistry; Engineering; Information Technology; Marine Science and Oceanography; Mathematics; Natural Resources; Physics)

Further Information: Also Belize City Campus

History: Founded August 2000 by the merger of the University College of Belize, Belize School of Nursing, Belize Teacher Training College.

Main Language(s) of Instruction: Spanish

Degrees and Diplomas: *Associate Degree*; *Bachelor's Degree*

Libraries: Yes
Last Updated: 21/03/12

PRIVATE INSTITUTIONS

GALEN UNIVERSITY

PO Box 177, Mile 62.5 Western Highway, Central Farm, San Ignacio, Cayo
Tel: +501 (824) 3226
Fax: +501 (824) 3723
EMail: admissions@galen.edu.bz
Website: http://www.galen.edu.bz

President: Nancy Adamson (2010-)
Tel: +501(824) 3226, Ext.106
EMail: nadamson@galen.edu.bz; vicepresident@galen.edu.bz

International Relations: Marion Cayetano, Vice-President, Planning EMail: planning@galen.edu.bz

Faculties
Arts and Social Sciences (Anthropology; Archaeology; Biological and Life Sciences; Botany; Chemistry; Computer Science; Cultural Studies; Development Studies; Economics; English; Environmental Studies; Mathematics; Political Sciences; Psychology; Religion; Sociology); **Business and Entrepreneurship** (Business Administration; Economics; Finance; Human Resources; International Business; International Relations; Management; Marketing); **Science and Technology** (Biology; Ecology; Engineering; Environmental Studies; Geology; Mathematics; Physics; Zoology)

History: Founded in 2003. Programmes offered jointly with University of Indianapolis

Governing Bodies: Board of Trustees

Academic Year: September to December; January to April; May to August. Students may enrol in any semester

Admission Requirements: (Undergraduate): High School Diploma, Cambridge First Certificate, 'O' Level Certificate or equivalent; Proof of English proficiency where necessary (TOEFL 500, IELT 5.0) SAT/ACT required. (Graduate studies): Original transcript of undergraduate degree. Proof of English proficiency where necessary

Fees: (Belize dollars): local students, undergraduate, 240.00 per credit hour; local students, postgraduate, 320.00. (US dollars, per credit hour): 240.00 overseas students, undergraduate; 320.00 overseas students, postgraduate

Main Language(s) of Instruction: English

International Co-operation: With universities in USA (University of Indianapolis)

Degrees and Diplomas: *Associate Degree*: Business Administration; Hospitality and Tourism Management, 2 yrs; *Bachelor's Degree*: Anthropology; Archaeology (BA); Environmental Science; Hospitality and Tourism Management; Business Administration; Economics; International Business; Marketing (BSc), 4 yrs. All degrees are awarded in partnership with the University of Indianapolis (USA)

Student Services: Academic counselling, Canteen, Employment services, Foreign student adviser, Handicapped facilities, Health services, Social counselling

Student Residential Facilities: Yes

Special Facilities: Local Maya ruins and caves used as field sites for Archaeology courses.

Libraries: Full library service
Last Updated: 09/03/11

Benin

STRUCTURE OF HIGHER EDUCATION SYSTEM

Description:

Higher education is provided by State and private institutions. The three-tier system based on the Bologna system and called LMD (for Licence - Master - Doctorat) is in the process of being implemented.

ADMISSION TO HIGHER EDUCATION

Admission to university-level studies:

Name of secondary school credential required: Baccalauréat de l'Enseignement Secondaire

Entrance exam requirements: Competitive examination in some cases (professional schools)

Other admission requirements: Prize-winners of national competitions (olimpiada) in various secondary-school subjects are exempt from entrance recruitment or examinations.

Foreign students admission:

Entrance exam requirements: Candidates must hold a secondary school-leaving certificate entitling them to enter higher education in their country. It must be officially recognized as being equivalent to a Polish maturity certificate by Polish local educational authorities or on the basis of a bilateral agreement on recognition. There are no entrance examinations for foreign students. However, in the case of fields of study in which special abilities are required, applicants must prove they possess them.

Language requirements: Candidates must attend a Polish language course preparing for higher studies organized by one of the institutions recommended by the Minister of National Education or obtain confirmation of the host institution that their command of Polish is sufficient to enrol. Some faculties also offer courses in foreign languages (mostly English or German).

RECOGNITION OF STUDIES

Bodies dealing with recognition:

Ministère de l'Enseignement supérieur et de la Recherche Scientifique - MESRS (Ministry of Higher Education and Scientific Research)
    Cotonou
    WWW: http://www.mesrs.bj/

NATIONAL BODIES

Ministère de l'Enseignement supérieur et de la Recherche Scientifique - MESRS (Ministry of Higher Education and Scientific Research)
    Minister: François Abiola
    Cotonou
    WWW: http://www.mesrs.bj/
Ministère de l'Enseignement secondaire et de la Formation technique et professionnelle - MESFP (Ministry of Secondary Education and Technical and Profesional Training)
    Minister: Natonde Ake
    Cotonou

Conseil consultatif de l'Enseignement supérieur
    Cotonou

Data for academic year: 2009-2010
Source: IAU from World Data on Education CD-ROM, International Bureau of Education, 2007 and documentation, 2009; National bodies updated in 2011.

INSTITUTIONS

PUBLIC INSTITUTIONS

ABOMEY-CALAVI UNIVERSITY
Université d'Abomey-Calavi (UAC)
01 BP 526, Calavi, Cotonou, Littoral
Tel: +229 36-00-74
Fax: +229 36-00-28
EMail: daa_uac@bj.refer.org
Website: http://www.uac.bj.refer.org/

Rector: Cossi Norbert Awanou (2006-) Tel: +229 36-00-28

Secretary-General: Ambroise Medegan Tel: +229 36-00-53

International Relations: Koko Dominique Sohounhloue
Tel: +229 36-11-19, Fax: +229 36-11-19
EMail: ph_3fr_tolin@yahoo.fr

Faculties
Agronomy *(Abomey-Calavi Campus)* (Agronomy; Animal Husbandry; Environmental Management; Food Technology; Nutrition; Rural Studies; Vegetable Production); **Arts and Humanities** (Anthropology; Archaeology; Arts and Humanities; Communication Studies; English; Geography; History; Literature; Modern Languages; Philosophy; Regional Planning; Sociology); **Economics and Management** (Economics; Management); **Health Sciences** (Medicine; Pharmacy; Social Work); **Law and Political Science** *(Abomey-Calavi Campus)* (Law; Political Sciences); **Science and Technology** (Biochemistry; Biology; Chemistry; Ecology; Geology; Mathematics; Natural Sciences; Physics; Technology)

Institutes
Arabic Language and Islamic Culture *(Abomey-Calavi Campus)* (Arabic; Islamic Studies); **Mathematics and Physics** *(Dangbo Campus)* (Mathematics; Physics); **Sports and Physical Education** *(Campus of Porto-Novo)* (Physical Education; Sports); **Technology** *(Campus of Lokossa)* (Civil Engineering; Computer Science; Electronic Engineering; Mechanics)

Schools
Applied Economics and Management *(National)* (Economics; Management); **Polytechnic** *(Abomey-Calavi Campus)* (Animal Husbandry; Biology; Computer Science; Electronic Engineering; Energy Engineering; Environmental Engineering; Mechanical Engineering; Radiology; Telecommunications Engineering); **Teacher Training** *(ENS, Campus of Porto Novo)* (Teacher Training); **Technical Teacher Training** *(ENS, Lokossa Campus)* (Teacher Training)

History: Founded 1970 as Université du Dahomey and incorporating departments of former Institut d'Enseignement supérieur du Bénin, established 1962. Acquired present status 1976 and present title 2000. A State Institution responsible to the Ministry of Higher Education and Scientific Research.

Governing Bodies: Conseil scientifique; Comité de Direction

Academic Year: October to July (October-January; January-March; April-July)

Admission Requirements: Secondary school certificate (baccalauréat) or equivalent

Fees: (CFA Francs): 6,200

Main Language(s) of Instruction: French

International Co-operation: With universities in Africa; Belgium; Canada; France; Germany; Netherlands; USA

Accrediting Agencies: African and Malagasy Council for Higher Education (CAMES)

Degrees and Diplomas: *Certificat d'Aptitude au Professorat de l'Enseignement Secondaire:* Teaching Qualification, secondary level (CAP), 2-4 yrs; *Diplôme d'Etudes Techniques Supérieures (DETS)*; *Diplôme d'Etudes Universitaires Générales:* Law; Economics, 2 yrs; *Diplôme Universitaire de Technologie:* Banking; Commerce; Management; Computer Science; Statistics, 3 yrs; *Diplôme Universitaire d'Etudes Littéraires:* Arts and Humanities, 2 yrs; *Diplôme Universitaire d'Etudes Scientifiques:* Natural Sciences; Technology, 2 yrs; *Licence/Licence professionnelle:* Law; Economics; Arts and Humanities; Natural Sciences; Technology, 1 yr following DEUG, DUEL, DUES; *Doctorat en Médecine:* Health Sciences, 7 yrs; *Ingénieur:* Polytechnics, Agronomy, 5 yrs; *Diplôme d'Etudes Supérieures Spécialisées:* Demography and Population, Natural Resources Management, 1 yr following Maîtrise; *Diplôme d'Etudes Approfondies:* Law; Economics; Arts and Humanities; Natural Sciences; Technology, 1 yr following Licence; *Maîtrise/Maîtrise professionnelle:* Law; Economics; Arts and Humanities; Natural Sciences; Technology, 1 yr following Licence; *Doctorat des Universités*

Student Services: Academic counselling, Canteen, Health services, Sports facilities

Student Residential Facilities: For 1,782 students

Libraries: Central Library, c. 46,000 vols; Agriculture, c. 10,000; Medicine, c. 7,000; Education, c. 5,000

Publications: Annales de la Faculté des Lettres, Arts et Sciences Humaines *(annually)*; Annales de la Faculté des Sciences Agronomiques *(quarterly)*; Bénin Médical *(3 per annum)*; Cahiers d'Etudes linguistiques *(biannually)*; Revue générale des Sciences juridiques, économiques et politiques *(quarterly)*

Press or Publishing House: Services des Publications Universitaires
Last Updated: 23/02/09

PARAKOU UNIVERSITY
Université de Parakou (UP)
BP 123, Parakou, Borgou
Tel: +229 23-61-07-12
Fax: +229 23-61-07-12
EMail: univ_parakou@borgou.net
Website: http://www.up.bj/

Rector: Simon Akpona (2006-)
Tel: +229 23-61-15-41 EMail: akponasimon@yahoo.fr

Secretary-General: Marc-Abel Ayedoun
Tel: +229 231-12-06 EMail: mayedoun@hotmail.com

International Relations: Nestor Sokpon
Tel: +229 97-16-49-91 EMail: nsokpon@yahoo.fr

Faculties
Agronomy *(Parakou Campus)* (Agronomy); **Economics and Management** *(Parakou Campus)* (Economics; Management); **Law and Political Science** *(Parakou Campus)* (Law; Political Sciences); **Medicine** *(Parakou Campus)* (Medicine)

Institutes
Technology *(IUT, Parakou Campus)* (Banking; Business Administration; Business Computing; Management; Technology)

Schools
Educational Sciences *(Natitingou Campus)* (Teacher Training)

History: Founded 2001 by Ministerial decree. Created from the breaking down of the National University of Benin into two national Universities: Abomey Calavi University and Parakou University in line with the Government's desire to accommodate the influx of upper six formers (holders of Baccalaureate) wishing to gain admission into higher institutions under adequate conditions.

Governing Bodies: Rector; Vice-Chancellors; General-Secretary

Admission Requirements: Baccalaureat

Fees: (CFA Francs): 15,000 (Classical Faculties); 260,000 to 418,000 (for Schools)

Main Language(s) of Instruction: French

International Co-operation: With universities in China; France (Orleans, Limoges, Tours); Belgium; Cameroon; Niger and Togo

Student Services: Academic counselling, Canteen, Health services, Language programs, Nursery care, Social counselling, Sports facilities

Special Facilities: 300 Laboratories

Libraries: Yes

Academic Staff 2007-2008	MEN	WOMEN	TOTAL
FULL-TIME	4,495	1,168	5,663
PART-TIME	24	4	28
Student Numbers 2007-2008			
All (Foreign Included)	4,378	1,131	5,509
FOREIGN ONLY	50	31	81

Last Updated: 05/05/09

PRIVATE INSTITUTIONS

ADVANCED SCHOOL OF ECONOMICS AND MANAGEMENT

Ecole supérieure d'Economie et de Gestion (ESEG)
02 BP 1092, Boulevard du Renouveau démocratique, Agontinkon,
Immeuble Ecobank Etoile 3ème Etage, Cotonou, Atlantique-littoral
Tel: +229 21-30-68-55
Fax: +229 95-96-43-91
EMail: eseg_africa@yahoo.com

Head: Ambroise Akpatcha

Programmes

Banking Administration (Administration; Banking); **Banking and Finance** (Banking; Finance); **Business Administration** (Business Administration); **Economic Policy** (Economic and Finance Policy); **International Business** (International Business); **Management of Decentralised Economies** (Economics; Management); **Management of Microfinance Institutions** (Business Administration; Finance)

History: Founded 2001.

Degrees and Diplomas: *Brevet de Technicien Supérieur; Licence/ Licence professionnelle; Maîtrise/Maîtrise professionnelle.* Also Diploma in Business Administration; Certificate in Economic and Professional English; Certificate in Advanced academic English
Last Updated: 21/03/12

AFRICAN UNIVERSITY OF TECHNOLOGY AND MANAGEMENT

Université Africaine de Technologie et de Management (UATM/GASA-FORMATION)
04 BP 1361, Cadjehoun, Cotonou, Atlantique
Tel: +229 21-30-86-87
Fax: +229 21-30-89-85
EMail: info@uatm-gasaformation.com
Website: http://www.uatm-gasaformation.com

Président: Théophane Ayi

Programmes

Administration and Business Management (Accountancy; Banking; Communication Studies; Finance; Human Resources; Insurance; International Business; International Relations; Management; Marketing); **Agronomy** (Agronomy); **Biotechnology** (Biotechnology; Food Technology; Industrial Engineering); **Economic Science** (Economics); **Electrical Engineering** (Computer Networks; Electrical Engineering; Software Engineering; Telecommunications Engineering); **Juridical Sciences**

Further Information: Also campuses in Agla, Akpakpa, Pahou and Porto-Novo.

Fees: (CFA Francs): BTS, 210,000-325,000 per annum; Licence, 170,000 per annum; Professional Licence, 365-000-430,000 per annum

Degrees and Diplomas: *Brevet de Technicien Supérieur; Diplôme Universitaire de Technologie; Licence/Licence professionnelle; Maîtrise/Maîtrise professionnelle; Doctorat des Universités*
Last Updated: 23/02/09

BENIN UNIVERSITY OF SCIENCE AND TECHNOLOGY

Université des Sciences et Technologies du Bénin (USTB)
03 BP 2332, Lot 413 bis Domaine Universitaire de Kpondéhou,
Cotonou, Atlantique
Tel: +229(21) 33-60-10
Fax: +229(21) 33-60-13
EMail: info@ustbenin.org

Président: Clautide Dohou
Tel: +229(21) 33-88-93, Fax: +229(21) 33-88-93

Secrétaire Général: Dieudonné Agbannekpo
Tel: +229(21) 33-26-11 EMail: agbovincent@yahoo.fr

International Relations: Nina Attignon, Directrice de l'Administration et des Relations Internationales
Tel: +229(21) 33-60-10 EMail: ninattignon@yahoo.fr

Faculties

Agronomy *(FASA)* (Agronomy) *Dean:* Serge Attignon; **Economics** *(FASE)* (Economics) *Dean:* Serge Percheron; **Fundamental and Applied Sciences** *(FAFSA)* (Biological and Life Sciences; Biotechnology; Chemistry; Earth Sciences; Mathematics; Physics; Technology) *Dean:* Clément Kouchade; **Humanities, Arts and Social Sciences** *(FLASS)* (Arts and Humanities; Chinese; English; Geography (Human); German; History; Philosophy; Social Sciences; Sociology; Spanish) *Dean:* François Kouakou; **Law** *(FAD)* (Administration; International Relations; Law; Political Sciences) *Dean:* Anani Houessou; **Management** *(FASG) Dean:* Serge Percheron

Higher Schools

Applied Informatics *(ESIA)* (Business Computing; Computer Engineering; Computer Science) *Director:* Guy Hounsa; **Civil Engineering, Mining and Geology** *(ESTPMG)* (Civil Engineering; Construction Engineering; Mechanical Engineering; Production Engineering; Surveying and Mapping) *Director:* Clément Koutchade; **Communication Studies** *(ESCOM)* (Communication Studies; Multimedia) *Director:* Serge Bléhoué Brou; **Industrial Technology** *(ESTI)* (Automation and Control Engineering; Chemistry; Computer Engineering; Computer Networks; Electrical Engineering; Electronic Engineering; Energy Engineering; Industrial Engineering; Maintenance Technology; Thermal Engineering) *Director:* Gaston Edah; **Management and Business Administration** *(ESMAE)* (Accountancy; Administration; Banking; Business Administration; Business and Commerce; Finance; Human Resources; International Business; Management; Marketing; Safety Engineering; Secretarial Studies) *Director (Acting):* Angèle Renaud-Dohou

History: Founded 1996. Acquired present status 2002.

Governing Bodies: Conseil d'Administration; Conseil d'Université

Academic Year: October to June

Admission Requirements: Secondary school certificate (baccalauréat) or foreign equivalent

Main Language(s) of Instruction: French; English; German; Spanish; Chinese

International Co-operation: With universities in France and China

Accrediting Agencies: African and Malagasy Council for Higher Education (CAMES)

Degrees and Diplomas: *Diplôme Universitaire de Technologie; Licence/Licence professionnelle:* 3 yrs; *Ingénieur:* 5 yrs; *Maîtrise/ Maîtrise professionnelle:* 5 yrs; *Doctorat des Universités:* 3 yrs following Maîtrise

Student Services: Academic counselling, Canteen, Employment services, Foreign student adviser, Foreign Studies Centre, Handicapped facilities, Health services, Nursery care, Social counselling, Sports facilities

Student Residential Facilities: 2 private halls of residence (forc. 630 students)

Special Facilities: Art Gallery

Libraries: 8,482 vols

Publications: Le Manager, Information on Management *(biannually)*; Message, Scientific *(biannually)*

Press or Publishing House: USTB-Info

Academic Staff 2007-2008	MEN	WOMEN	TOTAL
FULL-TIME	147	51	**198**
PART-TIME	318	70	**388**
STAFF WITH DOCTORATE			
FULL-TIME	47	19	**66**
PART-TIME	103	15	**118**
Student Numbers 2007-2008			
All (Foreign Included)	2,847	951	**3,798**
FOREIGN ONLY	803	215	**1,018**

Part-time students, 187. **Distance students**, 1,228. **Evening students**, 1,253.
Last Updated: 11/12/08

CATHOLIC UNIVERSITY WESTERN AFRICA

Université Catholique de l'Afrique de l'Ouest
Unité Universitaire de Cotonou, 04 BP 928, Cotonou
Tel: +(229) 21-30-51-18
Fax: +(229) 2130- 51-17
EMail: ucao@ucaobenin.com
Website: http://www.ucaobenin.com

President: Père Pierre Able Dago

Institutes
Pontifical Institute John Paul II (Family Studies)

Units
Cotonou *(UUBC)* (Accountancy; Advertising and Publicity; Business Administration; Business and Commerce; Business Computing; Communication Studies; Economics; Environmental Studies; Insurance; International Business; Law; Secretarial Studies; Transport Management)

Fees: (CFA Francs): 350,000 per annum

Degrees and Diplomas: *Diplôme d'Etudes Universitaires Générales*; *Licence/Licence professionnelle*; *Maîtrise/Maîtrise professionnelle*
Last Updated: 09/03/11

COLLEGE OF SURVEYING AND MAPPING

Ecole supérieure des Ingénieurs Géomètres Topographes (ESIGT)
03 BP 1941, Jéricho, Cotonou
Tel: +229 21-32-08-64 +229 954-212-70
Fax: +229 21-32-08-64

Managing Director: Constantin Bah
EMail: bah_constantin@yahoo.fr

Administrative Officer: Armand Folly

International Relations: Constantin Bah, Managing Director

Programmes
Surveying and Mapping (Surveying and Mapping)
History: Founded 2001.

Admission Requirements: Engineers: BTS, Licence, Master in Science

Fees: (CFA Francs): 600,000 per annum (Social fee), 2m. (Tuition)

Main Language(s) of Instruction: French

International Co-operation: With Ecole Supérieure des Géomètres Topographes de France (ESTG)

Accrediting Agencies: Ministry of Higher Education and Scientific Research (MESRS)

Degrees and Diplomas: *Ingénieur*: 5 yrs+6 months of practical training

Student Services: Academic counselling, Employment services, Foreign student adviser, Health services, Language programs, Nursery care, Sports facilities

Libraries: Yes

Publications: L'arpenteur, Related to surveying *(annually)*

Academic Staff 2008-2009	MEN	WOMEN	TOTAL
FULL-TIME	6	1	**7**
PART-TIME	10	1	**11**

Last Updated: 28/04/09

HIGHER INSTITUTE OF VOCATIONAL EDUCATION

Institut supérieur de Formation professionnelle (ISFOP)
01 BP, Cotonou, Littoral 1206
Tel: +229 21-30-36-18
EMail: isfop@nomade.fr

Head: Marius Dakpogan EMail: mariusdakpogan@yahoo.fr

Programmes
Accountancy and Management (Accountancy; Management); **Agricultural Production** (Agriculture); **Bank Management** (Banking); **Banking and Corporate Finance** (Banking; Finance); **Business Administration** (Business Administration); **Business Computing** (Business Computing); **Marketing and Commercial Action** (Marketing); **Regional Planning** (Regional Planning)

History: Founded 1993.

Degrees and Diplomas: *Brevet de Technicien Supérieur*; *Licence/Licence professionnelle*; *Master*
Last Updated: 23/02/09

HOUDEGBE NORTH AMERICAN UNIVERSITY BENIN (HNAUB)

06 BP 2080, Cotonou 229
Tel: +229 21-33-21-27 +229 90-90-27-77
Fax: +229 21-33-35-88
EMail: hnaub@hnaub.org; hnaub_cotonou@hotmail.com
Website: http://www.houdegbeuniversity.org

Chancellor and President: Octave Cossi Houdegbe (2001-)
Tel: +229 95-15-10-49, Fax: +229 21-33-35-88
EMail: hnaub-cotonou@hotmail.com

Administrator: Apollinaire Hacheme
Tel: +229 95-01-05-03 EMail: hachemepo@yahoo.fr

International Relations: Victorin Degbo, Special Assistant of Chancellor Tel: +229 97-68-46-34 EMail: degbovic@yahoo.fr

Institutes
Languages and Translation (English; French; German; Modern Languages; Secretarial Studies; Spanish; Translation and Interpretation) *Division Head*: Innocent Arire Mako

Schools
Business Administration and Economics *(Léon Sullivan School)* (Accountancy; Banking; Business Administration; Economics; Finance; Management; Marketing; Sociology) *Dean*: Francis Kent-Akibor; **International Affairs and Political Sciences** *(Dr. Kwame Nkrumah School)* (Education; International Relations; Law; Political Sciences; Public Administration) *Dean*: André Corneille Zanou; **Law** *(Kessington School)* (Commercial Law; International Law; Law; Maritime Law; Private Law; Public Law) *Dean*: Soares Ladipo; **Medicine and Pharmacy** *(Dr. Maryam Babanguida School)* (Biochemistry; Medicine; Nursing; Pharmacy) *Provost*: Samuel Hanan; **Science and Information Technology** (Computer Engineering; Computer Science; Information Sciences; Information Technology; Technology) *Dean*: David Abiona

History: Founded 2001. Acquired present status 2002.

Governing Bodies: Board of Governors

Admission Requirements: GCE ('O') Level, West African School Certificate or Baccalaureate (BAC)

Fees: (CFA Francs): 1m-1.5m per annum, including room and board (where applicable)

Main Language(s) of Instruction: English, French

International Co-operation: With universities in Canada; Germany and USA

Accrediting Agencies: Ministry of Higher Education and Scientific Research (MESRS); National Universities Commission (NUC)

Degrees and Diplomas: Bachelor's degree, 4 yrs, BSc (Management; Accountancy; Marketing; Economics; Finance; Human Resources; Computer Science; Nursing; Biology; Toxicology; Biochemistry; Chemistry); Bachelor's degree, 4 yrs, BA (Arts and Humanities); Master's degree, 2 yrs (Languages; Political Science; Sociology; Mass Communication; Accountancy; Business Administration; International Relations; Management; Community Health; Environmental Health Sciences)

Student Services: Academic counselling, Canteen, Cultural centre, Foreign student adviser, Health services, Social counselling, Sports facilities

Student Residential Facilities: Staff and student Apartments (single/double occupancies)

Libraries: Under construction; access to the US Cultural Center Library

Academic Staff 2008-2009	MEN	WOMEN	TOTAL
FULL-TIME	31	3	**34**
PART-TIME	26	3	**29**
STAFF WITH DOCTORATE			
FULL-TIME	8	–	**8**
PART-TIME	4	–	**4**
Student Numbers 2008-2009			
All (Foreign Included)	621	696	**1,317**
FOREIGN ONLY	611	688	**1,299**

Part-time students, 309.
Last Updated: 14/08/09

INTERNATIONAL POLYTECHNIC UNIVERSITY OF BENIN

Université Polytechnique Internationale du Bénin (UPIB)
Étoile Rouge, 02 BP 8133, Cotonou, Atlantique-Littoral
Tel: +229 21-32-83-95 +229 21-32-83-96
Website: http://www.cepib-formation.com

Head: Valère K. Glele

Programmes
Accountancy and Management; Banking and Finance (Banking; Finance); **Business Computing and Corporate Communication** (Business Computing; Communication Studies); **Communication, Advertising and New Media; Electronics** (Electronic Engineering); **Engineering** (Communication Studies; Finance; Management; Marketing); **Human Resources, Management and Social Relations** (Human Resources; Management; Social Studies); **Industrial Informatics and Maintenance** (Business Computing; Industrial Maintenance); **Informatics** (Computer Science); **Insurance** (Insurance); **Management; Marketing and Commercial Action; Marketing and Commercial Communication** (Advertising and Publicity; Communication Studies; Marketing); **Marketing, Communication and Commercial Strategy; Secretarial Studies** (Secretarial Studies); **Telecommunications Studies; Tourism and Leisure; Transports and Logistics** (Transport and Communications; Transport Management)

History: Founded 1992.

Fees: (CFA Francs): BTS, 50,000; fees, 320,000. Licence, 50,000; fees, 520,000-740,000. Postgraduate, 60,000; fees, 680,000-720,000

Degrees and Diplomas: *Diplôme Universitaire de Technologie; Licence/Licence professionnelle; Master*
Last Updated: 23/02/09

LE CITOYEN POLYTECHNIC INSTITUTE

Institut Polytechnique Le Citoyen (IPC)
01 BP 3524, C 156 lot O, rue du Commissariat de Cadjehoun, Domaine le Citoyen, Cotonou, Littoral
Tel: +229 21-30-51-06 +229 90-90-39-70
Fax: +229 21-30-23-73

Head: Abraham Voglozin

Programmes
Accountancy/Management; Corporate Banking and Finance; Development Communication; Education/Pedagogy (Education; Pedagogy); **Financial Resources Management; Human Resources Management** (Human Resources); **Secretarial Studies** (Secretarial Studies)

History: Founded 1998.

Degrees and Diplomas: *Brevet de Technicien Supérieur; Licence/ Licence professionnelle; Diplôme d'Etudes Supérieures Spécialisées; Maîtrise/Maîtrise professionnelle*

PIGIER BÉNIN
01 BP 2411 RP, Carré 10 - rue 503, Antikanmey Cotonou, Cotonou, Littoral
Tel: +229 21-31-16-44
Fax: +229 21-31-30-47
EMail: pigiercotonou@yahoo.fr
Website: http://www.cie-formation.com

Directeur général: Henri Tafou
Directeur pédagogique: Gérard Akindes
International Relations: Charles Hounnidé, Head of Marketing

Programmes
Accountancy and Management; Accountancy Audit and Management Control (Accountancy; Management); **Bilingual Executive Assistant; Commercial Action; Corporate Banking and Finance; Finance and Expertise** (Finance); **Journalism and Communication; Negociation and Multimedia Communication** (Communication Studies; Multimedia); **Secretarial Studies** (Secretarial Studies)

History: Founded 1993.
Admission Requirements: Baccalauréat or Licence
Fees: (CFA Francs): 800,000 per annum
Main Language(s) of Instruction: French and English
Degrees and Diplomas: *Brevet de Technicien Supérieur*: 2 yrs; *Licence/Licence professionnelle (Diplôme supérieur de spécialité)*: 3 yrs; *Master*: 5 yrs
Student Services: Foreign student adviser, Health services, Nursery care
Libraries: Yes

Academic Staff 2008-2009	MEN	WOMEN	TOTAL
FULL-TIME	86	14	**100**
STAFF WITH DOCTORATE			
FULL-TIME	27	2	**29**
Student Numbers 2008-2009			
All (Foreign Included)	350	200	**550**
FOREIGN ONLY	75	50	**125**

Evening students, 208.
Last Updated: 15/07/09

PROTESTANT UNIVERSITY OF WESTERN AFRICA

Université Protestante d'Afrique de l'Ouest (UPAO)
01 BP 176, 1er Arrondissement Ahouanticomè, Porto Novo, Ouémé
Tel: +229 20-21-29-30
Fax: +229 20-21-29-62
EMail: upaoben@intnet.bj

Rector: Marcellin S. Dossou (2002-)
Director of Academic Services: Timothée A. Gandonou
International Relations: Gaéton-Pierre Avademe, Director, Finance and Administration

Institutes
Accountancy and Finance Management (Accountancy; Finance; Management); **Education Sciences** (Educational Sciences; Pedagogy); **Human Resources Management** (Human Resources; Management); **Theology** (Theology)

History: UPAO belongs to four churches in three countries and was founded as a Theological college in 1924 before acquiring university status in 2003.
Academic Year: September to June
Admission Requirements: Secondary school certificate (Baccalauréat)
Fees: (CFA Francs): Registration, 300,000-500,000 per annum; students sent by member churches, 75%
Main Language(s) of Instruction: French, English
International Co-operation: With ASTHEOL (Association des Institutions d'Enseignement théologique en Afrique occidentale)
Accrediting Agencies: ASTHEOL; University of Benin and Private Universities Association

Degrees and Diplomas: *Licence/Licence professionnelle*: Theology, Science of Education, Accounting and Finance Management, Human Resource Management, 3 yrs; *Maîtrise/Maîtrise professionnelle*: Theology, Science of Education, Accounting and Finance Management, Human Resource Management, 4 yrs

Student Services: Academic counselling, Health services, Nursery care, Social counselling, Sports facilities

Student Residential Facilities: For 25 students

Libraries: Yes

Press or Publishing House: C.L.E. Yaoundé

Academic Staff *2008-2009*	MEN	WOMEN	TOTAL
FULL-TIME	56	6	62
PART-TIME	4	3	7
STAFF WITH DOCTORATE			
FULL-TIME	23	3	26
PART-TIME	7	2	9
Student Numbers *2008-2009*			
All (Foreign Included)	55	35	90
FOREIGN ONLY	12	4	16

Last Updated: 17/06/09

SCHOOL OF COMMERCE AND MANAGEMENT
Haute Ecole de Commerce et de Management (HECM)
01 BP 3842, Lot 485 Bar Tito, Cotonou Oueme-Plateau
Tel: +229 21-32-57-28
EMail: contact@hecm-afrique.net
Website: http://www.hecm-benin.net

Directeur: Natondé Ake

Programmes
Accountancy and Management (Accountancy; Management); **Administration and Human Resources Management** (Administration; Human Resources; Management); **Banking and Finance** (Banking; Finance); **Bureautics and Secretarial Studies; Business Computing; Communication and Commercial Negociation; Corporate Communication; Electronics** (Electronic Engineering); **Finance and Management Control** (Finance; Management); **Food Chemistry and Quality Control** (Chemistry; Food Science); **Human Resources Management** (Human Resources; Management); **Industrial Informatics and Maintenance** (Business Computing; Industrial Maintenance); **Journalism** (Journalism); **Management Informatics and NICT** (Business Computing; Information Technology; Management); **Marketing and Commercial Action** (Business and Commerce; Marketing); **Tourism and Leisure** (Leisure Studies; Tourism)

History: Founded 1999.

Admission Requirements: Secondary school leaving certificate (Baccalauréat); Bachelor for graduate programmes.

Fees: (CFA Francs): BTS, 395,000 per annum; Licence, 650,000 per annum.

Degrees and Diplomas: *Brevet de Technicien Supérieur (BTS)*; *Licence/Licence professionnelle*; *Master*
Last Updated: 03/02/09

UNIVERSITY INSTITUTE OF BENIN
Institut universitaire du Bénin (IUB)
06 BP 3116, Aïdjèdo, rue du Centre d'Accueil Mgr Parisot, Cotonou, Littoral 06
Tel: +229 21-32-81-97 +229 97-10-37-89
Fax: +229 21-32-78-32
EMail: secretariat@iubformations.org
Website: http://www.iubformations.org

Président: Albert Gandonou
Tel: +229 97-47-72-90 EMail: gandalert@yahoo.fr

Departments
Communication Studies (Communication Studies) *Director*: Hounpati Capo; **Computer Engineering** (Computer Engineering) *Director*: Fantodji; **French Language** (French; Literature; Translation and Interpretation) *Director*: Albert Gandonou; **Sociology** (Sociology) *Director*: Francis Akindès

History: Founded 2002.

Academic Year: October to December (October-December; January-March; April-June)

Admission Requirements: Baccalauréat

Main Language(s) of Instruction: French

International Co-operation: With universities in Côte d'Ivoire and Nigeria

Degrees and Diplomas: *Ingénieur*: Computer Science, 5 yrs; *Diplôme d'Etudes Supérieures Spécialisées*: Communication Studies; Human Resources; Development Studies and Management; Banking; Finance; Insurance (DESS), 5 ans; *Master*

Student Services: Language programs, Nursery care, Sports facilities

Libraries: Central library; E-library

Academic Staff *2008-2009*	MEN	WOMEN	TOTAL
FULL-TIME	2	1	3
PART-TIME	–	–	3
STAFF WITH DOCTORATE			
FULL-TIME	–	–	1
PART-TIME	–	–	3
Student Numbers *2008-2009*			
All (Foreign Included)	40	11	51
FOREIGN ONLY	9	5	14

Part-time students, 3. **Distance students**, 7. **Evening students**, 41.
Last Updated: 30/07/09

UNIVERSITY OF APPLIED SCIENCES AND MANAGEMENT
Université des Sciences appliquées et du Management (USAM)
221/224 rue et n°144 Accron-Gogankomey, Porto-Novo, Oueme 01 BP 3582
Tel: +229 20-21-54 +229 90-90-05-32
Fax: +229 22-54-05-31
EMail: info@univ-usam.net

Institutes
Advanced Business Studies *(IHEC)* (Business Administration); **Alternative and Continuous Training** (Continuing Education); **Applied Sciences and Technology** (Natural Sciences; Technology); **Political and Social Sciences Rights** *(IDSPS)* (Political Sciences; Social Sciences)

History: Founded 2003. Acquired present status 2004.

Main Language(s) of Instruction: French, English

Degrees and Diplomas: *Brevet de Technicien Supérieur*; *Licence/Licence professionnelle*; *Master*
Last Updated: 16/10/09

VERECHAGUINE A.K. SCHOOL OF CIVIL ENGINEERING
Ecole supérieure de Génie Civil Verechaguine (ESGC VAK)
02 BP 244, C/753 Gbegamey, Cotonou, Atlantique
Tel: +229 90-92-33-31 +229 97-97-00-96
Fax: +229 21-30-69-08
EMail: secretariat_general_vak@yahoo.fr
Website: http://www.verechaguine.com

Directeur: Gérard Léopold Gbaguidi Aisse
Tel: +229 21-30-69-17 EMail: dg_vak@yahoo.fr

Chef de Service Administratif et Financier: Svetlana Gbaguidi
Tel: +229 21-30-69-17

International Relations: Jeanne-Marie Menou, Chef de Service
Tel: +229 21-30-69-17

Programmes
Civil Engineering (Civil Engineering)

Admission Requirements: Secondary school certificate (baccalauréat); DT(BTP,DPB)

Main Language(s) of Instruction: French

International Co-operation: With IUT and EPAC (Benin); Université de Limoges (France); Consortium EG@

Accrediting Agencies: Ministry of Higher Education and Scientific Research; Direction des Etablissements Privés d'Enseignement Supérieur

Degrees and Diplomas: *Brevet de Technicien Supérieur*: Civil Engineering; Topography; Surveying and Mapping (DT-BTP; DT-BPB), 2 yrs; *Licence/Licence professionnelle*: Civil Engineering; Topography; Surveying and Mapping (LGCI), 3 yrs; *Master*. Also Diplôme de Technicien (3 yrs)

Student Services: Health services, Language programs, Social counselling, Sports facilities

Libraries: Yes

Academic Staff *2008-2009*	MEN	WOMEN	TOTAL
FULL-TIME	30	1	**31**
PART-TIME	50	2	**52**
STAFF WITH DOCTORATE			
FULL-TIME	10	2	**12**
PART-TIME	–	–	**20**
Student Numbers *2008-2009*			
All (Foreign Included)	652	40	**692**
FOREIGN ONLY	32	4	**36**

Evening students, 30.
Last Updated: 05/06/09

Bhutan

STRUCTURE OF HIGHER EDUCATION SYSTEM

Description:

Higher education is under the responsibility of the Royal University of Bhutan for planning, curriculum development and administration of public institutions whereas the Ministry of Education selects students for international scholarships, designs and implements higher education policy.

Stages of studies:

University level first stage: Bachelor's degree
Bachelor's degrees are conferred in Arts, Commerce, Science and IT after four years to students who have passed the Class XII examinations.

University level second stage: Postgraduate diploma/certificate
Different postgraduate degrees are conferred mostly in education and business studies.

ADMISSION TO HIGHER EDUCATION

Admission to university-level studies:

Name of secondary school credential required: Bhutan Higher Secondary Education Certificate

NATIONAL BODIES

Ministry of Education

Minister: Thakur Singh Powdyel
Director, Department of Adult and Higher Education: Maina Kharga
P.O.Box 112
Thimphu
Fax: +975(2) 325 183
WWW: http://www.education.gov.bt
Role of national body: The Ministry of Education is responsible for selecting students for international scholarship; designing and implementing higher education policies.

Royal University of Bhutan

Vice-Chancellor: Pema Thinley
P.O. Box 708
Thimphu
Tel: +975(2) 336 454
Fax: +975(2) 336 453
WWW: http://www.rub.edu.bt
Role of national body: The Royal University of Bhutan is responsible for planning, curriculum development and administration of public higher education.

Data for academic year: 2006-2007
Source: IAU from Ministry of Education website, Bhutan, 2007. Bodies updated in 2011.

INSTITUTIONS

ROYAL UNIVERSITY OF BHUTAN (RUB)

PO Box 708, Lower Motithang, Semtokha, Thimphu
Tel: +975(2) 336-454 +975(2) 336-523 +975(2) 336-524
Fax: +975(2) 336-453 +975(2) 336-456
EMail: tandindorji@hotmail.com
Website: http://www.rub.edu.bt

Vice-Chancellor: Pema Thinley (2007-)
Tel: +975(2) 336-451, Fax: +975(2) 336-453
EMail: vc_rub@rub.edu.bt; pemathinley_2005@yahoo.com

Registrar: Kezang Doma
Tel: +975(2) 336-457 EMail: registrarRUB@druknet.bt

International Relations: Phintsho Choeden, Director, Research
and External Relations
Tel: +975(2) 336-455 EMail: phintsho@druknet.bt

Colleges
Business Studies *(Gedu, Chukha)* (Business Administration;
Business and Commerce) *Head*: Lhatu Jamba; **Education** *(Paro)*
(Education; Teacher Training) *Head*: Thubten Gyatsho; **Education**
(Samtse) (Education; Teacher Training) *Head*: Kaylzang Tshering;
Natural Resources *(Lobesa, Thimphu)* (Agriculture; Animal Hus-
bandry; Forestry) *Head*: Dorji Wangchuk; **Science and Technol-
ogy** *(Phuentsholing, Chukha)* (Civil Engineering; Electrical
Engineering; Electronic Engineering; Telecommunications Engi-
neering) *Head*: Nidup Dorji; **Sherubtse** *(Kanglung, Trashigang)*
(Arts and Humanities; Biological and Life Sciences; History; Infor-
mation Technology; Natural Sciences; Political Sciences; Sociology)
Head: Singye Namgyel

Institutes
Health Sciences *(Thimphu, Changzamto)* (Health Sciences; Med-
ical Technology; Midwifery; Nursing) *Head*: Chencho Dorji; **Lan-
guage and Cultural Studies** *(Semtokha, Thimphu)* (Cultural
Studies; Native Language) *Head*: Lungten Gyatso; **Polytechnic**
(Dewathang, Samdrup, Jongkhar) (Civil Engineering; Electrical
Engineering; Mechanical Engineering) *Head*: Kezang Chhodar;
Traditional Medicine *(Thimphu, Kawajangsa)* (Traditional Eastern
Medicine) *Dean*: Dorji Wangchuk

History: Founded 2003 by Royal Decree. A federated organization
of ten member colleges and institutes.

Governing Bodies: University Council

Academic Year: July to June or February to December, depending
on each college or institute.

Admission Requirements: Secondary School Certificate

Main Language(s) of Instruction: English

International Co-operation: with institutions in Australis, Canada,
USA, India

Degrees and Diplomas: *Diploma*: Civil Engineering; Electrical
Engineering; Mechanical Engineering; Agriculture; Forestry; Animal
Husbandry; Leadership and Management; Nursing and Midwifery;
Traditional Medicine; Dzongkha, 2-3 yrs; *Bachelor's Degree*: Busi-
ness Administration; Civil and Electrical Engineering; (BBA; BE);
English; Dzongkha; Information Technology; Mathematics; Physics;
Chemistry; Biology (BEd), 4 yrs; *Bachelor's Degree*: Computer
Science; Physical Science; Life Science; Traditional Medicine (BSc;
BSc(Hons)), 3-5 yrs; *Bachelor's Degree*: Dzongkha and English;
Dzongkha and Geography; English and Geography; English and
Environmental Science; Geography and Economics; Economics
and Environmental Studies; Dzongkha (BA), 3 yrs; 4 yrs double
degree; *Master of Education*: School Management and Leadership
(MEd), 5 yrs (part time); *Postgraduate Diploma*: English; Mathe-
matics (PGD), 3 yrs (part time). Also Postgraduate Certificate in
Mathematics (2 yrs)

Student Services: Academic counselling, Canteen, Cultural centre,
Employment services, Foreign student adviser, Foreign Studies
Centre, Handicapped facilities, Health services, Language pro-
grams, Nursery care, Social counselling, Sports facilities

Student Residential Facilities: Yes

Libraries: Yes

Publications: Building Our Institutional Futures, Seminar papers
(other/irregular); Journal of Research and Development, Research
journal *(annually)*; Men-jong So-rig, Journal of Herbal Medicine
(annually); Rabsel, Research and non-research based articles on
educational issues *(biannually)*; Rig-Gter, Academic research journal *(annually)*; Sherub Doenme: Academic Journal of Sherubtse
College, Academic journal *(other/irregular)*; The Personal Helicon,
Creative writing magazine *(annually)*; Yonten, Writings on educational themes as monographs *(other/irregular)*

Academic Staff 2008-2009	MEN	WOMEN	TOTAL
FULL-TIME	650	179	**829**
STAFF WITH DOCTORATE FULL-TIME	20	–	**20**

Student Numbers 2008-2009			
All (Foreign Included)	3,296	1,755	**5,051**

Part-time students, 400. **Distance students**, 319.
Last Updated: 19/02/09

Bolivia

STRUCTURE OF HIGHER EDUCATION SYSTEM

Description:

Higher education is offered in universities, higher technical institutions and teacher-training colleges. There are different kinds of universities: public and autonomous universities, with 70% of the student population; state universities and private universities. The Comité Ejecutivo de la Universidad Boliviana (CEUB) is responsible for the public and autonomous universities, which are the only ones entitled to public national funds. It also coordinates and puts into practice the decisions of the supreme governing body, the Congreso Nacional de Universidades. Private universities, most of which were created after 1985, are organized in an association, the Asociacíon Nacional de Universidades Privadas (ANUP), founded in 1992, but are supervised by the Ministry of Education and Culture.

Stages of studies:

University level first stage: *Bachillerato, Licenciatura*
The Bachillerato en Ciencias or Artes is awarded in professional careers by public universities after four years' study. The Licenciatura is awarded after five years.

University level second stage: *Diplomado, Especialización, Maestría, Doctorado*
Post-graduate courses are offered after at least one year of study. The Maestría may be obtained two years after the Licenciatura, after three for the Doctorado.

University level third stage: *Doctor en Ciencias Médicas*
Post-graduate degree that can be obtained after the especializacion.

ADMISSION TO HIGHER EDUCATION

Admission to university-level studies:

Name of secondary school credential required: Diploma de Bachiller en Humanidades

Entrance exam requirements: University entrance examination (Pre-Grado)

Foreign students admission:

Entrance exam requirements: Foreign students must hold a Secondary School Leaving Certificate equivalent to the Diploma de Bachiller. Some universities require an entrance examination (Pre-Grado).

Entry regulations: Students should hold a visa

Language requirements: Students should be proficient in Spanish.

NATIONAL BODIES

Ministerio de Educación (Ministry of Education)
Minister: Roberto Iván Aguilar Gómez
Vice-Minister, Higher Education: Armando Terrazas Calderón
Av. Arce No 2147
Casilla de correo 3116
La Paz
Tel: +591(2) 244 2144
Fax: +591(2) 244 4814
WWW: http://www.minedu.gob.bo/

Comité Ejecutivo de la Universidad Boliviana (Executive Committee of the Boliviana University)
Executive Secretary: Eduardo Cortez Baldivieso
Av. Arce Esq.Pinilla No 2606 y Hnos Manchego No 2559
La Paz

Tel: +591(2) 243 5258
Fax: +591(2) 243 5267
WWW: http://www.ceub.edu.bo/

Data for academic year: 2006-2007
Source: IAU from Ministry of Education and Culture website, 2007; Bodies updated in 2011.

INSTITUTIONS

PUBLIC INSTITUTIONS

AMAZONIAN UNIVERSITY OF PANDO
Universidad Amazónica de Pando (UAP)
Avenida Tte. Cnl. Cornejo N° 77, Cobija, Nicolás Suarez
Tel: +591(842) 2411 +591(842) 2135
Fax: +591(842) 2411
EMail: uap@uap.edu.bo
Website: http://www.uap.edu.bo/

Rector: René Mamani Quisbert (2007-)
Tel: +591(842) 2136
EMail: remamqui@hotmail.com; rectorado@uap.edu.bo

Director Administrativo Financiero: Marco Blanco Saraiva
Tel: +591(842) 2134, Fax: +591(842) 2134
EMail: daf@uap.edu.bo; msaraiva5@hotmail.com

International Relations: Ariz Humerez Alves, Secretario General
EMail: sg@uap.edu.bo

Academies
Las Piedras (Accountancy; Business Administration; Tourism)

Areas
Biology and Natural Sciences (Aquaculture; Biology; Fishery; Forestry; Natural Sciences); **Economics and Finance** (Accountancy; Business Administration; Economics); **Health Science** (Health Sciences); **Law and Political Science** (Law; Political Sciences); **Science and Technology** (Civil Engineering; Computer Engineering; Industrial Engineering; Natural Sciences; Technology); **Social Science** (Physical Therapy)

Institutes
Technology *(Puerto Rico)* (Aquaculture; Computer Engineering; Crop Production; Fishery; Nursing)
History: Founded 1993.
Governing Bodies: Consejo Universitario; Gobierno Universitario Docente-Estudiantil
Academic Year: February to December
Admission Requirements: Secondary school certificate (bachillerato) and entrance examination or pre-university courses (curso preuniversitario)
Fees: (Bolivianos): Nationals, 100 per semester; 200 per annum; foreign students, 800 per semester, 1,600 per annum
Main Language(s) of Instruction: Spanish
Degrees and Diplomas: *Técnico Universitario Medio (TUM)*: 2 yrs; *Técnico Universitario Superior (TUS)*: 3 yrs; *Licenciatura (LIC.)*: 5 yrs
Student Services: Academic counselling, Cultural centre, Health services, Language programs, Social counselling, Sports facilities
Special Facilities: Museum of Natural History 'Pedro Villalobos'
Libraries: Central Library
Last Updated: 05/03/09

APIAGÛAIKI TÛPA INDIGENOUS UNIVERSITY
Universidad Indígena Apiagûaiki Tûpa
Kuruyuki, Chuquisaca

Faculties
Fishery (Fishery); **Forestry** (Forestry); **Petroleum and Gas Engineering** (Petroleum and Gas Engineering); **Veterinary Science** (Veterinary Science)
History: Founded 2008.
Main Language(s) of Instruction: Guarani
Degrees and Diplomas: *Licenciatura*: Petroleum and Gas Egineering; Forestry; Fishery; Veterinary Science
Last Updated: 20/04/09

AUTONOMOUS UNIVERSITY OF BENI
Universidad Autónoma del Beni 'José Ballivián' (UAB)
Casilla Postal 38, Avenida 6 de Agostos N° 5715, Calle Sucre, Trinidad, Beni
Tel: +591(3) 462-1590 +591(3) 462-0744
Fax: +591(3) 462-0236
EMail: rector@uabjb.edu.bo
Website: http://www.uabjb.edu.bo/uab

Rector: Luis Carlos Zambrano Aguirre (2010-)
Secretario General: Nelson Yañez Roca
EMail: secretariogeneral@uabjb.edu.bo

Faculties
Agriculture (Agricultural Engineering; Agriculture; Animal Husbandry; Civil Engineering); **Animal Husbandry** (Animal Husbandry; Cattle Breeding; Veterinary Science); **Economics** (Accountancy; Business Administration; Economics); **Forestry** (Forestry); **Health Sciences** (Biochemistry; Health Sciences; Nursing; Pharmacy); **Humanities and Education Sciences** (Education; Pedagogy; Tourism); **Law and Political and Social Science** (Communication Studies; Law; Political Sciences)

Institutes
Arts
History: Founded 1967 as Universidad Técnica del Beni 'Mariscal José Ballivián', acquired present title and status 2005.
Main Language(s) of Instruction: Spanish
Degrees and Diplomas: *Técnico Universitario Medio*; *Licenciatura*; *Maestría*
Libraries: c. 10,000 vols

Student Numbers *2009*: Total: c. 15,000
Last Updated: 09/03/11

CASIMIRO HUANCA INDIGENOUS UNIVERSITY
Universidad Indígena Casimiro Huanca
Chimore, Cochabamba

Faculties
Fishery (Fishery); **Food Technology** (Food Technology); **Forestry** (Forestry); **Tropical Agriculture** (Tropical Agriculture)
History: Founded 2008.

Main Language(s) of Instruction: Quechua

Degrees and Diplomas: *Licenciatura*: Tropical Agriculture; Food Technology; Forestry; Fishery

Last Updated: 20/04/09

EL ALTO PUBLIC UNIVERSITY
Universidad Pública de El Alto
Av. Sucre s/n Zona Villa Esperanza, El Alto, La Paz
Tel: +59 (12) 284-4177
Website: http://www.upea.edu.bo

Rector: Damaso Quispe

Faculties
Accountancy (Accountancy); **Agricultural Engineering** (Agricultural Engineering); **Architecture** (Architecture); **Business Administration** (Business Administration; Economics); **Development Studies** (Development Studies); **Educational Sciences** (Education; Educational Sciences); **Engineering** (Civil Engineering; Electronic Engineering; Petroleum and Gas Engineering; Systems Analysis); **Law** (Law); **Linguistics** (Linguistics); **Medicine** (Dentistry; Medicine); **Nursing** (Nursing); **Social Communication** (Communication Studies; Social Sciences); **Sociology** (Sociology); **Veterinary Science** (Veterinary Science)

History: Founded 2000.

Main Language(s) of Instruction: Spanish

Degrees and Diplomas: *Licenciatura*: Agricultural Engineering; Civil Engineering; Business Engineering, System Analysis; Electronic Engineering; Petroleum and Gas Engineering, 10 sem; *Licenciatura*: Business Administration; Architecture; Education; Development Studies; Social and Communication Studies; Accountancy; Law; Economics; Nursing; Linguistics; Medicine; Dentistry; Sociology; Social Work; Veterinary Science, 5 yrs

Last Updated: 11/03/11

GABRIEL RENÉ MORENO AUTONOMOUS UNIVERSITY
Universidad Autónoma Gabriel René Moreno (UAGRM)
Casilla Postal 702, Plaza 24 de Septiembre - Acera Oeste,
Santa Cruz, Santa Cruz de la Sierra
Tel: +591(3) 336-5533
Fax: +591(3) 334-2160
EMail: uagrm@uagrm.edu.bo
Website: http://www.uagrm.edu.bo

Rector: Reymi Ferreira Justiniano (2008-)
EMail: rectorado@uagrm.edu.bo

Secretario General: Marcia Rivero Añez

Vice-Rector: Oscar Callejas Saldías

Faculties
Accountancy (Accountancy) *Dean*: Richard Moreno Suárez; **Agriculture** (Agricultural Engineering; Agriculture; Agronomy; Biology; Forestry) *Dean*: Nelson Rodríguez Méndez; **Economics and Finance** (Business Administration; Business and Commerce; Economics; Finance) *Dean*: David Valverde Quiroz; **Exact Sciences and Technology** (Chemical Engineering; Civil Engineering; Computer Engineering; Electrical Engineering; Environmental Engineering; Food Science; Industrial Engineering; Mechanical Engineering; Petroleum and Gas Engineering; Physics; Technology); **Habitat, Arts and Design** (Design; Fine Arts; Interior Design); **Health Sciences** (Biochemistry; Health Sciences; Medicine; Nursing; Pharmacy); **Humanities** (Arts and Humanities; Communication Studies; Educational Sciences; Modern Languages; Philology; Psychology; Sociology); **Integral Del Chaco** (Accountancy; Agricultural Engineering; Computer Engineering; Nursing; Petroleum and Gas Engineering); **Integral Del Norte** (Accountancy; Computer Engineering; Finance; Industrial Engineering; Law; Medicine; Nursing; Petroleum and Gas Engineering; Veterinary Science); **Law, Political and Social Sciences** (International Relations; Law; Political Sciences; Social Sciences; Social Work); **Polytechnic** (Construction Engineering; Electrical Engineering; Electronic Engineering; Engineering; Mechanical Engineering; Surveying and Mapping; Technology); **Technology** *(Universitario Vallegrande)* (Agriculture); **Veterinary Science** (Veterinary Science)

History: Founded 1880 as Universidad de Santo Tomás de Aquino, became autonomous in 1911. A State institution.

Academic Year: February to December (February-June; July-December)

Admission Requirements: Secondary school certificate (bachillerato) and entrance examination

Main Language(s) of Instruction: Spanish

Degrees and Diplomas: *Técnico Universitario Superior*: Technical Studies, 3-4 yrs; *Licenciatura*: Accountancy; Animal Husbandry and Veterinary Medicine; Business Administration; Chemical Engineering; Civil Engineering; Economics; Law; Tropical Agriculture, Agriculture Engineering, 5 yrs; *Especialización no médica*

Student Residential Facilities: Yes

Libraries: Central Library, c. 70,000 vols; Campus library, c. 20,000

Press or Publishing House: Imprenta Universitaria

Academic Staff 2009	TOTAL
FULL-TIME	400
PART-TIME	c. 1,100

Student Numbers 2009	
All (Foreign Included)	c. 60,000

Last Updated: 04/03/09

JUAN MISAEL SARACHO AUTONOMOUS UNIVERSITY
Universidad Autónoma Juan Misael Saracho (UAJMS)
Casilla Postal 51, Avenida Victor Paz E. No 149, Tarija, Cercado
Tel: +591(4) 66431-10
Fax: +591(4) 61123-22
EMail: rector@uajms.edu.bo
Website: http://www.uajms.edu.bo

Rector: Carlos Cabrera Iñiguez
Tel: +591(66) 331-10 EMail: rector@mail.uajms.edu.bo

Secretaria General: Ana Rosa Lopez Reynoso
Tel: +591(66) 339-12 EMail: secun@uajms.edu.bo

International Relations: Eduardo Trigo
Tel: +591(66) 432-32 EMail: ppaunesco@mail.uajms.edu.bo

Departments
Morpho-physiology and Pathology (Pathology; Physiology)

Faculties
Agriculture and Forestry (Agriculture; Agronomy; Forestry); **Dentistry** (Dentistry); **Economics and Finance** (Accountancy; Business Administration; Economics; Finance; Statistics); **Health Sciences** (Health Sciences); **Humanities**; **Law and Political Sciences**; **Science and Technology** (Architecture; Chemical Engineering; Civil Engineering; Computer Engineering; Food Science; Mathematics and Computer Science; Technology)

Programmes
Journalism (Journalism)

History: Founded 1946. A State institution.

Governing Bodies: Consejo Universitario

Academic Year: March to December (March-July; August-December)

Admission Requirements: Secondary school certificate (bachillerato) and entrance examination

Fees: (US Dollars): Registration, c. 1,600; foreign students, c. 3,300 per annum

Main Language(s) of Instruction: Spanish

International Co-operation: Participates in the IESALC/UNESCO and CEPES-HU-CU programmes

Degrees and Diplomas: *Técnico Universitario Superior*: Accountancy; Accountancy and Cooperatives, 4 yrs; *Técnico Universitario Superior*: Agriculture and Stockraising; Agronomy; Veterinary Science and Zootechnics, 3 yrs; *Licenciatura*: Agriculture; Architecture; Auditing; Biochemistry and Pharmacy; Business Administration; Chemical Engineering; Civil Engineering; Computer Engineering; Dentistry; Economics; Food Science; Forestry; Law; Modern Languages; Nursing; Psychology, 5 yrs

Student Services: Health services, Sports facilities

Student Residential Facilities: Yes

Special Facilities: Observatorio Astronómico Nacional; Museo Histórico 'Cnl. José E. Méndez'. Casa de la Cultura. Canal de TV; Radio

Libraries: Central Library, c. 36,000 vols

Publications: Revista Nueva Economía *(biennially)*; Tercer Milenio *(monthly)*

Press or Publishing House: Imprenta Universitaria
Last Updated: 04/03/09

MARISCAL SUCRE PEDAGOGICAL UNIVERSITY
Universidad Pedagógica Mariscal Sucre
Avenida del Maestro No. 331, Sucre, Chuquisaca
Tel: +591(4) 646-2669 +591(4) 646-0391
Fax: +591(4) 645-3890
EMail: upedagogica@upedagogica.edu.bo
Website: http://upedagogica.edu.bo/

Rector: Otto Poppe Daza EMail: rectorado@upedagogica.edu.bo

Vice-Rectora: Sonia Alcocer Mayorga
EMail: vicerrectorado@upedagogica.edu.bo

Faculties
Educational Sciences (Education; Educational Sciences; Preschool Education; Primary Education; Secondary Education; Teacher Training)

History: Founded 1999.

Main Language(s) of Instruction: Spanish

Degrees and Diplomas: *Técnico Universitario Superior*: Education; Arts and Humanities; Natural Sciences; *Licenciatura*: Educational Sciences
Last Updated: 11/03/11

NATIONAL UNIVERSITY OF SIGLO VEINTE
Universidad Nacional de Siglo XX (UNSXX)
C.Campero No 36, Llallagua-Potosí
Tel: +591(2) 582-0222
Fax: +591(2) 582-2591
Website: http://www.unsxx.edu.bo/

Rector: Miltón Gomez Mamani

Secretario General: Ernesto Clani López

Areas
Health Sciences (Biochemistry; Dentistry; Laboratory Techniques; Nursing; Pharmacy); **Social Sciences** (Communication Studies; Educational Sciences; Law); **Technology** (Automotive Engineering; Computer Engineering; Electrical Engineering; Mechanical Engineering)

History: Founded in 1985.

Main Language(s) of Instruction: Spanish

Degrees and Diplomas: *Técnico Universitario Superior*; *Licenciatura*
Last Updated: 11/03/11

ROYAL, PONTIFICAL UNIVERSITY SAN FRANCISCO XAVIER OF DE CHUQUISACA
Universidad Mayor, Real y Pontificia de San Francisco Xavier de Chuquisaca
Casilla Postal 212, Calle Junín esq. Estudiantes, Sucre, Chuquisaca
Tel: +591(4) 64533-08
Fax: +591(4) 64553-08
EMail: r_internacionales@usfx.edu.bo
Website: http://www.usfx.edu.bo

Rector: Walter Arízaga CervantesFax: +591(4) 64415-41
EMail: rector@usfx.edu.bo

Vicerrector: Eduardo Rivero Zurita
Tel: +591(4) 64535-04, Fax: +591(4) 64810-80
EMail: vcerector@usfx.edu.bo

Faculties
Accountancy (Accountancy); **Agronomy** (Agricultural Engineering; Agriculture; Animal Husbandry; Crop Production; Forest Products; Forestry; Fruit Production; Natural Resources; Veterinary Science; Zoology); **Biochemistry and Pharmacy** (Biochemistry; Pharmacy); **Dentistry** (Dentistry); **Economics and Administration** (Administration; Economics); **Humanities** (Arts and Humanities; Education; Modern Languages; Pedagogy; Psychology; Tourism); **Law, Political and Social Sciences** (Law; Political Sciences; Social Sciences); **Medical Technology** (Laboratory Techniques; Medical Technology; Nutrition; Physical Therapy); **Medicine** (Biochemistry; Dentistry; Health Sciences; Medicine; Nursing; Pharmacy; Physical Therapy; Radiology); **Nursing** (Nursing); **Technical** (Automation and Control Engineering; Construction Engineering; Electrical and Electronic Engineering; Engineering; Industrial Engineering; Mechanical Engineering; Technology); **Technology** (Architecture; Chemical Engineering; Civil Engineering; Computer Engineering; Electrical Engineering; Food Technology; Industrial Engineering; Mechanical Engineering; Systems Analysis; Technology; Telecommunications Engineering)

History: Founded 1624 by Father Juan de Frías y Herrán of the Society of Jesus and by Papal Bull and Royal Decree. Higher education came under State control 1852 and the University was reorganized and granted autonomous status 1930.

Governing Bodies: Claustro Universitario; Consejo Universitario; Asambleas de Facultades; Consejos Directivos

Academic Year: March to December (March-August; September-December)

Admission Requirements: Secondary school certificate (bachillerato) or equivalent and entrance examination

Main Language(s) of Instruction: Spanish

Degrees and Diplomas: *Técnico Universitario Superior*; *Licenciatura*; *Especialización no médica*; *Diplomado*; *Maestría*; *Doctorado*

Student Residential Facilities: Yes

Special Facilities: Museum of Colonial Art; Museum of Anthropology; Museum of Modern Art

Libraries: University Library, c. 60,000 vols; specialized faculty and school libraries, c. 20,000

Publications: Boletín de la Universidad popular; Boletín del Museo Antropológico; Boletín del Museo Colonial 'Charcas'; Ciencias políticas y sociales; Revista de la Facultad de Ciencias económicas; Revista de la Facultad de Ciencias médicas; Revista de la Facultad de Derecho; Revista del Instituto de Sociología Boliviana
Last Updated: 10/03/11

SAN SIMÓN UNIVERSITY
Universidad Mayor de San Simón (UMSS)
Casilla 992, Avenida Oquendo y Sucre, Cochabamba
Tel: +591(4) 422-0717
Fax: +591(4) 452-2114
EMail: rector@umss.edu.bo
Website: http://www.umss.edu.bo

Rector: Juan Ríos del Prado

Vice Rector: Walter Lopez Valenzuela EMail: vice@umss.edu.bo

International Relations: Luis Arteaga Weill
Tel: +591(4) 452-4779 EMail: dric@umss.edu.bo

Faculties
Agriculture and Animal Husbandry (Agriculture; Agronomy; Animal Husbandry; Forestry; Veterinary Science) *Dean*: Juan Villaroel Soliz; **Architecture** (Architecture; Graphic Design; Interior Design; Tourism) *Dean*: Carlos Felipe Guzmán Montaño; **Biochemistry and Pharmacy** (Biochemistry; Pharmacy); **Dentistry** (Dentistry) *Dean*: Wilma Ferrufino Guevara; **Economics** (Accountancy; Administration; Economics; Statistics) *Dean*: Alex Torrico Lara; **Humanities and Education** (Arts and Humanities; Bilingual and Bicultural Education; Educational Sciences; Linguistics; Psychology; Social Sciences; Social Work) *Dean*: Elena Ferrufino Coqueugniot; **Law and Political Science** (Law; Political Sciences) *Dean*: Ana Maria Fernandez; **Medicine** (Medicine; Nutrition; Physical Therapy) *Dean*: Franco Ibarra Gomez; **Nursing** (Nursing); **Science and Technology** (Biology; Chemical Engineering; Chemistry; Civil Engineering; Computer Engineering; Computer Science; Electrical and Electronic Engineering; Industrial Engineering; Mathematics; Mechanical Engineering; Natural Sciences; Physics; Technology) *Dean*: Julio Medina Gamboa; **Social Sciences** (Social Sciences; Sociology)

Institutes

Polytechnic (Agricultural Equipment; Civil Engineering; Construction Engineering; Food Science; Industrial Chemistry; Mechanical Engineering; Nursing; Statistics)

Schools

Agriculture (Agriculture; Agronomy); **Forestry** (Forestry)

History: Founded 1832 as School of Science and Arts. Granted autonomous status by law 1930. The University is financed by the State. It is part of the Bolivian Public University System.

Governing Bodies: Consejo Universitario; Consejos Directivos of the faculties, Career Council

Academic Year: February to December (February-June; July-December)

Admission Requirements: Secondary school certificate (bachillerato) and entrance examination

Fees: (Bolivianos): 100-800 (fees vary according to faculty)

Main Language(s) of Instruction: Spanish

International Co-operation: Member of CRISCOS, UNAMAZ, OUI, ANDRES BELLO, MERCOSUR, AECI

Degrees and Diplomas: *Técnico Universitario Superior*; *Licenciatura*: in all subjects, 4-5 yrs

Student Services: Canteen, Health services, Language programs, Sports facilities

Special Facilities: Archaeological Museum

Libraries: 8 Faculty libraries, c. 57,303 vols

Press or Publishing House: Imprenta Universitaria

Last Updated: 10/03/11

SIMÓN BOLÍVAR ANDEAN UNIVERSITY

Universidad Andina Simón Bolívar (UASB)
Casilla postal 545, Calle R. Audiencia No. 73, Sucre, Chuquisaca
Tel: +591(4) 646-0265
Fax: +591(4) 646-0833
EMail: info@uasb.edu.bo
Website: http://www.uasb.edu.bo

Rector: Rafael Vergara Sandoval (2010-)

Programmes

Communication and Journalism *(La Paz)* (Communication Studies; Journalism; Social Studies); **Culture and Literature**; **Development Studies** *(La Paz)* (Development Studies); **Economics and Administration** (Banking; Business Administration; Environmental Engineering; Finance; Town Planning); **Economics and Management** *(La Paz)* (Business Administration; Economics; Insurance; International Business; Management); **Education and Political Science** (Communication Studies; Distance Education; Education; Educational Technology; Information Sciences; Latin American Studies; Political Sciences); **Health Sciences** *(La Paz)* (Health Sciences); **Health Sciences** (Health Sciences); **Human Rights** (Human Rights); **Law** *(La Paz)* (Law); **Law** (Law)

Further Information: Branches in La Paz, Santa Fe de Bogotá (Colombia), Quito (Ecuador) and Caracas (Venezuela)

Degrees and Diplomas: *Especialización no médica*; *Diplomado*; *Maestría*; *Doctorado*
Last Updated: 10/03/11

TECHNICAL UNIVERSITY OF ORURO

Universidad Técnica de Oruro (UTO)
Casilla Postal 49, Avenida 6 de Octubre 1209, Oruro
Tel: +591(2) 525-01-00
Fax: +591(2) 524-22-15
EMail: webmaster@uto.edu.bo
Website: http://www.uto.edu.bo

Rector: Pablo Zubieta Arce
Tel: +591(2) 527-71-01 EMail: rector@uto.edu.bo

Secretario General: Gino Gonzalo Martínez Guzman
EMail: striagal@uto.edu.bo

International Relations: José Cortes Gumucio
Tel: +591(252) 757-98 EMail: dpic@uto.edu.bo

Faculties

Agriculture and Stockbreeding *(Oruro, Challapta)* (Agricultural Engineering; Agriculture; Cattle Breeding; Veterinary Science) *Dean*: Fernando Mendizabal Jara; **Architecture and Town Planning** (Architecture; Town Planning) *Dean*: Fernando Mendizabal Jara; **Economics, Finance and Administration** (Accountancy; Administration; Economics; Finance) *Dean*: Augusto Vela Ch.; **Engineering** *(National)* (Architecture; Chemical Engineering; Civil Engineering; Computer Engineering; Electrical Engineering; Electronic Engineering; Geological Engineering; Industrial Engineering; Mechanical Engineering; Metallurgical Engineering; Mining Engineering; Systems Analysis) *Dean*: David Emilio Ismael Rojas; **Health Sciences** (Cardiology; Epidemiology; Nursing; Public Health; Surgery) *Dean*: Oscar Rodrigo Balladares; **Law, Political and Social Sciences** (Law; Political Sciences; Social Sciences) *Dean*: Vidal Villarroel Vega; **Technical Studies** (Technology) *Dean*: Francisco Lazarte Martinez

Further Information: Branches in Oruro and Challapta

History: Founded 1892 as provincial University. Became autonomous in 1937. Formerly known as the Universidad Autónoma de San Agustín. Financed by the State.

Governing Bodies: Consejo Supremo Universitario; Consejos Facultativos

Academic Year: January to December

Admission Requirements: Secondary school certificate (bachillerato en humanidades) and entrance examination

Fees: (US Dollars): 200 per annum

Main Language(s) of Instruction: Spanish

International Co-operation: With universities in Cuba and Peru

Degrees and Diplomas: *Técnico Universitario Superior*: Technical Studies, 3 yrs; *Licenciatura*: Agriculture (Perito Agrícola); Auditing; Chemistry (Químico); Civil Engineering (Ingeniero Civil); Economics; Electrical Engineering (Ingeniero Eléctrico); Law (Abogado); Mechanical Engineering (Ingeniero Mecánica); Metallurgy (Ingeniero Metalurgista); Mining (Ingeniero de Minas); *Maestría*; *Doctorado*. Professional Titles are awarded in the same fields as Licenciatura. Also Técnico, technical studies

Student Services: Academic counselling, Cultural centre, Health services, Language programs, Social counselling, Sports facilities

Student Residential Facilities: Some

Special Facilities: Museum of History and Folklore; Archaeology Museum; Mineralogy Museum. Botanical Garden. Cultural House

Libraries: Central Library, c. 9,100 vols; Law, c. 11,000; Economics, c. 7,500; Engineering, c. 10,000; Agriculture, c. 1,550; Polytechnic, c. 6,000

Publications: Cultura Boliviana *(quarterly)*; Revista de Agronomía *(annually)*; Revista de Derecho *(annually)*; Revista de Metalurgía *(annually)*

Press or Publishing House: Editora Universitaria
Last Updated: 03/03/09

TOMÁS FRÍAS AUTONOMOUS UNIVERSITY

Universidad Autónoma Tomás Frías (UATF)
Casilla Postal 36, Av. Del Maestro-Av. Cívica s/n, Potosí
Tel: +591(2) 622-7300
Fax: +591(2) 622-6663
EMail: uatf-rpi@cotapnet.bo
Website: http://www.uatf.edu.bo

Rector: Roberto Borquez EMail: rectoruatf@cotapnet.com.bo

Faculties

Agriculture and Animal Husbandry (Agronomy; Animal Husbandry) *Dean*: Rodolfo Puch Cabrera; **Arts** (Music; Visual Arts) *Dean*: Luis Torrico Gamarra; **Economics and Finance** (Accountancy; Administration; Economics; Finance) *Dean*: Octavio Martinez Chura; **Engineering** (Civil Engineering; Construction Engineering; Surveying and Mapping) *Dean*: Mario Ortubé Parra; **Geological Engineering** (Geological Engineering); **Health Sciences** (Medicine; Nursing); **Humanities and Social Sciences** (Linguistics; Social Work; Tourism); **Law** (Law); **Mining Engineering** (Mining Engineering); **Pure Science** (Chemistry; Information Sciences; Mathematics; Physics; Statistics); **Technology** (Electrical and Electronic Engineering; Mechanical Engineering)

History: Founded 1892, the University was at first attached to the Universidad Francisco Xavier Sucre but became independent and autonomous. Acquired present title and status 1937.

Governing Bodies: Consejo Universitario; Comisión Académica

Academic Year: February to December (January-July; July-December)

Admission Requirements: Secondary school certificate (bachiller) and entrance examination

Main Language(s) of Instruction: Spanish

International Co-operation: Participates in the AECI programme

Accrediting Agencies: Comité Ejecutivo de la Universidad Boliviana (CEUB)

Degrees and Diplomas: *Técnico Universitario Superior*: Accountancy; Chemistry; Construction Engineering; Electronic and Electrical Engineering; Mathematics; Mechanical Engineering; Physics; Surveying; Fine Arts; Music; Tourism, 3-4 yrs; *Licenciatura*: Accountancy; Business Administration; Economics; Law; Agricultural Engineering; Civil Engineering; Electronic and Electrical Engineering; Mechanical Engineering; Mining Engineering; Veterinary Medicine; Chemistry; Information Science; Linguistics; Mathematics; Physics; Statistics; Social Work; Tourism; Fine Arts; Music; Medicine; Nursing, 5 yrs; *Diplomado*: Education; Geology; Marketing; Metallurgy; Statistics, 1-2 yrs; *Maestría*: 1-2 yrs

Student Services: Academic counselling, Canteen, Cultural centre, Health services, Language programs, Nursery care, Social counselling, Sports facilities

Special Facilities: University Museum 'Ricardo Bohorquez'; Mineralogy Museum; Art Museum; Meteorology Museum; TV Network

Libraries: Central Library, 19,337 vols; Engineering, 7,075; Economics, 5,224; Law, 5,006; Agriculture and Animal Husbandry, 1,366; Technology, 579; Arts, 506; Accountancy, 566

Publications: Libros de texto, Research

Press or Publishing House: University Press

Last Updated: 09/03/11

TUPAK KATARI INDIGENOUS UNIVERSITY

Universidad Indígena Tupak Katari
Warisata, La Paz
Tel: +561(2) 222-3576
EMail: unintiqulla@hotmail.com

Rector: Benecio Quispe

Faculties
Agronomy of the Altiplano (Agronomy); **Food Technology** (Food Technology); **Textile Technology** (Textile Technology); **Veterinary Science** (Veterinary Science)

History: Founded 2008.

Main Language(s) of Instruction: Aymara

Degrees and Diplomas: *Licenciatura*: Agronomy; Food Technology; Textile Technology; Veterinary Science
Last Updated: 10/03/11

UNIVERSITY OF SAN ANDRÉS

Universidad Mayor de San Andrés (UMSA)
Casilla Postal 6042, Monoblock, Avenida Villazón 1995, La Paz
Tel: +591(2) 2441-690
EMail: webmaster@umsa.bo
Website: http://www.umsa.bo/

Rectora: Teresa Rescala Nemtala
Tel: +591(2) 2440-211 EMail: rector@umsa.bo

Secretario General (a.I.): Germán Montaño

Faculties
Agronomy (Agricultural Engineering; Agriculture; Agronomy); **Architecture, Art, Design and Town Planning** (Architecture; Design; Fine Arts; Urban Studies); **Dentistry** (Dentistry); **Economics and Finance** (Business Administration; Economics; Finance); **Engineering** (Civil Engineering; Electrical Engineering; Food Technology; Industrial Engineering; Mechanical Engineering; Petroleum and Gas Engineering); **Geology** (Environmental Engineering; Geography; Geology); **Humanities and Education** (Education; History; Library Science; Linguistics; Literature; Philosophy; Psychology; Tourism); **Law and Political Science** (Law; Political Sciences); **Medicine** (Dietetics; Medical Technology; Medicine; Nursing; Nutrition); **Pharmacy and Biochemistry** (Biochemistry; Pharmacy); **Pure and Natural Sciences** (Biology; Chemistry; Computer Science; Ecology; Mathematics; Physics; Statistics); **Social Sciences** (Anthropology; Archaeology; Communication Studies; Social Work; Sociology); **Technology** (Air Transport; Industrial Chemistry; Mechanical Equipment and Maintenance; Surveying and Mapping)

Institutes
Altitude Studies *(Bolivian)* (Mountain Studies); **Genetics** (Genetics) *Director*: Edwin Mollinedo; **Hydraulics** (Hydraulic Engineering) *Director*: Jorge Molina Carpio; **Sanitary Engineering** (Environmental Engineering) *Director*: José Díaz Benavente

Programmes
Biological Sciences *(Graduate)* (Biological and Life Sciences; Biotechnology) *Director*: Roger Carnavajal; **Bolivian Studies** *(Graduate)* (Hispanic American Studies) *Director*: Raúl Calderón Jemio; **Chemistry of Natural Products** *(Graduate)* (Chemistry) *Director*: Luisa Balderrama; **Ecology and Conservation** (Ecology; Environmental Studies) *Director*: Monica Moraez Ramirez; **Public Health and Social Medicine** *(Graduate)* (Public Health; Social and Preventive Medicine) *Director*: Jaime Evia; **Sanitary Engineering** (Sanitary Engineering); **Town Planning** (Development Studies; Town Planning) *Director*: David Barrientos Zapata

History: Founded 1830, acquired present title 1972. An autonomous institution financially supported by the State and by special taxes.

Governing Bodies: Consejo Universitario

Academic Year: February to December

Admission Requirements: Secondary school certificate (bachillerato) and entrance examination

Main Language(s) of Instruction: Spanish

Degrees and Diplomas: *Técnico Universitario Superior*: Technical Studies, 2-3 yrs; *Licenciatura*: 4-5 yrs; *Diplomado*; *Maestría*: Agricultural Development, Public Health, Development Studies, Higher Education, a further 2 yrs. Also Especializaciones

Student Services: Academic counselling, Cultural centre, Health services, Nursery care, Social counselling, Sports facilities

Student Residential Facilities: Yes

Special Facilities: Archivo Histórico. El Planetario Max Schreier. Observatorio de Chacaltaya. Museo de Historia Natural. Herbario Nacional de Bolivia

Libraries: Central Library, c. 120,000 vols; Economics, c. 5,000; Law, c. 13,000; Sociology, c. 7,000; Architecture, c. 1,500; Genetics, c. 8,000; Exact and Natural Sciences, c. 6,000; Technology, c. 8,000; Health Sciences, c. 9,000; Humanities, c. 10,000

Publications: Revista, Memoria Universitaria *(annually)*
Last Updated: 10/03/11

PRIVATE INSTITUTIONS

ADVENTIST UNIVERSITY OF BOLIVIA

Universidad Adventista de Bolivia (UAB)
Av. Simón I. Patiño Km 1, Vinto, Cochabamba
Tel: +591 (4) 426-3330
Fax: +591 (4) 426-3336
EMail: info@uab.edu.bo
Website: http://www.uab.edu.bo

Rector: Franz Rios Flores EMail: rector@uab.edu.bo

Vicerrector Académico: Edual Santos
EMail: esantos@uab.edu.bo

Colleges
Adventist

Faculties
Economics (Accountancy; Administration; Business Administration; Economics) *Dean*: Ruth Cabrera Borda; **Education** (Education; Pedagogy; Physical Education; Psychology); **Engineering**

(Computer Engineering; Engineering; Systems Analysis); **Health Sciences** (Health Sciences); **Theology** (Theology)

Institutes
Adventist Teacher Training (Teacher Trainers Education)
History: Founded 1928. Acquired present status 1998.
Main Language(s) of Instruction: Spanish
Degrees and Diplomas: *Técnico Universitario Superior*; *Licenciatura*; *Maestría*: Education Administration; Administration
Last Updated: 05/03/09

AQUINAS UNIVERSITY BOLIVIA
Universidad De Aquino Bolivia (UDABOL)
Pasaje Isaac Eduardo no 2643, Capitan Ravelo, La Paz
Tel: +591(2) 441-044
Fax: +591(2) 441-873
EMail: aquino@udabol.edu.bo
Website: http://www.udabol.edu.bo
Rector: Antonio Saavedra

Faculties
Architecture and Tourism (Architecture; Tourism); **Economics and Finance** (Accountancy; Business and Commerce; Economics; Finance; Marketing); **Health Sciences** (Biochemistry; Dentistry; Medicine; Nursing; Pharmacy; Physical Therapy); **Science and Technology** (Petroleum and Gas Engineering; Systems Analysis; Technology; Telecommunications Engineering); **Social and Human Sciences** (Communication Studies; International Relations; Law; Psychology; Social Sciences)
Further Information: Also branches in Cochabamba, Oruro and Santa Cruz
History: Founded 1995. Acquired present status 2001.
Main Language(s) of Instruction: Spanish
Degrees and Diplomas: *Técnico Universitario Superior*; *Licenciatura*: 9-12 sem; *Maestría*
Last Updated: 10/03/11

BETHESDA UNIVERSITY
Universidad Bethesda
Av. Alemana Calle Chomono # 3650 (3er Anillo Externo), Santa Cruz, Santa Cruz de la Sierra
Tel: +561(3) 341-6200
Fax: +561(3) 342-4614
EMail: info@unibeth.edu.bo
Website: http://www.unibeth.edu.bo

Faculties
Computer Engineering (Computer Engineering); **Social Communication** (Communication Studies; Social Sciences); **Social Work** (Social Work); **Theology** (Theology)
History: Founded 2006.
Main Language(s) of Instruction: Spanish
Degrees and Diplomas: *Técnico Universitario Superior*: Computer Engineering; Social Communication; Social Work; Theology, 3 yrs; *Licenciatura*: Computer Engineering; Social Communication; Social Work; Theology, 5 yrs
Last Updated: 20/04/09

BOLIVAR UNION UNIVERSITY
Universidad Unión Bolivariana (UB)
Av. 6 de Marzo entre Calles 5 y 6, El Alto, La Paz
Tel: +591(2) 282-3513
Fax: +591(2) 2822-389
EMail: dtic@ub.edu.bo
Website: http://www.ub.edu.bo/
Rector: Gonzalo Sánchez Almanza EMail: gsarector@ub.edu.bo
Director Acádemico: Rodolfo Revollo Loza

Faculties
Economics and Finance (Accountancy; Business Administration; Economics; Finance; International Business; International Relations; Marketing; Psychology; Public Administration; Sociology; Statistics; Taxation); **Education and Humanities** (Arts and

Humanities; Curriculum; Education; Educational Psychology; Educational Sciences; Educational Technology; International and Comparative Education; Latin American Studies; Modern Languages; Pedagogy; Social Studies; Sociology); **Engineering** (Computer Engineering; Computer Networks; Engineering; English; Mathematics; Physics; Software Engineering; Statistics); **Law, Social and Political Sciences** (Law; Political Sciences; Social Sciences)
History: Acquired present status 2004.
Degrees and Diplomas: *Licenciatura*: 5 yrs
Last Updated: 05/10/07

BOLIVIAN AMAZONIAN UNIVERSITY
Universidad de la Amazonía Boliviana (UNAB)
Av. Nicolás Suárez N° 171, Riberalta, Beni
Tel: +591(3) 852-3600
Fax: +591(3) 852-2705

Programmes
Agribusiness (Agricultural Business); **Business Administration** (Business Administration); **Communication Sciences** (Communication Studies); **Law** (Law); **Pedagogy** (Pedagogy); **Tourism** (Tourism)
Further Information: Also branch in Guayaramerin
History: Founded 1996.
Main Language(s) of Instruction: Spanish
Degrees and Diplomas: *Técnico Universitario Superior*; *Licenciatura*

BOLIVIAN EVANGELICAL UNIVERSITY
Universidad Evangélica Boliviana (UEB)
Casilla 4027, Santa Cruz, Santa Cruz de la Sierra
Tel: +591(3) 3560-990
EMail: ueb@ueb.edu.bo
Website: http://www.ueb.edu.bo
Vicerrector Académico: Hermes Cayalo Cossio
Rector: Timoteo Sánchez Bejarano

Faculties
Agriculture, Forestry and Veterinary Science (Agriculture; Forestry; Veterinary Science); **Business Studies** (Accountancy; Administration); **Communication and Culture** (Communication Studies; English; Music); **Health Sciences** (Biochemistry; Clinical Psychology; Dietetics; Health Sciences; Nursing; Nutrition; Pharmacy); **Science and Technology** (Electronic Engineering; Technology); **Theology, Education and Social Sciences** (Educational Sciences; Psychology; Social Sciences; Social Work; Theology)
History: Founded 1982. Acquired present status 1985.
Main Language(s) of Instruction: Spanish
Degrees and Diplomas: *Técnico Universitario Superior*: 3 yrs; *Licenciatura*: 5 yrs; *Maestría*
Last Updated: 10/03/11

BOLIVIAN PRIVATE UNIVERSITY, COCHABAMBA
Universidad Privada Boliviana (UPB)
Km 6.5 Camino antiguo a Quillacollo, Cochabamba
Tel: +591(4) 426-8287
Fax: +591(4) 426-8288
EMail: upb@upb.edu
Website: http://www.upb.edu
Rector: Manuel Olave Sarmiento EMail: molave@upb.edu
Secretario General: Juan Antonio Fernández Léon
International Relations: Edwin Durán EMail: eduran@upb.edu

Colleges
Graduate Studies (Business Administration; Commercial Law)

Faculties
Engineering and Architecture (Architecture; Civil Engineering; Computer Science; Engineering; Industrial Engineering; Petroleum and Gas Engineering; Production Engineering; Systems Analysis) *Dean*: Cesar Villagomez; **Entrepreneurial Sciences and Law**

(Business Administration; Business and Commerce; Communication Studies; Economics; Finance; Graphic Design; Law; Marketing)

Research Centres
Economics Research (Economics); **Energy** (Energy Engineering); **Entrepreneurship** (Business Administration)

Further Information: Also branches in La Paz, Santa Cruz, Oruro and Tarija

History: Founded 1992 by the Federation of Private Entrepreneurs of Cochabamba and the Confederation of Private Entrepreneurs of Bolivia.

Governing Bodies: Board of Directors

Academic Year: February to December

Admission Requirements: Diploma de Bachiller en Humanidades, Prueba de Aptitud Académica of the College Board

Main Language(s) of Instruction: Spanish and English

International Co-operation: With universities in USA, Netherlands, Austria, Costa Rica, Colombia, Chile

Accrediting Agencies: Bolivian Government; Vice-Ministry of Higher Education

Degrees and Diplomas: *Licenciatura*: Engineering; Architecture; Business Administration; Economics; Graphic Design; Commerce; Finance; Law, 4-5 yrs; *Maestría*: Business Administration; International Business; Commercial Law, 1 yr; *Doctorado*

Student Services: Academic counselling, Canteen, Employment services, Language programs, Social counselling, Sports facilities

Student Residential Facilities: None

Libraries: Yes
Last Updated: 10/03/09

BOLIVIAN UNIVERSITY OF COMPUTER SCIENCE
Universidad Boliviana de Informática (UBI)
Rosendo Villa No. 146 al 150, Sucre, Chuquisaca
Tel: +591(4) 644-76-70 +591(4) 644-31-61
Fax: +591(4) 644-76-70
EMail: info@ubi.edu.bo
Website: http://www.ubi.edu.bo/

Rector: René Pasquier

Programmes
Agroindustry Engineering (Agricultural Engineering); **Agronomy** (Agronomy); **Architecture** (Architecture); **Auditing** (Accountancy); **Civil Engineering** (Civil Engineering); **Commercial Engineering** (Business and Commerce); **Hardware Engineering** (Computer Engineering); **Law** (Law); **Medicine** (Medicine); **Social Work** (Social Work); **Software Engineering** (Software Engineering); **Systems Engineering** (Systems Analysis); **Veterinary Science** (Veterinary Science); **Zootechniques** (Zoology)

Further Information: Also branches in El Alto and La Paz

History: Founded 1994.

Main Language(s) of Instruction: Spanish

Degrees and Diplomas: *Técnico Universitario Medio*; *Técnico Universitario Superior*; *Licenciatura*
Last Updated: 10/03/11

BOLIVIAN UNIVERSITY OF TECHNOLOGY
Universidad Tecnológica Boliviana (UTB)
Calle Colombia N° 154, Zona San Pedro, La Paz
Tel: +591(2) 235-7734
Fax: +591(2) 239-0731
EMail: infolp@utb.edu.bo
Website: http://www.utb.edu.bo

Rector: Kenny La Fuente Cámara EMail: napaza@utb.edu.bo

Director Académico: Luis Copa Soto

Programmes
Commerce (Business Administration; Business and Commerce); **Ecology and Environmental Engineering**; **Finance and Banking**; **Information Systems** (Information Management); **International Business** (International Business); **Law** (Law); **Systems Engineering** (Computer Engineering); **Taxation** (Taxation)

History: Founded 1993.
Degrees and Diplomas: *Técnico Universitario Medio*; *Técnico Universitario Superior*; *Licenciatura*; *Maestría*
Last Updated: 12/03/09

CENTRAL UNIVERSITY
Universidad Central (UNICEN)
Casilla Postal 4853, Calle Santivañez No 216, Cochabamba
Tel: +591(4) 4252-987
Fax: +591(4) 4254-613
EMail: unicen@unicen.edu.bo
Website: http://www.unicen.edu.bo

Rector: Ramiro Bustamente García EMail: rector@unicen.edu.bo

Secretario General: Jorge Porcel Porcel
EMail: sgral@unicen.edu.bo

Programmes
Accountancy (Accountancy); **Advertising and Marketing** (Advertising and Publicity; Marketing); **Business Administration** (Business Administration); **Commercial Engineering** (Business and Commerce; Finance); **Educational Sciences** (Educational Sciences); **Journalism** (Journalism); **Law** (Law); **Physiotherapy and Rehabilitation** (Physical Therapy; Rehabilitation and Therapy); **Psychology** (Psychology); **Social Work** (Social Work); **Tourism and Hotel Management** (Hotel Management; Tourism)

Further Information: Also branch in La Paz

History: Founded 1990.

Main Language(s) of Instruction: Spanish

Degrees and Diplomas: *Técnico Universitario Superior*; *Licenciatura*. Also postgrados
Last Updated: 10/03/11

CHRISTIAN UNIVERSITY OF BOLIVIA
Universidad Cristiana de Bolivia (UCEBOL)
Casilla postal 3449, Km 5 Carr.al Norte, Santa Cruz, Santa Cruz de la Sierra
Tel: +591(3) 342-6311
Fax: +591(3) 342-2356
EMail: info@ucebol.edu.bo
Website: http://www.ucebol.edu.bo

Rector: Eun Shil Chung

Programmes
Agricultural Engineering (Agricultural Engineering; Agronomy); **Biochemistry and Pharmacy** (Biochemistry; Pharmacy); **Business Administration** (Business Administration); **Commercial Engineering** (Business and Commerce); **Computer Engineering** (Computer Engineering); **Dentistry** (Dentistry); **Educational Sciences and Pedagogy** (Educational Sciences; Pedagogy); **Medicine and Surgery** (Medicine; Surgery); **Physiotherapy** (Physical Therapy); **Theology** (Theology); **Tourism** (Tourism)

History: Founded 1990.

Main Language(s) of Instruction: Spanish

Degrees and Diplomas: *Licenciatura*; *Especialización médica*
Last Updated: 10/03/11

COSMOS PRIVATE TECHNICAL UNIVERSITY
Universidad Técnica Privada Cosmos
Av. Blanco Galindo Km 71/2, Florida Norte, Cochabamba
Tel: +591(4) 4370352
Fax: +591(4) 4370325
EMail: info@unitepc.edu.bo
Website: http://www.unitepc.edu.bo

Rector: Javier Hugo Terceros Cortez

Vicerrector: Hugo Fuentes Rojas

Faculties
Administration, Social Sciences and Law (Administration; Law; Social Sciences); **Educational Sciences** (Educational Sciences; Pedagogy); **Engineering** (Engineering); **Health Sciences** (Health Sciences)

Further Information: Also branch in El Alto

History: Founded 1993.

Main Language(s) of Instruction: Spanish

Degrees and Diplomas: *Técnico Universitario Superior*; *Licenciatura*; *Diplomado*; *Maestría*

Last Updated: 12/03/09

CUMBRE PRIVATE UNIVERSITY
Universidad Privada Cumbre
Av. Cañoto 580, Santa Cruz, Santa Cruz de la Sierra
Tel: +591(3) 3330-088
Fax: +591(3) 336-1319
EMail: info@cumbre.edu.bo
Website: http://www.cumbre.edu.bo/

Rectora: Salome Nasica Azogue

Vicerrector Académico: Samir Makaren Chavez

Faculties
Business Administration (Accountancy; Business Administration; Business and Commerce; International Business); **Law** (Law); **Science and Technology** (Computer Engineering); **Social Communication** (Communication Studies)

History: Founded 2001.

Main Language(s) of Instruction: Spanish

Degrees and Diplomas: *Técnico Universitario Superior*; *Licenciatura*; *Diplomado*

Last Updated: 11/03/11

DEL CHACO PRIVATE UNIVERSITY
Universidad Privada Del Chaco
Casilla N°: 09 Barrio Central, Comercio N° 955 Colegio 12 de Agosto Yacuiba, Tarija, Cercado
Tel: +591(4) 682-4371
Fax: +591(4) 683-8730

Rector: Oriel Sánchez

Faculties
Agricultural Engineering (Agricultural Engineering); **Commercial Engineering** (Business and Commerce); **Computer Engineering** (Computer Engineering); **Law** (Law); **Social Communication**

History: Founded 2008.

Degrees and Diplomas: *Licenciatura*: Social Communication; Law; Agroindustrial Engineering; Business and Commerce; Computer Engineering;

Last Updated: 20/04/09

DOMINGO SAVIO S.A. PRIVATE UNIVERSITY
Universidad Privada Domingo Savio S.A. (UPDS)
Av. Beni Tercer Anillo Externo, Santa Cruz de la Sierra, Santa Cruz de la Sierra
Tel: +591(3) 342-6600
Fax: +591(3) 342-6820
EMail: universidad@upds.edu.bo
Website: http://www.upds.edu.bo/

Rector: Silverio Márquez Tavera

International Relations: Isabel Estrada, Secretaria General
Tel: +591(3) 342-6600, Ext: 211 EMail: iestrada@upds.edu.bo

Faculties
Business Administration (Business Administration); **Humanities and Social Sciences** (Arts and Humanities; Communication Studies; Education; Educational Sciences; International Relations; Law; Pedagogy; Political Sciences; Psychology; Public Relations; Social and Community Services; Tourism); **Technology** (Technology)

Schools
Management (Management)

Further Information: Also branch in Tarija and Potosi

History: Founded 2000.

Main Language(s) of Instruction: Spanish

Degrees and Diplomas: *Diplomado*; *Maestría*; *Doctorado*

Last Updated: 11/03/09

FRANZ TAMAYO PRIVATE UNIVERSITY
Universidad Privada Franz Tamayo
Calle Héroes del Acre N°1855, esq. Landaeta, Casilla No 4780, La Paz
Tel: +591(2) 487-700 +591(2) 487-744
Fax: +591(2) 492-395
EMail: unifranz@unifranz.edu.bo
Website: http://newsite.unifranz.edu.bo

Rector Nacional: Pedro Sáenz Muñoz

Faculties
Design and Technology Crossroads (Advertising and Publicity; Architecture; Graphic Design; Marketing); **Economics and Business** (Accountancy; Business Administration; Economics; Hotel and Restaurant); **Engineering** (Finance; Systems Analysis); **Health Sciences** (Biochemistry; Dentistry; Medicine; Nursing; Pharmacy); **Law and Social Sciences** (Civil Law; Criminal Law; Law)

Programmes
Biochemistry and Pharmacy (Biochemistry; Pharmacy); **Educational Sciences** (Education; Educational Sciences); **Environmental Engineering** (Environmental Engineering); **Psychology** (Psychology); **Systems Engineering** (Computer Engineering)

Further Information: Branches in El Alto, Santa Cruz and Cochabamba

History: Founded 1993.

Main Language(s) of Instruction: Spanish

Degrees and Diplomas: *Técnico Universitario Superior*; *Licenciatura*; *Especialización no médica*; *Maestría*

Last Updated: 11/03/11

LA SALLE UNIVERSITY
Universidad La Salle (ULS)
Av. Arequipa No. 8578, La Florida, La Paz
Tel: +591(2) 272-3588 +591(2) 277-3672
Fax: +591(2) 277-3671
EMail: sprado@uls.edu.bo; prodriguez@uls.edu.bo
Website: http://www.uls.edu.bo/

Rector: José Antonio Diez Medina EMail: jdiezmedina@uls.edu.bo

Vicerrector Académico: José Gil Iñiguez EMail: jgil@uls.edu.bo

Programmes
Accountancy (Accountancy); **Commerce and Business Administration** (Business Administration; Business and Commerce); **Education** (Education); **Law** (Law); **Psychology** (Psychology); **Systems Engineering** (Computer Engineering); **Tourism** (Tourism)

Further Information: Also branch in El Alto

History: Founded 2003.

Main Language(s) of Instruction: Spanish

Degrees and Diplomas: *Técnico Universitario Superior*; *Licenciatura*; *Diplomado*

Last Updated: 10/03/11

LATIN AMERICAN PRIVATE OPEN UNIVERSITY
Universidad Privada Abierta Latinoamericana (UPAL)
Av. América N° 524, Cochabamba
Tel: +591(4) 486-100
Fax: +591(4) 116-857
EMail: upal@upal.edu
Website: http://www.upal.edu

Rector: Henry Maldonado EMail: hemaldo@hotmail.com

Programmes
Biochemistry and Pharmacy (Biochemistry; Pharmacy); **Dentistry** (Dentistry); **Marketing** (Marketing); **Medicine** (Medicine); **Physiotherapy** *(Oruro)* (Physical Therapy); **Psychology** (Psychology)

Further Information: Also branch in Oruro

History: Founded 1990.

Governing Bodies: University Council

Admission Requirements: Bachiller and prueba de aptitud académica or equivalent

Fees: (US Dollars): 440-750

Main Language(s) of Instruction: Spanish

International Co-operation: With universities in Brazil and Peru

Degrees and Diplomas: *Técnico Universitario Superior*: 3 yrs; *Licenciatura*: 5 yrs; *Maestría*

Student Services: Foreign student adviser, Health services, Sports facilities

Special Facilities: Anatomy Museum

Publications: Revista Cientifica Voces *(biennially)*

Last Updated: 11/03/11

LATIN AMERICAN UNIVERSITY
Universidad Latinoamericana (ULAT)
Uruguay N° E 836 entre 16 de Julio y Oquendo, Cochabamba
Tel: +591(4) 4221-004
Fax: +591(4) 4504126
EMail: latinoamericana@ulat.edu.bo
Website: http://www.ulat.edu.bo

Rector: Mario Israel Sánchez Balderama

Faculties
Economics (Accountancy; Economics); **Education and Law** (Education; Educational Sciences; Law); **Health Sciences** (Dentistry; Medicine; Nursing); **Science and Technology** (Civil Engineering; Geological Engineering; Surveying and Mapping; Systems Analysis)

History: Founded 2003.

Main Language(s) of Instruction: Spanish

Degrees and Diplomas: *Licenciatura*; *Diplomado*; *Maestría*
Last Updated: 10/03/11

LOYOLA UNIVERSITY
Universidad Loyola
Av. Busch No. 1191, Edificio El Sauce, La Paz
Tel: +591(2) 224-522
Fax: +591(2) 224-522
EMail: uloyola@loyola.edu.bo
Website: http://www.loyola.edu.bo

Rector: Humberto Mendizábal Orellana
EMail: rector@loyola.edu.bo

Secretario General: Juan Morales EMail: secgral@loyola.edu.bo

Faculties
Administration, Economics and Finance (Accountancy; Administration; Business Administration; Business and Commerce; Economics; Finance); **Natural Sciences** (Agronomy; Environmental Engineering; Food Technology; Natural Sciences; Veterinary Science; Zoology); **Social Sciences** (Communication Studies; Law; Music; Social Sciences); **Technology** (Civil Engineering; Electronic Engineering; Industrial Engineering; Mechanical Engineering; Systems Analysis; Technology)

History: Founded 1995.

Main Language(s) of Instruction: Spanish

Degrees and Diplomas: *Licenciatura*; *Diplomado*; *Maestría*
Last Updated: 10/03/11

MATEO KULJIS BUSINESS UNIVERSITY
Universidad Empresarial Mateo Kuljis
Casilla Postal 2321, Calle 24 de Septiembre no 455, Santa Cruz,
Santa Cruz de la Sierra
Tel: +591(3) 332-2211
Fax: +591(3) 336-5173
EMail: universidad@unikuljis.edu.bo

Rector: Ivo Kuljis Futchner

Programmes
Accountancy (Accountancy); **Business Administration** (Business Administration); **Economics and International Commerce** (Business and Commerce; Economics; International Business); **Finance** (Finance); **Foreign Trade** (International Business); **Law** (Law); **Marketing and Advertising** (Advertising and Publicity; Marketing);

Programme Analysis (Systems Analysis); **Systems Engineering** (Engineering; Systems Analysis)

History: Founded 2000.

Degrees and Diplomas: *Técnico Universitario Superior*: Accountancy; Marketing; Business Administration: International Business; Computer Engineering, 2 yrs; *Licenciatura*: Accountancy; Advertising and Publicity; Business Administration; Engineering; Jounalism; Communication Studies; Economics; Law, 4 yrs; *Diplomado*: Marketing; Finance; Computer Networks

NATIONAL UNIVERSITY OF ECOLOGY
Universidad Nacional Ecológica
Campus Universitario "Los Olivos", Km. 5 Carretera a Cotoca,
Santa Cruz, Santa Cruz de la Sierra
Tel: +591(3) 349-9199
EMail: uecologica@uecologica.edu.bo
Website: http://www.uecologica.edu.bo/

Rector: Jerjes Justiniano Talavera

Programmes
Biochemistry (Biochemistry); **Dentistry** (Dentistry); **Environmental Engineering** (Environmental Engineering); **Food Technology** (Food Technology); **Medicine** (Medicine); **Nursing** (Nursing); **Nutrition** (Nutrition); **Physical Therapy** (Physical Therapy)

History: Founded 1999.

Main Language(s) of Instruction: Spanish

Degrees and Diplomas: *Técnico Universitario Superior*; *Licenciatura*; *Diplomado*; *Maestría*
Last Updated: 11/03/11

NATIONAL UNIVERSITY OF THE EAST
Universidad Nacional del Oriente
Calle España N° 368 Esq. Florida, Santa Cruz,
Santa Cruz de la Sierra
Tel: +591(3) 333-7577
Fax: +591(3) 337-7951
EMail: uno@uno.edu.bo
Website: http://www.uno.edu.bo

Rector: Luis Zeballos Paredes EMail: zeballos99@hotmail.com

Faculties
Economics and Finance; **Health Sciences** (Biochemistry; Dental Technology; Dentistry; Health Sciences; Nursing; Pharmacy; Physical Therapy; Rehabilitation and Therapy); **Technology** (Forestry; Systems Analysis; Technology)

Further Information: Also branch in Montero

History: Founded 1997.

Main Language(s) of Instruction: Spanish

Degrees and Diplomas: *Técnico Universitario Superior*; *Licenciatura*

NUESTRA SEÑORA DE LA PAZ UNIVERSITY
Universidad Nuestra Señora de La Paz (UNSLP)
Casilla N° 5995, Calle Presbítero Medina N° 2412, La Paz
Tel: +591(2) 242-323
Fax: +591(2) 241-0255
EMail: unslp@unslp.edu.bo
Website: http://www.unslp.edu.bo/

Rector: Jorge Paz Navajas

Vicerrector Administrativo: Fernando Rodríguez Antezana

Faculties
Administration and Economics (Administration; Economics); **Architecture and Design** (Architecture; Design; Interior Design); **Engineering** (Environmental Engineering; Food Technology; Industrial Engineering; Systems Analysis); **Medicine** (Medicine); **Odontology** (Dentistry); **Political and Social Sciences** (International Relations; Political Sciences; Public Administration; Social Sciences)

History: Founded 1992.

Main Language(s) of Instruction: Spanish

Degrees and Diplomas: *Técnico Universitario Superior; Licenciatura; Maestría*
Last Updated: 11/03/11

NUR UNIVERSITY
Universidad Nur
Av. Cristo Redentor no 100, Santa Cruz, Santa Cruz de la Sierra
Tel: +591(3) 336-3939
Fax: +591(3) 331-1850
EMail: info@nur.edu
Website: http://www.nur.edu

Rector: Manutcher Shoaie EMail: rectorado@nur.edu

Programmes
Accountancy (Accountancy); **Administration** (Administration); **Agricultural Economics** (Agricultural Economics); **Finance** (Finance); **International Relations** (International Relations); **Law** (Law); **Marketing** (Marketing); **Public Relations** (Public Relations); **Social Communication** (Communication Studies); **Systems Engineering** (Systems Analysis); **Tourism for Sustainable Development** (Tourism)

Further Information: Also branches in La Paz, Sucre and Cochabamba

History: Founded 1984.

Main Language(s) of Instruction: Spanish

Degrees and Diplomas: *Técnico Universitario Superior; Licenciatura; Especialización no médica; Maestría*
Last Updated: 10/03/09

PRIVATE UNIVERSITY OF ORURO
Universidad Privada de Oruro (UNIOR)
C. Junín N° 348 esq. Potosí, Oruro
Tel: +591(2) 527-3780
Fax: +591(2) 528-0745
EMail: informaciones@unior.edu.bo
Website: http://www.unior.edu.bo

Rectora: Maria Beatriz Cortez EMail: rectorado@unior.edu.bo

Vicerrector Académico: Felipe Alfredo Ayala Dorado
EMail: academico@unior.edu.bo

Vicerrectora Administrativa: Asunción Ramirez Aliendre
EMail: viceadmin@unior.edu.bo

Programmes
Accountancy (Accountancy); **Business Administration** (Business Administration; Management); **Law** (Law); **Medicine** (Medicine); **Nursing** (Nursing); **Odontology** (Dentistry); **Systems Engineering** (Computer Engineering)

History: Founded 1999.

Degrees and Diplomas: *Técnico Universitario Superior; Licenciatura*
Last Updated: 10/03/09

PRIVATE UNIVERSITY OF SANTA CRUZ DE LA SIERRA
Universidad Privada de Santa Cruz de la Sierra (UPSA)
Casilla Postal 2944, Av. Paraguay 4° anillo, Santa Cruz de la Sierra, Santa Cruz de la Sierra
Tel: +591(3) 346-4000
Fax: +591(3) 346-5757
EMail: informacion@upsa.edu.bo
Website: http://www.upsa.edu.bo

Rector: Lauren Müller de Pacheco
EMail: laurenmuller@upsa.edu.bo

Secretario General: Roberto Antelo Scott
EMail: robertoantelo@upsa.edu.bo

Faculties
Architecture, Design and Town Planning (Architecture; Building Technologies; Industrial Design; Interior Design; Landscape Architecture) *Dean*: Victor Hugo Limpias; **Business Studies** (Accountancy; Advertising and Publicity; Business Administration; Business

and Commerce; Economics; Finance; Human Resources; International Business; Marketing) *Dean*: Mary Esther Parada; **Engineering** (Civil Engineering; Computer Engineering; Computer Networks; Electronic Engineering; Engineering; Industrial Engineering; Petroleum and Gas Engineering; Systems Analysis; Telecommunications Engineering) *Dean*: Javier Alanoca G.; **Humanities and Communication** (Communication Studies; Fashion Design; Graphic Design; Journalism; Psychology) *Dean*: Ingrid Steinbach de Loza; **Law** (Law) *Dean*: Fernando Nuñez

Programmes
Higher Education (Higher Education)

History: Founded 1984.

Main Language(s) of Instruction: Spanish

International Co-operation: With universities in USA, Europe and Latin America

Degrees and Diplomas: *Técnico Universitario Superior*: 7 sem.; *Licenciatura*: 10 sem.; *Especialización no médica*; *Diplomado*; *Maestría*: 4 sem.
Last Updated: 11/03/09

PRIVATE UNIVERSITY OF THE VALLEY
Universidad Privada del Valle
Av. Ayacucho 256, Cochabamba
Tel: +591(4) 431-8800
Fax: +591(4) 431-5886
EMail: relinternational@univalle.edu
Website: http://www.univalle.edu

Rector: Gonzalo Ruiz Martínez EMail: rectoradocba@univalle.edu

International Relations: Marco Vélez Ocampo V.
EMail: relinternacional@univalle.edu

Faculties
Architecture *(La Paz)* (Architecture; Town Planning); **Architecture** *(Trinidad)* (Architecture; Town Planning); **Architecture** *(Cochabamba)* (Architecture; Town Planning); **Architecture** *(Sucre)* (Architecture; Town Planning); **Computer Science** *(Cochabamba)* (Computer Science); **Computer Science** *(Sucre)* (Computer Science); **Computer Science** *(La Paz)* (Computer Science); **Electronics** (Biomedical Engineering; Computer Science; Electronic Engineering; Systems Analysis); **Electronics** *(Cochabamba)* (Electronic Engineering); **Engineering** *(Sucre)*; **Engineering** *(Cochabamba)* (Aeronautical and Aerospace Engineering; Chemical Engineering; Civil Engineering; Electrical Engineering; Food Science; Industrial Engineering); **Health Sciences** *(Cochabamba)* (Health Sciences); **Health Sciences** *(La Paz)* (Biochemistry; Dentistry; Health Sciences; Medicine; Pharmacy); **Social Sciences and Administration** *(La Paz)* (Accountancy; Business Administration; Business and Commerce; Communication Studies; Economics; Finance; Hotel Management; International Business; Journalism; Law; Marketing; Psychology; Tourism); **Social Sciences and Administration** *(Sucre)* (Accountancy; Business Administration; Business and Commerce; Communication Studies; Economics; Finance; Hotel Management; International Business; Journalism; Law; Marketing; Psychology; Tourism); **Social Sciences and Administration** *(Cochabamba)* (Accountancy; Business Administration; Business and Commerce; Communication Studies; Economics; Finance; Hotel Management; International Business; Journalism; Law; Marketing; Psychology; Tourism); **Social Sciences and Administration** *(Trinidad)* (Administration; Social Sciences)

Further Information: Central Campus in Cochabamba. Branches in La Paz, Chuquisaca and Beni

History: Founded 1988.

Main Language(s) of Instruction: Spanish

Degrees and Diplomas: *Diplomado*: E-Business; Higher Education; Law; Administration; Computer Networks; *Maestría*: Business Administration; Marketing; Finance; Commercial Law; Information Technology; Computer Science; Food Science; Pharmacy; Social Psychology; Engineering; Higher Education; *Doctorado*: Educational Sciences; Economics and Administration
Last Updated: 11/03/09

PROUNIVERSIDAD PRIVATE UNIVERSITY
Universidad Privada Prouniversidad
Avenida Ecuador No 2475, entre Belisario Salinas y Muñoz Cornejo, La Paz
Tel: +591(2) 410-632
EMail: prouni@entelnet.bo
Website: http://www.uta.cl/prouniversidad

Rector: Juan Cariaga Osario

Vicerrector: Adolfo Linares Arraya

Programmes
Business Administration (Business Administration); **Economics** (Economics)

Degrees and Diplomas: *Licenciatura*

ROYAL UNIVERSITY
Universidad Real
Capitan Ravelo 2329, Sopocachi, La Paz
Tel: +591(2) 443-635
EMail: info@universidadreal.edu.bo
Website: http://www.ureal.edu.bo

Rector: Marcelo Gozalvez Gonzáles
EMail: mgozalvez@ureal.edu.bo

Vicerrectora: Giovanna Torres Salvador
EMail: gtorres@ureal.edu.bo

Programmes
Audiovisual Communication (Communication Studies); **Computer Science** (Computer Science); **Financial Administration** (Administration; Finance); **International Trade** (International Business); **Law** (Law); **Marketing** (Marketing); **Tourism and Management** (Tourism)

History: Founded 1999.

Main Language(s) of Instruction: Spanish

Degrees and Diplomas: *Técnico Universitario Superior*: Marketing; English; Tourism and Hotel Management; *Licenciatura*: Marketing; Business Computing; Law; International Business; Cinema and Television; Finance; Tourism & Hotel Management
Last Updated: 11/03/11

SAINT PAUL UNIVERSITY
Universidad Saint Paul
Calle Yanacocha No. 875, La Paz
Tel: +591(2) 228-0787
Fax: +591(2) 228-0787
EMail: info@usp.edu.bo; uni_saintpaul@hotmail.com
Website: http://www.usp.edu.bo/

Rector: Juan Paz Villarroel Rodríguez
EMail: jpwillarroel@hotmail.com

Faculties
Economics (Accountancy; Business Administration; Economics; Finance); **Engineering** (Civil Engineering; Electronic Engineering; Food Technology; Industrial Engineering; Systems Analysis); **Health Sciences** (Dentistry; Health Sciences; Medicine; Nursing); **Law** (Law)

History: Founded 2003.

Main Language(s) of Instruction: Spanish

Degrees and Diplomas: *Técnico Universitario Superior*; *Licenciatura*
Last Updated: 05/03/09

COCHABAMBA CAMPUS
Cocahamba
Tel: +591(4) 425-2165
EMail: jpvvillarroel@hotmail.com
Website: http://www.usp.edu.bo

Faculties
Dentistry; **Law** (Law); **Medicine** (Medicine); **Nursing** (Nursing); **System Analysis** (Computer Engineering; Systems Analysis)

Degrees and Diplomas: *Licenciatura*: Medicine; Dentistry; Nursing; Computer Engineering; Law

SALESIAN UNIVERSITY OF BOLIVIA
Universidad Salesiana de Bolivia
Casilla postal 13102, Avda. Chacaltaya N. 1258 (Esq. Ramos Gavilán, Plaza Don Bosco), La Paz
Tel: +591(2) 230-5210
Fax: +591(2) 230-5111
EMail: arandap@usalesiana.edu.bo
Website: http://www.usalesiana.edu.bo

Rector: Thelían Argeo Corona Cortés

Vicerrector: José Manuel Rojas

International Relations: Pablo Aranda Manrique
Tel: +591(2) 230-5844 EMail: aranda@hotmail.com

Programmes
Accountancy (Accountancy); **Educational Sciences** (Education; Physical Education); **Law** (Law); **Systems Engineering** (Systems Analysis)

Further Information: Also branch in Camiri

History: Founded 1998.

Main Language(s) of Instruction: Spanish

Degrees and Diplomas: *Técnico Universitario Superior*, *Licenciatura*; *Diplomado*; *Maestría*
Last Updated: 11/03/09

SAN FRANCISCO DE ASÍS UNIVERSITY
Universidad San Francisco de Asís (USFA)
Casilla postal 5772, Av. 20 de Octubre esq. Belisario Salinas, La Paz
Tel: +591(2) 440-894
Fax: +591(2) 443-773
EMail: info@usfa.edu.bo
Website: http://www.usfa.edu.bo/

Rector: Boris Crespo Toranzo
EMail: bcrespo@usfa.edu.bo; rectorado@usfa.edu.bo

Programmes
Business Administration (Business Administration); **Commerce** (Business and Commerce); **Educational Sciences** (Educational Sciences); **Journalism** (Journalism); **Law** (Law); **Preschool and Primary Education** (Preschool Education; Primary Education); **Psychology** (Psychology); **Social Communication** (Communication Studies); **Systems Analysis** (Systems Analysis); **Systems Engineering** (Computer Engineering); **Urban Studies** (Urban Studies)

Further Information: Also branch in Tupiza

History: Founded 1998.

Main Language(s) of Instruction: Spanish

Degrees and Diplomas: *Técnico Universitario Superior*, *Licenciatura*; *Maestría*
Last Updated: 11/03/09

SAN PABLO BOLIVIAN CATHOLIC UNIVERSITY
Universidad Católica Boliviana San Pablo (UCB)
Casilla Postal 4805, Av. 14 de Septiembre N° 4807 Obrajes, La Paz
Tel: +591(2) 278-3148
Fax: +591(2) 278-3932
EMail: mhoyos@ucb.edu.bo
Website: http://www.ucb.edu.bo

Rector Nacional: Hans van den Berg
Tel: +591(2) 278-3148 EMail: rector@ucb.edu.bo

Vicerrector Académico: Edwin Claros Arispe
Tel: +591(2) 278-5152 EMail: claros@ucb.edu.bo

Secretario General: Mario Hoyos Tel: +591(2) 278-5152

International Relations: Jimena Sainz
Tel: +591(2) 278-2222 EMail: rrppint@ucb.edu.bo

Centres
Radio and Television Training Service for Development *(SECRAD)* (Radio and Television Broadcasting)

Departments
Architecture (Architecture); **Communication Studies** (Communication Studies; Information Technology; Public Relations); **Edu-**

cation (Education); **Graphic Design and Visual Communication** (Communication Arts; Design; Fine Arts; Graphic Design; Visual Arts); **Law** (Law) *Head*: Antonio Peres Velasco; **Political Sciences** (Political Sciences); **Psychology** (Psychology)

Faculties
Economics and Finance (Economics; Finance); **Exact Sciences and Engineering** (Engineering; Science Education)

Institutes
Democracy (Political Sciences); **Professional Ethics Studies** (Ethics); **Socio-Economic Research** (Economics; Social Studies)

Schools
Business Administration (Business Administration)

History: Founded 1966. A public institution under the administration of the Conferencia Episcopal de Bolivia.

Governing Bodies: Junta Directiva, Conferencia Episcopal de Bolivia

Academic Year: January to December (January-June; August-December)

Admission Requirements: Secondary school certificate (bachillerato) and entrance examination

Main Language(s) of Instruction: Spanish

Degrees and Diplomas: *Técnico Universitario Superior*: 3 yrs; *Licenciatura*: 5 yrs; *Especialización no médica*: 1 yr; *Diplomado*: 1 yr; *Maestría*: 2 yrs; *Doctor en Ciencias Médicas*: Medicine, 7 yrs; *Doctorado*: 3 yrs

Student Services: Canteen, Cultural centre, Health services, Language programs, Sports facilities

Special Facilities: Laboratories; Classrooms with data show; multimedia and internet services, WIFI in campus

Libraries: Central Library, c. 42,000 vols

Last Updated: 09/03/11

COCHABAMBA CAMPUS

Casilla Postal 4105, Avenida América, Esq. General Galindo, Tupuraya, Cochabamba
Tel: +591(4) 293-100
Fax: +591(4) 291-145
Website: http://www.ucbcba.edu.bo

Rector regional: Rene Santa Cruz Rodríguez
Tel: +591(4) 429-2717 EMail: santacrz@ucbcba.edu.bo

Academic Regional Head: Luis Alberto Vaca

Centres
Computer Science and Education (Computer Science); **Radio and Television Training Service for Development** *(SECRAD)* (Radio and Television Broadcasting)

Departments
Business Administration, Economics and Finance (Business Administration; Economics; Finance); **Education** (Education); **Exact Sciences and Engineering** (Engineering; Science Education); **Radio and Audiovisual Techniques** (Radio and Television Broadcasting); **Social Sciences** (Social Sciences)

Institutes
Bioethics (Biology; Ethics); **Missiology** (Missionary Studies); **Research in Applied Computer Science** (Computer Science); **Theological Studies** (Theology)

History: Founded 1971.

Main Language(s) of Instruction: Spanish

Student Services: Canteen, Cultural centre, Health services, Language programs, Sports facilities

Special Facilities: Pastoral activities; Multimedia; WIFI on campus

Libraries: 39,588 vols

SANTA CRUZ CAMPUS

Casilla Postal 3201, Calle España 368, Santa Cruz
Tel: +591(3) 337-815
Fax: +591(3) 332-389
Website: http://www.ucbscz.edu.bo

Rector regional: Jorge Ybarnegaray Urquidi
Tel: +591(3) 344-2999, Fax: +591(3) 344-2999
EMail: rector@ucbscz.edu.bo

Academic Regional Head: María Josefina Ortíz

Departments
Administration, Economics and Finance (Administration; Economics; Finance); **Architecture** (Architecture); **Education and Teacher Training** (Education; Teacher Training); **Educational Psychology** (Educational Psychology); **Exact Sciences and Engineering** (Engineering; Science Education); **Medicine** (Medicine); **Ondotology** (Dentistry)

Institutes
Ethics Studies (Ethnology)

History: Founded 1993.

Main Language(s) of Instruction: Spanish

Student Services: Canteen, Cultural centre, Health services, Language programs, Sports facilities

Special Facilities: Pastoral activities; Laboratories; Multimedia, WIFI on campus

Libraries: 8,000 vols

TARIJA CAMPUS

Calle Colón no 0734, Tarija
Tel: +591(4) 664-7971
EMail: secre@ucbtja.edu.bo
Website: http://www.ucbtja.edu.bo

Rector regional: Marco Antonio Limarino
EMail: vice@ucbtja.edu.bo

Academic Regional Head: Jaime Calderón

Departments
Architecture (Architecture); **Business Administration** (Business Administration); **Civil Engineering and Exact Sciences** (Civil Engineering; Science Education); **Law** (Law); **Public Accountancy** (Accountancy); **Social Communication** (Communication Studies); **Systems Engineering** (Systems Analysis); **Telecommunications Engineering** (Telecommunications Engineering)

History: Founded 1999.

Main Language(s) of Instruction: Spanish

Student Services: Canteen, Cultural centre, Health services, Sports facilities

Special Facilities: Pastoral activities; Laboratories;Multimedia; WIFI on Campus

Libraries: 3,519 vols

TECHNOLOGICAL PRIVATE UNIVERSITY OF SANTA CRUZ
Universidad Tecnológica Privada de Santa Cruz (UTEPSA)
Casilla postal 4146, 3er Anillo Interno entre Av. Busch y Av. San Martin, Santa Cruz, Santa Cruz de la Sierra
Tel: +591(3) 341-1919, Ext: 1640
Fax: +591(3) 341-1919
EMail: utepsa@utepsa.edu
Website: http://www.utepsa.edu

Rector: Antonio Carvalho Suárez

Vicerrector, Administración y Finanzas: Hussein Rezvani
EMail: hrezvani@utepsa.edu

International Relations: Claudia Quezada, Vicerrector
EMail: cquezada@utepsa.edu; international@utepsa.edu

Departments
Special Programmes *Director*: Gonzalo Arce; **Technical Education** (English; French; Italian; Modern Languages; Portuguese; Spanish; Technology) *Director*: Mery Rios

Faculties
Economics, Finance and Administration *(FEFA)* (Accountancy; Administration; Advertising and Publicity; Business and Commerce; Economics; Finance; Human Resources; International Business; Marketing; Tourism) *Dean*: +Rafael Muñoz; **Electronic and**

Telecommunications Engineering (Business and Commerce; Computer Engineering; Computer Networks; Computer Science; Electronic Engineering; Industrial Engineering; Management Systems; Petroleum and Gas Engineering; Telecommunications Engineering) *Dean*: Rafael Muñoz; **Law** *Dean*: Rafael Muñoz

History: Founded 1994, acquired present status 2001.

Governing Bodies: Consejo Superior

Academic Year: February to December (February-July; August-December)

Admission Requirements: Secondary school certificate (bachillerato)

Fees: (US Dollars): 416 per semester

Main Language(s) of Instruction: Spanish

International Co-operation: With universities in Argentina; Cuba; Germany; Italy; Mexico; Panama and USA

Degrees and Diplomas: *Técnico Universitario Superior*; *Licenciatura*: 5 yrs; *Diplomado*; *Maestría*: 2 yrs following Licenciatura

Student Services: Academic counselling, Canteen, Cultural centre, Employment services, Foreign student adviser, Foreign Studies Centre, Handicapped facilities, Health services, Language programs, Nursery care, Sports facilities

Student Residential Facilities: No

Libraries: Yes

Press or Publishing House: Imprenta El Deber

Academic Staff *2008-2009*	TOTAL
FULL-TIME	40
PART-TIME	c. 30

Student Numbers *2008-2009*	
All (Foreign Included)	c. 8,000
FOREIGN ONLY	130

Last Updated: 12/03/09

UNITY UNIVERSITY
Universidad Unidad (UNIDAD)
Urcullo 647, Sucre, Chuquisaca
Tel: +591(4) 6460-409
Fax: +591(4) 6434-028
Website: http://www.uunidad.com/

Rector: Orlando Howard Nutt **EMail:** hwnutt@entelnet.bo

Vicerrector Administrativo: Johnny Andrade

Faculties
Humanities (Cultural Studies; Theology)

History: Founded 2007.

Main Language(s) of Instruction: Spanish

Degrees and Diplomas: *Licenciatura*
Last Updated: 11/03/11

UNIVERSITY FOR STRATEGIC RESEARCH IN BOLIVIA
Universidad para la Investigación Estratégica en Bolivia (UPIEB)
Av. Arce 2799, Edificio Fortaleza piso 6, Of. 601, La Paz
Tel: +591(2) 243-2582
Fax: +591(2) 243-5235
EMail: upieb@acelerate.com
Website: http://www.upieb.edu.bo/

Rector: Fernando Ríos Pérez
Tel: +591(2) 271-2458, **Fax:** +591(2) 243-1866
EMail: fernandorios@upieb.edu.bo

+591(2) 243-2582: Mario Yapu Condo
EMail: marioyapu@upieb.edu.bo

Programmes
Economics (Economics); **Social Sciences** (Peace and Disarmament; Social Sciences)

History: Founded 2002.

Main Language(s) of Instruction: Spanish

International Co-operation: With the Ecole des Hautes Etudes en Sciences Sociales (France)

Degrees and Diplomas: *Especialización no médica*; *Diplomado*: Social Studies; Educational Research; Social Sciences, 6 months; *Maestría*: Social Sciences; Educational Research

Student Residential Facilities: None

Libraries: Yes

Publications: Formación y Desarrollo, magazine about Educational Research *(biennially)*
Last Updated: 11/03/11

UNIVERSITY OF THE ANDES
Universidad de Los Andes (UNANDES)
Avenida los Leones No 10, Zona Obrajes, La Paz
Tel: +591(2) 278-7308 +591(2) 278-7135
Fax: +591(2) 278-7308
EMail: unandes@udelosandes.edu.bo
Website: http://www.udelosandes.edu.bo

Rector: Roberto Oblitas Zamora

Faculties
Automotive Engineering (Automotive Engineering); **Business** (Business Administration; Business and Commerce; Business Computing; Management; Marketing; Public Administration); **Gastronomy and Hotel Management** (Cooking and Catering; Hotel and Restaurant; Hotel Management); **Law** (Law)

History: Founded 2002.

Main Language(s) of Instruction: Spanish

Degrees and Diplomas: *Técnico Universitario Superior*; *Licenciatura*
Last Updated: 10/03/11

UNIVERSITY OF THE CORDILLERA
Universidad de la Cordillera
Chaco No 1161, La Paz
Tel: +591(2) 215-2278 +591(2) 241-6973
EMail: unicor@ucordillera.edu.bo
Website: http://www.ucordillera.edu.bo

Programmes
Intercultural and Dialogue Studies (Cultural Studies); **Social Sciences** (Social Sciences)

History: Founded 1997.

Main Language(s) of Instruction: Spanish

Degrees and Diplomas: *Licenciatura*; *Maestría*

Bosnia and Herzegovina

STRUCTURE OF HIGHER EDUCATION SYSTEM

Description:

According to the Framework Law on Higher Education in BiH ("Official Gazette of BiH", No. 59/07), higher education institutions in Bosnia and Herzegovina comprise universities and colleges. The title "university" is limited to the higher education institutions undertaking both teaching and research, offering academic degrees in all three cycles, while the title "college" (visoka skola) is limited to higher education institutions accredited to offer first cycle diplomas and degrees. All higher education activities are subject to national (Republic Srpska) or cantonal (in the Federation of B&H) laws. Access to higher education is granted to all students having completed four years of secondary school.

Stages of studies:

University level first stage: *First cycle*
The first cycle leading to the academic title of completed undergraduate studies (Bachelor's degree) is obtained after three to four years of full time study following upon a secondary school leaving certificate. It is valued between 180 and 240 ECTS credit points. Studies in Medical Sciences are longer and valued 360 ECTS credit points.

University level second stage: *Second cycle*
The second cycle leads to the academic title of Master or equivalent. It is obtained after the completion of undergraduate studies and one or two years' study and has a value of 60 to 120 ECTS credit points, in such a way that the total number of credits obtained when adding the ones obtained in the first cycle amounts to 300 ECTS points.

University level third stage: *Third cycle*
The third cycle leads to the academic degree of Doctor or equivalent. The studies last for three years and are valued 180 ECTS credit points. The public defence of a doctoral thesis is required.

ADMISSION TO HIGHER EDUCATION

Foreign students admission:

Definition of foreign student: All those who are not in possession of Bosnia and Herzegovina's citizenship.

RECOGNITION OF STUDIES

Quality assurance system:

The Agency for Development of Higher Education and Quality Assurance, as an autonomous administrative organization, assists the relevant education authorities in the process of accreditation and licensing of higher education institutions, establish criteria and standards for quality assurance, provide advice and recommendations for removal of drawbacks in the quality of studies and higher education institutions, and the like.

Bodies dealing with recognition:

Agencija za Razvoj Visokog Obrazovanja i Osiguranje Kvaliteta Bosne i Hercegovine (Agency for the Development of Higher Education and Quality Assurance)
Vojvode Stepe Stepanovića Blvd. 11
Banjaluka 78000
Tel: +387(51) 430 510
Fax: +387(51) 462 302
EMail: info@hea.gov.ba
WWW: http://www.hea.gov.ba

Centar za Informiranje i Priznavanje Dokumenta iz Područja/Oblasti Visokog Obrazovanja (Centre for Information and Recognition of Qualifications in Higher Education)
Kneza Branimira 12
Mostar 88000
Tel: +387(36) 333 980
Fax: + 387(36) 333 991
WWW: http://www.cip.gov.ba

NATIONAL BODIES

Ministarvo Civilnih Poslova BiH (Ministry of Civil Affairs of Bosnia and Herzegovina)
Minister: Sredoje Nović
TRG BiH 1
Sarajevo 71000
Tel: +387(33) 492 532
EMail: zorica.rulj@mcp.gov.ba
WWW: http://www.mcp.gov.ba/

Federalno Ministarstovo Obrazovanja i Nauke (Federal Ministry of Education and Science)
Minister: Damir Mašić
Assistant Minister, Higher Education: Predrag Mitrović
Dr. Ante Starčevića bb
Mostar
Tel: +387(36) 355 700
Fax: +387(36) 355 742
EMail: info@fmon.gov.ba
WWW: http://www.fmon.gov.ba/
Role of national body: The Ministry coordinates the 10 cantonal education ministries.

Ministarstvo Prosvjete i Kulture (Ministry of Education)
Minister: Anton Kasipović
Trg Republike Srpske 1
Banja Luka

Agencija za Razvoj Visokog Obrazovanja i Osiguranje Kvaliteta Bosne i Hercegovine (Agency for the Development of Higher Education and Quality Assurance)
Director: Husein Nanić
Public Relations Adviser: Slavica Škoro
Vojvode Stepe Stepanovića Blvd. 11
Banjaluka 78000
Tel: +387(51) 430 510
Fax: +387(51) 462 302
EMail: info@hea.gov.ba
WWW: http://www.hea.gov.ba
Role of national body: The Agency for the Development of Higher Education and Quality Assurance, as an autonomous administrative organization, shall among other things assist the relevant education authorities in the process of accreditation and licensing of higher education institutions, establish criteria and standards for quality assurance, provide advice and recommendations for removal of drawbacks in the quality of studies and higher education institutions, and the like.

Centar za Informiranje i Priznavanje Dokumenta iz Područja/Oblasti Visokog Obrazovanja (Centre for Information and Recognition of Qualifications in Higher Education)
Director: Dženan Omanović
Kneza Branimira 12
Mostar 88000
Tel: +387(36) 333 980
Fax: + 387(36) 333 991
WWW: http://www.cip.gov.ba

Data for academic year: 2012-2013
Source: IAU from Ministry of Civil Affairs of Bosnia and Herzegovina, Education Sector, 2009, updated from CIP and Ministry websites, 2012.

INSTITUTIONS

PUBLIC INSTITUTIONS

DŽEMAL BIJEDIĆ UNIVERSITY OF MOSTAR
Univerzitet Džemal Bijedić, Mostar
USRC "Mithad Hudjur Hujka", Mostar 88 104
Tel: +387(36) 570-727
Fax: +387(36) 570-032
EMail: info@unmo.ba
Website: http://www.unmo.ba

Rektor: Fuad Ćatović (2011-)
Tel: +387(36) 571-197 EMail: Fuad.Catovic@unmo.ba

Secretary General: Zoran Kazazić
Tel: +387(36) 570-090 EMail: Zoran.Kazazic@unmo.ba

Academies
Teacher Training (Pedagogy)

Departments
Information Technology (Information Technology)

Faculties
Agro-Mediterranean (Agriculture; Mediterranean Studies); **Business Management** (Business Administration); **Civil Engineering** (Civil Engineering); **Humanities** (Arts and Humanities; Communication Studies; English; History; Theatre); **Law** (Law); **Mechanical Engineering** (Mechanical Engineering)

History: Founded 1977. Previously the Advanced School for Pedagogy. Since 1994, the University has been divided into two parts.

Governing Bodies: University Council

Admission Requirements: Secondary school certificate

Fees: (Konvertibilna Marka): 100 per annum for full-time; part-time, 800

Main Language(s) of Instruction: Bosanski, Hrvatski, Srpski

International Co-operation: With universities in Austria, England, Belgium, Spain, France, Netherlands, Turkey, Serbia and Montenegro

Degrees and Diplomas: *Bakalaureat*: Civil Engineering; Economics; Humanities; Law; Mechanical Engineering; Information Technologies; Mediterranean Agriculture; Teacher Training, 3-4 yrs; *Magistra*

Student Services: Canteen, Language programs

Publications: Monografija; Pregledi Predavanja
Last Updated: 23/09/11

UNIVERSITY OF BANJA LUKA
Univerzitet u Banjoj Luci
Bulevar vojvode Petra Bojovića 1A, Banja Luka 78000
Tel: +387(51) 321-112
Fax: +387(51) 315-694
EMail: info@unibl.rs
Website: http://www.unibl.org

Rektor: Stanko Stanić EMail: mirjanicd@blic.net

Generalni Sekretar: Dušanka Dragić Tel: +387(51) 218-1997

Academies
Arts (Fine Arts; Music; Theatre)

Faculties
Agriculture; **Architecture and Civil Engineering** (Architecture; Civil Engineering); **Economics** (Economics); **Electrical Engineer-**
ing (Computer Science; Electrical Engineering; Information Technology; Power Engineering; Telecommunications Engineering); **Forestry** (Forestry); **Law** (Law); **Mathematics and Natural Sciences** (Mathematics; Natural Sciences); **Mechanical Engineering** (Mechanical Engineering); **Medicine** (Medicine); **Mining** (Mining Engineering); **Philology** (Philology); **Philosophy** (Philosophy); **Physical Education and Sports** (Physical Education; Sports); **Political Science** (Political Sciences); **Technology** (Biotechnology; Environmental Engineering; Food Technology; Technology; Textile Technology)

Institutes
Genetic Resources (Genetics)

History: Founded 1975, incorporating faculties formerly attached to the University of Sarajevo. Since 1994, the University has been assisted by the University of the Arts, Belgrade and other universities from Serbia and Montenegro.

Governing Bodies: University Council and Academic Council

Academic Year: October to September

Admission Requirements: Svjedočanstvo and entrance examination

Fees: (Konvertibilna Marka): 300 per semester

Main Language(s) of Instruction: Serbian

International Co-operation: Participates in the Tempus Programme

Degrees and Diplomas: *Bakalaureat*; *Magistra*; *Doktora*

Student Services: Cultural centre, Health services, Sports facilities

Student Residential Facilities: Yes
Last Updated: 23/09/11

UNIVERSITY OF BIHAĆ
Univerzitet u Bihaću
Pape Ivana Pavla II 2/II, Bihać 77000
Tel: +387(37) 222-022
Fax: +387(37) 222-022
EMail: rektorat@unbi.ba
Website: http://www.unbi.ba

Rektor: Refik Šahinović EMail: refik.sahinovic@unbi.ba

Generalni Sekretar: Asija Cucak EMail: asija.cucak@unbi.ba

International Relations: Ekrem Pehlić
EMail: ekrem.pehlic@unbi.ba

Colleges
Medicine (Medicine); **Nursing** (Nursing)

Faculties
Biotechnology (Biotechnology); **Economics** (Economics); **Education** *(Islamic)* (Education); **Law** (Law); **Pedagogy** (Pedagogy); **Technical Engineering** (Engineering; Technology)

History: Founded 1997.

Governing Bodies: Administrative Board; Scientific Council

Admission Requirements: Secondary school certificate (Maturska Svjedodzba)

Main Language(s) of Instruction: Bosnian

Degrees and Diplomas: *Bakalaureat*: a further 1-2 yrs; *Magistra*; *Doktora*

Student Services: Academic counselling, Canteen, Cultural centre, Health services, Nursery care, Sports facilities

Student Residential Facilities: Yes

Libraries: Central Library with English Language Resource Centre

Publications: Research Papers, Human Rights Conflict Prevention Centre *(biannually)*
Last Updated: 23/09/11

UNIVERSITY OF EAST SARAJEVO
Univerzitet u Istočnom Sarajevu
Vuka Karadžića 30, Lukavica, Istočno Sarajevo 71123
Tel: +387(57) 340-464
Fax: +387(57) 340-263
EMail: univerzitet@paleol.net
Website: http://www.unssa.rs.ba

Rector: Mitar Novaković
Tel: +387(57) 320-155, Fax: +387(57) 340-263

Academies
Fine Arts *(Trebinje)*; **Music** (Music); **Theology** *(Srbinje)* (Theology)

Faculties
Agriculture (Agriculture); **Dental Medicine** *(Foca)* (Dentistry); **Economics** *(Brcko)*; **Economics** *(Pale)* (Economics); **Electrical Engineering**; **Foreign Trade** *(Bijeljina)*; **Law** *(Pale)* (Law); **Mechanical Engineering**; **Medicine** *(Foca)* (Medicine); **Orthodox Theology** *(St. Basil of Ostrog (Foca))*; **Philosophy** *(Pale)* (Philosophy); **Production and Management** *(Trebinje)* (Management; Production Engineering); **Sports** *(Pale)*; **Teacher Training** *(Bijeljina)*; **Technology** *(Zvornik)* (Technology); **Transport and Traffic Engineering** *(Doboj)* (Transport Engineering; Transport Management)
Last Updated: 23/09/11

UNIVERSITY OF MOSTAR
Sveučilište u Mostaru
Trg hrvatskih velikana 1, Mostar 88000
Tel: +387(36) 310-778
Fax: +387(36) 320-885
EMail: mail@sve-mo.ba
Website: http://www.sve-mo.ba

Rektor: Vlado Majstorović
Tel: +387(36) 327-885 EMail: rektor@sve-mo.ba

Academies
Fine Arts (Art History; Fine Arts; Graphic Design; Painting and Drawing; Sculpture)

Faculties
Agronomy (Agricultural Economics; Agriculture; Animal Husbandry; Food Technology; Plant and Crop Protection); **Civil Engineering** (Civil Engineering; Construction Engineering; Design; Industrial Engineering; Production Engineering); **Computer Engineering and Mechanical Engeenering** (Computer Engineering; Information Technology; Mechanical Engineering); **Economics** (Accountancy; Economics; Finance; Management; Marketing); **Health Science** (Health Sciences; Nursing; Physical Therapy; Radiology); **Law** (Law); **Medicine** (Medicine); **Natural Science and Pedagogy** (Archaeology; Art History; Biology; Chemistry; Computer Science; Education; English; Geography; German; History; Journalism; Latin; Literature; Mathematics; Music; Pedagogy; Physics; Preschool Education; Primary Education; Psychology; Slavic Languages; Teacher Training); **Philosophy** (Philosophy)

History: Founded 1977, acquired present title 1992.
Main Language(s) of Instruction: Croatian
International Co-operation: Participates in Tempus
Degrees and Diplomas: *Bakalaureat*; *Magistra*; *Doktora*
Student Residential Facilities: Yes
Libraries: Yes
Last Updated: 23/09/11

UNIVERSITY OF SARAJEVO
Univerzitet u Sarajevu
Obala Kulina Bana 7/II, Sarajevo 71000
Tel: +387(33) 663-392
Fax: +387(33) 663-393
EMail: rektorat@unsa.ba
Website: http://www.unsa.ba

Rektor: Faruk Čaklovika EMail: kabinet.rektora@unsa.ba
Secretary General: Zoran Selesković
Tel: +387(71) 668-250, Fax: +387(71) 668-252
EMail: zseleskovic@unsa.ba
International Relations: Ljiljana Šulentić, Coordinator, International Cooperation
Tel: +387(33) 668-454, Fax: +387(33) 215-504
EMail: rektoratms@unsa.ba

Academies
Drama (Acting; Theatre); **Fine Arts** (Fine Arts); **Music** (Music); **Pedagogy** (Pedagogy)

Faculties
Agriculture (Agriculture); **Architecture and Town Planning** (Architecture; Town Planning); **Civil Engineering** (Civil Engineering); **Criminology** (Criminology); **Dentistry** (Dentistry); **Economics** (Economics); **Electrical Engineering** (Automation and Control Engineering; Computer Science; Electrical Engineering; Electronic Engineering; Information Sciences; Telecommunications Engineering; Telecommunications Services); **Forestry** (Forestry; Horticulture); **Law** (Law); **Mechanical Engineering** (Automotive Engineering; Mechanical Engineering; Production Engineering; Wood Technology); **Medicine** (Medicine); **Natural Sciences and Mathematics** (Biology; Chemistry; Geography; Mathematics; Natural Sciences; Physics); **Pharmacy** (Pharmacy); **Philosophy** (Education; English; Germanic Languages; History; Library Science; Literature; Middle Eastern Studies; Philosophy; Psychology; Romance Languages; Slavic Languages; Sociology); **Physical Education** (Physical Education); **Political Science** (Journalism; Military Science; Political Sciences; Social Work; Sociology); **Transport and Communication** (Transport and Communications; Transport Engineering); **Veterinary Medicine** (Veterinary Science)

Institutes
Crime against Humanity Research and International Law (Criminology; International Law); **Genetic Engineering and Biotechnology** (Biotechnology; Genetics); **History** (History); **Oriental Research** (Oriental Studies)

Schools
Nursing (Nursing)

History: Founded 1949.
Governing Bodies: Senate
Academic Year: September to June
Admission Requirements: Secondary school certificate (Maturska Svjedodzba) or recognized equivalent and entrance examination
Fees: None
Main Language(s) of Instruction: Bosnian
Degrees and Diplomas: *Bakalaureat*: 3-4 yrs; *Magistra*: 1-2 yrs; *Doktora*: by thesis
Student Services: Canteen, Cultural centre, Health services
Student Residential Facilities: Yes
Libraries: University and National Library
Publications: Bibliography of Doctoral Thesis; Lecture Review *(annually)*
Last Updated: 23/09/11

UNIVERSITY OF TUZLA
Univerzitet u Tuzli
Muharema Fizovića Fiska 6, Tuzla, Tuzla Canton 75000
Tel: +387(35) 300-500
Fax: +387(35) 300-547
EMail: rektorat@untz.ba
Website: http://www.untz.ba

Rektor: Enver Halilović
General Secretary: Jasmina Berbič Tel: +387(35) 300-502
International Relations: Mensura Aščerić, Vice-Rector
Tel: +387(35) 300-506, Fax: +387(35) 300-528

Academies
Drama (Acting; Film)

Faculties

Economics (Accountancy; Finance; Management; Marketing) *Dean*: Reuf Kapić; **Electrical Engineering** (Computer Engineering; Power Engineering); **Law** (Law); **Mechanical Engineering** (Mechanical Engineering; Power Engineering; Production Engineering); **Medicine** (Medicine); **Mining, Geology and Civil Engineering** (Civil Engineering; Geology; Health Sciences; Hydraulic Engineering; Mining Engineering; Safety Engineering); **Pharmacy** (Pharmacy); **Philosophy** (Computer Science; English; Foreign Languages Education; German; History; Journalism; Literature; Pedagogy; Psychology; Slavic Languages; Social Work; Teacher Training; Technology Education; Turkish); **Science** (Biology; Chemistry; Geography; Mathematics; Physics); **Special Education and Rehabilitation** (Rehabilitation and Therapy; Special Education); **Sport and Physical Education** (Physical Education; Sports); **Technology** (Chemical Engineering; Ecology; Environmental Engineering; Food Technology)

History: Founded 1976, incorporating former faculties of the University of Sarajevo. Became Faculty of Mining 1960, Faculty of Medicine 1976. Acquired present status and title 2000.

Governing Bodies: University Senate

Academic Year: September to June (September-February; February-June)

Admission Requirements: Secondary school diploma (Maturska Svjedodzba)

Fees: (Konvertibilna Marka): 1,200-4,000 per annum

Main Language(s) of Instruction: Bosnian, Serbian, Croatian

International Co-operation: Participates in Tempus, WUS, FP6, Cost, World Bank Project

Degrees and Diplomas: *Bakalaureat*: Economics (BCs); Electrical Engineering, Mechanichal Engineering, Technology, Mining, Geology, Civil Engineering (B.Sc.); History, Journalism, Pedagogy, Psychology, Social Work; Law (BA); Mathematics Education, Physics Education, Chemistry Education, Biology Education, Geography Education; Slavic language Education, English Language Education, Turkish Language Education, German Language and Literature Education, Sport Education, 4 yrs; *Magistra*; *Doktora*: Medicine, 6 yrs

Student Services: Canteen, Cultural centre, Employment services, Handicapped facilities, Health services, Sports facilities

Libraries: 5 university libraries.
Last Updated: 23/09/11

UNIVERSITY OF ZENICA

Univerzitet u Zenici (UNZE)
Fakultetska 1, Zenica, Zenica-Doboj Canton 72000
Tel: +387(32) 449-420
Fax: +387(32) 449-425
EMail: rektorat@unze.ba
Website: http://www.unze.ba

Rector: Sabahudin Ekinovic (2005-)
EMail: sabahudin.ekinovic@unze.ba

Secretay General: Medina Mediha ARNAUT Arnaut
Tel: +387(32) 449-425 EMail: mediha.arnaut@unze.ba

International Relations: Darko Petkovic
Tel: +387(32) 449-145 EMail: dpetkovic@mf.unze.ba

Centres

Global Understanding of Law; Social and Inter-religion Researches

Faculties

Economics (Accountancy; Business Administration; Economics); **Education** (Arts and Humanities; Computer Science; Education; Educational Sciences; Literature; Mathematics; Mathematics and Computer Science; Modern Languages; Teacher Training); **Health** (Health Administration; Medicine); **Islamic Pedagogy** (Islamic Studies; Religion; Religious Education); **Law** (Law); **Mechanical Engineering** (Maintenance Technology; Mechanical Engineering); **Metallurgy and Materials Science** (Engineering; Materials Engineering; Metal Techniques; Metallurgical Engineering; Mining Engineering; Production Engineering; Technology; Vocational Counselling; Welfare and Protective Services; Wood Technology)

Institutes

Metallurgy *(Kemal Kapetanovic)* (Electrical and Electronic Engineering; Environmental Engineering; Mechanical Engineering; Metal Techniques; Metallurgical Engineering; Polymer and Plastics Technology)

History: Founded 2000.

Governing Bodies: Senate; Senate Commissions; Board of Trustees

Admission Requirements: Secondary school certificate or equivalent

Fees: (Euros): 750-1,000 per semester for postgraduate courses

Main Language(s) of Instruction: Bosnian, Serbian and Croatian

International Co-operation: With universities in Spain, Germany, Italy, USA, Austria, Turkey, Slovenia, Croatia, Thailand, Norway, Denmark, United Kingdom, Ireland, Serbia and Montenegro. Participates in various programmes including Tempus, Phare, DAAD, WUS, SUS, CARDS, Konrad Adenauer, Fulbright

Degrees and Diplomas: *Bakalaureat*: Foreign Language Teaching; Law; Economy, 4 yrs; *Bakalaureat*: Mechanical Engineering; Metallurgy Engineering; Materials Engineering; Environmental Engineering, 5 yrs; *Magistra*

Student Services: Academic counselling, Canteen, Handicapped facilities, Health services, Language programs, Nursery care, Sports facilities

Student Residential Facilities: For c. 400 students

Special Facilities: Art Gallery; Movie Studio

Libraries: Yes

Publications: Didakticki Putokazi - Didactical Trends *(quarterly)*; Mechanical Engineering Journal *(quarterly)*
Last Updated: 23/09/11

PRIVATE INSTITUTIONS

AMERICAN UNIVERSITY IN BOSNIA AND HERZEGOVINA

Americki Univerzitet u Bosni i Hercegovini (AUBIH)
Fra Anđela Zvizdovića 1, Sarajevo 71000
Tel: +387(33) 296-415
Fax: +387(33) 296-416
EMail: contact@aubih.edu.ba
Website: http://www.aubih.edu.ba

President: Denis Prcic

Academies

Modern Art *(American)* (Graphic Arts; Graphic Design; Journalism; Media Studies; Multimedia)

Colleges

International Law *(Banja Luka)* (International Law)

Institutes

Research and Development (Comparative Law; Economics; European Studies; Information Technology; Media Studies; Public Administration)

Schools

Economics *(American)* (Economics; Finance; International Business; International Economics; Marketing; Sales Techniques); **Government** *(American)* (International Law; International Relations; Political Sciences; Public Administration); **Technology** *(American)* (Industrial Management; Information Technology)

Further Information: Also branches in Banja Luka, Mostar and Tuzla

Academic Year: October-mid January; February-May

Degrees and Diplomas: *Bakalaureat*; *Magistra*; *Doktora*. Some degrees are issued by the State University of New York
Last Updated: 21/12/09

BANJA LUKA COLLEGE
Visoka škola Banja Luka koledž
Ulica Miloša Obilića br. 30, Banja Luka
Tel: +387(51) 433-010
Fax: +387(51) 433-815
EMail: info@blc.edu.ba
Website: http://www.blc.edu.ba

Programmes
Aeronautics (Aeronautical and Aerospace Engineering); **Business Administration** (Business Administration; Economics; Management); **Computer Science** (Computer Science; Information Technology); **NGO and Social Activities Management**; **Public Administration** (Public Administration)

Degrees and Diplomas: *Bakalaureat*
Last Updated: 22/12/09

BANJA LUKA COLLEGE OF COMMUNICATIONS KAPPA PHI
Komunikološki koledž u Banjaluci
Vojvođanska 2, Banja Luka 78000
Tel: +387(51) 321-200
Fax: +387(51) 321-201
EMail: informacije@kfbl.edu.ba
Website: http://www.blcc.edu.ba/

Director: Aleksandar Bogdanic

Programmes
Communication Studies (Advertising and Publicity; Communication Studies; Journalism; Public Relations); **Design** (Design; Graphic Design); **English** (English)

History: Founded 2000.
Main Language(s) of Instruction: South Slavic
Degrees and Diplomas: *Bakalaureat*
Last Updated: 23/12/09

COLLEGE OF MEDICAL CARE
Koledž zdravstvene njege
Pavlovica put bb, Bijeljina 76300
Tel: +387(55) 351-101
Fax: +387(55) 351-101
EMail: info@ubn.rs.ba
Website: http://www.ubn.rs.ba

Director: Ljiljana Tomic

Programmes
Nursing (Nursing); **Pharmacy** (Pharmacy)
Degrees and Diplomas: *Bakalaureat*
Last Updated: 23/09/11

HIGH COLLEGE FOR APPLIED AND LAW SCIENCES PROMETEJ
Visoka škola za primjenjene i pravne nauke Prometej
Knjaza Miloša 10a, Banja Luka
Tel: +387(51) 315-780
Fax: +387(51) 315-820
EMail: prometej@prometejbl.com
Website: http://www.prometejbl.com/

Direktor: Aleksa Macanovic

Programmes
Economics (Economics)
Degrees and Diplomas: *Bakalaureat*
Last Updated: 22/12/09

INDEPENDENT UNIVERSITY OF BANJA LUKA
Nezavisni Univerzitet Banja Luka
Ulica Veljka Mlađenovića 12 E, Banja Luka 78000
Tel: +387(51) 456-600
Fax: +387(51) 456-602
EMail: info@nubl.org
Website: http://www.nubl.org/

Rector: Dorde Mikic

Faculties
Computer Science (Computer Science; Software Engineering); **Ecology** (Ecology); **Economics** (Accountancy; Banking; Business Administration; Economics; Finance; Insurance; Management); **Political Sciences** (Political Sciences); **Social Sciences** (Social Sciences)

Degrees and Diplomas: *Bakalaureat*; *Magistra*
Last Updated: 23/09/11

INTERNATIONAL BURCH UNIVERSITY (IBU)
Francuske revolucije bb. Ilidža, Sarajevo 71210
Tel: +387(33) 782-100
Fax: +387(33) 782-131
EMail: info@ibu.edu.ba
Website: http://www.ibu.edu.ba

Rector: Huseyin Padem EMail: hpadem@ibu.edu.ba

Faculties
Economics (Business Administration; Economics; Management); **Education** (Education; English; Literature; Turkish); **Engineering and Information Technology** (Bioengineering; Engineering; Genetics; Information Technology)

History: Founded 2008.
Admission Requirements: High School Diploma
Fees: (Euros): 1,500-3,600 depending on programmes
International Co-operation: With universities in USA
Degrees and Diplomas: *Bakalaureat*; *Magistra*; *Doktora*
Student Services: Canteen, Sports facilities
Student Residential Facilities: Yes
Special Facilities: Computer and Information Club,Theatre Club
Libraries: Yes
Last Updated: 23/09/11

INTERNATIONAL UNIVERSITY OF SARAJEVO
Internacionalni Univerzitet u Sarajevu (IUS)
Paromlinska 66, Sarajevo 71000
Tel: +387(33) 720 600
Fax: +387(33) 720 625
EMail: info@ius.edu.ba
Website: http://www.ius.edu.ba/

Rector: Hilmi Ünlü EMail: rector@ius.edu.ba

Faculties
Arts and Social Sciences (Cultural Studies; Political Sciences; Social Sciences; Visual Arts); **Business Administration** (Economics; International Relations; Leadership; Management); **Engineering and Natural Sciences** (Bioengineering; Biology; Computer Engineering; Computer Science; Industrial Engineering; Materials Engineering; Microelectronics)

Schools
English Language (English)
History: Founded 2004.
Governing Bodies: Board of Trustees and Executive Board
Academic Year: September to June
Degrees and Diplomas: *Bakalaureat*; *Magistra*; *Doktora*
Libraries: Yes

Student Numbers *2009-2010*: Total: c. 800
Last Updated: 23/09/11

INTERNATIONAL UNIVERSITY OF TRAVNIK
Internacionalni Univerzitet Travnik
Bunar bb, - Dolac, Travnik 72 270
Tel: +387(30) 540-586
Website: http://www.iu-travnik.com

Rector: Ibrahim Jusufranic

Faculties

Ecology (Ecology); **Economic and Technical Logistics** (Management); **Economics** (Banking; Economics; Finance; Management; Marketing; Tourism); **Media and Communications** (Media Studies); **Traffic Engineering** (Transport Engineering)

History: Founded 2006. Acquired present status and title 2010.

Degrees and Diplomas: *Bakalaureat*; *Magistra*; *Doktora*
Last Updated: 26/09/11

JANJOS COLLEGE OF INFORMATICS AND MANAGEMENT

Koledž za informatiku i menadžment Janjoš
Trg Majora Karlice 1, Prijedor 79000
Tel: +387(52) 241-960
Fax: +387(52) 241-960
EMail: info@koledzprijedor.org
Website: http://www.koledzprijedor.org

Director: Duro Mikic

Programmes

Business Informatics (Business Computing); **Management** (Banking; Business Administration; Finance; Management; Marketing; Public Administration)

Main Language(s) of Instruction: Bosnian/Croatian/Serbian

Degrees and Diplomas: *Bakalaureat*
Last Updated: 23/09/11

PANEUROPEAN UNIVERSITY APEIRON

Panevropski univerzitet Apeiron
Pere Krece 13, Banja Luka 78102
Tel: +387(51) 430-890
Fax: +387(51) 430-891
EMail: info@apeiron-uni.eu
Website: http://www.apeiron-uni.eu/

Rector: Danelišen Dragan
Tel: +387(51) 430-922 EMail: risto.k@apeiron-uni.eu

Vice-Rector: Esad Jakupovic

Colleges

Business Economics (Banking; Business Administration; Finance; Management; Public Administration); **Computer Science** (Computer Education; Computer Science; Information Technology); **Health Care and Nursing** (Health Administration; Health Sciences; Medical Technology; Nursing; Occupational Therapy; Physical Therapy; Sanitary Engineering); **Law** (Commercial Law; Law); **Philology** (Philology); **Sports** (Sports; Sports Management)

History: Founded 2007.

Degrees and Diplomas: *Bakalaureat*; *Magistra*; *Doktora*
Last Updated: 22/03/12

SARAJEVO SCHOOL OF SCIENCE AND TECHNOLOGY (SSST)

Bistrik 7, Sarajevo 71000
Tel: +387(33) 563-030
Fax: +387(33) 563-033
EMail: admissions@ssst.edu.ba
Website: http://ssst.edu.ba/

President: Ejup Ganic

Departments

Computer Science (Computer Science); **Economics** (Economics); **Engineering** (Electrical and Electronic Engineering; Energy Engineering; Engineering; Environmental Engineering; Mathematics; Mechanical Engineering); **Information Systems** (Information Technology; Systems Analysis); **Modern Languages** (English; German); **Political Sciences and International Relations** (International Relations; Political Sciences)

Institutes

Conflict Resolution, Responsibility and Reconciliation *(Balkan)* (Peace and Disarmament)

History: Founded 2004.

Degrees and Diplomas: *Bakalaureat*. In cooperation with the University of Buckingham, SSST organizes postgraduate study for a Master of Science (MSc) and Doctor's degree
Last Updated: 23/09/11

SLOBOMIR P UNIVERSITY

Slobomir P Univerzitet
PF 70, Pavlovica put bb, Slobimir 76300
Tel: +387(55) 231-101
Fax: +381(55) 231-176
EMail: info@spu.ba
Website: http://www.spu.ba

Rector: Desanka Trakilovic EMail: desanka.trakilovic@spu.ba

Academies

Arts (Cinema and Television; Design; Graphic Design; Music; Theatre); **Fiscal** (Taxation)

Faculties

Economics and Management (Business Computing; Economics; Management; Marketing); **Information Technology** (Information Technology); **Law** (Law); **Phillology** (English; Philology)

History: Founded 2003.

Degrees and Diplomas: *Bakalaureat*; *Magistra*; *Doktora*

Libraries: Yes
Last Updated: 23/09/11

UNIVERSITY FOR BUSINESS ENGINEERING AND MANAGEMENT (PIM)

Univerzitet za Poslovni Inženjering i Menadžment
Ulici despota Stefana Lazarevića bb, Banja Luka
Tel: +387(51) 378-290
EMail: info@fakultetpim.com
Website: http://www.fakultetpim.com/

Rector: Zarko Pavic EMail: zarkopavic@yahoo.com

Pro-Rector: Ilija Dzombic EMail: idzombic@yahoo.com

Programmes

Economics (Economics); **Finance and Banking** (Banking; Finance); **Graphic Arts and Design** (Design; Graphic Arts; Industrial Design); **Law** (Law); **Management** (Management); **Marketing** (Marketing); **Psychology** (Psychology)

History: Founded 2003. Acquired present status 2007.
Last Updated: 22/03/12

UNIVERSITY OF BUSINESS STUDIES

Univerzitet za Poslovne Studije
Ul. Jovana Dučića br. 25, Banja Luka 78000
Tel: +387(51) 222-537
EMail: ups@univerzitetps.com
Website: http://www.univerzitetps.com/

Rector: Milorad Zivanovic

Faculties

Applied Economics (Economics); **Business and Financial Studies** (Business Administration; Finance); **Ecology** (Ecology); **Information Technology and Design** (Information Technology); **Law** (Law); **Tourism and Hostelry** (Hotel Management; Tourism)

History: Founded 2005.

Degrees and Diplomas: *Bakalaureat*; *Magistra*
Last Updated: 22/03/12

UNIVERSITY OF TRAVNIK

Univerzitet u Travniku
Aleja Konzula 5, Travnik 72270
Tel: +387(30) 541-061
EMail: rasim.dacic@fmt.ba
Website: http://www.fmt.ba

Rector: Rasim Dacic Tel: +387(61) 172-158

Faculties

Graphic Arts (Graphic Arts); **Kinesiology** (Physical Therapy); **Law** (Law); **Tourism Management** (Management; Tourism)

Degrees and Diplomas: *Bakalaureat; Magistra*
Last Updated: 23/09/11

UNIVERSITY SINERGIJA

Univerzitet Sinergija
Raje Baničića, Bijeljina
Tel: +387(55) 213-132
Fax: +387(55) 224-571
EMail: office@sinergija.edu.ba
Website: http://www.sinergija.edu.ba

Rector: Milovan Stanišic EMail: mstanisic@sinergija.edu.ba

Faculties
Business Administration (Accountancy; Business Administration; Marketing); **Business Computing** (Business Computing); **Civil Security** (Civil Security); **Cosmetology and Aesthetics** (Aesthetics; Cosmetology); **Economics** (Economics); **Law** (Law); **Philology** (Philology)

Degrees and Diplomas: *Bakalaureat; Magistra.* MBA programmes with Lincoln University
Last Updated: 23/09/11

VITEZ UNIVERSITY

Sveučilište/Univerzitet "VITEZ" Travnik
Ulica školska 23, Travnik 72270
Tel: +387(30) 519-750
Fax: +387(30) 519-759
EMail: info@unvi.edu.ba
Website: http://out.edu.ba/

Rector: Nikola Grabovac

Faculties
Business Economics (Accountancy; Agricultural Management; Banking; Business Administration; Economics; Finance; Insurance; Management; Marketing; Public Administration; Tourism); **Business Informatics** (Business Computing; Computer Science; Information Technology); **Health Care** (Gynaecology and Obstetrics; Health Administration; Health Sciences; Nursing; Occupational Therapy; Physical Therapy); **Law** (Law)

Degrees and Diplomas: *Bakalaureat; Magistra; Doktora*
Libraries: Yes
Last Updated: 23/09/11

Botswana

STRUCTURE OF HIGHER EDUCATION SYSTEM

Description:

Higher education falls under the mandate of the Tertiary Education Council. In 2008, the Council prepared the White Paper on Tertiary Education that is used in the on-going redrafting of the Tertiary Education Act. Higher education is offered at both public and private institutions.

Stages of studies:

University level first stage: *First degree*
Bachelor's degrees are offered after four years' study.

University level second stage: *Postgraduate level*
At postgraduate level, there are one-year Postgraduate programmes and one-and-a-half to two-and-a-half year Master programmes. A PhD (Doctor of Philosophy) may be obtained after the Master's degree and a minimum period of three years' research devoted to preparing a thesis.

ADMISSION TO HIGHER EDUCATION

Admission to university-level studies:

Name of secondary school credential required: Botswana General Certificate of Secondary Education
Minimum score/requirement: Grade B

Foreign students admission:

Definition of foreign student: All students who are not Botswana nationals.

Quotas: At University level all foreign students are free to apply.

Entrance exam requirements: Candidates must be holders of a Senior Secondary School Certificate or the Cambridge Overseas School Certificate or the General Certificate of Education (GCE), Ordinary ('O') level.

Entry regulations: Visas are required for some countries.

Language requirements: Students must be proficient in English.

RECOGNITION OF STUDIES

Quality assurance system:

The Tertiary Education Council (TEC) is responsible for the registration of tertiary institutions and the quality assurance of programmes of learning.

Bodies dealing with recognition:

Tertiary Education Council - TEC
Private Bag BR 108
Gaborone
Tel: +267 390 0679
Fax: +267 390 1481
EMail: info@tec.org.bw
WWW: http://www.tec.org.bw/

NATIONAL BODIES

Ministry for Education and Skills Development
Minister: Pelonomi Venson-Moiti
Private Bag 005
Gaborone

Tel: +267 365 5491/ 391 1453
Fax: +267 395 1624/ 390 7035
WWW: http://www.moe.gov.bw/

Tertiary Education Council - TEC
Chairperson: Jacob R. Swartland
Executive Secretary: Patrick D. Molutsi
Private Bag BR 108
Gaborone
Tel: +267 390 0679
Fax: +267 390 1481
EMail: info@tec.org.bw
WWW: http://www.tec.org.bw/
Role of national body: Parastatal body responsible for the coordination of higher education and for the determination and maintenance of standards of teaching, examination and research in higher education institutions in Botswana.

Data for academic year: 2009-2010
Source: IAU from Tertiary Education Council Website, Botswana, 2009; National bodies, 2011.

INSTITUTIONS

UNIVERSITY OF BOTSWANA (UB)
Private Bag 0022, Gaborone
Tel: +267(31) 355-0000
Fax: +267(31) 395-6591
EMail: webadmin@mopipi.ub.bw
Website: http://www.ub.bw

Vice-Chancellor: Bojosi Khebetu Otlhogile (2003-)
Tel: +267(31) 355-2032, Fax: +267(31) 318-4747
EMail: vc@mopipi.ub.bw

Director, Public Affairs: Mhitshane Reetsang (2009-)
Tel: +267(31) 355-2286, Fax: +267(31) 391-2420
EMail: directorpa@mopipi.ub.bw

International Relations: Francis Youngman, Deputy Vice Chancellor, Student Affairs (2005-2015)
Tel: (267) 355 2032, Fax: (267) 390 4243
EMail: dvcaa@mopipi.ub.bw

Centres
Academic Development; Continuing Education

Faculties
Business (Accountancy; Business Administration; Business and Commerce; Finance; Management); **Education** (Adult Education; Education; Educational Administration; Educational Sciences; Home Economics; Nursing; Physical Education; Primary Education; Science Education; Secondary Education; Special Education); **Engineering and Technology** (Architecture; Civil Engineering; Construction Engineering; Design; Electrical Engineering; Electronic Engineering; Engineering; Industrial Design; Mechanical Engineering; Mining Engineering; Regional Planning; Technology; Town Planning); **Health Sciences** (Environmental Studies; Health Sciences; Midwifery; Nursing); **Humanities** (African Languages; Archaeology; Arts and Humanities; English; Environmental Studies; French; History; Information Management; Information Sciences; Library Science; Media Studies; Religious Studies; Sociology; Theology); **Science** (Biological and Life Sciences; Biology; Chemistry; Computer Science; Environmental Studies; Geology; Information Management; Mathematics; Microbiology; Natural Sciences; Physics; Statistics); **Social Sciences** (Accountancy; Demography and Population; Development Studies; Economics; Law; Political Sciences; Psychology; Public Administration; Social Sciences; Social Work; Statistics)

Research Centres
Harry Oppenheimer Okavango; Research and Development

Schools
Graduate Studies; Medicine (Medicine)

Further Information: Also Legal Clinic and Business Clinic

History: Founded 1964 as University of Basutoland, Bechuanaland and Swaziland. Acquired present status and title 1982.

Governing Bodies: University Council

Academic Year: August to May (August-December; January-May)

Admission Requirements: Botswana General Certificate of Secondary Education (BGCSE); Cambridge Overseas School Certificate (COSC) or General Certificate of Education (GCE) or recognized foreign equivalent. Direct entrance to second year on completion of studies in another tertiary Institution

Fees: (Pula): c. 9,350-16,780 per annum; foreign students, 14,025-33,560

Main Language(s) of Instruction: English

Degrees and Diplomas: *Certificate*: Adult Education; Archives and Record Management; Library and Information Studies; Criminal Justice; Law; Mining Engineering; Population Studies; Social Work; Statistics, 2 yrs; *Bachelor's Degree*: Accountancy (BAcc); Arts (BA); Education (Physical) (BEd); Education (Primary Level) (BEd); Education (Special) (BEd); Finance (BAF); Library and Information Sciences (BLis); Management; Marketing (BBA); Nursing (BNS); Science (BSc); Social Work (BSW), 4 yrs; *Bachelor's Degree*: Civil Engineering; Electrical and Electronic Engineering; Mechanical Engineering (BEng); Law (LLB), 5 yrs; *Bachelor's Degree*: Education (BEd), 2 yrs following BA or BSc, or holders of DipSecEd with credit, 2 yrs; *Master's Degree*: Arts (MA); Education (MEd); Science (MSc), a further 1 1/2-2 1/2 yrs; *Master's Degree*: Law (LLM), a further 1-2 1/2 yrs; *Master's Degree*: Philosophy; *Post-Graduate Diploma*: Education, 1 yr; *PhD*: 4 yrs full-time; 8 yrs part-time

Student Services: Academic counselling, Canteen, Employment services, Foreign Studies Centre, Handicapped facilities, Health services, Social counselling, Sports facilities

Student Residential Facilities: Yes

Libraries: Central Library, 436,122 vols, 1,130 subscriptions to periodicals, 30,305 pamphlets

Academic Staff *2008*	MEN	WOMEN	TOTAL
FULL-TIME	493	210	**703**
Student Numbers *2008*			
All (Foreign Included)	7,882	6,538	**14,420**

Last Updated: 29/05/09

BOTSWANA COLLEGE OF AGRICULTURE (BCA)

Private Bag 0027, Gaborone
Tel: +267(31) 365-0100
Fax: +267(31) 392-8753
Website: http://www.bca.bw

Principal: E.J. Kemsley (1991-)

Centres
In-service and Continuing Education

Departments
Agricultural Economics, Education and Extension *(AEE)* (Agricultural Economics; Agricultural Education) *Head*: M. Mahabile; **Agricultural Engineering and Land Planning** *(AEL)* (Agricultural Education; Agricultural Engineering; Agricultural Equipment; Agriculture; Food Science; Harvest Technology; Power Engineering; Soil Science; Water Management) *Head*: C. Patrick; **Animal Science and Production** (Animal Husbandry; Cattle Breeding; Zoology) *Head*: J. M. Kamau; **Basic Sciences** (Biology; Botany; Chemistry; Mathematics; Natural Sciences; Physics) *Head*: R. M. Njogu; **Crop Science and Production** (Agronomy; Crop Production; Forestry; Horticulture; Plant and Crop Protection; Soil Science) *Head*: S. Macahacha

History: Founded 1967 as Botswana Agricultural College. Acquired present status and title 1991.

Degrees and Diplomas: *Certificate*; *Bachelor's Degree*; *Master's Degree*

Brazil

STRUCTURE OF HIGHER EDUCATION SYSTEM

Description:

Higher education is under the responsibility of the Ministry of Education (MEC). It is provided in public federal, state, municipal or confessional and private universities and other higher education institutions, foundations, federations and independent establishments. It is organized at two levels: graduação (undergraduate) programmes which take usually from 3 to 5 years of study and Pós-graduação (graduate) programmes lasting 2 to 6 years. A project of academic reform is underway to increase the participation rate and improve access in higher education.

Stages of studies:

University level first stage: *Graduação*
The first stage of higher education leads to the award of a Bacharelado which is usually obtained after four to six years of study, depending on the institution and the field of study (Odontology and Agriculture, four years; Architecture and Law, five years; Medicine, six years). The Licenciatura is generally awarded after three to four years' study to students who wish to become school teachers or enter graduate studies. It can be obtained at the same time as the Bacharelado.

University level second stage: *Pós-graduação*
The second stage leads to the Mestrado awarded upon completion of two to four years' study following upon the Bacharelado or Licenciatura to students who have followed a certain number of courses, passed examinations and submitted a thesis. The Doutorado, the highest degree, is awarded upon completion of four to six years' study and the submission of a thesis following upon the Mestrado.

ADMISSION TO HIGHER EDUCATION

Admission to university-level studies:

Name of secondary school credential required: Diploma de Técnico de Nivel Medio

Name of secondary school credential required: Certificado de Ensino Médio

Minimum score/requirement: 3 in Portuguese, 3 in another discipline and above 1 in all the others

For entry to: All courses

Name of secondary school credential required: Diploma de Técnico de Segundo Grau

Name of secondary school credential required: Certificado de Auxiliar Técnico

Entrance exam requirements: Concurso Vestibular with 3 as minimum mark in Portuguese, 3 in another discipline and over 1 in all the others .

Numerus clausus/restrictions: A Numerus clausus is applied if/when there are more candidates than available places. Overall achievement in secondary school and the Matura or final examination results are taken into account. According to the Regulations on Studies of Foreigners, the number of foreign students must not exceed 5% of all full-time study places available (and 50% of part-time study places).

Other admission requirements: Good knowledge of Portuguese.

Foreign students admission:

.Entrance exam requirements: Foreign students must hold a secondary-school-leaving certificate that is recognized by the Ministry of Education and pass an examination (Concurso Vestibular) comprising papers in Portuguese language and Brazilian History and Geography. Students from Latin American and African countries which have signed cultural agreements with Brazil are exempted from this examination and from paying tuition fees.

Language requirements: Foreign students must have a good command of Portuguese.

RECOGNITION OF STUDIES

Quality assurance system:

Quality assessment for undergraduate courses is carried out regularly by the institutions and annually by the INEP (Instituto Nacional de Estudos e Pesquisas Educacionais Anísio Teixeira). For graduate courses, the evaluation is carried out by the CAPES (Coordenação de Aperfeiçoamento de Pessoal de Nível Superior).

Special provisions for recognition:

Recognition for university level studies: Access to university-level studies is based on secondary school certification and the passing of examination in each unity of institution.

For access to advanced studies and research: Graduate study diploma.

For exercising a profession: Professional diploma.

NATIONAL BODIES

Ministério da Educação - MEC (Ministry of Education)
Minister: Fernando Haddad
Secretary, Higher Education: Luiz Cláudio Costa
Esplanada dos Ministérios
Bloco L
Brasília 70047-900
Tel: +55(61) 2022 7501
Fax: +55(61) 2022 7500
EMail: ai@mec.gov.br
WWW: http://portal.mec.gov.br/
Role of national body: Administration of education in the country.

Coordenação de Aperfeiçoamento de Pessoal de Nível Superior - CAPES (Commission for Improvement of Personnel in Higher Education)
President: Jorge Almeida Guimarães
Ministry of Education, Caixa Postal 365
Brasilia 70359-970
Tel: +55(61) 2104-8873/ 2104-8801
EMail: brpr@capes.gov.br
WWW: http://www.capes.gov.br
Role of national body: The CAPES is responsible for the evaluation of the Pós-graduação level; the promotion of international cooperation; and the dissemination of academic research.

Instituto Nacional de Estudos ePesquisas Educacionais Anísio Teixeira - INEP
President: Malvina Tania Tuttman
Director, Higher Education Evaluation: Claudia Maffini Griboski
SRTVS, Quadra 701, Bloco M, Edifício Sede do Inep
Brasilia 70340-909
WWW: http://www.inep.gov.br/

Conselho de Reitores das Universidades Brasileiras - CRUB (Council of Rectors of Brazilian Universities)
President: Ricardo Motta Miranda
Secretary-General: Dalva Maria de Mello
SEP/NORTE
Q. 516 conj. D
Brasília, DF 70770-545
Tel: +55(61) 3349 9010
Fax: +55(61) 3274 4621
EMail: crub@crub.org.br
WWW: http://www.crub.org.br

Associação Nacional dos Dirigentes das Instituições Federais de Ensino Superior - ANDIFES
President: João Luiz Martins
Executive Secretary: Gustavo Henrique de Sousa Balduino
SCS, Quadra 01, Bloco K, Ed. Denasa, N° 30, 8° Andar
Brasilia 70398-900

Tel: +55(61) 3321 6341
Fax: +55(61) 3321 4425
EMail: andifes@andifes.org.br
WWW: http://www.andifes.org.br
Role of national body: Represents federal higher education institutions.

Associação Brasileira das Universidades Comunitárias - ABRUC
President: Vilmar Thomé
Executive Secretary: José Carlos Aguilera
SEPN Quadra 516, Conjunto D
Brasilia 70770-524
Fax: +55(61) 3347 4951
EMail: se@abruc.org.br
WWW: http://www.abruc.org.br/

Data for academic year: 2007-2008
Source: IAU from Ministry of Education and SESU websites, 2007; Bodies updated 2011

INSTITUTIONS

PUBLIC INSTITUTIONS

ALAGOAS STATE UNIVERSITY OF HEALTH SCIENCES

Universidade Estadual de Ciências da Saúde de Alagoas (UNCISAL)
Rua Jorge de Lima 113, Trapiche da Barra, Maceió,
Alagoas 57010-382
Tel: +55(82) 3326-6505
EMail: ecmal@zipmail.com.br
Website: http://www.uncisal.edu.br
Reitora: Rozangela Maria de Almeida Fernandes Wyszomirska
EMail: reitoriauncisal@yahoo.com.br

Faculties
Medicine (Medicine); **Nursing** (Nursing); **Occupational Therapy** (Occupational Therapy); **Phonaudiology** (Speech Therapy and Audiology); **Physiotherapy** (Physical Therapy)

Schools
Health *(Technical)* (Health Sciences)
History: Founded 1970
Main Language(s) of Instruction: Portuguese
Degrees and Diplomas: *Bacharelado*; *Especialização/Aperfeiçoamento*
Last Updated: 26/05/10

CELSO SUCKOW DA FONSECA FEDERAL CENTRE OF TECHNOLOGICAL EDUCATION

Centro Federal de Educação Tecnológica Celso Suckow da Fonseca (CEFET/RJ)
Avenida Maracanã 229, Maracanã, Rio de Janeiro,
Rio de Janeiro 20271-110
Tel: +55(21) 2568-8890
Fax: +55(21) 2204-0978
EMail: sespi@cefet-rj.br
Website: http://www.cefet-rj.br
Director: Miguel Badenes Pradhes Filho (2003-)
EMail: badenes@cefet-rj.br

Units
Maracanã (Automation and Control Engineering; Civil Engineering; Computer Science; Electrical Engineering; Electronic Engineering; Environmental Management; Industrial Management; Mechanical Engineering; Production Engineering; Telecommunications Engineering); **Nova Friburgo** (Physics; Tourism); **Nova Iguaçu** (Automation and Control Engineering; Industrial Engineering; Production Engineering); **Petrópolis** (Physics; Tourism)
Further Information: Also branches in Maria da Graça and Nova Iguaçu
History: Founded 1909. Acquired present status 1978.
Academic Year: March to December
Admission Requirements: Secondary school certificate
Main Language(s) of Instruction: Portuguese
International Co-operation: With universities in Germany and France
Accrediting Agencies: Ministério de Educação (MEC), Coordenação Nacional de Aperfeiçoamento de Pessoal de Nível Superior (CAPES); Instituto Nacional de Estudos e Pesquisas Educacionais (INEP)
Degrees and Diplomas: *Tecnólogo*; *Bacharelado*; *Licenciatura*; *Mestrado*: Technonlogy; Science and Mathematics Education; Mechanical Engineering and Materials Technology; Electrical Engineering; Science, Technology and Education
Student Services: Academic counselling, Canteen, Employment services, Foreign student adviser, Handicapped facilities, Health services, Language programs, Nursery care, Sports facilities
Student Residential Facilities: No
Libraries: Central Library
Publications: Tecnologia & Cultura *(biennially)*
Last Updated: 22/04/10

DARCY RIBEIRO STATE UNIVERSITY OF THE NORTH OF THE STATE OF RIO DE JANEIRO

Universidade Estadual do Norte Fluminense Darcy Ribeiro (UENF)
Avenida Alberto Lamego 2000, Horto, Campos dos Goytacazes,
Rio de Janeiro 28015620
Tel: +55(24) 2726-3150
Fax: +55(24) 2726-1505
EMail: uenf@uenf.br
Reitor: Almy Junior Cordeiro de Carvalho

Centres
Agriculture and Stockraising Sciences and Technology (Agricultural Engineering; Agriculture; Cattle Breeding) *Head*: Silverio

Freitas; **Biosciences and Biotechnology** (Biological and Life Sciences; Biotechnology) *Head*: Carlos Rezende; **Human Sciences** (Social Sciences) *Head*: Arno Vogel; **Science and Technology** (Natural Sciences; Technology) *Head*: Paulo Nagipe

History: Founded 1990. A State institution.

Academic Year: Secondary school certificate and entrance examination

Fees: None

Main Language(s) of Instruction: Portuguese

International Co-operation: With universities in United Kingdom, USA, Netherlands, Portugal, Germany, Canada, France.

Degrees and Diplomas: *Bacharelado*; *Licenciatura*; *Especialização/Aperfeiçoamento*; *Mestrado*; *Doutorado*

Student Services: Cultural centre, Language programs, Social counselling, Sports facilities
Last Updated: 25/05/10

FACULTIES OF THE EDUCATIONAL FOUNDATION OF MOCOCA

Faculdades da Fundação de Ensino de Mococa (FAFEM)
Av. Monsenhor Demóstenes P. B. Pontes, 2.131 - Jd. São José, Mococa, São Paulo 13.737-632
Tel: +55(19) 3656-5516
EMail: comunica@fafem.com.br
Website: http://www.fafem.com.br

Diretora: Marcilene dos Santos

Courses

Accountancy (Accountancy); **Administration** (Administration); **Computer Science** (Computer Science); **Literature** (Literature); **Pedagogy** (Pedagogy)

History: Founded 1972 as Instituto de Ensino Superior de Mococa. Acquired present status and title 2002.

Main Language(s) of Instruction: Portuguese

Degrees and Diplomas: *Bacharelado*; *Licenciatura*
Last Updated: 29/06/10

FACULTY OF AGRICULTURE OF ARARIPINA

Faculdade de Ciências Agrárias de Araripina (FACIAGRA)
Avenida Florentino Alves Batista, S/n Campus Universitário Centro, Araripina, PE 56280000
Tel: +55(81) 3873-1001
Fax: +55(81) 3873-1001
EMail: aeda@htnet.com.br
Website: http://www.portalaeda.com.br/

Diretora: Maria Darticlea Albuquerque Lima Modesto

Courses

Agronomy (Agriculture; Agronomy)

History: Founded 1986

Main Language(s) of Instruction: Portuguese

Degrees and Diplomas: *Bacharelado*
Last Updated: 06/12/07

FACULTY OF ANICUNS

Faculdade de Anicuns
Avenida Bandeirantes, n° 1140, Setor Roosevelt, Anicuns, Goiás 76170-000
Tel: +55(62) 3564-1499
Fax: +55(62) 3564-2522
EMail: fea@internetional.com.br
Website: http://www.faculdadeanicuns.edu.br

Diretor: Jadir Gonçalves Rodrigues

Courses

Accountancy (Accountancy); **Business Administration** (Business Administration); **Geography** (Geography); **Graduate Studies**; **History** (History); **Law** (Law); **Pedagogy** *(FECHA)*
Further Information: Also Rodovia campus.

History: Founded 1985

Main Language(s) of Instruction: Portuguese

Degrees and Diplomas: *Bacharelado*; *Licenciatura*; *Especialização/Aperfeiçoamento*
Last Updated: 01/07/10

FACULTY OF APPLIED AND SOCIAL SCIENCES OF PETROLINA

Faculdade de Ciências Aplicadas e Sociais de Petrolina (FACAPE)
Campus Universitário, s/n, Vila Eduardo, Petrolina, Pernambuco 56328-903
Tel: +55(81) 3866-3200 +55(81) 3866-3257
Fax: +55(81) 3866-3204 +55(81) 3866-3253
EMail: direcao@facape.br
Website: http://www.facape.br/

Diretora Acadêmica: Ruth de Souza Dias Ferreira

Courses

Accountancy (Accountancy); **Administration** (Administration); **Computer Science** (Computer Science); **Economics** (Economics); **Foreign Trade** (International Business); **Graduate Studies**; **Law** (Law); **Secretarial Studies** (Secretarial Studies); **Tourism** (Tourism)

History: Founded 1976

Main Language(s) of Instruction: Portuguese

Degrees and Diplomas: *Bacharelado*; *Especialização/Aperfeiçoamento*
Last Updated: 02/07/10

FACULTY OF APPLIED SCIENCES OF LIMOEIRO

Faculdade de Ciências Aplicadas do Limoeiro (FACAL)
Av. Jerônimo Heráclio, n° 81, Centro, Limoeiro, PE 55700-000
Tel: +55(81) 3628-1397
Fax: +55(81) 3628-1397
EMail: facal@facal.edu.br
Website: http://www.facal.edu.br

Diretor: Cícero Benedito de Arruda

Courses

Accountancy (Accountancy); **Administration** (Administration); **Graduate Studies** (Management; Marketing; Public Administration)

History: Founded 1973 as Faculdade de Ciências da Administração do Limoeiro.

Main Language(s) of Instruction: Portuguese

Degrees and Diplomas: *Bacharelado*: 4 yrs; *Especialização/Aperfeiçoamento*
Last Updated: 02/07/10

FACULTY OF ARTS OF PARANA

Faculdade de Artes do Paraná (FAP)
Rua dos Funcionários 1357, Cabral, Curitibá, Paraná 80035050
Tel: +55(41) 3250-7300
Fax: +55(41) 3250-7301
EMail: fapr@fapr.br
Website: http://www.fapr.br/

Diretora: Rosane Schlögel

Courses

Cinema and Video (Film; Video); **Dance** (Dance); **Graduate Studies**; **Music** (Art Therapy; Jazz and Popular Music; Music); **Musicotherapy** (Art Therapy; Music); **Popular Music** (Jazz and Popular Music); **Scenic Arts** (Theatre); **Theatre** (Theatre); **Visual Arts** (Visual Arts)

History: Founded 1967

Degrees and Diplomas: *Bacharelado*; *Licenciatura*; *Especialização/Aperfeiçoamento*
Last Updated: 01/07/10

FACULTY OF EDUCATION, SCIENCES AND LETTERS OF PARAISO DO TOCANTINS

Faculdade de Educação, Ciências e Letras de Paraiso do Tocantins (FECIPAR)
Rua L, 20, Setor Interlagos, Paraíso do Tocantins, TO 77600-000
Tel: +55(63) 3602-6649
EMail: fepar@fecipar.br
Website: http://fecipar.edu.br/v2

Diretor: Luis da Silva César Jr

Courses
Accountancy (Accountancy); **Administration** (Administration; Business Administration); **Letters** (Literature); **Pedagogy** (Pedagogy)

History: Founded 1993.

Main Language(s) of Instruction: Portuguese

Degrees and Diplomas: *Bacharelado*; *Especialização/Aperfeiçoamento*
Last Updated: 02/08/10

FACULTY OF HUMAN AND APPLIED SOCIAL SCIENCES OF CABO DE SANTO AGOSTINHO

Faculdade de Ciências Humanas e Sociais Aplicadas do Cabo de Santo Agostinho (FACHUCA)
Rua Sebastião Joventino, S/N, Destilaria, Cabo de Santo Agostinho, PE 54500-000
Tel: +55(81) 3521-0400 +55(81) 3524-0707
Fax: +55(81) 3521-0483
EMail: factuta@uol.com.br
Website: http://www.fachuca.edu.br

Diretor: Joaquim Severino da Silva Filho

Courses
Administration (Administration); **Commerce** (Business and Commerce); **Graduate Studies** *(Lato Sensu)*; **History**

History: Founded 1992

Main Language(s) of Instruction: Portuguese

Degrees and Diplomas: *Bacharelado*; *Licenciatura*; *Especialização/Aperfeiçoamento*
Last Updated: 05/07/10

FACULTY OF HUMAN SCIENCES OF SERTÃO CENTRAL

Faculdade de Ciências Humanas do Sertão Central (FACHUSC)
Rua Antônio Filgueira Sampaio 134, Augusto Sampaio, Salgueiro, PE 56000000
Tel: +55(81) 3871-6040
Fax: +55(81) 3871-6040
EMail: fachusc2000@yahoo.com.br

Diretor: Francisco Avelar Sampaio Ulisses

Courses
History (History); **Literature** (Literature); **Pedagogy** (Pedagogy)

History: Founded 1984.

Main Language(s) of Instruction: Portuguese

Degrees and Diplomas: *Licenciatura*
Last Updated: 10/12/07

FACULTY OF HUMAN SCIENCES OF THE VALLEY OF PIRANGA

Faculdade de Ciências Humanas do Vale do Piranga (FAVAP)
Rua Cantídio Drumond 92, Centro, Ponte Nova, Minas Gerais 35430-006
Tel: +55(31) 3817-4503
Fax: +55(31) 3817-4503
EMail: fach@pontenet.com.br

Diretor: Luiz Raimundo

Courses
Geography (Geography); **History** (History); **Literature** (Literature)

History: Founded 1974.

Main Language(s) of Instruction: Portuguese

Degrees and Diplomas: *Licenciatura*
Last Updated: 10/12/07

FACULTY OF LAW OF CONSELHEIRO LAFAIETE

Faculdade de Direito de Conselheiro Lafaiete (FDCL)
Rua Lopes Franco 1001 - Blocos C /D, Centro, Conselheiro Lafaiete, Minas Gerais 36400-000
Tel: +55(31) 3769-1919
Fax: +55(31) 3769-1919
EMail: fdcl@fdcl.edu.br
Website: http://www.fdcl.edu.br

Diretor: Hamilton Junqueira

Courses
Law (Law)

History: Founded 1970

Main Language(s) of Instruction: Portuguese

Degrees and Diplomas: *Bacharelado*
Last Updated: 22/03/10

FACULTY OF LAW OF FRANCA

Faculdade de Direito de Franca (FDF)
Caixa Postal 282, Avenida Major Nicácio 2377, São José, Franca, São Paulo 14401-135
Tel: +55(16) 3724-4500
Fax: +55(16) 3724-4195
EMail: secretaria.fdf@direitofranca.br
Website: http://www.direitofranca.br

Diretor: Euclides Celso Berardo

Courses
Law (Law)

History: Founded 1958

Main Language(s) of Instruction: Portuguese

Degrees and Diplomas: *Bacharelado*
Last Updated: 06/07/10

FACULTY OF LAW OF SÃO BERNARDO DO CAMPO

Faculdade de Direito de São Bernardo do Campo (FDSBC)
Autarquia Municipal, Rua Java 425 Jardim do Mar, São Bernardo do Campo, São Paulo 09750-650
Tel: +55(11) 4123-0222
Fax: +55(11) 4123-0222
EMail: diretoria@direitosbc.br
Website: http://www.direitosbc.br

Diretor: Marcelo José Ladeira Mauad

Courses
Graduate Studies (Commercial Law; Law; Public Law); **Law** (Administrative Law; Civil Law; Commercial Law; Constitutional Law; Criminal Law; Economics; Forensic Medicine and Dentistry; International Law; Labour Law; Law; Philosophy; Sociology)

History: Founded 1964

Main Language(s) of Instruction: Portuguese

Degrees and Diplomas: *Bacharelado*; *Especialização/Aperfeiçoamento*
Last Updated: 06/07/10

FACULTY OF MEDICINE OF JUNDIAÍ

Faculdade de Medicina de Jundiaí (FMJ)
Rua Francisco Telles 250, Vila Arens, Caixa Postal 1295, Jundiaí, São Paulo 13202550
Tel: +55(11) 4587-1095
Fax: +55(11) 4587-1095
EMail: fmj@fmj.br
Website: http://www.fmj.br

Diretor: Itibagi Rocha Machado

Courses
Medicine (Medicine); **Nursing** (Nursing)
History: Founded 1968
Main Language(s) of Instruction: Portuguese
Degrees and Diplomas: *Bacharelado*; *Especialização/Aperfeiçoamento*
Last Updated: 09/07/10

FACULTY OF MEDICINE OF MARILIA
Faculdade de Medicina de Marília (FAMEMA)
Avenida Monte Carmelo 800, Vila Fragata, Marília,
São Paulo 17519030
Tel: +55(14) 3402-1835
Fax: +55(14) 3413-2594
EMail: info@famema.br
Website: http://www.famema.br
Diretor Geral: José Augusto Alves Ottaiano

Courses
Medicine (Medicine); **Nursing** (Nursing)
History: Founded 1967.
Main Language(s) of Instruction: Portuguese
Degrees and Diplomas: *Bacharelado*; *Especialização/Aperfeiçoamento*
Last Updated: 09/07/10

FACULTY OF MEDICINE OF SÃO JOSÉ DO RIO PRETO
Faculdade de Medicina de São José do Rio Preto (FAMERP)
Avenida Brigadeiro Faria Lima 5416, Vila São Pedro,
São José do Rio Prêto, São Paulo 15090000
Tel: +55(17) 3201-5700
Fax: +55(17) 3229-1777
EMail: secretariageral@famerp.br
Website: http://www.famerp.br
Diretor: Humberto Liedtke Junior (2005-)

Courses
Medicine (Medicine); **Nursing** (Nursing)
History: Founded 1974
Main Language(s) of Instruction: Portuguese
Degrees and Diplomas: *Bacharelado*; *Especialização/Aperfeiçoamento*; *Mestrado*; *Doutorado*
Last Updated: 09/07/10

FACULTY OF MUSIC OF ESPIRITO SANTO
Faculdade de Música do Espírito Santo (EMES)
Praça Américo Poli Monjardim, 60 Centro, Vitória,
Espirito Santo 29010340
Tel: +55(27) 3132-1099
Fax: +55(27) 3222-1326
EMail: aacademica@fames.es.gov.br
Website: http://www.fames.es.gov.br
Diretor: Edilson Barboza EMail: direcao@fames.es.gov.br

Courses
Music (Music)
History: Founded 1952.
Main Language(s) of Instruction: Portuguese
Degrees and Diplomas: *Bacharelado*; *Licenciatura*
Last Updated: 09/07/10

FACULTY OF PHILOSOPHY AND HUMANITIES OF GOIATUBA
Faculdade de Filosofia e Ciências Humanas de Goiatuba (FAFICH)
Rodovia GO 320 Km 01, Jardim Santa Paula, Campus Unversitário,
Goiatuba, Goiás 75600000
Tel: +55(64) 3495-1560 +55(64) 3495-2919
Fax: +55(64) 3495-2919
EMail: fafich@ig.com.br
Website: http://www.fafich.org.br
Diretora: Dulcimar Rosa Ferreira EMail: dulce@fafich.org.br

Courses
Accountancy (Accountancy); **Administration** (Administration);
Graduate Studies (Physical Education); **Law** (Law); **Literature**
(English; Literature; Portuguese); **Nursing** (Nursing); **Pedagogy**
(Pedagogy); **Physical Education** (Physical Education)
History: Founded 1988
Main Language(s) of Instruction: Portuguese
Degrees and Diplomas: *Bacharelado*; *Licenciatura*; *Especialização/Aperfeiçoamento*
Last Updated: 08/07/10

FACULTY OF PHILOSOPHY, SCIENCE AND LETTERS OF ALEGRE
Faculdade de Filosofia, Ciências e Letras de Alegre (FAFIA)
Rua Belo Amorim, n° 100, Centro, Alegre, ES 29500-000
Tel: +55(27) 3552-1412
Fax: +55(27) 3552-1412
EMail: fafia@fafia.edu.br
Website: http://www.fafia.edu.br
Diretora: Vera Lúcia de Souza Vieira

Courses
Biological Sciences; **Biology** (Biology); **Graduate Studies**; **History** (History); **Literature** (Literature); **Mathematics** (Mathematics);
Nursing (Nursing); **Pedagogy** (Pedagogy); **Pharmacy** (Pharmacy);
Psychology (Psychology)
History: Founded 1967
Degrees and Diplomas: *Bacharelado*; *Licenciatura*; *Especialização/Aperfeiçoamento*
Last Updated: 08/07/10

FACULTY OF PHILOSOPHY, SCIENCE AND LETTERS OF MANDAGUARI
Faculdade de Filosofia, Ciências e Letras de Mandaguari (FAFIMAN)
Rua Renê Táccola, 152, Centro, Caixa Postal, 100, Mandaguari,
PR 86975000
Tel: +55(44) 3233-1356
Fax: +55(44) 3233-2411
EMail: secretaria@fafiman.br
Website: http://www.fafiman.br
Diretor: Ivan Carlos de Moraes EMail: icmoraes@fafiman.br

Courses
Accountancy (Accountancy); **Administration** (Administration);
Agricultural Business (Agricultural Business); **Biological Sciences**; **Computer Science** (Computer Science); **English and Portuguese Literature** (English; Literature; Portuguese); **Graduate Studies** (Accountancy; Biology; Educational Psychology; Educational Technology; English; Environmental Management; Environmental Studies; Ethics; History; Marketing; Mathematics Education; Natural Resources; Physical Education; Political Sciences; Portuguese; Sociology; Spanish; Special Education); **History** (History);
Mathematics (Mathematics); **Nursing** (Nursing); **Pedagogy** (Pedagogy); **Physical Education** (Physical Education)
History: Founded 1966
Main Language(s) of Instruction: Portuguese
Degrees and Diplomas: *Bacharelado*; *Licenciatura*; *Especialização/Aperfeiçoamento*. Also MBA.
Last Updated: 08/07/10

FACULTY OF SCIENCE AND TECHNOLOGY OF BIRIGUI

Faculdade de Ciências e Tecnológia de Birigui (FATEB)
Rua Antônio Simões, 04, Centro, Birigüi, São Paulo 16200-027
Tel: +55(18) 3649-2200
Fax: +55(18) 3649-2201
EMail: fateb@fateb.br
Website: http://www.fateb.br

Diretor Geral: Pedro Ângelo Cintra

Courses
Accountancy (Accountancy); **Administration** (Administration); **Graduate Studies** (Education; Educational Sciences); **Industrial Design** (Industrial Design); **Information Systems** (Computer Science); **Literature** (Literature); **Mathematics** (Mathematics); **Pedagogy** (Pedagogy)

History: Founded 1985.

Degrees and Diplomas: *Bacharelado*; *Licenciatura*. Also Postgraduate Diploma.
Last Updated: 02/07/10

FACULTY OF SCIENCE OF THE FOUNDATION TECHNOLOGICAL INSTITUTE OF OSASCO

Faculdade de Ciências da Fundação Instituto Tecnológico de Osasco (FAC-FITO)
Rua Angélica 100, Jardim das Flores, Osasco,
São Paulo 06132-380
Tel: +55(11) 3652-3094
EMail: fac@fito.br
Website: http://www.fito.br/facfito/index.htm

Diretor: Olímpio Murilo Capeli Murilo Capeli

Courses
Accountancy (Accountancy); **Administration** (Administration); **Computer Science** (Computer Science); **Economics** (Economics); **Electrical Engineering** (Electrical Engineering); **Music** (Music); **Pedagogy** (Pedagogy); **Social Communication** (Communication Arts)

History: Founded 1965.

Main Language(s) of Instruction: Portuguese

Degrees and Diplomas: *Bacharelado*; *Licenciatura*
Last Updated: 02/07/10

FACULTY OF SOCIAL SCIENCES OF PALMARES

Faculdade de Ciências Sociais dos Palmares
Br 101 K 186 Sul s/n, Palmares, PE 55540-000
Tel: +55(81) 3661-1876
EMail: facip_educ@hotmail.com

Diretor: Paulo de Assis Mendes da Silva

Courses
Administration (Administration)

History: Founded 2004.

Main Language(s) of Instruction: Portuguese

Degrees and Diplomas: *Bacharelado*
Last Updated: 30/07/10

FACULTY OF TECHNOLOGY OF AMERICANA

Faculdade de Tecnologia de Americana (FATEC-AM)
Avenida Nossa Senhora de Fátima 567, Nossa Senhora de Fátima,
Americana, São Paulo 13478540
Tel: +55(19) 3468-1049 +55(19) 3468-11216
Fax: +55(19) 3468-1049
EMail: direcao@fatec.edu.br
Website: http://www.fatec.br

Diretor: Rafael Ferreira Alves

Courses
Business Administration (Business Administration); **Data Processing** (Data Processing); **Logistics and Transports** (Transport Management); **Systems Analysis and Information Technology** (Computer Science; Information Technology); **Textile Technology** (Textile Technology)

History: Founded 1986.

Main Language(s) of Instruction: Portuguese

Degrees and Diplomas: *Tecnólogo*; *Bacharelado*; *Licenciatura*
Last Updated: 08/07/10

FACULTY OF TECHNOLOGY OF JAHU

Faculdade de Tecnologia de Jahu (FATEC-JAHU)
Rua Frei Galvão, Jardim Pedro Ometto, Jahu, São Paulo 17212599
Tel: +55(14) 3622-8280 +55(14) 3622-8220
Fax: +55(14) 3622-8280 +55(14) 3622-8224
EMail: diretoria@fatecjahu.edu.br
Website: http://www.fatecjahu.edu.br

Diretor: Antonio Eduardo Assis Amorim

Courses
Computer Science (Computer Science); **Construction and Maintenance of River Navigation Systems** (Maintenance Technology; Water Management); **Postgraduate** (Postgraduate); **Technology** (Technology); **Transport Management** (Transport Management)

History: Founded 1990.

Main Language(s) of Instruction: Portuguese

Degrees and Diplomas: *Tecnólogo*; *Especialização/Aperfeiçoamento*
Last Updated: 08/07/10

FACULTY OF TECHNOLOGY OF JUNDIAÍ

Faculdade de Tecnologia de Jundiaí (FATEC JUNDIAÍ)
Av. União dos Ferroviários, 1760, Jundiaí, SP 13201-160
Tel: +55(11) 4522-7549
Fax: +55(11) 4523-0092
Website: http://fatecjd.edu.br/

Director: Antonio César Galhardi

Courses
Computer Science (Computer Science); **Events Management** (Public Relations; Tourism); **Graduate Studies** (Business Administration; Business and Commerce); **Logistics** (Transport Management)

Degrees and Diplomas: *Tecnólogo*; *Especialização/Aperfeiçoamento*
Last Updated: 23/08/10

FACULTY OF TECHNOLOGY OF PRAIA GRANDE

Faculdade de Tecnologia de Praia Grande (FATECPG)
Praça 19 de janeiro, 144, Praia Grande, SP 11700-100
Tel: +55 (13) 3591-1303 +55(13) 3591-6968
Website: http://www.fatecpg.com.br/

Courses
Business Computing (Business Computing); **Graduate Studies** (Business and Commerce; Management); **International Business** (International Business)

Degrees and Diplomas: *Tecnólogo*; *Especialização/Aperfeiçoamento*. Also MBA.
Last Updated: 23/08/10

FACULTY OF TECHNOLOGY OF SÃO JOSÉ DO RIO PRETO

Faculdade de Tecnologia de São José do Rio Preto (FATECRP)
Rua Fernandópolis, 2510, Eldorado, São José do Rio Preto,
SP 15043-020
Tel: +55 (17) 3219-1433
EMail: ouvidoria@fatecriopreto.edu.br
Website: http://www.fatecriopreto.edu.br/

Diretor: Waldir Barros Fernandes Jr.

Courses
Agribusiness (Agricultural Business); **Business Computing** (Business Computing); **Graduate Studies** (Computer Science)

Degrees and Diplomas: *Tecnólogo*; *Especialização/Aperfeiçoamento*
Last Updated: 23/08/10

FACULTY OF TECHNOLOGY OF SÃO PAULO

Faculdade de Tecnológia de São Paulo (FATEC-SP)
Pça. Cel. Fernando Prestes, 30, Bom Retiro, São Paulo,
São Paulo 1124060
Tel: +55(11) 3322-2200 +55(11) 3322-2249
Fax: +55(11) 3315-0383
EMail: ataa@fatecsp.br
Website: http://www.fatecsp.br

Diretor: Luciana Reyes Pires Kassab EMail: secdir@fatecsp.br

Courses

Civil and Construction Engineering (Civil Engineering; Construction Engineering; Hydraulic Engineering; Seismology; Technology); **Data Processing**; **Hydraulic and Environmental Engineering**; **Materials and Electronic Engineering** (Electronic Engineering; Materials Engineering); **Mechanical Engineering and Welding** (Mechanical Engineering; Metal Techniques); **Mechanics** (Mechanics); **Mechanics and Production Engineering**; **Office Automation and Secretarial Studies** (Business Computing; Secretarial Studies); **Postgraduate**; **Precision Mechanics** (Mechanics)

History: Founded 1973.

Main Language(s) of Instruction: Portuguese

Degrees and Diplomas: *Tecnólogo*; *Especialização/Aperfeiçoamento*
Last Updated: 08/07/10

FACULTY OF TECHNOLOGY OF SOROCABA

Faculdade de Tecnológia de Sorocaba (FATEC-SO)
Av. Engenheiro Carlos Reinaldo Mendes, 2015, Alto da Boa Vista,
Sorocaba, São Paulo 18013280
Tel: +55(15) 3238-5266
Fax: +55(15) 3228-2443
EMail: diretoria@fatecsorocaba.edu.br
Website: http://www.fatecsorocaba.edu.br

Diretor: Antonio Carlos de Oliveira (1998-)
Tel: +55(15) 3238-5260

Courses

Biomedical Systems (Medical Technology); **Data Processing** (Data Processing); **Logistics** (Transport Management); **Mechanics** (Polymer and Plastics Technology; Production Engineering); **Plastics Production** (Polymer and Plastics Technology); **Systems Analysis and Development** (Systems Analysis)

History: Founded 1970

Main Language(s) of Instruction: Portuguese

Degrees and Diplomas: *Tecnólogo*. Also Postgraduate Diploma.
Last Updated: 27/09/10

FEDERAL CENTRE OF TECHNOLOGICAL EDUCATION OF MINAS GERAIS

Centro Federal de Educação Tecnológica de Minas Gerais (CEFET-MG)
Avenida Amazonas 5253, Nova Suiça, Belo Horizonte,
Minas Gerais 30421-169
Tel: +55(31) 3319-7002
Fax: +55(31) 3319-7009
EMail: gabinete@adm.cefetmg.br
Website: http://www.cefetmg.br

Diretor Geral: Flávio Antônio dos Santos

Courses

Administration; **Automation and Control Engineering** (Automation and Control Engineering); **Automation and Industrial Engineering** (Automation and Control Engineering; Industrial Engineering); **Chemical Technology**; **Civil Engineering** (Civil Engineering); **Computer Engineering** (Computer Engineering); **Electrical Engineering** (Electrical Engineering); **Environmental Engineering**; **Materials Engineering**; **Mechanical Engineering**; **Mechatronics Engineering** (Electronic Engineering; Mechanical Engineering); **Quality and Normalisation** (Safety Engineering); **Radiology** (Radiology); **Teacher Training** (Teacher Training)

Further Information: Also branches in Leopoldina, Araxá and Divinópolis

History: Founded 1909. Acquired present status 1982.

Degrees and Diplomas: *Tecnólogo*; *Bacharelado*; *Licenciatura*; *Especialização/Aperfeiçoamento*; *Mestrado*
Last Updated: 23/04/10

FEDERAL INSTITUTE OF EDUCATION, SCIENCE AND TECHNOLOGY OF ALAGOAS

Instituto Federal de Educação, Ciência e Tecnologia de Alagoas (IFAL)
Rua Barão de Atalaia, s/n° - Poço, Maceió, Alagoas 57020-510
Tel: +55(82) 2126-7012 +55(82) 2126-7050
Fax: +55(82) 2126-7019
EMail: cefet@cefet-al.br; secgab@cefet-al.br
Website: http://www.cefet-al.br

Diretor-Geral: Roland dos Santos Gonçalves

Courses

Civil Engineering (Civil Engineering); **Food Science and Technology** (Food Science; Food Technology); **Hotel Management**; **Information Systems**; **Interior Design** (Interior Design); **Tourism**; **Town Planning** (Town Planning)

Further Information: Also Marechal Deodoro, Palmeira dos Índios and Satuba units.

History: Founded 1999 as Centro Federal de Educação Tecnológica de Alagoas. Acquired present title following merger with Escola Agrotécnica Federal de Satuba 2008.

Degrees and Diplomas: *Tecnólogo*; *Bacharelado*; *Mestrado*

Academic Staff

STAFF WITH DOCTORATE: Total 19
Last Updated: 23/04/10

FEDERAL INSTITUTE OF EDUCATION, SCIENCE AND TECHNOLOGY OF BAHIA

Instituto Federal de Educação, Ciência e Tecnologia da Bahia (IFBA)
Rua Emídio dos Santos s/n, Barbalho, Salvador, Bahia 40300010
Tel: +55(71) 2102-9400
Website: http://www.portal.ifba.edu.br

Diretora Geral: Aurina Oliveira Santana EMail: dgeral@cefetba.br

Departments

Applied Sciences (Applied Chemistry; Applied Mathematics; Applied Physics; Computer Science; Engineering); **Electrical and Electronic Engineering** (Electrical and Electronic Engineering); **Human Sciences and Languages**; **Industrial Engineering** (Industrial Engineering); **Mechanical and Materials Engineering** (Materials Engineering; Mechanical Engineering)

History: Founded 1993 as Centro Federal de Educação Tecnológica da Bahia. Acquired present title 2008.

Main Language(s) of Instruction: Portuguese

Degrees and Diplomas: *Tecnólogo*; *Bacharelado*; *Licenciatura*; *Especialização/Aperfeiçoamento*; *Mestrado*
Last Updated: 23/03/10

FEDERAL INSTITUTE OF EDUCATION, SCIENCE AND TECHNOLOGY OF CEARÁ

Instituto Federal de Educação, Ciência e Tecnologia do Ceará (IFCE)
Avenida Treze de Maio, 2081, Benfica, Fortaleza, Ceará 60040531
Tel: +55(85) 3307-3666
Fax: +55(85) 3307-3711
EMail: reitoria@ifce.edu.br
Website: http://www.ifce.edu.br

Reitor: Cláudio Ricardo Gomes de Lima

Campuses

Acaraú; **Canindé**; **Cedro** (Electronic Engineering; Engineering; Mathematics; Mechanical Engineering); **Crateús**; **Crato**; **Fortaleza** (Adult Education; Chemistry; Civil Engineering; Computer Engineering; Computer Networks; Electronic Engineering; Engineering; Environmental Engineering; Environmental Management; Fine Arts; Folklore; Hotel and Restaurant; Mathematics; Mechanical

Engineering; Performing Arts; Physics; Sports Management; Telecommunications Engineering; Theatre; Tourism; Visual Arts); **Iguatu**; **Juazeiro do Norte** (Automation and Control Engineering; Civil Engineering; Construction Engineering; Electronic Engineering; Engineering; Environmental Engineering; Mathematics; Physical Education); **Limoeiro do Norte** (Agricultural Business; Automation and Control Engineering; Electronic Engineering; Environmental Studies; Food Science; Irrigation; Mechanical Engineering; Nutrition; Public Health); **Maracanaú**; **Quixadá**; **Sobral** (Adult Education; Automation and Control Engineering; Electronic Engineering; Environmental Studies; Food Technology; Irrigation; Mechanical Engineering; Physics; Public Health)

Further Information: Also extensions in Aracati, Baturité, Camocim, Caucaia, Jaguaribe, Morada Nova, Tabuleiro do Norte, Tauá, Tianguá, Ubajara.

History: Founded 1999 as Centro Federal de Educação Tecnológica do Ceará. Acquired present status and title 2008.

Main Language(s) of Instruction: Portuguese

Degrees and Diplomas: *Tecnólogo*; *Bacharelado*; *Licenciatura*; *Especialização/Aperfeiçoamento*; *Mestrado*
Last Updated: 06/05/10

FEDERAL INSTITUTE OF EDUCATION, SCIENCE AND TECHNOLOGY OF ESPÍRITO SANTO

Instituto Federal de Educação, Ciência e Tecnologia do Espírito Santo (IFES)
Avenida Vitória 1729, Jucutuquara, Vitória, Espirito Santo 29040-780
Tel: +55(27) 3331-2110
Fax: +55(27) 3331-2222
EMail: gabinete@ifes.edu.br; gps@ifes.edu.br
Website: http://www.ifes.edu.br
Reitor: Denio Rebello Arantes

Campuses
Alegre; **Cariacica** (Production Engineering); **Colatina** (Computer Networks; Environmental Studies); **Serra** (Automation and Control Engineering; Computer Networks; Computer Science; Information Sciences); **Vitória** (Chemistry; Electrical Engineering; Environmental Engineering; Mathematics; Metal Techniques; Metallurgical Engineering)

Courses
Graduate Studies (PRAPPG) (Adult Education; Computer Science; Education; Materials Engineering; Metallurgical Engineering; Occupational Health; Production Engineering; Public Administration; Teacher Trainers Education)

History: Founded 1999 as Centro Federal de Educação Tecnológica do Espírito Santo (CEFET/ES). Acquired present status and title 2008 following merger with Escola Agrotécnicas de Alegre, Escola de Colatina and Escola de Santa Teresa.

Main Language(s) of Instruction: Portuguese

Degrees and Diplomas: *Tecnólogo*; *Licenciatura*; *Especialização/Aperfeiçoamento*; *Mestrado*
Last Updated: 06/05/10

FEDERAL INSTITUTE OF EDUCATION, SCIENCE AND TECHNOLOGY OF FARROUPILHA

Instituto Federal de Educação, Ciência e Tecnologia Farroupilha (IFFARROUPILHA)
Rua Esmeralda, 430, Faixa Nova, Camobi, Santa Maria, RS 97110-767
Tel: +55(55) 3257-1114
Fax: +55(55) 3257-1263
Website: http://www.iffarroupilha.edu.br
Reitor: Carlos Alberto Pinto da Rosa
EMail: capr@iffarroupilha.edu.br

Courses
Agricultural Business (Agricultural Business); **Agricultural Engineering** (Agricultural Engineering); **Agroindustry**; **Biological Sciences** (Biological and Life Sciences); **Chemistry** (Chemistry);

Computer Science (Computer Science); **Crop Production** (Crop Production); **Food Science** (Food Science); **Graduate Studies**; **Mathematics** (Mathematics); **Public Administration** (Public Administration); **Systems Analysis and Development** (Systems Analysis); **Systems for the Internet** (Computer Science); **Zootechnics** (Animal Husbandry)

Further Information: Also following Campuses: Alegrete, Júlio de Castilhos, Panambi, São Borja, Santa Rosa, Santo Augusto, São Vicente do Sul

History: Founded 2002 as Centro Federal Tecnológico de São Vicente do Sul - CEFETSVS. Acquired present status and title 2008 following merger with Escola Agrotécnica Federal de Alegrete, Unidade Descentralizada de Júlio de Castilhos e Unidade Descentralizada de Santo Augusto em uma nova instituição federal de ensino.

Degrees and Diplomas: *Tecnólogo*; *Licenciatura*; *Especialização/Aperfeiçoamento*
Last Updated: 05/05/10

FEDERAL INSTITUTE OF EDUCATION, SCIENCE AND TECHNOLOGY OF GOIÁNIA

Instituto Federal de Educação, Ciência e Tecnologia de Goiás (IFG)
Rua 75 No 46, Goiânia, Goiás 74055-110
Tel: +55(62) 3227-2700
Fax: +55(62) 3213-1451
EMail: gabinete@cefetbo.br
Website: http://www.cefetgo.br/
Diretor Geral: Paulo César Pereira (2005-)

Campuses
Inhumas; **Itumbiara** (Chemistry); **Jataí** (Technology); **Uruaçu** (Chemical Engineering; Chemistry; Construction Engineering; Environmental Engineering; Hotel and Restaurant; Industrial Engineering; Information Technology; Mining Engineering; Surveying and Mapping; Telecommunications Engineering; Tourism; Transport and Communications)

Courses
Automation and Control Engineering (Automation and Control Engineering); **History** (History); **Literature** (Literature; Portuguese); **Technology** (Technology); **Young and Adult Training** (PROEJA) (Cooking and Catering)

History: Founded 1909 as Escolas de Aprendizes Artífices. Became Escola Técnica Federal de Goiás 1965. Became Centro Federal de Educação Tecnológica de Goiás (CEFET-GO) 1999. Acquired present status and title 2008.

Degrees and Diplomas: *Tecnólogo*; *Bacharelado*; *Licenciatura*
Last Updated: 23/04/10

FEDERAL INSTITUTE OF EDUCATION, SCIENCE AND TECHNOLOGY OF GOIANO

Instituto Federal de Educação, Ciência e Tecnologia Goiano (IFGOIANO)
Rua C-137 Qd 567 Lt 05 Sala 03, Nova Suíça, GO 74003-901
Tel: +55(62) 3274-2006
Fax: +55(62) 3274-2006
Website: http://www.ifgoiano.edu.br
Reitor: José Donizete Borges EMail: reitoria@ifgoiano.edu.br

Campuses
Ceres (Administration; Agronomy; Biological and Life Sciences; Computer Science); **Iporá**; **Morrinhos** (Agronomy; Chemistry; Computer Science); **Rio Verde** (Agricultural Business; Agronomy; Animal Husbandry; Biological and Life Sciences; Chemistry; Crop Production; Environmental Engineering; Food Technology); **Urutaí** (Agricultural Engineering; Agronomy; Biological and Life Sciences; Food Technology; Information Technology; Mathematics; Systems Analysis; Water Management)

History: Founded 2002 as Centro Federal de Educação Tecnológica de Rio Verde. Acquired present status and title 2008.

Degrees and Diplomas: *Tecnólogo*; *Bacharelado*; *Licenciatura*; *Especialização/Aperfeiçoamento*: Biodiesel; *Mestrado*: Biological Sciences. Also Engenheiro Agronomo
Last Updated: 05/05/10

FEDERAL INSTITUTE OF EDUCATION, SCIENCE AND TECHNOLOGY OF MARANHÃO

Instituto Federal de Educação, Ciência e Tecnologia do Maranhão (IFMA)
Avenida Getúlio Vargas 4, Monte Castelo, São Luís,
Maranhão 65030-005
Tel: +55(98) 3218-9001
Fax: +55(98) 3218-9001
EMail: gabinete@ifma.edu.br
Website: http://www.ifma.edu.br

Reitor: José Ferreira Costa EMail: zecosta@ifma.edu.br

Campuses
Açailândia; **Alcântara** (Tourism); **Buriticupu** (Biology; Public Administration); **Centro Histórico**; **Codó** (Agriculture; Chemistry; Mathematics); **Imperatriz** (Physics); **Maracanã**; **Monte Castelo** (Agriculture; Biology; Chemistry; Civil Engineering; Computer Science; Electrical Engineering; Environmental Engineering; Industrial Engineering; Information Sciences; Materials Engineering; Mathematics; Mechanical Engineering; Physics; Telecommunications Engineering; Water Management); **Monte Castelo**; **Santa Inês**; **Zé Doca** (Chemistry; Food Science)

History: Founded 1989 as Centro Federal de Educação Tecnológica do Maranhão (CEFET-MA). Acquired present status and title 2008 following merger with Escola Agrotécnicas Federais de Codó, Escola de São Luís and Escola de São Raimundo das Mangabeiras é Autarquia.

Main Language(s) of Instruction: Portuguese

Degrees and Diplomas: *Bacharelado*; *Licenciatura*; *Especialização/Aperfeiçoamento*; *Mestrado*
Last Updated: 06/05/10

FEDERAL INSTITUTE OF EDUCATION, SCIENCE AND TECHNOLOGY OF MATO GROSSO

Instituto Federal de Educação, Ciência e Tecnologia de Mato Grosso (IFMT)
Rua Comandante Costa, 1144, Ed. Tarcom - Sala 12, Centro,
Cuiabá, MT 78020-400
Tel: +55(65) 3624-5577
EMail: gabinete@dg.cefetmt.br
Website: http://www.ifmt.edu.br

Reitor: José Bispo Barbosa

Courses
Agronomy (Agronomy); **Graduate Studies** (Computer Networks; Education); **Mathematics** (Mathematics); **Physics** (Physics); **Technological Studies** (Agricultural Business; Automation and Control Engineering; Computer Networks; Computer Science; Environmental Management; Systems Analysis); **Zootechnics** (Zoology)

Further Information: Also campuses in Barra do Garças, Cuiabá - Bela Vista, Cáceres, Confresa, Cuiabá, Juína, Campo Novo do Parecis, Pontes e Lacerda, Rondonópolis, São Vicente.Also Distance Education programmes.

History: Founded 2008 through merger of Centro Federal de Educação Tecnológica de Mato Grosso, Centro Federal de Educação Tecnológica de Cuiabá, and Escola Agrotécnica Federal de Cáceres.

Degrees and Diplomas: *Tecnólogo*; *Bacharelado*; *Licenciatura*; *Especialização/Aperfeiçoamento*
Last Updated: 12/07/10

FEDERAL INSTITUTE OF EDUCATION, SCIENCE AND TECHNOLOGY OF MINAS GERAIS

Instituto Federal de Educação, Ciência e Tecnologia de Minas Gerais (IFMG)
Av. Professor Mário Werneck 2590, Buritis,
Belo Horizonte 30575-180
Tel: + (31) 2511-0632
EMail: gabinete@ifmg.edu.br
Website: http://www.ifmg.edu.br

Diretor Geral: Caio Mário Bueno Silva

Courses
Administration (Administration); **Agronomy** (Agronomy); **Conservation and Restoration** (Restoration of Works of Art); **Electrical Engineering** (Electrical Engineering); **Financial Management** (Finance); **Food Science** (Food Science); **Forestry** (Forestry); **Geography** (Geography); **Internet Systems** (Computer Science); **Management Process** (Management); **Mathematics** (Mathematics); **Physics** (Physics); **Quality Engineering** (Safety Engineering); **Systems Analysis and Development** (Systems Analysis); **Tourism** (Tourism); **Zootechnics** (Zoology)

Further Information: Also São João Evangelista, Governador Valadares, Congonhas and Formiga campuses.

Degrees and Diplomas: *Tecnólogo*; *Bacharelado*; *Licenciatura*
Last Updated: 04/05/10

FEDERAL INSTITUTE MINAS GERAIS - OURO PRETO CAMPUS

CÂMPUS OURO PRETO

Rua Pandiá Calógeras, 898 - Bauxita, Ouro Prêto,
Minas Gerais 35400-000
Tel: +55(31) 3559-2100
Fax: +55(31) 3551-5227
EMail: gabinete@cefetop.edu.br
Website: http://www.cefetop.edu.br

Diretor-Geral: Caio Mário Bueno Silva
Vice-Diretor: Arthur Versiani Machado

Courses
Conservation and Restoration; **Environmental Management** *(Postgraduate)* (Environmental Management); **Geography** (Geography); **Quality Management** (Safety Engineering)

History: Founded 2002. Formerly know as Centro Federal de Educação Tecnológica de Ouro Preto (Federal Centre of Technological Education of Ouro Preto).

Degrees and Diplomas: *Tecnólogo*; *Licenciatura*; *Especialização/Aperfeiçoamento*

FEDERAL INSTITUTE OF EDUCATION, SCIENCE AND TECHNOLOGY OF MINAS GERAIS - BAMBUÍ CAMPUS

CÂMPUS BAMBUÍ

Fazenda Varginha s/n - Rodovia Bambuí/Medeiros Km 05,
Caixa Postal 05, Bambuí, Minas Gerais 38900000
Tel: +55(37) 3431-4900
Fax: +55(37) 3431-4900
EMail: campus.bambui@ifmg.edu.br
Website: http://www.cefetbambui.edu.br

Diretor Geral: Flávio Vasconcelos Godinho

Courses
Administration (Business Administration; Health Administration; Small Business); **Agronomy** (Agronomy); **Food Science** (Food Science); **Graduate Studies** (Adult Education; Environmental Studies; Finance; Safety Engineering); **Physics** (Physics); **Production Engineering** (Production Engineering); **Systems Analysis and Development** (Computer Networks; Computer Science; Systems Analysis); **Tourism** (Tourism); **Zootechnics** (Animal Husbandry)

History: Became Centro Federal de Educação Tecnológica – CEFET 2002. Became campus of Instituto Federal de Educação, Ciência e Tecnologia Minas Gerais – IFMG 2008.

Degrees and Diplomas: *Tecnólogo*; *Bacharelado*; *Licenciatura*: Physics; *Especialização/Aperfeiçoamento*

FEDERAL INSTITUTE OF EDUCATION, SCIENCE AND TECHNOLOGY OF NORTHERN MINAS GERAIS

Instituto Federal de Educação, Ciência e Tecnologia do Norte de Minas Gerais (IFNMG)
Rua Gabriel Passos 259, Centro, Montes Claros,
Minas Gerais 39400-112
Tel: +55(38) 3621-1100
Fax: +55(38) 3621-1572
EMail: reitor@ifnmg.edu.br
Website: http://www.ifnmg.edu.br

Diretor Geral: Paulo César Pinheiro de Azevedo
EMail: dg@cefetjanuaria.edu.br

Courses

Administration (Administration; Business Administration); **Agricultural and Environmental Engineering** (Agricultural Engineering; Environmental Engineering); **Agronomy**; **Biology** (Biology); **Chemistry** (Chemistry); **Irrigation** (Irrigation); **Mathematics** (Mathematics); **Physics** (Physics); **Systems Analysis and Development** (Computer Science; Systems Analysis)

Further Information: Also Araçuai, Arinos, Januária and Salinas campuses.

History: Founded 1960 as Escola Agrotécnica de Januária-MG. Renamed Colégio Agrícola de Januária 1964. Transformed into Centro Federal de Educação Tecnológica de Januária - CEFET 2002. Acquired present status and title 2008 following merger with Escola Agrotécnica Federal de Salinas.

Degrees and Diplomas: *Tecnólogo*; *Bacharelado*; *Licenciatura*; *Especialização/Aperfeiçoamento*
Last Updated: 23/04/10

FEDERAL INSTITUTE OF EDUCATION, SCIENCE AND TECHNOLOGY OF NORTHERN RIO GRANDE

Instituto Federal de Educação, Ciência e Tecnologia do Rio Grande do Norte (IFRN)
Avenida Senador Salgado Filho 1559, Tirol, Natal,
Rio Grande do Norte 59015000
Tel: +55(84) 4005-2600
EMail: acs@cefetrn.br; gabinete@cefetrn.br
Website: http://www.ifrn.edu.br

Reitor: Belchior de Oliveira Rocha

Campuses

Apodi; **Caicó** (Physics); **Currais Novos**; **Ipanguaçu**; **João Câmara**; **Macau** (Biology); **Mossoró**; **Natal - Central**; **Natal - Zona Norte**; **Pau dos Ferros** (Chemistry); **Santa Cruz** (Computer Science; Heating and Refrigeration; Mathematics; Mechanical Engineering; Physics)

History: Founded 1999 as Centro Federal de Educação Tecnológica do Rio Grande do Norte (CEFET/RN). Acquired present status and title 2008.

Main Language(s) of Instruction: Portuguese

Degrees and Diplomas: *Tecnólogo*; *Licenciatura*; *Especialização/Aperfeiçoamento*
Last Updated: 06/05/10

FEDERAL INSTITUTE OF EDUCATION, SCIENCE AND TECHNOLOGY OF PARÁ

Instituto Federal de Educação, Ciência e Tecnologia do Pará (IFPA)
Travessa Mariz e Barros, 2220, Belém, Pará 66093-090
Tel: +55(91) 3228-1719
Fax: +55(91) 3226-9710
EMail: cefetpa@cefetpa.br
Website: http://www.ifpa.edu.br

Reitor: Edson Ary de Oliveira Fontes

Campuses

Abaetetuba; **Altamira**; **Belém** (Automation and Control Engineering; Biology; Chemistry; Education; Engineering; Environmental Studies; Geography; Materials Engineering; Mathematics; Physics; Public Administration; Public Health; Systems Analysis; Telecommunications Engineering); **Bragança** (Physics); **Castanhal** (Agronomy; Aquaculture); **Conceiçao de Araguaia** (Education); **Itaituba**; **Marabá**; **Rural Marabá**; **Santarém**; **Tucuruí** (Biology; Computer Science; Education; Geography; Pedagogy; Physics)

History: Founded 1999 as Centro Federal de Educação Tecnológica do Pará (CEFET/PA). Acquired present status and title 2008.

Main Language(s) of Instruction: Portuguese

Degrees and Diplomas: *Tecnólogo*; *Licenciatura*; *Especialização/Aperfeiçoamento*
Last Updated: 06/05/10

FEDERAL INSTITUTE OF EDUCATION, SCIENCE AND TECHNOLOGY OF PARAÍBA

Instituto Federal de Educação, Ciência e Tecnologia da Paraíba (IFPB)
Avenida Primero de Maio 720, Jaguaribe, João Pessoa,
Paraíba 58015430
Tel: +55(83) 241-2200 +55(83) 241-2201
Fax: +55(83) 241-1434
EMail: cefetpb@cefetpb.edu.br
Website: http://www.cefetpb.edu.br

Reitor: João Batista de Oliveira Silva

Courses

Administration (Administration); **Automation and Industrial Engineering**; **Chemistry** (Chemistry); **Computer Networks** (Computer Networks); **Construction Engineering** (Construction Engineering); **Electrical Engineering** (Electrical Engineering); **Geoprocessing**; **Interior Design** (Interior Design); **Real Estate** (Real Estate); **Systems for Internet** (Computer Networks; Computer Science); **Telecommunications Engineering**

Further Information: Also branch in Cajazeiras and Campina Grande.

History: Founded 1909. Became CEFET – Centro Federal de Educação Tecnológica da Paraíba 1999. Acquired present title following merger with Escola Agrotécnica Federal de Souza 2008.

Degrees and Diplomas: *Tecnólogo*; *Bacharelado*; *Licenciatura*
Last Updated: 22/04/10

FEDERAL INSTITUTE OF EDUCATION, SCIENCE AND TECHNOLOGY OF PERNAMBUCO

Instituto Federal de Educação, Ciência e Tecnologia de Pernambuco (IFPE)
Avenida Professor Luiz Freire 500, Cidade Universitária, Recife,
Pernambuco 50740540
Tel: +55(81) 2125-1600
Fax: +55(81) 3271-2338
EMail: gabinete@reitoria.ifpe.edu.br
Website: http://www.ifpe.edu.br

Diretor-Geral: Sérgio Gaudêncio Portela de Melo

Campuses

Afogados da Ingazeira; **Barreiros**; **Belo Jardim** (Agricultural Business; Computer Science; Nursing); **Caruaru**; **Garanhuns**; **Ipojuca** (Automation and Control Engineering; Chemistry; Industrial Engineering; Occupational Health); **Pesqueira** (Construction Engineering; Electronic Engineering; Mathematics; Nursing; Physics); **Recife** (Environmental Management; Graphic Design; Production Engineering; Radiology; Systems Analysis; Tourism); **Vitória** (Agricultural Business; Agriculture; Animal Husbandry)

History: Founded 1999 as Centro Federal de Educação Tecnológica de Pernambuco. Acquired present and status 2008.

Degrees and Diplomas: *Tecnólogo*; *Bacharelado*; *Licenciatura*
Last Updated: 04/05/10

FEDERAL INSTITUTE OF EDUCATION, SCIENCE AND TECHNOLOGY OF PIAUÍ

Instituto Federal de Educação, Ciência e Tecnologia do Piauí (IFPI)
Praça da Liberdade 1597, Prédio A - Sala 61 Centro, Teresina,
Piauí 64000040
Tel: +55(86) 3215-5224
Fax: +55(86) 3215-5206
EMail: cefetpi@cefetpi.br
Website: http://www.ifpi.edu.br

Reitor: Francisco das Chagas Santana

Campuses

Corrente; **Floriano** (Biological and Life Sciences; Mathematics; Systems Analysis); **Parnaíba**; **Picos** (Chemistry; Physics); **Piripiri**; **Teresina - Central**; **Teresina Zona Sul**

Programmes

Escola Técnica Aberta do Brasil *(ETAPI - IFPI)* (Administration; Computer Science)

History: Founded 1999 as Centro Federal de Educação Tecnológica do Piauí (CEFET/PI). Acquired present status and title 2008.

Main Language(s) of Instruction: Portuguese

Degrees and Diplomas: *Tecnólogo*; *Bacharelado*; *Licenciatura*; *Especialização/Aperfeiçoamento*

Last Updated: 06/05/10

FEDERAL INSTITUTE OF EDUCATION, SCIENCE AND TECHNOLOGY OF RIO DE JANEIRO

Instituto Federal de Educação, Ciência e Tecnologia do Rio de Janeiro (IFRJ)

Rua Lúcio Tavares 1045, Nilópolis, Rio de Janeiro 26530-060
Tel: +55(21) 2691-9803
Fax: +55(21) 2691-1181
EMail: progradresponde@ifrj.edu.br; propesq@ifrj.edu.br
Website: http://www.ifrj.edu.br

Reitor: Fernando Cesar Pimentel Gusmão
EMail: reitoria@cefeteq.br

Courses
Biotechnology (Biotechnology); **Chemical Processes** (Chemistry; Industrial Chemistry); **Chemistry**; **Cultural Production** (Cultural Studies); **Environmental Management** (Environmental Management); **Management of Industrial Production** (Industrial Management); **Mathematics** (Mathematics); **Natural Products Chemistry**; **Occupational Therapy**; **Pharmacy** (Pharmacy); **Physical Therapy** (Physical Therapy); **Physics**; **Science Education** *(Postgraduate)* (Science Education)

Further Information: Also Unidades Paracambi and Rio de Janeiro

History: Founded 1999 as Centro Federal de Educação Tecnológica de Química de Nilópolis. Acquired present status and title 2008.

Degrees and Diplomas: *Tecnólogo*; *Bacharelado*; *Licenciatura*; *Especialização/Aperfeiçoamento*

Last Updated: 04/05/10

FEDERAL INSTITUTE OF EDUCATION, SCIENCE AND TECHNOLOGY OF RORAIMA

Instituto Federal de Educação, Ciência e Tecnologia de Roraima (IFRR)

Av Capitão Júlio Bezerra, 1392, Aparecida, Boa Vista, Roraima 69303340
Tel: +55(95) 3624-1224
Fax: +55(95) 3624-1224
EMail: gabinete.reitoria@ifrr.edu.br
Website: http://www.ifrr.edu.br

Reitor: Edvaldo Pereira da Silva EMail: reitor@ifrr.edu.br

Campuses
Amajari; **Boa Vista** (Environmental Studies; Health Administration; Literature; Physical Education; Public Health; Spanish; Systems Analysis; Tourism); **Novo Paraíso**

History: Founded 2002 as Centro Federal de Educação Tecnológica de Roraima (CEFET-RR). Acquired present status and title 2008.

Degrees and Diplomas: *Tecnólogo*; *Licenciatura*; *Especialização/ Aperfeiçoamento*

Last Updated: 05/05/10

FEDERAL INSTITUTE OF EDUCATION, SCIENCE AND TECHNOLOGY OF SANTA CATARINA

Instituto Federal de Educação, Ciência e Tecnologia de Santa Catarina (IF-SC)

Av. Mauro Ramos, 755, Centro, Florianópolis, Santa Catarina 88020-300
Tel: +55(48) 3224-2557
Fax: +55(48) 3224-2557
EMail: ouvidoria@cefetsc.edu.br
Website: http://www.ifsc.edu.br/

Reitora: Consuelo Aparecida Sielski Santos
Tel: +55(48) 3877-9002
EMail: consuelo@ifsc.edu.br; reitoria@ifsc.edu.br

Courses
Chemistry (Chemistry); **Graduate Studies** *(Lato Sensu)* (Education; Electronic Engineering; Health Sciences; Public Health; Science Education; Translation and Interpretation); **Graduate Studies** *(Stricto Sensu)* (Electronic Engineering); **Physics**; **Technological Studies**

Further Information: Also Distance Education programmes.

History: Founded 1909 as Escola de Aprendizes Artífices de Santa Catarin. Became Liceu Industrial de Florianópolis 1937. Transformed into Escola Industrial de Florianópolis 1942. Name changed to Escola Industrial Federal de Santa Catarina 1965. Became Escola Técnica Federal de Santa Catarina (ETF-SC) 1968. Transformed into Centro Federais de Educação Tecnológica (CEFET-SC) 1994. Acquired present title and status 2008.

Degrees and Diplomas: *Tecnólogo*; *Licenciatura*; *Especialização/ Aperfeiçoamento*; *Mestrado*

Last Updated: 12/07/10

FEDERAL INSTITUTE OF EDUCATION, SCIENCE AND TECHNOLOGY OF SÃO PAULO

Instituto Federal de Educação, Ciência e Tecnologia de São Paulo (IFSP)

Rua Pedro Vicente 625, Canindé, São Paulo, São Paulo 01109010
Tel: +55(11) 2763-7500
Fax: +55(11) 2763-7650
EMail: gab@cefetsp.br; drg@cefetsp.br
Website: http://www.ifsp.edu.br

Reitor: Garabed Kenchian

Courses
Automation and Control Engineering; **Biological Sciences** (Biological and Life Sciences); **Chemistry** (Chemistry); **Civil Engineering**; **Electrical Systems** (Electrical Engineering); **Electronic Systems**; **Geography**; **Graduate Studies**; **Industrial Electronics**; **Industrial Production Management**; **Mathematics** (Mathematics); **Mechanical Fabrication** (Mechanical Engineering); **Mechanical Production** (Mechanical Engineering); **Physics** (Physics); **Process Management**; **Systems Analysis and Development** (Systems Analysis); **Tourism** (Tourism)

Further Information: Also following Campuses: São Paulo, Cubatão, Sertãozinho, Guarulhos, Caraguatatuba, São João da Boa Vista, Bragança Paulista, Salto, São Roque, São Carlos, Campos do Jordão.

History: Founded 1999 as Centro Federal de Educação Tecnológica de São Paulo. Acquired present status and title 2008.

Main Language(s) of Instruction: Portuguese

Degrees and Diplomas: *Tecnólogo*; *Bacharelado*; *Licenciatura*; *Especialização/Aperfeiçoamento*; *Mestrado*: Automation and Control Engineering

Last Updated: 05/05/10

FEDERAL INSTITUTE OF EDUCATION, SCIENCE AND TECHNOLOGY OF SERGIPE

Instituto Federal de Educação, Ciência e Tecnologia de Sergipe (IFS)

Avenida Engenheiro Gentil Tavares da Mota, 1166, Bairro Getúlio Vargas, Aracaju, Sergipe 49055260
Tel: +55(79) 3711-3100
Fax: +55(79) 3711-3155
EMail: direcao@ifs.edu.br
Website: http://www.ifs.edu.br

Reitor: Cleiton José da Silva

Courses
Automation and Control Engineering (Automation and Control Engineering); **Civil Engineering** (Civil Engineering); **Ecotourism** (Tourism); **Environmental Studies**; **Mathematics**

History: Founded 2002 as Centro Federal de Educação Tecnológica de Sergipe (CEFETSE). Acquired present status and title 2008.

Degrees and Diplomas: *Tecnólogo*; *Bacharelado*; *Licenciatura*

Last Updated: 05/05/10

FEDERAL INSTITUTE OF EDUCATION, SCIENCE AND TECHNOLOGY OF SERTÃO PERNAMBUCANO

Instituto Federal de Educação, Ciência e Tecnologia do Sertão Pernambucano
Rodovia BR 235 Km 22, Projeto Senador Nilo Coelho N4,
Zona Rural, Petrolina, Pernambuco 56300000
Tel: +55(87)3863-2330 +55(87) 3862-3800
Fax: +55(87) 3862-3800
Website: http://www.ifsertao-pe.edu.br

Diretor-Geral: Sebastião Rildo Fernandes Diniz
EMail: rildo.diniz@ifsertao-pe.edu.br

Courses
Chemistry (Chemistry); **Irrigated Fruit Culture**; **Physics** (Physics); **Semi-Arid Fruit Production** *(Postgraduate)* (Fruit Production); **Vegetal Origin Food** (Physics); **Vitiviniculture and Oenology**

Further Information: Also Petrolina Campus.

History: Founded 1999 from Escola Agrotécnica Federal Dom Avelar Vilela. Formerly known as Centro Federal de Educação Tecnológica de Petrolina (CEFET-Petrolina).

Main Language(s) of Instruction: Portuguese

Degrees and Diplomas: *Tecnólogo; Licenciatura; Especialização/ Aperfeiçoamento*
Last Updated: 04/05/10

FEDERAL INSTITUTE OF EDUCATION, SCIENCE AND TECHNOLOGY OF SOUTHERN RIO GRANDE - BENTO GONÇALVES CAMPUS

Instituto Federal de Educação, Ciência e Tecnologia do Rio Grande do Sul - Campus Bento Gonçalves (IFRS)
Avenida Osvaldo Aranha, 540, Bairro Juventude da Enologia,
Bento Gonçalves, RS 95700-000
Tel: +55(54) 3455-3200
Fax: +55(54) 3455-3246
EMail: gabinete@bento.ifrs.edu.br
Website: http://bento.ifrs.edu.br/site/index.php

Reitora: Cláudia Schiedeck Soares de Souza

Courses
Graduate Studies (Viticulture); **Mathematics**; **Pedagogy** (Pedagogy); **Physics**; **Teacher Training** (Teacher Training); **Technical Studies**

Further Information: Also Distance Education programmes.

History: Founded 1959 as Colégio de Viticultura e Enologia de Bento Gonçalves. Changed name to Escola Agrotécnica Federal Presidente Juscelino Kubistchek 1985. Became Centro Federal de Educação Tecnológica de Bento Gonçalves (Cefet-BG) 2002. Acquired present status and title 2008.

Degrees and Diplomas: *Tecnólogo; Licenciatura; Especialização/ Aperfeiçoamento*
Last Updated: 12/07/10

FEDERAL INSTITUTE OF EDUCATION, SCIENCE AND TECHNOLOGY OF THE AMAZON

Instituto Federal de Educação, Ciência e Tecnologia do Amazonas (IFAM)
Avenida Sete de Setembro 1975 Centro, Mánaus,
Amazonas 69020120
Tel: +55(92) 3621-6700
EMail: gabinete@cefetam.edu.br
Website: http://www.ifam.edu.br

Reitor: João Martins Dias

Courses
Advertising and Publicity (Advertising and Publicity); **Biology**; **Chemical Processes**; **Chemistry** (Chemistry); **Construction Engineering** (Construction Engineering); **Electronic Systems**
(Electronic Engineering); **Food Science** (Food Science); **Industrial Mechatronics**; **Software Engineering** (Software Engineering); **Telecommunications Engineering** (Telecommunications Engineering)

Further Information: Also following campuses: Manaus – Centro, Manaus - Distrito Industial, Coari, São Gabriel da Cachoeira, Manaus - Zona Leste, Presidente Figueiredo, Lábrea, Tabatinga, Parintins

History: Founded 2001 as Centro Federal de Educação Tecnológica do Amazonas. Acquired present status and title 2008.

Main Language(s) of Instruction: Portuguese

Degrees and Diplomas: *Tecnólogo; Licenciatura; Especialização/ Aperfeiçoamento*
Last Updated: 05/05/10

FEDERAL INSTITUTE OF EDUCATION, SCIENCE AND TECHNOLOGY OF THE SOUTH OF RIO GRANDE

Instituto Federal de Educação, Ciência e Tecnologia Sul-Rio-Grandense (IFSUL)
Rua Gonçalves Chaves 3798, Bairro Centro, Pelotas,
Rio Grande do Sul 96015-560
Tel: +55(53) 3309-1750
Fax: +55(53) 3309-1766
EMail: reitoria@ifsul.edu.br
Website: http://www.cefetrs.tche.br

Reitor: Antônio Carlos Barum Brod

Campuses
Bagé; **Camaquã**; **Charqueadas**; **Passo Fundo** (Computer Science); **Pelotas** (Automation and Control Engineering; Computer Science; Education; Electrical Engineering; Environmental Management; Environmental Studies; Industrial Engineering; Modern Languages; Telecommunications Engineering); **Sapucaia do Sul** (Industrial Management; Mechanics); **Venâncio Aires**

History: Founded 1999 as Centro Federal de Educação Tecnológica de Pelotas. Acquired present status and title 2008.

Degrees and Diplomas: *Tecnólogo; Bacharelado; Especialização/ Aperfeiçoamento*
Last Updated: 04/05/10

FEDERAL INSTITUTE OF EDUCATION, SCIENCE AND TECHNOLOGY OF THE SOUTHEAST OF MINAS GERAIS

Instituto Federal de Educação, Ciência e Tecnologia do Sudeste de Minas Gerais
Avenida Francisco Bernardino, 165, Centro, Juiz de For a,
Minas Gerais 36013-100
Tel: +55(32) 3216-2366
Fax: +55(32) 3216-2366
EMail: gabinete@ifsudeste.edu.br
Website: http://www.ifsudeste.edu.br

Reitor: Mário Sérgio Costa Vieira
EMail: mario.sergio@ifsudeste.edu.br

Campuses
Barbacena; **Juiz de Fora** (Electronic Engineering; Mechanical Engineering; Physics); **Muriaé** (Administration; Fashion Design); **Rio Pomba**

History: Founded 1964 as Ginásio Agrícola de Rio Pomba. Became Colégio Agrícola de Rio Pomba 1968. Became Escola Agrotécnica Federal de Rio Pomba - MG 1979. Transformed into Centro Federal de Educação Tecnológica de Rio Pomba 2002. Acquired present status and title 2008.

Degrees and Diplomas: *Tecnólogo; Bacharelado; Licenciatura; Especialização/Aperfeiçoamento*
Last Updated: 05/05/10

FEDERAL INSTITUTE OF EDUCATION, SCIENCE AND TECHNOLOGY OF THE STATE OF RIO DE JANEIRO

Instituto Federal de Educação, Ciência e Tecnologia Fluminense (IF FLUMINENSE)
Rua Doutor Siqueira 273, Parque Dom Bosco, Campos dos Goytacazes, Rio de Janeiro 28030-130
Tel: +55(22) 2726-2800 +55(22) 2733 3244
Fax: +55(22) 2733-3079
EMail: webmaster@iff.edu.br
Website: http://www.iff.edu.br

Reitora: Cibele Daher Botelho Monteiro

Courses

Bacharelado; **Graduate Studies** (Adult Education; Computer Science; Cultural Studies; Design; Environmental Engineering; Environmental Studies; Geography; Literature; Marketing; Systems Analysis; Teacher Training); **Licenciatura** (Biology; Chemistry; Geography; Mathematics; Natural Sciences; Physics); **Technical Studies** (Automation and Control Engineering; Construction Engineering; Electrical Engineering; Electronic Engineering; Industrial Engineering; Information Technology; Mechanics; Occupational Health; Road Engineering; Safety Engineering; Telecommunications Engineering); **Technology** (Computer Science; Electrical Engineering; Graphic Design; Industrial Maintenance; Systems Analysis; Technology; Telecommunications Engineering); **Young and Adults Education** (EJA)

Further Information: Also Centro, Guarus, Cabo Frio, Macae, Bom Jesus do Itabapoana, and Itaperuna campuses.

History: Founded 1909 as Escolas de Aprendizes e Artífices. Became Centro Federal de Educação Tecnológica de Campos 1999. Transformed into Instituto Federal de Educação, Ciência e Tecnologia Fluminense 2008.

Degrees and Diplomas: Tecnólogo; Bacharelado; Licenciatura; Especialização/Aperfeiçoamento; Mestrado
Last Updated: 23/04/10

FEDERAL INSTITUTE OF EDUCATION, SCIENCE AND TECHNOLOGY OF TRIÂNGULO MINEIRO

Instituto Federal de Educação, Ciência e Tecnologia do Triângulo Mineiro (F TRIÂNGULO)
Rua Tupaciguara n° 117, Bairro São Benedito, Uberaba, Minas Gerais 38020-160
Tel: +55(34) 3326-1100
EMail: reitor@iftriangulo.edu.br; pi.reitoria@iftriangulo.edu.br
Website: http://www.iftriangulo.edu.br

Reitor: Eurípedes Ronaldo Ananias Ferreira

Campuses

Ituiutaba (Agricultural Business; Computer Science); **Paracatu** (Computer Science; Electronic Engineering); **Uberaba** (Agricultural Engineering; Animal Husbandry; Chemistry; Environmental Management; Food Technology; Social Sciences; Systems Analysis); **Uberlândia**

History: Founded 2002 as Centro Federal de Educação Tecnológica de Uberaba (CEFET Uberaba). Acquired present status and title 2008 following merger with Escola Agrotécnica Federal de Uberlândia.

Degrees and Diplomas: Tecnólogo; Bacharelado; Licenciatura; Especialização/Aperfeiçoamento
Last Updated: 05/05/10

FEDERAL RURAL UNIVERSITY OF PERNAMBUCO

Universidade Federal Rural de Pernambuco (UFRPE)
Rua Dom Manoel de Medeiros S/n Dois Irmãos, Recife, Pernambuco 52171900
Tel: +55(81) 3320.6011
EMail: reitoria@reitoria.ufrpe.br
Website: http://www.ufrpe.br

Reitor: Valmar Corrêa de Andrade EMail: valmarc@ufrpe.br

Departments

Agronomy (Agriculture; Agronomy); **Animal Husbandry** (Animal Husbandry); **Biology** (Biology); **Chemistry** (Chemistry); **Education** (Education); **Fishery and Aquaculture** (Aquaculture; Fishery); **Home Economics** (Home Economics); **Letters and Human Sciences** (Arts and Humanities); **Mathematics** (Mathematics); **Morphology and Animal Physiology** (Zoology); **Physics** (Physics); **Rural Technology** (Agricultural Engineering); **Statistics and Computer Science** (Computer Science; Statistics); **Veterinary Medicine** (Veterinary Science)

History: Founded 1912 as School, became University by State decree 1947, acquired status as Federal Institution 1956. Under the jurisdiction of the Ministry of Education and Sports.

Governing Bodies: Conselho Universitário; Conselho de Curadores; Conselho de Ensino, Pesquisa e Extensão

Academic Year: March to December (March-June; August-December)

Admission Requirements: Secondary school certificate and entrance examination

Main Language(s) of Instruction: Portuguese

Degrees and Diplomas: Bacharelado: Agricultural Engineering, 5-6 yrs; Bacharelado: Animal Husbandry; Fishery; Forestry; Social Sciences, 4-6 yrs; Bacharelado: Biology, 4-5 yrs; Licenciatura: Home Economics; Science, 4-5 yrs; Mestrado: a further 1-4 yrs; Doutorado. Also teaching qualifications

Student Residential Facilities: Yes

Libraries: Central Library, c. 41,155 vols

Publications: Anais; Caderno Omega

Press or Publishing House: Imprensa Universitária
Last Updated: 19/05/10

FEDERAL RURAL UNIVERSITY OF RIO DE JANEIRO

Universidade Federal Rural do Rio de Janeiro (UFRRJ)
BR 465 - Km 7, Seropédica, Rio de Janeiro 23890000
Tel: +55(21) 2682-1210
Fax: +55(21) 2682-1120
EMail: gabinete@ufrrj.br
Website: http://www.ufrrj.br

Reitor: Ricardo Motta Miranda

Vice-Reitora: Ana Maria Dantas Soares

Institutes

Agronomy (Agronomy; Geology) Director: Elson de Carvalho Viegas; **Animal Husbandry** (Animal Husbandry) Director: Nelson Jorge Moraes Matos; **Biology** (Biology) Director: Marcos Antônio José dos Santos; **Education** (Agriculture; Education; Physical Education) Director: Alda Maria Magalhães D. Silva; **Exact Sciences** (Chemistry; Mathematics; Physics) Director: Eliza Helena de Souza Farias; **Forestry** (Forestry) Director: Ricardo da Silva Pereira; **Human and Social Sciences** (Administration; Economics; Home Economics; Social Sciences) Director: Silvestre Prado de Souza Neto; **Technology** (Chemical Engineering; Food Science; Technology) Director: Luis Otávio Nunes da Silva; **Veterinary Medicine** (Veterinary Science) Director: Laerte Grisi

History: Founded 1910 as Universidade Rural do Brasil, acquired present status and title 1965. A State institution under the jurisdiction of and financially supported by the Ministry of Education and Sports.

Governing Bodies: Conselho Universitário; Conselho de Ensino, Pesquisa e Extensão; Conselho de Curadores

Academic Year: March to December (March-July; August-December)

Admission Requirements: Secondary school certificate and entrance examination

Fees: None

Main Language(s) of Instruction: Portuguese

Degrees and Diplomas: Bacharelado: 4 yrs; Licenciatura: 3-4 yrs; Mestrado: a further 2 1/2 yrs; Doutorado: a further 4 yrs. Also combined Licenciatura and Bacharelado, 3 1/2-4 yrs

Student Services: Academic counselling, Canteen, Foreign student adviser, Health services, Language programs, Sports facilities

Student Residential Facilities: Yes

Libraries: Central Library, c. 42,600 vols

Publications: Revista Universidade Rural. Série Ciências da Vida *(biannually)*; Revista Universidade Rural. Série Ciências Exactas e da Terra *(biannually)*; Revista Universidade Rural. Série Ciências Humanas *(biannually)*
Last Updated: 14/12/07

FEDERAL RURAL UNIVERSITY OF THE AMAZON
Universidade Federal Rural da Amazônia (UFRA)
Avenida Presidente Tancredo Neves 2501, Terra Firme, Belém, Pará 66077530
Tel: +55(91) 3274-3493 +55(91) 3274-0900
Fax: +55(91) 3274-3814
EMail: reitoria@ufra.edu.br
Website: http://www.ufra.edu.br/

Reitor: Sueo Numazawa

Faculties
Agronomy (Agronomy); **Fishery** (Fishery); **Forestry Engineering**; **Veterinary Science** (Veterinary Science); **Zoology** (Zoology)

History: Founded 1943 as Escola de Agronomia da Amazônia. Became Faculdade de Ciências Agrárias do Pará 1973. Acquired present title and status 2002.

Degrees and Diplomas: *Bacharelado*; *Licenciatura*; *Mestrado*; *Doutorado*
Last Updated: 19/05/10

FEDERAL RURAL UNIVERSITY OF THE SEMI-ARID REGION
Universidade Federal Rural do Semi-Árido (UFERSA)
BR 110 - Km 47 Bairro Pres. Costa e Silva, Mossoró, Rio Grande do Norte 59625900
Tel: +55(84) 312-2100 +55(84) 312-2121
Fax: +55(84) 312-2499
EMail: ufersa@ufersa.edu.br
Website: http://www2.ufersa.edu.br

Reitor: Josivan Barbosa Menezes EMail: reitor@ufersa.edu.br

Departments
Agricultural Technology and Social Sciences (Agricultural Engineering; Agronomy; Social Sciences); **Animal Sciences** (Veterinary Science; Zoology); **Botany** (Botany; Horticulture; Plant Pathology); **Environmental Studies**

History: Founded 1967 as Escola Superior de Agricultura de Mossoró. Acquired present status and title 2005.

Main Language(s) of Instruction: Portuguese

Degrees and Diplomas: *Bacharelado*; *Especialização/Aperfeiçoamento*; *Mestrado*; *Doutorado*
Last Updated: 19/05/10

FEDERAL UNIVERSITY OF ABC
Universidade Federal do ABC
Rua Santa Adélia, 166 - Bairro Bangu, Santo André, São Paulo 09.210-170
Tel: +55(11) 4996-3166
EMail: prograd@ufabc.edu.br
Website: http://www.ufabc.edu.br

Reitor: Helio Waldman

Centres
Engineering, Modelling and Applied Social Sciences (Engineering; Social Sciences); **Mathematics, Computer and Cognitive Sciences** (Cognitive Sciences; Computer Science; Mathematics); **Natural and Human Sciences** (Biology; Chemistry; Physics)

History: Founded 2005.

Main Language(s) of Instruction: Portuguese

Degrees and Diplomas: *Bacharelado*; *Licenciatura*; *Mestrado*; *Doutorado*
Last Updated: 20/05/10

FEDERAL UNIVERSITY OF ACRE
Universidade Federal do Acre (UFAC)
Campus Universitário, BR 364 / Km 4, Distrito Industrial, Rio Branco, Acre 69915900
Tel: +55(68) 3901-2500
EMail: reitoria@ufac.br
Website: http://www.ufac.br

Reitora: Olinda Batista Assmar Tel: +55(68) 229-5735 / 1534

Departments
Agronomy; **Economics**; **Education**; **Engineering**; **Geography**; **Health Sciences**; **History**; **Law** (Law); **Literature**; **Mathematics and Statistics**; **Natural Sciences**; **Philosophy and Social Sciences**; **Physical Education and Sports**

History: Founded 1971.

Admission Requirements: Secondary school certificate and entrance examination

Main Language(s) of Instruction: Portuguese

Degrees and Diplomas: *Bacharelado*; *Licenciatura*; *Especialização/Aperfeiçoamento*; *Mestrado*; *Doutorado*

Student Services: Canteen
Last Updated: 20/05/10

FEDERAL UNIVERSITY OF ALAGOAS
Universidade Federal de Alagoas (UFAL)
Km 97, Tabuleiro dos Martins, Maceió, Alagoas 57072900
Tel: +55(82) 3214-1002
Fax: +55(82) 3214-1700
EMail: gr@reitoria.ufal.br
Website: http://www.ufal.edu.br

Reitora: Ana Dayse Rezende Dorea Tel: +55(82) 3214-1006

Centres
Agriculture (Agricultural Economics; Agriculture; Animal Husbandry; Engineering); **Applied Social Sciences** (Accountancy; Economics; Social Sciences; Social Work); **Biological Sciences** (Biological and Life Sciences); **Education** (Education); **Exact and Natural Sciences** (Applied Mathematics; Chemistry; Geography; Geology; Mathematics; Meteorology; Natural Sciences; Physics; Surveying and Mapping); **Exact Sciences and Technology** (Architecture; Building Technologies; Chemical Engineering; Civil Engineering; Energy Engineering; Structural Architecture; Technology; Transport Engineering; Water Management); **Health Sciences** (Dentistry; Health Sciences; Medicine; Nursing; Nutrition; Physical Education; Social and Preventive Medicine; Surgery); **Human Sciences** (Arts and Humanities; Communication Studies; History; Literature; Modern Languages; Music; Pedagogy; Philosophy; Social and Community Services; Social Sciences; Theatre); **Law** (Law)

Further Information: Also University Hospital

History: Founded 1961. Reorganized 1983 and faculties and institutes replaced by academic centres. A State institution financed by the Federal Government.

Governing Bodies: Conselho Universitário

Academic Year: April to December (April-July; September-December)

Admission Requirements: Secondary school certificate and competitive entrance examination

Main Language(s) of Instruction: Portuguese

Degrees and Diplomas: *Bacharelado*: Accountancy; Administration; Animal Husbandry; Chemistry; Computer Science; Economics; Journalism; Juridical Sciences; Psychology; Public Relations, 4-5 yrs; *Bacharelado*: Agricultural Engineering; Architecture; Chemical Engineering; Civil Engineering; Dentistry; Medicine; Meteorology; Nursing; Nutrition; Social Work, 4-6 yrs; *Bacharelado*: Biology; Geography; Mathematics; Social Sciences, 4 yrs; *Licenciatura*: Biology; Education; Geography; History; Letters; Mathematics; Philosophy; Physical Education; Scenic Arts; Social Sciences, 4 yrs; *Licenciatura*: Music, 6 yrs; *Especialização/Aperfeiçoamento*: 8 months; *Mestrado*: Administration; Chemistry and Biotechnology; Development and Environmental Studies; Linguistics; Physics, a further 2 yrs; *Doutorado*: Linguistics, 4 yrs

Student Services: Academic counselling, Canteen, Cultural centre, Health services, Sports facilities

Special Facilities: Museum of Anthropology and Folklore; Natural History Museum. Art Gallery

Libraries: Central Library, 130,000 vols

Press or Publishing House: Edufal/Imprensa e Editora Universitária

FEDERAL UNIVERSITY OF ALFENAS
Universidade Federal de Alfenas (UNIFAL-MG)
Rua Gabriel Monteiro da Silva 714, Centro, Alfenas,
Minas Gerais 37130000
Tel: +55(35) 3299-1061
Fax: +55(35) 3299-1063
EMail: reitoria@unifal-mg.edu.br
Website: http://www.unifal-mg.edu.br

Reitor: Paulo Márcio de Faria e Silva
EMail: paulo.silva@unifal-mg.edu.br

Faculties
Dentistry (Dentistry); **Nutrition**; **Pharmacy** (Pharmacy)

Institutes
Biomedicine; **Exact Sciences** (Mathematics; Physics)

Schools
Nursing (Nursing)

History: Founded 1914 as Escola de Farmácia e Odontologia de Alfenas. Acquired present status and title 2005.

Degrees and Diplomas: *Bacharelado*: Biotechnology; Biological Sciences; Computer Science; Nursing; Pharmacy; Geography; Physics; Mathematics; Nutrition; Odontology; Pedagogy; Chemistry; *Licenciatura*: Biological Sciences; Geography; Physics; Mathematics; Chemistry; *Especialização/Aperfeiçoamento*: Clinical Analysis; Dentistry; Dental Technology and Surgery; *Mestrado*: Pharmaceutical Sciences; *Doutorado*
Last Updated: 25/05/10

FEDERAL UNIVERSITY OF AMAPÁ
Universidade Federal do Amapá (UNIFAP)
Rod. Juscelino Kubitschek, KM-02 - Jardim Marco Zero, Macapá,
Amapá 68902280
Tel: +55(96) 3312-1700
EMail: unifap@unifap.br
Website: http://www.unifap.br

Reitor: José Carlos Tavares Carvalho EMail: reitor@unifap.br

Courses
Architecture and Town Planning (Architecture; Town Planning); **Arts**; **Arts and Humanities**; **Biological and Life Sciences**; **Education**; **Electrical Engineering** (Electrical Engineering); **Environmental Studies**; **Geography**; **History**; **Law**; **Literature**; **Mathematics**; **Medicine**; **Nursing**; **Pedagogy**; **Pharmacy** (Pharmacy); **Physical Education**; **Physics** (Physics); **Social Sciences**
History: Founded 1990.

Admission Requirements: Secondary school certificate and entrance examination

Main Language(s) of Instruction: Portuguese

Degrees and Diplomas: *Bacharelado*; *Licenciatura*; *Especialização/Aperfeiçoamento*; *Mestrado*
Last Updated: 20/05/10

FEDERAL UNIVERSITY OF AMAZONAS
Universidade Federal do Amazonas (UFAM)
Avenida General Rodrigo Otávio Jordão Ramos 3000, Campus
Universitário, Coroado II, Mánaus, Amazonas 69077000
Tel: +55(92) 3647-4314 +55(92) 3647-4415
Fax: +55(92) 3647-4314
EMail: gabinete@ufam.edu.br
Website: http://www.ufam.edu.br

Reitora: Márcia Perales Mendes da Silva Tel: +55(92) 3644-1602

Centres
Environmental Sciences (Environmental Studies)

Faculties
Agrarian Sciences (Agricultural Engineering; Agriculture; Fishery; Forestry); **Dentistry** (Dentistry); **Education** (Education); **Law** (Law; Private Law; Public Law); **Medicine**; **Pharmacy**; **Physical Education** (Physical Education); **Social Studies** (Accountancy; Administration; Economics; Social Studies); **Technology** (Civil Engineering; Electrical Engineering; Graphic Design; Industrial Design; Technology)

Institutes
Biological Sciences (Biological and Life Sciences; Biotechnology; Nautical Science; Parasitology); **Exact Sciences** (Chemistry; Data Processing; Geology; Mathematics; Natural Sciences; Physics; Statistics); **Human Sciences and Languages** (Arts and Humanities; Geography; History; Journalism; Library Science; Modern Languages; Philosophy; Social Sciences; Social Work)

Schools
Nursing (Nursing)

Further Information: Campuses: Centro Universitário de Coari, Centro Universitário de Itacoatiara, Centro Universitário de Humaitá, Centro Universitário de Parintins, Centro Universitário de Benjamin Constant. Also Getúlio Vargas University Hospital

History: Founded 1909 as Escola Universitária Livre de Manáos. Later became Universidade de Manáos. Became Universidade do Amazonas 1962 and Universidade Federal do Amazonas 2002.

Governing Bodies: Conselho Universitário

Academic Year: March to November (March-June; August-November)

Admission Requirements: Secondary school certificate and entrance examination

Fees: None

Main Language(s) of Instruction: Portuguese

Degrees and Diplomas: *Bacharelado*: 4-6 yrs; *Licenciatura*: 4-6 yrs; *Especialização/Aperfeiçoamento*: 6 months-2 yrs (in co-operation with the Instituto Nacional de Pesquisa da Amazônia-INPA); *Mestrado*: a further 1-3 yrs; *Doutorado*: 2-4 yrs

Student Services: Canteen, Foreign student adviser, Handicapped facilities, Sports facilities

Student Residential Facilities: Yes

Special Facilities: Amazonian Museum. Hamnemamam Bacellar Art Centre

Libraries: Central Library, c. 183,500 vols; specialized libraries, c. 23,700 vols

Publications: Ciências Agrárias, Agrarian Sciences *(bimonthly)*; Ciências Humanas, Human Sciences; Ciências Tecnológicas, Technological Sciences; Revista da Universidade; Séries: Ciências da Saúde, Health Sciences

Press or Publishing House: Imprensa Universitária
Last Updated: 20/05/10

FEDERAL UNIVERSITY OF BAHIA
Universidade Federal da Bahia (UFBA)
Rua Augusto Viana S/n Palacio da Reitoria, Canela, Salvador,
Bahia 40110060
Tel: +55(71) 263-7000 +55(71) 263-7030
Fax: +55(71) 263-7027
EMail: reitor@ufba.br
Website: http://www.ufba.br

Reitora: Dora Rosa Leal (2010-)

Areas
Arts; **Biological and Health Sciences** (Biological and Life Sciences; Dentistry; Marine Science and Oceanography; Medicine; Natural Sciences; Nursing; Nutrition; Pharmacy; Speech Therapy and Audiology; Veterinary Science); **Literature** (Literature); **Philosophy and Human Sciences** (Accountancy; Administration; Archaeology; Communication Studies; Cultural Studies; Economics; History; Law; Library Science; Museum Studies; Pedagogy; Philosophy; Physical Education; Psychology; Secretarial Studies; Social Sciences); **Physics, Mathematics and Technology** (Architecture; Chemical Engineering; Chemistry; Civil Engineering; Computer Science; Electrical Engineering; Geography; Geology; Geophysics; Industrial Chemistry; Marine Science and Oceanography;

Mathematics; Mechanical Engineering; Mining Engineering; Physics; Sanitary Engineering; Statistics; Town Planning)

History: Founded 1575 by the Society of Jesus, became University 1946 incorporating other institutions. Reorganized 1968. A State Institution under the jurisdiction of the Ministry of Education and Sports.

Governing Bodies: Assembleía Universitária; Conselho de Curadores; Conselho de Coordenação; Conselho Universitário

Academic Year: February to December (February-June; August-December)

Admission Requirements: Secondary school certificate and entrance examination

Main Language(s) of Instruction: Portuguese

Degrees and Diplomas: *Bacharelado*: Accountancy; Architecture; Engineering; Geology; Medicine; Midwifery; Museology; Music Composition and Conducting; Music Instruments; Nursing; Nutrition; Pedagogy; Public Administration; Secretarial Studies; Singing; Theatre; Veterinary Medicine, 4-6 yrs; *Bacharelado*: Biology; Chemistry; Geography; History; Languages; Letters; Mathematics; Philosophy; Physics; Psychology; Social Sciences, 4-5 yrs; *Bacharelado*: Dance; *Licenciatura*: Ballet; Music; Science, 4 yrs; *Licenciatura*: Biology; Chemistry; Geography; History; Languages; Letters; Mathematics; Philosophy; Physics; Psychology; Social Sciences, 4-5 yrs; *Mestrado*; *Doutorado*

Student Residential Facilities: Yes

Special Facilities: Museu de Arte Sacra; Archaeology and Ethnology Museum; Afro-Brazilian Museum

Libraries: Central Library, c. 538,000 vols; Bahian Studies, c. 30,000; 32 teaching sections libraries

Publications: Publications of the Faculties and Institutes

Press or Publishing House: Gráfica Universitária
Last Updated: 25/05/10

FEDERAL UNIVERSITY OF CAMPINA GRANDE

Universidade Federal de Campina Grande
Avenida Aprigio Veloso 882, Bodocondo, Campina Grande,
Paraíba 58019-900
Tel: +55(83) 3310-1000
EMail: reitoria@reitoria.ufcg.edu.br
Website: http://www.ufcg.edu.br
Reitor: Thompson Fernandes Mariz

Centres
Biological and Health Sciences (Child Care and Development; Health Sciences; Medicine; Surgery); **Education and Health** *(Cuité Campus)*; **Electrical and Computer Engineering; Food Processing** (Food Science; Food Technology); **Health and Rural Technology** *(Patos Campus)* (Biology; Forest Management; Veterinary Science); **Humanities; Legal and Social Sciences** *(Souza Campus)*; **Science and Technology** (Chemical Engineering; Industrial Design; Materials Engineering; Mathematics; Mechanical Engineering; Physics; Production Engineering); **Teacher Training** *(Cajazeiras - Paraíba Campus)* (Teacher Training); **Technology and Natural Resources** (Natural Resources; Technology)

Further Information: Also branches in Patos, Sousa, Cajazeiras, Cuité

History: Founded 2002.

Main Language(s) of Instruction: Portuguese

Degrees and Diplomas: *Bacharelado*; *Licenciatura*; *Especialização/Aperfeiçoamento*; *Mestrado*; *Doutorado*
Last Updated: 25/05/10

FEDERAL UNIVERSITY OF CEARÁ

Universidade Federal do Ceará (UFC)
Avenida da Universidade 2853, Benfica, Fortaleza,
Ceará 60020181
Tel: +55(85) 4009 7301
Fax: +55(85) 4009 7303
EMail: prplufc@ufc.br
Website: http://www.ufc.br
Reitor: Jesualdo Pereira Farias EMail: reitor@ufc.br

Centres
Science *(Pici)* (Analytical Chemistry; Biochemistry; Biology; Computer Science; Mathematics; Natural Sciences; Physics); **Agrarian Sciences** *(Pici)* (Agricultural Engineering; Agriculture; Food Science; Soil Science); **Humanities** (Arts and Humanities; Computer Science; History; Literature; Philosophy; Psychology; Social Sciences); **Technology** *(Pici)* (Architecture; Chemical Engineering; Electrical Engineering; Environmental Engineering; Hydraulic Engineering; Mechanical Engineering; Structural Architecture; Technology; Town Planning; Transport Engineering)

Faculties
Economics (Economics) *Head*: Maria da Glória Arraes Peter; **Education** (Education); **Law** (Law); **Medicine** *(Porangabuçu)*; **Pharmacy, Dentistry and Nursing** *(Porangabuçu) Head*: Haroldo César Pinheiro Beltrão

Institutes
Culture and Art; Marine Sciences

Further Information: Also 'Walter Cantídio' University Hospital. 'Assis Chateaubriand' Maternity Hospital . Psychology Clinic. Portuguese Courses for foreign students

History: Founded 1954. A State institution financed by the Federal Government.

Governing Bodies: Conselho Universitário

Academic Year: March to December (March-July; August-December)

Admission Requirements: Secondary school certificate or equivalent and entrance examination

Fees: None

Main Language(s) of Instruction: Portuguese

Degrees and Diplomas: *Bacharelado*: 4 yrs; *Bacharelado*: Medicine, 6 yrs; *Licenciatura*: 4 yrs; *Licenciatura*: Medicine, 6 yrs; *Mestrado*: a further 2 yrs; *Doutorado*

Student Services: Canteen, Cultural centre, Foreign student adviser, Health services, Sports facilities

Special Facilities: Art Museum; 'José de Alencar House' Museum; 'Eusébio de Oliveira' Museum. Theatre. Auditorium. Radio Station

Libraries: Total, c. 189,000 vols

Publications: Arquivos de Ciências do Mar; Ciências Agronômicas; Educação em Debate; Engenharia; Geologia; Letras; Odontologia; Olhar Midiático *(biannually)*; Psicologia; Revista de Ciências Sociais *(biannually)*; Revista de Medicina *(biannually)*
Last Updated: 20/05/10

FEDERAL UNIVERSITY OF ESPÍRITO SANTO

Universidade Federal do Espírito Santo (UFES)
Avenida Fernando Ferrari 514 S/n Campus Universitário,
Goiabeiras, Vitória, Espírito Santo 29060900
Tel: +55(27) 4009-2770
Fax: +55(27) 4009-2818
EMail: reitoria@npd.ufes.br
Website: http://www.ufes.br
Reitor: Rubens Rasseli Tel: +55(27) 3335-2222

Centres
Agrarian Sciences (Agriculture; Agronomy; Animal Husbandry; Biology; Chemical Engineering; Computer Science; Floriculture; Food Technology; Geology; Industrial Engineering; Mathematics; Nutrition; Pharmacy; Physics; Veterinary Science; Zoology); **Arts** (Advertising and Publicity; Architecture; Fine Arts; Industrial Design; Journalism; Music; Town Planning; Visual Arts); **Education** (Cultural Studies; Education; Modern Languages; Pedagogy; Political Sciences); **Exact Sciences; General Studies** (Biology; Chemistry; Earth Sciences; Literature; Modern Languages; Philosophy; Physics; Psychology; Social Sciences; Statistics); **Human and Natural Sciences** (Biology; Development Studies; Ecology; Geography; History; Literature; Modern Languages; Natural Resources; Philosophy; Psychology; Social Sciences); **Law and Economics** (Business Administration; Communication Studies; Economics; Law; Library Science); **Physical Education and Sport** (Physical Education; Sports); **Technology** (Civil Engineering; Computer Science; Electrical Engineering; Environmental Engineering; Industrial Engineering; Mechanical Engineering; Production Engineering; Technology)

Further Information: Also Teaching Hospital

History: Founded 1954 as a State University incorporating existing colleges. Became a Federal Institution 1961 and reorganized 1966. Financed by the Federal Government.

Governing Bodies: Conselho Universitário; Conselho de Ensino e Pesquisa

Academic Year: March to December (March-July; August-December)

Admission Requirements: Secondary school certificate and entrance examination

Fees: None

Main Language(s) of Instruction: Portuguese

Degrees and Diplomas: *Bacharelado*: 4-8 yrs; *Licenciatura*: 4-8 yrs; *Mestrado*; *Doutorado*

Special Facilities: Museu Solar Monjardim; Museu Santa Luzia; Museu dos Reis Magos

Libraries: Central Library, c. 95,000 vols; Biomedicine, c. 9,000; Agriculture, c. 12,500

Publications: Revista de Cultura

Press or Publishing House: Gráfica Imprensa Universitária
Last Updated: 20/05/10

FEDERAL UNIVERSITY OF GOIÁS
Universidade Federal de Goiás (UFG)
Rodovia Goiânia-Nerópolis km 12, Prédio ICB IV, Campus
Samambaia, Goiânia, Goiás 74001970
Tel: +55(62) 3521-1000
Fax: +55(62) 3521-1200
EMail: reitora@reitora.ufg.br
Website: http://www.ufg.br

Reitor: Edward Madureira Brasil
Tel: +55(62) 3521-1146 EMail: reitoria@reitoria.ufg.br

Faculties
Communication and Library Sciences (Advertising and Publicity; Communication Studies; Journalism; Library Science; Public Relations); **Dentistry** (Dentistry); **Education** (Education); **Human Sciences and Letters** (Communication Studies; History; Modern Languages; Philosophy; Social Sciences); **Law** (Law); **Medicine** (Medicine); **Nursing** (Nursing); **Nutrition** (Nutrition); **Pharmacy** (Pharmacy); **Physical Education** (Physical Education)

Institutes
Chemistry (Chemistry)

Schools
Agriculture (Agriculture); **Engineering** (Building Technologies; Construction Engineering; Electronic Engineering; Engineering; Hydraulic Engineering; Sanitary Engineering; Systems Analysis); **Veterinary Medicine** (Veterinary Science)

History: Founded 1960. An autonomous institution under the jurisdiction of the Ministry of Education and Sports.

Governing Bodies: Conselho Universitário; Conselho de Curadores

Academic Year: February to December (February-June; August-December)

Admission Requirements: Secondary school certificate and entrance examination

Main Language(s) of Instruction: Portuguese

Degrees and Diplomas: *Bacharelado*: Agronomy; Biological Sciences; Civil Engineering; Electrical Engineering; Law; Veterinary Medicine, 5 yrs; *Bacharelado*: Art Education; Chemistry; Computer Science; Dentistry; Geography; History; Library Science; Mathematics; Modern Languages; Musical Instrument (Piano); Nursing and Midwifery; Nutrition; Pedagogy; Pharmacy; Philosophy; Physical Education; Physics; Singing; Social Communication; Social Sciences; Visual Arts, 4 yrs; *Bacharelado*: Medicine, 6 yrs; *Mestrado*: Agrarian Law; Biology; Brazilian Education; Genetics and Plant Improvement; History of Agrarian Societies; Language and Linguistics; Mathematics; Tropical Medicine, a further 2-3 yrs; *Doutorado*

Student Residential Facilities: Yes

Special Facilities: Museum of Anthropology. Planetarium. University Radio

Libraries: Central Library, c. 100,000 vols

Publications: Anais da Escola de Agronomia e Veterinaria *(annually)*; Boletim do Pessoal *(monthly)*; Revista da Faculdade de Direito *(biannually)*; Revista de Patologia Tropical *(quarterly)*; Revista do Instituto de Ciências Humanas e Letras *(quarterly)*; Revista Goiana de Artes *(biannually)*; Revista Goiana de Medicina *(quarterly)*; Revistas

Press or Publishing House: Centro Editorial e Gráfico da UFG-CEGRAF
Last Updated: 13/12/07

FEDERAL UNIVERSITY OF GRANDE DOURADOS FOUNDATION
Fundaçao Universidade Federal da Grande Dourados (UFGD)
Rua João Rosa Goes N° 1761, Vila Progresso, P.O. Box 322,
Dourados, Mato Grosso do Sul 79.825-070
Tel: +55(67) 3411-3600 +55(67) 3411-3601
Fax: +55(67) 3411-3637
EMail: reitoria@ufgd.edu.br
Website: http://www.ufgd.edu.br

Rector: Damião Duque de Farias

Pro-Rector, Administration and Planning: Silvana de Abreu
EMail: proap@ufgd.edu.br

International Relations: Cesar Augusto Silva da Silva, International Relations Officer

Faculties
Administration, Accountancy and Economics (Accountancy; Administration; Economics); **Agrarian Sciences**; **Biological and Environmental Sciences** (Biological and Life Sciences; Biotechnology; Environmental Studies); **Communication, Arts and Letters** (Arts and Humanities; Literature; Theatre); **Education** (Education; Indigenous Studies; Pedagogy; Physical Education); **Exact Sciences and Technology** (Chemistry; Energy Engineering; Food Technology; Information Technology; Mathematics; Production Engineering; Technology); **Health Sciences**; **Human Sciences**; **Law and International Relations** (International Relations; Law)

History: Founded 2005.

Main Language(s) of Instruction: Portuguese

Degrees and Diplomas: *Licenciatura*; *Especialização/Aperfeiçoamento*: Administration; Law; Teacher Training; Linguistics; Civil Security; *Mestrado*: Agronomy; Environmental Sciences and Technology; Education; Entomoly and Biodiversity Preservation; Geography; History Literature; Zoology; *Doutorado*: Agronomy
Last Updated: 17/06/10

FEDERAL UNIVERSITY OF HEALTH SCIENCES OF PORTO ALEGRE
Universidade Federal de Ciências de Saúde de Porto Alegre (UFCSPA)
Rua Sarmento Leite 245, Centro, Porto Alegre,
Rio Grande do Sul 90050170
Tel: +55(51) 3226-7913
Fax: +55(51) 3224-8822 +55(51) 3224-8178
Website: http://www.ufcspa.edu.br

Reitora: Miriam da Costa Oliveira EMail: reitora@ufcspa.edu.br

Departments
Basic Health Sciences (Health Sciences); **Clinical Medicine** (Medicine); **Clinical Surgery**; **Community Health**; **Diagnosis Methods**; **Gynaecology and Obstetrics** (Gynaecology and Obstetrics); **Health Education and Information**; **Nursing**; **Nutrition**; **Paediatrics**; **Pathology and Forensic Medicine** (Forensic Medicine and Dentistry; Pathology); **Physiotherapy** (Physical Therapy); **Psychology** (Psychology); **Speech Therapy**

History: Founded 1961 as Fundação Faculdade Federal de Ciências Médicas de Porto Alegre. Acquired present status and title 2008.

Main Language(s) of Instruction: Portuguese

297

Degrees and Diplomas: *Bacharelado*; *Especialização/Aperfeiçoamento*; *Mestrado*; *Doutorado*
Last Updated: 04/06/10

FEDERAL UNIVERSITY OF ITAJUBÁ
Universidade Federal de Itajubá (UNIFEI)
Caixa Postal 50, Itajubá, Minas Gerais 37500-903
Tel: +55(35) 3629-1101
Fax: +55(35) 3622-3596
EMail: vestibular@unifei.edu.br
Website: http://www.efei.edu.br/

Reitor: Renato de Aquino Faria Nunes

Institutes
Electrical and Energy Engineering; **Exact Sciences** (Chemistry; Mathematics; Mathematics and Computer Science; Physics); **Information Systems**; **Mechanical Engineering**; **Natural Resources** (Environmental Engineering; Natural Resources); **Production Engineering and Management**

History: Founded 1913 as Instituto Eletrotécnico e Mecânico de Itajubá. Became Escola Federal de Engenharia de Itajubá en 1968. Acquired present title and status 2002.

Degrees and Diplomas: *Bacharelado*; *Licenciatura*; *Especialização/Aperfeiçoamento*; *Mestrado*; *Doutorado*
Last Updated: 25/05/10

FEDERAL UNIVERSITY OF JUIZ DE FORA
Universidade Federal de Juiz de Fora (UFJF)
Reitoria, Campus Universitário, Juiz de Fora,
Minas Gerais 36036900
Tel: +55(32) 3229-3902
Fax: +55(32) 3229-3933
Website: http://www.ufjf.br

Reitor: Henrique Duque de Miranda Chaves Filho (2006-)
Tel: +55(32) 3215-6245 EMail: gabinete@ufjf.edu.br

Vice-Reitor: José Luiz Rezende Pereira

Faculties
Administration (Administration; Economics); **Communication** (Communication Studies; Journalism); **Dentistry** (Dentistry); **Economics**; **Education** (Education); **Engineering** (Architecture; Civil Engineering; Construction Engineering; Electrical Engineering; Energy Engineering; Engineering; Environmental Engineering; Mechanical Engineering; Production Engineering; Town Planning; Transport Engineering); **Law** (Law); **Letters**; **Medicine** (Medicine); **Nursing**; **Pharmacy and Biochemistry** (Biochemistry; Pharmacy); **Physical Education** (Physical Education; Sports); **Social Services**

Institutes
Arts and Design (Design; Fashion Design; Music; Performing Arts; Visual Arts); **Biological Sciences** (Biology); **Exact Sciences** (Architecture; Chemistry; Mathematics; Mathematics and Computer Science; Physics; Statistics); **Human Sciences** (Arts and Humanities; Geography; History; Philosophy; Psychology; Social Sciences; Tourism); **Literature and Language Studies**

History: Founded 1960 by the Federal Government, incorporating five private institutions.

Academic Year: February to December (February-June; August-December)

Admission Requirements: Secondary school certificate and entrance examination

Fees: None

Main Language(s) of Instruction: Portuguese

Degrees and Diplomas: *Bacharelado*: Architecture; Civil Engineering; Electrical Engineering; Law, 5 yrs; *Bacharelado*: Dentistry; Economics; Journalism; Pharmacy; Tourism, 4 yrs; *Bacharelado*: Medicine, 6 yrs; *Licenciatura*: Biology; Chemistry; Design and Plastic Arts; Education; Geography; History; Literature; Mathematics; Philosophy; Physical Education; Physics, 4 yrs; *Especialização/Aperfeiçoamento*; *Mestrado*; *Doutorado*

Special Facilities: Seven Museums. Laboratories. Theatres
Libraries: c. 20,000 vols

Publications: Boletim do Centro de Biologia de Reprodução; Educação em Foco; Etica e Filosofia Política; Instrumento, Educação; Ipotesi, Estudios Literários; Libertas, Revista do Serviço Social; Locus, Revista de História; Lumina; Numen, Pesquisa em Religião; Revista Brasileira de Zoociências; Revista de Engenharia; Veredas, Estudos Linguísticos
Last Updated: 25/05/10

FEDERAL UNIVERSITY OF LAVRAS
Universidade Federal de Lavras (UFLA)
Campus Universitário, Lavras, Minas Gerais 37200000
Tel: +55(35) 3829-1502
Fax: +55(35) 3829-1100
EMail: proad@ufla.br
Website: http://www.ufla.br

Reitor: Antônio Nazareno Guimarães Mendes

Departments
Administration and Economics; **Agriculture**; **Biology**; **Chemistry**; **Computer Science** (Computer Science); **Education**; **Engineering**; **Entomology**; **Exact Sciences** (Mathematics; Statistics); **Food Sciences**; **Forestry**; **Physical Education**; **Phytopathology**; **Soil Sciences**; **Veterinary Medicine**; **Zoology**

History: Founded 1908 as Instituto Gammon. Became Escola Superior de Agricultura de Lavras, acquired present status and title 1994.

Degrees and Diplomas: *Bacharelado*; *Licenciatura*; *Especialização/Aperfeiçoamento*; *Mestrado*; *Doutorado*
Last Updated: 21/05/10

FEDERAL UNIVERSITY OF MARANHÃO
Universidade Federal do Maranhão (UFMA)
AV. Dos Portugueses, s/n, São Luís, Maranhão 65085-580
Tel: +55(98) 217-8011 +55(98) 217-8094
Fax: +55(98) 217-8026
EMail: procin@ufma.br
Website: http://www.ufma.br

Reitor: Natalino Salgado Filho (2007-)

Centres
Biological and Health Sciences (Biological and Life Sciences; Dentistry; Health Sciences; Medicine; Nursing; Pharmacy; Physical Education); **Exact Sciences and Technology** (Chemistry; Computer Science; Electrical Engineering; Industrial Design; Mathematics; Physics; Technology); **Human Sciences**; **Social Sciences** (Accountancy; Economics; Hotel Management; Law; Library Science; Pedagogy; Social and Community Services; Social Sciences)

History: Founded 1966. An autonomous institution financially supported by the Federal Government. Acquired present status 1969.

Academic Year: March to December (March-June; August-December)

Admission Requirements: Secondary school certificate and entrance examination

Main Language(s) of Instruction: Portuguese

Degrees and Diplomas: *Bacharelado*: Accountancy; Dentistry (Cirurgião dentista); Economics; Industrial Chemistry (Químico industrial); Industrial Design (Desenhista Industrial); Library Science; Mathematics; Pharmaceutical Bio-chemistry (Farmacêutico-Bioquímico); Social Communication; Social Work (Assistente social), 4 yrs; *Bacharelado*: Electrical Engineering (Engenheiro Eletricista); Law, 5 yrs; *Bacharelado*: Pharmacy (Farmacêutico), 3 yrs; *Licenciatura*: Chemistry; Design and Plastic Arts; Education; History; Letters; Mathematics; Physical Education; Physics, 4 yrs; *Especialização/Aperfeiçoamento*; *Mestrado*

Student Residential Facilities: Yes

Libraries: Central Library, c. 73,030 vols; Medicine, c. 3,290; Nursing, c. 1,080; Dentistry and Pharmacy, c. 1,870
Last Updated: 19/05/10

FEDERAL UNIVERSITY OF MATO GROSSO

Universidade Federal de Mato Grosso (UFMT)
Avenida Fernando Corrêa da Costa, S/n Cidade Universitária,
Caxipó da Ponte, Cuiabá, Mato Grosso 78060-900
Tel: +55(65) 3615-8203
Fax: +55(65) 3615-8204
EMail: ufmt@cpd.br
Website: http://www.ufmt.br

Reitora: Maria Lúcia Cavalli Neder (2008-)
Tel: +55(65) 3615-8301 EMail: reitor@ufmt.br

Faculties
Administration and Economics (Administration; Economics);
Agriculture and Veterinary Medicine (Agriculture; Tropical Agriculture; Veterinary Science); **Engineering** (Engineering); **Forestry Engineering** (Forestry); **Law** (Law); **Medical Sciences** (Health Sciences; Medicine); **Nursing and Nutrition** (Nursing; Nutrition); **Physical Education** (Physical Education)

Institutes
Biosciences (Biochemistry; Biomedicine; Biophysics); **Education** (Education); **Exact Sciences** (Mathematics and Computer Science; Physics); **Human and Social Sciences** (Anthropology; Arts and Humanities; Geography; History; Social Sciences; Social Work; Sociology); **Languages** (Arts and Humanities; Communication Studies; Modern Languages)

Further Information: Also University Hospital 'Júlio Muller'. Campuses at: Rondonópolis, Médio Araguaia

History: Founded 1970, incorporating the Federal Faculty of Law, founded 1934, the Faculty of Philosophy, Science and Letters of Mato Grosso and the Institute of Science and Letters of Cuiabá. A State institution financed by the Federal Government and responsible to the Ministry of Education and Sports.

Governing Bodies: Conselho de Administração

Academic Year: March to December (March-July; August-December)

Admission Requirements: Secondary school certificate and entrance examination

Main Language(s) of Instruction: Portuguese, French, Spanish

Degrees and Diplomas: *Bacharelado*: 4 yrs; *Licenciatura*: 4 yrs; *Mestrado*: a further 2 yrs; *Doutorado*: 4 yrs

Student Services: Canteen, Cultural centre, Sports facilities

Student Residential Facilities: Yes

Special Facilities: Museu Rondon (ethnographic exhibition of the Indian population of the region). Audiovisual documentation of pre-Columbian cultures

Libraries: Central Library, c. 205,300 vols

Press or Publishing House: University Press
Last Updated: 21/05/10

FEDERAL UNIVERSITY OF MATO GROSSO DO SUL

Universidade Federal de Mato Grosso do Sul (UFMS)
Campus de Campo Grande, S/n Cidade Universitária,
Campo Grande, Mato Grosso do Sul 79070900
Tel: +55(67) 787-3833 +55(67) 787-2491
Fax: +55(67) 787-1081
EMail: reitor@nin.ufms.br
Website: http://www.ufms.br

Reitor: Manoel Peró

Campuses
Aquidauana (Geography; History; Natural Sciences)

Centres
Biological and Health Sciences (Biological and Life Sciences; Dentistry; Health Sciences; Medicine; Pharmacy; Veterinary Science); **Exact Sciences and Technology** (Civil Engineering; Computer Science; Electrical Engineering; Mathematics; Natural Sciences; Physics; Technology); **Human and Social Sciences** (Administration; Arts and Humanities; Communication Studies; Education; Physical Education; Social Sciences)

Departments
Corumbá (Accountancy; Administration; Arts and Humanities; Biology; Education; Geography; History; Mathematics; Psychology); **Dourados** (Accountancy; Agriculture; Arts and Humanities; Education; Geography; History; Mathematics); **Três Lagoas** (Arts and Humanities; Biology; Education; Geography; History; Mathematics)

History: Founded 1969 as Faculty of Pharmacy and Dentistry, became Institute of Biology 1966, State University 1970, and Federal University 1979.

Academic Year: March to December (March-June; August-December)

Admission Requirements: Secondary school certificate and entrance examination

Main Language(s) of Instruction: Portuguese

Degrees and Diplomas: *Bacharelado*: Civil and Electrical Engineering (Engenheiro civil e elétrico); Dentistry (Cirurgião dentista); Journalism (Jornalista); Pharmaceutical Bio-chemistry (Farmacêutico bioquímico); Veterinary Medicine (Médico veterinário), 4 yrs; *Bacharelado*: Civil Engineering (Engenheiro civil), 5 yrs; *Bacharelado*: Medicine (Médico), 6 yrs; *Bacharelado*: Pharmacy (Farmacêutico geral), 3 yrs; *Licenciatura*: Chemistry; Education; Geography; History; Letters; Mathematics; Physical Education and Sports; Physics; Plastic Arts; Psychology, 3 yrs; *Especialização/Aperfeiçoamento*; *Mestrado*; *Doutorado*

Libraries: Total, c. 131,000 vols

Publications: Revista Científica e Cultural
Last Updated: 13/12/07

FEDERAL UNIVERSITY OF MINAS GERAIS

Universidade Federal de Minas Gerais (UFMG)
Avenida Presidente Antônio Carlos 6627, Reitoria Pampulha,
Belo Horizonte, Minas Gerais 31270-901
Tel: +55(31) 3499-4124
Fax: +55(31) 3499-4130
EMail: gabinete@reitoria.ufmg.br
Website: http://www.ufmg.br

Reitor: Clélio Campolina Diniz EMail: reitor@ufmg.br

Faculties
Actuarial Sciences; **Agronomy** (Agronomy); **Dentistry** (Dentistry); **Economics** (Accountancy; Business Administration; Demography and Population; Economics); **Education** (Education); **Law** (Law); **Letters** (Literature; Modern Languages); **Medicine** (Medicine); **Pharmacy** (Pharmacy); **Philosophy and Humanities** (Anthropology; Arts and Humanities; History; Philosophy; Political Sciences; Psychology; Sociology); **Physiotherapy** (Physical Therapy)

Institutes
Agrarian Sciences (Agronomy); **Biology** (Biology); **Exact Sciences** (Mathematics and Computer Science; Natural Sciences); **Geosciences** (Geography; Geology; Tourism)

Schools
Architecture (Architecture; Town Planning); **Engineering** (Civil Engineering; Electrical Engineering; Hydraulic Engineering; Mechanical Engineering; Production Engineering); **Fine Arts** (Cinema and Television; Fashion Design; Fine Arts; Restoration of Works of Art; Theatre; Visual Arts); **Information Sciences** (Archiving; Information Sciences; Library Science; Museum Studies); **Music** (Music); **Nursing** (Nursing); **Physical Education** (Physical Education); **Veterinary Medicine** (Veterinary Science)

History: Founded 1927 as a University incorporating Institutions established between 1892 and 1911. Reorganized 1968. A State institution financed by the Federal Government and responsible to the Ministry of Education and Sports.

Governing Bodies: Conselho Universitário

Academic Year: February to December (February-June; August-December)

Admission Requirements: Secondary school certificate and entrance examination

Fees: (Reais): 250 per semester

Main Language(s) of Instruction: Portuguese

International Co-operation: With universities in Canada, USA, Italy, Belgium, England, France, Germany, Netherlands, Portugal, Spain and Hungary.

Degrees and Diplomas: *Bacharelado*: Accountancy; Actuarial Sciences; Agronomy; Architecture; Business Administration; Computer Science; Dentistry; Economics; Education; Engineering; Geology; Law; Music; Occupational Therapy; Pharmacy; Physiotherapy; Veterinary Medicine, 5 yrs; *Bacharelado*: Biology; Chemistry; Ecology; Fine Arts; Journalism; Letters; Library Science; Mathematics; Nursing; Philosophy; Physical Education; Physics; Psychology; Statistics; Tourism; Zoology, 4 yrs; *Bacharelado*: History, 3 yrs; *Bacharelado*: Medicine, 6 yrs; *Especialização/Aperfeiçoamento*: 1 yr; *Mestrado*: a further 2 yrs; *Doutorado*: 4 yrs

Student Services: Academic counselling, Canteen, Cultural centre, Employment services, Foreign student adviser, Health services, Language programs, Nursery care, Social counselling, Sports facilities

Special Facilities: Natural History Museum. Botanical Garden. Cultural Centre. Astronomical Observatory. Audio-Visual Centre. Museum of Morphological Sciences

Libraries: Central Library, c. 800,000 vols; libraries of the Schools and Faculties

Publications: Diversa *(monthly)*; Sistemático *(monthly)*

Press or Publishing House: Editora da UFMG
Last Updated: 21/05/10

FEDERAL UNIVERSITY OF OURO PRÊTO
Universidade Federal de Ouro Prêto (UFOP)
Rua Diogo de Vasconcelos 122, Centro, Ouro Prêto,
Minas Gerais 35400000
Tel: +55(31) 3559-1100
Fax: +55(31) 3559-1228
EMail: reitoria@cpd.ufop.br
Website: http://www.ufop.br

Reitor: João Luiz Martins Tel: +55(31) 3559-1210

Departments
Law (Law); **Museology** (Museum Studies); **Tourism** (Tourism)

Institutes
Biological and Exact Sciences (Biological and Life Sciences; Chemistry; Computer Science; Mathematics; Physics); **Philosophy, Arts and Culture** (Arts and Humanities; Cultural Studies; Music; Philosophy; Theatre); **Social and Human Sciences** *(Mariana)* (Arts and Humanities; History; Law; Social Sciences)

Schools
Mining Engineering (Civil Engineering; Geological Engineering; Metallurgical Engineering; Mining Engineering; Production Engineering); **Nutrition** (Nutrition); **Pharmacy** (Biochemistry; Pharmacy)

Further Information: Campuses at Mariana and Morro do Cruzeiro

History: Founded 1969 incorporating Escola de Minas de Ouro Prêto, founded 1876 as Escola de Farmácia e Bioquímica, 1839. Under the jurisdiction of the Ministry of Education and Sports and financially supported by the Federal Government.

Governing Bodies: Conselho Universitário; Conselho de Ensino, Pesquisa e Extensão

Academic Year: March to November (March-June; August-November)

Admission Requirements: Secondary school certificate and entrance examination

Main Language(s) of Instruction: Portuguese

Degrees and Diplomas: *Bacharelado*: 4 yrs; *Licenciatura*: 4 yrs; *Especialização/Aperfeiçoamento*; *Mestrado*; *Doutorado*

Student Services: Academic counselling, Canteen, Cultural centre, Employment services, Foreign student adviser, Health services, Nursery care, Social counselling, Sports facilities

Student Residential Facilities: Yes

Special Facilities: Museum of Mineralogy. Museum of Science and Technology

Libraries: Total, c. 30,000 vols

Publications: Revista da Escola de Farmácia; Revista de Escola de Minas
Press or Publishing House: Editora da UFOP
Last Updated: 21/05/10

FEDERAL UNIVERSITY OF PARÁ
Universidade Federal do Pará (UFPA)
Rua Augusto Corréa 01, Prédio da Reitoria - 3° andar, Belém,
Pará 66075110
Tel: +55(91) 3211-1112
Fax: +55(91) 3211-1675
EMail: proplan@ufpa.br
Website: http://www.ufpa.br

Reitor: Carlos Edilson de Almeida Maneschy
Tel: +55(91) 211-1112 EMail: reitor@ufpa.br

Centres
Biological Sciences (Biological and Life Sciences); **Education** (Education; Pedagogy; Physical Education); **Exact and Natural Sciences** (Chemistry; Mathematics and Computer Science; Natural Sciences; Physics; Statistics); **Letters and Arts** (Advertising and Publicity; Art Education; Arts and Humanities; Journalism; Literature); **Philosophy and Human Sciences** (Arts and Humanities; Geography; History; Philosophy; Psychology); **Socio-Economic Studies** (Accountancy; Administration; Economics; Social Studies; Tourism); **Technology** (Engineering; Technology)

History: Founded 1957 and comprising previously existing faculties. Reorganized 1970-71 with a structure comprising centres for professional education. An autonomous institution, financially supported by the State and responsible to the Ministry of Education and Sports.

Academic Year: March to December (March-June; August-December)

Admission Requirements: Secondary school certificate and competitive entrance examination

Fees: None

Main Language(s) of Instruction: Portuguese

Degrees and Diplomas: *Bacharelado*: Accountancy (Contador); Administration (Técnico em Administração); Bio-chemical Analysis (Farmacêutico bioquímico Analista clínico); Dentistry (Odontólogo); Economics (Economista); Geology (Geólogo); Industrial Chemistry (Químico industrial); Social Work (Assistente social), 4 yrs; *Bacharelado*: Architecture (Arquitecto); Chemical Engineering (Engenheiro químico); Civil Engineering (Engenheiro civil); Electronic Engineering (Engenheiro electrônico); Electrotechnical Engineering (Engenheiro electrotécnico); Law; Mechanical Engineering (Engenheiro mecânico), 5 yrs; *Bacharelado*: Commercial Pharmacy (Farmacêutico comercial), 3 yrs; *Bacharelado*: Medicine (Médico), 6 yrs; *Licenciatura*: Education; Geography; History; Letters; Mathematics; Physics; Social Sciences, 4 yrs; *Licenciatura*: Library Science, 3 yrs; *Mestrado*; *Doutorado*

Publications: Revista de Ciências Jurídicas, Econômicas e Sociais; Revista de Ciências Médicas; Revista de Letras e Artes
Last Updated: 19/05/10

FEDERAL UNIVERSITY OF PARAÍBA
Universidade Federal da Paraíba (UFPB)
Cidade Universitária, Campus I, Castelo Branco III, João Pessoa,
Paraíba 58059900
Tel: +55(83) 3216-7150
Fax: +55(83) 3225-1901
EMail: gabinete@reitoria.ufpb.br
Website: http://www.ufpb.br

Reitor: Rômulo Soares Polari EMail: reitor@reitoria.ufpb.br

Pró-Reitor Administrativo: Múcio S. Souto
Tel: +55(83) 3216-7410, Fax: +55(83) 3216-7561
EMail: mucio@pra.ufpb.br

International Relations: Timothy D. Ireland
Tel: +55(83) 3216-7156 EMail: aai@reitoria.ufpb.br

Centres
Agrarian Sciences *(CCA - Aréia)* (Agriculture; Agronomy; Animal Husbandry); **Applied Social Sciences** *(CCSA)* (Accountancy; Administration; Economics; Library Science; Social Sciences); **Education** *(CE)* (Education; Educational and Student Counselling;

Pedagogy); **Exact and Natural Sciences** *(CCEN)* (Biology; Chemistry; Computer Science; Ecology; Geography; Mathematics; Natural Sciences; Physics); **Health and Biological Sciences** *(CCBS, Campina Grande)* (Biology; Child Care and Development; Health Sciences; Social and Preventive Medicine; Surgery); **Health and Rural Technology** *(CSTR, Patos)* (Agricultural Engineering; Forestry; Health Sciences; Mathematics and Computer Science; Natural Sciences; Veterinary Science); **Health Sciences** *(CCS)* (Dentistry; Health Sciences; Medicine; Nursing; Nutrition; Pharmacy; Physical Education); **Human Sciences, Letters and Arts** *(CCHLA)* (Arts and Humanities; Communication Studies; Fine Arts; History; Literature; Modern Languages; Music; Philosophy; Psychology; Social Sciences; Social Work; Tourism); **Humanities** *(CH, Campina Grande)* (Administration; Arts and Humanities; Economics; Education; Fine Arts; Geography; History; Literature; Media Studies; Social Sciences); **Law** *(CCJ)* (Law); **Science and Technology** *(CCT, Campina Grande)* (Agricultural Engineering; Chemical Engineering; Civil Engineering; Computer Engineering; Computer Science; Electrical Engineering; Geology; Industrial Design; Materials Engineering; Mathematics; Mechanical Engineering; Meteorology; Mining Engineering; Natural Sciences; Physics; Statistics; Technology); **Social and Juridical Science** *(CCJS, Souza)*; **Teacher Training** *(CFP, Cajazeiras)* (Geography; History; Literature; Mathematics; Natural Sciences; Pedagogy; Teacher Training); **Technology** (Architecture; Civil Engineering; Food Science; Industrial Chemistry; Materials Engineering; Mechanical Engineering; Production Engineering; Technology); **Technology Training** *(CFT, Bananeiras)* (Technology Education)

Further Information: Also Teaching Hospitals (João Pessoa and Campina Grande)

History: Founded 1955, incorporating Faculties established 1947-52, acquired present status 1960. Reorganized 1974 with a structure comprising Centres for professional education situated in 7 campuses.

Academic Year: March to December (March-June; August-December)

Admission Requirements: Secondary school certificate and entrance examination

Main Language(s) of Instruction: Portuguese

International Co-operation: With universities in Africa, Europe, Latin and North America, and Japan

Degrees and Diplomas: *Bacharelado*: Accountancy (Contador); Administration (Administração); Agronomy (Agrónomo); Animal Husbandry (Zootecnista); Architecture (Arquitecto); Art and Media; Biology; Chemistry; Computer Science; Dentistry (Odontologo); Economics (Economista); Engineering (Engenheiro); Geography; Industrial Chemistry (Químico industrial); Industrial Design (Desenho industrial); Law (Direito); Library Science (Biblioteconomio); Mathematics; Medicine (Médico); Music; Nursing (Enfermera); Nutrition (Nutrição); Pharmacy (Farmacêutico); Philosophy; Physics; Psychology (Psicólogo); Social Sciences; Technical Studies (Técnico); Tourism; *Licenciatura*: Art Education; Chemistry; Education; Geography; History; Letters; Mathematics; Philosophy; Physical Education; Physics; Science; Social Sciences; Statistics; *Mestrado*; *Doutorado*

Student Services: Academic counselling, Canteen, Cultural centre, Employment services, Foreign student adviser, Handicapped facilities, Health services, Language programs, Nursery care, Social counselling, Sports facilities

Libraries: Central Library, 132,346 vols; libraries of the campuses, 266,251

Publications: Informaçâo e Sociedade, Information and Science review *(biannually)*; Revista brasileira de Saúde, Health and Medicine Journal *(biannually)*; Revista brasiliera de Engenharia agrícola e ambiental, Agricultural and Environmental Engineering Journal *(biannually)*; Temas em Educaçâo, Education publication *(annually)*

Press or Publishing House: Editora Universitária UFPB
Last Updated: 25/05/10

Reitor: Zaki Akel Sobrinho
Tel: +55(41) 3360-5001 EMail: gabinetereitor@ufpr.br

Academies

Agrarian Sciences (Agronomy; Forestry; Veterinary Science); **Applied Social Sciences** (Accountancy; Economics; International Business; Management; Social Sciences); **Biological Sciences** (Anatomy; Biochemistry; Biological and Life Sciences; Botany; Cell Biology; Entomology; Genetics; Physical Education; Physiology; Zoology); **Education** (Education; Pedagogy); **Exact Sciences** (Chemistry; Computer Science; Mathematics; Natural Sciences; Physics; Statistics); **Health Sciences** (Dentistry; Health Sciences; Medicine; Nursing; Nutrition; Pharmacology); **Humanities, Arts and Languages** (Arts and Humanities; Communication Studies; History; Industrial Design; Library Science; Literature; Philosophy; Psychology; Social Sciences; Tourism); **Law** (Law); **Technology** (Architecture; Chemical Engineering; Civil Engineering; Electrical Engineering; Geography; Geology; Mechanical Engineering; Surveying and Mapping; Technology; Town Planning)

Research Centres

Administration (Administration); **Applied Psychology** (Psychology); **Bone Marrow Transplant Studies** (Medicine); **Dermatology and Infectology** *('Souza Araújo')* (Dermatology); **Economics** (Economics); **Education** *(CEPED)* (Education); **Electronic Microscopy** (Electronic Engineering); **Engineering** *(CESEC)* (Engineering); **Environment and Development** (Development Studies; Environmental Engineering); **Food Processing** (Food Technology); **Hydromechanics** *('Parigot de Souza')* (Mechanics); **Marine Biology** (Marine Biology); **Nephrology** (Nephrology); **Veterinary Medicine and Animal Husbandry** (Animal Husbandry; Veterinary Science)

Schools

Technical Studies (Accountancy; Computer Science; Nursing; Periodontics; Technology)

Further Information: Also Clinical Hospital

History: Founded 1911, became Federal University 1950. Reorganized 1974 with a structure comprising sectors for professional education. An autonomous institution, but financially supported by the State, and under the jurisdiction of the Ministry of Education and Sports.

Governing Bodies: Conselho de Ensino e Pesquisa; Conselho Universitário; Conselho de Curadores; Conselho Administrativo

Academic Year: March to December (March-June; August-December)

Admission Requirements: Secondary school certificate and entrance examination, or entrance through international exchange programme

Fees: None

Main Language(s) of Instruction: Portuguese

Degrees and Diplomas: *Bacharelado*: 4 yrs; *Licenciatura*: 4 yrs; *Mestrado*: a further 2-4 yrs; *Doutorado*: 2-4 yrs

Student Services: Academic counselling, Canteen, Cultural centre, Foreign student adviser, Handicapped facilities, Health services, Language programs, Sports facilities

Student Residential Facilities: For c. 110 women students

Special Facilities: Archaeology and Ethnology Museum of Paraná. University Theatre. Art Gallery. Experimental Farm Centre

Libraries: Central library, c. 279,410 vols

Publications: Acta Biologica of Paraná; Agrarian Department Journal; Anthropology; DENS, Odontology; Food Processing and Research Centre; Geosciences of Paraná; Journal of Human Sciences; Nerítica, Marine Biology; Pesticides; Pharmaceutic Rostrum; The College of Law Magazine; The Economics Magazine; The Language Magazine *(annually)*

Press or Publishing House: Editora da UFPR
Last Updated: 19/05/10

FEDERAL UNIVERSITY OF PARANÁ

Universidade Federal do Paraná (UFPR)
Rua XV de Novembro 1299, Reitoria, Centro, Curitibá,
Paraná 80060000
Tel: +55(41) 3360-5000 +55(41) 3360-5121
Fax: +55(41) 3360-5126
EMail: vicerei@ufpr.br
Website: http://www.ufpr.br

FEDERAL UNIVERSITY OF PELOTAS

Universidade Federal de Pelotas (UFPEL)
Campus Universitário, Capão do Leão, Pelotas,
Rio Grande do Sul 96010900
Tel: +55(53) 3275-7104
Fax: +55(53) 3275-9023
EMail: reitor@ufpel.edu.br
Website: http://www.ufpel.edu.br/

Reitor: Antonio Cesar Goncalves Borges
Tel: +55(53) 3275-7104, Fax: +55(53) 3275-7404

Pró-Reitor Administrativo: Francisco Carlos Gomes Luzzardi-Francisco Carlos Gomes Luzzardi
Tel: +55(53) 3275-7204, Fax: +55(53) 3275-7407

International Relations: Candida Beatriz Borges Zambrano
Tel: +55(53) 3225-4183, Fax: +55(53) 3222-0354
EMail: dipiprec@ufpel.edu.br

Centres
Engineering; Technological Development (Biotechnology; Geological Engineering; Hydraulic Engineering; Materials Engineering; Mineralogy; Petroleum and Gas Engineering)

Conservatories
Music (Music)

Faculties
Administration and Tourism; Agronomy (Eliseu Maciel) (Agronomy; Animal Husbandry); **Architecture and Town Planning** (Architecture; Building Technologies; Town Planning); **Education** (Education; Pedagogy) Director: Avelino da Rosa Oliveira; **Home Economics** (Food Science; Home Economics); **Law** (Law); **Medicine** (Medicine); **Meteorology** (Meteorology); **Nursing and Obstetrics** (Gynaecology and Obstetrics; Nursing); **Nutrition** (Nutrition); **Odontology** (Dentistry); **Veterinary Science** (Veterinary Science)

Higher Schools
Physical Education (Physical Education)

Institutes
Arts and Design (Cinema and Television; Dance; Graphic Design; Music; Musical Instruments; Theatre; Visual Arts); **Biology** (Anatomy; Biological and Life Sciences; Botany; Genetics; Microbiology; Parasitology; Pharmacology; Physiology; Zoology) Director: Gladis Aver Ribeiro; **Chemistry and Geoscience** (Chemistry; Earth Sciences); **Human Sciences** (Anthropology; Arts and Humanities; Economics; Geography; Geography (Human); History; Museum Studies); **Physics and Mathematics** (Computer Engineering; Computer Science; Mathematics; Physics); **Sociology and Political Science** (Philosophy; Political Sciences; Sociology)

History: Founded 1883 as Escola Imperial de Medicina Veterinária e Agricultura, became Escola de Agronomia Eliseu Maciel 1926, Universidade Rural do Sul 1960, Universidade Federal Rural do Rio Grande do Sul 1967, and acquired present title and status 1969. Under the jurisdiction of the Ministry of Education and Sports and financially supported by the Federal Government.

Governing Bodies: Conselho Universitário; Conselho Diretor; Conselho Coordenador de Pesquisa, Ensino e Extensão

Academic Year: March to December (March-July; August-December)

Admission Requirements: Secondary school certificate or equivalent and entrance examination

Fees: None

Main Language(s) of Instruction: Portuguese

International Co-operation: With universities in Spain, Mexico, Cuba and Belgium. Also participates in PCI and Alpha programmes

Degrees and Diplomas: Bacharelado: Agricultural Engineering; Biological Sciences; Chemistry; Clothing Production Administration; Computer Science; Economics; Food Science; Hospital and Hotel Administration; Meteorology; Music; Nursing and Obstetrics; Nutrition (Nutricionista); Painting; Physical Education; Social Sciences; Tourism; Visual Arts (Graphic Design; Painting; Sculpture; Engraving), 4 yrs; Bacharelado: Agronomy; Architecture and Urbanism (Arquitecto); Dentistry (Cirurgião dentista); Veterinary Medicine (Médico veterinário), 5 yrs; Bacharelado: Law; Medicine (Médico), 6 yrs; Licenciatura: Arts (Drawing and Graphic Computation); Arts (Music); Arts (Visual Arts); Biological Sciences; Chemistry; English Language and Literature; Mathematics; Pedagogy; Philosophy; Physical Education; Physics; Portuguese and French; Portuguese Language and Literature; Social Sciences; Spanish Language and Literature; Visual Arts, 4 yrs; Licenciatura: Geography; History, 5 yrs; Especialização/Aperfeiçoamento: Administration (Enterprise Management with Emphasis on Agribusiness); Arts (Cultural Patrimony Artifacts Conservation); Brazilian Contemporaneous Literature; Drawing (Computational Graphics); Education; Endodontics

and Dentistry; Environmental Chemistry; Environmental Law; Family Health; Food Science (Fruit and Vegetable Technology); Irrigated Rice Seeds Production); Mathematics; Musical Therapy; Nursing; Philosophy (Moral and Political Philosophy); Physical Education (Sports Training and School Physical Education); Seeds Science and Technology); Sociology and Politics; Surgery; Oral and Maxillofacial Traumatology; Work Safety Engineering, 12-18 months; Mestrado: Agro-Industrial Science and Technology; Agronomy (Plant Breeding; Fruit Production; Plant Production and Soils); Domestic Economy; Education; Endodontics and Dentistry; Epidemiology; Meteorology, 2-3 yrs; Mestrado: Odontology (Surgery, Oral and Maxillofacial Traumatology); Phytosanity (Entomology and Phytopatology); Plant Physiology; Seeds Science and Technology); Veterinary Medicine; Zootechnics, 12-18 months; Doutorado: Agricultural Biotechnology; Agro-Industrial Science and Technology; Agronomy; Epidemiology; Phytosanity (Entomology and Phytopathology); Seeds Science and Technology; Zootechnics, 4 yrs. Also Medical Residency, 2-3 yrs

Student Services: Academic counselling, Canteen, Handicapped facilities, Health services, Language programs, Nursery care, Social counselling, Sports facilities

Student Residential Facilities: Yes

Special Facilities: Leopoldo Gotuzzo Museum of Art, Carlos Ritter Museum of Natural Sciences

Libraries: Faculty and Institute Libraries: Agrarian Sciences, 34,412 vols; Science and Technology, 21,743 vols; Social Sciences, 42,273 vols; Law, 18,265 vols; Dentistry, 9,921 vols; Medicine, 9,038 vols; Physical Education, 3,332 vols; Agro-technical School, 9,418 vols

Publications: Cadernos de Educação (annually); Dissertatio (annually); História da Educação (annually); RAM - Revista Acadêmica de Medicina (annually); Revista Brasileira de Agrociência (biannually); Revista das Ciências Sociais (annually)
Last Updated: 21/05/10

FEDERAL UNIVERSITY OF PERNAMBUCO
Universidade Federal de Pernambuco (UFPE)
Avenida Professor Moraes Rego 1235, Campus Universitário,
Cidade Universitária, Recife, Pernambuco 5067091
Tel: +55(81) 2126-8000
Fax: +55(81) 2126-8029
EMail: alins@ufpe.br
Website: http://www.ufpe.br

Reitor: Amaro Henrique Pessoa Lins (2003-)
Tel: +55(81) 2126-8001, Fax: +55(81) 2126-8029
EMail: reitor@ufpe.br

International Relations: Suzana Monteiro
Tel: +55(81) 2126-8118 EMail: cci@ufpe.br

Centres
Applied Social Sciences (Accountancy; Actuarial Science; Administration; Economics; Secretarial Studies; Social Sciences; Social Work; Tourism); **Arts and Communication** (Architecture; Arts and Humanities; Communication Studies; Design; Fine Arts; Journalism; Music; Town Planning); **Biology** (Anatomy; Biochemistry; Biology; Biophysics; Botany; Embryology and Reproduction Biology; Genetics; Histology; Pharmacology; Physiology; Zoology); **Computer Science; Education** (Education; Educational Sciences; Philosophy of Education; Psychology); **Exact and Natural Sciences** (Chemistry; Mathematics; Mathematics and Computer Science; Natural Sciences; Physics; Statistics); **Health Sciences** (Dentistry; Health Sciences; Neurology; Nursing; Nutrition; Pathology; Pharmacy; Physical Therapy; Psychiatry and Mental Health; Social and Preventive Medicine; Tropical Medicine); **Juridical Sciences** (Law); **Philosophy and Human Sciences** (Arts and Humanities; Geography; History; Philosophy; Psychology; Social Sciences); **Technology and Geosciences** (Chemical Engineering; Civil Engineering; Electrical and Electronic Engineering; Geology; Industrial Engineering; Marine Science and Oceanography; Mechanical Engineering; Nuclear Engineering; Surveying and Mapping; Systems Analysis; Technology)

Further Information: Also Clinical Hospital

History: Founded 1946 as Universidade do Recife, incorporating Faculties established 1827-1941. Acquired present title 1965. Under the jurisdiction of the Ministry of Education and Sports and financially supported by the Federal Government.

Academic Year: March to December (March-June; August-December)

Admission Requirements: Secondary school certificate and entrance examination

Main Language(s) of Instruction: Portuguese

International Co-operation: With universities in France, Spain, Portugal, United Kingdom, Germany, The Netherlands, USA, Canada.

Degrees and Diplomas: *Bacharelado*: 3 1/2-4 yrs; *Licenciatura*: 3-4 yrs; *Especialização/Aperfeiçoamento*; *Mestrado*; *Doutorado*

Student Residential Facilities: Yes

Libraries: Central Library, c. 352,652 vols

Publications: Cadernos de Serviço Social *(biannually)*; Clio, History and Geography *(biennially)*; Econômia e Desenvolvimento *(biannually)*; Estudos de Sociologia *(biennially)*; Estudos Filosóficos *(biennially)*; Política Hoje *(biennially)*; Revista Administração Escolar *(biennially)*; Revista Arte e Comunicação *(biannually)*; Revista Biológica Brasílicas *(biennially)*; Revista de Geografia *(biennially)*; Revista de Oceanografia *(biennially)*; Revista Estudos Universitários *(biennially)*

Last Updated: 21/05/10

FEDERAL UNIVERSITY OF PIAUÍ
Universidade Federal do Piauí (UFPI)
Campus Universitário, Ministro Petrônio Portela, Bairro Ininga,
Teresina, Piauí 64049550
Tel: +55(86) 3215-5625 +55(86) 3215-5621
Fax: +55(86) 3215-5880
EMail: ufpinet@ufpi.br
Website: http://www.ufpi.br

Reitor: Luiz de Sousa Santos Júnior (2004-)
Tel: +55(86) 3237-1362

Centres
Agrarian Sciences (Agricultural Engineering; Agriculture; Soil Science; Veterinary Science; Zoology); **Education** (Education; Music; Visual Arts); **Health Sciences** (Biochemistry; Dentistry; Health Sciences; Medicine; Nursing; Nutrition; Pharmacology; Physiology); **Human Sciences and Letters** (Accountancy; Administration; Arts and Humanities; Economics; Geography; History; Law; Philosophy; Social and Community Services; Social Sciences); **Natural Sciences** (Archaeology; Biology; Chemistry; Computer Science; Mathematics; Natural Sciences; Physics; Statistics); **Technology** (Architecture; Electrical Engineering; Geology; Hydraulic Engineering; Mechanical Engineering; Production Engineering; Technology; Transport and Communications)

History: Founded 1973. Under the jurisdiction of the Ministry of Education and Sports and financially supported by the Federal Government.

Governing Bodies: Conselho Universitário

Academic Year: March to November (March-June; August-November)

Admission Requirements: Secondary school certificate and entrance examination

Fees: None

Main Language(s) of Instruction: Portuguese

Degrees and Diplomas: *Bacharelado*: Accountancy; Agricultural Technology; Agriculture; Art; Business Administration; Cattle-raising; Civil Engineering; Construction; Economics; Education; Law; Nursing; Nutrition; Rural Administration; Social Service; Veterinary Medicine, 2-8 yrs; *Bacharelado*: Dentistry, 4-6 yrs; *Bacharelado*: Medicine, 5-9 yrs; *Licenciatura*: Biology; Chemistry; Commerce; Education; Geography; History; Letters; Mathematics; Philosophy; Physical Education; Physics; Science; Social Studies, 2 1/2-8 yrs; *Mestrado*; *Doutorado*

Libraries: Central Library, c. 80,880 vols
Last Updated: 19/05/10

FEDERAL UNIVERSITY OF RIO DE JANEIRO
Universidade Federal do Rio de Janeiro (UFRJ)
Av. Pedro Calmon, n° 500 - Prédio da Reitoria - 2° andar, Cidade
Universitária, Rio de Janeiro, Rio de Janeiro 21941590
Tel: +55(21) 2562-2010
Fax: +55(21) 2560-1805
EMail: reitoria@reitoria.ufrj.br
Website: http://www.ufrj.br

Reitor: Aloisio Teixeira

Centres
Arts and Letters *(CLA)* (Architecture; Architecture and Planning; Arts and Humanities; Fine Arts; Music; Town Planning); **Health Sciences** (Health Sciences); **Legal and Economic Sciences** *(CCJE)* (Economics; Law); **Mathematics and Natural Sciences** *(CCMN)* (Mathematics; Natural Sciences); **Philosophy and Humanities** *(CFCH)* (Arts and Humanities; Communication Studies; Education; Philosophy; Psychology; Social Sciences; Social Work); **Technology** *(CT)* (Technology)

Institutes
Biological and Health Sciences *(ICB)* (Biological and Life Sciences; Health Sciences); **Biology** (Biology); **Biophysics** *(IBCCF)* (Biophysics); **Chemistry** *(IQ)* (Chemistry); **Child Care and Education** *(IPPMG)* (Child Care and Development; Education); **Economics** *(IE)* (Economics); **Geosciences** *(IGEO)* (Earth Sciences); **Gynaecology** (Gynaecology and Obstetrics); **Macromolecules** *(IMA)* (Physics); **Mathematics** (Mathematics; Statistics); **Microbiology** (Microbiology); **Neurology** (Neurology); **Nutrition** (Nutrition); **Philosophy and Social Sciences** *(IFCS)* (Philosophy; Social Sciences); **Physics** (Physics); **Pneumology and Pthisis** (Health Sciences); **Psychiatry** (Psychiatry and Mental Health); **Psychology** (Psychology); **Regional and Urban Planning Research** *(IPPUR)* (Architecture; Regional Planning; Town Planning)

Schools
Architecture and Urban Planning *(FAU)* (Architecture; Town Planning); **Business Administration** *(COPPEAD, Graduate)* (Business Administration); **Business Administration and Accountancy** (Accountancy; Business Administration); **Chemistry** *(EQ)* (Chemistry); **Communication** *(ECO)* (Communication Studies); **Dentistry** (Dentistry); **Education** (Education); **Engineering** *(COPPE, Graduate)* (Chemical Engineering; Civil Engineering; Computer Engineering; Electrical Engineering; Engineering; Marine Engineering; Materials Engineering; Mechanical Engineering; Metallurgical Engineering; Nuclear Engineering; Production Engineering; Systems Analysis; Transport Engineering); **Engineering** (Civil Engineering; Electrical Engineering; Electronic Engineering; Engineering; Graphic Arts; Hydraulic Engineering; Industrial Engineering; Marine Engineering; Mechanical Engineering; Metallurgical Engineering; Naval Architecture; Nuclear Engineering; Sanitary Engineering; Structural Architecture); **Fine Arts** *(EBA)* (Fine Arts); **Law** (Law); **Letters** (Arts and Humanities; Classical Languages; English; German; Latin; Linguistics; Literature; Oriental Languages; Philology; Portuguese; Slavic Languages); **Medicine** (Medicine); **Music** (Music); **Nursing** *(EEAN)* (Nursing); **Pharmacy** (Pharmacy); **Physical Education and Sports** *(EEFD)* (Physical Education; Sports); **Social Service** (Social Work)

Units
Community Health Studies *(NESC)* (Health Sciences); **Health Education** *(NUTES)* (Health Education); **National Museum Studies** (Anthropology; Botany; Entomology; Geology; Paleontology); **Natural Products Research** *(NPPN)* (Ecology)

Further Information: Also 3 University Hospitals: Clementino Fraga Filho, São Francisco and Maternity

History: Founded 1920, reorganized 1937 as Universidade do Brasil with autonomous status. Acquired present title 1965.

Governing Bodies: Conselho de Curadores

Academic Year: March to December (March-June; August-December)

Admission Requirements: Secondary school certificate and entrance examination

Main Language(s) of Instruction: Portuguese

International Co-operation: UNESCO Chair on Sustainable Development

Degrees and Diplomas: *Bacharelado*: Civics; Clarinet, 7 yrs; *Bacharelado*: Medicine, 6 yrs; *Bacharelado*: Psychology, 5 yrs; *Licenciatura*: 3-5 yrs; *Mestrado*; *Doutorado*: by thesis

Student Services: Health services, Nursery care, Sports facilities

Student Residential Facilities: Yes

Special Facilities: Museu Nacional. Observatório do Valongo

Libraries: Biblioteca Central e Sistema de Bibliotecas e Informações (SIBI), 3m. vols, 43 Libraries

Press or Publishing House: University Press

Last Updated: 19/05/10

FEDERAL UNIVERSITY OF RIO GRANDE DO NORTE

Universidade Federal do Rio Grande do Norte (UFRN)
Avenida Senador Salgado Filho 3000, Campus Universitário,
Lagoa Nova, Natal, Rio Grande do Norte 59078970
Tel: +55(84) 3215-3119
Fax: +55(84) 3215-3131
EMail: gabinete@reitoria.ufrn.br
Website: http://www.ufrn.br

Reitor: José Ivonildo do Rêgo (2003-)

Vice-Rector: Nilsen Carvalho FilhoFax: +55(84) 3215-3131

International Relations: Djalma Marinho Pereira
Tel: +55(84) 3215-3114, Fax: +55(84) 3215-3202
EMail: assint@reitoria.ufrn.br

Centres

Applied Social Sciences *(CCSA)* (Accountancy; Administration; Economics; Law; Library Science; Pedagogy; Social Work; Tourism); **Bioscience** (Biochemistry; Biology; Botany; Cell Biology; Ecology; Genetics; Marine Science and Oceanography; Parasitology; Physiology; Zoology); **Earth and Exact Sciences** *(CCET)* (Computer Engineering; Computer Science; Geology; Materials Engineering; Mathematics; Physics; Statistics); **Health Sciences** *(CCS)* (Dentistry; Gynaecology and Obstetrics; Medicine; Nursing; Nutrition; Pharmacy; Physical Education; Physical Therapy); **Higher Education** *(CERES - Regional)*; **Human Sciences, Letters and Arts** *(CCHLA)* (Arts and Humanities; Communication Studies; Fine Arts; Geography; History; Philosophy; Psychology; Social Sciences); **Natural Sciences** *(CB)* (Aquaculture; Biological and Life Sciences; Biomedicine); **Technology** (Architecture; Chemical Engineering; Civil Engineering; Electrical Engineering; Mechanical Engineering; Production Engineering; Technology; Textile Technology; Town Planning; Zoology)

Further Information: Also 4 University Hospitals

History: Founded 1958 incorporating previously existing Faculties. Became federal institution and acquired present title 1960. Reorganized 1968 - faculties became academic departments

Governing Bodies: Rector; Vice-Rector; Office for Planning and General Coordination

Academic Year: March to December (March-June; August-December)

Admission Requirements: Secondary school certificate and entrance examination

Fees: None

Main Language(s) of Instruction: Portuguese

International Co-operation: None

Degrees and Diplomas: *Bacharelado*: Administration; Aquaculture; Architecture and Urbanism; Documentation Techniques; Biomedicine; Social Communication; Biology; Accountancy; Computer Science; Economics; Social Sciences; Cooperativism; Law; Art Education; Physical Education; Ecology; Arts & Humanities; Mathematics; Medicine; Music; Nutrition; Odontology; Pedagogy; Psychology; Chemistry; Radiology; Social Services; Tourism; Zootechnology; Gynecology & Obstetrics; Civil Engineering; Mechanical Engineering; Electrical Engineering; Computer Engineering; Chemical Engineering; Production Engineering; Textile Engineering; Statistics; Pharmacy; Philosophy; Physics; Physiotherapy; Geography; *Mestrado*: Administration; Accountancy; Economics; Education; Social Services; Social Sciences; Modern Languages; Philosophy; Geography; Psycology; Architecture & Urbanism; Electrical Engineering; Chemical Engineering; Production Engineering; Sanitary Engineering; Dentistry & Odontology; Oral Pathology; Nursing; Health Sciences; Pharmacy; Sanitary Engineering; Computer Systems; Physics; Chemistry; Earth Sciences; Geophysics; Natural Science; Bioecological Aquaculture; Psychobiology; Genetics & Molecular Biology; Biochemistry; *Doutorado*: Education; Social Sciences; Electrical Engineering; Chemical Engineering; Physics; Materials Engineering; Geodynamics and Geophysics; Psychobiology; Oral Pathology; Health Sciences

Student Services: Academic counselling, Cultural centre, Employment services, Foreign student adviser, Health services, Language programs, Nursery care, Social counselling, Sports facilities

Student Residential Facilities: Yes, 8 dormitories

Special Facilities: Câmara Cascudo Anthropology Museum. Marine Biology Museum. Climatological Station. Fine Arts and Culture Centre. Television Channel

Libraries: 138,928 vols; 279,423 magazines; 4,431 Periodical subscriptions

Publications: Educação e Saúde, Medicine *(monthly)*; Educação em Questão, Education *(monthly)*; Vivência, CCHLA *(monthly)*

Press or Publishing House: Editora Universitária

Last Updated: 19/05/10

FEDERAL UNIVERSITY OF RIO GRANDE DO SUL

Universidade Federal do Rio Grande do Sul (UFRGS)
Avenida Paulo Gama 110, Térreo Faroupilha, Porto Alegre,
Rio Grande do Sul 90040060
Tel: +55(51) 3316-7000
EMail: ufrgs@ufrgs.br
Website: http://www.ufrgs.br

Reitor: Carlos Alexandre Netto EMail: reitor@gabinete.ufrgs.br

Faculties

Agronomy (Agriculture; Agronomy; Forestry; Horticulture; Plant and Crop Protection; Soil Science; Zoology); **Architecture** (Architecture; Design; Town Planning); **Dentistry** (Dentistry; Surgery); **Economics** (Accountancy; Actuarial Science; Economics; International Relations); **Education** (Curriculum; Education); **Law** (Law); **Library Science and Journalism** (Advertising and Publicity; Journalism; Library Science; Museum Studies; Public Relations); **Medicine** (Medicine); **Pharmacy** (Pharmacy); **Veterinary Science** (Veterinary Science)

Institutes

Arts (Music; Theatre; Visual Arts); **Basic Health Sciences** (Biochemistry; Microbiology; Pharmacology; Physiology); **Bioscience** (Biology; Biotechnology; Botany; Ecology; Genetics; Molecular Biology; Zoology); **Chemistry** (Chemistry); **Food Science and Technology** (Food Science; Food Technology); **GeoSciences** (Earth Sciences; Geography; Geology; Mineralogy; Paleontology; Petroleum and Gas Engineering); **Hydrology Research** (Water Science); **Informatics** (Information Sciences); **Letters** (Arts and Humanities); **Mathematics** (Mathematics); **Philosophy and Humanities** (Arts and Humanities; History; Philosophy; Political Sciences; Social Sciences); **Physics** (Physics) *Director*: Claúdio Scherer; **Psychology**

Schools

Administration; **Engineering** (Automation and Control Engineering; Civil Engineering; Computer Engineering; Engineering; Environmental Engineering; Physical Engineering); **Nursing** (Nursing); **Physical Education** (Physical Education)

History: Founded 1934 as Universidade do Pôrto Alegre, incorporating faculties established 1896-1910. Acquired present status and title 1965.

Governing Bodies: Conselho Universitário; Conselho de Coordenação de Ensino e da Pesquisa

Academic Year: March to November (March-June; August-November)

Admission Requirements: Secondary school certificate and entrance examination

Main Language(s) of Instruction: Portuguese

Degrees and Diplomas: *Bacharelado*: Accountancy; Actuarial Sciences; Biology; Business Administration; Chemistry; Computer Sciences; Drama; Economics; Geography; History; Journalism;

Letters; Library Science; Mathematics; Philosophy and Human Sciences; Physics; Plastic Arts; Administration; Agricultural Engineering; Dentistry; Nursing; Public Administration; Social Sciences; Stastistics, 4 yrs; *Bacharelado*: Architecture; Engineering; Geology; Pharmacy; Psychology; Veterinary Medicine; Music; Law, 5 yrs; *Bacharelado*: Medicine, 6 yrs; *Licenciatura*: Biology; Chemistry; Education; Gography; History; Letters; Mathematics; Philosophy; Physics; Science; Social Sciences, 4 yrs; *Licenciatura*: Physical Education, 3 yrs; *Mestrado*; *Doutorado*. Also teaching qualifications

Student Services: Academic counselling, Canteen, Language programs, Nursery care, Social counselling, Sports facilities

Student Residential Facilities: Yes

Special Facilities: Theatre. Cinema. Agronomic Experimental Station (Experimental Farm). Observatory

Libraries: Central Library, c. 405,000 vols; 28 branch libraries, c. 486,340

Publications: Aplicação Review *(annually)*

Press or Publishing House: Gráfica e Editora da Universidade
Last Updated: 19/05/10

FEDERAL UNIVERSITY OF RIO GRANDE FOUNDATION

Fundação Universidade Federal do Rio Grande (FURG)
Avenida Itália km 8, Carreiros, Rio Grande, Rio Grande 96201900
Tel: +55(53) 3233-6730
Fax: +55(53) 3230-2248
EMail: reitoria@furg.br
Website: http://www.furg.br

Reitor: Joao Carlos Brahm Cousin

Faculties
Law (Law); **Medicine** (Anatomy; Medicine; Pathology; Physiology; Surgery)

Institutes
Biology; **Economics, Administration and Accountancy** (Accountancy; Administration; Business Administration; Economics; Transport Management); **Education** (Behavioural Sciences; Education); **Human Sciences and Information**; **Letters and Arts** (Arts and Humanities; Linguistics; Literature; Modern Languages); **Mathematics, Statistics and Physics** (Mathematics; Physics; Statistics); **Oceanography** (Marine Science and Oceanography)

Schools
Chemistry and Food Science (Chemistry; Food Science; Food Technology); **Computer Science**; **Engineering**; **Nursing** (Nursing)

Further Information: Also University Hospital

History: Founded 1969 incorporating previously existing Faculties of Industrial Engineering, Law, Philosophy, Science and Letters, Political and Economic Sciences. A State Institution under the jurisdiction of the Ministry of Education and Sports.

Governing Bodies: Conselho Universitário

Academic Year: March to November (March-June; August-November)

Admission Requirements: Secondary school certificate and competitive entrance examination

Main Language(s) of Instruction: Portuguese

Degrees and Diplomas: *Bacharelado*: Accountancy; Biological Sciences; Business Administration; Chemical Engineering; Chemistry; Civil Engineering; Computer Engineering; Economy; Education; Food Engineering; Geography; History; Letters; Mathematics; Mechanical Engineering; Nursing and Midwifery; Oceanology; Physics; Plastic Arts, 4-5 yrs; *Bacharelado*: Law; Medical Sciences, 6 yrs; *Licenciatura*: 4-6 yrs; *Mestrado*: Applied Mathematics; Environmental Education; Food Engineering; Physical Engineering; Physiological Sciences; Science in Oceanography; *Doutorado*: Oceanography. The Licenciatura is awarded in the same fields as the Bacharelado

Student Services: Canteen, Nursery care, Sports facilities

Special Facilities: Museu Oceanográfico. Museu Antártico. University Radio. Oceanographic Vessel. Aquaculture Sea Station

Libraries: Central Library, c. 60,000 vols

Publications: Ambiente e Educação, Environmental Education; Artexto, Letters and Arts; Atlântica, Oceanography; Biblos, Library Science and History; Juris, Law; Momento, Education; Sinergia, Economy, Administration and Accountancy; Vitale, Health Sciences

Press or Publishing House: Editora e Gráfica da FURG
Last Updated: 17/06/10

FEDERAL UNIVERSITY OF RONDÔNIA FOUNDATION

Fundação Universidade Federal de Rondônia (UNIR)
BR 364 km 95, Porto Velho, Rondônia 78900500
Tel: +55(69) 2182-2100
EMail: reitoria@unir.br
Website: http://www.unir.br

Reitor: José Januário de Oliveira Amaral

Units
Applied Social Sciences (Accountancy; Administration; Economics; Law; Library Science); **Health Sciences** (Medicine; Nursing; Physical Education; Psychology); **Human Sciences** (Archaeology; Educational Sciences; Fine Arts; History; Modern Languages; Philosophy; Social Sciences); **Science and Technology** (Biology; Chemistry; Civil Engineering; Computer Science; Electrical Engineering; Geography; Mathematics; Physics)

Further Information: Also campuses in Ariquemes, Cacoal, Guajará-Mirim, Ji-Paraná, Porto Velho, Rolim de Moura e Vilhena

History: Founded 1982.

Admission Requirements: Secondary school certificate and entrance examination (vestibular)

Main Language(s) of Instruction: Portuguese

Degrees and Diplomas: *Bacharelado*: Business Administration, 5 yrs; *Licenciatura*: Humanities, 4 yrs; *Especialização/Aperfeiçoamento*; *Mestrado*; *Doutorado*

Student Services: Academic counselling, Canteen, Cultural centre, Foreign student adviser, Language programs, Social counselling

Libraries: Central Library

Publications: Cadernos de Criação, Humanities periodical *(quarterly)*; Presença, Geosciences periodical *(biannually)*
Last Updated: 17/06/10

FEDERAL UNIVERSITY OF RORAIMA

Universidade Federal de Roraima (UFRR)
Campus Paricarana, Av. Cap. Enê Garcêz, n° 2413 Bairro Aeroporto, Boa Vista, Roraima 69304-000
Tel: +55(95) 3621-3100 +55(95) 3621-3102
Fax: +55(95) 3621-3101
EMail: reitoria@ufrr.br
Website: http://www.ufrr.br

Reitor: Roberto Ramos Santos
Tel: +55(95) 3621-3102 EMail: robertoramos@ufrr.br

Centres
Administration and Law; **Agriculture**; **Biological and Health Sciences**; **Communication and Letters** (Journalism; Literature; Modern Languages); **Computer Science** (Computer Science); **Education**; **Health Sciences** (Medicine); **Human Sciences**; **Science and Technology**

Institutes
Geosciences (Geology)

History: Founded 1985.

Academic Year: March to December (March-June; August-December)

Admission Requirements: Secondary school certificate and entrance examination

Fees: None

Main Language(s) of Instruction: Portuguese

International Co-operation: Also participates in Unibral programme

Degrees and Diplomas: *Bacharelado*: 4 yrs; *Licenciatura*: 4 yrs; *Especialização/Aperfeiçoamento*: 1 yr; *Mestrado*

Student Services: Canteen, Health services, Language programs, Nursery care, Sports facilities

Special Facilities: University Television

Libraries: Central Library

Publications: Texts and Discussions, Journal of Philosophy and Social Sciences *(biannually)*

Press or Publishing House: Federal University of Roraima Press

Last Updated: 21/05/10

FEDERAL UNIVERSITY OF SANTA CATARINA

Universidade Federal de Santa Catarina (UFSC)

Caixa Postal 476, Campus Universitário, Trindade, Florianópolis,
Santa Catarina 88040900
Tel: +55(48) 3721-9000
Fax: +55(48) 3234-4069
EMail: gabinete@reitoria.ufsc.br
Website: http://www.ufsc.br

Reitor: Alvaro Toubes Prata (2008-) Tel: +55(48) 3331-9572

Centres

Agrarian Sciences (Agricultural Engineering; Agriculture; Animal Husbandry; Aquaculture; Food Science; Food Technology; Plant and Crop Protection; Rural Planning; Rural Studies); **Biological Sciences** (Anatomy; Biochemistry; Biological and Life Sciences; Pharmacology; Physiology); **Communication and Expression** (Arts and Humanities; Communication Studies; English; French; German; Italian; Journalism; Linguistics; Literature; Portuguese); **Education** (Child Care and Development; Documentation Techniques; Education; Library Science; Pedagogy); **Health Sciences** (Dentistry; Health Sciences; Medicine; Nursing; Nutrition; Pharmacy); **Law** (Law); **Philosophy and Human Sciences** (Anthropology; Arts and Humanities; Cultural Studies; Environmental Studies; Geography; Geography (Human); History; Philosophy; Political Sciences; Psychology; Social Sciences; Sociology); **Physics and Mathematics** (Chemistry; Mathematics; Physics); **Socio-Economic Studies** (Accountancy; Business Administration; Economics; Social Studies; Social Work); **Sports** (Sports); **Technology** (Architecture; Automation and Control Engineering; Chemical Engineering; Civil Engineering; Computer Science; Electrical Engineering; Environmental Engineering; Food Technology; Mechanical Engineering; Production Engineering; Safety Engineering; Sanitary Engineering; Statistics; Technology; Town Planning; Transport and Communications; Transport Engineering)

History: Founded 1960 and comprising previously existing Faculties. Reorganized 1970 with a structure comprising Centres for professional Education and Centres of basic Studies. An autonomous Institution financially supported by the State and responsible to the Ministry of Education and Sports.

Governing Bodies: Conselho Universitário; Conselho de Ensino, Pesquisa e Extensão

Academic Year: March to December (March-June; August-December)

Admission Requirements: Secondary school certificate and entrance examination

Main Language(s) of Instruction: Portuguese

Degrees and Diplomas: *Bacharelado*: 3-4 yrs; *Licenciatura*: 3-4 yrs; *Especialização/Aperfeiçoamento*; *Mestrado*; *Doutorado*

Student Services: Academic counselling, Canteen, Cultural centre, Employment services, Foreign student adviser, Health services, Nursery care, Social counselling, Sports facilities

Special Facilities: Anthropology Museum; Marine Museum. Biological Garden. Art Gallery. Movie Studies. Observatory

Libraries: Central Library and branch libraries, total, c. 310,000 vols

Publications: Biotemas; Ciências de Saúde *(biannually)*; Ciências Humanas; Fragmentos; Geosul; Ilha do Desterro; Katalysis; Perspectiva; Poité; Principia; Seqüência; Travessia *(biannually)*

Press or Publishing House: Editora da Universidade

Last Updated: 21/05/10

FEDERAL UNIVERSITY OF SANTA MARIA

Universidade Federal de Santa Maria (UFSM)

Avenida Roraima, n° 1000, Cidade Universitária, Bairro Camobi,
Santa Maria, Rio Grande do Sul 97105900
Tel: +55(55) 3220-8000
Fax: +55(55) 3220-8001
EMail: gabinete@adm.ufsm.br
Website: http://www.ufsm.br

Reitor: Felipe Martins Müller

Centres

Arts and Letters (Fine Arts; Industrial Design; Linguistics; Literature; Music; Philology; Visual Arts); **Education** (Educational Administration; Special Education; Teacher Training); **Health Sciences** (Dentistry; Medicine; Nursing; Occupational Therapy; Pharmacy; Physical Therapy; Public Health; Speech Therapy and Audiology); **Natural and Exact Sciences** (Biology; Chemistry; Geography; Mathematics; Meteorology; Physics); **Physical Education and Sports** (Physical Education; Sports); **Rural Sciences** (Agricultural Equipment; Agronomy; Animal Husbandry; Crop Production; Food Science; Forestry; Horticulture; Soil Science; Veterinary Science); **Social and Human Sciences** (Accountancy; Administration; Advertising and Publicity; Archiving; Economics; Information Management; Journalism; Law; Philosophy; Political Sciences; Psychology; Public Relations; Social Sciences; Sociology); **Technology** (Architecture; Chemical Engineering; Civil Engineering; Computer Science; Electrical Engineering; Hydraulic Engineering; Mechanical Engineering; Production Engineering; Technology; Town Planning)

History: Founded 1960, incorporating existing Faculties created since 1931. Reorganized 1970 with a structure comprising Centres for Professional Education. A State institution under the jurisdiction of the Ministry of Education and Sports.

Governing Bodies: Conselho Universitário; Conselho de Curadores; Conselho de Ensino, Pesquisa e Extensão

Academic Year: March to December (March-July; August-December)

Admission Requirements: Secondary school certificate and entrance examination

Main Language(s) of Instruction: Portuguese

International Co-operation: Participates in Alfa programme

Degrees and Diplomas: *Bacharelado*: Accountancy; Agronomy (Agrónomo); Animal Science (Zootecnista); Civil Engineering (Engenheiro Civil); Dentistry (Cirurgião dentista); Law; Veterinary Medicine (Médico veterinário), 5 yrs; *Bacharelado*: Biology; Chemistry; Communication; Economics; Education; Forestry Engineering (Engenheiro florestal); Geography; History; Industrial Chemistry; Letters; Mathematics; Music; Pharmacy (Farmacêutico); Philosophy; Physical Education; Plastic Arts; Speech Therapy and Audiology (Fonoaudiólogo), 4 yrs; *Bacharelado*: Medicine (Médico), 6 yrs; *Licenciatura*: Physics, 3 yrs; *Especialização/Aperfeiçoamento*; *Mestrado*: Agricultural Education; Agronomy; Animal Science; Education; Electrical Engineering; Mechanical Engineering; Rural Engineering; Veterinary Medicine, 2 yrs; *Doutorado*

Student Services: Academic counselling, Canteen, Health services, Language programs, Nursery care, Sports facilities

Student Residential Facilities: For 1,807 students

Special Facilities: History Museum 'Gama D'Eça'; University Hospital; TV and Radio Station; Exhibition and Events Centre

Libraries: 146,789 vols

Publications: Boletim de Pessoal; Caderno Adulto; Caderno de Educação Especial; Caderno de Ensino; Ensino e Pesquisa; Geografi; Pesquisa e Extensão; Revista Ciência Florestal; Revista Ciência Natura; Revista Ciência Rural; Revista Ciências Biomédicas; Revista do Centro de Tecnologia; Revista do Curso de Farmácia

Last Updated: 21/05/10

FEDERAL UNIVERSITY OF SÃO CARLOS

Universidade Federal de São Carlos (UFSCAR)

Rodovia Washington Luís, Km 235, Monjolinho, São Carlos,
São Paulo 13565905
Tel: +55(16) 3351-8111
Fax: +55(16) 3261-2081
EMail: reitoria@power.ufscar.br
Website: http://www.ufscar.br

Reitor: Targino de Araújo Filho
Tel: +55(16) 3260-8101, Fax: +55(16) 3261-4846
EMail: reitor@power.ufscar.br

Pró-Reitor de Administração: Manoel Fernando Martins
Tel: +55(16) 3260-8013, Fax: +55(16) 3261-5464
EMail: rss@power.ufscar.br

Centres

Agricultural Sciences (Agricultural Economics; Agricultural Engineering; Agriculture; Biotechnology; Environmental Studies; Natural Resources); **Education and Human Sciences** (Arts and Humanities; Communication Studies; Education; Educational Sciences; Information Sciences; Psychology; Social Sciences); **Exact Sciences and Technology** (Chemical Engineering; Chemistry; Civil Engineering; Computer Science; Materials Engineering; Mathematics; Natural Sciences; Physics; Production Engineering; Statistics; Technology); **Health Sciences and Biology** (Anatomy; Biology; Botany; Ecology; Genetics; Health Sciences; Nursing; Occupational Therapy; Pathology; Physical Education; Physical Therapy; Physiology)

Further Information: Also Campus in Araras

History: Founded 1960 as Universidade Federal de São Paulo, acquired present title 1968. A State institution under the jurisdiction of the Ministry of Education and Sports.

Governing Bodies: Conselho Universitário

Academic Year: March to December (March-June; August-December)

Admission Requirements: Secondary school certificate and entrance examination

Fees: None

Main Language(s) of Instruction: Portuguese

Degrees and Diplomas: *Bacharelado*: Engineering; Education; Social Sciences; Natural Sciences; Information Sciences; Mathematics and Computer Science; Perfoming Arts; Agriculture, 4-5 yrs; *Licenciatura*: 5 yrs; *Especialização/Aperfeiçoamento*; *Mestrado*: Engineering; Education; Social Sciences; Natural Sciences; Mathematics and Computer Science; Philosophy, 2-3 yrs; *Doutorado*: 4-5 yrs

Student Services: Academic counselling, Canteen, Cultural centre, Foreign student adviser, Handicapped facilities, Health services, Language programs, Nursery care, Social counselling, Sports facilities

Student Residential Facilities: For 378 students

Special Facilities: Ecological Park. Multimedia Studio

Libraries: Biblioteca Comunitária, 182,287 vols

Publications: Revista Univerciência

Press or Publishing House: Editora da Universidade Federal de São Carlos (EDUFSCar)

Last Updated: 21/05/10

FEDERAL UNIVERSITY OF SÃO JOÃO DEL REI

Universidade Federal de São João del Rei (UFSJ)
Campus Santo Antonio Centro, Praça Frei Orlando 170, Centro, São João del Rei, Minas Gerais 36307352
Tel: +55(32) 3379-2340 +55(32) 3379-2341
Fax: +55(32) 3379-2525
EMail: reitoria@ufsj.edu.br
Website: http://www.ufsj.edu.br/

Reitor: Helvecio Luiz Reis (2008-)

Departments

Biosystems Engineering (Bioengineering); **Computer Science** (Computer Science); **Economics** (Economics); **Educational Sciences** (Educational Sciences); **Electrical Engineering** (Electrical Engineering; Engineering); **Geography** (Geography); **Literature, Arts and Culture** (Cultural Studies; Journalism; Literature; Theatre); **Mathematics and Statistics** (Mathematics; Statistics); **Mechanical Engineering** (Mechanical Engineering); **Music** (Music; Music Education; Musical Instruments; Singing); **Natural Sciences** (Biology; Chemistry; Electrical Engineering; Mathematics; Mechanical Engineering; Physics); **Philosophy and Methods** (Philosophy); **Physical Education and Health** (Health Sciences; Physical Education); **Psychology** (Psychology); **Social Sciences** (Social Sciences); **Thermal and Fluid Sciences** (Thermal Engineering)

History: Founded 1986.

Main Language(s) of Instruction: Portuguese

Degrees and Diplomas: *Bacharelado*; *Especialização/Aperfeiçoamento*; *Mestrado*; *Doutorado*
Last Updated: 21/05/10

FEDERAL UNIVERSITY OF SÃO PAULO

Universidade Federal de São Paulo (UNIFESP)
Rua Botucatú 740, Vila Clementino, São Paulo, São Paulo 4023900
Tel: +55(11) 5549-7699
Fax: +55(11) 5576-4313
EMail: reitoria@unifesp.br
Website: http://www.unifesp.br

Reitor: Walter Manna Albertoni (2009-)
EMail: walter.albertoni@unifesp.br

Secretario Geral: Stephan Geocze
Tel: +55(11) 5549-7890 EMail: geocze@epm.br

International Relations: Benjamin Israel Kopelman, International Relations Coordinator
Tel: +55(11) 5576-4769 EMail: bkopelman@terra.com.br

Departments

Biochemistry (Biochemistry; Molecular Biology) *Head*: Misako U. Sampaio; **Biophysics** (Biophysics; Physical Chemistry) *Head*: Clovis Ryuichi Nakaie; **Dermatology** (Dermatology; Parasitology) *Head*: Maurício M.A. Alchorne; **Diagnostic Medical Imaging** (Medical Technology; Treatment Techniques) *Head*: Henrique Manoel Lederman; **Gynaecology and Obstetrics** (Gynaecology and Obstetrics) *Head*: Edmund C. Baracat; **Health Informatics** (Distance Education; Information Technology) *Head*: Daniel Sigulem; **Immunology, Microbiology, Parasitology** (Cell Biology; Immunology; Microbiology; Parasitology) *Head*: Nobuko Yoshida; **Medicine** (Cardiology; Endocrinology; Gastroenterology; Gerontology; Haematology; Medicine; Nephrology; Parasitology; Pneumology; Rheumatology) *Head*: Durval R. Borges; **Morphology** (Anatomy; Biology; Embryology and Reproduction Biology; Genetics; Histology) *Head*: Eduardo Katchburian; **Neurology, Neurosurgery** (Neurology) *Head*: João Antonio M. Nobrega; **Nursing** (Midwifery; Nursing; Public Health) *Head*: Lucila A.C. Vianna; **Ophthalmology** (Ophthalmology) *Head*: José Carlos Reys; **Orthopaedics and Traumatology** (Orthopaedics; Surgery) *Head*: José Laredo Filho; **Otorhinolaryngology and Human Communication Disorders** (Communication Disorders; Otorhinolaryngology; Speech Therapy and Audiology) *Head*: Jacy Perissinoto; **Paediatrics** (Community Health; Gastroenterology; Immunology; Nutrition; Paediatrics; Rheumatology) *Head*: Ulysses Fagundes Neto; **Pathology** (Anatomy; Ethics; Law; Pathology; Surgery) *Head*: Osvaldo Giannotti Filho; **Pharmacology** (Endocrinology; Pharmacology) *Head*: Antônio José Lapa; **Physiology** (Physiology) *Head*: Luiz Eugênio A.M. Mello; **Preventive Medicine** (Epidemiology; Social and Preventive Medicine; Statistics) *Head*: José Eduardo C. Moncau; **Psychiatry** (Psychiatry and Mental Health; Psychology) *Head*: Luiz Antonio N. Martins; **Psychobiology** (Biology; Pharmacology) *Head*: Sérgio Tufik; **Surgery** (Anaesthesiology; Plastic Surgery; Surgery; Urology) *Head*: Enio Buffolo

Further Information: Also Hospital São Paulo, Hospital Municipal 'Vereador José Stropoli' and Hospital Geral de Pirajussara. Specific courses and programmes for graduate students

History: Founded 1938 as Escola Paulista de Medicina. Acquired present status and title 1994.

Governing Bodies: Conselho Universitário

Academic Year: February to December (February-June; August-December)

Admission Requirements: Secondary school certificate and entrance examination

Fees: None

Main Language(s) of Instruction: Portuguese

Accrediting Agencies: Ministry of Education of Brazil

Degrees and Diplomas: *Bacharelado*: Biomedical Sciences; Medicine; Nursing; Optical Technology; Speech Therapy and Audiology, 3-6 yrs; *Bacharelado*: Medicine; *Mestrado*: Epidemiology; Human Communication Disorders; Medical Basic Sciences; Medical Sciences; Nursing; Nutrition; Rehabilitation, a further 3 yrs; *Doutorado*: Human Communication Disorders; Medical Basic Sciences; Medical Sciences; Nursing; Nutrition; Rehabilitation, a further 3 yrs following Mestrado

Student Services: Academic counselling, Canteen, Cultural centre, Health services, Nursery care, Social counselling, Sports facilities

Student Residential Facilities: For 55 Men and 38 Women students

Special Facilities: Museu Histórico da Escola Paulista de Medicina. Museu do Índio

Libraries: Biblioteca Regional de Medicina, 12,723 vols. Databanks

Publications: Folia Médica (quarterly); Revista do Hospital São Paulo, Official Journal of the Sociedade paulista para Desenvolvimento da Medicina (annually)

Student Numbers 2009-2010: Total: c. 14,000
Last Updated: 28/01/10

FEDERAL UNIVERSITY OF SERGIPE
Universidade Federal de Sergipe (UFS)
Cidade Universitária Prof. "José, Aloísio de Campos, Av. Marechal Rondon, s/n Jardim Rosa Elze, São Cristovão, Sergipe 49100000
Tel: +55(79) 3212-6600
Fax: +55(79) 3212-6474
EMail: proad@ufs.br
Website: http://www.ufs.br

Reitor: Josué Modesto dos Passos Subrinho
Tel: +55(79) 3212-6404 EMail: reitor@ufs.br

Centres
Applied Social Sciences (Accountancy; Administration; Economics; Law; Social and Community Services; Social Sciences); **Biological and Health Sciences** (Biological and Life Sciences; Dentistry; Health Sciences; Medicine; Nursing; Nutrition; Physical Education); **Education and Humanities** (Arts and Humanities; Education; Geography; History; Philosophy; Psychology; Social Sciences); **Exact Sciences and Technology** (Chemical Engineering; Chemistry; Civil Engineering; Information Sciences; Mathematics; Natural Sciences; Physics; Statistics; Technology)

History: Founded 1967. Reorganized 1978 with a structure comprising centres for professional education. An autonomous institution financially supported by the State and responsible to the Ministry of Education and Sports.

Governing Bodies: Conselho Universitário; Conselho do Ensino e da Pesquisa

Academic Year: March to December (March-June; August-December)

Admission Requirements: Secondary school certificate and entrance examination

Main Language(s) of Instruction: Portuguese

Degrees and Diplomas: *Bacharelado*: Accountancy; Administration; Economics, 6 yrs; *Bacharelado*: Agriculture; Chemical Engineering (Engenheiro químico); Civil Engineering (Engenheiro civil); Law; Nursing (Enfermeiro); Psychology, 5 yrs; *Bacharelado*: Biology; Chemistry; Geography; Industrial Chemistry (Químico industrial); Physics; Social Service, 4 yrs; *Bacharelado*: Computer Science, 3 1/2 yrs; *Bacharelado*: Dentistry (Cirurgião dentista), 4 1/2 yrs; *Bacharelado*: Social Science, 3 yrs; *Licenciatura*: Biology; Chemistry; Education; Geography; History; Letters; Mathematics; Physics, 4 yrs; *Especialização/Aperfeiçoamento*: 2 yrs; *Mestrado*: a further 2 yrs; *Doutorado*

Student Residential Facilities: Yes

Special Facilities: Museu de Antropologia

Libraries: Central Library, c. 79,130 vols

Publications: Geonordeste
Last Updated: 20/05/10

FEDERAL UNIVERSITY OF THE BAY OF BAHIA
Universidade Federal do Recôncavo da Bahia (UFRB)
Campus Universitario da UFRB, Cruz das Almas, Bahia 44380-000
Tel: +55(75) 3621-2350
Fax: +55(75) 3621-9095
EMail: gabinete@urfb.edu.br
Website: http://www.ufrb.edu.br

Reitor: Paulo Gabriel Nacif

Centres
Agrarian, Environmental and Biological Sciences (Agronomy; Biology; Business Administration; Fishery; Forestry; Veterinary Science; Zoology); **Arts, Humanities and Literature** (Cachoeira); **Exact and Technological Sciences**; **Health Sciences** (Santo

Antônio de Jesus) (Nursing; Nutrition; Psychology); **Teacher Training** *(Amargosa)*

History: Founded 2005.

Main Language(s) of Instruction: Portuguese

Degrees and Diplomas: *Bacharelado*; *Licenciatura*; *Mestrado*; *Doutorado*
Last Updated: 19/05/10

FEDERAL UNIVERSITY OF THE PAMPAS
Universidade Federal do Pampa (UNIPAMPA)
Rua Melanie Granier, 48, Bagé, Rio Grande do Sul 96400-500
Tel: +55(53) 3247-4549
EMail: reitoria@unipampa.edu.br
Website: http://www.unipampa.edu.br

Rector: Maria Beatriz Luce
Tel: +55(53) 3247-4549 EMail: reitora@unipampa.edu.br

Pro-Rector, Administration: Éverton Bonow
Tel: +55(53) 3241-7483 EMail: everton.bonow@unipampa.edu.br

Campuses
Alegrete (Civil Engineering; Computer Science; Electrical Engineering; Mechanical Engineering); **Bagé** (Arts and Humanities; Chemical Engineering; Chemistry; Computer Engineering; Energy Engineering; English; Environmental Engineering; Food Technology; Literature; Mathematics; Physics; Portuguese; Production Engineering; Spanish); **Caçapava do Sul; Dom Pedrito** (Agricultural Business; Bioengineering; Zoology); **Itaqui** (Agricultural Engineering; Agronomy); **Jaguarão; Santana do Livramento; São Borja** (Advertising and Publicity; Journalism; Political Sciences; Social and Community Services; Social Sciences); **São Gabriel** (Agricultural Engineering; Biological and Life Sciences; Biotechnology; Environmental Management; Forest Biology; Forestry); **Uruguaiana**

History: Founded 2008.

Main Language(s) of Instruction: Portuguese

Degrees and Diplomas: *Licenciatura*; *Especialização/Aperfeiçoamento*: Literature and Languages; *Mestrado*
Last Updated: 17/06/10

FEDERAL UNIVERSITY OF THE STATE OF RIO DE JANEIRO
Universidade Federal do Estado do Rio de Janeiro (UNIRIO)
Avenida Pasteur 296, Urca, Rio de Janeiro, Rio de Janeiro 22290240
Tel: +55(21) 2543-5615
Fax: +55(21) 2543-5615
EMail: planejamento@unirio.br
Website: http://www.unirio.br

Reitora: Malvina Tania Tuttman EMail: reitora@unirio.br

Centres
Arts and Letters (Art Education; Arts and Humanities; Modern Languages; Music; Theatre); **Biological and Health Sciences** (Biological and Life Sciences; Health Sciences; Medicine; Nursing; Nutrition); **Humanities** (Archiving; Arts and Humanities; Documentation Techniques; Educational Sciences; Law; Library Science; Museum Studies); **Technological Sciences** (Technology)

History: Founded 1969 as Federação das Escolas Federais Isoladas do Estado Guanabara. Acquired present status and title 1979. Under the jurisdiction and financially supported by the Federal Government.

Governing Bodies: Conselho Universitário; Conselho de Ensino e Pesquisa; Conselho de Curadores

Academic Year: March to December (March-June; August-December)

Admission Requirements: Secondary school certificate and entrance examination

Main Language(s) of Instruction: Portuguese

Degrees and Diplomas: *Bacharelado*: 3-6 yrs; *Licenciatura*: 3-6 yrs; *Especialização/Aperfeiçoamento*; *Mestrado*: a further 2 yrs; *Doutorado*

Libraries: Central Library, c. 12,400 vols; other libraries, total, c. 43,000 vols

Publications: Catálogo da Produção Técnica-Científica e Artística (*annually*)

Press or Publishing House: Printing Office
Last Updated: 20/05/10

FEDERAL UNIVERSITY OF THE STATE OF RIO DE JANEIRO

Universidade Federal Fluminense (UFF)
Rua Miguel de Frias 9, 7° Andar, Icaraí, Niterói,
Rio de Janeiro 24220008
Tel: +55(21) 2629-5000
Fax: +55(21) 2629-5207
EMail: gabinete@gar.uff.br
Website: http://www.uff.br

Reitor: Roberto de Souza Salles
Tel: +55(21) 2629-5205 +55(21) 2629-5206 EMail: reitor@uff.br

Vice-Reitor: Emmanuel Paiva de Andrade
Tel: +55(21) 2629-5236 EMail: vicereitor@uff.br

Centres
Applied Social Studies (Accountancy; Administration; Economics; Education; Law; Social and Community Services; Social Work; Tourism); **General Studies** (Anthropology; Arts and Humanities; Biology; Chemistry; Classical Languages; Communication Studies; Earth Sciences; History; Literature; Mathematics; Modern Languages; Philosophy; Physics; Political Sciences; Psychology; Social Studies); **Medical Science** (Dentistry; Health Sciences; Medicine; Nursing; Nutrition; Pharmacy; Veterinary Science); **Technology** (Architecture and Planning; Chemical Engineering; Civil Engineering; Computer Science; Engineering; Industrial Engineering; Mechanical Engineering; Production Engineering; Town Planning)

Faculties
Administration, Accountancy and Tourism (Accountancy; Administration; Tourism); **Dentistry** (Dentistry); **Economics** (Economics); **Education** (Education); **Law** (Law); **Medicine** (Medicine); **Nutrition** (Nutrition); **Pharmacy** (Pharmacy); **Veterinary Science** (Veterinary Science)

Higher Schools
Ildefonso Bastos Borges *(Founded as Bom Jesus do Itabapoana)* (Agriculture); **Nilo Peçanha** (Agriculture)

Institutes
Arts and Social Communication (Advertising and Publicity; Archiving; Arts and Humanities; Cinema and Television; Communication Studies; Cultural Studies; Documentation Techniques; Journalism; Library Science; Marketing; Media Studies); **Biology** (Biology; Cell Biology; Immunology; Marine Biology; Molecular Biology; Neurosciences); **Biomedicine** (Biomedicine); **Chemistry** (Chemistry); **Computer Science** (Computer Science); **Earth Sciences** (Earth Sciences; Geography; Geology; Geophysics); **Humanities and Philosophy** (Anthropology; Arts and Humanities; History; Philosophy; Political Sciences; Psychology; Social Sciences; Sociology); **Languages and Literature** (Classical Languages; Literature; Modern Languages); **Mathematics** (Mathematics); **Physics** (Physics)

Schools
Architecture and Town Planning (Architecture; Town Planning); **Engineering** (Chemical Engineering; Engineering; Industrial Engineering; Mechanical Engineering; Metallurgical Engineering; Production Engineering; Telecommunications Engineering); **Nursing** (Nursing); **Social Service** (Social and Community Services)

Units
Advanced Studies *('José Veríssimo', Oriximiná - Pará)* (Development Studies); **Veterinary Science** *(Iguaba)* (Veterinary Science)

Further Information: Four campuses and other unities in Niterói, and in 16 other municipalities of the state of Rio de Janeiro. Also University Hospital and reference centre for AIDS. Portuguese courses for foreign students. Study abroad programmes

History: Founded 1960 as Federal University of the State of Rio de Janeiro, acquired present title 1965. Reorganized 1983. An autonomous institution.

Governing Bodies: Conselho Universitário; Conselho de Curadores; Conselho de Ensino e Pesquisa

Academic Year: March to December (March-July; August-December)

Admission Requirements: Secondary school certificate and entrance examination

Main Language(s) of Instruction: Portuguese

Accrediting Agencies: Ministry of Education and Sports

Degrees and Diplomas: *Bacharelado*: 4-6 yrs; *Especialização/ Aperfeiçoamento*: 2 yrs; *Mestrado*: Anthropology; Architecture and Town Planning; Cardiology; Chemistry; Civil Engineering; Civil and Population Defence; Computer Science; Dental Pathology; Dentistry; Earth Sciences (Geochemistry); Economy; Education; Experimental Pathology; Environmental Science; Geography; History; International Relations; Letters and Literature; Management Systems; Marine Biology and Geophysics; Mathematics; Mechanical Engineering; Medical Science; Metallurgical Engineering; Microbiology and Applied Parasitology; Neurology; Nursing; Neuro-Immunology; Organic Chemistry; Paediatrics and Child Studies; Physics; Political Science; Production Engineering; Psychology; Science of Arts; Science of Information; Social Communication; Social Policies; Sociology and Law; Telecommunications Engineering; Veterinary Clinic and Surgery; Veterinary Hygiene, 2 yrs; *Doutorado*: Anthropology; Civil Engineering; Computer Science; Earth Sciences; Geochemistry; Economy; Education; Experimental Pathology; Geography; History; Letters and Literature; Marine Biology; Marine Geology and Geophysics; Mechanical Engineering; Metallurgical Engineering; Neurology; Neuro-Immunology; Organic Chemistry; Pathological Anatomy; Physics; Science of Information; Social Communication; Veterinary Clinic and Surgery; Veterinary Hygiene, 4 yrs. Also Teaching Degrees in all fields, 4-5 yrs

Student Services: Academic counselling, Canteen, Cultural centre, Foreign student adviser, Health services, Nursery care, Social counselling, Sports facilities

Special Facilities: Art-Cinema. Theatre. National Symphony Orchestra. String Quartet. UFF Choir. UFF Ancient Music Group. Audiovisual Centre

Libraries: Libraries of the Centres and Faculties, total, c. 492,000 vols

Publications: Antropolitica, Anthropology and Social Sciences Journal; Confluências, Sociology and Law Journal; Contracampo, Social Communication Journal; Econômia, Economic Sciences Journal; Engevista, Engineering Sciences Journal; Gênero, Gender Studies Journal; Gragoatá, Language and Literature Journal; Medicina do Esporte, Sports Medicine Journal; Movimento, Education Faculty Journal; Poiesis, Science of Arts Journal; Revista de Ciências Médicas, Medical Sciences Journal; Revista de Ciências Veterinárias, Veterinary Sciences Journal; Revista de Psicologia, Psychology Journal; Tempo, History Journal

Press or Publishing House: EDUFF - Editora Universitária da UFF - University Publisher; NIU - Núcleo Imprensa Universitária - University Press
Last Updated: 19/05/10

FEDERAL UNIVERSITY OF THE TRIÂNGULO MINEIRO

Universidade Federal do Triângulo Mineiro (UFTM)
Rua Frei Paulino 30, Abadia, Uberaba, Minas Gerais 38025180
Tel: +55(34) 3318-5004
Fax: +55(34) 3312-1487
EMail: reitoria@reitoria.uftm.edu.br
Website: http://www.uftm.edu.br

Reitor: Virmondes Rodrigues Júnior (2010-)

Institutes
Biological and Natural Sciences; **Education and Arts**; **Exact Sciences and Technology** (Chemical Engineering; Civil Engineering; Electrical Engineering; Environmental Engineering; Mathematics; Mechanical Engineering; Physics; Production Engineering); **Health Sciences** (Biomedicine; Nursing; Nutrition; Occupational Therapy; Physical Therapy); **Human and Social Sciences** (Geography; History; Literature; Psychology; Social and Community Services)

History: Founded 1953 as Faculdade de Medicina do Triângulo Mineiro. Acquired present status and title 2005.

Main Language(s) of Instruction: Portuguese

Degrees and Diplomas: *Bacharelado*; *Especialização/Aperfeiçoamento*; *Mestrado*; *Doutorado*
Last Updated: 19/05/10

FEDERAL UNIVERSITY OF THE VALLEY OF SAN FRANCISCO

Universidade Federal do Vale do Sao Francisco
Av. José de Sá Maniçoba, S/N -Centro, Petrolina,
Pernambuco 56304-917
EMail: reitoria@univasf.edu.br
Website: http://www.univasf.edu.br

Reitor: José Weber Freire Macedo

Courses
Administration (Administration); **Archaeology and Heritage Preservation**; **Engineering** (Agricultural Engineering; Civil Engineering; Computer Engineering; Electrical Engineering; Environmental Engineering; Mechanical Engineering; Production Engineering); **Medicine** (Medicine); **Nursing** (Nursing); **Psychology**; **Veterinary Science** (Veterinary Science); **Zoology** (Zoology)

History: Founded 2002.

Main Language(s) of Instruction: Portuguese

Degrees and Diplomas: *Bacharelado*; *Mestrado*
Last Updated: 19/05/10

FEDERAL UNIVERSITY OF THE VALLEYS OF JEQUITINHONHA AND MUCURI

Universidade Federal dos Vales do Jequitinhonha e Mucuri (UFVJM)
Rua da Glória 187 Centro, Diamantino, Mato Grosso 39100000
Tel: +55(38) 3531-1811 +55(38) 3531-1024
Fax: +55(38) 3531-1024 +55(38) 3531-1030
EMail: fafeod@fafeod.br
Website: http://www.fafeod.br

Reitor: Pedro Ângelo Almeida Abreu

Faculties
Agrarian Sciences (Agronomy; Forest Management; Zoology); **Applied and Exact Social Sciences** (Accountancy; Administration; Economics; Mathematics; Social and Community Services); **Biology and Health Sciences** (Biology; Dentistry; Nursing; Nutrition; Pharmacy; Physical Education; Physical Therapy); **Exact Sciences and Technology**; **Human Sciences** (English; Geography; History; Literature; Pedagogy; Spanish; Tourism)

Institutes
Humanities (Geography; History; Literature; Pedagogy; Tourism); **Science and Technology** (Technology); **Science and Technology of Mucuri** (Civil Engineering; Hydraulic Engineering; Production Engineering)

History: Founded 1953 as Faculdade Federal de Odontologia de Diamantina. Became Faculdades Federais Integradas de Diamantina 2002. Acquired present status and title 2005.

Main Language(s) of Instruction: Portuguese

Degrees and Diplomas: *Bacharelado*; *Licenciatura*; *Especialização/Aperfeiçoamento*; *Mestrado*
Last Updated: 19/05/10

FEDERAL UNIVERSITY OF TOCANTINS

Universidade Federal do Tocantins
Av. NS 15, ALCNO 14, Bloco IV, 109 Norte, Palmas, Tocantins
Tel: +55(63) 3232- 8012
Fax: +55(63) 3232-8039
EMail: proad@uft.edu.br
Website: http://www.site.uft.edu.br/

Reitor: Alan Barbiero EMail: reitor@uft.edu.br

Courses
Accountancy; **Administration** (Administration); **Architecture and Town Planning** (Architecture; Town Planning); **Computer Science** (Computer Science); **Economics** (Economics); **Environmental Engineering**; **Food Engineering** (Food Technology); **Law** (Law); **Pedagogy**; **Social Communication**

Further Information: Also campuses at Araguaína, Arraias, Gurupi, Miracema, Porto Nacional and Tocantinópolis

History: Founded 2000.

Main Language(s) of Instruction: Portuguese

Degrees and Diplomas: *Bacharelado*; *Especialização/Aperfeiçoamento*; *Mestrado*; *Doutorado*
Last Updated: 19/05/10

FEDERAL UNIVERSITY OF UBERLÂNDIA

Universidade Federal de Uberlândia (UFU)
Avenida Engenheiro Diniz 1178, 3° Andar, Martins, Uberlândia,
Minas Gerais 38401136
Tel: +55(34) 3239-4810
Fax: +55(34) 3235-0099
EMail: celso@reito.ufu.br
Website: http://www.ufu.br

Reitor: Alfredo Júlio Fernandes Neto Tel: +55(34) 3239-4810

Faculties
Accountancy (Accountancy); **Architecture, Town Planning and Design**; **Arts, Philosophy and Social Sciences** (Music; Philosophy; Social Sciences; Theatre; Visual Arts); **Business and Administration** (Public Administration); **Chemical Engineering** (Chemical Engineering); **Civil Engineering** (Civil Engineering); **Computer Science**; **Dentistry**; **Education**; **Electrical Engineering** (Electrical Engineering); **Integrated Sciences** *(Pontal)* (Administration; Biology; Chemistry; Geography; History; Mathematics; Pedagogy; Physics; Production Engineering); **Law** (Law); **Mathematics**; **Medicine** (Medicine; Nursing; Nutrition); **Physical Education**; **Veterinary Science** (Veterinary Science)

Institutes
Agrarian Sciences (Agricultural Engineering; Environmental Engineering; Plant and Crop Protection; Plant Pathology; Soil Science); **Biology**; **Biomedicine** (Biomedicine; Immunology; Microbiology; Parasitology; Pharmacology; Physiology); **Chemistry** (Chemistry); **Economics** (Economics; Finance; International Relations); **Genetics and Biochemistry** (Biochemistry; Genetics); **Geography** (Geography); **History**; **Literature and Linguistics** (Linguistics; Literature); **Physics** (Physics); **Psychology**

Further Information: Three campuses. Also University Hospitals

History: Founded 1974, incorporating previously existing faculties. Recognized as a federal institution 1978.

Governing Bodies: Conselho Universitário

Academic Year: March to December (March-June; August-December)

Admission Requirements: Secondary school certificate or equivalent and entrance examination

Main Language(s) of Instruction: Portuguese

Degrees and Diplomas: *Bacharelado*: Accountancy; Administration; Economics; Law; Psychology, 4-7 yrs; *Bacharelado*: Architecture and Town Planning; Arts; Biological Sciences; Computer Sciences; Decoration; Dentistry; Education; Engineering; Medicine; Music; Philosophy; Scenic Arts; Veterinary Medicine; Visual Communication, 4-9 yrs; *Licenciatura*: Art; Design and Plastic Arts; Education; Geography; History; Letters; Music; Physical Education; Science; Social Studies, 2-7 yrs; *Especialização/Aperfeiçoamento*; *Mestrado*; *Doutorado*

Student Services: Canteen, Cultural centre, Employment services, Sports facilities

Special Facilities: Museu do Índio. Museu de Minerais e Rochas. Museu de Biociências. Art Gallery

Libraries: Total, c. 157,100 vols

Publications: Centro de Ciências Biomédicas; Economia; Letras e Letras; Psicologia e Trânsito

Press or Publishing House: Editora da Universidade
Last Updated: 20/05/10

FEDERAL UNIVERSITY OF VIÇOSA
Universidade Federal de Viçosa (UFV)
Avenida Peter Henry Rolfs S/n, Reitoria Campus Universitário,
Viçosa, Minas Gerais 36570-000
Tel: +55(31) 3899-2328
EMail: reitoria@ufv.br
Website: http://www.ufv.br

Reitor: Luiz Claudio Costa Tel: +55(31) 3899-2796

Centres
Agriculture (Agricultural Economics; Agricultural Engineering;
Agriculture; Forestry; Plant Pathology; Soil Science; Zoology);
Biological and Health Sciences (Biochemistry; Biological and Life
Sciences; Biology; Botany; Health Sciences; Medicine; Micro-
biology; Molecular Biology; Nursing; Nutrition; Physical Education;
Veterinary Science; Zoology); **Exact Sciences and Technology**
(Architecture; Chemistry; Civil Engineering; Computer Science;
Electrical Engineering; Food Technology; Mathematics; Physics;
Production Engineering; Town Planning); **Human Sciences, Let-
ters and Arts** (Accountancy; Administration; Arts and Humanities;
Business and Commerce; Economics; Education; Geography;
History; Home Economics; Law; Linguistics)
History: Founded 1922 as College of Agriculture, became Uni-
versidade Rural do Estado de Minas Gerais 1948 by State decree.
Reorganized as a federal University with present title 1969.
Governing Bodies: Conselho Universitário; Conselho de Ensino,
Pesquisa e Extensão
Academic Year: February to December (February-July; August-
December)
Admission Requirements: Secondary school certificate and
entrance examination
Main Language(s) of Instruction: Portuguese
Degrees and Diplomas: *Bacharelado*: 4-5 yrs; *Especialização/
Aperfeiçoamento*; *Mestrado*: a further 1-2 yrs; *Doutorado*: 2-4 yrs
Student Residential Facilities: For 1,382 students
Special Facilities: Museum. Art Gallery. Biological Garden
Libraries: Central Library, 243,997 vols
Publications: Revista Ação Ambiental; Revista Arvore; Revista
Brasileira de Ciência do Solo; Revista Brasileira de Zootecnia;
Revista Ceres; Revista do Direito; Revista Economia Rural; Revista
Engenharia na Agricultura; Revista Glaukus; Revista Mineira de
Educação Fisica; Revista Oikos; Revista Planta Daninha
Press or Publishing House: Divisão de Grafica Universitária
Last Updated: 20/05/10

FOUNDATION OF EDUCATION FOR WORK OF MINAS GERAIS
Fundação de Educação para o Trabalho de Minas Gerais (UTRAMIG)
Avenida Afonso Peña 3400, Cruzeiro, Belo Horizonte,
Minas Gerais 30130009
Tel: +55(31) 3263-7500
EMail: vicepresidencia@utramig.mg.gov.br
Website: http://www.utramig.mg.gov.br/

Presidente: Rosane Marques Crespo Costa
EMail: presidencia@utramig.mg.gov.br

Courses
Biology (Biology); **Chemistry** (Chemistry); **Mathematics** (Mathe-
matics); **Physics** (Physics); **Technology**
History: Founded 1965. Acquired present title 1972.
Main Language(s) of Instruction: Portuguese
Degrees and Diplomas: *Licenciatura*
Last Updated: 18/06/10

GARANHUNS HIGHER EDUCATION QUANGO
Autarquia do Ensino Superior de Garanhuns (AESGA)
Avenida Caruaru 508, São José, Garanhuns, PE 55295380
Tel: +55(87) 3761-1596
Fax: +55(87) 3761-1596 +55(81) 3762-6691
EMail: aesga@faga.edu.br
Website: http://www.aesga.edu.br

Presidente: Eliane Simões Vilar (1995-)

Faculties
Administration Sciences *(FAGA)* (Administration; Business
Administration; Health Administration; Marketing; Tourism);
Applied Social and Human Sciences *(FAHUG)* (Modern Lan-
guages; Secretarial Studies); **Law** *(FDG)* (Law)

Programmes
Graduate Studies
History: Founded 1976
Main Language(s) of Instruction: Portuguese
Degrees and Diplomas: *Bacharelado*; *Especialização/Aperfeiçoa-
mento*
Last Updated: 09/03/10

HIGHER EDUCATION CENTRE OF ARCOVERDE
Centro de Ensino Superior de Arcoverde (AESA/CESA)
Rua Gumercindo Cavalcanti, 420 Prédio São Cristovão, Arcoverde,
PE 56500000
Tel: +55(87) 821-0574 +55(87) 821-0530
Fax: +55(87) 821-1579
EMail: aesa@aesa-cesa.br
Website: http://www.aesa-cesa.br

Diretora: Maria da Penha de Queiroz Moraes (1997-)

Courses
Biology (Biology); **Geography**; **History**; **Literature** (English;
Literature; Portuguese); **Mathematics** (Mathematics); **Physical
Education**

Faculties
Nursing *(FENFA)* (Nursing)
History: Founded 1969.
Degrees and Diplomas: *Licenciatura*
Last Updated: 22/03/10

HIGHER EDUCATION CENTRE OF CONSELHEIRO LAFAIETE
Centro de Ensino Superior de Conselheiro Lafaiete (CES-CL)
Rua Lopes Franco 1001, Conselheiro Lafaiete,
Minas Gerais 36400-000
Tel: +55(31) 3762-0840
Fax: +55(31) 3761-2223
EMail: ces@ces-cl.edu.br
Website: http://www.ces-cl.edu.br

Diretor Geral: Antônio Efigênio Antunes

Faculties
Applied Social Sciences *(FACESA)* (Social Work); **Economic
Science** *(FACEL)*; **Electrical Engineering** *(FACEC)* (Electrical
Engineering)
History: Founded 2000.
Main Language(s) of Instruction: Portuguese
Degrees and Diplomas: *Bacharelado*
Last Updated: 25/03/10

HIGHER EDUCATION CENTRE OF THE SAN FRANCISCO VALLEY
Centro de Ensino Superior do Vale São Francisco (CESVASF)
Rua Coronel Trapiá 202, Térreo Centro, Belém do São Francisco,
PE 56440000
Tel: +55(81) 3876-1248
EMail: cesvasf@cesvasf.com.br
Website: http://www.cesvasf.com.br/

Diretor: Rosimary Torres Alves

Courses
Biology; **Geography** (Geography); **Graduate Studies**; **History**
(History); **Literature**; **Mathematics** (Mathematics); **Physics**
History: Founded 1984.
Main Language(s) of Instruction: Portuguese

Degrees and Diplomas: *Licenciatura*; *Especialização/Aperfeiçoamento*
Last Updated: 22/04/10

HIGHER EDUCATION UNION OF NOVA MUTUM

União de Ensino Superior de Nova Mutum (UNINOVA)
Av. Das Arapongas 1384N, Centro, Nova Mutum, MT 78450000
Tel: +55(65) 3308-2010
Fax: +55(65) 3308-2224
EMail: uninova@uninova.edu.br
Website: http://uninova.edu.br

Diretor: Dario Almudi Neto

Courses
Administration (Accountancy; Administration); **Agronomy**; **Modern Languages** (English; Literature; Modern Languages; Portuguese); **Pedagogy** (Pedagogy)

History: Founded 1994.

Degrees and Diplomas: *Bacharelado*; *Licenciatura*; *Especialização/Aperfeiçoamento*
Last Updated: 09/06/10

INSTITUTE OF EDUCATION OF GOIANA

Instituto Superior de Educação de Goiana (ISEG)
Rua Poco Rei, s/n, Centro, Goiana, PE 55900-000
Tel: +55(81) 3626-0517
EMail: ffpg@uol.com.br
Website: http://www.ffpg.edu.br

Diretor: Lourenço Benedito Bezerra

Courses
Literature (Literature); **Teacher Training** (Teacher Training)
Degrees and Diplomas: *Licenciatura*
Last Updated: 27/09/10

INSTITUTE OF EDUCATION OF RIO DE JANEIRO

Instituto Superior de Educação do Rio de Janeiro (ISERJ)
Rua Clarimundo de Melo 847, Quintino, Rio de Janeiro,
Rio de Janeiro 21311280
Tel: +55(21) 2597-9513
Fax: +55(21) 2557-9513
EMail: presidencia@faetec.rj.gov.br

Diretora Geral: Sandra Regina Pinto dos Santos

Courses
Education and Teacher Training

History: Founded 1998 as institute of the Fundação de Apoio à Escola Técnica (FAETEC).

Degrees and Diplomas: *Licenciatura*
Last Updated: 29/11/07

INSTITUTE OF EDUCATION OF TRÊS RIOS

Instituto Superior de Educação Três Rios
Rua Marechal Deodoro, 117, Centro, Três Rios, RJ 25802-220
Tel: +55(24) 2251-3099 +55(24) 2252-4651 +55(24) 2252-0698
Fax: +55(24) 2255-4574
EMail: ise.tresrios@faetec.rj.gov.br
Website: http://www.faetec.rj.gov.br/

Courses
Teacher Training (Teacher Training)
Degrees and Diplomas: *Licenciatura*
Last Updated: 28/09/10

INSTITUTE OF TECHNOLOGY IN COMPUTER SCIENCE OF RIO DE JANEIRO

Instituto Superior de Tecnologia em Ciências da Computação do Rio de Janeiro (IST-RIO)
Rua Clarimundo de Melo, 847, Quintino Bocaiúva, Rio de Janeiro,
RJ 21311-280
Tel: +55(21) 2332-4048
Fax: +55(21) 2332-4048
EMail: ist-rio@faetec.rj.gov.br
Website: http://www.faetec.rj.gov.br/ist-rio

Courses
Graduate Studies (Information Technology); **Undergraduate Studies** (Systems Analysis)

Degrees and Diplomas: *Tecnólogo*. Also Postgraduate Diploma.
Last Updated: 28/09/10

INTEGRATED FACULTIES OF ADAMANTINA

Faculdades Adamantinenses Integradas (FAI)
Rua Nove de Julho 730/40, Centro, Adamantina, SP 17800000
Tel: +55(18) 3522-1002
Fax: +55(18) 3522-1002
EMail: fai@fai.com.br
Website: http://www.fai.com.br

Diretor: Roldão Simione (1997-)

Areas
Agrarian Sciences; **Biological Sciences** (Biology; Dentistry; Food Science; Gerontology; Nursing; Nutrition; Pharmacy; Physical Education; Physical Therapy; Veterinary Science); **Exact Sciences** (Computer Science; Data Processing; Industrial Design; Mathematics); **Human Sciences** (Administration; Advertising and Publicity; Economics; Geography; History; Journalism; Law; Literature; Pedagogy; Psychology; Social and Community Services; Special Education)

History: Founded 1967. Acquired present status 1999.
Main Language(s) of Instruction: Portuguese

Degrees and Diplomas: *Bacharelado*; *Especialização/Aperfeiçoamento*
Last Updated: 30/06/10

INTEGRATED FACULTIES OF MINEIROS

Faculdades Integradas de Mineiros (FIMES)
Rua 22 Esquina c/ Avenida 21 s/n, Setor Aeroporto, Mineiros,
GO 75830000
Tel: +55(62) 3661-1970
Fax: +55(62) 3661-1970
EMail: fimes@fimes.edu.br
Website: http://www.fimes.edu.br/

Diretora: Ita de Fátima Assis EMail: ita@fimes.edu.br

Institutes
Administration and Computer Science (Administration; Information Sciences; Law; Marketing; Public Administration); **Agricultural Science**; **Education** (Art Education; Literature; Pedagogy)

History: Founded 1993.
Main Language(s) of Instruction: Portuguese

Degrees and Diplomas: *Bacharelado*; *Licenciatura*; *Especialização/Aperfeiçoamento*
Last Updated: 23/06/10

MILITARY ENGINEERING INSTITUTE

Instituto Militar de Engenharia (IME)
Praça General Tibúrcio 80, Praia Vermelha, Rio de Janeiro,
RJ 22290-270
Tel: +55(21) 2546-7080
Website: http://www.ime.eb.br/

Comandante: Amir Elias Abdalla Kurban

Courses
Graduate Studies (Chemical Engineering; Computer Engineering; Electrical and Electronic Equipment and Maintenance; Engineering; Materials Engineering; Mechanical Engineering; Nuclear

Engineering; Surveying and Mapping; Transport Engineering); **Undergraduate Studies** (Chemical Engineering; Computer Engineering; Construction Engineering; Electrical Engineering; Materials Engineering; Mechanical Engineering; Surveying and Mapping)

History: Founded 1811 as Academia Real Militar. Succesively changed its name to Imperial Academia Militar (1822), Academia Militar da Corte (1832), Escola Militar (1840) and Escola Central (1858). The school of military engineering started its activities in 1930. Changed name to Escola Técnica do Exército in 1933. Merged with Instituto Militar de Tecnologia and acquired present title 1959. Started admitting civilians in 1964 and women in 1997.

Degrees and Diplomas: *Bacharelado*; *Especialização/Aperfeiçoamento*; *Mestrado*; *Doutorado*
Last Updated: 22/09/10

MUNICIPAL HIGHER EDUCATION INSTITUTE OF ASSIS

Instituto Municipal de Ensino Superior de Assis (IMESA)
Avenida São Cristovão 635, Vila Rodrigues, Assis, SP 19800000
Tel: +55(18) 3322-6744
Fax: +55(18) 3322-6219
EMail: femasecr@femanet.com.br
Website: http://www.fema.edu.br/
Diretora: Márcia Valéria Seródio Carbone (1998-)

Courses
Administration; **Advertising** (Advertising and Publicity); **Computer Science** (Computer Science); **Data Processing** (Data Processing); **Industrial Chemistry** (Chemistry; Industrial Chemistry); **Journalism**; **Law**; **Mathematics**; **Nursing**; **Systems Analysis**
History: Founded 1988.
Main Language(s) of Instruction: Portuguese
Degrees and Diplomas: *Bacharelado*; *Licenciatura*; *Especialização/Aperfeiçoamento*
Last Updated: 15/06/10

MUNICIPAL INSTITUTE OF HIGHER EDUCATION OF CATANDUVA

Instituto Municipal de Ensino Superior de Catanduva (IMES)
Avenida Daniel Dalto s/n – (Rodovia Washington Luis - SP 310 - Km 382), Catanduva, São Paulo 15800970
Tel: +55(17) 3531-2200
Fax: +55(17) 3531-2205
EMail: secretaria@fafica.br
Website: http://www.fafica.br
Diretora: Cibelle Rocha Abdo

Courses
Accountancy (Accountancy); **Advertising** (Advertising and Publicity); **Biology**; **Computer Science** (Computer Science); **Dentistry** (Dentistry); **Geography** (Geography); **History** (History); **Journalism** (Journalism); **Law** (Law); **Literature** (Literature); **Mathematics** (Mathematics); **Pedagogy** (Pedagogy); **Physiotherapy**
History: Founded 1967 as Faculdade de Filosofia, Ciências e Letras de Catanduva. Acquired present status and title 2000.
Main Language(s) of Instruction: Portuguese
Degrees and Diplomas: *Bacharelado*; *Especialização/Aperfeiçoamento*
Last Updated: 14/06/10

MUNICIPAL INSTITUTE OF HIGHER EDUCATION OF MATAO

Instituto Matonense Municipal de Ensino Superior (IMMES)
Av. Habib Gabriel, 1360 Residencial Olivio Benassi, Matao, São Paulo
Tel: +55(16) 3384-1851
Fax: +55(16) 3384-1851
EMail: immes@immes.br
Website: http://www.immes.edu.br/

Diretor General: Carlos Henrique Gileno (2007-)
EMail: carlosgileno@immes.edu.br

Courses
Administration (Administration; Marketing); **Law**
History: Founded 1998.
Main Language(s) of Instruction: Portuguese
Degrees and Diplomas: *Bacharelado*
Last Updated: 15/06/10

MUNICIPAL INSTITUTE OF HIGHER EDUCATION OF SÃO MANUEL

Instituto Municipal de Ensino Superior de São Manuel (IMESSM)
Rua Quintino Bocaiuva s/n, Distrito Aparecida, São Manuel, São Paulo 18650000
Tel: +55(14) 6841-3766
Fax: +55(14) 6841-3766
EMail: secretaria@imessm.edu.br
Website: http://www.imessm.edu.br
Diretor: Marcelo Totti

Courses
Literature (Literature); **Pedagogy**; **Psychology** (Psychology)
History: Founded 1972 as Faculdade de Filosofia, Ciências e Letras de São Manuel. Acquired present status and title 1982.
Main Language(s) of Instruction: Portuguese
Degrees and Diplomas: *Bacharelado*; *Especialização/Aperfeiçoamento*
Last Updated: 14/06/10

MUNICIPAL UNIVERSITY CENTRE OF SÃO JOSÉ

Centro Universitário Municipal de São José (USJ)
Rua Koesa, 305 - Kobrasol, São José, Santa Catarina 88102-310
Tel: +55(48) 3247-6071
EMail: reitoria@usj.edu.br
Website: http://www.usj.edu.br
Reitor: Solange Sprandel da Silva

Courses
Accountancy (Accountancy); **Administration** (Administration); **Graduate Studies** (Civil Security); **Pedagogy**; **Religious Studies**
History: Founded 2005.
Main Language(s) of Instruction: Portuguese
Degrees and Diplomas: *Bacharelado*; *Licenciatura*; *Especialização/Aperfeiçoamento*
Last Updated: 15/06/10

MUNICIPAL UNIVERSITY OF SÃO CAETANO DO SUL

Universidade Municipal de São Caetano do Sul (IMES)
Avenida Goiás 3400, Barcelona, São Caetano do Sul, São Paulo 09550051
Tel: +55(11) 4239-3200
Fax: +55(11) 4239-3275
EMail: jovanov@uscs.edu.br
Website: http://www.uscs.edu.br
Reitor: Silvio Augusto Minciotti

Graduate Schools
Technology (Environmental Management; Finance; Human Resources; Information Technology; Management)

Schools
Business (Accountancy; Administration; Economics); **Communication**; **Computer Science** (Computer Science); **Education** (Pedagogy); **Health Sciences**; **Law**
History: Founded 1967. Acquired present status 2004.
Main Language(s) of Instruction: Portuguese
Degrees and Diplomas: *Tecnólogo*; *Bacharelado*; *Licenciatura*; *Especialização/Aperfeiçoamento*; *Mestrado*; *Doutorado*
Last Updated: 10/05/10

NATIONAL INSTITUTE OF EDUCATION FOR THE DEAF

Instituto Nacional de Educação de Surdos (INES)
Rua das Laranjeiras, 232, Laranjeiras, Rio de Janeiro,
RJ 22240-001
Tel: +55(21) 2285-7546 +55(21) 2285-7949
Fax: +55(21) 2285-7692
EMail: dirge@ines.gov.br
Website: http://www.ines.gov.br/

Courses
Pedagogy (Pedagogy)
Degrees and Diplomas: *Licenciatura*
Last Updated: 22/09/10

NATIONAL SCHOOL OF STATISTICS

Escola Nacional de Ciências Estatísticas (ENCE)
Rua André Cavalcanti 106, Bairro Santa Teresa, Rio de Janeiro,
Rio de Janeiro 20231050
Tel: +55(21) 2142-4677
Fax: +55(21) 2142-0501
EMail: ence@ibge.gov.br
Website: http://www.ence.ibge.gov.br/

Coordenador Geral: Sérgio da Costa Côrtes

Courses
Environmental and Territorial Management *(Postgraduate Lato Sensu)* (Environmental Management); **Population Studies and Social Research** *(Postgraduate Stricto Sensu)*; **Statistics** (Statistics)
History: Founded 1956
Main Language(s) of Instruction: Portuguese
Degrees and Diplomas: *Bacharelado*; *Especialização/Aperfeiçoamento*; *Mestrado*
Last Updated: 18/06/10

PALHOÇA MUNICIPAL FACULTY

Faculdade Municipal de Palhoça (FMP)
Rua Maria Theodora Haeming, 48, Passa Vinte, Palhoça 88133-155
Tel: +55(48) 3341-0616 +55(48) 3342-1833
EMail: fmp@fmpsc.edu.br
Website: http://www.fmpsc.edu.br

Diretora executiva: Mariah Terezinha Nascimento Pereira
EMail: mariahnascimento@terra.com.br

Courses
Administration; Pedagogy
History: Founded 2005.
Main Language(s) of Instruction: Portuguese
Degrees and Diplomas: *Bacharelado*: 4 yrs
Last Updated: 05/07/10

PRESIDENT KENNEDY INSTITUTE OF HIGHER EDUCATION - TRAINING CENTRE FOR EDUCATION PROFESSIONALS

Instituto de Educação Superior Presidente Kennedy - Centro de Formação de Profissionais de Educação
Rua Jaguarari 2100, Natal, Rio Grande do Norte 59064-500
Tel: +55(84) 3232- 6231
Fax: +55(84) 3232-6238
EMail: ifesp@rn.gov.br
Website: http://www.kennedy.rn.gov.br/

Diretor: Onilson Rodrigues de Oliveira

Courses
Literature (Literature); **Mathematics** (Mathematics); **Teacher Training** (Teacher Training)
History: Founded 1965 as Instituto de Educação Presidente Kennedy succeeding the Instituto de Educação de Natal. Acquired present name 2001.
Main Language(s) of Instruction: Portuguese
Degrees and Diplomas: *Licenciatura*
Last Updated: 17/06/10

PROFESSOR FRANCO MONTORO MUNICIPAL FACULTY

Faculdade Municipal Professor Franco Montoro (FMPFM)
Rua dos Estudantes s/n - Bairro Cachoeira de Cima, Mogi-Guaçu,
São Paulo 13840970
Tel: +55(19) 3891-5303
EMail: fmpfm@fmpfm.edu.br
Website: http://www.fmpfm.edu.br/

Diretor: Estéfano Vizconde Veraszto

Courses
Administration (Administration); **Chemical Engineering** (Chemical Engineering); **Computer Science** (Computer Science); **Environmental Engineering**; **Nutrition** (Nutrition); **Psychology** (Psychology)
History: Founded 1998.
Main Language(s) of Instruction: Portuguese
Degrees and Diplomas: *Bacharelado*
Last Updated: 05/07/10

PROFESSOR PAULO NEVES DE CARVALHO SCHOOL OF GOVERNMENT

Escola de Governo Professor Paulo Neves de Carvalho (EG)
Alameda das Acácias, n° 70, São Luís, Belo Horizonte,
Minas Gerais 31275-150
Tel: +55(31) 3448-9593
Fax: +55(31) 3448-9613
EMail: eg.fjp@fjp.mg.gov.br
Website: http://eg.fjp.mg.gov.br/

Diretor Geral: Afonso Henriques Borges Ferreira

Courses
Public Administration (Public Administration)
Further Information: Also Av. Brasil campus.
History: Founded 1992
Degrees and Diplomas: *Bacharelado*; *Especialização/Aperfeiçoamento*; *Mestrado*
Last Updated: 18/06/10

REGIONAL UNIVERSITY OF BLUMENAU

Universidade Regional de Blumenau (FURB)
Rua Antonio da Veiga 140, Victor Konder, Blumenau,
Santa Catarina 89012900
Tel: +55(47) 3321-0200
Fax: +55(47) 3322-8818
EMail: proen@furb.br
Website: http://www.furb.br

Reitor: Eduardo Deschamps **EMail:** edudes@furb.br

Centres
Applied Social Sciences (Accountancy; Administration; Economics; Leisure Studies; Tourism); **Communication and Human Sciences** (Advertising and Publicity; Communication Studies; Fashion Design; History; Religion; Secretarial Studies; Social Sciences; Social Work); **Education Sciences** (Arts and Humanities; Education; English; Pedagogy; Portuguese; Spanish); **Health Sciences** (Biochemistry; Dentistry; Health Sciences; Medicine; Pharmacy; Physical Education; Physical Therapy; Psychology); **Juridical Sciences** (Law); **Natural and Exact Sciences** (Biology; Chemistry; Computer Science; Mathematics; Natural Sciences); **Technology** (Architecture; Chemical Engineering; Civil Engineering; Electrical Engineering; Electronic Engineering; Forest Management; Forestry; Mechanical Engineering; Production Engineering; Technology; Telecommunications Engineering; Town Planning)

Institutes
Environmental Research (Environmental Studies); **Social Research** (Social Studies); **Technological Research** (Technology)

Laboratories
Informatics (Computer Science); **Languages** (Modern Languages)
Further Information: Also Psychology Clinic; Physiotherapy Ambulatory; University Ambulatory and 4 Cancer Clinics

History: Founded 1968. Under the supervision of the Fundação Universidade Regional de Blumenau.

Governing Bodies: Conselho Universitário; Conselho de Ensino, Pesquisa e Extensão

Academic Year: January to December (January-June; August-December)

Admission Requirements: Secondary school certificate and entrance examination

Main Language(s) of Instruction: Portuguese

International Co-operation: With universities in Germany, Chile, Argentina, Portugal, USA; Spain

Degrees and Diplomas: *Tecnólogo*: Data Processing Technology (Tecnólogo em Processamento de Dados), 3 yrs; *Bacharelado*: Accountancy; Administration; Economics, 4 yrs; *Bacharelado*: Chemical Engineering (Engenheiro químico); Civil Engineering (Engenheiro civil); Law, 5 yrs; *Bacharelado*: Odontology, 41/2 yrs; *Licenciatura*: Art Education; Biology; Chemistry; Education; Letters; Mathematics; Physical Education, 4 yrs; *Licenciatura*: Biological Sciences, 4 1/2 yrs; *Especialização/Aperfeiçoamento*; *Mestrado*; *Doutorado*

Student Services: Academic counselling, Canteen, Foreign student adviser, Health services, Language programs, Social counselling, Sports facilities

Student Residential Facilities: None

Libraries: Central Library, c. 380,000 vols

Publications: Dynamisis: Revista Tecno-científica *(quarterly)*; Revista de Divulgação Cultural *(3 per annum)*; Revista de Estudos Ambientais *(3 per annum)*; Revista de Negócios *(quarterly)*; Revista Jurídica *(biennially)*

Last Updated: 07/05/10

REGIONAL UNIVERSITY OF CARIRI

Universidade Regional do Cariri (URCA)
Rua Coronel Antônio Luiz 1161, Pimenta, Crato, Ceará 63100000
Tel: +55(88) 3102-1212
Fax: +55(88) 3102-1271
EMail: urca@urca.br
Website: http://www.urca.br

Reitor: Plácido Cidade Nuvens EMail: gabinete@urca.br

Centres
Applied Social Studies (Social Studies); **Health Sciences** (Health Sciences); **Humanities** (Arts and Humanities); **Science and Technology** (Mathematics and Computer Science; Natural Sciences; Technology)

Institutes
Ecology (Ecology); **Socio-Cultural Studies and Research** (Social Studies); **Technology** (Technology)

History: Founded 1986.

Academic Year: February to December (February-June; August-December)

Admission Requirements: Secondary school certificate and entrance examination

Main Language(s) of Instruction: Portuguese

Degrees and Diplomas: *Bacharelado*: 4 yrs; *Licenciatura*: 4 yrs; *Especialização/Aperfeiçoamento*; *Mestrado*

Special Facilities: Natural History Museum; Paleontology Museum. House of English, French and Portuguese Cultures

Libraries: Central Library; Luiz de Carvalho Maia Library; Guilherme Capaneme Library

Last Updated: 07/05/10

RUBENS LARA FACULTY OF TECHNOLOGY

Faculdade de Tecnológia Rubens Lara (FATEC/BS)
Avenida Bartolomeu de Gusmão, 110, Aparecida, Santos,
SP 11045-908
Tel: +55(13) 3227-6003 +55(13) 3227-6020
Fax: +55(13) 3227-6003 +55(13) 3227-6213
EMail: fatecbs@fatecbs.edu.br; orita_fatecbs@yahoo.com.br
Website: http://www.fatecbs.edu.br

Diretor: Paulo Roberto Schroeder de Souza

Courses
Graduate Studies (Systems Analysis); **Undergraduate Studies** (Business Administration; Business Computing; Data Processing; Information Technology; Systems Analysis; Transport Management)

History: Founded 1986. Formerly known as Faculdade de Tecnológia da Baixada Santista.

Degrees and Diplomas: *Tecnólogo*; *Especialização/Aperfeiçoamento*

Last Updated: 14/12/07

SÃO PAULO STATE UNIVERSITY

Universidade Estadual Paulista Júlio de Mesquita Filho (UNESP)
Rua Quirino de Andrade, 215, Centro - CEP, São Paulo,
São Paulo 01049-010
Tel: +55(11) 5627-0439
Fax: +55(11) 5627-0134
EMail: arex@reitoria.unesp.br
Website: http://www.unesp.br

Acting President: Júlio Cezar Durigan (2010-)
Tel: +55(11) 5627-0519 EMail: reitor@unesp.br

International Relations: José Celso Freire Junior, Head of International Relations
Tel: +55(11) 5627-0439 EMail: jcfreire@reitoria.unesp.br

Faculties
Mirandópolis *(Mirandópolis)*

Institutes
Biological and Exact Sciences and Languages *(São José do Rio Preto)* (Arts and Humanities; Biochemistry; Biomedicine; Biophysics; Mathematics; Physics); **Biological Sciences** *(Botucatu)* (Biochemistry; Biomedicine; Biophysics); **Biological Sciences** *(Rio Claro)* (Biochemistry; Biomedicine; Biophysics); **Chemistry** *(Araraquara)* (Chemistry)

Schools
Agriculture *(Botucatu)* (Agriculture); **Agriculture** *(Registro)*; **Agriculture and Veterinary Sciences** *(Jaboticabal)* (Agriculture; Veterinary Science); **Animal Sciences** *(Dracena)* (Animal Husbandry; Veterinary Science); **Architecture, Arts and Communication** *(Bauru)* (Architecture; Arts and Humanities; Communication Studies; Design; Journalism; Public Relations; Radio and Television Broadcasting); **Biological Sciences** *(São Vicente)* (Biological and Life Sciences); **Business** *(Tupã)* (Business and Commerce); **Dentistry** *(São José dos Campos)* (Dentistry); **Dentistry** *(Araraquara)* (Dentistry); **Dentistry** *(Araçatuba)* (Dentistry); **Engineering** *(Bauru)* (Engineering); **Engineering** *(Ilha Solteira)* (Engineering); **Engineering** *(Guaratinguetá)* (Engineering); **Engineering** *(Sorocaba)* (Engineering); **Geography** *(Ourinhos)* (Geography); **Geological and Exact Sciences** *(Rio Claro)* (Earth Sciences; Mathematics and Computer Science; Physics); **History, Law and Social Services** *(Franca)* (History; Law; Social and Community Services; Social Sciences); **Medicine** *(Botucatu)* (Medicine); **Pharmacy** *(Araraquara)* (Pharmacy); **Philosophy and Social Sciences** *(Marília)* (Anthropology; Economics; Educational Psychology; Information Sciences; Natural Sciences; Philosophy; Political Sciences; Sociology; Special Education); **Science** *(Bauru)* (Mathematics and Computer Science; Natural Sciences); **Science and Languages** *(Assis)* (Arts and Humanities; Mathematics and Computer Science; Modern Languages; Natural Sciences); **Science and Languages** *(Araraquara)* (Arts and Humanities; Mathematics and Computer Science; Modern Languages; Natural Sciences); **Science and Technology** *(Presidente Prudente)* (Natural Sciences; Technology); **Tourism** *(Rosana)* (Tourism); **Veterinary Medicine and Animal Science** *(Botucatu)* (Animal Husbandry; Veterinary Science); **Wood Engineering** *(Itapeva)*

Further Information: Also Teaching Hospital and 2 Veterinary Hospitals

History: Founded 1976, incorporating previously existing faculties established 1923-1966. An autonomous institution under the jurisdiction of and financially supported by the State of São Paulo.

Governing Bodies: Conselho de Ensino; Pesquisa e Extensão de Serviços à Comunidade

Academic Year: February to December (February-June; August-December)

Admission Requirements: Secondary school certificate or equivalent, and entrance examination
Fees: Tuition, none

Main Language(s) of Instruction: Portuguese

Degrees and Diplomas: *Bacharelado*: Agronomy; Animal Husbandry; Law; Pharmacy; Veterinary Medicine, 5-8 yrs; *Bacharelado*: Architecture and Planning; Engineering, 5-9 yrs; *Bacharelado*: Biology; Chemistry; Communication Studies; Community Services; Computer Science; Ecology; Economics; Geography; History; Industrial Design; Letters; Mathematics; Music; Physical Education; Public Administration; Social Sciences; Social Service, 4-7 yrs; *Bacharelado*: Dentistry; Psychology, 4-9 yrs; *Bacharelado*: Fine Arts; Nursing, 4-6 yrs; *Bacharelado*: Medicine, 6-9 yrs; *Bacharelado*: Nutrition, 5-7 yrs; *Bacharelado*: Physiotherapy; Statistics, 4-8 yrs; *Bacharelado*: Speech Therapy and Audiology, 4-5 yrs; *Licenciatura*: Art Education; Biology; History; Letters; Mathematics; Music; Pedagogy; Philosophy; Physical Education; Social Sciences, 4-7 yrs; *Licenciatura*: Chemistry; Education, 4 yrs; *Licenciatura*: Geography, 5-7 yrs; *Licenciatura*: Physics, 4-8 yrs; *Licenciatura*: Psychology, 5-9 yrs; *Mestrado*; *Doutorado*. Also dual degrees, Bacharelado/Licenciatura (Biology, Geology, Mathematics, Physics, Social Sciences)

Student Services: Academic counselling, Canteen, Cultural centre, Employment services, Foreign student adviser, Foreign Studies Centre, Handicapped facilities, Health services, Language programs, Nursery care, Social counselling, Sports facilities

Student Residential Facilities: Yes

Libraries: Central Library (São Paulo), 1,854,379 vols. 24 specialized libraries, total, 553,367 vols

Publications: Alfa, Linguistics *(annually)*; Alimentos e Nutrição *(annually)*; Arba, Review of Biomedical Sciences *(annually)*; Arte UNESP *(annually)*; Científica, Agronomy *(biannually)*; Didática, Education *(annually)*; Eclética Química *(annually)*; Geociêncas *(biannually)*; Historia *(annually)*; Naturalia, Biology *(annually)*; Perspectivas, Social Sciences *(annually)*; Revista de Ciencias Farmacêuticas *(biannually)*; Revista de Engenharia e Ciências Aplicadas *(annually)*; Revista de Geografia *(annually)*; Revista de Matematica e Nutrição *(annually)*; Revista de Odontologia da UNESP *(biannually)*; Transformação, Philosophy *(annually)*; Veterinária e Zootecnia *(annually)*

Press or Publishing House: Editora da UNESP (UNESP Publishing House)

Student Numbers *2011-2012*: Total 50,000
Last Updated: 25/05/10

SCHOOL OF ENGINEERING OF PIRACICABA

Escola de Engenharia de Piracicaba (EEP)
Avenida Monsenhor Martinho Salgot 560 Areião, Piracicaba,
São Paulo 13414-040
Tel: +55(19) 3412-1100
Fax: +55(19) 3421-3244
EMail: secretar@eep.br
Website: http://www.eep.br
Diretor: José Carlos Chitolina EMail: jcchito@eep.br

Courses
Administration (Administration); **Civil Engineering**; **Computer Science** (Computer Science); **Environmental Engineering**; **Mechanical Engineering** (Mechanical Engineering); **Mechanical Fabrication** (Mechanical Equipment and Maintenance); **Mechatronic Engineering**
History: Founded 1968
Main Language(s) of Instruction: Portuguese
Degrees and Diplomas: *Bacharelado*
Last Updated: 18/06/10

SCHOOL OF MUSIC AND FINE ARTS OF PARANA

Escola de Música e Belas Artes do Paraná (EMBAP)
Rua Comendador Macedo, 254, Curitibá, Paraná 80030-060
Tel: +55(41) 3026-0029
Fax: +55(41) 3017-2070
EMail: embap@embap.br
Website: http://www.embap.br
Diretora: Anna Maria Lacombe Feijó (1997-)

Courses
Fine Arts; **Graduate Studies** (Art History; Music; Music Education); **Music**
History: Founded 1954.
Main Language(s) of Instruction: Portuguese
Degrees and Diplomas: *Bacharelado*; *Licenciatura*; *Especialização/Aperfeiçoamento*; *Mestrado*
Last Updated: 18/06/10

SCHOOL OF PHYSICAL EDUCATION OF CRUZEIRO

Escola Superior de Educação Física de Cruzeiro (ESEFIC)
Rua Dr José Rodrigues Alves Sobrinho 191, Vila Celestina,
Cruzeiro, SP 12710-410
Tel: +55(12) 3144-1850
Fax: +55(12) 3144-1865
EMail: esefic@esefic.br
Website: http://www.esefic.br
Diretora: Rita de Cassia Rigotti Vilela Monteiro

Courses
Graduate Studies *(Lato Sensu)* (Physiology; Sports); **Nursing**; **Pedagogy**; **Physical Education** (Physical Education); **Physiotherapy**
History: Founded 1973
Main Language(s) of Instruction: Portuguese
Degrees and Diplomas: *Bacharelado*; *Licenciatura*; *Especialização/Aperfeiçoamento*
Last Updated: 23/06/10

SCHOOL OF PHYSICAL EDUCATION OF JUNDIAÍ

Escola Superior de Educação Física de Jundiaí (ESEFJ)
Rua Dr. Rodrigo Soares de Oliveira, s/no, Anhangabaú, Jundiaí,
São Paulo 13208120
Tel: +55(11) 4521-7955
Fax: +55(11) 4521-7955
EMail: educacaofisica@esef.br
Website: http://www.esef.br/
Diretor: Fernando Balbino

Courses
Graduate Studies (Dance; Physical Education; Sports; Sports Management); **Physical Education** (Physical Education)
History: Founded 1974.
Main Language(s) of Instruction: Portuguese
Degrees and Diplomas: *Bacharelado*; *Licenciatura*; *Especialização/Aperfeiçoamento*
Last Updated: 23/06/10

SOUTHWEST BAHIA STATE UNIVERSITY

Universidade Estadual do Sudoeste da Bahia (UESB)
Estrada do Bem Querer km 04, Zona Rural, Vitória da Conquista,
Bahia 45083900
Tel: +55(73) 4324 8728
Fax: +55(73) 3424 8624
EMail: uesb@uesb.br
Website: http://www.uesb.br
Reitor: Abel Rebouças São José

Areas
Agrarian Sciences; **Applied Social Sciences**; **Engineering**; **Exact and Earth Sciences** (Biology; Chemistry; Computer Science; Earth Sciences; Mathematics; Physics); **Health Sciences** (Biology; Nursing; Physical Education; Physical Therapy); **Human Sciences**
History: Founded 1980, incorporating previously existing faculties. Recognized by the Federal Government 1987.
Academic Year: March to December (March-July; September-December)

Admission Requirements: Secondary school certificate and entrance examination

Main Language(s) of Instruction: Portuguese

Degrees and Diplomas: *Bacharelado*: 4-5 yrs; *Licenciatura*: 4-5 yrs; *Especialização/Aperfeiçoamento*; *Mestrado*

Libraries: Total, c. 28,500 vols

Last Updated: 25/05/10

STATE FACULTY OF ECONOMICS OF APUCARANA

Faculdade Estadual de Ciências Econômicas de Apucarana (FECEA)
Rodovia do Café BR 376, S/n Rodovia Vila Nova, Apucarana, Paranà 86800970
Tel: +55(43) 3423-7277
Fax: +55(43) 3423-7277
EMail: fecea@fecea.br
Website: http://www.fecea.br

Diretor: Vanderley Ceranto EMail: vceranto@fecea.br

Departments

Accountancy (Accountancy); **Administration**; **Economics** (Economics); **Human Sciences**

History: Founded 1959.

Main Language(s) of Instruction: Portuguese

Degrees and Diplomas: *Bacharelado*; *Especialização/Aperfeiçoamento*; *Mestrado*

Last Updated: 26/10/07

STATE FACULTY OF EDUCATION, SCIENCE AND LETTERS OF PARANAVAÍ

Faculdade Estadual de Educação, Ciências e Letras de Paranavaí (FAFIPA)
Avenida Gabriel Esperidião s/n, Campus Universitário 'Frei Urico Goevert', Jardim Morumbi, Paranavaí, Paraná 87703000
Tel: +55(44) 423-3210
Fax: +55(44) 423-2178
EMail: fafipa@fafipa.br
Website: http://www.fafipa.br

Diretor: José Paszczuk

Departments

Accountancy (Accountancy); **Administration**; **Biology**; **Education** (Education); **Geography** (Geography); **History** (History); **Letters** (Literature); **Nursing**; **Physical Education** (Physical Education); **Social Sciences**

History: Founded 1965

Main Language(s) of Instruction: Portuguese

Degrees and Diplomas: *Bacharelado*; *Licenciatura*; *Especialização/Aperfeiçoamento*; *Mestrado*

Last Updated: 07/07/10

STATE FACULTY OF PHILOSOPHY, SCIENCE AND LETTERS OF PARANAGUÁ

Faculdade Estadual de Filosofia, Ciências e Letras de Paranaguá (FAFIPAR)
Rua Comendador Côrreia Junior 117, Centro, Paranaguá, Paraná 83203280
Tel: +55(41) 3423-3644
Fax: +55(41) 3423-1611 +55(41) 3424-3844
EMail: fafipar@fafipar.br

Diretor: Antonio Alpendre da Silva

Courses

Accountancy (Accountancy); **Administration** (Administration); **Biology**; **History** (History); **Letters**; **Mathematics**; **Pedagogy**

History: Founded 1956.

Main Language(s) of Instruction: Portuguese

Degrees and Diplomas: *Bacharelado*

Last Updated: 07/07/10

STATE FACULTY OF PHILOSOPHY, SCIENCE AND LETTERS OF UNIÃO DA VITÓRIA

Faculdade Estadual de Filosofia, Ciências e Letras de União da Vitória (FAFI)
Praça Coronel Amazonas s/n, Centro, União da Vitória, PR 84600000
Tel: +55(42) 3522-4433
Fax: +55(42) 3522-4433
EMail: fafi@net-uniao.com.br; fafiuv@uol.com.br
Website: http://www.fafiuv.br/

Diretor: Valderlei Garcias Sanches

Courses

Biology; **Chemistry**; **Geography** (Geography); **History** (History); **Letters**; **Mathematics** (Mathematics); **Pedagogy** (Pedagogy); **Philosophy** (Philosophy)

History: Founded 1956.

Main Language(s) of Instruction: Portuguese

Degrees and Diplomas: *Bacharelado*; *Licenciatura*; *Especialização/Aperfeiçoamento*

Last Updated: 07/07/10

STATE FACULTY OF SCIENCE AND LITERATURE OF CAMPO MOURÃO

Faculdade Estadual de Ciências e Letras de Campo Mourão (FECILCAM)
Avenida Comendador Norberto Marcondes 733, Centro, Campo Mourão, PR 87303100
Tel: +55(44) 3518-1880
EMail: fecilcam@fecilcam.br
Website: http://www.fecilcam.br

Diretor: Antonio Carlos Aleixo

Courses

Accountancy (Accountancy); **Administration** (Administration); **Agricultural Engineering** (Agricultural Engineering); **Economics** (Economics); **Geography** (Geography); **Letters** (Literature); **Mathematics** (Mathematics); **Pedagogy**; **Tourism and the Environment** (Environmental Studies; Tourism)

History: Founded 1972.

Main Language(s) of Instruction: Portuguese

Degrees and Diplomas: *Bacharelado*; *Licenciatura*; *Especialização/Aperfeiçoamento*

Last Updated: 07/07/10

STATE UNIVERSITY CENTRE OF THE WESTERN ZONE

Centro Universitario Estadual da Zona Oeste
Avenida Manuel Caldeira de Alvarenga, 1203, Campo Grande, RJ 23070-200
EMail: reitoria@uezo.rj.gov.br
Website: http://www.uezo.rj.gov.br

Reitor: Roberto Soares de Moura

Courses

Biology; **Computer Science**; **Pharmacy** (Pharmacy); **Production Engineering** (Production Engineering)

Main Language(s) of Instruction: Portuguese

Degrees and Diplomas: *Bacharelado*

Libraries: Yes

Last Updated: 09/07/10

STATE UNIVERSITY OF ALAGOAS

Universidade Estadual de Alagoas (UNEAL)
Av. Governador Luiz Cavalcante, s/n, Arapiraca, Alagoas 57500000
Tel: +55(82) 3530-3382
Fax: +55(82) 3530-3382
Website: http://www.uneal.edu.br

Reitora: Laudirege Fernandes Lima

Courses

Accountancy (Accountancy); **Administration** (Business Administration); **Biology**; **Geography** (Geography); **History** (History); **Law** (Law); **Literature** (Literature); **Mathematics** (Mathematics); **Pedagogy** (Pedagogy); **Public Administration**; **Social Studies** (Social Studies)

Further Information: Also campuses at Santana do Ipanema, Palmeira dos Índios, São Miguel dos Campos and União dos Palmares

History: Founded 1994. Acquired present status and title 2006.

Main Language(s) of Instruction: Portuguese

Degrees and Diplomas: *Bacharelado*; *Licenciatura*; *Especialização/Aperfeiçoamento*
Last Updated: 27/05/10

⊿⊿ STATE UNIVERSITY OF CAMPINAS

Universidade Estadual de Campinas (UNICAMP)
Cidade Universitária 'Zeferino Vaz' Barão Geraldo, C.P.6194,
Campinas, São Paulo 13083970
Tel: +55(19) 3521-4720
Fax: +55(19) 3788-4789
EMail: cori@reitoria.unicamp.br
Website: http://www.unicamp.br

President: Fernando Ferreira Costa (2009-2013)
Tel: +55(19) 3521-4702, Fax: +55(19) 3521-4789
EMail: fernando@reitoria.unicamp.br; pfister@reitoria.unicamp.br

Communications director: Clayton Levy
EMail: clayton@reitoria.unicamp.br

International Relations: Leandro Russovski Tessler, Director of International Relations
Tel: +55(19) 3521-4702, Fax: +55(19) 3788-4701
EMail: tessler@reitoria.unicamp.br

Centres

Chemistry, Biology and Agriculture; **Contemporary Music** (Music); **Energy Planning**; **Food Research**; **Gender Studies**; **Information Technology Applied to Education**; **Integration and Cultural Dissemination** (Cultural Studies); **Logic, Epistemology and the History of Science** (History; Logic; Philosophy); **Molecular Biology and Genetic Engineering**; **Petroleum Studies**; **Population Studies** (Demography and Population); **Public Policy Studies**; **Regional Documentation** (Regional Studies); **SemiConductor Components**; **Strategic Studies**; **Studies on Public Opinion**; **Studies on Sound Communication**

Faculties

Agricultural Engineering (Agricultural Engineering); **Chemical Engineering** (Chemical Engineering); **Civil Engineering, Architecture and Town Planning** (Architecture; Civil Engineering; Town Planning); **Dentistry** *(de Piracicaba)* (Dentistry; Surgery); **Education** (Education; Pedagogy); **Electrical Engineering and Computer Science** (Computer Engineering; Electrical Engineering); **Food Engineering** (Food Technology; Nutrition); **Mechanical Engineering** (Mechanical Engineering); **Medical Sciences** (Health Sciences; Medicine); **Physical Education** (Physical Education)

Institutes

Arts (Dance; Multimedia; Music; Theatre; Visual Arts); **Biology** (Biology); **Chemistry** (Chemistry); **Computer Science** (Computer Science); **Economics** (Economics); **Geosciences** (Earth Sciences; Geography; Geology); **Language Studies**; **Mathematics, Statistics and Computer Science** (Computer Science; Mathematics; Statistics); **Philosophy and Humanities** (Anthropology; Arts and Humanities; History; Philosophy; Political Sciences; Sociology); **Physics** (Physics)

Research Centres

Agriculture Meteorology and Climate; **Development of Creativity**; **Environmental Studies** (Environmental Studies); **Theatrical** (Theatre)

Further Information: Also University Clinical Hospital, Advanced Centre for Technological Education, Technical School of Campinas and Technical School of Limeira

History: Founded 1962 by the State legislature of São Paulo as an autonomous institution.

Governing Bodies: University Board; University Council

Academic Year: March to December (March-June; August-December)

Admission Requirements: Secondary school certificate and entrance examination

Main Language(s) of Instruction: Portuguese

International Co-operation: With universities in France, Spain, Portugal, Italy, Germany, United Kingdom, Japan, Argentina, Chile, Uruguay and USA.

Accrediting Agencies: Coordination for the Improvement of Higher Education Personnel Foundation, National Council for Scientific and Technological Development, State of São Paulo Research Foundation

Degrees and Diplomas: *Bacharelado*: 4-6 yrs; *Licenciatura*: 4-6 yrs; *Especialização/Aperfeiçoamento*; *Mestrado*: a further 2-3 yrs; *Doutorado*: 3 yrs and by thesis

Student Services: Academic counselling, Canteen, Employment services, Foreign student adviser, Handicapped facilities, Health services, Language programs, Nursery care, Social counselling, Sports facilities

Special Facilities: Art Gallery, TV Studio

Libraries: c. 500,000 vols

Publications: Journal de Unicamp, Publication of articles from several research areas *(weekly)*

Press or Publishing House: Editora UNICAMP
Last Updated: 27/05/10

STATE UNIVERSITY OF CEARÁ

Universidade Estadual do Ceará (UECE)
Avenida Paranjana 1700, Campus do Itaperi, Serrinha, Fortaleza,
Ceará 60740000
Tel: +55(85) 3101-8600
EMail: reitoira@uece.br
Website: http://www.uece.br

Reitor: Francisco de Assis Moura Araripe

Centres

Applied Social Studies (Social Studies); **Health Sciences** (Health Sciences; Nursing); **Humanities** (Arts and Humanities); **Science and Technology** (Mathematics and Computer Science; Natural Sciences; Technology)

Faculties

Education *(Crateus, Itapipoca)* (Education); **Education, Science and Letters** *(Sertão Central, Iguatu)* (Arts and Humanities; Education; Natural Sciences); **Philosophy** *(Dom Auréliano Matos)* (Philosophy); **Veterinary Science** (Veterinary Science)

Institutes
Biomedicine

Further Information: Also University Hospital

History: Founded 1975, incorporating previously existing private institutions. A State institution financed by the Federal Government.

Governing Bodies: Conselho Universitário; Conselho de Pesquisa, Ensino e Extensão

Academic Year: March to December (March-July; August-December)

Admission Requirements: Secondary school certificate and entrance examination

Main Language(s) of Instruction: Portuguese

Degrees and Diplomas: *Bacharelado*: 3-5 yrs; *Licenciatura*: 3-7 yrs; *Especialização/Aperfeiçoamento*; *Mestrado*; *Doutorado*

Libraries: Central Library, c. 25,000 vols
Last Updated: 26/05/10

STATE UNIVERSITY OF FEIRA DE SANTANA

Universidade Estadual de Feira de Santana (UEFS)
BR 116 Km 3 Norte, Campus Universitário, Novo Horizonte,
Feira de Santana, Bahia 44031460
Tel: +55(75) 224-8200 +55(75) 224 8001
Fax: +55(75) 224-2284
EMail: reitor@uefs.br
Website: http://www.uefs.br

Reitor: José Carlos Barreto de Santana

Departments

Applied Social Sciences (Accountancy; Administration; Economics; Law); **Biology** (Biochemistry; Biology; Biophysics; Cell Biology; Genetics; Histology; Immunology; Molecular Biology; Parasitology; Pathology; Pharmacology); **Education** (Education; Pedagogy); **Exact Sciences** (Chemistry; Geology; Mathematics and Computer Science; Physics; Statistics); **Health Sciences** (Dentistry; Health Sciences; Nursing; Pharmacy; Physical Education); **Human Sciences and Philosophy** (Arts and Humanities; Geography; History; Philosophy); **Letters and Arts** (Arts and Humanities; Literature); **Technology** (Civil Engineering; Computer Engineering; Food Technology)

History: Founded 1970 by the State legislature of Bahia, recognized by the Federal Government 1976.

Governing Bodies: Conselho Académico; Conselho Superior de Ensino, Pesquisa e Extensão

Academic Year: March to December (March-July; August-December)

Admission Requirements: Secondary school certificate and entrance examination

Main Language(s) of Instruction: Portuguese

Degrees and Diplomas: *Bacharelado*: Accountancy; Administration; Civil Engineering; Economics; Nursing, 4 yrs; *Licenciatura*: Languages and Letters; Science; Social Studies, 4 yrs; *Mestrado*; *Doutorado*

Libraries: c. 340,000 vols
Last Updated: 26/05/10

STATE UNIVERSITY OF GOIÁS
Universidade Estadual de Goiás (UEG)
Campus BR 153 - Km 98 Caixa Postal 459, Anápolis, Goiás 75110380
Tel: +55(62) 3328-1178
Fax: +55(62) 3328-1179
EMail: gabinete@ueg.br
Website:http://www.ueg.br

Reitor: Luiz Antônio Arantes
Tel: +55(62) 3313-3461 EMail: reitor@ueg.br

Courses

Accountancy (Accountancy); **Administration** (Administration; Agricultural Management; Hotel Management; Tourism); **Agricultural Engineering** (Agricultural Engineering); **Architecture and Planning** (Architecture and Planning); **Chemistry** (Chemistry); **Civil Engineering** (Civil Engineering); **Data Processing Technology** (Data Processing); **Economics** (Economics); **History and Geography** (Geography; History); **Industrial Chemistry** (Industrial Chemistry); **Letters** (Arts and Humanities; English; Portuguese); **Mathematics** (Mathematics); **Pedagogy** (Education; Pedagogy); **Pharmacy** (Biochemistry; Biology; Pharmacy)

History: Founded 1961 as Faculdade de Ciências Econômicas de Anápolis, became Universidade Estadual de Anápolis 1990 and acquired present status and title 1999. A State institution.

Admission Requirements: Secondary school certificate and entrance examination

Main Language(s) of Instruction: Portuguese

Degrees and Diplomas: *Tecnólogo*: 3 yrs; *Bacharelado*: 4-5 yrs; *Licenciatura*: 4 yrs; *Especialização/Aperfeiçoamento*; *Mestrado*
Last Updated: 26/05/10

STATE UNIVERSITY OF LONDRINA
Universidade Estadual de Londrina (UEL)
Rodovia Celso Gárcia Cid / PR 445, Km 380, Campus Universitário, Londrina, Paraná 86051-990
Tel: +55(43) 3371-4000
Fax: +55(43) 3328-4440
EMail: apcdaai@uel.br
Website: http://www.uel.br

Reitor: Cesar Antonio Caggiano Santos
Tel: +55(43) 3371-4311 EMail: reitoria@uel.br

Centres

Agriculture (Agriculture; Agronomy; Food Science; Food Technology; Veterinary Science; Zoology); **Applied Social Studies** (Accountancy; Administration; Business Administration; Economics; Law; Social and Community Services; Social Studies); **Biological Sciences** (Anatomy; Biological and Life Sciences; Biomedicine; Histology; Microbiology; Pathology; Physiology; Psychology); **Education, Communication Studies, and Arts** (Archiving; Art Education; Communication Studies; Display and Stage Design; Education; Fashion Design; Graphic Design; Library Science; Music; Pedagogy; Performing Arts; Theatre); **Exact Sciences** (Biochemistry; Chemistry; Computer Science; Geography; Geology; Mathematics; Physics; Statistics); **Health Sciences** (Dentistry; Health Sciences; Medicine; Nursing; Pharmacy; Physical Therapy); **Human Sciences and Letters** (English; History; Literature; Modern Languages; Native Language; Philosophy; Portuguese; Social Sciences; Spanish); **Physical Education and Sports** (Physical Education; Sports); **Technology and Town Planning** (Architecture and Planning; Civil Engineering; Construction Engineering; Electrical Engineering; Electronic Engineering; Technology; Town Planning)

Further Information: Also University Hospital, Veterinary Hospital, and 3 clinics

History: Founded 1970 incorporating previously existing State faculties. The University is constituted as a State Foundation.

Governing Bodies: Conselho Universitário; Conselho de Ensino, Pesquisa e Extensão; Conselho Administrativo; Conselho de Curadores

Academic Year: February to December (February-June; August-December)

Admission Requirements: Secondary school certificate or recognized foreign equivalent and entrance examination

Main Language(s) of Instruction: Portuguese

Degrees and Diplomas: *Bacharelado*: Accountancy; Administration (Técnico em Administração); Biology; Biomedicine; Chemistry; Computer Science; Economics; Fashion Design; Geography; Graphic Design; Letters; Library Science; Mathematics; Nursing (Enfermeiro); Physics; Physiotherapy (Fisioterapéuta); Psychology; Social Communication; Social Sciences; Social Work (Assistente social); Sports and Physical Education; Theatre, 4 yrs; *Bacharelado*: Agricultural Engineering (Engenheiro agrônomo); Architecture (Arquitecto e Urbanista); Civil Engineering; Electronic Engineering; Dentistry (Cirurgião dentista); Law; Pharmacy (Farmacêutico); Veterinary Medicine (Médico veterinário), 5 yrs; *Licenciatura*: Art Education; Chemistry; Geography; History; Letters; Mathematics; Music; Pedagogy; Philosophy; Physics; Psychology; Social Sciences, 4 yrs; *Licenciatura*: Physical Education, 3 yrs; *Especialização/Aperfeiçoamento*; *Mestrado*: 4 yrs; *Doutorado*

Student Services: Canteen, Foreign student adviser, Handicapped facilities, Health services, Nursery care, Social counselling, Sports facilities

Student Residential Facilities: Yes

Special Facilities: Historical Museum; Entomology Museum; Botanical Museum; Human Remains Museum. Exhibition Hall 'Celso Garcia Cid'

Libraries: Central Library, c. 89,000 vols

Publications: Biosaúde *(biennially)*; Boletim do Centro de Letras e Ciências Humanas *(biennially)*; Discursos Fotográficos *(annually)*; Entretexto *(annually)*; Geografia: Revista do Departamento de Geociências *(biennially)*; Mediações *(biennially)*; Olho Mágico *(quarterly)*; Scientia Iuris *(annually)*; Semina *(quarterly)*; Semina - Ciências Biológicas e da Saúde *(annually)*; Semina - Ciências Exatas e Tecnológicas *(biennially)*; Semina - Ciências Sociais e Humanas *(annually)*; Signun: Estudo da Linguagem *(biennially)*

Press or Publishing House: Editora EUEL. (Estudante da Universidade Estadual de Londrina)
Last Updated: 26/05/10

STATE UNIVERSITY OF MARANHÃO
Universidade Estadual do Maranhão (UEMA)
Cidade Universitária Paulo VI, S/n Campus Universitário Tirirical, Caixa Potal 09, São Luís, Maranhão 65055-310
Tel: +55(98) 245-5461; +55(98) 245-6708
Fax: +55(98) 245-5882
EMail: waldirmaranhao@uema.br
Website: http://www.uema.br

Reitor: José Augusto Silva Oliveira

Centres

Advanced Studies *(Presidente Dutra)* (Zoology); **Advanced Studies** *(Santa Inês)* (Literature; Pedagogy); **Advanced Studies** *(Balsas)* (Literature; Mathematics; Nursing); **Advanced Studies** *(Imperatriz)* (Administration; Biology; Chemistry; Education; Geography; History; Literature; Mathematics; Philosophy; Physics; Social Sciences); **Advanced Studies** *(Caxias)* (Biology; Chemistry; Education; Geography; History; Literature; Mathematics; Philosophy; Physics; Social Sciences); **Advanced Studies** *(Timon)*; **Advanced Studies** *(Bacabal)*; **Agronomy**; **Applied Social Sciences**; **Education, Exact and Natural Sciences** (Biology; Chemistry; Computer Science; Education; Geography; History; Literature; Mathematics; Philosophy; Physical Education); **Technology**

History: Founded 1973.

Admission Requirements: Admission Examination

Fees: None

Main Language(s) of Instruction: Portuguese

Degrees and Diplomas: *Bacharelado*: Administration; Agronomy; Architecture; Veterinary, 5 yrs; *Licenciatura*: Administration of Agricultural and Cooperative; Biology; Chemistry; Geography; History; Letters; Mathematics; Nursing; Nursing and Obstetrics; Pedagogy; Physics, 4 yrs; *Licenciatura*: Medicine, 6 yrs; *Mestrado*: 2 yrs

Student Services: Sports facilities

Student Residential Facilities: Yes

Special Facilities: no

Publications: Pesquisa em Foco, Scientific magazine *(biennially)*
Last Updated: 26/05/10

STATE UNIVERSITY OF MARINGÁ

Universidade Estadual de Maringá (UEM)
Avenida Colombo 5790, Escritório de Cooperação Internacional Bloco 101, Sala 09, Maringá, Paraná 87020900
Tel: +55(44) 3261-4441 +55(44) 3261-4238
Fax: +55(44) 3263-4820
EMail: sec-eci@uem.br
Website: http://www.uem.br

Reitor: Décio Sperandio (2007-) EMail: dsperandio@uem.br

International Relations: Elza Kimura Grimshaw, Head of International Cooperation Office EMail: ekimura@uem.br

Centres
Agronomy (Agriculture; Agronomy; Animal Husbandry); **Arts and Humanities** (Arts and Humanities; History; Linguistics; Literature; Philosophy); **Business Administration** (Accountancy; Administration; Business Administration; Secretarial Studies); **Education** (Education; Physical Education); **Engineering**; **Health Sciences** (Dentistry; Health Sciences; Medicine; Nursing; Pharmacy); **Law** (Law); **Mathematics and Computer Science** (Computer Science; Mathematics; Statistics); **Natural Sciences** (Biochemistry; Biology; Cell Biology; Chemistry; Genetics; Physics); **Social Sciences** (Economics; Geography; Psychology; Social Sciences)

History: Founded 1970, incorporating previously existing State faculties. A State foundation.

Governing Bodies: Conselho Universitário; Conselho de Ensino, Pesquisa e Extensão; Conselho de Administração; Conselho de Curadores

Academic Year: February to December (February-June; August-December)

Admission Requirements: Secondary school certificate and entrance examination

Main Language(s) of Instruction: Portuguese

Degrees and Diplomas: *Bacharelado*: Accountancy; Agricultural Engineering; Agronomy; Animal Science; Architecture; Chemical Engineering; Civil Engineering; Economics; Food Engineering; Law; Mechanical Engineering; Pharmaceutical Biochemistry; Production Engineering; Psychology; Textile Engineering, 5 yrs; *Bacharelado*: Administration; Chemistry; Civil Construction; Computer Science; Dentistry; Environmental Technology; Fashion; Music; Nursing and Midwifery; Pedagogy; Pharmacy; Philosophy; Trilingual Executive Secretariat, 4 yrs; *Bacharelado*: Food Technology, 3 yrs;

Bacharelado: Medicine, 6 yrs; *Licenciatura*: Biology; Geography; History; Mathematics; Physics; Science; Social Studies, 4 yrs; *Licenciatura*: Languages; Physical Education, 5 yrs; *Mestrado*: Administration; Agronomy; Animal Science; Biology; Chemical Engineering; Chemistry; Clinical Analysis; Computer Science; Ecology in Water Environment; Economy; Education; Genetics; Geography; Health Sciences; History; Languages; Law; Mathematics; Nursing; Pharmacy; Physics; *Doutorado*: Agronomy; Animal Science; Biology; Chemical Engineering; Chemistry; Ecology in Water Environment

Special Facilities: Museu da Bacia do Paraná

Libraries: c. 2,194,341 units

Press or Publishing House: Imprensa Universitária/University Press
Last Updated: 04/04/08

STATE UNIVERSITY OF MATO GROSSO DO SUL

Universidade Estadual de Mato Grosso do Sul (UEMS)
Cidade Universitária, Rodovia Dourados, Itahum Km 12 Cidade Universitaria, Aeroporto, Dourados, Mato Grosso do Sul 79804970
Tel: +55(67) 3411-9000
Fax: +55(67) 3411-9004
EMail: reitoria@uems.br
Website: http://www.uems.br

Reitor: Gilberto José de Arruda
Tel: +55(67) 3411-9001 EMail: luiz@uems.br

Centres
Biological Sciences and Health Services; **Human and Social Sciences** *Head*: Nívea Margareth Rosa do Nascimento; **Technology and Exact Sciences** *Head*: Antonio Zanforlin

History: Founded 1993. Acquired present status 1994.

Admission Requirements: Secondary school certificate and entrance examination

Fees: None

Main Language(s) of Instruction: Portuguese

Degrees and Diplomas: *Bacharelado*: Law; Administration; Animal Husbandry; Agronomy, 5 yrs; *Licenciatura*: Modern Languages; Mathematics; Physics; Biology; Chemistry; Pedagogy; Geography; History, 4 yrs; *Especialização/Aperfeiçoamento*

Student Services: Academic counselling, Canteen, Cultural centre, Employment services, Social counselling, Sports facilities

Special Facilities: Observatory; Language, Computing, Natural Sciences and Video-Conference labs
Last Updated: 13/12/07

STATE UNIVERSITY OF MONTES CLAROS

Universidade Estadual de Montes Claros (UNIMONTES)
Avenida Doutor Ruy Braga, S/n Campus Universitário, Professor Darcy Ribeiro Vila, Montes Claros, Minas Gerais 39401089
Tel: +55(38) 3229-8000
Fax: +55(38) 3229-8102
EMail: reitoria@unimontes.br
Website: http://www.unimontes.br

Reitor: Paulo César Gonçalves de Almeida
EMail: reitor@unimontes.br

Centres
Applied Social Sciences (Accountancy; Administration; Economics; Law; Social and Community Services; Social Sciences); **Biology and Health Sciences** (Biology; Biomedicine; Dentistry; Medicine; Nursing; Physical Education); **Exact Sciences and Technology** (Agricultural Business; Agronomy; Chemistry; Computer Science; Mathematics; Zoology); **Human Sciences**

Institutes
Education

History: Founded 1971, acquired present status 1984.

Main Language(s) of Instruction: Portuguese

Degrees and Diplomas: *Bacharelado*; *Licenciatura*; *Especialização/Aperfeiçoamento*; *Mestrado*
Last Updated: 26/05/10

STATE UNIVERSITY OF PARAÍBA
Universidade Estadual da Paraíba (UEPB)
Rua Baraúnas, 351 - Bairro Universitário, Campina Grande,
Paraíba 58100001
Tel: +55(83) 341-3300
EMail: reitoria@uepb.edu.br
Website: http://www.uepb.edu.br

Reitora: Marlene Alves Sousa Luna
Tel: +55(83) 333-1240, Fax: +55(83) 341-4509

Centres
Agrarian and Environmental Sciences *(Lagoa Seca)*; **Biological and Health Sciences** (Biological and Life Sciences; Dentistry; Health Sciences; Nursing; Pharmacy; Physical Education; Physical Therapy; Psychology); **Biology and Applied Social Sciences** *(João Pessoa)* (Archiving; Biology; International Relations); **Education** (Arts and Humanities; Education; Geography; History; Pedagogy); **Exact and Applied Sciences** *(Patos)* (Administration; Chemistry; Computer Science; Mathematics; Physics); **Human and Agrarian Sciences** *(Catolé do Rocha)* (Agronomy; Literature); **Human and Exact Sciences** *(Monteiro)* (Accountancy; Literature; Mathematics); **Humanities** *(Guarabira)* (Arts and Humanities; Geography; History; Law; Literature; Pedagogy); **Science and Technology** (Chemistry; Industrial Chemistry; Mathematics; Natural Sciences; Physics; Statistics; Technology)

History: Founded 1966.

Governing Bodies: Conselho Universitário

Academic Year: August to December

Admission Requirements: Secondary school certificate and entrance examination

Fees: None

Main Language(s) of Instruction: Portuguese

Degrees and Diplomas: *Bacharelado*: 7 sem; *Licenciatura*; *Especialização/Aperfeiçoamento*; *Mestrado*: a further 2-3 yrs; *Doutorado*

Special Facilities: Museu de Arte Assis Chateaubriand

Libraries: Total, c. 66,600 vols

Press or Publishing House: Gráfica Universitária
Last Updated: 27/05/10

STATE UNIVERSITY OF PIAUÍ
Universidade Estadual do Piauí (UESPI)
Rua João Cabral, Pirajá, Teresina, Piauí 64002150
Tel: +55(86) 213-5195 +55(86) 213-5224
Fax: +55(86) 213-2733
EMail: ascom@uespi.br
Website: http://www.uespi.br/

Reitor: Carlos Alverto Pereira da Silva Tel: +55(86) 213-5757

Centres
Education, Communication and Arts (Communication Studies; Education); **Health Sciences** (Health Sciences; Medicine; Nursing; Physical Education; Physical Therapy; Psychology); **Human Sciences and Letters** (English; Geography; History; Literature; Portuguese; Spanish); **Natural Sciences**; **Social and Applied Sciences** (Accountancy; Administration; Insurance; Law; Library Science; Tourism); **Technology and Town Planning** (Civil Engineering; Computer Science; Electrical Engineering)

Further Information: Also campuses in Campo Maior, Corrente, Floriano, Parnaiba, Picos, Piripiri, São Raimundo, Nonato (among 25 throughout the State)

History: Founded 1988. Under supervision of the Fundação de Apoio ao Desenvolvimento da Educação do Estado do Piauí (FADEP).

Academic Year: March to December (March-June; August-December)

Admission Requirements: Secondary school certificate and entrance examination

Main Language(s) of Instruction: Portuguese

Degrees and Diplomas: *Bacharelado*: 4-5 yrs; *Licenciatura*: 4 yrs; *Especialização/Aperfeiçoamento*

Student Services: Canteen, Employment services, Foreign student adviser, Health services, Language programs, Sports facilities

Libraries: Central Library, 16,000 vols
Last Updated: 25/05/10

STATE UNIVERSITY OF PONTA GROSSA
Universidade Estadual de Ponta Grossa (UEPG)
Avenida Carlos Cavalcanti 4748, Campus de Uvaranas,
Reitoria de Uvaranas, Ponta Grossa, Paraná 84030-900
Tel: +55(42) 3220-3000
Fax: +55(42) 3220-3233
EMail: uepg@uepg.br
Website: http://www.uepg.br

Reitor: João Carlos Gomes
Tel: +55(42) 3220-3232 EMail: reitoria@uepg.br

Centres
Agriculture and Technology (Agricultural Engineering; Agriculture; Agronomy; Civil Engineering; Computer Science; Construction Engineering; Crop Production; Entomology; Farm Management; Food Science; Food Technology; Forestry; Geological Engineering; Harvest Technology; Horticulture; Industrial Engineering; Machine Building; Materials Engineering; Soil Conservation; Soil Science; Systems Analysis; Technology; Transport Engineering; Water Science; Zoology); **Biology** (Biochemistry; Biological and Life Sciences; Biology; Dental Hygiene; Dental Technology; Dentistry; Health Sciences; Oral Pathology; Orthodontics; Periodontics; Pharmacy; Physical Education; Toxicology); **Exact Sciences** (Analytical Chemistry; Chemistry; Earth Sciences; Geography; Geophysics; Inorganic Chemistry; Mathematics; Natural Sciences; Organic Chemistry; Physical Chemistry; Physics; Statistics); **Human Sciences** (Arts and Humanities; Classical Languages; History; Linguistics; Literature; Modern Languages; Native Language; Teacher Trainers Education; Tourism); **Law** (Civil Law; Commercial Law; Human Rights; Labour Law; Law; Public Law); **Social Sciences** (Accountancy; Administration; Business Administration; Business and Commerce; Communication Studies; Comparative Politics; Economic and Finance Policy; Economic History; Economics; Family Studies; International Business; International Economics; Journalism; Marketing; Public Administration; Radio and Television Broadcasting; Social Problems; Social Sciences; Social Studies; Social Work)

Further Information: Campuses at: Telêmaco Borba, Palmeira, Castro, São Mateus do Sul, Uvaranas

History: Founded 1970, incorporating Faculties of Philosophy, Science and Languages, Pharmacy, Dentistry, Law, Economics and Business Administration.

Governing Bodies: Conselho Universitário

Academic Year: March to November (March-June; August-November)

Admission Requirements: Secondary school certificate and entrance examination

Fees: None

Main Language(s) of Instruction: Portuguese

International Co-operation: With universities in USA, Japan, Portugal, United Kingdom, Italy, Bolivia, Cuba.

Degrees and Diplomas: *Bacharelado*: 4-5 yrs; *Licenciatura*: 4-5 yrs; *Especialização/Aperfeiçoamento*: 1 yr; *Mestrado*: 2-3 yrs; *Doutorado*

Student Services: Academic counselling, Canteen, Cultural centre, Employment services, Health services, Nursery care, Social counselling, Sports facilities

Student Residential Facilities: For c. 60 students

Special Facilities: Historical Museum. Art Gallery. Observatory

Libraries: Central Library, 169,420 vols

Press or Publishing House: University Press
Last Updated: 26/05/10

STATE UNIVERSITY OF RIO GRANDE DO SUL
Universidade Estadual do Rio Grande do Sul
Rua 7 de Setembro, 1156 - Centro, Porto Alegre,
Rio Grande do Sul 90.010-191
Tel: +55(51) 3288-9000
EMail: proens@uergs.edu.br
Website: http://www.uergs.edu.br

Reitor: Carlos Alberto Martins Callegaro
EMail: reitoria@uergs.edu.br

Areas

Exact Sciences and Engineering (Automation and Control Engineering; Biotechnology; Computer Engineering; Energy Engineering; Mechanical Engineering); **Human Sciences** (Administration; Dance; Health Administration; Music; Pedagogy; Theatre; Visual Arts); **Life Sciences and Environment**

History: Founded 2001.

Main Language(s) of Instruction: Portuguese

Degrees and Diplomas: *Bacharelado*; *Licenciatura*; *Especialização/Aperfeiçoamento*
Last Updated: 25/05/10

STATE UNIVERSITY OF RORAIMA
Universidade Estadual de Roraima
Rua Sete de Setembro 231, Boa Vista, Roraima 69306-530
Tel: +55(95) 2121-0909
EMail: reitoria@uerr.edu.br
Website: http://www.uerr.edu.br

Reitor: Raimundo Nonato Vilarins

Courses

Accountancy *(Alto Alegre, Caracaraí, São Luiz do Anauá, Rorainópolis)* (Accountancy); **Administration** *(Boa Vista, Iracema, Normandia, São João da Baliza)* **Agronomy** *(Alto Alegre, Rorainópolis, Normandia)* (Agronomy); **Biology** *(Mucajaí, Boa Vista)*; **Chemistry** *(Rorainópolis, Boa Vista)*; **Computer Science** *(Caracaraí, Pacaraima)*; **Foreign Trade** *(Pacaraima)* (International Business); **Forestry Engineering** *(São João da Baliza)* (Forestry); **Geography** (Geography); **History** *(Boa Vista, São Luiz do Anauá)* (History); **Law** *(Boa Vista, Caracaraí)* (Law); **Literature** *(Boa Vista, Bonfim, Mucajaí , Rorainópolis, Pacaraima)* **Mathematics** *(Boa Vista, Caracaraí, São João da Baliza, Rorainópolis)* (Mathematics); **Nursing** *(Alto Alegre, Boa Vista)*; **Pedagogy** *(Boa Vista, Caracaraí, Normandia, Rorainópolis, São Luiz do Anauá)* (Pedagogy); **Philosophy** *(Boa Vista, Rorainópolis)* (Philosophy); **Physical Education** *(Mucajai)* (Physical Education); **Physics**; **Public Safety** (Safety Engineering); **Social Services** *(Mucajaí)*; **Sociology** *(Boa Vista, São João da Baliza)* (Sociology); **Tourism** *(Caracaraí, Pacaraima)*

History: Founded 2005.

Main Language(s) of Instruction: Portuguese

Degrees and Diplomas: *Bacharelado*; *Licenciatura*; *Especialização/Aperfeiçoamento*; *Mestrado*
Last Updated: 26/05/10

STATE UNIVERSITY OF SANTA CRUZ
Universidade Estadual de Santa Cruz (UESC)
Rodovia Ilhéus Itabuna Km 16 S/n Salobrinho, Ilhéus, Bahia 45650000
Tel: +55(73) 3680-5002
Fax: +55(73) 3689-1126
EMail: reitoria@uesc.br
Website: http://www.uesc.br

Reitor: Antônio Joaquim Bastos Da Silva Tel: +55(73) 3680-5001

Centres

Documentation and Regional Memory Studies (Archiving; Regional Studies) *Director:* Janete Ruiz de Macedo; **Social Studies** (Social Studies)

Departments

Administration and Accountancy (Accountancy; Administration); **Agricultural and Environmental Sciences** (Agriculture; Agronomy; Environmental Studies; Geography; Veterinary Science); **Biology** (Biology; Biomedicine); **Economics** (Business Administration; Economics); **Education** (Education); **Exact Sciences and Technology** (Chemistry; Mathematics and Computer Science; Physics; Production Engineering; Technology); **Health Sciences** (Health Sciences); **Law** (Law); **Letters and Arts** (Arts and Humanities; Literature; Modern Languages; Radio and Television Broadcasting); **Philosophy and Human Sciences** (Arts and Humanities; History; Philosophy; Social Sciences); **Portuguese Studies** (Portuguese) *Director:* Patricia Kátia de Costa Pina

History: Founded 1972. A State institution.

Academic Year: March to December

Admission Requirements: Secondary school certificate and entrance examination

Main Language(s) of Instruction: Portuguese

International Co-operation: With universities in: Canada, Cuba, France, Germany, Mozambique, Spain, USA

Degrees and Diplomas: *Bacharelado*: Accountancy; Administration; Agronomy; Biological Sciences; Computer Science; Economics; Law; Mass Communication; Mathematics; Nursing; Physics; Veterinary Medicine, 4 yrs; *Bacharelado*: Medicine, 6 yrs; *Licenciatura*: Biological Sciences; Chemistry; Geography; History; Letters and Arts; Mathematics; Pedagogy; Philosophy; Physics, 4 yrs; *Especialização/Aperfeiçoamento*: Archiving; Pedagogical Application of Computers; Pediatrical Nursing; Regional History; Teaching of Reading and Writing, 3 sem; *Especialização/Aperfeiçoamento*: Economics of Cooperative Entreprises; Education Management; Hotel Management; Radio and TV Scenario, 1 yr; *Mestrado*: Culture and Tourism; Genetics and Molecular Biology; Regional Development and Environment, 2 yrs; *Doutorado*: Education, 4 yrs

Student Services: Academic counselling, Canteen, Cultural centre, Foreign student adviser, Language programs, Sports facilities

Special Facilities: Discovery Museum; Colonial House Museum; Green House Museum.

Libraries: 8,100 vols

Publications: Especiaria, Humanities and Sciences Journal *(biannually)*; Kàwé, African-Brazilian Studies *(biannually)*

Press or Publishing House: Editus
Last Updated: 26/05/10

STATE UNIVERSITY OF THE CENTRE-WEST
Universidade Estadual do Centro-Oeste (UNICENTRO)
Rua Salvatore Renna - Padre, Salvador, 875 - Santa Cruz, Santa Cruz, Guarapuava, Paraná 85010990
Tel: +55(42) 622-4600 +55(42) 621-1000
Fax: +55(42) 623-8644
EMail: tais@unicentro.br
Website: http://www.unicentro.br

Reitor: Vitor Hugo Zanette Tel: +55(42) 621-1008

Centres

Agrarian and Environmental Sciences (Agriculture; Biology; Forestry; Geography); **Applied Social Sciences** (Accountancy; Administration; Economics; Secretarial Studies; Social Sciences; Social Work); **Exact Sciences and Technology** (Chemistry; Engineering; Food Science; Mathematics; Physics; Systems Analysis); **Health Sciences** (Health Sciences; Nursing; Nutrition; Physical Therapy); **Human Sciences, Letters and Arts** (Advertising and Publicity; Arts and Humanities; Education; English; History; Journalism; Literature; Mass Communication; Philosophy; Portuguese; Spanish)

Further Information: Campus at Irati, and branches at Laranjeiras do Sul, Pitanga, Prudentópolis and Chopinzinho. Also Polytechnic Centre (CEDETEG)

History: Founded 1990 incorporating existing faculties. Acquired present status 1997. A State institution.

Academic Year: February to November (February-June; August-November)

Admission Requirements: Secondary school certificate and entrance examination

Fees: None

Main Language(s) of Instruction: Portuguese, English, French, Italian, Spanish

International Co-operation: With universities in Portugal, Spain, Mexico, USA and Japan

Accrediting Agencies: Parana State Government

Degrees and Diplomas: *Bacharelado*; *Licenciatura*: 4-5 yrs; *Especialização/Aperfeiçoamento*; *Mestrado (MS)*; *Doutorado (Dr.)*

Student Services: Academic counselling, Canteen, Cultural centre, Employment services, Foreign student adviser, Handicapped facilities, Health services, Language programs, Sports facilities

Special Facilities: Natural Science Museum. Movie Theatre. Radio station

Libraries: 7 libraries

Publications: Analecta *(biannually)*; Revista Guairacá *(annually)*

Press or Publishing House: Editora Universitária

Last Updated: 26/05/10

STATE UNIVERSITY OF THE NORTH OF PARANA

Universidade Estadual do Norte do Paraná (UENP)
Avenida Getulio Vargas, 850, Centro, Jacarézinho,
Paranà 86400000
Tel: +55(43) 3542-8098
EMail: gabinete@uenp.edu.br
Website: http://www.uenp.edu.br

Reitor: Fernando José Penteado

Faculties
Law *(do Norte Pioneiro)* (Law); **Luiz Meneghel** (Agronomy; Biology; Computer Science; Nursing; Veterinary Science); **Philosophy, Science and Literature** *(Cornélio Procópio)* (Accountancy; Administration; Biology; Economics; Education; Geography; Literature; Mathematics; Pedagogy; Social Sciences); **Philosophy, Science and Literature**; **Physical Education and Physiotherapy** (Physical Education; Physical Therapy)

History: Founded 2006.

Main Language(s) of Instruction: Portuguese

Degrees and Diplomas: *Bacharelado*; *Licenciatura*; *Especialização/Aperfeiçoamento*; *Mestrado*

Last Updated: 25/05/10

STATE UNIVERSITY OF THE VALLEY OF THE ACARAU

Universidade Estadual do Vale do Acaraú (UVA)
Avenida da Universidade 850, Betânia, Sobral, Ceará 62040370
Tel: +55(88) 677-4243 +55(88) 677-2222
Fax: +55(88) 677-4229
EMail: gabinetereitor@uvanet.br
Website: http://www.uvanet.br/ceps/

Reitor: Antonio Colaço Martins
Tel: +55(88) 677-4223 EMail: reitoria@uvanet.br

Centres
Agrarian and Biological Sciences; **Applied Social Sciences** (Accountancy; Administration; Social Sciences); **Education** (Education); **Exact Sciences and Technology** (Analytical Chemistry; Applied Mathematics; Computer Science; Inorganic Chemistry; Organic Chemistry; Physics; Soil Science); **Health Sciences**; **Human Sciences** (Geography; History); **Law**; **Letters**; **Philosophy and Religion** (Philosophy; Religious Studies)

Further Information: Also campuses at: Nova Russas, Camocim, Tianguá, Santa Quitéria, Canindé, Acaraú, Três Lagoas.

History: Founded 1968, acquired present status 1994.

Admission Requirements: Secondary school certificate and entrance examination

Main Language(s) of Instruction: Portuguese

Degrees and Diplomas: *Bacharelado*: 4 yrs; *Licenciatura*: 4 yrs; *Especialização/Aperfeiçoamento*: 2 yrs; *Mestrado*

Student Services: Academic counselling, Canteen, Cultural centre, Employment services, Foreign student adviser, Handicapped facilities, Health services, Language programs, Nursery care, Social counselling, Sports facilities

Student Residential Facilities: Yes

Libraries: Central Library; sectorial libraries

Publications: Essentia *(bimonthly)*

Press or Publishing House: Edições UVA

Last Updated: 25/05/10

STATE UNIVERSITY OF WESTERN PARANÁ

Universidade Estadual do Oeste do Paraná (UNIOESTE)
Caixa Postal 801, Rua Universitária 1619, Jardim Universitário,
Cascavel, Paraná 85814110
Tel: +55(45) 3220-3000
Fax: +55(45) 3324-4590
EMail: gabinete@unioeste.br
Website: http://www.unioeste.br/

Reitor: Luiz Orlando Alcibíades

Campuses
Cascavel (Accountancy; Agricultural Engineering; Biological and Life Sciences; Civil Engineering; Computer Science; Dentistry; Economics; Health Sciences; Literature; Mathematics; Medicine; Nursing; Pedagogy; Pharmacy; Physical Therapy); **Foz do Iguaçu** (Accountancy; Administration; Computer Science; Electrical Engineering; Hotel Management; Law; Literature; Mathematics; Nursing; Pedagogy; Tourism); **Francisco Beltrão**; **Marechal Cândido Rondon** (Accountancy; Administration; Agriculture; Agronomy; Geography; History; Law; Literature; Physical Education; Social Sciences; Zoology); **Toledo**

History: Founded 1987 as State Foundation Federation of Higher Education of West Parana, incorporating four Municipal Faculties. Became Foundation State University of West Parana 1988, and acquired present status and title 1994. Now composed of 5 campuses.

Governing Bodies: Conselho Universitário (COU); Conselho de Ensino, Pesquisa e Extensão (CEPE)

Academic Year: February to November

Admission Requirements: Secondary school certificate and entrance examination

Main Language(s) of Instruction: Portuguese

Degrees and Diplomas: *Bacharelado*: 4-6 yrs; *Licenciatura*: 4-5 yrs; *Mestrado*

Student Services: Canteen, Cultural centre, Employment services, Health services, Sports facilities

Special Facilities: Academic Farm 'Pato Bragado'

Libraries: Total, 225,851 vols

Publications: Ciências Sociais Aplicadas, Magazine; Faz Ciência, Magazine; Línguas e Letras, Magazine; Plural Space Journal; Sciences Sociais em Perspectiva, Magazine; Temas & Matizes, Magazine; Time of Science, Magazine; Times Históricos Magazine; Varia Scientia, Magazine

Last Updated: 25/05/10

TEACHER TRAINING FACULTY OF AFOGADOS DA INGAZEIRA

Faculdade de Formação de Professores de Afogados da Ingazeira (FAFOPAI)
Rua Doutor Osvaldo Gouveia s/n Centro, Afogados da Ingazeira,
PE 56800-000
Tel: +55(81) 838-1579 +55(81) 838-1765
Fax: +55(81) 838-1579
EMail: aedai@zaz.com.br

Diretora: Maria José Acioly Paz de Moura

Courses
History (History); **Literature** (Literature); **Mathematics** (Mathematics); **Pedagogy** (Pedagogy)

History: Founded 1986.

Main Language(s) of Instruction: Portuguese

Degrees and Diplomas: *Licenciatura*. Also Postgraduate Diploma.

Last Updated: 08/07/10

TEACHER TRAINING FACULTY OF ARARIPINA

Faculdade de Formação de Professores de Araripina (FAFOPA)
Campus Universitário, Avenida Florentino Alves Batista s/n Centro,
Araripina, PE 56280000
Tel: +55(81) 3873-1001
Fax: +55(81) 3873-1001
EMail: fafopa@bol.com.br
Website: http://www.portalaeda.com.br

Diretor: Maria Cleide Gualter Alencar Arraes

Courses

Biology; **Geography** (Geography); **History**; **Literature** (Literature)

History: Founded 1979

Main Language(s) of Instruction: Portuguese

Degrees and Diplomas: *Licenciatura*
Last Updated: 05/12/07

TEACHER TRAINING FACULTY OF GOIANA

Faculdade de Formação de Professores de Goiana (FFPG)
Anexo, Rua Poço do Rei s/n Centro, Goiânia, Goiás 55900-000
Tel: +55(81) 3626-0740
Fax: +55(81) 3626-0517
EMail: ffpg@uol.com.br
Website: http://www.ffpg.com.br

Diretor: Lourenço Benedito Bezerra

Courses

Biology (Biology); **Geography**; **History**; **Mathematics**; **Pedagogy** (Pedagogy)

History: Founded 1972

Main Language(s) of Instruction: Portuguese

Degrees and Diplomas: *Licenciatura*
Last Updated: 09/07/10

TEACHER TRAINING FACULTY OF MATA SUL

Faculdade de Formação de Professores da Mata Sul (FAMASUL)
BR 101 Sul Km 117, Campus Universitário, Engenho São Manoel, Palmares, PE 55540-000
Tel: +55(81) 3661-1755
Fax: +55(81) 3661-0823
EMail: aemasul-famasul@bol.com.br
Website: http://www.aemasul.com

Diretor: Francisco Elpídio Câmara Silveira

Courses

Biological Sciences (Biological and Life Sciences); **Chemistry**; **Geography** (Geography); **Graduate Studies**; **History** (History); **Literature** (Literature); **Mathematics** (Mathematics)

History: Founded 1972

Main Language(s) of Instruction: Portuguese

Degrees and Diplomas: *Licenciatura*; *Especialização/Aperfeiçoamento*
Last Updated: 08/07/10

TEACHER TRAINING FACULTY OF SERRA TALHADA

Faculdade de Formação de Professores de Serra Talhada (FAFOPST)
Avenida Alfonso Magalhães, S/n Apt° Centro, Serra Talhada, PE 56900-000
Tel: +55(81) 3831-2311
Fax: +55(81) 3831-2698
EMail: aeset@fafopst.com.br

Diretora: Inaldo Dioniso Neto

Courses

Biological Sciences; **Geography**; **History**; **Literature** (English; Literature); **Mathematics**; **Physical Education** (Physical Education)

History: Founded 1983

Main Language(s) of Instruction: Portuguese

Degrees and Diplomas: *Licenciatura*
Last Updated: 09/07/10

TECHNICAL INSTITUTE OF AERONAUTICAL ENGINEERING

Instituto Tecnólogico de Aeronáutica (ITA)
Praça Marechal Eduardo Gomes 50 Vila das Acácias, São José dos Campos, São Paulo 12228900
Tel: +55(12) 3947-5732
Fax: +55(12) 3941-3500
EMail: chefeidg@ita.br
Website: http://www.ita.br

Reitor: Reginaldo dos Santos EMail: reitor@ita.br

Courses

Engineering (Aeronautical and Aerospace Engineering; Civil Engineering; Computer Engineering; Electronic Engineering; Mechanical Engineering)

History: Founded 1950.

Main Language(s) of Instruction: Portuguese

Degrees and Diplomas: *Bacharelado*; *Mestrado*; *Doutorado*
Last Updated: 14/06/10

TECHNOLOGICAL FEDERAL UNIVERSITY OF PARANÁ

Universidade Tecnológica Federal do Paraná (UTFPR)
Avenida Sete de Setembro 3165, Rebouças, Curitibá, Paraná 80230901
Tel: +55(41) 3310-4545
EMail: gadircwb@cefetpr.br
Website: http://www.cefetpr.br

Reitor: Carlos Eduardo Cantarelli (2008-)
EMail: falecomoreitor@utfpr.edu.br

Departments

Biology and Chemistry (Biology; Chemistry); **Civil Engineering** (Civil Engineering); **Communication Studies** (Communication Studies); **Computer Science** (Computer Science); **Economics and Administration** (Administration; Economics); **Electronic Engineering and Telecommunications Engineering**; **Industrial Design** (Industrial Design); **Mathematics**; **Mechanical Engineering** (Mechanical Engineering); **Physical Education**; **Physics** (Physics); **Social Studies** (Social Studies); **Technology** (Technology)

Further Information: Also campuses at Curitiba, Campo Mourão, Cornélio Procópio, Medianeira, Pato Branco/ Dois Vizinhos e Ponta Grossa

History: Founded 1909. Acquired present name and status 1998.

Degrees and Diplomas: *Bacharelado*; *Licenciatura*: 4 yrs; *Especialização/Aperfeiçoamento*; *Mestrado*: a further 2 yrs; *Doutorado*
Last Updated: 06/05/10

UNIRG FACULTY

Faculdade UNIRG
Alameda Madrid 545, Jardim Sevilha, Gurupi, TO 77410470
Tel: +55(63) 3612-7500
EMail: ascom@unirg.edu.br
Website: http://www.unirg.edu.br

Diretor: Ezemi Nunes Moreira

Courses

Accountancy; **Administration** (Administration); **Advertising** (Advertising and Publicity); **Computer Science** (Computer Science); **Dentistry**; **Journalism** (Journalism); **Law**; **Literature**; **Medicine**; **Nursing** (Nursing); **Pedagogy** (Pedagogy); **Pharmacy** (Pharmacy); **Physical Education** (Physical Education); **Physiotherapy** (Physical Therapy); **Psychology**

History: Founded 1985

Main Language(s) of Instruction: Portuguese

Degrees and Diplomas: *Bacharelado*; *Licenciatura*; *Especialização/Aperfeiçoamento*
Last Updated: 30/06/10

UNIVERSITY CENTRE OF FRANCA
Centro Universitario de Franca (UNI-FACEF)
Avenida Major Nicácio, 2443, Bairro São José, Franca,
São Paulo 14401-135
Tel: +55(16) 3713-4688
Fax: +55(16) 3722-4688
EMail: facef@facef.br
Website: http://www.facef.br

Reitor: Alfredo José Machado Neto
Tel: +55(16) 3722-4104, Fax: +55(16) 3722-4688
EMail: reitoria@facef.br

Courses
Accountancy (Accountancy); **Administration** (Administration); **Advertising and Publicity**; **Economics** (Economics); **Graduate Studies** *(Stricto Sensu - Mestrado)* (Development Studies; Regional Planning); **Graduate Studies** *(Lato Sensu - MBA)*; **Graduate Studies** *(Lato Sensu - Especializações)*; **Information Systems** (Information Sciences); **Literature** (Literature); **Mathematics** (Mathematics); **Psychology**; **Tourism** (Tourism); **Tourism and Hotel Management** (Hotel Management; Tourism)

History: Founded 1951 as Faculdade de Ciências Econômicas e Administrativas de Franca

Main Language(s) of Instruction: Portuguese

Degrees and Diplomas: *Bacharelado*; *Licenciatura*; *Especialização/Aperfeiçoamento*; *Mestrado*. Also MBA.
Last Updated: 27/05/10

UNIVERSITY CENTRE OF UNIÃO DA VITÓRIA
Centro Universitário de União da Vitória
Avenida Bento Munhoz da Rocha Neto, 3856, São Basílio Magno,
União da Vitória, PR 84600000
Tel: +55(42) 3522-1837
Fax: +55(42) 3522-1837
EMail: uniuv@uniuv.edu.br
Website: http://www.face.br

Diretor: Jairo Vicente Clivatti

Courses
Accountancy; **Administration** (Administration); **Advertising and Publicity**; **Architecture and Urbanism**; **Business Computing** (Business Computing); **Civil Engineering**; **Computer Science** (Computer Science); **Economics** (Economics); **Environmental Engineering** (Environmental Engineering); **Executive Secretarial Studies**; **Graduate Studies** (Accountancy; Business Administration; Business and Commerce; Communication Studies; Computer Networks; Dance; Environmental Engineering; Finance; Forestry; Health Administration; Hotel Management; Human Resources; Information Technology; International Business; Marketing; Physical Education; Preschool Education; Primary Education; Production Engineering; Public Administration; Secretarial Studies; Special Education; Sports; Tourism); **Industrial Engineering** *(da Madeira)*; **Journalism**; **Physical Education** (Physical Education); **Tourism**

Further Information: Also São Mateus do Sul campus.

History: Founded 1974

Degrees and Diplomas: *Bacharelado*; *Licenciatura*; *Especialização/Aperfeiçoamento*. Also MBA.
Last Updated: 31/05/10

UNIVERSITY OF BRASÍLIA
Universidade de Brasília (UNB)
Campus Universitário Darcy Ribeiro S/n Reitoria Asa Norte,
Brasília, DF 70910900
Tel: +55(61) 3307-2022
Fax: +55(61) 3272-0003
EMail: unb@unb.br
Website: http://www.unb.br

Reitor: José Geraldo de Sousa Junior Tel: +55(61)307-2210

Centres
Advanced Multidisciplinary Studies (African American Studies; Asian Studies; Child Care and Development; Ethics; Gerontology; Higher Education; Human Rights; Modern Languages; Peace and Disarmament; Public Administration; Public Health; Regional Studies; Rural Studies; Social Policy; Statistics; Technology; Urban Studies; Women's Studies); **Condensed Matter Physics** (Mechanics; Physics); **Human Transport Resources Development** (Applied Mathematics; Human Resources; Management; Transport and Communications); **Integrated Territorial Planning** (Architectural and Environmental Design; Architecture and Planning; Regional Planning; Town Planning); **Open, Continuing and Distance Education**; **Sustainable Development** (Development Studies; Ecology; Economics; Environmental Studies; History); **Technological Development Support**; **Tourism** (Hotel and Restaurant; Tourism); **Urban Planning** (Town Planning)

Faculties
Agronomy and Veterinary Medicine (Agronomy; Veterinary Science); **Applied Social Studies** (Accountancy; Archiving; Business Administration; Documentation Techniques; Information Sciences; Library Science; Public Administration; Social Studies); **Architecture and Town Planning** (Architecture; Town Planning; Urban Studies); **Communication** (Advertising and Publicity; Cinema and Television; Journalism; Radio and Television Broadcasting; Telecommunications Engineering); **Economics, Administration, Accountancy and Information and Documentation Science** (Accountancy; Administration; Economics; Information Sciences; Library Science); **Education** (Education; Educational Administration); **Health Sciences** (Dentistry; Health Sciences; Nursing; Nutrition; Pharmacy; Public Health); **Law** (Law); **Medicine** (Anatomy; Gynaecology and Obstetrics; Medicine; Paediatrics; Pathology; Surgery; Tropical Medicine); **Physical Education** (Physical Education); **Technology** (Civil Engineering; Electrical Engineering; Forestry; Mechanical Engineering; Technology)

Institutes
Art (Art History; Fine Arts; Industrial Design; Music; Painting and Drawing; Performing Arts; Sculpture; Theatre; Visual Arts); **Biological Sciences** (Anatomy; Biological and Life Sciences; Botany; Cell Biology; Ecology; Genetics; Physiology; Plant Pathology; Zoology); **Chemistry** (Analytical Chemistry; Chemistry; Inorganic Chemistry; Organic Chemistry; Physical Chemistry; Science Education); **Exact Sciences** (Computer Science; Mathematics; Statistics); **Geosciences** (Geochemistry; Geology; Mineralogy; Petroleum and Gas Engineering; Seismology); **Human Sciences** (Arts and Humanities; Economics; Geography; History; Philosophy; Social Work); **International Relations** (International Relations; Political Sciences); **Letters** (Arts and Humanities; Classical Languages; English; French; Linguistics; Literature; Native Language; Portuguese; Translation and Interpretation); **Physics** (Atomic and Molecular Physics; Nuclear Physics; Physics); **Psychology** (Clinical Psychology; Developmental Psychology; Educational Psychology; Psychology; Social Psychology); **Social Sciences** (Anthropology; Caribbean Studies; Latin American Studies; Social Sciences; Sociology)

Programmes
Foreign Languages (Education; Modern Languages; Portuguese)

Further Information: Also University Hospital

History: Founded 1962. The University is constituted as a State Foundation.

Governing Bodies: Conselho Director

Academic Year: March to December (March-July; August-December)

Admission Requirements: Secondary school certificate and entrance examination

Main Language(s) of Instruction: Portuguese

Degrees and Diplomas: *Bacharelado*: 4-7 yrs; *Licenciatura*: 4-7 yrs; *Especialização/Aperfeiçoamento*; *Mestrado*: a further 1-3 yrs; *Doutorado*: a further 1-5 yrs

Student Services: Academic counselling, Canteen, Cultural centre, Employment services, Foreign student adviser, Foreign Studies Centre, Handicapped facilities, Health services, Language programs, Nursery care, Social counselling, Sports facilities

Student Residential Facilities: Yes

Special Facilities: Science Museum. Seismologic Observatory. House of Latin American Culture. 'Dois Candangos' Movie Studio. 'Água Limpa' Farm. Biological Experimental Station

Libraries: Central Library, total, c. 579,100 vols. 12,500 thesis on Latin America subjects

Publications: Diogens *(biannually)*; Documentação Atualidade Política *(quarterly)*; Revista Humanidades *(quarterly)*

Press or Publishing House: Editora Universidade de Brasília

Last Updated: 07/06/10

UNIVERSITY OF PERNAMBUCO
Universidade de Pernambuco (UPE)

Avenida Agamenon Magalhães, S/n Santo Amaro, Recife,
Pernambuco 50100010
Tel: +55(81) 3416-4141
Fax: +55(81) 3416-4129
EMail: prograd@upe.br
Website: http://www.upe.br

Reitor: Carlos Fernando de Araújo Calado
EMail: reitor@reitoria.upe.br

Faculties

Administration; Biology; Dentistry; Medical Sciences; Nursing *(Nossa Senhora das Graças)*; Teacher Training *(Garanhuns, Petrolina, Nazaré da Mata)*

Higher Schools

Physical Education

Schools

Polytechnic

History: Founded 1960.

Admission Requirements: Secondary school certificate and entrance examination

Main Language(s) of Instruction: Portuguese

Degrees and Diplomas: *Bacharelado*; *Licenciatura*; *Especialização/Aperfeiçoamento*; *Mestrado*; *Doutorado*

Student Services: Canteen

Last Updated: 04/06/10

UNIVERSITY OF RIO VERDE
Universidade de Rio Verde

Caixa Postal 104, Campus Universitário - Fazenda
'Fontes do Saber', Rio Verde, GO 75901970
Tel: +55(62) 3620-2200
Fax: +55(62) 3620-2201
EMail: secretaria@fesurv.br
Website: http://www.fesurv.br/

Reitor: Sebastião Lázaro Pereira **EMail:** spereira@fesurv.br

Faculties

Accountancy (Accountancy); Administration (Administration; Business Administration); Agronomy; Biology; Computer Science (Computer Science); Design (Design); Economics; Environmental Engineering (Environmental Engineering); Geography (Geography); Law; Literature (Literature); Mathematics (Mathematics); Mechanical Engineering (Mechanical Engineering); Mechanical Engineering; Nursing (Nursing); Nutrition; Pedagogy (Pedagogy); Pharmacy and Biochemistry (Biochemistry; Pharmacy); Physical Education; Physiotherapy; Psychology; Veterinary Medicine; Zoology

History: Founded 1980.

Degrees and Diplomas: *Bacharelado*; *Licenciatura*; *Especialização/Aperfeiçoamento*; *Mestrado*

Last Updated: 03/06/10

UNIVERSITY OF SÃO PAULO
Universidade de São Paulo (USP)

Rua da Reitoria 109, Cidade Universitária Butantã, São Paulo,
São Paulo 05508-900
Tel: +55(11) 3091-3500
Fax: +55(11) 3815-5665
EMail: gr@usp.br
Website: http://www.usp.br

Reitor: João Grandino Rodas (2009-)

Provost for Culture and Extension: Ruy Alberto Corrêa Altafim

Secretária Geral: Maria Fidela de Lima Navarro
Tel: +55(11) 3091-3414, Fax: +55(11) 3815-2741

International Relations: Adnei Melges de Andrade, Vice-Rector, International Relations
Tel: +55(11) 3091-2249, Fax: +55(11) 3814-7342
EMail: ccint@usp.br

Centres

Marine Biology (Marine Biology) *Director*: Alvaro Esteves Migotto; **Nuclear Power in Agriculture** (Nuclear Engineering) *Director*: Virgilio Franco do Nascimento Filho

Faculties

Animal Husbandry and Food Engineering *(Pirassununga)* (Animal Husbandry; Food Science); **Architecture and Urbanism** (Architecture; Design; Town Planning); **Economics, Administration and Accountancy** *(Ribeirão Preto)* (Accountancy; Administration; Economics); **Economics, Administration and Accountancy**; **Education** (Education; Pedagogy); **Law** (Civil Law; Commercial Law; Criminal Law; Forensic Medicine and Dentistry; International Law; Labour Law; Law); **Law** *(Ribeirão Preto)* (Law); **Medicine** (Cardiology; Dermatology; Gastroenterology; Medicine; Pneumology; Surgery); **Medicine** *(Ribeirão Preto)* (Medicine); **Odontology** (Dentistry); **Odontology** *(Bauru)* (Dentistry); **Odontology** *(Ribeirão Preto)* (Dentistry); **Pharmaceutical Sciences** (Food Science; Nutrition; Pharmacy); **Pharmaceutical Sciences** *(Ribeirão Preto)* (Pharmacy); **Philosophy, Arts, and Human Sciences** (Anthropology; Arts and Humanities; Classical Languages; Comparative Literature; History; Linguistics; Literature; Modern Languages; Oriental Languages; Philosophy; Political Sciences; Psychology; Social Sciences; Sociology); **Philosophy, Science, and Letters** *(Ribeirão Preto)* (Biology; Chemistry; Education; Geology; Mathematics; Natural Sciences; Philosophy; Physics; Psychology); **Public Health** (Epidemiology; Nutrition; Public Health); **Veterinary Medicine and Animal Husbandry** (Animal Husbandry; Pathology; Veterinary Science)

Institutes

Advanced Studies (Environmental Studies; History; International Studies); **Astronomy, Geophysics and Atmospheric Science** (Astronomy and Space Science; Geophysics; Seismology); **Biomedical Sciences** (Biomedicine; Cell Biology; Immunology; Microbiology; Pathology); **Biosciences** (Biochemistry; Biomedicine; Biophysics); **Brazilian Studies** (Latin American Studies); **Chemistry** (Chemistry); **Chemistry** *(São Carlos)* (Chemistry); **Electrotechnical and Power Engineering** (Electrical and Electronic Engineering; Power Engineering); **Geosciences** (Geology; Mineralogy); **International Relations**; **Mathematical Sciences and Computers** *(São Carlos)* (Computer Science; Mathematics); **Mathematics and Statistics** (Mathematics; Statistics); **Oceanography** (Marine Science and Oceanography); **Physics** *(São Carlos)* (Physics); **Physics** (Physics); **Psychology** (Psychology); **Tropical Medicine** (Tropical Medicine)

Schools

Agriculture *(Luiz de Queiroz, Piracicaba)* (Agricultural Business; Agriculture; Biology; Entomology; Floriculture; Nutrition; Plant Pathology; Soil Science); **Arts, Sciences and Humanities**; **Communications and Arts** (Cinema and Television; Documentation Techniques; Fine Arts; Journalism; Library Science; Music; Painting and Drawing; Performing Arts; Public Relations; Publishing and Book Trade; Radio and Television Broadcasting; Sculpture; Theatre; Tourism); **Engineering** *(São Carlos)* (Architecture and Planning; Electrical Engineering; Engineering; Geological Engineering; Hydraulic Engineering; Materials Engineering; Mechanical Engineering; Sanitary Engineering; Structural Architecture; Transport and Communications); **Engineering** *(Lorena)*; **Nursing** *(Ribeirão Preto)* (Nursing); **Nursing** (Nursing); **Physical Education** (Physical Education); **Physical Education** *(Ribeirão Preto)* (Physical Education); **Polytechnic** (Civil Engineering; Computer Engineering; Engineering; Hydraulic Engineering; Mechanical Engineering; Metallurgical Engineering; Mining Engineering; Naval Architecture; Production Engineering; Sanitary Engineering; Structural Architecture; Technology; Transport and Communications; Transport Engineering)

Further Information: Also 2 University Hospitals at São Paulo and Bauru

History: Founded 1934. An autonomous institution under the jurisdiction of and financially supported by the State of São Paulo.

Governing Bodies: Conselho Universitário

Academic Year: March to December (March-June; August-December)

Admission Requirements: Secondary school certificate and entrance examination

Fees: None

Main Language(s) of Instruction: Portuguese

International Co-operation: 363 exchange programmes: 225 in Europe, mainly with France, Germany, Portugal, Italy and Spain; 56 in North America, mainly with the USA; 7 in Central America and the Caribbean; 50 in South America, mainly with Argentina, Chile and Colombia; 4 in Australia and 1 in New Zealand; 14 in Asia, mainly with Japan and 6 in Africa, mainly with Mozambique

Accrediting Agencies: Ministério da Educação

Degrees and Diplomas: *Bacharelado*: 4-6 yrs; *Licenciatura*: 4-6 yrs; *Especialização/Aperfeiçoamento*; *Mestrado*: max. of 4 yrs; *Doutorado*: max. of 5 yrs

Student Services: Academic counselling, Canteen, Cultural centre, Foreign student adviser, Foreign Studies Centre, Handicapped facilities, Health services, Language programs, Nursery care, Social counselling, Sports facilities

Special Facilities: Archaeology and Ethnology Museum; Museum of Contemporary Art; Zoology Museum; Paulista Museum

Libraries: Integrated Library System of 40 libraries

Publications: Almanack Braziliense *(biannually)*; Anais do Museu Paulista: História e Cultura Material; Arquivos de Zoologia *(biannually)*; Boletim de Botânica *(annually)*; Brazilian Journal of Oceanography; Brazilian Journal of Veterinary Research and Animal Science *(bimonthly)*; Brazilian Oral Research *(quarterly)*; Cadernos CERU; Cadernos de Psicologia Social do Trabalho; Clinics *(bimonthly)*; Comunicação e Educação *(quarterly)*; Educação e Pesquisa *(3 per annum)*; Estilos de Clínica *(biannually)*; Estudos Avançados *(3 per annum)*; Estudos Econômicos *(quarterly)*; Fisioterapia e Pesquisa; Geologia USP - Série Científica; Journal of Applied Oral Science; Journal of Comparative Biology; Paisagem e Ambiente; Papéis Avulsos de Zoologia *(3 per annum)*; Pesquisa em Edução Ambiental *(biannually)*; Psicologia USP *(quarterly)*; Resenhas *(biannually)*; Revista Acolhendo a Alfabetização em Países de Língua Portuguesa *(biannually)*; Revista Brasileira de Ciências Farmacêuticas *(quarterly)*; Revista Brasileira de Crescimento e Desenvolvimento Humano *(biannually)*; Revista Brasileira de Edução Física e Esporte *(quarterly)*; Revista da Escola de Enfermagem da USP *(quarterly)*; Revista da Faculdade de Direito; Revista de Administração da USP *(quarterly)*; Revista de Antropologia; Revista de História *(biannually)*; Revista de Psiquiatria Clínica; Revista de Saúde Pública *(bimonthly)*; Revista de Terapia Ocupacional; Revista Discurso; Revista do Instituto de Estudos Brasileiros *(biannually)*; Revista do Instituto de Medicina Tropical de São Paulo *(bimonthly)*; Revista do Museu de Arqueologia e Etnologia *(annually)*; Revista Latino-Americana de Enfermagem *(bimonthly)*; Revista Literatura e Sociedade *(annually)*; Revista Paidéia; Revista Tempo Social *(biannually)*; Revista USP *(quarterly)*; Saúde e Sociedade; Scientia Agricola *(bimonthly)*

Press or Publishing House: Editora da Universidade de São Paulo (EDUSP)

Last Updated: 03/06/10

UNIVERSITY OF SOUTH SANTA CATARINA
Universidade do Sul de Santa Catarina (UNISUL)
Avenida José Acácio Moreira 787, Dehon, Tubarão, Santa Catarina 88704-900
Tel: +55(48) 3621-3000
Fax: +55(48) 3621-3036
EMail: unisul@unisul.br
Website: http://www.unisul.br

Reitor: Ailton Nazareno Soares EMail: reitor@unisul.br

Vice Reitor: Sebastião Salésio Herdt EMail: salesio.herdt@unisul.br

Centres
Biology and Health Sciences (Biochemistry; Biology; Dentistry; Medicine; Nursing; Nutrition; Pharmacy; Physical Education; Physical Therapy; Psychology; Sports; Veterinary Science); **Exact, Agricultural and Engineering Sciences**; **Human Sciences,**

Literature and Arts (Geography; History; Literature; Pedagogy); **Social and Applied Sciences**

Further Information: Campuses at Tubarão, Araranguá, Grande Florianópolis e Norte da Ilha

History: Founded 1964 as Instituto Municipal de Ensino Superior, acquired present status and title 1989.

Governing Bodies: Conselho Universitário; Câmara de Gestão

Academic Year: March to December (March-July; August-December)

Admission Requirements: Secondary school certificate and entrance examination

Fees: (Reais): 9,000 per annum

Main Language(s) of Instruction: Portuguese

International Co-operation: With universities in France, Italy, Argentina, Mexico, Spain, Portugal, United Arab Emirates

Degrees and Diplomas: *Bacharelado*: 4-5 yrs; *Licenciatura*: 4-5 yrs; *Especialização/Aperfeiçoamento*: 1 1/2 yrs; *Mestrado*: a further 2 yrs; *Doutorado*: a further 3 yrs

Student Services: Academic counselling, Cultural centre, Employment services, Foreign student adviser, Language programs, Nursery care, Social counselling, Sports facilities

Special Facilities: Museum; Centro de Convivência Cultural

Libraries: 209,963 vols; 89,803 titles

Publications: Cadernos da Integração; Gestão Empresarial; Linguagem em (Dis)curso *(annually)*; Revista Episteme *(biennially)*; Revista Juridíca da Unisul *(annually)*
Last Updated: 31/05/10

UNIVERSITY OF TAUBATÉ
Universidade de Taubaté (UNITAU)
Rua Quatro de Março 432, Centro, Taubaté, São Paulo 12020270
Tel: +55(12) 3625-4100
Fax: +55(12) 3632-7660
EMail: reitoria@unitau.br
Website: http://www.unitau.br

Reitora: Maria Lucila Junqueira Barbosa

Departments
Agronomy (Agronomy); **Architecture and Town Planning** (Architecture; Town Planning); **Biology** (Biology); **Civil Engineering** (Civil Engineering); **Computer Science** (Computer Science; Data Processing); **Dentistry** (Dentistry); **Economics and Administration** (Administration; Economics); **Electrical Engineering** (Electrical Engineering); **Law** (Law); **Mathematics and Physics**; **Mechanical Engineering** (Mechanical Engineering); **Medicine** (Medicine); **Nursing** (Nursing); **Pedagogy** (Pedagogy); **Physical Education** (Physical Education); **Psychology** (Psychology); **Social Communication** (Communication Studies); **Social Science and Letters** (Arts and Humanities; Geography; History; Literature; Philosophy; Social Sciences); **Social Service** (Social Work)

Further Information: Also University Hospital

History: Founded 1974.

Admission Requirements: Secondary school certificate and entrance examination

Main Language(s) of Instruction: Portuguese

Degrees and Diplomas: *Bacharelado*; *Licenciatura*; *Especialização/Aperfeiçoamento*; *Mestrado*; *Doutorado*
Last Updated: 03/06/10

UNIVERSITY OF THE AMAZON STATE
Universidade do Estado do Amazonas
Avenida Djalma Batista 3578, Mánaus, Amazonas 69050020
Tel: +55(92) 3214-5770
EMail: faleconosco@uea.edu.br
Website: http://www.uea.edu.br

Reitor: Carlos Eduardo de Souza Gonçalves
EMail: ceduardo@uea.edu.br

Centres
Humid Tropics

Schools

Arts and Tourism (Conducting; Dance; Music; Musical Instruments; Singing; Tourism); **Health Sciences**; **Social Sciences** (Law; Public Administration); **Teacher Training**; **Technology**

Further Information: Also Centro de Estudos Superiores de Itacoatiara; Centro de Estudos Superiores de Parintins; Centro de Estudos Superiores de Tabatinga; Centro de Estudos Superiores de Tefé; Centro de Estudos Superiores de Lábrea; Núcleo de Ensino Superior de Boca de Acre; Núcleo de Ensino Superior de Carauari; Núcleo de Ensino Superior de Coari; Núcleo de Ensino Superior de Eirunepé; Núcleo de Ensino Superior de Humaitá; Núcleo de Ensino Superior de Manacapuru; Núcleo de Ensino Superior de Manicoré; Núcleo de Ensino Superior de Maués; Núcleo de Ensino Superior de Novo Aripuanã; Núcleo de Ensino Superior de Presidente Figueiredo; Núcleo de Ensino Superior de São Gabriel da Cachoeira.

History: Founded 1974.

Main Language(s) of Instruction: Portuguese

Degrees and Diplomas: *Tecnólogo*; *Bacharelado*; *Licenciatura*; *Especialização/Aperfeiçoamento*; *Mestrado*; *Doutorado*
Last Updated: 01/06/10

UNIVERSITY OF THE EXTREME SOUTH OF SANTA CATARINA

Universidade do Extremo Sul Catarinense (UNESC)
Caixa Postal 3167, Universitário, Avenida Universitária 1105,
Criciúma, Santa Catarina 88806000
Tel: +55(48) 3431-2500
Fax: +55(48) 3431-2750
EMail: reitoria@unesc.rct-sc.br
Website: http://www.unesc.rct-sc.br

Reitor: Gildo Volpato

Units

Applied Social Sciences (Accountancy; Administration; Economics; Law; Secretarial Studies); **Health Sciences** (Health Sciences; Medicine; Nursing; Nutrition; Pharmacy; Physical Therapy; Psychology); **Humanities, Science and Education** (Biology; Education; Environmental Studies; Geography; History; Literature; Mathematics; Pedagogy; Physical Education; Visual Arts); **Science, Engineering and Technology** (Agricultural Engineering; Architecture; Chemical Engineering; Computer Science; Engineering; Environmental Engineering; Materials Engineering; Town Planning)

History: Founded 1970, acquired present status 1997.

Admission Requirements: Secondary school certificate and entrance examination

Fees: (Reais): 400-1,800 per month

Main Language(s) of Instruction: Portuguese

Degrees and Diplomas: *Tecnólogo*: 3-5 yrs; *Bacharelado*: 5 yrs; *Licenciatura*: 4 yrs; *Especialização/Aperfeiçoamento*: 2 yrs; *Mestrado*: Environmental Sciences, 2 yrs; *Doutorado*

Student Services: Academic counselling, Canteen, Employment services, Language programs, Social counselling, Sports facilities

Special Facilities: Languages Laboratory; Zoology Museum; Information Technology Laboratories

Libraries: yes
Last Updated: 01/06/10

UNIVERSITY OF THE STATE OF AMAPÁ

Universidade do Estado do Amapá (UEAP)
Av. Presidente Vargas, n° 650, Macapá, Amapá 68906970
Tel: +55(96) 2101-0506 +55(96) 2101-0524
EMail: ueap@ueap.ap.gov.br
Website: http://www.ueap.ap.gov.br

Rector: José Maria de Silva

Pro-Rector, Planning and Administration: Geany Guimarães

Courses

Chemistry (Chemistry); **Design** (Design); **Fishery** (Fishery); **Forestry**; **Literature** (English; French; Literature; Modern Languages;

Spanish); **Pedagogy**; **Philosophy**; **Production Engineering** (Production Engineering)

History: Founded 2006.

Degrees and Diplomas: *Tecnólogo*: Design, 3 yrs; *Bacharelado*; *Licenciatura*: 8-16 sem. Also Professional Degrees in Engineering, 4 yrs.
Last Updated: 02/06/10

UNIVERSITY OF THE STATE OF BAHIA

Universidade do Estado da Bahia (UNEB)
Rua Silveira Martins, 2.555 - Cabula, Salvador, Bahia 41195001
Tel: +55 (71) 3117-2200
Fax: +55 (71) 3117-2387
EMail: uneb@uneb.br
Website: http: //www.uneb.br

Reitora: Lourisvaldo Valentim da Silva
Tel: +55 (71) 3117-2353, Fax: +55 (71) 3117-2387
EMail: valentim@uneb.br

Vice Reitora: Amélia Tereza Santa Rosa Maraux
EMail: vicereitoria@listas.uneb.br

Centres

Canadian Studies (Canadian Studies) *Coordenador*: Edson Miranda; **Italian Studies** (European Studies) *Coordenador*: Gianni Boscolo; **Japanese Studies** (Asian Studies) *Coordenadora*: Midore Inomata Santana; **Latin American Studies** *Coordenadora*: Maria Carmen de Farias; **Spanish Studies** *Coordenadora*: Maria Eunice Victal e Castro

Departments

Agronomy *(Médio São Francisco)* (Agronomy); **Education** *(Senhor do Bonfim, Serrinha, Guanambi)* (Education); **Exact and Earth Sciences** (Chemistry; Earth Sciences; Industrial Design; Production Engineering; Systems Analysis; Town Planning); **Health Sciences and Food Studies** (Food Science; Health Sciences); **Human Sciences** *(Juazeiro)* (Journalism; Pedagogy); **Philosophy, Science and Letters** *(Juazeiro, Caetité)* (Arts and Humanities; Mathematics and Computer Science; Natural Sciences; Philosophy); **Teacher Training** *(Alagoinhas, Jacobina, Santo António de Jesus)* (Teacher Training); **Technical Studies** (Technology)

Further Information: Campuses at: Salvador, Camaçari, Alagoinhas, Santo Antonio de Jesus, Valença, Ipiaú, Eunápolis, Teixeira de Freitas, Brumado, Guanambi, Caetité, Barreiras, Bom Jesus da Lapa, Seabra, Itaberaba, Serrinha, Conceição do Coité, Jacobina, Irecê, Xique-Xique, Senhor do Bomfim, Euclides da Cunha, Paulo Afonso, Juazeiro

History: Founded 1983 incorporating various Escolas Superiores. Acquired present status and title 1995.

Governing Bodies: Conselho Universitário, Conselho Superior de Ensino, Pesquisa e Extenção; Conselho de Curadores; Conselho de Administração

Academic Year: March to December (March-July; August-December)

Admission Requirements: Secondary school certificate and entrance examination

Fees: None

Main Language(s) of Instruction: Portuguese

Degrees and Diplomas: *Bacharelado*; *Licenciatura*; *Especialização/Aperfeiçoamento*; *Mestrado*

Student Services: Canteen, Cultural centre, Foreign student adviser, Foreign Studies Centre, Language programs, Social counselling

Special Facilities: Museum of Science and Technology

Libraries: Central Library, c. 43,500 vols. 17 sectorial libraries

Publications: Caderno de Extensão *(annually)*; Caderno de Pesquisa *(annually)*; Revista Canadart *(biannually)*; Revista da FAEEBA; Revista de Canudos *(biannually)*; Revista de Letras da F.F.P.A. *(annually)*; Revista Logos *(annually)*

Press or Publishing House: Gráfica da UNEB

UNIVERSITY OF THE STATE OF MATO GROSSO

Universidade do Estado de Mato Grosso (UNEMAT)
Avenida Tancredo Neves 1095, Cavalhada, Caceres,
Mato Grosso 78200000
Tel: +55(65) 3221-0000
EMail: coordecom@unemat.br
Website: http://www.unemat.br

Reitor: Taisir Mahmudo Karim

Faculties
Education (Education); **Exact Sciences** (Mathematics; Physics); **Law** (Commercial Law; Law)

Institutes
Human, Social and Applied Sciences (Architecture; Geography; History; Social Sciences; Tourism); **Modern Languages** (Modern Languages); **Natural Sciences and Technology** (Natural Sciences; Technology)

Further Information: Also campuses in Alta Floresta, Alto Araguaia, Barra do Bugres, Cáceres, Colíder, Juara, Luciara, Pontes e Lacerda, Nova Xavantina, Sinop, Tangará da Serra.

History: Founded 1978.

Main Language(s) of Instruction: Portuguese

Degrees and Diplomas: *Bacharelado*; *Licenciatura*
Last Updated: 02/06/10

UNIVERSITY OF THE STATE OF MINAS GERAIS

Universidade do Estado de Minas Gerais (UEMG)
Praça da Liberdade S/n Funcionários, Belo Horizonte,
Minas Gerais 30140010
Tel: +55(31) 3273-4611
Fax: +55(31) 3273-6647
EMail: uemg@uemg.br
Website: http://www.uemg.br

Reitora: Janete Gomes Barreto Paiva
EMail: Janete.Paiva@uemg.br

Faculties
Education; **Philosophy, Sciences and Letters** *(Carangola)*; **Public Policies** *(Tancredo Neves)* (Finance; Human Resources; Management)

Foundations
Education *(Vale do Jequitinhonha)* (Arts and Humanities; Education; Educational Administration; Educational and Student Counselling; English; History; Literature; Mathematics; Music; Musical Instruments; Pedagogy; Portuguese; Singing); **Higher Education** *(Passos - FESP)* (Accountancy; Administration; Advertising and Publicity; Agronomy; Arts and Humanities; Biological and Life Sciences; Business Administration; Civil Engineering; Computer Science; Education; Engineering; Environmental Engineering; Fashion Design; Higher Education; History; Journalism; Law; Mathematics; Nursing; Nutrition; Pedagogy; Philosophy; Physical Education; Social and Community Services)

Schools
Design; **Education** *(Patos)* (Education); **Education** *(Varginha)* (Education); **Education** *(Vale do Jequitinhanha)* (Education); **Education** *(Divinópolis)* (Education); **Education** *(Ituiutaba)* (Education); **Education** *(Lavras)* (Education); **Education** *(Campanha da Pincesa)*; **Guignard**; **Music**

Further Information: Associated campuses at Campanha, Carangola, Diamantina, Divinópolis, Ituiutaba, Lavras, Passos, Patos de Minas and Varginha

History: Founded 1994.

Admission Requirements: Secondary school certificate and entrance examination

Main Language(s) of Instruction: Portuguese

Degrees and Diplomas: *Bacharelado*: 4-5 yrs; *Licenciatura*: Teacher Training, 4 yrs; *Especialização/Aperfeiçoamento*; *Mestrado*; *Doutorado*

Student Services: Academic counselling, Canteen, Cultural centre, Handicapped facilities
Libraries: Central Library

Publications: Cadernos de Educação *(bimonthly)*; Revista Literária *(biannually)*
Last Updated: 12/12/07

UNIVERSITY OF THE STATE OF PARA

Universidade do Estado do Pará (UEPA)
Rua do Una 156, Telégrafo, Belém, Pará 66113070
Tel: +55(91) 3244-5460
Fax: +55(91) 3244-5460
EMail: vicereit@uepa.br
Website: http://www2.uepa.br/uepa_site

Reitora: Marília Brasil Xavier EMail: reitor@uepa.br

Centres
Biological and Health Sciences; **Natural Sciences and Technology**; **Social Sciences and Education**

History: Founded 1993.

Admission Requirements: Secondary school certificate and entrance examination

Main Language(s) of Instruction: Portuguese

Degrees and Diplomas: *Bacharelado*; *Licenciatura*; *Especialização/Aperfeiçoamento*; *Mestrado*; *Doutorado*
Last Updated: 01/06/10

UNIVERSITY OF THE STATE OF RIO DE JANEIRO

Universidade do Estado do Rio de Janeiro (UERJ)
Rua São Francisco Xavier 524, Maracanã, Rio de Janeiro,
Rio de Janeiro 20559900
Tel: +55(21) 2587-7720
Fax: +55(21) 2284-5033
EMail: datauerj@uerj.br
Website: http://www.uerj.br

Reitor: Ricardo Vieiralves de Castro
Tel: +55(21) 2587-7720, Fax: +55(21) 2284-5033
EMail: reitoria@uerj.br

Office Manager: Maria Eugênia Mosconi de Gouvêa
Tel: +55(21) 2587-7720, Fax: +55(21) 2284-5033
EMail: mosconi@uerj.br

International Relations: Jerônimo Rodrigues de Moraes Neto, International Relations Director
Tel: +55(21) 2587-7869 EMail: dci@uerj.br

Centres
Biomedical Studies (Biological and Life Sciences; Dentistry; Dietetics; Medicine; Nursing; Public Health; Surgery) *Head*: Maria Therezinha Nóbrega da Silva; **Education and Humanities** (Classical Languages; Educational Sciences; Fine Arts; Journalism; Mass Communication; Modern Languages; Performing Arts; Psychology; Sports; Teacher Training) *Head*: Maricélia Bispo Pereira; **Social Sciences** (Bulgarian; Economics; Finance; History; Law; Philosophy; Social and Community Services; Social Sciences) *Head*: Rosangela Martins Alcântara Zagaglia; **Technology** (Chemistry; Engineering; Geography; Geology; Industrial Design; Marine Science and Oceanography; Mathematics and Computer Science; Physics; Statistics) *Head*: Antonio Carlos Moreira da Rocha

Faculties
Administration and Finance (Accountancy; Administration; Business Administration; Finance); **Dentistry**; **Economics** (Economics); **Education** (Educational Sciences; Teacher Training); **Education** *(Baixada Fluminense; campus located at Duque de Caxias City)* (Educational Sciences; Teacher Training); **Engineering**; **Geology** (Biology; Chemical Engineering; Chemistry; Earth Sciences; Geography; Geology; Marine Science and Oceanography; Surveying and Mapping); **Law**; **Medical Sciences** (Medicine; Public Health; Rehabilitation and Therapy; Surgery; Treatment Techniques); **Nursing** (Nursing); **Social Communication**; **Social Services**; **Teacher Training** *(São Gonçalo; campus located at São Gonçalo City)*; **Technology** *(campus located at the city of Resende)*

Institutes
Application *(Fernando Rodrigues da Silveira)*; **Arts**; **Biology** *(Roberto Alcântara Gomes)* (Biology); **Chemistry** (Chemistry);

329

Geography (Geography); **Letters** (Literature); **Mathematics and Statistics** (Mathematics; Statistics); **Nutrition**; **Philosophy and Human Sciences** (History; Philosophy; Social Sciences); **Physical Education and Sports**; **Physics** (Physics); **Polytechnic** *(Nova Friburgo)* (Engineering); **Psychology** (Psychology); **Social Medicine** (Medicine; Public Health)

Schools
Industrial Design (Industrial Design)

Further Information: Also Pedro Ernesto University Hospital; campus at Ilha Grande

History: Founded 1950.

Governing Bodies: The University Council; The Higher Education and Research Council

Academic Year: March to December (March-June; August-December)

Admission Requirements: Secondary school certificate and entrance examination

Fees: None

Main Language(s) of Instruction: Portuguese

International Co-operation: With universities in USA, Germany, France, Italy, Portugal, Spain, Netherlands, Israel, China, Argentina, Uruguay, Canada and Japan

Degrees and Diplomas: *Bacharelado*: Accountancy; Biological and Life Sciences; Business Administration; Computer Sciences; Economic Sciences; Geography; History; Languages; Law; Mass Communication; Philosophy; Physics; Psychology; Social Sciences, 4-5 yrs; *Bacharelado*: Chemical Engineering; Dentistry; Education; Engineering; Geology; Industrial Design; Mechanical Engineering; Medicine; Nursing; Nutrition; Oceanography; Production Engineering; Psychology; Social and Community Services; Statistics, 4-6 yrs; *Licenciatura*: Artistic Education; Biological and Life Sciences; Chemistry; Education; Geography; History; Languages; Mathematics; Philosophy; Physical Education; Physics; Psychology; Social Sciences; Teacher Training, 4-5 yrs; *Mestrado*: Accountancy; Biology; Civil Engineering; Clinical and Experimental Physiopathology; Community Health; Computer Engineering; Computer Modelling; Dentistry; Economic Sciences; Education; Environmental Engineering; Geography; Hydrographical Basin Analysis; Languages; Law; Mass Communication; Medical Sciences; Cardiology; Endocrinology; Nephrology; Urology; Microbiology; Morphology; Nursing; Philosophy; Physics; Political History; Psychoanalysis; Social and Community Services; Social Sciences; Social Psychology; Sports Sciences, 2 yrs; *Doutorado*: Biology; Clinical and Experimental Physiopathology; Community Health; Computer Modelling; Dentistry; Education; Hydrographical Basin Analysis; Languages; Law; Medical Sciences; Morphology; Philosophy; Physics; Social Sciences; Social Psychology (PhD), 3-4 yrs

Student Services: Academic counselling, Canteen, Cultural centre, Employment services, Foreign student adviser, Handicapped facilities, Health services, Language programs, Nursery care, Social counselling, Sports facilities

Special Facilities: Odylo Costa Filho Theatre; Noel Rosa Theatre; Candido Portinari Gallery; Art Gallery of the Odylo Costa Filho Theatre Hall; Acoustic Shell Theatre.

Libraries: 21 libraries, 158,681 vols

Publications: Boletim Aconteceh, Bulletin of the Education and Humanities Centre *(monthly)*; Cadernos de Antropologia e Imagem, Publication on the use of images in the Social Sciences *(biennially)*; Cadernos de Graduação, Publication of the Graduation Sub-Rectory on higher education *(other/irregular)*; Cadernos do Fórum de Debates, Publication of the studies presented at the Annual Forum on Ancient History *(annually)*; Cadernos do IME, Publication of the Mathematics and Statistics Institute *(biennially)*; Concinnitas, Publication of the Arts Institute *(biennially)*; Geo-UERJ, Publication of the Geography Department, Geosciences Institute *(biennially)*; Interseções: Revista de Estudos Interdisciplinares, Studies on the interdisciplinarity of the human sciences *(biennially)*; Physis-Revista de Saùde Coletiva, Papers on community health and related matters *(biennially)*; Projeto Jornal Philia, Publication of the History Department of the Philosophy and Human Sciences Institute *(biennially)*; Publicação da Jornada de História Antiga, Publication of the studies presented at the Annual Ancient History Meeting *(annually)*; Revista de Enfermagem da UERJ, Papers of the Nursing Faculty *(3 per annum)*; Revista de Estudos Transdisciplinares,

Publication of the Philosophy and Human Sciences Institute *(annually)*; Revista do HUPE, Publication of the Pedro Ernesto University Hospital *(biennially)*; Revista Em Pauta, Publication of the Social Service Faculty on social sciences and relared areas *(biennially)*; Revista Estudos e Pequisas em Psicologia, Studies and research on psychology by the Psychology Institute *(biennially)*; Revista Logos, Publication of the Social Communication Faculty *(biennially)*; Revista Open to Discussion, Publication of the Languages Institute *(other/irregular)*; Revista Tamoios, Publication of the Education Faculty of Baixada Fluminese on Geography and Education Themes *(annually)*; Revista Textos sobre Envelhecimento, Publication of texts on ageing *(biennially)*; Revista Thauma, Publication of the Philosophy Department, Institute of Philosophy and Human Sciences *(annually)*; Revistas Espaço e Cultura, Publication of the Geosciences Institute *(biennially)*; Saùde e Sociedade, Recent research on community health themes *(other/irregular)*; Série de Estudos em Saùde Colevita, Studies on community health and related matters *(annually)*; Teias, Publication of the Faculty of Education, Social and Human Sciences, Arts and Culture. *(biennially)*; UERJ em Questão, Journal of the scientific production of the University *(quarterly)*

Press or Publishing House: ED-UERJ-UERJ's Publishing House
Last Updated: 01/06/10

UNIVERSITY OF THE STATE OF RIO GRANDE DO NORTE

Universidade do Estado do Rio Grande do Norte (UERN)
Rua Almino Afonso 478, Sede da Reitoria, Centro, Mossoró,
Rio Grande do Norte 59610210
Tel: +55(84) 3315-2139
Fax: +55(84) 3315-2108
EMail: reitoria@uern.br
Website: http://www.uern.br

Reitor: Milton Marques de Medeiros (1997-)

Faculties
Arts and Humanities (Arts and Humanities; Literature; Modern Languages; Music); **Economics** (Accountancy; Administration; Economics; Environmental Management; Tourism); **Education** (Education; Pedagogy); **Exact and Natural Sciences** (Biology; Computer Science; Mathematics; Natural Sciences; Physics); **Health Sciences**; **Law** (Law); **Nursing** (Nursing); **Philosophy and Social Sciences** (Advertising and Publicity; Geography; History; Journalism; Philosophy; Radio and Television Broadcasting; Social Sciences); **Physical Education** (Physical Education); **Social Work** (Social Work)

History: Founded 1968.

Academic Year: March to December (March-June; August-December)

Admission Requirements: Secondary school certificate and entrance examination

Main Language(s) of Instruction: Portuguese

Degrees and Diplomas: *Bacharelado*: 3-7 yrs; *Licenciatura*: 3-7 yrs; *Especialização/Aperfeiçoamento*; *Mestrado*
Last Updated: 01/06/10

UNIVERSITY OF THE STATE OF SANTA CATARINA

Universidade do Estado de Santa Catarina (UDESC)
Caixa Postal 6021, Avenida Madre Benvenuta 2007, Itacorubi,
Florianópolis, Santa Catarina 88035-001
Tel: +55(48) 3321-8000
Fax: +55(48) 3334-6000
EMail: r4sl@udesc.br
Website: http://www.udesc.br

Reitor: Sebastião Iberes Lopes Melo EMail: reitor@udesc.br

Vice-Reitor: Antonio Heronaldo de Sousa EMail: j2ahs@udesc.br

International Relations: Sónia Pereira Laus
Tel: +55(48) 3231-1550

Centres
Administration and Management *(ESAG)* (Administration; Business Administration; Economics; Management); **Agriculture and Veterinary Medicine** *(Lages)* (Agriculture; Agronomy;

Environmental Engineering; Forestry; Veterinary Science); **Art** *(CEART)* (Art Education; Design; Fashion Design; Fine Arts; Graphic Design; Industrial Design; Music; Painting and Drawing; Sculpture; Theatre); **Education** *(Planalto Norte)* (Information Sciences; Mechanical Engineering); **Health Sciences and Sports** *(CEFID)* (Health Sciences; Physical Education; Physical Therapy; Sports); **Higher Education** *(Ibarama)*; **Higher Education** *(Região Sul, Laguna)*; **Human Sciences and Education** (Geography; History; Pedagogy); **Technology** *(Joinville)* (Chemistry; Civil Engineering; Computer Science; Data Processing; Electrical Engineering; Mathematics; Mechanical Engineering; Physics; Technology)

History: Founded 1965.

Governing Bodies: University Council

Academic Year: March to December (March-June; August-December)

Admission Requirements: Secondary school certificate and entrance examination

Fees: None

Main Language(s) of Instruction: Portuguese

International Co-operation: With universities in Portugal; Spain; Germany; Argentina

Degrees and Diplomas: *Tecnólogo*: 3 yrs; *Bacharelado*: 4 yrs; *Especialização/Aperfeiçoamento*: 1 yr; *Mestrado*: a further 2-4 yrs; *Doutorado*: a further 2-4 yrs

Student Services: Canteen, Cultural centre, Foreign student adviser, Health services, Sports facilities

Student Residential Facilities: None

Special Facilities: Art Gallery

Libraries: Central Library, c. 54,000 vols

Publications: Universidade e Desenvolvimento, Journal of Cultural and Scientific information
Last Updated: 02/06/10

UNIVERSITY OF TOCANTINS
Universidade do Tocantins (UNITINS)
108 Sul Alameda 11 Lote 03 Centro, Palmas, Tocantins 77020-122
Tel: +55(63) 3218-2941
Fax: +55(63) 3218-2942
EMail: unitins@unitins.br
Website: http://www.unitins.br

Reitor: André Luiz de Matos Gonçalves

Departments
Accountancy (Accountancy); **Administration**; **Economics** (Economics); **Environment Engineering** (Environmental Engineering); **Law** (Law); **Pedagogy**; **Social Services** (Social and Community Services)

Further Information: Campuses at Araguaína, Arraias, Colinas, Guaraí, Gurupí, Miracema, Paraíso, Porto Nacional and Tocantinópolis

History: Founded 1990. A State institution.

Main Language(s) of Instruction: Portuguese

Degrees and Diplomas: *Tecnólogo*; *Bacharelado*; *Licenciatura*; *Especialização/Aperfeiçoamento*
Last Updated: 31/05/10

VALE DO IGUAÇU FACULTY OF DOIS VIZINHOS
Faculdade Vizinhança Vale do Iguaçu (VIZIVALI)
Rua Pedro Alvares Cabral 905, Dois Vizinhos, PR 85660000
Tel: +55(46) 3536-4438
Fax: +55(46) 3536-4438
EMail: ailson.texeira@unics.edu.br
Website: http://www.vizivali.edu.br

Director: Paulo Fernando Diel EMail: paulo.diel@cpea.br

Courses
Administration (Administration); **Advertising** (Advertising and Publicity); **Computer Technology** (Computer Science; Software Engineering); **Letters** (Literature); **Pedagogy** (Pedagogy); **Visual Arts**
History: Founded 1999.

Main Language(s) of Instruction: Portuguese
Degrees and Diplomas: *Bacharelado*; *Especialização/Aperfeiçoamento*
Last Updated: 30/06/10

VIRTUAL UNIVERSITY OF THE STATE OF MARANHÃO
Universidade Virtual do Estado do Maranhão (UNIVIMA)
Rua Portugal, 221, Reviver, São Luís, Maranhão 65010-480
Tel: +55(98) 3266-4602
Fax: +55(98)3266-4666
EMail: gabinete@univima.ma.gov.br
Website: http://www.univima.ma.gov.br

Rector: Othon de Carvalho Bastos

Centres
Technological Capability *(CETECMA)* (Technology); **Vocational Technology** (Technology)

Courses
Mathematics (Mathematics)
History: Founded 2003.
Main Language(s) of Instruction: Portuguese
Degrees and Diplomas: *Licenciatura*: 8 sem.; *Mestrado*
Last Updated: 06/05/10

VITÓRIO CARDASSI MUNICIPAL INSTITUTE OF HIGHER EDUCATION OF BEBEDOURO
Instituto Municipal de Ensino Superior de Bebedouro Vitório Cardassi (IMESB)
Rua Nelson Domingos Madeira 300, Parque Eldorado, Bebedouro, São Paulo 14700000
Tel: +55(17) 3345-9366
Fax: +55(17) 3345-9361
EMail: imesb@imesb.br
Website: http://www.imesb.br

Diretor: Alexandre Marques Mendes
EMail: ales.mendes@terra.com.br

Courses
Accountancy (Accountancy); **Administration** (Administration); **Advertising**; **Economics**; **Journalism**; **Law**; **Radio** (Radio and Television Broadcasting); **Social Services** (Social and Community Services)
History: Founded 1988.
Main Language(s) of Instruction: Portuguese
Degrees and Diplomas: *Bacharelado*
Last Updated: 14/06/10

PRIVATE INSTITUTIONS

15TH AUGUST FACULTY
Faculdade XV de Agosto (FAQ)
Avenida Quinze de Agosto 1210, Centro, Socorro, São Paulo 13960000
Tel: +55(19) 3895-1107
Fax: +55(19) 3895-1107
EMail: almir@faculdadexvdeagosto.edu.br
Website: http://www.faculdadexvdeagosto.edu.br

Diretor: Ruben Pal Lins Filho

Courses
Administration (Business Administration; Environmental Management; Hotel Management)
History: Founded 2001.
Main Language(s) of Instruction: Portuguese
Degrees and Diplomas: *Bacharelado*
Last Updated: 30/06/10

A VEZ DO MESTRE INSTITUTE

Instituto a Vez do Mestre
Rua do Carmo 07, Rio de Janeiro, RJ 20011-020
Tel: +55(21)2531-1344
EMail: arduini@vezdomestre.edu.br
Website: http://www.avm.edu.br

Diretor: Fernando Arduini Ayres.

Areas
Education (Educational Administration; Environmental Studies; Higher Education; Human Resources; Preschool Education; Special Education)

Courses
Law (Law)

History: Founded 2006.

Main Language(s) of Instruction: Portuguese

Degrees and Diplomas: *Especialização/Aperfeiçoamento*
Last Updated: 23/09/10

ABEU UNIVERSITY CENTRE

Abeu - Centro Universitário (UNIABEU)
Rua Itaiara 301, Bloco A, Centro, Belford Roxo,
Rio de Janeiro 26113-400
Tel: +55(21) 2104-0460
Fax: +55(21) 2662-1535
EMail: prmc@abeu.com.br; pesquisador@abeu.edu.br
Website: http://www.uniabeu.edu.br

Reitor: Júlio César Furtado dos Santos

Courses
Accountancy (Accountancy); **Administration** *(Angra dos Reis)* (Administration); **Administration** (Administration); **Arts and Humanities** *(Nilópolis)* (Arts and Humanities; English; Portuguese); **Arts and Humanities** *(Nilópolis)* (Arts and Humanities; Literature; Portuguese); **Biological and Life Sciences** (Biological and Life Sciences); **Computer Networks** *(Nova Iguaçu)* (Computer Networks); **Graduate Studies** (Anatomy; Bible; Business Administration; Christian Religious Studies; Computer Networks; Cultural Studies; Educational Administration; Educational and Student Counselling; Environmental Management; Finance; Higher Education; Human Resources; Literature; Marketing; Mathematics Education; Nursing; Pedagogy; Pharmacy; Physical Education; Physical Therapy; Physiology; Social Policy; Sports; Systems Analysis; Transport Management); **History** *(Nilópolis)* (History); **Law** *(Nilópolis)* (Law); **Mathematics** *(Nilópolis)*; **Nursing**; **Pedagogy** *(Nilópolis)* (Pedagogy); **Pharmacy** (Pharmacy); **Physical Education**; **Systems Analysis and Development** *(Angra dos Reis)* (Systems Analysis); **Systems Analysis and Development** *(Nova Iguaçu)*

History: Founded 1972. Formerly known as Abeu Faculdades Integradas.

Main Language(s) of Instruction: Portuguese

Degrees and Diplomas: *Bacharelado*; *Licenciatura*; *Especialização/Aperfeiçoamento*. Also MBA.
Last Updated: 19/05/10

AD1 FACULTY

Faculdade AD1
Setor de Industria E Abastecimento Trecho O2 Lotes 1510/1540,
Guará, DF
Tel: +55(61)3433-3000
EMail: secretaria@itecad1.com.br
Website: http://www.AD1.br

Diretora Geral: Sena Aparecida de Siqueira

Courses
Events Management; **Fashion Design**; **Fashion Marketing** *(Postgraduate Studies)*; **Interior Design** *(Postgraduate Studies)*

History: Founded 1998.

Main Language(s) of Instruction: Portuguese

Degrees and Diplomas: *Tecnólogo*; *Bacharelado*; *Especialização/Aperfeiçoamento*
Last Updated: 23/06/10

ADELMAR ROSADO FACULTY

Faculdade Adelmar Rosado (FAR)
Rua Gonçalo Cavalcante, 2858, Cabral, Teresina, Piauí 64000600
Tel: +55(86) 3213-2524 +55(86) 2106-2606
Fax: +55(86) 2106-2606
EMail: diretor.far@portalfar.edu.br
Website: http://www.portalfar.edu.br

Diretor: Lomanto Delba Moreira Rosado

Courses
Administration; **Social Services**

History: Founded 1999.

Main Language(s) of Instruction: Portuguese

Degrees and Diplomas: *Bacharelado*; *Especialização/Aperfeiçoamento*
Last Updated: 04/01/08

ADVENTIST FACULTY OF HORTOLÂNDIA

Faculdade Adventista de Hortolândia
Rua Pastor Hugo Gegembauer, 265, Parque Ortolândia,
Hortolândia, SP 13184-010
Tel: +55(19) 2118-8011
EMail: faleconosco-ht@unasp.edu.br
Website: http://www.iasp.br/ensinosuperior/Default.aspx

Diretor Geral: Alacy Mendes Barbosa

Courses
Administration (Administration); **Information Systems** (Information Technology); **Pedagogy** (Pedagogy); **Physical Education** (Physical Education)

Degrees and Diplomas: *Bacharelado*; *Licenciatura*
Last Updated: 16/07/10

ADVENTIST INSTITUTE OF PARANA

Instituto Adventista Paranaense (IAP - FAP)
Caixa Postal 1528, Maringá, Paraná 87001970
Tel: +55(44) 3236-8000
Fax: +55(44) 3236-8000
EMail: adm@iap.org.br
Website: http://www.iap.org.br

Diretor Geral: Flavio Machado Pasini
EMail: flavio.pasini@iap.org.br

Courses
Administration (Administration); **Educational Administration** *(Postgraduate)* (Educational Administration); **Information Systems** (Systems Analysis); **Nursing** (Nursing); **Speech Therapy**

History: Founded 1949. Acquired present status 2001.

Main Language(s) of Instruction: Portuguese

Degrees and Diplomas: *Bacharelado*; *Especialização/Aperfeiçoamento*: Educational Administration
Last Updated: 17/06/10

ADVENTIST UNIVERSITY CENTRE OF SÃO PAULO

Centro Universitário Adventista de São Paulo (UNASP)
Estrada de Itapecerica, 5859, São Paulo, São Paulo 05828-001
Tel: +55(11) 2128-6000
EMail: faleconosco-sp@unasp.edu.br
Website: http://www.unasp.br

Reitor: Euler Pereira Bahia (1998-)
Tel: +55(11) 5822-6167, Fax: +55(11) 5822-6198
EMail: euler.bahia@sp.unasp.edu.br; reitoria@unasp.edu.br

Courses
Accountancy (Accountancy); **Administration** (Administration); **Arts and Humanities**; **Arts Education**; **Biological Sciences**; **Civil Engineering** (Construction Engineering); **Computer Networks**; **Computer Science** (Computer Science); **Database** (Data Processing); **Graduate Studies** *(São Paulo)* (Education; Educational Administration; Environmental Management; Gynaecology and Obstetrics; Health Administration; Health Sciences; Mathematics Education; Nursing; Physical Education; Physical Therapy; Phy-

siology; Public Health); **Graduate Studies** *(Hortolândia)*; **Graduate Studies** *(Engenheiro Coelho)*; **History**; **Information Systems**; **Law** (Private Law); **Mathematics** (Mathematics Education); **Nursing** (Nursing); **Nutrition** (Nutrition); **Pedagogy**; **Physical Education** (Sports); **Physical Therapy**; **Psychology**; **Social Communication**; **Systems Analysis and Development**; **Systems for Internet** (Computer Science); **Theology**; **Translation and Interpretation** (Translation and Interpretation)

History: founded 1915, acquired present status 1999.

Governing Bodies: Sponsor (Conselho Deliberativo); Rector; Advisor of Education, Searches and Extension (Consepe); University Superior Advice (Consu); Vice-rector for Academic Affairs; Vice-rector for Campus; Vice-rector for Administrative Affairs

Academic Year: February to December

Admission Requirements: Entrance Exam

Fees: (Reais): 9,300 per semester

Main Language(s) of Instruction: Portuguese

International Co-operation: With universities in Argentina; Chile; UAE; Germany; Mexico; Peru; Russian Federation

Accrediting Agencies: Adventist Accreditation Agency

Degrees and Diplomas: *Bacharelado*; *Licenciatura*; *Mestrado*; *Doutorado*

Student Services: Academic counselling, Canteen, Cultural centre, Employment services, Handicapped facilities, Health services, Language programs, Nursery care, Social counselling, Sports facilities

Student Residential Facilities: Yes

Special Facilities: Art Academy; Temple; Restaurant; Museum; Radio Studio

Libraries: Library; multimedia; Internet Acces; magazines; scientific review; Workshops and events

Publications: Acta Científica, Magazine in Human Sciences *(biennially)*; Escola Adventista, Magazine about Education affairs that promote concepts and works about Education *(biennially)*

Press or Publishing House: Inmprensa Universitária UNAS-PRESS

Last Updated: 20/05/10

AEI-OSE FACULTIES - HIGHER EDUCATIONAL ORGANIZATION

AEI-OSE Faculdades - Organização Superior de Ensino
Rua Silva Jardim, 234, Centro, Itapetininga, São Paulo 18200-010
Tel: +55(15) 3275-7400
EMail: aei@aei.com.br
Website: http://www.aei.com.br

Diretor: Omar Jose Ozi

Faculties
Accountancy *(FCCI)* (Accountancy; Business Administration; Computer Science); **Administration** (Administration); **History** (History); **Information Systems** (Computer Science; Data Processing; Information Sciences; Systems Analysis); **Mathematics**; **Pedagogy** (Pedagogy); **Philosophy, Sciences and Literature** *(FFCLI)* (Arts and Humanities; English; History; Literature; Mathematics; Natural Sciences; Portuguese; Social Sciences; Writing); **Social Sciences**

History: Founded 1966 as Faculdade de Ciências Contábeis Itapetininga.

Main Language(s) of Instruction: Portuguese

Degrees and Diplomas: *Bacharelado*; *Licenciatura*
Last Updated: 05/03/10

AFFIRMATIVE FACULTY

Faculdade Afirmativo (FAFI)
Rua Coronel Pimenta Bueno 534, Dom Aquino, Cuiabá,
Mato Grosso 78015380
Tel: +55(65) 2123-9700
Fax: +55(65) 2123-9735
EMail: fafi.cba@terra.com.br
Website: http://www.afirmativo.com.br

Diretor Geral: Cecilió Francisco das Neves Pinto

Courses
Administration; **Law** (Law); **Pedagogy** (Pedagogy); **Secretarial Studies** (Secretarial Studies); **Social Communication**; **Speech Therapy** (Speech Therapy and Audiology); **Systems Analysis** (Systems Analysis); **Tourism** (Tourism)

History: Founded 1998

Degrees and Diplomas: *Bacharelado*; *Especialização/Aperfeiçoamento*
Last Updated: 30/06/10

AGES FACULTY

Faculdade AGES (AGES)
Avenida Universitária, 23 - Bairro Parque das Palmeiras,
Paripiranga, Bahia 48430-000
Tel: +55(75) 3279-2210
EMail: ageswilson@infonet.com.br
Website: http://www.faculdadeages.com.br

Diretor Geral: José Wilson dos Santos

Courses
Accountancy (Accountancy); **Administration** (Administration; Information Management); **Graduate Studies** (Foreign Languages Education; Human Resources; Literature; Native Language Education); **Law**; **Literature** (Literature; Portuguese); **Nursing** (Nursing); **Pedagogy** (Pedagogy); **Physical Education**; **Psychology** (Psychology)

History: Founded 2001.

Main Language(s) of Instruction: Portuguese

Degrees and Diplomas: *Bacharelado*; *Licenciatura*; *Especialização/Aperfeiçoamento*
Last Updated: 23/06/10

ALBERT EINSTEIN FACULTY

Faculdade Albert Einstein (FALBE)
Sgas 905 Conjunto B/Parte, Bloco 5, 1° e 2° Pavimentos,
Plano Piloto, Brasília, DF 70390-050
Tel: +55 (61) 3244-7061
EMail: diretor@falbe.edu.br

Diretor Geral: Milton Justus

Courses
Administration (Administration; Physical Education); **Information Systems** (Information Technology); **Mathematics** (Mathematics); **Physical Education**

Degrees and Diplomas: *Bacharelado*; *Licenciatura*
Last Updated: 16/07/10

ALBERT EINSTEIN FACULTY OF SÃO PAULO

Faculdade Albert Einstein de São Paulo (FAESP)
Rua Guaiuba, 268, Interlagos, SP 04810-110
Tel: +55(11) 5668-1500 +55(11) 5668-1504
EMail: faleconosco@einstein24h.com.br
Website: http://www.faesp.com.br/

Diretor: Flávio Perciotto

Courses
Administration (Administration); **Graduate Studies** (Education; Educational Psychology; Higher Education; Human Resources); **Pedagogy**; **Technological Studies** (Computer Networks; Human Resources; Safety Engineering; Systems Analysis)

Degrees and Diplomas: *Tecnólogo*; *Bacharelado*; *Especialização/Aperfeiçoamento*
Last Updated: 19/07/10

ALBERT EINSTEIN FACULTY OF SCIENCE AND TECHNOLOGY

Faculdade de Ciências e Tecnologia Albert Einstein (FACTAE)
Avenida Alberto Passos, 294, Centro, Cruz das Almas,
BA 44380-000
Tel: +55(75) 3621-9232
Fax: +55(75) 3621-9232
EMail: factae@factae.edu.br
Website: http://www.factae.edu.br/

Diretor Geral: Alino Matta Santana

Courses
Accountancy (Accountancy); **Administration** (Administration); **Pedagogy** (Pedagogy); **Tourism**
Degrees and Diplomas: *Bacharelado*
Last Updated: 20/07/10

ALBERT EINSTEIN INSTITUTE OF EDUCATION
Instituto Superior de Educação Albert Einstein (ISALBE)
Sgas 905 Conjunto B/Parte, s/n, Bloco 5, 1° e 2° Pavimentos, Plano Piloto, Brasília, DF 70390-050
Tel: +55(61) 3443-5271 +55(61) 3443-5330
EMail: diretorfalbe@falbe.edu.br

Diretor Geral: Milton Justus

Programmes
Pedagogy; **Teacher Training** (Pedagogy; Teacher Training)
Degrees and Diplomas: *Licenciatura*
Last Updated: 23/09/10

ALDETE MARIA ALVES FACULTY
Faculdade Aldete Maria Alves (FAMA)
Avenida Paranaiba 1295, Centro, Iturama, Minas Gerais 38280000
Tel: +55(34) 3411-9700
Fax: +55(34) 3411-9705
EMail: secretaria@facfama.edu.br
Website: http://www.facfama.edu.br

Diretora Geral: Caroline Freitas Stabile

Courses
Accountancy; **Administration** (Administration); **Graduate Studies** (Accountancy; Agricultural Business; Business Administration; Business and Commerce; Criminal Law; Educational Administration; Educational Psychology; Higher Education; Labour Law; Law; Public Health; Rehabilitation and Therapy); **Law** (Law); **Pedagogy** (Pedagogy)

History: Founded 1998

Main Language(s) of Instruction: Portuguese

Degrees and Diplomas: *Bacharelado; Licenciatura; Especialização/Aperfeiçoamento*
Last Updated: 23/06/10

ALFA BRASIL FACULTY
Faculdade Alfa Brasil (FAAB)
Rua Jacarezinho, 800, Bairro São Cristóvão, Cascavel, PR 85816-010
Tel: +55(45) 3035-7766
EMail: alfajr@terra.com.br; profbraz@yahoo.com.br
Website: http://www.faculdadealfabrasil.edu.br/

Diretor: Adilson José Siqueira

Courses
Administration; **Graduate Studies** (Computer Networks; Information Technology); **Technological Studies**
Degrees and Diplomas: *Tecnólogo; Bacharelado; Especialização/Aperfeiçoamento.* Also MBA.
Last Updated: 19/07/10

ALFA FACULTY
Faculdade Alfa (FA)
Rua Bartolomeu Dias, 205, Não há, Vila Oceânica III / Aviação, Praia Grande, SP 11702-620
Tel: +55(13) 3481-4510
EMail: joaohilton@uol.com.br; emanuelcardososilva@yahoo.com.br
Website: http://www.faculdadealfa.edu.br/

Diretor Geral: João Hilton Sayeg de Siqueira

Courses
Graduate Studies (Educational Administration; Educational Psychology; Native Language Education); **Literature** (English; Litera-

ture; Portuguese); **Pedagogy**; **Technological Studies** (Finance; Small Business; Transport Management)
Degrees and Diplomas: *Tecnólogo; Licenciatura; Especialização/Aperfeiçoamento*
Last Updated: 19/07/10

ALFA FACULTY OF TECHNOLOGY OF UMUARAMA
Faculdade de Tecnologia ALFA de Umuarama
Rua Desembargador Antônio Franco Ferreira da Costa, 3678 - Centro, Umuarama, PR 87.501-200
Tel: +55(44) 3622-2562
EMail: marcos@faculdadealfaumuarama.com.br
Website: http://www.faculdadealfaumuarama.com.br

Diretor: Jair Antonio Rodrigues
EMail: jair@faculdadealfaumuarama.com.br

Courses
Business Studies (Business Administration); **Education** *(Postgraduate)* (Education); **Health** (Health Administration; Health Sciences); **Law** *(Postgraduate)*; **Marketing** (Marketing)

Main Language(s) of Instruction: Portuguese

Degrees and Diplomas: *Tecnólogo; Especialização/Aperfeiçoamento; Mestrado*
Libraries: Yes
Last Updated: 19/08/10

ALFACASTELO FACULTY
Faculdade Alfacastelo (FCGB)
Rod. Castelo Branco Km 265, Saida 26 B Trevo de Barueri, Jardim Reginalice, Barueri, São Paulo 06407-000
Tel: +55(11) 4198-9822
Fax: +55(11) 4163-2836
EMail: alfacastelo@alfacastelo.br; cesb@cesb.br
Website: http://www.alfacastelo.br

Diretor: Egberto Franco **EMail:** egberto.franco@alfacastelo.br

Courses
Accountancy; **Administration** (Accountancy; Administration; Business Computing; Commercial Law; Economics; English; Finance; Human Resources; Information Sciences; Management; Marketing; Mathematics; Psychology; Sociology; Spanish; Statistics); **Graduate Studies** (Business and Commerce); **Pedagogy** (Pedagogy)

History: Founded 2000. Formerly known as Faculdade de Ciências Gerenciais de Barueri.

Main Language(s) of Instruction: Portuguese

Degrees and Diplomas: *Bacharelado.* Also MBA.
Last Updated: 24/06/10

ALFONSIAN FACULTIES AND COLLEGE
Faculdades e Colégio Aphonsiano (IAESUP)
Avenida Manoel Monteiro 55, Bairro Santuário, Trindade, Goias 75380000
Tel: +55(62) 3505-1913
Fax: +55(62) 3505-1913
EMail: aphon@terra.com.br
Website: http://www.aphonsiano.edu.br

Diretor Geral: Marcos Antonio de Queiroz

Courses
Accountancy; **Administration**; **Economics** (Economics); **Law**; **Pedagogy**

History: Founded 1999 as Instituto Aphonsiano de Ensino Superior. Acquired present title 2000.

Main Language(s) of Instruction: Portuguese

Degrees and Diplomas: *Bacharelado; Especialização/Aperfeiçoamento*
Last Updated: 29/06/10

ALFREDO NASSER FACULTY

Faculdade Alfredo Nasser (UNIFAN)
Avenida Bela Vista 26, Jardim Esmeraldas, Aparecida de Goiania,
Goiás 74905-020
Tel: +55(62) 3094-9494
Fax: +55(62) 3094-9714
EMail: anesgo@terra.com.br
Website: http://www.unifan.edu.br

President: Alcides Ribeiro Filho **EMail:** presidencia@unifan.edu.br

Centres
Languages (English; Portuguese; Spanish)

Courses
Graduate Studies

Higher Institutes
Education (ISE)

Institutes
Applied Social Sciences (ICSA); Health Sciences (ICS); Juridical Sciences (ICJ) (Law)

History: Founded 2000 as Escola Alfredo Nasser de Ensino Superior. Acquired present title and status 2005.

Main Language(s) of Instruction: Portuguese

Degrees and Diplomas: Bacharelado; Licenciatura; Especialização/Aperfeiçoamento
Last Updated: 24/06/10

ALLIANCE FACULTY

Faculdade Aliança
Rua Sao Pedro, 965, Centro, Teresina, Piauí 64001-260
Tel: +55(86) 3194-1800
EMail: comunicacao@faculdadealianca.com.br
Website: http://www.faculdadealianca.com.br

Diretora: Lívia Guimarães Pacheco

Courses
Biomedicine; Nursing; Physical Education (Physical Education); Physiotherapy (Physical Therapy)

History: Founded 2007 as Centro Integrado de Educação Superior do Piauí - CIESPI. Acquired present title 2009.

Main Language(s) of Instruction: Portuguese

Degrees and Diplomas: Bacharelado
Libraries: Yes
Last Updated: 12/07/10

ALMEIDA RODRIGUES FACULTY

Faculdade Almeida Rodrigues
Rua Quinca Honório Leão, 1030, Morada do Sol,
Rio VerdeCEP 75.909-030, Goiás
Tel: +55 (64) 3620-4700
Fax: +55 (64) 3620-4717
Website: http://www.faculdadefar.com.br

Diretora: Alba de Almeida Rodrigues

Courses
Administration; Law; Pedagogy (Pedagogy)

History: Founded 2002.

Main Language(s) of Instruction: Portuguese

Degrees and Diplomas: Bacharelado; Licenciatura; Especialização/Aperfeiçoamento
Libraries: Biblioteca Helena Risoline de Almeida
Last Updated: 12/07/10

ALMEIDA RODRIGUES INSTITUTE OF EDUCATION

Instituto Superior de Educação Almeida Rodrigues (ISEAR)
Rua Quinca Honório leão, 1030, Morada do Sol, Rio Verde,
GO 75909-030
Tel: +55(64) 3620-4700
Fax: +55(64) 3620-4717
EMail: isear@faculdadefar.com.br
Website: http://www.faculdadefar.com.br/

Courses
Pedagogy (Pedagogy); Teacher Training (Teacher Trainers Education)

History: Founded 2002.

Degrees and Diplomas: Licenciatura
Last Updated: 23/09/10

ALTERNATIVE FACULTY OF HIGHER EDUCATION OF AGRESTE

Faculdade Alternativa de Ensino Superior do Agreste
Rua Mal Floriano Peixoto, 98, Baixao, Arapiraca
Tel: +55(82) 3530-4019
EMail: soesa@ibest.com.br

Diretora: Antonia Barbosa Pereira dos Santos

Courses
Pedagogy; Tourism

Main Language(s) of Instruction: Portuguese

Degrees and Diplomas: Bacharelado; Licenciatura
Last Updated: 12/07/10

ALTERNATIVE HIGHER EDUCATION SCHOOL

Escola de Ensino Superior Alternativo
Rua Ipatinga 82, Barcelona, Serra, ES 29166-210
Tel: +55(27) 3241-9093
Fax: +55(27) 3241-9093

Diretora: Patrícia Gonçalves Oliveira

Courses
Information Systems (Information Technology); Literature; Literature - Portuguese; Pedagogy (Pedagogy)

Degrees and Diplomas: Bacharelado; Licenciatura
Last Updated: 13/07/10

ALVES FARIA FACULTIES

Faculdades Alves Faria (ALFA)
Avenida Perimental Norte 4.129, Vila João Vaz, Goiânia,
Goiás 74445190
Tel: +55(62) 3272-5000
Fax: +55(62) 3272-5002
EMail: alfa@alfa.br
Website: http://www.alfa.br

Diretor Superintendente: Nelson de Carvalho Filho

Courses
Accountancy (Accountancy); Administration (Business Administration; Marketing; Public Administration); Advertising; Civil Engineering; Computer Engineering (Computer Engineering); Economics; Electrical Engineering (Electrical Engineering); Information Sciences (Information Sciences); Journalism (Journalism); Law (Law); Mechanical Engineering (Mechanical Engineering); Pedagogy (Pedagogy); Psychology (Psychology); Telecommunications Engineering; Tourism (Tourism)

History: Founded 2000.

Main Language(s) of Instruction: Portuguese

Degrees and Diplomas: Bacharelado; Especialização/Aperfeiçoamento; Mestrado
Last Updated: 30/06/10

ALVORADA FACULTY OF BRASILIA

Faculdade Alvorada de Brasilia
SEUPN W3 516 bl "E" ed. Carlton Center, Asa Norte, Brasília,
DF 70770-520
Tel: +55(61) 3425-5600
EMail: faculdade@alvorada.com.br
Website: http://www.alvorada.com.br

Diretor Geral: Anderson José Campos de Andrade

Courses
Graduate Studies

Faculties
Computer Science and Data Processing *(FAIPD)* (Computer Science; Data Processing); **Physical Education and Sports** *(FAEFD)* (Accountancy; Administration; Advertising and Publicity; Biological and Life Sciences; Economics; English; History; Journalism; Law; Literature; Mathematics; Nursing; Nutrition; Pedagogy; Pharmacy; Physical Education; Physical Therapy; Portuguese; Psychology; Secretarial Studies; Tourism)

History: Founded 1992

Degrees and Diplomas: *Bacharelado*; *Licenciatura*; *Especialização/Aperfeiçoamento*
Last Updated: 24/06/10

ALVORADA PLUS INSTITUTE OF EDUCATION
Instituto Superior de Educação Alvorada Plus (ISEAP)
Rua Professor Conrado de Deo, 41, Campo Limpo, São Paulo,
SP 05788-360
Tel: +55(11) 5841-6664
Fax: +55(11) 5841-3782
Website: http://www.alvoradaplus.com.br/

Diretor: Guy José Leite

Courses
Administration (Administration); **Literature** (Literature); **Pedagogy** (Pedagogy); **Portuguese** (Portuguese); **Spanish** (Spanish)
Degrees and Diplomas: *Bacharelado*; *Licenciatura*
Last Updated: 23/09/10

AMADEUS FACULTY
Faculdade Amadeus
Rua Estáncia 937, Centro, Aracaju
Tel: +55(79) 2105-2050
EMail: :secretaria@faculdadeamadeus.com.br
Website: http://www.faculdadeamadeus.com.br

Diretor: José Augusto do Nascimento

Courses
Accountancy (Accountancy); **Administration** (Administration); **Pedagogy** (Pedagogy)
History: Founded 2003.
Main Language(s) of Instruction: Portuguese
Degrees and Diplomas: *Bacharelado*; *Licenciatura*; *Especialização/Aperfeiçoamento*
Libraries: Yes
Last Updated: 12/07/10

AMEC TRABUCO FACULTY
Faculdade Amec Trabuco
Rua Santa Clara - Convento do Desterro s/n - Entrada pelo estacionamento da Av. Joana Angélica, Salvador, BA 40040-450
Tel: +55(71) 2203-4012
EMail: famec@faculdadeamectrabuco.com.br
Diretor: Aloysio Rios Trabuco

Courses
Administration (Administration; Finance; Marketing); **Engineering** (Engineering; Environmental Engineering)
History: Founded 2004.
Main Language(s) of Instruction: Portuguese
Degrees and Diplomas: *Bacharelado*; *Especialização/Aperfeiçoamento*
Last Updated: 25/08/10

AMERICAN UNION FACULTY
Faculdade União Americana
Rua Massaranduba, 130, Nova Parnamirim, Parnamirim,
RN 59150-000
Tel: +55(84) 3608-2030
EMail: secretaria@uniaoamericana.edu.br
Website: http://www.uniaoamericana.edu.br/

Diretora Geral: Tarcimária Gomes
EMail: direcao@uniaoamericana.edu.br

Courses
Accountancy (Accountancy); **Administration** (Administration); **Tourism** (Tourism)
Degrees and Diplomas: *Bacharelado*. Also Postgraduate Diploma.
Last Updated: 21/09/10

ANCHIETA FACULTY
Faculdade Anchieta
Avenida Senador Vergueiro 505, Jardim do Mar,
São Bernardo do Campo, São Paulo 09750000
Tel: +55(11) 2823-1000
EMail: secretaria@faculdadeanchieta.com.br
Website: http://www.faculdadeanchieta.com.br

Diretor Geral: Carlos Rivera Ferreira
Tel: +55(11) 2823-1008 EMail: diretoria@portalenchieta.com.br

Courses
Accountancy; **Administration**; **Electronic Engineering** (Electronic Engineering); **Environmental Management** (Environmental Management); **Events Management**; **Financial Management**; **Graduate Studies** (Automation and Control Engineering; Business Administration; Data Processing; Educational Administration; Educational Psychology; Educational Sciences; Environmental Studies; Finance; Higher Education; Human Resources; Industrial and Organizational Psychology; Information Management; Information Technology; International Relations; Literature; Management; Marketing; Portuguese; Public Administration; Sales Techniques; Transport Management); **Human Resources** (Human Resources); **Industrial Automation** (Automation and Control Engineering); **Information Technology**; **International Business** (International Business); **Law** (Law); **Literature** (Literature); **Logistics**; **Management Process**; **Marketing**; **Pedagogy**; **Production Engineering** (Production Engineering); **Psychology** (Psychology); **Tourism** (Tourism)
History: Founded 2000.

Degrees and Diplomas: *Bacharelado*; *Licenciatura*; *Especialização/Aperfeiçoamento*. Also MBA.
Last Updated: 24/06/10

ANCHIETA FACULTY OF HIGHER EDUCATION OF PARANA
Faculdade Anchieta de Ensino Superior do Paraná
Rua Pedro Gusso, 4150 - Cidade Industrial, Curitiba,
Paraná 81315-000
Tel: +55(41) 3346-4548
Website: http://www.faesppr.edu.br

Diretor: Evaldo Benedito Graboski

Courses
Accountancy (Accountancy); **Administration** (Administration); **Environmental Engineering** (Environmental Engineering); **Information Systems**; **Pedagogy**
Degrees and Diplomas: *Bacharelado*; *Licenciatura*; *Especialização/Aperfeiçoamento*
Libraries: Biblioteca Julieta Padrilha Graboski
Last Updated: 12/07/10

ANCHIETA FACULTY OF RECIFE
Faculdade Anchieta do Recife
Rua Professor Aurélio de Castro Cavalcanti, 511 Boa Viagem,
Recife, PE
Tel: +55(81) 3328-1481
EMail: contato@faculdadeanchietape.com.br
Website: http://www.faculdadeanchietape.com.br/site/

Head: Lígia Gomes Monteiro EMail: ligiamonteiro@terra.com.br

Courses
Pedagogy
History: Founded 1999 as Instituto Superior de Educação Anchieta. Acquired present title 2008.
Main Language(s) of Instruction: Portuguese
Degrees and Diplomas: *Licenciatura*; *Especialização/Aperfeiçoamento*
Last Updated: 14/03/11

ANGEL VIANNA FACULTY
Faculdade Angel Vianna
Rua Jornalista Orlando Dantas, 2, Botafogo, Rio de Janeiro
Tel: +55(21) 2551-0099
Website: http://www.escolaangelvianna.com.br/novo/default.asp
Diretora: Angel Vianna

Courses
Dance

Degrees and Diplomas: *Bacharelado; Licenciatura; Especializa-ção/Aperfeiçoamento*
Last Updated: 12/07/10

ANGLICAN FACULTY OF ERECHIM
Faculdade Anglicana de Erechim
Av. Sete de Setembro, 44 - Centro, Erechim, RS 99700-000
Tel: +55(54) 2107-7800
Website: http://www.faers.com.br

Courses
Administration; Design (Fashion Design); Pedagogy; Systems Analysis

Main Language(s) of Instruction: Portuguese

Degrees and Diplomas: *Bacharelado; Licenciatura; Especializa-ção/Aperfeiçoamento*
Last Updated: 12/07/10

ANGLO-AMERICAN INSTITUTE OF EDUCATION OF FOZ DO IGUACU
Instituto Superior de Educação Anglo-Americano de Foz do Iguaçu (ISEAA)
Avenida Paraná, 5661, Vila A, Foz do Iguaçu, PR 85860-590
Tel: +55(45) 3028-3232
Fax: +55(45) 3028-3698
EMail: angloamericano.ffi@angloamericano.edu.br
Website: http://www.angloamericano.edu.br/

Reitor: Paulo César Martinez y Alonso
EMail: reitorpauloalonso@angloamericano.edu.br

Courses
Pedagogy (Pedagogy)

Degrees and Diplomas: *Licenciatura*
Last Updated: 24/09/10

ANGLO-AMERICAN INTEGRATED FACULTIES
Faculdades Integradas Anglo-Americano (FIAA)
Avenida das Américas, 2603 - Barra da Tijuca, Rio de Janeiro,
Rio de Janeiro 22631002
Tel: +55(21) 3388-9133
Fax: +55(21) 3388-9132
EMail: angloamericano.frj@angloamericano.edu.br
Website: http://www.angloamericano.edu.br

Diretor: Paulo César Martinez y Alonso
EMail: reitorpauloalonso@angloamericano.edu.br

Courses
Computer Networks (Computer Networks); Computer Science (Computer Science); Environmental Management (Environmental Management); International Business (International Business); International Relations (International Relations); Letters (Literature); Marketing (Marketing); Pedagogy (Pedagogy); Systems Analysis

Further Information: Also campuses in Foz do Iguaçu, João Pessoa, Caxias do Sul, Passo Fundo, Campina Grande, Chapeco and Bagé

History: Founded 1997

Main Language(s) of Instruction: Portuguese

Degrees and Diplomas: *Tecnólogo; Bacharelado; Especialização/Aperfeiçoamento*
Last Updated: 29/06/10

ANGLO-LATIN FACULTY
Faculdade Anglo Latino (FAL)
Rua Muniz de Souza 1051, Prédio, Aclimação, São Paulo,
São Paulo 01534-001
Tel: +55(11) 3209-9311
Fax: +55(11) 3209-8914
EMail: secfal@faculdadeanglolatino.com.br

Diretor: Sergio Antonio Pereira Leite Salles Arcuri
EMail: sergioarcuri@faculdadeanglolatino.com.br

Courses
Accountancy; Administration; Law (Law); Pedagogy; Social Communication (Advertising and Publicity; Journalism; Public Relations)

History: Founded 1998.

Main Language(s) of Instruction: Portuguese

Degrees and Diplomas: *Bacharelado; Licenciatura*
Last Updated: 14/03/11

ANHANGUERA EDUCACIONAL S.A.
Alameda Maria Teresa, 2000 Sala 6, Dois Corregos,
Valinhos, 13278-181
Tel: +55(19) 3512-1700
EMail: carbonari@uol.com.br
Website: http://www.unianhanguera.edu.br/home/index.php
Diretor: Antonio Carbonari Netto

Courses
Accountancy; Administration (Administration); Agronomy (Agronomy); Arts (Fine Arts); Biology (Biology); Biomedicine (Biomedicine); Computer Science (Computer Science); Design (Design; Interior Design); Engineering (Automation and Control Engineering; Civil Engineering; Electrical and Electronic Engineering; Mechanical Engineering; Production Engineering); Geography (Geography); History (History); Law (Law); Letters (Literature; Translation and Interpretation); Mathematics (Mathematics); Nursing (Nursing); Nutrition (Nutrition); Pedagogy (Pedagogy); Pharmacy (Pharmacy); Physical Education (Physical Education); Physiotherapy (Physical Therapy); Social Communication (Advertising and Publicity; Public Relations); Systems Analysis (Systems Analysis); Tourism (Tourism); Visual Arts (Visual Arts)

Further Information: Faculties in Anápolis (GO), Bauru (SP), Belo Horizonte (MG), Campinas (SP), Campo Grande (MS), Caxias do Sul (RS) Cuiabá (MT), Dourados (MS),Indaiatuba (SP), Itapecerica da Serra (SP), Jacareí (SP), Joinville (SC), Jundiaí (SP), Leme (SP),Limeira (SP), Matão (SP), Osasco (SP), Passo Fundo (RS), Pelotas (RS), Pindamonhangaba (SP), Piracicaba (SP), Pirassununga (SP), Ponta Porã (MS), Ribeirão Preto (SP), Rio Claro (SP), Rio Grande (RS), Rondonópolis (MT),Santa Bárbara d'Oeste (SP), Santo André (SP), São Caetano do Sul (SP), São José dos Campos (SP), São Paulo (SP) -Brigadeiro, São Paulo (SP) - Campo Limpo, São Paulo (SP) - Pirituba, Sertãozinho (SP), Sorocaba (SP),Sumaré (SP), Taboão da Serra (SP), Taguatinga (DF) - Brasília, Taguatinga (DF) - FACNET, Taguatinga (DF) - Santa Terezinha, Taubaté (SP), Valinhos (SP), Valparaíso de Goiás (GO)

History: Founded 2003.

Main Language(s) of Instruction: Portuguese

Degrees and Diplomas: *Bacharelado; Licenciatura; Especialização/Aperfeiçoamento; Mestrado*
Last Updated: 20/07/10

ANHANGUERA UNIVERSITY CENTRE
Centro Universitário Anhangüera (UNIFIAN)
Rua Waldemar Silenci 340, Cidade Jardim, Leme,
São Paulo 13614-370
Tel: +55(19) 3571-5717
Fax: +55(19) 3571-5717
EMail: daex.aesa@unianhanguera.edu.br;
supdca.leme@unianhanguera.edu.br
Website: http://www.unianhanguera.edu.br

Diretor: Débora Cristina Siqueira Aceti
EMail: debora.acetti@unianhanguera.edu.br

Courses

Administration (Administration); **Biological and Life Sciences** (Biological and Life Sciences); **Computer Science** (Computer Science); **Graduate Studies** (Accountancy; Animal Husbandry; Business Administration; Business and Commerce; Computer Networks; Educational Psychology; Energy Engineering; Environmental Management; Law; Nursing; Physiology; Special Education; Telecommunications Engineering; Veterinary Science); **Law** (Law); **Nursing**; **Physical Education** (Physical Education); **Physical Therapy**; **Production Engineering** (Production Engineering); **Psychology** (Psychology); **Social Communication** (Advertising and Publicity); **Social Services** (Social and Community Services); **Sugar and Alcohol Production** (Agriculture); **Veterinary Medicine** (Veterinary Science)

History: Founded 1994.

Main Language(s) of Instruction: Portuguese

Degrees and Diplomas: *Tecnólogo*; *Bacharelado*; *Licenciatura*; *Especialização/Aperfeiçoamento*. Also postgraduate and MBA programmes.
Last Updated: 20/05/10

ANHANGUERA UNIVERSITY CENTRE OF CAMPO GRANDE

Centro Universitário Anhanguera de Campo Grande (UNAES)
Rua Fernando Corrêa da Costa, 1800, Bairro Dr. João Rosa Pires, Campo Grande, Mato Grosso do Sul 79004-311
Tel: +55(67) 3316-6000
Fax: +55(67) 3316-6060
EMail: snl@unaes.br
Website: http://www.unaes.br

Reitora: Leocádia Aglaé Petry Leme Tel: +55(67) 3316-6011

Campuses

I; II (Administration; Automation and Control Engineering; Mechanical Engineering; Nursing; Physical Therapy; Production Engineering)

Courses

Graduate Studies (Accountancy; Agricultural Business; Agriculture; Animal Husbandry; Business and Commerce; Business Computing; Civil Law; Commercial Law; Communication Studies; Computer Networks; Computer Science; Criminal Law; Dermatology; Education; Educational Administration; Educational and Student Counselling; Educational Psychology; Energy Engineering; English; Environmental Management; Gerontology; Graphic Design; Health Administration; Higher Education; Industrial and Organizational Psychology; Industrial Management; Information Management; Information Technology; Interior Design; International Relations; Journalism; Labour Law; Law; Literature; Marketing; Nursing; Nutrition; Physical Therapy; Physiology; Public Administration; Public Law; Real Estate; Rehabilitation and Therapy; Safety Engineering; Special Education; Sports; Systems Analysis; Telecommunications Engineering; Translation and Interpretation; Transport Management; Veterinary Science)

History: Founded 1994 as Faculdade de Campo Grande. Acquired present title and status 2009.

Main Language(s) of Instruction: Portuguese

Degrees and Diplomas: *Tecnólogo*; *Bacharelado*; *Licenciatura*; *Especialização/Aperfeiçoamento*
Last Updated: 27/05/10

ANHANGUERA UNIVERSITY CENTRE OF SÃO PAULO

Centro Universitário Anhanguera de São Paulo (UNIBERO)
Avenida Brigadeiro Luis Antônio, 871, Bela Vista, São Paulo, São Paulo 01317-001
Tel: +55(11) 607-0071 +55(11) 326-5650
Fax: +55(11) 607-0071 +55(11) 3107-6618
EMail: reitoria.unibero@unianhanguera.edu.br
Website: http://www.unibero.edu.br/

Reitor: Valmor Bolan EMail: reitor@unibero.edu.br

Courses

Administration; **Advertising and Publicity**; **Arts and Humanities and Spanish** (Arts and Humanities; Spanish); **Arts and Humanities and Translation** (Arts and Humanities; English; Translation and Interpretation); **Digital Design** (Design); **International Relations** (International Relations); **Law** (Law); **Mechanical Engineering**; **Pedagogy**; **Social Service** (Social and Community Services); **Specific Training** (Business and Commerce); **Technological Studies**; **Tourism**

History: Founded 1971. Became Centro Universitário Ibero-Americano (UNIBERO) 1998. Acquired present title 2010.

Main Language(s) of Instruction: Portuguese

Degrees and Diplomas: *Tecnólogo*; *Bacharelado*; *Licenciatura*
Last Updated: 14/06/10

ANHANGUERA-UNIDERP UNIVERSITY

Universidade Anhanguera-Uniderp
Rua Ceará 333, Miguel Couto, Campo Grande, Mato Grosso do Sul 79003010
Tel: +55(67) 3348 - 8000
Fax: +55(67) 3341-9210
EMail: uniderp@uniderp.br
Website: http://www.uniderp.br

Reitor: Guilherme Marback Neto Tel: +55(67) 348-8002

Programmes

Administration; **Agronomy**; **Architecture and Planning**; **Arts and Humanities**; **Biological and Life Sciences**; **Communication Studies**; **Computer Science**; **Data Processing**; **Dentistry**; **Engineering**; **Geography**; **Law**; **Mathematics**; **Physical Therapy**; **Psychology**; **Tourism**; **Veterinary Science**
History: Founded 1976. Acquired present title 2008.
Admission Requirements: Secondary school certificate and entrance examination

Main Language(s) of Instruction: Portuguese

Degrees and Diplomas: *Bacharelado*; *Licenciatura*; *Mestrado*
Last Updated: 08/06/10

ANHEMBI MORUMBI UNIVERSITY

Universidade Anhembi Morumbi (UAM)
Rua Casa do Ator 90, Térreo Vila Olímpia, São Paulo, São Paulo 4546000
Tel: +55(11) 3847-3000
Fax: +55(11) 3841-9547
EMail: reit.rei@anhembi.br
Website: http://www.anhembi.br

President: Gabriel Mário Rodrigues (1997-)
EMail: gmr2@anhembi.br

Chief Executive Officer: Angela Regina de Paula Freitas
EMail: angela@anhembri.br

International Relations: Liliane Kafler, International Office Manager Tel: +55(11) 3847-3107 EMail: lilianekafler@anhembi.br

Schools

Arts, Architecture, Design and Fashion (Architecture; Dance; Design; Fashion Design; Media Studies; Music; Theatre; Town Planning); **Beauty Therapy**; **Business and Law** (Administration; International Business; International Relations; Law; Marketing); **Communication**; **Education** (Literature; Pedagogy); **Engineering and Technology**; **Health and Well-being** (Biology; Chiropractic; Nursing; Nutrition; Pharmacy; Physical Education; Physical Therapy; Psychology); **Medicine**; **Tourism and Hospitality** (Aeronautical and Aerospace Engineering; Hotel Management; Tourism); **Veterinary Medicine** (Veterinary Science)

History: Founded 1972, acquired present status 1997.

Admission Requirements: Secondary School certificate

Main Language(s) of Instruction: Portuguese, English

Degrees and Diplomas: *Bacharelado*; *Licenciatura*; *Especialização/Aperfeiçoamento*; *Mestrado*

Student Services: Academic counselling, Canteen, Employment services, Foreign student adviser, Handicapped facilities, Health services, Language programs, Nursery care, Social counselling, Sports facilities
Last Updated: 08/06/10

ANÍSIO TEIXEIRA FACULTY OF FEIRA DE SANTANA

Faculdade Anísio Teixeira de Feira de Santana (FAT)
Rua Juracy Magalhães 222, Ponto Central, Feira de Santana,
Bahia 44032-620
Tel: +55(75) 3616-9455
Fax: +55(75) 3616-9455
EMail: fat@fat.edu.br
Website: http://www.fat.edu.br

Diretor Presidente: Antonio Walter Moraes Lima

Courses
Accountancy; **Administration** (Administration); **Advertising and Publicity**; **Computer Networks** (Computer Networks); **Graduate Studies** (Accountancy; Communication Studies; Higher Education; Marketing; Medicine; Public Health; Speech Therapy and Audiology); **Journalism** (Journalism); **Law** (Law); **Nursing**; **Psychology** (Nursing); **Veterinary Medicine** (Veterinary Science)

History: Founded 2001.

Main Language(s) of Instruction: Portuguese

Degrees and Diplomas: *Bacharelado*; *Especialização/Aperfeiçoamento*
Last Updated: 24/06/10

ANÍSIO TEIXEIRA HIGHER EDUCATION CENTRE

Centro de Ensino Superior Anísio Teixeira (CESAT)
Avenida Desembargador Mario da Silva Nunes 1000,
Jardim Limoeiro, Serra, ES 29164-240
Tel: +55(27) 3041-7070 +55(27) 3041-7056
Fax: +55(27) 3041-7067
EMail: cesat@cesat.br
Website: http://www.cesat.br

Diretor Geral: Fabio Vassallo Mattos

Courses
Arts and Humanities; **Business Administration** (Business Administration); **Design** (Design); **Graduate Studies**; **History** (History); **Law** (Civil Law; Commercial Law; Constitutional Law; Criminal Law; Labour Law; Law; Private Law; Public Law); **Library Sciences**; **Mathematics** (Mathematics); **Political Science** (Political Sciences); **Secretarial Studies** (Secretarial Studies)

History: Founded 1999.

Main Language(s) of Instruction: Portuguese

Degrees and Diplomas: *Tecnólogo*; *Bacharelado*; *Especialização/ Aperfeiçoamento*
Last Updated: 22/03/10

ANÍSIO TEIXEIRA INSTITUTE OF EDUCATION

Instituto Superior de Educação Anísio Teixeira (ISEAT)
Avenida São Paulo, 3996, Vila Rosário, Ibirité, MG 32400-000
Tel: +55(31) 3521-9501
Fax: +55(31) 3533-2157
EMail: densino@fha.mg.gov.br

Courses
Graduate Studies (Educational Administration; Literacy Education; Pedagogy; Physical Education; Special Education); **Undergraduate Studies** (Biological and Life Sciences; English; Literature; Mathematics; Pedagogy; Physical Education)

Degrees and Diplomas: *Licenciatura*. Also Postgraduate Diploma.
Last Updated: 24/09/10

ANÍSIO TEIXEIRA INSTITUTE OF HUMAN AND SOCIAL SCIENCES

Instituto Superior de Ciências Humanas e Sociais Anísio Teixeira (ISAT)
Rua Dr. Francisco Portela, 2772, Zé Garoto, São Gonçalo,
RJ 24435-000
Tel: +55(21) 2712-6559
Fax: +55(21) 2605-1201
EMail: isat@isat.edu.br
Website: http://www.isat.edu.br/

Courses
Graduate Studies (Art Education; Business Administration; Educational Administration; Educational Psychology; English; History; Human Resources; Literacy Education; Mathematics Education; Petroleum and Gas Engineering; Translation and Interpretation); **Undergraduate Studies** (English; Literature; Pedagogy; Portuguese; Spanish; Translation and Interpretation)

Degrees and Diplomas: *Licenciatura*. Also Postgraduate Diploma.
Last Updated: 23/09/10

ANITA GARIBALDI FACULTY

Faculdade Anita Garibaldi
Rua Luiz Fagundes 1.680, Sao José, SC 88106-000
Tel: +55(48) 3343-2600
EMail: cesag@cesusc.edu.br

Diretor: Marison Luiz Soares

Courses
Accountancy (Accountancy); **Administration** (Administration); **Law** (Law); **Pedagogy** (Pedagogy); **Social Communication** (Advertising and Publicity; Public Relations); **Social Services** (Social and Community Services)

History: Founded 2004.

Main Language(s) of Instruction: Portuguese

Degrees and Diplomas: *Bacharelado*
Last Updated: 25/08/10

ANTONINO FREIRE INSTITUTE OF EDUCATION

Instituto Superior de Educação Antonino Freire (ISEAF)
Praça Firmina Sobreira, s/n, Matinha, Teresina, PI 64002-190
Tel: +55(86) 3216-3271
EMail: iseaf2004@yahoo.com.br
Website: http://www.iseaf.pi.gov.br/

Diretora Geral: Regina Cele Bonfim de Saboia Paz

Courses
Teacher Training (Teacher Training)

Degrees and Diplomas: *Licenciatura*
Last Updated: 24/09/10

ANTÔNIO EUFRÁSIO DE TOLEDO INTEGRATED FACULTIES OF PRESIDENTE PRUDENTE

Faculdades Integradas Antônio Eufrásio de Toledo de Presidente Prudente (FIAETPP)
Praça Raul Furquim 09, Vila Furquim, Presidente Prudente,
São Paulo 19030430
Tel: +55(18) 3901-4000
Fax: +55(18) 3901-4009
EMail: toledo@unitoledo.br
Website: http://www.unitoledo.br

Diretor Geral: Milton Pennacchi

Courses
Accountancy (Accountancy); **Administration** (Administration); **Economics** (Economics); **Law** (Law); **Social Services**

History: Founded 1961.

Main Language(s) of Instruction: Portuguese

Degrees and Diplomas: *Bacharelado*; *Especialização/Aperfeiçoamento*; *Mestrado*
Last Updated: 29/06/10

ANTÔNIO MENEGHETTI FACULTY

Faculdade Antônio Meneghetti
Rua Recanto Maestro, São João Polêsine 97230-000
EMail: amf@faculdadeam.edu.br
Website: http://www.faculdadeam.edu.br/institucional

Courses
Administration (Administration); **Information Systems**

Main Language(s) of Instruction: Portuguese

Degrees and Diplomas: *Bacharelado*; *Mestrado*
Last Updated: 12/07/10

APARÍCIO CARVALHO INTEGRATED FACULTIES

Faculdades Integradas Aparício Carvalho (FIMCA)
Rua das Araras 241, Jardim Eldorado, Porto Velho,
Rondônia 78912640
Tel: +55(69) 3227-8900
Fax: +55(69) 3227-0273
EMail: fimca@fimca.com.br
Website: http://www.fimca.com.br

Diretor Geral: Aparicio Carvalho de Moraes (1996-)
EMail: direcaogeral@fimca.com.br

Courses
Accountancy (Accountancy); **Administration**; **Agronomy** (Agronomy); **Architecture and Town Planning** (Architecture; Town Planning); **Biological and Life Sciences**; **Biomedicine** (Biomedicine); **Dentistry** (Dentistry); **Gastronomy** (Cooking and Catering); **Hospital Management**; **Medicine**; **Nursing** (Nursing); **Occupational Therapy** (Occupational Therapy); **Pharmacy** (Pharmacy); **Physical Therapy**; **Social Services** (Social and Community Services); **Tourism** (Tourism); **Veterinary Science** (Veterinary Science)

History: Founded 1998.

Main Language(s) of Instruction: Portuguese

Degrees and Diplomas: *Bacharelado*; *Licenciatura*; *Especialização/Aperfeiçoamento*
Last Updated: 29/06/10

APOGEU FACULTY

Faculdade Apogeu
Quadra 29 Lote 39/43 Setor Centra, Gama, DF 72405-290
EMail: secretaria@faculdadeapogeu.com.br
Website: http://www.faculdadeapogeu.com.br/apogeu/
principal.php

Diretor: Ademir Rodrigues Alves

Courses
Administration (Administration)

Main Language(s) of Instruction: Portuguese

Degrees and Diplomas: *Bacharelado*; *Especialização/Aperfeiçoamento*

Libraries: Yes
Last Updated: 13/07/10

APOIO FACULTY

Faculdade Apoio
Rua Praia de Itaparica s/n, Quadra 23, Vilas do Atlântico,
Lauro de Freitas, BA 42700-000
Tel: +55(71) 3379-6702
EMail: faculdadeapoio@faculdadeapoio.com.br
Website: http://www.faculdadeapoio.com.br

Diretor: José Vicente Cardoso Santos

Courses
Administration (Administration); **Law** (Law); **Production Engineering** (Production Engineering); **Teacher Training** (Teacher Training)

History: Founded 2004.

Main Language(s) of Instruction: Portuguese

Degrees and Diplomas: *Bacharelado*
Last Updated: 13/07/10

APRENDIZ CENTRE OF ADVANCED STUDIES

Centro de Estudos Superiores Aprendiz (CESA)
Avenida Bias Fortes, 2, Centro, Barbacena 36200-068
Tel: +55(32) 3333-0860
EMail: aprendiz@barbacena.com.br
Website: http://www.aprendiz.edu.br/

Reitora: Cristiane Nascimento

Courses
Law (Law); **Tourism** (Tourism)
Degrees and Diplomas: *Bacharelado*
Last Updated: 14/03/11

ARAGUAIA FACULTY

Faculdade Araguaia (FARA)
Rua 18, 81, Centro, Goiânia, Goiás 74030040
Tel: +55(62) 3224-8829
Fax: +55(62) 3224-8829
EMail: fara@faculdadearaguaia.edu.br
Website: http://www.faculdadearaguaia.edu.br/pgs/index.php

Diretor Presidente: Amaldo Cardoso Freire

Direção Administrativa: Ana Angélica Cardoso Freire
EMail: angelica@faculdadearaguaia.edu.br

Courses
Accountancy; **Administration**; **Advertising and Publicity** (Advertising and Publicity); **Biology**; **Environmental Engineering** (Environmental Engineering); **Graduate Studies**; **Journalism**; **Pedagogy** (Pedagogy); **Physical Education**

Further Information: Also Bueno Unit.

History: Founded 2001.

Degrees and Diplomas: *Bacharelado*; *Licenciatura*; *Especialização/Aperfeiçoamento*
Last Updated: 24/06/10

ARCHANGEL MICHAEL OF ARAPIRACA HIGHER EDUCATION CENTRE

Centro de Ensino Superior Arcanjo Mikael de Arapiraca (CESAMA)
Rua Gazeta de Alagoas, 85, Brasília, Arapiraca 57300-020
Tel: +55(82) 3530-1462
EMail: cesama.cesama@bol.com.br
Website: http://www.cesama.com/

Diretor Geral: Cícero Torres Sobrinho

Courses
Law

Degrees and Diplomas: *Bacharelado*
Last Updated: 12/07/10

ARCHDIOCESE OF DOM LUCIANO MENDES FACULTY

Faculdade Arquidiocesana Dom Luciano Mendes
Rodovia dos Inconfidentes, Km 108 s/n, Mariana, MG
Tel: +55(31) 3558-1439
EMail: famariana@famariana.edu.br
Website: http://www.famariana.edu.br/

Diretor: Paulo Vicente R. Nobre

Courses
Philosophy

Degrees and Diplomas: *Bacharelado*
Last Updated: 13/07/10

AREA 1 - FACULTY OF SCIENCE AND TECHNOLOGY

ÁREA1 - Faculdade de Ciência e Tecnológia (AREA1)
Av. Paralela, 3172, Salvador, Bahia 41720-200
Tel: +55(71) 2106-3911
EMail: area1@area1.br
Website: http://www.area1.br/

Diretor Geral: Ítalo Ghignone

Courses
Computer Engineering; **Electrical Engineering** (Electrical Engineering); **Environmental Engineering** (Environmental Engineering); **Graduate Studies** (Automation and Control Engineering; Civil Engineering; Computer Networks; Electrical Engineering; Environmental Engineering; Petroleum and Gas Engineering; Safety Engineering); **Mechatronic Engineering** (Electronic Engineering); **Production Engineering**

History: Founded 1999.

Main Language(s) of Instruction: Portuguese

Degrees and Diplomas: *Bacharelado*; *Especialização/Aperfeiçoamento*

Last Updated: 02/07/10

ARMANDO ÁLVARES PENTEADO FOUNDATION

Fundação Armando Álvares Penteado (FAAP)
Rua Alagoas 903, Prédio 5, Pacaembu, São Paulo,
São Paulo 1242001
Tel: +55(11) 3662-1662 +55(11) 3662-1130
Fax: +55(11) 3662-1662 +55(11) 3662-1173
EMail: adm.secretaria@faap.br
Website: http://www.faap.br

Diretor: Henrique Vailati Neto

Centres
Strategic Studies (Military Science)

Faculties
Administration (Administration; Hotel Management); **Communication and Marketing** *(FACOM-FAAP)*; **Computer Science** *(FCI-FAAP)* (Computer Science); **Economics** *(FEC-FAAP)* (Economics; International Relations); **Engineering** *(FEFAAP)* (Chemical Engineering; Civil Engineering; Electrical Engineering; Mechanical Engineering); **Law** *(FAD-FAAP)* (Law); **Visual Arts and Architecture** (Architecture; Art Education; Cultural Studies; Design; Fashion Design)

Further Information: Also campuses in Sao José dos Campos and Ribeirao Preto

History: Founded 1947.

Main Language(s) of Instruction: Portuguese

Degrees and Diplomas: *Bacharelado*; *Especialização/Aperfeiçoamento*; *Mestrado*

Last Updated: 18/06/10

ARNALDO HORACIO FERREIRA FACULTY

Faculdade Arnaldo Horacio Ferreira
Rua: Para - 2.280, Luis Eduardo Magalhães, BA 47.850-000
Tel: +55(77) 3628 - 9900
Fax: +55(77) 3628 - 9917
EMail: angelica@josewalter.adv.br
Website: http://www.faahf.edu.br/site

Diretora: Maria Angélica Cardoso Ferreira de Sousa

Courses
Accountancy (Accountancy); **Administration** (Administration); **Agronomy**; **Law** (Law); **Letters**; **Pedagogy**; **Production Engineering**

History: Founded 2005.

Main Language(s) of Instruction: Portuguese

Degrees and Diplomas: *Bacharelado*; *Especialização/Aperfeiçoamento*; *Mestrado*

Last Updated: 13/07/10

ARNALDO JANSSEN FACULTY

Faculdade Arnaldo Janssen
Praça João Pessoa, 200, Funcionários, Belo Horizonte,
MG 30140-020
Tel: +55(31) 3524-5001
Website: http://www.faculdadearnaldo.edu.br

Diretor: Renê Luiz Paulino de Oliveira

Courses
Administration (Administration; Management); **Law** (Law)

History: Founded 2001.

Main Language(s) of Instruction: Portuguese

Degrees and Diplomas: *Bacharelado*; *Especialização/Aperfeiçoamento*

Last Updated: 28/07/10

ARTHUR SÁ EARP NETO FACULTY/ FACULTY OF MEDICINE OF PETRÓPOLIS

Faculdade Arthur Sá Earp Neto/ Faculdade de Medicina de Petrópolis (FMP/FASE)
Av. Barão do Rio Branco, 1003 - Centro, Petrópolis,
Rio de Janeiro 25716970
Tel: +55(24) 2231-1818
EMail: ambe@fmpfase.edu.br
Website: http://www.fmpfase.edu.br

Supervisora Geral: Maria Isabel de Sá Earp de Resende Chaves (1998-)

Courses
Administration (Administration; Health Administration; Information Management; Information Sciences); **Graduate Studies** (Health Administration; Nutrition; Psychology; Public Health; Rehabilitation and Therapy); **Medicine** (Medicine); **Nursing**; **Nutrition** (Nutrition)

History: Founded ad Faculdade de Medicina de Petrópolis 1967. Faculdade Arthur Sá Earp Neto founded 1998

Degrees and Diplomas: *Bacharelado*; *Licenciatura*; *Especialização/Aperfeiçoamento*

Last Updated: 24/06/10

ARTS FACULTY

Faculdade Pensar
Praça Marconi 04, Salvador, BA 41830-200
Tel: +55(71) 3345-2419
EMail: jvcs.jvcs@gmail.com

Diretor: José Carlos . do Carmo

Courses
Administration (Administration); **Teacher Training** (Teacher Training)

History: Founded 2006.

Main Language(s) of Instruction: Portuguese

Degrees and Diplomas: *Bacharelado*

Last Updated: 22/09/10

ASA FACULTY OF BRUMADINHO

Faculdade ASA de Brumadinho
MG 040, KM 49, Brumadinho, Minas Gerais 35460-000
Tel: +55(31) 3571-9300
EMail: faculdadeasa@br.inter.net
Website: http://www.faculdadeasa.com.br

Diretora Geral: Sonia Aparecida Barcelos

Courses
Accountancy; **Administration** (Administration; Business Administration); **Graduate Studies** (Accountancy; Educational Psychology; Finance; Pedagogy; Preschool Education); **History**; **Law** (Law); **Literature**; **Technical Studies**

History: Founded 2001.

Main Language(s) of Instruction: Portuguese

Degrees and Diplomas: *Tecnólogo*; *Bacharelado*; *Licenciatura*; *Especialização/Aperfeiçoamento*

Last Updated: 24/06/10

ASCES FACULTY - HIGHER EDUCATION ASSOCIATION OF CARUARU

Faculdade ASCES - Associação Caruaruense de Ensino Superior (ASCES)
Avenida Portugal 584, Santa Maria, Caruaru, PE 55016400
Tel: +55(81) 2103-2000
EMail: asces@asces.edu.br
Website: http://www.asces.edu.br

Diretor Presidente: Paulo Muniz Lopez

Courses
Environmental Engineering (Environmental Engineering); **Graduate Studies**; **International Relations**; **Physical Education**; **Public Administration**; **Social Service** (Social Work; Welfare and Protective Services)

Faculties
Agreste de Pernambuco *(FAAPE)* (Biomedicine; Dentistry; Nursing; Pharmacy; Physical Therapy); **Law** *(FADICA)* (Law); **Odontology** *(FOC)*

History: Founded 1959. Acquired present status 2005.

Degrees and Diplomas: *Bacharelado*; *Especialização/Aperfeiçoamento*
Last Updated: 05/03/10

ASMEC INTEGRATED FACULTIES OF OURO FINO

Faculdades Integradas ASMEC Ouro Fino (FAECO)
Avenida Prof Dr. Antônio Eufrásio de Toledo 100, Jardim dos Ipes, Ouro Fino, Minas Gerais 37570000
Tel: +55(35) 3441-1617
Fax: +55(35) 3441-2608
EMail: asmec@asmec.br
Website: http://www.asmec.br

Diretor Presidente: Guilherme Bernades Filho
EMail: guilherme@asmec.br

Faculties
Economics; **Philosophy, Science and Literature** (Biology; Chemistry; Geography; Literature; Pedagogy; Physical Education); **Technology**

Higher Institutes
Education (Mathematics; Nutrition; Physical Therapy)

History: Founded 1974 as Faculdade de Filosofia, Ciências e Letras de Ouro Fino. Acquired present status 1998.

Main Language(s) of Instruction: Portuguese

Degrees and Diplomas: *Bacharelado*; *Licenciatura*; *Especialização/Aperfeiçoamento*
Last Updated: 30/06/10

ASSESC INTEGRATED FACULTIES

Faculdades Integradas ASSESC (FASSESC)
Rodovia SC 401 Km 01 407, Itacurubi, Florianópolis, Santa Catarina 88030000
Tel: +55(48) 3202-6000
Fax: +55(48) 3202-6042
EMail: assesc@assesc.edu.br
Website: http://www.assesc.edu.br/index2.php

Diretor: Maurício Silveira Ulysséa

Courses
Administration; **Gastronomy**; **Hotel Management** (Hotel Management); **Social Communication** (Media Studies; Public Relations); **Tourism**

History: Founded 1994. Acquired present status 2002.

Main Language(s) of Instruction: Portuguese

Degrees and Diplomas: *Bacharelado*; *Especialização/Aperfeiçoamento*; *Mestrado*
Last Updated: 29/06/10

ASSIS GURGACZ FACULTY

Faculdade Assis Gurgacz (FAG)
Avenida das Torres, 500, Loteamento FAG, Cascavel, Paraná 85812080
Tel: +55(45) 3321-3900
Fax: +55(45) 3321-3902
EMail: fag@fag.edu.br
Website: http://www.fag.edu.br

Diretor Geral: Sergio de Angelis

Courses
Accountancy; **Administration**; **Advertising and Publicity** (Advertising and Publicity); **Agronomy** (Agronomy); **Architecture and Town Planning** (Architecture; Town Planning); **Biology**; **Civil Engineering** (Civil Engineering); **Engineering - Automation, Control and TelecommunicationsEngineering** (Automation and Control Engineering; Telecommunications Engineering); **Graduate Studies** (Biological and Life Sciences; Biology; Business Education; Cinema and Television; Communication Studies; Constitutional

Law; Education; Educational Administration; Educational Psychology; Engineering; Finance; Higher Education; History; Human Resources; Marketing; Nursing; Nutrition; Pharmacology; Philosophy; Photography; Physical Therapy; Plant and Crop Protection; Preschool Education; Safety Engineering; Sociology; Soil Science; Special Education; Toxicology); **Journalism** (Journalism); **Law** (Law); **Mechanical Engineering**; **Medicine** (Medicine); **Nursing**; **Nutrition** (Nutrition); **Pedagogy** (Pedagogy); **Pharmacy** (Pharmacy); **Phonoaudiology**; **Physical Education** (Physical Education); **Physiotherapy**; **Psychology** (Psychology); **Veterinary Medicine**

History: Founded 1997.

Main Language(s) of Instruction: Portuguese

Degrees and Diplomas: *Bacharelado*; *Licenciatura*; *Especialização/Aperfeiçoamento*
Last Updated: 24/06/10

ASSIS SCHOOL OF PHYSICAL EDUCATION

Escola de Educação Física de Assis (EEFA)
Av. Dr. Dória, n° 260, Vila Ouro Verde 19816-230
Tel: +55(18) 3302-2552
Fax: +55(18) 3302-2552
EMail: secretariafac@ieda.edu.br
Website: http://189.126.166.100/PHP/edf.php

Courses
Physical Education

Degrees and Diplomas: *Licenciatura*
Last Updated: 13/07/10

ASSOCIATED FACULTIES OF SAO PAULO

Faculdades Associadas de São Paulo (FASP)
Avenida Paulista 2000, São Paulo, São Paulo 01310-200
Tel: +55(11) 3016-0233
EMail: secretaria@fasp.br
Website: http://www.fasp.br

Diretor: Nilton Trama

Courses
Administration; **Computer Science**

History: Founded 1974

Main Language(s) of Instruction: Portuguese

Degrees and Diplomas: *Bacharelado*; *Especialização/Aperfeiçoamento*; *Mestrado*
Last Updated: 30/06/10

ASSOCIATED FACULTIES OF UBERABA

Faculdades Associadas de Uberaba (FAZU)
Avenida do Tutuna 720, Uberaba, Minas Gerais 38061500
Tel: +55(34) 3318-4188
Fax: +55(34) 3318-4188
EMail: fazu@fazu.br
Website: http://www.fazu.br

Diretora Geral: Dionir Dias de Oliveira Andrade (1997-)

Courses
Agronomy (Agronomy); **Food Processing** (Food Technology); **Zoology**

History: Founded 1975 as Faculdade de Agronomia e Zootecnia de Uberaba.

Main Language(s) of Instruction: Portuguese

Degrees and Diplomas: *Bacharelado*; *Especialização/Aperfeiçoamento*
Last Updated: 30/06/10

ASSOCIATED SCHOOL OF GOIÁS

Escola Superior Associada de Goiânia (ESUP)
Avenida Antonio Fidélis, 515, Parque Amazônia, Goiânia, GO 74840-090
Tel: +55(62) 3931-4400
Fax: +55(62) 3931-4434
EMail: esup@esup.edu.br
Website: http://www.esup.edu.br

Diretor Academico da Unidade de Educação: Luiz Antônio Ribeiro de Sousa

Courses

Administration (Administration; Business Administration); **Graduate Studies** (Business Administration); **Law**

Degrees and Diplomas: *Bacharelado*; *Especialização/Aperfeiçoamento*
Last Updated: 15/07/10

ASSUNÇÃO UNIVERSITY CENTRE
Centro Universitário Assunção (UNIFAI)
Rua Nazaré, 993, Ipiranga, São Paulo 04263100
Tel: +55(11) 6166-8555
EMail: iesp@fai.br
Website: http://www.unifai.br

Reitor: José Benedito Simão (1995-)

Courses

Accountancy (Accountancy); **Administration** *(Vila Mariana)* (Administration); **Archiving** (Archiving); **Computer Engineering**; **Computer Science**; **Geography** *(Vila Mariana)* (Geography); **Graduate Studies**; **History** *(Vila Mariana)* (History); **Language and Literature** *(Vila Mariana)*; **Law** *(Vila Mariana)* (Law); **Library Studies** *(Vila Mariana)*; **Mathematics** *(Vila Mariana)* (Mathematics); **Pedagogy** *(Vila Mariana)* (Pedagogy); **Philosophy**; **Secretarial Studies** *(Vila Mariana)* (Secretarial Studies); **Social Sciences** *(Vila Mariana)* (Anthropology; Geography; History; Political Sciences; Social Sciences; Sociology); **Social Service**; **Tourism** (Tourism)

History: Founded 1971. Acquired present title and status 2000.
Main Language(s) of Instruction: Portuguese
Degrees and Diplomas: *Bacharelado*; *Licenciatura*; *Especialização/Aperfeiçoamento*; *Mestrado*
Last Updated: 20/05/10

ATENAS FACULTY
Faculdade Atenas
Rua Euridamas Avelino de Barros, 60 - Lavrado, Paracatu, MG 38600-000
Tel: +55(38) 3672-3737
EMail: faculdade@atenas.edu.br
Website: http://www.atenas.edu.br

Diretor: Hiran Costa Rabelo

Courses

Administration (Administration); **Information Systems**; **Law**; **Medicine** (Medicine); **Nutrition** (Nutrition); **Physical Education**
Main Language(s) of Instruction: Portuguese
Degrees and Diplomas: *Bacharelado*; *Licenciatura*; *Especialização/Aperfeiçoamento*
Libraries: Yes
Last Updated: 13/07/10

ATENAS MARANHENSE FACULTY
Faculdade Atenas Maranhense (FAMA)
Avenida São Luís Rei de França, n° 32, Turú, São Luís, Maranhão
Tel: +55(98) 2108-6000
Fax: +55(98) 2108-6011
EMail: faculdade@fama.br
Website: http://www.fama.br

Diretora Geral: Zenira Massoli Fiquene

Courses

Accountancy; **Administration** (Administration; Finance; Human Resources; Marketing; Technology; Transport Management); **Executive Secretary** (Secretarial Studies); **Graduate Studies** (Acupuncture; Business Administration; Development Studies; Educational Administration; Educational Psychology; English; Environmental Management; Health Administration; Higher Education; History; Hotel Management; Information Management; International Business; Justice Administration; Literacy Education; Literature; Management; Mathematics; Occupational Health; Portuguese; Production Engineering; Psychology; Public Administration; Safety Engineering; Secretarial Studies; Small Business;

Statistics; Tourism); **Literature** (English; Literature; Portuguese; Spanish); **Pedagogy**; **Tourism** (Tourism)
History: Founded 2000.
Fees: (Reals)
Main Language(s) of Instruction: Portuguese
Degrees and Diplomas: *Bacharelado*; *Licenciatura*; *Especialização/Aperfeiçoamento*
Last Updated: 24/06/10

ATENAS MARANHENSE FACULTY OF IMPERATRIZ
Faculdade Atenas Maranhense de Imperatriz (FAMA)
Monte Castelo 161, Centro, Imperatriz, MA 65900000
Tel: +55(99) 2101-6000
EMail: faculdade@famaitz.edu.br
Website: http://www.famaitz.edu.br

Diretor Geral: Antonio Cláudio dos Santos Júnio

Courses

Administration; **Graduate Studies**; **Tourism** (Tourism)
History: Founded 1999.
Main Language(s) of Instruction: Portuguese
Degrees and Diplomas: *Bacharelado*; *Especialização/Aperfeiçoamento*
Last Updated: 24/06/10

ATHENAEUM INSTITUTE OF EDUCATION
Instituto Superior de Educação Ateneu (ISEAT)
Rua Professor Annor Silva, 106, Coqueiral de Itaparica, Vila Velha, ES 29102-160
Tel: +55(27) 3319-1617
Fax: +55(27) 3319-1617
EMail: ateneu-es@ig.com.br

Courses

Mathematics (Mathematics); **Pedagogy** (Pedagogy)
Degrees and Diplomas: *Licenciatura*
Last Updated: 24/09/10

ATHENEUM FACULTY
Faculdade Ateneu
Avenida Coletor Antonio Gadelha 621, Fortaleza, CE 60871-170
Tel: +55 (85) 3276-2032
EMail: cfb@fortalnet.com.br
Website: http://www.fate.edu.br/v3

Diretor: Claudio Ferreira Bastos

Courses

Accountancy (Accountancy); **Administration** (Administration); **Health** *(Postgraduate)* (Health Sciences); **Law** *(Postgraduate)* (Law)
Further Information: Also campuses in Vila Velha and Tiangua
Degrees and Diplomas: *Bacharelado*; *Especialização/Aperfeiçoamento*
Libraries: Yes
Last Updated: 23/08/10

ATLANTIC FACULTY
Faculdade Atlântico
Rua Engenheiro João Carvalho de Aragão, n° 69, Atalaia, Aracaju, SE
Tel: +55(79) 3243-1435
EMail: faculdadeatlantico@infonet.com.br
Website: http://www.faculdadeatlantico.com.br

Diretora: Jaciara Cordeiro de Oliveira Lisbôa

Courses

Letters (Literature); **Pedagogy** (Pedagogy)
History: Founded 1990 as Centro Educacional Atlântico. Acquired present status and title 2002.
Main Language(s) of Instruction: Portuguese

Degrees and Diplomas: *Licenciatura*; *Especialização/Aperfeiçoamento*

Libraries: Biblioteca Central Josefa Ribeiro Lisbôa
Last Updated: 20/08/10

AUGUSTO MOTTA UNIVERSITY CENTRE
Centro Universitário Augusto Motta (UNISUAM)
Avenida Paris, 72, Bonsucesso, Rio de Janeiro,
Rio de Janeiro 21041-020
Tel: +55(21) 3882-9797 +55(21) 3882-9702
Fax: +55(21) 2564-2244
EMail: reitoria@unisuam.edu.br
Website: http://www.unisuam.edu.br

Reitor: Arapuan Medeiros da Motta Netto

Courses
Accountancy; **Administration**; **Advertising and Publicity** (Advertising and Publicity); **Architecture and Urbanism** (Architecture; Town Planning); **Arts and Humanities** (Arts and Humanities; Literature; Portuguese); **Arts and Humanities**; **Biological and Life Sciences** (Biological and Life Sciences); **Civil Engineering** (Civil Engineering); **Computer Science** (Computer Science); **Esthetics and Cosmetics**; **Gastronomy** (Cooking and Catering); **Graduate Studies** (Business Administration; Civil Law; Cooking and Catering; Law; Nursing; Nutrition; Occupational Health; Physical Education; Physical Therapy; Portuguese; Social and Community Services; Structural Architecture); **History**; **Informatics**; **Journalism**; **Law**; **Logistics**; **Marketing**; **Mathematics** (Mathematics); **Nursing**; **Nutrition** (Nutrition); **Pedagogy**; **Petroleum and Gas Engineering** (Petroleum and Gas Engineering); **Pharmacy** (Pharmacy); **Physical Education**; **Physical Therapy** (Physical Therapy); **Production Engineering** (Production Engineering); **Psychology** (Psychology); **Social Service** (Social and Community Services); **Tourism**

History: Founded 1970.

Main Language(s) of Instruction: Portuguese

Degrees and Diplomas: *Tecnólogo*; *Bacharelado*; *Licenciatura*. Also postgraduate programmes and MBA.
Last Updated: 20/05/10

AUM FACULTY
Faculdade Aum
Avenida Dom aquino n° 38, Centro, Cuiabá, MT 8015-200
Tel: +55(65) 3052-8120
EMail: assessoria.uam@terra.com.br
Website: http://www.faculdadeaum.com

Diretor: Dirceu do Nascimento

Courses
Biomedicine (Biomedicine); **Nursing**; **Physical Education** (Physical Education); **Psychology** (Psychology)

History: Founded 2008.

Main Language(s) of Instruction: Portuguese

Degrees and Diplomas: *Bacharelado*
Last Updated: 15/07/10

AUTONOMOUS FACULTY OF LAW OF SAO PAULO
Faculdade Autônoma de Direito de São Paulo (FADISP)
Rua João Moura 313, Pinheiros, São Paulo, SP
Tel: +55(11) 3061-0212
EMail: fadisp@fadisp.edu.br
Website: http://www.fadisp.com.br

Diretor: Nelson de Carvalho Filho

Courses
Law (Civil Law; Commercial Law; Criminal Law; Law)

History: Founded 2001.

Main Language(s) of Instruction: Portuguese

Degrees and Diplomas: *Bacharelado*; *Especialização/Aperfeiçoamento*; *Mestrado*; *Doutorado*

Libraries: Yes
Last Updated: 13/07/10

AUXILIUM INSTITUTE OF EDUCATION
Instituto Superior de Educação Auxilium (ISE AUXILIUM)
Avenida Nicolau Zarvos 754, Jardim Santa Clara, 1° Andar, Lins,
São Paulo 16401300
Tel: +55(14) 522-2733 +55(14) 522-2725
Fax: +55(14) 522-6025 +55(14) 522-6026
EMail: fal@fallins.edu.br

Diretora Presidente: Maria Aparecida Marin (1992-)

Courses
Arts and Humanities; **Biology** (Biology); **Chemistry**; **Education** (Education); **History** (History); **Mathematics**; **Physics** (Physics)

History: Founded 1957 as Faculdade Auxilium.

Main Language(s) of Instruction: Portuguese

Degrees and Diplomas: *Licenciatura*
Last Updated: 29/11/07

AVANTIS FACULTY
Faculdade Avantis
Av. Marginal Leste, n° 3600, KM 132 - Bairro dos Estados,
Balneário Camboriú, SC 88.339-125
Tel: +55(47) 3363-0631
EMail: bella@avantis.edu.br
Website: http://www.avantis.edu.br

Diretora: Isabel Regina Depine Poffo

Courses
Accountancy; **Administration** (Administration; Business Administration; Marketing); **Computer Science**; **Physical Education** (Physical Education); **Psychology** (Psychology)

History: Founded 2002.

Main Language(s) of Instruction: Portuguese

Degrees and Diplomas: *Bacharelado*; *Licenciatura*; *Especialização/Aperfeiçoamento*
Last Updated: 13/07/10

AVILA FACULTY
Faculdade Avila
Rua T-64 N° 881 Qd 157 Lt 1E - Setor Bueno, Goiania,
GO 74230-040
Website: http://www.faculdadeavila.com.br

Diretor Geral: Laercio Galvao de Oliveira Avila

Courses
Accountancy (Accountancy); **Administration** (Administration)

History: Founded 2002.

Main Language(s) of Instruction: Portuguese

Degrees and Diplomas: *Bacharelado*; *Especialização/Aperfeiçoamento*; *Mestrado*
Last Updated: 13/07/10

BAGOZZI FACULTY
Faculdade Bagozzi
Rua Caetano Marchesini 952, Curitiba, PR 81070-110
Tel: +55(41) 3521-2727
EMail: faculdade@faculdadebagozzi.edu.br
Website: http://www.faculdadebagozzi.edu.br

Diretor: Douglas Oliani

Courses
Administration (Administration); **Pedagogy** (Pedagogy); **Philiosophy** (Philosophy); **Social Services** (Social and Community Services)

History: Founded 2001.

Main Language(s) of Instruction: Portuguese

Degrees and Diplomas: *Bacharelado*; *Especialização/Aperfeiçoamento*; *Mestrado*

Libraries: Yes
Last Updated: 09/09/10

BAHIA ADVENTIST UNIVERSITY

Faculdades Adventista da Bahia (FADBA)
BR 101 Km 201, Estrada de Capoeiruçu, Cachoeira,
Bahia 44300000
Tel: +55(75) 3425-8000
EMail: info@adventista.edu.br
Website: http://www.adventista.edu.br

Diretor: Gilberto Damasceno da Silva
EMail: diretor.geral@adventista.edu.br

Faculties
Administration; **Pedagogy**; **Physical Therapy** (Physical Therapy); **Psychology and Nursing** (Nursing; Psychology); **Theology** (Theology)

Schools
Music (Music)

History: Founded 1998. Formerly known as Instituto Adventista de Ensino do Nordeste (Adventist Institute of Education of the North East).

Main Language(s) of Instruction: Portuguese

Degrees and Diplomas: *Bacharelado*; *Especialização/Aperfeiçoamento*
Last Updated: 30/06/10

BAHIA FACULTY OF LAW AND MANAGEMENT

Faculdade Baiana de Direito e Gestão
Rua Visconde de Itaborahy 989, Amaralina, Salvador, BA
Tel: +55(71) 3205-7700
EMail: contato@faculdadebaianadedireito.com.br
Website: http://www.faculdadebaianadedireito.com.br

Diretor: Guilherme Cortizo Bellintani

Courses
Accountancy (Accountancy); **Administration** (Administration); **Law** (Law); **Pedagogy** (Pedagogy); **Tourism** (Tourism)

History: Founded 2004.

Main Language(s) of Instruction: Portuguese

Degrees and Diplomas: *Bacharelado*; *Especialização/Aperfeiçoamento*
Last Updated: 31/08/10

BAHIA FACULTY OF SCIENCE

Faculdade Baiana de Ciências (FABAC)
Estrada do Coco, Km 45, Lauro de Freitas, Bahia 42700-000
Tel: +55(71) 3505-4599
Fax: +55(71) 3505-4599
EMail: Fabac@fabac.com.br
Website: http://www.fabac.edu.br

Superintendente Executivo (CEO): Jânyo Diniz

Courses
Graduate Studies (Business Administration; Criminology; Human Resources; Law; Public Administration; Real Estate); **Law** (Law)

History: Founded 1998

Main Language(s) of Instruction: Portuguese

Degrees and Diplomas: *Bacharelado*. Also Postgraduate Diploma.
Last Updated: 29/06/10

BAHIA SCHOOL OF ADMINISTRATION

Escola Bahiana de Administração (EBA)
Avenida Dom João VI 275, Brotas, Salvador, Bahia 40290-000
Tel: +55(71) 276-8246 +55(71) 276-8247
Fax: +55(71) 357-0218
EMail: fdbc@fbdc.edu.br
Website: http://www.ebah.com.br/eba

Diretora: Sonia Rapold

Courses
Administration (Administration)

History: Founded 1997

Degrees and Diplomas: *Bacharelado*

Last Updated: 04/01/08

BAHIA SCHOOL OF MEDICINE AND PUBLIC HEALTH

Escola Bahiana de Medicina e Saúde Pública (EBMSP)
Av. Dom João IV, 274, Salvador, Bahia 40290-000
Tel: +55(71) 2101-1900
Fax: +55(71) 3356-1936
EMail: fbdc@bahiana.edu.br
Website: http://www.bahiana.edu.br

Diretora: Maria Luisa Carvalho Soliani

Courses
Biomedicine (Biomedicine); **Graduate Studies** (Dental Technology; Dentistry; Nursing; Periodontics; Physical Therapy; Public Health; Surgery); **Graduate Studies** *(Stricto Sensu)* (Dentistry; Health Sciences; Medicine; Neurosciences; Periodontics; Stomatology; Virology); **Medicine** (Medicine); **Nursing** (Nursing); **Occupational Therapy**; **Odontology** (Dentistry); **Physiotherapy**; **Psychology** (Psychology)

History: Founded 1953

Degrees and Diplomas: *Bacharelado*; *Especialização/Aperfeiçoamento*; *Mestrado*
Last Updated: 18/06/10

BAHIA SCHOOL OF STATISTICS

Escola Superior de Estatística da Bahia (ESEB)
Rua Arquimedes Gonçalves 32, Jardim Baiano, Salvador,
Bahia 40050-300
Tel: +55(71) 3321-3028
Fax: +55(71) 3321-1906
EMail: esebsecretaria@veloxmail.com.br

Diretor: Jorge Fernandes da Luz Alves

Courses
Statistics (Statistics)

History: Founded 1953.

Main Language(s) of Instruction: Portuguese

Degrees and Diplomas: *Bacharelado*
Last Updated: 23/06/10

BAPTIST FACULTY OF MINAS GERAIS

Faculdade Batista de Minas Gerais (FBMG)
Rua Varginha, 630 - Bairro Floresta, Belo Horizonte,
Minas Gerais 31110-130
Tel: +55(31) 3429-7232
EMail: faleconosco@sistemabatista.edu.br
Website: http://www.faculdadebatista.com.br/

Diretora: Christina Rocha

Courses
Accountancy; **Administration** (Administration; Educational Administration; Marketing; Public Administration); **Graduate Studies** (Accountancy; Business and Commerce; Civil Law; Criminal Law; Educational Administration; Finance; Law; Management; Marketing; Philosophy; Theology); **Law**; **Theology** (Bible; Pastoral Studies; Theology)

History: Founded 1999.

Main Language(s) of Instruction: Portuguese

Degrees and Diplomas: *Bacharelado*; *Especialização/Aperfeiçoamento*
Last Updated: 29/06/10

BAPTIST FACULTY OF RIO DE JANEIRO

Faculdade Batista do Rio de Janeiro
Rua José Higino, 416 - Caixa Postal, 24060, Rio de Janeiro,
RJ 20510-412
Tel: +55(21) 2570-1833
Website: http://www.fabat.com.br

Diretor: Israel Belo de Azevedo

Courses
Music; **Pedagogy** (Pedagogy); **Theology** (Theology)

History: Founded 2000 as Faculdade de Ciências da Educação. Acquired present title 2004.

Main Language(s) of Instruction: Portuguese

Degrees and Diplomas: *Bacharelado*; *Licenciatura*

Last Updated: 15/07/10

BAPTIST FACULTY OF SERRA

Faculdade Batista da Serra (FABAVI)
Rua 1D - N° 80 - Civit II, Serra, ES 29165680
Tel: +55(27) 3434-6200
EMail: webmail@fabavi.br
Website: http://www.fabavi.br

Diretor: Rogério Moreira Scheidegger

Courses

Administration (Administration); **Advertising and Publicity** (Advertising and Publicity); **Biological Sciences** (Biological and Life Sciences); **Graduate Studies** (Administration; Biological and Life Sciences; Education; Energy Engineering; Health Sciences; Law; Physical Education; Technology); **Journalism** (Journalism); **Law**; **Nursing** (Nursing); **Pedagogy** (Pedagogy); **Technological Studies** (Computer Networks; Petroleum and Gas Engineering)

Further Information: Also Vila Velha, Vitória and Guarapari Units.

History: Founded 1999.

Degrees and Diplomas: *Tecnólogo*; *Bacharelado*; *Licenciatura*; *Especialização/Aperfeiçoamento*

Last Updated: 29/06/10

BAPTIST INSTITUTE OF HIGHER EDUCATION OF ALAGOAS

Instituto Batista de Ensino Superior de Alagoas
Av Aristeu de Andrade, 256 Farol, Maceió, AL
Tel: +55(82) 3221-5636
EMail: ibesa@ibesa.com.br
Website: http://www.ibesa.com.br

Diretor: Gilson Nobre dos Santos

Faculties

Physical Education (Physical Education)

History: Founded 2001.

Main Language(s) of Instruction: Portuguese

Degrees and Diplomas: *Bacharelado*; *Especialização/Aperfeiçoamento*

Libraries: Yes

Last Updated: 22/09/10

BAPTIST SCHOOL OF THE AMAZON

Escola Superior Batista do Amazonas (ESBAM)
Rua Leonor Teles, 153, Conjunto Abílio Nery, Adrianópolis,
Mánaus, Amazonas 69057-510
Tel: +55(92) 3236-6936
Fax: +55(92) 3236-7244
EMail: esbam@esbam.edu.br
Website: http://www.esbam.edu.br

Diretora Geral: Sandra Miranda de Queiroz
EMail: sandra@esbam.edu.br

Courses

Accountancy; **Biology** (Biology); **Business Administration** (Administration; Business Administration); **Graduate Studies** *(Lato Sensu)*; **Information Systems**; **Law**; **Literature** (English; Literature; Portuguese; Spanish); **Mathematics** (Mathematics); **Pedagogy**; **Psychology** (Psychology); **Social Services** (Social and Community Services); **Veterinary Medicine** (Veterinary Science)

History: Founded 2000.

Main Language(s) of Instruction: Portuguese

Degrees and Diplomas: *Bacharelado*; *Licenciatura*; *Especialização/Aperfeiçoamento*

Last Updated: 18/06/10

BARÃO DE MAUÁ UNIVERSITY CENTRE

Centro Universitário Barão de Mauá (UFBM)
Rua Ramos de Azevedo, 423, Jardim Paulista, Ribeirão Preto,
São Paulo 14090180
Tel: +55(16) 3603-6600
Fax: +55(16) 3618-6102
EMail: info@baraodemaua.com.br
Website: http://www.baraodemaua.br

Reitora: Maria Célia Pressinatto

Centres

Distance Education (Educational Psychology; Higher Education; Special Education)\

Courses

Administration (Administration); **Architecture and Urbanism**; **Arts and Humanities** (Arts and Humanities; English; Portuguese); **Arts Education**; **Biological Sciences** (Biological and Life Sciences); **Biomedicine** (Biomedicine); **Computer Science** (Computer Science; Mathematics and Computer Science); **Environmental Engineering** (Environmental Engineering); **Geography**; **Graduate Studies** *(MBA)* (Accountancy; Business Administration; Business and Commerce; Finance; Information Technology; Marketing); **Graduate Studies** *(Especialização)*; **History**; **Journalism** (Journalism); **Law** (Law); **Medicine** (Medicine); **Nursing** (Nursing); **Pedagogy** (Pedagogy); **Pharmacy** (Pharmacy); **Pharmacy** (Pharmacy); **Physical Therapy**; **Production Engineering** (Production Engineering); **Psychology** (Psychology); **Social and Community Services** (Social and Community Services); **Social Communication** (Advertising and Publicity); **Technological Studies** (Agricultural Business; Computer Science; Cooking and Catering; Environmental Management); **Theatre**; **Tourism** (Tourism); **Veterinary Science**

History: Founded 1968.

Degrees and Diplomas: *Tecnólogo*; *Bacharelado*; *Licenciatura*; *Especialização/Aperfeiçoamento*. Also MBA.

Last Updated: 21/05/10

BARDDAL FACULTIES

Faculdades Barddal
Avenida Madre Benvenuta 416, Trindade, Florianopolis,
Santa Catarina 88036500
Tel: +55(48) 3234-2344
Fax: +55(48) 3234-2344
EMail: loual@barddal.br
Website: http://www.barddal.br

Diretor: Dascomb Barddal

Courses

Accountancy; **Administration** (Administration); **Architecture and Town Planning** (Architecture; Town Planning); **Design** (Design); **Information Systems**

History: Founded 1999.

Main Language(s) of Instruction: Portuguese

Degrees and Diplomas: *Bacharelado*; *Especialização/Aperfeiçoamento*; *Mestrado*

Last Updated: 29/06/10

BARNABITA CENTRE OF HIGHER EDUCATION - FATHER MACHADO FACULTY

Centro de Educação Superior Barnabita - Faculdade Padre Machado
Av. do Contorno n° 6475 - Savassi, Belo Horizonte,
Minas Gerais 30110-039
Tel: +55(31) 3116-0800
Fax: +55(31) 3221-0707
EMail: contato@padremachado.edu.br
Website: http://www.padremachado.edu.br

Diretor: Aldir Remígio de Oliveira Leite

Courses

Administration

Main Language(s) of Instruction: Portuguese

Degrees and Diplomas: *Bacharelado*

Last Updated: 22/03/10

BARON OF PIRATININGA - AES FACULTY

Faculdade Barão de Piratininga - AES
Avenida Três de Maio N°: 127, Bairro Centro, São Roque,
SP 18134-000
Tel: +55(11) 4784-9777
EMail: silvia.donnini@aes.edu.br
Website: http://www.aes.edu.br

Courses
Information Systems (Computer Science); **Letters**; **Mathematics**; **Pedagogy**; **Physical Education**
Further Information: Also branch in Sorocaba
History: Founded 1999.
Main Language(s) of Instruction: Portuguese
Degrees and Diplomas: *Bacharelado*; *Licenciatura*
Libraries: Yes
Last Updated: 16/07/10

BARON OF RIO BRANCO FACULTY

Faculdade Barão do Rio Branco
Br 364 Km 02, Alameda Hungria, 200, Jardim Europa II, Rio Branco,
AC 69911-900
Tel: +55(68) 3213-7070
EMail: marco.brandao@uninorteac.com.br

Diretor: Rodrigo Calvo Galindo

Courses
Accountancy (Accountancy); **Administration** (Administration); **Architecture and Town Planning** (Architecture; Town Planning); **Dentistry** (Dentistry); **Law** (Law); **Nursing** (Nursing); **Physical Education** (Physical Education); **Physiotherapy** (Physical Therapy); **Psychology** (Psychology); **Social Sciences** (Social Sciences)
History: Founded 2002.
Main Language(s) of Instruction: Portuguese
Degrees and Diplomas: *Bacharelado*; *Licenciatura*
Last Updated: 16/09/10

BARRIGA VERDE UNIVERSITY CENTRE

Centro Universitario Barriga Verde (UNIBAVE)
Rua Pe. João Leonir DalÍAlba, Bairro Murialdo, Orleans,
SC 88870-000
Tel: +55(48) 3466-0192
Fax: +55(48) 3466-0192
EMail: secretaria@unibave.net
Website: http://www.unibave.net
Diretor: Celso de Oliveira Souza

Courses
Accountancy (Accountancy); **Administration** (Administration); **Agricultural Business** (Agricultural Business); **Agronomy** (Agronomy); **Ceramic Engineering** (Ceramics and Glass Technology; Engineering); **Graduate Studies** (Alternative Medicine; Business Administration; Education; Educational Administration; Educational Psychology; Educational Sciences; Environmental Management; Environmental Studies; Finance; Health Administration; Human Resources; Law; Linguistics; Literature; Marketing; Mathematics Education; Pedagogy; Public Administration; Special Education); **Information Systems**; **Law**; **Mathematics** (Mathematics); **Museology**; **Nursing** (Nursing); **Pedagogy**; **Pharmacy** (Pharmacy); **Physical Education** (Physical Education); **Production Engineering**; **Psychology** (Psychology); **Veterinary Medicine**
History: Founded 1998.
Main Language(s) of Instruction: Portuguese
Degrees and Diplomas: *Bacharelado*; *Especialização/Aperfeiçoamento*
Last Updated: 21/05/10

BARROS MELO INTEGRATED FACULTIES

Faculdades Integradas Barros Melo (CESBAM)
Avenida Transamazônica 405, Jardim Brasil II, Olinda,
Pernambuco 53300240
Tel: +55(81) 3426-3950
Fax: +55(81) 3241-4352
EMail: faleconosco@barrosmelo.edu.br
Website: http://www.aeso.br

Diretora: Ivânia Maria de Barros Melo

Courses
Administration (Administration; Business Administration); **Advertising** (Advertising and Publicity); **Information Systems**; **Journalism** (Journalism); **Law** (Law); **Photography** (Photography); **Plastic Arts**; **Sound Engineering** (Sound Engineering (Acoustics)); **Telecommunications** (Telecommunications Engineering)
History: Founded 1996.
Degrees and Diplomas: *Bacharelado*; *Especialização/Aperfeiçoamento*
Libraries: Yes
Last Updated: 29/06/10

BELO HORIZONTE INSTITUTE OF HIGHER EDUCATION

Instituto Belo Horizonte de Ensino Superior
Rua Albita, 131 - Cruzeiro, Belo Horizonte, MG 30310-160
Tel: +55(31) 3226-2549
EMail: marcioacbarros@yahoo.com.br
Website: http://www.ibhes.edu.br

Diretor: Geraldo Magela Alves

Courses
Accountancy (Accountancy); **Administration** (Administration); **Law** (Law); **Social Communication** (Advertising and Publicity); **Tourism** (Tourism)
History: Founded 2003.
Main Language(s) of Instruction: Portuguese
Degrees and Diplomas: *Bacharelado*
Last Updated: 22/09/10

BENNETT METHODIST UNIVERSITY CENTRE

Centro Universitário Metodista Bennett
Rua Marquês de Abrantes, 55, Flamengo, RJ 22230-060
Tel: +55(21) 3509-1000
EMail: deise.marques@bennett.br
Website: http://www.bennett.br/bennett.php?codSegmento=3
Reitor: Roberto Pontes da Fonseca

Courses
Administration; **Architecture and Urbanism**; **International Relations** (International Relations); **Law** (Law); **Nutrition** (Nutrition); **Pedagogy**; **Physical Education** *(Licenciatura)* (Physical Education); **Physical Education** (Physical Education); **Theology**; **Visual Arts**
Degrees and Diplomas: *Bacharelado*; *Licenciatura*
Last Updated: 13/07/10

BERTHIER INSTITUTE OF PHILOSOPHY

Instituto Superior de Filosofia Berthier (IFIBE)
Rua Senador Pinheiro, 350, Vila Rodrigues, Passo Fundo,
RS 99070-220
Tel: +55(54) 3045-3277
EMail: ifibe@ifibe.edu.br
Website: http://www.ifibe.edu.br/
Diretor Geral: JoséAndré da Costa

Courses
Human Rights (Human Rights); **Philosophy** (Philosophy)
History: Founded 1981.
Main Language(s) of Instruction: Portuguese
Degrees and Diplomas: *Bacharelado*; *Especialização/Aperfeiçoamento*
Last Updated: 14/03/11

BÉTHENCOURT DA SILVA FACULTY

Faculdade Béthencourt da Silva (FABES)
Rua Frederico Silva 86, 7° Andar Centro, Praça Onze,
Rio de Janeiro, Rio de Janeiro 20230-210
Tel: +55(21) 2277-7600
Fax: +55(21) 2242-2343
EMail: fabes@fabes.com.br
Website: http://www.fabes.com.br

Diretora: Maysa de Lacerda Freire (1997-)

Courses
Accountancy (Accountancy); **Administration; Civil Construction**
(Civil Engineering); **Electronics** (Electrical and Electronic Engineering); **Graduate Studies**

History: Founded 1981.

Main Language(s) of Instruction: Portuguese

Degrees and Diplomas: *Bacharelado*; *Licenciatura*; *Especialização/Aperfeiçoamento*
Last Updated: 29/06/10

BEZERRA DE ARAÚJO FACULTY

Faculdade Bezerra de Araújo (FABA)
Rua Viúva Dantas 501, Campo Grande, Rio de Janeiro,
Rio de Janeiro 23052090
Tel: +55(21) 2413-1017
EMail: direcaofaba@bezerradearaujo.com.br
Website: http://www.bezerradearaujo.com.br

Diretora Geral: Maria José Bezerra de Araújo

Courses
Graduate Studies (Acupuncture; Nursing; Nutrition; Pharmacology); **Nursing** (Nursing); **Nutrition** (Nutrition); **Pharmacy; Physiotherapy** (Physical Therapy)

Further Information: Also Tijuca and Carius units.

History: Founded 1999.

Main Language(s) of Instruction: Portuguese

Degrees and Diplomas: *Bacharelado*; *Especialização/Aperfeiçoamento*
Last Updated: 29/06/10

BI FACULTY CAMPINAS

Faculdade Bi Campinas
Rua José Paulino 1.369, Campinas, SP 13013-001
Tel: +55(19) 3739-6420
EMail: info@bifgv.com.br

Diretor: Heliomar Manoel Quaresma

Courses
Economics (Economics); **Production Engineering** (Production Engineering)

History: Founded 2008.

Main Language(s) of Instruction: Portuguese

Degrees and Diplomas: *Bacharelado*
Last Updated: 31/08/10

BLAURO CARDOSO DE MATTOS INSTITUTE OF HIGHER EDUCATION

Instituto de Ensino Superior Blauro Cardoso de Mattos
Rua Ipatinga, 82, Barcelona, Serra, ES 29.160-120
Tel: +55(27) 3318-3079
EMail: faserra@faserra.edu.br
Website: http://www.faserra.edu.br

Diretor: Márcio Rosetti de Castro

Courses
Accountancy (Accountancy)

History: Founded 2000.

Main Language(s) of Instruction: Portuguese

Degrees and Diplomas: *Bacharelado*; *Especialização/Aperfeiçoamento*

Libraries: Yes
Last Updated: 24/09/10

BLESSED SACRAMENT FACULTY

Faculdade Santíssimo Sacramento (FSSS)
Rua Marechal Deodoro, 118, Alagoinhas, BA 48005-020
Tel: +55(75) 3182-3182
Fax: +55(75) 3182-3181
EMail: fsssalagoinhas@gmail.com
Website: http://www.fsssacramento.br/

Diretora Geral: Lúcia Maria Sá Barreto de Freitas

Courses
Graduate Studies (Accountancy; Education; Educational Administration; Finance; Higher Education; Information Management; Linguistics; Literature; Management; Marketing; Pedagogy; Petroleum and Gas Engineering; Physical Education; Public Administration; Special Education; Transport Management); **Undergraduate Studies** (Accountancy; Administration; Pedagogy; Production Engineering; Psychology; Tourism)

Degrees and Diplomas: *Bacharelado*; *Licenciatura*; *Especialização/Aperfeiçoamento*. Also MBA.
Last Updated: 07/09/10

BLUE CROSS FACULTY

Faculdade Cruz Azul
Av. Dr. Luís Carlos, 1000, Bairro da Penha, São Paulo 03405-100
Tel: +55(11) 2091-3005
EMail: paulo.menegucci@craz.com.br
Website: http://www.facraz.edu.br

Diretor: José Paulo Menegucci

Courses
Accountancy (Accountancy); **Administration** (Administration)

History: Founded 2008.

Main Language(s) of Instruction: Portuguese

Degrees and Diplomas: *Bacharelado*

Libraries: Yes
Last Updated: 23/07/10

BOA VIAGEM FACULTY

Faculdade Boa Viagem (FBV)
Rua Jean Émile Favre, 422, Imbiribeira, Recife,
Pernambuco 51190-540
Tel: +55(81) 3081-4444
Fax: +55(81) 3465-3929
EMail: fbv@fbv.br
Website: http://www.fbv.br

Diretor: Ary Avellar Diniz

Courses
Accountancy (Accountancy); **Advertising and Publicity** (Advertising and Publicity); **Business Administration** (Business Administration); **Computer Science; Economics** (Economics; Finance); **Fashion Design** (Fashion Design); **Graduate Studies** *(Stricto Sensu)* (Business Administration); **Graduate Studies** *(Lato Sensu)* (Civil Law; Fashion Design; Finance; Interior Design; Labour Law; Law; Management; Marketing; Public Administration; Software Engineering; Transport Management); **Hotel Management; Interior Design** (Interior Design); **Law** (Law); **Physical Education** (Physical Education); **Production Engineering**

Institutes
Child Maternity - Pernambuco *(FBV-IMIP)* (Child Care and Development)

History: Founded 1999

Main Language(s) of Instruction: Portuguese

Degrees and Diplomas: *Bacharelado*; *Especialização/Aperfeiçoamento*; *Mestrado*. Also MBA.
Last Updated: 29/06/10

BOAS NOVAS FACULTY

Faculdade Boas Novas
Avenida General Rodrigo Octávio Jordão Ramos N° 1.655,
Centro de convenções Canaã, Japiim, Manaus, AM 69077-000
Tel: +55(92) 3237-2214
EMail: mariajose@faculdadeboasnovas.edu.br
Website: http://www.faculdadeboasnovas.edu.br

Diretor: Jônatas Câmara

Courses

Administration (Administration; Pedagogy); **Pedagogy**; **Social Communication** (Journalism); **Theology** (Theology)

History: Founded 2005.

Main Language(s) of Instruction: Portuguese

Degrees and Diplomas: *Bacharelado*; *Licenciatura*; *Especialização/Aperfeiçoamento*

Last Updated: 15/09/10

BOM JESUS DO ITABAPOANA INSTITUTE OF EDUCATION

Instituto Superior de Educação Bom Jesus do Itabapoana (ISEBJI)
Rua Aristides Figueiredo, 147, Centro, Bom Jesus do Itabapoana, RJ 28360-000
Tel: +55(22) 3831-7076
Fax: +55(22) 3831- 6859
EMail: ise.bjitabapoana@faetec.rj.gov.br
Website: http://www.faetec.rj.gov.br/

Courses

Teacher Training (Teacher Training)

Degrees and Diplomas: *Licenciatura*

Last Updated: 24/09/10

BORGES DE MENDONÇA FACULTIES

Faculdades Borges de Mendonça
Rua Deodoro 204, Florianopolis, SC 88010-020
Tel: +55(48) 3222-0504
EMail: thomas@borgesdemendonca.edu.br
Website: http://www.bm.edu.br

Diretor: Thomas de Mendonça

Courses

Accountancy (Accountancy); **Administration** (Administration); **Public Administration** (Public Administration)

History: Founded 1999.

Main Language(s) of Instruction: Portuguese

Degrees and Diplomas: *Bacharelado*; *Especialização/Aperfeiçoamento*

Last Updated: 23/08/10

BRASILIA FACULTY OF SAO PAULO

Faculdade Brasília de São Paulo
Rua Angá 395, Vila Formosa, São Paulo, São Paulo 03360000
Tel: +55(11) 6211-0066
EMail: faculdade@brasiliasp.br

Diretora Geral: Ayako Kuba Sakamoto (1993-)

Courses

Administration; **Information Systems** (Computer Science); **Pedagogy**; **Physical Education** (Physical Education); **Visual Arts** (Visual Arts)

History: Founded 1998.

Degrees and Diplomas: *Tecnólogo*; *Bacharelado*; *Especialização/Aperfeiçoamento*

Libraries: Yes

Last Updated: 21/09/07

BRAZ CUBAS UNIVERSITY

Universidade Braz Cubas (UBC)
Rua Francisco Rodrigues Filho 1233, Campus Universitário, Mogilar, Mogi das Cruzes, São Paulo 08773380
Tel: +55(11) 4791-8000
Fax: +55(11) 4790-3844
EMail: gabinete@brazcubas.br
Website: http://www.brazcubas.br

Reitor: Maurício Chermann Tel: +55(11) 4790-2256

Areas

Architecture and Design (Architecture; Interior Design; Town Planning); **Business and Law** (Accountancy; Administration; Finance; Human Resources; Law; Marketing); **Communication** (Advertising and Publicity; Communication Studies; Journalism; Multimedia); **Education** (Art Education; Arts and Humanities; Biology; History; Literature; Mathematics; Pedagogy); **Engineering** (Automation and Control Engineering; Computer Engineering; Engineering; Environmental Engineering; Mechanical Engineering); **Health** (Dentistry; Nursing; Optometry; Pharmacy; Physical Therapy; Psychology)

History: Founded 1952. Acquired present status 1985.

Academic Year: February to December (February-June; August-December)

Admission Requirements: Secondary school certificate and entrance examination

Main Language(s) of Instruction: Portuguese

Degrees and Diplomas: *Bacharelado*; *Licenciatura*; *Especialização/Aperfeiçoamento*; *Mestrado*

Last Updated: 08/06/10

BRAZIL ASSOCIATED FACULTY

Faculdade Associada Brasil
Rua Madre Emilie de Villeneuve, 331, Vila Mascote, SP
Tel: +55(11) 5677-1150
EMail: sec@faculdadebrasil.edu.br
Website: http://www.faculdadebrasil.edu.br/new

Reitor: José Feuser

Courses

Administration; **Advertising** (Advertising and Publicity); **Pedagogy**; **Tourism**

Main Language(s) of Instruction: Portuguese

Degrees and Diplomas: *Bacharelado*

Last Updated: 13/07/10

BRAZILIAN AMAZONIA INTEGRATED FACULTY

Faculdade Integrada Brasil Amazônia (FIBRA)
Av. Alcindo Cacela, 675, Umarizal, Belém, PA 66060-000
Tel: +55(91) 3266-3110 +55(91) 3226-5040 +55(91) 3226-9471
EMail: fibrapa@yahoo.com.br
Website: http://www.fibrapara.edu.br/

Diretora Geral: María Isabel Amazonas

Courses

Graduate Studies (Accountancy; African Studies; Art Education; Business Administration; Criminal Law; Criminology; Cultural Studies; Educational Administration; Educational Psychology; English; Environmental Management; Environmental Studies; Geography; History; Human Rights; International Business; Labour Law; Literature; Management; Mathematics; Natural Resources; Occupational Health; Portuguese; Science Education; Special Education; Tourism; Translation and Interpretation); **Undergraduate Studies** (Administration; English; Geography; History; Law; Literature; Pedagogy; Portuguese; Public Administration; Translation and Interpretation)

Degrees and Diplomas: *Bacharelado*; *Licenciatura*; *Especialização/Aperfeiçoamento*

Last Updated: 01/09/10

BRAZILIAN BAPTIST FACULTY

Faculdade Batista Brasileira (FBB)
Rua Altino Seberto de Barros, 140, Itaigara, Bahia 41850050
Tel: +55(71) 3505-3434
EMail: fbb@fbb.br
Website: http://www.fbb.br

Reitor: Bispo Átila Brandão EMail: reitoria@fbb.br

Courses

Accountancy (Accountancy); **Administration** (Administration); **Law** (Law); **Pedagogy** (Pedagogy); **Philosophy** (Philosophy); **Theology** (Theology)

History: Founded 1996.

Main Language(s) of Instruction: Portuguese

Degrees and Diplomas: *Bacharelado*; *Licenciatura*. Also Post-gaduate Diplomas.

Last Updated: 29/06/10

BRAZILIAN FACULTY

Faculdade Brasileira (UNIVIX)
Rua José Alves, n° 301, Goiabeiras, Vitória,
Espirito Santo 29075-080
Tel: +55(27) 3335-5666
EMail: atendimento@univix.br
Website: http://www.univix.br

Diretor: Alexandre José Serafim

Courses

Administration (Administration); **Architecture and Urbanism**; **Civil Production Engineering** (Production Engineering); **Computer Engineering** (Computer Engineering); **Electrical Engineering** (Electrical Engineering); **Graduate Studies** (Business Administration; Cosmetology; Electrical Engineering; Engineering; Environmental Management; Industrial Engineering; Nursing; Petroleum and Gas Engineering; Pharmacology; Pharmacy; Psychology; Surveying and Mapping); **Law** (Law); **Medicine** (Medicine); **Nursing**; **Pharmacy**; **Psychology**

History: Founded 1999

Main Language(s) of Instruction: Portuguese

Degrees and Diplomas: *Bacharelado*; *Especialização/Aperfeiçoamento*

Last Updated: 29/06/10

BRAZILIAN FACULTY OF EDUCATION AND CULTURE

Faculdade Brasileira de Educacão e Cultura
Av. Paranaíba, 374 - Centro, Goiânia, GO 74020-010
Tel: +55(62) 4012-0000
Website: http://www.fabecbrasil.edu.br

Diretor: Deusvolmi Silveira Rabelo

Courses

Accountancy (Accountancy); **Administration**

History: Founded 2005.

Main Language(s) of Instruction: Portuguese

Degrees and Diplomas: *Bacharelado*; *Especialização/Aperfeiçoamento*

Libraries: Yes

Last Updated: 15/07/10

BRAZILIAN FACULTY OF EXACT SCIENCES, HUMANITIES AND SOCIAL SCIENCES FABRAI

Faculdade Brasileira de Ciências Exatas, Humanas e Sociais - Fabrai (FABRAI)
Av. dos Andradas, 436, Centro, Belo Horizonte,
Minas Gerais 30120-010
Tel: +55(31) 3446-7788
EMail: fabrai@fabrai.brfabrai@fabrai.br
Website: http://www.fabrai.br

Diretor: José Eustáquio Ribeiro Vieira (1997-)

Courses

Accountancy (Accountancy); **Administration** (Administration); **Graduate Studies**; **Information Systems**; **Pedagogy** (Pedagogy); **Social Communication - Public Relations** (Public Relations); **Technological Studies** (Chemistry; Electronic Engineering; Human Resources; Systems Analysis; Transport Management)

Further Information: Also São Cristóvão and Centro II units.

History: Founded 1992

Degrees and Diplomas: *Tecnólogo*; *Bacharelado*; *Especialização/ Aperfeiçoamento*. Also MBA.

Last Updated: 29/06/10

BRAZILIAN FACULTY OF JURIDICAL SCIENCE

Faculdade Brasileira de Ciências Jurídicas (FBCJ)
Praça da República, 50, Térreo Centro, Rio de Janeiro,
Rio de Janeiro 20211-351
Tel: +55(21) 3077-0500
Fax: +55(21) 3077-0517
EMail: cpd@suesc.com.br
Website: http://www.suesc.com.br

Diretor: Heny Penilla da Silva

Courses

Law (Law)

History: Founded 1952

Main Language(s) of Instruction: Portuguese

Degrees and Diplomas: *Bacharelado*

Last Updated: 29/06/10

BRAZILIAN INSTITUTE OF TECHNOLOGY AND SCIENCE

Instituto Brasiliense de Tecnologia e Ciência (IBTC)
SGAS/SUL, Quadra 913, S/n Conjunto B (IBTC), ASA SUL,
Brasília, DF 70390-130
Tel: +55(61) 3345-9144
Fax: +55(61) 3345-9134
Website: http://www.ibtc.edu.br

Diretor: Fábio Nogueira Carlucci **EMail:** fncarlucci@uol.com.br

Courses

Administration (Administration)

History: Founded 1998.

Main Language(s) of Instruction: Portuguese

Degrees and Diplomas: *Bacharelado*

Last Updated: 28/09/10

BRAZILIAN MUSIC CONSERVATOIRE

Conservatorio Brasileiro de Música (CBM/CEU)
Avenida Graça Aranha 57, 12° Andar, Centro, Rio de Janeiro,
Rio de Janeiro 20030-002
Tel: +55(21) 3478-7600
EMail: cbm@cbm-musica.org.br
Website: http://www.cbm-musica.org.br

Diretora Geral: Cecilia Conde (1998-)

Courses

Art Therapy (Art Therapy); **Conducting**; **Music** (Music; Music Education; Music Theory and Composition; Musical Instruments); **Singing** (Singing)

History: Founded 1936.

Main Language(s) of Instruction: Portuguese

Degrees and Diplomas: *Bacharelado*; *Licenciatura*; *Especialização/Aperfeiçoamento*

Last Updated: 18/06/10

BRAZILIAN SCHOOL OF ECONOMICS AND FINANCE

Escola Brasileira de Economia e Finanças (EBEF)
Praia de Botafogo, 190, 11° Andar, Botafogo, Rio de Janeiro,
RJ 22253-900
Tel: +55 (21) 2559-5814
EMail: gradeco@fgv.br
Website: http://www5.fgv.br/graduacao_novo/curso.aspx?curso=4

Courses

Economics (Economics)

History: Founded 2002.

Degrees and Diplomas: *Bacharelado*

Last Updated: 13/07/10

BRAZILIAN SCHOOL OF PUBLIC AND BUSINESS ADMINISTRATION

Escola Brasileira de Administração Pública e de Empresas (FGV/EBAPE)
Praia de Botafogo, 190, 3°, 4° e 5° andares, Rio de Janeiro, RJ 22253-900
EMail: direcao.ebape@fgv.br
Website: http://www.ebape.fgv.br

Diretor: Flávio Carvalho de Vasconcelos
Tel: +55(21) 3799-5711 EMail: flavio.vasconcelos@fgv.br

Courses
Administration (Administration); **Business Administration** (Business Administration); **Management**

History: Founded 1952.

Main Language(s) of Instruction: Portuguese

Degrees and Diplomas: *Bacharelado*; *Mestrado*; *Doutorado*. Also Post-doctorate Programme in Administration.
Last Updated: 14/03/11

BRAZILIAN VIRTUAL UNIVERSITY INSTITUTE

Instituto Universidade Virtual Brasileira (IUVB)
Av. Dr. Cardoso de Melo, 1666, Conjunto 81, São Paulo, SP 04548-005
Tel: +55(11) 9983-1403
Fax: +55(11) 9983-1403
EMail: info@uvb.com.br
Website: http://www.uvb.com.br/

Diretor Geral: Karl Albert Diniz de Souza EMail: karl@unama.br

Courses
Graduate Studies (Criminology; Fiscal Law; Law); **Undergraduate Studies** (Administration)

History: Founded 2003.

Degrees and Diplomas: *Bacharelado*; *Especialização/Aperfeiçoamento*
Last Updated: 29/09/10

BUSINESS ADMINISTRATION SCHOOL

Escola Superior de Administração de Empresas (INEA)
Rua Laurent Martins, 329, Jardim Esplanada, São José dos Campos, SP 12242-431
Tel: +55(12) 2134-9199 +55(11) 4501-9706
Fax: +55(12) 2134-9199 +55(11) 4501-9720
EMail: francisco.borges@veris.edu.br;
valquiria.dumere@veris.edu.br; everton.marques@veris.edu.br

Courses
Accountancy (Accountancy); **Administration** (Administration)

Degrees and Diplomas: *Bacharelado*
Last Updated: 15/07/10

BUSINESS SCHOOL OF THE STATE OF BAHIA

Escola de Negócios do Estado da Bahia
Rua Barão de Cotegipe, 1414, Centro, Feira de Santana, BA 44025-030
Tel: +55(75) 3225-5253
Fax: +55(75) 3221-2925
EMail: eneb@eneb.edu.br
Website: http://www.eneb.edu.br/

Diretor Executivo: Saulo Bispo dos Reis

Courses
Accountancy (Accountancy); **Administration** (Administration); **Graduate Studies** (Accountancy; Higher Education); **Pedagogy** (Pedagogy); **Production Engineering**

History: Founded 2000.

Degrees and Diplomas: *Bacharelado*; *Licenciatura*; *Especialização/Aperfeiçoamento*
Last Updated: 15/07/10

BUTANTA INDEPENDENT FACULTY

Faculdade Independente Butantá (FIB)
Avenida Eng. Heitor Antonio Eiras Garcia 509, Jardim Bonfiglioli, São Paulo, São Paulo 5588000
Tel: +55(11) 3735-4592
Fax: +55(11) 3735-4592
EMail: fibsecretaria@hotmail.com
Website: http://www.fibutanta.br

Diretor Geral: Edson de Oliveira Peixoto

Courses
Accountancy (Accountancy); **Advertising** (Advertising and Publicity); **Business Administration**; **Secretarial Studies**; **Tourism**

History: Founded 1999

Main Language(s) of Instruction: Portuguese

Degrees and Diplomas: *Bacharelado*
Last Updated: 07/07/10

CALAFIORI FACULTY

Faculdade Calafiori
Av. José Pio de Oliveira, n° 10, Cidade Jardim Industrial, São Sebastião do Paraíso, MG 37.950-000
Tel: +55(35) 3558-6261
EMail: uniesp@paraisonet.com.br
Website: http://www.uniespmg.edu.br

Diretora Acadêmica: Angelita Bérgamo Pimenta Borges

Courses
History (History); **Pedagogy** (Pedagogy); **Physical Education** (Physical Education)

History: Founded 2002.

Main Language(s) of Instruction: Portuguese

Degrees and Diplomas: *Licenciatura*
Last Updated: 27/09/10

CÂMARA CASCUDO FACULTY

Faculdade Câmara Cascudo
Av. Alexandrino de Alencar, 708, Alecrim, Natal, RN 59030-350
Tel: +55(84) 3198-1600
Website: http://www.fcamaracascudo.com.br/home.htm

Diretor: Josué Viana de Oliveira Neto

Courses
Accountancy; **Administration** (Administration); **Computer Networks** (Computer Networks); **Hotel Management**; **Human Resource Management** (Human Resources; Management); **Law** (Law); **Marketing** (Marketing); **Petroleum and Gas** (Petroleum and Gas Engineering); **Production Engineering** (Production Engineering); **Systems Analysis** (Systems Analysis); **Tourism** (Tourism)

History: Founded 2002.

Main Language(s) of Instruction: Portuguese

Degrees and Diplomas: *Bacharelado*; *Especialização/Aperfeiçoamento*
Last Updated: 16/07/10

CAMBURY FACULTY

Faculdade Cambury
Av. T-2 n. 3531, Setor Sol Nascente, Goiânia, Goiás 74410-220
Tel: +55(62) 3236-3000
EMail: cambury@cambury.br
Website: http://www.cambury.br

Diretor: Giuseppe Vecci

Courses
Advertising (Advertising and Publicity); **Business Administration**; **Cosmetology** (Cosmetology); **Events Management** (Public Relations); **Gastronomy**; **Graduate Studies** (Advertising and Publicity; Cinema and Television; Communication Studies; Cooking and Catering; Management; Marketing; Safety Engineering); **Human Resource Management** (Human Resources); **Information Technology**; **Interior Design** (Interior Design); **Jewellery Design**

(Jewelry Art); **Law**; **Marketing** (Marketing); **Photography** (Photography)

Faculties
Formosa

History: Founded 1994.

Main Language(s) of Instruction: Portuguese

Degrees and Diplomas: *Tecnólogo*; *Bacharelado*. Also Postgraduate Diplomas
Last Updated: 29/06/10

CAMILO CASTELO BRANCO UNIVERSITY

Universidade Camilo Castelo Branco (UNICASTELO)
Rua Carolina Fonseca 584, Itaquera, São Paulo,
São Paulo 8230030
Tel: +55(11) 6170-0023
Fax: +55(11) 205-8226
EMail: unicastelo@unicastelo.br
Website: http://www.unicastelo.br

Reitor: Gilberto Luiz Moraes Selber (2006-)
EMail: reitoria@unicastelo.br

Courses
Accountancy; **Administration**; **Architecture and Town Planning**; **Arts and Humanities**; **Biology**; **Biomedical Engineering** (Biomedical Engineering); **Civil Engineering**; **Communication Studies**; **Education**; **Environmental Engineering**; **Environmental Studies**; **Information Sciences**; **Law**; **Mathematics**; **Occupational Therapy**; **Physical Education**; **Physiotherapy**; **Production Engineering** (Production Engineering); **Religious Sciences**; **Social and Community Services**; **Social Sciences** (Social Sciences); **Veterinary Science**

History: Founded 1989.

Main Language(s) of Instruction: Portuguese

Degrees and Diplomas: *Bacharelado*; *Licenciatura*; *Especialização/Aperfeiçoamento*; *Mestrado*; *Doutorado*
Last Updated: 08/06/10

CAMILO FILHO INSTITUTE

Instituto Camillo Filho (ICF)
Rua Napoleão Lima 1175, Jockey Club, Teresina, Piauí 64049220
Tel: +55(86) 3216-8800
Fax: +55(86) 3216-8817
EMail: icf@icf.edu.br
Website: http://www.icf.edu.br

Diretor Geral: Marcelino Leal Barroso de Carvalho

Courses
Administration (Administration); **Architecture and Town Planning**; **Fine Arts** (Fine Arts); **Law**; **Social Services** (Social and Community Services)

History: Founded 2000.

Main Language(s) of Instruction: Portuguese

Degrees and Diplomas: *Bacharelado*; *Especialização/Aperfeiçoamento*; *Mestrado*; *Doutorado*
Last Updated: 17/06/10

CAMOES INTEGRATED FACULTIES

Faculdades Integradas Camões
Avenida Jaime Reis N° 531, Alto São Francisco, Curitiba,
PR 80510-010
Tel: +55(41) 3302-5301
EMail: rafaelmichelotto@hotmail.com
Website: http://www.camoes.edu.br

Diretora: Melissa Micheletto

Courses
Accountancy (Accountancy); **Administration**
History: Founded 2000.

Main Language(s) of Instruction: Portuguese

Degrees and Diplomas: *Bacharelado*; *Especialização/Aperfeiçoamento*
Last Updated: 13/09/10

CAMPANHA DA PRINCESA CULTURAL FOUNDATION

Fundação Cultural Campanha da Princesa (FCCP)
Rua Padre Natuzzi, 53, Centro, Campanha, MG 37400-000
Tel: +55(35) 3261-2020
EMail: fpv@paivadevilhena.com.br
Website: http://www.paivadevilhena.edu.br/

President: Ivan Ferrer Maia

Faculties
Exact and Human Sciences da Campanha (Information Technology; Management); **Philosophy, Sciences and Literature Nossa Senhora de Sion** *(FAFI/SION)* (English; Geography; History; Literature; Pedagogy)

History: Founded 1966 as Fundação Universidade da Campanha. Acquired present title 1974. Maintains AFI SION (Faculdade de Filosofia Ciências e Letras Nossa Senhora de Sion), FACEHUC (Faculdade de Ciências Exatas e Humanas da Campanha).

Degrees and Diplomas: *Tecnólogo*; *Bacharelado*; *Licenciatura*. Also Postgraduate Diploma.
Last Updated: 23/07/10

CAMPO GRANDE FACULTY

Faculdade Campo Grande
Av. Afonso Pena, 275, Amambaí, Campo Grande, MS
Tel: +55(67) 3384-6949
EMail: diretoriaicg@ig.com.br
Website: http://www.icges.edu.br

Diretor: Ivan Reatte

Courses
Accountancy (Accountancy); **Administration** (Administration); **Computer Science** (Computer Science); **Law** (Law); **Pedagogy** (Pedagogy); **Physiotherapy** (Physical Therapy); **Social Communication** (Advertising and Publicity); **Tourism** (Tourism)

History: Founded 2002 as Instituto Campo Grande de Ensino Superior. Acquired present title 2010.

Main Language(s) of Instruction: Portuguese

Degrees and Diplomas: *Bacharelado*

Libraries: Yes
Last Updated: 22/09/10

CAMPO REAL FACULTY

Faculdade Campo Real (UNICAMPO)
Rua Comendador Norberto1299, Santa Cruz, Guarapuava,
Paraná 85015240
Tel: +55(42) 3621-5200
Fax: +55(42) 3621-5200
EMail: diretor@camporeal.edu.br
Website: http://www.camporeal.edu.br

Diretor: Antonio Cezar Ribas Pacheco
EMail: pacheco@unicampo.edu.br

Courses
Administration; **Advertising** (Advertising and Publicity); **Agricultural Engineering** (Agricultural Engineering); **Biomedicine**; **Law** (Law); **Letters**; **Nutrition**; **Production Engineering** (Production Engineering); **Psychology** (Psychology)

History: Founded 2000.

Degrees and Diplomas: *Bacharelado*; *Especialização/Aperfeiçoamento*; *Mestrado*
Last Updated: 29/06/10

CAMPOS DE ANDRADE UNIVERSITY CENTRE

Centro Universitário Campos de Andrade (UNIANDRADE)
R. João Scuissiato, 1, Santa Quitéria, Curitibá, Paraná 80310-310
Tel: +55(41) 3219-4290
Fax: +55(41) 3223-8919
EMail: uniandrade@uniandrade.br
Website: http://www.uniandrade.br

Reitor: José Campos de Andrade

Areas
Applied Social, Human and Legal Sciences (Postgraduate); Health Sciences (Postgraduate) (Health Administration; Health Sciences; Nursing; Occupational Health; Public Health); Licenciatura (Postgraduate)

Centres
Distance Education

Courses
Accountancy; Administration; Arts and Humanities (Arts and Humanities; Portuguese; Spanish); Arts and Humanities; Biology (Biology); Computer Science (Computer Science); Economics (Economics); Fashion Design (Fashion Design); Geography (Geography); History; Information Systems; Law; Library Science (Library Science); Mathematics (Mathematics); Media - Advertising (Advertising and Publicity; Media Studies); Media - Journalism (Journalism; Media Studies); Media - Public Relations (Media Studies; Public Relations); Nursing (Nursing); Nutrition (Nutrition); Pedagogy (Pedagogy); Pharmacy (Pharmacy); Philosophy (Philosophy); Physical Education (Physical Education); Physical Therapy (Physical Therapy); Physics (Physics); Secretarial Studies (Secretarial Studies); Technological Studies (Computer Networks; Cosmetology; Environmental Management; Hotel and Restaurant; Human Resources; Interior Design; International Business; Management; Marketing; Occupational Health; Secretarial Studies; Software Engineering; Systems Analysis; Transport Management); Tourism (Tourism)

Further Information: Also campuses in Ponta Grossa and Maringá

History: Founded 1999.

Degrees and Diplomas: Tecnólogo; Bacharelado; Licenciatura; Especialização/Aperfeiçoamento; Mestrado

Last Updated: 21/05/10

CAMPOS SALLES INTEGRATED FACULTIES
Faculdades Integradas Campos Salles (FICS)
Rua Nossa Senhora da Lapa 270/284 Lapa, São Paulo, São Paulo 05072000
Tel: +55(11) 3649-7000
EMail: cs@cs.edu.br
Website: http://www.campossalles.br

Diretor: Eduardo Césere Baságlia

Courses
Accountancy (Accountancy); Administration; Computer Science (Computer Science); Economics (Economics); International Business (International Business); Law (Law); Pedagogy (Pedagogy)

History: Founded 1971

Main Language(s) of Instruction: Portuguese

Degrees and Diplomas: Bacharelado; Licenciatura; Especialização/Aperfeiçoamento
Last Updated: 24/06/10

CÂNDIDO MENDES FACULTY OF VITORIA
Faculdade Cândido Mendes de Vitória (FACAM)
Av. Leitão da Silva 2055, Itararé, Vitória 29044-565
Tel: +55(27) 3315-4280
EMail: contato@candidomendesvitoria.br
Website: http://www.ucam.edu.br/institucional/detalheunidade. asp?id=16

Diretor: Alexandre Gazé

Courses
Accountancy (Accountancy); Administration (Administration; Environmental Management)

History: Founded 1999. Unit of the Universidade Candido Mendes.

Main Language(s) of Instruction: Portuguese

Degrees and Diplomas: Bacharelado
Last Updated: 29/06/10

CANDIDO MENDES UNIVERSITY - RIO DE JANEIRO
Universidade Candido Mendes (UCAM)
Rua da Assembléia 10, Centro, Rio de Janeiro, Rio de Janeiro 20011901
Tel: +55(21) 2531-2000
EMail: enunes@candidomendes.edu.br
Website: http://www.candidomendes.edu.br

Reitor: Cândido Antônio Mendes de Almeida (1998-)
Tel: +55(21) 531-2310, Fax: +55(21) 533-4782
EMail: cmendes@candidomendes.edu.br

Pró-Reitor de Administração, Jurídico, Financeiro: Jair Fialho Abrunhosa

International Relations: José Raimundo Romeo
Tel: +55(21) 531-2496, Fax: +55(21) 531-1336

Institutes
Business Administration and Law (Niterói, Nova Friburgo, Ipanema, Centro, Campos dos Goytacazes) (Business Administration; Law)

Research Institutes
Political Science and Sociology (IUPERJ, Botafogo) (Political Sciences; Sociology)

Schools
Fashion Design (Fashion Design); Interior Design

Further Information: Also 12 centres for study and research

History: Founded 1919, acquired present status 1997. Under the supervision of the Sociedade Brasileira de Instrucção, founded 1902, and recognized by the federal authorities.

Governing Bodies: Conselho Universitário

Academic Year: February to December (February-June; August-December)

Admission Requirements: Secondary school certificate and entrance examination

Main Language(s) of Instruction: Portuguese

Degrees and Diplomas: Bacharelado: Accountancy; Administration; Economics; Law, 4-5 yrs; Mestrado: Economics; Political Science; Sociology, a further 2-3 yrs; Doutorado: Political Science; Sociology, 4-5 yrs

Student Services: Academic counselling, Canteen, Cultural centre, Employment services, Health services, Social counselling, Sports facilities

Special Facilities: Mineralogy Museum. Cultural Centres. Art Galleries

Libraries: Total, c. 62,000 vols

Publications: Arche, Political, Social and Economic Sciences (3 per annum); Archetypon, Political, Social and Economic Sciences (3 per annum); Dados, Social Sciences (quarterly)

CANTAREIRA FACULTY
Faculdade Cantareira (FIC)
Rua Marcos Arruda 729, Belém, São Paulo, São Paulo 3020000
Tel: +55(11) 6090-5900
Fax: +55(11) 6090-5900
EMail: fic@cantareira.br
Website: http://www.cantareira.br

Diretor Geral: Paulo Meinberg

Courses
Administration (Administration); Advertising (Advertising and Publicity); Agronomy; Graduate Studies (Especialização) (Agricultural Business; Law; Marketing; Music Education); Graduate Studies (MBA); Law (Law); Music (Music)

History: Founded 1998

Main Language(s) of Instruction: Portuguese

Degrees and Diplomas: Bacharelado; Especialização/Aperfeiçoamento. Also MBA.
Last Updated: 29/06/10

CAPITAL UNIVERSITY CENTRE
Centro Universitário Capital (UNICAPITAL)
Rua Ibipetuba, n° 42/130, Parque da Mooca, São Paulo,
São Paulo 03127-180
Tel: +55(11) 2065-1000
Fax: +55(11) 2065-1000
EMail: unicapital@unicapital.edu.br
Website: http://www.capital.br

Reitor: Adriano Augusto Fernandes

Courses
Accountancy (Accountancy); **Actuarial Sciences**; **Arts and Humanities** (English; Literature; Portuguese; Spanish); **Business Administration**; **Electrical Engineering** (Electrical Engineering); **Environmental Management**; **Graduate Studies**; **Human Resources** (Human Resources); **Industrial Automation** (Automation and Control Engineering); **Information Systems**; **Law** (Law); **Pedagogy** (Pedagogy); **Physiotherapy**; **Psychology**; **Statistics**

History: Founded 1969 as Faculdade Pais de Barros. Acquired present status and title 1999.

Main Language(s) of Instruction: Portuguese

Degrees and Diplomas: *Tecnólogo*; *Bacharelado*; *Licenciatura*; *Especialização/Aperfeiçoamento*
Last Updated: 21/05/10

CARIOCA UNIVERSITY CENTRE
Centro Universitário Carioca (UNICARIOCA)
Avenida Paulo de Frontin 568, Rio Comprido, Rio de Janeiro,
Rio de Janeiro 20261-243
Tel: +55(21) 2563-1919
EMail: dirrc@unicarioca.br
Website: http://www.unicarioca.edu.br

Reitor: Celso Niskier (1996-)

Courses
Accountancy (Accountancy); **Advertising and Publicity**; **Computer Science** (Computer Science); **Design**; **Education** (Education; Pedagogy); **Graduate Studies** (Computer Education; Computer Networks; Computer Science; Design; Higher Education; Information Management); **Journalism** (Journalism); **Technological Studies** (Business and Commerce; Computer Networks; Environmental Management; Human Resources; Marketing; Occupational Health; Systems Analysis)

Further Information: Also Méier, Bento Ribeiro and Jacarepaguá Units

History: Founded 1990.

Main Language(s) of Instruction: Portuguese

Degrees and Diplomas: *Tecnólogo*; *Bacharelado*; *Licenciatura*. Also Postgraduate Programmes and MBA.
Last Updated: 21/05/10

CARLOS GOMES FACULTY OF MUSIC
Faculdade de Música Carlos Gomes (FMCG)
Rua Paula Ney 521, Vila Mariana, São Paulo, São Paulo 04107021
Tel: +55(11) 5081-7445
Fax: +55(11) 5081-7331
EMail: fmcg@fmcg.com.br
Website: http://www.fmcg.com.br/

Diretora: Sônia Regina Albano de Lima

Courses
Music (Music; Music Theory and Composition; Singing)
History: Founded 1963
Main Language(s) of Instruction: Portuguese
Degrees and Diplomas: *Bacharelado*; *Licenciatura*
Last Updated: 11/12/07

CARLOS QUEIROZ FACULTY OF PHILOSOPHY, SCIENCE AND LETTERS
Faculdade de Filosofia, Ciências e Letras Carlos Queiroz
Avenida Coronel Clementino Gonçalves 1561, Vila São Judas Tadeu, Santa Cruz do Rio Pardo, São Paulo 18900000
Tel: +55(14) 3372-1173
Fax: +55(14) 3372-4073
EMail: fafil.oapec@argon.com.br
Website: http://www.fascfafil.com.br

Diretora Acadêmica: Adélia de Paula Pimentel (1986-)

Courses
Business Administration (Business Administration); **Literature**; **Pedagogy** (Pedagogy)
History: Founded 1971
Main Language(s) of Instruction: Portuguese
Degrees and Diplomas: *Bacharelado*; *Licenciatura*; *Especialização/Aperfeiçoamento*
Last Updated: 08/07/10

CÁSPER LÍBERO FACULTY
Faculdade Cásper Líbero
Avenida Paulista, 900, 5° Andar, Bela Vista, São Paulo,
São Paulo 01310-940
Tel: +55(11) 3170-5883
Fax: +55(11) 3170-5891
EMail: diretoria@facasper.com.br
Website: http://www.facasper.com.br

Diretora: Tereza Vitalli
Tel: +55(11) 3170-5811 **EMail:** tereza@facasper.com.br

Courses
Advertising and Publicity (Advertising and Publicity); **General Culture**; **Graduate Studies**; **Journalism** (Journalism); **Public Relations**; **Radio and TV** (Radio and Television Broadcasting)
History: Founded 1947
Main Language(s) of Instruction: Portuguese
Degrees and Diplomas: *Bacharelado*; *Especialização/Aperfeiçoamento*; *Mestrado*
Last Updated: 29/06/10

CASTELLI SCHOOL OF HOSTELRY
Castelli Escola Superior de Hotelaria
Avenida Osvaldo Aranha 994, Centro, Canela, RS 95680000
Tel: +55(54) 3282-1460
Fax: +55(54) 3282-1460
EMail: castelli@castelli.edu.br
Website: http://www.castelli.edu.br/

Diretor: Geraldo Castelli

Courses
Hotel Management (Hotel Management)
History: Founded 1987. Acquired present status 2000.
Main Language(s) of Instruction: Portuguese
Degrees and Diplomas: *Bacharelado*; *Especialização/Aperfeiçoamento*
Last Updated: 09/03/10

CASTELO BRANCO FACULTY
Faculdade Castelo Branco
Avenida Brasil 1303 Maria das Graças, Colatina, ES 29705-100
Tel: +55(27)2102-6000
EMail: secretaria@funcab.br
Website: http://www.funcab.br

Diretor Administrativo: Elodilson Sabadini

Areas
Business and Law (Accountancy; Administration; Economics; Law); **Education**

History: Founded 2001 as Faculdades Integradas Castelo Branco. Acquired present title 2008.

Main Language(s) of Instruction: Portuguese

Degrees and Diplomas: *Bacharelado*; *Licenciatura*; *Especialização/Aperfeiçoamento*; *Mestrado*

Libraries: Yes

Last Updated: 20/07/10

CASTELO BRANCO UNIVERSITY - RIO DE JANEIRO

Universidade Castelo Branco (UCB)
Avenida Santa Cruz 1631, Realengo, Rio de Janeiro,
Rio de Janeiro 21710250
Tel: +55(21) 2406-7700
EMail: reitoria@castelobranco.br
Website: http://www.castelobranco.br

Reitor: Daniela Gusmão

Departments
Accountancy (Accountancy); **Administration** (Administration); **Biology** (Biology); **Computer Science** (Computer Science); **Data Processing Technology** (Data Processing); **Law** (Law); **Letters** (Arts and Humanities); **Mathematics** (Mathematics); **Physical Education** (Physical Education); **Physiotherapy** (Physical Therapy); **Social Communication** (Communication Studies); **Social Work** (Social and Community Services); **Veterinary Medicine** (Veterinary Science)

Faculties
Agricultural and Environmental Sciences (Agriculture; Environmental Studies); **Philosophy** *(Campos de Goytacazes)* (Philosophy)

History: Founded 1994 as Faculdade de Educação, Ciências e Letras Marechal Castelo Branco and Faculdade de Educação Física da Guanabara. Became Faculdades Integradas Castelo Branco 1976 and acquired present status and title 1994.

Academic Year: February to December (February-July; August-December)

Admission Requirements: Secondary school certificate

Main Language(s) of Instruction: Portuguese

Degrees and Diplomas: *Bacharelado*; *Licenciatura*; *Especialização/Aperfeiçoamento*; *Mestrado*

Student Services: Canteen, Cultural centre, Employment services, Health services, Sports facilities

Special Facilities: Theatre

Libraries: Biblioteca 'Manuel Bandeira', c. 40,010 vols

Publications: Boletim da Qualidade *(bimonthly)*; Boletim Desenvolvimento Gerencial *(bimonthly)*

Last Updated: 30/10/07

CASTRO ALVES FACULTY

Faculdade Castro Alves (FCA)
Rua Marechal Andréa, N° 265, Pituba, Salvador, Bahia 41820090
Tel: +55(71) 3205-2200
Fax: +55(71) 3248-7485
EMail: castroalves@castroalves.br
Website: http://www.castroalves.br

Diretor: Jair de Oliveira Santos

Courses
Accountancy (Accountancy); **Administration**; **Graduate Studies** (Accountancy; Finance; Human Resources; Marketing; Transport Management); **Psychology** (Psychology); **Tourism** (Tourism)

History: Founded 1999.

Main Language(s) of Instruction: Portuguese

Degrees and Diplomas: *Bacharelado*; *Especialização/Aperfeiçoamento*; *Mestrado*

Last Updated: 29/06/10

CATHEDRAL FACULTY

Faculdade Cathedral (FACES)
Av. Luís Canuto Chaves, 293, Caçari, Boa Vista,
Roraima 69307-053
Tel: +55(95) 2121-3460
EMail: cathedral@cathedral.edu.br
Website: http://www.cathedral.edu.br

Head: Bismarck Duarte Diniz EMail: bismarck@cathedral.edu.br

Faculties
Água Boa - Mato Grosso (Accountancy; Administration; Agricultural Business; Business and Commerce; Environmental Management; Health Administration; History; Human Resources; Industrial Management; Literature; Management; Marketing; Pedagogy; Portuguese; Public Relations; Social and Community Services; Systems Analysis; Teacher Training); **Barra do Garças - Mato Grosso** (Accountancy; Administration; Agricultural Business; Finance; Higher Education; Law; Marketing; Pedagogy; Systems Analysis); **Boa Vista - Roraima**; **Distance Education** *(EAD)* (Administration; Political Sciences; Theology)

Further Information: Also Distance Education Programmes with UNOPAR, ESAB and COC.

History: Founded 2001.

Main Language(s) of Instruction: Portuguese

Degrees and Diplomas: *Tecnólogo*; *Bacharelado*; *Licenciatura*; *Especialização/Aperfeiçoamento*

Last Updated: 30/06/10

CATHOLIC FACULTY OF ANAPOLIS

Faculdade Católica de Anápolis
Cidade Jardim, Rua 5, 580, Anápolis, GO 75080-730
Tel: +55(62) 3943-1048
Website: http://www.catolicadeanapolis.com.br

Diretora: Adriana Rocha Vilela Arantes

Courses
Administration (Administration); **Philosophy**; **Theology** (Theology)

History: Founded 1995 as Faculdade de Filosofia São Miguel Arcanjo. Acquired present title 2008.

Main Language(s) of Instruction: Portuguese

Degrees and Diplomas: *Bacharelado*; *Licenciatura*; *Especialização/Aperfeiçoamento*

Last Updated: 16/07/10

CATHOLIC FACULTY OF CARIRI

Faculdade Católica do Cariri
Rua Cel. Antônio Luiz, 1068, Pimenta, Crato, CE 63105-000
Tel: +55(88) 3586-9050
Website: http://www.catolicadocariri.edu.br

Reitor: Fernando Panico

Courses
Philosophy

Main Language(s) of Instruction: Portuguese

Degrees and Diplomas: *Bacharelado*; *Licenciatura*; *Especialização/Aperfeiçoamento*

Last Updated: 16/07/10

CATHOLIC FACULTY OF CEARA

Faculdade Católica de Ceará
Avenida Duque de Caixas 101, Fortaleza, Ceará 60.035-110
Tel: +55(85) 4009-6272
EMail: dg.fcc@marista.edu.br
Website: http://www.catolicaceara.edu.br/

Diretor: Ailton dos Santos Arruda

Courses
Advertising; **Fashion Design** (Fashion Design); **Marketing** (Marketing); **Physical Education**

History: Founded 1913 as Colégio Marista Cearense. Became Faculdade Marista Fortaleza 2003. Acquired present title 2006.

Main Language(s) of Instruction: Portuguese

Degrees and Diplomas: *Bacharelado*; *Licenciatura*; *Especialização/Aperfeiçoamento*

Last Updated: 19/07/10

CATHOLIC FACULTY OF ECONOMICS OF BAHIA

Faculdade Católica de Ciências Econômicas da Bahia (FACCEBA)
Rua da Mangueira 15, Nazaré, Salvador, Bahia 40050001
Tel: +55(71) 3243-5832
Fax: +55(71) 3321-0616
EMail: facceba@facceba.net
Website: http://www.facceba.com.br

Diretor: José Augusto Guimarães (1998-)

Courses
Economics (Economics)
History: Founded 1960.

Main Language(s) of Instruction: Portuguese

Degrees and Diplomas: *Bacharelado*; *Especialização/Aperfeiçoamento*; *Mestrado*

Last Updated: 27/09/07

CATHOLIC FACULTY OF NOSSA SENHORA DAS VITÓRIAS

Faculdade Católica Nossa Senhora das Vitórias
Rua Augusto Severo 200 - Centro, Assu, RN 59650-000
EMail: fcensv@fcproneves.edu.br
Website: http://www.fcproneves.edu.br/assu/

Diretora geral: Maricélia Almaida de Farias

Courses
Accountancy (Accountancy); **Business Administration**
History: Founded 2004.

Main Language(s) of Instruction: Portuguese

Degrees and Diplomas: *Bacharelado*; *Especialização/Aperfeiçoamento*

Libraries: Yes
Last Updated: 19/07/10

CATHOLIC FACULTY OF NOSSA SENHORA DES NEVES

Faculdade Católica Nossa Senhora des Neves
Praça Pedro II, 1055 - Alecrim, Natal, RN 59030-400
EMail: diracad.nsn@fcproneves.edu.br
Website: http://www.fcproneves.edu.br/neves

Diretora: Maria Araújo de Medeiros

Courses
Accountancy; **Administration** (Administration); **Social Services**
History: Founded 2004.

Main Language(s) of Instruction: Portuguese

Degrees and Diplomas: *Bacharelado*
Last Updated: 19/07/10

CATHOLIC FACULTY OF POUSO ALEGRE

Faculdade Católica de Pouso Alegre
Avenida Monsenhor Mauro Tommasini 75, Pouso Alegre, MG 37550-000
EMail: secretaria@facapa.edu.br
Website: http://www.facapa.edu.br

Diretor: Dionísio Ailton Pereira

Courses
Philosophy (Philosophy); **Theology**
History: Founded 2003.

Main Language(s) of Instruction: Portuguese

Degrees and Diplomas: *Bacharelado*; *Especialização/Aperfeiçoamento*

Libraries: Yes
Last Updated: 16/07/10

CATHOLIC FACULTY OF RONDONIA

Faculdade Católica de Rondônia
Rua Gonçalves Dias, 290 - Centro, Porto Velho, RO 76801-132
EMail: fabioheck@hotmail.com
Website: http://www.fcrondonia.com.br

Diretor: Fabio Rychecki Hecktheuer

Courses
Philosophy; **Postgraduate** (Administration; Education; Law)
History: Founded 2007.

Main Language(s) of Instruction: Portuguese

Degrees and Diplomas: *Bacharelado*; *Mestrado*; *Doutorado*
Last Updated: 16/07/10

CATHOLIC FACULTY OF TOCANTINS

Faculdade Católica do Tocantins
Av. Teotônio Segurado - 1402 Sul Cj. 01, Palmas, TO 77061-002
Tel: +55 (63) 3221-2100
EMail: clarete@catolica-to.edu.br
Website: http://www.cecb.edu.br/ubec/publicacao/engine.wsp?tmp.sitio=20

Diretora Geral: C. Clarete de Itoz

Courses
Accountancy; **Administration**; **Agronomy** (Agronomy); **Information Systems** (Computer Science); **Law** (Law)
History: Founded 2003.

Main Language(s) of Instruction: Portuguese

Degrees and Diplomas: *Bacharelado*; *Licenciatura*; *Especialização/Aperfeiçoamento*; *Mestrado*
Last Updated: 14/03/11

CATHOLIC FACULTY OF UBERLANDIA

Faculdade Católica de Uberlândia
Rua Padre Pio, 300, Osvaldo Rezende 38.400-386
EMail: contato@catolicaonline.com.br
Website: http://www.catolicaonline.com.br/portal

Diretor: Sérgio de Siqueira Camargo
EMail: diretor@catolicaonline.com.br

Areas
Applied Social Sciences (Administration; Journalism; Law; Social and Community Services); **Engineering** (Safety Engineering); **Health** (Health Sciences); **Human Sciences** (Geography; History; Pedagogy; Philosophy; Theology); **Letters** (Literature)
History: Founded 2002.

Main Language(s) of Instruction: Portuguese

Degrees and Diplomas: *Bacharelado*; *Licenciatura*; *Especialização/Aperfeiçoamento*
Last Updated: 16/07/10

CATHOLIC SALESIAN AUXILIUM UNIVERSITY CENTRE

Centro Universitário Católico Salesiano Auxilium (UNISALESIANO)
Rua Dom Bosco 265, Centro, Araçatuba, São Paulo 16400-505
Tel: +55(14) 3533-6200
EMail: academico@unisalesiano.edu.br
Website: http://www.unisalesiano.edu.br

Diretor: Paulo Fernando Vendrame

Courses
Accountancy (Accountancy); **Administration** (Administration); **Arts and Humanities** (Arts and Humanities; English; Literature; Portuguese); **Chemistry** (Chemistry); **Distance Education**; **Environmental Management** (Administration; Environmental Management); **Graduate Studies** (Accountancy; Business Administration; Higher Education; Labour Law; Law; Literature; Mathematics Education; Orthopaedics; Physical Therapy; Portuguese;

Public Health; Sports); **History** (History); **Internet Systems**; **Nursing**; **Occupational Health**; **Pedagogy** (Pedagogy); **Physical Education** (Physical Education); **Physiotherapy** (Physical Therapy); **Psychology**

History: Founded 1974 as Faculdade de Ciências Contábeis e Atuariais da Alta Noroeste. Acquired present title 2005.

Main Language(s) of Instruction: Portuguese

Degrees and Diplomas: *Tecnólogo*; *Bacharelado*. Also postgraduate programmes and MBA.
Last Updated: 21/05/10

CATHOLIC UNIVERSITY CENTRE OF THE SOUTH WEST OF PARANA

Centro Universitário Católico do Sudoeste do Paraná (UNICS)
Rodovia PRT 280, Trevo da Codapar, Palmas, Paraná 85555-000
Tel: +55(46) 3263-8100
EMail: secretaria@unics.edu.br
Website: http://www.unics.edu.br

Reitora: Ivania Marini Piton

Areas
Agrarian Science (Agriculture; Agronomy; Forestry); **Applied Social Sciences** (Accountancy; Administration; Law); **Biology** (Biology); **Engineering** (Civil Engineering); **Exact and Earth Sciences** (Chemistry; Computer Science; Mathematics; Physics); **Health Sciences**; **Human Sciences**; **Linguistics, Literature and Arts** (English; Literature; Spanish; Visual Arts)

Courses
Graduate Studies *(Lato sensu - Especialização)* (Accountancy; Arts and Humanities; Literature); **Graduate Studies** *(Stricto Sensu - Mestrado)*; **Technical Studies** (Nursing; Occupational Health)

History: Founded 1967 as Faculdade de Filosofia, Ciências e Letras de Palmas. Became Faculdades Integradas Católicas de Palmas 2001. Became Centro Universitário Diocesano do Sudoeste do Paraná – UNICS 2004. Acquired present title 2008.

Main Language(s) of Instruction: Portuguese

Degrees and Diplomas: *Bacharelado*; *Licenciatura*; *Especialização/Aperfeiçoamento*; *Mestrado*
Last Updated: 01/06/10

CATHOLIC UNIVERSITY OF BRASÍLIA

Universidade Católica de Brasília (UCB)
QS 07 Epct Lote 01, Águas Claras, Brasília, DF 72022900
Tel: +55(61) 3356-9000
EMail: leao@ucb.br
Website: http://www.ucb.br

Reitor: José Romualdo Degasperi

Areas
Applied Social Sciences (Accountancy; Administration; Advertising and Publicity; Communication Studies; Economics; International Relations; Journalism; Law; Social Sciences); **Education and Humanities**; **Life Sciences** (Biological and Life Sciences; Biomedicine; Dentistry; Medicine; Nursing; Nutrition; Pharmacy; Physical Therapy; Psychology); **Science and Technology** (Agricultural Business; Biomedical Engineering; Computer Science; Data Processing; Environmental Engineering; Information Management; Production Engineering)

Further Information: Also second campus for postgraduate students

History: Founded 1974 as Faculdade Católica de Ciências Humanas (FCCH). Reorganized 1981 as Faculdades Integradas da Católica de Brasília (FICB), acquired present status and title 1994. A private institution under the supervision of the União Brasiliense de Educação e Cultura.

Academic Year: February to December (February-June; August-December)

Admission Requirements: Secondary school certificate and entrance examination (vestibular)

Degrees and Diplomas: *Bacharelado*: Accountancy; Economic Science, 5-7 yrs; *Bacharelado*: Administration, 3-6 yrs; *Bacharelado*: Computer Sciences; Social Communication, 4 1/2-9 yrs;

Bacharelado: Dentistry; Law; Psychology, 5-8 yrs; *Bacharelado*: Environmental Engineering; International Relations; Nutrition, 4-8 yrs; *Bacharelado*: Physiotherapy, 5-9 yrs; *Licenciatura*: Biology; Chemistry, 4-6 yrs; *Licenciatura*: Data Processing, 3-6 yrs; *Licenciatura*: Letters; Mathematics; Pedagogy; Philosophy; Physical Education; Physics, 4-8 yrs; *Especialização/Aperfeiçoamento*; *Mestrado*: Education; *Doutorado*

Student Services: Canteen, Cultural centre, Health services, Sports facilities

Libraries: Biblioteca Central, c. 247,100 vols

Publications: Cadernos da Católica; Revista Universa

Press or Publishing House: Editora Universa
Last Updated: 08/06/10

CATHOLIC UNIVERSITY OF GOIÁS

Universidade Católica de Goiás (UCG)
Avenida Universitária 1440, Setor Universitário, Goiânia,
Goiás 74605010
Tel: +55(62) 3946-1155
EMail: ucg@ucg.br
Website: http://www.ucg.br

Reitor: Wolmir Therezio Amado
Tel: +55(62) 227-1004 +55(62) 227-1002

Centres
Biological Research and Study (Biological and Life Sciences); **Economic Research** (Economics); **Foreign Languages** (English; Foreign Languages Education; French; Modern Languages; Portuguese; Spanish); **Youth Village Research**

Departments
Accountancy (Accountancy); **Animal Husbandry** (Animal Husbandry); **Arts and Architecture** (Architecture; Fine Arts); **Biology** (Biology); **Biomedical Sciences** (Biomedicine); **Business Administration** (Business Administration); **Civil Engineering** (Civil Engineering); **Computer Science** (Computer Science); **Economics** (Economics); **Education** (Education); **History, Geography and Social Sciences** (Geography; History; Social Sciences); **Languages** (English; Modern Languages; Portuguese; Secretarial Studies); **Law Sciences** (Law); **Mathematics** (Food Technology; Mathematics; Physics); **Nursing** (Nursing); **Philosophy and Theology** (Philosophy; Theology); **Physical Education** (Physical Education); **Psychology** (Psychology); **Social Service** (Social Work); **Speech Pathology** (Speech Therapy and Audiology)

Institutes
Humid Tropics (Geography); **Prehistory and Anthropology** (Anthropology; Prehistory)

History: Founded 1959. A non-profit private Institution administered by the Catholic Archdiocese of Goiânia.

Governing Bodies: Conselho Universitário

Academic Year: March to December (March-July; August-December)

Admission Requirements: Secondary school certificate and entrance examination

Main Language(s) of Instruction: Portuguese

International Co-operation: Participates in the Intercampus Programme in Spain

Degrees and Diplomas: *Bacharelado*: Accountancy; Architecture; Bilingual Executive Secretarial Studies; Biology; Biomedicine; Civil Engineering; Computer Sciences; Economics; Education; Engineering; Food Technology; Geography; History; Law; Mathematics; Nursing; Philosophy; Physics; Portuguese; Portuguese-English; Psychology; Public and Business Administration; Social Service; Speech Pathology and Audiology; Zootechnics; *Especialização/Aperfeiçoamento*; *Mestrado*; *Doutorado*

Student Services: Canteen, Cultural centre, Health services, Social counselling, Sports facilities

Special Facilities: Anthropology Museum; Archaeology Museum; History Museum

Libraries: Central Library

Publications: Estudos, magazine *(bimonthly)*

Press or Publishing House: Divisão Gráfica e Editorial da UGC
Last Updated: 08/06/10

CATHOLIC UNIVERSITY OF PELOTAS

Universidade Católica de Pelotas (UCPEL)
Rua Felix da Cunha 412, Centro, Pelotas,
Rio Grande do Sul 96010000
Tel: +55(532) 2128-8000
EMail: ucpel@phoenix.ucpel.tche.br
Website: http://www.ucpel.tche.br

Reitor: Alencar Mello Proença
Tel: +55(532) 284-8220, Fax: +55(532) 222-9447

Pro-Reitor Administrativo: Carlos Ricardo Gass Sinnott
Tel: +55(532) 284-8221, Fax: +55(532) 222-9447

International Relations: Fabio Rychecki Hecktheuer, Assessor
Tel: +55(532) 284-8295, Fax: +55(532) 225-3105

Centres
Education and Communication (Advertising and Publicity; Fashion Design; History; Journalism; Literature; Mathematics; Pedagogy; Tourism); **Law, Economics and Social Sciences**; **Life and Health Sciences**; **Polytechnic**

Institutes
Philosophy; **Religious Studies** (Biology; Ethics); **Theology** (Theology)

Further Information: Also University Hospital

History: Founded 1960. A private Institution under the supervision of the Sociedade Pelotense de Assistência e Cultura, but receives financial support from the Federal Government.

Governing Bodies: Superior Council; University Council

Academic Year: March to November

Admission Requirements: Secondary school certificate or foreign equivalent and entrance examination

Main Language(s) of Instruction: Portuguese

International Co-operation: Programmes: Foundation Carolina (Spain); ALBAN (Communised Europe); Financial Institutions: DAAD (Germany); AECI (Spain); FULBRIGHT (USA); Countries: Spain, Portugal, Germany, Italy, Australia, Chile, Colombia, Uruguay, Argentina.

Accrediting Agencies: CNPq; FAPERGS; CAPES

Degrees and Diplomas: *Bacharelado*: 4-5 yrs; *Bacharelado*: Civil Engineering (Engenheiro civil); Electrical Engineering (Engenheiro electricista); Law (Avogado); Medicine (Médico); Pharmaceutical Biochemistry (Farmacêutico e Bioquímico); Psychology (Psicólogo); Social Work (Assistente social), 5 yrs; *Bacharelado*: Physiotherapy, 4-5 yrs; *Bacharelado*: Social Communication, 4 yrs; *Licenciatura*: 3-4 yrs; *Especialização/Aperfeiçoamento*; *Mestrado*; *Doutorado*

Student Services: Academic counselling, Canteen, Cultural centre, Handicapped facilities, Health services, Language programs, Nursery care, Social counselling, Sports facilities

Student Residential Facilities: no

Special Facilities: Museum; Art Gallery; TV Studio; Radio; Auditorium

Libraries: Central Library, 86,996 vols

Publications: ECO Revista, Communications Studies *(biennially)*; Linguagem & Ensino *(biennially)*; Razão e Fé, themes about Religion *(biennially)*; Revista da Escola de Direito *(annually)*; Revista da Escola de Medicina *(biennially)*; Sociedade em Debate, themes about social and community services *(quarterly)*

Press or Publishing House: Editora da Universidade Católica de Pelotas - EDUCAT
Last Updated: 07/06/10

CATHOLIC UNIVERSITY OF PERNAMBUCO

Universidade Católica de Pernambuco (UNICAP)
Rua do Príncipe 526, Campus Universitário, Unicap-Boa Vista,
Recife, Pernambuco 50050-900
Tel: +55(81) 2199-4000
Fax: +55(81) 3423-0541
EMail: asseplan@unicap.br
Website: http://www.unicap.br

Reitor: Pedro Rubens Ferreira Oliveira, S.J. (2006-)
Tel: +55(81) 3216-4110 EMail: prubens@unicap.br

Pro-Rector: Altamir Soares de Paula
Tel: +55(81) 3216-4142, Fax: +55(81) 3216-4231
EMail: altamir@unicap.br

International Relations: Paulo Gaspar de Meneses, S.J.
Tel: +55(81) 3216-4110 EMail: pmeneses@unicap.br

Centres
Biology and Health Sciences (Biology; Occupational Therapy; Physical Therapy; Psychology; Speech Therapy and Audiology); **Law** (Law); **Science and Technology** (Architecture; Chemical Engineering; Civil Engineering; Environmental Engineering; Mathematics; Mathematics and Computer Science; Natural Sciences; Physics; Technology; Town Planning); **Social Sciences** (Accountancy; Administration; Advertising and Publicity; Economics; Journalism; Public Relations; Social and Community Services; Social Sciences; Tourism); **Theology and Human Sciences** (Arts and Humanities; History; Literature; Philosophy; Theology)

History: Founded 1951 incorporating Faculty of Economics, established 1942, Faculty of Philosophy, 1943, and School of Engineering, 1912. Reorganized 1973 with a structure comprising centres for professional education. A private institution under the supervision of the Society of Jesus and recognized by the Federal Government.

Governing Bodies: Conselho Superior; Conselho de Ensino e Pesquisa; Conselho Universitário

Academic Year: February to December (February-June; August-December)

Admission Requirements: Secondary school certificate and entrance examination

Fees: (Real): 295-729.26 per month according to courses

Main Language(s) of Instruction: Portuguese

International Co-operation: With universities in France, Spain, Belgium, Chile, USA, Ecuador, Colombia, Venezuela, Uruguay, El Salvador, Peru, Guatemala and Portugal.

Degrees and Diplomas: *Bacharelado*: Accountancy; Business Administration; Economics; Industrial Chemistry; Journalism; Public Relations; Publicity and Advertising; Social Sciences; Speech Therapy (Fonoaudiólogo); Telecommunications, 4-7 yrs; *Bacharelado*: Architecture and Town Planning; Psychology (Psicólogo), 5-9 yrs; *Bacharelado*: Chemical Engineering; Civil Engineering, 6-9 yrs; *Bacharelado*: Chemistry, 4 1/2-7 yrs; *Bacharelado*: Computer Science; Law; Statistics, 5-8 yrs; *Bacharelado*: Environmental Engineering, 5 1/2-9 yrs; *Bacharelado*: Letters; Philosophy, 3 1/2-7 yrs; *Bacharelado*: Occupational Therapy; Physiotherapy, 5-7 1/2 yrs; *Bacharelado*: Physics; Theology, 5-7 yrs; *Bacharelado*: Tourism, 3-4 yrs; *Licenciatura*: Biological Sciences; History; Letters; Mathematics; Pedagogy; Physics, 3 1/2-7 yrs; *Licenciatura*: Chemistry; Social Sciences, 3-7 yrs; *Licenciatura*: Philosophy, 4-7 yrs; *Licenciatura*: Psychology, 5-7 yrs; *Especialização/Aperfeiçoamento*; *Mestrado*; *Doutorado*

Student Services: Academic counselling, Canteen, Cultural centre, Employment services, Foreign student adviser, Handicapped facilities, Health services, Social counselling, Sports facilities

Special Facilities: Museum of Archaeology

Libraries: Biblioteca Central 'Padre Aloisio Mosca de Carvalho', c. 222,389 vols

Publications: Ágora Filosófica *(biennially)*; Interlocuções *(biennially)*; Jus Et Fides *(biennially)*; Revista Economia Negócios e Financias *(biennially)*; Revista Educacão Teorias e Prácticas *(biennially)*; Revista Química e Tecnologia *(biennially)*; Revista Symposium *(biennially)*; Revista Teologia e Ciencia de Religião *(biennially)*
Last Updated: 07/06/10

CATHOLIC UNIVERSITY OF PETRÓPOLIS

Universidade Católica de Petrópolis (UCP)
Rua Benjamin Constant 213, Centro, Petrópolis,
Rio de Janeiro 25610130
Tel: +55(24) 2244-4000
Fax: +55(24) 2242-7747
EMail: reitoria@ucp.br
Website: http://www.ucp.br

Reitor: José Luiz Rangel Sampaio Fernandes EMail: reitor@ucp.br

Centres
Applied Social Sciences (Accountancy; Administration; Economics; Marketing; Tourism); **Engineering and Computer Science**

(Civil Engineering; Electrical Engineering; Engineering; Hydraulic Engineering; Mechanical Engineering; Production Engineering; Thermal Engineering); **Health Sciences** (Biomedicine; Physical Education; Physical Therapy; Psychology); **Law** (Law); **Theology and Humanities** (Arts and Humanities; History; Literature; Mathematics; Pedagogy; Philosophy; Theology)

History: Founded as Faculty of Law 1953, became University 1961 with the Diocesan Bishop as Grand Chancellor. Receives some financial support from the Federal Government.

Governing Bodies: Conselho Superior de Administração e Finanças; Conselho de Patronos; Conselho Universitário; Conselho de Coordenação de Ensino e Pesquisa

Academic Year: February to December (February-June; August-December)

Admission Requirements: Secondary school certificate and entrance examination

Main Language(s) of Instruction: Portuguese

Degrees and Diplomas: *Tecnólogo*; *Bacharelado*: 8-10 sem; *Licenciatura*; *Mestrado*

Student Residential Facilities: Yes

Libraries: Central Library, c. 120,200 vols

Publications: Revista U.C.P.

Press or Publishing House: Private Press
Last Updated: 07/06/10

CATHOLIC UNIVERSITY OF SALVADOR
Universidade Católica de Salvador (UCSAL)
Largo do Campo Grande, 07 - Campo Grande, Salvador,
Bahia 40040220
Tel: +55(71) 3324-7610
Fax: +55(71) 3328-0162
EMail: reitoria@ucsal.br
Website: http://www.ucsal.br

Reitor: José Carlos Almeida da Silva (1986-)
Tel: +55(71) 324-7503

Faculties
Economics (Economics); **Education** (Education); **Law** (Law); **Nursing** (Nursing)

Institutes
Exact and Natural Sciences (Mathematics and Computer Science; Natural Sciences; Physics); **Letters** (Arts and Humanities; Communication Studies; Secretarial Studies); **Music** (Music); **Philosophy** (Philosophy); **Theology** (Theology)

Schools
Accountancy (Accountancy); **Biology** (Biology); **Business Administration** (Business Administration); **Engineering** (Engineering); **Physical Education and Sports** (Physical Education; Sports); **Social Service** (Social Work)

History: Founded 1961.

Academic Year: January to December (January-June; August-December)

Admission Requirements: Secondary school certificate and entrance examination

Main Language(s) of Instruction: Portuguese

Degrees and Diplomas: *Bacharelado*: 8-10 sem; *Bacharelado*: Social work (Assistente social), 3 yrs; *Licenciatura*: 8-10 sem; *Especialização/Aperfeiçoamento*; *Mestrado*

Libraries: Central Library, c. 75,000 vols
Last Updated: 07/06/10

CATHOLIC UNIVERSITY OF SANTOS
Universidade Católica de Santos (UNISANTOS)
Rua Euclides da Cunha 241, Pompéia, Santos,
São Paulo 11065902
Tel: +55(13) 3205-5540
Fax: +55(13) 3205-5555 +55(13) 3205-5622
EMail: secgeral@unisantos.com.br
Website: http://www.unisantos.com.br

Reitor: Marcos Medina Leite Tel: +55(13) 3205-5545

Centres
Communication and Arts (Advertising and Publicity; Architecture; Journalism; Public Relations; Town Planning); **Educational Sciences**; **Exact Sciences and Technology** (Biotechnology; Chemistry; Civil Engineering; Computer Networks; Computer Science; Electrical Engineering; Environmental Engineering; Environmental Management; Petroleum and Gas Engineering; Production Engineering; Systems Analysis); **Health Sciences** (Cooking and Catering; Gynaecology and Obstetrics; Nursing; Nutrition; Pharmacy; Physical Therapy); **Languages**; **Law and Applied Social Sciences**

History: Founded 1986. A private institution under the jurisdiction of the Sociedade Visconde de São Leopoldo.

Admission Requirements: Secondary school certificate and entrance examination

Main Language(s) of Instruction: Portuguese

Degrees and Diplomas: *Bacharelado*; *Licenciatura*; *Especialização/Aperfeiçoamento*; *Mestrado*

Libraries: Central Library, c. 58,000 vols
Last Updated: 07/06/10

CATUAÍ FACULTY
Faculdade Catuaí
Av. Bento Munhoz da Rocha Neto 210, Cambe, PR 86186-000
Tel: +55(43) 3253-5454
EMail: direcaoacademica@ices.edu.br
Website: http://www.ices.edu.br

Diretora: Maria Izabel Baptista Alabarces

Courses
Administration (Administration); **Law** (Law); **Pedagogy** (Pedagogy)

Degrees and Diplomas: *Bacharelado*; *Especialização/Aperfeiçoamento*

Libraries: Biblioteca Prof. Dr. João Francisco Gonsalez
Last Updated: 22/09/10

CBES - CBES FACULTY
Faculdade CBES - CBES
Rua Doutor Muricy, 380 - Centro, Curitiba, PA 80010-120
Tel: +55(11) 5585-0060
EMail: tadeu.diretoria@cbes.edu.br
Website: http://www.cbes.edu.br

Diretora: Gillian Alonso Arruda EMail: gaa@pontocritico.com.br

Courses
Administration (Administration); **Nursing** (Nursing)

Further Information: Also branches in Belém, Porto Alegre and Sao Paulo

History: Founded 2001.

Main Language(s) of Instruction: Portuguese

Degrees and Diplomas: *Bacharelado*; *Especialização/Aperfeiçoamento*
Last Updated: 19/07/10

CCAA FACULTY
Faculdade CCAA
Av. Marechal Rondon 1460 Bairro Riachuelo, Rio de Janeiro, RJ
Tel: +55(21) 2156-5000
EMail: presidencia@grupoccaa.com.br
Website: http://www.faculdadeccaa.com.br/

Diretora: Eliane Faial

Courses
Administration (Administration); **Letters** (Literature); **Marketing**; **Social Communication** (Advertising and Publicity; Journalism; Multimedia)

History: Founded 2005.

Main Language(s) of Instruction: Portuguese

Degrees and Diplomas: *Bacharelado*; *Especialização/Aperfeiçoamento*; *Mestrado*
Last Updated: 19/07/10

CDL FACULTY OF TECHNOLOGY OF FORTALEZA

Faculdade de Tecnologia CDL de Fortaleza
Rua 25 de Março, 882 - Centro, Fortaleza, Ceará 60060-120
Tel: +55(85) 3433-3045
Fax: +55(85) 3433-3044
EMail: faleconosco@faculdadecdl.edu.br
Website: http://www.faculdadecdl.edu.br/

Diretor Geral: Honório Pinheiro

Courses
Commercial Management (Business and Commerce; Management); **Graduate Studies** (Administration; Banking; Management; Marketing); **Logistics** (Transport Management)

Degrees and Diplomas: *Tecnólogo.* Also MBA.
Last Updated: 20/08/10

CECAP FACULTY

Faculdade CECAP (CECAP)
Shin. QI 9/11 Lote B, Area Especial, Lago Norte, Brasília, DF 71515205
Tel: +55(61) 3468-9000
EMail: cecap@cecap.com.br
Website: http://www.cecap.com.br

Diretora: Katia Carneiro EMail: katia@cecap.com.br

Courses
Administration (Administration); **Graduate Studies**; **Pedagogy**; **Secretarial Studies**; **Tourism**

History: Founded 1999.

Main Language(s) of Instruction: Portuguese

Degrees and Diplomas: *Bacharelado*; *Licenciatura*; *Especialização/Aperfeiçoamento*
Last Updated: 30/06/10

CELER FACULTIES

Celer Faculdades
BR 282, quilômetro 528, Xaxim, SC 89825-000
Tel: +55(49) 3353-8787
Fax: +55(49) 3353-8751
EMail: sec@celer.com.br
Website: http://www.celer.com.br

Diretora: Ioli Rossatto

Courses
Accountancy (Accountancy); **Administration** (Administration; Advertising and Publicity; Business Administration); **Administration** (Administration); **Administration** (Administration); **Fashion Design** (Design; Fashion Design); **Graduate Studies**; **Journalism**; **Law** (Law); **Pedagogy** (Pedagogy); **Physical Education** (Physical Education); **Psychology** (Psychology); **Social Communication** (Mass Communication); **Tourism, Hotel and Event Management** (Hotel Management; Tourism)

History: Founded 1998.

Main Language(s) of Instruction: Portuguese

Degrees and Diplomas: *Bacharelado*; *Licenciatura*; *Especialização/Aperfeiçoamento*. Also MBA Programmes offered in Marketing and International Business.
Last Updated: 19/03/10

CÉLIA HELENA SCHOOL OF ARTS

Escola Superior de Artes Célia Helena
Avenida São Gabriel, 462, Itaim Bibi, São Paulo, SP 01435-000
Tel: +55(11) 3884-8294
Fax: +55(11) 3884-8214
EMail: contato@celiahelena.com.br
Website: http://www.celiahelena.com.br/

Diretora: Lígia Cortez

Courses
Theatre (Theatre)

Degrees and Diplomas: *Bacharelado*
Last Updated: 15/07/10

CELSO LISBOA UNIVERSITY CENTRE

Centro Universitário Celso Lisboa (CEUCEL)
Rua 24 de Maio, 797, Sampaio, Rio de Janeiro, Rio de Janeiro 20950-092
Tel: +55(21) 3289-4722
Fax: +55(21) 3289-4749
EMail: ceucel@ceucel.com.br
Website: http://www.celsolisboa.com.br

Reitora: Ana Carolina Lisboa EMail: reitoria@celsolisboa.edu.br

Courses
Accountancy (Accountancy); **Administration** (Administration); **Biology** (Biology); **Environmental Engineering** (Environmental Engineering); **Esthetics and Cosmetology**; **Graduate Studies**; **Human Resource Management** (Human Resources); **Informatics** (Computer Science); **Information Technology** (Information Technology); **Marketing**; **Nursing** (Nursing); **Nutrition** (Nutrition); **Pedagogy**; **Pharmacy** (Pharmacy); **Phonaudiology**; **Physical Education**; **Physiotherapy**; **Psychology** (Psychology); **Sports and Leisure Management**

History: Founded 1971.

Main Language(s) of Instruction: Portuguese

Degrees and Diplomas: *Tecnólogo*; *Licenciatura*; *Especialização/Aperfeiçoamento*. Also MBA.
Last Updated: 21/05/10

CENACAP FACULTY OF TECHNOLOGY

Faculdade de Tecnologia Cenacap (CENACAP)
SHCGN 714/715 - BLOCO B - Lote 10, Asa Norte, Brasília, DF 70760-795
Tel: +55(61) 3347-1094
Fax: +55(61) 3347-1094
EMail: cenacap@cenacap.com.br
Website: http://www.cenacap.com.br/

Diretor Geral: João Viegas

Courses
Administration (Administration); **Graduate Studies** (Anatomy; Health Sciences; Medical Technology; Radiology); **Nursing** (Nursing); **Radiology** (Radiology)

Degrees and Diplomas: *Tecnólogo*; *Bacharelado*; *Especialização/Aperfeiçoamento*
Last Updated: 20/08/10

CENECIST FACULTY OF BENTO GONÇALVES

Faculdade Cenecista de Bento Gonçalves (FACEBG)
Rua Arlindo Franklin Barbosa 460, Bairro São Roque, Bento Gonçalves, RS 95700000
Tel: +55(54) 3452-4422
Fax: +55(54) 3452-4422
EMail: secretaria@facebg.com.br
Website: http://www.facebg.com.br/

Diretor: Vercino Franzoloso (1998-)
EMail: vercino@cnecbento.com.br

Courses
Administration (Administration); **Advertising and Publicity** (Advertising and Publicity); **Graduate Studies** (Human Resources; Marketing; Production Engineering); **Nursing** (Nursing); **Nutrition** (Nutrition); **Physical Therapy** (Physical Therapy); **Tourism** (Tourism)

History: Founded 1998 as Centro de Ensino Superior de Bento Gonçalves. Acquired present status and title 2004.

Main Language(s) of Instruction: Portuguese

Degrees and Diplomas: *Bacharelado*; *Especialização/Aperfeiçoamento*
Last Updated: 30/06/10

CENECIST FACULTY OF BRASILIA

Faculdade Cenecista de Brasilia
QNM 30, Módulos H, I e J, Ceilândia, Brasilia, DF 72210-300
EMail: diretor@faceb.edu.br
Website: http://www.faceb.edu.br/faceb/index.shtml

Diretora: Maria Elvira de Melo Oliveira

Courses
Administration (Administration); **Information Systems** (Computer Science); **Letters**; **Pedagogy** (Pedagogy); **Social Services** (Social and Community Services)

History: Founded 2000.

Main Language(s) of Instruction: Portuguese

Degrees and Diplomas: *Bacharelado*; *Especialização/Aperfeiçoamento*

Libraries: Biblioteca Professor Roni Krauthein
Last Updated: 19/07/10

CENECIST FACULTY OF CAMPO LARGO

Faculdade Cenecista de Campo Largo (FACECLA)
Rua Rui Barbosa 541, Centro, Campo Largo, Paranà 83601-140
Tel: +55(41) 3116-3300
Fax: +55(41) 3116-3300
EMail: faculdade@presidentekennedy.br
Website: http://www.facecla.com.br

Diretor: Vitor Hugo Strozzi

Courses
Accountancy; **Administration** (Administration); **Graduate Studies** (Educational Psychology; Special Education); **Information Systems**; **Law** (Law); **Pedagogy** (Pedagogy)

History: Founded 1999 as Faculdade Cenecista Presidente Kennedy.

Main Language(s) of Instruction: Portuguese

Degrees and Diplomas: *Bacharelado*; *Licenciatura*. Also Posgraduate Diploma.
Last Updated: 30/06/10

CENECIST FACULTY OF FORTALEZA

Faculdade Cenecista de Fortaleza
Rua General Piragibe, 242 - Parquelândia, Fortaleza, CE 60450-250
Tel: +55(85) 3243-6778
EMail: cnec@cnec.br
Website: http://www.cnecce.com.br/facefor.php

Presidente: Alexandre José dos Santos

Courses
Accountancy (Accountancy); **Tourism** (Tourism)

Degrees and Diplomas: *Bacharelado*
Last Updated: 19/07/10

CENECIST FACULTY OF ILHA DO GOVERNADOR

Faculdade Cenecista da Ilha do Governador (ABEU)
Capitão Lemos Cunha, Estrada do Galeão, s/n, Ilha do Governador, Rio de Janeiro 21941-291
Tel: +55(21) 3975-6804 +55(21) 3975-6807
EMail: direcao@facig-rj.com.br
Website: http://www.facig-rj.com.br

Diretor: Eduardo Moreira Dias

Courses
Administration; **Graduate Studies** (Education; Educational Administration; Educational Psychology; English; Environmental Management; Occupational Health; Portuguese; Public Administration; Public Health); **Information Systems** (Information Management); **Pedagogy**

History: Founded 1977.

Main Language(s) of Instruction: Portuguese

Degrees and Diplomas: *Bacharelado*; *Licenciatura*; *Especialização/Aperfeiçoamento*
Last Updated: 30/06/10

CENECIST FACULTY OF ITABORAÍ

Faculdade Cenecista de Itaboraí (FACNEC)
Rua Presidente Costa e Silva, 212, Centro, Itaboraí, Rio de Janeiro 24800-000
Tel: +55(21) 2635-3512
Fax: +55(21) 2635-3512
EMail: adm@facnet-ita.br
Website: http://www.facnec-ita.br

Diretor: Marco Aurélio Togatlian

Courses
Administration (Administration); **Graduate Studies** (Business Administration; Business Education; Educational Administration; Educational Psychology; Higher Education; Hotel Management; Human Resources; Management; Mathematics; Rehabilitation and Therapy; Special Education; Statistics; Tourism; Transport Management); **Literature**; **Mathematics**; **Pedagogy** (Pedagogy)

History: Founded 1998

Main Language(s) of Instruction: Portuguese

Degrees and Diplomas: *Bacharelado*; *Licenciatura*; *Especialização/Aperfeiçoamento*
Last Updated: 30/06/10

CENECIST FACULTY OF ITUBERA

Faculdade Cenecista de Ituberá
Rua Olegário Martins 267 - Centro, Ituberá, BA 45435-000
Tel: +55(73) 3256-2222
EMail: ensinosuperior@cnec.br

Diretora: Carmen de Brito Bahia

Courses
History (History); **Letters** (Literature)

History: Founded 2006.

Main Language(s) of Instruction: Portuguese

Degrees and Diplomas: *Bacharelado*
Last Updated: 19/07/10

CENECIST FACULTY OF JOINVILLE

Faculdade Cenecista de Joinville (ESAN)
Rua Coronel Francisco Gomes 1290, Anita Garibaldi, Joinville, Santa Catarina 89202-250
Tel: +55(47) 3431-0900
EMail: deborah@fcj.com.br
Website: http://www.fcj.com.br

Diretor Geral: Félix José Negherbon
Tel: +55(47) 3431-0900 EMail: felix@fcj.com.br

Courses
Business and Commerce (Business Administration; Business and Commerce); **Business and International Commerce** (Business and Commerce; International Business); **Graduate Studies** (Accountancy; Business Administration; Commercial Law; Finance; Management; Marketing; Transport Management); **Information Systems**; **Law** (Law); **Management**; **Marketing**; **Technological Studies**; **Tourism** (Tourism)

History: Founded 2000.

Main Language(s) of Instruction: Portuguese

Degrees and Diplomas: *Tecnólogo*; *Bacharelado*; *Especialização/Aperfeiçoamento*
Last Updated: 30/06/10

CENECIST FACULTY OF NOVA PETROPÓLIS

Faculdade Cenecista de Nova Petropólis
Rua 28 de Fevereiro, 100 - Centro, Nova Petrópolis, RS 95150-000
Tel: +55(54) 3281 1067
EMail: secretaria@facenp.com.br
Website: http://www.facenp.com.br

Diretor: José Daniel Tavares EMail: diretor@facenp.com.br

Courses
Accountancy (Accountancy); **Administration** (Administration)

History: Founded 2003.

Main Language(s) of Instruction: Portuguese

Degrees and Diplomas: *Bacharelado*

Libraries: Biblioteca Cecília Meireles

Last Updated: 19/07/10

CENECIST FACULTY OF OSÓRIO

Faculdade Cenecista de Osório (FACOS)
Rua 24 de Maio, 141, Centro, Osório, RS 95520-000
Tel: +55(51) 3663-1763
EMail: facos@facos.edu.br
Website: http://www.facos.edu.br

Diretor: Adelar Hengemühle

Courses

Accountancy (Accountancy); Administration; Biological Sciences (Biological and Life Sciences); Computer Science; Geography (Geography); Graduate Studies; History (History); Law (Law); Literature; Mathematics (Mathematics); Pedagogy (Pedagogy); Physical Education (Physical Education); Teacher Training (Teacher Training)

History: Founded 1987.

Main Language(s) of Instruction: Portuguese

Degrees and Diplomas: *Bacharelado*; *Licenciatura*; *Especialização/Aperfeiçoamento*

Last Updated: 30/06/10

CENECIST FACULTY OF RIO BONITO

Faculdade Cenecista de Rio Bonito
Av. 7 de maio, 383 - Centro, Rio Bonito, RJ
Tel: +55(21) 2734-0222
EMail: cnec@cnecmonsenhor.com.br
Website: http://www.facerb.edu.br

Diretor: Carlos Alberto de Moura Machado

Courses

Administration (Administration)

Main Language(s) of Instruction: Portuguese

Degrees and Diplomas: *Bacharelado*

Last Updated: 20/07/10

CENECIST FACULTY OF RONDONÓPOLIS

Faculdade Cenecista de Rondonópolis
Av. Sothero Silva, 428 V. Aurora, Rondonópolis, MT 78740-040
EMail: cnec.facer@terra.com.br
Website: http://www.cnecfacer.com.br

Diretor: Reinaldo Mesquita Cassiano

Courses

Accountancy (Accountancy); Administration (Administration); Journalism (Journalism); Social Services

History: Founded 2004.

Main Language(s) of Instruction: Portuguese

Degrees and Diplomas: *Bacharelado*; *Especialização/Aperfeiçoamento*; *Mestrado*

Libraries: Biblioteca Felipe Tiago Gomes

Last Updated: 20/07/10

CENECIST FACULTY OF SENHOR DO BONFIM

Faculdade Cenecista de Senhor do Bonfim
Praça Dr Simões Filho 22, Senhor do Bonfim, BA
Tel: +55(74) 3541-4011
EMail: faculdadecenecistasb@hotmail.com
Website: http://www.facesb.com.br

Diretora: Vera Lúcia Gonçalves

Courses

History (History); Letters

History: Founded 2007.

Main Language(s) of Instruction: Portuguese

Degrees and Diplomas: *Licenciatura*

Last Updated: 20/07/10

CENECIST FACULTY OF SETE LAGOAS

Faculdade Cenecista de Sete Lagoas (FCSL)
Rua Pedro Gabriel de Lima, 20, Jardim Arizona, Sete Lagoas,
Minas Gerais 35700-377
Tel: +55(31) 3779-2270
EMail: secretaria@fcsl.edu.br
Website: http://www.fcsl.edu.br/

Diretor Geral: Eder Luiz Bolson
EMail: diretoria@fcsl.edu.br; eder@fcsl.edu.br

Courses

Administration (Administration); Graduate Studies (Educational Administration); Information Systems (Information Sciences; Information Technology)

History: Founded 2001.

Main Language(s) of Instruction: Portuguese

Degrees and Diplomas: *Bacharelado*. Also Postgraduate diploma.

Last Updated: 30/06/10

CENECIST FACULTY OF SINOP

Faculdade Cenecista de Sinop
Av. das Avencas n.° 200, Sinop, MG 78550-000
Tel: +55(66) 3531-7816
EMail: facenop@terra.com.br
Website: http://www.facenop.com.br

Diretora: Liliana Inês Weber

Courses

Journalism

History: Founded 2004.

Main Language(s) of Instruction: Portuguese

Degrees and Diplomas: *Bacharelado*; *Especialização/Aperfeiçoamento*

Libraries: Yes

Last Updated: 20/07/10

CENECIST FACULTY OF VARGINHA

Faculdade Cenecista de Varginha (FACECA)
Rua Professor Felipe Tiago Gomes, 173, Varginha,
Minas Gerais 37006-020
Tel: +55(35) 3690-8900
EMail: secretaria@faceca.br
Website: http://www.faceca.br

Diretor: Marco Antônio de Araújo (1998-) Tel: +55(35) 3690-8944

Courses

Accountancy (Accountancy); Administration (Administration; Business Administration; Marketing); Graduate Studies *(Lato Sensu)* (Accountancy; Business Administration; Civil Law; Labour Law); Graduate Studies *(Stricto Sensu)* (Administration); Information Systems (Information Sciences); Law (Law); Production Engineering (Production Engineering)

History: Founded 1970 as Faculdade de Ciências Econômicas, Contábeis e Administrativas de Varginha. Acquired present title 2000.

Main Language(s) of Instruction: Portuguese

Degrees and Diplomas: *Bacharelado*; *Especialização/Aperfeiçoamento*; *Mestrado*. Also MBA.

Last Updated: 30/06/10

CENECIST FACULTY OF VILA VELHA

Faculdade Cenecista de Vila Velha (FACEVV)
Avenida Vitória Régia 2950, Ibes, Vila Velha,
Espírito Santo 29108-660
Tel: +55(27) 3329-9838
Fax: +55(27) 3329-9838
EMail: facevv@facevv.edu.br
Website: http://www.facevv.edu.br

Diretor: Maria da Penha Passos Colusse

Courses

Administration (Administration; Business Administration); Pedagogy (Pedagogy)

History: Founded 2000.

Main Language(s) of Instruction: Portuguese

Degrees and Diplomas: *Bacharelado*; *Licenciatura*

Last Updated: 30/06/10

CENECIST HIGHER EDUCATION CENTRE OF FARROUPILHA

Centro de Ensino Superior Cenesista de Farroupilha (CESF)

Rua 14 de Julho 339, Centro, Farroupilha, RS 95180-000
Tel: +55(54) 3268-2288
Fax: +55(54) 3268-2733
EMail: cneccesf@terra.com.br
Website: http://www.cesfar.edu.br

Diretor: Luiz Fernando Felicetti (1997-)

Courses

Administrative Management; **Business Administration** (Business Administration; Real Estate); **Finance**; **Graduate Studies** (Education; Educational Psychology; Leisure Studies; Management; Marketing; Tourism); **Information Systems** (Information Management; Management); **Law** (Law); **Management** (Business Administration; Management); **Teacher Training** (Teacher Training); **Tourism**; **Transport Management**

History: Founded 1996.

Main Language(s) of Instruction: Portuguese

Degrees and Diplomas: *Bacharelado*; *Licenciatura*; *Especialização/Aperfeiçoamento*

Last Updated: 22/03/10

CENECIST INSTITUTE OF HIGHER EDUCATION OF SANTO ÂNGELO

Instituto Cenecista de Ensino Superior de Santo Ângelo (IESA)

Rua Doutor João Augusto Rodrigues 471, Centro Sul, Santo Ângelo, RS 98801015
Tel: +(55) 3313-1922
Fax: +(55) 3313-1745
EMail: iesa@iesanet.com.br; ensinosuperior@cnec.br
Website: http://www.iesanet.com.br

Diretor: Júlio César Lindemann

Courses

Accountancy (Accountancy); **Administration**; **Biomedicine** (Biomedicine); **Law** (Law); **Pedagogy**; **Physical Therapy** (Physical Therapy)

History: Founded 1998 incorporating the Faculties of Law, Administration and Accountancy of Santo Angelo.

Main Language(s) of Instruction: Portuguese

Degrees and Diplomas: *Bacharelado*; *Licenciatura*; *Especialização/Aperfeiçoamento*; *Mestrado*

Last Updated: 16/06/10

CENTRAL FACULTY OF CRISTALINA

Faculdade Central de Cristalina (FACEC)

Rua Jovino de Paiva Esquina Com Getúlio Vargas s/n Aeroporto, Cristalina, GO 73850-000
Tel: +55(61) 3612-6063
Fax: +55(61) 3612-5824
EMail: facec@brturbo.com.br
Website: http://www.facec.edu.br

Diretora: Ana Maria Trintinalha Molena

Courses

Administration (Administration); **Computer Networks** (Computer Networks); **Graduate Studies**; **Hospital Management** (Health Administration); **Law**; **Literature** (Literature); **Mathematics** (Mathematics); **Pedagogy** (Pedagogy); **Secretarial Studies** (Secretarial Studies)

History: Founded 2001.

Main Language(s) of Instruction: Portuguese

Degrees and Diplomas: *Bacharelado*; *Licenciatura*; *Especialização/Aperfeiçoamento*

Last Updated: 30/06/10

CENTRE FOR HIGHER EDUCATION AND DEVELOPMENT

Centro de Ensino Superior e Desenvolvimento (CESED)

Rua Luiza Bezerra Motta 200, Catole, Campina Grande, Paraíba 58104600
Tel: +55(83) 2101-8100 +55(83) 2101-8800
Fax: +55(83) 3337-1999
EMail: facisa@uol.com.br; fcm@cesed.br
Website: http://cesed.br

Diretora Presidente: Gisele Bianca Nery Gadelha

Faculties

Applied Social Sciences *(FACISA)* (Administration; Architecture; Business Administration; Information Sciences; Law; Tourism; Town Planning) *Directora*: Yara Macedo Lyra; **Medical Sciences** *(FCM)* (Medicine; Nursing; Physical Therapy) *Diretor*: Dalton Roberto Benevides Gadelha

Higher Schools

Civil Aviation *(ESAC)* (Air Transport) *Diretor*: Dalton Roberto Benevides Gadelha

History: Founded 1997.

Degrees and Diplomas: *Bacharelado*; *Especialização/Aperfeiçoamento*. Also MBA degree.

Last Updated: 22/04/10

CENTRE FOR TECHNICAL AND HIGHER EDUCATION OF WESTERN PARANA - EDUCATIONAL UNION OF THE MIDDLE WESTERN REGION OF PARANA

Centro Técnico-Educacional Superior do Oeste Paranaense - União Educacional do Médio Oeste Paranaense (UNIMEO/CTESOP)

Avenida Brasil 1441, Jardim Paraná, Assis Chateaubriand, Paraná 85935000
Tel: +55(44) 3528-2337
Fax: +55(44) 3528-2337
EMail: unimeo@unimeo.edu.br
Website: http://www.ctesop.com.br

Diretor Geral: Fabrício Jacob Begosso
EMail: fabricio@unimeo.com.br

Courses

Administration (Administration); **Distance Education**; **Geography** (Geography); **Graduate Studies** (Business and Commerce; Computer Networks; Computer Science; Educational Psychology; Geography; Higher Education; History; Human Resources; Marketing; Mathematics Education; Special Education; Transport Management); **History**; **Information Systems** (Information Technology); **Literature** (Literature; Spanish); **Mathematics** (Mathematics); **Pedagogy** (Pedagogy); **Tourism** (Tourism)

History: Founded 1985 as Centro Técnico-Educacional Superior do Oeste Paranaense. Acquired present status and title 1997.

Main Language(s) of Instruction: Portuguese

Degrees and Diplomas: *Bacharelado*; *Licenciatura*; *Especialização/Aperfeiçoamento*

Last Updated: 19/05/10

CENTRE OF ADVANCED STUDIES OF MACEIÓ

Centro de Estudos Superiores de Maceió (CESMAC)

Rua Cônego Machado 918, Farol, Maceió, Alagoas 57021160
Tel: +55(82) 3221-5007
Fax: +55(82) 3221-0402
EMail: asppe@fejal.br; ccsa@fejal.com.br
Website: http://www.fejal.br

Diretor Geral: João Rodrigues Sampaio Filho

Faculties

Applied Social Sciences *(FCSA)*; **Biological and Health Sciences** *(FCBS)*; **Education and Communication** *(FECOM)*; **Exact**

Sciences and Technology *(FACET)*; **Human Sciences** *(FCH)*; **Law** *(FADIMA)* (Law)

History: Founded 1973.

Degrees and Diplomas: *Bacharelado*; *Licenciatura*; *Especialização/Aperfeiçoamento*
Last Updated: 22/04/10

CERES FACULTY
Faculdade Ceres
Av. Anisio Haddad, 6751 - Jardim Morumbi,
São José do Rio Preto, SP
Tel: +55 (17) 3201-8200
EMail: faceres@faceres.com.br
Website: http://www.faceres.com.br

Diretor: Adalberto Miranda Distassi
EMail: diretoria@faceres.com.br

Courses
Administration (Administration); **Letters**; **Mathematics**; **Nursing**; **Pedagogy**; **Psychology**; **Social Sciences** (Social Sciences); **Social Services**

History: Founded 2002.

Main Language(s) of Instruction: Portuguese

Degrees and Diplomas: *Bacharelado*; *Especialização/Aperfeiçoamento*

Libraries: Yes
Last Updated: 20/07/10

CERES INSTITUTE OF EDUCATION
Instituto Superior de Educação Ceres (ISECERES)
Av. Anísio Haddad, 6751, Jardim Morumbi, São José do Rio Preto,
SP 15093-000
Tel: +55(17) 3201-8200
Fax: +55(17) 3201-8200
EMail: faceres@faceres.com.br
Website: http://www.faceres.com.br/

Diretor Geral: Adalberto Miranda Distassi
EMail: diretoria@faceres.com.br

Courses
Undergraduate Studies (English; Literature; Pedagogy; Social Sciences; Teacher Training)

History: Founded 2002.

Degrees and Diplomas: *Licenciatura*
Last Updated: 24/09/10

CESPI CORPORATE FACULTY
Faculdade Corporativa Cespi
Rua Joaquim Franco da Silva, 100/140 - Distrito Industrial,
Piraju, SP
Tel: +55(14) 3351-8955
EMail: diretoria@facespi.com.br
Website: http://www.unicespi.com.br

Diretor: Edson José dos Santos

Courses
Administration (Administration); **Pedagogy** (Pedagogy)
History: Founded 2004.

Main Language(s) of Instruction: Portuguese

Degrees and Diplomas: *Bacharelado*; *Especialização/Aperfeiçoamento*
Last Updated: 23/07/10

CETEP FACULTY OF TECHNOLOGY
Faculdade de Tecnologia Cetep (CETEP)
Rua Francisco Torres, 768, Curitiba, PR 80060-130
Tel: +55 (41) 3362-1705
Fax: +55 (41) 3362-7924
EMail: diretoria@cetepensino.com.br
Website: http://www.cetepensino.com.br/

President: Elio Vitiuk

Courses
Electronic Engineering (Electronic Engineering); **Graduate Studies** (Automotive Engineering; Environmental Management; Industrial Management; Public Administration; Safety Engineering; Technology Education); **Mechatronics** (Automation and Control Engineering); **Quality Management** (Safety Engineering)

History: Founded 1986.

Degrees and Diplomas: *Tecnólogo*; *Especialização/Aperfeiçoamento*
Last Updated: 20/08/10

CHAFIC FACULTY
Faculdade CHAFIC
Rua David Eid N° 111/241, Jardim Consórcio, São Paulo,
SP 04438-000
Tel: +55(11) 5563-2717
EMail: diretor@faculdadechafic.com.br
Website: http://www.faculdadechafic.com.br/modules/rep/?id=13

Diretor: Cristovão Carlos Cunha

Courses
Accountancy *(FAMATER)* (Accountancy); **Business Administration** (Business Administration); **History** (History); **Pedagogy** (Pedagogy); **Tourism** (Tourism)

History: Founded 2001.

Main Language(s) of Instruction: Portuguese

Degrees and Diplomas: *Bacharelado*; *Licenciatura*; *Especialização/Aperfeiçoamento*

Libraries: Yes
Last Updated: 16/09/10

CHAFIC FACULTY
Faculdade Chafic
Rua Irmãos Pila 144 Tucuruvi, São Paulo, SP 02308-000
Tel: +55(11) 6952-8666
EMail: diretor@faculdadechafic.com.br
Website: http://www.faculdadechafic.com.br

Diretor: Cristovão Carlos Cunha

Courses
Accountancy (Accountancy); **Business Administration**; **History** (History); **Pedagogy**; **Tourism**

History: Founded 2005.

Main Language(s) of Instruction: Portuguese

Degrees and Diplomas: *Bacharelado*; *Licenciatura*

Libraries: Yes
Last Updated: 20/07/10

CHRIST THE LORD EVANGELICAL FACULTY
Faculdade Evangélica Cristo Rei
Avenida José Florêncio Luz 88, Jaicos, PI 64575-000
Tel: +55(89) 3457-1305
EMail: fecr@fecr.com.br
Website: http://www.fecr.com.br

Diretor: Francisco Cecílio de Sousa

Courses
Accountancy (Accountancy); **Biology** (Biology); **History** (History); **Pedagogy** (Pedagogy); **Portuguese Literature** (Literature)

History: Founded 2010.

Main Language(s) of Instruction: Portuguese

Degrees and Diplomas: *Licenciatura*; *Especialização/Aperfeiçoamento*
Last Updated: 25/08/10

CHRIST THE LORD FACULTY
Faculdade Cristo Rei
PR 160, km 04, Conjunto Universitário, Cornélio Procópio, PR
Tel: +55(43) 3524-3301
EMail: diretoria@faccrei.edu.br
Website: http://www.faccrei.edu.br

Diretor: José Antonio da Conceição

Courses

Administration (Administration; Agricultural Business; Environmental Management; Finance; International Business; Marketing); **Journalism** (Journalism); **Law** (Law); **Tourism** (Tourism)

History: Founded 2001.

Main Language(s) of Instruction: Portuguese

Degrees and Diplomas: *Bacharelado*; *Especialização/Aperfeiçoamento*; *Mestrado*

Last Updated: 23/07/10

CHRISTUS FACULTY

Faculdade Christus (FAPFOR)

Rua Israel Bezerra 630, 8° Andar, Dionísio Torres, Fortaleza, Ceará 60135460
Tel: +55(85) 3461-2020
Fax: +55(85) 3461-2020
EMail: fc@christus.br
Website: http://www.fchristus.com.br/

Diretor: Roberto de Carvalho Rocha (1995-)

Courses

Accountancy (Accountancy); **Administration**; **Graduate Studies** (Accountancy; Business Administration; Business and Commerce; Civil Law; Educational Psychology; Gerontology; Health Sciences; Labour Law; Management; Medicine; Pedagogy; Physical Therapy; Psychology; Public Health; Rehabilitation and Therapy; Toxicology); **Information Systems** (Information Sciences; Information Technology); **Law** (Law); **Medicine** (Medicine); **Pedagogy**; **Physiotherapy**

Further Information: Also Dom Luís and Parque Ecológico campuses.

History: Founded 1994.

Main Language(s) of Instruction: Portuguese

Degrees and Diplomas: *Bacharelado*; *Licenciatura*; *Especialização/Aperfeiçoamento*. Also MBA.

Last Updated: 30/06/10

CHRISTUS FACULTY OF PIAUÍ

Christus Faculdade do Piauí (CHRISFAPI)

Rua Acelino Resende, 132, Fonte dos Matos, Piripiri, PI 64260-000
Tel: +55(86) 3276-2981
Fax: +55(86) 3276-2981
EMail: chrisfapi@chrisfapi.com.br; chrisfapi@hotmail.com
Website: http://www.chrisfapi.com.br

Diretora Geral: Maria do Carmo Amaral Brito

Courses

Accountancy (Accountancy); **Administration** (Administration); **Graduate Studies** (Accountancy; Educational Administration; Educational Psychology; Environmental Management; Health Administration; Higher Education; History; Labour Law; Literacy Education; Portuguese; Psychiatry and Mental Health; Public Health; Rehabilitation and Therapy); **Law** (Law); **Nursing** (Nursing)

Degrees and Diplomas: *Bacharelado*; *Especialização/Aperfeiçoamento*

Last Updated: 13/07/10

CIMAN FACULTY

Faculdade Ciman

Área Especial 16/17 N°: s/n Lado Leste / Região Administrativa II, Setor Central Gama, Brasilia, DF 72405-165
Tel: +55(61) 3385-5956
EMail: faculdadeciman@faculdadeciman.com.br
Website: http://www.ciman.com.br

Diretor: Eduardo Afonso de Medeiros Parente

Courses

Geography (Geography); **History** (History); **Letters** (Literature); **Pedagogy** (Pedagogy)

History: Founded 2005.

Main Language(s) of Instruction: Portuguese

Degrees and Diplomas: *Bacharelado*; *Licenciatura*
Last Updated: 23/07/10

CIMO FACULTY

Faculdade CIMO

Bráz Baltazar, 123. Caiçara- esq. c/ R. do Trevo, 140, Belo Horizonte, MG 30770-580
Tel: +55(31) 3464-1584
EMail: comunicacao@cimobh.com.br
Website: http://www.faculdadecimo.com.br

Diretora: Giselda Maria Moreira Garcia

Courses

Fashion Design

History: Founded 2004.

Main Language(s) of Instruction: Portuguese

Degrees and Diplomas: *Bacharelado*; *Especialização/Aperfeiçoamento*

Last Updated: 23/07/10

CIODONTO FACULTY

Faculdade CIODONTO (FAISA)

Av. Antônio Volpato, 1488, Centro, Sarandi, PR 87111-010
Tel: +55(44) 3035-2909
EMail: faleconosco@ciodonto.edu.br
Website: http://www.faculdadeciodonto.com.br/02.institucional.htm

Diretora Geral: Doris Camargo Martins de Andrade
EMail: doris@ciodonto.edu.br

Courses

Accountancy; **Administration** (Accountancy; Administration; International Business); **Information Systems**

History: Founded 2000 as Faculdade Sarandi. Acquired present title 2010.

Main Language(s) of Instruction: Portuguese

Degrees and Diplomas: *Bacharelado*; *Especialização/Aperfeiçoamento*

Last Updated: 01/07/10

CITY OF SALVADOR FACULTY

Faculdade Cidade do Salvador

Praça da Inglaterra, n° 2, Comércio, Salvador, BA 40.015-140
Tel: +55 (71) 3254-6000
EMail: jacymatos@faculdadedacidade.edu.br
Website: http://portal.faculdadedacidade.edu.br

Diretor: Renato José de Argolo Pinheiro

Courses

Accountancy (Accountancy); **Advertising** (Advertising and Publicity); **Business Administration** (Business Administration); **Fashion Design** (Fashion Design); **Journalism** (Journalism); **Law** (Law); **Pedagogy** (Pedagogy); **Product Design** (Design); **Psychology** (Psychology); **Tourism** (Tourism)

History: Founded 2004.

Main Language(s) of Instruction: Portuguese

Degrees and Diplomas: *Bacharelado*; *Especialização/Aperfeiçoamento*

Libraries: Biblioteca José Soares Pinheiro
Last Updated: 23/07/10

CLARETIAN UNIVERSITY CENTRE OF BATATAIS

Centro Universitário Claretiano de Batatais (UNICLAR)

Rua Dom Bosco 466, Castelo, Batatais, São Paulo 14300-000
Tel: +55(16) 3660-1777
Fax: +55(16) 3761-5030
EMail: secretariat@claretiano.edu.br; proreitoracad@claretiano.edu.br
Website: http://www.claretiano.edu.br

Reitor: Sérgio Ibanor Piva (1997-)

Areas
Health; **Management** (Administration; Secretarial Studies); **Teacher Training**; **Technology** (Human Resources; Information Technology; Marketing; Systems Analysis; Transport Management)

Courses
Distance Education; **Postgraduate** (Advertising and Publicity; Art Education; Biological and Life Sciences; Business Administration; Business Education; Communication Studies; Computer Networks; Computer Science; Data Processing; Educational Administration; Educational Psychology; English; Environmental Management; Ethics; Finance; Human Resources; Labour Law; Law; Literature; Marketing; Mathematics Education; Native Language Education; Nursing; Occupational Health; Philosophy; Physical Education; Physical Therapy; Physiology; Primary Education; Science Education; Sociology; Special Education; Sports; Sports Management; Translation and Interpretation; Writing)

History: Founded 1970.

Main Language(s) of Instruction: Portuguese

Degrees and Diplomas: *Bacharelado*; *Licenciatura*; *Especialização/Aperfeiçoamento*. Also MBA.
Last Updated: 25/05/10

CNEC CAPIVARI
CNEC Capivari (FACECAP)
Rua Barão do Rio Branco 374, Centro, Capivari, SP 13360-000
Tel: +55(19) 3492-8888
Fax: +55(19) 3492-8880
EMail: cnec@cneccapivari.br
Website: http://www.fc.edu.br

Diretora: Ana Maria Reginato

Courses
Accountancy; **Administration** (Administration); **Graduate Studies** (Business Administration; Educational Administration; Educational Psychology); **Information Systems** (Information Management; Information Sciences); **Pedagogy**

History: Founded 1978

Main Language(s) of Instruction: Portuguese

Degrees and Diplomas: *Bacharelado*; *Especialização/Aperfeiçoamento*
Last Updated: 18/06/10

COC FACULTIES
Faculdades COC
Rua Abraão Issa Halack 980, Ribeirânia, Ribeirão Preto, São Paulo 14096160
Tel: +55(16) 3603-9800
Fax: +55(16) 3603-9942
EMail: faculdadescoc@coc.com.br
Website: http://www.unicoc.edu.br

Diretor: Reginaldo Arthus

Courses
Administration (Administration); **Advertising and Publicity** (Advertising and Publicity); **Architecture and Town Planning** (Architecture; Town Planning); **Computer Science** (Computer Science); **Engineering**; **Journalism** (Journalism); **Law** (Law); **Physical Education** (Physical Education); **Physical Therapy** (Physical Therapy)

History: Founded 1998.

Main Language(s) of Instruction: Portuguese

Degrees and Diplomas: *Bacharelado*; *Licenciatura*; *Especialização/Aperfeiçoamento*
Last Updated: 29/06/10

CONTEMPORARY FACULTY OF AMAZONIA
Faculdade Atual de Amazônia
Rua Jornalista Humberto Silva, nº 308, Bairro União, Boa Vista, Roraima 69313-792
Tel: +55(95) 2121-5500
EMail: actual@technet.com.br
Website: http://www.faculdadeatual.edu.br

Diretor Geral: Adriano Ramos Remor

Courses
Accountancy; **Business Administration**; **Computer Science** *(Licenciatura)*; **Graduate Studies**; **Information Systems**; **Law** (Law); **Pedagogy** *(Licenciatura)*; **Social Communication - Advertising and Publicity** (Advertising and Publicity); **Social Communication - Journalism**; **Social Service** (Social and Community Services); **Technological Studies** (Agricultural Business; Environmental Management; Graphic Design; International Business; Management; Public Administration; Public Relations; Secretarial Studies)

History: Founded 2001.

Main Language(s) of Instruction: Portuguese

Degrees and Diplomas: *Tecnólogo*; *Bacharelado*; *Licenciatura*; *Especialização/Aperfeiçoamento*; *Mestrado*. Also MBA.
Last Updated: 24/06/10

CONTESTADO UNIVERSITY
Universidade do Contestado (UNC)
Rua Atílio Faoro, 221 - Caixa Postal - 17, Caçador, Santa Catarina 89500000
Tel: +55(49) 3561-2600
Fax: +55(49) 3561-2608
EMail: reitoria@unc.br
Website: http://www.unc.br

Reitor: José Alceu Valério

Departments
Accountancy (Accountancy); **Administration** (Administration); **Agriculture** (Agriculture); **Biology** (Biology); **Computer Science** (Computer Science; Data Processing); **Design**; **Education** (Education); **Electrical Engineering** (Electrical Engineering); **Forestry Engineering** (Forestry); **Fruit Growing** (Fruit Production); **History** (History); **Horticulture Engineering** (Horticulture); **Law** (Law); **Letters** (Arts and Humanities); **Nursing and Midwifery** (Midwifery; Nursing); **Physical Education** (Physical Education); **Physiotherapy** (Physical Therapy); **Production Engineering** (Production Engineering); **Psychology** (Psychology); **Sciences** (Mathematics; Natural Sciences); **Social Communication** (Radio and Television Broadcasting); **Social Services** (Social and Community Services); **Veterinary Medicine** (Veterinary Science); **Visual Arts**

Further Information: Campuses in Caçador, Canoinhas, Concórdia, Curitibanos and Mafra

History: Founded 1997. A Municipal institution.

Admission Requirements: Secondary school certificate and entrance examination

Main Language(s) of Instruction: Portuguese

Degrees and Diplomas: *Bacharelado*; *Licenciatura*; *Especialização/Aperfeiçoamento*; *Mestrado*
Last Updated: 03/06/10

COSTA BRAGA FACULTY OF ADMINISTRATION AND ACCOUNTANCY COSTA BRAGA
Faculdade de Ciências Administrativas e Contábeis Costa Braga (FCB)
Rua Desembargador Bandeira de Melo, 492, Sto Amaro, São Paulo, SP 4743-001
Tel: +55(11) 3477-3541
Fax: +55(11) 3477-3541
EMail: diretoriacostabraga@terra.com.br

Courses
Accountancy (Accountancy); **Administration** (Administration)

History: Founded 1972.

Main Language(s) of Instruction: Portuguese

Degrees and Diplomas: *Bacharelado*
Last Updated: 15/03/11

COSTA BRAGA FACULTY OF EDUCATION
Faculdade de Educação Costa Braga (FCB)
Rua Desembargador Bandeira de Melo 492, São Paulo,
São Paulo 4743-001
Tel: +55(11) 3477-3541
EMail: diretoriacostabraga@terra.com.br

Diretor Administrativo: Sidney Costa Carneiro Braga

Courses
Accountancy (Accountancy); **Administration** (Administration);
International Business; **Pedagogy**
History: Founded 1989
Main Language(s) of Instruction: Portuguese
Degrees and Diplomas: *Bacharelado*

COTEMIG FACULTY
Faculdade Cotemig (COTEMIG)
Rua Santa Cruz 546, Bairro Barroca, Belo Horizonte,
Minas Gerais 30431228
Tel: +55(31) 3371-3051
Fax: +55(31) 3371-1187
EMail: dac@cotemig.com.br
Website: http://www.cotemig.com.br

Diretor Presidente: Marcos Lúcio do Bom Conselho

Courses
Computer Science (Computer Science); **Information Systems**;
Technological Studies
History: Founded 1999
Main Language(s) of Instruction: Portuguese
Degrees and Diplomas: *Tecnólogo*; *Bacharelado*
Last Updated: 30/06/10

COTIA INSTITUTE OF HIGHER EDUCATION - ASSOCIATED FACULTY OF COTIA
Instituto de Ensino Superior de Cotia - Faculdade Associada de Cotia (IESC/FAAC)
Rua Nelson Raineri 630, Lajeado, Cotia, SP 06700560
Tel: +55(11) 4616-0770
EMail: secretaria@faac.br
Website: http://www.faac.br/

Diretora: Margarida Cecilia Corréa Nogueira Rocha
EMail: dir@faac.br

Courses
Administration (Administration); **Computer Science** (Computer Networks); **Literature** (Literature); **Marketing** (Marketing); **Nursing** (Nursing); **Pedagogy** (Pedagogy); **Physical Education** (Physical Education); **Tourism**; **Visual Arts**
History: Founded 1999.
Main Language(s) of Instruction: Portuguese
Degrees and Diplomas: *Bacharelado*; *Licenciatura*; *Especialização/Aperfeiçoamento*
Last Updated: 16/06/10

DAMAS FACULTY OF CHRISTIAN INSTRUCTION
Faculdade Damas da Instrução Crista
Av. Rui Barbosa, 1426-B - Graças, Recife, PE
Tel: +55(81) 3426-5026
EMail: diretoria@faculdadedamas.edu.br
Website: http://www.faculdadedamas.edu.br

Diretora: Maria Arcione Viera

Courses
Architecture and Town Planning (Architecture; Landscape Architecture; Town Planning); **International Relations** (International Relations); **Law** (Law)
History: Founded 2005.
Main Language(s) of Instruction: Portuguese
Degrees and Diplomas: *Bacharelado*; *Especialização/Aperfeiçoamento*
Last Updated: 26/07/10

DAMÁSIO DE JESUS FACULTY OF LAW
Faculdade de Direito Damásio de Jesus
Rua da Glória 195, Liberdade, São Paulo, SP 01510-001
Tel: +55(11) 3164-6600
Website: http://fddj.damasio.edu.br

Diretor: Damásio de Jesus

Courses
Law (Civil Law; Commercial Law; Criminal Law)
History: Founded 2002.
Main Language(s) of Instruction: Portuguese
Degrees and Diplomas: *Bacharelado*; *Especialização/Aperfeiçoamento*
Last Updated: 02/08/10

DARCY RIBEIRO FACULTY OF TECHNOLOGY
Faculdade de Tecnologia Darcy Ribeiro (FTDR)
Avenida Heráclito Graça, 400, Centro, Fortaleza, CE 60140-060
Tel: +55(85) 3535-1555 +55(85) 3535-1575
Fax: +55(85) 3535-1555
EMail: edson@ftdr.com.br
Website: http://www.ftdr.com.br/

Diretor Geral: Antônio Colaço Martins Filho

Courses
Financial Management (Finance); **Graduate Studies** (Art Education; Education; Educational Administration; Educational Psychology; Environmental Management; Management); **Human Resources** (Human Resources); **Management** (Management); **Marketing** (Marketing); **Tourism** (Tourism)
History: Founded 2004.
Main Language(s) of Instruction: Portuguese
Degrees and Diplomas: *Tecnólogo*; *Especialização/Aperfeiçoamento*. Also MBA.
Last Updated: 14/03/11

DECISION FACULTY
Faculdade Decisão (FADE)
Avenida Doutor Cláudio José Gueiros Leite 2939, Paulista,
Pernambuco 53437-000
Tel: +55(81) 3434-4018
EMail: fade@fade.edu.br
Website: http://www.fade.edu.br/

Diretor Geral: José Pereira Valadares de Sousa Neto

Courses
Accountancy; **Administration**; **Pedagogy** (Pedagogy)
History: Founded 2000.
Main Language(s) of Instruction: Portuguese
Degrees and Diplomas: *Bacharelado*; *Licenciatura*; *Especialização/Aperfeiçoamento*
Last Updated: 08/07/10

DIOCESAN FACULTY OF SÃO JOSÉ
Faculdade Diocesana São José
Estrada do Sao Francisco - 1576 Bairro Vitória, Rio Branco,
AC 69 909-021
Tel: +55(68) 3224-5756
EMail: fadisi.acre@hotmail.com
Website: http://fadisi.webs.com

Diretor: Joaquin Pertiñez Fernandez

Courses
Philosophy (Philosophy)
History: Founded 2005.
Main Language(s) of Instruction: Portuguese
Degrees and Diplomas: *Bacharelado*; *Especialização/Aperfeiçoamento*
Last Updated: 14/03/11

DOCTOR LEÃO SAMPAIO FACULTY OF APPLIED SCIENCES

Faculdade de Ciências Aplicadas Doutor Leão Sampaio (FLS)
Avenida Padre Cicero, 2830, Triangulo, Juazeiro do Norte,
CE 63041-140
Tel: +55(88) 2101-1000
Fax: +55(88) 2101-1001
EMail: ouvidoria@leaosampaio.edu.br
Website: http://www.leaosampaio.edu.br

Diretor Presidente: Jaime Romero de Souza
EMail: jaimeromero@leaosampaio.edu.br

Courses
Accountancy; **Administration** (Administration); **Biomedicine** (Biomedicine); **Graduate Studies** (Accountancy; Acupuncture; Administrative Law; Biochemistry; Business and Commerce; Cell Biology; Civil Law; Communication Studies; Constitutional Law; Criminal Law; Dermatology; Education; Educational Administration; Educational Psychology; Environmental Management; Finance; Food Technology; Gerontology; Haematology; Health Administration; Health Sciences; Higher Education; International Business; Labour Law; Law; Management; Marketing; Microbiology; Molecular Biology; Nursing; Pharmacology; Physical Therapy; Physiology; Portuguese; Psychiatry and Mental Health; Psychology; Public Health; Rehabilitation and Therapy; Safety Engineering; Social Policy; Transport Management); **Human Resources** (Human Resources); **Nursing** (Nursing); **Physical Education**; **Physical Therapy** (Physical Therapy); **Psychology** (Psychology); **Social Service** (Social and Community Services); **Systems Analysis and Development** (Systems Analysis)

Further Information: Also Ensino Saúde and Ensino Lagoa Seca Units.

Degrees and Diplomas: *Bacharelado*; *Licenciatura*; *Especialização/Aperfeiçoamento*
Last Updated: 20/07/10

DOCTUM FACULTIES

Faculdades Doctum (FADIL)
Avenida Getúlio Vargas 635, Centro, Leopoldina, MG 36700000
Tel: +55(33) 3441-7162
Fax: +55(33) 3321-2122
EMail: decom@doctumleo.com.br
Website: http://www.doctum.com.br

Diretor: Cláudio Cezar Azevedo de Almeida Leitão

Units
Cataguases (Information Sciences; Nursing); **Guarapari**; **Iúna** (Accountancy; Administration; Pedagogy; Teacher Training); **Leopoldina**; **Teófilo Otoni** (Accountancy; Administration; Information Sciences; Law; Nursing; Nutrition; Physical Education; Psychology; Social Work)

History: Founded 1936 as Sociedade Colégio Caratinga. Acquired present status 2000.

Main Language(s) of Instruction: Portuguese

Degrees and Diplomas: *Bacharelado*; *Licenciatura*; *Especialização/Aperfeiçoamento*; *Mestrado*
Last Updated: 29/06/10

DOM AQUINO CATHOLIC FACULTY OF CUIABA

Faculdade Católica Dom Aquino de Cuiabá
Rua Alexandre Barros, 387 - Coxipó da Ponte, Cuiabá,
MT 78080-030
Tel: +55(65) 3611-1739
EMail: pemorales@terra.com.br
Website: http://www.catolicamt.com.br

Diretor: Osvaldo dos Santos

Courses
Business Administration; **Information Systems**

History: Founded 2005.

Main Language(s) of Instruction: Portuguese

Degrees and Diplomas: *Bacharelado*
Last Updated: 19/07/10

DOM BOSCO CATHOLIC UNIVERSITY

Universidade Católica Dom Bosco (UCDB)
Avenida Tamandaré 6000, Jardim Seminário, Campo Grande,
Mato Grosso do Sul 79117900
Tel: +55(67) 3312-3800
Fax: +55(67) 3312-3301
EMail: webmaster@ucdb.br
Website: http://www.ucdb.br

Reitor: José Marinoni (1997-)

Courses
Accountancy (Accountancy); **Administration** (Administration; International Business; Small Business); **Animal Husbandry**; **Biology** (Biology); **Computer Engineering** (Computer Engineering); **Economics** (Economics); **Geography**; **History**; **Law** (Law); **Letters** (Arts and Humanities; English; Portuguese); **Mathematics** (Applied Mathematics; Mathematics); **Nutrition** (Nutrition); **Occupational Therapy**; **Pedagogy** (Education; Pedagogy); **Philosophy**; **Phonoaudiology**; **Physical Education and Sports** (Physical Education; Sports); **Physiotherapy** (Physical Therapy); **Psychology** (Psychology); **Real Estate**; **Sanitary and Environmental Engineering**; **Social Communication**; **Social Service** (Social and Community Services); **Tourism** (Tourism)

History: Founded 1961

Admission Requirements: Secondary school certificate and entrance examination

Main Language(s) of Instruction: Portuguese

Degrees and Diplomas: *Bacharelado*; *Licenciatura*; *Especialização/Aperfeiçoamento*; *Mestrado*

Student Services: Canteen
Last Updated: 07/06/10

DOM BOSCO EDUCATIONAL ASSOCIATION

Associação Educacional Dom Bosco (AEDB)
Av. Darci Ribeiro (antiga Resende/Riachuelo) 2535,
Campo de Aviação, Resende, RJ 27523-000
Tel: +55(24) 3383-9000
Fax: +55(24) 3383-9000
EMail: sec@aedb.br
Website: http://www.aedb.br

Faculties
Economics, Administration and Computer Science *(Dom Bosco)* (Administration; Communication Studies; Computer Science; Economics; Software Engineering); **Engineering** *(Resende - FER)*; **Philosophy, Science and Literature** *(FFCLDB)*

Programmes
Graduate Studies *(CPGE)*

History: Founded 1968.

Main Language(s) of Instruction: Portuguese

Degrees and Diplomas: *Tecnólogo*; *Bacharelado*; *Especialização/Aperfeiçoamento*. Also MBA
Last Updated: 08/03/10

DOM BOSCO FACULTY

Faculdade Dom Bosco (FDB)
Avenida das Torres 500, Loteamento Fag, Cascavel,
Paraná 85800000
Tel: +55(41) 3321-3900
Fax: +55(45) 3321-3902
EMail: fag@fag.edu.br
Website: http://www.dombosco.fag.edu.br

Diretor Geral: Sérgio De Angelis

Courses
Air Transport; **Computer Networks** (Computer Networks); **Education** (Education; Pedagogy; Special Education); **Environmental Management** (Environmental Management); **Marketing** (Marketing)

History: Founded 1999

Degrees and Diplomas: *Tecnólogo*; *Licenciatura*
Last Updated: 08/07/10

DOM BOSCO FACULTY OF EDUCATION, SCIENCE AND ARTS OF MONTE APRAZIVEL

Faculdade de Educação, Ciências e Artes 'Dom Bosco' de Monte Aprazivel (FAECA DOM BOSCO)
Rua Augusto Chiesa, 679, Monte Aprazivel, São Paulo 15150000
Tel: +55(17) 3275-1736
Fax: +55(17) 3275-1736
EMail: secfaculdade@faeca.com.br;
domboscosecretaria@fn.com.br
Website: http://www.faeca.com.br

Diretor: Vanderlei Pereira (1997-)

Courses

Accountancy (Accountancy); **Administration** (Administration); **Arts and Humanities** (Arts and Humanities); **Biological and Life Sciences**; **Graduate Studies**; **History** (History); **Law**; **Mathematics**; **Pedagogy** (Pedagogy); **Sugar Alcohol Production**

History: Founded 1973.

Degrees and Diplomas: *Bacharelado*; *Licenciatura*; *Especialização/Aperfeiçoamento*
Libraries: c. 20.000 vols.
Last Updated: 07/07/10

DOM BOSCO FACULTY OF HIGHER EDUCATION

Faculdade de Ensino Superior Dom Bosco
Avenida Quinze de Novembro, 57, Cornélio Procópio, PR
Tel: +55(43) 3523-2494
EMail: faculdadedombosco@bol.com.br
Website: http://www.facdombosco.edu.br/

Diretora: Jorgina Helena Lopes de Azevedo

Courses

Administration (Administration); **Law** (Law); **Pedagogy** (Pedagogy); **Pharmacy** (Pharmacy); **Physical Education** (Physical Education)

Degrees and Diplomas: *Bacharelado*; *Licenciatura*; *Especialização/Aperfeiçoamento*
Libraries: Yes
Last Updated: 04/08/10

DOM BOSCO HIGHER EDUCATION UNIT

Unidade de Ensino Superior Dom Bosco (UNDB)
Av. Colares Moreira, 443, Renascença II, São Luís, MA 65075-970
Tel: +55(98) 4009-7070
Fax: +55(98) 3235-4062
EMail: nti@dbosco.com.br
Website: http://www.undb.com.br/

Diretora Geral: Maria Izabel Rodrigues Pereira

Courses

Graduate Studies (Accountancy; Business Administration; Constitutional Law; Educational Administration; Educational Psychology; Fiscal Law; Higher Education; Law; Psychoanalysis; Public Administration); **Undergraduate Studies** (Accountancy; Administration; Civil Engineering; Information Sciences; Law; Pedagogy; Physical Education; Production Engineering; Tourism)

Degrees and Diplomas: *Bacharelado*; *Licenciatura*. Also Postgraduate diploma and MBA.
Last Updated: 29/09/10

DOM BOSCO SALESIAN FACULTY

Faculdade Salesiana Dom Bosco
Av. Epaminondas, 57, Centro, Manaus, AM 69010-090
Tel: +55(92) 2125-4690
EMail: cesar@fsdb.edu.br
Website: http://www.fsdb.edu.br/

Diretor Executivo: César Lobato Brito

Courses

Graduate Studies (Accountancy; Business Administration; Education; Educational Administration; Educational Psychology; Environmental Management; Environmental Studies; Finance; Gerontology; Higher Education; Management; Marketing; Pedagogy); **Undergraduate Studies** (Accountancy; Administration; Pedagogy; Philosophy; Social and Community Services)

Degrees and Diplomas: *Bacharelado*; *Licenciatura*. Also Postgraduate diploma.
Last Updated: 06/09/10

DOM BOSCO SALESIAN FACULTY OF PIRACICABA

Faculdade Salesiana Dom Bosco de Piracicaba
Rua Boa Morte, 1835, Centro, Piracicaba, SP
Tel: +55(19) 3437-3877
EMail: info.dbf@db-piracicaba.com.br
Website: http://www.domboscofaculdade.com.br/capa.asp?ScreenWidth=512

Diretor: José Ailton Trindade

Courses

Graduate Studies (Business Administration; Educational Administration; Finance; Literacy Education; Management; Marketing; Preschool Education; Transport Management); **Undergraduate Studies** (Administration; Information Sciences; Pedagogy)

History: Founded 2004.

Degrees and Diplomas: *Bacharelado*; *Licenciatura*. Also Postgraduate diploma and MBA.
Last Updated: 06/09/10

DOM HELDER CÂMARA SCHOOL

Escola Superior Dom Helder Câmara
Rua Álvares Maciel, 628, Sta. Efigênia, Belo Horizonte, MG 30150-250
Tel: +55(31) 2125-8800
Fax: +55(31) 2125-8818
EMail: contato@domhelder.edu.br
Website: http://www.domhelder.edu.br/

Diretor: Paulo Umberto

Courses

Graduate Studies *(Lato Sensu)* (Civil Security; Police Studies); **Graduate Studies** *(Stricto Sensu)* (Constitutional Law); **Law** (Administrative Law; Civil Law; Commercial Law; Constitutional Law; Criminal Law; Fiscal Law; International Law; Labour Law; Law)

History: Founded 1998.

Degrees and Diplomas: *Bacharelado*; *Especialização/Aperfeiçoamento*; *Mestrado*
Last Updated: 16/07/10

DOM ORIONE CATHOLIC FACULTY

Faculdade Católica Dom Orione
Rua Santa Cruz, 557. Centro -, Araguaína, TO 77804-090
Tel: +55(63) 3414-3355
EMail: diretoriaacademica@catolicaorione.edu.br
Website: http://www.catolicaorione.edu.br/site

Diretor: Francisco de Assis da Silva Alfenas

Courses

Administration (Administration); **Law** (Law)

History: Founded 2005.

Main Language(s) of Instruction: Portuguese

Degrees and Diplomas: *Bacharelado*; *Especialização/Aperfeiçoamento*
Last Updated: 19/07/10

DOM PEDRO II INTEGRATED FACULTIES

Faculdades Integradas Dom Pedro II
Av. Bady Bassitt, 3777, Imperial, São José do Rio Prêto, São Paulo 15015700
Tel: +55(17) 2139-1600
Fax: +55(17) 2139-1640
EMail: dompedro@dompedro.com.br
Website: http://www.dompedro.com.br

Diretor: Luiz Alberto Ismael Junior
EMail: ismael@dompedro.edu.br

Courses
Administration (Administration); Architecture and Town Planning; Civil Engineering (Civil Engineering); Economics (Economics)

History: Founded 2003.

Main Language(s) of Instruction: Portuguese

Degrees and Diplomas: Bacharelado; Mestrado
Last Updated: 23/06/10

DON DOMENICO FACULTY
Faculdade Don Domênico
Rua Dr. Arthur Costa Filho 20, Vila Maia, Guaruja,
São Paulo 11401970
Tel: +55(13) 3389-7000
Fax: +55(13) 3389-7017
EMail: secretariafaculdade@dondomenico.com.br
Website: http://www.faculdadedondomenico.edu.br

Diretor: Manoel Fernando Passaes

Courses
Administration; Geography; History (History); Letters (Literature); Pedagogy (Pedagogy); Tourism (Tourism)

History: Founded 1972.

Main Language(s) of Instruction: Portuguese

Degrees and Diplomas: Bacharelado; Licenciatura; Especialização/Aperfeiçoamento
Last Updated: 07/07/10

DR ARISTIDES DE CARVALHO SCHLOBACH HIGHER EDUCATION INSTITUTE OF TAQUARITINGA
Instituto Taquaritinguense de Ensino Superior Dr Aristides de Carvalho Schlobach (ITES)
159 Praça Dr. Horácio Ramalho, Centro, Taquaritinga,
São Paulo 15900000
Tel: +55(16) 3253-3169 +55(16) 3253-3170
Fax: +55(16) 3253-3169 +55(16) 3253-3170
EMail: ites@ites.com.br
Website: http://www.ites.com.br/index.php

Diretora: Ligiane Raimundo Gomes

Courses
Accountancy (Accountancy); Administration (Administration); Agronomy (Agronomy); Pedagogy; Psychology (Psychology)

History: Founded 1998.

Main Language(s) of Instruction: Portuguese

Degrees and Diplomas: Bacharelado
Last Updated: 14/06/10

DR. EDMUNSO ULSON UNIVERSITY CENTRE OF ARARAS
Centro Universitario de Araras Dr Edmunso Ulson (FCLA)
Avenida Ernani Lacerda de Oliveira 100, Parque Santa Cândida,
Araras, São Paulo 13603112
Fax: +55(19) 3542-7373
EMail: secretaria@unar.edu.br
Website: http://www.unar.edu.br

Reitora: Maria Terezinha P.B. Ulson

Courses
Accountancy; Administration (Administration); Advertising; Architecture and Town Planning; Art Education; Arts and Humanities (English; Literature; Spanish); Civil Engineering; Executive Secretarial Studies (Secretarial Studies); Geography (Geography); History; Information Systems (Information Sciences); Interior Design (Interior Design); Journalism (Journalism); Law (Law); Mathematics (Mathematics); Pedagogy; Philosophy (Philosophy); Production Engineering; Sociology (Sociology); Teacher Training (Teacher Training); Tourism

History: Founded 1971 as Faculdade de Ciências e Letras de Araras.

Main Language(s) of Instruction: Portuguese

Degrees and Diplomas: Bacharelado; Licenciatura; Especialização/Aperfeiçoamento; Mestrado; Doutorado
Last Updated: 07/01/08

DR. FRANCISCO MAEDA FACULTY
Faculdade Dr. Francisco Maeda (FAFRAM)
Rodovia Jerônimo Nunes Macedo Km 01, Campus Agronomia
Aeroporto, Ituverava, São Paulo 14500000
Tel: +55(16) 3729-9000
EMail: fafram@feituverava.com.br
Website: http://www.feituverava.com.br/fafram/

Diretor: Márcio Pereira

Courses
Agronomy (Agronomy); Computer Science (Computer Science); Law; Veterinary Science (Veterinary Science)

History: Founded 1987

Main Language(s) of Instruction: Portuguese

Degrees and Diplomas: Bacharelado; Especialização/Aperfeiçoamento
Last Updated: 07/07/10

DR. LEOCÁDIO JOSÉ CORREIA FACULTY
Faculdade Dr. Leocádio José Correia (FALEC)
Rua José Antônio Leprevost 331, Santa Candida, Curitibá,
Paraná 82640070
Tel: +55(41) 256-5717
Fax: +55(41) 256-5717
EMail: falec@falec.br
Website: http://www.falec.br

Diretor: Enio José Coimbra de Carvalho

Courses
Business Administration; Pedagogy; Spiritual Theology (Theology)

History: Founded 2000.

Main Language(s) of Instruction: Portuguese

Degrees and Diplomas: Bacharelado; Especialização/Aperfeiçoamento
Last Updated: 07/07/10

DRUMMOND FACULTY
Faculdade Drummond
Rua Professor Pedreira de Fraitas 405/415, Tatuapé, São Paulo,
São Paulo 03312000
Tel: +55(11) 6941-1488
Fax: +55(11) 6941-1488
EMail: drummond@drummond.com.br
Website: http://www.drummond.com.br

Diretor: Osmar Basílio (1998-)

Courses
Accountancy (Accountancy); Administration; Computer Science (Computer Science); Electronic Engineering (Automation and Control Engineering; Electronic Engineering); Graduate Studies (Accountancy; Business Administration; Communication Studies; Educational Administration; Engineering; Finance; Higher Education; Human Resources; Industrial and Organizational Psychology; International Business; Marketing; Public Health); Information Systems (Information Technology); Law (Law); Production Engineering; Technology (Advertising and Publicity; Automation and Control Engineering; Computer Networks; Fashion Design; Finance; Graphic Design; Health Administration; Human Resources; Information Technology; International Business; Leisure Studies; Management; Marketing; Real Estate; Sports; Sports Management; Systems Analysis; Tourism; Transport Management)

History: Founded 1998.

Main Language(s) of Instruction: Portuguese

Degrees and Diplomas: Bacharelado; Especialização/Aperfeiçoamento
Last Updated: 07/07/10

DULCINA DE MORAES FACULTY OF ARTS
Faculdade de Artes Dulcina de Moraes (FADM)
SDS Bloco C N°. 30/64, Edifício FBT, Brasília, DF 70392-902
Tel: +55(61) 3224-5369
Fax: +55(61) 3224-5369
EMail: fadmweb@fadm.com.br
Website: http://www.fadm.com.br
Diretora: Lúcia Andrade EMail: lucia@dulcina.art.br

Courses
Acting (Acting); **Fine Arts**; **Graduate Studies** (Art History; Theatre); **Scenic Arts** (Theatre); **Theatre Direction** (Theatre)
History: Founded 1980
Main Language(s) of Instruction: Portuguese
Degrees and Diplomas: *Bacharelado*; *Licenciatura*; *Especialização/Aperfeiçoamento*
Last Updated: 01/07/10

DYNAMIC FACULTY OF THE FALLS
Faculdade Dinâmica das Cataratas (UDC)
Rua Castelo Branco 349, Centro, Foz do Iguacu, PR 85852010
Tel: +55(45) 3523-6900
Fax: +55(45) 3523-6900
EMail: udc@udc.edu.br
Website: http://www.udc.edu.br
Diretora: Rosicler Hauggedo Prado
Secretária Geral: Ivana Maria Hauagge Humenhuk

Courses
Administration (Administration; Finance; Health Administration; Public Administration); **Architecture and Urbanism** (Architecture and Planning; Town Planning); **Education** (Education; Educational Administration; Educational and Student Counselling; Educational Psychology; Environmental Studies; Higher Education; Special Education); **Engineering**; **Information Systems** (Information Management); **Languages**; **Law** (Civil Law; Criminal Law; Law; Public Law); **Pedagogy** (Pedagogy); **Social Communication**; **Tourism**
History: Founded 1999.
Main Language(s) of Instruction: Portuguese
Degrees and Diplomas: *Bacharelado*; *Licenciatura*; *Especialização/Aperfeiçoamento*; *Mestrado*
Last Updated: 08/07/10

DYNAMIC FACULTY OF THE VALLEY OF PIRANGA
Faculdade Dinâmica do Vale do Piranga
Rua G n° 205, Quadra E, Paraíso, Ponte Nova, MG 35430-000
Tel: +55(31) 3817-2010
EMail: joseclaudio@faculdadedinamica.com.br
Website: http://www.faculdadedinamica.com.br
Diretor: José Cláudio Maciel de Oliveira.

Courses
Law (Law); **Pharmacy** (Pharmacy)
History: Founded 2006.
Main Language(s) of Instruction: Portuguese
Degrees and Diplomas: *Bacharelado*
Libraries: Yes
Last Updated: 20/09/10

EÇA DE QUEIROS FACULTY
Faculdade Eça de Queiros
Via de Acesso João de Góes, 2335, Bloco A, Jardim Alvorada, Jandira, SP 06612-000
Tel: +55(11) 4081-8400
EMail: secretaria@faceq.edu.br
Website: http://www.faceq.edu.br
Diretor Geral: Mauro César Gonçalves

Courses
Administration (Administration); **Letters** (Literature); **Pedagogy** (Pedagogy); **Social Communication** (Advertising and Publicity; Communication Studies)
History: Founded 2005.
Main Language(s) of Instruction: Portuguese
Degrees and Diplomas: *Bacharelado*; *Licenciatura*. Also Cursos de Pós-Graduação lato sensu
Libraries: Yes
Last Updated: 14/03/11

EDUCATION CENTRE OF ALTA PAULISTA
Centro de Ensino da Alta Paulista (CEALPA)
Avenida Internacional 3000, Centro, Lucélia, São Paulo 17780000
Tel: +55(18) 3551-1849
EMail: cealpa@terra.com.br
Website: http://www.cealpa.cesd.br
Diretor: Gilson João Parizoto

Courses
Administration and Accountancy *(CEALPA)* (Accountancy; Administration); **Management** (Management)
History: Founded 1972
Main Language(s) of Instruction: Portuguese
Degrees and Diplomas: *Bacharelado*
Last Updated: 22/03/10

EDUCATIONAL FACULTY OF ARAUCÁRIA
Faculdade Educacional de Araucária
Av. das Araucárias, 3803 -, Araucária, PR
Tel: +55(41) 3643-1551
EMail: murilo@facear.edu.br
Website: http://www.facear.edu.br/new/index.asp
Diretor: Murilo Martins de Andrade

Areas
Biological and Health Sciences (Biomedicine; Nursing; Nutrition; Physical Therapy); **Exact Sciences and Technology** (Civil Engineering; Computer Science; Production Engineering; Systems Analysis); **Social and Legal Sciences** (Administration; Law)

Courses
Letters (Literature); **Pedagogy**
History: Founded 2001.
Main Language(s) of Instruction: Portuguese
Degrees and Diplomas: *Bacharelado*; *Licenciatura*; *Especialização/Aperfeiçoamento*; *Mestrado*
Libraries: Yes
Last Updated: 24/08/10

EDUCATIONAL FACULTY OF LAPA
Faculdade Educacional da Lapa (FAEL)
Rodovia Deputado Olívio Belich s/n - Km 30, Lapa, PR 83750000
Tel: +55(41) 3622-5551
EMail: diretoria@fael.edu.br
Website: http://www.fael.edu.br
Diretor: Luiz Carlos Borges da Silveira

Courses
Administration; **Pedagogy**
History: Founded 1998
Main Language(s) of Instruction: Portuguese
Degrees and Diplomas: *Bacharelado*; *Licenciatura*; *Especialização/Aperfeiçoamento*
Last Updated: 07/07/10

EDUCATIONAL FACULTY OF MATELÂNDIA

Faculdade Educacional de Matelândia
R. Marechal Floriano, 964 Centro, Matelândia, PR 85887-000
Tel: +55(45) 3262-1000
EMail: fama@matelnet.com.br
Website: http://www.faculdadematelandia.edu.br

Diretor: Amauri de Lima

Courses
Administration (Administration); **Information Systems** (Computer Science)

History: Founded 2008.

Main Language(s) of Instruction: Portuguese

Degrees and Diplomas: *Bacharelado*; *Especialização/Aperfeiçoamento*

Libraries: Yes
Last Updated: 20/09/10

EDUCATIONAL FACULTY OF MEDIANEIRA

Faculdade Educacional de Medianeira (FACEMED)
Rua Rio Branco 367, Centro, Medianeira, Paraná 85884000
Tel: +55(45) 3264-3050
Fax: +55(45) 3264-4725
EMail: facemed@facemed.edu.br

Diretor Geral: Bruno Erno Steckling

Courses
Administration (Administration; Agricultural Business; Marketing); **Law** (Law); **Literature** (Literature); **Social Services** (Social and Community Services)

History: Founded 2000.

Main Language(s) of Instruction: Portuguese

Degrees and Diplomas: *Bacharelado*; *Licenciatura*
Last Updated: 29/10/07

EDUCATIONAL FACULTY OF PONTA GROSSA - UNIÃO

Faculdade Educacional de Ponta Grossa - UNIÃO
Rua Tibúrcio Pedro Ferreira 55, Ponta Grossa, PR 84010-090
Tel: +55(42) 3220-9999
EMail: uniao@uniao.edu.br
Website: http://www.uniao.edu.br

Head: Marco Antônio Razouk **EMail:** marco@uniao.edu.br

Courses
Administration (Administration); **Information Systems** (Computer Science); **Law** (Law)

History: Founded 2001.

Main Language(s) of Instruction: Portuguese

Degrees and Diplomas: *Bacharelado*

Libraries: Yes
Last Updated: 24/08/10

EDUCATIONAL FOUNDATION OF ALÉM PARAÍBA

Fundação Educacional de Além Paraíba
Rua Isabel Herdy Alves 305, São José Além Paraíba, MG 36660-000
Tel: +55(32) 3462-7030
EMail: fundacaoap@ig.com.br
Website: http://www.feap.edu.br

Presidente: José Alves Fortes

Faculties
Health Sciences *(Archimedes Theodoro)* (Nursing; Nutrition; Physical Education; Physical Therapy); **Law and Management** *(Alves Fortes)* (Administration; Civil Engineering; Law); **Management** *(Bicas)* (Management); **Philosophy, Science and Letters** *(Professora Nair Fortes Abu-Merhy)* (Geography; History; Literature; Mathematics; Pedagogy)

Institutes
Education *(Carlos Chagas)* (Pedagogy); **Education** *(Nair Fortes Abu-Merhy)* (Biology; Environmental Studies; Physical Education); **Education** *(Bicas)* (Pedagogy); **Education** *(Matias Barbosa)* (Pedagogy)

History: Founded 1973.

Main Language(s) of Instruction: Portuguese

Degrees and Diplomas: *Bacharelado*; *Licenciatura*; *Especialização/Aperfeiçoamento*
Last Updated: 27/07/10

EDUCATIONAL FOUNDATION OF DUQUE DE CAXIAS

Fundação Educacional de Duque de Caxias (FFCLDC)
Avenida Presidente Kennedy 9422 São Bento, Duque de Caxias, Rio de Janeiro 25045-000
Tel: +55(21) 2671-3669 +55(21) 2671-0888
Fax: +55(21) 2671-5568
EMail: secretaria@feuduc.edu.br
Website: http://www.feuduc.edu.br

Diretora: Sandra Mara de Souza Furtado
EMail: diretoria@feuduc.edu.br

Courses
Biology; **Geography**; **Graduate Studies** (Archaeology; Contemporary History; Environmental Studies; Geography; Mathematics; Microbiology; Pathology; Portuguese; Special Education); **History** (History); **Information Systems** (Information Technology); **Literature**; **Mathematics** (Mathematics)

History: Founded 1969

Main Language(s) of Instruction: Portuguese

Degrees and Diplomas: *Bacharelado*; *Licenciatura*; *Especialização/Aperfeiçoamento*
Last Updated: 08/07/10

EDUCATIONAL FOUNDATION OF FERNANDÓPOLIS

Fundação Educacional de Fernandópolis (FEF)
Avenida Teotónio Vilela, s/n Campus Universitarió, Fernandópolis, SP 15600000
Tel: +55(17) 3465-0000
EMail: secretaria@fef.br
Website: http://www.fef.br

Presidente: Paulo Sérgio do Nascimento

Courses
Accountancy (Accountancy); **Administration** (Accountancy; Administration; Marketing); **Aesthetics and Cosmetics**; **Arts and Humanities** (Arts and Humanities); **Biology** (Biology); **Biomedicine** (Biomedicine); **Chemistry**; **Economics**; **Environmental Engineering** (Environmental Engineering); **Food Technology**; **Information Systems** (Information Management); **Journalism**; **Mathematics**; **Nursing**; **Nutrition** (Nutrition); **Occupational Therapy**; **Pedagogy** (Pedagogy); **Pharmacy** (Pharmacy); **Phonaudiology** (Speech Therapy and Audiology); **Physical Education** (Physical Education); **Physics**; **Physiotherapy** (Physical Therapy); **Psychology** (Psychology); **Social Services** (Social and Community Services)

History: Founded 1997

Main Language(s) of Instruction: Portuguese

Degrees and Diplomas: *Bacharelado*; *Licenciatura*; *Especialização/Aperfeiçoamento*; *Mestrado*
Last Updated: 18/06/10

EDUCATIONAL INSTITUTE OF ASSIS

Instituto Educacional de Assis (IEDA)
Avenida Doutor Dória 204, Vila Ouro Verde, Assis, SP 19816230
Tel: +55(18) 3323-2552
Fax: +55(18) 3323-2552 +55(18) 3323-2224
EMail: ieda@ieda.edu.br
Website: http://www.ieda.edu.br

Diretor: Tacito Ferreira do Amaral (1998-)

Faculties
Accountancy *(FCCA)* (Accountancy); **Administration** (Administration); **Pedagogy** *(FAEDA)* (Pedagogy); **Physical Education** (Physical Education)

History: Founded 1970

Main Language(s) of Instruction: Portuguese

Degrees and Diplomas: *Bacharelado*; *Especialização/Aperfeiçoamento*

Last Updated: 15/06/10

EDUCATIONAL INSTITUTE OF CASTRO

Instituto Educacional de Castro (INEC)
Praça Sant'Ana do Iapó, 15, Centro, Castro, PR 84165-490
EMail: facastro@facastro.edu.br
Website: http://www.facastro.edu.br/

Diretor Geral: Edson Rubens Gaspari
EMail: edson@facastro.edu.br

Courses
Graduate Studies (Animal Husbandry; Computer Science; Education; Educational Administration; Literature; Management; Portuguese; Public Administration); **Undergraduate Studies** (Accountancy; Agricultural Business; Business Administration; English; Human Resources; Information Technology; Literature)

History: Founded 2001.

Degrees and Diplomas: *Tecnólogo*; *Bacharelado*; *Licenciatura*. Also Postgraduate Diploma.

Last Updated: 22/09/10

EDUCATIONAL INSTITUTE OF MONTE ALTO

Instituto Educacional de Monte Alto (IEMA)
Rua Wady Elias 191, Caixa Postal 381, Jardim Alvorada, Monte Alto, São Paulo 15910000
Tel: +55(16) 3242-7399
Fax: +55(16) 3242-1213
EMail: iema@terra.com.br
Website: http://www.fan.edu.br

Diretora: Marciane Paulatti Nogueira Ulian
Vice-Diretor: Éder Paulatti Nogueira

Faculties
Administration and Business *(FAN)* (Administration; Business and Commerce); **Pedagogy** *(FAM)* (Education; Educational Administration; Pedagogy)

History: Founded 1995. Acquired present status 2001.

Main Language(s) of Instruction: Portuguese

Degrees and Diplomas: *Tecnólogo*; *Licenciatura*; *Mestrado*
Last Updated: 15/06/10

EDUCATIONAL QUANGO OF BELO JARDIM

Autarquia Educacional do Belo Jardim
Sítio Inhumas s/n, Estrada de Serra dos Ventos, Belo Jardim, PE 55150-000
EMail: aeb@3serv.com.br
Website: http://www.aeb.edu.br

Diretora: Bernardina Santos Araújo de Sousa

Courses
Administration (Administration); **Biology** (Biology); **History** (History); **Letters** (Literature); **Mathematics** (Mathematics); **Nursing** (Nursing); **Pedagogy** (Pedagogy)

Main Language(s) of Instruction: Portuguese

Degrees and Diplomas: *Bacharelado*; *Licenciatura*; *Especialização/Aperfeiçoamento*

Libraries: Yes
Last Updated: 03/08/10

EDUCATIONAL UNION OF BRASILIA

União Educacional de Brasília (UNEB)
SGAS - Avenida W5 Sul Quadra 910 32 Bloco D, Asa Sul, Brasília, DF 70390100
Tel: +55(61) 3445-3344
Fax: +55(61) 3443-1204
EMail: uneb@uneb.com.br
Website: http://www.uneb.com.br

Diretora: Layse de Campos Moreira Gomes (1998-)

Diretor Acadêmico: Glauco dos Santos Lopes

Areas
Management (Accountancy; Administration; Business Administration; Economics; Environmental Management; Finance; Health Administration; International Business; Public Administration); **Technology**

History: Founded 1981.

Degrees and Diplomas: *Bacharelado*; *Licenciatura*; *Especialização/Aperfeiçoamento*
Last Updated: 09/06/10

EDUCATIONAL UNION OF HIGHER EDUCATION OF THE MÉDIO TOCANSIS REGION

União Educacional de Ensino Superior do Médio Tocansis
Avenida Alfredo Nasser, n°. 843, Centro, Paraíso do Tocantins, TO 77.600.000
EMail: sabrina@unest.edu.br
Website: http://www.unest.edu.br

Diretora: Sabrina Ribeiro de Santana

Faculties
Administration (Administration; Business Administration); **Information Systems** (Computer Science); **Law** (Law)

History: Founded 2003.

Main Language(s) of Instruction: Portuguese

Degrees and Diplomas: *Bacharelado*

Libraries: Yes
Last Updated: 27/07/10

EDUVALE FACULTY OF AVARÉ

Faculdade Eduvale de Avaré
Av. Pref. Misael Euphrásio Leal, 347 - Jardim América, Avaré, SP 18705-050
Tel: +55(14) 3733-8585
EMail: eduvale@eduvaleavare.com.br
Website: http://www.eduvaleavare.com.br

Diretor: Evandro Marcio de Oliveira.

Courses
Administration (Administration); **Agronomy** (Agronomy); **Biology** (Biology); **Law** (Law); **Nursing** (Nursing); **Social Communication** (Advertising and Publicity; Public Relations)

Degrees and Diplomas: *Bacharelado*
Last Updated: 24/08/10

EGÍDIO JOSÉ DA SILVA FACULTY OF TECHNOLOGY

Faculdade de Tecnologia Egídio José da Silva (FATEGIDIO)
Rua Jalile Naaman, 70, Grão Pará, Teófilo Otoni, MG
Tel: +55(33) 3522-6030
Fax: +55(33) 3522-5833
EMail: secretaria@fategidio.com.br
Website: http://www.fategidio.com.br/

Courses
Graduate Studies (Agricultural Business; Distance Education; Education; Environmental Studies; Information Technology; Law; Management; Marketing; Public Administration; Transport Management); **Hospital Management** (Health Administration); **Medical Radiology** (Radiology)

Further Information: Also Eunápolis and Porto Seguro Units.

Degrees and Diplomas: *Tecnólogo*. Also Postgraduate Diploma and MBA.

Last Updated: 24/08/10

EINSTEIN FACULTY
Faculdade Einstein
Rua a Quadra D Lote 26 S/n, Loteamento Seper Clube, Stella Maris, Salvador, BA 41150-060

Diretor: José Nilton Carvalho Pereira

Courses
Administration (Administration)

History: Founded 2007.

Main Language(s) of Instruction: Portuguese

Degrees and Diplomas: *Bacharelado*

Last Updated: 30/08/10

EINSTEIN INTEGRATED FACULTIES OF LIMEIRA
Faculdades Integradas Einstein de Limeira (FIEL)
Rua Jatobá, 200, Vila Queiroz, Limeira, São Paulo 13480000
Tel: +55(19) 3444-6612
EMail: diracademica@faculdadeespirita.com.br
Website: http://www.fiel.edu.br/novo

Diretora Presidente: Silvia Affonso Leite

Courses
Administration (Administration); **Biomedicine** (Biomedicine); **Civil Engineering**; **Electrical Engineering**; **Nursing**; **Pedagogy** (Pedagogy); **Physical Education**; **Physiotherapy** (Physical Therapy); **Production Engineering**; **Psychology** (Psychology); **Teacher Training**

History: Founded 1995.

Main Language(s) of Instruction: Portuguese

Degrees and Diplomas: *Bacharelado*; *Especialização/Aperfeiçoamento*; *Mestrado*

Last Updated: 23/06/10

ELVIRA DAYRELL INSTITUTE OF EDUCATION
Instituto Superior de Educação Elvira Dayrell
Rodovia de Ligaçao DA BR 120/259 - KM 001, Virginópolis, MG 39.730-000
Tel: +55(33) 3416-2121
EMail: argemirolessa@yahoo.com.br
Website: http://www.iseed.edu.br/

Diretor: Argemiro Afonso Dumont Lessa

Courses
Administration (Administration); **Biology** (Biology); **Geography** (Geography); **History** (History); **Letters** (Literature); **Mathematics** (Mathematics); **Nursing** (Nursing); **Pedagogy** (Pedagogy); **Physical Education** (Physical Education)

History: Founded 2003.

Main Language(s) of Instruction: Portuguese

Degrees and Diplomas: *Bacharelado*; *Licenciatura*; *Especialização/Aperfeiçoamento*

Last Updated: 28/09/10

ENERGY FACULTIES
Faculdades Energia (FEAN)
Rua Henrique Lage, 560, Criciúma, Santa Catarina 88010450
Tel: +55(48) 3431-2031
Fax: +55(48) 3431-2003
EMail: contato@fasc.com.br
Website: http://www.faculdadesenergia.com.br

Diretor Geral: Fabiula Sanvido Martins

Courses
Accountancy; **Administration** (Administration); **Graphic Design** (Graphic Design); **Information Systems**; **Pedagogy** (Pedagogy)

History: Founded 2000.

Main Language(s) of Instruction: Portuguese

Degrees and Diplomas: *Tecnólogo*; *Bacharelado*; *Especialização/Aperfeiçoamento*; *Mestrado*

Last Updated: 16/03/11

ENIAC FACULTY
Faculdade ENIAC
Rua Força Pública 89, Guarulhos, SP 07012-030
Tel: +55(11) 6472-5500
EMail: mant@eniac.com.br
Website: http://www.eniac.com.br

Diretor: Ruy Guerios

Courses
Administration (Administration); **Information Systems** (Computer Science); **Mechatronic Engineering** (Electronic Engineering; Mechanical Engineering); **Production Engineering** (Production Engineering); **Social Communication** (Advertising and Publicity; Public Relations)

History: Founded 2001.

Main Language(s) of Instruction: Portuguese

Degrees and Diplomas: *Bacharelado*; *Especialização/Aperfeiçoamento*

Last Updated: 24/08/10

ENIAC-FAPI FACULTY OF TECHNOLOGY
Faculdade de Tecnologia ENIAC-FAPI (ENIAC)
Rua Força Pública, 89, Centro, Guarulhos, SP 07012-030
EMail: mant@eniac.com.br
Website: http://www.eniac.com.br/

Courses
Administration (Administration); **Distance Postgraduate Studies** (Distance Education; Educational Administration; Educational Psychology; Law; Management); **Graduate Studies** (Automation and Control Engineering; Business and Commerce; Computer Networks; Finance; Human Resources; Information Technology; Management; Marketing; Safety Engineering; Transport Management); **Information Systems** (Information Sciences); **Mechatronics Engineering** (Electronic Engineering; Mechanical Engineering); **Production Engineering** (Production Engineering); **Social Communication - Advertising and Publicity** (Advertising and Publicity); **Social Communication - Public Relations** (Public Relations); **Technical Studies** (Computer Networks; Computer Science; Data Processing; Electronic Engineering; Environmental Management; Finance; Hotel Management; Human Resources; Industrial Management; Management; Marketing; Safety Engineering; Transport Management)

Degrees and Diplomas: *Tecnólogo*; *Bacharelado*. Also Postgraduate Diploma and MBA.

Last Updated: 24/08/10

EQUIPE DARWIN FACULTY OF TECHNOLOGY
Faculdade de Tecnologia Equipe Darwin
QS 07 Rua 400, Lote 01, Aguas Claras, Brasilia, DF
Tel: +55(61) 3356-0900
Fax: +55(61) 3356-6926
Website: http://www.faculdadedarwin.com/

Diretor Geral: José Marcelino da Silva

Courses
Computer Networks (Computer Networks); **Graduate Studies** (Administration; Administrative Law; Business Administration; Civil Law; Civil Security; Computer Networks; Criminal Law; Education; Educational Administration; Educational Psychology; Environmental Management; Geography; Gynaecology and Obstetrics; Health Sciences; Higher Education; History; Human Resources; Labour Law; Management; Occupational Health; Physical Education; Public Administration; Real Estate; Special Education); **Institutional Communication** (Communication Studies); **Marketing** (Marketing); **Public Administration** (Public Administration)

History: Founded 2005.

Main Language(s) of Instruction: Portuguese

Degrees and Diplomas: *Tecnólogo*. Also Postgraduate Diploma and MBA.

Last Updated: 24/08/10

EQUIPE FACULTY
Faculdade Equipe
Av. Sapucaia, 1376, Sapucaia do Sul, RS 93210-240
Tel: +55(51) 3474-4515
EMail: contato@faculdadesequipe.com.br
Website: http://www.faculdadesequipe.com.br

Diretor: Joaquim Francisco Muller de Paula
EMail: joaquim@faculdadesequipe.com.br

Courses
Accountancy (Accountancy); **Administration** (Administration); **Letters** (Literature); **Pedagogy** (Pedagogy)

History: Founded 1989 as Escola Técnica Equipe. Acquired present status and title 2001.

Main Language(s) of Instruction: Portuguese

Degrees and Diplomas: *Bacharelado*
Last Updated: 24/08/10

EQUIPE INSTITUTE OF EDUCATION
Instituto Superior de Educaçao Equipe
Av. Sapucaia, 1376, Sapucaia do Sul, RS
Tel: +55(51) 3474-4515
EMail: joaquim@faculdadesequipe.com.br
Website: http://www.faculdadesequipe.com.br

Diretor: Joaquim Francisco Muller de Paula

Courses
Accountancy (Accountancy); **Administration** (Administration); **Letters** (Literature); **Pedagogy** (Pedagogy)

History: Founded 2002.

Main Language(s) of Instruction: Portuguese

Degrees and Diplomas: *Bacharelado*; *Licenciatura*
Last Updated: 28/09/10

ERNESTO RISCALI FACULTY
Faculdade Ernesto Riscali
Rua Bruno Riscali 569, Olimpia, SP 15400-000
Tel: +55(17) 3281-8982
EMail: secretaria_faer@terra.com.br
Website: http://www.faer.edu.br/

Diretora: Maria Justina Boitar Riscali

Courses
Administration (Administration); **Letters** (Literature); **Mathematics** (Mathematics); **Pedagogy** (Pedagogy)

History: Founded 2000.

Main Language(s) of Instruction: Portuguese

Degrees and Diplomas: *Bacharelado*
Libraries: Yes
Last Updated: 26/08/10

ESEFAP FACULTIES
Faculdades ESEFAP (ESEFAP)
Rua Mandaguaris 274, Térreo Centro, Tupã, São Paulo 17600060
Tel: +55(14) 3496-1218
Fax: +55(14) 3496-1218
EMail: esefap@esefap.edu.br
Website: http://www.esefap.edu.br

Diretor: Robinson Moisés Salerno Ricci

Courses
Nursing (Nursing); **Nutrition** (Nutrition); **Physical Education** (Physical Education)

History: Founded 1970 as Escola Superior de Educação Física da Alta Paulista. Acquired present title 2004.

Main Language(s) of Instruction: Portuguese

Degrees and Diplomas: *Bacharelado*; *Licenciatura*; *Especialização/Aperfeiçoamento*
Last Updated: 29/06/10

ESIC BUSINESS AND MARKETING SCHOOL
Escola Superior de Gestão Comercial e Marketing (ESIC)
Rua Padre Dehon, 814, Hauer, Curitiba, PR 81630-090
Tel: +55(41) 3376-1417
Fax: +55(41) 3376-1417
EMail: academico@esic.br; diretor@esic.br
Website: http://www.esic.br/

Diretor Geral: Simón Reyes Martínez Córdova

Courses
Administration (Administration; Business Administration; Marketing); **Graduate Studies** (Advertising and Publicity; Business Administration; Communication Studies; Finance; Human Resources; International Relations; Management; Marketing)

Degrees and Diplomas: *Bacharelado*. Also specialised Master and MBA.
Last Updated: 16/07/10

ESPAM FACULTIES
Faculdades ESPAM
Quadra 04 Area Reservada 01, Sobradinho, Brasília, DF 73025400
Tel: +55(61) 3487-7100
Fax: +55(61) 3487-7100
EMail: secretaria@espam.edu.br
Website: http://www.espam.edu.br

Diretor: Duilio Reis Canedo

Courses
Accountancy *(Planalta)*; **Administration**; **Computer Science** (Computer Science); **History** (History); **Law**; **Literature**; **Mathematics** (Mathematics); **Pedagogy**

History: Founded 2001.

Main Language(s) of Instruction: Portuguese

Degrees and Diplomas: *Bacharelado*; *Especialização/Aperfeiçoamento*; *Mestrado*
Last Updated: 29/06/10

ESPERANÇA INSTITUTE OF HIGHER EDUCATION
Instituto Esperança de Ensino Superior (IESPES)
Rua Coaracy Nunes 3315, Caranazal, Santarem, PA 68040100
Tel: +55(91) 3591-760 +55(93) 3523-91762
Fax: +55(91) 3529-1761
EMail: iespes@iespes.edu.br
Website: http://www.iespes.edu.br

Diretora: Irene Escher

Courses
Administration (Administration); **Journalism**; **Nursing** (Nursing); **Pedagogy** (Pedagogy; Teacher Training); **Pharmacy** (Pharmacy); **Philosophy** (Philosophy); **Psychology** (Psychology); **Religion**; **Tourism** (Tourism)

History: Founded 1999.

Main Language(s) of Instruction: Portuguese

Degrees and Diplomas: *Tecnólogo*; *Bacharelado*; *Licenciatura*; *Especialização/Aperfeiçoamento*; *Mestrado*
Last Updated: 15/06/10

ESPÍRITA INTEGRATED FACULTIES
Faculdades Integradas Espírita (FIES)
Rua Tobias de Macedo Júnior 333, Santo Inácio, Curitibá, Paraná 82010340
Tel: +55(41) 3111-1717
Fax: +55(41) 3335-3423
EMail: diracademica@faculdadeespirita.com.br
Website: http://www.unibem.br/

Diretora Geral: Neyda Nerbass Ulysséa
EMail: dirgeral@faculdadeespirita.com.br

Courses
Agricultural Engineering (Agricultural Engineering); **Biological and Life Sciences** (Biological and Life Sciences; Biology);

Education (Education; Educational Administration; Pedagogy; Physical Education); **Geography** (Geography); **History** (History); **Nutrition** (Nutrition); **Physical Therapy**; **Physics** (Astronomy and Space Science; Physics); **Social Services** (Social and Community Services); **Zoology** (Zoology)

History: Founded 1975

Main Language(s) of Instruction: Portuguese

Degrees and Diplomas: *Bacharelado*; *Licenciatura*; *Especialização/Aperfeiçoamento*
Last Updated: 23/06/10

ESTAÇAO BUSINESS SCHOOL

Av. Sete de Setembro, 2775 5° andar, Curitiba, PR 80230-010
Tel: +55(41) 2101-8800
EMail: estacao@ebs.edu.br
Website: http://www2.estacaopr.com.br

Diretor: Judas Tadeu Grassi Mendes

Courses
Administration (Administration); **Business Education** (Business Education); **Commercial Law** (Commercial Law)

Main Language(s) of Instruction: Portuguese

Degrees and Diplomas: *Bacharelado*; *Mestrado*
Last Updated: 26/08/10

ESTÁCIO DE SÁ FACULTY OF BELO HORIZONTE

Faculdade Estácio de Sá de Belo Horizonte
Avenida Francisco Sales 23, Floresta, Belo Horizonte,
Minas Gerais 30150220
Tel: +55(31) 3279-7700
Fax: +55(31) 3212-6022
EMail: estaciodesa@bh.estacio.br
Website: http://www.bh.estacio.br

Diretor: Érico Ribeiro

Courses
Administration (Administration); **Advertising**; **Economics** (Economics); **Law** (Law); **Nursing**; **Physical Education** (Physical Education); **Physiotherapy** (Physical Therapy); **Tourism** (Tourism)

History: Founded 2000.

Main Language(s) of Instruction: Portuguese

Degrees and Diplomas: *Bacharelado*; *Especialização/Aperfeiçoamento*
Last Updated: 07/07/10

ESTÁCIO DE SÁ FACULTY OF CAMPO GRANDE

Faculdade Estació de Sá de Campo Grande
Rua Venâncio Borges do Nascimento, 377 - Jd. TV Morena,
Campo Grande, MS 79050-700
EMail: jcfernandes@fes.br
Website: http://www.fes.br

Programmes
Accountancy; **Administration** (Administration); **Advertising** (Advertising and Publicity); **Environmental Engineering** (Environmental Engineering); **Information Technology** (Information Technology); **Journalism** (Journalism); **Law** (Law); **Pharmacy** (Pharmacy); **Physiotherapy** (Physical Therapy); **Systems Analysis** (Systems Analysis)

Main Language(s) of Instruction: Portuguese

Degrees and Diplomas: *Bacharelado*
Last Updated: 14/03/11

ESTÁCIO DE SÁ FACULTY OF OURINHOS

Faculdade Estácio de Sá de Ourinhos (FAESO)
Avenida Luís Saldanha Rodrigues, S/n Quadra C1 - A Nova
Ourinhos, Ourinhos, São Paulo 19900910
Tel: +55(14) 3302-5000
Fax: +55(14) 3326-9109
EMail: angelamarinho@faeso.edu.br
Website: http://www.faeso.edu.br

Diretor: Marcelo Sylvino

Courses
Administration; **Law** (Law); **Nursing**; **Physical Education** (Physical Education); **Physiotherapy** (Physical Therapy); **Tourism** (Tourism)

History: Founded 1999.

Main Language(s) of Instruction: Portuguese

Degrees and Diplomas: *Bacharelado*; *Licenciatura*; *Especialização/Aperfeiçoamento*
Last Updated: 07/07/10

ESTÁCIO DE SÁ FACULTY OF SANTA CATARINA

Faculdade Estácio de Sá de Santa Catarina (FESSC)
Avenida Leoberto Leal 431, Barreiros, São José,
Santa Catarina 88117001
Tel: +55(48) 3381-8001
Fax: +55(48) 3381-8016
EMail: sc.estacio@sc.estacio.br
Website: http://www.sc.estacio.br/portal

Diretor: Luis Carlos Martinhago Schlichting

Courses
Administration; **Advertising** (Advertising and Publicity); **Fashion Design** (Fashion Design); **Journalism** (Journalism); **Law**; **Nursing** (Nursing); **Pharmacy** (Pharmacy); **Physiotherapy** (Physical Therapy); **Speech Therapy** (Speech Therapy and Audiology); **Tourism** (Tourism)

History: Founded 2000.

Main Language(s) of Instruction: Portuguese

Degrees and Diplomas: *Bacharelado*; *Especialização/Aperfeiçoamento*
Last Updated: 07/07/10

ESTÁCIO DE SÁ FACULTY OF VITORIA

Faculdade Estácio de Sá de Vitória (FESV)
Rua Herwan Modenesi Wanderley Q1 L6, Jardim Camburi, Vitória,
Espirito Santo 29090640
Tel: +55(27) 3395-1100
Fax: +55(27) 3395-1100
EMail: targueta@es.estacio.br
Website: http://www.es.estacio.br

Diretora Geral: Márcia Cristina Targueta Souza Cruz

Courses
Administration (*Postgraduate*); **Advertising and Publicity**; **Journalism** (Journalism); **Law** (Law); **Pedagogy** (Education; Pedagogy); **Physical Education**; **Physical Therapy**; **Tourism** (Tourism)

Further Information: Also branch in Vila Velha

History: Founded 2000.

Main Language(s) of Instruction: Portuguese

Degrees and Diplomas: *Bacharelado*; *Licenciatura*; *Especialização/Aperfeiçoamento*
Last Updated: 07/07/10

ESTÁCIO DE SÁ UNIVERSITY

Universidade Estácio de Sá (UNESA)
Rua do Bispo 83, Rio Comprido, Rio de Janeiro, Rio de Janeiro
20261-060
Tel: +55(21) 2503-7000
Fax: +55(21) 3325-9959
EMail: vr.graduacao@estacio.br
Website: http://www.estacio.br

Reitor: Gilberto Mendes de Oliveira Castro (1997-)
Tel: +55(21) 2433-9700, Fax: +55(21) 2433-9722
EMail: gmoc@estacio.br

Vice-Reitor: José Roberto Vasconcelos
Tel: +55(21) 2433-9700 EMail: jroberto@estacio.br

International Relations: Wandyr Hagge Siqueira, Director, International Relations

Tel: +55(21) 2433-9700, Fax: +55(21) 2430-9722
EMail: wandyr@estacio.br

Courses

Accountancy (Accountancy; Business Administration); **Administration** *(Campuses Campos dos Goytacazes, Petrópolis, Resende)* (Administration; Business Administration); **Architecture and Town Planning** (Architecture; Town Planning); **Audiology and Speech Pathology**; **Biology** (Biology); **Chemistry** (Chemistry); **Cinema and Television** (Cinema and Television; Performing Arts); **Civil Engineering** (Civil Engineering; Engineering); **Cooking and Catering** *(Polytechnic)*; **Data Processing** *(Campos dos Goytacazes, Nova Friburgo)* (Data Processing; Engineering); **Dentistry**; **Economics** (Economics; Social Sciences); **Electrical Engineering** (Computer Engineering; Electrical Engineering; Engineering); **Entrepreneurial Management and Information Technology** *(Polytechnic)* (Information Technology; Management); **Fashion Design** *(Polytechnic)* (Design; Fashion Design; Fine Arts); **Food Engineering** (Food Technology); **Graphic Design** *(Polytechnic)* (Design; Fine Arts; Graphic Design); **History**; **Hotel Management** *(Petrópolis)*; **Industrial Design** (Design; Fine Arts; Industrial Design); **International Relations** *(Niterói)* (International Studies); **Law** *(Cabo Frio, Campos dos Goytacazes, Nova Friburgo, Petrópolis, Resende)* (Law); **Letters** *(Campos dos Goytacazes, Niterói, Nova Friburgo, Petrópolis)*; **Marketing** *(Niterói)* (Marketing); **Mathematics**; **Medicine** (Health Sciences; Medicine); **Nursing** *(Campos dos Goytacazes, Nova Friburgo)*; **Nutrition** (Nutrition); **Pedagogy** *(Campos dos Goytacazes, Niterói, Nova Friburgo, Resende)* (Education; Educational Sciences; Pedagogy); **Petroleum and Gas Engineering** *(Polytechnic)*; **Pharmacy** *(Campos dos Goytacazes)* (Health Sciences; Pharmacy); **Photography** *(Polytechnic)* (Fine Arts; Photography; Visual Arts); **Physical Education** *(Campos dos Goytacazes, Niterói, Nova Friburgo)* (Physical Education); **Physical Therapy** *(Niterói, Nova Friburgo, Campos dos Goytacazes)*; **Production Engineering**; **Psychology** *(Campos dos Goytacazes, Nova Friburgo)* (Psychology); **Radiology** *(Polytechnic)* (Radiology); **Scenery Design and Theatre Lighting** *(Polytechnic)* (Display and Stage Design; Fine Arts; Theatre); **Social Communication** *(Niterói, Nova Friburgo)*; **Theatre Interpretation** *(Polytechnic)* (Acting; Performing Arts; Theatre); **Tourism**; **Trilingual Executive Secretariat** (English; French; Secretarial Studies; Spanish); **Veterinary Medicine** (Veterinary Science)

Further Information: Also University Hospital; Dental Clinics; Physiotherapy Clinics; Animal Care Centre. Research and Training Centres in almost all undergraduate areas

History: Founded 1970 as Law School, acquired present title and status 1988.

Governing Bodies: Conselho Universitário; Conselho de Ensino, Pesquisa e Extensão

Academic Year: February to December (February-June; August-December)

Admission Requirements: Secondary school certificate and entrance examination

Fees: (Reais): 4,000-22,000 per annum

Main Language(s) of Instruction: Portuguese

International Co-operation: Member of the Associated Universities of Latin America, UNIAAL. Also 32 exchange agreements with foreign institutions

Degrees and Diplomas: *Bacharelado*: 3-5 yrs; *Licenciatura*: 4 yrs; *Especialização/Aperfeiçoamento*: 1 yr; *Mestrado*: Law; Administration; Education; Dentistry; Medicine, 2-2 1/2 yrs; *Doutorado*

Student Services: Academic counselling, Canteen, Cultural centre, Employment services, Foreign student adviser, Handicapped facilities, Health services, Language programs, Social counselling, Sports facilities

Special Facilities: TV and Video Production Studio. Cinema. Journalism Training Centre. Graphic Design Office. Legal Advice Office. Flying School. Art Galleries

Libraries: Central Library and 41 local Libraries

Publications: ADM made, Journal of The Master's Course in Administration Entrepreneurial Development *(annually)*; Juris Poesis, Journal of Law *(biannually)*; Methodus, Scientific and Cultural Journal *(annually)*

Last Updated: 31/05/10

ESUCRI FACULTIES

Faculdades ESUCRI (ESUCRI)
Rua Gonçalves Ledo 185 Centro, Criciúma,
Santa Catarina 88802180
Tel: +55(48) 437-2060
Fax: +55(48) 437-2060
EMail: esucri@esucri.com.br
Website: http://www.esucri-univer.com.br

Diretor: Everaldo José Tiscoski

Courses

Accountancy; **Administration** (Administration; Business Administration); **Foreign Trade**; **Information Systems**; **Nursing** (Nursing); **Psychology**

History: Founded 1999 as Escola Superior de Criciúma. Acquired present title 2000.

Main Language(s) of Instruction: Portuguese

Degrees and Diplomas: *Bacharelado*; *Especialização/Aperfeiçoamento*

Last Updated: 02/11/07

ESUDA FACULTY OF HUMAN SCIENCES

Faculdade de Ciências Humanas ESUDA (FCHE)
Rua Bispo Cardoso Ayres, s/n - Santo Amaro, Recife,
Pernambuco 50050480
Tel: +55(81) 3412-4242
Fax: +55(81) 3412-4242
EMail: esuda@esuda.com.br
Website: http://www.esuda.com.br

Presidente: Wilson José Macedo Barreto (1997-)

Courses

Accountancy; **Administration** (Administration; Management; Marketing); **Architecture**; **Economics**; **Graduate Studies** (Accountancy; Architecture; Business Administration; Civil Engineering; Commercial Law; Community Health; Economics; Environmental Management; Finance; Interior Design; International Business; Labour Law; Landscape Architecture; Law; Management; Marketing; Neurological Therapy; Psychology; Psychotherapy; Town Planning; Transport Management); **Psychology** (Psychology)

Further Information: Also Distance Education Courses.

History: Founded 1974.

Main Language(s) of Instruction: Portuguese

Degrees and Diplomas: *Bacharelado*; *Especialização/Aperfeiçoamento*

Last Updated: 05/07/10

ETEP FACULTIES

ETEP Faculdades
Av. Barão do Rio Branco, 882, Jardim Esplanada,
São José dos Campos, São Paulo 12242800
Tel: +55(12) 3947-2200
Fax: +55(12) 3922-1850
EMail: marta.esteves@etep.edu.br
Website: http://www.etep.edu.br

Diretor: Thiago Rodrigues Pêgas

Courses

Administration (Administration); **Aeronautical Engineering** (Aeronautical and Aerospace Engineering); **Computer Engineering** (Computer Engineering); **Electrical Engineering** (Electrical Engineering); **Mechanical and Industrial Engineering** (Industrial Engineering; Mechanical Engineering); **Mechatronic Engineering** (Electronic Engineering; Mechanical Engineering); **Production Engineering** (Production Engineering); **Short-term Studies** (Business and Commerce; Computer Networks; Computer Science; Data Processing; Electronic Engineering; Finance; Human Resources; Industrial Management; Management; Systems Analysis; Transport Management); **Technical Studies** (Computer Science; Electronic Engineering; Mechanical Engineering)

Further Information: Also campuses in São José dos Campos, Taubaté and São Paulo.

History: Founded 1989.

Main Language(s) of Instruction: Portuguese

Degrees and Diplomas: *Diploma de Técnico de Nivel Medio*; *Bacharelado*; *Licenciatura*

Last Updated: 23/06/10

EUCLID FACULTY OF CUNHA

Faculdade Euclides da Cunha
Avenida Dep. Eduardo Vicente Nasser, 1020,
São José do Rio Pardo, SP
Tel: +55(19) 3608-4704
EMail: vicediretora@feucriopardo.edu.br
Website: http://www.feucriopardo.edu.br

Diretora: Isabela Custódio Talora Bozzini
EMail: diretor@feucriopardo.edu.br

Courses
Art (Fine Arts); **Biology** (Biology); **Geography** (Geography); **History** (History); **Letters** (Literature); **Mathematics** (Mathematics); **Pedagogy** (Pedagogy); **Physical Education** (Physical Education); **Physics** (Physics)

History: Founded 1964 as Faculdade de Filosofia, Ciências e Letras de São José do Rio Pardo. Acquired present title 2005.

Main Language(s) of Instruction: Portuguese

Degrees and Diplomas: *Bacharelado*; *Especialização/Aperfeiçoamento*

Libraries: Yes

Last Updated: 05/08/10

EUCLIDES DA CUNHA FACULTY OF EDUCATION OF THE STATE OF ACRE

Faculdade de Educaçao Acreano Euclides da Cunha
Rua do Aviário N°204, Bairro Aviário, Rio Branco, AC 69900-000
Tel: +55(68) 3224-7395
EMail: caa.souza@uol.com.br

Diretor: Carlos Alberto Alves de Souza

Courses
Geography (Geography); **History** (History)

History: Founded 2006.

Main Language(s) of Instruction: Portuguese

Degrees and Diplomas: *Licenciatura*

Last Updated: 02/08/10

EUCLIDES FERNANDES INTEGRATED FACULTY

Faculdade Integrada Euclides Fernandes
Rua Padre Altino Freire 63, Centro, Jequié, BA 45200000
Tel: +55(73) 3525-2971
EMail: ceteje@sst.com.br
Website: http://www.fief.com.br/index.php

Diretor: Euclides Nunes Fernandes

Courses
Accountancy *(FCCJ)* (Accountancy); **Administration**; **Economics** *(FCEJ)* (Economics)

History: Founded 1990. Formerly Faculdades Integradas de Jequié.

Main Language(s) of Instruction: Portuguese

Degrees and Diplomas: *Bacharelado*; *Especialização/Aperfeiçoamento*

Last Updated: 23/06/10

EUGENE GOMES INSTITUTE OF EDUCATION

Instituto Superior de Educação Eugênio Gomes
Rua Manoel Oliveira e Silva 127 - Campus Universitário, Ipirá, BA 44600-000
Tel: +55(75) 3254-3280
EMail: fundal@fundal.org.br
Website: http://www.fundal.org.br

Diretor: Antonio Almeida e Silva

Courses
Pedagogy (Pedagogy)

History: Founded 2004.

Main Language(s) of Instruction: Portuguese

Degrees and Diplomas: *Licenciatura*

Last Updated: 01/10/10

EURIPIDES UNIVERSITY CENTRE OF MARILIA

Centro Universitario Eurípides de Marília (UNIVEM)
Avenida Hygino Muzy Filho 529, Campus Universitãrio, Marília, São Paulo 17525901
Tel: +55(14) 2105-0800
Fax: +55(14) 3413-2516
EMail: marketing@univem.edu.br
Website: http://www.fundanet.br

Reitor: Luiz Carlos de Macedo Soares
Tel: +55(14) 2105-0845 EMail: reitor@univem.edu.br

Courses
Accountancy (Accountancy); **Administration** (Administration); **Commercial Management** (Business and Commerce); **Computer Networks**; **Computer Science** (Computer Science); **Graphic Design** (Graphic Design); **Human Resources** (Human Resources); **Industrial Production Management**; **Information Systems** (Information Sciences); **Information Technology Management** (Information Technology); **Interior Design** (Interior Design); **Law** (Law); **Literature** (English; Literature; Portuguese); **Logistics** (Transport Management); **Managerial Process** (Management); **Mathematics**; **Production Engineering**

History: Founded 1974

Main Language(s) of Instruction: Portuguese

Degrees and Diplomas: *Tecnólogo*; *Bacharelado*; *Licenciatura*; *Mestrado*: Law

Last Updated: 02/06/10

EURO-AMERICAN UNIVERSITY CENTRE

Centro Universitário Euro-Americano (UNIEURO)
Avenida das Nações, Trecho 0, Conjunto 5, Brasília, DF 70200-001
Tel: +55(61) 3445-5888 +55(61) 3445-5700
Fax: +55(61) 3445-5747
EMail: centrouniversitario@unieuro.edu.br
Website: https://www.unieuro.edu.br

Reitor: Myriam Christiano Maia Gonçalves
EMail: myriam@unieuro.edu.br

Pró-Reitora Administrativa: Flávia Marão Fecury
EMail: miguelfecury@unieuro.edu.br

Courses
Accountancy (Accountancy); **Administration** (Administration); **Advertising and Publicity** (Advertising and Publicity); **Architecture and Town Planning**; **Biomedicine**; **Graduate Studies**; **Graduate Studies** *(Stricto Sensu)*; **Information Systems**; **International Relations** (International Relations); **Journalism**; **Law** (Law); **Literature**; **Nursing**; **Nutrition**; **Pedagogy** (Pedagogy); **Pharmacy**; **Physical Education** *(Licenciatura)* (Physical Education); **Physical Education**; **Physical Therapy** (Physical Therapy); **Technological Studies** (Computer Networks; Construction Engineering; Cooking and Catering; Fashion Design; Finance; Heritage Preservation; Human Resources; Interior Design; Management; Marketing; Public Administration; Real Estate)

History: Founded 1998.

Main Language(s) of Instruction: Portuguese

Degrees and Diplomas: *Tecnólogo*; *Bacharelado*; *Licenciatura*; *Especialização/Aperfeiçoamento*; *Mestrado*

Last Updated: 02/06/10

EUROPAN FACULTY

Faculdade EUROPAN
Ruaé Howard A. Acheson Jr. 393, Jardim da Glória, Granja Viana, Cotia, SP 06711280
Tel: +55(11) 4612-8325
Fax: +55(11) 4612-8319
EMail: info@europan.com.br
Website: http://www.europan.com.br

Diretora Geral: Rita Carolino

Courses

Accountancy (Accountancy); **Administration** (Administration); **Advertising** (Advertising and Publicity); **Computer Science** (Computer Science); **Letters** (Literature); **Pedagogy** (Pedagogy); **Physical Education**

History: Founded 2000.

Main Language(s) of Instruction: Portuguese

Degrees and Diplomas: *Bacharelado*; *Licenciatura*
Last Updated: 07/07/10

EUROPEAN FACULTY OF ADMINISTRATION AND MARKETING
Faculdade Européia de Administraçao e Marketing
Rua Cândido Ferreira 343, Jaboatão dos Guararapes,
PE 54400-080
Tel: +55(81) 3461-4008
EMail: diretorexecutivo@faculdadeeuropeia.com.br
Website: http://www.fepamnet.com

Diretor: Caetano Alves

Courses

Marketing Administration (Administration; Business Administration; Finance; Marketing)

History: Founded 2002.

Main Language(s) of Instruction: Portuguese

Degrees and Diplomas: *Bacharelado*; *Mestrado*
Last Updated: 26/08/10

EVANGELICAL FACULTY OF BRASILIA
Faculdade Evangélica de Brasília
SGAS 910 Cj E - ASA SUL, AE 04 Setor J - Taguatinga- Norte,
Brasilia, DF
Tel: +55(61)3491-1620
EMail: coord.administracao@fe.edu.b
Website: http://www.fe.edu.br/fesite

Diretora: Dalma Arruda

Courses

Administration (Administration); **Letters** (Literature); **Pedagogy** (Pedagogy); **Theology** (Theology)

History: Founded 2005.

Main Language(s) of Instruction: Portuguese

Degrees and Diplomas: *Bacharelado*; *Licenciatura*; *Especializa-ção/Aperfeiçoamento*

Libraries: Yes
Last Updated: 30/08/10

EVANGELICAL FACULTY OF GOIANÉSIA
Faculdade Evangélica de Goianésia
Av. Brasil, N° 1000 - Covoa, Goianésia, GO 76380-000
Tel: +55(62) 3353-6260
EMail: evangelica@evangelicagoianesia.com.br
Website: http://www.evangelicagoianesia.edu.br

Diretor: José Mateus dos Santos

Courses

Accountancy (Accountancy); **Administration** (Administration); **Law** (Law)

History: Founded as Faculdade Betel de Goianésia.

Main Language(s) of Instruction: Portuguese

Degrees and Diplomas: *Bacharelado*; *Especialização/Aperfeiçoa-mento*; *Mestrado*
Last Updated: 15/07/10

EVANGELICAL FACULTY OF PARANA
Faculdade Evangélica do Paraná (FEPAR)
Rua Padre Anchieta 2770, Bairro Bigorrilho, Curitibá,
Paranà 80730000
Tel: +55(11) 3240-5500
Fax: +55(11) 3240-5500
EMail: fepar@fepar.edu.br
Website: http://www.fepar.edu.br

Diretor: Arnaldo Luiz Miró Rebello EMail: drgeral@fepar.edu.br

Courses

Environmental Management; **Medicine** (Medicine); **Nursing** (Nursing); **Nutrition**; **Physiotherapy** (Physical Therapy); **Psychology** (Psychology); **Theology** (Theology); **Veterinary Science** (Veterinary Science)

History: Founded 1969.

Main Language(s) of Instruction: Portuguese

Degrees and Diplomas: *Bacharelado*; *Especialização/Aperfeiçoa-mento*; *Mestrado*; *Doutorado*
Last Updated: 07/07/10

EVANGELICAL FACULTY OF PIAUÍ
Faculdade Evangélica do Piauí
Rua Treze de Maio, 2660 Bairro Pio XII, Teresina, PI 64018-285
Tel: +55(86) 3218-1329
EMail: faepi@faepi.com.br
Website: http://www.faepi.com.br/novo/

Diretor: Antonio de Freitas Melo

Areas

Computer Science *(Postgraduate)* (Computer Networks; Software Engineering); **Education** *(Postgraduate)* (Biology; Chemistry; Dance; Education; Educational Administration; Environmental Studies; Geography; Physical Education; Physics; Preschool Education; Religious Education); **Health** *(Postgraduate)* (Biology; Nursing; Nutrition; Psychiatry and Mental Health; Social and Community Services); **Law** *(Postgraduate)* (Civil Law; Commercial Law; Labour Law)

Courses

Pedagogy (Pedagogy); **Theology** (Theology)

History: Founded 1992 as Instituto Bíblico Pentecostal de Teresina. Acquired present status and title 2004.

Main Language(s) of Instruction: Portuguese

Degrees and Diplomas: *Bacharelado*; *Especialização/Aperfeiçoa-mento*; *Mestrado*

Libraries: Yes
Last Updated: 27/08/10

EVANGELICAL FACULTY OF SALVADOR
Faculdade Evangélica de Salvador
Av. Antônio Carlos Magalhães, n.° 3749, 2.° andar, Pituba,
Salvador, BA 41850-000
Tel: +55(71) 3333-5446
EMail: diretoria@facesa.com.br
Website: http://www.facesa.com.br

Diretor: Ivan Pitzer

Courses

Music (Music); **Pedagogy** (Pedagogy)

History: Founded 2001.

Main Language(s) of Instruction: Portuguese

Degrees and Diplomas: *Licenciatura*; *Especialização/Aperfeiçoa-mento*

Libraries: Yes
Last Updated: 25/08/10

EVANGELICAL FACULTY OF THE MID-NORTH REGION

Faculdade Evangélica do Meio Norte
Rua Nova, 429 - Centro, Coroatá, MA 65415-000
Tel: +55(99) 3641-2812
EMail: faeme_ieb@hotmail.com
Website: http://www.faeme.com.br

Diretor: Osiel Gomes da Silva EMail: drosiel@hotmail.com

Courses
Philosophy (Education; Philosophy)
History: Founded 2002.
Main Language(s) of Instruction: Portuguese
Degrees and Diplomas: *Licenciatura*; *Especialização/Aperfeiçoamento*
Last Updated: 30/08/10

EVILÁSIO FORMIGA FACULTY

Faculdade Evilásio Formiga
Rua Martins Moreira 652, Cajazeiras, PB 58900-000
Tel: +55(83)3531-3788
EMail: ramosformiga@bol.com.br

Diretora: Aparecida de Lourdes Ramos Formiga

Courses
Administration (Administration); **Social Services** (Social and Community Services)
History: Founded 2007.
Main Language(s) of Instruction: Portuguese
Degrees and Diplomas: *Bacharelado*
Last Updated: 30/08/10

EVOLUTION FACULTY

Faculdade Evoluçao
Avenida Varangüera 623, São Roque, SP 18130-340
Tel: +55(11) 4784-7040
EMail: diretoria-sp@uniesp.edu.br
Website: http://www.uniesp.edu.br/saoroque

Diretor: Carlos Roberto Sanches de Oliveira

Courses
Administration (Administration); **Law** (Law)
History: Founded 2002.
Main Language(s) of Instruction: Portuguese
Degrees and Diplomas: *Bacharelado*
Last Updated: 16/09/10

EVOLUTION FACULTY OF TECHNOLOGY

Faculdade de Tecnologia Evolução
R. Pedro I, 1276, Centro, Fortaleza, CE 60135-101
Tel: +55(85) 3308-1010 +55(85) 3308-1000
EMail: paulocavalcanti@evolucao.com.br
Website: http://www.faculdadeevolucao.edu.br/

Diretor Geral: Paulo Cavalcanti

Courses
Business Administration (Business Administration); **Computer Networks** (Computer Networks); **Graduate Studies** (Administration; Education; Health Sciences; Information Technology; Law); **Marketing** (Marketing); **Systems Analysis and Development** (Systems Analysis)
Degrees and Diplomas: *Tecnólogo*; *Especialização/Aperfeiçoamento*. Also MBA.
Last Updated: 24/08/10

EVOLUTIVE FACULTY

Faculdade Evolutivo (FACE)
Avenida Heráclito Graça 826, Centro, Fortazela, Ceará 60140061
Tel: +55(85) 226-8554
Fax: +55(85) 252-2832
EMail: face@evolutivo.com.br
Website: http://www.faceonline.com.br

Diretor: George da Justa Feijáo

Courses
Administration (Business Administration); **Social Communication**; **Tourism**
History: Founded 1999.
Main Language(s) of Instruction: Portuguese
Degrees and Diplomas: *Bacharelado*
Last Updated: 07/07/10

EXPERT FACULTY OF TECHNOLOGY

Faculdade Tecnológia Expert (FATEX)
Rua Pedro Ivo, 504, Centro, Curitiba, PR 80010-020
Tel: +55(41) 3022-5599
Fax: +55(41) 3022-5599
EMail: faculdade@expert.edu.br; giancarlo@expert.edu.br

Head: Giancarlo de Cristo Leite

Courses
Graduate Studies (Accountancy; Criminology; Finance; Public Administration); **Undergraduate Studies** (Finance; Information Technology; Management; Marketing)
Degrees and Diplomas: *Tecnólogo*. Also MBA.
Last Updated: 09/09/10

EXPOENTE FACULTY

Faculdade Expoente (UNIEXP)
Rua Carlos de Campos, 1090, Boa Vista, Curitiba, PR 82560-430
Tel: +55(41) 3312-4100
EMail: faculdadeexpoente@expoente.com.br
Website: http://www.faculdadeexpoente.edu.br/

Courses
Graduate Studies (Art Education; Computer Networks; Distance Education; Educational Administration; Educational Psychology; Educational Technology; Environmental Management; Health Administration; Higher Education; Humanities and Social Science Education; Information Technology; Management; Public Relations); **Undergraduate Studies** (Administration; Information Sciences; Marketing; Pedagogy)
History: Founded 2002 as Unidade de Ensino Superior Expoente (UniExp).
Degrees and Diplomas: *Bacharelado*; *Licenciatura*; *Especialização/Aperfeiçoamento*. Also MBA.
Last Updated: 29/09/10

EXPONENTIAL FACULTY

Faculdade Exponencial (FIE)
Avenida Nereu Ramos 3777-D, Térreo Seminário, Chapecó, Santa Catarina 89813000
Tel: +55(49) 3322-5882
Fax: +55(49) 3322-5882
EMail: faculdade@exponencial.br
Website: http://www.exponencial.br

Diretor Geral: Elio Antonio Maldaner

Courses
Accountancy; **Administration**; **Computer Science**; **Law** (Law)
History: Founded 2000.
Main Language(s) of Instruction: Portuguese
Degrees and Diplomas: *Bacharelado*; *Especialização/Aperfeiçoamento*
Last Updated: 07/07/10

FACCAT FACULTY

Faculdade FACCAT
Rua Cherentes 36 - Tèrreo e Superior, Tupa, SP 17600-090
Tel: +55(14) 3496 2620
EMail: faccat@faccat.com.br
Website: http://www.faccat.com.br/portal

Diretor: Celso Kawano

Courses
Accountancy (Accountancy); **Administration** (Administration); **Advertising** (Advertising and Publicity); **Architecture and Town Planning** (Architecture; Town Planning); **Computer Science** (Computer Science); **Economics** (Economics); **Information Systems** (Computer Science); **Pedagogy** (Pedagogy)

History: Founded 1970.

Main Language(s) of Instruction: Portuguese

Degrees and Diplomas: *Bacharelado*; *Licenciatura*; *Especialização/Aperfeiçoamento*

Libraries: Yes
Last Updated: 27/08/10

FACET FACULTIES
FACET Faculdades
Rua Marechal Floriano Peixoto 470, Centro, Curitibá,
Paraná 80010130
Tel: +55(41) 3223-6860
Fax: +55(41) 3223-6860
EMail: facet@facet.br
Website: http://www.facet.br
Diretora: Maria Eliza Reis

Courses
Graduate Studies *(Lato Sensu)*

Faculties
Sciences and Technology *(Paraná)*; **Social and Appplied Sciences** *(Paraná)* (Accountancy; Business Administration)

History: Founded 1998

Main Language(s) of Instruction: Portuguese

Degrees and Diplomas: *Bacharelado*; *Especialização/Aperfeiçoamento*. Also MBA.
Last Updated: 23/06/10

FACMIL FACULTY
Faculdade FACMIL
Rua Fritz Jacobs, 1134 - Boa Vista, São José do Rio Preto,
SP 15093-130
Tel: +55(17) 3216-2079
EMail: contato@facmil.com.br
Website: http://www.facmil.com.br
Diretor: Julio César Menegaz EMail: juliomenegaz@hotmail.com

Courses
Administration (Administration); **Law** (Law)

Main Language(s) of Instruction: Portuguese

Degrees and Diplomas: *Bacharelado*; *Especialização/Aperfeiçoamento*
Last Updated: 25/08/10

FACULTIES OF ATIBAIA
Faculdades Atibaia (FAAT)
Avenida Nove de Julho 298, Térreo, Centro, Atibaia,
São Paulo 12940580
Tel: +55(11) 4413-1671
EMail: faat@faat.edu.br
Website: http://www.faat.com.br
Diretor: Júlio César Ribeiro EMail: dirpres@faat.edu.br

Faculties
Applied Social Sciences (Accountancy; Administration; Advertising and Publicity; Journalism; Law; Public Relations); **Education** (Literature; Pedagogy; Teacher Training)

History: Founded 1971

Main Language(s) of Instruction: Portuguese

Degrees and Diplomas: *Bacharelado*; *Especialização/Aperfeiçoamento*
Last Updated: 30/06/10

FACULTIES OF CEARA
Faculdades Cearenses
Av. João Pessoa 3884. Damas, Fortaleza, CE 60450680
Tel: +55(85) 3201-7000
EMail: ouvidoria@faculdadescearenses.edu.br
Website: http://www.faculdadescearenses.edu.br
Diretor: José Luiz Torres Mota

Areas
Human and Social Sciences (Accountancy; Administration; Advertising and Publicity; Journalism; Law; Pedagogy; Social and Community Services; Tourism)

History: Founded 2002.

Main Language(s) of Instruction: Portuguese

Degrees and Diplomas: *Bacharelado*; *Especialização/Aperfeiçoamento*
Last Updated: 19/07/10

FACULTIES OF DISCOVERY
Faculdades do Descobrimento
Rua da Mata s/n, Santa Cruz Cabralia, BA 45807-000
Tel: +55(73) 3672-1641
EMail: facdesco@uol.com.br
Website: http://www.facdesco.edu.br
Diretor: Fernando Moura Neto.

Courses
Accountancy (Accountancy); **Administration** (Administration); **Computer Science** (Computer Science); **Tourism** (Tourism)

History: Founded 2002.

Main Language(s) of Instruction: Portuguese

Degrees and Diplomas: *Bacharelado*
Last Updated: 20/09/10

FACULTIES OF DRACENA
Faculdades de Dracena (UNIFADRA)
Avenida Alcides Chacon Couto 395, Metrópole, Dracena,
São Paulo 17900000
Tel: +55(18) 3821-9000
Fax: +55(18) 3821-9001
EMail: info@fundec.com.br
Website: http://fundec.edu.br/unifadra
Diretor: Wander Dorival Ramos (1998-)

Courses
Arts and Humanities; **Biological and Life Sciences**; **Computer Science**; **Education** (Art Education; Education; Pedagogy; Physical Education); **Mathematics**; **Nursing** (Nursing); **Psychology** (Psychology); **Social Services** (Social and Community Services)

History: Founded 1997.

Degrees and Diplomas: *Bacharelado*; *Licenciatura*; *Especialização/Aperfeiçoamento*
Last Updated: 29/06/10

FACULTIES OF FÁTIMA DO SUL
Faculdades de Fátima do Sul
Rua Antonio Barbosa n°1010, Jardim Universitário, Fátima do Sul,
MS 79700-000
Tel: +55(67) 3467-7100
Fax: +55(67) 3467-7100
Website: http://www.fafsnet.com
Diretor Geral: Paulo César Schotten
EMail: pcschotten@hotmail.com

Courses
Accountancy; **Administration**; **Graduate Studies**; **Literature** (English; Literature; Portuguese); **Nursing**; **Pedagogy**

History: Founded 1988.

Main Language(s) of Instruction: Portuguese

Degrees and Diplomas: *Bacharelado*; *Licenciatura*; *Especialização/Aperfeiçoamento*
Last Updated: 01/07/10

FACULTIES OF GUARAPUAVA
Faculdades Guarapuava
Rua Novo Ateneu 1015, Vale do Jordão, Guarapuava,
Paraná 85015-180
Tel: +55(42) 3621-7000
EMail: fg@almix.com.br
Website: http://www.faculdadesguarapuava.br
Diretor Geral: Jamil Abdanur Junior

Courses
Administration (Administration); **Environmental Studies**; **Law**;
Tourism
History: Founded 2000.
Main Language(s) of Instruction: Portuguese
Degrees and Diplomas: *Bacharelado; Especialização/Aperfeiçoamento*
Last Updated: 29/06/10

FACULTIES OF ITAPIRANGA
Faculdade de Itapiranga (SEI/FAI)
Rua Carlos Kummer, 100, Bairro Universitário, Itapiranga,
SC 89896-000
Tel: +55(49) 3678-8700
Fax: +55(49) 3677-0707
EMail: seifai@seifai.edu.br
Website: http://www.seifai.edu.br
Presidente: Tarcísio Kummer

Courses
Accountancy (Accountancy); **Administration** (Administration;
Human Resources; International Business; Marketing); **Agronomy**;
Food Technology (Food Technology); **Graduate Studies** (Business Administration; Civil Law; Crop Production; Development Studies; Education; Management; Public Administration); **Law**
(Law); **Mathematics** (Mathematics); **Pedagogy** (Pedagogy; Teacher Training); **Veterinary Science** (Veterinary Science)
History: Founded 2001.
Main Language(s) of Instruction: Portuguese
Degrees and Diplomas: *Tecnólogo; Bacharelado; Licenciatura;
Especialização/Aperfeiçoamento*
Libraries: Also MBA.
Last Updated: 09/07/10

FACULTIES OF OLIVEIRA
Faculdades de Oliveira
Rua Benjamim Guimarães, 35, Centro, Oliveira, MG 35540-000
Tel: +55(37) 3331-4075
EMail: feolfeol@yahoo.com.br
Website: http://www.feol.com.br
Diretor: Euler José Fonseca

Courses
Administration (Administration); **Information Systems** (Computer Science); **Law** (Law); **Letters** (Literature); **Pedagogy** (Pedagogy)
History: Founded 2000.
Main Language(s) of Instruction: Portuguese
Degrees and Diplomas: *Bacharelado; Licenciatura; Especialização/Aperfeiçoamento*
Libraries: Biblioteca José Aldo dos Santos
Last Updated: 29/09/10

FACULTIES OF PEDRO LEOPOLDO
Faculdades Pedro Leopoldo
Rua Teófilo Calazans de Barros 100 Santo Antônio da Barra,
Pedro Leopoldo, MG 33600000
Tel: +55(31) 33661-2111
Fax: +55(31) 3661-2686
EMail: secretaria@unipel.edu.br
Website: http://www.unipel.edu.br

Diretora Geral: Zélia de Cerqueira Barbosa (1996-)
EMail: zeliacerqueira@unipel.edu.br

Courses
Accountancy (Accountancy); **Administration** (Administration);
Computer Science; **History** (History); **Law** *(FADIPEL)* (Law);
Literature (Literature); **Mathematics** (Mathematics); **Teacher Training**; **Technology**
History: Founded 1975.
Main Language(s) of Instruction: Portuguese
Degrees and Diplomas: *Bacharelado; Especialização/Aperfeiçoamento; Mestrado*
Last Updated: 21/06/10

FACULTIES OF SANTOS DUMONT
Faculdades de Santos Dumont
Avenida Presidente Getúlio Vargas 547 Centro, Santos Dumont,
MG 36240000
Tel: +55(32) 3251-3817 +55(32) 3251-3752
Fax: +55(32) 3251-3817
EMail: fsd@cabangu.com.br
Website: http://www.fsd.edu.br
Presidente: Misael Geraldo Souza Camargo

Faculties
Administration *(FACIG)* (Accountancy; Administration; Business Administration; Computer Science; International Business); **Law**
(FCJSD); **Tourism** *(FACTURSD)*
Institutes
Teacher Training *(ISESD)*
History: Founded 1996.
Main Language(s) of Instruction: Portuguese
Degrees and Diplomas: *Bacharelado; Especialização/Aperfeiçoamento*
Last Updated: 29/06/10

FACULTIES OF TAQUARA
Faculdades de Taquara (FIT)
Avenida Oscar Martins Rangel 4500, 3° Piso Fogao Gaucho,
Taquara, RS 95600000
Tel: +55(51) 3541-6600
Fax: +55(51) 3541-6626
EMail: faccat@faccat.br
Website: http://www.faccat.br
Diretor: Delmar Henrique Backes

Courses
Accountancy; **Administration** (Administration); **Computer Science**
(Computer Science); **Engineering**; **History**; **Literature**; **Mathematics**
(Mathematics); **Pedagogy**; **Production Engineering**; **Psychology**
(Psychology); **Social Communication** (Advertising and Publicity;
Public Relations); **Tourism** (Tourism)
History: Founded 2001.
Main Language(s) of Instruction: Portuguese
Degrees and Diplomas: *Bacharelado; Licenciatura; Especialização/Aperfeiçoamento*
Last Updated: 29/06/10

FACULTIES OF TATUÍ
Faculdades de Tatuí
Rua Oracy Gomes 665, Térreo, Centro, Tatuí, São Paulo 18270000
Tel: +55(15) 3251-1573
Fax: +55(15) 3251-6777
EMail: asseta@asseta.com.br
Website: http://www2.asseta.com.br
Diretor: Acassil José de Oliveira Camargo (1998-)

Faculties
Industrial Design (Industrial Design); **Philosophy, Sciences and Letters** *(FAFICILE)* (Art Education; Arts and Humanities; Design; Educational Administration; Educational and Student Counselling; Fine Arts; Geography; History; Pedagogy; Philosophy; Social Sciences)

History: Founded 1971 as Faculdade de Filosofia, Ciências e Letras de Tatuí.

Main Language(s) of Instruction: Portuguese

Degrees and Diplomas: Licenciatura; Especialização/Aperfeiçoamento

Last Updated: 29/06/10

FACULTIES OF THE CENTRE OF PARANA
Faculdades do Centro do Paraná
Av. Universitária, s/n - Km 05 Linha Cantu - Campus Julio Podolan, Pitanga, PR 85200-000
Tel: +55(42) 3646-5555
EMail: administracao@ucppitanga.edu.br
Website: http://www.ucppitanga.edu.br

Courses
Accountancy (Ivaiporã) (Accountancy); **Administration** (Administration); **Administration** (Ivaiporã) (Administration); **Agricultural Business** (Agricultural Business); **Agricultural Business** (Ivaiporã) (Agricultural Business); **Biomedicine** (Ivaiporã) (Biomedicine); **Financial Management** (Ivaiporã) (Finance); **Information Systems** (Computer Science); **Law** (Law); **Letters** (Literature); **Marketing** (Ivaiporã) (Marketing); **Nursing** (Ivaiporã) (Nursing); **Physical Education** (Physical Education); **Physics** (Physics); **Social Services** (Social and Community Services)

History: Founded 2002.

Main Language(s) of Instruction: Portuguese

Degrees and Diplomas: Bacharelado; Licenciatura; Especialização/Aperfeiçoamento; Mestrado

Libraries: Biblioteca Professora Dirce Merlin Cleve
Last Updated: 05/08/10

FACULTIES OF THE PLATEAU
Faculdades Planalto (IESPLAN/FACPLAN)
Avenida W5 Sul-Eq 708/907 Conj. B, S/n Asa Sul, Brasília, DF 70390079
Tel: +55(61) 3443-2769
Fax: +55(61) 3443-2933
EMail: ceplanalto@tba.com.br
Website: http://www.iesplan.br

Diretor: Reinaldo Hermedo Poersch

Courses
Administration (Administration; Economics; Hotel Management; International Business; Marketing; Public Administration); **Architecture and Town Planning**; **Civil Engineering**; **Law** (Law); **Letters** (Arts and Humanities; Literature; Portuguese)

Institutes
Higher Education (Higher Education)

History: Founded 1999.

Main Language(s) of Instruction: Portuguese

Degrees and Diplomas: Bacharelado; Licenciatura
Last Updated: 21/06/10

FACULTIES OF THE PROFESSOR PAULO MARTINS SCHOOL
Faculdades Escola Superior Professor Paulo Martins (ESPAM)
Quadra 04 Área Reservada 01 - Região Administrativa V, Sobradinho, Brasilia, DF 73025-040
Tel: +55(61) 3487-7100
EMail: secretaria@espam.edu.br
Website: http://www.espam.edu.br

Diretor Administrativo: Duilio Reis Canedo

Faculties
Administration (Administration)

Higher Institutes
Education (ISPAM) (Education)

Higher Schools
Accountancy and Mathematics (Planaltina) (Accountancy; Mathematics)
Last Updated: 19/07/10

FACULTIES OF THE RIO GRANDE
Faculdades Rio-grandenses (FARGS)
Rua Tupi 200 Passo da Areia, Porto Alegre, Rio Grande do Sul 91030520
Tel: +55(51) 3341-2512
Fax: +55(51) 3341-2512
EMail: fargs@fargs.br; secretaria@fargs.br
Website: http://www.fargs.br

Diretor: Marcelo Mantelli (1994-)

Courses
Administration; **Hotel Management** (Hotel and Restaurant); **Law**; **Systems Analysis**; **Tourism** (Tourism)

History: Founded 1993

Main Language(s) of Instruction: Portuguese

Degrees and Diplomas: Bacharelado; Especialização/Aperfeiçoamento

Last Updated: 21/06/10

FACULTIES OF THE VALLEY OF CARANGOLA
Faculdades Vale do Carangola
Praça dos Estudantes, 23 - Santa Emilia, Carangola, MG 36800-000
Tel: +55(32) 3741-1969
EMail: sac@carangola.br
Website: http://www.carangola.br

Reitor: Dijon Moraes Junior

Courses
Administration (Administration); **Biology** (Biology); **Geography** (Geography); **History** (History); **Information Systems** (Computer Science); **Letters** (Literature); **Mathematics** (Mathematics); **Pedagogy** (Pedagogy); **Social Services** (Social and Community Services); **Tourism** (Tourism)

History: Founded 1970 as Faculdade de Filosofia, Clências e Letras de Carangola. Acquired present title 2007.

Main Language(s) of Instruction: Portuguese

Degrees and Diplomas: Bacharelado; Licenciatura; Especialização/Aperfeiçoamento

Libraries: Yes
Last Updated: 27/09/10

FACULTY CENTRE OF THE STATE OF SAO PAULO
Faculdade Centro Paulista
Av Prefeito Alberto Alves Casemiro, 1.747 - Jd Ternura, Ibitinga, SP 14940-000
Tel: +55(16) 3341-5800
EMail: facep@facep.edu.br
Website: http://www.facep.edu.br

Diretor: Akiro Chinen

Courses
Administration (Administration); **Letters** (Literature); **Pedagogy** (Pedagogy)

Degrees and Diplomas: Bacharelado; Licenciatura; Especialização/Aperfeiçoamento
Last Updated: 20/07/10

FACULTY CENTRE OF MATO GROSSO
Faculdade Centro Mato-Grossense
Rua Rui Barbosa 380, Sorisso, MT 78890-000
Tel: +55(66)3544-4932
EMail: facem@facem.com.br
Website: http://www.facem.com.br: 4,028/facemSite/

Diretora: Jurassa Cristina Mayer Ceron
EMail: ju.ceron@yahoo.com.br

Courses

Agronomy (Agronomy); **Physical Education** (Physical Education)

Main Language(s) of Instruction: Portuguese

Degrees and Diplomas: *Bacharelado*
Last Updated: 20/07/10

FACULTY CENTRE OF SAO PAULO

Faculdade Centro Paulistano
Rua Álves Penteado N°: 208/216 Largo do Café, São Paulo,
SP 01012-905
Tel: +55(11) 2173.4700
EMail: ckto@terra.com.b

Diretor: José Fernando Pinto da Costa
EMail: fernando.costa@uniesp.edu.br

Courses

Accountancy (Accountancy); **Administration** (Administration); **Letters** (Literature); **Pedagogy** (Pedagogy); **Social Communication** (Advertising and Publicity)

Main Language(s) of Instruction: Portuguese

Degrees and Diplomas: *Bacharelado*; *Licenciatura*
Last Updated: 20/07/10

FACULTY FOR THE DEVELOPMENT OF PERNAMBUCO

Faculdade para o Desenvolvimento de Pernambuco
Rua Dr. José Maria n° 1106, Recife, PE 52.041-000
Tel: +55(81) 3265-5020
EMail: fadepe@fadepe.com.br
Website: http://www.fadepe.com.br

Diretor: Aluízio Bezerra de Albuquerque Filho
EMail: aluiziof@terra.com.br

Courses

Administration (Administration)

History: Founded 2002.

Main Language(s) of Instruction: Portuguese

Degrees and Diplomas: *Bacharelado*. Also pos-graduação

Libraries: Yes
Last Updated: 09/09/10

FACULTY FOR THE DEVELOPMENT OF THE SOUTH EAST OF THE STATE OF TOCANTINS

Faculdade para o Desenvolvimento do Sudeste Tocantinense
Praça Aurélio Antonio Araújo n° 2, Centro, Dianópolis-,
TO 77.300–000
Tel: +55(63) 3692-1949
EMail: fades@fades.com.br
Website: http://www.fades.com.br

Diretora: Grazziella Povoa Costa Rodrigues

Courses

Accountancy (Accountancy); **Administration** (Administration)

History: Founded 2005.

Main Language(s) of Instruction: Portuguese

Degrees and Diplomas: *Bacharelado*; *Especialização/Aperfeiçoamento*
Last Updated: 09/09/10

FACULTY FOR THE DEVELOPMENT OF THE STATE AND OF THE PANTANAL OF MATO GROSSO

Faculdade para o Desenvolvimento do Estado e do Pantanal Mato-Grossense
Avenida Beira Rio 3045, Cuiaba, MT 78065-780
Tel: +55(65) 3316-4026
EMail: adonias@unirondon.br
Website: http://www.unipanmt.com.br

Diretor: Adonias Gomes de Almeida

Courses

Administration (Administration); **Law** (Law)

History: Founded 2004.

Main Language(s) of Instruction: Portuguese

Degrees and Diplomas: *Bacharelado*
Last Updated: 09/09/10

FACULTY FOR THE INTEGRATION OF HIGHER EDUCATION OF THE SOUTHERN CONE

Faculdade de Integração do Ensino Superior do Cone Sul
Av. Presidente Vargas, 561 - Centro, Garibaldi, RS 95720-000
Tel: +55(54) 3462-8300
EMail: fisul@fisul.edu.br
Website: http://www.fisul.edu.br

Diretora: Marlene Helena Nichel EMail: marlene@fisul.edu.br

Courses

Accountancy (Accountancy); **Administration** (Administration); **Commercial Management** (Business and Commerce; Management); **Human Resource Management** (Human Resources; Management); **Social Services** (Social and Community Services); **Tourism Management** (Management; Tourism)

History: Founded 2004.

Main Language(s) of Instruction: Portuguese

Degrees and Diplomas: *Bacharelado*; *Especialização/Aperfeiçoamento*

Libraries: Biblioteca Giuseppe Garibaldi
Last Updated: 06/08/10

FACULTY FOR THE INTEGRATION OF THE SERTÃO

Faculdade de Integração do Sertão
Rua Comandante Superior 841, Serra Talhada, PE
Tel: +55(87) 3831-1472
EMail: penha.oliveira@serratalhada.net
Website: http://www.fis.edu.br

Diretora: Maria da Penha Oliveira Bezzera

Courses

Accountancy (Accountancy); **Business Administration** (Business Administration); **Law** (Law); **Nursing** (Nursing)

History: Founded 2006.

Main Language(s) of Instruction: Portuguese

Degrees and Diplomas: *Bacharelado*
Last Updated: 06/08/10

FACULTY OF ACCOUNTANCY AND ADMINISTRATION OF AVARE

Faculdade de Ciências Contábeis e Administrativas de Avaré (FACCAA)
Praça Padre Tavares, 46, Avaré, São Paulo 18700140
Tel: +55(14) 3732-0981
EMail: faccaa@faccaa.br
Website: http://www.faccaa.br

Diretor Presidente: Mauro Guilherme de Almeida Righi

Courses

Accountancy (Accountancy); **Administration** (Administration)

History: Founded 1975

Main Language(s) of Instruction: Portuguese

Degrees and Diplomas: *Bacharelado*; *Especialização/Aperfeiçoamento*
Last Updated: 04/10/07

FACULTY OF ACCOUNTANCY AND ADMINISTRATION OF CACHOEIRO DE ITAPEMIRIM

Faculdade de Ciências Contábeis e Administrativas de Cachoeiro de Itapemirim (FACCACI)
Rod. Cachoeiro X Alegre km 8, ES 482, Morro Grande, Cachoeiro de Itapemirim, ES 29312220
Tel: +55(28) 3511-8955
EMail: faccaci@uol.com.br
Website: http://www.faccaci.edu.br/

Diretor: Mário Pires Martins Filho

Courses
Accountancy; Administration; Graduate Studies (Business Administration)

History: Founded 1970

Degrees and Diplomas: *Bacharelado*. Also MBA.
Last Updated: 02/07/10

FACULTY OF ACCOUNTANCY AND ADMINISTRATION OF THE JURUENA VALLEY

Faculdade de Ciências Contábeis e de Administração do Vale do Juruena (AJES)
Avenida Gabriel Müller, s/n, AJES - Faculdades do Vale do Juruena, Módulo I, Juína, MT 78320-000
Tel: +55(66) 3566-1875
EMail: clodis@ajes.edu.br; secretaria@ajes.edu.br
Website: http://www.ajes.edu.br

Reitor: Clodis Antonio Menegaz.

Courses
Accountancy (Accountancy); Administration; Geography (Geography); Law (Law); Letters (Literature); Mathematics (Mathematics); Nursing (Nursing); Pedagogy (Pedagogy); Psychology (Psychology); Social Communication (Communication Studies); Theology (Theology)

History: Founded 2005.

Main Language(s) of Instruction: Portuguese

Degrees and Diplomas: *Bacharelado*; *Especialização/Aperfeiçoamento*
Last Updated: 20/07/10

FACULTY OF ACCOUNTANCY OF AFONSO CLAÚDIO

Faculdade de Ciências Contábeis de Afonso Claúdio
Rua Ute Gastin de Padua 49, Afonso Claúdio, ES 29600-000
Tel: +55(27) 3735-2411
Fax: +55(27) 3735-2433
EMail: robertoadministra@gmail.com

Diretor: Roberto Alexandre Alcantara

Courses
Accountancy (Accountancy)
History: Founded 2000.
Main Language(s) of Instruction: Portuguese
Degrees and Diplomas: *Bacharelado*
Last Updated: 04/12/07

FACULTY OF ACCOUNTANCY OF PONTE NOVA

Faculdade de Ciências Contábeis de Ponte Nova (FACCO)
Rua dos Vereadores 177, Sumaré, Ponte Nova, Minas Gerais 35430039
Tel: +55(31) 3817-2580 +55(31) 3817-2494
Fax: +55(31) 3817-2580
EMail: facco@pontenet.com.br
Website: http://facco.neuronium.com.br

Diretor Acadêmico: José Geraldo da Silva

Courses
Accountancy (Accountancy)
History: Founded 1978
Main Language(s) of Instruction: Portuguese
Degrees and Diplomas: *Bacharelado*
Last Updated: 02/07/10

FACULTY OF ACCOUNTANCY OF RECIFE

Faculdade de Ciências Contábeis de Recife (FACCOR)
Avenida Ministro Marcos Freire 2855, Olinda, Pernambuco 53130-540
Tel: +55(81) 3495-0504
EMail: marcioacbarros@yahoo.com.br
Website: http://www.fape-pe.edu.br/FAPEIV/index.asp

Diretor: Newton Roberto Gregorio de Moraes
EMail: newton_moraes@uol.com.br

Courses
Accountancy
History: Founded 1992.
Main Language(s) of Instruction: Portuguese
Degrees and Diplomas: *Bacharelado*
Last Updated: 02/07/10

FACULTY OF ACCOUNTANCY OF VITORIA

Faculdade Vitoriana de Ciências Contábeis (FVCC)
Avenida Nossa Senhora da Penha 1800, Barro Vermelho, Vitória, Espirito Santo 29045400
Tel: +55(27) 325-0244 +55(27) 325-0229
Fax: +55(27) 324-1500
EMail: favi@favi.com.br
Website: http://www.favi.br

Diretor: Rodrigo Cambará Arantes Garcia de Paiva

Courses
Accountancy (Accountancy)
History: Founded 1990.
Main Language(s) of Instruction: Portuguese
Degrees and Diplomas: *Bacharelado*
Last Updated: 30/06/10

FACULTY OF ACRE

Faculdade do Acre
Br 364 Km 02 N°200, Alameda Hungria, Jardim Europa II, Rio Branco, AC 69911-900
Tel: +55(68) 3213-7070
EMail: marco.brandao@uninorteac.com.br

Diretor: Rodrigo Calvo Galindo

Courses
Biology (Biology); History (History); Letters (Literature); Social Communication (Advertising and Publicity); Social Services (Social and Community Services)

History: Founded 2002.
Main Language(s) of Instruction: Portuguese
Degrees and Diplomas: *Bacharelado*
Last Updated: 20/09/10

FACULTY OF ADMINISTRATION - ITPAC

Faculdade de Administração - ITPAC
Avenida Filadélfia, 568 - Setor Oeste, Araguaína, TO
Tel: +55(63) 3411- 8500
EMail: itpac@itpac.br
Website: http://www.itpac.br

Diretor: Bonifácio José Tamm de Andrada

Courses
Accountancy (Accountancy); Administration (Administration); Dentistry (Dentistry); Information Management (Information Management); Law (Law); Medicine (Medicine); Nursing (Nursing); Pedagogy (Pedagogy); Pharmacy (Pharmacy); Physical Education (Physical Education)

History: Founded 1998.

Main Language(s) of Instruction: Portuguese

Degrees and Diplomas: *Bacharelado*; *Licenciatura*; *Especialização/Aperfeiçoamento*; *Mestrado*
Last Updated: 26/07/10

FACULTY OF ADMINISTRATION AND ACCOUNTANCY OF SÃO ROQUE

Faculdade de Administração e Ciências Contábeis de São Roque (FACSÃO ROQUE)
Rua Sotero de Souza, 104, Centro, São Roque,
São Paulo 18130-200
Tel: +55(11) 4719-9300
Fax: +55(11) 4719-9302
EMail: fac@facsaoroque.br
Website: http://www.facsaoroque.br

Diretor: Eduardo Storópoli (1996-)

Courses

Accountancy; Administration; Human Resources (Human Resources); Information Technology; Law; Pedagogy

History: Founded 1995.

Main Language(s) of Instruction: Portuguese

Degrees and Diplomas: *Tecnólogo*; *Bacharelado*; *Licenciatura*. Also Postgraduate diplomas offered through Universidad Nove de Julho (UNINOVE).
Last Updated: 01/07/10

FACULTY OF ADMINISTRATION AND ARTS OF LIMEIRA

Faculdade de Administração e Artes de Limeira (FAAL)
Av. Eng Antônio Eugênio Lucatto, 2515, Limeira,
São Paulo 13485-905
Tel: +55(19) 3444-3240
Fax: +55(19) 3444-3239
EMail: secretaria@faal.com.br
Website: http://www.faal.com.br

Diretor Geral: Sebastião Orlando da Silva
EMail: orlando@faal.com.brorlando@faal.com.br

Courses

Administration; Graduate Studies (Advertising and Publicity; Design; Environmental Management; Higher Education; Human Resources; Landscape Architecture; Marketing; Mathematics); Graphic Design; Mathematics (Mathematics); Product Design (Industrial Design); Technological Studies; Visual Arts (Visual Arts)

History: Founded 2001.

Main Language(s) of Instruction: Portuguese

Degrees and Diplomas: *Tecnólogo*; *Bacharelado*; *Licenciatura*; *Especialização/Aperfeiçoamento*
Last Updated: 01/07/10

FACULTY OF ADMINISTRATION AND COMMERCE IN RIBEIRÃO PRETO

Faculdade de Administração e Negócios em Ribeirão Preto
Avenida Presidente Kennedy, 1693, Ribeirânia, Ribeirão Preto,
SP 14096-340
Tel: +55(16) 2138-1868
EMail: diretoria@reges.com.br
Website: http://www.ribeiraopreto.cesd.br/

Diretor: Ângelo Alberto Colucci Filho

Courses

Administration; Graduate Studies (Accountancy; Business Administration; Finance; Health Administration; Human Resources; Marketing; Public Relations; Small Business)

Degrees and Diplomas: *Bacharelado*. Also MBA.
Last Updated: 19/07/10

FACULTY OF ADMINISTRATION AND COMMERCE OF SERGIPE

Faculdade de Administração e Negócios de Sergipe (FANESE)
Avenida Delmiro Gouveia, 3701, Shopping Riomar - 2° Piso,
Aracaju, Sergipe 49035-800
Tel: +55(79) 3234-6350
EMail: fanese@infonet.com.br
Website: http://www.fanese.com.br

Diretor Geral: Ionaldo Vieira Carvalho
EMail: ionaldo@fanese.edu.br

Courses

Administration (Administration); Computer Science; Graduate Studies; Law; Production Engineering (Production Engineering); Technological Studies

History: Founded 1997

Main Language(s) of Instruction: Portuguese

Degrees and Diplomas: *Bacharelado*; *Especialização/Aperfeiçoamento*. Also MBA.
Last Updated: 01/07/10

FACULTY OF ADMINISTRATION AND COMPUTER SCIENCE

Faculdade de Administração e Informática (FAI)
Avenida Antônio de Cássia, 472, Jardim Santo Antônio,
Santa Rita do Sapucai, Minas Gerais 37540-000
Tel: +55(35)3473-3000
EMail: fai@fai-mg.br
Website: http://www.fai-mg.br

Diretor: Aldo Ambrósio Morelli (1995-) EMail: aldo@fai-mg.br

Courses

Administration (Administration); Graduate Studies; Information Systems (Information Technology); Pedagogy (Pedagogy)

History: Founded 1971.

Main Language(s) of Instruction: Portuguese

Degrees and Diplomas: *Bacharelado*; *Licenciatura*; *Especialização/Aperfeiçoamento*
Last Updated: 01/07/10

FACULTY OF ADMINISTRATION AND EDUCATION OF VITORIA

Faculdade Capixaba de Administração e Educação (UNICES)
Avenida Vitória 800, Vitória, Espirito Santo 29050141
Tel: +55(27) 3223-9100
EMail: diretoria@unices.com.br
Website: http://www.unices.com.br

Diretor: Luiz Guilherme Gazzinelli Cruz

Courses

Administration (Administration); Pedagogy

History: Founded 2001.

Main Language(s) of Instruction: Portuguese

Degrees and Diplomas: *Bacharelado*; *Licenciatura*
Last Updated: 29/06/10

FACULTY OF ADMINISTRATION AND TECHNOLOGY

Faculdade de Ciências Administrativas e de Tecnologia (FATEC-RO)
Avenida Governador Jorge Teixera, 3500, Setor Industrial,
Porto Velho, Rondônia 78906100
Tel: +55(69) 3217-9314
EMail: diretoria@fatec-ro.br
Website: http://www.fatec-ro.br

Diretor: Marco Antônio de Faria

Courses

Accountancy (Accountancy); Administration (Administration; Business Administration; Health Administration); Graduate Studies

(Accountancy; Business Education; Educational Psychology; Higher Education); **Information Systems** (Information Technology); **Pedagogy** (Educational Administration; Educational and Student Counselling; Pedagogy); **Systems for Internet** (Computer Science)

History: Founded 1994.

Main Language(s) of Instruction: Portuguese

Degrees and Diplomas: *Tecnólogo*; *Bacharelado*; *Especialização/ Aperfeiçoamento*

Last Updated: 10/10/07

FACULTY OF ADMINISTRATION OF ALAGOANA - HIGHER EDUCATION INSTITUTE OF ALAGOANA

Faculdade Alagoana de Administração - Instituto de Ensino Superior de Alagoas (FAA-IESA)
UNIDADE I - Av. Eng. Paulo Brandão Nogueira, 160, Loteamento Stela Maris, Jatiúca, Maceió, Alagoas 57036550
Tel: +55(82) 304-5200
Fax: +55(82) 304-5208
EMail: faa.al@uol.com.br
Website: http://www.aesa.edu.br

Diretora Geral: Conceição Gomes de Oliveira

Courses
Accountancy (Accountancy); **Administration** (Administration; Business Administration; Hotel Management; Human Resources; International Business; Marketing); **Advertising and Publicity**; **Computer Science**; **Law** (Law); **Physiotherapy** (Physical Therapy); **Technological Studies**; **Tourism** (Tourism)

Further Information: Also Farol Unit.

History: Founded 1994.

Main Language(s) of Instruction: Portuguese

Degrees and Diplomas: *Tecnólogo*; *Bacharelado*: 4 yrs
Last Updated: 23/06/10

FACULTY OF ADMINISTRATION OF CAMPINA VERDE

Faculdade de Administração de Campina Verde
Avenida Onze N°: 566 Centro, Campina Verde, MG 38270-000
Tel: +55(34) 3412-4319
EMail: menegaz@unirp.edu.br

Diretor: Julio César Menegaz de Almeida

Courses
Administration (Administration)
History: Founded 2004.

Main Language(s) of Instruction: Portuguese

Degrees and Diplomas: *Bacharelado*
Last Updated: 26/07/10

FACULTY OF ADMINISTRATION OF CAMPO BELO

Faculdade de Administração de Campo Belo
Rua Projetada, s/n°, Arnaldos, Campo Belo, MG 37270-000
Tel: +55(35) 3832-7855
EMail: cemes@stratus.com.br

Diretora: Ana Maria Almeida

Courses
Administration (Administration; Business Administration)
History: Founded 2001.

Main Language(s) of Instruction: Portuguese

Degrees and Diplomas: *Bacharelado*
Last Updated: 27/07/10

FACULTY OF ADMINISTRATION OF CURVELO

Faculdade de Ciências Administrativas de Curvelo (FACIAC)
Rua João Pessoa 88, 2° Andar, Centro, Curvelo, Minas Gerais 35790000
Tel: +55(38) 3721-3945
Fax: +55(38) 3721-3945
EMail: fac@rznet.com.br
Website: http://www.fac.br

Diretor: Marcus Vinícius Guimarães de Freitas (1996-)
EMail: diretoria@fac.br

Courses
Administration (Administration); **Commerce and Investment** *(Postgraduate - Lato Sensu)* (Business and Commerce)

History: Founded 1997.

Main Language(s) of Instruction: Portuguese

Degrees and Diplomas: *Bacharelado*: 4 yrs; *Especialização/ Aperfeiçoamento*
Last Updated: 02/07/10

FACULTY OF ADMINISTRATION OF MARIANA

Faculdade de Administração de Mariana
Rua Dom Silvério N° 161, Mariana 35420-000
Tel: +55(31) 3558 - 2673
EMail: femar@uai.com.br

Diretor: José Jarbas Ramos Filho.

Courses
Administration (Administration; Business Administration)
History: Founded 2004.

Main Language(s) of Instruction: Portuguese

Degrees and Diplomas: *Bacharelado*
Last Updated: 20/08/10

FACULTY OF ADMINISTRATION OF MINAS GERAIS

Faculdade de Estudos Administrativos de Minas Gerais (FEAD-MINAS)
Rua Cláudio Manoel, 1162, Savassi, Belo Horizonte, Minas Gerais 30140-100
Fax: +55(31) 4009-0900
EMail: fead@fead.br
Website: http://www.fead.br

Diretor Geral: José Roberto Franco Tavares Paes (1998-)

Courses
Accountancy *(EAD)* (Accountancy); **Administration** *(EAD)* (Administration); **Administration** (Business Administration); **Agronomy** (Agronomy); **Economics** (Economics); **Graduate Studies** *(Stricto Sensu)* (Administration; Business Administration; Economics); **Graduate Studies** *(Lato Sensu)*; **Law**; **Odontology** (Dentistry); **Phonoaudiology**; **Psychology**; **Tourism** (Tourism); **Veterinary Medicine** (Veterinary Science); **Zootechnics** (Animal Husbandry)

Further Information: Also five other units (Pós-graduação; Centro de Biotecnologia, Hospital Veterinário, Núcleo de Educação a Distância; Centro FEAD de Fonoaudiologia; Fazenda Experimental FEAD; Saúde - Odontologia e Psicologia - Núcleo de Assistência Judiciária); Distance Education Centers in Belo Horizonte, Rio de Janeiro, Goiâni, Vitória, Aracajú and São Paulo.

History: Founded 1998 as Faculdade de Administração de Empresas. Acquired present title 1999.

Degrees and Diplomas: *Bacharelado*; *Especialização/Aperfeiçoamento*; *Mestrado*. Also MBA.
Last Updated: 08/07/10

FACULTY OF ADMINISTRATION OF SANTA CRUZ DO RIO PARDO

Faculdade de Administração de Santa Cruz do Rio Pardo (FASC)
Avenida Coronel Clementino Gonçalves 1561, São Judas Tadeu, Santa Cruz do Rio Pardo, São Paulo 18900000
Tel: +55(14) 3372-1173
Fax: +55(14) 3372-4073
EMail: fafil.oapec@argon.com.br
Website: http://www.oapec.com.br/faculdade/administracao.htm
Diretora: Adelia de Paula Pimentel

Courses
Business Administration; **Literature**; **Pedagogy** (Pedagogy)
History: Founded 2000.
Main Language(s) of Instruction: Portuguese
Degrees and Diplomas: *Bacharelado*; *Licenciatura*. Also Postgraduate diplomas.
Last Updated: 01/07/10

FACULTY OF ADMINISTRATION OF SANTO ANTÔNIO DO MONTE

Faculdade de Administração de Santo Antônio do Monte
Rua Aristides Cabral 123, Santo Antônio do Monte, MG 35560-000
Tel: +55(37) 3281-1402
EMail: samec@isimples.com.br
Diretora: Margarete de Lourdes Resende

Courses
Administration (Administration)
History: Founded 2005.
Main Language(s) of Instruction: Portuguese
Degrees and Diplomas: *Bacharelado*
Last Updated: 01/09/10

FACULTY OF ADMINISTRATION OF THE CITY OF GOVERNADOR VALADARES

Faculdade de Administração de Governador Valadares (FAGV)
Rua José de Tassis 350, Vila Bretas, Governador Valadares, Minas Gerais 35030-250
Tel: +55(33) 3212-6777
EMail: faleconosco@fagv.com.br
Website: http://www.fagv.com.br
Diretor: Gervald De Aguiar Trindade

Courses
Administration (Administration)
History: Founded 1975.
Main Language(s) of Instruction: Portuguese
Degrees and Diplomas: *Especialização/Aperfeiçoamento*
Last Updated: 26/03/12

FACULTY OF ADMINISTRATION, SCIENCE, EDUCATION AND LETTERS

Faculdade de Administração, Ciêncas, Educação e Letras (FACEL)
Avenida Vicente Machado, 156, Centro, Curitibá, Paraná 80420010
Tel: +55(41) 3324-1115
Fax: +55(41) 3324-1115
EMail: facel@facel.com.br
Website: http://www.facel.com.br
Diretor: Wagner Tadeu dos Santos Gaby

Courses
Accountancy; **Administration**; **Distance Postgraduate Studies** (Accountancy; Administration; Literature; Pedagogy; Philosophy; Psychology; Theology); **English Literature** (English; Literature); **Graduate Studies** (Accountancy; Administration; Literature; Pedagogy; Psychology); **Pedagogy** (Pedagogy); **Philosophy** (Philosophy); **Psychology**; **Spanish Literature**; **Technological Studies**

(Human Resources; Marketing; Secretarial Studies; Transport Management); **Theology** (Theology)
History: Founded 1999
Main Language(s) of Instruction: Portuguese
Degrees and Diplomas: *Tecnólogo*; *Bacharelado*; *Licenciatura*; *Especialização/Aperfeiçoamento*. Also MBA.
Last Updated: 01/07/10

FACULTY OF ADVANCED STUDIES OF MINAS GERAIS - FEAD

Faculdade de Estudos Superiores de Minas Gerais - FEAD
Rua Cláudio Manoel 1162, Belo Horizonte, MG 30140-100
Tel: +55(31) 4009-0900
EMail: fead@fead.br
Website: http://www.fead.br
Diretor: José Roberto Franco Tavares Paes

Courses
Accountancy (Accountancy); **Administration** (Administration); **Agronomy** (Agricultural Engineering; Agronomy); **Dentistry** (Dentistry); **Economics** (Economics); **Law** (Law); **Psychology** (Psychology); **Speech Therapy** (Speech Therapy and Audiology); **Tourism** (Tourism); **Veterinary Science** (Veterinary Science); **Zoology** (Zoology)
History: Founded 2001.
Main Language(s) of Instruction: Portuguese
Degrees and Diplomas: *Bacharelado*; *Especialização/Aperfeiçoamento*; *Mestrado*
Libraries: Yes
Last Updated: 05/08/10

FACULTY OF ADVANCED STUDIES OF PARA

Faculdade de Estudos Avançados do Pará
Av. Augusto Montenegro Km 04 N°4120 Parque Verde, Belém, PA 66.635-110
Tel: +55(91) 3202-8000
EMail: socorro@feapa.com.br
Website: http://www.feapa.com.br
Diretora: Maria do Socorro Costa Do Nascimento

Courses
Accountancy (Accountancy); **Administration** (Administration); **Advertising** (Advertising and Publicity); **Graphic Design** (Graphic Design); **Information Systems** (Computer Science); **Journalism** (Journalism); **Tourism** (Tourism)
History: Founded 2000.
Main Language(s) of Instruction: Portuguese
Degrees and Diplomas: *Bacharelado*; *Especialização/Aperfeiçoamento*
Libraries: Yes
Last Updated: 05/08/10

FACULTY OF AGRIBUSINESS OF PARAÍSO DO NORTE

Faculdade de Agronegócio Paraíso do Norte (FAPAN)
Rua Olavo Bilac 78, Centro, Paraíso do Norte, PR 87780-000
Tel: +55(44) 3431-2211 +55(44) 3431-1212
EMail: sara@fapanpr.edu.br
Website: http://www.fapanpr.edu.br/
Diretor Geral: Marco Aurelio Claudiano da Silva
EMail: marco@fapanpr.edu.br

Courses
Accountancy (Accountancy); **Administration** (Administration); **Graduate Studies** (Accountancy; Administration; Education)
Degrees and Diplomas: *Bacharelado*. Also Postgraduate diploma.
Last Updated: 19/07/10

FACULTY OF AGRICULTURAL AND ENVIRONMENTAL SCIENCES

Faculdade de Ciências Agro-Ambientais (FAGRAM)
Avenida Brasil 9727, Olaria, Rio de Janeiro,
Rio de Janeiro 21030000
Tel: +55(21) 3866-8090 +55(21) 2561-8684
EMail: fagram@fagram.edu.br
Website: http://www.fagram.edu.br/

Diretor Geral: Octavio Junqueira Mello Alvarenga

Courses
Zootechnics (Agriculture; Animal Husbandry)

History: Founded 1994.

Main Language(s) of Instruction: Portuguese

Degrees and Diplomas: *Bacharelado*
Last Updated: 02/07/10

FACULTY OF AGRICULTURAL ENGINEERING OF PIRASSUNUNGA

Faculdade de Engenharia de Agrimensura de Pirassununga (FEAP)
Avenida dos Acadêmicos 1, Posto de Monta, Pirassununga,
São Paulo 13630000
Tel: +55(19) 3561-3845
Fax: +55(19) 3562-8822
EMail: feap@feap.com.br
Website: http://www.feap.com.br

Diretor Geral: Antônio Moacir Rodrigues Nogueira (1997-)

Courses
Agrimensure Engineering (Agricultural Engineering; Engineering; Surveying and Mapping)

History: Founded 1972

Main Language(s) of Instruction: Portuguese

Degrees and Diplomas: *Bacharelado*; *Especialização/Aperfeiçoamento*
Last Updated: 26/03/12

FACULTY OF AGRONOMY AND FORESTRY ENGINEERING OF GARÇA

Faculdade de Agronomia e Engenharia Florestal de Garça (FAEF)
Rua das Flores 740, Labienópolis, Garça, São Paulo 17400-000
Tel: +55(14) 3407-8000
EMail: faef@faef.br
Website: http://www.faef.br

Presidente: Wilson Shimizu

Courses
Accountancy (Accountancy); **Administration** (Business Administration); **Agronomy** (Agronomy); **Computer Science** (Computer Science); **Forestry Engineering**; **Law**; **Pedagogy**; **Psychology** (Psychology); **Tourism**; **Veterinary Science**

History: Founded 1989

Main Language(s) of Instruction: Portuguese

Degrees and Diplomas: *Bacharelado*; *Especialização/Aperfeiçoamento*; *Mestrado*
Last Updated: 10/10/07

FACULTY OF ÁGUAS EMENDADAS

Faculdade das Águas Emendadas
Av. Independência - Bloco C- Salas 12/13 - Edifício Plaza Shopping - Planaltina, Brasilia, DF 73320-000
Tel: +55(61) 3489-0582
EMail: jupasaeducacionais@uol.com.br
Website: http://www.faedf.edu.br

Diretor: Rubem José Boff

Courses
Administration (Administration); **Letters** (Literature); **Mathematics** (Mathematics)

History: Founded 2006.

Main Language(s) of Instruction: Portuguese
Degrees and Diplomas: *Bacharelado*; *Licenciatura*
Libraries: Yes
Last Updated: 26/07/10

FACULTY OF AGUDOS

Faculdade de Agudos (FAAG)
Avenida Celso Morato Leite 1200, Caixa Postal 40, Agudos,
SP 17120-000
Tel: +55(14) 3262-9400
Fax: +55(14) 3262-9401
EMail: faag@faag.com.br
Website: http://www.faag.com.br

Diretora: Lúcia Helena Aravechia de Oliveira

Courses
Administration; **Graduate Studies** (Business Administration; Education; Educational Administration; Environmental Management; Finance; Industrial Management; Management; Special Education); **Pedagogy** (Pedagogy); **Production Engineering** (Production Engineering); **Tourism**

Degrees and Diplomas: *Bacharelado*; *Licenciatura*; *Especialização/Aperfeiçoamento*. Also MBA.
Last Updated: 19/07/10

FACULTY OF ALAGOAS

Faculdade de Alagoas (FAL)
Rua Pio XII 70, Jatiúca, Maceió, Alagoas 57035-560
Tel: +55(82) 3214-6800
Fax: +55(82) 2123-2059
EMail: fal@fal.br
Website: http://www.fal.br

Diretora: Edriene Teixeira da Silva **EMail:** edriene@fal.br

Courses
Administration (Administration); **Information Systems** (Information Technology); **Law** (Law); **Nursing** (Nursing); **Physical Education** (Physical Education); **Physiotherapy** (Physical Therapy); **Technological Studies** (Computer Networks; Environmental Management; Finance; International Business; Marketing; Public Administration; Secretarial Studies); **Tourism** (Tourism); **Trilingual Secretarial Studies** (Modern Languages; Secretarial Studies)

History: Founded 1999.

Main Language(s) of Instruction: Portuguese

Degrees and Diplomas: *Tecnólogo*; *Bacharelado*; *Licenciatura*; *Especialização/Aperfeiçoamento*
Last Updated: 01/07/10

FACULTY OF ALMENARA

Faculdade de Almenara (ALFA)
Rua Vereador Virgílio Mendes Lima, 847, São Pedro, Almenara,
MG 39900-000
Tel: +55(33) 3721-1098
Fax: +55(33) 3721-1098
EMail: alfa.caldeira@yahoo.com.br
Website: http://www.faculdadealfa.com.br/

Diretor: Mauricio Almeida Caldeira Mourão

Courses
Nursing (Nursing)

Degrees and Diplomas: *Bacharelado*
Last Updated: 19/07/10

FACULTY OF AMAMBAI

Faculdade de Amambai
Rua Pe. Anchieta, 100, Vila Copacabana, Amambai, MS 79990000
Tel: +55(67) 3481-1355
Fax: +55(67) 3481-1355
EMail: atendimento@fiama.edu.br
Website: http://www.fiama.edu.br/

Diretor geral: Sérgio Périus

Courses

Accountancy; **Administration**; **Graduate Studies**; **Pedagogy** (Pedagogy)

History: Founded 1998

Main Language(s) of Instruction: Portuguese

Degrees and Diplomas: *Bacharelado*; *Licenciatura*; *Especialização/Aperfeiçoamento*
Last Updated: 01/07/10

FACULTY OF AMERICAN INTERACTION
Faculdade Interação Americana (FAT)
Rua Odeon 150, Vila Alcântara, São Bernardo do Campo,
São Paulo 9720290
Tel: +55(11) 4335-5070
Fax: +55(11) 4127-5923
EMail: fia@fia.edu.br
Website: http://www.tapajos.br

Diretor Geral: Oswaldo Accursi

Courses

Administration (Administration; Business Administration; Marketing); **Computer Science** (Computer Science); **Letters** (Literature); **Mathematics** (Mathematics)

History: Founded 1989 as Faculdade Tapajós. Acquired present title 2001.

Main Language(s) of Instruction: Portuguese

Degrees and Diplomas: *Bacharelado*; *Licenciatura*; *Especialização/Aperfeiçoamento*; *Mestrado*
Last Updated: 06/07/10

FACULTY OF AMERICANA
Faculdade de Americana (FAM)
Rua Joaquim Boer, 733, Jardim Luciene, Americana,
São Paulo 13477-360
Tel: +55(19) 3478-2449
Fax: +55(19) 3478-2449
EMail: fam@fam.br
Website: http://www.fam.br

Diretor Geral: Florindo Corral

Courses

Accountancy; **Administration** (Administration); **Biological Sciences**; **Computer Science** (Computer Science); **Electrical Engineering** (Electrical Engineering); **Environmental Engineering** (Environmental Engineering); **Law** (Law); **Literature** (English; Literature; Portuguese; Spanish); **Nursing** (Nursing); **Nutrition** (Nutrition); **Pedagogy**; **Pharmacy** (Pharmacy); **Physical Education** (Physical Education); **Physical Therapy** (Physical Therapy); **Psychology** (Psychology); **Social Commmunciation - Public Relations and Communication** (Communication Studies; Public Relations); **Technological Studies** (Transport Management)

History: Founded 1999.

Main Language(s) of Instruction: Portuguese

Degrees and Diplomas: *Bacharelado*; *Licenciatura*
Last Updated: 01/07/10

FACULTY OF AMPERE
Faculdade de Ampére
Rua dos Andradas 144, Centro, Ampére, Parana
Tel: +55(46) 3547-3031
EMail: atendimento@famper.com.br
Website: http://www.famper.com.br

Diretora: Terezinha dos Santos Reichert

Courses

Administration; **Arts** (Dance; Folklore; Music; Painting and Drawing; Theatre); **Letters** (Literature); **Pedagogy** (Pedagogy); **Social Services**

History: Founded 2005.

Main Language(s) of Instruction: Portuguese

Degrees and Diplomas: *Bacharelado*; *Licenciatura*; *Especialização/Aperfeiçoamento*; *Mestrado*

Libraries: Yes
Last Updated: 12/07/10

FACULTY OF APPLIED SCIENCES OF CASCAVEL
Faculdade de Ciências Aplicadas de Cascavel (FACIAP)
Avenida Brasil, 7210, Centro, Cascavel, PR 85810-000
Tel: +55(45) 3219-4411
EMail: projetos@unipan.br
Website: http://www.unipan.br/portal/

Secretaria Acadêmica: Eunice Rodrigues Valle Parada

Courses

Accountancy (Accountancy); **Administration** (Administration); **Computer Science** (Computer Science); **Engineering**; **Environmental Engineering** (Environmental Engineering); **Environmental Management** (Environmental Management); **Executive Secretarial Studies**; **Literature**; **Literature - English**; **Literature - Spanish** (Literature; Spanish); **Management Process** (Management); **Music**; **Pedagogy**; **Physical Education** (Physical Education); **Psychology** (Psychology); **Social Services** (Social and Community Services); **Visual Arts** (Visual Arts)

History: Founded 1995.

Main Language(s) of Instruction: Portuguese

Degrees and Diplomas: *Tecnólogo*; *Bacharelado*; *Licenciatura*
Last Updated: 20/07/10

FACULTY OF APPLIED SCIENCES OF SAO PAULO
Faculdade Paulista de Ciências Aplicadas
Av. Brigadeiro Luiz Antônio, 1224 - Bela Vista, São Paulo,
SP 01318-001
Tel: +55(11) 3287-4455
EMail: verapiza.diretora@fpa.art.br
Website: http://www.fpa.art.br/administracao

Diretora: Vera Toledo Piza.

Courses

Business Administration (Business Administration)

History: Founded 2004.

Main Language(s) of Instruction: Portuguese

Degrees and Diplomas: *Bacharelado*
Last Updated: 22/09/10

FACULTY OF APPLIED SCIENCES OF THE VALLEY OF SÃO LOURENÇO
Faculdade de Ciências Sociais Aplicadas do Vale de São Lourenço (EDUVALE)
Rua Caiçara 2114, Centro, Jaciara, Mato Grosso 78820000
Tel: +55(65) 3461-1864
Fax: +55(65) 36461-1377
EMail: eduvale@vsp.com.br
Website: http://www.eduvalesl.edu.br

Diretora: Ana Claudia Gutierrez de Oliveira R. Daleffe
EMail: anaclaudia.edu@vspmail.com.br

Courses

Accountancy (Accountancy); **Administration** (Administration); **Pedagogy** (Pedagogy)

History: Founded 1986

Main Language(s) of Instruction: Portuguese

Degrees and Diplomas: *Bacharelado*; *Especialização/Aperfeiçoamento*; *Mestrado*
Last Updated: 05/12/07

FACULTY OF APPLIED SOCIAL SCIENCES OF BELO HORIZONTE

Faculdade de Ciências Sociais Aplicadas de Belo Horizonte
Av. Antônio Carlos, 521 - 2° e 3° andares - Lagoinha, Belo Horizonte, MG 31.210-010
Tel: +55 (31) 3421-2207
EMail: facisa@facisa.com.br
Website: http://www.facisa.com.br/novo_site

Diretor: Antônio Baião de Amorim

Courses
Accountancy (Accountancy); Administration (Administration); Letters (Literature); Pedagogy (Pedagogy)

History: Founded 2002.

Main Language(s) of Instruction: Portuguese

Degrees and Diplomas: *Bacharelado*; *Licenciatura*
Last Updated: 29/07/10

FACULTY OF APPLIED SOCIAL SCIENCES OF CASCAVEL

Faculdade de Ciências Sociais Aplicadas de Cascavel (UNIVEL)
Avenida Tito Muffato, 2317, Bairro Santa Cruz, Cascavel, Paraná 85806-080
Tel: +55(45) 3036-3636
Fax: +55(45) 3036-3638
EMail: desenvolvimento@univel.br
Website: http://www.univel.br

Diretora Geral: Viviane da Silva

Courses
Accountancy (Accountancy); Administration (Administration); Graduate Studies (Accountancy; Administration; Business Administration; Business and Commerce; Civil Law; Human Resources; Law; Management; Marketing); Journalism (Journalism); Law (Law); Library Economics (Economics; Library Science); Technological Studies (Business and Commerce; Environmental Management; Finance; Human Resources; Safety Engineering; Systems Analysis; Transport Management)

History: Founded 1995

Main Language(s) of Instruction: Portuguese

Degrees and Diplomas: *Tecnólogo*; *Bacharelado*; *Especialização/ Aperfeiçoamento*. Also MBA.
Last Updated: 06/07/10

FACULTY OF APPLIED SOCIAL SCIENCES OF EXTREMA

Faculdade de Ciências Sociais Aplicadas de Extrema (FAEX)
Estrada Municipal Pedro Rosa da Silva s/n, Extrema, Minas Gerais 37640-000
Tel: +55(35) 3435-3988
Fax: +55(35) 3435-4414
EMail: faex@faex.edu.br
Website: http://www.faex.edu.br

Directora: Terezinha Aparecida Monteiro Onisto
EMail: diretoria@faex.edu.br

Secretária Geral: Eliana Aparecida Del Col Lopes
EMail: secretaria@faex.edu.br

Courses
Accounting (Accountancy); Administration; Automation and Control Engineering (Automation and Control Engineering); Graduate Studies (Business Administration; Educational Psychology; Finance; Higher Education; Human Resources; Transport Management); Law; Pedagogy (Educational Administration; Pedagogy); Production Engineering; Technical Studies (Environmental Studies; Marketing; Nursing; Secretarial Studies); Technological Studies (Electronic Engineering; Human Resources; Industrial Management; Safety Engineering; Systems Analysis)

History: Founded in 1999. Acquired present status 2002.

Admission Requirements: Secondary School Leaving Certificate
Main Language(s) of Instruction: Portuguese
Accrediting Agencies: Ministério da Educação
Degrees and Diplomas: *Tecnólogo*; *Bacharelado*; *Licenciatura*; *Especialização/Aperfeiçoamento*. Also MBA.
Libraries: Yes
Last Updated: 06/07/10

FACULTY OF APPLIED SOCIAL SCIENCES OF MARABA

Faculdade de Ciências Sociais Aplicadas de Marabá
Quadra 08 Lote 01 - Loteamento Novo Progresso s/n, Marabá, PA 68514-000
Tel: +55(94) 3321-4010
EMail: mendonca-filho@uol.com.br
Website: http://www.facimab.edu.br

Diretor: Valnir de Souza Soares.

Courses
Accountancy (Accountancy); Administration (Administration; Educational Administration); Education *(Parauapebas)* (Education); Finance *(Tucumã)* (Finance); Health Administration *(Parauapebas)* (Health Administration); History *(Tucuruí)* (History); Physical Education *(Tucuruí)* (Physical Education); Resource Managament *(Tucumã)* (Management)

Degrees and Diplomas: *Bacharelado*; *Especialização/Aperfeiçoamento*
Last Updated: 30/07/10

FACULTY OF APPLIED SOCIAL SCIENCES OF THE SOUTH OF MINAS GERAIS

Faculdade de Ciências Sociais Aplicadas do Sul de Minas Gerais (FACESM)
Av. Presidente Tancredo de Almeida Neves, 45, Itajubá, Minas Gerais 37504066
Tel: +55(35) 3629-5700
Fax: +55(35) 3629-5705
EMail: facesm@facesm.br
Website: http://www.facesm.br

Diretor Geral: Hector Gustavo Arango

Courses
Accountancy (Accountancy); Administration (Administration); Economics (Economics); Graduate Studies (Accountancy; Administration; Business and Commerce; Development Studies; Economics; Finance; Health Administration; Human Resources; Industrial Management; International Business; International Relations; Management; Marketing; Public Administration; Safety Engineering; Transport Management)

History: Founded 1966 as Faculdade de Ciências Econômicas do Sul de Minas.

Main Language(s) of Instruction: Portuguese

Degrees and Diplomas: *Bacharelado*; *Especialização/Aperfeiçoamento*. Also MBA.
Last Updated: 06/07/10

FACULTY OF APPLIED SOCIAL STUDIES OF VIANA

Faculdade de Estudos Sociais Aplicados de Viana (FESAV)
Km 11 Rodovia Br 101, Lar Esc Genoveva Machado, Bairro Universal, Viana, ES 29135-000
Tel: +55(27) 3344-1533
Fax: +55(27) 3344-1499
EMail: fesav@terra.com.br
Website: http://www.fesav.com.br/

Diretor: José Alexandre de Souza Gadioli

Courses
Accountancy (Accountancy); Administration (Administration); Pedagogy

History: Founded 1995

Main Language(s) of Instruction: Portuguese

Degrees and Diplomas: *Bacharelado*; *Especialização/Aperfeiçoamento*

Last Updated: 16/11/07

FACULTY OF APUCARANA

Faculdade de Apucarana

Rua Osvaldo de Oliveira, 600, Jardim Eliane, Igrejinha, Apucarana, Paraná 86811-500

Tel: +55(43) 3033-8900

EMail: fap@fap.com.br

Website: http://www.fap.com.br/

Diretora Geral: Joseane Balan da Silva

Courses

Administration (Administration); **Biology** (Biology); **Graduate Studies** (Biological and Life Sciences; Computer Science; Cooking and Catering; Educational Administration; Educational Psychology; Educational Sciences; Law; Marketing; Nursing; Physical Therapy; Special Education); **Information Systems**; **Law** (Law); **Mathematics**; **Nursing** (Nursing); **Nutrition**; **Pedagogy**; **Physiotherapy**; **Tourism**

History: Founded 1999.

Main Language(s) of Instruction: Portuguese

Degrees and Diplomas: *Bacharelado*; *Licenciatura*; *Especialização/Aperfeiçoamento*

Last Updated: 01/07/10

FACULTY OF ARACAJU

Faculdade de Aracaju

Rua Oscar Valois Galvão, 355, Conj. Leite Neto - Grageru, Aracaju, SE 49027-220

Tel: +55(79) 3217-7476

EMail: diretoriafaser@infonet.com.br

Website: http://www.unilist.com.br/facar/instituto/destaques.asp

Diretor: Adailton Vilela de Almeida

Courses

Accountancy (Accountancy); **Administration** (Administration); **Law** (Law); **Social Communication** (Advertising and Publicity); **Tourism** (Tourism)

History: Founded 2005 as Instituto Aracaju de Ensino e Cultura. Acquired present title 2010.

Main Language(s) of Instruction: Portuguese

Degrees and Diplomas: *Bacharelado*; *Licenciatura*

Last Updated: 27/09/10

FACULTY OF ARAÇATUBA

Faculdade de Araçatuba

Rua Sarjob Mendes, 244, Jardim Icaray, Araçatuba, SP 16020-360

Tel: +55(18) 3622-4686

Fax: +55(18) 3622-4686

EMail: fernando@uniesp.edu.br; ckto@terra.com.br

Website: http://www.uniesp.edu.br/aracatuba

Courses

Administration (Administration)

History: Founded 2007.

Main Language(s) of Instruction: Portuguese

Degrees and Diplomas: *Bacharelado*

Last Updated: 19/07/10

FACULTY OF ARACRUZ

Faculdade de Aracruz (FAACZ)

Rua Professor Berílio Basílio dos Santos, nº 180, Centro, Aracruz, ES 29194-910

Tel: +55(27) 3302-8000

Fax: +55(27) 3302-8001

EMail: secretaria@fsjb.edu.br

Website: http://www.faacz.com.br

Diretora: Vera Lúcia Cuzzuol

Courses

Accountancy; **Administration** (Administration); **Architecture and Urbanism** (Architecture; Town Planning); **Chemical Engineering** (Chemical Engineering); **Graduate Studies** (*Lato Sensu*) (Accountancy; Business Administration; Communication Studies; Educational Psychology; Engineering; Environmental Management; Environmental Studies; Finance; Higher Education; Law; Management; Petroleum and Gas Engineering; Safety Engineering; Town Planning); **Graduate Studies** (*Stricto Sensu*) (Environmental Engineering); **Law** (Law); **Mechanical Engineering** (Mechanical Engineering); **Pedagogy**

History: Founded 1989 as Faculdade de Ciências Humanas de Aracruz (FACHA). Acquired present status and title 2005.

Degrees and Diplomas: *Bacharelado*; *Licenciatura*; *Especialização/Aperfeiçoamento*; *Mestrado*

Last Updated: 01/07/10

FACULTY OF ARAPOTI

Faculdade Arapoti (FATI)

Rua das Rosas 001, Arapoti, PR 84990-000

Tel: +55(43) 3557-2566

Fax: +55(43) 3557-2566

EMail: fati@faculdadearapoti.com.br

Website: http://www.faculdadearapoti.com.br

Diretor: Ivan Siqueira Filho

Courses

Administration (Administration); **Nursing** (*Técnico*); **Pedagogy**

History: Founded 1999.

Main Language(s) of Instruction: Portuguese

Degrees and Diplomas: *Tecnólogo*; *Bacharelado*; *Licenciatura*. Postgraduate Programmes offered through Academia Brasileira de Ciências da Educação – ABRASCE.

Last Updated: 24/06/10

FACULTY OF ARTS OF SAO PAULO

Faculdade Paulista de Artes (FPA)

Av. Brigadeiro Luiz Antônio, 1224 - Bela Vista, São Paulo, São Paulo 1321000

Tel: +55(11) 3287-4455

Fax: +55(11) 3287-4455

EMail: fp.artes@terra.com.br

Website: http://www.fpa.art.br/

Diretora: Vera Toldedo Piza **EMail:** verapiza.diretora@fpa.art.br

Courses

Dance; **Fashion Design** (Fashion Design); **Industrial Design** (Industrial Design); **Music** (Music); **Music Therapy** (Art Therapy); **Plastic Arts** (Fine Arts); **Scenic Arts** (Theatre)

History: Founded 1974.

Main Language(s) of Instruction: Portuguese

Degrees and Diplomas: *Bacharelado*; *Licenciatura*; *Especialização/Aperfeiçoamento*

Last Updated: 05/07/10

FACULTY OF ARTS, SCIENCE AND TECHNOLOGY

Faculdade de Artes, Ciências e Tecnologias (FACET)

Rua Rubem Berta, 128, Pituba, Salvador, BA 41820-040

Tel: +55(71) 3347-5000 +55(71) 3248-1274

EMail: facet@facetba.com.br

Website: http://www.facetba.com.br/

Diretor Geral: Edgar Melo

Courses

Administration (Administration); **Law** (Law)

Degrees and Diplomas: *Bacharelado*; *Especialização/Aperfeiçoamento*

Last Updated: 19/07/10

FACULTY OF ARUJÁ
Faculdade de Arujá (FAR)
Avenida João Manoel, 1200, Bairro dos Fontes, Arujá,
SP 07400-000
Tel: +55(11) 4652-2646
EMail: atendimento@faculdadedearuja.edu.br
Website: http://www.faculdadedearuja.edu.br

Diretor: Roberto Jorge Mattar

Courses
Accountancy (Accountancy); **Administration** (Administration); **Graduate Studies** (Education; Educational Administration; Educational Psychology); **Pedagogy** (Pedagogy)

Degrees and Diplomas: *Bacharelado*; *Licenciatura*; *Especialização/Aperfeiçoamento*
Last Updated: 19/07/10

FACULTY OF AURIFLAMA
Faculdade de Auriflama (FAACI)
Via de Acesso Sp 310 Arthur Fornazari Neto, Km 28, Limoeiro, Auriflama, SP 15350-000
Tel: +55(17) 3482-4410
Fax: +55(17) 3482-4410
EMail: secretaria_fau@hotmail.com
Website: http://www.faculdadedeauriflama.com.br/

Diretor Geral: João Ângelo Segantin
EMail: faudiretor@hotmail.com

Courses
Accountancy (Accountancy); **Administration** (Administration); **Graduate Studies** (Accountancy); **Literature** (English; Literature; Portuguese); **Pedagogy** (Pedagogy); **Technical Studies**

History: Founded 2007.

Main Language(s) of Instruction: Portuguese

Degrees and Diplomas: *Certificado de Auxiliar Técnico*; *Bacharelado*; *Licenciatura*; *Especialização/Aperfeiçoamento*
Last Updated: 19/07/10

FACULTY OF BAHIA
Faculdade da Bahia
Largo da Calçada, 01 - Calçada, Salvador, BA 40.411-366
Tel: +55(71) 3312-4000
EMail: diretoria.geral@fab.edu.br
Website: http://www.fab.edu.br

Diretor: Joselito Viana

Courses
Administration (Administration); **Business Administration** (Business Administration); **Human Resources Management** (Human Resources; Management); **Information Technology** (Information Technology)

Main Language(s) of Instruction: Portuguese

Degrees and Diplomas: *Bacharelado*; *Especialização/Aperfeiçoamento*; *Mestrado*
Last Updated: 26/07/10

FACULTY OF BAIXO PARNAIBA
Faculdade do Baixo Parnaiba
Avenida Ataliba Vieira de Almeida 1452, Chapadinha, MA 65500-000
Tel: +55(98) 3471-1356
EMail: iscde@terra.com.br
Website: http://www.fapeduca.com.br

Diretora: Raimunda Nonata Fortes Braga

Courses
Administration (Administration); **Letters** (Literature); **Pedagogy** (Pedagogy)

History: Founded 2005 as Instituto Superior das Ciências da Educação do Baixo Parnaíba. Acquired present status and title 2007.

Main Language(s) of Instruction: Portuguese

Degrees and Diplomas: *Bacharelado*; *Licenciatura*; *Especialização/Aperfeiçoamento*

Libraries: Biblioteca Professora Lusimar Ferreira
Last Updated: 30/08/10

FACULTY OF BALSAS
Faculdade de Balsas (UNIBALSAS)
BR 230 – Km 05, Balsas, MA 65800-000
Tel: +55(99) 3541-2194
Fax: +55(99) 3541-2194
EMail: ouvidoria@unibalsas.edu.br
Website: http://www.unibalsas.edu.br/

Diretor Geral: Márcio Honaiser **EMail:** dir.geral@unibalsas.edu.br

Courses
Accountancy (Accountancy); **Administration** (Administration); **Graduate Studies**; **Information Systems** (Information Technology); **Law** (Law)

Degrees and Diplomas: *Bacharelado*; *Especialização/Aperfeiçoamento*
Last Updated: 19/07/10

FACULTY OF BARRETOS
Faculdade Barretos
Avenida 23 n° 055, Centro, Barretos, São Paulo 14780-320
Tel: +55(17) 3323-1112
Fax: +55(17) 3323-1112
EMail: mantenedora@unibarretos.com.br;
secretaria@unibarretos.com.br
Website: http://www.unibarretos.com.br

Diretor Geral: Chade Rezek Neto

Courses
Administration; **Graduate Studies**; **History**; **Information Systems** (Information Sciences); **Law** (Law)

History: Founded 2002.

Main Language(s) of Instruction: Portuguese

Degrees and Diplomas: *Bacharelado*; *Licenciatura*; *Especialização/Aperfeiçoamento*. Also MBA.
Last Updated: 29/06/10

FACULTY OF BELÉM
Faculdade de Belém (FABEL)
Travessa Aristides Lobo, 897, Reduto, Belém, PA 66053-040
Tel: +55(91) 3201-1300 +55(91) 3201-1318
Fax: +55(91) 3201-1309
EMail: fabel@fabelnet.com.br
Website: http://www.fabelnet.com.br

Diretor Geral: Ivan Guilherme de la Rocque Pinho

Courses
Accountancy; **Administration** (Administration); **Graduate Studies** *(Distance Learning)* (Accountancy; Administration; Banking; Computer Science; Education; Educational Psychology; Finance; Health Sciences; Human Resources; Law; Marketing; Mathematics; Political Sciences; Psychoanalysis; Psychology; Telecommunications Engineering; Theology; Transport Management); **Graduate Studies** *(Lato Sensu)*; **Law** (Law); **Technological Studies** (Finance; Marketing; Public Administration); **Tourism** (Tourism)

Degrees and Diplomas: *Tecnólogo*; *Bacharelado*; *Especialização/Aperfeiçoamento*. Also MBA.
Last Updated: 20/07/10

FACULTY OF BELFORD ROXO
Faculdade de Belford Roxo (FABEL)
Rua Virgilina Bicchieri, 61, Centro, Belford Roxo, Rio de Janeiro 26113510
Tel: +55(21) 2662-0066
EMail: info@fabel.edu.br
Website: http://www.fabel.edu.br/

Diretora Geral: Katia Maria Soares (1995-)

Courses

Administration (Administration); **Computer Science** (Computer Science); **Pedagogy** (Pedagogy)

History: Founded 1995

Main Language(s) of Instruction: Portuguese

Degrees and Diplomas: *Tecnólogo*; *Bacharelado*; *Licenciatura*
Last Updated: 01/07/10

FACULTY OF BERTIOGA
Faculdade Bertioga
Avenida Manoel da Nóbrega, 966, Jardim Lido, Bertioga
Tel: +55(13) 3317-3444
EMail: faculdadesbertioga@uol.com.br
Website: http://www.faculdadebertioga.com.br/contato.html

Diretor: Fernando Sena Rodrigues

Courses

Administration (Administration); **Law**; **Pedagogy**; **Tourism** (Tourism)

History: Founded 2003.

Main Language(s) of Instruction: Portuguese

Degrees and Diplomas: *Bacharelado*; *Licenciatura*; *Especialização/Aperfeiçoamento*
Last Updated: 16/07/10

FACULTY OF BIOLOGICAL AND HEALTH SCIENCES
Faculdade de Ciências Biológicas e da Saúde (FACISA)
Avenida Maria de Paula Santana, n° 3815, Bairro Silvestre, Viçosa, MG 36570-000
Tel: +55(31) 3899-8000
Fax: +55(31) 3899-8000
EMail: univicosa@univicosa.com.br
Website: http://www.univicosa.com.br/

Diretora: Adriana Silva Fialho Cambuí

Areas
Health Sciences (Nursing; Nutrition; Pharmacy; Physical Therapy; Psychology; Veterinary Science); **Technology** (Computer Networks; Computer Science; Environmental Studies; Marketing; Small Business)

Courses
Graduate Studies

Degrees and Diplomas: *Tecnólogo*; *Bacharelado*; *Especialização/ Aperfeiçoamento*. Also MBA.
Last Updated: 20/07/10

FACULTY OF BIOMEDICAL SCIENCES OF CACOAL
Faculdade de Ciências Biomédicas de Cacoal (FACIMED)
Avenida Cuiabá, 3087, Jardim Clodoaldo, Cacoal, RO 78976-005
Tel: +55(69) 3441-1950
EMail: assessoria_presidencia@facimed.com.br
Website: http://www.facimed.edu.br/

Diretora: Sandra Marques

Courses
Agricultural Business (Agricultural Business); **Biological Sciences** (Biological and Life Sciences); **Chemistry**; **Cooperative Management**; **Environmental Management** (Environmental Management); **Graduate Studies** (Accountancy; Agricultural Business; Business Administration; Economics; Education; Educational Administration; Educational and Student Counselling; Educational Psychology; Environmental Management; Gynaecology and Obstetrics; Health Administration; Human Resources; Literacy Education; Management; Mathematics and Computer Science; Nursing; Pharmacology; Physical Therapy; Physiology; Public Administration; Public Health; Science Education; Zoology); **Human Resources**; **Mathematics**; **Medicine** (Medicine); **Nursing**; **Odontology** (Dentistry); **Pharmacy and Biochemistry**; **Physical Education** (Physical Education); **Physical Therapy**; **Physics**;

Psychology (Psychology); **Veterinary Science** (Veterinary Science)

History: Founded 2002.

Degrees and Diplomas: *Tecnólogo*; *Bacharelado*; *Licenciatura*; *Especialização/Aperfeiçoamento*
Last Updated: 20/07/10

FACULTY OF BIRIGUI
Faculdade Birigui
Rua João Escanhuela 133, Birigui, SP 16204-142
Tel: +55(18) 3642-7808
Fax: +55(18) 3642-7808
EMail: mantenedora@uniesp.edu.br
Website: http://www.uniesp.edu.br/birigui

Courses
Accountancy; **Administration** (Administration); **Geography** (Geography); **History**; **Law** (Law); **Letters** (Literature); **Mathematics** (Mathematics); **Pedagogy** (Pedagogy); **Visual Arts**

History: Founded 2001.

Main Language(s) of Instruction: Portuguese

Degrees and Diplomas: *Bacharelado*; *Licenciatura*
Last Updated: 15/07/10

FACULTY OF BUSINESS ACTIVITIES OF TERESINA
Faculdade das Atividades Empresariais de Teresina (FAETE)
Avenida Dr. Nicanor Barreto, 4381, Vale Quem Tem, Teresina, Piauí 64057-355
Tel: +55(86) 3214-9500
Fax: +55(86) 3214-9500
EMail: info@faete.edu.br
Website: http://www.faete.edu.br/

Diretor Geral: Walter Pereira da Cunha

Courses
Administration (Administration); **Information Systems**; **Law** (Law); **Tourism** (Tourism)

History: Founded 2000.

Main Language(s) of Instruction: Portuguese

Degrees and Diplomas: *Bacharelado*; *Especialização/Aperfeiçoamento*
Last Updated: 30/06/10

FACULTY OF BUSINESS AND FINANCIAL STUDIES OF NATAL
Faculdade de Ciências Empresariais e Estudos Costeiros de Natal (FACEN)
Avenida Prudente de Morais, 3510, Lagoa Nova, Natal, Rio Grande do Norte 59063-200
Tel: +55(84) 3206-4013 +55(84) 3206-2195
EMail: facenm@yahoo.com.br
Website: http://www.facen.com.br

Diretor: Érico Rodrigues Bacelar

Courses
Administration (Administration); **Pedagogy**

Further Information: Also Liberdade, José de Alencar and Jequitibás campuses.

History: Founded 2000.

Main Language(s) of Instruction: Portuguese

Degrees and Diplomas: *Tecnólogo*; *Bacharelado*. Also Licenciatura degree offered through the Instituto Natalense de Educação Superior (INAES).
Last Updated: 05/07/10

FACULTY OF BUSINESS SCIENCES
Faculdade de Ciências Empresariais (FACEMP)
Travessa XV de Novembro, 89A, Centro, Santo Antônio de Jesus,
BA 44573-045
Tel: +55(75) 3631-3180
Website: http://www.facemp.edu.br/

Diretor: Antônio Carlos Lé Martini

Courses
Accountancy (Accountancy); **Administration** (Administration); **Graduate Studies** (Accountancy; Business Administration; Environmental Management; Finance; Health Administration; Management); **Pedagogy** (Pedagogy)

History: Founded 2002.

Degrees and Diplomas: *Bacharelado*; *Licenciatura*; *Especialização/Aperfeiçoamento*
Last Updated: 23/07/10

FACULTY OF CABRÁLIA
Faculdade Cabrália
Rua da Mata 1-b, Santa Cruz Cabrália, BA 45087-000
Tel: +55(73) 3672-1594
Fax: +55(73) 3672-1589.
EMail: diretoria@faculdadecabralia.edu.br
Website: http://www.faculdadecabralia.edu.br

Diretor: Roldão Luiz de Almeida Coelho
EMail: rcoelho@neurodiag.com.br

Courses
Nursing (Nursing)

History: Founded 2008.

Main Language(s) of Instruction: Portuguese

Degrees and Diplomas: *Bacharelado*
Last Updated: 15/07/10

FACULTY OF CALDAS NOVAS
Faculdade de Caldas Novas (UNICALDAS)
Portal do Lago, Quadra: 09, Lotes: 01 a 28, Loteamento Portal do
Lago, Caldas Novas, Goias 75690-000
Tel: +55(64) 3453-7880
Fax: +55(64) 3453-7880
EMail: unicaldas@unicaldas.edu.br
Website: http://www.unicaldas.edu.br

Diretora: Íris Gonzaga Menezes

Courses
Accountancy (Accountancy); **Administration** (Administration); **Biology** (Biology); **Environmental Engineering** (Environmental Engineering); **Graduate Studies**; **Information Systems**; **Law** (Law); **Pedagogy** (Pedagogy)

History: Founded 1999.

Degrees and Diplomas: *Bacharelado*; *Licenciatura*; *Especialização/Aperfeiçoamento*
Last Updated: 01/07/10

FACULTY OF CAMPINA GRANDE
Faculdade de Campina Grande (FAC-CG)
Praça Coronel Antônio Pessoa, 111, Centro, Campina Grande,
PB 58400-262
Tel: +55(83) 3321-4601
Fax: +55(83) 3321-4601
EMail: uescg@uol.com.br
Website: http://www.unescfaculdade.com.br/

Diretora Presidente: Ana Lígia Costa Feliciano
EMail: ligiafeliciano@unescfaculdades.com.br

Courses
Accountancy (Accountancy); **Administration**; **Commercial Management** (Business and Commerce; Management); **Graduate Studies** (Accountancy; Law; Occupational Health; Public Administration); **Law** (Law); **Marketing**; **Nursing** (Nursing); **Physical Therapy** (Physical Therapy)

Further Information: Also Alto Branco and Prata Units.

Degrees and Diplomas: *Tecnólogo*; *Bacharelado*; *Especialização/Aperfeiçoamento*
Last Updated: 20/07/10

FACULTY OF CAMPINA GRANDE DO SUL
Faculdade de Campina Grande do Sul (FACSUL)
Rua Prof. Duílio Calderari, N° 600, Jardim Paulista,
Caixa Postal n° 530, Campina Grande do Sul, Paraíba 83430-000
Tel: +55(41) 3679-1022
Fax: +55(41) 3679-6873
EMail: facsul@facsul.edu.br
Website: http://www.facsul.edu.br

Diretor: Antônio Carlos Banzzatto

Courses
Administration; **Graduate Studies** (Education; Environmental Management; Public Administration); **Information Technology** (Information Technology); **Pedagogy** (Pedagogy)

History: Founded 2001.

Main Language(s) of Instruction: Portuguese

Degrees and Diplomas: *Tecnólogo*; *Bacharelado*; *Licenciatura*; *Especialização/Aperfeiçoamento*
Last Updated: 01/07/10

FACULTY OF CAMPO LIMPO PAULISTA
Faculdade Campo Limpo Paulista (FACCAMP)
Rua Guatemala, n°167, Jardim America, Campo Limpo Paulista,
São Paulo 13231-230
Tel: +55(11) 4812-9400
EMail: secretaria@faccamp.br
Website: http://www.faccamp.br

Diretora: Patrícia Gentil Passos

Courses
Accountancy; **Administration**; **Advertising and Publicity**; **Chemistry** (Chemistry); **Computer Science** (Computer Science); **Electrical Engineering**; **Electrical Engineering** (Electrical Engineering; Telecommunications Engineering); **Geography** (Geography); **Graduate Studies** *(Stricto Sensu)* (Administration); **Graduate Studies** *(Lato Sensu)* (Arts and Humanities; Business Administration; Computer Networks; Education; Educational Psychology); **History**; **Journalism**; **Law** (Law); **Literature** (Literature); **Mathematics** (Mathematics); **Music**; **Nursing** (Nursing); **Pedagogy** (Pedagogy); **Pharmacy** (Pharmacy); **Physics**; **Production Engineering** (Production Engineering); **Radio and Television Broadcasting**; **Systems Analysis** (Systems Analysis); **Technological Studies**

History: Founded 1999.

Main Language(s) of Instruction: Portuguese

Degrees and Diplomas: *Tecnólogo*; *Bacharelado*; *Licenciatura*; *Especialização/Aperfeiçoamento*; *Mestrado*
Last Updated: 29/06/10

FACULTY OF CAMPO VERDE
Faculdade de Campo Verde (FCV)
Av. Brasilia, 1010, Centro, Campo Verde, MT 78840-000
Tel: +55(66) 3419-1918
EMail: campoverde@unirondon.br

Diretor Geral: Adonias Gomes de Almeida

Courses
Administration (Administration)

History: Founded 2003.

Main Language(s) of Instruction: Portuguese

Degrees and Diplomas: *Bacharelado*
Last Updated: 20/07/10

FACULTY OF CAMPOS ELISEOS
Faculdade Campos Eliseos (FCE)
Rua Vitorino Carmilo, 664, Campos Elíseos, São Paulo,
São Paulo 01153000
Tel: +55(11) 3661-5400
Fax: +55(11) 3661-5400
EMail: atendimento@fce.edu.br
Website: http://www.fce.edu.br

Presidente: Sônia Fonseca (1995-) EMail: presidencia@fce.edu.br

Courses
Accountancy; **Administration**; **Graduate Studies** (Accountancy; Business Administration; Finance; Management; Small Business)
Further Information: Also Tatuapé unit.
History: Founded 1994 as Faculdade de Ciências do Estado de São Paulo. Became Faculdade de Administração de Empresas do Estado de São Paulo – FAESP 1997. Now Faculdade Campos Elíseos.
Degrees and Diplomas: *Bacharelado*; *Especialização/Aperfeiçoamento*
Last Updated: 29/06/10

FACULTY OF CAPIM GROSSO
Faculdade Capim Grosso (FABES)
Rua Floresta, s/n, Sede, Loteamento Pousada das Mangueiras,
Capim Grosso, BA 44695-000
Tel: +55(74) 3651-1543 +55(74) 3651-1586
EMail: fabes@faculdadecapimgrosso.com.br
Website: http://www.faculdadecapimgrosso.com.br/

Diretor: Dario Loureiro Guimarães

Courses
Accountancy (Accountancy); **Administration**; **Pedagogy** (Pedagogy)
History: Founded 2003.
Main Language(s) of Instruction: Portuguese
Degrees and Diplomas: *Bacharelado*
Last Updated: 18/03/11

FACULTY OF CAPIVARI
Faculdade Capivari
Av. Nações Unidas - 500, Santo André, Capivari de Baixo,
SC 88745-000
EMail: secretaria@fucap.edu.br
Website: http://www.fucap.edu.br

Diretor: Expedito Michels

Courses
Accountancy; **Administration**
Main Language(s) of Instruction: Portuguese
Degrees and Diplomas: *Bacharelado*; *Especialização/Aperfeiçoamento*
Last Updated: 16/07/10

FACULTY OF CARIACICA
Faculdade de Cariacica (UNIEST)
Rua Antônio Peixoto s/ n°, Cariacica, ES 29146-785
Tel: +55(27) 3286-2551 +55(27) 3286-2652
EMail: uniest@uniest.com.br
Website: http://www.uniest.com.br

Diretor: Leonardo Barth

Courses
Accountancy (Accountancy); **Administration**; **Design** (Design); **Electrical Engineering**; **Graduate Studies** (Accountancy; Business Administration; Finance; Management)
History: Founded 2001.
Main Language(s) of Instruction: Portuguese
Degrees and Diplomas: *Bacharelado*. Also Postgraduate Diploma.
Last Updated: 01/07/10

FACULTY OF CASA BRANCA
Faculdade Casa Branca (FACAB)
Rodovia Sp 340 - Km 240 s/n - Rodovia Casa Branca, Casa Branca,
São Paulo 13700-000
Tel: +55(19) 3671-2145 +55(19) 3674-0101
Fax: +55(19) 3671-2145
EMail: facab@facab.br
Website: http://www.facab.br

Diretor: Jamil Zogbi

Courses
Administration (Administration; Business Administration); **Graduate Studies** (Biotechnology; Business Administration; Linguistics; Literature; Management; Portuguese; Speech Therapy and Audiology; Transport Management); **Law**; **Pedagogy** (Education; Pedagogy); **Radiology** (Radiology); **Tourism** (Hotel Management; Tourism)
History: Founded 1996.
Main Language(s) of Instruction: Portuguese
Degrees and Diplomas: *Tecnólogo*; *Bacharelado*; *Licenciatura*; *Especialização/Aperfeiçoamento*
Last Updated: 29/06/10

FACULTY OF CASCAVEL
Faculdade de Cascavel (FADEC)
Rua Rio Grande do Sul 675, Cascavel, Paraná 85806970
Tel: +55(45) 3038-4101
Fax: +55(45) 3038-4101
EMail: inespaula@certto.com.br
Website: http://www.fadec.edu.br

Diretora Geral: Inês Aparecida de Paula Dias

Courses
Administration (Administration); **Pedagogy**
History: Founded 2000.
Main Language(s) of Instruction: Portuguese
Degrees and Diplomas: *Bacharelado*
Last Updated: 07/12/07

FACULTY OF CASTANHAL
Faculdade de Castanhal (FCAT)
Rodovia BR-316, s/n, Km 60, Castanhal, PA 68740-420
Tel: +55(91) 3311-3400
EMail: fcat@fcat.edu.br
Website: http://www.fcat.com.br/

Diretor Geral: Mário Alves do Nacimento Neto

Courses
Accountancy; **Administration**; **Agricultural Business** (Agricultural Business); **Computer Networks** (Computer Networks); **Graduate Studies**; **Law** (Law); **Marketing** (Marketing)
History: Founded 2007.
Degrees and Diplomas: *Tecnólogo*; *Bacharelado*; *Especialização/Aperfeiçoamento*
Last Updated: 20/07/10

FACULTY OF CASTELO
Faculdade de Castelo (FACASTELO)
Av. Nicanor Marques s/n, Castelo, ES 29360-000
Tel: +55(27) 3542-2253 +55(27)3542-2291
Fax: +55(27) 3542-2253 +55(27)3542-2291
EMail: facastelo@terra.com.br
Website: http://www.facastelo.br

Diretor: Gilson Mendes da Cruz

Courses
Business Administration (Business Administration); **Law** (Law); **Veterinary Medicine** (Veterinary Science)
History: Founded 1999.
Main Language(s) of Instruction: Portuguese
Degrees and Diplomas: *Bacharelado*
Last Updated: 01/07/10

FACULTY OF CENTRAL BRAZIL
Faculdade Brasil Central
Qc 08, Lt 7/16, Mansões Village, Aguas Lindas, GO
Tel: +55(61) 3613-0423
EMail: diretoracademico@fbc.edu.b
Website: http://www.fbc.edu.br

Diretor: Cicero P. Silva

Courses
Accountancy (Accountancy); **Business Administration** (Business Administration); **Pedagogy** (Pedagogy)

History: Founded 2006.

Main Language(s) of Instruction: Portuguese

Degrees and Diplomas: *Bacharelado*
Last Updated: 15/07/10

FACULTY OF CENTRO LESTE
Faculdade do Centro Leste (UCL)
Avenida Guarapari 17, Valparaiso, Serra, ES 29164120
Tel: +55(27) 3328-2828
Fax: +55(27) 3328-2828
EMail: contato@ucl.br
Website: http://www.ucl.br

Diretor: Klinger Marcos Barbosa Alves

Courses
Administration (Administration); **Automation and Control** (Automation and Control Engineering); **Computer Science** (Computer Science); **Petroleum Engineering**; **Product Design** (Design); **Production Engineering**

History: Founded 2000.

Main Language(s) of Instruction: Portuguese

Degrees and Diplomas: *Bacharelado*; *Especialização/Aperfeiçoamento*; *Mestrado*
Last Updated: 08/07/10

FACULTY OF CERES
Faculdade de Ceres (FACERES)
Avenida Brasil, Quadra 13, Setor Morada Verde, Ceres, GO 76300-000
Tel: +55(62)3323-1040
EMail: ouvidoria@facer.edu.br
Website: http://www.faceres.edu.br/

Diretor: Marcos Terra Iacovelo

Courses
Administration; **Nursing**; **Pharmacy** (Pharmacy)

Degrees and Diplomas: *Bacharelado*. Also Postgraduate Diploma.
Last Updated: 20/07/10

FACULTY OF CERRADOS PIAUIENSES
Faculdade do Cerrados Piauienses (FCP)
Avenida Joaquina Nogueira de Oliveira, S/n Sitio IBC Aeroporto, Corrente, PI 64980000
Tel: +55(89) 573-1101 +55(89) 573-1500
Fax: +55(89) 573-1101 +55(89) 573-1500
EMail: diretoria@faculdadedocerrado.com.br
Website: http://www.faculdadedocerrado.com.br

Diretor: Marcos Aurelio De Araújo Alves

Courses
Accountancy; **Administration** (Accountancy; Administration; Business Administration); **Law** (Law); **Letters**

History: Founded 2000.

Main Language(s) of Instruction: Portuguese

Degrees and Diplomas: *Bacharelado*; *Licenciatura*

Libraries: Biblioteca Desembargador Heli Sobral
Last Updated: 08/07/10

FACULTY OF CHAPADAO DO SUL
Faculdade de Chapadao do Sul
Rua Vinte e Oito, n° 615, Parque União, Chapadao do Sul, MS 79560-000
EMail: soeco@brturbo.com.br
Website: http://www.fachasul.com.br/

Diretor: Wilton Paulino Junior

Courses
Accountancy (Accountancy); **Administration** (Administration)

History: Founded 2002.

Main Language(s) of Instruction: Portuguese

Degrees and Diplomas: *Bacharelado*; *Especialização/Aperfeiçoamento*

Libraries: Biblioteca Prof. Therezinha de Oliveira Pauli
Last Updated: 27/07/10

FACULTY OF COLIDER
Faculdade de Colider (FACIDER)
Avenida Senador Julio Campos 995 - Loteamento TREVO, Colider, MT 78500000
Tel: +55(66) 541-1080 +55(66) 541-1081
Fax: +55(66) 541-1082
EMail: sei-cesu@vsp.com.br
Website: http://www.sei-cesucol.edu.br

Diretora Geral: Roze Mirian Saldanha

Courses
Administration (Administration); **Law** (Law); **Nursing**; **Pharmacy**; **Physical Education**; **Sequential Studies** (Agricultural Business; Health Administration; Journalism)

History: Founded 2001.

Main Language(s) of Instruction: Portuguese

Degrees and Diplomas: *Bacharelado*
Last Updated: 06/07/10

FACULTY OF COMMUNICATION, TECHNOLOGY AND TOURISM OF OLINDA
Faculdade de Comunicação, Tecnologia e Turismo de Olinda
Av. Getúlio Vargas, n° 1.360, Bairro Novo, Olinda, PE
EMail: falecom@facottur.org
Website: http://www.facottur.org/

Diretor: Daniel Moraes Rêgo de Lucena

Courses
Management (Business Administration; Human Resources; Marketing); **Tourism** (Tourism)

History: Founded 1999.

Main Language(s) of Instruction: Portuguese

Degrees and Diplomas: *Bacharelado*
Last Updated: 30/07/10

FACULTY OF COMPUTER SCIENCE - FATEC
Faculdade de Informática - FATEC
Rua do Progresso 441, Soledade, Recife, PE
Tel: +55(81) 3445-5055
EMail: fatec@fatecpe.com.br
Website: http://fatecpe.com.br/www2/

Courses
Computer Science (Computer Science)

History: Founded 2001.

Main Language(s) of Instruction: Portuguese

Degrees and Diplomas: *Bacharelado*; *Especialização/Aperfeiçoamento*

Libraries: Biblioteca Professor Marcelo Santos
Last Updated: 06/08/10

FACULTY OF COMPUTER SCIENCE AND ADMINISTRATION OF SAO PAULO

Faculdade de Informática e Administração Paulista (FIAP)
Avenida Lins de Vasconcelos 1264 Aclimação, São Paulo,
São Paulo 01538-001
Tel: +55(11) 3385- 8010
Website: http://www.fiap.com.br

Diretora: Fabiula Alves Pimentel Baraúna
EMail: fabiula@fiap.com.br

Courses
Administration (Administration; Information Technology); **Administration**; **Computer Engineering**; **Graduate Studies**; **Information Systems**; **Technological Studies** (Computer Networks; Computer Science; Data Processing; Information Technology; Systems Analysis)

Further Information: Also Aclimação, Av. Paulista and Alphaville Units.

History: Founded 1991.

Main Language(s) of Instruction: Portuguese

Degrees and Diplomas: *Tecnólogo*; *Bacharelado*. Also MBA and certificate courses.
Last Updated: 09/07/10

FACULTY OF COMPUTER SCIENCE OF MONTES CLAROS

Faculdade de Computação de Montes Claros
Rua Olegário Silveira, 30. Centro., Montes Claros,
MG +55(38) 3221-2319
EMail: facomp@facomp.edu.br
Website: http://www.facomp.edu.br/facomp

Diretor: Luiz Carlos Pires dos Santos

Courses
Computer Networks (Computer Networks); **Information Systems** (Computer Science); **Systems Analysis** (Systems Analysis)

History: Founded 2005.

Main Language(s) of Instruction: Portuguese

Degrees and Diplomas: *Tecnólogo*; *Especialização/Aperfeiçoamento*
Last Updated: 30/07/10

FACULTY OF CONCHAS

Faculdade de Conchas
Rua Itaipu, 157 Vila Seminário, Conchas, SP 18570-000
Tel: +55(14) 3845-1618
EMail: facon@faculdadeconchas.com.br
Website: http://www.faculdadeconchas.com.br/faleconosco.html

Diretor: Paulo Nunes de Almeida

Courses
Pedagogy (Pedagogy)

History: Founded 2009.

Main Language(s) of Instruction: Portuguese

Degrees and Diplomas: *Licenciatura*. Also postgraduate degrees
Last Updated: 30/07/10

FACULTY OF CONCORDIA

Faculdade Concórdia
Rua Anita Garibaldi N° 3185, Acesso Contorno Norte, Bairro:
Primavera, Concórdia, SC 89700-000
EMail: secretaria@facc.com.br
Website: http://www.facc.com.br/

Diretor: César Antônio Schwertz

Courses
Accountancy (Accountancy); **Administration** (Administration); **Architecture and Town Planning** (Architecture; Town Planning); **Social Services** (Social and Community Services)

History: Founded 2002.

Main Language(s) of Instruction: Portuguese

Degrees and Diplomas: *Bacharelado*
Last Updated: 23/07/10

FACULTY OF DENTISTRY OF MANAUS

Faculdade de Odontologia de Manaus (FOM)
Avenida Getúlio Vargas n°. 1311 Centro, Mánaus,
Amazonas 69065001
Tel: +55(92) 3087-5659
EMail: f.o.m@uol.com.br
Website: http://www.fom.edu.br

Diretor Geral: Oscar Isamu Shirata

Courses
Dentistry (Dentistry)

History: Founded 2000.

Main Language(s) of Instruction: Portuguese

Degrees and Diplomas: *Bacharelado*
Last Updated: 09/07/10

FACULTY OF DENTISTRY OF RECIFE

Faculdade de Odontologia do Recife
Rua Artur Coutinho 143, Recife, PE 50100-280
Tel: +55(81) 3221-3325
EMail: coogradfor@yahoo.com.br
Website: http://www.for.edu.br

Diretora: Sônia Maria de Souza Fonteles

Courses
Dentistry (Dentistry)

History: Founded 2002.

Main Language(s) of Instruction: Portuguese

Degrees and Diplomas: *Bacharelado*
Last Updated: 10/08/10

FACULTY OF DIADEMA

Faculdade Diadema (FAD)
Av. Alda 831, Diadema, SP 09910-170
Tel: +55(11) 4056-5651
EMail: secretaria@fadnet.br
Website: http://www.uniesp.edu.br/diadema/conhecaUnidade.asp

Diretor Geral: Gilmar Getúlio Silveira Garagorry

Courses
Accountancy (Accountancy); **Administration** (Administration); **International Business** (International Business); **Law**; **Literature**; **Marketing** (Marketing); **Pedagogy**; **Physical Education**; **Tourism**

History: Founded 1999.

Main Language(s) of Instruction: Portuguese

Degrees and Diplomas: *Tecnólogo*; *Bacharelado*; *Licenciatura*; *Especialização/Aperfeiçoamento*
Last Updated: 08/07/10

FACULTY OF ECONOMICS AND FINANCE OF RIO DE JANEIRO

Faculdade de Economia e Finanças do Rio de Janeiro (FEFRJ)
Praça da República 50, Centro, Rio de Janeiro,
Rio de Janeiro 20211-351
Tel: +55(21) 3077-0508
Fax: +55(21) 3077-0517
EMail: cpd@suesc.com.br
Website: http://www.web.suesc.com.br/fefrj/

Diretor: Luiz Carlos Araújo de Abreu Texeira (1995-)

Courses
Accountancy (Accountancy); **Administration**

History: Founded 1916.

Main Language(s) of Instruction: Portuguese

Degrees and Diplomas: *Bacharelado*
Last Updated: 11/12/07

FACULTY OF ECONOMICS OF THE MINING TRIANGLE

Faculdade de Ciências Econômicas do Triângulo Mineiro (FCETM)
Avenida Afrânio Azevedo 1610, Bairro Universitário, Uberaba, Minas Gerais
Tel: +55(34) 3314-8383
EMail: fcetm@fcetm.br
Website: http://www.fcetm.br

Diretor: Marcos Juliano Bordon

Courses
Accountancy (Accountancy); **Administration** (Administration); **Economics** (Economics); **Graduate Studies** (Accountancy; Business Administration; Civil Engineering; Environmental Management; Finance; Human Resources; Information Technology; Marketing; Public Administration; Transport Management)

History: Founded 1966.

Main Language(s) of Instruction: Portuguese

Degrees and Diplomas: *Bacharelado*; *Especialização/Aperfeiçoamento*. Also MBA.

Libraries: Yes
Last Updated: 16/03/11

FACULTY OF ECONOMICS, ADMINISTRATION AND ACCOUNTANCY OF DIVINÓPOLIS

Faculdade de Ciências Econômicas, Administrativas e Contábeis de Divinópolis (FACED)
Praça do Mercado, 191, Divinópolis, Minas Gerais 35500-048
Tel: +55(37) 3512-2000
Fax: +55(37) 3229-8811
EMail: faced@faced.br
Website: http://www.faced.br

Diretora Acadêmica: Elizabeth Guimarães

Courses
Accountancy; **Administration**; **Fashion Design** (Fashion Design); **Graduate Studies** *(IPPEX)* (Accountancy; Fashion Design; Finance; Health Administration; Marketing); **Law**; **Psychology**; **Social Service**

History: Founded 1967 as Faculdade de Ciências Contábeis de Divinópolis.

Main Language(s) of Instruction: Portuguese

Degrees and Diplomas: *Bacharelado*. Also postgraduate diploma and MBA.
Last Updated: 05/07/10

FACULTY OF EDUCATION - UNICIDADE

Faculdade de Educação - UNICIDADE (FDE)
R. Nestor Gomes, 130, Vitória, Espirito Santo 29015-150
Tel: +55(27) 3222-5750
EMail: direcaoacademica06@yahoo.com.br
Website: http://www.unicidade.edu.br

Diretor Executivo: Roberto Alexandre Alcantara

Courses
Education (Education; Educational Administration); **Graduate Studies**

History: Founded 2001.

Degrees and Diplomas: *Licenciatura*; *Especialização/Aperfeiçoamento*
Last Updated: 07/07/10

FACULTY OF EDUCATION AND ADMINISTRATION OF VILHENA

Faculdade de Educação e Ciências Administrativas de Vilhena (FECAV)
Av. Liliana Gonzaga, 1265, Nova Vilhena, Cx Postal 138, Vilhena, RO 78995-000
Tel: +55(69) 3322-2822 +55(69) 3322-3336
Fax: +55(69) 3322-2822
EMail: avec@avec.br
Website: http://www.avec.br

Diretora: Maria Zenilda de Souza

Courses
Accountancy; **Administration** *(FCGV)*; **Graduate Studies**; **Law** (Law); **Pedagogy**

History: Founded 1989.

Main Language(s) of Instruction: Portuguese

Degrees and Diplomas: *Bacharelado*; *Licenciatura*. Also MBA.
Last Updated: 07/07/10

FACULTY OF EDUCATION AND COMMUNICATION OF THE STATE OF SAO PAULO

Faculdade Paulista de Educação e Comunicação
Rua Raimundo Santiago, 114 - Centro, Ibiúna, SP 18150-000
Tel: +55(15) 3248-4535
EMail: fapec@ibiuna.com.br
Website: http://www.fapec-isei.com.br

Diretora: Maria da Glória Costa Ribeiro Piletti
EMail: gloria@fapec-isei.com.br

Courses
Pedagogy (Pedagogy); **Teacher Training** (Teacher Training)

History: Founded 1998.

Main Language(s) of Instruction: Portuguese

Degrees and Diplomas: *Licenciatura*; *Especialização/Aperfeiçoamento*

Libraries: Biblioteca Universitária "Cecília Meirelles
Last Updated: 10/09/10

FACULTY OF EDUCATION AND CULTURE OF CEARA

Faculdade de Ensino e Cultura do Ceará
Rua Caetano Ximenes Aragão, 110, Bairro Eng. Luciano Cavalcante, Fortazela, Ceará 60813-620
Tel: +55(85) 4009-3400
Fax: +55(85) 4009-3437
EMail: marcioacbarros@yahoo.com.br
Website: http://www.iesc.edu.br

Diretora Geral: Rita Maria Silveira da Silva
Tel: +55(85) 8848-7464 EMail: ritamsilveira@gmail.com

Courses
Administration (Administration; Business Administration; Hotel Management; Human Resources; Marketing; Systems Analysis); **Hotel Management** (Hotel Management); **Law** (Law); **Nursing**; **Pharmacy** (Pharmacy); **Physiotherapy**; **Social Communication** (Advertising and Publicity); **Technological Studies**; **Tourism** (Tourism)

History: Founded 2001.

Main Language(s) of Instruction: Portuguese

Degrees and Diplomas: *Tecnólogo*; *Bacharelado*
Last Updated: 08/07/10

FACULTY OF EDUCATION AND TECHNOLOGY OF THE REGION OF SÃO PAULO DAS MISSÕES

Faculdade de Educação e Tecnologia da Região Missioneira
Av. do Comércio, 1508 - Centro, São Paulo das Missões, RS 97980-000
Tel: +55 (55) 3563-1433
EMail: altaherbst@yahoo.com.br
Website: http://www.fetremis.edu.br/site

Diretora: Rosicler Maria Herbst

Courses
Environmental Studies (Environmental Studies); **Pedagogy** (Educational Administration; Pedagogy; Special Education)

History: Founded 2005.

Main Language(s) of Instruction: Portuguese

Degrees and Diplomas: *Licenciatura*; *Especialização/Aperfeiçoamento*
Last Updated: 02/08/10

FACULTY OF EDUCATION AND THE ENVIRONMENT

Faculdade de Educação e Meio Ambiente
Av. Machadinho, 4.349 Setor 06, Ariquemes, RO 78.932-125
Tel: +55(69) 3536-6600
EMail: faema@faema.edu.br
Website: http://www.faema.edu.br

Diretor: Airton Leite Costa

Courses
Chemistry (Chemistry); **Nursing** (Nursing); **Pharmacy** (Pharmacy); **Physics** (Physics); **Physiotherapy** (Physical Therapy); **Psychology** (Psychology)

Degrees and Diplomas: *Bacharelado*; *Licenciatura*
Libraries: Biblioteca "Julio Bordignon"
Last Updated: 02/08/10

FACULTY OF EDUCATION OF BACABAL

Faculdade de Educação de Bacabal
Rua 12 de Outubro, 377, Centro, Bacabal, MA 65700-000
Tel: +55(99) 3621-1962
EMail: ouvidoria@febac.com.br
Website: http://www.febac.com.br/site

Diretor: Neyderman Amorim EMail: neyderman@febac.com.br

Courses
Administration (Administration); **Nursing** (Nursing); **Nutrition** (Nutrition); **Pharmacy** (Pharmacy)

History: Founded 2007.
Main Language(s) of Instruction: Portuguese
Degrees and Diplomas: *Bacharelado*; *Especialização/Aperfeiçoamento*
Last Updated: 02/08/10

FACULTY OF EDUCATION OF BOM DESPACHO

Faculdade de Educação de Bom Despacho (FACEB)
Br 262 - Km 480 S/N, Caixa Postal 160, Bom Despacho, MG 35600-000
Tel: +55(37) 3521-9550
Fax: +55(37) 3521-9595
EMail: pedagogiafaceb@bdonline.com.br
Website: http://www.unipacbomdespacho.com.br/v2/Pedag/Pedagogia/Faceb

Diretora: Débora Guerra

Courses
Education (Education; Educational Administration; Pedagogy)

Degrees and Diplomas: *Licenciatura*
Last Updated: 07/07/10

FACULTY OF EDUCATION OF COLORADO DO OESTE

Faculdade de Educação de Colorado do Oeste (FAEC)
Caixa Postal 21, Avenida Paulo de Assis Ribeiro, 5681, Centro, Colorado do Oeste, RO 78996-000
Tel: +55(69) 3341-2275
Fax: +55(69) 3341-2327
EMail: faec@avec.br
Website: http://www.faec.br

Diretora: Valéria Arenhardt (1998-)

Courses
Administration; **Pedagogy** (Pedagogy); **Technical Studies** (Nursing)

History: Founded 1998
Main Language(s) of Instruction: Portuguese
Degrees and Diplomas: *Bacharelado*; *Licenciatura*
Last Updated: 07/07/10

FACULTY OF EDUCATION OF COSTA RICA

Faculdade de Educação de Costa Rica (FECRA)
Rua Ambrasina Paes Coelho, 1054, Centro, Costa Rica, MS 79550000
Tel: +55(67) 3247-1101
Fax: +55(67) 3247 1101
EMail: fecra@terra.com.br
Website: http://www.fecra.edu.br

Diretora Geral: Evair Gomes Oliveira

Courses
Administration; **Graduate Studies** (Agricultural Business; Education; Higher Education; Human Resources); **Literature** (Arts and Humanities; Literature); **Pedagogy**

History: Founded 1998
Degrees and Diplomas: *Bacharelado*; *Licenciatura*; *Especialização/Aperfeiçoamento*
Last Updated: 07/07/10

FACULTY OF EDUCATION OF ITABORAÍ

Faculdade de Educação de Itaboraí (FEITA)
Avenida Antônio Gomes, 1250, Prédio Parque Royal, Itaboraí, Rio de Janeiro 24800-000
Tel: +55(21) 2639-1253
Fax: +55(21) 2639-1234
EMail: semeita@ig.com.br; vf.ss@hotmail.com; magaldri@ig.com.br

Diretor: Marcelo Souza Paula

Courses
Education (Education); **Pedagogy** (Pedagogy)
History: Founded 1974
Main Language(s) of Instruction: Portuguese
Degrees and Diplomas: *Licenciatura*
Last Updated: 11/01/08

FACULTY OF EDUCATION OF JARU

Faculdade de Educação de Jaru (UNICENTRO)
Avenida Otaviano Pereira Neto, s/n, Setor 02, Jaru, RO 76890-000
Tel: +55(69) 3521-5606
Fax: +55(69) 3521-5606
EMail: unicentro@wol-net.com.br
Website: http://www.unicentroro.edu.br

Diretor Geral: Juarez Eduardo de Toledo Prado

Courses
Accountancy; **Administration** (Administration); **Biology** (Biology); **Environmental Management** (Environmental Management); **Graduate Studies**; **Pedagogy** (Pedagogy); **Social Service** (Social and Community Services)

History: Founded 2001.
Main Language(s) of Instruction: Portuguese
Degrees and Diplomas: *Bacharelado*; *Licenciatura*; *Especialização/Aperfeiçoamento*
Last Updated: 07/07/10

FACULTY OF EDUCATION OF OSVALDO CRUZ

Faculdade de Educação de Osvaldo Cruz (FEOCRUZ)
Rua Chile 501, Jardim das Bandeiras, Osvaldo Cruz, São Paulo 17700-000
Tel: +55(18) 3528-4706
Fax: +55(18) 3528-4706
EMail: feocruz@feocruz.edu.br
Website: http://www.feocruz.edu.br

Diretor: Jayme Gonzaga da Silva Filho

Courses
Administration (Administration); **Graduate Studies** (Business and Commerce; Educational Psychology; Marketing); **Literature** (English; Literature; Portuguese); **Pedagogy**

History: Founded 1998.

Main Language(s) of Instruction: Portuguese

Degrees and Diplomas: *Bacharelado*; *Licenciatura*; *Especialização/Aperfeiçoamento*. Also MBA.

Last Updated: 07/07/10

FACULTY OF EDUCATION OF PORTO VELHO

Faculdade de Educação de Porto Velho
Avenida Mamoré, bairro Cascalheira, n° 1520, Porto Velho,
Rondônia 78919-541
Tel: +55(69) 3733-5000
Fax: +55(69) 3733-5001
EMail: diracademica@uniron.edu.br
Website: http://www.uniron.edu.br

Diretor: Juarez Américo do Prado (1997-)

Units
Administration (Accountancy; Business Administration; Human Resources); **Architecture** (Architecture; Town Planning); **Biological and Agricultural Sciences** (Agronomy; Biological and Life Sciences; Zoology); **Communication** (Advertising and Publicity; Journalism); **Education** (Literature; Pedagogy); **Health Sciences** (Nursing; Physical Therapy); **Law** (Law); **Technology** (Computer Networks; Systems Analysis)

History: Founded 1995

Main Language(s) of Instruction: Portuguese

Degrees and Diplomas: *Bacharelado*; *Licenciatura*; *Especialização/Aperfeiçoamento*; *Mestrado*

Last Updated: 16/03/11

FACULTY OF EDUCATION OF SÃO BRAZ

Faculdade de Educação São Braz
Rua Antônio Escorsin, 1.650, no bairro São Braz, Curitiba,
PR 82300-490
EMail: isal@isal.com.br
Website: http://www.isal.com.br

Diretora: Vera Lúcia Pacheco

Courses
Accountancy (Accountancy); **Administration** (Administration); **Letters** (Literature); **Mathematics** (Mathematics); **Pedagogy** (Pedagogy); **Social Services** (Social and Community Services)

History: Founded 2004.

Main Language(s) of Instruction: Portuguese

Degrees and Diplomas: *Bacharelado*; *Licenciatura*; *Especialização/Aperfeiçoamento*

Last Updated: 03/08/10

FACULTY OF EDUCATION OF TANGARÁ DA SERRA

Faculdade de Educação de Tangará da Serra (FACEDUTS)
Rua José Corsino 1037-W, 1° Andar, Parque das Mansões,
Tangará da Serra, MT 78300-000
Tel: +55(65) 3326-4650
Fax: +55(65) 3326-4650
EMail: facitec@terra.com.br
Website: http://www.faceduts.com.br

Diretor: Wilson Dalto (1988-)

Courses
Pedagogy

History: Founded 1988.

Main Language(s) of Instruction: Portuguese

Degrees and Diplomas: *Licenciatura*; *Especialização/Aperfeiçoamento*

Last Updated: 07/07/10

FACULTY OF EDUCATION, ADMINISTRATION AND TECHNOLOGY OF IBAITI

Faculdade de Educação, Administração e Tecnológia de Ibaiti (FEATI)
Av. Tertuliano de Moura Bueno, 1400, Bairro Flamenguinho, Ibaiti,
PR 84900-000
Tel: +55(43) 3546-1263
Fax: +55(43) 3546-1263
EMail: feati@feati.com.br
Website: http://www.feati.com.br

Diretora: Edmilsa Bonin Braga

Courses
Administration; **Graduate Studies**; **Information Systems** (Information Technology); **Law** (Law); **Pedagogy** (Pedagogy)

History: Founded 2000.

Main Language(s) of Instruction: Portuguese

Degrees and Diplomas: *Bacharelado*; *Especialização/Aperfeiçoamento*. Also MBA.

Last Updated: 07/07/10

FACULTY OF EDUCATION, SCIENCE AND TECHNOLOGY

Faculdade de Educação, Ciência e Tecnologia
Avenida Mangalô N° 2385, Bairro Morada do Sol, Goiânia,
GO 74085-010
Tel: +55(62) 3293-1993
EMail: valotto@valottoconsultoria.com.br

Diretor: Adriano Franco Valotto

Courses
Administration (Administration)

Main Language(s) of Instruction: Portuguese

Degrees and Diplomas: *Bacharelado*

Last Updated: 03/08/10

FACULTY OF EDUCATIONAL EXCELLENCE OF RIO GRANDE DO NORTE - SUDERN

Faculdade de Excelência Educacional do Rio Grande do Norte - SUDERN
Rua Doutor Hernani Hugo Gomes, 90 - Capim Macio, Natal,
RN 59082-270
Tel: +55(84) 4008-0354
EMail: fatern@digizap.com.br
Website: http://www.fatern.edu.br

Diretor: Francisco Sidney Nogueira de Brito

Courses
Administration (Administration); **Advertising** (Advertising and Publicity); **Computer Networks** (Computer Networks); **Financial Management** (Finance); **Nursing** (Nursing); **Physical Therapy** (Physical Therapy); **Social Services** (Social and Community Services); **Systems Analysis** (Systems Analysis)

History: Founded 2007.

Main Language(s) of Instruction: Portuguese

Degrees and Diplomas: *Bacharelado*; *Especialização/Aperfeiçoamento*

Last Updated: 05/08/10

FACULTY OF EDUCATIONAL SCIENCES

Faculdade de Ciências Educacionais (FACE)
Rua Maria Consuelo, 123, Graça, Valença, BA 45400-000
Tel: +55(75) 3641-6898 +55(75) 3641-6899
Fax: +55(75) 3641-6898 +55(75) 3641-6899
EMail: contato@facebahia.com
Website: http://www.facebahia.edu.br

Diretor Geral: Dario Loureiro Guimarães

Courses
Administration (Administration); **Graduate Studies** (Adult Education; Educational Administration; Educational Psychology; Environmental Management; Higher Education; Linguistics; Literature;

Management; Marketing; Mathematics Education; Social and Community Services; Special Education; Teacher Training); **Literature** (Literature; Portuguese); **Mathematics** (Mathematics); **Pedagogy** (Pedagogy)

Degrees and Diplomas: *Bacharelado*; *Licenciatura*; *Especialização/Aperfeiçoamento*
Last Updated: 23/07/10

FACULTY OF EDUCATIONAL SCIENCES AND INTEGRATED SYSTEMS

Faculdade de Ciências Educacionais e Sistemas Integrados (FACESI)
Rodovia BR 369, Km 134, Ibiporã, PR 86200-000
Tel: +55(43) 3258-7991
Fax: +55(43) 3258-7991
EMail: facesi@facesi.edu.br
Website: http://www.facesi.edu.br/

Diretor Geral: Edgar Augusto Miguel Monteiro

Courses
Administration (Administration); **Graduate Studies** (Business Administration; Educational Psychology); **Marketing** (Marketing); **Pedagogy** (Pedagogy)

History: Founded 2005.

Main Language(s) of Instruction: Portuguese

Degrees and Diplomas: *Bacharelado*. Also pós-graduação
Last Updated: 16/03/11

FACULTY OF EDUCATIONAL SCIENCES OF SERGIPE

Faculdade de Ciências Educacionais de Sergipe (FCES)
Avenida Delmiro Gouveia, 800, Aracaju, SE 49035-810
Tel: +55(79) 3234-6380
Fax: +55(79) 2105-8000
EMail: efreitas@infonet.com.br
Website: http://www.faceeducar.com.br/

Diretor Geral: André Monteiro Freitas
EMail: andre.freitas@globo.com

Courses
Pedagogy (Pedagogy); **Petroleum and Gas Engineering** (Petroleum and Gas Engineering); **Theology** (Theology)

History: Founded 2005.

Main Language(s) of Instruction: Portuguese

Degrees and Diplomas: *Tecnólogo*; *Bacharelado*; *Licenciatura*
Last Updated: 23/07/10

FACULTY OF ENGINEERING OF MINAS GERAIS

Faculdade de Engenharia de Minas Gerais (FEAMIG)
Rua Aquiles Lobo, 524, Bairro Floresta, Belo Horizonte,
Minas Gerais 30150-160
Tel: +55(31) 3274-1974
Fax: +55(31) 3274-5006
EMail: secretaria@feamig.br
Website: http://www.feamig.br

Diretor: Fabiano José dos Santos

Courses
Graduate Studies (Civil Engineering; Environmental Engineering; Safety Engineering); **Land Surveying Engineering** (Agricultural Engineering; Surveying and Mapping); **Production Engineering**

Further Information: Also Gameleira Unit.

History: Founded 1974 as Escola Superior de Agrimensura de Minas Gerais. Acquired present title and status 1991.

Main Language(s) of Instruction: Portuguese

Degrees and Diplomas: *Bacharelado*; *Especialização/Aperfeiçoamento*
Last Updated: 07/07/10

FACULTY OF ENGINEERING OF SÃO PAULO

Faculdade de Engenharia São Paulo (FESP)
Avenida Nove de Julho 5520, Jardim Europa, São Paulo,
São Paulo 01406-200
Tel: +55(11) 3061-5022
Fax: +55(11) 3061-5022
EMail: fesp@sesp.edu.br
Website: http://www.fesp.br

Diretor Geral: Guilherme Gaspar Silva Dias

Courses
Civil Engineering (Civil Engineering); **Electrical Engineering** (Electrical Engineering); **Metallic Structures** (Metal Techniques)

History: Founded 1975

Main Language(s) of Instruction: Portuguese

Degrees and Diplomas: *Tecnólogo*; *Bacharelado*
Last Updated: 07/07/10

FACULTY OF ENGINEERING OF SOROCABA

Faculdade de Engenharia de Sorocaba (FACENS)
Rodovia Senador José Ermírio de Moraes, 1425, Castelinho km 15 -
Alto da Boa Vista, Sorocaba, São Paulo 18087-125
Tel: +55(15) 3238-1188
Fax: +55(15) 3238-1188
EMail: facens@facens.br
Website: http://www.facens.br

Diretor: José Alberto Deluno **EMail:** deluno@facens.br

Courses
Graduate Studies (Business and Commerce; Environmental Management; Industrial Management; Safety Engineering; Transport Management); **Undergraduate Studies**

History: Founded 1976

Main Language(s) of Instruction: Portuguese

Degrees and Diplomas: *Bacharelado*; *Especialização/Aperfeiçoamento*. Also MBA.
Last Updated: 07/07/10

FACULTY OF ESCADA

Faculdade da Escada
rua Coronel Antônio Marques, 67, Escada, PE 55.500-000
Tel: +55(81) 3534-2034
EMail: nilbemoreira.faesc@hotmail.com
Website: http://www.faesc.com

Diretor: Nilbe Maria Moreira de Oliveira

Courses
Administration (Administration); **Letters** (Literature); **Pedagogy** (Pedagogy); **Tourism** (Tourism)

History: Founded 2002.

Main Language(s) of Instruction: Portuguese

Degrees and Diplomas: *Bacharelado*; *Licenciatura*; *Especialização/Aperfeiçoamento*; *Mestrado*
Last Updated: 26/07/10

FACULTY OF ESPIRITO SANTO - UNICAPE

Faculdade Espirito Santense - UNICAPE
Rua São Jorge, 335 - Campo Grande, Cariacica, ES 29150-525
Tel: +55(27) 2122-0700
EMail: adrianapelicioni@faesa.br
Website: http://unicape.faesa.br

Diretor: Alexandre Nunes Theodoro **EMail:** diretorgeral@faesa.br

Courses
Administration (Administration); **Management and Business** (Business Education; Management)

History: Founded 2000.

Main Language(s) of Instruction: Portuguese

Degrees and Diplomas: *Bacharelado*; *Especialização/Aperfeiçoamento*

Libraries: Yes
Last Updated: 26/08/10

FACULTY OF FRUTAL
Faculdade Frutal
Rua Nova Ponte 439, Frutal, MG 38200-000
Tel: +55(34) 3423-8566
EMail: frutal@faculdadefaf.com.br
Website: http://www.sofes.edu.br
Diretor: Randall Freitas Stabile

Courses
Administration (Administration; Business Administration; Marketing); **Nutrition** (Nutrition); **Pedagogy** (Pedagogy); **Social Services** (Social and Community Services)
History: Founded 2005.
Main Language(s) of Instruction: Portuguese
Degrees and Diplomas: *Bacharelado*; *Especialização/Aperfeiçoamento*
Libraries: Yes
Last Updated: 27/08/10

FACULTY OF GUANAMBI
Faculdade Guanambi
Rua Vasco da Gama, N° 317 - A, Guanambi, BA 46430-000
Tel: +55 (77) 3451-8400
EMail: edilmacotrim@uol.com.br
Website: http://www.portalfg.com.br
Diretor: Felipe Gabriel Duarte

Courses
Accountancy (Accountancy); **Administration** (Administration); **Biomedicine** (Biomedicine); **Law** (Law); **Nursing** (Nursing); **Nutrition** (Nutrition); **Pharmacy** (Pharmacy); **Physiotherapy** (Physical Therapy)
History: Founded 2002.
Main Language(s) of Instruction: Portuguese
Degrees and Diplomas: *Bacharelado*; *Especialização/Aperfeiçoamento*
Libraries: Biblioteca Dr. Wilson Thomé Sardinha
Last Updated: 19/08/10

FACULTY OF GUARARAPES
Faculdade de Guararapes (FAG)
R. Alfredo Pacheco, 750, Guararapes, São Paulo 16700-000
Tel: +55(18) 3406-9200
Fax: +55(18) 3406-2800
EMail: mantenedora@uniesp.edu.br; ilma.lorencetti@uniesp.edu.br
Website: http://www.uniesp.edu.br/guararapes
Diretor: Joaquim Santiago Filho

Courses
Administration (Administration); **Literature** (English; Literature; Portuguese); **Pedagogy** (Pedagogy)
Degrees and Diplomas: *Bacharelado*; *Licenciatura*
Last Updated: 09/07/10

FACULTY OF GUARUJÁ
Faculdade do Guarujá (FACC)
Avenida Miguel Mussa Gaze 247, Guaruja, São Paulo 11431120
Tel: +55(13) 3383-8273
EMail: diretoria-fagu@uniesp.edu.br
Website: http://www.uniesp.edu.br
Diretor Geral: José Fernando Pinto da Costa

Courses
Administration; **Computer Science**; **Law** (Law); **Marketing** (Marketing); **Nursing**; **Telecommunications Engineering**; **Tourism** (Tourism)
History: Founded 1978. Acquired present status 1999.
Main Language(s) of Instruction: Portuguese
Degrees and Diplomas: *Tecnólogo*; *Bacharelado*
Last Updated: 04/01/08

FACULTY OF HEALTH AND HUMAN ECOLOGY
Faculdade da Saúde e Ecologia Humana (FASEH)
Rua São Paulo 958, Jardim Alterosa, Vespasiano, Minas Gerais 33200-000
Tel: +55(31) 2138-2900
Fax: +55(31) 2138-2909
EMail: faseh@faseh.edu.br
Website: http://www.faseh.edu.br
Diretor: Assuero Rodrigues da Silva EMail: diretoria@faseh.edu.br

Courses
Medicine; **Nursing** (Nursing); **Physiotherapy** (Physical Therapy)
History: Founded 2001.
Main Language(s) of Instruction: Portuguese
Degrees and Diplomas: *Bacharelado*: 4 yrs
Last Updated: 30/06/10

FACULTY OF HEALTH OF SÃO PAULO
Faculdade de Saúde de São Paulo
Rua Antônio Veronese, 850 – Jd. Brasília – Penápolis, São Paulo, SP 16300-000
Tel: +55(18) 3653-6100
EMail: fassp@fassp.edu.br
Website: http://www.fassp.edu.br
Diretor: Ulisses Bueno Marques Jr

Courses
Nursing (Nursing); **Physiotherapy** (Physical Therapy)
History: Founded 2005.
Main Language(s) of Instruction: Portuguese
Degrees and Diplomas: *Bacharelado*; *Especialização/Aperfeiçoamento*
Last Updated: 16/08/10

FACULTY OF HEALTH SCIENCES
Faculdade de Ciências da Saúde (FASU/ACEG)
Rua das Flores 740, Labienópolis, Garca, São Paulo 17400-000
Tel: +55(14) 3407-8000
Fax: +55(14) 3407-8001
EMail: faef@faef.br
Website: http://www.faef.br
Diretor: Sidney da Silva Pereira Bissoli (2003-)

Courses
Psychology
History: Founded 2001.
Degrees and Diplomas: *Bacharelado*; *Especialização/Aperfeiçoamento*; *Mestrado*
Last Updated: 18/06/08

FACULTY OF HEALTH SCIENCES OF CAMPOS GERAIS
Faculdade de Ciências da Saúde de Campos Gerais (FACICA)
Rua Santa Terezinha, 389, Centro, Campos Gerais, MG 37160-000
Tel: +55(35) 3853-1914
EMail: contato@facica.com.br
Website: http://www.facica.edu.br/
Diretor: Dilermando Rabelo

Courses
Biological Sciences (Biological and Life Sciences); **Graduate Studies** (Educational Psychology); **Nursing** (Nursing); **Pedagogy** (Pedagogy); **Pharmacy** (Pharmacy)
Degrees and Diplomas: *Bacharelado*; *Licenciatura*; *Especialização/Aperfeiçoamento*
Last Updated: 22/07/10

FACULTY OF HEALTH SCIENCES OF SAO PAULO

Faculdade de Ciências da Saúde de São Paulo (FACIS)
Rua Dona Inácia Uchoa, 399, Vila Mariana, São Paulo,
São Paulo 04110-021
Tel: +55(11) 5084-3141
Fax: +55(11) 5084-3141
EMail: info@facis.edu.br; secretariageral@facis.edu.br
Website: http://www.facis.edu.br

Diretora: Maria de Lourdes de Paula Gomes Brunini

Courses
Biological Sciences (Biological and Life Sciences); **Graduate Studies**
History: Founded 1998.
Main Language(s) of Instruction: Portuguese
Degrees and Diplomas: *Bacharelado*; *Licenciatura*; *Especialização/Aperfeiçoamento*
Last Updated: 02/07/10

FACULTY OF HEALTH SCIENCES OF SERRA

Faculdade de Ciências da Saúde da Serra (FABAVI)
Rua 1D, 80, Civit II, Serra, ES 29165-157
Tel: +55(27) 3328-6283
EMail: andrea.oliveira@fabavi.br; adrianosalvador@fabavi.br
Website: http://www.fabavi.br/

Diretor: Wesley Bastos de Souza

Courses
Nursing (Nursing)
Degrees and Diplomas: *Bacharelado*
Last Updated: 22/07/10

FACULTY OF HEALTH SCIENCES OF UNAÍ

Faculdade de Ciências da Saúde de Unaí (FACISA-UNAI)
Av. Governador Valadares, 1441, Centro, Unaí, MG 38610-000
Tel: +55(38) 3677-6030
EMail: contato@facisaunai.com.br
Website: http://facisaunai.com.br/

Courses
Nursing; **Social Services** (Social and Community Services); **Veterinary Science** (Veterinary Science)
History: Founded 2008.
Main Language(s) of Instruction: Portuguese
Degrees and Diplomas: *Bacharelado*. Also Postgraduate Diploma.
Last Updated: 16/07/10

FACULTY OF HIGHER EDUCATION OF CATALAO - CESUC FACULTY

Faculdade de Ensino Superior de Catalao - Faculdade CESUC
Catalão, GO
Tel: +55(64) 3441-6200
EMail: cesuc@cesuc.br
Website: http://www.cesuc.br

Diretor: Paulo Antonio Lima **EMail:** lima@cesuc.br

Courses
Administration; **Law** (Law)
History: Founded 2005.
Main Language(s) of Instruction: Portuguese
Degrees and Diplomas: *Bacharelado*; *Especialização/Aperfeiçoamento*; *Mestrado*
Last Updated: 04/08/10

FACULTY OF HIGHER EDUCATION OF FLORIANO

Faculdade de Ensino Superior de Floriano
Rua Nogueira Paranagá, 508 - Manguinha, Floriano, PI 64800-00
Tel: +55(89) 3521-6512
EMail: faesf@faesfpi.com.br
Website: http://www.faesfpi.com.br/afaesf.asp

Diretora: Elza Waquim Bucar de Almeida Nunes

Courses
Accountancy (Accountancy); **Administration** (Administration); **Law** (Law); **Nursing** (Nursing); **Nutrition** (Nutrition); **Pharmacy and Biochemistry** (Biochemistry; Pharmacy); **Physiotherapy** (Physical Therapy)
History: Founded 2003.
Main Language(s) of Instruction: Portuguese
Degrees and Diplomas: *Bacharelado*; *Especialização/Aperfeiçoamento*
Last Updated: 04/08/10

FACULTY OF HIGHER EDUCATION OF MARECHAL CÂNDIDO RONDON - ISEPE RONDON

Faculdade de Ensino Superior de Marechal Cândido Rondon - ISEPE RONDON
Rua Sete de Setembro 2341, Jd. Alvorada,
Marechal Cândido Rondon, PR 85960-000
Tel: +55(45) 3284-7400
EMail: secretaria@iseperondon.com.br
Website: http://www.isepe.com.br

Diretor: João César Silveira Portela

Courses
Administration (Administration); **Law** (Law)
History: Founded 2001.
Main Language(s) of Instruction: Portuguese
Degrees and Diplomas: *Bacharelado*
Last Updated: 05/08/10

FACULTY OF HIGHER EDUCATION OF PARAIBA

Faculdade de Ensino Superior da Paraiba
Av. Flávio Ribeiro Coutinho, 805, 3° Piso - Manaíra Shopping,
Manaíra, João Pessoa, PB
Tel: +55(83) 2106-6175
EMail: atendimento@fespfaculdades.com.br
Website: http://www.fespfaculdades.com.br/

Diretora: Maria Goretti de Assis Laier

Courses
Accountancy (Accountancy); **Administration** (Administration); **Law** (Law)
History: Founded 1997.
Main Language(s) of Instruction: Portuguese
Degrees and Diplomas: *Bacharelado*; *Especialização/Aperfeiçoamento*; *Mestrado*
Libraries: Yes
Last Updated: 03/08/10

FACULTY OF HIGHER EDUCATION OF PARANA

Faculdade de Educação Superior do Paraná
Rua Dr. Faivre, 141, Centro, Curitiba, PR
Tel: +55(41) 3028-6500
EMail: secretaria@fesppr.br
Website: http://www.fesppr.br

Presidente: Antonio Carlos Morozowski

Courses
Accountancy (Accountancy); **Administration** (Administration); **Economics** (Economics); **Foreign Trade** (International Business); **Information Systems** (Computer Science); **Law** (Law)

History: Founded 1974 as Instituto de Ciências Sociais do Paraná. Acquired present title 2010.

Main Language(s) of Instruction: Portuguese

Degrees and Diplomas: *Bacharelado*; *Especialização/Aperfeiçoamento*; *Mestrado*

Last Updated: 23/09/10

FACULTY OF HIGHER EDUCATION OF PIAUÍ
Faculdade de Ensino Superior do Piauí (FAESPI)
Rua Primeiro de Maio 2235, Primavera, Teresina, Piauí 64002-510
Tel: +55(86) 2107-2200
Fax: +55(86) 2107-2200
EMail: faespi.edu@gmail.com
Website: http://www.faespi.com.br

Diretor Geral: Gislan Vieira de Sousa

Courses
Graduate Studies (Administration; Educational Psychology; Educational Technology; Higher Education; Human Resources; Rehabilitation and Therapy; Special Education); **Information Systems** (Information Technology); **Law** (Law); **Pedagogy**; **Phonoaudiology** (Speech Therapy and Audiology)

History: Founded 2001.

Main Language(s) of Instruction: Portuguese

Degrees and Diplomas: *Bacharelado*; *Licenciatura*; *Especialização/Aperfeiçoamento*

Last Updated: 08/07/10

FACULTY OF HIGHER EDUCATION OF PIEMONTE DA CHAPADA
Faculdade de Educação Superior do Piemonte da Chapada
Cantiliano Rios N°: s/n, BA 417 Km 15, Contornolândia, Serrolândia, BA 44710-000
Tel: +55(74) 3631-2253
EMail: funcegemm@bol.com.br

Diretor: Geziel Moreira Jordão

Courses
Administration (Administration); **Pedagogy** (Pedagogy)
History: Founded 2005.

Main Language(s) of Instruction: Portuguese

Degrees and Diplomas: *Bacharelado*
Last Updated: 03/08/10

FACULTY OF HIGHER EDUCATION OF RORAIMA
Faculdade Roraimense de Ensino Superior (FARES)
Avenida Juscelino kubitschek, 300, Canarinho, Boa Vista, RR 69306-535
Tel: +55(95) 2121-5701
Fax: +55(95) 2121-5700
EMail: fares@fares.edu.br
Website: http://www.fares.edu.br/

Diretor Geral: José Mozart de Holanda Pinheiro

Courses
Graduate Studies (Agriculture; Higher Education; International Business); **Undergraduate Studies** (Administration; Agronomy; Economics; Nursing; Pedagogy)

Degrees and Diplomas: *Bacharelado*; *Licenciatura*; *Especialização/Aperfeiçoamento*
Last Updated: 06/09/10

FACULTY OF HIGHER EDUCATION OF SÃO MIGUEL DO IGUAÇU
Faculdade de Ensino Superior de São Miguel do Iguaçu (FAESI)
Rua Valentim Celeste Palavro, 1501, São Miguel do Iguaçu, PR 85877000
Tel: +55(45) 3565-3181
Fax: +55(45) 3565-3181
EMail: faesi@faesi.com.br
Website: http://www.faesi.com.br/2007

Diretora: Andréa Stefânia Sereni Ghellere
EMail: andrea@faesi.com.br

Courses
Accountancy (Accountancy); **Administration**; **Geography**; **Graduate Studies**; **Information Systems**; **Physical Education**; **Rural Tourism**; **Teacher Training** *(EI)* (Teacher Training); **Teacher Training** *(AI)*; **Tourism** (Tourism)

History: Founded 2000.

Main Language(s) of Instruction: Portuguese

Degrees and Diplomas: *Bacharelado*; *Licenciatura*; *Especialização/Aperfeiçoamento*
Last Updated: 08/07/10

FACULTY OF HIGHER EDUCATION OF THE INNER STATE OF SAO PAULO
Faculdade de Ensino Superior do Interior Paulista
Avenida Antonieta Altenfelder, 65 Distrito Industrial, Marília, SP 17512-130
Tel: +55(14) 3481-7737
EMail: faif@faef.br
Website: http://www.faip.edu.br/index.html

Diretora: Dayse Maria Alonso Shimizu

Courses
Administration (Administration); **Fashion Design** (Fashion Design)

History: Founded 2007.

Main Language(s) of Instruction: Portuguese

Degrees and Diplomas: *Bacharelado*
Last Updated: 05/08/10

FACULTY OF HIGHER EDUCATION OF THE REUNITED AMAZON
Faculdade de Ensino Superior da Amazônia Reunida
Rodovia PA 287, Km 15 | Cx Postal 131, Redenção, PA
Tel: +55(94) 424-5133
EMail: administrativo@fesar.com.br
Website: http://www.fesar.com.br

Diretor: Nayjla Lane

Courses
Administration (Administration); **Biomedicine** (Biomedicine); **Law** (Law); **Pedagogy** (Pedagogy); **Zoology** (Zoology)

History: Founded 2004.

Main Language(s) of Instruction: Portuguese

Degrees and Diplomas: *Bacharelado*
Libraries: Yes
Last Updated: 03/08/10

FACULTY OF HUMAN AND EXACT SCIENCES OF SERTÃO DO SÃO FRANCISCO
Faculdade de Ciências Humanas e Exatas do Sertão do São Francisco
Rua Cel Trapiá, 201 - Centro, Belém do São Francisco, PE 56440.000
Tel: +55(87)3876 1460
EMail: facesf@hotmail.com
Website: http://www.facesf.com.br

Diretor: Licinio Lustosa

Courses

Law (Law)

History: Founded 2007.

Main Language(s) of Instruction: Portuguese

Degrees and Diplomas: *Bacharelado*

Libraries: Biblioteca Professor Edson Lustosa Cantarelli

Last Updated: 29/07/10

FACULTY OF HUMAN AND HEALTH SCIENCES

Faculdade de Ciências Humanas e da Saude
Br 365 - Km 407 S/N, Patos de Minas, MG 38700-000
Tel: +55(34) 3821-5900
EMail: diretora@sespa.edu.br
Website: http://www.sespa.edu.br

Diretora: Terezinha de Deus Fonseca

Courses

Geography (Geography); **Nutrition** (Nutrition); **Physical Education** (Physical Education); **Psychology** (Psychology); **Tourism**

History: Founded 2003.

Main Language(s) of Instruction: Portuguese

Degrees and Diplomas: *Bacharelado*; *Licenciatura*

Last Updated: 29/07/10

FACULTY OF HUMAN AND SOCIAL SCIENCES

Faculdade de Ciências Humanas e Sociais (FCHS)
Rua Mariz e Barros 612, Tijuca, Rio de Janeiro,
Rio de Janeiro 5041001
Tel: +55(21) 2567-1185 +55(21) 2569-3849
Fax: +55(21) 2567-3849
EMail: secretariaisabel@ig.com.br
Website: http://www.institutoisabel.com.br/faculdade.
asp?faculdade=1

Diretora: Eulalia Schiavo

Courses

Pedagogy (Pedagogy)

History: Founded 1973

Degrees and Diplomas: *Licenciatura*

Last Updated: 05/07/10

FACULTY OF HUMAN AND SOCIAL SCIENCES

Faculdade de Ciências Humanas e Sociais (FUCAMP)
Av. Brasil Oeste, s/n, Jardim Zenith II, Monte Carmelo,
Minas Gerais 38500-000
Tel: +55(34) 842-5272
Fax: +55(34) 842-2330
EMail: fucamp@fucamp.com.br
Website: http://www.fucamp.com.br

Diretora Presidente: Guilherme Marcos Ghelli

Courses

Administration (Administration); **Agronomy** (Agronomy); **Biological Sciences**; **Graduate Studies** *(MBA)* (Accountancy; Business Administration; Finance; Human Resources; Marketing; Public Health); **Graduate Studies** *(Especializações)*; **Law** (Law); **Literature** (English; Literature; Portuguese); **Pedagogy** (Pedagogy); **Systems for Internet** (Information Technology)

History: Founded 2000.

Degrees and Diplomas: *Bacharelado*; *Licenciatura*; *Especialização/Aperfeiçoamento*. Also MBA.

Last Updated: 05/07/10

FACULTY OF HUMAN SCIENCES OF AGUAI

Faculdade de Ciências Humanas de Aguai (FACHA)
Olinda Silveira Cruz Braga 200, Prédio 5 Paque Interlagos, Aguai,
SP 13860000
Tel: +55(19) 3652-4344
Fax: +55(19) 3652-5345
EMail: faculdade@aguai.edu.br
Website: http://www.aguai.edu.br

Diretora Geral: Ellen Rose Bentley

Courses

Graduate Studies (Educational Psychology; Health Education; Higher Education; Literacy Education; Preschool Education; Social Work; Special Education); **Pedagogy** (Educational Administration; Educational and Student Counselling; Pedagogy); **Social Services** (Social and Community Services)

History: Founded 2001.

Main Language(s) of Instruction: Portuguese

Degrees and Diplomas: *Bacharelado*; *Licenciatura*. Also Postgraduate Diploma.

Last Updated: 05/07/10

FACULTY OF HUMAN SCIENCES OF CRUREIZO

Faculdade de Ciências Humanas de Cruzeiro
Rua dos Andradas, 1039 - Vila Brasil, Crureizo, SP 12703-030
Tel: +55(12) 3143-3866
EMail: faciccruzeiro@uol.com.br
Website: http://www.faciccruzeiro.com.br

Courses

Accountancy (Accountancy); **Administration** (Administration; Finance; Human Resources; Management); **Law** (Civil Law; Commercial Law; Criminal Law; Labour Law; Law); **Production Engineering** (Chemistry; Computer Science; Design; Management; Marketing; Materials Engineering; Physics; Production Engineering)

History: Founded 2006.

Main Language(s) of Instruction: Portuguese

Degrees and Diplomas: *Bacharelado*; *Especialização/Aperfeiçoamento*

Last Updated: 29/07/10

FACULTY OF HUMAN SCIENCES OF CURVELO

Faculdade de Ciências Humanas de Curvelo (FACIC)
Avenida J.K. 1441, Jóquei Clube, Curvelo, Minas Gerais 35790000
Tel: +55(38) 3722-2600
Fax: +55(38) 3722-2600
EMail: facic@facic.br
Website: http://www.facic.br

Diretor Geral: Leonardo Paiva Martins de Oliveira
EMail: diretoria@facic.br

Courses

Graduate Studies (Business Education; Educational and Student Counselling; Educational Psychology; Educational Technology; Mathematics; Tourism; Zoology); **History** (History); **Literature**; **Nursing** (Nursing); **Science**

History: Founded 1975.

Main Language(s) of Instruction: Portuguese

Degrees and Diplomas: *Bacharelado*; *Licenciatura*; *Especialização/Aperfeiçoamento*

Last Updated: 05/07/10

FACULTY OF HUMAN SCIENCES OF GARÇA

Faculdade de Ciências Humanas de Garça (FAHU)
Rua das Flores 740, Labienópolis, Garça, São Paulo 174000-000
Tel: +55(14) 3704-8000
Fax: +55(14) 3704-8001
EMail: faef@faef.br
Website: http://www.faef.br

Diretora: Dayse Maria Alonso Shimizu

Courses

Pedagogy (Pedagogy); **Tourism** (Tourism)

History: Founded 1999.

Degrees and Diplomas: *Bacharelado*; *Licenciatura*

Last Updated: 05/07/10

FACULTY OF HUMAN SCIENCES OF OLINDA
Faculdade de Ciências Humanas de Olinda (FACHO)
Rodovia PE 15 Km 36, Ouro Preto, Olinda, Pernambuco 53250770
Tel: +55(81) 3429-4046
Fax: +55(81) 3429-4100
EMail: facho@facho.br
Website: http://www.facho.br

Diretor: José Adailson de Medeiros

Courses
Graduate Studies (Art Therapy; Curriculum; Education of the Socially Disadvantaged; Educational Psychology; Literacy Education; Psychology; Social Work); **Literature**; **Nursing**; **Pedagogy** (Pedagogy); **Psychology** (Psychology); **Tourism** (Tourism)
History: Founded 1973
Main Language(s) of Instruction: Portuguese
Degrees and Diplomas: *Bacharelado*; *Licenciatura*; *Especialização/Aperfeiçoamento*
Last Updated: 05/07/10

FACULTY OF HUMAN SCIENCES OF PERNAMBUCO
Faculdade de Ciências Humanas de Pernambuco (FCHPE)
Avenida João de Barros 561, Boa Vista, Recife, Pernambuco 50050-180
Tel: +55(81) 3221-4423
Fax: +55(81) 3421-4100
EMail: sopece@sopece.br
Website: http://www.sopece.br

Diretora Vice-Presidente: Osita Moraes Pinto Ferreira
EMail: osita@sopece.br

Courses
Accountancy; **Administration** (Administration); **Law** (Law)
History: Founded 1987
Main Language(s) of Instruction: Portuguese
Degrees and Diplomas: *Bacharelado*
Last Updated: 05/07/10

FACULTY OF HUMAN SCIENCES OF THE VALLEY OF RIO GRANDE
Faculdade de Ciências Humanas do Vale do Rio Grande (EDUVALE)
Av. Gov. Dr. Adhemar Pereira de Barros, 1.200, Distrito Industrial, Olimpia, São Paulo 15400-000
Tel: +55(17) 3281-4372
Fax: +55(17) 3281-4364
EMail: secretariageral@eduvale.br
Website: http://www.eduvale.br

Diretora: Lucia de Fatima Zangirolami Souza

Courses
Administration (Administration); **Chemistry**; **Labour Safety** (Safety Engineering)
History: Founded 1990
Main Language(s) of Instruction: Portuguese
Degrees and Diplomas: *Bacharelado*. Also Technical diploma.
Last Updated: 05/07/10

FACULTY OF HUMAN SCIENCES OF VITÓRIA
Faculdade de Ciências Humanas de Vitória (FCHV)
Rua Padre Antonio /Ribeiro Pinto 142, Ed. FAVIX, Vitória, Espirito Santo 29052-290
Tel: +55(27) 3225-4004 +55(27) 3026-949
Fax: +55(27) 3225-0370
EMail: direcao@metropolitanavix.com.br
Website: http://www.favix.com.br
Diretor: Carlos Coutinho Batalha (1990-)

Courses
Accountancy (Accountancy); **Administration** (Administration; Business Administration; Hotel and Restaurant; Human Resources; Information Sciences; International Business; Transport Management); **Arts and Humanities** (Arts and Humanities); **Education** (Education; Teacher Training); **Postgraduate** (Accountancy; Transport Management)
History: Founded 1986.
Main Language(s) of Instruction: Portuguese
Degrees and Diplomas: *Bacharelado*; *Licenciatura*; *Especialização/Aperfeiçoamento*; *Mestrado*
Last Updated: 12/12/07

FACULTY OF HUMAN, HEALTH, EXACT AND JURIDICAL SCIENCES OF TERESINA - CENTRE OF UNIFIED EDUCATION OF TERESINA
Faculdade de Ciências Humanas, Saúde, Exatas e Jurídicas de Teresina - Centro de Ensino Unificado de Teresina (CEUT)
Avenida dos Expedicionários 790 São João, Teresina, Piauí 64046700
Tel: +55(86) 4009-4300
Fax: +55(86) 3232-4888
EMail: fatima@ceut.com.br
Website: http://www.ceut.com.br

Diretor: Honório José Nunes Bona (1994-)
EMail: honoriobona@ceut.com.br

Courses
Accountancy; **Administration**; **Advertising and Publicity** (Advertising and Publicity); **Computer Science**; **Executive Secretary**; **Graduate Studies**; **Journalism**; **Law** (Law); **Nursing** (Nursing); **Nutrition**; **Physical Therapy**
History: Founded 1994.
Main Language(s) of Instruction: Portuguese
Degrees and Diplomas: *Bacharelado*; *Especialização/Aperfeiçoamento*
Last Updated: 22/04/10

FACULTY OF IGARASSU
Faculdade de Igarassú (FACIG)
Rodovia BR 101 Norte Km 25, Cerntro, Igarassu, PE 53600000
Tel: +55(81) 3543-1636
Fax: +55(81) 3543-1205
EMail: facig@facig-pe.edu.br
Website: http://facig-pe.edu.br

Diretor: Walfredo Uchoa Cavalcanti **EMail:** diretor@facig-pe.com.br

Courses
Accountancy (Accountancy); **Administration** (Administration); **Law**; **Mathematics**; **Pedagogy** (Pedagogy)
History: Founded 1998
Main Language(s) of Instruction: Portuguese
Degrees and Diplomas: *Bacharelado*; *Licenciatura*. Also Postgraduate diploma.
Last Updated: 09/07/10

FACULTY OF ILHA SOLTEIRA
Faculdade de Ilha Solteira (FIS)
Alameda Bahia 490 C Centro, Ilha Solteira, São Paulo 15385000
Tel: +55(18) 3743-3905
Fax: +55(18) 3743-3906
EMail: faisa@projetonet.com.br
Website: http://www.faisa.com.br
Diretor Geral: Osmar Martins de Oliveira

Courses
Administration (Administration; Business and Commerce; Human Resources; Marketing); **Graduate Studies** *(Lato Sensu)*; **Pedagogy**
History: Founded 2000.
Main Language(s) of Instruction: Portuguese

Degrees and Diplomas: *Bacharelado*; *Licenciatura*; *Especialização/Aperfeiçoamento*
Last Updated: 09/07/10

FACULTY OF IMPERATRIZ
Faculdade de Imperatriz (FACIMP)
Av. Prudente de Morais, s/nº, Residencial Kubitscheck, Imperatriz, MA 65900-000
Tel: +55(98) 3525-1775
Fax: +55(98) 3524-8298
EMail: facimp@facimp.edu.br
Website: http://www.facimp.edu.br

Diretora Geral: Dorlice Souza Andrade
EMail: gabinete@facimp.edu.br

Courses
Accountancy (Accountancy); **Economics** (Economics); **Graduate Studies** (Accountancy; Educational Technology; Higher Education; Public Health; Systems Analysis); **Information Systems** (Computer Science); **Law**; **Nursing** (Nursing); **Odontology** (Dentistry); **Pedagogy** (Pedagogy); **Pharmacy** (Pharmacy); **Zootechnics** (Animal Husbandry)

History: Founded 2001.

Main Language(s) of Instruction: Portuguese

Degrees and Diplomas: *Bacharelado*; *Licenciatura*; *Especialização/Aperfeiçoamento*
Last Updated: 09/07/10

FACULTY OF INDUSTRIAL DESIGN OF MAUÁ
Faculdade de Desenho Industrial de Mauá (FADIM)
Rua Alonso Vasconcelos Pacheco, 1621, Vila Bocaina, Mauá, São Paulo 9310380
Tel: +55(11) 4516-2166 +55(11) 4547-4688
Fax: +55(11) 4547 4688
EMail: secretaria@fadim.edu.br
Website: http://www.fadim.edu.br/

Diretora: Rosane Andréa Tartuce

Courses
Environmental Management; **Fashion Design** (Fashion Design); **Human Resources Management** (Human Resources); **Industrial Design** (Industrial Design)

History: Founded 1975

Main Language(s) of Instruction: Portuguese

Degrees and Diplomas: *Tecnólogo*; *Bacharelado*
Last Updated: 06/07/10

FACULTY OF INHUMAS
Faculdade de Inhumas
Avenida Monte Alegre 100 - Qd 03 Lt 11/37, Inhumas, GO 75400-000
Tel: +55(62) 3514-5050
EMail: contato@facmais.com.br
Website: http://www.facmais.edu.br

Diretor: Celmar Laurindo de Freitas

Courses
Accountancy (Accountancy); **Administration** (Administration); **Nursing** (Nursing)

History: Founded 2006.

Main Language(s) of Instruction: Portuguese

Degrees and Diplomas: *Bacharelado*; *Especialização/Aperfeiçoamento*
Last Updated: 06/08/10

FACULTY OF INTEGRATED THEOLOGY
Faculdade de Teologia Integrada
Br 101 Km 425 s/n, Igarassu, PE 53640-900
Tel: +55(81)3088-1907
EMail: faculdadefatin@hotmail.com
Website: http://www.fatin.com.br

Diretora: Cleide Gomes Vianna

Courses
Business Administration (Business Administration); **Theology** (Theology)

History: Founded 2005.

Main Language(s) of Instruction: Portuguese

Degrees and Diplomas: *Bacharelado*; *Especialização/Aperfeiçoamento*

Libraries: Yes
Last Updated: 30/08/10

FACULTY OF INTENSIVE TECHNOLOGY
Faculdade de Tecnologia Intensiva (FATECI)
Rua Barão de Aratanha, 51, Centro, Fortaleza, CE 60050-070
Tel: +55(85) 3253-7050
Fax: +55(85) 3253-7050
EMail: fateci@fateci.com.br
Website: http://www.fateci.com.br/

Diretor Geral: Clauder Ciarlini Filho **EMail:** clauder@fateci.com.br

Courses
Biomedicine (Biomedicine); **Environmental Management** (Environmental Management); **Gastronomy Management** (Hotel and Restaurant); **Graduate Studies** (Cooking and Catering; Educational Psychology; Health Administration; Health Education; Medicine; Psychoanalysis; Psychology; Radiology; Safety Engineering); **Hospital Management** (Health Administration); **Nursing** (Nursing); **Pharmacy** (Pharmacy); **Phonoaudiology** (Speech Therapy and Audiology); **Physical Therapy** (Physical Therapy); **Radiology** (Radiology); **Real Estate** (Real Estate)

Degrees and Diplomas: *Tecnólogo*; *Especialização/Aperfeiçoamento*
Last Updated: 25/08/10

FACULTY OF IPORA
Faculdade de Iporá
Rua Serra Cana Brava Qd. 02 Lt 04 nº 512 Jd. Novo Horizonte II, Iporá, GO 76200-000
Tel: +55(64) 3674-5181
EMail: fai@faculdadedeipora.com.br
Website: http://www.faculdadedeipora.com.br

Diretora: Angela Maria Leonel Ferreira Moura.

Courses
Accountancy (Accountancy); **Administration** (Administration)

History: Founded 2005.

Main Language(s) of Instruction: Portuguese

Degrees and Diplomas: *Bacharelado*; *Especialização/Aperfeiçoamento*
Last Updated: 06/08/10

FACULTY OF ITAITUBA
Faculdade de Itaituba
Av. Gov. Fernando Guilhon, nº 895 - Bairro Jardim Das Araras, Itaituba, PA 68180-110
Tel: +55(93) 3518-4319
EMail: fai@unifaitb.edu.br
Website: http://www.unifaitb.edu.br

Diretor: Abel Huyapuam de Sá Almeida

Courses
Accountancy (Accountancy); **Business Administration** (Business Administration); **History** (History); **Letters** (Literature); **Pedagogy** (Pedagogy)

History: Founded 2003.

Main Language(s) of Instruction: Portuguese

Degrees and Diplomas: *Bacharelado*; *Especialização/Aperfeiçoamento*
Last Updated: 06/08/10

FACULTY OF ITANHAEM
Faculdade Itanhaém (FAITA)
Av. Emb.Pedro de Toledo, 196 Centro, Itanhaem, SP 11740000
Tel: +55(13) 3426-5040
Fax: +55(13) 3426-5040
EMail: secretaria@faita.edu.br
Website: http://www.faita.edu.br

Diretor: Paulo Sergio Lourenço

Courses
Accountancy (Accountancy); **Administration**; **Tourism**
History: Founded 1998.
Main Language(s) of Instruction: Portuguese
Degrees and Diplomas: *Bacharelado*
Last Updated: 06/07/10

FACULTY OF ITAPECERICA DA SERRA
Faculdade de Itapecerica da Serra
Estrada dos Maciéis, 198/210, Bairro: Embu Mirim,
Itapecerica da Serra, SP
Tel: +55 (11) 4668-6767
EMail: falefit@faculdadefit.edu.br
Website: http://www.faculdadefit.edu.br

Diretora: Margarida Cecília Corrêa Nogueira Rocha

Courses
Administration (Administration); **Letters** (Literature); **Pedagogy** (Pedagogy)
History: Founded 2006.
Main Language(s) of Instruction: Portuguese
Degrees and Diplomas: *Bacharelado*; *Licenciatura*; *Especialização/Aperfeiçoamento*
Last Updated: 06/08/10

FACULTY OF ITAPETININGA
Faculdade de Itapetininga
Rua Izolina de Moraes 727, Itapetininga, SP 18206-320
Tel: +55(15) 3272 6126
EMail: objetivoitape@bol.com.br

Diretora: Telma de Melo Almada Lobo

Courses
Information Systems (Computer Science)
History: Founded 2004.
Main Language(s) of Instruction: Portuguese
Degrees and Diplomas: *Bacharelado*
Last Updated: 06/08/10

FACULTY OF ITÁPOLIS
Faculdade de Itápolis (FACITA)
Rua Mário de Souza Castro, 200, (Prolongamento da Rua
Ricieri Antonio Vessoni), Jardim Santa Mônica, Itápolis,
São Paulo 14900-000
Tel: +55(16) 3263-9210
Fax: +55(16) 3262-3173
EMail: facita@facita.edu.br
Website: http://www.facita.edu.br

Diretor: Maria José Jacomelli Próspero

Courses
Administration; **Graduate Studies** *(Lato Sensu)*; **Pedagogy** (Pedagogy)
History: Founded 1999
Degrees and Diplomas: *Bacharelado*; *Licenciatura*; *Especialização/Aperfeiçoamento*
Last Updated: 09/07/10

FACULTY OF JABOTICABAL
Faculdade de Jaboticabal
Rua Juca Quito 618, Jaboticabal, SP 14870-260
Tel: +55(16) 3202-3844
EMail: diretoria@fajab.com.br
Website: http://www.fajab.com.br

Diretor: Edwin Kenji Takeuti

Courses
Administration (Administration); **Information Management** (Information Management); **Rural Administration** (Rural Planning)
History: Founded 2001.
Main Language(s) of Instruction: Portuguese
Degrees and Diplomas: *Bacharelado*
Last Updated: 06/08/10

FACULTY OF JAGUARIAÍVA
Faculdade Jaguariaíva
Rua Santa Catarina, n° 04, bairro: Jardim Nossa Senhora de
Fátima, Jaguariaíva, PR 84200-000
Tel: +55(43) 3535-2830
EMail: fajar@fajar.edu.br
Website: http://www.fajar.edu.br

Diretor: José Carlos de Carvalho **EMail:** josecarlos@fajar.edu.br

Courses
Forestry Engineering (Forestry); **Law** (Law)
History: Founded 2002.
Main Language(s) of Instruction: Portuguese
Degrees and Diplomas: *Bacharelado*; *Especialização/Aperfeiçoamento*
Libraries: Yes
Last Updated: 01/09/10

FACULTY OF JAGUARIÚNA
Faculdade de Jaguariúna (FAJ)
Rua Amazonas 504, Jardim Dom Bosco, Jaguariúna,
São Paulo 13820000
Tel: +55(19) 3837-8800
Fax: +55(19) 3867-1000
EMail: secretaria@faj.br
Website: http://www.faj.br

Diretor Geral: Ricardo Tannus **EMail:** diretor@faj.br

Courses
Accountancy; **Administration**; **Automation and Control Engineering**; **Computer Science**; **Environmental Engineering** (Environmental Engineering); **Events Management** (Public Relations); **Food Engineering** (Food Technology); **Graduate Studies** (Anaesthesiology; Animal Husbandry; Business Administration; Dentistry; Health Administration; Public Health; Safety Engineering; Surgery; Veterinary Science); **Industrial Automation**; **Law** (Law); **Logistics** (Transport Management); **Marketing** (Marketing); **Nursing** (Nursing); **Nutrition** (Nutrition); **Physical Education** (Physical Education); **Physical Therapy** (Physical Therapy); **Production Engineering** (Production Engineering); **Psychology** (Psychology); **Tourism** (Tourism); **Veterinary Medicine** (Veterinary Science)
Further Information: Also two other Units: Hospital-Escola Veterinário and Interclínicas.
History: Founded 2000.
Degrees and Diplomas: *Tecnólogo*; *Bacharelado*; *Licenciatura*; *Especialização/Aperfeiçoamento*. Also MBA.
Last Updated: 09/07/10

FACULTY OF JANDAIA DO SUL
Faculdade de Jandaia do Sul (FAFIJAN)
Rua Dr. João Maximiano 426, Térreo, Centro, Jandaia do Sul,
PR 86900000
Tel: +55(43) 3432-4141
Fax: +55(43) 3432-4141
EMail: fafijan@fafijan.br
Website: http://www.fafijan.br

Diretor: Italo Tasso

Courses

Accountancy (Accountancy); **Biology** (Biology); **Business Administration** (Business Administration); **Geography** (Geography); **Letters** (Literature); **Marketing**; **Pedagogy** (Pedagogy); **Psychology** (Psychology); **Quality Management** (Management)

History: Founded 1966 as Faculdade de Filosofia, Ciências e Letras de Jandaia do Sul.

Degrees and Diplomas: *Bacharelado*; *Licenciatura*; *Especialização/Aperfeiçoamento*; *Mestrado*
Last Updated: 09/07/10

FACULTY OF JAU
Faculdade Jauense
Rua Edgard Ferraz, 41 - Centro, Jau, SP 17201-440
Tel: +55(14) 3602-7799
EMail: fajau@fajau.com.br
Website: http://www.fajau.com.br/fajau.html

Diretora: Monica Abed Zaher

Courses

Business Administration (Business Administration); **Systems Analysis** (Systems Analysis)

History: Founded 2007.

Main Language(s) of Instruction: Portuguese

Degrees and Diplomas: *Bacharelado*
Last Updated: 01/09/10

FACULTY OF JOSÉ BONIFACIO
Faculdade de José Bonifacio (FJB)
Avenida Joaquim Moreira da Silva 3200, José Bonifacio, São Paulo 15200000
Tel: +55(17) 3245-4045
EMail: uibe@fjb.com.br
Website: http://www.fjb.com.br

Diretor: Neide Romani Covre

Courses

Administration; **Letters** (Literature); **Pedagogy** (Pedagogy)

History: Founded 1999.

Main Language(s) of Instruction: Portuguese

Degrees and Diplomas: *Bacharelado*; *Licenciatura*; *Especialização/Aperfeiçoamento*; *Mestrado*

Libraries: Biblioteca Professor José Gonzaga da Silva Neto
Last Updated: 09/07/10

FACULTY OF JUAZEIRO DO NORTE
Faculdade de Juazeiro do Norte
Rua São Francisco 1224, Juazeiro do Norte, CE 63010-210
Tel: +55(88) 3511-1852
EMail: fjn@fjn.edu.br
Website: http://www.fjn.edu.br/

Diretor: José Marcondes Macêdo Landim

Courses

Accountancy (Accountancy); **Information Systems** (Computer Science); **Nursing** (Nursing); **Pharmacy** (Pharmacy)

History: Founded 2003.

Main Language(s) of Instruction: Portuguese

Degrees and Diplomas: *Bacharelado*; *Especialização/Aperfeiçoamento*

Libraries: Biblioteca Central Patativa do Assaré
Last Updated: 06/08/10

FACULTY OF JURIDICAL SCIENCES AND MANAGEMENT OF GARÇA
Faculdade de Ciências Jurídicas e Gerenciais de Garça (FAEG)
Rua das Flores 740, Labienópolis, Garça, São Paulo 17400-000
Tel: +55(14) 3407-8000
Fax: +55(14) 3407-8001
EMail: faef@faef.br
Website: http://www.faef.br

Diretor: Jozébio Esteves Gomes

Courses

Accountancy; **Administration** (Administration; Business Administration; International Business; Management); **Information Systems**; **Law** (Law)

History: Founded 1998

Degrees and Diplomas: *Bacharelado*. Also M.B.A. in Administration and Marketing
Last Updated: 12/12/07

FACULTY OF JURIDICAL SCIENCES, MANAGEMENT AND EDUCATION
Faculdade de Ciências Jurídicas, Gerenciais e Educação de Sinop (FIS)
Avenida Brasília 955 Setor Industrial, Sinop, MT 78550000
Tel: +55(65) 3531-0916
Fax: +55(65) 3531-1000
EMail: unicsnp@terra.com.br

Diretor Presidente: Altamiro Belo Galindo

Courses

Accountancy; **Administration** (Administration); **Biology**; **Computer Networks**; **Law** (Law); **Postgraduate** (Business Administration; Civil Law; Finance; Information Management; Laboratory Techniques)

History: Founded 1999

Degrees and Diplomas: *Bacharelado*; *Licenciatura*; *Especialização/Aperfeiçoamento*
Last Updated: 12/12/07

FACULTY OF LAW AND SOCIAL SCIENCES OF LESTE DE MINAS
Faculdade de Direito e Ciências Sociais do Lests de Minas
Avenida Marcionília Breder Sathler N°: 1, Reduto, MG 36920-000
Tel: +55(33) 3378-4000
EMail: secretaria@fadileste.edu.br
Website: http://www.fadileste.edu.br/2010

Diretor: João Paulo Hott

Courses

Information Systems (Computer Science); **Law** (Law); **Letters** (Literature); **Mathematics** (Mathematics); **Pedagogy** (Pedagogy)

History: Founded 1989.

Main Language(s) of Instruction: Portuguese

Degrees and Diplomas: *Bacharelado*
Libraries: Yes
Last Updated: 02/08/10

FACULTY OF LAW OF CACHOEIRO DO ITAPEMIRIM
Faculdade de Direito de Cachoeiro do Itapemirim (FDCI)
Rodovia ES 482 - Cachoeiro x Alegre, Km 05 - Morro Grande, Cachoeiro de Itapemirim, ES 29313-210
Tel: +55(27) 2101-0311
Fax: +55(27) 2101-0330
EMail: fdci@fdci.br
Website: http://www.fdci.br

Diretor: Humberto Dias Viana (1996-)
EMail: humbertoviana@fdci.br

Courses
Law (Law); **Magistrate Career** (Law)
History: Founded 1965.
Degrees and Diplomas: *Bacharelado*; *Especialização/Aperfeiçoamento*
Last Updated: 06/07/10

FACULTY OF LAW OF CARANGOLA

Faculdade de Direito de Carangola
Praça dos Estudantes N°23, Santa Emília, Carangola,
MG 36800-000
EMail: funcec@uai.com.br

Courses
Law (Law)
History: Founded 2007.
Main Language(s) of Instruction: Portuguese
Degrees and Diplomas: *Bacharelado*
Last Updated: 02/08/10

FACULTY OF LAW OF FRANCISCO BELTRÃO

Faculdade de Direito de Francisco Beltrão (CESUL)
Av. Antônio de Paiva Cantelmo, 1222, Centro, Francisco Beltrão,
PR 85601-270
Tel: +55(46) 3524-4242
Fax: +55(46) 3524-4242
EMail: cesul@cesul.br
Website: http://www.cesul.br

Diretor: Roseli T. Michaloksi Alves **EMail:** marlon@cesul.br

Courses
Law
History: Founded 2000.
Main Language(s) of Instruction: Portuguese
Degrees and Diplomas: *Bacharelado*; *Especialização/Aperfeiçoamento*
Last Updated: 06/07/10

FACULTY OF LAW OF ITABIRA

Faculdade de Direito de Itabira
Rua Francisco Ozório de Menezes 520, Itabira, MG 35900-597
Tel: +55(31) 3834-7000
EMail: censi@censi.edu.br

Diretor: Arlélio de Carvalho Lage

Courses
Law (Law)
History: Founded 2002.
Main Language(s) of Instruction: Portuguese
Degrees and Diplomas: *Bacharelado*
Last Updated: 10/08/10

FACULTY OF LAW OF ITU

Faculdade de Direito de Itú (FADITU)
Avenida Tiradentes, 1817, Itú, São Paulo 13300000
Tel: +55(11) 4024-9500
Fax: +55(11) 4024-1114 +55(11) 4024-2933
EMail: faditu@faditu.com.br
Website: http://www.faditu.com.br

Diretor: Mário Antônio Duarte **EMail:** diretoria@faditu.com.br

Courses
Graduate Studies (Civil Law; Commercial Law; Criminal Law; Environmental Studies; Higher Education; Labour Law; Public Law); Law (Law)
History: Founded 1969
Degrees and Diplomas: *Bacharelado*; *Especialização/Aperfeiçoamento*. Also MBA.
Last Updated: 06/07/10

FACULTY OF LAW OF SANTA MARIA

Faculdade de Direito de Santa Maria
Rua Duque de Caxias 2319, Santa Maria, RS 97060
Tel: +55(55) 3220-2500
EMail: fadisma@fadisma.com.br
Website: http://www.fadisma.com.br

Diretor: Eduardo de Assis Brasil Rocha
EMail: eduardo@fadisma.com.br

Courses
Law (Commercial Law; International Law; Law; Private Law)
History: Founded 2003.
Main Language(s) of Instruction: Portuguese
Degrees and Diplomas: *Bacharelado*; *Especialização/Aperfeiçoamento*
Libraries: Biblioteca Ministro Eros Roberto Grau
Last Updated: 02/08/10

FACULTY OF LAW OF SOROCABA

Faculdade de Direito de Sorocaba (FADI)
Rua Doutora Ursulina Lopes Torres 123, Vergueiro, Sorocaba,
São Paulo 18035380
Tel: +55(15) 2105-1234
Fax: +55(15) 2105-1234
EMail: secretaria@fadi.br
Website: http://www.fadi.br

Diretor: José de Mello Junqueira

Courses
Graduate Studies; Law (Law)
History: Founded 1957
Main Language(s) of Instruction: Portuguese
Degrees and Diplomas: *Bacharelado*; *Especialização/Aperfeiçoamento*
Last Updated: 06/07/10

FACULTY OF LAW OF THE SOUTH OF MINAS

Faculdade de Direito do Sul de Minas (FDSM)
Av. Dr. João Beraldo, 1075, Bairro Saúde, Pouso Alegre,
Minas Gerais 37550-000
Tel: +55(35) 3449 8100
Fax: +55(35) 3449-8102
EMail: fdsm@fdsm.edu.br
Website: http://www.fdsm.edu.br

Diretor: Rafael Tadeu Simões
Tel: +(35) 3449-8101 **EMail:** diretoria@fdsm.edu.br

Courses
Graduate Studies *(Lato Sensu)* (Civil Law; Constitutional Law); **Graduate Studies** *(Stricto Sensu)*; Law (Law)
History: Founded 1969
Main Language(s) of Instruction: Portuguese
Degrees and Diplomas: *Bacharelado*; *Especialização/Aperfeiçoamento*; *Mestrado*
Last Updated: 06/07/10

FACULTY OF LAW OF THE VALLEY OF THE DOCE RIVER

Faculdade de Direito do Vale do Rio Doce
Rua Dom Pedro II, 244 – Centro, Governador Valadares,
MG 35010-090
Tel: +55(33) 3271-2004
EMail: fadivale@fadivale.edu.br
Website: http://www.fadivale.edu.br/

Diretor: Alcyr Nascimento

Courses
Law (Civil Law; Criminal Law; Labour Law; Public Law)
History: Founded 1969.
Main Language(s) of Instruction: Portuguese

Degrees and Diplomas: *Bacharelado*; *Especialização/Aperfeiçoamento*

Libraries: Yes
Last Updated: 02/08/10

FACULTY OF LAW OF THE UPPER STATE OF SAO PAULO - FACULTY OF THE UPPER STATE OF SAO PAULO

Faculdade de Direito da Alta Paulista - Faculdade da Alta Paulista (FADAP)
Rua Mandaguaris 1010, Térreo, Centro, Tupã, São Paulo 17604000
Tel: +55(14) 3441-1862
Fax: +55(14) 3441-1862
EMail: secretaria@fadap.br
Website: http://www.fadap.br

Diretor: Carlos Roberto Marsiglia de Figueiredo

Courses
Administration (Administration); **Computer Networks** (Computer Networks); **Hotel Management** (Hotel Management); **Law** *(FADAP)* (Law); **Literature**; **Nursing**; **Physiotherapy**; **Psychology** (Psychology); **Tourism** (Tourism); **Web Design** (Computer Science)

History: Founded 1970 as Faculdade de Direito da Alta Paulista. Added Faculdade da Alta Paulista at a later stage.

Main Language(s) of Instruction: Portuguese

Degrees and Diplomas: *Bacharelado*; *Especialização/Aperfeiçoamento*
Last Updated: 29/06/10

FACULTY OF LAW OF VARGINHA

Faculdade de Direito de Varginha (FADIVA)
Rua José Gonçalves Pereira, 112 Vila Pinto, Varginha, Minas Gerais 37010-500
Tel: +55(35) 3221-1900
EMail: diretoria@fadiva.edu.br
Website: http://www.fadiva.edu.br

Diretor: Álvaro Vani Bemfica

Courses
Graduate Studies (Civil Law; Constitutional Law); **Law** (Criminal Law; International Law; Labour Law; Law; Political Sciences)

History: Founded 1966.

Main Language(s) of Instruction: Portuguese

Degrees and Diplomas: *Bacharelado*; *Especialização/Aperfeiçoamento*
Last Updated: 06/07/10

FACULTY OF LIFE SCIENCES

Faculdade Ciências da Vida
Rua Campinas, 417, Bairro Canaan, Sete Lagoas
EMail: contato@cienciasdavida.com.br
Website: http://www.cienciasdavida.com.br

Diretor: Valcir Farias

Courses
Nursing (Nursing); **Nutrition** (Nutrition); **Psychology** (Psychology)

History: Founded 2006.

Main Language(s) of Instruction: Portuguese

Degrees and Diplomas: *Bacharelado*; *Especialização/Aperfeiçoamento*
Last Updated: 23/07/10

FACULTY OF LUÍS EDUARDO MAGALHÃES

Faculdade de Luís Eduardo Magalhães
Av. Padre Anchieta, Quadra 06. Lote 01.02 e 03.,
Bairro Vereda Tropical, Luís Eduardo Magalhães, BA
Tel: +55(77) 3628-4446
EMail: secretaria@filem.edu.br
Website: http://www.filem.edu.br

Diretor: Antonio Corrêa Junior

Courses
Information Systems (Computer Science); **Law** (Law); **Pedagogy** (Pedagogy)

History: Founded 2005.

Main Language(s) of Instruction: Portuguese

Degrees and Diplomas: *Bacharelado*; *Especialização/Aperfeiçoamento*

Libraries: Yes
Last Updated: 02/09/10

FACULTY OF LUZ CITY

Faculdade Cidade Luz
Alameda Bahia 490D, Ilha Solteiro, SP 15385-000
Tel: +55 (18) 3743-3905
EMail: faculdade.faciluz@terra.com.br
Website: http://www.faciluz.com.br

Diretor: Osmar Martins de Oliveira

Courses
Law (Law)

History: Founded 2003.

Main Language(s) of Instruction: Portuguese

Degrees and Diplomas: *Bacharelado*
Last Updated: 23/07/10

FACULTY OF MACAPA

Faculdade de Macapá
Rod. Duque de Caxias, Km 05, Cabralzinho, Macapá-, AP 68.906720
Tel: +55(96) 2101-0400
EMail: d.academica@faculdadedemacapa.com.br
Website: http://www.faculdadedemacapa.com.br

Diretor: Rodrigo Tarcísio Biazon

Courses
Accountancy (Accountancy); **Administration** (Administration); **Architecture and Town Planning** (Architecture; Town Planning); **Biology** (Biology); **Computer Networks** (Computer Networks); **Dentistry** (Dentistry); **Environmental Management** (Environmental Management); **History** (History); **Law** (Law); **Letters** (Literature); **Mathematics** (Mathematics); **Nursing** (Nursing); **Physical Education** (Physical Education); **Physiotherapy** (Physical Therapy); **Psychology** (Psychology); **Social Sciences** (Social Sciences); **Social Services** (Social and Community Services)

History: Founded 2001.

Main Language(s) of Instruction: Portuguese

Degrees and Diplomas: *Bacharelado*; *Licenciatura*; *Especialização/Aperfeiçoamento*; *Mestrado*

Libraries: Yes
Last Updated: 09/08/10

FACULTY OF MACEIO

Faculdade de Maceió
Rua Fernandes de Barros 161, Maceio, AL 57020-020
Tel: +55(82) 3336 9700
EMail: dir.academica@fama-al.com.br
Website: http://www.fama-al.com.br

Diretor: José Luitgard Moura de Figueiredo

Courses
Accountancy (Accountancy); **Administration** (Administration); **Law** (Law); **Tourism** (Tourism)

History: Founded 2001.

Main Language(s) of Instruction: Portuguese

Degrees and Diplomas: *Bacharelado*
Last Updated: 29/07/10

FACULTY OF MANAGEMENT
Faculdade de Ciências Gerenciais
Praça dos Estudantes, 23, Santa Emilia, Carangola, MG 36800-000

Courses
Accountancy (Accountancy)
History: Founded 2007.
Main Language(s) of Instruction: Portuguese
Degrees and Diplomas: *Bacharelado*
Last Updated: 23/07/10

FACULTY OF MANAGEMENT
Faculdade de Ciências Gerenciais
Rua Maria Rosa da Silva 151, São Joaquim da Barra,
SP 14600-000
Tel: +55(16) 3818-3271
EMail: facig@terra.com.br

Diretor: Josimar Santos Rosa

Courses
Accountancy (Accountancy); **Administration** (Administration);
Tourism (Tourism)
History: Founded 2008.
Main Language(s) of Instruction: Portuguese
Degrees and Diplomas: *Bacharelado*
Last Updated: 31/08/10

FACULTY OF MANAGEMENT OF BAHIA
Faculdade de Ciências Gerenciais da Bahia
Rua das Hortênsias, 696, Pça. Ana Lúcia Magalhães, Itaigara,
Salvador, BA
EMail: diretora@unicenid.edu.br
Website: http://www.unicenid.edu.br

Diretora: Maria Eugênia Viana da Silva Barroso

Courses
Accountancy (Accountancy); **Business Administration** (Business
Administration)
History: Founded 2002.
Main Language(s) of Instruction: Portuguese
Degrees and Diplomas: *Bacharelado*; *Mestrado*
Last Updated: 28/07/10

FACULTY OF MANAGEMENT OF BARÃO DE JUNDIAÍ
Faculdade de Ciências Gerenciais Barão de Jundiaí
Avenida Jundiaí, 1465 - Jardim Ana Maria, Jundiaí, SP 13208-053
Tel: +55(11) 4522-2212
EMail: secretaria.jundiai@cesd.br
Website: http://www.jundiai.cesd.br

Courses
Administration (Administration)
History: Founded 2006.
Main Language(s) of Instruction: Portuguese
Degrees and Diplomas: *Bacharelado*
Libraries: Biblioteca Liliana Gonzaga
Last Updated: 28/07/10

FACULTY OF MANAGEMENT OF COTIA
Faculdade de Ciências Gerenciais de Cotia (FCG)
Rua Howard A. Acheson Jr, 393 -Granja Viana, Cotia, SP 6708230
Tel: +55(11) 4612-8325
Fax: +55(11) 4612-8325
EMail: cesc@cesc.br; mec@cesc.br

Diretor: José Jorge Perealta

Courses
Administration (Administration)
History: Founded 1998
Main Language(s) of Instruction: Portuguese
Degrees and Diplomas: *Bacharelado*
Last Updated: 19/10/07

FACULTY OF MANAGEMENT OF MANHUAÇU
Faculdade de Ciências Gerenciais de Manhuaçu
Av. Getulio Vargas 733 Coqueiro, Manhuaçu, MG
Tel: +55(33) 3331-7000
EMail: facig@uai.com.br
Website: http://www.facig.edu.br/

Diretor: Thales Hannas

Courses
Accountancy (Accountancy); **Administration** (Administration;
Agricultural Business); **Civil Engineering** (Civil Engineering);
Construction Engineering (Construction Engineering); **Environmental Management** (Environmental Management); **Marketing**
(Marketing); **Mathematics** (Mathematics); **Social Services** (Social
and Community Services); **Systems Analysis** (Systems Analysis)
History: Founded 2000.
Main Language(s) of Instruction: Portuguese
Degrees and Diplomas: *Bacharelado*; *Mestrado*
Libraries: Biblioteca Dr. Jorge Hannas
Last Updated: 28/07/10

FACULTY OF MANAGEMENT OF SETE LAGOAS
Faculdade Setelagoana de Ciências Gerenciais (FASCIG)
Avenida Marechal Castelo Branco, 3870, Jardim Universitário,
Sete Lagoas, MG 35702-134
Tel: +55(31) 3774-9991
EMail: facgeraes@uai.com.br

Courses
Administration (Administration)
History: Founded 2002.
Main Language(s) of Instruction: Portuguese
Degrees and Diplomas: *Bacharelado*
Last Updated: 09/09/10

FACULTY OF MANAGEMENT OF VOTUPORANGA
Faculdade de Ciências Gerenciais em Votuporanga
Rua Amazonas, 4125 - Centro, Votuporanga, SP 15500-003
Tel: +55(17) 3405-1212
EMail: votuporanga@cesd.br
Website: http://www.votuporanga.cesd.br

Diretor: José Gonzaga da Silva Neto

Courses
Administration (Administration)
History: Founded 2006.
Main Language(s) of Instruction: Portuguese
Degrees and Diplomas: *Bacharelado*; *Mestrado*
Libraries: Biblioteca Liliana Gonzaga
Last Updated: 31/08/10

FACULTY OF MANTENA
Faculdade de Mantena
Rua Sete de Setembro, 644. Centro, Mantena, MG 35.290-000
Tel: +55(33) 3241-2147
EMail: direcao@famamg.edu.br
Website: http://www.famamg.edu.br

Diretora: Izabel Cristina Cunha de Araújo Mol

Courses
Administration (Administration); **Social Services** (Social and
Community Services)

History: Founded 2001.

Main Language(s) of Instruction: Portuguese

Degrees and Diplomas: *Bacharelado*

Last Updated: 09/08/10

FACULTY OF MARANHÃO

Faculdade de Maranhão

Rua dos Bicudos, Qd. 21, Lotes 23 e 24 - Renascença II, São Luis, MA 65075-090
Tel: +55(98) 3227-1238
EMail: direcao@facam-ma.com.br
Website: http://www.facam-ma.com.br

Diretor: Carlos César Branco Bandeira

Courses
Accountancy (Accountancy); **Administration** (Administration); **Law** (Law); **Nursing** (Nursing); **Pedagogy** (Pedagogy); **Tourism** (Tourism)

History: Founded 2006.

Main Language(s) of Instruction: Portuguese

Degrees and Diplomas: *Bacharelado*

Libraries: Yes

Last Updated: 23/08/10

FACULTY OF MARINGA

Faculdade Maringá (CESPAR)

Avenida Prudente de Moraes 815 Zona 07, Maringá, Paraná 87010020
Tel: +55(44) 3027-1100
Fax: +55(44) 3027-1200
EMail: faculdadesmaringa@faculdadesmaringa.br
Website: http://www.faculdadesmaringa.br

Diretor: Amaury Antônio Meller (1997-)
EMail: meller@faculdadesmaringa.br

Courses
Administration; **Journalism**; **Law**

History: Founded 1998

Main Language(s) of Instruction: Portuguese

Degrees and Diplomas: *Bacharelado; Especialização/Aperfeiçoamento; Mestrado*

Last Updated: 06/07/10

FACULTY OF MARKETING AND BUSINESS STUDIES

Faculdade de Marketing e Negocios

Av das Américas, 505, Morada da Colina, Uberlândia, MG 38411-126
Tel: +55(34) 3254-1213
EMail: posgraduacao@uniessa.com.br
Website: http://www.uniessa.com.br

Diretora: Vanessa de Sousa Rabelo

Courses
Administration (Administration; Agricultural Business; Business Administration; Health Administration); **Design** (Design; Interior Design)

History: Founded 2004.

Main Language(s) of Instruction: Portuguese

Degrees and Diplomas: *Bacharelado; Especialização/Aperfeiçoamento*

Libraries: Yes

Last Updated: 09/08/10

FACULTY OF MAUA

Faculdade de Mauá

Rua Vitorino Dell Antonia, 349 - Vila Noêmia, Mauá, SP 09370-570
Tel: +55(45) 12-6100
EMail: faleconosco@facmaua.edu.br
Website: http://www.facmaua.edu.br

Diretor: José Alechsandre dos Santos Lima

Courses
Accountancy (Accountancy); **Administration** (Administration); **Finance** (Finance); **Information Systems** (Computer Science); **Management** (Management); **Nursing** (Nursing); **Nutrition** (Nutrition); **Pedagogy** (Pedagogy); **Physical Education** (Physical Education); **Social Services** (Social and Community Services)

History: Founded 2001.

Main Language(s) of Instruction: Portuguese

Degrees and Diplomas: *Bacharelado; Licenciatura; Especialização/Aperfeiçoamento*

Libraries: Yes

Last Updated: 09/08/10

FACULTY OF MEDICAL AND PARAMEDICAL SCIENCES OF THE STATE OF RIO DE JANEIRO

Faculdade de Ciências Médicas e Paramédicas Fluminense (SEFLU)

Rua Pracinha Wallace Paes Leme, 1338, Centro, Nilópolis, Rio de Janeiro 26525-045
Tel: +55(21) 2792-0352
Fax: +55(21) 2691-0559
EMail: ouvidoria@seflu.com.br; secretaria@seflu.com.br
Website: http://www.seflu.com.br

Diretora: Lana de Oliveira Goulart **EMail:** diretoria@seflu.com.br

Courses
Graduate Studies (Physical Therapy; Psychology); **Physiotherapy** (Physical Therapy); **Psychology** (Psychology)

History: Founded 1985.

Main Language(s) of Instruction: Portuguese

Degrees and Diplomas: *Bacharelado; Especialização/Aperfeiçoamento*

Last Updated: 06/07/10

FACULTY OF MEDICINE AND HEALTH OF JUIZ DE FOR A

Faculdade de Ciências Médicas e da Saúde de Juiz de Fora

BR 040 - KM 796 - Salvaterra, Juiz de Fora, MG
Tel: +55(32) 2101-5000
EMail: analice@suprema.edu.br
Website: http://www.suprema.edu.br

Diretor: José Paixão de Souza

Courses
Dentistry (Dentistry); **Medicine** (Medicine); **Nursing** (Nursing); **Pharmacy** (Pharmacy); **Physiotherapy** (Physical Therapy)

History: Founded 2002.

Main Language(s) of Instruction: Portuguese

Degrees and Diplomas: *Bacharelado; Especialização/Aperfeiçoamento*

Last Updated: 29/07/10

FACULTY OF MEDICINE OF ABC

Faculdade de Medicina do ABC (FMABC)

Av. Lauro Gomes, 2.000 - Bairro Vila Sacadura Cabral, Santo André, São Paulo 09060-870
Tel: +55(11) 4993-5400
EMail: diretoria@fmabc.br
Website: http://www.fmabc.br

Diretor: Luiz Henrique Camargo Paschoal

Courses
Environmental Health Management (Health Administration); **Medicine** (Medicine); **Nursing** (Nursing); **Nutrition**; **Occupational Therapy**; **Pharmacy** (Pharmacy); **Physiotherapy** (Physical Therapy)

History: Founded 1969

Main Language(s) of Instruction: Portuguese

Degrees and Diplomas: *Bacharelado; Especialização/Aperfeiçoamento; Mestrado*

Last Updated: 09/07/10

FACULTY OF MEDICINE OF BARBACENA

Faculdade de Medicina de Barbacena (FAME)
Praça Presidente Antônio Carlos 08, São Sebastião, Barbacena,
Minas Gerais 36202336
Tel: +55(32) 3339-2950
EMail: fame@funjob.edu.br
Website: http://www.funjob.edu.br

Diretor: Marco Aurélio Bernardes de Carvalho

Courses
Medicine (Medicine)

History: Founded 1971

Main Language(s) of Instruction: Portuguese
Last Updated: 09/07/10

FACULTY OF MEDICINE OF CAMPOS

Faculdade de Medicina de Campos (FMC)
Avenida Doutor Alberto Torres 217 Térreo Centro, Campos dos
Goytacazes, Campos dos Goytacazes, Rio de Janeiro 28035580
Tel: +55(24) 2733-2211
Fax: +55(24) 2733-2211
EMail: fmc@fmc.br
Website: http://www.fmc.br

Diretor: Nélio Artiles Freitas

Courses
Medicine (Medicine); **Pharmacy**

History: Founded 1967.

Main Language(s) of Instruction: Portuguese

Degrees and Diplomas: *Bacharelado*; *Especialização/Aperfeiçoamento*
Last Updated: 09/07/10

FACULTY OF MEDICINE OF ITAJUBÁ

Faculdade de Medicina de Itajubá (FMIT)
Avenida Renno Júnior 368, São Vicente, Itajubá,
Minas Gerais 37502138
Tel: +55(35) 3621-4545 +55(35) 3621-4666
Fax: +55(35) 3621-4555
EMail: secretaria@aisi.edu.br
Website: http://www.aisi.edu.br

Diretor: Sérgio Visoni Vargas

Courses
Medicine (Medicine); **Nutrition** (Nutrition)

History: Founded 1968

Main Language(s) of Instruction: Portuguese

Degrees and Diplomas: *Bacharelado*; *Especialização/Aperfeiçoamento*
Last Updated: 09/07/10

FACULTY OF MEDICINE OF JUAZEIRO DO NORTE

Faculdade de Medicina de Juazeiro do Norte (FMJ)
Av. Tenente Raimundo Rocha s/n - Bairro Planalto, Juazeiro do
Norte, CE 63011970
Tel: +55(88) 2101-9000
EMail: atendimento@fmj-ce.edu.br
Website: http://www.fmj-ce.edu.br

Diretora: Angela Massayo Ginbo-Lima

Courses
Medicine

History: Founded 2000.

Main Language(s) of Instruction: Portuguese

Degrees and Diplomas: *Bacharelado*; *Especialização/Aperfeiçoamento*
Last Updated: 09/07/10

FACULTY OF MEDICINE OF MINAS GERAIS

Faculdade de Ciências Médicas de Minas Gerais (FCMMG)
Alameda Ezequiel Dias, 275 - 3 ° Andar, Centro, Belo Horizonte,
Minas Gerais 30130-110
Tel: +55(31) 3248-7100
Fax: +55(31) 3248-7132
EMail: fcmmg@fcmmg.br
Website: http://www.fcmmg.br

Diretor: Ludércio Rochas de Oliveira

Courses
Graduate Studies (Acupuncture; Biotechnology; Cardiology; Dermatology; Gerontology; Medicine; Nursing; Nutrition; Occupational Health; Osteopathy; Paediatrics; Pathology; Physical Therapy; Physiology; Psychology; Psychotherapy; Public Health; Rehabilitation and Therapy; Speech Therapy and Audiology; Surgery; Urology); **Medicine** (Medicine); **Nursing** (Nursing); **Occupational Therapy**; **Physiotherapy** (Physical Therapy); **Psychology** (Psychology)

History: Founded 1951.

Degrees and Diplomas: *Bacharelado*; *Especialização/Aperfeiçoamento*
Last Updated: 06/07/10

FACULTY OF MEDICINE OF PARAIBA

Faculdade de Ciências Médicas da Paraíba
Praça Dom Ulrico, 56, Centro, João Pessoa, PB 58010-740
Tel: +55(83) 3044-0300
EMail: cienciasmedicas@cienciasmedicas.com.br
Website: http://www.cienciasmedicas.com.br

Diretor: Othamar Batista Gama

Courses
Medicine (Medicine); **Nursing** (Nursing); **Pharmacy** (Pharmacy); **Physiotherapy** (Physical Therapy); **Psychology** (Psychology)

History: Founded 2002.

Main Language(s) of Instruction: Portuguese

Degrees and Diplomas: *Bacharelado*; *Especialização/Aperfeiçoamento*
Last Updated: 29/07/10

FACULTY OF MEDICINE OF SANTA CASA DE SÃO PAULO

Faculdade de Ciências Médicas da Santa Casa de São Paulo (FCMSCSP)
Rua Dr. Cesário Motta Jr. n ° 61, São Paulo, São Paulo 01221-020
Tel: +55(11) 3367-7700
Fax: +55(11) 3367-7833
EMail: diretoria@fcmscsp.edu.br
Website: http://www.fcmscsp.edu.br

Diretor: Ermani Geraldo Rolim (1996-)

Courses
Graduate Studies *(Lato Sensu)* (Nursing); **Graduate Studies** *(Stricto Sensu)*; **Medicine** (Community Health; Gynaecology and Obstetrics; Health Sciences; Medicine; Orthopaedics; Otorhinolaryngology; Surgery); **Nursing** (Nursing); **Speech Therapy**

History: Founded 1963

Degrees and Diplomas: *Bacharelado*; *Especialização/Aperfeiçoamento*; *Mestrado*; *Doutorado*. Also Pots-doutorado course.
Last Updated: 06/07/10

FACULTY OF MILAGRES CEARÁ

Faculdade de Milagres Ceará
Avenida Santana 270, Milagres, CE 63250-000
Tel: +55(88) 3553-1100
EMail: profmsfernandes@hotmail.com

Diretor: Geraldo Tacidálio Fernandes

Courses
Administration (Administration); **Letters** (Literature)

History: Founded 2005.

Main Language(s) of Instruction: Portuguese

Degrees and Diplomas: *Bacharelado*

Last Updated: 09/08/10

FACULTY OF MINAS
Faculdade de Minas (FAMINAS)
Av. Cristiano Ferreira Varella, 655 - Bairro Universitário, Muriaé,
MG 36880-000
Tel: +55(32) 3729-7500
EMail: secretaria@faminas.edu.br
Website: http://www.faminas.edu.br/principal

Courses
Accountancy (Accountancy); **Administration** (Administration); **Advertising** (Advertising and Publicity); **Biomedicine** (Biomedicine); **Information Sciences** (Computer Science); **Journalism** (Journalism); **Law** (Law); **Music** (Music); **Nursing** (Nursing); **Nutrition** (Nutrition); **Occupational Therapy** (Occupational Therapy); **Pedagogy** (Pedagogy); **Pharmacy** (Pharmacy); **Physical Education** (Physical Education); **Physiotherapy** (Physical Therapy); **Psychology** (Psychology); **Social Services** (Social and Community Services); **Tourism** (Tourism)

Further Information: Also branch in Belo Horizonte

Main Language(s) of Instruction: Portuguese

Degrees and Diplomas: *Bacharelado; Licenciatura; Especialização/Aperfeiçoamento; Mestrado*

Libraries: Yes

Last Updated: 09/08/10

FACULTY OF MINEIROS
Faculdade Mineirense
Praça Deputado José Alves de Assis 58, Mineiros, GO 75830-000
Tel: +55(64) 3672 0007
EMail: potrichrezendefama@uol.com.br
Website: http://www.famafaculdade.com.br

Diretor: Alessandro Rogério Barros de Rezende
EMail: dir.geral@famafaculdade.com.br

Courses
Dentistry (Dentistry); **Nursing** (Nursing); **Nutrition** (Nutrition); **Pharmacy** (Pharmacy); **Physiotherapy** (Physical Therapy)

History: Founded 2007.

Main Language(s) of Instruction: Portuguese

Degrees and Diplomas: *Bacharelado*

Last Updated: 06/09/10

FACULTY OF MORUMBI SUL
Faculdade Morumbi Sul (FMS)
Rua Nossa Senhora do Bom Conselho 351, Morumbi Sul,
São Paulo, São Paulo 5763470
Tel: +55(11) 5818-0600
Fax: +55(11) 5818-0600
EMail: faleconosco@morumbisul.com.br
Website: http://www.morumbisul.com.br

Diretor Pedagógico: Paulo Dyrker Silveira Elesbam

Courses
Administration (Administration); **Pedagogy** (Pedagogy)

History: Founded 1999

Main Language(s) of Instruction: Portuguese

Degrees and Diplomas: *Bacharelado; Licenciatura; Especialização/Aperfeiçoamento*

Last Updated: 05/07/10

FACULTY OF NANUQUE
Faculdade de Nanuque
Rua Nelício Cordeiro, s/n° - Bairro: Israel Pinheiro, Nanuque,
MG 39860-000
Tel: +55(33) 3621-5100
EMail: fanan@fanan.edu.br
Website: http://www.fanan.edu.br

Diretora: Rute Ferreira Tolentino Gusmão

Courses
Administration (Administration); **Chemistry** (Chemistry); **Computer Science** (Computer Science); **Environmental Engineering** (Environmental Engineering); **Information Systems** (Computer Science); **Nursing** (Nursing); **Pedagogy** (Pedagogy); **Pharmacy** (Pharmacy); **Physical Education** (Physical Education); **Physiotherapy** (Physical Therapy)

History: Founded 2003.

Main Language(s) of Instruction: Portuguese

Degrees and Diplomas: *Bacharelado; Licenciatura; Especialização/Aperfeiçoamento; Mestrado*

Last Updated: 09/08/10

FACULTY OF NATAL
Faculdade de Natal (FAL)
Alameda das Mansões 2110, Candelária, Natal,
Rio Grande do Norte 59067010
Tel: +55(84) 3615-8000
Fax: +55(84) 3615-8003
EMail: secretaria@falnatal.com.br
Website: http://www.falnatal.com.br

Diretora Geral: Leideana Galváo Bacurau de Farias

Courses
Accountancy; **Administration**; **Information Systems** (Computer Science; Information Management); **Law** (Law); **Pedagogy** (Pedagogy)

History: Founded 1998.

Main Language(s) of Instruction: Portuguese

Degrees and Diplomas: *Bacharelado; Licenciatura; Especialização/Aperfeiçoamento; Mestrado*

Last Updated: 09/07/10

FACULTY OF NORTH PIONEIRO
Faculdade do Norte Pioneiro (FANORPI)
Rod. Br. 153, Km 40, S/n Parque de Exposições, Dr. Alicio Dias dos
Reis, Santo Antonio da Platina, PR 86430000
Tel: +55(43) 3534-4177
Fax: +55(43) 3534-4177
EMail: fanorpi@fanorpi.com.br
Website: http://www.fanorpi.com.br

Diretor: Carlos Vinícius Maluly EMail: cvmaluly@fanorpi.com.br

Courses
Accountancy (Accountancy); **Advertising** (Advertising and Publicity); **Business Administration**; **Economics**; **Fashion Design**; **Hotel Management** *(Jacarezinho)* (Hotel Management); **Journalism** (Journalism); **Law** (Law); **Marketing** (Marketing); **Pedagogy**; **Tourism** *(Jacarezinho)* (Tourism)

Further Information: Also branch in Jacarezinho

History: Founded 1999

Main Language(s) of Instruction: Portuguese

Degrees and Diplomas: *Tecnólogo; Bacharelado; Especialização/Aperfeiçoamento*

Last Updated: 08/07/10

FACULTY OF NOVA VENÉCIA
Faculdade de Nova Venécia (UNIVEN)
Rua Jacobina 165, São Francisco, Nova Venécia, ES 29830000
Tel: +55(27) 3752-2811
EMail: univen@univen.edu.br
Website: http://www.univen.edu.br

Diretor: Tadeu Antônio de Oliveira Penina
EMail: tadeup@univen.edu.br

Courses
Accountancy; **Administration** (Administration; Business Administration; International Business; Systems Analysis); **Law** (Law); **Letters**; **Nursing**; **Pedagogy** (Pedagogy); **Petroleum and Gas**; **Production Engineering**; **Social Services** (Social and Community Services)

History: Founded 1999.

Main Language(s) of Instruction: Portuguese

Degrees and Diplomas: *Tecnólogo*; *Bacharelado*; *Licenciatura*; *Especialização/Aperfeiçoamento*
Last Updated: 09/07/10

FACULTY OF NOVO HAMBURGO - IENH FACULTY

Faculdade Novo Hamburgo - Faculdade IENH
Rua Frederico Mentz 526 - Prédio, Novo Hamburgo, RS 93525-360
Tel: +55(51) 3594-3022
EMail: faculdade@ienh.com.br
Website: http://www.ienh.com.br/

Diretor: Seno Leonhardt

Courses
Administration (Administration); **Biology** (Biology)
History: Founded 2007.
Main Language(s) of Instruction: Portuguese
Degrees and Diplomas: *Bacharelado*; *Licenciatura*
Libraries: Biblioteca Ernest Sarlet
Last Updated: 08/09/10

FACULTY OF OLINDA

Faculdade de Olinda (FOCCA)
Rua do Bonfim 37 Térreo Carmo, Olinda, Pernambuco 53120090
Tel: +55(81) 3429-3696
Fax: +55(81) 3429-5965
EMail: focca@focca.com.br
Website: http://www.focca.com.br

Diretora Presidente: Antonieta Alves Chiappetta

Courses
Accountancy (Accountancy); **Business Administration** (Administration; Business Administration); **Geography/Environment**; **Law** (Law); **Letters**; **Secretarial Studies**
History: Founded 1972.
Main Language(s) of Instruction: Portuguese
Degrees and Diplomas: *Bacharelado*; *Licenciatura*; *Especialização/Aperfeiçoamento*; *Mestrado*
Last Updated: 09/07/10

FACULTY OF ORLÂNDIA

Faculdade de Orlândia
Avenida 15 255 A, Orlândia, SP 14620-000
Tel: +55(16) 3826-9888
EMail: fao@fao.com.br
Website: http://www.fao.com.br

Diretor: Clóvis de Souza Dias

Courses
Administration (Administration); **Agricultural Business** (Agricultural Business)
History: Founded 2001.
Main Language(s) of Instruction: Portuguese
Degrees and Diplomas: *Bacharelado*; *Especialização/Aperfeiçoamento*
Libraries: Yes
Last Updated: 10/08/10

FACULTY OF OURO PRETO DO OESTE

Faculdade de Ouro Preto do Oeste
Rua Marechal Castelo Branco N°: 184, Incra, Ouro Preto do Oeste, RO 78950-000
Tel: +55(69) 3461-4278
EMail: adriancury@unescnet.br
Website: http://www.uneouro.edu.br

Diretor: Antonio Carlos da Silva

Courses
Information Systems (Computer Science); **Letters** (Literature); **Mathematics** (Mathematics); **Social Sciences** (Social Sciences)
History: Founded 2001.
Main Language(s) of Instruction: Portuguese

Degrees and Diplomas: *Bacharelado*
Last Updated: 06/08/10

FACULTY OF PARÁ DE MINAS

Faculdade de Pará de Minas (FAPAM)
Rua Ricardo Marinho 110, São Geraldo, Pará de Minas, MG 35660398
Tel: +55(37) 3236-1308
Fax: +55(37) 3236-1308
EMail: fapam@nwm.com.br
Website: http://www.nwm.com.br/fapam

Diretor: Geraldo Fernandes Fonte Boa

Courses
Administration; **Agricultural Business**; **Biology** (Biology); **Information Technology**; **Law**; **Letters** (Literature); **Mathematics**; **Nursing** (Nursing); **Nutrition** (Nutrition); **Pedagogy** (Pedagogy)
History: Founded 1976.
Main Language(s) of Instruction: Portuguese
Degrees and Diplomas: *Bacharelado*; *Licenciatura*; *Especialização/Aperfeiçoamento*
Last Updated: 09/07/10

FACULTY OF PARANA

Faculdade Paranaense
Rua Dom Pedro II 400, Jardim Horácio Cabral, Rolândia, PR 86600000
Tel: +55(43) 3255-8500
Fax: +55(43) 3255-8503
EMail: pos@faccar.com.br
Website: http://www.faccar.com.br

Diretor: José Roberto Beffa (1997-)

Courses
Accountancy (Accountancy); **Administration** (Administration; Business Administration); **Law**; **Letters** (Literature)
History: Founded 1973 as Faculdade de Ciências Contábeis e Administrativas de Rôlandia. Acquired present status and title 2001.
Main Language(s) of Instruction: Portuguese
Degrees and Diplomas: *Bacharelado*; *Especialização/Aperfeiçoamento*
Libraries: Biblioteca "Algacyr Munhoz Maeder"
Last Updated: 05/07/10

FACULTY OF PATO BRANCO

Faculdade de Pato Branco (FADEP)
Rua Benjamin Borges dos Santos 21, Fraron, Pato Branco, Paraná 85503350
Tel: +55(46) 3220-3000
Fax: +55(46) 3220-3000
EMail: fadep@fadep.br
Website: http://www.fadep.br

Diretor: Eliseu Miguel Bertelli

Courses
Administration (Administration); **Law** (Law); **Nursing**; **Nutrition**; **Pedagogy**; **Physical Education** (Physical Education); **Physiotherapy** (Physical Therapy); **Psychology** (Psychology); **Social Communication** (Advertising and Publicity; Journalism)
History: Founded 2000.
Main Language(s) of Instruction: Portuguese
Degrees and Diplomas: *Bacharelado*; *Licenciatura*; *Especialização/Aperfeiçoamento*; *Mestrado*
Last Updated: 09/07/10

FACULTY OF PATROCINIO - IESP

Faculdade de Patrocínio - IESP
Rua Professor Hugo Machado da Silveira, 520, Distrito Industrial, Patrocínio, MG 38740-000
Tel: +55(34) 3831-1258
EMail: secretaria@faculdadeiesp.com.br
Website: http://www.faculdadeiesp.com.br

Diretor: Rodolpho Bernardi Neto

Courses
Administration (Administration); **Agricultural Business** (Agricultural Business); **Systems Analysis** (Systems Analysis)
Main Language(s) of Instruction: Portuguese
Degrees and Diplomas: *Bacharelado*; *Especialização/Aperfeiçoamento*
Last Updated: 10/08/10

FACULTY OF PAULÍNIA
Faculdade de Paulínia
Rua Nelson Prodócimo n° 495 - Jardim Bela Vista, Paulínia,
SP 13140-000
Tel: +55(19) 3874-4035
EMail: secretaria@facp.com.br
Website: http://www.facp.com.br

Diretor: Nelson Gentil

Courses
Accountancy (Accountancy); **Administration** (Administration); **Chemistry** (Chemistry); **Law** (Law); **Pedagogy** (Pedagogy); **Production Engineering** (Production Engineering)
History: Founded 2001.
Main Language(s) of Instruction: Portuguese
Degrees and Diplomas: *Bacharelado*; *Especialização/Aperfeiçoamento*
Libraries: Yes
Last Updated: 10/08/10

FACULTY OF PEDAGOGY - ANAEC
Faculdade de Pedagogia - ANAEC
Avenida Eurico Soares Andrade N°: 730, Centro, Nova Andradina,
MS 79750-000
Tel: +55(67) 3441-1379
EMail: anaec@anaec.com.br

Diretora: Vera Lucia Martinez Battistetti

Courses
Pedagogy (Pedagogy)
History: Founded 1998.
Main Language(s) of Instruction: Portuguese
Degrees and Diplomas: *Licenciatura*
Last Updated: 10/08/10

FACULTY OF PEDAGOGY OF AFONSO CLÁUDIO
Faculdade de Pedagogia de Afonso Claudio (ISEAC)
Rua Ute Amelia Gastim Padua 49, São Tarcisco, Afonso Claúdio,
ES 29600000
Tel: +55(27) 3735-2411
Fax: +55(27) 3735-2433
EMail: robertoadministra@gmail.com

Diretor: Roberto Alexandre Alcantara

Courses
Pedagogy (Pedagogy)
History: Founded 1999.
Main Language(s) of Instruction: Portuguese
Degrees and Diplomas: *Licenciatura*
Last Updated: 09/07/10

FACULTY OF PEDAGOGY OF DORES DO INDAIÁ
Faculdade de Pedagogia de Dores do Indaía
Praça Santuário 04, Dores do Indaiá, MG 35610-000
Tel: +55(37) 3551-3627
EMail: fapedi@indanet.com.br

Diretora: Herlaine Patrícia de Oliveira

Courses
Pedagogy (Educational Administration; Pedagogy)
History: Founded 2002.
Main Language(s) of Instruction: Portuguese
Degrees and Diplomas: *Licenciatura*
Last Updated: 10/08/10

FACULTY OF PERUÍBE
Faculdade Peruíbe
Avenida Darcy Fonseca, n° 530, bairro Jardim dos Prados, Peruíbe,
SP 11750-000
Tel: +55(13)3828-2840
EMail: scelisul@scelisul.com.br
Website: http://www.faculdadeperuibe.com.br

Diretor: Aderbal Alfredo Calderari Bernardes

Courses
Pedagogy (Pedagogy)
History: Founded 2006.
Main Language(s) of Instruction: Portuguese
Degrees and Diplomas: *Licenciatura*
Last Updated: 10/09/10

FACULTY OF PHILOSOPHY, SCIENCE AND LETTERS
Faculdade de Filosofia, Ciências e Letras (FAFIL)
Rua Eurico Dutra, 64, Santa Rita, PB 58301-055
Tel: +55(83) 3229-1479
Fax: +55(83) 3229-1479
EMail: iespa@ig.com.br
Website: http://iespa.edu.br

Diretor: Francisco de Paula Melo Aguiar

Courses
Literature (Literature; Portuguese)
History: Founded 1971
Main Language(s) of Instruction: Portuguese
Degrees and Diplomas: *Licenciatura*
Last Updated: 08/07/10

FACULTY OF PHILOSOPHY, SCIENCE AND LETTERS OF ALTO SÃO FRANCISCO
Faculdade de Filosofia, Ciências e Letras do Alto São Francisco (FASF)
Avenida Laerton Paulinelli, 153, Bairro Monsenhor Pareiras, Luz,
Minas Gerais 35595-000
Tel: +55(37) 3421-9006
EMail: fasf@catedralnet.com.br
Website: http://www.fasf.edu.br

Diretor: Enrico dos Santos Veloso

Courses
Accountancy; **Administration** (Administration); **Advertising and Publicity**; **Biology** (Biology); **Chemistry**; **Environmental Management** (Environmental Management); **Graduate Studies** (Business Administration; Educational Psychology; Environmental Management; Environmental Studies; Leadership; Mathematics Education; Portuguese); **Literature** (Literature); **Mathematics** (Mathematics); **Pharmacy** (Pharmacy); **Psychology** (Psychology)
History: Founded 1974 as part of the Catholic University of Minas Gerais. Acquired present status and title 1985.
Main Language(s) of Instruction: Portuguese
Degrees and Diplomas: *Tecnólogo*; *Bacharelado*; *Licenciatura*; *Especialização/Aperfeiçoamento*. Also MBA.
Last Updated: 08/07/10

FACULTY OF PHILOSOPHY, SCIENCE AND LETTERS OF BOA ESPERANÇA

Faculdade de Filosofia, Ciências e Letras de Boa Esperança (FAFIBE)
Av. Gov. Aureliano Chaves, 192, Jardim Nova Esperança,
Boa Esperança, Minas Gerais 37170-000
Tel: +55(35) 3851-1223
Fax: +55(35) 3851-1891
EMail: secretaria@fafibemg.edu.br
Website: http://www.fafibemg.edu.br

Diretora: Jussara Figueiredo de Oliveira
EMail: direcao.fafibe@fafibemg.edu.br

Courses
Environmental Management (Environmental Management); **Geography** (Geography); **History** (History); **Literature**; **Mathematics**; **Pedagogy**
History: Founded 1978
Main Language(s) of Instruction: Portuguese
Degrees and Diplomas: *Licenciatura*
Last Updated: 30/11/07

FACULTY OF PHILOSOPHY, SCIENCE AND LETTERS OF CAJAZEIRAS

Faculdade de Filosofia, Ciências e Letras de Cajazeiras (FAFIC)
Rua Padre Ibiapina, s/n, Centro, Cajazeiras, Paraiba 58900-000
Tel: +55(83) 3531-3500
Fax: +55(83) 3531-3500
EMail: fafic@fescfafic.edu.br
Website: http://fescfafic.edu.br

Diretor: Agripino Ferreira de Assis

Courses
Accountancy; **Law**; **Philosophy**; **Social Services** (Social and Community Services)
History: Founded 1970
Main Language(s) of Instruction: Portuguese
Degrees and Diplomas: *Bacharelado*; *Licenciatura*
Last Updated: 08/07/10

FACULTY OF PHILOSOPHY, SCIENCE AND LETTERS OF CARUARU

Faculdade de Filosofia, Ciências e Letras de Caruaru (FAFICA)
Rua Azevedo Coutinho s/n, Térreo, Petrópolis, Caruaru, PE 55030902
Tel: +55(81) 3721-2611
EMail: fafica@fafica.com
Website: http://www.fafica.com

Diretor Geral: Everaldo Fernandes da Silva (1994-)
EMail: everaldo@fafica.com

Courses
Accountancy (Accountancy); **Administration**; **Commercial Management** (Business and Commerce); **Computer Networks** (Computer Networks); **Graduate Studies** (Accountancy; Adult Education; Business Administration; Computer Networks; Economics; Education; Educational Administration; Educational Psychology; Finance; Geography; History; Industrial and Organizational Psychology; Law; Modern Languages; Native Language Education; Public Administration; Real Estate; Sociology; Software Engineering; Special Education; Teacher Training; Transport Management); **History** (History); **Literature** (Literature; Modern Languages); **Pedagogy** (Pedagogy); **Philosophy** (Philosophy); **Systems Analysis** (Systems Analysis)
History: Founded 1960
Main Language(s) of Instruction: Portuguese
Degrees and Diplomas: *Bacharelado*; *Licenciatura*; *Especialização/Aperfeiçoamento*. Also MBA.
Last Updated: 08/07/10

FACULTY OF PHILOSOPHY, SCIENCE AND LETTERS OF IBITINGA

Faculdade de Filosofia, Ciências e Letras de Ibitinga (FAIBI)
Rua Roque Raineri, 81, Jd. Centenário, Ibitinga,
São Paulo 14940-000
Tel: +55(16) 3342-7303
Fax: +55(16) 3342-7303
EMail: faibi@faibi.com.br
Website: http://www.faibi.com.br

Diretora: Leonilda Marquesi Costa

Courses
Administration (Administration); **Pedagogy** (Pedagogy); **Tourism** (Tourism)
History: Founded 2001.
Main Language(s) of Instruction: Portuguese
Degrees and Diplomas: *Bacharelado*; *Licenciatura*
Last Updated: 08/07/10

FACULTY OF PHILOSOPHY, SCIENCE AND LETTERS OF ITUVERAVA

Faculdade de Filosofia, Ciências e Letras de Ituverava (FAFIL)
Rua Flauzino Barbosa Sandoval, 1259, Cidade Universitária,
Ituverava, São Paulo 14500-000
Tel: +55(16) 3729-9000
Fax: +55(16) 3729-3199
EMail: ffcl@feituverava.com.br
Website: http://www.feituverava.com.br/ffcl/

Diretor: José Ignácio Azevedo Filho

Courses
Administration (Administration); **Biology** (Biology); **Graduate Studies** (Biological and Life Sciences; Education; Educational Psychology; Finance; History; Linguistics; Literacy Education; Literature; Management; Marketing; Mathematics Education; Special Education); **History** (History); **Literature** (English; Literature; Portuguese); **Mathematics** (Mathematics); **Pedagogy**
History: Founded 1971
Main Language(s) of Instruction: Portuguese
Degrees and Diplomas: *Bacharelado*; *Licenciatura*; *Especialização/Aperfeiçoamento*
Last Updated: 08/07/10

FACULTY OF PHILOSOPHY, SCIENCE AND LETTERS OF MACAÉ

Faculdade de Filosofia, Ciências e Letras de Macaé (FAFIMA)
Rua Tenente Rui Lopes Ribeiro 200, Centro, Macaé,
Rio de Janeiro 27910-330
Tel: +55(24) 2762-1457
Fax: +55(24) 2762-1457
EMail: fafima@fafima.br
Website: http://www.fafima.br

Diretora: Cláudia de Magalhães Bastos Leite

Courses
Geography; **Graduate Studies**; **History** (History); **Literature** (English; Literature; Portuguese); **Mathematics**; **Occupational Safety** (Occupational Health); **Pedagogy**
History: Founded 1973
Main Language(s) of Instruction: Portuguese
Degrees and Diplomas: *Tecnólogo*; *Licenciatura*; *Especialização/Aperfeiçoamento*
Last Updated: 08/07/10

FACULTY OF PHILOSOPHY, SCIENCE AND LETTERS OF PENÁPOLIS

Faculdade de Filosofia, Ciências e Letras de Penápolis (FAFIPE)
Avenida São José 400, Vila Martins, Penápolis, SP 16300-000
Tel: +55(18) 3654-7690
Fax: +55(18) 3652-2340
EMail: funepe@funepe.edu.br
Website: http://www.funepe.edu.br

Diretora: Fabiana Ortiz Tanoue de Mello
EMail: fabiana@funepe.edu.br

Courses
Accountancy; **Administration** (Administration); **Agricultural Business** (Agricultural Business); **Biology** (Biology); **Graduate Studies**; **Information Systems** (Information Technology); **Literature**; **Mathematics**; **Pedagogy** (Pedagogy); **Physics**; **Psychology** (Psychology); **Visual Arts**

History: Founded 1966.

Main Language(s) of Instruction: Portuguese

Degrees and Diplomas: *Tecnólogo*; *Bacharelado*; *Licenciatura*; *Especialização/Aperfeiçoamento*
Last Updated: 08/07/10

FACULTY OF PHILOSOPHY, SCIENCE AND LETTERS OF PIRAJÚ

Faculdade de Filosofia, Ciências e Letras de Pirajú (FAFIP)
Rua João Hailer, 408, Centro, Pirajú, São Paulo 18800-000
Tel: +55(14) 3351-3255 +55(14) 3351-1025
Fax: +55(14) 3351-3255
EMail: secretaria@fafip.edu.br
Website: http://www.fafip.edu.br

Diretor: Renato Dardes Barberio

Courses
History (History); **Pedagogy**
History: Founded 1973
Main Language(s) of Instruction: Portuguese

Degrees and Diplomas: *Licenciatura*; *Especialização/Aperfeiçoamento*
Last Updated: 08/07/10

FACULTY OF PHYSICAL EDUCATION OF BARRA BONITA

Faculdade de Educação Física de Barra Bonita (FAEFI)
Av. Narcisa Chesini Ometto, 3555, Barra Bonita,
São Paulo 17340000
Tel: +55(14) 3642-1044
Fax: +55(14) 3604-1200
EMail: prof.nono@funbbe.br; coordenacaofaefi@funbbe.br
Website: http://www.funbbe.br/Default.aspx?alias=www.funbbe.br/faefi

Diretor: José Norberto Basso Junior

Courses
Graduate Studies (Physical Education; Sports); **Physical Education** (Physical Education)
History: Founded 1972.
Main Language(s) of Instruction: Portuguese

Degrees and Diplomas: *Licenciatura*; *Especialização/Aperfeiçoamento*
Last Updated: 07/07/10

FACULTY OF PHYSICAL EDUCATION OF THE CRISTÁ DE MOÇOS ASSOCIATION OF SOROCABA

Faculdade de Educação Física da Associação Cristá de Moços de Sorocaba (FEFISO)
Rua da Penha 680, Centro, Sorocaba, São Paulo 18010002
Tel: +55(15) 3234-9115
EMail: fefiso@fefiso.edu.br
Website: http://www.fefiso.edu.br

Diretora: Mirian Aparecida Ribeiro Borba Leme (1998-)

Courses
Physical Education
History: Founded 1971.
Main Language(s) of Instruction: Portuguese

Degrees and Diplomas: *Bacharelado*; *Licenciatura*; *Especialização/Aperfeiçoamento*
Last Updated: 07/07/10

FACULTY OF PIAU

Faculdade Piauiense
Avenida Jóquei Clube, 710, Teresina, PI 64049-240
Tel: +55(86) 3133-2616
EMail: comunicacao@fapteresina.com.br
Website: http://www.fapteresina.com.br

Diretora: Roselane Moita Pierot

Courses
Accountancy (Accountancy); **Administration** (Administration); **History** (History); **Law** (Law); **Pedagogy** (Pedagogy); **Tourism** (Tourism)

History: Founded 2001.
Main Language(s) of Instruction: Portuguese

Degrees and Diplomas: *Bacharelado*; *Licenciatura*; *Especialização/Aperfeiçoamento*
Libraries: Yes
Last Updated: 10/09/10

FACULTY OF PIMENTA BUENO

Faculdade de Pimenta Bueno (FAP)
Avenida Castelo Branco 780, Bairro Pioneiros, Pimenta Bueno, RO 78984000
Tel: +55(69) 3451-4100
EMail: direcao@fap-pb.com.br
Website: http://www.fap-pb.com.br

Diretor Geral: Aécio Alves Pereira

Courses
Administration; **Computer Science** (Computer Science); **Letters**; **Pedagogy** (Pedagogy)

History: Founded 1999.
Main Language(s) of Instruction: Portuguese

Degrees and Diplomas: *Bacharelado*; *Especialização/Aperfeiçoamento*
Last Updated: 11/10/07

FACULTY OF PINDAMONHANGABA

Faculdade de Pindamonhangaba
Rodovia Presidente Eurico Gaspar Dutra s/n - Km 99,
Pindamonhangaba, SP 12422-970
Tel: +55(12) 3648-8323
EMail: secretaria@fapi.br
Website: http://www.fapi.br

Diretor: Luís Otávio Palhari

Areas
Biological Sciences (Dentistry; Nutrition; Pharmacy; Physical Education; Physical Therapy); **Exact Sciences** (Chemical Engineering; Information Sciences); **Human Sciences** (Administration; Pedagogy)

History: Founded 2002.
Main Language(s) of Instruction: Portuguese

Degrees and Diplomas: *Bacharelado*; *Licenciatura*; *Especialização/Aperfeiçoamento*
Libraries: Yes
Last Updated: 10/08/10

FACULTY OF PIRACANJUBA
Faculdade de Piracanjuba (FAP)
Avenida Amym Daher s/n - Esquina c/ Rod. GO-217, Piracanjuba, GO 75640000
Tel: +55(64) 3405-2113
Fax: +55(64) 3405-2113
EMail: fap@fapgoias.com.br
Website: http://www.fapgoias.com.br

Diretor: Ariston José de Araújo

Courses
Accountancy; **Administration** (Administration; Agricultural Business; Business Administration; Environmental Management); **Literature**

History: Founded 2000.
Main Language(s) of Instruction: Portuguese
Degrees and Diplomas: *Bacharelado*; *Licenciatura*; *Especialização/Aperfeiçoamento*
Last Updated: 09/07/10

FACULTY OF PONTA PORÃ
Faculdade de Ponta Porã (FAP)
Rua Antônio João 1675, Centro, Ponta Porã, Mato Grosso do Sul 79900000
Tel: +55(67) 3431-1002
Fax: +55(67) 3431-1002
EMail: fap@fap.br
Website: http://www.fap.br

Diretora Geral: Labibe Esther Esgaib Kayatt (1989-)

Courses
Accountancy; **Administration** (Administration); **Geography** (Geography); **History** (History); **Letters**

History: Founded 1988.
Main Language(s) of Instruction: Portuguese
Degrees and Diplomas: *Bacharelado*; *Licenciatura*
Last Updated: 09/07/10

FACULTY OF PORTO ALEGRE
Faculdade Porto-Alegrenses (FAPA)
Avenida Manoel Elias 2001, Bairro Morro Santana, Porto Alegre, Rio Grande do Sul 91240261
Tel: +55(51) 3386-3033
Fax: +55(51) 3386-1009
EMail: fapa@fapa.com.br
Website: http://www.fapa.com.br

Diretor: Darci Sanfelici

Courses
Accountancy (Accountancy); **Administration** (Administration); **History** (History); **Letters** (Literature); **Pedagogy** (Pedagogy); **Science/Mathematics**

History: Founded 1975.
Main Language(s) of Instruction: Portuguese
Degrees and Diplomas: *Bacharelado*; *Licenciatura*; *Especialização/Aperfeiçoamento*; *Mestrado*
Last Updated: 02/07/10

FACULTY OF PORTO VELHO
Faculdade de Porto Velho (FIP)
Rua Paulo Freire 4767, Bairro Flodoaldo Pontes Pinto, Porto Velho, Rondônia 78908790
Tel: +55(69) 3221-6000
EMail: contato@portovelho.br
Website: http://www.portovelho.br/2009/

Diretor: Milton Peluccio

Courses
Administration (Administration); **Computer Science** (Computer Science); **Pedagogy** (Pedagogy)

History: Founded 2001.
Main Language(s) of Instruction: Portuguese
Degrees and Diplomas: *Bacharelado*; *Especialização/Aperfeiçoamento*
Last Updated: 09/07/10

FACULTY OF PRESIDENT EPITÁCIO
Faculdade de Presidente Epitácio
Rua Pernambuco 17-05, Centro, Presidente Epitácio, São Paulo 19470000
Tel: +55(18) 3281-4800
EMail: secretaria-fape@uniesp.edu.br
Website: http://www.uniesp.edu.br/epitacio

Diretor Presidente: José Fernando Pinto da Costa (1998-)

Courses
Accountancy (Accountancy); **Administration** (Administration); **Computer Science** (Computer Science); **Law** (Law); **Literature** (Literature); **Pedagogy** (Pedagogy); **Secretarial Studies** (Secretarial Studies); **Tourism** (Tourism); **Translation** (Translation and Interpretation)

History: Founded 1998
Main Language(s) of Instruction: Portuguese
Degrees and Diplomas: *Bacharelado*; *Especialização/Aperfeiçoamento*
Last Updated: 09/07/10

FACULTY OF PRESIDENT PRUDENTE
Faculdade de Presidente Prudente (FAPEPE)
Avenida Presidente Prudente 6093, Presidente Prudente, São Paulo 19053-210
Tel: +55(18) 3918-9800
Website: http://www.uniesp.edu.br/prudente/

Diretora: Maria Helena Bueno

Courses
Accountancy (Accountancy); **Administration**; **Literature**; **Pedagogy** (Pedagogy); **Secretarial Studies** (Secretarial Studies); **Tourism**; **Translation** (Translation and Interpretation)

History: Founded 2001.
Main Language(s) of Instruction: Portuguese
Degrees and Diplomas: *Bacharelado*
Last Updated: 09/07/10

FACULTY OF PRESIDENT VENCESLAU
Faculdade de Presidente Venceslau (FAPREV)
Rua Piracicaba, n° 47 - Jardim Coroados, Presidente Venceslau, São Paulo 19400000
Tel: +55(18) 3271-2373
Fax: +55(18) 3271-3100
EMail: fafipreve@fafiprev.edu.br
Website: http://www.uniesp.edu.br/venceslau/

Diretora: Aldora Maia Veríssimo

Courses
Administration (Administration); **Geography**; **History** (History); **Literature** (Literature); **Mathematics** (Mathematics); **Pedagogy**; **Postgraduate** (Educational Psychology; Higher Education; Literature; Preschool Education)

History: Founded 1972. Merged with Faculdade de Filosofia, Ciências e Letras de Presidente Venceslau 2008.
Main Language(s) of Instruction: Portuguese
Degrees and Diplomas: *Bacharelado*; *Licenciatura*. Also postgraduate degree courses.
Last Updated: 21/04/10

FACULTY OF QUATRO MARCOS
Faculdade de Quatro Marcos
Avenida Projetada II, 205, Jardim das Oliveiras, São José dos
Quatro Marcos, MT 78285-000
Tel: +55(65) 3251-3005
EMail: faleconosco@fqm.edu.br
Website: http://www.fqm.edu.br/new/site/index.php

Diretor: Evandro Luiz Echeverria
EMail: evandro.echeverria@fqm.edu.br

Courses
Nursing (Nursing); **Pharmacy** (Pharmacy); **Psychology** (Psychology)
History: Founded 2006.
Main Language(s) of Instruction: Portuguese
Degrees and Diplomas: *Bacharelado*; *Especialização/Aperfeiçoamento*
Libraries: Yes
Last Updated: 10/08/10

FACULTY OF RANCHARIA
Faculdade Ranchariense (FRAN)
Avenida Pedro de Toledo, 1149, Vila Guaçu, Rancharia,
SP 19600-000
Tel: +55(18) 3265-5100
Fax: +55(18) 3265-5038
EMail: fran@fran.edu.br
Website: http://www.fran.edu.br/

Courses
Administration (Administration); **Pedagogy** (Pedagogy); **Physical Education** (Physical Education)
History: Founded 2002.
Degrees and Diplomas: *Bacharelado*; *Licenciatura*
Last Updated: 03/09/10

FACULTY OF REALAZA
Faculdade de Realeza (CESREAL)
Rodovia PR 281 Km 2, Realaza, PR 85770000
Tel: +55(46) 3543-4444
EMail: cesreal@cesreal.br
Website: http://www.cesreal.br

Head: Fabio Holmes Lins

Courses
Accountancy (Accountancy); **Administration**
History: Founded 2001.
Main Language(s) of Instruction: Portuguese
Degrees and Diplomas: *Bacharelado*
Last Updated: 09/07/10

FACULTY OF REGIONAL DEVELOPMENT AND INTEGRATION
Faculdade de Desenvolvimento e Integração Regional
Rua Prof. Ivani Batista Silva, 29, Nova Santa Cruz,
Santa Cruz do Capibaribe, PE 55190-000
Tel: +55(81) 3731-0300
EMail: diretoria@fadire.edu.br
Website: http://www.fadire.edu.br

Diretor: Joaquim Bezerra

Courses
Accountancy (Accountancy); **Administration** (Administration); **Fashion Design** (Fashion Design)
Main Language(s) of Instruction: Portuguese
Degrees and Diplomas: *Bacharelado*; *Especialização/Aperfeiçoamento*; *Mestrado*
Last Updated: 30/07/10

FACULTY OF REHABILITATION OF THE ASCE
Faculdade de Reabilitação da ASCE (FRASCE)
Rua Uarumã 80, Higienópolis, Rio de Janeiro,
Rio de Janeiro 21050660
Tel: +55(21) 3866-0029
EMail: frasce@uol.com.br
Website: http://www.frasce.edu.br

Diretor: Liborni Siqueira

Courses
Administration; Computer Science; Foreign Trade (International Business); **Pedagogy** (Pedagogy); **Physiotherapy** (Physical Therapy)
History: Founded 1977.
Main Language(s) of Instruction: Portuguese
Degrees and Diplomas: *Bacharelado*; *Licenciatura*; *Especialização/Aperfeiçoamento*
Last Updated: 09/07/10

FACULTY OF RESEARCH AND HIGHER EDUCATION OF THE STATE OF SAO PAULO
Faculdade Paulista de Pesquisa e Ensino Superior
Av. Brigadeiro Luis Antonio 277 - 8°, 9°, 10° e 11° andares,
São Paulo, SP 01317-000
Tel: +55(11) 3115-5434
EMail: fappes@fappes.edu.br
Website: http://www.fappes.edu.br

Diretor: Leandro Berchielli

Courses
Administration (Administration; Business Administration); **Law** *(Postgraduate)*
History: Founded 2006.
Main Language(s) of Instruction: Portuguese
Degrees and Diplomas: *Bacharelado*; *Especialização/Aperfeiçoamento*; *Mestrado*
Libraries: Yes
Last Updated: 10/09/10

FACULTY OF RIBAS DO RIO PARDO
Faculdade Superior de Ribas do Rio Pardo (FASURP)
Avenida Aureliano Moura Brandão, 1605, Jardim Vista Alegre,
Ribas do Rio Pardo, MS 79180-000
EMail: rosamosso@rede21.com

Courses
Pedagogy (Pedagogy)
Degrees and Diplomas: *Licenciatura*
Last Updated: 09/09/10

FACULTY OF ROLIM DE MOURA
Faculdade de Rolim de Moura
Lote 79 B Gleba 14 do Projeto Integrado de Colonização s/n,
Rolim de Moura, RO 78987-000
Tel: +55(69)3442-4004
EMail: farolrm@hotmail.com
Website: http://www.farolrm.com.br

Diretora: Benta Idavina Ferreira Pepinelli Peres

Courses
Accountancy (Accountancy); **Administration** (Administration); **Geography** (Geography); **History** (History); **Information Systems** (Computer Science); **Law** (Law); **Pedagogy** (Pedagogy); **Psychology** (Psychology); **Tourism** (Tourism)
History: Founded 2003.
Main Language(s) of Instruction: Portuguese
Degrees and Diplomas: *Bacharelado*; *Especialização/Aperfeiçoamento*
Last Updated: 10/08/10

FACULTY OF RONDÔNIA
Faculdade de Rondônia (FARO)
Br 364 Km 65 s/n, Campus FARO, Porto Velho,
Rondônia 78914751
Tel: +55(69) 217-5100
Fax: +55(69) 222-1888
EMail: secretaria@faro.edu.br
Website: http://www.faro.edu.br

Presidente: Neórico Alves de Souza
EMail: presidencia@faro.edu.br

Courses
Accountancy (Accountancy); **Administration**; **Civil Engineering** (Civil Engineering); **Forestry Engineering** (Forestry); **Law**; **Nursing** (Nursing); **Pedagogy** (Pedagogy); **Social Communication**
History: Founded 1988.
Main Language(s) of Instruction: Portuguese
Degrees and Diplomas: *Bacharelado*; *Licenciatura*; *Especialização/Aperfeiçoamento*
Last Updated: 09/07/10

FACULTY OF ROSEIRA
Faculdade de Roseira
Rodovia Presidente Dutra, Km 77, Roseira Velha, SP 12580-000
Tel: +55(12) 3646-2071
EMail: pasin@bjp.com.br
Website: http://www.faculdaderoseira.com.br

Diretor: Jorge Pasin de Oliveira

Courses
Environmental Engineering (Environmental Engineering)
History: Founded 2008.
Main Language(s) of Instruction: Portuguese
Degrees and Diplomas: *Bacharelado*; *Especialização/Aperfeiçoamento*; *Mestrado*
Last Updated: 16/08/10

FACULTY OF SABARÁ
Faculdade de Sabará (SOECS)
Rodovia Mgt05 (Sabará-BH) Km 14, 1084, Sede Própria Caieira-Sabará MG, Belo Horizonte, Minas Gerais 34555000
Tel: +55(31) 3241-2891
Fax: +55(31) 3241-7204
EMail: soecs@faculdadedesabara.br
Website: http://www.faculdadedesabara.edu.br

Reitor: Mário de Lima Guerra

Courses
Administration; **Law** (Law); **Letters** (Literature)
History: Founded 1998
Main Language(s) of Instruction: Portuguese
Degrees and Diplomas: *Bacharelado*; *Especialização/Aperfeiçoamento*
Last Updated: 09/07/10

FACULTY OF SAINT BENEDICT OF RIO DE JANEIRO
Faculdade de São Bento do Rio de Janeiro (FSB/RJ)
Rua Dom Gerardo, 42 / 6° andar, Rio de Janeiro, RJ 20090-030
Tel: +55(21) 2206-8281
EMail: info@faculdadesaobento.org.br
Website: http://www.faculdadesaobento.org.br/

President: Antonio Lopes

Courses
Graduate Studies (Art History; Business Education; Ethics; Law; Medieval Studies; Philosophy; Portuguese; Religious Studies; Theology); **Undergraduate Studies** (Philosophy; Theology)
Degrees and Diplomas: *Bacharelado*. Also Postgraduate diploma.
Last Updated: 07/09/10

FACULTY OF SAINT CATHERINE
Faculdade de Santa Catarina (FASC)
Avenida Salvador Di Bernardi, 503, Campinas, São José,
SC 88101-201
Tel: +55(48) 3878-5000
Website: http://www.fasc.edu.br/

Diretor Geral: Geraldo Majela Ferreira de Macedo

Courses
Undergraduate Studies (Accountancy; Administration; Advertising and Publicity; Law; Pedagogy; Tourism)
History: Founded 2002.
Degrees and Diplomas: *Bacharelado*; *Licenciatura*
Last Updated: 06/09/10

FACULTY OF SANTA FÉ
Faculdade de Santa Fé (CESSF)
Avenida João Pessoa 300, Cutim Anil, São Luís,
Maranhão 65040001
Tel: +55(98) 3243-3530
Fax: +55(98) 3243-6959
EMail: contato@faculdadesantafe.com.br
Website: http://www.santafe.edu.br

Head: Marilourdes Maranhão Mussalém

Courses
Geography (Geography); **History**; **Literature** (Literature); **Pedagogy** (Pedagogy); **Philosophy**
History: Founded 2000.
Main Language(s) of Instruction: Portuguese
Degrees and Diplomas: *Licenciatura*; *Especialização/Aperfeiçoamento*
Last Updated: 09/07/10

FACULTY OF SÃO BENTO
Faculdade de São Bento
Largo de São Bento, s/n, São Paulo, SP
Tel: +55(11) 3328-8796
EMail: filosofiasb@uol.com.br
Website: http://www.saobento.org.br

Courses
Philosophy (Philosophy); **Theology** (Theology)
History: Founded 1946 as Faculdade de Filosofia São Bento. Acquired present status and title 2002.
Main Language(s) of Instruction: Portuguese
Degrees and Diplomas: *Licenciatura*; *Especialização/Aperfeiçoamento*
Libraries: Biblioteca do Mosteiro de São Bento
Last Updated: 16/08/10

FACULTY OF SÃO BERNARDO DO CAMPO
Faculdade de São Bernardo do Campo
Rua Américo Brasiliense 449, Centro, São Bernardo do Campos,
São Paulo 09715020
Tel: +55(11) 4335-3277
Fax: +55(11) 4335-4875
EMail: fasb@facsaobernardo.com.br
Website: http://www.facsaobernardo.com.br

Diretor Executivo: Ariovaldo José Pecora (1994-)

Courses
Administration (Administration; Environmental Management; Information Technology; Marketing); **Chemical Engineering** (Chemical Engineering); **Letters** (Literature); **Pedagogy**; **Social Studies**; **Teacher Training** (Teacher Training)
History: Founded 1970 as Faculdade de Filosofia, Ciências e Letras de São Bernardo do Campo. Acquired present status and title 2002.
Main Language(s) of Instruction: Portuguese
Degrees and Diplomas: *Bacharelado*; *Licenciatura*; *Especialização/Aperfeiçoamento*
Last Updated: 08/07/10

FACULTY OF SÃO JOSÉ DOS CAMPOS - BILAC
Faculdade de São José dos Campos - BILAC
Rua Francisco Paes, 84 . Centro, São José dos Campos 12200-000
Tel: +55(12) 3947-2200
EMail: marta.esteves@csa.edu.br
Website: http://www.bilac.com.br

Courses
Accountancy (Accountancy); **Administration** (Administration); **Pedagogy** (Pedagogy)
Degrees and Diplomas: *Bacharelado*
Last Updated: 16/08/10

FACULTY OF SÃO LOURENÇO
Faculdade de São Lourenço
Rua Madame Schimidt 90 Federal, São Lourenço,
Minas Gerais 37470000
Tel: +55(35) 3332-3355
Fax: +55(35) 3332-3355
EMail: info@faculdadesantamarta.br
Website: http://www.faculdadesaolourenco.com.br/
Diretor: Guilherme Bernardes

Courses
Accountancy (Accountancy); **Administration** (Accountancy; Administration; Marketing); **Biology**; **Computer Networks** (Computer Networks); **Environmental Management** (Environmental Management); **Gastronomy** (Cooking and Catering); **Geography** (Geography); **History** (History); **Information Systems** (Information Management); **Languages** (English; Literature; Modern Languages; Portuguese); **Law** (Law); **Nursing** (Nursing); **Nutrition** (Nutrition); **Pedagogy**; **Physical Education** (Physical Education); **Social Services**; **Tourism and Hotel Management** (Hotel and Restaurant; Hotel Management; Tourism)
History: Founded 1992 as Faculdade Santa Marta. Acquired present status and title 2007.
Main Language(s) of Instruction: Portuguese
Degrees and Diplomas: *Bacharelado*; *Licenciatura*; *Especialização/Aperfeiçoamento*
Last Updated: 08/07/10

FACULTY OF SÃO LUÍS
Faculdade São Luís
Rua Grande, 1455, Diamante, São Luís, MA 65020-250
Tel: +55(98) 3214-6400
EMail: geraldo@facsaoluis.br
Website: http://www.facsaoluis.br/paginas/Default.aspx
Diretor: Geraldo Demosthenes Siqueira

Courses
Accountancy (Accountancy); **Administration** (Administration); **Advertising** (Advertising and Publicity); **Biomedicine** (Biomedicine); **Journalism** (Journalism); **Law** (Law); **Nursing** (Nursing); **Nutrition** (Nutrition); **Physical Education** (Physical Education); **Tourism** (Tourism)
History: Founded 2001.
Main Language(s) of Instruction: Portuguese
Degrees and Diplomas: *Bacharelado*; *Licenciatura*; *Especialização/Aperfeiçoamento*
Libraries: Biblioteca Prof. José Maria Ramos Martins
Last Updated: 29/07/10

FACULTY OF SÃO SEBASTIÃO
Faculdade de São Sebastião (FASS)
Rua Agripino José do Nascimento, 177, Vila Amélia, São Sebastião,
SP 11600-000
Tel: +55(12) 3893-3100
EMail: fass@fass.edu.br
Website: http://www.fass.edu.br/

Courses
Undergraduate Studies (Administration; Hotel Management; Law; Literature; Pedagogy; Tourism)

Degrees and Diplomas: *Bacharelado*; *Licenciatura*
Last Updated: 08/09/10

FACULTY OF SCIENCE AND EDUCATION OF ESPIRITO SANTO
Faculdade de Ciências e Educação do Espírito Santo (UNIVES)
Avenida Maruípe, n° 2.535, Bairro Santa Marta, Vitória,
Espirito Santo 29045-231
Tel: +55(27) 3324-4343
Fax: +55(27) 3324-4343
EMail: unives@unives.br
Website: http://www.unives.edu.br
Diretor Geral: Adriano Aguiar Araújo

Courses
Administration; **Graduate Studies** (Business Education; Education; Educational Administration; Educational Psychology; Educational Technology; Health Administration; Higher Education; Literacy Education; Management; Petroleum and Gas Engineering; Public Administration; Rehabilitation and Therapy; Small Business; Special Education); **Pedagogy** *(AUFES)*
History: Founded 2000.
Main Language(s) of Instruction: Portuguese
Degrees and Diplomas: *Bacharelado*; *Licenciatura*; *Especialização/Aperfeiçoamento*. Also MBA.
Last Updated: 02/07/10

FACULTY OF SCIENCE AND EDUCATION OF RUBIATABA
Faculdade de Ciências e Educação de Rubiataba (FACER)
Avenida Jataí, 110 - Centro, Rubiataba, GO 76350-000
Tel: +55(62) 3325-1749
Fax: +55(62) 3325-1749
EMail: secretaria@facer.edu.br
Website: http://www.facer.edu.br
Diretora: Zita Pires de Andrade (1998-)

Courses
Administration (Administration); **History**; **Law**; **Marketing** (Marketing); **Tourism**
History: Founded 1997.
Main Language(s) of Instruction: Portuguese
Degrees and Diplomas: *Bacharelado*; *Licenciatura*; *Especialização/Aperfeiçoamento*
Last Updated: 19/09/07

FACULTY OF SCIENCE AND LETTERS - ACADEMY OF EDUCATION
Faculdade de Ciências e Letras - Academia de Ensino
Rua Romeu do Nascimento, 777, Jardim Portal da Colina,
Sorocaba, SP 18047-410
Tel: +55(15) 3331-7201
Fax: +55(15) 3331-7201
Website: http://www.aes.edu.br/

Courses
Graduate Studies; **Information Systems** (Information Technology); **Literature** (Literature); **Mathematics** (Mathematics); **Pedagogy** (Pedagogy); **Physical Education** (Physical Education); **Technological Studies** (Business and Commerce; Computer Networks; Finance; Human Resources; Management; Systems Analysis; Transport Management)
Degrees and Diplomas: *Tecnólogo*; *Bacharelado*; *Licenciatura*. Also Postgraduate diploma.
Last Updated: 22/07/10

FACULTY OF SCIENCE AND LETTERS OF BRAGANÇA PAULISTA

Faculdade de Ciências e Letras de Bragança Paulista
Avenida Francisco Samuel Lucchesi Filho, 770, Penha,
Bragança Paulista, São Paulo 12929-600
Tel: +55(11) 4035-7800
Fax: +55(11) 4035-7802
EMail: faculdade@fesb.br
Website: http://www.fesb.br

Diretora: Lúcia Inês Ribas de Souza Siqueira
EMail: diretoria@fesb.edu.br

Courses
Art Education (Art Education); **Biology** (Biology); **Chemistry** (Chemistry); **Geography** (Geography); **Graduate Studies**; **History** (History); **Literature**; **Mathematics** (Mathematics); **Nutrition** (Nutrition); **Pedagogy**; **Physical Education** (*Bacharelado*) (Physical Education); **Physical Education**; **Veterinary Science** (Veterinary Science)

History: Founded 1967
Main Language(s) of Instruction: Portuguese
Degrees and Diplomas: *Bacharelado*; *Licenciatura*; *Especialização/Aperfeiçoamento*
Last Updated: 18/03/11

FACULTY OF SCIENCE AND TECHNOLOGY

Faculdade de Ciência e Tecnologia (FACITEC)
Avenida Presidente Kennedy, 2300, Jardim Itália, Palotina,
PR 85950-000
Tel: +55(44) 3649-9002 +55(44) 3649-9024
EMail: uespar@uespar.edu.br
Website: http://www.uespar.edu.br/

Diretor: Edelar Bulegon EMail: direcao@uespar.edu.br

Courses
Accountancy (Accountancy); **Administration** (Administration); **Graduate Studies** (Accountancy); **Technological Studies** (Marketing; Systems Analysis)

History: Founded 2003.
Degrees and Diplomas: *Tecnólogo*; *Bacharelado*; *Especialização/Aperfeiçoamento*
Last Updated: 20/07/10

FACULTY OF SCIENCE AND TECHNOLOGY OF BRASÍLIA

Faculdade de Ciências e Tecnologia de Brasília (FACITEB)
SD/Sul Bloco L, 30, Edifício Miguel Badya, Asa Sul, Brasília,
DF 70394-901
EMail: mariifel@hotmail.com

Diretora Geral: Mariana Costa Feliciano

Courses
Accountancy (Accountancy); **Administration** (Administration); **Commercial Management** (Business and Commerce); **Nursing** (Nursing); **Pedagogy** (Pedagogy)

Degrees and Diplomas: *Tecnólogo*; *Bacharelado*; *Licenciatura*
Last Updated: 22/07/10

FACULTY OF SCIENCE AND TECHNOLOGY OF MARANHÃO

Faculdade de Ciências e Tecnologia do Maranhão (FACEMA)
Rua Aarão Reis, 1000, Centro, Caxias, MA 65606-020
Tel: +55(99) 3422-6800
EMail: facema@facema.edu.br
Website: http://facema.edu.br/

Diretora Geral: Aryzaltina Silva Penha

Courses
Administration (Administration); **Graduate Studies** (Adult Education; Business Administration; Business Education; Education; Higher Education; Management; Public Health; Teacher Trainers

Education); **Nursing** (Nursing); **Pedagogy** (Pedagogy); **Physical Therapy** (Physical Therapy)

Degrees and Diplomas: *Bacharelado*; *Licenciatura*; *Especialização/Aperfeiçoamento*
Last Updated: 23/07/10

FACULTY OF SCIENCE AND TECHNOLOGY OF NATAL

Faculdade de Ciências e Tecnologia de Natal (FACITEN)
Rua Coronel Estevam, 1415, Alecrim, Natal, RN 59035-000
EMail: unipbmec@gmail.com

Courses
Administration (Administration); **Nursing** (Nursing)
Degrees and Diplomas: *Bacharelado*
Last Updated: 22/07/10

FACULTY OF SCIENCE AND TECHNOLOGY OF TERESINA

Faculdade de Ciências e Tecnologia de Teresina (FACET)
Rua Areolino de Abreu, 1941, Centro, Teresina, PI 64000-180
Tel: +55(86) 3221-2115
Fax: +55(86) 3221-2115
EMail: facetpi@facetpi.com.br
Website: http://www.facetpi.com.br/

Diretor Geral: Bartolomeu Ramos Pinto
EMail: bartolomeu.ramos@facetpi.com.br

Courses
Accountancy (Accountancy); **Administration** (Administration); **Graduate Studies** (Accountancy; Educational Psychology; Higher Education)

History: Founded 2001.
Degrees and Diplomas: *Bacharelado*; *Especialização/Aperfeiçoamento*
Last Updated: 23/07/10

FACULTY OF SCIENCE AND TECHNOLOGY OF THE VALLEY

Faculdade de Ciências e Tecnologia do Vale (FCTVALE)
Rua dos Pioneiros, 46, Centro, Rio do Sul, SC 89160-000
EMail: epozes@yahoo.com

Diretor Presidente: Edmundo Pozes da Silva

Courses
Accountancy (Accountancy); **Administration** (Administration); **Marketing** (Marketing)
Degrees and Diplomas: *Tecnólogo*; *Bacharelado*
Last Updated: 23/07/10

FACULTY OF SCIENCE AND TECHNOLOGY OF UNAÍ

Faculdade de Ciências e Tecnologia de Unaí (FACTU)
Rua Rio Preto, No 422, Centro, Unaí, Minas Gerais 38610-000
Tel: +55(38) 3676-6222
Fax: +55(38) 3676-6222
EMail: factu@factu.br
Website: http://www.factu.br

Diretor Geral: Adalberto Lucas Capanema

Courses
Accountancy (Accountancy); **Agronomy** (Agronomy); **Information Systems** (Information Technology); **Law** (Law); **Nursing** (Nursing); **Pedagogy** (Pedagogy); **Physical Education**; **Visual Arts** (Visual Arts)

History: Founded 1997.
Main Language(s) of Instruction: Portuguese
Degrees and Diplomas: *Bacharelado*; *Licenciatura*; *Especialização/Aperfeiçoamento*
Last Updated: 05/07/10

FACULTY OF SCIENCE OF BAHIA

Faculdade de Ciências da Bahia (FACIBA)
Rua direta da Piedade, 02, Piedade, Salvador, BA
Tel: +55(71) 3321-0251 +55(71) 3011-0251
Fax: +55(71) 3321-0251 +55(71) 3011-0251
EMail: faciba@faciba.com.br
Website: http://www.faciba.com.br/

Diretor Presidente: Afonso Santana de Miranda

Courses
Graduate Studies *(Stricto Sensu)* (Administration; Education); **Graduate Studies** *(Lato Sensu)* (Administration; Applied Linguistics; Business Administration; Development Studies; Educational Administration; Educational Psychology; Environmental Management; German; Higher Education; Management; Mathematics Education; Rehabilitation and Therapy; Special Education; Transport Management); **Philosophy**

Degrees and Diplomas: *Bacharelado*; *Especialização/Aperfeiçoamento*; *Mestrado*
Last Updated: 20/07/10

FACULTY OF SCIENCE OF BRASÍLIA

Faculdade de Ciências de Brasília
Projeção, QE 20 A/E Guará, Brasília, DF 71015-057
Tel: +55(61) 3381-3000
Fax: +55(61) 3381-3000
EMail: faculdade@projecao.br
Website: http://www.facibra.com.br/facibra002/

Courses
Administration (Administration); **Computer Networks** (Computer Networks); **Data Processing** (Data Processing); **Logistics** (Transport Management); **Systems Analysis and Development** (Systems Analysis); **Tourism** (Tourism); **Tourism Management** (Tourism)

Degrees and Diplomas: *Tecnólogo*; *Bacharelado*
Last Updated: 22/07/10

FACULTY OF SCIENCE OF GUARULHOS

Faculdade de Ciências de Guarulhos (FACIG)
Avenida Guarulhos, 1844, Vila Augusta, Guarulhos, SP 07025-000
Tel: +55(11) 2414-0827
EMail: secretaria@faculdadefacig.com.br
Website: http://www.faculdadefacig.com.br/

Diretor Geral: Ki Bong Lee

Courses
Accountancy (Accountancy); **Administration** (Administration); **Graduate Studies** (Dental Technology; Dentistry; Dermatology); **Nursing** (Nursing)

Degrees and Diplomas: *Bacharelado*; *Especialização/Aperfeiçoamento*
Last Updated: 22/07/10

FACULTY OF SCIENCE OF TIMBAÚBA

Faculdade de Ciências de Timbaúba (FACET)
Av. Antonio Xavier de Morais, 3, Sapucaia, Timbaúba, PE 55870-000
Tel: +55(81) 3631-0752
EMail: facet@bol.com.br
Website: http://www.faculdadedetimbauba.com.br/

Diretor: Luiz Rodrigues de Souza

Courses
Accountancy (Accountancy); **Law** (Law)

Degrees and Diplomas: *Bacharelado*
Last Updated: 22/07/10

FACULTY OF SCIENCE OF WENCESLAU BRAZ

Faculdade de Ciências de Wenceslau Braz (FACIBRA)
Avenida Augusto Paschoal da Silva, 670, Vila Getúlio Vargas, Wenceslau Braz, PR 84950-000
Tel: +55(43) 3528-3194
Fax: +55(43) 3528-1938
EMail: facibra@facibra.edu.br
Website: http://www.facibra.edu.br

Diretor: Wilson Nery

Courses
Administration (Administration); **Graduate Studies** (Educational Psychology; Environmental Management; Special Education); **Pedagogy** (Pedagogy)

History: Founded 1998.

Main Language(s) of Instruction: Portuguese

Degrees and Diplomas: *Bacharelado*; *Licenciatura*; *Especialização/Aperfeiçoamento*
Last Updated: 02/07/10

FACULTY OF SCIENCE, CULTURE AND EXTENSION OF RIO GRANDE DO NORTE

Faculdade de Ciênciãs, Cultura e Extensão do Rio Grande do Norte (FACEX)
Rua Orlando Silva, 2897 - Capim Macio, Natal, Rio Grande do Norte 59080-020
Tel: +55(84) 3235-1415
Fax: +55(84) 3235-1433
EMail: secretaria@facex.com.br
Website: http://www.facex.com.br/2007

Diretor Acadêmico: Raymundo Gomes Vieira
EMail: vieira@facex.com.br

Courses
Accountancy; **Administration** (Administration); **Biology** (Biology); **Graduate Studies** (Business Administration; Business and Commerce; Civil Security; Education; Educational Administration; Environmental Studies; Finance; Higher Education; Literacy Education; Management; Marketing; Microbiology; Natural Resources; Parasitology; Public Administration; Public Health; Social and Community Services; Social Work); **Law**; **Nursing** (Nursing); **Pedagogy**; **Psychology**; **Secretarial Studies** (Secretarial Studies); **Social Services**; **Technological Studies** (Finance; Hotel Management; Human Resources; Marketing; Public Administration); **Tourism**

History: Founded 1981.

Main Language(s) of Instruction: Portuguese

Degrees and Diplomas: *Bacharelado*; *Licenciatura*; *Especialização/Aperfeiçoamento*. Also MBA.
Last Updated: 06/07/10

FACULTY OF SCIENCE, EDUCATION AND THEOLOGY OF THE NORTH OF BRAZIL

Faculdade de Ciências, Educação e Teologia do Norte do Brasil
Avenida dos Bandeirantes, 900, Pricumã, Boa Vista, RR 69309-100
Tel: +55(95) 3625-5477
EMail: faceten@click21.com.br
Website: http://www.faceten.edu.br

Diretora: Rita de Cassia Duarte Sampaio

Courses
Pedagogy (Pedagogy); **Philosophy** (Philosophy); **Religious Sciences** (Religious Studies); **Theology**

Institutes
Education (Education)

History: Founded 2002.

Main Language(s) of Instruction: Portuguese

Degrees and Diplomas: *Bacharelado*; *Especialização/Aperfeiçoamento*

Libraries: Yes
Last Updated: 30/07/10

FACULTY OF SCIENCE, LETTERS AND EDUCATION OF THE NORTHWEST OF PARANA

Faculdade de Ciências, Letras e Educaçao do Noroeste do Paraná
Rua Wenceslau Braz N° 1399, esquina c/ Av. São Paulo, Centro, Loanda, PR 87900-000
Tel: +55(44) 3425-1109
EMail: inovohorizonte@brturbo.com.br
Website: http://www.novohorizonte.edu.br/ensino/4038/
Diretor: Darci Cruz Camacho

Courses
Accountancy (Accountancy); **Letters** (Literature); **Mathematics** (Mathematics); **Pedagogy** (Pedagogy); **Social Services** (Social and Community Services)
History: Founded 2000.
Main Language(s) of Instruction: Portuguese
Degrees and Diplomas: *Bacharelado*; *Licenciatura*; *Especialização/Aperfeiçoamento*
Last Updated: 30/07/10

FACULTY OF SCIENCE, TECHNOLOGY AND EDUCATION

Faculdade de Ciência, Tecnologia e Educação (FACITE)
Rua Emílio Marques, 298, Loteamento do Parque de Exposição, Santa Maria da Vitória, BA 47640-000
EMail: facinst25@yahoo.com.br; gilvanetenp@hotmail.com
Diretor Geral: Gilvanete Nunes Pereira

Courses
Administration (Administration); **Pedagogy** (Pedagogy)
Degrees and Diplomas: *Bacharelado*; *Licenciatura*
Last Updated: 20/07/10

FACULTY OF SECOND OF JULY

Faculdade Dois de Julho (F2J)
Avenida Leovigildo Filgueiras 81, Garcia, Salvador, Bahia 40100000
Tel: +55(71) 3114-3400
Fax: +55(71) 3114-3406
EMail: faculdade@fdj.com.br
Website: http://www.fdj.com.br
Diretor: Josué da Silva Mello

Courses
Administration; **Advertising and Marketing** (Advertising and Publicity; Marketing); **Electrical Engineering** (Electrical Engineering); **Journalism** (Journalism); **Law** (Law)
History: Founded 2000.
Main Language(s) of Instruction: Portuguese
Degrees and Diplomas: *Bacharelado*; *Especialização/Aperfeiçoamento*; *Mestrado*
Last Updated: 08/07/10

FACULTY OF SELVIRIA

Faculdade de Selviria (FAS)
Avenida Goiás 900 Centro, Selviria, MS 79590000
Tel: +55(67) 579-1048
Fax: +55(67) 579-1269
EMail: fas.escritorio@terra.com.br
Website: http://www.fas.edu.br
Diretor Geral: Gentil Fernandes Marques EMail: gentil@fas.edu.br

Courses
Administration; **Social Communication**; **Theology**; **Tourism**
History: Founded 2000.
Main Language(s) of Instruction: Portuguese
Degrees and Diplomas: *Bacharelado*; *Especialização/Aperfeiçoamento*
Last Updated: 08/07/10

FACULTY OF SERGIPE

Faculdade de Sergipe
Rua Urquiza Leal 538, Aracaju, SE 49020-490
EMail: fasedir@fase-se.edu.br
Diretor: Ruy Gomes Chaves

Courses
Administration (Administration; Hotel Management; Human Resources; International Business; Marketing); **Law** (Law); **Nursing** (Nursing); **Nutrition** (Nutrition); **Physical Education** (Physical Education); **Physiotherapy** (Physical Therapy); **Psychology** (Psychology); **Tourism** (Tourism)
History: Founded 2002.
Main Language(s) of Instruction: Portuguese
Degrees and Diplomas: *Bacharelado*; *Licenciatura*; *Especialização/Aperfeiçoamento*; *Mestrado*; *Doutorado*
Libraries: Yes
Last Updated: 16/08/10

FACULTY OF SERRA GAUCHA

Faculdade da Serra Gaúcha (FSG)
Rua os Dezoito do Forte, 2366, Caxias do Sul, Rio Grande do Sul 95020-472
Tel: +55(54) 2101-6000
Fax: +55(54) 2101-6017
EMail: fsg@fsg.br
Website: http://www.fsg.br
Diretor: João dal Bello

Courses
Accountancy (Accountancy); **Administration** (Administration; Finance; Human Resources; International Business; Marketing; Systems Analysis); **Architecture and Urbanism** (Architecture; Town Planning); **Biomedicine** (Biomedicine); **Civil Engineering**; **Design** (Design); **Graduate Studies**; **Law** (Law); **Nursing** (Nursing); **Physical Education** (Physical Education); **Physiotherapy** (Physical Therapy); **Production Engineering** (Production Engineering); **Psychology** (Psychology)
History: Founded 1999.
Main Language(s) of Instruction: Portuguese
Degrees and Diplomas: *Bacharelado*; *Licenciatura*; *Especialização/Aperfeiçoamento*. Also MBA.
Last Updated: 30/06/10

FACULTY OF SERTÁOZINHO

Faculdade de Sertáozinho (FASERT)
Avenida António Paschoal 1954, São José, Sertáozinho, SP 14170700
Tel: +55(16) 2105-3555
EMail: fasert@fasert.com.br
Website: http://www.fasert.com.br
Diretora Geral: Rosemary Aparecida Amorim Merli
EMail: rosemarymerli@fasert.com.br

Courses
Administration; **Literature** (Literature); **Pedagogy**
History: Founded 2000.
Main Language(s) of Instruction: Portuguese
Degrees and Diplomas: *Bacharelado*; *Especialização/Aperfeiçoamento*
Last Updated: 15/10/07

FACULTY OF SOCIAL AND AGRARIAN SCIENCES OF ITAPEVA

Faculdade de Ciências Sociais e Agrárias de Itapeva (FAIT)
Rodovia Francisco Alves Negrão, SP 258, km 285, Bairro Pilão D'Água, Itapeva, São Paulo 18412000
Tel: +55(15) 3526-8888
Fax: +55(15) 3526-8881
EMail: direcao@fait.edu.br
Website: http://www.fait.edu.br
Diretora: Simone da Silva Gomes Cardoso

Courses

Administration; **Agronomy**; **Forestry Engineering**; **Information Systems** (Information Technology); **Law** (Law); **Nursing**; **Occupational Therapy**; **Pedagogy** (Pedagogy); **Pharmacy** (Pharmacy); **Physical Education** (Physical Education); **Physical Therapy**; **Postgraduate** (Business Administration; Educational Psychology; Environmental Management); **Social Service**; **Veterinary Science** (Veterinary Science)

History: Founded 1999

Degrees and Diplomas: *Bacharelado*: 4 yrs; *Licenciatura*: 4 yrs; *Especialização/Aperfeiçoamento*. Also MBA.
Last Updated: 06/07/10

FACULTY OF SOCIAL AND APPLIED SCIENCES OF DIAMANTINO

Faculdade de Ciências Sociais e Aplicadas de Diamantino (UNED)
Rua Rui Barbosa n.° 535, Jardim Eldorado, Diamantino, Mato Grosso 78400-000
Tel: +55(65) 3336-1001
Fax: +55(65) 3336-1446
EMail: presidente@uned.edu.br
Website: http://www.uned.edu.br

Diretora Geral: Marineze de Araújo Meira

Courses

Administration (Administration); **Graduate Studies** (Business and Commerce; Business Education; Constitutional Law; Environmental Studies; Health Administration; Health Sciences; Higher Education; Management; Physical Education; Sports); **Law** (Law); **Nursing**; **Physical Education** (Physical Education)

History: Founded 2001.

Main Language(s) of Instruction: Portuguese

Degrees and Diplomas: *Bacharelado*; *Licenciatura*; *Especialização/Aperfeiçoamento*. Also MBA.
Last Updated: 06/07/10

FACULTY OF SOCIAL SCIENCES OF FLORIANÓPOLIS

Faculdade de Ciências Sociais de Florianópolis (FCSA/CESUSC)
Rodovia Sc 401, Km 10 s/n, Trevo de Santo Antônio de Lisboa, Florianópolis, Santa Catarina 88050-001
Tel: +55(48) 3239-2600
EMail: mec@cesusc.com.br
Website: http://www.cesusc.edu.br

Diretora Geral: Betina Ines Backes

Courses

Administration (Administration); **Graduate Studies** (Administration; Administrative Law; Civil Law; Criminal Law; Environmental Management; Labour Law; Law; Psychoanalysis; Psychology; Public Administration; Real Estate); **Interior Design**; **Law** (Law); **Psychology**

History: Founded 2000.

Degrees and Diplomas: *Bacharelado*; *Especialização/Aperfeiçoamento*. Also MBA.
Last Updated: 06/07/10

FACULTY OF SOCIAL SERVICES OF SÃO CAETANO DO SUL

Faculdade Paulista de Serviço Social de São Caetano do Sul (FAPSS-SCS)
Avenida Paraíso 600 Vila Gerti, São Caetano do Sul, São Paulo 9571200
Tel: +55(11) 4238-6922
Fax: +55(11) 4238-6423
EMail: fapss-sc@fapss.br
Website: http://www.fapss.br

Diretor: Danilo Vieiro

Courses

Social Services (Social Work)
History: Founded 1972.

Main Language(s) of Instruction: Portuguese

Degrees and Diplomas: *Bacharelado*; *Especialização/Aperfeiçoamento*
Last Updated: 05/07/10

FACULTY OF SOCIAL SERVICES OF SAO PAULO

Faculdade Paulista de Serviço Social (FAPSS)
Rua Lopes Chaves 273 275 Barra Funda, São Paulo, São Paulo 01154010
Tel: +55(11) 3666-0246
Fax: +55(11) 3826-1925
EMail: fapss@fapss.br
Website: http://www.fapss.br

Diretor: Heliton Betetto (1997-)

Courses

Social Services (Social Work)
History: Founded 1940.

Main Language(s) of Instruction: Portuguese

Degrees and Diplomas: *Bacharelado*; *Especialização/Aperfeiçoamento*
Last Updated: 05/07/10

FACULTY OF SORRISO

Faculdade de Sorriso
Avenida Noemia Tonello Dalmolin, 2499 - Bairro Universitário - Caixa Postal 475, Sorriso, MT 78890-000
Tel: +55(66) 3545-7600
EMail: fais@fais.com.br
Website: http://www.fais.com.br

Diretora: Natal da Silva Rego

Courses

Accountancy (Accountancy); **Administration** (Administration); **Law** (Law); **Nursing** (Nursing); **Pedagogy** (Pedagogy)

History: Founded 2001.

Main Language(s) of Instruction: Portuguese

Degrees and Diplomas: *Bacharelado*; *Especialização/Aperfeiçoamento*

Libraries: Yes
Last Updated: 17/08/10

FACULTY OF SOUTH AMERICA

Faculdade Sul D'América
Rua Iguaçu Qd. 109 lt. 15/13, Vila Brasília, Aparecida de Goiânia, GO 74900-000
Tel: +55(62) 3548-3333
EMail: suldamerica@suldamerica.edu.br
Website: http://www.suldamerica.edu.br/

Diretor Presidente: Valdemar Moreira de Souza

Courses

Graduate Studies (Educational Psychology; Management; Marketing; Public Administration; Transport Management); **Undergraduate Studies** (Administration; History)

History: Founded 2005.

Degrees and Diplomas: *Bacharelado*; *Licenciatura*; *Especialização/Aperfeiçoamento*
Last Updated: 09/09/10

FACULTY OF SUSTAINABLE DEVELOPMENT OF CRUZEIRO DO SUL - IEVAL

Faculdade de Desenvolvimento Sustentável de Cruzeiro do Sul - IEVAL
Rodovia BR 307, Km 9 - Bairro Boca da Alemanha - Caixa Postal 66, Cruzeiro do Sul, AC 69980-000
Tel: +55(68) 3311-1500
EMail: ieval@avec.br
Website: http://www.avec.br/ieval/site

Diretor: João Maria Fagundes Weiber

Courses

Accountancy (Accountancy); **Administration** (Administration)

History: Founded 2002.

Main Language(s) of Instruction: Portuguese

Degrees and Diplomas: *Bacharelado*

Last Updated: 30/07/10

FACULTY OF TABOÃO DA SERRA
Faculdade Taboão da Serra (FTS)
Rodovia Régis Bittencourt, 199, Taboão da Serra,
São Paulo 06763460
Tel: +55(11) 4788-7978
EMail: uniuniversitario@uol.com.br
Website: http://www.fts.com.br

Diretora: Sandra Aparecida Simões

Courses

Accountancy; **Business Administration**; **Education**; **Environmental Education and Management**; **Geography**; **History** (History); **Information Systems** (Information Management); **Law** (Civil Law; Criminal Law; Law); **Mathematics**; **Modern Languages** (English; Modern Languages; Portuguese); **Nursing** (Nursing); **Public and Family Health**; **Tourism** (Hotel and Restaurant; Hotel Management; Tourism); **Visual Arts** (Visual Arts)

History: Founded 2000.

Main Language(s) of Instruction: Portuguese

Degrees and Diplomas: *Bacharelado*; *Licenciatura*; *Especialização/Aperfeiçoamento*

Last Updated: 29/06/10

FACULTY OF TECHNOLOGICAL AND SOCIAL SCIENCES
Faculdade de Ciências Sociais e Tecnológicas (FACITEC)
Csg 09, lotes 15/16 - Taguatinga, Brasília, DF 72035-509
Tel: +55(61) 3356-8150
EMail: facitec@facitec.br; elaine@facitec.br
Website: http://www.facitec.br

Diretor Geral: Bráulio Pereira Lins

Courses

Accountancy (Accountancy); **Administration** (Administration); **Advertising and Publicity**; **Computer Networks**; **Graduate Studies** (Architecture; Business Education; Cinema and Television; Civil Law; Communication Studies; Food Science; Higher Education; Law; Management; Mathematics; Portuguese; Public Law; Public Relations; Software Engineering; Special Education; Statistics; Transport Management); **Information Systems** (Information Technology); **Information Systems** (Information Sciences); **Journalism** (Journalism); **Law** (Law); **Pedagogy** (Pedagogy); **Production Engineering** (Production Engineering); **Systems for Internet** (Information Technology); **Tourism**; **Tourism Management** (Tourism)

History: Founded 2001.

Degrees and Diplomas: *Bacharelado*; *Licenciatura*; *Especialização/Aperfeiçoamento*

Last Updated: 06/07/10

FACULTY OF TECHNOLOGY AND SCIENCE
Faculdade de Tecnológia e Ciências
Av. Luís Viana Filho, n° 8812, Paralela, Salvador, Bahia 41741590
Tel: +55(71) 3281-8000 +55(71) 3254-6666
Fax: +55(71) 3281-8019
EMail: dilcelia@ftc.br
Website: http://www.ftc.br

Diretor Geral: Humberto Santos Filho

Courses

Administration; **Biomedicine** (Biomedicine); **Design** (Fashion Design); **Education** (Physical Education); **Engineering**; **Environmental Management** (Environmental Management); **Health and Social Sciences** (Biomedicine; Dentistry; Medicine; Nutrition; Pharmacy; Physical Therapy; Psychology); **Law** (Law); **Natural Sciences**; **Physical Therapy**; **Social Communication and Information Sciences** (Advertising and Publicity; Cinema and Television; Communication Studies; Information Management; Journalism; Media Studies; Public Relations; Video)

Further Information: Campuses: Feira de Santana, Vitória da Conquista, Itabuna and Jequié

History: Founded 2000.

Main Language(s) of Instruction: Portuguese

Degrees and Diplomas: *Tecnólogo*; *Bacharelado*; *Licenciatura*

Last Updated: 08/07/10

FACULTY OF TECHNOLOGY AND SCIENCE OF FEIRA DE SANTANA
Faculdade de Tecnologia e Ciências de Feira de Santana (FTC)
Rua Artêmia Pires, SIM, Feira de Santana, BA 44043-590
Tel: +55(75) 3602-7000
Website: http://portal.ftc.br/index.php?option=com_frontpage&Itemid=94

Diretor Geral: Heraldo José Morais Silva

Courses

Accountancy (Accountancy); **Administration** (Administration); **Civil Engineering** (Civil Engineering); **Environmental Engineering** (Environmental Engineering); **Information Systems** (Information Sciences); **Nursing** (Nursing); **Nutrition** (Nutrition); **Physical Therapy** (Physical Therapy); **Psychology** (Psychology); **Veterinary Medicine** (Veterinary Science)

Degrees and Diplomas: *Bacharelado*

Last Updated: 24/08/10

FACULTY OF TECHNOLOGY AND SCIENCE OF ITABUNA
Faculdade de Tecnologia e Ciências de Itabuna (FTC)
Praça José Bastos, 55, Centro, Itabuna, BA 45600-081
Tel: +55(73) 3214-2400
Website: http://portal.ftc.br/index.php?option=com_frontpage&Itemid=96

Diretor Geral: Cristiano Lôbo

Courses

Administration (Administration); **Advertising and Publicity** (Advertising and Publicity); **Civil Engineering** (Civil Engineering); **Environmental Engineering** (Environmental Engineering); **Information Systems** (Information Sciences); **Journalism** (Journalism); **Law** (Law); **Nursing** (Nursing); **Nutrition** (Nutrition); **Physical Education** (Physical Education); **Physical Therapy** (Physical Therapy); **Psychology** (Psychology)

Degrees and Diplomas: *Bacharelado*

Last Updated: 24/08/10

FACULTY OF TECHNOLOGY AND SCIENCE OF JEQUIÉ
Faculdade de Tecnologia e Ciências de Jequié (FTC)
Rua Antônio Orrico, 357, São Judas Tadeu, Jequié, BA 45204-010
Tel: +55(73) 3527-8100
EMail: ftc.jeq@ftc.br
Website: http://portal.ftc.br/index.php?option=com_frontpage&Itemid=97

Diretor Geral: José Carlos Martins Oliveira

Courses

Administration (Administration); **Advertising and Publicity** (Advertising and Publicity); **Information Systems** (Information Sciences); **Journalism** (Journalism); **Nursing** (Nursing); **Psychology** (Psychology)

Degrees and Diplomas: *Bacharelado*

Last Updated: 24/08/10

FACULTY OF TECHNOLOGY AND SCIENCE OF NORTHERN PARANÁ

Faculdade de Tecnologia e Ciências do Norte do Paraná (FATECIE)

Rua Getúlio Vargas, 333, Paranavaí, PR 87709-000
Tel: +55(44) 3422-0716
Fax: +55(44) 3422-0716
Website: http://fatecie.com/

Diretor Geral: Gilmar de Oliveira

Courses

Administration (Administration); **Environmental Management** (Environmental Management); **Graduate Studies** (Business Administration; Computer Science; Environmental Studies; Higher Education; Management; Marketing); **Marketing** (Marketing)

Degrees and Diplomas: Tecnólogo. Also Postgraduate diploma.
Last Updated: 24/08/10

FACULTY OF TECHNOLOGY AND SCIENCE OF VITÓRIA DE CONQUISTA

Faculdade de Tecnologia e Ciências de Vitória de Conquista (FTC)

Rua Ubaldino Figuera, 200, Exposição, Vitória de Conquista, BA 45020-510
Tel: +55(77) 3422-8800
Website: http://portal.ftc.br/index.php?option=com_frontpage&Itemid=95

Diretor: Sérgio Magalhães EMail: smagalhaes.vic@ftc.br

Courses

Administration (Administration); **Advertising and Publicity** (Advertising and Publicity); **Civil Engineering** (Civil Engineering); **Information Systems** (Information Sciences); **Law** (Law); **Nursing** (Nursing); **Nutrition** (Nutrition); **Physical Education** (Physical Education); **Physical Therapy** (Physical Therapy); **Psychology** (Psychology)

Degrees and Diplomas: Bacharelado
Last Updated: 24/08/10

FACULTY OF TECHNOLOGY IN HOSTELRY, GASTRONOMY AND TOURISM OF SÃO PAULO

Faculdade de Tecnologia em Hotelaria, Gastronomia e Turismo de São Paulo (HOTEC)

Rua das Palmeiras, 117, 122 e 184, São Paulo, SP 01226-010
Tel: +55(11) 3246-2888
EMail: secretaria@hotec.com.br
Website: http://www.hotec.com.br/

Courses

Environmental Management (Environmental Management); **Events** (Public Relations; Tourism); **Gastronomy** (Cooking and Catering); **Graduate Studies** (Business and Commerce; Cooking and Catering; Higher Education; Public Relations; Service Trades); **Hospital Hostelry** (Health Administration; Hotel Management); **Hotel Management** (Hotel Management); **Human Resources** (Human Resources); **Nutrition** (Nutrition); **Tourism** (Tourism)

Degrees and Diplomas: Tecnólogo; Bacharelado. Also Postgraduate Diploma.
Last Updated: 24/08/10

FACULTY OF TECHNOLOGY OF ALAGOAS

Faculdade de Tecnologia de Alagoas (FAT/AL)

Av. Presidente Roosevelt, 1200, Serraria, Maceió, AL 57045-150
Tel: +55(82) 3328-7000
Website: http://www.fat-al.edu.br/

Courses

Advertising and Publicity (Advertising and Publicity); **Cooperatives Management** (Management); **Financial Management** (Finance); **Graduate Studies** (Accountancy; Criminology; Leisure Studies; Management; Marketing; Safety Engineering; Software Engineering; Sports Management; Transport Management); **Human Resources** (Human Resources); **Marketing** (Marketing); **Social and Sportive Events Management** (Public Relations);

Systems Analysis and Development (Systems Analysis); **Tourism** (Tourism)

History: Founded 2002 as Centro de Educação Tecnológica de Alagoas – CET/AL. Acquired present status and title 2004.

Degrees and Diplomas: Tecnólogo. Also Postgraduate Degrees and MBA.
Last Updated: 20/08/10

FACULTY OF TECHNOLOGY OF CACHOEIRO DE ITAPEMIRIM

Faculdade de Tecnologia Cachoeiro de Itapemirim (FACI)

Rua Amâncio Silva, 40, Arariguaba, Cachoeiro de Itapemirim, ES 29305-470
Tel: +55(28) 3521-6450
EMail: faci-direcao@faci.edu.br
Website: http://www.faci.edu.br

Courses

Human Resources (Human Resources); **Information Systems Management** (Information Management); **Ornamental Rock** (Geology)

Degrees and Diplomas: Tecnólogo. Also Postgraduate Diploma.
Last Updated: 20/08/10

FACULTY OF TECHNOLOGY OF CATALÃO

Faculdade de Tecnologia de Catalão (FATECA)

Rua Prof. Paulo Lima, 100, Catalão, GO
Tel: +55(64) 3441-6200
EMail: cesuc@cesuc.br
Website: http://www.fateca.edu.br/

Diretora: Maria Eleonora de O. Scalia

Courses

Graduate Studies (Civil Law; Finance; Higher Education; Human Resources; Information Technology; Management; Production Engineering; Transport Management); **Systems for Internet** (Computer Science)

History: Founded 2004.

Degrees and Diplomas: Tecnólogo; Especialização/Aperfeiçoamento. Also MBA.
Last Updated: 20/08/10

FACULTY OF TECHNOLOGY OF GUARATINGUETÁ

Faculdade de Tecnológia de Guaratinguetá (FATEC GT)

Av. Prof. João Rodrigues Alckmin, 1501, Jd. Esperança, Guaratingueta, SP 12517-475
Tel: +55(12) 3126-3921 +55(12) 3125-7785 +55(12) 3126-4849
Fax: +55(12) 3532-5110 +55(12) 3126-3921
EMail: secretaria@fatecguaratingueta.edu.br; fatecgt@uol.com.br
Website: http://www.fatecguaratingueta.edu.br

Diretor: Severino Antônio Moreira Barbosa
EMail: diretoria@fatecguaratingueta.edu.br

Courses

Graduate Studies (Management); **Undergraduate Studies** (Business Administration; Computer Science; Finance; Information Technology; Management; Systems Analysis; Transport Management)

History: Founded 1994.

Degrees and Diplomas: Tecnólogo. Also Postgraduate Diploma.
Last Updated: 27/09/10

FACULTY OF TECHNOLOGY OF INDAIATUBA

Faculdade de Tecnológia de Indaiatuba (FATEC-ID)

Rua Dom Pedro I, 65, Cidade Nova, Indaiatuba, SP 13334-100
Tel: +55(19) 3885-1923
EMail: fatecid@fatecindaiatuba.edu.br
Website: http://www.fatecid.com.br

Diretor: Luiz Antonio Daniel
EMail: diretoria@fatecindaiatuba.edu.br

Courses

Graduate Studies (E-Business/Commerce; Transport Management); **Undergraduate Studies** (Business Administration; Computer Networks; Data Processing; Information Sciences; Information Technology; International Business; Management; Marketing; Secretarial Studies; Transport Management)

History: Founded 1994.

Degrees and Diplomas: *Tecnólogo*; *Especialização/Aperfeiçoamento*
Last Updated: 27/09/10

FACULTY OF TECHNOLOGY OF JARAGUÁ DO SUL

Faculdade de Tecnologia de Jaraguá do Sul (FATEJ)
Rua Major Julio Ferreira, Vila Lalau, Jaraguá do Sul, SC
Tel: +55(47) 2107-4700
EMail: cribak@fatej.com.br
Website: http://www.fatej.com.br/

Courses

Financial Management (Finance; Management); **Marketing** (Marketing)

Degrees and Diplomas: *Tecnólogo*; *Especialização/Aperfeiçoamento*
Last Updated: 20/08/10

FACULTY OF TECHNOLOGY OF PALMAS

Faculdade de Tecnologia de Palmas (FATEP)
Centro comercial Wilson Vaz 104 sul, salas 225, Palmas, TO
Tel: +55(63) 3215-8240
EMail: fatep@ftp.edu.br
Website: http://www.ftp.edu.br
Diretor Geral: Edival Jacinto da Silva

Courses

Events Management (Public Relations); **Graduate Studies** (Educational Administration; Family Studies; Health Administration; Pedagogy; Psychoanalysis; Public Relations; Theology)

Further Information: Also Pole in Guaraí.

Degrees and Diplomas: *Tecnólogo*. Also Postgraduate Diploma and MBA.
Last Updated: 23/08/10

FACULTY OF TECHNOLOGY OF PIAUI

Faculdade de Tecnológia do Piaui (FATEPI)
Rua 1° de Maio 2235, Bairro Primavera, Teresina, Piauí 64002510
Tel: +55(86) 2107-2200
Fax: +55(86) 2107-2200
EMail: fatepi@fatepi.com.br
Website: http://www.fatepi.com.br/
Diretor Geral: Gislan Vieira de Sousa

Courses

Information Systems; **Law** (Law; Public Law); **Pedagogy** (Educational Administration; Educational Psychology; Environmental Studies; Special Education); **Speech Therapy** (Speech Therapy and Audiology)

History: Founded 1999.

Degrees and Diplomas: *Bacharelado*; *Licenciatura*; *Especialização/Aperfeiçoamento*
Last Updated: 08/07/10

FACULTY OF TECHNOLOGY OF PIRACICABA

Faculdade de Tecnologia de Piracicaba (FATEP)
R. Silva Jardim, 1763, Cidade Alta, Piracicaba, SP 13419-140
Tel: +55(19) 3432-9957
EMail: marcos@fateppiracicaba.edu.br
Website: http://www.fateppiracicaba.edu.br/

Courses

Graduate Studies (Accountancy; Agriculture; Business Administration; Education; Educational Psychology; Finance; Industrial Management; Information Technology; Management; Marketing;

Safety Engineering; Social Policy; Transport Management); **Human Resources** (Human Resources); **Industrial Production Management** (Industrial Management); **Logistics** (Transport Management); **Marketing** (Marketing); **Sugar Alcohols Production** (Agriculture)

History: Founded 2007.

Degrees and Diplomas: *Tecnólogo*; *Especialização/Aperfeiçoamento*. Also MBA.
Last Updated: 23/08/10

FACULTY OF TECHNOLOGY OF PONTA PORÃ

Faculdade de Tecnologia de Ponta Porã (FATEP)
Rua Antônio João 1675, Centro, Ponta Porã,
Mato Grosso do Sul 79900000
Tel: +55(67) 3431-1002
Fax: +55(67) 3431-1002
EMail: fapp@click21.com.br
Diretora Geral: Labibe Esther Esgaib Kayatt

Courses

Civil Engineering

History: Founded 1998

Degrees and Diplomas: *Bacharelado*
Last Updated: 08/07/10

FACULTY OF TECHNOLOGY OF RIO CLARO

Faculdade de Tecnologia de Rio Claro (CBTA)
Rodovia Washington Luiz Km 1733, Rio Claro, SP 13501-600
Tel: +55(19) 3533 7073
Fax: +55(19) 3533 7073
EMail: cbta@cbta.edu.br
Website: http://www.cbta.edu.br/
Diretor: Carlos Renato Gherarde Lins
EMail: carlosl@sistemained.com.br

Courses

Distance Education (Finance; History; Human Resources; Marketing; Mathematics; Safety Engineering; Transport Management); **Environmental Management** (Environmental Management); **Financial Management** (Finance); **Graduate Studies** (Business and Commerce; Environmental Management; Finance; Industrial and Organizational Psychology; Industrial Management; Management; Marketing; Transport Management); **Human Resources** (Human Resources); **Industrial Production Management** (Industrial Management); **Logistics** (Transport Management); **Marketing** (Marketing); **Systems Analysis and Development** (Systems Analysis)

Degrees and Diplomas: *Tecnólogo*; *Licenciatura*. Also MBA.
Last Updated: 23/08/10

FACULTY OF TECHNOLOGY OF TAUBATÉ

Faculdade de Tecnologia de Taubaté (ETEP)
R. José Olegário de Barros, 1350, Vila das Graças, Taubaté,
SP 12060-400
Tel: +55(12) 3947-2200
Website: http://www.etep.edu.br/

Courses

Administration (Administration); **Aeronautical Engineering** (Aeronautical and Aerospace Engineering); **Computer Engineering** (Computer Engineering); **Electrical Engineering** (Electrical Engineering); **Mechanical Industrial Engineering** (Industrial Engineering; Mechanical Engineering); **Mechatronics Engineering** (Electronic Engineering; Mechanical Engineering); **Production Engineering** (Production Engineering)

History: Founded 1956 as Escola Técnica Professor Everardo Passos. Changed name to EEI - Escola de Engenharia Industrial 1968 and to FACAP - Faculdade de Ciências Aplicadas 1987. Acquired present title 2004.

Degrees and Diplomas: *Tecnólogo*; *Bacharelado*
Last Updated: 02/09/10

FACULTY OF TECHNOLOGY OF TERESINA
Faculdade de Tecnologia de Teresina (CET)
Rua Firmino Pires, 527, Centro/Norte, Teresina, PI 64001-070
Tel: +55(86) 3221-0079 +55(86) 3226-1933
EMail: cet@cet.edu.br
Website: http://www.cet.edu.br/

Courses
Biomedicine (Biomedicine); **Computer Networks** (Computer Networks); **Data Bases** (Data Processing); **Financial Management** (Finance); **Food Engineering** (Food Technology); **Graduate Studies** (Higher Education; Software Engineering); **Human Resources** (Human Resources); **Nursing** (Nursing); **Pharmacy** (Pharmacy); **Systems for Internet** (Computer Science)

Further Information: Also São Cristóvão campus.

Degrees and Diplomas: *Tecnólogo*; *Bacharelado*; *Especialização/ Aperfeiçoamento*
Last Updated: 23/08/10

FACULTY OF TECHNOLOGY OF THE AMAZON
Faculdade de Tecnologia da Amazônia (FAZ)
Av. Almirante Barroso, 777, Marco, Belém, PA 66093-020
Tel: +55(91) 3344-0700
EMail: coord.comunicacao@faz.edu.br
Website: http://www.faz.edu.br

Diretor Geral: Suely Melo de Castro Menezes
EMail: diretoriageral@faz.edu.br; suelymenezes@idepa.com.br

Courses
Advertising and Publicity (Advertising and Publicity); **Computer Networks** (Computer Networks); **Financial Management** (Finance); **Graphic Design** (Graphic Design); **Human Resources** (Human Resources); **institutional Communication** (Communication Studies); **Logistics** (Transport Management); **Marketing** (Marketing); **Private Security Management** (Protective Services); **Radiology** (Radiology); **Real Estate** (Real Estate); **Systems Analysis and Development** (Systems Analysis); **Telecommunications Engineering** (Telecommunications Engineering)

History: Founded 2002 as Centro de Educação Tecnológica da Amazônia - CFAZ. Acquired present status and Title 2004.

Degrees and Diplomas: *Tecnólogo*; *Especialização/Aperfeiçoamento*
Last Updated: 20/08/10

FACULTY OF TECHNOLOGY OF THE NORTH EAST
Faculdade de Tecnologia do Nordeste (FATENE)
Rua Matos Vasconcelos, 1626, Damas, Fortaleza, CE 60426-110
Tel: +55(85) 3299-2829
Fax: +55(85) 3299-2822
EMail: fatene@fatene.edu.br
Website: http://www.fatene.edu.br/

Courses
Graduate Studies *(Caucaia)* (Accountancy; Educational Administration; Educational Psychology; History; Management; Occupational Health; Physical Education; Public Health); **Graduate Studies** *(Fortaleza)* (Accountancy; Business Administration; Computer Science; Contemporary History; Distance Education; Education; Educational Psychology; Health Administration; Human Resources; Special Education); **Graduate Studies** *(Itapipoca)* (Business Administration; History; Mathematics Education; Physical Education; Public Health); **Nursing** (Nursing); **Physical Education** (Physical Education); **Social Service** (Social and Community Services); **Technological Studies** (Computer Science; Finance; Information Technology; Marketing; Systems Analysis)

Degrees and Diplomas: *Tecnólogo*; *Bacharelado*; *Licenciatura*; *Especialização/Aperfeiçoamento*. Also MBA.
Last Updated: 23/08/10

FACULTY OF TECHNOLOGY OF UNIUOL
Faculdade de Tecnologia do Uniuol (UNIUOL)
Av. Epitácio Pessoa, 4657, Tambaú, João Pessoa, PB
Tel: +55(83) 3241-9904
Website: http://www.uniuol.com.br/

Courses
Commercial Management (Business and Commerce); **Financial Management** (Finance); **Graduate Studies** (Educational Administration; Finance; Management; Safety Engineering; Transport Management); **Marketing** (Marketing)

Degrees and Diplomas: *Tecnólogo*. Also Postgraduate Degree.
Last Updated: 24/08/10

FACULTY OF TECHNOLOGY OF VITORIA
Faculdade Vitoriana de Tecnologia (FAVI)
Avenida Nossa Senhora da Penha 1800, Barro Vermelho, Vitória, Espirito Santo 29045400
Tel: +55(27) 3325-0244 +55(27) 3325-0229
Fax: +55(27) 324-1500
EMail: favi@favi.com.br
Website: http://www.favi.br

Diretor: Rodrigo Cambará Arantes Garcia de Paiva

Courses
Information Systems
History: Founded 1986
Main Language(s) of Instruction: Portuguese
Degrees and Diplomas: *Bacharelado*
Last Updated: 30/06/10

FACULTY OF TECHNOLOGY, SCIENCE AND EDUCATION
Faculdade de Tecnologia, Ciências e Educação
Av. Painguás, 225/243 - Jd. Urupê, Pirassununga, SP 13630-250
Tel: +55(19) 3561-1543
EMail: fatece@fatece.edu.br
Website: http://www.fatece.edu.br

Diretor: Claudio Romualdo

Courses
Administration (Administration); **Computer Science** (Computer Science); **Mathematics** (Mathematics); **Pedagogy** (Pedagogy)
History: Founded 2006.
Main Language(s) of Instruction: Portuguese
Degrees and Diplomas: *Bacharelado*; *Especialização/Aperfeiçoamento*; *Mestrado*
Libraries: Biblioteca Paulo Freire
Last Updated: 21/09/10

FACULTY OF TELÊMACO BORBA
Faculdade de Telêmaco Borba (FATEB)
Rua Arthur Bernardes 140, Socomin, Telêmaco Borba, PR 84265390
Tel: +55(42) 3271-8000
Fax: +55(42) 3271-8000
EMail: fatebtb@fatebtb.edu.br
Website: http://www.fatebtb.edu.br

Diretor: Wilson José Tim Pontara
EMail: timpontara@fatebtb.edu.br

Courses
Accountancy; **Administration** (Accountancy; Administration); **Chemical Engineering**; **Law** (Law); **Letters** (English; Literature; Portuguese; Spanish); **Pedagogy** (Education; Pedagogy); **Tourism** (Tourism)

History: Founded 2000.
Main Language(s) of Instruction: Portuguese
Degrees and Diplomas: *Bacharelado*; *Licenciatura*; *Especialização/Aperfeiçoamento*; *Mestrado*
Last Updated: 08/07/10

FACULTY OF THE AMAZON
Faculdade da Amazônia
BR 316 Km 7, n° 590, Ananindeua, PA
Tel: +55(91) 3255-2236
EMail: faculdadedaamazonia@bol.com.br
Website: http://www.faculdadedaamazonia.com.br

Courses
Accountancy (Accountancy); **Administration** (Administration); **History** (History); **Letters** (Literature); **Pedagogy** (Pedagogy)
History: Founded 2004.
Main Language(s) of Instruction: Portuguese
Degrees and Diplomas: *Bacharelado*; *Licenciatura*; *Especialização/Aperfeiçoamento*
Libraries: Biblioteca Tapajoara
Last Updated: 26/07/10

FACULTY OF THE AMAZON
Faculdade do Amazonas (IAES)
Rua Pará, 5464 Ed. José Frota - São Geraldo, Mánaus, Amazonas 69050010
Tel: +55(92) 3584-6068
Fax: +55(92) 3584-6067
EMail: iaes@vivax.com.br
Website: http://www.iaes.com.br/
Diretora: Zobélia Maria de Souza Lopes

Courses
Dentistry (Dentistry)
History: Founded 2001.
Main Language(s) of Instruction: Portuguese
Degrees and Diplomas: *Bacharelado*; *Especialização/Aperfeiçoamento*; *Mestrado*; *Doutorado*
Last Updated: 08/07/10

FACULTY OF THE AMERICAS
Faculdade das Américas
R. Augusta, 973 - Metrô Consolação
Tel: +55(11) 3257-4088
EMail: academico@faculdadedasamericas.com
Website: http://www.fam2010.com.br/site
Diretora: Leila Mejdalina Pereira

Courses
Administration (Administration); **Advertising** (Advertising and Publicity); **Law** (Law); **Pedagogy** (Pedagogy)
History: Founded 1998.
Main Language(s) of Instruction: Portuguese
Degrees and Diplomas: *Bacharelado*; *Licenciatura*; *Especialização/Aperfeiçoamento*
Libraries: Yes
Last Updated: 26/07/10

FACULTY OF THE BRAZIL INSTITUTE
Faculdade do Instituto Brasil (FIBRA)
Br 060/153 3400 - KM 97, Anápolis, Goiás 75133050
Tel: +55(62) 3313-3500
EMail: secretaria@fibra.edu.br
Website: http://www.fibra.edu.br/v2/
Diretor: Maryam Mikhael

Courses
Accountancy (Accountancy); **Biomedicine** (Biomedicine); **Business Administration** (Accountancy; Agricultural Business; Business Administration; Finance; International Business; Marketing); **International Relations** (International Relations); **Law** (Labour Law; Law); **Nursing** (Nursing); **Nutrition** (Consumer Studies; Nutrition); **Pharmacy** (Pharmacy); **Physiotherapy** (Physical Therapy)

History: Founded 2001.
Degrees and Diplomas: *Bacharelado*; *Especialização/Aperfeiçoamento*
Last Updated: 08/07/10

FACULTY OF THE BRAZILIAN ACADEMY OF EDUCATION AND CULTURE
Faculdade da Academia Brasileira de Educação e Cultura
Av. Rio Branco, 277, 1° Andar - Centro, Rio de Janeiro, RJ
Tel: +55(21) 3504-0348
EMail: gestor@fabecrj.edu.br
Website: http://www.fabecrj.edu.br
Diretor: Luiz Claudio Barbosade Oliveira

Courses
Accountancy (Accountancy)
History: Founded 2005.
Main Language(s) of Instruction: Portuguese
Degrees and Diplomas: *Bacharelado*; *Especialização/Aperfeiçoamento*
Last Updated: 23/07/10

FACULTY OF THE CITY OF COROMANDEL
Faculdade Cidade de Coromandel (FCC)
Avenida Adolfo Timóteo da Silva 433, Brasil Novo, Coromandel, Minas Gerais 385500-000
Tel: +55(34) 3841-3405
Fax: +55(34) 3841-3405
EMail: fcc@fcc.edu.br
Website: http://www.fcc.edu.br
Diretor: Paulo César de Souza

Courses
Administration; **Graduate Studies** (Lato Sensu); **Literature** (Literature); **Nursing**; **Pedagogy** (Pedagogy); **Physical Education**
History: Founded 2000.
Main Language(s) of Instruction: Portuguese
Degrees and Diplomas: *Bacharelado*; *Licenciatura*; *Especialização/Aperfeiçoamento*
Last Updated: 30/06/10

FACULTY OF THE CITY OF GUANHÃES
Faculdade Cidade de Guanhães
Br 259 – Km 2, Bairro Nova União, Guanhães, MG 39.740.000
EMail: mailto:facig@portalfacig.com.br
Website: http://www.portalfacig.com.br
Diretor: Argemiro Afonso Dumont Lessa
Last Updated: 22/07/10

FACULTY OF THE CITY OF JOÃO PINHEIRO
Faculdade Cidade de João Pinheiro
Av. Zico Dornelas, 380 - Santa Cruz II, João Pinheiro, MG 38770-000
Tel: +55(38) 3561-3900
EMail: ideasp@terra.com.br
Website: http://www.fcjp.edu.br
Diretor: Paulo Cesar de Sousa

Institutes
Education (Biology; Chemistry; Geography; History; Literature; Mathematics; Pedagogy; Physical Education); **Health** (Biomedicine; Nursing; Physical Therapy); **Science and Technology** (Business Administration)
History: Founded 2002.
Main Language(s) of Instruction: Portuguese
Degrees and Diplomas: *Bacharelado*; *Licenciatura*; *Especialização/Aperfeiçoamento*
Libraries: Yes
Last Updated: 22/07/10

FACULTY OF THE CITY OF PATOS DE MINAS

Faculdade Cidade de Patos de Minas
Rua Major Gote, Centro, Patos de Minas, MG 38700-000
Tel: +55(34) 3818-2300
EMail: administrativo@unifpm.edu.br
Website: http://www.faculdadepatosdeminas.com

Diretor: Paulo de Sousa

Courses
Administration (Administration); **Biology** (Biology); **Biomedicine** (Biomedicine); **Chemistry** (Chemistry); **Dentistry** (Dentistry); **Mathematics** (Mathematics); **Nursing** (Nursing); **Nutrition** (Nutrition); **Pharmacy** (Pharmacy); **Physical Education** (Physical Education); **Physiotherapy** (Physical Therapy); **Psychology** (Psychology)

History: Founded 2005.

Main Language(s) of Instruction: Portuguese

Degrees and Diplomas: *Bacharelado*; *Licenciatura*; *Especialização/Aperfeiçoamento*

Libraries: Yes
Last Updated: 23/07/10

FACULTY OF THE CITY OF SANTA LUZIA

Faculdade da Cidade de Santa Luzia (FACSAL)
Avenida Beira Rio, 2000, Dist. Industrial III, Caixa Postal 3423,
Santa Luzia, MG 33040-260
Tel: +55(31) 3079-9000
Fax: +55(31) 3079-9000
EMail: facsal@facsal.br
Website: http://www.facsal.br

Diretor: Daniel Ramalho Marques

Courses
Accountancy (Accountancy); **Administration** (Administration); **Biological Sciences**; **Information Systems**; **Law** (Law); **Literature**; **Nursing** (Nursing); **Nutrition** (Nutrition); **Pedagogy** (Pedagogy); **Physical Education** (Physical Education); **Physiotherapy** (Physical Therapy); **Social Communication - Advertising and Publicity**; **Technological Studies** (Computer Networks; Marketing); **Tourism**

History: Founded 2000.

Main Language(s) of Instruction: Portuguese

Degrees and Diplomas: *Tecnólogo*; *Bacharelado*; *Licenciatura*
Last Updated: 30/06/10

FACULTY OF THE EDUCATIONAL CENTRE OF MINEIRO

Faculdade do Centro Educacional Mineiro
Rua Eufrates, 30, Alípio de Melo, Belo Horizone, MG
Tel: +55(31) 3474-3702
EMail: contato@facembh.com.br
Website: http://www.facembh.com.br

Diretora: Jane Lovalho Mourão

Courses
Accountancy (Accountancy); **Administration** (Administration)
History: Founded 2009.
Main Language(s) of Instruction: Portuguese
Degrees and Diplomas: *Bacharelado*
Libraries: Yes
Last Updated: 30/08/10

FACULTY OF THE EDUCATIONAL FOUNDATION OF ARAÇATUBA

Faculdade da Fundação Educacional Araçatuba (FAC-FEA)
Rua São Marcos 349, Jardim Sumaré, Araçatuba,
São Paulo 16015-280
Tel: +55(18) 3608-5272
EMail: fcea@terra.com.br
Website: http://www.feata.edu.br/

Diretor: Pascoal Manfredi Neto
Tel: +55(18) 3622-8262 **EMail:** facfea.diretor@terra.com.br

Courses
Administration (Administration); **Biological Sciences**; **Economics** (Economics); **Graduate Studies** (*Lato sensu*) (Educational Psychology; Psychoanalysis; Public Administration; Special Education); **Mathematics** (Mathematics); **Pedagogy**; **Psychology** (Psychology)

History: Founded 1989

Main Language(s) of Instruction: Portuguese

Degrees and Diplomas: *Bacharelado*; *Licenciatura*; *Especialização/Aperfeiçoamento*
Last Updated: 30/06/10

FACULTY OF THE ENVIRONMENT AND TRADE TECHNIQUES

Faculdade do Medio Ambiente e de Tecnologia de Negocios
Sia/Sul, Trecho 02, Lotes 1.510 / 1.540 N°: s/n, Região
Administrativa X, Guará, Brasília, DF 71200-020
Tel: +55(61) 3433-3000
EMail: secretaria@famatec.edu.br
Website: http://www.famatec.edu.br

Diretora: Alessandra Maria Frisso

Courses
Accountancy (Accountancy); **Administration** (Administration)
History: Founded 2006.

Main Language(s) of Instruction: Portuguese

Degrees and Diplomas: *Bacharelado*; *Especialização/Aperfeiçoamento*; *Mestrado*
Libraries: Yes
Last Updated: 17/09/10

FACULTY OF THE FRONTIER

Faculdade da Fronteira
Rodovia PRT 163, Km 01, s/n, Barracão, PR 85.700-000
Tel: +55(49) 3644-1684
EMail: sec@faf.edu.br
Website: http://www.faf.edu.br

Diretora: Lucila Mai

Courses
Accountancy (Accountancy); **Administration** (Administration); **Letters** (Literature); **Mathematics** (Mathematics); **Pedagogy** (Pedagogy)

History: Founded 1999.

Main Language(s) of Instruction: Portuguese

Degrees and Diplomas: *Bacharelado*; *Licenciatura*; *Especialização/Aperfeiçoamento*
Libraries: Yes
Last Updated: 26/07/10

FACULTY OF THE FUTURE

Faculdade do Futuro
Rua Duarte Peixoto 259, Manhuacu, MG 36900-000
Tel: +55(33) 3331-1214
EMail: secretaria@faculdadedofuturo.edu.br
Website: http://www.faculdadedofuturo.edu.br

Diretor: Flávio José Ribeiro de Almeida

Courses
Biology (Biology); **Nursing** (Nursing); **Pharmacy** (Pharmacy); **Physical Education** (Physical Education)

History: Founded 2003.

Main Language(s) of Instruction: Portuguese

Degrees and Diplomas: *Licenciatura*; *Especialização/Aperfeiçoamento*

Libraries: Biblioteca Professora Ivonne Ribeiro de Almeida
Last Updated: 30/08/10

FACULTY OF THE INTERIOR OF THE STATE OF SAO PAULO

Faculdade do Interior Paulista (FIP)
Rua Joao Gerem 275 Vila Operária, Barra Bonita,
São Paulo 17340000
Tel: +55(14) 3604-1200
Fax: +55(14) 3604-1200
EMail: secretariafunbbe@bol.com.br
Website: http://www.funbbe.br/Default.aspx?
alias=www.funbbe.br/fip

Diretor: José Norberto Basso Junior

Courses
Business Administration (Agricultural Business; Business Administration; Small Business); **Information Systems**; **Tourism** (Tourism)

History: Founded 2000.

Degrees and Diplomas: *Bacharelado*; *Especialização/Aperfeiçoamento*
Last Updated: 08/07/10

FACULTY OF THE LAKES REGION

Faculdade da Região dos Lagos (FERLAGOS)
Avenida Júlia Kubitschek 80, Jardim Flamboyant, Cabo Frio,
Rio de Janeiro 28905000
Tel: +55(24) 2645-6100
Fax: +55(24) 2643-0485
EMail: secretaria@ferlagos.br
Website: http://www.ferlagos.br

Diretor: Carlos Alberto Sepúlveda Alves
EMail: direcao@ferlagos.br

Courses
Graduate Studies (Art Education; Business Administration; Cultural Studies; Educational Administration; Educational Psychology; English; Environmental Management; Finance; Geography; History; Human Resources; Literacy Education; Marketing; Mathematics; Mathematics Education; Petroleum and Gas Engineering; Physical Education; Portuguese; Rehabilitation and Therapy; Translation and Interpretation)

Higher Institutes
Education *(ISE)* (Biology; English; Geography; Literature; Mathematics; Portuguese; Spanish)

Institutes
Administration and Economic Sciences *(IACE)* (Accountancy; Administration)

History: Founded 1979.

Main Language(s) of Instruction: Portuguese

Degrees and Diplomas: *Bacharelado*; *Licenciatura*; *Especialização/Aperfeiçoamento*
Last Updated: 30/06/10

FACULTY OF THE MID-PARNAIBA REGION

Faculdade do Médio Parnaíba
Rua 18 de Setembro 293 - Ao lado do Emater, São Pedro do Piauí,
PI 64430-000
Tel: +55(86)3280-1149
EMail: faculdadefamep@yahoo.com.br
Website: http://www.famep-pi.com.br

Diretor: Washington Aluisio Gomes de Oliveira

Courses
Accountancy (Accountancy); **Biology** (Biology); **History** (History); **Nursing** (Nursing)

History: Founded 2006.

Main Language(s) of Instruction: Portuguese

Degrees and Diplomas: *Bacharelado*; *Especialização/Aperfeiçoamento*

Libraries: Yes
Last Updated: 23/08/10

FACULTY OF THE MUNDIAL FOUNDATION

Faculdade Mundial
Avenida Paulista, 2.200 – 12° andar, São Paulo, SP 01310-300
EMail: fundacaomundial@fundacaomundial.com.br
Website: http://www.faculdademundial.com.br

Diretor: José Abrão

Courses
Public Relations (Public Relations); **Social Communication** (Advertising and Publicity)

History: Founded 2009.

Main Language(s) of Instruction: Portuguese

Degrees and Diplomas: *Bacharelado*
Last Updated: 07/09/10

FACULTY OF THE NATIONAL INSTITUTE OF POST-GRADUATE STUDIES OF CAMPINAS

Faculdade do Instituto Nacional de Pós-Graduaçao de Campinas
Avenida Coronel Silva Teles N°: 700, Anexo ao Colégio Madre
Cecília, Cambuí, Campinas, SP 13024-001
Tel: +55(19) 2102-5656
EMail: secretaria.camp@inpg.edu.br
Website: http://www.inpg.edu.br/homesite/default.asp

Presidente: José Leônidas Olinquevitch

Courses
Administration (Administration; Finance; Human Resources; Management)

Further Information: Also branch in São José dos Campos

History: Founded 2004.

Main Language(s) of Instruction: Portuguese

Degrees and Diplomas: *Bacharelado*; *Especialização/Aperfeiçoamento*; *Mestrado*
Last Updated: 21/09/10

FACULTY OF THE NAUTICAL CLUB OF MOGI DAS CRUZES

Faculdade do Clube Náutico Mogiano (FCNM)
Rua Cabo Diogo Oliver 758, Mogi das Cruzes, São Paulo 8773000
Tel: +55(11) 4791-7100
EMail: nautico@nautico.edu.br
Website: http://www.nautico.edu.br

Diretor: Ademir Pimentel Fernandes

Courses
Physical Education (Physical Education); **Physical Therapy** (Physical Therapy)

History: Founded 1972.

Main Language(s) of Instruction: Portuguese

Degrees and Diplomas: *Bacharelado*; *Licenciatura*
Last Updated: 08/07/10

FACULTY OF THE NORTE NOVO REGION OF APUCARANA

Faculdade do Norte Novo de Apucarana
Av. Zilda Seixas do Amaral, 4350 - Pq. Industrial Norte, Apucarana,
PR 86806-380|
Tel: +55(43) 3420-1700
EMail: facnopar@facnopar.com.br
Website: http://www.facnopar.com.br

Diretor: Danilo Lemos Freire

Courses
Law (Law); **Pedagogy** (Pedagogy); **Social Communication** (Advertising and Publicity; Journalism; Public Relations)

History: Founded 2001.

Main Language(s) of Instruction: Portuguese

Degrees and Diplomas: *Bacharelado*; *Licenciatura*; *Especialização/Aperfeiçoamento*; *Mestrado*

Libraries: Yes
Last Updated: 17/09/10

FACULTY OF THE NORTH OF GOIAS

Faculdade do Norte Goiano
Rua Floriano Peixoto 28, Porangatu, GO 76550-000
Tel: +55(62) 3224-7674
EMail: deciocl@hotmail.com
Website: http://www.facporangatu.com.br

Diretor: Decio Correa Lima

Courses
Administration (Administration); **Nursing** (Nursing)

History: Founded 2006.

Main Language(s) of Instruction: Portuguese

Degrees and Diplomas: *Bacharelado*; *Especialização/Aperfeiçoamento*
Last Updated: 23/08/10

FACULTY OF THE NORTH WEST OF MINAS

Faculdade do Noroeste de Minas (FINOM)
Rodavia MG 188-Km 167, Bairro Fazendinha, Paracatu,
Minas Gerais 38600000
Tel: +55(61) 3671-2454
Fax: +55(61) 3671-2454
EMail: finom@finom.br
Website: http://www.finom.edu.br/index.asp

Diretor Geral: William José Ferreira

Courses
Accountancy (Accountancy); **Agronomy**; **Civil Engineering** (Civil Engineering); **Electrical Engineering** (Electrical Engineering); **Environmental Engineering** (Environmental Engineering); **Food Processing** (Food Technology); **Geography**; **History** (History); **Law** (Law); **Mathematics** (Mathematics); **Mining Engineering**; **Pedagogy**; **Physics** (Physics); **Production Engineering** (Production Engineering); **Systems Analysis** (Systems Analysis); **Telecommunications Engineering** (Telecommunications Engineering)

History: Founded 1987.

Main Language(s) of Instruction: Portuguese

Degrees and Diplomas: *Bacharelado*; *Licenciatura*; *Especialização/Aperfeiçoamento*
Last Updated: 08/07/10

FACULTY OF THE NORTH WEST OF PARANA

Faculdade do Noroeste Paranaense
Av. Brasil, n 1382, Nova Esperança, PR 87600-000
Tel: +55(44) 3252-1122
EMail: contato@fanp.com.br
Website: http://portal.fanp.com.br

Diretora: Marlene Meneguetti Afonso

Courses
Administration (Administration); **Pedagogy** (Pedagogy); **Social Services** (Social and Community Services)

History: Founded 1997.

Main Language(s) of Instruction: Portuguese

Degrees and Diplomas: *Bacharelado*; *Licenciatura*; *Especialização/Aperfeiçoamento*
Libraries: Yes
Last Updated: 23/08/10

FACULTY OF THE PANTANAL

Faculdade do Pantanal
Av. Sete de Setembro, s/n, Bairro DNER, Cáceres, MT 78200-000
Tel: +55(65) 3223-1777
EMail: direcao@fap-pb.com.br
Website: http://www.fapan.edu.br

Diretor: Aécio Alves Pereira

Courses
Administration (Administration); **Information Sciences** (Computer Science); **Psychology** (Psychology)

History: Founded 2007.

Main Language(s) of Instruction: Portuguese

Degrees and Diplomas: *Bacharelado*; *Licenciatura*; *Especialização/Aperfeiçoamento*
Last Updated: 23/08/10

FACULTY OF THE PEOPLE

Faculdade do Povo
Rua Barão de Itapetininga, 163 - Edifício Louza,
1 andar - República, São Paulo, SP 01042-001
Tel: +55(11) 3355-4040
EMail: atendimento@fapsp.com.br
Website: http://www.facdopovo.com.br

Diretor: Eber Cocareli

Courses
Social Communication (Advertising and Publicity; Journalism; Radio and Television Broadcasting)

History: Founded 2009.

Main Language(s) of Instruction: Portuguese

Degrees and Diplomas: *Bacharelado*

Libraries: Biblioteca Dr. R.R. Soares
Last Updated: 20/08/10

FACULTY OF THE REGION OF PIAUI

Faculdade Piauiense (FAP)
Avenida Pinheiro Machado 2611, Rodoviária, Parnaiba,
PI 64210010
Tel: +55(86) 323-4148
Fax: +55(86) 323-3250
EMail: altair.marinho@fapparnaiba.com.br
Website: http://www.phb.fap.com.br

Diretora Geral: Rosany Correa
EMail: rosany.correa@fapparnaiba.com.br

Courses
Accountancy; **Administration**; **Computer Science**; **Law** (Law); **Nursing** (Nursing); **Nutrition**; **Pedagogy** (Pedagogy); **Physiotherapy** (Physical Therapy)

History: Founded 2000.

Main Language(s) of Instruction: Portuguese

Degrees and Diplomas: *Bacharelado*; *Especialização/Aperfeiçoamento*; *Mestrado*
Last Updated: 05/07/10

FACULTY OF THE SERIDO

Faculdade do Seridó
Rua Prefeito Alcindo Gomes 679, Currais Novos, RN 59380-000
Tel: +55(84) 3412-3377
EMail: max_rosan@hotmail.com
Website: http://www.faculdadedoserido.com.br

Diretora: Cléa Maria Galvão Bacurau
EMail: cleabac@yahoo.com.br

Courses
Accountancy (Accountancy); **Tourism** (Tourism)

History: Founded 2005.

Main Language(s) of Instruction: Portuguese

Degrees and Diplomas: *Bacharelado*; *Especialização/Aperfeiçoamento*
Last Updated: 20/08/10

FACULTY OF THE SERRANA REGION

Faculdade da Região Serrana
Rua Hermann Röelke, 230 - Centro, Santa Maria de Jetibá,
ES 29.645-000
Tel: +55(27)3263-2010
EMail: farese@farese.edu.br
Website: http://www.farese.edu.br

Diretor: Arildo Castelluber

Courses

Accountancy (Accountancy); **Administration** (Administration); **Forestry** (Forestry); **Mathematics** (Mathematics); **Pedagogy** (Pedagogy)

History: Founded 2000.

Main Language(s) of Instruction: Portuguese

Degrees and Diplomas: *Bacharelado*; *Licenciatura*; *Especialização/Aperfeiçoamento*; *Mestrado*

Libraries: Biblioteca Graça Aranha
Last Updated: 26/07/10

FACULTY OF THE SOUTH EAST OF GOIAS

Faculdade do Sudeste Goiano
Avenida Lino Sampaio, 79, Centro, Pires do Rio, GO
Tel: +55(64) 3461-1891
EMail: fasug@fasug.edu.br
Website: http://www.fasug.edu.br/

Diretor: Pedro José Martins de Araújo

Courses

Accountancy (Accountancy); **Business Administration** (Business Administration); **Law** (Law); **Teacher Training** (Teacher Training)

History: Founded 2002.

Main Language(s) of Instruction: Portuguese

Degrees and Diplomas: *Bacharelado*
Last Updated: 20/08/10

FACULTY OF THE SOUTH OF BAHIA

Faculdade do Sul da Bahia (FASB)
Rua Graciliano Viana, 79, Bela Vista, Teixeira de Freitas,
BA 45995000
Tel: +55(73) 3292-4820
EMail: ffassis@ffassis.edu.br
Website: http://www.ffassis.edu.br

Diretora: Lay Alves Ribeiro

Courses

Accountancy; **Administration**; **Biomedicine**; **Human Resource Management** (Human Resources); **Law**; **Marketing** (Marketing); **Mechatronic Engineering** (Electronic Engineering; Mechanical Engineering); **Nursing** (Nursing); **Pedagogy** (Pedagogy); **Production Engineering** (Production Engineering); **Systems Analysis** (Systems Analysis); **Tourism** (Tourism)

History: Founded 2001.

Main Language(s) of Instruction: Portuguese

Degrees and Diplomas: *Tecnólogo*; *Bacharelado*; *Licenciatura*; *Especialização/Aperfeiçoamento*; *Mestrado*
Last Updated: 08/07/10

FACULTY OF THE SOUTH OF BRAZIL

Faculdade Sul Brasil (FASUL)
Avenida Ministro Cime Lima 2565, Jardim Coopagro, Toledo,
PR 85903590
Tel: +55(45) 3278-2002
Fax: +55(45) 3278-2002
EMail: fasul@fasul.com.br
Website: http://www.fasul.edu.br

Diretor: João Luis Seimetz

Courses

Accountancy (Accountancy); **Business Administration**; **Computer Science** (Computer Science); **Management**; **Pedagogy** (Pedagogy); **Secretarial Studies** (Secretarial Studies); **Social Communication**; **Tourism** (Tourism)

History: Founded 2000.

Main Language(s) of Instruction: Portuguese

Degrees and Diplomas: *Bacharelado*; *Especialização/Aperfeiçoamento*; *Mestrado*
Last Updated: 09/10/07

FACULTY OF THE SOUTH WEST OF SAO PAULO

Faculdade Sudoeste Paulistano (FASUP)
Avenida Professor Francisco Morato 1900, Butantã, São Paulo,
São Paulo 05512200
Tel: +55(11) 3721-5243
Fax: +55(11) 3721-8926
EMail: fasup@fasup.edu.br
Website: http://www.fasup.edu.br

Diretor Geral: Jorge Bastos

Courses

Accountancy (Accountancy); **Business Administration** (Administration; Business Administration); **Letters** (Literature); **Pedagogy** (Pedagogy)

History: Founded 1997.

Main Language(s) of Instruction: Portuguese

Degrees and Diplomas: *Bacharelado*; *Especialização/Aperfeiçoamento*
Last Updated: 13/11/07

FACULTY OF THE SOUTH WEST OF THE STATE OF SAO PAULO

Faculdade Sudoeste Paulista (FSP)
Av. Prefeito Celso Ferreira da Silva, 1001, Avaré,
São Paulo 18.707-150
Tel: +55(14) 3732-5020
Fax: +55(14) 3732-5020
EMail: fsp@fspnet.com.br
Website: http://www.fspnet.com.br/principal.asp

Diretor: Alexandre José Braga Chaddad

Areas

Applied Social Sciences; **Health Sciences** (Biomedicine; Nursing; Pharmacy; Physical Therapy; Psychology); **Human Sciences** (Accountancy; Administration; Law; Secretarial Studies; Tourism)

History: Founded 1999.

Main Language(s) of Instruction: Portuguese

Degrees and Diplomas: *Bacharelado*; *Especialização/Aperfeiçoamento*; *Mestrado*
Last Updated: 30/06/10

FACULTY OF THE VALLEY OF CRITARÉ

Faculdade Vale do Cricaré
Rua Venezuela, 01, Bairro Universitário, São Mateus,
ES 29.937-900
Tel: +55 (27) 3313-0000
EMail: ivc@ivc.br
Website: http://www.ivc.br/pages/principal.php

Diretor: José Fernandes Magnago de Jesus

Courses

Accountancy (Accountancy); **Administration** (Administration); **Law** (Law); **Pedagogy** (Pedagogy); **Social Communication** (Advertising and Publicity); **Tourism** (Tourism)

History: Founded 1997.

Main Language(s) of Instruction: Portuguese

Degrees and Diplomas: *Bacharelado*; *Especialização/Aperfeiçoamento*; *Mestrado*

Libraries: Yes
Last Updated: 13/09/10

FACULTY OF THE VALLEY OF GORUTUBA

Faculdade Vale do Gorutuba
Avenida Tancredo de Almeida Neves 302-F -, Nova Porteirinha,
MG 39525-000
Tel: +55(38)3834-1027
EMail: secretaria@favag.com.br
Website: http://www.favag.edu.br

Diretor: Vanilson Almeida Nascimento
EMail: vanilsonalmeida@favag.com.br

Courses

Business Administration (Business Administration); **Law** (Law); **Nursing** (Nursing); **Pedagogy** (Pedagogy); **Social Services** (Social and Community Services)

Degrees and Diplomas: *Bacharelado*; *Licenciatura*; *Especialização/Aperfeiçoamento*

Libraries: Biblioteca Professora Luizita Aparecida
Last Updated: 13/09/10

FACULTY OF THE VALLEY OF JAGUARIBE

Faculdade do Vale do Jaguaribe (FVJ)
Rua Coronel Alexandrino 563, Centro, Aracati,
Estado do Ceará 62800000
Tel: +55(88) 3421-9750
Fax: +55(88) 3421-9758
EMail: fvj@fvjr.br
Website: http://www.fvj.br

Diretora Geral: Suely Marza Melo

Courses

Administration (Administration); **Letters** (Literature); **Nursing**; **Pedagogy** (Pedagogy); **Social Services** (Social and Community Services); **Tourism** (Tourism)

History: Founded 1999.

Main Language(s) of Instruction: Portuguese

Degrees and Diplomas: *Bacharelado*; *Licenciatura*; *Especialização/Aperfeiçoamento*
Last Updated: 08/07/10

FACULTY OF THE VALLEY OF SALGADO

Faculdade Vale do Salgado
Rua Monsenhor Frota, 609, Centro, Icó, CE
Tel: +55(88) 3561-2760
EMail: petrola@secrel.com.br
Website: http://www.fvs.edu.br/

Diretor: Casemiro Dutra de Medeiros Junior

Courses

Accountancy (Accountancy); **Administration** (Administration); **Nursing** (Nursing); **Social Services** (Social and Community Services)

History: Founded 2002.

Main Language(s) of Instruction: Portuguese

Degrees and Diplomas: *Bacharelado*; *Especialização/Aperfeiçoamento*
Last Updated: 13/09/10

FACULTY OF THE VILLAGE OF CARAPICUIBA

Faculdade da Aldeia de Carapicuíba
Estrada da aldeinha, 245 - JD Marilu, Carapicuíba, SP
Tel: +55(11) 4146-5775
EMail: faculdadealdeia@terra.com.br
Website: http://www.falc.edu.br/site2

Diretor: Walter Alves Pereira

Courses

Accountancy (Accountancy); **Business Administration** (Business Administration); **Law** (Law); **Letters** (Literature); **Nursing** (Nursing); **Pedagogy** (Pedagogy)

History: Founded 2002.

Main Language(s) of Instruction: Portuguese

Degrees and Diplomas: *Bacharelado*; *Licenciatura*

Libraries: Yes
Last Updated: 23/07/10

FACULTY OF THE WESTERN AMAZON

Faculdade da Amazônia Occidental
Estrada Dias Martins, 894, Jardim Primavera, Rio Branco,
Acre 69912-470
Tel: +55(68) 2106-8200
EMail: fale.conosco@faao.com.br
Website: http://www.faao.com.br

Diretor Geral: Luiz Antonio Campos Correa
EMail: luiz.antonio@faao.com.br

Courses

Accountancy *(FIRB)*; **Administration** *(FIRB)* (Administration; International Business); **Architecture**; **Graduate Studies**; **Law** (Law); **Psychology** (Psychology); **Secretarial Studies** *(FIRB)*; **Social Services** (Social and Community Services); **Tourism** (Tourism); **Visual Arts** (Visual Arts)

History: Founded 1998.

Main Language(s) of Instruction: Portuguese

Degrees and Diplomas: *Bacharelado*; *Licenciatura*; *Especialização/Aperfeiçoamento*
Last Updated: 30/06/10

FACULTY OF THEOLOGY OF BOA VISTA

Faculdade de Teologia de Boa Vista
Avenida Mario Homem de Melo N°: 2744, Liberdade, Boa Vista,
RR 69303-010
Tel: +55(95) 3626-8457
EMail: fatebov@technet.com.br

Diretor: Osmar de Souza Corrêa

Courses

Pedagogy (Educational Administration; Pedagogy); **Theology** (Theology)

History: Founded 2001.

Main Language(s) of Instruction: Portuguese

Degrees and Diplomas: *Bacharelado*; *Licenciatura*
Last Updated: 20/09/10

FACULTY OF TIMBAÚBA

Faculdade de Timbaúba
Av. Antônio Xavier de Moraes, 03/05 - Sapucaia, Timbaúba,
PE 55870000
Fax: +55(81) 3631-0752
EMail: falecom@faculdadedetimbauba.com.br
Website: http://www.faculdadedetimbauba.edu.br

Diretor: Luiz Rodrigues da Souza

Courses

Accountancy; **Administration** (Administration); **Law** (Law); **Pedagogy**

History: Founded 1997

Main Language(s) of Instruction: Portuguese

Degrees and Diplomas: *Bacharelado*; *Licenciatura*
Last Updated: 08/07/10

FACULTY OF TRÊS DE MAIO

Faculdade Três de Maio (SETREM)
Avenida Santa Rosa 2405, Centro, Três de Maio, RS 98910000
Tel: +55(55) 3535-1011
Fax: +55(55) 3535-1011
EMail: setrem@setrem.com.br
Website: http://www.setrem.com.br/

Diretor: Flavio Magedanz

Courses

Administration (Administration; Finance; Marketing); **Agronomy** (Agricultural Engineering; Agronomy); **Computer Networks**; **Fashion Design** (Fashion Design); **Information Systems** (Information Management; Information Technology); **Nursing**; **Pedagogy** (Education; Educational Administration; Pedagogy); **Production Engineering** (Production Engineering); **Psychology** (Psychology)

History: Founded 1976. Acquired present status 1999.

Main Language(s) of Instruction: Portuguese

Degrees and Diplomas: *Bacharelado*; *Licenciatura*; *Especialização/Aperfeiçoamento*
Last Updated: 30/06/10

FACULTY OF TUPI PAULISTA - CESTUPI

Faculdade de Tupi Paulista - CESTUPI
Rua Arcebispo Lemieux, 250 - Centro, Tupi Paulista, SP 17930-000
Tel: +55(18) 3851-1310
EMail: secretaria.cestupi@cesd.br
Website: http://www.cestupi.cesd.br

Diretor: Antonio Luiz Pioltine

Courses
Administration (Administration; Environmental Management);
Pedagogy (Pedagogy)
History: Founded 2002.
Main Language(s) of Instruction: Portuguese
Degrees and Diplomas: *Bacharelado*; *Especialização/Aperfeiçoamento*
Libraries: Biblioteca Liliana Gonzaga
Last Updated: 30/08/10

FACULTY OF VENDA NOVA DO IMIGRANTE

Faculdade Venda Nova do Imigrante
Av. Ângelo Altoé, 888, Santa Cruz, Venda Nova do Imigrante,
ES 29375-000
Tel: +55(28) 3546-3349
EMail: secretaria@faveni.edu.br
Website: http://faveni.edu.br

Diretor: Aldezir Fuzari

Courses
Accountancy (Accountancy); **Administration** (Administration);
Pedagogy (Pedagogy)
History: Founded 2000.
Main Language(s) of Instruction: Portuguese
Degrees and Diplomas: *Bacharelado*; *Mestrado*
Libraries: Yes
Last Updated: 13/09/10

FACULTY OF VETERINARY MEDICINE AND ZOOTECHNOLOGY

Faculdade de Medicina Veterinária e Zootecnica (FAMED)
Rua das Flores 740, Labienópolis, Garca, São Paulo 17400000
Tel: +55(14) 3407-8000
Fax: +55(14) 3407-8001
EMail: faef@faef.br
Website: http://www.faef.edu.br

Diretor: Paulo César Gonçalves dos Santos

Courses
Veterinary Sciences (Animal Husbandry; Veterinary Science;
Zoology)
History: Founded 2000.
Degrees and Diplomas: *Bacharelado*; *Especialização/Aperfeiçoamento*
Last Updated: 12/12/07

FACULTY OF VIÇOSA

Faculdade de Viçosa (FDV)
Rua Milton Bandeira 380 4° e 5°, Andares Centro, Viçosa,
Minas Gerais 36570000
Tel: +55(31) 3891-5054
Fax: +55(31) 3891-5054
EMail: faculdadevicosa@faculdadevicosa.com.br
Website: http://www.faculdadevicosa.com.br/site

Diretor: Heleno do Nascimento Santos

Courses
Administration; **Advertising** (Advertising and Publicity); **Computer Science** (Computer Science); **Pedagogy** (Pedagogy); **Physical Education** (Physical Education); **Production Engineering** (Production Engineering)
History: Founded 2001.
Main Language(s) of Instruction: Portuguese
Degrees and Diplomas: *Bacharelado*; *Licenciatura*; *Especialização/Aperfeiçoamento*; *Mestrado*
Last Updated: 08/07/10

FACULTY OF VINHEDO

Faculdade de Vinhedo (FV)
Avenida Benedito Storani 470, Centro, Vinhedo, São Paulo
13280000
Tel: +55(19) 3886-6144
Fax: +55(19) 3886-6144
EMail: info@faculdadedevinhedo.com.br
Website: http://www.faculdadedevinhedo.com.br

Diretor Geral: José Norberto Comune

Courses
Administration (Administration); **Computer Science**; **Letters**;
Pedagogy (Pedagogy); **Physical Education** (Physical Education);
Tourism
History: Founded 2000.
Main Language(s) of Instruction: Portuguese
Degrees and Diplomas: *Bacharelado*; *Licenciatura*
Last Updated: 08/07/10

FACULTY OF VITORIA

Faculdade de Vitória (UVV VITÓRIA)
Rua Coração de Maria 315, Vitória, Espirito Santo 29055770
Tel: +55(27) 3421-2266
Fax: +55(27) 3421-2266
EMail: uvv@uvv.br
Website: http://www.uvv.br/unidades/uvv_vitoria.asp

Diretor Geral: Giulianno de Oliveira Bresciani

Courses
Administration
History: Founded 2001.
Degrees and Diplomas: *Bacharelado*
Last Updated: 13/12/07

FACVEST INTEGRATED FACULTIES

Faculdades Integradas FACVEST
Avenida Marechal Floriano 947, Centro, Lages,
Santa Catarina 88501103
Tel: +55(49) 225-0747
Fax: +55(49) 225-0747
EMail: univest@matrix.com.br
Website: http://www.sle.br

Diretor Geral: Geovani Broering

Areas
Applied Social Sciences (Accountancy; Administration; Advertising and Publicity; Economics; Journalism; Photography; Public Relations); **Exact Sciences** (Computer Science; Mathematics);
Health Sciences (Biology; Nursing; Pharmacy; Physical Education; Physical Therapy; Psychology; Veterinary Science); **Human Sciences** (History; Pedagogy); **Law** (Law)
History: Founded 2002.
Main Language(s) of Instruction: Portuguese
Degrees and Diplomas: *Bacharelado*; *Licenciatura*; *Especialização/Aperfeiçoamento*
Last Updated: 22/06/10

FAFIBE INTEGRATED FACULTIES

Faculdades Integradas Fafibe (FAFIBE)
Rua Professor Orlando França de Carvalho 325, Centro,
Bebedouro, São Paulo 14701070
Tel: +55(17) 3344 7100
Fax: +55(17) 3344-7101
EMail: fafibe@fafibe.br
Website: http://www.fafibe.br

Diretora: Iná Izabel Faria Soares de Oliveira

Courses
Accountancy; **Administration** (Administration); **Biology**; **History** (History); **Information Systems**; **Law** (Law); **Letters** (English; Modern Languages; Portuguese; Spanish); **Mathematics**; **Nursing** (Nursing); **Pedagogy** (Pedagogy); **Physical Education**; **Physiotherapy** (Physical Therapy); **Psychology**

History: Founded 1970

Main Language(s) of Instruction: Portuguese

Degrees and Diplomas: *Bacharelado; Licenciatura; Especialização/Aperfeiçoamento*
Last Updated: 22/06/10

FAMA FACULTY OF TECHNOLOGY
Faculdade de Tecnologia FAMA (FAMA)
Rua Benfica, 126, Madalena, Recife, PE 50720-635
Tel: +55(81) 3081-0596
Fax: +55(81) 3227-0982
EMail: coordenacao@escolademarketing.com.br
Website: http://www.escolademarketing.com.br/

President: José Lavanère Lemos

Courses
Administration (Administration); **Advertising and Publicity** (Advertising and Publicity); **Commercial Management** (Business and Commerce; Management); **Graduate Studies** (Advertising and Publicity; Management; Marketing; Photography; Transport Management); **Human Resources** (Human Resources)

Degrees and Diplomas: *Tecnólogo; Especialização/Aperfeiçoamento.* Also MBA.
Last Updated: 24/08/10

FAPAN FACULTY
Faculdade FAPAN
Av. Fco. Prestes Maia, 116 Centro, São Bernardo do Campo, SP 09770-000
Tel: +55(11) 4337-2400
EMail: fapan@fapan.com.br
Website: http://www.fapan.com.br/novosite/pagina1.htm

Diretor: Matias Alves Correia

Courses
Law (Law)

History: Founded 2002.

Main Language(s) of Instruction: Portuguese

Degrees and Diplomas: *Bacharelado*

Libraries: Biblioteca Prof. Ms. Carlos Alberto Cruz
Last Updated: 27/08/10

FARIAS BRITO FACULTY
Faculdade Farias Brito (FFB)
Rua Castro Monte 1364, Varjota, Fortazela, Ceará 60175230
Tel: +55(85) 3486-9090
EMail: daa@faculdadefb.com.br
Website: http://www.ffb.edu.br

Diretor Geral: Tales de Sá Cavalcante

Courses
Administration (Administration); **Computer Science** (Computer Science); **Law**; **Marketing** (Marketing)
History: Founded 2001.

Main Language(s) of Instruction: Portuguese

Degrees and Diplomas: *Bacharelado; Especialização/Aperfeiçoamento*
Last Updated: 07/07/10

FASE FACULTY
Faculdade FASE (FASE)
Rua Ipatinga, 82, Bairro Barcelona, Serra, ES 29.166-210
Tel: +55(27) 3338-3799
Fax: +55(27) 3338-3799
EMail: fase@fase.br
Website: http://www.fase.br

Diretor Geral: Carlos Fernando Barbosa

Courses
Administration; **Education** (Education; Pedagogy; Primary Education)

Further Information: Also Afonso Claudio and Manaus units
History: Founded 1999.

Main Language(s) of Instruction: Portuguese

Degrees and Diplomas: *Bacharelado; Licenciatura; Especialização/Aperfeiçoamento*
Last Updated: 07/07/10

FASIPE FACULTY
Faculdade FASIPE
Rua Carine 11, Sinop, MT 78550-000
Tel: +55(66) 3517-1320
EMail: faculdadefasipe@terra.com.br
Website: http://www.fasipe.com.br

Diretora: Dalvinethe Matilde Campos Pinto

Courses
Accountancy (Accountancy); **Administration** (Administration; Agricultural Business; Finance; Marketing); **Biomedicine** (Biomedicine); **Journalism** (Journalism); **Law** (Law); **Nursing** (Nursing); **Physical Education** (Physical Education); **Psychology** (Psychology); **Tourism** (Tourism)

History: Founded 2001.

Main Language(s) of Instruction: Portuguese

Degrees and Diplomas: *Bacharelado; Especialização/Aperfeiçoamento*

Libraries: Yes
Last Updated: 27/08/10

FATEF FACULTY
Faculdade FATEF
Avenida Presidente Wilson 1013, Gonzaguinha, São Vicente, São Paulo 11320001
Tel: +55(13) 3467-6776 +55(13) 3467-6109
Fax: +55(13) 3467-6776
EMail: fatef@fortec.g12.br
Website: http://www.fortec.g12.br

Diretor: Nelson Simões Filho

Courses
Industrial Engineering and Automation (Automation and Control Engineering; Industrial Engineering); **Information Systems**; **Mechatronics** (Electronic Engineering; Mechanical Engineering)

Further Information: Also Unidade Cubatão, Unidade Praia Grande

History: Founded 2001.

Main Language(s) of Instruction: Portuguese

Degrees and Diplomas: *Tecnólogo; Bacharelado*
Last Updated: 08/07/10

FATEP FACULTY OF TECHNOLOGY
Faculdade de Tecnologia FATEP (FATEP)
Av. 25, n° 148, Ruas 1 e 0, Cidade Jardim, Rio Claro, SP 13501-110
Tel: +55(19) 3533-1605
EMail: fatep@fatep.com
Website: http://www.fatep.com/

Diretor Geral: Moacir Martins Junior

Courses
Environmental Health (Health Sciences); **Graduate Studies** (Business Administration; Ceramics and Glass Technology; Finance; Law; Marketing; Safety Engineering); **Private Security Management** (Protective Services); **Quality Management** (Safety Engineering)

Degrees and Diplomas: *Tecnólogo.* Also MBA.
Last Updated: 25/08/10

FATIMA FACULTY

Faculdade Fátima
Rua Alexandre Fleming N°: 454, Madureira, Caxias do Sul, RS
Tel: +55(54) 3535-7322
EMail: direcao@faculdadefatima.com.br
Website: http://www.faculdadefatima.com.br

Diretor: Virvi Ramos

Courses
Administration (Administration); **Nursing** (Nursing); **Nutrition** (Nutrition); **Speech Therapy** (Speech Therapy and Audiology)

History: Founded 2003.

Main Language(s) of Instruction: Portuguese

Degrees and Diplomas: *Bacharelado*; *Especialização/Aperfeiçoamento*

Libraries: Yes
Last Updated: 08/09/10

FAYAL CENECIST INSTITUTE OF HIGHER EDUCATION

Instituto Cenecista Fayal de Ensino Superior (IFES)
Avenida Adolfo Konder, 2000, Bairro São Vicente, Itajai, Santa Catarina 88303140
Tel: +55(47) 3248-2421
Fax: +55(47) 3248-2421
EMail: ifes@ifes.com.br
Website: http://www2.ifes.com.br/webifes/home.aspx

Diretor: Tarcísio Tomazoni

Courses
Accountancy (Accountancy); **Administration**; **Advertising**; **Graphic Design** (Graphic Design); **Pedagogy** (Pedagogy); **Teacher Training** (Teacher Training); **Tourism** (Tourism)

History: Founded 2000.

Main Language(s) of Instruction: Portuguese

Degrees and Diplomas: *Bacharelado*; *Especialização/Aperfeiçoamento*
Last Updated: 17/06/10

FEB UNIVERSITY CENTRE

Centro Universitario FEB
Avenida Professor Roberto Frade Monte 389, Bairro Aeroporto, Barretos, São Paulo 14783-226
Tel: +55(17) 3322-6411
Fax: +55(17) 3322-6205
EMail: feb@feb.br
Website: http://www.feb.br

Diretor: Álvaro Fernandez Gomes
EMail: reitoria@feb.br; afgomes@feb.br

Courses
Administration (Administration); **Agronomy** (Agronomy); **Biology** (Biology); **Chemical Engineering** (Chemical Engineering); **Chemical Technology**; **Chemistry** (Chemistry); **Civil Engineering**; **Electrical Engineering**; **Electrical Engineering**; **Environmental Engineering** (Environmental Engineering); **Graduate Studies** *(Stricto Sensu)* (Dentistry); **Graduate Studies** *(Lato Sensu)* (Civil Law; Computer Networks; Criminal Law; Finance; Labour Law; Rehabilitation and Therapy; Safety Engineering; Social Policy; Surgery); **Information Systems** (Information Sciences); **Law** (Law); **Mathematics**; **Mechanical Engineering** (Mechanical Engineering); **Odontology** (Dentistry); **Pedagogy** (Pedagogy); **Pharmacy**; **Physical Education** (Physical Education); **Physics** (Physics); **Production Engineering**; **Social Services** (Social and Community Services); **Zootechniccs** (Animal Husbandry)

History: Founded 1996

Main Language(s) of Instruction: Portuguese

Degrees and Diplomas: *Bacharelado*; *Licenciatura*; *Especialização/Aperfeiçoamento*; *Mestrado*
Last Updated: 02/06/10

FECAP UNIVERSITY CENTRE

**Centro Universitário
FECAP (FECAP)**
Av. Liberdade, 532, Liberdade, SP 01502-001
Tel: +55(11) 3272-2222 +55(11) 3272-2273
Fax: +55(11) 3272-2208
EMail: relacionamento@fecap.br
Website: http://www.fecap.br

Reitor: Sérgio de Gouvêa Franco EMail: reitoria@fecap.br

Courses
Accountancy; **Administration**; **Advertising and Publicity** (Advertising and Publicity); **Economics** (Economics); **Executive Secretary**; **Graduate Studies** *(Stricto Sensu)* (Accountancy); **Graduate Studies** *(Lato Sensu)* (Accountancy; Banking; Business Administration; Educational Administration; Finance; Human Resources; Marketing; Public Administration); **International Relations** (International Relations); **Public Relations** (Public Relations)

Degrees and Diplomas: *Bacharelado*; *Especialização/Aperfeiçoamento*; *Mestrado*. Also MBA.
Last Updated: 12/07/10

FEEVALE UNIVERSITY CENTRE

**Centro Universitário
Feevale (FEEVALE)**
RS-239, 2755, Novo Hamburgo, Rio Grande do Sul 93352-000
Tel: +55(51) 3586-8800
Fax: +55(51) 3586-8836
EMail: feevale@feevale.br
Website: http://www.feevale.br

Reitor: Ramon Fernando da Cunha EMail: reitoria@feevale.br

International Relations: Paula Casari Cundari, Head, International Relations EMail: paulacc@feevale.br

Courses
Graduate Studies *(Lato Sensu)* (Accountancy; Art Therapy; Business Administration; Communication Studies; Cosmetology; Gerontology; Health Administration; Health Sciences; Literature; Marketing; Microbiology; Modern Languages; Music; Occupational Health; Philosophical Schools; Psychology; Safety Engineering; Sports; Toxicology; Visual Arts); **Graduate Studies** *(Stricto Sensu)* (Cultural Studies; Environmental Studies; Materials Engineering; Social and Community Services)

Institutes
Applied Social Sciences *(ICSA)*; **Exact Sciences and Technology** *(ICET)* (Architecture; Chemical Engineering; Computer Science; Construction Engineering; Design; Electronic Engineering; Environmental Management; Farm Management; Industrial Engineering; Information Sciences; Mechanical Engineering; Production Engineering; Town Planning); **Health Sciences** *(ICS)*; **Human Sciences, Letters and Arts** *(ICHLA)* (Art Education; Art Therapy; Arts and Humanities; Educational Psychology; History; Pedagogy; Psychology; Teacher Training; Visual Arts)

History: Founded 1970. Acquired present status 1999.

Academic Year: February-July; August-December

Fees: (Reais) 249.45 per credit

Main Language(s) of Instruction: Portuguese

International Co-operation: With institutions in Argentina; Belgium; Canada; Chile; Spain; USA; Mexico; Paraguay; Portugal; Uruguay

Degrees and Diplomas: *Tecnólogo*; *Bacharelado*; *Licenciatura*; *Especialização/Aperfeiçoamento*; *Mestrado*; *Doutorado*: Environmental Quality;

30w?>Special Facilities: Technological Park of Sinos Valley; Art Museum

Libraries: 65,926 vols

Publications: Jornal da Feevale *(monthly)*

Press or Publishing House: Editora Feevale
Last Updated: 02/06/10

FERNÃO DIAS FACULTY
Faculdade Fernão Dias
Rua Euclides da Cunha, 70, Centro, Osasco, SP 06016-030
Tel: +55(11) 3681-7614
EMail: faculdade@faculdadefernaodias.edu.br
Website: http://www.faculdadefernaodias.edu.br

Diretor: Saburo Matsubara

Courses
Accountancy (Accountancy); **Administration** (Administration); **Law** (Law); **Letters** (Literature); **Mathematics** (Mathematics); **Pedagogy** (Pedagogy)

History: Founded 2001.

Main Language(s) of Instruction: Portuguese

Degrees and Diplomas: *Bacharelado*; *Licenciatura*; *Especialização/Aperfeiçoamento*
Last Updated: 16/09/10

FIAM FAAM UNIVERSITY CENTRE
Centro Universitario FIAM FAAM (UNIFIAM-FAAM)
Rua Taguá 150 Prédio 1, Liberdade, São Paulo,
São Paulo 01508010
Tel: +55(11) 3346-6200
EMail: reitoria@fiamfaam.br
Website: http://www.fiamfaam.br/

Reitora: Labibi Elias Alves da Silva

Courses
Advertising and Publicity (Advertising and Publicity); **Architecture and Town Planning** (Architecture; Town Planning); **Graduate Studies** *(Stricto Sensu)* (Law); **Graduate Studies** *(Lato Sensu)*; **Journalism** (Journalism); **Music**; **Radio, TV and Video** (Radio and Television Broadcasting; Video); **Technologial Studies** (Cinema and Television; Interior Design; Photography; Radio and Television Broadcasting; Video)

Further Information: Also centro, Morumbi, Vila Mariana 1 and Vila Mariana 2 campuses.

History: Founded 1972 as Faculdades Integradas Alcântara Machado. Acquired present status and title 2002.

Main Language(s) of Instruction: Portuguese

Degrees and Diplomas: *Tecnólogo*; *Bacharelado*; *Licenciatura*; *Especialização/Aperfeiçoamento*; *Mestrado*
Last Updated: 03/06/10

FIEO UNIVERSITY CENTRE
Centro Universitário FIEO (UNIFEO)
Avenida Franz Voegeli, 300, Vila Yara, Osasco,
São Paulo 06020190
Tel: +55(11) 3651-9999
Fax: +55(11) 3651-9999 ramal 9700
EMail: reitoria@unifieo.br
Website: http://www.unifieo.br

Reitor and Pró-Reitor Administrativo: José Cassio Soares Hungria **Tel:** +55(11) 3651-9933

Courses
Accountancy (Accountancy); **Administration**; **Advertising and Publicity** (Advertising and Publicity); **Arts and Humanities** (Arts and Humanities; English; Latin; Linguistics; Portuguese); **Biological Sciences** (Biological and Life Sciences); **Chemistry**; **Computer Engineering** (Computer Engineering); **Computer Science** (Computer Science); **Digital Design** (Design); **Geography** (Geography); **Graduate Studies** *(Stricto Sensu)*; **Graduate Studies** *(Lato Sensu)*; **History** (History); **Information Systems** (Information Sciences); **International Trade and Business** (International Business); **Journalism** (Journalism); **Law** (Law); **Mathematics** (Mathematics); **Pedagogy** (Pedagogy); **Pharmacy**; **Physical Education** (Physical Education); **Physical Therapy** (Physical Therapy); **Psychopedagogy** (Educational Psychology); **Technological Studies** (Banking; Business and Commerce; Computer Networks; Finance; Hotel Management; Human Resources; Secretarial Studies; Systems Analysis; Transport Management); **Telecommunications Engineering** (Telecommunications Engineering)

Further Information: Also Narciso (law) and Wilson Campuses
History: Founded 1969.
Main Language(s) of Instruction: Portuguese

Degrees and Diplomas: *Tecnólogo*; *Bacharelado*; *Licenciatura*; *Especialização/Aperfeiçoamento*; *Mestrado*. Also MBA.
Last Updated: 03/06/10

FIGUEIREDO COSTA FACULTY
Faculdade Figueiredo Costa
Av. Cícero de Toledo 427, Maceio, AL 57022-150
Tel: +55(82) 3326-8069
EMail: fic@unifal.edu.br

Diretor: Sérgio Tadeu Regis Costa

Courses
Administration (Administration); **Environmental Engineering** (Environmental Engineering); **Production Engineering** (Production Engineering)

History: Founded 2004.

Main Language(s) of Instruction: Portuguese

Degrees and Diplomas: *Bacharelado*; *Especialização/Aperfeiçoamento*
Libraries: Yes
Last Updated: 26/08/10

FILADELFIA FACULTY
Faculdade Filadélfia
Av. Capitão Salomão 121 A, Ribeirão Preto, SP 14085-440
Tel: +55(16) 3211 - 4400
EMail: fafil@fafil.com.br
Website: http://www.fafil.com.br

Diretora: Eliazer Lopes de Moura

Courses
Pedagogy (Pedagogy)

Main Language(s) of Instruction: Portuguese

Degrees and Diplomas: *Licenciatura*
Libraries: Yes
Last Updated: 16/09/10

FILADELFIA UNIVERSITY CENTRE
Centro Universitário Filadélfia (UNIFIL)
Av. Juscelino Kubitscheck, 1626 Centro, Londrina,
Paraná 86020-000
Tel: +55(43) 3375-7400
Fax: +55(43) 3375-7412
EMail: unifil@filadelfia.br
Website: http://www.unifil.br

Reitor: Eleazar Ferreira **EMail:** reitor@filadelfia.br

Areas
Agrarian Sciences; **Applied Social Sciences** (Accountancy; Administration; Architecture; Law; Town Planning); **Biological Sciences** (Biological and Life Sciences); **Engineering**; **Exact Sciences** (Computer Science; Information Sciences); **Health Sciences** (Biomedicine; Nursing; Nutrition; Pharmacy; Physical Education; Physical Therapy); **Humanities**

Courses
Graduate Studies (Business Administration; Education; Educational Psychology; Health Sciences; Human Resources; Interior Design; Nursing; Nutrition; Psychology; Public Health; Software Engineering; Special Education); **Technological Studies** (Cooking and Catering; Cosmetology; Environmental Management; Transport Management)

History: Founded 1972 as Centro de Estudos Superiores de Londrina (Cesulon). Acquired present status and title 2001.

Main Language(s) of Instruction: Portuguese

Degrees and Diplomas: *Tecnólogo*; *Bacharelado*; *Especialização/Aperfeiçoamento*. Also MBA.
Last Updated: 03/06/10

FLAMA FACULTY - FSSSL

Faculdade Flama - FSSSL
Rua Pedro Correia nᵒs 318, 330, 370 s/n, Vila Meriti,
Duque de Caxias, RJ 25020-160
Tel: +55(21) 2782-8278
EMail: faculdadeflama@faculdadeflama.edu.br
Website: http://www.faculdadeflama.edu.br

Diretor: José Garrido

Courses
Administration (Administration); **Social Services** (Social and Community Services)

History: Founded 1997.

Main Language(s) of Instruction: Portuguese

Degrees and Diplomas: *Bacharelado*
Last Updated: 16/09/10

FLAMINGO FACULTY

Faculdade Flamingo
Avenida Francisco Matarazzo 913, Perdizes, São Paulo,
São Paulo 05001350
Tel: +55(11) 2117-4500
Fax: +55(11) 2117-4524
EMail: info@grupoflamingo.com
Website: http://www.grupoflamingo.com

Diretor: Anadyr Nogueira França Filho

Areas
Computer Science (Computer Networks; Systems Analysis); **Education**; **Industry** (Automation and Control Engineering); **Management** (Accountancy; Administration; Business Administration; Finance; Human Resources; Management; Marketing)

History: Founded 2000.

Main Language(s) of Instruction: Portuguese

Degrees and Diplomas: *Bacharelado*; *Especialização/Aperfeiçoamento*
Last Updated: 29/06/10

FLEMING FACULTIES

Faculdades Fleming (FCCG)
Rua Dona Maria Umbelina Couto 58, Bairro Guanabara, Campinas,
São Paulo 13090110
Tel: +55(19) 3744-4000
Fax: +55(19) 3744-4010
EMail: fleming@setanet.com.br
Website: http://www.faculdadesfleming.com.br

Diretora: Angela Corrêa da Silva

Courses
Accountancy (Accountancy); **Administration** (Administration)

History: Founded 1999.

Main Language(s) of Instruction: Portuguese

Degrees and Diplomas: *Bacharelado*; *Especialização/Aperfeiçoamento*
Last Updated: 29/06/10

FLORENCE INSTITUTE OF HIGHER EDUCATION

Instituto Florence de Ensino Superior
Rua Rio Branco, nᵒ 216, Centro, São Luís, MA 65040-270
Tel: +55(98) 3878-2120
Fax: +55(98) 3878-2120
EMail: florencesuperior@gmail.com
Website: http://www.florencesuperior.com.br

Diretora Geral: Rita Ivana Barbosa Gomes

Courses
Graduate Studies (Educational Administration; Educational Psychology; Nursing; Pedagogy; Pharmacy; Psychiatry and Mental Health; Public Health); **Undergraduate Studies** (Nursing; Pharmacy)

Further Information: Also Cohab unit.

History: Founded 2000.

Degrees and Diplomas: *Bacharelado*. Also Postgraduate Diploma.
Last Updated: 22/09/10

FORTIUM FACULTY

Faculdade Fortium
Setor de Rádio e Televisão Norte Conjunto P 1ᵒ Subsolo s/n,
Edifício Brasília Rádio Center, Asa Norte, Brasília, DF 70710-200
Tel: +55(61) 9295-9945
EMail: reuzi@fortium.com.br
Website: http://www.fortium.edu.br

Diretora: Ruthe Prates Barroso

Courses
Administration (Administration); **Biology** (Biology); **Chemistry** (Chemistry); **Computer Science** (Computer Science); **Design** (Design); **Law** (Law); **Letters** (Literature); **Philosophy** (Philosophy); **Social Communication** (Communication Studies)

History: Founded 2008.

Main Language(s) of Instruction: Portuguese

Degrees and Diplomas: *Bacharelado*; *Licenciatura*; *Especialização/Aperfeiçoamento*; *Mestrado*
Libraries: Yes
Last Updated: 16/09/10

FOUNDATION FOR HIGHER EDUCATION AND COMMUNICATION OF MACHADO

Fundação Machadense de Ensino Superior e Comunicação
Rodóvia BR 267 Km 3, S/n Distrito Industrial Parque Industrial,
Machado, Minas Gerais 37750000
Tel: +55(35) 3295-9800
Fax: +55(35) 3295-9801
EMail: fumesc@fumesc.com.br
Website: http://www.fumesc.com.br

Diretor: Cleuton Pereira Gonçalves

Faculties
Administration (Administration); **Law** (Law)

History: Founded 2001.

Main Language(s) of Instruction: Portuguese

Degrees and Diplomas: *Bacharelado*; *Especialização/Aperfeiçoamento*; *Mestrado*
Last Updated: 29/11/07

FRANCISCAN INSTITUTE OF HIGHER EDUCATION

Instituto de Ensino Superior Franciscano (IESF)
Rua 22 Quadra 07, 10, Maiobão, Paço do Lumiar, MA 65130-000
Tel: +55(98) 3237-1007
EMail: cefran@elo.com.br

Courses
Pedagogy (Pedagogy)

Degrees and Diplomas: *Licenciatura*
Last Updated: 22/09/10

FRANCISCAN UNIVERSITY CENTRE

Centro Universitário Franciscano (UNIFRA)
Rua dos Andradas, 1614, Centro, Santa Maria,
Rio Grande do Sul 97010-032
Tel: +55(55) 3220-1200
Fax: +55(55) 3222-6484
EMail: reitoria@unifra.br
Website: http://www.unifra.br

Reitora: Irani Rupolo (1997-) **Tel:** +55(55) 3220-1200

Pró-Reitor Administrativo: Inacir Pederiva

Courses
Administration; **Advertising and Publicity**; **Architecture and Town Planning**; **Biomedicine**; **Chemistry** (Chemistry); **Computer Science** (Computer Science); **Design**; **Economics**; **Environ-**

mental Engineering; **Geography** (Geography); **Graduate Studies** *(Lato Sensu)* (Business Administration; Communication Studies; Educational Psychology; Environmental Management; Health Administration; Marketing; Pharmacy; Public Health; Safety Engineering; Welfare and Protective Services); **Graduate Studies** *(Stricto Sensu)* (Mathematics Education; Science Education); **History** (History); **Information Systems** (Information Sciences); **Journalism**; **Law** (Law); **Literature** (Literature; Portuguese); **Literature**; **Materials Engineering**; **Mathematics** (Mathematics); **Nursing** (Nursing); **Nutrition**; **Occupational Therapy** (Occupational Therapy); **Odontology** (Dentistry); **Pedagogy** (Pedagogy); **Pharmacy** (Pharmacy); **Philosophy** (Philosophy); **Physical Therapy** (Physical Therapy); **Physics** (Physics); **Psychology** (Psychology); **Social Service** (Social and Community Services); **Technical Studies** (Nursing); **Tourism** (Tourism)

History: Founded 1955. Acquired present status 1998.

Academic Year: March to December (March-July; August-December)

Admission Requirements: Secondary school leaving certificate and Vestibular

Fees: (Reais) 9,125.82 per semester

Main Language(s) of Instruction: Portuguese

Accrediting Agencies: SESU/MEC

Degrees and Diplomas: *Bacharelado*; *Licenciatura*; *Especialização/Aperfeiçoamento*; *Mestrado*

Student Services: Academic counselling, Canteen, Handicapped facilities, Language programs

Student Residential Facilities: None

Libraries: 128,814 vols; 50,708 vols

Publications: Disciplinarum Scientia *(annually)*; Vidya *(biennially)*
Last Updated: 03/06/10

FRASSINETTI FACULTY OF RECIFE
Faculdade Frassinetti do Recife (FAFIRE)
Avenida Conde da Boa Vista 921 Boa Vista, Recife,
Pernambuco 50060002
Tel: +55(81) 2122-3500
Fax: +55(81) 3423-3066
EMail: comunica@fafire.br
Website: http://www.fafire.br

Diretora: Maria das Graças Soares da Costa

Courses
Administration (Administration); **Biology** (Biology); **Letters** (Literature); **Pedagogy** (Pedagogy); **Psychology**; **Tourism**

History: Founded 1941as Faculdade de Filosofia do Recife.

Main Language(s) of Instruction: Portuguese

Degrees and Diplomas: *Bacharelado*; *Licenciatura*; *Especialização/Aperfeiçoamento*
Last Updated: 07/07/10

FUCAPE BUSINESS SCHOOL
Avenida Fernando Ferrari 1358, Vitoria, ES 29075-010
Tel: +55 (27) 4009 4444
EMail: fucape@fucape.br
Website: http://www.fucape.br

Diretor: Aridelmo Teixeira

Courses
Accountancy (Accountancy); **Administration** (Administration); **Economics** (Economics)

History: Founded 2004.

Main Language(s) of Instruction: Portuguese

Degrees and Diplomas: *Bacharelado*; *Mestrado*; *Doutorado*

Libraries: Yes
Last Updated: 25/08/10

FUCAPI-CESF INSTITUTE OF HIGHER EDUCATION
Instituto de Ensino Superior FUCAPI-CESF (FUCAPI-CESF)
Avenida Governador Danilo Areosa 381, Distrito Industrial, Mánaus, Amazonas 69075351
Tel: +55(92) 2127-3066
Fax: +55(92) 3613-2655
EMail: direcaocesf@fucapi.br
Website: http://portal.fucapi.edu.br/cesf/

Diretor: Antônio Luiz da Silva Maués

Courses
Administration (Administration); **Computer Engineering**; **Computer Science** (Computer Science); **Digital Interface Design** (Computer Science); **Electrical Engineering** (Electrical Engineering); **Environmental Engineering**; **Systems Analysis** (Systems Analysis); **Telecommunications Engineering**

History: Founded 1998.

Main Language(s) of Instruction: Portuguese

Degrees and Diplomas: *Bacharelado*; *Especialização/Aperfeiçoamento*; *Mestrado*
Last Updated: 15/06/10

FUMEC UNIVERSITY
Universidade FUMEC
Rua Cobre, 200, Bairro Cruzeiro, Belo Horizonte,
Minas Gerais 30310190
Tel: +55(31) 3228-3000
EMail: fumec@fumec.br
Website: http://www.fumec.br

Reitor: Antonio Tomé Loures

Faculties
Business Administration (Accountancy; Administration; Computer Science; Food Science; Hotel Management; Telecommunications Engineering); **Engineering and Architecture** (Aeronautical and Aerospace Engineering; Architecture; Civil Engineering; Design; Engineering; Environmental Engineering; Production Engineering; Telecommunications Engineering; Town Planning); **Health Sciences** (Health Sciences; Nursing; Occupational Therapy; Physical Therapy; Speech Therapy and Audiology); **Human Sciences** (Advertising and Publicity; Arts and Humanities; Journalism; Law; Pedagogy; Physical Education; Psychology)

History: Founded 1965. Became Centro Universitário FUMEC 2000 following merger of Faculdade de Ciências Econômicas, Administrativas e Contábeis de Belo Horizonte (FACE), Faculdade de Ciências Humanas (FCH) e Faculdade de Engenharia e Arquitetura (FEA). Acquired present status 2005.

Degrees and Diplomas: *Tecnólogo*; *Bacharelado*; *Especialização/Aperfeiçoamento*; *Mestrado*; *Doutorado*
Last Updated: 11/05/10

FUNCESI FACULTIES
Faculdades FUNCESI
Rodovia MG 03 - s/n Córrego Seco, Areão, Itabira, MG 35900021
Tel: +55(31) 3831-6055
Fax: +55(31) 3839-3600
EMail: secretariat@funcesi.br
Website: http://www.funcesi.br

Diretor: Nélio de Alvarenga Fonseca

Courses
Accountancy; **Administration**; **Biology** (Biology); **Biomedicine**; **Computer Science**; **Engineering**; **Geography**; **History** (History); **Law** (Law); **Literature** (Literature); **Mathematics** (Mathematics); **Nursing** (Nursing); **Nutrition** (Nutrition); **Pharmacy** (Pharmacy); **Physiotherapy**; **Tourism** (Tourism)

Faculties
Administration and Accountancy *(Faculdade de Ciêcias Administrativas e Contábeis de Itabira (FACCI))* (Accountancy; Administration); **Health Sciences** *(Faculdade Itabirana de Saúde (FISA))* (Health Sciences); **Human Sciences** *(Faculdade de Ciências Humanas de Itabira (FACHI))*; **Science and Technology**

Development *(Faculdade Itabirana de Desenvolvimento das Ciências e Tecnologias (FATEC))* (Environmental Engineering; Information Management; Production Engineering)

Higher Institutes
Education *(Instituto Superior de Educação de Itabira (ISEI))* (Arts and Humanities; Biological and Life Sciences; English; Geography; History; Mathematics)

History: Founded 1994

Degrees and Diplomas: *Bacharelado; Especialização/Aperfeiçoamento; Mestrado*
Last Updated: 27/03/12

FUNDETEC FACULTY OF TECHNOLOGY
Faculdade de Tecnologia FUNDETEC (FATEF)
Alameda Nothmann, 598, Campos Elíseos, São Paulo,
SP 01216-000
Tel: +55(11) 3222-6969
EMail: juliana.grasso@fundacaofundetec.org.b
Website: http://www.faculdadefundetec.com.br/

Courses
Commercial Management (Business and Commerce); **Environmental Management** (Environmental Management); **Financial Management** (Finance); **Graduate Studies** (International Business; Management; Marketing); **Hospital Management** (Health Administration); **Hotel Management** (Hotel Management); **Human Resources** (Human Resources); **Information Technology** (Information Technology); **International Business** (International Business); **Logistics** (Transport Management); **Management Process** (Management); **Marketing** (Marketing); **Public Administration** (Public Administration); **Quality Management** (Safety Engineering); **Telecommunications Engineering** (Telecommunications Engineering); **Tourism** (Tourism)

History: Founded 2006.
Main Language(s) of Instruction: Portuguese
Degrees and Diplomas: *Tecnólogo; Especialização/Aperfeiçoamento*
Last Updated: 25/08/10

GAMA AND SOUZA FACULTY
Faculdade Gama e Souza (FGS)
Rua Leopoldina Rego 502 Olária, Rio de Janeiro, Rio de Janeiro
21021521
Tel: +55(21) 2564-1168 +55(21) 560-6884
Fax: +55(21) 2564-1168
EMail: gamaesouza@openlink.com.br
Website: http://www.gamaesouza.edu.br

Diretora: Peralva de Miranda Delgado

Courses
Accountancy (Accountancy); **Administration** (Administration); **Computer Science** (Computer Science); **Economics** (Economics); **Law**; **Literature** (Literature); **Pedagogy** (Pedagogy); **Science** (Mathematics); **Tourism**

History: Founded 1998.
Main Language(s) of Instruction: Portuguese
Degrees and Diplomas: *Bacharelado; Licenciatura; Especialização/Aperfeiçoamento*
Last Updated: 07/07/10

GAMA FILHO UNIVERSITY - RIO DE JANEIRO
Universidade Gama Filho (UGF)
Rua Manoel Vitorino, 553, Prédio ON 4° Andar, Piedade,
Rio de Janeiro, Rio de Janeiro 20748900
Tel: +55(21) 2599-7125 +55(21) 2599-7126
Fax: +55(21) 2599-1448
EMail: vrac@ugf.br
Website: http://www.ugf.br

Reitora: Maria José Mesquita Cavalleiro de Macedo Wehling
Tel: +55(21) 2599-7272, Fax: +55(21) 2289-8394
EMail: reitoria@ugf.br

Centres
Exact Sciences and Technology (Architecture; Automation and Control Engineering; Cinema and Television; Civil Engineering; Computer Engineering; Computer Networks; Electrical Engineering; Engineering; Industrial Design; Information Technology; Marketing; Mathematics; Mechanical Engineering; Petroleum and Gas Engineering; Production Engineering; Taxation; Telecommunications Engineering); **Health Sciences** (Biology; Biomedicine; Dentistry; Medicine; Nursing; Nutrition; Pharmacy; Physical Education; Physical Therapy; Psychology); **Social Sciences and Humanities** (Accountancy; Administration; Communication Studies; Geography; History; Law; Management; Philosophy; Social Sciences)

History: Founded 1939. A private institution recognized by the Federal Government and administered by the Sociedade Universitária Gama Filho. Acquired present status 1972.

Governing Bodies: Conselho Universitário; Conselho de Ensino e Pesquisa

Academic Year: March to December (March-June; August-December)

Admission Requirements: Secondary school certificate and entrance examination

Fees: (Reais): 295. 44-1,624 per month
Main Language(s) of Instruction: Portuguese
International Co-operation: With universities in Portugal, France and USA.

Degrees and Diplomas: *Tecnólogo*: Auditing and Taxation; Marketing, 2 yrs; *Tecnólogo*: Automation and Control Engineering; Telecommunication Networks, 3 yrs; *Tecnólogo*: Information Technology; Petroleum and Gas Engineering; Computer Networks; Cinema and Television, 2 1/2 yrs; *Bacharelado*: Architecture; Law; Psychology, 5 yrs; *Bacharelado*: Business Administration; Computer Science; Biological and Life Science; Accountancy; Communication Studies; Engineering; Nursing; Nutrition, 4 yrs; *Bacharelado*: Industrial Design; Pharmacy, 3 yrs; *Bacharelado*: Medicine, 6 yrs; *Licenciatura*: História; Education, 3 1/2 yrs; *Licenciatura*: Physical Education; Physiotherapy; Arts and Humanities; Mathematics; Odontology, 4 yrs; *Mestrado*: Physical Education; Law; Philosophy, a further 2 yrs; *Doutorado*: Physical Education; Law; Philosophy, a further 4 yrs

Student Services: Academic counselling, Canteen, Cultural centre, Employment services, Handicapped facilities, Health services, Language programs, Nursery care, Social counselling, Sports facilities
Student Residential Facilities: None
Special Facilities: University Museum; Art Gallery; Theatre; Auditorium
Libraries: 248,326 vols
Publications: Caderno Cientifico do Mestrado e Doutorado em Direito *(biennially)*; Ethica-Cadernos Académicos *(biannually)*; Légein *(annually)*; Mente social *(biennially)*; Motus Corporis *(biennially)*; Revista Ciências Biológicas *(quarterly)*; Revista Ciências Humanas *(quarterly)*; Revista Ciências Sociais *(biennially)*; Revista Cientifica do Instituto de Pesquisas Biomédicas Gonzaga da Gama Filho *(biennially)*; Scientia Sexualis *(quarterly)*
Press or Publishing House: Gráfica TEJU
Last Updated: 11/05/10

GAMALIEL FACULTY OF THEOLOGY, PHILOSOPHY AND HUMAN SCIENCES
Faculdade de Teologia, Filosofia e Ciências Humanas Gamaliel
Rua 1s/n, Esquina com a Rua W-1, Jardim Marilucy, Tucuruí,
PA 68459-490
Tel: +55(94) 3787-1010
EMail: revocelio@hotmail.com
Website: http://www.faculdadegamaliel.com.br

Diretor: Ocelio Nauar de Araujo

Courses
Administration (Administration); **Law** (Law); **Theology** (Theology)
History: Founded 2002.
Main Language(s) of Instruction: Portuguese

Degrees and Diplomas: *Bacharelado*; *Especialização/Aperfeiçoamento*

Libraries: Yes
Last Updated: 20/09/10

GAMMON PRESBYTERIAN FACULTY
Faculdade Presbiteriana Gammon (FAGAM)
Praça Doutor Augusto Silva 616, Centro, Lavras,
Minas Gerais 37200000
Tel: +55(35) 6133-3821 +55(35) 6133-6114
Fax: +55(35) 821-6114
EMail: unigammon@gammon.br
Website: http://www.fagammon.edu.br

Diretor: Sergio Wagner de Oliveira

Courses
Administration (Administration); **Computer Science** (Computer Science); **Physical Education**; **Tourism**

History: Founded 1990

Main Language(s) of Instruction: Portuguese

Degrees and Diplomas: *Bacharelado*; *Especialização/Aperfeiçoamento*

Last Updated: 02/07/10

GENNARI AND PEARTREE FACULTY
Faculdade Gennari e Peartree
Rodovia Comandante João Ribeiro de Barros (Bauru-Jaú), km 207,
Parque da Colina, Pederneiras, SP 17280-000
Tel: +55(14) 3284-4999
EMail: fgp@fgp.com.br
Website: http://www.fgp.com.br

Diretor: Carlos Alberto Guerini Comini

Courses
Business Administration (Business Administration); **Information Systems** (Computer Science)

History: Founded 2001.

Main Language(s) of Instruction: Portuguese

Degrees and Diplomas: *Bacharelado*

Libraries: Yes
Last Updated: 25/08/10

GERALDO DI BIASE UNIVERSITY CENTRE
Centro Universitário Geraldo Di Biase
Rua Deputado Geraldo Di Biase, 81, Aterrado, Volta Redonda,
Rio de Janeiro 27213-080
Tel: +55(24) 3345-1700
EMail: ferp@ferp.br
Website: http://www.ferp.br

Reitor: Mário César Di Biase

Centres
Technological Studies - NGT *(Barra do Piraí)* (Environmental Management; Human Resources; Transport Management); **Technological Studies - NGT** *(Volta Redonda)*

Courses
Graduate Studies *(Barra do Piraí)* (Business Education; Educational Administration; Portuguese); **Graduate Studies** *(Volta Redonda)* (Architecture; Biochemistry; Business Education; Commercial Law; Contemporary History; Data Processing; Ecology; Educational Administration; Educational Psychology; English; Environmental Studies; Finance; Geography; Geography (Human); Higher Education; History; Human Resources; Information Technology; Interior Design; Law; Literature; Mathematics Education; Microbiology; Natural Resources; Pedagogy; Portuguese; Public Administration; Religion; Safety Engineering; Small Business; Town Planning; Translation and Interpretation; Transport Management); **Graduate Studies** *(Nova Iguaçu)*

Higher Institutes
Education - ISE *(Volta Redonda)* (Biological and Life Sciences; Computer Science; English; Geography; History; Literature; Mathematics; Pedagogy; Portuguese; Spanish); **Education - ISE** *(Barra do Piraí)* (Biological and Life Sciences; Computer Science; English; History; Literature; Pedagogy; Physical Education; Portuguese; Theatre; Visual Arts)

Institutes
Exact, Earth Sciences and Engineering - ICETE *(Nova Iguaçu)* (Civil Engineering; Environmental Engineering; Production Engineering); **Exact, Earth Sciences and Engineering - ICETE** *(Barra do Piraí)*; **Health Sciences - ICS** *(Barra do Piraí)* (Biomedical Engineering; Nursing); **Social and Human Sciences - ICSH** *(Barra do Piraí)* (Accountancy; Administration; Social and Community Services); **Social and Human Sciences - ICSH** *(Volta Redonda)*

Further Information: Also Barra do Piraí and Nova Iguaçu campuses.

History: Founded 1967 as Fundação Educacional Rosemar Pimentel. Acquired present status and title 2005.

Main Language(s) of Instruction: Portuguese

Degrees and Diplomas: *Tecnólogo*; *Bacharelado*; *Licenciatura*; *Especialização/Aperfeiçoamento*. Also MBA.
Last Updated: 03/06/10

GEREMÁRIO DANTAS FACULTY
Faculdade Geremário Dantas
Rua Cândido Benício, 159, Campinho, Rio de Janeiro,
RJ 21320-061
Tel: +55(21) 2108-7901
EMail: ouvidoria@fgd.edu.br
Website: http://www.fgd.edu.br/

Diretora Geral: Irmã Marisa Aquino

Courses
Graduate Studies (Education; Educational Psychology; Philosophy; Preschool Education; Religious Education; Sociology); **Undergraduate Studies** (Literature; Pedagogy; Portuguese; Spanish)

Degrees and Diplomas: *Licenciatura*. Also Postgraduate diploma.
Last Updated: 31/08/10

GLOBAL FACULTY OF UMUARAMA
Faculdade Global de Umuarama (FGU)
Rua Farroupilha, 2582, Umuarama, PR 87505-100
Tel: +55(44) 3621-4700
EMail: faculglobal@uol.com.br
Website: http://www.fgu.edu.br/

Diretor Geral: Antonio de Oliveira Filho

Courses
Graduate Studies (Education; Educational Administration; Educational Psychology; Environmental Management; Foreign Languages Education; Higher Education; Literature; Native Language Education; Special Education; Writing); **Undergraduate Studies** (Biological and Life Sciences; Literature; Pedagogy; Speech Therapy and Audiology)

History: Founded 1977. Became Colégio centro de Educação Global 1992. Acquired present status and title 2001.

Degrees and Diplomas: *Licenciatura*. Also Postgraduate diploma.
Last Updated: 31/08/10

GOVERNOR OZANAM COELHO FACULTY
Faculdade Governador Ozanam Coelho (FAGOC)
Rua Dr Adjalme da Silva Botelho 20, Bairro Seminário, Uba,
Minas Gerais 36500000
Tel: +55(32) 3531-2370
Fax: +55(32) 3531-2370
EMail: barbieri@uai.com.br
Website: http://www.fagoc.br

Diretor Geral: Marcelo Oliveira Andrade **EMail:** marcelo@fagoc.br

Courses
Accountancy (Accountancy); **Business Administration** (Business Administration); **Computer Science** (Computer Science); **Physical Education** (Physical Education); **Social Communication - Journalism**

History: Founded 1999.

Degrees and Diplomas: *Bacharelado*; *Licenciatura*; *Especialização/Aperfeiçoamento*
Last Updated: 30/06/10

GRANBERY METHODIST FACULTY
Faculdade Metodista Granbery (FAMEG)
Rua Batista de Oliveira 1145, Centro, Juiz de Fora,
Minas Gerais 36010530
Tel: +55(32) 3215-1833
Fax: +55(32) 3213-4893
EMail: faculdade@granbery.com
Website: http://www.granbery.edu.br/

Diretor Geral: Roberto Pontes da Fonseca

Courses
Administration; **Information Systems** (Information Management); **Law**; **Pedagogy** (Education; Pedagogy); **Physical Education** (Physical Education)

History: Founded 1998.

Main Language(s) of Instruction: Portuguese

Degrees and Diplomas: *Bacharelado*; *Licenciatura*; *Especialização/Aperfeiçoamento*
Last Updated: 06/07/10

GRANDE ABC UNIVERSITY - SÃO CAETANO DO SUL
Universidade do Grande ABC (UNIABC)
Avenida Industrial 3330, Campestre, São Caetano do Sul,
São Paulo 09080511
Tel: +55(11) 4232-3233 +55(11) 4991-9800
Fax: +55(11) 4232-3477 +55(11) 4991-9818
EMail: reitoria@uniabc.br
Website: http://www.uniabc.br

Reitor: Azurem Ferrreira Pinto (1995-)
Tel: +55(11) 4991-9824 EMail: reitor@uniabc.br

Courses
Accountancy (Accountancy); **Architecture and Town Planning** (Architecture; Town Planning); **Biology** (Biology); **Communication Studies** (Communication Studies); **Computer Science** (Computer Science); **Education** (Education); **Engineering Management** (Engineering Management); **History** (History); **Law** (Law); **Mathematics** (Mathematics); **Mechanical Engineering** (Mechanical Engineering); **Mechanics** (Mechanics); **Nursing** (Nursing); **Nutrition** (Nutrition); **Pharmacy** (Pharmacy); **Physical Education** (Physical Education); **Physiotherapy** (Physical Therapy); **Psychology** (Psychology); **Tourism** (Tourism); **Veterinary Science** (Veterinary Science)

History: Founded 1969.

Admission Requirements: Secondary school certificate and entrance examination

Main Language(s) of Instruction: Portuguese

Degrees and Diplomas: *Tecnólogo*; *Bacharelado*; *Licenciatura*; *Especialização/Aperfeiçoamento*; *Mestrado*
Last Updated: 01/06/10

GRANDE VITÓRIA FACULTY
Faculdade Grande Vitória (UNFGV)
Rua São José 199, Jardim Limoeiro, Serra, ES 29164220
Tel: +55(27) 3328-8555
Fax: +55(27) 3328-8555
EMail: unfgv@terra.com.br

Head: Francisco Luiz Feu Rosa Pavan

Courses
Administration

History: Founded 1999.

Main Language(s) of Instruction: Portuguese

Degrees and Diplomas: *Bacharelado*
Last Updated: 01/02/08

GUAIANÁS FACULTY
Faculdade Guaianás
Rua Otelo Augusto Ribeiro, 411, Guaianases, São Paulo,
SP 08412-000
Tel: +55(11) 2016-9600
EMail: secretariageral@faculdadeguaianas.com.br
Website: http://www.faculdadeguaianas.com.br/

Diretor: Osvair Lima de Castro
EMail: osvair@faculdadeguaianas.com.br

Courses
Accountancy (Accountancy); **Administration** (Administration); **Human Resources** (Human Resources); **Literature** (Literature); **Pedagogy** (Pedagogy)

History: Founded 2005. Acquired present title 2009.

Main Language(s) of Instruction: Portuguese

Degrees and Diplomas: *Tecnólogo*; *Bacharelado*; *Licenciatura*
Last Updated: 31/08/10

GUAIRACÁ FACULTY
Faculdade Guairacá
Rua XV de Novembro, 7050, Centro, Guarapuava, PR 85010-000
Tel: +55(42) 3622-2000
EMail: contato@faculdadeguairaca.edu.br
Website: http://www.faculdadeguairaca.edu.br/

Diretor Geral e Pedagógico: Juarez Matias Soares
EMail: soares@faculdadeguairaca.edu.br

Courses
Graduate Studies (Educational Psychology; Environmental Management; Family Studies; Gerontology; Health Sciences; Native Language Education; Occupational Health; Pedagogy; Physical Education; Social Welfare; Sports); **Undergraduate Studies** (Biological and Life Sciences; Mathematics; Nursing; Pedagogy; Physical Education; Physical Therapy; Psychology; Social and Community Services; Systems Analysis)

History: Founded 2006.

Degrees and Diplomas: *Tecnólogo*; *Bacharelado*; *Licenciatura*; *Especialização/Aperfeiçoamento*
Last Updated: 31/08/10

GUARÁ ORGANISATION OF EDUCATION
Organização Guará de Ensino (OGE)
Avenida Pedro de Toledo 195, Pavimento Inferior, Vila Paraiba,
Guaratinguetá, São Paulo 12515690
Tel: +55(12) 3125-2911
Fax: +55(12) 3125-2284
EMail: oge@oge.edu.br
Website: http://www.oge.edu.br

Diretora: Maria Lúcia Bittencourt Zollner Machado Jacupino

Faculties
Accountancy *(FACEG)*; **Administration** (Administration); **Pedagogy**

History: Founded 1974.

Main Language(s) of Instruction: Portuguese

Degrees and Diplomas: *Bacharelado*; *Especialização/Aperfeiçoamento*
Last Updated: 14/06/10

GUARAÍ FACULTY
Faculdade Guaraí (FAG)
Av JK n 2541 Bloco VII, Setor Universitário, Guaraí, TO 77700-000
Tel: +55(63) 3464-1289
Fax: +55(63) 3464-1289
EMail: marceloterra-to@hotmail.com
Website: http://www.faculdadeguarai.edu.br/

Diretor: Marcelo Alves Terra

Courses
Agronomy (Agronomy); **Biomedicine** (Biomedicine); **Business Administration** (Business Administration); **Literature** (Literature); **Nursing** (Nursing); **Pedagogy** (Pedagogy)

Degrees and Diplomas: *Bacharelado*; *Licenciatura*
Last Updated: 31/08/10

GUARULHOS UNIVERSITY

Universidade Guarulhos (UNG)
Praça Tereza Cristina, 1, Centro, Guarulhos, São Paulo 07023070
Tel: +55(11) 6464-1700
Fax: +55(11) 6464-1727
EMail: ung@server.ung.br
Website: http://www.ung.br
Reitora: Dumara Coutinho Tokunaga Sameshima
Tel: +55(11) 6464-1650 EMail: reitor@ung.br

Areas
Applied Social Sciences; **Biological and Health Sciences** (Biological and Life Sciences; Health Sciences); **Exact Sciences and Technology** (Engineering; Mathematics and Computer Science; Natural Sciences; Physics; Technology); **Human and Social Sciences** (Advertising and Publicity; Geography; History; Industrial Design; Journalism; Law; Literature; Pedagogy; Psychology; Social Sciences; Visual Arts)

History: Founded 1970 as Faculdade de Filosofia, Ciências e Letras 'Farias Brito'. Became Centros Integrados 'Farias Brito' 1982, and acquired present status and title 1986. A private institution.

Governing Bodies: Conselho Universitário; Conselho de Ensino, Pesquisa e Extensão

Academic Year: February to December (February-June; August-December)

Admission Requirements: Secondary school certificate and entrance examination

Fees: (Reais) 1,443-7,333 per semester

Main Language(s) of Instruction: Portuguese

International Co-operation: With universities in Spain, United States

Degrees and Diplomas: *Bacharelado*: 8-10 semesters; *Licenciatura*: 8 semesters; *Especialização/Aperfeiçoamento*; *Mestrado*

Student Services: Canteen, Cultural centre, Employment services, Foreign student adviser, Handicapped facilities, Health services, Language programs, Nursery care, Social counselling, Sports facilities

Special Facilities: Museu e Laboratório de Estudos de Minerais, Rochas e Fósseis

Libraries: Central Library, c. 85,972 vols

Publications: Revista Universidade Guarulhos *(bimonthly)*

Press or Publishing House: Editora Universidade Guarulhos
Last Updated: 11/05/10

HEART OF JESUS INSTITUTE OF EDUCATION

Instituto Superior de Educação Coração de Jesus (ISECJ)
Rua Barão da Boa Esperença, 594, Catumbi, Três Pontas, MG 37190-000
Tel: +55(35) 3265-6163
EMail: ecjobjetivo@trespontas.com.br

Courses
Biological Sciences (Biological and Life Sciences)
Degrees and Diplomas: *Licenciatura*
Last Updated: 24/09/10

HÉLIO ALONSO INTEGRATED FACULTIES

Faculdades Integradas Hélio Alonso (FACHA)
Rua Muniz Barreto 51, Botafogo, Rio de Janeiro, Rio de Janeiro 22251090
Tel: +55(21) 2102-3100
EMail: secgeral@facha.br
Website: http://www.facha.edu.br
Diretor Geral: Hélio Alonso
EMail: presidencia@helioalonso.com.br

Courses
Law (Law); **Social Communication** (Advertising and Publicity; Journalism; Public Relations; Radio and Television Broadcasting); **Tourism** (Tourism)

Further Information: Also Centro campus, Botafogo campus and Meir campus

History: Founded 1972

Main Language(s) of Instruction: Portuguese

Accrediting Agencies: Ministério da Educação

Degrees and Diplomas: *Bacharelado*: Journalism; Public Relations; Tourism, 4 yrs; *Bacharelado*: Law, 5 yrs; *Especialização/ Aperfeiçoamento*
Last Updated: 22/06/10

HÉLIO ROCHA FACULTY

Faculdade Hélio Rocha
Rua Fernando Menezes de Góes 570, Pituba, Salvador, Bahia 41820035
Tel: +55(71) 2101-5000
Fax: +55(71) 2101-5000
EMail: fhr@heliorocha.com.br
Website: http://www.heliorocha.com.br
Diretor Geral: Hélio Rocha

Courses
Administration (Administration); **Advertising** (Advertising and Publicity); **Computer Science**; **Editorial Production** (Publishing and Book Trade); **Tourism**

History: Founded 2001.

Main Language(s) of Instruction: Portuguese

Degrees and Diplomas: *Bacharelado*
Last Updated: 07/07/10

HERMÍNIO OMETTO DE ARARRAS UNIVERSITY CENTRE

Centro Universitário Hermínio Ometto de Araras (UNIARARAS)
Avenida Doutor Maximiliano Baruto 500, s/n Jardim Universitário, Araras, São Paulo 13607-339
Tel: +55(19) 3543-1400
Fax: +55(19) 3543-1412
EMail: secretaria@uniararas.br
Website: http://www.uniararas.br
Reitor: José Antonio Mendes EMail: josemendes@uniararas.br

Areas
Education (Chemistry; Mathematics; Pedagogy; Physics); **Engineering**; **Health Sciences** (Biology; Biomedicine; Dentistry; Nursing; Pharmacy; Physical Education; Physical Therapy); **Humanities** (Accountancy; Administration; Psychology); **Information Systems** (Information Sciences); **Technology** (Chemical Engineering; Computer Networks; Cosmetology; Environmental Management; Finance; Food Science; Human Resources; Industrial Management; Marketing; Safety Engineering; Transport Management)

Courses
Graduate Studies *(Stricto Sensu)* (Biomedicine; Orthodontics); **Graduate Studies** *(Lato Sensu)* (Acupuncture; Agriculture; Alternative Medicine; Biological and Life Sciences; Biotechnology; Business Administration; Cosmetology; Dentistry; Educational Administration; Educational Psychology; Educational Sciences; Finance; Food Technology; Gerontology; Haematology; Higher Education; Immunology; Information Technology; Molecular Biology; Nursing; Orthodontics; Orthopaedics; Pedagogy; Pharmacology; Pharmacy; Physical Therapy; Psychiatry and Mental Health; Public Health; Rehabilitation and Therapy; Science Education; Sports; Surgery; Toxicology; Transport Management; Veterinary Science)

History: Founded 1973

Main Language(s) of Instruction: Portuguese

Degrees and Diplomas: *Tecnólogo*; *Bacharelado*; *Licenciatura*; *Especialização/Aperfeiçoamento*; *Mestrado*. Also MBA.
Last Updated: 03/06/10

HERRERO FACULTY OF TECHNOLOGY
Faculdade de Tecnologia Herrero (FATEC)
Rua Álvaro Andrade, 345, Curitiba, PR 80610-240
Tel: +55(41) 3016-1930
Fax: +55(41) 3026-8411
EMail: infocursos@herrero.com.br; herrero@herrero.com.br
Website: http://www.herrero.com.br/

Diretor Geral: Sergio Herrero Moraes
EMail: direcao@herrero.com.br

Courses
Graduate Studies (Dental Technology; Dentistry; Nursing; Orthodontics; Periodontics); **Hospital Management** (Health Administration); **Nursing** (Nursing); **Occupational Safety** (Safety Engineering)

Degrees and Diplomas: *Tecnólogo*; *Bacharelado*; *Especialização/ Aperfeiçoamento*
Last Updated: 25/08/10

HIGHER EDUCATION ASSOCIATION OF PIAUÍ
Associação de Ensino Superior do Piauí (AESPI)
Rua Gov. Joca Pires 1000, Fátima, Piauí 64046470
Tel: +55(86) 3233-6666
Fax: +55(86) 3232-7676
EMail: aespi@aespi.br; ouvidoria@aespi.br
Website: http://www.aespi.br

Faculties
Administration *(FAT)*; **Data Processing** *(FPPD)*

Institutes
Higher Education *(IEST)* (Accountancy; Advertising and Publicity; Law; Nursing; Physical Therapy)

Further Information: Also campus in São Cristóvão
History: Founded 1992
Main Language(s) of Instruction: Portuguese
Degrees and Diplomas: *Tecnólogo*; *Bacharelado*
Last Updated: 08/03/10

HIGHER EDUCATION CENTRE - FLORIANÓPOLIS
Centro de Educação Superior - Florianópolis (UNICA)
Rua Salvatina Feliciano dos Santos 525, Itacurubi, Florianópolis, Santa Catarina 88034-600
Tel: +55(48) 3239-4700
Fax: +55(48) 3334-6437
EMail: unica@sociesc.com.br; diredu@unica.br
Website: http://www.sociesc.org.br/pt/unica

Courses
Accountancy (Accountancy; Business Administration); **Administration**; **Business and Commerce** (Business Administration; Business and Commerce); **Graduate Studies** (Accountancy; Architecture; Business Administration; Business and Commerce; Management; Marketing; Real Estate; Safety Engineering; Software Engineering); **Human Resources** (Business Administration; Human Resources); **Management Process** (Business Administration; Management); **Marketing** (Marketing); **Production Engineering**

History: Founded 1998.

Degrees and Diplomas: *Tecnólogo*; *Bacharelado*; *Especialização/ Aperfeiçoamento*. Also MBA. Postgraduate Courses are offered by Instituto Superior Tupy (IST) and Fundação Getulio Vargas
Last Updated: 22/03/10

HIGHER EDUCATION CENTRE OF AMAPÁ
Centro de Ensino Superior do Amapá (CEAP)
Rodovia Duca Serra, Via 17, n° 350, Alvorada, Macapá, Amapá 68906720
Tel: +55(96) 3261-2133
Fax: +55(96) 3261-1401
EMail: ceap@ceap.br
Website: http://www.ceap.br

Diretor: Leonil de Aquino Pena Amanajas EMail: diretor@ceap.br

Courses
Accountancy (Accountancy); **Administration**; **Architecture and Town Planning** (Architecture; Town Planning); **Design**; **Economics**; **Graduate Studies**; **Law**; **Physical Education** (Physical Education); **Secretarial Studies** (Secretarial Studies)

History: Founded 1992.

Main Language(s) of Instruction: Portuguese

Degrees and Diplomas: *Bacharelado*; *Licenciatura*: Physical Education; *Especialização/Aperfeiçoamento*
Last Updated: 22/04/10

HIGHER EDUCATION CENTRE OF BLUMENAU
Centro de Educação Superior de Blumenau (CESBLU)
Rua Capitão Santos 145, Garcia, Blumenau, Santa Catarina 89020062
Tel: +55(47) 3222-1980
Fax: +55(47) 3222-1980
EMail: cesb@cesblu.br; secretariageral@cesblu.br
Website: http://www.cesblu.br

Diretor Geral: Raul Otto Laux

Courses
Administration (Administration); **Computer Networks**; **Databases** (Data Processing); **Digital Systems** (Computer Science); **Law**; **Marketing** (Marketing)

History: Founded 1998.

Main Language(s) of Instruction: Portuguese

Degrees and Diplomas: *Tecnólogo*; *Bacharelado*; *Mestrado*
Last Updated: 22/03/10

HIGHER EDUCATION CENTRE OF CAMPOS GERAIS
Centro de Ensino Superior dos Campos Gerais (CESCAGE)
AvenidaCarlos Cavalcanti 8000, Uvaras, Ponta Grossa, Paraná 84030-000
Tel: +55(42) 3219-8000
EMail: cescage@cescage.com.br
Website: http://www.cescage.edu.br/site

Diretora: Julia Streski Fagundes Cunha

Courses
Administration (Administration); **Advertising and Publicity**; **Agronomy** (Agronomy); **Construction Engineering** (Construction Engineering); **Electrical Engineering**; **Environmental Management** (Environmental Management); **Graduate Studies** (Acupuncture; Agricultural Business; Business Administration; Civil Law; Cooking and Catering; Dental Hygiene; Dentistry; Environmental Management; Finance; Higher Education; Marketing; Nutrition; Orthodontics; Physical Therapy; Public Health; Rehabilitation and Therapy; Safety Engineering; Surgery; Transport Management); **Law**; **Nursing**; **Nutrition**; **Odontology** (Dental Technology); **Pharmacy**; **Physical Therapy** (Physical Therapy); **Veterinary Science** (Veterinary Science)

History: Founded 1999.

Main Language(s) of Instruction: Portuguese

Degrees and Diplomas: *Tecnólogo*; *Bacharelado*; *Licenciatura*; *Especialização/Aperfeiçoamento*
Last Updated: 23/06/10

HIGHER EDUCATION CENTRE OF CATALÃO
Centro de Ensino Superior de Catalão (CESUC)
Rua Prof. Paulo Lima, 100, Catalão, GO 75706420
Tel: +55(62) 3441-6200
Fax: +55(64) 3441-6200
EMail: cesuc@cesuc.br
Website: http://www.cesuc.br/

Diretora Geral: Maria Eleonora de Oliveira Scalia

Courses
Accountancy; **Administration** (Administration; Marketing); **Administration of Information System** (Information Management); **Graduate Studies** (Business Administration; Education;

Engineering; Human Resources; Law; Management; Marketing; Production Engineering; Transport Management); **Law** (Law); **Physiotherapy**

Faculties
Technology *(FATECA)* (Computer Science)

History: Founded 1984.

Main Language(s) of Instruction: Portuguese

Degrees and Diplomas: *Tecnólogo*; *Bacharelado*; *Especialização/ Aperfeiçoamento*. Also MBA degree
Last Updated: 22/03/10

HIGHER EDUCATION CENTRE OF DRACENA - DRACENA FACULTY OF ADMINISTRATION

Centro de Ensino Superior de Dracena - Faculdade de Ciências Gerenciais de Dracena (CESD)
Rodovia Engenho Byron Azevedo Nogueira, S/n Km Zero Vila Barros, Dracena, São Paulo 17900000
Tel: +55(18) 5821-9099
Fax: +55(18) 5821-9099
EMail: cesd@cesd.br; secretaria@cesd.br
Website: http://www.cesd.br
President: José Gonzaga Da Silva Neto

Courses
Accountancy; **Administration** *(FCGD)* (Administration); **Graduate Studies**; **Law**; **Tourism** (Tourism)

History: Founded 1995.

Main Language(s) of Instruction: Portuguese

Degrees and Diplomas: *Bacharelado*; *Especialização/Aperfeiçoamento*. Also MBA
Last Updated: 25/03/10

HIGHER EDUCATION CENTRE OF FOZ DO IGUAÇU

Centro de Ensino Superior de Foz do Iguaçu (CESUFOZ)
Avenida Paraná 3695 Jardim Central, Foz do Iguaçu, PR 85863-720
Tel: +55(45) 3522-1727
Fax: +55(45) 3522-1714
EMail: secretaria@cesufoz.br
Website: http://www.cesufoz.edu.br
Diretor Geral: Edson Gaspar EMail: direcao@cesufoz.br

Faculties
Economics and Data Processing *(FEPI)* (Computer Science; Data Processing; Economics); **Physical Education** *(FEFFI)*

Institutes
Higher Education *(IESFI)* (Accountancy; Administration; Advertising and Publicity; Business Administration; Communication Studies; Computer Networks; Graphic Design; Health Administration; Human Resources; International Business; Law; Management; Marketing; Multimedia; Nursing; Pharmacy; Physical Therapy; Psychology; Sports Management; Tourism)

History: Founded 1993.

Main Language(s) of Instruction: Portuguese

Degrees and Diplomas: *Tecnólogo*; *Bacharelado*; *Licenciatura*: Physical Education;
Last Updated: 25/03/10

HIGHER EDUCATION CENTRE OF ILHÉUS - FACULTY OF ILHÉUS

Centro de Ensino Superior de Ilhéus - Faculdade de Ilhéus (CESUPI)
Rod. Ilhéus-Olivença, km 25, Jardim Atlântico, Ilhéus, Bahia
Tel: +55(73) 2101-1700
Fax: +55(73) 2101-1709
EMail: cesupi@faculdadedeilheus.com.br
Website: http://www.faculdadedeilheus.com.br
Diretor Geral: Almir Milanesi

Courses
Accountancy (Accountancy); **Administration** (Administration); **Graduate Studies** (Business Administration; Finance; Management; Public Administration); **Law** (Law); **Nursing**; **Nutrition**

History: Founded 2002.

Main Language(s) of Instruction: Portuguese

Degrees and Diplomas: *Bacharelado*; *Especialização/Aperfeiçoamento*
Last Updated: 25/03/10

HIGHER EDUCATION CENTRE OF JATAÍ

Centro de Ensino Superior de Jataí (CESUT)
Rua Santos Dumont 1200, Setor Oeste, Jataí, GO 75804-045
Tel: +55(64) 2102-1050 +55(64) 3631-2466
Fax: +55(64) 3631-2524
EMail: cesut@cesut.edu.br
Website: http://www.cesut.edu.br
Diretor: Evaristo Anania de Paula (1990-)

Courses
Administration (Administration); **Graduate Studies**; **Law** (Law)

History: Founded 1994.

Main Language(s) of Instruction: Portuguese

Degrees and Diplomas: *Bacharelado*; *Especialização/Aperfeiçoamento*
Last Updated: 25/03/10

HIGHER EDUCATION CENTRE OF JUIZ DE FORA

Centro de Ensino Superior de Juiz de Fora (CES-JF)
Rua Halfeld 1179, Centro, Juiz de Fora, Minas Gerais 36016000
Tel: +55(32) 2102-7700
Fax: +55(32) 2102-7738
EMail: cesjf@cesjf.br
Website: http://www.cesjf.br
Reitor: José Carlos Aguiar de Souza
Tel: +55(32) 2102-6011 EMail: reitoriasec@cesjf.br

Courses
Architecture and Town Planning (Architecture; Town Planning); **Biology** (Biological and Life Sciences; Biology; Natural Sciences); **Computer Science**; **Cuisine**; **Fashion Design** (Fashion Design); **Geography** (Geography); **History**; **Literature**; **Mathematics**; **Media Studies** (Communication Studies; Media Studies); **Pedagogy** (Pedagogy); **Philosophy**; **Psychology** (Psychology); **Speech Therapy** (Speech Therapy and Audiology); **Telecommunications Engineering** (Telecommunications Engineering); **Theology** (Theology)

Programmes
Graduate Studies

History: Founded 1972.

Main Language(s) of Instruction: Portuguese

Degrees and Diplomas: *Tecnólogo*; *Bacharelado*; *Licenciatura*; *Especialização/Aperfeiçoamento*; *Mestrado*
Last Updated: 26/03/10

HIGHER EDUCATION CENTRE OF PRIMAVERA

Centro de Ensino Superior de Primavera (CESPRI)
Rua Diamantina Quadra 132, S/n Distrito de Primavera, Rosana, São Paulo 19274000
Tel: +55(18) 3284-1600 +55(18) 3284-2015
Fax: +55(18) 3284-1600
EMail: dircespri@uol.com.br
Website: http://www.cespri.br
Diretor: José Wanderley Correa da Silva

Courses
Accountancy (Accountancy); **Administration**; **Environmental Management**; **Occupational Safety** (Occupational Health); **Pedagogy**

Programmes

Clinical and Institutional Psychopedagogy *(Postgraduate)* (Psychology); **Distance Education** *(EAD)* (Accountancy; Administration; Banking; Computer Science; Education; Educational Psychology; Finance; Health Education; Human Resources; Law; Marketing; Mathematics; Political Sciences; Psychoanalysis; Psychology; Telecommunications Engineering; Theology; Transport Management)

History: Founded 1999.

Degrees and Diplomas: *Tecnólogo*; *Bacharelado*; *Especialização/ Aperfeiçoamento*. Also MBA (distance education)
Last Updated: 21/04/10

HIGHER EDUCATION CENTRE OF SÃO GOTARDO

Centro de Ensino Superior de São Gotardo
Avenida Francisco Resende Filho 35, São Gotardo, MG 38800-000
Tel: +55(34) 3671-3862
EMail: livro_dae@hotmail.com
Website: http://www.cesg.edu.br/

Diretor: João Eduardo Lopes Queiroz

Courses

Administration (Administration); **Pedagogy** (Pedagogy); **Production Engineering** (Production Engineering)
History: Founded 2000.
Main Language(s) of Instruction: Portuguese
Degrees and Diplomas: *Bacharelado*; *Especialização/Aperfeiçoamento*
Last Updated: 28/07/10

HIGHER EDUCATION CENTRE OF THE VALLEY OF PARNAÍBA

Centro de Ensino Superior do Vale do Parnaíba (CESVALE)
BR 343 Km 04, Estrada Teresina-Altos 68, Teresina, Piauí 64000-010
Tel: +55(86) 3232-5079
EMail: cesvale@cesvale.com.br
Website: http://www.cesvale.com.br

Diretor: Francisco Gabriel Batista

Courses

Accountancy; **Administration** (Administration); **Graduate Studies** (Accountancy; Advertising and Publicity; Finance; Health Administration; Hotel Management; Human Resources; Marketing; Mathematics; Occupational Health; Pedagogy; Physical Education; Portuguese; Psychology; Public Administration; Small Business; Tourism; Town Planning); **Law**
History: Founded 1985.
Degrees and Diplomas: *Bacharelado*; *Especialização/Aperfeiçoamento*
Last Updated: 22/04/10

HIGHER EDUCATION CENTRE OF UBERABA

Centro de Ensino Superior de Uberaba
Av. Randolfo Borges Júnior, 1250, Univerdecidade, Uberaba, Minas Gerais 38066-005
Tel: +55(34) 3312-9897
EMail: cesube@cesube.edu.br
Website: http://www.cesube.edu.br

Academic Diretor: Neivaldo Miranda Carneiro

Courses

Art Education; **Biology** (Biology); **Civil Engineering** (Civil Engineering); **Environmental Management** *(Postgraduate Studies)* (Environmental Management); **Geography**; **Pedagogy**; **Physical Education**; **Social Sciences**
History: Founded 1999.
Main Language(s) of Instruction: Portuguese
Degrees and Diplomas: *Bacharelado*; *Licenciatura*. Also Postgraduate degree course.
Last Updated: 22/04/10

HIGHER EDUCATION CENTRE OF VALENÇA

Centro de Ensino Superior de Valença (CESVA)
Rua Sargento Victor Hugo 161, Bairro Fátima, Valença, RJ 27600000
Tel: +55(24) 2453-1888
Fax: +55(24) 2453-1888
EMail: ouvidoria@faa.edu.br
Website: http://www.faa.edu.br

Presidente: José Rogério Moura de Almeida Filho

Courses

Arts and Humanities (Arts and Humanities; Literature; Philosophy); **Economics** (Economics); **Graduate Studies** (Dentistry; Education; Law; Physical Education; Physical Therapy; Veterinary Science); **History** (History); **Law** (Law); **Mathematics**; **Medicine** (Medicine); **Nursing** (Nursing); **Odontology** (Dentistry); **Pedagogy** (Pedagogy); **Systems Analysis**; **Veterinary Science** (Veterinary Science)
History: Founded 1966.
Main Language(s) of Instruction: Portuguese
Degrees and Diplomas: *Bacharelado*; *Especialização/Aperfeiçoamento*; *Mestrado*
Last Updated: 22/04/10

HIGHER EDUCATION CENTRE OF VITÓRIA

Centro de Ensino Superior de Vitória (CESV)
Rua Wellington de Freitas 265, Jardim Camburi, Vitória, Espirito Santo 29090-240
Tel: +55(27) 3041-0111
Fax: +55(27) 3041-0106
EMail: cesv@cesv.br
Website: http://www.cesv.br/

Presidente: Wanderlino Evilasio Siqueira

Courses

English Literature (Arts and Humanities; English; Literature); **Law** (Constitutional Law; Law); **Literature** (Arts and Humanities; Literature); **Portuguese Literature**; **Social Communication** (Communication Studies; Social Sciences); **Spanish Literature**
History: Founded 1998.
Main Language(s) of Instruction: Portuguese
Degrees and Diplomas: *Bacharelado*; *Licenciatura*; *Especialização/Aperfeiçoamento*
Last Updated: 22/04/10

HIGHER EDUCATION FOUNDATION OF CLEVELANDIA

Fundação de Ensino Superior de Clevelândia
Rua Coronel Manoel Ferreira Bello, 270 - Centro, Caixa Postal 43, Clevelândia, PR 85530-000
Tel: +55(46) 3252-3399
EMail: danilo@fescpr.edu.br
Website: http://www.fescpr.edu.br

Diretor: Danilo Leão

Courses

Administration (Administration); **Geography** (Geography)
History: Founded 2001.
Main Language(s) of Instruction: Portuguese
Degrees and Diplomas: *Bacharelado*; *Licenciatura*; *Especialização/Aperfeiçoamento*; *Mestrado*
Last Updated: 22/09/10

HIGHER EDUCATION FOUNDATION OF PASSOS

Fundaçao de Ensino Superior de Passos
Av. Juca Stockler, 1130, Belo Horizonte, Passos, MG 37900-106
Tel: +55(35) 3529-6015
EMail: projetos@fespmg.edu.br
Website: http://www.fespmg.edu.br

Diretor: Dácio Lemos Martins **EMail:** dacio.martins@fespmg.edu.br

Courses

Accountancy (Accountancy); **Advertising** (Advertising and Publicity); **Agronomy** (Agronomy); **Biology** (Biology); **Business Administration** (Business Administration); **Civil Engineering** (Civil Engineering); **Environmental Engineering** (Environmental Engineering); **Fashion and Design** (Design; Fashion Design); **History** (History); **Information Systems** (Computer Science); **Journalism** (Journalism); **Law** (Law); **Letters** (Literature); **Mathematics** (Mathematics); **Nursing** (Nursing); **Nutrition** (Nutrition); **Pedagogy** (Pedagogy); **Physical Education** (Physical Education); **Production Engineering** (Production Engineering); **Social Services** (Social and Community Services)

History: Founded 2002.

Main Language(s) of Instruction: Portuguese

Degrees and Diplomas: *Bacharelado*; *Licenciatura*; *Especialização/Aperfeiçoamento*

Libraries: Biblioteca Eng° Oto Lopes de Figueiredo
Last Updated: 16/09/10

HIGHER EDUCATION FOUNDATION OF THE CENTRE-SOUTH REGION

Fundação de Ensino Superior da Região Centro-Sul (FUNDASUL)
Avenida Cônego Luiz Walter Hanquet 151 Centro, Camaqua, RS 96180000
Tel: +55(51) 3671-5905
Fax: +55(51) 3671-1855
EMail: fundasul@fundasul.br
Website: http://www.fundasul.br

Diretor: Rubem Carlos Serafini Machado

Faculties

Accountancy and Administration *(Camaqüense)* (Accountancy; Administration); **Teacher Training** *(FAFOPEE)* (Biology; English; Literature; Mathematics Education; Portuguese; Science Education; Teacher Training)

History: Founded 1999

Main Language(s) of Instruction: Portuguese

Degrees and Diplomas: *Bacharelado*; *Licenciatura*; *Especialização/Aperfeiçoamento*
Last Updated: 18/06/10

HIGHER EDUCATION INSTITUTE OF AMERICANA

Instituto de Ensino Superior de Americana (IESA)
Avenida Paulista 1526, Nossa Senhora de Fátima, Americana, São Paulo 13478580
Tel: +55(19) 3468-2844
Fax: +55(19) 3468-1310
Website: http://www.iesam.edu.br/

Diretor Geral: Edson Barbosa dos Santos

Courses

Accountancy; **Business Administration**; **Computer Science** (Computer Science); **Tourism**

History: Founded 1998

Main Language(s) of Instruction: Portuguese

Degrees and Diplomas: *Bacharelado*
Last Updated: 16/06/10

HIGHER EDUCATION INSTITUTE OF BRASILIA

Instituto de Educação Superior de Brasilía
Campus Jovanina Rimoli, SGAN Quadra 609 - Módulo D - Av. L2 Norte, Brasília, DF 72450070
Tel: +55(61) 3448-9800
EMail: iesb@iesb.br
Website: http://www.iesb.br/

Diretora Geral: Eda Machado Coutinho

Diretor Acadêmico: Teobaldo Rivas

Courses

Administration; **Computer Science**; **Engineering**; **Hotel and Restaurant**; **International Relations**; **Law** (Law); **Pedagogy** (Pedagogy); **Psychology** (Psychology); **Radiology** (Radiology); **Secretarial Studies** (Secretarial Studies); **Social Communication** (Advertising and Publicity; Cinema and Television; Communication Arts; Communication Studies; Journalism; Marketing; Media Studies; Public Relations); **Tourism** (Tourism)

History: Founded 2001.

Degrees and Diplomas: *Bacharelado*; *Licenciatura*; *Especialização/Aperfeiçoamento*
Last Updated: 17/06/10

HIGHER EDUCATION INSTITUTE OF ITAPIRA

Instituto de Ensino Superior de Itapira (IESI)
Avenida Rio Branco 99, Centro, Itapira, São Paulo 13970070
Tel: +55(19) 3863-2106
Fax: +55(19) 3863-4191
EMail: iesi@unip.br
Website: http://www.iesi.edu.br/

Diretor: Ulisses Feres da Silva

Courses

Accountancy (Accountancy); **Administration** (Administration; Business Administration); **Computer Science** (Computer Science); **Law** (Law); **Nursing** (Nursing); **Pedagogy**; **Physiotherapy** (Physical Therapy); **Social Communication** (Communication Studies); **Systems Analysis**; **Tourism**

History: Founded 1999.

Degrees and Diplomas: *Bacharelado*
Last Updated: 16/06/10

HIGHER EDUCATION INSTITUTE OF JOINVILLE

Instituto de Ensino Superior de Joinville (IESVILLE)
Rua Campos Salles 850, Glória, Joinville, Santa Catarina 89217100
Tel: +55(47) 3453-2828
Fax: +55(47) 3453-2929
EMail: margariane@iesville.com.br
Website: http://www.iesville.com.br/

Diretor Geral: Taury Rocha Ramos

Courses

Accountancy (Accountancy); **Administration** (Administration; Business Administration; Marketing); **Communication Studies**; **Education and Pedagogy**; **Finance and Taxation** (Finance; Taxation); **Information Systems** (Information Management); **Multimedia Production** (Multimedia); **Transport Management** (Transport Management)

History: Founded 2001.

Main Language(s) of Instruction: Portuguese

Degrees and Diplomas: *Bacharelado*; *Especialização/Aperfeiçoamento*; *Mestrado*
Last Updated: 16/06/10

HIGHER EDUCATION INSTITUTE OF PARAIBA

Instituto de Educação Superior da Paraíba (IESP)
Avenida João Maurício 1819, João Pessoa, Paraíba 58037010
Tel: +55(83) 2106-3828
Fax: +55(83) 2106-3827
EMail: secretaria@iesp.edu.br
Website: http://www.iesp.edu.br/

Diretor Geral: José Edinaldo de Lima

Diretora Acadêmica: Maria Elinete Taurino Guedes

Courses

Accountancy (Accountancy); **Administration**; **Information Systems**; **Law** (Law); **Nursing** (Nursing); **Production Engineering**; **Social Communication** (Advertising and Publicity; Communication Studies); **Tourism**

History: Founded 1998.

Degrees and Diplomas: *Bacharelado*; *Especialização/Aperfeiçoamento*

Last Updated: 17/06/10

HIGHER EDUCATION INSTITUTE OF RIO VERDE/ OBJETIVO FACULTY

Instituto de Ensino Superior de Rio Verde / Faculdade Objetivo (IESRIVER)
Rua 12 de Outubro s/n Quadra Lote 2, Jardim Adriana, Rio Verde, GO 75906577
Tel: +55(62) 3621-3539
Fax: +55(62) 3621-4543
EMail: objetivo@arasoft.com.br
Website: http://www.faculdadeobjetivo.com.br

Director Administrativo: Fábio Buzzi Ferraz
EMail: fabio@faculdadeobjetivo.com.br

Diretora Acadêmica: Adriana Casarin
EMail: adriana@faculdadeobjetivo.com.br

Courses
Administration (Administration; Business Administration; Information Management; International Business; Marketing); **Law** (Law); **Nursing**; **Physiotherapy** (Physical Therapy); **Social Communication** (Advertising and Publicity; Communication Studies); **Tourism** (Tourism)

History: Founded 1999.

Main Language(s) of Instruction: Portuguese

Degrees and Diplomas: *Bacharelado*

Last Updated: 16/06/10

HIGHER EDUCATION INSTITUTE OF TAUBATE

Instituto Taubaté de Ensino Superior (ITES)
Rua Bahia, 44 - Jardim dos Estados, Taubate, São Paulo 12020200
Tel: +55(12) 3635-4553
Fax: +55(12) 3635-4553
EMail: naotem@naotem.com.br
Website: http://www.ites.edu.br

Diretor: Izidro José de Paiva Medeiros

Courses
Administration; Computer Science; Nursing; Physiotherapy; Social Communication (Advertising and Publicity); **Tourism**

History: Founded 1999.

Main Language(s) of Instruction: Portuguese

Degrees and Diplomas: *Bacharelado*

Last Updated: 14/06/10

HIGHER EDUCATION INSTITUTE OF THE FUNLEC

Instituto de Ensino Superior da Funlec (IESF)
Rua Coronel Calcido Arantes 322 Cachoeira II, Campo Grande, Mato Grosso do Sul 79040450
Tel: +55(67) 3901-2878
Fax: +55(67) 3901-2872
EMail: secretaria.iesfcg@funlec.com.br
Website: http://www.funlec.com.br

Diretor Geral: José Carlos Pesente

Courses
Administration *(Bonito Campus)* (Administration); **Library Science** (Library Science); **Pedagogy** (Pedagogy); **Secretarial Studies** (Secretarial Studies); **Tourism** *(Bonito Campus)* (Tourism); **Tourism** (Physical Education); **Visual Arts** (Visual Arts)

Further Information: Also Bonito Campus.

History: Founded 1997.

Degrees and Diplomas: *Bacharelado*; *Especialização/Aperfeiçoamento*

Last Updated: 16/06/10

HIGHER EDUCATION INSTITUTE OF THE NORTH EAST

Instituto de Ensino Superior do Nordeste (IESNE)
Rua Dr Messias de Gusmão 211 - Próxima ao Campo do CRB, Ponta Verde, Maceió, Alagoas 57030460
Tel: +55(82) 3033-5548
Fax: +55(82) 3377-9090
EMail: celsoguerreiro@yahoo.com.br

Diretor: Agripino Celso Guerreiro Barbosa

Courses
Accountancy

History: Founded 1999.

Main Language(s) of Instruction: Portuguese

Degrees and Diplomas: *Bacharelado*

Last Updated: 16/06/10

HIGHER EDUCATION INSTITUTE OF THE PROVINCE OF PERNAMBUCO

Instituto Pernambuco de Ensino Superior (IPESU)
Av. Ministro Marcos Freire, 2855 - Casa Caiada, Recife, Pernambuco 50670000
Tel: +55(81) 3453-0051
Fax: +55(81) 3453-335833
EMail: ipesupioxii@veloxmail.com.br
Website: http://www.ipes.edu.br

Diretor: Newton Roberto Gregório de Moraes

Courses
Accountancy (Accountancy); **Administration** (Business Administration; Marketing); **Tourism** (Tourism)

History: Founded 2001.

Main Language(s) of Instruction: Portuguese

Degrees and Diplomas: *Bacharelado*

Last Updated: 14/06/10

HIGHER EDUCATION SOCIETY OF THE NORTH EAST

Sociedade de Ensino Universitário do Nordeste (SEUNE)
Avenida Dom Antônio Brandão 204, Farol, Maceió, Alagoas 57021190
Tel: +55(82) 3336-2640
EMail: seune@seune.com.br
Website: http://www.seune.edu.br

Diretor: Sebastião José Palmeira (1998-)

Courses
Administration (Administration; Business Administration); **Law** (Law); **Nursing** (Nursing)

Faculties
Accountancy (Accountancy)

History: Founded 1998.

Main Language(s) of Instruction: Portuguese

Degrees and Diplomas: *Bacharelado*

Last Updated: 09/06/10

HIGHER INSTITUTE OF THE COAST OF PARANA

Instituto Superior do Litoral do Paraná (ISULPAR)
Rua Coronel José Lobo 800, Costeira, Paranaguá, Paraná 83203310
Tel: +55(41) 3423-3415
Fax: +55(41) 3423-3415
EMail: secretaria@isulpar.com.br
Website: http://www.isulpar.com.br/

Diretor: Ivan de Medeiros Petry Maciel

Courses
Administration; **Computer Science** (Computer Science); **Geography**; **Law** (Law); **Pedagogy** (Pedagogy); **Tourism** (Tourism)
History: Founded 2000.
Main Language(s) of Instruction: Portuguese
Degrees and Diplomas: *Bacharelado*; *Especialização/Aperfeiçoamento*
Last Updated: 14/06/10

HOLY CROSS INTEGRATED FACULTIES OF CURITIBA
Faculdades Integradas Santa Cruz de Curitiba (FARESC)
Rua Afiffe Mansur, 565, Novo Mundo, Curitibá, Paraná 81050-180
Tel: +55(41) 3346-1414
EMail: santacruz@santacruz.br
Website: http://www.santacruz.br

Diretor: José Antonio Soares (1997-)

Courses
Accountancy (Accountancy); **Administration** (Administration); **Economics** (Economics); **Information Sciences** (Information Sciences); **Law**; **Letters** (English; Literature; Portuguese); **Pedagogy** (Pedagogy); **Tourism** (Tourism)
History: Founded 1992.
Main Language(s) of Instruction: Portuguese
Degrees and Diplomas: *Bacharelado*; *Licenciatura*; *Especialização/Aperfeiçoamento*
Last Updated: 22/06/10

HOLY SPIRIT METHODIST FACULTY
Faculdade Metodista do Espírito Santo
Rua Castelo Branco 1803, Centro, Vila Velha,
Espírito Santo 29100040
Tel: +55(27) 3200-4358
Fax: +55(27) 3399-5851
EMail: coordenacaoadm@metodistaes.edu.br
Website: http://www.metodistaes.edu.br

Diretor: Miguel Ângelo Três (1998-) EMail: Miguel Angelo Tres
Vice Diretor: Hugo Luiz de Souza EMail: hsouza@univila.br

Courses
Administration (Administration; International Business; Marketing); **Information Systems**; **Pedagogy** (Pedagogy); **Social Communication** (Advertising and Publicity); **Social Services** (Social and Community Services)

Faculties
Law

History: Founded 1998 incorporating the Faculdade de Ciências Econômicas e Administrativas de Vila Velha, the Faculdade de Vila Velha, the Faculdade de Ciências Sociais de Ibiraçu and the Faculdade de Direito de Vila Velha. Acquired present title through merger with Faculdades UNIVILA 2008.
Degrees and Diplomas: *Bacharelado*; *Especialização/Aperfeiçoamento*; *Mestrado*
Last Updated: 14/12/07

HORIZONS FACULTY
Faculdade Horizontes
Rua Conselheiro Crispiniano, 116/120, Centro, São Paulo,
SP 05794-330
Tel: +55(11) 5843-5500

Diretor Presidente: José Fernando Pinto da Costa

Courses
Accountancy (Accountancy); **Administration** (Administration); **Law** (Law); **Nursing** (Nursing); **Pedagogy** (Pedagogy); **Physical Education** (Physical Education)
Degrees and Diplomas: *Bacharelado*; *Licenciatura*
Last Updated: 31/08/10

HORIZONTINA FACULTY
Faculdade Horizontina (FAHOR)
Rua Buricá, 725, Horizontina, RS 98920-000
Tel: +55(55) 3537-2066
EMail: fahor@fahor.com.br
Website: http://www.fahor.com.br/

Diretor: Sedelmo Desbessel EMail: sedelmo@fahor.com.br

Courses
Economics (Economics); **Mechanical Engineering** (Mechanical Engineering); **Production Engineering** (Production Engineering)
Degrees and Diplomas: *Bacharelado*. Also Postgraduate diploma.
Last Updated: 01/09/10

HUMAN TALENT FACULTY
Faculdade Talentos Humanos
Rua Manoel Gonçalves de Rezende, 230 - Vila São Cristóvão,
Uberaba, MG
Tel: +55(34) 3311-9800
EMail: facthus@facthus.edu.br
Website: http://www.facthus.edu.br

Diretor: Cláudio Nascimento de Oliveira

Courses
Accountancy (Accountancy); **Biomedicine** (Biomedicine); **Control and Automation** (Automation and Control Engineering); **Electrical Engineering** (Electrical Engineering); **Environmental Engineering** (Environmental Engineering); **Information Systems** (Computer Science); **Law** (Law); **Mechanical Engineering** (Mechanical Engineering); **Nursing** (Nursing); **Physiotherapy** (Physical Therapy); **Speech Therapy** (Speech Therapy and Audiology); **Telecommunications** (Telecommunications Engineering)
History: Founded 2004.
Main Language(s) of Instruction: Portuguese
Degrees and Diplomas: *Bacharelado*
Libraries: Biblioteca Diva Saraiva
Last Updated: 17/08/10

IAPEC FACULTY OF TECHNOLOGY
Faculdade de Tecnologia IAPEC (IAPEC)
Av. Tiradentes, 858, Jardim Shangri-la A, Londrina, PR 86070-000
Tel: +55(43) 3347-3121
EMail: secretaria@iapec.com.br
Website: http://www.iapec.com.br/

Diretor Geral: Sergio Henrique Toledo

Courses
Computer Networks (Computer Networks); **Distance Studies** (Business and Commerce; Finance; Industrial Management; International Business; Management; Marketing; Pedagogy; Public Administration; Secretarial Studies; Transport Management); **Graduate Studies** (Accountancy; Art Education; Business Administration; Civil Law; Education; Educational Psychology; Environmental Management; Foreign Languages Education; Health Administration; Higher Education; Human Resources; Humanities and Social Science Education; Journalism; Law; Management; Marketing; Mathematics Education; Native Language Education; Occupational Health; Production Engineering; Public Administration; Public Health; Science Education; Secretarial Studies; Special Education)
Degrees and Diplomas: *Tecnólogo*; *Licenciatura*. Also Postgraduate Diploma offered through Faculdade Internacional de Curitiba (Facinter).
Last Updated: 25/08/10

IBGEN FACULTY - BRAZILIAN INSTITUTE OF COMMERCIAL MANAGEMENT

Faculdade IBGEN - Instituto Brasileiro de Gestão de Negócios (IBGEN)
Rua Barão do Amazonas, 46, Petrópolis, Porto Alegre,
RS 90670-000
Tel: +55(51) 3332-0202
Fax: +55(51) 3327-6620
EMail: ibgen@ibgen.com.br; contato@ibgen.com.br
Website: http://www.ibgen.com.br/

Courses
Graduate Studies (Accountancy; Business Administration; Commercial Law; Communication Studies; Finance; Health Administration; Human Resources; Information Technology; International Business; Management; Marketing; Safety Engineering; Service Trades; Transport Management); **Undergraduate Studies** (Administration; Finance; Human Resources; Information Sciences; Information Technology; Psychology)

History: Founded 1996. Acquired present status 2004.

Degrees and Diplomas: *Tecnólogo*; *Bacharelado*. Also MBA.
Last Updated: 01/09/10

IBGM/FGM FACULTY OF TECHNOLOGY, MANAGEMENT & MARKETING

Faculdade de Tecnologia, Gestão & Marketing - IBGM/FGM
Rua Joaquim Felipe, 250, Boa Vista, Recife, PE 50050-340
Tel: +55(81) 3231-7771
Fax: +55(81) 3231-5712
EMail: ouvidoria@ibgm.org
Website: http://www.ibgm.org/

Courses
Graduate Studies (Business Administration; Communication Studies; Industrial and Organizational Psychology; International Business; Leadership; Management; Transport Management); **Human Resources** (Human Resources); **Logistics** (Transport Management); **Management Process** (Management); **Marketing** (Marketing)

Degrees and Diplomas: *Tecnólogo*; *Especialização/Aperfeiçoamento*
Last Updated: 25/08/10

IBIRAPUERA UNIVERSITY

Universidade Ibirapuera (UNIB)
Avenida Iraí 297, Moema, São Paulo, São Paulo 4082000
Tel: +55(11) 5091-1155
EMail: reitoria@ibirapuera.br
Website: http://www.ibirapuera.br

Reitor: Jorge Bastos (1996-) Tel: +55(11) 5543-1911

Areas
Business (Accountancy; Administration; Communication Studies; Law; Tourism); **Education** (Biology; Chemistry; Literature; Mathematics; Pedagogy; Physical Education); **Health Sciences**; **Technology**

History: Founded 1971. Acquired present status 1992.

Admission Requirements: Secondary school certificate and entrance examination

Main Language(s) of Instruction: Portuguese

Degrees and Diplomas: *Bacharelado*; *Licenciatura*; *Especialização/Aperfeiçoamento*; *Mestrado*
Last Updated: 11/05/10

IBITURUNA FACULTY OF HEALTH

Faculdade de Saúde Ibituruna
Avenida Nice, 99 - Ibituruna, Montes Claros, MG 39401-303
Tel: +55(38) 3690-6600
EMail: itagiba.castro@fasi.edu.br
Website: http://www.fasi.edu.br

Diretor: Itagiba de Castro Filho

Courses
Biology (Biology); **Biomedicine** (Biomedicine); **Nursing** (Nursing); **Nutrition** (Nutrition); **Pharmacy** (Pharmacy); **Psychology** (Psychology)

History: Founded 2004.

Main Language(s) of Instruction: Portuguese

Degrees and Diplomas: *Bacharelado*; *Especialização/Aperfeiçoamento*

Libraries: Yes
Last Updated: 16/08/10

IBMEC FACULTY

Faculdade IBMEC (IBMEC)
Rua Paraíba, 330 - 4o andar, Edifício Séculus Business Center,
Belo Horizonte, Minas Gerais 30130-140
Tel: +55 (31) 3247-5757
Fax: +55(31) 3247-5777
EMail: contactcenter@ibmecmg.br
Website: http://www.ibmecrj.br/sub/mg

Presidente: Eduardo Wurzmann

Units
Brasília (Accountancy; Administration; Business Administration; Economics; Finance; International Relations; Public Administration); **Minas Gerais** (Administration; Economics; International Relations); **Rio de Janeiro**

History: Founded 1985.

Main Language(s) of Instruction: Portuguese

Degrees and Diplomas: *Bacharelado*; *Mestrado*. Also MBA
Last Updated: 07/07/10

IBRAFEM FACULTY OF BUSINESS ADMINISTRATION

Faculdade de Administração de Empresas Ibrafem-IBRAFEM
Rodovia do Açúcar, km 152, Rio das Pedras, SP
Tel: +55(19) 3493-9999
EMail: diretoria@faculdadeibrafem.edu.br
Website: http://www.ibrafem.com.br/conheca/faculdade.html

Diretor: Sergio Augusto Lucke

Courses
Business Administration (Business Administration)
History: Founded 2005.
Main Language(s) of Instruction: Portuguese
Degrees and Diplomas: *Bacharelado*
Last Updated: 27/07/10

IBRATEC FACULTY OF TECHNOLOGY

Faculdade de Tecnologia IBRATEC (UNIBRATEC)
Av. Marechal Mascarenhas de Morais, 4989, Imbiribeira, Recife,
PE 51150-002
Tel: +55(81) 3339-0998
EMail: aldo.moura@unibratec.edu.br;
wagner.pinheiro@unibratec.edu.br
Website: http://www.unibratec.edu.br/

Courses
Computer Networks (Computer Networks); **Graduate Studies** (Information Management; Information Technology; Management; Software Engineering); **Graphic Design** (Graphic Design); **Systems Analysis and Development** (Systems Analysis)

Further Information: Also João Pessoa Campus.

History: Founded 1994.

Degrees and Diplomas: *Tecnólogo*. Also Postgraduate diploma.
Last Updated: 25/08/10

IDC FACULTY
Faculdade IDC (IDC)
Rua Vicente da Fontoura, 1578, Porto Alegre, RS 90640-002
Tel: +55(51) 3028-4888
EMail: idc@idc.org.br
Website: http://www.idc.org.br/

Diretor: Sérgio Almeida de Figueiredo

Courses
Graduate Studies (Civil Law; Commercial Law; Criminal Law; Fiscal Law; Labour Law; Public Law); **Philosophy** (Philosophy)

History: Founded 1962 as Instituto Social Cristão de Reforma de Estruturas – ISCRE. Acquired present title 1973. Acquired present status 2005.

Degrees and Diplomas: *Bacharelado; Especialização/Aperfeiçoamento.* Also MBA.
Last Updated: 01/09/10

IDEAL FACULTY
Faculdade Ideal (FACI)
Rua dos Munducurus 1427, Batista Campos, Belém,
Pará 66025660
Tel: +55(91) 3323-6000
Fax: +55(91) 3323-6001
EMail: faci@grupoideal.com.br
Website: http://www.grupoideal.com.br/faci

Diretor: José Dos Santos

Courses
Accountancy (Accountancy); **Administration**; **Civil Engineering** (Civil Engineering); **Computer Engineering** (Computer Engineering); **Law** (Law); **Pedagogy** (Pedagogy)

History: Founded 1999.

Main Language(s) of Instruction: Portuguese

Degrees and Diplomas: *Bacharelado; Licenciatura; Especialização/Aperfeiçoamento*
Last Updated: 07/07/10

IDEAU FACULTY
Faculdade IDEAU
Borges de Medeiros, 2113 Bairro Champagnet, Getúlio Vargas,
RS 99.900-000
Tel: +55(54) 3341-6600
EMail: ideau@ideau.com.br
Website: http://www.ideau.com.br

Diretor: Flávio Carlos Barro

Courses
Accountancy (Accountancy); **Administration** (Administration); **Agronomy** (Agronomy); **Pedagogy** (Pedagogy); **Physical Education** (Physical Education); **Tourism** (Tourism)

History: Founded 2004.

Main Language(s) of Instruction: Portuguese

Degrees and Diplomas: *Bacharelado; Especialização/Aperfeiçoamento; Mestrado*
Last Updated: 19/08/10

IESA FACULTY
Faculdade IESA (IESA)
Rua Delfim Moreira 40 Centro, Santo André, São Paulo 09015070
Tel: +55(11) 4438-9962
Fax: +55(11) 4438-9277
EMail: iesa@iesa.edu.br
Website: http://www.uniesp.edu.br/santoandre

Diretor: Neuza Aparecida Garcia Hashiguchi

Courses
Accountancy (Accountancy); **Administration** (Administration); **Arts and Humanities** (Arts and Humanities); **Business Administration** (Business Administration); **Computer Science** (Computer Science); **Finance** (Finance); **Human Resources** (Human Resources); **Information Management** (Information Management);

Measurement and Precision Engineering (Measurement and Precision Engineering); **Pedagogy** (Pedagogy)

Degrees and Diplomas: *Tecnólogo; Bacharelado; Licenciatura; Especialização/Aperfeiçoamento*
Last Updated: 30/11/07

IESCO FACULTY
Faculdade IESCO
CSG 09 Lotes 15/16 - 2° Andar Taguatinga, Brasília, DF 72120470
Tel: +55(61) 3037-5858
Fax: +55(61) 3037-5858
EMail: iesco@iesco.com.br
Website: http://www.iesco.edu.br

Diretor Geral: Braulio Pereira Lins

Courses
Administration; **Letters**; **Philosophy** (Philosophy)

History: Founded 2001.

Main Language(s) of Instruction: Portuguese

Degrees and Diplomas: *Bacharelado; Licenciatura; Especialização/Aperfeiçoamento*
Last Updated: 07/07/10

IESGO FACULTIES
Faculdades IESGO
Av. Brasília, n.° 2001 Centro, Formosa, GO 73813-010
Tel: +55(61) 3642-1900
EMail: iesgo@iesgo.edu.br
Website: http://www.iesgo.edu.br

Diretor Presidente: José Albino Filho

Courses
Administration (Administration); **Computer Science** (Computer Networks; Computer Science); **Law** (Law); **Literature** (Literature); **Mathematics** (Mathematics); **Nursing** (Nursing); **Pedagogy**

History: Founded 2000.

Main Language(s) of Instruction: Portuguese

Degrees and Diplomas: *Bacharelado; Licenciatura; Especialização/Aperfeiçoamento*
Last Updated: 29/06/10

IGUAÇU FACULTY
Faculdade Iguaçu
Avenida Botucaris, 1590, Bairro Santa Cruz, Capanema,
PR 85760-000
Tel: +55(46) 3552-1464
Fax: +55(46) 3552-1464
EMail: faculdade.iguacu@yahoo.com.br
Website: http://www.faculdadeiguacu.edu.br/

Diretora: Andreza Piton Farina

Courses
Administration (Administration); **Graduate Studies** (Special Education); **Information Systems** (Information Sciences)

History: Founded 2004.

Main Language(s) of Instruction: Portuguese

Degrees and Diplomas: *Bacharelado.* Also Postgraduate diploma.
Last Updated: 01/09/10

IGUAÇU UNIVERSITY - NOVA IGUAÇU
Universidade Iguaçu (UNIG)
Avenida Abílio Augusto Távora 2134, Redenção, Nova Iguaçu,
Rio de Janeiro 26260000
Tel: +55(21) 2765-4000
EMail: unig@unig.br
Website: http://www.unig.br

Reitor: Antonio José Mayhé Raunheitti **EMail:** reitoria@unig.br

Centres
Community Health Studies (Community Health); **Environmental Studies** (Environmental Studies); **Law and Society Research** (Law; Social Studies)

Faculties
Biological and Health Sciences (Biological and Life Sciences; Dentistry; Health Sciences; Medicine; Pharmacy; Physical Education; Physical Therapy; Speech Therapy and Audiology); **Education and Letters** (Arts and Humanities; Education; Literature; Modern Languages; Philosophy); **Exact Sciences and Technology** (Chemistry; Computer Engineering; Computer Science; Data Processing; Mathematics; Natural Sciences; Physics; Technology); **Law and Applied Social Sciences** (Accountancy; Administration; Economics; Law)

Laboratories
Educational Technology (Educational Technology)

Further Information: Also University Hospital

History: Founded 1969 as Faculdade de Filosofia, Ciências e Letras; Incorporated other Faculties and acquired present status and title 1993. A private institution under the supervision of the Sociedade de Ensino Superior da Nova Iguaçu.

Governing Bodies: Conselho Universitário

Academic Year: March to December

Admission Requirements: Secondary school certificate and competitive entrance examination

Main Language(s) of Instruction: Portuguese

Degrees and Diplomas: *Bacharelado*; *Licenciatura*; *Mestrado*: Business Administration; Juridical Sciences

Special Facilities: Native Plants Vivarium

Publications: Revista da UNIG *(quarterly)*
Last Updated: 11/05/10

IMPACTA FACULTY OF TECHNOLOGY
Faculdade Impacta Tecnologia (FIT)
Rua Arabé, 71, Vila Clementino, São Paulo, SP 04042-070
Tel: +55(11) 3262-5007
EMail: impacta@proeduc.org
Website: http://www.impacta.edu.br/

Diretor Geral: Célio Antunes de Souza

Courses
Graduate Studies (Business Administration; Computer Science; Design; Graphic Design; Information Management; Information Technology; Law; Management; Marketing; Safety Engineering; Software Engineering); **Undergraduate Studies** (Administration; Computer Networks; Computer Science; Data Processing; Design; Information Sciences; Public Administration)

Degrees and Diplomas: *Tecnólogo*; *Bacharelado*; *Especialização/Aperfeiçoamento*
Last Updated: 01/09/10

INCONFIDÊNCIA FACULTY
Faculdade Inconfidência (FI)
Rua Santa Rita Durão, 1160, Funcionários, Belo Horizonte, MG 30140-908
Tel: +55(31) 4009-0931
EMail: joseroberto@fead.br

Reitor: Jamis Prado de Oliveira

Courses
Occupational Therapy; **Physical Therapy** (Physical Therapy)
History: Founded 2006.
Main Language(s) of Instruction: Portuguese
Degrees and Diplomas: *Bacharelado*
Last Updated: 01/09/10

INDEPENDENT FACULTY OF THE NORTH EAST
Faculdade Independente do Nordeste
Avenida Luís Eduardo Magalhães, 1305, Candeias, Vitória da Conquista, BA 45055-030
Tel: +55(77) 3161-1000
EMail: celianevesfainor@gmail.com
Website: http://www.fainor.com.br/
Diretor Geral: Edgard Larry Andrade Soares

Courses
Graduate Studies (Educational Administration; Higher Education; Management; Physical Therapy; Toxicology; Transport Management); **Undergraduate Studies** (Accountancy; Administration; Architecture; Computer Engineering; Dentistry; Electrical Engineering; Law; Nursing; Pharmacy; Physical Therapy; Production Engineering)

History: Founded 2001.

Degrees and Diplomas: *Bacharelado*; *Especialização/Aperfeiçoamento*. Also MBA.
Last Updated: 01/09/10

INEDI - CESUCA FACULTY
Faculdade INEDI - CESUCA
Rua Silvério Manoel da Silva, 160, Bairro Colinas, Cachoeirinha, RS 94940-243
Tel: +55(51) 3396-1000
Fax: +55(51) 3396-1000
EMail: cesuca@cesuca.edu.br
Website: http://www.cesuca.com.br/

Diretor Geral: Antonio Carlos Peixoto da Silva
EMail: direcaogeral@cesuca.edu.br

Courses
Accountancy (Accountancy); **Administration** (Administration); **Mathematics** (Mathematics); **Pedagogy** (Pedagogy); **Psychology** (Psychology)

Degrees and Diplomas: *Bacharelado*; *Licenciatura*
Last Updated: 01/09/10

INESC FACULTIES
Faculdades INESC
Rua Celina Lisboa Frederico 142, Centro, Unaí, Minas Gerais 38610000
Tel: +55(38) 3677-4747
EMail: inesc@inesc.br
Website: http://www.inesc.br

Diretor: Romualdo Neiva Gonzaga

Courses
Accountancy (Accountancy); **Agro-industrial Production Engineering** (Agricultural Engineering); **Business Administration** (Business Administration); **Computer Science** (Computer Science); **Law**; **Pedagogy** (Pedagogy)

History: Founded 1994.

Main Language(s) of Instruction: Portuguese

Degrees and Diplomas: *Bacharelado*; *Especialização/Aperfeiçoamento*; *Mestrado*
Last Updated: 29/06/10

INESP FACULTY - NATIONAL INSTITUTE OF EDUCATION AND RESEARCH
Faculdade INESP - Instituto Nacional de Ensino e Pesquisa
Av. Getúlio Dornelles Vargas, 1340, Jardim Primavera, Jacareí, SP 12308-390
Tel: +55(12) 3962-2800 +55(12) 3951-9524
EMail: inesp@inesp.edu.br
Website: http://www.inesp.edu.br/

Diretor Geral: Álvaro Ferreira Lisboa Jr.

Courses
Graduate Studies (Accountancy; Health Administration; Management; Marketing; Physiology; Rehabilitation and Therapy; Transport and Communications; Transport Management); **Undergraduate Studies** (Business Administration)

Degrees and Diplomas: *Bacharelado*; *Especialização/Aperfeiçoamento*. Also MBA.
Last Updated: 01/09/10

INFNET INSTITUTE
Instituto INFNET
Rua São José, 90, 2° piso, Rio de Janeiro, RJ 20010-020
Tel: +55(21) 2122 8800
EMail: infnet@infnet.edu.br
Website: http://www.infnet.edu.br/

Diretor: Eduardo Ramos

Courses
Graduate Studies (Computer Networks; Computer Science; Data Processing; Design; E-Business/Commerce; Information Technology; Marketing; Software Engineering; Video)

Schools
Communication and Digital Design (Advertising and Publicity; Graphic Design); **Information Technology** (Computer Networks; Information Technology; Software Engineering)

Degrees and Diplomas: *Tecnólogo*; *Bacharelado*. Also Postgraduate diploma and MBA.
Last Updated: 16/03/11

INFÓRIUM FACULTY OF TECHNOLOGY
Faculdade de Tecnologia Infórium
Rua dos Timbiras, 1532, Lourdes, Belo Horizonte, MG 30140-060
Tel: +55(31) 2103-2103
EMail: inforium@inforium.com.br
Website: http://www.inforium.com.br/

Courses
Graduate Studies (Business Administration; Information Technology); **Undergraduate Studies** (Computer Networks; Finance; Health Administration; Human Resources; Information Sciences; Software Engineering; Transport Management)

Further Information: Also João Pinheiro Campus.

History: Founded 1999 as Escola Técnica Infórium. Acquired present title and status 2003.

Degrees and Diplomas: *Tecnólogo*; *Bacharelado*. Also Postgraduate Diploma.
Last Updated: 01/09/10

INGA FACULTY
Faculdade Ingá (UNINGA)
Avenida Colombo 9.727, Km 130, Maringá, Paraná 87070810
Tel: +55(44) 3225-5009
Fax: +55(44) 3225-5009
EMail: uninga@uninga.br
Website: http://www.uninga.br

Diretor: Ricardo Benedito de Oliveira EMail: diretoria@uninga.br

Courses
Biology (Biology); **Biomedicine** (Biomedicine); **Dentistry** (Dentistry); **Medicine** (Medicine); **Nursing**; **Nutrition** (Nutrition); **Pharmacy**; **Physical Education** (Physical Education); **Physiotherapy** (Physical Therapy); **Psychology** (Psychology); **Social Services** (Social and Community Services); **Speech Therapy**

History: Founded 1999.

Main Language(s) of Instruction: Portuguese

Degrees and Diplomas: *Bacharelado*; *Licenciatura*; *Especialização/Aperfeiçoamento*; *Mestrado*
Last Updated: 06/07/10

INSTITUTE OF ADVANCED STUDIES OF THE AMAZON
Instituto de Estudos Superiores da Amazônia (IESAM)
Avenida Gov. José Malcher 1148, Nazaré, Belém, Pará 66055260
Tel: +55(91) 4005-5400
Fax: +55(91) 4005-5407
EMail: iesam@iesam.com.br
Website: http://www.iesam.com.br

Diretor: Antônio Marcos de Lima Araújo

Courses
Accountancy (Accountancy); **Administration** (Administration; Agricultural Business; Environmental Management); **Cinema and**

Television (Cinema and Television); **Design** (Design); **Economics** (Economics); **Engineering** (Automation and Control Engineering; Computer Engineering; Computer Networks; Engineering; Telecommunications Engineering); **Information Systems**; **Social Communication**; **Tourism** (Tourism)

History: Founded 2000.

Main Language(s) of Instruction: Portuguese

Degrees and Diplomas: *Tecnólogo*; *Bacharelado*; *Especialização/Aperfeiçoamento*; *Mestrado*
Last Updated: 15/06/10

INSTITUTE OF AGRICULTURAL SCIENCES
Instituto Superior de Ciências Agrárias (ISAP)
Rodovia MG 352, s/n, km 35, Zona Rural, Pitangui, MG 35650-000
Tel: +55(37) 3271-4004
EMail: isap@funedi.edu.br
Website: http://www1.funedi.edu.br/funedi/novo/index.php/isapprincipal.html

Presidente: Gilson Soares

Courses
Agronomy (Agronomy)
Degrees and Diplomas: *Bacharelado*
Last Updated: 23/09/10

INSTITUTE OF APPLIED HUMAN AND SOCIAL SCIENCES OF ABAETÉ
Instituto Superior de Ciências Humanas e Sociais Aplicadas de Abaeté (ISAB)
Rua João Gonçalves, 197, Bairro Amazonas, Abaeté, MG 35620-000
Tel: +55(37) 3541-2172
EMail: isab@funedi.edu.br
Website: http://www1.funedi.edu.br/funedi/novo/index.php/isab.html

Courses
Accountancy (Accountancy); **Administration** (Administration); **Social Services** (Social and Community Services)

History: Founded 2001.

Degrees and Diplomas: *Bacharelado*
Last Updated: 23/09/10

INSTITUTE OF APPLIED THEOLOGY
Instituto Superior de Teologia Aplicada (INTA)
Rua Coronel Antônio Rodrigues Magalhães, 359, Dom Expedito Lopes, Caixa Postal, 10, Sobral, CE 62050-100
Tel: +55(88) 3614-3232
Fax: +55(88) 3614-3232
EMail: inta2@zipmail.com.br
Website: http://www.inta.edu.br/

Diretor Geral: Oscar Rodriguez Junior

Courses
Undergraduate Studies (History; Nursing; Nutrition; Pedagogy; Pharmacy; Physical Education; Physical Therapy; Social and Community Services; Teacher Training; Theology; Veterinary Science)

History: Founded 2003.

Degrees and Diplomas: *Bacharelado*; *Licenciatura*
Last Updated: 28/09/10

INSTITUTE OF EDUCATION
Instituto Superior de Educação (ISED-TRÊS PONTAS)
Pça. D' Aparecida, 57, Centro, Três Pontas, MG 37190-000
EMail: rondineli@unis.edu.br
Website: http://portal.unis.edu.br/

Courses
Pedagogy (Pedagogy)
Degrees and Diplomas: *Licenciatura*
Last Updated: 23/09/10

INSTITUTE OF EDUCATION AND CULTURE OF CUIABA

Instituto Cuiabá de Ensino e Cultura
Rua Oswaldo da Silva Corrêa e Rua Santa Filomena, 621,
Santa Marta, Cuiabá, MT 78048-005
Tel: +55(65) 3621-2000
EMail: marcioacbarros@yahoo.com.br
Website: http://www.icec.edu.br

Diretor: Pedro Américo Frugoli

Courses
Accountancy (Accountancy); **Administration** (Administration);
Computer Science (Computer Science); **Law** (Law); **Physiotherapy** (Physical Therapy); **Social Communication** (Advertising and Publicity); **Tourism** (Tourism)

History: Founded 2002.

Main Language(s) of Instruction: Portuguese

Degrees and Diplomas: *Bacharelado*

Libraries: Biblioteca Mãe Bonifácia
Last Updated: 27/09/10

INSTITUTE OF EDUCATION AND HIGHER EDUCATION OF CAMPINAS

Instituto de Educação e Ensino Superior de Campinas
Rua Antônio Ferreira Laranja, 57, Jd Garcia (paralela à Av. Jhon
Boyd Dunlop), Campinas, SP 13061-100
Tel: +55(19) 3227-6152
EMail: coordenacaogeral@iescamp.com.br
Website: http://www.iescamp.com.br/capa

Diretora: Maria José Di Santo Navarro

Courses
Administration (Administration); **Pedagogy** (Pedagogy)

History: Founded 2005.

Main Language(s) of Instruction: Portuguese

Degrees and Diplomas: *Bacharelado*; *Licenciatura*

Libraries: Yes
Last Updated: 23/09/10

INSTITUTE OF EDUCATION AND HIGHER EDUCATION OF SAMAMBAIA

Instituto de Educação e Ensino Superior de Samambaia
Qn 406 A/E N°: 01, Região Administrativa XII, Samambaia, Brasília,
DF 72310-060
Tel: +55(61) 3358-5057
EMail: faculdadesiesa@terra.com.br

Diretor: Jaime de Lima Damasceno

Courses
Accountancy (Accountancy); **Administration** (Administration);
History (History); **Letters** (Literature); **Pedagogy** (Pedagogy)

History: Founded 2001

Main Language(s) of Instruction: Portuguese

Degrees and Diplomas: *Bacharelado*; *Licenciatura*
Last Updated: 27/09/10

INSTITUTE OF EDUCATION AND RESEARCH OF ITUIUTABA

Instituto Superior de Ensino e Pesquisa de Ituiutaba (ISEPI)
Rua Geraldo Moisés da Silva, s/n, Campus Universitario, Ituiutaba,
MG 38302-192
Tel: +55(34) 3271-9922
EMail: isepi@ituiutaba.uemg.br
Website: http://www.ituiutaba.uemg.br/isepi.php

Courses
Undergraduate Studies (Agrobiology; Computer Engineering;
Electrical Engineering; Information Sciences; Information Technology; Law; Pedagogy; Psychology)

Degrees and Diplomas: *Tecnólogo*; *Bacharelado*
Last Updated: 28/09/10

INSTITUTE OF EDUCATION AND RESEARCH OF THE STATE OF SAO PAULO

Instituto Paulista de Ensino e Pesquisa (IPEP)
Rua Maria Paula 35 1°, Andar Bela Vista, São Paulo,
São Paulo 01319001
Tel: +55(11) 3107-3558
EMail: rcc.sp@ipep.edu.br
Website: http://www.ipep.edu.br

Diretor: Erico Rodrigues Bacelar

Courses
Administration (Administration); **Advertising**; **Computer Science**
(Computer Science); **Information Systems**; **Radio, TV and Multimedia**

Faculties
Technology (*Campinas - FATEC CAMPINAS*); **Technology** (*Sao Paulo - FATEC SP*)

Further Information: Also campuses in Campinas and Natal.
History: Founded 1992.

Degrees and Diplomas: *Bacharelado*; *Licenciatura*; *Mestrado*
Last Updated: 14/06/10

INSTITUTE OF EDUCATION AND TECHNOLOGY

Instituto de Educação e Tecnologias
Rua Portugal, 15, Comércio, Salvador, BA
Tel: +55(71) 3242-0929
Website: http://www.inet.edu.br

Diretor: Waldeck Ornélas

Courses
Letters (Literature); **Pedagogy** (Pedagogy)

History: Founded 2005.

Main Language(s) of Instruction: Portuguese

Degrees and Diplomas: *Licenciatura*

Libraries: Yes
Last Updated: 23/09/10

INSTITUTE OF EDUCATION OF BARRETOS

Instituto Superior de Educação de Barretos (ISEB)
Rua 6, N° 963, Barretos, SP 14780-713
Tel: +55(17) 3322-7258 +55(17) 3324-5729
Fax: +55(17) 3324-5729
EMail: iseb@isebarretos.edu.br
Website: http://www.isebarretos.edu.br/

Courses
Graduate Studies (Education; Educational Psychology; Special
Education); **Undergraduate Studies** (English; Literature; Pedagogy; Spanish)
Last Updated: 24/09/10

INSTITUTE OF EDUCATION OF BICAS

Instituto Superior de Educação de Bicas (ISEB)
Rua Áurea Aliada Pereira Lanha, 107, Centro, Bicas, MG 36600-000
Tel: +55(32) 3271-1043
EMail: isebfeap@hotmail.com
Website: http://www.faculdadebicas.adm.br/

Diretora: Eliane Abdo Barreto

Courses
Pedagogy (Pedagogy)

Degrees and Diplomas: *Licenciatura*
Last Updated: 24/09/10

INSTITUTE OF EDUCATION OF CAJAZEIRAS

Instituto Superior de Educação de Cajazeiras
Avenida Brasil, s/n, Rodovia PB 393, Jardim Adalgisa, Cajazeiras,
PB 58900-000
Tel: +55(83) 3531-3011
Fax: +55(83) 3531-3011
EMail: iseccajazeiras@bol.com.br

Courses
Pedagogy (Pedagogy)
Degrees and Diplomas: *Licenciatura*
Last Updated: 24/09/10

INSTITUTE OF EDUCATION OF CAMPO VERDE

**Instituto Superior de Educação de Campo Verde
(ISE - CAMPO VERDE)**
Avenida Brasília, 1010, Centro, Campo Verde, MT 78840-000
Tel: +55(66) 3419-1918
EMail: campoverde@unirondon.br

Diretor Geral: Adonias Gomes de Almeida

Courses
Pedagogy (Pedagogy)
Degrees and Diplomas: *Licenciatura*
Last Updated: 27/09/10

INSTITUTE OF EDUCATION OF CAXIAS

Instituto Superior de Educação de Caxias (ISEC)
Rua Coronel Libânio Lobo, 805, Centro, Caxias, MA 65608-010
Tel: +55(99) 3521-2905 +55(99) 3421-6106
EMail: fai@faionline.com.br
Website: http://www.faionline.com.br/

Courses
Teacher Training (Teacher Training)
Last Updated: 27/09/10

INSTITUTE OF EDUCATION OF FLORESTA

Instituto Superior de Educação de Floresta (ISEF)
Avenida Deputado Audemar Ferraz, 98, Centro, Floresta,
PE 56400-000
Tel: +55(87) 3877-1509
EMail: isef_floresta@hotmail.com

Diretora: Maria Auxiliadora Marquim Nogueira Cornélio.

Courses
Pedagogy (Pedagogy); Teacher Training (Teacher Training)
Degrees and Diplomas: *Licenciatura*
Last Updated: 27/09/10

INSTITUTE OF EDUCATION OF GUARATUBA

**Instituto Superior de Educação de Guaratuba
(ISEPE-GUARATUBA)**
Rua Joaquim Menelau de Almeida Torres, 101, Piçarras,
Guaratuba, PR 83280-000
Tel: +55(41) 3442-8500
Fax: +55(41) 3442-8500
EMail: direcao@isepeguaratuba.com.br
Website: http://www.isepe.com.br

Diretor: Luis Machaliszyn Filho

Courses
Graduate Studies (Agricultural Business; Art Education; Art Therapy; Business Education; Dance; Distance Education; Ecology; Education; Educational Administration; Environmental Management; Foreign Languages Education; Gerontology; Health Sciences; Higher Education; History; Information Technology; Mathematics Education; Native Language Education; Pharmacy; Physical Education; Psychiatry and Mental Health; Public Health; Rehabilitation and Therapy; Social and Community Services; Social Policy; Social Welfare; Special Education; Sports; Transport Management); **Undergraduate Studies** (Administration; Law; Pedagogy)

Degrees and Diplomas: *Bacharelado*; *Licenciatura*; *Especialização/Aperfeiçoamento*. Also MBA.
Last Updated: 27/09/10

INSTITUTE OF EDUCATION OF IGUAPE

Instituto Superior de Educação de Iguape (ISE IGUAPE)
Avenida Ademar de Barros, 1070, Porto do Ribeira, Iguape,
SP 11920-000
Tel: +55(13) 3841-4966
Fax: +55(13) 3841-4966
EMail: secretariafisa@scelisul.com.br
Website: http://www.fisa.edu.br/

Diretor Presidente: Aderbal Alfredo Calderari Bernardes

Courses
Pedagogy (Pedagogy); **Special Education** (Special Education)
History: Founded 2005.
Main Language(s) of Instruction: Portuguese
Degrees and Diplomas: *Licenciatura*. Also Postgraduate Diploma.
Last Updated: 27/09/10

INSTITUTE OF EDUCATION OF ITAPERUNA

Instituto Superior de Educação de Itaperuna (ISEI)
Rua Aloísio Dias Moreira, 320, Presidente Costa e Silva, Itaperuna,
RJ 28300-000
Tel: +55(22) 3822-4315
Fax: +55(22) 3822-5722
EMail: ise.itaperuna@faetec.rj.gov.br
Website: http://www.faetec.rj.gov.br/iseitaperuna/

Diretora: Helena Marina de Moraes Won-Held.

Courses
Literacy Education (Literacy Education); **Teacher Training** (Teacher Training)
History: Founded 2001.
Main Language(s) of Instruction: Portuguese
Degrees and Diplomas: *Licenciatura*. Also Postgraduate Diploma.
Last Updated: 27/09/10

INSTITUTE OF EDUCATION OF IVOTI

Instituto Superior de Educaçao Ivoti
rua Júlio Hauser n°171, bairro 7 de Setembro, Ivoti, RS 93900-000
Tel: +55(51) 3563-8600
EMail: isei@isei.edu.br
Website: http://www.isei.edu.br

Diretor: Manfredo Carlos Wachs

Courses
Pedagogy (Pedagogy)
History: Founded 2002.
Main Language(s) of Instruction: Portuguese
Degrees and Diplomas: *Licenciatura*; *Especialização/Aperfeiçoamento*
Libraries: Biblioteca Machado de Assis
Last Updated: 28/09/10

INSTITUTE OF EDUCATION OF JANAÚBA

Instituto Superior de Educação de Janaúba
Rua Pio Xii 100, Janaúba, MG 39440-000
Tel: +55(38) 3821-1070
EMail: isejan@isejan.com.br
Website: http://www.isejan.com.br/index2.htm

Diretora: Marielle de Almeida Cavalcanti Araújo

Courses
Geography (Geography); **Letters** (Literature); **Teacher Training** (Teacher Training)
History: Founded 2003.
Main Language(s) of Instruction: Portuguese
Degrees and Diplomas: *Bacharelado*; *Licenciatura*; *Especialização/Aperfeiçoamento*
Last Updated: 27/09/10

INSTITUTE OF EDUCATION OF JUNQUEIRÓPOLIS

Instituto Superior de Educacão de Junqueirópolis
Rua Piauí, 801 – Distrito Comercial e Industrial, Junqueirópolis,
SP 17890-000
Tel: +55(18) 3842-1636
EMail: secretaria.unialpa@cesd.br
Website: http://www.unialpa.cesd.br
Diretora: Cleide Alves de Arruda

Courses
Letters (Literature); **Pedagogy** (Pedagogy)
History: Founded 2002.
Main Language(s) of Instruction: Portuguese
Degrees and Diplomas: *Licenciatura*
Libraries: Biblioteca Liliana Gonzaga
Last Updated: 27/09/10

INSTITUTE OF EDUCATION OF NOVA ANDRADINA

Instituto de Ensino de Nova Andradina
Rua Alcides Menezes de Farias n° 1067 - Centro, Nova Andradina,
MS 79750-000
Website: http://www.iesna.com.br
Diretor: Valentim Loli

Courses
Administration (Administration); **Education** *(Postgraduate)* (Education); **Health** *(Postgraduate)*
History: Founded 1988.
Main Language(s) of Instruction: Portuguese
Degrees and Diplomas: *Bacharelado*; *Especialização/Aperfeiçoamento*
Libraries: Yes
Last Updated: 18/03/11

INSTITUTE OF EDUCATION OF PARANA

Instituto Superior de Educação do Paraná
Rua Monte Castelo 375, Cianorte, PR 87200-000
Tel: +55(44) 3225 - 1197
EMail: insep@fnsep.edu.br
Website: http://www.fainsep.edu.br/
Diretor: Argemiro Aluísio Karling

Courses
Pedagogy (Pedagogy)
History: Founded 2004.
Main Language(s) of Instruction: Portuguese
Degrees and Diplomas: *Licenciatura*; *Especialização/Aperfeiçoamento*
Libraries: Yes
Last Updated: 28/09/10

INSTITUTE OF EDUCATION OF PESQUEIRA

Instituto Superior de Educação de Pesqueira
Rua José Nepomuceno das Neves 47, 51 e 57, Pesqueira,
PE 55200-000
Tel: +55(87)3835-1211
EMail: isepnet@hotmail.com
Website: http://www.isepnet.com.br
Diretor: Luiz Henrique Dinize Silva

Courses
Letters (Literature); **Pedagogy** (Pedagogy); **Philosophy** (Philosophy)
History: Founded 2002.
Main Language(s) of Instruction: Portuguese
Degrees and Diplomas: *Licenciatura*; *Especialização/Aperfeiçoamento*; *Mestrado*
Last Updated: 29/09/10

INSTITUTE OF EDUCATION OF SALGUEIRO

Instituto Superior de Educação de Salgueiro
Rua Prof♀ Maria Nita de Oliveira, 169 –Bairro Divino Espírito Santo,
Salgueiro, PE
Tel: +55(87) 3871-0940
EMail: educaises@zipmail.com.br
Website: http://www.iseseduca.com.br
Diretora: Solange Nunes de Sousa e Oliveira

Courses
Pedagogy (Pedagogy); **Philosophy** (Philosophy)
History: Founded 2002.
Main Language(s) of Instruction: Portuguese
Degrees and Diplomas: *Licenciatura*; *Especialização/Aperfeiçoamento*
Last Updated: 27/09/10

INSTITUTE OF EDUCATION OF SANTO ANTÔNIO DE PÁDUA

Instituto Superior de Educação de Santo Antônio de Pádua
Km 25 da Rodovia Rj 186 S/N, Antigo Parque de Exposição Gov.
Chagas Freitas, Divinéia, Santo Antônio de Pádua, RJ 28470-000
EMail: ise.padua@faetec.rj.gov.br
Website: http://www.faetec.rj.gov.br
Diretora: Maria Cristina Souza Machado

Courses
Teacher Training (Teacher Training)
Degrees and Diplomas: *Licenciatura*
Last Updated: 28/09/10

INSTITUTE OF EDUCATION OF SÃO PAULO

Instituto Paulista de Ensino (FIPEN)
Rua Euclides da Cunha, 377, Centro, Osasco, SP 06016-030
Tel: +55(11) 3133-5408
Fax: +55(11) 3133-5446
Website: http://www.fipen.edu.br/

Courses
Administration (Administration); **Human Resources** (Human Resources)
Degrees and Diplomas: *Tecnólogo*; *Bacharelado*
Last Updated: 23/09/10

INSTITUTE OF EDUCATION OF SAO PAULO - SINGULARIDADES

Instituto Superior de Educação de São Paulo - SINGULARIDADES
Av. Brigadeiro Faria Lima, 386 Pinheiros, São Paulo, SP 05426-200
Tel: +55(11) 3034-5445
EMail: singularidades@singularidades.com.br
Website: http://www.singularidades.com.br/
Diretora: Gisela Wajskop

Courses
Pedagogy (Pedagogy)
History: Founded 2001.
Main Language(s) of Instruction: Portuguese
Degrees and Diplomas: *Licenciatura*
Last Updated: 28/09/10

INSTITUTE OF EDUCATION OF SERRA

Instituto Superior de Educação da Serra (FABAVI)
Rua 1d Ue-I, Lote 02, 80, Setor Centro Industrial da Grande Vitória -
CIVIT, CIVIT II, Serra, ES 29161-848
Tel: +55(27) 3328-6283
Fax: +55(27) 3328-6283
EMail: Bernadete.Passos@FABAVI.br
Website: http://www.fabavi.br

Courses
Undergraduate Studies (Biological and Life Sciences; Physical Education)

Degrees and Diplomas: *Licenciatura*
Last Updated: 24/09/10

INSTITUTE OF EDUCATION OF THE VALLEY OF THE JURUENA

Instituto Superior de Educação do Vale do Juruena
Avenida Gabriel Müller s/n, Módulo I, Juína 78320-000
Tel: +55(66) 3566-1875
EMail: secretaria@ajes.edu.br
Website: http://www.ajes.edu.br

Diretor: Clodis Antonio Menegaz EMail: clodis@ajes.edu.br

Courses
Geography (Geography); **Letters** (Literature); **Mathematics** (Mathematics); **Pedagogy** (Pedagogy); **Psychology** (Psychology); **Theology** (Theology)

History: Founded 2005.

Main Language(s) of Instruction: Portuguese

Degrees and Diplomas: *Licenciatura*; *Especialização/Aperfeiçoamento*
Last Updated: 01/10/10

INSTITUTE OF EDUCATION OF THE WESTERN ZONE

Instituto Superior de Educação da Zona Oeste (ISE ZONA OESTE)
Rua Manoel Caldeira de Alvarenga, 1203, Quintino-Bocaiúva, Rio de Janeiro, RJ 23070-200
EMail: ise.uezo@faetec.rj.gov.br
Website: http://www.faetec.rj.gov.br/

Courses
Teacher Training (Teacher Training)

Degrees and Diplomas: *Licenciatura*
Last Updated: 24/09/10

INSTITUTE OF GRADUATE AND UNDERGRADUATE STUDIES

IPOG - Instituto de Pós-Graduação e Graduação (IPOG)
Rua T-55 Qd 96 lt 11, n.580, Setor Bueno, Goiânia, GO 74215-170
Tel: +55(62) 3945-5050
Fax: +55(62) 3945-5050
EMail: cursos@ipog.edu.br
Website: http://www.ipog.edu.br/

Diretor: Paulo José Santana

Courses
Graduate Studies (Agricultural Business; Architecture; Business Administration; Business and Commerce; Civil Law; Constitutional Law; Construction Engineering; Cosmetology; Criminal Law; Criminology; Economics; Education; Engineering; Environmental Engineering; Environmental Management; Environmental Studies; Finance; Health Administration; Health Sciences; Higher Education; Information Technology; Interior Design; Leadership; Management; Marketing; Occupational Health; Pharmacy; Safety Engineering; Transport Management); **Undergraduate Studies** (Administration)

History: Founded 2001.

Degrees and Diplomas: *Bacharelado*. Also Postgraduate diploma and MBA.
Last Updated: 29/09/10

INSTITUTE OF HEALTH SCIENCES

Instituto Superior de Ciências da Saúde (INCISA)
Av. Barão Homem de Melo, 4324, Estoril, Belo Horizonte, MG 30450-250
Tel: +55(31) 3297-7960
EMail: imamterapias@imamterapias.com.br
Website: http://www.incisaimam.com.br/brasil/

Diretor Geral: Paulo César Barbosa Noleto
EMail: diretorgeral@incisaimam.com.br

Courses
Graduate Studies (Acupuncture; Biotechnology; Dietetics; Management; Pharmacology; Physical Therapy; Traditional Eastern Medicine; Water Management); **Undergraduate Studies** (Biological and Life Sciences; Environmental Management)

Further Information: Also Ipatinga and Juiz de Fora units.

Degrees and Diplomas: *Tecnólogo*; *Bacharelado*; *Licenciatura*. Also Postgraduate Diploma.
Last Updated: 23/09/10

INSTITUTE OF HIGHER EDUCATION AND ADVANCED TRAINING OF VITORIA

Instituto de Ensino Superior e Formação Avançada de Vitória (IESFAVI)
Avenida Nossa Senhora da Penha 1800, Vermelho, Vitória, Espirito Santo 29045400
Tel: +55(27) 3325-0244
Fax: +55(27) 3324-1500
EMail: favi@favi.br
Website: http://www.favi.br/IESFAVI/index.asp

Diretor: Rodrigo Cambará Arantes Garcia de Paiva
EMail: direcao@favi.br

Courses
Administration (Administration; Hotel Management; Human Resources; International Business; Marketing; Systems Analysis); **Computer Science** (Computer Science); **Law** (Law); **Pedagogy** (Pedagogy); **Physiotherapy** (Physical Therapy); **Psychology**; **Social Communication**; **Tourism** (Tourism)

History: Founded 2000.

Main Language(s) of Instruction: Portuguese

Degrees and Diplomas: *Tecnólogo*; *Bacharelado*
Last Updated: 15/06/10

INSTITUTE OF HIGHER EDUCATION IN PROFESSIONAL TRAINING

Instituto de Ensino Superior de Formação Profissional
Rua Tibiriçá N°870, Centro, Ribeirão Preto, SP 14010-090
EMail: ceforp@coc.com.br

Diretor: Durval Antunes Filho

Courses
Letters (Literature)

History: Founded 2007.

Main Language(s) of Instruction: Portuguese

Degrees and Diplomas: *Licenciatura*
Last Updated: 27/09/10

INSTITUTE OF HIGHER EDUCATION OF ACRE

Instituto de Ensino Superior do Acre (IESACRE)
Travessa Ponta Pora 100 - Capoeira, Rio Branco, Acre 69910900
Tel: +55(68) 3223-4331
EMail: aesacre@uol.com.br
Website: http://www.iesacre.edu.br

Diretor Geral: Sergio Guimaraes da Costa Florido

Courses
Administration (Administration); **Journalism**; **Social Services** (Social and Community Services); **Systems Analysis** (Systems Analysis)

History: Founded 1999.

Main Language(s) of Instruction: Portuguese

Degrees and Diplomas: *Bacharelado*
Last Updated: 16/06/10

INSTITUTE OF HIGHER EDUCATION OF AMAPÁ

Instituto de Ensino Superior do Amapá (IESAP)
Avenida Feliciano Coelho, 125, Trem, Macapá, AP 68901-025
Tel: +55(96) 3222-6400 +55 (96) 3222-6605
Fax: +55(96) 3222-6403
EMail: iesap@iesap.edu.br
Website: http://www.iesap.edu.br/

Diretor Administrativo: José Adauto Teixeira Rodrigues

Courses
Graduate Studies (Educational and Student Counselling; English; French; Higher Education; Hotel Management; Management; Pedagogy; Tourism); **Undergraduate Studies** (English; French; Literature; Pedagogy; Philosophy; Spanish; Tourism; Translation and Interpretation)

Degrees and Diplomas: *Bacharelado*; *Licenciatura*; *Especialização/Aperfeiçoamento*
Last Updated: 21/09/10

INSTITUTE OF HIGHER EDUCATION OF BAHIA

Instituto Baiano de Ensino Superior
Rua Luiz Portela da Silva, 628 - Itaigara, Salvador, BA
Tel: +55(71) 3496-4050
EMail: ibesbahia@yahoo.com.br
Website: http://www.ibes.edu.br

Diretor: Daniel Jorge dos Santos Branco Borges

Courses
Accountancy (Accountancy); **Administration** (Administration); **Computer Science** (Computer Science); **Law** (Law); **Physiotherapy** (Physical Therapy); **Social Communication** (Advertising and Publicity); **Tourism** (Tourism)

History: Founded 2002.
Main Language(s) of Instruction: Portuguese
Degrees and Diplomas: *Bacharelado*
Last Updated: 22/09/10

INSTITUTE OF HIGHER EDUCATION OF BAURU

Instituto de Ensino Superior de Bauru (IESB)
Alfredo Ruiz, n° 3-53 Bairro Centro, Bauru, São Paulo 17015120
Tel: +55(14) 4009-8800
Fax: +55(14) 223-8574
EMail: said@iesbpreve.com.br
Website: http://www.iesbpreve.com.br

Diretor: Said Yusuf Abu Lawi

Courses
Accountancy (Accountancy); **Administration** (Business Administration; International Business); **Design**; **Law** (Law); **Letters**; **Pedagogy**

History: Founded 2001.
Main Language(s) of Instruction: Portuguese
Degrees and Diplomas: *Bacharelado*; *Licenciatura*
Last Updated: 16/06/10

INSTITUTE OF HIGHER EDUCATION OF BLUMENAU

Instituto Blumenauense de Ensino Superior (IBES)
Rua Pandiá Calógeras, 272, Blumenau, Santa Catarina 8901040
Tel: +55(47) 2111-2900
Fax: +55(47) 2111-2900
EMail: u@unibes.com.br
Website: http://www.unibes.edu.br

Diretor Presidente: Anselmo Medeiros

Courses
Accountancy (Accountancy); **Administration**; **Advertising** (Advertising and Publicity); **Foreign Trade** (International Business); **International Relations** (International Relations); **Journalism**

(Journalism); **Law** (Law); **Marketing**; **Physical Education** (Physical Education); **Psychology** (Psychology); **Public Relations** (Public Relations); **Secretarial Studies**; **Tourism** (Tourism)

History: Founded 2000.

Degrees and Diplomas: *Bacharelado*; *Especialização/Aperfeiçoamento*; *Mestrado*
Last Updated: 17/06/10

INSTITUTE OF HIGHER EDUCATION OF CURITIBA

Instituto de Ensino Superior de Curitiba
Rua Engenheiro Benedito Mário da Silva N°35, Cajuru, Curitiba, PR 82970-000
Tel: +55(41) 3015-4601
EMail: marcioacbarros@yahoo.com.br

Diretor: Jorge Brihy Junior

Courses
Accountancy (Accountancy); **Administration** (Administration); **Social Communication** (Advertising and Publicity); **Tourism** (Tourism)

History: Founded 2007.
Main Language(s) of Instruction: Portuguese
Degrees and Diplomas: *Bacharelado*
Last Updated: 27/09/10

INSTITUTE OF HIGHER EDUCATION OF GARÇA

Instituto de Ensino Superior de Garça (IESG)
Rua América 281, Labienópolis, Garça, São Paulo 17400000
Tel: +55(14) 3406-1108
Fax: +55(14) 3406-1108
EMail: secretaria@iesg.edu.br
Website: http://www.iesg.edu.br

Diretor Geral: João Cassettari

Courses
Accountancy (Accountancy); **Administration**; **Letters**; **Mathematics**; **Pedagogy** (Pedagogy)

History: Founded 1999.
Main Language(s) of Instruction: Portuguese
Degrees and Diplomas: *Bacharelado*; *Licenciatura*; *Especialização/Aperfeiçoamento*; *Mestrado*
Last Updated: 16/06/10

INSTITUTE OF HIGHER EDUCATION OF ITAPETININGA

Instituto Itapetiningano de Ensino Superior (IIES)
Rua Isolina de Morais Rosa 727, Vila Nastri, Itapetininga, São Paulo 18206320
Tel: +55(15) 3275-8700
EMail: diretoria@ites.edu.br
Website: http://www.iies.edu.br

Diretor: Carlos Eduardo Fernandes d'Andretta

Courses
Accountancy (Accountancy); **Administration** (Administration; Marketing); **Advertising**; **Law** (Law); **Tourism**

History: Founded 1998.
Main Language(s) of Instruction: Portuguese
Degrees and Diplomas: *Bacharelado*
Last Updated: 15/06/10

INSTITUTE OF HIGHER EDUCATION OF JOÃO MONLEVADE

Instituto de Ensino Superior de João Monlevade (IES/FUNCEC)

Rua 16 24, Prédio 1, Vila Tanque, João Monlevade,
Minas Gerais 35930408
Tel: +55(31) 3852-4000 +55(31) 3852-4216
Fax: +55(31) 3852-4434
EMail: iesfuncec@funcec.br
Website: http://www.funcec.br

Diretor Geral: Alessandro Moreira Lima

Courses

Accountancy; **Administration**; **Environmental Studies**; Journalism (Journalism); **Law**; **Literature** (Literature); **Pedagogy**

History: Founded 1972.

Main Language(s) of Instruction: Portuguese

Degrees and Diplomas: *Bacharelado*; *Especialização/Aperfeiçoamento*

Last Updated: 16/06/10

INSTITUTE OF HIGHER EDUCATION OF MARANHÃO

Instituto de Estudos Superiores do Maranhão (IESMA)

Rua do Rancho, 110, Centro, São Luís, MA 65010-010
Tel: +55(98) 3231-3235
EMail: iesma@terra.com.br
Website: http://www.iesma.com.br/

Diretor Geral: Abraão Marques Colins **EMail:** amcolins@elo.com.br

Courses

Graduate Studies (Education; Educational Psychology; Gerontology; Higher Education; History; Management; Philosophy; Religious Education); **Undergraduate Studies** (Philosophy; Religious Studies; Theology)

History: Founded 1984 as Centro Teológico do Maranhão (CETEMA). Acquired present title 1999.

Degrees and Diplomas: *Bacharelado*; *Licenciatura*; *Especialização/Aperfeiçoamento*

Last Updated: 22/09/10

INSTITUTE OF HIGHER EDUCATION OF MATO GROSSO

Instituto de Ensino Superior de Mato Grosso

Rua Santa Filomena, 621, Santa Marta, Cuiabá, MT
Tel: +55(65) 3621-8959
EMail: assessoriadareitoria@yahoo.com.br
Website: http://www.unilist.com.br/iesmt

Diretor: Jorge Brihy Junior

Courses

Accountancy (Accountancy); **Administration** (Administration); **Social Communication** (Advertising and Publicity); **Tourism** (Tourism)

History: Founded 2007.

Main Language(s) of Instruction: Portuguese

Degrees and Diplomas: *Bacharelado*

Libraries: Yes
Last Updated: 24/09/10

INSTITUTE OF HIGHER EDUCATION OF MINAS GERAIS

Instituto de Ensino Superior de Minas Gerais

Av. São Sebastião n° 968, Bairro Estudantil, Sabinópolis,
MG 39750-000
Tel: +55(33) 3423-1017.
EMail: uessaltdaa@hotmail.com
Website: http://www.iesmig.com.br

Diretor: Evandro José de Pinho

Courses

Biology (Biology); **Nursing** (Nursing)

History: Founded 2006.

Main Language(s) of Instruction: Portuguese

Degrees and Diplomas: *Bacharelado*
Last Updated: 24/09/10

INSTITUTE OF HIGHER EDUCATION OF NORTHERN RIO GRANDE

Instituto de Ensino Superior do Rio Grande do Norte (IESRN)

Av. Prudente de Morais, 4.890, Lagoa Nova, Natal, RN 59077-000
Tel: +55(84) 3234-3637
Website: http://www.unilist.com.br/iesrn/

Diretora Geral: Josefa Iluminata de Macedo Borba
Tel: +55(84) 3234-3,551; +55(84) 3234-3533
EMail: iluminataborba@yahoo.com.br

Courses

Undergraduate Studies (Accountancy; Administration; Advertising and Publicity; Tourism)

Degrees and Diplomas: *Bacharelado*
Last Updated: 21/09/10

INSTITUTE OF HIGHER EDUCATION OF OLINDA

Instituto de Ensino Superior de Olinda

Av. Sigismundo Gonçalves, 375 Carmo, Olinda, PE
Tel: +55(81) 3492-9701
EMail: newton_moraes@uol.com.br
Website: http://www.unilist.com.br/ieso

Diretor: Newton Roberto Gregório de Moraes

Courses

Administration (Administration); **Law** (Law); **Social Communication** (Advertising and Publicity)

History: Founded 2002.

Main Language(s) of Instruction: Portuguese

Degrees and Diplomas: *Bacharelado*
Last Updated: 27/09/10

INSTITUTE OF HIGHER EDUCATION OF PARAISÓPOLIS

Instituto de Educação Superior de Paraisópolis

Rua Cumbica 37, Paraisópolis, MG 37660-000
Tel: +55(35) 3651-1139
EMail: fep@sbs-net.com.b

Diretor: Luiz Gonzaga da Rosa

Courses

Teacher Training (Teacher Training)

History: Founded 2003.

Main Language(s) of Instruction: Portuguese

Degrees and Diplomas: *Licenciatura*
Last Updated: 27/09/10

INSTITUTE OF HIGHER EDUCATION OF PIEDADE

Instituto de Ensino Superior de Piedade

Rua José Braz Moscow, n° 252, bairro Piedade,
Jaboatão dos Guararapes, PE 54410-390
Tel: +55(81) 3361-1941
EMail: marcioacbarros@yahoo.com.br
Website: http://www.fape-pe.edu.br/FAPEIII/index.asp

Diretor: Newton Moraes

Courses

Administration (Administration); **Social Communication** (Advertising and Publicity); **Tourism** (Tourism)

History: Founded 2002.

Main Language(s) of Instruction: Portuguese

Degrees and Diplomas: *Bacharelado*

Libraries: Biblioteca Francisco Brennand
Last Updated: 27/09/10

INSTITUTE OF HIGHER EDUCATION OF POUSO ALEGRE

Instituto de Educação Superior de Pouso Alegre
Rua Ver. Antonio Augusto Ribeiro, 95, Centro, Pouso Alegre,
MG 37550-000
Tel: +55(35) 3421-2891
EMail: asmec@asmec.br
Website: http://www.asmecpa.com.br

Courses
Administration (Administration); **Pedagogy** (Pedagogy)
History: Founded 2009.
Main Language(s) of Instruction: Portuguese
Degrees and Diplomas: *Bacharelado*; *Licenciatura*; *Especialização/Aperfeiçoamento*
Last Updated: 27/09/10

INSTITUTE OF HIGHER EDUCATION OF RONDÔNIA

Instituto de Ensino Superior de Rondônia (IESUR)
Avenida Capitão Sílvio 2738 - Fundos c/ Rua Rio Negro,
Ariquemes, Rondônia 78932000
Tel: +55(69) 3535-5005
Fax: +55(69) 3535-5008
EMail: iesur@faarnet.com.br
Website: http://www.faar.edu.br

Diretor: Ivanilde José Rosique

Courses
Administration (Administration; Business Administration); **Computer Science** (Computer Science); **Law**; **Psychology** (Psychology)
History: Founded 2001.
Main Language(s) of Instruction: Portuguese
Degrees and Diplomas: *Bacharelado*; *Especialização/Aperfeiçoamento*
Last Updated: 16/06/10

INSTITUTE OF HIGHER EDUCATION OF THE FUPESP

Instituto de Ensino Superior da Fupesp
Rua Aldo Moretti N°181, Jardim Ouro Negro, Paulínia,
SP 13140-000
EMail: superint@fupespp.gov.br

Courses
Administration
History: Founded 2003.
Main Language(s) of Instruction: Portuguese
Degrees and Diplomas: *Bacharelado*
Last Updated: 24/09/10

INSTITUTE OF HIGHER EDUCATION OF THE GREATER FLORIANÓPOLIS

Instituto de Ensino Superior da Grande Florianópolis (IES)
Rua Vereador Walter Borges 424, Campinas, São José,
Santa Catarina 88101030
Tel: +55(48) 241-0674 +55(48) 241-4343
Fax: +55(48) 241-0674
EMail: iesalpha@intergate.com.br
Website: http://www.ies.edu.br

Diretor: Geraldo Majela Ferreira de Macedo

Courses
Accountancy; **Administration** (Business Administration; Hotel Management; Human Resources; Information Management; Marketing); **Advertising** (Advertising and Publicity); **Computer Science** (Computer Science); **Law** (Law); **Physiotherapy** (Physical Therapy); **Social Services**; **Tourism**
History: Founded 1999.
Main Language(s) of Instruction: Portuguese
Degrees and Diplomas: *Bacharelado*; *Especialização/Aperfeiçoamento*
Last Updated: 16/06/10

INSTITUTE OF HIGHER EDUCATION OF THE WEST OF THE STATE OF SAO PAULO

Instituto de Ensino Superior do Oeste Paulista (IESOP)
Avenida 23 55, Centro, Barretos, São Paulo 14781343
Tel: +55(17) 3325-2200
Fax: +55(17) 3325-2204
EMail: marcioacbarros@yahoo.com.br
Website: http://www.iesop.edu.br

Diretor: Antonio Mauro Alves

Courses
Tourism (Tourism)
History: Founded 1999.
Main Language(s) of Instruction: Portuguese
Degrees and Diplomas: *Bacharelado*
Last Updated: 16/06/10

INSTITUTE OF PHILOSOPHY AND THEOLOGY OF GOIÁS

Instituto de Filosofia e Teologia de Goiás (IFITEG)
7a Avenida, 531, Setor Leste Universitário, Goiânia, GO 74603-030
Tel: +55(62) 3218-3280 +55(62) 9183-1004
EMail: secretariageral@ifite.edu.br
Website: http://www.ifiteg.edu.br/

Diretor Geral: Juracy Cipriano da Silva

Courses
Graduate Studies (Art Therapy; Cinema and Television; Fashion Design; Management; Philosophy); **Undergraduate Studies** (Philosophy; Theology)
History: Founded 1982.
Degrees and Diplomas: *Bacharelado*; *Licenciatura*; *Especialização/Aperfeiçoamento*
Last Updated: 22/09/10

INSTITUTE OF SOCIAL AND HUMAN SCIENCES

Instituto de Ciências Sociais e Humanas - Januária (INCISOH)
Praça Tiradentes 164, Centro, Januária, Minas Gerais 39480000
Tel: +55(38) 3621-1403
Fax: +55(38) 3621-2056
EMail: ceiva@comnt.com.br
Website: http://www.ceiva.com.br

Diretora: Denise de Alkmim Falcão (1996-)

Courses
Geography (Geography); **History** (History); **Portuguese Literature**; **Teacher Training** (Teacher Training); **Tourism** (Tourism)
History: Founded 1995.
Main Language(s) of Instruction: Portuguese
Degrees and Diplomas: *Bacharelado*; *Licenciatura*; *Especialização/Aperfeiçoamento*
Last Updated: 17/06/10

INTEGRAL DIFFERENTIAL FACULTY

Faculdade Integral Diferencial (FACID)
Rua Rio Poty 2381, Horto Florestal, Teresina, Piauí 64051210
Tel: +55(86) 3216-7900
EMail: comunicacao@facid.com.br
Website: http://www.facid.com.br

Diretor Geral: Paulo Raimundo Machado Vale

Courses
Computer Science; **Dentistry** (Dentistry); **Law** (Law); **Medicine**; **Nursing** (Nursing); **Physiotherapy** (Physical Therapy); **Psychology** (Psychology)

History: Founded 2001.

Main Language(s) of Instruction: Portuguese

Degrees and Diplomas: *Bacharelado*; *Especialização/Aperfeiçoamento*; *Mestrado*
Last Updated: 06/07/10

INTEGRAL FACULTY OF TECHNOLOGY
Faculdade de Tecnologia Integral (CETI)
Avenida Marechal Floriano, 1226, Centro, Curitiba, PR 80230-110
Tel: +55(41) 3027-7554
Fax: +55(41) 3027-7554
EMail: assessoriaexecutiva@integralsien.com.br
Website: http://www.integralsien.com.br/

Courses
Financial Management (Finance); **Graduate Studies** (Accountancy; Finance; Management)

Degrees and Diplomas: *Tecnólogo*. Also MBA.
Last Updated: 25/08/10

INTEGRATED ADVENTIST FACULTIES OF MINAS GERAIS
Faculdades Integradas Adventistas de Minas Gerais (FADMINAS)
Rua Joaquim Gomes Guerra 590 Bairro Kennedy, Lavras, Minas Gerais 37200000
Tel: +55(35) 3822-3933
Fax: +55(35) 3822-3933
EMail: iaemg@iaemg.org; fiamg@iaemg.org.br
Website: http://www.iaemg.org.br
Diretor: Waldomiro Domingos dos Passos

Courses
Administration (Administration)
History: Founded 1999.

INTEGRATED BRAZILIAN FACULTIES - BOITUVA CAMPUS
Faculdades Integradas Brasileiras – campus Boituva (FIB)
Rodovia SP 129 Km 14, Campo de Boituva, Boituva, São Paulo 18550000
Tel: +55(15) 3363-3932
EMail: contato@fibsp.edu.br
Website: http://www.boituva.br
Diretor: Olavo Lázaro Munhoz Soares Filho

Courses
Accountancy (Accountancy); **Business Administration** (Business Administration); **Law** (Law); **Pedagogy** (Pedagogy)
History: Founded 2001 as Faculdades Integradas de Boituva. Acquired present title 2008.

Main Language(s) of Instruction: Portuguese

Degrees and Diplomas: *Bacharelado*; *Especialização/Aperfeiçoamento*
Last Updated: 17/06/10

INTEGRATED FACULTIES OF ANGELES
Faculdades Integradas de Angeles
Avenida da Saudade N°757, Vila Estádio, Araçatuba, SP 16020-070
EMail: deangeles@deangeles.com.br
Diretor: Valmir Leonardo Dos Santos

Courses
Administration (Administration); **Pedagogy** (Pedagogy)
History: Founded 2003.

Main Language(s) of Instruction: Portuguese

Degrees and Diplomas: *Bacharelado*; *Licenciatura*
Last Updated: 27/09/10

INTEGRATED FACULTIES OF ARIQUEMES
Faculdades Integradas de Ariquemes (FIAR)
Avenida Guaporé 3577, Setor Institucional, Setor 6, Ariquemes, Rondônia 78932000
Tel: +55(69) 3535-5977
Fax: +55(69) 3535-5977
EMail: fiar@fiar.com.br
Website: http://www.fiar.com.br
Diretor: Gilmar Utzig

Courses
Accountancy (Accountancy); **Administration**; **Biology** (Biology); **Geography** (Geography); **History**; **Letters**; **Mathematics** (Mathematics); **Pedagogy** (Pedagogy); **Tourism** (Tourism)

History: Founded 1990

Main Language(s) of Instruction: Portuguese

Degrees and Diplomas: *Bacharelado*; *Licenciatura*; *Especialização/Aperfeiçoamento*
Last Updated: 24/06/10

INTEGRATED FACULTIES OF BAURU
Faculdades Integradas de Bauru (FIB)
Rua Rodolfina dias Domingues 11, Quinta Ranieri, Jardim Ferraz, Bauru, São Paulo 17056100
Tel: +55(14) 3106-6200
Fax: +55(14) 3106-6200
EMail: contato@fibbauru.br
Website: http://www.fibbauru.br
Diretor Geral: José Augusto Vieira Ranieri

Courses
Administration (Administration); **Advertising** (Advertising and Publicity); **Agronomy** (Agronomy); **Biomedicine**; **Law** (Law); **Physical Education** (Physical Education); **Physiotherapy** (Physical Therapy); **Tourism** (Tourism)

History: Founded 1998.

Main Language(s) of Instruction: Portuguese

Degrees and Diplomas: *Tecnólogo*; *Bacharelado*; *Licenciatura*; *Especialização/Aperfeiçoamento*
Last Updated: 24/06/10

INTEGRATED FACULTIES OF BOTUCATU
Faculdades Integradas de Botucatu (FIB)
Avenida Leonardo Villas Boas 351, Vila Nova Botucatu, Botucatu, SP 18608901
Tel: +55(14) 6821-2500
Fax: +55(14) 6821-2500
EMail: secretaria@unifac.com.br
Website: http://www.unifac.com.br
Diretora Geral: Cecília B. Pires Tavares de Anderlini (1997-)
EMail: diretoria@unifac.com.br

Courses
Accountancy (Accountancy); **Administration** (Administration); **Economics** (Economics); **Letters**; **Pedagogy**; **Physical Education** (Physical Education); **Social Services**; **Tourism** (Tourism)
History: Founded 1993.

Main Language(s) of Instruction: Portuguese

Degrees and Diplomas: *Bacharelado*; *Licenciatura*; *Especialização/Aperfeiçoamento*; *Mestrado*
Last Updated: 24/06/10

INTEGRATED FACULTIES OF BRAZIL
Faculdades Integradas do Brasil (UNIBRASIL)
Rua Konrad Adenauer 442, Turumá, Curitibá, Paraná 82820540
Tel: +55(41) 361-4200
Fax: +55(41) 361-4200
EMail: unibrasil@unibrasil.com.br
Website: http://www.unibrasil.com.br
Diretor: Sérgio Ferraz de Lima

Schools
Administration (Accountancy; Administration; Tourism); **Communication Studies** (Advertising and Publicity; Design; Journalism; Public Relations); **Education and Humanities**; **Health Sciences** (Biology; Biomedicine; Nursing; Nutrition; Pharmacy; Physical Therapy; Psychology); **Law and International Relations** (International Relations; Law)

History: Founded 2000.

Main Language(s) of Instruction: Portuguese

Degrees and Diplomas: *Bacharelado*; *Especialização/Aperfeiçoamento*; *Mestrado*
Last Updated: 23/06/10

INTEGRATED FACULTIES OF CACOAL
Faculdades Integradas de Cacoal
Rua dos Esportes 1038, Incra, Cacoal, RO 78.976-215
Tel: +55(69) 3441-4503
Fax: +55(69) 3441-7002
EMail: unesc@unescnet.br
Website: http://www.unescnet.br

Diretor: Ismael Cury

Courses
Accountancy (Accountancy); **Business Administration**; **Computer Science** (Computer Science); **Economics**; **Environmental Engineering** (Environmental Engineering); **Law**; **Literature** (Literature); **Pedagogy** (Pedagogy); **Psychology** (Psychology); **Theology** (Theology)

History: Founded 1985.

Main Language(s) of Instruction: Portuguese

Degrees and Diplomas: *Bacharelado*; *Licenciatura*; *Especialização/Aperfeiçoamento*
Last Updated: 24/06/10

INTEGRATED FACULTIES OF CAMPO GRANDE
Faculdades Integradas Campo-Grandenses
Estrada da Caroba 685, Campo Grande, Rio de Janeiro, Rio de Janeiro 23085590
Tel: +55(21) 2413-5230 +55(21) 2413-5216
Fax: +55(21) 2413-5230 +55(21) 2413-5211
EMail: feuc@feuc.br
Website: http://www.feuc.br

Diretor: Hélio Rosa de Araújo

Courses
Computer Science; **Geography** (Geography); **History**; **Letters** (Literature); **Mathematics**; **Pedagogy** (Pedagogy); **Social Sciences** (Social Sciences)

History: Founded 1960 as Faculdade de Filosofia de Campo Grande. Acquired present status and title 2005.

Main Language(s) of Instruction: Portuguese

Degrees and Diplomas: *Bacharelado*; *Licenciatura*; *Especialização/Aperfeiçoamento*; *Mestrado*
Last Updated: 24/06/10

INTEGRATED FACULTIES OF CARATINGA
Faculdades Integradas de Caratinga (FIC)
Rua João Pinheiro 168, Centro, Caratinga, Minas Gerais 35300037
Tel: +55(33) 3321-2122
Fax: +55(33) 3321-1976
EMail: diretoria@doctum.com.br
Website: http://www.ficmg.edu.br

Diretor: Cláudio Cézar Azevedo de Almeida Leitão

Courses
Accountancy (Accountancy); **Computer Science** (Computer Science); **Engineering**; **Law** (Law); **Social Communication** (Communication Studies; Journalism; Public Relations); **Social Services** (Social Work); **Tourism** (Tourism)

History: Founded 1972. Acquired present status and title 2000.

Main Language(s) of Instruction: Portuguese

Degrees and Diplomas: *Bacharelado*; *Especialização/Aperfeiçoamento*
Last Updated: 24/06/10

INTEGRATED FACULTIES OF CASSILANDIA
Faculdades Integradas de Cassilândia (FIC)
Rua Martiniano José de Moura 470, Vila Pernambuco, Cassilândia, MS 79540000
Tel: +55(67) 3596-5538
EMail: secretaria@ficms.com.br
Website: http://www.ficms.com.br

Diretora: Dinorá Ferreira de Oliveira Fazio (1997-)

Courses
Business Administration (Administration; Business Administration); **Pedagogy**

History: Founded 1988.

Degrees and Diplomas: *Bacharelado*; *Especialização/Aperfeiçoamento*
Last Updated: 24/06/10

INTEGRATED FACULTIES OF CATAGUASES
Faculdades Integradas de Cataguases (FAFIC)
Rua Romualdo Menezes, S/n Menezes, Cataguases, Minas Gerais 36773084
Tel: +55(32) 3421-3109
EMail: secretaria@fafic.com.br
Website: http://www.fafic.com.br

Diretora: Ana Brígida Moreira Costa Cruz Couto
EMail: anabrigida@fafic.com.br

Courses
Administration (Administration); **Biology**; **Geography and Environment** (Environmental Studies; Geography); **History**; **Letters** (Literature); **Pedagogy** (Pedagogy); **Production Engineering**

History: Founded 1965.

Main Language(s) of Instruction: Portuguese

Degrees and Diplomas: *Bacharelado*; *Licenciatura*
Last Updated: 24/06/10

INTEGRATED FACULTIES OF COXIM
Faculdades Integradas de Coxim (FICO)
Rua Piaui 220, Morada Alto de São Pedro, Coxim, MS 79400000
Tel: +55(67) 3291-1406
Fax: +55(67) 3291-1406
EMail: fico@citinet.com.br
Website: http://www.uniderp.br/fico

Diretor Geral: Marcos Rodrigues Marques (1996-)
EMail: marcosmarques@mail.uniderp.br

Courses
Literature (Literature); **Tourism**

History: Founded 1996.

Main Language(s) of Instruction: Portuguese

Degrees and Diplomas: *Bacharelado*; *Licenciatura*
Last Updated: 24/06/10

INTEGRATED FACULTIES OF CRUZEIRO
Faculdades Integradas de Cruzeiro (FIC)
Rua Dom Bosco 35, Centro, Cruzeiro, SP 12701250
Tel: +55(12) 3141 1600
EMail: iesc@iconet.cxom.br
Website: http://www.ficsp.edu.br/index.php

Diretora: Betsy Grinberg (1991-)

Courses
Administration (Administration); **Geography** (Geography); **History** (History); **Letters** (Literature); **Pedagogy** (Pedagogy)

History: Founded 1972.

Main Language(s) of Instruction: Portuguese

Degrees and Diplomas: *Bacharelado*; *Especialização/Aperfeiçoamento*
Last Updated: 24/06/10

INTEGRATED FACULTIES OF DIAMANTINO

Faculdades Integradas de Diamantino (FID)
Rua Almirante Batista das Neves 1112, Centro, Diamantino,
Mato Grosso 78400000
Tel: +55(65) 3336-1133
Fax: +55(65) 3336-2709
EMail: fid@jkm.com.br
Website: http://www.fidedu.com.br

Diretor: Geraldo Magela

Courses
Accountancy (Accountancy); **Administration** (Administration);
Computer Science; **Letters** (Literature); **Pedagogy** (Pedagogy)

History: Founded 1989.

Main Language(s) of Instruction: Portuguese

Degrees and Diplomas: *Bacharelado*; *Especialização/Aperfeiçoamento*; *Mestrado*
Last Updated: 24/06/10

INTEGRATED FACULTIES OF ESPIRITO SANTO

**Faculdades Integradas Espírito Santenses
(FIESA)**
Rua Anselmo Serrat 199, Ilha de Monte Belo, Vitória,
Espirito Santo 29040410
Tel: +55(27) 2122-4100
Fax: +55(27) 2122-4139
EMail: faesa@faesa.br
Website: http://www.basf-cc.com.br

Diretor: Alexandre Nunes Theodoro (1990-)

Areas
Computer Science (Computer Networks; Computer Science);
Design (Fashion Design; Interior Design); **Education** (Biology;
Chemistry; Pedagogy; Physical Education); **Engineering** (Environmental Engineering; Production Engineering); **Law** (Law); **Management**; **Medical and Health Sciences** (Dentistry; Nursing;
Nutrition; Occupational Therapy; Psychology; Speech Therapy and
Audiology); **Social Communication** (Advertising and Publicity;
Journalism; Radio and Television Broadcasting)

Further Information: Also Campus II: Faculdades de Saúde e Meio
Ambiente, Faculdade de Educação e Comunicação Social (Vitória)
and Campus III: Faculdade Espírito-Santense (Cariacica)

History: Founded 1972.

Main Language(s) of Instruction: Portuguese

Degrees and Diplomas: *Bacharelado*; *Especialização/Aperfeiçoamento*
Last Updated: 17/03/11

INTEGRATED FACULTIES OF FÁTIMA DO SUL

**Faculdades Integradas de Fátima do Sul
(FIFASUL)**
Rua Tenente Antônio João 1410, Centro, Fátima do Sul,
MS 79700000
Tel: +55(67) 467-1307 +55(67) 467-1200
Fax: +55(67) 467-1344 +55(67) 467-1201
EMail: cer@fifasul.br

Diretor: Lauro Andrei Monteiro de Carvalho

Courses
Accountancy (Accountancy); **Administration** (Administration);
Literature (Literature); **Nursing**; **Pedagogy**; **Physical Education**
(Physical Education)

History: Founded 1980.

Main Language(s) of Instruction: Portuguese

Degrees and Diplomas: *Bacharelado*; *Especialização/Aperfeiçoamento*
Last Updated: 24/06/10

INTEGRATED FACULTIES OF HUMAN SCIENCES, HEALTH AND EDUCATION OF GUARULHOS

**Faculdades Integradas de Ciências Humanas, Saúde e
Educação de Guarulhos**
Rua Barão de Mauá 600, Centro, Guarulhos, São Paulo 07012040
Tel: +55(11) 6409-3533
Fax: +55(11) 6409 3533
EMail: documenta@fg.edu.br
Website: http://www.faculdadesdeguarulhos.edu.br

Diretora: Aparecida Najar (1995-)

Courses
Biology (Biology); **Business Administration**; **Geography** (Geography); **History** (History); **Letters** (Literature); **Mathematics**
(Mathematics); **Nursing** (Nursing); **Pedagogy** (Pedagogy); **Physiotherapy** (Physical Therapy); **Psychology** (Psychology)

History: Founded 1971.

Main Language(s) of Instruction: Portuguese

Degrees and Diplomas: *Bacharelado*; *Licenciatura*; *Especialização/Aperfeiçoamento*
Last Updated: 24/06/10

INTEGRATED FACULTIES OF ITAPETININGA

Faculdades Integradas de Itapetininga (FII)
Caixa Postal 24, Rodovia Raposo Tavares Km 162, S/n Campus,
Nova Itapetininga, Itapetininga, São Paulo 18203340
Tel: +55(15) 3376-9300
EMail: fii@fkb.br
Website: http://www.fkb.br

Diretor Geral: Eliel Ramos Maurício (1997-)

Courses
Administration (Administration); **Law** (Law); **Physical Education**
(Physical Education); **Public Relations**; **Social Communication**
(Communication Studies)

History: Founded 1968.

Main Language(s) of Instruction: Portuguese

Degrees and Diplomas: *Bacharelado*
Last Updated: 23/06/10

INTEGRATED FACULTIES OF ITARARÉ

Faculdades Integradas de Itararé
Rua João Batista Veiga 1725 Cruzeiro, Itararé, SP 18460000
Tel: +55(15) 3531-8484
Fax: +55(15) 3531-8484
EMail: fafit@itapevanet.com.br
Website: http://www.fafitfacic.com.br/

Diretor: Heron Conrado do Carmo Ferreira
EMail: diretor@fafitfacic.com.br

Courses
Accountancy (Accountancy); **Administration** (Administration;
Agricultural Business); **Computer Science** (Computer Science);
Law (Law); **Letters**; **Mathematics** (Mathematics); **Pedagogy**;
Physical Education; **Tourism** (Tourism)

History: Founded 1973.

Main Language(s) of Instruction: Portuguese

Degrees and Diplomas: *Tecnólogo*; *Bacharelado*; *Licenciatura*;
Especialização/Aperfeiçoamento; *Mestrado*
Last Updated: 23/06/10

INTEGRATED FACULTIES OF JACAREPAGUÁ

Faculdades Integradas de Jacarepaguá (FIJ)
Ladeira da Freguesia 196 Freguesia, Jacarepaguá, Rio de Janeiro,
Rio de Janeiro 22760090
Tel: +55(21) 3392-6646
Fax: +55(21) 3392-6503
EMail: fij@fij.br
Website: http://www.fij.br

Diretora Geral: Angela Jorge (1996-)

Courses

Accountancy; **Administration** (Administration); **Computer Science** (Computer Science); **Data Processing**; **Environmental Engineering** (Environmental Engineering); **Nursing** (Nursing); **Physical Education** (Physical Education); **Tourism** (Tourism)

History: Founded 1973 as Faculdade Maria Magalhães Pinto. Acquired present status and title 1989.

Main Language(s) of Instruction: Portuguese

Degrees and Diplomas: *Bacharelado*; *Especialização/Aperfeiçoamento*

Last Updated: 17/03/11

INTEGRATED FACULTIES OF JAÚ

Faculdades Integradas de Jaú (FIJ)
Rua Tenente Navarro 642, Chacara Miraglia, Jaú, SP 17207310
Tel: +55(14) 2104-3366
Fax: +55(14) 2104-3301
EMail: fundacao@fjaunet.com.br
Website: http://www.fjaunet.com.br/Fundacao/sl?id=28

Head: Cleusa Camillo Atique

Courses

Accountancy (Accountancy); **Administration** (Administration); **Computer Science** (Computer Science); **Geography** (Geography); History (History); **Law** (Law); **Literature** (Literature); **Mathematics** (Mathematics); **Nursing**; **Pedagogy**; **Social Communication** (Advertising and Publicity; Journalism)

History: Founded 1999.

Main Language(s) of Instruction: Portuguese

Degrees and Diplomas: *Bacharelado*; *Especialização/Aperfeiçoamento*

Last Updated: 23/06/10

INTEGRATED FACULTIES OF NAVIRAÍ

Faculdades Integradas de Naviraí (FINAV)
Rua Laurentino Pires de Arruda 220 Jardim Progresso, Naviraí, MS 79950000
Tel: +55(67) 461-2380
Fax: +55(67) 461-2380
EMail: finav@terra.com.br
Website: http://www.finav.br

Diretor: Ivolim Monteiro de Carvalho

Courses

Accountancy *(FACINAV)* (Accountancy); **Administration** (Administration); **Geography** (Geography); **Literature**; **Pedagogy**

History: Founded 1987.

Main Language(s) of Instruction: Portuguese

Degrees and Diplomas: *Bacharelado*; *Especialização/Aperfeiçoamento*

Last Updated: 23/06/10

INTEGRATED FACULTIES OF NOVA ANDRADINA

Faculdades Integradas de Nova Andradina (FINAN)
Avenida António Joaquim de Moura Andrade 338, Centro, Nova Andradina, MS 79750000
Tel: +55(67) 3441-1558
Fax: +55(67) 3441-1991
EMail: finan@finan.com.br
Website: http://www.finan.com.br

Diretor: Gláucio Hashimoto

Courses

Accountancy (Accountancy); **Administration** (Administration); Law; **Pedagogy** *(FENA)* (Pedagogy); **Tourism** *(FATUR)* (Tourism)

History: Founded 1998.

Main Language(s) of Instruction: Portuguese

Degrees and Diplomas: *Bacharelado*. Also postgraduate diplomas

Last Updated: 17/03/11

INTEGRATED FACULTIES OF OURINHOS

Faculdades Integradas de Ourinhos (FIO)
Rodovia BR153 Km339 + 400m, Bairro Água do Cateto, Ourinhos, São Paulo 19900011
Tel: +55(14) 3302-6400
Fax: +55(14) 3302-6401
EMail: secretaria@fio.edu.br
Website: http://fio.edu.br

Diretor: Bianor Costa Freire Colchesqui

Courses

Administration (Accountancy; Administration; Business Administration; International Business; Marketing; Public Administration); **Agronomy** (Agronomy); **Architecture and Urbanism**; **Biology** (Biology); **Fine Arts** (Fine Arts); **Geography** (Geography); **Hotel and Restaurant** (Hotel and Restaurant; Hotel Management); **Information Systems** (Information Management); **Law** (Law); **Modern Languages** (English; Modern Languages; Portuguese); **Nursing** (Nursing); **Pedagogy**; **Pharmacy** (Pharmacy); **Psychology** (Industrial and Organizational Psychology; Psychology); **Tourism** (Tourism); **Veterinary Science**

History: Founded 1970.

Main Language(s) of Instruction: Portuguese

Degrees and Diplomas: *Bacharelado*; *Licenciatura*; *Especialização/Aperfeiçoamento*; *Mestrado*

Last Updated: 23/06/10

INTEGRATED FACULTIES OF PARANAIBA

Faculdades Integradas de Paranaíba (FIPAR)
Rua Maclino de Queiroz 270, Jardim Redentora, Paranaiba, MS 79500000
Tel: +55(17) 3668-1945
Fax: +55(17) 3668-1945
EMail: fipar@netsite.com.br
Website: http://www.fipar.edu.br

Diretor: Edna Mendes de Medeiros

Courses

Accountancy; **Administration**; **Computer Science**; **Letters** (Literature); **Pedagogy**

History: Founded 1995.

Main Language(s) of Instruction: Portuguese

Degrees and Diplomas: *Bacharelado*; *Especialização/Aperfeiçoamento*

Last Updated: 23/06/10

INTEGRATED FACULTIES OF PATOS

Faculdades Integradas de Patos
Rua José Gomes Alves, S/n Térreo, Centro, Patos, PB 58700250
Tel: +55(83) 3421-2819
EMail: ffmascarenhas@uol.com.br
Website: http://www.ffm.com.br

Diretor: João Leuson Palmeira Gomes Alves

Courses

Biomedicine (Biomedicine); **Computer Science** (Computer Science); **Economics** (Economics); **Geography**; **History** (History); **Journalism** (Journalism); **Law** (Law); **Literature** (Literature); **Nursing**; **Pedagogy** (Pedagogy); **Physiotherapy**

History: Founded 1967 as Faculdade de Ciências Econômicas de Patos.

Main Language(s) of Instruction: Portuguese

Degrees and Diplomas: *Bacharelado*; *Especialização/Aperfeiçoamento*

Last Updated: 23/06/10

INTEGRATED FACULTIES OF PONTA PORÃ

Faculdades Integradas de Ponta Porã (FIP)
Rua Tiradentes 349, Centro, Ponta Porã, Mato Grosso do Sul 79900000
Tel: +55(67) 431-5851
EMail: recepcaofip@mail.uniderp.br
Website: http://www.uniderp.br/fip

Diretor Geral: Anibal Bess Formighieri

Courses
Administration (Administration; Marketing); **Computer Science** (Computer Science); **Law**; **Literature** (Literature)
History: Founded 1997.
Degrees and Diplomas: *Bacharelado*
Last Updated: 06/11/07

INTEGRATED FACULTIES OF RIBEIRÃO PIRES

Faculdades Integradas de Ribeirão Pires (FIRP)
Rua Coronel Oliveira Lima 3345 Parque Aliança, Ribeirão Pires, Säo Paulo 09404000
Tel: +55(11) 4828-2347
Fax: +55(11) 4828-5513
EMail: firp@firp.edu.br
Website: http://www.firp.edu.br

Diretora: Vera Ferro de Carvalho EMail: diretoria@firp.edu.br

Courses
Business Administration (Business Administration); **History** (History); **Letters** (English; History; Portuguese); **Mathematics** (Mathematics); **Pedagogy** (Pedagogy); **Physical Education**
History: Founded 1999 incorporating the Faculdade de Ciências e Letras de Ribeirão Pires and the Faculdade de Educação Física.
Main Language(s) of Instruction: Portuguese
Degrees and Diplomas: *Bacharelado*; *Licenciatura*
Last Updated: 23/06/10

INTEGRATED FACULTIES OF RIO CLARO

Faculdades Integradas Claretianas (FIC)
Avenida Santo Antônio Maria Claret 1724 Cidade Claret, Rio Claro, São Paulo 13503250
Tel: +55(19) 2111-6000
EMail: irani@claretanias.br
Website: http://www.claretianas.br

Diretor Geral: Luiz Claudemir Botteon

Secretária Geral: Irani Algisi

Diretor Acadêmico: Sávio Carlos Desan Scopinho

Courses
Administration; **Engineering** (Electrical and Electronic Engineering; Mechanical Engineering); **Environmental Management**; **Health** (Physical Education); **Information Systems** (Information Management); **Law** (Law); **Social Communication** (Advertising and Publicity; Journalism); **Teacher Training**
History: Founded 1970.
Degrees and Diplomas: *Bacharelado*; *Licenciatura*; *Especialização/Aperfeiçoamento*; *Mestrado*
Last Updated: 24/06/10

INTEGRATED FACULTIES OF RONDONÓPOLIS

Faculdades Integradas de Rondonópolis (FAIR)
Rua Floriano Peixoto 597, Centro, Rondonópolis, MT +55(66) 3411-0500
Tel: +55(66) 3411-0503
EMail: fair@unir-roo.br

Diretor Geral: Ernando Cabral Machado

Courses
Agronomy (Agronomy); **Business Administration** (Accountancy; Administration; Secretarial Studies); **Computer Science**; **Law** (Law); **Letters** (Literature)
History: Founded 1999 incorporating the Escola Superior de Informática de Rondonópolis and the Escola Superior de Ciências Contábeis de Rondonópolis.
Main Language(s) of Instruction: Portuguese
Degrees and Diplomas: *Tecnólogo*; *Bacharelado*; *Licenciatura*
Last Updated: 23/06/10

INTEGRATED FACULTIES OF SANTA FÉ DO SUL

Faculdades Integradas de Santa Fé do Sul (FUNEC)
Rua Oito, 854 - Centro, Santa Fé do Sul, São Paulo 15775000
Tel: +55(17) 3631-1046
EMail: fisadir@funecfisa.br
Website: http://www.funecsantafe.edu.br

Diretora: Eliana Izabel Scurciatto Fernandes

Courses
Administration; **Biology**; **Dentistry** (Dentistry); **Environmental Management** (Environmental Management); **Law**; **Letters**; **Mathematics**; **Nursing**; **Pedagogy**; **Physical Education** (Physical Education); **Physiotherapy**; **Social Services**; **Tourism**
History: Founded 1998.
Main Language(s) of Instruction: Portuguese
Degrees and Diplomas: *Bacharelado*; *Licenciatura*; *Especialização/Aperfeiçoamento*
Last Updated: 23/06/10

INTEGRATED FACULTIES OF SANTO ANDRÉ

Faculdades Integradas de Santo André (FEFISA)
Rua Clélia 161, Santo André, São Paulo 09130-010
Tel: +55(11) 4451-0700
Fax: +55(11) 4451-0700 +55(11) 4452-2435
EMail: info@fefisa.com.br
Website: http://www.fefisa.com.br

Diretora: Dinah Kohjuk Zekcer (1996-)

Courses
Nutrition (Nutrition); **Physical Education** (Physical Education); **Physiotherapy**
History: Founded 1973.
Main Language(s) of Instruction: Portuguese
Degrees and Diplomas: *Bacharelado*; *Licenciatura*; *Especialização/Aperfeiçoamento*
Last Updated: 23/06/10

INTEGRATED FACULTIES OF SÃO CARLOS

Faculdades Integradas de São Carlos (FADISC)
Rua Doutor Marino da Costa 786, Vila Nery, São Carlos, São Paulo 13560970
Tel: +55(16) 3362-4300
Fax: +55(16) 3362-4316
EMail: fadisc@fadisc.edu.br
Website: http://www.fadisc.edu.br

Diretor: Fábio Pereira Honda

Courses
Business Administration (Business Administration); **Computer Science**; **Engineering** (Civil Engineering; Engineering; Production Engineering); **Law** (Law); **Literature**; **Secretarial Studies**
Main Language(s) of Instruction: Portuguese
Degrees and Diplomas: *Bacharelado*; *Especialização/Aperfeiçoamento*
Last Updated: 23/06/10

INTEGRATED FACULTIES OF SAO PAULO

Faculdades Integradas de São Paulo (FISP)
Rua Engenheiro Isaac Milder 355 Morumbi, São Paulo, São Paulo 5688010
Tel: +55(11) 3758-3009
Fax: +55(11) 3758-7477
EMail: fisp@fisp.br
Website: http://www.fisp.br

Diretor Geral: Labibi Elias Alves da Silva (1998-)

Courses
Law; **Mechatronic Engineering** (Electronic Engineering; Mechanical Engineering); **Production Engineering** (Production Engineering)
History: Founded 1998.

Main Language(s) of Instruction: Portuguese

Degrees and Diplomas: *Bacharelado*; *Especialização/Aperfeiçoamento*; *Mestrado*

Last Updated: 23/06/10

INTEGRATED FACULTIES OF TÁNGARA DA SERRA

Faculdades Integradas de Tangará da Serra (FITS)
Avenida Brasil 2350 - N, Caixa Postal 211, Jardim Europa,
Tángara da Serra, MT 78300000
Tel: +55(65) 3326-6615
Fax: +55(65) 3326-7272
EMail: unitas@unitas.edu.br
Website: http://www.unitas.edu.br

Diretora Geral: Daniella Freire Krakhecke
EMail: daniella@unitas.edu.br

Diretora Acadêmica: Rosecler Goulart Pereira
EMail: diretoriaacademica@unitas.edu.br

Courses
Administration (Accountancy; Administration; Agricultural Business; Business Administration; Secretarial Studies); **Communication Studies** (Communication Studies); **Engineering** (Software Engineering); **Law** (Law); **Pedagogy**; **Tourism**

History: Founded 2000.

Main Language(s) of Instruction: Portuguese

Degrees and Diplomas: *Tecnólogo*; *Bacharelado*; *Licenciatura*; *Especialização/Aperfeiçoamento*

Last Updated: 23/06/10

INTEGRATED FACULTIES OF TAPAJÓS

Faculdades Integradas do Tapajós (ISES)
Rua Rosa Vermelha 335, Bairro Aeroporto Velho, Santarem,
PA 68010200
Tel: +55(91) 523-5088 +55(91) 523-1933
Fax: +55(91) 523-1989
EMail: fit@fit.br
Website: http://www.fit.br

Diretor: Helvio Moreira Arruda EMail: helvio@fit.br

Centres
.**Applied Social Sciences** (Accountancy; Administration; Advertising and Publicity; Economics; Journalism; Law; Social and Community Services); **Biological and Health Sciences**; **Exact Sciences and Technology** (Computer Networks; Computer Science)

History: Founded 1985 as Instituto Santareno de Ensino Superior.

Main Language(s) of Instruction: Portuguese

Degrees and Diplomas: *Bacharelado*; *Especialização/Aperfeiçoamento*

Last Updated: 23/06/10

INTEGRATED FACULTIES OF TERRA DE BRASILIA

Faculdades Integradas da Terra de Brasília (FTB)
Quadra 203 - Área Especial Lote 32 Recanto das Emas,
S/n Recanto das Emas, Brasília, DF 72610300
Tel: +55(61) 3333-9126
Fax: +55(61) 3333-9127
EMail: info@ftb.edu.br
Website: http://www.ftb.br

Diretora: Vanderci Carrara

Courses
Administration (Administration); **Agronomy** (Agronomy); **Biology**; **Food Processing** (Food Science; Food Technology); **History** (History); **Literature** (Literature); **Mathematics** (Mathematics); **Pedagogy**; **Tourism** (Tourism); **Veterinary Science** (Veterinary Science); **Zoology**

History: Founded 1999.

Main Language(s) of Instruction: Portuguese

Degrees and Diplomas: *Bacharelado*; *Especialização/Aperfeiçoamento*

Last Updated: 25/09/07

INTEGRATED FACULTIES OF THE CERTO UNION OF HIGHER EDUCATION

Faculdades Integradas da União de Ensino Superior Certo
Setor D Sul, Area Especial 06, Blocos I e II, Samdu Sul,
Região Administrativa III, Brasília, DF 72020600
Tel: +55(61) 3352-4996
Fax: +55(61) 3352-6404 +55(61) 3352-6209
EMail: unicerto@unicerto.com.br
Website: http://www.unicerto.com.br

Diretora: Mirian Rodrigues Nogueira Pereira

Courses
Administration (Administration); **Computer Science** (Computer Science); **Literature**; **Secretarial Studies** (Secretarial Studies)

History: Founded 2001.

Main Language(s) of Instruction: Portuguese

Degrees and Diplomas: *Bacharelado*; *Licenciatura*

Last Updated: 24/06/10

INTEGRATED FACULTIES OF THE EDUCATIONAL UNION OF PLANALTO CENTRAL

Faculdades Integradas da União Educacional do Planalto Central (FACIPLAC)
SHIS - QI 7 - Bloco E - Lago Sul, Brasília, DF
Tel: +55(61) 3248-5100
EMail: uniplac@uniplac.br
Website: http://www.uniplac.br

Diretor: Apparecido dos Santos

Faculties
Accountancy (Accountancy); **Architecture and Town Planning** (Architecture; Town Planning); **Business Administration** (Business Administration); **Computer Science**; **Dentistry** (Dentistry); **Law** (Law); **Medicine** (Medicine); **Nursing** (Nursing); **Pharmacy**; **Physiotherapy** (Physical Therapy); **Veterinary Science** (Veterinary Science)

History: Founded 1985.

Main Language(s) of Instruction: Portuguese

Degrees and Diplomas: *Bacharelado*; *Especialização/Aperfeiçoamento*; *Mestrado*

Last Updated: 24/06/10

INTEGRATED FACULTIES OF THE HEART OF JESUS

Faculdades Integradas Coração de Jesus
Rua Siqueira Campos, 483 – Centro, Santo André, SP 09020-240
Tel: +55(11) 4433-7477
EMail: joseroberto@fainc.com.br
Website: http://www.fainc.com.br

Diretora: Silvia Irene Pela EMail: diretora@fainc.com.br

Faculties
Art Education (Design; Fine Arts; Music; Theatre); **Library Studies** (Library Science); **Nutrition** (Nutrition); **Social Communication** (Advertising and Publicity)

History: Founded 1976.

Main Language(s) of Instruction: Portuguese

Degrees and Diplomas: *Bacharelado*; *Especialização/Aperfeiçoamento*

Libraries: Yes
Last Updated: 13/09/10

INTEGRATED FACULTIES OF THE STATE OF SÃO PAULO

Faculdades Integradas Paulista
Rua Serra de Jairé, 658, Belenzinho, São Paulo,
São Paulo 5007001
Tel: +55(11) 6823-4151
Fax: +55(11) 3862-6951
EMail: diretoria@ape.edu.br
Website: http://www.fipsp.edu.br

Diretor: João Alberto Fiorini Filho

Courses
Administration (Administration); **Biology**; **Computer Science** (Computer Science); **Letters**; **Mathematics** (Mathematics); **Pedagogy**
History: Founded 2005 through merger of Faculdade Batista de Administração e Informática and Faculdade Batista de Educação.

Main Language(s) of Instruction: Portuguese

Degrees and Diplomas: *Bacharelado*; *Licenciatura*; *Especialização/Aperfeiçoamento*
Last Updated: 22/06/10

INTEGRATED FACULTIES OF THE VALLEY OF RIBEIRA

Faculdades Integradas do Vale do Ribeira (FIVR)
Rua Oscar Yoshiaki Magário, S/n Térreo, Jardim Das Palmeiras, Registro, SP 11900000
Tel: +55(13) 6821-6122
Fax: +55(13) 6821-3571
EMail: scelisul@scelisul.com.br
Website: http://www.scelisul.com.br

Diretor Geral: Venâncio dos Santos Lopes
EMail: venacio@scelisul.com.br

Courses
Accountancy (Accountancy); **Biology** (Biology); **Business Administration**; **Chemistry** (Chemistry); **Computer Networks** (Computer Networks); **History** (History); **Law** (Law); **Letters**; **Mathematics** (Mathematics); **Pedagogy**; **Physical Education**; **Systems Analysis**
History: Founded 2000.

Main Language(s) of Instruction: Portuguese

Degrees and Diplomas: *Bacharelado*; *Licenciatura*; *Especialização/Aperfeiçoamento*
Last Updated: 23/06/10

INTEGRATED FACULTIES OF THE VALLEY OF THE IVAI

Faculdades Integradas do Vale do Ivaí (UNIVALE)
Avenida Minas Gerais 651 Centro, Ivaiporã, Paraná 86870000
Tel: +55(43) 3472-1414
Fax: +55(43) 3472-1414
EMail: dtecnica@univale.com.br
Website: http://www.univale.com.br

Diretora: Neila F. Estigarribia **EMail:** secuni@univale.com.br

Courses
Accountancy (Accountancy); **Administration** (Administration); **Law**; **Letters** (Literature); **Pedagogy** (Pedagogy); **Systems Analysis** (Systems Analysis)

Institutes
Estudos Avançados e Pós-Graduação (Administration; Education; Health Sciences)
History: Founded 1995.

Main Language(s) of Instruction: Portuguese

Degrees and Diplomas: *Bacharelado*; *Especialização/Aperfeiçoamento*
Last Updated: 23/06/10

INTEGRATED FACULTIES OF TRÊS LAGOAS

Faculdades Integradas de Três Lagoas (FITL)
Avenida Ponta Porã 2750, Distrito Industrial, Três Lagoas, MS 79610320
Tel: +55(67) 521-4761 +55(67) 521-9218
Fax: +55(67) 521-0327
EMail: aems@aems.com.br
Website: http://www.aems.com.br

Diretora Geral: Maria Lúcia Atique Gabriel (1998-)

Courses
Accountancy (Accountancy); **Administration** (Administration); **Advertising**; **Journalism** (Journalism); **Law** (Law); **Nursing** (Nursing); **Nutrition** (Nutrition); **Pedagogy** (Pedagogy); **Physical Education** (Physical Education); **Physiotherapy** (Physical Therapy); **Public Relations** (Public Relations); **Secretarial Studies**; **Social Services**; **Tourism** (Tourism)

History: Founded 1994.

Main Language(s) of Instruction: Portuguese

Degrees and Diplomas: *Bacharelado*; *Especialização/Aperfeiçoamento*; *Mestrado*
Last Updated: 23/06/10

INTEGRATED FACULTIES OF UPIS

Faculdades Integradas da Upis (UPIS)
SEP Sul EQ 712/912, S/n Conjunto A, Asa Sul, Brasília, DF 70390125
Tel: +55(61) 3445-6700
Fax: +55(61) 3346-8473
EMail: rodolpho@upis.br
Website: http://www.upis.br

Diretor Presidente: Vicente Nogueira Filho (1998-)

Courses
Accountancy (Accountancy); **Administration** (Administration; Hotel Management; Marketing); **Agronomy** (Agronomy); **Computer Science** (Computer Science; Data Processing); **Economics** (Economics); **Geography** (Geography); **History** (History); **Secretarial Studies** (Secretarial Studies); **Tourism** (Tourism); **Veterinary Medicine** (Veterinary Science); **Zoology** (Zoology)

History: Founded 1971.

Main Language(s) of Instruction: Portuguese

Degrees and Diplomas: *Tecnólogo*; *Bacharelado*; *Especialização/Aperfeiçoamento*; *Mestrado*
Last Updated: 24/06/10

INTEGRATED FACULTIES OF VÁRZEA GRANDE

Faculdades Integradas de Várzea Grande (FIAVEC)
Rua Artur Bernadses 525, Ipase, Várzea Grande, Mato Grosso 78125100
Tel: +55(65) 3686-3730
Fax: +55(65) 3686-1902
EMail: ive@bol.com.br
Website: http://www.ive.edu.br

Diretor: José Carlos de Mello

Courses
Journalism (Journalism); **Pedagogy** (Pedagogy)
History: Founded 2001.

Main Language(s) of Instruction: Portuguese

Degrees and Diplomas: *Bacharelado*; *Especialização/Aperfeiçoamento*
Last Updated: 05/10/07

INTEGRATED FACULTIES OF VITORIA

Faculdades Integradas de Vitória (FDV)
Rua Doutor João Carlos de Sousa 779, Santa Luzia, Vitória, Espirito Santo 29045410
Tel: +55(27) 3041-3672
Fax: +55(27) 3041-3663
EMail: secretaria@fdv.br
Website: http://www.fdv.br

Diretor: Antonio José Ferreira Abikair

Diretora Acadêmica: Paula Castello Miguel

International Relations: Igor Rodrigues Britto

EMail: internacional@fdv.br

Courses

Law (Civil Law; Ethics; Law; Public Law)

History: Founded 1995.

Main Language(s) of Instruction: Portuguese

Degrees and Diplomas: *Bacharelado*; *Licenciatura*; *Especialização/Aperfeiçoamento*; *Mestrado*

Last Updated: 23/06/10

INTEGRATED FACULTIES OF VITÓRIA DE SANTO ANTÃO

Faculdades Integradas de Vitória de Santo Antão (FAINTVISA)

Jardim São Vicente Ferrer 71, Cajá, Vitória de Santo Antão, PE 55600000

Tel: +55(81) 3523-1020

Fax: +55(81) 3523-1608

EMail: faintvisa@faintvisa.com.br

Website: http://www.faintvisa.com.br/v7/

Diretora: Maria das Gracas Malheiros De Souza Carneiro da Cunha

Courses

Administration (Administration); **Biology** (Biology); **Geography** (Geography); **History** (History); **Literature** (Literature); **Mathematics**; **Pedagogy** (Pedagogy); **Pharmacy** (Pharmacy); **Psychology** (Psychology); **Secretarial Studies** (Secretarial Studies); **Tourism**

History: Founded 1972 as Faculdade de Formação de Professores da Vitória de Santo Antão. Acquired present status and title 2003.

Main Language(s) of Instruction: Portuguese

Degrees and Diplomas: *Bacharelado*; *Licenciatura*; *Especialização/Aperfeiçoamento*

Last Updated: 23/06/10

INTEGRATED FACULTY OF ARAGUATINS

Faculdade Integrada de Araguatins (FAIARA)

Praça Rui Barbosa, 972, Centro, Araguatins, TO 77950-000

Tel: +55(63) 3474-2623

EMail: faiara_febip@yahoo.com.br

Website: http://faiara.com/

Courses

Graduate Studies (Educational Technology; Public Administration); **Undergraduate Studies** (Business Administration; Literature; Pedagogy)

Degrees and Diplomas: *Bacharelado*; *Licenciatura*. Also Postgraduate Diploma.

Last Updated: 02/09/10

INTEGRATED FACULTY OF BRAZIL

Faculdade Integrada do Brasil (FAIBRA)

Rua Simplício Mendes, 867, Centro Sul, Teresina, PI 64000-110

Tel: +55(86) 3218-1329 +55(86) 9925-5599

Fax: +55(86) 3236-1425

EMail: faibrateresina@hotmail.com

Reitor: Amilton Pereira

Courses

Pedagogy (Pedagogy)

History: Founded 2006.

Main Language(s) of Instruction: Portuguese

Degrees and Diplomas: *Bacharelado*

Last Updated: 02/09/10

INTEGRATED FACULTY OF CAMPO MOURÃO

Faculdade Integrado de Campo Mourão (CIES)

Avenida Irmãos Pereira 670, Caixa Postal 695, Centro, Campo Mourão, PR 87301010

Tel: +55(44) 523-1982

Fax: +55(44) 523-1982

EMail: gies@grupointegrado.br

Website: http://www.grupointegrado.br/index.php

Diretor Geral: Goro Saito

Courses

Administration; **Agronomy** (Agronomy); **Biology** (Biology); **International Relations** (International Relations); **Law** (Law); **Nursing** (Nursing); **Nutrition**; **Pedagogy** (Pedagogy); **Pharmacy**; **Physical Education**; **Systems Analysis** (Systems Analysis); **Veterinary Science**

History: Founded 1998.

Main Language(s) of Instruction: Portuguese

Degrees and Diplomas: *Bacharelado*; *Licenciatura*; *Especialização/Aperfeiçoamento*; *Mestrado*

Last Updated: 06/07/10

INTEGRATED FACULTY OF CEARA

Faculdade Integrada do Ceará (FIC)

Rua Vicente Linhares 308, Aldeota, Fortaleza, Ceará 60135270

Tel: +55(85) 4005-9990

Fax: +55(85) 4005-9953

EMail: fic@fic.br

Website: http://www.fic.br

Diretora Geral: Ana Flávia Alcântara Rocha Chaves

Courses

Accountancy (Accountancy); **Administration** (Administration; Hotel Management; International Business; Marketing); **Advertising** (Advertising and Publicity); **Computer Science** (Computer Science); **Journalism**; **Law** (Law); **Physical Education** (Physical Education); **Physiotherapy** (Physical Therapy); **Tourism** (Tourism)

History: Founded 1998.

Main Language(s) of Instruction: Portuguese

Degrees and Diplomas: *Bacharelado*; *Especialização/Aperfeiçoamento*

Last Updated: 29/10/07

INTEGRATED FACULTY OF GRANDE FORTALEZA

Faculdade Integrada da Grande Fortaleza (FGF)

Av. Porto Velho, 401, João XXIII, Fortaleza, CE 60525-571

Tel: +55(85) 3299-9900

Fax: +55(85) 3496-4384

EMail: fgf@fgf.edu.br

Website: http://www.fgf.edu.br/

Diretor Geral: José Liberato Barrozo Filho

Courses

Undergraduate Studies (Accountancy; Business Administration; Computer Science; Journalism; Law; Literature; Nursing; Physical Education; Teacher Training)

History: Founded 2000.

Degrees and Diplomas: *Bacharelado*; *Licenciatura*

Last Updated: 02/09/10

INTEGRATED FACULTY OF HIGHER EDUCATION OF COLINAS

Faculdade Integrada de Ensino Superior de Colinas (FIESC)

Rua Goianésia 1132 Novo Planalto, Colinas do Tocantins, TO 77760000

Tel: +55(63) 3476-2705

Fax: +55(63) 3476-1855

EMail: fiesc@fecolinas.edu.br

Website: http://www.fiesc.edu.br

Diretor Geral: Cleivane Peres dos Reis

Courses

Accountancy; **Geography** (Geography); **History** (History); **Law**; **Letters** (Literature); **Pedagogy** (Pedagogy); **Social Services**

History: Founded 2000.

Main Language(s) of Instruction: Portuguese

Degrees and Diplomas: *Bacharelado*; *Licenciatura*; *Especialização/Aperfeiçoamento*

Libraries: Biblioteca Americano do Brasil de Oliveira

Last Updated: 06/07/10

INTEGRATED FACULTY OF PERNAMBUCO

Faculdade Integrada de Pernambuco (FACIPE)

Rua José Osório, 76, Madalena, Recife, PE 50610-280
Tel: +55(81) 3073-8877
EMail: facipe@facipe.edu.br
Website: http://home.facipe.edu.br/

Diretor Geral: Walter Tenório Ferreira

Courses

Graduate Studies (Civil Security; Finance; Law; Real Estate); **Undergraduate Studies** (Administration; Cosmetology; Finance; Law; Management; Nursing; Radiology; Tourism)

History: Founded 2001.

Degrees and Diplomas: *Tecnólogo*; *Bacharelado*; *Especialização/Aperfeiçoamento*. Also MBA.

Last Updated: 02/09/10

INTEGRATED FACULTY OF RECIFE

Faculdade Integrada do Recife (FIR)

Avenida Eng. Abdias de Carvalho 1678, Madalena, Recife, Pernambuco 50720635
Tel: +55(81) 3227-83000
Fax: +55(81) 3227-8308
EMail: fir@fir.br
Website: http://www.fir.br

Diretor Geral: Cristiane Hengler EMail: chengler@fir.br

Courses

Administration; **Computer Science** (Computer Networks; Software Engineering); **International Relations** (International Relations); **Law** (Law); **Physiotherapy**; **Psychology**; **Speech Therapy** (Speech Therapy and Audiology); **Tourism** (Tourism)

History: Founded 1998.

Main Language(s) of Instruction: Portuguese

Degrees and Diplomas: *Bacharelado*; *Licenciatura*; *Especialização/Aperfeiçoamento*

Last Updated: 06/07/10

INTEGRATED FACULTY OF THE FALLS

Faculdade Integrada das Cataratas

Rua David Muffato, 367, Jardim Comercial das Bandeiras, Foz do Iguaçu, PR 85864-390
Tel: +55(45) 3520-1900
EMail: udc@udc.edu.br
Website: http://www.udc.edu.br

Courses

Administration (Administration); **Management** (Management)

Degrees and Diplomas: *Tecnólogo*; *Bacharelado*

Last Updated: 02/09/10

INTEGRATED INSTITUTE OF HIGHER EDUCATION - EDUCATIONAL FOUNDATION OF THE NORTH EAST OF MINAS GERAIS

Instituto de Ensino Superior Integrado - Fundação Educacional Nordeste Mineiro (IESI/FENORD)

Rua Teodolindo Pereira 111, Grão Pará, Teófilo Otoni, Minas Gerais 39800000
Tel: +55(33) 3522-2745
Fax: +55(33) 522-2745
EMail: fato@fenord.com.br
Website: http://www.fenord.com.br

Diretora: Eliane Scofleld Ferreira Miglio

Faculties

Administration; **Law**; **Philosophy, Science and Literature** (Literature; Mathematics; Pedagogy; Philosophy)

Institutes

Education (Teacher Training)

History: Founded 1990

Main Language(s) of Instruction: Portuguese

Degrees and Diplomas: *Bacharelado*

Last Updated: 15/06/10

INTEGRATED NATIONAL FACULTIES

Faculdades Integradas Nacional (FINAC)

Avenida Saturnino Rangel Mauro 1401, Jardim da Penha, Vitória, Espirito Santo 29060770
Tel: +55(27) 2123-2900
EMail: faculdadenacional1@yahoo.com.br
Website: http://www.finac.br

Diretor: Alexandre Zamprogno

Courses

Accountancy (Accountancy); **Administration** (Administration); **Architecture and Planning** (Architecture and Planning); **Economics**; **Law** (Law)

History: Founded 1999.

Main Language(s) of Instruction: Portuguese

Degrees and Diplomas: *Bacharelado*

Last Updated: 22/06/10

INTEGRATED REGIONAL FACULTIES OF AVARÉ

Faculdades Integradas Regionais de Avaré (FIRA)

Praça Prefeito Romeu Bretas 163, Centro, Avaré, São Paulo 18700902
Tel: +55(14) 3732-1133
Fax: +55(14) 3732-0799
EMail: secretaria@frea.edu.br
Website: http://www.fira.edu.br/

Diretor: Emerson Calil Rossetti EMail: direcaofira@frea.edu.br

Courses

Arts (Art Education; Cultural Studies; Design; Education; Visual Arts); **Biology** (Biology); **Chemistry** (Chemistry); **Letters** (Literature); **Mathematics**; **Pedagogy**; **Physical Education**

History: Founded 1969 as Faculdade de Ciências e Letras de Avaré. Acquired present status and title 2001.

Main Language(s) of Instruction: Portuguese

Degrees and Diplomas: *Bacharelado*; *Especialização/Aperfeiçoamento*

Last Updated: 22/06/10

INTEGRATION FACULTY - WESTERN ZONE

Faculdade Integração - Zona Oeste (FIZO)

Avenida Franz Voegeli 900, Vila Yara, Osasco, São Paulo 6020190
Tel: +55(11) 3681-0440
Fax: +55(11) 3681-0440
EMail: daex.aesa@unianhanguera.edu.br

Diretor Geral: Roberto Orlando Stersi Filho

Courses

Accountancy (Accountancy); **Administration**; **Law**; **Literature**; **Pedagogy** (Pedagogy); **Social Communication** (Advertising and Publicity; Journalism); **Teacher Training**; **Tourism** (Tourism)

History: Founded 1999.

Main Language(s) of Instruction: Portuguese

Degrees and Diplomas: *Bacharelado*; *Licenciatura*

INTEGRATION FACULTY TIETÊ

Faculdade Integração Tietê (FIT)
Rua Santa Terezinha, 425, Tietê 18530-000
Tel: +55 (15) 3282-7501 +55(15) 3282-7548
EMail: tatianajacob@faculdadetiete.com.br
Website: http://www.faculdadetiete.com.br/

Courses

Graduate Studies (Accountancy; Educational Administration; Educational Psychology; Finance; Health Administration; Human Resources; Nursing; Physiology; Public Health); **Undergraduate Studies** (Accountancy; Administration; Biomedicine; Literature; Nursing; Pedagogy; Physical Education; Production Engineering; Tourism)

Degrees and Diplomas: *Bacharelado*; *Licenciatura*; *Especialização/Aperfeiçoamento*
Last Updated: 01/09/10

INTERAMERICAN FACULTY OF PORTO VELHO - UNIRON

Faculdade Interamericana de Porto Velho - UNIRON
Avenida Mamoré, n° 1520, Cascalheira, Porto Velho,
RO 78919-541
Tel: +55(69) 3733-5000
EMail: diracademica@uniron.edu.br
Website: http://www.uniron.edu.br/

Faculties

Architecture (Architecture; Town Planning); **Biological and Agrarian Sciences** (Agronomy; Animal Husbandry; Biological and Life Sciences; Environmental Management); **Communication** (Advertising and Publicity; Journalism); **Education** (Literature; Pedagogy); **Graduate Studies** (Accountancy; Administrative Law; Architecture; Art History; Business Administration; Civil Law; Communication Studies; Computer Networks; Criminal Law; Criminology; Educational Psychology; Electrical Engineering; Environmental Management; Environmental Studies; Finance; Fiscal Law; Gynaecology and Obstetrics; Health Sciences; Higher Education; Human Resources; International Business; Journalism; Justice Administration; Labour Law; Law; Literature; Management; Nursing; Occupational Health; Oncology; Pedagogy; Political Sciences; Portuguese; Private Law; Psychology; Public Administration; Public Health; Rehabilitation and Therapy; Safety Engineering; Spanish; Special Education); **Health Sciences** (Nursing; Physical Therapy); **Law** (Law); **Managerial Sciences** (Accountancy; Business Administration; Business and Commerce; Human Resources; Public Administration); **Technology** (Computer Networks; Information Technology)

Further Information: Also UNIRON Shopping Unit.

History: Founded 1995. Became UNIRON 1999. Authorised 2001.

Degrees and Diplomas: *Tecnólogo*; *Bacharelado*; *Licenciatura*. Also Postgraduate Studies.
Last Updated: 02/09/10

INTERLAGOS FACULTY OF EDUCATION AND CULTURE

Faculdade Interlagos de Educação e Cultura (FINTEC)
Avenida Jangadeiro 111/445 Interlagos, São Paulo,
São Paulo 4815020
Tel: +55(11) 5666-2256
Fax: +55(11) 5666-6747
EMail: fintec@fac-interlagos.br
Website: http://www.fac-interlagos.br/

Diretor: João Jorge Peralta (1995-) EMail: dperalta@sti.com.br

Courses

Accountancy (Accountancy); **Administration**; **Computer Science** (Computer Science); **Law** (Law); **Letters**; **Mathematics** (Mathematics); **Pedagogy** (Pedagogy); **Physical Education** (Physical Education); **Physiotherapy**; **Tourism** (Tourism)

History: Founded 1995.

Degrees and Diplomas: *Bacharelado*; *Especialização/Aperfeiçoamento*
Last Updated: 06/07/10

INTERMUNICIPAL FACULTY OF THE NORTHWEST OF PARANA

Faculdade Intermunicipal do Noroeste do Paraná (FACINOR)
Rua Mato Grosso 240, Loanda, PR 87900000
Tel: +55(44) 3425-1037
Fax: +55(44) 3425-1037
EMail: facinor@facinor.br
Website: http://www.facinor.br

Diretor: Agenor de Oliveira Duarte

Courses

Administration (Administration); **Agricultural Business** (Agricultural Business); **Business Computing** (Business Computing); **Literature** (Literature); **Nursing** (Nursing); **Pedagogy** (Education; Pedagogy)

History: Founded 1999.

Main Language(s) of Instruction: Portuguese

Degrees and Diplomas: *Tecnólogo*; *Bacharelado*; *Licenciatura*; *Especialização/Aperfeiçoamento*; *Mestrado*
Last Updated: 06/07/10

INTERNATIONAL FACULTY OF BUSINESS SCIENCES

Faculdade Internacional de Ciências Empresariais (FICE)
R. Sergipe, 1000, Savassi, Belo Horizonte, MG 30130-171
Tel: +55(31) 3284-0558
EMail: fice@fice.com.br
Website: http://www.fice.com.br/

Courses

Administration (Administration)

Degrees and Diplomas: *Bacharelado*
Last Updated: 02/09/10

INTERNATIONAL FACULTY OF CURITIBA

Faculdade Internacional de Curitiba (FACINTER)
Rua do Rosário 169, Terréo Centro, Curitibá, Paraná 80020110
Tel: +55(41) 2102-3365
Fax: +55(41) 2102-3365
EMail: facinter@facinter.br
Website: http://www.facinter.br

Diretor: Wilson Picler

Diretor Acadêmico: João Correia Defreitas

Areas

Business *(Instituto Brasileiro de Pós-Graduação e Extensão (IBPEX), Postgraduate)*; **Education** *(Instituto Brasileiro de Pós-Graduação e Extensão (IBPEX), Postgraduate)*; **Health Sciences** *(Instituto Brasileiro de Pós-Graduação e Extensão (IBPEX), Postgraduate)*

History: Founded 2000.

Degrees and Diplomas: *Bacharelado*; *Licenciatura*; *Especialização/Aperfeiçoamento*
Last Updated: 11/12/07

INTERNATIONAL FACULTY OF TECHNOLOGY

Faculdade de Tecnologia Internacional (FATEC INTERNACIONAL)
Rua Saldanha Marinho, 131, Praça Tiradentes, Centro, Curitiba, PR 80410-150
Tel: +55(41) 2102-7944
Fax: +55(41) 2102-7961
EMail: vilmaaguiar@grupouninter.com.br; igormarques@grupouninter.com.br; pi@grupouninter.com.br
Website: http://www.fatecinternacional.com.br/

Diretor Geral: Wilson Picler

Courses

Commercial Management (Business and Commerce); **Distance Education** (Business and Commerce; Finance; Industrial Management; International Business; Management; Marketing; Pedagogy; Public Administration; Secretarial Studies; Transport Management); **Distance Postgraduate Studies** (Accountancy; Administration; Art Education; Business Administration; Civil Law; Educational and Student Counselling; Educational Psychology; Foreign Languages Education; Health Administration; Higher Education; Human Resources; Journalism; Law; Management; Marketing; Mathematics Education; Native Language Education; Occupational Health; Production Engineering; Public Administration; Public Health; Science Education; Secretarial Studies; Small Business; Special Education; Teacher Training); **Financial Management** (Finance); **Graduate Studies** *(Presential)* (Accountancy; Administration; Adult Education; African Studies; Agricultural Business; Art Education; Art Therapy; Business Administration; Business and Commerce; Business Education; Chemistry; Civil Engineering; Civil Law; Commercial Law; Communication Studies; Cosmetology; Criminal Law; Criminology; Dentistry; Design; Economics; Education; Educational Administration; Educational Psychology; Engineering; English; Environmental Management; Environmental Studies; Epidemiology; Fiscal Law; Folklore; Food Science; Foreign Languages Education; French; Gender Studies; Genetics; Gerontology; Gynaecology and Obstetrics; Health Administration; Health Education; Health Sciences; History; Hotel Management; Humanities and Social Science Education; Immunology; Industrial Management; Information Management; Information Technology; International Business; Labour Law; Law; Literature; Management; Marketing; Mathematics Education; Mining Engineering; Molecular Biology; Music Education; Neurology; Nursing; Nutrition; Occupational Health; Oncology; Orthopaedics; Pedagogy; Petroleum and Gas Engineering; Pharmacology; Pharmacy; Physical Education; Physical Therapy; Physiology; Political Sciences; Portuguese; Production Engineering; Psychiatry and Mental Health; Psychology; Psychotherapy; Public Administration; Public Health; Public Law; Radiology; Real Estate; Rehabilitation and Therapy; Religious Education; Safety Engineering; Science Education; Secretarial Studies; Social and Community Services; Social and Preventive Medicine; Sociology; Spanish; Special Education; Sports; Telecommunications Engineering; Theology; Tourism; Toxicology; Transport Management; Tropical Medicine); **Industrial Production Management** (Industrial Management); **International Business** (International Business); **Labour Safety** (Safety Engineering); **Logistics** (Transport Management); **Managerial Process** (Business Administration); **Marketing** (Marketing); **Systems Analysis and Development** (Systems Analysis); **Systems for Internet** (Computer Science)

History: Founded 2002.

Degrees and Diplomas: *Tecnólogo*; *Licenciatura*; *Especialização/ Aperfeiçoamento*. Also MBA.
Last Updated: 26/08/10

INTERNATIONAL FACULTY OF THE DELTA
Faculdade Internacional do Delta
Rua Bel Benjamin Constant, n° 540, Centro, Parnaíba, PI 64200-370
Tel: +55(86) 3322-5062
EMail: moses@sobral.org
Website: http://www.intafid.com.br/
Diretor Geral: Oscar Rodrigues Junior

Courses
Graduate Studies (Art Education; Biology; Business Administration; Business and Commerce; Civil Law; Computer Networks; Constitutional Law; Education; Educational Administration; Educational Psychology; Educational Technology; English; Health Administration; Health Sciences; Higher Education; History; Human Resources; Labour Law; Literacy Education; Literature; Marketing; Mathematics Education; Nutrition; Occupational Health; Physical Education; Physics; Physiology; Portuguese; Public Health; Rehabilitation and Therapy; Religious Education; Science Education; Social and Community Services; Social Policy; Sociology; Software Engineering; Spanish; Special Education; Sports; Tourism); **Undergraduate Studies** (History; Social and Community Services)

Degrees and Diplomas: *Bacharelado*; *Licenciatura*; *Especialização/Aperfeiçoamento*. Also Postgraduate diploma and MBA.
Last Updated: 02/09/10

INTESP FACULTY OF ELECTRICAL ENGINEERING
Faculdade INTESP de Engenharia Eletrica
Avenida Rui Barbosa 540, Centro, Ipaucu, São Paulo 18950000
Tel: +55(14) 3344-1157
Fax: +55(14) 3344-1157
EMail: intesp-eletrica@uol.com.br
Website: http://www.intesp.edu.br
Diretora: Maria Luiza Egreja Alves Lima

Courses
Electrical Engineering
History: Founded 2001.
Main Language(s) of Instruction: Portuguese
Degrees and Diplomas: *Bacharelado*; *Especialização/Aperfeiçoamento*
Last Updated: 06/07/10

IPH FACULTY OF ADMINISTRATION
Faculdade de Administração IPH
Avenida Duquesa de Goiás 262, Real Parque - Morumbi, São Paulo, São Paulo 5686001
Tel: +55(11) 3787-0120
Fax: +55(11) 3787-5571
EMail: iphfaculdade@iph.com.br
Diretor Geral: Domingos Marcos Flávio Fiorentini (1997-)

Courses
Administration (Banking; Business Administration; Finance; Health Administration; International Business; Marketing; Sports Management)
History: Founded 1973.
Main Language(s) of Instruction: Portuguese
Degrees and Diplomas: *Bacharelado*; *Especialização/Aperfeiçoamento*
Last Updated: 04/10/07

IPIRANGA FACULTY
Faculdade Ipiranga (FA)
Avenida Almirante Barroso, 777, Belém, PA 66093-020
Tel: +55(91) 3344-0700
Website: http://www.faculdadeipiranga.com.br
Diretora Geral: Suely Melo de Castro Menezes

Courses
Graduate Studies (Accountancy; Business Administration; Development Studies; Education; Educational Administration; Educational Psychology; Educational Technology; Environmental Studies; Higher Education; History; Human Resources; Literacy Education; Mathematics Education; Pedagogy); **Undergraduate Studies** (Administration; Advertising and Publicity; Business and Commerce; Communication Studies; Cosmetology; Graphic Design; Journalism; Management; Pedagogy; Public Administration; Systems Analysis; Telecommunications Engineering; Tourism)

Further Information: Also Cabanagem campus.

Degrees and Diplomas: *Tecnólogo*; *Bacharelado*; *Licenciatura*; *Especialização/Aperfeiçoamento*; *Mestrado*. Also MBA.
Last Updated: 02/09/10

IPITANGA INTEGRATED FACULTIES - UNIBAHIA
Faculdades Integradas Ipitanga - Unibahia
Avenida Luiz Tarquínio s/n, Qd A, Lot. 06 e 07, Pitangueiras, Lauro de Freitas, BA 42700-000
Tel: +55(71) 2202-3600
EMail: assessoria@unibahia.edu.br
Website: http://www.unibahia.br
Diretora: Ana Maria de Barros Santos Soares

Courses
Administration (Administration; Computer Science; Health Administration; Marketing); **Mechanical Engineering** (Mechanical Engineering); **Pedagogy** (Pedagogy); **Social Communication**

(Journalism; Public Relations); **Telecommunications Engineering** (Telecommunications Engineering)

History: Founded 1998.

Main Language(s) of Instruction: Portuguese

Degrees and Diplomas: *Bacharelado*; *Licenciatura*

Last Updated: 15/09/10

IPUC FACULTY OF TECHNOLOGY
Faculdade de Tecnologia IPUC (FATIPUC)
Avenida Guilherme Schell, 5000, Centro, Canoas, RD 92310-000
Tel: +55(51) 2103-3000
EMail: ipuc@ipuc.com.br
Website: http://www.ipuc.com.br/

Courses
Graduate Studies (Grammar); **Portuguese Language and Literature** (Literature; Portuguese); **Radiology** (Radiology)

Degrees and Diplomas: *Tecnólogo*; *Licenciatura*; *Especialização/ Aperfeiçoamento*

Last Updated: 26/08/10

ISAAC NEWTON FACULTY
Faculdade Isaac Newton (FACINE)
Avenida Sete de Setembro, n° 1477, Centro, Salvador, BA 40000-000
Tel: +55(71) 3491-1399 +55(71) 3012-4141
EMail: marimeir@ufba.br
Website: http://www.isaacnewton.edu.br/

Courses
Administration (Administration); **Social Communication** (Advertising and Publicity; Public Relations)

Degrees and Diplomas: *Bacharelado*. Also Postgraduate diploma.

Last Updated: 02/09/10

ISCA FACULTIES OF LIMEIRA
ISCA Faculdades de Limeira
Via 147 Limeira-Piracicaba Km 04 - Cruz do Padre, Limeira, São Paulo 13482383
Tel: +55(19) 3404-4700
Fax: +55(19) 3404-4707
EMail: isca@alie.br
Website: http://home.alie.br/sites/iscafaculdades

Diretora Geral: Rosely Berwerth Pereira

Courses
Accountancy (Accountancy); **Administration** (Administration); **Advertising and Publicity** (Advertising and Publicity); **Chemistry**; **Economics** (Economics); **Electrical Engineering**; **Environmental Engineering** (Environmental Engineering); **Geography**; **Journalism** (Journalism); **Law** (Law); **Pedagogy**; **Social Sciences** (Social Sciences); **Social Services** (Social and Community Services)

History: Founded 1970.

Degrees and Diplomas: *Bacharelado*; *Licenciatura*; *Especialização/Aperfeiçoamento*; *Mestrado*

Last Updated: 14/06/10

ISEIB FACULTIES
Faculdades ISEIB
Rua Lírio Brant 511, Montes Claros, MG 39401-063
Tel: +55(38)3222-9444
EMail: assomc@uai.com.br
Website: http://www.iseib.com.br

Diretor: Carlos Felipe Silveira e Oliveira

Courses
Administration (Administration); **Biology** (Biology); **Chemistry** (Chemistry); **Geography** (Geography); **History** (History); **Letters** (Literature); **Mathematics** (Mathematics); **Pedagogy** (Pedagogy); **Physics** (Physics)

Further Information: Also campuses in Belo Horizonte and Betim

History: Founded 2008.

Main Language(s) of Instruction: Portuguese

Degrees and Diplomas: *Bacharelado*; *Especialização/Aperfeiçoamento*; *Mestrado*

Libraries: Biblioteca Central Professor Padre Sebastião Raymundo de Castro

Last Updated: 31/08/10

ITALIAN-BRAZILIAN UNIVERSITY CENTRE
Centro Universitario Ítalo-Brasileira
Avenida João Dias, 2046, São Paulo, São Paulo 04724-003
Tel: +55(11) 5645-0099
Fax: +55(11) 5645-0103
EMail: secretariageral@italo.br
Website: http://www.italo.br

Reitor: Marcos Antônio Gagliardi Cascino EMail: reitor@italo.br

Pró-Reitor Acadêmico: Luiz Carlos Pereira de Souza

International Relations: Alfredo Grimaldi, Diretor de Relações Internacionais EMail: ri@italo.br

Courses
Accountancy; **Administration**; **Arts and Humanities** (Arts and Humanities; English; Portuguese; Spanish); **Biological Sciences** (Biological and Life Sciences); **Geography** (Geography); **Graduate Studies** (Accountancy; Banking; Business Administration; Civil Law; Communication Studies; Education; Educational Administration; Educational Psychology; Environmental Studies; Finance; Health Administration; Human Rights; Industrial and Organizational Psychology; Marketing; Molecular Biology; Nursing; Nutrition; Pedagogy; Physical Education; Psychiatry and Mental Health; Real Estate; Rehabilitation and Therapy; Teacher Training; Theology); **Nursing** (Nursing); **Pedagogy** (Pedagogy); **Philosophy** (Philosophy); **Physical Education** (Physical Education); **Physiotherapy** (Physical Therapy); **Social Service** (Social and Community Services); **Sociology** (Sociology); **Technological Studies** (Data Processing; Finance; Human Resources; Industrial Management; Information Technology; International Business; Marketing; Radiology; Secretarial Studies; Small Business; Systems Analysis; Transport Management); **Visual Arts** (Visual Arts)

History: Founded 1972 as Faculdade Ítalo Brasileira. Acquired present status and title 2006.

Degrees and Diplomas: *Bacharelado*; *Licenciatura*; *Especialização/Aperfeiçoamento*

Last Updated: 14/06/10

ITECNE FACULTIES OF CASCAVEL
Faculdades Itecne de Cascavel
Avenida Brasil, 8607, Coqueiral, Cascavel, PR 85807-030
Tel: +55(45) 3226-0110
Fax: +55(45) 3226-0110
EMail: faculdade@itecnecascavel.com.br
Website: http://www.itecne.com.br/

Diretor Geral: Ivo José Triches

Courses
Graduate Studies (Accountancy; Adult Education; Agricultural Business; Art Education; Art Therapy; Business Administration; Education; Educational Administration; Educational Psychology; Environmental Management; Family Studies; Finance; Foreign Languages Education; Geography; Higher Education; History; Information Technology; Law; Literacy Education; Literature; Management; Mathematics Education; Medieval Studies; Native Language Education; Nursing; Occupational Health; Philosophy; Physical Education; Preschool Education; Psychiatry and Mental Health; Psychology; Public Administration; Public Health; Rehabilitation and Therapy; Religious Education; Science Education; Social Work; Special Education; Teacher Training; Transport Management); **Undergraduate Studies** (Agricultural Business; Social and Community Services)

Degrees and Diplomas: *Tecnólogo*; *Bacharelado*; *Especialização/Aperfeiçoamento*. Also MBA.

Last Updated: 30/09/10

ITOP FACULTY
Faculdade ITOP
Quadra ACSUSE 40, Conjunto 02, Lote 16 - AV NS-02, Palmas,
TO 77000-000
Tel: +55(63)3214-7345
EMail: munizap@hotmail.com
Website: http://www.itopedu.com.br

Diretor: Muniz Araújo Pereira

Courses
Accountancy (Accountancy); **Administration** (Administration);
Letters (Literature); **Pedagogy** (Pedagogy)

History: Founded 2008.

Main Language(s) of Instruction: Portuguese

Degrees and Diplomas: *Bacharelado*; *Especialização/Aperfeiçoamento*; *Mestrado*
Last Updated: 01/09/10

IZABELA HENDRIX METHODIST UNIVERSITY CENTRE
Centro Universitário Metodista Izabela Hendrix (IMIH)
Rua da Bahia 2020, Praça da Liberdade, Belo Horizonte,
Minas Gerais 30160-012
Tel: +55(31) 3244-7200
EMail: cae@metodistademinas.edu.br
Website: http://www.metodistademinas.edu.br/novo/
centrouniversitario.php

Diretor Geral e Reitor: Marcio de Moraes (2005-)

Pró-Reitor Administrativo: Fabiano Dalforno Teixeira

Courses
Accountancy (Accountancy); **Administration**; **Architecture and Urbanism** (Architecture; Town Planning); **Biological Sciences**; **Biomedicine** (Biomedicine); **Civil Engineering**; **Communication** (Advertising and Publicity; Journalism); **Environmental Engineering** (Environmental Engineering); **Environmental Management**; **Graduate Studies**; **Interior Design** (Interior Design); **Law** (Law); **Marketing** (Marketing); **Music**; **Nursing**; **Nutrition** (Nutrition); **Pedagogy** (Pedagogy); **Phonaudiology** (Speech Therapy and Audiology); **Physical Education**; **Physiotherapy**; **Production Engineering** (Production Engineering); **Social Services** (Social and Community Services); **Systems Analys and Development** (Systems Analysis); **Theology** (Theology)

History: Founded 1904 as Instituto Metodista Izabela Hendrix. Accredited as university centre 2002.

Admission Requirements: Secondary school certificate and entrance examination (Vestibular)

Fees: (US Dollars): 2,700 per annum

Main Language(s) of Instruction: Portuguese

International Co-operation: With universities in Argentina; France; Uruguay and USA

Degrees and Diplomas: *Tecnólogo*; *Bacharelado*: 4 yrs; *Licenciatura*; *Especialização/Aperfeiçoamento*: 2 yrs

Student Services: Cultural centre, Foreign student adviser, Handicapped facilities, Nursery care, Social counselling, Sports facilities

Special Facilities: Theatre

Libraries: Two libraries, 40,000 vols

Publications: A Tocha, Bulletin *(biennially)*
Last Updated: 15/06/10

JANGADA FACULTY
Faculdade Jangada
Rua Presidente Epitácio Pessoa 676, Jaraguá do Sul,
SC 89251-100
Tel: +55(47) 3371-0202
EMail: academica@faculdadejangada.com.br
Website: http://www.faculdadejangada.com.br

Diretor: Luiz Carlos Duarte de Souza
EMail: dir.geral@faculdadejangada.com.br

Courses
Biology (Biology); **Nursing** (Nursing); **Physical Education** (Physical Education)

History: Founded 2004.

Main Language(s) of Instruction: Portuguese

Degrees and Diplomas: *Bacharelado*; *Licenciatura*; *Especialização/Aperfeiçoamento*

Libraries: Yes
Last Updated: 01/09/10

JAPI FACULTY OF HIGHER EDUCATION
Faculdade Japi de Ensino Superior
Rua Lobo Rezende, 100, Centro, Jundiaí, São Paulo 13201789
Tel: +55(11) 4521-0186
Fax: +55(11) 4586-2817
EMail: info@japi.br
Website: http://www.japi.br

Diretora: Rute Maria Pozzi Casati

Courses
Administration (Administration); **Chemical Engineering**; **Literature**; **Pedagogy**

History: Founded 2000.

Main Language(s) of Instruction: Portuguese

Degrees and Diplomas: *Bacharelado*; *Especialização/Aperfeiçoamento*
Last Updated: 26/11/07

JARDIM FACULTY OF TECHNOLOGY
Faculdade de Tecnologia Jardim (FATEJ)
Rua Almirante Protógenes, 68, Bairro Jardim, Santo André,
SP 09090-760
Tel: +55(11) 4436-6489 +55(11) 4992-3822
EMail: fatej@fatej.edu.br
Website: http://www.fatej.edu.br/

Reitora: Arleide Braga

Courses
Graduate Studies (Social Welfare); **Pension Management** (Management); **Security Management** (Protective Services)

Degrees and Diplomas: *Tecnólogo*; *Especialização/Aperfeiçoamento*
Last Updated: 26/08/10

JESUIT FACULTY OF PHILOSOPHY AND THEOLOGY
Faculdade Jesuíta de Filosofia e Teologia (FAJE)
Avenida Doutor Cristiano Guimarães 2127 Planalto, Belo Horizonte,
Minas Gerais 31720300
Tel: +55(31) 3115-7000
Fax: +55(31) 3115-7015
EMail: faje@faculdadejesuita.edu.br
Website: http://www.cesjesuit.br

Reitor: Jaldemir VitórioFax: reitor@faculdadejesuita.edu.br

Departments
Philosophy *(Ecclesiastical)*; **Theology** *(Ecclesiastical)*

Higher Institutes
Education (Education; Philosophy)

History: Founded 1992. Acquired present title 2005.

Main Language(s) of Instruction: Portuguese

Degrees and Diplomas: *Bacharelado*; *Licenciatura*; *Especialização/Aperfeiçoamento*; *Mestrado*
Last Updated: 06/07/10

JESUS MARIA JOSÉ FACULTY

Faculdade Jesus Maria José (FAJESU)
Qng 46 - Área Especial 08, Região Administrativa III, Brasília,
DF 72130400
Tel: +55(61) 3354-1838
Fax: +55(61) 3354-0498
EMail: secretaria@fajesu.com.br
Website: http://webadm.fajesu.org/fajesu/New_Site/

Diretora: Maria da Silva Maciel EMail: diretoria@fajesu.edu.br

Courses
Administration (Administration); **Computer Science** (Computer Networks; Computer Science; Software Engineering); **Literature** (Literature); **Mathematics** (Mathematics); **Pedagogy** (Pedagogy); **Secretarial Studies** (Secretarial Studies)

History: Founded 1999.

Main Language(s) of Instruction: Portuguese

Degrees and Diplomas: *Bacharelado*; *Licenciatura*; *Especialização/Aperfeiçoamento*
Last Updated: 06/07/10

JOAN OF ARC FACULTY

Faculdade Joana d'Arc
Avenida Professor Francisco Morato N°: 5.000, Vila Sônia,
São Paulo, SP 05520-300
Tel: +55(11) 3751-2050
EMail: marciacorreia@alfa.br

Diretor: José Carlos Pomarico

Courses
Accountancy (Accountancy); **Administration** (Administration)
History: Founded 2002.

Main Language(s) of Instruction: Portuguese

Degrees and Diplomas: *Bacharelado*
Last Updated: 03/09/10

JOÃO ALFREDO DE ANDRADE HIGHER EDUCATION INSTITUTE

Instituto de Ensino Superior João Alfredo de Andrade (IJAA)
Avenida Tanus Saliba 468, Centro, Juatuba,
Minas Gerais 35675000
Tel: +55(31) 3535-8142
Fax: +55(31) 3535-8849
EMail: ijaa@ijaa.br
Website: http://www.jandrade.edu.br

Diretor Geral: Cláudia Matos Diniz

Courses
Accountancy (Accountancy); **Administration** (Administration); **Advertising and Publicity** (Advertising and Publicity); **Journalism**; **Law** (Law); **Sales Techniques** (Sales Techniques)
History: Founded 1999.

Degrees and Diplomas: *Tecnólogo*; *Bacharelado*
Last Updated: 15/06/10

JOÃO CALVINO FACULTY

Faculdade João Calvino
Av. Ahylon Macêdo, 1029 - Morada Nobre, Barreiras, BA 47806-180
Tel: +55(77) 3613-1514
EMail: cetai@cetai.com.br
Website: http://www.cetai.com.br

Diretor: Flávio Morais Leite

Courses
Philosophy (Anthropology; History; Philosophy; Sociology); **Theology** (Theology)
History: Founded 2000.

Main Language(s) of Instruction: Portuguese

Degrees and Diplomas: *Bacharelado*; *Licenciatura*; *Especialização/Aperfeiçoamento*
Libraries: Yes
Last Updated: 16/09/10

JOAQUIM NABUCO FACULTY

Faculdade Joaquim Nabuco
Av. Senador Salgado Filho S/N - Centro, Paulista, PE 53.401-440
Tel: +55(81) 2121-5999
Website: http://www.joaquimnabuco.edu.br/home/indexNabuco/

Diretor: Inácio Feitosa Neto EMail: inacio@sereducacional.com.br

Courses
Accountancy (Accountancy; Pedagogy); **Administration** (Administration; Marketing); **Information Systems** (Computer Science); **Law** (Law); **Pedagogy**; **Social Communication** (Advertising and Publicity; Journalism); **Tourism** (Tourism)

Further Information: Also branch in Recife

History: Founded 2007.

Main Language(s) of Instruction: Portuguese

Degrees and Diplomas: *Bacharelado*; *Licenciatura*; *Especialização/Aperfeiçoamento*
Libraries: Yes
Last Updated: 16/09/10

JOHN PAUL II FACULTY

Faculdade João Paulo II
Rua Bartolomeu de Gusmão 531, Marilia, SP 17506-280
Tel: +55(14) 3414-1965
EMail: sec.geral@fajopa.edu.br
Website: http://www.fajopa.edu.br

Diretor: Maurílio Alves Rodrigues (2008-)

Courses
Philosophy (Philosophy); **Theology** (Theology)
History: Founded 2003.

Main Language(s) of Instruction: Portuguese

Degrees and Diplomas: *Bacharelado*; *Licenciatura*
Libraries: Yes
Last Updated: 21/09/10

JOHN XXIII FACULTY

Faculdade João XXIII
Avenida Penha de França 35, Penha, São Paulo,
São Paulo 03606010
Tel: +55(11) 6192-8400
Website: http://joao23.educacional.net/

Diretor: Osmar Basilio

Courses
Administration (Administration); **Law** (Law); **Pedagogy**; **Production Engineering** (Production Engineering)
History: Founded 2001.

Main Language(s) of Instruction: Portuguese

Degrees and Diplomas: *Bacharelado*; *Licenciatura*; *Especialização/Aperfeiçoamento*
Last Updated: 08/07/10

JORGE AMADO UNIVERSITY CENTRE

Centro Universitário Jorge Amado (UNIJORGE)
Avenida Luis Vania Filho 6775, Paralela, Salvador,
Bahia 41745-130
Tel: +55(71) 3534-8000
Fax: +55(71) 3206-8099
EMail: rbrito@fja.adm.br
Website: http://www.fja.edu.br

Reitor/ Diretor Geral: Sílvio Bello

Courses
Bacharelado (Accountancy; Administration; Advertising and Publicity; Architecture; Chemical Engineering; Civil Engineering; Computer Engineering; Electrical Engineering; English; Environmental Engineering; Graphic Design; History; Information Sciences; International Relations; Journalism; Law; Literature; Materials Engineering; Mechanical Engineering; Nursing; Nutrition; Petroleum and Gas Engineering; Physical Education; Physical Therapy; Physics; Portuguese; Production Engineering; Psychology; Radio and

Television Broadcasting; Speech Therapy and Audiology; Telecommunications Engineering; Town Planning); **Graduate Studies** (Architecture; Behavioural Sciences; Business Administration; Business and Commerce; Computer Science; Cultural Studies; Design; Ecology; Fashion Design; Finance; Higher Education; History; Information Technology; Marketing; Modern Languages; Nursing; Psychology; Rehabilitation and Therapy; Safety Engineering; Software Engineering; Transport Engineering); **Licenciatura** (Biological and Life Sciences; English; Geography; History; Mathematics; Pedagogy; Physical Education; Physics; Portuguese; Spanish); **Technological Studies** (Business and Commerce; Cinema and Television; Communication Studies; Computer Networks; Cooking and Catering; Environmental Management; Fashion Design; Finance; Health Administration; Hotel Management; Human Resources; Interior Design; International Business; Leisure Studies; Management; Marketing; Multimedia; Occupational Health; Performing Arts; Photography; Real Estate; Safety Engineering; Software Engineering; Sports Management; Transport Management)

History: Founded 1998.

Main Language(s) of Instruction: Portuguese

Degrees and Diplomas: *Bacharelado*; *Licenciatura*; *Especialização/Aperfeiçoamento*. Also MBA.
Last Updated: 14/06/10

JOSÉ AUGUSTO VIEIRA FACULTY
Faculdade José Augusto Vieira
Praça Nossa Sra. Aparecida, 40, Bairro Cidade Nova, Lagarto, SE
Tel: +55(79) 3631-9210
EMail: fijav@marata.com.br
Website: http://www.fjav.com.br

Diretora: M♀. Silmere Alves Santos de Souza

Courses
Accountancy (Accountancy); **Administration** (Administration); **Geography** (Geography); **History** (History); **Information Systems** (Computer Science); **Letters** (Literature); **Mathematics** (Mathematics); **Production Engineering** (Production Engineering); **Social Services** (Social and Community Services)

History: Founded 2004.

Main Language(s) of Instruction: Portuguese

Degrees and Diplomas: *Bacharelado*; *Licenciatura*; *Especialização/Aperfeiçoamento*
Last Updated: 01/09/10

JOSÉ DO ROSÁRIO VELLANO UNIVERSITY
Universidade José do Rosário Vellano (UNIFENAS)
Rodóvia MG 179 km 0, Campus Universitário, Alfenas, Minas Gerais 37130000
Tel: +55(35) 3299-3000 +55(35) 3299-3257
Fax: +55(35) 3299-3800
EMail: unifenas@unifenas.br
Website: http://www.unifenas.br

Reitora: Maria do Rosário Araújo Valeno (2008-)
Tel: +55(35) 3299-3157, Fax: +55(35) 3299-3811

Executive Manager: Paulo Tadeu Barroso Salles
Tel: +55(35) 3299-3148, Fax: +55(35) 3299-3284
EMail: paulo.salles@unifenas.br

International Relations: Sebastião M. Franco de Carvalho
Tel: +55(35) 3299-3257

Faculties
Agriculture (Agriculture; Agronomy; Animal Husbandry); **Architecture, Civil Engineering and Computer Science** (Architecture; Civil Engineering; Computer Science; Town Planning); **Dentistry, Speech Therapy and Audiology** (Dental Technology; Dentistry; Speech Therapy and Audiology); **Education** (Education); **Law** (Law); **Management** (Management); **Medicine** (Health Sciences; Medicine); **Pharmacy, Nutrition and Biomedicine** (Biomedicine; Nutrition; Pharmacy); **Physiotherapy and Nursing** (Nursing; Physical Therapy); **Psychology** (Psychology); **Veterinary Medicine**

Further Information: Also Alzira Velano Universitarian Hospital

History: Founded 1965 as Faculdades Integradas da Região de Alfenas, became University of Alfenas 1988. Under the supervision of the Fundação de Ensino e Tecnologia de Alfenas. Acquired present title 2002.

Governing Bodies: Conselho Direccão
Academic Year: February to December (February-June; August-December)
Admission Requirements: Secondary school certificate and entrance examination
Main Language(s) of Instruction: Portuguese
International Co-operation: With University of Miami
Accrediting Agencies: Conselho Nacional de Educação; Conselho Estadual de Educação de Minas Gerais; Fundação CAPES

Degrees and Diplomas: *Bacharelado*: 4-6 yrs; *Licenciatura*: 4-6 yrs; *Mestrado*: a further 2 yrs; *Doutorado*
Student Services: Academic counselling, Canteen, Cultural centre, Employment services, Handicapped facilities, Health services, Social counselling, Sports facilities
Special Facilities: Biological Garden. Veterinary Clinic. Waters Laboratory and Treatment Service
Libraries: 127,286 vols
Last Updated: 11/05/10

BELO HORIZONTE CAMPUS
CÂMPUS DE BELO HORIZONTE
Belo Horizonte, Minas Gerais 31110-110
Tel: +55(31) 3422-4111
Fax: +55(31) 3422-4638
EMail: belohorizonte@unifenas.br

Gestor: Fuad Haddad (2000-)

Faculties
Law; **Management** (Management); **Medicine** (Medicine); **Nutrition and Health Sciences**

CAMPO BELO CAMPUS
CÂMPUS DE CAMPO BELO
Al. Roberto Assunção, s/n, Bairro El Dorado, Campo Belo, Minas Gerais 37270-000
Tel: +55(35) 3832-6462
Fax: +55(35) 3831-2582
EMail: cbelo@unifenas.br
Website: http://www.unifenas.br

Gestor: Gilberto de Sousa Filho (1993-)
Tel: +55(35) 3291-4443, Fax: +55(35) 3291-4443
EMail: gilberto@unifenas.br

Faculties
Law (Law); **Nursing**; **Physiotherapy** *Coordinator*: Anadely A. da Silva
History: Founded 1972.

DIVINÓPOLIS CAMPUS
CÂMPUS DE DIVINÓPOLIS
Rua Antônio Olímpio de Morais 2100, Bairro Santa Clara, Divinópolis, Minas Gerais 35500-091
Tel: +55(37) 3222-3314
Fax: +55(37) 3212-7888
EMail: hudson.bianchini@unifenas.br
Website: http://www.unifenas.br

Gestor: Hudson Bianchini (2000-)

Faculties
Biomedicine (Biomedicine); **Fashion Design** (Fashion Design); **Nutrition** (Nutrition); **Pharmacy** (Pharmacy); **Physiotherapy** (Physical Therapy); **Radiology** (Radiology)
History: Founded 1999.

POÇOS DE CALDAS CAMPUS
CÂMPUS DE POÇOS DE CALDAS
Rodóvia Geraldo Martins Costa s/n, Jardim Kennedy, Poços de Caldas, Minas Gerais 37700-970
Tel: +55(35) 3713-4400
Fax: +55(35) 3712-3507
EMail: pocos@unifenas.br
Website: http://www.unifenas.br

Gestor: Gilberto de Sousa Filho (1993-)
Tel: +55(35) 3291-4443, Fax: +55(35) 3291-4443
EMail: gilberto@unifenas.br

Faculties
Law (Law); **Management**; **Nursing** (Nursing); **Nutrition** (Nutrition); **Pharmacy**
History: Founded 1972.

VARGINHA CAMPUS
CÂMPUS DE VARGINHA

Praça do Estudante, 2000, Varginha, Minas Gerais 37002-970
Tel: +55(35) 3212-7766
Fax: +55(35) 3212-7957
EMail: varginha@unifenas.br
Website: http://www.unifenas.br

Gestor: Fuad Haddad (2000-)

Faculties
Dentistry and Pharmacy; **Nursing** (Nursing); **Psychology**; **Radiology** (Radiology)

JOSÉ LACERDA JR FACULTY OF APPLIED SCIENCES
Faculdade José Lacerda Filho de Ciências Applicadas (FACOLJA)
Avenida Francisco Alves de Souza 500, Centro, Ipojuca,
PE 55590000
Tel: +55(81) 3551-1221
Fax: +55(81) 3551-1370
EMail: falcoja@falcoja.com.br
Website: http://www.fajolca.edu.br

Diretora: Lais da Fonseca Lacerda

Courses
Accountancy; **Administration**; **Pedagogy** (Pedagogy)
History: Founded 1999.
Main Language(s) of Instruction: Portuguese
Degrees and Diplomas: *Bacharelado*
Last Updated: 06/07/10

JUDGE SAVIO BRANDAO INTEGRATED FACULTIES
Faculdades Integradas Desembargador Sávio Brandao
Rua Arthur Bernardes, s/n, Várzea Grande, MT 78125-100
Tel: +55(65) 3363-1900
EMail: maxleao@unic.br
Website: http://www.unic.br/amec

Diretor: Maximilliam Mayolino Leão

Courses
Business Administration (Business Administration); **Law** (Law)
History: Founded 1994.
Main Language(s) of Instruction: Portuguese
Degrees and Diplomas: *Bacharelado*
Last Updated: 15/09/10

JUSCELINO KUBITSCHEK FACULTIES
Faculdades Juscelino Kubitschek (FJK)
Qs1 rua 212 lotes 11/15 - Águas Claras-DF, Brasília, DF 71950550
Tel: +55(61) 3352-6290
Fax: +55(61) 3352-3626
EMail: diretoria@faculdadejk.com.br
Website: http://www.faculdadejk.edu.br

Diretor: Eurico Monteiro de Alarcão Junior

Courses
Administration (Administration); **Advertising and Publicity** (Advertising and Publicity); **Biology**; **Biomedicine** (Biomedicine); **Journalism** (Journalism); **Languages** *(Valparaíso campus)* (Mod-

ern Languages); **Law**; **Nursing** (Nursing); **Nutrition** (Nutrition); **Pedagogy**; **Pharmacy** (Pharmacy); **Public Relations** (Public Relations)
Further Information: Also Taguatinga and Valparaíso campuses
History: Founded 1999.
Main Language(s) of Instruction: Portuguese
Degrees and Diplomas: *Bacharelado*; *Licenciatura*; *Especialização/Aperfeiçoamento*
Last Updated: 10/12/07

JUVÊNCIO TERRA FACULTY
Faculdade Juvêncio Terra (JTS)
Avenida Otávio Santos 158, Recreio, Vitória da Conquista,
Bahia 45020750
Tel: +55(77) 3425-1696
Fax: +55(77) 3425-1696
EMail: administrativo@juvencioterra.edu.br
Website: http://www.juvencioterra.edu.br

Diretora: Maria Lucia Cajazeira Mendes
EMail: dgeral@juvencioterra.edu.br

Courses
Administration (Administration); **Computer Science** (Computer Science); **Philosophy** (Philosophy); **Psychology** (Psychology); **Secretarial Studies** (Secretarial Studies); **Social Communication**
History: Founded 1999.
Main Language(s) of Instruction: Portuguese
Degrees and Diplomas: *Bacharelado*; *Especialização/Aperfeiçoamento*
Libraries: Biblioteca Rosália Figueira Silveira
Last Updated: 06/07/10

KENNEDY FACULTIES
Faculdades Kennedy
Rua José Dias Vieira 46, Rio Branco, Belo Horizonte,
Minas Gerais 31535040
Tel: +55(31) 3408-2350
Fax: +55(31) 3408-2391
EMail: kennedy@gold.com.br
Website: http://www.kennedy.br

Diretor Geral: João Evangelista Alves de Paula (1996-)

Courses
Administration (Administration; Marketing; Sports Management); **Civil Engineering** *(Escola de Engenharia Kennedy)*; **Education** (Education; Pedagogy); **Law** (Law); **Mining Engineering**; **Production Engineering**
History: Founded 1964 as Escola de Engenharia Civil Kennedy.
Main Language(s) of Instruction: Portuguese
Degrees and Diplomas: *Bacharelado*; *Especialização/Aperfeiçoamento*
Last Updated: 21/06/10

KENNEDY FACULTY
Faculdade Kennedy (FK)
Rua Paracatu 115, Nossa Senhora da Conceição, João Monlevade,
Minas Gerais 35930032
Tel: +55(31) 3851-3030
Fax: +55(31) 3851-3030
EMail: kennedy@kennedyjm.edu.br
Website: http://www.kennedyjm.edu.br

Diretor: Antônio Henriques de Albuquerque

Courses
Computer Science
History: Founded 2001.
Main Language(s) of Instruction: Portuguese
Degrees and Diplomas: *Bacharelado*; *Especialização/Aperfeiçoamento*
Last Updated: 06/07/10

KURIOS FACULTY
Faculdade Kurios
Avenida Dr. Argeu Gurgel B. Herbest 960, Maranguape,
CE 61940-000
Tel: +55(85)3341-0562
EMail: contato@fak.edu.br
Website: http://www.fak.edu.br

Diretor: Augusto Ferreira da Silva Neto

Courses
Administration (Administration); **Letters** (Literature); **Theology** (Theology)

History: Founded 2002.

Main Language(s) of Instruction: Portuguese

Degrees and Diplomas: *Bacharelado*; *Licenciatura*; *Especialização/Aperfeiçoamento*

Libraries: Yes
Last Updated: 01/09/10

LA SALLE FACULTY OF MANAUS
Faculdade La Salle de Manaus
Av. Dom Pedro I, 151, Manaus, AM 69040-040
Tel: +55(92) 3655-1200
EMail: lasalle.manaus@lasalle.edu.br
Website: http://www.unilasalle.edu.br/manaus

Diretor: Valério Menegat

Courses
Accountancy (Accountancy); **Business Administration** (Business Administration); **Information Systems** (Computer Science); **International Relations** (International Relations); **Physical Education** (Physical Education)

Further Information: Also branches in Lucas do Rio Verde and Estrela

History: Founded 2004.

Main Language(s) of Instruction: Portuguese

Degrees and Diplomas: *Bacharelado*; *Licenciatura*; *Especialização/Aperfeiçoamento*; *Mestrado*

Libraries: Biblioteca La Salle
Last Updated: 02/09/10

LA SALLE INSTITUTE OF EDUCATION
Instituto Superior de Educação La Salle
Rua Gastão Gonçalves N°79, Santa Rosa, Niterói, RJ 24240-030
Tel: +55(21) 2199-6600
EMail: unilasalle-rj@unilasalle-rj.edu.br
Website: http://www.lasallerj.org

Courses
Computer Science (Computer Science); **History** (History); **Information Sciences** (Computer Science); **Pedagogy** (Pedagogy)

History: Founded 2001.

Main Language(s) of Instruction: Portuguese

Degrees and Diplomas: *Licenciatura*
Last Updated: 01/10/10

LA SALLE INSTITUTE OF HUMANITIES AND PHILOSOPHY
Instituto Superior de Ciências Humanas e Filosofia La Salle (ISCHF LA SALLE)
Rua Gastão Gonçalves, 79, Santa Rosa, Niterói, RJ 24240-120
Tel: +55(21) 2199-6600
EMail: unilasalle-rj@unilasalle-rj.edu.br
Website: http://www.lasallerj.org/

Courses
Undergraduate Studies (Accountancy; Administration; International Relations; Law)

Degrees and Diplomas: *Bacharelado*; *Mestrado*
Last Updated: 23/09/10

LA SALLE UNIVERSITY CENTRE
Centro Universitário La Salle (UNILASALLE)
Avenida Victor Barreto, 2288, Centro, Canoas,
Rio Grande do Sul 92010-000
Tel: +55(51) 3476-8500
Fax: +55(51) 3472-3511
EMail: unilasalle@lasalle.edu.brou
Website: http://www.unilasalle.edu.br

Reitor: Paulo Fossatti

Pró-Reitora Acadêmica: Vera Lúcia Ramirez

Areas
Linguistics and Literature, Arts; **Applied Social Sciences**; **Biological Sciences** (Biology); **Engineering**; **Exact and Earth Sciences** (Chemistry; Computer Education; Computer Science; Mathematics; Physics); **Health Sciences**; **Human Sciences**

Courses
Graduate Studies *(Lato Sensu)*; **Graduate Studies** *(Stricto Sensu)*; **Technological Studies** (Computer Networks; Computer Science; Finance; Human Resources; Industrial Design; Management)

Faculties
Estrelas; **Lucas do Rio Verde** (Accountancy; Administration; Law; Tourism); **Manaus**; **Niterói** (Accountancy; Administration; Computer Science; History; International Relations; Law; Pedagogy)

Further Information: Also other services available in Health; Social and Company Sciences

History: Founded 1972 as Centro Educacional La Salle de Ensino Superior - CELES. Acquired present status and title 1998.

Governing Bodies: Sociedade Porvir Cientifico

Admission Requirements: School Certificate (in Portuguese); Identity Documents

Fees: (Reals): For 2 subject-matter, 328.38 per month

Main Language(s) of Instruction: Portuguese

International Co-operation: With universities in Argentina, Chile, Colombia, USA, Spain, France, Mexico, Uruguay

Accrediting Agencies: Ministério da Educaçào e Cultura (MEC - Ministry of Culture and Education)

Degrees and Diplomas: *Tecnólogo*; *Bacharelado*; *Licenciatura*; *Especialização/Aperfeiçoamento*; *Mestrado*. Also MBA.

Student Services: Academic counselling, Canteen, Cultural centre, Employment services, Foreign student adviser, Handicapped facilities, Health services, Language programs, Nursery care, Social counselling, Sports facilities

Student Residential Facilities: Yes

Libraries: Yes

Publications: Cadernos La Salle; La Salle - Revista de educaçào, ciência e cultura, A multi-disciplinary academic-scientific publication in several languages *(biennially)*; Revista Diálogos, Thematic Magazine *(annually)*

Press or Publishing House: Centro Editorial
Last Updated: 15/06/10

LATIN AMERICAN FACULTY - IJUÍ UNIT
Faculdade América Latina - Unidade Ijuí (FAL - IJUÍ)
Rua 13 de maio, 67, Centro, Ijuí, RS 98700-000
Tel: +55(55) 3333-2476
Website: http://www.americalatina.edu.br/home.
php?cod_unidade=2

Diretora: Sílvia B. Vilasfam

Courses
Graduate Studies (Business Administration; Educational Administration; Industrial and Organizational Psychology); **Undergraduate Studies** (Accountancy; Administration)

History: Formerly known as Faculdade Rio Claro.

Degrees and Diplomas: *Bacharelado*; *Especialização/Aperfeiçoamento*
Last Updated: 06/09/10

LATIN AMERICAN FACULTY OF EDUCATION

Faculdade Latino Americana de Educação (FLATED)
Rua Dona Leopoldina, 907 – Centro, Fortazela, Ceará 60015051
Tel: +55(85) 3454-1299
EMail: flated@flated.edu.br
Website: http://www.flated.edu.br

Diretora: Maria do Socorro de Sousa

Courses
Administration; **Pedagogy** (Pedagogy); **Tourism**
History: Founded 2000. Moved in 2004.
Main Language(s) of Instruction: Portuguese
Degrees and Diplomas: *Bacharelado*; *Especialização/Aperfeiçoamento*
Last Updated: 06/07/10

LEMOS DE CASTRO FACULTY OF COMPUTER SCIENCE

Faculdade de Informática Lemos de Castro (FILC)
Rua Carolina Machado, 304, Rio de Janeiro,
Rio de Janeiro 21351-021
Tel: +55(21) 3390-0101 +55(21) 2450-1799
Fax: +55(21) 450-1666
EMail: filc@lemosdecastro.br; lemos@lemosdecastro.br
Website: http://www.lemosdecastro.br/Filc/cfrmCur.htm

Diretor: Délio Torres de Castro

Courses
Computer Science (Computer Science; Information Technology)
History: Founded 1999
Main Language(s) of Instruction: Portuguese
Degrees and Diplomas: *Bacharelado*
Last Updated: 09/07/10

LEONARDO DA VINCI UNIVERSITY CENTRE

Centro Universitário Leonardo da Vinci (UNIASSELVI)
Rodovia BR 470 Km 71, 1040, Benedito, Indaial, SC 89130000
Tel: +55(47) 3281-9000
Fax: +55(47) 3281-9090
EMail: asselvi@asselvi.com.br
Website: http://www.uniasselvi.com.br

Diretor Geral: José Tafner

Courses
Accountancy (Accountancy); **Advertising and Publicity** (Advertising and Publicity); **Architecture and Urbanism** (Architecture; Town Planning); **Arts and Humanities**; **Civil Engineering** (Civil Engineering); **Design-Fashion**; **Electrical Engineering** (Electrical Engineering); **Electrical Engineering - Telecommunications**; **Environmental Engineering** (Environmental Engineering); **Finance**; **Geography** (Geography); **Human Resources** (Human Resources); **Information Systems**; **International Business** (International Business); **Law**; **Marketing**; **Mechanical Engineering**; **Physical Education**; **Production Engineering** (Production Engineering)
Further Information: Also branch in Blumenau
History: Founded 1999. Transformed into Faculdades Integradas do Vale do Itajaí 2000. Acquired university status and title 2004. Authorised to offer distance courses 2005. Integrated in the UNIASSELVI group 2008.
Degrees and Diplomas: *Bacharelado*; *Licenciatura*
Last Updated: 15/06/10

LIBERTAS - INTEGRATED FACULTIES

Libertas - Faculdades Integradas (LIBERTAS)
Avenida Wenceslau Bras, 1018, Pavimento Térreo e Pavimento Superior, Lagoinha, São Sebastião do Paraíso, MG 37950-000
Tel: +55(35) 3531-1998
Fax: +55(35) 3531-1328
EMail: ceduc2008@hotmail.com
Website: http://www.fecom.edu.br/

Courses
Graduate Studies (Accountancy; Administrative Law; Business Administration; Computer Science; Finance; Health Administration; Public Health; Software Engineering); **Undergraduate Studies** (Accountancy; Administration; Information Sciences; Law; Nursing)
Degrees and Diplomas: *Bacharelado*; *Especialização/Aperfeiçoamento*. Also MBA.
Last Updated: 29/09/10

LIONS FACULTY

Faculdade Lions
Rua Armogaste Jose da Silveira n° 350 - Setor Fama, Goiania, GO
Tel: +55(62) 3211-1151
EMail: faclions@faclions.com.br
Website: http://www.faclions.org/v1

Diretor: Eurípides Rossi Camilo

Courses
Administration (Administration); **Advertising** (Advertising and Publicity); **Hotel Management** (Hotel Management); **Law** (Law); **Tourism** (Tourism)
History: Founded 2002.
Main Language(s) of Instruction: Portuguese
Degrees and Diplomas: *Bacharelado*; *Especialização/Aperfeiçoamento*
Libraries: Yes
Last Updated: 02/09/10

LITERATUS FACULTY

Faculdade Literatus
Av. Constatino Nery, n° 3693, Chapada, Manaus, AM 69050-001
Tel: +55(92) 3622-3503
EMail: fal_cel@vivax.com.br
Website: http://www.literatus.edu.br/home/index.php

Diretor: Alcirene Maria da Silva Cursino

Courses
Administration (Administration); **Biomedicine** (Biomedicine); **Nursing** (Nursing); **Nutrition** (Nutrition); **Radiology** (Radiology)
History: Founded 2007.
Main Language(s) of Instruction: Portuguese
Degrees and Diplomas: *Bacharelado*; *Especialização/Aperfeiçoamento*
Last Updated: 02/09/10

LOGATTI FACULTIES ARARAQUARA

Faculdades Logatti Araraquara (FIAR)
Avenida Brasil 782, Centro, Araraquara, São Paulo 14801050
Tel: +55(16) 3301-2410
Fax: +55(16) 3301-2411
EMail: logatti@logatti.edu.br
Website: http://www.logatti.edu.br

Diretor: Walter Logatti Filho (1997-) EMail: walter@logatti.edu.br

Courses
Administration (Administration); **Agricultural Engineering**; **Civil Engineering** (Civil Engineering); **Computer Engineering** (Computer Engineering); **Computer Science** (Computer Science); **Electrical Engineering** (Electrical Engineering); **Environmental Engineering** (Environmental Engineering)
History: Founded 1966.
Main Language(s) of Instruction: Portuguese
Degrees and Diplomas: *Bacharelado*; *Especialização/Aperfeiçoamento*
Last Updated: 21/06/10

LOGOS THEOLOGICAL FACULTY OF HUMANITIES AND SOCIAL SCIENCES

Faculdade Teológica de Ciências Humanas e Sociais Logos (FAETEL)
Rua Padre Adelino, 700, Belenzinho, São Paulo, SP 03303-000
Tel: +55(11) 2081-4486
Fax: +55(11) 2081-4486
EMail: faetel@faetel.edu.br
Website: http://www.faetel.edu.br/

President: Alcino Lopes de Toledo

Courses
Graduate Studies (Educational Psychology; Higher Education; Religious Studies); **Undergraduate Studies** (Theology)
History: Founded 1983 as Faculdade de Educação Teológica.
Degrees and Diplomas: *Bacharelado*; *Licenciatura*; *Especialização/Aperfeiçoamento*
Last Updated: 09/09/10

LOURENÇO FILHO FACULTY

Faculdade Lourenço Filho (FLF)
Rua Barão do Rio Branco 2101, Centro, Fortaleza, Ceará 60025062
Tel: +55(85) 4009-6060
Fax: +55(85) 4009-6001
EMail: roberta@flf.edu.br
Website: http://www.flf.edu.br

Diretor: Antônio Figueiras Lima Filho (1998-)

Courses
Accountancy; **Computer Science** (Computer Science)
History: Founded 1997.
Main Language(s) of Instruction: Portuguese
Degrees and Diplomas: *Bacharelado*
Last Updated: 09/10/07

LS FACULTY

Faculdade Ls
Setor D Sul "5", Taguatinga Sul, Brasilia, DF 72.020-111
Tel: +55(61) 3352-2294
EMail: mada@ls.edu.br
Website: http://www.ls.edu.br/faculdade/?id=1

Diretor: Luiz Antônio de França

Courses
Letters (Literature); **Nursing** (Nursing)
History: Founded 2005.
Main Language(s) of Instruction: Portuguese
Degrees and Diplomas: *Bacharelado*; *Licenciatura*; *Especialização/Aperfeiçoamento*
Libraries: Yes
Last Updated: 02/09/10

LUCIANO FEIJÃO FACULTY

Faculdade Luciano Feijão
Avenida Dom José 325 - Anexo B, Sobral, CE 62010-290
Tel: +55(88) 3611-3100
EMail: isabelpontes@lucianofeijao.com.br
Website: http://www.flucianofeijao.com.br

Diretora: Isabel de Aguiar Pontes

Courses
Administration (Administration); **Law** (Law)
History: Founded 2004.
Main Language(s) of Instruction: Portuguese
Degrees and Diplomas: *Bacharelado*
Libraries: Yes
Last Updated: 02/09/10

LUIZ MENDES FACULTY OF ACCOUNTANCY

Faculdade de Ciências Contábeis Luiz Mendes (LUMEN)
Rua Maria Alves da Rocha, 51, Aeroclube, João Pessoa,
PB 58040-040
Tel: +55(83) 3243-8380
EMail: lumensecretaria@hotmail.com
Website: http://www.lumenfaculdades.edu.br/

Diretor: Ambrosio Elias de Araújo Pontes

Courses
Accountancy (Accountancy); **Administration**; **Graduate Studies**
History: Founded 2002.
Degrees and Diplomas: *Bacharelado*; *Especialização/Aperfeiçoamento*
Last Updated: 20/07/10

LUSÍADA UNIVERSITY CENTRE

Centro Universitário Lusíada (UNILUS)
Armando de Salles Oliveira, 150, Boqueirão, Santos,
São Paulo 11050071
Tel: +55(13) 3235-1311
Fax: +55(13) 3221-4488
EMail: unilus@lusiada.br
Website: http://www.lusiada.br

Reitor: Nelson Teixeira (1998-)

Courses
Administration; **Biomedicine** (Biomedicine); **Graduate Studies** *(Stricto Sensu)* (Medicine); **Graduate Studies** *(Lato Sensu)*; **International Relations**; **Medicine**; **Nursing** (Nursing); **Pedagogy**; **Phonoaudiology** (Speech Therapy and Audiology); **Physical Therapy** (Physical Therapy); **Technological Studies**
History: Founded 1966.
Main Language(s) of Instruction: Portuguese
Degrees and Diplomas: *Tecnólogo*; *Bacharelado*; *Licenciatura*; *Especialização/Aperfeiçoamento*; *Mestrado*
Last Updated: 15/06/10

LUTHERAN INSTITUTE AND EDUCATIONAL CENTRE - BOM JESUS

Instituto Superior e Centro Educacional Luterano - Bom Jesus (BOM JESUS/IELUSC)
Rua Alexandre Dohler 56 Centro, Joinville,
Santa Catarina 89201260
Tel: +55(47) 3433-0155
Fax: +55(47) 3433-4737
EMail: ielusc@ielusc.br
Website: http://www.ielusc.br/

Diretor: Tito Lívio Lermen (1996-)

Courses
Nursing (Nursing); **Nutrition** (Nutrition); **Physical Education** (Physical Education); **Social Communication**
History: Founded 1995
Main Language(s) of Instruction: Portuguese
Degrees and Diplomas: *Bacharelado*
Last Updated: 14/06/10

LUTHERAN UNIVERSITY OF BRAZIL

Universidade Luterana do Brasil (ULBRA)
Av. Farroupilha, n° 8001 · Bairro São José, Canoas,
Rio Grande do Sul 92425-900
Tel: +55(51) 3477-4000
Fax: +55(51) 3477-1313
EMail: ulbra@ulbra.br
Website: http://www.ulbra.br

Reitor: Marcos Fernando Ziemer
Tel: +55(51) 477-2222, Fax: +55(51) 477-9111

Areas
Applied Social Sciences; **Education, Science and Art** (Arts and Humanities; Communication Studies; Education; Geography; History; Modern Languages; Philosophy; Physical Education; Theol-

ogy; Tourism; Visual Arts); **Health Sciences** (Biochemistry; Dentistry; Health Sciences; Medicine; Nursing; Optometry; Pharmacy; Physical Therapy; Psychology; Radiology; Speech Therapy and Audiology; Veterinary Science); **Technology and Computer Science** (Agriculture; Architecture; Automotive Engineering; Chemical Engineering; Civil Engineering; Computer Networks; Computer Science; Electrical Engineering; Environmental Engineering; Environmental Management; Fashion Design; Industrial Design; Technology; Textile Technology)

Further Information: Campuses at Cachoeira do Sul, Carazinho, Gravataí, Guaíba, Santa Maria, São Jerônimo and Torres, Ji-Parana, Manaus, Palmas, Santarém, Itumbiara and Porto Velho. Also 2 University Hospitals at Pôrto Alegre ('Lutheran Hospital') and Tramandaí

History: Founded 1964 as Canõas College of Administration Sciences, became University 1989. Maintained by the Comunidade Evangelica Luterana São Paulo.

Governing Bodies: Conselho de Ensino, Pesquisa e Extensão; Conselho Administrativo

Academic Year: March to December (March-July; August-December)

Admission Requirements: Secondary school certificate and entrance examination

Main Language(s) of Instruction: Portuguese

Degrees and Diplomas: *Bacharelado*: 4-6 yrs; *Licenciatura*: 4-6 yrs; *Especialização/Aperfeiçoamento*: 1-1/2-2 yrs; *Mestrado*: 2-2 1/2 yrs; *Doutorado*: 3-6 yrs

Student Services: Academic counselling, Canteen, Cultural centre, Employment services, Foreign student adviser, Handicapped facilities, Health services, Nursery care, Social counselling, Sports facilities

Special Facilities: Natural Science Museum. Radio Station. Movie Studio

Libraries: 'Martin Luther' Central Library, c. 250,000 vols

Publications: Aletheia, Psychology *(biannually)*; Caesura, Humanities and Social Sciences *(biannually)*; Logos, Revista de Divulgação Científica *(biannually)*; Opinio jure, Law *(biannually)*; Stomatos, Dentistry *(biannually)*

Press or Publishing House: Editora da Universidade Luterana do Brasil

Last Updated: 11/05/10

LUZWEL FACULTY OF ADMINISTRATION AND ACCOUNTANCY

Faculdade de Administração e Ciências Contábeis Luzwell (LUZWELL)
Avenida Chibaras 74, Moema, São Paulo, São Paulo 04076-000
Tel: +55(11) 5051-1611
EMail: facluzwell@facluzwell.br
Website: http://www.facluzwell.br

Diretor: José Rage Zaher (1996-)

Courses
Accountancy; **Administration** (Administration)
History: Founded 1972.
Main Language(s) of Instruction: Portuguese
Degrees and Diplomas: *Bacharelado*
Last Updated: 09/01/08

MACAPAENSE INSTITUTE OF HIGHER EDUCATION

Instituto Macapaense de Ensino Superior (IMMES)
Rua Jovino Dinoá, 2085, Centro, Macapá, AP 68900-075
Tel: +55(96) 3223-4244
Fax: +55(96) 3223-4244
EMail: diretoriaacademica@immes.com.br
Diretor Geral: Mateus Freire Leite

Courses
Undergraduate Studies (Administration; Agricultural Engineering; Agronomy; Dentistry; Engineering; Nutrition; Pharmacy; Physical Therapy; Psychology; Social and Community Services)
Degrees and Diplomas: *Bacharelado*
Last Updated: 22/09/10

MACHADO DE ASSIS FACULTY

Faculdade Machado de Assis (FAMA)
Praça Marquês do Herval 4, Santa Cruz, Rio de Janeiro,
Rio de Janeiro 23510140
Tel: +55(21) 3395-5166
Fax: +55(21) 3395-0944
EMail: sap@famanet.br
Website: http://www.famanet.br

Diretor: Jacob Gribbler Neto EMail: diretorgeral@famanet.br

Courses
Accountancy (Accountancy); **Administration** (Administration); **Letters** (Literature); **Mathematics**; **Tourism** (Tourism)
History: Founded 1998.
Main Language(s) of Instruction: Portuguese
Degrees and Diplomas: *Bacharelado*; *Licenciatura*; *Especialização/Aperfeiçoamento*; *Mestrado*
Last Updated: 06/07/10

MACHADO DE ASSIS FACULTY OF TECHNOLOGY

Faculdade de Tecnologia Machado de Assis (FAMA)
Rua Waldir de Jesus, 99, Capão Raso, Curitiba, PR 81130-11
Tel: +55(41) 3248-2885 +55(41) 3015-0954
EMail: secretariacr@sema.edu.br
Website: http://www.sema.edu.br/

Diretor Geral: Fábio Marcello Sorgon
EMail: direcao@sema.edu.br; sorgon@yahoo.com

Courses
Accountancy (Accountancy); **Administration** (Administration); **Biology** (Biology); **Environmental Management** (Environmental Management); **Financial Management** (Finance); **Graduate Studies** (Business and Commerce; Educational Administration; Educational Psychology); **History** (History); **Human Resources** (Human Resources); **International Business** (International Business); **Literature** (Literature); **Logistics** (Transport Management); **Marketing** (Marketing); **Mathematics** (Mathematics); **Social Services** (Social and Community Services)
Further Information: Also Santa Cândida and Fazenda Rio Grande campuses.
Degrees and Diplomas: *Tecnólogo*; *Bacharelado*; *Licenciatura*; *Especialização/Aperfeiçoamento*
Last Updated: 26/08/10

MACHADO DE ASSIS INTEGRATED FACULTIES

Faculdades Integradas Machado de Assis (FIMA)
Rua Santos Dumont 820, Centro, Santa Rosa, RS 98900000
Tel: +55(55) 3511-3800
EMail: secretariafaculdades@fema.com.br
Website: http://www.fema.com.br

Diretor: Antonio Roberto L. Ternes

Courses
Accountancy; **Administration** (Administration); **Law**; **Social Services** (Social and Community Services); **Visual Arts and Design** (Design; Visual Arts)
History: Founded 2001.
Main Language(s) of Instruction: Portuguese
Degrees and Diplomas: *Bacharelado*; *Especialização/Aperfeiçoamento*
Last Updated: 22/06/10

MACHADO SOBRINHO FACULTY

Faculdade Machado Sobrinho
Rua Pedro Celeste S/n, Bairro Cruzeiro do Sul, Juiz de Fora,
Minas Gerais 36030140
Tel: +55(32) 3234-1436
Fax: +55(32) 3234-1444
EMail: secfac@machadosobrinho.com.br
Website: http://www.machadosobrinho.com.br

Diretor: José Luiz de Souza Botti

Courses
Accountancy (Accountancy); **Administration** (Administration); **Pedagogy** (Pedagogy); **Production Engineering** (Production Engineering); **Psychology**

History: Founded 1969.

Main Language(s) of Instruction: Portuguese

Degrees and Diplomas: *Bacharelado*; *Especialização/Aperfeiçoamento*
Last Updated: 06/07/10

MACKENZIE PRESBYTERIAN UNIVERSITY

Universidade Presbiteriana Mackenzie (MACKENZIE)
Rua da Consolação 896, Campus São Paulo, Vila Buarque,
São Paulo, São Paulo 1239902
Tel: +55(11) 2114-8391 +55(11) 2114-1618
Fax: +55(11) 3259-6405
EMail: secgeral@mackenzie.br; acoi@mackenzie.br
Website: http://www.mackenzie.br

Reitor: Manassés Claudino Fonteles
Tel: +55(11) 2114-8170, Fax: +55(11) 3214-3102

Centres
Applied Social Sciences; **Communication and Letters** (Advertising and Publicity; Art History; Arts and Humanities; Cultural Studies; Fine Arts; Journalism); **Health Sciences and Biology**; **Science and Humanities** (Arts and Humanities; Chemistry; Mathematics; Pedagogy; Philosophy; Physics)

Faculties
Architecture and Urbanism (Architectural and Environmental Design; Architecture; Town Planning; Urban Studies); **Computer Science** (Computer Science; Information Management); **Law** (Economics; Law; Political Sciences)

Schools
Engineering (Civil Engineering; Electrical Engineering; Engineering; Materials Engineering; Mechanical Engineering; Production Engineering); **Theology** (Religion; Theology)

History: Founded as College by American Presbyterian missionaries 1870. Became University and recognized by the State 1952. A private institution, under the jurisdiction of the Federal Government. Since 1961, affiliated to the Brazilian Presbyterian Church.

Governing Bodies: Conselho Universitário

Academic Year: February to December (February-June; August-December)

Admission Requirements: Secondary school certificate and competitive entrance examination

Main Language(s) of Instruction: Portuguese

International Co-operation: With universities in France; Portugal; Romania; Spain and USA. Also participates in the Red Latinoamericana

Degrees and Diplomas: *Tecnólogo*: 3 yrs; *Bacharelado*: Accountancy; Business Administration; Economics; Foreign Commerce; Industrial Design; Languages and Education; Publicity and Marketing; Science; Visual Communication, 4 yrs; *Bacharelado*: Architecture; Engineering; Law; Psychology, 5 yrs; *Licenciatura*: Arts; Languages and Education; Science, 3 yrs; *Especialização/Aperfeiçoamento*; *Mestrado*: Development Studies; Letters; Arts and Culture History; Business Administration; Electrical Engineering; Religion; Architecture and Urbanism; Politics and Economics; *Doutorado*: Letters; Business Administration; Architecture and Urbanism;

Student Services: Academic counselling, Canteen, Cultural centre, Handicapped facilities, Health services, Social counselling, Sports facilities
Special Facilities: Observatory. TV and Radio Studio
Libraries: Biblioteca 'George Alexander', 71,460 vols
Press or Publishing House: Gráfica Universitária
Last Updated: 07/05/10

MADEIRA MAMORÉ FACULTY

Faculdade Madeira Mamoré
Avenida Costa e Silva 4137, Porto Velho, RO 78905-010
Tel: +55(69) 3222-7877
EMail: mardonin@hotmail.com

Diretora: Flora Maria Castelo Branco Correia Santos

Courses
Administration (Administration)

History: Founded 2003.

Main Language(s) of Instruction: Portuguese

Degrees and Diplomas: *Bacharelado*
Last Updated: 02/09/10

MADRE CELESTE SCHOOL

Escola Superior Madre Celeste (ESMAC)
Cidade Nova VIII, Estrada da Providência, 10, Ananindeua,
PA 67110-000
Tel: +55(91) 3273-1558
Fax: +55(91) 3273-1558
EMail: esmac@esmac.com.br
Website: http://www.esmac.com.br/

Diretora Geral: Iranilse Pinheiro

Courses
Accountancy (Accountancy); **Administration** (Administration); **Graduate Studies** (Art Education; Business Education; Educational Technology; Health Administration; Higher Education; History; Jewelry Art; Management; Mathematics; Pedagogy; Spanish; Visual Arts); **History** (History); **Hospital Administration** (Health Administration); **Law** (Law); **Literature** (English; Literature; Portuguese); **Management** (Management); **Mathematics**; **Nursing** (Nursing); **Pedagogy**; **Physical Education**; **Visual Arts**

Degrees and Diplomas: *Tecnólogo*; *Bacharelado*; *Licenciatura*; *Especialização/Aperfeiçoamento*
Last Updated: 16/07/10

MAGISTER FACULTY

Faculdade Magister
Avenida Nossa Senhora do Sabará 1300, Santo Amaro, São Paulo,
São Paulo 4686001
Tel: +55(11) 5633-4000
EMail: lucinei@magister.com.br
Website: http://www.magister.edu.br/

Diretor Geral: Alberto Palos Martinho

Courses
Administration (Administration; Business Administration; International Business; Marketing); **Literature** (Literature); **Pedagogy** (Pedagogy)

History: Founded 1999.

Main Language(s) of Instruction: Portuguese

Degrees and Diplomas: *Bacharelado*; *Especialização/Aperfeiçoamento*
Last Updated: 21/06/10

MAGSUL FACULTIES

Faculdades Magsul
Avenida Presidente Vargas 725, Centro, Ponta Porã,
Mato Grosso do Sul 79900000
Tel: +55(67) 3431-2107 +55(67) 3431-2124
Fax: +55(67) 3431-2107 +55(67) 3431-2120
EMail: magsul@pontapora.com.br
Website: http://www.magsul-ms.com.br

Diretora Geral: Maria de Fatima Viegas Josgrilbert

Courses
Accountancy (Accountancy); **Arts and Humanities** (Arts and Humanities); **Biological Sciences** (Biological and Life Sciences); **Pedagogy** (Education; Pedagogy); **Physical Education**; **Visual Arts**

History: Founded 1986.

Degrees and Diplomas: *Bacharelado*; *Licenciatura*; *Especialização/Aperfeiçoamento*
Last Updated: 21/06/10

MANCHESTER INSTITUTE OF HIGHER EDUCATION OF THE STATE OF SAO PAULO
Instituto Manchester Paulista de Ensino Superior (IMAPES)
Rua da Penha 620, Centro, Sorocaba, São Paulo 18010002
Tel: +55(15) 2101-3800
EMail: info@imapes.br
Website: http://www.imapes.br

Diretor: Nelson Raul da Cunha Fonseca **EMail:** nraul@imapes.br

Courses
Administration; International Business; Human Resources; Information Sciences; Chemistry (Administration; Chemistry; Human Resources; Information Sciences; International Business)

History: Founded 1999.

Main Language(s) of Instruction: Portuguese

Degrees and Diplomas: *Bacharelado*; *Especialização/Aperfeiçoamento*

MARANHENSE INSTITUTE OF EDUCATION AND CULTURE
Instituto Maranhense de Ensino e Cultura (IMEC)
Av. Ignácio Mourão Rangel, s/n°, Quadra 18, Parque Renascença, Jaracati, São Luís, MA 65071-680
Tel: +55(98) 3236-1307
EMail: marcioacbarros@yahoo.com.br
Website: http://www.unilist.com.br/imec/index.asp

Diretor Secretário: Fernando Di Gênio Barbosa

Courses
Undergraduate Studies (Accountancy; Administration; Advertising and Publicity; Tourism)
Last Updated: 22/09/10

MARIA MILZA FACULTY
Faculdade Maria Milza
Praça Manoel Caetano da Rocha Passos, 308 - Centro, Cruz das Almas, BA 44380-000
Tel: +55(75) 3621 - 1710
EMail: adm@mariamilza.com.br
Website: http://www.famam.com.br

Diretor: Weliton Antonio Bastos de Almeida

Courses
Administration (Administration); **Biomedicine** (Biomedicine); **Geography** (Geography); **History** (History); **Nursing** (Nursing); **Pedagogy** (Pedagogy); **Pharmacy** (Pharmacy); **Physical Education** (Physical Education)

History: Founded 2004.

Main Language(s) of Instruction: Portuguese

Degrees and Diplomas: *Bacharelado*; *Licenciatura*; *Especialização/Aperfeiçoamento*

Libraries: Yes
Last Updated: 02/09/10

MARIA THEREZA INTEGRATED FACULTIES
Faculdades Integradas Maria Thereza (FAMATH)
Rua Visconde do Rio Branco 869, São Domingos, Niterói, Rio de Janeiro 24240006
Tel: +55(21) 2620-0660 +55(21) 2620-0219
Fax: +55(21) 2620-6830
EMail: famath@famath.com.br
Website: http://www.famath.com.br

Diretor Geral: Oswaldo Salles Lima (1998-)

Courses
Biology (Biology); **Marine Biology**; **Pedagogy** (Pedagogy); **Physical Education** (Physical Education); **Psychology** (Psychology)

History: Founded 1975.

Main Language(s) of Instruction: Portuguese

Degrees and Diplomas: *Bacharelado*; *Especialização/Aperfeiçoamento*
Last Updated: 22/06/10

MÁRIO DA ANDRADE FACULTY
Faculdade Mário de Andrade
Rua Clélia, 965 - Lapa, São Paulo, SP 05042-000
Tel: +55(11) 3873-2899
EMail: atendimento@mariodeandrade.com.br
Website: http://www.mariodeandrade.com.br/faculdade

Courses
Administration (Administration); **Finance Management** (Finance); **Information Systems** (Computer Science)

History: Founded 2000.

Main Language(s) of Instruction: Portuguese

Degrees and Diplomas: *Bacharelado*; *Mestrado*
Last Updated: 02/09/10

MARIO SCHENBERG FACULTY
Faculdade Mario Schenberg
Estrada Municipal do Espigão, 1413, Cotia, SP 06710-500
Tel: +55(11) 4613 6200
EMail: informacoes@fms.edu.br
Website: http://www.fms.edu.br/

Diretora: Aparecida Maria Clapis de Paula

Courses
Administration (Administration); **Biomedicine** (Biomedicine); **Civil Engineering** (Civil Engineering); **Gastronomy** (Cooking and Catering); **Law** (Law); **Marketing** (Marketing); **Nursing** (Nursing); **Pedagogy** (Pedagogy); **Physical Education** (Physical Education)

History: Founded 2006.

Main Language(s) of Instruction: Portuguese

Degrees and Diplomas: *Bacharelado*; *Especialização/Aperfeiçoamento*
Last Updated: 02/09/10

MARIST FACULTY
Faculdade Marista
Rua Jorge Tasso Neto, 318, Apipucos, Recife, PE
Tel: +55(81) 4009-7777
EMail: fmr@marista.edu.br
Website: http://www.maristaspe.com

Diretor: João Marcelo Sombra

Courses
Administration (Administration); **Advertising** (Advertising and Publicity); **Human Resources** (Human Resources); **Law** (Law)

History: Founded 2002.

Main Language(s) of Instruction: Portuguese

Degrees and Diplomas: *Bacharelado*; *Especialização/Aperfeiçoamento*

Libraries: Yes
Last Updated: 03/09/10

MARSHAL RONDON FACULTY

Faculdade Marechal Rondon (FMR)
Viscinal Dr Nilo Lisboa Chavasco 5000, Chacara Saltinho,
São Manuel, São Paulo 18650000
Tel: +55(14) 6841-3830
Fax: +55(14) 6841-3830
EMail: fmr@fmr.edu.br
Website: http://www.fmr.edu.br

Diretor: Eduardo Storópoli

Courses
Administration (Administration); **Law** (Law); **Nursing** (Nursing);
Physiotherapy (Physical Therapy)
History: Founded 2000.
Main Language(s) of Instruction: Portuguese
Degrees and Diplomas: *Bacharelado*
Last Updated: 26/11/07

MARTHA FALCÁO FACULTY

Faculdade Martha Falcáo (FMF)
Rua Natal 300, Adrianópolis, Mánaus, Amazonas 69050790
Tel: +55(92) 2121-0900
EMail: secfmf@infs.com.br
Website: http://www.faculdademarthafalcao.com.br/

Diretor: Fernando Matos de Souza Neto

Courses
Accountancy; **Administration**; **Advertising** (Advertising and
Publicity); **Design** (Design); **Journalism** (Journalism); **Law** (Law);
Pedagogy (Pedagogy); **Psychology**; **Social Services** (Social and
Community Services)
History: Founded 1999.
Main Language(s) of Instruction: Portuguese
Degrees and Diplomas: *Bacharelado*; *Licenciatura*; *Especializa-*
ção/Aperfeiçoamento
Last Updated: 06/07/10

MARY AUXILIARY SALESIAN FACULTY

Faculdade Salesiana Maria Auxiliadora (FSMA)
Rua Monte Elisio s/n, Visconde de Araújo, Macaé,
Rio de Janeiro 27943180
Tel: +55(22) 2772-0010
Fax: +55(22) 2762-0358
EMail: secretaria@salesiana.edu.br
Website: http://www.salesiana.edu.br/2010

Diretora Geral: Irmã Maria Léa Ramos

Courses
Administration (Administration); **Advertising** (Advertising and
Publicity); **Chemical Engineering** (Chemical Engineering); **Com-**
puter Science (Computer Science); **Journalism**; **Production**
Engineering (Production Engineering); **Psychology** (Psychology)
History: Founded 2001.
Main Language(s) of Instruction: Portuguese
Degrees and Diplomas: *Bacharelado*; *Especialização/Aperfeiçoa-*
mento
Last Updated: 02/07/10

MARY THE IMMACULATE INTEGRATED FACULTIES

Faculdades Integradas Maria Imaculada (FIMI)
Rua Maringá, 450 - Parque Taquaral, Piracicaba,
São Paulo 13423-514
Tel: +55(19) 3414-2003
Fax: +55(19) 3861-4066
EMail: mariaimaculada@mariaimaculada.br
Website: http://www.mariaimaculada.br

Diretora Geral: Raphaela Carrozzo Scardua (1991-)

Courses
Administration (Administration); **History**; **Industrial Chemistry**;
Literature (Literature); **Pedagogy**; **Pharmacy** (Pharmacy); **Sci-**

ence (Biology; Chemistry; Mathematics); **Social Services** (Social
and Community Services)
Further Information: Also Mogi Guçu campus
History: Founded 1991.
Main Language(s) of Instruction: Portuguese
Degrees and Diplomas: *Bacharelado*
Last Updated: 22/06/10

MATER CHRISTI FACULTY OF SCIENCE AND TECHNOLOGY

Faculdade de Ciências e Tecnológia Mater Christi
(FCTMC)
Rua Ferreira Itajubá, 745, Santo Antonip, Mossoró,
Rio Grande do Norte 59619140
Tel: +55(84) 3422-0500
Fax: +55(84) 3422-0530
EMail: faculdade@materchristi.edu.br
Website: http://materchristi.edu.br

Diretora geral: Maria Auxiliadora Tenório Pinto de Azevêdo

Courses
Accountancy; **Administration** (Administration); **Graduate Stu-**
dies (Finance; Law; Petroleum and Gas Engineering; Safety Engi-
neering); **Information Systems**; **Law** (Law)
History: Founded 2001.
Main Language(s) of Instruction: Portuguese
Degrees and Diplomas: *Bacharelado*; *Especialização/Aperfeiçoa-*
mento. Also MBA.
Last Updated: 05/07/10

MATER DEI FACULTY

Faculdade Mater Dei (FMD)
Avenida Tupi, 3091, Centro, Pato Branco, Paraná 85505000
Tel: +55(46) 3224-2882
Fax: +55(46) 3224-2882
EMail: facmater@whiteduck.psi.br
Website: http://materdei.ceicom.com.br

Diretor: Guido Victor Guerra

Courses
Administration; **Architecture and Town Planning** (Architecture;
Town Planning); **Computer Science** (Computer Science; Software
Engineering); **Law** (Law)
History: Founded 1999.
Main Language(s) of Instruction: Portuguese
Degrees and Diplomas: *Bacharelado*; *Especialização/Aperfeiçoa-*
mento
Last Updated: 06/07/10

MATERDEI INSTITUTE OF HIGHER EDUCATION

Instituto de Ensino Superior Materdei (IES-MATERDEI)
Av. Leonardo Malcher, 1176, Centro, Manaus, AM 69010-170
Tel: +55(92) 2101-0800
Fax: +55(92) 2101-0813
EMail: iesmaterdei@iesmaterdei.com.br
Website: http://www.iesmaterdei.com.br/

Diretor Geral: Luis Eduardo Sarmiento Lozano

Courses
Nursing (Nursing)
Degrees and Diplomas: *Bacharelado*
Last Updated: 22/09/10

MAUA FACULTY OF BRASILIA

Faculdade Mauá de Brasilia
Colônia Agrícola Vicente Pires 54 - salas 101/132, Brasilia,
DF 72110-800
Tel: +55(61) 3397-5251
EMail: dilcia@mauadf.com.br
Website: http://www.mauadf.com.br

Diretor: Roberto Pereira Teles

Courses

Administration (Administration); **Letters** (Literature); **Physical Education** (Physical Education); **Visual Arts** (Visual Arts)

History: Founded 2005.

Main Language(s) of Instruction: Portuguese

Degrees and Diplomas: *Bacharelado*; *Licenciatura*; *Especialização/Aperfeiçoamento*; *Mestrado*

Last Updated: 03/09/10

MAURICIO DE NASSAU FACULTY
Faculdade Mauricio de Nassau
Rua Guilherme Pinto, 114 - Graças | Rua Fernandes Vieira, 110 - Boa Vista, Recife, PE 52011-210
Tel: +55(81) 3413-4611
EMail: janguie@esbj.com.br
Website: http://www.mauriciodenassau.edu.br

Diretor: Janguiê Diniz

Courses

Accountancy (Accountancy); **Administration** (Administration); **Advertising** (Advertising and Publicity); **Architecture and Town Planning** (Architecture; Town Planning); **Biomedicine** (Biomedicine); **Digital Cinema** (Cinema and Television); **Environmental Engineering** (Environmental Engineering); **Hotel Management** (Hotel Management); **Information Systems** (Computer Science); **Journalism** (Journalism); **Law** (Law); **Nursing** (Nursing); **Nutrition** (Nutrition); **Pharmacy** (Pharmacy); **Physical Education** (Physical Education); **Physiotherapy** (Physical Therapy); **Psychology** (Psychology); **Radio and Television** (Radio and Television Broadcasting); **Telecommunications Engineering** (Telecommunications Engineering); **Tourism** (Tourism)

Further Information: Also branches in João Pessoa, Campina Grande, Natal, Salvador and Maceio

History: Founded 2003.

Main Language(s) of Instruction: Portuguese

Degrees and Diplomas: *Bacharelado*; *Licenciatura*; *Especialização/Aperfeiçoamento*; *Mestrado*

Libraries: Yes
Last Updated: 03/09/10

MAX PLANCK FACULTY
Faculdade Max Planck
R. Rêmulo Zoppi, 434 - Vila Areal, Indaiatuba, SP 13333-090
Tel: +55(19) 3825-0514
EMail: diretoria@facmaxplanck.edu.br
Website: http://www.seufuturonapratica.com.br/portal/index.php?id=1451

Courses

Administration (Administration; Business Administration; International Business); **Engineering** (Automation and Control Engineering; Production Engineering); **Law** (Law); **Letters** (Literature); **Nursing** (Nursing); **Nutrition** (Nutrition); **Pedagogy** (Pedagogy); **Physical Education** (Physical Education); **Veterinary Science** (Veterinary Science)

Degrees and Diplomas: *Bacharelado*; *Licenciatura*; *Especialização/Aperfeiçoamento*

Last Updated: 03/09/10

MENDES DE ALMEIDA INSTITUTE
Instituto Superior Mendes de Almeida (IMA)
Rua Renascer da Terceira Idade, s/n, Jardim Campomar, Rio das Ostras, RJ 28890-000
Tel: +55(22) 2764-7107 +55(22) 2764-3173
Fax: +55(22) 2764-3173
EMail: atendimento@ima.edu.br

Courses

Undergraduate Studies (Administration; Law; Production Engineering; Tourism)

Degrees and Diplomas: *Bacharelado*. Also Postgraduate Diploma offered through Faculdade Cenescista de Itaboraí (FACNEC).

Last Updated: 28/09/10

MERCURIO FACULTY
Faculdade Mercúrio
Rua Mercúrio 293 e 1.631, Rio de Janeiro, RJ 21532-470
Tel: +55(21) 2474-8000
EMail: famerc@famerc.com.br
Website: http://www.faculdademercurio.edu.br

Diretora: Nisia Fatima Sousa Gomes Gama

Courses

Administration (Administration; Business Administration); **Information Systems** (Computer Science); **Physical Education** (Physical Education)

History: Founded 2001.

Main Language(s) of Instruction: Portuguese

Degrees and Diplomas: *Bacharelado*; *Licenciatura*; *Especialização/Aperfeiçoamento*

Libraries: Biblioteca Rui Barbosa
Last Updated: 03/09/10

META FACULTY
Faculdade Meta (FAMETA)
Rua Rubens Carneiro, 536, Abrahão Alab, Rio Branco, AC 69907-170
Tel: +55(68) 3226-1501 +55(69) 8112-7866
Fax: +55(69) 3451-4200 +55(68) 3226-1501
EMail: direcao@athenaseducacional.com.br, rosangela@athenaseducacional.com.br
Website: http://www.fameta.com.br

Courses

Administration (Administration); **Biological and Life Sciences** (Biological and Life Sciences); **Graduate Studies** (Environmental Management; Fiscal Law; Higher Education; International Business; Labour Law; Management; Public Health; Transport Management); **Information Systems** (Information Sciences); **Pedagogy** (Pedagogy)

History: Founded 1978 as colégio Meta.

Degrees and Diplomas: *Bacharelado*; *Licenciatura*. Also postgraduate diploma.

Last Updated: 06/09/10

META FACULTY OF TECHNOLOGY OF AMAPÁ
Faculdade de Tecnologia do Amapá - META (FACULDADE META)
Rua Pedro Siqueira n° 333, Jardim Marco Zero, Macapá, AP 68903-151
Tel: +55(96) 3241-6636
Website: http://www.meta.edu.br/

Courses

Computer Networks (Computer Networks); **Edifice Building** (Building Technologies); **Graduate Studies** (Business Administration; Computer Networks; Educational Psychology; Higher Education; Law; Systems Analysis); **Radiology** (Radiology); **Systems for Internet** (Computer Science)

Degrees and Diplomas: *Tecnólogo*; *Especialização/Aperfeiçoamento*. Also MBA.

Last Updated: 23/08/10

METHODIST FACULTY
Faculdade Metodista
Rua 9 de Julho 175, Centro, Birigui, São Paulo 16200060
Tel: +55(18) 3642-7808
Fax: +55(18) 3642-7808
EMail: faibi@issnet.edu.br
Website: http://www.faculdademetodista.edu.br

Diretor: Luiz Carlos Lemos Junior

Courses

Accountancy (Accountancy); **Administration** (Administration); **Secretarial Studies** (Secretarial Studies)

History: Founded 1998 as Faculdade de Administração e Informática de Birigüi.

Main Language(s) of Instruction: Portuguese

Degrees and Diplomas: *Bacharelado*; *Especialização/Aperfeiçoamento*

Last Updated: 06/07/10

METHODIST FACULTY OF ITAPEVA
Faculdade Metodista de Itapeva
Rua Prefeito Felipe Marinho 110, Jardim Ferrari, Itapeva, SP
Tel: +55(15) 3521-9520
EMail: zuleide.leite@metodista.br
Website: http://www.metodista.br/itapeva

Diretor: Marcio de Moraes

Courses

Accountancy (Accountancy); **History/Geography** (Geography; History); **Letters** (Literature)

History: Founded 1995.

Main Language(s) of Instruction: Portuguese

Degrees and Diplomas: *Bacharelado*; *Licenciatura*; *Especialização/Aperfeiçoamento*

Libraries: Yes
Last Updated: 03/09/10

METHODIST FACULTY OF SANTA MARIA
Faculdade Metodista de Santa Maria (FAMES)
Rua Doutor Turi 2003, Prédio Centro, Santa Maria,
Rio Grande do Sul 97050180
Tel: +55(55) 3028-7000
Fax: +55(55) 3028-7007
EMail: adriana@ipametodista.edu.br
Website: http://www.metodistadosul.edu.br/fames/capa/
apresentacao.php

Diretora: Adriana Rivoire Menelli de Oliveira

Courses

Administration (Administration; Health Administration); **Computer Science** (Computer Science); **Health Management** (Health Administration); **Law**; **Literature** (Literature); **Physical Education**

History: Founded 1998.

Main Language(s) of Instruction: Portuguese

Degrees and Diplomas: *Bacharelado*; *Licenciatura*
Last Updated: 06/07/10

METHODIST UNIVERSITY CENTRE
Centro Universitário Metodista (IPA)
Rua Cel. Joaquim Pedro Salgado, 80, Bairro Rio Branco,
Porto Alegre, RS 90420-060
Tel: +55(51) 3316-1300
EMail: direcao.geral@metodistadosul.edu.br
Website: http://www.metodistadosul.edu.br/centro_universitario/
capa/default.php

Reitor: Roberto Pontes da Fonseca

Courses

Accountancy; **Administration**; **Advertising**; **Analysis and Systems Development** (Systems Analysis); **Architecture and Urbanism** (Architecture; Town Planning); **Biological Sciences**; **Biomedicine** (Biomedicine); **Civil Engineering**; **Computer Engineering**; **Education**; **English**; **Fashion Design** (Fashion Design); **Graduate Studies** *(Stricto Sensu)* (Biological and Life Sciences; Rehabilitation and Therapy); **Graduate Studies** *(Lato Sensu)*; **History** (History); **Hospital Administration** (Health Administration); **Interior Design** (Interior Design); **International Business**; **Journalism** (Journalism); **Law**; **Mathematics** (Mathematics); **Music** (Music); **Nursing** (Nursing); **Nutrition** (Nutrition); **Occupa-**tional Therapy; **Pharmacy** (Pharmacy); **Philosophy**; **Phonoaudiology**; **Physical Education** (Physical Education); **Physiotherapy** (Physical Therapy); **Portuguese** (Portuguese); **Production Engineering** (Production Engineering); **Psychology**; **Social Service** (Social and Community Services); **Tourism**

Further Information: Also: Colégio Metodista Americano, Dona Leonor, DC Shopping, Instituto Metodista Centenário, Instituto União de Uruguaiana da Igreja Metodista.

Degrees and Diplomas: *Bacharelado*; *Licenciatura*; *Especialização/Aperfeiçoamento*; *Mestrado*. Also MBA.
Last Updated: 17/03/11

METHODIST UNIVERSITY OF PIRACICABA
Universidade Metodista de Piracicaba (UNIMEP)
Rodovia do Açucar km 156 S/n Campus Taquaral, Piracicaba,
São Paulo 13400911
Tel: +55(19) 3124-1515
Fax: +55(19) 3124-1500
EMail: unimep@unimep.br
Website: http://www.unimep.br

Reitor: Clovis Pinto de Castro
Tel: +55(19) 3124-1600 EMail: reitoria@unimep.br

Faculties

Business and Management (Accountancy; Administration; Business and Commerce; Economics; Hotel Management; International Business; Management; Tourism); **Communication** (Advertising and Publicity; Communication Studies; Journalism; Public Relations; Radio and Television Broadcasting); **Dentistry** *(Lins)* (Dentistry); **Engineering, Architecture and Town Planning** (Architecture; Automation and Control Engineering; Chemical Engineering; Engineering; Food Technology; Industrial Chemistry; Industrial Engineering; Mechanical Engineering; Production Engineering; Town Planning); **Exact and Natural Sciences** (Computer Science; Information Technology; Management Systems; Mathematics; Natural Sciences; Systems Analysis); **Health Sciences** (Nursing; Nutrition; Pharmacy; Physical Education; Physical Therapy; Speech Therapy and Audiology); **Human Sciences** (Education; English; History; Modern Languages; Music; Pedagogy; Philosophy; Portuguese; Psychology); **Law** (Law); **Religious Studies** (Religious Studies)

Further Information: Also Samaritan Evangelical Hospital. Senior Citizens University, Piracicaba Music School, Martha Watts Cultural Centre and several units and laboratories.

History: Founded 1881 as Primary School by the American Methodist Mission, became Faculdade de Ciências Econômicas, Contábeis e Administração de Emprêsas 1964. Faculty of Education added 1966 and Faculty of Law 1970. Became University with present structure 1975. An autonomous institution under the jurisdiction of the national Ministry of Education and Sports.

Governing Bodies: Conselho Diretor; Conselho Universitário; Conselho de Ensino e Pesquisa

Academic Year: February to December (February-June; August-December)

Admission Requirements: Secondary school certificate and Entrance Examination.

Main Language(s) of Instruction: Portuguese

International Co-operation: With universities in Angola, Argentina, Arab countries, Bolivia, Belgium, Cap Verde, Canada, Chile, United Kingdom, France, Germany, Japan, Mexico, Mozambique, Netherlands, Portugal, USA, Spain and Zimbabwe.

Degrees and Diplomas: *Tecnólogo*: Technology, 2 1/2-3 yrs; *Bacharelado (BA; BSc)*: 4-5 yrs; *Licenciatura*: 4-5 yrs; *Mestrado*: a further 2 yrs; *Doutorado*: a further 2-3 yrs

Student Services: Canteen, Cultural centre, Foreign student adviser, Foreign Studies Centre, Handicapped facilities, Health services, Language programs, Social counselling, Sports facilities

Special Facilities: Jair de Araújo Lopes Museum. University Theatre. Lodging Centre. Martha Watts Cultural Centre.

Libraries: 'Taquaral' Library, 125,558 vols; 'Santa Bárbara d'Oeste' Library, 34,552 vols; 'Lins' Library, 24,041 vols. Special Research Collections

Publications: Cadernos de Direito *(biannually)*; Revista Brasileira de Educação Especial *(biannually)*; Revista da Faculdade de

Odontologia de Lins *(biannually)*; Revista de Ciência e Tecnologia *(biannually)*; Revista Impulso, Journal of social and human sciences *(quarterly)*; Saúde em Revista *(biannually)*

Press or Publishing House: Editora UNIMEP
Last Updated: 11/05/10

METHODIST UNIVERSITY OF SÃO PAULO
Universidade Metodista de São Paulo (UMESP)
Rua Alfeu Tavares, 149, Rudge Ramos, São Bernardo do Campo, São Paulo 9640000
Tel: +55(11) 4366-5600
Fax: +55(11) 4366-5768
EMail: sgeral@metodista.br
Website: http://www.metodista.br

Reitor: Márcio de Moraes
Tel: +55(11) 4366-5510 EMail: marcio@metodista.br

Colleges
Philosophy and Religious Sciences (Philosophy; Religion)

Courses
Graduate

Schools
Administration (Administration; Business and Commerce; Finance; International Business); **Advertising and Tourism** (Advertising and Publicity; Tourism); **Biological and Health Sciences** (Biological and Life Sciences; Biology; Biomedicine; Health Sciences; Nutrition); **Economics and Accountancy** (Accountancy; Economics); **Education and Teacher Training** (Education; Pedagogy; Special Education; Teacher Training); **Exact Sciences and Technology** (Computer Science; Mathematics; Software Engineering; Technology); **Journalism and Public Relations** (Journalism; Public Relations); **Law**; **Odontology** (Dentistry); **Physical Education and Physiotherapy** (Physical Education; Physical Therapy); **Radio and Television**; **Theology** (Theology); **Veterinary Science** (Veterinary Science)

Further Information: Also Veterinary Hospital

History: Founded 1971 as Methodist Institute of Higher Education, integrating Methodist School of Theology, founded 1938. Acquired present status and title 1997.

Academic Year: January to December

Admission Requirements: Secondary school certificate and entrance examination

Fees: (US Dollars): 200-700 per month

Main Language(s) of Instruction: Portuguese

Degrees and Diplomas: *Bacharelado*: 4 yrs; *Especialização/Aperfeiçoamento*; *Mestrado*; *Doutorado*

Student Services: Academic counselling, Canteen, Cultural centre, Employment services, Nursery care, Sports facilities

Special Facilities: Radio and TV studio. Theatre

Libraries: 'Jalmar Bowden' Library, 120,000 vols
Last Updated: 17/12/07

MÉTODO FACULTY OF SAO PAULO
Faculdade Método de São Paulo
Av. Jabaquara, 1314, São Paulo, SP 04046-200
Tel: +55(11) 5074-1010
EMail: famesp@famesp.edu.br
Website: http://www.famesp.edu.br/

Diretora: Lígia Marini Lacrimanti

Courses
Pedagogy (Pedagogy)
History: Founded 2007.
Main Language(s) of Instruction: Portuguese
Degrees and Diplomas: *Licenciatura*; *Especialização/Aperfeiçoamento*
Libraries: Yes
Last Updated: 08/09/10

METROPOLITAN FACULTY
Faculdade Metropolitana (POLIFUCS)
Avenida Deputado João Leão, Loteamento Joquei Clube s/n, Centro, Lauro de Freitas, Bahia 42700000
Tel: +55(71) 3288-2588
EMail: edna@ufba.br
Website: http://www.polifucs.br

Diretor Geral: José de Brito Alves

Courses
Social Communication
History: Founded 2000.
Main Language(s) of Instruction: Portuguese
Degrees and Diplomas: *Bacharelado*

METROPOLITAN FACULTY - UNESSA
Faculdade Metropolitana - unessa
Rua: Araras, 241 Bairro: Jardim Eldorado, Porto Velho, RO 78912-640
Tel: +55(69) 3026-1020
EMail: fimca@fimca.com.br
Website: http://www.metropolitana-ro.com.br

Diretora: Maria Silvia Fonseca Ribeiro Carvalho de Moraes

Courses
Letters (Literature); **Pedagogy** (Pedagogy); **Physical Education** (Physical Education)
History: Founded 2002.
Main Language(s) of Instruction: Portuguese
Degrees and Diplomas: *Licenciatura*
Libraries: Yes
Last Updated: 03/09/10

METROPOLITAN FACULTY OF BELO HORIZONTE
Faculdade Metropolitana de Belo Horizonte (METROPOLITANA -BH)
Rua Paracatu 1385, Santo Agostinho, Belo Horizonte, Minas Gerais 30180091
Tel: +55(31) 3295-5006
Fax: +55(31) 3295-5006
EMail: secretariageral@metropolitanabh.com.br
Website: http://www.metropolitanabh.com.br

Diretor: Rogério Monteiro Barbosa

Courses
Administration (Administration); **Advertising and Publicity** (Advertising and Publicity); **Education** (Environmental Studies; Pedagogy); **Information Systems** (Information Management); **Law** (Commercial Law; Law; Public Law); **Psychology** (Psychology); **Tourism** (Tourism)
History: Founded 2001.
Degrees and Diplomas: *Bacharelado*; *Licenciatura*; *Especialização/Aperfeiçoamento*
Last Updated: 05/07/10

METROPOLITAN FACULTY OF CAIEIRAS
Faculdade Metropolitana de Caieiras
Rua México 100, Caieiras, SP 07700-000
Tel: +55(11) 4445-4255
EMail: juridico@panelliarruda.com.br
Website: http://www.unicaieiras.com.br

Diretor: Wladimir Panelli

Courses
Accountancy (Accountancy); **Administration** (Administration); **Pedagogy** (Pedagogy)
History: Founded 2005.
Main Language(s) of Instruction: Portuguese
Degrees and Diplomas: *Bacharelado*; *Licenciatura*; *Especialização/Aperfeiçoamento*; *Mestrado*
Libraries: Yes
Last Updated: 06/09/10

METROPOLITAN FACULTY OF CAMAÇARI

Faculdade Metropolitana de Camaçari (FAMEC)
Avenida Eixo Urbano Central, S/n Prédio Centro, Camaçari,
BA 42800000
Tel: +55(71) 2101-3250
EMail: facmecnet@uol.com.br
Website: http://www.famec.edu.br/afamec.htm

Diretora: Celene Maria de Oliveira Santos (1998-)

Courses
Administration (Administration); **Biology**; **Chemistry**; **Environmental Engineering** (Environmental Engineering); **Law**; **Letters** (Literature); **Mathematics** (Mathematics); **Nursing**; **Oceanography** (Marine Science and Oceanography); **Pedagogy** (Pedagogy); **Physics** (Physics); **Physiotherapy** (Physical Therapy); **Production Engineering**; **Psychology** (Psychology); **Social Communication** (Public Relations); **Teacher Training** (Teacher Training)

History: Founded 1998.

Main Language(s) of Instruction: Portuguese

Degrees and Diplomas: *Bacharelado*; *Licenciatura*; *Especialização/Aperfeiçoamento*; *Mestrado*
Last Updated: 05/07/10

METROPOLITAN FACULTY OF CURITIBA

Faculdade Metropolitana de Curitiba (FAMEC)
Avenida Rui Barbosa 5881, Afonso Pena, São José dos Pinhais,
PR 83040550
Tel: +55(41) 3593-1200
Fax: +55(41) 3593-1200
EMail: dgeral@famec.com.br
Website: http://www.famec.com.br

Diretor Geral: Almeri Paulo Finger

Courses
Accountancy (Accountancy); **Administration** (Administration); **Computer Science** (Computer Networks; Computer Science); **Law**; **Pedagogy**; **Tourism** (Tourism)

History: Founded 1999.

Main Language(s) of Instruction: Portuguese

Degrees and Diplomas: *Bacharelado*; *Licenciatura*; *Especialização/Aperfeiçoamento*; *Mestrado*
Last Updated: 05/07/10

METROPOLITAN FACULTY OF GRANDE FORTALEZA

Faculdade Metropolitana da Grande Fortaleza
R. Conselheiro Estelita, 500/Centro, Fortaleza, CE 60010-260
Tel: +55(85) 3206-6400
EMail: fametro@fametro.com.br
Website: http://www.fametro.com.br

Diretor: Luis Antonio Rabelo Cunha

Courses
Accountancy (Accountancy); **Administration** (Administration); **Nursing** (Nursing)

History: Founded 2002.

Main Language(s) of Instruction: Portuguese

Degrees and Diplomas: *Bacharelado*; *Especialização/Aperfeiçoamento*
Libraries: Yes
Last Updated: 06/09/10

METROPOLITAN FACULTY OF GRANDE RECIFE

Faculdade Metropolitana da Grande Recife (UNESJ)
Avenida Barreto de Menezes 809 Jaboata dos Guararapes, Recife,
Pernambuco 51030390
Tel: +55(81) 3361-0620
Fax: +55(81) 3343-4086
EMail: metropolitana@metropolitana.edu.br
Website: http://www.metropolitana.edu.br

Diretor: Anternor Geraldo Zanetti Ferreira

Courses
Accountancy; **Administration** (Administration); **Advertising** (Advertising and Publicity); **Law**; **Tourism** (Tourism)

History: Founded 2001.

Main Language(s) of Instruction: Portuguese

Degrees and Diplomas: *Bacharelado*; *Especialização/Aperfeiçoamento*
Last Updated: 05/07/10

METROPOLITAN FACULTY OF GUARAMIRIM

Faculdade Metropolitana de Guaramirim (FAMEG)
Rodovia BR 280 Km 60 15885, Imigrantes, Guaramirim,
SC 89270000
Tel: +55(47) 3373-2000
Fax: +55(47) 3373-2000
EMail: fameg@fameg.edu.br
Website: http://www.fameg.edu.br

Diretor: Gonter Bartel
EMail: diretor.fameg@grupouniasselvi.com.br

Courses
Accountancy (Accountancy); **Administration** (Administration; Finance; Human Resources; International Business; Marketing); **Computer Networks** (Computer Networks); **Design** (Fashion Design); **Law** (Law); **Mathematics** (Mathematics); **Production Engineering** (Production Engineering); **Psychology** (Psychology); **Social Communication** (Advertising and Publicity); **Social Service** (Social and Community Services); **Systems Analysis and Development** (Systems Analysis); **Teacher Training** (Teacher Training); **Tourism** (Tourism)

History: Founded 2000.

Main Language(s) of Instruction: Portuguese

Degrees and Diplomas: *Tecnólogo*; *Bacharelado*; *Licenciatura*
Last Updated: 05/07/10

METROPOLITAN FACULTY OF MANAUS

Faculdade Metropolitana de Manaus
Av. Constantino Nery Nr. 3.000, Chapada, Manaus, AM 69050-001
Tel: +55(92) 3642-3770
EMail: secad@fametro.edu.br
Website: http://www.fametro.edu.br/

Diretora: Cinara Cardoso

Areas
Exact Sciences (Architecture; Computer Science; Town Planning); **Health** (Nursing; Nutrition; Physical Education; Psychology); **Human Sciences** (Accountancy; Administration; Law; Pedagogy; Social and Community Services; Tourism)

History: Founded 2002.

Main Language(s) of Instruction: Portuguese

Degrees and Diplomas: *Bacharelado*; *Especialização/Aperfeiçoamento*
Libraries: Yes
Last Updated: 06/09/10

METROPOLITAN FACULTY OF MARABA

Faculdade Metropolitana de Marabá
Rodovia BR 230, Km 05, S/N, Marabá, PA 68507-765
Tel: +55(94) 2101-3950
EMail: diretoria@faculdademetropolitana.com.br
Website: http://www.faculdademetropolitana.com.br

Diretor: Iramar Ricardo Paulini
EMail: iramar@faculdademetropolitana.com

Courses
Accountancy (Accountancy); **Administration** (Administration; Finance; Human Resources; Marketing); **Computer Networks** (Computer Networks); **Graphic Design** (Graphic Design); **Infor-**

mation Systems (Computer Science); **Production Engineering** (Production Engineering); **Visual Arts** (Visual Arts)

History: Founded in 2006.

Main Language(s) of Instruction: Portuguese

Degrees and Diplomas: *Bacharelado*; *Especialização/Aperfeiçoamento*

Libraries: Yes
Last Updated: 06/09/10

METROPOLITAN FACULTY OF MARINGA

Faculdade Metropolitana de Maringá (UN IFAMMA)
Av. Mauá, 2854 - Centro, Maringá, Paraná 87070810
Tel: +55(44) 2101-5555
Fax: +55(44) 2101-5551
EMail: unifamma@unifamma.edu.br
Website: http://www.unifamma.edu.br/

Diretor: Lupércio Cascone

Courses
Accountancy (Accountancy); **Administration** (Administration; Agricultural Business; Business and Commerce; Finance; Human Resources); **Law** (Law); **Secretarial Studies** (Secretarial Studies); **Social Communication** (Advertising and Publicity; Public Relations); **Social Services** (Social and Community Services)

History: Founded 2000.

Main Language(s) of Instruction: Portuguese

Degrees and Diplomas: *Bacharelado*; *Especialização/Aperfeiçoamento*; *Mestrado*
Last Updated: 05/07/10

METROPOLITAN FACULTY OF RIO DO SUL

Faculdade Metropolitana de Rio do Sul
Rodovia Br 470 Km 140 5.253, Rio do Sul, SC 89160-000
Tel: +55(47) 3521-8510
EMail: gerencia.academica@famesul.com.br
Website: http://www.grupouniasselvi.com.br/pt_br/
index.php?unidade=5

Diretor: Marlon Jackson Tafner **EMail:** marlon@asselvi.com.br

Courses
Administration (Administration; Finance; Human Resources; Marketing); **Fashion Design** (Fashion Design); **Information Systems** (Computer Science)

History: Founded 2006.

Main Language(s) of Instruction: Portuguese

Degrees and Diplomas: *Bacharelado*; *Licenciatura*; *Especialização/Aperfeiçoamento*

Libraries: Biblioteca Dante Alighieri
Last Updated: 06/09/10

METROPOLITAN FACULTY OF THE AMAZON

Faculdade Metropolitana de Amazônia
Avenida Visconde de Souza Franco, n° 72, bairro Reduto
(Doca, Belém, PA
Tel: +55(91) 3222-7560
EMail: ass@famaz.com.br
Website: http://www.famaz.edu.br

Diretor: Shen Paul Ming Jen

Courses
Accountancy (Accountancy); **Administration** (Administration); **Nursing** (Nursing)

History: Founded 2007.

Main Language(s) of Instruction: Portuguese

Degrees and Diplomas: *Bacharelado*

Libraries: Yes
Last Updated: 08/09/10

METROPOLITAN FACULTY OF THE PLANALTO NORTE REGION

Faculdade Metropolitana do Planalto Norte
Rua Senador Felipe Schmidt, 1355 - Centro, Canoinhas
Tel: +55(47) 3622 - 6063
EMail: fameplan@fameplan.com.br
Website: http://www.fameplan.com.br

Diretora: Rosane Godoi Sati

Courses
Administration (Administration; Agricultural Business; Human Resources; International Business; Marketing); **Education** *(Postgraduate)* (Education); **Management** *(Postgraduate)* (Management)

History: Founded 2006.

Main Language(s) of Instruction: Portuguese

Degrees and Diplomas: *Bacharelado*; *Especialização/Aperfeiçoamento*

Libraries: Biblioteca Presidente Getulio Vargas
Last Updated: 06/09/10

METROPOLITAN INSTITUTE OF HIGHER EDUCATION

Instituto Metropolitano de Ensino Superior (IMES)
Avenida Marechal Cândido Rondon, 850, Veneza I, Ipatinga,
MG 35164314
Tel: +55(31) 3822-1905
Fax: +55(31) 3822-1905
EMail: direg.dirac@famevaco.br
Website: http://famevaco.br

Presidente: Carlos Haroldo Piancastelli

Courses
Medicine (Medicine)

History: Founded 2001.

Main Language(s) of Instruction: Portuguese

Degrees and Diplomas: *Bacharelado*
Last Updated: 15/06/10

METROPOLITAN UNIVERSITY CENTRE OF SÃO PAULO

Centro Universitário Metropolitano de São Paulo (FIG-UNIMESP)
Rua Dr. Sólon Fernandes, 155, Vila Rosalia, Guarulhos,
SP 07072-080
Tel: +55(11) 3544-0333
Fax: +55(11) 3544-0333
EMail: sec.geral@fig.br
Website: http://www.fig.br/

Reitor: Antonio Darci Pannocchia

Courses
Accountancy (Accountancy); **Administration** (Administration); **Art Education** (Art Education); **Biological Sciences** (Biological and Life Sciences); **Biological Sciences** *(Licenciatura)*; **Chemistry** (Chemistry); **Economics**; **Geography**; **History**; **Information Systems**; **Law** (Law); **Literature** (English; Literature; Portuguese; Spanish); **Mathematics** (Mathematics); **Nutrition** (Nutrition); **Pedagogy** (Pedagogy); **Philosophy**; **Physical Education** (Physical Education); **Physical Education** (Physical Education); **Physics** (Physics); **Social Sciences** (Social Sciences); **Technological Studies**

Degrees and Diplomas: *Tecnólogo*; *Bacharelado*; *Licenciatura*
Last Updated: 13/07/10

METROPOLITAN UNIVERSITY OF SANTOS

Universidade Metropolitana de Santos (UNIMES)
Rua da Constituição 374, Vila Nova, Santos, São Paulo 11015470
Tel: +55(13) 3233-3400
Fax: +55(13) 3235-2990
EMail: vera.raphaelli@unimes.com.br
Website: http://www.unimes.br

Reitora: Renata Garcia de Siqueira Viegas da Cruz (1996-)

Courses

Accountancy (Accountancy); **Business Administration** (Accountancy; Business Administration; Finance; International Business; Marketing; Transport Management); **Economics** (Economics); **Engineering and Technology** (Food Science; Food Technology; Petroleum and Gas Engineering); **Health Sciences** (Dental Technology; Dentistry; Health Administration; Medicine; Nursing); **Law**; **Physical Education**; **Veterinary Science** (Veterinary Science)

History: Founded 1996.

Admission Requirements: Secondary school certificate and entrance examination

Main Language(s) of Instruction: Portuguese

Degrees and Diplomas: *Bacharelado*; *Licenciatura*; *Especialização/Aperfeiçoamento*; *Mestrado*; *Doutorado*
Last Updated: 10/05/10

MICHAELANGELO FACULTY
Faculdade Michelangelo
SCS Qd. 8 Bloco 'B' 60, 3° Andar, Shopping Venâncio 2000, Regiáo Administrativa I, Brasília, DF 70333900
Tel: +55(61) 3323-4168
Fax: +55(61) 3225-1816
EMail: faculdade@fmichelangelo.com.br
Website: http://www.michelangelo.edu.br

Diretor Geral: Stuart do Rêgo Barros Carício

Courses

Accountancy; **Administration** (Administration); **Computer Science**; **History**; **Letters** (Literature); **Pedagogy**; **Social Services** (Social and Community Services)

History: Founded 2000.

Main Language(s) of Instruction: Portuguese

Degrees and Diplomas: *Bacharelado*; *Licenciatura*; *Especialização/Aperfeiçoamento*; *Mestrado*
Last Updated: 05/07/10

MIGUEL DE CERVANTES INSTITUTE OF HIGHER EDUCATION
Instituto de Ensino Superior Miguel de Cervantes (IESMC)
Rua 17, 100, Jardim Araçagy I, São José de Ribamar, MA 65110-000
Tel: +55(98) 3238-1262 +55(98) 3238-3890
Fax: +55(98) 3334-4890 +55(98) 3334-4891
EMail: direcao@escoladomquixote.com.br

Diretor: Joaquim Freitas Carlos

Courses

Pedagogy (Pedagogy); **Tourism** (Tourism)
Degrees and Diplomas: *Bacharelado*; *Licenciatura*
Last Updated: 22/09/10

MILTON CAMPOS FACULTIES
Faculdades Milton Campos (FAMC)
Rua Milton Campos, 202, Vila da Serra, Nova Lima, MG 34000000
Tel: +55(31) 3286-7048
Fax: +55(31) 3286-1985
EMail: administracao@mcampos.br
Website: http://www.mcampos.br

Diretora: Lúcia Massara EMail: diretoria@mcampos.br

Faculties

Administration; **Law** (Law)
History: Founded 1998.

Main Language(s) of Instruction: Portuguese

Degrees and Diplomas: *Bacharelado*; *Especialização/Aperfeiçoamento*; *Mestrado*
Last Updated: 21/06/10

MINAS GERAIS FACULTY
Faculdade Minas Gerais (FAMIG)
Avenida do Contorno 10185, Belo Horizonte, Minas Gerais 30110-140
Tel: +55(31) 3421-6755
Fax: +55(31) 3421-5468
EMail: famig@famig.edu.br
Website: http://www.famig.edu.br

Diretor Geral: José Carlos de Oliveira Tavares
EMail: direcao@famig.edu.br

Courses

Administration (Administration); **Law** (Law)
History: Founded 2001.

Main Language(s) of Instruction: Portuguese

Degrees and Diplomas: *Bacharelado*
Last Updated: 05/07/10

MOACYR SREDER BASTOS UNIVERSITY CENTRE
Centro Universitário Moacyr Sreder Bastos (MSB)
Rua Engenheiro Trindade, 229, Campo Grande, Rio de Janeiro, Rio de Janeiro 23050-290
Tel: +55(21) 2413-5727
Fax: +55(21) 3394-4733
EMail: info@msb.br
Website: http://www.msb.br

Reitor: Adilson Rodrigues Pinto EMail: reitor@msb.br

Courses

Accountancy; **Administration** (Administration); **Arts and Humanities** (Arts and Humanities; English; Literature; Portuguese); **Geography** (Geography); **Graduate Studies** (Business Education; Civil Law; Computer Science; Criminal Law; Human Resources; Labour Law; Mathematics Education; Portuguese); **History** (History); **Information Systems** (Information Sciences); **Law**; **Mathematics** (Mathematics); **Pedagogy** (Pedagogy); **Physical Education** (Physical Education); **Physical Therapy** (Physical Therapy); **Physics** (Physics); **Social Communication**; **Social Communication** (Advertising and Publicity)

History: Founded 1970, acquired present status 1997.

Academic Year: February to December

Admission Requirements: Secondary school certificate and entrance examination

Fees: (Reais): 1,240-2,334 per semester

Main Language(s) of Instruction: Portuguese

Degrees and Diplomas: *Bacharelado*; *Licenciatura*; *Especialização/Aperfeiçoamento*

Student Services: Academic counselling, Canteen, Employment services, Language programs, Sports facilities

Special Facilities: Movie Studio. Theatre. Cultural Centre. Burle Marx Ecological Reserve

Libraries: Central Library

Publications: Pró-Ciência; Redes, Social Sciences *(biannually)*
Last Updated: 15/06/10

MODELO FACULTY
Faculdade Modelo
Rua Engenheiro Benedito Mário da Silva 95 - Prédio Térreo, Curitiba, PR 82970-000
Tel: +55(41) 3226-4545
EMail: luciana@facimod.com.br
Website: http://www.facimod.com.br

Diretor: Romeu Ferreira Ribas

Courses

Accountancy (Accountancy); **Administration** (Administration); **Pedagogy** (Pedagogy)
History: Founded 2004.

Main Language(s) of Instruction: Portuguese

Degrees and Diplomas: *Bacharelado*; *Especialização/Aperfeiçoamento*

Libraries: Yes
Last Updated: 06/09/10

MODULE FACULTY
Faculdade Módulo (FMP)
Rua Tito 1175 Lapa, São Paulo, São Paulo 05051001
Tel: +55(79) 3670-7070
EMail: fabiula@fiap.com.br
Website: http://www.faculdademodulo.com.br

Diretor: Wagner Sanchez

Courses
Administration; **Computer Science** (Computer Networks; Computer Science)

Faculties
Technology *(FTPM)* (Data Processing; Technology)
History: Founded 2000.
Main Language(s) of Instruction: Portuguese
Degrees and Diplomas: *Bacharelado*
Last Updated: 05/07/10

MODULE UNIVERSITY CENTRE
Centro Universitario Módulo (UNIMODULO)
Avenida Frei Pacífico Wagner 653, Centro, Caraguatatuba,
São Paulo 11660-903
Tel: +55(12) 3897-2000
Fax: +55(12) 3897-2021
EMail: modulo@modulo.edu.br
Website: http://www.modulo.br

Reitor: Daniel Carreira Filho

Courses
Graduate - Bacharelado (Accountancy; Administration; Advertising and Publicity; Architecture; Biological and Life Sciences; Information Sciences; Journalism; Law; Nursing; Physical Education; Production Engineering; Town Planning); **Graduate - Licenciatura** (Biological and Life Sciences; English; History; Literature; Mathematics; Pedagogy; Physical Education; Portuguese); **Graduate - Technological Studies** (Business and Commerce; Environmental Management; Human Resources; Interior Design; Multimedia; Petroleum and Gas Engineering; Public Administration; Real Estate; Systems Analysis; Tourism); **Graduate Studies** (Administration; Arts and Humanities; Biological and Life Sciences; Business and Commerce; Health Sciences; Natural Sciences; Technology)

History: Founded 1998.
Main Language(s) of Instruction: Portuguese
Degrees and Diplomas: *Tecnólogo*; *Bacharelado*; *Licenciatura*; *Especialização/Aperfeiçoamento*. Also MBA.
Last Updated: 15/06/10

MONTE SERRAT UNIVERSITY CENTRE
Centro Universitário Monte Serrat (UNIMONTE)
Avenida Rangel Pestana, 99, Vila Mathias, Santos,
São Paulo 11013551
Tel: +55(13) 3221-3466 +55(13) 3228-2100
Fax: +55(13) 3222-7521 +55(13) 3228 2131
EMail: unimonte@unimonte.br
Website: http://www.unimonte.br

Reitor: Ozires Silva

Courses
Accountancy (Accountancy); **Administration**; **Advertising and Publicity**; **Arts and Humanities** (Arts and Humanities; English; Literature; Portuguese); **Audiovisual** (Cinema and Television); **Biological Sciences** (Biological and Life Sciences); **Biomedicine** (Biomedicine); **Environmental Engineering** (Environmental Engineering); **Graduate Studies**; **Journalism**; **Law**; **Nursing** (Nursing); **Nutrition** (Nutrition); **Oceanography** (Marine Science and Oceanography); **Pedagogy** (Pedagogy); **Petroleum and Gas Engineering** (Petroleum and Gas Engineering); **Physical Education**; **Physical Therapy**; **Production Engineering** (Production Engineering); **Radio and Television**; **Social Services** (Social and Community Services); **Veterinary Science** (Veterinary Science)

History: Founded 1972.

Degrees and Diplomas: *Bacharelado*; *Licenciatura*; *Especialização/Aperfeiçoamento*. Also MBA.
Last Updated: 15/06/10

MONTEIRO LOBATO FACULTY
Faculdade Monteiro Lobato
Rua dos Andradas, 1180, Porto Alegre, RS 90020-007
Tel: +55(51) 3287-8000
EMail: monteirolobato@monteirolobato.com.br
Website: http://www.monteirolobato.com.br

Diretor: Bruno Eizerik

Courses
Accountancy (Accountancy); **Administration** (Administration)
History: Founded 2003.
Main Language(s) of Instruction: Portuguese
Degrees and Diplomas: *Bacharelado*; *Especialização/Aperfeiçoamento*
Libraries: Yes
Last Updated: 10/09/10

MONTENEGRO FACULTIES
Faculdades Montenegro
Avenida São Vicente de Paula 462, Térreo Centro, Ibicaraí,
Bahia 45745000
Tel: +55(73) 3242-1225
Fax: +55(73) 3242-1225
EMail: aemontenegro@ligmax.com.br
Website: http://www.faculdadesmontenegro.edu.br

Diretora: Waldir Pinto Montenegro Matos

Courses
Pedagogy *(FAEM)* (Pedagogy); **Physical Education** (Physical Education); **Secretarial Studies** (Secretarial Studies); **Tourism**
History: Founded 1989.
Main Language(s) of Instruction: Portuguese
Degrees and Diplomas: *Licenciatura*; *Especialização/Aperfeiçoamento*
Last Updated: 21/06/10

MONTES BELOS FACULTY
Faculdade Montes Belos
Av. Hermogenes Coelho, n° 340 - Setor Universitário,
São Luis de Montes Belos, GO 76100-000
Tel: +55(64) 3671-2814
EMail: aeco@fmb.edu.br
Website: http://www.fmb.edu.br

Diretor: Raimundo Fonseca Pinheiro

Courses
Accountancy (Accountancy); **Administration** (Administration); **Agronomy** (Agronomy); **Law** (Law); **Nursing** (Nursing); **Pedagogy** (Pedagogy); **Pharmacy** (Pharmacy); **Physiotherapy** (Physical Therapy)

History: Founded 2002.
Main Language(s) of Instruction: Portuguese
Degrees and Diplomas: *Bacharelado*; *Licenciatura*; *Especialização/Aperfeiçoamento*
Libraries: Yes
Last Updated: 08/09/10

MONTES CLAROS FACULTY OF SCIENCE AND TECHNOLOGY
Faculdade de Ciência e Tecnologia de Montes Claros
Avenida Deputado Esteves Rodrigués, 1637, Centro,
Montes Claros, MG 39400-215
Tel: +55 (38) 2104-5777
EMail: femc@femc.edu.br
Website: http://www.femc.edu.br/facit/index.php
Diretora Superintendente: Ângela Maria Carvalho Veloso

Courses

Automation and Control Engineering (Automation and Control Engineering); **Chemical Engineering** (Chemical Engineering); **Computer Engineering** (Computer Engineering); **Production Engineering** (Production Engineering); **Telecommunications Engineering** (Telecommunications Engineering)

Degrees and Diplomas: *Bacharelado*
Last Updated: 20/07/10

MONTESSORI FACULTY OF EDUCATION AND CULTURE

Faculdade de Educação e Cultura Montessori (FAMEC)
Avenida Jurucê 402, Moema, São Paulo, São Paulo 04080-001
Tel: +55(11) 4831-9724
Fax: +55(11) 4831-9729
EMail: ejrmontessori@yahoo.com.br; secretariageral@radial.br

Diretor Acadêmico: Claudemir Edson Viana (1997-)

Courses

Administration; **Advertising**; **Information Systems**; **Pedagogy**; **Theatre** (Theatre); **Tourism** (Tourism); **Visual Arts** (Visual Arts)

History: Founded 1997.

Main Language(s) of Instruction: Portuguese

Degrees and Diplomas: *Bacharelado*; *Licenciatura*; *Especialização/Aperfeiçoamento*
Last Updated: 16/11/07

MONTESSORI FACULTY OF IBIUNA

Faculdade Montessori de Ibiúna
Rodovia Bunjiro Nakao s/n - KM 665, Ibiúna, SP 18150-000
Tel: +55(15) 3248-1850
EMail: faculdadedeibiuna@yahoo.com.br
Website: http://www.fmi.edu.br

Diretora: Selma Ligeiro Rein **EMail:** selma@montessorinet.com.br

Courses

Administration (Administration); **Letters** (Literature); **Pedagogy** (Pedagogy); **Visual Arts** (Visual Arts)

History: Founded 2005.

Main Language(s) of Instruction: Portuguese

Degrees and Diplomas: *Bacharelado*; *Licenciatura*; *Especialização/Aperfeiçoamento*; *Mestrado*

Libraries: Yes
Last Updated: 06/09/10

MONTESSORI FACULTY OF SALVADOR

Faculdade Montessoriano de Salvador
Rua Abelardo Andrade de Carvalho, n°05 Boca do Rio, Salvador, BA 41.706-710
Tel: +55(71) 3371-5643
EMail: fama@montessoriano.com.br
Website: http://www.montessoriano.com.br/faculdade

Diretor: Juraci Saraiva Matos

Courses

Administration; **Pedagogy** (Pedagogy)

Degrees and Diplomas: *Bacharelado*; *Especialização/Aperfeiçoamento*
Last Updated: 07/09/10

MORAES JÚNIOR FACULTY

Faculdade Moraes Júnior (FMJ)
Rua Buenos Aires 283, Centro, Rio de Janeiro, Rio de Janeiro 20061003
Tel: +55(21) 2221-8200
EMail: ibc@ibc.br
Website: http://www.moraesjunior.edu.br

Diretor: Carlos Cesar Ferreira Vargas

Courses

Accountancy (Accountancy); **Administration** (Administration); **Economics** (Economics); **Law** (Law)

History: Founded 1965.

Main Language(s) of Instruction: Portuguese

Degrees and Diplomas: *Bacharelado*; *Especialização/Aperfeiçoamento*
Last Updated: 05/07/10

MOTHER TERESA FACULTY

Faculdade Madre Tereza
Rua Ubaldo Figueira 1777 - Nova Brasília, Santana, AP 68925-000
Tel: +55(96) 3281-2645
EMail: madretereza@madretereza.edu.br
Website: http://www.madretereza.edu.br

Diretora: Maria Borges Gomes
EMail: mariaborges@madretereza.edu.br

Courses

Administration (Administration); **Mathematics** (Mathematics); **Nursing** (Nursing)

History: Founded 2005.

Main Language(s) of Instruction: Portuguese

Degrees and Diplomas: *Bacharelado*
Last Updated: 02/09/10

MOTHER THAIS FACULTY

Faculdade Madre Thaís
Rua Madre Thaís, 197, Alto da Piedade, Ilhéus, BA
Tel: +55(73) 3634-6160
EMail: fmt@faculdademadrethais.com.br
Website: http://www.faculdademadrethais.com.br

Diretor: Eusínio Lavigne Gesteira

Courses

Administration (Administration; Environmental Management); **Nursing** (Nursing)

History: Founded 2004.

Main Language(s) of Instruction: Portuguese

Degrees and Diplomas: *Bacharelado*; *Especialização/Aperfeiçoamento*
Last Updated: 02/09/10

MOURA LACERDA UNIVERSITY CENTRE

Centro Universitário Moura Lacerda (IML)
Rua Padre Euclídes, 995, Campos Elíseos, Ribeirão Preto, São Paulo 14085-420
Tel: +55(16) 2101-1010
Fax: +55(16) 2101-1024
EMail: reitoria@mouralacerda.com.br
Website: http://www.mouralacerda.edu.br

Reitor: Glauco Eduardo Pereira Cortez

Courses

Accountancy (Accountancy); **Administration** *(Ribeirão Preto)* (Administration); **Administration** *(Jaboticabal)* (Administration); **Advertising and Publicity** (Advertising and Publicity); **Agronomy** (Agronomy); **Architecture and Town Planning** (Architecture and Planning); **Arts and Humanities** (Arts and Humanities; English; Literature; Portuguese; Spanish); **Civil Engineering** (Civil Engineering); **Computer Science**; **Economics** (Economics); **Electronic Engineering** (Electronic Engineering); **Fashion Design**; **Fine Arts** (Fine Arts); **Graduate Studies** *(Lato Sensu)*; **Graduate Studies** *(Stricto Sensu)*; **International Relations** (International Relations); **Law** (Law); **Mathematics** (Mathematics); **Pedagogy** (Pedagogy); **Philosophy**; **Physical Education** *(Jaboticabal)* (Physical Education); **Physical Education** *(Ribeirão Preto)*; **Production Engineering** (Production Engineering); **Technological Studies**; **Veterinary Science** (Veterinary Science)

History: Founded 1923. Acquired present status 1997.

Main Language(s) of Instruction: Portuguese

Degrees and Diplomas: *Tecnólogo*; *Bacharelado*; *Licenciatura*; *Especialização/Aperfeiçoamento*; *Mestrado*
Last Updated: 15/06/10

MOZARTEUM FACULTY OF SAO PAULO

Faculdade Mozarteum de São Paulo (FAMOSP)
Rua Nova dos Portugueses 365, Santa Terezinha, São Paulo,
São Paulo 2462080
Tel: +55(11) 6236-0788
Fax: +55(11) 6236-0788
EMail: mozarteum@mozarteum.br
Website: http://www.mozarteum.br

Diretor: Ormando de Maria Colacioppo (1997-)

Courses
Art Education (Art Education); **Business Administration** (Business Administration); **Music** (Music); **Pedagogy** (Pedagogy); **Singing** (Singing)
History: Founded 1973.

Main Language(s) of Instruction: Portuguese

Degrees and Diplomas: *Bacharelado*; *Licenciatura*; *Especialização/Aperfeiçoamento*
Last Updated: 05/07/10

MULTIEDUCATIONAL FACULTY

Faculdade Multieducativa
Eqnp 15/19 - Área Especial "F", Brasilia, DF 72241-576
Tel: +55(61) 3379-1213
EMail: multieducativa@terra.com.br

Diretor: Elmano Ferreira dos Santos

Courses
Information Systems (Computer Science); **Letters** (Literature)
History: Founded 2002.

Main Language(s) of Instruction: Portuguese
Degrees and Diplomas: *Bacharelado*
Last Updated: 07/09/10

MÚLTIPLO INSTITUTE OF HIGHER EDUCATION

Instituto de Ensino Superior Múltiplo (IESM)
Av. Boa Vista, nº700, Parque São Francisco, Timon,
MA +55(99) 3212-2185 +55(99) 3212-3869
Tel: +55(99) 3212-2185 +55(99) 3212-3869
EMail: iesm-faculdade@uol.com.br
Website: http://www.institutoiesm.com.br/

Diretor Geral: Rosilene Melo de Oliveira

Courses
Graduate Studies (Animal Husbandry; Irrigation; Physical Education); **Undergraduate Studies** (Accountancy; Animal Husbandry; English; Literature; Nursing; Pedagogy; Physical Education)
History: Founded 2004.

Degrees and Diplomas: *Bacharelado*; *Licenciatura*; *Especialização/Aperfeiçoamento*
Last Updated: 22/09/10

MUSIC CONSERVATOIRE OF SÃO PAULO

Conservatório Dramático Musical de São Paulo (CDMSP)
Avenida São João 269, Centro, São Paulo, São Paulo 01035000
Tel: +55(11) 3337-2111
Fax: +55(11) 3223-9231
EMail: cdmsp@cdmsp.edu.br
Website: http://www.cdmsp.edu.br

Diretor: Julio da Cruz Navega Neto

Areas
Music
History: Founded 1906.

Main Language(s) of Instruction: Portuguese
Degrees and Diplomas: *Bacharelado*
Last Updated: 19/10/07

MUSIC CONSERVATORY OF NITERÓI

Conservatório de Música de Niterói (CMN)
Rua São Pedro 96, Centro, Niterói, RJ 24020-051
Tel: +55(21) 2719-2330 +55(21) 2717-3545
Fax: +55(21) 2717-3585
EMail: conservatoriocmn@ig.com.br;
faleconosco@conservatoriocmn.com.br
Website: http://www.conservatoriocmn.com.br

Diretora: Ruth Vianna (1998-)

Courses
Art Education (Art Education); **Music** (Conducting; Music; Music Theory and Composition; Musical Instruments; Singing)
History: Founded 1965.

Degrees and Diplomas: *Bacharelado*; *Licenciatura*

NATAL FACULTY FOR THE DEVELOPMENT OF THE NORTHERN RIO GRANDE REGION

Faculdade Natalense Para o Desenvolvimento do Rio Grande do Norte (FARN)
Rua Prefeita Eliane Barros 2000, Tirol, Natal,
Rio Grande do Norte 59014540
Tel: +55(84) 211-8688 +55(84) 215-2917
Fax: +55(84) 211-8688
EMail: farn@farn.br
Website: http://www.farn.br

Diretor: Daladier Pessoa Cunha Lima (1999-)

Courses
Accountancy (Accountancy); **Administration** (Administration); **Information Sciences** (Information Sciences); **Law** (Law); **Marketing** (Marketing); **Nursing** (Nursing); **Nutrition** (Nutrition); **Physiotherapy**; **Psychology**
History: Founded 1998

Main Language(s) of Instruction: Portuguese

Degrees and Diplomas: *Bacharelado*; *Licenciatura*; *Especialização/Aperfeiçoamento*; *Mestrado*
Last Updated: 05/07/10

NATAL INSTITUTE OF HIGHER EDUCATION

Instituto Natalense de Educação Superior (INAES)
Rua Nossa Senhora da Conceição, 1255, Lagoa Seca, Natal,
RN 59054-120
Tel: +55(84) 3206-4013
Fax: +55(84) 3206-3856
EMail: naes@ipeprn.edu.br
Website: http://www.facen.com.br/inaes/inaes_main.php

Courses
Pedagogy (Pedagogy)

Degrees and Diplomas: *Licenciatura*
Last Updated: 22/09/10

NATIONAL FACULTY OF EDUCATION AND HIGHER EDUCATION OF PARANÁ

Faculdade Nacional de Educação e Ensino Superior do Paraná (FANEESP)
Rua das Araucárias, 5129, Thomaz Coelho, Araucária,
PR 83707-070
Tel: +55(41) 3552-1300
Fax: +55(41) 3552-1300
EMail: direcao@faneesp.edu.br
Website: http://www.faneesp.edu.br/

Diretora: Vergínia Aparecida Mariani

Courses
Administration (Administration); **Law** (Law); **Pedagogy** (Pedagogy)
History: Founded 2001.

Degrees and Diplomas: *Bacharelado*. Also Postgraduate Diploma.
Last Updated: 30/09/10

NATIONAL FACULTY OF THE NORTH OF PARANA

Faculdade Nacional do Norte do Paraná
Praça Madre Rafaela Ybarra 418, Marialva, PR 86990-000
Tel: +55(41) 2112-9005
EMail: elietti.svilela@terra.com.br

Diretor: Elietti de Souza Vilela

Courses
Administration (Administration)

Degrees and Diplomas: *Bacharelado*
Last Updated: 07/09/10

NATIONAL INSTITUTE OF TELECOMMUNICATIONS

Instituto Nacional de Telecomunicações (INATEL)
Avenida João de Camargo 510 Centro, Santa Rita do Sapucai,
Minas Gerais 37540000
Tel: +55(35) 4713-9200
Fax: +55(35) 3471-9314
EMail: inatel@inatel.br
Website: http://www.inatel.br

Diretor: Wander Wilson Chaves

Courses
Biomedical Engineering (Biomedical Engineering); **Computer Engineering** (Computer Engineering); **Computer Networks** (Computer Networks); **Digital Television** (Telecommunications Engineering); **Electrical Engineering**; **Telecommunications**

History: Founded 1965.

Main Language(s) of Instruction: Portuguese

Degrees and Diplomas: *Bacharelado*; *Especialização/Aperfeiçoamento*; *Mestrado*
Last Updated: 14/06/10

NATIONAL SCHOOL OF SECURITY

Escola Superior Nacional de Seguros (ESNS)
Rua Senador Dantas, 74, Subsolo, Loja, 2°, 3° e 4° andares,
Centro, Rio de Janeiro, RJ 20031-205
Tel: +55(21) 3380-1000 +55(21) 3380-1543
Fax: +55(21) 3380-1446
EMail: faleconosco@funenseg.org.br
Website: http://www.funenseg.org.br/

Diretor-Executivo: Renato Campos Martins Filho

Courses
Administration

Further Information: Units in Belo Horizonte, Blumenau, Brasília, Campinas, Curitiba, Goiânia, Porto Alegre, Recife, Ribeirão Preto, Salvador, Santos, São Paulo - Bela Vista, São Paulo – Paulista, Vitória. Also Distance Educaiton programmes

History: Founded 1971.

Degrees and Diplomas: *Bacharelado*. Also MBA.
Last Updated: 16/07/10

NATIONAL SENIOR FACULTY

Faculdade Nacional Sênior
Rua Talita Brezolin N° 1.13, Apucarana, PR 86802-390
EMail: unisenior@terra.com.br

Courses
Administration (Administration)

Degrees and Diplomas: *Bacharelado*
Last Updated: 10/09/10

NAZARENE FACULTY OF BRAZIL

Faculdade Nazarena do Brasil
Estrada da Rhodia, Km 15 em Barão Geraldo, Campinas,
SP 13085-000
Tel: +55(19) 3287-6053
EMail: contato@fnb.com.br
Website: http://www.fnb.edu.br

Diretor: Geraldo Nunes Filho

Courses
Administration (Administration); **Communication** (Journalism); **Pedagogy** (Pedagogy); **Theology** (Theology)

History: Founded 2008.

Main Language(s) of Instruction: Portuguese

Degrees and Diplomas: *Bacharelado*; *Licenciatura*

Libraries: Yes
Last Updated: 07/09/10

NETWORK FACULTY

Faculdade Network
Avenida Ampélio Gazzetta 2445, Jardim Lopes Iglesias,
Nova Odessa, SP 13460000
Tel: +55(19) 3466-2527
Fax: +55(19) 3466-2527
EMail: diretoriageral@colegionetwork.com.br
Website: http://www.nwk.edu.br

Diretora: Tânia Cristina Bassani Cecilio
EMail: diretoriageral@nwk.edu.br

Courses
Administration (Administration); **Computer Science** (Computer Science); **Pedagogy**

Further Information: Also campus in Sumaré

History: Founded 2000.

Main Language(s) of Instruction: Portuguese

Degrees and Diplomas: *Bacharelado*; *Licenciatura*; *Especialização/Aperfeiçoamento*
Last Updated: 05/12/07

NEW HORIZONS FACULTY

Faculdade Novos Horizontes
Rua Alvarenga Peixoto 1270, Belo Horizonte,
Minas Gerais 30220060
Tel: +55(31) 3293-7000
Fax: +55(31) 3291-6633
EMail: secretaria@unihorizontes.br
Website: http://www.unihorizontes.br

Diretora: Marlene Catarina de Oliveira Lopes Melo

Courses
Accountancy; **Administration**; **Law** (Law); **Social Services**

History: Founded 1999.

Main Language(s) of Instruction: Portuguese

Degrees and Diplomas: *Bacharelado*; *Especialização/Aperfeiçoamento*; *Mestrado*
Last Updated: 05/07/10

NEW MILLENNIUM FACULTY

Faculdade Novo Milénio (FNM)
Av. Santa Leopoldina no 840, Coqueiral de Itaparica, Vila Velha,
Espírito Santo 29102-040
Tel: +55(27) 3399-5555
Fax: +55(27) 3399-2973
EMail: novomilenio@gol.com.br
Website: http://www.novomilenio.br/

Diretor: Paulo Cézar de Araújo

Courses
Administration (Administration); **Cooking and Catering**; **Engineering** (Computer Engineering; Electrical Engineering; Engineering; Petroleum and Gas Engineering; Telecommunications Engineering); **Fashion Design** (Fashion Design); **Information**

Systems (Information Management); **Law** (Law); **Nursing** (Nursing); **Pedagogy** (Pedagogy); **Physiotherapy** (Physical Therapy); **Social Communication** (Advertising and Publicity; Communication Studies; Media Studies); **Social Services**; **Speech Therapy**; **Tourism** (Tourism)

History: Founded 1999.

Main Language(s) of Instruction: Portuguese

Degrees and Diplomas: *Bacharelado*; *Licenciatura*; *Especialização/Aperfeiçoamento*
Last Updated: 05/07/10

NEWTON PAIVA UNIVERSITY CENTRE

Centro Universitário Newton Paiva (UNICENTRO)
Rua José Cláudio Rezende, 80, Estoril, Minas Gerais 30190-052
Tel: +55(31) 3516-2411 +55(31) 3516-2410
Fax: +55(31) 3516-2340
EMail: newtonpaiva@newtonpaiva.br
Website: http://www.newtonpaiva.br

Reitor: Luis Carlos Souza Vieira

Secretário Geral: Carlos Wolney Mota Santos

Courses
Accountancy; **Advertising and Publicity** (Advertising and Publicity); **Architecture and Urbanism** (Architecture; Town Planning); **Arts and Humanities** *(Licenciatura)*; **Automation and Control Engineering** (Automation and Control Engineering); **Biological Sciences** (Biological and Life Sciences); **Business Administration**; **Chemical Engineering** (Chemical Engineering); **Civil Engineering**; **Economics** (Economics); **Electrical Engineering**; **Environmental Engineering** (Environmental Engineering); **Geography and Environmental Studies**; **Graduate Studies**; **Information Systems** (Information Sciences); **International Business**; **International Relations**; **Journalism**; **Law** (Law); **Mechanical Engineering**; **Nursing** (Nursing); **Nutrition**; **Odontology** (Dental Technology); **Pedagogy** *(Licenciatura)* (Pedagogy); **Pharmacy**; **Physical Therapy** (Physical Therapy); **Production Engineering**; **Psychology** (Psychology); **Public Relations**; **Technological Studies**; **Tourism** (Tourism)

Further Information: Also Carlos Luz: and Silva Lobo campuses.

History: Founded 1972, acquired present status 1997.

Academic Year: February to December (February-June; August-December)

Admission Requirements: Secondary school certificate and entrance examination

Main Language(s) of Instruction: Portuguese

Degrees and Diplomas: *Tecnólogo*; *Bacharelado*: 4 yrs; *Licenciatura*: 4 yrs; *Especialização/Aperfeiçoamento*: 1-2 yrs. Also MBA.

Student Services: Canteen, Employment services, Language programs, Sports facilities

Special Facilities: Radio and TV Laboratories

Libraries: 3 Libraries

Publications: Filosofia e Ciências Humanas *(biennially)*; Iniciacão Científica *(annually)*; Lácio *(biennially)*; Psique *(biennially)*; Vanguarda Econômica *(biennially)*
Last Updated: 16/06/10

NILTON LINS UNIVERSITY CENTRE

Centro Universitário Nilton Lins (UNINILTON LINS)
Av. Professor Nilton Lins, 3259, Parque das Laranjeiras, Flores, Mánaus, Amazonas 69058-030
Tel: +55(92) 3643-2000
Fax: +55(92) 3642-7742
EMail: uniniltonlins@niltonlins.br
Website: http://www.niltonlins.br

Reitora: Giselle Lins de Queiroz
Tel: +55 (92) 3643-2005, Fax: +55 (92) 3643 2005
EMail: glins@niltonlins.br

Vice-Reitora: Karla Pedrosa
Tel: +55 (92) 3643-2115, Fax: +55 (92) 3643-2113
EMail: karla@niltonlins.br

International Relations: Carlo Caitete, International Relations Officer

Tel: +55 (92) 3643-2092, Fax: +55 (92) 3643-2003
EMail: ccaitete@niltonlins.br

Areas
Applied and Social Sciences (Accountancy; Administration; Journalism; Tourism); **Biological and Health Sciences** (Dentistry; Medicine; Nursing; Nutrition; Pharmacy; Physical Therapy; Speech Therapy and Audiology); **Engineering and Technology**; **Exact and Earth Sciences** (Veterinary Science); **Human and Social Sciences** (Law; Psychology; Social and Community Services); **Licenciaturas**; **Technological Studies** (Computer Networks; Cooking and Catering; Environmental Management; Interior Design; Occupational Health; Petroleum and Gas Engineering; Safety Engineering; Transport Engineering)

Courses
Graduate Studies (Accountancy; Aquaculture; Biology; Business and Commerce; Civil Security; Communication Studies; Environmental Management; Finance; Higher Education; Human Resources; Human Rights; Law; Physical Therapy; Production Engineering; Social Policy; Speech Therapy and Audiology; Transport Management)

History: Founded 1986.

Academic Year: January to December

Admission Requirements: Secondary School Certificate

Main Language(s) of Instruction: Portuguese

International Co-operation: Portugal, Germany, Spain

Degrees and Diplomas: *Tecnólogo*; *Bacharelado*; *Licenciatura*; *Especialização/Aperfeiçoamento*; *Mestrado*. Alos MBA.

Student Services: Academic counselling, Canteen, Handicapped facilities, Health services, Nursery care, Social counselling, Sports facilities

Student Residential Facilities: None

Libraries: 2 main libraries
Last Updated: 16/06/10

NINTH OF JULY UNIVERSITY

Universidade Nove de Julho (UNINOVE)
Rua Guaranésia, 425, Vila Maria, Vila Maria, São Paulo, São Paulo 02117010
Tel: +55(11) 6633-9000
Fax: +55(11) 6967-1195
EMail: uninove@uninove.br
Website: http://www.uninove.br

Reitor: Eduardo Storópoli (1997-)

Areas
Administration (Accountancy; Administration; Economics; Management); **Applied Social Sciences** (Advertising and Publicity; Communication Studies; Journalism; Social Sciences; Tourism); **Education**; **Exact Sciences and Technology**; **Health Sciences** (Biochemistry; Biological and Life Sciences; Dentistry; Health Sciences; Nursing; Nutrition; Pharmacy; Physical Education; Physical Therapy; Psychology)

Centres
Technology and Specialized Training

History: Founded 1997. Acquired present status and title 2008. Formerly known as Centro Universitário Nove de Julho (Ninth of July University Centre).

Main Language(s) of Instruction: Portuguese

Degrees and Diplomas: *Licenciatura*; *Especialização/Aperfeiçoamento*; *Mestrado*; *Doutorado*
Last Updated: 10/05/10

NOBRE FACULTY OF FEIRA DE SANTANA

Faculdade Nobre de Feira de Santana
Avenida Maria Quitéria 2116, Feira de Santana, BA 44025-250
Tel: +55(75) 2102-9100
EMail: fan@fan.com.br
Website: http://www.fan.com.br

Diretor: Luciano Ribeiro Santos

Courses

Biomedicine (Biomedicine); **Electrical Engineering** (Electrical Engineering); **Law** (Law); **Mechanical Engineering** (Mechanical Engineering); **Nursing** (Nursing); **Nutrition** (Nutrition); **Physical Education** (Physical Education); **Physiotherapy** (Physical Therapy); **Psychology** (Psychology); **Social Services** (Social and Community Services); **Speech Therapy** (Speech Therapy and Audiology)

History: Founded 2001.

Main Language(s) of Instruction: Portuguese

Degrees and Diplomas: *Bacharelado*; *Especialização/Aperfeiçoamento*

Last Updated: 08/09/10

NORTE CAPIXABA FACULTY OF SÃO MATEUS - UNISAM

Faculdade Norte Capixaba de São Mateus - UNISAM
Rodovia Othovarino Duarte Santos s/n, Residencial Parque Washington, São Mateus, ES
EMail: tadeup@unisam.edu.br
Website: http://www.unisam.edu.br

Diretor: Tadeu Antônio de Oliveira Penina

Courses

Administration (Administration); **Chemical Engineering** (Chemical Engineering); **Civil Engineering** (Civil Engineering); **Mechanical Engineering** (Mechanical Engineering); **Pedagogy**; **Petroleum and Gas** (Petroleum and Gas Engineering); **Social Services** (Social and Community Services)

History: Founded 2006.

Main Language(s) of Instruction: Portuguese

Degrees and Diplomas: *Bacharelado*; *Licenciatura*. Pós-Graduação Lato Sensu

Last Updated: 17/03/11

NORTHEASTERN FACULTIES

Faculdades Nordeste (FANOR)
Av. Santos Dumont, 7800 - Dunas, Fortazela, Ceará 60135000
Tel: +55(85) 3052-4848
Fax: +55(85) 3052-4848
EMail: lourenco.filho@fanor.edu.br
Website: http://fanor.educacao.ws/institucional-fanor/

Diretor: Lourenço Rodrigues da Mata Filho

Courses

Accountancy; **Administration**; **Architecture** (Architecture); **Computer Science** (Computer Science); **Design** (Design); **Law**; **Nursing**; **Nutrition** (Nutrition); **Physical Education** (Physical Education); **Physiotherapy** (Physical Therapy); **Psychology** (Psychology); **Social Communication** (Advertising and Publicity; Journalism; Radio and Television Broadcasting); **Tourism** (Tourism)

Further Information: Also North Shopping campus

History: Founded 2001.

Main Language(s) of Instruction: Portuguese

Degrees and Diplomas: *Bacharelado*; *Especialização/Aperfeiçoamento*

Last Updated: 21/06/10

NOSSA CIDADE FACULTY

Faculdade Nossa Cidade
Av. Rui Barbosa, 605 – Centro, Carapicuíba, SP CEP 06310-390
Tel: +55(11) 4184-2515
EMail: FNC@FaculdadeNossaCidade.com.br
Website: http://www.faculdadenossacidade.com.br

Diretor: Joel Garcia de Oliveira

Courses

Administration (Administration); **Letters** (Literature); **Pedagogy** (Pedagogy); **Physical Education** (Physical Education)

Degrees and Diplomas: *Bacharelado*; *Licenciatura*; *Especialização/Aperfeiçoamento*

Libraries: Yes
Last Updated: 08/09/10

NOSSA SENHORA DOS ANJOS CENECIST FACULTY

Faculdade Cenecista Nossa Senhora dos Anjos
Rua Dr. José Loureiro da Silva, 1991, Gravataí, RS 94010-001
Tel: +55(51) 3488-1991
EMail: facensa@facensa.com.br
Website: http://www.facensa.com.br

Diretora: Eunice Carolina Ohlweiler de Oliveira

Courses

Accountancy (Accountancy); **Administration**; **Industrial Administration**; **Information Systems** (Computer Science); **Law** (Law)

History: Founded 2002.

Main Language(s) of Instruction: Portuguese

Degrees and Diplomas: *Bacharelado*; *Especialização/Aperfeiçoamento*

Libraries: Biblioteca Senador Paulo Sarasate
Last Updated: 20/07/10

NOVA ESPERANÇA FACULTIES OF NURSING AND MEDICINE

Faculdades de Enfermagem e Medicina Nova Esperança
Avenida Frei Galvão n°12, Gramame, João Pessoa, Paraiba 58067-695
Tel: +55(83) 2106-4777
Website: http://www.facene.com.br/V3

Diretor: Eitel Santiago

Courses

Medicine (Medicine); **Nursing** (Nursing)

History: Founded 2001.

Main Language(s) of Instruction: Portuguese

Degrees and Diplomas: *Bacharelado*; *Especialização/Aperfeiçoamento*

Libraries: Biblioteca Joacil de Brito Pereira
Last Updated: 03/08/10

NOVA ROMA FACULTY

Faculdade Nova Roma
Estrada do Bongi, 425 B - Afogados, Recife, PE 50830-260
Tel: +55(81) 2128-8000
EMail: leonardo@cbpe.com.br
Website: http://www.faculdadenovaroma.com.br

Diretor: Jose Folhadela dos Santos Neto

Courses

Accountancy (Accountancy); **Administration** (Administration); **Computer Science** (Computer Science)

History: Founded 2007.

Main Language(s) of Instruction: Portuguese

Degrees and Diplomas: *Bacharelado*; *Mestrado*. Also Pós-MBA

Libraries: Yes
Last Updated: 08/09/10

NOVAFAPI FACULTY

Faculdade NOVAFAPI (NOVAFAPI)
Rua Vitorino Orthiges Fernandes 6123, Bairro do Uruguai, Teresina, Piauí 64000000
Tel: +55(86) 2106-0700
Fax: +55(86) 2106-0740
EMail: novafapi@novafapi.com.br
Website: http://www.novafapi.com.br

Diretora: Cristina Maria Miranda de Sousa

Courses

Administration (Administration); **Biomedicine** (Biomedicine); **Civil Engineering** (Civil Engineering); **Dentistry** (Dentistry); **Fashion**

Design; **Law** (Law); **Medicine**; **Nursing** (Nursing); **Nutrition** (Nutrition); **Physical Education**; **Physiotherapy** (Physical Therapy); **Speech Therapy** (Speech Therapy and Audiology)

History: Founded 2000.

Main Language(s) of Instruction: Portuguese

Degrees and Diplomas: *Bacharelado*; *Especialização/Aperfeiçoamento*

Last Updated: 05/07/10

NURSING FACULTY OF THE ALBERT EINSTEIN ISRAELITE HOSPITAL

Faculdade de Enfermagem do Hospital Israelita 'Albert Einstein' (FEHIAE)
Av. Prof. Francisco Morato, 4293, São Paulo, São Paulo 05521-200
Tel: +55(11) 2151-1001 +55(11) 2151-6894
Fax: +55(11) 3746-1070
EMail: facenf@einstein.br
Website: http://www.einstein.br/ensino/faculdade-de-enfermagem/
Paginas/faculdade-de-enfermagem.aspx

Diretora: Olga Guilhermina Dias Farah

Courses
Nursing (Nursing)

History: Founded 1989

Main Language(s) of Instruction: Portuguese

Degrees and Diplomas: *Bacharelado*
Last Updated: 07/07/10

OBJETIVO INSTITUTE OF EDUCATION AND RESEARCH

Instituto de Ensino e Pesquisa Objetivo (IEPO)
ACSU-SE 40, Conjunto 02, Lote 07 Centro, Palmas,
Tocantins 77103040
Tel: +55(63) 3214-5387 +55(63) 3214-3471
EMail: objfac@uol.com.br
Website: http://www.iepo.edu.br

Diretor: Ronaldo Roberto Filho (1998-)

Courses
Administration; **Computer Science** (Computer Science); **Law** (Law); **Physiotherapy**; **Social Communication**; **Tourism** (Tourism)

History: Founded 1997

Degrees and Diplomas: *Tecnólogo*; *Bacharelado*
Last Updated: 16/06/10

OBJETIVO UNIFIED INSTITUTE OF HIGHER EDUCATION

Instituto Unificado de Ensino Superior Objetivo (IUESO)
Avenida T-02 1993, Setor Bueno, Goiânia, Goiás 74215010
Tel: +55(62) 3607-9000
Fax: +55(62) 3607-9025
EMail: objetivo@objetivo-goiania.br
Website: http://www.unilist.com.br/iueso/

Diretor: Eduardo Mendes Reed (1998-)

Courses
Administration (Administration; Business Administration; Systems Analysis); **Computer Science** (Computer Science); **Data Processing** (Data Processing); **Engineering** (Civil Engineering; Electrical and Electronic Engineering; Engineering); **Law**; **Pedagogy**; **Pharmacy**; **Social Communication** (Communication Studies); **Speech Therapy and Audiology** (Speech Therapy and Audiology); **Tourism** (Tourism); **Veterinary Science** (Veterinary Science)

History: Founded 1988.

Main Language(s) of Instruction: Portuguese

Degrees and Diplomas: *Bacharelado*; *Licenciatura*
Last Updated: 14/06/10

OCTOGON FACULTY

Faculdade Octógono (FOCO)
Rua Cel. Fernando Prestes 326, Centro, Santo André,
São Paulo 9020110
Tel: +55 4979-3718 +55 4438-5577
Fax: +55 4438-5577
EMail: info@foco.br

Diretor: Fernando Eduardo Peres

Courses
Administration (Administration; Business Administration; Marketing); **Tourism**

History: Founded 1999.

Main Language(s) of Instruction: Portuguese

Degrees and Diplomas: *Bacharelado*
Last Updated: 05/07/10

OLGA METTIG INTEGRATED FACULTIES

Faculdades Integradas Olga Mettig (FAMETTIG)
Rua da Mangueira 32, Prédio Nazaré, Salvador, Bahia 40040400
Tel: +55(71) 2108-1500
Fax: +55(71) 3332-1198
EMail: diretoria@famettig
Website: http://www.famettig.br

Diretora Geral: Eny kleyde Vasconcelos Farias

Faculties
Administration (Administration); **Pedagogy** (Pedagogy); **Tourism** (Tourism)

Institutes
Musical Education (Music Education)

History: Founded 1967.

Main Language(s) of Instruction: Portuguese

Degrees and Diplomas: *Bacharelado*; *Especialização/Aperfeiçoamento*
Last Updated: 22/06/10

OMNI FACULTY

Faculdade Omni
Av. 22 de Maio, 5.300 - Itaboraí, Rio de Janeiro
Tel: +55(21) 2635-2212
EMail: sociedadeomni@yahoo.com.br
Website: http://www.new9.faculdadeomni.com.br

Diretor: Luiz Paulo Moreira Lima

Courses
Accountancy (Accountancy); **Administration** (Administration); **History** (History); **Law** (Law); **Letters** (Literature); **Mathematics** (Mathematics)

Institutes
Education (Education)

History: Founded 2005.

Main Language(s) of Instruction: Portuguese

Degrees and Diplomas: *Bacharelado*; *Licenciatura*

Libraries: Yes
Last Updated: 09/09/10

OPET FACULTY

Faculdade Opet
Rua Nilo Peçanha 1635, Bom Retiro, Curitibá, Paraná 80520000
Tel: +55(41) 3028-2800
Fax: +55(41) 3028-2803
EMail: grupoopet@opet.com.br
Website: http://www.opet.com.br/

Diretor: José Antônio Karam

Courses
Accountancy (Accountancy) *Co-ordinator*: Juliana Loraine Falat Moreira; **Administration** (Administration) *Co-ordinator*: Estela Maris Trento Hein; **Law** (Law) *Co-ordinator*: Fernando Gustavo

Knoerr; **Social Communication** *Co-ordinator:* Alexandre Correia dos Santos

History: Founded 1999. Acquired present status 2008.

Main Language(s) of Instruction: Portuguese

Degrees and Diplomas: *Bacharelado; Licenciatura; Especialização/Aperfeiçoamento; Mestrado*

Last Updated: 05/07/10

ORIGENES LESSA FACULTY

Faculdade Origenes Lessa (FACOL)
Rod. Osny Matheus, Km. 108, Centro, Lencois Paulista,
SP 18683-900
Tel: +55(14) 3269-3939
EMail: secretaria@facol.br
Website: http://www.facol.br

Diretor Geral: Afonso Placca Filho

Courses
Administration (Administration); **Bioenergy** (Biotechnology); **Computer Science** (Computer Science); **Letters** (Literature); **Pedagogy**; **Physical Education**

History: Founded 1999.

Main Language(s) of Instruction: Portuguese

Degrees and Diplomas: *Tecnólogo; Bacharelado; Licenciatura; Especialização/Aperfeiçoamento*

Last Updated: 05/07/10

OSMAN DA COSTA LINS FACULTY

Faculdade Osman da Costa Lins (FACOL)
Rua do Estudante 85, Barrio Universitario, Vitória, PE 55612650
Tel: +55(81) 3523-0604
Fax: +55(81) 3523-0012
EMail: contato@facol.net
Website: http://www.facol.com

Diretor Presidente: Paulo Roberto Leite de Arruda

Courses
Administration (Administration); **Computer Science**; **Law** (Law); **Marketing**; **Pedagogy**; **Tourism**

History: Founded 1999 as Faculdade Escritor Osman da Costa Lins. Acquired present status and title 2001.

Main Language(s) of Instruction: Portuguese

Degrees and Diplomas: *Bacharelado; Licenciatura; Especialização/Aperfeiçoamento*

Last Updated: 05/07/10

OSWALDO CRUZ FACULTIES

Faculdades Oswaldo Cruz (FOC)
Rua Brigadeiro Galvão 540, Barra Funda, São Paulo,
São Paulo 01152000
Tel: +55(11) 3824-3660
Fax: +55(11) 3824-3660 +55(11) 3824-3102
EMail: secretariageral@oswaldocruz.br
Website: http://www.oswaldocruz.br

Presidente: Carlos Eduardo Quirino Simões de Amorim

Faculties
Administration, Economics and Accountancy (Accountancy; Administration; Economics); **Industrial Design** (Design; Industrial Design); **Pharmacy and Biochemistry** (Biochemistry; Pharmacy); **Social Communication** (Advertising and Publicity; Radio and Television Broadcasting); **Technology** *(Oswaldo Cruz)* (Computer Networks; Computer Science; Cosmetology; Environmental Management; Food Technology; Information Technology; Safety Engineering; Systems Analysis; Technology; Telecommunications Engineering)

Institutes
Education (Chemistry; Literature; Mathematics; Pedagogy; Physics)

Schools
Chemistry
History: Founded 1966.

Main Language(s) of Instruction: Portuguese

Degrees and Diplomas: *Bacharelado; Especialização/Aperfeiçoamento; Mestrado*

Last Updated: 21/06/10

OUR LADY APARECIDA FACULTY

Faculdade Nossa Senhora Aparecida (FANAP)
Avenida Pedro Luiz Ribeiro, Quadra 01, Lote 01, Chácara Santo Antônio, Gleba 04, Conjunto Bela Morada, Aparecida de Goiania,
Goiás 74916180
Tel: +55(62) 3277-1000
Fax: +55(62) 3277-1000
EMail: fanap@fanap.br
Website: http://www.fanap.br

Diretor: Frederico Lucas **EMail:** frederico@fanap.br

Courses
Accountancy (Accountancy); **Administration**; **Computer Science** (Computer Science); **Pedagogy** (Pedagogy); **Secretarial Studies** (Secretarial Studies)

History: Founded 1999

Main Language(s) of Instruction: Portuguese

Degrees and Diplomas: *Bacharelado; Especialização/Aperfeiçoamento*

Last Updated: 14/11/07

OUR LADY APARECIDA FACULTY OF PHILOSOPHY, SCIENCE AND LETTERS

Faculdade de Filosofia, Ciências e Letras Nossa Senhora Aparecida (FNSA)
Jordão Borghetti, 1260, Alto da Semar, Sertãozinho, SP 14170560
Tel: +55(16) 3946-4900
Fax: +55(16) 3945-3511
EMail: faculdade@semar.edu.br
Website: http://www.semar.edu.br

Diretor Geral: Paulo Sergio de Freitas Gomide

Courses
Administration (Administration; Marketing); **Graduate Studies**; **Literature**; **Pedagogy** (Pedagogy)

History: Founded 2000.

Main Language(s) of Instruction: Portuguese

Degrees and Diplomas: *Bacharelado; Licenciatura; Especialização/Aperfeiçoamento.* Also MBA.

Last Updated: 08/07/10

OUR LADY OF FATIMA FRANCISCAN INSTITUTE OF EDUCATION

Instituto Superior de Educação Franciscano Nossa Senhora de Fátima
SGAS - Q. 906 - CONJ. "F", Fornecido por Joomla!.
Valid XHTML and CSS., Brasília, DF 70390-060
Tel: +55(61) 3442-8650
Website: http://www.institutofatima.edu.br

Diretora: Inês Alves Lourenço

Courses
Pedagogy (Pedagogy); **Systems Analysis** (Systems Analysis)

History: Founded 2005.

Main Language(s) of Instruction: Portuguese

Degrees and Diplomas: *Bacharelado; Licenciatura; Especialização/Aperfeiçoamento*

Libraries: Biblioteca Rui Barbosa

Last Updated: 28/09/10

OUR LADY OF SION INSTITUTE OF EDUCATION

Instituto Superior de Educação Nossa Senhora de Sion
Alameda Presidente Taunay, 260, Batel, Curitiba, PR 80420-180
Tel: +55(41) 3019-6155
EMail: instituto@sion.arauc.br
Website: http://www.isenss.edu.br

Diretora: Martha Marques

Courses
History (History); **Pedagogy** (Pedagogy)
History: Founded 2002.
Main Language(s) of Instruction: Portuguese
Degrees and Diplomas: Licenciatura; Especialização/Aperfeiçoamento
Libraries: Yes
Last Updated: 28/09/10

OUR LADY OF THE PATRONAGE UNIVERSITY CENTRE

Centro Universitário Nossa Senhora do Patrocínio (CEUNSP)
Rua Madre Maria Basília 965, Centro, Itú, São Paulo 13300200
Tel: +55(11) 4013-9900
Fax: +55(11) 4023-0678
EMail: ceunsp@ceunsp.edu.br
Website: http://www.ceunsp.br

Reitor: Rubens Anganuzzi (1994-)

Faculties
Administration and Commerce (Administration; International Business; Secretarial Studies); **Communication and Arts**; **Education**; **Health and Life Sciences** (Biological and Life Sciences; Biomedicine; Nursing; Nutrition; Occupational Health; Pharmacy; Physical Education; Psychology; Social and Community Services; Speech Therapy and Audiology); **Hospitality** (Cooking and Catering; Hotel and Restaurant; Hotel Management; Tourism); **Law** (Law); **Management and Commerce** (Accountancy; Administration; Finance; Information Sciences; Management; Public Administration; Safety Engineering; Systems Analysis); **Technology** (Computer Networks; Computer Science; Environmental Management; Fashion Design; Human Resources; Marketing; Telecommunications Engineering; Transport Management)

Higher Institutes
Engineering, Architecture and Design; Postgraduate Studies and Research
Further Information: Also Campus Universitário São José, Campus Universitário Nossa Senhora do Mont Serrat, Campus Universitário Jesus de Nazareth, o Bom Pastor, Clínica de Fisioterapia e Nutrição, Clínica de Fonoaudiologia and Núcleo de Prática Jurídica.
History: Founded 1958, acquired present status and title 1998.
Degrees and Diplomas: Tecnólogo; Bacharelado; Licenciatura; Especialização/Aperfeiçoamento
Last Updated: 16/06/10

PADRÃO FACULTY

Faculdade Padrão
Rua Araponga 70, Jardim Vila Boa - Conjunto Novo Horizonte, Goiânia, GO 74030-010
Tel: +55(62) 258-6000
EMail: unidade1@faculdadepadrao.com.br
Website:http: //www.faculdadepadrao.com.br

Diretor: João Rodrigues de Paula Oliveira

Courses
Accountancy (Accountancy); **Administration** (Administration; Business Administration; Hotel Management; Marketing; Tourism); **Biomedicine** (Biomedicine); **Dance** (Dance); **History** (History); **Law** (Law); **Letters** (Literature); **Nursing** (Nursing); **Nutrition** (Nutrition); **Pedagogy** (Pedagogy); **Physical Education** (Physical Education); **Physiotherapy** (Physical Therapy)
History: Founded 1998.

Main Language(s) of Instruction: Portuguese
Degrees and Diplomas: Bacharelado; Licenciatura; Especialização/Aperfeiçoamento
Libraries: Yes
Last Updated: 09/09/10

PADRE ALBINO INTEGRATED FACULTIES

Faculdades Integradas Padre Albino
Rua dos Estudantes, 225, Catanduva, São Paulo 15.809 -144
Tel: +55(17) 3531-3200
EMail: diretoriageral@fipa.com.br
Website: http://www.fundacaopadrealbino.org.br/faculdades

Diretor: Nelson Jimenes

Courses
Administration; **Law** (Law); **Medicine** (Medicine); **Nursing** (Nursing); **Physical Education** (Physical Education)
History: Founded 1969 as Faculdade de Medicina de Catanduva (FAMECA). Acquired present status and title 2007.
Main Language(s) of Instruction: Portuguese
Degrees and Diplomas: Bacharelado; Especialização/Aperfeiçoamento
Last Updated: 22/06/10

PADRE ANCHIETA FACULTY OF CAJAMAR

Faculdade Padre Anchieta de Cajamar
Rua Lázaro Dalcin N°: 256, Cajamar, SP 07760-000
Tel: +55(11) 4408-3246
EMail: faccajamar@anchieta.br
Website: http://www.anchieta.br/cajamar

Diretor: Norberto Mohor Fornani

Courses
Accountancy (Accountancy); **Administration** (Administration)
History: Founded 2007.
Main Language(s) of Instruction: Portuguese
Degrees and Diplomas: Bacharelado; Especialização/Aperfeiçoamento; Mestrado
Libraries: Yes
Last Updated: 10/09/10

PADRE ANCHIETA FACULTY OF VÁRZEA PAULISTA

Faculdade Padre Anchieta de Várzea Paulista
Rua José Rabello Portella, n° 2364, Vila Popular, Várzea Paulista, SP
Tel: +55(11) 4596-6990
EMail: bhoff@anchieta.br
Website: http://www.anchieta.br/varzeapaulista/Faculdade

Diretor: Norberto Mohor Fornari

Courses
Accountancy (Accountancy); **Administration** (Administration); **Pedagogy** (Pedagogy)
Degrees and Diplomas: Bacharelado; Licenciatura; Mestrado
Libraries: Yes
Last Updated: 10/09/10

PADRE ANCHIETA INTEGRATED FACULTIES OF GUARAPARI

Faculdades Integradas Padre Anchieta de Guarapari (FAG)
Rodovia Jones Santos Neves 1000, Lagoa Funda, Guarapari, ES 29214000
Tel: +55(27) 3361-3993
EMail: fipag@fipag.br
Website: http://www.fipag.br

Diretor: João Everaldo Assis dos Santos

Courses
Accountancy (Accountancy); **Administration**; **Law** *(FADIG)*; **Pedagogy**; **Social Communication** *(FACOM)* (Advertising and Publicity; Public Relations); **Tourism**
History: Founded 1997.
Main Language(s) of Instruction: Portuguese
Degrees and Diplomas: *Bacharelado*; *Especialização/Aperfeiçoamento*
Last Updated: 02/10/07

PADRE ANCHIETA UNIVERSITY CENTRE
Centro Universitario Padre Anchieta
Rua Bom Jesus de Pirapora, 100/140, Jundiaí,
São Paulo 13207-270
Tel: +55(11) 4587-6165
Fax: +55(11) 4587-6165
EMail: fcecae@anchieta.br
Website: http://www.anchieta.br/unianchieta/default.asp
Diretor: Norberto Mohor Fornari

Courses
Bacharelados (Accountancy; Administration; Advertising and Publicity; Chemical Engineering; Civil Engineering; Economics; Electronic Engineering; Food Technology; Information Sciences; Law; Nursing; Nutrition; Occupational Therapy; Pharmacy; Physical Education; Physical Therapy; Production Engineering; Psychology); **Graduate Studies**; **Licenciaturas**; **Technological Studies** (Automation and Control Engineering; Chemistry; Environmental Management; International Business; Marketing; Polymer and Plastics Technology; Systems Analysis; Transport Management)
Further Information: Also Campus Prof. Pedro C. Fornari.
History: Founded 1966 as Faculdade de Ciências Econômicas, Contábeis e de Administração de Empresas Padre Anchieta. Acquired present status and title 2004.
Degrees and Diplomas: *Tecnólogo*; *Bacharelado*; *Licenciatura*; *Especialização/Aperfeiçoamento*; *Mestrado*. Also MBA.
Last Updated: 16/06/10

PALAS ATENA FACULTY
Faculdade Palas Atena (FPA)
Rua Bahia, 263 - Centro, Astorga, Parana 86.730.000
Tel: +55(44) 3234-7673
EMail: fpa@chnet.com.br
Website: http://www.palasatena.edu.br/
Diretor: Benner Luis Turini

Courses
Administration (Administration); **Pedagogy**
History: Founded 2000.
Main Language(s) of Instruction: Portuguese
Degrees and Diplomas: *Bacharelado*; *Licenciatura*; *Especialização/Aperfeiçoamento*
Last Updated: 05/07/10

PALAS ATENA FACULTY OF CHOPINZINHO
Faculdade Palas Atena de Chopinzinho (FPA)
Rua Frei Everaldo, 93, Centro, Chopinzinho, PR 85560-000
Tel: +55(46) 3242-2222
Fax: +55(46) 3242-2222
EMail: palasatena@wln.com.br
Diretor: Bener Luiz Turini

Courses
Administration (Administration); **Pedagogy** (Pedagogy)
Degrees and Diplomas: *Bacharelado*; *Licenciatura*
Last Updated: 30/09/10

PALOTINA FACULTY
Faculdade Palotina
Av. Pres. Vargas, 115, Bairro Patronato, Santa Maria,
RS 97020-001
Tel: +55(55) 3220-4575
EMail: fapas@fapas.edu.br
Website: http://www.fapas.edu.br
Diretor: Antônio Amélio Dalla Costa EMail: direção@fapas.edu.br

Courses
Administration (Administration); **Law** (Law); **Philosophy** (Philosophy); **Theology** (Theology)
History: Founded 2001.
Main Language(s) of Instruction: Portuguese
Degrees and Diplomas: *Bacharelado*; *Especialização/Aperfeiçoamento*
Libraries: Yes
Last Updated: 09/09/10

PAN AMERICAN FACULTY
Faculdade Pan Americana (FPA)
Avenida João Paulo II, 801, Fatima, Capanema 68700-050
Tel: +55(91) 3462-4548
EMail: fpa@fpa.edu.br
Website: http://fpa.edu.br/
Diretor Presidente: Dirceu Milani

Courses
Literature (Literature; Portuguese); **Pedagogy** (Pedagogy); **Philosophy** (Philosophy); **Theology** (Theology)
Degrees and Diplomas: *Bacharelado*; *Licenciatura*. Also Postgraduate Diploma.
Last Updated: 30/09/10

PANAMERICAN FACULTY OF JI-PARANÁ
Faculdade Panamericana de Ji-Paraná
Rodovia RO 135, Km 01 Estrada para Nova Londrina, Ji-Paraná,
RO 78960-000
Tel: +55(69) 3903-1500
EMail: basilioleandro@uniron.edu.br
Website: http://www.unijipa.edu.br/
Diretor: Basílio Leandro Pereira de Oliveira

Courses
Accountancy (Accountancy); **Business Administration** (Business Administration); **Pedagogy** (Pedagogy)
History: Founded 2007.
Main Language(s) of Instruction: Portuguese
Degrees and Diplomas: *Bacharelado*; *Licenciatura*; *Especialização/Aperfeiçoamento*
Libraries: Yes
Last Updated: 09/09/10

PARADISE FACULTY
Faculdade Paraíso (FAP)
Rua Visconde de Itaúna 2671, Paraíso, São Gonçalo,
Rio de Janeiro 24431005
Tel: +55(21) 2604-5666
Fax: +55(21) 2605-3259
EMail: informacoes@faculdadeparaiso.edu.br
Website: http://www.faculdadeparaiso.edu.br
Diretor: João Luis Alexandre Fiúsa

Courses
Administration (Administration); **Computer Science**; **Law** (Law); **Letters** (Literature); **Management**; **Pedagogy**; **Political Science** (Political Sciences); **Tourism** (Tourism)
History: Founded 2000.
Main Language(s) of Instruction: Portuguese
Degrees and Diplomas: *Bacharelado*; *Especialização/Aperfeiçoamento*; *Mestrado*
Last Updated: 05/07/10

PARAIBANO INSTITUTE OF RENOVATED EDUCATION

Instituto Paraibano de Ensino Renovado (INPER)
Rua Afonso Barbosa, 2011, Jardim Marizópolis, João Pessoa,
PB 58033-450
Tel: +55(83) 2106-9600
Website: http://www.inper-tec.com.br/

Courses
Undergraduate Studies (Accountancy; Advertising and Publicity;
Business Administration; Computer Science; Health Administration;
Human Resources; Information Sciences; Law; Marketing; Pedagogy; Physical Therapy; Tourism)
Degrees and Diplomas: *Tecnólogo*; *Bacharelado*
Last Updated: 23/09/10

PARQUE FACULTY

Faculdade Parque
Rua Silveira Martins n° 3806, Salvador, BA 41100-000
Tel: +55(71) 3230-5565
EMail: colegioparque@hotmail.com
Website: http://www.faculdadeparque.com.br
Diretor: Marcelo Sacramento de Araujo

Courses
Pedagogy (Pedagogy)
History: Founded 2007.
Main Language(s) of Instruction: Portuguese
Degrees and Diplomas: *Bacharelado*
Last Updated: 09/09/10

PASCHOAL DANTAS FACULTY

Faculdade Paschoal Dantas
Av. Afonso de Sampaio e Souza, 495 - Itaquera, São Paulo,
SP 08270-000
Tel: +55(11) 6741-5100
EMail: cpaschoald@uol.com.br
Website: http://www.faculdadepaschoaldantas.com.br
Diretora: Aparecida Maria Clapis de Paula

Courses
Business Administration (Business Administration); **Mathematics**
(Mathematics); **Nursing** (Nursing); **Pedagogy** (Pedagogy)
History: Founded 2008.
Main Language(s) of Instruction: Portuguese
Degrees and Diplomas: *Bacharelado*; *Licenciatura*; *Especialização/Aperfeiçoamento*
Libraries: Yes
Last Updated: 09/09/10

PAUL VI FACULTY OF PHILOSOPHY AND THEOLOGY

Faculdade de Filosofia e Teologia Paulo VI
Rodovia Pedro Eroles S/N - km 42, Mogi das Cruzes, SP 08701-970
Tel: +55(11) 4790-5660
EMail: faculdadepaulovi@uol.com.br
Diretor: Claudio Antonio Delfino

Courses
Philosophy (Philosophy); **Theology** (Theology)
History: Founded 2004.
Main Language(s) of Instruction: Portuguese
Degrees and Diplomas: *Bacharelado*
Last Updated: 06/08/10

PAULO FREIRE FACULTY OF TECHNOLOGY

Faculdade de Tecnologia Paulo Freire (FATEP-DF)
SHIN Centro de Atividades 2, Lote 21 Lago Norte, Brasília,
DF 71503-502
Tel: +55(61) 3031-6700
Website: http://www.efti.com.br/

Diretora Presidente: Patrícia Ferreira de Faria de Alencar
Courses
Computer Networks (Computer Networks); **Digital Games**
(Software Engineering); **Graduate Studies** (Computer Networks;
Information Management; Management); **Systems Analysis and Development** (Systems Analysis)
History: Founded 2002.
Degrees and Diplomas: *Tecnólogo*; *Especialização/Aperfeiçoamento*. Also MBA.
Last Updated: 26/08/10

PAULUS FACULTY OF TECHNOLOGY AND COMMUNICATION

Faculdade Paulus de Tecnologia e Comunicação
Rua Major Maragliano 191, São Paulo, SP 04017-030
Tel: +55(11) 2139-8500
EMail: secretaria@fapcom.com.br
Website: http://www.fapcom.com.br
Diretor: Manoel Conceição Quinta EMail: diretor@fapcom.com.br

Courses
Social Communication (Advertising and Publicity; Journalism;
Public Relations; Radio and Television Broadcasting)
History: Founded 2005.
Main Language(s) of Instruction: Portuguese
Degrees and Diplomas: *Bacharelado*
Libraries: Yes
Last Updated: 09/09/10

PEDRO II FACULTY

Faculdade Pedro II
Rua Areado, 437- Bairro Carlos Prates, Belo Horizonte,
MG 30710-530
Tel: +55(31) 3411-1214
EMail: coordenacaogeral@fape2.edu.br
Website: http://www.fape2.edu.br

Courses
Geography (Geography); **Letters** (Literature); **Mathematics**
(Mathematical Physics); **Pedagogy** (Pedagogy)
History: Founded 2006.
Main Language(s) of Instruction: Portuguese
Degrees and Diplomas: *Licenciatura*; *Especialização/Aperfeiçoamento*
Libraries: Yes
Last Updated: 09/09/10

PEDRO ROGÉRIO GARCIA FACULTY OF TECHNOLOGY

Faculdade de Tecnologia Pedro Rogério Garcia (FATTEP)
Rodovia Pedro Rogério Garcia 283 - Km 08, Distrito de Santo
Antônio, n° 8.100, Caixa Postal 820, Concórdia, SC 89700-000
Tel: +55(49) 3442-9656
EMail: jamir@fabet.com.br
Website: http://www.fabet.com.br/

Courses
Environmental Management (Environmental Management);
Executive Secretarial Studies (Secretarial Studies); **Graduate Studies** (Administration; Environmental Management; Environmental Studies; Finance; Management; Transport Management);
Logistics (Transport Management); **Managerial Process** (Management); **Specialised Studies** (Accountancy; Business and Commerce; Human Resources; Transport Management)
History: Founded 2005.
Degrees and Diplomas: *Tecnólogo*; *Especialização/Aperfeiçoamento*. Also Postgraduate Diploma.
Last Updated: 26/08/10

PEREIRA DE FREITAS FACULTY
Faculdade Pereira de Freitas
Rua Potiguar, 150 - Iguaçu, Ipatinga, MG +55(31) 3826-5198
EMail: faculdade@pereiradefreitas.com.br
Website: http://www.pereiradefreitas.com.br
Diretora Acadêmica: Margarida Lievore

Courses
Information Systems (Computer Science); **Letters** (Literature); **Mathematics** (Mathematics); **Physics** (Physics)
History: Founded 2002.
Main Language(s) of Instruction: Portuguese
Degrees and Diplomas: *Bacharelado*; *Licenciatura*
Libraries: Yes
Last Updated: 22/09/10

PESTALOZZI FACULTIES
Faculdades Pestalozzi (ESEHA)
Estrada Caetano Monteiro 857, Pendotiba, Niterói,
Rio de Janeiro 24320570
Tel: +55(21) 2616-0937
EMail: eseha@nitnet.com.br
Website: http://www.pestalozzi.org.br
Diretora: Lizair de Moraes Guarino (1985-)

Courses
Administration; **Dentistry** (Dentistry); **Occupational Therapy**; **Physiotherapy**; **Speech Therapy** (Speech Therapy and Audiology); **Visual Arts**
History: Founded 1985.
Main Language(s) of Instruction: Portuguese
Degrees and Diplomas: *Bacharelado*; *Especialização/Aperfeiçoamento*
Last Updated: 21/06/10

PHOENIX FACULTY OF HUMAN AND SOCIAL SCIENCES OF BRAZIL
Faculdade Phênix de Ciências Humanas e Sociais do Brasil
Avenida Goiás Nº1/7Quadras 111 e 112, Centro,
Santo Antônio do Descoberto, GO 72900-000
Tel: +55(61) 3626-1209
EMail: phenix.assesb@ibest.com.br
Website: http://www.faculdadephenix.org
Diretor: Moisés Dias da Silva

Courses
Letters (Literature); **Philosophy** (Philosophy)
History: Founded 2006.
Main Language(s) of Instruction: Portuguese
Degrees and Diplomas: *Licenciatura*; *Especialização/Aperfeiçoamento*
Libraries: Yes
Last Updated: 22/09/10

PINHALZINHO - HORUS FACULTY
Faculdade Pinhalzinho - HORUS
Rua Aracaju, 225, Centro, Pinhalzinho, SC 89870-000
Tel: +55(49) 3366-1890
EMail: secretaria@horus.edu.br
Website: http://www.horus.edu.br/
Diretor: Sergio Mazonetto

Courses
Accountancy (Accountancy); **Administration** (Administration); **Information Systems** (Information Sciences); **Physical Education** (Physical Education)
Degrees and Diplomas: *Bacharelado*; *Licenciatura*
Last Updated: 30/09/10

PINHEIRO GUIMARÃES FACULTY
Faculdade Pinheiro Guimarães (FAPG)
Rua Silveira Martins 151 Catete, Rio de Janeiro,
Rio de Janeiro 22221000
Tel: +55(21) 2556-7995
Fax: +55(21) 2205-0797
EMail: faculdade@pinheiroguimaraes.br
Diretor: Armando Santos Pinheiro Guimarães

Courses
Communication Studies
History: Founded 1987.
Main Language(s) of Instruction: Portuguese
Degrees and Diplomas: *Bacharelado*
Last Updated: 05/12/07

PIONEER FACULTY
Faculdade Bandeirantes (FABAN)
Rua Saldanha Marinho 915, Centro, Ribeirão Petro,
São Paulo 14010060
Tel: +55(16) 2111-0090
Fax: +55(16) 612-0090
EMail: caac@faban.com.br
Website: http://www.uniesp.edu.br/ribeiraopreto
Diretor Geral: Carlos Alberto Ferreira

Courses
Accountancy (Accountancy); **Administration**; **Advertising and Publicity** (Advertising and Publicity); **Economics**; **Graduate Studies** (Pedagogy); **Information Systems**; **Literature** (English; Literature; Portuguese; Spanish); **Mathematics** (Mathematics); **Pedagogy** (Pedagogy); **Production Engineering** (Production Engineering); **Theology** (Theology); **Tourism** (Tourism)
History: Founded 1997.
Main Language(s) of Instruction: Portuguese
Degrees and Diplomas: *Bacharelado*; *Especialização/Aperfeiçoamento*
Last Updated: 29/06/10

PIONEER UNIVERSITY OF SÃO PAULO
Universidade Bandeirante de São Paulo (UNIBAN)
Rua Maria Cândida 1813, Vila Guilherme, São Paulo,
São Paulo 02071013
Tel: +55(11) 6967-9000
Fax: +55(11) 6967-9000
EMail: lcosme@uniban.br
Website: http://www.uniban.br
Reitor: Heitor Pinto Filho (1997-)
Tel: +55(11) 6967-9003 EMail: reitoria@uniban.br

Institutes
Biological and Health Sciences; **Business and Administration** (Accountancy; Business Administration; Economics); **Communication and Arts**; **Computer Science** (Systems Analysis); **Polytechnic**; **Social and Human Sciences** (Biology; Chemistry; Geography; History; Law; Literature; Mathematics; Pedagogy; Philosophy; Physics; Social and Community Services)
History: Founded 1994.
Admission Requirements: Secondary school certificate and entrance examination
Main Language(s) of Instruction: Portuguese
Degrees and Diplomas: *Bacharelado*; *Licenciatura*; *Especialização/Aperfeiçoamento*; *Mestrado*
Libraries: Central Library, c. 67,000 vols
Last Updated: 08/06/10

PITAGORAS FACULTY OF BELO HORIZONTE
Faculdade Pitágoras de Belo Horizonte
Av. Prudente de Morais, n° 1.602 Cidade Jardim, Belo Horizonte,
Minas Gerais
Tel: +55(31) 2111-2000
EMail: diretoria_jardins@pitagoras.com.br
Website: http://www.faculdadepitagoras.com.br/BeloHorizonte/
Paginas/default.aspx

Diretor: Sandro Bonás

Courses
Accountancy; **Administration**; **Biology** (Biology); **Computer Science** (Computer Science); **Engineering**; **Law**; **Letters**; **Nursing** (Nursing); **Nutrition** (Nutrition); **Pedagogy**; **Pharmacy**; **Physical Education** (Physical Education); **Physiotherapy**; **Psychology**; **Social Communication** (Advertising and Publicity; Journalism); **Tourism** (Tourism)

Further Information: Also units at Betim, Vila da Serra, Vale do Aço, Sao Luis, Fadom, Divinopolis, Jundai, Londrina, Vitoria

Main Language(s) of Instruction: Portuguese

Degrees and Diplomas: *Bacharelado*; *Licenciatura*; *Especialização/Aperfeiçoamento*
Last Updated: 02/07/10

PITAGORAS FACULTY OF BETIM
Faculdade Pitágoras de Betim
Av. Juscelino Kubitscheck, 229, Centro, Betim, MG 32510-000
Tel: +55(31) 2101-9000
Website: http://www.faculdadepitagoras.com.br/Betim/

Diretora: Nívea Patrícia de Oliveira Batista

Courses
Accountancy (Accountancy); **Administration** (Administration); **Automation and Control Engineering** (Automation and Control Engineering); **Chemical Engineering** (Chemical Engineering); **Civil Engineering** (Civil Engineering); **Computer Science** (Computer Science); **Electrical Engineering**; **Environmental Engineering** (Environmental Engineering); **Graduate Studies** (Alternative Medicine; Health Sciences; Industrial Engineering; Nursing; Public Health); **Law**; **Mechanical Engineering** (Mechanical Engineering); **Nursing** (Nursing); **Pharmacy**; **Physical Education** (Physical Education); **Physiotherapy** (Physical Therapy); **Production Engineering**; **Psychology** (Psychology)

Main Language(s) of Instruction: Portuguese

Degrees and Diplomas: *Bacharelado*; *Licenciatura*; *Especialização/Aperfeiçoamento*
Last Updated: 02/07/10

PITAGORAS FACULTY OF DIVINÓPOLIS
Faculdade Pitágoras de Divinópolis
Rua Santos Dumont, 1001, Bairro Do Carmo, Divinópolis,
MG 35500-286
Tel: +55(37) 2101-4800
Fax: +55(37) 2101-4834
Website: http://www.faculdadepitagoras.com.br/divinopolis/

Diretor: Leandro Benedito Dizotti

Courses
Accountancy (Accountancy); **Administration** (Administration); **Automation and Control Engineering** (Automation and Control Engineering); **Civil Engineering** (Civil Engineering); **Computer Science** (Computer Science); **Electrical Engineering** (Electrical Engineering); **Environmental Engineering** (Environmental Engineering); **Graduate Studies** (Business and Commerce; Leadership; Management; Mass Communication; Transport Management); **Information Systems** (Information Sciences); **Law** (Law); **Mechanical Engineering** (Mechanical Engineering); **Nursing** (Nursing); **Pharmacy** (Pharmacy); **Production Engineering** (Production Engineering); **Social Communication** (Advertising and Publicity; Journalism)

Degrees and Diplomas: *Bacharelado*. Also MBA.
Last Updated: 30/09/10

PITAGORAS FACULTY OF FEIRA DE SANTANA
Faculdade Pitágoras de Feira de Santana
Rua Venezuela, 204, Capuchinhos, Feira de Santana,
BA 44052-030
Tel: +55(75) 3625-2031
Website: http://www.faculdadepitagoras.com.br/FeiradeSantana/

Courses
Administration (Administration); **Nursing** (Nursing); **Production Engineering** (Production Engineering)

Degrees and Diplomas: *Bacharelado*
Last Updated: 30/09/10

PITAGORAS FACULTY OF GUARAPARI
Faculdade Pitágoras de Guarapari
Rodovia Governador Jones dos Santos Neves, 1.000,
Lagoa Funda, Guarapari, ES 29214-005
Tel: +55(27) 3361-8300
Website: http://www.faculdadepitagoras.com.br/guarapari/

Courses
Accountancy (Accountancy); **Administration** (Administration); **Automation and Control Engineering** (Automation and Control Engineering); **Chemical Engineering** (Chemical Engineering); **Civil Engineering** (Civil Engineering); **Computer Science** (Computer Science); **Electrical Engineering** (Electrical Engineering); **Graduate Studies** (Accountancy; Business Administration; Finance; Health Administration; Higher Education; Management); **Law** (Law); **Mechanical Engineering** (Mechanical Engineering); **Nursing** (Nursing); **Pedagogy** (Pedagogy); **Pharmacy** (Pharmacy); **Physical Education** (Physical Education); **Production Engineering** (Production Engineering); **Social Communication** (Advertising and Publicity; Public Relations); **Tourism** (Tourism)

Degrees and Diplomas: *Bacharelado*; *Licenciatura*; *Especialização/Aperfeiçoamento*. Also MBA.
Last Updated: 30/09/10

PITAGORAS FACULTY OF IPATINGA
Faculdade Pitágoras de Ipatinga (FPI)
Rua Jequitibá, 401, Horto, Ipatinga, MG 35160-306
Tel: +55(31) 2136-2000
Website: http://www.faculdadepitagoras.com.br/Ipatinga/

Diretor: Gilberto Alves

Courses
Accountancy (Accountancy); **Administration** (Administration); **Automation and Control Engineering** (Automation and Control Engineering); **Civil Engineering** (Civil Engineering); **Electrical Engineering** (Electrical Engineering); **Graduate Studies** (Civil Law; Management; Safety Engineering); **Law** (Law); **Mechanical Engineering** (Mechanical Engineering); **Nursing** (Nursing); **Nutrition** (Nutrition); **Pedagogy** (Pedagogy); **Pharmacy** (Pharmacy); **Physical Education** (Physical Education); **Production Engineering** (Production Engineering); **Psychology** (Psychology)

Degrees and Diplomas: *Bacharelado*; *Licenciatura*; *Especialização/Aperfeiçoamento*. Also MBA.
Last Updated: 30/09/10

PITAGORAS FACULTY OF JUNDIAÍ
Faculdade Pitágoras de Jundiaí
Rua São Bento, 41, Centro, Jundiaí, SP 13201-033
Tel: +55(11) 2136-7000 +55(11) 2136-7022
Website: http://www.faculdadepitagoras.com.br/jundiai/

Head: Eduardo Rocha

Courses
Administration (Administration); **Automation and Control Engineering** (Automation and Control Engineering); **Chemical Engineering** (Chemical Engineering); **Civil Engineering** (Civil Engineering); **Graduate Studies** (Accountancy; Business Administration; Educational Psychology; Educational Sciences; Finance; Health Administration; Management; Nursing; Safety Engineering; Sports; Transport Management); **Mechanical Engineering** (Mechanical Engineering); **Pedagogy** (Pedagogy); **Pharmacy** (Pharmacy); **Production Engineering** (Production Engineering);

Psychology (Psychology); **Technological Studies** (Finance; Food Science; Human Resources; Industrial Management; Transport Management)

Degrees and Diplomas: *Tecnólogo*; *Bacharelado*; *Licenciatura*. Also Postgraduate Diploma and MBA.
Last Updated: 30/09/10

PITAGORAS FACULTY OF LONDRINA
Faculdade Pitágoras de Londrina
Rua Edwy Taques de Araújo, 1100, Londrina, Paraná 86047500
Tel: +55(43) 3373-7333
Fax: +55(43) 3373-7373
EMail: ump@ump.edu.br
Website: http://www.faculdadepitagoras.com.br/londrina/Paginas/default.aspx

Diretor: Marcos Jerônimo Goroski Rambalducci

Courses
Administration (Administration; International Business; Marketing); **Computer Science** (Computer Science); **Engineering**; **Law** (Law); **Nursing**; **Pedagogy**; **Psychology**; **Social Communication** (Advertising and Publicity; Journalism; Social Studies)

History: Founded 2001.

Main Language(s) of Instruction: Portuguese

Degrees and Diplomas: *Bacharelado*; *Licenciatura*; *Especialização/Aperfeiçoamento*
Last Updated: 05/07/10

PITAGORAS FACULTY OF NOVA LIMA
Faculdade Pitágoras de Nova Lima
Rua Paisagem, 220, Vila da Serra, Nova Lima, MG 34000-000
Website: http://www.faculdadepitagoras.com.br

Courses
Computer Science (Computer Science); **Production Engineering** (Production Engineering)

Degrees and Diplomas: *Bacharelado*; *Licenciatura*
Last Updated: 30/09/10

PITAGORAS FACULTY OF POÇOS DE CALDAS
Faculdade Pitágoras de Poços de Caldas
Avenida João Pinheiro, 1046, Centro, Poços de Caldas, MG 37701-386
Tel: +55(35) 2107-6000
Website: http://www.faculdadepitagoras.com.br/PocosdeCaldas/

Diretor: Carlos Renato Gherarde Lins

Courses
Accountancy (Accountancy); **Administration** (Administration); **Computer Science** (Computer Science); **Graduate Studies** (Accountancy; Business Administration; Business and Commerce; Educational Psychology; Educational Sciences; Finance; Health Administration; Human Resources; Nursing; Public Health; Safety Engineering); **Nursing** (Nursing); **Production Engineering** (Production Engineering); **Psychology** (Psychology)

Degrees and Diplomas: *Bacharelado*; *Especialização/Aperfeiçoamento*. Also MBA.
Last Updated: 30/09/10

PITAGORAS FACULTY OF SÃO LUÍS
Faculdade Pitágoras de São Luís
Av. Daniel De La Touche, 23, Olho D'água, São Luís, MA 65061-050
Tel: +55(98) 3878-8010
Website: http://www.faculdadepitagoras.com.br/SaoLuis/

Diretor: Samir Martins Maluf

Courses
Administration (Administration); **Civil Engineering** (Civil Engineering); **Computer Science** (Computer Science); **Graduate Studies** (Educational Administration; Educational Sciences; Higher Education; Production Engineering); **Nursing** (Nursing); **Pharmacy** (Pharmacy); **Production Engineering** (Production Engineering); **Psychology** (Psychology)

Degrees and Diplomas: *Bacharelado*; *Especialização/Aperfeiçoamento*
Last Updated: 30/09/10

PITAGORAS FACULTY OF TECHNOLOGY OF GUARAPARI
Faculdade Pitágoras de Tecnologia de Guarapari
Rua Manoel Lopes Gomide, 01, Muquiçaba, Guarapari, ES 29216-065
Tel: +55(27) 3361-3744
Fax: +55(27) 3361-3744
EMail: ddi@kroton.com.br
Website: http://www.faculdadepitagoras.com.br/

Courses
Administration (Administration); **International Business** (International Business); **Marketing** (Marketing)

Degrees and Diplomas: *Tecnólogo*; *Bacharelado*
Last Updated: 30/09/10

PITAGORAS FACULTY OF TEIXEIRA DE FREITAS
Faculdade Pitágoras de Teixeira de Freitas
Avenida Juscelino Kubitschek 3000 - Br 101 KM 8794, Teixeira de Freitas, BA 45996-220
Tel: +55(73) 3011-8300
EMail: factef@factef.com
Website: http://www.faculdadepitagoras.com.br/teixeiradefreitas/

Diretor: Célio Eduardo Nascimento

Courses
Administration (Administration); **Computer Science** (Computer Science); **Forestry Engineering** (Forestry); **Geography** (Geography); **Law** (Law); **Nursing** (Nursing); **Pedagogy** (Pedagogy); **Pharmacy** (Pharmacy); **Physical Education** (Physical Education)

History: Founded 2002.

Main Language(s) of Instruction: Portuguese

Degrees and Diplomas: *Bacharelado*; *Licenciatura*; *Especialização/Aperfeiçoamento*
Last Updated: 21/09/10

PITAGORAS FACULTY OF UBERLÂNDIA
Faculdade Pitágoras de Uberlândia
Avenida dos Vinhedos, 1200, Morada da Colina, Uberlândia, Minas Gerais 38411-159
Tel: +55(34) 3292-1900
Fax: +55(34) 3292-1932
EMail: uniminas@uniminas.br
Website: http://www.faculdadepitagoras.com.br

Diretor Presidente: Nestor Barbosa de Andrade

Courses
Accountancy (Accountancy); **Administration**; **Automation and Control Engineering** (Automation and Control Engineering); **Chemical Engineering** (Chemical Engineering); **Civil Engineering** (Civil Engineering); **Electrical Engineering** (Electrical Engineering); **Environmental Engineering** (Environmental Engineering); **Graduate Studies** (Agricultural Business; Biotechnology; Business Administration; Business and Commerce; Commercial Law; Criminology; Education; Educational Administration; Educational Psychology; Engineering; Environmental Studies; Health Administration; Health Sciences; Higher Education; Human Resources; Information Management; Information Technology; Labour Law; Management; Nursing; Physical Education; Production Engineering; Safety Engineering; Sports; Telecommunications Engineering); **information Systems**; **Law** (Law); **Mechanical Engineering** (Mechanical Engineering); **Nursing**; **Pedagogy** (Pedagogy); **Pharmacy** (Pharmacy); **Physical Education** (Physical Education); **Production Engineering**; **Psychology** (Psychology); **Technological Studies** (Business and Commerce; Communication Studies; Computer Networks; Finance; Human Resources; International Business; Transport Management); **Telecommunications Engineering** (Telecommunications Engineering)

History: Founded 2001. Formerly known as Faculdade de Ciências Aplicadas de Minas (FACIMINAS).

Main Language(s) of Instruction: Portuguese

Degrees and Diplomas: *Tecnólogo*; *Bacharelado*; *Licenciatura*; *Especialização/Aperfeiçoamento*; *Mestrado*
Last Updated: 02/07/10

PITAGORAS FACULTY OF VOTORANTIM-SOROCABA

Faculdade Pitágoras de Votorantim-Sorocaba
Av. Juscelino Kubitschek de Oliveira, 279, Protestantes, Votorantim, SP 18110-008
Tel: +55(15) 3416-7000
Website: http://www.faculdadepitagoras.com.br/ VotorantimSorocaba/

Diretor: Antonio Nunes

Courses
Administration (Administration); **Automation and Control Engineering** (Automation and Control Engineering); **Computer Science** (Computer Science); **Graduate Studies** (Business and Commerce; Management; Transport Management); **Journalism** (Journalism); **Mechanical Engineering** (Mechanical Engineering); **Production Engineering** (Production Engineering)

Degrees and Diplomas: *Bacharelado*. Also MBA.
Last Updated: 30/09/10

PIUS X FACULTY

Faculdade Pio Décimo (FPD)
Rua Estância 382 Terreo Centro, Aracaju, Sergipe 49010180
Tel: +55(79) 2106-3050
Fax: +55(79) 211-3363
EMail: faleconosco@piodecimo.com.br
Website: http://www.piodecimo.com.br

Diretor Geral: José Sebastiao dos Santos

Courses
Engineering (Chemical Engineering; Civil Engineering; Electrical Engineering); **Law**; **Letters** (Literature); **Pedagogy**; **Psychology**; **Veterinary Science**

History: Founded 1976.

Main Language(s) of Instruction: Portuguese

Degrees and Diplomas: *Bacharelado*; *Licenciatura*; *Especialização/Aperfeiçoamento*
Last Updated: 05/07/10

PIUS XII FACULTY

Faculdade PIO XII
Rua Bolivar de Abreu 48, Campo Grande, Cariacica, ES 29146330
Tel: +55(27) 3343-2563
Fax: +55(27) 3343-2563
EMail: faculdade@pioxil-es.com.br
Website: http://www.faculdade.pioxii-es.com.br

Diretor: Luciano Villaschi Chibib

Courses
Applied Social Sciences *(Espirito Santo)* (Accountancy; Administration; Business Administration; International Business; Law); **Biomedicine** *(Espirito Santo)* (Biomedicine)

History: Founded 1998.

Main Language(s) of Instruction: Portuguese

Degrees and Diplomas: *Bacharelado*: 4 yrs; *Bacharelado*: Law, 5 yrs; *Mestrado*

Libraries: Yes
Last Updated: 05/07/10

PLINIO LEITE UNIVERSITY CENTRE

Centro Universitário Plinio Leite (UNIPLI)
Rua Visconde do Rio Branco, 123, Centro, Niterói, Rio de Janeiro 24020000
Tel: +55(21) 2199-1441
Fax: +55(21) 2613-1281
EMail: plinioleite@nitnet.com.br
Website: http://www.unipli.com.br/siteunipli2/

Reitor: Hidiberto Ramos Cavalcanti de Albuquerque Júnior

Courses
Accountancy; **Administration**; **Architecture and Town Planning** (Architecture; Town Planning); **Arts and Humanities**; **Biomedicine** (Biomedicine); **Computer Science**; **Graduate Studies**; **Law**; **Nursing** (Nursing); **Nutrition** (Nutrition); **Pharmacy**; **Physical Therapy** (Physical Therapy); **Social Communication - Advertising and Publicity** (Advertising and Publicity); **Social Communication - Journalism** (Journalism); **Social Services**; **Technology Studies** (Communication Studies; Environmental Management; Fashion Design; Marketing; Tourism; Transport Management); **Tourism**; **Veterinary Medicine** (Veterinary Science)

Further Information: Also Niterói - Camboinhas, São Gonçalo and Itaboraí campuses.

History: Founded 1999.

Main Language(s) of Instruction: Portuguese

Degrees and Diplomas: *Tecnólogo*; *Bacharelado*; *Licenciatura*; *Especialização/Aperfeiçoamento*; *Mestrado*
Last Updated: 16/06/10

POLITEC FACULTY

Faculdade Politec
Rua da Agricultura, 4000, Santa Bárbara d' Oeste, SP 13454-005
Tel: +55(19) 3459-1000
Website: http://www.faculdadepolitec.edu.br/

Diretor Geral: Jaime Alfredo Klava

Courses
Undergraduate Studies (Automation and Control Engineering; Business Administration; Computer Networks; Cosmetology; Information Sciences; Pedagogy; Physical Education; Safety Engineering)

Degrees and Diplomas: *Tecnólogo*; *Bacharelado*; *Licenciatura*
Last Updated: 02/09/10

POLYTECHNIC FACULTY OF CAMPINAS

Faculdade Politécnica de Campinas (POLICAMP)
Rua Luiz Otávio, 1281, Campinas, SP 13087-570
Tel: +55(19) 3756-2300
Website: http://www.seufuturonapratica.com.br/portal/ index.php?id=99

Courses
Graduate Studies (Accountancy; Business Administration; Computer Networks; Finance; Industrial Design; Leadership; Management; Marketing; Public Relations; Software Engineering; Transport Management); **Undergraduate Studies** (Accountancy; Administration; Automation and Control Engineering; Communication Studies; Computer Networks; Electronic Engineering; Information Sciences; International Business; Law; Marketing; Production Engineering; Systems Analysis; Transport Management)

History: Founded 2003.

Degrees and Diplomas: *Tecnólogo*; *Bacharelado*. Also Postgraduate diploma and MBA.
Last Updated: 02/09/10

POLYTECHNIC FACULTY OF UBERLANDIA

Faculdade Politécnica de Uberlândia (FPU)
Avenida Fernando Vilela 839, Martins, Uberlândia, Minas Gerais 38400456
Tel: +55(34) 3217-9500
EMail: politecnica@nanet.com.br
Website: http://www1.fpu.com.br

Diretor: Eduardo Galassi Cunha EMail: eduardo@facpoli.edu.br

Courses

Computer Science; **Engineering**; **Law** (Law); **Management** (Accountancy; Administration; Finance; Human Resources; Industrial Management; Marketing)

History: Founded 2000.

Main Language(s) of Instruction: Portuguese

Degrees and Diplomas: *Tecnólogo*; *Bacharelado*; *Especialização/ Aperfeiçoamento*

Last Updated: 02/07/10

PONTIFICAL CATHOLIC UNIVERSITY OF CAMPINAS

Pontifícia Universidade Católica de Campinas (PUC-CAMPINAS)
Rodovia Dom Pedro I Km 136, S/n Parque das Universidades,
Campinas, São Paulo 13086900
Tel: +55(19) 3343-7000
EMail: reitoria@puc-campinas.edu.br
Website: http://www.puc-campinas.br

Reitor: Angela de Mendonça Engelbrecht (2010-)

Centres

Economics and Administration (Accountancy; Administration; Economics; International Business); **Exact Sciences, Environment and Technology** (Architecture; Chemistry; Civil Engineering; Computer Engineering; Computer Networks; Construction Engineering; Electrical Engineering; Environmental Engineering; Geography; Information Technology; Mathematics; Mathematics and Computer Science; Systems Analysis; Town Planning); **Human and Applied Sciences** (History; Law; Library Science; Pedagogy; Philosophy; Physical Education; Social and Community Services; Social Sciences; Theology); **Language and Communication** (Advertising and Publicity; Hotel Management; Journalism; Literature; Public Relations; Tourism; Visual Arts); **Life Sciences** (Biology; Dentistry; Medicine; Nursing; Nutrition; Occupational Therapy; Pharmacy; Physical Therapy; Psychology; Speech Therapy and Audiology)

Further Information: Also University hospital, 3 Health centres, Dentistry and Psychology clinics

History: Founded 1941 as Faculty of Philosophy, formally constituted as University and recognized by the State 1955. Raised to the rank of Catholic University 1955, and acquired present title 1972. A private university financially supported by 'Sociedade Campineira de Educação e Instrução'. The University is under the responsibilty of the Metropolitan Archbishop of Campinas, and is managed by its Grand Chancellor.

Governing Bodies: Conselho Universitário; Conselhos dos Centros Universitários (University Council); Academic Council; University Board

Academic Year: February to November (February-June; August-November)

Admission Requirements: Secondary school certificate and entrance examination

Fees: Vary according to courses

Main Language(s) of Instruction: Portuguese

International Co-operation: Alfa, PCI-AECI (Spain), and IAESTE programmes

Accrediting Agencies: Brazilian Government Agency (CAPES)

Degrees and Diplomas: *Bacharelado*: Accountancy; Administration; Advertising and Publicity; Chemistry; Biological Science; Dentistry; Economics; Social Sciences; Geography; History; Letters; Philosophy; Journalism; Library Science; Nursing; Nutrition; Occupational Therapy; Pharmaceutical Sciences; Public Relations; Social Service; Systems Analysis; Theology; Tourism; Visual Arts, 4 yrs; *Bacharelado*: Architecture and Town Planning; Civil Engineering; Computer Engineering; Electrical Engineering; Telecommunications Engineering; Environmental Engineering; Law; Physical Therapy; Psychology, 5 yrs; *Bacharelado*: Medicine, 6 yrs; *Bacharelado*: Religious Sciences, 3 yrs; *Licenciatura*: Biological Sciences; Geography; History; Letters; Mathematics and Physics; Pedagogy; Philosophy; Physical Education; Sports; Social Sciences; Teacher Training (Special Education); Visual Arts, 4 yrs; *Licenciatura*: Psychology, 5 yrs; *Mestrado*: Clinical Psychology; Computer Networks; Education; Educational Psychology; Library

Science; Social Philosophy; Ethics; Systems and Information Management; Telecommunications; Town Planning; *Doutorado*: Psychology

Student Services: Academic counselling, Canteen, Cultural centre, Employment services, Foreign student adviser, Handicapped facilities, Health services, Nursery care, Social counselling, Sports facilities

Special Facilities: Centro de Cultura e Arte. University Museum. TV Network and Studio. Art Gallery. Observatory.

Libraries: Central Library; Specialized Libraries, total, c. 210,000 vols

Publications: Cadernos da FACECA *(biennially)*; Cadernos de Serviço Social *(biennially)*; Cadernos do CCH *(biennially)*; Comunicarte *(biennially)*; Estudios de Psicologia *(quarterly)*; Humanitas *(biennially)*; Óculum Ensaios *(biennially)*; Phrónesis *(biennially)*; Reflexão *(biennially)*; Revista da Educação da PUC-Campinas *(biennially)*; Revista de Ciências Médicas *(bimonthly)*; Revista de Estudos do Curso de Jornalismo *(biennially)*; Revista de Letras *(biennially)*; Revista de Nutrição *(biennially)*; Revista Jurídica *(biennially)*; Revista Notícia Bibliográfica e Histórica *(bimonthly)*; Transinformação *(3 per annum)*

Last Updated: 14/06/10

PONTIFICAL CATHOLIC UNIVERSITY OF MINAS

Pontifícia Universidade Católica de Minas (PUC MINAS)
Avenida Dom José Gaspar, 500, Coração Eucarístico,
Belo Horizonte, Minas Gerais 30535-610
Tel: +55(31) 3319-4915; +55(31) 3319-4200; +55(31) 3319-4226
Fax: +55(31) 3319-4225
EMail: central@pucminas.br
Website: http://www.pucminas.br

Reitor: Joaquim Giovani Mol Guimarães

Departments

Architecture and Urbanism (Architecture; Town Planning); **International Relations** (International Relations; Sociology); **Mathematics and Statistics** (Mathematics; Statistics); **Physics** (Physics); **Physics and Chemistry** (Chemistry; Physics); **Psychology** (Psychology); **Social Communication** (Advertising and Publicity; Journalism; Public Relations); **Social Work** (Social Work); **Sociology** (Sociology)

Faculties

Law (Law) *Dean*: César Augusto de Castro Fiúza

Higher Schools

Teacher Qualification (Teacher Training)

Institutes

Biological and Health Sciences (Biological and Life Sciences; Dentistry; Nursing; Physical Therapy; Speech Therapy and Audiology); **Computer Science** (Computer Science; Information Sciences); **Economics and Management** (Accountancy; Business Administration; Economics); **Humanities** (English; Geography; History; Pedagogy; Philosophy; Portuguese; Religious Education; Special Education; Theology); **Polytechnic** (Automation and Control Engineering; Civil Engineering; Electrical Engineering; Electronic Engineering; Mechanical Engineering; Telecommunications Engineering)

Schools

Tourism (Tourism)

Units

Metropolitan Unit II - Contagem (Accountancy; Business Administration; Geography; Information Technology; International Business; Law; Social Work); **PUC/ Minas - Arcos** *(PUC/ Minas - Arcos)* (Advertising and Publicity; Business Administration; Communication Studies; Information Sciences; International Business; Journalism; Law; Psychology); **PUC/ Minas - Poços de Caldas** (Architecture and Planning; Business Administration; Civil Engineering; Computer Science; Electrical Engineering; Law; Pedagogy; Physical Therapy; Psychology; Tourism; Veterinary Science); **PUC/ Minas - São Gabriel** (Accountancy; Actuarial Science; Business Administration; Communication Studies; Computer Science; Information Sciences; Law; Management; Portuguese; Psychology; Social Sciences);

PUC/ Minas - Serro (Business Administration; Law); **PUC/Minas - Betim** (Biological and Life Sciences; Business Administration; English; Information Technology; Law; Mathematics; Nursing; Physical Therapy; Portuguese; Psychology; Veterinary Science)

History: Founded 1958, incorporating existing faculties and schools founded between 1943 and 1953. Title of Pontifical University conferred 1983.

Governing Bodies: University Council; Council of Teaching and Research

Academic Year: February to November (February-June; August-November)

Admission Requirements: Senior high school certificate and entrance examination

Main Language(s) of Instruction: Portuguese

International Co-operation: With universities in USA, Netherlands, Spain, United Kingdom, Canada and countries from Mercosur

Degrees and Diplomas: *Bacharelado*: 4-5 yrs; *Licenciatura*: 2-4 yrs; *Especialização/Aperfeiçoamento*: 5 months-2 yrs; *Mestrado*; *Doutorado*

Student Services: Academic counselling, Canteen, Cultural centre, Employment services, Foreign student adviser, Foreign Studies Centre, Handicapped facilities, Health services, Social counselling, Sports facilities

Special Facilities: Natural Science Museum; TV Studio

Libraries: Central Library, 208,332 vols and 116,614 titles. Connection with Biblodata (FGV), BIREME, IBICT, SUPRIR, IBGS, DATAPREV, CNEN and internet. All other units have libraries

Publications: Arquitetura *(annually)*; Caderno de Estudos Jurídicos *(annually)*; Caderno de Geografia *(biennially)*; Cadernos Cespuc de Pequisa, Portuguese-African-Brazilian studies publication *(biennially)*; Econonomia e Gestão *(biennially)*; Fronteira, Inititation in International Relations; Horizonte, Theological studies *(biennially)*; Psicologia em Revista *(biennially)*; Revista da Faculdade Mineira de Direito *(annually)*; Scripta, Postgraduate studies in Portuguese Language & Literature publication *(biennially)*
Last Updated: 11/06/10

PONTIFICAL CATHOLIC UNIVERSITY OF PARANÁ

Pontifícia Universidade Católica do Paraná (PUCPR)
Rua Imaculada Conceição 1155 Prado Velho, Curitibá, Paraná 80215901
Tel: +55(41) 3271-1505
Fax: +55(41) 3271-1726
EMail: siga@pucpr.br
Website: http://www.pucpr.br

Reitor: Clemente Ivo Juliatto (2002-)
Tel: +55(41) 3330-1505, Fax: +55(41) 3330-1726
EMail: reitor@rla01.pucpr.br

Pro-Reitor de Administração: Valdecir Cavalheiro
Tel: +55(41) 3330-1581, Fax: +55(41) 3330-1644

Centres
Applied Social Sciences; **Biology and Health Sciences** (Biology; Dentistry; Health Sciences; Medicine; Nursing; Nutrition; Pharmacy; Physical Therapy; Psychology; Speech Therapy and Audiology); **Exact and Technological Sciences** (Architecture and Planning; Chemical Engineering; Civil Engineering; Computer Engineering; Computer Science; Electrical Engineering; Engineering; Food Technology; Industrial Chemistry; Industrial Design; Mathematics; Mechanical Engineering; Production Engineering; Systems Analysis; Technology; Town Planning); **Juridical and Social Sciences** (Advertising and Publicity; Journalism; Law; Public Relations; Social and Community Services; Social Sciences; Tourism); **Theology and Human Sciences** (Arts and Humanities; English; Pedagogy; Philosophy; Physical Education; Portuguese; Religious Studies; Secretarial Studies; Theology)

Further Information: Also campuses in Londrina, Maringá and São José dos Pinhais

History: Founded 1959 incorporating institutions established between 1945 and 1956. Title of Pontifical University conferred 1985. A private institution under the supervision of the Sociedade Paranaense de Cultura and recognized by the Federal Government.

Governing Bodies: Conselho Universitário; Conselho de Administração; Conselho de Desenvolvimento; Conselho de Ensino e Extensão

Academic Year: February to December

Admission Requirements: Secondary school certificate or foreign equivalent and entrance examination

Fees: (Reais): 3,732-15,108 per annum; Graduate, 2,400-25,200

Main Language(s) of Instruction: Portuguese

International Co-operation: With universities in France, Italy, Germany

Accrediting Agencies: Ministry of Education

Degrees and Diplomas: *Bacharelado*: 2-6 yrs; *Especialização/Aperfeiçoamento*; *Mestrado*: Applied Informatics; Architecture and Town Planning; Dentistry; Economic and Social Law; Education; Mechanical Engineering; Medicine, a further 2-4 yrs; *Doutorado*: Applied Informatics, 2-4 yrs

Student Services: Canteen, Cultural centre, Employment services, Foreign student adviser, Health services, Language programs, Nursery care, Social counselling, Sports facilities

Student Residential Facilities: None

Special Facilities: Biology Museum. Herbarium. Art Gallery. TV Studio

Libraries: Central Library, 262,161 vols; São José dos Pinhais Campus Library, 34,331 vols; Londrina Campus, 88,885 vols

Publications: Changer, higher education *(biennially)*; Filosofia *(annually)*; Fisioterápia em Movimento *(biennially)*; Psicologia Argumento *(annually)*

Press or Publishing House: Editora Universitária Champagnat
Last Updated: 11/06/10

PONTIFICAL CATHOLIC UNIVERSITY OF RIO DE JANEIRO

Pontifícia Universidade Católica do Rio de Janeiro (PUC-RIO)
Rua Marquês de São Vicente 225, Gávea, Rio de Janeiro, Rio de Janeiro 22453900
Tel: +55(21) 3114-1001
EMail: hortal@puc-rio.br
Website: http://www.puc-rio.br

Reitor: Jesús Hortal (1995-)
Tel: +55(21) 3527-1120, Fax: +55(21) 3527-1145

Centres
Biological Sciences and Medicine (Biological and Life Sciences; Dentistry; Health Sciences; Medicine); **Science and Technology** (Chemistry; Civil Engineering; Computer Engineering; Computer Science; Electrical Engineering; Industrial Engineering; Materials Engineering; Mathematics; Mechanical Engineering; Metallurgical Engineering; Natural Sciences; Petroleum and Gas Engineering; Physics; Production Engineering; Technology; Telecommunications Engineering); **Social Sciences** (Advertising and Publicity; Business Administration; Cinema and Television; Communication Studies; Economics; Geography; History; Journalism; Law; Political Sciences; Social Sciences; Social Work; Sociology); **Theology and Humanities** (Architecture; Education; Fashion Design; Industrial Design; Media Studies; Philosophy; Psychology; Theology; Town Planning)

Further Information: Also International Students Programmes and Study Abroad Programmes (semester and academic year enrolment and double degree programmes). Intensive and regular courses of Portuguese as a foreign language

History: Founded 1940 by Cardinal D. Sebastião Leme and Father Leonel Franca, S.J. Acquired University status 1946. Title of Pontifical University conferred 1947. Under the supervision of the Society of Jesus and under the supreme authority of the Cardinal Archbishop of Rio de Janeiro as Grand Chancellor. Receives some financial support from the Federal Government.

Governing Bodies: Conselho de Curadores; Conselho Universitário

Academic Year: March to December (March-July; August-December)

511

Admission Requirements: Secondary school certificate and entrance examination

Fees: (US dollars): 6,000-11,000 per annum

Main Language(s) of Instruction: Portuguese

International Co-operation: With universities in Africa, Asia, Europe, Latin America and North America

Degrees and Diplomas: *Bacharelado*: 4 yrs; *Licenciatura*: 4 yrs; *Mestrado*: Business Administration; Chemistry; Civil Engineering; Computer Science; Design; Economics; Education; Electrical Engineering; History; International Relations; Language Studies and Linguistics; Law; Mathematics; Mechanical Engineering; Metallurgical Engineering; Metrology; Philosophy; Physics; Portuguese Language and Literature; Production Engineering; Psychology; Social Work; Theology, 2 yrs; *Doutorado*: Business Administration; Chemistry; Civil Engineering; Computer Science; Economics; Education; Electrical Engineering; History; Language Studies and Linguistics; Law; Mathematics; Mechanical Engineering; Metallurgical Engineering; Philosophy; Physics; Portuguese Language Literature; Production Engineering; Psychology; Theology, 4 yrs

Student Services: Academic counselling, Canteen, Cultural centre, Employment services, Foreign student adviser, Health services, Social counselling, Sports facilities

Special Facilities: Solar 'Grandjean de Montigny', preserved by the National Historical and Artistic Heritage Service (SPHAN) and restored to its original conception. Centro Loyola de Cultura e Fé

Libraries: Central Library and 4 libraries per academic area 500,000 vols

Publications: Contexto Internacional *(biannually)*; Criatividade; Direito, Estado e Sociedade; Estudos em Design; Gavea *(biannually)*; O que nos faz pensar; Psicologia Clínica; PUC-Ciência *(quarterly)*

Last Updated: 11/06/10

PONTIFICAL CATHOLIC UNIVERSITY OF RIO GRANDE DO SUL

Pontifícia Universidade Católica do Rio Grande do Sul (PUC-RS)
Avenida Ipiranga 6681, Partenon, Porto Alegre,
Rio Grande do Sul 90619-900
Tel: +55(51) 3320-3500
EMail: dircad@pucrs.br
Website: http://www.pucrs.br

Reitor: Joaquim Clotet (2005-) Tel: +55(51) 3320-3501

International Relations: Silvana Souza Silveira
Tel: +55(51) 3320-3660, Fax: +55(51) 3320-3885
EMail: aaii@pucrs.br

Faculties

Administration, Accountancy and Economics *(Uruguaiana)* (Accountancy; Business Administration; Economics; Hotel Management; Management; Marketing; Tourism); **Aeronautical Sciences** (Aeronautical and Aerospace Engineering); **Architecture and Town Planning** (Architecture; Design; Landscape Architecture; Town Planning); **Bioscience** (Biology; Cell Biology; Genetics; Molecular Biology; Zoology); **Chemistry** (Chemistry; Industrial Chemistry); **Computer Science** (Computer Engineering; Computer Science); **Dentistry** (Dentistry); **Education** (Education); **Engineering** (Automation and Control Engineering; Chemical Engineering; Civil Engineering; Computer Engineering; Electrical and Electronic Engineering; Mechanical Engineering; Technology); **Law** (Law), **Law** *(Uruguaiana)* (Law); **Letters** (Arts and Humanities; Linguistics; Literature; Modern Languages); **Mathematics** (Mathematics); **Medicine** (Medicine); **Nursing, Nutrition and Physiotherapy** (Nursing; Nutrition; Physical Therapy); **Pharmacy** (Pharmacy); **Philosophy and Human Sciences** (Arts and Humanities; Geography; History; Philosophy; Social Sciences); **Philosophy, Science and Humanities** *(Uruguaiana)* (Arts and Humanities; Mathematics and Computer Science; Natural Sciences; Philosophy); **Physical Education and Sports** (Physical Education; Sports); **Physics** (Physics); **Psychology** (Psychology); **Social Communications** (Communication Studies) *Division Head*: Santos Braga; **Social Services** (Social Work); **Theology** (Religion; Theology)

Institutes

Bioethics; **Environment**; **Geriatrics** (Gerontology) *Director*: Yukio Moriguchi; **Japanese Studies** (Japanese); **Music** (Music); **Scientific and Technological Research** (Natural Sciences; Technology); **Spanish Studies**; **Toxicology** (Toxicology)

Further Information: Also São Lucas University Hospital. Portuguese for foreign students. Centre for Nature Preservation and Research. Viamão and Zona Norte campuses

History: Founded 1931 by the Marist Brothers as Faculty of Economics. Incorporated Faculties and Schools established 1939. Acquired University status 1948, became Pontifical University 1950. An independent institution.

Governing Bodies: Conselho de Curadores (Board of Trustees); Conselho Universitário; Conselho de Coordenação, Ensino e Pesquisa

Academic Year: March to December (March-July; August-December)

Admission Requirements: Secondary school certificate or foreign equivalent and competitive entrance examination

Fees: (Reais): 1,856-5,433 per semester (20-35 per credit)

Main Language(s) of Instruction: Portuguese

Degrees and Diplomas: *Bacharelado*: Accountancy; Agriculture; Animal Husbandry; Architecture and Urban Planning; Business Administration; Dentistry; Economics; Engineering; Psychology; Systems Analysis; Veterinary Medicine, 10 sem; *Bacharelado*: Aeronautical Sciences; Philosophy, 6 sem; *Bacharelado*: Computer Science; Pharmacy; Physics, 9 sem; *Bacharelado*: Geography; History; Journalism; Letters; Mathematics; Pedagogy; Public Relations; Publicity; Social Sciences; Social Work; Tourism, 8 sem; *Bacharelado*: Law; Medicine, 12 sem; *Licenciatura*: Biology; Geography; History; Letters; Mathematics; Pedagogy; Social Studies; Theology, 8 sem; *Licenciatura*: Chemistry; Physics, 9 sem; *Licenciatura*: Philosophy, 6 sem; *Mestrado*: Bucco-Maxillofacial Surgery and Traumatology; Communications Media; Computer Science; Criminal Sciences; Dentistry; Education; Electrical Engineering; History; Law; Linguistics and Letters; Medical Clinic; Paediatrics; Philosophy; Psychology; Social Service; Zoology, a further 1-3 yrs; *Doutorado*: Buco-Maxillofacial Surgery and Traumatology; Clinical Stomatology; Education; History; Linguistics and Letters; Philosophy; Psychology; Zoology, by thesis, 2-4 yrs

Student Services: Academic counselling, Canteen, Cultural centre, Employment services, Foreign student adviser, Handicapped facilities, Health services, Social counselling, Sports facilities

Special Facilities: Museu de Ciências e Tecnologia

Libraries: Central Library, c. 238,150 vols

Publications: Análise *(quarterly)*; Biociência *(biannually)*; Comunicações do Museu de Ciências e Tecnologia *(biannually)*; Direito e Justiça *(annually)*; Divulgações do Museu de Ciências e Tecnologia *(biannually)*; Educação *(biannually)*; Estudos Ibero-Americanos *(biannually)*; Letras de Hoje *(quarterly)*; Odontociência *(biannually)*; Psico *(biannually)*; Revista do FAMECO *(biannually)*; Revista Medicina da PUCRS *(quarterly)*; Telecomunicação *(quarterly)*; Veritas *(quarterly)*

Press or Publishing House: EDIPUCRS
Last Updated: 11/06/10

PONTIFICAL CATHOLIC UNIVERSITY OF SÃO PAULO

Pontifícia Universidade Católica de São Paulo (PUCSP)
Rua Monte Alegre 984, Perdizes, São Paulo, São Paulo 05014901
Tel: +55(11) 3670-8000
EMail: reitoria@pucsp.br
Website: http://www.pucsp.br

Reitor: Dirceu de Mello
Tel: +55(11) 3670-8278, Fax: +55(11) 3670-8505

Faculties

Economics, Administration, Accountancy and Acturial Studies (Accountancy; Actuarial Science; Administration; Economics); **Education** (Pedagogy); **Exact Sciences and Technology** (Biomedical Engineering; Computer Science; Electrical Engineering; Mathematics; Physics; Production Engineering); **Human and Health Sciences** (Physical Therapy; Psychology; Speech Therapy and Audiology); **Law** (Law) *Director*: Marcelo Figueiredo Santos; **Medicine and Health** (Medicine; Nursing); **Philosophy, Communication, Letters and Art** (Advertising and Publicity; Art Criticism; Art History; Communication Studies; Journalism; Literature; Multimedia; Philosophy; Secretarial Studies); **Social Sciences** (Geography; History; International Relations; Social Sciences; Social Work; Tourism); **Theology** (Theology)

Institutes
Ageing Society Studies (Gerontology) *Co-ordinator*: Elizabeth Mercadante; **Language Research** (Linguistics) *Co-ordinator*: Elisabeth Brait; **Special Studies** *(Programmes for decentralized and disadvantaged areas) Director*: Mariângela Belfiori Wanderley; **Women's Studies** (Women's Studies) *Co-ordinator*: Maria Izilda Matos

Units
Communication Problems (Communication Disorders) *Director*: Alfredo Tabith

Further Information: Also 3 University Hospitals. Programa Estudante-Convênio do Ministério das Relações Exteriores do Brasil

History: Founded 1946, incorporating extra Faculties, including Faculties of Science, Philosophy and Literature, founded 1908, by the Episcopate of the Province of São Paulo and recognized by Government decree. Title of Pontifical University conferred 1947. Academic structure reorganized 1976. Responsible to the Fundação São Paulo with the Cardinal Archbishop of São Paulo as Grand Chancellor.

Governing Bodies: Conselho Superior; Conselho Universitário

Academic Year: February to December (February-June; August-December)

Admission Requirements: Secondary school certificate or foreign equivalent and entrance examination (Vestibular)

Fees: (Reais): 850,28-2,623.85 per month

Main Language(s) of Instruction: Portuguese

Degrees and Diplomas: *Bacharelado*: 4-6 yrs; *Licenciatura*: 4-6 yrs; *Mestrado*: 2-4 yrs; *Doutorado*: 4-6 yrs

Special Facilities: Museum. Videoteca. Museu da Cultura

Libraries: Central Library, c. 178,000 vols; Biomedical Library; Exact Sciences Library

Publications: Administração em diálogo *(annually)*; Cadernos de Administração *(annually)*; Cadernos Metrópole *(biannually)*; Cadernos PUC Economia *(biannually)*; Cognitio *(biannually)*; Distúrbios da Comunicação *(quarterly)*; Educação Matemática Pesquisa *(biannually)*; Estudos de Cinema *(annually)*; Hypnos *(biannually)*; Natureza Humana *(biannually)*; Projeto História *(biannually)*; Psicologia da Educação *(biannually)*; Psicologia Revista *(biannually)*; PUC-SP Ciências Biológicas e do Ambiente *(quarterly)*

Press or Publishing House: EDUC: Editora da Pontifícia Universidade Católica de São Paulo
Last Updated: 27/03/12

PORTAL FACULTY
Faculdade Portal
Rodovia RS 153, 555, Passo Fundo, RS 99034-600
Tel: +55(54) 3314-1055
EMail: secretaria@facportal.com.br
Website: http://www.facportal.com.br/
Diretor: Sigmundo Gomig

Courses
Distance Education (Education; Environmental Management; Management; Transport Management); **Graduate Studies** (Agricultural Business; Art Education; Civil Law; Education; Educational Administration; Environmental Studies; Finance; Higher Education; Safety Engineering; Social and Community Services; Tourism); **Undergraduate Studies** (Accountancy; Administration; Environmental Management; Information Sciences)

History: Founded 2003.
Degrees and Diplomas: *Tecnólogo*; *Bacharelado*; *Especialização/ Aperfeiçoamento*
Last Updated: 03/09/10

PORTO DAS ÁGUAS FACULTY
Faculdade Porto das Águas (FAPAG)
Rodovia SC 412 - Km 02, No 1499, Perequê, Porto Belo, SC 88210-000
Tel: +55(47) 3369-6200
Fax: +55(47) 3369-9543
EMail: direcao_academica@fapag.com.br
Website: http://www.fapag.com.br/

Courses
Graduate Studies (Environmental Management; Finance; Management; Tourism); **Undergraduate Studies** (Administration; Physical Education)
History: Founded 2005.
Degrees and Diplomas: *Bacharelado*; *Licenciatura*. Also MBA.
Last Updated: 03/09/10

PORTO SEGURO FACULTY
Faculdade Porto Seguro (FAPS)
Avenida Deputado João Rios, 269, Centro, Iúna, ES 29390-000
Tel: +55(28) 3545-2715
EMail: faps@faps.edu.br
Diretor Geral: Maria da Penha Barros Pereira

Courses
Administration (Administration)
Degrees and Diplomas: *Bacharelado*
Last Updated: 03/09/10

PORTO SEGURO INSTITUTE OF EDUCATION
Instituto Superior de Educação Porto Seguro
Avenida Deputado João Rios N° 269, Centro, Iúna, ES 29390-000
Tel: +55(28) 3545-2715
EMail: faps@faps.edu.br
Diretora: Maria Da Penha Barros Pereira

Courses
Pedagogy (Pedagogy)
History: Founded 2003
Main Language(s) of Instruction: Portuguese
Degrees and Diplomas: *Licenciatura*
Last Updated: 29/09/10

PORTUGUESE-BRAZILIAN FACULTY
Faculdade Luso-Brasileira
Avenida Congresso Eucarístico Internacional 01, Carpina, PE 55815-150
Tel: +55(81) 3621-0668
EMail: maurifalub@crape.com.br
Website: http://www.falub.edu.br/v2/
Diretor: Mauri Vieira Costa

Courses
Accountancy (Accountancy); **Administration** (Administration); **Letters** (Literature); **Pedagogy** (Pedagogy)
History: Founded 2001.
Main Language(s) of Instruction: Portuguese
Degrees and Diplomas: *Bacharelado*
Libraries: Biblioteca Professor Francisco Igino Barbosa Lima Sobrinho
Last Updated: 02/09/10

POSITIVO UNIVERSITY
Universidade Positivo (UNICENP)
Rua Professor Pedro Viriato Parigot de Souza, Curitibá, Paraná 81280330
Tel: +55(41) 3317-3000
Fax: +55(41) 3317-3030 +55(41) 3317-3082
EMail: secretaria@unicenp.edu.br
Website: http://www.unicenp.br
Reitor: José Pio Martins

Schools

Biological and Health Sciences (Biological and Life Sciences; Dentistry; Health Sciences; Medicine; Nutrition; Pharmacy; Physical Education; Physical Therapy; Psychology); **Human and Applied Social Sciences** (Accountancy; Administration; Advertising and Publicity; Economics; International Business; Journalism; Law; Marketing; Pedagogy; Social Sciences; Tourism); **Technology and Exact Sciences** (Architecture and Planning; Civil Engineering; Computer Engineering; Electrical Engineering; Industrial Design; Information Sciences; Mechanical Engineering)

History: Founded 1998. Acquired present status and title 2008. Formerly know as Centro Universitário Positivo (Positive University Centre).

Main Language(s) of Instruction: Portuguese

Degrees and Diplomas: *Bacharelado*; *Especialização/Aperfeiçoamento*; *Mestrado*; *Doutorado*
Last Updated: 07/05/10

POTIGUAR DA PARAÍBA FACULTY

Faculdade Potiguar da Paraíba (FPB)
Av. Monsenhor Walfredo Leal, 512, Tambiá, João Pessoa,
PB 58020-540
Tel: +55(83) 3133-2900
Fax: +55(83) 3133-2920
EMail: direcaogeralfpb@fpb.edu.br
Website: http://www.fpb.edu.br/

Diretor Geral: Silvio de Mendon Furtado

Courses

Administration (Administration); **Commercial Management** (Business and Commerce); **Law** (Law); **Managerial Projects** (Management); **Public Administration** (Public Administration)

History: Founded 2005.

Degrees and Diplomas: *Tecnólogo*; *Bacharelado*
Last Updated: 03/09/10

POTIGUAR UNIVERSITY - NATAL

Universidade Potiguar (UNP)
Avenida Senador Salgado Filho 1610, Lagoa Nova, Natal,
Rio Grande do Norte 59056000
Tel: +55(84) 3215-1234
EMail: reitoria@unp.br
Website: http://www.unp.br

Reitora: Sâmela Soraya Gomes de Oliveira Tel: +55(84) 215-1245

Schools

Communication and Arts; **Education** (English; History; Literature; Pedagogy; Portuguese); **Engineering and Exact Sciences** (Architecture; Civil Engineering; Computer Engineering; Computer Networks; Environmental Engineering; Petroleum and Gas Engineering; Production Engineering; Town Planning); **Health** (Biology; Dentistry; Medicine; Nursing; Nutrition; Occupational Therapy; Pharmacy; Physical Education; Physical Therapy; Psychology; Social Welfare; Speech Therapy and Audiology); **Hospitality and Gastronomy** (Cooking and Catering; Tourism); **Law**; **Management**

Further Information: Also Environmental Education Centre at Pitangui

History: Founded 1981 as Faculdade de Administração, Ciências Contábeis e Ciências Econômicas. Acquired present status and title 1996.

Admission Requirements: Secondary school certificate and entrance examination

Main Language(s) of Instruction: Portuguese

Degrees and Diplomas: *Bacharelado*; *Licenciatura*; *Especialização/Aperfeiçoamento*; *Mestrado*
Last Updated: 07/05/10

PRAXIS FACULTY

Faculdade Práxis (FIPEP)
Rua Dr. Antonio Bento 113, Santo Amaro, São Paulo,
São Paulo 04750000
Tel: +55(11) 5687-2245
Fax: +55(11) 5687-2245
EMail: faculdadepraxis@uol.com.br

Diretor Geral: Luiz Amaro de Araujo Lima

Courses

Nursing; **Pedagogy**
History: Founded 2001.

Main Language(s) of Instruction: Portuguese

Degrees and Diplomas: *Licenciatura*. Also professional diploma in Nursing (4 yrs)
Last Updated: 02/07/10

PRESIDENT ANTÔNIO CARLOS FACULTY - ITPAC PORTO NACIONAL

Faculdade Presidente Antônio Carlos - ITPAC Porto Nacional
Rua Antônio Aires Primo, 2398, Centro, Porto Nacional,
TO 77500-000
Tel: +55(63) 3363-1674
EMail: contabilidade@itpacporto.com.br
Website: http://www.itpacporto.com.br/

Courses

Administration (Administration); **Architecture and Urbanism** (Architecture; Town Planning); **Civil Engineering** (Civil Engineering); **Medicine** (Medicine); **Nursing** (Nursing); **Odontology** (Dentistry); **Physical Therapy** (Physical Therapy); **Social Communication** (Communication Studies)

Degrees and Diplomas: *Bacharelado*
Last Updated: 03/09/10

PRESIDENT ANTONIO CARLOS INSTITUTE OF THE STATE OF TOCANTINS

Instituto Tocantinense Presidente Antônio Carlos (ITPAC)
Avenida Filadélfia 568, Setor Oeste, Araguaína, TO 77816530
Tel: +55(63) 3411-8500
Fax: +55(63) 3411-8502
EMail: itpac@itpac.br
Website: http://www.itpac.br

Diretor: Bonifácio José Tamm de Andrada

Courses

Accountancy (Accountancy); **Administration** (Administration); **Dentistry**; **Information Sytem** (Information Sciences); **Law**; **Medicine** (Medicine); **Nursing** (Nursing); **Pedagogy** (Pedagogy; Teacher Training); **Pharmacy** (Pharmacy); **Physical Education** (Physical Education)

History: Founded 1998.

Main Language(s) of Instruction: Portuguese

Degrees and Diplomas: *Bacharelado*: 4-6 yrs; *Licenciatura*: 4 yrs; *Especialização/Aperfeiçoamento*: a further 2 yrs
Last Updated: 14/06/10

PRESIDENT ANTÔNIO CARLOS UNIVERSITY

Universidade Presidente Antônio Carlos (UNIPAC)
Rua Monsenhor José Augusto 203 São José, Barbacena,
Minas Gerais 36205018
Tel: +55(32) 3693-8865
EMail: falecom@unipac.br
Website: http://www.unipac.br

Reitor: Bonifácio José Tamm de Andrada EMail: reitoria@unipac.br

Courses

Accountancy (Accountancy); **Administration** (Administration); **Communication Studies**; **Computer Science**; **Data Processing** (Data Processing); **Education** (Education); **History** (History); **Information Technology**; **Law** (Law); **Mathematics** (Mathematics); **Medicine** (Medicine); **Nutrition**; **Physiotherapy**; **Socal and Community Services**; **Speech Therapy and Audiology**; **Tourism**

Faculties

Philosophy, Science and Letters *(Deputado José Laviola - FAFICIL)* (Arts and Humanities; English; Portuguese); **Philosophy, Sciences and Letters** *(Congonhas - FAFIC)* (Arts and Humanities; Educational Administration; Educational and Student Counselling; Pedagogy; Philosophy; Social Sciences)

History: Founded 1963. Acquired present status 1997.

Admission Requirements: Secondary school certificate and entrance examination

Main Language(s) of Instruction: Portuguese

Degrees and Diplomas: *Tecnólogo*; *Bacharelado*; *Licenciatura*; *Mestrado*

Last Updated: 07/05/10

PRESIDENT TANCREDO DE ALMEIDA NEVES INSTITUTE OF HIGHER EDUCATION

Instituto de Ensino Superior Presidente Tancredo de Almeida Neves (IPTAN)
Avenida Leite de Castro 1101, São João del Rei,
Minas Gerais 36305044
Tel: +55(32) 3379-2724
Fax: +55(32) 3379-2724
EMail: iptan@iptan.edu.br
Website: http://www.iptan.edu.br

Diretora: Mirian Moreira V. Silva

Courses
Accountancy (Accountancy); **Administration** (Administration); **Law**; **Nursing** (Nursing); **Physical Education** (Physical Education)

History: Founded 2000.

Main Language(s) of Instruction: Portuguese

Degrees and Diplomas: *Bacharelado*

Last Updated: 16/06/10

PRISMA FACULTY

Faculdade Prisma (FAP)
Av. Coronel Prates, n° 16, Centro, Montes Claros, MG 39400-104
Tel: +55(38) 3229-1900
EMail: faculdade@prisma.edu.br
Website: http://www.prisma.edu.br/

Diretor Geral: Manoel José Pereira Neto

Courses
Chemistry (Chemistry); **Commercial Management** (Business and Commerce); **Physics** (Physics)

History: Founded 2008.

Degrees and Diplomas: *Tecnólogo*; *Licenciatura*

Last Updated: 03/09/10

PROCESSUS FACULTY

Faculdade Processus
Avenida das Araucárias, 4400, Águas Claras, Brasília,
DF 71936-250
Tel: +55(61) 3563-3247 +55(61) 3562-6343
EMail: ouvidoria@institutoprocessus.com.br
Website: http://www.institutoprocessus.com.br/

Diretora Acadêmica: Claudine Fernandes de Araújo
EMail: claudine@institutoprocessus.com.br

Courses
Graduate Studies (Commercial Law; Criminal Law; Labour Law; Portuguese; Public Law); **Undergraduate Studies** (Finance; Law; Secretarial Studies)

Further Information: Also Asa Sul and Planaltina campuses.

Degrees and Diplomas: *Tecnólogo*; *Bacharelado*. Also Postgraduate Diploma.

Last Updated: 03/09/10

PROF. LUIZ ROSA FACULTY OF TECHNOLOGY

Faculdade de Tecnologia Prof. Luiz Rosa (FATEC PRFOF. LUIZ ROSA)
Rua Senador Fonseca, 1182, Centro, Jundiaí, SP 13201-789
Tel: +55(11) 4583-1600
Fax: +55(11) 4583-1603
EMail: romilda@luizrosa.edu.br
Website: http://www.luizrosa.edu.br/fatec/

Diretor: Fernando Leme do Prado

Courses
Accountancy (Accountancy); **Administration** (Administration); **Environmental Management** (Environmental Management); **Financial Management** (Finance); **Graduate Studies** (Business Administration; Business and Commerce; Environmental Management; Finance; Industrial Management; Management; Marketing; Public Administration; Transport Management); **Human Resources** (Human Resources); **Institutional Communication** (Communication Studies); **Logistics** (Transport Management); **Marketing** (Marketing); **Production Management** (Industrial Management); **Systems Analysis and Development** (Systems Analysis)

History: Founded 1917 as Escola Prof. Luiz Rosa. Acquired present status and title 2001.

Degrees and Diplomas: *Tecnólogo*; *Bacharelado*. Also MBA.

Last Updated: 26/08/10

PROFESSOR JOSÉ DE SOUZA HERDY UNIVERSITY OF GRANDE RIO

Universidade do Grande Rio Professor José de Souza Herdy
Rua Professor José de Sousa Herdy, 1160 - Bairro 25 de Agosto,
Duque de Caxias, Rio de Janeiro 25071-200
Tel: +55(21) 2672-7777
EMail: faleconosco@unigranrio.edu.br
Website: http://www.unigranrio.br

Reitor: Arody Cordeiro Herdy **EMail:** reitoria@unigranrio.com.br

Schools
Applied Social Sciences; **Education, Science, Letters, Arts and Humanities** (Education; History; Literature; Mathematics; Pedagogy; Visual Arts); **Health Sciences**; **Science and Technology** (Computer Science; Petroleum and Gas Engineering; Production Engineering)

History: Founded 1970 as Faculdades Unidas Grande Rio. Acquired present status and title 1994.

Main Language(s) of Instruction: Portuguese

Degrees and Diplomas: *Bacharelado*; *Licenciatura*; *Especialização/Aperfeiçoamento*; *Mestrado*

Last Updated: 01/06/10

PROFESSOR LUCIA DANTAS INSTITUTE OF EDUCATION

Instituto Superior de Educação Professora Lúcia Dantas
QNN 29 Área Especial A s/n, Ceilândia Norte, Brasília,
DF 72225-290
EMail: isel@ad1.br

Courses
Teacher Training (Teacher Training)

Degrees and Diplomas: *Licenciatura*

Last Updated: 29/09/10

PROFESSOR MIGUEL ÂNGELO DA SILVA SANTOS FACULTY

Faculdade Professor Miguel Ângelo da Silva Santos (FEMASS)
R. Aluísio da Silva Gomes, 50, Granja dos Cavaleiros, Macaé,
RJ 27930-560
Tel: +55(22) 2796-2500
EMail: femass@funemac.edu.br
Website: http://www.funemac.edu.br/

Courses
Administration (Administration); **Information Systems** (Information Sciences); **Production Engineering** (Production Engineering)

Degrees and Diplomas: *Bacharelado*

Last Updated: 03/09/10

PROGRAMUS INSTITUTE OF EDUCATION
Instituto Superior de Educação Programus
Rua Moraes 310, Agua Branca, PI 64460-000
Tel: +55(86) 3282-1175
EMail: lsepro@isepro.com.br
Website: http://www.isepro.com.br

Diretor: Eloan Coimbra Lima

Courses
Pedagogy (Pedagogy)
History: Founded 2004.

Main Language(s) of Instruction: Portuguese

Degrees and Diplomas: *Licenciatura*; *Especialização/Aperfeiçoamento*

Libraries: Yes
Last Updated: 29/09/10

PROJECTION FACULTY
Faculdade Projeção (FAPRO)
Area Especial 5/6 Setro C, Taguatinga, Brasília, DF 72115700
Tel: +55(61) 3451-3888
Fax: +55(61) 3561-0201
EMail: faculdadeprojecao@projecao.br
Website: http://www.projecao.br/faculdade/default.htm

Diretor: Lauri Tadeu Correa Martins

Schools
Business (Accountancy; Administration; Advertising and Publicity); **Law and Social Sciences** (Law); **Teacher Training** (Geography; History); **Technology** (Information Technology)

History: Founded 2000.

Main Language(s) of Instruction: Portuguese

Degrees and Diplomas: *Bacharelado*; *Especialização/Aperfeiçoamento*
Last Updated: 02/07/10

PROMOVE FACULTIES
Faculdades Promove
Av. João Pinheiro, 164, Belo Horizonte, Minas Gerais 30130180
Tel: +55(31) 2103-2103
Fax: +55(31) 2103-2103
EMail: faculdade@faculdadepromove.br
Website: http://www.faculdadepromove.br

Diretor Geral: Milton Cabral Moreira

Courses
Administration (Administration; Marketing; Sports Management); **Law** *(Promove)* (Law); **Nursing**; **Social Communication** (Advertising and Publicity; Publishing and Book Trade)

Further Information: Also branch in Sete Lagoas
History: Founded 1999.

Main Language(s) of Instruction: Portuguese

Degrees and Diplomas: *Bacharelado*; *Especialização/Aperfeiçoamento*; *Mestrado*
Last Updated: 21/06/10

PRUDENTE DE MORAES FACULTY
Faculdade Prudente de Moraes (FPM)
Rua Professor José Benedicto Gonçalves 309, Rancho Grande, Itú, São Paulo 13300000
Tel: +55(11) 4024-1902
Fax: +55(11) 4024-3777
EMail: fpm@fpm.edu.br
Website: http://www.fpm.edu.br

Diretor Geral: Luiz Roberto da Silveira Castro (1998-)

Courses
Administration; **Advertising**; **Journalism** (Journalism)
History: Founded 1990.

Main Language(s) of Instruction: Portuguese

Degrees and Diplomas: *Bacharelado*; *Especialização/Aperfeiçoamento*; *Mestrado*
Last Updated: 02/07/10

PYTHAGORAS INTEGRATED FACULTIES
Faculdades Integradas Pitágoras (FIP-MOC)
Rua Monte Pascoal 284, Montes Claros, Minas Gerais
Tel: +55(38) 3214-7100
Fax: +55(38) 3212 1002
EMail: secretaria@fip-moc.edu.br
Website: http://www.fip-moc.edu.br

Diretora: Maria de Fátima Turano

Courses
Advertising (Advertising and Publicity); **Biomedicine** (Biomedicine); **Design**; **Engineering**; **Law** (Law); **Medicine** (Medicine); **Nursing** (Nursing); **Pedagogy** (Pedagogy); **Pharmacy** (Pharmacy); **Physiotherapy** (Physical Therapy); **Psychology** (Psychology); **Tourism and Hotel Management**

History: Founded 2000.

Main Language(s) of Instruction: Portuguese

Degrees and Diplomas: *Bacharelado*; *Licenciatura*; *Especialização/Aperfeiçoamento*
Last Updated: 22/06/10

QUARESMA BI SOCIAL FACULTY
Faculdade Bi Social Quaresma
Avenida Frederico Ozannan N°: 6.000, loja 2.475 Maxi Shopping, Jardim Florestal, Jundiaí, SP 13215-700
Tel: +55(11)4583-8300
EMail: antoniomotta@mail.com

Diretor: Heliomar Manoel Quaresma

Courses
Accountancy (Accountancy); **Administration** (Administration); **Environmental Management** (Environmental Management); **Financial Management** (Finance); **Information Technology Management** (Information Technology); **Management** (Management); **Pedagogy** (Pedagogy)

History: Founded 2004.

Main Language(s) of Instruction: Portuguese

Degrees and Diplomas: *Bacharelado*
Last Updated: 31/08/10

QUEEN OF PEACE CATHOLIC FACULTY OF ARAPUTANGA
Faculdade Católica Rainha da Paz de Araputanga (FCARP)
Avenida 23 de Maio, N° 02, Araputanga, MT 78260-000
Tel: +55(65) 3261-1314
Fax: +55(65) 3261-2341
EMail: fcarp@fcarp.edu.br
Website: http://www.fcarp.edu.br

Diretora: Marilza Larranhagas da Cruz

Courses
Graduate Studies

Departments
Accountancy (Accountancy); **Administration**; **Information Systems** (Computer Science); **Law** (Law); **Physical Education**

History: Founded 1999.

Main Language(s) of Instruction: Portuguese

Degrees and Diplomas: *Bacharelado*; *Licenciatura*; *Especialização/Aperfeiçoamento*
Last Updated: 30/06/10

QUIRINÓPOLIS FACULTY
Faculdade Quirinópolis
Av. Quirino Cândido de Moraes, 38, Centro, Quirinópolis,
GO 75860-000
Tel: +55(64) 3651-2214
EMail: contato@faculdadequirinopolis.com.br
Website: http://www.faculdadequirinopolis.com.br/

Courses
Administration (Administration); **Environmental Management** (Environmental Management); **Law** (Law); **Nursing** (Nursing)

History: Founded 2005.

Degrees and Diplomas: *Tecnólogo*; *Bacharelado*
Last Updated: 03/09/10

R. SÁ FACULTY
Faculdade R. Sá
Br 316, Km 3025 s/n, Picos, PI 64600-000
Tel: +55(89) 3421-6032
EMail: iesrsa@iesrsa.com.br
Website: http://www.iesrsa.esab.edu.br/

Diretor: Raimundo Sá Urtiga Filho

Courses
Administration (Administration); **Information Systems**; **Pedagogy** (Pedagogy)

History: Founded 2006.

Main Language(s) of Instruction: Portuguese

Degrees and Diplomas: *Bacharelado*; *Especialização/Aperfeiçoamento*; *Mestrado*
Last Updated: 23/09/10

RADIAL FACULTY OF CURITIBA
Faculdade Radial Curitiba
Avenida Senador Souza Naves, 1715, Cristo Rei, Curitiba, PR
Tel: +55(41) 3592-2700
EMail: secretariageral@radial.br
Website: http://portal.estacio.br/unidades/faculdade-radial-curitiba.aspx

Diretor Presidente: Eduardo Alcalay

Courses
Accountancy (Accountancy); **Administration** (Administration); **Electrical Engineering** (Electrical Engineering); **Law** (Law); **Production Engineering** (Production Engineering)

History: Founded 2003.

Degrees and Diplomas: *Bacharelado*
Last Updated: 03/09/10

RADIAL FACULTY OF TECHNOLOGY OF SANTO ANDRÉ
Faculdade de Tecnologia Radial Santo André
Rua das Esmeraldas, 67, Bairro Jardim, Santo André,
SP 09090-770
Tel: +55(11) 4932-2000
Website: http://portal.estacio.br/unidades/faculdade-de-tecnologia-radial-santo-andre.aspx

Courses
Financial Management (Finance); **Graduate Studies** (Business Administration; Transport Management); **Human Resources** (Human Resources); **International Business** (International Business); **Logistics** (Transport Management); **Marketing** (Marketing)

Degrees and Diplomas: *Tecnólogo*. Also MBA.
Last Updated: 27/08/10

RADIAL UNIVERSITY CENTRE
Centro Universitário Radial (UNIRADIAL)
Rua Promotor Gabriel Netuzzi Perez 108, Santo Amaro, São Paulo,
São Paulo 04743020
Tel: +55(11) 5541-5533
EMail: secretariaf@radial.br
Website: http://www.radial.br

Diretor: Carlos Rivera Ferreira

Courses
Bacharelado (Accountancy; Administration; Advertising and Publicity; Electrical Engineering; Environmental Engineering; Fashion Design; Information Sciences; Journalism; Law; Petroleum and Gas Engineering; Physical Education; Production Engineering); **Graduate Studies**; **Licenciatura** (History; Literature; Mathematics; Pedagogy; Physical Education; Visual Arts); **Technological Studies** (Automation and Control Engineering; Communication Studies; Computer Networks; Environmental Management; Fashion Design; Finance; Graphic Design; Human Resources; Information Technology; International Business; Management; Marketing; Secretarial Studies; Systems Analysis; Transport Management)

History: Founded 1980.

Degrees and Diplomas: *Tecnólogo*; *Bacharelado*; *Licenciatura*; *Especialização/Aperfeiçoamento*. Also MBA.
Last Updated: 17/06/10

RAIMUNDO MARINHO FACULTY
Faculdade Raimundo Marinho
Avenida Durval de Góes Monteiro, 8501, Tabuleiro dos Martins,
Maceió, AL 57200-000
Tel: +55(82) 3325-9574
EMail: contato@frm.edu.br
Website: http://www.frm.edu.br/

President: Lysia Ramalho Marinho

Courses
Administration *(Penedo)* (Administration); **Administration** *(Maceió)*; **Law** *(Penedo)* (Law); **Law** *(Maceió)* (Law); **Nursing**; **Pedagogy** *(Maceió)* (Pedagogy); **Pedagogy** *(Penedo)* (Pedagogy); **Postgradaute Studies**; **Social Service** (Social and Community Services)

History: Founded 1999 as Faculdade de Ciências Sociais Aplicadas de Penedo (FCSAP). Merged with Faculdade de Formação de Professores (FFPP) and Faculdade de Ciências Jurídicas de Alagoas (FCJAL) 2010.

Main Language(s) of Instruction: Portuguese

Degrees and Diplomas: *Bacharelado*; *Licenciatura*; *Especialização/Aperfeiçoamento*. Also MBA.
Last Updated: 06/07/10

RAÍZES FACULTY
Faculdade Raízes
Rua Floriano Peixoto, N° 900, Centro, Anápolis, GO 75024-030
Tel: +55(62) 3099-5094
EMail: jesse@unievangelica.edu.br
Website: http://www.faculdaderaizes.com.br/

Courses
Law (Law)

History: Founded 2002.

Degrees and Diplomas: *Bacharelado*
Last Updated: 03/09/10

RATIO - PHILOSOPHICAL AND THEOLOGICAL FACULTY
Ratio - Faculdade Teológica e Filosófica (RATIO)
Avenida Visconde do Rio Branco, 2801, Joaquim Távora,
Fortaleza, CE 60055-171
Tel: +55(85) 3253-4801
Fax: +55(85) 3253-4801
EMail: secacademica@ratio.edu.br
Website: http://www.ratio.edu.br/

Courses
Undergraduate Studies (Public Administration; Social and Community Services); **Undergraduate Studies** (Psychology; Safety Engineering; Social and Community Services)

Degrees and Diplomas: *Bacharelado*; *Especialização/Aperfeiçoamento*. Also MBA.
Last Updated: 29/09/10

BRAZIL–Private Institutions

RED BALLOON INSTITUTE OF EDUCATION
Instituto Superior de Educação Balão Vermelho (ISEBV)
Avenida Bandeirantes, 800, Mangabeiras, Belo Horizonte,
MG 30315-000
EMail: balao@balaovermelho.com.br

Courses
Teacher Training (Teacher Training)
Degrees and Diplomas: *Licenciatura*
Last Updated: 24/09/10

REDENTOR FACULTY
Faculdade Redentor (FACREDENTOR)
Rodovia BR 356, número 25, Bairro Cidade Nova, Itaperuna,
RJ 28300-000
Tel: +55 (22) 3811-0111
EMail: pi@redentor.edu.br
Website: http://www.redentor.edu.br/

Diretor: Heitor Antonio da Silva

Courses
Administration (Administration); **Architecture and Urbansim** (Architecture; Town Planning); **Biological and Life Sciences** (Biological and Life Sciences); **Civil Engineering** (Civil Engineering); **Graduate Studies** (Acupuncture; Administration; Computer Networks; Education; Educational Administration; Educational and Student Counselling; Educational Psychology; Engineering Management; Environmental Management; Finance; Higher Education; Hotel Management; Law; Leisure Studies; Management; Medicine; Nursing; Public Administration; Safety Engineering; Social Policy; Software Engineering; Sports; Tourism); **Information Systems** (Information Sciences); **Mechanical Engineering** (Mechanical Engineering); **Nursing** (Nursing); **Nutrition** (Nutrition); **Phonoaudiology** (Speech Therapy and Audiology); **Physical Therapy** (Physical Therapy); **Production Engineering** (Production Engineering); **Social Service** (Social and Community Services)

Degrees and Diplomas: *Bacharelado*; *Especialização/Aperfeiçoamento*. Also Postgraduate Diploma and MBA.
Last Updated: 03/09/10

REGIONAL COMMUNITY UNIVERSITY OF CHAPECÓ
Universidade Comunitária Regional de Chapecó (UNOCHAPECO)
Avenida Senador Attílio Fontana, 591-E, Bairro Efapi,
P.O. Box 1141, Chapecó, Santa Catarina 89809-000
Tel: +55(49) 3321-8000
EMail: viceplan@unochapeco.edu.br
Website: http://www.unochapeco.edu.br

Reitor: Odilon Luiz Poli **EMail:** gabreitor@unochapeco.edu.br
Vice-Rector for Administration: Sady Mazzioni
EMail: viceadm@unochapeco.edu.br

Areas
Exact and Environmental Sciences; Health Sciences; Human Sciences and Law; Social and Applied Sciences
Further Information: Also campuses in São Lourenço do Oeste and Xaxim.
History: Founded 2002.
Main Language(s) of Instruction: Portuguese
Degrees and Diplomas: *Tecnólogo*; *Bacharelado*: 4-5 yrs; *Especialização/Aperfeiçoamento*; *Mestrado*; *Doutorado*
Last Updated: 07/06/10

REGIONAL FACULTY OF ALAGOINHAS
Faculdade Regional de Alagoinhas (FARAL)
Rua Altino Ribeiro Rocha da Cruz, s/n, Alagoinhas Velhas,
Alagoinhas, BA
Tel: +55(75) 3422-8900
EMail: unirb@unirb.edu.br
Website: http://www.unirb.edu.br/

Courses
Graduate Studies (Law; Public Health); **Law** (Law); **Nursing** (Nursing); **Nutrition** (Nutrition); **Physical Education** (Physical Education); **Physical Therapy** (Physical Therapy); **Psychology** (Psychology)

Degrees and Diplomas: *Bacharelado*; *Licenciatura*; *Especialização/Aperfeiçoamento*
Last Updated: 03/09/10

REGIONAL FACULTY OF BAHIA
Faculdade Regional da Bahia (UNIRB)
Av. Tamburugy, 474, Patamares, Salvador, BA 41680-430
EMail: unirb@unirb.edu.br
Website: http://www.unirb.edu.br/

Courses
Graduate Studies (Administration; Educational Administration; Gerontology; Law; Midwifery; Oncology; Physical Education; Physical Therapy; Psychology; Public Health; Rehabilitation and Therapy); **Undergraduate Studies** (Accountancy; Biomedicine; Business Administration; Chemical Engineering; Computer Networks; Cooking and Catering; Dentistry; Environmental Engineering; Journalism; Law; Nursing; Nutrition; Occupational Health; Pedagogy; Physical Education; Physical Therapy; Production Engineering; Psychology; Public Administration; Radiology; Social and Community Services; Software Engineering; Speech Therapy and Audiology; Systems Analysis; Tourism)

Degrees and Diplomas: *Tecnólogo*; *Bacharelado*; *Licenciatura*; *Especialização/Aperfeiçoamento*
Last Updated: 03/09/10

REGIONAL FACULTY OF PHILOSOPHY, SCIENCES AND LITERATURE OF CANDEIAS
Faculdade Regional de Filosofia, Ciências e Letras de Candeias (FAC)
Rod BA 522, Km 8, Fazenda Caroba, Candeias, BA 43813-300
Tel: +55(71) 3602-9256
EMail: iescfac@iescfac.edu.br
Website: http://www.iescfac.edu.br/

Courses
Graduate Studies (Advertising and Publicity; Business Administration; Business Education; Cultural Studies; Distance Education; Ecology; Education; Educational Administration; Educational Psychology; Educational Technology; English; Environmental Management; Geography; Health Administration; Higher Education; History; Industrial and Organizational Psychology; Information Management; Information Sciences; Law; Leisure Studies; Literacy Education; Literature; Management; Marketing; Mathematics Education; Native Language Education; Nursing; Pedagogy; Philology; Philosophy; Physical Education; Physiology; Portuguese; Psychology; Public Administration; Public Health; Rehabilitation and Therapy; Science Education; Social and Community Services; Social Policy; Sociology; Spanish; Special Education; Sports; Tourism; Transport Management; Writing); **Undergraduate Studies** (Administration; Information Sciences; Nursing; Pedagogy)

Degrees and Diplomas: *Tecnólogo*; *Bacharelado*; *Licenciatura*. Also Postgraduate diploma jointly offered with Cidade Especializações.
Last Updated: 03/09/10

REGIONAL FACULTY OF RIACHÃO DO JACUÍPE
Faculdade Regional de Riachão do Jacuípe
Rua Manoel Mascarenhas, 98, Barra, Riachão do Jacuípe,
BA 44640-000
Tel: +55(75) 3264-1839
Fax: +55(75) 3264-1839
EMail: gilsonivo@gmail.com
Website: http://www.farj-edu.com/

Reitora: Vitoria De Cassía Teixeira Fernandes

Courses
Graduate Studies (Art Education; Biochemistry; Biology; Chemistry; Civil Law; Computer Networks; Computer Science;

Constitutional Law; Criminal Law; Cultural Studies; Education; Educational Administration; Educational Psychology; Educational Technology; English; Environmental Studies; Fiscal Law; Gender Studies; Geography; Health Administration; Higher Education; History; Human Resources; Labour Law; Literature; Mathematics Education; Native Language Education; Nutrition; Occupational Health; Performing Arts; Physical Education; Physics; Physiology; Portuguese; Psychiatry and Mental Health; Public Administration; Public Health; Religious Education; Religious Studies; Science Education; Secondary Education; Social and Community Services; Social Policy; Sociology; Software Engineering; Spanish; Special Education; Sports; Welfare and Protective Services); **MBA** (Business Administration; Business and Commerce; Health Administration; Human Resources; Small Business; Tourism); **Undergraduate Studies** (Accountancy; Administration; Law; Pedagogy; Psychoanalysis; Religious Studies; Systems Analysis; Theology)

Degrees and Diplomas: *Bacharelado*. Also Postgraduate diploma and MBA.
Last Updated: 03/09/10

REGIONAL FACULTY OF RIBEIRA DO POMBAL

Faculdade Regional de Ribeira do Pombal (FARRP)
Br-110- Km 07 Ribeira do Pombal, s/n, Pombalzinho,
Ribeira do Pombal, BA 48400-00
Tel: +55(75) 3276-1731
Fax: +55(75) 3276-1731
EMail: diretoriacademica@farrp.edu.br

Courses
Accountancy (Accountancy); **Administration** (Administration); **English** (English); **Literature** (Literature); **Pedagogy** (Pedagogy)

Degrees and Diplomas: *Bacharelado*; *Licenciatura*
Last Updated: 03/09/10

REGIONAL FACULTY OF SERRANA

Faculdade Regional Serrana (FUNPAC)
BR 262 kM 110, São João de Viçosa, Venda Nova do Imigrante,
ES 2937-5000
Tel: +55(28) 3546-6451
Fax: +55(28) 3546-6622
EMail: direcao@funpac.com.br
Website: http://www.funpac.com.br/
Diretor: Miguel Angelo Tres

Courses
Administration (Administration); **Pedagogy** (Pedagogy); **Social Services** (Social and Community Services)

Degrees and Diplomas: *Bacharelado*; *Licenciatura*
Last Updated: 03/09/10

REGIONAL INTEGRATED UNIVERSITY OF UPPER URUGUAI AND MISSIONS

Universidade Regional Integrada do Alto Uruguai e das Missões (URI)
Avenida Sete de Setembro 1558 2° e 3° Andar, Centro, Erechim,
Rio Grande do Sul 99700000
Tel: +55(54) 3522-1255
Fax: +55(54) 3522-1255
EMail: gabinete@reitoria.uri.br
Website: http://www.uri.reitoria.br
Reitor: Bruno Ademar Mentges **EMail:** mentges@reitoria.uri.br

Departments
Agronomy (Agronomy); **Applied Social Sciences**; **Biology** (Biology); **Computer Science and Engineering** (Computer Engineering; Computer Science); **Exact and Earth Sciences** (Chemistry; Earth Sciences; Natural Sciences); **Health Sciences** (Dentistry; Health Sciences; Nutrition); **Human Sciences**; **Linguistics, Letters and Arts** (Arts and Humanities; Linguistics; Literature; Philosophy)

History: Founded 1992.

Admission Requirements: Secondary school certificate and entrance examination

Main Language(s) of Instruction: Portuguese

Degrees and Diplomas: *Bacharelado*; *Licenciatura*; *Especialização/Aperfeiçoamento*; *Mestrado*
Student Residential Facilities: For c. 40 students
Last Updated: 07/05/10

REGIONAL UNIVERSITY CENTRE OF ESPIRITO SANTO DO PINHAL

Centro Regional Universitário de Espirito Santo do Pinhal (UNIPINHAL)
Avénida Hélio Vergueiro Leite, Jardim Universitário,
Espirito Santo do Pinhal, São Paulo 13990-970
Tel: +55(19) 3651-9600 +55(19) 3651-9610
Fax: +55(19) 3651-9616
EMail: reitoriaadministrativa@unipinhal.edu.br
Website: http://www.unipinhal.edu.br/
Reitor: José Eduardo Vergueiro Neves

Programmes
Administration; **Agricultural Engineering**; **Arts and Humanities** (Arts and Humanities; English; Portuguese); **Biological Sciences** (Biological and Life Sciences); **Biomedicine**; **Computer Engineering**; **Computer Science** (Computer Science); **Environmental Engineering**; **Food Technology**; **Graduate Studies** (Higher Education; Physical Education); **Law** (Civil Law; Commercial Law; Law); **Mechatronics Engineering**; **Nursing** (Nursing); **Pharmacy**; **Physical Education** (Physical Education); **Physical Therapy** (Physical Therapy); **Production Engineering** (Production Engineering); **Short-term Studies**; **Social Communication - Advertising and Publicity** (Advertising and Publicity); **Tourism**; **Veterinary Science** (Veterinary Science)

History: Founded 1966.

Degrees and Diplomas: *Tecnólogo*; *Bacharelado*; *Licenciatura*; *Especialização/Aperfeiçoamento*
Last Updated: 06/05/10

REGIONAL UNIVERSITY OF THE NORTHWEST OF THE STATE OF RIO GRANDE DO SUL

Universidade Regional do Noroeste do Estado do Rio Grande do Sul (UNIJUI)
Caixa Postal 560, Rua do Comércio 3000, Ijuí,
Rio Grande do Sul 98700-000
Tel: +55(55) 3332-0200
Fax: +55(55) 3332-9100
EMail: eronitab@unijui.tche.br
Website: http://www.unijui.tche.br
Reitor: Gilmar Antônio Bedin

Departments
Administration (Business Administration); **Agrarian Studies** (Agriculture); **Biology and Chemistry** (Biology; Chemistry); **Economics and Accountancy** (Accountancy; Economics); **Health Sciences** (Cosmetology; Health Sciences; Nursing; Nutrition; Pharmacy); **Juridical Studies** (Law); **Languages, Arts and Communication** (Advertising and Publicity; Communication Studies; Design; Literature; Visual Arts); **Pedagogy** (Pedagogy); **Philosophy and Psychology** (Philosophy; Psychology); **Physics, Statistics and Mathematics** (Mathematics; Physics; Statistics); **Social Sciences** (Geography; History; Social Sciences; Sociology); **Technology** (Computer Engineering; Electronic Engineering; Mechanical Engineering; Technology)

Institutes
Regional Rural Development *(IRDeR)* (Regional Planning; Rural Planning) *Head:* Jaime Wünsch

Research Centres
International Economics and Agriculture Market (Agricultural Business; Agricultural Management; International Economics) *Coordinator:* Argemiro Luis Brum

History: Founded 1957 as Faculty of Philosophy, Science and Letters. Acquired present status and title 1985. A private institution under the supervision of the Fundação de Integração, Desenvolvimento e Educação do Noroeste do Estado.

Governing Bodies: Conselho Universitário

Academic Year: March to December (March-July; August-December)

Admission Requirements: Secondary school certificate and entrance examination

Fees: (Reais): 3,200 per semester

Main Language(s) of Instruction: Portuguese

Degrees and Diplomas: *Bacharelado*: Accountancy; Business Administration; Economics; Law, 5 yrs; *Especialização/Aperfeiçoamento*; *Mestrado*: Education; Mathematics, a further 2 yrs. Also Teaching Qualifications

Student Services: Canteen, Foreign student adviser, Health services, Sports facilities

Special Facilities: Museu Antropológico

Libraries: Central Library, 107,324 vols

Publications: Ciência e Ambiente *(biannually)*; Contexto e Educação *(other/irregular)*; Direito em Debate *(annually)*; Espaços da Escola *(quarterly)*; Município e Saúde *(biannually)*

Press or Publishing House: SEDIGRAF-Serviços de Editoração e Gráfica

Last Updated: 07/05/10

REINALDO RAMOS FACULTY

Faculdade Reinaldo Ramos (CESREI)
Rua Almeida Barreto, 242, Centro, Campina Grande, PB
Tel: +55(83) 3341-7997
EMail: cesrei@cesrei.com.br
Website: http://www.cesrei.com.br/

Diretor Geral: Cleumberto Reinaldo Ramos

Courses
Advertising and Publicity (Advertising and Publicity); **Graduate Studies** (Advertising and Publicity; Business Administration; Environmental Management; Graphic Design; Management; Marketing; Mass Communication; Media Studies; Public Administration; Teacher Training); **Law** (Law)

Degrees and Diplomas: *Bacharelado*. Also Postgraduate diploma.
Last Updated: 03/09/10

RENAISSANCE FACULTIES OF SÃO PAULO

Faculdades Renascença de São Paulo
Rua Álvares Penteado, 139/184/216/231, Centro - Largo do Café, São Paulo, São Paulo 01121000
Tel: +55(11) 2173-4700
EMail: secretaria-sp@uniesp.edu.br
Website: http://www.uniesp.edu.br/sp

Diretor: José Marta Filho

Courses
Accountancy (Accountancy); **Administration** (Administration; Marketing); **Computer Science**; **Hotel Management** (Hotel Management); **Law**; **Secretarial Studies** (Secretarial Studies); **Tourism** (Tourism)

Further Information: Also Unidade Centro Novo, Unidade Brooklin

History: Founded 1973 as Faculdades Hebraico Brasileira Renascença. Acquired present status and title 2005.

Main Language(s) of Instruction: Portuguese

Degrees and Diplomas: *Bacharelado*; *Especialização/Aperfeiçoamento*
Last Updated: 23/11/07

REUNITED FACULTY

Faculdade Reunida (FAR)
Avenida Brasil Sul n° 1065, Ilha Solteira, São Paulo 15385000
Tel: +55(18) 3742-5333
Fax: +55(18) 3743-2051
EMail: far@faculdadereunida.com.br
Website: http://www.faculdadereunida.com.br

Diretora Geral: Zilca Fernandes Marques

Courses
Hotel Management; **Pedagogy** (Pedagogy); **Social Services** (Social and Community Services)

History: Founded 2000.

Main Language(s) of Instruction: Portuguese

Degrees and Diplomas: *Bacharelado*; *Especialização/Aperfeiçoamento*
Last Updated: 08/10/07

RIO BRANCO INTEGRATED FACULTIES

Faculdades Integradas Rio Branco (FRB)
Rua Capitão José Inácio do Rosário 133, Lapa, São Paulo, São Paulo 05038070
Tel: +55(11) 3879-3100
Fax: +55(11) 3879-3100 +55(11) 3879-2524
EMail: faculdades@riobrancofac.edu.br
Website: http://www.riobrancofac.edu.br/

Diretor Geral: Custódio Pereira

Courses
Administration (Administration; Business Administration); **Information Sciences** (Information Sciences); **International Relations**; **Law** (Law); **Literature** (Arts and Humanities; Literature); **Pedagogy** (Education; Pedagogy); **Social Communication** (Advertising and Publicity; Journalism; Radio and Television Broadcasting); **Tourism**

History: Founded 2001.

Degrees and Diplomas: *Bacharelado*; *Especialização/Aperfeiçoamento*; *Mestrado*
Last Updated: 22/06/10

RIO DE JANEIRO SCHOOL OF LAW

Escola de Direito do Rio de Janeiro (FGV DIREITO RIO)
Praia de Botafogo, 190, 13° andar, Rio de Janeiro, RJ 22250-900
Tel: + 55(21) 3799-5301
Fax: + 55(21) 3799-5335
EMail: maria.freitas@fgv.br
Website: http://direitorio.fgv.br

Diretor: Joaquim Falcão

Courses
Graduate Studies (Commercial Law; Fiscal Law; Law); **Law**

Degrees and Diplomas: *Bacharelado*; *Especialização/Aperfeiçoamento*; *Mestrado*
Last Updated: 13/07/10

RIO SONO FACULTY

Faculdade Rio Sono (RISO)
Rua 04, 350, Centro, Pedro Afonso, TO 77710-000
Tel: +55(63) 3466-2429
EMail: risoedusuperior@yahoo.com

Presidente: Pedro Pires Filho

Courses
Administration (Administration); **Agricultural Business** (Agricultural Business)

Degrees and Diplomas: *Tecnólogo*; *Bacharelado*
Last Updated: 06/09/10

RIO VERDE VALLEY UNIVERSITY

Universidade Vale do Rio Verde (UNINCOR)
Avenida Castelo Branco 82, Chácara das Rosas, Três Corações, Minas Gerais 37410000
Tel: +55(35) 3239-1000
Fax: +55(35) 3239-1238
EMail: unincor@unincor.br
Website: http://www.unincor.br

Reitor: Adair Ribeiro

Courses
Accountancy (Accountancy); **Administration** (Administration); **Agronomy** (Agronomy); **Arts and Humanities** (Arts and Humanities); **Biology** (Biology); **Chemistry** (Chemistry); **Computer Science** (Computer Science); **Dentistry** (Dentistry); **Education** (Education); **Geography** (Geography); **History** (History); **Law** (Law); **Library Science** (Library Science); **Mathematics** (Mathematics); **Pedagogy** (Pedagogy); **Pharmacy** (Pharmacy);

Philosophy (Philosophy); **Physical Therapy** (Physical Therapy); **Psychology** (Psychology); **Speech Therapy and Audiology** (Speech Therapy and Audiology); **Tourism** (Tourism); **Veterinary Science** (Veterinary Science)

Further Information: Also campuses at Caxambu, São Gonçalo do Sapucai

History: Founded 1967 as Faculdade de Filosofia, Ciências e Letras de Três Corações, acquired present status and title 1998.

Admission Requirements: Secondary school certificate and entrance examination

Main Language(s) of Instruction: Portuguese

Degrees and Diplomas: *Bacharelado*; *Licenciatura*; *Especialização/Aperfeiçoamento*; *Mestrado*; *Doutorado*
Last Updated: 17/12/07

RITTER DOS REIS UNIVERSITY CENTRE
Centro Universitário Ritter dos Reis (UNIRITTER)
Rua Orfanotrófio 555, Alto Teresópolis, Porto Alegre,
Rio Grande do Sul 90840-440
Tel: +55(51) 3230-3333
Fax: +55(51) 3230-3317
EMail: ritter@ritterdosreis.br
Website: http://www.ritterdosreis.br

Diretor Geral: Flávio Romeu d'Almeida Reis

Courses
Administration (Administration); **Architecture and Urbanism** (Architecture; Town Planning); **Computer Science** (Information Sciences; Systems Analysis); **Design** (Fashion Design; Graphic Design; Industrial Design); **Graduate Studies** *(Lato Sensu)* (Architecture; Civil Law; Commercial Law; Computer Science; Design; Educational Psychology; English; Interior Design; Labour Law; Law; Linguistics; Literature; Marketing; Pedagogy; Tourism; Town Planning); **Graduate Studies** *(Stricto Sensu)* (Design; Linguistics; Literature); **Law** (Law); **Law** *(Canoas Campus)*; **Literature** (English; Literature; Portuguese); **Pedagogy** (Pedagogy)

History: Founded 1971.

Main Language(s) of Instruction: Portuguese

Degrees and Diplomas: *Tecnólogo*; *Bacharelado*; *Licenciatura*; *Especialização/Aperfeiçoamento*; *Mestrado*
Last Updated: 17/06/10

RUI BARBOSA INTEGRATED FACULTIES
Faculdades Integradas Rui Barbosa (FIRB)
Rua Rodrigues Alves 756 Centro, Andradina, São Paulo 16900900
Tel: +55(18) 3722-7788
Fax: +55(18) 3722-2602
EMail: fam@firb.br
Website: http://www.firb.br

Diretor Geral: Flávio Antônio Moreira (1998-)

Courses
Accountancy (Accountancy); **Geography** (Geography); **History** (History); **Letters** (Literature); **Pedagogy** (Pedagogy)

History: Founded 1969

Main Language(s) of Instruction: Portuguese

Degrees and Diplomas: *Bacharelado*; *Licenciatura*; *Especialização/Aperfeiçoamento*
Last Updated: 22/06/10

RUI BARBOSA LUTHERAN FACULTY
Faculdade Luterana Rui Barbosa
Rua D. Pedro n° 1151. Caixa Postal: 04, Marechal Cândido Rondon,
PR 85.960-000
Tel: +55(45) 3254-2175
EMail: falurb@falurb.edu.br
Website: http://www.falurb.edu.br

Diretor: Neander Kloss

Courses
Administration (Administration)
History: Founded 2002.

Main Language(s) of Instruction: Portuguese
Degrees and Diplomas: *Bacharelado*; *Mestrado*
Libraries: Yes
Last Updated: 02/09/10

RUY BARBOSA FACULTY
Faculdade Ruy Barbosa (FRBA)
Rua Theodomiro Batista 422, Rio Vermelho, Salvador,
Bahia 41940320
Tel: +55(71) 3205-1700
Fax: +55(71) 3205-1705
EMail: diretoriaacademica@frb.br
Website: http://www.frb.edu.br

Diretor Geral: Rogério Flores da Silva

Courses
Architecture and Town Planning (Architecture; Town Planning); **Business Administration** (Administration; Business Administration); **Computer Science**; **Law** (Law); **Psychology** (Psychology)

History: Founded 1990.

Main Language(s) of Instruction: Portuguese

Degrees and Diplomas: *Bacharelado*; *Especialização/Aperfeiçoamento*; *Mestrado*
Last Updated: 02/07/10

SABERES FACULTY
Faculdade Saberes
Av. Cezar Helal, 1180, 2° Andar, Praia do Suá, Vitória 29052-231
Tel: +55(27) 3227-8203
EMail: graduacao@saberes.edu.br
Website: http://www.saberes.edu.br/

Diretor Geral: Alacir de Araújo Silva

Courses
Graduate Studies (Applied Linguistics; Art Therapy; Communication Studies; Cultural Studies; Educational Administration; Educational Psychology; Environmental Management; Family Studies; Fine Arts; Gerontology; History; Literacy Education; Literature; Mathematics Education; Modern Languages; Psychology; Special Education; Town Planning); **Undergraduate Studies** (English; History; Literature; Portuguese)

Degrees and Diplomas: *Licenciatura*. Also Postgraduate diploma.
Last Updated: 06/09/10

SAINT AMELIA FACULTIES
Faculdades Santa Amélia (SECAL)
Rua Barão do Cerro Azul 827, Centro, Ponta Grossa,
Paraná 84010210
Tel: +55(42) 3220-6700
Fax: +55(42) 225-2424
EMail: nucleo@secal.edu.br
Website: http://www.secal.edu.br

Diretora: Isaura Cristina Andrade Aguiar

Courses
Accountancy; **Administration**; **Journalism** (Journalism); **Law** (Law); **Literature** (Literature); **Pedagogy**; **Tourism** (Tourism)

History: Founded 2001.

Main Language(s) of Instruction: Portuguese

Degrees and Diplomas: *Bacharelado*; *Licenciatura*
Last Updated: 02/07/10

SAINT ANNA FACULTY OF SALTO
Faculdade SantAnna de Salto (FASAS)
Avenida Tranquilo Gianini, 801, Saída 44 da Rodovia Santos
Dumont, Salto, SP 13320-000
Tel: +55(11) 4028-1929
Fax: +55(11) 4028-1929
EMail: info@santanna.br
Website: http://www.unisantanna.br/site/institucional/
campus.aspx?id=8

Courses

Graduate Studies (Administration); **Undergraduate Studies** (Administration; Tourism)

Degrees and Diplomas: *Bacharelado*; *Especialização/Aperfeiçoamento*
Last Updated: 07/09/10

SAINT ANNA INSTITUTE OF EDUCATION

Instituto Superior de Educação SantAna (ISESA)
Rua Senador Pinheiro Machado, 189, Centro, Ponta Grossa,
PR 84010-310
Tel: +55(42) 3224-0301
EMail: secretaria@iessa.edu.br
Website: http://www.iessa.edu.br/

Courses

Undergraduate Studies (Pedagogy; Philosophy; Physical Education; Teacher Training)

Degrees and Diplomas: *Licenciatura*
Last Updated: 28/09/10

SAINT ANTHONY FACULTY

Faculdade Santo Antônio (FSA)
Rua Conselheiro Junqueira, s/n, Rua do Catu, Alagoinhas,
BA 48090-020
Tel: +55(75) 3421-4733
Fax: +55(75) 3421-4733
EMail: contato@fsaa.edu.br
Website: http://www.fsaa.edu.br/

Diretor Geral: Wagner Monteiro Mendonça

Courses

Undergraduate Studies (Accountancy; Administration; Biomedicine; Nursing; Pedagogy; Physical Therapy)

Degrees and Diplomas: *Bacharelado*; *Licenciatura*
Last Updated: 07/09/10

SAINT ANTHONY INSTITUTE OF HIGHER EDUCATION

Instituto de Ensino Superior Santo Antônio (INESA)
Rua Papa João XXIII, 1100, Iririú, Joinville, SC 89227-301
Tel: +55(47) 3145-5000
EMail: inesa@inesa.com.br
Website: http://www.inesa.com.br

Diretor Geral: Rafael Thomazi Bratti

Courses

Undergraduate Studies (Administration; Pedagogy)

Degrees and Diplomas: *Bacharelado*; *Licenciatura*
Last Updated: 22/09/10

SAINT ANTHONY OF PADUA FACULTY

Faculdade Santo Antônio de Pádua (FASAP)
R. Coronel Olivier, 60, Centro, Santo Antônio de Pádua, RJ
Tel: +55(22) 3853-3393
Fax: +55(22) 3853-3393
EMail: fasap@fasap.com.br
Website: http://www.fasap.com.br/

Diretor Geral: Francisco Simonini da Silva

Courses

Graduate Studies (Business Administration); **Undergraduate Studies** (Administration; Law; Nursing; Physical Education)

History: Founded 2002.

Degrees and Diplomas: *Bacharelado*; *Licenciatura*. Also MBA.
Last Updated: 07/09/10

SAINT AUGUSTINE FACULTY

Faculdade Santo Agostinho (FACSA)
Rua Palmares, 3, Loteamento Cajueiro, Conceição, Ipiaú,
BA 45570-000
Tel: +55(73) 3531-3344
EMail: facsa@facsa.com.br
Website: http://www.facsa.com.br/

Diretora Geral: Ana Ruth Bastos de Mattos Lima

Courses

Graduate Studies (Accountancy; Adult Education; Business Administration; Education; Educational Administration; Educational Psychology; Environmental Management; Health Administration; Health Sciences; History; Literature; Management; Mathematics Education; Nursing; Occupational Health; Portuguese; Public Administration; Public Health); **Undergraduate Studies** (History)

Degrees and Diplomas: *Licenciatura*. Also Postgraduate diploma and MBA.
Last Updated: 07/09/10

SAINT AUGUSTINE FACULTY

Faculdade Santo Agostinho (FSA)
Av. Valter Alencar, 665, São Pedro, Teresina, Piauí 64046080
Tel: +55(86) 3215-8700
Fax: +55(86) 3215-8710
EMail: fsa@fsanet.com.br
Website: http://www.fsanet.com.br/site/

Diretora Geral: Yara Lira

Courses

Accountancy (Accountancy); **Administration** (Administration); **Journalism**; **Law** (Law); **Nursing** (Nursing); **Nutrition** (Nutrition); **Pedagogy** (Pedagogy); **Physiotherapy** (Physical Therapy); **Production Engineering**; **Psychology** (Psychology); **Teacher Training** (Teacher Training)

History: Founded 1998.

Main Language(s) of Instruction: Portuguese

Degrees and Diplomas: *Bacharelado*; *Licenciatura*; *Especialização/Aperfeiçoamento*
Last Updated: 01/07/10

SAINT AUGUSTUS FACULTY

Faculdade Santo Augusto (FAISA)
Avenida Angelo Santi, s/n, Getúlio Vargas, Santo Augusto,
RS 98590-000
Tel: +55(55) 3781-4103
EMail: leandrosperotto@yahoo.com.br
Website: http://www.faisaceleiro.com.br/

Courses

Graduate Studies *(Unidade Ijuí/Rs E Região)* (Law; Public Health); **Graduate Studies** *(Unidade Cruz Alta/Rs E Região)* (Agronomy); **Graduate Studies** *(Unidade Porto Alegre/Rs E Região)* (Education); **Graduate Studies** *(Unidade Santo Augusto/Rs E Região)* (Management); **Graduate Studies** *(Unidade Chapecó/Sc E Região)* (Agriculture; Agronomy; Animal Husbandry; Environmental Management; Food Technology; Nutrition); **Graduate Studies** *(Unidade Cascavel / Pr E Região)* (Food Technology; Nutrition); **Undergraduate Studies** (Accountancy; Administration)

Degrees and Diplomas: *Bacharelado*. Also Postgraduate diploma and MBA.
Last Updated: 07/09/10

SAINT AUGUSTUS FACULTY OF IGUAPE

Faculdade Iguapense Santo Augusto
Avenida Ademar de Barros, 1070, Porto do Ribeira, Iguape,
SP 11920-000
Tel: +55(13) 3841-4966
EMail: faculdadeiguapense@uol.com.br
Website: http://www.fisa.edu.br/

Diretor-Secretário: Aderbal Alfredo Calderari Bernarde

Courses

Graduate Studies (Special Education); **Pedagogy** (Pedagogy)

Degrees and Diplomas: *Licenciatura*. Also Postgraduate diploma.
Last Updated: 01/09/10

SAINT BENEDICT FACULTY OF BAHIA
Faculdade São Bento da Bahia
Avenida Sete de Setembro, 30/32, Centro, Salvador, BA 40060-001
Tel: +55(71) 3322-4746
EMail: faculdade@saobento.org
Website: http://www.saobento.org/Faculdade/
Diretor: Clenio de Araújo Carvalho

Courses
Graduate Studies (Educational Administration; Educational Psychology; Heritage Preservation; Higher Education; History; Management; Philosophy; Portuguese; Psychology; Social Work; Theology); **Undergraduate Studies** (History; Philosophy; Psychology; Theology)

Degrees and Diplomas: *Bacharelado*; *Licenciatura*; *Especialização/Aperfeiçoamento*
Last Updated: 07/09/10

SAINT CAMILO FACULTIES - RIO DE JANEIRO
Faculdades São Camilo - Rio de Janeiro
Rua Doutor Satamini 245, Prédio, Tijuca, Rio de Janeiro,
Rio de Janeiro 20270233
Tel: +55(21) 2117-4200
EMail: diretorgeral@saocamilo-rj.br
Website: http://www.saocamilo-rj.br
Diretora Geral: Gilceia Maria Lodi

Courses
Administration (Business Administration; Health Administration)

Faculties
Nursing *(Luiza de Marillac - FELM)* (Anatomy; Health Administration; Nursing; Physiology)
History: Founded 1942.
Main Language(s) of Instruction: Portuguese

Degrees and Diplomas: *Bacharelado*; *Especialização/Aperfeiçoamento*; *Mestrado*
Last Updated: 18/06/10

SAINT CAMILO FACULTY
Faculdade São Camilo
Rua Visconde de Itaborai 102 Amaralina, Salvador,
Bahia 41900000
Tel: +55(71) 3205-3552
Fax: +55(71) 3240-1845
EMail: saocamilo@saocamilo-ba.br
Website: http://www.saocamilo-ba.br
Diretor Geral: Antônio Celso Pasquini Celso Pasquini

Courses
Administration (Administration; Health Administration); **Biology** (Biology); **Nursing** (Nursing)
History: Founded 1997.
Main Language(s) of Instruction: Portuguese

Degrees and Diplomas: *Bacharelado*; *Licenciatura*; *Especialização/Aperfeiçoamento*; *Mestrado*
Last Updated: 01/07/10

SAINT CAMILO FACULTY
Faculdade São Camilo (FASC-MG)
Avenida Assis Chateaubriand, 218, Floresta, Belo Horizonte,
MG 30150-100
Tel: +55(31) 3308-6820
Fax: +55(31) 3308-6820
Website: http://www.saocamilo-mg.br/
Diretor: Henrique Pinto dos Santos

Courses
Graduate Studies (Accountancy; Anatomy; Biotechnology; Food Science; Gerontology; Health Administration; Industrial Design;

Nursing; Nutrition; Occupational Health; Physical Therapy; Public Health; Radiology; Rehabilitation and Therapy); **Undergraduate Studies** (Administration; Radiology)

Degrees and Diplomas: *Tecnólogo*; *Bacharelado*; *Especialização/Aperfeiçoamento*
Last Updated: 07/09/10

SAINT CATHERINE FACULTY
Faculdade Santa Catarina (FASC)
Estrada do Arraial, 2740, Tamarineira, Recife, PE 52051-380
Tel: +55(81) 3334-1160
EMail: fasc@faculdadesantacatarina.com.br
Website: http://www.faculdadesantacatarina.com.br
Diretor Geral: Alexandre Barros Fonseca

Courses
Undergraduate Studies (Accountancy; Administration; Pedagogy)
History: Founded 2003.

Degrees and Diplomas: *Bacharelado*; *Licenciatura*
Last Updated: 06/09/10

SAINT CECILIA FACULTY
Faculdade Santa Cecília (FASC)
Praça Barão do Rio Branco 59 Centro, Pindamonhangaba,
SP 12400280
Tel: +55(12) 3642-5755
Fax: +55(12) 3642-5537
EMail: secretaria@fascpinda.com.br
Website: http://www.fascpinda.com.br
Diretora: Lenita de Azeredo Freitas

Courses
Art Education (Design; Fine Arts; Theatre); **Music** (Music)
History: Founded 1975 as Faculdade de Música Santa Cecília. Acquired present title and status 2000.
Main Language(s) of Instruction: Portuguese

Degrees and Diplomas: *Bacharelado*; *Licenciatura*; *Especialização/Aperfeiçoamento*
Last Updated: 02/07/10

SAINT CECILIA INSTITUTE OF HIGHER EDUCATION
Instituto de Ensino Superior Santa Cecília (IESC)
rua Floracy da Silva Barros, n°288, Alto do Cruzeiro, Arapiraca,
AL 57312-500
Tel: +55(82) 3530-3168
EMail: daa@isesc.edu.br
Website: http://www.isesc.edu.br/
Diretora Geral: Deusdeth Barbosa da Silva
EMail: direção@isesc.edu.br

Courses
Graduate Studies (Higher Education); **Undergraduate Studies** (Law; Pedagogy; Social and Community Services)

Degrees and Diplomas: *Bacharelado*; *Licenciatura*. Also Postgraduate Diploma.
Last Updated: 22/09/10

SAINT CECÍLIA UNIVERSITY
Universidade Santa Cecília (UNISANTA)
Rua Oswaldo Cruz 266, Boqueirão, Santos, São Paulo 11045907
Tel: +55(13) 3202-7100
Fax: +55(13) 3234-5297
EMail: scecilia@usc.stcecilia.br; scecilia@unisanta.br
Website: http://www.unisanta.br
Reitora: Sílvia Ângela Texeira Penteado (1996-)
Tel: +55(13) 3232-4010 EMail: silvia@unisanta.br

Centres
Computer Science (Computer Science)

Departments
Extension

Faculties
Civil Engineering (Civil Engineering); **Commerce and Administration** (Administration; Business and Commerce); **Dentistry** (Dentistry); **Education and Human Sciences** (Arts and Humanities; Education); **Industrial Engineering** (Industrial Engineering); **Physical Education** (Physical Education); **Plastic Arts** (Painting and Drawing; Sculpture); **Science and Technology** (Mathematics and Computer Science; Natural Sciences; Technology)

History: Founded 1961 as College, became Instituto Superior de Educação Santa Cecília 1969 and acquired present status and title 1996. A private Institution recognized by the Federal Government and administered by the Sociedade Universitária de Santos.

Academic Year: February to December (February-June; August-December)

Admission Requirements: Secondary school certificate and entrance examination

Main Language(s) of Instruction: Portuguese

Degrees and Diplomas: *Bacharelado*: Administration; Biology; Business Administration; Computer Sciences; Industrial Design (Desenhista industrial); Visual Communication (Comunicação visual), 4 yrs; *Bacharelado*: Dentistry (Cirurgião dentista), 5 yrs.; *Bacharelado*: Engineering (Engenheiro), 5-6 yrs; *Licenciatura*: Art Education, 2 yrs; *Licenciatura*: Education; Physical Education; Science; Social Studies, 3 yrs; *Especialização/Aperfeiçoamento*; *Mestrado*

Special Facilities: Museu de Conchas; Museu Didático e do Folclore

Libraries: Biblioteca 'Martins Fontes', c. 45,500 vols
Last Updated: 07/05/10

SAINT CROSS FACULTY
Faculdade Santa Cruz (FACRUZ)
Rua Júlia Aragão, 307, Centro, Santa Cruz do Capibaribe, PE 55190-000
Tel: +55(81) 3731-4364
EMail: cesac.facruz@ig.com.br

Diretor: Miguel Guedes de Brito

Courses
Administration (Administration)

Degrees and Diplomas: *Bacharelado*
Last Updated: 06/09/10

SAINT DOROTHY FACULTY OF PHILOSOPHY
Faculdade de Filosofia 'Santa Dorotéia' (FFSD)
Rua Monsenhor Miranda, 86 – Centro, Nova Friburgo, Rio de Janeiro 28610-230
Tel: +55(24) 2522-2900
Fax: +55(24) 2522-3930
EMail: diretoria@ffsd.br
Website: http://www.ffsd.br

Diretora: Celma Calvão da Silva (1998-)

Courses
Geography (Geography); **Graduate Studies** (Computer Networks; Education; Educational Administration; Educational Psychology; English; Environmental Studies; History; Management; Mathematics; Portuguese); **History**; **Literature**; **Literature** (Literature; Spanish; **Literature**; **Pedagogy** (Pedagogy); **Science**; **Secretarial Studies**; **Systems Analysis**

History: Founded 1967.

Main Language(s) of Instruction: Portuguese

Degrees and Diplomas: *Tecnólogo*; *Bacharelado*; *Licenciatura*; *Especialização/Aperfeiçoamento*
Last Updated: 08/07/10

SAINT DOROTHY FACULTY OF THE AMAZON
Faculdade Santa Dorotéia do Amazonas
Av. Joaquim Nabuco, 1097, Centro, Manaus, AM 69020-030
EMail: stdoroteia@argo.com.br

Courses
Pedagogy (Pedagogy); **Social Communication** (Advertising and Publicity)

Degrees and Diplomas: *Bacharelado*; *Licenciatura*
Last Updated: 06/09/10

SAINT EMILY FACULTY
Faculdade Santa Emília
Av. Augusto Moreira, 1704 e 1502, Casa Caiada, Olinda, PE
Tel: +55(81) 3431-4433
EMail: leonidas@fasefaculdade.edu.br
Website: http://fasefaculdade.edu.br/

Courses
Graduate Studies (Business Administration; Business and Commerce; Cultural Studies; Educational Psychology; Environmental Management; Forensic Medicine and Dentistry; History; Labour Law; Management; Marketing; Petroleum and Gas Engineering; Safety Engineering); **Undergraduate Studies** (Administration; Information Sciences)

Further Information: Also Cabugá campus.

Degrees and Diplomas: *Bacharelado*; *Especialização/Aperfeiçoamento*. Also MBA.
Last Updated: 06/09/10

SAINT FRANCIS FACULTY - PIUMHI
Faculdade São Francisco - Piumhi
Rua Severo Veloso, 1880, Bairro Nova Esperança, Piumhi, MG 37.925-000
Tel: +55(37) 3371-5022
EMail: diretor@ceasf.com.br
Website: http://www.ceasf.com.br

Diretor: Hilberto Carvalho de Lopes EMail: direito@ceasf.com.br

Courses
Accountancy (Accountancy); **Administration** (Administration); **Environmental Management** (Environmental Management); **Law** (Law); **Nursing** (Nursing); **Pedagogy** (Pedagogy)

History: Founded 2002.

Main Language(s) of Instruction: Portuguese

Degrees and Diplomas: *Bacharelado*; *Licenciatura*

Libraries: Biblioteca Maria Aparecida Ferreira de Freitas
Last Updated: 29/09/10

SAINT FRANCIS FACULTY OF BARREIRAS
Faculdade São Francisco de Barreiras (FASB)
BR 135 Km 01 n° 2341, Bairro Boa Sorte, Barreiras, BA 47805270
Tel: +55(77) 3613-8800
Fax: +55(77) 3613-8824
EMail: fasb@fasb.edu.br
Website: http://www.fasb.edu.br

Diretor: Tadeu Sergio Bergamo EMail: iaesb@fasb.edu.br

Courses
Accountancy; **Administration** (Accountancy; Administration; International Business); **Agronomy** (Agronomy); **Law**; **Nursing**; **Pedagogy** (Pedagogy); **Physical Education** (Physical Education); **Physiotherapy** (Physical Therapy); **Psychology** (Clinical Psychology; Educational Psychology; Industrial and Organizational Psychology; Psychology); **Social Communication** (Advertising and Publicity; Communication Studies; Journalism); **Systems Analysis** (Systems Analysis)

History: Founded 1999.

Main Language(s) of Instruction: Portuguese

Degrees and Diplomas: *Bacharelado*; *Licenciatura*; *Especialização/Aperfeiçoamento*
Last Updated: 01/07/10

SAINT FRANCIS FACULTY OF EDUCATION
Faculdade de Educação São Francisco (FAESF)
Rua Abílio Monteiro 1751, Engenho, Pedreiras, MA 65725000
Tel: +55(99) 3642-1678
Fax: +55(99) 3642-1678
EMail: faesf@faesf.com.br; c.saofrancisco@zipmail.com.br
Website: http://www.faesf.com.br

Diretor: Aldeñora Veloso Medeiros

Courses
Administration; **Geography** (Geography); **Literature**; **Nursing** (Nursing); **Pedagogy** (Pedagogy)
History: Founded 1990.
Degrees and Diplomas: *Bacharelado*; *Licenciatura*; *Especialização/Aperfeiçoamento*
Last Updated: 07/07/10

SAINT FRANCIS FACULTY OF JUAZEIRO
Faculdade São Francisco de Juazeiro
Rua Paraíso, n° 800, Santo Antonio, Juazeiro, BA 48903-050
Tel: +55(74) 3611- 7672 +55(74) 3612-7579
EMail: vivan@fasj.edu.br
Website: http://www.fasj.edu.br/

Diretor Presidente: Tadeu Sergio Bergamo
EMail: iaesb@fasb.edu.br

Courses
Undergraduate Studies (Administration; Advertising and Publicity)
Degrees and Diplomas: *Bacharelado*
Last Updated: 07/09/10

SAINT FRANCIS FACULTY OF PIUMHI
Faculdade São Francisco de Piumhi
Rua Severo Veloso, 1880, Nova Esperança, Piumhi, MG 37925-000
Tel: +55(37) 3371-5022 +55(37) 3371-4289
EMail: falecom@ceasf.com.br
Website: http://www.ceasf.com.br/

Courses
Distance Education (Accountancy; Social and Community Services); **Undergraduate Studies** (Administration; Law; Nursing)
History: Founded 2002.
Degrees and Diplomas: *Bacharelado*
Last Updated: 07/09/10

SAINT FRANCIS OF ASSISI FACULTY
Faculdade São Francisco de Assis
Rua Rio Negro, 386, Tonetto, Nova Xavantina, MT 78690-000
Tel: +55(66) 3438-1582
Fax: +55(66) 3438-2456
EMail: fasfa@fasfa.com.br
Website: http://www.fasfa.com.br/

Courses
Undergraduate Studies (Accountancy; Administration; Pedagogy)
Degrees and Diplomas: *Bacharelado*; *Licenciatura*
Last Updated: 07/09/10

SAINT FRANCIS OF ASSISI FACULTY
Faculdade São Francisco de Assis (UNIFIN)
Avenida Sertório, 253, Navegantes, Porto Alegre, RS 91020-001
Tel: +55(51) 3362-1771 +55(51) 3337-0428
EMail: secretaria@unifin.com.br
Website: http://www.unifin.com.br/

Diretor: José Luiz dos Santos **EMail:** joseluiz@unifin.com.br

Courses
Graduate Studies (Accountancy; Business Administration; Finance; Management; Marketing); **Undergraduate Studies** (Accountancy; Administration)
Degrees and Diplomas: *Bacharelado*; *Especialização/Aperfeiçoamento*
Last Updated: 07/09/10

SAINT FRANCIS OF ASSISI SCHOOL
Escola São Francisco de Assis (ESFA)
Rua Bernardino Monteiro, 700, Dois Pinheiros, Santa Tereza, ES 29650-000
Tel: +55(27) 3259-1322
Fax: +55(27) 3259-1322
EMail: esfa@esfa.edu.br
Website: http://www.esfa.edu.br/

Diretor Geral: Ricardo Acevedo Diaz

Courses
Biology (Biology); **Biomedicine**; **Dentistry**; **Environmental Health**; **Graduate Studies** (Environmental Studies; Pharmacology; Pharmacy; Physical Education; Sports); **Pharmacy** (Pharmacy); **Physical Education** (Physical Education); **veterinary Science**
History: Founded 1998. Acquired present title 2004.
Main Language(s) of Instruction: Portuguese
Degrees and Diplomas: *Bacharelado*; *Licenciatura*; *Especialização/Aperfeiçoamento*
Last Updated: 18/06/10

SAINT FRANCIS UNIVERSITY
Universidade São Francisco (USF)
Avenida José de Souza Campos, 1547 - 11°, Edificio Norte, Sul Business Center, Campinas, São Paulo 13025320
Tel: +55(19) 3754-3300 +55(11) 4034-8269
Fax: +55(19) 3254-0490 +55(11) 4034-8007
EMail: secretariageral@saofrancisco.edu.br
Website: http://www.saofrancisco.edu.br

Reitor: Hector Edmundo Huanay Escobar
EMail: reitoria@saofrancisco.edu.br

Institutes
Anthropology *(Franciscan, IFAN)* (Anthropology; Comparative Religion; Religious Studies; Social Problems; Sociology)

Units
Biological and Health Sciences (Biological and Life Sciences; Dentistry; Health Sciences; Medicine; Nursing; Pharmacy; Physical Therapy; Speech Therapy and Audiology); **Exact and Technological Sciences** *(Itatiba and Pari-São Paulo Campuses)* (Architecture; Civil Engineering; Computer Engineering; Electrical and Electronic Engineering; Mathematics; Mechanical Engineering); **Legal, Human and Social Sciences** *(Itatiba, Campinas and Pari-São Paulo Campuses)* (Arts and Humanities; Education; Law; Modern Languages; Philosophy; Psychology; Social and Community Services; Social Sciences; Teacher Training); **Management Sciences** *(Bragança Paulista, Itatiba, Campinas and Pari-São Paulo Campuses)* (Accountancy; Business Administration; Hotel Management; Management; Tourism)
Further Information: Also Teaching Hospital; Dental and Psychology Clinics
History: Founded 1976 as Faculdades Franciscanas under the supervision of the Third Order of Saint Francis of Assisi (Casa de Nossa Senhora da Paz). Acquired present status and title 1985.
Governing Bodies: Chancelaria; Conselho Universitário; Conselho Superior de Ensino, Pesquisa e Extensão; Conselho Acadêmico; Diretoria
Academic Year: February to December (February-June; August-December)
Admission Requirements: Secondary school certificate and entrance examination
Fees: (Reais): Tuition, c. 370-2,120 per month
Main Language(s) of Instruction: Portuguese
International Co-operation: With universities in America, Europe and Asia
Degrees and Diplomas: *Bacharelado*: Architecture and Urbanism; Dentistry; Engineering; Law; Psychology, 5 yrs; *Bacharelado*: Hotel Management; Management; Nursing; Pedagogy; Physiotherapy; System Analysis; Tourism, 4 yrs; *Bacharelado*: Mathematics; Philosophy, 3 yrs; *Bacharelado*: Medical Sciences, 6 yrs; *Bacharelado*: Pharmacy, 4 1/2 yrs; *Licenciatura*: Psychology, 4 yrs; *Especialização/Aperfeiçoamento*; *Mestrado*: Education; Pharmacy; Psychology, a further 2 yrs; *Doutorado*

Student Services: Academic counselling, Canteen, Cultural centre, Employment services, Foreign student adviser, Foreign Studies Centre, Health services, Social counselling, Sports facilities

Student Residential Facilities: None

Libraries: Bragança Paulista's Campus, Central Library, Law School Library, Tourism Library, 115,753 vols; Itatiba Campus, 36,532; São Paulo's Campus, 41,534; Campinas Campus, 446

Publications: Cadernos do IFAN, Psychological Journal (quarterly); Educação e Ensino-USF, Education (biannually); Horizontes, Human Sciences Journal (biannually); Lecta, Biological Journal (biannually); Psico-USF, Psychology (biannually)

Last Updated: 06/05/10

SAINT GABRIEL FACULTY
Faculdade São Gabriel (FSG)
Avenida Mirtes Melão 700, Teresina, Piauí 64049220
Tel: +55(86) 3233-8400
Fax: +55(86) 3233-8404
EMail: diretoriageral@unesc.com.br
Website: http://www.unesc.com.br

Diretora Geral: Cristina Maria do Vale e Silva

Courses
Accountancy (Accountancy); **Law**; **Nursing**; **Radiology** (Radiology)

History: Founded 1998.

Degrees and Diplomas: Bacharelado
Last Updated: 13/11/07

SAINT HELENA FACULTY
Faculdade Santa Helena (FASH)
Rua Demócrito de Souza Filho, 452, Madalena, Recife, Pernambuco 52110010
Tel: +55(81) 3226-1464
Fax: +55(81) 3226-1464
EMail: fsh@fsh.edu.br
Website: http://www.fsh.edu.br/

Diretor: Marcelo Pimentel

Courses
Accountancy; **Administration** (Administration; Business Administration; Human Resources; Marketing); **Tourism** (Hotel and Restaurant; Hotel Management; Tourism)

History: Founded 1999.

Main Language(s) of Instruction: Portuguese

Degrees and Diplomas: Bacharelado; Mestrado
Last Updated: 02/07/10

SAINT IPHIGENY FACULTY OF COMMUNICATION -VEREDAS FACULTY
Faculdade de Comunicação Social Santa Efigênia - Faculdade Veredas
Br 040 N°: 18.400, Bairro Gagé, Conselheiro Lafaiete, MG 36400-000
EMail: secretaria@faculdadeveredas.com.br

Courses
Social Communication (Advertising and Publicity; Journalism; Public Relations)

History: Founded 2004

Main Language(s) of Instruction: Portuguese

Degrees and Diplomas: Bacharelado
Last Updated: 30/07/10

SAINT IZILDINHA FACULTY
Faculdade Santa Izildinha (FIESI)
Rua Tetis, s/n, São Paulo, São Paulo 08330-485
Tel: +55(11) 2141-5618
EMail: diretoria@staizildinha.com.br
Website: http://www.fiesi.com.br

Diretor: Aparecido dos Santos

Courses
Administration (Administration); **Geography**; **History**; **Information Systems** (Computer Science); **Literature** (Literature); **Mathematics**; **Pedagogy**

History: Founded 2001.

Main Language(s) of Instruction: Portuguese

Degrees and Diplomas: Bacharelado; Licenciatura; Especialização/Aperfeiçoamento
Last Updated: 02/07/10

SAINT JOSÉ FACULTY
Faculdades São José (FASJ)
Rua Marechal Soares d'Andrea 90 Realengo, Rio de Janeiro, Rio de Janeiro 21710180
Tel: +55(21) 3331-3695
Fax: +55(21) 3332-0047
EMail: reitoria@saojose.br
Website: http://www.saojose.br

Diretor Geral: Antonio José Zaib (1997-)

Courses
Accountancy; **Administration** (Administration; Business Administration); **Biology** (Biology); **Computer Science** (Computer Science); **Dentistry** (Dentistry); **Law** (Law); **Pedagogy** (Pedagogy); **Physiotherapy** (Physical Therapy); **Tourism** (Tourism)

History: Founded 1980.

Main Language(s) of Instruction: Portuguese

Degrees and Diplomas: Bacharelado; Especialização/Aperfeiçoamento; Mestrado
Last Updated: 18/06/10

SAINT JUDE THADDEUS FACULTY - RIO DE JANEIRO
Faculdade São Judas Tadeu - Rio de Janeiro (FSJT)
Rua Clarimundo de Melo 79 Encantado, Rio de Janeiro, Rio de Janeiro 20740321
Tel: +55(21) 3296-5000
Fax: +55(21) 2592-3493
EMail: sjtcpd@easynet.com.br
Website: http://www.sjt.com.br

Diretor Geral: Geraldo Moreira Santana (1980-)

Courses
Administration (Accountancy; Administration; Business Administration; Environmental Management; Human Resources; Marketing; Tourism); **Arts and Humanities**; **Education** (Education; Educational Psychology; Higher Education; Primary Education); **Social Services**; **Systems Analysis**

History: Founded 1974.

Degrees and Diplomas: Bacharelado; Licenciatura; Especialização/Aperfeiçoamento; Mestrado
Last Updated: 07/12/07

SAINT JUDE THADDEUS FACULTY OF PINHAIS
Faculdade São Judas Tadeu de Pinhais (FAPI)
Av. Camilo Di Lellis, 1151, Pinhais, PR Pinhais
Tel: +55(41) 3667-6000
EMail: fapi@onda.com.br
Website: http://www.revista.fapi-pinhais.edu.br/inicio/

Courses
Graduate Studies (Education; Educational Administration; Educational Psychology; Educational Technology; Health Administration; Leadership; Literacy Education; Literature; Mathematics Education; Pedagogy; Public Health; Special Education); **Undergraduate Studies** (Administration; Law; Literature; Pedagogy; Social and Community Services)

Degrees and Diplomas: Bacharelado; Licenciatura; Especialização/Aperfeiçoamento
Last Updated: 07/09/10

SAINT JUDE THADDEUS INSTITUTE OF EDUCATION

Instituto Superior de Educação São Judas Tadeu (ISESJT)
Rua Félix Pacheco, 530, Centro, Floriano, PI 64800-000
Tel: +55(89) 3522-2444
Fax: +55(89) 3522-2444
EMail: isesjt@yahoo.com.br
Website: http://isesjtfloriano.com.br/

Diretora Geral: Albertina Gomes da Costa Tel: +55(89) 3522-3065

Courses
Graduate Studies (Education; Educational Administration; Educational and Student Counselling; Geography; Higher Education; History; Literature; Science Education); **Undergraduate Studies** (Pedagogy)

History: Founded 2003.

Degrees and Diplomas: *Licenciatura*; *Especialização/Aperfeiçoamento*
Last Updated: 28/09/10

SAINT JUDE THADDEUS INTEGRATED FACULTIES

Faculdades Integradas São Judas Tadeu (SJT)
Rua Dom Diogo de Souza 100, Cristo Redentor, Porto Alegre, Rio Grande do Sul 91350000
Tel: +55(51) 3340-7888
Fax: +55(51) 3340-2568
EMail: saojudas@saojudastadeu.com.br
Website: http://www.saojudastadeu.com.br

Diretor: Sandra Diamantina Mierczynski (1997-)

Courses
Accountancy (Accountancy); **Administration** (Administration); **Law**; **Pedagogy**; **Physical Education** (Physical Education)

History: Founded 1970.

Main Language(s) of Instruction: Portuguese

Degrees and Diplomas: *Bacharelado*; *Especialização/Aperfeiçoamento*
Last Updated: 22/06/10

SAINT JUDE THADDEUS UNIVERSITY

Universidade São Judas Tadeu (USJT)
Rua Taquarí 546, Mooca, São Paulo, São Paulo 03166000
Tel: +55(11) 6099-1933
EMail: daa@usjt.br
Website: http://www.usjt.br

Reitor: José Christiano Altenfelder S. Mesquita (2001-)
Tel: +55(11) 6099-1999 EMail: paulapeduto@usjt.br

Faculties
Arts and Humanities, Communication and Education (Advertising and Publicity; Architecture; Arts and Humanities; Communication Studies; Education; Industrial Design; Journalism; Literature; Town Planning; Translation and Interpretation); **Biology and Health Sciences** (Biology; Health Sciences; Nutrition; Pharmacy; Physical Education; Physical Therapy); **Exact Sciences and Technology** (Civil Engineering; Engineering; Mathematics and Computer Science; Mechanical Engineering; Natural Sciences; Production Engineering; Technology); **Human and Social Sciences** (Accountancy; Administration; Economics; Philosophy; Psychology; Secretarial Studies; Tourism); **Law** (Law)

History: Founded 1971 as Faculdades, acquired present title 1989.

Academic Year: February to December

Admission Requirements: Secondary school certificate and entrance examination

Main Language(s) of Instruction: Portuguese

Degrees and Diplomas: *Bacharelado*: 4-5 yrs; *Licenciatura*: 2 yrs; *Especialização/Aperfeiçoamento*; *Mestrado*

Student Services: Academic counselling, Canteen, Employment services, Handicapped facilities, Health services, Language programs, Nursery care, Social counselling, Sports facilities

Libraries: c. 147,000 vols
Publications: Revista Integração, Scientific Journal *(biannually)*
Last Updated: 06/05/10

SAINT LOUIS FACULTY

Faculdade São Luis (FSL)
Rua Haddock Lobo 400, São Paulo, São Paulo 01414902
Tel: +55(11) 3138-9747
Fax: +55(11) 3214-3577
EMail: diretoria@faculdadesaoluis.br

Diretor: Alfonso Carlos Palacio y Larrauri

Courses
Accountancy (Accountancy); **Administration** (Administration); **Economics** (Economics)

History: Founded 1948.

Main Language(s) of Instruction: Portuguese

Degrees and Diplomas: *Bacharelado*; *Especialização/Aperfeiçoamento*
Last Updated: 29/07/10

SAINT LOUIS FACULTY

Faculdade São Luiz (FSL)
Av das Comunidades, 233, Centro, Brusque, SC 88350-970
Tel: +55(47) 3396-7919
EMail: fsl@faculdadesaoluiz.edu.br
Website: http://www.faculdadesaoluiz.edu.br/

Diretor Geral: Claudio Marcio Piontkewicz

Courses
Graduate Studies (Art Therapy; Business Administration); **Undergraduate Studies** (Philosophy)

History: Founded 2000.

Degrees and Diplomas: *Bacharelado*; *Especialização/Aperfeiçoamento*. Also MBA.
Last Updated: 08/09/10

SAINT LOUIS FACULTY OF EDUCATION OF JABOTICABAL

Faculdade de Educação São Luis de Jaboticabal
Rua Floriano Peixoto, 839-873, Centro, Jaboticabal, São Paulo 14870-370
Tel: +55(16) 3209-1800
Fax: +55(16) 3209-2120
EMail: saoluis@saoluis.br
Website: http://www.saoluis.br

Diretora: Irace Miriam de Castro Martins (1973-)

Courses
Administration (Administration); **Art Education** (Art Education); **Arts and Humanities** (Arts and Humanities; English; Literature; Portuguese); **Arts and Humanities** (Arts and Humanities; English; Literature; Spanish); **Biological Sciences** (Biological and Life Sciences); **Geography** (Geography); **Graduate Studies** (Administrative Law; Agricultural Business; Art Education; Communication Arts; Computer Science; Cultural Studies; Education; Educational Administration; Educational Psychology; Environmental Studies; Health Administration; Health Education; Health Sciences; Higher Education; History; Human Resources; Labour Law; Law; Literacy Education; Management; Mathematics Education; Nursing; Pedagogy; Philosophy; Portuguese; Preschool Education; Public Administration; Public Health; Spanish; Special Education; Teacher Training); **History** (History); **Information Systems** (Information Technology); **Law** (Law); **Mathematics** (Mathematics; Mathematics and Computer Science); **Nursing**; **Pedagogy** (Pedagogy); **Philosophy** (Philosophy); **Social Communication** (Advertising and Publicity); **Trilingual Executive Secretary**

History: Founded 1972

Degrees and Diplomas: *Bacharelado*: 4 yrs; *Licenciatura*: 3 yrs; *Especialização/Aperfeiçoamento*. Also MBA.
Last Updated: 07/07/10

SAINT LOUIS OF FRANCE FACULTY
Faculdade São Luis de França (FSL)
Rua Laranjeiras 1838, Getulio Vargas, Aracaju, Sergipe 49055380
Tel: +55(79) 3214-3990
Fax: +55(79) 3214-6300
EMail: atendimento@faculdadesaoluis.com.br
Website: http://www.faculdadesaoluisdefranca.com.br

Diretor: Jeferson Fonseca de Moraes

Courses
Administration (Administration); **Letters** (Literature); **Pedagogy** (Pedagogy)

History: Founded 1997.

Main Language(s) of Instruction: Portuguese

Degrees and Diplomas: *Bacharelado*; *Especialização/Aperfeiçoamento*
Last Updated: 01/07/10

SAINT LUCAS FACULTY
Faculdade São Lucas (FSL)
Rua Alexandre Guimaráes 1927, Areal, Porto Velho,
Rondônia 78916450
Tel: +55(69) 3211-8001
Fax: +55(69) 3211-8058
EMail: faculdade@saolucas.edu.br
Website: http://www.saolucas.edu.br

Diretora Geral: Maria Eliza de Aguiar e Silva

Courses
Administration (Business Administration; Health Administration); **Biology**; **Biomedicine** (Biomedicine); **Dentistry** (Dentistry); **Law**; **Medicine**; **Nursing** (Nursing); **Nutrition** (Nutrition); **Physiotherapy**; **Speech Therapy** (Speech Therapy and Audiology); **Tourism** (Tourism)

History: Founded 1999.

Main Language(s) of Instruction: Portuguese

Degrees and Diplomas: *Bacharelado*; *Especialização/Aperfeiçoamento*; *Mestrado*
Last Updated: 01/07/10

SAINT LUCY FACULTY
Faculdade Santa Lúcia (FCACSL)
Rua Doutor Ulhoa Cintra, 351, Centro, Mogi-Mirim, SP 13800-970
Tel: +55(19) 3806-3996
EMail: santalucia@santalucia.br
Website: http://www.santalucia.br/

Diretor Presidente: Roberto Raphael Carrozzo Scardua

Courses
Graduate Studies (Accountancy; Business Administration; Business and Commerce; Law; Management; Marketing; Transport Management); **Undergraduate Studies** (Accountancy; Administration; Information Sciences; Law; Social and Community Services)

History: Founded 1994.

Degrees and Diplomas: *Bacharelado*; *Especialização/Aperfeiçoamento*. Also MBA.
Last Updated: 06/09/10

SAINT MARC FACULTY
Faculdade São Marcos (FASAMAR)
Rua Antônio Aires Primo, 2697, Centro, Porto Nacional,
TO 77500-000
Tel: +(63) 3363 -2922
EMail: faculdadesaomarcos@bol.com.br

Courses
Undergraduate Studies (Administration; Pedagogy)

Degrees and Diplomas: *Bacharelado*; *Licenciatura*
Last Updated: 08/09/10

SAINT MARCELINA FACULTY
Faculdade Santa Marcelina (FASM)
Rua Doutor Emílio Ribas 89, Perdizes, São Paulo,
São Paulo 5006020
Tel: +55(11) 3824-5800
Fax: +55(11) 3824-5818
EMail: fasm@fasm.edu.br
Website: http://www.fasm.edu.br

Diretora: Angela Rivero (1997-)

Courses
Accountancy *(Itaquera)*; **Administration** *(Itaquera)*; **Art Education** (Art Education); **Fashion Design** (Design; Fashion Design); **International Relations** (International Relations); **Music** (Music); **Nursing** *(Itaquera)* (Nursing); **Nutrition** *(Itaquera)* (Nutrition); **Physiotherapy** *(Itaquera)*; **Plastic Arts** (Fine Arts)

History: Founded 1981.

Main Language(s) of Instruction: Portuguese

Degrees and Diplomas: *Bacharelado*; *Especialização/Aperfeiçoamento*; *Mestrado*
Last Updated: 02/07/10

SAINT MARY FACULTY
Faculdade Santa Maria (FSM)
Rodovia BR, 230, Cajazeiras, PB 58900-000
Tel: +55(83) 3531-1365
Fax: +55(83) 3531-1365
EMail: ouvidoria@fsm.edu.br
Website: http://www.fsm.edu.br/

Diretora: Ana Costa Goldfarb **EMail:** anagoldfarb@bol.com.br

Courses
Graduate Studies (Gerontology; Gynaecology and Obstetrics; Nursing; Physical Therapy; Public Health); **Undergraduate Studies** (Administration; Nursing; Pharmacy; Physical Therapy; Social and Community Services)

History: Founded 2000.

Degrees and Diplomas: *Bacharelado*; *Especialização/Aperfeiçoamento*
Last Updated: 06/09/10

SAINT MARY FACULTY
Faculdade Santa Maria (FSM)
Rua Padre Bernadino Pessoa, N° 512, Boa Viagem, Recife,
PE 51020 - 210
Tel: +55(81) 3465-0702
Fax: +55(81) 3465-0723
Website: http://www.fsm.com.br/

Diretor Presidente: Luis Otávio Cavalcanti
EMail: lotavio@fsm.com.br

Courses
Graduate Studies (Computer Networks; International Relations; Management; Psychoanalysis); **Undergraduate Studies** (Administration; Information Sciences)

History: Founded 2001.

Degrees and Diplomas: *Bacharelado*; *Especialização/Aperfeiçoamento*
Last Updated: 06/09/10

SAINT MICHAEL FACULTY
Faculdade São Miguel (FSL)
Rua Dom Bosco 1308, Boa Vista, Recife, Pernambuco 50070-070
Tel: +55(81) 3221-3702
Fax: +55(81) 3222-0916
EMail: atendimento@faculdadesaomiguel.com.br
Website: http://www.quapin.com.br/saomiguel/

Diretora: Manoelita Alves Chiappetta

Courses
Administration; **Economics** (Economics); **Education** (Education); **Letters** (Literature); **Nursing** (Nursing); **Nutrition** (Nutrition); **Physiotherapy**

History: Founded 2001.

Main Language(s) of Instruction: Portuguese

Degrees and Diplomas: *Bacharelado*; *Licenciatura*; *Especialização/Aperfeiçoamento*; *Mestrado*

Last Updated: 01/07/10

SAINT PASTOUS FACULTY OF TECHNOLOGY

Faculdade de Tecnologia Saint Pastous

Rua São Luiz 132, 4° andar, Santana, Porto Alegre, RS 90620-170

Tel: +55(51) 3219-3699

EMail: fundacao@saintpastous.org.br

Website: http://www.saintpastous.org.br/

Courses

Radiology (Radiology)

Degrees and Diplomas: *Tecnólogo*. Also Postgraduate Diploma.

Last Updated: 27/08/10

SAINT PAUL FACULTY

Faculdade São Paulo (FACSP)

Av. Liberdade N° 808, Liberdade, São Paulo, SP 01502-001

Tel: +55(11) 3277-6887

Fax: +55(11) 3277-6887

EMail: secretaria@facsp.com.br

Website: http://www.facsp.edu.br/

Courses

Undergraduate Studies (Accountancy; Administration; Computer Networks; Information Technology; Marketing; Pedagogy)

Degrees and Diplomas: *Tecnólogo*; *Bacharelado*; *Licenciatura*

Last Updated: 08/09/10

SAINT PAUL FACULTY

Faculdade São Paulo (FSP)

Avenida 25 de Agosto, 6961, São Cristóvão, Rolim de Moura, RO 78987-000

Tel: +55(69) 3442-1001

Fax: +55(69) 3442-6346

President: Iêda Pacheco Chaves

Courses

Information Systems (Information Sciences)

Degrees and Diplomas: *Bacharelado*

Last Updated: 08/09/10

SAINT PETER INTEGRATED FACULTIES

Faculdades Integradas São Pedro (FAESA)

Rodovia Serrafim Derenzi 3115, Inhanguetá, São Pedro, Espirito Santo 29030-026

Tel: +55(27) 3331-4500

EMail: secretaria2@faesa.br

Website: http://www.faesa.br

Diretor Geral: Alexandre Nunes Theodoro (1995-)

Areas

Education (Biology; Education; Pedagogy; Physical Education); **Health Sciences** (Dentistry; Health Sciences; Medicine; Nursing; Nutrition; Occupational Therapy; Psychology; Speech Therapy and Audiology); **Social Communication**

History: Founded 1994.

Main Language(s) of Instruction: Portuguese

Degrees and Diplomas: *Bacharelado*; *Licenciatura*; *Especialização/Aperfeiçoamento*

Last Updated: 22/06/10

SAINT SAVIOUR FACULTY

Faculdade São Salvador (FSS)

Rua dos Algibebes, 6/12, Comércio, Salvador, BA 40015-060

Tel: +55(71) 2106-2733

Fax: +55(71) 3328-2333 +55(71) 2101-2333

EMail: fssal@terra.com.br

Website: http://www.saosalvador.edu.br/

Diretor Geral: Gilberto C. Martins

Tel: +55(71) 2101-2,333; +55(71) 3328-2333

EMail: gmartins@saosalvador.edu.br

Courses

Graduate Studies (Accountancy; Business Administration; Environmental Management; Finance; Management; Nursing; Public Health; Transport Management); **Technological Studies** (Business and Commerce; Finance; Human Resources; Management); **Undergraduate Studies** (Accountancy; Administration; Law; Nursing; Nutrition; Physical Therapy; Tourism)

Degrees and Diplomas: *Tecnólogo*; *Bacharelado*. Also Postgraduate diploma and MBA.

Last Updated: 08/09/10

SAINT THOMAS AQUINAS FACULTY

Faculdade São Tomás de Aquino (FACESTA)

Avenida Muniz Falcão, s/n, São Francisco, Palmeira dos Índios, AL 57600-060

Tel: +55(82) 3421-1060

EMail: facesta@bol.com.br

Diretor: Antônio Melo de Almeida

Courses

Undergraduate Studies (Philosophy; Physical Education; Teacher Training)

Degrees and Diplomas: *Licenciatura*

Last Updated: 08/09/10

SAINT THOMAS AQUINAS FACULTY

Faculdade São Tomaz de Aquino (FSTA)

Av. Juracy Magalhães, n° 115, Rio Vermelho Rua Lima e Silva, Salvador, BA 41940-060

Tel: +55(71) 2104-3333

Fax: +55(71) 2104-3319

EMail: salles@fsta.edu.br

Website: http://www.fsta.edu.br/

Courses

Undergraduate Studies (Accountancy; Administration; Journalism; Law; Mass Communication; Nursing; Pedagogy; Tourism)

Further Information: Also Liberdade and Itapoã campuses.

Degrees and Diplomas: *Bacharelado*; *Licenciatura*

Last Updated: 08/09/10

SAINT ÚRSULA UNIVERSITY

Universidade Santa Úrsula (USU)

Rua Fernando Ferrari 75, Botafogo, Rio de Janeiro, Rio de Janeiro 22231040

Tel: +55(21) 2554-2500

EMail: reitoria@usu.br

Website: http://www.usu.br

Reitor: George Bittencourt Doyle Maia (2004-)

Tel: +55(21) 2554-8036

Chanceler: Maria de Fátima Maron Ramos

Centres

Human and Social Sciences (Arts and Humanities; Social Sciences)

Institutes

Architecture and Arts (Architecture; Town Planning); **Biology and Environmental Sciences** (Biology; Environmental Studies; Nutrition); **Computer Science** (Computer Science; Library Science); **Economics and Management** (Accountancy; Administration; Economics; Management); **Education and Letters** (Pedagogy); **Exact Sciences and Technology** (Civil Engineering; Electrical Engineering; Mechanical Engineering); **Law**; **Mathematics** (Mathematics); **Psychology and Psychoanalysis** (Psychoanalysis; Psychology); **Theology and Philosophy** (Philosophy; Theology)

Research Centres

Biology (Biology); **Economics and Management** *(ICEG)* (Economics; Management); **Mathematics** (Mathematics)

History: Founded 1939 by the Ursulines as Catholic Faculty of Education, Science and Letters. Acquired University status 1975. A private institution under the supervision of the Associação Universitária Santa Úrsula.

Governing Bodies: Conselho Superior de Administração; Conselho Universitário; Conselho de Ensino e Pesquisa

Academic Year: March to November (March-June; August-November)

Admission Requirements: Secondary school certificate and entrance examination

Main Language(s) of Instruction: Portuguese

Degrees and Diplomas: *Bacharelado*: 4-5 yrs; *Bacharelado*: Architecture; Engineering; Nutrition; Psychology, 4-5 yrs; *Licenciatura*: 3-4 yrs; *Especialização/Aperfeiçoamento*; *Mestrado*

Libraries: Central Library, c. 70,000 vols; Theology, c. 15,000; Biology, c. 6,800; ICEG, c. 5,500; Informative, c. 15,000; History, c. 20,000

Publications: Espaço-Cadernos de Cultura; Série Documentos e Letra *(biannually)*

Press or Publishing House: Serviço Gráfico. Editora
Last Updated: 07/05/10

SAINT VINCENT FACULTY
Faculdade São Vicente (FASVIPA)
Rua Padre Soares Pinto, 314, Centro, Pão de Açúcar,
AL 57400-000
Tel: +55(82) 3624-1862
Fax: +55(82) 3624-1862
EMail: fasvipa@hotmail.com

Courses
Undergraduate Studies (Chemistry; Nursing; Pedagogy)

Degrees and Diplomas: *Bacharelado*; *Licenciatura*
Last Updated: 08/09/10

SALESIAN FACULTY OF PINDAMONHANGABA
Faculdade Salesiana de Pindamonhangaba (FASP)
Rua São João Bosco, 873, Santana, Pindamonhangaba,
SP 12403-010
Tel: +55(12) 3645-3535
Fax: +55(12) 3642-1551
EMail: mrezende@unisal-lorena.br

Courses
Administration (Administration); **Teacher Training** (Teacher Training)

Degrees and Diplomas: *Bacharelado*; *Licenciatura*
Last Updated: 06/09/10

SALESIAN FACULTY OF SANTA TERESA
Faculdade Salesiana de Santa Teresa (FSST)
Rua Dom Aquino, 1119, Centro, Corumbá, MS 79301-970
Tel: +55(67) 3234-2600
EMail: faculdade@steresa.org.br
Website: http://www.fsst.edu.br/

Courses
Economics (Economics); **Graduate Studies** (Accountancy); **Law** (Law)

Degrees and Diplomas: *Bacharelado*. Postgraduate diploma offered jointly with Universidade Católica Dom Bosco (UCDB virtual).
Last Updated: 06/09/10

SALESIAN FACULTY OF THE NORTH EAST
Faculdade Salesiana do Nordeste (FASNE)
Rua Dom Bosco 551, Boa Vista, Recife, Pernambuco 50070070
Tel: +55(81) 2129-5900
Fax: +55(81) 2129-5900
EMail: fasne@fasne.edu.br
Website: http://www.fasne.edu.br
Diretor: Robson Barros da Costa

Courses
Accountancy (Accountancy); **Administration**; **Biology**; **Law** (Law); **Physical Education** (Physical Education); **Tourism**
History: Founded 2000.
Main Language(s) of Instruction: Portuguese
Degrees and Diplomas: *Bacharelado*; *Licenciatura*; *Especialização/Aperfeiçoamento*
Last Updated: 02/07/10

SALESIAN FACULTY OF VITÓRIA
Faculdade Salesiana de Vitória (UNISALES)
Avenida Vitória 950, Forte São João, Vitória,
Espirito Santo 29017950
Tel: +55(27) 3331-8500
Fax: +55(27) 3222-3829
EMail: faculdade@salesiano.com.br
Website: http://www.faculdadesalesiana.edu.br/imprensa/noticias.asp
Diretor: Juper Laurindo Crispino

Courses
Administration; **Biology** (Biology); **Education**; **Information Systems** (Information Management); **Nursing** (Nursing); **Nutrition** (Nutrition); **Pharmacy**; **Philosophy** (Philosophy); **Physiotherapy** (Physical Therapy); **Psychology** (Psychology); **Social Services** (Social and Community Services); **Software Engineering** (Software Engineering)
History: Founded 2000.
Main Language(s) of Instruction: Portuguese
Degrees and Diplomas: *Bacharelado*; *Licenciatura*; *Especialização/Aperfeiçoamento*
Last Updated: 02/07/10

SALESIAN INSTITUTE OF PHILOSOPHY
Instituto Salesiano de Filosofia (INSAF)
Avenida Abdias de Carvalho 1855, Bongi, Recife,
Pernambuco 50830000
Tel: +55(81) 2129-4000
Fax: +55(81) 2129-4001
EMail: secretaria@insaf.com.br
Website: http://www.insaf.com.br/home/?principal
Diretor Presidente: Anderson de Alencar Menezes

Courses
Philosophy (Philosophy)
History: Founded 2001.
Main Language(s) of Instruction: Portuguese
Degrees and Diplomas: *Licenciatura*
Last Updated: 14/06/10

SALESIAN UNIVERSITY CENTRE OF SÃO PAULO
Centro Universitário Salesiano de São Paulo (UNISAL)
Av. de Cillo, n° 3.500, Americana, São Paulo 13467-600
Tel: +55(19) 3471-9700
Fax: +55(19) 3471-9716
EMail: secretaria.geral@unisal.br
Website: http://www.unisal.br
Reitor: Edson Donizetti Castilho

Courses
Accountancy *(Americana / Maria Auxiliadora)*; **Administration** *(Americana / Maria Auxiliadora; Campinas / São José; Lorena / São Joaquim; São Paulo / Santa Teresinha)* (Administration); **Advertising and Publicity** *(Americana / Dom Bosco)* (Advertising and Publicity); **Automation and Control Engineering** *(Americana / Dom Bosco; Campinas / São José)*; **Automotive Systems** *(Campinas / São José)*; **Computer Science** *(Lorena / São Joaquim)* (Computer Science); **Electrical Engineering - Electronic Engineering** *(Campinas / São José)*; **Electrical Engineering - Telecommunciations Engineering** *(Campinas / São José)* (Electrical Engineering; Telecommunications Engineering); **Environmental Engineering** *(Americana / Dom Bosco)*; **Fashion**

(Americana / Dom Bosco); **Geography** (Lorena / São Joaquim) (Geography); **History** (Lorena / São Joaquim); **Hotel Management** (Lorena / São Joaquim) (Hotel Management); **Industrial Automation** (Campinas / São José); **Information Systems** (Americana / Dom Bosco) (Information Sciences); **Law** (Americana / Maria Auxiliadora; Campinas / Liceu Salesiano; Lorena / São Joaquim; São Paulo / Santa Teresinha) (Law); **Mathematics** (Lorena / São Joaquim) (Mathematics); **Pedagogy** (Americana / Maria Auxiliadora; Lorena / São Joaquim; São Paulo / Santa Teresinha) (Pedagogy); **Philosophy** (Lorena / São Joaquim) (Philosophy); **Postgraduate Lato Sensu** (Americana / Maria Auxiliadora) (Accountancy; Administrative Law; Business and Commerce; Civil Law; Communication Studies; Computer Networks; Criminal Law; Data Processing; Distance Education; Education; Educational Administration; Educational Psychology; Environmental Management; Finance; Information Technology; Labour Law; Law; Management; Marketing; Public Administration; Safety Engineering; Software Engineering; Systems Analysis; Transport Management); **Postgraduate Lato Sensu** (Campinas / São José) (Accountancy; Agricultural Business; Automotive Engineering; Business and Commerce; Computer Science; Cultural Studies; Education; Educational Psychology; Electronic Engineering; Engineering; Finance; Gerontology; Health Administration; History; International Relations; Management; Marketing; Mechanical Engineering; Pedagogy; Philosophy; Production Engineering; Safety Engineering; Software Engineering; Telecommunications Engineering; Transport Management); **Postgraduate Lato Sensu** (São Paulo / Santa Teresinha) (Business and Commerce; Commercial Law; Education; Educational Administration; Educational and Student Counselling; International Law; Law; Marketing; Pedagogy); **Postgraduate Lato Sensu** (Campinas / Liceu Salesiano) (Civil Law; Commercial Law; Human Rights); **Postgraduate Lato Sensu** (Lorena / São Joaquim) (Biotechnology; Business and Commerce; Civil Law; Commercial Law; Educational Administration; Educational Psychology; Environmental Management; Environmental Studies; Finance; Industrial Management; Information Technology; International Business; Labour Law; Law; Management; Marketing; Mathematics Education; Psychoanalysis; Public Administration; Public Law; Rehabilitation and Therapy; Transport Management); **Postgraduate Lato Sensu** (São Paulo / Pio Xi); **Postgraduate Stricto Sensu** (Americana / Maria Auxiliadora) (Administration; Education); **Postgraduate Stricto Sensu** (Lorena / São Joaquim) (Law); **Psychology** (Americana / Maria Auxiliadora; Lorena / São Joaquim) (Psychology); **Social Services** (Americana / Maria Auxiliadora) (Social and Community Services); **Systems for Internet** (Lorena / São Joaquim); **Theology** (São Paulo / Pio Xi); **Tourism** (Lorena / São Joaquim) (Tourism)

History: Founded 1952.

Degrees and Diplomas: Tecnólogo; Bacharelado; Licenciatura; Especialização/Aperfeiçoamento; Mestrado. Also MBA.
Last Updated: 17/06/10

SALGADO DE OLIVEIRA UNIVERSITY

Universidade Salgado de Oliveira (UNIVERSO)
Rua Lambari 10, Térreo Trindade, São Gonçalo,
Rio de Janeiro 24456420
Tel: +55(21) 3712-9559
EMail: universo@universo.edu.br
Website: http://www.universo.g12.br

Reitora: Marlene Salgado de Oliveira (1997-)
Tel: +55(21) 2620-5206

Courses
Accountancy (Accountancy); **Administration** (Administration); **Art Education**; **Arts and Humanities** (Arts and Humanities); **Biological and Life Sciences** (Biological and Life Sciences); **Chemistry** (Chemistry); **Communication Studies** (Communication Studies); **Dentistry**; **Design**; **Economics**; **Education** (Education); **Fashion Design**; **Fine Arts** (Fine Arts); **Food Technology** (Food Technology); **Geography** (Geography); **History** (History); **Law** (Law); **Mathematics** (Mathematics); **Nutrition** (Nutrition); **Physical Education** (Physical Education); **Physical Therapy** (Physical Therapy); **Psychology**; **Statistics** (Statistics); **Systems Analysis** (Systems Analysis)

Further Information: Also campuses in Salvador, Recife, Niterói, Juiz de Fora, Goiânia, Campos dos Goytacazes, Belo Horizonte
History: Founded 1976. Acquired present status 1993.

Admission Requirements: Secondary school certificate and entrance examination
Main Language(s) of Instruction: Portuguese
Degrees and Diplomas: Bacharelado; Licenciatura; Especialização/Aperfeiçoamento; Mestrado
Last Updated: 07/05/10

SALVADOR INSTITUTE OF EDUCATION AND CULTURE

Instituto Salvador de Ensino e Cultura (ISEC)
Avenida Magalhães Neto, 571, Loteamento Aquarius, Pituba,
Salvador, BA 41810-011
Tel: +55(71) 3496-4150

Courses
Undergraduate Studies (Accountancy; Administration; Advertising and Publicity; Computer Science; Information Technology; Law; Pedagogy; Physical Therapy; Tourism)

Degrees and Diplomas: Tecnólogo; Bacharelado; Licenciatura
Last Updated: 23/09/10

SALVADOR UNIVERSITY

Universidade Salvador (UNIFACS)
Rua Ponciano Oliveira 126, Garibaldi, Salvador, Bahia 40225300
Tel: +55(71) 3273-9550
Fax: +55(71) 3273-9501
EMail: areitoria@unifacs.br
Website: http://www.unifacs.br

Reitor: Manoel Joaquim de Barros Sobrinho (1997-)
Tel: +55(71) 245-0911

Departments
Applied Social Sciences (Accountancy; Administration; Economics; International Business; Law; Tourism); **Engineering and Architecture**; **Exact Sciences and Communication** (Advertising and Publicity; Computer Science; Design; Literature; Marketing; Public Relations; Systems Analysis); **Human and Health Sciences** (Psychology)

History: Founded 1972 as Escola de Administração de Empresas da Bahia, acquired present status 1997.
Academic Year: March to December
Admission Requirements: Secondary school certificate and entrance examination
Fees: (Reais): 497.70-698.20 per month
Main Language(s) of Instruction: Portuguese
Degrees and Diplomas: Bacharelado: 4 yrs; Licenciatura: 4 yrs
Student Services: Academic counselling, Canteen, Cultural centre, Language programs, Social counselling, Sports facilities
Libraries: Central Library. 5 sectorial libraries
Publications: De Hoje a Oito; Pré-textos para Discussão, Academic Reports (biannually)
Last Updated: 07/05/10

SANTA ANNA UNIVERSITY CENTRE

Centro Universitário Sant'Anna (UNISANT'AN)
Rua Voluntários da Pátria 257, Santana, São Paulo,
São Paulo 02011000
Tel: +55(11) 2175-8000
EMail: info@santanna.br
Website: http://www.santanna.br

Reitor: Leonardo Placucci

Courses
Accountancy; **Administration** (Administration); **Arts and Humanities** (Arts and Humanities; English; Literature; Modern Languages; Portuguese); **Biology**; **Computer Engineering** (Computer Engineering); **Computer Science** (Computer Science); **Economics**; **Electrical Engineering** (Electrical Engineering); **Geography** (Geography); **Graduate Studies** (Business and Commerce; Communication Studies; Computer Networks; Education; Educational Psychology; English; Environmental Studies; Finance; Management; Marketing; Nursing; Physiology; Public Relations; Rehabilitation and Therapy; Spanish; Transport Management); **History**

(History); **Mathematics**; **Music**; **Nursing**; **Pedagogy** (Pedagogy); **Physical Education**; **Physical Therapy** (Physical Therapy); **Production Engineering**; **Social Communication - Advertising and Publicity** (Advertising and Publicity); **Social Communication - Journalism**; **Social Communication - Public Relations** (Public Relations); **Social Communication - Radio and Television** (Radio and Television Broadcasting); **Sociology**; **Technological Studies** (Aeronautical and Aerospace Engineering; Business and Commerce; Computer Networks; Cosmetology; Environmental Management; Fashion Design; Graphic Design; Hotel Management; Human Resources; International Business; Marketing; Photography; Public Relations; Radiology; Systems Analysis); **Tourism**

Further Information: Also Shopping Aricanduva and Salto campuses.

History: Founded 1970.

Main Language(s) of Instruction: Portuguese

Degrees and Diplomas: *Tecnólogo*; *Bacharelado*; *Licenciatura*; *Especialização/Aperfeiçoamento*
Last Updated: 17/06/10

SANTA BARBARA FACULTY OF HIGHER EDUCATION

Faculdade de Ensino Superior Santa Barbara
Rua Xi de Agosto 2.900, Tatui, SP 18277-000
Tel: +55(15) 3259-4024
EMail: aejc@uol.com.br
Website: http://www.faesb.com.br/portal

Diretor: Antonio David Julian

Courses
Accountancy (Accountancy); **Administration** (Administration); **Agronomy** (Agronomy); **Information Systems** (Computer Science); **Nursing** (Nursing)

History: Founded 2006.

Main Language(s) of Instruction: Portuguese

Degrees and Diplomas: *Bacharelado*; *Especialização/Aperfeiçoamento*; *Mestrado*
Last Updated: 04/08/10

SANTA CATARINA ASSOCIATION OF EDUCATION - GUILHERME GUIMBALA FACULTY

Associação Catarinense de Ensino - Faculdade Guilherme Guimbala (ACE)
Rua São José 490, Anita Garibaldi, Joinville,
Santa Catarina 89202-010
Tel: +55(47) 3026-4000
Fax: +55(47) 3026-4000
EMail: ace@ace.br
Website: http://www.ace.br

Diretor: Norberto Schwarz

Courses
Education; Graduate Studies; Information Systems; Law (Commercial Law; Law); Occupational Therapy; Physical Therapy

Faculties
Psychology (Psychology)

History: Founded 1973.

Main Language(s) of Instruction: Portuguese

Degrees and Diplomas: *Bacharelado*; *Licenciatura*; *Especialização/Aperfeiçoamento*. Also MBA
Last Updated: 05/03/10

SANTA CRUZ INSTITUTE OF EDUCATION

Instituto Superior de Educação Santa Cruz
Rua Júlia Aragão N°307, Centro, Santa Cruz do Capibaribe,
PE 55190-000
Tel: +55(81) 3731-4364
EMail: cesac.facruz@ig.com.br

Diretor: Miguel Guedes de Brito

Courses
Pedagogy (Pedagogy)

History: Founded 2004.

Main Language(s) of Instruction: Portuguese

Degrees and Diplomas: *Licenciatura*
Last Updated: 29/09/10

SANTA EMÍLIA DE RODAT FACULTY

Faculdade Santa Emília de Rodat (FASER)
Praça Caldas Brandão, s/n Praça Tambia, João Pessoa,
Paraíba 58023650
Tel: +55(83) 3214-4820
EMail: covese@faser.edu.br
Website: http://www.faser.edu.br

Diretora: Maria da Gloria Uchoa dos Santos

Courses
Biomedicine; **Cosmetics** (Cosmetology); **Nursing** (Nursing); **Radiology** (Radiology)

History: Founded 1961.

Main Language(s) of Instruction: Portuguese

Degrees and Diplomas: *Bacharelado*; *Especialização/Aperfeiçoamento*
Last Updated: 02/07/10

SANTA LÚCIA ASSOCIATION FOR EDUCATION AND ASSISTANCE

Associação Educacional e Assistencial Santa Lúcia (AEDASLU)
Rua Doutor Ulhoa Cintra, 351, Centro, Mogi-Mirim,
São Paulo 13800970
Tel: +55(19) 3806-3996
Fax: +55(19) 3860-3996
EMail: santalucia@santalucia.br
Website: http://www.santalucia.br

Faculties
Administrative Sciences and Accountancy (FCACSL - Santa Lúcia) (Accountancy; Administration; Business Administration; Business and Commerce; Finance; Human Resources; Information Sciences; Marketing; Social and Community Services; Transport Management); **Law** (Mogi Mirim) (Law)

History: Founded 1990.

Main Language(s) of Instruction: Portuguese

Degrees and Diplomas: *Bacharelado*; *Especialização/Aperfeiçoamento*: Business Administration (MBA)
Last Updated: 09/03/10

SANTA MARCELINA FACULTY OF PHILOSOPHY, SCIENCE AND LETTERS

Faculdade de Filosofia, Ciências e Letras Santa Marcelina (FAFISM)
Praça Annina Bisegna, 40, Centro, Muriaé, Minas Gerais 36880-000
Tel: +55(32) 3721-1026
Fax: +55(32) 3722-4355
EMail: fafism@fafism.com.br
Website: http://www.fafism.com.br

Diretora: Irmã Christina Maria Pastore (1995-)

Courses
Biological Sciences; **Geography**; **Graduate Studies** (Chemistry; Computer Science; Education; English; Environmental Studies; Literature; Mathematics; Modern Languages; Physics; Portuguese); **History**; **Literature** (Literature); **Pedagogy**; **Sciences - Chemistry**; **Sciences - Mathematics** (Mathematics; Teacher Training); **Sciences - Physics**; **Systems Analysis** (Systems Analysis)

History: Founded 1961.

Main Language(s) of Instruction: Portuguese

Degrees and Diplomas: *Tecnólogo*; *Licenciatura*; *Especialização/Aperfeiçoamento*
Last Updated: 08/07/10

SANTA MARINA FACULTY
Faculdade Santa Marina
AV. Guilherme Giorgi, 430 – Vila Carrão, São Paulo, SP 03422-001
Tel: +55(11) 2296-2400
EMail: santamarina@santamarina.edu.br
Website: http://www.santamarina.edu.br

Diretor Administrativo: Paulo Gaspar

Courses
Pedagogy (Pedagogy)
History: Founded 2003.
Main Language(s) of Instruction: Portuguese
Degrees and Diplomas: *Licenciatura*
Last Updated: 29/09/10

SANTA RITA DE CÁSSIA FACULTY
Faculdade Santa Rita de Cássia (UNIFASC)
Avenida Adelina Alves Vilela, 393, Jardim Primavera, Itumbiara,
GO 75524-680
Tel: +55(64) 3404-9020
EMail: unifasc@netsite.com.br
Website: http://www.unifasc.com.br/

Diretora Executiva: Marta Furtado Freire

Courses
Graduate Studies (Administration; Agricultural Business; Business
Administration; Education; Educational Psychology; Higher Educa-
tion; Labour Law; Management; Marketing; Nursing; Pedagogy;
Safety Engineering; Special Education); **Undergraduate Studies**
(Administration; Pedagogy; Radiology)
Main Language(s) of Instruction: Portuguese
Degrees and Diplomas: *Tecnólogo; Bacharelado; Licenciatura.*
Also Postgraduate diploma.
Last Updated: 07/09/10

SANTA RITA DE CÁSSIA INSTITUTE OF EDUCATION
Instituto Superior de Educação Santa Rita de Cássia
Rua Dr. Valdivino Vaz N°292, Ed. Antares, Centro, Itumbiara,
GO 75503-420
EMail: unifasc@netsite.com.br

Courses
Pedagogy (Pedagogy)
Last Updated: 29/09/10

SANTA RITA FACULTY
Faculdade Santa Rita (FACEAS)
Avenida Jaçanã 648, São Paulo, São Paulo 2273001
Tel: +55(11) 6241-0777
EMail: santarita@santarita.br
Website: http://www.santarita.br

Diretor: Anunciato Storopoli Neto (1996-)

Courses
Accountancy (Accountancy); **Administration** (Administration;
Business Administration; Human Resources; Marketing); **Law**
(Law); **Nursing** (Nursing); **Pedagogy** (Pedagogy)
History: Founded 1994.
Main Language(s) of Instruction: Portuguese
Degrees and Diplomas: *Tecnólogo; Bacharelado; Licenciatura;
Especialização/Aperfeiçoamento*
Last Updated: 01/07/10

SANTA RITA FACULTY
Faculdade Santa Rita (FASAR)
Estrada Real Km 2, S/n Caixa Postal 26, Conselheiro Lafaiete,
Minas Gerais 36400000
Tel: +55(31) 3763-2001
Fax: +55(31) 3763-2001
EMail: fasar@fasar.com.br
Website: http://www.fasar.com.br/

Diretora: Maria da Paz Fonseca e Costa

Courses
Administration (Administration); **Economics**; **Education** (Educa-
tion; Pedagogy; Physical Education); **Geography**; **Languages**
(Literature; Modern Languages; Portuguese; Translation and Inter-
pretation); **Nursing** (Nursing); **Nutrition** (Nutrition); **Production
Engineering** (Production Engineering); **Tourism** (Tourism)
History: Founded 1998.
Main Language(s) of Instruction: Portuguese
Degrees and Diplomas: *Bacharelado; Licenciatura*
Last Updated: 01/07/10

SANTA RITA FACULTY
Faculdade Santa Rita (FASAR)
Rua Doutor Mário Florence 144, Jardim Aeroporto, Novo Horizonte,
São Paulo 14960000
Tel: +55(17) 3542-6004
Fax: +55(17) 3542-3434
EMail: fasar@novonet.com.br
Website: http://www.fasar.edu.br/

Diretor: Eduardo Nemi Costa

Courses
Administration (Administration; Business Administration); **Education** *(Postgraduate)*; **Literature** (English; Literature; Modern Languages; Portuguese)
Degrees and Diplomas: *Bacharelado; Licenciatura; Especializa-
ção/Aperfeiçoamento*
Last Updated: 01/07/10

SANTA TERESINHA CATHOLIC FACULTY
Faculdade Católica Santa Teresinha
Rua Visitador Fernandes 78, Caico, RN 59300-000
Tel: +55(84) 3417-2316
EMail: diracad.st@fcproneves.edu.br
Website: http://www.fcproneves.edu.br/caico

Diretora: Suzanna Lago Nobre

Courses
Administration (Administration; Business Administration); **Tour-
ism**
History: Founded 2004.
Main Language(s) of Instruction: Portuguese
Degrees and Diplomas: *Bacharelado; Especialização/Aperfeiçoa-
mento*
Last Updated: 19/07/10

SANTA TEREZINHA FACULTY
Faculdade Santa Terezinha (CEST)
Avenida Casemiro Júnior 12, Anil, São Luís, Maranhão 65045180
Tel: +55(98) 3213-8000
Fax: +55(98) 3213-8040
EMail: cest@cest.com.br
Website: http://www.cest.edu.br

Diretor Geral: Expedito Alves de Melo

Courses
Law; **Nursing**; **Nutrition** (Nutrition); **Occupational Therapy**
(Occupational Therapy); **Physiotherapy** (Physical Therapy);
Speech Therapy
History: Founded 1998.
Main Language(s) of Instruction: Portuguese
Degrees and Diplomas: *Bacharelado; Especialização/Aperfeiçoa-
mento*
Last Updated: 01/07/10

SANTA TEREZINHA FACULTY

Faculdade Santa Terezinha (CEUTAG)
QNJ 17 s/n Lotes 01/05 Taguatinga, Brasília, DF 72140170
Tel: +55(61) 3475-2244
Fax: +55(61) 3475-4496
EMail: diretoria.santaterezinha@unianhanguera.edu.br

Diretor: Expedito Alves de Melo

Courses
Administration; **Education** (Education; Educational Administration; Educational and Student Counselling; Educational Psychology; Higher Education; Literature; Mathematics Education; Primary Education; Sports); **Environmental Studies** (Environmental Studies); **Fine Arts** (Fine Arts); **Information Systems** (Data Processing; Information Management); **Mathematics** (Mathematics); **Pedagogy**; **Psychology** (Clinical Psychology; Industrial and Organizational Psychology; Psychology)

History: Founded 1998.

Degrees and Diplomas: *Bacharelado*; *Licenciatura*; *Especialização/Aperfeiçoamento*
Last Updated: 01/07/10

SANTA TEREZINHA FACULTY OF EDUCATION

Faculdade de Educação Santa Terezinha
Rua Perimetral Castelo Branco, 116 - Pq Anhanguera,
Imperatriz, MA
Tel: +55(99) 2101-0880
EMail: ffest@bol.com.br
Website: http://www.fest.edu.br

Diretora: Roza Maria Soares da Silva

Courses
Economics (Economics); **Law** (Law); **Pedagogy** (Pedagogy)
History: Founded 2002.

Main Language(s) of Instruction: Portuguese

Degrees and Diplomas: *Bacharelado*; *Licenciatura*; *Especialização/Aperfeiçoamento*
Libraries: Biblioteca Roza Maria Soares da Silva
Last Updated: 03/08/10

SANTO AGOSTINHO FACULTIES

Faculdades Santo Agostinho (FASA)
Av. Universitária, s/n JK, Montes Claros, MG 39404-006
Tel: +55(38) 3690-3690
EMail: facet@santoagostinho.edu.br;
fadisa@santoagostinho.edu.br; facisa@santoagostinho.edu.br
Website: http://www.fasa.edu.br

Areas
Exact Sciences and Technology (Architecture; Automation and Control Engineering; Computer Networks; Construction Engineering; Electrical Engineering; Environmental Engineering; Information Technology; Production Engineering; Town Planning); **Health Science** (Nursing; Pharmacy); **Human Sciences** (Administration; Law; Pedagogy; Social and Community Services)

Courses
Graduate Studies (Business Administration; Cardiology; Civil Law; Cosmetology; Educational Administration; Educational Psychology; Environmental Studies; Gerontology; Health Administration; Human Resources; Law; Marketing; Music Education; Occupational Health; Pedagogy; Public Administration; Rehabilitation and Therapy; Social Policy; Town Planning; Toxicology)

Further Information: Also campus II (Av. Osmane Barbosa, 937 JK) and Campus III (Av. Donato Quintino, 90 Cidade Nova).

History: Founded 2002, the Faculties are: Faculdade de Ciências Exatas e Tecnológicas Santo Agostinho - FACET; Faculdade de Direito Santo Agostinho - FADISA; Faculdade de Ciências Sociais Aplicadas Santo Agostinho - FACISA; Instituto Superior de Educação Santo Agostinho - ISA; Faculdade de Saúde e Desenvolvimento Humano Santo Agostinho - FS (founded 2005).

Degrees and Diplomas: *Tecnólogo*; *Bacharelado*; *Licenciatura*; *Especialização/Aperfeiçoamento*. Also MBA.
Last Updated: 23/07/10

SÃO CAMILO UNIVERSITY CENTRE

Centro Universitário São Camilo (UNISC)
Avenida Nazaré 1501, Ipiranga, São Paulo, São Paulo 04263200
Tel: +55(11) 2588-4000
Fax: +55(11) 6215-2361
EMail: info@scamilo.br
Website: http://www.scamilo.edu.br

Reitor: Christian de Paul de Barchifontaine (1997-)
Tel: +55(11) 6169-4003 EMail: cpb@scamilo.br

Direitor: Antônio Celso Pasquini
Tel: +55(11) 6915-9070 EMail: cristina@saocamilo.br

International Relations: Grazia Maria Guerra
Tel: +55(11) 3861-3400, Fax: +55(11) 3861-3400
EMail: grazia@saocamilo.br

Courses
Graduate Studies *(MBA)*; **Graduate Studies** *(Espeicalização)*; **Graduate Studies** *(Mestrado)*; **Potsgraduate Studies** *(Doutorado)*; **Technical Studies** (Nursing; Radio and Television Broadcasting); **Undergraduate Studies** (Biology; Biomedicine; Business Administration; Cooking and Catering; Health Administration; Medicine; Nursing; Nutrition; Occupational Therapy; Pedagogy; Pharmacy; Philosophy; Physical Therapy; Psychology; Radiology)

Further Information: Also Ipiranga 2 and Pompéia campuses.

History: Founded 1976, acquired present status 1997.

Academic Year: February-June; August-December

Admission Requirements: Secondary school certificate and entrance examination

Fees: (Reais): 362.30-903.06

Main Language(s) of Instruction: Portuguese

Degrees and Diplomas: *Tecnólogo*; *Bacharelado*; *Licenciatura*; *Especialização/Aperfeiçoamento*; *Mestrado*: Bioethics; *Doutorado*: Bioethics;

Student Services: Canteen, Cultural centre, Handicapped facilities

Libraries: 77,000 vols, 1,257 periodicals

Publications: Cadernos - Centro Universitário São Camilo; O Mundo da Saúde *(bimonthly)*
Last Updated: 17/06/10

SÃO CAMILO UNIVERSITY CENTRE - ESPÍRITO SANTO

Centro Universitário São Camilo - Espírito Santo (SÃO CAMILO-ES)
Rua São Camilo de Léllis, 01, Paraíso, Cachoeiro de Itapemirim, ES 29304-910
Tel: +55(28) 3526-5911
EMail: sg@saocamilo-es.br
Website: http://www.saocamilo-es.br/centrouniversitario/

Reitor: João Batista Gomes de Lima

Courses
Accountancy (Accountancy); **Administration** (Administration); **Biological Sciences**; **Biological Sciences** *(Licenciatura)*; **Chemistry**; **English Literature**; **Geography** *(Licenciatura)* (Geography); **Geography** (Geography); **Graduate Studies** (Accountancy; Business Administration; Communication Studies; Educational Psychology; Environmental Management; Ethics; Geography; Gerontology; Health Administration; Higher Education; History; Human Resources; Information Technology; International Business; Law; Marine Biology; Marketing; Mathematics Education; Nursing; Nutrition; Pedagogy; Physical Education; Physical Therapy; Portuguese; Public Health; Religious Education; Software Engineering); **History** (History); **Information Systems** (Information Technology); **Law** (Law); **Mathematics** (Mathematics); **Nursing** (Nursing); **Nutrition** (Nutrition); **Pedagogy**; **Pharmacy** (Pharmacy); **Physical Education** *(Licenciatura)* (Physical Education); **Physical Education**; **Physical Therapy** (Physical Therapy); **Physics** (Physics); **Portuguese Literature**; **Psychology**; **Social Communication - Advertising** (Advertising and Publicity); **Social Communication - Journalism** (Journalism); **Technical Studies**; **Technological Studies** (Petroleum and Gas Engineering; Systems Analysis; Tourism)

Further Information: Also Campus II (IPA), Vitória Unit and Crato Training Centre.

Degrees and Diplomas: *Tecnólogo*; *Bacharelado*; *Licenciatura*; *Especialização/Aperfeiçoamento*. Also MBA.
Last Updated: 13/07/10

SÃO CARLOS FACULTY

Faculdade São Carlos (FASC)
Rua João Pessoa 59 Centro, São Bernardo do Campo,
São Paulo 09715000
Tel: 591(11) 3699-9038
Fax: 591(11) 3699-9038
EMail: vice.reitoria@uniban.br

Diretor: Milton Linhares

Courses
Accountancy (Accountancy)
Last Updated: 01/07/10

SÃO FRANCISCO DE ASSIS INSTITUTE OF HIGHER EDUCATION OF TEÓFILO OTONI

Instituto de Educação Superior São Francisco de Assis de Teófilo Otoni
Rua Antônio Onofre, 750 - Marajoara, Teófilo Otoni, MG 39803-077
Tel: +55(33) 3523-1742
EMail: iesfato@iesfato.com.br
Website: http://www.iesfato.com.br

Courses
Social Communication (Journalism); **Social Services** (Social and Community Services)
History: Founded 2004.
Main Language(s) of Instruction: Portuguese
Degrees and Diplomas: *Bacharelado*
Last Updated: 24/09/10

SÃO FRANCISCO FACULTY OF TECHNOLOGY

Faculdade de Tecnologia São Francisco (FATESF)
Av. Siqueira Campos, 1174, Centro, Jacareí, SP 12307-000
Tel: +55(12) 3955-3380
EMail: fatesf@fatesf.com.br
Website: http://www.fatesf.edu.br

Diretor: Pio Torre Flores

Courses
Administration (Administration; Transport Management); **Automation and Control Engineering** (Automation and Control Engineering); **Computer Engineering** (Computer Engineering)
Degrees and Diplomas: *Bacharelado*
Last Updated: 27/08/10

SÃO FRANCISCO FACULTY OF TECHNOLOGY

Faculdade de Tecnologia São Francisco (UNESF)
Praça Joaquim Alves de Souza n° 40 Bambé, Barra de São Francisco, 29.800-000 29800-000
Tel: +55(27) 3756-2797
EMail: secretaria@faculdadesaofrancisco.com.br
Website: http://faculdadesaofrancisco.com.br/

Diretor Geral: Jair Gomes de Souza

Courses
Business Administration (Administration; Business Administration); **Graduate Studies** (Adult Education; Art Education; Art Therapy; Biology; Business Administration; Cultural Studies; Education; Educational Administration; Educational and Student Counselling; Educational Psychology; English; Environmental Management; Environmental Studies; Geography; Health Administration; Higher Education; History; Human Resources; Literacy Education; Literature; Mathematics; Mathematics Education; Occupational Health; Philosophy; Physical Education; Portuguese; Public Administration; Public Health; Religious Education; Secretarial Studies; Social and Community Services; Sociology; Spanish; Special Education; Statistics); **Human Resources** (Human Resources); **Systems Analysis** (Systems Analysis)

Degrees and Diplomas: *Tecnólogo*; *Bacharelado*. Also Postgrafuate Diploma
Last Updated: 27/08/10

SÃO FRANCISCO INSTITUTION OF EDUCATION

Instituição de Ensino São Francisco
Av. Rodrigo Mazon 601, Bairro Guaçu PQ. Real, Mogi Guaçu, SP 13.840-000
Tel: +55(19) 3841-6405
EMail: iesf@sfrancisco.com.br
Website: http://www.sfrancisco.com.br

Diretor: Marcos Antonio

Courses
Administration (Administration); **Nursing** (Nursing); **Nutrition** (Nutrition); **Social Services** (Social and Community Services)
History: Founded 2003.
Main Language(s) of Instruction: Portuguese
Degrees and Diplomas: *Bacharelado*; *Especialização/Aperfeiçoamento*
Libraries: Yes
Last Updated: 22/09/10

SÃO GERALDO FACULTY

Faculdade São Geraldo (FSG)
Rua 13 de maio, 40, São Geraldo, Cariacica 29146-724
Tel: +55(27) 3421-9770 +55(27) 3421-9769
Fax: +55(27) 3421-9771
EMail: faculdade@saogeraldo.edu.br
Website: http://www.saogeraldo.edu.br/faculdade/index.php

Diretor: Moacir Lelis

Courses
Graduate Studies (Accountancy; Business Administration; Education; Educational Administration; Educational Psychology; Law; Public Administration; Special Education); **Undergraduate Studies** (Administration; Information Sciences; Law; Pedagogy)

Degrees and Diplomas: *Bacharelado*; *Licenciatura*; *Especialização/Aperfeiçoamento*
Last Updated: 07/09/10

SÃO JOSÉ DOS COCAIS MARANHENSE FACULTY

Faculdade Maranhense São José dos Cocais (FSJ)
Rua 01, n° 290, Loteamento Boa Vista, Timon, MA 65636-720
Tel: +55(99) 3212-5538
EMail: fsj@sjc.edu.br
Website: http://www.sjc.edu.br/

Diretor Geral: Herbert Lago

Courses
Accountancy (Accountancy); **Administration** (Administration); **Law** (Law)
History: Founded 2005.
Degrees and Diplomas: *Bacharelado*
Last Updated: 07/09/10

SÃO LEOPOLDO INSTITUTE OF MUSIC

Instituto Superior de Música de São Leopoldo (ISM)
Rua Amadeo Rossi, 467, Morro do Espelho, São Leopoldo, RS 93030-220
EMail: isaec@isaec.com.br

Courses
Music (Music)
Degrees and Diplomas: *Bacharelado*
Last Updated: 28/09/10

SÃO LEOPOLDO MANDIC FACULTY OF DENTISTRY

Faculdade de Odontologia São Leopoldo Mandic
Rua Dr. José Rocha Junqueira, 13, Ponte Preta, Campinas,
SP 13045-755
Tel: +55(19) 3211-3600
EMail: faleconosco@slmandic.edu.br
Website: http://www.slmandic.com.br

Diretor: José Luiz Cintra Junqueira

Courses
Dentistry (Dentistry)

Further Information: Also units in Unidade Belo Horizonte, Brasília, Curitiba, Fortaleza, Itapetininga, Porto Alegre, Rio de Janeiro, São Paulo, Vila Velha

History: Founded 2003.

Main Language(s) of Instruction: Portuguese

Degrees and Diplomas: *Bacharelado*; *Especialização/Aperfeiçoamento*; *Mestrado*; *Doutorado*

Libraries: Biblioteca São Leopoldo Mandic
Last Updated: 10/08/10

SÃO MARCOS FACULTY

Faculdade São Marcos (FALSM)
Rua Dr. Mário Totta 260, Vila Agritter, Alvorada, RS 94820400
Tel: +55(51) 3483-4621
Fax: +55(51) 3442-9378
EMail: faculdade@saomarcos.br
Website: http://www.saomarcos.br

Diretor: Ari Pfluck

Courses
Administration (Administration); **Human Resources** (Human Resources); **Management** (Management)

History: Founded 2000.

Degrees and Diplomas: *Bacharelado*
Last Updated: 06/07/10

SÃO MARCOS UNIVERSITY

Universidade São Marcos (UNIMARCO)
Avenida Nazaré 900, Ipiranga, São Paulo, São Paulo 4262100
Tel: +55(11) 3471-5700
EMail: info@smarcos.br
Website: http://www.smarcos.br

Reitor: Ernani Bicudo de Paula (2001-) Fax: +55(11) 6914-1384
EMail: reitoria@smarcos.br

Secretária Geral: Célia Aparecida Jussani
Tel: +55(11) 3491-0500, Fax: +55(11) 3491-0529
EMail: cjussani@smarcos.br

International Relations: Luciane de Paula Chermann
Tel: +55(11) 3491-0514, Fax: +55(11) 3491-0529
EMail: dri@smarcos.br

Courses
Accountancy (Accountancy; Business Administration); **Administration** (Administration); **Agronomy** (Agriculture; Agronomy; Animal Husbandry); **Architecture and Town Planning** (Architecture; Town Planning); **Chemical Engineering**; **Computer Engineering** (Computer Engineering; Computer Science); **Environmental Engineering** (Environmental Engineering) *Head*: Maria Therezina Monteiro; **Hotel Management** (Hotel Management); **Law** (Law); **Nursing** (Nursing); **Pedagogy** (Education; Educational Administration; Educational Sciences; Pedagogy; Preschool Education; Primary Education; Teacher Trainers Education); **Petroleum Engineering** (Petroleum and Gas Engineering); **Production Engineering** (Production Engineering); **Psychology** (Clinical Psychology; Psychology; Social Sciences) *Head*: Lucia Ghiringhello; **Social Sciences and Communication** (Advertising and Publicity; Communication Studies; Information Sciences; Journalism; Social Sciences) *Head*: Philadelpho Menezes; **Tourism** (Tourism) *Head*: Paulo Flores; **Veterinary Science** (Veterinary Science)

History: Founded 1971 as a College of Humanities. Acquired present status 1994.

Academic Year: February to December

Admission Requirements: Secondary school certificate and entrance examination

Fees: (Reais): 3,105 per semester; postgraduate, 2,560

Main Language(s) of Instruction: Portuguese

Degrees and Diplomas: *Bacharelado*: 4-5 yrs; *Licenciatura*: 3 yrs; *Especialização/Aperfeiçoamento*; *Mestrado*: a further 2 yrs; *Doutorado*

Student Services: Academic counselling, Canteen, Cultural centre, Employment services, Foreign Studies Centre, Health services, Language programs

Libraries: Biblioteca 'Laura Prestes Barra', 68,201 vols

Publications: Interações, Psychology *(biannually)*; Juridical Studies *(biannually)*; Psychê, Psychoanalysis *(biannually)*

Press or Publishing House: UniMarco Editora
Last Updated: 06/05/10

SÃO PAULO FACULTY SCHOOL OF LAW

**Faculdade Escola Paulista de Direito
(FACULDADE EPD)**
Av. Liberdade, 956, São Paulo, São Paulo 01502001
Tel: +55(11) 3277-6887
Fax: +55(11) 3277-2822
Website: http://www.facepd.com.br/

Diretor Geral: Gerson Kiste

Courses
Accountancy (Accountancy); **Administration** (Administration)

History: Founded 1994.

Main Language(s) of Instruction: Portuguese

Degrees and Diplomas: *Bacharelado*
Last Updated: 07/07/10

SÃO PAULO SCHOOL OF ECONOMICS

Escola de Economia de São Paulo (EESP)
Rua Itapeva, 474, 13° andar, Bela Vista, São Paulo, SP 01332-000
Tel: +55(11) 3799-3350
Fax: +55(11) 3799-3357
EMail: economia@fgv.br
Website: http://www.eesp.fgv.br/

Diretor: Yoshiaki Nakano

Courses
Economics; Graduate Studies

Degrees and Diplomas: *Bacharelado*; *Mestrado*; *Doutorado*. Also MBA and Post-doctorate courses.
Last Updated: 13/07/10

SÃO PAULO SCHOOL OF LAW

Escola de Direito de São Paulo (DIREITO GV)
Rua Rocha, 233, 8° andar, Bela Vista, São Paulo, SP 01330-000
Tel: +55(11) 3799-3306
Fax: +55(11) 3799-3701
EMail: direitogv@fgv.br
Website: http://www.fgv.br/direitogv/

Diretor: Ary Oswaldo Mattos Filho EMail: ary.mattos@fgv.br

Vice-Diretor Administrativo: Paulo Clarindo Goldschmidt
EMail: paulo.goldschmidt@fgv.br

Courses
Law

Degrees and Diplomas: *Bacharelado*; *Especialização/Aperfeiçoamento*; *Mestrado*
Last Updated: 13/07/10

SÃO VICENTE DE PAULA FACULTY OF NURSING

Faculdade de Enfermagem São Vicente de Paula
Av. Rio Grande do Sul - 1169 - Bairro dos Estados,
João Pessoa, PB
Tel: +55(83) 3243-7878
EMail: fesvip@fesvip.com.br
Website: http://www.fesvip.com.br

Diretor: Elzir Pontes de Miranda

Courses
Nursing (Nursing)

History: Founded 1999 as Escola de Enfermagem São Vicente de Paula (EESVP). Acquired present status and title 2006.

Main Language(s) of Instruction: Portuguese

Degrees and Diplomas: *Bacharelado*

Libraries: Yes
Last Updated: 03/08/10

SATC FACULTY

Faculdade SATC (FASATC)
Rua Pascoal Meller, 73, Universitário, Criciúma, SC 88805-380
Tel: +55(48) 3431-7500
Fax: +55(48) 3431-7501
EMail: copefa@satc.edu.br
Website: http://www.portalsatc.com/satcportal/site/educacao2.
asp?i_categoria=2&i_subcategoria=
3&area=8&secaoedu=0&titulo=%27Faculdade%20SATC%27

Courses
Graduate Studies (Business Administration; Design; Geology; Industrial Engineering; Management; Production Engineering; Public Administration; Surveying and Mapping); **Undergraduate Studies** (Automation and Control Engineering; Electrical Engineering; Graphic Design; Industrial Management; Journalism; Mechanical Engineering; Telecommunications Engineering)

Degrees and Diplomas: *Tecnólogo*; *Bacharelado*. Also Postgraduate diploma.
Last Updated: 08/09/10

SAVONITTI FACULTY

Faculdade Savonitti
Rua Miguel Cortez, 50, Tropical Shopping, Vila Melhado,
Araraquara, SP 14807-066
Tel: +55(16) 3333-7071
Fax: +55(16) 3333-7071
EMail: savonitti@savonitti.com.br
Website: http://savonitti.com.br/

Diretor Geral: Henrique Savonitti

Courses
Law (Law)

Degrees and Diplomas: *Bacharelado*
Last Updated: 08/09/10

SCHOOL OF ADMINISTRATION AND MANAGEMENT

Escola Superior de Administração e Gestão (ESAGS)
Av. Industrial, 1455, Santo André, SP 09090-030
Tel: +55(11) 4433-6161
EMail: esag@esag.edu.br
Website: http://www.esags.edu.br

Diretora: Regina Célia Alem Jorge Socolowski

Courses
Administration

Further Information: Also Unit in Santos.

History: Founded 2000.
Last Updated: 15/07/10

SCHOOL OF ADMINISTRATION OF SÃO PAULO

Escola Superior Paulista de Administração
Rua João Gonçalves, 471, Centro, Guarulhos, SP 07010-010
Tel: +55(11) 2087-7090
EMail: contato@espa.edu.br
Website: http://www.espa.edu.br

Diretor Geral: Paulo Amorim Futami

Courses
Administration; **Graduate Studies** (Accountancy; Management); **Technological Studies** (Finance; Management)

Degrees and Diplomas: *Tecnólogo*; *Bacharelado*; *Especialização/ Aperfeiçoamento*
Last Updated: 16/07/10

SCHOOL OF ADMINISTRATION, LAW AND ECONOMICS

Escola Superior de Administração, Direito e Escola Superior de Administração, Direito e Economia (ESADE)
Rua General Vitorino, 25, Porto Alegre, RS 90020-171
Tel: +55(51) 3254-1111
EMail: esade@esade.com.br
Website: http://www.esade.com.br/

Diretor Geral: Carlos A. M. Klein

Courses
Accountancy (Accountancy); **Administration** (Administration); **Economics**; **Graduate Studies** (Industrial and Organizational Psychology; International Business; Journalism; Law; Management; Sports Management; Teacher Training); **Law** (Law); **Psychology** (Psychology); **Technologial Studies**

Further Information: Also Cidade Baixa Unit.

Degrees and Diplomas: *Tecnólogo*; *Bacharelado*; *Especialização/ Aperfeiçoamento*. Also MBA.
Last Updated: 15/07/10

SCHOOL OF ADMINISTRATION, MARKETING AND COMMUNICATION OF CAMPINAS

Escola Superior de Administração, Marketing e Comunicação de Campinas (ESAMC)
Rua José Paulino 1345 Centro, Campinas, São Paulo 13013001
Tel: +55(19) 3231-0614
Fax: +55(19) 3231-0614
EMail: rosely.godoy@esamc.edu
Website: http://www.esamc.br

Presidente: Luiz Gracioso

Courses
Executive MBA (Accountancy; Business Administration; Communication Studies; Finance; Human Resources; Industrial Management; International Business; Marketing; Public Relations; Transport Management); **Graduate Studies**; **Technological Studies** (Business and Commerce; Finance; Human Resources; Management; Marketing; Transport Management)

Faculties
Commerce, Law and Communication (Accountancy; Advertising and Publicity; Business Administration; Economics; Fashion Design; Graphic Design; International Relations; Journalism; Law; Marketing; Public Relations); **Education**; **Engineering**

Further Information: Also units in Brasília, Salvador, Sao Paulo - Perdisez, Santos, Sorocaba and Uberlândia

Main Language(s) of Instruction: Portuguese

Degrees and Diplomas: *Tecnólogo*; *Bacharelado*; *Licenciatura*; *Especialização/Aperfeiçoamento*. Also MBA
Last Updated: 18/06/10

SCHOOL OF ADVANCED SCIENTIFIC STUDIES OF SANTA CASA DE MISERICÓRDIA DE VITÓRIA

Escola Superior de Ciências da Santa Casa de Misericórdia de Vitória (EMESCAM)
Avenida Nossa Senhora da Penha, Santa Luiza, Vitória,
Espirito Santo 29045402
Tel: +55(27) 3334-3509
Fax: +55(27) 3334-3509
EMail: emescam@emescam.br
Website: http://www.emescam.br

Diretor: Claudio Medina da Fonseca

Courses
Graduate Studies (Development Studies; Social Policy); **Graduate Studies** *(Lato Sensu)* (Genetics; Gerontology; Homeopathy; Medicine; Nephrology; Nursing; Nutrition; Oncology; Pharmacy; Physical Therapy; Public Health; Rehabilitation and Therapy; Social Policy; Toxicology); **Medicine** (Medicine); **Nursing**; **Pharmacy**; **Physiotherapy** (Physical Therapy); **Social Services**

History: Founded 1968.

Main Language(s) of Instruction: Portuguese

Degrees and Diplomas: *Bacharelado*; *Especialização/Aperfeiçoamento*; *Mestrado*
Last Updated: 23/06/10

SCHOOL OF AGRICULTURAL MEASUREMENT ENGINEERING

Escola de Engenharia de Agrimensura (EEA)
Avenida Joana Angélica, 1381, Nazaré, Bahia
Tel: +55(71) 2103-5922
Fax: +55(71) 3321-5694
EMail: euridez@hotmail.com
Website: http://www.eeemba.br

Diretor Presidente: Dirval Campos de Carvalho

Courses
Agricultural Engineering (Agricultural Engineering); **Graduate Studies**

Further Information: Also Brotas Unit.

History: Founded 1974.

Main Language(s) of Instruction: Portuguese

Degrees and Diplomas: *Bacharelado*; *Especialização/Aperfeiçoamento*
Last Updated: 18/06/10

SCHOOL OF AGRONOMY OF PARAGUAÇÚ PAULISTA

Escola Superior de Agronomia de Paraguaçú Paulista (ESAPP)
Rua Prefeito Jayme Monteiro, 791, Centro, Paraguaçu Paulista,
SP 19700-000
Tel: +55(18) 3361-9492
EMail: fundacao@funge.com.br
Website: http://www.funge.com.br/

Diretora: Juliana Parisotto Poletine

Courses
Agronomy (Agronomy); **Zootechnics** (Animal Husbandry)

Degrees and Diplomas: *Bacharelado*
Last Updated: 15/07/10

SCHOOL OF AMAZONIA

Escola Superior da Amazônia (ESAMAZ)
Av. José Bonifácio, 893, São Bráz, Belém, PA 66063-010
Tel: +55(91) 4005-0505
Fax: +55(91) 3259-6744
Website: http://www.esamaz.com
Diretor Geral: Luzimar Reinaldo Barros Gonçalves

Courses
Administration; **Biomedicine** (Biomedicine); **Computer Networks** (Computer Networks); **Data Processing**; **Environmental Management** (Environmental Management); **Geography** (Geography); **Graduate Studies** (Accountancy; Alternative Medicine; Business Administration; Communication Studies; Computer Networks; Computer Science; Cosmetology; Data Processing; Education; Environmental Management; Health Sciences; Higher Education; Information Technology; Literature; Neurosciences; Nursing; Physical Therapy; Rehabilitation and Therapy; Speech Therapy and Audiology); **Hospital Management** (Health Administration); **Literature**; **Logistics**; **Marketing**; **Nursing** (Nursing); **Nutrition**; **Occupational Therapy**; **Odontology** (Dentistry); **Pedagogy** (Pedagogy); **Pharmacy**; **Phonoaudiology** (Speech Therapy and Audiology); **Physical Education**; **Physical Therapy** (Physical Therapy); **Portuguese** (Portuguese); **Private Security Management** (Protective Services); **Psychology** (Psychology); **Quality Management**; **Social Sciences** (Social Sciences); **Social Services**; **Tourism** (Tourism)

Degrees and Diplomas: *Tecnólogo*; *Bacharelado*; *Licenciatura*; *Especialização/Aperfeiçoamento*. Also MBA.
Last Updated: 15/07/10

SCHOOL OF BUSINESS ADMINISTRATION OF SAO PAULO

Escola de Administração de Empresas de São Paulo (EAESP-FGV)
Avenida Nove de Julho, 2029, Bela Vista, São Paulo,
São Paulo 01313-902
Tel: +55(11) 3799-7777
Fax: +55(11) 3284-1789
EMail: midori@fgvsp.br; cavin@fgv.br
Website: http://www.fgv.br/eaesp

Diretora: Maria Tereza Leme Fleury **EMail:** mtereza.fleury@fgv.br

Courses
Business Administration (Business Administration); **Graduate Studies** *(Stricto Sensu)* (Business Administration; Public Administration); **Graduate Studies** *(Lato Sensu)*; **Public Administration** (Public Administration)

History: Founded 1963.

Main Language(s) of Instruction: Portuguese

Degrees and Diplomas: *Bacharelado*; *Especialização/Aperfeiçoamento*; *Mestrado*; *Doutorado*. Also MBA.
Last Updated: 18/06/10

SCHOOL OF BUSINESS AND COMPUTER STUDIES

Escola Superior de Estudos Empresariais e Informática (ESEEI)
Rua Jaime Reis, 531A, Alto São Franscisco, Curitibá,
Paraná 80215-170
Tel: +55(41) 4063-8220
Fax: +55(41) 4063-8220
EMail: diretoria@eseei.edu.br
Website: http://www.spet.br

Diretor Presidente: Joaquim Manoel Monteiro Vauverde

Courses
Advertising; **Data Processing** (Data Processing); **Digital Media**; **Graduate Studies** (Building Technologies; Civil Engineering; Telecommunications Engineering); **IT Infrastructure** (Information Technology); **Journalism**; **Public Relations**; **Radio and Television**; **Software Engineering** (Software Engineering)

History: Founded 1989.

Main Language(s) of Instruction: Portuguese

Degrees and Diplomas: *Bacharelado*; *Especialização/Aperfeiçoamento*. Also MBA.
Last Updated: 23/06/10

SCHOOL OF CIVIL AVIATION
Escola Superior de Aviação Civil (ESAC)
Rua Luiza Bezerra Motta, 200, Catolé, Campina Grande,
SP 58104-600
Tel: +55(83) 2101-8100
Fax: +55(83) 3337-1999
EMail: esac@cesed.br
Website: http://www.cesed.br/portal/faculdades/esac.php

Diretor: Dalton Roberto Benevides Gadelha
Tel: +55(83) 2101-8801

Courses
Aeronautical Sciences (Aeronautical and Aerospace Engineering;
Air Transport)

Degrees and Diplomas: *Bacharelado*
Last Updated: 15/07/10

SCHOOL OF CORPORATE EDUCATION
Escola Superior de Educação Corporativa (ESEC)
Rua João Grumiche, 2069, Roçado, São José, SC 88108-100
Tel: +55(48) 3258-8955
EMail: divair@gmail.com

Reitora: Divair Maria Terna Gomes

Courses
Accountancy (Accountancy); **Administration** (Administration);
Management Process - Business Administration (Business
Administration; Management); **Secretarial Studies** (Secretarial
Studies); **Social Services** (Social and Community Services)

History: Founded 2002.
Main Language(s) of Instruction: Portuguese
Degrees and Diplomas: *Tecnólogo*; *Bacharelado*
Last Updated: 14/03/11

SCHOOL OF ENGINEERING AND MANAGEMENT OF SAO PAULO
Escola Superior de Engenharia e Gestão de São Paulo (ESEG)
Rua Vergueiro, 1951, Vila Mariana, São Paulo, SP 04101-000
Tel: +55(11) 2187-1230
Fax: +55(11) 2187-1271
EMail: fale_conosco@eseg.edu.br
Website: http://www.eseg.edu.br/

Diretor Geral: João Carlos Passoni

Courses
Administration (Administration); **Graduate Studies** (Business
Administration; Finance; Information Technology); **Information
Systems**; **Production Engineering** (Production Engineering)

Further Information: Also Valinhos campus.

Degrees and Diplomas: *Bacharelado*; *Especialização/Aperfeiçoamento*
Last Updated: 16/07/10

SCHOOL OF ENVIRONMENTAL STUDIES
Escola Superior em Meio Ambiente (ESMA)
Rua 155 No 253, Bairro Bela Vista, Iguatama,
Minas Gerais 38910-000
Tel: +55(37) 3353-2222
Fax: +55(37) 3353-2110
EMail: esma@esma.edu.br
Website: http://www.esma.edu.br

Diretor Administrativo: Lucivane Lamounier Faria

Courses
Administration - Environmental Management (Administration;
Environmental Management); **Biological Sciences** (Biological and
Life Sciences); **Biomedicine** (Biomedicine)

History: Founded 1995.
Main Language(s) of Instruction: Portuguese
Degrees and Diplomas: *Bacharelado*; *Licenciatura*
Last Updated: 23/06/10

SCHOOL OF HEALTH SCIENCES
Escola Superior de Ciências da Saúde (ESCS)
SMHN Quadra 03, conjunto A, Bloco 1 Edifício Fepecs, Brasília,
DF 70710-907
EMail: escs@saude.df.gov.br
Website: http://www.escs.edu.br/

Diretor Geral: Mourad Ibrahim Belaciano (2001-)

Courses
Graduate Studies (Public Health); **Medicine**; **Nursing** (Nursing)

Degrees and Diplomas: *Bacharelado*; *Especialização/Aperfeiçoamento*
Last Updated: 16/07/10

SCHOOL OF MARKETING
Escola Superior de Marketing
Rua Benfica, 126, Madalena, PE 50720001
Tel: +55(81) 3081-0596
EMail: esm@escolademarketing.com.br
Website: http://www.escolademarketing.com.br

Diretora Acadêmica: Ana Carla Lemos de Assis
EMail: diretoria.academica@escolademarketing.com.br

Courses
Administration (Administration); **Advertising and Publicity**
(Advertising and Publicity); **Commercial Management** (Business
and Commerce); **Graduate Studies**; **Human Resources** (Human
Resources)

History: Founded 1974.
Main Language(s) of Instruction: Portuguese
Degrees and Diplomas: *Bacharelado*; *Especialização/Aperfeiçoamento*. Also MBA.
Last Updated: 23/06/10

SCHOOL OF PHYSICAL EDUCATION OF MUZAMBINHO
Escola Superior de Educação Física de Muzambinho (ESEFM)
Rua Dinah 75, Jardim Canaã, Muzambinho,
Minas Gerais 37890-000
Tel: +55(35) 3571-2205
Fax: +55(35) 3571-1155
EMail: secretaria@efmuzambinho.org.br
Website: http://www.efmuzambinho.org.br

Diretor: Ronaldo Rommel Antinori

Courses
Graduate Studies *(Lato Sensu)* (Physical Education); **Physical
Education** (Physical Education)

History: Founded 1969.
Main Language(s) of Instruction: Portuguese
Degrees and Diplomas: *Bacharelado*; *Licenciatura*; *Especialização/Aperfeiçoamento*
Last Updated: 23/06/10

SCHOOL OF PROPAGANDA AND MARKETING OF PORTO ALEGRE
Escola Superior de Propaganda e Marketing de Porto Alegre (ESPM)
Rua Guilherme Schel 350, Santo Antonio, Porto Alegre,
Rio Grande do Sul 90640-040
Tel: +55(51) 3217-1988
Fax: +55(51) 3219-1988
EMail: graduacao-rs@espm.br
Website: http://www.espm.br

Presidente: Roberto Whitaker Penteado

Courses
Administration (Administration); **Design** (Design); **Graduate Studies** (Business Administration; Business and Commerce; Finance;

Leadership; Marketing); **International Relations** (International Relations); **Social Communication - Advertising and Publicity**

Further Information: Also branches in Sao Paulo, Rio de Janeiro, Brasilia, Alphaville and Campinas

History: Founded 1999.

Main Language(s) of Instruction: Portuguese

Degrees and Diplomas: *Bacharelado*; *Especialização/Aperfeiçoamento*. Also MBA.

Last Updated: 23/06/10

SCHOOL OF PUBLIC MINISTRY

Fundação Escola Superior do Ministério Público (FMP)
Rua Coronel Genuíno, 421, 6° Andar, Porto Alegre, RS 90010-350
Tel: +55(51) 3027-6565
Fax: +55(51) 3027-6565
EMail: fmp@fmp.com.br
Website: http://www.fmp.com.br/

Diretor: Anízio Pires Gavião Filho

Courses
Graduate Studies

Faculties
Law (Law)

Degrees and Diplomas: *Bacharelado*; *Especialização/Aperfeiçoamento*
Last Updated: 16/07/10

SCHOOL OF PUBLIC RELATIONS

Escola Superior de Relações Públicas (ESURP)
Avenida Conselheiro Rosa e Silva 839/773, Aflitos, Recife, Pernambuco 52020-220
Tel: +55(81) 3427-8600
Fax: +55(81) 3427-8620
EMail: direcao@esurp.edu.br
Website: http://www.esurp.edu.br

Diretora: Maria de Fátima Serrão Schuler Vilarôco

Courses
Graduate Studies (Communication Studies; Environmental Engineering; Management; Marketing; Public Relations; Secretarial Studies); **Public Relations** (Public Relations); **Secretarial Studies** (Secretarial Studies)

History: Founded 1973

Degrees and Diplomas: *Bacharelado*; *Especialização/Aperfeiçoamento*
Last Updated: 23/06/10

SCHOOL OF SOCIAL SCIENCES

Escola Superior de Ciências Sociais (FGV/CPDOC)
Praia de Botafogo, 190, 14° andar, Botafogo, Rio de Janeiro, RJ 22253-900
Tel: +55(21) 3799-5676 +55(21) 3799-5677
Fax: +55(21) 3799-5679
EMail: faleconosco.cpdoc@fgv.br
Website: http://cpdoc.fgv.br/escs/

Coordenador: Carlos Eduardo Sarmento
EMail: carlos.sarmento@fgv.br

Courses
History (Cultural Studies; History; International Relations; Social Policy); **Social Sciences**

History: Founded 2005.

Degrees and Diplomas: *Bacharelado*; *Licenciatura*
Last Updated: 16/07/10

SCHOOL OF SOCIOLOGY AND POLITICAL SCIENCE OF SÃO PAULO FOUNDATION

Fundação Escola de Sociologia e Política de São Paulo (FESPSP)
Rua General Jardim, 522, 1° Andar, Vila Buarque, São Paulo, SP 01223-010
Tel: +55(11) 3868-6901
Fax: +55(11) 3868-6924
EMail: fespsp@fespsp.org.br; edileine@fespsp.org.br
Website: http://www.fespsp.org.br/

Diretor Geral: Waltercio Zanvettor (1996-)
Tel: +55(11) 3868-6903 EMail: waltercio@fespsp.org.br

Secretary General: Ana Flávia Guimarães
Tel: +55(11) 3123-7802, Fax: +55(11) 3123-7831
EMail: anaflavia@fespsp.org.br

International Relations: Almiro Vicente Heitor, Financial Director
Tel: +55(11) 3868-6904 EMail: almiro@fespsp.org.br

Schools
Administration (Business Administration); **Library Science and Information Sciences** (Information Sciences; Library Science); **Sociology and Politics** (Anthropology; Political Sciences; Sociology)

History: Founded 1933 as Escola de Sociologia e Política (ESP). Acquired present status 1946.

Admission Requirements: Secondary school certificate and entrance examination.

Fees: (Reais): 3,986.10 per semester

Main Language(s) of Instruction: Portuguese

Accrediting Agencies: Ministry of Education (MEC)

Degrees and Diplomas: *Bacharelado*: Sociology and Political Science; Library and Information Sciences; Administration (ESP; FaBCI; FAD); *Especialização/Aperfeiçoamento*: 18 mths

Student Services: Academic counselling, Canteen, Cultural centre, Employment services, Handicapped facilities

Special Facilities: Computer Laboratory

Libraries: Central Library

Academic Staff 2010-2011	MEN	WOMEN	TOTAL
FULL-TIME	24	47	71
STAFF WITH DOCTORATE FULL-TIME	11	14	25
Student Numbers 2010-2011			
All (Foreign Included)	388	552	940

Last Updated: 01/10/10

SCHOOL OF TECHNOLOGY AND EDUCATION OF PORTO FERREIRA

Escola Superior de Tecnologia e Educação de Porto Ferreira (ESPF)
rua Padre Nestor C. Maranhão, 40, Jd. Aeroporto, Porto Ferreira, São Paulo 13660-000
Tel: +55(19) 3585-6111 +55(19) 3589-6111
Fax: +55(19) 3585-6200
EMail: milani@unicep.com.br
Website: http://www.asser.com.br/portoferreira

Diretor: Waldomiro Bordini Racy
EMail: waldomiro.racy@yahoo.com.br

Courses
Exact Sciences (Information Sciences; Materials Engineering); **Graduate Studies**; **Human Sciences** (Administration; Pedagogy)

History: Founded 1980.

Main Language(s) of Instruction: Portuguese

Degrees and Diplomas: *Bacharelado*; *Licenciatura*; *Especialização/Aperfeiçoamento*
Last Updated: 23/06/10

SCHOOL OF TECHNOLOGY AND EDUCATION OF RIO CLARO

Escola Superior de Tecnológia e Educação de Rio Claro (ESRC)
Rua 7, 1193, Centro, Rio Claro, São Paulo 13500-200
Tel: +55(19) 3525-2945
Fax: +55(19) 3523-2001
EMail: rioclaro@asser.com.br
Website: http://www.asser.edu.br/rioclaro/index.html

Diretor: Artur Darezzo Filho

Courses
Exact Sciences; **Graduate Studies**; **Health and Biological Sciences** (Nutrition; Physical Education; Physical Therapy); **Human Sciences** (Administration; Architecture; Pedagogy; Town Planning)
History: Founded 1980.
Main Language(s) of Instruction: Portuguese
Degrees and Diplomas: *Bacharelado*; *Licenciatura*; *Especialização/Aperfeiçoamento*. Also MBA.
Last Updated: 23/06/10

SCHOOL OF THE CITY - FACULTY OF ARCHITECTURE AND URBANISM

Escola da Cidade - Faculdade de Arquitetura e Urbanismo
Rua General Jardim, 65/51, Vila Buarque, São Paulo, SP 01223-011
Tel: +55(11) 3258-8108
Fax: +55(11) 3258-8108
EMail: escoladacidade@escoladacidade.edu.br
Website: http://www.escoladacidade.edu.br

Diretor: Ciro Pirondi

Courses
Architecture and Urbanism
Degrees and Diplomas: *Bacharelado*; *Especialização/Aperfeiçoamento*
Last Updated: 13/07/10

SCHOOL OF THEOLOGY

Escola Superior de Teologia
Rua Amadeo Rossi, 467, Morro do Espelho, São Leopoldo, RS 93030-220
Tel: +55(51) 2111-1400
Fax: +55(51) 2111-1411
EMail: est@est.edu.br
Website: http://www.est.edu.br/

Reitor: Oneide Bobsin

Courses
Graduate Studies; **Musical Therapy**; **Theology** (Theology)
Degrees and Diplomas: *Bacharelado*; *Especialização/Aperfeiçoamento*; *Mestrado*; *Doutorado*
Last Updated: 16/07/10

SEAMA FACULTY

Faculdade Seama (SEAMA)
Avenida Nações Unidas 1201, Laguinho, Macapá, Amapá 68908170
Tel: +55(96) 3223-7393
Fax: +55(96) 3223-7393
EMail: seama@seama.edu.br
Website: http://www.seama.edu.br

Diretor: Carlos Edemar Scapin

Courses
Advertising (Advertising and Publicity); **Biomedicine** (Biomedicine); **Computer Networks**; **Computer Science** (Computer Science); **Information Systems** (Computer Science); **Journalism**; **Law** (Law); **Nursing** (Nursing); **Nutrition** (Nutrition); **Physiotherapy** (Physical Therapy); **Psychology**; **Public Relations** (Public Relations); **Speech Therapy** (Speech Therapy and Audiology); **Tourism**

History: Founded 2000.
Main Language(s) of Instruction: Portuguese
Degrees and Diplomas: *Bacharelado*; *Especialização/Aperfeiçoamento*
Last Updated: 01/07/10

SENA AIRES FACULTY OF SCIENCE AND EDUCATION

Faculdade de Ciências e Educação Sena Aires (FACESA)
Rua Acre Quadra 02 Lotes 17/18 Chácaras, Anhanguera, Valparaiso de Goias, Goias 72870-000
Tel: +55(61) 3627-4200
Fax: +55(61) 3627-4200
EMail: facesa@senaaires.com.br
Website: http://www.senaaires.com.br/facesa/faculdade.html

Diretor: Josias Leite de Freitas Júnior
EMail: josias@senaaires.com.br

Courses
Biomedicine; **Graduate Studies**; **Nursing** (Nursing); **Pharmacy**; **Physiotherapy**
History: Founded 2000.
Main Language(s) of Instruction: Portuguese
Degrees and Diplomas: *Bacharelado*; *Especialização/Aperfeiçoamento*
Last Updated: 02/07/10

SENAC FACULTY OF TECHNOLOGY BLUMENAU

Faculdade de Tecnologia SENAC Blumenau
Av. Brasil, 610 - Ponta Aguda, Blumenau, SC 89010-971
Tel: +55(47) 3035-9999
Fax: +55(47) 3035-9999
Website: http://sc.senac.br/open.php?outros=home&opc=010

Diretora: Elita Grosch Maba

Courses
Graduate Studies (Accountancy; Management; Marketing); **Information Technology Management** (Information Technology); **Logistics** (Transport Management); **Management** (Management); **Occupational Safety** (Safety Engineering)
Degrees and Diplomas: *Tecnólogo*. Also Postgraduate Diploma.
Last Updated: 27/08/10

SENAC FACULTY OF TECHNOLOGY CAÇADOR

Faculdade de Tecnologia SENAC Caçador
Rua Sete de Setembro, 169, Centro, Caçador, SC 89500-000
Tel: +55(49) 3563-0349
EMail: cacador@sc.senac.br
Website: http://www.sc.senac.br/open.php?outros=home&opc=023

Diretor: Fabiano Battisti Archer **EMail:** fabiano@sc.senac.br

Courses
Graduate Studies (Business Administration; Finance; Management); **Management** (Management)
Degrees and Diplomas: *Tecnólogo*; *Especialização/Aperfeiçoamento*
Last Updated: 27/08/10

SENAC FACULTY OF TECHNOLOGY CHAPECÓ

Faculdade de Tecnologia SENAC Chapecó
Rua Castro Alves, 298E, Bairro São Cristóvão, Chapecó, SC 89803-110
Tel: +55(49) 3361-5000
Fax: +55(49) 3361-5000
Website: http://www.sc.senac.br/open.php?outros=home&opc=013

Diretora: Silvana Marcon **EMail:** silvanamarcon@sc.senac.br

Courses

Graduate Studies (Information Management; Management); **Human Resources** (Human Resources); **Logistics** (Transport Management); **Management** (Management)

Last Updated: 27/08/10

SENAC FACULTY OF TECHNOLOGY DF

Faculdade de Tecnologia SENAC DF (FAC SENAC DF)
SEUP Sul, EQS 703/903 Lote A, Brasília, DF 70390-039
Tel: +55(61) 3217-8821
Website: http://www.facsenac.edu.br

Diretora Geral: Flávia Furtado Rainha Silveira
EMail: flavia.silveira@senacdf.com.br

Courses

Commercial Management (Business and Commerce); **Graduate Studies** (Business Administration; Commercial Law; Data Processing; Design; Higher Education; Human Resources; Information Management; Management; Transport Management); **Human Resources** (Human Resources); **Information Technology Management** (Information Technology); **Marketing** (Marketing)

Degrees and Diplomas: *Tecnólogo*; *Especialização/Aperfeiçoamento*. Also Posgraduate Diploma and MBA.

Last Updated: 27/08/10

SENAC FACULTY OF TECHNOLOGY FLORIANÓPOLIS

Faculdade de Tecnologia SENAC Florianópolis
Rua Silva Jardim, 360, Prainha, Florianópolis, SC 88020-200
Tel: +55(48) 3229-3200
Fax: +55(48) 3229-3200
Website: http://www.sc.senac.br/open.
php?outros=home&opc=009

Courses

Commercial Management (Business and Commerce); **Distance Postgraduate Education** (Distance Education; Educational Administration; Environmental Studies; Food Science; Information Technology; Visual Arts); **Graduate Studies** (Information Management; Management; Marketing; Transport Management); **Information Technology Management** (Information Technology); **Management** (Management)

Degrees and Diplomas: *Tecnólogo*. Also Postgraduate Diploma.

Last Updated: 27/08/10

SENAC FACULTY OF TECHNOLOGY GOIÁS

Faculdade de Tecnologia SENAC Goiás
Av. Independência, N° 1002, St. Leste Vila Nova, Goiânia, GO 74645-010
Tel: +55(62) 3524-4800
EMail: faculdadesenac@go.senac.br
Website: http://www.go.senac.br/faculdade/index.php

Diretor Geral: Lionisio Pereira dos Santos Filho
EMail: lionisio@go.senac.br

Courses

Graduate Studies *(Distance Education)* (Cultural Studies; Distance Education; Educational Administration; Environmental Studies; Food Science; Information Technology; Visual Arts); **Graduate Studies** (Business Administration; Business and Commerce; Computer Networks; Computer Science; Educational Administration; Tourism); **Undergraduate Studies** (Business and Commerce; Environmental Management; Graphic Design; Information Management; Information Technology; Tourism)

Degrees and Diplomas: *Tecnólogo*; *Especialização/Aperfeiçoamento*

Last Updated: 27/08/10

SENAC FACULTY OF TECHNOLOGY JARAGUÁ DO SUL

Faculdade de Tecnologia SENAC Jaraguá do Sul
Rua dos Imigrantes, n° 410, Vila Rau, Jaraguá do Sul, SC 89254-430
Tel: +55(47) 3275-8400
Fax: +55(47) 3275-8404
Website: http://www.sc.senac.br/open.
php?outros=home&opc=020

Diretor: Mauricio Anisio Ferreira

Courses

Graduate Studies (Management; Software Engineering); **Undergraduate Studies** (Information Technology; Management)

Degrees and Diplomas: *Tecnólogo*. Also Postgraduate Diploma.

Last Updated: 27/08/10

SENAC FACULTY OF TECHNOLOGY OF RIO GRANDE DO SUL

Faculdade de Tecnologia SENAC do Rio Grande do Sul (SENAC/RS)
Rua Coronel Genuíno, 130, Porto Alegre, RS 90010-150
Tel: +55(51) 3022-1044
EMail: fatec_poa@senacrs.com.br
Website: http://portal.senacrs.com.br/faculdades/index.asp

Diretor: Roberto Sarquis Berte **EMail:** rsberte@senacrs.com.br

Courses

Computer Networks (Computer Networks); **Fashion Design** (Fashion Design); **Financial Management** (Finance); **Graduate Studies** (Finance; Information Management); **Hotel Management** (Hotel Management); **Human Resources** (Human Resources); **Marketing** (Marketing); **Systems Analysis and Development** (Systems Analysis)

Degrees and Diplomas: *Tecnólogo*; *Especialização/Aperfeiçoamento*

Last Updated: 27/08/10

SENAC FACULTY OF TECHNOLOGY PASSO FUNDO

Faculdade de Tecnologia SENAC Passo Fundo
Av. Sete de Setembro, 1045, Passo Fundo, RS 99010-122
Tel: +55(54) 3313-4599
EMail: senacpfundo@senacrs.com.br
Website: http://portal.senacrs.com.br/faculdades/index.
asp?unidade=14

Diretora: Nara Beatriz Lopes Pires da Luz
EMail: nlpires@senacrs.com.br

Courses

Graduate Studies (Marketing; Transport Management); **Undergraduate Studies** (Systems Analysis)

Degrees and Diplomas: *Tecnólogo*; *Especialização/Aperfeiçoamento*

Last Updated: 27/08/10

SENAC FACULTY OF TECHNOLOGY PELOTAS

Faculdade de Tecnologia SENAC Pelotas (FATEC SENAC PELOTAS)
Rua Gonçalves Chaves, 602, Pelotas, RS 96015-560
Tel: +55(53) 3225-6918
EMail: fatecpelotas@senacrs.com.br
Website: http://portal.senacrs.com.br/faculdades/index.
asp?unidade=78

Diretora: Nara Beatriz Lopes Pires da Luz
EMail: nlpires@senacrs.com.br

Courses

Graduate Studies (Hotel Management; Transport Management); **Undergraduate Studies** (Computer Networks; Management; Marketing; Systems Analysis)

Degrees and Diplomas: *Tecnólogo*; *Especialização/Aperfeiçoamento*

Last Updated: 27/08/10

SENAC FACULTY OF TECHNOLOGY RIO

Faculdade de Tecnologia SENAC Rio
(FATEC SENAC RIO)
Rua Santa Luzia, 735 - 2° Andar, Centro, Rio de Janeiro, RJ
Tel: +55(21) 2517-9200 / 9268 / 9238
Fax: +55(21) 2517-9284
Website: http://fatec.rj.senac.br/

Diretora: Ana Alice Pinto

Courses

Graduate Studies (Business Administration; Distance Education; Education; Environmental Management; Graphic Design; Health Administration; Management; Software Engineering); **Undergraduate Studies** (Computer Networks; Computer Science; Graphic Design; Telecommunications Engineering; Tourism; Transport Management)

Degrees and Diplomas: *Tecnólogo*; *Especialização/Aperfeiçoamento*. Also MBA.
Last Updated: 27/08/10

SENAC FACULTY OF TECHNOLOGY SÃO MIGUEL DO OESTE

Faculdade de Tecnologia SENAC São Miguel do Oeste
Rua Sete de Setembro, 1415, Centro, São Miguel do Oeste, SC 89900-000
Tel: +55(49) 3621-0055
Website: http://www.sc.senac.br/open.php?outros=home&opc=018

Diretor: Adilson José de Almeida

Courses

Graduate Studies (Business Administration); **Undergraduate Studies** (Business and Commerce)

Degrees and Diplomas: *Tecnólogo*. Also Postgraduate Diploma.
Last Updated: 30/08/10

SENAC FACULTY OF TECHNOLOGY TUBARÃO

Faculdade de Tecnologia SENAC Tubarão
Av. Marcolino Martins Cabral, 2100, Vila Moema, Tubarão, SC 88705-000
Tel: +55(48) 3632-2428
Fax: +55(48) 3626-5831
Website: http://www.sc.senac.br/open.php?outros=home&opc=019

Diretora: Marisa Martini Ramos

Courses

Distance Education (Cultural Studies; Distance Education; Environmental Studies; Food Science; Information Technology; Tourism; Visual Arts); **Graduate Studies** (Business Administration; Information Management); **Undergraduate Studies** (Human Resources; Management)

Further Information: Also distance education programmes

Degrees and Diplomas: *Tecnólogo*; *Especialização/Aperfeiçoamento*
Last Updated: 30/08/10

SENAC MINAS FACULTY

Faculdade Senac Minas
Rua das Paineiras, 1300, Jardim Eldorado, Contagem, MG 32310-400
Tel: +55(31) 3048-9800
Fax: +55(31) 3048-9801
Website: http://www.mg.senac.br/faculdade

Courses

Graduate Studies (Accountancy; Business Administration; Educational Technology; Environmental Management; Finance; Health Administration; Hotel and Restaurant; Hotel Management; Information Technology; Management; Marketing; Public Administration; Public Health; Transport Management); **Undergraduate Studies** (Accountancy; Administration; Safety Engineering)

Further Information: Also unitsd in Araxá, Barbacena, Belo Horizonte, Contagem, Coronel Fabriciano, Governador Valadares, Guaxupé, Itabira, Juiz de Fora, Montes Claros, Oliveira, Poços de Caldas, Pouso Alegre, São Sebastião do Paraíso, Uberaba e Varginha.

History: Founded 2004.

Degrees and Diplomas: *Tecnólogo*; *Bacharelado*; *Especialização/Aperfeiçoamento*. Also MBA.
Last Updated: 08/09/10

SENAC PERNAMBUCO FACULTY

Faculdade Senac Pernambuco (SENACPE)
Av. Visconde de Suassuna, n° 500, Santo Amaro, Recife, PE 50050-540
Tel: +55(81) 3413-6655
EMail: faculdade@pe.senac.br
Website: http://www.faculdadesenacpe.edu.br/

Diretor Regional: Sylvio Romero de Souza Ribeiro

Courses

Distance Postgraduate Education (Cultural Studies; Distance Education; Educational Administration; Environmental Management; Food Science; Information Technology; Retailing and Wholesaling; Visual Arts); **Graduate Studies** (Business and Commerce; Fashion Design; Higher Education; Public Relations); **Undergraduate Studies** (Administration; Fashion Design; Hotel and Restaurant; Public Relations; Service Trades)

Degrees and Diplomas: *Tecnólogo*; *Bacharelado*; *Especialização/Aperfeiçoamento*
Last Updated: 08/09/10

SENAC RS FACULTY

Faculdade Senac RS
Rua Coronel Genuíno, 358, Centro, Porto Alegre, RS 90010-350
Tel: +55(51) 3212-4444
EMail: faculdadesenac@senacrs.com.br
Website: http://portal.senacrs.com.br/faculdades/index.asp?Unidade=65

Diretor: Roberto Sarquis Berte **EMail:** rsberte@senacrs.com.br

Courses

Distance Postgraduate Studies (Cultural Studies; Distance Education; Educational Administration; Environmental Studies; Food Science; Information Technology; Retailing and Wholesaling; Visual Arts); **Graduate Studies** (Finance; Information Management); **Undergraduate Studies** (Administration)

Degrees and Diplomas: *Bacharelado*; *Especialização/Aperfeiçoamento*
Last Updated: 08/09/10

SENAC UNIVERSITY CENTRE

Centro Universitário Senac (SENAC)
Av. Engenheiro Eusébio Stevaux, 823, Santo Amaro, São Paulo, São Paulo 04696-000
Tel: +55(11) 5682-7300
Fax: +55(11) 5682-7441
EMail: campussantoamaro@sp.senac.br
Website: http://www.sp.senac.br

Diretor: Luiz Francisco de A. Salgado

Courses

Extension; **Graduate**; **Graduate Studies** *(Stricto Sensu)*; **Graduate Studies** *(Lato Sensu)*

Further Information: Also São Paulo State Units (Campos do Jordão, Águas de São Pedro, Araraquara, Araçatuba, Barretos, Bauru, Bebedouro, Botucatu, Campinas, Catanduva, Franca, Guaratinguetá, Itapetininga, Itapira, Itu, Jaboticabal, Jaú, Jundiaí, Limeira, Marília, Mogi Guaçu, Piracicaba, Presidente Prudente, Ribeirão Preto, Rio Claro, Santos, Sorocaba, São Carlos, São José do Rio Preto, São José dos Campos, São João da Boa Vista, Taubaté, Votuporanga) and Greater São Paulo Units (24 de Maio, Consolação, Francisco Matarazzo, Guarulhos, Itaquera, Jabaquara, Lapa Faustolo, Lapa Scipião, Lapa Tito, Nove de Julho, Osasco, Penha, Santa Cecília, Santana, Santo Amaro, Santo André, Tatuapé, Tiradentes, Vila Prudente).

History: Created in 1946 as administrative commercial training centres. Previously individual faculties (Faculdade Senac de Ciências Exatas e Tecnologia; Faculdade Senac de Communicação e Artes; Faculdade Senac de Educação Ambiental; Faculdade Senac de Moda; Faculdade Senac de Turismo e Hotelaria de Águas de São Pedro; Faculdade Senac de Turismo e Hotelaria de Campos do Jordão; Faculdade Senac de Turismo e Hotelaria de São Paulo) merged to form current institution. Obtained current title and status 2004.

Academic Year: February to December

Admission Requirements: Undergraduate, Vestibular exam and High School Certificate; Postgraduate and Research Programmes, Entrance exam, interview and Undergraduate degree; Extension Programmes, Entrance exam and Undergraduate degree

Fees: (Reais): 490.00 to 1.500.00 per month

Main Language(s) of Instruction: Portuguese

International Co-operation: with universities in Canada, UK, France, Portugal, Australia, Spain. Also with European University Association

Accrediting Agencies: MEC/CAPES

Degrees and Diplomas: *Tecnólogo*: 2 yrs; *Bacharelado*: 4 yrs; *Licenciatura*; *Especialização/Aperfeiçoamento*; *Mestrado*: a further 2 yrs

Student Services: Canteen, Employment services, Foreign student adviser, Foreign Studies Centre, Language programs, Nursery care, Sports facilities

Student Residential Facilities: None

Special Facilities: Film Studio; Design Labs; Industrial Kitchens; Convention Centre

Libraries: Yes.

Publications: INTERFACEHS *(3 per annum)*
Last Updated: 17/06/10

SENAI CETIND FACULTY OF TECHNOLOGY
Faculdade de Tecnologia SENAI CETIND
Avenida Luiz Tarquínio Pontes, 938, Aracuí, Lauro de Freitas, BA 42700-000
Tel: +55(71) 3379-8201
EMail: sacsenai@fieb.org.br
Website: http://www.ead.fieb.org.br/portal_faculdades/faculdade-cetind/apresentacao-cetind.html

Gestor: Carlos Roberto Oliveira de Sousa

Courses
Graduate Studies (Communication Studies; Environmental Studies; Occupational Health; Water Management); **Undergraduate Studies** (Environmental Studies)

Degrees and Diplomas: *Tecnólogo*; *Especialização/Aperfeiçoamento*
Last Updated: 30/08/10

SENAI CIMATEC FACULTY OF TECHNOLOGY
Faculdade de Tecnologia SENAI CIMATEC
Avenida Orlando Gomes, 1845, Piatã, Salvador, BA 41650-010
Tel: +55(71) 3462-9580 +55(71) 3462-8517
EMail: miltoncruz54@hotmail.com
Website: http://ead.fieb.org.br/portal_faculdades/faculdade-cimatec/apresentacao-cimatec.html

Gestor: Leone Peter Correia da Silva Andrade

Courses
Graduate Studies (Automation and Control Engineering; Automotive Engineering; Electrical Engineering; Energy Engineering; Engineering; Heating and Refrigeration; Industrial Design; Industrial Engineering; Industrial Management; Management; Metal Techniques; Metallurgical Engineering; Polymer and Plastics Technology; Transport Management); **Undergraduate Studies** (Automotive Engineering; Electronic Engineering; Industrial Management; Management; Mechanical Engineering; Metal Techniques; Polymer and Plastics Technology; Transport Management)

Degrees and Diplomas: *Tecnólogo*; *Bacharelado*; *Especialização/ Aperfeiçoamento*; *Mestrado*. Also MBA.
Last Updated: 30/08/10

SENAI FACULTY OF ENVIRONMENTAL TECHNOLOGY
Faculdade Senai de Tecnologia Ambiental
Av. José Odorizzi, 1555, Assunção, São Bernardo do Campo, SP 09861-000
Tel: +55(11) 4109-9499
EMail: senaimarioamato@sp.senai.br
Website: http://www.sp.senai.br/meioambiente

Courses
Graduate Studies (Environmental Studies; Law); **Undergraduate Studies** (Environmental Engineering; Polymer and Plastics Technology)

Degrees and Diplomas: *Tecnólogo*. Also Postgraduate Diploma.
Last Updated: 08/09/10

SENAI FACULTY OF GRAPHIC TECHNOLOGY
Faculdade Senai de Tecnológia Gráfica
Rua Bresser 2315, Mooca, São Paulo, São Paulo 03162030
Tel: +55(11) 6097-6333
Fax: +55(11) 6097-6318
EMail: senaigrafica@sp.senai.br
Website: http://www.sp.senai.br

Diretor: Manoel Manteigas de Oliveira

Courses
Graphic Design (Graphic Design; Printing and Printmaking)
History: Founded 1997.

Degrees and Diplomas: *Tecnólogo*; *Especialização/Aperfeiçoamento*
Last Updated: 01/07/10

SENAI FACULTY OF MECHATRONIC TECHNOLOGY
Faculdade Senai de Tecnológia Mecatrônica (SENAI)
Rua Niteroi 180, Centro, São Caetano do Sul, São Paulo 09510200
Tel: +55(11) 4228-3355
Fax: +55(11) 4228-3326
EMail: senaimecatronica@sp.senai.br
Website: http://www.sp.senai.br

Diretor: Marcos Cardozo Pereira

Courses
Engineering (Automation and Control Engineering; Computer Engineering; Electronic Engineering; Engineering; Industrial Engineering; Production Engineering; Robotics)
History: Founded 1999.

Degrees and Diplomas: *Tecnólogo*; *Especialização/Aperfeiçoamento*
Last Updated: 01/07/10

SENAI FACULTY OF SAO PAULO
Faculdade Senai de São Paulo (SENAI)
Rua Anhaia 1321, Bom Retiro, São Paulo, SP 01130-000
Tel: +55(11) 3361-3787
Fax: +55(11) 3361-3787 +55(11) 3361-3212
EMail: senaivestuario@sp.senai.br; mandato@sp.senai.br
Website: http://www.sp.senai.br/vestuario

Diretor: Marcelo Costa

Courses
Clothes Production (Fashion Design); **Graduate Studies** (Fashion Design)
History: Founded 2000.

Main Language(s) of Instruction: Portuguese

Degrees and Diplomas: *Tecnólogo*; *Especialização/Aperfeiçoamento*
Last Updated: 28/09/10

SENAI FACULTY OF TECHNOLOGY ANCHIETA
Faculdade de Tecnologia SENAI Anchieta
Rua Gandavo, 550, Vila Mariana, São Paulo, SP 04023-001
Tel: +55(11) 5579-7426
EMail: senaianchieta@sp.senai.br
Website: http://www.sp.senai.br/eletronica

Courses
Graduate Studies (Design); **Undergraduate Studies** (Electronic Engineering)
Degrees and Diplomas: *Tecnólogo*. Also Postgraduate diploma.
Last Updated: 30/08/10

SENAI FACULTY OF TECHNOLOGY BLUMENAU
Faculdade de Tecnologia SENAI Blumenau
Rua São Paulo n° 1147, Victor Konder, Blumenau, SC 89012-001
Tel: +55(47) 3321-9600
EMail: blumenau@sc.senai.br
Website: http://www.sc.senai.br/siteinstitucional/servicos/unidade

Courses
Graduate Studies (Automation and Control Engineering; Communication Studies; Fashion Design; Textile Technology; Water Management); **Undergraduate Studies** (Automation and Control Engineering; Environmental Management; Mechanical Engineering; Textile Technology)
Degrees and Diplomas: *Tecnólogo*. Also Postgraduate Diploma.
Last Updated: 30/08/10

SENAI FACULTY OF TECHNOLOGY FLORIANÓPOLIS
Faculdade de Tecnologia SENAI Florianopolis
Rodovia SC 401 3730 Saco Grande, Florianópolis, Santa Catarina 88032005
Tel: +55(48) 3239-5800
Fax: +55(42) 3239-5802
EMail: ctai@ctai.rct-sc.br
Website: http://www.sc.senai.br
Diretor: João Roberto Lorenzett

Courses
Computer Networks; **Industrial Automation** (Automation and Control Engineering); **Telecommunications** (Telecommunications Engineering)
History: Founded 1998.
Main Language(s) of Instruction: Portuguese
Degrees and Diplomas: *Tecnólogo*; *Especialização/Aperfeiçoamento*
Last Updated: 08/07/10

SENAI FACULTY OF TECHNOLOGY JOINVILLE
Faculdade de Tecnologia SENAI Joinville
Rua Arno Waldemar Döhler, 957, Bairro Zona Ind. Norte, Joinville, SC 89218-155
Tel: +55(47) 3441-7600 +55(47) 3441-7700
Fax: +55(47) 3441-7740
EMail: joinville@sc.senai.br
Website: http://www.sc.senai.br/siteinstitucional/servicos/unidade/index/cidade/16/pgcursoaberto/2/

Courses
Graduate Studies (Automation and Control Engineering; Mechanical Engineering; Software Engineering); **Undergraduate Studies** (Automation and Control Engineering; Computer Networks; Industrial Management; Mechanical Engineering)
Degrees and Diplomas: *Tecnólogo*; *Especialização/Aperfeiçoamento*
Last Updated: 31/08/10

SENAI FACULTY OF TECHNOLOGY OF MANAGEMENT DEVELOPMENT
Faculdade de Tecnologia SENAI de Desenvolvimento Gerencial (FATESG)
Rua 227-A, n° 95, Setor Leste Universitário, Goiânia, GO 74610-155
Tel: +55(62) 3269-1200
Fax: +55(62) 3269-1233
EMail: fatesg.senai@sistemafieg.org.br
Website: http://www.senaigo.com.br/

Courses
Graduate Studies (Agricultural Business; Business Administration; Computer Networks; Construction Engineering; Environmental Management; Industrial Management; Information Technology; International Business; Transport Management); **Undergraduate Studies** (Computer Networks; Systems Analysis)
Degrees and Diplomas: *Tecnólogo*; *Especialização/Aperfeiçoamento*. Also MBA.
Last Updated: 31/08/10

SENAI FACULTY OF TECHNOLOGY OF PORTO ALEGRE
Faculdade de Tecnologia SENAI de Porto Alegre (FATEC SENAI)
Avenida Assis Brasil, 8450, Sarandi, Porto Alegre, RS 91140-000
Tel: +55(51) 3347-8400
EMail: faculdadesenai@senairs.org.br
Website: http://www.senairs.org.br/fatec/
Diretor: Clovis Leopoldo Reichert

Courses
Graduate Studies (Computer Networks; Construction Engineering; Energy Engineering; Environmental Management); **Undergraduate Studies** (Automation and Control Engineering; Telecommunications Engineering)
Degrees and Diplomas: *Tecnólogo*. Also Postgraduate Studies.
Last Updated: 31/08/10

SENAI-CETIQT FACULTY
Faculdade Senai-Cetiqt (SENAI-CETIQT)
Rua Dr Manoel Cotrim 195, Prédio Anexo - 6° Andar, Riachuelo, Rio de Janeiro, Rio de Janeiro 20961040
Tel: +55(21) 2582-1000
Fax: +55(21) 2241-0495
EMail: dg@cetiqt.senai.br
Website: http://www.cetiqt.senai.br
Diretor Geral: Alexandre Figueira Rodrigues

Courses
Design (Design; Fashion Design; Textile Design); **Fine Arts**; **Textile Engineering** (Textile Technology)
Further Information: Riachuelo and Barra campuses
History: Founded 1997
Main Language(s) of Instruction: Portuguese
Degrees and Diplomas: *Bacharelado*; *Licenciatura*; *Especialização/Aperfeiçoamento*
Last Updated: 01/07/10

SERRA DA MESA FACULTY
Faculdade Serra da Mesa (FASEM)
Av. JK, Qd. U5, Setor Sul II, Uruaçu, GO
Tel: +55(62) 3357-7272
EMail: secretaria@fasem.edu.br
Website: http://www.fasem.edu.br/
Diretor geral: Rodrigo Gabriel Moisés
EMail: diretoriageral@fasem.edu.br

Courses
Graduate Studies (Accountancy; Environmental Management; Finance; Higher Education; Information Technology; Management); **Undergraduate Studies** (Administration; Information Technology)

Degrees and Diplomas: *Tecnólogo*; *Bacharelado*; *Especialização/ Aperfeiçoamento*
Last Updated: 08/09/10

SERRA DO CARMO FACULTY
Faculdade Serra do Carmo (FASEC)
Quadra 103 Norte, Rua de Pedestre NO - 3, n.26, Centro, Palmas,
TO 77001-016
Tel: +55(63) 3216-6000
Fax: +55(63) 3216-6007
EMail: leandro.schneider@serradocarmo.edu.br

Courses
Undergraduate Studies (Accountancy; Administration; Law)
Degrees and Diplomas: *Bacharelado*
Last Updated: 08/09/10

SERRA DOS ORGÃOS UNIVERSITY CENTRE
Centro Universitario Serra dos Orgãos (UNIFESO)
Avenida Alberto Torres 111 Alto, Teresópolis,
Rio de Janeiro 25964000
Tel: +55(21) 2641-7000
EMail: dirger@feso.br
Website: http://www.feso.br

Reitor: Luis Eduardo Possidente Tostes (1997-)
EMail: reitor@feso.br

Courses
Accountancy (Accountancy); **Administration** (Administration); **Biological Sciences**; **Computer Science** (Computer Science); **Environmental Engineering** (Environmental Engineering); **Graduate Studies**; **Law**; **Mathematics**; **Medicine** (Medicine); **Nursing**; **Odontology** (Dentistry); **Pedagogy** (Pedagogy); **Pharmacy**; **Physical Therapy**; **Production Engineering** (Production Engineering); **Veterinary Science**

Further Information: Also Quinta do Paraíso, FESO PRO ARTE and HCTCO campuses.
History: Founded 1970.
Main Language(s) of Instruction: Portuguese
Degrees and Diplomas: *Bacharelado*; *Licenciatura*; *Especialização/Aperfeiçoamento*. Also MBA.
Last Updated: 17/06/10

SERRANA FACULTY OF HIGHER EDUCATION
Faculdade Serrana de Ensino Superior (FASEP)
Quadra 13, Área Especial Reservada, 3, Sobradinho, Brasília,
DF 73040-130
Tel: +55(61) 3487-5246
Fax: +55(61) 3487-4231
EMail: contacto@fasep.edu.br
Website: http://www.fasep.edu.br/

Diretor-Presidente: João Carlos Coelho de Medeiros

Courses
Graduate Studies *(Stricto Sensu)* (Business Administration); **Graduate Studies** *(Lato Sensu)* (Accountancy; Agricultural Business; Educational Administration; Environmental Management; Finance; Management; Mathematics Education; Public Administration; Real Estate); **Undergraduate Studies** (Accountancy; Administration; Finance)

History: Founded 2000.
Degrees and Diplomas: *Tecnólogo*; *Bacharelado*; *Especialização/ Aperfeiçoamento*; *Mestrado*. Also MBA.
Last Updated: 08/09/10

SERRANA REGIONAL FACULTY OF EDUCATION
Faculdade de Educação Regional Serrana
Br 262 Km 110 N°: s/n, Distrito de São João de Viçosa, Conceição
do Castelo, ES 29370-000
Tel: +55(28) 3546-6451
EMail: direcao@univeneto.edu.br
Website: http://www.univeneto.edu.br

Diretor: Hugo Luis de Souza

Courses
Administration (Administration); **Pedagogy**; **Social Services** (Social and Community Services)
History: Founded 2001
Main Language(s) of Instruction: Portuguese
Degrees and Diplomas: *Bacharelado*; *Licenciatura*
Last Updated: 03/08/10

SETE LAGOAS FACULTY OF MINAS GERAIS
Faculdade Sete Lagoas de Minas Gerais (FSLMG)
Rua Doutor Pena, 35, Centro, Sete Lagoas, MG 35700-032
Tel: +55(31) 3779-2700
Fax: +55(31) 3779-2700
Website: http://www.promovesetelagoas.com.br/

Courses
Undergraduate Studies (Administration; Advertising and Publicity; Environmental Management; Human Resources; Industrial Management; Transport Management)
History: Founded 2001.
Degrees and Diplomas: *Tecnólogo*; *Bacharelado*
Last Updated: 09/09/10

SEVENTH OF SEPTEMBER FACULTY
Faculdade Sete de Setembro (FA7)
Rua Alm. Maximiniano da Fonseca, 1395 - Eng. Luciano
Cavalcante, Fortazela, Ceará 60811 - 020
Tel: +55(85) 4006-7600
Fax: +55(85) 4006-7614
EMail: fa7@guy.eti.br
Website: http://www.fa7.edu.br

Diretor: Ednilton Soárez

Courses
Accountancy (Accountancy); **Administration**; **Graphic Design** (Graphic Design); **Information Systems** (Computer Science); **Law**; **Pedagogy**; **Real Estate** (Real Estate); **Social Communication** (Advertising and Publicity; Journalism)
History: Founded 2000.
Main Language(s) of Instruction: Portuguese
Degrees and Diplomas: *Bacharelado*; *Especialização/Aperfeiçoamento*
Last Updated: 30/06/10

SEVENTH OF SEPTEMBER FACULTY
Faculdade Sete de Setembro (FASETE)
Av. Vereador José Moreira, n° 1000, Centro, Paulo Afonso,
BA 48601-180
Tel: +55(75) 3501-0777
Fax: +55(75) 3501-0777
Website: http://www.fasete.edu.br/

Diretor Geral: Gilberto Gomes de Oliveira

Courses
Graduate Studies (Adult Education; Applied Linguistics; Business Administration; Education; Educational Technology; English; Environmental Management; Finance; Health Administration; Literature; Management; Marketing; Portuguese; Tourism); **Undergraduate Studies** (Administration; Information Sciences; Law; Literature; Tourism)
Degrees and Diplomas: *Bacharelado*; *Licenciatura*; *Especialização/Aperfeiçoamento*
Last Updated: 09/09/10

SEVERINO SOMBRA UNIVERSITY
Universidade Severino Sombra (USS)
Av. Expedicionário Oswaldo de Almeida Ramos, 280, Centro,
Vassouras, Rio de Janeiro 27700000
Tel: +55(24) 2471-8225
Fax: +55(24) 2471-2223
EMail: reitoria@uss.br
Website: http://www.uss.br

Reitor: José Antônio da Silva
Tel: +55(24) 2471-2223 EMail: reitor@uss.br

Centres
Exact, Technological and Natural Sciences; Health Sciences;
Philosophy, Literature and Humanities

Further Information: Also University Hospital

History: Founded 1968.

Admission Requirements: Secondary school certificate and
entrance examination

Main Language(s) of Instruction: Portuguese

Degrees and Diplomas: Bacharelado; Licenciatura; Especializa-
ção/Aperfeiçoamento; Mestrado

Student Services: Academic counselling, Canteen, Cultural centre,
Employment services, Handicapped facilities, Health services,
Nursery care, Social counselling, Sports facilities

Student Residential Facilities: For c. 30 students

Publications: Caminhos da Historia (annually); Revista do Mestrado de História (annually)
Last Updated: 06/05/10

SEVIGNE INTEGRATED FACULTIES
Faculdades Integradas Sévigné
Rua Duque de Caxias, Porto Alegre, RS 90010-283
Tel: +55(51) 3225-7499
EMail: ise@sevigne.g12.br

Diretora: Véra Fátima Dullius

Courses
Pedagogy (Pedagogy)

History: Founded 2005.

Main Language(s) of Instruction: Portuguese

Degrees and Diplomas: Licenciatura
Last Updated: 15/09/10

SILVA AND SOUZAFACULTY
Faculdade Silva e Souza (FISS)
Estrada dos Três Rios 385, Rio de Janeiro,
Rio de Janeiro 22745-004
Tel: +55(21)) 2456-2069
EMail: silvaesouza@silvaesouza.com.br
Website: http://www.silvaesouza.com.br/aspbase/cursos.asp?
secao=33452334&pagina=1

Diretor: Anley Sleiman da Costa

Courses
Architecture and Town Planning (Architecture; Town Planning);
Environmental Engineering (Environmental Engineering); Safety
Engineering (Tijuca Unit) (Safety Engineering)

History: Founded 1971.

Main Language(s) of Instruction: Portuguese

Degrees and Diplomas: Bacharelado; Especialização/Aperfeiçoa-
mento; Mestrado
Last Updated: 30/06/10

SIMONSEN INTEGRATED FACULTIES
Faculdades Integradas Simonsen (FEFIS)
Rua Ibitiuva 151, Padre Miguel, Rio de Janeiro,
Rio de Janeiro 21715400
Tel: +55(21) 2406-6464
Fax: +55(21) 2406-6464
EMail: simonsen@simonsen.br
Website: http://www.simonsen.br

Diretor Geral: Celso Murilo Menezes da Costa
Diretor Acadêmico: Cezar Di Blazio

Courses
Accountancy (Accountancy); Administration (Administration);
Geography (Geography); History (History); Law (Law); Letters
(Literature); Pedagogy (Pedagogy)

History: Founded 1971.

Main Language(s) of Instruction: Portuguese

Degrees and Diplomas: Bacharelado; Licenciatura; Especializa-
ção/Aperfeiçoamento
Last Updated: 22/06/10

SINERGIA FACULTY
Faculdade Sinergia
Av. Prefeito Cirino Adolfo Cabral, 199, Bairro São Pedro,
Navegantes, SC 88375-000
Tel: +55(47) 3342-9700
Fax: +55(47) 3342-9723
EMail: sinergia@sinergia.edu.br
Website: http://www.sinergia.edu.br

Diretor Geral: Giancarlo Moser

Courses
Graduate Studies (Educational and Student Counselling; Man-
agement); Undergraduate Studies (Accountancy; Administration;
Law; Pedagogy)

History: Founded 2001 as CESNA – Centro de Ensino Superior
Navegantes. Acquired present title 2002.

Degrees and Diplomas: Bacharelado; Licenciatura; Especializa-
ção/Aperfeiçoamento. Also MBA.
Last Updated: 09/09/10

SINOP FACULTY
Faculdade Sinop (FASIP)
Avenida Magda Cassia Pissinatti, 69, Residencial Florença, Sinop,
MT 78550-000
Tel: +55(66) 3531-1320
EMail: fasip@terra.com.br

Diretor Geral: Deivison Benedito Campos Pinto

Courses
Undergraduate Studies (Administration; Law; Tourism)

Degrees and Diplomas: Bacharelado
Last Updated: 09/09/10

SOARES DE OLIVEIRA INTEGRATED FACULTIES
Faculdades Integradas Soares de Oliveira (FISO)
Avenida Vinte e Nove 783, Térreo, Centro, Barretos,
São Paulo 14780350
Tel: +55(17) 3321-5733
Fax: +55(17) 3321-5733
EMail: fatima@soaresoliveira.br
Website: http://www.soaresoliveira.br

Diretor Geral: Milton Diniz Soares de Oliveira (1998-)
EMail: aceb@soaresoliveira.br

Faculties
Accountancy (Accountancy); Data Processing (Data Processing);
Graduate Studies (Pedagogy); Pedagogy (Pedagogy)

History: Founded 1973. Formerly known as Faculdade de Educação 'Antonio Augusto Reis Neves'.

Degrees and Diplomas: Tecnólogo; Licenciatura; Especialização/
Aperfeiçoamento

SOCIAL FACULTY OF BAHIA
Faculdade Social da Bahia (FSBA)
Av. Oceânica, n° 2717, Ondina, Salvador, BA 40170-010
Tel: +55(71) 4009-2840 +55(71) 4009-2841
Website: http://www.faculdadesocial.edu.br/

Diretor Geral: Antônio Alberto Freitas

Courses
Graduate Studies (Communication Studies; Education; Educational Psychology; Gynaecology and Obstetrics; Human Resources; Industrial and Organizational Psychology; Journalism; Management; Nursing; Physical Education; Physical Therapy; Psychology; Public Health; Rehabilitation and Therapy; Sports; Urology); **Undergraduate Studies** (Administration; Advertising and Publicity; Journalism; Law; Pedagogy; Physical Education; Physical Therapy; Psychology; Theatre; Theology)

Degrees and Diplomas: *Bacharelado*; *Licenciatura*; *Especialização/Aperfeiçoamento*. Also MBA.
Last Updated: 09/09/10

SOGIPA FACULTY OF PHYSICAL EDUCATION
Faculdade SOGIPA de Educação Física
Rua Barão do Cotegipe, 400, Porto Alegre, RS 90154-020
Tel: +55(51) 3325-7381 +55(51) 3326-1811
EMail: faculdade@faculdadesogipa.edu.br
Website: http://www.faculdadesogipa.edu.br/

Diretor Administrativo: Milton Sonza Dri

Courses
Graduate Studies (Sports; Sports Management); **Physical Education** (Physical Education)

Degrees and Diplomas: *Bacharelado*; *Especialização/Aperfeiçoamento*
Last Updated: 09/09/10

SOUTH AMERICA FACULTY
Faculdade Sudamérica
Avenida Eudaldo Lessa, n° 627, Popular, Cataguases, MG
Tel: +55(32) 3422-7879
Fax: +55(32) 3422-7879
EMail: contato@sudamerica.edu.br
Website: http://www.sudamerica.edu.br/

Diretor Geral: Alcino Leite Antonucci

Courses
Undergraduate Studies (Accountancy; Law; Physical Education; Physical Therapy)

History: Founded 1999.

Degrees and Diplomas: *Bacharelado*; *Licenciatura*
Last Updated: 09/09/10

SOUTH AMERICAN FACULTY
Faculdade Sul-Americana (FASAM)
BR 153, Km 502, Jardim da Luz, Goiânia, GO 74850-370
Tel: +55(62) 3219-4000 +55(62) 3219-4001
Fax: +55(62) 3219-4009
Website: http://www.fasam.edu.br/

Diretora Geral: Milena Silveira Saraiva Maldonado

Courses
Graduate Studies (Higher Education); **Undergraduate Studies** (Administration; Advertising and Publicity; Information Sciences; Journalism; Law; Pedagogy; Public Relations)

History: Founded 2001.

Degrees and Diplomas: *Bacharelado*; *Licenciatura*; *Especialização/Aperfeiçoamento*
Last Updated: 09/09/10

SOUTH FLUMINENSE FACULTY
Faculdade Sul Fluminense (FASF)
Rua Alberto Rodrigues, 39, Jardim Amália I, Volta Redonda, RJ 27251-220
Tel: +55(24) 3337-8001
EMail: fasf@colegioict.com.br
Website: http://www.fasfsul.edu.br/

Diretor Geral: Claudio A. Menchise
EMail: claudio@colegioict.com.br

Courses
Graduate Studies (Administration; Business Administration; Higher Education; Human Resources; Management; Marketing; Safety Engineering; Transport Management); **Undergraduate Studies** (Administration; Electronic Engineering; Human Resources; Industrial Management; Transport Management)

Degrees and Diplomas: *Tecnólogo*; *Bacharelado*. Also Postgraduate diploma and MBA.
Last Updated: 09/09/10

SOUTHERN FACULTY
Faculdade Meridional
Rua Senador Pinheiro 304, Passo Fundo, RS 99070-220
Tel: +55(54) 3045-6100
EMail: imed@imed.edu.br
Website: http://www.imed.edu.br

Diretor: Eduardo Capellari

Courses
Administration (Administration); **Architecture and Town Planning** (Architecture; Town Planning); **Dentistry** (Dentistry); **Information Systems** (Computer Science); **Law** (Law); **Psychology** (Psychology)

History: Founded 2004.

Main Language(s) of Instruction: Portuguese

Degrees and Diplomas: *Bacharelado*; *Especialização/Aperfeiçoamento*; *Mestrado*
Last Updated: 03/09/10

SOUTHERN METHODIST EDUCATION NETWORK
Rede Metodista de Educação do Sul
Rua Coronel Joaquim Pedro Salgado 80, Terréo Rio Brabco, Rio Branco, Porto Alegre, Rio Grande do Sul 90420060
Tel: +55(51) 3331-3000
Fax: +55(51) 3316-1272
EMail: direcaogeral@ipametodista.edu.br
Website: http://www.metodistadosul.edu.br

Diretora: Carolina Reschke Fulcher (1990-)

Faculties
Health Sciences *(FCS - IPA)* (Health Sciences); **Law** *(FADIPA)* (Law)

History: Founded 1971

Degrees and Diplomas: *Bacharelado*; *Especialização/Aperfeiçoamento*; *Mestrado*

SOUZA MARQUES FACULTIES
Faculdades Souza Marques
Avenida Ernani Cardoso 335/345 Cascadura, Rio de Janeiro, Rio de Janeiro 21310310
Tel: +55(21) 2128-4900
Fax: +55(21) 350-5981
EMail: ftesm@ism.com.br
Website: http://www.souzamarques.br/2006/index.php

Diretor: Francisco Michel

Courses
Accountancy (Accountancy); **Administration** *(FCCASM)* (Accountancy; Administration); **Biology** (Biology); **Chemistry** (Chemistry); **Civil Engineering**; **Letters** (Literature); **Mechanical Engineering** (Mechanical Engineering); **Nursing** *(EESM)* (Nursing); **Pedagogy**

Schools
Medicine *(EMSM)* (Medicine)

History: Founded 1985.

Degrees and Diplomas: *Bacharelado*; *Licenciatura*; *Especialização/Aperfeiçoamento*
Last Updated: 18/06/10

SPEI FACULTIES
Faculdades SPEI
Alaémeda DR. Carlos de Carvalho 256, Centro, Curitibá,
Paraná 80410180
Tel: +55(41) 3321-3131
Fax: +55(41) 3321-3131
EMail: spei@spei.br
Website: http://www.spei.br

Presidente: Ailton Renato Dörl

Courses
Accountancy; **Administration**; **Computer Science**
History: Founded 1983
Main Language(s) of Instruction: Portuguese
Degrees and Diplomas: *Tecnólogo*; *Bacharelado*; *Especialização/ Aperfeiçoamento*
Last Updated: 18/06/10

ST. AUGUSTINE INSTITUTE OF EDUCATION OF TERESINA
Instituto Superior de Educação Santo Agostinho de Teresina (ISA)
Avenida Valter Alencar, 665, Sao Pedro, Teresina, PI 64019-625
Tel: +55(86) 3215-8700
EMail: reccursos@fsanet.com.br
Website: http://www.fsanet.com.br/

Courses
Pedagogy (Pedagogy); **Teacher Training** (Teacher Training)
Degrees and Diplomas: *Licenciatura*
Last Updated: 28/09/10

STELLA MARIS CATHOLIC FACULTY
Faculdade Católica Stella Maris
Avenida Antonio Justo, 3.180, Fortaleza, CE 60165-090
Tel: +55(85) 4008-4455
EMail: catolicafortaleza@catolicafortaleza.com.br

Diretor: Claudio Pimentel da Silva

Courses
Accountancy (Accountancy); **Administration** (Administration); **International Relations**
History: Founded 2005.
Main Language(s) of Instruction: Portuguese
Degrees and Diplomas: *Bacharelado*
Last Updated: 19/07/10

STELLA MARIS INTEGRATED FACULTIES OF ANDRADINA
Faculdades Integradas Stella Maris de Andradina (FISMA)
Rua Amazonas 571, Stella Maris, Andradina, São Paulo 16901-160
Tel: +55(18) 3702-3702
Fax: +55(18) 3702-3702
EMail: fisma@fea.br
Website: http://www.fea.br/FISMA/graduacao.htm

Diretora: Cristina Lacerda Soares Petrarolha Silva
EMail: petrarolha@fea.br

Courses
Biotechnology (Biotechnology); **Physical Education** (Physical Education); **Systems Analysis** (Data Processing; Systems Analysis); **Veterinary Science**
History: Founded 1977
Main Language(s) of Instruction: Portuguese
Degrees and Diplomas: *Bacharelado*; *Especialização/Aperfeiçoamento*
Last Updated: 22/06/10

STUDENT HOUSE FACULTY
Faculdade Casa do Estudante
Rua Mário Pimentel Rocha, 213, Bairro Nova Aracruz, Aracruz
Tel: +55(27) 3256-2319
EMail: facefaculdade@terra.com.br
Website: http://facefaculdade.com.br/site

Diretor: Antônio Eugênio Cunha

Courses
Administration (Administration); **Law** (Law)
Main Language(s) of Instruction: Portuguese
Degrees and Diplomas: *Bacharelado*; *Especialização/Aperfeiçoamento*
Libraries: Yes
Last Updated: 16/07/10

SUMARÉ FACULTY
Faculdade Sumaré (ISES)
1121 Rua Capote Valente, Sumaré, São Paulo, São Paulo 5409003
Tel: +55(11) 3061-7999
Fax: +55(11) 3061-7999
EMail: facsumare@ises.com.br
Website: http://www.facsumare.com.br

Diretor: João Paulo dos Santos Netto

Courses
Accountancy; **Administration** (Administration); **Computer Science**; **Information Systems** (Computer Science); **Secretarial Studies** (Secretarial Studies)
History: Founded 1999.
Main Language(s) of Instruction: Portuguese
Degrees and Diplomas: *Bacharelado*; *Licenciatura*; *Especialização/Aperfeiçoamento*; *Mestrado*
Last Updated: 29/06/10

TÁHIRIH FACULTY
Faculdade Táhirih (FT)
Rua Leonora Armstrong, n°09, Bloco A, São José IV, Manaus, AM 69084-598
Tel: +55(92) 3249-9500 +55(92) 3249-9503
Fax: +55(92) 3648-5545
EMail: adcam@adcam.org.br
Website: http://www.adcam.org.br/?pg=facu_tahirih

Diretora: Suzan Sami Ramos

Courses
Undergraduate Studies (Administration; Pedagogy; Social and Community Services)
History: Founded 2002.
Degrees and Diplomas: *Bacharelado*; *Licenciatura*
Last Updated: 09/09/10

TAMANDARÉ FACULTY
Faculdade Tamandaré (FAT)
Rua T-27 N° 1374, Setor Bueno, Goiânia, GO 74210-030
Tel: +55(62) 3946-2248
Fax: +55(62) 3946-2248
Website: http://www.faculdadetamandare.com/

Diretor administrativo: Augusto Cezar Casseb

Courses
Undergraduate Studies (Administration; Computer Engineering; Computer Science; Marketing; Physical Therapy; Sales Techniques)
Degrees and Diplomas: *Bacharelado*
Last Updated: 09/09/10

TANCREDO NEVES FACULTY
Faculdade Tancredo Neves (FTN)
Avenida Divino Salvador 856/876, Moema, São Paulo,
São Paulo 04078013
Tel: +55(11) 5052-4600
Fax: +55(11) 5052-3881
EMail: tancredo@tancredo.br

Diretora: Lígia Maria Venturelli Fioravante

Courses
Administration; Computer Science; International Relations; Systems Analysis
History: Founded 1999.
Main Language(s) of Instruction: Portuguese
Degrees and Diplomas: *Bacharelado*
Last Updated: 29/06/10

TAPAJOS FACULTY
Faculdade Tapajós
Av. Transamazônica, 479, Bela Vista, Itaituba, PA 68180-230
Tel: +55(93) 3518-2519
EMail: sertfat@bol.com.br
Website: http://www.fatfaculdade.com.br

Diretor: Jadir Emilio Fank

Courses
Accountancy (Accountancy); **Administration** (Administration)
History: Founded 2005.
Main Language(s) of Instruction: Portuguese
Degrees and Diplomas: *Bacharelado*
Libraries: Yes
Last Updated: 23/09/10

TEACHING AND RESEARCH CENTRE OF MACHADO
Centro Superior de Ensino e Pesquisa de Machado (CESEP)
Av Dr Athayde Pereira de Souza 730, Machado,
Minas Gerais 37750-000
Tel: +55(35) 3295-9500
Fax: +55(35) 3295-9540
EMail: secretaria@fem.com.br
Website: http://www.fem.com.br

Diretora: Sônia Regina Alvim Negreti

Courses
Accountancy; Agronomy (Agronomy); **Biology** (Biology); **Computer Networks** (Computer Networks); **Environmental Management** (Environmental Management); **Geography; History** (History); **Literature; Marketing** (Marketing); **Mathematics** (Mathematics); **Nursing** (Nursing); **Nutrition; Pedagogy; Physical Education** (Physical Education); **Social Services**
History: Founded 1968.
Degrees and Diplomas: *Tecnólogo; Bacharelado; Licenciatura*
Last Updated: 19/05/10

TECBRASIL FACULTY OF TECHNOLOGY
Faculdade de Tecnologia Tecbrasil
Rua Gustavo Ramos Sehbe N°107, Cinquentenário, Caxias do Sul,
RS 95012-669
Tel: +55(54) 3027-1300
EMail: claudio@ftec.com.br
Website: http://www.ftec.com.br

Diretor: Claudino José Meneguzzi Júnior

Courses
Computer Engineering (Computer Engineering); **Production Engineering** (Production Engineering)
Further Information: Also branches in Bento Gonçalves, Porto Alegre and Novo Hamburgo
History: Founded 2002.
Main Language(s) of Instruction: Portuguese

Degrees and Diplomas: *Bacharelado; Especialização/Aperfeiçoamento*
Last Updated: 20/09/10

TECHNOLOGICAL FACULTY OF COMMERCE
Faculdade de Tecnologia do Comércio (FATEC-COMERCIO)
Avenida João Pinheiro 515, Funcionários, Belo Horizonte,
MG 30130-180
Tel: +(31) 3249-1839
Fax: +(31) 3249-1835
EMail: alexandre.franca@fateccomercio.edu.br
Website: http://www.fateccomercio.edu.br/

Diretor Geral: Salvador Ohana

Courses
Distance Education (Business and Commerce; Management; Mathematics; Safety Engineering; Sales Techniques; Small Business); **Financial Management** (Finance); **Graduate Studies** (Accountancy; Administration; Business and Commerce; Computer Science; Finance; Human Resources; Marketing; Transport Management); **Human Resources** (Human Resources); **Logistics** (Transport Management); **Marketing** (Marketing)
Degrees and Diplomas: *Tecnólogo; Especialização/Aperfeiçoamento*
Last Updated: 23/08/10

TECHNOLOGICAL INSTITUTE OF APPLIED SOCIAL AND HEALTH SCIENCES OF THE OUR LADY HELP EDUCATIONAL CENTRE
Instituto Tecnológico e das Ciências Sociais Aplicadas e da Saúde do Centro Educ. N. Sr♀ Auxiliadora (ITCSAS/CENSA)
Rua Salvador Correa, 139, Centro, Campos dos Goytacazes,
RJ 28035-310
Tel: +55(22) 2726-2727
Fax: +55(22) 2726-2720
EMail: ise-censa@censanet.com.br
Website: http://www.isecensa.edu.br/

Diretora Geral: Suraya Benjamin Chaloub

Courses
Undergraduate Studies (Administration; Architecture; Mechanical Engineering; Nursing; Physical Education; Physical Therapy; Production Engineering; Psychology)
Degrees and Diplomas: *Bacharelado; Licenciatura*
Last Updated: 29/09/10

TECHNOLOGICAL INSTITUTE OF CARATINGA
Instituto Tecnológico de Caratinga (ITC)
Praça Cesário Alvim, 110, 5° andar, Centro, Caratinga,
MG 35300-036
Tel: +55(33) 3322-6321 +55(33) 3322-6322 +55(33) 9912-9787
Fax: +55(33) 3321-7559
EMail: diretoria@doctum.edu.br
Website: http://www.doctum.com.br/

Courses
Undergraduate Studies (Civil Engineering; Electrical Engineering)
Degrees and Diplomas: *Bacharelado*
Last Updated: 29/09/10

TECSOMA FACULTIES
Faculdades Tecsoma (FATEC)
Rua Orlando Ulhoa Batista 380 A, Vila Alvorada, Paracatu,
Minas Gerais 38600000
Tel: +55(38) 3671-5827
Fax: +55(38) 3671-5827
EMail: tecsoma@tecsoma.br
Website: http://www.tecsoma.br

Diretor Geral: Nidelson Teixeira Falcão

Courses

Administration; **Biology**; **Literature** (Literature); **Nursing** (Nursing); **Physiotherapy** (Physical Therapy)

History: Founded 1999.

Main Language(s) of Instruction: Portuguese

Degrees and Diplomas: *Bacharelado*

Last Updated: 18/06/10

TERESA MARTIN INTEGRATED FACULTIES

Faculdades Integradas Teresa Martin (FATEMA)
Rua Antonieta Leitão 129, Freguesia do Ô, São Paulo,
São Paulo 02925160
Tel: +55(11) 3931-2755
Fax: +55(11) 3931-2755
EMail: fatema@fatema.br
Website: http://www.fatema.br

Diretora: Helyett Melantonio

Courses

Administration; **Biology** (Biology); **Computer Networks**; **Computer Science** (Computer Science); **Geography** (Geography); **History** (History); **Law**; **Letters** (Arts and Humanities; Literature); **Mathematics** (Mathematics); **Pedagogy**

History: Founded 1999.

Main Language(s) of Instruction: Portuguese

Degrees and Diplomas: *Bacharelado*; *Licenciatura*

Last Updated: 21/06/10

TERESA OF AVILA INTEGRATED FACULTIES - LORENA

Faculdades Integradas Teresa d'Avila - Lorena (FATEA)
Avenida Peixoto de Castro 539, Vila Celeste, Lorena,
São Paulo 12606580
Tel: +55(12) 2124-2888 +55(12) 21242-830
Fax: +55(12) 3153-2688
EMail: secretaria-fatea@fatea.br
Website: http://www.fatea.br

Diretora: Olga de Sá EMail: olgasa@fatea.br

Courses

Administration (Administration; Advertising and Publicity; Business Administration; Finance; Human Resources; Public Relations); **Art Education** (Art Education; Fine Arts); **Biology** (Biology); **Computer Science** (Computer Science); **Decoration** (Interior Design); **Industrial Design**; **Letters** (Literature); **Library Science** (Library Science); **Nursing** (Nursing); **Pedagogy** (Pedagogy); **Social Communication**; **Speech Therapy**

Programmes
Home Economics

History: Founded 1975

Main Language(s) of Instruction: Portuguese

Degrees and Diplomas: *Bacharelado*; *Especialização/Aperfeiçoamento*

Last Updated: 21/06/10

TERRA NORDESTE FACULTY

Faculdade Terra Nordeste
Coronel Correia, 1119, Soledade, Caucaia, CE 61600-000
Tel: +55(85) 3299-2829
EMail: fatene@fatene.edu.br
Website: http://www.fatene.edu.br/

Courses

Undergraduate Studies (Nursing; Physical Education; Social and Community Services)

Degrees and Diplomas: *Bacharelado*

Last Updated: 09/09/10

THATHI FACULTIES

Faculdades Thathi
Avenida Joaquim Pompeu de Toledo 75, Araçatuba,
São Paulo 16015640
Tel: +55(2118) 623-6014
Fax: +55(2118) 623-6014
EMail: faculdadesthathi@coc.com.br
Website: http://www.faculdadesthathi.com.br/

Diretor: Luiz Antônio Rodrigues Martinez

Courses

Administration (Administration); **Computer Engineering** (Computer Engineering); **Computer Science**

History: Founded 1999.

Main Language(s) of Instruction: Portuguese

Degrees and Diplomas: *Bacharelado*: 4 yrs

Last Updated: 26/09/07

THEREZA PORTO MARQUES FACULTY OF EDUCATION

Faculdade de Educação Thereza Porto Marques (FAETEC)
Rua São Sebastião 25, Centro, Jacarei, São Paulo 12308320
Tel: +55(12) 3954-4231
Fax: +55(12) 3952-4231
EMail: secfac@faetec.br; roberto@faetec.br
Website: http://www.faetec.br

Diretora: Thereza Porto Marques (1985-)

Courses

Education (Literature; Pedagogy; Portuguese; Visual Arts); **Graduate Studies** (Educational Administration; Educational Psychology; Special Education)

History: Founded 1988

Main Language(s) of Instruction: Portuguese

Degrees and Diplomas: *Licenciatura*; *Especialização/Aperfeiçoamento*

Libraries: Ludmila Saharovsky Library

Last Updated: 07/07/10

THEREZA PORTO MARQUES FACULTY OF TECHNOLOGY

Faculdade de Tecnologia Thereza Porto Marques (FAETEC)
Rua São Sebastião 25, Centro, Jacarei, São Paulo 12308320
Tel: +55(12) 352-4231
Fax: +55(12) 352-4231
EMail: roberto@faetec.br
Website: http://www.faetec.br

Diretora: Thereza Porto Marques (1993-)

Courses
Technology

History: Founded 1988.

Main Language(s) of Instruction: Portuguese

Degrees and Diplomas: *Tecnólogo*; *Licenciatura*; *Especialização/ Aperfeiçoamento*

Last Updated: 08/07/10

THOMAS CRUZ INSTITUTE OF MAIRIPORÃ

Instituto Mairiporã Thomas Cruz (IMENSU)
Av. Dr. Thomaz Rodrigues da Cruz, 1113, Mairiporã, SP 07600-000
Tel: +55(11) 4604-2999
Fax: +55(11) 4604-2999
EMail: iim@im.br
Website: http://www.im.br

Diretor: Thomaz Melo Cruz (1997-)

Faculties

Administration (Administration); **Information Systems**; **Literature**; **Physical Education** (Physical Education)

History: Founded 1963.

Main Language(s) of Instruction: Portuguese
Degrees and Diplomas: *Bacharelado*; *Licenciatura*
Last Updated: 15/06/10

TIBIRIÇÁ INTEGRATED FACULTIES
Faculdades Integradas Tibiriçá (FIT)
Rua Líbero Badaró, 616 (Prédio 1) Centro, São Paulo,
São Paulo 01029010
Tel: +55(11) 3105-5155
Fax: +55(11) 3105-5155
EMail: fati@fati.br
Website: http://www.fati.br

Diretor: Davi Chermann

Courses
Accountancy; **Administration**; **Computer Science** (Computer Science); **Foreign Trade** (Business and Commerce); **Literature** (Literature); **Pedagogy**

History: Founded 2000.

Degrees and Diplomas: *Bacharelado*; *Especialização/Aperfeiçoamento*
Last Updated: 14/11/07

TIJUCUSSU FACULTY
Faculdade Tijucussu
Rua Martim Francisco, 488, Santa Paula, São Caetano do Sul,
SP 09541-330
Tel: +55(11) 4224-9490
EMail: secretaria@factijucussu.edu.br
Website: http://www.factijucussu.edu.br/

Diretor Geral: Alvaro Barbosa Da Silva Junior

Courses
Undergraduate Studies (Accountancy; Administration; Dance; Law; Literature; Pedagogy; Social and Community Services)

History: Founded 1997 as Colégio Tijucussu Pueri Domus Escolas Associadas. Acquired present status and title 2002.

Degrees and Diplomas: *Bacharelado*; *Licenciatura*
Last Updated: 21/09/10

TIRADENTES INTEGRATED FACULTY
Faculdade Integrada Tiradentes (FITS)
Av. Comendador Gustavo Paiva, 5017, Cruz das Almas, Maceió,
AL 57031-530
Tel: +55(82) 3311-3100
EMail: dario_arcanjo@fits.edu.br
Website: http://www.fits.edu.br/

Courses
Graduate Studies (Accountancy; Acupuncture; Business Administration; Civil Engineering; Civil Law; Finance; Health Administration; Information Technology; Law; Management; Physical Education; Physical Therapy; Physiology; Psychiatry and Mental Health; Public Administration; Safety Engineering; Transport and Communications; Transport Management); **Undergraduate Studies** (Accountancy; Administration; Advertising and Publicity; Biological and Life Sciences; Biomedicine; Finance; Human Resources; Information Technology; Journalism; Law; Nursing; Physical Therapy; Psychology; Public Administration; Social and Community Services)

History: Founded 2006.

Degrees and Diplomas: *Tecnólogo*; *Bacharelado*; *Licenciatura*; *Especialização/Aperfeiçoamento*. Also MBA.
Last Updated: 02/09/10

TIRADENTES UNIVERSITY
Universidade Tiradentes (UNIT)
Avenida Murilo Dantas 300, Farolândia, Aracaju, Sergipe 49032490
Tel: +55(79) 3218-2100
Fax: +55(79) 3218-2111
EMail: reitoria@unit.br
Website: http://www.unit.br

Reitor: Jouberto Uchôa de Mendonça (1994-)

Centres
Administration (Administration; Business Administration; Human Resources; Marketing; Systems Analysis)

Programmes
Biological and Health Sciences (Biological and Life Sciences; Biomedicine; Dentistry; Health Sciences; Nursing; Pharmacy; Psychology); **Computer Sciences** (Computer Science; Information Management; Robotics); **Economics and Accountancy** (Accountancy; Economics; Finance; Industrial and Production Economics; Management); **Education and Vocational Studies** (Education; Geography; History; Physical Education; Vocational Education); **Law** (Law); **Letters** (Arts and Humanities); **Mathematics and Statistics** (Mathematics; Statistics); **Social Communication** (Advertising and Publicity; Communication Studies; Journalism; Public Relations); **Social Sciences** (Social Sciences; Tourism); **Technology and Arts** (Architecture; Design; Fine Arts; Technology; Town Planning)

History: Founded 1972, acquired present status 1994.

Academic Year: February to December (February-June; August-December)

Main Language(s) of Instruction: Portuguese

Degrees and Diplomas: *Bacharelado*: 4-5 yrs; *Licenciatura*: 3-4 yrs; *Especialização/Aperfeiçoamento*: 1yr; *Mestrado*: 2-3 yrs

Student Residential Facilities: For c. 6,380 students

Special Facilities: Memorial of Sergipe Museum. Institute of Technology and Research. Central Biomedical Laboratory. Health and Education Centre

Libraries: Jacinto Uchôa Library, c. 139,000 vols

Publications: Fragmenta *(bimonthly)*
Last Updated: 19/01/07

TOBIAS BARRETO FACULTY
Faculdade Tobias Barreto (FTB)
Rua Riachuelo, 1071, São José, Aracaju, SE
Tel: +55(79) 3217-3073
Fax: +55(79) 3217-3073
Website: http://www.ftb-se.edu.br/

Diretor Geral: João Severo Filho **EMail:** diretoria@ftb-se.edu.br

Courses
Graduate Studies (Accountancy; Construction Engineering; Education; Higher Education; History; Industrial Design; Information Technology; Linguistics; Literature; Management; Marketing; Transport Management); **Undergraduate Studies** (Administration; Literature; Portuguese)

Degrees and Diplomas: *Bacharelado*; *Licenciatura*. Also Postgraduate diploma and MBA.
Last Updated: 21/09/10

TOLEDO INSTITUTION OF EDUCATION
Instituição Toledo de Ensino
Praça Nove de Julho 1-51, Térreo, Vila Pacifico, Bauru,
São Paulo 17050790
Tel: +55(14) 2107-5000
EMail: ite@ite.com.br
Website: http://www.ite.edu.br

Diretor: José Roberto Martins Segalla

Courses
Accountancy (Accountancy); **Administration** (Administration; Business Administration); **Aeronautics** (Aeronautical and Aerospace Engineering); **Economics** (Economics); **Law** (Law); **Social Services** (Social and Community Services)

Further Information: Also branches in Botucatu and Ibitinga

History: Founded 1950 as Escola Técnica de Bauru.

Main Language(s) of Instruction: Portuguese

Degrees and Diplomas: *Bacharelado*; *Especialização/Aperfeiçoamento*; *Mestrado*; *Doutorado*
Last Updated: 17/06/10

TOLEDO UNIVERSITY CENTRE
Centro Universitario Toledo
Rua Antônio Afonso de Toledo, 595, Araçatuba,
São Paulo 16015-270
Tel: +55(18) 3636-7000
EMail: secretariageral@toledo.br
Website: http://www.toledo.br

Diretor Geral: Bruno Roberto Pereira de Toledo (2006-)

Areas
Commerce (Accountancy; Administration; Human Resources); **Communication and Design**; **Education** (English; History; Literature; Pedagogy; Portuguese; Spanish); **Health Sciences** (Nutrition; Physical Education); **Humanities** (Law); **Technology** (Information Technology)

Courses
Graduate Studies (Accountancy; Administration; Administrative Law; Advertising and Publicity; Agricultural Business; Business Administration; Business and Commerce; Civil Law; Commercial Law; E-Business/Commerce; Educational Psychology; Finance; Health Sciences; Higher Education; Human Resources; Industrial and Organizational Psychology; Labour Law; Literacy Education; Literature; Marketing; Nutrition; Physical Education; Physiology; Portuguese; Preschool Education; Special Education; Transport Management); **Graduate Studies** *(Mestrado)* (Law)

History: Founded 1966 as Faculdade de Filosofia, Ciências e Letras de Araçatuba. Acquired present status and title 2004.

Main Language(s) of Instruction: Portuguese

Degrees and Diplomas: *Bacharelado*; *Licenciatura*; *Especialização/Aperfeiçoamento*; *Mestrado*: Law. Also MBA
Last Updated: 17/06/10

TORRICELLI INTEGRATED FACULTIES
Faculdades Integradas Torricelli
Rua do Rosário 300, Centro, Guarulhos, São Paulo 7110-080
Tel: +55(11) 2107-1900
Website: http://www.torricelli.edu.br/

Diretor Geral: Aparecido Djalma da Silva
EMail: diretoria_faculdade@torricelli.edu.br

Areas
Biology and Health; **Exact Sciences and Technology** (Automation and Control Engineering; Electrical Engineering; Information Sciences; Production Engineering); **Human and Social Sciences** (Accountancy; Administration; Advertising and Publicity; Journalism; Law; Literature; Pedagogy; Public Relations; Tourism)

History: Founded 2002.

Main Language(s) of Instruction: Portuguese

Degrees and Diplomas: *Bacharelado*; *Licenciatura*; *Especialização/Aperfeiçoamento*
Last Updated: 21/06/10

TREVISAN FACULTY
Faculdade Trevisan (FAT)
Rua Bela Cintra 934, Cerqueira César, São Paulo,
São Paulo 01415000
Tel: +55(11) 3138-5200
Fax: +55(11) 3138-5231
EMail: trevisan@trevisan.com.br
Website: http://www.faculdadetrevisan.com.br

Diretor: Fernando Augusto Trevisan

Courses
Accountancy (Accountancy); **Business Administration** (Business Administration); **International Relations** (International Relations); **Marketing** (Marketing)

Further Information: Also branches in Rio de Janeiro and Ribeirão Bonito

History: Founded 1999.

Main Language(s) of Instruction: Portuguese

Degrees and Diplomas: *Licenciatura*; *Especialização/Aperfeiçoamento*; *Mestrado*
Last Updated: 30/06/10

TRIÂNGULO MINEIRO FACULTY
Faculdade Triângulo Mineiro (FTM)
Avenida Geraldo Alves Tavares 1980, Campus Universitario,
Ituiutaba, Minas Gerais 38302134
Tel: +55(34) 3269-8200
Fax: +55(34) 3269-8200
EMail: ftm@ftm.edu.br
Website: http://www.ftm.edu.br

Diretor: Wesley do Amaral Prado **EMail:** direcao@ftm.edu.br

Courses
Accountancy; **Administration** (Administration); **Social Communication** (Advertising and Publicity); **Tourism** (Tourism)

History: Founded 1970.

Main Language(s) of Instruction: Portuguese

Degrees and Diplomas: *Bacharelado*; *Mestrado*
Last Updated: 30/06/10

TRIÂNGULO UNIVERSITY CENTRE
Centro Universitário do Triângulo (UNITRI)
Av. Nicomedes Alves dos Santos, 4545, Bairro Gávea, Uberlândia,
Minas Gerais 38411-106
Tel: +55(34) 4009-9053
Fax: +55(34) 4009-9125
EMail: cpa@unitri.edu.br
Website: http://www.unitri.edu.br

Reitora: Marlene Salgado de Oliveira
Tel: +55(34) 4009-9041, Fax: +55(34) 4009-9125
EMail: reitoria@unitri.edu.br

Courses
Accountancy; **Administration**; **Advertising and Publicity** (Advertising and Publicity); **Architecture and Urbanism** (Architecture and Planning; Town Planning); **Biology** (Biology); **Civil Engineering** (Civil Engineering); **Computer Science**; **Fashion Design** (Fashion Design); **Graduate Studies** (Accountancy; Agricultural Business; Business Administration; Business and Commerce; Data Processing; Educational Sciences; Finance; History; Hotel Management; Journalism; Marketing; Nursing; Pedagogy; Physical Therapy; Safety Engineering; Software Engineering; Tourism); **Information Systems** (Information Sciences); **Journalism** (Journalism); **Law**; **Literature** (English; Literature; Portuguese); **Nursing** (Nursing); **Nutrition** (Nutrition); **Odontology** (Dentistry); **Pedagogy** (Pedagogy); **Pharmacy** (Pharmacy); **Physical Education** (Physical Education); **Physical Therapy** (Physical Therapy); **Production Engineering** (Production Engineering); **Psychology** (Psychology); **Social Services**; **Technological Studies** (Aesthetics; Agricultural Business; Business Administration; Cinema and Television; Civil Security; Computer Networks; Cooking and Catering; Finance; Software Engineering; Transport Management); **Tourism and Hotel Management** (Hotel and Restaurant; Service Trades; Tourism)

Further Information: Also campus in Araguari.

History: Founded 1990. Acquired present status 1997.

Degrees and Diplomas: *Tecnólogo*; *Bacharelado*; *Licenciatura*; *Especialização/Aperfeiçoamento*
Last Updated: 02/06/10

TUIUTI UNIVERSITY OF PARANÁ
Universidade Tuiuti do Paraná (UTP)
Rua Sydnei Antonio Rangel Santos, 238, Santo Inácio, Curitibá,
Paraná 82010330
Tel: +55(41) 3331-7700
EMail: gabinete@utp.br
Website: http://www.utp.br

Reitor: Luiz Guilherme Rangel Santos (1997-)
Tel: +55(41) 331-7702 EMail: reitor@utp.br

Secretário Geral: Bruno Carneiro da Cunha
EMail: bruno.diniz@utp.br

Faculties
Aeronautical Sciences; **Agrarian Sciences**; **Applied Social Sciences**; **Biological and Health Sciences**; **Exact Sciences and Technology**; **Human Sciences, Letters and Arts**; **Law**

History: Founded 1973, acquired present status 1997.

Admission Requirements: Secondary school certificate and entrance examination

Main Language(s) of Instruction: Portuguese

Degrees and Diplomas: *Bacharelado*; *Licenciatura*; *Especialização/Aperfeiçoamento*; *Mestrado*; *Doutorado*
Last Updated: 06/05/10

TUPY HIGHER INSTITUTE
Instituto Superior Tupy (IST)
3333 Rua Albano Schmidt, Boa Vista, Joinville,
Santa Catarina 89201972
Tel: +55(47) 3461-0243
Fax: +55(47) 3461-0114
EMail: ist@sociesc.com.br
Website: http://www.sociesc.org.br/ensino/ist/index.htm

Diretor: Wesley Masterson Belo de Abreu
EMail: wesley@sociesc.org.br

Courses
Administration (Administration); **Computer Science** (Computer Engineering; Computer Networks; Computer Science; Information Management; Information Technology); **Law** (Law); **Management** (Accountancy; Management; Safety Engineering; Transport Management); **Pedagogy** (Pedagogy)

History: Founded 1997.

Degrees and Diplomas: *Bacharelado*; *Licenciatura*; *Especialização/Aperfeiçoamento*; *Mestrado*
Last Updated: 14/06/10

TUPY HIGHER INSTITUTE OF FLORIANÓPOLIS
Instituto Superior Tupy de Florianópolis (IST FLORIANÓPOLIS)
Rua Salvatina Feliciana dos Santos, 525, Itacorubi, Florianópolis,
SC 88034-001
Tel: +55(48) 3239-4700
Fax: +55(48) 3239-4700
EMail: unica@sociesc.org.br
Website: http://www.sociesc.org.br/pt/unica/

Courses
Production Engineering (Production Engineering)
Last Updated: 29/09/10

UIRAPURU FACULTY
Faculdade Uirapuru
Romeu do Nascimento, 247, Jd. Panorama, Sorocaba,
SP 18031-005
Tel: +55(15) 3412-4300
Website: http://colegio.uirapuru.edu.br/UirapuruSuperior/Web/Home/Default.aspx

Courses
Graduate Studies (Business and Commerce; Educational Administration; Educational Psychology; Information Technology; Sports); **Undergraduate Studies** (Administration; Business and Commerce; Chemistry; Computer Networks; Finance; Fine Arts; Geography; History; Human Resources; Literature; Marketing; Mathematics; Pedagogy; Physical Education; Physics; Systems Analysis; Transport Management)

History: Founded through the merger of Faculdade de Tecnologia Uirapuru and Instituto Superior de Educação Uirapuru.

Degrees and Diplomas: *Tecnólogo*; *Bacharelado*; *Licenciatura*; *Especialização/Aperfeiçoamento*. Also MBA.
Last Updated: 21/09/10

UNA FACULTY OF CONTAGEM
Faculdade Una de Contagem
Avenida João César de Oliveira, 6620, Beatriz, Contagem,
MG 32040-000
Tel: +55(31) 3514-5000
Website: http://www.una.br/institucional/nossas-unidades/una-contagem-8

Courses
Graduate Studies (Business and Commerce; Management; Transport Management); **Undergraduate Studies** (Accountancy; Computer Networks; Finance; Human Resources; Management; Marketing; Transport Management)

Degrees and Diplomas: *Tecnólogo*; *Bacharelado*. Also MBA.
Last Updated: 21/09/10

UNA UNIVERSITY CENTRE
Centro Universitário UNA (FCG-UNA)
Rua Aimores 1451, bairro Lourdes, Belo Horizonte,
Minas Gerais 30140-071
Tel: +55(31) 3235-7300
Fax: +55(31) 3379-1250
EMail: una@una.br
Website: http://www.una.br

Diretor: Geraldo Magela Teixeira EMail: reitoria@una.br

Courses
Graduate Studies *(Lato Sensu)* (Aesthetics; Biological and Life Sciences; Cinema and Television; Communication Studies; Cultural Studies; Earth Sciences; Education; Engineering; Environmental Management; Health Sciences; History; Law; Management; Social Work; Technology); **Graduate Studies** *(Stricto Sensu)* (Development Studies; Environmental Studies; Social Work; Tourism); **Technological Studies** *(UNATEC)* (Aeronautical and Aerospace Engineering; Agricultural Business; Air Transport; Business and Commerce; Computer Networks; Computer Science; Cosmetology; Environmental Management; Fashion Design; Finance; Graphic Design; Health Administration; Human Resources; Industrial Management; Interior Design; Management; Marketing; Public Administration; Real Estate; Safety Engineering; Systems Analysis; Tourism; Transport Management); **Undergraduate Studies**

Further Information: Also Liberdade, Barreiro, Barro Preto, Raja, Guajajaras, Contagem campuses.

History: Founded 1961

Degrees and Diplomas: *Tecnólogo*; *Bacharelado*; *Licenciatura*; *Especialização/Aperfeiçoamento*; *Mestrado*
Last Updated: 17/06/10

UNIÃO BUSINESS SCHOOL
Faculdade União (UBS)
Rua Frei Mont, 445, Vila Aricanduva, São Paulo, SP 03505-010
Tel: +55(11) 2092-3777
Fax: +55(11) 2092-3777
EMail: uniao@faculdadeuniao.edu.br
Website: http://www.faculdadeuniao.edu.br/

Diretora: Edna Aparecida Vieira dos Santos

Courses
Graduate Studies (Business and Commerce; Finance; Human Resources; Management; Marketing); **Undergraduate Studies** (Administration)

Further Information: Also Av. Paulista and Penha units.

Degrees and Diplomas: *Bacharelado*. Also Postgraduate Diploma.
Last Updated: 21/09/10

UNIBR - FACULTY OF SÃO VICENTE
UNIBR - Faculdade de São Vicente (FSV)
Avenida Capitão Mor Aguiar 798 Centro, São Vicente,
São Paulo 11310200
Tel: +55(13) 3569-8200
Fax: +55(13) 3569-8215
EMail: beth@unibr.com.br
Website: http://www.unibr.com.br

Diretor Geral: Valdir José Lanza EMail: valdirlanza@unibr.com.br

Courses
Accountancy (Accountancy); **Administration** (Administration; Public Administration); **International Business**; **Literature**; **Logistics** (Transport Management); **Marketing** (Marketing); **Mathematics** (Mathematics); **Pedagogy and Teacher Training**;

Teacher Training (Teacher Training); **Tourism**; **Visual Arts** (Visual Arts)

History: Founded 2001. Formerly know as Faculdade Integração (Integration Faculty).

Main Language(s) of Instruction: Portuguese

Degrees and Diplomas: *Bacharelado*

Last Updated: 09/06/10

UNICE - HIGHER EDUCATION

UNICE - Ensino Superior

Rua Dona Leopoldina 912, Centro, Fortaleza, Ceará 60110001
Tel: +55(85) 3226-6446
Fax: +55(85) 3221-1132
EMail: unice@unice.br
Website: http://www.unice.br

Diretor Geral: Fabio Luiz Tartuce Filho

Diretor Acadêmico: Hamilton Vale Leitão

Faculties
Computer Science (Computer Networks; Computer Science; Software Engineering); **Human Sciences** *(FCHFOR)*; **Information Technology** *(FATI)* (Information Technology); **Technology** *(FCTFOR)*

Institutes
Higher Education *(Fortaleza - IESF)*

History: Founded 1990.

Main Language(s) of Instruction: Portuguese

Degrees and Diplomas: *Bacharelado*; *Especialização/Aperfeiçoamento*; *Mestrado*

Last Updated: 09/10/07

UNICESP INTEGRATED FACULTIES

Faculdades Integradas Unicesp

QE 11 Area Especial 'C' 'D', S/n Guará I, Brasília, DF 71020621
Tel: +55(61) 3383-9500
Fax: +55(61) 3383-9524
EMail: unicesp@unicesp.edu.br
Website: http://www.unicesp.edu.br

Diretora Geral: Elaine Fagundes

Courses
Accountancy (Accountancy); **Administration** (Administration); **Biomedicine**; **Civil Aviation** (Aeronautical and Aerospace Engineering); **Computer Networks** (Computer Networks); **Environmental Management** (Environmental Management); **Finance Management**; **Hospital Management** (Health Administration); **Hotel Management**; **Human Resource Management** (Human Resources); **Law** (Law); **Literature**; **Marketing** (Marketing); **Nursing** (Nursing); **Pedagogy** (Pedagogy); **Social Communication** (Advertising and Publicity; Journalism)

History: Founded 1995. Acquired present status and title 2003.

Main Language(s) of Instruction: Portuguese

Degrees and Diplomas: *Bacharelado*; *Especialização/Aperfeiçoamento*; *Mestrado*

Last Updated: 21/06/10

UNIFAE UNIVERSITY CENTRE

UniFAE Centro Universitário (UNIFAE)

Rua 24 de Maio 135, 5° Andar, Centro, Curitibá, Paraná 80230-090
Tel: +55(41) 2105-1450
Fax: +55(41) 2105-4195
EMail: pro.reitoria@fae.edu
Website: http://www.fae.edu

Reitor: Nelson José Hilesheim (2007-)
Tel: +55 (41) 2105-4122, Fax: +55 (41) 2105-4195
EMail: nelsonh@bomjesus.br; reitoria@fae.edu

Secretary-General: Vicente Keller
Tel: +55 (41) 2105-4154, Fax: +55 (41) 2105-4195
EMail: vkeller@fae.edu

International Relations: Areta Galat, International Relations Officer
Tel: +55 (41) 2105-4444, Fax: +55 (41) 2105-4445
EMail: aretagallat@fae.edu

Programmes
Accountancy (Accountancy); **Administration** (Administration); **Economics** (Economics); **Environmental Engineering**; **Industrial Design** (Industrial Design); **International Business**; **Law** (Law); **Mechanical Engineering**; **Production Engineering** (Production Engineering); **Psychology** (Psychology); **Social Communication** (Advertising and Publicity)

Further Information: Also Cristo Rei Campus

History: Founded 1957. Previously known as Faculdades Bom Jesus. 1998 became FAE Business School. Acquired current title and status 2005.

Main Language(s) of Instruction: Portuguese

International Co-operation: With universities in USA, Spain, Germany

Accrediting Agencies: Ministry of Education and Culture (MEC)

Degrees and Diplomas: *Tecnólogo*: Internet Systems; Transport Management; Human Resources; Finance; Marketing, 2 - 2.5 yrs; *Bacharelado*: Administration; Accounting; Economics; Mass Communication; Industrial Design; Philosophy; International Business;, 4 yrs; *Bacharelado*: Law; Production Engineering; Environmental Engineering, 5 yrs; *Especialização/Aperfeiçoamento*; *Mestrado*

Student Services: Academic counselling, Canteen, Employment services, Foreign student adviser, Foreign Studies Centre, Health services, Language programs, Social counselling, Sports facilities

Special Facilities: Computer labs; Theatre

Libraries: c. 54,000 vols.

Publications: FAE Business, Debates and professional forums about successful management companies *(quarterly)*; Scintilla, Philosophy and Mediaeval Studies *(3 per annum)*

Last Updated: 08/06/10

UNIFIED EUROPEAN INSTITUTE OF BRAZIL

Instituto Unificado Europeu do Brasil (IUNEBRASIL)

Rodovia Br 104 Km 62, s/n, Pólo Comercial de Caruaru, Nova Caruaru, Caruaru, PE 55014-170
Tel: +55(81) 3725-5009
EMail: iune@iunebrasil.edu.br

Diretor Geral: José Manuel dos Santos Henriques

Courses
Undergraduate Studies (Dentistry; Nursing; Pharmacy; Physical Therapy; Psychology)

Degrees and Diplomas: *Bacharelado*

Last Updated: 29/09/10

UNIFIED FACULTIES OF FOZ DO IGUAÇU

Faculdades Unificadas de Foz do Iguaçu (UNIFOZ)

Alameda Rui Ferrera 164, Centro, Foz do Iguaçu, PR 85851400
Tel: +55(45) 3574-2611
Fax: +55(45) 3523-0809
EMail: unifoz@foznet.com.br
Website: http://www.unifoz.com.br

Presidente: Rogério Tuma

Courses
Administration; **Hotel Management** (Hotel Management); **Law**

History: Founded 1993

Main Language(s) of Instruction: Portuguese

Degrees and Diplomas: *Bacharelado*; *Especialização/Aperfeiçoamento*

Last Updated: 18/06/10

UNIGRAN CAPITAL FACULTY
Faculdade UNIGRAN Capital
Rua José Antônio, 1941, Monte Castelo, Campo Grande,
MS 79010-190
Tel: +55(67) 3389-3389
Fax: +55(67) 3384-1102
EMail: seccapital@unigran.br
Website: http://www.unigrancapital.com.br/

Diretora Geral: Márcia Rita Trindade Leite Malheiros
EMail: direcaounigrancapital@unigran.br

Courses
Distance Education (Accountancy; Administration; Advertising and Publicity; Agricultural Business; Distance Education; Educational Psychology; Environmental Management; Higher Education; Information Sciences; Linguistics; Literature; Pedagogy; Real Estate; Social and Community Services; Systems Analysis; Theology); **Graduate Studies** (Cosmetology; Education; Human Resources; Information Sciences; Marketing; Physical Education; Public Health); **Undergraduate Studies** (Cosmetology; Nursing; Physical Education)

History: Founded 2007.

Degrees and Diplomas: *Tecnólogo*; *Bacharelado*; *Licenciatura*. Also Postgraduate Diploma.
Last Updated: 21/09/10

UNIGRANRIO UNIVERSITY
Universidade Unigranrio (UNIGRANRIO)
25 de Agosto - Duque de Caxias, Rio de Janeiro 25071-202
Tel: +55(21) 2672-7777
Fax: +55(21) 2673-1911
EMail: daa@unigranrio.edu.br
Website: http://www.unigranrio.br

Reitor: Arody Cordeiro Herdy (1998-)
Tel: +55(21) 2672-7712
EMail: arody@unigranrio.br; reitoria@unigranrio.com.br

Institutes
Biosciences (Biology); **Exact and Natural Sciences** (Chemistry; Mathematics; Natural Sciences); **Humanities** (Arts and Humanities; English; History; Portuguese; Social and Community Services; Spanish)

Schools
Accountancy and Economics (Accountancy; Administration; Business and Commerce; Economics); **Computer Science, Telematics and Information** (Business Administration; Computer Science; Data Processing; Information Sciences; Telecommunications Services); **Dentistry** (Dentistry); **Education** (Art Education; Education; Pedagogy); **Law** (Civil Law; Criminal Law; History; Human Rights; Law); **Management and Business** (Administration; Business Administration; Management; Secretarial Studies); **Medicine** (Medicine); **Nursing** (Nursing); **Pharmacy** (Pharmacy); **Physical Education** (Physical Education); **Physiotherapy** (Physical Therapy); **Veterinary Science** (*Silva Jardim*) (Veterinary Science)

History: Founded 1972, acquired present status 1994.

Governing Bodies: Conselho Universitário; Conselho de Ensino e Pesquisa

Admission Requirements: Secondary school certificate and entrance examination

Fees: (US Dollars): 1,500-7,000 per annum

Main Language(s) of Instruction: Portuguese

Degrees and Diplomas: *Bacharelado*: Accountancy; Administration; Chemistry; Computer Science; Nursing; Physiotherapy, 4 yrs; *Bacharelado*: Biology, 3 yrs; *Bacharelado*: Dentistry; Veterinary Medicine, 4 1/2 yrs; *Bacharelado*: Law, 5 yrs; *Bacharelado*: Medicine, 6 yrs; *Bacharelado*: Pharmacy, 4 1/2 yrs; *Licenciatura*: Mathematics; Portuguese Literature; Portuguese-English; Portuguese-Spanish, 3 yrs; *Licenciatura*: Pedagogy, 4 yrs; *Especialização/Aperfeiçoamento*; *Mestrado*

Student Services: Canteen, Cultural centre, Employment services, Health services, Language programs, Sports facilities

Libraries: Total, 120,000 vols

Publications: Caderno de Contabilidade e Economia *(biannually)*; Caderno de Direito *(biannually)*; Caderno de Enfermagem, (Research Issues in Nursing) *(biannually)*; Caderno de Gestão *(biannually)*; Caderno de Meio Ambiente, (Research Issues in Biology and Ecology) *(biannually)*; Caderno de Odontologia *(biannually)*; Caderno Técnico-Científico de Medicina Veterinária, (Research Issues in Veterinary Medicine) *(biannually)*; Paidéia, (Research Issues in Humanities) *(biannually)*
Last Updated: 06/05/10

UNILAGOS FACULTY
Faculdade Unilagos
Avenida Saldanha Marinho, 85, Mangueirinha, PR 85540-000
Tel: +55(46) 3243-1371 +55(46) 3243-2822
Fax: +55(46) 3243-1371
Website: http://www.unilagos.com.br/

Diretora Geral: Aline Fernandes Galli

Courses
Technological Studies (Environmental Management; Systems Analysis); **Undergraduate Studies** (Administration; Mathematics; Pedagogy; Social and Community Services; Visual Arts)

Degrees and Diplomas: *Tecnólogo*; *Bacharelado*; *Licenciatura*. Also Postgraduate Diploma.
Last Updated: 21/09/10

UNIME FACULTY
Faculdade Unime (UNIME)
Avenida Luís Tarquínio Pontes 600, Centro, Lauro de Freitas,
Bahia 42700000
Tel: +55(71) 3378-8900
Fax: +55(71) 3378-8900
EMail: unime@unime.com.br
Website: http://www.unime.com.br

Diretor: Marcelino Galindo

Faculties
Agrarian and Health Sciences (Agricultural Business; Biology; Dentistry; Multimedia; Nursing; Nutrition; Pharmacy; Physical Education; Physical Therapy; Psychology; Radiology; Speech Therapy and Audiology; Veterinary Science); **Education and Communication** *(FEC)* (Education; Educational Sciences; English; Literature; Pedagogy; Portuguese; Teacher Training); **Exact Sciences and Technology** (Architecture; Computer Networks; Computer Science; Electrical Engineering; Information Technology; Systems Analysis; Technology; Urban Studies); **Law** *(FCJ)* (Law); **Social Sciences** *(FCS)*

History: Founded 2000.

Degrees and Diplomas: *Tecnólogo*; *Bacharelado*; *Licenciatura*; *Especialização/Aperfeiçoamento*; *Mestrado*
Last Updated: 30/06/10

UNION FACULTY OF GOYAZES
Faculdade União de Goyazes (FUG)
Rodovia Go-060 Km 19, 3184, Setor Laguna Parque, Trindade,
GO 75380-000
Tel: +55(62) 3506-9300
EMail: secretaria@fug.edu.br
Website: http://www.fug.edu.br/

Diretor Geral: Carlos Augusto de Oliveira Botelho

Courses
Graduate Studies (Sports); **Undergraduate Studies** (Biological and Life Sciences; Biomedicine; Nursing; Nutrition; Occupational Therapy; Pharmacy; Physical Education; Physical Therapy)

Degrees and Diplomas: *Bacharelado*; *Licenciatura*; *Especialização/Aperfeiçoamento*
Last Updated: 21/09/10

UNION OF FACULTIES OF ALTA FLORESTA

União das Faculdades de Alta Floresta (UNIFLOR)
Av. Leandro Adorno s/n, Alta Floresta, MT
Tel: +55(66) 3521-1676
Fax: +55(66) 3521-4320
EMail: uniflor@uniflor.edu.br
Website: http://www.uniflor.edu.br

Diretor: José Antonio Tobias (1997-)

Campuses
Administration (Administration)

Courses
Accountancy (Accountancy); **Law** (Law); **Literature**; **Pedagogy** *(FEAFLOR)* (Arts and Humanities; English; Higher Education; Humanities and Social Science Education; Pedagogy; Portuguese); **Tourism** (Tourism)

Further Information: Also campus in Guarantã do Norte.

History: Founded 1997

Main Language(s) of Instruction: Portuguese

Degrees and Diplomas: *Bacharelado*; *Licenciatura*; *Especialização/Aperfeiçoamento*; *Mestrado*; *Doutorado*
Last Updated: 09/06/10

UNION OF FACULTIES OF JUSSARA

União das Faculdades de Jussara (UNIFAJ)
Rodovia BR 70 Km 5 Zona Rural, Saída para Goiás, Jussara, GO 76270000
Tel: +55(62) 3373-1219
Fax: +55(62) 3373-1219
EMail: presidencia@unifaj.edu.br
Website: http://www.unifaj.edu.br

Diretora: Leila de Fátima Lopes (1998-)

Courses
Accountancy; **Administration** (Administration); **Commercial Administration** (Business and Commerce); **Law** (Law)

History: Founded 1998

Main Language(s) of Instruction: Portuguese

Degrees and Diplomas: *Tecnólogo*; *Bacharelado*; *Especialização/Aperfeiçoamento*
Last Updated: 09/06/10

UNION OF FACULTIES OF THE GREAT LAKES

União das Faculdades dos Grandes Lagos (UNILAGO)
Rua Eduardo Nielsen 960, Jardim Aeroporto, São José do Rio Prêto, São Paulo 15001970
Tel: +55(17) 3203-6166
Fax: +55(17) 3203-6154
EMail: unilago@unilago.com.br
Website: http://www.unilago.com.br

Diretora Geral: Maria Lúcia Atique Gabriel (1998-)

Courses
Administration (Administration); **Advertising**; **Biomedicine** (Biomedicine); **Food Processing** (Food Technology); **Information Systems**; **Journalism** (Journalism); **Law** (Law); **Nursing** (Nursing); **Nutrition** (Nutrition); **Pedagogy** (Pedagogy); **Pharmacy** (Pharmacy); **Physical Education**; **Physiotherapy** (Physical Therapy); **Psychology** (Psychology); **Public Relations** (Public Relations); **Secretarial Studies** (Secretarial Studies); **Social Services** (Social and Community Services); **Tourism**; **Translation and Interpretation** (Literature; Translation and Interpretation)

History: Founded 1986.

Main Language(s) of Instruction: Portuguese

Degrees and Diplomas: *Bacharelado*; *Especialização/Aperfeiçoamento*; *Mestrado*
Last Updated: 09/06/10

UNION OF SCHOOLS OF PARAÍSO

União de Escolas Superiores Paraíso (UNIESP)
Avenida Santo Amaro 4039, Brooklin, São Paulo, São Paulo 4555002
Tel: +55(11) 556-11313
Fax: +55(11) 556-11313
EMail: vaurene@hoyler.edu.br
Website: http://www.hoyler.edu.br

Diretor: Jabes Oliveira Moura (1995-)

Courses
Accountancy *(Hortolândia)* (Accountancy); **Administration**; **Advertising** *(Hortolândia)* (Advertising and Publicity); **Computer Science** (Computer Networks; Computer Science); **Journalism** *(Hortolândia)* (Journalism); **Literature** *(Vargem Grande Paulista)* (Literature); **Pedagogy** *(Vargem Grande Paulista)* (Pedagogy); **Teacher Training** *(Vargem Grande Paulista)*

Faculties
Human Resources

Further Information: Also following campuses: Araçatuba, Birigui, Guararapes, Hortolândia, Mirandópolis, Presidente Epitácio, Presidente Prudente, Presidente Venceslau, Ribeirão Preto, São Roque, Sorocaba, Taquaritinga, Vargem Grande.

History: Founded 1985.

Main Language(s) of Instruction: Portuguese

Degrees and Diplomas: *Bacharelado*; *Especialização/Aperfeiçoamento*
Last Updated: 17/10/07

UNION OF SCHOOLS OF THE FAIMI EDUCATION GROUP

União das Escolas do Grupo FAIMI de Educação (FAIMI)
Avenida Luís Fernando Moreira, 1005, Mirassol, São José 15130-000
Tel: +55(17) 3253-9110
Fax: +55(17) 3253-9119
EMail: FAIMI@FAIMI.edu.br
Website: http://www.faimi.edu.br

Diretor Geral: Alvaro José Almeida Simões Branco (1998-)

Courses
Administration (Administration; Business Administration; Finance; Human Resources; Marketing); **Design** (Design); **Education** (Education; Educational Psychology; Pedagogy; Physical Education); **Information Systems** (Information Management); **Languages**; **Law**; **Nursing**

History: Founded 1998. Acquired present title 2006. Formerly known as Faculdade Integrada de Mirassol (Integrated Faculty of Mirassol).

Main Language(s) of Instruction: Portuguese

Degrees and Diplomas: *Bacharelado*; *Licenciatura*; *Especialização/Aperfeiçoamento*
Last Updated: 09/06/10

UNION OF SCHOOLS OF THE FUNESO

União das Escolas Superiores da FUNESO (UNESF)
Campus Universitário da Funeso, S/n Jardim Fragoso, Olinda, Pernambuco 53060770
Tel: +55(81) 3439-1990
Fax: +55(81) 3439-3694
EMail: funeso@funeso.com.br
Website: http://www.funeso.com.br

Diretor Geral: Mário Marques de Santana

Diretora Acadêmica: Francisca Zuleide Duarte de Souza

Centres
Arts and Humanities (Administration; Arts and Humanities; History; Modern Languages; Pedagogy); **Exact and Natural Sciences**; **Health Sciences** (Health Sciences; Nursing; Speech Therapy and Audiology)

History: Founded 1971.

Degrees and Diplomas: *Bacharelado*; *Licenciatura*; *Especialização/Aperfeiçoamento*
Last Updated: 09/06/10

UNION OF THE AMERICAS FACULTY
Faculdade União das Américas
Avenida Tarquínio Joslin Santos 1000, Jardim Universitário das Américas, Foz do Iguaçu, PR 85870400
Tel: +55(45) 2105-9000
Fax: +55(45) 2105-9033
EMail: uniamerica@uniamerica.br
Website: http://www.uniamerica.br

Diretor: Wildenilson Sinhorini Vieira da Silva
EMail: direcao@uniamerica.br

Courses
Biomedicine (Biomedicine); **Environmental Engineering**; **Nursing** (Nursing); **Nutrition**; **Physical Education**; **Physiotherapy**; **Psychology** (Psychology)

History: Founded 2001.

Degrees and Diplomas: *Bacharelado*; *Licenciatura*; *Especialização/Aperfeiçoamento*; *Mestrado*
Last Updated: 30/06/10

UNION OF THE AMERICAS INSTITUTE OF EDUCATION
Instituto Superior de Educação União das Américas (UNIAMÉRICA)
Avenida Tarquínio Joslin Santos, 1000, Jardim Universitário, Foz do Iguaçu, PR 85870-901
Tel: +55(45) 2105-9000
Fax: +55(45) 2105-9000
EMail: direcao@uniamerica.br
Website: http://www.uniamerica.br

Courses
Pedagogy (Pedagogy); **Teacher Training** (Teacher Training)

Degrees and Diplomas: *Licenciatura*
Last Updated: 28/09/10

UNIRONDON UNIVERSITY CENTRE
Centro Universitário UNIRONDON
Avenida Beira Rio 3001, Jardim Europa, Cuiabá, Mato Grosso 78065780
Tel: +55(65) 3316-4000
EMail: adonias@unirondon.br
Website: http://www.unirondon.br

Diretora Geral: Luzia Guimarães (1997-)
Tel: +11(65) 3316-4024 +11(65) 3316-4078

Courses
Accountancy; **Administration**; **Advertising and Publicity**; **Biology** *(Licenciatura)* (Biology); **Biomedicine** (Biomedicine); **Computer Science**; **Journalism** (Journalism); **Law**; **Nursing** (Nursing); **Pedagogy** *(Licenciatura)*; **Technological Studies** (Business and Commerce; Finance; Information Management; Public Administration; Radiology; Real Estate; Systems Analysis); **Tourism**

History: Founded 2004.

Main Language(s) of Instruction: Portuguese

Degrees and Diplomas: *Tecnólogo*; *Bacharelado*; *Licenciatura*; *Especialização/Aperfeiçoamento*
Last Updated: 18/06/10

UNISSA FACULTY OF SARANDI
Faculdade UNISSA de Sarandi (UNISSA)
Rua Machado de Assis, S/n Jardim Universitário, Sarandi, PR 87111970
Tel: +55(44) 3264-6000
Fax: +55(44) 3264-6000
EMail: dp.unissa@hotmail.com
Website: http://www.unissa.edu.br

Diretor Geral: José Jorge Zabloski

Courses
Accountancy (Accountancy); **Administration** (Accountancy; Administration); **Geography**; **Pedagogy**

History: Founded 1999.

Main Language(s) of Instruction: Portuguese

Degrees and Diplomas: *Bacharelado*; *Especialização/Aperfeiçoamento*
Last Updated: 30/06/10

UNISULBAHIA INTEGRATED FACULTIES
UNISULBAHIA Faculdades Integradas (UNISULBAHIA)
Rodovia BR 367 Km 14, Eunápolis, Bahia 45820000
Tel: +55(73) 281-4342
Fax: +55(73) 281-1477
EMail: unece@unece.br
Website: http://www.unisulbahia.edu.br

Diretor Presidente: Ademilde Maria Alves da Silva Fadini

Courses
Accountancy; **Administration** (Administration); **Computer Science**; **Law** (Law); **Nursing** (Nursing); **Pedagogy** (Pedagogy); **Physical Education** (Physical Education); **Physiotherapy** (Physical Therapy); **Tourism**

History: Founded 2000.

Main Language(s) of Instruction: Portuguese

Degrees and Diplomas: *Bacharelado*
Last Updated: 23/06/10

UNIT OF HIGHER EDUCATION OF FEIRA DE SANTANA
Unidade de Ensino Superior de Feira de Santana
Avenida Presidente Dutra, s/n - Capuchinhos, Feira de Santana, BA 44.052-000
Tel: +55(75) 2101-5656
EMail: unef@unef.edu.br
Website: http://www.unef.edu.br

Diretor: Newton Oliveira EMail: newton@unef.edu.br

Courses
Administration (Administration); **Advertising** (Advertising and Publicity); **Journalism** (Journalism)

History: Founded 1999 as Faculdade de Ensino Superior da Cidade de Feira de Santana. Acquired present title 2002.

Main Language(s) of Instruction: Portuguese

Degrees and Diplomas: *Bacharelado*; *Especialização/Aperfeiçoamento*
Last Updated: 03/08/10

UNIT OF HIGHER EDUCATION OF SOUTHERN MARANHÃO
Unidade de Ensino Superior do Sul do Maranhão (IESMA)
Rua São Pedro, S/N, Jd. Cristo Rei, Imperatriz, MA 65907-070
Tel: +55(99) 2101-0202
Fax: +55(99) 2101-0203
Website: http://www.unisulma.edu.br/

Presidente: Lula Almeida

Courses
Undergraduate Studies (Administration; Biological and Life Sciences; Law; Nursing; Nutrition; Physical Education; Social and Community Services)

History: Founded 2004.

Main Language(s) of Instruction: Portuguese

Degrees and Diplomas: *Bacharelado*; *Licenciatura*
Last Updated: 17/03/11

UNITED FACULTIES OF PERNAMBUCO

Faculdades Unidas de Pernambuco (ESUSPE)
Av. Norte, 80, Santo Amaro, Recife, Pernambuco 50040-200
Tel: +55(81) 3222-5015
Fax: +55(81) 3221-7903
EMail: faupe@alae.com.br
Website: http://www.alae.com.br/faupe/home/

Diretora: Gabriela Martin Ávila

Courses
Accountancy (Accountancy); Administration (Administration); Building Technologies (Architecture; Town Planning); Interior Design (Interior Design)

History: Founded 1984

Main Language(s) of Instruction: Portuguese

Degrees and Diplomas: *Bacharelado*; *Especialização/Aperfeiçoamento*; *Mestrado*
Last Updated: 18/06/10

UNITED FACULTIES OF THE NORTH OF MINAS

Faculdades Unidas do Norte de Minas (FUNORTE)
Avenida Osmane Barbosa 11.111 JK, Montes Claros,
Minas Gerais 39404006
Tel: +55(38) 3690-3027
Fax: +55(38) 3690-3055
EMail: funorte@connect.com.br

Diretor: Ruy Adriano Borges Muniz

Courses
Administration (Administration); Civil Engineering; Food Processing (Food Technology); Geography (Geography); History; Journalism (Journalism); Literature (Literature); Pedagogy (Pedagogy); Pharmacy; Social Services (Social and Community Services); Teacher Training (Teacher Training); Tourism

Institutes
Health Sciences *(ICS)*

History: Founded 1997.

Main Language(s) of Instruction: Portuguese

Degrees and Diplomas: *Bacharelado*; *Especialização/Aperfeiçoamento*; *Mestrado*; *Doutorado*
Last Updated: 26/11/07

UNITED FACULTIES OF THE VALLEY OF ARAGUAIA

Faculdades Unidas do Vale do Araguaia
Rua Moreira Cabral 1000, Setor Mariano, Barra do Garças,
MT 78600000
Tel: +55(65) 3401-1602
Fax: +55(65) 3401-1602 +55(65) 3401-1212
EMail: contato@univar.edu.br
Website: http://www.univar.edu.br

Diretor Presidente: Marcelo Antôncio Fuster Soler (1997-)

Courses
Accountancy (Accountancy); Administration (Administration); History; Nursing (Nursing); Nutrition; Pedagogy (Pedagogy); Pharmacy (Pharmacy); Physical Education (Physical Education); Physiotherapy (Physical Therapy); Social Services (Social and Community Services); Systems Analysis

History: Founded 1993

Main Language(s) of Instruction: Portuguese

Degrees and Diplomas: *Bacharelado*; *Especialização/Aperfeiçoamento*; *Mestrado*
Last Updated: 18/06/10

UNITED FACULTY OF CAMPINAS

Faculdade Unida de Campinas (FACUNICAMPS)
R. Pouso Alto, 892, esq. com Av. Castelo Branco, Setor Campinas,
Goiânia, GO 74525-020
Tel: +55(62) 3091-6600
Fax: +55(62) 3091-6600
EMail: diretoria@unicamps.com.br
Website: http://www.unicamps.com.br/

Courses
Graduate Studies (Accountancy; Civil Law; Criminal Law; Educational Psychology; Finance; Higher Education; Labour Law; Marketing; Neurosciences; Pharmacology; Rehabilitation and Therapy); Undergraduate Studies (Accountancy; Business Administration; Nursing)

Degrees and Diplomas: *Bacharelado*; *Especialização/Aperfeiçoamento*
Last Updated: 21/09/10

UNITED FACULTY OF PARAÍBA

Faculdade Unida da Paraíba (UNIPB)
Avenida Monsenhor Walfredo Leal, 512, Tambiá, João Pessoa,
PB 58020-540
Tel: +55(83) 3133-2900
Fax: +55(83) 3133-2920
Website: http://www.unipb.com.br/

Diretor Geral: Silvio de Mendonça Furtado

Courses
Environmental Engineering (Environmental Engineering); Nursing (Nursing); Nutrition (Nutrition)

History: Founded 2005 as Instituto de Ensino Superior e Pesquisa "Lynaldo Cavalcanti". Acquired present status and title 2006.

Degrees and Diplomas: *Bacharelado*
Last Updated: 29/09/10

UNITED FACULTY OF SUZANO

Faculdade Unida de Suzano (UNISUZ)
Rua José Correia Gonçalves 57, Centro, Suzano,
São Paulo 08675130
Tel: +55(11) 4746-7300
EMail: diretoria@unisuz.com.br
Website: http://www.unisuz.com.br

Diretor: Nazih Youssef Franciss

Courses
Accountancy; Administration (Administration); Finance; Information Systems; Law (Law); Letters; Marketing (Marketing); Mathematics (Mathematics); Pedagogy (Pedagogy); Physical Education (Physical Education)

History: Founded 1999.

Main Language(s) of Instruction: Portuguese

Degrees and Diplomas: *Tecnólogo*; *Bacharelado*; *Licenciatura*; *Especialização/Aperfeiçoamento*
Last Updated: 30/06/10

UNITED FACULTY OF VITÓRIA

Faculdade Unida de Vitória
Rua Engenheiro Fábio Ruschi, n° 161, Bento Ferreira, Vitória,
ES 29050-670
Tel: +55(27) 3325-2071
EMail: faculdadeunida@faculdadeunida.com.br
Website: http://www.faculdadeunida.com.br/

Diretor Geral: Wanderley Pereira da Rosa

Courses
Graduate Studies (Bible; Family Studies; Nursing; Pharmacology; Philosophy; Psychoanalysis; Religious Studies; Sports); Undergraduate Studies (Theology)

History: Founded 1997 as Faculdade Teológica Unida - FTU. Acquired present title 2007.

Degrees and Diplomas: *Bacharelado*; *Especialização/Aperfeiçoamento*

Last Updated: 21/09/10

UNITED METROPOLITAN FACULTIES

Faculdades Metropolitanas Unidas (UNIFMU)

Campus Liberdade, Avenida Liberdade 654, São Paulo, São Paulo 1508010
Tel: +55(11) 3207-0733
Fax: +55(11) 3209-4589
EMail: gabinete_reitoria@fmu.br
Website: http://www.fmu.br

Reitora: Labibi Elias Alves da Silva

Areas

Applied Social Sciences, Humanities and Arts (Design; Fashion Design; History; Hotel Management; Literature; Pedagogy; Social and Community Services; Tourism); **Biological and Health Sciences** (Art Therapy; Biomedicine; Dentistry; Music; Nursing; Nutrition; Pharmacy; Physical Education; Physical Therapy; Psychology; Speech Therapy and Audiology; Veterinary Science); **Exact Sciences, Technology and Agrarian Sciences** (Accountancy; Actuarial Science; Computer Science; Economics); **Legal and Social Sciences**

History: Founded 1968.

Main Language(s) of Instruction: Portuguese

Degrees and Diplomas: *Tecnólogo*; *Bacharelado*; *Licenciatura*; *Especialização/Aperfeiçoamento*; *Mestrado*

Last Updated: 21/06/10

UNIVATES UNIVERSITY CENTRE

Centro Universitário Univates (UNIVATES)

Rua Avelino Tallini, 171-B. Universitário, Lajeado, RS 95900-000
Tel: +55(51) 3714-7000
Fax: +55(51) 3714-7001
EMail: campus@univates.br
Website: http://www.univates.br

Reitor: Ney José Lazzari **EMail:** nlazzari@univates.br

Provost: Oto Roberto Moerschbaecher
EMail: ihuppes@univates.br

International Relations: Isabel Körbes Scapini
EMail: aaii@univates.br

Courses

Graduate Studies *(Stricto Sensu)* (Environmental Studies; Science Education); **Graduate Studies** *(Lato Sensu)* (Accountancy; Business Administration; Business and Commerce; Commercial Law; Dance; Ecology; Finance; Food Technology; Health Sciences; Industrial Management; International Relations; Labour Law; Law; Management; Marketing; Oncology; Physical Therapy; Physiology; Rehabilitation and Therapy; Safety Engineering; Special Education; Tourism; Water Management); **Technological Studies**; **Undergraduate Studies**

History: Founded 1972. Acquired present status 1997.

Governing Bodies: Council of Education and Research

Academic Year: March to December (March-July; August-December)

Admission Requirements: Secondary education certificate and entrance examination

Main Language(s) of Instruction: Portuguese

International Co-operation: With universities in Chile, Germany, Portugal

Accrediting Agencies: Federal Ministry of Education

Degrees and Diplomas: *Bacharelado*; *Licenciatura*; *Especialização/Aperfeiçoamento*; *Mestrado*. Also Teaching Qualification

Student Services: Academic counselling, Canteen, Cultural centre, Employment services, Foreign student adviser, Language programs, Social counselling, Sports facilities

Student Residential Facilities: None

Special Facilities: Natural Sciences Museum, Art Gallery

Libraries: Total, c. 60,000 vols

Publications: Estudio y Debate

Last Updated: 18/06/10

UNIVERSITAS FACULTIES

Faculdades Universitas

Rua Vereador Henrique Soler, 229 – Ponta da Praia, Santos, SP
Tel: +55(13) 3269-0012
EMail: unimant@iron.com.br
Website: http://www.faculdadesuniversitas.com.br

Courses

Administration (Administration)

History: Founded 2008.

Main Language(s) of Instruction: Portuguese

Degrees and Diplomas: *Bacharelado*

Libraries: Yes

Last Updated: 21/09/10

UNIVERSITY CENTRE - BENNETT METHODIST INSTITUTE

Centro Universitario - Instituto Metodista Bennett

Rua Marques de Abrantes 55 Flamengo, Rio de Janeiro, Rio de Janeiro 22230-060
Tel: +55(21) 3509-1000
Fax: +55(21) 3509-1000 +55(21) 3509-1055
EMail: imb@bennett.br
Website: http://www.bennett.br

Reitor: Roberto Pontes da Fonseca

Courses

Administration (Administration; Human Resources); **Architecture and Urbanism**; **Art Education**; **International Relations**; **Law** (Law); **Nutrition**; **Pedagogy** (Pedagogy); **Physical Education** (Physical Education); **Theology**

History: Founded 1978 as Faculdades Integradas Bennett. Acquired present status and title 2004.

Degrees and Diplomas: *Bacharelado*; *Licenciatura*

Last Updated: 19/05/10

UNIVERSITY CENTRE OF AMPARO

Centro Universitário Amparense

Rodovia "João Beira" SP 95, Km 465, Caixa Postal 118, Amparo, São Paulo 13905-529
Tel: +55(19) 3907-9870
Fax: +55(19) 3808-9662
EMail: info@unifia.edu.br
Website: http://www.unifia.edu.br

Diretora: Aderbal Alfredo Bernarde Calderari
EMail: reitoria@unifia.edu.br

Courses

Accountancy (Accountancy); **Administration** (Administration); **Arts and Humanities** (Arts and Humanities); **Biology** (Biology); **Biomedicine** (Biomedicine); **Civil Engineering** (Civil Engineering); **Envir** (Environmental Management); **Graduate Studies** (Accountancy; Business Administration; Educational Psychology; Environmental Studies; Higher Education; Physical Education); **Human Resources** (Human Resources); **Industrial Chemistry** (Industrial Chemistry); **Industrial Production Management** (Industrial Management); **Logistics**; **Marketing** (Marketing); **Nursing** (Nursing); **Nutrition**; **Pedagogy** (Pedagogy); **Physical Education**; **Production Engineering** (Production Engineering); **Quality Management**; **Social Services**; **Systems Analysis and Development** (Systems Analysis); **Workplace Safety** (Occupational Health)

History: Founded 1971.

Main Language(s) of Instruction: Portuguese

Degrees and Diplomas: *Bacharelado*; *Licenciatura*. Also Postgraduate programmes.

Last Updated: 20/05/10

UNIVERSITY CENTRE OF ANÁPOLIS

Centro Universitário de Anápolis (UNIEVANGÉLICA)
Avenida Universitária Km. 35, Cidade Universitária, Anápolis,
Goiás 75070-290
Tel: +55(62) 3310-6600
Fax: +55(62) 3318-1120
EMail: unievangelica@unievangelica.edu.br
Website: http://www.unievangelica.edu.br

Reitor: Carlos Hassel Mendes da Silva

Courses

Administration (Administration); **Biology** (Biology); **Civil Engineering** (Civil Engineering); **Computer Science** (Computer Science); **Graduate Studies**; **Information Systems** (Information Management); **Law** (Law); **Mathematics** (Mathematics); **Mechanical Engineering** (Mechanical Engineering); **Medicine** (Medicine); **Modern Languages** (English; Portuguese; Spanish); **Nursing** (Nursing); **Odontology**; **Pedagogy** (Pedagogy); **Pharmacy** (Pharmacy); **Physical Education** (Physical Education); **Physical Therapy**; **Technological Studies**

History: Founded 1961.

Main Language(s) of Instruction: Portuguese

Degrees and Diplomas: *Tecnólogo*; *Bacharelado*; *Licenciatura*; *Especialização/Aperfeiçoamento*; *Mestrado*. Also MBA.
Last Updated: 26/05/10

UNIVERSITY CENTRE OF ARARAQUARA

Centro Universitário de Araraquara (UNIARA)
Rua Carlos Gomes, n.° 1338, Centro, Araraquara,
São Paulo 14801-340
Tel: +55(16) 3201-7100
Fax: +55(16) 3232-1921
EMail: uniara@uniara.com.br; marketing@uniara.com.br
Website: http://www.uniara.com.br

Reitor: Luiz Felipe Cabral Mauro (1997-)

Pró-Reitoria Administrativa: Fernando Soares Mauro

Courses

Administration (Administration); **Advertising and Publicity** (Advertising and Publicity); **Agronomy**; **Architecture and Urbanism**; **Bioenergetic Engineering** (Bioengineering; Energy Engineering); **Biology**; **Biomedicine** (Biomedicine); **Civil Engineering** (Civil Engineering); **Computer Engineering** (Computer Engineering); **Digital Design** (Design); **Economics** (Economics); **Electrical Engineering**; **Fonoaudiology**; **Graduate Studies** (Business Administration; Civil Law; Commercial Law; Computer Science; Criminal Law; Development Studies; Ecology; Environmental Management; Finance; Gerontology; Human Resources; Industrial Management; International Business; International Relations; Labour Law; Law; Management; Marketing; Nutrition; Orthodontics; Physical Education; Physical Therapy; Production Engineering; Safety Engineering; Sports; Surgery; Tourism); **Information Systems** (Information Sciences); **Journalism** (Journalism); **Law**; **Mechatronics Engineering** (Electronic Engineering; Mechanical Engineering); **Medicine** (Medicine); **Nursing** (Nursing); **Nutrition** (Nutrition); **Occupational Therapy** (Occupational Therapy); **Odontology** (Dentistry); **Pedagogy**; **Pharmacy** (Pharmacy); **Physical Education** (Physical Education); **Physical Therapy** (Physical Therapy); **Production Engineering** (Production Engineering); **Psychology** (Psychology); **Technological Studies** (Business Administration; Computer Science; Cosmetology; Fashion Design; Finance; Human Resources; Marketing)

History: Founded 1969. Acquired present status 1997.

Academic Year: February to December

Admission Requirements: Secondary school certificate and SAT examination (vestibular)

Main Language(s) of Instruction: Portuguese

Accrediting Agencies: Ministry of Education and Culture

Degrees and Diplomas: *Tecnólogo*; *Bacharelado*: 4 yrs; *Licenciatura*: 4-5 yrs; *Especialização/Aperfeiçoamento*; *Mestrado*. Also MBA.

Student Services: Canteen, Cultural centre, Handicapped facilities, Health services

Student Residential Facilities: None

Special Facilities: Art gallery. Movie studio. Radio station. Basalto Ecology Park

Libraries: Yes

Publications: Revista UNIARA *(biennially)*
Last Updated: 26/05/10

UNIVERSITY CENTRE OF BAHIA

Centro Universitario da Bahia (FIB)
Rua Xingu 179, Jardim Atalaia Stiep, Salvador, Bahia 41770130
Tel: +55(71) 2107-8100
EMail: fib@fib.br
Website: http://www.fib.br

Diretor Geral: Oseas Vieira Guedes

Courses

Accountancy (Accountancy); **Administration** (Administration); **Advertising** (Advertising and Publicity); **Computer Science** (Computer Science); **Engineering**; **Graduate Studies** (Administration; Civil Security; Dermatology; Environmental Management; Health Administration; Human Resources; Law; Management; Marketing; Medicine; Nursing; Nutrition; Petroleum and Gas Engineering; Safety Engineering; Transport Management); **Hotel Management** (Hotel Management); **Information Systems** (Information Sciences); **International Relations**; **Journalism** (Journalism); **Law**; **Marketing** (Marketing); **Nursing** (Nursing); **Nutrition** (Nutrition); **Pedagogy** (Pedagogy); **Pharmacy** (Pharmacy); **Physiotherapy** (Physical Therapy); **Professional Studies**; **Psychology** (Psychology); **Secretarial Studies**; **Social Services** (Social and Community Services); **Tourism**

History: Founded 1997

Degrees and Diplomas: *Tecnólogo*; *Bacharelado*; *Licenciatura*; *Especialização/Aperfeiçoamento*. Also MBA.
Last Updated: 25/05/10

UNIVERSITY CENTRE OF BARRA MANSA

Centro Universitário de Barra Mansa (UBM)
Rua Vereador Pinho de Carvalho, 267, Centro, Barra Mansa,
Rio de Janeiro 27330-550
Tel: +55(24) 3325-0222
Fax: +55(24) 3323-3690
EMail: ubm@ubm.br
Website: http://www.ubm.br

Reitor: Guilherme de Carvalho Cruz (2004-)
Tel: +55(24) 3325-0222, Fax: +55(24) 3323-3690
EMail: reitor@ubm.br

Pro-Reitor Administration: Feres Nader
Tel: +55(24) 3325-0222, Fax: +55(24) 3323-3690
EMail: pro.adm@ubm.br

International Relations: Terry Vincent McIntyre, Coordinator,
International Programmes
Tel: +55(24) 3325-0262, Fax: +55(24) 3323-9565
EMail: terry.mcintyre@ubm.br

Courses

Accountancy; **Administration**; **Arts and Humanities** (Arts and Humanities; English; Spanish); **Automation and Control Engineering**; **Biological and Life Sciences**; **Computer Engineering** (Computer Graphics; Computer Networks; Data Processing; Software Engineering); **Computer Science** (Computer Science); **Educational Sciences** (Pedagogy); **Geography** (Geography (Human)); **Graduate Studies** (Acupuncture; Art Education; Art History; Biological and Life Sciences; Communication Studies; Data Processing; Dietetics; Economics; Education; Educational Administration; Electronic Engineering; English; Environmental Management; Environmental Studies; Finance; Gerontology; History; Human Resources; Industrial and Organizational Psychology; Industrial Management; Information Technology; Literature; Management; Marketing; Mathematics Education; Mechanical Engineering; Nursing; Nutrition; Philosophy; Physical Education; Physical Therapy; Portuguese; Public Administration; Public Health; Rehabilitation and Therapy; Spanish; Statistics; Theatre; Transport Management); **History** (History); **Law** (Private Law; Public Law); **Mathematics** (Mathematics); **Music** (Music); **Nursing**; **Nutrition** (Nutrition); **Pedagogy**; **Petroleum and Gas Engineering**; **Pharmacy**; **Physical Education** (Physical Education); **Physical Therapy** (Physical

Therapy); **Production Engineering** (Production Engineering); **Psychology**; **Social Communication**; **Technological Studies** (Environmental Management; Human Resources; Industrial Management; Safety Engineering; Tourism; Transport Management); **Veterinary Medicine** (Veterinary Science); **Visual Arts** (Painting and Drawing; Photography; Sculpture)

Further Information: Also Cicuta Unit and Barra Mansa campus.

History: Founded 1961.

Governing Bodies: Barra Mansa Society of Higher Education

Academic Year: February to December

Admission Requirements: High School Diploma and Vestibular (university entrance exam)

Fees: (Reais): 304-1,173 per month

Main Language(s) of Instruction: Portuguese

International Co-operation: With universities in USA.

Accrediting Agencies: Federal Ministry of Education and Culture (MEC)

Degrees and Diplomas: *Tecnólogo*; *Bacharelado*; *Licenciatura*; *Especialização/Aperfeiçoamento*. Also MBA.

Student Services: Academic counselling, Canteen, Cultural centre, Foreign student adviser, Handicapped facilities, Health services, Language programs, Sports facilities

Student Residential Facilities: None

Special Facilities: Art Gallery; Museum; Rapido Museum (copies of art works). Judicial Training Centre; Cultural Centre; Theatre.

Libraries: 43,151 vols; c. 500 periodicals; c. 450 CDs; c. 1,800 videos

Publications: Caderno de Cultura Referencia *(quarterly)*; Revista Cientifica

Last Updated: 26/05/10

UNIVERSITY CENTRE OF BELO HORIZONTE

Centro Universitário de Belo Horizonte (UNIBH)
Rua Diamantina 567, 2° Andar, Lagoinha, Belo Horizonte,
Minas Gerais 31110320
Tel: +55(31) 3423-9495
Fax: +55(31) 3423-9499
EMail: unibh@unibh.br
Website: http://www.unibh.br

Reitora: Sueli Maria Baliza Dias EMail: ffaria@unibh.br

Pró-Reitor Administrativo: Wellington José da Cunha
EMail: praf@unibh.br

Departments

Biological, Environmental and Health Sciences *(DCBAS)*; **Communication Sceinces** *(DCC)*; **Exact Sciences and Technology** *(DCET)* (Architecture; Chemical Engineering; Civil Engineering; Computer Networks; Computer Science; Construction Engineering; Cosmetology; Electrical Engineering; Environmental Engineering; Environmental Management; Food Technology; International Business; Mathematics; Production Engineering; Telecommunications Engineering; Town Planning); **Graduate Studies** (Business and Commerce; Communication Studies; Environmental Management; Food Technology; Human Resources; Information Technology; Marketing; Physical Therapy; Radio and Television Broadcasting; Sports; Transport Management); **Human Sciences, Letters and Arts** *(DCHLA)* (Arts and Humanities; History; Pedagogy; Social and Community Services); **Juridical, Political and Managerial Sciences** *(DCJPG)* (Accountancy; Administration; International Relations; Law); **Technology** (Civil Security; Computer Science; Fashion Design; Graphic Design; Information Technology; Marketing; Multimedia; Public Administration; Safety Engineering)

Further Information: Also Diamantina, Estoril and Lourdes campuses.

History: Founded 1970.

Main Language(s) of Instruction: Portuguese

Degrees and Diplomas: *Bacharelado*; *Licenciatura*; *Especialização/Aperfeiçoamento*; *Mestrado*. Also MBA.
Last Updated: 26/05/10

UNIVERSITY CENTRE OF BRASILIA

Centro Universitário de Brasília (UNICEUB)
Eqn. 707/907 Conjunto, Campus do CEUB, Asa Norte, Brasília,
DF 70790-075
Tel: +55(61) 3966-1385 +55(61) 3966-1384
Fax: +55(61) 3273-0503
EMail: nucleo.informacoes@uniceub.br
Website: http://www.uniceub.br

Reitor: Getúlio Américo Moreira Lopes

Courses

Accountancy (Accountancy); **Administration**; **Advertising and Publicity** (Advertising and Publicity); **Architecture and Urbanism**; **Arts and Humanities**; **Biology** (Biology); **Biomedicine**; **Civil Engineering** (Civil Engineering); **Communication and Marketing** (Communication Studies; Marketing); **Computer Engineering**; **Computer Science**; **Geography** (Geography); **Graduate Studies** (Commercial Law; Communication Studies; Criminal Law; Environmental Studies; Genetics; Higher Education; History; Immunology; Information Technology; International Relations; Labour Law; Law; Management; Marketing; Physical Therapy; Portuguese; Psychoanalysis; Psychology; Public Health; Public Law; Social Studies; Software Engineering); **History** (History); **International Relations** (International Relations); **Journalism** (Journalism); **Law** (Law); **Nursing** (Nursing); **Nutrition** (Nutrition); **Pedagogy** (Pedagogy); **Physical Education** (Physical Education); **Physical Therapy** (Physical Therapy); **Psychology** (Psychology); **Technological Studies** (Management; Systems Analysis)

Programmes
Mestrado and Doutorado

History: Founded 1968 as Centro de Ensino Unificado de Brasília. Acquired present title and status 1990.

Main Language(s) of Instruction: Portuguese

Degrees and Diplomas: *Tecnólogo*; *Bacharelado*; *Licenciatura*; *Mestrado*; *Doutorado*. Also postgraduate courses.
Last Updated: 26/05/10

UNIVERSITY CENTRE OF BRUSQUE

Centro Universitário de Brusque (UNIFEBE)
Rua Dorval Luz 123, Bairro Santa Terezinha, PO Box 1501,
Brusque, Santa Catarina 88352-400
Tel: +55(47) 3211-7000
Fax: +55(47) 3211-7000
EMail: reitoria@unifebe.edu.br
Website: http://www.unifebe.edu.br

Rector: Maria de Lourdes Busnardo Tridapalli (1998-)

Pró-Reitor Administration: Antônio Carlos Schlindwein
Tel: +55(47) 3211-7231 EMail: vice@unifebe.edu.br

International Relations: Eliane Tejera Lisbôa, Assessora of International Relations EMail: asrii@unifebe.edu.br

Courses

Accountancy; **Administration** (Administration); **Business Administration**; **Commercial Management**; **Fashion Design** (Fashion Design); **Graduate Studies** (Business Administration; Fashion Design; Textile Design); **History** (History); **Industrial Process Technology-Electromechanics** (Hydraulic Engineering; Industrial Engineering); **Information Sciences** (Information Sciences); **Law** (Law); **Literature** (Literature); **Logistics**; **Pedagogy** (Pedagogy); **Physical Education** (Physical Education); **Production Engineering** (Production Engineering); **Real Estate** (Real Estate); **Textile Production** (Textile Technology)

History: Founded 1973. Acquired present status 2003.

Governing Bodies: University Council

Academic Year: February to December

Admission Requirements: Secondary school diploma and entrance examination

Fees: (Reais): c. 319.80 per month

Main Language(s) of Instruction: Portuguese

International Co-operation: With universities in France and Italy

Degrees and Diplomas: *Tecnólogo*; *Bacharelado*; *Licenciatura*; *Especialização/Aperfeiçoamento*. Also MBA.

Student Services: Academic counselling, Canteen, Handicapped facilities

Special Facilities: Central Auditorium

Libraries: Central Library

Publications: Revista da Unifebe, Review of Scientific publications of Unifebe *(annually)*

Last Updated: 27/05/10

UNIVERSITY CENTRE OF CARATINGA

Centro Universitário de Caratinga (FUNEC)
Avenida Moacyr de Mattos 87, 1° Andar, Centro, Caratinga,
Minas Gerais 35300-047
Tel: +55(33) 3329-4500
EMail: cae@funec.br
Website: http://www.funec.br

Reitor: Antônio Fonseca da Silva
Tel: +55(33) 3329-4509 EMail: reitoria@funec.br

Courses
Accountancy (Accountancy); **Actuarial Sciences** (Actuarial Science); **Administrative Sciences** (Administration); **Arts and Humanities** (Arts and Humanities; English; French; Portuguese; Spanish); **Biological Sciences** (Biological and Life Sciences); **Chemistry** (Chemistry); **Computer Science**; **Cultural Production** (Cultural Studies); **Economics** (Economics); **Fonaudiology** (Speech Therapy and Audiology); **Geography** (Geography); **Graduate Studies** *(Lato Sensu)* (Business Administration; Business Education; Educational Administration; Environmental Management; Health Sciences; Nutrition; Pharmacology; Physical Education; Physiology; Public Health; Science Education); **Graduate Studies** *(Strictro Sensu)* (Education; Environmental Studies; Health Sciences; Modern Languages; Natural Sciences; Rehabilitation and Therapy); **Healt and Environmental Engineering** (Environmental Engineering); **History** (History); **Industrial and Technological Production Engineering** (Production Engineering); **Information Systmes**; **Mathematics** (Mathematics); **Medicine** (Medicine); **Nursing** (Nursing); **Nutrition** (Nutrition); **Pedagogy**; **Pharmacy** (Pharmacy); **Phsyical Therapy** (Physical Therapy); **Physical Education** (Physical Education); **Physics**; **Psychology** (Psychology); **Religious Studies** (Religious Studies); **Teacher Training** (Teacher Training)

History: Founded 1968.

Main Language(s) of Instruction: Portuguese

Degrees and Diplomas: *Bacharelado*; *Licenciatura*; *Especialização/Aperfeiçoamento*; *Mestrado*
Last Updated: 27/05/10

UNIVERSITY CENTRE OF CENTRAL SÃO PAULO

Centro Universitário Central Paulista (UNICEP SÃO CARLOS)
Rua Pedro Bianchi 111, Vila Alpes, São Carlos,
São Paulo 13570300
Tel: +55(16) 3363-2111
Fax: +55(16) 3272-6019
EMail: asser@asser.com.br
Website: http://www.unicep.com.br

Diretor Geral: Dorival Marcos Milani

Areas
Exact Sciences (Computer Engineering; Electrical Engineering; Information Sciences; Mathematics; Production Engineering); **Health and Biological Sciences** (Biology; Biomedicine; Nursing; Nutrition; Pharmacy; Physical Education; Physical Therapy; Psychology); **Human Sciences** (Accountancy; Administration; Advertising and Publicity; Architecture; History; Law; Literature; Pedagogy; Tourism; Town Planning); **Technological Studies** (Agriculture; Hotel and Restaurant; Radiology; Tourism)

Courses
Graduate Studies (Accountancy; Business Administration; Environmental Management; Finance; Law; Marketing; Safety Engineering; Town Planning; Transport Management)

Further Information: Also Miguel Petroni campus.

History: Founded 1974.

Main Language(s) of Instruction: Portuguese

Degrees and Diplomas: *Tecnólogo*: Radiology; Aeronautical Maintenance; *Bacharelado*; *Licenciatura*; *Especialização/Aperfeiçoamento*. Also MBA.
Last Updated: 21/05/10

UNIVERSITY CENTRE OF CERRADO PATROCÍNIO

Centro Universitário do Cerrado Patrocínio (UNICERP)
Rua Artur Botelho, s/n, Campus Universitário, Patrocíno,
Minas Gerais 38740000
Tel: +55(34) 3839-3737
Fax: +55(34) 3839-3737
EMail: unicerp@unicerp.edu.br
Website: http://www.unicerp.edu.br

Diretora: Iêda Pereira de Magalhães Martins

Courses
Accountancy; **Administration**; **Agribusiness**; **Agronomy**; **Biology**; **Information Systems** (Information Sciences); **Interior Design** (Interior Design); **Literature**; **Mathematics**; **Nursing**; **Nutrition** (Nutrition); **Pedagogy** (Pedagogy); **Phonoaudiology**; **Physical Education**; **Physiotherapy** (Physical Therapy); **Postgraduate**; **Psychology** (Psychology)

History: Founded 1997 as Faculdades Integradas de Patrocínio. Acquired present status and title 2005.

Main Language(s) of Instruction: Portuguese

Degrees and Diplomas: *Tecnólogo*; *Bacharelado*; *Licenciatura*. Also Postgraduate degree courses.
Last Updated: 01/06/10

UNIVERSITY CENTRE OF CURITIBA

Centro Universitário Curitiba (UNICURITIBA)
Rua Chile 1678 - Prédio, Curitibá, Paraná 80220-181
Tel: +55(41) 3213-8770
Fax: +55(41) 3213-8726
EMail: diretoria.fic@aena.br; processolegal@unicuritiba.edu.br
Website: http://www.unicuritiba.edu.br/

Reitor: Eric David Cohen

Pró-Reitor Acadêmico: Rainer Czajkowski

Secretária-Geral: Alison Regina Mazza

Courses
Administration (Accountancy; Administration; Human Resources; Marketing); **Advertising and Publicity** (Advertising and Publicity); **Financial Management** (Finance; Management); **Graduate Studies** (Administrative Law; Business Administration; Business and Commerce; Civil Law; Commercial Law; Communication Studies; Criminal Law; International Business; Law; Leadership; Marketing; Occupational Health; Sports Management; Transport Management); **Graphic Design** (Graphic Design); **Human Resources** (Human Resources); **Industrial Design**; **Industrial Production Management**; **Interior Design** (Interior Design); **International Relations**; **Journalism** (Journalism); **Law** (Law); **Logistics**; **Marketing**; **Mestrado** (Commercial Law); **Quality Management**; **Tourism**

History: Founded 2001.

Degrees and Diplomas: *Bacharelado*; *Licenciatura*; *Especialização/Aperfeiçoamento*; *Mestrado*. Also MBA.
Last Updated: 25/05/10

UNIVERSITY CENTRE OF ESPIRITO SANTO

Centro Universitário do Espirito Santo (UNESC)
Av. Fioravante Rossi, 2930, Bairro Martinelli, Colatina,
Espírito Santo 29703-900
Tel: +55(27) 3723-3000 +55(27) 2101-3000
Fax: +55(27) 3723-3000 +55(27) 2101-3000
EMail: revista@unesc.br
Website: http://www.unesc.br

Reitor: João Bosco de Castro Teixeira

Courses

Accountancy (Accountancy); **Administration** (Administration); **Civil Engineering** (Civil Engineering); **Graduate Studies** (Accountancy; Business Administration; Civil Law; Commercial Law; Computer Networks; Criminal Law; Gerontology; Health Administration; Health Sciences; Higher Education; Industrial and Organizational Psychology; Labour Law; Nutrition; Physical Therapy; Public Health; Public Law; Software Engineering; Water Management); **Information Systems** (Information Technology); **Law** (Law); **Mechanical Engineering** (Mechanical Engineering); **Medicine** (Medicine); **Nursing** (Nursing); **Nutrition** (Nutrition); **Pedagogy** (Pedagogy); **Pharmacy** (Pharmacy); **Physical Education** *(Bacharelado & Licenciatura)* (Physical Education); **Physical Therapy**; **Teacher Training** (Teacher Training); **Technological Studies** (Agricultural Business; Cosmetology; Fashion Design; Systems Analysis); **Telecommunications Engineering** (Telecommunications Engineering); **Veterinary Medicine** (Veterinary Science)

Further Information: Also Campus in Serra.

History: Founded 1997. Acquired present status 2000.

Main Language(s) of Instruction: Portuguese

Degrees and Diplomas: *Tecnólogo; Bacharelado; Licenciatura; Especialização/Aperfeiçoamento.* Also postgraduate degrees and MBA.

Last Updated: 01/06/10

UNIVERSITY CENTRE OF FINE ARTS OF SAO PAULO

Centro Universitário Belas Artes de São Paulo (FEBASP)

Rua Dr. Álvaro Alvin, 76 Vila Mariana, São Paulo,
São Paulo 4018-010
Tel: +55(11) 5576-7300
Fax: +55(11) 5549-7985
EMail: paulo.cardim@belasartes.br
Website: http://www.belasartes.br/

Reitor: Paulo Antonio Gomes Cardim

Courses

Advertising and Publicity (Advertising and Publicity); **Architecture and Town Planning** (Architecture; Town Planning); **Fashion Design** (Fashion Design); **Graduate Studies** (Architecture; Ceramic Art; Cinema and Television; Communication Studies; Design; Display and Stage Design; Educational Administration; Higher Education; Human Rights; International Relations; Museum Studies; Photography; Public Relations; Video); **Graphic Design** (Graphic Design); **Interior Design**; **International Relations** (International Relations); **Public Relations**; **Radio and TV** (Radio and Television Broadcasting); **Teacher Training** (Teacher Training); **Visual Arts** (Visual Arts)

History: Founded 1925. Acquired present status and title 2002.

Main Language(s) of Instruction: Portuguese

Degrees and Diplomas: *Bacharelado; Licenciatura; Especialização/Aperfeiçoamento*
Last Updated: 21/05/10

UNIVERSITY CENTRE OF FORMIGA

Centro Universitario de Formiga (UNIFOR-MG)

Avenida Dr. Arnaldo de Senna 328, Bairro Água Vermelha,
Formiga, Minas Gerais 37570-000
Tel: +55(37) 3329-1400
EMail: unifor@uniformg.edu.br
Website: http://www.uniformg.edu.br

Reitor: Marco Antonio de Souza Leão

Courses

Accountancy; **Administration** (Administration); **Architecture and Urbanism**; **Arts and Humanities**; **Arts and Humanities** (Arts and Humanities; English; Portuguese); **Biological Science** (Biological and Life Sciences); **Chemistry** (Chemistry); **Civil Engineering** (Civil Engineering); **Computer Science** (Computer Science); **Environmental Engineering** (Environmental Engineering); **Graduate Studies** (Accountancy; Business Administration; Marketing); **Law** (Law); **Library Science** (Library Science); **Nursing** (Nursing); **Nutrition** (Nutrition); **Pedagogy** (Pedagogy); **Physical Education**

(Bacharelado); **Physical Education** *(Licenciatura)* (Physical Education); **Physical Therapy** (Physical Therapy); **Production Engineering** (Production Engineering); **Social Service** (Social and Community Services); **Veterinary Science**

History: Founded 1974.

Main Language(s) of Instruction: Portuguese

Degrees and Diplomas: *Bacharelado; Licenciatura.* Also MBA.
Last Updated: 27/05/10

UNIVERSITY CENTRE OF GOIAS

Centro Universitário de Goiás (UNI-ANHANGÜERA)

Rua Professor Lázaro Costa 456, Cidade Jardim, Goiânia,
Goiás 74415420
Tel: +55(62) 3246-1400
Fax: +55(62) 3246-1444
EMail: anhanguera@anhanguera.edu.br
Website: http://www.fach.br

Reitor: Jovenny Sebastião Cândido de Oliveira

Courses

Accountancy (Accountancy); **Administration**; **Advertising and Publicity** (Advertising and Publicity); **Agronomy**; **Biological Sciences** (Biological and Life Sciences); **Chemistry**; **Computer Engineering**; **Economics**; **Graduate Studies** *(Lato Sensu)* (Accountancy; Agricultural Business; Agricultural Engineering; Biological and Life Sciences; Biology; Biotechnology; Business Administration; Business Education; Civil Law; Commercial Law; Communication Studies; Cosmetology; Ecology; Education; Educational Administration; Educational Psychology; Environmental Management; Finance; Higher Education; Human Resources; Information Management; Irrigation; Laboratory Techniques; Labour Law; Landscape Architecture; Management; Marketing; Occupational Health; Pharmacy; Plant and Crop Protection; Psychiatry and Mental Health; Public Administration; Public Health; Public Law; Real Estate; Safety Engineering; Software Engineering; Statistics; Transport Management); **Graduate Studies** *(Stricto Sensu)*; **Law**; **Pedagogy** (Pedagogy); **Technological Studies**

History: Founded 1973 as Faculdade Anhangüera. Acquired present status and title 2004.

Degrees and Diplomas: *Tecnólogo; Bacharelado; Licenciatura; Especialização/Aperfeiçoamento; Mestrado*
Last Updated: 27/05/10

UNIVERSITY CENTRE OF HIGHER EDUCATION OF THE AMAZON

Centro Universitario de Ensino Superior do Amazonas (CIESA)

Rua Pedro Dias Leme 203, Flores, Mánaus, Amazonas 69058-818
Tel: +55(92) 3643-4200
Fax: +55(92) 3642-4243
EMail: ciesa@ciesa.br
Website: http://www.ciesa.br

Reitor: Valdecir Antonio Simão EMail: valdecir.simao@ciesa.br

Courses

Accountancy (Accountancy); **Administration**; **Computer Science** (Computer Science); **Economics** (Economics); **Graduate Studies** (Business Administration; Business and Commerce; Law); **Law**; **Pedagogy** (Pedagogy); **Public Relations** (Public Relations); **Secretarial Studies**; **Technological Studies**; **Tourism**

History: Founded 1974.

Main Language(s) of Instruction: Portuguese

Degrees and Diplomas: *Tecnólogo; Bacharelado*: 4 yrs; *Especialização/Aperfeiçoamento.* Aslo MBA.
Last Updated: 27/05/10

UNIVERSITY CENTRE OF ITAJUBÁ

Centro Universitário de Itajubá (FEPI)

Avenida Doutor Antônio Braga Filho 687, Varginha, Itajubá,
Minas Gerais 37501-002
Tel: +55(35) 3629-8400
Fax: +55(35) 3629-8400
EMail: universitas@fepi.br
Website: http://www.fepi.br

Reitor: Erwin Rolf Mádisson Júnior

Courses

Arts and Humanities; **Biological Sciences** (Biological and Life Sciences); **Civil Engineering** (Civil Engineering); **Graduate Studies**; **Industrial Automation** (Automation and Control Engineering); **Information Systems**; **Law** (Law); **Mechanical Manufacture** (Mechanical Equipment and Maintenance; Metal Techniques); **Pedagogy**; **Pharmacy**; **Physical Education** (Physical Education); **Physical Therapy** (Physical Therapy); **Production Engineering** (Production Engineering); **Psychology**; **Veterinary Medicine**

Further Information: Also Brasópolis, Borda da Mata and Natércia Units.

History: Founded 1965.

Main Language(s) of Instruction: Portuguese

Degrees and Diplomas: *Tecnólogo*; *Bacharelado*; *Licenciatura*; *Especialização/Aperfeiçoamento*
Last Updated: 28/05/10

UNIVERSITY CENTRE OF JALES

Centro Universitário de Jales (UNIJALES)
Avenida Francisco Jales 1851, Centro, Jales, São Paulo 15700000
Tel: +55(17) 3622-1620
EMail: unijales@unijales.edu.br
Website: http://www.unijales.edu.br/unijales
Diretora: Maria Christina Fuster Soler Bernardo (1995-)

Courses

Accountancy; **Administration** (Administration); **Arts and Humanities** (Arts and Humanities; Portuguese; Spanish); **Arts and Humanities** (Arts and Humanities; English; Portuguese); **Biological and Life Sciences** (Biological and Life Sciences); **Geography** (Geography); **Graduate Studies** (Accountancy; Agriculture; Business Administration; Dance; Education; Educational Administration; Educational Psychology; English; Environmental Management; Finance; Fine Arts; History; Information Management; Information Sciences; Literature; Mathematics Education; Music; Physical Education; Portuguese; Public Administration; Public Health; Social and Community Services; Spanish; Sports; Sports Management); **History** (History); **Information Systems** (Information Sciences); **Mathematics** (Mathematics); **Nursing**; **Pedagogy** (Pedagogy); **Pharmacy**; **Physical Education**; **Physical Therapy** (Physical Therapy); **Social Services** (Social and Community Services); **Tourism**; **Visual Arts - Art Education** (Art Education; Visual Arts)

History: Founded 1970.

Degrees and Diplomas: *Bacharelado*; *Licenciatura*; *Especialização/Aperfeiçoamento*. Also MBA.
Last Updated: 28/05/10

UNIVERSITY CENTRE OF JARAGUÁ DO SUL

Centro Universitário de Jaraguá do Sul (UNERJ)
Caixa Postal 251, Rua dos Imigrantes, 500, Vila Rau, Jaraguá do Sul, Santa Catarina 89254-430
Tel: +55(47) 3275-8200
Fax: +55(47) 3275-8200
EMail: reitoria@unerj.br
Website: http://www.unerj.br

Reitora: Pedra Santana Alves

Pró-Reitor de Administração: Paulo Onildo de Matos

International Relations: Pedro Guilherme Kraus
Tel: +55(47) 3275-8232, Fax: +55(47) 3275-8200
EMail: pgkraus@unerj.br

Centres

Applied Social and Juridical Sciences (Accountancy; Administration; Business Administration; Human Resources; International Business; Law; Marketing; Transport and Communications); **Art and Technology** (Architectural Restoration; Architecture and Planning; Automation and Control Engineering; Design; Electrical Engineering; Environmental Management; Fashion Design; Food Technology; Mechanical Engineering; Production Engineering; Systems Analysis; Town Planning); **Humanities and Education**

Courses

Graduate Studies

History: Founded 1973. Acquired present status 2000.
Governing Bodies: Board of Directors
Academic Year: March to December
Admission Requirements: Examination
Main Language(s) of Instruction: Portuguese
International Co-operation: With universities in USA; Spain; Chile; Portugal; Germany; Mexico; Argentina; Italy
Accrediting Agencies: Ministry of Education; Conselho Estadual de Educação
Degrees and Diplomas: *Tecnólogo*; *Bacharelado*; *Licenciatura*; *Especialização/Aperfeiçoamento*; *Mestrado*
Student Services: Canteen, Language programs, Sports facilities
Libraries: Yes
Publications: Saberes *(quarterly)*
Last Updated: 28/05/10

UNIVERSITY CENTRE OF JOÃO PESSOA

Centro Universitário de João Pessoa (UNIPE)
Campus do Unipê BR 230 Km, Água Fria, João Pessoa, Paraíba 58053-000
Tel: +55(83) 2106-9200
Fax: +55(83) 3231-1130
EMail: info@unipe.br
Website: http://www.unipe.br

Reitor: José Loureiro Lopes
Tel: +55(83) 2106-9202 / 9240 EMail: sramalho@unipe.br

Courses

Accountancy (Accountancy); **Administration**; **Architecture and Town Planning**; **Computer Science**; **Fashion Design**; **Fonaudiology** (Speech Therapy and Audiology); **Graduate Studies** *(MBA)* (Business Administration; Computer Science); **Graduate Studies** *(Especializações)*; **Information Technology Management** (Information Technology); **Law**; **Nursing** (Nursing); **Odontology** (Dentistry); **Physical Education**; **Physical Therapy** (Physical Therapy); **Psychology**; **Systems for Internet** (Computer Science)

History: Founded 1997.

Main Language(s) of Instruction: Portuguese

Degrees and Diplomas: *Tecnólogo*; *Bacharelado*; *Especialização/ Aperfeiçoamento*. Also MBA.
Last Updated: 28/05/10

UNIVERSITY CENTRE OF LAVRAS

Centro Universitário de Lavras (UNILAVRAS)
Rua Padre José Poggel, 506, Centenário, Minas Gerais 37200000
Tel: +55(800) 283-2833
EMail: reitoria@unilavras.edu.br
Website: http://www.unilavras.edu.br

Reitora: Christiane Amaral Lunkes Argenta

Courses

Biology (Biology); **Civil Engineering** (Civil Engineering); **Graduate Studies**; **Graduate Studies - Licenciatura** (Biological and Life Sciences; Chemistry; Pedagogy; Teacher Training); **Industrial Chemistry** (Industrial Chemistry); **Law**; **Nursing**; **Nutrition** (Nutrition); **Odontology** (Dentistry); **Pharmacy** (Pharmacy); **Physiotherapy**; **Production Engineering**; **Psychology**; **Technological Studies**

History: Founded 1968.

Main Language(s) of Instruction: Portuguese

Degrees and Diplomas: *Tecnólogo*; *Bacharelado*; *Licenciatura*; *Especialização/Aperfeiçoamento*
Last Updated: 28/05/10

UNIVERSITY CENTRE OF LESTE MINAS GERAIS

Centro Universitário do Leste de Minas Gerais (UNILESTE-MG)

Av Tancredo de Almeida Neves, 3500, Bairro Universitário,
Coronel Fabriciano, Minas Gerais 35170-056
Tel: +55(31) 3846-5500
Fax: +55(31) 3846-5524
EMail: unilestemg@unilestemg.br
Website: http://www.unilestemg.br

Reitor: Genésio Zeferino da Silva Filho
Tel: +55(31) 3846-7901, Fax: +55(31) 3846-7953
EMail: reitoria@unilestemg.br

Areas
Applied Social Sciences; **Educational Sciences** (English; Geography; History; Literature; Pedagogy; Philosophy; Portuguese); **Exact Sciences** (Automation and Control Engineering; Chemical Engineering; Civil Engineering; Computer Science; Electrical Engineering; Environmental Engineering; Materials Engineering; Mechanical Engineering; Metallurgical Engineering; Production Engineering); **Health Sciences** (Biological and Life Sciences; Health Sciences; Nursing; Nutrition; Pharmacy; Physical Education; Physical Therapy; Psychology)

Courses
Graduate Studies *(Mestrado)* (Industrial Engineering); **Graduate Studies** *(Especialização)* (Accountancy; Administration; Architecture; Art Management; Automation and Control Engineering; Biological and Life Sciences; Biomedicine; Business Administration; Business and Commerce; Business Education; Clinical Psychology; Communication Studies; Dental Technology; Ecology; Education; Educational Administration; Educational Psychology; Engineering; English; Environmental Management; Finance; Gerontology; Health Administration; Higher Education; Human Resources; Industrial and Organizational Psychology; Industrial Engineering; Law; Literacy Education; Literature; Marketing; Mathematics Education; Metal Techniques; Metallurgical Engineering; Nursing; Nutrition; Orthodontics; Pedagogy; Periodontics; Pharmacology; Physical Therapy; Psychiatry and Mental Health; Psychoanalysis; Psychology; Public Administration; Public Health; Public Law; Safety Engineering; Sports; Telecommunications Engineering; Transport Management; Water Management); **Technological Studies** (Computer Networks; Environmental Management; Management; Metal Techniques; Metallurgical Engineering)

History: Founded 1972

Governing Bodies: Faculdade de Engenharia

Academic Year: February to December

Admission Requirements: High school diploma

Fees: (Reais): 3,000 per semester (depending on course)

Main Language(s) of Instruction: Portuguese

International Co-operation: With universities in Portugal, France and Italy.

Degrees and Diplomas: *Tecnólogo*; *Bacharelado*; *Licenciatura*; *Especialização/Aperfeiçoamento*; *Mestrado*. Also MBA.

Student Services: Academic counselling, Canteen, Cultural centre, Foreign student adviser, Handicapped facilities, Health services, Language programs, Social counselling, Sports facilities

Student Residential Facilities: None

Special Facilities: Museum; Photographic Studio; Radio and Television Laboratory; Software Development Laboratory.

Libraries: Yes

Publications: Doxa (Scientific Journal), Technical articles, Research papers *(biennially)*
Last Updated: 01/06/10

UNIVERSITY CENTRE OF LINS

Centro Universitário de Lins (UNILINS)

Avenida Nicolau Zarvos, 1925, Jardim Aeroporto, Lins,
São Paulo 16401-371
Tel: +55(14) 3533-3200
Fax: +55(14) 3533-3248
EMail: unilins@unilins.edu.br
Website: http://www.unilins.edu.br

Reitor: Milton Léo EMail: reitoria@unilins.edu.br

Courses
Administration (Administration); **Automation and Control Engineering - Mechatronics**; **Civil Engineering** (Civil Engineering); **Computer Engineering** (Computer Engineering); **Electronic Engineering**; **Electrotechnical Engineering** (Electrical and Electronic Engineering; Electronic Engineering); **Environmental Engineering**; **Executive Secretarial Studies**; **Graduate Studies** (Advertising and Publicity; Agricultural Business; Automation and Control Engineering; Business Administration; Computer Science; Environmental Studies; Health Sciences; Higher Education; Human Resources; Industrial Chemistry; Information Sciences; International and Comparative Education; Law; Safety Engineering; Social Policy; Social Work; Structural Architecture; Surveying and Mapping; Transport Engineering); **Information Systems** (Information Sciences); **Marketing** (Marketing); **Nursing**; **Social Services** (Social and Community Services); **Technological Studies**

History: Founded 1964, acquired present status 2001.

Main Language(s) of Instruction: Portuguese

International Co-operation: With Fundação Eduardo dos Santos based in Luanda, Angola

Degrees and Diplomas: *Tecnólogo*; *Bacharelado*; *Especialização/Aperfeiçoamento*. Also MBA.

Student Services: Academic counselling, Canteen, Cultural centre, Employment services, Foreign student adviser, Foreign Studies Centre, Handicapped facilities, Health services, Language programs, Nursery care, Social counselling, Sports facilities

Student Residential Facilities: Yes

Special Facilities: Movie studio

Libraries: Yes

Publications: Estudos e Pesquisas; Jornal de Olho na Fundação *(biennially)*; Revista Científica *(annually)*
Last Updated: 28/05/10

UNIVERSITY CENTRE OF MARANHÃO

Centro Universitário do Maranhão (UNICEUMA)

Rua Josué Montello, n°1, Bairro Renascença II, São Luís,
Maranhão 65075-120
Tel: +55(98) 3214-4277
Fax: +55(98) 3235-3265
EMail: ceuma@ceuma.br
Website: http://www.ceuma.br

Reitora: Cristina Nitz da Cruz

Areas
Engineering (Architecture; Environmental Engineering; Production Engineering; Town Planning); **Exact Sciences** (Information Sciences; Information Technology); **Health Sciences** (Biology; Dentistry; Medicine; Nursing; Nutrition; Occupational Health; Pharmacy; Physical Education; Physical Therapy; Speech Therapy and Audiology); **Human Sciences** (Accountancy; Administration; Advertising and Publicity; English; Law; Literature; Pedagogy; Portuguese; Psychology; Social and Community Services; Spanish)

Courses
Graduate Studies *(Stricto Sensu - Mestrado)* (Biology; Dentistry); **Graduate Studies** *(L.ato Sensu)*; **Technological Studies** (Business Administration; Construction Engineering; Cooking and Catering; Cosmetology; Fashion Design; Interior Design; Marketing; Real Estate; Systems Analysis)

Further Information: Also Cohama, Anil, Bacabal, Imperatriz and Timon Units.

History: Founded 1992.

Main Language(s) of Instruction: Portuguese

Degrees and Diplomas: *Tecnólogo*; *Bacharelado*; *Licenciatura*; *Especialização/Aperfeiçoamento*; *Mestrado*. Also MBA.
Last Updated: 02/06/10

UNIVERSITY CENTRE OF MARINGÁ

Centro Universitário de Maringá (CESUMAR)
Avenida Guedner, 1610, Jardim Aclimação, Maringá,
Paraná 87050-390
Tel: +55(44) 3027-6360
EMail: info@cesumar.br
Website: http://www.cesumar.br

Reitor: Wilson de Matos Silva (1998-) EMail: reitor@cesumar.br

Courses
Accountancy (Accountancy); **Administration**; **Advertising** (Advertising and Publicity); **Agricultural Business** (Agricultural Business); **Agronomy**; **Architecture**; **Biological Sciences**; **Biomedicine**; **Civil Engineering** (Civil Engineering); **Commercial Management** (Business and Commerce); **Computer Networks** (Computer Networks); **Computer Science**; **Cosmetology** (Cosmetology); **Electrical Engineering**; **English Literature** (English; Literature); **Environmental Engineering** (Environmental Engineering); **Fashion Design** (Fashion Design); **Fonaudiology** (Speech Therapy and Audiology); **Gastronomy** (Cooking and Catering); **Graduate Studies** (Accountancy; Administration; Communication Arts; Computer Science; Dentistry; Education; Engineering; Environmental Studies; Fashion Design; Health Sciences; Law; Nutrition; Physical Education; Psychology; Veterinary Science; Visual Arts); **Graduate Studies** (Stricto Sensu - Mestrado) (Law); **Graduate Studies** (MBA) (Business Administration; Marketing); **Human Resources** (Human Resources); **Industrial Automation** (Automation and Control Engineering); **Information Systems**; **Integral Administration** (Administration); **Interior Design**; **International Business**; **Journalism**; **Law**; **Marketing**; **Mechatronic Engineering** (Electronic Engineering; Mechanical Engineering); **Nursing** (Nursing); **Nutrition** (Nutrition); **Odontology** (Dentistry); **Pedagogy** (Pedagogy); **Pharmacy** (Pharmacy); **Physical Education** (Physical Education); **Physiotherapy** (Physical Therapy); **Psychology**; **Social Services**; **Spanish Literature** (Literature; Spanish); **Systems Analysis** (Systems Analysis); **Technological Studies** (Agriculture; International Business; Marketing; Real Estate); **Theology**; **Tourism** (Tourism); **Veterinary Science** (Veterinary Science); **Visual Arts** (Visual Arts)

History: Founded 1990.

Degrees and Diplomas: Tecnólogo; Bacharelado; Licenciatura; Especialização/Aperfeiçoamento; Mestrado. Also MBA.
Last Updated: 28/05/10

UNIVERSITY CENTRE OF NORTHERN SÃO PAULO

Centro Universitário do Norte Paulista (UNORP)
Rua Ipiranga, 3460, Jardim Alto Rio Prêto, São José do Rio Prêto,
São Paulo 15020-040
Tel: +55(17) 3203-2500
Fax: +55(17) 3203-2515
EMail: deluca@unorp.br
Website: http://www.unorp.br

Reitor: Eudes Quintino de Oliveira Junior
EMail: eudesojrreitor@unorp.br

Pró-Reitor Administrativo: Augusto Cezar Casseb
EMail: accasseb@unorp.br

Courses
Accountancy (Accountancy); **Administration**; **Agronomy**; **Architecture and Urbanism** (Architecture; Town Planning); **Arts and Humanities** (Arts and Humanities; English; Portuguese; Spanish; Translation and Interpretation); **Biological and Life Sciences** (Biological and Life Sciences); **Biomedicine** (Biomedicine); **Chemical Engineering**; **Civil Engineering** (Civil Engineering); **Computer Engineering** (Computer Engineering); **Computer Science** (Computer Science); **Electrical Engineering**; **Gastronomy and Events** (Cooking and Catering); **Graduate Studies** (Accountancy; Administration; Agriculture; Civil Law; Communication Studies; Criminal Law; Curriculum; Dental Technology; Dentistry; Education; Finance; Forensic Medicine and Dentistry; Health Sciences; Higher Education; Human Resources; Labour Law; Marketing; Orthodontics; Pedagogy; Periodontics; Physical Education; Physical Therapy; Portuguese; Psychology; Public Administration; Radiology; Special Education; Stomatology; Tourism); **Information Systems** (Information Sciences); **Labour Safety Engineering**; **Law** (Law); **Nur-**

sing; **Nutrition** (Nutrition); **Occupational Therapy** (Occupational Therapy); **Odontology** (Dentistry); **Pedagogy**; **Pharmacy** (Pharmacy); **Phonoaudiology**; **Physical Education** (Physical Education); **Physiotherapy** (Physical Therapy); **Production Engineering** (Production Engineering); **Psychology** (Psychology); **Social Communication** (Mass Communication); **Technological Studies** (Advertising and Publicity; Agricultural Business; Agricultural Management; Cosmetology; Ecology; Environmental Management; Fashion Design; Finance; Graphic Design; Hotel Management; Human Resources; International Business; Jewelry Art; Marketing; Real Estate; Safety Engineering; Systems Analysis; Tourism; Transport Management); **Telecommunications Engineering** (Telecommunications Engineering)

History: Founded 1972 as Faculdade Riopretense de Filosofia, Ciências e Letras, acquired present status and title 1996.

Academic Year: February to December

Admission Requirements: Secondary school certificate

Main Language(s) of Instruction: Portuguese

Degrees and Diplomas: Tecnólogo; Bacharelado; Licenciatura; Especialização/Aperfeiçoamento

Student Services: Canteen, Cultural centre, Handicapped facilities, Sports facilities

Special Facilities: Studio. Multimedia Laboratory. Language Laboratory

Libraries: Total, 40,000 items

Publications: Leia Já, Pedagogy articles and general information (monthly)
Last Updated: 02/06/10

UNIVERSITY CENTRE OF PARÁ

Centro Universitário do Pará (CESUPA)
Avenida Nazaré 630, Nazaré, Belém, Pará 66035-170
Tel: +55(91) 4009-2100
Fax: +55(91) 4009-2116
EMail: cesupa@cesupa.br
Website: http://www.cesupa.br

Reitor: João Paulo do Valle Mendes

Areas
Applied Sciences; **Biological and Health Sciences** (Biology; Dentistry; Environmental Studies; Medicine; Nursing; Nutrition; Pharmacy; Physical Therapy); **Exact Sciences and Technology** (Computer Networks; Computer Science; Data Processing; Information Sciences; Production Engineering; Systems Analysis)

Courses
Graduate Studies

Further Information: Also José Malcher, Almirante Barroso, Oliveira Belo campuses.

History: Founded 1989.

Main Language(s) of Instruction: Portuguese

Degrees and Diplomas: Tecnólogo; Bacharelado; Licenciatura; Especialização/Aperfeiçoamento
Last Updated: 02/06/10

UNIVERSITY CENTRE OF PATOS DE MINAS

Centro Universitário de Patos de Minas (UNIPAM)
Rua Major Gote, 808, Bairro Caiçaras, Patos de Minas,
Minas Gerais 38702-054
Tel: +55(34) 3823-0300 +55(34) 3822-1599
Fax: +55(34) 3822-1312
EMail: webmaster@fepam.br
Website: http://www.unipam.edu.br

Reitor: Raul Scher

Pró-Reitor de Planejamento, Administração e Finanças: Milton Roberto de Castro Teixeira

Courses
Accountancy (Accountancy); **Administration** (Administration); **Agronomy** (Agronomy); **Arts and Humanities** (Arts and Humanities; Literature); **Biological Sciences** (Biological and Life Sciences); **Chemcial Engineering** (Chemical Engineering); **Chemistry** (Chemistry); **Civil Engineering** (Civil Engineering);

Environmental Engineering (Environmental Engineering); Executive Secretarial Studies (Secretarial Studies); Graduate Studies; History (History); Information Systems (Information Sciences); Law; Mathematics; Medicine; Nursing (Nursing); Nutrition (Nutrition); Pedagogy (Pedagogy); Pharmacy; Physical Education (Physical Education); Physical Therapy; Physics (Physics); Production Engineering (Production Engineering); Psychology (Psychology); Social Communication - Advertising and Publicity (Advertising and Publicity); Social Communication - Journalism (Journalism); Technological Studies (Agricultural Business; Business and Commerce); Zootechnics

History: Founded 2001.

Degrees and Diplomas: Tecnólogo; Bacharelado; Licenciatura; Especialização/Aperfeiçoamento. Also postgraduate studies
Last Updated: 28/05/10

UNIVERSITY CENTRE OF RIO PRÊTO

Centro Universitário de Rio Prêto (UNIRP)
Rua Yvette Gabriel Atique 45, Boa Vista, São José do Rio Prêto, São Paulo 15025-400
Tel: +55(17) 3211-3000
Fax: +55(17) 3211-3199
EMail: reitoria@unirpnet.com.br
Website: http://www.unirpnet.com.br

Reitor: Halim Atique Júnior (1998-)

Courses

Accountancy (Accountancy); Administration; Architecture and Town Planning (Architecture; Town Planning); Art Education; Biology (Biology); Computer Engineering; Computer Science (Computer Science); Economics; Electrical Engineering; Fashion Design (Fashion Design); Graduate Studies (Accountancy; Administration; Animal Husbandry; Biotechnology; Business and Commerce; Civil Law; Commercial Law; Communication Studies; Criminal Law; Dentistry; Educational Psychology; Environmental Management; Fashion Design; Finance; Higher Education; Human Resources; Information Technology; Labour Law; Literature; Marketing; Mathematics Education; Nutrition; Pharmacy; Physical Education; Special Education; Veterinary Science); Law (Law); Mathematics; Nursing (Nursing); Nutrition; Odontology (Dentistry); Pedagogy (Pedagogy); Pharmacy (Pharmacy); Physical Education (Physical Education); Physiotherapy (Physical Therapy); Social Communication (Advertising and Publicity; Journalism); Technological Studies (Agriculture; Cosmetology; Environmental Management; Information Technology; Safety Engineering); Veterinary Science (Veterinary Science)

History: Founded 1965.

Main Language(s) of Instruction: Portuguese

Degrees and Diplomas: Tecnólogo; Bacharelado; Licenciatura; Especialização/Aperfeiçoamento. Also MBA.
Last Updated: 31/05/10

UNIVERSITY CENTRE OF SANTO ANDRÉ

Centro Universitário de Santo André (UNIA)
Rua Senador Flaquer, 456/459, Centro, Santo André, São Paulo 09010-160
Tel: +55(11) 4435-8899
Fax: +55(11) 4992-2963
EMail: secretaria@unia.br
Website: http://www.unia.br

Diretor: Paulo Rolim Rosa
EMail: paulo.rosa@unianhanguera.edu.br

Courses

Accountancy (Accountancy); Administration (Accountancy; Administration; Communication Studies; Economics; Finance; Human Resources; International Relations; Law; Mathematics; Transport Management); Arts and Humanities (Arts and Humanities; English; Linguistics; Literature; Portuguese); Biological Sciences (Anatomy; Biochemistry; Biological and Life Sciences; Biophysics; Cell Biology; Chemistry; Ecology; Embryology and Reproduction Biology; Genetics; Histology; Immunology; Law; Mathematics; Organic Chemistry; Parasitology; Physiology; Zoology); Computer Science (Computer Science; Data Processing; Mathematics; Software Engineering); Executive Secretarial Stu-

dies; Graduate Studies; Law; Mechanical Engineering (Mechanical Engineering); Nursing (Nursing); Pedagogy; Production Engineering; Psychology; Social Services (Social and Community Services); Technological Studies (Advertising and Publicity; Automation and Control Engineering; Business and Commerce; Computer Science; Electronic Engineering; Environmental Management; Finance; Health Administration; Human Resources; Interior Design; International Business; Management; Marketing; Mechanical Engineering; Public Administration; Radiology; Safety Engineering; Systems Analysis; Transport Engineering)

History: Founded 1969.

Degrees and Diplomas: Tecnólogo; Bacharelado; Licenciatura; Especialização/Aperfeiçoamento. Also MBA.
Last Updated: 31/05/10

UNIVERSITY CENTRE OF SETE LAGOAS

Centro Universitario de Sete Lagoas (UNIFEMM)
Av. Marechal Castelo Branco 2765, Santo António, Sete Lagoas, Minas Gerais 35701242
Tel: +55(31) 2106-2106
Fax: +55(31) 2106-2101
EMail: comunicacao@unifemm.edu.br
Website: http://www.unifemm.edu.br

Diretor: Antônio Fernandino de Castro Bahia Filho
EMail: falecomreitor@unifemm.edu.br

Courses

Accountancy (Accountancy); Administration (Administration); Arts and Humanities (Arts and Humanities; English; Literature; Portuguese; Spanish); Biological Sciences (Biological and Life Sciences); Economic Sciences (Economics); Environmental Engineering (Environmental Engineering); Geography (Geography); Graduate Studies; History; Information Management (Information Management); Law (Law); Mathematics (Mathematics); Metallurgical Engineering; Nursing (Nursing); Nutrition (Nutrition); Pedagogy (Pedagogy); Physical Education (Physical Education); Physics (Physics); Production and Mechanical Engineering (Mechanical Engineering; Production Engineering); Public Administration (Public Administration); Social Services; Technological Studies

History: Founded 1999 as Faculdades FEMM. Acquired present status and title 2006.

Degrees and Diplomas: Tecnólogo; Bacharelado; Licenciatura; Especialização/Aperfeiçoamento
Last Updated: 31/05/10

UNIVERSITY CENTRE OF THE ARAXA PLATEAU

Centro Universitário do Planalto de Araxá (UNIARAXÁ)
Av. Ministro Olavo Drummond, 5, Campus Universitário, São Geraldo, Araxa, Minas Gerais 38180-084
Tel: +55(34) 3669-2000
Fax: +55(34) 3669-2002
EMail: uniaraxa@uniaraxa.edu.br
Website: http://www.uniaraxa.edu.br

Reitor: Válter Gomes EMail: reitoria@uniaraxa.edu.br

Vice Reitora: Lídia Maria de Oliveira Jordão Rocha da Cunha

Higher Institutes
Education/Technology (ISE/T) (Business Administration; Computer Science; Human Resources; Marketing; Pedagogy)

Institutes
Exact and Human Sciences (ICEH); Health Sciences (ICS) (Biological and Life Sciences; Biology; Nursing; Physical Education; Physical Therapy)

History: Founded 1999 as Faculdades Integradas do Alto Paranaíba, following merger of the Faculdade de Filosofia do Alto Paranaíba, the Faculdade de Ciências Gerenciais do Alto Paranaíba and the Faculdade de Direito do Alto Paranaíba. Acquired present status and title 2002.

Degrees and Diplomas: Tecnólogo; Bacharelado; Licenciatura; Especialização/Aperfeiçoamento
Last Updated: 02/06/10

UNIVERSITY CENTRE OF THE CITY
Centro Universitário da Cidade (UNIVERCIDADE)
Rua José Bonifácio 140, Rio de Janeiro, Rio de Janeiro 20770-240
Tel: +55(21) 2536-5040
Fax: +55(21) 2536-5047
EMail: info@univercidade.br
Website: http://www.univercidade.br

Reitor: Ronald Guimarães Levinsohn

Courses
Accountancy (Accountancy); **Administration** (Administration); **Advertising and Publicity**; **Arts and Humanities** (Arts and Humanities; English; Literature; Portuguese; Spanish); **Biology**; **Computer Networks** (Computer Networks); **Computer Science** (Computer Science); **Dance** (Dance); **Environmental Engineering** (Environmental Engineering); **Graduate Studies** (Business Administration; Business and Commerce; Cardiology; Civil Law; Commercial Law; Computer Networks; Computer Science; Dance; Educational Psychology; Finance; Health Administration; Human Resources; Industrial Management; Journalism; Law; Marketing; Nursing; Physical Therapy; Public Law; Sales Techniques; Service Trades; Telecommunications Engineering; Theatre); **Hotel Management** (Hotel Management); **Industrial Design**; **Information Systems** (Information Sciences); **International Relations**; **Journalism** (Journalism); **Law**; **Leisure and Sports Management**; **Marketing**; **Nursing** (Nursing); **Pedagogy**; **Physical Education** (Physical Education); **Physical Therapy** (Physical Therapy); **Production Engineering**; **Systems Analysis and Development**; **Telecommunications Engineering** (Telecommunications Engineering); **Theatre** (Theatre); **Tourism** (Tourism)

History: Founded 1971 as Centro Unificado Professional, incorporating various faculties. Acquired present status and title 1998.

Main Language(s) of Instruction: Portuguese and English

Degrees and Diplomas: *Tecnólogo*; *Bacharelado*; *Licenciatura*. Also postgraduate courses and MBA.

Student Services: Academic counselling, Cultural centre, Employment services, Handicapped facilities, Language programs
Last Updated: 25/05/10

UNIVERSITY CENTRE OF THE DEVELOPMENT OF THE CENTRE WEST
Centro Universitário de Desenvolvimento do Centro Oeste (UNIDESC)
Km. 16 da BR-040, Luziania, GO 72870000
Tel: +55(61) 3878-3100
EMail: unidesc@unidesc.edu.br
Website: http://www.unidesc.com

Reitor: Luiz Pinto Fernandes

Courses
Accountancy (Accountancy); **Administration**; **Arts and Humanities**; **Biological Sciences**; **Biomedicine** (Biomedicine); **Executive Secretarial Studies**; **Fashion Design** (Fashion Design); **History** (History); **Information System** (Information Sciences); **Law** (Law); **Mathematics** (Mathematics); **Nursing** (Nursing); **Pedagogy** (Pedagogy); **Pharmacy** (Pharmacy); **Physical Education**; **Technological Studies**; **Veterinary Medicine** (Veterinary Science)

Further Information: Also campus in Valparaíso de Goiás.
History: Founded 1990.

Degrees and Diplomas: *Tecnólogo*; *Bacharelado*; *Licenciatura*; *Especialização/Aperfeiçoamento*
Last Updated: 27/05/10

UNIVERSITY CENTRE OF THE EDUCATIONAL FOUNDATION OF GUAXUPÉ
Centro Universitário da Fundação Educacional Guaxupé (FACEG)
Avenida Dona Floriana 463 Térreo, Centro, Guaxupé, Minas Gerais 37800-000
Tel: +55(35) 3551-5267
Fax: +55(35) 3551-5267
EMail: secretaria@unifeg.edu.br
Website: http://www.unifeg.edu.br

Reitor: Antônio Roberto Ezau Dos Santos

Courses
Accountancy (Accountancy); **Administration**; **Advertising and Publicity** (Advertising and Publicity); **Arts and Humanities - Portuguese/English**; **Biological Sciences**; **Child Education** (Education); **Computer Science**; **Environmental Sciences** (Biological and Life Sciences; Environmental Studies); **Graduate Studies**; **Industrial Chemistry** (Industrial Chemistry); **International Business** (International Business); **Journalism**; **Law** (Law); **Nursing** (Nursing); **Pedagogy**; **Philosophy** (Philosophy); **Physical Education**; **Physical Therapy** (Physical Therapy); **Production and Quality Engineering** (Production Engineering; Safety Engineering); **Social Services** (Social and Community Services)

History: Founded 1965.

Degrees and Diplomas: *Bacharelado*; *Licenciatura*; *Especialização/Aperfeiçoamento*. Also MBA.
Last Updated: 25/05/10

UNIVERSITY CENTRE OF THE FEDERAL DISTRICT
Centro Universitario do Distrito Federal (UDF)
SEP/SUL EQ 704/904 - CONJ A, Brasília, DF 70390-045
Tel: +55(61) 3704-8888
EMail: udf@udf.edu.br
Website: http://www.udf.edu.br

Reitor: Renato Caiado de Rezende

Courses
Accountancy (Accountancy); **Administration** (Administration); **Civil Engineering** (Civil Engineering); **Graduate Studies** (Accountancy; Administrative Law; Aesthetics; Business Administration; Civil Law; Criminal Law; Finance; Fiscal Law; Higher Education; History; Information Technology; Leadership; Management; Marketing; Pedagogy; Public Administration; Real Estate; Transport Management); **Information Sytems**; **International Relations** (International Relations); **Law** (Law); **Literature** (English; Literature; Portuguese); **Mechanical Engineering** (Mechanical Engineering); **Pedagogy** (Pedagogy); **Political Sciences** (Political Sciences); **Public Administration** (Public Administration)

Further Information: Also Short-term Study programmes.

History: Founded 1967. Integrated into the Grupo Educacional Cruzeiro do Sul de São Paulo 2008.

Degrees and Diplomas: *Bacharelado*; *Licenciatura*; *Especialização/Aperfeiçoamento*. Also MBA.
Last Updated: 12/07/10

UNIVERSITY CENTRE OF THE FEDERAL DISTRICT PLATEAU - UNIPLAN
Centro Universitário Planaltodo Distrito Federal - Uniplan (UNIPLAN)
Setor de Grandes Áreas - Sga, 913, Lotes 54/55 - Bloco H, Asa Sul, Brasília, DF 70390-130
Tel: +55 (61) 345-9100
EMail: marcioacbarros@yahoo.com.br
Website: http://www.uniplandf.edu.br

Diretor Secretário: Jorge Brihy Junior

Courses
Administration; **Architecture and Urbanism** (Architecture; Town Planning); **Business Administration** (Business Administration); **Business Administration and Control** (Accountancy; Business Administration); **Civil Engineering** (Civil Engineering); **Communication and Digital Illustration** (Communication Arts); **Computer Science** (Computer Science); **Corporate Communication** (Communication Studies); **Economics**; **Evnet Management**; **Graphic Design** (Graphic Design); **Hospital Management**; **Human Resources**; **Information Technology Management** (Information Technology); **Interior Design**; **International Business** (International Business); **Law** (Law); **Marketing**; **Mercadological Management** (Business Administration); **Multimedia** (Multimedia); **Mutlimedia Production** (Multimedia); **Nursing** (Nursing); **Pedagogy**; **Pharmacy** (Pharmacy); **Phonoaudiology** (Speech Therapy and Audiology); **Physical Education**; **Physical Therapy**; **Real**

Estate (Real Estate); **Social Communication** (Advertising and Publicity); **Sports Management** (Sports Management)

Degrees and Diplomas: *Tecnólogo*; *Bacharelado*; *Licenciatura*; *Especialização/Aperfeiçoamento*
Last Updated: 13/07/10

UNIVERSITY CENTRE OF THE FEI

Centro Universitário da FEI (UNIFEI)
Avenida Humberto de Alencar, Castelo Branco 3972, Assunção, São Bernardo do Campo, São Paulo 09850901
Tel: +55(11) 4353-2900
Fax: +55(11) 4109-5994
EMail: info_fei@fei.edu.br
Website: http://www.fei.edu.br

Courses
Graduate Studies (Accountancy; Administration; Automation and Control Engineering; Automotive Engineering; Business Administration; Chemistry; Energy Engineering; Environmental Management; Finance; Health Administration; Heating and Refrigeration; Human Resources; Industrial Management; Information Technology; International Business; Management; Marketing; Mechanics; Metallurgical Engineering; Occupational Health; Safety Engineering; Textile Design; Transport and Communications; Transport Management)

Departments
Administration; **Chemical Engineering** (Chemical Engineering); **Civil Engineering**; **Computer Science** (Computer Science; Mathematics); **Electrical Engineering**; **Mathematics** (Mathematics); **Mechanical Engineering** (Mechanical Engineering); **Metallurgical and Materials Engineering** (Materials Engineering; Metallurgical Engineering); **Physics**; **Production Engineering** (Production Engineering); **Social and Juridical Sciences** (Law; Social and Community Services); **Textile Engineering** (Textile Technology)

Further Information: Also campus Liberdade.

History: Founded 1972.

Admission Requirements: Secondary school certificate, certificate of regularity for military obligation (for Brazilians)

Fees: (Real) for Engineering: day course - 5,566.20 per semester; evenining course 4,641; for Administration: 3,240; for Computer Science: 4,152

Main Language(s) of Instruction: Portuguese

Accrediting Agencies: Ministry of Education

Degrees and Diplomas: *Bacharelado*; *Especialização/Aperfeiçoamento*; *Mestrado*
Last Updated: 25/05/10

UNIVERSITY CENTRE OF THE GRANDE DOURADOS REGION

Centro Universitário da Grande Dourados (UNIGRAN)
Rua Balbina de Matos, 2121, Jardim Universitário, Dourados, Mato Grosso do Sul 79824900
Tel: +55(67) 3411-4141
Fax: +55(67) 3411-4167
EMail: webmaster@unigran.br
Website: http://www.unigran.br

Reitora: Rosa Maria d'Amato de Déa (1996-)
EMail: rosa@unigran.br

Courses
Distance Education (Accountancy; Administration; Advertising and Publicity; Agricultural Business; Arts and Humanities; Business and Commerce; Educational Psychology; Environmental Management; Higher Education; Information Sciences; Modern Languages; Pedagogy; Real Estate; Social and Community Services; Systems Analysis; Theology); **Graduate Studies**; **Technological Studies** (Advertising and Publicity; Agriculture; Cosmetology)

Faculties
Administration and Accountancy (Accountancy; Administration; Advertising and Publicity; Agricultural Business; Journalism); **Biological and Health Sciences**; **Education**; **Exact and Earth Sciences** (Agronomy; Architecture; Computer Science; Town Planning); **Law** (Law; Social and Community Services)

History: Founded 1976, Acquired present status and title 1998.

Academic Year: February to December

Admission Requirements: Secondary school certificate and entrance examination

Fees: (Reais): 150-400 per month

Main Language(s) of Instruction: Portuguese

Degrees and Diplomas: *Bacharelado*; *Licenciatura*. Also postgraduate courses.

Student Services: Academic counselling, Canteen, Employment services, Handicapped facilities, Nursery care, Sports facilities

Libraries: Total, 60,000 vols

Publications: Revista Jurídica, Issues and articles on Law *(biannually)*
Last Updated: 26/05/10

UNIVERSITY CENTRE OF THE MAUÁ INSTITUTE OF TECHNOLOGY

Centro Universitário do Instituto Mauá de Tecnologia (CEUN-IMT)
Praça Mauá 1, Mauá, São Caetano do Sul, São Paulo 09580-900
Tel: +55(11) 4239-3000
Fax: +55(11) 4239-3131
EMail: cp@maua.br
Website: http://www.maua.br

Reitor: Otavio de Mattos Silvares (2000-)
Tel: +55(11) 4329-3022 EMail: otavioms@maua.br

Campuses
Automation and Control Engineering (Automation and Control Engineering); **São Paulo** (Administration)

Courses
Administration (Administration); **Chemical Engineering** (Chemical Engineering); **Civil Engineering**; **Electrical Engineering** (Electrical Engineering); **Engineering** (Engineering); **Environmental Management**; **Food Engineering** (Food Technology); **Graduate Studies** *(São Paulo Campus)* (Administration; Business Administration; Environmental Management; Management; Marketing; Transport Management); **Graduate Studies** *(São Caetano do Sul Campus)*; **Information Technology Management**; **Marketing** (Marketing); **Mechanical Engineering** (Mechanical Engineering); **Mechanical Production Engineering** (Production Engineering); **Process Management** (Management); **Product Design** (Industrial Design)

History: Founded as Mauá Engineering School in 1962. Acquired present status 2000.

Governing Bodies: Higher Council; Council of Education

Academic Year: February to December (February-June; August-December)

Admission Requirements: High school certificate and entrance examination

Fees: (Reais): Faculty of Engineering, Day students 11,100 per annum; Evening students 9,300; Faculty of Administration, 10,100 per annum

Main Language(s) of Instruction: Portuguese

International Co-operation: With universities in Portugal and USA.

Accrediting Agencies: Ministry of Education

Degrees and Diplomas: *Tecnólogo*; *Bacharelado*; *Especialização/Aperfeiçoamento*; *Mestrado*. Also MBA.

Student Services: Academic counselling, Canteen, Employment services, Sports facilities

Libraries: Central Library at Caetano do Sul campus and section library at Mauá School of Administration at São Paulo campus
Last Updated: 01/06/10

UNIVERSITY CENTRE OF THE NORTH

Centro Universitario do Norte (UNINORTE)
Rua Dez de Julho 873, Centro, Mánaus, Amazonas 69010-060
Tel: +55(92) 3212-5000
Fax: +55(92) 3212-5010
EMail: extensao@objetivomao.br
Website: http://www.uninorte.com.br

Diretora: Maria Hercília Tribuzy de Magalhães Cordeiro (1998-)

Courses

Accountancy; **Administration** (Administration); **Architecture and Town Planning**; **Biology** (Biology); **Civil Engineering** (Civil Engineering); **Computer Networks** (Computer Networks); **Computer Science** (Computer Science); **Databases**; **Economics** (Economics); **Electrical Engineering** (Electrical Engineering); **Environmental Engineering** (Environmental Engineering); **Esthetics and Cosmetics** (Cosmetology); **Geography** (Geography); **Graduate Studies** *(Lato Sensu)* (Accountancy; Administration; Advertising and Publicity; Architecture; Archiving; Biological and Life Sciences; Chemistry; Cosmetology; Dentistry; Design; Economics; Education; Engineering; Geography; History; Information Technology; Interior Design; Law; Literature; Management; Marketing; Mass Communication; Naval Architecture; Nursing; Pedagogy; Pharmacy; Physical Education; Physical Therapy; Portuguese; Psychology; Secretarial Studies; Social and Community Services; Speech Therapy and Audiology; Tourism); **Graduate Studies** *(Stricto Sensu)* (Accountancy; Administration; Law; Social and Community Services; Tourism); **Graphic Design** (Graphic Design); **History** (History); **International Relations**; **Law** (Law); **Literature - English** (English; Literature); **Literature - Portuguese**; **Literature - Spanish** (Literature; Spanish); **Marketing**; **Mechanical Engineering** (Mechanical Engineering); **Mechanical Production Engineering** (Mechanical Engineering); **Nursing** (Nursing); **Nutrition** (Nutrition); **Odontology**; **Pedagogy** (Pedagogy); **Petroleum and Gas** (Petroleum and Gas Engineering); **Pharmacy**; **Phonoaudiology** (Speech Therapy and Audiology); **Physical Education** (Physical Education); **Physiotherapy**; **Production Engineering** (Production Engineering); **Psychology** (Psychology); **Quality Management** (Safety Engineering); **Sciences - Chemistry** (Chemistry); **Sciences - Mathematics** (Mathematics); **Sciences - Physics** (Physics); **Social Communication - Advertising and Publicity** (Advertising and Publicity); **Social Communication - Journalism**; **Social Communication - Radialism** (Radio and Television Broadcasting); **Social Services**; **Software Development**; **Systems Analysis and Development**; **Telecommunications Engineering**; **Tourism**

Further Information: Also distance education programmes.

History: Founded 1998 as Instituto Cultural de Ensino do Amazonas. Acquired present title and status 2004.

Main Language(s) of Instruction: Portuguese

Degrees and Diplomas: *Tecnólogo*; *Bacharelado*; *Licenciatura*; *Especialização/Aperfeiçoamento*; *Mestrado*
Last Updated: 02/06/10

UNIVERSITY CENTRE OF THE OCTÁVIO BASTOS EDUCATION FOUNDATION

Centro Universitário Fundação de Ensino Octávio Bastos (UNIFEOB)

Rua General Osório 433, Centro, São João da Boa Vista, São Paulo 13870000
Tel: +55(19) 3634-3300
Fax: +55(19) 3634-3328
EMail: presidencia@feob.br
Website: http://www.unifeob.edu.br

Reitor: João Otávio Bastos Junqueira

Pró-Reitor Acadêmico: José Elias Isaac

Courses

Accountancy (Accountancy); **Administration**; **Arts and Humanities**; **Biology**; **Chemistry** (Chemistry); **Geography** (Geography); **Graduate Studies**; **History** (History); **Information Systems** (Information Sciences); **Law**; **Mathematics** (Mathematics); **Nursing** (Nursing); **Pedagogy** (Pedagogy); **Philosophy**; **Physical Therapy** (Physical Therapy); **Physics**; **Social Sciences**; **Technological Studies** (Agricultural Business; Business and Commerce; Environmental Management; Finance; Human Resources; Industrial Management; International Business; Management; Marketing; Public Administration; Safety Engineering; Transport Management); **Veterinary Science** (Veterinary Science)

History: Founded 2001

Degrees and Diplomas: *Tecnólogo*; *Bacharelado*; *Licenciatura*; *Especialização/Aperfeiçoamento*
Last Updated: 03/06/10

UNIVERSITY CENTRE OF THE SANTO ANDRÉ FOUNDATION

Centro Universitário Fundação Santo André (FSA)

Avenida Príncipe de Gales 821, Bairro Príncipe de Gales, Santo André, São Paulo 09060-650
Tel: +55(11) 4979-3300
Fax: +55(11) 4990-2048
EMail: fsa@fsa.br
Website: http://www.fsa.br

Reitor: Oduvaldo Cacalano

Pró-Reitor de Administração e Planejamento: Flávio Morgado

Courses

Graduate Studies (Administration; Banking; Business Administration; Communication Studies; Distance Education; Education; Educational Psychology; Electronic Engineering; Energy Engineering; Engineering; Environmental Management; Finance; Geography; Health Administration; History; Information Sciences; Information Technology; International Business; International Relations; Journalism; Linguistics; Literature; Management; Marketing; Mathematics Education; Mechanical Engineering; Public Law; Safety Engineering; Science Education; Social Sciences; Software Engineering; Special Education; Statistics; Telecommunications Engineering; Transport Management)

Faculties

Economics and Administration *(Faeco)* (Accountancy; Administration; Economics; Health Administration; International Relations); **Engineering** *(Faeng - Eng. Celso Daniel)* (Computer Engineering; Electronic Engineering; Engineering; Environmental Engineering; Materials Engineering; Mechanical Engineering; Production Engineering); **Philosophy, Science and Letters** *(Fafil)* (Biology; Chemistry; Computer Science; English; Geography; History; Information Sciences; Literature; Mathematics; Pedagogy; Physics; Portuguese; Social Sciences)

History: Founded 1962. Acquired present status 2000.

Main Language(s) of Instruction: Portuguese

International Co-operation: With Universidade Autônoma do Caribe, Universidade Simon Bolívar (Barranquilla, Colombia) and the Consulate of Cape Verde

Degrees and Diplomas: *Bacharelado*; *Licenciatura*; *Especialização/Aperfeiçoamento*. Also MBA.

Student Services: Academic counselling, Canteen, Employment services, Foreign student adviser, Language programs, Nursery care
Last Updated: 03/06/10

UNIVERSITY CENTRE OF THE SOUTH OF MINAS

Centro Universitário do Sul de Minas (UNIS)

Avenida Cel. José Alves, 256, Vila Pinto, Varginha, Minas Gerais 37010-540
Tel: +55(35) 3219-5000
Fax: +55(35) 3219-5251
EMail: unis@unis.edu.br
Website: http://portal.unis.edu.br

Reitor: Stéfano Barra Gazzola

Courses

Administration (Administration; International Business); **Biomedicine** (Biomedicine); **Civil Engineering** (Civil Engineering); **Computer Science** (Computer Science); **Distance Postgraduate Studies**; **Graduate Studies**; **Mechanical Engineering** (Mechanical Engineering); **Nursing**; **Nutrition** (Nutrition); **Pedagogy** (Pedagogy); **Physical Education** (Physical Education); **Physical Therapy** (Physical Therapy); **Production Engineering** (Production Engineering); **Social Communication - Advertising and Publicity**; **Social Communication - Journalism** (Journalism); **Social Services** (Social and Community Services); **Technological Studies** (Automation and Control Engineering; Environmental Management; Human Resources; Management; Systems Analysis; Transport Management)

Further Information: Also campuses in Cabo Verde, Nova Resende, Silvianópolis and Três Pontas

History: Founded 1996.

Main Language(s) of Instruction: Portuguese

Degrees and Diplomas: *Tecnólogo*; *Bacharelado*; *Licenciatura*. Also Postgraduate Sudies and MBA.

Last Updated: 02/06/10

UNIVERSITY CENTRE OF THE STATE OF RIO DE JANEIRO

Centro Universitario Fluminense (UNIFLU)

Rua Tenente Coronel Cardoso 349, Campos dos Goytacazes, Rio de Janeiro 28053000

Tel: +55(22) 2101-3350
Fax: +55(24) 2101-3353
EMail: ouvidoria@uniflu.edu.br
Website: http://www.uniflu.edu.br

Reitor: Levi Quaresma

Courses
Graduate Studies

Faculties
Law *(UNIFLU/FDC)* (Law); **Odontology** *(UNIFLU/FOC)* (Dentistry); **Philosophy** *(UNIFLU/FAFIC)*

History: Founded 1961

Main Language(s) of Instruction: Portuguese

Degrees and Diplomas: *Bacharelado*; *Especialização/Aperfeiçoamento*; *Mestrado*

Last Updated: 03/06/10

UNIVERSITY CENTRE OF THE STATE OF SAO PAULO

Centro Universitário Paulistano

Rua Madre Cabrini 38, Vila Mariana, São Paulo, São Paulo 04020001

Tel: +55(11) 5549-3033 +55(11) 5549-3035
Fax: +55(11) 5549-3033 +55(11) 5549-3049
EMail: unipaulistana@unipaulistana.edu.br
Website: http://www.unipaulistana.edu.br

Diretor: Azurem Ferreira Pinto

Pró-reitora Acadêmica: Rosangela Calixto

Courses
Accountancy; **Administration**; **Architecture and Urbanism** (Architecture; Town Planning); **Biological Sciences**; **Chemistry**; **Graduate Studies**; **Information Systems** (Information Management); **Letters** (English; Literature; Portuguese); **Mathematics**; **Mechanical Engineering**; **Nursing** (Nursing); **Pedagogy** (Pedagogy); **Production Engineering** (Production Engineering); **Psychology**; **Technological Studies** (Business and Commerce; Computer Networks; Finance; Health Administration; Human Resources; Occupational Health; Public Administration; Systems Analysis; Transport Management)

History: Founded 1972.

Degrees and Diplomas: *Tecnólogo*; *Bacharelado*; *Licenciatura*; *Especialização/Aperfeiçoamento*

Last Updated: 16/06/10

UNIVERSITY CENTRE OF VÁRZEA GRANDE

Centro Universitário de Várzea Grande (UNIVAG)

Av. Dom Orlando Chaves, 2655 Bairro Cristo Rei, Várzea Grande, Mato Grosso 78118-900

Tel: +55(65) 3688-6000
Fax: +55(65) 3685-6000
EMail: univag@univag.com.br
Website: http://www.univag.com.br

Diretor Geral: Dráuzio Antônio Medeiros (1986-)

Courses
Accountancy (Accountancy); **Administration** (Accountancy; Administration; Business Administration; International Business; Management; Marketing); **Agronomy** (Agronomy); **Arts and Humanities** (Arts and Humanities; Geography (Human); History; Philosophy; Sociology); **Biological Sciences** (Biological and Life Sciences); **Environmental Engineering**; **Food Engineering** (Food Technology); **Graduate Studies** (Administration; Biotechnology;

Botany; Business Education; Communication Studies; Data Processing; Higher Education; Information Technology; Labour Law; Law; Literacy Education; Management; Mathematics; Molecular Biology; Pharmacology; Political Sciences; Portuguese; Preschool Education; Public Administration; Public Health; Speech Therapy and Audiology; Zoology); **Information Systems** (Information Sciences); **Law** (Law); **Literature**; **Mathematics** (Mathematics; Mathematics and Computer Science); **Nursing**; **Odontology** (Dentistry); **Pedagogy** (Pedagogy); **Pharmacy** (Pharmacy); **Phonaudiology** (Speech Therapy and Audiology); **Physical Education** (Physical Education); **Physical Therapy**; **Psychology** (Psychology); **Social Communication**; **Social Services** (Social and Community Services); **Technological Studies**; **Tourism** (Tourism)

History: Founded 1989

Main Language(s) of Instruction: Portuguese

Degrees and Diplomas: *Tecnólogo*; *Bacharelado*; *Licenciatura*; *Especialização/Aperfeiçoamento*. Also MBA.

Last Updated: 31/05/10

UNIVERSITY CENTRE OF VILA VELHA

Centro Universitário Vila Velha (UVV)

Rua Commissário José Dantas de Melo, 21, Boa Vista, Vila Velha, Espírito Santo 29102-770

Tel: +55(27) 3421-2001
Fax: +55(27) 3320-2029
EMail: uvv@uvv-es.br
Website: http://www.uvv.br

Reitor: Manoel Ceciliano Salles de Almeida

International Relations: Tarina Macedo, Associate Director International Affairs
Tel: +55(27) 3320-2032, Fax: +55(27) 3320-2029
EMail: tarina@uvv.br

Areas
Applied Human and Social Sciences; **Exact Sciences and Engineering**; **Health and Agrarian Sciences** (Animal Husbandry; Biological and Life Sciences; Dentistry; Medicine; Nursing; Nutrition; Pharmacy; Physical Education; Physical Therapy; Speech Therapy and Audiology; Veterinary Science)

Courses
Graduate Studies *(Lato Sensu)*; **Graduate Studies** *(Stricto Sensu)*; **Technological Studies** (Cooking and Catering; Cosmetology; Environmental Studies; Fashion Design; Human Resources; Industrial Design; Marine Transport; Occupational Health; Petroleum and Gas Engineering; Transport Management)

Further Information: Also N. Sra da Penha, Praia da Costa, Vitória and Guaçuí campuses.

History: Founded 1976.

Admission Requirements: Secondary school certificate and entrance examination (Vestibular)

Fees: (Reais): 6,000 per annum; 3,000 per semester

Main Language(s) of Instruction: Portuguese

Accrediting Agencies: Ministry of Education

Degrees and Diplomas: *Tecnólogo*; *Bacharelado*: 4-5 yrs; *Especialização/Aperfeiçoamento*; *Mestrado*. Also MBA.

Student Services: Academic counselling, Canteen, Cultural centre, Employment services, Foreign student adviser, Handicapped facilities, Health services, Language programs, Nursery care, Sports facilities

Libraries: 69,000 vols

Publications: Scientia *(biannually)*

Last Updated: 18/06/10

UNIVERSITY CENTRE OF VOLTA REDONDA

Centro Universitário de Volta Redonda (UNIFOA)

Avenida Paulo Erlei Alves Abrantes, 1325, Três Poços, Volta Redonda, Rio de Janeiro 27240-560

Tel: +55(24) 3340-8400
Fax: +55(24) 3340-8404
EMail: foa@foa.org.br
Website: http://www.unifoa.edu.br

Reitor: Alexandre Fernandes Habibe

Courses

Accountancy; **Administration** (Administration); **Advertising and Publicity**; **Biological Sciences** (Biological and Life Sciences; Biotechnology); **Civil Engineering**; **Design** (Design; Industrial Design); **Electrical Engineering** (Electrical Engineering); **Environmental Engineering**; **Graduate Studies** *(Stricto Sensu)* (Environmental Management; Health Sciences; Materials Engineering); **Graduate Studies** *(Lato Sensu)* (Accountancy; Business and Commerce; Civil Law; Communication Studies; Comparative Literature; Computer Networks; Computer Science; Dental Technology; Dentistry; Education; Finance; Higher Education; Industrial Engineering; Industrial Management; Information Technology; Linguistics; Management; Mechanical Engineering; Nursing; Nutrition; Occupational Health; Physical Therapy; Psychiatry and Mental Health; Public Health; Radiology; Rehabilitation and Therapy; Safety Engineering; Sports; Surgery); **History** (History); **Information Systems** (Computer Science); **Journalism**; **Law** (Law); **Literature**; **Mechanical Engineering** (Mechanical Engineering); **Medicine** (Medicine); **Nursing**; **Nutrition** (Nutrition); **Odontology** (Dentistry); **Physical Education**; **Physical Therapy** (Physical Therapy); **Production Engineering** (Production Engineering); **Social Service**; **Technological Studies**

Further Information: Also Aterrado, Colina, Vila, and Tangerinal campuses.

History: Founded 1968.

Degrees and Diplomas: *Tecnólogo*; *Bacharelado*; *Licenciatura*; *Especialização/Aperfeiçoamento*; *Mestrado*
Last Updated: 31/05/10

UNIVERSITY CENTRE OF VOTUPORANGA

Centro Universitário de Votuporanga (UNIFEV)
Rua Pernambuco 4196, Centro, Votuporanga,
São Paulo 15500-006
Tel: +55(17) 3405-9999
Fax: +55(17) 3422-4510
EMail: reitoria.ceuv@votuporanga.com.br
Website: http://www.fev.edu.br/

Reitor: Marcelo Ferreira Lourenço

Courses

Accountancy; **Administration**; **Advertising and Publicity** (Advertising and Publicity); **Architecture and Urbanism** (Architecture; Town Planning); **Biological Sciences**; **Biomedicine** (Biomedicine); **Chemistry**; **Clothing Production** (Clothing and Sewing); **Commercial Management** (Business and Commerce); **Computer Engineering** (Computer Engineering); **Cooking and Catering** (Cooking and Catering); **Education** (Education); **Electrical and Electronic Engineering** (Electrical and Electronic Engineering); **Electrical Engineering** (Electrical Engineering); **Environmental Management** (Environmental Management); **Furniture Production** (Furniture Design); **Geography** (Geography); **Hospitality** (Hotel and Restaurant); **Human Resources**; **Industrial Production**; **Information Systems**; **Journalism**; **Law** (Law); **Literature**; **Logistics**; **Marketing** (Marketing); **Mathematics** (Mathematics); **Mechanical Fabrication**; **Multimedia Production**; **Nursing**; **Nutrition** (Nutrition); **Pharmacy** (Pharmacy); **Physical Education**; **Physical Therapy** (Physical Therapy); **Physics** (Physics); **Physics** (Physics); **Postgradute Studies**; **Psychology** (Psychology); **Quality Management** (Safety Engineering); **Social Work**; **Sugarcane Production** (Agriculture)

Further Information: Also Cidade Universitária campus.
History: Founded 1966. Acquired present status and title 1997.
Main Language(s) of Instruction: Portuguese
Degrees and Diplomas: *Tecnólogo*; *Bacharelado*; *Licenciatura*; *Especialização/Aperfeiçoamento*. Also MBA.
Last Updated: 01/06/10

UNIVERSITY FOR THE DEVELOPMENT OF THE UPPER VALLEY OF THE ITAJAI

Universidade para o Desenvolvimento do Alto Vale do Itajaí (UNIDAVI)
Rua Doutor Guilherme Gemballa 13, Jardim América,
Rio do Sul, Santa Catarina 89160000
Tel: +55(47) 3531-6000
Fax: +55(47) 3531-6001
EMail: unidavi@unidavi.edu.br
Website: http://www.unidavi.edu.br

Reitor: Viegand Eger EMail: reitor@unidavi.edu.br

Courses

Biology (Biology); **Computer Networks** (Computer Networks); **Food Processing** (Food Technology); **Industrial Chemistry** (Industrial Chemistry); **Literature** (Literature); **Tourism** (Tourism)

History: Founded 1966.

Main Language(s) of Instruction: Portuguese

Degrees and Diplomas: *Bacharelado*; *Especialização/Aperfeiçoamento*; *Mestrado*
Last Updated: 10/05/10

UNIVERSITY FOUNDATION OF ITAPERUNA

Fundaçao Universitaria de Itaperuna
Rua Silva Jardim 775, Marechal Castelo Branco, Itaperuna, RJ
Tel: +55(22) 3824-6274
EMail: funita@funita.edu.br
Website: http://www.funita.edu.br

Presidente: Marcelo Padilha

Courses

Physical Education (Physical Education)

History: Founded 1999.

Main Language(s) of Instruction: Portuguese

Degrees and Diplomas: *Licenciatura*

Libraries: Yes
Last Updated: 29/09/10

UNIVERSITY OF AMAZONIA

Universidade da Amazônia (UNAMA)
Avenida Alcindo Cacela 287, Térreo Umarizal, Belém,
Pará 66060902
Tel: +55(91) 4009-3000
EMail: planeja@unama.br
Website: http://www.unama.br

Reitor: Antonio de Carvalho Vaz Pereira
Tel: +55(91) 210-3001 EMail: reitor@unama.br

Vice Reitor: Henrique Heidtmann Neto EMail: vicereitor@unama.br

Centres

Applied Social Studies; **Education and Human Sciences** (Educational Sciences; Literature; Pedagogy; Secretarial Studies; Social and Community Services; Social Sciences); **Health and Biological Sciences** (Biological and Life Sciences; Health Sciences; Occupational Therapy; Physical Therapy; Psychology; Speech Therapy and Audiology); **Technology and Mathematics** (Architecture; Civil Engineering; Computer Science; Data Processing; Environmental Engineering; Production Engineering; Sanitary Engineering; Town Planning; Visual Arts)

History: Founded 1974.

Admission Requirements: Secondary school certificate and entrance examination

Main Language(s) of Instruction: Portuguese

Degrees and Diplomas: *Bacharelado*; *Licenciatura*; *Especialização/Aperfeiçoamento*; *Mestrado*
Last Updated: 07/06/10

UNIVERSITY OF CAXIAS DO SUL

Universidade de Caxias do Sul (UCS)
Rua Francisco Getúlio Vargas 1130 Bloco A Petrópolis,
Caxias do Sul, Rio Grande do Sul 95070560
Tel: +55(54) 3289-9000
EMail: informa@ucs.br
Website: http://www.ucs.br

Reitor: Isidoro Zorzi (2006-) Tel: +55(54) 212-1660

Centres

Administration (Administration; Business Administration); **Agronomy and Biological Sciences** (Agronomy; Biological and Life Sciences); **Applied Social Sciences** *(Região dos Vinhedos)* (Accountancy; Administration; Economics; International Business; Law; Tourism); **Arts and Architecture** (Architecture; Fashion Design; Town Planning; Visual Arts); **Communication** (Communication Studies); **Computer Science and Technology** (Computer Science; Information Technology); **Economics, Accountancy and International Business** (Accountancy; Economics; International Business); **Exact Sciences and Technology** (Mathematics and Computer Science; Natural Sciences; Technology); **Exact Sciences, Natural Sciences and Technology** *(Região dos Vinhedos)* (Biology; Data Processing; Design; Electrical Engineering; Information Sciences; Mechanical Engineering; Production Engineering); **Health Sciences** (Medicine; Nursing; Nutrition; Pharmacy; Physical Education; Physical Therapy); **Human Sciences** (Arts and Humanities; Geography; History; Literature; Psychology; Secretarial Studies; Social and Community Services); **Human Sciences and Education** *(Região dos Vinhedos)* (Geography; Literature; Pedagogy; Physical Education); **Law** (Law); **Philosophy and Education** (Education; Philosophy)

History: Founded 1967, incorporating previously existing Faculties. A private Institution constituted as a Foundation and recognized by the Federal Government.

Academic Year: March to December (March-July; August-December)

Admission Requirements: Secondary school certificate and entrance examination

Main Language(s) of Instruction: Portuguese

Degrees and Diplomas: *Bacharelado:* 4-5 yrs; *Bacharelado:* Engineering, 5 yrs; *Bacharelado:* Medicine, 6 yrs; *Bacharelado:* Nursing; School Inspection, 4 yrs; *Licenciatura:* 4-5 yrs; *Especialização/Aperfeiçoamento:* 2 yrs; *Mestrado; Doutorado*

Special Facilities: Natural Science Museum. Art Gallery

Libraries: c. 80,000 vols

Publications: Revista Chronos *(biannually)*

Press or Publishing House: Editora da Universidade de Caxias do Sul
Last Updated: 07/06/10

UNIVERSITY OF CRUZ ALTA
Universidade de Cruz Alta (UNICRUZ)
Rua Andrade Neves 308, Centro, Cruz Alta,
Rio Grande do Sul 98025810
Tel: +55(55) 3321-1500
Fax: +55(55) 3321-1500
EMail: reitoria@unicruz.edu.br
Website: http://www.unicruz.edu.br

Reitora: Elizabeth Fontoura Dorneles

Departments
Agronomy (Agronomy); **Architecture and Town Planning** (Architecture; Town Planning); **Informatics** (Information Sciences); **Nursing** (Nursing); **Pharmacy** (Pharmacy); **Physiotherapy** (Physical Therapy); **Social Communication** (Communication Studies); **Social Services** (Social and Community Services)

Faculties
Law (Law); **Philosophy, Science and Letters** (Arts and Humanities; Biology; Education; English; History; Mathematics; Natural Sciences; Philosophy; Portuguese; Social Studies; Spanish); **Physical Education** (Physical Education); **Political Science and Economics** (Accountancy; Administration; Economics; Political Sciences)

History: Founded 1964. Acquired present status and title 1993.

Academic Year: March to December (March-June; August-December)

Admission Requirements: Secondary school certificate and entrance examination

Main Language(s) of Instruction: Portuguese

Degrees and Diplomas: *Bacharelado:* 4 yrs; *Licenciatura; Especialização/Aperfeiçoamento*

Libraries: c. 20,000 vols
Last Updated: 04/06/10

UNIVERSITY OF CRUZEIRO DO SUL
Universidade Cruzeiro do Sul (UNICSUL)
Avenida Dr Ussiel Cirilo 225, São Miguel Paulista, São Paulo,
São Paulo 08060-070
Tel: +55(11) 6137-5760
Fax: +55(11) 6137-5760
EMail: unicsul@unicsul.br
Website: http://www.unicsul.br

Reitora: Sueli Cristina Marquesi (1976-)
EMail: sueli.marquesi@unicsul.br

Centres
Administrative Sciences and Business (Accountancy; Administration; Advertising and Publicity; Business Administration; Business and Commerce; Communication Studies; Economics; Hotel Management; Human Resources; International Business; Journalism; Marketing; Public Relations; Radio and Television Broadcasting; Secretarial Studies; Tourism); **Biological and Health Sciences** (Biological and Life Sciences; Biology; Dentistry; Health Sciences; Nursing; Nutrition; Physical Education; Physical Therapy; Psychology; Veterinary Science); **Exact Sciences and Technology** (Architecture; Civil Engineering; Computer Education; Computer Networks; Computer Science; Data Processing; Electrical Engineering; Information Management; Mathematics; Mathematics Education; Mechanical Engineering; Multimedia; Systems Analysis; Technology); **Human and Social Sciences** (Art Education; Arts and Humanities; Education; Education of the Handicapped; Educational Administration; Educational and Student Counselling; English; Foreign Languages Education; Geography; History; Music; Musical Instruments; Native Language Education; Pedagogy; Preschool Education; Primary Education; Singing; Social Sciences; Social Work; Spanish; Visual Arts)

History: Founded 1973 as Faculdade de Administração e Ciências Contábeis São Miguel Paulista. Became Faculdades Integradas Cruzeiro do Sul 1992, incorporating Faculdades de Ciências e Letras, Processamento de Dados, Música and Faculdade Santos Dumont. Acquired present status and title 1993.

Governing Bodies: Conselho de Centros (CONCEN); Conselho de Ensino, Pesquisa e Extensão (Teaching, Research and Extension Council); Conselho Universitário (CONSU); Education Ministry

Academic Year: February to December

Admission Requirements: Secondary school certificate and entrance examination

Fees: (Reais): 547 to 1,582 per semester

Main Language(s) of Instruction: Portuguese

International Co-operation: With universities in Angola and Cuba. Also participates in the Organização Universitária Interamericana (OUI) programmes

Degrees and Diplomas: *Tecnólogo:* Data Processing; Computer Networks; Information Systems; Website Development; Hotel Management; Human Resources Management, 2-3 yrs; *Bacharelado:* Communication Studies; Music; Architecture; Biology; Nursing; Physiotherapy; Nutrition; Veterinary Medicine; Dentistry; Psychology; Law; Engineering; Computer Science; Administration; Accountancy; Social Work; Tourism; Secretarial Studies; Economics; Physical Education, 4-5 yrs; *Licenciatura:* Mathematics Education; Computer Education; Biology; Physical Education; Pedagogy; Geography; History; Foreign Languages Education; Native Language Education; Visual Arts, 3-4 yrs; *Especialização/Aperfeiçoamento; Mestrado; Doutorado*

Student Services: Academic counselling, Canteen, Cultural centre, Employment services, Foreign student adviser, Foreign Studies Centre, Handicapped facilities, Health services, Language programs, Nursery care, Social counselling, Sports facilities

Special Facilities: Radio and TV Studio; Art Centre; Music and Dance; Dental Clinic; Physiotherapy Clinic; Law Office; Psychology Clinic; Laboratories (Computer, Health Sciences, Languages, Technology, etc)

Libraries: Haddock Lobo Library, c. 140,000 vols, on-line catalogue

Publications: Revista UNICSUL *(biannually)*
Last Updated: 07/06/10

UNIVERSITY OF CUIABÁ
Universidade de Cuiabá (UNIC)
Avenida Beira Rio 3100, Jardim Europa, Cuiabá,
Mato Grosso 78015480
Tel: +55(65) 3615-1000
Fax: +55(65) 3615-1100
EMail: unic@zaz.com.br
Website: http://www.unic.br

Reitor: Altamiro Belo Galindo (1994-) Tel: +55(65) 615-1000

Faculties

Accountancy (Accountancy); **Administration**; **Aesthetics and Cosmetics** (Cosmetology); **Agronomy** (Agricultural Engineering; Agronomy); **Architecture, Town Planning, Engineering and Fine Arts** (Architecture; Civil Engineering; Construction Engineering; Electrical Engineering; Environmental Engineering; Interior Design; Production Engineering; Safety Engineering; Town Planning); **Biology**; **Civil Aviation**; **Dentistry**; **Education**; **Landscape Architecture** (Landscape Architecture); **Law**; **Medicine**; **Nursing**; **Nutrition**; **Pharmacy**; **Physical Education**; **Physiotherapy**; **Psychology**; **Science and Technology**; **Social Communication**; **Social Services** (Social and Community Services); **Veterinary Science** (Veterinary Science)

History: Founded 1988.

Admission Requirements: Secondary school certificate and entrance examination

Main Language(s) of Instruction: Portuguese

Degrees and Diplomas: *Bacharelado*; *Licenciatura*; *Especialização/Aperfeiçoamento*; *Mestrado*
Last Updated: 04/06/10

UNIVERSITY OF FORTALEZA
Universidade de Fortaleza (UNIFOR)
Avenida Washington Soares 1321, Edson Queiroz, Fortaleza,
Ceará 60811341
Tel: +55(85) 3477-3000
Fax: +55(85) 3477-3055
EMail: reitoria@unifor.br
Website: http://www.unifor.br

Reitor: Carlos Alberto Batista Mendes de Sousa
Tel: +55(85) 477-3001

Diretor Administrativo: Stenival José Alves Bezerra

Centres

Administration (Accountancy; Administration; Economics; Tourism); **Health Sciences** (Dentistry; Health Sciences; Nursing; Occupational Therapy; Pharmacy; Physical Education; Physical Therapy; Speech Therapy and Audiology); **Human Sciences** (Arts and Humanities; Law; Mass Communication; Pedagogy; Psychology; Sociology); **Technology** (Civil Engineering; Computer Science; Electrical and Electronic Engineering; Mechanical Engineering; Technology)

History: Founded 1973. Under the supervision of the Fundação Edson Queiroz. A private Institution recognized by the Federal Government.

Academic Year: February to December (February-July; August-December)

Admission Requirements: Secondary school certificate and entrance examination

Main Language(s) of Instruction: Portuguese

Degrees and Diplomas: *Bacharelado*: Accountancy; Administration; Architecture; Civil Engineering; Computer Sciences; Dentistry; Economics; Information Sciences; Law; Mechanical and Electrical Engineering; Nursing; Occupational Therapy; Pedagogy; Pharmacy; Physical Education; Physiotherapy; Psychology; Social Sciences; Speech Therapy and Audiology; Tourism; *Especialização/Aperfeiçoamento*; *Mestrado*; *Doutorado*

Student Services: Nursery care, Sports facilities

Libraries: Central Library, c. 114,500 vols

Publications: Pensar *(biannually)*; Revista do Centro de Ciências Administrativas *(biannually)*; Revista do Centro de Ciências da Saúde *(biannually)*; Revista Humanidades *(biannually)*; Revista Tecnologia *(biannually)*

Press or Publishing House: Gráfica Unifor
Last Updated: 04/06/10

UNIVERSITY OF FRANCA
Universidade de Franca (UNIFRAN)
Avenida Doutor Armando Salles Oliveira 201, Campus
Universitário, Parque Universitário, Franca, São Paulo 14404600
Tel: +55(16) 3711-8888
Fax: +55(11) 3711-8886
EMail: reitoria@unifran.br
Website: http://www.unifran.br

Reitora: Rosalinda Chedian Pimentel Tel: +55(16) 3711-8851

Areas

Biological and Health Sciences (Biology; Biomedicine; Dentistry; Nursing; Nutrition; Pharmacy; Physical Education; Physical Therapy; Psychology; Speech Therapy and Audiology; Veterinary Science); **Exact Sciences and Technology** (Chemical Engineering; Chemistry; Civil Engineering; Computer Science; Electrical Engineering; Mathematics; Mechanical Engineering; Physics; Production Engineering); **Human Sciences and Arts** (Advertising and Publicity; Architecture; Art Education; Design; Fashion Design; Geography; Graphic Design; History; Journalism; Literature; Pedagogy; Town Planning); **Law and Applied Social Sciences** (Accountancy; Administration; Law)

History: Founded 1972.

Admission Requirements: Secondary school certificate and entrance examination

Main Language(s) of Instruction: Portuguese

Degrees and Diplomas: *Bacharelado*; *Licenciatura*; *Especialização/Aperfeiçoamento*; *Mestrado*; *Doutorado*

Student Services: Canteen
Last Updated: 04/06/10

UNIVERSITY OF ITAÚNA
Universidade de Itaúna (UI)
Rodóvia MG, 431 Km 45, Campus Verde, Itaúna,
Minas Gerais 35680142
Tel: +55(37) 3249-3000
Fax: +55(37) 3249-3062
EMail: uit@uit.br
Website: http://www.uit.br

Reitor: Faiçal David Freire Chequer (1998-)
Tel: +55(37) 3249-3003

Areas

Biology and Health Sciences (Biology; Dentistry; Medicine; Nursing; Nutrition; Pharmacy; Physical Education; Physical Therapy); **Exact and Earth Sciences and Technology** (Chemistry; Computer Science; Electronic Engineering; Mechanical Engineering; Production Engineering); **Human and Applied Social Sciences** (Accountancy; Administration; Architecture; Law; Literature; Pedagogy; Town Planning)

Further Information: Also Almenara campus

History: Founded 1965, acquired present status and title 1997.

Admission Requirements: Secondary school certificate and entrance examination

Main Language(s) of Instruction: Portuguese

Degrees and Diplomas: *Bacharelado*; *Licenciatura*; *Especialização/Aperfeiçoamento*; *Mestrado*

Student Services: Canteen
Last Updated: 04/06/10

UNIVERSITY OF MARÍLIA
Universidade de Marília (UNIMAR)
Avenida Higyno Muzzy Filho 1001, Bloco I, Campus Universitário,
Marília, São Paulo 17525902
Tel: +55(14) 2105-4000
EMail: falecom@unimar.br
Website: http://www.unimar.br

Reitor: Márcio Mesquita Serva (1988-)
Tel: +55(14) 433-6269 EMail: reitoria@unimar.br

Pró-Reitora: Maria Beatriz B. Moraes Trazzi
Tel: +55(14) 421-4121

International Relations: Regina Lúcia Ottaiano Losasso Serva
Tel: +55(14) 433-6269 EMail: reitoria@unimar.br

Faculties

Agrarian Sciences (Agricultural Engineering; Animal Husbandry; Veterinary Science) *Director:* Helmuth Kieckhöfer; **Communication, Education and Tourism** (Advertising and Publicity; Communication Studies; Education; Journalism; Modern Languages; Pedagogy; Tourism) *Director:* Suely Villibor Flory; **Dentistry** (Dentistry) *Director:* Valdir Gouveia Garcia; **Engineering, Architecture**

and Technology (Architecture; Civil Engineering; Computer Science; Data Processing; Electrical Engineering; Engineering; Mechanical Engineering; Production Engineering; Technology; Town Planning) *Director*: Odair Laurindo Filho; **Health Sciences** (Biology; Health Sciences; Nutrition; Pharmacy; Physical Education; Physical Therapy; Psychology; Speech Therapy and Audiology) *Director*: Armando Castello Branco Jr.; **Human Sciences** (Accountancy; Economics; Management; Social and Community Services) *Director*: Cláudia de Pádua Sabia; **Law** (Law) *Director*: Jussara Suzy Assis Nasser Borges Ferreira; **Medicine** (Medicine; Nursing) *Director*: Carlos Eduardo Bueno

Further Information: Also Veterinary Hospital; Clinical Analysis Laboratory; Psychological Clinic; Speech Therapy and Audiology Clinic; Informatics Laboratories; Dental Clinic; Model Factory for Pharmaceutical Products and 2 Hospitals

History: Founded 1956 as school, acquired present status and title 1988.

Academic Year: February to December (February-June; August-December)

Admission Requirements: Secondary school certificate and entrance examination

Fees: (Reais): 366-2,900 per month

Main Language(s) of Instruction: Portuguese

Degrees and Diplomas: *Bacharelado*: 4-6 yrs; *Bacharelado*: Technology, 3-4 yrs; *Licenciatura*: 3-4 yrs; *Especialização/Aperfeiçoamento*; *Mestrado*

Student Services: Academic counselling, Canteen, Cultural centre, Employment services, Foreign student adviser, Handicapped facilities, Health services, Language programs, Nursery care, Social counselling, Sports facilities

Student Residential Facilities: Yes

Special Facilities: Anatomy Museum. Television and Radio Studio

Libraries: Central Library

Publications: Human Sciences Review *(annually)*; Law Review *(annually)*; Odontological Review *(annually)*; UNIMAR Ciências, Scientific Magazine

Last Updated: 30/10/07

UNIVERSITY OF MOGI DAS CRUZES
Universidade de Mogi das Cruzes (UMC)
Avenida Dr. Cândido Xavier Almeida Souza 200, Mogi das Cruzes, São Paulo 08780911
Tel: +55(11) 4798-7051
Fax: +55(11) 4799-1569
EMail: reitoria@umc.br
Website: http://www.umc.br

Reitora: Regina Coeli Bezerra de Melo Nassri (2002-)

Secretary-General: Claudio da Silva Nicoliche
Tel: +55(11) 4798-7294, Fax: +55(11) 4798-7082
EMail: silva@umc.br

Divisions
Business Studies; **Exact Sciences** (Architecture; Chemical Engineering; Chemistry; Civil Engineering; Computer Science; Electrical Engineering; Mechanical Engineering; Production Engineering; Town Planning); **Health Sciences** (Biology; Dentistry; Medicine; Nursing; Nutrition; Pharmacy; Physical Education; Physical Therapy; Psychology); **Human Sciences** (Advertising and Publicity; Journalism; Law; Literature; Pedagogy; Visual Arts)

Units
Biochemical Research (Biochemistry) *Head*: Flávio Aparecido Rodrigues; **Biotechnology** (Biotechnology); **Environmental Sciences** (Environmental Studies) *Head*: Nelson Durán; **Social Sciences** (Social Sciences) *Head*: Adolfo Ignacio Calderón Flores; **Technological Research** (Technology) *Head*: Annie France Slaets

History: Founded 1962, incorporating previously existing faculties. A private institution under the supervision of the Organização Mogiana de Educação e Cultura, with didactic-scientific, disciplinary, administrative and financial autonomy.

Governing Bodies: Conselho Universitário

Academic Year: February to December (February-June; August-December)

Admission Requirements: Secondary school certificate and entrance examination

Fees: (Reais): 2,838-13,103 per semester

Main Language(s) of Instruction: Portuguese

Degrees and Diplomas: *Tecnólogo*: Automation; Information Systems; Environmental Studies; Tourism; Marketing; Industrial Production; Development of Software Systems; Agribusiness; Logistics; Graphic Production; Private and Public Management, 6 sem; *Bacharelado*: Architecture; Town Planning; Engineering; Mathematics; Chemistry; Computer Science; Biological and Life Sciences; Biomedicine; Medicine; Nursing; Nutrition; Pharmacy; Physical Therapy; Psychology; Administration; Law; Communication Studies; Accountancy; Physical Education, 8-12 sem; *Licenciatura*: Mathematics; Biological and Life Sciences; Physical Education; Psychology; Arts and Humanities; Pedagogy, 6-8 sem; *Especialização/Aperfeiçoamento*; *Mestrado*: Biotechnology; Biomedical Engineering, 4 sem; *Doutorado*: Biotechnology; Biomedical Engineering, 6 sem

Student Services: Academic counselling, Canteen, Cultural centre, Employment services, Handicapped facilities, Health services, Nursery care, Social counselling, Sports facilities

Libraries: Central Library, 110,217 vols

Last Updated: 04/06/10

UNIVERSITY OF NORTHERN PARANÁ
Universidade Norte do Paraná (UNOPAR)
Avenida Paris 675, Jardim Piza, Londrina, Paraná 86041140
Tel: +55(43) 3371-7838
Fax: +55(43) 3371-7721
EMail: unopar@unopar.br
Website: http://www.unopar.br

Reitora: Elisabeth Laffranchi EMail: reitoria@unopar.br

Areas
Biological and Health Sciences (Biological and Life Sciences; Dentistry; Nursing; Nutrition; Pharmacy; Physical Education; Physical Therapy; Speech Therapy and Audiology; Veterinary Science); **Business Administration and Social Sciences** (Accountancy; Administration; Business Administration; Hotel Management; Human Resources; Law; Marketing; Secretarial Studies; Tourism); **Exact Sciences and Technology** (Aeronautical and Aerospace Engineering; Agricultural Business; Architecture; Automation and Control Engineering; Chemistry; Computer Engineering; Electrical Engineering; Engineering; Food Technology; Industrial Chemistry; Industrial Design; Natural Sciences; Systems Analysis; Technology; Town Planning); **Human Sciences, Education, Communication and Arts** (Arts and Humanities; Communication Studies; Education; Fine Arts; Journalism; Pedagogy; Social and Community Services; Social Sciences; Theology; Visual Arts)

Further Information: Also campuses in Arapongas and Bandeirrantes

History: Founded 1972.

Admission Requirements: Secondary school certificate and entrance examination

Main Language(s) of Instruction: Portuguese

Degrees and Diplomas: *Tecnólogo*; *Bacharelado*; *Licenciatura*; *Especialização/Aperfeiçoamento*; *Mestrado*
Last Updated: 10/05/10

UNIVERSITY OF PARANÁ
Universidade Paranaense (UNIPAR)
Praça Mascarenhas de Moraes S/n Centro, Umuarama, Paraná 87502210
Tel: +55(44) 3621-2828
Fax: +55(44) 3621-2830
EMail: degpa@unipar.br
Website: http://www.unipar.br

Reitor: Cândido Garcia
Tel: +55(44) 621-2828 r/1223 EMail: candido@unipar.br

Institutes
Applied Social Sciences (Social Sciences); **Biological, Medical and Health Sciences** (Biology; Health Sciences; Medicine); **Education** (Education); **Exact, Agrarian, Technological and Earth**

Sciences (Agriculture; Earth Sciences; Mathematics and Computer Science; Physics; Technology); **Human Sciences, Linguistics, Letters and Arts** (Arts and Humanities; Fine Arts; Modern Languages)

Further Information: Campuses at Toledo, Guaíra, Paranavaí, Cianorte and Cascavel. Also Veterinary Hospital

History: Founded 1972 as Faculty of Umuarama, became Faculdades Integradas de Umurama 1990 incorporating already existing faculties. Acquired present status and title 1993.

Admission Requirements: Secondary school certificate and entrance examination

Main Language(s) of Instruction: Portuguese

Degrees and Diplomas: *Bacharelado*: Accountancy; Administration; Advertising and Publicity; Architecture; Information Systems; International Business; Journalism; Law; Marketing; Tourism and Hotel Management, 4-5 yrs; *Bacharelado*: Dentistry; Nursing; Nutrition; Pharmacy; Physical Therapy, 4 yrs; *Bacharelado*: Veterinary Medicine, 5 yrs; *Licenciatura*: Biotechnology; History; Mathematics; Pedagogy; Portuguese - English; Portuguese - Spanish, 3-4 yrs; *Especialização/Aperfeiçoamento*; *Mestrado*. Also combined Licenciatura and Bacharelado, 4-5 yrs, in Physical Education, Psychology, Industrial Chemistry

Student Services: Academic counselling, Canteen, Cultural centre, Employment services, Handicapped facilities, Health services, Language programs, Social counselling, Sports facilities

Special Facilities: Farm School. Medicinal Herbarium. Geology Museum

Libraries: Campus libraries

Publications: Akropolis - Revista de Ciências Humanas da UNIPAR *(quarterly)*; Arquivos de Ciências da Saúde da UNIPAR *(quarterly)*; Arquivos de Ciências Veterinárias e Zoologia da UNIPAR *(biannually)*; Revista de Ciências Empresariais da UNIPAR *(biannually)*; Revista de Ciências Jurídicas e Sociais da UNIPAR *(biannually)*

Last Updated: 10/05/10

UNIVERSITY OF PASSO FUNDO
Universidade de Passo Fundo (UPF)
Campus I - Km 171 - BR 285, São José, Passo Fundo,
Rio Grande do Sul 99001970
Tel: +55(54) 3316-8100
Fax: +55(54) 3316-8125
EMail: reitoria@upf.tche.br
Website: http://www.upf.tche.br

Reitor: Rui Getúlio Soares

Centres
Agronomical Extension and Research *(Cepagro)* (Agronomy); **Applied Psychology** *(CPA)* (Psychology); **Environmental Science and Technology** *(CCTAM)* (Environmental Engineering); **Food Research** (Food Science); **Historical Research of Rio Grande do Sul** *(CPH-RS)* (History); **Literature and Multimedia Reference** (Literature; Multimedia); **Regional Economics and Administration** *(CEA)* (Administration; Economics); **Regional Education** *(CRE)* (Education); **Regional Studies and Activities for Ageing** (Gerontology; Regional Studies)

Faculties
Agronomy and Veterinary Medicine (Agronomy; Veterinary Science); **Arts and Communication** (Advertising and Publicity; Fine Arts; Information Sciences; Journalism; Music; Visual Arts); **Dentistry** (Dentistry); **Economics, Administration and Accountancy** (Accountancy; Administration; Business Administration; Economics); **Education** (Education; Educational Technology; Pedagogy); **Engineering and Architecture** (Architecture; Civil Engineering; Electrical Engineering; Engineering; Environmental Engineering; Food Technology; Mechanical Engineering; Town Planning); **Law** (Law); **Medicine** (Medicine; Speech Therapy and Audiology); **Physical Education and Physiotherapy** (Physical Education; Physical Therapy)

Institutes
Biology (Biology; Health Sciences; Nursing; Nutrition; Pharmacy); **Exact and Earth Sciences** (Chemistry; Earth Sciences; Geography; Mathematics; Mathematics and Computer Science;

Physics); **Philosophy and Human Sciences** (Arts and Humanities; History; Literature; Philosophy; Psychology)

Units
Architecture and Town and Community Development *(Naduc)* (Architecture; Development Studies; Town Planning); **Electronics** *(NE)* (Electronic Engineering); **Interdisciplinary Studies of Natural Products** *(Nipron)*; **Law** *('Teixeira de Freitas')* (Law); **Mechanical Technology** *(NTM)* (Mechanical Engineering); **Special Education** *(NEE)* (Special Education)

Further Information: Branches at Carazinho, Casca, Lagoa Vermelha, Palmeira das Missões, Soledade and Sarandi

History: Founded 1968 incorporating Faculty of Law, established 1956 and Faculties of Philosophy and Political Science, established 1957. A private institution recognized by the federal government.

Governing Bodies: Conselho Universitário

Academic Year: March to December (March-July; August-December)

Admission Requirements: Secondary school certificate and entrance examination

Main Language(s) of Instruction: Portuguese

Degrees and Diplomas: *Bacharelado*: 3-6 yrs; *Licenciatura*; *Especialização/Aperfeiçoamento*; *Mestrado*; *Doutorado*

Student Services: Academic counselling, Canteen, Cultural centre, Employment services, Foreign student adviser, Language programs, Sports facilities

Student Residential Facilities: Yes

Special Facilities: 'Augusto Ruscht' Zoobotanical Museum. 'Ruth Schneider' Visual Arts Museum. Zoological Garden

Libraries: Central Library, c. 83,882 vols

Publications: Cesta Básica *(monthly)*; Espaço Pedagógico *(annually)*; Justiça do Direito *(biannually)*; Revista da Faculdade de Odontologia *(biannually)*; Revista de Filosofia e Ciências Humanas *(biannually)*; Teoria e Evidência Econômica *(biannually)*

Press or Publishing House: Gráfica e Editora UPF

Last Updated: 04/06/10

UNIVERSITY OF RIBEIRÃO PRÊTO
Universidade de Ribeirão Prêto (UNAERP)
Avenida Costábile Romano 2201, Ribeirânia, Ribeirão Preto,
São Paulo 14096380
Tel: +55(16) 3603-7000
Fax: +55(16) 3603-7073
EMail: unaerp@unaerp.br
Website: http://www.unaerp.br

Reitora: Elmara Lúcia de Oliveira Bonini Corauci (1997-)
Tel: +55(16) 3603-6815, Fax: +55(16) 3603-7005
EMail: ecorauci@unaerp.br

International Relations: Teobaldo Rivas
Tel: +55(16) 3603-7087 EMail: trivas@unaerp.br

Areas
Exact Sciences (Chemical Engineering; Computer Science; Production Engineering; Systems Analysis); **Health Sciences** (Dentistry; Health Sciences; Medicine; Nursing; Nutrition; Pharmacy; Physical Education; Physical Therapy; Psychology); **Human Sciences** (Administration; Advertising and Publicity; International Business; International Relations; Journalism; Law; Music; Pedagogy; Social and Community Services; Tourism; Translation and Interpretation)

History: Founded 1924. A private institution under the jurisdiction of the Associação de Ensino de Ribeirão Prêto.

Academic Year: February to June and August to December

Admission Requirements: Secondary school certificate and entrance examination

Main Language(s) of Instruction: Portuguese

International Co-operation: With universities in USA; Australia; Germany; Argentina; Cuba; Portugal

Accrediting Agencies: Ministério da Educação (MEC)

Degrees and Diplomas: *Bacharelado*: 4 and 5 yrs; *Licenciatura*; *Especialização/Aperfeiçoamento*: 1 yr; *Mestrado*: 2 to 4 yrs; *Doutorado*

Student Services: Academic counselling, Canteen, Cultural centre, Foreign student adviser, Handicapped facilities, Health services, Language programs, Social counselling, Sports facilities
Last Updated: 03/06/10

UNIVERSITY OF SANTA CRUZ DO SUL
Universidade de Santa Cruz do Sul (UNISC)
Avenida Independência 2293, Universitário, Santa Cruz do Sul, Rio Grande do Sul 96815900
Tel: +55(51) 3717-7300
Fax: +55(51) 3717-1855
EMail: info@unisc.br
Website: http://www.unisc.br

Reitor: Vilmar Thomé (2006-)
Tel: +55(51) 717-7304 EMail: reitoria@unisc.br

Departments
Accountancy (Accountancy); **Administration** (Administration; Business Administration; Finance; Marketing); **Biology and Pharmacy** (Biology; Pharmacy); **Computer Science** (Computer Science); **Economics** (Agricultural Engineering; Economics); **Education** (Education); **Engineering, Architecture and Agronomy** (Agricultural Engineering; Architecture; Civil Engineering; Electrical Engineering; Production Engineering; Town Planning); **History and Geography** (Architecture; Geography; History; Tourism; Town Planning); **Human Sciences** (Philosophy; Social and Community Services); **Law** (Law); **Liberal Arts** (Arts and Humanities; English; Modern Languages; Native Language; Spanish); **Mathematics** (Mathematics); **Nursing and Odontology** (Dentistry; Nursing); **Physical Education and Health Sciences** (Nutrition; Physical Education; Physical Therapy; Sports); **Physics and Chemistry** (Chemistry; Physics); **Psychology** (Psychology); **Social Communication** (Advertising and Publicity; Communication Studies; Journalism; Public Administration)

Research Centres
Accountancy *(CEC)* (Accountancy); **Archaeology** *(CEPA)* (Archaeology); **Business Administration** *(CEPAD)* (Business Administration); **Economics** *(CEPE)* (Economics); **Law** *(CEPE-JUR)* (Law); **Regional Development** *(CEPEDER)* (Development Studies); **Science** *(CECIUNISC)* (Natural Sciences); **Social Studies** *(NUPES)* (Social Studies); **Technological Modernization** *(Pole)* (Technology); **Urban Planning and Town Management** *(NPU)* (Town Planning; Urban Studies)

History: Founded 1964, incorporating existing Faculties, acquired present status and title 1993. A communitary non Governmental Institution administered by the Santa Cruz do Sul Pro-Instruction Association.

Academic Year: March to November (March-July; August-November)

Admission Requirements: Competitive entrance examination

Main Language(s) of Instruction: Portuguese

Degrees and Diplomas: *Bacharelado*; *Licenciatura*; *Especialização/Aperfeiçoamento*; *Mestrado*; *Doutorado*

Student Services: Academic counselling, Canteen, Cultural centre, Employment services, Foreign student adviser, Foreign Studies Centre, Handicapped facilities, Health services, Language programs, Nursery care, Social counselling, Sports facilities

Special Facilities: TV and Radio Studio

Libraries: Central Library, c. 138,500 vols

Publications: Ágora, History and Geography *(biannually)*; Barbarói, Human Sciences and Psychology *(biannually)*; Caderno de Pesquisa-Série Botânica, Botanics and Biology *(biannually)*; Estudos do CEPA *(biannually)*; Estudos do CEPE, Economics *(biannually)*; REDES, Regional Development *(biannually)*; Reflexão e Ação, Education *(biannually)*; Revista do Direito, Law *(biannually)*; SIGNO, Liberal Arts *(biannually)*; Tecno-lógica *(biannually)*

Press or Publishing House: Editora da Universidade de Santa Cruz do Sul (EDUNISC)
Last Updated: 03/06/10

UNIVERSITY OF SANTO AMARO
Universidade de Santo Amaro (UNISA)
Rua Professor Enéas de Siqueira Neto, 340 - Jardim das Imbuias - Sto. Amaro, São Paulo, São Paulo 04829-300
Tel: +55(11) 5545-8800
Fax: +55(11) 5522-7844
EMail: sdutra@unisa.br
Website: http://www.unisa.br

Reitor: Darci Gomes do Nascimento

Areas
Biological Sciences; **Exact Sciences** (Environmental Engineering; Production Engineering; Systems Analysis); **Human Sciences**

Further Information: Also Teaching Hospital; Veterinary Hospital. Dental Clinic. Psychology Clinic

History: Founded 1968 as Faculdades de Santo Amaro. Acquired present status and title 1994. A private Institution.

Governing Bodies: Organização Santamarense de Educação e Cultura (OSEC)

Academic Year: February to December

Admission Requirements: Secondary school certificate (Vestibular) and entrance examination

Fees: (Reais): 4,200-18,000 per annum

Main Language(s) of Instruction: Portuguese

International Co-operation: With universities in Cuba and USA.

Accrediting Agencies: Ministry of Education and Culture

Degrees and Diplomas: *Bacharelado*: 4-6 yrs; *Licenciatura*: 4-5 yrs; *Especialização/Aperfeiçoamento*: 1-2 yrs; *Mestrado*: 2-3 yrs; *Doutorado*: 2-3 yrs. Also Master of Business Administration 2 yrs

Student Services: Academic counselling, Canteen, Cultural centre, Foreign student adviser, Handicapped facilities, Health services, Social counselling, Sports facilities

Student Residential Facilities: None

Special Facilities: Anatomy Museum. Herbarium.

Libraries: Milton Soldani Afonso Library, c. 103,000 vols

Publications: Biological *(biannually)*; Direito *(annually)*; Humanas *(biannually)*; Verbum *(annually)*

Press or Publishing House: Editora UNISA
Last Updated: 03/06/10

UNIVERSITY OF SOROCABA
Universidade de Sorocaba (UNISO)
Rodóvia Raposo Tavares S/n km 925, Jardim Novo Eldorado, Sorocaba, São Paulo 18023000
Tel: +55(15) 2101-7000
EMail: uniso@uniso.br
Website: http://www.uniso.br

Reitor: Fernando de Sá Del Fiol EMail: fernando.fiol@uniso.br

Pró-Reitor Acadêmico: José Martins de Oliveira Jr
EMail: jose.oliveira@prof.uniso.br

Centres
Applied Social Sciences (Accountancy; Administration; Advertising and Publicity; Design; Economics; Hotel Management; International Business; Journalism; Law; Social Sciences; Tourism); **Biological and Health Sciences** (Biochemistry; Biological and Life Sciences; Biotechnology; Health Sciences; Nursing; Nutrition; Occupational Therapy; Pharmacy); **Engineering and Architecture** (Architecture; Automation and Control Engineering; Chemical Engineering; Civil Engineering; Computer Engineering; Electrical Engineering; Environmental Engineering; Production Engineering); **Exact and Earth Sciences** (Chemistry; Computer Science; Information Sciences; Mathematics; Physics; Systems Analysis); **Human Sciences** (Education; History; Philosophy); **Linguistics, Letters and Arts** (Dance; Literature; Music; Theatre; Visual Arts)

Further Information: Also Câmpus Seminário, Câmpus Trujillo and Câmpus Tietê

History: Founded 1950, became Faculdade de Filosofia, Ciências e Letras 1954 and acquired present status and title 1994.

Academic Year: February-June; August-December

Admission Requirements: Secondary school certificate and entrance examination

Fees: (Reais) c. 3,000 per semester

Main Language(s) of Instruction: Portuguese

International Co-operation: With universities in the United States, Spain

Accrediting Agencies: Ministry of Education

Degrees and Diplomas: *Bacharelado*: 4-5 yrs; *Licenciatura*: 4 yrs; *Especialização/Aperfeiçoamento*: 1 1/2 yrs; *Mestrado*: Education, 1 1/2 yrs

Student Services: Academic counselling, Canteen, Foreign student adviser, Foreign Studies Centre, Handicapped facilities, Health services, Language programs, Nursery care, Social counselling, Sports facilities

Publications: Quaestio - Revista de Estudos de Educação *(biannually)*; Revista de Estudos Universitários *(biannually)*; Revista UNISO *(annually)*

Last Updated: 03/06/10

UNIVERSITY OF THE CAMPANHA REGION
Universidade da Região da Campanha (URCAMP)
Avenida Tupy Silveira 2099, Centro, Bagé,
Rio Grande do Sul 96400110
Tel: +55(532) 3242-8244
Fax: +55(532) 3242-8898
EMail: urcamp@attila.urcamp.tche.br
Website: http://attila.urcamp.tche.br

Reitor: Francisco Arno Vaz da Cunha Tel: +55(532) 42-8244

Centres
Economics and Computer Science (Accountancy; Computer Science; Economics); **Education Sciences, Communication and Arts** (Advertising and Publicity; Art Education; Journalism; Literature; Mathematics; Pedagogy; Physical Education; Social Sciences); **Exact and Environmental Sciences**; **Health Sciences** (Nursing; Nutrition; Pharmacy; Physical Therapy; Psychology); **Law**; **Rural Studies** (Agronomy; Veterinary Science)

Further Information: Campuses at Alegrete, Caçapava, Dom Pedrito, Sant'Ana do Livramento, São Borja and São Gabriel. Also University Hospital

History: Founded 1955.

Admission Requirements: Secondary school certificate and entrance examination

Main Language(s) of Instruction: Portuguese

Degrees and Diplomas: *Bacharelado*; *Licenciatura*; *Especialização/Aperfeiçoamento*; *Mestrado*; *Doutorado*

Student Services: Canteen

Student Residential Facilities: For c. 300 students
Last Updated: 07/06/10

UNIVERSITY OF THE CITY OF SÃO PAULO
Universidade Cidade de São Paulo (UNICID)
Rua Cesário Galeno 448/475, Tatuapé, São Paulo,
São Paulo 03071000
Tel: +55(11) 6190-1200
Fax: +55(11) 6190-1415
EMail: cidadesp@cidadesp.edu.br
Website: http://www.unicid.br

Head: Rubens Lopes da Cruz (2002-)
Tel: +55(11) 6190-1410, Fax: +55(11) 6190-1415
EMail: rcruz@unicid.br

International Relations: Marcelo Naddeo
Tel: +55(11) 6190-1446, Fax: +55(11) 6190-1415
EMail: mnaddeo@unicid.br

Areas
Architecture and Town Planning (Architecture; Town Planning); **Business Studies** (Accountancy; Administration); **Computer Science** (Computer Science); **Education**; **Engineering**; **Health Sciences**; **Law** (Law); **Social Communication** (Advertising and Publicity; Journalism); **Tourism** (Tourism)

History: Founded 1972.

Admission Requirements: Secondary school certificate and entrance examination

Fees: (Reais): 600,000; fees vary according to courses

Main Language(s) of Instruction: Portuguese

Degrees and Diplomas: *Tecnólogo*: Management; Telecommunications; Environmental Studies, 2 - 3 1/2 yrs; *Bacharelado*: Medicine; Dentistry; Physiotherapy; Social Communication; Teacher Training, 3 - 6 yrs; *Licenciatura*: History; Geography; Mathematics; Chemistry; Education; Letters, 3 - 4 yrs; *Especialização/Aperfeiçoamento*: all fields, 1 1/2 - 2 yrs; *Mestrado*: Education; Physiotherapy; Dentistry, 2 yrs

Student Services: Academic counselling, Canteen, Employment services, Handicapped facilities, Health services, Social counselling

Special Facilities: Art Gallery; Theatre

Libraries: Yes
Last Updated: 07/06/10

UNIVERSITY OF THE REGION OF JOINVILLE
Universidade da Região de Joinville (UNIVILLE)
Campus Universitário S/n, Caixa Postal 246, Bom Retiro, Joinville,
Santa Catarina 89223900
Tel: +55(47) 3461-9000
Fax: +55(47) 3473-0131
EMail: univille@univille.edu.br
Website: http://www.univille.br

Reitora: Paulo Ivo Koehntopp
Tel: +55(47) 461-9011 +55(47)461-9081
EMail: reitoria@univille.edu.br

Vice-Reitor: Wilmar Anderle Tel: +55(47) 461-9011

International Relations: Cristala Athanazio Buschle, Assessora de Relações Internacionais
Tel: +55(47) 461-9051 EMail: critala@univille.edu.br

Departments
Accountancy (Accountancy); **Administration** (Administration; Business Administration; Industrial Management; Marketing; Transport Management); **Biology** (Biology; Marine Biology); **Chemical Engineering** (Chemical Engineering); **Computer Science**; **Dentistry**; **Design**; **Economics** (Economics); **Environmental Engineering**; **Foreign Trade** (International Business); **Geography** (Geography); **History** (History); **Law**; **Literature**; **Mathematics** (Mathematics); **Mechanical Engineering** (Mechanical Engineering); **Medicine**; **Pedagogy** (Education; Pedagogy); **Pharmacy**; **Physical Education** (Education; Physical Education); **Psychology**; **Visual Arts**

Further Information: Distance Education courses offered

History: Founded 1967. Acquired present status 1996. A Municipal Institution.

Admission Requirements: Secondary school certificate and entrance examination

Main Language(s) of Instruction: Portuguese

International Co-operation: With universities in Spain, France, Germany, Chile, United Kingdom and Italy

Degrees and Diplomas: *Bacharelado*; *Licenciatura*; *Especialização/Aperfeiçoamento*; *Mestrado*

Student Services: Academic counselling, Canteen, Employment services, Foreign student adviser, Handicapped facilities, Nursery care, Sports facilities
Last Updated: 07/06/10

UNIVERSITY OF THE RIO DOS SINOS VALLEY
Universidade do Vale do Rio dos Sinos (UNISINOS)
Avenida Unisinos 950, Barrio Cristo Rei, São Leopoldo,
Rio Grande do Sul 93022-000
Tel: +55(51) 3590-8237
Fax: +55(51) 3590-8289
EMail: intercambio@unisinos.br
Website: http://www.unisinos.br

President: Marcelo Fernandes de Aquino (2006-)
Pró-Reitor Acadêmico: Pedro Gilberto Gomes

Institutes

Anchietano; **Computer Science**; **Humanitas Unisinos** *(IHU)*; **Languages** (French; German; Italian; Japanese; Latin; Modern Languages; Spanish); **Research** *(Planarias)*

Schools
Design

History: Founded 1954 as Faculdade de Filosofia, Ciências e Letras. A private Institution under the supervision of the Society of Jesus. Acquired present status 1969, and recognized 1983. Reorganized with a structure comprising centres for Professional Education.

Governing Bodies: University Board

Academic Year: February to December (February-July; August-December)

Admission Requirements: Secondary school certificate and entrance examination

Fees: (Reais): c. 1,093.97 per subject, per semester

Main Language(s) of Instruction: Portuguese

International Co-operation: Participates in the Programa de Cooperação Inter-universitária, which includes universities in Spain and Latin America, Rede AUSJAL, Rede Deusto, Rede Alfa, RECOAGESDEL, Rede GAFRA, FIUC

Degrees and Diplomas: *Bacharelado*: 3-9 yrs; *Licenciatura*: 3-7 yrs; *Especialização/Aperfeiçoamento*: 1-2 yrs; *Mestrado*: 2 yrs; *Doutorado*: 2-4 yrs

Student Services: Academic counselling, Canteen, Cultural centre, Employment services, Foreign student adviser, Handicapped facilities, Health services, Language programs, Nursery care, Social counselling, Sports facilities

Special Facilities: Geology Museum; Archaeology Museum. Audio-visual Centre. TV and Radio Studio

Libraries: Central Library, c. 700,000 vols. Videotapes. Maps

Publications: Acta Biologica Leopoldensia *(biennially)*; Arquitetura Unisinos *(biennially)*; Ciências Sociais da Unisinos *(biennially)*; Controvérsia *(biennially)*; Educação Unisinos *(biennially)*; Entrelinhas *(biennially)*; Estudos Jurídicos *(3 per annum)*; Estudos Tecnológicos-Engenharia *(biennially)*; Filosofia Unisinos *(biennially)*; Fronteiras *(quarterly)*; História Unisinos *(3 per annum)*; Perspectiva Econômica *(quarterly)*; Revista AV *(biennially)*; Revista BASE *(3 per annum)*; Revista Calidoscopio *(3 per annum)*; Revista GAEA *(biennially)*; Scientia *(biennially)*; Verso e Reverso *(3 per annum)*

Press or Publishing House: UNISINOS Press; UNISINOS Publishing House

Last Updated: 31/05/10

UNIVERSITY OF THE SACRED HEART
Universidade do Sagrado Coração (USC)
Rua Irmã Arminda, Jardim Brasil, Bauru, São Paulo 17011-160
Tel: +55(14) 3235-7003
Fax: +55(14) 3235-7325
EMail: reitoria@usc.br
Website: http://www.usc.br

Reitora: Elvira Milani (2005-)
Tel: +55(14) 3235-7003, Fax: +55(14) 3235-7325

Areas
Exact and Applied Social Sciences (Advertising and Publicity; Communication Studies; Journalism; Public Relations; Tourism); **Health Sciences** (Biochemistry; Biological and Life Sciences; Biology; Dentistry; Health Sciences; Nursing; Nutrition; Occupational Therapy; Pharmacy; Physical Therapy; Speech Therapy and Audiology); **Human Sciences** (English; Fine Arts; Geography; History; Music; Music Education; Musical Instruments; Pedagogy; Philosophy; Portuguese; Psychology; Spanish; Theatre; Translation and Interpretation)

Centres
Research and Postgraduation

Further Information: Also Clinics: Physiotherapy; Dental; Psychology; Speech Therapy

History: Founded 1953 as Faculdade de Filosofia, Ciências e Letras do Sagrado Coração de Jesus. Acquired present status

1986. A private Catholic institution under the supervision of the Instituto das Apóstolas do Sagrado Coração.

Academic Year: February to December (February-June; August-December)

Admission Requirements: Secondary school certificate and entrance examination (Vestibular)

Main Language(s) of Instruction: Portuguese

Degrees and Diplomas: *Tecnólogo*: 2 yrs; *Bacharelado*: 4-5 yrs; *Licenciatura*: 4-5 yrs; *Especialização/Aperfeiçoamento*; *Mestrado*; *Doutorado*

Student Services: Academic counselling, Canteen, Cultural centre, Employment services, Foreign student adviser, Handicapped facilities, Health services, Social counselling, Sports facilities

Special Facilities: Zoology Museum; Natural Sciences Museum; Anatomy Museum. Art Gallery. Theatre. History Centre. Art Centre

Libraries: Central Library 'Cor Jesu', c. 210,000 vols

Publications: Cadernos de Divulgação Cultural *(annually)*; Revista Mimesis *(annually)*; Revista Salusvita *(annually)*

Press or Publishing House: Editora do Sagrado Coração - EDUSC

Last Updated: 31/05/10

UNIVERSITY OF THE SANTA CATARINA PLATEAU
Universidade do Planalto Catarinense (UNIPLAC)
Avenida Castelo Branco 170, Universitário, Lages,
Santa Catarina 88509900
Tel: +55(49) 3251-1022
Fax: +55(49) 3251-1051
EMail: uniplac@uniplac.net
Website: http://www.uniplac.net/

Reitor: Gilberto Borges de Sá

Departments
Applied Social Sciences; **Biological and Health Sciences**; **Exact and Technological Sciences**; **Human Sciences, Letters and Arts**; **Law**

History: Founded 1998.

Main Language(s) of Instruction: Portuguese

Degrees and Diplomas: *Bacharelado*; *Licenciatura*; *Especialização/Aperfeiçoamento*; *Mestrado*
Last Updated: 31/05/10

UNIVERSITY OF THE SAPUCAI VALLEY
Universidade do Vale do Sapucai (UNIVAS)
Avenida Pref. Tuany Toledo, 470, Pouso Alegre,
Minas Gerais 37550000
Tel: +55(35) 3449-2300
EMail: reitoria@univas.edu.br
Website: http://www.univas.edu.br

Reitor: Virgínio Cândido Tosta de Souza

Faculties
Health Sciences *(Dr. José Antônio Garcia Coutinho)*; **Philosophy, Science and Literature** *(Eugênio Pacelli)*

History: Founded 1964 as Fundação Universidade do Vale do Sapucaí. Acquired present status and title 1999.

Main Language(s) of Instruction: Portuguese

Degrees and Diplomas: *Bacharelado*; *Especialização/Aperfeiçoamento*; *Mestrado*
Last Updated: 31/05/10

UNIVERSITY OF THE STATE OF SÃO PAULO
Universidade Paulista (UNIP)
Rua Doutor Bacelar 1212, Mirandópolis, São Paulo,
São Paulo 04026002
Tel: +55(11) 577-3184 +55(11) 577-4000
Fax: +55(11) 275-1541
Website: http://www.unip.br

Reitor: João Carlos di Genio Tel: +55(11) 5586-4031

Institutes
Exact Sciences and Technology (Aeronautical and Aerospace Engineering; Architecture; Chemical Engineering; Computer Science; Electrical Engineering; Engineering; Industrial Design; Mathematics; Mechanical Engineering; Telecommunications Engineering; Town Planning); **Health Sciences** (Biology; Biomedicine; Dentistry; Health Sciences; Nursing; Nutrition; Pharmacy; Physical Education; Physical Therapy; Speech Therapy and Audiology; Veterinary Science; Zoology); **Human Sciences** (Fashion Design; Hotel Management; Pedagogy; Psychology; Secretarial Studies; Tourism); **Social Sciences and Communication** (Accountancy; Administration; Advertising and Publicity; Economics; Journalism; Law; Marketing; Social Sciences; Translation and Interpretation)

Further Information: Also 6 campuses in other cities in the State of São Paulo

History: Founded 1972 as Instituto Unificado Paulista de Ensino Superior. Acquired present status 1988.

Governing Bodies: Conselho Universitário; Conselho de Ensino e Pesquisa; Conselho de Curadores

Academic Year: February to December

Admission Requirements: Secondary school certificate and entrance examination

Main Language(s) of Instruction: Portuguese

Degrees and Diplomas: *Bacharelado*; *Licenciatura*; *Especialização/Aperfeiçoamento*; *Mestrado*; *Doutorado*

Student Services: Academic counselling, Canteen, Employment services, Nursery care, Sports facilities

Libraries: 22,525 vols

Press or Publishing House: Centro de Recursos Educacionais (CERED)

Last Updated: 07/05/10

UNIVERSITY OF THE VALLEY OF ITAJAÍ
Universidade do Vale do Itajaí (UNIVALI)
Rua Uruguai 458, Centro, Itajaí, Santa Catarina 88-302-202
Tel: +55(47) 3341-7500
EMail: reitoria@univali.br
Website:http://www.univali.br

Reitor: Mário Cesar dos Santos (2010-)

Centres
Applied Social Sciences-Communication, Tourism and Leisure *(Balneário Camboriú, Florianópolis, Itajaí)* (Advertising and Publicity; Architecture; Cooking and Catering; Cosmetology; Fashion Design; Graphic Design; Hotel Management; Industrial Design; Interior Design; Journalism; Multimedia; Music; Photography; Tourism; Town Planning); **Applied Social Sciences-Management** *(Balneário Camboriú, Balneário de Piçarras, Biguaçu, Itajaí, São José, Tijucas)* (Accountancy; Administration; Economics; International Business; Transport Management); **Health Sciences** *(Biguaçu, Itajaí)* (Dentistry; Medicine; Nursing; Pharmacy; Psychology; Speech Therapy and Audiology); **Law and Social Sciences** *(Balneário Camboriú, Biguaçu, Itajaí, São José, Tijucas)* (International Relations; Law; Political Sciences; Social Sciences); **Technological Earth and Sea Science** *(Florianópolis, Itajaí, São José, Tijucas)* (Biological and Life Sciences; Civil Engineering; Computer Engineering; Computer Science; Environmental Engineering; Marine Science and Oceanography; Naval Architecture)

History: Founded 1989, incorporating previously existing faculties. Under the supervision of the Municipal authorities.

Academic Year: February to December (February-June; July-December)

Admission Requirements: Secondary school certificate or equivalent and entrance examination

Main Language(s) of Instruction: Portuguese

International Co-operation: Student exchange programmes with European and Latin American universities

Degrees and Diplomas: *Bacharelado*: 4 yrs; *Licenciatura*: 4 yrs; *Especialização/Aperfeiçoamento*; *Mestrado*: a further 2 yrs; *Doutorado*: 4 yrs

Student Services: Academic counselling, Canteen, Employment services, Foreign student adviser, Health services, Language programs, Social counselling, Sports facilities

Student Residential Facilities: no

Special Facilities: Ocean Museum. UNIVALI Museum; Theatre; Foreign Trade Consultancy; Consultancy for Law Students Training

Libraries: Total, c. 170,000 vols

Publications: Novos Estudos Jurídicos, Periodical of the Masters' Degree Programme in Law *(biennially)*; Turismo Visão e Ação, Periodical of the Masters' Degree Programme in Tourism and Hotel Management *(biennially)*

Press or Publishing House: Editora da UNIVALI

Last Updated: 31/05/10

UNIVERSITY OF THE VALLEY OF PARAIBA
Universidade do Vale do Paraíba (UNIVAP)
São José dos Campos, São Paulo 12244-000
Tel: +55(12) 3947-1056
Fax: +55(12) 3949-1334
EMail: gabinete@univap.br
Website: http://www.univap.br

Reitor: Baptista Gargione Filho (2004-) EMail: baptista@univap.br

Pró-Reitor Administrativo: Airton Teixeira
Tel: +55(12) 3947-1074, Fax: +55(12) 3949-2397
EMail: teixeira@univap.br

International Relations: Antonio de Souza Teixeira Jr
Tel: +55(12) 3947-1036, Fax: +55(12) 3947-1211
EMail: texjr@univap.br

Faculties
Applied Social Sciences and Communication (Accountancy; Administration; Advertising and Publicity; Fashion Design; Journalism; Radio and Television Broadcasting; Social and Community Services; Tourism); **Computer Engineering** *Dean:* Luiiz Alberto Vieira Dias; **Education and Arts**; **Engineering, Architecture and Town Planning** (Aeronautical and Aerospace Engineering; Architecture; Civil Engineering; Electrical and Electronic Engineering; Environmental Engineering; Materials Engineering; Town Planning); **Health Sciences**; **Law**

Further Information: Also campus at Urbanova

History: Founded 1954.

Academic Year: February to November

Admission Requirements: Secondary school certificate and entrance examination

Fees: (US Dollars): 1,000 per semester

Main Language(s) of Instruction: Portuguese

International Co-operation: With universities in Denmark, Peru, Spain

Degrees and Diplomas: *Bacharelado*: 4-5 yrs; *Mestrado*: 2 yrs; *Mestrado*: Education, 3-4 yrs; *Doutorado*: minimum 2 yrs

Student Services: Academic counselling, Canteen, Cultural centre, Language programs, Nursery care, Sports facilities

Libraries: Total, 105,000 vols

Publications: Revista UNIVAP *(biennially)*

Last Updated: 31/05/10

UNIVERSITY OF THE WEST OF SAO PAULO
Universidade do Oeste Paulista (UNOESTE)
Rua José Bongiovani 700, Cidade Universitária, Campus Universitário, Presidente Prudente, São Paulo 19050680
Tel: +55(18) 3229-1000
Fax: +55(18) 3229-1013
EMail: unoeste@apec.unoeste.br
Website:http://www.unoeste.br

Reitora: Ana Cardoso Maia de Oliveira Lima
Tel: +55(18) 3229-1000

Faculties
Animal Husbandry and Agriculture (Agriculture; Animal Husbandry); **Civil Engineering** (Civil Engineering); **Computer Science** (Computer Science); **Dentistry** (Dentistry); **Health Sciences** (Health Sciences; Physical Therapy; Psychology); **Law, Administration, and Accountancy** (Accountancy; Administration; Law); **Medicine** (Medicine); **Pharmacy and Biochemistry** (Biochemistry; Pharmacy); **Science, Letters, and Education** (Arts and Huma-

nities; Education; Mathematics and Computer Science; Natural Sciences); **Veterinary Medicine** (Veterinary Science)

History: Founded 1974, incorporating previously existing Faculties. Under the supervision of the Associação Prudentina de Educação e Cultura.

Academic Year: February to December (February-June; August-December)

Admission Requirements: Secondary school certificate and entrance examination

Main Language(s) of Instruction: Portuguese

Degrees and Diplomas: *Bacharelado*; *Licenciatura*; *Especialização/Aperfeiçoamento*; *Mestrado*

Student Residential Facilities: Yes

Libraries: Biblioteca Nair Fortes Abu-Mehri, c. 70,500 vols

Publications: Scientific Magazine *(annually)*

Last Updated: 01/06/10

UNIVERSITY OF UBERABA
Universidade de Uberaba (UNIUBE)
Av. Guilherme Ferreira, 217 Bairro Centro, Campus Universitário II, Uberaba, Minas Gerais 38055500
Tel: +55(34) 3319-6600
EMail: uniube@uniube.br
Website: http://www.uniube.br

Reitor: Marcelo Palmério (1996-)
Tel: +55(34) 3311-8811 EMail: marcelo.palmerio@uniube.br

Superintendente: Alaor Vilela
Tel: +55(34) 3321-6600, Fax: +55(34) 3321-6332
EMail: alaor.vilela@uniube.br

International Relations: José Neto EMail: jose.peres@uniube.br

Areas
Agronomy and Veterinary Science (Agriculture; Veterinary Science); **Applied Social Sciences** (Accountancy; Administration; Advertising and Publicity; Biology; Journalism; Law; Literature; Mathematics; Pedagogy; Social and Community Services; Social Sciences; Tourism); **Engineering and Computer Science** (Architecture; Chemical Engineering; Civil Engineering; Computer Engineering; Electrical Engineering; Environmental Engineering; Production Engineering; Systems Analysis; Town Planning); **Medicine and Health Sciences**

Further Information: Also campus in Uberlandia

History: Founded 1965, acquired present status and title 1988.

Academic Year: February to December

Admission Requirements: Secondary school certificate and entrance examination

Main Language(s) of Instruction: Portuguese

International Co-operation: With University of Alberta, Canada

Degrees and Diplomas: *Tecnólogo*: Architecture; Dentistry; Veterinary Medicine, 10 sem; *Tecnólogo*: Medicine, 12 sem; *Bacharelado*: Administration; Biological Sciences; Social Communication and Journalism; Social Communication and Publicity; Tourism, 4 yrs; *Bacharelado*: Aeronautical Sciences, 6 sem; *Bacharelado*: Civil Engineering; Computer Engineering; Electrical Engineering; Industrial Pharmacy; Information Systems; Nursing; Nutrition; Occupational Therapy; Physical Education; Physical Therapy; Social Work; Speech Therapy and Audiology, 8 sem; *Bacharelado*: Law, 10 sem; *Licenciatura*: Biological Sciences; Chemistry; History; Letters; Mathematics; Pedagogy, 4 yrs; *Licenciatura*: Psychology, 5 yrs; *Especialização/Aperfeiçoamento*; *Mestrado*

Student Services: Canteen, Cultural centre, Employment services, Handicapped facilities, Health services, Language programs, Sports facilities

Student Residential Facilities: No

Publications: Jornal Revelação, Social Communication and Journalism Journal *(weekly)*; Revista Profissão Docente, Scientific online journal of Education

Last Updated: 03/06/10

UNIVERSITY OF WEST SANTA CATARINA
Universidade do Oeste de Santa Catarina (UNOESC)
Rua Getúlio Vargas, 2125, Flor da Serra, Chapecó, Santa Catarina 89600000
Tel: +55(49) 3551-2000
EMail: reitoria@unoesc.edu.br
Website: http://www.unoesc.edu.br

Reitor: Aristides Cimadon EMail: reitor@unoesc.edu.br

Departments
Administration; **Biological and Health Sciences**; **Communication**; **Education**; **Human and Social Sciences**; **Law**; **Process Engineering**; **Psychology**

Institutes
Regional Socio-Economic Studies *(IESER)*

History: Founded 1968. A Municipal institution.

Admission Requirements: Secondary school certificate and entrance examination

Main Language(s) of Instruction: Portuguese

Degrees and Diplomas: *Bacharelado*; *Licenciatura*; *Especialização/Aperfeiçoamento*; *Mestrado*

Student Services: Canteen

Student Residential Facilities: Yes

Last Updated: 01/06/10

UNOPEC FACULTIES
Faculdades UNOPEC
Rua Zephiro Puccinelli 1281, Jardim Morada do Sol, Indaiatuba, São Paulo 13348060
Tel: +55(19) 3875-8529
Fax: +55(19) 3875-8152
EMail: info@opec.com.br
Website: http://www.unopecsp.com.br/mantenedora/historia/

Diretor Geral: José Roberto Neves Souto Mayor (1995-)

Courses
Accountancy (Accountancy); **Administration**; **Computer Science** (Computer Science); **International Relations**; **Pedagogy** *(FECGI)*; **Social Communication** (Advertising and Publicity); **Tourism** (Tourism)

Faculties
Education and Administrative Sciences *(Sumaré, Sao Paulo)*

Further Information: Also branches in Sao Paulo and Sumare

History: Founded 1995

Main Language(s) of Instruction: Portuguese

Degrees and Diplomas: *Bacharelado*; *Especialização/Aperfeiçoamento*

Last Updated: 18/06/10

UNYAHNA INSTITUTE OF HIGHER EDUCATION OF SALVADOR
Instituto de Educação Superior Unyahna de Salvador (IESUS)
Rua Bicuiba s/n, Alameda Patamares, Patamares, Salvador, Bahia 41680440
Tel: +55(71) 3367-8425
Fax: +55(71) 3367-8457
EMail: iesus@unyahna.br
Website: http://www.unyahna.br

Diretora: Dilza Coelho Mendes

Courses
Administration (Accountancy; Administration; Business Administration; International Business; Marketing); **Economics** (Economics); **Law**; **Tourism** (Tourism)

Further Information: Also branches in Barreiras and Luis Eduardo Magalhães

History: Founded 1998.

Degrees and Diplomas: *Bacharelado*; *Especialização/Aperfeiçoamento*

Last Updated: 17/06/10

URUBUPUNGÁ INTEGRATED FACULTIES

Faculdades Integradas Urubupungá (FACCUR)
Avenida Coronel Jonas Alves de Mello 1660, Térreo Centro,
Pereira Barreto, SP 15370000
Tel: +55(18) 3704-4242
Fax: +55(18) 3704-4222
EMail: fiu@fiu.com.br
Website: http://www.fiu.com.br

Presidente: José Alexandrino Filho

Programmes
Business Administration; **Education** (Education; Educational Psychology; Higher Education; Pedagogy; Teacher Training); **Hotel Management** (Hotel Management); **Mathematics**

History: Founded 1995.

Main Language(s) of Instruction: Portuguese

Degrees and Diplomas: *Bacharelado*
Last Updated: 11/10/07

VALE DO IVAÍ INTEGRATED FACULTIES

Faculdades Integradas do Vale do Ivaí (FEIVAI)
Av. Minas Gerais, 651, Centro, Ivaiporã, Paraná 86870-000
Tel: +55(43) 3472-1414 +55(43) 3472-1210
Fax: +55(43) 3472-1414
EMail: secretaria@univale.com.br
Website: http://www.univale.com.br

Diretora Geral: Neila Francisca Estigarribia (1987)

Courses
Accountancy (Accountancy); **Administration**; **Graduate Studies**; **Law** (Law); **Literature** (Arts and Humanities; English; Literature; Portuguese); **Pedagogy** (Education; Pedagogy); **Systems Analysis**

History: Founded as Faculdade de Educação de Ivaiporã (FEIVAI) 1987. Acquired present title following merger with Faculdade de Ciências Humanas and União das Escolas Superiores do Vale do Ivaí 2003.

Degrees and Diplomas: *Bacharelado*; *Licenciatura*; *Especialização/Aperfeiçoamento*
Last Updated: 07/07/10

VALE DO SALGADO INSTITUTE OF EDUCATION

Instituto Superior de Educação Vale do Salgado (IVS)
Rua Monsenhor Frota, 609, Centro, Icó, CE 63430-000
Tel: +55(88) 5612-760
EMail: petrola@secrel.com.br
Website: http://www.fvs.edu.br/

Courses
Pedagogy (Pedagogy); **Teacher Training** (Teacher Training)

Degrees and Diplomas: *Licenciatura*
Last Updated: 28/09/10

VALLEY OF IGUAÇU HIGHER EDUCATION UNIT

Unidade de Ensino Superior Vale do Iguaçu (UNIGUACU)
Rua Padre Saporiti 717, Rio da Areia, União da Vitória,
PR 84600000
Tel: +55(42) 3522-6192
Fax: +55(42) 3522-6192
EMail: cac_marta@uniguacu.edu.br; assessoria@uniguacu.edu.br
Website: http://www.uniguacu.edu.br

Presidente: Nelson Ronaldo Pedroso

Courses
Administration (Administration); **Agronomy** (Agronomy); **Biomedicine** (Biomedicine); **Computer Science** (Computer Science); **Law** (Law); **Nursing**; **Nutrition** (Nutrition); **Pharmacy** (Pharmacy); **Physical Education**; **Physiotherapy** (Physical Therapy); **Social Services** (Social and Community Services; Social Sciences); **Veterinary Science** (Veterinary Science)

History: Founded 2001.

Degrees and Diplomas: *Bacharelado*; *Licenciatura*; *Especialização/Aperfeiçoamento*
Last Updated: 08/06/10

VALLEY OF THE RIO DOCE UNIVERSITY

Universidade Vale do Rio Doce (UNIVALE)
Rua Moreira Sales 850, Campus I Vila Bretas, Governador
Valadares, Minas Gerais 35030390
Tel: +55(33) 3279-5200
EMail: fpf@univale.br
Website: http://www.univale.br

Reitora: Ana Angélica Gonçalves Leão (2007-)
EMail: reitoria@univale.br

Centres
Agriculture (Agriculture; Agronomy); **Biological and Health Sciences** (Biological and Life Sciences; Dentistry; Health Sciences; Pharmacy); **Exact and Technological Sciences** (Accountancy; Civil Engineering; Computer Science; Electrical Engineering; Industrial Chemistry; Information Technology; Mathematics; Mechanical Engineering; Technology); **Human Sciences** (Advertising and Publicity; Arts and Humanities; Commercial Law; Criminal Law; Education; Graphic Design; History; Journalism; Preschool Education; Primary Education; Psychology; Radio and Television Broadcasting; Social and Community Services; Social Sciences; Tourism)

Further Information: Also Armando Vieira and Antônio Rodrigues Coelho Campuses.

History: Founded 1968.

Admission Requirements: Secondary school certificate and entrance examination

Main Language(s) of Instruction: Portuguese

Degrees and Diplomas: *Bacharelado*; *Licenciatura*; *Especialização/Aperfeiçoamento*; *Mestrado*
Last Updated: 17/12/07

VASCO DE GAMA FACULTY

Faculdade Vasco de Gama
Avenida Vasco da Gama 2787 A, Salvador, BA 40240-090
Tel: +55(71) 3261-1658
EMail: lhaba14@hotmail.com
Website: http://www.faculdadevascodagama.com.br

Diretor: Luiz Henrique de Jesus Almeida

Courses
Accountancy (Accountancy); **Administration** (Administration); **Social Communication** (Advertising and Publicity); **Social Pedagogy** (Pedagogy); **Social Services** (Social and Community Services); **Tourism** (Tourism)

History: Founded 2005.

Main Language(s) of Instruction: Portuguese

Degrees and Diplomas: *Bacharelado*; *Especialização/Aperfeiçoamento*; *Mestrado*

Libraries: Yes
Last Updated: 13/09/10

VEIGA DE ALMEIDA UNIVERSITY

Universidade Veiga de Almeida (UVA)
Rua Ibituruna 108, Tijuca, Rio de Janeiro, Rio de Janeiro 20271901
Tel: +55(21) 2574-8800
Fax: +55(21) 2568-2165
EMail: sstijuca@uva.br
Website: http://www.uva.br

Reitor: Mário Veiga de Almeida Júnior (1995-)

Centres
Biological and Health Sciences (Biology; Dentistry; Nursing; Nutrition; Physical Education; Physical Therapy; Psychology; Speech Therapy and Audiology); **Engineering and Technology** (Aeronautical and Aerospace Engineering; Civil Engineering; Computer Science; Electrical and Electronic Engineering; Production Engineering); **Human Sciences**; **Social Sciences** (Accountancy;

Administration; Advertising and Publicity; Communication Studies; Journalism; Law; Social and Community Services; Tourism)

History: Founded 1972. Acquired present status 1992.

Admission Requirements: Secondary school certificate and entrance examination

Main Language(s) of Instruction: Portuguese

Degrees and Diplomas: *Bacharelado*; *Licenciatura*; *Especialização/Aperfeiçoamento*; *Mestrado*
Last Updated: 06/05/10

VERA CRUZ INSTITUTE OF EDUCATION
Instituto Superior de Educação Vera Cruz
(ISE VERA CRUZ)
Rua Baumann, 73, Vila Leopoldina, São Paulo, SP 05318-000
Tel: +55(11) 3838-5992
Fax: +55(11) 3838-5999
EMail: eventos@veracruz.edu.br
Website: http://veracruz.edu.br/?frame=paginas.php&unidade=4

Courses
Graduate Studies (Education; Literacy Education; Pedagogy; Portuguese); **Undergraduate Studies** (Pedagogy)

Degrees and Diplomas: *Licenciatura*; *Especialização/Aperfeiçoamento*
Last Updated: 28/09/10

VERDE CITY FACULTY
Faculdade Cidade Verde
Avenida Horácio Raccanello Filho, 5950, Novo Centro, Maringá, PR
Tel: +55(44) 3028-4416
EMail: barbieri@fcv.edu.br
Website: http://fcv.edu.br
Diretor: José Carlos Barbieri

Courses
Accountancy (Accountancy); **Administration** (Administration); **Economics** (Economics)

History: Founded 2005.

Main Language(s) of Instruction: Portuguese

Degrees and Diplomas: *Bacharelado*; *Especialização/Aperfeiçoamento*; *Mestrado*
Last Updated: 23/07/10

VERIS FACULTIES
Veris Faculdades
Avenida Paulista, 302/306, Conjuntos 1050607080901001 10120 e 130, Bela Vista, São Paulo, SP 01310-000
Tel: +55(11) 4501-9706 +55(11) 4501-9775
Fax: +55(11) 4501-9720
EMail: valquiria.dumere@veris.edu.br;
francisco.borges@veris.edu.br; everton.marques@veris.edu.br
Website: http://www.veris.com.br/

Courses
Accountancy (Accountancy); **Administration** (Administration); **Advertising and Publicity** (Advertising and Publicity); **Automation and Control Engineering** (Automation and Control Engineering); **Biomedicine** (Biomedicine); **Chemical Engineering** (Chemical Engineering); **Chemical Processes** (Chemistry); **Chemistry** (Chemistry); **Civil Engineering** (Civil Engineering); **Commercial Management - Equinoculture** (Business and Commerce); **Commercial Management - Fashion** (Business and Commerce); **Computer Engineering** (Computer Engineering); **Computer Networks** (Computer Networks); **Computer Science** (Computer Science); **Data Base** (Data Processing); **Financial Management** (Finance); **Graduate Studies** (Accountancy; Automation and Control Engineering; Business Administration; Business and Commerce; Business Education; Civil Law; Commercial Law; Communication Studies; Data Processing; Educational Psychology; Finance; Human Resources; Information Management; Information Technology; Management; Marketing; Software Engineering; Transport Management); **Human Resources** (Human Resources); **Information Systems** (Information Sciences); **Law** (Law); **Logistics** (Transport Management); **Marketing** (Marketing); **Nutrition**

(Nutrition); **Pedagogy** (Pedagogy); **Physical Education** (Physical Education); **Physical Education and Sports** (Physical Education; Sports); **Physical Therapy** (Physical Therapy); **Physics** (Physics); **Public Relations** (Public Relations); **Social Service** (Social and Community Services); **Systems Analysis and Development** (Systems Analysis); **Systems for Internet** (Computer Science); **Web Development** (Computer Science)

Further Information: Also Campinas, São José dos Campos and Sorocaba campuses.

History: Founded 2001 as Grupo Ibmec Educacional. Unification of the following brands: IBTA, Imapes, Uirapuru and Metrocamp.

Degrees and Diplomas: *Tecnólogo*; *Bacharelado*; *Licenciatura*. Also Postgraduate Diploma and MBA.
Last Updated: 25/08/10

VÉRTICE FACULTY
Faculdade Vértice
Rua Bernardo Torres 180, Matipo, MG 35357-000
Tel: +55(31) 8422-9956
EMail: lfsleutjes@hotmail.com
Website: http://www.faculdadevertice.com.br
Diretor: Lucio Flávio Sleutjes

Courses
Accountancy (Accountancy); **Administration** (Administration); **Agronomy** (Agronomy); **Nursing** (Nursing); **Pharmacy** (Pharmacy); **Physical Education** (Physical Education); **Veterinary Science** (Veterinary Science)

History: Founded 2007.

Main Language(s) of Instruction: Portuguese

Degrees and Diplomas: *Bacharelado*; *Licenciatura*; *Especialização/Aperfeiçoamento*; *Mestrado*

Libraries: Biblioteca Alice Virgínia Muratori Gardingo
Last Updated: 13/09/10

VIANNA JÙNIOR INSTITUTE
Instituto Vianna Jùnior
Avenida dos Andradas 415, Centro, Juiz de Fora,
Minas Gerais 36036000
Tel: +55(32) 3239-2940
Fax: +55(32) 3239-2906
EMail: viannajr@viannajr.edu.br
Website: http://www.viannajr.edu.br
Diretor: Henderson Marques Lopez

Courses
Administration (Administration); **Business Administration** (Business Administration; Management); **Economics** (Economics); **Environmental Management**; **Law**

Faculties
Software Engineering

History: Founded 1970 as Faculdade de Ciências Juridicas e Sociais de Vianna Junior. Acquired present title 2005.

Main Language(s) of Instruction: Portuguese

Degrees and Diplomas: *Bacharelado*; *Especialização/Aperfeiçoamento*
Last Updated: 14/06/10

VICENTINA FACULTY
Faculdade Vicentina
Avenida Jaime Reis, 531A - Alto São Francisco, Curitiba,
PR 80510-020
Tel: +55(41) 3079-7716
EMail: direcao@favic.com.br
Website: http://www.favic.com.br
Diretor: André Marmilicz EMail: andremar@mps.com.br

Courses
Philosophy (Philosophy); **Theology** (Theology)

History: Founded 2006.

Main Language(s) of Instruction: Portuguese

Degrees and Diplomas: *Bacharelado*; *Especialização/Aperfeiçoamento*
Last Updated: 13/09/10

VIÇOSA SCHOOL OF HIGHER STUDIES
Escola de Estudos Superiores de Viçosa (ESUV)
Rua Doutor Gerhardus Lambertus Voorpostel, n° 10,
Bairro Liberdade, Viçosa, Minas Gerais 36570-000
Tel: +55(31) 3892-6767
EMail: contato@esuv.com.br
Website: http://www.esuv.com.br

Diretor Geral: Vicente Batista Lima Júnior
EMail: diretoria@esuv.com.br

Courses
Accountancy (Accountancy); **Graduate Studies** (Accountancy; Law; Public Administration); **Law** (Law); **Social Services** (Social and Community Services)

Degrees and Diplomas: *Bacharelado*; *Especialização/Aperfeiçoamento*. Also MBA.
Last Updated: 15/07/10

VICTOR HUGO FACULTY
Faculdade Victor Hugo
Av. Dom Pedro II, 135 - Centro, São Lourenço, MG
Tel: +55(35) 3332-2700
EMail: secretaria@victorhugo.edu.br
Website: http://www.victorhugo.edu.br/web

Diretor: Adolfo Cherman Direzenchi

Courses
Administration (Administration); **Pedagogy** (Pedagogy)
History: Founded 2007.
Main Language(s) of Instruction: Portuguese
Degrees and Diplomas: *Bacharelado*; *Especialização/Aperfeiçoamento*; *Mestrado*
Libraries: Yes
Last Updated: 13/09/10

VISCOUNT OF CAIRU FOUNDATION
Fundação Visconde de Cairu (FVC)
Rua do Salete 50, Barris, Salvador, Bahia 40070200
Tel: +55(71) 2108-8503
Fax: +55(71) 2108- 8511
EMail: cairu@cairu.br
Website: http://www.cairu.br

Diretor: Antônio Carrera Trigo

Courses
Administration; **Tourism** (Tourism)

Faculties
Accountancy *(FACIC)* (Accountancy)

Institutes
Education (Education; Pedagogy)
History: Founded 1999.

Main Language(s) of Instruction: Portuguese
Degrees and Diplomas: *Bacharelado*; *Especialização/Aperfeiçoamento*
Last Updated: 30/06/10

WENCESLAU BRAZ NURSING SCHOOL
Escola de Enfermagem Wenceslau Braz (EEWB)
Avenida Cesário Alvim, 566, Centro, Itajubá,
Minas Gerais 37500000
Tel: +55(35) 3622-0930
Fax: +55(35) 3622-1043
EMail: eewb@eewb.br
Website: http://www.eewb.br

Diretor Geral: José Vitor da Silva

Courses
Nursing (Nursing)
History: Founded 1954.
Main Language(s) of Instruction: Portuguese
Degrees and Diplomas: *Bacharelado*; *Especialização/Aperfeiçoamento*
Last Updated: 18/06/10

ZACARIAS DE GÓES FACULTY
Faculdade Zacarias de Góes
Rua A Loteamento Jardim Grimaldi s/n, Valença, BA 45400-000
Tel: +55(75) 3641-5000
EMail: vitorino.coor@fazag.com.br
Website: http://www.fazag.com.br/_2009

Diretor: Vitorino Ferreira de Souza Filho

Areas
Exact Sciences (Accountancy; Computer Science); **Health** (Nursing; Physical Education; Physical Therapy); **Human Sciences** (Administration; Literature; Pedagogy; Tourism)

Degrees and Diplomas: *Bacharelado*; *Licenciatura*
Last Updated: 13/09/10

ZUMBI DOS PALMARES FACULTY
Faculdade Zumbi dos Palmares
Av. Santos Dumont, 843, Armênia, São Paulo, SP 01101-000
Tel: +55(11) 3229-4590
EMail: vestibular@zumbidospalmares.edu.br
Website: http://www2.zumbidospalmares.edu.br

Diretor: Jarbas Nascimento

Courses
Administration (Administration); **Law** (Law); **Pedagogy** (Pedagogy); **Social Communication** (Advertising and Publicity)
History: Founded 2000.
Main Language(s) of Instruction: Portuguese
Degrees and Diplomas: *Bacharelado*
Libraries: Yes
Last Updated: 13/09/10

Brunei Darussalam

STRUCTURE OF HIGHER EDUCATION SYSTEM

Description:

Students who have adequate and relevant O-level results may proceed to the pre-university level. At this level, most students follow a two-year course leading to the GCE Advanced level (A-level) examination. Those who complete A-level courses with adequate and relevant passes may be eligible for entry to local universities or be awarded scholarships for further studies abroad. The minimum period of university studies (local universities) is normally four academic years. Higher education is provided by universities and technical and vocational institutes and colleges. The Ministry of Education is responsible for all education levels.

Stages of studies:

University level first stage: Bachelor's degree
The main stage of higher education leads, after studies lasting between four and six years, to the Bachelor's degree (Bachelor of Arts, Bachelor of Science, Bachelor of Engineering, Bachelor of Commerce, Bachelor of Arts Education, etc...) in such fields as Education, Business Studies, Arts and Social Sciences, Medicine, Pure Science, Engineering, IT, Arabic Language, Brunei Studies, Syariah and Usuluddin.

University level second stage: Master's degree, Postgraduate certificate in Education
A Master's degree is conferred after one to two years' study beyond the Bachelor's degree. It can be awarded through coursework and a project or through coursework and a dissertation, or through dissertation only. The Postgraduate certificate in Education is awarded after one to one and a half years' study beyond the Bachelor's degree. Other Postgraduate programmes are also offered.

University level third stage: Doctorate
PhD programmes are available in all faculties.

ADMISSION TO HIGHER EDUCATION

Admission to university-level studies:

Name of secondary school credential required: Brunei/Cambridge Advanced Level Certificate of Education

For entry to: All undergraduate programmes.Minimum marks: Depends on the programme applied.

Alternatives to credentials: "A" level equivalents such as the International Baccalaureate or a pass in year 1 or an undergraduate programme from a recognized university abroad.

Other admission requirements: 2 "A" levels at specified grades in relevant subjects or their equivalent. English "O" level or TOEFL 550 or IELTS 6.5.

Foreign students admission:

Definition of foreign student: Foreign students are non-Bruneian citizens residing in Brunei or students directly arriving from abroad and/or students holding a green identity card enrolled in any of the ITB academic programmes and universities in Brunei Darussalam.

Quotas: Two students having applied for a Brunei government scholarship per programme. ITB welcomes fee-paying international students subject to meeting the admission and entry requirements and seat availability.

Entry regulations: Successful applicant must have a valid travel document (passport) with a valid visa to enter Brunei Darussalam. Once registered as a university student, he/she is required to have a valid student pass issued by the Brunei Immigration and Registration Dept. For entry to the Institut Brunei Darussalam, the necessary qualifications follow the Brunei Darussalam Technical and Vocational Education Council's (BDTVEC) policies, and must be approved by the Brunei Darussalam National Accreditation Council. (MKPK). To apply for a scholarship from the Government, applicants can contact:
- Brunei Darussalam Embassies/ High Commissions in the capitals of ASEAN Member countries;
- Commonwealth agencies in the student's home country;

- Scholarships and Training Unit, Permanent Secretary Office, Ministry of Education;
or look at the website of the Ministry of Foreign Affairs and Trade at http://www.mfa.gov.bn/scholarship/index.htm.

Health requirements: Foreign students are required to pass a medical fitness test with a certified government doctor.

Language requirements: Foreign students must have either a grade Jayyid grade or above for Islamic language programmes or a "O" level in Malay language for Malay medium programmes or a "O" level in English language for English medium programmes or TOEFL 550 or IELTS 6.5.

RECOGNITION OF STUDIES

Quality assurance system:

The Brunei Darussalam National Accreditation Council (BDNAC), a unit under the Ministry of Education, is in charge of the recognition of local and overseas higher education institutions/universities and their courses/programmes.

Bodies dealing with recognition:

Majlis Kebangsaan Pengiktirafan Kelulusan - MKPK, Negara Brunei Darussalam (Brunei Darussalam National Accreditation Council - BDNAC)

Room B211, Block B, Level 2
Ministry of Education Building
Old Airport Road
Berakas 3510
Tel: +673 238 1133 ext 2209/2210
Fax: +673 238 1238
EMail: mkpk@moe.edu.bn
WWW: http://www.moe.gov.bn/departments/accreditation/index.htm

NATIONAL BODIES

Ministry of Education

Minister: Awang Haji Abu Bakar Haji Apong
Permanent Secretary, Higher Education: Mohd Daud bin Haji Mahmud
Old Airport Road
Berakas 3510
Tel: +673 238 1133
Fax: +673 238 0101
EMail: da@moe.edu.bn
WWW: http://www.moe.edu.bn

Majlis Kebangsaan Pengiktirafan Kelulusan - MKPK, Negara Brunei Darussalam (Brunei Darussalam National Accreditation Council - BDNAC)

Executive Secretary: Datin Hjh Khadijah Hj Akbar
Room B211, Block B, Level 2
Ministry of Education Building
Old Airport Road
Berakas 3510
Tel: +673 238 1133 ext 2209/2210
Fax: +673 238 1238
EMail: mkpk@moe.edu.bn
WWW: http://www.moe.gov.bn/departments/accreditation/index.htm
Role of national body: To evaluate the status and quality of qualifications awarded by local and overseas institutions; To establish appropriate accreditation guidelines and to publish directories of qualifications and institutions accredited by the Government of His Majesty The Sultan and Yang Di Pertuan of Brunei

Darussalam; To set up, if necessary, appropriate committees to assist the Council in the evaluation and assessment of qualifications in various subjects or disciplines; To act upon matters relating to the Council's responsibilities either as directed by His Majesty the Sultan and Yang Di Pertuan of Brunei Darussalam or if and when the Council considers it appropriate and necessary to do so; To review status of any qualifications as and when the Council sees it fit or necessary.

Data for academic year: 2010-2011
Source: IAU from Department of Planning Development and Research, Ministry of Education, Brunei Darussalam, 2010. Bodies, 2011.

INSTITUTIONS

UNIVERSITY OF BRUNEI DARUSSALAM

Universiti Brunei Darussalam
Tungku Link Road, Gadong BE 1410
Tel: +673(2) 463-001
Fax: +673(2) 461-003
EMail: admi@admin.ubd.edu.bn
Website: http://www.ubd.edu.bn

Vice-Chancellor: Hj Zulkarnain bin Haji Hanafi
Tel: +673(2) 460-957, Fax: +673(2) 240-519
EMail: chanclry@admin.ubd.edu.bn; hihd@admin.ubd.edu.bn

Registrar and Secretary (Acting): Awang Haji Jalil Bin Haji Mail
EMail: registr@admin.ubd.edu.bn; jalil@admin.ubd.edu.bn

International Relations: Rosna Ramly
Tel: +673(2) 463-062, Fax: +673(2) 463-062
EMail: ioenquiry@admin.ubd.edu.bn; rosramly@lc.ubd.edu.bn

Academies
Brunei Studies (Asian Studies) *Director*: Hj Serbini bin Hj Matahir

Centres
Educational Technology (Educational Technology) *Head*: Hj Andy Azhar Sura; **Information Communication Technology** (Computer Networks; Computer Science; Information Technology; Telecommunications Engineering) *Director*: Yong Chee Tuan; **Islamic Banking, Finance and Management** (Banking; Finance; Management) *Director*: Hjh Salma binti Hj Noor Mohamad; **Kuala Belalong Field Studies** *Head*: Kamariah binti Hj Abu Salim; **Language** (Modern Languages) *Director*: Saidai bin Hj Hitam; **Library** (Library Science) *Chief*: Hj Suhaimi bin Abdul Karim; **Postgraduate Studies, Research and Development** *Dean*: Diana Cheong

Faculties
Arts and Social Sciences (Anthropology; Applied Linguistics; Arts and Humanities; English; Geography; History; Linguistics; Literature; Malay; Social Sciences; Sociology) *Dean*: Ampuan Hj Brahim bin Ampuan Hj Tengah; **Business, Economics and Policy Studies** (Business Administration; Economics; Management; Political Sciences; Public Administration) *Dean*: Azman bin Ahmad; **Science** (Biology; Chemistry; Engineering; Mathematics; Natural Sciences; Petroleum and Gas Engineering; Physics) *Dean*: Zohran binti Hj Sulaiman

Institutes
Education *(Sultan Hassanai Bolkiah)* (Art Education; Education; Educational Psychology; Mathematics Education; Native Language Education; Preschool Education; Science Education; Social Sciences; Teacher Training) *Dean*: Hj Junaidi bin Hj Abd Rahman; **Islamic Studies** *(Sultan Haji Omar Ali Saifuddien)* (Arabic; Islamic Law; Islamic Studies) *Dean*: Hjh Saadiah binti Derma Wijaya Hj Tamit; **Medicine** (Biomedicine; Medicine; Midwifery; Nursing) *Director*: Zulkarnain bin Hj Hanafi

Sections
Student Affairs *Dean*: Hj Mohamed bin Damit

History: Founded 1985.

Governing Bodies: Council; Senate

Academic Year: August to May (August-December; January-May)

Admission Requirements: General Certificate of Education (GCE) 'A' levels, International Baccalaureate (I.B.), or equivalent

Fees: (Brunei Dollars): 3,000-4,000 per annum; graduate, c. 10,000

Main Language(s) of Instruction: Malay, English, Arabic

Degrees and Diplomas: *Bachelor's Degree*; *Postgraduate Certificate*; *Master's Degree*; *Ph.D.*

Student Residential Facilities: Yes

Libraries: 600,000 vols; 3,200 periodical subscriptions; special collections
Last Updated: 08/01/07

Bulgaria

STRUCTURE OF HIGHER EDUCATION SYSTEM

Description:

Higher education is provided by higher schools - universities, specialized higher schools (academies, institutes etc.) - and independent colleges. Some universities and colleges are private. Higher education is regulated by the 1995 Law on Higher Education (latest amendment 2010) and the Law for the development of academic staff (May 2010).

Stages of studies:

University level first stage: Bakalavr (Bachelor)
This stage of study at higher education institutions lasts for at least four years of regular study with at least 240 credits and leads to the Bachelor's degree (Bakalavr) in many fields. It is a first cycle degree according to the Bologna process and corresponds to level 6 in the EQF and to level 5A in ISCED-97. This is a degree created by the Higher Education Act of 1995. However, there are some fields where the Bachelor does not exist and where studies lead directly to the second stage of studies (Master's degree level)- e.g. Law, Medicine, Dental Medicine, Pharmacy, Architecture, Veterinary Medicine.

University level second stage: Magistr (Master)
This stage of study amounts to at least 300 credits and lasts for five to six years of regular study following upon secondary education or one year after a Bachelor's degree. Students must (usually) complete a thesis and pass a state examination. It is a second cycle degree according to the Bologna process and corresponds to level 7 in the EQF and to level 5A in ISCED-97.
The former Diplom za Visse Obrazovanie, awarded before the 1995 law, is officially regarded as equivalent to the Master's.

University level third stage: Doktor (Doctor)
This stage is the third cycle of the higher education system and leads to the title of Doctor. It corresponds to level 8 in the EQF and to level 6 in ISCED-97. It is obtained on the basis of individual research and after the defence of a thesis. It replaces the former Kandidat na Naukite (Candidate of the Sciences). The Higher Education Act of 1995 grants all Kandidat na Naukite holders the rights of a holder of a Doctor's degree.

Distance higher education:
Ordinance on the state requirements for distance education at higher schools /Decree by the Council of Ministers # 292 of 2004/ – it establishes the state requirements for the organizing of distance education, the organization of the teaching/learning process, the use of technological
devices, the conditions for ensuring quality.

ADMISSION TO HIGHER EDUCATION

Admission to university-level studies:

Name of secondary school credential required: Diploma za Sredno Obrazovanie

For entry to: University/ Specialized Higher School

Numerus clausus/restrictions: Yes

Other admission requirements: For less demanded specialities, candidates may enrol on the basis of document submission, graded according to academic record.

Foreign students admission:

Definition of foreign student: Students who are not Bulgarian citizens.

Quotas: Quotas are defined each year according to the needs of the higher education institutions.

Entrance exam requirements: Foreign students must hold a Secondary School Leaving Certificate equivalent to the Bulgarian Secondary School Leaving Certificate and must be officially admitted by the Ministry of Education and Science.

Entry regulations: Candidates should have a valid passport or a visa and be recommended by qualified persons and institutions in their home country.

Language requirements: A pre-university year of studies in the Bulgarian language is required. Examinations take place after 1 year of studies in the Bulgarian language at the Institute for Foreign Students.

RECOGNITION OF STUDIES

Quality assurance system:

The National Evaluation and Accreditation Agency at the Council of Ministers evaluates universities, specialized higher schools and colleges and accredits their programmes.

Bodies dealing with recognition:

Natzionalen tzentar za informatzia I dokmentatzia (National Centre for Information and Documentation - NACID)
Executive Director: Vanya Grashkina
Secretary: Verzhinia Cankova
Chief, Academic Recognition/Regulated Professions: Kostadin Tonev
52 A, MD. GM Dimitrov Blvd.
Sofia 1125
Tel: +359(2) 871 3863
Fax: +359(2) 971 3120
EMail: nacid@nacid-bg.net
WWW: http://www.nacid.bg/
Deals with credential recognition for entry to institution: Yes
Deals with credential recognition for entry to profession: Yes

Nazionalna agenzia za ozeniavane i akreditazia - NAOA (National Evaluation and Accreditation Agency)
125 Tsarigradsko shose Blvd, bl. 5,fl. 4, north wing
Sofia 1113
Tel: +359(2) 807 7811
Fax: +359(2) 971 2068
EMail: info@neaa.government.bg
WWW: http://www.neaa.government.bg

NATIONAL BODIES

Ministerstvo na obrazovanieto, mladezhta i naukata (Ministry of Education, Youth and Science)
Minister: Sergei Simeonov Ignatov
Secretary: Krasimir Vulchev
Director: Iliana Hristova
2A, Dondukov Bld.
Sofia 1000
Tel: +359(2) 921 7799
Fax: +359(2) 988 2485
WWW: http://www.minedu.government.bg
Role of national body: Executive body in charge of the implementation of the national higher education policy.

Nazionalna agenzia za ozeniavane i akreditazia - NAOA (National Evaluation and Accreditation Agency)
Chairman: Boyan Biolchev
Director: Stoyanka Kireva
125 Tsarigradsko shose Blvd, bl. 5,fl. 4, north wing
Sofia 1113
Tel: +359(2) 807 7811
Fax: +359(2) 971 2068
EMail: info@neaa.government.bg
WWW: http://www.neaa.government.bg

Role of national body: NAQA is the specialized national body for quality assurance, evaluation and accreditation of HEIs' activities: teaching, research, etc. according to their specific features. There are two types of accreditation: institutional accreditation and programme accreditation. The evaluation and accreditation criteria used are consistent with the Higher Education Act and adopted State requirements. NAQA also evaluates projects for the establishment or transformation of schools and colleges as well as for the opening of new academic streams.

Data for academic year: 2010-2011
Source: IAU from the National Center for Information and Documentation (NACID), 2010, Bodies updated in 2011.

INSTITUTIONS

PUBLIC INSTITUTIONS

ACADEMY OF MUSIC, DANCE AND FINE ARTS
Akademija za muzikalno i tanzovo izkustvo
2 Todor Samodumov Str., 4025 Plovdiv
Tel: +359(32) 601-441
Fax: +359(32) 631-688
EMail: office@artacademyplovdiv.com
Website: http://www.artacademyplovdiv.com

Rector: Vassilka Yoncheva
Tel: +359(32) 601-442 EMail: amti_rektor@evrocom.net

Departments
Postgraduate Studies (Dance; Music)

Faculties
Folklore Music, Choreography and Visual Arts (Art Education; Conducting; Dance; Musical Instruments; Musicology; Painting and Drawing; Visual Arts)

History: Founded 1964 as Pedagogical Faculty, became Pedagogical Institute of Music 1972. Acquired present status and title 1995.

Governing Bodies: General Assembly

Academic Year: September to May (September-December; February-May)

Admission Requirements: Secondary school certificate (Diploma za zavarsheno sredno obrazovanie) and entrance examination

Main Language(s) of Instruction: Bulgarian

Degrees and Diplomas: *Bakalavr (BA)*: 4 yrs; *Magistr (MA)*: a further yr; *Doktor (PhD)*

Student Services: Canteen, Cultural centre, Health services, Sports facilities

Special Facilities: Art gallery, Museum

Libraries: c. 18,150 vols; c. 7,500 records and tapes
Last Updated: 19/09/11

AGRICULTURAL UNIVERSITY
Agraren Universitet (AU)
12 Mendeleev Boulevard, 4000 Plovdiv
Tel: +359(32) 654-200
Fax: +359(32) 633-157
EMail: info@au-plovdiv.bg
Website: http://www.au-plovdiv.bg

Rector: Dimitar Grekov (2007-)
Tel: +359(32) 633-232, Fax: +359(32) 633-157
EMail: rector@au-plovdiv.bg

International Relations: Dora Ivanova
Tel: +359(32) 654-303 EMail: inter@au-plovdiv.bg

Departments
Languages and Sport (Bulgarian; Modern Languages; Physical Education; Sports)

Faculties
Agronomy *("Saint Dimitrius of Thessaloniki")* (Agronomy; Animal Husbandry; Biochemistry; Botany; Crop Production; Farm Management; Plant and Crop Protection; Soil Science); **Economics** (Accountancy; Agricultural Business; Agricultural Economics; Agriculture; Tourism); **Horticulture and Viticulture** (Agricultural Engineering; Horticulture; Viticulture); **Plant Protection and Agroecology** (Agriculture; Chemistry; Ecology; Entomology; Microbiology; Plant and Crop Protection)

Further Information: Experimental fields - 185 ha, Experimental Wine-cellar

History: Founded 1945 as Higher Institute of Agriculture, acquired present status and title 2001.

Academic Year: September to June

Admission Requirements: Secondary school certificate (Diploma za zavarsheno sredno obrazovanie), or foreign equivalent

Main Language(s) of Instruction: Bulgarian

Degrees and Diplomas: *Bakalavr*: 4 yrs; *Magistr*: a further 1-2 yrs; *Doktor (PhD)*: a further 3-3 1/2 y after the Master's degree by PhD thesis

Student Services: Canteen, Sports facilities

Student Residential Facilities: 3 Student hostels for 800 students

Publications: Scientific Works *(quarterly)*
Last Updated: 19/09/11

ANGEL KANČEV RUSE UNIVERSITY
Rusenski universitet Angel Kančev (RU)
8 Studentska Str., 7017 Ruse
Tel: +359(82) 888-465
Fax: +359(82) 845-362
EMail: secretary@ru.acad.bg
Website: http://www.ru.acad.bg

Rector: Hristo Beloev (2007-)
Tel: +359(82) 888-465 EMail: rector@ru.acad.bg

Secretary-General: Tania Grozeva
Tel: +359(82) 888-258 EMail: tgrozeva@ru.acad.bg

International Relations: Todorka Todorova
EMail: cicm@ru.acad.bg

Departments
Physical and Occupational Therapy (Occupational Therapy; Physical Therapy)

Faculties
Transport Engineering (Automotive Engineering; Transport and Communications; Transport Engineering) *Dean*: Rosen Ivanov; **Agricultural Mechanization** (Agricultural Engineering; Agricultural Equipment; Ecology; Hydraulic Engineering; Industrial Design; Thermal Engineering) *Division Head*: Plamen Kangalov; **Business and Management** (Business and Commerce; Economics; European Studies; Management); **Electrical and Electronic Engineering and Automation** (Automation and Control Engineering;

Electrical and Electronic Engineering; Physics; Telecommunications Engineering); **Law** (Law); **Mechanical and Manufacturing Engineering** (Mechanical Engineering; Production Engineering); **Natural Sciences and Education** (Bulgarian; Information Technology; Mathematics; Pedagogy; Physical Education; Social Sciences; Sports); **Pedagogy** (Pedagogy) *Dean*: Margarita Teodosieva

Further Information: Branches in Razgrad and Silistra

History: Founded 1946 as Higher Technical School, acquired present status and title 1995.

Governing Bodies: General Assembly; Academy Board

Academic Year: September to June (September-January; February-June)

Admission Requirements: Secondary school certificate (Diploma za zavarsheno sredno obrazovanie) and entrance examination

Fees: (Leva): native students,180-230 per annum; (Euros): foreign students, 1,800-2,400

Main Language(s) of Instruction: Bulgarian

International Co-operation: Participates in Erasmus; Comenius; Minerva; Leonardo da Vinci; 5th and 6th Framework programme; CEEPUS; DAAD; NATO and Stablility Pact

Accrediting Agencies: Bureau Veritas Quality International (BVQI); National Agency for Evaluation and Accreditation

Degrees and Diplomas: *Profesionalen Bakalavr*: Technology, 3 yrs; *Bakalavr*: 4 yrs; *Magistr*: a further 2-4 yr; *Magistr*. Law, a further 5 yrs; *Doktor*: a further 4 yrs by thesis following Bakalaur; *Doktor (PhD)*: a further 3 yrs by thesis following Master

Student Services: Canteen, Cultural centre, Employment services, Foreign student adviser, Foreign Studies Centre, Health services, Language programs, Social counselling, Sports facilities

Student Residential Facilities: For c. 1,800 students

Libraries: Total, c. 306,650 vols

Publications: Nauchni Trudove

Press or Publishing House: Pečantna Baza
Last Updated: 20/09/11

D.A. TSENOV ACADEMY OF ECONOMICS - SVIŠTOV

Stopanska akademija 'Dimitr Čenov' Svištov
2 Emanuil Čakarov Str., 5250 Svištov
Tel: +359(631) 609-07
Fax: +359(631) 604-72
EMail: rectorat@uni-svishtov.bg
Website: http://www.uni-svishtov.bg

Rector: Velichko Adamov Yonov
Tel: +359(631) 604-91 EMail: rector@uni-svishtov.bg

Registrar: Ventsislav Tanev
Tel: +359(631) 604-93 EMail: pomrektor@uni-svishtov.bg

International Relations: Agop Sarkisyan
Tel: +359(631) 604-50
EMail: agop@uni-svishtov.bg; mvip@uni-svishtov.bg

Centres
Distance Learning *(CDL)* (Banking; Business and Commerce; Economics; Insurance; International Economics) *Director*: Andrei Zahariev

Faculties
Accountancy (Accountancy; Economic and Finance Policy; Economic History; Mathematics; Statistics); **Management and Marketing** (Business Administration; Business and Commerce; Information Technology; International Economics; International Relations; Management; Marketing); **Production and Commercial Business** (Agricultural Economics; Business and Commerce; Industrial and Production Economics; Industrial Management)

Institutes
Postgraduate Qualification and Retraining; **Scientific Research** *(ISR)* (Accountancy; Economic and Finance Policy; Finance; Information Technology; Insurance; Management; Marketing; Political Sciences; Social Studies; Social Welfare)

Schools
Finance (Economic and Finance Policy; Finance; Social Welfare)

Further Information: Branches in Loveč, Plovdiv, Botevgrad, College of Economics and Management, Svishtov

History: Founded 1936, as Higher Institute of Finance and Economics, acquired present status and title 1995.

Governing Bodies: Academic Council

Academic Year: September to June (September-December; February-June)

Admission Requirements: Secondary school certificate (Diploma za zavarsheno sredno obrazovanie), and entrance examination

Fees: (Leva): c. 40 per semester

Main Language(s) of Instruction: Bulgarian

International Co-operation: With universities in United Kingdom, Austria

Accrediting Agencies: National Agency for Evaluation and Accreditation; Lloyd Register Quality Assurance

Degrees and Diplomas: *Profesionalen Bakalavr*: Economics, 3 yrs; *Bakalavr (BA)*: 4 yrs; *Magistr (MA)*: a further 1 1/2 yrs; *Doktor (PhD)*: a further 3 yrs by thesis following Master

Student Services: Academic counselling, Canteen, Cultural centre, Health services, Sports facilities

Student Residential Facilities: Hostels for 1,800 students

Special Facilities: Museum of the History of the Academy. Theatre

Libraries: 'Prof. Nikola Mihov' Library

Publications: Business Management *(quarterly)*; Economic World Library *(quarterly)*; Narodostopanski Archiv, Records of National Economy *(quarterly)*

Press or Publishing House: 'D. Čenov' Publishing House
Last Updated: 20/09/11

INTERNATIONAL BUSINESS SCHOOL

Meždunarodno vische biznes učiliše (IBS)
14, Gurko Str., 2140 Botevgrad
Tel: +359 723-688 12
EMail: info@ibsedu.bg
Website: http://www.ibsedu.bg

Rector: Ruslan Penchev
Tel: +359 723-68812 EMail: rpenchev@ibsedu.com

Deputy-Rector: Bojidar Guioshev EMail: bgyoshev@ibsedu.bg

International Relations: Nadya Gaydarska
Tel: +359(2) 987-0292 EMail: ngaydarska@ibsedu.bg

Programmes
Accountancy and Audit (Accountancy); **Business Administration** (Business Administration); **Business Finance** (Finance); **International Economic Relations** (International Economics); **International Management and Business Development**; **Project Management** (Management); **Tourism** (Tourism)

History: Founded 1991. Acquired present status 2002.

Main Language(s) of Instruction: Bulgarian, English

International Co-operation: With Seattle University (USA)

Degrees and Diplomas: *Bakalavr*; *Magistr*; *Doktor*
Last Updated: 19/09/11

KONSTANTIN PRESLAVSKI UNIVERSITY OF SHUMEN

Šumenski universitet 'Episcop Konstantin Preslavski'
115 Universitetska Str., 9700 Šoumen
Tel: +359(54) 832-101
Fax: +359(54) 830-371
EMail: int.rel@shu-bg.net
Website: http://www.shu-bg.net

Rector: Margarita Georgieva (2007-)
Tel: +359(54) 830-350, Ext.101 EMail: rector@shu-bg.net

Vice-Rector (Finance and Administration): Dobrimir Enčev

International Relations: Ivaylo Ivanov

Centres
Astronomy (Astronomy and Space Science); **Bulgarian Language Teaching to Foreigners** (Bulgarian); **Educational Management**; **Postgraduate Education and Qualification** *(Varna)*; **Teacher Information and Qualification** *(Varna)* (Teacher Training)

Faculties

Arts and Humanities (Arts and Humanities; Bulgarian; English; German; History; Modern Languages; Philology; Theology); **Education** (Art Education; Pedagogy); **Mathematics, Informatics and Economics** (Computer Science; Economics; Mathematics); **Natural Sciences** (Biology; Chemistry; Physics); **Technical Sciences** (Technology)

History: Founded 1971 as Higher Pedagogical Institute, acquired present status and title 1996.

Governing Bodies: Senate

Academic Year: September to June (September-December; February-June)

Admission Requirements: Secondary school certificate (Diploma za zavarsheno sredno obrazovanie)

Main Language(s) of Instruction: Bulgarian

Degrees and Diplomas: *Bakalavr*. 4 yrs; *Magistr*. a further 1 1/2 yr; *Doktor (PhD)*: a further 3 yrs by thesis

Student Residential Facilities: For c. 1,000 students

Libraries: Central Library, c. 200,000 vols; Modern Languages Specialized library, c. 5,000 vols

Press or Publishing House: Konstantin Preslavski Publishing House

Academic Staff 2008-2009	TOTAL
FULL-TIME	400
PART-TIME	300
STAFF WITH DOCTORATE	
FULL-TIME	c. 220

Student Numbers 2008-2009	
All (Foreign Included)	c. 7,000

Last Updated: 20/11/09

KRUSTYO SARAFOV NATIONAL ACADEMY OF THEATRE AND FILM ARTS

Nacionalna akademia za teatralno i filmovo izkustvo 'Krustyo Sarafov' (NATFIZ)
108-A Rakovsky Str., 1000 Sofia
Tel: +359(2) 987- 9866
Fax: +359(2) 989-7389
EMail: natfiz@bgcict.acad.bg
Website: http://natfiz.bg

Rector: Lubomir Halatchev Tel: +359(2) 987-9866

Administrative Director: Ivan Alexandrov Tel: +359(2) 989-8757

Faculties

Screen Arts (Cinema and Television; Film; Photography; Video); **Stage Arts** (Acting; Display and Stage Design; Theatre)

History: Founded 1948 as Higher Institute of Theatrical Art, acquired present status and title 1995. A State Institution.

Governing Bodies: Rectorate

Academic Year: October to June (October-January; February-June)

Admission Requirements: Secondary school certificate (Diploma za zavarsheno sredno obrazovanie)

Fees: (US Dollars): Foreign students, Theatre department, 4,500 per annum; Film department, 8,000

Main Language(s) of Instruction: Bulgarian

International Co-operation: Participates in the Tempus and Socrates programmes

Accrediting Agencies: National Agency for Evaluation and Accreditation

Degrees and Diplomas: *Bakalavr*. Arts (BA), 4 yrs; *Magistr*. Arts (MA), a further 2 yrs; *Doktor (PhD)*: a further 2 yrs by thesis following Master
Last Updated: 18/01/12

LYUBEN KARAVELOV HIGHER SCHOOL OF CIVIL ENGINEERING

Vische stroitelno utchilichte 'Ljuben Karavelov' - Sofia (VSU)
175 Suhodolska Str., 1373 Sofia
Tel: +359(2) 802-9191
Fax: +359(2) 802-9188
EMail: vsu@vsu.bg
Website: http://www.vsu.bg

Rector: Georgi Godinyachki
Tel: +359(2) 802- 9191 EMail: rector@vsu.bg

International Relations: Neli Yordanova
EMail: intoffice.vsu@gmail.com

Faculties

Architecture (Architecture); **Construction Engineering** (Construction Engineering)

History: Founded 1928 as Professional School for Army Corps' Engineers. HSCE was transformed from a military into a civilian state institution of higher education. Acquired present title and status 2000.

Degrees and Diplomas: *Profesionalen Bakalavr*. 3 yrs; *Bakalavr*. 4 yrs; *Magistr*. 1 1/2 yrs following Bachelor; *Doktor (PhD)*

Student Services: Canteen, Sports facilities

Student Residential Facilities: 3 student dormitories

Special Facilities: Computer Centre, Laboratories

Libraries: Yes
Last Updated: 24/11/09

MEDICAL UNIVERSITY - PLEVEN

Medicinski universitet - Pleven (MUPL)
1 St Kliment Ohridski Str., 5800 Pleven
Tel: +359(64) 884-101
Fax: +359(64) 801-603
EMail: rector@mu-pleven.bg
Website: http://www.mu-pleven.bg/

Rector: Grigor Gorchev (2004-)
Tel: +359(64) 800-728, Fax: +359(64) 801-603

Vice-Rector for Academic Affairs: Petyo Bochev
EMail: vice-rector-edu@mu-pleven.bg

International Relations: Regina Komsa-Penkova
EMail: iro@mu-pleven.bg

Colleges

Medical Sciences *(Veliko Tarnovo)* (Medicine; Nursing); **Medical Sciences** *(Rousse)* (Medicine); **Medical Sciences** *(Pleven)* (Medicine)

Faculties

Health Care (Gynaecology and Obstetrics; Immunology; Laboratory Techniques; Nursing; Orthopaedics; Physical Therapy); **Medicine** (Medicine); **Public Health** (Health Administration; Midwifery; Nursing; Occupational Therapy; Public Health)

Further Information: Branches in Rousse and Véliko Turnovo for the Medical College. Also Institute Hospital

History: Founded 1974 as independent Institute.

Governing Bodies: Council

Academic Year: September to May (September-December; February-May)

Admission Requirements: Secondary school certificate (Diploma za zavarsheno sredno obrazovanie) or foreign equivalent and entrance examination. One year preparatory courses in Bulgarian language for foreign students. For students of the Faculty of Nursing - Speciality 'Management of Nursing Care', Diploma from a medical college and a minimum of 5 years of practice in health institutions

Fees: (Euros): 3,343 per annum

Main Language(s) of Instruction: Bulgarian

International Co-operation: With universities in Germany

Accrediting Agencies: National Agency for Evaluation and Accreditation

Degrees and Diplomas: *Bakalavr*. Nursing (BC), 3 yrs; *Magistr*. Medicine (MD), 6 yrs; *Magistr*. Nursing (MD), 2 yrs; *Doktor*. Medicine (PhD), 2-4 yrs

Student Services: Academic counselling, Canteen, Employment services, Foreign student adviser, Health services, Social counselling, Sports facilities

Student Residential Facilities: 2 student hostels for c. 1,050 students

Special Facilities: Anatomy Museum. Audio-Video Centre

Libraries: Central Medical Library, c. 85,000 vols

Student Numbers *2009* — **TOTAL**
All (Foreign Included) — **2,044**
FOREIGN ONLY — **275**
Last Updated: 19/09/11

MEDICAL UNIVERSITY - PLOVDIV
Medicinski Universitet - Plovdiv
15A Vassil Aprilov Str., 4002 Plovdiv
Tel: +359(32) 443-839
Fax: +359(32) 442-194
EMail: vicer_ms@meduniversity-plovdiv.bg
Website: http://www.meduniversity-plovdiv.bg

Rector: Stefan Kostyanev (2003-)
Tel: +359(32) 602-507, Fax: +359(32) 602-534
EMail: rector@meduniversity-plovdiv.bg

International Relations: Mariana Murdjeva, Vice-Rector of International Relations Tel: +359(32) 602-201

Colleges
Medicine (Midwifery; Nursing)

Departments
Foreign Languages (Modern Languages)

Faculties
Medicine (Medicine); **Pharmacy** (Pharmacy); **Public Health** (Anthropology; Economics; Epidemiology; Ethics; Health Administration; Hygiene; Law; Psychology; Public Health; Statistics); **Stomatology** (Dentistry; Stomatology)

Further Information: Also Teaching Hospitals

History: Founded 1945.

Governing Bodies: Council

Academic Year: September to July (September-January; February-July)

Admission Requirements: Secondary school certificate (Diploma za zavarsheno sredno obrazovanie) and entrance examination

Main Language(s) of Instruction: Bulgarian

Degrees and Diplomas: *Bakalavr:* Healthcare Management, 2 1/2 yrs following compulsory education in Health Sciences in a college; *Bakalavr:* Nursing; Midwifery, 4 yrs; *Magistr:* Dentistry, 6 yrs, 10 sem and 9 months practical work; *Magistr:* Medicine, 6 yrs, 10 sem and 1 yr clinical rotations; *Magistr:* Pharmacy, 5 yrs, 9 sem and 6 months practical work; *Doktor (PhD).* Also Professional Degree (3yrs)

Student Services: Academic counselling, Canteen, Foreign student adviser, Health services, Social counselling, Sports facilities

Student Residential Facilities: Hostels

Libraries: c. 190,000 vols

Publications: Folia Medica *(quarterly)*
Last Updated: 20/09/11

MEDICAL UNIVERSITY - SOFIA
Medicinski universitet - Sofia
15, Akad. Ivan Geshov Blvd., Sofia
Tel: +359(2) 915-2149
Fax: +359(2) 953-1174
EMail: glavsec@mu-sofia.bg
Website: http://mu-sofia.bg

Rector: Vanyo Mitev
Tel: +359(2) 541-715, Fax: +359(2) 541-715
EMail: mitev@medfac.acad.bg

Colleges
Medicine *(Vratsa)* (Medicine); **Medicine** *(Sofia)* (Medicine)

Departments
Languages and Sports (Modern Languages; Sports)

Faculties
Medicine (Anatomy; Biochemistry; Biology; Chemistry; Histology; Medicine; Microbiology; Pathology; Pharmacology; Physics; Physiology; Surgery); **Pharmacy** (Pharmacy); **Public Health** (Public Health)

Further Information: Also 4 Teaching Hospitals

History: Founded 1917 as a Faculty of Medicine at Sofia University, became independent 1950 as Medical Academy with departments of Medicine and Dentistry, joined by the Department of Pharmacy 1951. Acquired present status 2006.

Governing Bodies: Academic Council

Academic Year: September to June (September-January; February-June)

Admission Requirements: Secondary school certificate (Diploma za zavarsheno sredno obrazovanie) or recognized foreign equivalent

Main Language(s) of Instruction: Bulgarian

Degrees and Diplomas: *Bakalavr; Magistr:* Medicine, 6 yrs; *Magistr:* Pharmacy, 5 yrs; *Doktor:* Medicine, a further 3 yrs following Master

Student Services: Canteen, Foreign student adviser, Health services, Sports facilities

Student Residential Facilities: For c. 1,100 students

Libraries: Central Medical Library

Publications: Acta Medica Bulgarica *(biannually)*
Last Updated: 20/09/11

NEOFIT RILSKI SOUTH-WEST UNIVERSITY
Yugo-zapaden universitet 'Neofit Rilski' (SWU)
66 Ivan Mihajlov Str., 2700 Blagoevgrad
Tel: +359(73) 885-505
Fax: +359(73) 885-516
EMail: info@aix.swu.bg
Website: http://www.swu.bg

Rector: Iliya Mirchev
Tel: +359(73) 885-501, Fax: +359(73) 885-516
EMail: mirchev@swu.bg

International Relations: Georgieva Dobrinka, Vice-Rector
Tel: +359(73) 885-504 EMail: vr_ir@swu.bg

Colleges
Technology (Electronic Engineering; Mechanical Engineering; Telecommunications Engineering; Textile Technology)

Faculties
Arts (Acting; Art Education; Cinema and Television; Cultural Studies; Dance; Fashion Design; Industrial Design; Music Education; Performing Arts; Photography; Singing; Theatre) *Dean:* Rumen Poterov; **Economics** (Accountancy; Business Administration; Finance; Management; Marketing; Tourism) *Dean:* Chavdar Nikolov; **Law and History** (Administration; Administrative Law; Anthropology; Business Administration; Civil Law; Constitutional Law; Criminal Law; Criminology; Finance; Health Administration; History; International Law; International Relations; Law; Medicine; Pedagogy; Psychology; Public Administration; Public Law; Public Relations; Religious Studies; Social Policy; Sociology) *Dean:* Sofka Mateeva; **Natural Sciences and Mathematics** (Chemistry; Computer Engineering; Computer Science; Ecology; Environmental Studies; Geography; Inorganic Chemistry; Mathematics Education; Organic Chemistry; Pedagogy; Physics; Teacher Training) *Dean:* Borislav Yurukov; **Pedagogy** (Educational Administration; Humanities and Social Science Education; Modern Languages; Pedagogy; Physical Education; Physical Therapy; Preschool Education; Primary Education; Psychology; Social and Community Services; Social Psychology; Special Education; Sports; Technology Education) *Dean:* Russi Rusev; **Philology** (Applied Linguistics; Bulgarian; English; Foreign Languages Education; Modern Languages; Philology; Slavic Languages); **Philosophy** (Community Health; Philosophy; Political Sciences; Psychotherapy; Social and Community Services; Social Work; Speech Therapy and Audiology) *Dean:* Georgi Apostolov, **Social Health and Sport** *Dean:* Stoian Ivanov

Further Information: Branches in Kjustendil, Dupnica, Targovište, Smoljan

History: Founded 1975 as an affiliate faculty of Sofia St. Kliment Ohridski University, reorganized as Higher Institute of Education 1983, an independent Institution. Acquired present status and title 1995. Acquired institutional accreditation 2001.

Governing Bodies: General Assembly; Academic Council; Rector

Academic Year: September to June (September-January; February-June)

Admission Requirements: Secondary Education Diploma in Bulgarian (Diploma za zavarsheno sredno obrazovanie); Diploma from High School, translated and legalized in Bulgarian Language

Fees: (Euros): 3,000 per annum; (Leva): 6,000 per annum

Main Language(s) of Instruction: Bulgarian; English for some programmes

International Co-operation: With universities in Austria; Italy; France; Belgium; Greece; Sweden

Accrediting Agencies: National Agency for Evaluation and Accreditation

Degrees and Diplomas: *Profesionalen Bakalavr*: Techology (S), 3 yrs; *Bakalavr (B)*: 4 yrs; *Magistr (M)*: a further yr; *Doktor (PhD)*: a further 3 yrs after Master

Student Services: Academic counselling, Canteen, Cultural centre, Foreign student adviser, Foreign Studies Centre, Health services, Language programs, Social counselling, Sports facilities

Student Residential Facilities: Hostels for c. 900 students

Special Facilities: Yes

Libraries: Central Library, Faculty Libraries

Publications: South-West Pages, Magazine of Humanities published by the Faculty of Philosophy *(quarterly)*

Press or Publishing House: Yes
Last Updated: 24/11/09

N.Y. VAPTSAROV NAVAL ACADEMY

Vische voennomorsko utchilichte 'N.Y. Vaptsarov'
Vassil Drumev Blvd. 73, 9026 Varna
Tel: +359(52) 552-228
Fax: +359(52) 303-163
EMail: info@naval.acad.bg
Website: http://www.naval-acad.bg

Rector: Dimitar Angelov

Courses
Deck Officers (Information Technology; Maritime Law; Nautical Science; Physics); **Engineers for the Navy** (Engineering Drawing and Design; Information Technology; Mechanical Engineering; Metal Techniques; Physics); **Fleet and Port Technologists and Managers** (Marine Transport; Naval Architecture); **Marine Engineers** (Marine Engineering); **Naval Communication Officers** (Computer Science; Electronic Engineering; Physics); **Naval Warfare Officers** (Nautical Science); **Ocean Engineers** (Marine Engineering); **Ship Repairs Technologists** (Naval Architecture)

History: Founded 1881.

Academic Year: October to June

Fees: (Euros): 400-600 per annum for citizens from EU member states; 2,900 per annum for non EU citizens.

Main Language(s) of Instruction: Bulgarian

Degrees and Diplomas: *Bakalavr; Magistr*
Last Updated: 21/09/11

PAISSII HILENDARSKI UNIVERSITY - PLOVDIV

Plovdivski universitet 'Paisii Hilendarski' (PU)
24 Tsar Assen Str., 4000 Plovdiv
Tel: +359(32) 261-363
Fax: +359(32) 635-049
EMail: pduniv@uni-plovdiv.bg
Website: http://www.uni-plovdiv.bg

Rector: Zapryan Kozludzhov
Tel: +359(32) 261-444 EMail: rector@uni-plovdiv.bg

Colleges
Khardzali *(Liuben Karavelov)* (Mathematics; Natural Sciences; Pedagogy; Philology; Social Sciences); **Smolyan** (Biology; Bulgarian; Chemistry; English; Geography; History; Mathematics and Computer Science; Preschool Education; Tourism); **Smolyan Technical** (Electrical Engineering; Machine Building; Transport Engineering)

Faculties
Biology (Bioengineering; Biology; Biotechnology; Botany; Chemistry; Ecology; Environmental Studies; Microbiology; Molecular Biology; Physiology; Zoology); **Chemistry** (Analytical Chemistry;

Chemistry; Computer Engineering; Inorganic Chemistry; Physics); **Economics and Social Sciences** (Agricultural Economics; Agricultural Management; Business Administration; Economics; Human Resources; International Business; Management; Marketing; Political Sciences; Public Administration; Social Sciences); **Education** (Acting; Art Education; Education; Education of the Socially Disadvantaged; Foreign Languages Education; Humanities and Social Science Education; Jazz and Popular Music; Physical Education; Preschool Education; Primary Education; Psychology); **Languages and Literature** (Bulgarian; Central European Studies; English; French; German; Greek; History; Literature; Philology; Polish; Russian; Serbocroatian; Slavic Languages; Spanish); **Law** (Law); **Mathematics and Computer Science** (Applied Mathematics; Computer Networks; Mathematics; Mathematics and Computer Science); **Philosophy and History** (Ethnology; History; Philosophy; Sociology); **Physics** (Mathematical Physics; Nuclear Physics; Physical Engineering; Physics; Solid State Physics)

Further Information: Also Technical College in the town of Smolyan and affiliated College in Smolyan and Kardzhali.

History: Founded 1961 as Teacher Training Institute, acquired present status and title 1972. A State institution with the right of autonomy.

Governing Bodies: General Assembly, comprising 290 members; Academic Council, comprising 45 members

Academic Year: September to June (September-December; February-June)

Admission Requirements: Secondary school certificate (diploma za zavarsheno sredno obrazovanie), and entrance examination

Fees: (US Dollars): Tuition, 3,000 per annum; part-time students, 2,000-3,000

Main Language(s) of Instruction: Bulgarian

International Co-operation: Participates in the Socrates; Erasmus; Minerva; Komenski; Lingua; Leonardo; 6FP and COST programmes

Accrediting Agencies: National Agency for Evaluation and Accreditation

Degrees and Diplomas: *Bakalavr (BA)*: 4 yrs; *Magistr (MA)*: a further yr. Also Teaching Qualifications, 4 yrs

Student Services: Academic counselling, Canteen, Foreign student adviser, Language programs, Sports facilities

Student Residential Facilities: Yes

Special Facilities: Audio-visual Centre

Libraries: Central Library, c. 248,200 vols

Publications: Naučni Trudove *(other/irregular)*

Press or Publishing House: University Publishing House
Last Updated: 20/09/11

PROF. ASSEN ZLATAROV UNIVERSITY - BOURGAS

Universitet 'Prof. Dr. Assen Zlatarov' - Burgas (BTU)
1 Prof. Jakimov Str., 8010 Burgas
Tel: +359(56) 860-041
Fax: +359(56) 880-249
EMail: office@btu.bg
Website: http://www.btu.bg

Rector: Petko Petkov
Tel: +359(56) 880-249, Fax: +359(56) 683-178
EMail: rector@btu.bg

Colleges
Medicine (Medical Auxiliaries; Medicine; Nursing; Rehabilitation and Therapy); **Technical Studies** (Computer Engineering; Electrical and Electronic Engineering; Marketing; Mechanical Engineering; Mechanical Equipment and Maintenance; Technology; Transport Engineering); **Tourism** (Hotel Management; Tourism)

Departments
Teaching of Foreign Languages (English; Foreign Languages Education; French; Slavic Languages)

Faculties
Natural Sciences (Analytical Chemistry; Chemistry; Ecology; Environmental Studies; Inorganic Chemistry; Natural Sciences;

Organic Chemistry; Physics); **Social Sciences** (Accountancy; Business Administration; Economics; Foreign Languages Education; Industrial Management; Information Technology; Management; Marketing; Pedagogy; Preschool Education; Primary Education; Social Sciences; Tourism); **Technical Sciences** (Biotechnology; Chemical Engineering; Inorganic Chemistry; Materials Engineering; Organic Chemistry)

Sections
Research

History: Founded 1963 as Higher Institute of Chemical Technology, acquired present status and title 1995.

Governing Bodies: Academic Council

Academic Year: October to June

Admission Requirements: Secondary school certificate (Diploma za zavarsheno sredno obrazovanie)

Fees: (Euros): 2,800 per annum

Main Language(s) of Instruction: Bulgarian and English

International Co-operation: With universities in Russian Federation, United Kingdom, France, Germany.

Accrediting Agencies: National Agency for Evaluation and Accreditation

Degrees and Diplomas: *Profesionalen Bakalavr*: Hotel and Restaurant Management; Mechanical and Equipment Engineering; Transport Equipment and Technology; Electronics; Electrical Engineering; Computer Equipment and Technology; Marketing; Nursing; Rehabilitation Therapy; Medical Auxiliary; Tourism Management, 3 yrs; *Bakalavr*: Organic Chemistry; Biotechnology; Inorganic Chemistry; Chemical Engineering; Materials Technology and Materials Science; Business Administration; Marketing; Tourism; Industrial Management; Pre-school and Primary School Pedagogy; Pre-school Pedagogy and a Foreign Language; Primary School Pedagogy and a Foreign Language; Social Pedagogy; Chemistry; Ecology and Environmental Protection, 4 yrs; *Magistr*: Organic and Inorganic Chemistry; Chemical Engineering; Materials Technology and Materials Science; Business Administration; Tourism; Pre-school and Primary School Pedagogy; Chemistry; Ecology and Environmental Protection, a further 1 1/2 yrs; *Doktor (PhD)*: a further 3 yrs following Magistr and 4 yrs following Bakalavr

Student Services: Academic counselling, Canteen, Employment services, Foreign student adviser, Foreign Studies Centre, Health services, Language programs, Nursery care, Sports facilities

Student Residential Facilities: 3 students hostels for c. 1,300 students

Libraries: Science Library, c. 160,000 vols
Last Updated: 20/09/11

PROF. DR. PARASKEV STOYANOV MEDICAL UNIVERSITY - VARNA
Medicinski universitet 'Prof. Dr. Paraskev Stoyanov' - Varna
55, Marin Drinov Str., 9002 Varna
Tel: +359(52) 677-020
Fax: +359(52) 677-020
EMail: international_relations@mu-varna.bg
Website: http://www.mu-varna.bg/muVarna

Rector: Anelia Klisarova
Tel: +359(52) 225-622 EMail: kalisarova@mu-varna.bg

International Relations: Aneta Dokova
Tel: +359(52) 677-019 EMail: dokova@mu-varna.bg

Colleges
Medicine *(Šoumen, Dobrič)* (Medicine)

Faculties
Dentistry (Dentistry); **Medicine** (Anatomy; Embryology and Reproduction Biology; Histology; Medicine; Orthopaedics; Pathology; Physiology); **Pharmacy** (Pharmacy); **Public Health** (Health Administration; Health Sciences; Public Health)

Further Information: Also University Hospitals (St Marina, St Anna)

History: Founded 1961 as Higher Institute of Medicine, acquired present status 1995.

Governing Bodies: University Council

Academic Year: September to June (September-December; February-June)

Admission Requirements: Secondary school certificate (Diploma za zavarsheno sredno obrazovanie)

Main Language(s) of Instruction: Bulgarian, English

International Co-operation: Participates in the Erasmus programme

Degrees and Diplomas: *Profesionalen Bakalavr*: Health Care, 3 yrs; *Bakalavr*: Health Management, 4 yrs; *Magistr*: Health Management, a further yr; *Magistr*: Medicine, 6 yrs

Student Services: Academic counselling, Canteen, Health services, Social counselling, Sports facilities

Student Residential Facilities: For c. 470 students

Libraries: University Library, c. 190,000 vols

Publications: Biomedical Reviews *(annually)*; Scripta Scientifica Medica *(annually)*
Last Updated: 19/09/11

PROF. PANČO VLADIGEROV NATIONAL ACADEMY OF MUSIC
Natsionalna muzikalna akademija 'Prof. Pančo Vladigerov' (NMA)
94 Evlogi Georgiev Blvd., 1505 Sofia
Tel: +359(2) 442-197
Fax: +359(2) 944-1454
EMail: info@nma.bg
Website: http://nma.bg/

Rector: Dimitar Momtchilov
Tel: +359(2) 943-4862, Fax: +359(2) 364-677

Vice-Rector: Pravda Atanasova Goranova Tel: +359(2) 944-1449

International Relations: Petya Kissimova Tel: +359(2) 470-181

Faculties
Composition, Theory and Conducting (Conducting; Music Theory and Composition; Musicology; Sound Engineering (Acoustics)); **Instruments** (Musical Instruments); **Vocal Studies** (Dance; Jazz and Popular Music; Opera; Singing)

History: Founded 1921 as Bulgarian State Conservatory, became National Academy of Music in 1995, acquired present status and title 2006.

Governing Bodies: Rector's Council; Academic Council

Academic Year: September to June

Admission Requirements: Secondary school certificate (Diploma za zavarsheno sredno obrazovanie), and competitive entrance examination

Fees: (US Dollars): Preliminary Courses, 2,200 per annum; specialized courses, 600 per month; tuition, 4,000 per annum; Master and postgraduate degrees, 6,000

Main Language(s) of Instruction: Bulgarian, English

International Co-operation: Participates in the Erasmus and Socrates programmes

Accrediting Agencies: National Agency for Evaluation and Accreditation

Degrees and Diplomas: *Bakalavr (BSc)*: 4 yrs; *Magistr (MSc)*: a further yr

Student Services: Academic counselling, Canteen, Employment services, Foreign student adviser, Foreign Studies Centre, Health services, Language programs

Student Residential Facilities: Hostel c. 570 students

Libraries: c. 80,000 vols
Last Updated: 20/09/11

ST. CYRIL AND ST. METHODIUS UNIVERSITY OF VÉLIKO TURNOVO

Vélikoturnovski universitet Sv. Sv. Kiril i Metodi (VTU)
2 Teodossi Turnovski Str., 5003 Véliko Turnovo
Tel: +359(62) 618-221
Fax: +359(62) 628-023
EMail: mbox@uni-vt.bg
Website: http://www.uni-vt.bg

Rector: Plamen Anatoliev Legkostup (2007-)
Tel: +359(62) 620-189, Fax: +359(62) 618-399
EMail: rector@uni-vt.bg

Vice-Rector for Academic Affairs: Petko Stefanov Petkov
EMail: p.petkov@uni-vt.bg

International Relations: Bagrelia Borissova, Vice-Rector, International Relations and Internal Cooperation
Tel: +359(62) 618-247, Fax: +359(62) 618-612
EMail: b.borisova@uni-vt.bg

Colleges

Education *(Pleven)* (Bulgarian; Business Administration; Education; Environmental Studies; Finance; Geography; Geography (Human); History; Philosophy; Preschool Education; Primary Education); **Education** *(Vratza)* (Education)

Faculties

Economics (Accountancy; Business Administration; Economics; Finance; Foreign Languages Education; International Business; International Economics; Library Science; Management; Marketing; Social and Community Services; Tourism); **Education** (Computer Education; Computer Science; Education; Foreign Languages Education; Information Technology; Mathematics; Mathematics Education; Music Education; Pedagogy; Physical Education; Preschool Education; Primary Education; Psychology; Social Psychology; Sports); **Fine Arts** (Fine Arts; Graphic Arts; Graphic Design; Painting and Drawing; Visual Arts); **History** (Archaeology; Geography; History; Medieval Studies); **Law** (Law); **Mathematics and Informatics** (Computer Science; Information Technology; Mathematics); **Modern Languages** (Applied Linguistics; Bulgarian; Central European Studies; Classical Languages; English; English Studies; French; French Studies; German; Germanic Studies; Information Sciences; Library Science; Linguistics; Literature; Oriental Languages; Philology; Romance Languages; Russian; Slavic Languages); **Orthodox Theology** (Bible; Orthodox Theology; Religious Art; Theology); **Philosophy** (Cultural Studies; Foreign Languages Education; Philosophy; Political Sciences; Psychology; Sociology)

History: Founded 1963 as Teacher Training Institute, acquired present status and title 1971. A State Institution.

Governing Bodies: Senate

Academic Year: September to June (September-December; February-June)

Admission Requirements: Secondary school certificate (diploma za zavarsheno sredno obrazovanie) and entrance examination

Fees: (Euros): Overseas students, 2,200 full-time, 1,300 part-time per annum

Main Language(s) of Instruction: Bulgarian

International Co-operation: With universities throughout Europe, Africa, Asia and USA. Also participates in Socrates, Leonardo, Tempus and Ceepus programmes

Accrediting Agencies: National Agency for Evaluation and Accreditation

Degrees and Diplomas: *Bakalavr.* 4 yrs; *Magistr.* a further 1-2.5 yrs; *Doktor.* 2-4 yrs. Also Teaching Qualifications

Student Services: Academic counselling, Canteen, Foreign student adviser, Health services, Language programs, Nursery care, Sports facilities

Student Residential Facilities: Yes

Special Facilities: Ronsar Museum; Museum of Fine Arts

Libraries: Central Library, c. 153,000 vols; Philological Reading Room, c. 1,000 vols; History, c. 1,000 vols; Ideological Centre, c. 5,000 vols; Specialized textbooks, c. 10,000 vols; also Faculties and Foreign Languages Centres Libraries

Publications: Archives of Historical and Geographical Research *(quarterly)*; Epohi, History Journal *(monthly)*; Pedagogičeski Almanač, Pedagogical Journal *(biannually)*; Proglass, Philology Journal *(quarterly)*; Trudove na VTU Kiril i Metodii, Works of the University of Véliko Turnovo *(annually)*
Last Updated: 21/09/11

ST. IVAN RILSKI UNIVERSITY OF MINING AND GEOLOGY

Minno-geoložki universitet Sv. Ivan Rilski (MGU)
Stoyan Edrev Str., 1700 Sofia
Tel: +359(2) 806-0269
Fax: +359(2) 962-5931
EMail: staf@mgu.bg
Website: http://www.mgu.bg

Rector: Lyuben Ivanov Totev
Tel: +359(2) 962-7224 EMail: rector@mgu.bg

Vice-Rector for Education: Vyara Georgieva Pozhidaeva
Tel: +359(2) 862-1146 EMail: vpojidaeva@abv.bg

International Relations: Stefka Dimitrova Pristavova, Vice-Rector for International collaboration and Science Research
Tel: +359(2) 962-5161 EMail: stprist@mgu.bg

Departments

Humanities (Arts and Humanities)

Faculties

Geology (Ecology; Environmental Management; Geology; Geophysics; Petroleum and Gas Engineering); **Mining Electromechanics** (Automation and Control Engineering; Electrical Engineering; Mining Engineering; Petroleum and Gas Engineering); **Mining Technology** (Industrial Management; Mineralogy; Mining Engineering; Surveying and Mapping)

History: Founded 1953. Acquired present status and title 2005.

Governing Bodies: Academic Board

Academic Year: September to July

Admission Requirements: Secondary school certificate (Diploma za zavarsheno sredno obrazovanie), and entrance examination

Fees: (Euros): 1,650-3,300 per annum

Main Language(s) of Instruction: Bulgarian, English

International Co-operation: Participates in the Tempus, Ceepus, Socrates and Copernicus programmes.

Accrediting Agencies: National Agency for Evaluation and Accreditation

Degrees and Diplomas: *Profesionalen Bakalavr.* 3 yrs; *Bakalavr (BSc):* 4 yrs; *Magistr (MSc):* a further 1 1/2 yr; *Doktor (PhD):* a further 3 yrs by thesis following Master

Student Services: Academic counselling, Canteen, Foreign student adviser, Foreign Studies Centre, Handicapped facilities, Health services, Language programs, Nursery care, Social counselling, Sports facilities

Student Residential Facilities: Yes

Special Facilities: Museum of Geology and Paleontology.

Libraries: Specialized library, 92,500 vols

Publications: Annual of the University of Mining and Geology "St. Ivan Rilski", Scientific Journal with research developments *(annually)*

Press or Publishing House: University Publishing House
Last Updated: 20/09/11

ST. KLIMENT OHRID SOFIA UNIVERSITY

Sofiiski universitet Sv. Kliment Ohridski (SU)
15 Tsar Osvoboditel Blvd., 1504 Sofia
Tel: +359(2) 930-8200
Fax: +359(2) 946-0255
EMail: rectorsoffice@admin.uni-sofia.bg
Website: http://www.uni-sofia.bg

Rector: Ivan Ilchev
Tel: +359(2) 987-3996 EMail: rector@uni-sofia.bg

Departments

Language Learning (Bulgarian; Modern Languages); **Sports** (Physical Education; Sports); **Teacher Training** (Teacher Training)

Faculties

Biology (Animal Husbandry; Anthropology; Biochemistry; Biological and Life Sciences; Biology; Biophysics; Biotechnology; Botany; Cell Biology; Ecology; Embryology and Reproduction Biology; Environmental Studies; Genetics; Histology; Inorganic Chemistry; Limnology; Marine Biology; Microbiology; Molecular Biology; Organic Chemistry; Physiology; Plant Pathology; Zoology); **Chemistry** (Analytical Chemistry; Chemistry; Inorganic Chemistry; Organic Chemistry; Physical Chemistry; Polymer and Plastics Technology; Thermal Physics); **Classical and Modern Philology** (American Studies; Classical Languages; English Studies; Foreign Languages Education; German; Germanic Studies; Modern Languages; Philology; Romance Languages; Scandinavian Languages; Spanish); **Economics and Business Administration** (Business Administration; Economics); **Education** (Education; Educational Administration; Pedagogy); **Geology and Geography** (Geography; Geology; Tourism); **History** (Ancient Civilizations; Archaeology; Archiving; Central European Studies; History; Modern History); **Journalism and Mass Communication** (Journalism; Mass Communication; Printing and Printmaking; Public Relations; Publishing and Book Trade; Radio and Television Broadcasting); **Law** (Administrative Law; Civil Law; Constitutional Law; Criminal Law; History of Law; International Law; International Relations; Law); **Mathematics and Informatics** (Applied Mathematics; Computer Education; Computer Graphics; Computer Science; Information Technology; Mathematics; Mathematics Education; Statistics; Systems Analysis); **Medicine** (Medicine); **Philosophy** (Aesthetics; Cultural Studies; Developmental Psychology; Educational Psychology; Ethics; Experimental Psychology; Information Sciences; Library Science; Logic; Philosophical Schools; Philosophy; Political Sciences; Psychology; Public Administration; Social Psychology; Sociology); **Physics** (Applied Physics; Astronomy and Space Science; Atomic and Molecular Physics; Electronic Engineering; Geophysics; Laser Engineering; Meteorology; Microelectronics; Nuclear Physics; Optics; Physics; Power Engineering; Radiophysics; Solid State Physics; Thermal Physics); **Preschool and Primary School Education** (Preschool Education; Primary School Education); **Slavic Studies** (Ancient Civilizations; Bulgarian; Central European Studies; Eastern European Studies; Educational Sciences; Literature; Native Language Education; Russian; Slavic Languages); **Theology** (Bible; Canon Law; Christian Religious Studies; History of Religion; New Testament; Orthodox Theology; Theology)

Institutes

Human and Social Sciences (*Germanicum*) (Arts and Humanities; German; Germanic Studies; Social Sciences)

Further Information: Also Regional Centre of Distance Education

History: Founded 1888 as Higher School of Education with one Faculty, reorganized as University 1904 and acquired present title 1905 with the number of Faculties increasing to seven by 1938. Reorganized 1944, when the Faculties of Medicine and Agriculture were detached from the University and established as separate Institutions. Acquired present title and status 2004. A State Institution.

Governing Bodies: University Council, comprising the Rector and 5 Pro-Rectors; Faculty Councils

Academic Year: September to June (September-December; February-June)

Admission Requirements: Secondary school certificate (diploma za zavarsheno sredno obrazovanie) and entrance examination

Fees: (US Dollars): Foreign students, c. 3,000 per annum

Main Language(s) of Instruction: Bulgarian, English

International Co-operation: Participates in the Tempus programme

Accrediting Agencies: National Agency for Evaluation and Accreditation

Degrees and Diplomas: *Bakalavr.* 4 yrs; *Magistr.* a further yr; *Doktor (PhD):* a further 3 yrs and thesis

Student Services: Academic counselling, Canteen, Cultural centre, Employment services, Foreign student adviser, Health services, Language programs, Nursery care, Social counselling, Sports facilities

Student Residential Facilities: Yes

Special Facilities: History Museum, Palaeontology Museum, Art gallery, Radio Studio

Libraries: University Library; Online catalogue

Press or Publishing House: University Printing House

Last Updated: 20/09/11

TECHNICAL UNIVERSITY OF GABROVO

Tehničeski universitet Gabrovo (TUG)
4 Hadji Dimitar Str., 5300 Gabrovo
Tel: +359(66) 827-777
Fax: +359(66) 801-155
EMail: info@tugab.bg
Website: http://www.tugab.bg

Rector: Deshka Markova
Tel: +359(66) 801-144
EMail: rector@tugab.bg; markova@tugab.bg

International Relations: Lyubomir Lazov, Vice-Rector
Tel: 359(66) 800-671 EMail: lazov@tugab.bg

Faculties

Economics (Business and Commerce; Economics; Industrial Management; Marketing; Public Administration; Social Work); **Electrical Engineering and Electronics** (Automation and Control Engineering; Computer Engineering; Electrical and Electronic Engineering; Environmental Engineering; Power Engineering; Telecommunications Engineering); **Mechanical and Precision Engineering** (Environmental Engineering; Hydraulic Engineering; Industrial Design; Industrial Engineering; Instrument Making; Machine Building; Materials Engineering; Measurement and Precision Engineering; Mechanical Engineering; Power Engineering; Textile Technology)

History: Founded 1964 as Higher Institute of Mechanical and Electrical Engineering, acquired present status and title 1995.

Governing Bodies: Academic Board; General Assembly

Academic Year: September to July

Admission Requirements: Secondary school certificate (Diploma za zavarsheno sredno obrazovanie) and entrance examination

Fees: (Leva): 235 per semester

Main Language(s) of Instruction: Bulgarian

International Co-operation: With universities in Germany; Netherlands; United Kingdom; Spain; Russian Federation; Ukraine; Poland; Romania; Serbia; Montenegro; Switzerland; Austria and Lithuania

Accrediting Agencies: National Agency for Evaluation and Accreditation

Degrees and Diplomas: *Bakalavr.* Engineering; Business Administration; Social Sciences, 4 yrs; *Magistr.* Engineering, a further 1-1 1/2 yrs; *Doktor.* 3 yrs

Student Services: Academic counselling, Canteen, Cultural centre, Employment services, Foreign student adviser, Health services, Language programs, Social counselling, Sports facilities

Student Residential Facilities: 5 Hostels

Libraries: University Library

Publications: Journal of Technical University of Gabrovo (*quarterly*); Proceedings from Conferences (*annually*)

Press or Publishing House: University Publishing House

Part-time students, 3,000.
Last Updated: 20/09/11

TECHNICAL UNIVERSITY OF SOFIA

Tehničeski universitet Sofija (TUS)
8 Kliment Ohridski Str., 1000 Sofia
Tel: +359(2) 8623-073
Fax: +359(2) 8683-215
EMail: office_tu@tu-sofia.bg
Website: http://www.tu-sofia.bg

Rector: Marin Hristov
Tel: +359(2) 965-2450 EMail: rector@tu-sofia.bg

Administrative Director: Valentin Dimitrov
Tel: +359(2) 683-046, Fax: +359(2) 683-215
EMail: valdim@tu-sofia.bg

International Relations: Elko Tzekov
Tel: +359(2) 987-7870, Fax: +359(2) 987-7870
EMail: int.dept@tu-sofia.bg

Centres
Continuing Education (Business and Commerce; Law; Management; Meteorology)

Departments
Applied Physics (Applied Physics); **Foreign Languages and Applied Linguistics** (Applied Linguistics; Linguistics; Modern Languages); **Physical Education and Sports** (Physical Education; Sports)

Faculties
Applied Mathematics and Information Science (Applied Mathematics; Computer Science); **Automatics** (Automation and Control Engineering; Electrical Engineering; Production Engineering; Systems Analysis); **Computer Systems and Control** (Computer Engineering; Computer Science); **Electrical Engineering** (Electrical Engineering); **Electronic Engineering and Technology** (Chemistry; Microelectronics; Power Engineering; Technology); **Engineering** *(In English)* (Engineering); **Engineering** *(In French)* (Engineering); **Machine Technology** (Machine Building; Mechanical Engineering; Metal Techniques; Metallurgical Engineering); **Management** (Economics; Industrial Engineering; Industrial Management); **Mechanical Engineering** (Automation and Control Engineering; Mechanical Engineering; Production Engineering); **Power Engineering and Power Machines** (Heating and Refrigeration; Hydraulic Engineering; Nuclear Engineering; Power Engineering; Textile Technology; Thermal Engineering); **Telecommunication Engineering** (Telecommunications Engineering); **Transport** (Air Transport; Automotive Engineering; Railway Transport; Transport and Communications)

History: Founded 1945. Acquired present status and title 1995.

Governing Bodies: Academic Senate

Academic Year: September to June (September-January; February-June)

Admission Requirements: Secondary school certificate and entrance examination

Fees: (Leva): 200 per annum; foreign students, US$ 3,000

Main Language(s) of Instruction: Bulgarian

International Co-operation: With universities in Germany, France, United Kingdom

Degrees and Diplomas: *Bakalavr*: 4 yrs; *Magistr*: 1-2 yrs following Bakalavr; *Doktor (PhD)*: a further 3 yrs

Student Services: Academic counselling, Canteen, Foreign student adviser, Health services, Language programs, Sports facilities

Student Residential Facilities: Yes

Special Facilities: Museum, Computer Centre

Libraries: Central Library

Publications: Annals of the Technical University of Sofia *(annually)*

Press or Publishing House: Izdatelstvo i Pechatna baza
Last Updated: 20/09/11

PLOVDIV BRANCH
61 Sankt Peterburg Blvd., 4000 Plovdiv
Tel: +359(32) 633-250 +359(32) 633-251
Fax: +359(32) 633-156

Director: Ludmul Genov
Tel: +359(32) 626-886, Fax: +359(32) 626-886

Boards Of Study
Special Training (Automation and Control Engineering; Electronic Engineering; Mechanical Engineering; Production Engineering; Systems Analysis; Transport Engineering)

Faculties
Electronics and Automatics (Automation and Control Engineering; Electronic Engineering); **Mechanical and Device Engineering** (Mechanical Engineering)

History: Founded 1945, acquired present status and title 1986.

SLIVEN BRANCH
59 Burgasko Šose Bvd., 8800 Sliven
Tel: +359(2) 448-9114

Director: Penka Genova (2000-)

Faculties
Pedagogy Engineering (Applied Mathematics; Chemistry; Information Sciences; Mechanical Engineering; Physics; Science Education; Teacher Trainers Education) *Dean*: E. Ratz

TECHNICAL UNIVERSITY OF VARNA
Tehničeski universitet Varna (TU-VARNA)
1 Studentska Str., Vassil Levski district, 9010 Varna
Tel: +359(52) 302-444
Fax: +359(52) 302-771
EMail: rector@tu-varna.acad.bg
Website: http://www.tu-varna.acad.bg

Rector: Ovid Farhi

International Relations: Velko Naumov, Vice-Rector
Tel: +359(52) 383-422, Fax: +359(52) 302-442
EMail: fs_centre@tu-varna.acad.bg

Colleges
Technical Studies (Automation and Control Engineering; Chemical Engineering; Information Technology; Mechanical Engineering; Transport Engineering); **Technology** *(City of Dobrich)* (Agricultural Engineering; Automation and Control Engineering; Electronic Engineering; Information Technology; Mechanical Engineering)

Departments
Foreign Languages

Faculties
Computer Systems and Automatics (Applied Mathematics; Artificial Intelligence; Automation and Control Engineering; Computer Networks; Mathematics and Computer Science); **Electrical Engineering** (Electrical Engineering; Power Engineering); **Electronics** (Electronic Engineering; Telecommunications Engineering); **Marine Sciences and Ecology** (Ecology; Engineering Management; Marine Science and Oceanography; Marine Transport; Nautical Science); **Mechanical Engineering and Technologies** (Building Technologies; Industrial Design; Machine Building; Metal Techniques); **Shipbuilding** (Building Technologies; Marine Engineering; Naval Architecture; Thermal Engineering)

History: Founded 1962 as Institute of Mechanical and Electrical Engineering, acquired present status and title 1995.

Governing Bodies: Academic Council; Rector's Board, comprising the Rector, Vice-Rectors and Deans of Faculties

Academic Year: September to July

Admission Requirements: Secondary school certificate (Diploma za zavarsheno sredno obrazovanie) and entrance examination

Fees: (US Dollars): 2,000-3,000 per annum

Main Language(s) of Instruction: Bulgarian

International Co-operation: With universities in Belgium, Finland, France, Germany, Greece, Poland, Portugal, Romania, Russian Federation, Turkey, United Kingdom, USA. Also participates in Leonardo da Vinci, Tempus and Phare programmes

Accrediting Agencies: National Agency for Evaluation and Accreditation

Degrees and Diplomas: *Profesionalen Bakalavr*: 3 yrs; *Bakalavr (B.Sc)*: 4 yrs; *Magistr (M.Sc)*: 5 yrs; *Doktor (PhD)*: 3 yrs after M.Sc. Also Diplom za Visše Obrazovanie 5 yrs

Student Services: Canteen, Employment services, Foreign student adviser, Foreign Studies Centre, Health services, Sports facilities

Student Residential Facilities: Hostel for 1,600 students

Special Facilities: TV Studio

Libraries: Central Library, c. 235,700 vols

Publications: Acta Universitatis Pontica Euxinus *(biennially)*

Press or Publishing House: Printing House (Pečatna Baza)

Academic Staff *2008-2009*	TOTAL
FULL-TIME	600
PART-TIME	50
STAFF WITH DOCTORATE	
FULL-TIME	c. 220
Student Numbers *2008-2009*	
All (Foreign Included)	c. 6,500
FOREIGN ONLY	180

Part-time students, 1,500.

THE NATIONAL ACADEMY OF ARTS

Nacionalna hudojestvena akademija (NAA)

1 Šipka Str., 1000 Sofia
Tel: +359(2) 988-1702
Fax: +359(2) 987-8064
EMail: art_academy@yahoo.com
Website: http://www.nha-bg.org/

Rector: Svetoslav Kokalov Tel: +359(2) 988-1701

International Relations: Mitko Dinev
Tel: +359(2) 987-8177 +359(2) 987-3328

Faculties

Applied Arts (Ceramic Art; Design; Display and Stage Design; Fashion Design; Fine Arts; Glass Art; Industrial Design; Metal Techniques; Restoration of Works of Art; Textile Design); **Fine Arts** (Art History; Fine Arts; Graphic Arts; Painting and Drawing; Printing and Printmaking; Sculpture)

History: Founded 1896 as Higher School of Drawing (Fine Arts), acquired present title 1921. A State institution.

Governing Bodies: Academic Council

Academic Year: October to June (October-January; February-June)

Admission Requirements: Secondary school certificate (Diploma za zavarsheno sredno obrazovanie) and entrance examination

Fees: (Euros) 148-197 per annum; foreign students, 3,000-4,000, specialisations, 400 per month, Bulgarian language course, 2,000 per annum

Main Language(s) of Instruction: Bulgarian

International Co-operation: With universities in Austria, Germany, Finland, Portugal, Spain, United Kingdom, Italy, Greece, Netherlands, France, Belgium, China. Also participates in the Tempus, Socrates/Erasmus programmes

Accrediting Agencies: National Agency for Evaluation and Accreditation

Degrees and Diplomas: *Bakalavr*: Fine Arts; Applied and Industrial Arts (BA), 4 yrs; *Magistr*: Art History; Restoration of Works of Art, a further 1 yr; *Magistr*: Fine Arts; Applied and Industrial Arts (MA), a further 1 1/2 yrs; *Doktor*: Fine Arts; Applied and Industrial Arts, a further 3 yrs following MA. Also Professional qualification certificate, following specialisations

Student Services: Academic counselling, Cultural centre, Foreign student adviser, Health services, Language programs, Social counselling, Sports facilities

Student Residential Facilities: Yes

Special Facilities: Museum. Auditoriums. Computer Centre. Laboratories

Libraries: Main Library with 2 branches

Academic Staff *2008-2009*	TOTAL
FULL-TIME	200
STAFF WITH DOCTORATE	
FULL-TIME	c. 20
Student Numbers *2008-2009*	
All (Foreign Included)	c. 1,000
FOREIGN ONLY	150

Last Updated: 20/09/11

TODOR KABLECHKOV UNIVERSITY OF TRANSPORT

Vische transportno utchilichte 'Todor Kablechkov'

Geo Milev Str. 158, 1574 Sofia
Tel: +359(2) 970-9240
Fax: +359(2) 970-9242
EMail: office@vtu.bg
Website: http://www.vtu.bg/

Rector: Peter Kolev Kolev EMail: rector@vtu.bg

International Relations: Nentcho Nenov, Vice-Rector, Research and International Relations
Tel: +359(2) 970-9335, Fax: +359(2) 970-9325
EMail: nnenov@vtu.bg

Faculties

Communication and Electrical Equipment (Computer Science; Electrical Engineering; Mathematics; Physics; Power Engineering; Telecommunications Engineering); **Machinery and Construction Technologies in Transport** (Building Technologies; Machine Building; Mechanical Engineering; Transport and Communications; Transport Engineering); **Transport Management** (Arts and Humanities; Machine Building; Transport Economics; Transport Management)

History: Founded 1958 as Railway College. Renamed Todor Kableshkov Higher Military School of Transport 1984. Demilitarized and renamed as Todor Kableshkov Higher School of Transport 2000.

Main Language(s) of Instruction: Bulgarian

Degrees and Diplomas: *Profesionalen Bakalavr, Bakalavr, Magistr, Doktor*
Last Updated: 21/09/11

TRAKIA UNIVERSITY

Trakiyski universitet

Studentski Grad, 6000 Stara Zagora
Tel: +359(42) 670-204
Fax: +359(42) 672-009
EMail: intern@uni-sz.bg
Website: http://www.uni-sz.bg

Rector: Ivan Stankov
Tel: +359(42) 670-204 EMail: rector@uni-sz.bg

Secretary-General: Tsonka Kasnakova
Tel: +359(42) 699-205 EMail: kasnakova@uni-sz.bg

International Relations: Veselina Gadjeva, Vice-Rector
Tel: +359(42) 673-004 EMail: vgadjeva@mf.uni-sz.bg

Colleges

Medicine *(Stara Zagora)* (Nursing; Rehabilitation and Therapy); **Technology** *(Yambol)* (Agricultural Equipment; Automation and Control Engineering; Electronic Engineering; Food Technology; Machine Building; Maintenance Technology; Textile Technology)

Departments

Information & In-service Teacher Training (Art Education; Computer Education; Foreign Languages Education; Humanities and Social Science Education; Literacy Education; Mathematics Education; Music Education; Native Language Education; Physical Education; Preschool Education; Primary Education; Secondary Education; Teacher Trainers Education; Technology Education)

Faculties

Agriculture *(with experimental station)* (Agricultural Engineering; Agronomy; Animal Husbandry; Aquaculture; Ecology; Fishery); **Economics** (Agricultural Economics; Banking; Economics; Finance; Regional Planning; Rural Studies); **Education** (Education; Pedagogy); **Medicine** (Medicine; Social and Community Services; Social Welfare; Social Work); **Veterinary Medicine** (Veterinary Science)

Further Information: University Hospital; Preparatory courses for foreign students; Experimental Farm; Training-Experimental Base(Medicine), Haskovo

History: Founded 1995, incorporating the former Higher Institute of Medicine and Higher Institute of Animal Production and Veterinary Medicine. Three Medical Colleges affiliated to Trakia University 1997.

Governing Bodies: General Assembly; Academic Council composed of 45 members; Rector; Vice-Rectors

Academic Year: September to July (September-December; February-July)

Admission Requirements: Secondary school certificate (zrelostno svidetelstvo), or equivalent

Fees: (Euros): Foreign students, Bachelor, 1,000-2,000 per annum; Master, 1,000-3,300; Doctorate, 1,500-5,000; Specialist, 500-2,600; Bulgarian Language courses, 2,000

Main Language(s) of Instruction: Bulgarian

International Co-operation: Participates in the Erasmus programme with universities in Germany, France, Italy, Greece, Slovak Republic, Czech Republic, Turkey. Participates in Leonardo programme with Universities in Italy and Spain.

Accrediting Agencies: National Agency for Evaluation and Accreditation

Degrees and Diplomas: *Bakalavr:* Animal Husbandry; Agricultural Economics; Agronomy; Agricultural Engineering; Rural Planning and Regional Planning; Environmental Studies; Special Education; Primary Education; Preschool Education Foreign Languages Education; Social Work; Public Health (Bachelor's Degree); Farm Management; Machine and Instrument Building; Agricultural Equipment; Maintenance Technology; Textile Technology; Electronic Engineering; Automation and Control Engineering; Food Technology (Bachelor's Degree), 3 yrs; *Magistr (MA):* a further 2 yrs following Bachelor's Degree; *Magistr:* Medicine; Veterinary Science (MA), 6 yrs; *Doktor (PhD):* a further 3 yrs following Master's Degree

Student Services: Academic counselling, Canteen, Cultural centre, Employment services, Foreign student adviser, Foreign Studies Centre, Health services, Language programs, Nursery care, Social counselling, Sports facilities

Student Residential Facilities: Yes. Capacity of 1,660 beds

Special Facilities: Animal Production Museum; Veterinary Medicine Museum

Libraries: Total, c. 380,000 vols; Bulgarian, English, French, Russian and German periodical subscriptions.

Publications: Bulgarian Journal of Veterinary Medicine *(quarterly)*; Trakia Journal of Sciences *(quarterly)*

Last Updated: 20/09/11

UNIVERSITY OF ARCHITECTURE, CIVIL ENGINEERING AND GEODESY

Universitet po Arhitektura, Stroitelstvo i Geodezia (UACEG)
1 Hristo Smirnenski Blvd., 1046 Sofia
Tel: +359(2) 963-5245
Fax: +359(2) 865-6863
EMail: aceadm@uacg.bg
Website: http://www.uacg.bg

Rector: Krasimir Petrov
Tel: +359(2) 866-1967 EMail: k_petrov_fhe@uacg.bg

Assistant Rector: Dimitar Nikolaev Vitanov
Tel: +359(2) 866-1257 EMail: vitanov_adm@uacg.bg

International Relations: Boyan Milchev Georgiev, Vice-Rector
Tel: +359(2) 866-5810, Fax: +359(2) 963-1796
EMail: boyangeo_far@uacg.bg

Centres
Open and Continuing Education *(COCE)* (Business Administration; Business and Commerce; Civil Engineering; Computer Engineering; Computer Science; Construction Engineering; Engineering Drawing and Design; International Business; International Economics; International Law; International Relations; Management; Real Estate; Systems Analysis) *Director:* Kosta Apostolov Mladenov

Departments
Applied Linguistics *Director:* Atanaska Stoicheva Miteva; **Applied Linguistics and Physical Education** (Applied Linguistics; Physical Education)

Faculties
Architecture (Architecture; Architecture and Planning; Interior Design; Landscape Architecture; Regional Planning; Rural Planning; Town Planning); **Geodesy** (Engineering; Geological Engi-

neering; Soil Science; Surveying and Mapping); **Hydraulic Engineering** (Civil Engineering; Environmental Engineering; Hydraulic Engineering; Irrigation; Waste Management; Water Management); **Structural Engineering** (Building Technologies; Construction Engineering; Structural Architecture); **Transportation Engineering** (Railway Engineering; Road Engineering; Transport Engineering)

History: Founded 1942 as Higher Technical School, reorganized as State Polytechnic 1945 and as Higher Institute of Civil Engineering 1953. Became Higher Institute of Architecture and Civil Engineering (VIAS) 1977 and University of Architecture, Civil Engineering and Geodesy 1990. Acquired present status 1995.

Governing Bodies: General Assembly; Academic Council, comprising 45 members

Academic Year: September to June (September-January; February-June)

Admission Requirements: Secondary school certificate (diploma za zavarsheno sredno obrazovanie)

Fees: (Leva): 155 per semester; (Euros): foreign students, 2,000 for the preparatory year; 3,000 per annum for full time course

Main Language(s) of Instruction: Bulgarian. Also German for Hydraulic Engineering and Transportation Engineering degree courses

International Co-operation: With universities in France, Germany, Austria; Greece; Poland; Russian Federation; Sweden and United Kingdom. Also participates in Socrates/Erasmus, Leonardo da Vinci, the 5th and 6th Framework Programme of Eu for Scientific Research; the Central European Exchange Programme for University (Ceepus); the scientific programme of NATO

Accrediting Agencies: National Agency for Evaluation and Accreditation

Degrees and Diplomas: *Bakalavr:* Urban Planning, 4 yrs; *Magistr:* Architecture, 5 1/2 yrs; *Magistr:* Civil Engineering and Geodesy, 5 yrs; *Doktor:* Architecture; Civil Engineering and Geodesy, a further 3 yrs by thesis following Master

Student Services: Canteen, Foreign student adviser, Health services, Sports facilities

Student Residential Facilities: For 2,675 students

Libraries: Central Technical Library

Press or Publishing House: Printing House of UACEG
Last Updated: 18/01/12

UNIVERSITY OF CHEMICAL TECHNOLOGY AND METALLURGY

Himiko-tehnologičen i metalurgičen universitet (UCTM)
8 St. Kliment Ohridski Str., 1756 Sofia
Tel: +359(2) 816-3120
Fax: +359(2) 868-5488
EMail: rectorat@uctm.edu
Website: http://www.uctm.edu

Rector: Mitko Georgiev EMail: uctm.rector@uctm.edu

Secretary-General: Ludmil Fachikov EMail: fachikov@uctm.edu

International Relations: Ivan Pentchev
Tel: +359(2) 8163-111 EMail: pentchev@uctm.edu

Faculties
Chemical and Systems Engineering (Automation and Control Engineering; Biotechnology; Chemical Engineering; Ecology; Environmental Studies; Industrial Management; Information Technology); **Chemical Technology** (Chemical Engineering; Inorganic Chemistry; Leather Techniques; Paper Technology; Polymer and Plastics Technology; Textile Technology; Wood Technology); **Metallurgy and Material Sciences** (Materials Engineering; Metallurgical Engineering)

History: Founded 1953 as Institute of Chemical Technology, acquired present status and title 1995.

Governing Bodies: Academic Council

Academic Year: September to June

Admission Requirements: Secondary school certificate (Diploma za zavarsheno sredno obrazovanie), and entrance examination (chemistry or mathematics)

Main Language(s) of Instruction: Bulgarian

Accrediting Agencies: National Agency for Evaluation and Accreditation

Degrees and Diplomas: *Bakalavr (BSc)*: 4 yrs; *Magistr (MSc)*: a further 2 yrs; *Doktor (PhD)*: a further 3 yrs by thesis following Master

Libraries: c. 66,000 vols

Publications: Journal of the University of Chemical Technology and Metallurgy *(quarterly)*

Last Updated: 19/09/11

UNIVERSITY OF ECONOMICS - VARNA
Ikonomičeski universitet, Varna (UE-VARNA)
77 Kniaz Boris I Blvd., 9002 Varna
Tel: +359(52) 225-351
Fax: +359(52) 235-680
EMail: int_relations@ue-varna.bg
Website: http://www.ue-varna.bg

Rector: Plamen Blagov Iliev EMail: rector@ue-varna.bg

Vice-Rector for Academic Affairs: Evgeni Petrov Stanimirov EMail: eugstan@abv.bg

International Relations: Violeta Janeva Dimitrova
Tel: +359(52) 660-358, Fax: +359(52) 660-358
EMail: violeta_dimitrova@mail.ue-varna.bg

Centres
Information Technology (Information Technology) *Director*: Alexander Frantsev

Colleges
Tourism (European Languages; International Economics; Slavic Languages; Tourism)

Departments
Foreign Languages (European Languages; Modern Languages; Slavic Languages)

Faculties
Computer Science (Computer Science; Econometrics; Mathematics; Physical Education; Sports; Statistics); **Economics** (Agricultural Economics; Business and Commerce; Economics; Industrial and Production Economics; Management); **Finance and Accountancy** (Accountancy; Finance); **Management** (International Economics; International Relations; Management; Marketing; Tourism)

History: Founded 1920 as Higher School of Commerce, acquired present status and title 1994.

Governing Bodies: Academic Council

Academic Year: September to May (September-December; February-May)

Admission Requirements: Secondary school certificate (Diploma za zavarsheno sredno obrazovanie), and entrance examination

Fees: (Bulgarian Leva): 200-260 per annum; Foreign students, US$ 2,500

Main Language(s) of Instruction: Bulgarian

International Co-operation: Participates in the Tempus, Erasmus, Leonardo, Scopes, CDG and CEP programmes

Accrediting Agencies: National Agency for Evaluation and Accreditation

Degrees and Diplomas: *Bakalavr*: Economics; Management; Computer Science (BA), 4 yrs; *Magistr*: Economics; Management (MA), a further yr; *Doktor*: Economics; Management (PhD), 3 yrs by thesis

Student Services: Academic counselling, Canteen, Cultural centre, Employment services, Foreign student adviser, Health services, Nursery care, Social counselling, Sports facilities

Student Residential Facilities: For c. 800 students

Special Facilities: Movie studio

Libraries: University Library, c. 250,000 vols

Press or Publishing House: University Publishing House
Last Updated: 19/09/11

UNIVERSITY OF FOOD TECHNOLOGY
Universitet po hranitelni technologii (UFT)
26 "Maritza" Blvd., 4002 Plovdiv
Tel: +359(32) 643-005
Fax: +359(32) 644-102
EMail: uht@uft-plovdiv.bg
Website: http://uft-plovdiv.bg/

Rector: Georgi Valtchev (2003-) EMail: g_valtchev@abv.bg

Registrar: Volodya Kamenov Tel: +359(32) 644-242

International Relations: Zheljazko Simov, Vice Rector of International Cooperation
Tel: +359(32) 643-007 EMail: vicerector_inter@uft-plovdiv.bg

Centres
Francophone (Food Technology; Technology Education); **Language Training**; **Physical Education and Sports**; **Scientific Research and Development Activities** (Food Science)

Faculties
Economics (Business Administration; Economics; Industrial and Production Economics; Tourism); **Technical** (Automation and Control Engineering; Computer Engineering; Electrical and Electronic Equipment and Maintenance; Engineering; Heating and Refrigeration; Mechanical Engineering); **Technology** (Analytical Chemistry; Biochemistry; Biotechnology; Dairy; Food Technology; Heating and Refrigeration; Inorganic Chemistry; Microbiology; Oenology; Plant and Crop Protection; Technology)

History: Founded 1953 as Higher Institute of Food and Flavour Industries, acquired present title and status 2003.

Governing Bodies: General Assembly; Academic Council

Academic Year: September to May (September-December; February-May)

Admission Requirements: Secondary school certificate (Diploma za zavarsheno sredno obrazovanie)

Fees: (Euros): Foreign students, 3,000 per annum for full-time Bachelor and Master; 4,500 per annum for PhD

Main Language(s) of Instruction: English

International Co-operation: With universities in the European Union; China; Russian Federation; Ukraine. Also participates in the Tempus, Socrates-Erasmus and Leonardo programmes.

Accrediting Agencies: National Agency for Evaluation and Accreditation

Degrees and Diplomas: *Bakalavr*: Food Technology; Biotechnology; Engineering; Business Administration; Industrial Management; Tourism (BSc), 4 yrs; *Magistr*: Food Technology; Biotechnology; Engineering; Business Administration; Industrial Management; Tourism; Ecology; Environmental Safety (MSc), a further 1 1/2 yr; *Doktor*: Food Science and Technology (PhD), 3 yrs

Student Services: Academic counselling, Canteen, Employment services, Foreign student adviser, Health services, Language programs, Social counselling, Sports facilities

Student Residential Facilities: For 1,500 students

Libraries: c. 150,000 vols

Publications: Scientific Works of UFT

Academic Staff *2008-2009*	TOTAL
FULL-TIME	c. 210

Student Numbers *2008-2009*	
All (Foreign Included)	c. 3,200
FOREIGN ONLY	60

Part-time students, 1,000.
Last Updated: 23/11/09

UNIVERSITY OF FORESTRY - SOFIA
Lesotehničeski universitet - Sofia (LTU)
10 St. Kliment Ohridski Blvd., 1756 Sofia
Tel: +359(2) 962-5997
Fax: +359(2) 622-830
EMail: zhelev@ltu.bg
Website: http://www.ltu.bg

Vice-Chancellor: Peter Zhelev Stoyanov

International Relations: Michael Andreev
Tel: +3559(2) 862-3059 EMail: mandreev@abv.bg

Centres
Postgraduate Studies (Agronomy; Ecology; Forestry; Handicrafts; Industrial Management; Landscape Architecture; Modern Languages; Pedagogy; Veterinary Science) *Director:* Nikola Ivanov

Departments
Computer Systems and Informatics (Computer Networks; Computer Science) *Head:* Jordan Konstandinov

Faculties
Agronomy (Agriculture; Agronomy; Crop Production; Forest Biology; Horticulture); **Business Administration** (Business Administration; Economics; Industrial Management; Marketing); **Ecology and Landscape Architecture** (Ecology; Landscape Architecture; Plant Pathology); **Forest Industry** (Forest Economics; Forest Management; Forestry; Furniture Design; Wood Technology); **Forestry** (Forest Management; Forest Products; Forestry; Soil Science) *Dean:* Miko Milev; **Veterinary Medicine** (Veterinary Science)

Further Information: Also Scientific Research Department

History: Founded 1925 as Forestry Department of Sofia University 'St. Kliment Ochridski', reorganized as Higher Technical Institute of Forestry, an autonomous institution. Acquired present status and title 1995.

Academic Year: October to June

Fees: (US Dollars): 3,000 per annum

International Co-operation: Participates in Erasmus, Leonardo da Vinci, Tempus

Degrees and Diplomas: *Bakalavr:* Science, 4 yrs; *Magistr:* Science, a further 1-1/2 yrs; *Doktor (PhD):* a further 3 yrs by thesis following Master

Student Services: Canteen, Cultural centre, Language programs

Student Residential Facilities: Hostels

Special Facilities: Museum. Biological Garden. Animal Treatment and Training Clinic. Experimental and Training Forest Ranges. Information Centre.

Libraries: University Library, c. 108,000 vols

Publications: Forestry Ideas, Magazine; Management and Sustainable Development, Magazine; Woodworking and Furniture Production, Magazine

Press or Publishing House: Publishing Division

Academic Staff 2009	TOTAL
FULL-TIME	300
STAFF WITH DOCTORATE	
FULL-TIME	30
PART-TIME	c. 20

Student Numbers 2009	
All (Foreign Included)	c. 2,200
FOREIGN ONLY	80

Part-time students, 150.
Last Updated: 18/01/12

UNIVERSITY OF NATIONAL AND WORLD ECONOMY
Universitet za nacionalno i svetovno stopanstvo (UNWE)
Studentski Grad 'Hristo Botev', 1756 Sofia
Tel: +359(2) 819-5211
Fax: +359(2) 962-3903
EMail: secretary@unwe.acad.bg
Website: http://www.unwe.acad.bg

Rector: Statty Stattev
Tel: +359(2) 962-3812 EMail: sstattev@unwe.acad.bg

Vice-Rector for Scientific Research and International Projects: Plamen Mishev EMail: mishevp@unwe.acad.bg

Faculties
Applied Informatics and Statistics (Business Computing; Communication Studies; Econometrics; Information Technology; Statistics); **Business** (Agricultural Business; Business Administration; Economics; Real Estate); **Economics of Infrastructure** (Commu-

nication Studies; Economics; Media Studies; Transport Economics); **Finance and Accountancy** (Accountancy; Finance); **General Economics** (Economics; Human Resources; Social Policy; Sociology); **International Economy and Politics** (International Business; International Relations; Political Sciences); **Law** (Criminal Law; Law; Private Law; Public Law); **Management and Administration** (Business Administration; Management; Marketing; Public Administration; Regional Studies)

Further Information: Also affiliated branch (Economics and Management) in Haskovo

History: Founded 1947 as Higher Institute of Economics, acquired present status and title 1995.

Academic Year: October to June (October-January; March-June)

Main Language(s) of Instruction: Bulgarian

Accrediting Agencies: National Agency for Evaluation and Accreditation

Degrees and Diplomas: *Bakalavr:* 4 yrs; *Magistr:* a further 1-2 yrs; *Doktor (PhD):* a further 2 yrs by thesis following Master

Student Services: Canteen, Foreign student adviser, Health services, Sports facilities

Student Residential Facilities: For c. 4,500 students

Libraries: c. 430,000 vols

Publications: Alternativi; Ikonomist; Trudove

Press or Publishing House: University Publishing House 'Stopanstvo'. University Press
Last Updated: 18/01/12

VARNA FREE UNIVERSITY "CHERNORIZETS HRABAR"
Varnenski svoboden universitet 'Chernorizeth Hrarbar' (VFU)
"Chaika" Resort Complex, 9007 Varna
Tel: +359(52) 356-088
Fax: +359(52) 356-088
EMail: rector@vfu.bg
Website: http://www.vfu.bg

Rector: Anna Nedyalkova (1997-)

Vice-Rector for Academic Affairs: Galya Gercheva
Tel: +359(52) 357-066, Fax: +359(52) 357-066
EMail: gercheva@vfu.bg

International Relations: Pavel Pavlov, Vice-Rector for Research Work Tel: +359(52) 357-066 EMail: pavlov_p@vfu.bg

Centres
Distance Learning *(Smolyan)*

Departments
Foreign Language Teaching (Modern Languages)

Faculties
Architecture (Architecture; Arts and Humanities; Construction Engineering; Fine Arts; Urban Studies); **Economics** (Administration; Economics; Management; Political Sciences); **Law** (Economics; Law; Psychology; Social Studies)

Institutes
Technology (Technology)

Further Information: Also Campus in Smolyan

History: Founded 1991, officially recognized 1995.

Governing Bodies: Academic Council

Academic Year: October to June (October-January; February-June)

Admission Requirements: Secondary school certificate (Diploma za zavarsheno sredno obrazovanie)

Fees: (Euros): 2,000-2,500 per annum

Main Language(s) of Instruction: Bulgarian

International Co-operation: Participates in the FP6, Fare, Socrates, Leonardo, Cost, Interreg Programmes

Accrediting Agencies: National Agency for Evaluation and Accreditation

Degrees and Diplomas: *Bakalavr:* 4 yrs; *Magistr:* a further yr; *Doktor (PhD):* a further 2 yrs by thesis following Master

Student Services: Academic counselling, Canteen, Cultural centre, Foreign student adviser, Handicapped facilities, Health services, Language programs, Nursery care, Sports facilities

Student Residential Facilities: For c. 400 students

Special Facilities: Art Gallery. Media Centre. Computer Halls

Libraries: c. 120,000 vols

Publications: Science Almanach, Scientific and cultural academic and students publications and studies *(annually)*
Last Updated: 21/09/11

VASSIL LEVSKI NATIONAL SPORTS ACADEMY
Nacionalna sportna akademija Vassil Levski (NSA)
Studentski Grad Darvenitza, 1700 Sofia
Tel: +359(2) 962-0460
Fax: +359(2) 629-007
EMail: intrelations@nsa.bg
Website: http://nsa.bg

Rector: Latchezar Dimitrov
Tel: +359(2) 962-0458 EMail: rector@nsa.bg

International Relations: Daniela Dasheva, Vice-Rector of International Relations
Tel: +359(2) 868- 6087 EMail: dani_dash@yahoo.com

Faculties
Coaches (Biochemistry; Physiology; Sports; Sports Management); **Physiotherapy** (Physical Therapy; Rehabilitation and Therapy; Sports; Sports Medicine); **Teachers** (Anatomy; Pedagogy; Psychology; Sociology; Sports)

History: Founded 1942 as Higher Institute of Physical Culture, acquired present status and title 1995.

Governing Bodies: General Assembly; Academic Council

Academic Year: September to June

Admission Requirements: Secondary school certificate (Diploma za zavarsheno sredno obrazovanie), and a year of preparation course in the Language Training Centre

Fees: (Euros): 3,000 per annum

Main Language(s) of Instruction: Bulgarian

International Co-operation: With universities in Germany; France; Belgium; Greece; Finland; Spain; Portugal. Also participates in the Socrates and Erasmus programmes

Accrediting Agencies: National Agency for Evaluation and Accreditation

Degrees and Diplomas: *Bakalavr.* Physical Education; Sports; Kinesitherapy/Physiotherapy (BSc), 4 yrs; *Magistr.* Sports; Kinesitherapy/Physiotherapy (MSc), a further yr; *Doktor.* Physical Education; Sports; Kinesitherapy/Physiotherapy (PhD), 3 yrs full-time, 4 yrs part-time

Student Services: Academic counselling, Canteen, Health services, Language programs, Social counselling, Sports facilities

Student Residential Facilities: Hostels for 1,343 students

Libraries: NSA Library, 128,000 vols

Publications: NSA International Annual Scientific Conference *(annually)*; Sport and Science *(monthly)*

Academic Staff	TOTAL
FOREIGN ONLY	250

Part-time students, 600.
Last Updated: 20/09/11

PRIVATE INSTITUTIONS

AMERICAN UNIVERSITY IN BULGARIA
Amerikanski universitet v Bulgaria (AUBG)
2700 Blagoevgrad
Tel: +359(73) 888-307
Fax: +359(73) 888-344
EMail: president@aubg.bg
Website: http://www.aubg.bg
President: David Huwiler (2007-) EMail: dhuwiler@aubg.bg

Registrar: Tania Markova EMail: tania@aubg.bg

International Relations: Pavlina Pavlova
Tel: +359(73) 885-556, Fax: +359(73) 888-399
EMail: pavlinap@aubg.bg

Centres
Education and Culture *(AUBG Elieff Centre, Sofia)* (European Studies)

Departments
Arts, Languages and Literature (Arts and Humanities; English; Fine Arts; Literature; Modern Languages; Philosophy; Religion; Writing); **Business** (Business Administration); **Computer Science** (Computer Science; Information Technology); **Economics** (Economics); **History and Civilizations** (Anthropology; European Studies; History; Philosophy; Religion); **Journalism and Mass Communication** (Journalism; Mass Communication); **Mathematics and Science** (Mathematics and Computer Science; Natural Sciences); **Political Science and European Studies** (European Studies; International Relations; Political Sciences; Psychology; Sociology)

History: Founded in 1991. First American-style liberal arts institution in Eastern Europe, established as a joint venture between the US and Bulgarian governments, the Open Society Institute and the University of Maine

Governing Bodies: Board of Directors

Academic Year: August to May (August-December; January-May)

Admission Requirements: College Board SAT Examination. TOEFL test (minimum 550)

Fees: (US Dollars): c. 6,800 per annum

Main Language(s) of Instruction: English

International Co-operation: With universities in Germany, Netherlands, Ireland, Greece, Poland, Slovak Republic, Sweden, Spain, France, Austria, Belgium, Hungary, Italy. Also participates in Erasmus and is a member of ISEP.

Accrediting Agencies: New England Association of Schools and Colleges (NEASC); National Agency for Evaluation and Accreditation

Degrees and Diplomas: *Bakalavr.* Business Administration; Economics; Journalism and Mass Communication; Political Science and International Relations; Mathematics; Computer Science; European Studies; European Studies; History and Civilizations; Information Systems (BA), 4 yrs. Executive MBA program (a 16 month program) offered by AUBG's Elieff Center for Education and Culture in Sofia

Student Services: Academic counselling, Canteen, Employment services, Foreign student adviser, Handicapped facilities, Health services, Language programs, Social counselling, Sports facilities

Student Residential Facilities: For c. 885 students

Libraries: c. 101,701 monographs, 1,940 periodical titles, 1,681 CD-Roms, 8,005 microfilm titles, more than 374 music and videocassettes. It is also a World Bank document depository.

Academic Staff *2008-2009*	TOTAL
FULL-TIME	50
PART-TIME	20
STAFF WITH DOCTORATE	
FULL-TIME	40
PART-TIME	c. 10

Student Numbers *2008-2009*	
All (Foreign Included)	c. 1,100
FOREIGN ONLY	300

Last Updated: 19/09/11

BURGAS FREE UNIVERSITY
Burgaski svoboden universitet (BFU)
101 Aleksandrovska Str., 8000 Burgas
Tel: +359(56) 900-501
Fax: +359(56) 813-905
EMail: maria@bfu.bg
Website: http://www.bfu.bg

Rector: Petko Stanokov Chobanov (1996-)
Tel: +359(56) 900-500 EMail: chobanov@bfu.bg

Vice-Rector for Academic Affairs: Milen Baltov
EMail: mbaltov@bfu.bg

International Relations: Galya Hristozova
EMail: hristozova@bfu.bg

Faculties
Business and Management (Accountancy; Business Administration; Finance; Management; Marketing); **Computer Science and Engineering** (Business Computing; Computer Engineering; Computer Networks; Computer Science; Electrical and Electronic Engineering; Industrial Management; Technology); **Humanities** (Bulgarian; English; Journalism; Philology; Primary Education; Public Relations; Social Work) *Dean*: Evelina Dineva; **Legal Studies** (Administrative Law; Civil Law; Commercial Law; Constitutional Law; Criminal Law; European Union Law; Fiscal Law; History of Law; International Law; International Relations; Labour Law; Law; Political Sciences; Public Administration; Public Law)

Further Information: Also Foreign Languages Centre. Centre for Telematics and Information Support. Multimedia Centre for Teaching Foreign Languages. 7 Centres for Further Education

History: Founded 1991 by the Burgas Academic Association. Acquired status of Higher Educational Institution by the Act of the Great National Assembly.

Governing Bodies: General Assembly; Academic Council

Academic Year: October to June (October-January; February-June)

Admission Requirements: Secondary school certificate (diploma za zavarsheno sredno obrazovanie) or recognized foreign equivalent and entrance examination

Fees: (Leva): 620,000 per semester; part-time 500,000; Foreign students, Euro 3,200 per annum

Main Language(s) of Instruction: Bulgarian

International Co-operation: Participates in Tempus S-JEP projects and Socrates/Erasmus programme

Accrediting Agencies: National Agency for Evaluation and Accreditation

Degrees and Diplomas: *Bakalavr*: 4 yrs; *Magistr*: a further 1-2 yrs

Student Services: Academic counselling, Canteen, Cultural centre, Social counselling, Sports facilities

Special Facilities: Radio Club

Libraries: University Library

Publications: Juridical Collection *(biannually)*

Press or Publishing House: University Publishing House
Last Updated: 19/09/11

COLLEGE OF TELECOMMUNICATIONS AND POST - SOFIA

Kolej po telekomunikatsii I pochti-Sofia
1 Akad. Stefan Mladenov Str., 1700 Sofia
Tel: +359(2) 623-021
Fax: +359(2) 623-025
EMail: rector@hctp.acad.bg
Website: http://english.hctp.acad.bg

Rector: Ivan Kurtev
Tel: +359(2) 862-2893, Fax: +359(2) 806-2227

International Relations: Anna Otsetova
Tel: +359(2) 806-2124, Fax: +359(2) 806-2227
EMail: aotsetova@hctp.acad.bg

Departments
Management and Informatics in Telecommunications and Posts (Management; Telecommunications Engineering); **Telecommunication and Computer Science** (Computer Networks; Software Engineering; Telecommunications Engineering); **Telecommunication Technologies** (Computer Networks; Computer Science; Electrical Engineering; Electronic Engineering; English); **Wireless Communications and Broadcasting** (Communication Studies; Computer Engineering; Computer Networks; Information Sciences; Radio and Television Broadcasting)

History: Founded 1922.

Degrees and Diplomas: *Bakalavr*. Also postgraduate studies

Student Services: Sports facilities
Last Updated: 25/11/09

EUROPEAN COLLEGE OF ECONOMICS AND MANAGEMENT

Evropejski kolej po iknomika i upravlenie
18 Zadruga Str., Krim 1, 4004 Plovdiv
Tel: +359(32) 672-362
Fax: +359(32) 677-004
EMail: info@ecem.org
Website: http://www.ecem.org

Rector: Tsvetan Kolev (2008-)

Departments
Administration and Management (Business Administration; Management); **Economics** (Economics); **Foreign Languages** (Modern Languages); **Mathematics and Informatics** (Mathematics and Computer Science)

History: Founded 2001.

Degrees and Diplomas: *Bakalavr*

Libraries: Yes
Last Updated: 05/01/12

EUROPEAN POLYTECHNIC UNIVERSITY

23 "StSt. Kiril and Metodiy" Str, 2300 Pernik
Tel: +359(76) 600-773
EMail: office@epu.bg
Website: http://epu.bg

Rector: Hristo Hristov

Departments
Humanities and Social Sciences (Arts and Humanities; Business Administration; Management)

Schools
Architecture and Civil Engineering (Architecture; Civil Engineering; Construction Engineering); **Engineering and Natural Sciences** (Computer Networks; Computer Science; Energy Engineering; Software Engineering; Telecommunications Engineering)

History: Founded 2010.

Main Language(s) of Instruction: English

Degrees and Diplomas: *Bakalavr, Magistr*
Last Updated: 20/09/11

INTERNATIONAL BUSINESS SCHOOL

14, Gurko Street, 2140 Botevgrad
EMail: ngaydarska@ibsedu.bg
Website: http://www.ibsedu.com

Rector: Ruslan Penchev EMail: rpenchev@ibsedu.bg

Programmes
Accountancy and Control (Accountancy; Finance); **Business Administration** (Business Administration); **International Economics** (International Economics); **Tourism** (Tourism)

History: Founded in 1991 as a Bulgarian-Dutch college of economics and management. Acquired present status and title 2002.

Main Language(s) of Instruction: Bulgarian and English

Degrees and Diplomas: *Bakalavr, Magistr*
Last Updated: 23/09/11

NEW BULGARIAN UNIVERSITY

Nov Bulgarski Universitet (NBU)
21 Montevideo Str., 1618 Sofia
Tel: +359(2) 811-0482
Fax: +359(2) 811-0248
EMail: info@nbu.bg
Website: http://www.nbu.bg

Rector: Ljudmil Gueorgiev
Tel: +359(2) 811-0247, Fax: +359(2) 955-6078

Executive Director: George Tekev
Tel: +359(2) 811-0223, Fax: +359(2) 955-6078
EMail: gtekev@nbu.bg

International Relations: Elena Hazarbasanova, Director
Tel: +359(2) 811-0222, Fax: +359(2) 811-0260
EMail: ehazarbasanova@nbu.bg

Centres

Anthropological and Field Research (Anthropology; Development Studies; Regional Studies; Rural Studies; Social Sciences; Urban Studies); **Assessment** (Advertising and Publicity; Business Administration; Business and Commerce; Ecology; Economics; Environmental Management; International Business; International Economics; Management; Marketing; Private Administration; Secretarial Studies; Small Business); **Cognitive Sciences** *(Central Eastern European)* (Behavioural Sciences; Cognitive Sciences; Social Sciences); **Human Relations** *(Bulgarian)* (Educational Psychology; Family Studies; Humanities and Social Science Education; Social Problems; Social Work); **Public Administration** (Administration; Art Management; Government; Institutional Administration; Management; Public Administration; Social and Community Services; Welfare and Protective Services); **Semiotic Studies** *(South-Eastern European)* (Aesthetics; Ethics; Gender Studies; Linguistics; Logic; Metaphysics; Philosophical Schools; Philosophy; Psycholinguistics; Speech Studies; Writing) *Director.* Maria Popova

Departments

Anthropology (Anthropology; Arts and Humanities; Comparative Religion; East Asian Studies; History of Religion; Social Policy; Social Studies; Sociology); **Archaeology** (Archaeology; Prehistory); **Biomedical Sciences** (Biomedicine; Health Administration; Natural Sciences); **Cinema, Advertising and Show Business** (Advertising and Publicity; Cinema and Television; Film; Graphic Design; Painting and Drawing; Performing Arts; Photography; Video; Visual Arts); **Cognitive Sciences and Psychology** (Clinical Psychology; Cognitive Sciences; Communication Disorders; Communication Studies; Developmental Psychology; Experimental Psychology; Psychoanalysis; Psychology; Social Psychology; Social Sciences); **Design and Architecture** (Architecture; Fashion Design; Glass Art; Interior Design; Textile Design); **Earth and Environment Sciences** (Botany; Crystallography; Earth Sciences; Ecology; Environmental Studies; Geochemistry; Geography; Geology; Geophysics; Marine Biology; Mineralogy; Natural Resources; Seismology; Toxicology); **Economics and Business Administration** (Accountancy; Banking; Business Administration; Business and Commerce; Economic and Finance Policy; Economic History; Economics; Finance; International Economics; Labour and Industrial Relations; Management; Management Systems; Marketing; Statistics; Taxation; Tourism); **Fine Arts** (Art Management; Ceramic Art; Design; Fashion Design; Fine Arts; Painting and Drawing; Sculpture; Textile Design); **Foreign Languages and Literatures** (Adult Education; Arabic; Bulgarian; English; Foreign Languages Education; Foreigners Education; French; German; Italian; Native Language Education; Spanish; Terminology; Translation and Interpretation; Writing); **History** (Central European Studies; Contemporary History; Heritage Preservation; History; History of Societies; Modern History); **History of Culture** (Ancient Civilizations; Art Criticism; Art History; Central European Studies; Cultural Studies; Ethnology; Heritage Preservation; Medieval Studies; Philosophical Schools); **Informatics** (Applied Mathematics; Artificial Intelligence; Business Computing; Computer Engineering; Computer Graphics; Computer Science; Information Management; Information Technology; Medical Technology; Software Engineering; Systems Analysis; Technology); **Law** (Administrative Law; Canon Law; Civil Law; Commercial Law; Comparative Law; Constitutional Law; Criminal Law; European Union Law; Fiscal Law; History of Law; Human Rights; International Law; Justice Administration; Labour Law; Law); **Mass Communication** (Advertising and Publicity; Communication Arts; Information Sciences; Journalism; Mass Communication; Media Studies; Multimedia; Public Relations; Radio and Television Broadcasting); **Mediterranean and Eastern Studies** (Ancient Civilizations; Comparative Religion; History; History of Religion; Jewish Studies; Medieval Studies; Mediterranean Studies; Oriental Studies; Tourism); **Musical Arts** (Conducting; Dance; Folklore; Jazz and Popular Music; Music; Music Education; Music Theory and Composition; Musical Instruments; Musicology; Opera; Performing Arts; Singing); **New Bulgarian Studies** (Bulgarian; Cultural Studies; Linguistics; Literature; Native Language; Slavic Languages); **Philosophy and Sociology** (Philosophy; Sociology); **Political Science** (Comparative Politics; European Studies; International Relations; Political Sciences); **Telecommunications** (Postal Services; Tele-communications Engineering); **Theatre** (Acting; Conducting; Dance; Display and Stage Design; Theatre)

Schools

Basic Education (Education); **Graduate Studies** (Arts and Humanities; Communication Studies; Humanities and Social Science Education); **Management** (Engineering Management; Environmental Management; Hotel Management; Human Resources; Industrial Management; Leadership; Management; Management Systems; Store Management); **Undergraduate Studies** (Arts and Humanities; Communication Studies; Humanities and Social Science Education)

History: Founded 1991. Acquired present status 1991. A private Institution.

Governing Bodies: Board of Trustees; Academic Council

Academic Year: October to July

Admission Requirements: Secondary school certificate (Diploma za zavarsheno sredno obrazovanie) or foreign equivalent, and competitive entrance examination

Fees: (Euros): 2,700 per annum for Bachelor and Master Programmes, (1,500 for citizens from Macedonia and Palestine)

Main Language(s) of Instruction: Bulgarian, English

International Co-operation: With universities in United Kingdom, France, Italy, Spain, Germany, Belgium, Netherlands, Switzerland, Portugal, Austria, Poland, Hungary, Czech Republic, Slovenia, Macedonia, Greece, Romania, Turkey, Finland, Israel, Russian Federation, Estonia, Norway, Sweden, USA and Canada. Also participates in the Tempus, Ceepus, Leonardo da Vinci, Hesp, Socrates, Jean Monnet programmes.

Accrediting Agencies: National Agency for Evaluation and Accreditation

Degrees and Diplomas: *Profesionalen Bakalavr.* 3 yrs; *Bakalavr.* 4 yrs; *Magistr.* a further 1 or 2 yrs; *Doktor (PhD)*: a further 3 yrs by thesis

Student Services: Academic counselling, Canteen, Foreign student adviser, Foreign Studies Centre, Health services, Language programs, Social counselling, Sports facilities

Special Facilities: Internet; 18 Laboratories; 5 Special rooms

Libraries: c. 150 000 vols

Publications: Proceedings 'Archaeology' *(annually)*; Proceedings 'Mass Communication' *(annually)*; 'Sledva', Review *(quarterly)*

Academic Staff 2009	TOTAL
FULL-TIME	400
PART-TIME	1,000
STAFF WITH DOCTORATE	
FULL-TIME	c. 150

Student Numbers 2009	
All (Foreign Included)	c. 12,000
FOREIGN ONLY	100

Part-time students, 1,600. **Distance students,** 1,800.
Last Updated: 20/09/11

UNIVERSITY OF AGRIBUSINESS AND RURAL DEVELOPMENT
Zemedelski kolej
78 Dunav Blvd., 4000 Plovdiv
Tel: +359(32) 650-551
Fax: +359(32) 650-355
EMail: agri_college@mail.bg
Website: http://www.agricollege.com/menu/home1.htm

Rector: Dimitar Dimitrov

Programmes

Agricultural Economics (Agricultural Economics); **Agrotechnologies** (Agriculture; Animal Husbandry; Plant and Crop Protection); **Business Administration** (Business Administration); **Economics of Tourism** (Economics; Tourism); **Horticulture and Wine Production**

History: Founded 1922 as Agricultural College. Acquired present status and title 2011.

Degrees and Diplomas: *Bakalavr*

UNIVERSITY OF LIBRARIAN KNOWLEDGE AND INFORMATION TECHNOLOGY – SOFIA

Spetsializirano vische utchilichte po bibliotekoznanie I informatzionni technologii
119 Tzarigradsko Chausee Bvld., 1784 Sofia
Tel: +359(2) 790-166
Fax: +359(2) 790-081
EMail: unibit@unibit.bg
Website: http://www.unibit.bg

Programmes
Information Technology (Information Technology); **Library Science** (Library Science); **Typographical Communications** (Communication Arts)

Degrees and Diplomas: *Bakalavr, Magistr, Doktor*
Last Updated: 05/01/12

VUZF UNIVERSITY

Vische utchilichte po zastrahovane i finansi
29 Panajot Volov Str., Sofia
EMail: vazov@vuzf.bg
Website: http://www.vuzf.bg

President: Grigorii Vazov

Programmes
Accountancy and Accountancy Analysis (Accountancy); **Euro-economics** (Economics); **Finance** (Finance); **Financial Audit** (Finance); **Insurance and Social Insurance** (Insurance)

History: Founded 2002.

Degrees and Diplomas: *Bakalavr.* 4 yrs; *Magistr*
Last Updated: 05/01/12

Burkina Faso

STRUCTURE OF HIGHER EDUCATION SYSTEM

Description:

Higher education is provided by universities and several higher education institutions, both public and private, the latter since 2004. The universities are autonomous institutions under the jurisdiction of the Ministère des Enseignements secondaire, supérieur et de la Recherche scientifique. In 1996, the Institut universitaire de Technologie, the Institut de Développement rural and the Ecole supérieure d'Informatique were transferred to Bobo-Dioulasso to constitute the Centre universitaire Polytechnique de Bobo-Dioulasso which is now the Université Polytechnique de Bobo-Dioulasso. In 1996-97, the Institut des Sciences de l'Education was transferred to Koudougou and is now called the Université de Koudougou. Several other universities should be created in the near future in the capital city (University of Ouaga II), Fada N'Gourma and Ouahigouya.

Stages of studies:

University level first stage: *Premier cycle*
The first stage of university studies leads to the Diplôme d'Etudes universitaires générales (DEUG) after two years. In Health Sciences, the first stage leads to the premier cycle d'études médicales (PCEM) and, at the Institut universitaire de Technologie, it leads to the Diplôme universitaire de Technologie (DUT). The new Licence, a degree awarded after three years' study, is progressively being introduced.

University level second stage: *Deuxième cycle*
The second stage leads after one year to the Licence. One year after the Licence, the Maîtrise may be obtained in some fields. In Medicine, the second stage lasts for four years. In Engineering, it leads after three years' further study to the Diplôme d'Ingénieur.
The Master, a degree awarded after two years' study after the new Licence is progressively being introduced.

University level third stage: *Troisième cycle*
The third stage leads after one year to the Diplôme d'Etudes supérieures spécialisées (DESS) and to the Diplôme d'Etudes approfondies (DEA), and after two years following the DEA, to the Doctorat de troisième Cycle. After three to five years following the DEA, the Doctorat or the Doctorat d'Etat is conferred in some fields of study. In Medicine, the Doctorat d'Etat en Médecine is awarded after one further year following the four-year second cycle. The new Doctorat, a degree awarded after three to four years' study and research after the Master is progressively being introduced.

ADMISSION TO HIGHER EDUCATION

Admission to university-level studies:

Name of secondary school credential required: Baccalauréat

Entrance exam requirements: From the academic year 2004/2005 onwards, there are no entrance examinations. Applicants' ranking is based on their secondary school grades and their érettségi vizsga (secondary school leaving examination) results or based solely on the latter, considering the interest of the applicant.

Other admission requirements: An aptitude test (e.g. teacher training) or practical examinations (e.g. in arts, sports, etc) is required for some study programmes.

Foreign students admission:

Entrance exam requirements: For admission to courses leading to Alapfokozat (Bachelor degree) or Mesterfokozat (Master degree in one tier long cycle, undivided programme): Foreign students must hold a Secondary School Leaving Certificate or its equivalent (issued after the completion of 12 years of study or eleven years if primary and secondary education comprise eleven years in that particular country and entitles its holder to apply for admission to a higher education institution in the given country). The admission to some programmes can be based on additional aptitude test or practical examination. For admission to courses leading to Mesterfokozat (Master degree): Alapfokozat (Bachelor degree) or its equivalent is required. For admission to doctorate courses: Mesterfokozat (Master degree) or its equivalent is required. Additional requirements for admittance to mesterképzés (Master courses) and doktori képzés (doctorate courses) are determined by the higher education institutions.

Entry regulations: Conditions vary according to relations with the country of origin.

Language requirements: Students must have a good command of French.

RECOGNITION OF STUDIES

Bodies dealing with recognition:

Ministère des Enseignements secondaire, supérieur et de la Recherche scientifique - MESSRS (Ministry of Secondary and Higher Education and Scientific Research)

> BP 7047
> Ouagadougou 03
> Tel: +226 7021 2389
> Fax: +266 5033 2626
> WWW: http://www.messrs.gov.bf

NATIONAL BODIES

Ministère des Enseignements secondaire, supérieur et de la Recherche scientifique - MESSRS (Ministry of Secondary and Higher Education and Scientific Research)

> Minister: Albert Ouédraogo
> BP 7047
> Ouagadougou 03
> Tel: +226 7021 2389
> Fax: +266 5033 2626
> WWW: http://www.messrs.gov.bf

Data for academic year: 2009-2010
Source: IAU from MESSRS Website, 2009. National bodies 2011.

INSTITUTIONS

PUBLIC INSTITUTIONS

INTERNATIONAL CENTRE FOR RESEARCH-DEVELOPMENT OF ANIMAL HUSBANDRY IN SUBHUMID ZONES

Centre international de Recherche-Développement sur l'Elevage en Zone subhumide (CIRDES)
01 BP 454, Bobo-Dioulasso 01
Tel: +226 20-97-20-53
Fax: +226 20-97-23-20
EMail: cirdes@ird.bf
Website: http://www.cirdes.org

Directeur général: Abdoulaye S. Gouro
EMail: dgcirdes@fasonet.bf

Research Units
Animal Husbandry and Environment *(UREEN)* (Animal Husbandry; Biotechnology; Epidemiology; Parasitology); **Animal Production** *(URPAN)* (Animal Husbandry); **Parasitology** *(URBIO)* (Epidemiology; Parasitology)

Degrees and Diplomas: *Diplôme d'Etudes supérieures spécialisées*; *Diplôme d'Etudes approfondies*; *Doctorat de troisième Cycle (PhD)*. Also postgraduate training at MSc and PhD levels
Publications: La Lettre du CIRDES; Rapport d'Activité scientifique *(annually)*
Last Updated: 02/07/09

INTERNATIONAL INSTITUTE FOR WATER AND ENVIRONMENTAL ENGINEERING

Institut international d'Ingénierie de l'Eau et de l'Environnement (2IE)
BP 594, Rue de la Science, Ouagadougou 01
Tel: +226 50-49-28-00
Fax: +226 50-49-28-01
EMail: 2ie@2ie-edu.org; desa@2ie-edu.org
Website: http://www.2ie-edu.org

Directeur Général: Paul Giniès
Tel: +226 50-49-28-14
EMail: pal.ginies@eieretsher.org; dg@2ie-edu.org

Directeur, Administration et Finance: Jacques Muhet
EMail: jacques.andre.muhet@eier.org

International Relations: Abibou Ciss

Programmes
Agricultural Engineering; **Civil Engineering**; **Computer Science**; **Environmental Engineering** (Environmental Engineering); **Hydraulic Engineering** (Hydraulic Engineering); **Industrial and Energy Engineering**; **Sanitary Engineering** (Sanitary Engineering); **Water Management**

Further Information: Branch in Kamboinse.

History: Founded 1968. Acquired present status and title after merger between Ecole inter-Etats d'Ingénieurs de l'Equipement rural and Ecole inter-Etats des Techniciens supérieurs de l'Hydraulique et de l'Equipement rural. Known as Groupe EIER-ETSHER (EIER-ETSHER Group) until 2006.

Main Language(s) of Instruction: French

International Co-operation: With universities in France and Switzerland

Degrees and Diplomas: *Licence*: Civil Engineering; Construction Engineering; Hydraulic Engineering; Water Management, 1 yr; *Diplôme d'Ingénieur*: Engineering; *Doctorat d'Etat*. Also Master and Master spécialisé

Student Services: Academic counselling, Cultural centre, Health services, Social counselling, Sports facilities

Publications: Sud Sciences et Technologie *(biennially)*
Last Updated: 24/08/09

NATIONAL SCHOOL FOR ADMINISTRATION AND MAGISTRACY
Ecole nationale d'Administration et de Magistrature
03 B.P. 7024, Ouagadougou
Tel: +226 50-31-42-64
Fax: +226 50-30-66-11
EMail: enam@cenatrin.bf
Website: http://www.enam.gov.bf

Directeur: Moctar Tall

Programmes
Communication (Communication Studies); **Management** (Management); **National Economy** (Economics); **Political Science** (Political Sciences); **Public Administration** (Public Administration); **Public Finance** (Finance); **Social Sciences** (Social Sciences)

History: Founded 1960.

Main Language(s) of Instruction: French
Last Updated: 27/04/07

POLYTECHNIC UNIVERSITY OF BOBO-DIOULASSO
Université Polytechnique de Bobo-Dioulasso (UPB)
01 B.P. 1091, Bobo-Dioulasso, 01 Houet
Tel: +226 20-98-06-35
Fax: +226 20-97-25-77
EMail: info@univ-bobo.bf
Website: http://www.univ-bobo.bf

Président: George Anicet Ouédraogo (2012-)
Tel: +226 20-97-05-57

Secretary General: Abdoul Rahamane Sawadogo
EMail: abdouraso@yahoo.fr

International Relations: Irenée Somda, Director
Tel: +226 70 28-66-35, Fax: +226 20 98-25-77
EMail: ireneesomda@yahoo.fr

Higher Schools
Computer Science *(ESI)* (Computer Science; Mathematics; Statistics)

Institutes
Exact and Applied Sciences *(ISEA)* (Applied Mathematics; Applied Physics; Mathematics; Physics); **Life and Natural Science** *(ISNV)*; **Medical Science** *(INSSA)*; **Rural Development** *(IDR)* (Agricultural Economics; Agriculture; Animal Husbandry; Forestry; Rural Studies; Social Studies; Sociology); **Technology** *(IUT)*

(Electrical Engineering; Management; Mechanical Engineering; Mechanical Equipment and Maintenance; Secretarial Studies; Technology)

History: Founded 1995 as Centre universitaire polytechnique de Bobo-Dioulasso. Acquired present status 1997.

Academic Year: October to July

Admission Requirements: Secondary school certificate (baccalauréat)

Fees: (CFA Francs): 15,000 per annum; foreign students 200,500 per annum

Main Language(s) of Instruction: French

International Co-operation: With universities in France, Canada, Netherlands, Côte d'Ivoire, Niger, Austria, Sweden, Denmark, Spain

Degrees and Diplomas: *Brevet de Technicien supérieur*: Technology, 2 yrs; *Diplôme universitaire de Technologie*: Business; Commerce; Finance; Accountancy, 2 yrs; *Licence*: Civil Engineering, 3 yrs; *Diplôme d'Ingénieur*: Computer Science; Rural Development; Agronomy; Animal Husbandry; Forestry; Sociology; Rural Economics, 5 yrs; *Diplôme d'Etudes approfondies*: 6 yrs; *Doctorat de troisième Cycle*: Agronomy; Animal Science; Computing; Forestry; Health, 8 yrs

Student Services: Canteen, Health services, Social counselling, Sports facilities

Student Residential Facilities: Yes

Academic Staff *2007-2008*	MEN	WOMEN	TOTAL
FULL-TIME	95	6	101
PART-TIME	169	11	180
STAFF WITH DOCTORATE			
FULL-TIME	2	–	2
PART-TIME	169	11	180
Student Numbers *2007-2008*			
All (Foreign Included)	1,147	441	1,588
FOREIGN ONLY	18	6	24

Last Updated: 07/05/09

UNIVERSITY OF KOUDOUGOU
Université de Koudougou
BP 376, Koudougou
Tel: +226 50-44-01-22
Fax: +226 50-44-01-19
EMail: info@univ-koudougou.bf
Website: http://www.univ-koudougou.bf/

Président: Bila Gérard Segda

Vice-Président: Missa Barro

Secrétaire Général: M. Sompougdou

Institutes
Technology *(IUT)* (Accountancy; Business Administration; Finance; Hotel Management; Secretarial Studies)

Schools
Teacher Training *(ENS)* (Education; Educational Administration; Educational and Student Counselling; Pedagogy; Physical Education; Secondary Education; Teacher Training; Technology Education)

Units
Arts and Humanities (Geography (Human); History; Literature; Psychology); **Economics and Management** (Agricultural Economics; Economics; Environmental Studies; Management)

History: Founded 2005 incorporating the Ecole normale supérieure de Koudougou.

Main Language(s) of Instruction: French

Degrees and Diplomas: *Certificat d'Aptitude au Professorat de l'Enseignement technique*; *Licence*; *Certificat d'Aptitude au Professorat de l'Enseignement secondaire*; *Maîtrise*

Student Numbers *2008-2009*: Total 4,713
Last Updated: 24/08/09

UNIVERSITY OF OUAGA II

Université Ouaga II
BP 417, Ouagadougou 12
EMail: univ_ouaga2@yahoo.fr

Departments
Economics and Management (Economics; Management); **Law and Political Science** (Law; Political Sciences)
History: Founded 2007.

Academic Staff *2008-2009*: Total 291
Student Numbers *2008-2009*: Total 10,719
Last Updated: 31/08/09

UNIVERSITY OF OUAGADOUGOU

Université de Ouagadougou
B.P. 7021, Ouagadougou, 03 Kadiogo
Tel: +226 50 30-70-64/65
Fax: +226 50 30-72-42
EMail: info@univ-ouaga.bf
Website: http://www.univ-ouaga.bf

Président: Jean-Gustave Kabré
Tel: +226 50 30-16-36, Fax: +226 50 30-72-42
EMail: president@univ-ouaga.bf

Faculties
Applied and Exact Sciences (Applied Mathematics; Chemistry; Computer Science; Mathematics; Physics); **Economics and Management** (Agricultural Economics; Business Administration; Economics; Management); **Health Sciences** (Health Sciences; Medical Technology; Medicine; Pharmacy); **Humanities** (Archaeology; Arts and Humanities; Geography (Human); History; Philosophy; Psychology; Sociology); **Languages, Arts, and Communication** (African Studies; Archaeology; Arts and Humanities; Communication Studies; Cultural Studies; English; Fine Arts; German; Journalism; Linguistics; Literature; Modern Languages); **Law and Political Science** (International Law; Law; Political Sciences; Private Law; Public Law); **Life and Earth Sciences** (Biochemistry; Biological and Life Sciences; Earth Sciences; Geology; Microbiology; Physiology; Plant and Crop Protection)

Institutes
Arts and Crafts *(Burkinabe)* (Accountancy; Banking; Business and Commerce; Computer Networks; Finance; Insurance; Secretarial Studies); **Demography** (Demography and Population); **Science**

(Biological and Life Sciences; Earth Sciences; Mathematics; Physics)

History: Founded 1965 as Ecole normale supérieure, became Centre d'Enseignement supérieur 1969. Acquired present title and status 1974. Reorganized 1985, 1991 and 1997. An autonomous institution under the jurisdiction of the Ministry of Education and Culture.

Governing Bodies: Conseil d'Administration; Assemblée; Conseil de l'Université

Academic Year: September to June (September-December; January-March; April-June)

Admission Requirements: Secondary school certificate (baccalauréat) or recognized equivalent and entrance examination

Main Language(s) of Instruction: French

Degrees and Diplomas: *Diplôme d'Etudes universitaires générales*: 2 yrs; *Diplôme universitaire de Technologie*: 2 yrs; *Certificat d'Aptitude au Professorat de l'Enseignement technique*: 3 yrs; *Certificat d'Aptitude au Professorat des Collèges d'Enseignement général*: 3 yrs; *Licence*: 1 yr following DEUG; *Diplôme d'Etudes supérieures spécialisées*: 1 yr following Maîtrise; *Maîtrise*: 1 yr following Licence; *Diplôme d'Etudes approfondies*: 1 yr following Maîtrise; *Doctorat d'Etat en Médecine*: Medicine, 6 yrs; *Doctorat de troisième Cycle*: Chemistry; Linguistics; Mathematics; *Doctorat de troisième Cycle*: Economics, 5 yrs following DEA; *Certificat d'Etudes spécialisées (CES)*: Surgery, 3 yrs following Doctorat d'Etat en Médecine; *Doctorat d'Etat*

Student Services: Canteen, Cultural centre, Health services, Social counselling

Special Facilities: Experimental Fields at Gampela and Leo

Libraries: Central Library, c. 75,000 vols; libraries of the Faculties, c. 25,250 vols

Publications: Annales de l'Ecole supérieure des Lettres et des Sciences humaines *(annually)*; Annales de l'Université (Série A: Sciences humaines et sociales, Série B: Sciences exactes) *(annually)*; Bulletin du Laboratoire universitaire pour la Tradition orale *(quarterly)*; La Revue du CEDRES; Revue Burkinabe de Droit *(biannually)*

Press or Publishing House: Direction des Presses Universitaires (DPU)

Academic Staff *2007-2008*: Total 484
Student Numbers *2007-2008*: Total 30,467
Last Updated: 31/08/09

Burundi

STRUCTURE OF HIGHER EDUCATION SYSTEM

Description:

Public higher education is mainly provided by the Université du Burundi which enjoys administrative and management autonomy. It is administered by a Rector appointed by the President of the Republic for four years. Policy-making is the responsibility of a Governing Board appointed by the President of the Republic and representing the major spheres of activity concerning higher education development. Several private universities exist.

Stages of studies:

University level first stage: *Premier cycle*
The first stage of study for the Licence lasts for two years and leads to the Candidature.
In Medicine, the professional title of Docteur en Médecine is awarded after seven years of study. In Civil Engineering, courses last for five years and four years in Industrial Engineering.

University level second stage: *Second cycle*
A further two years' study beyond the Candidature leads to the Licence.
A Certificat d'Etudes specialisées can follow a degree of Docteur en Médecine. Courses last for 5 years.

University level third stage: *Troisième cycle*
A Diplôme d'Etudes approfondies (DEA) -a research-oriented degree - is conferred in one year following upon the Licence or the Diplôme d'Ingénieur. A Diplôme d'Etudes supérieures spécialisées (DESS) - a profesional-oriented degree - is also conferred in one year following upon the Licence or the Diplôme d'Ingénieur.
A Certificat d'Etudes specialisées can follow a degree of Docteur en Médecine. Courses last for 5 years.

ADMISSION TO HIGHER EDUCATION

Admission to university-level studies:

Name of secondary school credential required: Diplôme de fin des Humanités

Minimum score/requirement: Varies according to year

Alternatives to credentials: An Examen d'Etat is required for the University of Burundi.

Foreign students admission:

Entrance exam requirements: Foreign students must have followed seven years' general education or hold a technician's diploma.

Entry regulations: They must hold a visa and a residence permit.

Language requirements: Good knowledge of French

RECOGNITION OF STUDIES

Bodies dealing with recognition:

Commission Nationale d'Equivalence des Diplômes, Titres Scolaires et Universitaires
PO Box 1990
Bujumbura
Tel: +257 225112/5514

Special provisions for recognition:

Recognition for university level studies: The holder of a foreign credential must submit the following data to the "Commission d'Equivalence des Titres et Diplômes universitaires": curriculum vitae specifying the duration of the training abroad; total number of hours of all the training modules; contents of training programmes; methods of assessment, and a certified copy of the original credential.

For access to advanced studies and research: Same as above.

NATIONAL BODIES

Ministère de l'Enseignement supérieur et de la Recherche scientifique (Ministry of Higher Education and Scientific Research)

Minister: Julien Nimubona

BP 1990

Bujumbura

Fax: +257 22 3755

Role of national body: Central administration and coordination body.

Data for academic year: 2008-2009

Source: IAU from Base Curie, Min. des Affaires étrangères et européennes, France, 2007 and the Country Report on the Development of Education prepared for the International Conference on Education by the Ministry of Education of Burundi, 2008. National body updated 2011.

INSTITUTIONS

PUBLIC INSTITUTIONS

HIGHER INSTITUTE OF BUSINESS ADMINISTRATION

Institut supérieur de Gestion des Entreprises (ISGE)
BP 2450, Bujumbura
Tel: +257(22) 4698 +257(21) 4875
Fax: +257(22) 1785

Directeur général: Damien Karerwa

Programmes
Business Administration (Business Administration)
History: Founded 1987.
Main Language(s) of Instruction: French
Degrees and Diplomas: *Diplôme*. Also Diplôme d'études supérieures spécialisées (DESS)
Last Updated: 02/05/07

UNIVERSITY OF BURUNDI

Université du Burundi
BP 1550, Bujumbura
Tel: +257(22) 0979
Fax: +257(22) 3288
EMail: rectorat@ub.edu.bi
Website: http://www.ub.edu.bi

Président: Alexandre Hatungimana
Tel: +257(21) 9838, Fax: +257(22) 7534 +257(22) 3288
EMail: rectorat@biblio.ub.edu.bi

Faculties
Agronomy (Agronomy); **Applied Sciences** (Applied Chemistry; Applied Mathematics; Applied Physics; Natural Sciences); **Arts and Humanities** (African Languages; Arts and Humanities; English; French; Geography; History; Literature); **Economics and Administration** (Administration; Economics); **Law** (Law); **Medicine** (Medicine); **Psychology and Education** (Education; Psychology); **Science** (Mathematics and Computer Science; Natural Sciences)

Higher Institutes
Agriculture *(Gitega)* (Agriculture); **Commerce** (Business and Commerce); **Technical Studies** (Technology)

Institutes
Pedagogy (Pedagogy); **Physical Education and Sports** (Physical Education; Sports)

History: Founded 1960, incorporating the Institut agronomique du Rwanda-Urundi, previously Faculty of Agriculture of the Université officielle du Congo Belge founded 1958 and the Centre universitaire Rumuri founded 1960. Title of Université officielle de Bujumbura adopted 1964, acquired present title 1977. Largely financed by the State.

Governing Bodies: Conseil d'Administration comprising 15 members, appointed by the President of the Republic

Academic Year: October to July (October-December; January-April; April-July)

Admission Requirements: Secondary school certificate (Certificat d'Humanités complètes) or foreign equivalent

Main Language(s) of Instruction: French

Degrees and Diplomas: *Candidature*: Agriculture; Arts and Humanities; Economics and Social Sciences; Education and Psychology; Law; Medical Sciences; Physical Education; Pure and Applied Sciences, 2 yrs; *Candidature*: Civil Engineering, 3 yrs; *Diplôme*: Commerce; Journalism; Teacher Training, 2 yrs; *Ingénieur industriel*: Agriculture, 3-4 yrs; *Doctorat en Médecine*: Medicine, 6 yrs; *Ingénieur de Conception*: Agronomy; Civil Engineering, 5 yrs; *Licence*: Administration; Arts and Humanities; Economics; Education; Law; Mathematics and Physics; Physical Education; Psychology; Pure and Applied Sciences, 2 yrs following Candidature; *Diplôme d'Etudes approfondies*: Agricultural Planning; Management Systems; Mathematics; Physics; *Diplôme de Spécialité*: Medicine; *Certificat d'Etudes spécialisées*

Student Residential Facilities: Yes

Libraries: c. 100,000 vols

Publications: Revue de l'Université (Séries: Sciences humaines; Sciences exactes, naturelles, et médicales)

Last Updated: 06/08/09

PRIVATE INSTITUTIONS

LIGHT UNIVERSITY OF BUJUMBURA

Université Lumière de Bujumbura (ULBU)
BP 1368, Campus Mutanga Nord, Bujumbura
Tel: +257(22) 235-549
Fax: +257(22) 229-275
EMail: ulbu@cbinf.com
Website: http://www.ulbu.bi

Recteur: Grégoire Njejimana
Tel: +257(22) 236-800 EMail: greg2007njeji@yahoo.com
Vice-Recteur: Charles Kabwigiri Tel: +257(22) 259-001
International Relations: Grégoire Njejimana, Rector

Faculties

Business Administration *Dean*: Josette Ngendakumana; **Communication** (Cinema and Television; Communication Studies); **Computer Science**; **Law** *Dean*: Deo Ntahonkiriye; **Management**; **Theology** (Theology) *Dean*: P. Ntukamazina

Further Information: Also Kinindo Campus

History: Founded 2000.

Governing Bodies: Board of Directors

Academic Year: October to July (October-December; January-March; April-July)

Admission Requirements: High School Diploma

Fees: (Burundi Francs): 255,000

Main Language(s) of Instruction: French, English

International Co-operation: With Laval University, Canada (Distance education mode)

Accrediting Agencies: Ministry of National Education

Degrees and Diplomas: *Licence*: 4 yrs. Also Maitrise and Master

Student Services: Academic counselling, Canteen, Cultural centre, Foreign student adviser, Foreign Studies Centre, Language programs, Social counselling, Sports facilities

Libraries: Yes

Academic Staff 2008-2009	MEN	WOMEN	TOTAL
FULL-TIME	13	3	16
PART-TIME	100	24	124
STAFF WITH DOCTORATE			
FULL-TIME	2	–	2
PART-TIME	26	1	27
Student Numbers 2008-2009			
All (Foreign Included)	1,029	991	2,020
FOREIGN ONLY	87	33	120

Distance students, 40. **Evening students**, 50.
Last Updated: 17/08/09

UNIVERSITY OF LAKE TANGANYIKA

Université du Lac Tanganyika (ULT)
BP 5403, 6, Avenue des Palmiers, Bujumbura
Tel: +257(22) 243-645
Website: http://ult.bi

Recteur: Jean-Baptiste Bahama

Faculties
Applied Economics and Management; **Computer Science** (Computer Science); **Law** (Law); **Political, Social and Administrative Sciences** (Administration; Political Sciences; Social Sciences)

History: Founded 2000.

Degrees and Diplomas: *Licence*
Last Updated: 27/04/07

UNIVERSITY OF NGOZI

Université de Ngozi
BP 137, Ngozi
Tel: +257(30) 2171 +257(24) 1636
Fax: +257(30) 2259 +257(24) 1451
EMail: uningozi@yahoo.fr
Website: http://www.univ-ngozi.org/

Recteur: Apollinaire Bangayimbaga
Tel: +257(92) 5246, Fax: +257(30) 2259

Vice-Recteur: Bonaventure Bangurambona
EMail: bbangur@yahoo.fr

Faculties

Agronomy (Accountancy; Agricultural Economics; Agricultural Equipment; Agricultural Management; Agriculture; Agronomy; Animal Husbandry; Biochemistry; Biology; Botany; Chemistry; Economics; Entomology; Food Technology; Forestry; Genetics; Geography; Geology; Inorganic Chemistry; Limnology; Mathematics; Mechanics; Meteorology; Microbiology; Mineralogy; Physics; Physiology; Sociology; Soil Science; Statistics; Surveying and Mapping; Water Science; Zoology); **Arts and Humanities** (Arts and Humanities; Computer Science; Grammar; Greek (Classical); Latin; Linguistics; Literature; Philosophy; Phonetics; Psychology; Social Sciences; Sociology; Spanish; Swahili; Translation and Interpretation; Writing); **Law, Economics and Administration**; **Mathematics and Computer Science** (Accountancy; Computer Engineering; Computer Networks; Computer Science; Electrical and Electronic Engineering; Physics; Software Engineering; Statistics; Technology; Telecommunications Engineering); **Medicine**

Institutes

Health Sciences (Anaesthesiology; Anatomy; Biochemistry; Cardiology; Cell Biology; Chemistry; Child Care and Development; Dermatology; Dietetics; Endocrinology; English; Epidemiology; French; Gastroenterology; Genetics; Gynaecology and Obstetrics; Haematology; Health Administration; Health Education; Histology; Hygiene; Immunology; Laboratory Techniques; Microbiology; Molecular Biology; Nephrology; Neurology; Nursing; Nutrition; Ophthalmology; Otorhinolaryngology; Paediatrics; Pathology; Pharmacology; Philosophy; Physical Therapy; Physiology; Pneumology; Psychiatry and Mental Health; Psychology; Radiology; Rheumatology; Stomatology)

History: Founded 1999.

Governing Bodies: General Assembly; Board of Directors; Council; Management Committee

Admission Requirements: Secondary school certificate

Fees: (Burundi Francs): 200,000 per annum

Main Language(s) of Instruction: French; English

International Co-operation: With universities in Belgium; Democratic Republic of Congo; Italy; Rwanda; Spain and Uganda

Degrees and Diplomas: *Ingénieur industriel*: Computer Science, 3 yrs; *Doctorat en Médecine*: Medicine, 7 yrs; *Ingénieur de Conception*: Agronomy, 5 yrs; *Licence*: Translation and Interpretation; Economics; Health Sciences; Business and Commerce; Law, 4 yrs

Student Services: Academic counselling, Health services, Social counselling, Sports facilities

Libraries: Yes
Last Updated: 17/02/09

UNIVERSITY OF THE GREAT LAKES

Université des Grands Lacs (UGL)
BP 2310, Bujumbura
Tel: +257(24) 3554
Fax: +257(27) 2020
EMail: webmaster@ult.bi
Website: http://www.ult.bi/

Recteur: Sylvère Suguru
International Relations: Nicodème Niyongabo

Faculties
Administration and Business Management (Administration; Business Administration); **Education**

History: Founded 2000.

Cambodia

STRUCTURE OF HIGHER EDUCATION SYSTEM

Description:

The Ministry of Education, Youth and Sport has overall responsibility for higher education institutions, but some institutions are responsible to other Ministries (Labour, Agriculture, Health, etc). Higher education institutions are either public or private.

Stages of studies:

University level first stage: *Licence, Bachelor's degree*
Studies leading to the Bachelor's degree or equivalent (eg. Licence) last for at least four years. In general, study programmes are divided into two sequences. The first lasts for one year and provides general education (foundation year or common courses) and the last offers specialization or professional education. Students follow their respective course programmes in the first and second sequence and sit for examinations during and at the end of each stage. They graduate when they have successfully passed all examinations. They must also pass a final examination.

University level second stage: *Master*
Masters are awarded after one to two years' study following upon a Bachelor's degree.

University level third stage: *Ph.D.*
Ph.Ds are awarded after three years of study and a thesis following upon a Master's degree.

ADMISSION TO HIGHER EDUCATION

Admission to university-level studies:

Name of secondary school credential required: Certificate of Upper Secondary Education

Name of secondary school credential required: Baccalauréat

Alternatives to credentials: Equivalent to Baccalauréat or Certificate of upper secondary education.

Entrance exam requirements: Grade 12 results are used for selecting students.

Foreign students admission:

Definition of foreign student: Students who are not Cambodian and are studying in Cambodia.

Quotas: Based on MOU with other countries.

Entrance exam requirements: Meet criteria of MOU. Students should have credentials that are equivalent to the Baccalauréat or Certificate of upper secondary education.

Entry regulations: Visa and financial guarantees (supported by Royal Government of Cambodia).

Language requirements: The national language of instruction is Khmer but English is also used in most higher education institutions.

RECOGNITION OF STUDIES

Quality assurance system:

The Accreditation Committee of Cambodia was established by the will of Royal Decree No. NS/RKT/0303/129 dated 31 March 2003 to ensure and improve the quality of higher education institutions in Cambodia and meet international standards through accreditation.

NATIONAL BODIES

Ministry of Education, Youth and Sports

Minister: Im Sethy

80, Preah Norodom Blvd

Phnôm Penh

Tel: +855(23) 217 253

Fax: +855(23) 212 512

WWW: http://www.moeys.gov.kh

Accreditation Committee of Cambodia

Chairman: Sok An

Building of the Office of the Council of Ministers #41,

Russian Federation Blvd

Phnom Penh

Tel: +855(23) 224 620

EMail: info@acc.gov.kh

WWW: http://www.acc.gov.kh/

Data for academic year: 2006-2007

Source: IAU from SEAMEO (http://www.seameo.org/); France diplomatie (http://www.diplomatie.gouv.fr/); and UK Naric (http://www.naric.org.uk/) websites, 2007. Bodies updated in 2011.

INSTITUTIONS

PUBLIC INSTITUTIONS

CAMBODIAN UNIVERSITY OF HEALTH SCIENCES

Sakal Vityalay Vitya Sas Sokha Phibal (UHSC/USSC)

73 Monivong Boulevard, Sangkat Sras Chak, Khan Daun, Phnom Penh

Tel: +855(23) 430-591

Fax: +855(23) 430-186

EMail: uhsc@univ-sante.edu.kh

Website: http://www.univ-sante.edu.kh

Rector: Sophal Oum (2005-)

Tel: +855(23) 430-715 EMail: sophanna@univ-sante.edu.kh

Vice-Rector: Sophanna Youk

Tel: +855(23) 430-715 EMail: sophanna@univ-sante.edu.kh

International Relations: Tharith Seang, Director, International Relations and Cooperation

Tel: +855(23) 430-732 EMail: tharith_seang@univ-sante.edu.kh

Faculties

Dentistry (Dentistry); **Medicine** (Medicine); **Pharmacology** (Pharmacology; Pharmacy)

Schools

Nursing (Nursing)

History: Founded 1946 as School for Medical Officers; became Faculty of Medicine, Pharmacy and Dentistry in 1980. Acquired current status and title 2001.

Governing Bodies: Administrative Board

Admission Requirements: Secondary school certificate (baccalauréat)

Fees: (US Dollars): 850 - 1,200 per annum

Main Language(s) of Instruction: Khmer, French and English

International Co-operation: With universities in France

Accrediting Agencies: Ministry of Education, Youth and Sport

Degrees and Diplomas: *Bachelor's Degree*: Nursing, 4 yrs; *Professional Diploma*: Dental Surgery (BDS), 7 yrs; *Professional Diploma*: Medicine (General) (MD), 8 yrs; *Professional Diploma*: Medicine (Specialist) (MD), 10 yrs; *Professional Diploma*: Pharmacy (DPharm) (Pharmacist), 5 yrs; *Master's Degree*: Public Dental Health; Orthodontics, 10-11 yrs; *PhD's Degree*: Pharmacy, 9 yrs. Also Diploma in Nursing, Midwifery, Medical Lab Technology and Physiotherapy (3 yrs)

Student Services: Canteen, Language programs, Nursery care

Student Residential Facilities: None

Libraries: Four Libraries

Academic Staff 2009-2010	MEN	WOMEN	TOTAL
FULL-TIME	120	76	**196**
PART-TIME	96	72	**168**

Student Numbers 2009-2010			
All (Foreign Included)	3,251	2,928	**6,179**

Last Updated: 11/06/10

CHENLA UNIVERSITY

No.43 St.231, Phnom Penh 12159

Tel: +855(23) 883-269

EMail: info@chenla-edu.org

History: Founded 2007.

Accrediting Agencies: Ministry of Education, Youth and Sport

Degrees and Diplomas: *Bachelor's Degree*; *Master's Degree*

Last Updated: 06/09/10

CITY UNIVERSITY

N° 6A, Yothapol Khemarak Phoumin (St. 271), Phnom Penh 12102

EMail: cu_education@yahoo.com

History: Founded 2005.

Accrediting Agencies: Ministry of Education, Youth and Sport

Degrees and Diplomas: *Bachelor's Degree*; *Master's Degree*

Last Updated: 06/09/10

ECONOMICS AND FINANCE INSTITUTE (EFI)

N° 60 Daun Penh (St. 92), Phnom Penh
Tel: +855(23) 430-556 +855(23) 428-624
Fax: +855(23) 430-168
EMail: efi@camnet.com.kh
Website: http://www.efi.edu.kh

Programmes
Economics (Economics); **Finance** (Finance)

History: Founded 2002.

Accrediting Agencies: Ministry of Economy and Finance

Degrees and Diplomas: *Bachelor's Degree*; *Master's Degree*
Last Updated: 03/09/10

MAHARISHI VEDIC UNIVERSITY

Chea Sim University of Kamchaymear (CSKU)
GPO Box 865, No.152 Norodom Blvd, Phnom Penh 12302
Tel: +855(23) 210-743
Website: http://www.csuk.edu.kh/

Faculties
Agriculture (Agricultural Management; Agriculture; Agronomy; Rural Planning); **Management** (Accountancy; Human Resources; Marketing)

Further Information: Also campuses in Kampong Cham and Prey Veng.

History: Founded 1993 as Sakal Vityalay ved Maharishi (Maharishi Vedic University) by agreement between the Ministry of Education, Youth and Sports and Australian Aid for Cambodia Fund (AACF) to provide education to rural youth. Acquired current title 2008.

Academic Year: October to July (October-March; April-July)

Admission Requirements: Entrance examination

Main Language(s) of Instruction: Khmer

Accrediting Agencies: Ministry of Education, Youth and Sport

Degrees and Diplomas: *Bachelor's Degree*: Management; Agricultural Science, 4 yrs; *Master's Degree*: Business Administration; Agriculture (Economic and Rural Development), further 2 yrs

Student Services: Academic counselling, Employment services, Health services, Social counselling, Sports facilities

Student Residential Facilities: For c. 500 students

Libraries: M.V.U. Library, Kamchai Mear, c. 8,000 vols
Last Updated: 11/06/10

MEAN CHEY UNIVERSITY

No 5 National Road, Sangkat Teuk Thla, Sisophon, Banteay Mean Chey
EMail: info@mcu.edu.kh
Website: http://www.mcu.edu.kh/

Rector: Choeun Tauch

Faculties
Agriculture and Food Processing (Agricultural Engineering; Agriculture; Agronomy; Environmental Management; Environmental Studies; Natural Resources; Veterinary Science); **Business Management** (Accountancy; Banking; Finance; Management; Marketing); **Humanities, Arts and Languages** (English; History; Japanese; Korean; Literature; Native Language; Thai Languages); **Science and Technology** (Biology; Chemistry; Civil Engineering; Electrical Engineering; Information Technology; Mathematics; Physics); **Social Science and Community Development** (Economics; Educational Sciences; Law; Philosophy; Political Sciences; Public Administration; Sociology)

History: Founded 2007.

Accrediting Agencies: Ministry of Education, Youth and Sport

Degrees and Diplomas: *Bachelor's Degree*; *Master's Degree*
Last Updated: 11/06/10

NATIONAL INSTITUTE OF BUSINESS (NIB)

Street 61, Sangkat Wat Phnom, Khan Daun Penh, Phnom Penh 12202
Tel: +855(23) 430-812
Fax: +855(23) 430-810
EMail: nib@nib.edu.kh
Website: http://www.nib.edu.kh/

Programmes
Accounting (Accountancy); **Business Administration** (Business Administration)

Further Information: Traditional and Open Learning Institution

History: Founded 1979 as School of Central Commercial Technique. Acquired present status and title 2001.

Main Language(s) of Instruction: Khmer

Accrediting Agencies: Ministry of Labour and Vocational Training

Degrees and Diplomas: *Bachelor's Degree*: Business Administration; Accountancy; *Master's Degree*: Business Administration. In-Class and E-Learning courses
Last Updated: 03/09/10

NATIONAL TECHNICAL TRAINING INSTITUTE (NTTI)

Russian Boulevard, Sangkat Teukthla, Khan Sen Sok, Phnom Penh 12102
Tel: +855(23) 883-039 +855(12) 669-953
Fax: +855(23) 883-039
EMail: info@ntti.edu.kh
Website: http://www.ntti.edu.kh/

Director: Yok Sothy

Programmes
Engineering (Engineering); **Management** (Management); **Technology** (Construction Engineering; Electrical Engineering; Heating and Refrigeration)

History: Founded 1999.

Accrediting Agencies: Ministry of Labour and Vocational Training

Degrees and Diplomas: *Diplôme universitaire de Technologie (DUT)*: 2 yrs; *Bachelor's Degree*: Civil Engineering; Electrical Engineering; Business Information Technology, 4 yrs; *Master's Degree*: Civil Engineering; Electrical Engineering, a further 2 yrs
Last Updated: 01/06/10

NATIONAL UNIVERSITY OF MANAGEMENT

Sakal Vityalay Cheath Kroup Krorng (NUM)
Corner of Monivong Blvd and Christopher Howes St (St n° 96), Kh. Daun Penh, Phnom Penh
Tel: +855(23) 427-105
Fax: +855(23) 427-105
EMail: num@num.edu.kh
Website: http://num.edu.kh/

Rector: Thong Iv

Vice-Director, Administration, Personnel and Accounting: Sahak Vann EMail: vannsahak@num.edu.kh

International Relations: Buntheoun Seng, Vice-Rector
EMail: s_buthoeun@yahoo.com

Programmes
Accountancy (Accountancy); **Economics** (Economics); **Foreign Languages** (English; Japanese; Korean); **Human Resource Management** (Human Resources); **Information Technology** (Information Technology); **Law** (Law); **Management** (Management); **Marketing** (Marketing); **Tourism** (Tourism)

History: Created 1983 as National Institute of Management. Acquired present status and title 2004.

Governing Bodies: Board of Trustees

Admission Requirements: High School Certificate

Fees: (USD): 4,000 per annum

Main Language(s) of Instruction: Khmer

Accrediting Agencies: Ministry of Education, Youth and Sport

Degrees and Diplomas: *Bachelor's Degree*: Business Administration, 4 yrs; *Master's Degree*: Business Administration; Finance, a further 2 yrs; *PhD's Degree*: Business Administration. Also certificate

Academic Staff *2009-2010*	MEN	WOMEN	TOTAL
FULL-TIME	–	–	82
PART-TIME	–	–	343
STAFF WITH DOCTORATE			
FULL-TIME	–	–	11
PART-TIME	–	–	29
Student Numbers *2009-2010*			
All (Foreign Included)	8,569	6,496	15,065

Last Updated: 01/06/10

PREAH SIHANOUK RAJA BUDDHIST UNIVERSITY

Ministry of Cults and Religions, Preah Sisowath Quay, Sangkat Chey Chum Neas, Khan Daun Penh, Phnom Penh 12206
Tel: +855(23) 722-699 +855(23) 725-099
Fax: +855(23) 725-699

Faculties
Education and Information Technology (Education; Information Technology); **Khmer Literature** (Literature); **Pasi-Sanskrit and Foreign Languages** (Modern Languages; Sanskrit); **Philosophy and Religions** (Philosophy; Religion)

History: Founded 1954. Acquired present status 2006.

Accrediting Agencies: Ministry of Cults and Religions

Degrees and Diplomas: *Bachelor's Degree*; *Master's Degree*
Last Updated: 26/04/11

ROYAL ACADEMY OF CAMBODIA

PO Box 2070, Phnom Penh 12102
Tel: +855(23) 890-180 +855(23) 884-523
Fax: +855(23)221-408 +855(23) 884-523
EMail: hacademy@camnet.com.kh; racademy@camnet.com.kh
Website: http://www.rac.edu.kh/

Institutes
Biology, Medicine and Agriculture (Agriculture; Biology; Dentistry; Ecology; Fishery; Forestry; Medicine; Pharmacy; Water Management; Water Science); **Culture and Fine Arts** (Archaeology; Architecture; Cultural Studies; Fine Arts); **Humanities and Social Sciences** (Anthropology; Business and Commerce; Economics; Education; Ethics; Ethnology; Geography; History; Law; Management; Philosophy; Political Sciences; Psychology; Religion; Sociology; Urban Studies); **National Language** (Linguistics; Literature; Native Language; Translation and Interpretation); **Science and Technology** (Chemistry; Food Technology; Information Technology; Mathematics; Physics; Statistics; Technology)

History: Founded 1999. A research institution.

Accrediting Agencies: Council of Ministers

Degrees and Diplomas: *Master's Degree*; *PhD's Degree*
Last Updated: 06/09/10

ROYAL UNIVERSITY OF AGRICULTURE

Sakal Vityalay Phum Min Kasi Kam (RUA)
PO Box 2696, Dongkor District, Phnom Penh 12401
Tel: +855(23) 219-829
Fax: +855(23) 219-690
EMail: rua@camnet.com.kh
Website: http://www.rua.edu.kh/

Rector: Chan Nareth

Faculties
Agricultural Economics and Rural Development (Agricultural Business; Agricultural Economics; Rural Planning); **Agricultural Technology and Management** (Agricultural Engineering; Agricultural Equipment; Agricultural Management); **Agro-Industry** (Food Science; Harvest Technology); **Agronomy** (Agronomy; Crop Production; Horticulture; Plant and Crop Protection; Soil Science); **Animal Science and Veterinary Science** (Animal Husbandry; Veterinary Science); **Fisheries** (Fishery); **Forestry** (Forestry); **Land Management and Administration** (Farm Management)

History: Founded 1964. Acquired present status 1999.

Governing Bodies: Administration Council; Ministry of Agriculture, Forestry and Fisheries, Ministry of Economy and Finance

Admission Requirements: High School Certificate

Fees: (US Dollars): 370 per annum

Main Language(s) of Instruction: Khmer

International Co-operation: With universities in Thailand, Japan, Vietnam, Indonesia, Singapore, Korea, China, Belgium, Germany, France and Canada

Accrediting Agencies: Ministry of Education, Youth and Sport

Degrees and Diplomas: *Bachelor's Degree*; *Master's Degree*; *PhD's Degree*

Student Residential Facilities: Yes

Libraries: Documentation Centre and library in each faculty

Publications: Agriculture Magazine
Last Updated: 03/09/10

ROYAL UNIVERSITY OF LAW AND ECONOMICS

Mohavityalay Netesas neng Vecheasas sethakech (RULE)
Preah Monivong Boulevard, Phnom Penh
Tel: +855(23) 211-565
Fax: +855(12) 564-094
EMail: rector@rule.edu.kh
Website: http://www.rule.edu.kh

Rector: Ngoy Youk

Departments
Finance and Economics (Economics; Finance); **Public Law** (Public Law)

History: Founded 1948 as National Institute of Law, Politics and Economics. Acquired present status and title 2003.

Accrediting Agencies: Ministry of Education, Youth and Sport

Degrees and Diplomas: *Bachelor's Degree*; *Master's Degree*
Last Updated: 03/09/10

ROYAL UNIVERSITY OF PHNOM PENH

Sakal Vityalay Phoum min Phnom Penh (RUPP)
University Centre, Russian Federation Boulevard Khan Tuol Kork, Phnom Penh 12156
Tel: +855(12) 811-925
Fax: +855(23) 880-116
EMail: secretary@upp.edu.kh
Website: http://www.rupp.edu.kh

President: Lao Chhiv Eav (2005-)

Faculties
Science (Biology; Chemistry; Computer Science; Environmental Studies; Mathematics; Physics); **Social Sciences and Humanities** (Communication Studies; Geography; History; Literature; Media Studies; Philosophy; Psychology; Sociology; Tourism)

Institutes
Foreign Languages (Chinese; English; Foreign Languages Education; French; Japanese; Korean; Thai Languages)

History: Founded 1960 incorporating Faculties established between 1955 and 1959. Present title adopted 1996. A State institution responsible to the Ministry of Education, Youth and Sports. Acquired present status and title 1988.

Governing Bodies: Administration Council

Academic Year: September to June (September-January; February-June)

Admission Requirements: Secondary school certificate (baccalauréat), and entrance examination

Main Language(s) of Instruction: Khmer, French, English

International Co-operation: With universities in Japan, Australia, USA, France, Thailand, Italy, Philippines, Belgium, Germany, China, Republic of Korea, Singapore, Canada, United Kingdom, Indonesia

Accrediting Agencies: Ministry of Education, Youth and Sport

Degrees and Diplomas: *Bachelor's Degree*; *Master's Degree*

Student Services: Health services

Libraries: Hun Sen Library, c. 60,000 vols

Academic Staff *2007-2008*	MEN	WOMEN	**TOTAL**
FULL-TIME	329	144	**473**
Student Numbers *2007-2008*			
All (Foreign Included)	6,850	3,359	**10,209**

Last Updated: 03/09/10

SVAY RIENG UNIVERSITY

National Road N° 1, Chek Commune, Svay Rieng
Tel: +855(44) 395-539 +855(44) 715-776
Fax: +855(44) 715-778
EMail: info@sru.edu.kh
Website: http://www.sru.edu.kh

Rector: Saravuth Tum

Faculties

Agriculture (Agronomy; Rural Planning); **Arts, Humanities and Foreign Languages** (Arts and Humanities; English); **Business Administration**; **Science and Technology** (Computer Science; Mathematics); **Social Sciences** (Public Administration)

History: Founded 2005.

Main Language(s) of Instruction: Khmer and English

Accrediting Agencies: Ministry of Education, Youth and Sport

Degrees and Diplomas: *Bachelor's Degree*: 3-5 yrs; *Master's Degree*: a further 2 yrs

Last Updated: 11/06/10

UNIVERSITY OF BATTAMBANG

National Road No 5, Prek Preah Sdech Commune, Battambang, Battambang
Tel: +855(53) 952-905
Fax: +855(53) 952-905
EMail: info@ubb.edu.kh
Website: http://www.ubb.edu.kh/

Rector: Visalsok Touch

Faculties

Agriculture and Food Processing (Agriculture; Food Science; Food Technology; Veterinary Science; Zoology); **Arts, Humanities and Education** (Arts and Humanities; Cultural Studies; Education); **Business Administration and Tourism**; **Science and Technology** (Civil Engineering; Engineering; Information Technology; Nuclear Engineering); **Sociology and Community Development**

Institutes

Foreign Languages

History: Created 2007.

Accrediting Agencies: Ministry of Education, Youth and Sport

Degrees and Diplomas: *Bachelor's Degree*: 4 yrs; *Master's Degree*: a further 2 yrs

Last Updated: 11/06/10

PRIVATE INSTITUTIONS

ANGKOR UNIVERSITY

Borey Seang Nam, Phum Khna, Khum Chreav, Srok Siem Reap, Siem Reap
Tel: +855(92) 256-086
Fax: +855(63) 760-340
EMail: info@angkor.edu.kh
Website: http://www.angkor.edu.kh/html_english

Rector: Neak Oknha Seang Nam

Programmes

Accountancy and Finance (Accountancy; Finance); **Computer Science and Technology** (Computer Science; Technology); **Education and Manegement** (Educational Administration); **Foreign Languages** (Modern Languages); **Management** (Management); **Marketing** (Marketing); **Tourism and Hospitality** (Tourism)

History: Founded 2004.

Fees: (US Dollars): Undergraduate, 360 per annum; Master programme, 750 per annum

Accrediting Agencies: Ministry of Education, Youth and Sport

Degrees and Diplomas: *Bachelor's Degree*: 4 yrs; *Master's Degree*: 2 yrs

Last Updated: 14/06/10

ASIA EURO UNIVERSITY

Sakal Vityalay Asia Euro (AEU)
832 ABCD, Kampuchea Krom Blvd., Sangkat Teuk Laak I, Khan Toul Kork, Phnom Penh
Tel: +855(17) 797-799 +855(23) 998-124
EMail: info@aeu.edu.kh
Website: http://www.aeu.edu.kh/

Rector: Duong Leang

Faculties

Arts, Humanities and Languages (English); **Business** (Accountancy; Business Administration; Management); **Economics** (Banking; Economics; Finance); **Hotel Management and Tourism** (Hotel Management; Tourism); **Science And Information Technology** (Computer Networks; Computer Science)

History: Founded 2002 as Asia Euro Institute. Acquired present status and title 2005. Former name "Mohavityalay Asia Euro".

Main Language(s) of Instruction: Khmer

Accrediting Agencies: Ministry of Education, Youth and Sport

Degrees and Diplomas: *Bachelor's Degree*; *Master's Degree*. Also Associate Degree.

Last Updated: 03/09/10

BUILD BRIGHT UNIVERSITY (BBU)

Samdech Sothearos (St. 3) Grey building, riverside near Samdech Hun Sen Park, Phnom Penh 12301
Tel: +855(23) 987 700
Fax: +855(23) 987 900
EMail: internationalprogram@bbu.edu.kh; info@bbu.edu.kh
Website: http://www.bbu.edu.kh

President: Diep Seiha

Faculties

Business Management; **Education and Languages** (Modern Languages); **Engineering and Architecture**; **Law and Social Sciences**; **Science and Technology** (Computer Networks; Computer Science; Information Technology); **Tourism and Hospitality**

Further Information: Also study centres in Siem Reap, Sihanouk, Ratanakiri, Battambang, Takeo, Banteay Meanchey, and Stung Treng.

History: Founded 2000.

Accrediting Agencies: Ministry of Education, Youth and Sport

Degrees and Diplomas: *Bachelor's Degree*; *Master's Degree*; *PhD's Degree*

Last Updated: 14/06/10

CAMBODIAN MEKONG UNIVERSITY

Mohavityalay Mekong Kampochea (CMU)
9B, Street 271, Sangkat Tek Thla, Khan Russey Keo, Phnom Penh 12102
Tel: +855(23) 882-211
Fax: +855(12) 809-191
EMail: info@mekong.edu.kh
Website: http://www.mekong.edu.kh/

Chancellor: Ich Seng

Faculties

Arts, Humanities and Foreign Languages (American Studies; Arts and Humanities; Chinese; Education; English; Japanese; Modern Languages); **Economics** (Banking; Economics; Finance; Rural Planning); **Law** (Commercial Law; Law); **Management and Tourism** (Accountancy; Hotel Management; Human Resources; International Business; Management; Marketing; Real Estate; Tourism); **Science and Technology** (Architecture; Civil

Engineering; Computer Science; Technology); **Social Sciences** (Leadership; Management; Social Sciences)

History: Founded 2003.

Main Language(s) of Instruction: Khmer

Accrediting Agencies: Ministry of Education, Youth and Sport

Degrees and Diplomas: *Bachelor's Degree*; *Master's Degree*; *PhD's Degree*
Last Updated: 03/09/10

CAMBODIAN UNIVERSITY FOR SPECIALTIES (CUS)

N° 43 Street 231 Psar Doum Kor, Phnom Penh 12159
Tel: +855(23) 350-828
EMail: info@cus.edu.kh
Website: http://www.cus.edu.kh/

President: Sokhom Sdoueng

Faculties
Arts, Humanities and Linguistics (Educational Administration; Educational Psychology; Educational Sciences; English; Geography; History; Native Language); **Business Administration and Economics** (Accountancy; Advertising and Publicity; Banking; Business Administration; Economics; Finance; Hotel Management; Human Resources; International Business; Management; Marketing; Rural Planning; Tourism); **Engineering** (Civil Engineering; Computer Engineering; Computer Networks; Electrical and Electronic Engineering); **Science and Technology**; **Social Science and Law**; **Tourism and Hospitality**

Further Information: Also campuses in Kampong Cham, Siem Reap and Battambang.

History: Founded 2001.

Fees: (US Dollars): Undergraduate, 450 per annum; Master programmes, 900 per annum; Doctoral programmes, 1,500 per annum.

Accrediting Agencies: Ministry of Education, Youth and Sport

Degrees and Diplomas: *Bachelor's Degree*; *Master's Degree*; *PhD's Degree*
Last Updated: 14/06/10

CHAMROEUN UNIVERSITY OF POLY-TECHNOLOGY (CUP)

88, St. 150, Sangkat Toul Svayprey I, Khan Chamkarmon, Phnom Penh 12308
Tel: +855(23) 987-795
Fax: +855(23) 987-695
EMail: info@cup.edu.kh
Website: http://www.cup.edu.kh/

Rector: Chea Chamroeun

Faculties
Business and Finance; **Foreign Languages**; **Law** (Law)

History: Founded 2002.

Main Language(s) of Instruction: Khmer

International Co-operation: With Bansamjej Chaopraya Rajabhat University (BSRU), Thailand; Edith Cowan University, Australia; London Chamber of Commerce and Industry International (LCCI), United Kingdom

Accrediting Agencies: Ministry of Education, Youth and Sport

Degrees and Diplomas: *Bachelor's Degree*; *Master's Degree*; *PhD's Degree*
Last Updated: 14/06/10

HUMAN RESOURCES UNIVERSITY

Building 2, Street 163, Sangkat Olympic, Khan Chamkamorn, Phnom Penh
Tel: +855(23) 987 826
EMail: info@hru.edu.kh
Website: http://www.hru.edu.kh

Rector: Seng Phally

Faculties
Arts (Fine Arts); **Business Management and Tourism** (Accountancy; Banking; Business Administration; Finance; Management;

Marketing; Tourism); **Human Science and Foreign Languages** (Arts and Humanities; English; Geography; Modern Languages); **Law and Political Science** (Law; Political Sciences); **Science and Technology** (Natural Sciences; Technology); **Sociology and Economics** (Economics; Sociology)

History: Created 2005.

Accrediting Agencies: Ministry of Education, Youth and Sport

Degrees and Diplomas: *Bachelor's Degree*; *Master's Degree*; *PhD's Degree*
Last Updated: 03/09/10

IIC UNIVERSITY OF TECHNOLOGY (IICUT)

Building 650, National Road 2, Sankat Chak Angre Krom, Khan Mean Chey, Phnom Penh
Tel: +855(23) 425-148
Fax: +855(23) 425-149
EMail: info@iic.edu.kh
Website: http://www.iic.edu.kh

Rector: Chan Than Chhuon

Faculties
Arts, Humanities and Linguistics (Chinese; Communication Studies; English; Japanese); **Commerce** (Business and Commerce); **Economics** (Economics); **Mathematics and Science** (Computer Science; Information Technology; Mathematics); **Social Socience** (Political Sciences; Public Administration)

History: Created 2008.

Accrediting Agencies: Ministry of Education, Youth and Sport

Degrees and Diplomas: *Bachelor's Degree*; *Master's Degree*
Last Updated: 03/09/10

INSTITUTE OF TECHNOLOGY OF CAMBODIA
Vitya Satan Bachek Vichea Kampuchea (ITC)

PO Box 86, Pochentong Boulevard, Phnom Penh
Tel: +855(23) 880-370 +855(11) 878-207
Fax: +855(23) 880-369
EMail: info@itc.edu.kh
Website: http://www.itc.edu.kh

Director: Sackona Phoeurng

Director of Administration: San Penh

Departments
Chemical Engineering and Food Technology (Chemical Engineering; Food Technology); **Civil Engineering** (Civil Engineering); **Computer Science** (Computer Science); **Energy and Electrical Engineering** (Electrical Engineering; Energy Engineering); **Mechanical and Industrial Engineering** (Industrial Engineering; Mechanical Engineering); **Rural Engineering** (Agricultural Engineering)

History: Founded 1964.

Main Language(s) of Instruction: Khmer; French; English.

Accrediting Agencies: Ministry of Education, Youth and Sport

Degrees and Diplomas: *Bachelor's Degree*; *Master's Degree*. Also professional degree (Engineer and Higher Technician)
Last Updated: 11/06/10

INTERNATIONAL UNIVERSITY (IU)

Street 1986 & 1011, Sangkat Phnom Penh Thmey, Khan Sen Sok, Phnom Penh 12150
Tel: +855(23) 881-623 +855(17) 926-969
Fax: +855(23) 881-623
EMail: info@iu.edu.kh; iusabo@yahoo.com
Website: http://www.iu.edu.kh/

President: Uon Sabo **EMail:** iusabo@yahoo.com

Faculties
Agriculture and Rural Development (Agronomy; Development Studies; Rural Planning; Veterinary Science); **Business and Economics** (Banking; Business Administration; Finance; Hotel Management; Tourism); **Health Sciences** (Dentistry; Medicine; Midwifery; Nursing; Paediatrics; Pharmacy); **Humanities and Languages**; **Law** (Commercial Law; International Law; Law; Private Law; Public Law); **Nursing Sciences** (Midwifery; Nursing); **Science**

and Technology (Architecture; Civil Engineering; Computer Science; Environmental Management); **Social Sciences and Journalism**

History: Founded 2002.

Main Language(s) of Instruction: Khmer, English

Accrediting Agencies: Ministry of Education, Youth and Sport

Degrees and Diplomas: *Bachelor's Degree*: Civil Engineering; English Literature and Teaching; Educational Sciences; Linguistics; International Law; Commercial Law; Property Law; Private and Public Law; Management; Finance; Accountancy; Marketing; *Master's Degree*: Civil Engineering; Construction Informatics; International Business Management; Hotel Management and Tourism; Finance; Human Resources; International Law; Commercial Law; International Relations and Diplomacy; Educational Administration; English Literature; Public Health; Rural Development; Environmental Management; Political Science; Sociology; *PhD's Degree*: Philosophy; Technology; Science. Also Associate Degree.

Last Updated: 11/06/10

KHEMARAK UNIVERSITY

N° 41 Sang Kreach Tieng (St. 222), Phnom Penh 12301
Tel: +855(23) 223-415
Website: http://www.khemarak.com/

Rector: Sok Touch

Faculties

Agricultural Science and Rural Development (Agriculture; Rural Planning; Rural Studies); **Business Administration and Tourism** (Accountancy; Banking; Business Administration; Finance; Hotel Management; Management; Marketing; Tourism); **Educational Science** (Biology; Chemistry; Educational Administration; English; Geography; History; Literature; Mathematics; Native Language; Philosophy; Physics); **Humanities, Art and Linguistics** (Fine Arts; Linguistics; Psychology; Sociology); **Law and Economic Science** (Economics; Law); **Polictical Science and International Relations** (International Relations; Political Sciences); **Science, Technology and Information Science** (Computer Networks; Computer Science; Information Sciences; Information Technology; Mathematics)

History: Founded 2004.

Main Language(s) of Instruction: Khmer

Accrediting Agencies: Ministry of Education, Youth and Sport

Degrees and Diplomas: *Bachelor's Degree*; *Master's Degree*; *PhD's Degree*

Last Updated: 03/09/10

NORTON UNIVERSITY

Sakal Vityalay Norton (NU)
St. Keo Chinda, Chroy Changva, Reussey Keo, Phnom Penh
Tel: +855(12) 900-222 +855(23) 982-177 +855(23) 982-166
Fax: +855(23) 211-273
EMail: info@norton.edu.kh
Website: http://www.norton-u.com

Rector: Chan Sok Khieng
Tel: +855(23) 824-546, Fax: +855(23) 211-273
EMail: khieng_cvt@norton-u.com

Vice-Rector: Vannthoeun Ung
Tel: +855(12) 949-686 EMail: vannthoeun@gmail.com

Colleges

Arts, Humanities and Languages (English; Translation and Interpretation); **Science** (Architecture; Bridge Engineering; Civil Engineering; Computer Networks; Computer Science; Electrical and Electronic Engineering; Interior Design; Road Engineering; Town Planning); **Social Sciences** (Social Sciences)

Schools

Graduate Studies (Business Administration; English; Information Technology; Management)

Further Information: Also Branch in Phnom Penh (Banana Centre).

History: Founded 1996.

Governing Bodies: Governing Council; Academic Board

Academic Year: October to June (October-January; March-June)

Admission Requirements: Secondary school certificate baccalauréat

Fees: (US Dollars): Engineering, 500 per semester; other courses 480 per semester

Main Language(s) of Instruction: Khmer, English

International Co-operation: With institutions in the Philippines, UK and Thailand.

Accrediting Agencies: Ministry of Education, Youth and Sport

Degrees and Diplomas: *Bachelor's Degree*: Business Administration; Law; Hotel Management and Tourism; Teaching English as a Second Language; Translation and Interpretation; English Communication; Engineering; Architecture; Economics; Computer Science, 4 yrs; *Master's Degree*: Business Administration; Development Management; Information Technology; English

Student Services: Canteen, Language programs

Special Facilities: Movie studio

Libraries: c. 150,000 vols

Publications: Norton's Academic Research *(quarterly)*
Last Updated: 11/06/10

PANNASASTRA UNIVERSITY OF CAMBODIA (PUC)

No.92-94, Sothearos Blvd., Phnom Penh 12207
Tel: +855(23) 990-153
Fax: +855(23) 218-909
EMail: info@puc.edu.kh
Website: http://www.puc.edu.kh/

President: Chea San Chanthan (2004-)

Assistant Director: Chantha Puth EMail: puthchantha@puc.edu.kh

Faculties

Arts, Letters and Humanities (Arts and Humanities; Asian Studies; English); **Business and Economics** (Accountancy; Banking; Business Administration; Economics; Finance; Tourism); **Communication and Media Arts** (Communication Arts; Communication Studies; Journalism; Media Studies); **Education**; **Law and Public Affairs**; **Mathematics, Science and Engineering**; **Social Sciences and International Relations** (Development Studies; International Relations; Peace and Disarmament; Political Sciences; Social Sciences)

Institutes
Foreign Language

History: Founded 1997.

Fees: (US Dollars): 160-1,250 per term

Main Language(s) of Instruction: English

International Co-operation: With universities in USA, Europe, Asia-Pacific Region

Accrediting Agencies: Ministry of Labour and Vocational Training

Degrees and Diplomas: *Bachelor's Degree*; *Master's Degree*; *PhD's Degree*
Last Updated: 11/06/10

PNOMH PENH INTERNATIONAL UNIVERSITY (PPIU)

Building 36, St. 169, Sangkat Veal Vong, Khan 7 Makara, Phnom Penh 12253
Tel: +855(23) 999-908 +855(23) 999-907
EMail: info@ppiu.edu.kh
Website: http://www.ppiu.edu.kh

Rector: Tep Kolap

Faculties

Business; **English, Foreign Languages and Communication Studies** (Communication Studies; English; Foreign Languages Education); **Science and Engineering** (Computer Science; Information Management; Telecommunications Engineering)

History: Founded 2006 as a result of merger of the International Institute of Cambodia and the ASEAN University.

Fees: (US Dollars): Undergraduate, 390 per annum; graduate, 1,000-2,400

Main Language(s) of Instruction: Khmer

Accrediting Agencies: Ministry of Labour and Vocational Training

Degrees and Diplomas: *Bachelor's Degree; Master's Degree; PhD's Degree*

Last Updated: 14/06/10

SETEC UNIVERSITY (SETECU)

92, Russian Blvd, Khan Toul Kork, Phnom Penh 12102
Tel: +855(23) 880-612 +855(12) 395-190
EMail: info@setecu.com
Website: http://www.setecu.com/

Director: Sokveng Ngoun

Faculties
Information Technology (Business Administration; Computer Networks; Data Processing; Information Technology; Management); **Management Systems** (Business Administration; Computer Networks; English; Management Systems; Multimedia; Software Engineering)

Programmes
Design (Design)

History: Founded 2002.

Main Language(s) of Instruction: Khmer

Accrediting Agencies: Ministry of Education, Youth and Sport

Degrees and Diplomas: *Bachelor's Degree*: Management Systems; Business Administration and English; Computer and Local Area Networking; Software Engineering; Website and Multimedia Development; *Master's Degree*: Information Technology; Management; Database Administration; Application Development; Networking Technology. Also Associate Degree.

Last Updated: 11/06/10

UNIVERSITY OF CAMBODIA

P.O. Box 166, 143-145, Preah Norodom Boulevard, Phnom Penh 12000
Tel: +855(23) 993-274 +855(23) 993-275 +855(23) 993-276
Fax: +855(23) 993-284 +855(23) 994940
EMail: info@uc.edu.kh
Website: http://www.uc.edu.kh/

President: Kao Kim Hourn EMail: uc_president@uc.edu.kh

Colleges
Arts and Humanities (American Studies; Asian Studies; Communication Studies; Fine Arts; Journalism; Linguistics; Modern Languages; Performing Arts; Philosophy; Religious Studies); **Education** (Education; Educational Administration; Foreign Languages Education; Pedagogy); **Law** (International Law; Law; Private Law; Public Law); **Management** (Accountancy; Banking; Business Administration; Economics; Finance; Human Resources; International Business; Management; Marketing; Tourism); **Science and Technology** (Computer Science; Electronic Engineering; Information Technology; Technology; Telecommunications Engineering); **Social Sciences** (Development Studies; History; International Relations; Peace and Disarmament; Political Sciences; Public Administration)

History: Founded 2003.

Academic Year: September to September (September-January; February-June; June-September)

Main Language(s) of Instruction: English

Accrediting Agencies: Ministry of Education, Youth and Sports. Accredited by the Accreditation Committee of Cambodia

Degrees and Diplomas: *Bachelor's Degree; Master's Degree; PhD's Degree*

Last Updated: 03/09/10

UNIVERSITY OF MANAGEMENT AND ECONOMICS
Vitya Satan Krap Krang ning Sethakek (IME)

PO Box 303, Battambang, Battambang
Tel: +855(53) 952-160 +855(17) 868-386 +855(12) 723-794
Fax: +855(53) 953-160
EMail: information@ume.edu.kh; umecambodia@gmail.com; chanthy.ume@gmail.com
Website: http://www.ume.edu.kh/

President: Tun Pheakdey EMail: tunume@gamil.com

Schools
Agriculture and Rural Development (Agriculture; Agronomy; Rural Planning; Rural Studies); **Arts, Humanities and Foreign Languages** (English; Translation and Interpretation); **Engineering and Architecture** (Architecture; Engineering); **Law and Economics** (Economics; Law; Private Law; Public Law); **Management and Tourism** (Accountancy; Banking; Finance; Human Resources; International Business; Tourism); **Science and Technology** (Computer Networks; Computer Science; Information Technology)

Further Information: Also campuses in Posat, Kampot, Sihanukville, Kampong Cham and Banteay Meanchey.

History: Founded 2000 as Institute of Management and Economics. Acquired present status and title 2005.

Main Language(s) of Instruction: Khmer

Accrediting Agencies: Ministry of Education, Youth and Sport

Degrees and Diplomas: *Bachelor's Degree; Master's Degree*

Last Updated: 03/09/10

UNIVERSITY OF PUTHISASTRA

#55, St 180, Sangkat Boeung Raing, Khan Daun Penh, Phnom Penh
Tel: +855(23) 220-476 +855(16) 707-855 +855(17) 803-806
EMail: info@puthisastra.edu.kh
Website: http://www.puthisastra.edu.kh

Faculties
Arts and Languages (English; Social Studies; Translation and Interpretation); **Economics and Business** (Banking; Business Administration; Economics; Finance; Management); **Rural Development and Agriculture** (Agricultural Economics; Agriculture; Forestry; Natural Resources; Plant and Crop Protection; Rural Planning; Rural Studies); **Science and Technology** (Computer Science; Information Technology; Technology); **Social Science and Law** (Law; Social Sciences)

History: Created 2007.

Accrediting Agencies: Ministry of Education, Youth and Sport

Degrees and Diplomas: *Bachelor's Degree; Master's Degree*

Last Updated: 03/09/10

UNIVERSITY OF SOUTH EAST ASIA (USEA)

In front of Angkor High School, Siem Reap City
Tel: +855(63) 690-1696 +855(12) 428-889 +855(12) 886-476
EMail: info@usea.edu.kh
Website: http://www.usea.edu.kh/

Rector: Sein Sovanna

Faculties
Agricultural and Rural Development (Agricultural Business; Agricultural Economics; Agricultural Management; Marketing; Rural Planning; Rural Studies); **Economics, Business and Tourism** (Accountancy; Banking; Business Administration; Business and Commerce; Economics; Finance; Hotel Management; International Business; Management; Tourism); **Science and Technology** (Architecture; Civil Engineering; Information Technology; Mathematics); **Social Science and Law** (International Law; International Relations; Law; Political Sciences; Private Law; Public Administration; Public Law)

History: Created 2006.

Accrediting Agencies: Ministry of Education, Youth and Sport

Degrees and Diplomas: *Bachelor's Degree*; *Master's Degree*
Last Updated: 03/09/10

VANDA INSTITUTE OF ACCOUNTING (VIA)

N° 216-218 Mao Tse Toung (St. 245), Phnom Penh 12306
Tel: +855(23) 213-563
EMail: vanda@camnet.com.kh
Website: http://www.vanda.edu.kh/

Director: Vanda Heng

Programmes
Accountancy (Accountancy); **Political Science** (Political Sciences)

History: Founded 2001.

Main Language(s) of Instruction: Khmer

Accrediting Agencies: Ministry of Education, Youth and Sport

Degrees and Diplomas: *Bachelor's Degree*: Accounting; *Master's Degree*: Accounting; Auditing; Political Science
Last Updated: 03/09/10

WESTERN UNIVERSITY (WU)

3, Street 528, Sangkat Boeungkok I, Khan Toul Kork, Phnom Penh
Tel: +855(23) 990-699
Fax: +855(23) 990-699
EMail: info@western.edu.kh
Website: http://www.western.edu.kh/

Principal: Lauren Te

Departments
Business Administration (Business Administration); **Computer Science** (Computer Science); **Economics** (Economics); **Engineering** (Engineering); **English** (English); **Hotel and Tourism** (Hotel Management; Tourism); **Law** (Law); **Public Administration and Policy** (Public Administration)

History: Founded 2003.

Accrediting Agencies: Ministry of Education, Youth and Sport

Degrees and Diplomas: *Bachelor's Degree*; *Master's Degree*; *PhD's Degree*
Last Updated: 14/06/10

Cameroon

STRUCTURE OF HIGHER EDUCATION SYSTEM

Description:

Higher education is mainly provided by universities, specialized institutions and schools. The Minister in charge of higher education takes final policy decisions regarding universities, although each university has a governing council. Councils are responsible for personnel recruitment. The creation of departments, degrees, courses and changes in regulations must receive ministerial consent. Each university receives a budget from the State. The University of Buea is headed by a Vice-Chancellor who is appointed by the government and who, in turn, is chair of the Administrative Council. Other public universities are headed by a Rector. The Presidents of the Administrative Councils of Yaoundé I and II, Dschang, Ngaoundéré, and Douala Universities and the pro-chancellor of Buea University are nominated. Several higher education institutions do not fall directly under the Ministry of Higher Education, but the Minister must ascertain that they meet academic standards. Some are directly run by other Ministries or belong to the private sector.

Stages of studies:

University level first stage: Premier cycle
The Licence or Bachelor's degree are obtained after three years' study.

University level second stage: Deuxième cycle
The Master is conferred after a further two years' study following the Licence/Bachelor's degree. In Medicine, the Diplôme de Docteur en Médecine is conferred after six years.

University level third stage: Troisième cycle
A Diplôme d'Etudes approfondies (DEA) is conferred by the Francophone universities one year after the Maîtrise. A Master's with thesis is conferred by Anglophone universities one year after the Master's degree. A Doctorat or Doctor of Philosophy (PhD) degree is conferred 3 to 5 years after the DEA or the Master's with thesis.

ADMISSION TO HIGHER EDUCATION

Admission to university-level studies:

Name of secondary school credential required: General Certificate of Education Advanced Level

For entry to: Universities

Name of secondary school credential required: Baccalauréat

For entry to: Universities

Entrance exam requirements: Entrance Examination

Foreign students admission:

Definition of foreign student: Non-Cameroonian, non-member of CEMAC (Central African Economic Community).

Entrance exam requirements: Foreign students must hold a Baccalauréat or its equivalent, a scientific Baccalauréat or a General Certificate of Education Advanced Level or the Higher School Certificate and have passed the competitive examination of one of the schools.

Entry regulations: Visa, residence permit

Language requirements: Good knowledge of French or English. Language and orientation courses are offered.

RECOGNITION OF STUDIES

Quality assurance system:

The State is responsible for the higher education policy and its implementation. Private higher education institutions have to be authorized to open, registered to deliver courses and approved to grant national diplomas. Evaluations are compulsory for both public and private institutions.

NATIONAL BODIES

Ministère de l'Enseignement Supérieur (Ministry of Higher Education)
Minister: Jacques Fame Ndongo
B.P. 1739
Yaoundé
Tel: +237 2222 6759
Fax: +237 2222 9724
WWW: http://www.minesup.gov.cm

Data for academic year: 2009-2010
Source: IAU from the Ministry of Higher Education, Yaoundé, updated from the Ministry and Universities websites, 2010. Body, 2011.

INSTITUTIONS

PUBLIC INSTITUTIONS

INSTITUTE OF STATISTICS AND APPLIED ECONOMICS

Institut sous-régional de Statistique et d'Economie appliquée (ISSEA)
BP 294, Yaoundé, Centre
Tel: +237 2222-01-34
Fax: +237 2222-95-21
EMail: isseacemac@yahoo.fr
Website: http://www.issea-cemac.org

Directeur général: Leoncio Feliciano Esono Nze Oyana
EMail: lfesono@hotmail.com

Programmes
Continuing Education and Research in Applied Statistics and Economics *Director:* Robert Ngonthe; **Initial Training in Applied Statistics and Economics** (Economics; Statistics) *Director:* Jean Cleophas Ondo

History: Founded 1961. Acquired present status 1984.

Governing Bodies: Conseil d'Administration; Direction générale et Comité scientifique

Academic Year: October to June

Admission Requirements: First and second cycles, Secondary school leaving certificate with scientific major (Baccalauréat scientifique); 3rd cycle, Licence

Fees: (CFA Francs): Free for citizens from the Communauté Économique et Monétaire de l'Afrique Centrale (CEMAC); 1 m. for others

Main Language(s) of Instruction: French

International Co-operation: With all Statistics Schools of sub-saharian Africa (ENSEA Sénégal, ENSEA-Abidjan) and with institutions from the CEMAC sub-region

Accrediting Agencies: CEMAC Commission

Degrees and Diplomas: *Diplôme de Technicien supérieur:* Statistics and Applied Economics (TSS), 2 yrs; *Diplôme d'Ingénieur de Conception:* Statistics and Applied Economics (IAS), 3 yrs. Also Diploma in Statistics and Economic Engineering (Diplôme d'Ingénieur statisticien économiste - ISE), in 3 yrs

Student Services: Employment services

Student Residential Facilities: Apartments

Special Facilities: 2 Computer Rooms

Libraries: Yes

Academic Staff *2008-2009*	MEN	WOMEN	TOTAL
FULL-TIME	–	–	10
PART-TIME	–	–	50
STAFF WITH DOCTORATE			
FULL-TIME	–	–	3

Student Numbers *2008-2009*			
All (Foreign Included)	243	42	285

Last Updated: 09/06/09

INTERNATIONAL INSTITUTE OF INSURANCE

Institut international des Assurances (IIA)
BP 1575, Yaoundé, Centre
Tel: +237 2220-71-52
Fax: +237 2220-71-51
EMail: iia@cm.refer.org
Website: http://www.iiacameroun.com

Directeur général: Jean Raoul Yovo Dossou
EMail: dg@iiacameroun.com

Directeur administratif et financier: Luc Ze Ndong
EMail: daf@iiacameroun.com

International Relations: Paul Sarr EMail: de@iiacameroun.com

Programmes
Insurance Management and Studies *(International)* (Insurance)

History: Founded 1972. Acquired present status 1992.

Governing Bodies: Conseil d'Administration

Academic Year: December to November

Admission Requirements: DEUG for cycle II, MSTA; Master for cycle III, DESSA

Main Language(s) of Instruction: French

International Co-operation: CAMES; AUF; Association des Etablissements francophones de Formation à l'Assurance (AIEFFA)

Degrees and Diplomas: *Diplôme de Technicien supérieur:* Technology, 2 yrs; *Diplôme d'Etudes supérieures spécialisées (DESS):* Insurance; Management, 2 yrs

Student Services: Canteen, Cultural centre, Foreign student adviser, Health services, Sports facilities

Student Residential Facilities: Yes

Publications: Afrique Assurance, Research in the field of Insurance *(biannually)*

Student Numbers *2008-2009*	MEN	WOMEN	TOTAL
All (Foreign Included)	43	4	47

Last Updated: 10/08/09

NATIONAL ADVANCED SCHOOL OF POST AND TELECOMMUNICATIONS

Ecole nationale supérieure des Postes et Télécommunications (ENSPT)
BP 1186, Yaoundé, Centre
Tel: +237 2222-37-00
Fax: +237 2223-50-05
EMail: info@enspt-yaounde.net
Website: http://www.enspt-yaounde.net

Director: Pierre Tagne Noutouom Tel: +237 2222-37-23

Departments
Communications (Communication Studies); **Electronics, Computer Science and Telematics**; **Financing and Accountancy Services** (Accountancy; Finance); **General Studies**; **Local Networks** (Telecommunications Engineering); **Post Management** (Postal Services); **Technology and Electronics** (Electronic Engineering; Technology); **Telecommunications** (Telecommunications Engineering); **Transmissions and Radio Communications** (Radio and Television Broadcasting)

History: Founded 1969 as Ecole Fédérale des Postes et Télécommunications. Acquired present status and title 1982.

Governing Bodies: Board of Directors; Academic Board; Directorate

Degrees and Diplomas: *Diplôme d'Ingénieur de Conception*
Last Updated: 23/07/09

NATIONAL INSTITUTE OF YOUTH AND SPORT

Institut national de la Jeunesse et des Sports (INJS)
BP 1016, Yaoundé, Centre
EMail: secretariat@injs.org

Directeur: Daniel Ngoa Nguele

Departments
Administration and Management (Administration; Management); **Andragogy**; **Educational Technology**; **Physical Education** (Physical Education); **Psychopedagogy** (Pedagogy; Psychology); **Recreation** (Leisure Studies); **Sports Education** (Sports)

Divisions
Animation Science and Techniques; **Physical and Sport Sciences and Techniques** (Physical Education; Sports); **Specialized Studies**

Research Centres
Adult Education; **High Level Sports** (Sports); **Sports Medicine** (Medicine)

History: Founded 1960.

Main Language(s) of Instruction: French

Degrees and Diplomas: *Diplôme d'Etudes supérieures spécialisées (DESS)*. Also Diplôme de Conseiller Principal de Jeunesse et d'Animation (DCPJA); Diplôme de Conseiller de Jeunesse et d'Animation (DCJA); Certificat d'aptitude au Professorat d'Education Physique et Sportive I (CAPEPS I); Certificat d'aptitude au Professorat d'Education Physique et Sportive II (CAPEPS II)
Last Updated: 06/08/09

NATIONAL SCHOOL OF ADMINISTRATION AND MAGISTRACY

Ecole nationale d'Administration et de Magistrature (ENAM)
BP 7171, Yaoundé, Centre
Tel: +237 2222-13-08
Fax: +237 2222-92-95
Website: http://www.enam.cm

Directeur général: Benoît Ndong Soumhet Tel: +237 2222-91-95

Centres
Research and Documentation (Documentation Techniques; Library Science)

Divisions
Administration (Administration; Labour and Industrial Relations; Social Welfare); **Finance** (Accountancy; Finance; Taxation); **Information and Communications Technology**; **Legal Administration** (Justice Administration)

History: Founded 1959. Acquired present status 1995. Its mission is to train top-ranking civil servants and carry out applied research in order to develop government services and the judiciary.

Governing Bodies: Board of Directors

Admission Requirements: Secondary school certificate (baccalauréat) or equivalent and competitive entrance examination for Brevet; Undergraduate degree for Diploma course; Master's degree in Magistracy for Legal Administration

Fees: (CFA Francs): 120,000 per annum

Main Language(s) of Instruction: French, English

Accrediting Agencies: Ministry of Public Service and Administrative Reform

Degrees and Diplomas: Brevet de l'ENAM (1 yr), Diplôme de l'ENAM (2 yrs)

Student Services: Academic counselling, Canteen, Employment services, Foreign student adviser, Health services, Language programs, Social counselling, Sports facilities

Student Residential Facilities: None

Libraries: Yes

Publications: Journal de l'ENAM *(biannually)*
Last Updated: 10/06/09

NATIONAL SCHOOL OF PUBLIC WORKS

Ecole nationale supérieure des Travaux publics (ENSTP)
BP 510, Yaoundé, Centre 510
Tel: +237 2222-04-06
Fax: +237 2223-09-44
EMail: enstp@iccnet.cm

Directeur: George Nkeng Elambo (2000-)
Tel: +237 2222-18-16, Fax: +237 2222-18-16
EMail: gnkeng@yahoo.com

Directeur Adjoint: Jean-Pierre Mebenga

International Relations: Joseph René Nsegbe, Responsable de la Coopération Tel: +237 9990-99-98
EMail: nsegbe@hotmail.com

Departments
Civil Engineering (Civil Engineering) *Head*: Emmanuel Etonde Sosso; **Management** *Head*: Charles Ekwelgen; **Rural Engineering** *Head*: André Talla; **Surveying** *Head*: Georges Tchikou Tchuisseu; **Town Planning Engineering** *Head*: Alice Matcheubou

History: Founded 1984.

Academic Year: September to June

Admission Requirements: Secondary school certificate (GCE Advanced Level)

Fees: (CFA Francs): 235,000 per annum

Main Language(s) of Instruction: French, English

International Co-operation: With institutions in France and USA

Accrediting Agencies: Ministère des Travaux Publics

Degrees and Diplomas: Diplôme d'Ingénieur des Travaux: Civil Engineering; Rural Engineering; Surveying; Town Planning (3 yrs); Diplôme d'Ingénieur Manager (2 yrs)

Student Services: Academic counselling, Health services, Language programs, Social counselling, Sports facilities

Student Residential Facilities: None

Libraries: Yes

Academic Staff *2008-2009*	MEN	WOMEN	TOTAL
FULL-TIME	–	–	70
STAFF WITH DOCTORATE			
FULL-TIME	–	–	5
PART-TIME	–	–	2
Student Numbers *2008-2009*			
All (Foreign Included)	822	148	970
FOREIGN ONLY	28	2	30

Last Updated: 09/06/09

UNIVERSITY OF BUEA
Université de Buéa (UB)
PO Box 63, Buéa, South West Province
Tel: +237 3332-21-34
Fax: +237 3332-22-72
Website: http://www.ub.cm

Vice-Chancellor: Vincent Titanji Tel: +237 3332-27-06

Registrar: Samson Abangma

International Relations: Victor Julius Ngoh, Deputy Vice-Chancellor, Research and Cooperation

Faculties
Arts (English; French; History; Linguistics; Performing Arts) *Dean*: Albert Azeye; **Education** (Curriculum; Education; Educational Administration; Educational Psychology) *Dean*: André Mvesso; **Health Sciences** (Health Sciences; Laboratory Techniques; Medicine; Nursing; Surgery) *Dean*: Peter Ndoumbe; **Science** (Biochemistry; Botany; Chemistry; Environmental Studies; Geology; Mathematics; Microbiology; Physics; Zoology) *Dean*: Theresa Akenji; **Social and Management Sciences** (Accountancy; Anthropology; Banking; Economics; Finance; Gender Studies; Geography; Journalism; Law; Management; Mass Communication; Political Sciences; Sociology; Women's Studies) *Dean*: Martha Tumnde

Schools
Translation and Interpretation (Translation and Interpretation) *Director*: Emmanuel Chia

History: Founded 1985 as University Centre of Buea. Acquired present status and title 1993.

Governing Bodies: Council, comprising 26 members; Senate; Congregation

Academic Year: October to July (October-February; March-July)

Admission Requirements: Secondary school certificate and competitive entrance examination. Bachelor's Degree or recognized equivalent for School of Translation and Interpretation

Fees: (CFA Francs): Nationals, 50,000; Foreign students, 300,000-1m. per annum

Main Language(s) of Instruction: English

International Co-operation: With universities in USA; United Kingdom; Canada and France

Degrees and Diplomas: *Bachelor's Degree*: Arts (BA); Law (LLB); Science (BSc), 3 yrs; *Bachelor's Degree*: Medicine; Surgery (MBBS), 6 yrs; *Bachelor's Degree*: Women and Gender Studies; Medical Laboratory Science; Nursing (BSc), 4 yrs; *Master*: Arts; Science (MA; MSc), a further 2 yrs; *Postgraduate Diploma*: Education; Women and Gender Studies; Interpretation, 1 yr; *Doctorat/ Doctor of Philosophy*: 3-5 yrs

Student Services: Academic counselling, Canteen, Foreign student adviser, Health services, Language programs, Social counselling, Sports facilities

Student Residential Facilities: Yes (110 rooms)

Special Facilities: Language Laboratory; Interpretation Laboratory; Journalism Multimedia Centre; CISCO Network Academy; Information Technology Centre

Libraries: University of Buéa Library, c. 60,000 vols

Publications: Epasa Moto, Bilingual Journal of Language, Letters and Culture *(annually)*; Journal of Applied Social Sciences *(biannually)*

Academic Staff *2007-2008*	MEN	WOMEN	TOTAL
FULL-TIME	190	60	**250**
STAFF WITH DOCTORATE FULL-TIME	–	–	c. **140**
Student Numbers *2007-2008*			
All (Foreign Included)	4,870	5,050	c. **9,920**

Last Updated: 08/06/09

UNIVERSITY OF DOUALA
Université de Douala (UDLA)
BP 2701, Douala, Littoral
Tel: +237 3340-64-15
Fax: +237 3340-64-15
EMail: ud@univ-douala.com
Website: http://www.univ-douala.com

Recteur: Bruno Bekolo Ebé (2003-)
Tel: +237 3340-11-26, Fax: +237 3340-11-26
EMail: brunobekolo@univ-douala.com

Secrétaire général: Rémy Sylvestre Bouelet Ivaha Mbembe
Tel: +237 3340-58-62 EMail: remysylvestrebouelet@yahoo.fr

International Relations: Nicole C. Ndoko, Vice-Recteur, Recherche et Coopération
Tel: +237 3340-11-19, Fax: +237 3340-11-19
EMail: nicoleclaire_ndoko@yahoo.fr

Faculties
Arts and Humanities *(FLSH)* (African Languages; African Studies; Arts and Humanities; Bilingual and Bicultural Education; English; French; German; History; Literature; Philosophy; Spanish); **Economics and Applied Management** *(FSEGA)* (Econometrics; Economic and Finance Policy; Economics; Finance; Management; Marketing; Mathematics); **Industrial Engineering**; **Law and Political Science** *(FSJP)* (Law; Political Sciences; Private Law; Public Law); **Medicine and Pharmacy** (Biochemistry; Biology; Medicine; Pharmacy; Sports); **Science** *(FS)* (Biology; Chemistry; Computer Science; Mathematics; Natural Sciences; Physics)

Institutes
Technology *(IUT)* (Accountancy; Biology; Business Administration; Business and Commerce; Civil Engineering; Computer Science; Electrical and Electronic Engineering; Industrial Engineering; Secretarial Studies; Telecommunications Engineering)

Schools
Economics and Commerce *(ESSEC, Advanced Studies)*; **Teacher Training in Technical Education** *(ENSET, Advanced Studies)*

History: Founded 1977 as Centre Universitaire. Previously part of the University of Yaoundé. Acquired present status and title 1993.

Governing Bodies: Conseil d'Administration

Academic Year: October to July (October-December; January-March; April-July)

Admission Requirements: Competitive entrance examination following secondary school certificate (baccalauréat)

Fees: (CFA Francs): c. 50,000 per annnum; foreign students, c. 300,000-1m.

Main Language(s) of Instruction: French, English

Degrees and Diplomas: *Licence*; *Diplôme de Docteur*: Medicine; Pharmacy; *Master*; *Doctorat/Doctor of Philosophy*: Bioengineering; Physics; Economics; Administration; English; Spanish; German; French; African Languages; History; Geography; Comparative Literature; Philosophy; Sociology; Communication Studies; Industrial Engineering; Private Law; Public Law; Political Sciences

Student Services: Academic counselling, Canteen, Cultural centre, Health services, Social counselling, Sports facilities

Student Residential Facilities: Yes

Libraries: Central Library, c. 5,600 vols; libraries of the schools, c. 4,000

Last Updated: 02/06/09

UNIVERSITY OF DSCHANG
Université de Dschang (UDS)
BP 96, Dschang, West
Tel: +237 345-13-81
Fax: +237 345-13-81
EMail: udsrectorat@univ-dschang.com
Website: http://www.univ-dschang.org

Recteur: Anaclet Fomethe (2005-)

Secrétaire général: Marthe-Isabelle Atangana Abolo

International Relations: Ajaga Nji, Vice-Recteur, Recherche et Cooperation

Centres
Audiovisual (Cinema and Television)

Faculties
Agronomy and Agricultural Sciences *(FASA)* (Agricultural Engineering; Agriculture; Animal Husbandry; Biotechnology; Forestry; Rural Studies; Soil Science; Veterinary Science; Water Manage-

ment; Water Science); **Arts and Humanities** *(FLSH)* (African Studies; Arts and Humanities; French; Geography (Human); German; History; Italian; Linguistics; Philosophy; Psychology; Sociology; Spanish); **Economics and Management** *(FSEG)* (Agricultural Business; Economic and Finance Policy; Economics; Management); **Law and Political Science** *(FSJP)* (Human Rights; Law; Political Sciences; Private Law; Public Law) **Science** *(FS)* (Biochemistry; Chemistry; Earth Sciences; Geology; Mathematics and Computer Science; Natural Sciences; Physics)

Institutes

Fine Arts *(Foumban)*; **Technology** *(IUT Fotso Victor)* (Business and Commerce; Civil Engineering; Computer Engineering; Electrical and Electronic Engineering; Secretarial Studies; Technology)

History: Founded 1977 as Centre Universitaire. Previously part of the University of Yaoundé. Acquired present status and title 1993.

Governing Bodies: University Council

Academic Year: October to July (October-March; March-July)

Admission Requirements: Secondary school certificate (baccalauréat), or foreign equivalent at Advanced 'A' level. General Certificate of Education

Fees: (CFA Francs): Foreign students, 500,000-1m. per annum

Main Language(s) of Instruction: French, English

Accrediting Agencies: Ministry of Higher Education

Degrees and Diplomas: *Diplôme de Technicien supérieur:* Agriculture, 3 yrs; *Licence:* 3 yrs; *Diplôme d'Ingénieur de Conception:* Agronomy, 5 yrs; *Diplôme d'Etudes supérieures spécialisées (DESS):* Human Rights, a further 4 yrs; *Master:* Law; Literature; Science; Economics; *Diplôme d'Etudes approfondies (DEA):* a further 4 yrs; *Doctorat/Doctor of Philosophy:* Agronomy

Student Services: Academic counselling, Canteen, Cultural centre, Employment services, Handicapped facilities, Health services, Language programs, Sports facilities

Student Residential Facilities: For 2,000 students

Special Facilities: Computer Centre. Welfare Centre. Multimedia Centre

Libraries: Central Library, c. 50,000 vols

Publications: Jeune Afrique Economique *(monthly)*; Le Flamboyant *(monthly)*

Last Updated: 06/08/09

UNIVERSITY OF NGAOUNDÉRÉ
Université de Ngaoundéré (UNDERE)
BP 454, Ngaoundéré, Adamaoua
Tel: +237 2225-27-65
Fax: +237 2225-27-51

Recteur: Paul Henri Amvam Zollo (2003-)

Faculties

Arts and Humanities *(FALSH)* (African Studies; Anthropology; Arts and Humanities; Cultural Studies; Demography and Population; Development Studies; Environmental Studies; Geography (Human); History; International Relations; Literature; Modern Languages; Museum Studies; Psychology; Regional Planning; Social Sciences; Social Studies; Sociology; Tourism; Town Planning; Translation and Interpretation); **Economics and Management** *(FSEG)* (Accountancy; Banking; Economics; Finance; Human Resources; Insurance; International Economics; Management; Marketing); **Education** (Education); **Law and Political Science** *(FSJP)* (Commercial Law; Economic and Finance Policy; Finance; International Law; International Relations; Law; Political Sciences; Private Law; Public Law); **Science** *(FS)* (Biological and Life Sciences; Biology; Biomedicine; Chemistry; Civil Engineering; Earth Sciences; Electrical Engineering; Environmental Studies; Food Science; Geology; Mathematics and Computer Science; Mechanical Engineering; Medicine; Mining Engineering; Natural Sciences; Nutrition; Pharmacy; Physics)

Institutes

Technology *(IUT)* (Computer Science; Electrical and Electronic Engineering; Food Technology; Heating and Refrigeration; Maintenance Technology; Mechanical Engineering; Technology)

Schools

Agro-Industry *(ESAI)* (Agronomy; Food Science; Food Technology; Industrial Chemistry; Nutrition); **Chemical Engineering and**

Mineral Processing (Chemical Engineering; Materials Engineering); **Geology and Mining Prospecting** (Geology; Mining Engineering; Petroleum and Gas Engineering); **Veterinary Medicine and Animal Science** (Anatomy; Animal Husbandry; Histology; Microbiology; Parasitology; Pathology; Pharmacy; Physiology; Veterinary Science)

History: Founded 1982 as Centre Universitaire, acquired present status and title 1993. A State Institution.

Governing Bodies: Conseil de l'Université; Conseil d'Administration

Academic Year: October to July (October-February; March-July)

Admission Requirements: Secondary school certificate (baccalauréat), or foreign equivalent at Advanced ('A') level

Fees: (CFA Francs): Foreign students, undergraduate, 300,000-600,000 per annum; postgraduate, 3m.-5m.

Main Language(s) of Instruction: French, English

International Co-operation: With universities in Belgium, Chad, France, Germany, Norway and United Kingdom

Degrees and Diplomas: *Diplôme universitaire de Technologie (DUT):* Technology; Food Technology, 2 yrs; *Licence:* 3 yrs; *Diplôme d'Ingénieur de Conception:* Agroindustrial Sciences; *Diplôme d'Ingénieur de Conception:* Food Technology, 5 yrs; *Master:* 2 yrs; *Diplôme d'Etudes approfondies (DEA):* Management; Food Science; Geography; Process Engineering; Arts and Humanities, a further yr following Maîtrise; *Doctorat/Doctor of Philosophy:* Management; Food Science; Geography; Process Engineering; Arts and Humanities, 3-5 yrs

Student Services: Academic counselling, Canteen, Health services, Social counselling, Sports facilities

Student Residential Facilities: Yes

Libraries: Total, c. 50,000 vols

Publications: Annales de la FALSH, Arts and Humanities, Social Sciences *(biennially)*

Last Updated: 18/02/09

UNIVERSITY OF YAOUNDÉ I
Université de Yaoundé I (UY I)
BP 337, Yaoundé, Centre
Tel: +237 2222-07-44
Fax: +237 2222-13-20
EMail: uy.cdc@uninet.cm
Website: http://www.uy1.uninet.cm/

Recteur: Oumarou Bouba

Secrétaire général: Jean-Emmanuel Pondi
Tel: +237 2222-15-23, Fax: +237 2222-05-34

International Relations: Guy Tsala Ndzomo, Vice-Recteur, Recherche et Coopération
Tel: +237 2222-12-60, Fax: +237 2222-12-60
EMail: tako640@yahoo.ca

Centres
Biotechnology; **Information Technology**

Faculties

Arts, Letters and Humanities *(FALSH)* (African Languages; African Studies; Anthropology; Archaeology; Art History; Arts and Humanities; English; Fine Arts; Foreign Languages Education; French; Geography (Human); German; History; Italian; Performing Arts; Philosophy; Psychology; Sociology; Spanish; Tourism); **Medicine and Biomedical Studies** *(FSMB)* (Anaesthesiology; Anatomy; Behavioural Sciences; Biochemistry; Biology; Biomedicine; Botany; Cardiology; Dentistry; Dermatology; Embryology and Reproduction Biology; Endocrinology; Environmental Studies; Epidemiology; Gastroenterology; Gynaecology and Obstetrics; Haematology; Health Education; Medical Technology; Medicine; Microbiology; Nephrology; Nutrition; Ophthalmology; Otorhinolaryngology; Paediatrics; Parasitology; Pathology; Pharmacology; Pharmacy; Physiology; Pneumology; Psychiatry and Mental Health; Public Health; Radiology; Surgery; Venereology; Virology); **Science** *(FS)* (Applied Chemistry; Applied Physics; Biochemistry; Biology; Botany; Computer Science; Earth Sciences; Ecology; Geology; Inorganic Chemistry; Mathematics; Multimedia; Natural Sciences; Organic Chemistry; Parasitology; Petrology; Physics; Physiology; Seismology; Statistics; Zoology)

Schools

Polytechnic *(Ecole Nationale Supérieure Polytechnique (ENSP))* (Chemistry; Civil Engineering; Computer Engineering; Electrical Engineering; Engineering; Industrial Engineering; Mathematics; Mechanical Engineering; Physics; Technology; Telecommunications Engineering; Urban Studies); **Teacher Training** *(Ecole normale supérieure (ENS))* (Biology; Chemistry; Education; Educational Sciences; English; Foreign Languages Education; French; Geography; History; Mathematics Education; Philosophy; Physics; Secondary Education; Teacher Training)

History: Founded 1962, replacing the Institut national d'Etudes supérieures, founded 1961. Acquired present status and title 1993. A State institution responsible to the Ministry of Education.

Governing Bodies: Conseil de l'Université; Conseil d'Administration presided over by the Rector (Senate and Council).

Academic Year: October to August (October-February; March-August)

Admission Requirements: Secondary school certificate (baccalauréat) or foreign equivalent, and entrance examination (for Medicine and Engineering)

Fees: (CFA Francs): 50,000 per annum; foreign students, 600,000 per annum for Science and Technology; 300,000 for foreign students in Arts and Education

Main Language(s) of Instruction: French, English

International Co-operation: Participates in the Fulbright Grant programme

Degrees and Diplomas: *Licence*: Economics; Law; Letters; Letters (BA); Science; Science (BSc), 3 yrs; *Diplôme de Docteur*: Medicine (BM; BS), 6-7 yrs; *Diplôme d'Ingénieur de Conception*: Engineering (Dip.Ing), 5 yrs; *Master (MA; MSc)*: a further 2 yrs; *Doctorat/Doctor of Philosophy*: a further 2-3 yrs

Student Services: Academic counselling, Canteen, Employment services, Health services, Language programs, Social counselling, Sports facilities

Student Residential Facilities: Yes

Libraries: Central Library, c. 90,000 vols

Publications: Annales des Facultés *(annually)*; Revue Ecriture; Sosongo
Last Updated: 07/08/09

UNIVERSITY OF YAOUNDÉ II
Université de Yaoundé II (UY II)
BP 1365, Yaoundé, Centre
Tel: +237 2220-11-54
Fax: +237 7799-14-23
EMail: contact@universite-yde2.org
Website: http://www.universite-yde2.org/

Recteur: Jean Tabi Manga (2003-)

Secrétaire générale: Lisette Elomo Ntonga

International Relations: Georges E. Ekodeck

Faculties
Economics and Management *(FSEG)* (Economics; Management); **Law and Political Science** *(FSJP)* (Law; Political Sciences)

Higher Schools
Information and Communication Technologies *(ESSTIC)* (Information Sciences; Journalism; Mass Communication; Radio and Television Broadcasting)

Institutes
Demographic Training and Research *(IFORD)* (Demography and Population); **International Relations** *(IRIC)* (Banking; Finance; International Relations; Marketing)

Further Information: Also campus in Soa

History: Founded 1993.

Academic Year: October to July (October-December; January-March; April-July)

Admission Requirements: Secondary school certificate (baccalauréat) or foreign equivalent, and entrance examination

Main Language(s) of Instruction: French, English

Degrees and Diplomas: *Diplôme de Technicien supérieur*. Information, 2 yrs; *Diplôme de Technicien supérieur*. Journalism, 3 yrs; *Licence*: Economics; Law, 3 yrs; *Diplôme d'Etudes supérieures spécialisées (DESS)*; *Master*. Economics, a further 2 yrs; *Master*. International Relations; Political Science; *Master*. Law, a further 2 yr; *Diplôme d'Etudes approfondies (DEA)*; *Doctorat/Doctor of Philosophy*: International Relations, 4 yrs; *Doctorat/Doctor of Philosophy*: Law; Science, 2-4 yrs following Maîtrise

Libraries: Bibliothèque de l'Université
Last Updated: 24/07/09

PRIVATE INSTITUTIONS

ADVANCED INSTITUTE OF MANAGEMENT
Institut supérieur de Management (ISMA)
BP 5739, Douala, Littoral
Tel: +237 3343-12-51
Fax: +237 3343-12-59
EMail: isma@globalnet.com

Programmes
Commerce (Business and Commerce); **Management** (Management)

Degrees and Diplomas: *Brevet de Technicien Supérieur*; *Master*
Last Updated: 27/04/07

CATHOLIC UNIVERSITY OF CENTRAL AFRICA
Université catholique d'Afrique centrale (UCAC)
BP 11628, Yaoundé, Centre 11628
Tel: +237 2223-74-00
Fax: +237 2223-74-02
EMail: ucac.icy-nk@camnet.cm
Website: http://www.apdhac.org/ucac.html

Recteur: Christian Mofor (2005-)
Tel: +237 2223-74-01
EMail: recteuruca@camnet.cm; recteur@uca.ac

International Relations: Gilles Noudjag

Departments
Canon Law (Canon Law); **Philosophy** (Philosophy) *Dean*: Gabriel Ndinga

Faculties
Social Sciences and Management (Accountancy; Computer Science; Economics; Law; Management; Political Sciences; Social Sciences) *Dean*: Louis De Vaocelles; **Theology** (Theology) *Dean*: Antoine Babe

Higher Institutes
Technology *(IST/Pointe-Noire (Congo))* (Industrial Maintenance)

Research Groups
Artificial Intelligence and Management Sciences *(GRIAGES)* (Artificial Intelligence; Management) *Director*: Philippe Dubin; **Business and Culture** *(GREC)* (Business Administration; Cultural Studies) *Director*: Philippe Dubin

Schools
Nursing (Nursing)

History: Founded 1989, opened 1991.

Governing Bodies: Administrative Council; Private Council; Permanent Council; Academic Council

Academic Year: October to June (October-February; March-June)

Admission Requirements: Secondary school certificate (baccalauréat), or foreign equivalent

Fees: (CFA Francs): 365,000-825,000 per annum

Main Language(s) of Instruction: French

International Co-operation: With universities in France and Canada

Degrees and Diplomas: *Brevet de Technicien Supérieur*. Industrial Maintenance, 2 yrs; *Diplôme universitaire de Technologie (DUT)*: Management; Commerce; Marketing and Sales, 2 yrs; *Licence*: Management; Commerce; Marketing and Sales;

Socio-Anthropology; Political Science and Law; Human Resource Management; Business Administration (LEG, LICOD, LSS, LiPADE), 3 yrs; *Licence*: Philosophy; *Diplôme d'Ingénieur de Conception*: Industrial Maintenance, 5 yrs; *Master*. Finance and Accountancy, Commerce, Marketing and Sales, Human Rights and Humanitarian Action; Theology; Canon Law, 5 yrs; *Master*. Management; Social Anthropology; Political Science and Law; Human Resource Management; *Diplôme d'Etudes approfondies (DEA)*: Theology, 6 yrs; *Doctorat/Doctor of Philosophy*. Also Diplôme d'Etudes universitaires en Sciences infirmières (3 yrs), Master

Student Services: Academic counselling, Canteen, Foreign student adviser, Health services, Social counselling, Sports facilities

Student Residential Facilities: Yes

Libraries: 41,000 vols

Publications: Cahiers de l'UCAC *(annually)*

Press or Publishing House: Presses de l'UCAC (PUCAC)
Last Updated: 02/09/09

COSENDAI ADVENTIST UNIVERSITY
Université Adventiste Cosendai (AU-G/UAG)
Nanga-Eboko, Centre
Tel: + 237 2223-86-41
EMail: uacosendai@yahoo.fr
Website: http://www.uacosendai.net

Rector: Lucile Sabas (2003-)
Tel: + 237 7755-95-54
EMail: sabas_lucile@yahoo.fr; rector@uaconsendai.net

Administrative Officer: Pierre Ovono Nyolo
Tel: + 237 7768- 99-43 EMail: ovononyolo@yahoo.fr

Faculties
Educational Sciences *Dean*: Joseph Nkou; **Health Sciences** *Dean*: Marie Abemyl; **Management and Computer Science** *Dean*: Claude Mboulet Ndaki; **Theology** (Theology) *Dean*: Paul Ikouba

History: Founded in 1996. Acquired present status 2002.

Governing Bodies: Council; Board Committee; Administrative Committee

Admission Requirements: Baccalauréat

Fees: (CFA Francs): 400,000 per annum

Main Language(s) of Instruction: French and English

International Co-operation: With universities in USA and France

Accrediting Agencies: Ministry of Higher Education; Adventist Accrediting Association

Degrees and Diplomas: *Bachelor's Degree*: Business Administration (BA); Computer Science (BSc); Management and Church Administration (BBA); Theology (BTH), 3-4 yrs; *Bachelor's Degree*: Nursing (BNS); Science of Education (BA), 4 yrs; *Licence*; *Master*; *Doctorat/Doctor of Philosophy*

Student Services: Academic counselling, Canteen, Employment services, Health services, Nursery care, Sports facilities

Student Residential Facilities: Dormitories

Libraries: Yes
Last Updated: 02/05/07

HIGHER INSTITUTE OF TECHNOLOGY AND INDUSTRIAL DESIGN
Institut supérieur des Technologies et du Design Industriel (ISTDI)
BP 3001, Douala, Littoral
Tel: + 237 3300-13-92
Fax: + 237 3347-33-55
EMail: istdi@yahoo.fr
Website: http://www.istdi.com

Président: Paul Guimezap (2001-)
Tel: + 237 9991-92-91 EMail: guimezapp@yahoo.fr

Secretaire General: Cyrille Meukaleuni
Tel: + 237 5524-68-92 EMail: meukaleuni@yahoo.fr

International Relations: Martine Guimezap, Attachée de direction
Tel: + 237 9968-21-60 EMail: guimemart@yahoo.fr

Programmes
Business and Commerce and Management *Head*: Cyrille Meukaleuni; **Engineering** *Head*: Arthur Mangamtcheith; **Industrial Design** (Industrial Design; Wood Technology) *Head*: Armand Ndongmo Zébazé; **Technology** (Information Technology) *Head*: François Xavier Tekoudjou

Admission Requirements: Secondary school certificate (baccalauréat) and entrance examination

Fees: (CFA Francs): c. 600,000

Main Language(s) of Instruction: French

International Co-operation: With universities in France and Canada

Accrediting Agencies: ACDI

Degrees and Diplomas: *Brevet de Technicien Supérieur (BTS)*: 2 yrs; *Licence*: 1 yr; *Master*

Student Services: Academic counselling, Canteen, Employment services, Foreign Studies Centre, Language programs, Sports facilities

Student Residential Facilities: Yes

Special Facilities: Movie Studio

Libraries: Yes

Academic Staff *2008-2009*	MEN	WOMEN	TOTAL
FULL-TIME	14	8	**22**
PART-TIME	85	25	**110**

Student Numbers *2008-2009*			
All (Foreign Included)	836	230	**1,066**
FOREIGN ONLY	58	8	**66**

Evening students, 150.
Last Updated: 08/07/09

HIGHER SCHOOL OF SCIENCE AND TECHNIQUES
Ecole supérieure des Sciences et Techniques (ESSET)
BP 13244, Douala, Littoral
Tel: + 237 3341-14-53
EMail: esset.douala@camnet.cm
Website: http://www.essetcmr.com/

Directeur: Robert Womonou

Administrative Officer: Arouna Tapit

International Relations: Arnaud Lontsi

Programmes
Commerce and Management (Accountancy; Business Administration; Business Computing; Insurance; International Business; Secretarial Studies); **Industry and Technology** (Electrical Engineering; Electronic Engineering; Industrial Engineering; Maintenance Technology; Technology)

History: Founded 1997. Acquired present status 2002.

Admission Requirements: Baccalauréat

Fees: (CFA Francs): 260,000-1,500,000 per annum

Main Language(s) of Instruction: French and English

Degrees and Diplomas: *Diplôme de Technicien supérieur*; *Licence*; *Diplôme d'Ingénieur de Conception*; *Master*. Also Mastère spécialisé

Student Services: Academic counselling, Canteen, Employment services, Foreign student adviser, Foreign Studies Centre, Health services, Language programs, Sports facilities

Libraries: Yes

Academic Staff *2008-2009*	MEN	WOMEN	TOTAL
FULL-TIME	25	5	**30**
PART-TIME	3	–	**3**

Student Numbers *2008-2009*			
All (Foreign Included)	75	15	**90**

Part-time students, 45.
Last Updated: 05/06/09

HIGHER SIANTOU INSTITUTE

Institut Siantou Supérieur (ISS)
BP 04, Yaoundé, Centre
Tel: +237 9955-91-41
Website: http://www.siantou.com

Programmes

Accountancy (Accountancy); **Commerce**; **Communication** (Communication Studies; Journalism; Photography); **Economics** (Economics); **Electronic Engineering** (Electronic Engineering); **Law** (Law); **Management** (Management); **Mechanical Engineering** (Mechanical Engineering)

Degrees and Diplomas: *Brevet de Technicien Supérieur*; *Licence*; *Master*
Last Updated: 18/02/09

PANAFRICAN INSTITUTE FOR DEVELOPMENT IN CENTRAL AFRICA

Institut panafricain pour le Développement en Afrique Centrale (IPD-AC/PAID-CA)
BP 4078, Douala, Littoral
Tel: +237 3340-37-70
Fax: +237 3340-37-70
EMail: ipdac_ong@yahoo.fr

Directeur: Jacques Bakolon (2007-)
Tel: +237(77) 44-16-11 EMail: bakolonj@yahoo.fr

Institutes

Panafrican Development (Adult Education; African Studies; Development Studies; Library Science; Natural Resources; Rural Studies) *Director:* Ernest Zocli

History: Founded 1965, IPD-AC contributes to the development of regions through training, research and practical action, counselling, publication and institution development.

Governing Bodies: Conseil d'Administration

Academic Year: October to September

Admission Requirements: Secondary school certificate or equivalent

Main Language(s) of Instruction: French

Degrees and Diplomas: *Diplôme de Technicien supérieur:* Environmental Studies; Business Management; Finance; Natural Resources Management (DCTD), 2 yrs; *Licence:* Environmental Studies; Business Management; Finance; Natural Resources Management, 3 yrs; *Diplôme d'Etudes supérieures spécialisées (DESS):* Development Planning, Progamming and Management, 5 yrs; *Master:* Project Management; Sustainable Development. Also Certificat de fin de Formation, 1-7 months

Student Services: Academic counselling, Canteen, Health services, Sports facilities

Student Residential Facilities: None

Libraries: Main Library

Publications: Nouvelles de l'IPD-AC *(biannually)*
Last Updated: 24/04/09

PROTESTANT UNIVERSITY OF CENTRAL AFRICA

Université protestante d'Afrique Centrale
BP 4011, Yaoundé, Centre
Tel: +237 2221-26-90
Fax: +237 2220-53-24
EMail: rectorat@upac-edu.org
Website: http://www.upac-edu.org

Rector: Emmanuel Anya Anyambod Tel: +237 7774-54-46

General Secretary: M.C. Bouba Mbima
Tel: +237 2221-26-29; +237 77-78-21-58
EMail: mbimaj2000@yahoo.fr

International Relations: Emmanuel Anya Anyambod, Rector

Faculties
Social Sciences and International Relations

Programmes

Protestant Theology and Religious Sciences (Protestant Theology; Religious Studies)

History: Founded 1962. Previously known as Faculté de Théologie protestante de Yaoundé (Faculty of Protestant Theology).

Governing Bodies: Conseil d'Administration

Admission Requirements: Baccalauréat; Licence

Main Language(s) of Instruction: French

International Co-operation: With Universities in Switzerland (Université de Lausanne, Université de Genève, Faculté de Théologie de Neuchâtel), France (Université de Strasbourg, Faculté libre de Théologie de Montpellier, Faculté libre de Paris). Agreements with Université de Yaoundé I and Université de Yaoundé II (Soa)

Degrees and Diplomas: *Licence:* Theology; Peace and Disarmament and Development Studies, 3 yrs; *Master:* Theology; Peace and Disarmament and Development Studies, 2 yrs; *Doctorat/Doctor of Philosophy:* Theology, 3 yrs

Student Services: Academic counselling, Canteen, Employment services, Health services, Sports facilities

Student Residential Facilities: Accommodation for 78 students

Libraries: c. 23,000 vols.

Press or Publishing House: Flambeau

Academic Staff *2008-2009*	MEN	WOMEN	TOTAL
FULL-TIME	13	1	**14**
PART-TIME	29	3	**32**
Student Numbers *2008-2009*			
All (Foreign Included)	296	108	**404**
FOREIGN ONLY	30	15	**45**

Evening students, 10.
Last Updated: 05/05/09

SCHOOL OF MANAGEMENT

Ecole supérieure de Gestion (ESG)
BP 12489, Douala, Littoral
Tel: +237 3337-50-59 +237 3337-50-60
Fax: +237 3342-89-02
Website: http://esg-ista-univ.com/esg/index.html

Directeur général: Louis-Marie Djambou

Programmes
Commerce and Management; **Communication**

History: Founded 1993.

Degrees and Diplomas: *Licence*; *Master*
Last Updated: 02/09/09

UNIVERSITY COLLEGE OF TECHNOLOGY OF BUEA (UCT)

Buéa, South West Region PMB 63
Tel: +237(330) 93678
Fax: +237(333) 51177
EMail: info@uctbc.com
Website: http://www.uctbc.com/

President: Ebot Ntui Ogork (2004-)
Tel: +237(330) 09721, Fax: +237(333) 51177
EMail: cobmate@gmail.com

Registrar: Paul Abunaw Arrey EMail: registrar@uctbc.com

International Relations: Eric Kami EMail: international@uctb.com

Schools

Business Computing and Contemporary Management (Actuarial Science; Banking; Business Administration; Educational Administration; Environmental Management; Film; Finance; Information Management; Insurance; International Relations; Marketing; Mass Communication; Public Administration; Transport Management) *Dean:* Godfred Njimanted; **Engineering** *Dean:* Bilihka Ndjel

History: Created 2004. Acquired current status 2008.

Governing Bodies: Senate; Promotion Committee; Research and Evaluation Committee; College Congregation.

Academic Year: October to July

Fees: (CFA Francs): 300,000 - 400,000

Main Language(s) of Instruction: English

International Co-operation: With institutions in Nigeria

Accrediting Agencies: Ministry of Higher Education

Degrees and Diplomas: *Bachelor's Degree*: Engineering (BEng), 4 yrs; *Bachelor's Degree*: Technology (BTech), 3 yrs; *Master*. Also Advanced Professional Diploma (1 yr) and Higher Professional Diploma (2 yrs)

Student Services: Academic counselling, Canteen, Employment services, Foreign student adviser, Foreign Studies Centre, Health services, Language programs, Social counselling, Sports facilities

Student Residential Facilities: No.

Special Facilities: Engineering Laboratory.

Libraries: 5,000 books.

Academic Staff 2008-2009	MEN	WOMEN	TOTAL
FULL-TIME	–	–	73
STAFF WITH DOCTORATE			
FULL-TIME	–	–	8
PART-TIME	–	–	10
Student Numbers 2008-2009			
All (Foreign Included)	1,276	113	1,389
FOREIGN ONLY	–	–	19

Part-time students, 7. **Distance students**, 4. **Evening students**, 6.

Last Updated: 24/07/09

Canada

STRUCTURE OF HIGHER EDUCATION SYSTEM

Description:

In Canada, education is the responsibility of each province and territory. For specific information, consult the individual provincial/territorial descriptions of each educational system provided in the publication. Because ministers of education needed a forum in which to discuss issues of mutual concern, they established the Council of Ministers of Education, Canada (CMEC) in 1967.

ADMISSION TO HIGHER EDUCATION

Foreign students admission:

Definition of foreign student: Foreign (international) students are students who are neither Canadian citizens nor permanent residents of Canada, and are enrolled full time in a recognized academic, professional or vocational training course of study at a university, college or other educational institution in Canada.

Entrance exam requirements: Each institution may vary in its international admission requirements. Institutions may require the following documentation: official academic transcripts (some institutions may require them to be translated into English or French), proof of your country's equivalent of a Canadian secondary school or high school education, and completion of English or French Language requirements as requested by the institution.

Entry regulations: Before you come to study in Canada, you will need: a "Study Permit" if the programme of study you will be admitted to is longer than six months in duration, regardless of the length of your stay in Canada; a letter of acceptance from the school of your choice; proof that you have enough money to pay for school fees, living expenses and return transportation for yourself and any family members who come with you to Canada; to establish that you will return home at the end of your studies; to pass a medical exam if required; to be a law abiding citizen with no criminal record and not be a risk to the security of Canada and to qualify as a temporary resident in Canada, including holding a temporary resident visa (required for citizens of many countries). A small number of students do not require a Study Permit by virtue of their status in Canada (e.g. diplomats and their children); students should contact the nearest overseas Canadian diplomatic mission to confirm procedures and requirements.

Health requirements: Most education institutions require international students to buy health insurance in addition to their tuition fees; those that do not will require proof of independent health insurance coverage. Medical examinations are not required by institutions but may be required by Citizenship and Immigration Canada for students from a number of countries.

Language requirements: Students must be proficient in English or French. Many universities offer second language upgrading courses.

RECOGNITION OF STUDIES

Quality assurance system:

A brief description of Canada's post-secondary institutions and their quality assurance mechanisms is available at: http://www.cicic.ca/420/quality assurance in canada.canada

Bodies dealing with recognition:

Alliance of Credential Evaluation Services of Canada - ACSED (Alliance canadienne des services d'évaluation des diplômes)

Secretary: Yves E. Beaudin
95 St Clair Avenue West, Suite 1106
Toronto, Ontario M4V 1N6
Tel: +1(416) 962 9725
Fax: +1(416) 962 2800

EMail: info@cicic.ca
WWW: http://www.canalliance.org

Canadian Information Centre for International Credentials - CICIC (Centre d'information canadien sur les diplômes internationaux (CICDI))
National Coordinator: Yves E. Beaudin
95 St Clair Avenue West, Suite 1106
Toronto, Ontario M4V 1N6
Tel: +1(416) 962 9725
Fax: +1(416) 962 2800
EMail: info@cicic.ca
WWW: http://www.cicic.ca

NATIONAL BODIES

Council of Ministers of Education, Canada - CMEC (Conseil des Ministres de l'Éducation, Canada - CMEC)
Director General: Andrew Parkin
Coordinator, International Programmes: Antonella Manca-Mangoff
95 St Clair Avenue West, Suite 1106
Toronto, Ontario M4V 1N6
Tel: +1(416) 962 8100
Fax: +1(416) 962 2800
EMail: cmec@cmec.ca
WWW: http://www.cmec.ca
Role of national body: The Council of Ministers of Education, Canada (CMEC) is an intergovernmental body founded in 1967 by ministers of education to serve as: a forum to discuss policy issues; a mechanism through which to undertake activities, projects, and initiatives in areas of mutual interest; a means by which to consult and cooperate with national education organizations and the federal government; an instrument to represent the education interests of the provinces and territories internationally.

Canadian Bureau for International Education - CBIE
President and CEO: Karen McBride
220 Laurier West, Suite 1550
Ottawa, Ontario K1P 5Z9
Tel: +1(613) 237 4820
Fax: +1(613) 237 1073
EMail: info@cbie.ca
WWW: http://www.cbie.ca

Association des Universités de la Francophonie canadienne - AUFC
President: Kenneth McRoberts
260, rue Dalhousie, bureau 400
Ottawa, Ontario K1N 7E4
Tel: +1 (613) 244 5231
Fax: +1 (613) 244 0283
WWW: http://www.aufc.ca/
Role of national body: Membership organization of French-speaking universities.

Association of Atlantic Universities - AAU (Association des Universités de l'Atlantique)
President: Ray Ivany
Executive Director: Peter Halpin
Suite 403, 5657 Spring Garden Road
Halifax, Nova Scotia B3J 3R4
Tel: +1(902) 425 4230
Fax: +1(902) 425 4233
EMail: info@atlanticuniversities.ca

WWW: http://atlanticuniversities.ca/
Role of national body: Membership organization representing the university communities of New Brunswick, Newfoundland and Labrador, Nova Scotia and Prince Edward Island.

Association of Canadian Community Colleges - ACCC (Association des Collèges communautaires du Canada)

Chairperson: Ann Buller
President and CEO: James Knight
Suite 701 - 1 Rideau Street
Ottawa, Ontario K1N 8S7
Tel: +1(613) 746 2222
Fax: +1(613) 746 6721
EMail: info@accc.ca
WWW: http://www.accc.ca
Role of national body: Membership organization of Canadian colleges and cegeps.

Association of Registrars of the Universities and Colleges of Canada - ARUCC (Association des Registraires des Universités et Collèges du Canada)

President: Joanne Duklas
Secretary-Treasurer: Angelique Saweczko
WWW: http://www.arucc.ca

Association of Universities and Colleges of Canada - AUCC (Association des Universités et Collèges du Canada)

Chairperson: Michel Belley
President and CEO: Paul Davidson
Assistant Director: Gail Bowkett
600-350 Albert Street
Ottawa, Ontario K1R 1B1
Tel: +1(613) 563 1236
Fax: +1(613) 563 9745
EMail: info@aucc.ca
WWW: http://www.aucc.ca
Role of national body: To foster and promote the interests of higher education and university research.

Data for academic year: 2008-2009
Source: IAU from the Canadian Information Centre for International Credentials (CICIC), a unit of the Council of Ministers of Education, Canada (CMEC), 2008; National bodies 2010.

Canada - Alberta

STRUCTURE OF HIGHER EDUCATION SYSTEM

Description:

Higher education in Canada is the constitutional responsibility of the provinces. There are several types of institutions providing post secondary education in Alberta.

Stages of studies:

University level first stage: Baccalaureate degree/First Professional degree
Bachelor's degree programmes are offered at institutions that have received approval from the ministry responsible for advanced education. Institutions must meet specific quality requirements before they can offer degrees. Approved undergraduate degree programmes are currently offered at the four comprehensive Alberta universities, Alberta College of Art & Design, Grant MacEwan University, Mount Royal University, NAIT, SAIT, and 6 private institutions. Most undergraduate study leads to a "General" Bachelor's degree or an "Honours" or specialized degree (4 years and prescribed subject concentration). Degrees are normally titled in broad descriptive groups, e.g. Bachelor of Arts (B.A.) and Bachelor of Science (B.Sc.). In addition, there are other professional degree programmes that typically require specific high school prerequisites and four years of study, e.g. Bachelor of Science in Nursing (B.Sc.N.), Bachelor of Commerce (B.Comm.) and Bachelor of Education (B.Ed.). Vocationally-oriented applied Bachelor's degrees are also offered at 9 public colleges and technical institutes. First- and second-year university transfer courses and programmes are also offered by most publicly funded public colleges. As well, first professional degree programmes require prerequisite university studies followed by additional years of professional training, e.g. three years for a Juris Doctor(J.D.) and four years for Doctor of Medicine (M.D.) and Doctor of Dental Surgery (D.D.S.) degrees.

University level second stage: Master's degree
The Master's degree normally requires at least two years of study after completion of a Bachelor's degree or equivalent. A Master's degree may be thesis- or course-based, with some professional programmes consisting of non thesis options. Examples of Masters' degrees include the M.A., M.Sc., M.Ed., and M.B.A. Graduate level diplomas are considered an intermediate stage between the Bachelor's or first professional degree and the Master's degree.

University level third stage: Doctoral degree
The Doctoral degree is the highest academic qualification awarded by Alberta; it comprises the third stage of university level studies. This degree normally requires at least 3 to 6 years of study after the Bachelor's degree. The submission and defence of a major thesis (dissertation) are the principal requirements, and supplemental course work is usually required. The degree "Doctor of Philosophy" (Ph.D.) is the designation most commonly used to signify the Doctorate. It is a generic title applicable to degrees in most disciplines (the Doctorate should not be confused with certain first professional degrees, e.g. Doctor of Medicine, Doctor of Dental Surgery).

Distance higher education:
Athabasca University, an open university specializing in distance education, emphasizes an open admission policy and a personalized learning system. Its students are scattered across the country and internationally and use special home study materials, often supplemented by "paced delivery", Internet, audiotapes, work-shops, teleconference sessions, and television broadcasts. Anyone 16+ years of age can enrol, regardless of educational background. E CampusAlberta is a consortium of fifteen colleges and technical institutes that facilitates increased access to high-quality online learning opportunities, emphasizes community-based student support, and provides a collaborative online learning experience that spans the province. Alberta North is a partnership of seven post secondary institutions who work together to make education accessible in northern communities throughout Alberta and the Northwest Territories. The partners provide facilities, learning technologies, and support services to over 87 online learning sites called Community Access Points (CAP sites). At these sites, students can receive courses and programmes offered by many different post-secondary institutions.

ADMISSION TO HIGHER EDUCATION

Admission to university-level studies:

Name of secondary school credential required: High School Diploma

Alternatives to credentials: Post secondary institutions and private vocational providers determine specific programme based admission requirements. Admission requirements for mature (adult) students may vary by institution and by programme. Prior learning assessment and recognition (PLAR) may be used to determine credit or advanced standing for specific courses.

Other admission requirements: Admission averages required to enter an undergraduate programme, vary by institution, faculty, and programme. Admission to programmes that have enrolment limits may require competitive marks higher than the minimum admission requirements set out in the academic calendar. Mature applicants who do not meet normal admission requirements may be considered with differing qualifications. Competency in English is required of foreign students. Prospective students should consult the institution(s) of their choice for further details on admission.

Foreign students admission:

Definition of foreign student: Foreign (international) students are students who are neither Canadian citizens nor permanent residents of Canada, and are enrolled full-time in a recognized academic, professional or vocational training, or English as a Second Language programme of study at a university, college or other educational institution in Canada.

Entrance exam requirements: Each institution may vary in its international admission requirements. Contact the International Education or Admissions Office at the institution for specific details. Generally, institutions may require the following documentation: official academic transcripts translated into English (some institutions may require official transcripts be notarized, proof of your country's equivalent of a Canadian secondary school or high school education, and completion of English Language requirements as requested by the institution.

Entry regulations: Before you come to study in Canada, you will need: a "Study Permit" if the programme of study you will be admitted to is longer than six months in duration, regardless of the length of your stay in Canada; the letter of introduction that students received from the visa office when their study permit was approved (this letter contains the study permit reference number); a letter of acceptance from the school of your choice; proof that you have enough money to pay for school fees, living expenses and return transportation for yourself and any family members who come with you to Canada; to establish that you will return home at the end of your studies; to pass a medical exam if required; to be a law abiding citizen with no criminal record and not be a risk to the security of Canada and to qualify as a temporary resident in Canada, including holding a temporary resident visa (required for citizens of many countries). A small number of students do not require a Study Permit by virtue of their status in Canada (e.g. diplomats and their children); students should contact their home country embassy in Canada to confirm this requirement. See also http://www.cic.gc.ca/english/study/

Health requirements: Most education institutions require international students to buy health insurance in addition to their tuition fees; those that do not will require proof of independent health insurance coverage. Medical examinations are not required by institutions but may be required by Citizenship and Immigration Canada for students from a number of countries. Those intending to study and reside in Alberta for at least 12 months are eligible for free Alberta Health Care Insurance Plan (AHCIP) coverage for the period of their studies. Coverage begins on the date of arrival in Alberta, provided registration validation requirements are met.

Language requirements: Each institution's language requirements will vary but most institutions will require students to demonstrate English language proficiency (by presenting specific test results); otherwise students will be required to enrol in an English as a second language course if they have not met specific requirements. Contact the International Education or Admissions Office at the institution for specific details.

RECOGNITION OF STUDIES

Quality assurance system:

Approval of degree programmes under the Post-secondary Learning Act and the Approval of Programmes of Study Regulation follows a two-stage review process once the Minister receives a proposal. Stage 1 is a system coordination review of the proposed programme by the Ministry to make a determination of the need for the programme and how it fits with other programmes currently offered within Alberta's post-secondary system. Stage 2 is a quality review enacted if the Minister forwards the proposal to the Campus Alberta Quality Council. The Campus Alberta Quality Council (CAQC) is an arms-length quality assurance agency that reviews all proposals for new degrees to be offered in Alberta. It also monitors all new degree programmes.

Bodies dealing with recognition:

International Qualifications Assessment Service - IQAS

9th Floor, 108 Street Building

9942 - 108 Street

Edmonton, Alberta T5K 2J5

Tel: +1(780) 427 2655

Fax: +1(780) 422 9734

WWW: http://employment.alberta.ca/immigration/4512.html

Special provisions for recognition:

Recognition for university level studies: The Alberta Council on Admissions and Transfer (ACAT) is responsible for developing policies, guidelines, and procedures designed to facilitate transfer agreements among post-secondary institutions so that learners can move from one institution to another and receive credit for courses for which they have already demonstrated competence. An important activity of ACAT is to maintain a database of negotiated and approved transfer agreements between post-secondary institutions. This Information is accessible either by using the Online Alberta Transfer Guide or the annual printed Alberta Transfer Guide. More information is available at: www.transferalberta.ca.

PROVINCIAL BODIES

Alberta Advanced Education and Technology

Minister: Greg Weadick

324 Legislature Building 10800 - 97 Avenue

Edmonton, AB T5K 2B6

Tel: +1(780) 422 5400

EMail: AET.INFO@gov.ab.ca

WWW: http://www.advancededucation.gov.ab.ca

Role of national body: To provide the leadership, services & coordination necessary for the efficient development and functioning of an effective and responsive post-secondary learning system.

Campus Alberta Quality Council - CAQC

Director: Marilyn Patton

11th Floor, Commerce Place 10155 - 102 Street

Edmonton, AB T5J 4L5

Tel: +1(780) 427 8921

Fax: +1(780) 427 4185

WWW: http://www.caqc.gov.ab.ca/

Role of national body: To promote system development and integrity, review the quality and recommend degree programmes for approval, and monitor the quality of degree programmes within the post-secondary system.

Alberta Council on Admissions and Transfer - ACAT

11th Floor, Commerce Place 10155 - 102 Street

Edmonton, Alberta T5J 4L5

Tel: +1(780) 422 9021

Fax: +1(780) 422 3688
EMail: acat@gov.ab.ca
WWW: http://alis.alberta.ca/ps/ep/aas/ta/transferalberta.html
Role of national body: To provide leadership and direction in the improvement of educational opportunities for Alberta students through inter-institutional transfer and coordination.

Data for academic year: 2011-2012
Source: IAU from the Canadian Information Centre for International Credentials (CICIC), a unit of the Council of Ministers of Education, Canada (CMEC), on behalf of the Province of Alberta, 2011.

INSTITUTIONS

PUBLIC INSTITUTIONS

ATHABASCA UNIVERSITY (AU)

1 University Drive, Athabasca, Alberta T9S 3A3
Tel: +1(780) 675-6100 +1(800) 788-9041
Fax: +1(780) 675-6145
Website: http://www.athabascau.ca

President: Frits Pannekoek (2005-)
Tel: +1(780) 675-6108, Fax: +1(780) 675-6450
EMail: auprez@athabascau.ca; fritsp@athabascau.ca

Vice President, Finance and Administration: Ray Block
EMail: rblock@athabascau.ca

International Relations: Margaret Haughey, Vice-President, Academic
Tel: +1(780) 675-6447, Fax: +1(780) 675-6431
EMail: mhaughey@athabascau.ca

Centres
Distance Education (Distance Education; Educational Sciences; Educational Technology); **Learning Accreditation** *(PLAR)*; **Learning Design and Development**; **Research**

Faculties
Business (Accountancy; Business Administration; E-Business/Commerce; Finance; Human Resources; Leadership; Marketing); **Graduate Studies** (Business Administration; Distance Education; Educational Sciences; Educational Technology; Health Sciences; Heritage Preservation; Information Sciences; Law; Management; Nursing; Psychology); **Health Disciplines** (Health Sciences; Nursing; Psychology); **Humanities and Social Sciences** (Anthropology; Art History; Arts and Humanities; Canadian Studies; Communication Studies; Criminal Law; Cultural Studies; Education; Educational Sciences; English; Environmental Studies; Film; French; Gender Studies; Geography (Human); German; Government; Health Administration; Heritage Preservation; History; Human Resources; Indigenous Studies; International Studies; Labour and Industrial Relations; Labour Law; Law; Literature; Music; Philosophy; Political Sciences; Psychology; Public Administration; Religious Studies; Social and Community Services; Sociology; Spanish; Women's Studies; Writing); **Science and Technology** (Astronomy and Space Science; Biology; Chemistry; Computer Engineering; Computer Science; Environmental Studies; Geography; Geology; Health Sciences; Information Sciences; Laboratory Techniques; Mathematics; Nutrition; Physics; Software Engineering; Statistics)

Further Information: Traditional and Open Learning Institution. Also Learning Centres in Edmonton and Calgary and Centre for Innovative Management (CIM) in St. Albert.

History: Founded 1970. An open, distance education university funded by the Department of Advanced Education of the government of Alberta. Accepted first students 1973, and received permanent self-governing status under the Alberta University Act 1978.

Governing Bodies: Unicameral Governing Council; Academic Council

Academic Year: No terms. Admission is granted all year round in undergraduate programmes

Admission Requirements: Minimum age is 16 years old

Fees: (Can. Dollars): Undergraduate programmes, canadians permanent Residents of Alberta, 646 for a 3 credit course; For Canadian residents outside Alberta, per course, 751 (for Senior Canadian, 414/519 for a 3-credit course). Foreign students, 971 for a 3-credit course.

Main Language(s) of Instruction: English

Degrees and Diplomas: *Bachelor's Degree*; *Master's Degree*; *Doctoral Degree*. Also Post-Baccalaureate Diploma, 2,5 yrs.

Student Services: Academic counselling, Canteen, Handicapped facilities

Libraries: c. 130,000 vols and audiovisual items. Online access to more than 7,000 journals.

Publications: Bridging the Distance *(annually)*; Profiles in Research *(annually)*

Academic Staff 2010-2011	MEN	WOMEN	TOTAL
FULL-TIME	–	–	**1,200**
Student Numbers 2010-2011			
All (Foreign Included)	12,540	25,460	**38,000**

Last Updated: 15/12/10

GRANT MACEWAN UNIVERSITY

PO Box 1796, 10050 MacDonald Drive, Edmonton, Alberta T5J 2P2
Tel: +1(780) 497-5040
Fax: +1(780) 497-5001
EMail: info@macewan.ca
Website: http://www.macewan.ca/web/home/index.cfm

President and CEO: Paul Byrne
Tel: +1(780) 497-5402, Fax: +1(780) 497-5405

Centres
Arts and Communications (Art Management; Communication Studies; Design; Display and Stage Design; Fine Arts; Jazz and Popular Music; Journalism; Music; Musical Instruments; Theatre; Writing)

Faculties
Arts and Science (Anthropology; Arts and Humanities; Biological and Life Sciences; Chemistry; Chinese; Classical Languages; Computer Science; Earth Sciences; Economics; English; French; German; Greek (Classical); History; Japanese; Latin; Mathematics; Philosophy; Physics; Political Sciences; Psychology; Sociology; Spanish; Statistics); **Health and Community Studies** (Acupuncture; Child Care and Development; Criminal Law; Gerontology; Health Sciences; Law; Nursing; Occupational Therapy; Physical Therapy; Police Studies; Rehabilitation and Therapy; Social Work; Special Education; Speech Therapy and Audiology)

Schools
Business (Accountancy; Business Administration; Business and Commerce; Human Resources; Information Technology; Insurance; Law; Leadership; Library Science; Management; Public Relations)

History: Founded 1971 as Grant MacEwan College. Acquired present title 2009.

Fees: (Canadian Dollar): Bachelor's degree, domestic students, 6,220-9,537 per annum; international Students, 16,282-21,111 per annum. Applied Degree, domestic students, 5,137-6,783; International students, 5,137-16,618 per annum. Certificate/diplomas, Domestic students, 1,931-14,868 per annum; International students, 4,678-34,350 per annum.

Degrees and Diplomas: *Applied Degree*; *Bachelor's Degree*
Last Updated: 16/12/10

LAKELAND COLLEGE - ALBERTA (LC)

5707 College Drive, Vermillion, Alberta T9X 1K5
Tel: +1(780) 853-8400
Fax: +1(780) 853-7355
EMail: admissions@lakelandc.ab.ca
Website: http://www.lakelandc.ab.ca

President and Chief Executive Officer: Glenn Charlesworth
Tel: +1(780) 853-8400 Ext. 510

Programmes

Academic Upgrading (Adult Education); **Agricultural Sciences** (Agricultural Business; Agriculture; Animal Husbandry; Cattle Breeding; Crop Production; Veterinary Science; Zoology); **Business** (Accountancy; Agricultural Business; Business Administration; Finance; Management); **Continuing Education**; **Environmental Sciences** (Ecology; Environmental Management; Fishery; Tourism; Wildlife); **Fire and Emergency** (Fire Science; Protective Services); **Health and Wellness** (Nursing; Physical Therapy); **Human Services** (Child Care and Development; Education); **Interior Design** (Interior Design); **Tourism** (Tourism); **Trades and Technology** (Metal Techniques; Service Trades; Technology); **University Transfer** *(University of Alberta or University of Saskatchewan)* (Arts and Humanities; Business and Commerce; Dentistry; Education; Medicine; Pharmacy; Primary Education; Secondary Education; Veterinary Science)

Further Information: Also Lloydminster Campus.

Degrees and Diplomas: *Bachelor's Degree*. Applied Bachelor's degree, 2-3 rs post-diploma programme; Bachelor's degree (professional), 4 yrs.
Last Updated: 03/12/10

LETHBRIDGE COLLEGE

300 College Drive South, Lethbridge, Alberta T1K 1L6
Tel: +1(403) 320-3200
Fax: +1(403) 320-1461
EMail: info@lethbridgecollege.ab.ca
Website: http://www.lethbridgecollege.ab.ca

President and Chief Executive Officer: Tracy L. Edwards
Tel: +1(403) 320-3209 EMail: tracy.edwards@lethbridgecollege.ca

Areas

Academic Upgrading & Transition Programs (Biology; Chemistry; English; Mathematics; Physics); **Agriculture and Science** (Agricultural Equipment; Agriculture; Biotechnology; Fishery; Wildlife); **Alternative Energy** (Energy Engineering); **Apprenticeships** (Automotive Engineering; Cooking and Catering; Metal Techniques); **Automotives and Mechanics** (Agricultural Equipment; Automotive Engineering); **Business and Administration** (Administration; Business Administration; Information Technology; Management); **Communications and Media** (Communication Arts; Multimedia); **Computing and Information Technology** (Communication Arts; Computer Science; Information Technology; Multimedia; Surveying and Mapping); **Criminal Justice and Law** (Criminal Law; Fire Science; Law; Police Studies); **Culinary Arts and Hospitality** (Business Administration; Cooking and Catering); **Design** (Civil Engineering; Communication Arts; Computer Science; Design; Fashion Design; Information Technology; Interior Design; Marketing; Multimedia); **Education** (Preschool Education; Special Education); **Engineering** (Civil Engineering; Engineering; Surveying and Mapping); **Environment** (Biotechnology; Environmental Studies; Fishery; Natural Resources; Wildlife); **Fitness and Recreation** (Management; Sports); **Health** (Biotechnology; Health Sciences; Nursing); **Human Services** (Child Care and Development; Preschool Education; Rehabilitation and Therapy; Special Education); **Humanities, Psychology and Sociology** (Child Care and Development; Law; Police Studies); **Languages and English as a Second Language** (English); **Marketing** (Business Administration); **Outdoor Careers** (Energy Engineering; Environmental Studies; Fishery; Natural Resources; Wildlife); **Science** (Biotechnology); **Trades** (Agricultural Equipment; Automotive Engineering; Energy Engineering; Metal Techniques); **Transportation** (Agricultural Equipment; Automotive Engineering)

Further Information: Traditional and Open Learning Institution

History: Founded 1957 as Lethbridge Community College.

Degrees and Diplomas: *Bachelor's Degree*. Applied bachelor's degree (professional), 4 yrs; Bachelor of Nursing in partnership with University of Lethbridge, 4 yrs.
Last Updated: 02/12/10

MEDICINE HAT COLLEGE (MHC)

299 College Drive S.E., Medicine Hat, Alberta T1A 3Y6
Tel: +1(403) 529-3811 +1(866) 282-8394
Fax: +1(403) 504-3517
EMail: info@acd.mhc.ab.ca
Website: http://www.mhc.ab.ca

President: Ralph Weeks
Tel: +1(403) 529-3801, Fax: +1(403) 504-3510
EMail: weeks@mhc.ab.ca

Vice-President, Academic: Linda Schwatrz-Trivett
Tel: +1(403) 529-3802 EMail: lschwartz@mhc.ab.ca

Divisions

Adult Development (Adult Education; Biology; Chemistry; Computer Science; English; Mathematics; Physics); **Arts** (Arts and Humanities; Child Care and Development; Communication Studies; Criminal Law; Education; Fine Arts; Journalism; Law; Police Studies; Preschool Education; Social Work; Visual Arts); **Business** (Administration; Business Administration; Business and Commerce; Communication Studies; Management; Marketing; Tourism); **Health Studies** (Health Sciences; Nursing; Occupational Therapy; Paramedical Sciences; Physical Therapy; Social Work; Speech Therapy and Audiology); **International Education** (English); **Science** (Business Computing; Computer Graphics; Computer Science; Dental Hygiene; Dentistry; Engineering; Environmental Studies; Information Technology; Laboratory Techniques; Leadership; Medicine; Nutrition; Optometry; Pharmacy; Power Engineering; Tourism; Veterinary Science); **Trades** (Metal Techniques; Service Trades; Technology)

Further Information: Also Brooks Campus.

History: Founded 1965 as Medicine Hat Junior College. Acquired present title 1969.

Degrees and Diplomas: *Bachelor's Degree*. Applied Bachelor's degree (professional) 4 yrs; Bachelor's degree with University of Alberta, University of Calgary and Athabasca University; Bachelor of Professional Arts with Athabasca University.
Last Updated: 02/12/10

MOUNT ROYAL UNIVERSITY

4825 Mount Royal Gate, SW, Calgary, Alberta T3E 6K6
Tel: +1(403) 440-6111
Fax: +1(403) 240-6339
EMail: admissions@mtroyal.ca
Website: http://www.mtroyal.ca/

President: David Docherty (2011-)
Tel: +1(403) 440-6393 EMail: president@mtroyal.ca

Provost and Vice-President, Academic: Robin Fisher
Tel: +1(403) 440-6858 EMail: rfisher@mtroyal.ca

Vice-President, Administrative Services: Richard Roberts
Tel: +1(403) 440-6312 EMail: rroberts@mtroyal.ca

International Relations: Lorna Smith, Director, International Education
Tel: +1(403) 440-5004, Fax: +1(403) 440-5155
EMail: LSmith@mtroyal.ca; international@mtroyal.ca

Centres
Child Well-Being (Child Care and Development); **Iniskim** (Indigenous Studies)

Conservatories
Music *(Mount Royal)* (Jazz and Popular Music; Music; Music Theory and Composition; Musical Instruments; Singing)

Faculties
Arts (Anthropology; Art History; Arts and Humanities; Canadian Studies; Chinese; Classical Languages; Economics; English; French; German; Greek (Classical); History; Interior Design; Italian; Japanese; Latin; Linguistics; Modern Languages; Philosophy; Political Sciences; Psychology; Religious Studies; Romance Languages; Social Policy; Sociology; Spanish; Women's Studies); **Communication Studies** (Information Management; Journalism; Music; Public Relations; Radio and Television Broadcasting; Theatre); **Continuing Education** (Accountancy; Adult Education; Arabic; Business Administration; Child Care and Development; Chinese; Cinema and Television; Communication Studies; Computer Science; Data Processing; Design; English; Environmental Management; Film; Finance; French; German; Health Sciences; Human Resources; Insurance; Italian; Japanese; Leadership; Management; Marketing; Occupational Therapy; Petroleum and Gas Engineering; Photography; Physical Therapy; Police Studies; Portuguese; Public Relations; Real Estate; Rehabilitation and Therapy; Russian; Small Business; Spanish; Toxicology; Transport and Communications; Video; Visual Arts; Writing; Yoga); **Health and Community Studies** (Business Administration; Child Care and Development; Criminal Law; Forensic Medicine and Dentistry; Health Sciences; Nursing; Physical Education; Psychiatry and Mental Health; Rehabilitation and Therapy; Social Work; Tourism); **Science and Technology** (Biological and Life Sciences; Chemistry; Computer Science; Earth Sciences; Engineering; Environmental Studies; Information Sciences; Mathematics; Physics); **Teaching and Learning** (Education)

Institutes
Integrative Health (Health Sciences); **International Education/ Languages Institute** (Arabic; Chinese; Communication Studies; English; French; German; Italian; Japanese; Modern Languages; Portuguese; Russian; Spanish); **Nonprofit Studies** (Business Administration; Management); **Scholarship of Teaching and Learning**

Schools
Business *(Bissett)* (Accountancy; Business Administration; Finance; Human Resources; Insurance; International Business; Management; Marketing)

Further Information: Also Institute for Scholarship of Teaching and Learning; Centre for Child Well-Being; Also Holy Cross and Springbank campuses.

History: Founded 1911 as Mount Royal College. Acquired present title 2009.

Governing Bodies: Board of Governors; General Faculties Council

Admission Requirements: Secondary school certificate or recognized foreign equivalent; interview for some programmes

Fees: (Can. Dollars): Canadian/resident students, degree program (five courses), 2,507 per semester; International students, degree program (five courses), 5,641 per semester.

Main Language(s) of Instruction: English

International Co-operation: with more than 65 universities in Australia; Austria; Chile; China; Czech Republic; Estonia; Finland; France; Germany; Ghana; Japan; Malaysia; Mexico; New Zealand; Netherlands; Norway; Poland; Spain; Sri Lanka; Sweden; United Kingdom and USA. Also participates in the International Academic Mobility Program (Canada-European Union and North America)

Degrees and Diplomas: *Applied Degree*; *Bachelor's Degree*

Student Services: Academic counselling, Canteen, Cultural centre, Employment services, Handicapped facilities, Health services, Language programs, Nursery care, Social counselling, Sports facilities

Student Residential Facilities: Two residence complexes for 1,020 students

Special Facilities: Broadcasting and Music studios. Theatre. Organ Recital Hall

Libraries: 198,194 vols; Licensed databases, 179; Ebooks, 47,732

Academic Staff 2009-2010	MEN	WOMEN	TOTAL
FULL-TIME	–	–	387
PART-TIME	–	–	524
STAFF WITH DOCTORATE			
FULL-TIME	–	–	120
PART-TIME	–	–	70
Student Numbers 2009-2010			
All (Foreign Included)	5,315	8,860	14,175
FOREIGN ONLY	–	–	210

Part-time students, 3,732.
Last Updated: 05/04/11

NORTHERN ALBERTA INSTITUTE OF TECHNOLOGY (NAIT)
11762-106 Street N.W., Edmonton, Alberta T5G 2R1
Tel: +1(780) 471-6248
Fax: +1(780) 471-8490
EMail: registrar@nait.ab.ca
Website: http://www.nait.ab.ca

Acting President and CEO: David Janzen
Tel: +(780) 471-7704, Fax: +(780) 471-8583
EMail: president@nait.ca

Areas
Academic Upgrading (Business Administration; Engineering; Technology); **Animal Studies** (Business Administration; Veterinary Science); **Building Construction and Design** (Architecture; Building Technologies; Civil Engineering; Construction Engineering; Graphic Design; Interior Design; Materials Engineering; Mechanical Engineering); **Business Administration** (Accountancy; Banking; Business Administration; Finance; Human Resources; Management; Marketing); **Engineering and Applied Sciences** (Aeronautical and Aerospace Engineering; Architecture; Biological and Life Sciences; Biomedical Engineering; Building Technologies; Chemical Engineering; Computer Engineering; Computer Networks; Construction Engineering; Design; Electrical Engineering; Electronic Engineering; Energy Engineering; Engineering Management; Environmental Studies; Forestry; Geological Engineering; Instrument Making; Interior Design; Laboratory Techniques; Materials Engineering; Nanotechnology; Petroleum and Gas Engineering; Surveying and Mapping; Telecommunications Engineering); **Environment and Land Management** (Landscape Architecture); **Environmental Management** (Biological and Life Sciences; Chemical Engineering; Energy Engineering; Geological Engineering; Surveying and Mapping; Water Management); **Health** (Biomedical Engineering; Dental Technology; Dentistry; Laboratory Techniques; Medical Technology; Medicine; Radiology; Respiratory Therapy; Sports; Veterinary Science); **Health and Safety** (Engineering Management; Occupational Health); **Hospitality and Culinary Arts** (Cooking and Catering; Hotel and Restaurant); **Information Technology and Electronics** (Aeronautical and Aerospace Engineering; Computer Engineering; Computer Networks; Electrical Engineering; Electronic Engineering; Graphic Arts; Information Technology; Photography; Radio and Television Broadcasting; Telecommunications Engineering); **Mechanical and Industrial** (Aeronautical and Aerospace Engineering; Automotive Engineering; Building Technologies; Instrument Making; Mechanical Engineering; Petroleum and Gas Engineering; Power Engineering); **Media and Design** (Communication Arts; Graphic Arts; Media Studies; Photography; Radio and Television Broadcasting); **Recreation and Outdoors** (Landscape Architecture; Marine Transport; Sports); **Trades** (Aeronautical and Aerospace Engineering; Automotive Engineering; Business Administration; Marine Transport; Power Engineering; Service Trades)

Degrees and Diplomas: *Bachelor's Degree.* Bachelor's degree (professional) in Business Administration, 4 yrs; Applied Bachelor's degree and Bachelor of Technology, 2 yrs post-diplomas.

Academic Staff 2010-2011: Total: c. 3,300
Last Updated: 02/12/10

OLDS COLLEGE (OCCI)

4500-50 Street, Olds, Alberta T4H 1R6
Tel: +1(403) 556-8281 +1(800) 661-6537
Fax: +1(403) 556-4711
EMail: info@oldscollege.ca
Website: http://www.oldscollege.ab.ca

President: H.J. (Tom) Thompson

Areas

Agriculture (Agricultural Business; Finance; Management); **Animal Sciences** (Animal Husbandry; Veterinary Science); **Business** (Administration; Business Administration); **Fashion** (Marketing); **Horticulture** (Horticulture; Management); **Land and Environment** (Water Management); **Trades and Technology** (Agricultural Equipment; Agriculture; Metal Techniques; Service Trades)

Further Information: Also Calgary Campus.

Degrees and Diplomas: *Bachelor's Degree.* Applied Bachelor's degree (professional), 4 yrs.
Last Updated: 02/12/10

RED DEER COLLEGE (RDC)

PO Box 5005, 100 College Blvd., Red Deer, Alberta T4N 5H5
Tel: +1(403) 342-3300
Fax: +1(403) 340-8940
EMail: registrar@admin.rdc.ab.ca
Website: http://www.rdc.ab.ca

President: Joel Ward
Tel: +1(403) 342-3233, Fax: +1(403) 341-4899

Programmes

Arts *(University of Calgary)* (English; Psychology; Sociology); **Certificates and Diplomas** (Acting; Administration; Automotive Engineering; Business Administration; Child Care and Development; Computer Networks; Finance; Health Sciences; Laboratory Techniques; Music; Nursing; Performing Arts; Pharmacy; Service Trades; Social Work; Software Engineering; Sports; Theatre; Visual Arts); **Education** *(University of Alberta)* (Education); **General Studies** *(Athabasca University)*; **Motion Picture Arts**; **Nursing** *(University of Alberta)* (Nursing); **Social Work** *(University of Calgary)* (Social Work)

History: Founded 1963.

Degrees and Diplomas: *Bachelor's Degree.* Applied Bachelor's degree (professional), 4yrs; Bachelor's degree offered with Athabasca University, University of Alberta and University of Calgary.
Last Updated: 02/12/10

SOUTHERN ALBERTA INSTITUTE OF TECHNOLOGY (SAIT)

1301-16 Avenue N.W., Calgary, Alberta T2M 0L4
Tel: +1(403) 284-7248 +1(877) 284-7248
Fax: +1(403) 284-8940
EMail: registrar@sait.ab.ca
Website: http://www.sait.ab.ca

President and CEO: Irene Lewis
Tel: +1(403) 284-8581, Fax: +1(403) 284-8940

Vice-President, Academic: Gordon Nixon

Schools

Business (Accountancy; Business Administration; Finance; Information Management; Law; Management; Marketing); **Construction** (Architecture; Civil Engineering; Design; Surveying and Mapping); **Energy** *(MacPhail)* (Automation and Control Engineering; Chemical Engineering; Electrical Engineering; Environmental Engineering; Laboratory Techniques; Petroleum and Gas Engineering; Power Engineering); **Health and Public Safety** (Dentistry; Health Sciences; Information Technology; Medical Technology; Medicine; Pharmacy; Radiology; Rehabilitation and Therapy; Respiratory Therapy); **Hospitality and Tourism** (Cooking and Catering; Hotel and Restaurant; Tourism); **Information and Communications Technologies** (Electronic Engineering; Film; Information Sciences; Information Technology; Journalism; Library Science; Media Studies; Radio and Television Broadcasting; Video); **Manufacturing and Automation** (Automation and Control Engineering; Mechanical Engineering; Metal Techniques); **Transportation** (Aeronautical and Aerospace Engineering; Automotive Engineering; Business Administration; Railway Transport)

Further Information: Also Mayland Heights Campus and Art Smith Aero Centre for Training and Technology.

History: Founded as as the Provincial Institute of Technology and Art (PITA) in 1916. Renamed the Southern Alberta Institute of Technology (SAIT) 1960. Rebranded as SAIT Polytechnic in 2004.

Degrees and Diplomas: *Bachelor's Degree.* Bachelor's degree (professional), 4 yrs; Applied Bachelor's degree, 2 yrs following diploma.
Last Updated: 02/12/10

UNIVERSITY OF ALBERTA (U OF A)

114 St. 89 Ave, Edmonton, Alberta T6G 2E1
Tel: +1(780) 492-3111
Fax: +1(780) 492-7172
EMail: admissions.international@ualberta.ca
Website: http://www.ualberta.ca

President and Vice-Chancellor: Indira Samarasekera (2005-)
Tel: +1(780) 492-3212, Fax: +1(780) 492-9265
EMail: president@ualberta.ca; indira.samarasekera@ualberta.ca

Provost and Vice-President (Academic): Carl G. Amrhein
Tel: +1(780) 492-3920, Fax: +1(780) 492-1438
EMail: provost@ualberta.ca

International Relations: Britta Baron, Vice-Provost and Associate Vice-President (International)
Tel: +1(780) 492-5104, Fax: +1(780) 492-1438
EMail: britta.baron@ualberta.ca

Campuses

Augustana (Biology; Chemistry; Classical Languages; Computer Science; Development Studies; Economics; English; Environmental Studies; Fine Arts; French; Geography; German; Greek (Classical); History; Latin; Management; Mathematics; Modern Languages; Music; Physical Therapy; Physics; Political Sciences; Psychology; Religion; Scandinavian Languages; Social Sciences; Sociology; Spanish; Sports; Theatre; Visual Arts); **Saint-Jean** (Agriculture; Animal Husbandry; Arts and Humanities; Biological and Life Sciences; Business Administration; Canadian Studies; Earth Sciences; Ecology; Economics; Education; Engineering; Environmental Studies; History; Literature; Mathematics; Modern Languages; Natural Sciences; Nursing; Physics; Political Sciences; Primary Education; Psychology; Secondary Education; Sociology; Soil Management; Teacher Training)

Colleges

St. Joseph's (Ethics; Philosophy; Religious Education; Theology); **St. Stephen's** (Art Therapy; Pastoral Studies; Psychology; Theology)

Faculties

Agricultural, Life and Environmental Sciences (Agricultural Business; Agricultural Economics; Animal Husbandry; Ecology; Food Science; Food Technology; Forest Biology; Forest Economics; Forest Management; Horticulture; Natural Resources; Nutrition; Soil Science; Veterinary Science; Wildlife); **Arts** (African Studies; Ancient Civilizations; Anthropology; Arabic; Art History; Arts and Humanities; Comparative Literature; Criminology; Cultural Studies; Danish; Design; Economics; English; Environmental Studies; Film; Fine Arts; Folklore; French; German; History; Hungarian; Indic Languages; Information Sciences; International Studies; Italian; Linguistics; Literature; Mathematics; Medieval Studies; Middle Eastern Studies; Modern Languages; Music; Music Theory and Composition; Musicology; Norwegian; Peace and Disarmament; Persian; Philosophy; Polish; Political Sciences; Portuguese; Psychology; Religious Studies; Russian; Singing; Slavic Languages; Sociology; Spanish; Swahili; Swedish; Technology; Theatre; Translation and Interpretation; Visual Arts; Women's Studies); **Education** (Education; Educational Psychology; Educational Sciences; Natives Education; Physical Education; Primary Education; Secondary Education); **Engineering** (Biomedical Engineering; Chemical Engineering; Civil Engineering; Computer Engineering; Electrical Engineering; Engineering; Environmental Engineering; Materials Engineering; Mechanical Engineering; Mining Engineering; Petroleum and Gas Engineering); **Extension** (Acupuncture; Administration; Adult Education; Business Administration; Chinese; Communication Studies; Continuing Education; English; Fine Arts; French; German; Government; Human Resources; Information

Management; Information Technology; Insurance; Japanese; Management; Natural Resources; Occupational Health; Painting and Drawing; Spanish; Statistics; Writing); **Graduate Studies and Research** (Agricultural Economics; Agriculture; Ancient Civilizations; Anthropology; Applied Linguistics; Arts and Humanities; Biochemistry; Biological and Life Sciences; Biomedical Engineering; Business Administration; Canadian Studies; Cell Biology; Chemical Engineering; Chemistry; Civil Engineering; Communication Studies; Comparative Law; Computer Engineering; Computer Science; Cultural Studies; Dentistry; Design; Earth Sciences; East Asian Studies; Ecology; Economics; Education; Educational Psychology; Educational Sciences; Electrical Engineering; Engineering; English; Environmental Engineering; Environmental Studies; Fine Arts; Food Science; French; Genetics; German; Gynaecology and Obstetrics; Health Education; Health Sciences; History; Immunology; Information Sciences; Italian; Laboratory Techniques; Latin American Studies; Law; Library Science; Linguistics; Materials Engineering; Mathematics; Mechanical Engineering; Medicine; Microbiology; Modern Languages; Music; Natural Resources; Neurosciences; Nursing; Nutrition; Occupational Therapy; Oncology; Ophthalmology; Paediatrics; Pathology; Pharmacology; Pharmacy; Philosophy; Physical Education; Physical Therapy; Physics; Physiology; Political Sciences; Primary Education; Psychiatry and Mental Health; Psychology; Public Health; Radiology; Rehabilitation and Therapy; Religious Studies; Russian; Secondary Education; Slavic Languages; Sociology; Spanish; Speech Therapy and Audiology; Statistics; Surgery; Technology; Telecommunications Engineering; Theatre; Translation and Interpretation); **Law** (Law); **Medicine and Dentistry** (Anaesthesiology; Biochemistry; Biomedical Engineering; Cell Biology; Dental Hygiene; Dentistry; Genetics; Gynaecology and Obstetrics; Immunology; Laboratory Techniques; Medicine; Microbiology; Oncology; Ophthalmology; Paediatrics; Pathology; Pharmacology; Physiology; Psychiatry and Mental Health; Public Health; Radiology; Surgery); **Native Studies** (Native American Studies); **Nursing** (Nursing); **Pharmacy and Pharmaceutical Sciences** (Pharmacy); **Physical Education and Recreation** (Physical Education; Physical Therapy; Sports; Tourism); **Rehabilitation Medicine** (Occupational Therapy; Physical Therapy; Rehabilitation and Therapy; Speech Therapy and Audiology); **Science** (Biological and Life Sciences; Chemistry; Computer Science; Earth Sciences; Mathematics; Psychology; Statistics)

Schools

Business (*Alberta*) (Accountancy; Business Administration; Economics; Finance; Information Sciences; Law; Management; Marketing; Operations Research; Statistics); **Library and Information Studies** (Information Sciences; Library Science); **Public Health** (Behavioural Sciences; Epidemiology; Health Sciences; Occupational Health; Public Health)

Further Information: Also St. Joseph's College and St. Stephen's College for Theological Education. Campuses: South Campus and Michener Park, Augustana, Saint-Jean (French-language campus), Enterprise Square.

History: Founded 1908. A publicly supported, non-denominational, co-educational institution.

Governing Bodies: Board of Governors

Academic Year: September to April (September-December; January-April); Spring and Summer sessions available

Admission Requirements: Secondary school certificate or recognized foreign equivalent; post secondary transcrits; English language proficiency

Fees: (Can. Dollars): Undergraduate studies: Canadian students, 2,588.40-9,815.18 for Winter/Fall terms (full-time) or 1,035.36-19,630.36 for Winter/Fall terms (part-time); for Spring/Summer terms, 517.68-861.48 per 3 credit course or 1,035.36-1,722.96 per 6-credit course; International students: 8,997.60-14,725.52 for Winter/Fall terms (full-time) or 17,995.20-30,091-28 for Winter/Fall terms (part-time); for Spring/Summer terms 1,799.52-2,993.58 per 3 credit courses or 3,599.04-5,987.16 per 6-credit courses. Dentistry, Medicine programmes, 2,210.42-9,815.18 per term or 4,420.84-19,630.36; Postgraduate Medical Education, 942.16 per annum; DDS Advanced Placement Programmes, 3,849.11 per annum. Postgraduate studies: Canadian students, 3,643.20 (full-time) or 1,214.4 (part-time) for Winter/Fall terms; 2,893.28 (full-time) otr 1,196.64 (part-time) for Spring/Summer terms; International students, 7,286.40 (full-time) or 2,428 (part-time) for Winter/Fall terms; 4,786.56 (full-time) or 2,393.28 (part-time) for Spring/Summer

terms. MBA: Canadian students, 6,072 (full-time) or 12,214.40 (part-time); International students, 12,144 (full-time) or 2,428.80 (part-time).

Main Language(s) of Instruction: English. Also French at Faculté Saint-Jean

International Co-operation: With 165 institutions in 56 countries

Degrees and Diplomas: *Bachelor's Degree*; *Master's Degree*; *Doctoral Degree*. Also combined degree programmes, 4-5 yrs; Executive MBA, 2 yrs.

Student Services: Academic counselling, Employment services, Health services, Social counselling

Student Residential Facilities: For c. 4,000 students

Libraries: Total, 6,1m. vols; 1,5 m. maps; over 20,000 full text electronic journals

Press or Publishing House: University of Alberta Press

Academic Staff *2007-2008*	MEN	WOMEN	TOTAL
FULL-TIME	–	–	c. **3,300**
Student Numbers *2008-2009*			
All (Foreign Included)	16,576	20,424	c. **37,000**
FOREIGN ONLY	–	–	**1,280**

Part-time students, 3,530.
Note: Part-time students are not included in the total
Last Updated: 16/12/10

UNIVERSITY OF CALGARY (U OF C)

2500 University Drive North West, Calgary, Alberta T2N 1N4
Tel: +1(403) 220-5110
Fax: +1(403) 282-8413
EMail: uofcinfo@ucalgary.ca
Website: http://www.ucalgary.ca

President: Elizabeth Cannon (2010-2015)
Tel: +1(403) 220-5617, Fax: +1(403) 289-6800
EMail: president@ucalgary.ca

Provost and Vice-President (Academic): Alan Harrison
Tel: +1(403) 220-5464, Fax: +1(403) 289-6800
EMail: provost@ucalgary.ca

Associate Vice-Provost (Enrolment) and Registrar: David Johnston Tel: +1(403) 220-7993 EMail: registra@ucalgary.ca

International Relations: Carol Stewart, Vice-Provost (International) Tel: +1(403) 220-3672 EMail: vpi@ucalgary.ca

Centres

Advanced Technologies of Life Sciences *(CAT)* (Biological and Life Sciences; Biomedicine; Health Sciences; Veterinary Science); **Alberta Global Forum** (Communication Studies; Cultural Studies); **Bioengineering Research and Education** *(CBRE)* (Bioengineering); **Environmental Engineering Research and Education** *(CEERE)* (Energy Engineering; Environmental Engineering); **Gifted Education** (Special Education); **Health and Policy Studies** *(CHAPS)* (Public Health); **Information Security and Cryptography** (Computer Science; Mathematics); **Innovation Studies** *(THECIS)*; **Innovative Technology** *(Calgary - CCIT)*; **Institutional Research Information Services Solution** *(IRISS)* (Information Sciences); **Mathematics in Life Sciences** (Biological and Life Sciences; Ecology; Mathematics; Medicine); **Microsystems Engineering** *(CME)* (Engineering); **Military and Strategic Studies** *(CMSS)* (Military Science); **Pipeline Engineering** *(PEC)* (Mechanical Engineering; Petroleum and Gas Engineering); **Public Interest Accounting** *(CPIA)* (Accountancy); **Risk Studies**; **Social Work Research and Development** (Social Work); **Study of Higher Education** *(Canadian)* (Higher Education); **World Tourism Education and Research** (Tourism)

Faculties

Arts (African Studies; Anthropology; Archaeology; Art Education; Canadian Studies; Communication Studies; Cultural Studies; Dance; Development Studies; Earth Sciences; East Asian Studies; Economics; English; French; Geography; German; Greek (Classical); Heritage Preservation; History; Indigenous Studies; International Relations; International Studies; Italian; Latin; Latin American Studies; Law; Linguistics; Media Studies; Museum Studies; Music; Philosophy; Political Sciences; Psychology; Religious Studies; Slavic Languages; Sociology; Spanish; Technology; Theatre; Urban

Studies; Women's Studies); **Education** (Education; Psychology; Teacher Training); **Environmental Design** (Architecture; Design; Environmental Studies); **Graduate Studies** (Anthropology; Archaeology; Architecture; Arts and Humanities; Astronomy and Space Science; Biochemistry; Biological and Life Sciences; Biomedical Engineering; Business Administration; Cardiology; Chemical Engineering; Chemistry; Civil Engineering; Communication Studies; Computer Engineering; Computer Science; Continuing Education; Design; Earth Sciences; East Asian Studies; Economics; Education; Electrical Engineering; Energy Engineering; Engineering; English; Environmental Engineering; Fine Arts; French; Gastroenterology; Geography; German; Germanic Studies; Greek (Classical); History; Immunology; Italian; Latin; Law; Linguistics; Mathematics; Mechanical Engineering; Medicine; Microbiology; Military Science; Molecular Biology; Music; Natural Sciences; Neurosciences; Nursing; Petroleum and Gas Engineering; Philosophy; Physical Therapy; Physics; Political Sciences; Psycholinguistics; Psychology; Religious Studies; Respiratory Therapy; Slavic Languages; Social and Preventive Medicine; Social Work; Sociology; Spanish; Statistics; Surveying and Mapping; Theatre; Veterinary Science); **Kinesiology** (Anatomy; Health Sciences; Pedagogy; Physical Therapy; Physiology; Rehabilitation and Therapy); **Law** (Law); **Medicine** (Anatomy; Biochemistry; Cardiology; Cell Biology; Genetics; Gynaecology and Obstetrics; Health Sciences; Laboratory Techniques; Medicine; Microbiology; Molecular Biology; Neurosciences; Oncology; Paediatrics; Pathology; Pharmacology; Physiology; Psychiatry and Mental Health; Radiology; Rehabilitation and Therapy; Surgery; Veterinary Science); **Nursing** (Nursing); **Nursing - Qatar** *(Qatar)* (Nursing); **Science** (Astronomy and Space Science; Biological and Life Sciences; Chemistry; Computer Science; Earth Sciences; Environmental Studies; Mathematics; Nanotechnology; Natural Sciences; Physics; Statistics); **Social Work** (Social Work); **Veterinary Medicine** (Veterinary Science)

Institutes
Advanced Policy Research; **Biocomplexity and Informatics** (Biology; Molecular Biology); **Biogeoscience** (Biological and Life Sciences; Biology; Botany; Earth Sciences; Ecology; Environmental Engineering; Environmental Management; Environmental Studies; Geography; Neurosciences; Surveying and Mapping; Wildlife); **Bone and Joint Health** *(McCaig)* (Medicine; Rheumatology); **Gender Research** (Gender Studies); **Humanities** *(Calgary)* (Arts and Humanities); **Professional Communication** *(IPC)* (Communication Studies; Cultural Studies); **Quantum Information Science** (Applied Mathematics; Computer Science; Physics); **Space Research** (Astronomy and Space Science); **Sustainable Energy, Environment and Economy** (Economics; Energy Engineering; Environmental Studies); **United States Policy Research** (Economics; International Relations; Political Sciences)

Research Centres
Fine Arts *(CRFA)* (Fine Arts); **Informatics** (Computer Science); **Language** (Linguistics; Modern Languages); **Latin American** *(LARC)* (Latin American Studies)

Schools
Business *(Haskayne)* (Accountancy; Business Administration; Business and Commerce; Finance; Hotel and Restaurant; Human Resources; Information Sciences; International Business; Management; Marketing; Operations Research; Tourism); **Engineering** *(Schulich)* (Bioengineering; Biomedical Engineering; Chemical Engineering; Civil Engineering; Computer Engineering; Electrical Engineering; Engineering; Environmental Engineering; Mechanical Engineering; Petroleum and Gas Engineering; Software Engineering; Surveying and Mapping)

Units
Continuing Education (English)

Further Information: Also Consortium for Research in Elastic Wave Exploration Seismology

History: Founded 1960 as University of Alberta at Calgary, and acquired present status and title 1966.

Governing Bodies: Board of Governors; General Faculties Council

Academic Year: September to June (September-December; January-April; May-June). Also Summer Session (July-August)

Admission Requirements: Secondary school certificate or recognized foreign equivalent

Fees: (Can. Dollars): tuition fees for undergaduate programmes, 667.93 per course for Canadian students and 1,927.72 per course fro International students, except Medicine, 1,489.36 per course; Law, 6,485.59 for 6 courses for Canadian students and 20,400.67 for 6 courses for International students. Graduate programmes, 5,439.90-5,561.28 per programme for Canadian students except MBA, 11,148.36; for international students, 12,347.34 per programme, except MBA, 24,598.68

Main Language(s) of Instruction: English

International Co-operation: Participates in Erasmus and UMAP programmes

Degrees and Diplomas: *Bachelor's Degree*; *Master's Degree*; *Doctoral Degree*. Also Combined Degree Programmes (Bachelor/Master), 5 yrs; Postgraduate Medical Education; MBA

Student Services: Academic counselling, Canteen, Employment services, Foreign student adviser, Foreign Studies Centre, Handicapped facilities, Health services, Language programs, Nursery care, Social counselling, Sports facilities

Student Residential Facilities: Yes

Special Facilities: Nickle Arts Museum

Libraries: MacKimmie Library; Medical Library; Law Library; Business Library; Gallagher Library of Geology and Geophysics, total, c. 2m. vols; 3.6m. Microforms

Publications: Arctic, Arctic Institute of North America *(quarterly)*; Ariel *(quarterly)*; Canadian Ethnic Studies *(3 per annum)*; Canadian Journal of Law and Society *(annually)*; Canadian Journal of Philosophy *(quarterly)*; Canadian Review of American Studies *(3 per annum)*; Classical Views/Echos du Monde Classique, Department of Classics *(3 per annum)*; Grove, Department of English *(annually)*; International Journal of Drama and Theatre *(biennially)*; Journal of Child and Youth Care, Faculty of Social Work *(3 per annum)*; Journal of Comparative Family Studies *(3 per annum)*; Journal of Educational Thought *(3 per annum)*; Journal of Military and Strategic Studies *(biennially)*

Press or Publishing House: The University of Calgary Press

Academic Staff 2007-2008	TOTAL
FULL-TIME	c. **2,210**
Student Numbers 2007-2008	
All (Foreign Included)	**28,000**

Part-time students, 6,000.
Last Updated: 21/12/10

UNIVERSITY OF LETHBRIDGE (U OF L)
4401 University Drive, Lethbridge, Alberta T1K 3M4
Tel: +1(403) 329-2111
Fax: +1(403) 329-5159
EMail: inquiries@uleth.ca
Website: http://www.uleth.ca

President and Vice-Chancellor: Mike Mahon (2010-)
Tel: +1(403) 329-2201, Fax: +1(403) 329-2097
EMail: mike.mahon@uleth.ca

Vice-President (Finance and Administration): Nancy Walker
Tel: +1(403) 329-2207, Fax: +1(403) 380-2097
EMail: nancy.walker@uleth.ca

Faculties
Arts and Science (Agriculture; Anthropology; Archaeology; Art History; Biochemistry; Biological and Life Sciences; Biotechnology; Canadian Studies; Chemistry; Computer Science; Dentistry; Economics; Engineering; English; Environmental Studies; Food Science; French; Geography; German; History; Journalism; Law; Mathematics; Medicine; Museum Studies; Music; Native American Studies; Neurosciences; Nutrition; Optometry; Painting and Drawing; Philosophy; Physical Education; Physical Therapy; Physics; Political Sciences; Psychology; Regional Studies; Religious Studies; Social Sciences; Social Work; Sociology; Spanish; Surveying and Mapping; Theatre; Urban Studies; Veterinary Science; Women's Studies; Writing); **Education** (Curriculum; Education; Educational and Student Counselling; Educational Psychology; Special Education); **Fine Arts** (Art History; Display and Stage Design; Fine Arts; Media Studies; Museum Studies; Music; Performing Arts; Theatre); **Graduate Studies** (Arts and Humanities; Education; Educational and Student Counselling; Fine Arts; Health Sciences; Leadership;

Management; Music; Philosophy); **Health Sciences** (Health Sciences; Nursing; Public Health; Toxicology); **Management** *(Edmonton)* (Accountancy; Business Administration; Finance; Human Resources; International Business; Management; Marketing); **Management** *(Calgary)* (Accountancy; Government; International Business; Management); **Management** *(Lethbridge)* (Management)

Further Information: Also Language Centre providing non-credit programmes in English as a Second Language, and University level writing

History: Founded 1967.

Governing Bodies: Board of Governors; General Faculties Council

Academic Year: September to August (September-December; January-April; May-August)

Admission Requirements: Secondary school certificate or recognized foreign equivalent, with 65% or equivalent average (actual cut-off may vary from year to year depending on space available and demand)

Fees: (Can. Dollars): Undergraduate, 484 per course for Canadian students and 1,095 per course for International students; Graduate, Canadian Open studies students, 568 per course and International open studies students, 1,267 per course; Master and PhD programmes, 1,893.33 for Canadian students and 4,223.33 for International students; except for Master's degree in Management, 3,200 for Canadian students and 6,400 for International students; Part-time programmes, 1,230.67 for Canadian students and 2,745.17 for International students. Summer session, 284 for Canadian students and 633.50 for International students.

Main Language(s) of Instruction: English

Degrees and Diplomas: *Bachelor's Degree*; *Master's Degree*; *Doctoral Degree.* Also combined degree programmes (Bachelor in a chosen degree, and a Bachelor of Education), 5 yrs; Post-Diploma Bachelor's degree, 2yrs; Pre-Professional Transfer Programmes

Student Services: Academic counselling, Canteen, Cultural centre, Employment services, Foreign student adviser, Handicapped facilities, Health services, Language programs, Social counselling, Sports facilities

Student Residential Facilities: For c. 570 students

Special Facilities: Art Gallery; Aquatic Centre; Theatre; Recital Hall/Film Theatre; Observatory

Libraries: Central Library, total 1.4 m vols

Publications: Performing Arts Preview
Last Updated: 21/12/10

PRIVATE INSTITUTIONS

CANADIAN UNIVERSITY COLLEGE (CUC)

5415 College Avenue, Lacombe, Alberta T4L 2E5
Tel: +1(403) 782-3381 +1(800) 661-8129
Fax: +1(403) 782-3170
EMail: info@cauc.ca; admissions@cauc.ca
Website: http://www.cauc.ca

President: Mark Haynal EMail: mhaynal@cauc.ca

Vice-President, Student Services: Stacy Hunter
EMail: shunter@cauc.ca

Divisions
Arts (Art History; Ceramic Art; Design; English; French; History; Music; Painting and Drawing; Philosophy; Political Sciences; Religious Studies; Spanish); **Science** (Behavioural Sciences; Biochemistry; Biology; Chemistry; Computer Science; Engineering; Geology; Mathematics; Physical Education; Physics; Psychology; Social Work; Sociology)

Schools
Business (Accountancy; Business Administration; Human Resources; International Business; Management); **Education** (Art Education; Business Education; Education; Foreign Languages Education; Mathematics Education; Music Education; Native

Language Education; Physical Education; Primary Education; Religious Studies; Science Education; Secondary Education; Social Studies)

History: Founded 1907 as Alberta Seventh-day Adventist secondary school. The Board of Trustees authorized the establishment of a junior college 1919. Became known as Canadian Union College and statred offering its first four-year programme in Theology 1947. Acquired present title 1997.

Fees: (US Dollars): For US, Australian and Bermudian Students: Application Fee, 50; Tuition fee, 340 per credit or 10,880 for two semesters. For International Students: application fees, 200; Tuition fee, 340 per credit or 10,880 for two semesters.

Degrees and Diplomas: *Bachelor's Degree.* Bachelor's degree (Professional), 4 years.
Last Updated: 01/12/10

CONCORDIA UNIVERSITY COLLEGE OF ALBERTA (CUCA)

7128 Ada Boulevard, Edmonton, Alberta T5B 4E4
Tel: +1(780) 479-8481
Fax: +1(780) 477-1033
EMail: admits@concordia.ab.ca
Website: http://www.concordia.ab.ca

President: Gerald S. Krispin
Tel: +1(780) 479-9236, Fax: +1(780) 474-1933
EMail: gerald.krispin@concordia.ab.ca

Vice-President, Academics and Provost: Richard Willie
Tel: +1(780) 479-9215, Fax: +1(780) 474-1933
EMail: richard.willie@concordia.ab.ca

International Relations: A.L.A. (Tony) Norrad, Dean, Admissions and Finance Aid
Tel: +1(780) 479-9224 EMail: tony.norrad@concordia.ab.ca

Faculties
Arts (Art History; Arts and Humanities; English; Greek (Classical); Hebrew; History; Modern Languages; Music; Nursing; Philosophy; Political Sciences; Psychology; Religious Studies; Sociology; Theatre; Writing); **Continuing Education** (Accountancy; Behavioural Sciences; Biological and Life Sciences; Chemistry; Computer Science; Economics; English; Environmental Studies; Finance; Fine Arts; History; Management; Marketing; Mathematics; Musical Instruments; Nursing; Physics; Psychology; Social Studies; Spanish; Writing); **Education** (Education); **Graduate Studies** (Bible; Christian Religious Studies; Information Management; Information Sciences); **Professional Education** (Management; Public Health); **Science** (Biology; Chemistry; Earth Sciences; Environmental Studies; Forensic Medicine and Dentistry; Health Sciences; Mathematics and Computer Science; Physics)

History: Founded 1921. Became a degree-granting university 1987.

Governing Bodies: Board of Regents comprising 15 members

Academic Year: September to April (September-December; January-April). Also Spring/Summer Session (May-August)

Admission Requirements: Secondary school certificate or recognized foreign equivalent, including International Baccalaureate and Advanced Placement

Fees: (Can. Dollars): undergraduate programmes, 265 per credit; 3,315 per semester; Mandatory Fees (full-time), 389.23; International Student Fee, 191 per credit or 1,700 per semester.

Main Language(s) of Instruction: English

International Co-operation: With universities in Israel and Germany

Accrediting Agencies: Government of Alberta - Post-Secondary Learning Act (Alberta); Association of Universities and Colleges of Canada

Degrees and Diplomas: *Bachelor's Degree*; *Master's Degree*

Student Services: Academic counselling, Canteen, Employment services, Foreign student adviser, Handicapped facilities, Social counselling, Sports facilities

Student Residential Facilities: For 90 students

Libraries: 177,822 vols
Last Updated: 16/12/10

DEVRY INSTITUTE OF TECHNOLOGY - CALGARY (DEVRY)

2700 3rd Avenue S.E., Calgary, Alberta T2A 7WA
Tel: +1(403) 235-3450 +1(800) 363-5558
EMail: CAL-Webmaster@devry.edu
Website: http://www.cal.devry.ca

President: Ranil Herath

Registrar: Larry Wagner

Programmes
Business Administration (Business Administration; Communication Studies; Finance; Hotel and Restaurant; Industrial Management; Information Sciences; Management; Marketing; Sales Techniques; Small Business; Tourism); **Computer Engineering Technology** (Computer Engineering); **Computer Information Systems** (Business Administration; Computer Science; Data Processing; Information Sciences; Systems Analysis); **Electronics Engineering Technology** (Electronic Engineering); **Network and Communications Management** (Computer Science; Telecommunications Engineering)

Degrees and Diplomas: *Bachelor's Degree.* Bachelor's degree (Professional), 4 yrs.
Last Updated: 01/12/10

ST. MARY'S UNIVERSITY COLLEGE

14500 Bannister Road SE, Calgary, Alberta T2X 1Z4
Tel: +1(403) 531-9130
Fax: +1(403) 531-9136
EMail: admissions@stmu.ab.ca
Website: http://www.stmu.ab.ca

President: Terrence Downey
Tel: +1(403) 254-3701 EMail: Terry.Downey@stmu.ab.ca

Vice-President Academic and Dean: Mark Charlton
Tel: +1(403) 254-3771 EMail: Mark.Charlton@stmu.ab.ca

Programmes
Biological Sciences (Biological and Life Sciences); **Business/ Management** (Business Administration; Management); **Catholic Educators** (Educational Administration; Religious Education); **English** (English); **General Studies** (Arts and Humanities; Natural Sciences); **History** (History); **Psychology** (Psychology)

History: Founded 1986. Acquired present status and title 2004.

Governing Bodies: Board of Governors; Community Advisory Council; Academic Council

Academic Year: September to June

Admission Requirements: Secondary school certificate or recognized equivalent

Fees: (Can. Dollars): 2,745 per semester

Main Language(s) of Instruction: English

Accrediting Agencies: Campus Alberta Quality Council

Degrees and Diplomas: *Bachelor's Degree.* Bachelor of Arts in English, 4yrs; Bachelor of Education (Elementary), 2 yr after degree programme.

Student Services: Academic counselling, Canteen, Handicapped facilities, Sports facilities

Student Residential Facilities: None

Libraries: Central library and membership in the Alberta Library (TAL) and Integrated Library System (ILS)

Publications: Salvia, Student Academic Journal *(annually)*; Sight Lines, Literary Journal *(biennially)*

Press or Publishing House: St. Mary's University College Press
Last Updated: 03/12/10

THE KING'S UNIVERSITY COLLEGE (TKUC)

9125-50 Street North West, Edmonton, Alberta T6B 2H3
Tel: +1(780) 465-3500
Fax: +1(780) 465-3534
EMail: general-info@kingsu.ca; registrar@kingsu.ca
Website: http://www.kingsu.ca

President: Harry Fernhout EMail: president@kingsu.ca

Vice-President Academic: Harry Spaling
EMail: harry.spaling@kingsu.ca

Faculties
Arts (Art History; Display and Stage Design; English; History; Media Studies; Music; Music Theory and Composition; Musical Instruments; Musicology; Painting and Drawing; Philosophy; Singing; Theatre; Theology); **Education** (Education; Primary Education; Secondary Education); **Natural Sciences** (Astronomy and Space Science; Biology; Chemistry; Computer Science; Mathematics; Natural Sciences; Physics); **Social Sciences** (Business and Commerce; Economics; Geography; Management; Physical Education; Political Sciences; Psychology; Social Sciences; Sociology)

Programmes
Cross-Divisional Studies (Communication Arts; Economics; Environmental Studies; History; Political Sciences; Social Sciences)

Further Information: Also Study Abroad programmes: American, China, Latin American, Middle East, Dutch, Russian Studies Programmes; Los Angeles Film Studies Center; Oxford Honors Programme; Oxford Summer School Programme; Summer Institute of Journalism and others

History: Founded 1979 as The King's College. A private, co-educational Christian liberal arts institution offering undergraduate degrees accredited by the Government of Alberta since 1987. Acquired present title 1993.

Governing Bodies: Board of Governors, comprising 26 members; Senate, comprising 14 members

Academic Year: September to April (September-December; January-April)

Admission Requirements: Secondary school certificate with minimum 60% average in prescribed courses or recognized foreign equivalent. Proficiency in oral and written English. If English is applicant's second language, TOEFL score of 580+, or computer-based score of 237+, or IELTS score of 6.5. Requirements may include acceptable performance in entrance tests, such as ACT and SAT

Fees: (Can. Dollars): Tuition 6,696 per annum; Bachelor of Education, 6,810; Student fees 305

Main Language(s) of Instruction: English

Accrediting Agencies: Private Colleges Accreditation Board (Alberta); Association of Universities and Colleges in Canada; Council for Christian Colleges & Universities

Degrees and Diplomas: *Bachelor's Degree.* Bachelor's degree (professional), 4 yrs.

Student Services: Academic counselling, Canteen, Employment services, Foreign student adviser, Handicapped facilities, Social counselling, Sports facilities

Student Residential Facilities: For c. 260 students

Libraries: 76,000 vols
Last Updated: 03/12/10

Canada - British Columbia

STRUCTURE OF HIGHER EDUCATION SYSTEM

Description:

Higher education in Canada is the constitutional responsibility of the provinces. British Columbia's public post-secondary education system includes 25 public institutions: 11 universities, 11 colleges and three institutes. Universities in B.C. offer an array of undergraduate degree programmes and a range of programmes at the graduate level. Some also offer courses and programmes in trades, vocational and career technical studies leading to certificates and diplomas, as well as developmental programmes that prepare adult learners for post-secondary studies. Some universities undertake original and applied research in a range of disciplines, while others undertake applied research and scholarly activities in support of their programming. Colleges offer developmental programmes that prepare adult learners for post-secondary studies, as well as courses and programmes in trades, vocational, career technical and academic studies leading to certificates, diplomas, associate degrees and applied baccalaureate degrees. Institutes are organized according to career, vocational and technical specialties, covering a variety of occupations. They may offer credentials from certificates to degrees. One institute has an Aboriginal focus. All public post-secondary institutions are governed by boards comprised of provincially-appointed members and members elected by faculty, staff and students. Government also supports pre-employment, apprenticeship and vocational programmes. Private or out of province public institutions must receive authorization through provincial legislation in order to offer or grant degrees, or use the word "university" to indicate that an educational programme is available. 17 private post-secondary institutions (including two out of province public institutions) have legislative authority to offer and grant academic degrees and 14 private post-secondary institutions have legislative authority to offer and grant theological degrees. 349 private career training institutions offer certificate and diploma programmes in trades, technology, and vocational fields of study. In addition, there are a large number of private institutions operating in British Columbia that offer programmes such as language training, non-degree theological or recreational courses. These institutions are not required to register with PCTIA as they do not offer career training as defined in the Act; however, they may register on a voluntary basis.

Stages of studies:

University level first stage: *Bachelor's degree*
In B.C., universities, colleges and institutes all offer programming that leads to baccalaureate degrees. In the case of colleges, it is typically the first two years of a baccalaureate degree, as well as some applied baccalaureate degrees (e.g., Bachelor of Business Administration). Most undergraduate study leads to a "General" Bachelor's degree (minimum three years) or an "Honours" degree (4 years and prescribed subject concentration). Degrees are normally titled in broad descriptive groups, e.g. B.A. and B.Sc. Arts and Sciences programmes which consist of courses in the liberal arts, humanities, social or physical sciences. A two-year Associate degree in Arts and Science provides two-year transfer to the public universities. The first stage also includes undergraduate Diplomas (1-3 years of study) and short (up to 1 year) special Certificate programmes; these may enable entry to degree programmes and are frequently given in close cooperation with professional bodies. In addition, the first stage includes other professional programmes that typically require no university level prerequisites and four years of study, e.g. Bachelor of Science in Nursing, Bachelor Business Administration and Bachelor of Education. First stage includes first professional degree programmes requiring prerequisite university studies (generally a baccalaureate degree) followed by three years for a Bachelor of Law (LL.B.) while others, e.g. Doctor of Medicine (M.D.) and Doctor of Veterinary Medicine (D.V.M.), normally require four years.

University level second stage: *Master's degree*
The Master's degree normally requires at least one year's study after a Bachelor's degree or equivalent. Most Master's programmes, e.g. in Business Administration, require at least two years. A thesis is usually required, often course work as well. Examples are: M.A., M.Sc., M.Ed., and M.B.A.

University level third stage: *Doctoral degrees*
A Doctoral degree is the highest academic qualification and comprises the third stage of university level studies. This degree normally requires at least three years of study after the Master's degree; the submission and defence of a dissertation are the principal requirements, and supplemental course work is usually also required.

The degree "Doctor of Philosophy" (Ph.D.) is the designation most commonly used to signify the doctoral degrees. There are also doctoral programmes in professional areas that typically use the term "Doctorate". Doctoral degree-holders frequently use the title "Dr." (Doctoral degrees should not be confused with certain first professional degrees in the Health Sciences, e.g. Medicine, Veterinary Medicine and Dentistry). In B.C., Doctoral degrees are limited to 5 of the 11 public universities. Doctoral degrees in professional studies are becoming more common for third level studies in specific professional fields such as Doctor of Education (Ed.D).

Distance higher education:

British Columbia has a well developed system of distance education which provides a range of open learning services to learners in all regions of the province and beyond. The Thompson Rivers University has a provincial mandate for public open and distance education and has assumed the functions of the BC Open University and Open College. Other public post-secondary institutions and many private post-secondary institutions throughout the province also deliver a wide range of open learning programmes.

BCcampus is a collaboration of post-secondary institutions in British Columbia that provides a web-based central access point to public post-secondary distance learning resources. BCcampus also provides support services for learners, faculty and course developers, staff and administrators. BCcampus enhances access to and choices of quality post-secondary learning opportunities for all students, particularly those in rural and remote communities and those whose lives demand a more flexible schedule for their education. For additional information on BCcampus, visit: http://www.bccampus.ca

ADMISSION TO HIGHER EDUCATION

Admission to university-level studies:

Name of secondary school credential required: Certificate of Graduation

Name of secondary school credential required: Adult Education Graduation Program

Alternatives to credentials: Post-secondary institutions set their own admission policies.

Numerus clausus/restrictions: Post-secondary institutions set their own admissions policies.

Other admission requirements: Minimum score: Generally, at least C+ (67-72%). Proof of proficiency in the language of instruction. Some post-secondary institutions provide remedial courses or a transitional year programme, and most seek to admit a proportionately equitable mix of qualified applicants.

Foreign students admission:

Definition of foreign student: Foreign (International) Students are students who are not Canadian citizens, refugees or permanent residents of Canada, and are enrolled full time or part time in recognized academic, professional or vocational training or English as a Second Language programme course at a university, college or other educational institution in Canada.

Entrance exam requirements: Students applying to any post-secondary programme in B.C. must meet the admission requirements of the specific institution. Please contact the International Education or Admissions Office at the institution for specific details.

Entry regulations: Before students come to study in Canada, they need: a valid passport or travel document, the letter of introduction that students received from the visa office when their study permit was approved. This letter contains their study permit reference number; a letter of acceptance from the institution where students have been granted permission to study; proof that they have enough money to pay for school fees and living expenses; establishes that they will return home at the end of their studies; a valid temporary resident visa (required for citizens of many countries); and letters of reference or any other documents recommended by the visa office where students applied. A small number of students do not require a Study Permit by virtue of their status in Canada (e.g. diplomats and their children).

Health requirements: Medical examinations are required by Citizenship and Immigration Canada for students who plan to study in Canada longer than six months or studying and working in a school, hospital, day-care centre or other facility where it is important to protect public health.

Medical insurance is required for all students while they are in Canada. In B.C., basic health-care insurance coverage begins three months after they arrive in the province and apply to the B.C Medical Services Plan. Basic MSP health-care insurance covers things like visiting the doctor and going to the hospital. Students must have enough private health-care insurance to cover their entire stay in B.C. for shorter programmes (less than six months) or to cover the waiting period prior to receiving MSP coverage.

Language requirements: Students may need to demonstrate competence in the English language, generally by achieving a specified minimum score on an IELTS, TOEFL or English proficiency test. Please contact the International Education or Admissions Office at the institution for specific details.

RECOGNITION OF STUDIES

Quality assurance system:

Public post-secondary institutions have senates, education councils or other similar bodies which include appointed administration and elected student and faculty representatives. These bodies oversee academic matters, such as admission standards, curriculum and grading. The Private Career Training Institutions Agency offers a voluntary accreditation process to registered private career training institutions in which institutions undergo a more rigorous quality assurance process, including demonstrating they meet certain institutional and quality standards. The Degree Quality Assessment Board (the Board) reviews and makes recommendation to the Minister on new degree programmes, use of the word "university" in British Columbia.

Bodies dealing with recognition:

Degree Quality Assessment Board
PO Box 9177, Stn Prov Govt
Victoria, BC V8W 9H8
Tel: +1(250) 387 5163
WWW: http://www.aved.gov.bc.ca/degree-authorization/

International Credential Evaluation Service - ICES (at the British Columbia Institute of Technology)
3700 Willingdon Avenue
Burnaby, BC V5G 3H2
Tel: +1(604) 432 8800
Fax: +1(604) 435 7033
EMail: icesinfo@bcit.ca
WWW: http://www.bcit.ca/ices/
Services provided and students dealt with: ICES has service agreements with over 90 affiliations comprised of regulated professional organizations, government agencies and educational institutions in Canada. Sixteen B.C. public institutions use ICES' services for programme specific credential assessments. A formal ICES assessment provides recognition and credits for individuals to purse their career and to studies in Canada with minimal disruption or loss of previous educational and work experiences.

Special provisions for recognition:

Recognition for university level studies: Post-secondary institutions establish their own admissions criteria and make their own admissions decisions in response to individual applications. Any restrictions on admissions are determined by each institution based on given available teaching and other resources. Universities and other post-secondary institutions regularly assess and make decisions on foreign academic credentials for admission purposes. Additionally, the Canadian Information Centre for International credentials (CICIC) provides information and guidance on the recognition of foreign studies.

For access to advanced studies and research: Post-secondary institutions establish their own admissions criteria and make their own admissions decisions in response to individual applications. Any restrictions on admissions are determined by each institution based on given available teaching and other resources.

For exercising a profession: Access to most professions is governed by provincial and/or federal statutes and is restricted to Canadian citizens or immigrants accepted as permanent residents. Applicants must meet examination and/or practical training requirements set by the relevant professional body or provincial or federal licensing board. ICES has service agreements with over 90 affiliations comprised of regulated professional organizations, government agencies and educational institutions in Canada. A formal ICES assessment provides recognition and credits for individuals to purse their career and to studies in Canada with minimal disruption or loss of previous educational and work experiences.

PROVINCIAL BODIES

Ministry of Advanced Education

Minister: Naomi Yamamoto
PO Box 9080, Stn. Prov Govt
Victoria, BC V8W 9T2
Canada
Tel: +1(250) 952 0179
Fax: +1(250) 952-0260
EMail: AVED.GeneralInquiries@gov.bc.ca
WWW: http://www.gov.bc.ca/aved/index.html

BC Council on Admissions and Transfer - BCCAT

Executive Director: Robert Fleming
709-555 Seymour Street
Vancouver, BC V6B 3H6
Canada
Tel: +1(604) 412 7700
Fax: +1(604) 683 0576
EMail: info@bccat.ca
WWW: http://www.bccat.ca/

Role of national body: To develop, in cooperation with the various institutions of post-secondary education, policies that will facilitate successful admission and transfer of students within the British Columbia post-secondary education system.

Private Career Training Institutions Agency - PCTIA

Chairperson: Kelly Rainsforth
300-5172 Kingsway
Burnaby, BC V5H 2E8
Canada
Tel: +1(604) 660 4400
Fax: +1(604) 660 3312
EMail: info@pctia.bc.ca
WWW: http://pctia.bc.ca/

Role of national body: The Private Career Training Institutions Agency is a not-for-profit corporation which operates at arm's length from government. Established under the Private Career Training Institutions Act in November 2004, the objects of the Agency are:

• To provide consumer protection to the students and prospective students of registered institutions;

• To establish standards of quality that must be met by accredited institutions;

• To carry out, in the public interest, its powers, duties and functions under the Act, the Regulations and the Bylaws.

The legislation also provides for the Student Training Completion Fund which provides compensation to students affected by the closure of a registered institution.

Data for academic year: 2011-2012

Source: IAU from the Canadian Information Centre for International Credentials (CICIC), a unit of the Council of Ministers of Education, Canada (CMEC), on behalf of the Province of British Columbia, 2011.

INSTITUTIONS

PUBLIC INSTITUTIONS

BRITISH COLUMBIA INSTITUTE OF TECHNOLOGY (BCIT)

3700 Willingdon Avenue, Burnaby, British Columbia V5G 3H2
Tel: +1(604) 434-5734
Fax: +1(604) 434-6243
EMail: regweb@bcit.bc.ca
Website: http://www.bcit.ca

President: Don Wright
Tel: 604-432-8200, Fax: 604-432-7848 EMail: Don_Wright@bcit.ca

Schools

Business (Accountancy; Business Administration; Communication Studies; Design; Finance; Human Resources; Information Technology; Insurance; International Business; Journalism; Management; Marketing; Media Studies; Radio and Television Broadcasting; Real Estate; Sales Techniques; Tourism); **Computing and Academic Studies** (Accountancy; Chemistry; Computer

Networks; Computer Science; Criminology; English; Forensic Medicine and Dentistry; History; Information Technology; Literature; Mass Communication; Mathematics; Philosophy; Physics; Political Sciences; Sociology; Software Engineering); **Construction and the Environment** (Architecture; Building Technologies; Civil Engineering; Construction Engineering; Design; Ecology; Electrical Engineering; Energy Engineering; Engineering; Environmental Engineering; Fishery; Heating and Refrigeration; Interior Design; Metal Techniques; Mining Engineering; Natural Resources; Structural Architecture; Surveying and Mapping; Technology; Wildlife; Wood Technology); **Energy** (Automation and Control Engineering; Chemical Engineering; Computer Graphics; Electrical Engineering; Electronic Engineering; Energy Engineering; Fire Science; Heating and Refrigeration; Industrial Engineering; Machine Building; Mechanical Engineering; Petroleum and Gas Engineering; Polymer and Plastics Technology; Power Engineering; Robotics; Technology Education; Telecommunications Engineering); **Health Sciences** (Biomedical Engineering; Biotechnology; Cardiology; Food Technology; Genetics; Health Administration; Health Sciences; Laboratory Techniques; Medical Technology; Nursing; Occupational Health; Public Health; Radiology; Rehabilitation and Therapy); **Transportation** (Aeronautical and Aerospace Engineering; Automotive Engineering; Crafts and Trades; Maintenance Technology; Marine Engineering; Marine Transport; Railway Transport; Technology; Transport and Communications)

Further Information: Also Downtown Campus, Marine Campus, Aerospace Technology Campuses, Great Northern Way Campus and Satellite Locations (Burnaby, Surrey, North Vancouver, Langley, Kelowna, Coquitlam, Maple Ridge).

History: Founded 1961. Merged with Pacific Vocational Institute 1986 and amalgamated with Pacific Marine Training 1994. Acquired Polytechnic status 2004.

Fees: (Canadian Dollar): For Canadian students, Full-time degree programme tuition fees, 2,396-2,755; Technology programmes, 2,121-2,890 per term. For International students, degree programmes, 7,876-9,636; Technology programmes, 6,536-16,897.

International Co-operation: International partnerships span training, education and research initiatives in South America, Central America, Southeast Asia and Eastern Europe.

Degrees and Diplomas: *Certificate/Diploma*; *Associate Degree*. Bachelor of Technology (Professional), 4 yrs; Master's degree to be offered as of September 2011 term; Advanced diploma and Advanced speciality certificate.

Student Numbers *2009-2010*: Total: c. 48,000
Last Updated: 22/12/10

CAPILANO UNIVERSITY

2055 Purcell Way, Vancouver, British Columbia V7J 3H5
Tel: +1(604) 986-1911
Fax: +1(604) 984-4985
EMail: admissions@capilanou.ca
Website: http://www.capilanou.ca

President: Kris Bulcroft **EMail:** glee@capilanou.ca

Programmes
Business and Professional Studies (Accountancy; Business Administration; Business and Commerce; Communication Studies; Human Resources; International Business; Law; Management; Marketing; Public Administration; Tourism); **Fine and Applied Arts** (Acting; Art Therapy; Cinema and Television; Conducting; Design; Jazz and Popular Music; Media Studies; Music; Painting and Drawing; Performing Arts; Textile Design; Theatre; Video; Visual Arts); **Health and Education** (Art Therapy; Education; Health Sciences; Nursing; Preschool Education; Rehabilitation and Therapy; Special Education); **Liberal Arts** (Anthropology; Art History; Behavioural Sciences; Chinese; Criminology; Economics; English; French; Geography; German; History; Japanese; Linguistics; Philosophy; Political Sciences; Psychology; Sociology; Spanish; Women's Studies); **Science and Technology** (Astronomy and Space Science; Biology; Chemistry; Computer Science; Design; Engineering; Geography; Geology; Mathematics; Physical Education; Physics; Statistics); **Tourism and Outdoor Recreation** (Tourism)

Further Information: Also Squamish and Sunshine Coast Campuses.

History: Founded 1968 as Capilano College.

Degrees and Diplomas: *Certificate/Diploma*; *Associate Degree*. Bachelor's degree (professional), 4 yrs.

EMILY CARR UNIVERSITY OF ART AND DESIGN (ECUAD)

1399 Johnston Street, Granville Island, Vancouver, British Columbia V6H 3R9
Tel: +1(604) 844-3800 +1(800) 832-7788
Fax: +1(604) 844-3801
EMail: admissions@ecuad.ca
Website: http://www.ecuad.ca/

President and Vice Chancellor: Ron Burnett
Tel: +1(604) 844-3890 EMail: rburnett@ecuad.ca

Vice-President (Finance and Administration): Michael Clifford
Tel: +1(604) 844-3851 Ext.3851 EMail: mclifford@ecuad.ca

Faculties
Culture and Community (English; Film; Media Studies; Social and Community Services; Video; Visual Arts); **Design and Dynamic Media** (Design; Visual Arts); **Graduate Studies** (Design; Fine Arts; Media Studies; Visual Arts); **Visual Art and Material Practice** (Art History; Ceramic Art; Fine Arts; Media Studies; Painting and Drawing; Sculpture; Visual Arts)

History: Founded 1925. Acquired university status 2008. Formerly known as Emily Carr Institute of Art and Design.

Fees: (Canadian Dollar): tuition fees for Canadian students, 350.25 for a 3-credit class; For International students, 1,153.86 for a 3-credit class. Masters Programme, 5,791.05.

Degrees and Diplomas: *Bachelor's Degree*; *Master's Degree*

Academic Staff *2009-2010*	TOTAL
FULL-TIME	99

Student Numbers *2009-2010*	
All (Foreign Included)	1,828
FOREIGN ONLY	242

Last Updated: 22/12/10

KWANTLEN POLYTECHNIC UNIVERSITY

12666 - 72nd Avenue, Surrey, British Columbia V3W 2M8
Tel: +1(604) 599-2100
Fax: +1(604) 599-2086
EMail: info@kwantlen.ca
Website: http://www.kwantlen.ca

President and Vice Chancellor: David W. Atkinson
Tel: +1(604) 599-2078, Fax: +1(604) 599-2235
EMail: david.atkinson@kwantlen.ca

International Relations: Ron Maggiore, AVP, Strategic Enrolment Management
Tel: +1(604) 599-2905, Fax: +1(604) 598 2498
EMail: Ron.Maggiore@kwantlen.ca

Divisions
Science, Mathematics and Applied Sciences (Astronomy and Space Science; Biology; Chemistry; Engineering; Environmental Studies; Mathematics; Physics; Psychology)

Faculties
Academic and Career Advancement *(formerly College of Qualifying Studies)* (Adult Education; Child Care and Development; Communication Studies; English); **Community and Health Studies** (Gerontology; Health Sciences; Nursing; Psychiatry and Mental Health; Special Education); **Continuing Studies**; **Design** (Design; Fashion Design; Graphic Design; Interior Design); **Humanities** (Anthropology; Art History; Arts and Humanities; Ceramic Art; Chinese; Criminology; English; Fine Arts; French; Geography; German; History; Indic Languages; Japanese; Linguistics; Mathematics; Media Studies; Modern Languages; Music; Musical Instruments; Painting and Drawing; Philosophy; Photography; Political Sciences; Psychology; Sculpture; Singing; Sociology; Spanish; Visual Arts; Writing); **Professional Studies** (Communication Studies; Food Technology; Health Sciences; Nursing; Pharmacology; Surgery); **Social Sciences** (Anthropology; Asian Studies; Behavioural Sciences; Canadian Studies; Criminology; English; Geography; History; Journalism; Law; Political Sciences; Psychology; Social

Sciences; Social Work; Sociology); **Trades and Technology** (Automotive Engineering; Building Technologies; Electrical Engineering; Maintenance Technology; Metal Techniques; Technology)

Schools
Business (Accountancy; Administration; Business Administration; Business Computing; Communication Studies; Computer Science; Economics; Human Resources; Information Sciences; Information Technology; Law; Leadership; Management; Marketing; Public Relations); **Horticulture** (Horticulture; Landscape Architecture)

Further Information: Also Richmond, Langley and Cloverdale campuses. International Student Exchange Programme

History: Founded 1981 as Kwantlen University College, acquired present status and title 2008.

Governing Bodies: Board of Governors, comprising 14 members; Education Council

Academic Year: September to August (September-December; January-April; May-August)

Admission Requirements: Secondary school certificate or recognized foreign equivalent

Fees: (Can. Dollars): Open admission and selective entry Programmes, Tuition 121.15 per credit for Canadian students and 450.00 per credit for international students; Fixed term and full-time continuous intake programmes, 105.50 per week for Canadian students and 450.00 per week for International students; For other programmes, 121.15-181.66 per credit for Canadian students and 450.00 per credit for International students.

Main Language(s) of Instruction: English

International Co-operation: With universities in Finland, USA, Chile, India, China, Germany, Spain

Accrediting Agencies: Government of British Columbia

Degrees and Diplomas: *Certificate/Diploma*; *Associate Degree.* Also Bachelor's degree (professional), Bachelor of Applied Arts and Honours Bachelor's degree, 4yrs.

Student Services: Academic counselling, Canteen, Employment services, Foreign student adviser, Handicapped facilities, Social counselling, Sports facilities

Special Facilities: Cloverdale Trades and Technology Centre; British Columbia Horticulture Centre; Art Gallery; Nursing Simulation Labs; Music Concert Hall; Wellness Centre

Libraries: Total, c. 168,230 vols, 891 serial or periodical subscriptions, 12,450 back issues of periodicals; 7,440 audiovisual items
Last Updated: 22/12/10

ROYAL ROADS UNIVERSITY (RRU)

2005 Sooke Road, Victoria, British Columbia V9B 5Y2
Tel: +1(250) 391-2511 +1(800) 788-8028
Fax: +1(250) 391-2500
EMail: RRU-info@royalroads.ca
Website: http://www.royalroads.ca

President, Vice-Chancellor: Allan Cahoon (2007-)
Tel: +1(250) 391-2517 EMail: allan.cahoon@royalroads.ca

Vice President, Academic and Provost: Thomas Chase
Tel: +1(250) 391-2545 EMail: thomas.chase@royalroads.ca

Centres
Applied Leadership and Management (Development Studies; Health Administration; Human Resources; Leadership; Management); **Continuing Studies** (Business Administration; Communication Studies; Computer Science; Cultural Studies; Ecology; Education; Environmental Management; Environmental Studies; Fine Arts; Horticulture; Leadership; Performing Arts; Teacher Training; Tourism; Visual Arts; Writing); **Entrepreneurial Studies** *(Eric C. Douglass)* (Business Administration); **Health Leadership and Research** (Health Administration); **Livelihoods and Ecology** (Ecology; Forest Products; Natural Resources); **Robert Bateman** (Environmental Studies; Fine Arts)

Institutes
Values-Based Leadership *(Todd Thomas)* (Leadership)

Programmes
Interdisciplinary Studies (Leadership; Management; Social Sciences)

Schools
Business (Business Administration; Business and Commerce; Human Resources; International Business; Management; Tourism); **Communication and Culture** (Communication Studies; Educational Administration; Educational Technology); **Environment and Sustainability** (Communication Studies; Education; Environmental Management; Environmental Studies); **Leadership Studies** (Leadership); **Peace and Conflict Management** (Computer Science; Criminology; Law; Peace and Disarmament; Philosophy; Political Sciences; Public Administration; Safety Engineering; Social Work; Sociology); **Tourism and Hospitality Management** (Hotel Management; Tourism)

History: Founded 1995 by the Government of British Columbia. The institution offers a blend of web-based and classroom courses, or online only.

Governing Bodies: Board of Governors; Academic Council

Academic Year: September to August

Admission Requirements: Applicants may be assessed for admission to Royal Roads University on the basis of their formal academic training and/or on the skills, knowledge and background developed outside traditional learning structures; a minimum two years' post-secondary education at a recognized institution may be eligible for admission with a full credit transfer; Admission to postgraduate programmes require an undergraduate degree or equivalent, plus significant related work experience.

Fees: (Can. Dollars): PhD, 73,440; Master's degree Programmes, 20,000-36,470 for domestic students and 27,000-54,710 for international students; Bachelor's degree, 12,320-15,020 for domestic students or 24,640-30,040 for international students; Graduate Diploma programmes, 10,690-13,300 for domestic students or 16,040-19,950 for international students; Certificate Programmes, 5,500-9,500 for domestic students or 5,500-13,780 for international students.

Main Language(s) of Instruction: English

Accrediting Agencies: AUCC; WARUCC

Degrees and Diplomas: *Certificate/Diploma*; *Bachelor's Degree*; *Master's Degree*; *Doctoral Degree.* Also MBA in Executive Management.

Student Services: Academic counselling, Canteen, Employment services, Foreign student adviser, Handicapped facilities, Health services, Social counselling, Sports facilities

Student Residential Facilities: 147 dorm rooms and 33 en-suites for students and visitors; 10 housing complexes for faculty and staff

Libraries: Extensive collection of print, media, and electronic resources to support the University's unique programmes. It is also a member of the Electronic Library Network and the Council of Prairie and Pacific University Libraries.

Academic Staff *2008-2009*	MEN	WOMEN	TOTAL
FULL-TIME	130	233	**363**
PART-TIME	25	45	**70**
STAFF WITH DOCTORATE			
FULL-TIME	38	18	**56**
PART-TIME	–	1	**1**
Student Numbers *2008-2009*			
All (Foreign Included)	2,017	2,032	**4,049**
FOREIGN ONLY	–	–	**1,507**

Part-time students, 30.
Last Updated: 23/12/10

SIMON FRASER UNIVERSITY (SFU)

8888 University Drive, Burnaby, British Columbia V5A 1S6
Tel: +1(778) 782-3111
EMail: sfumpr@sfu.ca; gosfu@sfu.ca
Website: http://www.sfu.ca

President and Vice-Chancellor: Andrew Petter (2010-)
Tel: +1(778) 782-4641, Fax: +1(778) 782-4860
EMail: Petter@sfu.ca

Vice-President, Academic and Provost: Jon Driver
Tel: +1(778) 782-3925, Fax: +1(778) 782-5876
EMail: vpacad@sfu.ca

International Relations: Tim Rahilly, Associate Vice-President, Students and International
Tel: +1(604) 291-3583, Fax: +1(604) 291-4860
EMail: trahilly@sfu.ca

Faculties

Applied Sciences (Artificial Intelligence; Automation and Control Engineering; Biomedical Engineering; Computer Engineering; Computer Graphics; Computer Science; Data Processing; Electronic Engineering; Engineering; Geography; Mechanical Engineering; Microelectronics; Multimedia; Physical Engineering; Software Engineering; Surveying and Mapping); **Arts and Social Sciences** (Ancient Civilizations; Anthropology; Archaeology; Arts and Humanities; Asian Studies; Canadian Studies; Chinese; Cognitive Sciences; Criminology; Cultural Studies; Economics; English; Film; Gender Studies; German; Gerontology; Greek; Greek (Classical); History; International Studies; Japanese; Labour and Industrial Relations; Latin American Studies; Linguistics; Literature; Medieval Studies; Modern History; Modern Languages; Native American Studies; Persian; Philosophy; Political Sciences; Portuguese; Psychology; Religion; Social Sciences; Sociology; Spanish; Urban Studies; Women's Studies); **Business Administration** (Accountancy; Business Administration; Engineering Management; Finance); **Communication, Art and Technology** (Communication Studies; Computer Science; Cultural Studies; Dance; Design; Film; Fine Arts; Media Studies; Music; Music Theory and Composition; Musical Instruments; Political Sciences; Publishing and Book Trade; Technology; Theatre; Visual Arts); **Education** (Art Education; Curriculum; Education; Educational and Student Counselling; Educational Psychology; Educational Sciences; Educational Technology; English; Foreign Languages Education; Indigenous Studies; Mathematics; Natives Education; Physical Education; Secondary Education; Special Education; Teacher Training); **Environment** (Development Studies; Environmental Management; Environmental Studies; Geography; Geography (Human); Natural Resources; Surveying and Mapping; Urban Studies); **Health Sciences** (Behavioural Sciences; Biology; Chemistry; Epidemiology; Health Administration; Health Sciences; Molecular Biology; Occupational Health; Psychiatry and Mental Health; Public Health; Social and Preventive Medicine; Statistics; Toxicology); **Science** (Actuarial Science; Applied Mathematics; Applied Physics; Behavioural Sciences; Biochemistry; Biological and Life Sciences; Biology; Biophysics; Business Administration; Cell Biology; Chemistry; Computer Science; Earth Sciences; Ecology; Environmental Studies; Forestry; Geology; Health Education; Management; Marine Science and Oceanography; Mathematical Physics; Mathematics; Molecular Biology; Neurosciences; Nuclear Physics; Nutrition; Physical Therapy; Physics; Physiology; Rehabilitation and Therapy; Sports; Statistics; Toxicology)

History: Founded 1963. First students enrolled 1965. A downtown Vancouver campus (Simon Fraser University at Vancouver) opened 1989. Programmes at this campus focus on the advanced recurring educational needs of the urban population. The Surrey campus (Simon Fraser University Surrey) opened its doors in 2002 offering undegraduate and graduate programmes including innovative cohort programmes: Tech One, Science Year One and Explorations.

Governing Bodies: Senate, comprising 60 members; Board of Governors, comprising 15 members

Academic Year: January to December (January-April; May-August; September-December)

Admission Requirements: Secondary school certificate or recognized foreign equivalent

Fees: (Can. Dollars): Undergraduate tuition fee, 160.50-214 per unit for domestic students or 527.20-580.70 per unit for international students; Graduate tuition fees: Research programmes full-time fee , 1,597 per term; Premium Fee Programmes, 151.10-584 per unit; MBA 600 per unit.

Main Language(s) of Instruction: English

Degrees and Diplomas: *Certificate/Diploma*; *Bachelor's Degree*; *Master's Degree*; *Doctoral Degree.* Also Honour Bachelor's degree; Executive MBA; Double-Degree Programme.

Student Services: Academic counselling, Canteen, Employment services, Foreign Studies Centre, Handicapped facilities, Health services, Language programs, Nursery care, Sports facilities

Student Residential Facilities: For c. 1,660 students

Special Facilities: Collection of Archaeology and Ethnology Artifacts and Archives from various parts of world, with particular emphasis on Pacific North-West Coast indigenous peoples. Art Gallery. Marine Biology Station

Libraries: c. 1,5 m. vols; 1.2 m. titles on microform; 15,300 sound and audio records; 115,000 maps; 772 manuscripts; 6,150 print journal subscriptions; 35,100 electronic subscriptions

Publications: International History Review *(quarterly)*; Journal of Computational Intelligence *(quarterly)*

Academic Staff *2007-2008*: Total 720
STAFF WITH DOCTORATE Total: 720
Student Numbers *2007-2008*: Total: c. 23,650
Distance students, 3,310.
Last Updated: 23/12/10

THE UNIVERSITY OF BRITISH COLUMBIA (UBC)

2329 West Mall, Vancouver, British Columbia V6T 1Z4
Tel: +1(604) 822-2211
Fax: +1(604) 822-5055
EMail: student.information@ubc.ca; international.reception@ubc.ca
Website: http://www.ubc.ca

President and Vice-Chancellor: Stephen J. Toope (1997-)
Tel: +1(604) 822-8300, Fax: +1(604) 822-5055
EMail: presidents.office@ubc.ca

Provost and Vice President Academic: David H. Farrar
Tel: +1(604) 822-4948, Fax: +1(604) 822-3134
EMail: david.farrar@ubc.ca

International Relations: Helen Pennant, Executive Director, International Affairs
EMail: helen.pennant@ubc.ca; ubcintl@interchange.ubc.ca

Colleges

Health Disciplines (Health Sciences; Public Health); **Interdisciplinary Studies** (Applied Mathematics; Asian Studies; Biotechnology; Computer Graphics; Computer Science; Environmental Management; Environmental Studies; Ethics; European Studies; Fishery; Forest Economics; Gender Studies; Genetics; International Relations; Molecular Biology; Multimedia; Natural Resources; Neurosciences; Oncology; Pacific Area Studies; Peace and Disarmament; Public Health; Regional Planning; Statistics; Women's Studies)

Faculties

Applied Science (Architecture; Bioengineering; Biomedical Engineering; Chemical Engineering; Civil Engineering; Computer Engineering; Design; Electrical Engineering; Engineering; Environmental Engineering; Geological Engineering; Landscape Architecture; Materials Engineering; Mechanical Engineering; Mining Engineering; Nursing; Physical Engineering); **Arts** (Anthropology; Archiving; Art History; Arts and Humanities; Asian Studies; Central European Studies; Eastern European Studies; Economics; English; Film; Fine Arts; French; Gender Studies; Geography; History; Information Sciences; Italian; Journalism; Linguistics; Museum Studies; Music; Philosophy; Political Sciences; Psychology; Religious Studies; Social Work; Sociology; Spanish; Theatre; Visual Arts; Women's Studies; Writing); **Continuing Studies** (Business Administration; Chinese; Cooking and Catering; Development Studies; English; French; French Studies; Health Administration; Italian; Japanese; Law; Management; Marketing; Multimedia; Psychology; Spanish; Technology); **Dentistry** (Biological and Life Sciences; Dentistry; Health Sciences; Oral Pathology); **Education** (Curriculum; Education; Educational and Student Counselling; Educational Psychology; Educational Sciences; Foreign Languages Education; Literacy Education; Physical Education; Teacher Training); **Forestry** (Forest Management; Forest Products; Forestry; Wood Technology); **Graduate Studies** (Adult Education; Agricultural Economics; Ancient Civilizations; Anthropology; Archaeology; Architecture; Archiving; Art Education; Art History; Asian Studies; Astronomy and Space Science; Biochemistry; Bioengineering; Biomedical Engineering; Botany; Business Administration; Cell Biology; Chemical Engineering; Chemistry; Civil Engineering; Classical Languages; Computer Engineering; Computer Science; Cultural Studies; Curriculum; Dentistry; Development Studies; Economic History; Economics; Education; Educational Administration; Educational Sciences; Educational Technology; Electrical Engineering; English;

Environmental Management; Environmental Studies; Film; Fine Arts; Foreign Languages Education; Forestry; French; Gender Studies; Genetics; Geography; Geological Engineering; Geology; Geophysics; Germanic Studies; Health Administration; Health Sciences; Higher Education; History; Home Economics Education; Humanities and Social Science Education; Hygiene; Immunology; Information Sciences; Journalism; Landscape Architecture; Law; Library Science; Linguistics; Literacy Education; Literature; Marine Science and Oceanography; Materials Engineering; Mathematics; Mathematics Education; Measurement and Precision Engineering; Mechanical Engineering; Media Studies; Medical Technology; Medicine; Meteorology; Microbiology; Mining Engineering; Molecular Biology; Music; Music Education; Natural Resources; Neurosciences; Nursing; Nutrition; Occupational Health; Occupational Therapy; Oncology; Pacific Area Studies; Pathology; Pharmacology; Pharmacy; Philosophy; Physical Education; Physical Engineering; Physical Therapy; Physics; Political Sciences; Preschool Education; Psychology; Public Health; Rehabilitation and Therapy; Religious Studies; Science Education; Social Work; Sociology; Software Engineering; Soil Science; Spanish; Special Education; Speech Therapy and Audiology; Statistics; Surgery; Technology Education; Theatre; Women's Studies; Writing; Zoology); **Land and Food Systems** (Agricultural Economics; Biology; Botany; Ecology; Food Science; Health Sciences; Nutrition; Soil Science; Zoology); **Law** (Law); **Medicine** (Anaesthesiology; Biochemistry; Cardiology; Cell Biology; Dermatology; Endocrinology; Gastroenterology; Genetics; Gynaecology and Obstetrics; Haematology; Immunology; Laboratory Techniques; Medicine; Midwifery; Molecular Biology; Nephrology; Occupational Health; Occupational Therapy; Oncology; Ophthalmology; Orthodox Theology; Paediatrics; Pathology; Pharmacology; Physical Therapy; Physiology; Psychiatry and Mental Health; Public Health; Radiology; Rehabilitation and Therapy; Respiratory Therapy; Rheumatology; Speech Therapy and Audiology; Surgery; Urology); **Pharmaceutical Sciences** (Pharmacy); **Science** (Astronomy and Space Science; Botany; Chemistry; Computer Science; Earth Sciences; Immunology; Marine Science and Oceanography; Mathematics; Microbiology; Physics; Statistics; Zoology)

Schools

Business *(Sauder)* (Accountancy; Behavioural Sciences; Business Administration; Business and Commerce; Economics; Finance; Human Resources; Information Sciences; Law; Marketing; Operations Research; Real Estate; Transport Management)

Further Information: UBC is affiliated with several research institutes, centres, organizations, and hospitals, many of which are located on the university's main Point Grey campus. Details available at: http://www.ubc.ca/affiliated/index.html

History: Founded 1908 and incorporated by the Provincial Government. Admitted first students 1915 and moved to its present location at Point Grey 1925. The University operates under the authority of the University Act of the Province of British Columbia (RSBC, 1979), and is the second largest University in Canada.

Governing Bodies: Board of Governors, comprising 15 members; Senate comprising 88 members

Academic Year: September to August (September-December; January-April). Also Summer session (May-July; July-August)

Admission Requirements: Secondary school certificate or recognized foreign equivalent

Fees: (Can. Dollars): Undergraduate Degree Programmes, 150.60-223.14 per credit for domestic students and 703.93-788.72 per credit for international students; Specialized Undergraduate/Post-baccalaureate tuition (dentistry, medicine, law), 10,135.46-33,652.38 per year or 150.60-197.71 per credit for domestic students and 683.65-703.93 per credit for international students; Certificate Programmes, 1,393.42 per instalment or 1,070.98 per 3-credit course; Research Master's Degree Programmes, 4,180.26 per year for domestic students and 7,344 per year for international students; Professional Master's Degree Programmes, 2,461.02-30,405.75 per year for domestic students and 4,223.10-36,756 per year for international students; Executive MBA, 48,750 per year; Research Doctoral Degree Programmes, 4,180.26 per year for domestic students and 7,344 per year for international students; Professional Doctoral Degree Programmes, 4,781.22-25,372.44 per year for domestic students and 4,781.22-36,756 per year for international students.

Main Language(s) of Instruction: English

International Co-operation: For further information, please consult our website: www.interchange.ubc.ca/ubcintl/linkages

Degrees and Diplomas: *Certificate/Diploma*; *Bachelor's Degree*; *Master's Degree*; *Doctoral Degree*. The degrees of Doctor of Laws LLD(Honoris Causa), Doctor of Science, DSc (Honoris Causa) and Doctor of Letters, Dlitt (Honoris Causa) are the honorary degrees conferred from time to time by the Senate of the University upon persons who have achieved distinction in scholarship or public service. Also Certificates in Advanced Studies (Library, Archival and Information Studies) and Diplomas (Accountancy, Administration, Art History, Applied Creative Non-Fiction, Piano Studies, Computer Science, Education, Film Studies, Forestry, Linguistics, Aquaculture, Meteorology, Periodontics, Translation, Urban Land Economics); Also Combined Programmes and Dual Degrees.

Student Services: Academic counselling, Canteen, Employment services, Foreign student adviser, Foreign Studies Centre, Handicapped facilities, Health services, Language programs, Nursery care, Social counselling, Sports facilities

Student Residential Facilities: Yes

Special Facilities: Museum of Anthropology; Museum of Geological Sciences; Zoological Museum. Botany Collection and Herbarium. Fine Arts Gallery. Morris and Helen Belkin Art Gallery. Nitobe Garden. Asian Centre. International House. Norman McKenzie Centre for Fine Arts. Aquatic Centre. Disability Resource Centre. First Nations House of Learning. Chan Centre for the Performing Arts. Student Union Building Auditorium (Theatre); Frederic Wood Theatre; B.C.Tor Studio Theatre. Royal Bank Cinema; Liu Centre for the Study of Global Issues; Botanical Gardens

Libraries: Main Library. Specialized Libraries: Asian; Crane (for the visually-impaired); Data; Education; Fine Arts; Land Management; Law; MacMillan (Forestry); Agriculture and Food Sciences; Map; Mathematics; Music; Koerner (Humanities; Social Sciences); Social Work; Special Collections and University Archives, total c. 3.2m. Vols

Publications: Asia Pacific Report *(biannually)*; B.C. Studies *(quarterly)*; BC Asian Review *(annually)*; Canadian Journal of Civil Engineering *(bimonthly)*; Canadian Journal of Family Law *(biannually)*; Canadian Literature *(quarterly)*; Canadian Yearbook of International Law *(annually)*; Journal of Business Administration *(biannually)*; Pacific Affairs *(quarterly)*; PRISM International *(quarterly)*; Studies in Medieval and Renaissance History; University of British Columbia Law Review *(biannually)*

Press or Publishing House: University of British Columbia Press
Last Updated: 24/12/10

THOMPSON RIVERS UNIVERSITY (TRU)

Box 3010, 900 McGill Road, Kamloops, British Columbia V2C 5N3
Tel: +1(250) 828-5000
Fax: +1(250) 828-5006
EMail: admissions@tru.ca
Website: http://www.tru.ca

President and Vice-Chancellor: Alan Shaver (2010-)
Tel: +1(250) 828-5001 EMail: president@tru.ca

Vice-President, Administration and Finance: Cliff Neufeld
Tel: +1(250) 828-5012, Fax: +1(250) 828-5394
EMail: cneufeld@tru.ca

International Relations: Wesley J. Koczka, Associate Vice President, International and CEO Global Operations
Tel: +1(250) 828-1902 EMail: wes.koczka@shaw.ca

Faculties

Arts (Anthropology; Canadian Studies; Chinese; Economics; English; Fine Arts; French; Geography; German; History; Japanese; Journalism; Modern Languages; Performing Arts; Philosophy; Political Sciences; Psychology; Sociology; Spanish; Theatre; Visual Arts); **Human, Social and Educational Development** (Distance Education; Education; Foreign Languages Education; Physical Education; Preschool Education; Primary Education; Social Work; Special Education); **Law** (Law); **Science** (Animal Husbandry; Architectural and Environmental Design; Astronomy and Space Science; Automation and Control Engineering; Biological and Life Sciences; Biology; Cell Biology; Chemistry; Computer Engineering; Computer Science; Design; Ecology; Electronic Engineering; Engineering; Engineering Drawing and Design; Fine Arts; Geology;

Mathematics; Molecular Biology; Natural Resources; Physics; Respiratory Therapy; Statistics; Telecommunications Engineering)

Schools

Business and Economics *(SoBE)* (Accountancy; Business Administration; Computer Science; Economics; Finance; Human Resources; International Business; Management; Marketing); **Nursing** (Health Sciences; Nursing); **Tourism** (Cooking and Catering; Food Science; Hotel Management; Sports; Sports Management; Tourism); **Trades and Technology** (Horticulture; Metal Techniques; Service Trades; Technology; Water Management)

Further Information: Also Williams Lake Campus.

History: Founded 1970 as Cariboo College. Named the University College of the Cariboo (UCC) 1992. Acquired present status and title 2004.

Governing Bodies: Board of Governors

Academic Year: September to August (September-December; January-April; May-August)

Admission Requirements: Secondary school certificate or recognized foreign equivalent; English Language Assessment Test, TOEFL or IELTS for students whose first language is not English

Fees: (Canadian Dollars): Canadian citizens, 120.33 per credit; Master of Business Administration, 304.21 per credit; Master of Education, 1,912.50 per semester; Master of Science, 1,836 per semester. International Students, c. 6,900 per semester; 22,266 per programme for Master's degree programmes.

Main Language(s) of Instruction: English

Degrees and Diplomas: *Certificate/Diploma*; *Associate Degree*; *Bachelor's Degree*; *Master's Degree*

Student Services: Academic counselling, Canteen, Cultural centre, Employment services, Foreign student adviser, Foreign Studies Centre, Handicapped facilities, Health services, Nursery care, Social counselling, Sports facilities

Student Residential Facilities: For c. 900 students

Libraries: c. 249,000 vols and 5,000 periodical Subscriptions

Academic Staff *2007-2008*	TOTAL
FULL-TIME	750
PART-TIME	c. 200

Student Numbers *2007-2008*	
All (Foreign Included)	13,072
FOREIGN ONLY	1,270

Last Updated: 03/01/11

UNIVERSITY OF NORTHERN BRITISH COLUMBIA (UNBC)

3333 University Way, Prince George, British Columbia V2N 4Z9
Tel: +1(250) 960-5555
Fax: +1(250) 960-5791
EMail: registrar-info@unbc.ca
Website: http://www.unbc.ca

President: George Iwama (2009-)
Tel: +1(250) 960-5600, Fax: +1(250) 960-7301
EMail: president@unbc.ca

Vice-President Administration and Finance: Eileen Bray
Tel: +1(250) 960-5541, Fax: +1(250) 960-5659
EMail: braye@unbc.ca

International Relations: Carolyn Russell
Tel: +1(250) 960-5706, Fax: +1(250) 960-5546
EMail: russel1@unbc.ca

Colleges

Arts, Social and Health Sciences (Anthropology; Canadian Studies; Community Health; Economics; Education; English; Health Sciences; History; Indigenous Studies; International Studies; Native Language; Nursing; Political Sciences; Psychology; Rehabilitation and Therapy; Social Work; Women's Studies); **Science and Management** (Accountancy; Business Administration; Chemistry; Computer Science; Ecology; Environmental Engineering; Environmental Management; Environmental Studies; Finance; Geography; Human Resources; International Business; Leisure Studies; Marketing; Mathematics; Physics; Tourism)

Programmes

Continuing Studies (Christian Religious Studies; Forest Management; Human Resources; Management; Music Education; Occupational Health; Surveying and Mapping; Wildlife); **Graduate Studies** (Anthropology; Biology; Business Administration; Chemistry; Community Health; Computer Science; Economics; Education; English; Environmental Studies; Forestry; Gender Studies; Geography; Health Sciences; History; Indigenous Studies; International Studies; Leadership; Mathematics; Natural Resources; Nursing; Physics; Political Sciences; Psychology; Rehabilitation and Therapy; Social Work; Special Education; Tourism); **Northern Medical** (Anaesthesiology; Cardiology; Dermatology; Epidemiology; Ethics; Gynaecology and Obstetrics; Health Sciences; Law; Medicine; Ophthalmology; Orthopaedics; Paediatrics; Pharmacology; Psychiatry and Mental Health; Surgery)

Further Information: Also following campuses: Northwest (Prince Rupert), Peace River-Liard (Fort St. John) and South-Central (Quesnel).

History: Founded 1990.

Governing Bodies: Board of Governors, comprising 15 members; Senate, comprising 21 members

Academic Year: September to May (September-December; January-May)

Admission Requirements: Successful completion of an academic grade 12 programme (65% average)

Fees: (Can. Dollars): Tuition for undergraduate studies, 151.28 per credit hour; Foreign students, 529.47 per credit hour. Graduate studies, 864-922.18 per semester; MBA, 6,494.60 per semester.

Main Language(s) of Instruction: English

International Co-operation: With universities in Circumpolar North; Europe; Asia Pacific; North America

Accrediting Agencies: Association of Universities and Colleges of Canada; Association of Commonwealth Universities

Degrees and Diplomas: *Certificate/Diploma*; *Bachelor's Degree*; *Master's Degree*; *Doctoral Degree (PhD)*

Student Services: Academic counselling, Canteen, Cultural centre, Employment services, Foreign student adviser, Foreign Studies Centre, Handicapped facilities, Health services, Language programs, Nursery care, Social counselling, Sports facilities

Student Residential Facilities: For c. 580 students

Special Facilities: Art exhibitions in UNBC Library

Libraries: UNBC Library, 163,460 vols; microforms, 460,000; serials, 1,200; videos, 2,090; and more than 60 electronic databases

Academic Staff *2008-2009*	TOTAL
FULL-TIME	173
PART-TIME	292

Student Numbers *2008-2009*	
All (Foreign Included)	4,332
FOREIGN ONLY	308

Last Updated: 04/01/11

UNIVERSITY OF THE FRASER VALLEY (UFV)

33844 King Road, Abbotsford, British Columbia V2S 7M8
Tel: +1(604) 504-7441
Fax: +1(604) 855-7614
EMail: info@ufv.ca
Website: http://www.ufv.ca/

President: Mark Evered (2009-)
Tel: +1(604) 854-4608, Fax: +1(604) 853-7341
EMail: jill.smith@ufv.ca

Vice-President, Academic and Provost: Eric Davis
Tel: +1(604) 864-4630, Fax: +1(604) 853-7341
EMail: eric.davis@ufv.ca

Vice President of Administration: Tim Segger
EMail: eleanor.busse@ufv.ca

International Relations: Karola Stinson, Director of International Education Department
Tel: +1(604) 854-4544, Fax: +1(604) 855-7153
EMail: international@ufv.ca

Faculties

Access and Continuing Studies (Accountancy; Business Administration; Child Care and Development; Communication Studies; Computer Science; Dentistry; Education; English; Environmental Studies; Foreign Languages Education; Health Sciences; Horticulture; Human Resources; Law; Library Science; Management; Modern Languages; Nursing; Photography; Publishing and Book Trade; Service Trades; Technology; Writing); **Arts** (Chinese; Communication Studies; Criminal Law; Criminology; Cultural Studies; Economics; English; Fashion Design; French; Geography; Graphic Design; History; Indic Languages; Japanese; Journalism; Media Studies; Modern Languages; Native Language; Philosophy; Political Sciences; Psychology; Russian; Social Studies; Spanish; Theatre; Visual Arts); **Professional Studies** (Accountancy; Administration; Adult Education; Agricultural Management; Air Transport; Business Administration; Child Care and Development; Dental Hygiene; Dental Technology; Health Sciences; Information Technology; Library Science; Management; Marketing; Nursing; Preschool Education; Service Trades; Social and Community Services; Social Work; Teacher Trainers Education); **Science** (Biology; Chemistry; Computer Science; Engineering; Geography; Mathematics; Physical Education; Physical Therapy; Physics; Statistics); **Trades** (Agriculture; Air Transport; Architectural and Environmental Design; Automotive Engineering; Cooking and Catering; Electrical Engineering; Electronic Engineering; Jewelry Art; Metal Techniques; Technology; Wood Technology)

Schools

Graduate Studies (Criminal Law; Social Work)

Further Information: Also Campuses in Chilliwack, Mission, Hope, and India office in Chandigarh, India.

History: Founded 1974 as Fraser Valley College, a two-year community college. Became the University College of the Fraser Valley (UCFV) 1991. Acquired university status and present title 2008.

Academic Year: September to August (September-December; January-April; May-August)

Fees: (Canadian Dollars): Tuition, 123.78 per credit; Some programmes (Dental Hygiene, Nursing, Teacher Education) have special fees 2,706-18,041 per programme . Graduate studies, 509.23 per credit.

Main Language(s) of Instruction: English

International Co-operation: With universities in China, United Kingdom, Korea, Italy, India, Japan, Mexico and United Arab Emirates

Accrediting Agencies: British Columbia Ministry of Advanced Education; Canadian Bureau of International Education (CBIE); British Columbia Centre of International Education (BCCIE); Association of Universities and Colleges of Canada (AUCC); Association of Canadian Colleges (ACC)

Degrees and Diplomas: *Certificate/Diploma*; *Associate Degree*; *Bachelor's Degree*; *Master's Degree*. Also Honours Bachelor's degree.

Student Services: Academic counselling, Canteen, Foreign student adviser, Foreign Studies Centre, Handicapped facilities, Language programs, Social counselling, Sports facilities

Student Residential Facilities: Home stay programme offers by the International Education Department; On campus residence available as of September 2007.

Special Facilities: Art Gallery; Theatre; Student Activity Centre and Bookstore

Libraries: 2 Libraries

Academic Staff 2008-2009	MEN	WOMEN	TOTAL
FULL-TIME	243	432	**675**
PART-TIME	143	178	**321**
Student Numbers 2009-2010			
All (Foreign Included)	6,487	8,959	**15,446**
FOREIGN ONLY	449	300	**749**

Part-time students, 6,000.
Note: Part time = at least 60% course load
Last Updated: 04/01/11

UNIVERSITY OF VICTORIA (UVIC)

PO Box 1700, STN CSC, Victoria, British Columbia V8W 2Y2
Tel: +1(250) 721-7211
Fax: +1(250) 721-7212
EMail: admsinfo@uvic.ca
Website: http://www.uvic.ca

President and Vice-Chancellor: David H. Turpin (2000-)
Tel: +1(250) 721-7002, Fax: +1(250) 721-8654
EMail: pres@uvic.ca

University Secretary: Julia Eastman
Tel: +1(250) 721-8100, Fax: +1(250) 721-6223
EMail: usec@uvic.ca; jeastman@uvic.ca

International Relations: James P. Anglin, Director, International Affairs
Tel: +1(250) 472-4644, Fax: +1(250) 721-6542
EMail: oiadir@uvic.ca

Centres

Aboriginal Health Research; **Addictions Research of B.C.**; **Advanced Materials and Related Technology** *(CAMTEC)*; **Aging**; **Asia-Pacific Initiatives** *(CAPI)*; **Biomedical Research**; **Co-operative and Community-Based Economy**; **Forest Biology**; **Global Studies**; **Studies in Religion and Society**; **Youth and Society**

Divisions

Continuing Studies (Adult Education; Arts and Humanities; Business Administration; Canadian Studies; Community Health; Computer Science; Continuing Education; Dentistry; Distance Education; English; Environmental Management; Fine Arts; Foreign Languages Education; French; Health Sciences; Heritage Preservation; Indigenous Studies; Museum Management; Native Language; Occupational Health; Public Relations; Tourism); **Medical Sciences** (Medicine; Neurosciences)

Faculties

Education (Education; Health Education; Natives Education; Physical Education; Primary Education; Secondary Education; Teacher Training); **Engineering** (Computer Engineering; Computer Science; Electrical Engineering; Engineering; Mechanical Engineering; Software Engineering); **Fine Arts** (Art History; Fine Arts; Music; Music Education; Music Theory and Composition; Musical Instruments; Painting and Drawing; Photography; Sculpture; Theatre; Video; Visual Arts; Writing); **Graduate Studies** (Anthropology; Applied Linguistics; Art History; Asian Studies; Astronomy and Space Science; Biochemistry; Biology; Business Administration; Chemistry; Child Care and Development; Computer Engineering; Computer Science; Curriculum; Economics; Educational Psychology; Electrical Engineering; English; Environmental Studies; French; Geography; Germanic Studies; Greek (Classical); History; Indigenous Studies; Information Sciences; Italian; Latin; Law; Leadership; Linguistics; Marine Science and Oceanography; Mathematics; Mechanical Engineering; Microbiology; Music; Nursing; Pacific Area Studies; Peace and Disarmament; Philosophy; Physical Education; Physics; Political Sciences; Psychology; Public Administration; Russian; Social and Community Services; Social Work; Sociology; Spanish; Statistics; Theatre; Visual Arts; Writing); **Human and Social Development** (Child Care and Development; Indigenous Studies; Information Sciences; Nursing; Peace and Disarmament; Public Administration; Public Health; Social Policy; Social Work); **Humanities** (Asian Studies; English; Ethics; European Studies; Film; French; German; Germanic Studies; Greek (Classical); History; Indigenous Studies; Italian; Latin; Linguistics; Medieval Studies; Mediterranean Studies; Pacific Area Studies; Philosophy; Religious Studies; Slavic Languages; Social Studies; Spanish; Women's Studies; Writing); **Law** (Law); **Science** (Astronomy and Space Science; Biochemistry; Biology; Chemistry; Earth Sciences; Marine Science and Oceanography; Mathematics; Microbiology; Physics; Statistics); **Social Sciences** (Anthropology; Economics; Environmental Studies; Geography; Political Sciences; Psychology; Social Sciences; Sociology)

Institutes

Climate Solutions *(Pacific)*; **Coastal and Oceans Research**; **Dispute Resolution**; **Integrated Energy Systems** *(IESVic)*

Laboratories

Automation, Communication and Information Systems Research *(LACIR)*

Schools

Business *(Peter B. Gustavson)* (Business Administration; Business and Commerce; International Business; Management)

History: Founded 1903 as Victoria College in affiliation with McGill University, acquired present status and title 1963.

Governing Bodies: Board of Governors; Senate

Academic Year: September to August (September-December; January-April; May-August)

Admission Requirements: Secondary school certificate or recognized foreign equivalent

Fees: (Can. Dollars): Undergraduate Tuition, 317.74 per unit; international students, 1,028.12 per unit. Graduate tuition fees, 1,650.08 for Canadian students and 1,963.44 for International students. Exceptions: MBA, for Canadian students, 3,552.78 per term for daytime programme and 2,368.52 for evening programme; for international students 3,866.16 per term for daytime programme 2,577.44 per term for evening programme; Master's degrees in Global Business, Community Development, Health Informatics, Public Health and Double Degree Nursing and Health Information, 2,000-6,000 per term for Candian students and 2,380-7,666.68 for international students. Graduate diploma and certificates, 612-750 for Canadian students and 726.24-1,000 for International students.

Main Language(s) of Instruction: English

Degrees and Diplomas: *Certificate/Diploma*; *Bachelor's Degree*; *Master's Degree*; *Doctoral Degree (PhD)*. Also MBA; Honours Bachelor's degree; Concurrent degree programmes (JD/Master of Business Administration, JD/Master of Public Administration, JD/BCL (Civil Law Degree Graduates)).

Student Services: Academic counselling, Canteen, Cultural centre, Employment services, Foreign student adviser, Foreign Studies Centre, Handicapped facilities, Health services, Nursery care, Social counselling, Sports facilities

Student Residential Facilities: For 1,788 students

Special Facilities: Maltwood Art Museum and Gallery. Climenhaga Observatory. Glover Greenhouse Facility. Finnerty Gardens. Phoenix Theatre

Libraries: c. 1.8m. Vols

Academic Staff *2009-2010*	TOTAL
FULL-TIME	c. 800

Student Numbers *2009-2010*	
All (Foreign Included)	19,333
FOREIGN ONLY	182

Last Updated: 04/01/11

VANCOUVER ISLAND UNIVERSITY

900 Fifth Street, Nanaimo, British Columbia V9R 5S5
Tel: +1(250) 753-3245
Fax: +1(250) 755-8725
EMail: info@viu.ca
Website: http://www.viu.ca/

President and Vice-Chancellor: Ralph Nilson
Tel: +1(250) 740-6102, Fax: +1(250) 740-6555
EMail: Ralph.Nilson@viu.ca

Vice-President, Administration and Finance: Pat Eagar
Tel: +1(250) 740-6231, Fax: +1(250) 740-6489
EMail: Pat.Eagar@viu.ca

Vice-President Academic and Provost: David Witty
Tel: +1(250) 740-6436, Fax: +1(250) 740-6451
EMail: Michelle.Champagne@viu.ca

International Relations: Graham Pike, Dean, International Programmes Tel: +1(250) 740-6311 EMail: Graham.Pike@viu.ca

Areas

Art, Design and Performing Arts (Fine Arts; Graphic Design; Interior Design; Jazz and Popular Music; Music; Theatre; Visual Arts); **Business and Management** (Business Administration; Health Administration; Hotel and Restaurant; Leisure Studies; Management; Sports Management; Tourism); **Career and Academic Preparation** (Biology; Chemistry; Computer Science; Education; English; History; Mathematics; Natural Sciences; Physics; Psychology; Technology; Writing); **Education** (Education; Leadership; Special Education); **English-as-a-Second-Language** *(ESL)* (English); **First Nations** (Child Care and Development; Forestry; Natives Education; Sports Management); **Health** (Dental Hygiene; Dentistry; Health Administration; Health Sciences; Nursing); **High School Equivalency** *(ABE)* (Biology; Chemistry; Computer Science; Education; English; History; Mathematics; Natural Sciences; Physics; Psychology; Writing); **Human Services** (Child Care and Development; Horticulture; Leadership; Preschool Education; Social and Community Services; Special Education); **Humanities and Social Sciences** (Anthropology; Arts and Humanities; Biology; Business Administration; Chemistry; Computer Science; Criminology; Development Studies; Earth Sciences; Economics; English; Environmental Management; Geography; Graphic Design; History; Indigenous Studies; International Economics; Mathematics; Media Studies; Natural Resources; Philosophy; Physical Education; Political Sciences; Psychology; Romance Languages; Sociology; Theatre; Visual Arts; Welfare and Protective Services; Women's Studies; Writing); **Online/Distance Courses** (Biology; Business Computing; Child Care and Development; Energy Engineering; English; Geology; Gerontology; Health Administration; Journalism; Media Studies; Physical Education; Sports; Tourism; Writing); **Science and Technology** (Aquaculture; Biology; Chemistry; Computer Science; Earth Sciences; Engineering; Fishery; Forest Products; Geography; Horticulture; Information Technology; Mathematics; Natural Resources; Physics; Psychology); **Tourism, Recreation and Hospitality** (Hotel and Restaurant; Leisure Studies; Sports Management; Tourism); **Trades and Applied Technology** (Automotive Engineering; Business Computing; Cooking and Catering; Electrical Engineering; Heating and Refrigeration; Information Technology; Marine Transport; Metal Techniques; Road Engineering; Service Trades; Sports; Technology)

Faculties

Adult and Continuing Education (Animal Husbandry; Business Administration; Communication Studies; Fire Science; Forestry; Health Administration; Management; Marine Engineering; Psychiatry and Mental Health; Service Trades; Technology)

Programmes

Natural Resources Extension (Environmental Studies; Fishery; Geology; Water Science)

Further Information: Also campuses in Cowichan, Parksville - Qualicum, Powell River.

History: Founded 1969 as Malaspina College. Renamed Malaspina University-College 1989. Acquired present title 2008. A comprehensive university-college serving the central Vancouver Island region.

Governing Bodies: Education Council

Academic Year: September to May (September-December; January-May). Also Summer Session (May-August)

Admission Requirements: Secondary school certificate or equivalent. TOEFL test for foreign students with score of min. 550

Fees: (Can. Dollars): 126.12 per credit hour; International Students, 5,900 per semester. MBA programme, 18,500 per annum for Canadian students and 29,500 for International students.

Main Language(s) of Instruction: English

International Co-operation: With universities in Australia, New Zealand and Japan

Accrediting Agencies: Association of Universities and Colleges of Canada (AUCC)

Degrees and Diplomas: *Certificate/Diploma*; *Associate Degree*; *Bachelor's Degree*; *Master's Degree*

Student Services: Academic counselling, Canteen, Employment services, Foreign student adviser, Foreign Studies Centre, Handicapped facilities, Health services, Language programs, Nursery care, Social counselling, Sports facilities

Student Residential Facilities: For 400 students

Special Facilities: Natural History Museum. Nanaimo Art Gallery

Libraries: Nanaimo Campus Library, c. 110,000 vols

Student Numbers *2009-2010* | **TOTAL**
All (Foreign Included) — **18,243**
FOREIGN ONLY — **1,536**
Last Updated: 05/01/11

PRIVATE INSTITUTIONS

TRINITY WESTERN UNIVERSITY (TWU)

Trinity Western University, Work 7600 Glover Road, Langley,
British Columbia V2Y 1Y1
Tel: +1(604) 888-7511
Fax: +1(604) 513-2061
EMail: admissions@twu.ca
Website: http://www.twu.ca

President: Jonathan S. Raymond (2006-)
Tel: +1(604) 888-7511, Ext.2021 EMail: president@twu.ca

Registrar: Grant McMillan
Tel: +1(604) 513-2070, Fax: +1(604) 513-2096
EMail: registrar@twu.ca; grant.mcmillan@twu.ca

International Relations: Mark Charlton, International Liaison
Officer
Tel: +1(604) 888-7511, Ext. 3120, Fax: +1(604) 513-2018
EMail: charlton@twu.ca

Faculties

Humanities and Social Sciences (Arts and Humanities; Bible;
Canadian Studies; Chinese; Christian Religious Studies; Cultural
Studies; English; Environmental Studies; European Studies; French;
Geography; German; History; International Studies; Japanese; Lin-
guistics; Literature; Missionary Studies; Modern Languages; Philo-
sophy; Political Sciences; Psychology; Religious Studies; Russian;
Social Studies; Sociology; Spanish); **Natural and Applied Sciences**
(Biology; Biotechnology; Chemistry; Computer Science; Engineering;
Environmental Studies; Mathematics; Physics)

Programmes

ACTS Seminaries (Applied Linguistics; Christian Religious Studies;
Holy Writings; Religion; Social Problems; Theology)

Schools

Business (Accountancy; Business Administration; Communication
Studies; Finance; Human Resources; International Business; Lea-
dership; Management; Marketing; Sports Management); **Education**
(Art Education; Education; Humanities and Social Science Educa-
tion; Leadership; Mathematics Education; Native Language Edu-
cation; Primary Education; Science Education; Secondary
Education; Teacher Training); **Graduate Studies** (Bible; Business
Administration; English; Foreign Languages Education; History;
Leadership; Linguistics; Nursing; Philosophy; Psychology); **Human
Kinetics** (Leisure Studies; Physical Education; Physical Therapy;
Sports; Sports Management); **Nursing** (Nursing); **The Arts, Media
and Culture** (Acting; Art History; Communication Arts; Commu-
nication Studies; Design; Handicrafts; Leadership; Media Studies;
Music; Music Education; Musical Instruments; Painting and Draw-
ing; Photography; Printing and Printmaking; Religious Music;
Sculpture; Theatre; Writing)

Further Information: Also Extension Campuses: the Laurentian
Leadership Centre in Ottawa, TWU Bellingham in Bellingham,
Crows Nest Ecological Research Area on Salt Spring Island; Also
Irish, American, Latin American, and Russian Studies Programmes.
Oxford Summer School Programme. Los Angeles Film Studies
Centre.

History: Founded 1962 as Trinity Junior College, became Trinity
Western College 1972, and acquired present status and title 1985.

Governing Bodies: Board of Governors, comprising 21 members

Academic Year: September to April (September-December; January-April); Interweave: End-April to Mid-May, and August. Also
Summer Session (May-August)

Admission Requirements: Secondary school certificate or recognized foreign equivalent

Fees: (Can. Dollars): c. 7,500 per semester

Main Language(s) of Instruction: English

Degrees and Diplomas: *Certificate/Diploma*; *Bachelor's Degree*;
Master's Degree; *Doctoral Degree*: Ministry. Also concurrent programme to obtain a Bachelor of Arts or a Bachelor of Science
degree at the same time as a Bachelor of Education degree in five
years; Also Honours Bachelor's degree; Post-degree Bachelor's
degree Programme in Education, 2 yrs.

Student Services: Academic counselling, Canteen, Employment
services, Foreign student adviser, Handicapped facilities, Health
services, Social counselling, Sports facilities

Student Residential Facilities: On-campus housing for 842
students.

Libraries: Norma Marion Alloway Library, 210,000 print vols; 4,500
non-print vols; 20,000 electronic resources; 350,000 microform titles

Academic Staff *2007-2008* | **TOTAL**
FULL-TIME — **150**
PART-TIME — **c. 150**

Student Numbers *2007-2008*
All (Foreign Included) — **c. 4,000**
FOREIGN ONLY — **470**
Last Updated: 03/01/11

UNIVERSITY CANADA WEST (UCW)

950 King's Road, Victoria, British Columbia V8T 1W6
Tel: +1(250) 978-1800
Fax: +1(250) 978-1801
EMail: info@universitycanadawest.ca
Website: http://www.universitycanadawest.ca

President: Verna Magee-Shepherd
EMail: david.strong@universitycanadawest.ca

Registrar: Carolyn Jordan
EMail: registrar@universitycanadawest.ca

Programmes

English as a Second Language (English); **Graduate degree**
(Business Administration); **Online degree** (Business Administra-
tion; Business and Commerce; Communication Studies; Media
Studies); **Undergraduate degree** (Business and Commerce;
Communication Studies; Media Studies)

Further Information: Also Vancouver campus.

History: Founded 2004.

Fees: (Canadian Dollars): Canadian students, undergraduate fee,
495 per course and graduate fee, 2,160 per course; for international
students, undergraduate fee, 1,350 per course and graduate fee,
2,160 per course.

Accrediting Agencies: Ministry of Advanced Education and
Labour Market Development.

Degrees and Diplomas: *Bachelor's Degree*; *Master's Degree*.
Also accelerated MBA programme, 2 yrs; Degree Completion programme to obtain a Bachelor's degree.

Student Services: Academic counselling, Canteen, Handicapped
facilities, Health services, Nursery care, Sports facilities

Student Residential Facilities: None.
Last Updated: 03/01/11

Canada - Manitoba

STRUCTURE OF HIGHER EDUCATION SYSTEM

Description:

Higher education in Canada is the constitutional responsibility of the provinces. The main types of institutions providing higher education in Manitoba are universities, university colleges and colleges. The colleges provide diverse technical and vocational programmes leading to a certificate or diploma, and also offer Baccalaureate degrees with an applied focus, while the universities are degree-granting institutions. The one university college in the province offers degrees, certificates and diplomas. Colleges, university colleges and universities in Manitoba are independently administered institutions with full autonomy on admissions and all other academic matters. The governing bodies of universities and the university college are a mixture of provincial and institutional representatives and the college boards are all composed of provincial representatives.

In addition to the public post secondary institutions and various government-supported re-employment, apprenticeship and other vocational programmes there are also numerous private vocational or career training institutions.

Stages of studies:

University level first stage: Bachelor's degree
There are four public universities in Manitoba which offer undergraduate degree programmes; the University of Manitoba, the University of Winnipeg and Brandon University offer programmes in English, while the Collège universitaire de Saint Boniface is a French language institution. Most undergraduate study in Manitoba leads to a "General" Bachelor's degree (minimum 3 years) or an "Honours" degree (4 years and prescribed subject concentration). Degrees are normally titled in broad descriptive groups, e.g. B.A. and B.Sc. Universities also offer undergraduate diplomas (1 to 2 years of study) and short (up to 1 year) certificate programmes. Certificate programmes may enable entry to degree programmes and are frequently given in close cooperation with professional bodies. The undergraduate stage includes professional programmes that require no university-level prerequisites such as the Bachelor of Social Work (BSW) and the Bachelor of Commerce (B.Comm) and others that have prerequisite university studies such as the Bachelor of Law (LL.B) or a Doctor of Medicine (M.D.). In Manitoba, a Bachelor of Education degree is offered either as a five-year concurrent programme or a two-year after degree programme, which requires a three-year undergraduate degree prior to entering the programme. Manitoba has one private religious university which receives public funds, the Canadian Mennonite University (CMU). CMU offers one certificate programme, as well as Bachelor's and Master's level degrees. Programmes offered include general Arts, Music and Theology. These programmes are accepted for university transfer where agreements exist with Manitoba universities. Graduates of CMU have gone on to complete graduate studies in Canada and internationally. In Manitoba, there are three partially funded private degree-granting religious institutions; Providence College and Seminary, Steinbach Bible College and William and Catherine Booth University College. These colleges are special purpose institutions which offer certificates, diplomas and degrees, as well as seminary studies. General Arts, Science and some Religion programmes are accepted for university transfer where agreements exist with Manitoba universities. Graduates of private religious colleges in Manitoba have gone on to complete graduate studies in Canada and internationally.

University level second stage: Master's degree
Most graduate work is done at the University of Manitoba, although Brandon University, Collège universitaire Saint Boniface and the University of Winnipeg offer a limited number of Master's programmes. The Master's degree normally requires from one to two years' study after a four year Bachelor's degree or an Honours degree. A thesis or comprehensive examination is usually required in addition to course work. Examples are: M.A., M.Sc., M.Ed., M.B.A.

University level third stage: Doctorate
The Doctorate is the highest academic qualification awarded by Canadian universities and it comprises the third stage of university-level studies. This degree normally requires at least five years of study after the Bachelor's degree; the submission and defence of a major thesis (dissertation) are the principal requirements, and supplemental course work is usually also required. The degree "Doctor of Philosophy" (Ph.D.) is the designation

most commonly used to signify the Doctorate. It is a generic title, applicable to degrees in most disciplines (the Doctorate should not be confused with certain first professional degrees in the Health Sciences, e.g. Medicine, Veterinary Medicine and Dentistry). The University of Manitoba is the only doctoral degree-granting institution in Manitoba.

Distance higher education:

The University of Manitoba, the University of Winnipeg, Brandon University, Collège universitaire de Saint Boniface, Red River College, Assiniboine Community College and the University College of the North have been engaged in distance education learning programmes for many years. The three universities offer an Inter Universities North programme in Northern Manitoba, a programme that is coordinated by the University College of the North. Additionally, Campus Manitoba is a consortium of colleges and universities and UCN that offers degree programmes through distance technology to further expand accessibility to higher education for Manitobans in rural and remote areas.

ADMISSION TO HIGHER EDUCATION

Admission to university-level studies:

Name of secondary school credential required: High School Diploma/Diplôme d'études secondaires

Name of secondary school credential required: Mature Student High School Diploma

Alternatives to credentials: Universities set their own admission policies and requirements. These do not involve separate entrance examinations, and usually include flexibility for mature students, i.e. applicants aged 21 or more, who have not completed secondary school.

Numerus clausus/restrictions: Universities limit enrolment in professional programmes because of the number of allotted seats based on anticipated demand in the workforce as estimated by the professional bodies, e.g. Medicine. Percentage of students admitted varies with size of applicant pool. Order of preference: provincial residents, those of other provinces, and foreign students (in Medicine, about 25% of applicants across Canada are admitted).

Other admission requirements: Admission to some professional programmes (e.g. Medicine, Dentistry, Law) requires previous university education. Specific admission requirements may vary by field of study and by university and may include such factors as interviews and references.

Foreign students admission:

Definition of foreign student: Foreign (International) students are students who are neither Canadian citizens nor permanent residents of Canada, and are enrolled full-time in a recognized academic, professional or vocational training course at a university, college or other educational institution in Canada.

Entrance exam requirements: Institutions have their own policies on international students. The universities will accept international students on a pre-established list of high school equivalents. As well, students must provide proof of English language proficiency if the student's first language is not English (or French if attending CUSB). This may be done through various internationally accepted tests. A lack of proficiency in English or French will also be taken into account by the Canadian Immigration Office in the evaluation of the application.

Entry regulations: Before you come to study in Canada, you will need: a "Study Permit" if the programme of study you will be admitted to is longer than six months in duration, regardless of the length of your stay in Canada; a letter of acceptance from the school of your choice; proof that you have enough money to pay school fees and living expenses; to establish that you will return home at the end of your studies; to pass a medical exam if required; and to qualify as a temporary resident in Canada, including holding a temporary resident visa (required for citizens of many countries). A small number of students do not require a Study Permit by virtue of their status in Canada (e.g. diplomats and their children).

Health requirements: Most education institutions require international students to buy health insurance in addition to their tuition fees; those that do not will require proof of independent health insurance coverage. Medical examinations are not required by institutions but are required by Citizenship and Immigration Canada for students from many countries.

RECOGNITION OF STUDIES

Quality assurance system:

See: http://www.cicic.ca/567/quality-assurance-MB.canada

Bodies dealing with recognition:

Council on Post-Secondary Education - COPSE (Conseil de l'Enseignement Postsecondaire)

> 410-330 Portage
> Winnipeg, Manitoba R3C 0C4
> Tel: +1(204) 945 1833
> Fax: +1(204) 945 1841
> EMail: info@copse.mb.ca
> WWW: http://www.copse.mb.ca

Special provisions for recognition:

Recognition for university level studies: Universities establish their own admissions criteria and make their own admissions decisions in response to individual applications. Any restrictions on admission are determined by the institutions themselves, given available teaching and other resources, but in a few instances are a result of government policy. For restricted programmes, priority is usually given to provincial residents first, other Canadian residents, then international students.

Additionally, the Canadian Information Centre for International Credentials (CICIC) provides information and guidance on the recognition of foreign studies.

For access to advanced studies and research: In general, none. However, some high cost, limited enrolment programmes, e.g. Medicine and Dentistry, limit enrolment to Canadian citizens.

For exercising a profession: For each profession, anyone who has not obtained their credentials within Canada must meet specified educational, experience and language requirements and pass registration examinations. A special programme gives immigrants who are foreign-trained professionals improved access to acquiring Canadian experience by creating new full-time positions in certain areas for up to one year.

PROVINCIAL BODIES

Manitoba Advanced Education and Literacy (Enseignement postsecondaire et Alphabétisation Manitoba)

> Minister: Erin Selby
> 162 Legislative Building
> Manitoba R3C 0V8
> Canada
> Tel: +1(204) 945 3744
> Fax: +1(204) 945 4261
> EMail: mgi@gov.mb.ca
> WWW: http://www.edu.gov.mb.ca/ael/index.html
> *Role of national body*: Manitoba Advanced Education and Literacy (MAEL) is charged with the overall responsibility for Manitoba's system of adult and advanced education, including funding and identification of priorities for the literacy and adult education system, and the post-secondary system.

Council on Post-Secondary Education - COPSE (Conseil de l'Enseignement Postsecondaire)

> Chairperson: Curtis Nordman
> Secretary: Sid Rogers
> 410-330 Portage
> Winnipeg, Manitoba R3C 0C4
> Canada
> Tel: +1(204) 945 1833
> Fax: +1(204) 945 1841
> EMail: info@copse.mb.ca
> WWW: http://www.copse.mb.ca
> *Role of national body*: The Council on Post-Secondary Education, which reports to the minister, is legislatively charged with the responsibility of setting priorities and allocating funds for the Province's universities and

colleges. The Council plans and co-ordinates the development of a post-secondary education system in the province that promotes excellence in and accessibility to education, supports the co-ordination and integration of services and facilities, and promotes fiscal responsibility.

Data for academic year: 2011-2012

Source: IAU from the Canadian Information Centre for International Credentials (CICIC), a unit of the Council of Ministers of Education, Canada (CMEC), on behalf of the Province of Manitoba, 2011

INSTITUTIONS

PUBLIC INSTITUTIONS

BRANDON UNIVERSITY (BU)

270 18th Street, Brandon, Manitoba R7A 6A9
Tel: +1(204) 728-9520
Fax: +1(204) 726-4573
EMail: admissions@brandonu.ca
Website: http://www.brandonu.ca

President and Vice-Chancellor: Deborah C. Poff
Tel: Scott J. B. Lamont, Fax: +1(204) 729-9016
EMail: president@brandonu.ca; poffd@brandonu.ca

Vice President, Administration and Finance: Scott J. B. Lamont
Tel: +1(204) 727-9707, Fax: +1(204) 726-4573
EMail: lamont@brandonu.ca

International Relations: Anita Allan, Coordinator, Office of International Activities
Tel: +1(204) 727-7479, Fax: +1(204) 727-7471
EMail: allan@brandonu.ca

Faculties
Arts (Anthropology; Archaeology; Business Administration; Ceramic Art; Classical Languages; Design; Economics; English; French; Gender Studies; German; Greek (Classical); History; Indigenous Studies; Italian; Latin; Linguistics; Modern Languages; Native Language; Painting and Drawing; Philosophy; Political Sciences; Religion; Rural Planning; Sociology; Spanish; Theatre; Visual Arts; Women's Studies; Writing); **Education** (Curriculum; Education; Educational Administration; Education and Student Counselling; Educational Psychology; Music Education; Physical Education; Special Education; Teacher Training); **Graduate Studies** (Education; Music; Nursing; Rural Planning); **Health Studies** (Health Sciences; Nursing; Psychiatry and Mental Health; Psychology); **Music** (Jazz and Popular Music; Music; Music Education; Music Theory and Composition; Musical Instruments); **Science** (Agriculture; Astronomy and Space Science; Biology; Chemistry; Computer Science; Dentistry; Environmental Studies; Geography; Geology; Mathematics and Computer Science; Medicine; Optometry; Pharmacy; Physics; Psychology; Safety Engineering; Veterinary Science)

History: Founded 1899 as Brandon College, affiliated with the University of Manitoba, acquired present status and title 1967.

Governing Bodies: Board of Governors; Senate

Academic Year: September to April (September-December; January-April). Also Spring/Summer Session (May-August)

Admission Requirements: Secondary school certificate or recognized foreign equivalent, including International Baccalaureate

Fees: (Can. Dollars): Undergraduate Canadian students, 3,713-4,030 per annum; undergraduate international students, 5,989.80-6,363.60 per annum; graduate, 2,287.35-2,246.25 per annum

Main Language(s) of Instruction: English

Degrees and Diplomas: *University Certificate/Diploma*; *Bachelor's Degree*; *Master's Degree*; *Graduate Diploma/Certificate*. Also Honours Bachelor's degree, 4 yrs; Concurrent Bachelor's degree programmes, B.Ed./ and another degree, 5 yrs; Pre-professional degree programmes.

Student Residential Facilities: Yes

Special Facilities: B. J. Hales Museum of Natural History. Observatory

Libraries: c. 1,140,770 vols

Publications: Canadian Journal of Native Studies *(biannually)*; Community Report *(annually)*; Peace Research : The Canadian Journal of Peace Studies *(quarterly)*

Academic Staff 2007-2008	TOTAL
FULL-TIME	c. 460

Student Numbers 2009-2010	
All (Foreign Included)	3,203
FOREIGN ONLY	130

Part-time students, 1,077.
Last Updated: 05/01/11

ST. ANDREW'S COLLEGE (UNIVERSITY OF MANITOBA)

29 Dysart Road, Winnipeg, Manitoba R3T 2M7
Tel: +1(204) 474-8895
Fax: +1(204) 474-7624
EMail: st_andrews@umanitoba.ca
Website: http://www.umanitoba.ca/colleges/st_andrews/

Principal (Acting): Roman Bozyk

Faculties
Theology (Religion; Religious Music; Theology)

Degrees and Diplomas: *University Certificate/Diploma*; *Bachelor's Degree*; *Master's Degree*
Last Updated: 06/01/11

ST. JOHN'S COLLEGE (UNIVERSITY OF MANITOBA)

92 Dysart Road, Winnipeg, Manitoba R3T 2M5
Tel: +1(204) 474-8531
Fax: +1(204) 474-7610
EMail: stjohns_college@umanitoba.ca
Website: http://www.umanitoba.ca/colleges/st_johns/

Warden and Vice-Chancellor: Janet Hoskins
Tel: +1(204) 474-8529 EMail: j_hoskins@umanitoba.ca

Bursar and Executive Assistant to the Warden: Ivan Froese
Tel: +1(204) 474-8533 EMail: froesei@cc.umanitoba.ca

Faculties
Theology (Bible; Theology)

Institutes
Anglican Ministry (Protestant Theology)

Programmes
Biology (Biology); **Chemistry** (Chemistry); **History** (History); **Indigenous Studies** (Indigenous Studies); **Literature** (Literature); **Physical Chemistry** (Physical Chemistry); **Physics** (Physics); **Sociology** (Sociology); **Statistics** (Statistics)

History: Founded 1866.

Degrees and Diplomas: *University Certificate/Diploma*; *Bachelor's Degree*; *Master's Degree*; *Doctoral Degree*. Also Advanced Certificate, 3 yrs.
Last Updated: 06/01/11

ST. PAUL'S COLLEGE (UNIVERSITY OF MANITOBA)

70 Dysart Road, Winnipeg, Manitoba R3T 2M6
Tel: +(204) 474-8575
Fax: +(204) 474-7620
EMail: stpauls@umanitoba.ca
Website: http://www.umanitoba.ca/colleges/st_pauls/

Rector: Denic C. Bracken
Tel: +(204) 474-8581 EMail: bracken@cc.umanitoba.ca

Centres
Catholic Studies *(Jesuit)* (Catholic Theology); **Peace and Justice** *(Arthur V. Mauro)* (Peace and Disarmament)
History: Founded 1926.
Degrees and Diplomas: *Bachelor's Degree*; *Master's Degree*; *Doctoral Degree*

Student Numbers *2009-2010*: Total: c. 1,200
Last Updated: 07/01/11

THE UNIVERSITY OF WINNIPEG (UWINNIPEG)

515 Portage Avenue, Winnipeg, Manitoba R3B 2E9
Tel: +1(204) 786-7811
Fax: +1(204) 786-8656
EMail: info@uwinnipeg.ca
Website: http://www.uwinnipeg.ca

President and Vice-Chancellor: Lloyd Axworthy
Tel: +1(204) 786-9214, Fax: +1(204) 786-1693
EMail: president@uwinnipeg.ca

Vice-President (Finance and Administration): Bill Balan
Tel: +1(204) 786-9229 EMail: b.balan@uwinnipeg.ca

International Relations: Neil Besner, Vice-President (Research and International)
Tel: +1(204) 988-7104, Fax: +1(204) 786-8656
EMail: n.besner@uwinnipeg.ca

Divisions
Continuing Education (Arabic; Art Management; Business Computing; Chinese; Computer Science; Data Processing; Education; French; German; Hindi; Human Resources; Indigenous Studies; Information Technology; Italian; Japanese; Korean; Leadership; Management; Marketing; Portuguese; Public Relations; Russian; Software Engineering; Spanish)

Faculties
Arts (Classical Languages; Communication Studies; Criminal Law; Cultural Studies; East Asian Studies; English; Film; French; Gender Studies; German; Greek (Classical); History; Indigenous Studies; Italian; Latin; Literature; Modern Languages; Philosophy; Physical Therapy; Political Sciences; Psychology; Religion; Sociology; Spanish; Sports; Theatre; Women's Studies; Writing; **Business and Economics** (Business Administration; Economics; Finance); **Education** (Business Education; Education; Natives Education; Teacher Training); **Science** (Anthropology; Biochemistry; Biology; Chemistry; Computer Science; Engineering; Environmental Studies; Geography; Mathematics; Physics; Psychology; Statistics); **Theology** (Pastoral Studies; Religion; Theology)

Programmes
Pre-Professional Studies (Architecture; Chiropractic; Dental Hygiene; Dentistry; Engineering; Journalism; Law; Medical Technology; Medicine; Occupational Therapy; Optometry; Pharmacy; Physical Therapy; Respiratory Therapy; Social Work; Veterinary Science)

Further Information: Also 23 Academic Units, Centres, and Chairs: see http://www.uwinnipeg.ca/index/faculty-academic

History: Founded 1871 as Manitoba College by the Presbyterian Church and Wesley College by the Methodist Church 1877. Merged and became United Colleges 1938. Acquired present status and title 1967.

Governing Bodies: Board of Regents; Senate
Academic Year: September to August (September-December; January-April; May-August)
Admission Requirements: Secondary school certificate or recognized foreign equivalent
Fees: (Can. Dollars): Canadian students, 305.70-352.17 per 3 credit hours; international students, 1,100.73-1,269.27 per 3 credit hours.
Main Language(s) of Instruction: English
Degrees and Diplomas: *University Certificate/Diploma*; *Bachelor's Degree*; *Master's Degree*. Alo integrated Bachelor's degree of Education and Arts or Science, 5 yrs; After degree Bachelor's degree of Education programme, 2 yrs following undergraduate degree; Joint Master's Programmes with the University of Manitoba.
Student Services: Academic counselling, Canteen, Cultural centre, Employment services, Foreign student adviser, Handicapped facilities, Health services, Nursery care, Social counselling, Sports facilities
Student Residential Facilities: Student residences
Special Facilities: Art Gallery
Libraries: c. 750,000 items including books, periodicals, microfiche, and videos.

Academic Staff *2010-2011*	TOTAL
FULL-TIME	330
PART-TIME	c. 567
Student Numbers *2010-2011*	
All (Foreign Included)	9,860
FOREIGN ONLY	1,069

Last Updated: 07/01/11

UNIVERSITY COLLEGE OF SAINT-BONIFACE (UNIVERSITY OF MANITOBA)

Collège universitaire de Saint-Boniface (University of Manitoba) (CUSB)
200, avenue de la Cathédrale, Saint-Boniface, Manitoba R2H 0H7
Tel: +1(204) 233-0210
Fax: +1(204) 237-3240
EMail: stad@ustboniface.mb.ca
Website: http://www.ustboniface.mb.ca

Rectrice: Raymonde Gagné (2003-)
Tel: +1(204) 233-0210, Fax: +1(204) 237-3099
EMail: rgagne@ustboniface.mb.ca

Registraire: André Boucher
Tel: +1(204) 237-1818 Ext.408, Fax: +1(204) 235-4485
EMail: aboucher@ustboniface.mb.ca

International Relations: Robin Rooke, Coordonnatrice, Bureau international
Tel: +1(204) 237-1818 Ext.503, Fax: +1(204) 237-3240
EMail: international@cusb.ca; rrooke@ustboniface.mb.ca

Faculties
Arts (Anthropology; Arts and Humanities; Canadian Studies; Economics; English; French; Geography (Human); German; History; Literature; Mathematics; Modern Languages; Philosophy; Political Sciences; Psychology; Religious Studies; Social Sciences; Sociology; Spanish); **Business Administration** (Business Administration; Human Resources; International Business; Labour and Industrial Relations; Management; Marketing); **Education** (Curriculum; Education; Educational Administration; Educational and Student Counselling; Literacy Education; Native Language Education; Primary Education; Secondary Education); **Sciences** (Biochemistry; Chemistry; Computer Science; Mathematics; Microbiology; Physics; Statistics; Zoology); **Social Services** (Social and Community Services)

Programmes
Continuing Education (French; Spanish); **Distance Education** (Canadian Studies; Computer Science; Education; Translation and Interpretation)

Schools
Technical and Professional (Business Administration; Computer Science; Health Sciences; Multimedia; Nursing; Preschool

Education; Tourism); **Translation** (English; French; Translation and Interpretation)

History: Founded 1818. An affiliated college of the University of Manitoba.

Fees: (Can. Dollars): 3,500-4,300 per annum; Technical and professional programmes, 1,800-4,300 per annum.

Main Language(s) of Instruction: French

Degrees and Diplomas: *University Certificate/Diploma*; *Bachelor's Degree*; *Master's Degree*; *Graduate Diploma/Certificate*

Student Numbers *2009-2010*	**TOTAL**
All (Foreign Included)	**989**
FOREIGN ONLY	**235**

Last Updated: 06/01/11

UNIVERSITY OF MANITOBA (UM)

66 Chancellors Circle, Winnipeg, Manitoba R3T 2N2
Tel: +1(204) 474-8880
Fax: +1(204) 474-7536
EMail: admissions@umanitoba.ca
Website: http://www.umanitoba.ca

President and Vice-Chancellor: David T. Barnard (2008-)
Tel: +1(204) 474-9345, Fax: +1(204) 261-1318
EMail: president@umanitoba.ca

Vice-President (Administration): Deborah J. McCallum
Tel: +1(204) 474-8889, Fax: +1(204) 261-1318
EMail: vpadmin@umanitoba.ca

International Relations: James M. Dean, Executive Director, Office of International Relations
Tel: +1(204) 474-6835, Fax: +1(204) 474-7632
EMail: James_Dean@umanitoba.ca

Centres

Aging (Gerontology); **Agri-food Research in Health and Medicine** *(Canadian)* (Food Science); **Architectural Structures and Technology** *(C.A.S.T.)* (Architecture); **Breast Cancer Research and Diagnosis** *(Great-West Life Manitoba)* (Oncology); **Cell Biology** *(Manitoba)* (Cell Biology); **Defence and Security Studies** (Protective Services); **Earth Observation Science** *(CEOS)* (Earth Sciences); **Functional Foods and Nutraceuticals** *(RCFFN)* (Food Science); **Global Public Health** (Public Health); **Globalization and Cultural Studies** (Cultural Studies); **Health Policy** *(Manitoba)* (Health Sciences); **Hellenic Civilization** (Ancient Civilizations); **Human Models of Disease**; **Internet Innovation** (Information Technology); **Livestock and the Environment** *(Manitoba)* (Animal Husbandry); **Nursing and Health Research** *(MCNHR)* (Health Sciences; Nursing); **Professional and Applied Ethics** (Ethics); **Proteomics and Systems Biology** *(Manitoba)* (Biology); **Research and Treatment of Atherosclerosis** (Medicine; Rehabilitation and Therapy)

Divisions

Extended Education (Anthropology; Architecture; Arts and Humanities; Business Administration; Earth Sciences; Ecology; Engineering; English; Environmental Studies; Food Science; Geology; Indigenous Studies; Management; Modern Languages; Music; Native Language Education; Natural Resources; Natural Sciences; Nursing; Nutrition; Physics; Slavic Languages; Social Work; Sports; Sports Management; Writing)

Faculties

Agricultural and Food Sciences (Agricultural Business; Agricultural Economics; Agriculture; Animal Husbandry; Bioengineering; Biomedicine; Botany; Entomology; Environmental Engineering; Food Science; Soil Science; Veterinary Science); **Architecture** (Architectural and Environmental Design; Architecture; Design; Interior Design; Landscape Architecture; Town Planning); **Arts** (Adult Education; Anthropology; Arts and Humanities; Asian Studies; Canadian Studies; Catholic Theology; Central European Studies; Classical Languages; Criminology; Cultural Studies; Development Studies; Eastern European Studies; Economics; English; Film; French; Gender Studies; German; Greek (Classical); History; Icelandic; Indigenous Studies; Italian; Jewish Studies; Judaic Religious Studies; Labour and Industrial Relations; Labour Law; Latin; Latin American Studies; Leadership; Linguistics; Medieval Studies; Modern History; Philosophy; Political Sciences; Psy-

chology; Religion; Slavic Languages; Sociology; Spanish; Theatre; Women's Studies); **Dentistry** (Biology; Community Health; Dental Hygiene; Dentistry; Oral Pathology; Surgery); **Education** (Adult Education; Continuing Education; Education; Foreign Languages Education); **Engineering** (Aeronautical and Aerospace Engineering; Bioengineering; Civil Engineering; Computer Engineering; Design; Electrical Engineering; Engineering; Industrial Engineering; Mechanical Engineering); **Environment, Earth, and Resources** *(Clayton H. Riddell)* (Environmental Management; Environmental Studies; Geography; Geology; Geophysics; Natural Resources); **Graduate Studies** (Agricultural Business; Agricultural Economics; Anatomy; Animal Husbandry; Anthropology; Architectural and Environmental Design; Architecture and Planning; Astronomy and Space Science; Biochemistry; Bioengineering; Biological and Life Sciences; Biology; Botany; Canadian Studies; Cell Biology; Chemistry; Civil Engineering; Classical Languages; Community Health; Computer Engineering; Computer Science; Curriculum; Dentistry; Economics; Education; Educational Administration; Educational Psychology; Electrical Engineering; English; Entomology; Environmental Studies; Family Studies; Film; Fine Arts; Food Science; French; Genetics; Geography; Geology; German; Greek; Health Sciences; History; Icelandic; Immunology; Indigenous Studies; Interior Design; Italian; Landscape Architecture; Latin; Law; Linguistics; Management; Mathematics; Mathematics and Computer Science; Mechanical Engineering; Medical Auxiliaries; Microbiology; Music; Natural Resources; Nursing; Nutrition; Occupational Therapy; Oncology; Orthodontics; Pathology; Peace and Disarmament; Periodontics; Pharmacology; Pharmacy; Philosophy; Physical Therapy; Physics; Physiology; Political Sciences; Psychology; Public Administration; Public Health; Rehabilitation and Therapy; Religion; Slavic Languages; Social Sciences; Social Work; Sociology; Soil Science; Spanish; Statistics; Surgery; Textile Design; Theatre; Town Planning; Zoology); **Human Ecology** (Family Studies; Nutrition; Textile Design); **Kinesiology and Recreation Management** (Leisure Studies; Physical Education; Physical Therapy; Sports); **Law** *(Robson Hall)* (Administrative Law; Civil Law; Commercial Law; Constitutional Law; Criminal Law; History of Law; Law; Private Law; Public Law); **Medicine** (Anaesthesiology; Anatomy; Biochemistry; Cell Biology; Clinical Psychology; Community Health; Genetics; Gynaecology and Obstetrics; Health Education; Immunology; Medicine; Microbiology; Ophthalmology; Otorhinolaryngology; Paediatrics; Pharmacology; Physiology; Psychiatry and Mental Health; Radiology; Surgery); **Music** *(Marcel A. Desautels)* (Art History; Jazz and Popular Music; Music; Music Education; Music Theory and Composition; Musical Instruments; Singing); **Nursing** (Health Sciences; Nursing; Oncology); **Pharmacy** (Pharmacy); **Science** (Actuarial Science; Astronomy and Space Science; Biochemistry; Biological and Life Sciences; Biotechnology; Chemistry; Computer Science; Genetics; Mathematics; Microbiology; Physics; Psychology; Statistics); **Social Work** (Social Work)

Institutes

Cardiovascular Sciences (Cardiology); **Humanities** (Arts and Humanities); **Industrial Mathematical Sciences** (Mathematics); **Legal Research** (Law); **Theoretical Physics** *(with University of Winnipeg)* (Physics); **Transport** (Transport and Communications)

Laboratories

Applied Electromagnetics (Electrical Engineering); **Structural Engineering** *(W.R. McQuade)* (Engineering)

Programmes

University 1 (Accountancy; Agricultural Business; Agriculture; Anthropology; Applied Mathematics; Architectural and Environmental Design; Architecture; Art History; Arts and Humanities; Asian Studies; Astronomy and Space Science; Biological and Life Sciences; Biotechnology; Business Administration; Canadian Studies; Catholic Theology; Chemistry; Classical Languages; Computer Science; Dental Hygiene; Dentistry; Ecology; Economics; Education; Engineering; English; Entomology; Environmental Studies; Family Studies; Film; Fine Arts; Food Science; French; Gender Studies; Genetics; Geography; Geology; Geophysics; German; Greek (Classical); Health Sciences; History; Hungarian; Icelandic; Indigenous Studies; Italian; Jewish Studies; Labour and Industrial Relations; Latin; Law; Leisure Studies; Linguistics; Management; Marketing; Mathematics; Medicine; Microbiology; Music; Native Language; Natural Resources; Nursing; Nutrition; Occupational Therapy; Pharmacy; Philosophy; Physical Education; Physical Therapy; Physics; Polish; Political Sciences; Portuguese; Psychology;

Religion; Respiratory Therapy; Russian; Slavic Languages; Social Work; Sociology; Spanish; Statistics; Textile Design; Theatre; Veterinary Science; Women's Studies)

Research Centres

Aboriginal Health (Health Sciences); **Data** *(Manitoba)* (Data Processing); **Grain Storage** *(Canadian Wheat Board)* (Agriculture); **Higher Education and Development** *(CHERD)* (Development Studies; Higher Education); **RESOLVE** *(Prairie Research Network on Family Violence)* (Family Studies; Social Problems); **Spinal Cord** (Medicine)

Research Groups

Aquatic Biology (Biology); **Community Acquired Infections** (Community Health); **Composite Materials and Structures** (Materials Engineering); **Developmental Health** (Health Sciences); **Mood and Anxiety Disorders** (Psychology); **Psychiatric Neuroimaging** (Psychiatry and Mental Health)

Research Institutes

Health, Leisure and Human Performance (Health Sciences; Leisure Studies; Sports)

Schools

Agriculture (Agriculture; Crop Production; Fruit Production; Horticulture; Landscape Architecture; Vegetable Production); **Art** (Art History; Ceramic Art; Fine Arts; Graphic Design; Painting and Drawing; Photography; Printing and Printmaking; Sculpture; Video); **Business** *(I.H. Asper)* (Business Administration; Finance; Human Resources; Management; Marketing; Small Business); **Dental Hygiene** (Dental Hygiene); **Medical Rehabilitation** (Health Sciences; Occupational Therapy; Physical Therapy; Rehabilitation and Therapy; Respiratory Therapy)

Units

Aerospace Materials Engineering Facility (Aeronautical and Aerospace Engineering); **Crystallography and Mineralogy Research Facility** (Crystallography; Mineralogy); **Digital Image Analysis Facility**; **Nuclear Magnetic Resonance (NMR) Facility** (Nuclear Engineering); **Regional Materials and Surface Characterization Facility** *(Manitoba)* (Materials Engineering)

Further Information: Also Fort Garry Campus, Bannatyne Campus; William Norrie Centre; University of Manitoba Downtown: Aboriginal Education Centre (hosting the Division of Extended Education); National Centre for Livestock and Environment , agricultural research farm at Carman; field stations at Delta Marsh on Lake Manitoba, Star Lake in the Whiteshell, and Wallace Lake in eastern Manitoba.

History: Founded 1877 on the model of the University of London, as an examining and degree-conferring body. Appointed the first Professors 1904.

Governing Bodies: Board of Governors; Senate

Academic Year: September to April, Regular Session; May to June, Intersession; July to August, Summer-Day Session; May to July, Summer-Evening Session

Admission Requirements: Secondary school certificate or recognized foreign equivalent

Fees: (Can. Dollars): From 3,300 per annum

Main Language(s) of Instruction: English

Degrees and Diplomas: *University Certificate/Diploma; Bachelor's Degree; Master's Degree*: a further 1-3 yrs; *Graduate Diploma/Certificate; Doctoral Degree (PhD)*. Bachelor of Medicine: awarded concurrently to Medicine students who choose a research option

Student Services: Academic counselling, Canteen, Cultural centre, Employment services, Foreign student adviser, Foreign Studies Centre, Handicapped facilities, Health services, Language programs, Nursery care, Social counselling, Sports facilities

Student Residential Facilities: Yes

Special Facilities: Botany Museum. Geology Museum. Zoology Museum. Planetarium. Art Gallery. Theatre. Field Stations

Libraries: Total, 2m. vols

Press or Publishing House: University of Manitoba Press

Academic Staff *2010-2011*   **TOTAL**
FULL-TIME   3,661
Student Numbers *2010-2011*
All (Foreign Included)   27,476
FOREIGN ONLY   2,170
Last Updated: 20/01/11

PRIVATE INSTITUTIONS

CANADIAN MENNONITE UNIVERSITY (CMU)

500 Shaftsbury Boulevard, Winnipeg, Manitoba R3P 2N2
Tel: +1(204) 487-3300
Fax: +1(204) 487-3858
EMail: info@cmu.ca
Website: http://www.cmu.ca/

President: Gerald Gerbrandt EMail: ggerbrandt@cmu.ca

Registrar and Assistant Vice-President Academic: Wesley Toews EMail: wtoews@cmu.ca

International Relations: Paul Kroeker, Dean of International Programs EMail: pkroeker@cmu.ca

Programmes

Anthropology (Anthropology; Prehistory); **Biblical and Theological Studies** (Bible; Christian Religious Studies; Religion; Theology); **Biology** (Anatomy; Biological and Life Sciences; Biology; Physiology); **Business and Organizational Administration** (Accountancy; Administration; Business Administration; Finance; Human Resources; International Business; Leadership; Management; Small Business); **Chemistry** (Chemistry; Physical Chemistry); **Communications and Media** (Communication Studies; Graphic Design; Journalism; Mass Communication; Media Studies; Political Sciences; Radio and Television Broadcasting); **Computer Science** (Computer Science); **Counselling Studies** (Psychology; Social Sciences); **Disaster Recovery** (Social and Community Services; Social Sciences; Theology; Welfare and Protective Services); **Economics** (Economics; International Business; International Economics); **English** (English; Literature; Writing); **Geography** (Environmental Studies; Geography; Geography (Human)); **Graduate Studies** (Christian Religious Studies; Theology); **History** (History); **Intercultural Studies** (Social Sciences); **International Development Studies** (Development Studies; Economics; Religion); **Mathematics** (Mathematics); **Music** (Art Therapy; Music; Musical Instruments; Musicology); **Music Therapy** (Art Therapy; Music); **Peace and Conflict Transformation Studies** (Peace and Disarmament); **Philosophy** (Metaphysics; Philosophy); **Physics** (Mechanics; Physics); **Political Studies** (Development Studies; History; Human Rights; Media Studies; Philosophy; Political Sciences); **Practica** (Development Studies; Music; Pastoral Studies; Peace and Disarmament; Social Sciences; Theology); **Preprofessional Studies** (Agriculture; Dentistry; Ecology; Education; Law; Medicine; Nursing; Pharmacy; Physical Education; Rehabilitation and Therapy; Social Work); **Psychology** (Behavioural Sciences; Psychology); **Religion** (Religion); **Social Service** (Social and Community Services; Social Sciences); **Sociology** (Media Studies; Philosophy; Social Welfare; Sociology); **Theatre, Film, and Art** (Art History; Film; Literature; Theatre)

History: Founded 1998 through the amalgamation of three colleges: Mennonite Brethren Bible College/Concord College (est. 1944); Canadian Mennonite Bible College (est. 1947); and Menno Simons College (est. 1989)

Fees: (Canadian Dollar): Canadian tuition fees, undergraduate and graduate studies, 609 per 3 credit hour course; International tuition fees, 1,066 per 3 credit hour course.

Degrees and Diplomas: *University Certificate/Diploma; Bachelor's Degree; Master's Degree; Graduate Diploma/Certificate*

Publications: Direction, Publication addressing Biblical, theological, historical, ethical, and church-related issues. *(biannually)*; Peace Research Journal, Journal on issues of conflict, violence, poverty, just peace and human well-being. *(biannually)*; Vision, Publication to encourage theological reflection by church leaders on the identity, mission and practices of the church from an Anabaptist-Mennonite perspective. *(biannually)*
Last Updated: 05/01/11

PROVIDENCE COLLEGE AND THEOLOGICAL SEMINARY

10 College Crescent, Otterburne, Manitoba R0A 1G0
Tel: +1(204) 433-7488 +1(800) 668-7768
Fax: +1(204) 433-7158
EMail: info@prov.ca
Website: http://www.prov.ca

President: August Konkel EMail: august.konkel@prov.ca

Provost and Executive Vice President: David Johnson
EMail: David.Johnson@prov.ca

International Relations: John Johnson, International Student Services Coordinator EMail: john.Johnson@prov.ca

Departments
Biblical and Theological Studies (Bible; Theology)

Institutes
English Language *(ELI)* (English)

Programmes
Aviation (Air Transport); **Business Administration** (Accountancy; Business Administration; Commercial Law; Economics; Finance; Human Resources; Management; Marketing); **Church Ministries** (Christian Religious Studies; Theology); **Communications and Media** (Journalism; Mass Communication; Media Studies; Photography; Radio and Television Broadcasting; Writing); **Field Education** (Christian Religious Studies); **Humanities** (Arts and Humanities; Bible; English; History; Music; Music Theory and Composition; Musical Instruments; Musicology; Philosophy; Theatre; Theology); **Integrative Vocational Studies**; **Intercultural Studies** (Anthropology; Cultural Studies; Protestant Theology; Religion; Theology); **Mathematics** (Mathematics); **Music** (Art Therapy; Jazz and Popular Music; Music; Music Education; Musical Instruments; Religious Music; Singing); **Pre-Professional Studies** (Agriculture; Architecture; Dental Hygiene; Dentistry; Ecology; Education; Engineering; Environmental Studies; Fine Arts; Law; Management; Medicine; Music; Natural Resources; Natural Sciences; Nursing; Pharmacy; Physical Education; Rehabilitation and Therapy; Social Work); **Seminary** (Christian Religious Studies; Foreign Languages Education; Psychology; Religion; Theology); **Social Sciences** (Anthropology; Bible; Psychology; Social Sciences; Sociology; Theology); **Social Work** (Social Work); **Sociology** (Social Sciences; Sociology); **Teaching English to Speakers of Other Languages** *(TESOL)* (English; Foreign Languages Education); **Theatre** (Acting; Theatre); **Worship Studies** (Bible; Communication Studies; Fine Arts; Leadership; Music; Theology); **Youth Leadership** (Leadership)

History: Founded 1925 as Winnipeg Bible School. Became Winnipeg Bible Institute and College of Theology 1949. Formed Theological Seminary 1972. Became Providence College and Theological Seminary 1992.

Governing Bodies: Board of Governors

Academic Year: September to June (September-December; January-June)

Admission Requirements: High School Certificate or equivalent with 28 credits.

Fees: (Can. Dollars): Canadian and US Students, 3,150 per semester; International Students, 3,405 per semester. Room and Board, 700 per semester.

Main Language(s) of Instruction: English

Accrediting Agencies: Association of Biblical Higher Education (ABHE); TESOL program is accredited by TESL Canada.

Degrees and Diplomas: *University Certificate/Diploma*; *Bachelor's Degree*; *Master's Degree*; *Doctoral Degree*. Also Honours Bachelor's degree, 4 yrs.

Student Services: Academic counselling, Canteen, Employment services, Foreign student adviser, Language programs, Sports facilities

Student Residential Facilities: Yes.

Libraries: Over 60,000 vols

Publications: Didaskalia, Original research in academic and applied studies in History, Theology, Bible and Christian Education *(biennially)*

Academic Staff *2007-2008*	TOTAL
FULL-TIME	20
PART-TIME	30
STAFF WITH DOCTORATE	
FULL-TIME	c. 30

Student Numbers *2007-2008*	
All (Foreign Included)	c. 820
FOREIGN ONLY	50

Part-time students, 60.
Last Updated: 06/01/11

WILLIAM AND CATHERINE BOOTH COLLEGE

447 Web Place, Winnipeg, Manitoba R3B 2P2
Tel: +1(204) 947-6701 +1(877) 942-6684
Fax: +1(204) 942-3856
EMail: wcbc@boothcollege.ca; admissions@boothuc.ca
Website: http://www.boothcollege.ca/

President: Donald E. Burke
Tel: +1(204) 924-4871 EMail: dburke@boothcollege.ca

Programmes
Behavioural Sciences (Behavioural Sciences); **Business Administration** (Business Administration); **Christian Studies** *(Certificate Programme)* (Christian Religious Studies); **English and Film** (English; Film); **General Studies** (Arts and Humanities; Natural Sciences); **Liberal Arts** *(Certificate Programme)* (Arts and Humanities); **Religion** (Religion); **Social Work** (Social Work)

Further Information: Traditional and Open Learning Institution

Degrees and Diplomas: *University Certificate/Diploma*; *Bachelor's Degree*. Bachelor's degree (professional), 4 yrs.
Last Updated: 03/12/10

Canada - New Brunswick

STRUCTURE OF HIGHER EDUCATION SYSTEM

Description:

Higher education in Canada is the constitutional responsibility of the provinces. The two main types of institutions providing higher education are universities and colleges, which provides diverse technical and vocational programmes usually leading to a Certificate or Diploma. The former are degree-granting institutions, while the latter are not (although some offer university-level transfer courses). Besides various government support pre-employment, apprenticeship and other vocational programmes, there are also several private training organizations operating in New Brunswick (which are required to register under the Private Occupational Training Act). Universities are independently administered institutions with full autonomy on admissions and all other academic matters. New Brunswick provides funding to four public universities. Private universities do not receive government funding. There are three not-for-profit private chartered institutions operating in the Province. In 2001, New Brunswick adopted the Degree Granting Act, allowing private for-profit institutions to confer university degrees. To date, three institutions; Yorkville University, University of Fredericton and Meritus University have been designated to confer specific degree programmes.

Stages of studies:

University level first stage: *Bachelor's degree*
Most undergraduate study leads to a "general" Bachelor's degree (minimum 3 years) or an "Honours" degree (4 years and prescribed subject concentration). Degrees are normally titled in broad descriptive groups, e.g. B.A. and B.Sc. The first stage also includes undergraduate diplomas (1-3 years of study) and short (up to 1 year) special Certificate programmes; these may enable entry to degree programmes and are frequently given in close cooperation with professional bodies. In addition, the first stage includes other professional programmes that typically require no university-level prerequisites and 4 years of study, e.g. Bachelor of Science in Nursing (B.Sc.N) and Bachelor of Commerce (B.Comm.) and also first- and second-year university transfer programmes offered by provincially-supported community colleges.

University level second stage: *Master's degree*
The Master's degree normally requires at least one year's study after an Honours Bachelor's degree or equivalent. Some Master's programmes, e.g. in Business Administration, necessitate at least 2 years. A thesis is usually required, often course work as well. Examples are: M.A., M.Sc., M.Ed., M.B.A. Besides graduate level Diplomas (considered as intermediate between the Bachelor's or first professional degree and the Master's degree), the second stage also includes first professional degree programmes requiring prerequisite university studies - followed by perhaps 3 years for a Bachelor of Law (LL.B.) or typically 2 years for a Bachelor of Education (B.Ed.) while a few others normally require 4 years.

University level third stage: *Doctorate degree*
The Doctorate is the highest qualification awarded by Canadian universities and (in all provinces except Quebec) it comprises the third stage of university-level studies. This degree normally requires at least 3 years of study after the Bachelor's degree; the submission and defence of a major thesis (dissertation) are the principal requirements, and supplemental course work is usually also required. The degree "Doctor of Philosophy" (Ph.D) is the designation most commonly used to signify the Doctorate. It is a generic title, applicable to degrees in most disciplines (the Doctorate should not be confused with certain first professional degrees in the Health Sciences, e.g. Medicine, Veterinary Medicine and Dentistry). Universities may choose to allow a PhD graduate to pursue Post-Doctoral studies which do not lead to another degree and may be combined with entrance-level professorial responsibilities.

Distance higher education:
All universities and certain colleges in New Brunswick are currently offering distance education courses using various methods. Three private for-profit degree-granting institutions operate completely online.

ADMISSION TO HIGHER EDUCATION

Foreign students admission:

Definition of foreign student: Foreign (International) Students are students who are neither Canadian citizens nor permanent residents of Canada, and are enrolled full-time in a recognized academic, professional or vocational training course at a university, college or other educational institution in Canada.

Quotas: There is a quota applied at institutional and state level.

Entrance exam requirements: Generally, as for domestic students, a high school diploma or equivalent will be required.

Entry regulations: Before you come to study in Canada, you will need: a "Study Permit" if the programme of study you will be admitted to is longer than six months in duration, regardless of the length of your stay in Canada; a letter of acceptance from the school of your choice; proof that you have enough money to pay for school fees and living expenses; to establish that you will return home at the end of your studies; to pass a medical exam if required; and to qualify as a temporary resident in Canada, including holding a temporary resident visa (required for citizens of many countries). A small number of students do not require a Study Permit by virtue of their status in Canada (e.g. diplomats and their children).

Health requirements: Most education institutions require international students to buy health insurance in addition to their tuition fees; those that do not will require proof of independent health insurance coverage. Medical examinations are not required by institutions but are required by Citizenship and Immigration Canada for students from many countries.

Language requirements: A lack of proficiency in English or French will be taken into account by the Canadian immigration office in the evaluation of the application.

RECOGNITION OF STUDIES

Quality assurance system:

All four public universities consider possible transfer credit for applicable coursework completed at New Brunswick community colleges. However, the transfer potential of many college programmes is limited by their vocational and specialized character.

Special provisions for recognition:

Recognition for university level studies: Universities establish their own admissions criteria and make their own admissions decisions in response to individual applications. Any restrictions on admission are determined by the institutions themselves, given available teaching and other resources, but in a few instances are a result of government policy.

For access to advanced studies and research: In general none. However, if in some high cost or limited enrolment programmes, e.g. Law and Education, qualified applicants outnumber available enrolment capacity, then most universities will establish special admissions committees and provide for proportionately more Canadians than foreign applicants to be admitted.

For exercising a profession: In general none. For each profession, both Canadians and non-Canadians who studied abroad have to meet specified educational and experience requirements, and usually pass registration examinations. Non-Canadians may sometimes also need to pass language tests. Access to most professions is governed by provincial and/or federal statutes and is restricted to Canadian citizens or immigrants accepted as permanent residents. In addition to professional studies, applicants must also meet examination and/or practical training requirements set by the relevant professional body.

PROVINCIAL BODIES

Department of Post-Secondary Education, Training and Labour (Ministère de l'Education post-secondaire, Formation et Travail)

Minister: Martine Coulombe
Chestnut Complex
P.O. Box 6000
Fredericton, NB E3B 5H1
Canada

Tel: +1(506) 453 2597
Fax: +1(506) 453 3618
EMail: dpetlinfo@gnb.ca
WWW: http://www.gnb.ca/post-secondary

Maritime Provinces Higher Education Commission - MPHEC (Commission de l'Enseignement supérieur des Provinces maritimes - CESPM)

Chairperson: David Stewart
CEO: Mireille Duguay
82 Westmorland Street,
Suite 401, P.O. Box 6000
Fredericton, NB E3B 5H1
Canada
Tel: +1(506) 453 2844
Fax: +1(506) 453 2106
EMail: mphec@mphec.ca
WWW: http://www.mphec.ca/

Role of national body: Advisory body to assist the three Maritime provinces (N.B., N.S., P.E.I.) and institutions in achieving a more efficient and effective utilization of resources.

Data for academic year: 2011-2012
Source: IAU from The Canadian Information Centre for International Credentials (CICIC), a unit of the Council of Ministers of Education, Canada (CMEC), on behalf of the Province of New Brunswick, 2011

INSTITUTIONS

PUBLIC INSTITUTIONS

MOUNT ALLISON UNIVERSITY (MTA)

62 York Street, Sackville, New Brunswick E4L 1E4
Tel: +1(506) 364-2269
Fax: +1(506) 364-2272
EMail: admissions@mta.ca
Website: http://www.mta.ca

President: Robert Campbell (2006-)
Tel: +1(506) 364-2300, Fax: +1(506) 364-2299
EMail: rcampbell@mta.ca

Vice-President, Administration: David Stewart
Tel: +1(506) 364-2630, Fax: +(506) 364-2299
EMail: dstewart@mta.ca

International Relations: Ron G. Byrne, Vice-President, International and Student Affairs
Tel: +1(506) 364-2254, Fax: +1(506) 364-2263
EMail: rbyrne@mta.ca

Faculties
Arts (American Studies; Ancient Civilizations; Canadian Studies; Classical Languages; English; Fine Arts; French; French Studies; German; Germanic Studies; Greek (Classical); Hispanic American Studies; History; Japanese; Latin; Literature; Modern Languages; Music; Music Education; Music Theory and Composition; Musical Instruments; Philosophy; Psychology; Religious Studies; Spanish; Theatre; Women's Studies); **Science** (Air Transport; Biochemistry; Biology; Chemistry; Cognitive Sciences; Computer Networks; Computer Science; Environmental Studies; Geography; Mathematics; Mathematics and Computer Science; Physics; Psychology; Software Engineering); **Social Science** (Anthropology; Business and Commerce; Economics; Environmental Studies; Geography (Human); International Relations; Meteorology; Political Sciences; Social Sciences; Sociology)

History: Founded 1839 as Mount Allison Wesleyan Academy, became degree-granting Mount Allison Wesleyan College 1858,

and acquired present status and title 1886. Although conducted on a non-sectarian basis, the University is a Church-related institution (United Church of Canada). As such, it is interested in the all-round development of students.

Governing Bodies: Board of Regents

Academic Year: September to April (September-December; January-April)

Admission Requirements: Secondary school certificate or recognized foreign equivalent

Fees: (Can. Dollars): Full-Time tuition fees, 6,720 per annum for Canadian students and 14,110 per annum for international students.

Main Language(s) of Instruction: English

Degrees and Diplomas: *University Certificate/Diploma*; *Baccalaureate*; *Master's Degree*: Chemistry; Biochemistry

Student Services: Academic counselling, Canteen, Cultural centre, Employment services, Handicapped facilities, Language programs, Nursery care, Social counselling, Sports facilities

Student Residential Facilities: For c. 1,038 men and 730 women students

Special Facilities: Owens Art Gallery, with more than 2000 works in its permanent collection

Libraries: Ralph Pickard Bell Library, c. 849,980 vols. Alfred Whitehead Memorial Library, c. 31,730 vols

Publications: About Canada; Josiah Wood Lectures *(other/irregular)*

Last Updated: 20/01/11

UNIVERSITY OF MONCTON

Université de Moncton
Campus de Moncton, 18, avenue Antonine-Maillet, Moncton, New Brunswick E1A 3E9
Tel: +1(506) 858-4000
Fax: +1(506) 858-4379
EMail: info@umoncton.ca
Website: http://www.umoncton.ca

Recteur et Vice-Chancelier: Yvon Fontaine (2000-)
Tel: +1(506) 858-4111, Fax: +1(506) 858-4538
EMail: recteur@umoncton.ca

Secrétaire générale: Lynne M. Castonguay
Tel: +1(506) 858-4106, Fax: +1(506) 858-4096
EMail: lynne.castonguay@umoncton.ca

Vice-recteur à l'administration et aux ressources humaines:
Nassir El-Jabi
Tel: +1(506) 858-4117, Fax: +1(506) 858-4162
EMail: nassir.el-jabi@umoncton.ca@umoncton.ca

International Relations: Benoit Bourque, Directeur, Bureau des relations internationales
Tel: +1(506) 858-4826, Fax: +1(506) 863-2058
EMail: benoit.bourque@umoncton.ca

Faculties

Administration (Accountancy; Administration; Business Administration; Finance; International Business; Management; Marketing); **Arts and Social Sciences** (Arts and Humanities; Economics; English; French; Geography; German; Gerontology; Health Administration; History; Interior Design; Linguistics; Literature; Music; Philosophy; Political Sciences; Public Administration; Religious Studies; Social Sciences; Social Work; Sociology; Spanish; Theatre; Translation and Interpretation; Visual Arts); **Educational Sciences** (Education; Educational and Student Counselling; Educational Psychology; Educational Sciences; Primary Education; Secondary Education); **Engineering** (Civil Engineering; Electrical Engineering; Engineering; Industrial Engineering; Mechanical Engineering; Technology); **Forestry** *(Edmundston)* (Forestry); **Health Sciences and Community Services** (Family Studies; Food Science; Gerontology; Health Sciences; Leisure Studies; Nursing; Nutrition; Physical Education; Physical Therapy; Psychology; Social and Community Services; Tourism); **Law** (Administrative Law; Civil Law; Commercial Law; Law; Public Law); **Sciences** (Astronomy and Space Science; Biochemistry; Biological and Life Sciences; Biology; Chemistry; Computer Science; Laboratory Techniques; Mathematics; Physics; Radiology; Respiratory Therapy; Statistics)

Further Information: Also Edmunston and Shippagan campuses, where students can complete the first-cycle of their studies.

History: Founded 1864 as Saint Joseph College, acquired present status and title 1963. The University now has 3 campuses: Campus de Moncton, Campus d'Edmunston and Campus de Shippagan.

Governing Bodies: Conseil des gouverneurs, comprising 27 members; Sénat académique, comprising 42 members

Academic Year: May to April (May-August; September-December; January-April)

Admission Requirements: Secondary school certificate or recognized foreign equivalent

Fees: (Can. Dollars): 4,920 per annum; foreign students, 8,343.

Main Language(s) of Instruction: French

Degrees and Diplomas: *Baccalaureate*; *Master's Degree*; *Doctoral Degree*. For Bachelor of Common Law, LLB, Degree courses are either 3 yrs full-time following First Degree, by course of instruction, dissertion and examination, or for approved Civil Law graduates of a Canadian University, 2 sem. full-time; Also combined programmes, Master in Business Administration/Bachelor of Law, Master in Public Administration/Bachelor of Law, Master in Environmental Studies/Bachelor of Law (all in 4 yrs).

Student Residential Facilities: Yes

Special Facilities: Museum and Gallerie d'art Louise et Reuben-Cohen; La Grange (Theatre)

Libraries: c. 460,000 vols

Publications: Contact-Acadie; Egalité; La Revue de l'Université

Academic Staff *2007-2008*	TOTAL
FULL-TIME	c. 290

Student Numbers *2010-2011*	
All (Foreign Included)	c. 6,200

Part-time students, 1,370.
Note: Part-time students are not included in total
Last Updated: 21/01/11

UNIVERSITY OF NEW BRUNSWICK (UNB)

P.O. Box 4400, Fredericton, New Brunswick E3B 5A3
Tel: +1(506) 453-4666
Fax: +1(506) 453-4599
EMail: registrar@unb.ca
Website: http://www.unb.ca

President and Vice-Chancellor: Eddy Campbell (2009-)
Tel: +1(506) 453-4567, Fax: +1(506) 453-5158
EMail: president@unb.ca

Vice-President, Finance and Corporate Services: Daniel V. Murray
Tel: +1(506) 453-4797, Fax: +1(506) 447-3181
EMail: dmurray@unb.ca

International Relations: Gerhard Dueck, Director, International Relations
Tel: +1(506) 447-3151, Fax: +1(506) 453-5005
EMail: gdueck@unb.ca

Centres

Applied Statistics (Statistics); **Coastal Studies and Aquaculture** *(Saint John campus)* (Aquaculture; Coastal Studies); **Construction Technology Centre Atlantic, Inc.** *(CTCA)* (Construction Engineering); **Criminal Justice Studies** *(Saint John campus)* (Criminal Law); **Early Childhood; Educational Administration** *(New Brunswick)* (Educational Administration); **Electronic Commerce** *(Saint John campus)* (E-Business/Commerce); **Electronic Text** (Electronic Engineering); **Enhanced Teaching and Learning; Geodetic Engineering** *(CCGE)* (Surveying and Mapping); **Information Technology** *(ITC)* (Information Technology); **International Business and Entrepreneurship** (International Business; Management); **Management Development and Information** *(Saint John campus)* (Management); **Nuclear Energy Research, Inc.** (Nuclear Engineering); **Planetary and Space Science** (Astronomy and Space Science); **Promotion of Instructional Technology** (Educational Technology); **Property Studies; Second Language Education** (Foreign Languages Education); **Study of War and Society** *(Gregg)* (Peace and Disarmament); **Wood Science and Technology** (Forest Products; Wood Technology)

Chairs

Construction Engineering and Management *(M. Patrick Gillin)* (Construction Engineering; Management); **Environmental Design Engineering** *(NSERC)* (Environmental Engineering); **Highway Construction and Pavement Research** *(D.C. Campbell)* (Civil Engineering); **Nuclear Engineering** *(NSERC/NB Power/AECL)* (Nuclear Engineering); **Ocean Mapping** (Surveying and Mapping); **Power Plant Engineering** *(NB Power)* (Power Engineering); **Regional Economics** *(Vaughan)* (Economics); **Technology Management and Entrepreneurship** *(J. Herbert Smith/ACOA)* (Engineering Management); **Wildlife Ecology** *(NSERC/CWS Research)* (Ecology; Wildlife); **Women and the Law** *(Mary Louise Lynch)* (Law)

Colleges

Extended Learning (Administration; Adult Education; Business Administration; Education; Film; French; Health Sciences; Human Resources; Leadership; Management; Nursing; Rehabilitation and Therapy; Social Problems; Software Engineering; Spanish; Women's Studies); **Renaissance** (Economics; Leadership; Philosophy; Political Sciences); **Saint John** *(Saint John Campus)* (Cultural Studies; English)

Faculties

Arts (Ancient Civilizations; Anthropology; Arabic; Archaeology; Chinese; Classical Languages; Cultural Studies; Development Studies; Economics; English; Film; French; German; Germanic Studies; Greek (Classical); History; Japanese; Latin American Studies; Law; Literature; Modern Languages; Multimedia; Music; Philosophy; Political Sciences; Psychology; Russian; Social Problems; Sociology; Spanish; Theatre; Women's Studies; Writing); **Arts** *(Saint John Campus)* (Clinical Psychology; Communication Studies; Comparative Literature; Economics; English; French; History; Information Sciences; Linguistics; Philosophy; Political Sciences; Psychology; Social Sciences; Sociology; Spanish; Sports); **Business** *(Saint John Campus)* (Accountancy; Business Administration; E-Business/Commerce; Hotel and Restaurant; Management; Tourism); **Business Administration** (Business Administration; Engineering Management; Human Resources; Public Administration; Sports Management); **Computer Science** (Computer Science; Information Sciences; Software Engineering); **Education** (Adult Education; Art Education; Curriculum; Education; Educational Administration; Educational and Student Counselling; Foreign Languages Education; Humanities and Social Science Education; Literacy Education; Mathematics Education; Physical Education; Preschool Education; Science Education); **Engineering** (Chemical Engineering; Civil Engineering; Computer Engineering; Electrical Engineering; Engineering; Engineering Management; Forestry; Geological Engineering; Management; Mechanical Engineering; Software Engineering; Surveying and Mapping); **Forestry and Environmental Management** (Engineering; Environmental Management; Forestry); **Kinesiology** (Physical Therapy; Sports; Sports Management); **Law** (Administrative Law; Civil Law; Commercial Law; Constitutional Law; Criminal Law; Law); **Nursing** (Nursing); **Science** (Biology; Chemistry; Computer Science; Geochemistry; Geology; Mathematics; Physics; Psychology; Statistics); **Science, Applied Science and Engineering** *(Saint John Campus)* (Biology; Chemistry; Computer Science; Engineering; Health Sciences; Marine Biology; Mathematics; Nursing; Statistics)

Institutes
Biomedical Engineering (Biomedical Engineering); **Canadian Rivers** *(Fredericton and Saint John campuses)*; **Micmac - Maliseet**

Laboratories
Acoustics and Vibration (Sound Engineering (Acoustics)); **Advanced Computational Research and ACEnet** (Computer Science); **Advanced Machining**; **Advanced Plastics Manufacturing** (Polymer and Plastics Technology); **Architectural, Engineering and Construction Interactive Collaboration** (Architecture; Construction Engineering; Engineering); **Bio Signals** (Biological and Life Sciences); **Canadian Rivers Institute Research Facility** *(Saint John campus)*; **Computer Applications** (Computer Science); **Entomology** (Entomology); **Flow-Induced Vibration**; **Fluid Mechanics** (Mechanics); **Forest and Conservation Genomics and Biotechnology** (Biotechnology; Forest Management); **Forest Engineering/Geotechnical** *(Gillan)* (Forestry; Geological Engineering); **Geodetic Research** (Surveying and Mapping); **Geographic Information Systems** *(GIS)* (Surveying and Mapping); **Heat Transfer** (Heating and Refrigeration); **High-Resolution X-ray Microtomography** *(Micro-CT)*; **Integrated Forest Management** (Forest Management); **Magnetic Resonance Imaging**; **Manufacturing and Processing**; **Motion Analysis**; **Network Security**; **Nuclear Radiation** (Nuclear Engineering); **Robotics and Mechanisms** (Robotics); **Soils and Environmental Quality** (Environmental Management; Soil Conservation); **Stable Isotopes in Nature**; **Thermal Analysis Unit** (Thermal Engineering); **Threat-Material Detection**; **Tree Physiology/Biochemistry** (Biochemistry; Physiology)

Research Centres
Atlantic Cooperative Wildlife Ecology Research Network (Ecology; Wildlife); **CADMI Microelectronics, Inc.** (Microelectronics); **Environment and Sustainable Development** (Environmental Studies); **Environment and Sustainable Development** (Environmental Studies); **Family Violence** *(Muriel McQueen Fergusson)* (Social Problems); **Forest Watershed** *(NEXFOR/ BOWATER)*; **Noncommutative Geometry and Topology** (Mathematics); **Pulp and Paper Research and Education** *(Dr. Jack McKenzie Limerick)* (Paper Technology); **Youth, Science, Teaching and Learning - CRYSTAL Atlantique** *(NSERC CRYSTAL)*

Research Groups
Artificial Intelligence (Artificial Intelligence); **Automated Reasoning** (Automation and Control Engineering); **Canadian observatory on the justice system response to intimate partner violence** *(SSHRC Cluster)*; **Energy Conversion Engineering** (Energy Engineering); **Greater Fundy Ecosystem Project**; **Groundwater Studies** (Water Science); **Health and Education** *(HERG)* (Education; Health Sciences); **Industrial City in Transition: A Cultural and Environmental Inventory of Greater Saint John** *(SSHRC CURA)* (Environmental Studies); **Labour History in New Brunswick Project** *(SSHRC CURA)*; **Materials** (Materials Engineering); **Ocean Mapping Group** (Surveying and Mapping); **Parallel/Distributed Processing**; **Population Ecology**; **Sustain-**

able Power (Power Engineering); **Transportation** (Transport and Communications); **UNB/Bhutan Project**

Research Institutes
Chronic Illness (Health Sciences); **Social Policy** *(CRISP)* (Social Policy)

Research Units
Cooperative Fish and Wildlife (Wildlife); **Fish and Wildlife** *(NB Cooperative)* (Biology; Forestry; Wildlife)

Further Information: Also Saint John campus.

History: Founded 1785 as Provincial Academy of Liberal Arts and Sciences; incorporated by Royal Charter 1828 as King's College. Acquired present title 1859. Saint John campus founded 1964. New Brunswick Teachers College incorporated 1973.

Governing Bodies: Board of Governors

Academic Year: September to April (September-December; January-April)

Admission Requirements: Secondary school certificate or recognized foreign equivalent

Fees: (Can. Dollars): 5,621 per annum

Main Language(s) of Instruction: English

International Co-operation: Participates in c. 70 international agreements

Degrees and Diplomas: *University Certificate/Diploma*; *Baccalaureate*; *Master's Degree*; *Doctoral Degree*. Also concurrent degree programmes: Bachelor of Arts/Bachelor of Science (BA/BCS), 5 yrs and Bachelor of Arts/Bachelor of Computer Science (BA/BSc), 5 yrs; Professional development certificate programmes.

Student Services: Academic counselling, Canteen, Cultural centre, Employment services, Foreign student adviser, Foreign Studies Centre, Handicapped facilities, Health services, Language programs, Nursery care, Social counselling, Sports facilities

Student Residential Facilities: Yes

Special Facilities: Fredericton: UNB Art Centre. William Brydon Jack Observatory (1851). Sir Howard Douglas Hall (1826). Burden Academy (pre-1867). Ice House (1851). Neville Homestead (1876). Alumni Memorial Building. Aitken University Centre. Poet's Corner. Saint John: The Little Gallery. Canada Games Stadium

Libraries: Harriet Irvin Library, the Engineering and Science Libraries (Fredericton) 1,241,505 vols; Ward Chipman library (Saint John), 195,490 vols; Law Library (Fredericton) 126,617 vols

Publications: Acadiensis (Historical journal of the Atlantic Provinces) *(biennially)*; Canadian Journal of Regional Science, Interdisciplinary research on regional and urban issues issued by the Department of Economics; Journal of Conflict Studies, Publication of the Department for Conflict Studies; Qwerty, Publication of the Department of English *(3 per annum)*; The Fiddlehead, Canadian longest running literary journal

Academic Staff *2007-2008*	TOTAL
FULL-TIME	680
PART-TIME	c. 230
Student Numbers *2009-2010*	
All (Foreign Included)	c. **11,400**
FOREIGN ONLY	**1,400**

Part-time students, 1,960.
Last Updated: 24/01/11

PRIVATE INSTITUTIONS

CRANDALL UNIVERSITY

333 Gorge Road, Box 6004, Moncton, New Brunswick NB E1C 9L7
Tel: +1(506) 858-8970
Fax: +1(506) 858-9694
EMail: admissions@abu.nb.ca
Website: http://www.abu.nb.ca

President: Brian D. MacArthur
Tel: +1(506) 858-8970 Ext. 107 EMail: president@abu.nb.ca

Registrar: Sheldon MacLeod
Tel: +1(506) 858-8970 Ext. 103
EMail: sheldon.macleod@crandallu.ca

Programmes

Arts (Bible; Communication Studies; English; History; Management; Psychology; Religious Studies; Sociology); **Business** (Business Administration; Management); **Certificate** (Christian Religious Studies; English; Leadership); **Continuing Education** (Literacy Education; Management); **Education** (Education; Literacy Education); **Off-Site Study** (American Studies; Education; Environmental Studies; Film; Latin American Studies; Middle Eastern Studies; Russian); **Science** (Biology)

History: Founded 1949 as the United Baptist Bible Training School, both a Bible College and a High School. In transition as the emphasis changed to a post high school program, it became a Bible College and a Christian Junior Liberal Arts College 1968. Changed its name to Atlantic Baptist College 1970. Statrting offering Bachelor's degree in the early 1980s. Changed its name to Atlantic Baptist University 1996 before acquiring present title.

Degrees and Diplomas: *University Certificate/Diploma*; *Baccalaureate*. Bachelor's degree (professional), 4 yrs.

Last Updated: 22/02/07

ST. STEPHEN'S UNIVERSITY (SSU)

8 Main Street, St Stephen, New Brunswick E3L 3E2
Tel: +1(506) 466-1781
Fax: +1(506) 466-1783
EMail: ssu@ssu.ca
Website: http://www.ssu.ca

President: Robert J. Cheatley

Programmes

International Studies (International Studies); **Liberal Arts** (Ancient Civilizations; Arts and Humanities; History; International Studies; Literature; Philosophy; Psychology; Religious Studies); **Ministry** (Theology)

History: Founded 1975.

Fees: (Canadian dollars): Tuition fees for Bachelor of arts / international studies programmes, 5,065 per term; Ministry module programmes, 2,700 per module.

Degrees and Diplomas: *University Certificate/Diploma*: Ministry; *Baccalaureate*; *Master's Degree*: Ministry. Also Bachelor of Arts Honours.

Last Updated: 20/01/11

UNIVERSITY OF FREDERICTON

371 Queen Street, Suite 101, Fredericton, New Brunswick E3B 1B1
Tel: +1(506) 454-6232
Fax: +1(506) 455-1675
EMail: info@UniversityFredericton.ca
Website: http://www.universityfredericton.ca

Director and President: Don Roy

Institutes

Professional Learning (Environmental Engineering; Environmental Management; Industrial Design; Leadership; Rehabilitation and Therapy; Safety Engineering)

Schools

Business (Business Administration; Criminal Law; Leadership)

Fees: (Canadian Dollar): Tuition, 14,000 for MBA programme and 24,500 for Executive MBA programme.

Accrediting Agencies: The Province of New Brunswick in Canada.

Degrees and Diplomas: *Master's Degree.* Also Professional diploma

Last Updated: 21/01/11

YORKVILLE UNIVERSITY

1149 Smythe Street, Fredericton, New Brunswick E3B 3H4
Tel: +1(506) 454-1220 +1(866) 838-6542
Fax: +1(506) 454-1221
EMail: info@yorkvilleu.ca
Website: http://www.yorkvilleu.ca

President: Rick Davey

Dean of Academics: John McLaughlin
EMail: jmclaughlin@yorkvilleu.ca

Faculties

Behavioural Sciences (Behavioural Sciences; Psychology; Social Problems; Toxicology)

Further Information: Traditional and Open Learning Institution

History: Founded 2003. Acquired present status 2004.

Accrediting Agencies: New Brunswick Department of Education.

Degrees and Diplomas: *Master's Degree.* Also Post-graduate Diploma, 2-3 semesters following Master's degree.

Last Updated: 24/01/11

Canada - Newfoundland & Labrador

STRUCTURE OF HIGHER EDUCATION SYSTEM

Description:

Higher education in Canada is the constitutional responsibility of the provinces. In Newfoundland and Labrador, the institutions providing higher education are the provincially supported Memorial University of Newfoundland (MUN, categorized as a comprehensive university), and the College of the North Atlantic (CNA), which provides diverse technical and career-oriented certificate, apprenticeship and diploma programmes. As an affiliate of MUN, the Marine Institute (MI) provides training in all aspects of fisheries and marine technology. MUN is a full degree granting institution, while CNA is not (although it does offer university level transfer courses). MUN is an autonomous institution largely dependent on government for funding, whereas CNA is an agent of the crown. Besides MUN and CNA, there are also 25 provincially registered private training institutions which also provide technical and career oriented certificates and diplomas. Queen's College, a theology school, is a private not-for-profit institution, affiliated with MUN, and with the power to grant degrees qualifying recipients for ordination. Adult Basic Education (ABE) is a high school equivalency programme for adults who did not complete high school, and is part of the NL higher education system offered through the community college, private training institutions and community organizations.

Stages of studies:

University level first stage: Bachelor's degree
Most undergraduate study leads to a "General" (Pass) Bachelor's degree (4 years of full time study) or an "Honours" degree (additional year) as well as professional degrees in areas such as Business Administration, Engineering, Medicine, Nursing, Pharmacy, and Social Work. Degrees are normally titled in broad descriptive groups, e.g. B.A., B.Sc., B.N. The first stage also includes undergraduate diplomas (1-3 years of study) and short (up to 1 year) special certificate programmes. The Marine Institute of Memorial University offers Bachelor's degrees in Maritime Studies and Technology. In addition, first year university transfer courses are offered by CNA.

University level second stage: Master's degree
The Master's degree normally requires at least one year's study after a Bachelor's (Honours) degree or equivalent. Some Master's programmes, e.g. Business Administration, necessitate at least two years. A thesis is usually required supplemented by course work. Examples are: M.A., M.Sc., M.Ed., M.B.A. Besides graduate level diplomas (considered as intermediate between the Bachelor's or first professional degree and the Master's degree), the second stage also includes first professional degree programmes requiring prerequisite university studies (e.g. Doctor of Medicine (M.D.)). The Marine Institute of Memorial University offers a Master's degree in Maritime Studies, Technology Management, and Maritime Management.

University level third stage: Doctorate degree
The Doctorate is the highest academic qualification awarded by Canadian universities and (in all provinces except Quebec) it comprises the third stage of university level studies. This degree normally requires at least three years of study after the Master's degree; the submission and defence of a major thesis (dissertation); along with supplemental course work. The degree "Doctor of Philosophy" (Ph.D.) is the designation that is most commonly used to signify the Doctorate, although other designations exist (e.g., the degree of Doctor of Psychology (Psy.D.)). The doctoral degree is a generic title, applicable to degrees in most disciplines (the Doctorate should not be confused with certain first professional degrees in the Health Sciences, e.g. Medicine (M.D.), Veterinary Medicine and Dentistry).

Distance higher education:
Memorial University offers a variety of credit and non-credit courses that are available on-line, including more than 350 credit courses to complete degree programmes from 10 faculties and schools. Distance Education, Learning and Teaching Support (DELTS) offers distance programming in degree areas such as Business, Education, Health and maritime studies (www.distance.mun.ca/). Through the Professional Development and Conferencing Services, (www.med.mun.ca/pdcs), MUN also provides continuing medical education, distributed medical education, needs assessments, family practice skills enhancement, faculty development for

International Medical Graduates (IMG)/Family Practice (FP) preceptors and other tele-medicine services. College of the North Atlantic's Distributed Learning Service (DLS) (dls.cna.nl.ca) serves remote learners with over 300 courses and student enrolment from nearly 400 Newfoundland and Labrador communities, every Canadian province and territory, and international locations including Qatar. Many courses have credit transfer status with other colleges and universities. The Distributed Learning Service also provides customized e learning solutions to organizations and educational institutions worldwide. The Centre for Distance Learning and Innovation (CDLI) established by the Department of Education (www.cdli.ca) increases learning opportunities and career options for students, particularly those in small and isolated schools by developing and delivering e-learning programmes and services for students and teachers. In 2010/11, e-teachers are delivering 45 distance education courses to students in both the Anglophone and Francophone school districts.

ADMISSION TO HIGHER EDUCATION

Admission to university-level studies:

Name of secondary school credential required: High School Diploma

Alternatives to credentials: Secondary School Diploma. Alternatives: Memorial University sets admission policies and requirements for various categories of applicants including local high school students; high schools students from other Canadian provinces and abroad; mature students (aged 21 or more); Adult Basic Education (ABE) students; senior citizens (aged 60 or more); and transfer students.

Numerus clausus/restrictions: There is a numerus clausus at institutional level.

Other admission requirements: At least 70% overall average in select high school courses. Proof of proficiency in the language of instruction.

Foreign students admission:

Definition of foreign student: Foreign (International) Students are students who are neither Canadian citizens nor permanent residents of Canada and are enrolled full-time in a recognized academic, professional or vocational training course at a university, college or other educational institution in Canada.

Quotas: Neither MUN nor CNA set quotas for international students. Students are advised that admission to certain professional programmes (e.g. MUN Pharmacy) is highly competitive and selective. In some cases, priority is given to applicants who are bona fide residents of Newfoundland and Labrador.

Private training institutions are also involved in foreign student education and have their own admissions and quota policies for these students.

Entrance exam requirements: Generally, as for domestic students, a high school diploma or equivalent will be required.

Entry regulations: Before you come to study in Canada, you will need: a "Study Permit" if the programme of study you will be admitted to is longer than six months in duration, regardless of the length of your stay in Canada; a letter of acceptance from the school of your choice; proof that you have enough money to pay school fees and living expenses; to establish that you will return home at the end of your studies; to pass a medical exam if required; and to qualify as a temporary resident in Canada, including holding a temporary resident visa (required for citizens of many countries). A small number of students do not require a Study Permit by virtue of their status in Canada (e.g. diplomats and their children).). More at http://www.cic.gc.ca/english/study/

Health requirements: Most education institutions require international students to buy health insurance in addition to their tuition fees; those that do not will require proof of independent health insurance coverage. Medical examinations are not required by institutions but are required by Citizenship and Immigration Canada for students from many countries.

Language requirements: Both MUN and CNA require the Test of English as a Foreign Language (TOEFL) - minimum mark is 550 (written) or 213 (computer-based).

RECOGNITION OF STUDIES

Quality assurance system:

MUN: Before making a regulation providing for a new course of study or a change in an existing course of study, the Senate will refer to the appropriate faculty council and appropriate faculty of affiliated colleges or institutions for consideration. University programmes are accredited and reviewed by accrediting bodies where appropriate (e.g., nursing, medicine, etc).

CNA: The Board of Governors must assess the education and training needs of the Province and of the region in respect of which CNA is responsible for providing educational services, as those needs are perceived by community committees, local organizations, private citizens or other groups.

MUN and CNA have agreements that enable students to obtain transfer credit for some courses/programmes. All private training institutions must be registered, the superintendent of private training institutions reviews and approves every course of study prior to registration of the institutions, and the provincial government conducts yearly inspections. Provincial Apprenticeship and Certification Board accredits apprenticeship programmes offered by both public colleges and private training institutions to ensure standards are consistent across institutions delivering provincial curriculum.

Bodies dealing with recognition:

Department of Education
PO Box 8700
Confederation Building, West Block
100 Prince Philip Drive
St John's, NL A1B 4J6
Tel: +1(709) 729 5097
Fax: +1(709) 729 5896
EMail: education@gov.nl.ca
WWW: http://www.ed.gov.nl.ca/edu/

PROVINCIAL BODIES

Department of Education
Minister: Joan Burke
PO Box 8700
Confederation Building, West Block
100 Prince Philip Drive
St John's, NL A1B 4J6
Canada
Tel: +1(709) 729 5097
Fax: +1(709) 729 5896
EMail: education@gov.nl.ca
WWW: http://www.ed.gov.nl.ca/edu/
Role of national body: The Department of Education is responsible for early childhood learning, the K-12 system, post-secondary education and skills training, and adult literacy. The vision of the Department of Education is citizens with the values, knowledge and skills necessary to be productive and contributing members of society.

Data for academic year: 2011-2012
Source: IAU from the Canadian Information Centre for International Credentials (CICIC), a unit of the Council of Ministers of Education, Canada (CMEC), on behalf of the Province of Newfoundland and Labrador, 2011

INSTITUTIONS

PUBLIC INSTITUTIONS

MARINE INSTITUTE OF MEMORIAL UNIVERSITY OF NEWFOUNDLAND
Ridge Road campus, P.O. Box 4920, St John's,
Newfoundland A1C 5R3
Tel: +1(709) 778-0200 +1(800) 563-5799
Fax: +1(709) 778-0346
EMail: admissions@mi.mun.ca
Website: http://www.mi.mun.ca

Executive Director: Glen Blackwood
EMail: glenn.blackwood@mi.mun.ca

Manager, Regulatory Affairs and Administration: Margaret Allan
International Relations: Bill Chislett, Director M.I. International
Tel: +1(709) 778-0558, Fax: +1(709) 778-0371
EMail: bill.chislett@mi.mun.ca

Centres
Aquaculture and Seafood Development (Aquaculture; Fishery);
Fisheries Ecosystems Research (Fishery); **Marine Simulation**

(Marine Transport); **Offshore Safety and Survival** (Fire Science; Marine Transport; Petroleum and Gas Engineering; Safety Engineering); **Safety and Emergency Response Training** (Safety Engineering); **Sustainable Aquatic Resources** (Natural Resources)

Schools

Fisheries (Fishery); **Maritime Studies** (Business Administration; Economics; Human Resources; Marine Engineering; Marketing; Safety Engineering); **Ocean Technology** *(SOT)* (Marine Transport; Technology)

Further Information: Also OSSC, Marine Base and SERT (Stephenville) campuses.

History: Founded 1992. The Institute is affiliated with Memorial University of Newfounldland.

Fees: (Canadian Dollars): Tuition for Technician Diploma and Diploma of Technology Programs for Canadian citizens, 173.00 per course to a maximum of 690.00 per term; International students, 519.00 per course to a maximum of 2,070.00 per term. Technical Session fees for Canadian students, 173.00 per course to a maximum of 345.00; For International students Technical Session fees, 519.00 to a maximum of 1,035.00. Tuition for Advanced Diploma Programs for Canadian citizens, 345.00 per course to a maximum of 1,380.00 per term; International students, 690.00 per course to a maximum of 2,760.00 per term.

Degrees and Diplomas: *University Certificate/Diploma*; *Bachelor's Degree*; *Master's Degree*; *Graduate Diploma/Certificate*. Also Joint Diploma of Technology/Bachelor of Technology, 4yrs; Advanced certificates, 1 yr following a three-year diploma; Technical Certificates and Technicinan Diplomas.

Libraries: Dr. C.R. Barrett Library
Last Updated: 24/01/11

MEMORIAL UNIVERSITY OF NEWFOUNDLAND (MUN)

P.O. Box 4200, St John's, Newfoundland A1C 5S7
Tel: +1(709) 864-8000
Fax: +1(709) 864-4569
EMail: info@mun.ca
Website: http://www.mun.ca

President and Vice-Chancellor: Gary Kachanoski (2010-)
Tel: +1(709) 737-8212, Fax: +1(709) 737-2059
EMail: president@mun.ca

Vice-President, Administration and Finance: Kent Decker
Tel: +1(709) 737-8217, Fax: +1(709) 737-8028
EMail: vpadmin@mun.ca

International Relations: Sonja Knutson, Director, International Centre Tel: +1(709) 864-3288 EMail: sknutson@mun.ca

Bureaus
Student Volunteer

Centres
Academic Advising; **Allied Health Services** (Health Sciences); **Aquaculture and Seafood Development** (Aquaculture; Fishery); **Archaeology Unit** (Archaeology); **Atlantic Computational Excellence Network**; **Atlantic Provinces Council on the Sciences** *(APICS)*; **Botanical Garden**; **Campus Food Bank**; **Canadian Committee on Labour History** *(CCLH)* (History); **Canadian Marine Communications** *(CCMC)* (Marine Transport; Transport and Communications); **Career Development**; **C-CORE** (Hydraulic Engineering; Mining Engineering; Petroleum and Gas Engineering; Surveying and Mapping); **Childcare** (Child Care and Development); **Collaborative Health Professional Education**; **Computer Purchasing**; **Co-Operative Education Services** (Education); **Counselling** (Psychology); **CREAIT Network**; **Digital Media** (Media Studies); **Earth Resources Research** *(CERR)* (Natural Resources); **E-Learning Research** *(Killick)* (Distance Education); **Engineering One Help** *(Cahill)* (Engineering); **English Language Research** (English); **Gardiner** (Business Administration; E-Business/Commerce; Human Resources; Leadership; Management; Marketing); **Genesis Group**; **Harris** *(The Leslie Harris Centre of Regional Policy and Development)* (Development Studies; Regional Studies); **Institutional Analysis and Planning** *(CIAP)*; **International** (International Studies); **International Business Studies** *(CIBS)* (International Business); **International Nursing** (Nursing);

Marine Simulation (Marine Transport); **Marine Station** *(Bonne Bay)*; **Maritime History Archive** (History); **Math Learning** (Mathematics Education); **Memorial University of Newfoundland Botanical Garden**; **MI International**; **Newfoundland and Labrador Heritage** (Heritage Preservation); **Newfoundland Studies** *(J. R. Smallwood)* (Regional Studies); **Ocean Sciences** (Marine Science and Oceanography); **Offshore Safety and Survival** (Fire Science; Marine Transport; Safety Engineering); **Students with Disabilities** *(Blundun)*; **Sustainable Aquatic Resources** (Natural Resources); **Women's Resource** (Women's Studies); **Writing** (Writing)

Chairs
Women in Science and Engineering *(NSERC/Petro-Canada)* (Engineering; Natural Sciences)

Colleges
Sir Wilfred Grenfell (Arts and Humanities; Biology; Business Administration; Chemistry; Cultural Studies; Earth Sciences; English; Environmental Studies; Fine Arts; History; Mathematics; Natural Resources; Nursing; Physics; Primary Education; Psychology; Social Studies; Theatre; Tourism; Visual Arts)

Departments
Distance Education and Learning Technologies (Anthropology; Biology; Business Administration; Criminology; Curriculum; Earth Sciences; Economics; Education; Educational and Student Counselling; Educational Psychology; Engineering; English; Folklore; French; German; Higher Education; Law; Leadership; Leisure Studies; Library Science; Linguistics; Marine Engineering; Marine Science and Oceanography; Mathematics; Music; Nursing; Parks and Recreation; Philosophy; Physical Education; Physical Therapy; Police Studies; Political Sciences; Psychology; Public Administration; Regional Studies; Religious Studies; Russian; Social Work; Sociology; Spanish; Sports; Statistics; Technology; Women's Studies)

Divisions
Lifelong Learning (Accountancy; Business Administration; Communication Studies; Computer Networks; Criminology; Development Studies; Human Resources; Insurance; Leadership; Library Science; Management; Marketing; Public Administration; Public Relations; Regional Studies; Robotics; Transport and Communications; Writing)

Faculties
Arts (Ancient Civilizations; Anthropology; Archaeology; Arts and Humanities; Asian Religious Studies; Bible; Canadian Studies; Communication Studies; Constitutional Law; Criminal Law; Cultural Studies; Economics; English; Ethics; European Studies; Film; Folklore; Foreign Languages Education; French; Gender Studies; Geography; German; Greek (Classical); History; History of Law; History of Religion; Indigenous Studies; International Law; Islamic Theology; Judaic Religious Studies; Latin; Law; Linguistics; Literature; Medieval Studies; Music; New Testament; Philosophy; Police Studies; Political Sciences; Psychology; Regional Studies; Religious Studies; Russian; Sociology; Spanish; Theatre; Women's Studies); **Business Administration** (Business Administration; Business and Commerce; International Business; Labour and Industrial Relations; Management); **Education** (Adult Education; Computer Education; Curriculum; Education; Foreign Languages Education; French; Higher Education; Humanities and Social Science Education; Information Technology; Leadership; Literacy Education; Mathematics Education; Music; Music Education; Native Language Education; Natives Education; Primary Education; Psychology; Science Education; Secondary Education; Special Education; Teacher Training); **Engineering and Applied Science** (Civil Engineering; Computer Engineering; Electrical Engineering; Engineering; Engineering Management; Environmental Engineering; Mechanical Engineering; Naval Architecture; Petroleum and Gas Engineering); **Medicine** (Anaesthesiology; Biomedicine; Cardiology; Community Health; Epidemiology; Genetics; Gynaecology and Obstetrics; Immunology; Laboratory Techniques; Medicine; Nephrology; Neurosciences; Oncology; Orthopaedics; Paediatrics; Pathology; Psychiatry and Mental Health; Public Health; Radiology; Surgery); **Science** (Aquaculture; Atomic and Molecular Physics; Behavioural Sciences; Biochemistry; Biology; Chemistry; Cognitive Sciences; Computer Science; Earth Sciences; Environmental Studies; Food Science; Geography; Geology; Geophysics; Marine Biology; Marine

Science and Oceanography; Mathematics; Physics; Psychology; Social Psychology; Statistics)

Institutes
Labrador (Anthropology; Archaeology; English; Geography; Linguistics; Meteorology; Social Work); **Social and Economic Research** *(ISER)* (Economics; Social Sciences)

Laboratories
Language *(Digital Language Centre)* (Classical Languages; Danish; English; French; German; Greek (Classical); Irish; Italian; Latin; Linguistics; Russian; Spanish)

Research Centres
Ocean Engineering (Marine Engineering); **Study of Music, Media, and Place** *((MMaP))* (Media Studies; Music)

Schools
Graduate Studies (Administration; Ancient Civilizations; Anthropology; Aquaculture; Archaeology; Arts and Humanities; Asian Religious Studies; Atomic and Molecular Physics; Behavioural Sciences; Bible; Biochemistry; Biology; Business Administration; Cardiology; Chemistry; Christian Religious Studies; Civil Engineering; Cognitive Sciences; Computer Engineering; Computer Science; Conducting; Curriculum; Earth Sciences; Economics; Education; Electrical Engineering; Engineering; Engineering Management; English; Environmental Engineering; Environmental Management; Environmental Studies; Epidemiology; Ethics; Ethnology; Experimental Psychology; Fishery; Folklore; Food Science; Foreign Languages Education; French Studies; Genetics; Geography; Geology; Geophysics; German; Greek (Classical); Health Sciences; Higher Education; History; History of Religion; Immunology; Information Technology; Inorganic Chemistry; Islamic Theology; Labour and Industrial Relations; Latin; Leadership; Linguistics; Literature; Management; Marine Biology; Marine Engineering; Marine Science and Oceanography; Mathematics; Mechanical Engineering; Medicine; Music; Music Education; Musical Instruments; Musicology; Naval Architecture; Neurosciences; New Testament; Nursing; Oncology; Organic Chemistry; Parks and Recreation; Performing Arts; Petroleum and Gas Engineering; Pharmacy; Philosophy; Physical Therapy; Physics; Physiology; Political Sciences; Psychology; Public Health; Religious Studies; Social Psychology; Social Work; Sociology; Sports; Statistics; Women's Studies); **Human Kinetics and Recreation** (Administration; Curriculum; Parks and Recreation; Physical Education; Physical Therapy; Physiology; Psychology); **Music** (Art History; Conducting; Music; Music Education; Music Theory and Composition; Musical Instruments; Musicology); **Nursing** (Health Sciences; Nursing); **Pharmacy** (Pharmacy); **Social Work** (Social Work)

Further Information: Traditional and Open Learning Institution. Also affiliation with 4 major Teaching Hospitals (Eastern Health, Central Health, Western Health, Labrador-Grenfell Health). Other campuses: St. John's, Grenfell Campus in Corner Brook, Harlow (in Essex, England), Labrador Institute (Happy Valley-Goose Bay).

History: Founded 1925 as Memorial University College. Awarded degree-granting status and present title 1949. The only degree-granting post-secondary institution in the Province of Newfoundland and Labrador.

Governing Bodies: Board of Regents, comprising the Chancellor, President, Pro-Vice-Chancellor, 6 members elected by the Alumni Association, 17 members appointed by the government, and 2 full-time students, appointed by the government; Senate

Academic Year: September to August (September-December; January-April; May-August); also 6-week inter-session and 6-week summer session.

Admission Requirements: Secondary school certificate or recognized foreign equivalent, with minimum of 70% average. Proof of proficiency in English language

Fees: (Can. Dollars): Undergraduate tuition on Saint John's campus, 2,550 for two semesters (30 credit-hours) for Canadian students and 8,800 for two semesters (30 credit-hours) for International Students. Undergraduate tuition on Grenfell Campus, 255 per three credit hours for Canadian students and 969 per three credit hours for International students. Graduate tuition: for Canadian students,

323 per semester for Graduate Diploma, 733 per semester for Master's degree (except Master of Science in Medicine, 2,000 per semester) and 887 per semester for Ph.D; for International Students, 420 per semester for Graduate Diploma, 953 per semester for Master's degree (except Master of Science in Medicine, 2,000 per semester) and 887 per semester for Ph.D. Some programmes (Master of Applied Science, Business Administration, Engineering, Nursing, Public Health, Technology Management, Post-Masters Nurse Practitioner Graduate Diploma and Doctor of Philosophy (Management)) also require special fees in addition to afore mentionned: 1,460-34,000 per programme.

Main Language(s) of Instruction: English

International Co-operation: Cooperation with universities in Belgium, United Kingdom and USA

Degrees and Diplomas: *University Certificate/Diploma*; *Bachelor's Degree*; *Bachelor's Degree - Honours*; *Master's Degree*; *Graduate Diploma/Certificate*; *Doctoral Degree.* also Executive MBA

Student Services: Academic counselling, Canteen, Cultural centre, Employment services, Foreign student adviser, Handicapped facilities, Health services, Language programs, Nursery care, Social counselling, Sports facilities

Student Residential Facilities: For 1,380 students

Special Facilities: Botanical Garden; Art Gallery; Folklore and Language Archive, Aquarena, Centre for Newfoundland Studies

Libraries: Queen Elizabeth II Library; Sir Wilfred Grenfell College Library; Health Sciences Library, total, 2.5m. vols

Publications: Canadian Folklore/Folklore canadien *(biannually)*; Culture and Tradition *(annually)*; International Journal of Maritime History *(biannually)*; Labour/Le Travail *(biannually)*; Newfoundland Quarterly *(quarterly)*; Regional Languages Studies *(annually)*; Research Directory *(annually)*

Press or Publishing House: University Printing Services

Academic Staff *2010-2011*: Total 950
Student Numbers *2010-2011*: Total 17,604
Last Updated: 24/01/11

QUEEN'S COLLEGE (AFFILIATED WITH MEMORIAL UNIVERSITY OF NEWFOUNDLAND)

210 Prince Philip Drive, Suite 3000, St John's, Newfoundland A1B 3R6
Tel: +1(709) 753-0116 + (877) 753-0116
Fax: +1(709) 753-1214
EMail: queens@mun.ca
Website: http://www.mun.ca/queens

Provost and Vice-Chancellor: John Mellis EMail: Mellis@mun.ca

Programmes
Associate Studies (Bible; New Testament; Pastoral Studies; Religious Education; Theology); **Degree Studies** (Bible; Canon Law; History of Religion; Pastoral Studies; Religion; Religious Practice; Religious Studies; Theology); **Diploma Studies** (Bible; Christian Religious Studies; Religion; Religious Education; Theology); **Youth Ministry** (Religion; Theology)

History: Founded 1841 the Theological Institute. An affiliated College of Memorial University of Newfoundland.

Fees: (Canadian Dollar): Fee per course (three credit hours), 420; Intensive fee per course (three credit hours), 500; Associate in Theology, Fee per course (two credit hours), 280; Diploma in Theology and Ministry, Fee per semester, 330; Vocational Development Seminar (not applicable to full-time M.Div. and B.Th. students), 140; Clinical Pastoral Education: Basic or Advanced Unit Fee per unit (approx - varies by location), 1,700.

Degrees and Diplomas: *Bachelor's Degree*; *Master's Degree.* Also Honorary Degrees (Doctor of Divinity / Doctor of Canon Law and Doctor of Sacred Letters) awarded in recognition of distinguished service to the Church; Diploma programmes.
Last Updated: 25/01/11

Canada - Northwest Territories

STRUCTURE OF HIGHER EDUCATION SYSTEM

Description:

The Department of Education, Culture and Employment is responsible for postsecondary education in the Northwest Territories. It does not have its own university, though the Department contributes financially to students from the Territory pursuing university studies elsewhere in Canada. Aurora College provides postsecondary education and offers academic (including university transfer courses), business, trades (pre-employment and apprenticeship), career development, technical and vocational training programmes usually leading to a Certificate or Diploma. The College can grant degrees but has not to date. It has full autonomy on admissions and all other academic matters. The Boards of Governors are appointed by the Department of Education, Culture and Employment.

Stages of studies:

Non-university level:

There is one public college in the Northwest Territories, Aurora College. It has a central campus, two regional campuses, and a network of community learning centres. It was created through the Public Colleges Act on January 1, 1995, following the split of the former Arctic College. The College offers a full range of college-level programmes, including literacy and adult basic education, trades and technical training, labour market skill training, university preparation, one-year Certificate programmes, and two-year and three-year Diploma programmes. It also delivers in-service training for government employees and specialized training for third-party sponsors in the public and private sectors.

University level first stage:

Many of the courses in the College Diploma programmes are eligible for transfer credit with universities and professional associations across Canada. The College also offers selected university credit courses through its campuses. Aurora College offers a Bachelor in Science of Nursing in partnership with the University of Victoria. In addition, it offers a Licensed Practical Nurse programme that prepares students for the Canadian Practical Nurse Registration Examinations and a Community Health Representative programme.

Distance higher education:

The colleges are offering courses about technology-based education to prepare teachers as digital communications technology is introduced across the NWT. They are also offering a variety of courses through technology-based distance education, including courses in the Certificate in Adult Education Programme.

ADMISSION TO HIGHER EDUCATION

Foreign students admission:

Definition of foreign student: Foreign (International) Students are students who are neither Canadian citizens nor permanent residents of Canada and are enrolled full-time in a recognized academic, professional or vocational training course at a university, college or other educational institution in Canada.

Entrance exam requirements: Generally, as for domestic students, a high school diploma or equivalent will be required. A lack of proficiency in English or French will be taken into account by the Canadian Immigration Office in the evaluation of the application.

Entry regulations: Before you come to study in Canada, you will need: a "Study Permit" if the programme of study you will be admitted to is longer than six months in duration, regardless of the length of your stay in Canada; a letter of acceptance from the school of your choice; proof that you have enough money to pay school fees and living expenses; to establish that you will return home at the end of your studies; to pass a medical exam if required; and to qualify as a temporary resident in Canada, including holding a temporary resident visa (required for citizens of many countries). A small number of students do not require a Study Permit by virtue of their status in Canada (e.g. diplomats and their children).

Health requirements: Most education institutions require international students to buy health insurance in addition to their tuition fees; those that do not will require proof of independent health insurance coverage. Medical examinations are not required by institutions but are required by Citizenship and Immigration Canada for students from many countries.

RECOGNITION OF STUDIES

Quality assurance system:
See http://www.cicic.ca/573/quality-assurance-NT.canada

PROVINCIAL BODIES

Education, Culture and Employment
Minister: Jackson Lafferty
Director, Advanced Education: Laurie Morton
PO Box 1320
Yellowknife, NT X1A 2L9
Canada
Tel: +1(867) 920 3059
Fax: +1(867) 873 0456
EMail: Ashley_Green@gov.nt.ca
WWW: http://www.ece.gov.nt.ca
Role of national body: To coordinate the development and delivery of career programmes and services for adult education and training and postsecondary education.

Data for academic year: 2011-2012
Source: IAU from Canadian Information Centre for International Credentials (CICIC),Council of Ministers of Education of Canada (CMEC), 2011

Canada - Nova Scotia

STRUCTURE OF HIGHER EDUCATION SYSTEM

Description:

Higher education in Canada is the constitutional responsibility of the Provinces. The three main types of institutions are universities, community college and private career colleges. The universities are independent, degree granting institutions, with full autonomy on admission policies and all other academic matters. The Nova Scotia Community College (NSCC) provides a variety of post-secondary programmes usually leading to a Certificate or Diploma. It is a self-governing institution operating under the direction of a board of governors with a mandate to meet the Province's occupational training needs. The NSCC is accountable to government for matters of public concern, such as the appropriate use of tax dollars, admissions policy and tuition. Private career colleges are independently operated for profit business institutions that operate under regulations established by the province.

Stages of studies:

University level first stage: Bachelor's Degree
University level education in Nova Scotia is delivered through 11 publicly supported degree-granting institutions. Some of the Province's degree-granting institutions are highly specialized; others offer a broader range of undergraduate and graduate programmes. General undergraduate degrees at most universities in Nova Scotia require a minimum of 3 years of full-time study. Honours degrees, involving a higher level of concentration in the honours discipline and a higher level of academic performance generally require 4 years of full-time study. Most universities also offer diploma and certificate programmes in various specialized fields. These vary in length depending on the program and the institution.

University level second stage: Master's Degree
The Master's degree may take one or two years after an Honours degree (or equivalent) depending on the field of study. Some programmes require both course work and a thesis, while others require only course work. Degrees awarded include Master of Arts, Master of Science, Master of Business Administration and Master of Education. This stage also includes graduate level, or intermediate, diplomas (between a Bachelor's degree and a Master's degree).

University level third stage: Doctorate Degree (Ph.D.)
The Doctorate is the highest qualification awarded by Canadian universities and, in all provinces except Quebec, it comprises the third stage of university-level studies. This degree normally requires at least three years of study beyond a Bachelor's degree and the submission and defence of a dissertation. Course work is also usually required. The degree "Doctor of Philosophy" (Ph.D.). is a designation most commonly used to signify the Doctorate.

Distance higher education:
The private career colleges, community college and universities are active in providing distance education opportunities that lead to a Certificate, Diploma or Degree in a variety of programme areas through a number of different modes of delivery.

ADMISSION TO HIGHER EDUCATION

Admission to university-level studies:

Name of secondary school credential required: High School Graduation Diploma

Alternatives to credentials: Students are sometimes admitted with "mature student status". Prior learning assessment practices are also being introduced as an alternative means of assessing applicants.

Other admission requirements: 60% average in final year of secondary school studies in 5 appropriate academic subjects (most programmes have minimum grade point average). Universities set their admissions policies. Highly selective programmes require admissions qualifications that are higher than specified minimum. Proof of proficiency in language of instruction may be required. Some universities offer remedial courses or preparatory programmes.

Foreign students admission:

Definition of foreign student: Foreign (International) Students are students who are neither Canadian citizens nor permanent residents of Canada, and are enrolled full-time in a recognized academic, professional or vocational training course at a university, college or other educational institution in Canada.

Entrance exam requirements: Generally, as for domestic students, a high school diploma or equivalent will be required. A lack of proficiency in English or French will be taken into account by the Canadian immigration office in the evaluation of the application.

Entry regulations: Before you come to study in Canada, you will need: a "Study Permit" if the programme of study you will be admitted to is longer than six months in duration, regardless of the length of your stay in Canada; a letter of acceptance from the school of your choice; proof that you have enough money to pay school fees and living expenses; to establish that you will return home at the end of your studies; to pass a medical exam if required; and to qualify as a temporary resident in Canada, including holding a temporary resident visa (required for citizens of many countries). A small number of students do not require a "Study Permit" by virtue of their status in Canada (e.g. diplomats and their children).

Health requirements: Most education institutions require international students to buy health insurance in addition to their tuition fees; those that do not will require proof of independent health insurance coverage. Medical examinations are not required by institutions but are required by Citizenship and Immigration Canada for students from many countries.

RECOGNITION OF STUDIES

Quality assurance system:

The Maritime Provinces Higher Education Commission assesses programme quality through a quality assurance process for new programmes and monitors the institutions to ensure a quality assurance process is in place for existing programmes. Individual educational institutions are responsible for recognition/accreditation for credit transfer. As a result, practices vary by institution and programme. In general, the institutions use information from a variety of sources to assess academic credentials.

Special provisions for recognition:

Recognition for university level studies: In general none. Universities establish their own admissions criteria and make their own admissions decisions in response to individual applications. Any restrictions on admission are determined by the institutions themselves, given available teaching and other resources, but in a few instances are a result of government policy. Priority is usually given to provincial residents first, other Canadian residents, then foreign students.
Additionally, the Canadian Information Centre for International Credentials (CICIC) provides information and guidance on the recognition of foreign studies.

For access to advanced studies and research: In general none. However, if in some high cost, limited enrolment programmes, e.g. Medicine and Dentistry, qualified applicants outnumber available enrolment capacity, then most universities will establish special admissions committees and provide for proportionately more domestic than foreign applicants to be admitted.

For exercising a profession: In general none. For each profession, both Canadians and non-Canadians who studied abroad have to meet specified educational and experience requirements, and usually pass registration examinations. Non-Canadians may sometimes also need to pass language tests.

PROVINCIAL BODIES

Nova Scotia Department of Labour and Advanced Education
Minister: Marilyn More
PO Box 697,
5151 Terminal Road
Halifax, NS B3J 2T8
Canada

Tel: +1(902) 424 5301
Fax: +1(902) 424 0575
WWW: http://www.gov.ns.ca/lae/

Council of Nova Scotia University Presidents - CONSUP
Chairperson: John Harker
Suite 403,
5657 Spring Garden Road
Halifax, NS B3J 3R4
Canada
Tel: +1(902) 425 4230
Fax: +1(902) 425 4233
WWW: http://www.atlanticuniversities.ca/council-nova-scotia-university-presidents

Private Colleges Association of Nova Scotia
President: Jamie Hartling
WWW: http://www.pcans.ca/

Data for academic year: 2011-2012
Source: IAU from the Canadian Information Centre for International Credentials (CICIC), a unit of the Council of Ministers of Education, Canada (CMEC), on behalf of the Province of Nova Scotia, 2011

INSTITUTIONS

PUBLIC INSTITUTIONS

ACADIA UNIVERSITY

15 University Avenue, Wolfville, Nova Scotia B4P 2R6
Tel: +1(902) 542-2201 +1(902) 585-2201
Fax: +1(902) 585-7224
EMail: agi@acadiau.ca
Website: http://www.acadiau.ca

President and Vice-Chancellor: Ray Ivany (2009-)
Tel: +1(902) 585-1218, Fax: +1(902) 585-1077
EMail: president@acadiau.ca

Vice-President, Finance and Administration and Chief Financial Officer: Darrell Youden
Tel: +1(902) 585-1177, Fax: +1(902) 585-1077
EMail: darrell.youden@acadiau.ca

Academies
Environment *(Arthur Irving)* (Environmental Studies)

Colleges
Divinity (Bible; Christian Religious Studies; History of Religion; New Testament; Religion; Religious Education; Religious Studies; Theology)

Departments
Graduate Studies (Biology; Chemistry; Computer Science; Education; Educational Sciences; English; Geology; Mathematics; Parks and Recreation; Political Sciences; Psychology; Social Sciences; Sociology; Statistics; Surveying and Mapping); **Research**

Faculties
Arts (Ancient Civilizations; Art Therapy; Canadian Studies; Comparative Religion; Economics; English; Environmental Studies; French; German; Greek (Classical); Histology; History; Latin; Literature; Modern Languages; Music; Music Education; Music Theory and Composition; Musical Instruments; Musicology; Philosophy; Political Sciences; Singing; Sociology; Spanish; Theatre; Women's Studies); **Professional Studies** (Accountancy; Biology; Business Administration; Education; Marketing; Music Education; Nutrition; Parks and Recreation; Physical Therapy; Primary Education; Secondary Education; Technology Education); **Pure and Applied**

Science (Biology; Chemistry; Computer Science; Dietetics; Earth Sciences; Engineering; Environmental Studies; Mathematics; Nutrition; Physics; Psychology; Statistics)

Laboratories
Chemical Analysis and Bio-imaging *(CABL)* (Biological and Life Sciences; Chemistry); **Environmental Biogeochemistry** (Chemistry); **Eukaryotic Microbiology and Parasitology** (Microbiology; Parasitology); **Inorganic Photophysics and Biological Sciences** (Biological and Life Sciences; Physics); **Investigating Ultra-trace Organic Contaminants in the Environment**; **Photosciences**; **Plant Developmental Morphology and Systematics**; **Psychomotor Behaviour**

Research Centres
Analytical Research on the Environment *(CARE)* (Environmental Studies); **Estuarine Research** *(ACER)* (Coastal Studies); **Lifestyle Studies** *(CoLS)*; **Mathematical Modelling and Computation** *(ACMMaC)* (Mathematics); **Media** *(AMC)* (Media Studies); **Microstructural Analysis** *(ACMA)*; **Northeast Asia** *(NEARC)* (Asian Studies); **Organizational Research and Development** *(COR&D)*; **Sensory Research of Food** *(CSRF)* (Food Technology); **Social and Business Entrepreneurship** (Business Administration; Management); **Study of Ethnocultural Diversity** *(ACSED)* (Cultural Studies; Ethnology); **Wildlife and Conservation Biology** (Biology; Wildlife)

Research Units
K.C. Irving Environmental Science Centre and Harriet Irving Botanical Gardens (Botany; Environmental Studies)

History: Founded 1838 as Queen's College by the Nova Scotia Baptist Education Society, became Acadia College 1841. Incorporated 1891 by act of the Nova Scotia legislature with the powers of a university. Acquired present title 1891.

Governing Bodies: Board of Governors; Senate

Academic Year: September to April (September-December; January-April)

Admission Requirements: Secondary school certificate or recognized foreign equivalent, including International Baccalaureate

Fees: (Can. Dollars): Undergraduate tuition fees, 2,685-6,653 per term for Canadian students and 6,469-13,410 for International students; Masters programmes tuition fees, 4,373-6,355 per annum for Canadian Students (for Non Residents of Nova Scotia); .3,351-5,333 per annum for Canadian Students (for Qualifying Residents of Nova Scotia); 9,102-13,065 per annum for International students.

Main Language(s) of Instruction: English

Degrees and Diplomas: *Bachelor's Degree*; *Master's Degree*. Also Bachelor with Honours in Business Administration, Recreation Management and Kynesiology, 4 yrs. Also inter-university doctoral programme (PhD) in Educational Studies, 14 months, jointly offered with Mount Saint Vincent University and St. Francis Xavier University.

Student Services: Sports facilities

Student Residential Facilities: Yes

Special Facilities: Acadia University Art Gallery. Acadia Centre for Estuarine Research. Morton Centre. Bon Portage Island Centre

Libraries: Vaughan Memorial Library , c. 1m. Vols

Publications: Acadia Connections *(monthly)*

Academic Staff *2010-2011*: Total: c. 320
Student Numbers *2010-2011*: Total 3,485
Last Updated: 25/01/11

ATLANTIC SCHOOL OF THEOLOGY (SAINT MARY'S UNIVERSITY)

660 Francklyn Street, Halifax, Nova Scotia B3H 3B5
Tel: +1(902) 423-6939
Fax: +1(902) 492-4048
EMail: academicoffice@astheology.ns.ca;
advancement@astheology.ns.ca
Website: http://astheology.ns.ca/

President: Eric Beresford
Tel: +1(902) 423-6801 EMail: eberesford@astheology.ns.ca

Dean, Academic: David MacLachlan
Tel: +1(902) 496-7941 EMail: dmaclachlan@astheology.ns.ca

Programmes
Graduate Studies (Religion; Religious Studies; Theology); **Theological Studies** (Theology); **Youth Ministry** (Leadership)

History: Founded 1971. Affiliated with Saint Mary's University 2002.

Academic Year: August to May (August-December; January-May); Also Summer Term from June to August.

Fees: (Canadian Dollar): Full time tuition, 5,210 per annum.

Degrees and Diplomas: *Master's Degree*
Last Updated: 25/01/11

CAPE BRETON UNIVERSITY (CBU)

P.O.Box 5300, 1250 Grand Lake Road, Sydney,
Nova Scotia B1P 6L2
Tel: +1(902) 539-5300 +1(888) 959-9995
Fax: +1(902) 562-0119
EMail: registrar@cbu.ca
Website: http://www.cbu.ca

President and Vice-Chancellor: H. John Harker
Tel: 1+(902) 563-1333, Fax: +1(902) 562-0273
EMail: john_harker@cbu.ca

Vice-President, Student Services and Registrar: Alexis Manley
Tel: +1(902) 563-1650, Fax: +1(902) 563-1371

International Relations: Terry Gibbs, Director, Centre for International Studies
Tel: +1(902) 563-1274, Fax: +1(902) 563-1360
EMail: terry_gibbs@cbu.ca

Centres
Cape Breton Studies (Celtic Languages and Studies; Ethnology; Folklore; Music; Musicology) *Director*: Richard MacKinnon; **Children's Rights** (Human Rights); **International Studies**; **Natural History** (Biological and Life Sciences; Botany; Natural Sciences); **Philosophy and Religion** *(PAR)* (Philosophy; Religion); **Religion and Society** *(Abraham)* (Christian Religious Studies; Islamic Theology; Judaic Religious Studies; Religion); **Small Business Development** *(SBDC)* (Small Business); **Sustainability in Energy and the Environment** *(CSEE)* (Energy Engineering; Environmental Studies)

Groups
Petroleum Applications of Wireless Systems *(PAWS)* (Petroleum and Gas Engineering)

Institutes
Alexander Graham Bell; **Beaton** (Cultural Studies; Economics; Environmental Studies; History; Industrial and Production Economics; Labour and Industrial Relations; Political Sciences; Religious Studies; Rural Studies; Social Studies) *Director*: Catherine Arseneau; **Community Economic Development** *(CED)* (Development Studies); **Development of Energy and Sustainability** (Energy Engineering); **Ecosystem Research** *(Bras d'Or)* (Ecology); **Human Values and Technology** *(Tompkins)* (Technology); **Integrative Science and Health** *(IISH)*; **Louisbourg** (Education); **Small and Medium-sized Enterprise** *(SMEI)* (Small Business); **Tourism Development** *(International)* (Tourism)

Programmes
Online Education (Engineering; Environmental Studies; Hotel and Restaurant; Industrial Engineering; Protective Services; Public Administration; Public Health; Social and Community Services; Tourism)

Research Centres
Marketing (Marketing)

Schools
Arts and Social Sciences (Anthropology; Business Administration; Celtic Languages and Studies; Communication Studies; Cultural Studies; English; Environmental Studies; Fine Arts; Folklore; French; Health Sciences; Heritage Preservation; History; Literature; Management; Media Studies; Modern Languages; Musicology; Native American Studies; Native Language; Philosophy; Physical Education; Political Sciences; Psychology; Public Administration; Religious Studies; Social and Community Services; Social Sciences; Sociology; Spanish; Theatre; Women's Studies); **Business** *(Shannon)* (Accountancy; Business Administration; Development Studies; Economics; Finance; Hotel and Restaurant; Human Resources; Law; Marketing; Tourism); **Graduate and Professional Studies** (Art Education; Arts and Humanities; Biology; Business Administration; Chemistry; Curriculum; Education; Educational and Student Counselling; Educational Technology; Health Sciences; Information Technology; Mathematics; Microbiology; Nursing; Nutrition; Occupational Health; Public Health; Secondary Education; Social Sciences); **Science and Technology** (Agriculture; Automation and Control Engineering; Bioengineering; Biology; Chemical Engineering; Chemistry; Civil Engineering; Computer Engineering; Computer Science; Electrical Engineering; Electronic Engineering; Engineering; Environmental Studies; Geology; Industrial Engineering; Mathematics; Mechanical Engineering; Metallurgical Engineering; Mining Engineering; Petroleum and Gas Engineering; Physical Therapy; Physics; Psychology; Technology)

Further Information: Also Campus in Cairo (Canadian International College Egypt); Study Abroad and Exchange programmes (Contact Diane Toomey. Tel: +1(902) 563-1,278; E-mail: diane_-toomey@cbu.ca)

History: Founded 1974 by amalgamation of Saint Francis Xavier University's former Sydney campus (1951) and Nova Scotia Eastern Institute of Technology (1968). Acquired present status and title 2005.

Governing Bodies: Board of Governors; Senate

Academic Year: September to August (September-December; January-April; May-August)

Admission Requirements: Secondary school certificate or recognized foreign equivalent, including International Baccalaureate; TOEFL score of 550

Fees: (Can. Dollars): Undergraduate Courses, 566-620.50 per 3 credit course (Nova Scotia students and Out-of-Province Canadian Students receive a bursary the Province of Nova Scotia to be applied against tuition respectively in the amount of 128.30 and 26.10 per three credit course; International Students, 1,132 per 3 credit course or equivalent. Graduate tuition fees, 1,184 per 3 credit course for Canadian students and 1,750 per 3 credit course for International students.

Main Language(s) of Instruction: English

Degrees and Diplomas: *Bachelor's Degree*; *Master's Degree*. Also joint Bachelor of Arts Community Studies/Bachelor of Business Administration (BACS/BBA) degree program; Pre-MBA Program for International Students; Honours Bachelor's degree; two year programme for graduates with a relevant Bachelor's Degree or Technology Programme (first year of a joint 2-year post-diploma program is also offered in French in partnership with the Bathurst campus of the New Brunswick Community College).

Student Services: Academic counselling, Canteen, Cultural centre, Employment services, Foreign student adviser, Handicapped facilities, Health services, Nursery care, Social counselling, Sports facilities

Student Residential Facilities: MacDonald Residence, Cabot Residence, Alumni Hall and Harriss Hall (Total capcity of c. 570 beds)

Special Facilities: Art Gallery; Theatre

Libraries: c. 300,000 vols

Press or Publishing House: CBU Press

Academic Staff 2010-2011	TOTAL
FULL-TIME	100
PART-TIME	50
STAFF WITH DOCTORATE	
FULL-TIME	80
PART-TIME	c. 10
Student Numbers 2010-2011	
All (Foreign Included)	c. 3,500
FOREIGN ONLY	400

Last Updated: 25/01/11

DALHOUSIE UNIVERSITY (DAL)

1236 Henry Street, Halifax, Nova Scotia B3H 4R2
Tel: +1(902) 494-2211
Fax: +1(902) 494-2319
EMail: admissions@dal.ca
Website: http://www.dal.ca

President and Vice-Chancellor: Thomas Traves (1995-)
Tel: +1(902) 494-2511, Fax: +1(902) 494-1658
EMail: tom.traves@dal.da

Registrar: Asa Kachan
Tel: +1(902) 494-2450, Fax: +1(902) 494-1630
EMail: registrar@dal.ca

International Relations: Patricia Rodee, Director, International Research and Development (IRD) and International Liaison Officer (ILO)
Tel: +1(902) 494-1743, Fax: +1(902) 494-1595
EMail: pat.rodee@dal.ca

Colleges
Continuing Education (Adult Education; Engineering; English; Environmental Management; Fire Science; Information Technology; Leadership; Management; Occupational Health; Peace and Disarmament; Safety Engineering; Small Business; Writing)

Faculties
Architecture and Planning (Architecture and Planning; Arts and Humanities; Building Technologies; Design; Environmental Management; History; Landscape Architecture; Technology; Town Planning); **Arts and Social Sciences** (Acting; Ancient Civilizations; Anthropology; Arabic; Business Administration; Canadian Studies; Chinese; Cognitive Sciences; Contemporary History; Development Studies; Display and Stage Design; Engineering; English; Environmental Studies; European Studies; Film; French; Gender Studies; German; Greek (Classical); Health Sciences; History; Italian; Journalism; Latin; Law; Linguistics; Literature; Modern History; Music; Philosophy; Political Sciences; Religious Studies; Russian; Sociology; Spanish; Theatre; Women's Studies; Writing); **Computer Science** (Computer Science); **Dentistry** (Dental Hygiene; Dental Technology; Dentistry; Oral Pathology; Orthodontics; Periodontics; Surgery); **Engineering** (Bioengineering; Biomedical Engineering; Chemical Engineering; Civil Engineering; Computer Engineering; Electrical Engineering; Engineering; Environmental Engineering; Food Science; Food Technology; Industrial Engineering; Materials Engineering; Mathematics; Mechanical Engineering; Mining Engineering; Petroleum and Gas Engineering); **Graduate Studies**

(Agriculture; Anatomy; Ancient Civilizations; Anthropology; Architecture; Architecture and Planning; Biochemistry; Bioengineering; Biology; Biomedical Engineering; Biophysics; Business Administration; Chemical Engineering; Chemistry; Civil Engineering; Communication Disorders; Computer Engineering; Computer Science; Dental Technology; Dentistry; Development Studies; E-Business/Commerce; Earth Sciences; Economics; Electrical Engineering; Engineering; English; Environmental Engineering; Environmental Management; Environmental Studies; Finance; Food Science; Food Technology; French; German; Greek (Classical); Health Administration; Health Sciences; History; Immunology; Industrial Engineering; Information Management; Journalism; Latin; Law; Leisure Studies; Management; Marine Science and Oceanography; Materials Engineering; Mathematics; Mechanical Engineering; Medicine; Meteorology; Microbiology; Mining Engineering; Molecular Biology; Musicology; Neurosciences; Nursing; Occupational Therapy; Ophthalmology; Pathology; Periodontics; Petroleum and Gas Engineering; Pharmacology; Pharmacy; Philosophy; Physical Education; Physical Therapy; Physics; Physiology; Political Sciences; Psychology; Public Administration; Public Health; Rehabilitation and Therapy; Social Work; Sociology; Speech Therapy and Audiology; Statistics); **Health Professions** (Communication Disorders; Health Administration; Health Sciences; Leisure Studies; Nursing; Occupational Therapy; Ophthalmology; Pharmacy; Physical Therapy; Social Work); **Law** (Civil Law; Comparative Law; Constitutional Law; Criminal Law; International Law; Law; Maritime Law; Public Law); **Management** (Business Administration; Business and Commerce; E-Business/Commerce; Environmental Management; Finance; Information Management; Information Sciences; Library Science; Management; Natural Resources; Public Administration); **Medicine** (Anaesthesiology; Anatomy; Biochemistry; Biomedical Engineering; Biophysics; Cardiology; Dermatology; Endocrinology; Epidemiology; Ethics; Gastroenterology; Gerontology; Gynaecology and Obstetrics; Haematology; Immunology; Medicine; Microbiology; Molecular Biology; Nephrology; Neurology; Oncology; Ophthalmology; Orthopaedics; Otorhinolaryngology; Paediatrics; Pathology; Pharmacology; Physical Therapy; Physiology; Plastic Surgery; Psychiatry and Mental Health; Public Health; Radiology; Rehabilitation and Therapy; Respiratory Therapy; Rheumatology; Surgery; Urology); **Science** (Biochemistry; Biology; Chemistry; Earth Sciences; Economics; Environmental Studies; Immunology; Marine Biology; Marine Science and Oceanography; Mathematics; Meteorology; Microbiology; Molecular Biology; Neurosciences; Physics; Psychology; Statistics)

Further Information: Also Teaching Hospitals

History: Founded 1818. Acquired present status 1997 by merging with Technical University of Nova Scotia.

Governing Bodies: Board of Governors, comprising 25 members, including 3 student representatives; the Senate, comprising 72 members including 6 student representatives.

Academic Year: September to June (September-December; January-April; May-June). Also Summer Sessions (July-August)

Admission Requirements: Secondary school certificate or recognized foreign equivalent, including International Baccalaureate

Fees: (Can. Dollars): undergraduate tuition fee, 2,100-3,510 per term, except Pharmacy programme, 4,338 per term; International students have to pay an additional 3,630 per term. Graduate tuition fee, 6,381-9,110 per annum, except Masters of Occupational Therapy and Physiotherapy, 13,017 per annum; MBA, 19,000 per annum, Master's degree in Medical disciplines, 14,481 per annum. International Students, an additional 2,595-3,630 per annum.

Main Language(s) of Instruction: English

International Co-operation: With universities in Argentina, Australia, Cuba, Denmark, Dominican Republic, Fiji, Finland, France, Germany, Iceland, Italy, India, Jordan, Korea, Malaysia, Malta, Mexico, Netherlands, New Zealand, Norway, Russia, Singapore, Spain, Swaziland, Sweden, Taiwan, United Kingdom, United States of America, Zimbabwe. Also participates in the Canada-EU Community Program for Cooperation in Higher Education and Training (ATLANTIS) and in the North American Consortium on Legal Education (NACLE).

Degrees and Diplomas: *Bachelor's Degree*; *Master's Degree*; *Doctoral Degree*. Also Honours Bachelor's degree; Dual/Combined Degrees: Master of Library and Information Studies / Master of Public Administration, Master of Library and Information Studies / Master of Resource and Environmental Studies, Master of Library and Information Studies / Bachelor of Laws, Master of Public Administration / Bachelor of Laws

Student Services: Academic counselling, Canteen, Cultural centre, Employment services, Foreign student adviser, Foreign Studies Centre, Handicapped facilities, Health services, Language programs, Nursery care, Social counselling, Sports facilities

Student Residential Facilities: Several residences, c. 2,200 beds.

Special Facilities: Dalhousie Art Gallery. Dalplex. Dalhousie Arts Centre

Libraries: Killiam Library, Weldon Law Library, Kellog Health Sciences Library, Sevton Campus Library, total, c. 1,342,850 vols

Press or Publishing House: Dalhousie University Press

Academic Staff 2009-2010	MEN	WOMEN	TOTAL
FULL-TIME	–	–	1,012
STAFF WITH DOCTORATE			
FULL-TIME	–	–	931
Student Numbers 2009-2010			
All (Foreign Included)	7,512	9,181	16,693
FOREIGN ONLY	–	–	1,753

Last Updated: 26/01/11

MOUNT SAINT VINCENT UNIVERSITY (MSVU)

166 Bedford Highway, Halifax, Nova Scotia B3M 2J6
Tel: +1(902) 457-6788 +1(902) 457-6117
Fax: +1(902) 457-6498
EMail: admissions@msvu.ca
Website: http://www.msvu.ca

President and Vice-Chancellor: Ramona Lumpkin (2010-)
Tel: +1(902) 457-6131, Fax: +1(902) 457-0096
EMail: johnann.leblanc@msvu.ca

Vice-President, Administration: Brian Jessop
Tel: +1(902) 457-6742, Fax: +1(902) 445-3302
EMail: brian.jessop@msvu.ca

International Relations: Paula Barry, Manager, International Education Centre
Tel: +1(902) 457-6130 EMail: paula.barry@msvu.ca

Faculties
Arts and Science (Anthropology; Biology; Canadian Studies; Chemistry; Communication Studies; Computer Science; Cultural Studies; Economics; English; French; German; History; Library Science; Linguistics; Mathematics; Modern Languages; Peace and Disarmament; Philosophy; Physics; Political Sciences; Psychology; Religious Studies; Social Policy; Sociology; Spanish; Statistics; Women's Studies; Writing); **Education** (Continuing Education; Curriculum; Education; Educational Psychology; Literacy Education; Primary Education; Secondary Education; Teacher Training); **Professional Studies** (Business Administration; Child Care and Development; Family Studies; Gerontology; Hotel and Restaurant; Information Technology; Nutrition; Public Relations; Tourism)

Programmes
Distance Learning and Continuing Education (Business Administration; Child Care and Development; Educational Psychology; English; Hotel and Restaurant; Marketing; Psychology; Public Relations; Religious Studies; Tourism; Women's Studies)

Further Information: Also Study Abroad Programmes. Branch in Ontario

History: Founded 1873 as an academy. The Nova Scotia legislature granted Mount Saint Vincent College status to confer degrees 1925, making it the only independent Women's college in the British Commonwealth. Became Mount Saint Vincent University 1966. Current charter was approved to transfer ownership of the University from Sisters of Charity to the Board of Governors 1988.

Governing Bodies: Board of Governors, comprising 38 members; Senate, comprising 34 members, including 10 ex officio, 19 Faculty representatives, 5 student representatives

Academic Year: September to April (September-December; January-April)

Admission Requirements: Secondary school certificate or recognized foreign equivalent

Fees: (Can. Dollars): undergraduate tuition fee, 1,110 per unit of credit; Bachelor of Educational Sciences, 1,171 per unit of credit;

Graduate tuition fee, 1,523 per unit of credit, except School psychology (GSPY) courses, 1,623 per unit of credit; International students have to pay 1,059 per unit of credit in addition to regular tuition fees.

Main Language(s) of Instruction: English

Degrees and Diplomas: *Bachelor's Degree*; *Master's Degree*. Also inter-university doctoral programme (PhD) in Educational Studies, 14 months, jointly offered with Acadia University and St. Francis Xavier University.

Student Services: Academic counselling, Canteen, Employment services, Foreign student adviser, Health services, Language programs, Nursery care, Social counselling, Sports facilities

Student Residential Facilities: For 221 women students and 20 male students

Special Facilities: Mount Saint Vincent University Art Gallery; Mount Saint Vincent University Arboretum

Libraries: 201,170 vols

Publications: Atlantis (A Women's Studies Journal) *(biannually)*

Academic Staff 2009-2010	TOTAL
FULL-TIME	230
PART-TIME	150
STAFF WITH DOCTORATE	
FULL-TIME	120
PART-TIME	c. 30
Student Numbers 2009-2010	
All (Foreign Included)	c. 4,000
FOREIGN ONLY	450

Part-time students, 2,360. **Distance students**, 3,150.
Last Updated: 26/01/11

NOVA SCOTIA AGRICULTURAL COLLEGE (DALHOUSIE UNIVERSITY) (NSAC)

PO Box 550, Station Main, Truro, Nova Scotia B2N 5E3
Tel: +1(902) 893-6600
Fax: +1(902) 895-5529
EMail: reg@nsac.ca
Website: http://www.nsac.ns.ca

Co-President: Leslie MacLaren
Tel: +1(902) 893-6030 EMail: lmaclaren@nsac.ca

Co-President and Vice President, Administration: Bernie MacDonald
Tel: +1(902) 893-6034, Fax: +1(902) 893-4601
EMail: bmacdonald@nsac.ca

Registrar: Wayne Paquet
Tel: +1(902) 893-6722 EMail: wpaquet@nsac.ca

International Relations: Nancy Pitts, Associate Professor and Dean of Internationalization
Tel: +1(902) 893-6653, Fax: +1(902) 893-4939
EMail: npitts@nsac.ca

Departments
Business and Social Sciences (Agricultural Business; Agricultural Economics; Business Administration; International Business; Management); **Continuing and Distance Education** (Agricultural Equipment; Agriculture; Animal Husbandry; Botany; Farm Management; Horticulture); **Engineering** (Engineering; Environmental Management; Soil Management; Waste Management; Water Management); **Environmental Sciences** (Biology; Chemistry; Environmental Studies; Horticulture; Pest Management; Soil Management; Waste Management); **Plant and Animal Sciences** (Agronomy; Animal Husbandry; Aquaculture; Biotechnology; Botany; Crop Production; Food Science; Horticulture; Management; Physiology; Veterinary Science); **Research and Graduate Studies** (Agricultural Management; Agriculture; Animal Husbandry; Biochemistry; Botany; Chemistry; Crop Production; Ecology; Economics; Entomology; Environmental Studies; Fruit Production; Genetics; Natural Resources; Nutrition; Pathology; Pest Management; Physiology; Safety Engineering; Soil Conservation; Soil Management; Soil Science; Vegetable Production; Waste Management; Water Management)

History: Founded 1905, incorporating School of Agriculture and School of Horticulture.

Academic Year: September to April (September-December; January-April)

Admission Requirements: Equivalent of Canadian Grade 12 Diploma with high marks in English, Mathematics, Chemistry, and Biology or Physics

Fees: (Can. Dollars): Undergraduate tuition fees, 550 per course for Canadian students; Full-time Nova Scotia degree/technology programme students are eligible for a Nova Scotia Bursary of 1,283 based on a full course load (e.g. 10 courses per year for a degree student); Full-time non Nova Scotia Canadian degree and technology students will receive a 261 Nova Scotia Bursary; For international students, 1,100 per course. Graduate tuition fee, 2,418 per term for Canadian students and 4,148 per term for International students.

Main Language(s) of Instruction: English

International Co-operation: With universities in United Kingdom, Finland, Denmark, Norway, Czech Republic, Slovak Republic and Jamaica

Accrediting Agencies: Maritime Provinces Higher Education Commission

Degrees and Diplomas: *Bachelor's Degree*; *Master's Degree*. The Master of Science (MSc) degree is granted by Dalhousie University in association with Nova Scotia Agricultural College

Student Services: Academic counselling, Canteen, Employment services, Foreign student adviser, Handicapped facilities, Health services, Nursery care, Social counselling, Sports facilities

Student Residential Facilities: For c. 1,000 students

Libraries: MacRac Library, 23,000 vols
Last Updated: 26/01/11

NSCAD UNIVERSITY (NSCAD)

5163 Duke Street, Halifax, Nova Scotia B3J 3J6
Tel: +1(902) 444-9600
Fax: +1(902) 425-2420
EMail: admissions@nscad.ca
Website: http://nscad.ca

President: David B. Smith
Tel: +1(902) 494-8114, Fax: +1(902) 422-7562
EMail: president@nscad.ca

Registrar: Laurelle LeVert
Tel: +1(902) 494-8129, Fax: +1(902) 425-2987
EMail: registrar@nscad.ca

International Relations: John Mabley, Vice President, University Relations
Tel: +1(902) 444-7223, Fax: +1(902) 425-3240
EMail: universityrelations@nscad.ca

Divisions
Craft (Ceramic Art; Fine Arts; Handicrafts; Jewelry Art; Textile Design); **Design** (Design); **Fine Arts** (Fine Arts; Painting and Drawing; Printing and Printmaking; Sculpture); **Foundation Studies** (Computer Science; Design; Film; Metal Techniques; Painting and Drawing; Photography; Printing and Printmaking; Video; Visual Arts; Wood Technology); **Historical and Critical Studies** (Art History); **Media Arts** (Film; Fine Arts; Media Studies; Photography; Video; Visual Arts)

Schools
Extended Studies (Art Management; Ceramic Art; Computer Graphics; Computer Science; Design; Fashion Design; Fine Arts; Glass Art; Graphic Arts; Jewelry Art; Painting and Drawing; Paper Technology; Photography; Printing and Printmaking; Sculpture; Textile Design); **Graduate Studies** (Ceramic Art; Design; Film; Fine Arts; Handicrafts; Jewelry Art; Painting and Drawing; Performing Arts; Photography; Printing and Printmaking; Sculpture; Textile Design; Video)

History: Founded 1887 as Victoria School of Art and Design, became Nova Scotia College of Art 1925 and Nova Scotia College of Art and Design 1969. An independent institution of higher education. Students may also arrange to take courses at Dalhousie University and at other universities in Halifax. Acquired current title and status 2003.

Governing Bodies: Board of Governors

Academic Year: September to April (September-December; January-April). Also Summer session, May to August

Admission Requirements: Secondary school certificate or recognized foreign equivalent

Fees: (Can. Dollars): c. 5,500 per annum; c. 12,120 foreign students

Main Language(s) of Instruction: English

International Co-operation: With universities in USA; Ireland; United Kingdom; Portugal; France; Germany; Netherlands; Ghana; Korea; Australia; New Zealand; Japan; Mexico

Accrediting Agencies: Association of Universities and Colleges of Canada (AUCC)

Degrees and Diplomas: *Bachelor's Degree*; *Master's Degree*. Also Professional certificates.

Student Services: Academic counselling, Employment services, Foreign student adviser, Social counselling

Student Residential Facilities: No

Special Facilities: Anna Leonowens Art Gallery

Libraries: c. 32,000 vols; 115,000 slides
Last Updated: 27/01/11

SAINT MARY'S UNIVERSITY

923 Robie Street, Halifax, Nova Scotia B3H 3C3
Tel: +1(902) 420-5400
Fax: +1(902) 420-5561
EMail: service.centre@smu.ca
Website: http://www.smu.ca

President: J. Colin Dodds (2000-)
Tel: +1(902) 420-5401, Fax: +1(902) 420-5102
EMail: president@smu.ca; colin.dodds@smu.ca

Vice President, Administration: Gabrielle Morrison
Tel: +1(902) 420-5409, Fax: +1(902) 420-5566
EMail: gabe.morrison@smu.ca

International Relations: Maureen Woodhouse, Acting Director, International Activities Office
Tel: +1(902) 496-8794, Fax: +1(902) 420-5530
EMail: maureen.woodhouse@smu.ca

Centres
Atlantic Metropolis *(Immigration, Integration and Cultural Diversity)*; **Electron Microscopy Centre** *(EMC)*; **Ethics and Public Affairs** *(Canadian)* (Ethics); **Excellence in Accounting and Reporting for Co-operatives** *(CEARC)* (Accountancy); **Leadership Excellence** (Leadership); **Occupational Health and Safety** *(CN)* (Occupational Health); **Regional Geochemistry** *(Saint Mary's University)* (Geochemistry); **Spirituality and the Workplace**; **Students with Disabilities** *(Atlantic)*; **Study of Sport and Health** (Health Sciences; Sports)

Departments
Engineering (Bioengineering; Chemical Engineering; Civil Engineering; Electrical Engineering; Engineering; Environmental Engineering; Industrial Engineering; Mechanical Engineering; Metallurgical Engineering; Mining Engineering)

Divisions
Continuing Education (Accountancy; Business Administration; Canadian Studies; Chinese; Communication Studies; Finance; Forensic Medicine and Dentistry; Hispanic American Studies; Human Resources; Human Rights; Japanese; Leadership; Linguistics; Management; Mathematics Education; Peace and Disarmament; Spanish; Writing)

Faculties
Arts (Ancient Civilizations; Anthropology; Asian Studies; Business Administration; Canadian Studies; Chinese; Classical Languages; Criminology; Development Studies; Economics; English; Film; French; Gender Studies; Geography; German; Greek (Classical); Hispanic American Studies; History; Irish; Japanese; Latin; Linguistics; Mathematics; Modern Languages; Philosophy; Political Sciences; Psychology; Religious Studies; Sociology; Spanish; Theology; Women's Studies); **Education** (Education; Foreign Languages Education; Linguistics; Mathematics Education; Teacher Training); **Graduate Studies and Research** *(FGSR)* (Astronomy and Space Science; Business Administration; Canadian Studies; Criminology; Development Studies; Finance; Gender Studies;

History; Industrial and Organizational Psychology; Management; Philosophy; Psychology; Religious Studies; Theology; Women's Studies); **Science** (Applied Physics; Astronomy and Space Science; Astrophysics; Biology; Chemistry; Computer Science; Engineering; Environmental Studies; Forensic Medicine and Dentistry; Geography; Geology; Industrial and Organizational Psychology; Mathematics; Mathematics Education; Physics; Psychology)

Institutes
Computational Astrophysics (ICA) (Astrophysics)

Programmes
Coastal CURA (Coastal Studies); **Co-operative Education** (Accountancy; Anthropology; Biology; Business Administration; Business Computing; Chemistry; Computer Science; Economics; Environmental Studies; Finance; Geography; Geology; Human Resources; Information Technology; International Business; Labour and Industrial Relations; Management; Marketing; Mathematics; Psychology; Small Business); **English as a Second Language** (English; Foreign Languages Education)

Research Centres
ACEnet (Computer Science); **Astronomical Observatory** (Burke-Gaffney) (Astronomy and Space Science); **Community Based Environmental Monitoring Network** (CBEMN) (Environmental Management); **Environmental Analysis and Remediation** (CEAR) (Environmental Studies); **Maritime Provinces Spatial Analysis** (MP_SpARC)

Research Institutes
Gorsebrook (Canadian Studies; Regional Studies)

Schools
Business (Sobey) (Accountancy; Business Administration; Computer Science; Economics; Finance; Human Resources; Information Sciences; Information Technology; International Business; Labour and Industrial Relations; Management; Marketing)

History: Founded 1802 as Saint Mary's College, acquired present status and title 1841. From 1970, a public, non-denominational institution.

Governing Bodies: Board of Governors; Academic Senate

Academic Year: September to April (September-December; January-April). Also Summer Semesters.

Admission Requirements: Secondary school certificate or recognized foreign equivalent; TOEFL test for foreign students

Fees: (Can. Dollars): Undergraduate tuituon fees, 423.50-558 per half credit (3 credit hours) course for Canadian students (though the Nova Scotia University Student Bursary reduces the cost) and 981.50-1,116 per half credit (3 credit hours) course for International students. Graduate tuition fees: 3,075-6,150 for Candian students and 5,307-11,172 per annum for International students; except for MBA-CMA, 11,010 per programme, Master's degree in Finance, 31,700-34,300 per annum, executive MBA, 22,500 per annum; PhD, 3,750-5,000 per annum for Canadian students and 8,982-7,232 for International students.

Main Language(s) of Instruction: English

Degrees and Diplomas: Bachelor's Degree; Master's Degree; Doctoral Degree. Also Bachelor of Arts (Honours) degree; Executive MBA, 18 months; Accelerated MBA, 12-28 months; MBA-CMA, 24 months; Professional certificates.

Student Services: Academic counselling, Employment services, Foreign student adviser, Handicapped facilities, Health services, Nursery care, Social counselling, Sports facilities

Student Residential Facilities: Yes

Special Facilities: Burke-Gaffney Observatory; Art gallery; Gorsebrook Research Institute for Atlantic Canadian Studies; TESL Centre; The Tower (Athletics and Recreation)

Libraries: Patrick Power Library (434,551 vols; 590,557 micro-material; 20,127 non-print holdings); Member of Novanet Consortium of Libraries; the Atlantic Scholarly Information Network; Canadian Research Knowledge Network

Publications: Maroon and White; The Times

Academic Staff 2010-2011	TOTAL
FULL-TIME	420

Student Numbers 2010-2011	
All (Foreign Included)	c. 7,200
FOREIGN ONLY	1,580

Last Updated: 27/01/11

SAINT-ANNE UNIVERSITY
Université Sainte-Anne
1695, Route 1, Pointe-de-l'Eglise, Nova Scotia BOW 1MO
Tel: +1(902) 769-2114
Fax: +1(902) 769-2930
EMail: admission@ustanne.ednet.ns.ca
Website: http://www.usainteanne.ca

Recteur et Vice-chancelier: André Roberge (2001-)
Tel: +1(902) 769-2114, Ext. 300, Fax: +1(902) 769-3120
EMail: Andre.Roberge@usainteanne.ca

Registraire/Admissions: Murielle Comeau-Péloquin
Tel: +1(902) 769-2114, Ext. 216, Fax: +1(902) 769-2930
EMail: Murielle.ComeauPeloquin@usainteanne.ca

Centres
Acadian (Canadian Studies)

Faculties
Arts and Sciences (Canadian Studies; Education; English; Foreign Languages Education; French; Health Sciences; History; Primary Education; Public Health; Secondary Education; Social and Community Services; Translation and Interpretation); **Professional Programmes** (Accountancy; Business Administration; Education; English; Foreign Languages Education; French; Humanities and Social Science Education; International Business; Marketing; Mathematics Education; Native Language Education; Primary Education; Science Education; Secondary Education; Transport Management)

Programmes
Customized Language Training Services (Non-credited courses) (Chinese; English; French; Spanish)

Research Centres
Education (Education); **Minority Health** (Health Sciences); **Orality of Francophone minority of America** (Coframi) (Folklore)

Research Groups
Acadian Studies (GREA) (Canadian Studies)

Schools
French Immersion (Foreign Languages Education; French)

Further Information: Also campuses in Halifax, Petit-de-Grat, Saint-Joseph-du-Moine and Tusket.

History: Founded as College Sainte-Anne 1890 by Mgr. Blanche and the Fathers of the Congregation of Jesus and Mary (Eudists). Incorporated 1892 by an Act of the Nova Scotia legislature, and endowed with the power of conferring degrees. Acquired present title 1977.

Governing Bodies: Conseil des gouverneurs, comprising 20 members

Academic Year: September to June (September-December; January-April; May-June)

Admission Requirements: Secondary school certificate or recognized foreign equivalent. Acceptable knowledge of the French language necessary

Fees: (Can. Dollars): Registration fee, 90 per annum; Undergraduate tuition, 566-578 per 3 credit-course for Canadian students and 782 per 3 credit-course for International students. Graduate tuition, 755 per 3 credit-course for Canadian students and 961 per 3 credit-course for International students. Senior students (over 60 years old) are granted a 50% rebate on tuition fees.

Main Language(s) of Instruction: French

International Co-operation: With institutions in France, Canada, Mexico, USA

Accrediting Agencies: Association des Collèges communautaires du Canada (ACCC); Association des universités et collèges du Canada (AUCC); Association des universités de l'Atlantique (AUA); Association des universités de la francophonie canadienne (AUFC);

Association des registraires des universités et des collèges du Canada (ARUCC); Association de l'éducation permanente dans les universités de l'Atlantique (AEPUA); Association atlantique des registraires et officiers de l'admission (AAROA); Association des services aux étudiants des collèges et universités de l'Atlantique (ASECUA); Association des services aux étudiants des universités et collèges du Canada (ASEUCC); Agence universitaire de la francophonie (AUF); Council of Nova Scotia University Presidents (CONSUP); Conseil des programmes de langues secondes au Canada (CPLSC); Fédération canadienne des études humaines (FCEH); Fédération canadienne des sciences sociales (FCSS); Réseau des cégeps et collèges francophones du Canada (RCCFC); Réseau d'enseignement francophone à distance (REFAD).

Degrees and Diplomas: *Bachelor's Degree; Master's Degree*: Education. Some Baccalauréat degrees in Business Administration are offered in 2 years in collaboration with the Collège communautaire du Nouveau-Brunswick (CCNB); Integrated programme: Baccalauréat ès arts / Baccalauréat en éducation, 5 years.

Student Services: Academic counselling, Canteen, Cultural centre, Employment services, Handicapped facilities, Nursery care, Sports facilities

Student Residential Facilities: For c. 360 students

Special Facilities: Acadian Museum. Art Gallery

Libraries: Bibliothèque Louis R. Cormeau, c. 85,000 vols

Publications: Revue de l'Université Sainte-Anne *(annually)*

Press or Publishing House: Les Presses de l'Université Sainte-Anne

Last Updated: 28/01/11

ST. FRANCIS XAVIER UNIVERSITY (STFX)

PO Box 5000, Antigonish, Nova Scotia B2G 2W5
Tel: +1(902) 863-3300
Fax: +1(902) 867-5153
EMail: admit@stfx.ca
Website: http://www.stfx.ca

President and Vice-Chancellor: Sean E. Riley (1996-)
Tel: +1(902) 867-2188, Fax: +1(902) 867-5008
EMail: sriley@stfx.ca

Registrar: Timothy MacInnes
Tel: +1(902) 867-2160, Fax: +1(902) 867-5458
EMail: registr@stfx.ca

Academic Vice President and Provost: Mary McGillivray
EMail: mmcgilli@stfx.ca

Centres
Applied Petroleum Sciences (Petroleum and Gas Engineering); **Biofouling Research**; **Community Science** *(CSCA)*; **Logic and Information** (Information Sciences); **National Collaborating Centre for Determinants of Health** (Health Sciences); **Philosophy, Theology, and Cultural Traditions** (Cultural Studies; Philosophy; Theology); **Post-Communist Studies**; **Regional Studies** (Regional Studies); **Sports Nutrition and Exercise Metabolism** (Nutrition)

Faculties
Arts (Adult Education; Ancient Civilizations; Anthropology; Aquaculture; Asian Religious Studies; Bible; Canadian Studies; Catholic Theology; Celtic Languages and Studies; Christian Religious Studies; Classical Languages; Development Studies; Economics; English; Fine Arts; French; German; Greek (Classical); History; Jazz and Popular Music; Latin; Literature; Modern Languages; Music; Music Theory and Composition; Philosophy; Political Sciences; Psychology; Religious Studies; Sociology; Spanish; Women's Stu-

dies); **Business** *(Gerald Schwartz)* (Accountancy; Business Administration; Business Computing; Computer Science; Economics; Finance; Information Sciences; Information Technology; Leadership; Management; Marketing; Software Engineering); **Education** (Continuing Education; Curriculum; Education; French; Leadership; Literacy Education; Pedagogy; Physical Education; Primary Education; Secondary Education); **Science** (Aquaculture; Biology; Chemistry; Computer Science; Earth Sciences; Engineering; Environmental Studies; Mathematics; Nursing; Nutrition; Physical Education; Physical Therapy; Physics; Statistics)

Institutes
Coady International (Adult Education; Development Studies; Finance; Health Sciences; Leadership; Natural Resources)

Laboratories
Aquatic Plant Resources *(McLachlan)* (Plant and Crop Protection); **Behavioural Neuroscience** *(Dr. Karen Brebner and Dr. John McKenna)* (Behavioural Sciences; Neurosciences); **Comparative Biomechanics**; **Food Research** *(FRL)*; **Infant Action and Cognition**; **Infant Development** (Child Care and Development); **Invertebrate Neuroethology**; **Marine Ecology** (Ecology); **Parent and Child Interaction** (Child Care and Development); **SafetyNET-Rx Research**; **X-CELL Analytical Service**

Programmes
Climate Science *(CREATE Training Programs)* (Meteorology); **Graduate Studies** (Adult Education; Biology; Celtic Languages and Studies; Chemistry; Computer Science; Earth Sciences; Education; Physics)

Research Centres
ACEnet *(Atlantic Computational Excellence Network)* (Computer Science); **Culture and Human Development** *(CRCHD)*; **Environmental Sciences** *(ESRC)* (Environmental Studies); **Health Literacy in Rural Nova Scotia Research Project** (Health Sciences); **TPI [physics]** (Physics)

History: Founded 1853 as St. Francis Xavier College, Seminary 1855. Full university powers conferred by the province of Nova Scotia 1866.

Governing Bodies: Board of Governors; Senate

Academic Year: September to May (September-December; January-May)

Admission Requirements: Secondary school certificate or recognized foreign equivalent

Fees: (Can. Dollars): Tuition, 4,922 per annum for Nova Scotia Students, 5,944 for Non-Nova Scotia Students, 6,205 for International students.

Main Language(s) of Instruction: English, French, Scots Gaelic

Degrees and Diplomas: *Bachelor's Degree; Master's Degree*. Also Honours Bachelor's degree programmes; inter-university doctoral programme (PhD) in Educational Studies, 14 months, jointly offered with Acadia University and Mount Saint Vincent University.

Student Services: Academic counselling, Canteen, Cultural centre, Employment services, Foreign student adviser, Foreign Studies Centre, Handicapped facilities, Health services, Language programs, Nursery care, Social counselling, Sports facilities

Student Residential Facilities: Yes

Special Facilities: Art Gallery. Observatory. Theatre

Libraries: Angus L. MacDonald Library, c. 802,000 vols. Celtic special Collections. Marie Michael Library of the Coady International Institute

Last Updated: 27/01/11

Canada - Nunavut

STRUCTURE OF HIGHER EDUCATION SYSTEM

Description:

The Department of Education is responsible for post-secondary education in Nunavut. Although Nunavut does not have a university, Nunavut Arctic College, the only post-secondary institution in Nunavut, offers a variety of certificate, diploma, trades and university transfer programmes as well as two degree programmes in partnership with the University of Regina and Dalhousie University. Programme areas include Teacher Education, Nursing, Career Development, Environmental Technology and Management Studies. A Master of Education degree is also available through a partnership with the University of Prince Edward Island, St. Francis Xavier University, Nunavut Arctic College and the Department of Education. Programmes vary in length from eight weeks (trades programmes) to two years, but generally speaking, certificate programmes involve one year of full time studies, and diploma programmes in two years. In addition, Nunavut Arctic College provides adult basic education, skills development courses, trades training and contract training on behalf of local employers. Nunavut Arctic College has an established process to allow students to apply for course credits for previous learning and work experience. Nunavut Arctic College has transfer arrangements with a number of institutions in the south, including McGill University, Dalhousie University, Athabasca University, University of Manitoba and numerous Alberta institutions though their membership on the Alberta Council on Admissions and Transfer.

Stages of studies:

University level first stage: *Post-Secondary Programmes*
Many of the courses in the college diploma programmes are eligible for transfer credit with universities and professional associations throughout Canada. As well, the college offers selected university courses and programmes through agreements with approved degree granting institutions. Nunavut-based students can attend other post-secondary institutions within and outside of Canada.

Distance higher education:
The College offers a limited number of courses through technology-based distance education.

ADMISSION TO HIGHER EDUCATION

Admission to university-level studies:

Name of secondary school credential required: High School Graduation Diploma

Alternatives to credentials: Mature students not meeting the academic requirements – will demonstrate that they are 19 years or older and have been out of the K-12 school system for a minimum of one year; provide at least 2 letters of reference from persons able to assess the candidate's ability to proceed with post-secondary studies; provide a personal letter outlining the grounds for requesting mature student status; provide official transcripts documents showing formal and informal academic qualifications; and information about related work experience. An interview man be required.

Numerus clausus/restrictions: This applies to International and Out of Territory Students: acceptance of non-resident applicant will be limited by the maximum student capacity of the programme, the number of qualified applications received from Nunavut residents, and specific programme language requirements.

Foreign students admission:

Definition of foreign student: Foreign (International) Students are students who are neither Canadian citizens nor permanent residents of Canada and are enrolled full-time in a recognized academic, professional or vocational training course at a university, college or other educational institution in Canada.

Entrance exam requirements: Generally, as for domestic students, a high school diploma or equivalent will be required. A lack of proficiency in English or French will be taken into account by the Canadian Immigration Office in the evaluation of the application.

Entry regulations: Before you come to study in Canada, you will need: a "Study Permit" if the programme of study you will be admitted to is longer than six months in duration, regardless of the length of your stay in Canada; a letter of acceptance from the school of your choice; proof that you have enough money to pay school fees and living expenses; to establish that you will return home at the end of your studies; to pass a medical exam if required; and to qualify as a temporary resident in Canada, including holding a temporary resident visa (required for citizens of many countries). A small number of students do not require a Study Permit by virtue of their status in Canada (e.g. diplomats and their children).

Health requirements: Most education institutions require international students to buy health insurance in addition to their tuition fees; those that do not will require proof of independent health insurance coverage. Medical examinations are not required by institutions but are required by Citizenship and Immigration Canada for students from many countries.

RECOGNITION OF STUDIES

Quality assurance system:

The college has established its own academic evaluation policies, academic probation, attendance policies and policies relating to student conduct.

PROVINCIAL BODIES

Department of Education (Ministère de l'Education)

Deputy Minister: Kathy Okpik
Government of Nunavut,
PO Box 1000, Station 910,
2nd Floor Sivummut Building
Iqaluit, Nunavut X0A 0H0
Canada
Tel: +1(867) 975 5600
Fax: +1(867) 975 5605
WWW: http://www.edu.gov.nu.ca/

Data for academic year: 2011-2012
Source: IAU from the Canadian Information Centre for International Credentials (CICIC), a unit of the Council of Ministers of Education, Canada (CMEC), on behalf of the Province of Nunavut, 2011

Canada - Ontario

STRUCTURE OF HIGHER EDUCATION SYSTEM

Description:

Higher education in Canada is constitutionally the responsibility of the provinces. There are 19 provincially assisted universities and the Ontario College of Arts and Design and 24 provincially assisted colleges of applied arts and technology (CAATs).

Universities are degree granting institutions. Each institution has an Act of the Legislative Assembly and operates independently, determines its own academic and admissions policies, programmes and staff appointments. Several privately funded degree granting institutions also exist in Ontario. CAATs provide technical and vocational programmes usually leading to a Certificate or Diploma. In addition to certificate and diploma programmes, CAATs may also apply to the Minister of Training, Colleges and Universities for consent to offer a degree programme in an applied area of study. A combination of theory and applied skills training makes up the four year college applied degree programme model, which also includes a compulsory paid work term.

Pursuant to the Post-secondary Education Choice and Excellence Act 2000 (PSECE Act), all institutions – Ontario or out-of-province, public or private for-profit or not-for-profit – require either an act of the Legislative Assembly of Ontario or the consent of the Minister of Training, Colleges and Universities to offer and/or advertise a degree, programs or part of a program leading to a degree, or to call themselves a university or to advertise using the word "university" in Ontario. The act also allows CAATs to apply for a ministerial consent to offer a baccalaureate degree in an applied area of study. The act also enshrines in legislation the Post-secondary Education Quality Assessment Board. The Board is responsible for providing recommendations to the Minister on the academic rigour and institutional soundness of new degree granting proposals. The Board has established criteria against which it assesses applications for a Minister's consent prior to making its recommendations to the Minister for consideration.

The College Compensation and Appointments Council, a provincial government agency, appoints the governing bodies of the CAATs.

Besides various government supported pre-employment and apprenticeship programs, there are also many private career colleges which are required to register and have their vocational programs approved by the Ministry of Training, Colleges and Universities under the Private Career Colleges Act, 2005.

Stages of studies:

University level first stage: *Bachelor's Degree*
Most undergraduate study leads to a "General" Bachelor's Degree (minimum three years) or a "specialized" degree (four years and prescribed subject concentration). Degrees are normally titled in broad descriptive groups, e.g. Bachelor of Arts (B.A.) and Bachelor of Science (B.Sc.) The first stage also includes the undergraduate Diploma (one to three years of study) and short (up to one year) special certificate programmes; these may enable entry to degree programmes and are frequently given in close cooperation with professional bodies. In addition, the first stage includes other professional programmes that typically require no university level prerequisites and four years of study, e.g. Bachelor of Science in Nursing (B.Sc.N.), Bachelor of Commerce (B.Comm.). Finally, the Royal Military College of Canada, operated by the Federal Department of National Defence, is located in Kingston.

University level second stage: *Master's Degree*
The Master's Degree normally requires at least one year of study after a specialized Bachelor's Degree or equivalent. Most Master's programmes, e.g. in Business Administration, require two years of study. A thesis and course work are usually required. Graduate level Diplomas are considered an intermediate between a Bachelor's degree or first professional degree and the Master's Degree). The second stage also includes first professional degree programmes that demand prerequisite university studies e.g. professional Baccalaureate programmes (Bachelor of Law (LL.B.) and clinical Doctorates (Doctor of Medicine (M.D.); Doctor of Dental Surgery (DDS).

University level third stage: *Doctorate*
The research Doctorate is the highest academic qualification awarded by Ontario universities and it comprises the third stage of university-level studies. This degree normally requires at least three years of study after the

Bachelor's Degree; the submission and defence of a major thesis (dissertation) are the principal requirements, and supplemental course work is usually also required. The degree "Doctor of Philosophy" (Ph.D.) is the designation most commonly used to signify the Doctorate. It is a generic title, applicable to degrees in most disciplines. (The research Doctorate should not be confused with the "clinical" Doctorate, which is a first professional degree awarded in certain health science disciplines, e.g., M.D. in Medicine, D.D.S. in Dentistry and D.V.M. in Veterinary Medicine.)

Distance higher education:
Traditional "distance education" in which technology is used to connect learners and educators who are separated by time or distance is well developed with the majority of Ontario's colleges and universities offering courses and some complete programmes.

ADMISSION TO HIGHER EDUCATION

Admission to university-level studies:

Name of secondary school credential required: Secondary School Diploma

Alternatives to credentials: Varying credentials for mature students.

Other admission requirements: Overall average of 60% and six Grade 12 university (U) or university/college (M) courses. Universities and/or programmes often have additional specific requirements.

Foreign students admission:

Definition of foreign student: Foreign (International) Students are students who are neither Canadian citizens nor permanent residents of Canada, and are enrolled full-time in a recognized academic, professional or vocational training course at a university, college or other educational institution in Canada.

Quotas: Generally no. However, in a small number of professional programmes, there are limits to enrolment.

Entrance exam requirements: Generally, as for domestic students, a high school diploma or equivalent will be required. A lack of proficiency in English or French will be taken into account by the Canadian Immigration Office in the evaluation of the application.

Entry regulations: Before an international students can come to study in Canada, he or she will need: a "Study Permit" if the programme of study the individual is admitted to is longer than six months in duration, regardless of the length of your stay in Canada. In order to obtain a study permit, the student must provide: a letter of acceptance from the postsecondary institution; proof of enough money to pay school fees and living expenses; confirmation that the student will return home at the end of his of her studies; passing a medical exam if required; and qualification as a temporary resident in Canada, including holding a temporary resident visa (required for citizens of many countries). A small number of students do not require a Study Permit by virtue of their status in Canada (e.g. diplomats and their children).

Health requirements: Most education institutions require international students to buy health insurance in addition to their tuition fees; those that do not will require proof of independent health insurance coverage. Medical examinations are not required by institutions but are required by Citizenship and Immigration Canada for students from many countries.

RECOGNITION OF STUDIES

Quality assurance system:

There are more than 100 provincial standards which set the expected outcomes for college programs. The Ontario College Quality Assurance Service (OCQAS) implements and manages the self-regulatory quality assurance mechanism for Ontario's publicly supported colleges through the Credentials Validation Service (CVS) and the Program Quality Assurance Process Audit (PQAPA). The CVS ensures that all proposed new or modified certificate and diploma level programs of instruction conform to provincial standards. The PQAPA independently audits, on a cyclical basis, the colleges' quality assurance policies and procedures.

Once a university program receives approval from the University's Senate, the Undergraduate Program Review Audit Committee of the Council of Ontario Universities (reviews undergraduate programs only), and Ontario Council of Graduate Studies (reviews graduate programs only) review and approve the program proposal. Also, Multi-Year Accountability Agreements (MYAAs) are bilateral agreements signed by the executive heads of all publicly-supported colleges and universities and the government. The agreements outline the government's goals and commitments for access, quality and accountability, and the system-level measures and indicators that will be used to demonstrate clear and tangible results for the increased investment in postsecondary education.

Special provisions for recognition:

Recognition for university level studies: In general none. Universities establish their own admissions criteria and make their own admissions decisions in response to individual applications.

Additionally, the Canadian Information Centre for International Credentials (CICIC) provides information and guidance on the recognition of foreign studies.

For access to advanced studies and research: In general none.

For exercising a profession: In general, none. Both Canadians and non-Canadians who studied abroad have to meet specified educational, experience and language requirements, and usually pass registration examinations. The Comparative Education Service (CES) of the University of Toronto assesses foreign qualifications relating to numerous professions. Access to most professions is governed by provincial and/or federal statutes and is generally restricted to Canadian citizens or immigrants accepted as permanent residents. Applicants must also meet examination and/or practical training requirements set by the relevant professional body or provincial or federal licensing board.

PROVINCIAL BODIES

Ministry of Training, Colleges and Universities
Minister: John Milloy
Mowat Block / Edifice Mowat
900 Bay Street / 900, rue Bay
Toronto, Ontario M7A 1L2
Canada
Tel: +416 325 2929/ +800 387 5514
Fax: +416 325 6348
EMail: info@edu.gov.on.ca
WWW: http://www.edu.gov.on.ca/eng/tcu/
Role of national body: The Ministry of Training, Colleges and Universities is responsible for: developing policy directions for universities and colleges of applied arts and technology; planning and administering policies related to basic and applied research in this sector; authorizing universities to grant degrees; distributing funds allocated by the provincial legislature to colleges and universities; providing financial assistance programmes for post-secondary school students; defining courses of study at faculties of education; and registering private career colleges.

Council of Ontario Universities
President and CEO: Bonnie Patterson
Executive Director: Sharon Berman
180 Dundas St West
Suite 1100
Toronto, Ontario M5G 1Z8
Canada
Tel: +1(416) 979 2165 Ext. 221
Fax: +1(416) 979 8635
WWW: http://www.cou.on.ca/
Role of national body: The Council provides services to its University members and the community including research advocacy, communication and public affairs, and the central processing of university applications. The Council is comprised of Ontario University Presidents and is the primary advocacy group for the public university system.

Colleges Ontario
President and CEO: Linda Franklin
20 Bay Street, Suite 1600, Box 88

Toronto, ON M5J 2N8
Canada
Tel: +1(647) 258 7670
Fax: +1(647) 258 7699
EMail: savage@collegesontario.org
WWW: http://www.collegesontario.org/
Role of national body: Advocacy and marketing association of the 24 Colleges of Applied Arts and Technology of Ontario.

Data for academic year: 2008-2009
Source: IAU from the Canadian Information Centre for International Credentials (CICIC), a unit of the Council of Ministers of Education, Canada (CMEC), on behalf of the Province of Ontario, 2008. Credentials updated in 2010.

INSTITUTIONS

PUBLIC INSTITUTIONS

ALGONQUIN COLLEGE OF APPLIED ARTS AND TECHNOLOGY

1385 Woodroffe Avenue, Ottawa, Ontario K2G 1V8
Tel: +1(613) 727-4723
Fax: +1(613) 727-7684
EMail: AskAlgonquin@algonquincollege.com;
registrar@algonquincollege.com
Website: http://www.algonquincollege.com/
President: Robert C. Gillett

Centres
Career and Academic Access (Health Sciences)

Colleges
Algonquin *(Ottawa Valley)* (Administration; Arts and Humanities; Business Administration; Computer Science; Cooking and Catering; Forest Products; Nursing; Police Studies; Preschool Education; Social and Community Services)

Institutes
Algonquin College Heritage (Administration; Social Work); Language (English; Modern Languages); Police and Public Safety (Police Studies; Protective Services; Social and Community Services; Veterinary Science)

Schools
Advanced Technology (Aeronautical and Aerospace Engineering; Architecture; Biotechnology; Civil Engineering; Computer Engineering; Computer Science; Construction Engineering; Data Processing; Electrical Engineering; Information Technology; Mechanical Engineering; Microelectronics; Surveying and Mapping; Telecommunications Engineering; Water Management); Business (Accountancy; Administration; Business Administration; Finance; Human Resources; International Business; Law; Management; Marketing; Small Business); General Arts and Science (Communication Studies; Design; Environmental Studies; Health Sciences; Media Studies; Music; Nursing; Service Trades; Social and Community Services; Technology); Health and Community Studies (Dental Hygiene; Leisure Studies; Museum Studies; Nursing; Physical Therapy; Preschool Education; Respiratory Therapy; Social Work; Sports); Hospitality and Tourism (Cooking and Catering; Food Science; Hotel and Restaurant; Nutrition; Service Trades; Tourism); Media and Design (Advertising and Publicity; Graphic Design; Horticulture; Information Technology; Interior Design; Journalism; Media Studies; Multimedia; Music; Painting and Drawing; Photography; Public Relations; Radio and Television Broadcasting; Software Engineering; Theatre; Writing); Transportation and Building Trades (Automotive Engineering; Heating and Refrigeration; Maintenance Technology; Metal Techniques; Service Trades)

Further Information: Traditional and Open Learning Institution; Also Perth and Pembroke campuses.

Degrees and Diplomas: *Certificate/Diploma*; *Graduate Diploma/Certificate*. Bachelor's degree (professional), 4 yrs; Applied Bachelor's degree (professional), 4 yrs; Advanced Diploma, 3 yrs.
Last Updated: 03/12/10

ASSUMPTION UNIVERSITY (UNIVERSITY OF WINDSOR)

400 Huron Church Road, Windsor, Ontario N9B 3P4
Tel: +1(519) 973-7033
Fax: +1(519) 973-7089
EMail: cbertrand@assumptionu.ca
Website: http://www.assumptionu.ca
President and Vice-Chancellor: Paul J. Rennick
EMail: president@uwindsor.ca

Centres
Religion and Culture (Religion)

Departments
Theology (Pastoral Studies; Theology)

Programmes
Christian Culture Series (Christian Religious Studies)

History: Founded 1857 as Assumption College. Incorporated by an Act of the Parliament of Upper Canada, which received Royal Assent 1858. Affiliated with Western University (now the University of Western Ontario, London) 1919. Affiliated with Holy Names College 1934. Received university powers and ended the affiliation with the University of Western Ontario 1953. Acquired present name 1956. Accepted the Essex College as affiliated college 1954 and affiliated with Canterbury College 1957. Facilities and teaching faculty of Assumption University were integrated into the University of Windsor 1962. An independent University federated the University of Windsor since 1963.

Governing Bodies: Board of Governors; Senate; Board of Regents;

Degrees and Diplomas: *Master's Degree*
Last Updated: 28/01/11

BRESCIA UNIVERSITY COLLEGE (UNIVERSITY OF WESTERN ONTARIO)

1285 Western Road, London, Ontario N6G 1H2
Tel: +1(519) 432-8353
Fax: +1(519) 858-5137
EMail: brescia@uwo.ca
Website: http://www.brescia.uwo.ca/
Principal: Colleen Hanycz (2008-)
Tel: +1(519) 432-8353 Ext. 28263 EMail: chanycz@uwo.ca

Academic Dean: John Mitchell
Tel: +1(519) 432-8353 Ext. 28263 EMail: jbmitche@uwo.ca

International Relations: Christina Lord, International Student Program Coordinator
Tel: +1(519) 432-8353 Ext. 28012 EMail: clord3@uwo.ca

Divisions

Arts and Humanities (English; French; French Studies; Linguistics; Literature; Philosophy; Religious Education; Religious Studies); **Food and Nutritional Sciences** (Dietetics; Food Science; Food Technology; Nutrition); **Social Sciences** (Accountancy; Administration; Canadian Studies; Finance; History; Human Resources; Leadership; Management; Political Sciences; Psychology; Public Administration; Social Sciences); **Sociology and Family Studies** (Development Studies; Family Studies; Sociology)

Programmes

Graduate Studies (Food Science; Nutrition); **Health Sciences** (Health Sciences; Public Health); **Kinesiology** (Physical Therapy; Sports); **Pre-University** (Biology; Canadian Studies; Chemistry; English; French; Geography; Leadership; Mathematics; Religious Studies; Sociology; Spanish); **Scholar's Electives**

History: Founded 1919 as Brescia Hall. Became a separately incorporated not-for-profit corporation 2001. Acquired present title 2002.

Governing Bodies: Council of Trustees; College Council; Foundation Board.

Fees: (Canadian Dollar): Tuition fee, 6,234.35 (preliminary year and year 1) for Canadian and permanent residents; for International students, 10,674.35 in preliminary year and 17,325.35 in year 1.

International Co-operation: With institutions in the Netherlands, England and Barbados.

Degrees and Diplomas: *University Certificate/Diploma*: Community Development; *Bachelor's Degree*; *Master's Degree*

Student Residential Facilities: Students residence.

Academic Staff *2010-2011*	TOTAL
FULL-TIME	c. **70**

Student Numbers *2010-2011*	
All (Foreign Included)	**960**

Part-time students, 145.
Last Updated: 28/01/11

BROCK UNIVERSITY (BROCK U)

500 Glenridge Avenue, Saint Catharines, Ontario L2S 3A1
Tel: +1(905) 688-5550
Fax: +1(905) 688-2789
EMail: info@www.brocku.ca
Website: http://www.brocku.ca

President and Vice-Chancellor: Jack N. Lightstone
Tel: +1(905) 688-5550, Ext. 3333, Fax: +1(905) 688-1255
EMail: president@brocku.ca

Provost and Vice-President, Academic: Murray Knuttila
Tel: +1(905) 688-5550 Ext. 4121 EMail: mknuttila@brocku.ca

International Relations: John Kaethler, Director, International Services and Programs Abroad
Tel: +1(905) 688-5550 Ext. 3732 EMail: jkaethler@brocku.ca

Centres

Aboriginal Education and Research *(Tecumseh)* (Natives Education); **Digital Humanities** (Arts and Humanities; History; Literature; Modern Languages); **Healthy Development** (Physical Education; Sports); **Muscle Metabolism and Biophysics** (Biophysics; Physical Education; Public Health); **Sport Capacity** (Sports)

Faculties

Applied Health Sciences (Dental Hygiene; Health Sciences; Leisure Studies; Nursing; Parks and Recreation; Pharmacy; Physical Education; Physical Therapy; Public Health; Sports; Sports Management); **Business** (Accountancy; Administration; Business Administration; Management); **Education** (Adult Education; Education; Educational Sciences; Natives Education; Preschool Education; Teacher Training); **Graduate Studies** (Accountancy; Aesthetics; Ancient Civilizations; Applied Linguistics; Biological and Life Sciences; Biotechnology; Business Administration; Chemistry; Child Care and Development; Classical Languages; Comparative Literature; Computer Science; Cultural Studies; Earth Sciences; Economics; Education; Educational Sciences; English; Folklore; Geography; Greek (Classical); Health Sciences; History; Latin; Management; Mathematics; Philosophy; Physics; Political Sciences; Psychology; Rehabilitation and Therapy; Sociology; Statistics); **Humanities** (Aesthetics; Ancient Civilizations; Applied Linguistics; Art History; Arts and Humanities; Canadian Studies; Classical Languages; Communication Disorders; Comparative Literature; Computer Science; Cultural Studies; English; Fine Arts; Foreign Languages Education; French; French Studies; Greek (Classical); History; Italian; Latin; Latin American Studies; Literature; Medieval Studies; Modern History; Modern Languages; Multimedia; Music; Performing Arts; Philosophy; Portuguese; Spanish; Speech Therapy and Audiology; Theatre; Visual Arts; Writing); **Mathematics and Science** (Biochemistry; Biological and Life Sciences; Biomedicine; Biophysics; Biotechnology; Chemistry; Computer Networks; Computer Science; Earth Sciences; Education; Geology; Mathematics; Mathematics and Computer Science; Neurosciences; Oenology; Physics; Viticulture); **Social Sciences** (Child Care and Development; Communication Studies; Cultural Studies; Economics; Environmental Studies; Film; Folklore; Geography; Geography (Human); Information Technology; International Relations; Labour and Industrial Relations; Media Studies; Neurosciences; Philosophy; Political Sciences; Psychology; Public Administration; Public Law; Rehabilitation and Therapy; Social Psychology; Social Sciences; Sociology; Surveying and Mapping; Tourism; Women's Studies)

Institutes

Cool Climate Oenology and Viticulture (Oenology; Viticulture); **Electrophysiological Research** (Biological and Life Sciences; Physical Education; Physical Therapy; Psychology)

Research Centres

Lifespan Development *(Jack and Nora Walker)*; **Niagara Community Observatory** (Regional Studies)

Research Institutes

Humanities (Arts and Humanities); **Youth Studies** *(BRIYS)*

Further Information: Also Hamilton campus.

History: Founded 1964.

Governing Bodies: Board of Trustees comprising 21 lay members, 3 members of the Faculty, 3 students, 3 members of the permanent staff, the President and Vice-Chancellor and the Chancellor; Senate

Academic Year: Fall/Winter Session: September to April (September-December; January-April); Spring Session: May to June; Summer Session: July to August

Admission Requirements: Secondary school certificate or recognized foreign equivalent

Fees: (Can. Dollars): Undergraduate tuition, 5,404.30-6,209.30 per annum for Canadian students and 14,160.15 per annum for International students. Graduate tuition, 2,080.33-2,399.62 per term for Canadian students and 5,413.90-5,481.92 per term for International students.

Main Language(s) of Instruction: English

International Co-operation: With universities in Argentina; Australia; Austria; Bangladesh; Brazil; United Kingdom; China; Colombia; Cuba; Fiji; Finland; France; Germany; Ghana; India; Italy; Jamaica; Japan; Kenya; Republic of Korea; Malaysia; Malta; Martinique; Mauritius; Mexico; Netherlands; New Zealand; Nigeria; Pakistan; Philippines; Singapore; South Africa; Swaziland; Sweden; Switzerland; Tanzania; Thailand; Uganda; United States; Uruguay; Zimbabwe

Accrediting Agencies: Ministry of Training, Colleges and Universities of Ontario

Degrees and Diplomas: *University Certificate/Diploma*; *Bachelor's Degree*; *Bachelor's Degree - Honours*; *Master's Degree*; *Doctoral Degree*. Also Concurrent degrees in 5 yrs: Bachelor of Arts (Honours)/Bachelor of Education (Intermediate/Senior); Bachelor of Arts Child and Youth Studies (Honours)/Bachelor of Education (Primary/Junior); Bachelor of Arts - Integrated Studies (Honours)/Bachelor of Education (Junior/Intermediate); Bachelor of Physical Education (Honours)/Bachelor of Education (Intermediate/Senior); Bachelor of Physical Education (Honours)/Bachelor of Education (Junior/

Intermediate); Bachelor of Science (Honours)/Bachelor of Education (Intermediate/Senior); Bachelor of Science - Integrated Studies (Honours)/Bachelor of Education (Junior/Intermediate).

Student Services: Academic counselling, Canteen, Cultural centre, Employment services, Foreign student adviser, Foreign Studies Centre, Handicapped facilities, Health services, Language programs, Nursery care, Social counselling, Sports facilities

Student Residential Facilities: 6 residences with a total capacity of 2,389 beds.

Special Facilities: David S. Howes Theatre; Sean O'Sullivan Theatre; Art Gallery

Libraries: 2,194,400 vols

Publications: Research Directory *(biennially)*; Surgite *(quarterly)*

Press or Publishing House: Block Press

Academic Staff 2010-2011	MEN	WOMEN	TOTAL
FULL-TIME	–	–	**583**
Student Numbers 2010-2011			
All (Foreign Included)	7,508	10,369	**17,877**

Last Updated: 28/01/11

CARLETON UNIVERSITY (CU)

1125 Colonel By Drive, Ottawa, Ontario K1S 5B6
Tel: +1(613) 520-7400
Fax: +1(613) 520-7858
EMail: info@carleton.ca
Website: http://www.carleton.ca

President and Vice-Chancellor: Roseann O'Reilly Runte (2008-)
Tel: +1(613) 520-3801, Fax: +1(613) 520-4474
EMail: presidents_office@carleton.ca

Provost and Vice-President (Academic): Peter Ricketts
Tel: +1(613) 520-3806, Fax: +1(613) 520-2536
EMail: provost@carleton.ca

International Relations: Kimberly Matheson, Vice-President (Research and International)
Tel: +1(613) 520-3570, Fax: +1(613) 520-3945
EMail: vpri@carleton.ca

Centres

Community Innovation *(3CI)*; **Conflict Education and Research** *(CCER)* (Peace and Disarmament); **European Studies** *(CES)* (European Studies); **Indigenous Research, Culture, Language and Education** *(CIRCLE)* (Indigenous Studies); **Intelligence and Security Studies** *(CCISS)* (Protective Services); **International Migration and Settlement Studies** (Demography and Population); **Public History** *(CCPH)* (History); **Research and Education on Women and Work** *(CREWW)* (Education); **Security and Defence Studies** *(CSDS)* (Military Science); **Social and Cultural Analysis** *(Duncombe)* (Cultural Studies; Social Studies); **Study of Stress Processes and Stress Management** (Health Sciences); **Survey** *(CUSC)*; **Trade Policy and Law** *(CTPL)* (Law); **Transnational Cultural Analysis** *(CTCA)* (Cultural Studies); **Treaty Compliance** *(CCTC)*; **Values and Ethics** *(COVE)* (Ethics); **Visualization and Simulation** *(VSIM)*; **Voluntary Sector Research and Development** *(CVSRD)*

Faculties

Arts and Social Sciences (African Studies; Ancient Civilizations; Anthropology; Applied Linguistics; Arabic; Art History; Arts and Humanities; Canadian Studies; Child Care and Development; Chinese; Classical Languages; Cognitive Sciences; Communication Studies; Comparative Literature; Cultural Studies; Education; English; Environmental Studies; Film; Folklore; Foreign Languages Education; French; Gender Studies; Geography; German; Greek (Classical); Hebrew; History; Human Rights; Italian; Japanese; Jazz and Popular Music; Latin; Linguistics; Literature; Modern Languages; Music; Natives Education; Philosophy; Portuguese; Psychology; Religion; Russian; Social Problems; Sociology; Spanish; Surveying and Mapping; Women's Studies); **Engineering and Design** (Aeronautical and Aerospace Engineering; Architecture; Biomedical Engineering; Civil Engineering; Computer Engineering; Design; Electrical Engineering; Electronic Engineering; Energy Engineering; Engineering; Engineering Management; Environmental Engineering; Industrial Design; Information Technology; Materials Engineering; Mechanical Engineering; Software Engi-

neering; Telecommunications Engineering; Town Planning); **Graduate and Postdoctoral Affairs** (Aeronautical and Aerospace Engineering; Anthropology; Applied Linguistics; Applied Mathematics; Architecture; Art History; Biology; Biomedical Engineering; Business Administration; Canadian Studies; Chemistry; Civil Engineering; Cognitive Sciences; Communication Studies; Computer Engineering; Computer Science; Cultural Studies; Earth Sciences; Economics; Electrical and Electronic Engineering; Electrical Engineering; Energy Engineering; Engineering Management; English; Environmental Engineering; Environmental Studies; European Studies; Film; French; Gender Studies; Geography; Health Administration; History; Industrial Design; International Studies; Journalism; Law; Management; Materials Engineering; Mathematics; Mechanical Engineering; Music; Neurosciences; Peace and Disarmament; Philosophy; Physics; Political Sciences; Psychology; Public Administration; Religion; Russian; Social Work; Sociology; Statistics; Welfare and Protective Services; Women's Studies); **Public Affairs** (Asian Studies; Communication Studies; Criminal Law; Criminology; Economics; European Studies; Journalism; Law; Political Sciences; Public Administration; Russian; Social Work); **Science** (Biochemistry; Biological and Life Sciences; Biology; Business Computing; Chemistry; Computer Networks; Computer Science; Earth Sciences; Environmental Studies; Ethics; Forensic Medicine and Dentistry; Health Sciences; Information Sciences; Information Technology; Mathematics; Natural Sciences; Neurosciences; Physics; Software Engineering; Statistics; Technology)

Groups
Real Time and Distributed Systems

Institutes
Ottawa Medical Physics *(OMPI)*

Research Centres
Broadband Communications and Wireless Systems *(BCWS)* (Telecommunications Engineering); **Carleton Immersive Media Studio** *(CIMS)* (Media Studies); **Geomatics and Cartographic** *(GCRC)* (Surveying and Mapping); **Sustainable Energy** *(CSERC)* (Energy Engineering); **Technology Innovation** (Technology)

Research Institutes
Ottawa-Carleton Bridge *(OCBRI)*

Research Units
Innovation, Science and Environment Policy *(CRUISE)*

Schools
Business *(Sprott)* (Accountancy; Business Administration; Business and Commerce; Engineering Management; Finance; Information Sciences; International Business; Management; Marketing)

Further Information: Also a number of Study Abroad programmes as part of student/faculty exchange programmes. Contact Carleton International for further information

History: Founded 1942, incorporated as Ottawa Association for the Advancement of Learning, 1943, and reorganized as Carleton College 1952. Acquired present status and title 1957.

Governing Bodies: Board of Governors

Academic Year: September to May (September-December; January-May). Also Summer Session (May-August)

Admission Requirements: Secondary school certificate or recognized foreign equivalent

Fees: (Can. Dollars): Undegraduate tuition, 5,967.35-8,509.35 for Canadian students and 16,857.35-19,681.35 per annum for International students; Graduate tuition, 2,303.16-3,912.16 per term for Canadian students and 5,121.16-8,560.16 per term for International students.

Main Language(s) of Instruction: English

Degrees and Diplomas: *University Certificate/Diploma*; *Bachelor's Degree*; *Bachelor's Degree - Honours*; *Master's Degree*; *Doctoral Degree (PhD)*. Some Master's and Doctorates degree are offered through an Ottawa-Carleton Joint Institute.

Student Services: Academic counselling, Canteen, Cultural centre, Employment services, Foreign student adviser, Handicapped facilities, Health services, Language programs, Nursery care, Social counselling, Sports facilities

Student Residential Facilities: Residence with a 2,873 beds capacity

Special Facilities: Art Gallery. Radio and Television Broadcasting Facilities. Campus Radio Station

Libraries: c. 3m.vols, periodicals, government documents, maps, newspapers, musical scores, compact discs, microforms, archives and rare books

Press or Publishing House: Carleton University Press

Academic Staff *2009-2010*	TOTAL
FULL-TIME	849

Student Numbers *2009-2010*
All (Foreign Included) — 25,262

Part-time students, 5,021.
Last Updated: 28/01/11

CENTENNIAL COLLEGE OF APPLIED ARTS AND TECHNOLOGY

P.O. Box 631, Station A, Toronto, Ontario M1K 5E9
Tel: +1(416) 289-5000
Fax: +1(416) 439-7358
EMail: success@centennialcollege.ca
Website: http://www.centennialcollege.ca/

President: Ann Buller (2004-)
Tel: +1(416) 289-5289 EMail: ABuller@centennialcollege.ca

Schools
Advancement (Arts and Humanities; Biology; Chemistry; English; Logic; Mathematics; Natural Sciences; Social Sciences); **Business** (Accountancy; Administration; Business Administration; Finance; Human Resources; International Business; Law; Marketing); **Communications, Media and Design** (Advertising and Publicity; Design; Film; Fine Arts; Journalism; Media Studies; Radio and Television Broadcasting); **Community and Health Studies** (Child Care and Development; Food Science; Health Sciences; Leisure Studies; Nursing; Nutrition; Occupational Therapy; Paramedical Sciences; Pharmacy; Physical Therapy; Preschool Education; Social and Community Services; Social Work); **Continuing Education at Centennial College** (Accountancy; Administration; Adult Education; Aesthetics; Automotive Engineering; Behavioural Sciences; Business Administration; Business Computing; Chinese; Computer Networks; Computer Science; Data Processing; Design; Education; Electrical Engineering; English; Finance; Food Science; Foreign Languages Education; French; French Studies; Gerontology; Health Administration; Human Resources; Information Technology; Insurance; International Business; Labour and Industrial Relations; Law; Leadership; Management; Marketing; Mechanics; Nursing; Oncology; Ophthalmology; Paramedical Sciences; Preschool Education; Psychology; Public Relations; Real Estate; Rehabilitation and Therapy; Safety Engineering; Sales Techniques; Small Business; Software Engineering; Spanish; Technology; Toxicology; Translation and Interpretation; Transport Management; Writing); **Engineering Technology and Applied Science** *(SETAS)* (Architecture; Automation and Control Engineering; Biomedical Engineering; Biotechnology; Computer Engineering; Computer Networks; Design; Electrical Engineering; Electronic Engineering; Energy Engineering; Environmental Engineering; Heating and Refrigeration; Industrial Engineering; Laboratory Techniques; Maintenance Technology; Mechanical Engineering; Microbiology; Robotics; Software Engineering); **Hospitality, Tourism and Culture** (Cooking and Catering; Hotel Management; Tourism); **Transportation** (Air Transport; Automotive Engineering; Maintenance Technology; Mechanics; Road Transport; Safety Engineering; Transport and Communications; Transport Management)

History: Founded 1966.

Fees: (Canadian Dollar): Post-Secondary Programs, c. 2,320 for two semesters for domestic students and c. 10,400 for two semesters for International students. Bachelor of Science in Nursing (BScN), c. 5,300 for two semesters for domestic students and c. 16,160 for two semesters for International students. Applied Degree Programmes, 5,710-6,394.50 for two semesters for domestic students and c. 14,375 for two semesters for International students.

Degrees and Diplomas: *Certificate/Diploma*; *Graduate Diploma/Certificate*. Applied Bachelor's degree (professional), 4 yrs; Applied Bachelor's degree, 4yrs; College Advanced Diploma, 3 yrs.

Student Numbers *2009-2010*: Total 14,400
Last Updated: 06/12/10

CONESTOGA COLLEGE INSTITUTE OF TECHNOLOGY AND ADVANCED LEARNING

299 Doon Valley Drive, Kitchener, Ontario N2G 4M4
Tel: +1(519) 748-5220
Fax: +1(519) 748-3505
EMail: geninfo@conestogac.on.ca
Website: http://www.conestogac.on.ca/

President: John Tibbits
Tel: +1(519) 748-5220 Ext. 3500 EMail: jtibbits@conestogac.on.ca

Institutes
Language *(Conestoga Language)* (English)

Programmes
Postgraduate Studies (Accountancy; Computer Science; Environmental Engineering; Finance; Human Resources; Information Management; Information Technology; Journalism; Management; Marketing; Media Studies; Paramedical Sciences; Police Studies; Preschool Education; Public Relations; Wood Technology)

Schools
Business and Hospitality (Accountancy; Administration; Business Administration; Cooking and Catering; Finance; Health Administration; Hotel and Restaurant; Insurance; International Business; Management; Marketing; Public Administration; Retailing and Wholesaling; Service Trades; Social and Community Services; Tourism); **Career and Academic Access**; **Engineering and Information Technology** (Architecture; Automation and Control Engineering; Business Administration; Civil Engineering; Computer Engineering; Computer Networks; Computer Science; Construction Engineering; Design; Electrical Engineering; Electronic Engineering; Energy Engineering; Environmental Engineering; Information Technology; Interior Design; Mechanical Engineering; Media Studies; Metal Techniques; Robotics; Software Engineering; Technology; Telecommunications Engineering; Wood Technology); **Health and Life Sciences and Community Services** (Biotechnology; Computer Science; Criminal Law; Dietetics; Fire Science; Health Sciences; Law; Leisure Studies; Nursing; Occupational Therapy; Paramedical Sciences; Police Studies; Preschool Education; Respiratory Therapy; Social and Community Services; Social Work; Sports); **Liberal Studies** (Air Transport; Applied Mathematics; Arts and Humanities; Behavioural Sciences; Social Sciences); **Media and Design** (Advertising and Publicity; Communication Studies; Design; Graphic Design; Interior Design; Journalism; Marketing; Media Studies; Public Relations; Radio and Television Broadcasting; Visual Arts); **Trades and Apprenticeship** (Automotive Engineering; Construction Engineering; Cooking and Catering; Electrical Engineering; Maintenance Technology; Mechanical Engineering; Metal Techniques; Power Engineering)

Further Information: Also Guelph, Waterloo, Stratford, Cambridge and Ingersoll campuses.

History: Founded 1967.

Fees: (Canadian Dollar): Tuition Fees for local students, 2,300-9,720 for two semesters; International Student Tuition, 9,800-12,500 for two semesters.

Degrees and Diplomas: *Certificate/Diploma*; *Bachelor's Degree*. Applied Bachelor's degree (professional), 4 yrs; Bachelor's degree (profeesional) in Nursing, 4 yrs; Advanced College Diploma,

Student Numbers *2009-2010*: Total 8,500
Part-time students, 38,000.
Last Updated: 06/12/10

CONRAD GREBEL COLLEGE (UNIVERSITY OF WATERLOO)

140 Westmount Road North, Waterloo, Ontario N2L 3G6
Tel: +1(519) 885-0220
Fax: +1(519) 885-0014
EMail: congreb@uwaterloo.ca
Website: http://www.grebel.uwaterloo.ca

President: Henry Paetkau
Tel: +1(519) 885-0220, Ext.237 EMail: cgcpres@uwaterloo.ca

Courses
Arts/Fine Arts (Arts and Humanities; Film; Fine Arts; Folklore); **English** (English; Literature); **History** (History; History of Religion);

Peace and Conflict Studies (Peace and Disarmament); **Philosophy** (Ethics; Philosophy); **Religious Studies** (Bible; Christian Religious Studies; History of Religion; Holy Writings; Peace and Disarmament; Religious Music; Religious Studies; Theology); **Sociology** (Sociology)

Departments
Music (Conducting; Music; Music Theory and Composition; Opera)

Programmes
Continuing Education (Peace and Disarmament; Religious Studies); **Mennonite Studies** (Christian Religious Studies; History; Literature; Peace and Disarmament; Theology); **Theological Studies** (Bible; Catholic Theology; History of Religion; Theology)

Degrees and Diplomas: *University Certificate/Diploma*; *Bachelor's Degree*; *Master's Degree*: Theological Studies (MTS). Also Honours Bachelor's degree in Peace and Conflict Studies.
Last Updated: 31/01/11

DOMINICAN UNIVERSITY COLLEGE
Collège universitaire dominicain
96, Empress Avenue, Ottawa, Ontario K1R 7G3
Tel: +1(613) 233-5696
Fax: +1(613) 233-6064
EMail: info@dominicancollege.ca
Website: http://www.collegedominicain.ca

President: Gabor Csepregi
Tel: +1(613) 233-5696 poste 319, Fax: +1(613) 233-6064
EMail: gabor.csepregi@collegedominicain.ca

Vice-President: Maxime Allard
Tel: +1(613) 233-5696 poste 313
EMail: maxime.allard@collegedominicain.ca

Registrar: Hervé Tremblay
Tel: +1(613) 233-5696, Fax: +1(613) 233-6064
EMail: registraire@collegedominicain.ca

Faculties
Philosophy (Philosophy); **Theology** (Theology)

Institutes
Pastoral Theology (Pastoral Studies; Theology) *Head*: R.P. Daniel Cadrin

History: Founded 1967, previously established 1900 as 'Studium Generale' of the Order of Friars Preachers in Canada. A private university institution incorporated in the Province of Ontario since 1909. Previously known as the Collège Dominicain de Philosophie et de Théologie (Dominican College of Philosophy and Theology).

Governing Bodies: Conseil académique; Conseil d'administration

Academic Year: September to April (September-December; January-April). Also Summer Session (July)

Admission Requirements: 1 yr study in a Faculty of Arts of a recognized university, or foreign equivalent

Fees: (Can. Dollars): Undergraduate tuition, 1,715 per semester for Canadian students and 2,250 per semester for International students. Graduate tuition, 1,860 per semester for Canadian. Full-time students who are not Canadian citizens or landed immigrants must pay fees of 2,500 per year, additional to the above mentioned fees.

Main Language(s) of Instruction: French, English

Degrees and Diplomas: *University Certificate/Diploma*; *Bachelor's Degree*; *Master's Degree*; *Doctoral Degree (PhD)*

Student Residential Facilities: For c. 20 students

Libraries: c. 130,000 vols

Publications: Koinônia, Bulletin *(annually)*
Last Updated: 31/01/11

EMMANUEL COLLEGE OF VICTORIA UNIVERSITY (UNIVERSITY OF TORONTO)
75 Queen's Park Crescent, Toronto, Ontario M5S 1K7
Tel: +1(416) 585-4539
Fax: +1(416) 585-4516
EMail: ec.office@utoronto.ca
Website: http://www.emmanuel.utoronto.ca/

Principal: Mark G. Toulouse
Tel: +1(416) 585-4541, Fax: +1(416) 585-4516
EMail: m.toulouse@utoronto.ca

Programmes
Community and Health Ministries (Health Sciences); **Divinity** (Religion); **Muslim Studies** (Islamic Studies); **Pastoral Studies** (Pastoral Studies); **Religious Education** (Religious Education); **Sacred Music** (Religious Music); **Theology** (Theology)

History: Founded 1928 as Union College united with the Faculty of Theology of Victoria University.

Governing Bodies: Senate; Board of Regents.

Fees: (Canadian Dollar): Basic degree tuition, 2,074-3,111 per annum for Canadian students and 5,572-8,358 per annum for International students. Advanced degree tuition fee, 2,043-9,197 per annum for Canadian students and per annum 4,180-13,938 for International students.

Accrediting Agencies: Association of Theological Schools (ATS).

Degrees and Diplomas: *Certificate/Diploma*; *Master's Degree*; *Doctoral Degree*
Last Updated: 31/01/11

FANSHAWE COLLEGE OF APPLIED ARTS AND TECHNOLOGY
P.O. Box 7005, 1460 Oxford Street East, London, Ontario N5Y 5R6
Tel: +1(519) 452-4430
Fax: +1(519) 452-4420
EMail: registrar@fanshawec.on.ca
Website: http://www.fanshawec.on.ca/

President: Howard R. Rundle (1995-) Tel: +1(519) 452-4200

Schools
Applied Science and Technology (Biotechnology; Electrical Engineering; Electronic Engineering; Environmental Engineering; Heating and Refrigeration; Industrial Engineering; Laboratory Techniques; Mechanical Engineering; Metal Techniques; Technology); **Building Technology** (Architecture; Building Technologies; Civil Engineering; Construction Engineering; Technology); **Business** *(Lawrence Kinlin)* (Accountancy; Business Administration; Communication Studies; Finance; Health Administration; Human Resources; Insurance; International Business; Law; Leadership; Management; Marketing; Public Relations); **Contemporary Media** (Communication Studies; Film; Fine Arts; Journalism; Media Studies; Multimedia; Photography; Public Relations; Radio and Television Broadcasting; Theatre); **Design** (Fashion Design; Graphic Design; Horticulture; Interior Design; Landscape Architecture; Marketing; Surveying and Mapping; Town Planning); **Health Sciences and Nursing** (Anaesthesiology; Dental Hygiene; Dentistry; Health Sciences; Nursing; Paramedical Sciences; Pharmacy; Respiratory Therapy; Sports; Treatment Techniques); **Human Services** (Behavioural Sciences; Child Care and Development; Development Studies; Law; Leadership; Leisure Studies; Police Studies; Preschool Education; Protective Services; Social Work); **Information Technology** (Administration; Business Administration; Computer Science; Information Management; Law; Software Engineering); **Language and Liberal Studies** (Accountancy; Administration; Agricultural Equipment; Anaesthesiology; Architecture; Automotive Engineering; Behavioural Sciences; Biotechnology; Business Administration; Business Computing; Child Care and Development; Cinema and Television; Civil Engineering; Communication Studies; Computer Science; Construction Engineering; Cooking and Catering; Dental Hygiene; Dentistry; Development Studies; Electrical Engineering; Electronic Engineering; English; Environmental Engineering; Fashion Design; Film; Finance; Fine Arts; Food Science; Graphic Design; Health Sciences; Heating and Refrigeration; Horticulture; Hotel Management; Human Resources; Industrial Engineering; Information Management; Information Sciences; Insurance; Interior Design; International Business; Journalism; Laboratory Techniques; Landscape Architecture; Law; Leadership; Leisure Studies; Maintenance Technology; Management; Marketing; Mechanical Engineering; Media Studies; Medical Technology; Metal Techniques; Multimedia; Nursing; Nutrition; Paramedical

Sciences; Pharmacy; Photography; Police Studies; Power Engineering; Preschool Education; Public Relations; Radio and Television Broadcasting; Respiratory Therapy; Service Trades; Social Work; Sports; Surveying and Mapping; Technology; Telecommunications Engineering; Theatre; Tourism; Town Planning); **Motive Power Technology** (Agricultural Equipment; Automotive Engineering; Maintenance Technology; Technology); **Tourism and Hospitality** (Cooking and Catering; Hotel and Restaurant; Hotel Management; Nutrition; Tourism)

Further Information: Also James N. Allan Campus, St. Thomas/ Elgin Campus, Strathroy Centre, Woodstock Campus, Tillsonburg Centre.

Fees: (Canadian Dollar): year one, 3,225.82; year two, 3,214.56; year three and above, 3,198.68. For International students, 12,411.54 per annum.

Degrees and Diplomas: *Certificate/Diploma; Graduate Diploma/ Certificate.* Applied Bachelor's degree (professional), 4 yrs; College Advanced Diploma, 3 yrs.
Last Updated: 07/12/10

GEORGE BROWN COLLEGE OF APPLIED ARTS AND TECHNOLOGY (GBC)

P.O. Box 1015, Station B, Toronto, Ontario M5T 2T9
Tel: +1(416) 415-2000
Fax: +1(416) 415-4993
EMail: info@gbrownc.on.ca
Website: http://www.gbrownc.on.ca/

President: Anne Sado
Tel: +1(416) 415-5000 Ext. 4471, Fax: +1(416) 415-4641
EMail: asado@georgebrown.ca

Centres
Arts and Design (Dance; Design; Fashion Design; Jewelry Art; Performing Arts; Theatre); **Business** (Accountancy; Business Administration; Finance; Human Resources; International Business; Management; Marketing; Sports Management) **Community Services and Early Childhood** (Preschool Education; Social and Community Services; Special Education); **Construction and Engineering Technologies** (Architecture; Computer Engineering; Construction Engineering; Mechanical Engineering); **Continuous Learning** (Arabic; Business Administration; Chinese; Communication Studies; Computer Science; Cooking and Catering; Cosmetology; Electronic Engineering; English; Fashion Design; Film; French; German; Greek; Health Sciences; Hotel and Restaurant; Information Technology; Interior Design; Italian; Japanese; Jewelry Art; Management; Mechanical Engineering; Nursing; Photography; Portuguese; Protective Services; Russian; Service Trades; Social and Community Services; Spanish; Technology; Transport Management; Visual Arts); **Health Sciences** (Dental Hygiene; Dental Technology; Dentistry; Health Administration; Health Sciences; Medical Technology; Nursing); **Hospitality and Culinary Arts** (Cooking and Catering; Hotel and Restaurant; Tourism); **International and Immigrant Education** (Educational and Student Counselling; English; Teacher Training); **Preparatory and Liberal Studies** (Arts and Humanities; Cooking and Catering; Health Sciences; Hotel and Restaurant; Natural Sciences; Social and Community Services; Special Education)

Further Information: Traditional and Open Learning Institution

History: Founded 1967.

Fees: (Canadian Dollars): undegraduate diploma/certificate, 562-15,419; postgraduate degree, 3,237-14,213; Degree, 7,050-7,080.

Degrees and Diplomas: *Certificate/Diploma; Graduate Diploma/ Certificate.* Applied Bachelor's degree (professional), 4 yrs; Postgraduate programme, 1-4 semesters.

Academic Staff *2010-2011*	**TOTAL**
FULL-TIME	1,216
PART-TIME	1,862
Student Numbers *2010-2011*	
All (Foreign Included)	70,956
FOREIGN ONLY	2,070

Last Updated: 07/12/10

GEORGIAN COLLEGE OF APPLIED ARTS AND TECHNOLOGY

1 Georgian Drive, Barrie, Ontario L4M 3X9
Tel: +1(705) 728-1968
Fax: +1(705) 722-5123
EMail: inquire@georgianc.on.ca
Website: http://www.georgianc.on.ca/

President: Brian Tamblyn
Tel: +1(705) 728-1968 Ext. 1248, Fax: +1(705) 722-1559
EMail: btamblyn@georgianc.on.ca; lmcphee@georgianc.on.ca

Programmes
Aboriginal Studies (Development Studies; Natives Education); **Automotive Studies** (Business Administration; Management; Marketing; Mechanical Engineering); **Aviation Studies** (Air Transport); **Business Studies** (Accountancy; Administration; Advertising and Publicity; Air Transport; Business Administration; Hotel Management; Human Resources; International Business; Law; Management; Marketing; Tourism); **Community Studies** (Administration; Child Care and Development; Dental Hygiene; Dentistry; Development Studies; Environmental Engineering; Justice Administration; Natives Education; Paramedical Sciences; Physical Therapy; Police Studies; Preschool Education; Social Work; Technology; Toxicology; Veterinary Science); **Computer Studies** (Computer Engineering; Computer Networks; Computer Science); **Design and Visual Art Studies** (Advertising and Publicity; Design; Fine Arts; Graphic Design; Interior Design; Jewelry Art; Photography; Visual Arts); **Health Studies** (Communication Disorders; Dental Hygiene; Dentistry; Health Administration; Health Sciences; Nursing; Optometry; Paramedical Sciences; Physical Therapy; Toxicology; Veterinary Science); **Hospitality, Tourism and Recreation Studies** (Cooking and Catering; Hotel Management; Leisure Studies; Management; Tourism); **Skilled Trades and Apprenticeships** (Heating and Refrigeration; Maintenance Technology; Mechanics; Metal Techniques; Service Trades; Technology); **Social Sciences and Humanities** (Anthropology; Arts and Humanities; Gerontology; History; Law; Political Sciences; Psychology; Social Sciences; Social Work; Sociology); **Transportation Studies** (Business Administration; Marine Engineering; Marketing; Mechanical Engineering); **University and Graduate Studies** (Business Administration; Communication Disorders; Computer Networks; Human Resources; International Business; Jewelry Art; Management; Nursing; Paramedical Sciences; Police Studies; Rehabilitation and Therapy; Social Work; Toxicology)

Schools
Engineering Technology (Architecture; Automation and Control Engineering; Automotive Engineering; Civil Engineering; Electrical Engineering; Marine Engineering; Mechanical Engineering; Power Engineering; Service Trades; Technology); **Environmental Studies** (Environmental Engineering; Environmental Studies)

Further Information: Also Orillia and Owen Sound Campuses.

Fees: (Canadian Dollar): Domestic students, 1,470.90-5,312.14; International students, 4,598.97-9,410.65.

Degrees and Diplomas: *University Certificate/Diploma.* Bachelor's degree (professional), 4 yrs, offered in association with Laurentian University; Applied Bachelor's degree (professional), 4 yrs; Bachelor's degree in Nursing in association with Georgian College/York University; Postgraduate diplomas, 1-2 yrs following a two-year college diploma or university degree.
Last Updated: 07/12/10

HUMBER COLLEGE INSTITUTE OF TECHNOLOGY AND ADVANCED LEARNING

205 Humber College Boulevard, Etobicoke, Ontario M9W 5L7
Tel: +1(416) 675-3111
Fax: +1(416) 675-2427
EMail: enquiry@humber.ca
Website: http://www.humber.ca/

President: John Davies Tel: +1(416) 675-6622 Ext. 4853

Schools
Applied Technology (Civil Engineering; Computer Engineering; Computer Networks; Design; Electrical Engineering; Electronic Engineering; Heating and Refrigeration; Horticulture; Industrial Design; Interior Design; Landscape Architecture; Maintenance

Technology; Management; Mechanical Engineering; Service Trades; Telecommunications Engineering); **Business** (Accountancy; Business Administration; Cosmetology; E-Business/Commerce; Finance; Human Resources; International Business; Law; Management; Marketing; Public Administration; Tourism); **Creative and Performing Arts** (Acting; Jazz and Popular Music; Music; Publishing and Book Trade; Theatre; Writing); **Health Sciences** (Health Sciences; Medicine; Nursing; Occupational Health; Paramedical Sciences; Pharmacy; Preschool Education); **Hospitality, Recreation and Tourism** (Cooking and Catering; Hotel Management; Leisure Studies; Nutrition; Physical Therapy; Sports; Sports Management; Tourism); **Liberal Arts and Sciences** (Arts and Humanities; English); **Media Studies and Information Technology** (Advertising and Publicity; Computer Graphics; Film; Graphic Design; Information Technology; Journalism; Media Studies; Multimedia; Photography; Public Relations; Radio and Television Broadcasting; Visual Arts); **Social and Community Services** (Child Care and Development; Criminal Law; Police Studies; Social and Community Services)

Further Information: Traditional and Open Learning Institution. Also Humber Lakeshore and Humber Orangeville Campuses.

History: Founded 1967. Acquired present status 2003.

Fees: (Canadian Dollar): For Domestic Students, Total Fee Allocation, 873.48 per two semesters; For International Students, Tuition Costs 11,730 per two semesters.

Degrees and Diplomas: *University Certificate/Diploma*; *Graduate Diploma/Certificate.* Applied Bachelor's degree (professional), 4 yrs; Bachelor's degree (professional), 4yrs; Bachelor's degree in Nursing in collaboration with the University of New Brunswick, 4 yrs; Advanced Diplomas, 6 semesters.

Student Numbers *2010-2011*: Total: c. 22,000
Part-time students, 56,000.
Last Updated: 07/12/10

HUNTINGTON UNIVERSITY (LAURENTIAN UNIVERSITY)

935 Ramsey Lake Road, Sudbury, Ontario P3E 2C6
Tel: +1(705) 673-4126 +1(800) 461-6366
Fax: +1(705) 673-6917
EMail: bchristiansen@laurentian.ca
Website: http://www.huntington.laurentian.ca

President - Principal: Kevin McCormick
Tel: +1(705) 673-4126, Ext.209
EMail: kmccormick@huntingtonu.ca

Registrar, Executive Assistant and Secretary to the Board of Regents: Karen McBain EMail: kmcbain@huntingtonu.ca

Centres
Holistic Health; **Study of Research in Gerontology** (Gerontology); **Teaching and Learning** *(Lougheed)*

Programmes
Communication Studies (Communication Studies; Mass Communication); **Ethics** (Ethics; Philosophy; Religious Studies); **Gerontology** (Gerontology); **Graduate Studies** (Pastoral Studies); **Religious Studies** (Christian Religious Studies; Religion; Religious Studies); **Theology** (Theology)

History: Founded 1960.

Fees: (Canadian Dollar): undergraduate tuition fee for Canadian students, 5,090-5,286 for 30-credits (with the exception of Engineering 5,523-5,736); for International students, 12,509-16,440 for 36 credits. EAP (English Academic Preparation), 3,500 per term. Graduate tuition fee for Canadian students, 1,509-2,924 per semester; for International students, 2,600-5,387 per semester.

Degrees and Diplomas: *University Certificate/Diploma*: Ethics; *Bachelor's Degree*; *Master's Degree*: Pastoral Counselling. Also Honours Bachelor's degree in Communication Studies, 4 yrs.

Student Residential Facilities: Student residence.

Libraries: J.W. Tate library.

Student Numbers *2010-2011*: Total 2,300
Last Updated: 31/01/11

HURON UNIVERSITY COLLEGE (UNIVERSITY OF WESTERN ONTARIO) (HURON)

1349 Western Road, London, Ontario N6G 1H3
Tel: +1(519) 438-7224
Fax: +1(519) 438-3938
EMail: huron@uwo.ca
Website: http://www.huronuc.ca/

Interim Principal: Trish Fulton (2010-)
Tel: +1(519) 438-7224 Ext. 237, Fax: +1(519) 438-9981
EMail: tfulton@huron.uwo.ca

Registrar: Bonnie Crocker
Tel: +1(519) 438-7224 Ext. 285, Fax: +1(519) 438-3938
EMail: bcrocke2@huron.uwo.ca

International Relations: Theresa Hyland
Tel: +1(519) 438-7224 Ext. 317, Fax: +1(519) 438-3938
EMail: thyland@huron.uwo.ca

Faculties
Arts and Social Science (Accountancy; Administration; Asian Studies; Business Administration; Chinese; Economics; English; Finance; French; French Studies; History; Human Resources; International Studies; Japanese; Jewish Studies; Management; Mathematics; Philosophy; Political Sciences; Psychology; Religion; Sociology; Writing); **Theology** (Religious Studies; Theology)

Programmes
Non-Degree Studies (Theology)

History: Founded 1863 as Huron College. An affiliated institution of The University of Western Ontario. Acquired present status and title 2000.

Governing Bodies: Executive Board; Academic Council

Academic Year: September to May (September-December; January-May)

Fees: (Can. Dollars): Arts and Social Science, 5,196 per annum (Full-time Cdn); International Students, 14,084 per annum; Theology, 5,226 (Full-time Cdn); International Students, 14,114

Main Language(s) of Instruction: English

International Co-operation: With universities in Belize, France, Hong Kong, Japan, Republic of Korea, Malta, Mexico, Norway, Singapore, Sweden, United Kingdom and China

Degrees and Diplomas: *Bachelor's Degree*; *Master's Degree*. Also Honours Bachelor's degree, 4 yrs; Honors Bachelor in Business Administration (HBA) with Honors Specialization in Global Development studies/Globalization Studies/Global Culture Studies, 5 yrs.

Student Services: Academic counselling, Canteen, Cultural centre, Employment services, Foreign student adviser, Foreign Studies Centre, Health services, Language programs, Sports facilities

Student Residential Facilities: 3 residence buildings and 6 residence houses

Libraries: Huron University College Library (c. 165,000 vols). Access to all libraries at the University of Western Ontario.

Student Numbers *2009-2010*: Total 1,300

Note: I
Last Updated: 31/01/11

KNOX COLLEGE (UNIVERSITY OF TORONTO)

59 St. George Street, Toronto, Ontario M5S 2E6
Tel: +1(416) 978-4500
Fax: +1(416) 971-2133
EMail: knox.college@utoronto.ca
Website: http://www.utoronto.ca/knox/

Principal: J. Dorcas Gordon
Tel: +1(416) 978-4503 EMail: jd.gordon@utoronto.ca

Centres
Lay Education *(Ewart)* (Bible; Christian Religious Studies; Korean; Religious Education)

Programmes
Advanced Degree (Bible; History of Religion; Pastoral Studies; Theology); **Christian Faith and Life** (Bible; Christian Religious

Studies; New Testament; Religion; Religious Education; Theology); **Continuing Education** (Theology); **Divinity** (Bible; Christian Religious Studies; Theology); **Online Education** (Theology); **Religious Education** (Religious Education); **Theological Studies** (Theology)

History: Founded 1844. Chartered to grant degrees by the Government of Ontario in 1858.

Degrees and Diplomas: *Certificate/Diploma*; *Master's Degree*; *Doctoral Degree*

Student Residential Facilities: Student Residence with 103 beds (for 52 males and 51 females students).

Libraries: Caven Library, one of more than 30 libraries within the University of Toronto Library System (8.5 million vols).

Last Updated: 01/02/11

LA CITÉ COLLÉGIALE COLLEGE OF APPLIED ARTS AND TECHNOLOGY

Collège d'arts appliqués et de technologie La Cité collégiale

801 promenade de l'aviation, Ottawa, Ontario K1K 4R3
Tel: +1(613) 742-2483
Fax: +1(613) 742-2483
EMail: info@lacitec.on.ca; admissions@lacitec.on.ca
Website: http://www.lacitec.on.ca/

Presidente: Lise Bourgeois (2010-)
Tel: +1(613) 742-2483 Ext. 2000

Areas
Administration (Administration; Business Administration; Finance; Law; Marketing; Sales Techniques); **Arts and Design** (Fine Arts; Graphic Design; Interior Design; Photography); **Communication** (Advertising and Publicity; Public Relations); **Construction and Mechanics** (Automotive Engineering; Building Technologies; Electrical Engineering; Heating and Refrigeration; Mechanical Engineering; Metal Techniques; Technology); **Electronics** (Electronic Engineering); **Esthetics and Hairdressing** (Cosmetology; Service Trades); **Forestry and Environment** (Environmental Engineering; Forestry); **Health Sciences** (Biotechnology; Dental Hygiene; Dentistry; Health Sciences; Medical Auxiliaries; Paramedical Sciences; Physical Therapy; Physiology; Respiratory Therapy); **Hospitality** (Cooking and Catering; Hotel and Restaurant); **Housing and Town Planning** (Architecture; Civil Engineering); **Human Sciences** (Behavioural Sciences; Gerontology; Social Work; Special Education); **Informatics** (Computer Engineering; Computer Networks; Computer Science; Information Technology); **Media** (Journalism; Radio and Television Broadcasting); **Security** (Civil Security; Fire Science; Police Studies; Protective Services); **Tourism and Leisure** (Service Trades; Tourism)

Programmes
Preparatory Studies (Arts and Humanities; Biology; Chemistry; Communication Studies; English; Ethics; Mathematics; Philosophy; Physics; Psychology)

History: Founded 1990.

Fees: (Canadian Dollar): first year, 1,158.77 per term; second year, 1,145.16 per term; third year, 1,134.73 per term. International students additional fee, 3,880.73 per term.

Degrees and Diplomas: *Certificate/Diploma*. Applied Bachelor's degree (professional), 4 yrs; Postgraduate diploma, a further 1-2 yrs following college diploma or first university degree.
Last Updated: 08/12/10

LAKEHEAD UNIVERSITY

955 Oliver Road, Thunder Bay, Ontario P7B 5E1
Tel: +1(807) 343-8110
Fax: +1(807) 343-8023
EMail: info@lakeheadu.ca
Website: http://www.lakeheadu.ca

President and Vice-Chancellor: Brian Stevenson (2010-)
Tel: +1(807) 343-8200, Fax: +1(807) 346-7920
EMail: bstevens@lakeheadu.ca

Vice-President (Administration and Finance): Michael Pawlowski
Tel: +1(807) 343-8383, Fax: +1(807) 346-7992
EMail: michael.pawlowski@lakeheadu.ca

Centres
Analytical Services *(LUCAS)* (Archaeology; Environmental Studies; Forensic Medicine and Dentistry; Forest Products; Forestry; Mineralogy; Molecular Biology; Paleontology; Soil Science; Toxicology); **Application of Resource Information Systems** (Information Sciences); **Excellence for Children and Adolescents with Special Needs**; **Health Care Ethics** (Ethics; Health Sciences); **Northern Studies** (Nordic Studies)

Faculties
Business Administration (Accountancy; Business Administration; Business and Commerce; Finance; Human Resources; Information Sciences; Labour and Industrial Relations; Marketing; Secretarial Studies); **Education** (Communication Studies; Curriculum; Ecology; Education; English; Fine Arts; Foreign Languages Education; French; Gerontology; History; Human Resources; Information Technology; Leadership; Native Language Education; Natives Education; Natural Sciences; Parks and Recreation; Physical Therapy; Psychology; Religious Education; Special Education; Teacher Training; Women's Studies); **Engineering** (Automation and Control Engineering; Chemical Engineering; Civil Engineering; Computer Engineering; Electrical Engineering; Engineering; Environmental Engineering; Mechanical Engineering; Software Engineering); **Graduate Studies** (Automation and Control Engineering; Biology; Biotechnology; Business Administration; Chemistry; Computer Engineering; Computer Science; Economics; Education; Educational Sciences; Electrical Engineering; English; Environmental Engineering; Environmental Studies; Forestry; Geology; Gerontology; Health Sciences; History; Management; Mathematics; Nursing; Physical Therapy; Physics; Psychology; Public Health; Social Work; Sociology; Tourism; Women's Studies); **Health and Behavioural Sciences** (Behavioural Sciences; Gerontology; Health Sciences; Nursing; Physical Therapy; Psychology; Public Health; Social Work); **Natural Resources Management** (Botany; Ecology; Entomology; Environmental Management; Fire Science; Fishery; Forestry; Genetics; Management; Natural Resources; Pathology; Soil Science; Water Science; Wildlife; Wood Technology); **Science and Environmental Studies** (Anthropology; Biology; Chemistry; Computer Science; Economics; Environmental Studies; Geography; Geology; Information Technology; Mathematics; Molecular Biology; Physics; Water Science); **Social Sciences and Humanities** (Classical Languages; English; Finnish; French; German; Greek (Classical); History; Indigenous Studies; Italian; Latin; Modern Languages; Music; Musical Instruments; Nordic Studies; Parks and Recreation; Philosophy; Political Sciences; Singing; Social Sciences; Sociology; Spanish; Tourism; Visual Arts; Women's Studies)

Institutes
Globalization and Culture *(Advanced)*; **Social History** *(Lakehead)* (History)

Programmes
Biorefining Research Initiative; **Biotechnology Research** (Biotechnology)

Research Centres
Education and Research on Aging and Health (Gerontology; Health Sciences); **Rural and Northern Health** (Health Sciences); **Safe Driving** (Road Transport); **Tourism and Community Development** *(Lakehead University)* (Social and Community Services; Tourism)

Schools
Medicine *(Northern Ontario - NOSM)* (Anaesthesiology; Gerontology; Gynaecology and Obstetrics; Health Sciences; Medicine; Orthopaedics; Paediatrics; Psychiatry and Mental Health; Public Health; Social and Preventive Medicine; Surgery)

Further Information: Also Orillia Campus.

History: Founded 1946 as Lakehead Technical Institute, became Lakehead College of Arts, Science and Technology 1956 and acquired present status and title 1965.

Governing Bodies: Board of Governors, comprising 30 members; Senate, comprising 70 members

Academic Year: September to April (September-December; January-April)

Admission Requirements: Ontario secondary school diploma (OSSD) or equivalent

701

Fees: (Can. Dollars): Undergraduate tuition, 5,028-5,800 per annum for Canadian students and 13,600 per annum for International students. Graduate tuition fees, c. 2,100 per term for all programmes (except MBA, 4,935 per term) for Canadian students; c. 4,760 per term for all programmes (except MBA, 7,260 per term) for International students.

Main Language(s) of Instruction: English

International Co-operation: With universities in Finland; Sweden, Germany, France, England, Australia. Also participates in North 2 North and NAFTA programmes

Degrees and Diplomas: *University Certificate/Diploma*: Nursing; Palliative Care; Dementia Studies; Business Administration (Accountancy, Human Resources,...); Languages.; *Bachelor's Degree*; *Master's Degree*; *Graduate Diploma/Certificate*; *Doctoral Degree (PhD)*. Also Master of Business Administration (MBA), 1-3 yrs; Honours Bachelor degree, 4 yrs; Professional Year Bachelor of Education, 1 yr; Concurrent degrees in 4-5 yrs: Bachelor of Arts (General)/Bachelor of Education (Native Studies) (BA/BEd), Bachelor of Science (General)/ Bachelor of Education (Native Studies) (BSc/BEd), Bachelor of Arts/Bachelor of Education (Indigenous Learning Major) (BA/BEd), Honours Bachelor of Arts/Bachelor of Education (Indigenous Learning Major) (HBA/BEd) Honours Bachelor of Arts (Music)/Bachelor of Education programmes, Honours Bachelor of Fine Arts, (Visual Arts Major) Bachelor of Education I/S.

Student Services: Academic counselling, Canteen, Cultural centre, Employment services, Foreign student adviser, Foreign Studies Centre, Handicapped facilities, Health services, Social counselling, Sports facilities

Student Residential Facilities: For 1,341 students

Libraries: University Library (Chancellor Paterson and Education Library), total c. 920,000 vols

Publications: Agora; Publications of the Faculties

Press or Publishing House: In-House Publishing

Academic Staff 2007-2008	MEN	WOMEN	TOTAL
FULL-TIME	–	–	c. 300
Student Numbers 2008-2009			
All (Foreign Included)	3,149	4,260	7,409
FOREIGN ONLY	89	33	122

Part-time students, 1,161.
Last Updated: 01/02/11

LAURENTIAN UNIVERSITY/UNIVERSITÉ LAURENTIENNE (LU)

935 Ramsey Lake Road, Sudbury, Ontario P3E 2C6
Tel: +1(705) 675-1151 + 1(800) 461-4030
Fax: +1(705) 675-4891
EMail: admissions@laurentian.ca
Website: http://www.laurentian.ca

President: Dominic Giroux (2009-)
Tel: +1(705) 675-1151 Ext. 3410, Fax: +1(705) 673-6519
EMail: president@laurentian.ca; dominicgiroux@laurentian.ca

Acting Vice-President, Administration: Normand Lavallée
Tel: +1(705) 675-1151 Ext. 3438, Fax: +1(705) 671-3806
EMail: nlavallee@laurentian.ca

International Relations: Melissa Keeping, Director, Laurentian International
Tel: +1(705) 675-1151 Ext. 1556
EMail: mkeeping@laurentian.ca; international@laurentian.ca

Faculties
Humanities (Ancient Civilizations; Archaeology; Classical Languages; Communication Studies; Computer Science; English; Ethics; Ethnology; Fine Arts; Folklore; French; French Studies; Greek (Classical); History; Indigenous Studies; Italian; Latin; Literature; Mathematics; Mathematics and Computer Science; Media Studies; Modern Languages; Music; Native American Studies; Native Language; Philosophy; Religion; Religious Studies; Spanish; Speech Therapy and Audiology; Theatre; Women's Studies); **Management** *(Some Programmes are offered at Georgian College (Barrie) and St-Lawrence College (Kingston))* (Accountancy; Business Administration; Business and Commerce; Economics; Finance; Human Resources; Management; Marketing; Public Administration); **Pro-**

fessional Schools (Education; Educational Sciences; Health Education; Health Sciences; Leadership; Midwifery; Nursing; Physical Education; Physical Therapy; Psychology; Social Work; Sports; Sports Management; Theatre); **Science and Engineering** (Anthropology; Archaeology; Behavioural Sciences; Biochemistry; Biology; Biomedicine; Chemical Engineering; Chemistry; Civil Engineering; Computer Science; Earth Sciences; Ecology; Engineering; Environmental Studies; Ethnology; Forensic Medicine and Dentistry; Geography; Geology; Mathematics; Mechanical Engineering; Mineralogy; Mining Engineering; Neurosciences; Physics; Psychology; Radiology; Rehabilitation and Therapy; Surveying and Mapping; Zoology); **Social Sciences** (Anthropology; Earth Sciences; Economics; Geography (Human); Geology; Gerontology; Health Sciences; History; Labour and Industrial Relations; Law; Political Sciences; Psychology; Public Health; Social Sciences; Sociology)

Institutes
Franco-Ontarien *(IFO)*; **International Economic Policy** *(IEPI)* (International Economics); **Northern Ontario Research and Development** *(INORD)* (Regional Studies); **Sport Marketing** *(ISM)* (Marketing; Sports Management)

Laboratories
Elliot Lake Research Field Station (Environmental Studies; Inorganic Chemistry; Soil Science); **Laurentian University Mining Automation** *(LUMAL)* (Mining Engineering)

Research Centres
Association francophone pour le savoir *((ACFAS), Sudbury Section)* (French); **Geomechanics** *(GRC)* (Mining Engineering); **Human Development** *(CRHD)* (Administration; Business and Commerce; Geology; Indigenous Studies; Nursing; Philosophy; Psychology; Social Work; Sociology); **Humanities Research and Creativity** (Cultural Studies; Education; Fine Arts; History; Literature; Modern Languages; Music; Philosophy; Political Sciences); **Interdisciplinarity Research in Human Sciences** *(International - ICIRHS)* (Social Sciences); **Interdisciplinary Research in Law** *(International - ICIRL)* (Law), **Mineral Exploration** *(MERC)* (Earth Sciences; Geology); **Mining Materials** *(CIMMR)* (Mining Engineering); **Occupational Safety and Health** *(CROSH)* (Occupational Health); **Rural and Northern Health Research** *(CRaNHR)* (Health Sciences); **Social Justice and Policy** *(CRSJP)* (Social Policy); **Sudbury Neutrino Observatory** *(SNO)* (Astrophysics)

Research Groups
Mining Innovation, Rehabilitation and Applied Research Corporation *(MIRARCO)* (Environmental Management; Mining Engineering)

Units
Cooperative Freshwater Ecology *(CFEU)* (Ecology)

History: Founded 1960 as a non-denominational bilingual institution offering courses in both French and English.

Governing Bodies: Senate; Board of Governors

Academic Year: September to April (September-December; January-April)

Admission Requirements: Ontario secondary school diploma (OSSD) including a minimum of 6 Ontario Academic Courses (OAC's) with minimun overall average of 70%

Fees: (Canadian Dollar): Undergraduate tuition, 5,090-5,736 per annum for Canadian students and 12,509-16,440 for International students; EAP (English Academic Preparation), 3,500 per term; Graduate tuition fee, 1,509-2,924 per semester for Canadian students and 2,600-5,387 per semester for International students.

Main Language(s) of Instruction: English, French

Degrees and Diplomas: *University Certificate/Diploma*; *Bachelor's Degree*; *Master's Degree*; *Doctoral Degree (PhD)*. Also Honours Diploma, 4 yrs; MBA-CGA programme, 2 yrs; Concurrent programmes in 4-5 yrs: Bachelor of Education/Bachelor of Arts double degree, Bachelor of Education/Bachelor of Arts double degree - Music, Bachelor of Education/Bachelor of Arts double degree - Sport Psychology, Bachelor of Education/Bachelor of Physical and Health Education double degree - Health Promotion, Bachelor of Education/Bachelor of Physical and Health Education double degree - Outdoor Adventure Leadership, Bachelor of Education/Bachelor of Physical and Health Education double degree - Sport and Physical Education, Bachelor of Education/Bachelor of Science double degree - Science.

Student Services: Academic counselling, Canteen, Cultural centre, Employment services, Foreign student adviser, Handicapped facilities, Health services, Nursery care, Social counselling, Sports facilities

Student Residential Facilities: Yes

Libraries: J.N. Demarais Library, c. 1 m. vols

Press or Publishing House: Laurentian Press

Academic Staff *2007-2008*	TOTAL
FULL-TIME	393

Student Numbers *2010-2011*	
All (Foreign Included)	8,792
FOREIGN ONLY	299

Part-time students, 2,605.
Last Updated: 02/02/11

LOYALIST COLLEGE OF APPLIED ARTS AND TECHNOLOGY

Wallbridge-Loyalist Road, P.O. Box 4200, Belleville,
Ontario K8N 5B9
Tel: +1(613) 969-1913
Fax: +1(613) 962-1376
EMail: rabb@loyalistc.on.ca
Website: http://www.loyalistc.on.ca/

President: Maureen Piercy

Centres
Justice Studies (Law; Police Studies; Social and Community Services; Welfare and Protective Services)

Schools
Architecture and Building Sciences (Architecture; Civil Engineering; Construction Engineering; Surveying and Mapping); **Biosciences** (Biotechnology; Chemical Engineering; Environmental Engineering; Laboratory Techniques; Safety Engineering); **Business and Management Studies** (Accountancy; Business Administration; Cooking and Catering; Cosmetology; Hotel and Restaurant; Human Resources; Management; Marketing); **Health and Human Studies** (Arts and Humanities; Child Care and Development; Health Sciences; Leisure Studies; Mathematics; Military Science; Nursing; Paramedical Sciences; Preschool Education; Social Work; Sports); **Media Studies** (Advertising and Publicity; Design; Fine Arts; Journalism; Media Studies; Public Relations; Radio and Television Broadcasting); **Skills Training** (Automotive Engineering; Electrical Engineering; Industrial Engineering)

Further Information: Traditional and Open Learning Institution

History: Founded 1967.

Degrees and Diplomas: *Certificate/Diploma*; *Graduate Diploma/Certificate*. Also Postgraduate diploma, 1-2 yrs following college diploma or first university degree; Bachelor of Science in Nursing offered jointly with Brock University, 4yrs.
Last Updated: 08/12/10

MCMASTER DIVINITY COLLEGE (MCMASTER UNIVERSITY)

1280 Main Street West, Hamilton, Ontario L8S 4K1
Tel: +1(905) 525-9140
Fax: +1(905) 577-4782
EMail: divinity@mcmaster.ca
Website: http://www.macdiv.ca/home.php

President: Stanley E. Porter
Tel: +1(905) 525-9140 Ext. 23500 EMail: princpl@mcmaster.ca

Executive Assistant to the President and Academic Dean: Nina Thomas
Tel: +1(905) 525-9140 Ext. 23500 EMail: thomn@mcmaster.ca

Programmes
Christian Studies (Bible; Christian Religious Studies; New Testament; Religion; Theology); **Non-Degree Studies** (Bible; New Testament; Religion; Theology); **Professional Degrees** (Bible; Religion; Theology)

History: Founded 1881 as Toronto Baptist College. Acquired present status 1887 and present title 1988. Reorganised 1957.

Fees: (Canadian Dollar): tuition fees for Canadian students, 4,149.12-6,253.56 per annum; for International students, 4,169.04-8,788.80. Ph.D., 10,950.

Degrees and Diplomas: *Master's Degree*; *Doctoral Degree*. Also non-degree diploma and certifiactes.
Last Updated: 02/02/11

MCMASTER UNIVERSITY (MCMASTER)

1280 Main Street West, Hamilton, Ontario L8S4L8
Tel: +1(905) 525-9140
Fax: +1(905) 521-1504
EMail: arianol@mcmaster.ca
Website: http://www.mcmaster.ca

President and Vice-Chancellor: Patrick Deane (2010-)
Tel: +1(905) 525 9140 Ext.24340, Fax: +1(905) 522 3391
EMail: preswww@mcmaster.ca

Vice-President, Administration: Andrea Farquhar
Tel: +1(905) 525-9140 Ext. 23658, Fax: +1(905) 522-3391
EMail: farquhar@mcmaster.ca

International Relations: M.W.Luke Chan, Associate Vice-President (International Affairs)
Tel: +1(905) 525 9140 Ext. 24700, Fax: +1(905) 546 5212
EMail: avpint@mcmaster.ca

Centres
Ancient DNA *(McMaster)*; **Child Studies** *(Offord)* (Child Care and Development); **Climate Change** *(McMaster)* (Meteorology); **Emerging Device Technologies** (Technology); **Evaluation of Medicines** (Medicine); **Functional Genomics** (Genetics); **Gene Therapeutics** (Genetics); **Health Economics and Policy Analysis** (Economics); **Microbial Chemical Biology** (Biology); **Minimal Access Surgery** (Surgery); **Peace Studies** (Peace and Disarmament); **Probe Development and Commercialization**; **Spatial Analysis**; **Statistics Canada Research Data** (Statistics); **Surgical Invention and Innovation** (Surgery)

Faculties
Engineering (Biomedical Engineering; Business Computing; Chemical Engineering; Civil Engineering; Computer Engineering; Electrical Engineering; Electronic Engineering; Engineering; Engineering Drawing and Design; Engineering Management; Materials Engineering; Mechanical Engineering; Physics; Production Engineering; Software Engineering; Technology); **Health Sciences** (Anaesthesiology; Behavioural Sciences; Biochemistry; Biomedicine; Cardiology; Endocrinology; Epidemiology; Gastroenterology; Gerontology; Gynaecology and Obstetrics; Haematology; Health Sciences; Immunology; Medical Auxiliaries; Medicine; Microbiology; Molecular Biology; Nephrology; Neurology; Neurosciences; Nursing; Occupational Therapy; Oncology; Ophthalmology; Orthopaedics; Otorhinolaryngology; Paediatrics; Pathology; Physical Therapy; Plastic Surgery; Psychiatry and Mental Health; Radiology; Rehabilitation and Therapy; Respiratory Therapy; Rheumatology; Social and Preventive Medicine; Statistics; Surgery; Urology); **Humanities** (Acting; Ancient Civilizations; Archaeology; Art History; Asian Studies; Cinema and Television; Cognitive Sciences; Communication Studies; Comparative Literature; Cultural Studies; English; Film; Fine Arts; French; Gender Studies; German; Greek (Classical); History; Italian; Japanese; Latin; Linguistics; Literature; Modern Languages; Multimedia; Music; Music Education; Musical Instruments; Painting and Drawing; Peace and Disarmament; Performing Arts; Philology; Philosophy; Polish; Printing and Printmaking; Russian; Sculpture; Spanish; Theatre; Women's Studies); **Science** (Astronomy and Space Science; Behavioural Sciences; Biochemistry; Biology; Biomedicine; Biophysics; Cell Biology; Chemistry; Earth Sciences; Ecology; Environmental Studies; Geochemistry; Geography; Geography (Human); Mathematics; Neurosciences; Physical Therapy; Physics; Psychology; Radiology; Statistics; Water Science); **Social Sciences** (Accountancy; Anthropology; Archaeology; Asian Religious Studies; Behavioural Sciences; Bible; Business Administration; Christian Religious Studies; Cognitive Sciences; Cultural Studies; Earth Sciences; Economics; Environmental Studies; Experimental Psychology; Finance; Geography (Human); Gerontology; Health Sciences; International Business; International Relations; International Studies; Islamic Theology; Judaic Religious Studies; Labour and Industrial Relations;

Linguistics; Neurosciences; Political Sciences; Psychology; Public Administration; Religious Studies; Social Problems; Social Psychology; Social Sciences; Social Work; Sociology; Water Science)

Institutes
Applied Radiation Sciences *(McMaster - McIARS)*; **Automotive Research and Technology** *(McMaster - MacAUTO)* (Automotive Engineering); **Confucius** (Asian Studies; Chinese); **Energy Studies** *(McMaster)* (Energy Engineering); **Environment and Health** *(McMaster)* (Environmental Studies; Health Sciences); **Globalization and the Human Condition**; **Molecular Biology and Biotechnology** *(McMaster)* (Biotechnology; Molecular Biology); **Polymer Production Technology** *(McMaster)* (Polymer and Plastics Technology); **Respiratory Health** *(Firestone)* (Respiratory Therapy); **Transportation and Logistics** *(McMaster)* (Transport and Communications; Transport Management)

Programmes
Arts and Science (Biology; Chemical Engineering; Cultural Studies; East Asian Studies; Economics; Environmental Studies; Literature; Logic; Mathematics; Physics; Statistics; Technology; Western European Studies; Writing); **Globalization studies** *(Institute on Globalization and the Human Condition)* (International Studies); **Indigenous Studies** (Indigenous Studies)

Research Centres
Antimicrobial; **Bertrand Russell**; **Childhood Disability** *(CanChild)* (Rehabilitation and Therapy); **eBusiness** *(McMaster - MeRC)* (E-Business/Commerce); **Gerontological Health** *(R. Samuel McLaughlin)* (Gerontology); **Henderson**; **Management of Innovation and New Technology** (Engineering Management; Technology); **Medical Imagining Informatics** *(MIIRC@M)* (Medical Technology); **Network for Evaluation of Education and Training Technologies** (Educational Technology); **Promotion of Women's Health** (Women's Studies); **Pulp and Paper** *(McMaster)* (Paper Technology); **Steel** (Metal Techniques); **Surgical Outcomes** (Surgery)

Research Institutes
Child Health *(McMaster)* (Health Administration); **Infectious Disease** *(Michael G. DeGroote)* (Epidemiology); **Manufacturing** *(McMaster)* (Production Engineering); **Materials** *(Brockhouse)* (Materials Engineering); **Population Health** (Public Health); **Quantitative Studies in Economics and Population** (Demography and Population; Economics)

Schools
Business *(DeGroote)* (Accountancy; Business Administration; Business and Commerce; Engineering Management; Finance; Human Resources; Information Sciences; Management; Marketing); **Graduate Studies** (Ancient Civilizations; Anthropology; Astronomy and Space Science; Behavioural Sciences; Biochemistry; Biology; Biomedicine; Business Administration; Chemical Engineering; Chemistry; Civil Engineering; Classical Languages; Cognitive Sciences; Communication Studies; Computer Engineering; Cultural Studies; Earth Sciences; Economics; Electrical Engineering; Engineering; Engineering Management; English; French; Gender Studies; Geography; Gerontology; Greek (Classical); Health Administration; Health Sciences; History; Labour and Industrial Relations; Latin; Materials Engineering; Mathematics; Mechanical Engineering; Media Studies; Medical Technology; Metal Techniques; Neurosciences; Nuclear Engineering; Nursing; Occupational Therapy; Philosophy; Physical Therapy; Physics; Political Sciences; Psychology; Rehabilitation and Therapy; Religious Studies; Social Sciences; Social Work; Sociology; Software Engineering; Statistics; Surveying and Mapping)

Further Information: Also Teaching Hospitals

History: Founded 1887 in Toronto and located in Hamilton 1930. A non-denominational private foundation.

Governing Bodies: Board of Governors, comprising 37 members; Senate, comprising 66 members; University Planning Committee.

Academic Year: September to April (September-December; January-April)

Admission Requirements: Secondary school certificate or recognized foreign equivalent

Fees: (Can. Dollars): 5,582 - 7,748 per annum; foreign students, 13,693 - 20,611.

Main Language(s) of Instruction: English

International Co-operation: With institutions in 72 countries including Australia, Belgium, China, El Salvador, France, Italy, India, Japan, The Netherlands, Poland, Saudi Arabia, Singapore and the United Kingdom.

Degrees and Diplomas: *Bachelor's Degree*; *Master's Degree*; *Graduate Diploma/Certificate*: Advanced Neonatal Nursing; Gender Studies and Feminist Research; Health Services and Policy Research; Management of Innovation & New Technology; Nuclear Technology; Spatial Analysis and GIS; Steel Processing and Manufacturing; *Doctoral Degree*. Also MBA, 8-month Accelerated MBA, or self-directed Part-time MBA; Honours Bachelor degree, 4 yrs; Combined Honours programmes, ; Professional designations in Business; Engineering and Management Programme, Engineering and Society, 5 yrs; Honours Bachelor of Music or B.A. Combined Honours in Music; MD/PhD programme.

Student Residential Facilities: For c. 2,280 students

Libraries: c. 1.5m. vols; c. 1.25m. microform items. Mills Memorial Library for Humanities and Social Sciences; H.G. Thode Library of Science and Engineering; Health Sciences Library; Innis Library for Business; Lloyd Reeds Map Library

Publications: Journal of the Bertrand Russell Archives *(quarterly)*; Library Research News *(3 per annum)*; McMaster Nuclear Reactor Research Report *(annually)*; McMaster Times *(quarterly)*; McMaster University Medical Centre Report *(annually)*; Research Bulletin *(monthly)*

Academic Staff *2007-2008*: Total 1,434
STAFF WITH DOCTORATE: Total 1,386
Student Numbers *2009-2010*: Total 23,325
Last Updated: 03/02/11

NIAGARA COLLEGE
PO Box 1005, 300 Woodlawn Road, Welland, Ontario L3C 7L3
Tel: +1(905) 735-2211 Ext. 7559
Fax: +1(905) 736-6000
EMail: info@niagarac.on.ca
Website: http://www.niagarac.on.ca/

President: Daniel J. Patterson
Tel: +1(905) 641-2252 Ext. 4040
EMail: dpatterson@niagaracollege.ca

Areas
Academic and General Studies (Arts and Humanities; Behavioural Sciences; Design; Health Sciences; Literacy Education; Media Studies; Natural Sciences; Psychology; Social and Community Services); **Administrative Studies** (Administration; Health Administration; Information Management; Law); **Business and Entrepreneurship** (Accountancy; Business Administration; Hotel and Restaurant; Human Resources; International Business; Leadership; Management; Marketing; Military Science; Occupational Health; Safety Engineering; Sales Techniques; Small Business; Transport Management); **Community Studies** (Adult Education; Behavioural Sciences; Child Care and Development; Gerontology; Leisure Studies; Preschool Education; Psychology; Rehabilitation and Therapy; Social and Preventive Medicine; Social Work); **Computer Studies and Computer Engineering Technology** (Computer Engineering; Computer Networks; Computer Science; Software Engineering); **Construction Studies** (Civil Engineering; Construction Engineering); **Culinary Studies** *(Canadian and Food and Wine Institute)* (Cooking and Catering; Food Technology); **Electrical and Electronics Studies** (Electrical Engineering; Electronic Engineering); **Environmental Studies** (Energy Engineering; Environmental Engineering; Environmental Management; Surveying and Mapping); **Health Studies** (Dental Hygiene; Dentistry; Health Sciences; Nursing; Occupational Therapy; Paramedical Sciences; Pharmacy; Physical Therapy; Rehabilitation and Therapy; Sports); **Horticulture and Agribusiness** (Horticulture; Landscape Architecture; Viticulture); **Hospitality and Tourism** (Hotel and Restaurant; Tourism); **Language Studies** (English; French; Spanish); **Mechanical Studies** (Mechanical Engineering; Mechanics); **Media and Design** (Acting; Cinema and Television; Computer Science; Design; E-Business/Commerce; Film; Fine Arts; Graphic Design; Journalism; Media Studies; Photography; Public Relations; Radio and Television Broadcasting; Writing); **Motive Power Automotive Studies** (Automotive Engineering; Maintenance Technology); **Photonics Studies** (Engineering; Laser Engineering); **Policing**

and Security (Justice Administration; Law; Police Studies; Social and Community Services); **Skilled Trades, Apprenticeships and Pre-Apprenticeships** (Automotive Engineering; Cooking and Catering; Metal Techniques; Service Trades); **Spa and Salon Studies** (Cosmetology; Service Trades); **Welding Studies** (Metal Techniques); **Winery, Viticulture and Brewery Studies** (Brewing; Management; Marketing; Viticulture)

Further Information: Also Niagara College NOTL Campus.

Fees: (Canadian Dollar): 1,824-12,266 per annum.

Degrees and Diplomas: *Certificate/Diploma*; *Graduate Diploma/ Certificate.* Applied Bachelor's degree (Professional), 4 yrs; Advanced Diploma, 3 yrs.

Last Updated: 08/12/10

NIPISSING UNIVERSITY (NU)

100 College Drive, Box 5002, North Bay, Ontario P1B 8L7
Tel: +1(705) 474-3450
Fax: +1(705) 474-1947
EMail: nuinfo@nipissingu.ca
Website: http://www.nipissingu.ca

President and Vice-Chancellor: Lesley Lovett-Doust (2009-)
Tel: +1(705) 474-3461 Ext. 4286, Fax: +1(705) 495-3677
EMail: lld@nipissingu.ca

Vice-President, Finance, Administration and Strategic Capital Investments: Vicky Paine-Mantha
Tel: +1(705) 474-3450 Ext. 4289, Fax: +1(705) 495-2601
EMail: vickyp@nipissingu.ca

International Relations: Karen Strang, International Services and Programs Administrator
Tel: +1(705) 474-3461 Ext. 4105 EMail: karens@nipissingu.ca

Faculties

Applied and Professional Studies (Accountancy; Administration; Business Administration; Business and Commerce; Cell Biology; Child Care and Development; Commercial Law; Criminal Law; Criminology; Development Studies; Economics; English; Family Studies; Finance; Health Sciences; History; Human Resources; Information Sciences; International Business; Law; Management; Marketing; Mathematics; Medieval Studies; Molecular Biology; Nursing; Occupational Health; Philosophy; Small Business; Social Welfare; Statistics); **Arts and Science** (Adult Education; Ancient Civilizations; Art History; Arts and Humanities; Biology; Classical Languages; Computer Science; Cultural Studies; Education; English; Environmental Management; Environmental Studies; Family Studies; Fine Arts; Gender Studies; Geography; Geography (Human); Greek (Classical); Health Education; History; Human Rights; Indigenous Studies; Latin; Literature; Mathematics; Mathematics and Computer Science; Natives Education; Neurosciences; Painting and Drawing; Philosophy; Physical Education; Physical Therapy; Political Sciences; Psychology; Religion; Sculpture; Social Sciences; Social Work; Sociology; Surveying and Mapping; Writing)

Institutes
Applied Social Research *(IASR)* (Social Studies)

Research Centres
Education and the Arts *(Northern Canadian - NORCCREA)* (Education)

Schools
Education *(Schulich)* (Adult Education; Education; Health Education; Natives Education; Physical Education; Primary Education; Secondary Education)

Further Information: Also Muskoka and Brantford regional campuses.

History: Founded 1967 as University College affiliated with Laurentian University, acquired present status 1992.

Governing Bodies: Board of Governors, comprising 26 members; Academic Senate

Academic Year: September to April (September-December; January-April). Also Spring and Summer Sessions (Early May-Late June; July-Mid August)

Admission Requirements: Ontario secondary school diploma (OSSD) with minimum overall average of 60% in at least 6 Academic Credits, or recognized foreign equivalent. All student visa applicants or landed immigrant applicants for admission to Faculty of Arts and Science whose first or mother tongue is not English must supply proof of proficiency in English. TOEFL test with minimum score of 550 or MELAB with minimum score of 90%

Fees: (Can. Dollars): Bachelor of Arts and Science, 3,888-5,916 per annum; Bachelor of Business Administration and Computer Science, 4,144-6,972 per annum; Bachelor of Education, 5,815 per annum. Master's degree, 7,746.25-9,006.25. Tuition fee for International students, 464-537.50 per course.

Main Language(s) of Instruction: English

Degrees and Diplomas: *University Certificate/Diploma*; *Bachelor's Degree*; *Master's Degree.* Also Bachelor's degree with Combined Major, 3 yrs; Honours Bachelor's degree, 4 yrs; Advanced Bachelor's Degree in Education and Educational Leadership; Concurrent Bachelor of Arts/Bachelor of Education in English Studies, Geography, History, Mathematics, Computer Science, Psychology, 5 yrs; Professional Designations in Business (Accountancy, Human Resources); non-degree programmes.

Student Services: Academic counselling, Canteen, Employment services, Handicapped facilities, Health services, Social counselling, Sports facilities

Student Residential Facilities: For 362 students

Libraries: Education Centre Library, 476,875 vols

Publications: Nipissing Review *(annually)*

Academic Staff *2010-2011*	TOTAL
FULL-TIME	149
Student Numbers *2010-2011*	
All (Foreign Included)	4,838

Part-time students, 1,051.
Last Updated: 03/02/11

ONTARIO COLLEGE OF ART AND DESIGN (OCAD)

100 McCaul Street, Toronto, Ontario M5T 1W1
Tel: +1(416) 977-6000
Fax: +1(416) 977-6006
EMail: general@ocad.ca
Website: http://www.ocad.on.ca

President: Sara Diamond
Tel: +1(416) 977-6000 Ext. 300 EMail: sdiamond@ocad.ca

Vice-President, Academic: Sarah McKinnon
Tel: +1(416) 977-6000 Ext. 427 EMail: smckinnon@ocad.ca

International Relations: Susan Kemp, Coordinator, International Student Services and tudent Mobility/Exchange
Tel: +1(416) 977-6000 Ext. 293 EMail: international@ocad.ca

Courses
Continuing Studies (Art History; Design; Multimedia; Painting and Drawing; Photography; Sculpture); **DFI (Digital Futures Initiative)** (Media Studies; Multimedia); **Interdisciplinary Studies** (Media Studies; Technology; Visual Arts)

Faculties
Art (Art Criticism; Fine Arts; Media Studies; Painting and Drawing; Photography; Printing and Printmaking; Sculpture); **Design** (Advertising and Publicity; Ceramic Art; Design; Graphic Design; Handicrafts; Industrial Design; Jewelry Art; Painting and Drawing); **Liberal Studies** (Arts and Humanities; English; Mathematics; Natural Sciences; Social Sciences; Technology; Visual Arts)

Programmes
Aboriginal Visual Culture (Indigenous Studies; Visual Arts); **Alternative Studies** (Design; Fine Arts); **English Language** (English); **Graduate Studies** (Advertising and Publicity; Art Criticism; Art History; Design; Fine Arts; Media Studies)

Governing Bodies: Board of Governors, including 25 members; Academic Council.

Fees: (Canadian Dollar): Undergraduate tuition fee, 5,090-5,180 per annum for Canadian students and 15,280 per annum for International students; Graduate tuition fee, 4,725-5,248 per annum for Canadian students and 8,100-12,480 per annum for International students; Executive Masters Design-Advertising, 11,403 per annum for Canadian students and 13,736 per annum for International students.

Degrees and Diplomas: *Bachelor's Degree*; *Master's Degree*; *Graduate Diploma/Certificate*. Also Executive Master in Advertising (EMDes), a part-time two-year programme (seven-semester); non-degree programmes.

Academic Staff 2009-2010	MEN	WOMEN	TOTAL
FULL-TIME	63	45	108
PART-TIME	–	–	96
STAFF WITH DOCTORATE			
FULL-TIME	–	–	15

Student Numbers 2009-2010			
All (Foreign Included)	1,620	2,042	3,662
FOREIGN ONLY	63	123	186

Part-time students, 821.
Last Updated: 03/02/11

QUEEN'S UNIVERSITY (QUEEN'S)

99 University Avenue, Kingston, Ontario K7L 3N6
Tel: +1(613) 533-2000
Fax: +1(613) 533-6300
EMail: admissn@post.queensu.ca
Website: http://www.queensu.ca

Principal and Vice-Chancellor: Daniel Woolf (2009-)
Tel: +1(613) 533-2201, Fax: +1(613) 533-6838
EMail: Principal@QueensU.ca

Registrar: Jo-Anne Brady
Tel: +1(613) 533-2045, Fax: +1(613) 533-2068
EMail: bradyj@post.queensu.ca

International Relations: John Dixon, Vice-Provost, International
Tel: +1(613) 533-3208, Fax: +1(613) 533-6441
EMail: John.Dixon@queensu.ca

Centres
Advanced Materials and Manufacturing *(Queen's RMC)* (Materials Engineering; Production Engineering); **Biological Communication** (Biological and Life Sciences); **Geoengineering** (Geological Engineering); **Health Services and Policy Research** (Health Administration); **Industrial Relations** (Labour and Industrial Relations); **International Relations** (International Relations); **Manufacturing of Advanced Ceramics and Nanomaterials** (Ceramics and Glass Technology; Nanotechnology); **Monieson** (Economics; Human Resources; Management); **Neuroscience Studies** (Neurosciences); **Obesity Research and Education** (Dietetics); **Studies in Primary Care** (Health Sciences); **Study of Democracy** (Political Sciences); **Surveillance Studies**; **Water and the Environment** (Environmental Studies; Water Science)

Faculties
Arts and Science (Anatomy; Ancient Civilizations; Arabic; Archaeology; Art History; Asian Religious Studies; Astronomy and Space Science; Bible; Biochemistry; Biological and Life Sciences; Biology; Cell Biology; Chemistry; Chinese; Classical Languages; Cognitive Sciences; Computer Science; Design; Development Studies; Economics; English; Environmental Studies; Ethics; Film; Fine Arts; French Studies; Gender Studies; Geography; Geography (Human); Geological Engineering; Geology; German; Greek; Greek (Classical); Health Education; Health Sciences; Hebrew; Heritage Preservation; History; History of Religion; Immunology; Italian; Japanese; Jewish Studies; Latin; Linguistics; Literature; Mathematics; Mathematics and Computer Science; Media Studies; Microbiology; Music; Music Education; Music Theory and Composition; Musical Instruments; Musicology; Painting and Drawing; Pharmacology; Philosophy; Physical Education; Physical Engineering; Physical Therapy; Physics; Physiology; Political Sciences; Psychology; Religious Studies; Sociology; Software Engineering; Spanish; Statistics; Surveying and Mapping; Theatre; Theology; Toxicology); **Education** (Education; Natives Education; Primary Education; Teacher Training); **Engineering and Applied Science** (Chemical Engineering; Chemistry; Civil Engineering; Computer Engineering; Electrical Engineering; Engineering; Geological Engineering; Materials Engineering; Mathematics; Mechanical Engineering; Mining Engineering; Physics); **Health Sciences** (Anaesthesiology; Anatomy; Biochemistry; Cardiology; Cell Biology; Endocrinology; Epidemiology; Ethics; Gastroenterology; Gerontol-

ogy; Gynaecology and Obstetrics; Haematology; Health Sciences; Immunology; Medicine; Microbiology; Molecular Biology; Nephrology; Neurology; Nursing; Occupational Therapy; Oncology; Ophthalmology; Otorhinolaryngology; Paediatrics; Pathology; Pharmacology; Physical Therapy; Physiology; Plastic Surgery; Psychiatry and Mental Health; Public Health; Radiology; Rehabilitation and Therapy; Respiratory Therapy; Rheumatology; Surgery; Toxicology; Urology); **Law** (Civil Law; Commercial Law; Comparative Law; Constitutional Law; Criminal Law; Economics; European Union Law; Fiscal Law; Human Rights; International Law; Labour Law; Law; Private Law; Public Law)

Institutes
Energy and Environmental Policy *(Queen's)* (Energy Engineering; Environmental Engineering); **Intergovernmental Relations** (International Relations); **Study of Economic Policy** *(John Deutsch)* (Economic and Finance Policy)

Laboratories
High Performance Computing Virtual *(HPCVL)* (Computer Engineering)

Research Centres
Fuell Cell *(Queen's -RMC / FCRC)*; **Human Mobility** (Demography and Population); **Southern African** (African Studies); **Sudbury Neutrino Observatory**

Research Institutes
Cancer (Oncology)

Schools
Business (Accountancy; Business Administration; Business and Commerce; Data Processing; Economics; Finance; Human Resources; Information Sciences; International Business; Labour and Industrial Relations; Leadership; Management; Marketing; Operations Research; Small Business; Statistics; Taxation); **Graduate Studies** (Anatomy; Archaeology; Art History; Astronomy and Space Science; Biochemistry; Biology; Biomedical Engineering; Business Administration; Cell Biology; Chemical Engineering; Chemistry; Civil Engineering; Classical Languages; Computer Engineering; Computer Science; Cultural Studies; Development Studies; Economics; Education; Electrical Engineering; Engineering; English; Environmental Studies; Epidemiology; French Studies; Gender Studies; Geography; Geological Engineering; Geology; German; Greek (Classical); Health Sciences; Heritage Preservation; History; Immunology; Labour and Industrial Relations; Latin; Law; Management; Materials Engineering; Mathematics; Mechanical Engineering; Microbiology; Mining Engineering; Molecular Biology; Neurosciences; Nursing; Occupational Therapy; Oncology; Pathology; Pharmacology; Philosophy; Physical Engineering; Physical Therapy; Physics; Physiology; Political Sciences; Psychology; Public Administration; Public Health; Regional Planning; Rehabilitation and Therapy; Religious Studies; Sociology; Statistics; Town Planning; Toxicology); **Religion** (Asian Religious Studies; Christian Religious Studies; Islamic Theology; Religious Studies; Theology)

Further Information: Also Branch in British Columbia. Also distance education courses.

History: Founded 1841 by Royal Charter issued by Queen Victoria. Modelled on the University of Edinburgh, Scottish academic influences have helped to mould its character. A national institution privately endowed and privately controlled.

Governing Bodies: Senate, comprising 17 ex-officio Members, 17 students, and 34 faculty members; Board of Trustees, comprising 35 members and 3 ex-officio members

Academic Year: September to April (September-December; January-April)

Admission Requirements: Secondary school certificate or recognized foreign equivalent

Fees: (Can. Dollars): Undergraduate tuition, 5,135-13,170 per annum (18,228 for Medical studies programmes) for Canadian students and 17,135-26,504.50 per annum (65,000 for Medical studies programmes) for International studetns. Graduate tuition, 6,258-9,054 per annum for Canadian students and 9,883-18,300 per annum for International students. MBA, 65,000 for Canadian students and 70,000 for International students.

Main Language(s) of Instruction: English

International Co-operation: With universities in Australia, Belgium, Chile, China, Cuba, Denmark, United Kingdom, Finland, France, Germany, Hong Kong, Hungary, Italy, Japan, Mexico, Netherlands, New Zealand, Northern Ireland, Norway; Singapore, Sweden, Switzerland, Taiwan, USA

Degrees and Diplomas: *University Certificate/Diploma*; *Bachelor's Degree*; *Master's Degree*; *Graduate Diploma/Certificate*; *Doctoral Degree*. Also Honours Bachelor's degree, 4 yrs; Executive MBA, 16 months; Accelerated MBA, 12 months; Dual Degree Programme (5 yrs), allowing students to complete degrees from two different Faculties or Schools concurrently at Queen's University; Double degree: Master of Management - Global Management degree/ master's degree from one of Queen's University's international business school partners.

Student Services: Academic counselling, Canteen, Cultural centre, Employment services, Foreign student adviser, Foreign Studies Centre, Handicapped facilities, Health services, Language programs, Nursery care, Social counselling, Sports facilities

Student Residential Facilities: Yes

Special Facilities: Zoology Collection; Geology Science; Mineral Ethnology; Herbarium; Optical Observatory. Student Art Gallery; Agnes Etherington Art Gallery

Libraries: Main Library (Stauffer), total, c. 4.000,000 vols; also libraries of the faculties

Publications: Inventory of Research in Progress *(annually)*; Queen's Quarterly *(quarterly)*

Press or Publishing House: McGill-Queen's University Press

Academic Staff *2009-2010*	TOTAL
FULL-TIME	1,137
PART-TIME	1,436
Student Numbers *2009-2010*	
All (Foreign Included)	22,477
FOREIGN ONLY	1,413

Part-time students, 2,927.
Last Updated: 03/02/11

REGIS COLLEGE (UNIVERSITY OF TORONTO)

100 Wellesley Street, Toronto, Ontario M5S 2Z5
Tel: +1(416) 922-5474
Fax: +1(416) 922-2898
EMail: regis.registrar@utoronto.ca
Website: http://www.regiscollege.ca

President and Rector: Joseph G. Schner
Tel: +1(416) 922-5474 Ext. 222 EMail: joseph.schner@utoronto.ca

Registrar: Elaine Chu Tel: +1(416) 922-5474 Ext. 226

Programmes
Advanced Research (Religion; Theology); **Discovering Theology** (Theology); **Ecclesiastical Leadership** (Theology); **General Interest** (Christian Religious Studies; Philosophy; Theology); **Ministerial Preparation** (Philosophy; Religion; Theology); **Professional Development** (Religion; Theology)

Further Information: Associated Institutions: Alpha Sigma Nu, the Anishinabe Research Centre, Camp Ekon, Canadian Institute of Jesuit Studies, Faith Connections, Ignatius Jesuit Centre of Guelph - Loyola House, Jesuit Archives, Jesuit Communication Project, Jesuit Forum for Social Faith and Justice, Lonergan Research Institute, the Lupina Centre, Our Lady of Lourdes Parish, Society of Jesus, Toronto Institute for Pastoral Education (TIPE).

History: Founded 1930 as as the Jesuit Seminary / College of Christ the King. Acquired present status 1978.

Governing Bodies: Board of Governors; Academic Council.

Fees: (Canadian Dollars): Basic degree fee, 518.50 per 1-credit course for Canadian students and 1,393 per 1-credit course for Inernational students; Advanced degree fee, 518.50-1,547 per 1-credit couse for Canadian students and 1,393-2,322 per 1-credit course for International students.

Degrees and Diplomas: *Bachelor's Degree*; *Master's Degree*; *Graduate Diploma/Certificate*; *Doctoral Degree*. Also combined

Master of Divinity/Master of Arts in Theology (M.Div./M.A.); Licentiate in Sacred Theology (S.T.L.).

Student Residential Facilities: Student residence.

Student Numbers *2008-2009:* Total 65
Last Updated: 04/02/11

ROYAL MILITARY COLLEGE OF CANADA/ COLLÈGE MILITAIRE ROYAL DU CANADA (RMC)

PO Box 17000, Station Forces, Kingston, Ontario K7K 7B4
Tel: +1(613) 541-6000
Fax: +1(613) 542-3565
EMail: liaison@rmc.ca
Website: http://www.rmc.ca

Principal and Director of Studies/Principal et Directeur des Etudes: Joel Sokolsky (2008-)
Tel: +1(613) 541-6000 Ext. 3880, Fax: +1(613) 541-6039
EMail: principals.office@rmc.ca

Registrar: Raymond Stouffer
Tel: +1(613) 541-6000 Ext. 6302, Fax: +1(613) 542-3565

Centres
Language (English; French; Modern Languages)

Divisions
Continuing Studies *(DCS)* (Business Administration; Chemistry; Computer Science; Economics; English; French; History; Mathematics; Military Science; Physics; Political Sciences; Psychology); **Graduate Studies and Research** (Business Administration; Chemical Engineering; Chemistry; Civil Engineering; Computer Engineering; Computer Science; Electrical Engineering; Environmental Engineering; Environmental Studies; Materials Engineering; Mathematics; Mechanical Engineering; Military Science; Nuclear Engineering; Physics; Protective Services; Software Engineering)

Faculties
Arts (Business Administration; Economics; French; French Studies; History; Leadership; Linguistics; Military Science; Political Sciences; Psychology; Social Sciences); **Engineering** (Aeronautical and Aerospace Engineering; Chemical Engineering; Civil Engineering; Computer Engineering; Electrical Engineering; Engineering; Materials Engineering; Mechanical Engineering); **Science** (Astronomy and Space Science; Chemical Engineering; Chemistry; Computer Science; Marine Science and Oceanography; Materials Engineering; Mathematics; Mathematics and Computer Science; Physics; Sound Engineering (Acoustics))

History: Founded 1876.

Governing Bodies: Board of Governors

Academic Year: September to April (September-December; January-April)

Fees: (Can. Dollars): Undergraduate tuition, 1,695-2,325 per term for Canadian students and 8,000 per term for International students; Graduate tuition, 1,800-2,250 per term for Canadian students and 6,000-8,000 per term for International students.

Degrees and Diplomas: *University Certificate/Diploma*; *Bachelor's Degree*; *Master's Degree*; *Doctoral Degree*. Also Honours Bachelor's degree, 4 yrs.

Libraries: c. 250,000 vols; 1,200 journals; 1,800 audio-visual items, in both English and French
Last Updated: 04/02/11

RYERSON UNIVERSITY

350 Victoria Street, Toronto, Ontario M5B 2K3
Tel: +1(416) 979-5000
Fax: +1(416) 979-5221
EMail: inquiries@acs.ryerson.ca
Website: http://www.ryerson.ca

President: Sheldon H. Levy (2005-)
Tel: +1(416) 979-5002, Fax: +1(416) 979-5292
EMail: pres@ryerson.ca

Interim Asst VP, Marketing & Communications, Public Affairs: Bruce Piercey

Tel: +1(416) 979-5000 Ext.6638, Fax: +1(416) 979-5208
EMail: bpiercey@ryerson.ca

International Relations: Marsha Mceachruane, Director, RI and International Liaison Officer
Tel: +1(416) 979-5000 Ext. 6995, Fax: +1(416) 979-5352
EMail: mmceachr@ryerson.ca

Centres
Communication *(Rogers)* (Communication Studies); **Food Security** (Food Science); **Learning Technologies** (Educational Technology); **Research Data** (Data Processing); **Study of Commercial Activity** (Business and Commerce); **Urban Energy** (Energy Engineering); **Voluntary Sector Studies** (Management; Public Administration; Social Work)

Chairs
Management of Technological Change in Retailing (Engineering Management; Retailing and Wholesaling)

Faculties
Arts (Arts and Humanities; Business and Commerce; Criminal Law; Cultural Studies; Economics; English; Finance; French; Geography; Geography (Human); Government; History; International Economics; International Studies; Literature; Management; Philosophy; Political Sciences; Psychology; Public Administration; Religion; Social Sciences; Sociology); **Communication and Design** (Acting; Communication Arts; Communication Studies; Dance; Design; Fashion Design; Film; Interior Design; Journalism; Media Studies; Photography; Radio and Television Broadcasting; Theatre); **Community Services** (Child Care and Development; Food Science; Health Administration; Information Management; Midwifery; Nursing; Nutrition; Occupational Health; Public Health; Rehabilitation and Therapy; Rural Planning; Social Work; Town Planning); **Engineering, Architecture and Science** (Aeronautical and Aerospace Engineering; Applied Mathematics; Architecture; Biology; Biomedical Engineering; Chemical Engineering; Chemistry; Civil Engineering; Computer Engineering; Computer Science; Electrical Engineering; Engineering; Engineering Management; Industrial Engineering; Mathematics; Mechanical Engineering; Natural Sciences; Physics)

Institutes
Innovation and Technology Management *(IITM)* (Engineering Management); **Management and Technology** *(Diversity)* (Management; Technology); **Privacy and Cyber Crime** *(PCCI)* (Criminology); **Study of Corporate Social Responsibility** *(Ryerson - CSR)* (Sociology)

Laboratories
Analytical Centre *(Ryerson University)*; **Electric Drive Applications and Research** *(LEDAR)* (Electrical Engineering); **Experiential Design and Gaming Environments** *(EDGE)* (Software Engineering); **Human Factors Engineering** (Safety Engineering); **Human Factors in Amusement Safety** *(THRILL)* (Safety Engineering); **Network-Centric Applied Research Team** *(NCART)* (Computer Science; Information Sciences); **Propulsion Research Facility** (Aeronautical and Aerospace Engineering); **Robotics and Manufacturing Automation** (Automation and Control Engineering; Robotics); **Science of Music, Auditory Research and Technology** *(SMART)* (Music)

Research Centres
Caribbean *(Ryerson)* (Caribbean Studies); **GTA Forum - Planning**; **Human Factors in Amusement Safety** (Safety Engineering); **Immigration and Settlement** *(Joint Centre of Excellence for Research)* (Demography and Population); **Interdisciplinary Human Factors** (Safety Engineering); **Progressive Research Portal** *(sponsored by the CAW-Sam Gindin Chair in Social Justice and Democracy)*; **Social Reporting Network** *(Ryerson)* (Social Studies); **Toronto Region Statistics Canada** (Data Processing; Statistics)

Research Groups
Signal Analysis *(SAR)* (Electrical Engineering)

Research Institutes
International (International Business)

Research Laboratories
Heat Transfer (Heating and Refrigeration); **Infoscape** (Media Studies); **Multimedia** *(Ryerson University)* (Multimedia)

Schools
Graduate Studies *(Yeates)* (Aeronautical and Aerospace Engineering; Applied Mathematics; Architecture; Business Administration; Chemical Engineering; Civil Engineering; Communication Studies; Computer Engineering; Computer Networks; Computer Science; Construction Engineering; Cultural Studies; Demography and Population; Economics; Electrical Engineering; Engineering Management; Environmental Management; Fashion Design; Finance; International Economics; Journalism; Literature; Mechanical Engineering; Media Studies; Molecular Biology; Nursing; Nutrition; Philosophy; Photography; Physics; Preschool Education; Psychology; Public Administration; Social Policy; Social Work; Surveying and Mapping; Town Planning); **Management** *(Ted Rogers)* (Accountancy; Business Administration; Business Computing; Commercial Law; Economics; Finance; Hotel and Restaurant; Human Resources; Information Technology; International Business; Management; Marketing; Tourism)

History: Founded 1948 as Ryerson Institute of Technology, became Ryerson Polytechnic Institute 1963 and acquired present status and title 1993. Ryerson combines a traditional focus on theory with career-oriented emphasis on applicable skills-through laboratory work, field trips, outside projects, work experience, internships, regular contact with business and industry and work experience in the professional community.

Governing Bodies: Board of Governors, comprising 24 members; the Senate, comprising 51 members.

Academic Year: September to April (September-December; January-April). Also 2 seven week summer sessions

Admission Requirements: If graduating with OACs, most Ryerson programmes/schools encourage 70% or higher in six OACs, or equivalent, and include the required subject prerequisite within these averages. If graduating under the new curriculum effective 2003, most Ryerson programmes/schools encourage 70% or higher in a minimum of six Grade 12 U or U/C credits, and include the required subject prerequisite within these averages. Applicants from a country where English is not the first language, or where English is an official language but not the first language are required to provide proof of English proficiency at a satisfactory level. Eligibility for admission will be based on an assessment of academic and, when applicable, non-academic factors, such as audition, admission essay, interview, portfolio, etc. For the Diploma of Arts Programme and the pre-University Studies option, the minimum requirements is the OSSD.

Fees: (Can. Dollars): Undergraduate fees, 5,758.15-8,267.88 per annum for Canadian students and 17,498.19-19,148.43 per annum for International students; Master's degree, 4,785.03 per annum (Communication and Culture) to 19,479.30 per annum (MBA and Computer Networks) for Canadian students and 16,159.83-34,097.25 per annum for International students; PhD, 4,785.03 per annum (Communication and Culture) to 8,014.68 per annum (Engineering) for Canadian students and 16,159.86 to 17,295.27 per annum for International students.

Main Language(s) of Instruction: English

International Co-operation: With universities in Australia; Austria; Denmark; France; Germany; Hong Kong; Italy; Mexico; Netherlands; New Zealand; Sweden; United Kingdom; USA

Degrees and Diplomas: *University Certificate/Diploma*; *Bachelor's Degree*; *Master's Degree*; *Graduate Diploma/Certificate*; *Doctoral Degree*. PhD and Master's degree in Communication and Culture are jointly offered with York University.

Student Services: Academic counselling, Canteen, Cultural centre, Employment services, Foreign student adviser, Handicapped facilities, Health services, Nursery care, Social counselling, Sports facilities

Student Residential Facilities: For 840 students

Special Facilities: Ryerson Theatre. Recreation and Athletics Centre

Libraries: 1,483,708 vols (including volume equivalent for microfilm reels and microfiche items)

Publications: Eyeopener (during school year) *(weekly)*; Forum (during school year) *(monthly)*; Night Views (during school year)

(biweekly); Ryerson Magazine *(biannually)*; Ryersonian (during semester) *(weekly)*

Academic Staff *2009-2010* **TOTAL**
FULL-TIME 933
PART-TIME 180

Student Numbers *2009-2010*
All (Foreign Included) c. 28,000
FOREIGN ONLY 680
Last Updated: 07/02/11

SENECA COLLEGE OF APPLIED ARTS AND TECHNOLOGY

1750 Finch Avenue East, North York, Ontario M2J 2X5
Tel: +1(416) 491-5050
Fax: +1(416) 493-3958
EMail: admissions@senecac.on.ca; eileen.burns@senecac.on.ca
Website: http://www.senecac.on.ca/

President: David Agnew
Tel: +1(416) 491-5050 Ext. 7001, Fax: +1(905) 948-0578
EMail: president@senecac.on.ca

Sections
Visual Arts (Advertising and Publicity; Graphic Design; Media Studies; Photography; Public Relations; Radio and Television Broadcasting; Visual Arts)

Sectors
Academic Studies (Arts and Humanities; English; Natural Sciences; Technology); **Accounting** (Accountancy; Business Administration; Finance); **Administration** (Administration; Business Administration; Finance; International Business; Marketing); **Advertising** (Advertising and Publicity); **Analyst** (Accountancy; Business Administration; Computer Engineering; Computer Science; Information Technology; Marketing; Software Engineering; Transport Management); **Animal Care** (Veterinary Science); **Animation** (Visual Arts); **Aviation/Pilot** (Air Transport); **Business** (Accountancy; Business Administration; Finance; Human Resources; Insurance; International Business; Management; Marketing; Small Business; Transport Management); **CNC Programming** (Mechanical Engineering); **Communications** (Advertising and Publicity; Communication Studies; Film; Information Technology; Journalism; Library Science; Media Studies; Radio and Television Broadcasting; Visual Arts); **Community Service** (Child Care and Development; Fire Science; Gerontology; Leisure Studies; Preschool Education; Social Work); **Computers** (Computer Engineering; Computer Networks; Data Processing; Electronic Engineering; Visual Arts); **Customs** (Taxation; Transport Management); **Die Design** (Mechanical Engineering); **Early Childhood Education** (Child Care and Development; Preschool Education); **Education** (Arts and Humanities; English); **Electronics** (Computer Engineering; Electronic Engineering); **Emergency Services** (Fire Science); **Engineering/Technology** (Air Transport; Building Technologies; Civil Engineering; Computer Science; Electronic Engineering; Engineering; Fire Science; Mechanical Engineering); **Environmental Studies** (Civil Engineering; Environmental Engineering; Environmental Studies; Mechanical Engineering); **Esthetics/Spa** (Cosmetology); **Fashion** (Fashion Design); **Finance** (Accountancy; Business Administration; Finance); **Fire Alarm Inspection** (Fire Science; Technology); **Fire Fighter** (Fire Science; Technology); **Fire Investigation** (Fire Science; Technology); **Fire Prevention Officer** (Fire Science; Technology); **General Machinist** (Mechanical Engineering); **Government Service** (Administration; Business Administration; Finance; Justice Administration; Law; Public Administration); **Graphic Design** (Graphic Design); **Health Sciences** (Chemical Engineering; Nursing; Optometry; Rehabilitation and Therapy); **Human Resources** (Business Administration; Human Resources); **Illustration** (Painting and Drawing); **Insurance** (Business Administration; Finance; Insurance); **Landscaping/Horticulture** (Horticulture; Landscape Architecture); **Law/Legal Services** (Justice Administration; Law; Police Studies); **Life Skills/Employment Preparation** (Adult Education; Vocational Education); **Logistics** (Taxation; Transport Management); **Machine Design** (Machine Building; Mechanical Engineering); **Management** (Business Administration; Civil Engineering; Computer Networks; Finance; Fire Science; Management; Mechanical Engineering; Software Engineering); **Marketing** (Advertising and Publicity; Business Administration; Marketing); **Media** (Journalism; Media Studies; Radio and Television Broadcasting); **Mould Design** (Mechanical Engineering); **Mould Maker** (Mechanical Engineering); **Networking** (Automation and Control Engineering; Computer Engineering; Computer Networks; Computer Science; Electronic Engineering); **Photography** (Photography); **Policing** (Police Studies); **Preparatory Programs**; **Programming** (Computer Engineering; Computer Science; Data Processing); **Public Administration** (Justice Administration; Public Administration); **Recreation/Parks** (Environmental Management; Landscape Architecture; Leisure Studies); **Sales/Merchandising** (Advertising and Publicity; Business Administration; Cosmetology; Design; Graphic Design; Management; Marketing; Sales Techniques; Small Business; Visual Arts); **Science/Research** (Biotechnology; Forensic Medicine and Dentistry; Laboratory Techniques; Pharmacy); **Skilled Trades** (Mechanical Engineering); **Social Services** (Gerontology; Social Work); **Sprinkler Design** (Fire Science); **Technical** (Communication Studies; Data Processing); **Technician/Technology** (Biotechnology; Building Technologies; Chemical Engineering; Civil Engineering; Computer Networks; Fire Science; Laboratory Techniques; Mechanical Engineering); **Therapeutic Recreationist** (Rehabilitation and Therapy); **Tool and Die** (Mechanical Engineering); **Tourism/Leisure Services** (Hotel and Restaurant; Leisure Studies; Tourism)

Further Information: Also Buttonville, Jane, King, Markham, Newham, York and Community campuses.

Degrees and Diplomas: *Certificate/Diploma*; *Graduate Diploma/Certificate*. Bachelor's degree (professional), 4yrs; Applied Bachelor's degree (professional), 4yrs; Collaborative Bachelor's degree in Nursing with York University; Advanced Diploma, 3yrs.
Last Updated: 09/12/10

SHERIDAN COLLEGE INSTITUTE OF TECHNOLOGY AND ADVANCED LEARNING

1430 Trafalgar Road, Oakville, Ontario L6H 2L1
Tel: +1(905) 845-9430
Fax: +1(905) 815-4002
EMail: infosheridan@sheridaninstitute.ca
Website: http://www.sheridanc.on.ca/

President: Jeff Zabudsky (2009-)
Tel: +1(905) 845-9430 Ext. 4020
EMail: jeff.zabudsky@sheridaninstitute.ca

Schools
Animation, Arts and Design (Art History; Ceramic Art; Communication Arts; Computer Graphics; Crafts and Trades; Design; Film; Fine Arts; Glass Art; Information Technology; Interior Design; Journalism; Media Studies; Painting and Drawing; Performing Arts; Photography; Radio and Television Broadcasting; Sculpture; Theatre; Visual Arts); **Applied Computing and Engineering Sciences** (Architecture; Chemical Engineering; Chemistry; Computer Engineering; Computer Networks; Computer Science; Data Processing; Electrical Engineering; Electronic Engineering; Environmental Management; Information Sciences; Information Technology; Laboratory Techniques; Mechanical Engineering; Metal Techniques; Multimedia; Safety Engineering; Software Engineering; Systems Analysis; Technology; Telecommunications Engineering); **Business** (Accountancy; Administration; Advertising and Publicity; Banking; Business Administration; Finance; Human Resources; International Business; Law; Management; Marketing; Tourism); **Community and Liberal Studies** (Anatomy; Animal Husbandry; Arts and Humanities; Behavioural Sciences; Biology; Business Administration; Chemistry; Cosmetology; Education; English; Health Sciences; Mathematics; Pharmacy; Physiology; Preschool Education; Rehabilitation and Therapy; Social and Community Services; Social Sciences); **Workforce Development** (Biology; Chemistry; English; Mathematics)

Further Information: Traditional and Open Learning Institution. Also Davis and Mississauga campuses and Oakville Skills Training Centre.

History: Founded 1967.

Fees: (Canadian Dollar): Full-Time Tuition Fee, 1,135-1,160 per Term.

Degrees and Diplomas: *Certificate/Diploma*; *Applied Degree*; *University Certificate/Diploma*; *Bachelor's Degree*; *Graduate Diploma/Certificate*. Also advanced diploma, 2-3 yrs.

Student Numbers *2009-2010*: Total 16,000
Last Updated: 15/12/10

ST. AUGUSTINE'S SEMINARY (UNIVERSITY OF TORONTO)

2661 Kingston Road, Scarborough, Ontario M1M 1M3
Tel: +1(416) 261-7207
Fax: +1(416) 261-2529
EMail: tehil@web.net
Website: http://www.staugustines.on.ca/

Rector: A. Robert Nusca

Institutes
Theology (Anthropology; Bible; Christian Religious Studies; History of Religion; Religious Education; Religious Studies; Theology)

Programmes
Philosophy (Philosophy); **Religious Education** (MRE) (Religious Education); **Sacred Theology and Master of Divinity** (STB and Mdiv) (Religion; Theology); **Theological Studies** (Theology); **Theological Studies and Lay Ministry** (Religion; Theology)

History: Founded 1913.

Governing Bodies: Board of Governors; Academic Council; Formation Council.

Fees: (Canadian Dollar): tuition fee, 518.50 per course for Canadian students and 1,393 per course for International students.

Degrees and Diplomas: Bachelor's Degree; Master's Degree; Graduate Diploma/Certificate. Also Honors Master of Divinity Thesis, 1 yr; Non-degree Diploma Programmes.

Student Residential Facilities: Residence for candidates to the priesthood, the Priestly Formation Programme and the Diaconate Formation Programme.

Libraries: c. 39,000 vols; 170 periodicals and newspaper; collection of DVDs, videos and audio cassettes.
Last Updated: 07/02/11

ST. CLAIR COLLEGE OF APPLIED ARTS AND TECHNOLOGY

South Campus, 2000 Talbot Road West, Windsor, Ontario N9A 6S4
Tel: +1(519) 966-1656
Fax: +1(519) 972-3811
EMail: info@stclaircollege.ca
Website: http://www.stclaircollege.ca/

President: John A. Strasser
Tel: +1(519) 972-2701, Fax: +1(519) 966-3763
EMail: jstrasser@stclaircollege.ca

Campuses
Thames (Chatham) (Accountancy; Administration; Biology; Business Administration; Chemistry; Child Care and Development; Communication Studies; Computer Science; Cosmetology; Electrical Engineering; Justice Administration; Mathematics; Mechanical Engineering; Nursing; Occupational Therapy; Paramedical Sciences; Police Studies; Preschool Education; Protective Services; Welfare and Protective Services); **Wallaceburg** (James A. Burgess Skills Centre); **Windsor** (Accountancy; Administration; Advertising and Publicity; Architecture; Arts and Humanities; Automation and Control Engineering; Behavioural Sciences; Business Administration; Child Care and Development; Civil Engineering; Computer Networks; Computer Science; Construction Engineering; Cooking and Catering; Cosmetology; Dental Hygiene; Dentistry; Electrical Engineering; Electronic Engineering; Energy Engineering; English; Finance; Fire Science; Gerontology; Graphic Design; Health Sciences; Heating and Refrigeration; Horticulture; Hotel and Restaurant; Human Resources; Interior Design; International Business; Journalism; Justice Administration; Laboratory Techniques; Landscape Architecture; Law; Management; Marketing; Mechanical Engineering; Metal Techniques; Natural Sciences; Nursing; Paramedical Sciences; Pharmacy; Police Studies; Power Engineering; Preschool Education; Protective Services; Service Trades; Social and Community Services; Social Work; Taxation; Technology; Theatre; Tourism; Veterinary Science; Wood Technology)

Centres
Arts (Windsor) (Advertising and Publicity; Cooking and Catering; Criminal Law; Graphic Design; Hotel and Restaurant; Journalism; Law; Taxation; Tourism)

Further Information: Traditional and Open Learning Institution. Also Windsor - Downtown, MediaPlex, Chatham and Wallaceburg campuses.

History: Founded 1966.

Fees: (Canadian Dollar): Full-time Domestic, 2,320.00 for year one and 2,214.31 for year two and three; Full-time International, 9,588 per annum; Full-time USA, 6,050 per annum.

Degrees and Diplomas: Certificate/Diploma; Bachelor's Degree; Graduate Diploma/Certificate. Also College Advanced Diploma, 3 yrs
Last Updated: 15/12/10

ST. JEROME'S UNIVERSITY (UNIVERSITY OF WATERLOO) (SJU)

290 Westmount Road, North, Waterloo, Ontario N2L 3G3
Tel: +1(519) 884-8110
Fax: +1(519) 884-5759
EMail: webmaster@usjc.uwaterloo.ca
Website: http://www.sju.ca

President and Vice-Chancellor: David B. Perrin
Tel: +1(519) 884-8111, Ext.28245
EMail: dperrin@sju-serv1.uwaterloo.ca

Faculties
Arts (Accountancy; Anthropology; Arts and Humanities; Business Administration; Classical Languages; Communication Studies; Computer Science; Criminology; Development Studies; Eastern European Studies; Economics; English; Family Studies; Fine Arts; French Studies; Gender Studies; Geography; German; Greek (Classical); History; Human Resources; International Business; Latin; Latin American Studies; Law; Medieval Studies; Music; Philosophy; Political Sciences; Psychology; Religious Studies; Russian; Social Sciences; Sociology; Spanish; Speech Studies; Statistics; Theatre; Women's Studies); **Mathematics** (Accountancy; Business Administration; Computer Science; Insurance; Mathematics; Mathematics and Computer Science)

Programmes
Interdisciplinary (Cognitive Sciences; Criminology; Development Studies; East Asian Studies; Economics; Family Studies; Fine Arts; Gender Studies; Human Resources; International Studies; Jewish Studies; Law; Management; Medieval Studies; Peace and Disarmament; Performing Arts; Religion; Religious Music; Speech Studies; Women's Studies); **Master of Catholic Thought** (Catholic Theology)

Further Information: Also 3 affiliated colleges

History: Founded 1865 as St. Jerome's College, acquired present status and title 1959. A federated University College.

Governing Bodies: Board of Governors; the Senate (University of Waterloo).

Academic Year: September to August (September-December; January-April; May-August)

Fees: (Can. Dollars): tuition fees, c. 3,700-10,000 per annum; International students, c. 14,000-28,400 per annum.

Main Language(s) of Instruction: English

Degrees and Diplomas: Bachelor's Degree; Master's Degree. Degrees are offered by the University of Waterloo. Also Honours Bachelor's degree, 4 yrs; Double Degrees in 5 yrs jointly offered by University of Waterloo and Wilfred Laurier University: Business Administration/ Computer Science; Business Administration and Mathematics.

Student Services: Academic counselling, Canteen, Cultural centre, Handicapped facilities, Health services, Nursery care, Social counselling, Sports facilities

Libraries: 40,000 vols and periodicals and a variety of audiovisual and electronic resources.
Last Updated: 07/02/11

ST. PETER'S SEMINARY (UNIVERSITY OF WESTERN ONTARIO (KING'S UNIVERSITY COLLEGE))

1040 Waterloo Street North, London, Ontario N6A 3Y1
Tel: +1(519) 432-1824
Fax: +1(519) 432-0964
EMail: jslawik@uwo.ca
Website: http://www.stpetersseminary.ca/

Rector: Stevan A. Wlusek
Tel: +1(519) 432-1824 Ext. 213 EMail: swlusek@uwo.ca

Vice-Rector: Murray Watson
Tel: +1(519) 432-1824 Ext. 247 EMail: mwatson@dol.ca

Programmes
Diocesan Studies (Religion); **Non-degree Studies** (Adult Education); **Philosophy** (Philosophy); **Theology** (Theology)

History: Founded 1912.

Fees: (Canadian Dollar): Tuition fee, 5,181-6,297.94 per annum for Canadian students and 15,936 per annum for International students.

Degrees and Diplomas: *Bachelor's Degree; Master's Degree.* Also Non-degree Certificate in Adult Education.
Last Updated: 07/02/11

TRENT UNIVERSITY

1600 West Bank Drive, Peterborough, Ontario K9J 7B8
Tel: +1(705) 748-1011
Fax: +1(705) 748-1246
EMail: communications@trentu.ca
Website: http://www.trentu.ca

President and Vice-Chancellor: Steven E. Franklin (2009-)
Tel: +1(705) 748-1347, Fax: +1(705) 748-1657
EMail: kspearing@trentu.ca

Provost and Vice-President, Academic: Gary Boir
Tel: +1(705) 748-1011 Ext. 7695, Fax: +1(705) 748-1105
EMail: provost@trentu.ca

International Relations: Michael Allcott, Director, international Programmes
Tel: +1(705) 748-1314 EMail: michaelallcott@trentu.ca

Campuses
Oshawa (Anthropology; English; Environmental Studies; History; Literature; Natural Resources; Psychology; Sociology)

Centres
Community-Based Education *(Trent)* (Education); **Kawartha World Issues** (Education)

Departments
Ancient History and Classics (Ancient Civilizations; Archaeology; Classical Languages; Greek (Classical); Latin; Literature; Theatre); **Anthropology** (Anthropology; Archaeology; Biology; Cultural Studies; Linguistics); **Astronomy and Physics** (Astronomy and Space Science; Physics); **Biology** (Biology; Health Sciences); **Canadian Studies** (Canadian Studies); **Chemistry** (Analytical Chemistry; Biochemistry; Chemistry; Inorganic Chemistry; Organic Chemistry; Physical Chemistry); **Computing and Information Systems** *(COIS)* (Computer Science; Information Technology; Software Engineering); **Cultural Studies** (Comparative Literature; Cultural Studies; Film; Literature; Media Studies; Music; Social Sciences; Theatre; Visual Arts); **Economics** (Econometrics; Economics; Finance; International Business; Labour and Industrial Relations; Mathematics; Statistics); **English Literature** (English; Literature); **Geography** (Earth Sciences; Geography; Geography (Human); Meteorology; Natural Sciences; Soil Conservation; Soil Management; Surveying and Mapping; Town Planning; Water Science; Wildlife); **History** (History); **Indigenous Studies** (Indigenous Studies; Native American Studies; Native Language; Natives Education); **Mathematics** (Computer Science; Economics; Finance; Mathematical Physics; Mathematics; Statistics); **Modern Languages and Literatures** (French; German; Hispanic American Studies; Linguistics; Literature; Modern Languages); **Philosophy** (Ethics; Philosophy); **Politics** (Political Sciences); **Sociology** (Sociology); **Women's Studies** (Women's Studies)

Programmes
Biochemistry and Molecular Biology (Biochemistry; Molecular Biology); **Business Administration** (Business Administration; Development Studies; Human Resources; Management); **Chemical Physics** (Chemistry; Physics); **Computing and Physics** (Computer Science; Physics); **Concurrent Teacher Education** *(Queen's-Trent)* (Art Education; Computer Education; Foreign Languages Education; Humanities and Social Science Education; Mathematics Education; Native Language Education; Science Education; Teacher Training); **Degree Completion Options** *(for Students at Ontario Community Colleges)* (Biology; Business Administration; Chemistry; Computer Science; Environmental Studies; Information Technology; Natural Resources); **Diploma Studies** (Canadian Studies; Development Studies; Environmental Studies; Indigenous Studies; Native Language; Natives Education); **Ecological Restoration** (Ecology); **Emphasis** (Agriculture; Anthropology; Archaeology; Ethics; Food Science; International Economics; International Studies; Law; Linguistics; Medieval Studies; Modern History; Museum Studies; Nordic Studies; Political Sciences; Surveying and Mapping; Teacher Training); **Environmental Chemistry** (Chemistry; Environmental Studies); **Environmental Resource Science / Studies** *(ERS)* (Chemistry; Ecology; Environmental Studies; Indigenous Studies; Natural Resources); **Forensic Science** (Biology; Chemistry; Computer Science; Forensic Medicine and Dentistry; Physics; Political Sciences; Psychology; Sociology); **Indigenous Environmental Studies** *(IES)* (Environmental Studies; Indigenous Studies); **International Development Studies** (Cultural Studies; Development Studies; Economics; Environmental Studies; Gender Studies; History; Political Sciences; Social Problems; Social Studies); **International Political Economy** (International Economics); **International Students, Study Abroad** *(Trent International)* (Business Administration; Development Studies; Economics; Education; Forensic Medicine and Dentistry; Natural Sciences; Nursing; Social Sciences); **Professional Studies** (Business Administration; Education; Forensic Medicine and Dentistry; Nursing; Teacher Training); **Psychology** (Cognitive Sciences; Developmental Psychology; Neurosciences; Psychology); **Special Programs and Opportunities** *(including Trent-Fleming Joint Programmes)* (Teacher Training)

Schools
Education and Professional Learning (Art Education; Computer Education; Education; Foreign Languages Education; Natives Education; Science Education; Teacher Training); **Graduate Studies** (Ancient Civilizations; Anthropology; Astronomy and Space Science; Biological and Life Sciences; Canadian Studies; Chemistry; Classical Languages; Computer Science; Cultural Studies; Economics; Engineering; English; Environmental Studies; Geography; Greek (Classical); History; Indigenous Studies; Latin; Materials Engineering; Mathematics; Natural Resources; Physics; Political Sciences; Psychology); **Nursing** *(Trent/Fleming)* (Anatomy; Microbiology; Nursing; Pharmacology; Physiology)

Units
Trail Studies *(Trent-Fleming)* (Economics; Education; Environmental Studies; Health Sciences; Heritage Preservation; Parks and Recreation; Tourism)

Further Information: Also Oshawa campus.

History: Founded 1963 as an independent university with full degree-granting powers by an Act of the Ontario legislature which received Royal Assent in April 1963. Accepted first students 1964. Teaching takes the form of tutorial and seminar work in small groups. Undergraduates are expected to do considerable academic work outside term.

Governing Bodies: Senate; Board of Governors

Academic Year: September to April (September-December; January-April)

Admission Requirements: Secondary school certificate or recognized foreign equivalent

Fees: (Can.Dollars): Undergraduate tuition fees, 6,218.70-6,823.27 per annum for Canadian students and 16,416.83-17,021.40 per annum for International students; Graduate tuition fees, 6,321.37 per annum for Canadian students and 13,719.15 per annum for International students.

Main Language(s) of Instruction: English

Degrees and Diplomas: *University Certificate/Diploma; Bachelor's Degree; Master's Degree; Doctoral Degree.* Also Honours degree,

4 yrs; Joint Major Honours programme; compressed Honours degree programme in Nursing (B.Sc.N.), 3 yrs; Second Entry Professional Degrees.

Student Services: Academic counselling, Canteen, Cultural centre, Employment services, Foreign student adviser, Handicapped facilities, Health services, Nursery care, Sports facilities

Student Residential Facilities: Yes

Libraries: Thomas J. Bata Library, c. 525,000 vols; 280,000 microforms

Publications: Journal of Canadian Studies (quarterly)

Academic Staff 2010-2011	MEN	WOMEN	TOTAL
FULL-TIME	143	96	**239**
PART-TIME	–	–	**70**
STAFF WITH DOCTORATE			
FULL-TIME	–	–	**238**

Student Numbers 2010-2011			
All (Foreign Included)	2,734	4,940	**7,674**
FOREIGN ONLY	325	163	**488**

Part-time students, 1,311.
Last Updated: 08/02/11

UNIVERSITY OF GUELPH (U OF G)

50 Stone Road East, Guelph, Ontario N1G 2W1
Tel: +1(519) 824-4120
Fax: +1(519) 766-94881
EMail: admission@registrar.uoguelph.ca
Website: http://www.uoguelph.ca

President and Vice-Chancellor: Alastair Summerlee (2003-)
Tel: +1(519) 824-4120 Ext. 52200 EMail: president@uoguelph.ca

Provost and Vice-President (Academic): Maureen Mancuso
Tel: +1(519) 824-4120 Ext. 53845
EMail: m.mancuso@exec.uoguelph.ca

International Relations: Steven N. Liss, Associate Vice-President (Research Services)and International Liaison Officer
Tel: +1(519) 824-4120, Ext. 54124

Centres
Advanced Analysis (Biological and Life Sciences; Physics); **Agricultural Renewable Energy and Sustainability** (Agricultural Engineering; Energy Engineering); **Agri-Technology Commercialization** (Agricultural Engineering; Energy Engineering; Waste Management); **Aquaculture** (Aquaculture); **Arthritis Network Core Facility** (Canadian) (Rheumatology); **Bioproducts Discovery and Development** (Biological and Life Sciences); **Cooperative Wildlife Health** (Canadian) (Wildlife); **Couple and Family Therapy** (Social Problems); **Electrochemical Technology** (Chemical Engineering; Electronic Engineering); **Families, Work and Well-being**; **Food Safety Network** (Food Technology; Safety Engineering); **Food Technology** (Guelph - GFTC) (Food Technology); **Genetic Improvement of Livestock** (Animal Husbandry; Genetics); **Genomics Facility/Advanced Analysis** (Genetics); **Health and Performance** (Health Sciences; Sports Medicine); **Land and Water Stewardship** (Soil Management; Water Management); **Landscape Architecture Community Outreach** (Landscape Architecture); **Language and Literacy Research Network** (Canadian) (Education); **Mathematics of Information Technology and Complex Systems** (Information Technology; Mathematics); **Nuclear Magnetic Resonance** (Nuclear Physics); **Nutrition Modelling** (Nutrition); **Organization and Management Solution** (Human Resources; Psychology); **Poultry Welfare** (Meat and Poultry); **Psychological Services** (Psychology); **Public Health and Zoonoses** (Public Health); **Rural Wastewater** (Ontario) (Water Management); **Study of Animal Welfare** (Campbell) (Welfare and Protective Services); **Urban Systems Environment Design** (Environmental Engineering; Town Planning); **Veterinary Teaching Hospital** (Veterinary Science); **Water Safety and Security** (AquaSanitas) (Public Health; Water Management); **Weather Innovation** (Meteorology)

Colleges
Agriculture (Ontario) (Agricultural Economics; Agriculture; Animal Husbandry; Botany; Environmental Studies; Food Science; Horticulture; Landscape Architecture; Meat and Poultry; Plant and Crop Protection; Rural Planning; Rural Studies; Safety Engineering); **Arts**

(Art History; Caribbean Studies; Classical Languages; English; European Studies; Fine Arts; French; French Studies; German; Greek (Classical); History; Italian; Latin; Latin American Studies; Literature; Modern Languages; Music; Philosophy; Spanish; Theatre; Visual Arts); **Biological Science** (Biological and Life Sciences; Biology; Biomedicine; Biophysics; Cell Biology; Health Sciences; Molecular Biology; Neurosciences; Nutrition; Sports; Toxicology); **Management and Economics** (Agricultural Business; Business Administration; Business and Commerce; Economics; Environmental Studies; Finance; Hotel and Restaurant; Human Resources; Leadership; Management; Marketing; Public Administration; Real Estate; Tourism); **Physical and Engineering Science** (Applied Mathematics; Bioengineering; Biological and Life Sciences; Biology; Biomedical Engineering; Biophysics; Chemistry; Computer Engineering; Computer Science; Earth Sciences; Engineering; Environmental Engineering; Environmental Studies; Forest Biology; Geology; Hydraulic Engineering; Information Sciences; Mathematics; Mechanical Engineering; Meteorology; Natural Resources; Physics; Statistics); **Social and Applied Human Sciences** (Anthropology; Child Care and Development; Clinical Psychology; Cognitive Sciences; Criminal Law; Development Studies; Earth Sciences; Environmental Studies; Family Studies; Geography; Industrial and Organizational Psychology; Neurosciences; Nutrition; Political Sciences; Psychology; Public Administration; Social Problems; Social Psychology; Social Sciences; Sociology; Surveying and Mapping); **Veterinary Science** (Ontario) (Biology; Biomedical Engineering; Epidemiology; Immunology; Medicine; Microbiology; Parasitology; Pathology; Public Health; Veterinary Science)

Groups
Advanced Foods and Materials Network (AFMNet) (Biological and Life Sciences; Ethics; Food Science; Law); **Bioconversion Network** (Energy Engineering; Environmental Engineering)

Institutes
Biodiversity (Ontario) (Molecular Biology); **Comparative Cancer Investigation** (Oncology); **Ichthyology** (Axelrod) (Marine Biology); **Robotics and Intelligent Systems** (Artificial Intelligence; Robotics); **Turfgrass** (Guelph - GTI) (Horticulture)

Laboratories
Advanced Robotics and Intelligent Systems (Artificial Intelligence; Automation and Control Engineering; Robotics); **Aqualab** (Hagen) (Aquaculture; Biology; Ecology; Physiology; Toxicology); **Laboratory Services** (Food Technology)

Programmes
Graduate Studies (Agricultural Economics; Agriculture; Animal Husbandry; Anthropology; Aquaculture; Biology; Biomedical Engineering; Biophysics; Business Administration; Caribbean Studies; Cell Biology; Chemistry; Computer Science; Criminal Law; Criminology; Development Studies; Economics; Engineering; English; European Studies; Family Studies; Fine Arts; Food Science; Food Technology; French Studies; Geography; Health Sciences; History; Hydraulic Engineering; Landscape Architecture; Latin American Studies; Leadership; Literature; Management; Marketing; Mathematics; Meat and Poultry; Medicine; Molecular Biology; Natural Resources; Neurosciences; Nutrition; Philosophy; Physics; Political Sciences; Psychology; Public Health; Rural Planning; Rural Studies; Safety Engineering; Sociology; Statistics; Theatre; Toxicology; Veterinary Science; Visual Arts; Writing); **Research** (U of G / OMAFRA enhanced partnership) (Agriculture; Food Science); **University of Guelph-Humber** (Business Administration; Child Care and Development; Law; Media Studies; Physical Therapy; Psychology; Social and Community Services)

Research Centres
Agricultural Trade Policy and Competitive Research Network (Canadian) (Agricultural Business); **Arboretum Gene Bank** (Botany; Genetics); **Business Development Office** (Business Administration); **Controlled Environment Systems** (Environmental Studies); **International Leadership** (Leadership); **Metals in the Human Environment** (Environmental Studies); **Neutrino Observatory** (Sudbury) (Nuclear Engineering); **Pollination Initiative** (Canadian) (Biological and Life Sciences; Ecology; Entomology); **Shared Hierarchical Academic Research Computing Network** (SHARCNET) (Business Computing; Computer Science); **Transgenic Plant** (Guelph) (Botany; Genetics)

Research Institutes

Food Safety *(Canadian - CRIFS)* (Food Technology; Safety Engineering)

Research Units

Human Nutraceutical (Dietetics)

Further Information: Also Ontario Veterinary College Teaching Hospital. Affiliated with Collège d'Alfred, Kemptville College and Ridgetown College. Overseas study semesters in: London; Cracow; India; Latin America and Paris. 66 Study Abroad programmes in 27 countries. Open Learning Bureau offers Continuing Education, Open Learning Programmes, Distance Education and English as a Scond Language (ESL) University Preparation Programmes.

History: Founded 1964 comprising 3 colleges previously affiliated with the University of Toronto (Ontario Veterinary College, Ontario Agricultural College and Macdonald Institute).

Governing Bodies: Board of Governors; Senate

Academic Year: September-December; January-April; May-August

Admission Requirements: Ontario Secondary School Diploma (OSSD), or equivalent

Fees: (Can. Dollars): Undergraduate studies, 2,606-4,236 per semester for Canadian students and 8,461-25,598 per semester for international students. Graduate studies, 2,256-5,180 per semester for Canadian students and 5,420-5,720 per semester for international students.

Main Language(s) of Instruction: English

Degrees and Diplomas: *University Certificate/Diploma*; *Bachelor's Degree*; *Master's Degree*; *Graduate Diploma/Certificate*; *Doctoral Degree*. Also honours Bachelor's degree, 4 yrs; Double degree programmes (Bachelor's degree and Diploma) offered in 4 yrs through University of Guelph-Humber.

Student Services: Academic counselling, Canteen, Cultural centre, Employment services, Foreign student adviser, Foreign Studies Centre, Handicapped facilities, Health services, Language programs, Nursery care, Social counselling, Sports facilities

Student Residential Facilities: For 5,000 students

Special Facilities: MacDonald Stewart Art Centre. CFRU Radio. The Donald Forster Sculpture Park

Libraries: Total 3,108,788 items. CD-ROM public catalogue and online circulation system with remote access

Publications: Research Magazine

Academic Staff *2007-2008*	TOTAL
FULL-TIME	800
PART-TIME	c. 140

Student Numbers *2007-2008*	
All (Foreign Included)	c. 18,000

Last Updated: 21/02/11

UNIVERSITY OF ONTARIO INSTITUTE OF TECHNOLOGY (UOIT)

2000 Simcoe Street North, Oshawa, Ontario L1H 7K4
Tel: +1(905) 721-8668
Fax: +1(905) 721-3178
EMail: admissions@uoit.ca
Website: http://www.uoit.ca

President and Vice-Chancellor: Ronald Bordessa
Tel: +1(905) 721-8668 Ext. 3212 EMail: ron.bordessa@uoit.ca

Vice-President, Finance and CFO: Tom Austin
Tel: +1(905) 721-8668 Ext. 3796 EMail: tom.austin@uoit.ca

Provost and vice-president, Academic: Richard Marceau
Tel: +1(905) 721-8668 Ext. 3147 EMail: richard.marceau@uoit.ca

Faculties

Business and Information Technology (Accountancy; Business Administration; Business and Commerce; E-Business/Commerce; Finance; Human Resources; Information Technology; International Business; Management; Marketing; Transport Management); **Education** (Computer Education; Education; Mathematics Education; Science Education; Teacher Training); **Energy Systems and Nuclear Science** (Energy Engineering; Engineering; Health Sciences; Nuclear Engineering; Power Engineering; Safety Engineer-

ing); **Engineering and Applied Science** (Automotive Engineering; Electrical Engineering; Energy Engineering; Engineering; Mechanical Engineering; Nuclear Engineering; Production Engineering; Software Engineering); **Health Sciences** (Community Health; Dental Hygiene; Haematology; Health Sciences; Information Management; Laboratory Techniques; Microbiology; Nursing; Occupational Therapy; Pharmacy; Physical Therapy; Respiratory Therapy); **Science** (Applied Mathematics; Biological and Life Sciences; Chemistry; Computer Science; Forensic Medicine and Dentistry; Management; Materials Engineering; Mathematics; Physics); **Social Science and Humanities** (Arts and Humanities; Business and Commerce; Communication Studies; Constitutional Law; Criminology; Health Sciences; Human Rights; Labour Law; Law; Marketing; Media Studies; Police Studies; Social Policy; Social Sciences; Technology)

History: Founded 2002.

Governing Bodies: Board of Governors; Academic Council.

Fees: (Canadian Dollar): Undergraduate tuition, 5,140-8,082 per annum for Canadian students and 14,040-16,592 per annum for international students. Graduate tuition, 4,898-9,846 per annum for Canadian students and 9,450-18,375 per annum for international students.

Degrees and Diplomas: *Bachelor's Degree*; *Master's Degree*; *Graduate Diploma/Certificate*; *Doctoral Degree*. Also Honours Bachelor of Applied Science, 4 yrs; Concurrent BSc/BEd Five Year Teacher Education Programme, 5 yrs

Last Updated: 21/02/11

⌨ UNIVERSITY OF OTTAWA / UNIVERSITÉ D'OTTAWA (UOTTAWA)

Tabaret Hall, 75 Laurier Avenue East, Ottawa, Ontario K1N 6N5
Tel: +1(613) 562-5700
Fax: +1(613) 562-5323
EMail: infoservice@uOttawa.ca
Website: http://www.uottawa.ca

President: Allan Rock (2008-)
Tel: +1(613) 562-5809, Fax: +1(613) 562-5103
EMail: president@uOttawa.ca

Vice-Rector, Resources: Victor Simon
Tel: +1(613) 562-5822 EMail: vrres@uottawa.ca

International Relations: Gilles Breton, Associate Vice-President Academic (International) and Director of the International Office
Tel: +1(613) 562-5800 Ext. 1450, Fax: +1(613) 562-5100
EMail: uointl@uOttawa.ca; gbreton@uOttawa.ca

Centres

Advanced Research in Environmental Genomics *(CAREG)* (Genetics); **Catalysis Research and Innovation; Environmental Law and Global Sustainability** (Environmental Studies; Law); **Environmental Microbiology** *(CREM)* (Microbiology); **Governance** (Government); **Hazard Mitigation and Emergency Management** (Safety Engineering); **Human Rights Research and Education** (Human Rights); **Interdisciplinary Research on Citizenship and Minorities** *(CIRCEM)*; **International Policy Studies** *(CIPS)* (International Studies); **Law, Technology and Society** (Law; Technology); **Neural Dynamics** (Neurosciences); **Neuromuscular Disease** *(University of Ottawa)* (Medicine; Neurology; Pathology)

Departments

Professional Training Service (Communication Studies; Grammar; Management; Writing)

Faculties

Arts (Arabic; Art History; Art Management; Asian Studies; Canadian Studies; Celtic Languages and Studies; Classical Languages; Communication Studies; Conducting; English; English Studies; Environmental Studies; Ethics; Film; Fine Arts; Foreign Languages Education; French Studies; Geography; German; Greek (Classical); History; Indigenous Studies; Information Sciences; Italian; Jewelry Art; Journalism; Latin; Latin American Studies; Linguistics; Medieval Studies; Modern History; Music; Music Education; Philosophy; Political Sciences; Psycholinguistics; Public Relations; Religious Studies; Russian; Sociology; Spanish; Surveying and Mapping; Theatre; Translation and Interpretation; Visual Arts; Women's

Studies; Writing); **Education** (Canadian Studies; Cultural Studies; Education; Educational Administration; Educational and Student Counselling; Health Education; Higher Education; Literacy Education; Natives Education; Teacher Training; Technology Education; Women's Studies); **Engineering** (Aeronautical and Aerospace Engineering; Bioengineering; Biomedical Engineering; Chemical Engineering; Civil Engineering; Computer Engineering; Computer Science; E-Business/Commerce; Electrical Engineering; Engineering; Engineering Management; Environmental Engineering; Information Technology; Mechanical Engineering; Software Engineering); **Graduate and Postdoctoral Studies** (Administration; Anthropology; Behavioural Sciences; Biochemistry; Biology; Biomedical Engineering; Business Administration; Canadian Studies; Canon Law; Cell Biology; Chemical Engineering; Chemistry; Civil Engineering; Classical Languages; Communication Studies; Computer Engineering; Computer Science; Conducting; Criminology; Development Studies; E-Business/Commerce; Earth Sciences; Economic History; Economics; Education; Electrical Engineering; Engineering Management; English; Environmental Engineering; Epidemiology; Ergotherapy; Ethics; Fine Arts; French Studies; Genetics; Geography; Government; Greek; Health Administration; Health Education; Health Sciences; Higher Education; History; Immunology; Information Sciences; Information Technology; International Relations; Latin; Law; Linguistics; Management; Materials Engineering; Mathematics; Mechanical Engineering; Medical Technology; Medicine; Medieval Studies; Microbiology; Modern History; Molecular Biology; Music; Music Education; Neurosciences; Nursing; Pathology; Peace and Disarmament; Philosophy; Physical Therapy; Physics; Political Sciences; Production Engineering; Psychology; Public Administration; Public Health; Rehabilitation and Therapy; Religious Education; Religious Studies; Slavic Languages; Social and Community Services; Social Work; Sociology; Software Engineering; Spanish; Speech Therapy and Audiology; Statistics; Theatre; Theology; Toxicology; Translation and Interpretation; Visual Arts; Women's Studies); **Health Sciences** (Biophysics; Health Sciences; Leisure Studies; Nursing; Occupational Therapy; Parks and Recreation; Physical Therapy; Physiology; Psychology; Public Health; Social Sciences; Speech Therapy and Audiology; Sports; Sports Management); **Law** (Civil Law; Environmental Studies; Human Rights; International Law; Labour Law; Law); **Medicine** (Anaesthesiology; Biochemistry; Cardiology; Cell Biology; Community Health; Dermatology; Endocrinology; Epidemiology; Gastroenterology; Genetics; Gerontology; Gynaecology and Obstetrics; Haematology; Immunology; Laboratory Techniques; Medicine; Microbiology; Molecular Biology; Nephrology; Neurology; Oncology; Ophthalmology; Otorhinolaryngology; Paediatrics; Pathology; Physical Therapy; Plastic Surgery; Psychiatry and Mental Health; Public Health; Radiology; Rehabilitation and Therapy; Respiratory Therapy; Rheumatology; Surgery; Urology); **Science** (Biochemistry; Biological and Life Sciences; Biology; Biomedicine; Chemical Engineering; Chemistry; Computer Science; Earth Sciences; Economics; Environmental Studies; Geology; Geophysics; Mathematics; Pharmacy; Physics; Science Education; Statistics; Toxicology); **Social Sciences** (Anthropology; Civil Law; Clinical Psychology; Criminology; Development Studies; Economics; Experimental Psychology; French; Gerontology; Government; Human Rights; International Economics; International Studies; Law; Modern Languages; Peace and Disarmament; Political Sciences; Psychology; Public Administration; Social and Community Services; Social Sciences; Social Work; Sociology; Women's Studies)

Institutes

Brain and Mind *(University of Ottawa)* (Behavioural Sciences; Neurosciences); **Canadian Studies** (Canadian Studies); **Environment** (Environmental Studies); **Medical Devices Innovation** (Medical Technology); **Official Languages and Bilingualism** *(OLBI)* (English; French; Modern Languages); **Population Health** (Public Health); **Prevention of Crime** *(IPC)* (Criminal Law; Criminology; Police Studies); **Science, Society and Policy** *(ISSP)*; **Systems Biology** *(Ottawa)* (Biology); **Women's Studies** (Women's Studies)

Research Centres

Accounting *(CGA)* (Accountancy); **Biopharmaceuticals and Biotechnology** (Biotechnology; Pharmacy); **Educational and Community Services** *(CRECS)* (Education; Social and Community Services); **Emerging Pathogens** *(University of Ottawa)* (Epidemiology); **French Canadian Culture** (Canadian Studies; French

Studies); **Photonics** (Electrical and Electronic Engineering); **Sport in Canadian Society** (Sports); **Tax** *(CGA)* (Taxation)

Schools

Management *(Telfer)* (Accountancy; Business Administration; Business and Commerce; E-Business/Commerce; Finance; Health Administration; Human Resources; International Business; Leadership; Management; Marketing)

Further Information: Also 6 Teaching Hospitals

History: Founded 1848 as College of Bytown, became College of Ottawa 1933. Acquired present status and title 1965.

Governing Bodies: Board of Governors; Senate

Academic Year: September to August (September-December; January-April; May-August)

Admission Requirements: Senior secondary school diploma, or recognized foreign equivalent

Fees: (Can. Dollars): Undergraduate tuition, 6,094.90-7,911.92 per annum, except for national programmes in Common and Civil Law, 12,656.66-13,391.33 per annum and Medicine Programme, 19,019.19 per annum; Graduate tuition, 5,256.12-6,457.41 per annum, except MBA, 13,604 per annum and MHA, 10,541.70 per annum. For International students: undergraduate tuition, 16,443.63-20,363.28 per annum, except for national programmes in Common and Civil Law, 29,829.44; Graduate tuition, 9,157.41-11,516.41 per annum, except MBA, 21,542.66 per annum and MHA, 16,205.25 per annum.

Main Language(s) of Instruction: French; English

International Co-operation: With universities in Argentina; Australia; Belgium; Brazil; Canada; Chile; China - Hong Kong; Costa Rica; Denmark; Ecuador; France; Germany; Iceland; Ireland; Israel; Italy; Japan; Kenya; Korea; Lebanon; Mexico; Morocco; Norway; Peru; Poland; Romania; Senegal; Slovak Republic; Spain; Switzerland; Sweden; Taiwan; Thailand; Netherlands; Tunisia; Turkey; United Kingdom; USA; Uruguay and Venezuela

Accrediting Agencies: Association Canadienne des Orthophonistes et Audiologistes (ACOA), Health Services Administration (ACEHSA), American Psychological Association

Degrees and Diplomas: *University Certificate/Diploma; Bachelor's Degree; Master's Degree; Graduate Diploma/Certificate; Doctoral Degree (PhD).* Also Honours Bachelor's degree; Joint Honours Bachelor's degree; Executive MBA; Integrated programmes; Professional development programmes.

Student Services: Academic counselling, Canteen, Cultural centre, Employment services, Foreign student adviser, Foreign Studies Centre, Handicapped facilities, Health services, Language programs, Nursery care, Social counselling, Sports facilities

Student Residential Facilities: 2,880 places in seven different residences

Libraries: Central Library, (General, Medicine, Law and Education)

Press or Publishing House: Presses de l'Université d'Ottawa/ University of Ottawa Press

Academic Staff 2009-2010	MEN	WOMEN	TOTAL
FULL-TIME	–	–	**4,300**
PART-TIME	–	–	c. **830**

Student Numbers 2009-2010			
All (Foreign Included)	16,986	22,865	**39,851**
FOREIGN ONLY	–	–	**1,929**

Last Updated: 22/02/11

SAINT PAUL UNIVERSITY / UNIVERSITÉ SAINT PAUL

223 Main Street, Ottawa, Ontario K1S 1C4
Tel: +1(613) 236-1393 +1(800) 637-685
Fax: +1(613) 782-3005
EMail: info@ustpaul.ca
Website: http://www.ustpaul.ca

Rectrice: Chantal Beauvais (2009-)
Tel: +1(613) 236-1393, Fax: +1(613) 751-4020
EMail: rectrice-rector@ustpaul.ca

Registrar/Registraire: Claudette Dubé-Socqué
Tel: +1(613) 236-1393, Fax: +1(613) 782-3033
EMail: csocque@ustpaul.ca

Centres
Ethics (Ethics); **Lonergan** (Business Administration; Ethics; Peace and Disarmament; Religion); **Women and Christian Traditions** (Bible; Ethics; History; Pastoral Studies; Psychology; Religion; Theology)

Faculties
Canon Law (Administration; Canon Law); **Human Sciences** (Communication Studies; Peace and Disarmament; Psychology; Religious Studies); **Philosophy** (Arts and Humanities; Ethics; Philosophy; Theology); **Theology** (Christian Religious Studies; Ethics; Missionary Studies; Pastoral Studies; Religion; Religious Education; Religious Studies; Theology)

Institutes
Eastern Christian Studies *(Metropolitan Andrey Sheptytsky)* (Christian Religious Studies)

Research Centres
Conflict (Peace and Disarmament); **Religious History of Canada** (History of Religion)

History: Founded 1848 as College of Byton. A Federated institution whose degree-granting authority is held in abeyance with the University of Ottawa.

Governing Bodies: Senate; Council of Administration

Academic Year: September to April (September-December; January-April). Also Summer Session

Admission Requirements: Secondary school certificate or recognized equivalent

Fees: (Can. Dollars): Undergraduate tuiton, 2,043.60 per semester for Canadian students (part-time, 556,40) and 4,378.40 per semester for international students (part-time, 1,108.64); Graduate tuition, 2,178.80 per semester for Canadian students (part-time, 743.60) and 4,539.60 per semester for international students (part-time, 1,632.80).

Main Language(s) of Instruction: French, English

Degrees and Diplomas: *University Certificate/Diploma; Bachelor's Degree; Master's Degree; Graduate Diploma/Certificate; Doctoral Degree.* Also Honours Bachelor's degree programmes; Ecclesiastical Programmes (Bachelor's degree, Licenciate and Doctorate) in Philosophy.

Student Services: Academic counselling, Canteen, Employment services, Handicapped facilities, Social counselling

Student Residential Facilities: For c. 230 students

Libraries: c. 500,000 vols

Publications: Locos, A Journal of Eastern Christian Studies; Mission, Revue des Sciences de la Mission; Pastoral Sciences-Sciences pastorales; Studia Canonica; Theoforum

Press or Publishing House: Novalis

UNIVERSITY OF ST. MICHAEL'S COLLEGE (UNIVERSITY OF TORONTO) (USMC)

81 St. Mary Street, Toronto, Ontario M5S 1J4
Tel: +1(416) 926-1300
Fax: +1(416) 926-7276
Website: http://www.utoronto.ca/stmikes

President: Anne Anderson (2009-)
Tel: +1(416) 926-7147, Fax: +1(416) 926-7277
EMail: anne.anderson@utoronto

Principal: Mark McGowan EMail: mark.mcgowan@utoronto.ca

Divisions
Continuing Education (Leadership; Religion; Social Work)

Faculties
Theology *(Graduate Studies)* (Christian Religious Studies; Ecology; Leadership; Religion; Religious Education; Theology)

Institutes
Canadian Catholic Bioethics (Ethics); **Mediaeval Studies** *(Pontifical)* (Medieval Studies)

Programmes
Book and Media Studies (Media Studies; Publishing and Book Trade); **Celtic Studies** (Archaeology; Celtic Languages and Studies; Cultural Studies; Fine Arts; Folklore; Irish; Literature; Music); **Christianity and Culture** (Christian Religious Studies; Cultural Studies); **Medieval Studies** (Medieval Studies); **Religious Education** (Religious Education)

Further Information: Students registered at St Michael's College have full access to all of the more than 2,000 courses offered in over 300 programs by the Faculty of Arts and Science of the University of Toronto.

History: Founded 1852 as St. Michael's College, acquired present status and title 1958. A Federated University of the University of Toronto.

Governing Bodies: Collegium; Senate

Academic Year: September to April (September-December; January-April). Also Summer Sessions (May-June; July-August)

Admission Requirements: Secondary school certificate or recognized foreign equivalent

Fees: (Can. Dollars): Basic degree fees, 518.50 per course for Canadian students and 1,393 per course for international students. Advanced degree fees, 1,021-9,197 per annum, foreign students (Theology), 2,322-13,938 per annum.

Main Language(s) of Instruction: English

Degrees and Diplomas: *University Certificate/Diploma; Bachelor's Degree (BA); Master's Degree (MA); Graduate Diploma/Certificate; Doctoral Degree (PhD).* Also Concurrent Education programme in Religious Education that enables students to study simultaneously for a Bachelor of Arts degree (with a major in Christianity and Culture) and a Bachelor of Education, 5 yrs; joint degree programmes (MDiv/MRE and MDiv/MA) 4 yrs; Non-degree certificates.

Student Services: Academic counselling, Handicapped facilities, Social counselling

Student Residential Facilities: Yes

Libraries: c. 400,000 vols

Publications: Medieval Studies *(annually)*; Original texts, documents and commentaries regularly edited and published in field of Medieval research
Last Updated: 22/02/11

UNIVERSITY OF TORONTO (U OF T)

27 King's College Circle, Toronto, Ontario M5S 1A1
Tel: +1(416) 978-2011
Fax: +1(416) 978-7022
EMail: ut.info@utoronto.ca
Website: http://www.utoronto.ca/

President: David Naylor (2005-)
Tel: +1(416) 978-2121, Fax: +1(416) 971-1360
EMail: president@utoronto.ca

Vice-President (Human Resources and Equity): Angela Hildyard
Tel: +1(416) 978-4865, Fax: +1(416) 978-2592
EMail: angela.hildyard@utoronto.ca

International Relations: Lorna Jean Edmonds, Assistant Vice-President, International Relations
Tel: +1(416) 978-8828, Fax: +1(416) 978-4431
EMail: international.relations@utoronto.ca; lj.edmonds@utoronto.ca

Campuses
University of Toronto Mississauga (Accountancy; Ancient Civilizations; Anthropology; Arabic; Art History; Astronomy and Space Science; Behavioural Sciences; Biochemistry; Biology; Biotechnology; Business and Commerce; Canadian Studies; Cell Biology; Chemistry; Chinese; Cinema and Television; Commercial Law; Communication Studies; Computer Science; Criminal Law; Criminology; Cultural Studies; Earth Sciences; Ecology; Economics; English; Environmental Management; Environmental Studies; Finance; Fine Arts; French; French Studies; Gender Studies; Geography; Geology; German; Hindi; History; Human Resources; Information Sciences; Information Technology; International Relations; Italian; Labour and Industrial Relations; Latin; Law; Linguistics; Logic; Management; Marketing; Mathematical Physics; Mathematics; Molecular Biology; Neurology; Paleontology; Performing Arts; Persian; Philosophy; Physics; Physiology; Political Sciences; Psychology; Religion; Sanskrit; Science Education;

Sociology; Spanish; Statistics; Surveying and Mapping; Theatre; Visual Arts; Women's Studies; Writing); **University of Toronto Scarborough** (Anthropology; Arabic; Art History; Arts and Humanities; Astronomy and Space Science; Astrophysics; Biochemistry; Biological and Life Sciences; Biology; Business Administration; Cell Biology; Chemistry; Chinese; Cognitive Sciences; Computer Science; Ecology; Economics; English; Environmental Engineering; Environmental Studies; Geography; Health Sciences; Hindi; History; Information Technology; International Studies; Journalism; Latin; Linguistics; Management; Mathematics; Media Studies; Microbiology; Modern Languages; Molecular Biology; Music; Neurosciences; Performing Arts; Philosophy; Political Sciences; Psychology; Public Administration; Religion; Sanskrit; Social Sciences; Sociology; South and Southeast Asian Languages; Spanish; Statistics; Teacher Training; Urban Studies; Visual Arts; Women's Studies)

Centres

Aboriginal Studies (Indigenous Studies); **Academic Retiree**; **Bioethics** *(Joint)* (Ethics); **Cellular and Biomolecular Research** *(Terrence Donnelly)* (Cell Biology; Molecular Biology); **Cities** (Development Studies; Urban Studies); **Comparative Literature** (Comparative Literature); **Criminology** (Criminology); **Diaspora and Transnational Studies** (Geography (Human)); **Economics and Public Affairs** (Economics); **Environment** (Environmental Studies); **Ethics** (Ethics); **European, Russian and Eurasian Studies** (Eurasian and North Asian Languages; European Studies; Russian); **Forensic Science** (Forensic Medicine and Dentistry); **Global Affairs** *(Munk)* (American Studies; Asian Studies; Eastern European Studies; European Studies; Germanic Studies; International Studies; Latin American Studies; Pacific Area Studies; South Asian Studies; Southeast Asian Studies); **Global Change Science**; **Health Promotion** (Health Sciences); **History and Philosophy of Science and Technology** (History; Philosophy); **Humanities** *(Jackman)* (Arts and Humanities); **Industrial Relations and Human Resources** (Human Resources; Labour and Industrial Relations); **Innovation Law and Policy** *(CILP)* (Law); **International Health** (Health Sciences); **International Studies** (International Studies); **Medieval Studies** (Medieval Studies); **Molecular Medicine** *(McLaughlin)* (Medicine; Molecular Biology); **Neurobiology of Stress** *(UTSC)* (Neurosciences); **Nuclear Engineering** (Nuclear Engineering); **Peace and Conflict Studies** *(Trudeau)* (Peace and Disarmament); **Pulp and Paper** (Paper Technology); **Quantum Information and Quantum Control** *(CQIQC)* (Chemistry; Computer Science; Electrical Engineering; Materials Engineering; Mathematics; Physics); **Reformation and Renaissance Studies** (Modern History); **Research in Neurodegenerative Diseases** (Neurology); **Research in Women's Health** (Health Sciences); **Sexual Diversity Studies** (Gender Studies); **South Asian Studies** (South Asian Studies); **Study of Drama** *(Graduate)* (Theatre); **Study of France and the Francophone World** (French; French Studies); **Study of Pain** (Health Sciences); **Study of Religion** (Religion); **Study of United States** (American Studies); **Urban and Community Studies** (Social and Community Services; Urban Studies); **Urban Health Initiatives** (Health Sciences); **Urban Schooling** *(OISE/UT)* (Education); **Wilson** *(Faculty of Medicine)* (Medicine); **Women's Studies in Education** *(OISE/UT)* (Education; Women's Studies)

Faculties

Applied Science and Engineering (Aeronautical and Aerospace Engineering; Applied Chemistry; Bioengineering; Biomedical Engineering; Chemical Engineering; Civil Engineering; Computer Engineering; Electrical Engineering; Energy Engineering; Engineering; Environmental Engineering; Industrial Engineering; Materials Engineering; Mechanical Engineering; Mining Engineering; Nanotechnology); **Architecture, Landscape, and Design** *(John H. Daniels)* (Architecture; Design; Landscape Architecture); **Arts and Science** (Actuarial Science; African Studies; American Studies; Anthropology; Archaeology; Architecture; Art History; Artificial Intelligence; Arts and Humanities; Asian Religious Studies; Asian Studies; Astronomy and Space Science; Astrophysics; Biology; Business and Commerce; Canadian Studies; Caribbean Studies; Cell Biology; Celtic Languages and Studies; Chemistry; Christian Religious Studies; Cinema and Television; Classical Languages; Communication Studies; Comparative Literature; Computer Science; Criminology; East Asian Studies; Ecology; Economics; Electrical Engineering; English; Environmental Studies; Ethics; Eurasian and North Asian Languages; European Studies; Finance; Fine Arts;

Foreign Languages Education; French; French Studies; Gender Studies; Genetics; Geography; Geology; German; Government; Greek (Classical); Health Sciences; History; Human Resources; Hungarian; Immunology; Indigenous Studies; Inorganic Chemistry; International Economics; International Law; International Relations; International Studies; Italian; Jewish Studies; Korean; Labour and Industrial Relations; Latin; Latin American Studies; Law; Linguistics; Literature; Materials Engineering; Mathematics; Medieval Studies; Modern History; Multimedia; Optics; Pacific Area Studies; Peace and Disarmament; Philosophy; Physics; Political Sciences; Polymer and Plastics Technology; Portuguese; Psychiatry and Mental Health; Psychology; Public Administration; Publishing and Book Trade; Religion; Russian; Slavic Languages; Sociology; South Asian Studies; Spanish; Statistics; Theatre; Urban Studies; Visual Arts; Women's Studies; Writing; Zoology); **Dentistry** (Anaesthesiology; Dental Technology; Dentistry; Oral Pathology; Orthodontics; Periodontics; Surgery); **Forestry** (Ecology; Environmental Studies; Forest Biology; Forest Economics; Forest Management; Forestry); **Information** (Information Sciences; Museum Studies); **Law** (Commercial Law; Constitutional Law; Environmental Studies; International Law; Law); **Medicine** (Anaesthesiology; Biochemistry; Biology; Biomedical Engineering; Biophysics; Community Health; Genetics; Gynaecology and Obstetrics; Health Administration; Health Sciences; Immunology; Laboratory Techniques; Medical Auxiliaries; Medical Technology; Medicine; Nutrition; Occupational Health; Occupational Therapy; Oncology; Ophthalmology; Otorhinolaryngology; Paediatrics; Pathology; Pharmacology; Physical Therapy; Physiology; Psychiatry and Mental Health; Public Health; Radiology; Rehabilitation and Therapy; Speech Therapy and Audiology; Surgery; Toxicology); **Music** (Jazz and Popular Music; Music; Music Education; Music Theory and Composition; Musical Instruments; Musicology; Opera; Singing); **Nursing** *(Lawrence S. Bloomberg)* (Anaesthesiology; Health Sciences; Nursing); **Pharmacy** *(Leslie L. Dan)* (Chemistry; Molecular Biology; Pharmacy); **Physical Education and Health** (Health Education; Physical Education); **Social Work** *(Factor-Inwentash)* (Administration; Development Studies; Family Studies; Gerontology; Social Problems; Social Work; Welfare and Protective Services)

Institutes

Aerospace Studies (Aeronautical and Aerospace Engineering); **Asian** (Asian Studies); **Biomaterials and Biomedical Engineering** *(IBBME)* (Biomedical Engineering; Materials Engineering); **Child Study** *(ICS)* (Child Care and Development); **Cinema Studies** (Cinema and Television); **Communication and Culture** *(UTM)* (Communication Studies; Cultural Studies); **Drug Research** (Pharmacology); **Education** *(Ontario)* (Adult Education; Child Care and Development; Curriculum; Development Studies; Education; Educational Administration; Educational and Student Counselling; Educational Psychology; Foreign Languages Education; Higher Education; Philosophy of Education; Primary Education; Psychology; Secondary Education; Sociology; Teacher Training; Technology Education); **Emerging Communication Technology** (Biotechnology; Electronic Engineering; Information Technology; Nanotechnology; Optics); **European Studies** (European Studies); **Knowledge Media Design** *(KMDI)* (Media Studies); **Lassonde** (Geological Engineering; Geology); **Life Course and Aging** (Gerontology; Health Sciences; Psychology; Social Sciences); **Medical Science** *(IMS)* (Communication Studies; Ethics; Medicine; Radiology); **Music** *(Canadian)* (Music); **Optical Sciences** (Optics); **Policy Analysis** (Economics; Social Policy); **Risk Management** (Insurance); **Theoretical Astrophysics** *(Canadian)* (Astrophysics); **Theoretical Astrophysics** *(Canadian - CITA)* (Astrophysics); **Women's Studies and Gender Studies** (Gender Studies; Women's Studies)

Programmes

Transitional Year *(TYP)* (Arts and Humanities; English; Literature; Social Sciences)

Research Institutes

Dental (Dentistry); **Mathematical Science** *(Fields)* (Mathematics)

Schools

Continuing Studies (Accountancy; Advertising and Publicity; Arabic; Architecture; Business Administration; Chinese; Communication Studies; E-Business/Commerce; English; Environmental Studies; Finance; French; German; Germanic Languages; Greek; Health Sciences; Human Resources; Italian; Japanese; Korean;

Latin; Law; Leadership; Literature; Management; Marketing; Music; Persian; Philosophy; Polish; Portuguese; Public Relations; Religion; Romanian; Russian; Spanish; Translation and Interpretation; Turkish; Vietnamese; Visual Arts; Writing); **Global Affairs** *(Munk)* (American Studies; Asian Studies; Eurasian and North Asian Languages; European Studies; Hungarian; International Relations; International Studies; Korean; Latin American Studies; Pacific Area Studies; Peace and Disarmament; Russian; South Asian Studies); **Graduate Studies** (Accountancy; Adult Education; Aeronautical and Aerospace Engineering; Ancient Civilizations; Anthropology; Applied Chemistry; Architecture; Art History; Asian Studies; Astronomy and Space Science; Astrophysics; Biochemistry; Biology; Biomedical Engineering; Biophysics; Biotechnology; Cell Biology; Chemical Engineering; Chemistry; Cinema and Television; Civil Engineering; Classical Languages; Communication Studies; Community Health; Comparative Literature; Computer Engineering; Computer Science; Criminology; Cultural Studies; Curriculum; Dentistry; Design; Developmental Psychology; East Asian Studies; Ecology; Economics; Education; Educational Administration; Educational and Student Counselling; Educational Psychology; Electrical Engineering; English; Environmental Engineering; Environmental Studies; Ethics; Ethnology; Eurasian and North Asian Languages; European Studies; Finance; Foreign Languages Education; Forest Management; Forestry; French; Gender Studies; Genetics; Geography; Geology; German; Germanic Languages; Gerontology; Government; Greek (Classical); Health Administration; Health Sciences; Higher Education; History; Human Resources; Immunology; Indigenous Studies; Industrial Engineering; Information Sciences; International Relations; International Studies; Italian; Jewish Studies; Labour and Industrial Relations; Landscape Architecture; Latin; Law; Linguistics; Literature; Management; Materials Engineering; Mathematics; Mechanical Engineering; Medical Technology; Medicine; Medieval Studies; Middle Eastern Studies; Museum Studies; Music; Musical Instruments; Neurosciences; Nursing; Nutrition; Occupational Health; Occupational Therapy; Optics; Pacific Area Studies; Pathology; Pharmacology; Pharmacy; Philosophy; Philosophy of Education; Physical Therapy; Physics; Physiology; Political Sciences; Primary Education; Psychology; Public Administration; Public Health; Radiology; Rehabilitation and Therapy; Religion; Russian; Secondary Education; Slavic Languages; Social Welfare; Social Work; Sociology; South Asian Studies; Spanish; Speech Therapy and Audiology; Statistics; Town Planning; Toxicology; Visual Arts; Women's Studies); **Management** *(Joseph L. Rotman)* (Business Administration; Business and Commerce; Finance; Management); **Public Health** *(Dalla Lana)* (Behavioural Sciences; Community Health; Epidemiology; Health Sciences; Nutrition; Occupational Health; Psychiatry and Mental Health; Public Health; Social and Preventive Medicine; Statistics); **Public Policy and Governance** (Government; Public Administration; Social Policy)

Further Information: Also Mississauga and Scarborough campuses.

History: Founded as King's College at York 1827 by Royal Charter, in close collaboration with the Church of England. Became secularized and acquired present title 1849. University of St. Michael's College and Victoria University entered into federation with the University 1890, Trinity College was federated 1904. The University has 8 colleges: Innis, New, St. Michael's, Trinity, University, Victoria, Woodsworth.

Governing Bodies: Governing Council

Academic Year: September to August (September-December; January-May; May-June; July-August)

Admission Requirements: Secondary school certificate or recognized foreign equivalent

Fees: (Canadian Dollar): For Canadian students: Undergraduate tuition, 5,216-10,095 per annum; graduate tuition, 6,621-26,883 per annum (except Doctorate in Pharmacy, 33,120 per annum; MBA, 24,978-36,733 per annum). For international students: undergraduate tuition, 16,082-34,267 per annum; graduate tuition, 10,132-36,183 per annum (except Doctorate in Dentistry, 55,914 per annum; Doctorate in Medicine, 53,604 per annum; MBA, 33,000-48,293 per annum).

Main Language(s) of Instruction: English

Degrees and Diplomas: *University Certificate/Diploma*; *Bachelor's Degree*; *Master's Degree*; *Graduate Diploma/Certificate*; *Doctoral Degree (PhD)*. Also Concurrent Teacher Education Programmes; Collaborative Programmes (multidisciplinary programs that involve a wide range of graduate departments across the institution); Combined Programmes, two degree programmes within a reduced timeframe of four years (Juris Doctor and the Master of Information; Combined Doctor of Medicine/Doctor of Philosophy Programme); Professional Master's degree programmes in Health Sciences.

Student Services: Academic counselling, Canteen, Cultural centre, Employment services, Foreign student adviser, Foreign Studies Centre, Handicapped facilities, Health services, Language programs, Nursery care, Social counselling, Sports facilities

Student Residential Facilities: Yes

Special Facilities: Observatory; Two Art Galleries; Three Theatres

Libraries: Total, 14.8m vols (46 libraries). Thomas Fisher Rare Book Library (500,000 vols)

Press or Publishing House: University of Toronto Press

Academic Staff *2008-2009*	MEN	WOMEN	TOTAL
FULL-TIME	1,496	858	**2,354**
PART-TIME	–	–	c. **144**
Student Numbers *2009-2010*			
All (Foreign Included)	30,384	38,672	**69,056**
FOREIGN ONLY	3,421	3,340	**6,761**

Part-time students, 6,646.
Last Updated: 23/02/11

UNIVERSITY OF TRINITY COLLEGE (UNIVERSITY OF TORONTO)

6 Hoskin Avenue, Toronto, Ontario M5S 1H8
Tel: +1(416) 978-2522
Fax: +1(416) 978-2797
EMail: registrar@trinity.utoronto.ca
Website: http://www.trinity.utoronto.ca

Provost and Vice-Chancellor: Andy Orchard (2007-)
Tel: +1(416) 978-2689, Fax: +1(416) 978-2749
EMail: provost@trinity.utoronto.ca

Registrar and Director of Student Services: Bruce W. Bowden
Tel: +1(416) 978-2687, Fax: +1(416) 978-2831
EMail: bowden@trinity.utoronto.ca

Faculties
Divinity (Christian Religious Studies; Religion; Religious Music; Theology)

Programmes
Ethics, Society, and Law *(Interdisciplinary)* (Anthropology; Classical Languages; Criminology; Economics; Ethics; Geography; Law; Philosophy; Political Sciences; Religion; Sociology); **Immunology** *(Interdisciplinary)* (Immunology); **Independent Studies**; **International Relations** *(Interdisciplinary)* (Economics; History; International Relations; Political Sciences); **International Relations/ Peace and Conflict Studies** *(Joint specialist degree)* (International Relations; Peace and Disarmament)

History: Founded 1852 as Trinity College, the Church of England University in Canada. Became a Federated University of the University of Toronto 1904.

Academic Year: September to August (September-December; January-April; May-August)

Admission Requirements: Secondary school certificate or recognized foreign equivalent

Fees: (Can. Dollars): 3,196-3,250 per annum; foreign students, 8,000-10,000

Main Language(s) of Instruction: English

Degrees and Diplomas: *University Certificate/Diploma*; *Bachelor's Degree*; *Master's Degree*: Theology; *Doctoral Degree*: Theology

Student Services: Academic counselling, Handicapped facilities, Social counselling

Student Residential Facilities: 2 residences for 430 students.

Special Facilities: George Ignatieff Theatre

Libraries: c. 150,000 vols

Publications: Trinity University Review
Last Updated: 24/02/11

UNIVERSITY OF WATERLOO (UW)

200 University Avenue West, Waterloo, Ontario N2L 3G1
Tel: +1(519) 888-4567
Fax: +1(519) 888-8009
EMail: registrar@uwaterloo.ca
Website: http://www.uwaterloo.ca

President and Vice-Chancellor: Feridun Hamdullahpur (2010-)
Tel: +1(519) 888-4567 Ext. 32202, Fax: +1(519) 888-6337
EMail: president@uwaterloo.ca

Registrar: Kenneth Lavigne
Tel: +1(519) 888-4567, Ext. 2263, Fax: +1(519) 746-2882
EMail: klavigne@uwaterloo.ca

International Relations: Leo Rothenburg, Associate Vice President, International
Tel: +1(519) 888-4567 Ext. 35466 EMail: leoroth@uwaterloo.ca

Centres

Accounting Research and Education *(CARE)* (Accountancy); **Advanced Materials Joining** (Materials Engineering); **Advanced Studies in Finance** *(CASF)* (Finance); **Advancement of Co-operative Education** *(Waterloo - WatCACE)* (Education); **Advancement of Trenchless Technologies at Waterloo** *(CATT)* (Technology); **Applied Cryptographic Research** *(CACR)* (Mathematics and Computer Science); **Arts and Technology** *(Canadian - CCAT)* (Arts and Humanities; Technology); **Atmospheric Sciences** *(Waterloo)* (Earth Sciences; Environmental Studies); **Automotive Research** *(Waterloo - WatCAR)* (Automotive Engineering); **Business, Entrepreneurship and Technology** *(Conrad - CBET)* (Business Administration; Management; Technology); **Computational Mathematics in Industry and Commerce** *(CCMIC)* (Business Computing; Mathematics and Computer Science); **Contact Lens Research** *(CCLR)* (Optical Technology); **Control of Emerging Contaminants** (Environmental Studies); **Ecosystem Resilience and Adaptation** *(ERA)* (Ecology; Environmental Management); **Education in Mathematics and Computing** *(CEMC)* (Computer Education; Mathematics Education); **German Studies** *(Waterloo)* (German; Germanic Studies); **Heritage Resource** (Heritage Preservation); **Mental Health Research** *(CMHR)* (Psychiatry and Mental Health); **Pavement and Transportation Technology** *(CPATT)* (Transport Engineering); **Survey Research** *(SRC)* (Actuarial Science; Statistics); **Teaching Excellence** *(CTE)* (Teacher Training); **Theoretical Neuroscience** (Neurosciences)

Colleges

Conrad Grebel University *(Affiliated)* (Arts and Humanities; Bible; Christian Religious Studies; English; Fine Arts; History; Music; New Testament; Peace and Disarmament; Philosophy; Religious Studies; Sociology; Theology); **Renison University** *(Affiliated)* (Asian Studies; Chinese; Development Studies; Japanese; Korean; Psychology; Social Work; Sociology); **St. Jerome's University** *(Affiliated)* (Accountancy; Anthropology; Business Administration; Catholic Theology; Christian Religious Studies; Classical Languages; Cognitive Sciences; Communication Studies; Criminology; Development Studies; East Asian Studies; Eastern European Studies; Economics; English; Family Studies; Finance; Fine Arts; French Studies; Gender Studies; Geography; German; Greek (Classical); History; Human Resources; Insurance; International Studies; Italian; Jewish Studies; Latin; Latin American Studies; Law; Management; Mathematics; Mathematics and Computer Science; Medieval Studies; Music; Peace and Disarmament; Performing Arts; Philosophy; Political Sciences; Psychology; Religious Music; Religious Studies; Russian; Sociology; Spanish; Speech Studies; Theatre; Women's Studies); **St. Paul's University** *(Affiliated)* (Canadian Studies; Development Studies; English; Indigenous Studies; International Studies; Philosophy; Psychology; Religious Studies; Sociology)

Faculties

Applied Health Sciences (Gerontology; Health Sciences; Leisure Studies; Parks and Recreation; Physical Therapy); **Arts** (Accountancy; Acting; Ancient Civilizations; Anthropology; Archaeology; Art History; Art Management; Ceramic Art; Chinese; Classical Languages; Communication Studies; Criminology; Development Studies; Dutch; East Asian Studies; Eastern European Studies; Economics; English; Family Studies; Film; Finance; Fine Arts; French; French Studies; Gender Studies; German; Germanic Languages; Germanic Studies; Government; Greek (Classical); History; International Economics; Italian; Japanese; Jewish Studies; Latin; Latin American Studies; Law; Leadership; Literature; Media Studies; Medieval Studies; Music; Painting and Drawing; Peace and Disarmament; Philosophy; Polish; Political Sciences; Psychology; Religious Music; Religious Studies; Russian; Slavic Languages; Social Work; Sociology; Spanish; Speech Studies; Taxation; Theatre; Women's Studies; Writing); **Engineering** (Architecture; Automation and Control Engineering; Biotechnology; Chemical Engineering; Civil Engineering; Computer Engineering; Electrical Engineering; Electronic Engineering; Energy Engineering; Engineering; Engineering Management; Environmental Engineering; Fire Science; Geological Engineering; Management; Mechanical Engineering; Microwaves; Nanotechnology; Safety Engineering; Software Engineering); **Environment** (Design; Development Studies; Ecology; Economics; Environmental Management; Environmental Studies; Geography; Natural Resources; Political Sciences; Regional Planning; Sociology; Statistics; Surveying and Mapping; Tourism; Town Planning; Waste Management; Water Management); **Mathematics** (Actuarial Science; Applied Mathematics; Computer Science; Finance; Mathematical Physics; Mathematics; Mathematics and Computer Science; Statistics); **Science** (Astronomy and Space Science; Astrophysics; Biochemistry; Biology; Biophysics; Biotechnology; Cell Biology; Chemistry; Earth Sciences; Ecology; Environmental Studies; Genetics; Geochemistry; Geological Engineering; Geology; Geophysics; Mathematical Physics; Microbiology; Molecular Biology; Optics; Optometry; Pharmacology; Pharmacy; Physics; Physiology; Toxicology)

Institutes

Advanced Information Technology *(Nortel Networks - NNI)* (Information Technology); **Biochemistry and Molecular Biology** (Biochemistry; Molecular Biology); **Computer Research** *(ICR)* (Computer Science); **Groundwater Research** *(Waterloo - WIGR)* (Water Science); **Innovation Research** *(IIR)* (Management; Technology); **Insurance and Pension Research** *(IIPR)* (Insurance); **Nanotechnology** *(Waterloo)* (Nanotechnology); **Polymer Research** *(IPR)* (Polymer and Plastics Technology); **Quantum Computing** *(IQC)* (Computer Science); **Risk Research** *(IRR)* (Insurance); **Sustainable Energy** *(Waterloo - WISE)* (Energy Engineering); **Water** (Actuarial Science; Applied Mathematics; Biology; Chemical Engineering; Chemistry; Civil Engineering; Computer Science; Earth Sciences; Economics; Electronic Engineering; Engineering; Environmental Engineering; Environmental Management; Environmental Studies; Geography; Hydraulic Engineering; Mechanical Engineering; Natural Resources; Statistics; Water Science)

Research Institutes

Aging *(Schlegel - UW/ RIA)* (Gerontology); **Insurance, Securities and Quantitative Finance** *(Waterloo - WatRISQ)* (Finance; Insurance)

Further Information: Also Study Abroad programmes

History: Founded 1957 as Waterloo College Associate Faculties in association with Waterloo College (a Liberal Arts College operated by the Lutheran Church, later Waterloo Lutheran University, now Wilfrid Laurier University). Acquired present status and title 1959. The University of Waterloo Act was updated 1972.

Governing Bodies: Board of Governors; Senate

Academic Year: September to August (September-December; January-April; May-August)

Admission Requirements: Ontario Secondary school Diploma or recognized Canadian or foreign equivalent

Fees: (Can. Dollars): Undergraduate, 2,448-3,587 per quarter; co-operative programme, 2,919-5,911; foreign students, 8,366-9,113; foreign co-operative programme, 8,838-13,169. Graduate, 1,816 per term; foreign students, 4,590

Main Language(s) of Instruction: English

Accrediting Agencies: Association of Universities and Colleges of Canada; Ontario Council of Graduate Studies

Degrees and Diplomas: *University Certificate/Diploma; Bachelor's Degree; Master's Degree; Graduate Diploma/Certificate; Doctoral Degree (PhD).* Also Honours Bachelor's Degree awarded in most of the same fields of study as the Bachelor's Degree, 4-5 yrs.

Student Services: Academic counselling, Canteen, Cultural centre, Employment services, Foreign student adviser, Foreign Studies

Centre, Handicapped facilities, Health services, Language programs, Nursery care, Social counselling, Sports facilities

Student Residential Facilities: Yes

Special Facilities: Museum of Biology and Earth Sciences; Museum and Archives of Games; Museum of Optometry. Brubacher House. Humanities Theatre; Theatre of the Arts. Art Galleries. Observatory. Athletic facilities

Libraries: Dana Porter Library; Davis Centre Library; Map and Design Library; Optometry Library, total, c. 2,006,887 vols, 20,028 periodicals, 1,707,697 microforms, 1,178 audiovisual items

Publications: The New Quarterly *(quarterly)*

Academic Staff *2010-2011*	TOTAL
FULL-TIME	1,047

Student Numbers *2010-2011*	
All (Foreign Included)	32,505

Part-time students, 2,549.
Last Updated: 24/02/11

UNIVERSITY OF WESTERN ONTARIO (UWO)

1151 Richmond Street, London, Ontario N6A 3K7
Tel: +1(519) 661-2111
Fax: +1(519) 661-3388
EMail: reg_admissions@uwo.ca
Website: http://www.uwo.ca

President and Vice-Chancellor: Amit Chakma (2009-)
Tel: +1(519) 661-3106, Fax: +1(519) 661-3139
EMail: achakma@uwo.ca

Provost and Vice-President (Academic): Janice Deakin
Tel: +1(519) 661-3110 Ext. 83110, Fax: +1(519) 661-3676
EMail: provostvpa@uwo.ca

International Relations: Ted Hewitt, Vice-President (Research & International Relations)
Tel: +1(519) 661-3812 Ext. 83812 EMail: hewitt@uwo.ca

Colleges

Brescia University (Anthropology; Development Studies; Dietetics; English; Family Studies; Food Science; Food Technology; French; Health Sciences; History; Leadership; Management; Nutrition; Philosophy; Physical Therapy; Political Sciences; Psychology; Religious Studies; Sociology); **Huron University** *(Affiliated)* (Asian Studies; Business Administration; Chinese; Economics; English; French; French Studies; History; International Studies; Japanese; Jewish Studies; Management; Philosophy; Political Sciences; Psychology; Religious Studies; Theology); **King's University** *(Affiliated)* (Business Administration; Economics; English; Film; French; History; Italian; Literature; Mathematics; Modern Languages; Peace and Disarmament; Philosophy; Political Sciences; Psychology; Religious Studies; Social Work; Sociology; Spanish; Writing)

Faculties

Arts and Humanities (Arabic; Archaeology; Art Criticism; Art History; Arts and Humanities; Classical Languages; Communication Studies; Comparative Literature; Cultural Studies; English; Ethics; Film; Fine Arts; French; French Studies; Gender Studies; German; Greek (Classical); Hindi; History; Italian; Japanese; Korean; Latin; Linguistics; Literature; Mediterranean Studies; Modern Languages; Museum Studies; Philology; Philosophical Schools; Philosophy; Portuguese; Russian; Spanish; Speech Studies; Women's Studies; Writing); **Education** (Curriculum; Education; Educational Psychology; Educational Sciences; Leadership; Natives Education; Primary Education; Secondary Education; Special Education; Technology Education); **Engineering** (Chemical Engineering; Civil Engineering; Computer Engineering; Electrical Engineering; Electronic Engineering; Engineering; Environmental Engineering; Mechanical Engineering; Software Engineering); **Health Sciences** (Communication Disorders; Communication Studies; Health Sciences; Nursing; Occupational Therapy; Physical Therapy; Rehabilitation and Therapy); **Information and Media Studies** (Folklore; Information Sciences; Jazz and Popular Music; Journalism; Library Science; Media Studies); **Law** (Civil Law; Commercial Law; Comparative Law; International Law; Law; Private Law); **Music** *(Don Wright)* (Art History; Jazz and Popular Music; Music; Music Education; Music Theory and Composition; Musical Instruments; Musicology; Opera; Performing Arts; Singing); **Science** (Actuarial Science; Anatomy;

Applied Mathematics; Astronomy and Space Science; Biochemistry; Biological and Life Sciences; Biology; Biophysics; Cell Biology; Chemistry; Computer Science; Earth Sciences; Environmental Studies; Genetics; Geology; Geophysics; Immunology; Inorganic Chemistry; Materials Engineering; Mathematics; Mathematics and Computer Science; Microbiology; Organic Chemistry; Pathology; Pharmacology; Physics; Software Engineering; Statistics; Zoology); **Social Science** (Air Transport; American Studies; Anthropology; Archaeology; Canadian Studies; Cognitive Sciences; Criminology; Cultural Studies; Demography and Population; Economics; Ethnology; Finance; Gender Studies; Geography; History; Indigenous Studies; International Economics; International Relations; Jewish Studies; Latin American Studies; Linguistics; Management; Neurosciences; Philosophy; Political Sciences; Psychoanalysis; Psycholinguistics; Social Sciences; Sociology; Surveying and Mapping; Urban Studies; Women's Studies)

Programmes

London Regional Cancer *(Affiliated)* (Oncology)

Research Institutes

Lawson Health *(Affiliated)* (Health Sciences); **Robarts** (Dentistry; Engineering; Medicine)

Schools

Business *(Richard Ivey)* (Business Administration; Finance; Leadership; Management); **Graduate and Postdoctoral Studies** (Actuarial Science; American Studies; Anatomy; Anthropology; Applied Mathematics; Art History; Astronomy and Space Science; Biochemistry; Bioengineering; Biology; Biomedical Engineering; Biophysics; Business Administration; Cell Biology; Chemical Engineering; Chemistry; Civil Engineering; Classical Languages; Communication Disorders; Communication Studies; Comparative Literature; Computer Engineering; Computer Science; Demography and Population; Economics; Education; Electrical Engineering; English; Environmental Engineering; Environmental Studies; Epidemiology; Ethnology; Film; Fine Arts; Folklore; Food Science; French; Geography; Geology; Geophysics; Greek (Classical); Health Sciences; History; Immunology; Information Sciences; Jazz and Popular Music; Journalism; Latin; Law; Library Science; Linguistics; Management; Materials Engineering; Mathematics; Mechanical Engineering; Media Studies; Medicine; Microbiology; Music; Neurosciences; Nuclear Engineering; Nursing; Nutrition; Occupational Therapy; Orthodontics; Pathology; Pharmacology; Philosophy; Physical Therapy; Physics; Physiology; Political Sciences; Production Engineering; Psychology; Public Administration; Rehabilitation and Therapy; Social Work; Sociology; Spanish; Statistics; Theology; Toxicology; Visual Arts; Women's Studies); **Medicine and Dentistry** *(Schulich)* (Anaesthesiology; Anatomy; Biochemistry; Biology; Biomedical Engineering; Biophysics; Cell Biology; Dentistry; Engineering; Epidemiology; Gynaecology and Obstetrics; Immunology; Medicine; Microbiology; Neurology; Neurosciences; Oncology; Ophthalmology; Orthodontics; Otorhinolaryngology; Paediatrics; Pathology; Pharmacology; Physiology; Psychiatry and Mental Health; Rehabilitation and Therapy; Statistics; Surgery; Toxicology)

Further Information: Also two Teaching Hospitals: St. Joseph's Health Care London.

History: Founded 1878 as The Western University of London, Ontario. Acquired present status and title 1923.

Governing Bodies: Senate; Board of Governors

Academic Year: September to April (September-December; January-April); summer session, May to August

Admission Requirements: Secondary school certificate or recognized foreign equivalent. Specific requirements according to programme

Fees: (Can. Dollars): Undergraduate fees, 6,029.80-9,786.80 per annum (except Business, Law, Medicine and Dentistry: 14,337.80-58,313.80 per annum) for Canadian students and 16,903.80-21,693.80 per annum (except Business, Law, Medicine and Dentistry: 21,323.80-57,613.80 per annum) for international students; Graduate fees, 2,007.33-3,525.67 per term (except fro Dentistry 6,736.33 per term and Management, 27,500.00-35,000 per term) for Canadian students and 4,556.67-6,730 per term (except for Orthodontics, 15,050 per term) for international students.

Main Language(s) of Instruction: English
International Co-operation: Yes

Accrediting Agencies: Association of Universities and Colleges of Canada

Degrees and Diplomas: *University Certificate/Diploma*; *Bachelor's Degree*; *Master's Degree*; *Doctoral Degree*. Also Dual degrees (Concurrent degrees and Combined Degrees); Professional programmes and professional graduate programmes.

Student Services: Academic counselling, Canteen, Cultural centre, Employment services, Foreign student adviser, Foreign Studies Centre, Handicapped facilities, Health services, Language programs, Nursery care, Social counselling, Sports facilities

Student Residential Facilities: Yes

Special Facilities: Museum of Indian Archaeology (London); McIntoch Gallery, houses permanent collection of European, Canadian and American art; Observatory; Wind Tunnel

Libraries: Seven Libraries 3,085,319 vols; 3,883,392 microforms. Other Libraries

Publications: Academic Calendar, http://www.registrar.uwo.ca; Publications on the history of the University

Academic Staff *2010-2011*	**TOTAL**
FULL-TIME	c. **1,400**

Student Numbers *2010-2011*	
All (Foreign Included)	c. **35,000**
FOREIGN ONLY	**1,380**

Part-time students, 3,880.
Last Updated: 25/02/11

UNIVERSITY OF WINDSOR

401 Sunset Avenue, Windsor, Ontario N9B 3P4
Tel: + 1(519) 253-3000 + 1(519) 253-4232
Fax: + 1(519) 973-7050
EMail: registr@uwindsor.ca
Website: http://www.uwindsor.ca

President and Vice-Chancellor: Alan Wildeman (2008-)
Tel: + 1(519) 253-3000 Ext. 2000, Fax: + 1(519) 973-7070
EMail: president@uwindsor.ca

Provost and Vice-President, Academic: Leo Groarke
Tel: + 1(519) 253-3000 Ext. 4242, Fax: + 1(519) 561-1400
EMail: groarke@uwindsor.ca

International Relations: Bruce Tucker, Associate Vice-President, Academic Affairs
Tel: + 1(519) 253-3000 Ext. 2010, Fax: + 1(519) 561-1400
EMail: ucker1@uwindsor.ca

Centres
Automotive Research and Development (Automotive Engineering); **Business Advancement and Research** (Business Administration); **Canadian Aquatic Invasive Species Network** *(CAISN)* (Environmental Studies); **Catalysis and Materials Research** (Materials Engineering); **Community Based Research and Development** (Data Processing; Psychiatry and Mental Health); **Contemporary Studies in Accounting and Finance** *(Odette)* (Accountancy; Finance); **Excellence** *(AUTO21 Network)* (Automotive Engineering); **Executable Specifications of Grammars** (Grammar); **History of Health Communication - Cultures of Health** (Communication Studies; Health Sciences); **Imaging Research and Advanced Materials Characterization** (Engineering; Materials Engineering); **Intelligent Manufacturing Systems** (Production Engineering); **Inter-Faculty Programmes** (Arts and Humanities; Criminology; Environmental Studies; Forensic Medicine and Dentistry); **Lake Erie Millennium Network** (Ecology; Environmental Studies); **Materials and Surface Science** (Materials Engineering); **Smart Community Innovation**; **SpeechWeb Project** (Computer Science); **Statistical Consulting, Research and Learning Services** (Statistics); **Studies in Social Justice** (Human Rights); **Teaching and Learning** (Education; Teacher Training)

Courses
Distance Education (Accountancy; Art Management; Business Administration; Canadian Studies; Cell Biology; Economics; Finance; French; Genetics; International Law; Mathematical Physics; Microbiology; Public Administration; Sociology; Theatre)

Faculties
Arts and Social Sciences (Acting; Anthropology; Arabic; Art History; Art Management; Art Therapy; Arts and Humanities; Classical Languages; Communication Studies; Criminology; Cultural Studies; English; Film; Fine Arts; Foreign Languages Education; French; French Studies; German; Greek (Classical); History; Italian; Latin; Latin American Studies; Literature; Media Studies; Music; Music Theory and Composition; Musical Instruments; Philosophy; Political Sciences; Psychology; Social and Community Services; Social Work; Sociology; Spanish; Theatre; Visual Arts; Women's Studies); **Education** (Curriculum; Education; Educational Administration; Educational Sciences; Primary Education; Secondary Education; Teacher Training); **Engineering** (Automotive Engineering; Civil Engineering; Computer Engineering; Electrical Engineering; Engineering; Environmental Engineering; Industrial Engineering; Materials Engineering; Mechanical Engineering); **Graduate Studies** (Biochemistry; Biological and Life Sciences; Business Administration; Chemistry; Civil Engineering; Communication Studies; Computer Science; Criminology; Data Processing; Earth Sciences; Economics; Education; Electrical Engineering; English; Environmental Engineering; Environmental Studies; History; Industrial Engineering; Management; Materials Engineering; Mathematics; Mechanical Engineering; Nursing; Philosophy; Physical Therapy; Physics; Political Sciences; Production Engineering; Psychology; Social Work; Sociology; Statistics; Visual Arts); **Human Kinetics** (Physical Therapy; Sports; Sports Management); **Law** (Civil Law; Constitutional Law; Criminal Law; International Law; Law); **Nursing** (Health Sciences; Nursing); **Science** (Behavioural Sciences; Biochemistry; Biological and Life Sciences; Biology; Biotechnology; Chemistry; Cognitive Sciences; Computer Science; Earth Sciences; Econometrics; Economics; Environmental Studies; Information Technology; Mathematics; Mathematics and Computer Science; Mathematics Education; Neurosciences; Physics; Software Engineering; Statistics)

Groups
Developmental Group on Aging (Gerontology); **Signal and Information Processing** (Automation and Control Engineering; Computer Engineering; Electrical Engineering; Engineering; Robotics; Telecommunications Engineering)

Institutes
Diagnostic Imaging Research (Medical Technology); **Environmental Research** *(Great Lakes - GLIER)* (Environmental Studies); **North American Public Health** *(NAPHI - collaboration with Wayne State University)* (Public Health)

Laboratories
Clean Diesel Engine (Mechanical Engineering); **Computer Vision and Sensing Systems** (Computer Science); **Multi-purpose Environmental Modelling Facility** *(MEMF Lab)* (Environmental Studies)

Research Centres
Canadian-American (American Studies; Canadian Studies); **Data** *(Windsor)* (Data Processing); **Integrated Microsystems** (Computer Engineering; Electrical Engineering; Engineering); **Management of Intelligent Enterprise Systems, Security and Assurance** *(ARC-MIE)* (E-Business/Commerce; Insurance); **Reasoning, Argumentation and Rhetoric** (Communication Studies; Speech Studies); **Study of Violence against Women** *(Health)* (Women's Studies)

Research Groups
Animal Cognition (Zoology); **Feminist** (Women's Studies); **Humanities** (Arts and Humanities); **Light Metals Casting Technology** (Metal Techniques); **Operational** *(ORG)* (Operations Research); **Problem Gambling** (Behavioural Sciences); **Tribology of Lightweight Materials** (Materials Engineering); **Vehicle Dynamics and Control** (Automotive Engineering)

Research Institutes
Fluid Dynamics (Physics)

Schools
Business *(Odette)* (Accountancy; Business Administration; Business and Commerce; Business Computing; Finance; Human Resources; Industrial Management; International Business; Management; Marketing; Transport Management); **Medicine and Dentistry - Windsor Program** *(Schulich -)* (Dentistry; Medicine)

History: Founded 1857 as Assumption College, reorganized as Assumption University of Windsor 1953, affiliated with the Faculty of Arts and Science of University of Western Ontario 1919-1956. Acquired present title 1962.

Governing Bodies: Board of Governors; Senate

Academic Year: September to April (September-November; January-April)

Admission Requirements: Secondary school certificate or recognized foreign equivalent

Fees: (Can. Dollars): 2,500-3,000 per semester for Canadian students and 7,400-14,000 per semester for international students.

Main Language(s) of Instruction: English

Degrees and Diplomas: *University Certificate/Diploma; Bachelor's Degree; Master's Degree; Graduate Diploma/Certificate; Doctoral Degree (PhD).* Also concurrent programmes with Bachelor of Education; Combined Bachelor's degrees; Honours Bachelor's degrees and Combined Honours Bachelor's degrees, 4 yrs.

Student Services: Academic counselling, Canteen, Foreign student adviser, Foreign Studies Centre, Handicapped facilities, Health services, Language programs, Sports facilities

Student Residential Facilities: Yes

Libraries: Leddy Library; Paul Martin Law Library, total, 2.5m. Vols

Publications: Catalogue of Research and Scholarly Activity

Academic Staff 2008-2009	MEN	WOMEN	TOTAL
FULL-TIME	–	–	524
PART-TIME	–	–	280
STAFF WITH DOCTORATE			
FULL-TIME	–	–	c. 460
Student Numbers 2008-2009			
All (Foreign Included)	7,220	8,475	c. 15,695
FOREIGN ONLY	–	–	1,726

Part-time students, 3,760.
Last Updated: 25/02/11

VICTORIA UNIVERSITY (UNIVERSITY OF TORONTO)

73 Queen's Park Crescent, Toronto, Ontario M5S 1K7
Tel: +1(416) 585-4508
Fax: +1(416) 585-4584
EMail: applytovic@utoronto.ca
Website: http://www.vicu.utoronto.ca

President and Vice-Chancellor: Paul Gooch
Tel: +1(416) 585-4511, Fax: +1(416) 813-4072
EMail: vic.president@utoronto.ca; paul.gooch@utoronto.ca

Registrar: Susan McDonald
Tel: +1(416) 585-4405, Fax: +1(416) 585-4459
EMail: vic.registrar@utoronto.ca; s.mcdonald@utoronto.ca

International Relations: Caitriona Brennan, Coordinator, International Student Life and Study Abroad
Tel: +1(416) 585-4582 EMail: vic.international@utoronto.ca

Colleges
Emmanuel (Asian Religious Studies; Bible; History of Religion; Islamic Studies; New Testament; Pastoral Studies; Religion; Religious Education; Religious Music; Theology); **Victoria** (Architecture; Cinema and Television; Communication Studies; Comparative Literature; Education; Ethics; History; Linguistics; Literature; Logic; Modern History; Music; Philosophy; Political Sciences; Religious Studies; Teacher Training; Theatre; Visual Arts)

History: Founded 1836 as Upper Canada Academy at Cobourg, granted degree-conferring power as Victoria College 1841. Became a Federated University of the University of Toronto 1892.

Governing Bodies: Board of Regents; Senate

Academic Year: September to August (September-December; January-April; May-August)

Admission Requirements: Secondary school certificate or recognized foreign equivalent

Fees: (Can. Dollars): 1,160.37 per course; foreign students, 4,051.37; graduate, 11,400-27,000 per annum; graduate for foreign students, 16,800-37,839 per annum

Main Language(s) of Instruction: English

Degrees and Diplomas: *University Certificate/Diploma; Bachelor's Degree; Master's Degree; Doctoral Degree.* Also Concurrent Teacher Education Program (CTEP) that enables students to receive an Honours Bachelor of Arts or an Honours Bachelor of Science degree concurrently with a Bachelor of Education (B.Ed.) degree in 5 yrs.

Student Services: Academic counselling, Canteen, Handicapped facilities, Sports facilities

Student Residential Facilities: For 755 students

Special Facilities: Gardiner Museum of Ceramics

Libraries: Victoria University Library system, 294,990 vols; Microform items, 101,521; Victoria University United Church Archives, 7,410 monographs, 1,414 serial titles

Publications: The annual Senator Keith Davey Lecture, Liberal Politics and Thought *(annually)*

Academic Staff 2007-2008	MEN	WOMEN	TOTAL
FULL-TIME	10	5	15
PART-TIME	–	–	5
STAFF WITH DOCTORATE			
FULL-TIME	10	5	15
PART-TIME	–	–	5
Student Numbers 2007-2008			
All (Foreign Included)	1,340	2,590	**3,930**

Last Updated: 25/02/11

WATERLOO LUTHERAN SEMINARY (WILFRID LAURIER UNIVERSITY)

75 University Avenue West, Waterloo, Ontario N2L 3C5
Tel: +1(519) 884-0710 Ext. 3234
Fax: +1(519) 886-9351
EMail: swheeler@wlu.ca
Website: http://www.seminary.wlu.ca

Principal Dean and Registrar: David G. Pfrimmer
Tel: +1(519) 884-0710 Ext.3229 EMail: dpfrimmer@wlu.ca

Development and Administration Coordinator: Dorinda Kruger Allen
Tel: +1(519) 884-0710 Ext.3241, Fax: +1(519) 725-2434
EMail: dkrugerallen@wlu.ca

Programmes
Spiritual Care and Counselling (Psychology; Religious Studies); **Theological Education** (Christian Religious Studies; Pastoral Studies; Religion; Social Work; Theology)

History: Founded 1911.

Fees: (Canadian Dollar): 2,310-2,294 per annum for Canadian students and 4,971-4,976 per annum for international students.

Degrees and Diplomas: *Bachelor's Degree; Master's Degree; Graduate Diploma/Certificate; Doctoral Degree*
Last Updated: 25/02/11

WILFRID LAURIER UNIVERSITY (WLU)

75 University Avenue West, Waterloo, Ontario N2L 3C5
Tel: +1(519) 884-1970
Fax: +1(519) 886-9351
EMail: webmaster@wlu.ca
Website: http://www.wlu.ca

President and Vice-Chancellor: Max Blouw (2007-)
Tel: +1(519) 884-0710 Ext. 2443, Fax: +1(519) 884-2947
EMail: mknechtelbell@wlu.ca

Vice President, Finance and Administration: James S. Butler
Tel: +1(519) 884-0710 Ext. 2248 EMail: jbutler@wlu.ca

International Relations: Peter Donahue, Director and International Liaison Officer
Tel: +1(519) 884-0710 Ext. 6704, Fax: +1(519) 884-4507
EMail: pdonahue@wlu.ca

Campuses
Brantford (Child Care and Development; Contemporary History; Criminology; Education; Engineering Management; Health Administration; Health Sciences; Human Rights; Journalism; Law; Leadership; Psychology; Social Studies)

Centres

Community Research, Learning and Action *(CCRLA)* (Social and Community Services; Welfare and Protective Services); **Executive Development** *(Laurier)* (Finance; Leadership; Marketing; Technology; Transport Management); **Northwest Territories Partnership** *(Laurier)* (Environmental Studies); **Strategic Leadership** (Leadership); **Study of Nascent Entrepreneurship and the eXploitation of Technology** *(NeXt)* (Management)

Faculties

Arts (American Studies; Ancient Civilizations; Anthropology; Arabic; Archaeology; Asian Religious Studies; Christian Religious Studies; Classical Languages; Communication Studies; Cultural Studies; English; Environmental Studies; Film; French; Gender Studies; Geography; German; Greek; Greek (Classical); History; International Studies; Islamic Studies; Islamic Theology; Italian; Judaic Religious Studies; Latin; Literature; Medieval Studies; Mediterranean Studies; Middle Eastern Studies; Modern Languages; Philosophy; Political Sciences; Religion; Social Sciences; Sociology; Spanish; Women's Studies); **Education** (Education; Primary Education; Secondary Education; Teacher Training); **Graduate Studies** (Ancient Civilizations; Art Therapy; Biology; Business Administration; Chemistry; Communication Studies; Criminology; Cultural Studies; Economics; Education; English; Finance; Geography; Government; History; International Studies; Management; Mathematics; Philosophy; Physical Therapy; Political Sciences; Psychology; Religion; Religious Studies; Social Work; Sociology; Theology); **Music** (Art History; Art Therapy; Music; Music Education; Music Theory and Composition; Musical Instruments); **Science** (Analytical Chemistry; Biochemistry; Biology; Chemistry; Computer Science; Health Sciences; Inorganic Chemistry; Materials Engineering; Mathematics; Organic Chemistry; Physical Chemistry; Physical Education; Physical Therapy; Physics; Psychology); **Social Work** (Indigenous Studies; Social Work)

Institutes

Study of Contemporary Africa *(Tshepo)* (African Studies); **Water Science** *(Laurier)* (Water Science)

Research Centres

Cold Regions *(CRRC)* (Regional Studies); **International Migration** (Demography and Population)

Schools

Business and Economics *(Laurier)* (Accountancy; Business Administration; Economics; Finance; Human Resources; Management; Marketing; Operations Research); **International Affairs** *(Balsillie)* (Government; International Studies; Public Administration)

Further Information: Also Waterloo Lutheran Seminary.

History: Founded 1911 as Evangelical Lutheran Seminary of Canada, became Water College of Arts 1925, reorganized Waterloo Lutheran University 1960, and acquired present status and title 1973.

Governing Bodies: Board of Governors; Senate

Academic Year: September to August (September-December; January-April; May-August)

Admission Requirements: Secondary school certificate or recognized foreign equivalent

Fees: (Can. Dollars): domestic students, undergraduate programme, 2,606.70-4,704 per term; graduate programme, 2,281.95-2,923.45 per term; MBA, 7,200 per term. Foreign students, undergraduate programme, 7,475. 75-9,840 per term; graduate programme, 5,129.20 per term; MBA, 9,927.05 per term.

Main Language(s) of Instruction: English

Degrees and Diplomas: *University Certificate/Diploma; Bachelor's Degree; Master's Degree; Graduate Diploma/Certificate; Doctoral Degree.* Also Honours Bachelor's degrees, 4-5 yrs; Joint PhD; Consecutive Bachelor of Education.

Student Services: Academic counselling, Canteen, Cultural centre, Employment services, Foreign student adviser, Foreign Studies Centre, Handicapped facilities, Health services, Language programs, Social counselling, Sports facilities

Student Residential Facilities: For 2,495 students

Special Facilities: Robert Langen Art Gallery; Maureen Forrester Concert Hall; Women's Centre

Libraries:c. 1,7m. items, including 691,000 monographs and serials; 167,000 government documents; 700,000 microforms. Access to 6 m. items through TriUniversity Group of Libraries (Wilfrid Laurier University, University of Waterloo and University of Guelph)

Press or Publishing House: WLU Press

Academic Staff *2009-2010*	TOTAL
FULL-TIME	c. **620**

Student Numbers *2009-2010*	
All (Foreign Included)	**15,567**
FOREIGN ONLY	**360**

Part-time students, 1,541.
Last Updated: 28/02/11

WYCLIFFE COLLEGE (UNIVERSITY OF TORONTO)

5 Hoskin Avenue, Toronto, Ontario M5S 1H7
Tel: +1(416) 946-3535
Fax: +1(416) 979-0471
EMail: wycliffe.registrar@utoronto.ca
Website: http://www.wycliffecollege.ca/

Principal: George Sumner
Tel: +1(416) 946-3521 EMail: george.sumner@utoronto.ca

Registrar: Marie Soderlund Tel: +1(416) 946-3530

Programmes

Advanced Degree (Religion; Theology); **Basic Degree** (Christian Religious Studies; Religion; Theology)

History: Founded 1877.

Fees: (Canadian Dollar): Basic degree tuition fees, 518.50 per course for Canadian students and 1,393 per course for international students; Graduate studies, 518.50-1,547 per course for Canadian students and 1,393-2,322 per course for international students; Doctorate, 6,131-9,197 per annum for Canadian students and 9,291-13,938 per annum for international students.

Degrees and Diplomas: *Master's Degree; Graduate Diploma/Certificate; Doctoral Degree*
Last Updated: 28/02/11

YORK UNIVERSITY (YORKU)

4700 Keele Street, Toronto, Ontario M3J 1P3
Tel: +1(416) 736-2100
Fax: +1(416) 736-5700
EMail: infoserv@yorku.ca
Website: http://www.yorku.ca

President and Vice-Chancellor: Mamdouh Shoukri (2007-)
Tel: +1(416) 736-5200, Fax: +1(416) 736-5641
EMail: mshoukri@yorku.ca; president@yorku.ca

Vice-President Academic and Provost: Patrick J. Monahan
Tel: +1(416) 736-5280 Ext. 5528, Fax: +1(416) 736-5876
EMail: vpacad@yorku.ca

Vice-President Students: Robert J. Tiffin
Tel: +1(416) 736-5955, Fax: +1(416) 736-5990
EMail: vpstdnts@yorku.ca; rjtiffin©yorku.ca

International Relations: Lorna Wright, Associate Vice-President
Tel: +1(416) 736-5280, Fax: +1(416) 736-5876
EMail: lwright@yorku.ca

Campuses

Glendon (Business Administration; Canadian Studies; Communication Studies; Economics; English; Environmental Studies; Foreign Languages Education; French Studies; Health Sciences; International Studies; Law; Linguistics; Mathematics; Philosophy; Phonetics; Political Sciences; Psychology; Sociology; Spanish; Theatre; Translation and Interpretation; Women's Studies; Writing)

Centres

Asian Research *(YCAR)* (Asian Studies); **Atmospheric Chemistry** *(CAC)* (Meteorology); **Canadian Studies** *(Robarts)* (Canadian Studies); **CERIS - The Ontario Metropolis Project** *(Centre of Excellence)* (Demography and Population); **Education and Community** *(YCEC)* (Education); **Feminist Research** *(CFR)* (Women's Studies); **German and European Studies** *(Canadian - CCGES)* (European Studies; Germanic Studies); **International and Security**

Studies *(YCISS)* (International Studies; Welfare and Protective Services); **Jewish Studies** *(Israel and Golda Koschitzky - CJS)* (Jewish Studies); **Practical Ethics** *(CPE)* (Ethics); **Public Policy and Law** *(YCPPL)* (Public Administration; Public Law); **Refugee Studies** *(CRS)* (Demography and Population); **Transnational Human Rights, Crime and Security** *(Jack and Mae Nathanson)* (Criminology; Human Rights; Protective Services); **Vision Research** *(CVR)* (Ophthalmology)

Faculties

Education (Education; Environmental Studies; Higher Education; Jewish Studies; Mathematics Education; Preschool Education; Primary Education; Secondary Education; Special Education; Teacher Training); **Environmental Studies** *(FES)* (Environmental Studies); **Fine Arts** (Art History; Cinema and Television; Dance; Design; Film; Fine Arts; Music; Theatre; Visual Arts); **Graduate Studies** (Accountancy; Acting; Administration; Anthropology; Applied Linguistics; Art History; Art Management; Arts and Humanities; Asian Studies; Astronomy and Space Science; Biology; Business Administration; Caribbean Studies; Chemistry; Civil Security; Communication Studies; Computer Engineering; Computer Science; Cultural Studies; Dance; Demography and Population; Design; Development Studies; Earth Sciences; Economics; Education; Engineering; English; Environmental Studies; Ethics; European Studies; Film; French Studies; Geography; Germanic Studies; Health Sciences; Hebrew; Higher Education; History; Human Resources; Information Technology; International Studies; Jewish Studies; Latin American Studies; Law; Leadership; Linguistics; Management; Mathematics; Mathematics Education; Music; Neurosciences; Nursing; Philosophy; Physics; Political Sciences; Psychology; Public Administration; Real Estate; Rehabilitation and Therapy; Safety Engineering; Social Sciences; Social Studies; Social Work; Sociology; Statistics; Technology; Theatre; Translation and Interpretation; Visual Arts; Women's Studies); **Health** (Behavioural Sciences; Clinical Psychology; Developmental Psychology; Health Administration; Health Sciences; Neurosciences; Nursing; Physical Therapy; Physiology; Psychology; Rehabilitation and Therapy; Social Psychology; Sports Management); **Liberal Arts and Professional Studies** (Accountancy; Administration; Advertising and Publicity; African Studies; Amerindian Languages; Ancient Civilizations; Anthropology; Applied Linguistics; Arabic; Arts and Humanities; Bible; Business Administration; Canadian Studies; Caribbean Studies; Child Care and Development; Chinese; Classical Languages; Cognitive Sciences; Communication Studies; Criminology; Cultural Studies; Development Studies; East Asian Studies; Economics; English; Ethics; Ethnology; European Studies; Finance; Foreign Languages Education; French; French Studies; Gender Studies; Geography; German; Germanic Studies; Greek; Greek (Classical); Health Sciences; Hebrew; Hindi; History; Human Resources; Human Rights; Indic Languages; Indigenous Studies; Information Technology; International Studies; Italian; Japanese; Jewish Studies; Journalism; Korean; Labour and Industrial Relations; Latin; Latin American Studies; Law; Linguistics; Management; Marketing; Modern Languages; Philosophy; Polish; Political Sciences; Portuguese; Public Administration; Public Relations; Publishing and Book Trade; Radio and Television Broadcasting; Real Estate; Religious Studies; Russian; Safety Engineering; Social Sciences; Social Studies; Social Work; Sociology; South Asian Studies; Spanish; Swahili; Technology; Transport Management; Urban Studies; Women's Studies; Writing); **Science and Engineering** (Astronomy and Space Science; Biochemistry; Biology; Biomedicine; Biophysics; Biotechnology; Business Computing; Chemistry; Computer Engineering; Computer Science; Earth Sciences; Engineering; Environmental Studies; Geography; Geological Engineering; Mathematics and Computer Science; Mathematics Education; Meteorology; Multimedia; Physics; Software Engineering; Surveying and Mapping; Technology)

Institutes

City (Urban Studies); **Health Research** *(YIHR)* (Health Sciences); **Research and Innovation in Sustainability** *(IRIS)* (Environmental Studies); **Science and Technology Studies** *(iSTS)* (Arts and Humanities; Social Sciences; Technology); **Social Research** *(ISR)* (Social Studies)

Research Centres

Biomolecular Interactions *(CRBI)* (Molecular Biology); **Child and Youth Research** *(LaMarsh)* (Child Care and Development); **Earth and Space Science** *(CRESS)* (Astronomy and Space Science;

Earth Sciences; Robotics); **Language Contact** *(CRLC)* (Demography and Population; History; Linguistics; Musicology; Political Sciences; Psychology; Sociology); **Latin America and the Caribbean** *(CERLAC)* (Caribbean Studies; Latin American Studies); **Mass Spectrometry** *(CRMS)* (Chemistry); **Muscle Health** *(MHRC)* (Health Sciences; Sports); **Work and Society** *(CRWS)* (Labour and Industrial Relations)

Research Institutes

Global Migrations of African People *(Harriet Tubman)* (Demography and Population); **Learning Technologies** *(IRLT)* (Educational Technology)

Schools

Business *(Schulich)* (Business Administration; Finance; International Business; Management; Marketing; Public Administration); **Law** *(Osgoode Hall)* (Comparative Law; Fiscal Law; International Law; Justice Administration; Law)

Further Information: Also Glendon campus, Miles S. Nadal Management Centre and Osgoode Professional Development Centre.

History: Founded 1959. Established originally as affiliate of University of Toronto, the University moved to Glendon campus 1961. The University has 4 campuses in the City of Toronto.

Governing Bodies: Board of Governors; Senate

Academic Year: September to April (September-December; January-April). Summer Session: May-August

Admission Requirements: Ontario Secondary School Diploma (OSSD), or equivalent. A minumum of six Grade 12 U or M courses, including Grade 12 U English, all Faculty prerequisites and at least one Grade 12 U or M course from one of the following disciplines: Canadian and World Studies; Classical Languages and International Languages; French; Mathematics; Social Sicence and Humanities; or native Studies. Additional requirements for many programmes. Francophone applicants can present 12U French (FRA4U, FEF4U, or FIF4U). Combination of U and M courses and OACs accepted. Early conditional admission if strong grade 11 finals and/or interim Grade 12 results.

Fees: (Can. Dollars): Undergraduate programmes, 6,003-8,473 per annum; International students, 16,403-17,944.

Main Language(s) of Instruction: English

International Co-operation: With universities in 46 countries

Degrees and Diplomas: *University Certificate/Diploma; Bachelor's Degree; Master's Degree; Graduate Diploma/Certificate; Doctoral Degree.* Also Honours Bachelor's degrees, 4-5 yrs; Some certificates and diploma programmes are offered through affiliated Colleges Centennial College and Seneca College); the Faculty of Education offers a 4-yr Concurrent co registered BEd degree, a Concurrent co registered program in Jewish Teacher Education and a Concurrent co registered BEd (French) degree and a full-time and part-time Consecutive BEd programme running over an extended academic year; the school of Law offers combined programmes (Juris Doctor and Master of Business Administration, Environmental Studies, Philosophy, Law or Bachelor of Civil Law); the Business school also offers a 2-yr MBA programme in India, an Executive MBA, combined Master's degree in Business Administration/Fine Arts/Arts and Business and Law (MBA/Juris Doctor) in 3-4 yrs; the Faculty of Science and Engineering offers an International Bachelor of Science (exchange agreements in 32 countries).

Student Services: Academic counselling, Canteen, Employment services, Foreign student adviser, Foreign Studies Centre, Handicapped facilities, Health services, Language programs, Nursery care, Social counselling, Sports facilities

Student Residential Facilities: On-campus: 10 undergraduate residences (suite, single and double rooms) for 2,679 students. Boys and girls are separated. One and two-bedroom apartments for Bachelor holders, mature (21 yrs old and older) and married students. Off-campus Housing service.

Special Facilities: Petrie Astronomical Observatory; Burton Auditorium; Nat Taylor Cinema; York University Art Gallery; Albert and Lucy Boden Studio; Joseph G. Green Studio Theatre; Oscar Peterson Studio; Strate Dance Studio Theatre; L.L.O. Ordette Centre for Sculpture; Various college art galleries, Music halls and theatres. Centre for Vision Research. Dacary Hall. Joan and Martin Goldfarb Centre for Fine Arts

Libraries: York University's Keele and Glendon campuses: 5 major libraries (the Scott Library for Humanities, Social Sciences and Fine Arts, the Steacie Science Library, the Bronfman Business Library, the Law Library and the Frost Library). Also the University Archies and Special Collections, Sound and Moving Image Library and the Map Library (all located in the Scott Library building). Total: more than 2,5m. Vols, 100,000 electronic books, 9,000 active print journal subscriptions, 11,000 electronic journals and hundreds of other journal, government and statistical databases.

Publications: Canada Watch (*biennially*); Canadian Woman Studies Journal (*quarterly*)

Last Updated: 28/02/11

PRIVATE INSTITUTIONS

INSTITUTE FOR CHRISTIAN STUDIES

229 College Street, Suite 100, Toronto, Ontario M5T 1R4
Tel: +1(416) 979-2331 +1(888) 326-5347
Fax: +1(416) 979-2332
EMail: info@icscanada.edu
Website: http://www.icscanada.edu/

President: Chris Gort (2010-)
Tel: +1(416) 979-2331 Ext. 235 EMail: CGort@icscanada.edu

Director, Finance and Administration: Claire Veenstra
Tel: +1(416) 979-2331 Ext. 290 EMail: CVeenstra@icscanada.edu

Programmes
Philosophy (Aesthetics; Anthropology; Bible; Ethics; Philosophy; Theology); **Worldview Studies** (*MWS*) (Bible; Education; Philosophy)

Research Centres
Philosophy, Religion and Social Ethics (Ethics; Philosophy; Religion)

Further Information: Also Distance Education programmes.

History: Founded 1967.

Governing Bodies: Academic Council; Senate.

Degrees and Diplomas: *Master's Degree*; *Doctoral Degree (PhD)*

Last Updated: 31/01/11

ST. LAWRENCE COLLEGE OF APPLIED ARTS AND TECHNOLOGY (SLC)

100 Portsmouth Avenue, Kingston, Ontario K7L 5A6
Tel: +1(613) 544-5400
Fax: +1(613) 545-3923
EMail: dreamit@sl.on.ca; international@sl.on.ca
Website: http://www.stlawrencecollege.ca/

President and CEO: Chris Whitaker EMail: CWhitaker@sl.on.ca

Schools
Applied Arts (Adult Education; English; Fine Arts; Journalism; Mathematics; Music; Performing Arts; Visual Arts); **Business** (Accountancy; Administration; Advertising and Publicity; Business Administration; Graphic Design; Human Resources; Marketing); **Community Services** (Behavioural Sciences; Preschool Education; Psychology; Social Work); **Computer and Engineering Technology** (Automation and Control Engineering; Civil Engineering; Computer Networks; Energy Engineering; Thermal Engineer-

ing); **Graphic Design** (Graphic Design); **Health and Science** (Biotechnology; Health Administration; Laboratory Techniques; Medical Technology; Nursing; Veterinary Science); **Hospitality** (Hotel and Restaurant; Tourism); **Justice Studies** (Administration; Law; Police Studies; Social and Community Services); **Skilled Trades and Apprenticeships** (Automotive Engineering; Cooking and Catering; Mechanical Engineering; Metal Techniques; Service Trades)

Further Information: Aslo Brockville and Cornwall campuses.

History: Founded 1967.

Fees: (Canadian Dollar): Tuition fees for domestic students, 848.40-11,280 per annum; For International students, 500-22,609.98 per annum.

Degrees and Diplomas: *Certificate/Diploma*. Applied Bachelor's degree (professional) in Behavioural Psychology, 4 yrs; Bachelor's degree in Business Administration and Nursing from Laurentian University; College Advanced diploma, 3yrs.

Last Updated: 01/12/10

TYNDALE UNIVERSITY COLLEGE AND SEMINARY

25 Ballyconnor Court, Willowdale, Ontario M2M 4B3
Tel: +1(416) 226-6380 +1(877) 896-3253
Fax: +1(416) 226-6746
EMail: contact@tyndale.ca; admissions@tyndale.ca
Website: http://www.tyndale.ca/

President and Vice Chancellor: Gary V. Nelson (2010-)
EMail: bstiller@tyndale.ca

Programmes
Business Administration (Accountancy; Business Administration; Economics; Finance; Marketing); **Business Administration - International Development** (Accountancy; Business Administration; Finance; International Business; Management); **Christian Studies** (Christian Religious Studies); **Education** (Education; Primary Education; Secondary Education; Teacher Training); **English** (English; Literature); **Graduate Studies** (Bible; Christian Religious Studies; History of Religion; Leadership; Missionary Studies; Pastoral Studies; Religion; Theology); **History** (History); **Human Services - Early Childhood Education Track** (Child Care and Development; Preschool Education); **Human Services - Social Service Work Track** (Social and Community Services; Social Work); **Linguistics** (Bible; English; Linguistics; Literature; Philosophical Schools; Psychology); **Philosophy** (Ethics; Philosophy); **Psychology** (Behavioural Sciences; Psychology; Social Psychology); **Religious Education** (Pastoral Studies; Religion; Religious Education); **Religious Studies** (Bible; Religion; Religious Studies; Theology)

History: Founded 1894. Obtained current status 2003.

Fees: (Canadian Dollar): Undergraduate tuition, 1,296 per course (12,960 per annum); Graduate tuition, 1,113 per course (10,017 per annum).

Degrees and Diplomas: *Certificate/Diploma*; *Bachelor's Degree*; *Master's Degree*; *Graduate Diploma/Certificate*; *Doctoral Degree*: Ministry. Also Honours Bachelor's degrees.

Libraries: c. 159,000 vols

Student Numbers *2007-2008*: Total 1,499
Last Updated: 18/02/11

Canada - Prince Edward Island

STRUCTURE OF HIGHER EDUCATION SYSTEM

Description:

Higher education in Canada is the constitutional responsibility of the provinces. The two main institutions providing higher education on PEI are the University of Prince Edward Island and Holland College; the latter provides diverse technical and vocational programmes usually leading to a Certificate or Diploma. The University, independently administered with full autonomy on admissions and academic matters, offers mainly undergraduate degrees and houses the regional Atlantic Veterinary College. UPEI also offers postgraduate studies in Education, Science, Biology and Chemistry with the Master of Education in Leadership and Learning, the Master of Science in Biology and the Master of Science in Chemistry programmes having recently been added to its delivery options. The Atlantic Veterinary College provides undergraduate, graduate and continuing education in the field of Veterinary Medicine. Holland College provides technical and vocational programmes leading to a Certificate or Diploma. Besides various pre-employment, apprenticeship and vocational programmes, there are 13 private vocational or career training colleges registered with the PEI Department of Innovation and Advanced Learning. French post-secondary education programmes are delivered through College l'Acadie.

Stages of studies:

University level first stage: Bachelor's Degree
The courses offered by the University of Prince Edward Island lead to degrees in Arts, Science, Business Administration, Education, Music, Veterinary Medicine and Nursing.

University level second stage: Master's Degree
In 1999, UPEI was granted the authority to offer graduate level degrees. Since then, a Master of Education in Leadership and Learning (M.Ed), a Master of Science in Biology, a Master of Science in Chemistry, a Master of Arts in Island Studies, a Master of Applied Health Services Research, a Master of Nursing and a Master of Business Administration have been added to its offerings. In addition to the above mentioned programmes, UPEI offers a Master of Science (M.Sc.) programme through the Atlantic Veterinary College (which also primarily serves the other three Atlantic provinces of Nova Scotia, New Brunswick and Newfoundland, as well as international students). The first class was accepted in 1986 and about 50 students are admitted each year. The M.Sc. degree normally requires two years of training after an appropriate first degree.

University level third stage: Ph.D. Degree
The only Ph.D.-level programmes offered by the University of Prince Edward Island are in Veterinary Medicine and Education. A Ph.D in Educational Studies is available after the completion of a Master's degree in Education. Following the completion of the four-year Doctorate of Veterinary Medicine (DVM), some students continue on to also complete a Master's degree or PhD in Veterinary Medicine. The DVM programme, while often considered at doctoral level, is an initial degree programme and is provided through the Atlantic Veterinary College, which serves (primarily) the other three Atlantic Provinces.

Distance higher education:
UPEI, Holland College, and College Acadie offer some skills-based training through distance and open learning formats. Some private training schools also offer distance education programmes.

ADMISSION TO HIGHER EDUCATION

Admission to university-level studies:

Name of secondary school credential required: High School Graduation Diploma

Alternatives to credentials: The University of PEI sets its own admission policies and requirements. These do not involve separate entrance examinations, and usually include flexibility for mature students, i.e. applicants aged 21 who have been out of school for three years. Prior learning assessment and recognition (PLAR) and GED testing ares generally recognized.

Other admission requirements: Admission to university programmes usually includes attaining a certain average in high school and completion of certain academic subjects, besides holding a Gr. 12 certificate. Admission to some professional programmes (e.g. Medicine) may require previous university education. Specific admission requirements may vary by field of study and by university (and may include interviews and references).

Foreign students admission:

Definition of foreign student: Foreign (International) Students are students who are neither Canadian citizens nor permanent residents of Canada, and are enrolled full-time in a recognized academic, professional or vocational training course at a university, college or other educational institution in Canada.

Quotas: There are quotas at the institutional level for some programmes.

Entrance exam requirements: Generally, as for domestic students, a high school diploma or equivalent will be required. A lack of proficiency in English or French will be taken into account by the Canadian Immigration Office in the evaluation of the application. UPEI: International students must submit documents which prove that their qualifications are comparable to Canadian applicants. High school admission requirements include: successful completion of final examinations with an overall average of at least 65% or a standing of A, B, or C in at least five subjects. For BA, BBA: English, Mathematics, and three acceptable academic electives; for BSc: English, Mathematics, two Sciences and one acceptable academic elective. There are special requirements for Nursing, Education, Radiography, and Veterinary Medicine programmes. The same subject cannot be counted more than once when taken at more than one level (Advanced or Ordinary level). Students must have 12 years of elementary and secondary education and Senior Secondary Certificate, Higher School Certificate or matriculation as defined by home institution. Students are usually required to pass one of the following English language proficiency tests with a score at or above the acceptable minimum. TOEFL: 550 minimum on paper based test, or 213 minimum on computer based test; MELAB: 80 minimum; IELTS: 6,5 minimum - with a minimum of 6.0 in each category; and Can TEST: 4.5 minimum.

Entry regulations: Before you come to study in Canada, you will need: a "Study Permit" if the programme of study you will be admitted to is longer than six months in duration, regardless of the length of your stay in Canada; a letter of acceptance from the school of your choice; proof that you have enough money to pay for school fees and living expenses; to establish that you will return home at the end of your studies; to pass a medical exam if required; and to qualify as a temporary resident in Canada, including holding a temporary resident visa (required for citizens of many countries). A small number of students do not require a Study Permit by virtue of their status in Canada (e.g. diplomats and their children).

Health requirements: Most education institutions require international students to buy health insurance in addition to their tuition fees; those that do not will require proof of independent health insurance coverage. Medical examinations are not required by institutions but are required by Citizenship and Immigration Canada for students from many countries.

Language requirements: English language proficiency tests with a score at or above the acceptable minimum. TOEFL: 550 minimum on paper based test, or 213 minimum on computer based test; MELAB: 80 minimum; IELTS: 6,5 minimum with a minimum of 6.0 in each category; and Can TEST: 4.5 minimum.

RECOGNITION OF STUDIES

Quality assurance system:

Maritime Provinces Higher Education Commission reviews degree programmes at UPEI as a quality assurance measure. Holland College is ISO 9001:9008 certified and offers a student warranty guaranteeing that students will meet employers needs or will be offered retraining.

Bodies dealing with recognition:

Department of Innovation and Advanced Learning
Shaw Building, 5th Floor,
105 Rochford Street,
P.O. Box 2000
Charlottetown, PE C1A 7N8
Canada
Tel: +1(902) 368 4240
Fax: +1(902) 368 4242

EMail: rrryder@gov.pe.ca
WWW: http://www.gov.pe.ca/ial/index.php3

Special provisions for recognition:

Recognition for university level studies: In general, none. The University of PEI establishes its own admission criteria and makes decisions in response to individual applications. Any restrictions on admission are determined by the University, given available teaching and other resources, but in a few instances are a result of government policy. Additionally, the Canadian Information Centre for International Credentials (CICIC) provides information and guidance on the recognition of foreign studies.

For access to advanced studies and research: Admission to the Atlantic Veterinary College (which has only postgraduate programmes) at the University of Prince Edward Island is mainly restricted to Canadian citizens and permanent residents of the four Atlantic provinces (New Brunswick, Newfoundland, Nova Scotia and Prince Edward Island). However, there is a quota set for international students each year.

For exercising a profession: In general, none. For each profession, both Canadian and non-Canadians who studied abroad have to meet specified educational and experience requirements, and usually pass registration examinations. Non-Canadians may sometimes also need to pass a language test. Access to most professions is governed by provincial and/or federal statutes and is restricted to Canadian citizens or immigrants accepted as permanent residents. Usually, applicants must also meet examination and/or practical training requirements set by the relevant professional body or provincial or federal licensing board.

PROVINCIAL BODIES

Department of Innovation and Advanced Learning
Minister: Allan V. Campbell
Shaw Building, 5th Floor,
105 Rochford Street,
P.O. Box 2000
Charlottetown, PE C1A 7N8
Canada
Tel: +1(902) 368 4240
Fax: +1(902) 368 4242
EMail: rrryder@gov.pe.ca
WWW: http://www.gov.pe.ca/ial/index.php3
Role of national body: Provincial government department responsible for post-secondary and continuing education including the funding arrangements for UPEI, Holland College, College l'Acadie and the administration of the Private Training Schools Act. Representative of the Department sits on the board of Holland College, College l'Acadie and the Maritime Provinces Higher Education Commission.

Data for academic year: 2011-2012
Source: IAU from the Canadian Information Centre for International Credentials (CICIC), a unit of the Council of Ministers of Education, Canada (CMEC), on behalf of the Province of Prince Edward Island, 2011

INSTITUTIONS

PUBLIC INSTITUTIONS

UNIVERSITY OF PRINCE EDWARD ISLAND (UPEI)
550 University Avenue, Charlottetown, Prince Edward Island C1A 4P3
Tel: +1(902) 566-0439
Fax: +1(902) 566-0795
EMail: registrar@upei.ca
Website: http://www.upei.ca

President and Vice-Chancellor: Wade MacLauchlan
Tel: +1(902) 566-0400, Fax: +1(902) 628-4311
EMail: president@upei.ca; wmaclauchlan@upei.ca

Registrar: Kathleen Kielly
Tel: +1(902) 566-0628, Fax: +1(902) 566-0795
EMail: kkielly@upei.ca

Centres
Aquatic Virology Collaborating (Virology); **Bioactive Valuation (ACBV)** (Biological and Life Sciences); **Canadian Cooperative Wildlife Health** (Health Sciences; Wildlife); **Christianity and Culture** (Christian Religious Studies); **Education Research**

(Education); **Health and Biotechnology Management Research** (Biotechnology; Health Sciences); **Life-Long Learning** (Accountancy; Business Administration; Education; French; Health Sciences; Island Studies; Microbiology; Pathology; Radiology; Small Business; Veterinary Science); **Veterinary Epidemiological Research** (CVER) (Epidemiology; Veterinary Science)

Faculties

Arts (Ancient Civilizations; Anthropology; Arts and Humanities; Asian Studies; Canadian Studies; Classical Languages; Development Studies; Economics; English; Environmental Studies; Fine Arts; French; German; Greek (Classical); History; Island Studies; Journalism; Latin; Modern Languages; Music; Music Education; Philosophy; Political Sciences; Psychology; Public Administration; Religious Studies; Sociology; Spanish; Theatre; Women's Studies; Writing); **Education** (Adult Education; Education; Human Resources; International and Comparative Education; Leadership; Library Science; Natives Education); **Graduate Studies** (Business Administration; Education; Environmental Studies; Health Sciences; Island Studies; Leadership; Management; Materials Engineering; Molecular Biology; Veterinary Science); **Science** (Biology; Business Administration; Chemistry; Computer Science; Engineering; Environmental Studies; Family Studies; Information Technology; Mathematics; Nutrition; Physics; Psychology; Radiology; Statistics; Veterinary Science); **Veterinary** (Atlantic Veterinary College's - AVC) (Anaesthesiology; Animal Husbandry; Biomedicine; Cardiology; Cell Biology; Endocrinology; Environmental Studies; Epidemiology; Health Administration; Health Sciences; Immunology; Microbiology; Molecular Biology; Neurosciences; Parasitology; Pathology; Physiology; Public Health; Surgery; Toxicology; Veterinary Science; Virology; Zoology)

Groups

Children's Health and Applied Research (Child Care and Development)

Research Centres

Tourism (Tourism)

Research Groups

Animal Movement and Resource Selection (Zoology); **Interdisciplinary Research in Culture, Multimedia, Technology and Cognition** (CMTC) (Cognitive Sciences; Cultural Studies; Multimedia; Technology); **Neurosciences** (Neurosciences); **School Health** (Health Sciences)

Schools

Business (Accountancy; Business Administration; Hotel and Restaurant; International Business; Management; Tourism); **Nursing** (Nursing)

History: Founded 1969, a public, non-denominational university, formed by the merger of 2 institutions of higher learning, Prince of Wales College (founded 1834) and Saint Dunstan's University (founded 1855). Faculty of Veterinary Science established 1986.

Academic Year: September to April (September-December; January-April)

Admission Requirements: Secondary school certificate or recognized foreign equivalent

Fees: (Canadian Dollar): Canadian Students, 5,714-10,748 per annum; International Students, 11,499-52,243 per annum.

Main Language(s) of Instruction: English

Degrees and Diplomas: Certificate/Diploma; Bachelor's Degree; Master's Degree; Doctoral Degree. Also Honours Bachelor's degrees, 4 yrs; Executive-Style MBA, 23 months-6 yrs; Accelerated Bachelor of Business Administration, 3 yrs; Professional programmes in Business Administration and through the Centre for Life-Long Learning; Accelerated programme in Nursing, 2 yrs.

Student Services: Academic counselling, Canteen, Cultural centre, Employment services, Health services, Nursery care, Social counselling, Sports facilities

Student Numbers 2009-2010	TOTAL
All (Foreign Included)	c. 4,450
FOREIGN ONLY	450

Last Updated: 28/02/11

Canada - Quebec

STRUCTURE OF HIGHER EDUCATION SYSTEM

Description:

Higher education in Canada, as well as primary, secondary, vocational or technical education, are the constitutional responsibility of the provinces. In Quebec, higher education is delivered by two main types of institutions: colleges and universities. The Collèges d'enseignement général et professionnel (CEGEPs) are offering two different types of programmes: 2-year pre-university programmes leading to university and 3-year technical programmes mainly for entry into the labour market. There are 48 public CEGEPs (43 French-speaking and 5 English-speaking) located in large and medium cities of the province. There are also 25 private subsidized institutions under the responsibility of the Ministère de l'Éducation, du Loisir et du Sport (18 French-speaking; 3 English-speaking; 4 French-English-speaking). Some institutions are under the responsibility of other Ministries such as music conservatories or agricultural institutes. The programmes offered by these institutions are approved by the Ministère de l'Éducation, du Loisir et du Sport (MELS). There are also 32 private colleges under licence of the MELS. There are 18 universities organized as follows: 3 English-speaking degree-granting universities (McGill, Concordia and Bishop's); 15 French-speaking degree-granting universities (Laval, Montréal, École Polytechnique de Montréal,École des Hautes Études Commerciales de Montréal, Sherbrooke and the 10 institutions related to the Université du Québec network hereby located in the main cities of the province (Université du Québec à Montréal, Université du Québec à Rimouski, Université du Québec à Chicoutimi, Université du Québec à Trois Rivières, Université du Québec en Outaouais, Université du Québec en Abitibi Témiscamingue, École nationale d'administration publique, École de technologie supérieure, Institut national de la recherche scientifique, Télé-université). Except for the Université du Québec, created by an Act of the National Assembly of Quebec, each other institution has a private charter. Although the Québec government provides a major portion of their funding, these institutions operate independently in all academic matters (admission, programs of study, evaluation, management, staffing ...).

Stages of studies:

University level first stage: *Baccalauréat/Bachelor's Degree*
In Québec, the undergraduate university level usually leads to a Bachelor's degree after 3 or 4 years of study (Teacher Education, Engineering, Medicine). In English-universities, a bachelor programme can include a major and one minor or a choice of 3 certificates. Universities also offer short programmes, recognized by an undergraduate certificate.

University level second stage: *Maîtrise/Master's Degree*
In Québec, the graduate university level usually leads to a Master's degree normally requiring 2 years of study and a dissertation after a Bachelor's degree,. Universities also offer short one-year programmes recognized by a Diplôme d'études supérieures spécialisées (advanced graduate diploma). Graduate students include medical residents whose clinical training period may vary by specialty, with a minimum of 2 years.

University level third stage: *Doctorat/Ph.D./Doctorate*
Post-graduate studies lead to a PhD, requiring 3 years of study after the Master's degree and the submission of a major thesis (doctoral dissertation).

Distance higher education:
Some colleges and universities offer distance courses and programmes of study as part of their general education mandate. Furthermore, the Université du Québec is offering online only programmes through the Télé université (TELUQ) at all three university levels.At the same time, a consortium of colleges has created cegep@distance.

ADMISSION TO HIGHER EDUCATION

Admission to university-level studies:

Name of secondary school credential required: Diplôme d'études collégiales

For entry to: University

Alternatives to credentials: Universities set their own admission policies and requirements. These do not involve separate entrance examinations, and usually include flexibility for mature students, i.e. applicants aged 21 or more, who have not completed secondary school. Quebec universities have introduced "prior learning assessments" (PLA) in considering admission to some degree programmes.

Numerus clausus/restrictions: Universities decree numerus clausus in some programmes, mainly in the health sector. In medicine, a numerus clausus is decided by the Government, including a quota for foreign students.

Foreign students admission:

Definition of foreign student: Foreign (International) Students are students who are neither Canadian citizens nor permanent residents of Canada, and are enrolled full-time in a recognized academic, professional or vocational training course at a university, college or other educational institution in Canada.

Entry regulations: Before you come to study in Quebec, you will need: a "Certificat d'acceptation du Québec (CAQ)" from the Ministère de l'Immigration et des Communautés culturelles (MICC); a "Study Permit" from Citizenship and Immigration Canada (CIC) if the programme of study you will be admitted to is longer than six months in duration, regardless of the length of your stay in Canada; a letter of acceptance from the school of your choice; proof that you have enough money to pay school fees and living expenses; to establish that you will return home at the end of your studies; to pass a medical exam if required; and to qualify as a temporary resident in Canada, including holding a temporary resident visa (required for citizens of many countries). A small number of students do not require a Study Permit by virtue of their status in Canada (e.g. diplomats and their children).

Health requirements: Quebec requires foreign students to provide proof of health insurance. The universities offer a health insurance policy to foreign students. Medical examinations are not required by institutions but are required by Citizenship and Immigration Canada for students from many countries.

Language requirements: Universities offer language training programmes.

RECOGNITION OF STUDIES

Quality assurance system:

Recognition of studies is given by colleges (public and private) and by universities. For some professional bodies, additional requirements have to be met.

Special provisions for recognition:

Recognition for university level studies: In general, no special requirement. Universities establish their own admissions criteria and make their own admissions decisions in response to individual applications. Any restrictions on admission are determined by the institutions themselves, given available teaching and other resources. Additionally, the Canadian Information Centre for International Credentials (CICIC) provides information and guidance on the recognition of foreign studies.

For access to advanced studies and research: In general, no special requirements.

For exercising a profession: In Québec, adequate knowledge of French is required to practice any profession. The Office des professions and the Office de la langue française are responsible for the tests administered to candidates who come from outside Québec. Access to most professions is governed by provincial status and is restricted to Canadian citizens or immigrants accepted as permanent residents.

PROVINCIAL BODIES

Ministère de l'Education, du Loisir et du Sport
Minister: Line Beauchamp
1035, rue De La Chevrotière, 28e étage
Québec, Québec G1R 5A5
Canada
Tel: +1(418) 643 7095
Fax: +1(418) 646 6561
WWW: http://www.mels.gouv.qc.ca
Role of national body: To direct, promote and develop postsecondary, college and university education, including scientific research and development.

Ministère du Développement économique, de l'Innovation et de l'Exportation
Minister: Clément Gignac
710, place D'Youville, 3° étage
Québec, Québec G1R 4Y4
Canada
Tel: +1(418) 691 5950
Fax: +(418) 644 0118
WWW: http://www.mdeie.gouv.qc.ca/
Role of national body: To promote and develop the overall scientific and technological development required in the country, including applied research in colleges and university research.

Conseil supérieur de l'Education
President: Nicole Boutin
Secretary-General: Lucie Bouchard
1175, avenue Lavigerie, bureau 180
Québec, Québec G1V 5B2
Canada
Tel: +1(418) 643 3850
Fax: +1(418) 644 2530
EMail: panorama@cse.gouv.qc.ca
WWW: http://www.cse.gouv.qc.ca
Role of national body: To advise the Minister on the status of education and university research and needs in this area.

Conseil de la Science et de la Technologie (Council of Science and Technology)
President: Sylvie Dillard
Secretary-General: Brigitte Van Coillie-Tremblay
1150, Grande Allée Ouest, RC
Québec, Québec G1S 4Y9
Canada
Tel: +1(418) 691 5986
EMail: cst@cst.gouv.qc.ca
WWW: http://www.cst.gouv.qc.ca
Role of national body: To advise the Minister on overall scientific and technological development in Quebec.

Commission d'Evaluation de l'Enseignement collégial
President: Michel Lauzière
800, place d'Youville, 18° étage
Québec, Québec G1R 5P4
Canada
Tel: +1(418) 643 9938
Fax: +1(418) 643 9019
EMail: info@ceec.gouv.qc.ca
WWW: http://www.ceec.gouv.qc.ca
Role of national body: To act as an independent government organization whose evaluation mandate covers most aspects of college education, with special emphasis on student achievement and programmes of studies. Legislation attributes to the Commission the power to evaluate and make recommendations, as well as to exercise a declaratory power.

Association des Collèges privés du Québec - ACQP
President: Pierre L'Heureux
Director General: Guy Forgues
1940, boulevard Henri-Bourassa Est
Montréal, Québec H2B 1S2
Canada
Tel: +1(514) 381 8891
Fax: +1(514) 381 4086
EMail: acpq@cadre.qc.ca
WWW: http://www.acpq.net/

Role of national body: To act as the voice of 22 private subsidized colleges in order to promote education at college level.

Conférence des Recteurs et Principaux des Universités du Québec - CREPUQ (Conference of Rectors and Principals of Quebec Universities)

President: Denis Brière
Director General: Daniel Zizian
500, rue Sherbrooke Ouest, bureau 200
Montréal H3A 3C6
Canada
Tel: +1(514) 288 8524
Fax: +1(514) 288 0554
EMail: info@crepuq.qc.ca
WWW: http://www.crepuq.qc.ca/

Role of national body: To act as the voice of Quebec's universities, facilitate cooperation and information-sharing among universities, and coordinate assessment activities on study programmes.

Fédération des Cégeps

President: Patricia Hanigan
Director General: Gaëtan Boucher
500, boulevard Crémazie Est
Montréal, Québec H2P 1E7
Canada
Tel: +1(514) 381 8631
Fax: +1(514) 381 2263
EMail: comm@fedecegeps.qc.ca
WWW: http://www.fedecegeps.qc.ca

Role of national body: To promote education at the college level, and more specifically in the general and vocational colleges known as CEGEPs; the Fédération is the voice of 48 public CEGEPS in Québec.

Data for academic year: 2011-2012
Source: IAU from the Canadian Information Centre for International Credentials (CICIC), a unit of the Council of Ministers of Education, Canada (CMEC), on behalf of the Province of Québec, 2011.

INSTITUTIONS

PUBLIC INSTITUTIONS

BISHOP'S UNIVERSITY (BU)

2600 College St., Lennoxville, Québec J1M 1Z7
Tel: +1(819) 822-9600
Fax: +1(819) 822-9661
EMail: liaison@ubishops.ca
Website: http://www.ubishops.ca

Principal & Vice-Chancellor: Michael Goldbloom (2008-)
Tel: +1(819) 822-9600 Ext. 2611, Fax: +1(819) 822-1166
EMail: principal@ubishops.ca

Registrar: Yves Jodoin
Tel: +1(819) 822-9600 Ext. 2676 EMail: yves.jodoin@ubishops.ca

International Relations: Lillian Rogerson, Coordinator of International Students
Tel: +1(819) 822-9600 Ext. 2212, Fax: +1(819) 822-9616
EMail: lillian.rogerson@ubishops.ca

Centres
Entrepreneurship *(Dobson-Lagassé)* (Management)

Chairs
Representation of Algebras *(Maurice Auslander)* (Mathematics)

Divisions
Humanities (Art History; Arts and Humanities; Canadian Studies; Classical Languages; English; Film; Fine Arts; French Studies; German; Greek (Classical); History; Italian; Japanese; Jazz and Popular Music; Latin; Modern Languages; Music; Music Theory and Composition; Painting and Drawing; Philosophy; Religion; Sculpture; Spanish; Theatre; Writing); **Natural Sciences and Mathematics** (Biochemistry; Biology; Chemistry; Computer Science; Environmental Studies; Information Technology; Mathematics; Natural Sciences; Physics); **Social Sciences** (Criminology; Economics; Environmental Studies; Geography; Gerontology; International Economics; International Studies; Political Sciences; Psychology; Social Sciences; Sociology)

Groups
Modélisation en Imagerie, Vision et Réseaux de neurones (Neurosciences); **Plato** (Philosophy)

Programmes
Collaborative Studies *(BU / UdeS)* (Arts and Humanities; Chemical Engineering; Civil Engineering; Engineering); **Multidisciplinary Studies** (Business and Commerce; Environmental Studies; Information Technology; International Studies; Medicine; Social Studies; Sports)

Research Centres
Eastern Townships (Regional Studies)

Research Groups

Multi-scale Climate and Environmental Change (Environmental Studies; Meteorology); **Psychological Health and Well-being** (Health Sciences; Psychology)

Research Units

Crossing Borders Research Cluster (African Studies); **Modern History of Europe and Africa** (Modern History); **Stellar Astrophysics and Relativity Research Cluster** (Astrophysics)

Schools

Business *(Williams)* (Accountancy; Business Administration; Finance; Human Resources; International Business; Management; Marketing); **Continuing Education** (English; Fine Arts; Italian; Museum Studies; Painting and Drawing; Photography; Sculpture); **Education** (Art Education; Curriculum; Education; English; Foreign Languages Education; French; Humanities and Social Science Education; Leadership; Mathematics Education; Music Education; Native Language Education; Primary Education; Science Education; Secondary Education; Spanish; Teacher Training)

Further Information: Also Knowlton and St. Lambert campuses.

History: Founded 1843 as Bishop's College, constituted as a university by Royal Charter with power to confer degrees 1853. A small, residential, Liberal Arts university.

Governing Bodies: Senate

Academic Year: September to April (September-December; January-April). Also 2 Summer Sessions (May-August)

Admission Requirements: Collegial Diploma (DEC), or recognized foreign equivalent

Fees: (Can. Dollars): Tuition Fees for Quebec residents, 68.93 per credit (c. 1,030 per semester); Tuition Fees for Out-of-province residents, 188.92 per credit (c. 2,830 per semester); International fees, 482.05-538.65 per credit (c. 7,230-8,080 per semester).

Main Language(s) of Instruction: English

International Co-operation: With universities in USA, United Kingdom, France, and Switzerland

Degrees and Diplomas: *University Certificate/Diploma*; *Baccalauréat/Bachelor's Degree*; *Diplôme d'études supérieures spécialisées*; *Maîtrise/Master's Degree*. Also Honours Bachelor's degree; double majors in Liberal Arts combined with everything from Fine Art to Biology, from Music to Modern Languages, in Secondary Education and Music, and Education and a teaching discipline; Double-degree programme leading simultaneously to two Bachelor's degrees: a B.A. in Liberal Arts from Bishop's University (taught in English), and a B.Ing. (either Civil or Chemical Engineering), from the Université de Sherbrooke (taught in French).

Student Residential Facilities: Yes

Special Facilities: Art Collection

Libraries: c. 360,000 vols. Databases services (Dialog, Infoglobe, Infomart); Ph. Scowen Eastern Townships Collection; McKinnon Collection of Canadiana; Bel-Gard Collection

Publications: Bishop's Collects, Works in the University's Art Collection

Academic Staff *2009-2010*	MEN	WOMEN	TOTAL
FULL-TIME	–	–	c. **170**

Student Numbers *2009-2010*			
All (Foreign Included)	1,347	1,058	**2,405**
FOREIGN ONLY	–	–	**313**

Part-time students, 551.
Last Updated: 01/03/11

CONCORDIA UNIVERSITY

1455 Maisonneuve Blvd. West, Montréal, Québec H3G 1M8
Tel: +1(514) 848-2424
Fax: +1(514) 848-4546
Website: http://www.concordia.ca

President and Vice-Chancellor: Frederick H. Lowy (2011-)
Tel: +1(514) 848-2424, Ext. 4849, Fax: +1(514) 848-4546
EMail: president@concordia.ca; Frederick.Lowy@concordia.ca

Director, Media Relations: Christine Mota
Tel: +1(514) 848-2424 Ext. 4884, Fax: +1(514) 848-3383
EMail: chris.mota@concordia.ca

International Relations: Liselyn Adams, Associate Vice-President, International Relations
Tel: +1(514) 848-2424, Ext. 5429, Fax: +1(514) 848-4303
EMail: Liselyn.Adams@concordia.ca

Centres

Advanced Vehicle Engineering *(Concordia)* (Automotive Engineering); **Arts in Human Development** (Art Therapy; Fine Arts); **Biological Applications of Mass Spectrometry** (Biological and Life Sciences); **Broadcasting Studies** *(Concordia)* (Radio and Television Broadcasting); **Building Studies** (Building Technologies); **Composites** *(Concordia)* (Materials Engineering); **Continuing Education** (Business Administration; Communication Studies; Computer Science; Photography; Public Relations; Visual Arts); **Ethnographic Research and Exhibition in the Aftermath of Violence** (Human Rights; Museum Studies); **Innovation in Business Finance** *(Desjardins)* (Finance); **Investment and Trading** (Business Administration); **JMSB Executive** (Accountancy; Business Administration; Finance; Leadership; Management; Marketing); **Multidisciplinary Business Research** (Business Administration); **Oral History and Digital Storytelling** (History); **Pattern Recognition and Machine Intelligence** (Artificial Intelligence); **Recherche en Développement Humain** (Development Studies); **Signal Processing and Communications** (Computer Science); **Structural and Functional Genomics** (Genetics); **Studies in Behavioural Neurobiology** (Behavioural Sciences; Biology; Neurosciences); **Study of Learning and Performance** (Higher Education; Preschool Education; Primary Education; Secondary Education); **Sustainable Enterprise** *(David O'Brien)* (Management); **Technoculture, Art and Games** (Computer Science; Literature)

Courses

eConcordia (Accountancy; Business Administration; Chemistry; Christian Religious Studies; Communication Studies; Computer Science; Criminal Law; Cultural Studies; Economics; Ethics; Finance; Fine Arts; Human Rights; Information Management; Information Technology; Law; Leisure Studies; Management; Marketing; Mathematics; Political Sciences; Protective Services; Real Estate; Religion; Social Studies; Sociology; Statistics; Taxation; Urban Studies)

Faculties

Arts and Science (Actuarial Science; Adult Education; Ancient Civilizations; Anthropology; Applied Linguistics; Applied Mathematics; Arabic; Archaeology; Arts and Humanities; Behavioural Sciences; Biochemistry; Biology; Biophysics; Biotechnology; Canadian Studies; Cell Biology; Chemistry; Child Care and Development; Chinese; Classical Languages; Communication Studies; Cultural Studies; Ecology; Economics; Education; Educational Sciences; Educational Technology; English; Environmental Studies; Finance; Foreign Languages Education; French; French Studies; Gender Studies; Genetics; Geography; German; Greek (Classical); Histology; History; Italian; Jewish Studies; Journalism; Latin; Leisure Studies; Linguistics; Literature; Mathematics; Mathematics Education; Media Studies; Molecular Biology; Neurosciences; Philosophy; Physical Therapy; Physics; Physiology; Political Sciences; Preschool Education; Primary Education; Psychology; Public Administration; Rehabilitation and Therapy; Religion; Sociology; South Asian Studies; Spanish; Statistics; Theology; Town Planning; Translation and Interpretation; Urban Studies; Western European Studies; Women's Studies; Writing); **Engineering and Computer Science** (Aeronautical and Aerospace Engineering; Civil Engineering; Computer Engineering; Computer Networks; Computer Science; Construction Engineering; Electrical Engineering; Engineering; Environmental Engineering; Industrial Engineering; Information Sciences; Mechanical Engineering; Safety Engineering; Software Engineering); **Fine Arts** (Art Education; Art History; Art Therapy; Ceramic Art; Dance; Design; Display and Stage Design; Film; Fine Arts; Gender Studies; Jazz and Popular Music; Music; Music Theory and Composition; Musical Instruments; Painting and Drawing; Photography; Printing and Printmaking; Sculpture; Sound Engineering (Acoustics); Theatre)

Groups

Hardware Verification (Computer Engineering); **NanoScience** (Nanotechnology)

Institutes

Canadian Jewish Studies *(Concordia)* (Jewish Studies); **Community Entrepreneurship and Development** (Development Studies; Management); **Co-operative education** (Accountancy; Acting; Applied Mathematics; Art History; Biochemistry; Business Administration; Chemistry; Civil Engineering; Computer Science; Construction Engineering; Design; Economics; Electrical Engineering; Environmental Engineering; Finance; Fine Arts; French Studies; Human Resources; Industrial Engineering; Information Sciences; International Business; Management; Marketing; Mathematics; Mechanical Engineering; Physics; Safety Engineering; Software Engineering; Statistics); **Genocide and Human Rights Studies** *(Montreal)* (Human Rights); **Political Economy** *(Karl Polanyi)* (Political Sciences); **Research/Creation In Media Arts and Technologies** *(Hexagram-Concordia)* (Media Studies); **Studies in Canadian Art** *(Gail and Stephen A. Jarislowsky)* (Fine Arts)

Research Centres

Business Process Innovations *(Bell)* (Business Administration); **InterNeg** (Business Administration); **Molecular Modeling** (Molecular Biology)

Research Groups

New Rural Economy 2 *(Concordia Rural)* (Economics; Rural Studies)

Research Units

High Performance Computer Cluster Platform (Computer Science); **Solar Buildings Research Network** (Energy Engineering)

Schools

Business *(John Molson)* (Accountancy; Administration; Business Administration; Economics; Finance; Human Resources; Information Management; Insurance; International Business; Management; Marketing); **Canadian Irish Studies** (Irish); **Extended Learning** (Business Administration; Human Resources; Marketing); **Graduate Studies** (Accountancy; Administration; Adult Education; Aeronautical and Aerospace Engineering; Anthropology; Applied Linguistics; Art Education; Art History; Art Therapy; Arts and Humanities; Biochemistry; Biology; Biotechnology; Business Administration; Chemistry; Child Care and Development; Civil Engineering; Communication Studies; Computer Engineering; Computer Networks; Computer Science; Construction Engineering; Cultural Studies; Economics; Education; Educational Sciences; Educational Technology; Electrical Engineering; English; Environmental Engineering; Environmental Studies; Film; Fine Arts; Genetics; Geography; History; Industrial Engineering; Information Sciences; Jewish Studies; Journalism; Literature; Management; Mathematics; Mathematics Education; Mechanical Engineering; Media Studies; Musical Instruments; Philosophy; Physics; Political Sciences; Psychology; Public Administration; Religion; Safety Engineering; Social Sciences; Sociology; Software Engineering; Spanish; Theology; Translation and Interpretation; Urban Studies)

History: Founded 1974 by the merger of Sir George Williams University, founded 1948, and Loyola College of Montreal, incorporated 1896.

Governing Bodies: Board of Governors

Academic Year: Regular session, September to April (September-December; January-April); summer session, May to August).

Admission Requirements: Diploma of Collegial Studies (DEC) following successful completion of a 2-year pre-university course at a CEGEP (Collège d'Enseignement général et professionnel), or recognized equivalent

Fees: (Canadian Dollar): Undergraduate tuition, 2,067.90 per Fall and Winter term for Canadian, Quebec Resident; 5,667.60 per Fall and Winter term for Canadian, Non-Quebec Resident; 16,159.50-19,440 per Fall and Winter term for International Students. Master's degree, 4,980.81-6,728.66 per term for Quebec Residents; 10,380.36-13,928.06 per term for Non-Quebec Residents; 24,707.22-40,573.58 per term for International students. PhD programmes, 9,951.95-10,323.95 per term for Canadian, Quebec & Non-Quebec Residents; 44,105.06-44,477.06 per term for International Students. Other Graduate certificates and diploma programmes are the same that undergraduate tuitions except, 14,461.80-19,440 per Fall and Winter term for International Students.

Main Language(s) of Instruction: English

Degrees and Diplomas: *University Certificate/Diploma; Baccalauréat/Bachelor's Degree; Diplôme d'études supérieures spécialisées; Maîtrise/Master's Degree; Doctorat/Doctoral Degree (PhD).* Also Honours degrees; Accelerated MBA, 1-2 yrs; Executive MBA, 20 months.

Student Residential Facilities: For c. 200 full-time students

Libraries: c. 2,950,000 vols

Publications: Arts and Sciences' Connections; Concordia Journal; Concordia University Magazine; Engineering and Computer Science Faculty Quarterly; President's Report

Academic Staff 2009-2010	TOTAL
FULL-TIME	910
PART-TIME	673

Student Numbers 2009-2010	
All (Foreign Included)	39,904
FOREIGN ONLY	4,439

Part-time students, 14,050.
Note: Part-time students are included in total
Last Updated: 02/03/11

ENGINEERING SCHOOL - ETS (UNIVERSITY OF QUEBEC)

Ecole de Technologie supérieure (Université du Québec) (ETS)

1100, rue Notre-Dame Ouest, (angle Peel), Montréal,
Québec H3C 1K3
Tel: +1(514) 396-8800
Fax: +1(514) 396-8950
EMail: admission@etsmtl.ca
Website: http://www.etsmtl.ca

Directeur général: Yves Beauchamp (2003-2013)
Tel: +1(514) 396-8802, Fax: +1(514) 396-8539
EMail: yves.beauchamp@etsmtl.ca

Registraire: Stéphanie de Celles
Tel: +1(514) 396-8885, Fax: +1(514) 396-8831
EMail: registraire@etsmtl.ca

International Relations: Pierre L'Heureux, Directeur du Bureau des Relations internationales et du Recrutement étudiant
Tel: +1(514) 396-8809, Fax: +1(514) 396-8539
EMail: pierre.lheureux@etsmtl.ca

Centres

Thermal Technology/ Technologie thermique *(CTT)* (Thermal Engineering)

Departments

Automated Production Engineering (Automation and Control Engineering; Operations Research; Production Engineering; Sanitary Engineering; Transport Management); **Construction Engineering** (Bridge Engineering; Construction Engineering; Engineering Management; Environmental Engineering; Hydraulic Engineering); **Electrical Engineering** (Electrical Engineering; Energy Engineering; Microelectronics; Telecommunications Engineering); **Mechanical Engineering** (Aeronautical and Aerospace Engineering; Energy Engineering; Engineering; Industrial Management; Mechanical Engineering; Production Engineering; Safety Engineering); **Software Engineering and Information Technologies** (Engineering Management; Information Technology; Software Engineering)

Laboratories

Computer Systems Architecture *(LASI)* (Computer Engineering); **Control and Robotics/ Commande et de robotique** *(CoRo)* (Automation and Control Engineering; Robotics); **Design and Control of Production Systems/ Conception et contrôle des systèmes de production** *(C2SP)* (Production Engineering); **Management Networks and Telecommunications/ Gestion des réseaux informatiques et de télécommunications** *(LAGRIT)* (Computer Networks; Telecommunications Engineering); **Multimedia Communication in Telepresence/ Communication multimédia en téléprésence** *(Synchromedia)* (Multimedia; Telecommunications Engineering); **Pavement, Roads and Bituminous Materials/ Chaussées, routes et enrobés bitumineux** *(LUCREB)* (Road Engineering); **Production Technologies Integration/ Intégration des technologies de production** *(LITP)*

(Production Engineering); **Products, Processes, and Systems Engineering** *(P2SEL)* (Engineering); **Semantics and Cognitive Engineering** *(LiNCS)* (Cognitive Sciences); **Shape Memory Alloys and Intelligent Systems/ Alliages à mémoire et les systèmes intelligents** *(LAMSI)* (Artificial Intelligence); **Stress Analysis by Finite Element and Testing/Analyse des contraintes par éléments finis et expérimentation** *(ACEFE)* (Mechanical Engineering); **Telecommunications and Microelectronics Integration/ Communications et d'intégration de la microélectronique** *(LACIME)* (Microelectronics; Telecommunications Engineering)

Research Centres

Advanced Research in Telecommunications/ Recherche avancée en télécommunications *(COMunity/ COMunité)* (Telecommunications Engineering); **Development and Research on Structures and Rehabilitation/ Développement et recherche en structures et réhabilitation** *(DRSR)* (Bridge Engineering; Civil Engineering); **Experimental Station of Pilot Processes in Environment/ Station expérimentale des procédés pilotes en environnement** *(STEPPE)* (Environmental Engineering); **Machine Dynamics, Structures and Processes/ Dynamique des machines, des structures et des procédés** *(DYNAMO)* (Mechanical Engineering); **Occupational Safety/ Sécurité du travail** *(EREST)* (Safety Engineering)

Research Groups

Avionic and Navigation (Air Transport); **Development and Applied Research in Environmental Modeling/ Développement et en recherche appliquée à la modélisation environnementale** *(DRAME)* (Environmental Engineering); **Integration and Sustainable Development in Built Environment/ Intégration et développement durable en environnement bâti** *(GRIDD)* (Development Studies); **Power Electronics and Industrial Control/ Electronique de puissance et commande industrielle** *(GREPCI)* (Automation and Control Engineering; Electronic Engineering; Industrial Engineering; Power Engineering); **Production of Francis Turbine Shroud Ring/ Fabrication de couronnes de turbine Francis** (Hydraulic Engineering)

Research Laboratories

Active Control, Avionics and Aeroservoelasticity/ Commande active, avionique et aéroservoélasticité *(LARCASE)* (Aeronautical and Aerospace Engineering; **Imagery and Orthopedics/ Imagerie et orthopédie** *(LIO)* (Medical Technology; Orthopaedics); **Multimedia** *(LABMULTIMEDIA)* (Multimedia); **Software Engineering Management/ Génie logiciel** *(GELOG)* (Software Engineering)

History: Founded 1974. An Engineering School, part of the University of Quebec network specialized in applied engineering and technology. Cooperative education system with work-study programme.

Governing Bodies: Board of Directors

Academic Year: September to August (September-December; January-April; May-August)

Admission Requirements: Diploma of Collegial Studies (DEC) following successful completion of 3-year pre-university course in physical technology or technology of computer-controlled systems, at a CEGEP (Collège d'Enseignement général et professionnel) in Quebec, or recognized equivalent

Fees: (Canadian Dollar): Undergraduate tuition, 827.16 for Quebec Resident Canadian Students; 2,267.04 for Non-Quebec Resident Canadian Students; 6,463.80 for International students. Postgraduate tuition, 620.37 for Quebec Resident Canadian Students; 1,700.28 for Non-Quebec Resident Canadian Students; 4,338.54 for International students. PhD, 620.37 for Quebec Resident Canadian Students; 620.37 for Non-Quebec Resident Canadian Students; 3,892.68 for International students.

Main Language(s) of Instruction: French

International Co-operation: With Engineering Schools in Algeria; Argentina; Belgium; Benin; Brazil; China; Colombia; Ecuador; France; Germany; Hong Kong; Iceland; Italy; Lebanon; Morocco; Mexico; Netherlands; Poland; Russian Federation; Spain; Tunisia; United Kingdom; USA and Vietnam

Degrees and Diplomas: *University Certificate/Diploma*; *Baccalauréat/Bachelor's Degree*; *Diplôme d'études supérieures spécialisées*; *Maîtrise/Master's Degree*; *Doctorat/Doctoral Degree (Ph.D.)*

Student Services: Academic counselling, Canteen, Employment services, Foreign student adviser, Handicapped facilities, Social counselling, Sports facilities

Student Residential Facilities: For 850 students

Libraries: 65,000 vols and 18,000 e-books

Publications: L'ETS @ 360° *(biannually)*

Academic Staff 2007-2008	MEN	WOMEN	TOTAL
FULL-TIME	126	19	**145**
PART-TIME	182	26	**208**
STAFF WITH DOCTORATE			
FULL-TIME	96	16	**112**
PART-TIME	34	6	**40**

Student Numbers 2009-2010			
All (Foreign Included)	–	–	c. **5,500**
FOREIGN ONLY	–	–	**180**

Last Updated: 02/03/11

HEC MONTREAL (UNIVERSITY OF MONTREAL)

HEC Montréal (Université de Montréal) (HEC)
3000, chemin de la Côte-Sainte-Catherine, Montréal,
Québec H3T 2A7
Tel: +1(514) 340-6000
Fax: +1(514) 340-6411
EMail: registraire.info@hec.ca
Website: http://www.hec.ca

Director: Michel Patry
Tel: +1(514) 340-6300, Fax: +1(514) 340-6314
EMail: michel.patry@hec.ca

Secrétaire général: Jacques Nantel
Tel: +1(514) 340-6305, Fax: +1(514) 340-6899
EMail: jacques.nantel@hec.ca

International Relations: Federico Pasin, Directeur des activités internationales
Tel: +1(514) 340-6752, Fax: +1(514) 340-6907
EMail: federico.pasin@hec.ca

Centres

Computerization of Organizations *(Francophone - CEFRIO)* (Computer Science); **Financial Information** *(International Watch)* (Finance); **House of Technology for Training and Learning** *(MATI Montreal)* (Educational Technology); **Humanism, Management and Globalization** (Management); **International Association for Research in Entrepreneurship and SMEs** *(AIREPME)* (Management; Small Business); **International Business Families** *(McGill - HEC Montreal)* (International Business); **Logistics hub** (Transport Management); **Productivity and Prosperity** (Economics); **Promotion of Excellence in Municipal Management** (Management); **Studies in Management of Financial Services Cooperatives** *(Desjardins)* (Finance; Management); **Studies of Business Processes** *(CMA International)* (Business Administration)

Chairs

Arts Management *(Carmelle and Rémi Marcoux)* (Art Management); **Commercial Space and Customer Service Management** (Business and Commerce; Management); **Data Mining** (Data Processing); **E-Commerce** *(RBC Financial Group)* (E-Business/Commerce); **Entrepreneurship** *(Rogers—J.-A.-Bombardier)* (Management); **Ethical Management** (Management); **Game Theory and Management** (Management); **Governance and Forensic Accounting** (Accountancy; Government); **International Economics and Governance** (Government; International Economics); **International Strategic Management** *(Walter-J.-Somers)* (Management); **Leadership** *(Pierre-Péladeau)* (Leadership); **Learning and Teaching Technologies in Management Education** (Educational Technology); **Monetary Policy and Financial Markets** (Finance); **Research in Distribution Management** *(Canada)* (Transport Management); **Research in Information Technology Implementation and Management** *(Canada)* (Information Management; Information Technology); **Research in Information Technology in Health Care** *(Canada)* (Information Technology); **Research in Logistics and Transportation** *(Canada)* (Transport and Communications; Transport Management); **Research in Management of Employee Commitment and Performance** *(Canada)* (Management); **Research in Risk Management** *(Canada)*

(Insurance); **Research in Strategic Management in Pluralistic Settings** *(Canada)* (Management); **Retailing** *(Omer DeSerres)* (Retailing and Wholesaling); **Small and Medium-size Business Development and Succession** (Small Business); **Strategic Management of Information Technology** (Information Technology; Management); **Supply Management** (Transport Management)

Departments

Accounting Studies (Accountancy; Administration; Business Administration; Finance; Fiscal Law; Management; Taxation); **Finance** (Finance); **Human Resources Management** *(GRH)* (Business Administration; Human Resources; Management); **Information Technology** (Business Administration; Business Computing; E-Business/Commerce; Information Technology); **International Business** (Business Administration; International Business; Management); **Logistics and Operations Management** *(GOL)* (Management; Transport Management); **Management** (Administration; Art Management; Business Administration; Environmental Management; Management); **Marketing** (Administration; Business Administration; Business and Commerce; Management; Marketing; Retailing and Wholesaling; Sales Techniques); **Quantitative Methods for Management Development** *(MQG)* (Administration; Finance; Management; Transport Management)

Groups

Strategy as Practice Study (Management); **Women, Management and Organizations** (Management)

Institutes

Applied Economics *(IEA)* (Administration; Economics; Finance)

Laboratories

ERPsim (Business Administration)

Research Centres

Analysis on Organizations *(Interuniversity - CIRANO)* (Management); **Creation Management and Transfer** *(Mosaic)* (Management); **E-Finance** (Finance); **Enterprise Networks, Logistics and Transportation** *(Interuniversity - CIRRELT)* (Transport and Communications; Transport Management); **Families in Business** (Business Administration); **Globalization and Work** *(Interuniversity - CRIMT)* (International Economics); **Healthcare Management Hub** (Health Administration); **Life Cycle of Products, Processes and Services** *(Interuniversity - CIRAIG)* (Business Administration); **Organizational Transformation** *(CETO)* (Management); **Quantitative Economics** *(Interuniversity - CIREQ)* (Economics); **Risk, Economic Policies and Employment** *(Interuniversity - CIRPEE)* (Economics); **Social Innovations** *(CRISES)* (Welfare and Protective Services); **Work, Health and Organizational Effectiveness** *(CRITEOS)* (Management)

Research Groups

CHAIN (Transport Management); **Decision Analysis** *(GERAD)* (Management; Operations Research); **Education and Research on Management and Environment** *(GERM)* (Environmental Studies; Management); **Information Systems** *(GReSI)* (Information Sciences); **International Affairs** *(GRAI)* (International Business); **Non-profit, Community and Cultural Organizations** (Management); **Organizations Strategy** *(STRATEGOS)* (Management); **Sustainable Development** *(Interdisciplinary - GRIDD-HEC)* (Development Studies); **Use, Development and Transfer of Management Knowledge** (Management)

Further Information: Exchange Programme (Passeport pour le Monde)

History: Founded 1907 as Ecole des Hautes Etudes Commerciales de Montréal. Acquired present name 2002. Affiliated to the University of Montreal.

Governing Bodies: Board of Directors; International Board

Academic Year: September to July (September-December; January-May; May-July)

Admission Requirements: Depending on programmes; information available from the institution

Fees: (Canadian Dollar): Undergraduate tuition, 145.18-168.01 per credit for Quebec-resident students, 265.17-288 per credit for Non-Quebec-resident students, 614.90-637.73 per credit for international students. MBA, 6,700 for Quebec-resident students, 13,600 for Non-Quebec-resident students, 30,300 for international students. Master's degree, 1,142.31 per semester (for the 4 first semester and

then 761.81) for Quebec-resident students, 2,492.20 per semester (for the 4 first semester and then 761.81) for Non-Quebec-resident students, 5,790.03 per semester (for the 4 first semester and then 936.81) for international students. PhD, 1,400.56 per semester (for the 6 first semester and then 911.81) for Quebec-resident students and Non-Quebec-resident students, 6,854.41 per semester (for the 6 first semester and then 1,086.81) for international students.

Main Language(s) of Instruction: French, English, Spanish

International Co-operation: With 79 institutions

Accrediting Agencies: AMBA (The Association of MBA's - UK); European Quality Improvement System (EQUIS) of the European Foundation for Management Development (EFMD); AACSB International (United States)

Degrees and Diplomas: *University Certificate/Diploma*; *Baccalauréat/Bachelor's Degree*; *Diplôme d'études supérieures spécialisées (D.E.S.S.)*; *Maîtrise/Master's Degree*; *Doctorat/Doctoral Degree (Ph.D.)*. Also MBA

Student Services: Academic counselling, Canteen, Cultural centre, Employment services, Foreign student adviser, Foreign Studies Centre, Handicapped facilities, Health services, Language programs, Nursery care, Social counselling, Sports facilities

Student Residential Facilities: Yes

Special Facilities: Trading Room

Libraries: Myriam and J.-Robert Ouimet Library, 345,000 vols and more than 60 databases

Publications: Assurances, Insurance and Risk Management Journal *(quarterly)*; Gestion (Revue internationale), Management Journal *(quarterly)*; International Journal of Arts Management, Academic Journal on Arts and Cultural Organizations Management *(quarterly)*; International Management, Academic Journal on International Management *(quarterly)*

Last Updated: 03/03/11

LAVAL UNIVERSITY

Université Laval

2325, rue de l'Université, Québec, Québec G1V 0A6
Tel: +1(418) 656-2131 +1(418) 656-3333
Fax: +1(418) 656-5920
EMail: info@ulaval.ca
Website: http://www.ulaval.ca

Recteur: Denis Brière (2007-)
Tel: +1(418) 656-2272, Fax: +1(416) 656-7917
EMail: Denis.Briere@rec.ulaval.ca

Vice-Recteur exécutif et au développement: Éric Bauce
Tel: +1(418) 656-3573, Fax: +1(418) 656-7917
EMail: eric.bauce@vrex.ulaval.ca

International Relations: Monique Généreux, Responsable au développement et aux relations internationales
Tel: +1(418) 656-2131 poste 3917
EMail: monique.genereux@bi.ulaval.ca

Faculties

Agriculture and Food Sciences (Agricultural Business; Agricultural Economics; Agricultural Engineering; Agriculture; Agronomy; Animal Husbandry; Biology; Botany; Dietetics; Environmental Engineering; Food Science; Food Technology; Forest Products; Microbiology; Nutrition; Soil Science; Zoology); **Arts** (Ancient Civilizations; Archaeology; Archiving; Art History; Arts and Humanities; Chinese; Cinema and Television; Classical Languages; Communication Studies; English; English Studies; Ethnology; Foreign Languages Education; French; German; Grammar; Greek (Classical); History; Information Sciences; International Studies; Italian; Japanese; Journalism; Latin; Linguistics; Literature; Modern Languages; Museum Studies; Portuguese; Public Relations; Russian; Spanish; Terminology; Theatre; Translation and Interpretation; Writing); **Business Administration** (Accountancy; Business Administration; E-Business/Commerce; Finance; Information Management; Information Sciences; Insurance; International Business; Management; Marketing; Occupational Health; Real Estate; Small Business; Tourism); **Dentistry** (Dental Hygiene; Dentistry; Gerontology; Surgery); **Education** (Education; Educational Administration; Educational and Student Counselling; Educational Psychology; Educational Technology; Health Education; Humanities and Social Science Education; Mathematics Education; Native

Language Education; Pedagogy; Physical Education; Primary Education; Science Education; Secondary Education; Sports; Technology Education; Vocational Education); **Forestry and Geomatics** (Environmental Studies; Forest Biology; Forest Management; Forestry; Geography; Meteorology; Rural Studies; Surveying and Mapping; Urban Studies; Wood Technology); **Graduate Studies**; **Law** (Commercial Law; Environmental Studies; International Law; Law; Notary Studies); **Medicine** (Anaesthesiology; Anatomy; Biochemistry; Biomedicine; Cardiology; Cell Biology; Cognitive Sciences; Community Health; Endocrinology; Epidemiology; Ergotherapy; Gender Studies; Gynaecology and Obstetrics; Immunology; Medicine; Microbiology; Molecular Biology; Neurology; Neurosciences; Ophthalmology; Otorhinolaryngology; Paediatrics; Pathology; Physical Therapy; Physiology; Plastic Surgery; Psychiatry and Mental Health; Public Health; Radiology; Rehabilitation and Therapy; Social and Preventive Medicine; Speech Therapy and Audiology; Surgery; Toxicology; Urology); **Music** (Music; Music Education; Religious Music); **Nursing** (Cardiology; Community Health; Nursing); **Pharmacy** (Epidemiology; Pharmacology; Pharmacy); **Philosophy** (Ethics; Philosophy); **Planning, Architecture and Visual Arts** (Architecture; Art Education; Fine Arts; Graphic Design; Regional Planning; Town Planning; Visual Arts); **Science and Engineering** (Actuarial Science; Aeronautical and Aerospace Engineering; Biochemistry; Biology; Biotechnology; Chemical Engineering; Chemistry; Civil Engineering; Computer Engineering; Computer Science; Earth Sciences; Electrical Engineering; Engineering; Geological Engineering; Geology; Hydraulic Engineering; Industrial Engineering; Marine Science and Oceanography; Materials Engineering; Mathematics; Mechanical Engineering; Metallurgical Engineering; Microbiology; Mining Engineering; Natural Sciences; Optics; Physical Engineering; Physics; Polymer and Plastics Technology; Software Engineering; Statistics); **Social Sciences** (Anthropology; Clinical Psychology; Criminology; Cultural Studies; Economics; Gerontology; Human Resources; International Relations; Labour and Industrial Relations; Management; Mathematics; Philosophy; Political Sciences; Psychology; Public Administration; Social and Community Services; Social Sciences; Sociology; Women's Studies); **Theology and Religious Studies** (Classical Languages; Ethics; Hebrew; Oriental Languages; Pastoral Studies; Religious Studies; Sanskrit; Theology)

Institutes
International Studies *(Québec)* (International Studies)

Laboratories
'Mont Mégantic' Observatory *(OMM)*

Programmes
Continuous Education (Accountancy; Agricultural Management; Bible; Biotechnology; Computer Science; Development Studies; Educational Administration; English Studies; Ethics; Finance; Food Science; French; Geography; German; Grammar; Greek (Classical); History of Religion; Human Resources; Industrial Engineering; Information Management; Information Technology; International Business; International Law; Journalism; Latin; Law; Leadership; Management; Music; Occupational Health; Ophthalmology; Pastoral Studies; Pharmacy; Philosophy; Portuguese; Public Relations; Publishing and Book Trade; Real Estate; Religion; Religious Studies; Russian; Small Business; Social Psychology; Software Engineering; Statistics; Surveying and Mapping; Theology; Tourism; Toxicology; Vocational Education; Writing); **Distance Education** (Agrobiology; Animal Husbandry; Business Administration; Cognitive Sciences; Communication Studies; Computer Science; Cultural Studies; E-Business/Commerce; Ethnology; Food Technology; Forestry; French; Geography; Gerontology; Health Sciences; Horticulture; Information Sciences; Information Technology; Insurance; Law; Nutrition; Philosophy; Political Sciences; Religious Practice; Small Business; Theology)

Research Centres
Aboriginal Studies and Research *(CIERA)*; **Agricultural Economics** *(CREA)* (Agricultural Economics; Agronomy); **Algebric Mathematics Calculation** *(Interuniversity Centre, CICMA)*; **Brain, Behaviour and Neuropsychiatry** *(CRCN)* (Behavioural Sciences; Neurology; Psychiatry and Mental Health); **Cancer** *(CRC)* (Oncology); **Catalysis and Interfaces Properties** *(CERPIC)* (Organic Chemistry); **Concrete Technology** *(Interuniversity Research, CRIB)* (Building Technologies); **Education and Work Life** *(Interuniversity Research, CRIEVAT)*; **Energy Metabolism** *(CREME)*

(Physiology); **Forestry Biology** *(CRBF)* (Forest Biology); **Geomatics** *(CRG)*; **Horticulture** *(CRH)* (Horticulture); **Infectiology** *(CRI)* (Epidemiology); **Language Planning** *(International Research Centre, CIRAL)* (Linguistics; Modern Languages); **Languages, Arts and Popular Francophone Traditions of North America** *(CELAT)* (Canadian Studies; Cultural Studies; Folklore; French Studies; Modern Languages); **Macromolecules Sciences and Engineering** *(CERSIM)* (Molecular Biology); **Milk Science and Technology** *(STELA)* (Dairy; Technology); **Molecular Endocrinology and Oncology** *(CREMO)* (Endocrinology; Oncology); **Network Organisation Technologies** *(CENTOR)* (Computer Networks; Telecommunications Engineering); **Nordic Studies**; **Optics, Photonics and Laser** (Laser Engineering; Optics); **Protein, Function and Structure Engineering** *(CREFSIP)* (Physical Engineering); **Quebec Literature and Culture** *(Interuniversity Research; CRILCQ)* (Canadian Studies; Cultural Studies; Literature); **Quebec Studies** *(Interuniversity Centre, CIEQ)* (Canadian Studies; Cultural Studies; Social Sciences); **Regional Planning and Development** *(CRAD)* (Regional Planning; Rural Planning; Town Planning); **Rehabilitation and Social Integration** (Psychology; Rehabilitation and Therapy; Social Work); **Reproduction Biology** *(CRBR)* (Embryology and Reproduction Biology); **Research and Intervention on Academic Success** *(CRIRES)* (Educational Sciences); **Risk, Economic Policies and Employment** *(Interuniversity Research, CIRPEE)* (Economics; Finance); **Training and Teaching Professions** *(Interuniversity Research Centre (CRIFPE))* (Teacher Trainers Education; Teacher Training); **Violence Against Women and Family Violence**; **Youth and Families at Risk** *(JEFAR)* (Social Work)

Research Groups
Finite Element Methods *(Interdisciplinary Research Group, GIREF)* (Engineering; Mathematics); **Health Respiratory** *(GESER)* (Health Sciences); **Oral Ecology** *(GREB)*; **Psychosocial Inadaptation of the Child** *(GRIP)* (Child Care and Development; Educational Psychology); **Quebec Oceanographic Research** *(Interuniversity Group, Quebec-Ocean)* (Marine Science and Oceanography)

Further Information: Also 9 Teaching Hospitals. French courses for foreign students. 386 programmes. International, Work-Study and Entrepeneurial profiles integrated into many programmes.

History: Founded 1663 as Grand Séminaire de Québec. Granted royal Charter 1852. Granted a new charter by the Assemblée Nationale du Québec 1970; modified 1991. Financed by a Provincial Grant.

Governing Bodies: Board, comprising Rector, Executive Vice-Rector, 5 representatives of academic staff, 3 representatives of student body, 3 representatives of non-academic staff, 12 representatives of a broad cross-section of the public and 5 members without vote. University Council, comprising Rector, 5 Vice-Rectors, Secretary-General, 17 Deans, 27 representatives of academic staff, 8 representatives of student body, 3 representatives of non-academic staff, 1 representative of collegial level, 1 representative of External Research, 2 representative of Research sections and 6 members without vote

Academic Year: September to August (September-December; January-April; May-August)

Admission Requirements: Diploma of Collegial Studies (DEC) following successful completion of a 2-year pre-university course at a CEGEP (Collège d'Enseignement général et professionnel), or recognized equivalent

Fees: (Can. Dollars): Tuition fees, 2,592 per annum for Quebec residents, 6,192 per annum for other Canadian students and 2,592-16,684 per annum for international students.

Main Language(s) of Instruction: French

International Co-operation: More than 550 cooperation agreements with 65 countries

Degrees and Diplomas: *University Certificate/Diploma*; *Baccalauréat/Bachelor's Degree*; *Diplôme d'études supérieures spécialisées*; *Maîtrise/Master's Degree*; *Doctorat/Doctoral Degree (PhD)*. Also M.B.A.; Undergraduate and graduate microprogrammes.

Student Services: Academic counselling, Canteen, Cultural centre, Employment services, Foreign student adviser, Foreign Studies Centre, Handicapped facilities, Health services, Language programs, Nursery care, Social counselling, Sports facilities

Student Residential Facilities: 2,400 rooms

Special Facilities: Museum. Art Gallery. Botanical Garden. Movie Studio. Geological Garden. Theatre

Libraries: c. 3.4 m. vols; 24,000 periodical titles, and 585,000 audiovisual items

Press or Publishing House: Presses de l'Université Laval

Academic Staff 2009-2010	TOTAL
FULL-TIME	2,500
PART-TIME	100
STAFF WITH DOCTORATE	
FULL-TIME	c. 1,310

Student Numbers 2009-2010	
All (Foreign Included)	c. 45,000
FOREIGN ONLY	4,000

Part-time students, 14,000.
Last Updated: 22/03/11

MCGILL UNIVERSITY (MCGILL)

845 Sherbrooke Street West, Montréal, Québec H3A 2T5
Tel: +1(514) 398-4455
EMail: admissions@mcgill.ca
Website: http://www.mcgill.ca

Principal and Vice-Chancellor: Heather Munroe-Blum (2003-)
Tel: +1(514) 398-4180, Fax: +1(514) 398-4768
EMail: heather.munroe.blum@mcgill.ca

University Registrar and Executive Director, Enrolment Services: Kathleen Massey
Tel: +1(514) 398-3672 EMail: kathleen.massey@mcgill.ca

International Relations: Rose Goldstein, Vice-Principal, Research and International Relations
Tel: +1(514) 398-2995, Fax: +1(514) 398-8257
EMail: rose.goldstein@mcgill.ca

Centres

Continuing Education (Accountancy; Business Administration; Education; English; Finance; French; Health Sciences; Human Resources; Information Technology; Insurance; International Business; Leadership; Management; Marketing; Operations Research; Public Relations; Social Work; Spanish; Taxation; Translation and Interpretation; Transport Management)

Faculties

Agricultural and Environmental Sciences (Agricultural Economics; Agriculture; Animal Husbandry; Biochemistry; Bioengineering; Biological and Life Sciences; Biology; Botany; Dietetics; Ecology; Entomology; Environmental Engineering; Environmental Studies; Farm Management; Food Science; Food Technology; Forestry; Meteorology; Microbiology; Molecular Biology; Natural Resources; Nutrition; Soil Management; Soil Science; Tropical Agriculture; Water Management; Wildlife); **Arts** (African Studies; American Studies; Anthropology; Art History; Arts and Humanities; Canadian Studies; Caribbean Studies; Catholic Theology; Cinema and Television; Classical Languages; Cognitive Sciences; Communication Studies; Development Studies; East Asian Studies; Economics; Educational Psychology; English; French; Gender Studies; German; Greek (Classical); History; Italian; Jewish Studies; Labour and Industrial Relations; Latin; Latin American Studies; Linguistics; Literature; Middle Eastern Studies; Philosophy; Political Sciences; Religion; Russian; Slavic Languages; Social Work; Sociology; Spanish; Statistics; Women's Studies); **Dentistry** (Dentistry; Oral Pathology; Surgery); **Education** (Education; Educational and Student Counselling; Educational Psychology; Educational Sciences; Family Studies; Foreign Languages Education; Health Education; Human Resources; Indigenous Studies; Information Sciences; Jewish Studies; Leadership; Library Science; Music Education; Natives Education; Pedagogy; Physical Education; Physical Therapy; Physiology; Primary Education; Psychology; Secondary Education; Special Education; Teacher Training); **Engineering** (Architecture; Bioengineering; Biomedical Engineering; Chemical Engineering; Civil Engineering; Computer Engineering; Computer Science; Electrical Engineering; Energy Engineering; Engineering; Environmental Engineering; Hydraulic Engineering; Materials Engineering; Mechanical Engineering; Mechanics; Mining Engineering; Nanotechnology; Power Engineering; Software Engineering; Structural Architecture; Telecommunications Engineering; Town Planning; Transport Engineering); **Law** (Air and Space Law; Civil Law; Comparative Law; Environmental Studies; Ethics; European Union Law; Human Rights; International Law; Law; Private Law); **Management** (Accountancy; Business Administration; Health Administration; Industrial Management; Leadership; Management); **Medicine** (Anaesthesiology; Anatomy; Biochemistry; Biomedical Engineering; Cardiology; Cell Biology; Communication Disorders; Communication Studies; Dermatology; Endocrinology; Epidemiology; Gastroenterology; Genetics; Gerontology; Gynaecology and Obstetrics; Haematology; Immunology; Medicine; Microbiology; Nephrology; Neurology; Nursing; Occupational Health; Occupational Therapy; Oncology; Ophthalmology; Orthopaedics; Otorhinolaryngology; Paediatrics; Pathology; Pharmacology; Physical Therapy; Physiology; Plastic Surgery; Psychiatry and Mental Health; Radiology; Respiratory Therapy; Rheumatology; Social Studies; Statistics; Surgery; Urology); **Religious Studies** (Asian Religious Studies; Bible; Christian Religious Studies; Ethics; History of Religion; New Testament; Philosophy; Religion; Religious Studies; Theology); **Science** (Applied Mathematics; Astronomy and Space Science; Biochemistry; Biological and Life Sciences; Biology; Cell Biology; Chemistry; Clinical Psychology; Computer Science; Earth Sciences; Environmental Studies; Experimental Psychology; Geography; Geophysics; Immunology; Marine Science and Oceanography; Mathematics; Meteorology; Microbiology; Molecular Biology; Natural Sciences; Neurosciences; Physics; Psychology; Software Engineering; Statistics)

Programmes

Graduate and Postdoctoral Studies (Agricultural Economics; Agriculture; Anatomy; Anthropology; Architecture; Art History; Astronomy and Space Science; Biochemistry; Bioengineering; Biology; Biomedical Engineering; Biotechnology; Botany; Business Administration; Cell Biology; Chemical Engineering; Chemistry; Civil Engineering; Classical Languages; Communication Disorders; Communication Studies; Computer Engineering; Computer Science; Dentistry; Development Studies; Dietetics; Earth Sciences; East Asian Studies; Economics; Education; Educational and Student Counselling; Educational Psychology; Electrical Engineering; English; Environmental Engineering; Environmental Studies; Epidemiology; Ethics; European Studies; Food Science; French; Gender Studies; Genetics; Geography; German; Greek (Classical); History; Immunology; Information Sciences; Islamic Studies; Italian; Jewish Studies; Latin; Law; Linguistics; Literature; Management; Marine Science and Oceanography; Materials Engineering; Mechanical Engineering; Mechanics; Medical Technology; Meteorology; Microbiology; Mining Engineering; Music; Natural Resources; Neurosciences; Nursing; Nutrition; Occupational Health; Occupational Therapy; Oncology; Otorhinolaryngology; Parasitology; Pathology; Pharmacology; Philosophy; Physical Education; Physical Therapy; Physics; Physiology; Polish; Psychiatry and Mental Health; Psychology; Religious Studies; Russian; Slavic Languages; Social Studies; Social Work; Sociology; Spanish; Statistics; Surgery; Town Planning; Tropical Agriculture; Women's Studies; Zoology)

Schools

Music *(Schulich)* (Jazz and Popular Music; Music; Music Education; Music Theory and Composition; Musical Instruments; Musicology; Singing)

Further Information: For additional information see website. Also online courses.

History: Founded 1821 as University of McGill College. A corporation created by Royal Charter granted by the United Kingdom Crown and exercised through the Governor-General as 'visitor'.

Governing Bodies: Board of Governors; Senate

Academic Year: September to April (September-December; January-April)

Admission Requirements: Diploma of Collegial Studies (DEC) following successful completion of a 2-year pre-university course at a CEGEP (Collège d'Enseignement général et professionnel) in Quebec, or high school diploma with university entrance

Fees: (Can. Dollars): Undergraduate tuition, Quebec Students, 2,067.90-4,825.10 per annum; non-Quebec Canadians, 5,667.60-13,224.40 per annum; international students, 14,461.80-37,705.50 per annum. Graduate tuition, Quebec Students, 2,067.90 per annum; non-Quebec Canadians, 2,067.90-5,667.60 per annum; international students, 12,975.60-14,461.80 per annum.

Main Language(s) of Instruction: English (Students may write term papers and exams in French)

International Co-operation: With universities in the Americas, Asia and the Middle East, Europe and Oceania.

Accrediting Agencies: Association of Universities and Colleges of Canada

Degrees and Diplomas: *University Certificate/Diploma; Baccalauréat/Bachelor's Degree; Diplôme d'études supérieures spécialisées; Maîtrise/Master's Degree; Doctorat/Doctoral Degree.* Also Honours Bachelor's degree; Concurrent degree programmes in Science and Education; Joint Bachelor's degree programmes in Law and Business Administration/Social Work; Joint PhD McGill/Université de Montreal Programme in Social Work; MBA, Executive MBA; MBA in Japan.

Student Services: Academic counselling, Foreign student adviser, Handicapped facilities, Health services, Language programs, Nursery care, Social counselling, Sports facilities

Student Residential Facilities: For 3,325 students

Special Facilities: Redpath Museum (Botany, Entomology, Geology, Zoology); McCord Museum (Canadiana); Lyman Museum of Entomology; Rutherford Collection of Experimental Physics; Anatomical, Medicine and Pathology Facilities; Facility for Electron Microscopy Research; Institute for Cancer Research; CLUMEQ (Consortium Laval-UQAM-McGill and Eastern Quebec for high performance computing) Super Computer Centre; Brain Tumor Research Centre; Centre for Climate and Global Change Research; Emile Lods Agronomy Centre; Phytotron; Aerospace Medical Research Unit; Bellairs Research Institute in St. James, Barbados; Sheldon Biotechnology Centre; McConnell Brain Imaging Centre; R. Howard Webster Centre for Teaching and Research in Animal and Poultry Science; Centre for Translational Research in Cancer; Subarctic Research Station in Shefferville; McGill Arctic Research Station (MARS); Avian Science and Conservation Centre; Centre for Trace Element Analysis (Geochemical Laboratories); Centre for Biorecognition and Biosensors; Research Greenhouses at macdonals Campus Farm; Gault Nature Reserve and Mont St. Hilaire Biosphere Reserve; Brace Centre for Water Resources Management; McGill University and Genome Quebec Innovation Centre; Research Institute of the McGill University Health Centre (RIMUHC)

Libraries: McLennan Library (Humanities and Social Sciences); Blackader-Lauterman Library of Architecture and Art; Education Library; Edward Rosenthall Library of Mathematics and Statistics; Health Sciences Library; Islamic Studies Library; Law Library; Macdonald Campus Library (Agriculture and Environment); Howard Ross Management Library; Marvin Duchow Music Library; Osler Library (History of Medicine); Schulich Library of Science and Engineering; Birks Reading Room (Religious Studies); Walter Hitschfeld Environmental Earth Sciences Library; Life Sciences Library; Nahum Gelber Law Library

Publications: McGill International Journal of Sustainable Development Law and Policy; McGill Journal of Education; McGill Journal of Law and Health; McGill Journal of Medicine; McGill Law Journal

Press or Publishing House: McGill-Queen's University Press

Academic Staff *2010-2011*	TOTAL
FULL-TIME	1,627
STAFF WITH DOCTORATE FULL-TIME	1,538

Student Numbers *2010-2011*	
All (Foreign Included)	36,531
FOREIGN ONLY	7,294

Part-time students, 6,776.
Note: Doctoral staff totals do not include faculty with a terminal degree other than a doctorate.
Last Updated: 03/03/11

MONTREAL DIOCESAN THEOLOGICAL COLLEGE (MCGILL UNIVERSITY) (MDTC)

3475 University Street, Montréal, Québec H3A 2A8
Tel: +1(514) 849-3004
EMail: info@dio-mdtc.ca
Website: http://www.dio-mdtc.ca/

Principal: John Simons
Tel: +1(514) 849-3004 Ext. 222
EMail: jsimons@montreal.anglican.ca

Centres
Lay Education (Adult Education; Religious Education)

Programmes
Divinity (Pastoral Studies; Religion; Religious Studies; Theology); **Ministry** (New Testament; Religion; Theology); **Reading and Tutorial** (Ethics; History of Religion; Holy Writings; New Testament; Philosophy; Theology); **Theology** (New Testament; Theology)

Degrees and Diplomas: *Baccalauréat/Bachelor's Degree; Maîtrise/Master's Degree*
Last Updated: 03/03/11

NATIONAL INSTITUTE OF SCIENTIFIC RESEARCH (UNIVERSITY OF QUEBEC)

Institut national de la Recherche scientifique (Université du Québec) (INRS)
490, rue de la Couronne, Québec, Québec G1K 9A9
Tel: +1(418) 654-4677
Fax: +1(418) 654-3876
EMail: registrariat@adm.inrs.ca
Website: http://www.inrs.ca/

Directeur général: Daniel Coderre
Tel: +1(418) 654-2505, Fax: +1(418) 654-3876
EMail: daniel.coderre@adm.inrs.ca

Secrétaire générale: Lana Fiset
Tel: +1(418) 654-2508, Fax: +1(418) 654-3876
EMail: lana.fiset@adm.inrs.ca

International Relations: Dalida Poirier, Adjointe au Directeur Scientifique et Directrice du Service
Tel: +1(418) 654-3896, Fax: +1(418) 654-3858
EMail: dalida.poirier@adm.inrs.ca

Institutes
Armand Frappier *(Laval)* (Biological and Life Sciences; Biology; Health Sciences; Immunology; Microbiology; Virology)

Research Centres
Energy, Materials and Telecommunications *(Varennes)* (Chemistry; Energy Engineering; Laser Engineering; Materials Engineering; Physics; Telecommunications Engineering); **Urbanization, Culture and Society** (Cultural Studies; Demography and Population; Social Studies; Urban Studies); **Water, Earth and Environment** (Earth Sciences; Water Science)

History: Founded 1969. A Postgraduate Research Institute constituent of the University of Quebec.

Academic Year: September to August

Admission Requirements: University degree at Bachelor level

Fees: (Canadian Dollar): Tuition for Second Cycle Degree Programmes, Quebec Residents, 1,033.95 per term; non-Quebec residents, 2,833.80; International students, 7,230.90. Tuition for Third Cycle Degree Programmes, Quebec Residents and Non-Quebec Resident, 1,033,95; International students, 6,487.80 per term.

Main Language(s) of Instruction: French

Degrees and Diplomas: *Maîtrise/Master's Degree; Doctorat/Doctoral Degree*

Libraries: c. 60,000 vols

Academic Staff *2010-2011*	MEN	WOMEN	TOTAL
FULL-TIME	–	–	c. **150**
Student Numbers *2010-2011*			
All (Foreign Included)	350	350	c. **700**
FOREIGN ONLY	–	–	**230**

Last Updated: 03/03/11

NATIONAL SCHOOL OF PUBLIC ADMINISTRATION (UNIVERSITY OF QUEBEC)

Ecole nationale d'Administration publique (Université du Québec) (ENAP)

555, boul. Charest Est, Québec, Québec G1K 9E5
Tel: +1(418) 641-3000
Fax: +1(418) 641-3060
EMail: martine.gallant@enap.ca
Website: http://www.enap.ca

Directeur général: Marcel Proulx (2001-)
Tel: +1(418) 641-3000, Ext. 6500, Fax: +1(418) 641-3058
EMail: marcel.proulx@enap.ca

Directrice de l'Administration et Secrétaire Générale: Louise Laflamme

International Relations: Simon Chabot, Responsable des Relations Internationales
Tel: +1(418) 641-3000 poste 6232, Fax: +1(418) 641-3060
EMail: simon.chabot@enap.ca

Programmes

Second-Cycle Studies (Communication Studies; Finance; Government; Health Administration; Human Resources; Information Sciences; Information Technology; International Business; Management; Public Administration; Urban Studies); **Third-Cycle Studies** (Management; Public Administration)

Further Information: Also Branches in Montréal, Gatineau, Saguenay and Trois-Rivières. On-line short second-cycle programme in Public Management.

History: Founded 1969. A Postgraduate Constituent School of the University of Quebec.

Governing Bodies: Board of Trustees; Academic Senate

Academic Year: August to June (August-December; January-April; May-June)

Admission Requirements: Diploma of Collegial Studies (DEC) following successful completion of a 2-year pre-university course at a CEGEP (Collège d'Enseignement général et professionnel), or recognized equivalent

Fees: (Can. Dollars): tuition, 68.93 per credit for Quebec-resident Canadian students and 99.16 per credit for non-Quebec resident and international students.

Main Language(s) of Instruction: French

Degrees and Diplomas: *Diplôme d'études supérieures spécialisées; Maîtrise/Master's Degree; Doctorat/Doctoral Degree.* Also short degree programmes.

Student Services: Academic counselling, Employment services, Foreign student adviser, Handicapped facilities, Social counselling

Libraries: c. 102,000 vols

Academic Staff *2009-2010*: Total 335
Student Numbers *2009-2010*: Total 2,023
Last Updated: 02/03/11

POLYTECHNIC SCHOOL OF MONTREAL (UNIVERSITY OF MONTREAL)

Ecole polytechnique de Montréal (Université de Montréal)

Case postale 6079, succ. Centre-ville, Montréal, Québec H3C 3A7
Tel: +1(514) 340-4711
Fax: +1(514) 340-5836
EMail: registraire@polymtl.ca
Website: http://www.polymtl.ca

Directeur général: Christophe Guy (2007-)
Tel: +1(514) 340-4943, Fax: +1(514) 340-4600
EMail: christophe.guy@polymtl.ca

Registraire: Robert Vinet
Tel: +1(514) 340-4711 Ext. 4324, Fax: +1(514) 340-5836
EMail: robert.vinet@polymtl.ca

International Relations: Line Dubé, Directrice, Bureau des relations internationales (BRIN)
Tel: +1(514) 340-4711 poste, Fax: +1(514) 340-4222
EMail: line.dube@polymtl.ca; brin@polymtl.ca

Centres

Applied Research on Polymers and Composites (Polymer and Plastics Technology); **Characterization and Microscopy of Materials** *((CM)2)* (Metallurgical Engineering); **Continuing Education** (Aeronautical and Aerospace Engineering; Biomedical Engineering; Building Technologies; Civil Engineering; Construction Engineering; Development Studies; Display and Stage Design; Electrical Engineering; Engineering; Fire Science; Industrial Design; Industrial Engineering; Mechanical Engineering; Operations Research; Polymer and Plastics Technology; Production Engineering; Safety Engineering; Technology; Water Management); **Northern Engineering** *(CINEP)* (Engineering; Meteorology); **Research in Computational Thermochemistry** *(CRCT)* (Chemical Engineering; Safety Engineering); **Research in Radiofrequency Electronics** *(CREER)* (Electronic Engineering; Telecommunications Engineering); **Risque et Performance** (Industrial Engineering; Safety Engineering); **Water Treatment Technologies and Processes** *(Research, Development and Validation)* (Waste Management; Water Management)

Chairs

Drinking Water Treatment *(NSERC Industrial)* (Water Management); **Environment and Mine Wastes Management** *(NSERC-Polytechnique-UQAT Industrial)* (Mining Engineering; Waste Management; Water Management); **Fluid-Structure Interaction** *(BWC/AECL/NSERC Industrial)* (Mechanical Engineering); **Liquid Composite Molding Technological Network** *(RTMFLOT Software)* (Mechanical Engineering); **Methodology for Life Cycle Assessment** *(Industrial International)* (Chemical Engineering); **Next Generations Mobile Networking Systems** *(NSERC/Ericsson Industrial)* (Computer Engineering); **Nuclear Engineering** *(Hydro-Quebec Industrial)* (Nuclear Engineering); **Process Integration in the Pulp and Paper Industry** *(NSERC Environmental Design - I3P)* (Environmental Engineering; Paper Technology); **Research on Low Cost Composite Manufacturing for Automotive Applications** *(NSERC/GM Canada Industrial)* (Automotive Engineering; Production Engineering); **Research in Advanced Microelectronic Systems Architecture and Development** *(Canada)* (Microelectronics); **Research in Analysis, Characterization and Multidisciplinary Design Optimization of Complex Systems** *(Canada)* (Mechanical Engineering); **Research in Applied Metabolic Engineering** *(Canada)* (Chemical Engineering); **Research in Cartilage Tissue Engineering** *(Canada)* (Biomedical Engineering); **Research in Earthquake Resistance Design and Construction of Steel Structures** *(Canada)* (Civil Engineering); **Research in Ergonomic Intervention for the Prevention and Rehabilitation of Musculoskeletal Disorders** *(Canada - MSD)* (Industrial Engineering; Rehabilitation and Therapy); **Research in Fabricating Microsystems and Advanced Materials** *(Canada)* (Aeronautical and Aerospace Engineering; Automotive Engineering); **Research in Future Intelligent Radio-frequency Metamaterials** *(Canada)* (Electrical and Electronic Engineering); **Research in Future Photonics Systems** *(Canada)* (Materials Engineering; Technology); **Research in High Performance Composite Design and Manufacturing** (Mechanical Engineering); **Research in Hybrid Biomaterials for Innovative Regenerative Technologies** *(NSERC Piramal Industrial)* (Biomedical Engineering; Chemical Engineering); **Research in International Project Management** *(Jarislowsky/SNC-Lavalin)* (Management); **Research in Large Transportation Network Optimization** *(Canada)* (Applied Mathematics); **Research in Materials Micro/Nanoengineering Using Lasers** *(Canada)* (Materials Engineering); **Research in Mechanobiology of the Pediatric Musculoskeletal System** (Bioengineering); **Research in Micro/Nanosystem Development, Construction and Validation** *(Canada)* (Robotics); **Research in Microbial Contaminant Dynamics in Source Waters** *(Canada)* (Environmental Engineering; Water Science); **Research in Radio Frequency and Millimetric Wave Engineering** *(Canada)* (Electrical Engineering; Electronic Engineering); **Research in Smart Medical Devices** *(Canada - SMD)* (Biomedical Engineering; Electrical and Electronic Equipment and Maintenance; Electronic Engineering; Information Technology); **Research In Software Change and Evolution** *(Canada)* (Information Technology); **Research in Software Patterns and Patterns of Software** (Software Engineering); **Research in Spine Biomechanics** *(NSERC/Medtronic Industrial)* (Biomedical Engineering); **Research in the Theory, Manufacturing and Applications of Photonic Crystals** *(Canada)* (Electrical and Electronic Engineering); **Research on Evaluation and Implementation of Sustainability in Transportation** *(MOBILITÉ Chair)*

(Transport Engineering); **Research on innovations CAO/MAO in orthopedic engineering** *(Canada)* (Biomedical Engineering); **Research on Materials and Films for smart, Safe and Sustainable Packaging** *(NSERC/Saputo/Excel-Pac Industrial)* (Packaging Technology; Safety Engineering); **Research on Protein-enhanced biomaterials** *(Canada)* (Chemical Engineering); **Research on Technology Management** *(Canada)* (Industrial Engineering; Mathematics); **Sciences and Engineering Academic Teaching** (Engineering; Science Education)

Departments
Biomedical Engineering (Biomedical Engineering); **Chemical Engineering** (Biomedical Engineering; Biotechnology; Chemical Engineering; Energy Engineering; Engineering Management; Environmental Engineering; Paper Technology; Pharmacology; Polymer and Plastics Technology); **Civil, Geological and Mining Engineering** (Civil Engineering; Construction Engineering; Environmental Engineering; Geological Engineering; Mining Engineering; Transport Engineering); **Computer Engineering** (Computer Engineering; Computer Networks; Information Technology; Multimedia; Software Engineering); **Electrical Engineering** (Aeronautical and Aerospace Engineering; Automation and Control Engineering; Computer Engineering; Electrical Engineering; Energy Engineering; Engineering Management; Management; Microelectronics; Microwaves; Software Engineering; Telecommunications Engineering); **Engineering Physics** (Biomedical Engineering; Engineering; Nanotechnology; Nuclear Engineering; Physical Engineering); **Mathematics and Industrial Engineering** (Applied Mathematics; Engineering Management; Industrial Design; Industrial Engineering; Mathematics; Production Engineering; Safety Engineering; Transport Management); **Mechanical Engineering** (Aeronautical and Aerospace Engineering; Materials Engineering; Mechanical Engineering; Metallurgical Engineering)

Groups
Experimental and numerical engineering water flow *(GENIE EAU)* (Hydraulic Engineering; Safety Engineering); **Mechanical Components Analysis** *(GACM)* (Mechanical Engineering); **Nuclear Analysis** (Nuclear Engineering); **Ptidej** (Software Engineering); **Regroupement Québécois sur les Matériaux de Pointe** *(RQMP)* (Materials Engineering); **URPEI** (Chemical Engineering)

Laboratories
BioMEMS (Mechanical Engineering; Microelectronics); **Bioperformance Analysis and Innovation** (Biomedical Engineering); **Broadband Networks** *(Broadlab)* (Electrical Engineering); **Complex Applications Design and Implementation** (Computer Engineering); **Distributed open reliable systems analysis** *(DORSAL)* (Computer Engineering; Software Engineering); **Electrical Energy** (Electrical Engineering); **Environmental Engineering** (Environmental Engineering); **Epitaxy and Characterization of Compound Semiconductors** (Electronic Engineering; Physical Engineering); **Fiber Optics** (Physical Engineering); **Fluid Dynamics** *(LADYF)* (Hydraulic Engineering; Mechanics); **Functional Coating and Surface Engineering** (Physical Engineering); **Hydrogeology and Mining Environment** (Geological Engineering; Hydraulic Engineering); **LASEM** (Electrical Engineering); **Laser Processing** *(LPL)* (Laser Engineering); **Magnetics** (Physical Engineering); **Material Surface Analysis** *(LASM)* (Materials Engineering; Nanotechnology; Physical Engineering); **Micro and Nano Systems** (Microelectronics; Nanotechnology); **Microfabrication** (Physical Engineering); **Multi-scale Mechanics** (Mechanics); **NanoRobotics** (Nanotechnology; Robotics); **Nanostructures** (Nanotechnology); **Networking and Digital Geometry** *(MAGNU)* (Computer Engineering); **Neurotechnology** *(Polystim)* (Electrical Engineering); **New Materials for Energy and Electrochemistry** (Chemistry; Electronic Engineering; Energy Engineering; Materials Engineering); **Optoelectronics** (Physical Engineering); **Photo Acoustic Spectroscopy and Laser-Ultrasonics** *(PASLU)* (Laser Engineering; Physical Engineering); **Polynov** (Chemical Engineering); **Robotics** *(Ecole Polytechnique Montreal)* (Robotics); **SCRIBENS** (Electrical Engineering; Neurosciences); **SLOWPOKE** (Physical Engineering); **Software Engineering** (Software Engineering); **Spectroscopy of Materials and Nanostructures** (Materials Engineering; Nanotechnology); **Thermalhydraulics** (Nuclear Engineering)

Research Centres
Biomedical Science and Technologies *(GRSTB)* (Biomedical Engineering; Biomedicine); **Entreprise Networks, Logistics and**

Transportation *(Interuniversity -CIRRELT)* (Transport and Communications; Transport Management); **IDEA** (Aeronautical and Aerospace Engineering); **Life Cycle of Products, Processes and Services** *(Interuniversity - CIRAIG)* (Chemical Engineering; Industrial Design); **Microsystems Strategic Alliance** *(RESMIQ)* (Electrical Engineering); **Microwaves and Space Electronics** *(Advanced - POLY-GRAMES)* (Electronic Engineering; Microwaves); **Process Engineering - Biorefinery** *(CRIP)* (Chemical Engineering; Heating and Refrigeration; Petroleum and Gas Engineering); **SQUIRREL** (Software Engineering); **Technology for Training and Learning** *(Roland-Giguère House)* (Educational Technology)

Research Groups
Computational Engineering *(GRMIAO)* (Computer Engineering); **Decision Analysis** *(GERAD)* (Industrial Engineering; Mathematics; Operations Research); **MADITUC** (Civil Engineering); **Microelectronics and Microsystems** *(GR2M)* (Microelectronics); **Networking and Mobile Computing** *(GRIM)* (Computer Engineering; Computer Networks); **Perception and Robotics** *(GRPR)* (Robotics); **PolyPhotonic** (Electrical Engineering; Physical Engineering); **Product Development and Manufacturing** *(GRDFP)* (Mechanical Engineering; Production Engineering); **Structural Engineering** *(GRS)* (Civil Engineering; Safety Engineering); **Thin Film Physics and Technology** *(GCM)* (Physical Engineering)

Research Laboratories
Mobile Computing and Networking *(LARIM)* (Computer Engineering; Computer Networks); **Tightness Testing** *(TTRL)* (Mechanical Engineering); **Virtual Manufacturing** (Mechanical Engineering)

Research Units
Energy Efficiency and Sustainable Development of the Forest Biorefinery (Chemical Engineering; Environmental Engineering; Paper Technology)

History: Founded 1873.

Governing Bodies: Conseil d'Administration, comprising 11 members; Conseil académique, comprising 17 members

Academic Year: September to August (September-December; January-April; May-August)

Admission Requirements: Diplôme d'études collégiales (DEC) in Sciences. Baccalauréat français (Serie S)

Fees: (Can. Dollars): 1,800-3,000 per annum; foreign students, 9,300

Main Language(s) of Instruction: French

Degrees and Diplomas: *Baccalauréat/Bachelor's Degree; Diplôme d'études supérieures spécialisées; Maîtrise/Master's Degree; Doctorat/Doctoral Degree.* Graduate diploma programmes are called "Microprogrammes" and can be achieved in 3-6 terms.

Student Services: Academic counselling, Canteen, Cultural centre, Employment services, Foreign student adviser, Handicapped facilities, Health services, Nursery care, Social counselling, Sports facilities

Libraries: c. 200,000 vols.; 4,000 electronic periodicals; 50 databanks

Student Numbers 2009-2010	MEN	WOMEN	TOTAL
All (Foreign Included)	4,930	1,434	**6,364**

Last Updated: 02/03/11

PRESBYTERIAN COLLEGE (MCGILL UNIVERSITY)

3495 University Street, Montréal, Québec H3A 2A8
Tel: +1(514) 288-5256
Fax: +1(514) 288-8072
EMail: info@presbyteriancollege.ca
Website: http://www.presbyteriancollege.ca/

Principal: John A. Vissers EMail: jvissers@presbyteriancollege.ca

Courses
Christian Theology (Christian Religious Studies; Theology)

Programmes

Divinity (Christian Religious Studies; Ethics; History of Religion; Holy Writings; New Testament; Religion; Theology); **Lay Education** *(One Day Offsite)* (Theology); **Lay Leadership** (History of Religion; Holy Writings; Leadership; New Testament); **Theology** (Religious Studies; Theology)

History: Founded 1865.

Fees: (Canadian Dollar): tuition fee, 3,350 (335 per 3 credit course).

Degrees and Diplomas: *Baccalauréat/Bachelor's Degree; Maî-trise/Master's Degree.* The Master's degree in Divinity is awarded by the College in conjunction with the Montreal Diocesan Theological College and the United Theological College.
Last Updated: 03/03/11

UNITED THEOLOGICAL COLLEGE OF MONTREAL (MCGILL UNIVERSITY) (UTC)

3521, University Street, Montréal, Québec H3A 2A9
Tel: +1(514) 849-2042 +1(888) 849-2042
Fax: +1(514) 849-8634
EMail: admin@utc.ca
Website: http://www.utc.ca/

Principal: Philip L. Joudrey EMail: pjoudrey@utc.ca

Director of Studies: Elisabeth Jones EMail: erjones@utc.ca

Programmes

Continuing Education *(United Theological College/ Le Seminaire Uni)* (Christian Religious Studies; Theology); **Divinity** (Bible; Ethics; History of Religion; Pastoral Studies; Philosophy; Religion; Religious Studies; Theology); **Lay Education** (New Testament); **Sacred Theology** (Theology)

Fees: (Canadian Dollar): tuition fee, 2,750-3,450 per annum for Canadian students and 13,965 per annum for international students.

Main Language(s) of Instruction: English and French

Degrees and Diplomas: *Maîtrise/Master's Degree*
Last Updated: 03/03/11

UNIVERSITY OF MONTREAL

Université de Montréal (UDEM)
C.P. 6128, succursale Centre-ville, Montréal, Québec H3C 3J7
Tel: +1(514) 343-6111
Fax: +1(514) 343-5976
EMail: dcr@umontreal.ca
Website: http://www.umontreal.ca

Recteur/Rector: Guy Breton (2010-)
Tel: +1(514) 343-6776, Fax: +1(514) 343-2354
EMail: recteur@umontreal.ca; guy.breton@umontreal.ca

Secrétaire général: Alexandre Chabot
Tel: +1(514) 343-6800, Fax: +1(514) 343-2239
EMail: alexandre.chabot@umontreal.ca

International Relations: Joseph Hubert, Vice-recteur, Recherche et Affaires internationales
Tel: +1(514) 343-7270, Fax: +1(514) 343-2098
EMail: joseph.hubert@umontreal.ca

Departments

Kinesiology (Ethics; Health Education; Physical Education; Physical Therapy; Physiology)

Faculties

Arts and Sciences (Ancient Civilizations; Anthropology; Arabic; Art History; Arts and Humanities; Biochemistry; Biological and Life Sciences; Catalan; Chemistry; Chinese; Communication Studies; Comparative Literature; Computer Science; Criminology; Demography and Population; Economics; Educational Psychology; Educational Technology; English; Film; French; Geography; German; Germanic Studies; Greek; History; Information Sciences; Italian; Japanese; Labour and Industrial Relations; Library Science; Linguistics; Literature; Mathematics; Medieval Studies; Modern Languages; Operations Research; Philosophy; Physics; Political Sciences; Portuguese; Psychology; Social Sciences; Social Work; Sociology; Spanish; Statistics; Translation and Interpretation); **Continuing Education** (Advertising and Publicity; Child Care and Development; Communication Studies; Community Health; Computer Science; Criminology; Foreign Languages Education; French;

Gerontology; Health Administration; Health Sciences; Journalism; Labour and Industrial Relations; Law; Management; Multimedia; Psychiatry and Mental Health; Public Relations; Rehabilitation and Therapy; Social and Community Services; Social Problems; Translation and Interpretation; Writing); **Dentistry** (Biochemistry; Biomedicine; Community Health; Dental Technology; Dentistry; Immunology; Microbiology; Neurology; Orthodontics; Public Health; Stomatology); **Education** (Education; Educational Administration; Educational Psychology; Educational Sciences; Foreign Languages Education; French; International and Comparative Education; Mathematics Education; Physical Education; Preschool Education; Primary Education; Religious Education; Science Education; Secondary Education; Special Education; Teacher Training); **Environmental Design** (Architectural and Environmental Design; Architecture; Design; Industrial Design; Interior Design; Landscape Architecture; Software Engineering; Town Planning); **Graduate and Postdoctoral Studies** (Actuarial Science; Administration; Anaesthesiology; Anthropology; Architecture; Archiving; Art History; Arts and Humanities; Bible; Biochemistry; Biological and Life Sciences; Biology; Biomedical Engineering; Biomedicine; Cell Biology; Chemistry; Civil Law; Classical Languages; Clinical Psychology; Commercial Law; Communication Studies; Community Health; Comparative Literature; Computer Science; Conducting; Criminology; Curriculum; Demography and Population; Dentistry; Development Studies; E-Business/Commerce; Economics; Education; Educational Administration; Educational Psychology; English; English Studies; Environmental Management; Environmental Studies; Ethics; Film; Fiscal Law; Forensic Medicine and Dentistry; French; Genetics; Geography; German; Germanic Studies; Greek (Classical); Health Administration; Health Education; Health Sciences; Higher Education; History; Immunology; Information Sciences; Information Technology; International Economics; International Law; International Studies; Labour and Industrial Relations; Latin; Law; Library Science; Linguistics; Literature; Mathematics; Mathematics and Computer Science; Microbiology; Molecular Biology; Museum Studies; Music; Music Theory and Composition; Musical Instruments; Neurosciences; Notary Studies; Nursing; Nutrition; Occupational Health; Optometry; Oral Pathology; Paediatrics; Pathology; Pharmacology; Pharmacy; Philosophy; Physical Therapy; Physics; Physiology; Political Sciences; Psychology; Public Health; Radiology; Rehabilitation and Therapy; Religious Studies; Safety Engineering; Secondary Education; Social Sciences; Social Work; Sociology; Software Engineering; Spanish; Special Education; Speech Studies; Speech Therapy and Audiology; Statistics; Surveying and Mapping; Teacher Training; Theology; Town Planning; Toxicology; Translation and Interpretation; Veterinary Science; Virology); **Law** (Administrative Law; Civil Law; Commercial Law; Constitutional Law; Criminal Law; Fiscal Law; International Law; Labour Law; Law; Notary Studies); **Medicine** (Anaesthesiology; Biochemistry; Biomedicine; Cardiology; Community Health; Dermatology; Endocrinology; Gastroenterology; Genetics; Gerontology; Gynaecology and Obstetrics; Haematology; Health Administration; Immunology; Medicine; Microbiology; Molecular Biology; Nephrology; Neurology; Nutrition; Occupational Health; Oncology; Ophthalmology; Paediatrics; Pathology; Pharmacology; Physical Therapy; Physiology; Plastic Surgery; Psychiatry and Mental Health; Public Health; Radiology; Rehabilitation and Therapy; Respiratory Therapy; Rheumatology; Speech Therapy and Audiology; Surgery; Toxicology; Urology; Virology); **Music** (Art History; Conducting; Music; Music Theory and Composition; Musical Instruments; Musicology; Singing); **Nursing** (Cardiology; Health Administration; Health Education; Health Sciences; Nephrology; Nursing); **Pharmacy** (Biological and Life Sciences; Epidemiology; Pharmacology; Pharmacy); **Theology and Religious Studies** (Bible; Christian Religious Studies; Community Health; Ethics; Islamic Studies; Religious Studies; Theology); **Veterinary Medicine** (Biomedicine; Epidemiology; Food Technology; Immunology; Microbiology; Pathology; Pharmacology; Toxicology; Veterinary Science; Virology)

Schools

Optometry (Biomedicine; Neurosciences; Ophthalmology; Optometry; Paediatrics; Physiology; Psychology; Rehabilitation and Therapy); **Public Health** (Public Health)

History: Founded 1878 as a branch of Laval University. Became autonomous 1919 and acquired present status and title 1967. A public institution. The largest French-speaking university outside France.

Academic Year: September to August (September-December; January-April; May-August)

Admission Requirements: Diploma of Collegial Studies (DEC) following successful completion of a 2-year pre-university course at a CEGEP (Collège d'enseignement général et professionnel), or recognized equivalent

Fees: (Can. Dollars): Undergraduate tuition, 68.93 per credit for Quebec residents; 188.92 per credit for other Canadian residents; 482.06-581.78 per credit for international students; Graduate tuition, 1,033.95 per term for Quebec residents (except for Medicine programmes, 1,194.56 per term); 2,833.80 per term for other Canadian residents; 6,487.86-7,230.90 per term for international students.

Main Language(s) of Instruction: French. Students may write examinations in French or English

International Co-operation: With universities in France; Belgium; Switzerland; Italy; Spain; United Kingdom; Japan; Mexico; Chile; Argentina

Degrees and Diplomas: *University Certificate/Diploma*; *Baccalauréat/Bachelor's Degree*; *Diplôme d'études supérieures spécialisées*; *Maîtrise/Master's Degree*; *Doctorat/Doctoral Degree*. Also Honours Bachelor's degree; Joint degrees (Combined Honours Mathematics and Computer science; Combined programmes in Law; Postdoctoral fellows in Nursing.

Student Services: Academic counselling, Canteen, Cultural centre, Employment services, Foreign student adviser, Handicapped facilities, Health services, Nursery care, Social counselling, Sports facilities

Student Residential Facilities: For 1,200 students

Special Facilities: Mount Mégantic Astronomical Observatory. Botanical Garden, Biological Station

Libraries: Printed matter and microtexts, 5,144,228 items; periodical subscriptions, 44,653

Publications: Cahiers d'histoire; Circuit, revue nord-américaine de musique du XXe siècle; Forum; META, Journal des Traducteurs/Translator's Journal; Revue juridique Thémis; Sociologie et Sociétés

Press or Publishing House: University Press (Les Presses de l'Université de Montréal)

Academic Staff *2007-2008*	TOTAL
FULL-TIME	2,105
PART-TIME	c. 3,700

Student Numbers *2009-2010*	
All (Foreign Included)	c. 41,448
FOREIGN ONLY	6,657

Part-time students, 17,500.
Note: Part-time students are not included in the total
Last Updated: 04/03/11

UNIVERSITY OF QUEBEC
Université du Québec (UQ)
475, rue du Parvis, Québec, Québec G1K 9H7
Tel: +1(418) 657-3551
Fax: +1(418) 657-2132
EMail: communications@uquebec.ca
Website: http://www.uquebec.ca

Présidente: Sylvie Beauchamp (2009-2014)
Tel: +1(418) 657-4301, Fax: +1(418) 657-2132
EMail: sylvie.beauchamp@uquebec.ca; presidence@uquebec.ca

Secrétaire général: André G. Roy (2009-2014)
Tel: +1(418) 657-4307
EMail: andre.g.roy@uquebec.ca; sg@uquebec.ca

History: Founded 1968 by an Act of the National Assembly of the Province of Quebec, the University is the Province's first public university but it is self-governing and reports to the State each year. The University of Quebec groups 9 institutions (6 comprehensive universities, 1 research institute and 2 schools). The traditional university organization by Faculties and Schools has been replaced by a structure composed of 3 elements: Departments, Modules and Research Centres. The Module is responsible for administration of First Degree programmes (1er cycle) while Departments and Research Centres (concerned with higher Degrees) are respectively responsible for teaching and research of any given discipline.

Governing Bodies: Assemblée des Gouverneurs; Conseil des Etudes; Commission de Planification

Academic Year: September to April

Admission Requirements: Diploma of Collegial Studies (DEC) following successful completion of 2 yrs pre-university course at a CEGEP (Collège d'Enseignement général et professionnel), or recognized equivalent

Main Language(s) of Instruction: French

Degrees and Diplomas: *University Certificate/Diploma*; *Baccalauréat/Bachelor's Degree*; *Diplôme d'études supérieures spécialisées*; *Maîtrise/Master's Degree*; *Doctorat/Doctoral Degree (PhD)*. Also Attestation d'études de premier, deuxième et troisième cylces, and Doctorat de premier cycle.

Student Residential Facilities: Yes

Libraries: 2.5m. documents. Each Campus has its own Library

Press or Publishing House: Presses de l'Université du Québec

Academic Staff *2008-2009*: Total: c. 4,000
Student Numbers *2008-2009*: Total: c. 87,000
Note: Amalgamated statistics for all institutions gathered under the Univeristé du Québec.
Last Updated: 04/03/11

UNIVERSITY OF QUEBEC ABITIBI-TEMISCAMINGUE
Université du Québec en Abitibi-Témiscamingue (UQAT)
445 boul. de l'Université, Rouyn-Noranda, Québec J9X 5E4
Tel: +1(819) 762-0971
Fax: +1(819) 797-4727
EMail: information@uqat.ca
Website: http://www.uqat.ca

Rectrice: Johanne Jean (2004-)
Tel: +1(819) 762-0971 poste 2248, Fax: +1(819) 797-4727
EMail: Johanne.Jean@uqat.ca

Secrétaire général: Martine Rioux
Tel: +1(819) 762-0971 poste 2265, Fax: +1(819) 797-4727
EMail: Martine.Rioux@uqat.ca

Areas
Applied Sciences (Biology; Computer Science; Electronic Engineering; Engineering; Environmental Studies; Forest Management; Forestry; Geological Engineering; Geology; Information Technology; Mechanical Engineering; Mining Engineering; Multimedia); **Creation and New Media** (Cinema and Television; Computer Science; Fine Arts; Multimedia; Visual Arts) **Education** (Art Education; Education; Educational Administration; Fine Arts; Foreign Languages Education; Painting and Drawing; Pedagogy; Preschool Education; Primary Education; Secondary Education; Vocational Education); **Health Sciences** (Anaesthesiology; Cardiology; Health Sciences; Nursing; Occupational Health; Rehabilitation and Therapy); **Human and Social Development** (Art Therapy; Development Studies; Educational Psychology; Indigenous Studies; Peace and Disarmament; Psychology; Social Sciences; Social Work); **Management Sciences** (Accountancy; Administration; Business Administration; Development Studies; Finance; Health Administration; Human Resources; Management)

Further Information: Also following campuses: Amos, La Sarre, Mont-Laurier, Barraute-Senneterre, Val-d'Or, Chibougamau, Lebel-sur-Quévillon, Matagami-Radisson, Ville-Marie; Station de recherche du lac-Duparquet.

History: Active from 1970 as Services universitaires dans le Nord-Ouest québécois, reorganized as Direction des études universitaires dans l'Ouest québécois 1972, as Centre d'études universitaires dans l'Ouest québécois 1976, as Centre d'études universitaires en Abitibi-Témiscamingue 1981 and acquired present status and title 1983, a Constituent University of the University of Quebec.

Governing Bodies: Conseil d'Administration

Academic Year: September to August (September-December; January-April; May-August)

Admission Requirements: Diploma of Collegial Studies (DEC) following successful completion of a 2-year pre-university course at a CEGEP (Collège d'Enseignement général et professionnel), or recognized equivalent

Fees: (Can. Dollars): undergraduate tuition, 341.78 per course (3 credits) for Quebec residents; 710.81 per course for other Canadian students; 1,849.58 per course for international students. Graduate tuition, 373,78-1,250.90 per course for Quebec residents; 742.81-3,096.05 per course for other Canadian students; 1,699.90-7,881.50 per course for international students.

Main Language(s) of Instruction: French

Degrees and Diplomas: *University Certificate/Diploma; Baccalauréat/Bachelor's Degree; Diplôme d'études supérieures spécialisées; Maîtrise/Master's Degree; Doctorat/Doctoral Degree (PhD).* Also undergraduate and graduate short programmes (microprogrammes).

Student Services: Academic counselling, Canteen, Employment services, Foreign student adviser, Handicapped facilities, Social counselling, Sports facilities

Libraries: 130,000 vols

Academic Staff *2010-2011*: Total: c. 420

Student Numbers *2010-2011*: Total: c. 3,500

Distance students, 800. **Evening students**, 2,100.
Last Updated: 11/03/11

UNIVERSITY OF QUEBEC AT CHICOUTIMI

Université du Québec à Chicoutimi (UQAC)
555, boulevard de l'Université, Chicoutimi, Québec G7H 2B1
Tel: +1(418) 545-5011 +1(800) 463-9880
Fax: +1(418) 545-5012
EMail: Info_Programmes@uqac.ca
Website: http://www.uqac.ca

Recteur: Michel Belley (2002-)
Tel: +1(418) 545-5011 Ext. 5509 EMail: Michel_Belley@uqac.ca

Registraire: Claudio Zoccastello
Tel: +1(418) 545-5011 Ext. 2139
EMail: Claudio_Zoccastello@uqac.ca

International Relations: Martin Gauthier, Adjoint du recteur/ Secrétaire Exécutif/Affaires internationales
Tel: +1(418) 545-5011 Ext. 5685 EMail: Martin_Gauthier@uqac.ca

Centres
Studies on Mineral Resources *(CERM)* (Mineralogy)

Departments
Applied Science (Civil Engineering; Computer Engineering; Earth Sciences; Electrical Engineering; Engineering; Geological Engineering; Geology; Mechanical Engineering; Meteorology); **Arts and Letters** (Art Education; Art History; Arts and Humanities; Cinema and Television; Design; Fine Arts; Foreign Languages Education; French; Linguistics; Literature; Modern Languages; Spanish; Theatre; Video; Writing); **Basic Sciences** (Biology; Chemistry; Environmental Studies; Natural Resources; Natural Sciences); **Computer Science and Mathematics** (Computer Science; Information Technology; Mathematics); **Economics and Administrative Sciences** (Accountancy; Administration; Air Transport; Business Administration; Economics; Health Sciences; Hotel and Restaurant; Human Resources; Management; Marketing; Transport Management); **Educational Sciences** (Education; Educational Administration; Educational Sciences; Foreign Languages Education; Humanities and Social Science Education; Mathematics Education; Preschool Education; Primary Education; Psychology; Secondary Education; Special Education; Vocational Education); **Health Sciences** (Community Health; Health Education; Health Sciences; Industrial and Organizational Psychology; Nursing; Physical Education; Physical Therapy; Psychiatry and Mental Health; Psychology); **Humanities** (Anthropology; Archaeology; Archiving; Arts and Humanities; Communication Studies; Development Studies; Ethics; Geography; Government; Health Education; History; Indigenous Studies; International Studies; Medicine; Nursing; Philosophy; Physical Education; Political Sciences; Regional Planning; Regional Studies; Religious Studies; Social Work; Sociology; Tourism; Toxicology)

Laboratories
Analysis and Separation of Plant Species *(LASEVE)* (Botany); **Anthropology and Symbolic Ritual** *(Lerari)* (Anthropology);

Anti-Icing Materials *(International - LIMA)* (Materials Engineering); **Applied Geography** *(LERG)* (Geography); **Biodiversity Data from Quebec** *(CDBQ)* (Environmental Studies); **Change Management** *(Multidisciplinary - LEMC 2)* (Management); **Clearinghouse for Analysis of Innovations and Business Support** *(CAISEN)* (Business Administration); **Identification and Control of Electrical Machines** *(LICOM)* (Automation and Control Engineering; Electrical Engineering); **Identities, Communities and Memberships in Reconstruction** *(ICARE)* (Government; Social Studies); **Land Materials** *(Labmate)* (Materials Engineering); **Multi-and Interdisciplinary Research on the Ethical and Social Development of Nanotechnology** *(NBE)* (Nanotechnology); **Outdoor Research** *(LERPA)* (Tourism); **Personal Adjustment, Social and Neuropsychological** *(LAPERSONE)* (Psychology; Social and Community Services); **Quantitative Metallogeny** *(LAMEQ)* (Metallurgical Engineering); **Software Development** *(LDL)* (Software Engineering)

Research Centres
Aluminum *(CURAL CURAL)* (Metallurgical Engineering); **Atmospheric Icing and Engineering of Electrical Networks** *(International Agency)* (Electrical Engineering; Meteorology)

Research Groups
Creation and Community (Development Studies); **Informatics** *(GRI)* (Computer Science); **Process Engineering and Systems** *(GRIPS)* (Engineering Management); **Regional Response** *(GRIR)* (Regional Studies); **Renewable Energy and the Impact of Northern Climate** *(GREEN)* (Natural Resources); **Renewable Resources in the Boreal** *(GR 3 MB)* (Natural Resources); **Wood Thermotransformation** *(GRTB)* (Wood Technology)

Research Laboratories
Ambient Intelligence for Recognition of Activities *(LIAR)* (Household Management); **Computer and Office** *(ENBI)* (Business Computing; Computer Science); **Ethics** *(LARIEP)* (Ethics); **Organizational Governance** *(LARIGO)* (Government)

Research Units
Commercial Boreal Forest *(Consortium)* (Forest Management); **Educational Research** *(Regional Consortium - RRAC)* (Educational Sciences); **Mineral Exploration** *(Consortium - CONSOREM)* (Mineralogy); **Native American** *(Consortium)* (Native American Studies)

History: Founded 1969. A Constituent University of the University of Quebec.

Governing Bodies: Board of Directors (UQAC); Assembly of Governors (University of Quebec)

Academic Year: September to August (September-December; January-April; May-August)

Admission Requirements: Diploma of Collegial Studies (DEC) following successful completion of a 2-year pre-university course at a CEGEP (Collège d'Enseignement général et professionnel), or recognized equivalent

Fees: (Can. Dollars): Undergraduate tuition, 68.93 per credit for Quebec residents; 188.92 per credit for non-Qebec residents Canadian students; 482.06-538.65 for international students. Graduate tuition, 1,033.95 per term for Canadian students; 6,487.80 per term for international students.

Main Language(s) of Instruction: French

International Co-operation: With universities in Hungary, France, Morocco, Tunisia, Lebanon, China, Brazil

Degrees and Diplomas: *University Certificate/Diploma; Baccalauréat/Bachelor's Degree; Diplôme d'études supérieures spécialisées; Maîtrise/Master's Degree; Doctorat/Doctoral Degree (PhD)*

Student Services: Academic counselling, Canteen, Cultural centre, Employment services, Handicapped facilities, Health services, Language programs, Social counselling, Sports facilities

Student Residential Facilities: Yes

Special Facilities: Arts Gallery

Libraries: c. 147,110 vols. Virtual Library

Publications: Protee, Semiotics Theories and Practices *(3 per annum)*

Academic Staff *2008-2009*: Total 603

Student Numbers *2008-2009*: Total 6,207
Last Updated: 04/03/11

UNIVERSITY OF QUEBEC AT MONTREAL
Université du Québec à Montréal (UQAM)
Case postale 8888, succursale Centre-ville, Montréal,
Québec H3C 3P8
Tel: +1(514) 987-3000
Fax: +1(514) 987-7906
EMail: admission@uqam.ca
Website: http://www.uqam.ca

Recteur: Claude Corbo (2008-)
Tel: +1(514) 987-6116, Fax: +1(514) 987-8424
EMail: corbo.claude@uqam.ca

Secrétaire général: Normand Petitclerc
Tel: +1(514) 987-3046, Fax: +1(514) 987-0258
EMail: parent.pierre@uqam.ca

International Relations: Sylvain St-Amant, Directeur, Service des Relations internationales
Tel: +1(514) 987-7969, Fax: +1(514) 987-6506
EMail: st-amand.sylvain@uqam.ca

Chairs
By-Products Management (Industrial Management; Insurance); **Cancer Prevention and Treatment** (Nutrition; Oncology); **Changes on a Global Scale** *(UNESCO)* (Earth Sciences; Environmental Studies; Geophysics); **Cinema and Cultural Production Strategies** *(René-Malo)* (Cinema and Television; Film); **Communications and International Development** *(UNESCO-BELL Chair)* (Distance Education; Information Technology; International and Comparative Education; Mass Communication); **Cooperative Business** *(Guy-Bernier)* (Business and Commerce; Management); **Financial and Organisational Information** (Accountancy; Business Administration; Finance; Information Management); **Financial Services Management** (Finance; Human Resources; Information Technology); **Governance and Development Aid** *(C.-A.-Poissant)* (Development Studies; Economics; Finance; Government; Social Sciences); **History of Quebec** *(Hector-Fabre)* (Canadian Studies; History; International Relations); **Logistics and Management** *(CRSNG)* (Management; Technology); **Philosophy of Justice and Democratic Societies** *(UNESCO)* (Human Rights; Law; Philosophy; Political Sciences); **Professional Competence Management** (Human Resources; Labour and Industrial Relations; Management); **Public Relations** (Public Relations); **Real Estate** *(UQAM-SITQ Chair)* (Business and Commerce; Real Estate); **Social Responsibility and Sustainable Development** (Development Studies; Ethics; Social Problems); **Socio-Economic Studies** *(CESE)* (Economic and Finance Policy; Social Problems); **Strategic and Diplomatic Studies** *(Raoul-Dandurand)* (Comparative Politics; International Economics; International Relations); **Sustainable Forestry Management** *(CRSNG/UQAT/UQAM)* (Ecology; Environmental Management; Forest Economics; Forest Management); **Tourism** *(Transat)* (Tourism); **Training in Agri-food Market Globalization** *(Philippe Pariseault)* (Agricultural Economics; Agronomy); **Transnational Management** *(Bombardier)* (Industrial Management; International Business); **Urban Ecosystems Studies** (Ecology; Urban Studies)

Faculties
Arts (Architectural and Environmental Design; Architecture; Archiving; Art History; Communication Arts; Dance; Design; Education; Environmental Studies; Fine Arts; French; Geography; Graphic Design; Heritage Preservation; History; Information Management; Information Sciences; Jazz and Popular Music; Literature; Media Studies; Museum Studies; Music; Music Education; Performing Arts; Political Sciences; Regional Planning; Surveying and Mapping; Theatre; Tourism; Urban Studies; Visual Arts); **Communication** (Arabic; Asian Religious Studies; Asian Studies; Chinese; Cinema and Television; Communication Studies; Cultural Studies; French; German; Italian; Japanese; Journalism; Marketing; Mass Communication; Media Studies; Modern Languages; Portuguese; Public Relations; Radio and Television Broadcasting; Russian; Spanish); **Educational Sciences** (Adult Education; Education; Educational Sciences; Foreign Languages Education; French; Grammar; Mathematics Education; Pedagogy; Special Education); **Political Science and Law** (Administration; Communication Studies; International Law; International Relations; International Studies; Labour Law; Law; Political Sciences; Private Law; Public Administration; Social Sciences; Women's Studies); **Sciences** (Actuarial Science; Biochemistry; Biological and Life Sciences; Biology; Chemistry; Computer Networks;

Computer Science; Earth Sciences; Ecology; Environmental Studies; Ergotherapy; Geology; Health Education; Industrial Design; Mathematics; Mathematics Education; Meteorology; Microelectronics; Natural Resources; Physical Education; Physical Therapy; Physiology; Preschool Education; Software Engineering; Statistics; Telecommunications Engineering); **Social Sciences** (Ancient Civilizations; Cognitive Sciences; Gender Studies; Geography; Geography (Human); Gerontology; Grammar; History; Linguistics; Medieval Studies; Philosophy; Psychology; Religious Studies; Social Sciences; Social Work; Sociology; Surveying and Mapping; Women's Studies)

Higher Schools
Fashion (Fashion Design; Industrial Management)

Institutes
Health and Society (Health Sciences; Occupational Health)

Research Centres
Biology, Health, Society and Environment *(CINBIOSE)*; **BIOMED** (Biochemistry; Biomedical Engineering; Physiology); **Cognition Neuroscience** *(CNC)*; **Computer Mathematics and Combinatory Laboratory** *(LACIM)* (Applied Mathematics; Mathematics and Computer Science); **CRILICQ** (Canadian Studies; Cultural Studies; Literature); **Differential Geometry and Topology** *(CIRGET)*; **Environment Toxicology** *(TOXEN)* (Environmental Studies; Public Health; Toxicology); **FIGURA**; **Forestry Ecology Research** *(GREFi)* (Ecology; Forest Management; Forest Products); **Geochemistry and Geodynamics** *(GEOTOP-UQAM-McGill)* (Environmental Studies; Geochemistry; Geophysics; Marine Science and Oceanography; Meteorology); **Globalization and International Studies** *(CEIM)*; **Letters, Arts and Traditions Studies** *(CELAT)*; **Limnology and Marine Environment Research** *(GRIL)* (Environmental Management; Limnology; Marine Biology; Marine Science and Oceanography); **Mediatic Arts** *(CIAM)* (Fine Arts; Technology); **Regional Climate Modelling** *(ESCER)* (Meteorology); **Risk, Economic Policies and Employment** (Econometrics; Economic and Finance Policy); **Science and Technology** *(CIRST)* (History; Information Management; Social Studies; Technology); **Social Innovations** *(CRISES)* (Consumer Studies; Economic and Finance Policy; Labour and Industrial Relations; Public Administration; Social and Community Services)

Schools
Management *(ESG UQAM)* (Accountancy; Administration; Business Administration; Business Computing; Communication Studies; Cooking and Catering; E-Business/Commerce; Economics; Ethics; Fashion Design; Finance; Hotel and Restaurant; Hotel Management; Human Resources; Industrial Management; Information Sciences; Information Technology; Insurance; International Business; Leadership; Leisure Studies; Management; Marketing; Multimedia; Operations Research; Public Administration; Real Estate; Road Transport; Safety Engineering; Sales Techniques; Small Business; Statistics; Taxation; Tourism; Town Planning; Transport and Communications; Transport Management; Urban Studies)

History: Founded 1969, incorporating 5 existing institutions. The University gained 'associate university' status in the University of Quebec network 1989, giving it greater autonomy.

Governing Bodies: Board of Directors; Executive Committee

Academic Year: September to April (September-December; January-April)

Admission Requirements: Diploma of Collegial Studies (DEC) following successful completion of a 2-year pre-university course at a CEGEP (Collège d'Enseignement général et professionnel), or recognized equivalent (13 years of study); if only 12, one year of transition courses (30 credits) before admission to bachelor's programme; or 22 years of age and appropriate experience or basic university studies

Fees: (Canadian Dollars): Foreign students, 11,900 per annum

Main Language(s) of Instruction: French

International Co-operation: With universities in Argentina, Belgium, Brazil, Chile, China, Columbia, Côte d'Ivoire, Cuba, Czech Republic, Ecuador, Egypt, Finland, France, Germany, Guinea, Haïti, Honduras, Italy, Japan, Morocco, Mexico, Netherlands, Nigeria, Peru, Portugal, Romania, Spain, Sweden, Switzerland, Tunisia,

Turkey, Uruguay, United Kingdom, USA, Venzuela, Vietnam. Also participates in UNESCO programmes.

Accrediting Agencies: Association of Universities and Colleges of Canada (AUCC); European Foundation for Management Development (EQUIS); Conférence des Recteurs et des Principaux des Universités du Québec (CREPUQ)

Degrees and Diplomas: *University Certificate/Diploma*; *Baccalauréat/Bachelor's Degree*; *Diplôme d'études supérieures spécialisées (DESS)*; *Maîtrise/Master's Degree*; *Doctorat/Doctoral Degree (Ph.D)*. Also short undergraduate and graduate programmes.

Student Services: Academic counselling, Canteen, Cultural centre, Employment services, Foreign student adviser, Foreign Studies Centre, Handicapped facilities, Language programs, Social counselling, Sports facilities

Student Residential Facilities: Yes

Special Facilities: UQAM Gallery; UQAM Design Centre; the Agora de la danse; Alfred-Laliberté Studio-Theatre; The Coeur des Sciences (Enhancing and Promoting Science Centre); Pierre-Péladeau Centre (Performing Centre); Pierre-Mercure and Marie-Gérin-Lajoie performance halls.

Libraries: Bibliothèque Centrale de l'UQAM, c. 1,712,300 vols

Academic Staff *2009-2010*	TOTAL
FULL-TIME	1,006

Student Numbers *2009-2010*	
All (Foreign Included)	40,519
FOREIGN ONLY	2,465

Part-time students, 20,000.
Note: Part-time and TÉLUQ students are not included in total
Last Updated: 07/03/11

TÉLÉ-UNIVERSITÉ (TÉLUQ)

455, rue du Parvis, Québec, Québec G1K 9H6
Tel: +1(418) 657-2262
Fax: +1(418) 657-2094
EMail: info@teluq.uqam.ca
Website: http://www.teluq.uquebec.ca/

Directeur général: Raymond Duchesne (2008-)
EMail: DUCHESNE.Raymond@teluq.uqam.ca

Directeur des affaires administratives, par intérim: Paul Préseault EMail: PRESEAULT.Paul@teluq.uqam.ca

Units
Education (Adult Education; Distance Education; Education; Educational Technology; Information Technology); **Humanities, Arts and Communications** (Canadian Studies; Communication Studies; Developmental Psychology; English; Foreign Languages Education; French; Literature; Media Studies; Psychiatry and Mental Health; Psychology; Social Psychology; Social Sciences; Spanish; Translation and Interpretation); **Science and Technology** (Computer Science; Environmental Studies; Information Technology; Software Engineering; Wildlife); **Work, Economy and Management** (Accountancy; Administration; Business Administration; Development Studies; E-Business/Commerce; Finance; Health Administration; Human Resources; Insurance; Labour and Industrial Relations; Management; Occupational Health; Tourism)

Further Information: Also Montréal campus.

History: Founded 1972.

Fees: (Canadian Dollar): 290-390 per course.

Degrees and Diplomas: *University Certificate/Diploma*; *Baccalauréat/Bachelor's Degree*; *Diplôme d'études supérieures spécialisées*; *Maîtrise/Master's Degree*; *Doctorat/Doctoral Degree*

Academic Staff *2008-2009*: Total 520
Student Numbers *2008-2009*: Total 18,000

UNIVERSITY OF QUEBEC AT RIMOUSKI
Université du Québec à Rimouski (UQAR)
C. P. 3300, succ. A, 300, allée des Ursulines, Rimouski, Québec G5L 3A1
Tel: +1(418) 723-1986
Fax: +1(418) 724-1525
EMail: uqar@uqar.ca
Website: http://www.uqar.qc.ca

Recteur: Michel Ringuet (2003-)
Tel: +1(418) 724-1410 EMail: recteur@uqar.ca

Secrétaire général: Alain Caron
Tel: +1(418) 724-1416 EMail: secgen@uqar.ca

Registraire, par intérim: Denis Lebel
Tel: +1(418) 723-1986 poste 1432, Fax: +1(418) 724-1708
EMail: denis_lebel@uqar.ca

Departments
Arts and Humanities (Arts and Humanities; Cultural Studies; English; Ethics; French; History; Literature; Writing); **Biology, Chemistry and Geography** (Biology; Chemistry; Ecology; Environmental Studies; Geography; Marine Science and Oceanography; Physiology; Wildlife); **Mathematics, Computer Science and Engineering** (Computer Science; E-Business/Commerce; Electrical Engineering; Electronic Engineering; Energy Engineering; Engineering; Ethics; Management; Marine Science and Oceanography; Mathematics; Mechanical Engineering; Telecommunications Engineering); **Nursing** (Community Health; Health Sciences; Nursing; Psychiatry and Mental Health); **Psychology and Social Work** (Communication Studies; Psychology; Social Sciences; Social Work); **Societies, Territories and Development** (Development Studies; Public Administration; Regional Studies; Rural Studies; Social Problems; Social Studies)

Institutes
Marine Science *(Rimouski - ISMER)* (Biology; Computer Science; Ecology; Electrical Engineering; Environmental Studies; Geography; Marine Science and Oceanography; Mechanical Engineering; Physiology; Wildlife)

Research Centres
Forestry *(Multiregional)* (Forestry); **Marine and Island Environments** *(CERMIM - Affiliated)* (Environmental Studies); **Northern Studies** *(NEC)* (Environmental Studies); **Québec Aquaculture Network** *(RAQ)* (Aquaculture); **Quebec-Ocean** (Marine Science and Oceanography); **Spatial Development** *(CRTD)* (Development Studies)

Research Groups
Ethics *(ETHOS)* (Ethics); **Learning and Socialization** *(APPSO)* (Science Education); **Northern Environments** *(BOREAS)* (Environmental Studies); **Regional Development of Eastern Quebec** *(GRIDEQ - Interdisciplinary)* (Development Studies)

Research Laboratories
Biotechnology and Environmental Chemistry *(CRAB)* (Biotechnology; Chemistry; Environmental Studies); **Health in the Region** *(LASER)* (Health Sciences); **Production** *(PRL)* (Production Engineering); **Wind** *(LREE)* (Energy Engineering; Power Engineering)

Units
Educational Sciences *(Lévis Campus)* (Adult Education; Education; Educational Administration; Educational Psychology; Educational Sciences; Foreign Languages Education; Pedagogy; Preschool Education; Secondary Education); **Educational Sciences** *(Rimouski Campus)* (Education; Educational Administration; Educational Psychology; Educational Sciences; Preschool Education; Primary Education; Secondary Education; Vocational Education); **Management Sciences** *(Rimouski Campus)* (Accountancy; Administration; Biology; Computer Science; E-Business/Commerce; Electrical Engineering; Electronic Engineering; Finance; Geography; Human Resources; Management; Marine Transport; Marketing; Mechanical Engineering; Natural Resources; Taxation); **Management Sciences** *(Lévis Campus)* (Accountancy; Administration; Business Administration; Finance; Human Resources; Management; Marine Transport; Marketing; Taxation)

Further Information: Also campus in Lévis. Research Centres, Groups, Laboratories and Chairs

History: Founded as Centre d'Etudes universitaires de Rimouski, 1969. Acquired present status and title 1973. A Constituent University of the University of Quebec. Campus in Lévis.

Governing Bodies: Board of Governors

Academic Year: September to June (September-December; January-April; May-June)

Admission Requirements: Diploma of Collegial Studies (DEC) following successful completion of a 2-year pre-university course at a CEGEP (Collège d'Enseignement général et professionnel), or recognized equivalent

Fees: (Can. Dollars): Quebec students, 68.93 per credit; other Canadian students, 188.92 per credit; foreign students, 432.52-565.65 per credit.

Main Language(s) of Instruction: French

International Co-operation: With universities in Germany; Argentina; Belgium; Brazil; Egypt; France; Gabon; Morocco; Mauritania; Peru; Romania; Tunisia. Also participates in the CREPUQ and CIME programmes

Accrediting Agencies: Association of Universities and Colleges of Canada (AUCC); ADARUQ

Degrees and Diplomas: *University Certificate/Diploma*; *Baccalauréat/Bachelor's Degree*; *Diplôme d'études supérieures spécialisées*; *Maîtrise/Master's Degree*; *Doctorat/Doctoral Degree (PhD)*

Student Services: Academic counselling, Canteen, Employment services, Foreign student adviser, Handicapped facilities, Social counselling, Sports facilities

Student Residential Facilities: 270 rooms

Special Facilities: Art Gallery

Libraries: c. 400,000 vols and 4,152 periodicals, 250 bibliographical data bases

Academic Staff 2007-2008	TOTAL
FULL-TIME	c. 480

Student Numbers 2009-2010	
All (Foreign Included)	c. 6,000
FOREIGN ONLY	350

Last Updated: 10/03/11

UNIVERSITY OF QUEBEC AT TROIS-RIVIÈRES
Université du Québec à Trois-Rivières (UQTR)
3351, boul. des Forges, C.P. 500, Trois-Rivières, Québec G9A 5H7
Tel: +1(819) 376-5011
Fax: +1(819) 376-5210
EMail: crmultiservice@uqtr.ca
Website: http://www.uqtr.ca

Recteur: Ghislain Bourque
Tel: +1(819) 376-5000, Fax: +1(819) 376-5111
EMail: Ghislain.Bourque@uqtr.ca

Secrétaire général: André Gabias
Tel: +1(819) 376-5011, Ext. 2218, Fax: +1(819) 376-5029
EMail: Andre.Gabias@uqtr.ca

International Relations: Jacques E. Brisoux
Tel: +1(819) 376-5001, Fax: +1(819) 376-5167 EMail: dci@uqtr.ca

Departments
Accounting Studies (Accountancy); **Arts** (Art Education; Art History; Fine Arts; Glass Art; Theatre); **Chemical Engineering** (Chemical Engineering); **Chemistry-Biology** (Biochemistry; Biology; Biomedicine; Biophysics; Biotechnology; Cell Biology; Chemistry; Ecology; Environmental Studies; Midwifery); **Chiropractic** (Chiropractic); **Educational Sciences** (Education; Educational Administration; Educational Sciences; Mathematics Education; Native Language Education; Pedagogy; Primary Education; Science Education; Secondary Education; Technology Education); **Electrical and Computer Engineering** (Computer Engineering; Electrical Engineering; Energy Engineering); **Humanities** (Canadian Studies; Environmental Studies; Geography; History; Meteorology; Natural Resources; Surveying and Mapping); **Humanities and Social Communication** (Arts and Humanities; Communication Studies; French Studies; Literature; Writing); **Industrial Engineering** (Engineering; Industrial Engineering; Occupational Health); **Leisure Studies, Culture and Tourism** (Cultural Studies; Leisure Studies; Tourism); **Management Science** (Administration; Business

Administration; Finance; Human Resources; Labour and Industrial Relations; Management; Marketing; Operations Research; Protective Services; Small Business); **Mathematics and Computer Science** (Applied Mathematics; Computer Science; Mathematics; Mathematics and Computer Science; Mathematics Education); **Mechanical Engineering** (Mechanical Engineering); **Modern Languages and Translation** (English; Modern Languages; Spanish; Translation and Interpretation); **Nursing** (Nursing; Psychiatry and Mental Health; Public Administration); **Occupational Therapy** (Health Sciences; Occupational Therapy); **Philosophy** (Aesthetics; Philosophy); **Physical Activity Sciences** (Health Sciences; Physical Education; Physical Therapy; Podiatry); **Physics** (Computer Science; Materials Engineering; Physics); **Psychoeducation** (Educational Psychology; Social Psychology); **Psychology** (Gerontology; Psychology)

Laboratories
"Family-School-Community and Transversal Skills"; **Political and Cultural Analyses**; **Professional Integration in Teaching**; **Teaching of Media Studies** (Media Studies); **Vertebral Illnesses**

Research Centres
Pulp and Paper (Paper Technology); **Quebec Studies** *(Interdisciplinary)* (Canadian Studies; Regional Studies)

Research Groups
Aquatics (Aquaculture); **Cellular and Molecular Biopathologies** (Cell Biology; Molecular Biology; Pathology); **Child and Family Development** (Child Care and Development; Family Studies); **Communication and Speech** (Communication Studies; Speech Studies); **Energy and Biomolecular Information** (Biomedical Engineering; Energy Engineering); **Industrial Electronics** (Electronic Engineering)

Research Institutes
Hydrogen; **Small and Medium Business** (Business Administration; Small Business)

Research Laboratories
Business Performances (Business Administration); **French Youth Literatures of America** (Literature); **Gerontology** (Gerontology); **Mental Deficiencies** *(LARIDI)* (Psychiatry and Mental Health); **Mental Health** (Psychiatry and Mental Health); **Neurosciences** (Neurosciences); **Transdisciplinary and Interdisciplinary Studies and Research in Education** (Educational Research); **Visual Arts** (Visual Arts)

Schools
Engineering (Chemical Engineering; Computer Engineering; Electrical Engineering; Engineering; Industrial Engineering; Mechanical Engineering); **French** *(International)* (French)

History: Founded 1969. A Constituent University of the University of Quebec.

Governing Bodies: Ministère de l'Education, Gouvernement du Québec

Academic Year: September to August (September-December; January-April; May-August)

Admission Requirements: Diploma of Collegial Studies (DEC) following successful completion of a 2-year pre-university course at a CEGEP (Collège d'Enseignement général et professionnel), or recognized equivalent

Fees: (Can. Dollars): tuition for first and second cycle programmes, 216.78 per course (3 credits) for Quebec residents, 369.03 per course for other Canadian students and 1,239.39 per course for international students. Tuition for third cycle programmes, 216.78 per course for all Canadian students and 1,090.77 per course for international students.

Main Language(s) of Instruction: French

International Co-operation: Wth universities in France, Poland and Spain. Agreements for scientific cooperation with universities mainly in Europe, Western Europe and Latin America

Degrees and Diplomas: *University Certificate/Diploma*; *Baccalauréat/Bachelor's Degree*; *Diplôme d'études supérieures spécialisées*; *Maîtrise/Master's Degree*; *Doctorat/Doctoral Degree (PhD)*

Student Services: Academic counselling, Canteen, Employment services, Foreign student adviser, Handicapped facilities, Health services, Language programs, Nursery care, Social counselling, Sports facilities

Student Residential Facilities: Residence for 800 students.

Libraries: 350,000 vols

Academic Staff 2009-2010	TOTAL
FULL-TIME	1,200

Student Numbers 2009-2010	
All (Foreign Included)	12,500
FOREIGN ONLY	400

Last Updated: 11/03/11

UNIVERSITY OF QUEBEC IN OUTAOUAIS

Université du Québec en Outaouais (UQO)

283, boulevard Alexandre-Taché, C.P. 1250, succursale Hull,
Gatineau, Québec J8X 3X7
Tel: +1(819) 595-3900 +1(800) 567-1283
Fax: +1(819) 595-3924
EMail: registraire@uqo.ca
Website: http://www.uqo.ca

Recteur: Jean Vaillancourt (1995-)
Tel: +1(819) 595-3910, Fax: +1(819) 595-3924
EMail: rectorat@uqo.ca

Secrétaire général: Luc Maurice
Tel: +1(819) 595-3965 EMail: luc.maurice@uqo.ca

Departments
Accounting Studies (Accountancy; Business Administration; Finance; Management); **Administrative Sciences** (Administration; Commercial Law; Finance; Management; Marketing; Public Relations); **Computer and Engineering** (Computer Engineering; Computer Science; Information Management; Information Sciences; Information Technology); **Educational Sciences** (Art Education; Education; Educational Administration; Educational Sciences; Educational Technology; Preschool Education; Primary Education; Secondary Education); **Industrial Relations** (Human Resources; Industrial and Organizational Psychology; Labour and Industrial Relations; Occupational Health); **Language Studies** (Foreign Languages Education; Modern Languages; Translation and Interpretation); **Nursing** (Nursing); **Psychoeducation and Psychology** (Educational and Student Counselling; Psychology); **Social Sciences** (Communication Studies; Development Studies; Geography; History; Media Studies; Museum Studies; Occupational Health; Political Sciences; Social Sciences; Sociology); **Social Work** (Development Studies; Social Work)

Schools
Image Arts (Multidisciplinary) (Graphic Design; Museum Studies; Painting and Drawing; Visual Arts)

Further Information: Also Saint-Jérôme Campus.

History: Founded 1970 as Services universitaires dans le nord-ouest québécois, reorganized several times and acquired present status and title 2002. A Constituent University of the University of Quebec.

Governing Bodies: Commission des Etudes; Board of Directors

Academic Year: September to August (September-December; January-April; May-August)

Admission Requirements: Undergraduate programmes, Diploma of Collegial Studies (DEC) following successful completion of a 2-year pre-university course at a CEGEP (Collège d'enseignement général et professionnel), or recognized equivalent

Fees: (Can. Dollars): First cycle programmes tuition, 1,329.65 per term for Québec residents; 3,129.50 per term for other Canadian students; c. 7,560 per term for international students. Second cycle programmes tuition, 852.29 per term for Québec residents; 1,932.20 per term for other Canadian students; c. 4,583 per term for international students. Third cycle programmes tuition, 1,265.87 per term for Québec residents; 3,065.72 per term for other Canadian students; c. 4,580 per term for international students.

Main Language(s) of Instruction: French. Some graduate programmes in English

International Co-operation: With universities in Bulgaria; Chile; Spain; France; Mexico; Dominican Republic; Senegal

Degrees and Diplomas: University Certificate/Diploma; Baccalauréat/Bachelor's Degree; Diplôme d'études supérieures spécialisées; Maîtrise/Master's Degree; Doctorat/Doctoral Degree (PhD). Also undergraduate and graduate short programmes.

Student Services: Academic counselling, Canteen, Cultural centre, Employment services, Handicapped facilities, Nursery care, Social counselling, Sports facilities

Student Residential Facilities: Yes

Special Facilities: Art Gallery

Libraries: c. 221,000 vols (including monographs and periodicals); c. 22,100 microforms

Publications: Savoir Outaouais (biannually)

Press or Publishing House: Presses de l'Université du Québec

Academic Staff 2010-2011	TOTAL
FULL-TIME	193
PART-TIME	370
STAFF WITH DOCTORATE	
FULL-TIME	140
PART-TIME	c. 50

Student Numbers 2010-2011	
All (Foreign Included)	c. 5,700
FOREIGN ONLY	210

Part-time students, 2,600.
Last Updated: 17/03/11

UNIVERSITY OF SHERBROOKE

Université de Sherbrooke (UDES)

Cité Universitaire, Sherbrooke, Québec J1K 2R1
Tel: +1(819) 821-7686 +1(800) 267-8337
Fax: +1(819) 821-7966
EMail: information@usherbrooke.ca
Website: http://www.usherb.ca

Rectrice: Luce Samoisette (2009-)
Tel: +1(819) 821-8280, Fax: +1(819) 821-7966
EMail: rectrice@USherbrooke.ca

Directrice du Service des communications: Lucie Frenière
Tel: +1(819) 821-7388, Fax: +1(819) 821-7900
EMail: Lucie.Freniere@USherbrooke.ca

Vice-rectrice à l'administration: Joanne Roch
Tel: +1(819) 821-8281, Fax: +1(819) 821-8295
EMail: vra@USherbrooke.ca

International Relations: Jocelyne Faucher, Secrétaire générale et vice-rectrice aux relations internationales
Tel: +1(819) 821-8285, Fax: +1(819) 821-8295
EMail: Jocelyne.Faucher@USherbrooke.ca

Centres
Business (Business Administration); **Continuing Education** (Administration; Arts and Humanities; Business Administration; Chinese; Communication Studies; Computer Science; Education; Educational Administration; Engineering; Engineering Management; Environmental Studies; Ethics; Health Sciences; Information Technology; Law; Management; Medicine; Multimedia; Natural Sciences; Political Sciences; Rehabilitation and Therapy; Sports; Theology); **Environmental Training** (Environmental Management; Environmental Studies); **Monitoring of the Environment and Sustainable Development** (Observatory) (Development Studies; Environmental Management; Environmental Studies); **Research and Training in Disability Prevention** (Rehabilitation and Therapy); **Training in Gerontology** (Gerontology)

Faculties
Administration (Accountancy; Administration; Business Administration; Economics; Finance; Human Resources; Information Sciences; Management; Management Systems; Marketing); **Arts and Humanities** (Arts and Humanities; Communication Studies; Comparative Literature; Economics; English; Ethics; French; Geography; Gerontology; History; Music; Philosophical Schools; Political Sciences; Psychology; Social and Community Services; Social Sciences; Social Work; Surveying and Mapping); **Education** (Adult Education; Educational Administration; Educational and Student Counselling; Educational Psychology; Pedagogy; Preschool Education; Primary Education; Secondary Education; Special Education); **Engineering** (Aeronautical and Aerospace Engineering; Biotechnology; Chemical Engineering; Civil Engineering; Computer

Engineering; Electrical Engineering; Electronic Engineering; Mechanical Engineering); **Law** (Civil Law; International Law; Law; Notary Studies); **Medicine and Health Sciences** (Anaesthesiology; Anatomy; Biochemistry; Cardiology; Cell Biology; Community Health; Endocrinology; Environmental Studies; Gastroenterology; Gynaecology and Obstetrics; Haematology; Immunology; Medicine; Microbiology; Nephrology; Neurology; Nursing; Oncology; Ophthalmology; Otorhinolaryngology; Paediatrics; Pathology; Pharmacology; Physiology; Pneumology; Psychiatry and Mental Health; Public Health; Radiology; Rehabilitation and Therapy; Rheumatology; Surgery; Toxicology); **Physical Education and Sports** (Physical Education; Physical Therapy; Sports); **Religious Studies** (Ethics; Indigenous Studies; Pastoral Studies; Philosophy; Religious Studies; Theology); **Sciences** (Biochemistry; Biology; Chemistry; Computer Science; Mathematics; Natural Sciences; Physics)

Institutes
Entrepreneurship (Management); **Pharmacology** *(Sherbrooke)* (Pharmacology); **Research on Educational Practice** (Educational Sciences)

Programmes
Performa (Education; Educational and Student Counselling; Higher Education; Teacher Training; Vocational Education)

History: Founded 1954. Recognized as a Catholic University through a decree 1957.

Academic Year: September to August (September-December; January-April; May-August)

Admission Requirements: Diploma of Collegial Studies (DEC) following successful completion of a 2-year pre-university course at a CEGEP (Collège d'Enseignement général et professionnel), or recognized equivalent

Fees: (Can. Dollars): Tuition fee, 1,033.95 per term for Quebec students; 2,833.80 per term for non-Quebec resident Canadian students; 6,487.80-8,079.75 per term for international students.

Main Language(s) of Instruction: French

Degrees and Diplomas: *University Certificate/Diploma; Baccalauréat/Bachelor's Degree; Diplôme d'études supérieures spécialisées; Maîtrise/Master's Degree; Doctorat/Doctoral Degree (PhD).* Also Diploma in Environmental Management; Combined Bachelor's degree programmes (Law and Business/biological and Life Sciences); Post-doctoral floows in Law; MBA.

Student Services: Academic counselling, Canteen, Cultural centre, Employment services, Foreign student adviser, Foreign Studies Centre, Handicapped facilities, Health services, Nursery care, Social counselling, Sports facilities

Student Residential Facilities: For c. 1,230 students

Special Facilities: Art Gallery
Libraries: Total, c. 1,1 m. vols

Academic Staff *2010-2011:* Total: c. 6,700
Student Numbers *2010-2011:* Total: c. 37,000
Last Updated: 04/03/11

PRIVATE INSTITUTIONS

INSTITUTE OF THEOLOGICAL TRAINING OF MONTREAL

Institut de Formation Théologique de Montréal (IFTM)
2065, rue Sherbrooke Ouest, Montréal, Québec H3H 1G6
Tel: +1(514) 935-1169
Fax: +1(514) 935-5497
EMail: info@iftm.ca
Website: http://www.iftm.ca/

Recteur: Charles Langlois
Tel: +1(514) 935-1169 Poste 202, Fax: +1(514) 935-5497

Directeur des Services Administratifs et des Ressources Humaines: Maurice Lamoureux
Tel: +1(514) 935-1169 Poste 203, Fax: +1(514) 935-5497
EMail: m.lamoureux@iftm.ca

Departments
Pastoral Studies (Pastoral Studies); **Philosophy** (Philosophy); **Theology** (Bible; Theology)

History: Founded 1840 as Grand Seminary of Montreal. Became headquarters of the Faculty of Theology 1878. Attached to the Université Laval of Quebec it was then recognised as a Faculty of the University of Montreal as of 1920. Affiliated to the Faculty of Theology of the Pontifical University of Latran as of 1979 an to the Faculty of Philosophy of the Pontifical University of Latran as of 1986. The Centre for Theological Formation was transformed into an Institute was 1988 and acquired present title 1995. Granted the right to offer civil degrees 1998. Acquired autonomy 2009.

Fees: (Canadian Dollar): Undergraduate programmes, 75 per credit. Graduate programmes, 75 per credit; Memory work writing, 300 per semester; Memory work evaluation, 300 per semester.

Degrees and Diplomas: *University Certificate/Diploma; Baccalauréat/Bachelor's Degree; Diplôme d'études supérieures spécialisées; Maîtrise/Master's Degree*
Last Updated: 03/03/11

Canada - Saskatchewan

STRUCTURE OF HIGHER EDUCATION SYSTEM

Description:

Higher education in Canada is the constitutional responsibility of the provinces. In Saskatchewan, the Ministry of Advanced Education, Employment and Immigration has responsibility for higher education. The higher (post-secondary) system includes two universities with four federated and seven affiliated colleges; Saskatchewan Institute of Applied Science and Technology (SIAST), the Saskatchewan Indian Institute of Technologies (SIIT), Dumont Technical Institute (DTI), seven regional colleges and one inter provincial college under Alberta legislation, Lakeland College; the Saskatchewan Apprenticeship and Trade Certification Commission (SATCC); and many private vocational schools. The universities grant undergraduate and graduate degrees in the professions, Arts, Sciences, and Humanities. SIAST and SIIT deliver a wide range of Certificate and Diploma skill training programmes intended to lead directly to employment. SATCC contracts SIAST and other training institutions to deliver apprenticeship and technical training. Regional Colleges, located throughout the province in seven distinct geographic regions, broker university and SIAST credit courses, and other courses, through contracts with the credit granting institutions. The universities are autonomous institutions, governed by boards and responsible for their own administrative, academic, and financial affairs in accordance with the respective university Acts. SIAST, SATCC, and the regional colleges operate at arm's length from government under their own boards of directors and trustees, respectively. SIIT operates under the legislated authority of the Federation of Saskatchewan Indian Nations (FSIN). All parts of the higher education system are governed by acts of the provincial legislature. The Gabriel Dumont Institute of Native Studies and Applied Research Inc. (GDI) is the official education, research and development arm of the Métis Nation - Saskatchewan. GDI is affiliated with the University of Saskatchewan and the University of Regina and federated with SIAST. Its programs include the Saskatchewan Urban Native Teacher Education Program (SUNTEP), a four year, fully accredited Bachelor of Education program. The Dumont Technical Institute arm of GDI is responsible for Adult Basic Education, skills training, vocational and cultural programs. The Gabriel Dumont College arm of GDI offers the first two years of a Bachelor of Arts and Science degree. The Northern Teacher Education Program and Northern Professional Access College (NORTEP/PAC) is an off-campus institution that is accredited by the University of Saskatchewan and the University of Regina (and First Nations University of Canada). NORTEP/PAC currently offers four degree programs in Northern Saskatchewan; the four-year Bachelor of Education (B.Ed.) program; Education students may attend a fifth year and obtain a Bachelor of Arts (B.A.) as well; a Master's Program (M.ED) in Curriculum and Instruction; and NORPAC offers three years of university arts and sciences courses designed to prepare Northerners for entry into the two universities or other post-secondary programs.

Stages of studies:

University level first stage: Bachelor's degree
Most undergraduate study leads to a Bachelor's degree (minimum 3 or 4 years) or an "Honours" degree (minimum 4 years) with a major subject concentration. Degrees are normally labelled in broad descriptive groups such as Bachelor of Arts (B.A.) and Bachelor of Science (B.Sc.). The first stage also includes undergraduate Diplomas (1-3 years of study) and short (up to 1 year) special Certificate programs, frequently in close cooperation with professional bodies. Undergraduate professional programs that require no university level pre-requisites, such as Bachelor of Commerce (B.Com.), and Bachelor of Education (B.Ed.), require 4 years of study. Some first and second year university courses are offered by the universities off campus through provincially supported regional colleges, GDI, NORTEP/PAC, and SIAST.

University level second stage: Master's degree
The Master's degree normally requires two years of study after a Bachelor's degree or equivalent. A thesis and course-work are usually required. Examples are: Master of Arts (M.A.), Master of Science (M.Sc.), Master of Education (M.Ed.), and Master of Business Administration (M.B.A.). There are also graduate-level Diplomas (considered intermediate between the Bachelor's or first professional degree and the Master's degree). Second stage programs also includes first professional degree programs requiring one to two years of prerequisite

university studies, followed by three to four years, such as Bachelor of Law (LL.B.), Doctor of Medicine (M.D.) and Doctor of Veterinary Medicine (D.V.M.).

University level third stage: *Doctorate*
The Doctorate is the highest academic qualification awarded by universities and comprises the third stage of university level studies. This degree normally requires at least 3 years of study after the Master's degree; the submission and defence of a major thesis (dissertation) are the principal requirements, and supplemental course work. Doctor of Philosophy" (Ph.D.) is the generic title used to signify the Doctorate degrees in most disciplines. (The Doctorate should not be confused with titles attributed to certain first professional degrees in the health sciences, such as Medicine, Veterinary Medicine and Dentistry.)

Distance higher education:
Saskatchewan's credit-granting institutions offer a variety of online and other distance-delivery courses and programs. Regional colleges use various classroom-based and distance learning modalities to provide access and support to learners who reside off-campus.

ADMISSION TO HIGHER EDUCATION

Admission to university-level studies:

Name of secondary school credential required: High School Completion Certificate

Alternatives to credentials: Universities set their own admission policies and requirements. Some provision is made for special admission procedures such as mature students (e.g. 22 years of age or older) or probationary entrance for students who do not meet established academic entrance criteria. Some university faculties or colleges select only the most qualified applicants. Admission to some professional programs requires previous university education. Both universities and SIAST adhere to Recognition of Prior Learning practices and plan to expand upon this initiative (e.g. 2 + 2 program offerings internationally).

Numerus clausus/restrictions: There is a numerus clausus (quota system) established at the institutional level for specific programs.

Other admission requirements: Admission minimum is 65% average at the University of Regina and 70% average at the University of Saskatchewan from 5 or 7 specified subject areas dependent on selected study course.

Foreign students admission:

Definition of foreign student: Foreign (International) Students are students who are neither Canadian citizens nor permanent residents of Canada, and are enrolled in a recognized academic, professional or vocational training course at a university, college or other educational institution in Canada.

Quotas: There are quotas at the institutional level.

Entrance exam requirements: For undergraduate applicants: In general, applicants must be qualified to enter university in their home country. Admission is typically based on up to 6 secondary courses, will vary by credential and must include the specific courses required by their chosen faculty.
For graduate applicants: Applicants are required to have a four-year Honours degree, or equivalent, from a recognized college or university in an academic discipline relevant to the proposed field of study.
All applicants must provide evidence of English language proficiency. A lack of proficiency in English or French will be taken into account by the Canadian Immigration Office in the evaluation of the application.

Entry regulations: Before you come to study in Canada, you will need: a Study Permit unless your program of study is six months or less and can be completed within six months. To obtain a Study Permit you must meet the following requirements: have received an original acceptance letter from a university in Saskatchewan; be able to provide proof of enough money to pay for tuition and living costs for you and any accompanying family members; be able to prove that you will return to your home country after completing studies at a university in Saskatchewan; pass a medical examination if required; and meet other visitor requirements, including a visa if required. You must be a law abiding citizen with no criminal record and be of no risk to the security of Canada. You may have to provide a police certificate (it is not required for all countries). A small number of students do not require a Study Permit by virtue of their status in Canada (e.g. diplomats and their children).

Health requirements: International students attending the universities in Saskatchewan, are entitled to Provincial Health Coverage for no additional cost. Medical examinations are not required by institutions but are required by Citizenship and Immigration Canada for students from many countries.

Language requirements: All applicants must demonstrate an appropriate level of proficiency in the English language: TOEFL: Internet based – overall 0f 80; computer based – 213; paper based – 550; IELTS: band score of 6.5; CanTest: Listening – 4.5, reading – 4.5, Writing – 4.0; MELAB – 85; CAEL – 60; CELT - 60.

RECOGNITION OF STUDIES

Quality assurance system:

There are formalized credit transfer agreements between the universities and their federated or affiliated colleges and between SIAST and the two universities in selected program areas such as Nursing, Engineering and Commerce, as well as universities in other provinces.

Bodies dealing with recognition:

Ministry of Advanced Education, Employment and Immigration
Room 208, Legislative Building, 2405 Legislative Drive
Regina, Saskatchewan S4S 0B3
Canada
Tel: +1(306) 787 0341
Fax: +1(306) 787 6946
EMail: Linda.roy@gov.sk.ca
WWW: http://www.aeei.gov.sk.ca/

Special provisions for recognition:

Recognition for university level studies: In general, none. Universities establish their own criteria for recognition of studies in their institutions. Where quotas apply, space may be reserved for international students. Additionally, the Canadian Information Centre for International Credentials (CICIC) provides information and guidance on the recognition of foreign studies.

For access to advanced studies and research: Applications from international students are not accepted for undergraduate study in Education, Medicine, Physical Therapy or Veterinary Medicine at the University of Saskatchewan. No restrictions are imposed by the University of Regina.

For exercising a profession: In general, none. For each profession, both Canadian and non-Canadians who studied abroad have to meet specified educational and experience requirements, and usually pass registration examinations. Non-Canadians whose first language is not English, may sometimes also need to pass language testing. Access to most professions is governed by provincial and/or federal statutes and is restricted to Canadian citizens or immigrants accepted as permanent residents. Applicants must also meet examination and/or practical training requirements set by the relevant professional body or provincial or federal licensing board.

PROVINCIAL BODIES

Ministry of Advanced Education, Employment and Immigration
Minister of Advanced Education: Rob Norris
Room 208, Legislative Building, 2405 Legislative Drive
Regina, Saskatchewan S4S 0B3
Canada
Tel: +1(306) 787 0341
Fax: +1(306) 787 6946
EMail: Linda.roy@gov.sk.ca
WWW: http://www.aeei.gov.sk.ca/
Role of national body: The Ministry provides leadership and resources to foster a high quality advanced education and training system and provides employment and immigration services to develop a workforce that responds to the needs of Saskatchewan's people and economy.

Data for academic year: 2011-2012
Source: IAU from The Canadian Information Centre for International Credentials (CICIC), a unit of the Council of Ministers of Education, Canada (CMEC), on behalf of the Province of Saskatchewan, 2011

INSTITUTIONS

PUBLIC INSTITUTIONS

BRIERCREST COLLEGE AND SEMINARY

510 College Drive, Caronport, Saskatchewan S0H 0S0
Tel: +1(306) 756-3200
Fax: +1(306) 756-3366
EMail: info@briercrest.ca
Website: http://www.briercrest.ca/

President: Dwayne Uglem EMail: president@briercrest.ca

Programmes

Applied Linguistics: TESOL (Applied Linguistics; English; Foreign Languages Education); **Arts** (Bible; Christian Religious Studies; Economics; English; Fine Arts; History; Literature; Mathematics; Philosophy; Religion; Social Sciences; Theology); **Biblical Studies** (Bible; Classical Languages; Greek (Classical); Theology); **Business Administration** (Accountancy; Administration; Business Administration; Communication Studies; Economics; Finance; Human Resources; Information Management; Leadership; Management; Marketing; Operations Research); **Certificate** (Acting; Bible; Business Administration; Christian Religious Studies; Communication Studies; Computer Science; Economics; Fine Arts; Greek (Classical); Hebrew; History; Holy Writings; Linguistics; Mathematics; Modern Languages; Music; Native American Studies; New Testament; Philosophy; Psychology; Sociology; Sports; Theatre; Theology); **Christian Ministry** (Arts and Humanities; Bible; Family Studies; Pastoral Studies; Psychology; Religion; Religious Music; Theology); **Church and Culture** (Bible; Christian Religious Studies; History of Religion; Theology); **Education** (Education; Foreign Languages Education; History; Humanities and Social Science Education; Music Education; Physical Education; Primary Education); **Global Studies** (Anthropology; Bible; History; Religion; Sociology; Theology); **Graduate Studies** *(Seminary)* (Bible; Family Studies; Holy Writings; Leadership; Management; New Testament; Pastoral Studies; Psychology; Theology); **Humanities** (Art History; Arts and Humanities; English; Fine Arts; History; Literature; Music; Philosophy); **Music** (Art History; Music; Music Education; Musical Instruments; Religious Music; Singing); **Social Sciences** (Administration; Anthropology; Native American Studies; Psychology; Social Sciences; Sociology); **Theology** (Theology); **Youth Ministry** (Bible; Pastoral Studies; Psychology; Sociology; Theology)

Further Information: Traditional and Open Learning Insitution. Also Seminary.

History: Founded 1935 as Briercrest Bible Institute. Earned full accreditation 1976. Acquired present title 1982. Affiliated with University of Saskatchewan.

Governing Bodies: Board of Directors

Fees: (Canadian Dollar): 256 per credit hour.

Accrediting Agencies: Association for Biblical Higher Education (formerly the Accrediting Association of Bible Colleges).

Degrees and Diplomas: *Certificate/Diploma*; *Bachelor's Degree*; *Master's Degree*
Last Updated: 23/03/11

CAMPION COLLEGE (UNIVERSITY OF REGINA)

3737 Wascana Parkway, Regina, Saskatchewan S4S 0A2
Tel: +1(306) 586-4242
Fax: +1(306) 359-1200
EMail: campion.college@uregina.ca
Website: http://www.campioncollege.sk.ca

President: Benjamin Fiore
Tel: +1(306) 359-1212 EMail: Benjamin.Fiore@uregina.ca

Executive Director of Administration: Fred Marcia
Tel: +1(306) 359-1231 EMail: fred.marcia@uregina.ca

Departments

Astronomy (Astronomy and Space Science); **English** (English); **French** (French); **History** (History; Medieval Studies); **Humanities and Religious Studies** (Catholic Theology; Christian Religious Studies; Ecology; Jewish Studies; New Testament; Religion; Religious Studies; Theology); **Media Studies** (Film; Media Studies; Radio and Television Broadcasting); **Pastoral Studies** (Arts and Humanities; Pastoral Studies; Psychology; Religious Studies); **Philosophy and Classics** (Ancient Civilizations; Classical Languages; History; Latin; Metaphysics; Philosophy); **Political Science** (Comparative Politics; International Relations; Political Sciences); **Psychology** (Behavioural Sciences; Psychology; Social Psychology); **Statistics** (Statistics); **Theatre Studies** (Acting; Theatre)

History: Founded 1917 as Catholic College of Regina. Became a Junior College of the University of Saskatchewan 1923. A federated College of the University of Regina.

Governing Bodies: Board of Regents

Academic Year: September to August (September-December; January-April; May-June; July-August)

Admission Requirements: Secondary school certificate or recognized foreign equivalent

Fees: (Can. Dollars): Tuition fees for undergraduate Student, 4,410 per annum for canadian students; 13,230 per annum for international students.

Main Language(s) of Instruction: English

Degrees and Diplomas: *Certificate/Diploma*; *Bachelor's Degree*. Also Bachelor's degree (professional), 4 yrs; Honour Bachelor's degree; Advanced Certificate; Pre-Professional Programmes.

Student Services: Academic counselling, Canteen, Cultural centre, Handicapped facilities, Social counselling

Libraries: 50,000 vols

Student Numbers 2010-2011: Total: c. 1,000
Last Updated: 24/03/11

COLLEGE OF EMMANUEL AND ST. CHAD (UNIVERSITY OF SASKATCHEWAN)

114 Seminary Crescent, Saskatoon, Saskatchewan S7N 0X3
Tel: +1(306) 975-3753
Fax: +1(306) 934-2683
EMail: emmanuel.stchad@usask.ca
Website: http://www.usask.ca/stu/emmanuel/

Vice-Chancellor/Acting Principal: Bill Richards
EMail: wrichards@sasktel.net

Registrar: Colleen Walker EMail: colleen.walker@usask.ca

Programmes

Anglican Studies (Christian Religious Studies; Protestant Theology; Theology); **Distance Education** (Bible; Ethics; History of Religion; Holy Writings; Religious Education); **Divinity** *(Master's degree)* (Bible; Ethics; History of Religion; Pastoral Studies; Religion; Theology); **Sacred Theology** *(Master's degree offered in association with Lutheran Theological Seminary and St. Andrew's)* (Bible; Pastoral Studies; Theology); **Theological Studies** *(Master's degree)* (Bible; Ethics; Holy Writings; Religion; Theology); **Theology** (Bible; Ethics; History of Religion; Pastoral Studies; Theology)

Schools

Ministry *(Dr. William Winter)*

History: Founded 1879. Emmanuel College and St. Chad's College were amalgamated under the name of College of Emmanuel and St. Chad 1964.

Fees: (Canadian Dollar): 650 per 3 credit course.

Degrees and Diplomas: *Bachelor's Degree*; *Master's Degree*
Last Updated: 24/03/11

FIRST NATIONS UNIVERSITY OF CANADA (UNIVERSITY OF REGINA)

1 First Nations Way, Regina, Saskatchewan S4S 7K2
Tel: +1(306) 790-5950
Fax: +1(306) 790-5999
EMail: info@firstnationsuniversity.ca
Website: http://www.firstnationsuniversity.ca/

Interim President: Shauneen Pete
Tel: +1(306) 790-5950 Ext. 2100

Departments

English (Interdisciplinary Programmes) (English; Modern Languages; Writing); **Health Sciences and Nursing** (Professional Programmes) (Health Sciences; Nursing); **Indian Communication Arts** (INCA - Interdisciplinary Programmes) (Communication Arts; Leadership); **Indian Fine Arts** (Interdisciplinary Programmes) (Art History; Fine Arts); **Indian Languages, Literatures and Linguistics** (Interdisciplinary Programmes) (Amerindian Languages; Linguistics; Literature); **Indigenous Education** (Professional Programmes) (Native Language Education; Natives Education; Pedagogy; Philosophy; Primary Education; Secondary Education); **Indigenous Studies** (Interdisciplinary Programmes) (Indigenous Studies); **Science** (Interdisciplinary Programmes) (Environmental Studies; Health Sciences)

Schools

Business and Public Administration (SBPA - Professional Programmes) (Accountancy; Administration; Business Administration; Economics; Human Resources; Management; Marketing; Public Administration); **Dental Therapy** (National - Professional Programmes) (Dental Hygiene; Dentistry; Oral Pathology); **Indian Social Work** (ISW - Professional Programmes) (Social Work)

Further Information: Also campuses in Saskatoon and Prince Albert

History: Founded 1976 as Saskatchewan Indian Federated College (SIFC). A Federated College of the University of Regina.

Governing Bodies: Board of Governors

Academic Year: January to December (January-April; September-December). Also Spring/Summer Session (May-August)

Admission Requirements: Secondary level standing (24 credits) or equivalent. A minimum overall average of 65% is required for subjects used for admission. Canadian citizens or landed immigrants who satisfy the English proficiency requirement of the University of Regina may be admitted if applicants are at least 21 years of age

Fees: (Can. Dollars): c. 1,330 per semester

Main Language(s) of Instruction: English

Degrees and Diplomas: *University Certificate/Diploma; Bachelor's Degree; Master's Degree.* Also Honours Bachelor of Arts.

Student Services: Academic counselling, Canteen, Employment services, Foreign student adviser, Foreign Studies Centre, Handicapped facilities, Health services, Language programs, Nursery care, Social counselling, Sports facilities

Student Residential Facilities: Yes

Libraries: c. 50,000 items. Collection focuses on Indigenous Peoples of North, South and Central America
Last Updated: 24/03/11

LUTHER COLLEGE (UNIVERSITY OF REGINA)

3737 Wascana Parkway, Regina, Saskatchewan S4S 0A2
Tel: +1(306) 585-5333 +1(800) 588-4378
Fax: +1(306) 585-2949
EMail: lutheru@luthercollege.edu
Website: http://www.luthercollege.edu

President: Bryan Hillis (2010-)
Tel: +1(306) 585-5024 EMail: bryan.hillis@luthercollege.edu

Registrar: Mary Jesse
Tel: +1(306) 585-5083 EMail: mary.jesse@uregina.ca

Faculties

Arts (Arts and Humanities; Chinese; Criminal Law; Economics; Environmental Studies; French; French Studies; German; Health Sciences; International Studies; Japanese; Journalism; Law; Natural Resources; Police Studies; Spanish); **Fine Arts** (Arts and Humanities; Education; Fine Arts; Music; Music Education; Visual Arts); **Science** (Community Health; Computer Science; Health Sciences; Laboratory Techniques; Medical Technology)

Programmes

Pre-professional Studies (Chiropractic; Dentistry; Health Sciences; Journalism; Law; Medicine; Nutrition; Optometry; Pharmacy; Police Studies; Veterinary Science)

History: Founded 1914 as Luther Academy, acquired present status and title 1926. Officially federated with the University of Saskatchewan, Regina Campus 1968. Opened the doors to its new academic and residence buildings on the University of Regina campus in 1971. A Federated College of the University of Regina.

Governing Bodies: Board of Regents

Academic Year: September to April

Admission Requirements: Secondary school certificate or recognized foreign equivalent

Fees: (Can. Dollars): 1,933-2,044 per semester; foreign students 3,583-3,694 per semester

Main Language(s) of Instruction: English

Degrees and Diplomas: *University Certificate/Diploma; Bachelor's Degree.* Also Applied Professional Bachelor's degree (professional) in Human Justice, 4-5 yrs; Bachelors of Education/ Bachelors of Arts in English, French or history, 5 yrs; Honours Bachelor's degree, 4 yrs; Pre-professional Programmes, 1-3 yrs; Advanced Certificates.

Student Services: Academic counselling, Canteen, Social counselling

Student Residential Facilities: Residence for 214 students.

Libraries: Luther College Library, 14,000 vols
Last Updated: 25/03/11

LUTHERAN THEOLOGICAL SEMINARY (UNIVERSITY OF SASKATCHEWAN) (LTS)

114 Seminary Crescent, Saskatoon, Saskatchewan S7N 0X3
Tel: +1(306) 966-7850
Fax: +1(306) 966-7852
EMail: lutheran.seminary@usask.ca
Website: http://www.usask.ca/stu/luther/

President: Kevin A. Oglivie
Tel: +1(306) 966-7863 EMail: kevin.ogilvie@usask.ca

Registrar: Susan Avant
Tel: +1(306) 966-7856 EMail: susan.avant@usask.ca

Programmes

Diaconal Certificate (Bible; Ethics; History of Religion; Holy Writings; New Testament; Religious Education; Theology); **Divinity** (Classical Languages; Ethics; Greek (Classical); History of Religion; Holy Writings; New Testament; Religion; Theology); **Lutheran Formation Certificate** (Ethics; History of Religion; Pastoral Studies; Protestant Theology; Theology); **Sacred Theology** (STM) (Bible; Ethics; History of Religion; Pastoral Studies; Theology); **Theological Studies** (MTS) (Bible; Ethics; History of Religion; Holy Writings; New Testament; Pastoral Studies; Theology); **Theology** (Theology)

History: Founded 1968 through the merger between Lutheran College and Seminary (LCS) and the Luther Theological Seminary.

Governing Bodies: Board of Governors.

Fees: (Canadian Dollar): 650 per course, except Master of Sacred Theology (STM), 925 per course and Upgraded MDiv course, 750 per course.

Degrees and Diplomas: *University Certificate/Diploma; Bachelor's Degree; Master's Degree.* Also professional certificate programme.
Last Updated: 25/03/11

ST. ANDREW'S COLLEGE (UNIVERSITY OF SASKATCHEWAN)

1121 College Drive, Saskatoon, Saskatchewan S7N 0W3
Tel: +1(306) 966-8970
Fax: +1(306) 966-8981
EMail: reidb@duke.usask.ca
Website: http://www.usask.ca/stu/standrews/index.php

Principal: Lorne Calvert
Tel: +1(306) 966-8975 EMail: lorne.calvert@usask.ca

Registrar: Colleen Walker
Tel: +1(306) 966-5244 EMail: standrews.registrar@usask.ca

Programmes

Distance Education (Bible; Ethics; Holy Writings; Religious Education; Theology); **Divinity** (Bible; Ethics; Holy Writings; Pastoral

Studies; Theology); **Sacred Theology** (Theology); **Theological Studies** (Bible; Ethics; History of Religion; Holy Writings; Pastoral Studies; Theology); **Theology** (Bible; Ethics; History of Religion; Holy Writings; Pastoral Studies; Religious Education; Theology)

History: Founded as as the Presbyterian Theological College 1912. Acquired present title 1924.

Governing Bodies: Board; Academic Committee; College Council.

Fees: (Canadian Dollar): 650 per 3 credit hour course.

Accrediting Agencies: The Association of Theological Schools (ATS).

Degrees and Diplomas: *University Certificate/Diploma*; *Master's Degree*

Libraries: c. 36,000 vols and 134 periodical titles.

Last Updated: 28/03/11

ST. PETER'S COLLEGE (UNIVERSITY OF SASKATCHEWAN)

RPO Box 40, Muenster, Saskatchewan S0K 2Y0
Tel: +1(306) 682-7888
Fax: +1(306) 682-4402
EMail: spc@stpeters.sk.ca
Website: http://www.stpeterscollege.ca/

President: Glen Kobussen EMail: president@stpeters.sk.ca

Vice-President/Provost: Rob Harasymchuk
EMail: vicepresident@stpeters.sk.ca

Colleges
Agriculture and Bioresources (Agricultural Business; Agricultural Economics; Agricultural Management; Agriculture; Agrobiology; Agronomy; Animal Husbandry; Botany; Ecology; Food Science; Forestry; Microbiology; Natural Resources; Soil Science); **Arts and Science** (Art History; Arts and Humanities; Biology; Chemistry; Dentistry; Economics; English; Fine Arts; Geography; Health Sciences; History; Mathematics; Medicine; Music; Native American Studies; Natural Sciences; Nursing; Nutrition; Pharmacy; Philosophy; Physics; Political Sciences; Psychology; Religious Studies; Social Sciences; Sociology; Statistics; Theatre; Veterinary Science); **Kinesiology** (Physical Education; Physical Therapy; Physiology; Psychology; Sports)

Programmes
Writing (Writing)

Schools
Business *(Edwards)* (Business Administration; Business and Commerce; International Business)

History: Founded 1921. Affiliated to University of Saskatchewan 1926.

Fees: (Canadian Dollar): 2,370-3,270 per semester (450 per 3 credit units for Humanities and Social Sciences (e.g. English or Psychology) programmes; 465 per 3 credit units for Agriculture, Kinesiology, Mathematics, Statistics and Natural Sciences programmes; 630 per 3 credit units for Commerce programmes.

Degrees and Diplomas: *University Certificate/Diploma*; *Bachelor's Degree*. Also Combined B.Sc. (Kin) and B. Ed. degree programme, 5 yrs; Honours Bachelor's degree programme, 4 yrs; pre-professional year programmes in Health Sciences (Dentistry, Medicine, Nursing,...).

Last Updated: 28/03/11

UNIVERSITY OF REGINA (U OF R)

3737 Wascana Parkway, Regina, Saskatchewan S4S 0A2
Tel: +1(306) 585-4111
Fax: +1(306) 585-5203
EMail: admissions@uregina.ca;
international.admissions@uregina.ca
Website: http://www.uregina.ca

President and Vice-Chancellor: Vianne Timmons
Tel: +1(306) 585-4696, Fax: +1(306) 585-5200
EMail: The.President@uregina.ca

Vice-President (Administration): Dave Button
Tel: +1(306) 585-4386, Fax: +1(306) 585-5255
EMail: Dave.Button@uregina.ca

International Relations: Livia Castellanos, Director, Office of International Cooperation and Development
Tel: +1(306) 337-2477, Fax: +1(306) 337-3128
EMail: International.Relations@uregina.ca

Centres
Aging and Health *(CAH)* (Gerontology; Health Sciences); **Continuing Education** (Administration; Adult Education; Arts and Humanities; Continuing Education; Dance; Education; Engineering; English; Foreign Languages Education; Government; Leadership; Management; Marketing; Music; Musical Instruments; Native Language Education; Pastoral Studies; Performing Arts; Public Relations; Sales Techniques; Singing; Theatre; Writing); **International Education and Training** *(CIET)* (Educational Administration; Human Resources; International and Comparative Education); **Studies in Energy and Environment** *(CSEE)* (Energy Engineering; Environmental Studies; Meteorology); **Sustainable Communities** (Development Studies; Health Sciences)

Faculties
Arts (Ancient Civilizations; Anthropology; Arabic; Arts and Humanities; Chinese; Classical Languages; Economics; English; Environmental Studies; Fine Arts; French; Gender Studies; Geography; German; Greek (Classical); Health Sciences; History; Human Resources; Indigenous Studies; International Studies; Japanese; Journalism; Korean; Latin; Law; Linguistics; Literature; Modern Languages; Native Language; Natural Resources; Philosophy; Police Studies; Political Sciences; Psychology; Religious Studies; Social Studies; Sociology; Spanish; Women's Studies); **Education** (Adult Education; Art Education; Business Education; Curriculum; Education; Educational Administration; Educational Psychology; Health Education; Human Resources; Humanities and Social Science Education; Mathematics Education; Music Education; Natives Education; Physical Education; Primary Education; Religious Education; Science Education; Secondary Education; Special Education); **Engineering and Applied Science** (Electronic Engineering; Engineering; Environmental Engineering; Industrial Engineering; Petroleum and Gas Engineering; Production Engineering; Software Engineering); **Fine Arts** (Acting; Art History; Ceramic Art; Display and Stage Design; Film; Fine Arts; Media Studies; Music; Music Education; Music Theory and Composition; Musical Instruments; Painting and Drawing; Printing and Printmaking; Sculpture; Theatre; Visual Arts); **Graduate Studies and Research** (Anthropology; Biochemistry; Biology; Business Administration; Chemistry; Computer Science; Economics; Education; Engineering; English; Fine Arts; French; Gender Studies; Geography; Geology; Gerontology; Health Sciences; History; Indigenous Studies; Law; Linguistics; Mathematics; Media Studies; Music; Philosophy; Physical Therapy; Physics; Police Studies; Polish; Political Sciences; Psychology; Public Administration; Religious Studies; Social Studies; Social Work; Sociology; Statistics; Visual Arts; Women's Studies); **Kinesiology and Health Studies** (Gerontology; Health Sciences; Parks and Recreation; Physical Therapy; Sports); **Nursing** (Nursing); **Science** (Actuarial Science; Biochemistry; Biology; Cell Biology; Chemistry; Computer Science; Ecology; Geography; Geology; Mathematics; Molecular Biology; Physics; Statistics); **Social Work** (Social Work)

Graduate Schools
Business *(Kenneth Levene)* (Accountancy; Administration; Business Administration; Finance; Human Resources; International Business; Labour and Industrial Relations; Leadership; Management; Marketing); **Public Policy** *(Johnson-Shoyama)* (Health Administration; International Business; Management; Public Administration)

Institutes
French *(Institut français)* (French; French Studies); **Prairie Particle Physics** *(P3I)* (Physics)

Programmes
English as a Seconde Language *(ESL)* (English; Foreign Languages Education); **Prairie Adaptation Research Collaborative - University of Regina** *(PARC-UR)* (Agriculture; Environmental Studies; Forestry; Meteorology)

Research Centres
Applied Health *(Dr. Paul Schwann)* (Cardiology; Health Sciences; Medicine); **Canadian Plains** *(CPRC)* (Native American Studies); **Francophone Minority Communities** *(CRFM)* (French Studies);

Indigenous Peoples' Health *(IPHRC)* (Health Sciences; Indigenous Studies); **Research and Education for Solutions to Violence and Abuse** *(RESOLVE)* (Social Problems)

Research Institutes
Humanities *(HRI)* (Arts and Humanities)

Research Units
Saskatchewan Instructional Development *(SIDRU)* (Curriculum; Education; Educational Sciences); **Saskatchewan Population Health and Evaluation** *(SPHERU)* (Community Health; Health Sciences; Public Health); **Social Policy** *(SPR)* (Social Policy; Welfare and Protective Services); **Survey** (Data Processing; Surveying and Mapping)

Schools
Business *(Paul J. Hill)* (Accountancy; Business Administration; Finance; Human Resources; Management; Marketing)

Units
Community Research *(CRU)* (Social and Community Services)

Further Information: Also Subatomic Physics at Regina with Research Offshore

History: Founded 1911 as Regina College, Reorganized 1925 as University of Saskatchewan, 1959 as University of Saskatchewan, Regina Campus, and acquired present status and title 1974.

Governing Bodies: Senate; Board of Governors

Academic Year: September to April (September-December; January-April)

Admission Requirements: Secondary school certificate or recognized foreign equivalent

Fees: (Can. Dollars): Undergraduate tuition, 4,776-5,342 per annum for Canadian students and 13,596-14,162 per annum for international students; Graduate tuition, 3,245-11,783 per annum for Canadian students and 4,245-12,783 per annum for international students.

Main Language(s) of Instruction: English

International Co-operation: North America Mobility Programmes; EU-Canada Student Mobility Programmes; China; Mexico; Japan; Colombia; various countries in Europe

Degrees and Diplomas: *University Certificate/Diploma; Bachelor's Degree; Master's Degree; Doctoral Degree (PhD)*. Also Combined Degree BA/Badm, BA/BEd (French), Bachelor of Education/Bachelor of Science; Honours Bachelor's degree; Advanced Certificates (Undergraduate); Professional Certificate Programmes.

Student Services: Academic counselling, Canteen, Employment services, Foreign student adviser, Handicapped facilities, Health services, Language programs, Nursery care, Social counselling, Sports facilities

Student Residential Facilities: Yes

Special Facilities: Norman Mackenzie Art Gallery concentrates on Canadian history and contemporary art with special interest in Western Canadian, 19th and 20th century European art, and aspects of contemporary American and European works of art

Libraries: c. 1.7m. items in monograph and journal collections; c. 754,000 microform items. Federated collections, c. 72,700 vols

Publications: UResearch *(biennially)*; Wascana Review (literary journal)

Academic Staff 2010-2011	TOTAL
FULL-TIME	506
STAFF WITH DOCTORATE FULL-TIME	c. 376
Student Numbers 2010-2011	
All (Foreign Included)	c. 12,267
FOREIGN ONLY	1,040

Part-time students, 3,154.
Last Updated: 28/03/11

UNIVERSITY OF SASKATCHEWAN (U OF S)
107 Administration Place, Saskatoon, Saskatchewan S7N 5A2
Tel: +1(306) 966-4343
Fax: +1(306) 975-1026
EMail: registrar@usask.ca
Website: http://www.usask.ca

President: Peter MacKinnon (1999-)
Tel: +1(306) 966-6612, Fax: +1(306) 966-4530
EMail: peter.mackinnon@usask.ca

University Secretary: Lea Pennock
Tel: +1(306) 966-4633 EMail: lea.pennock@usask.ca

Director, University Communications: Carla Vipond
Tel: +1(306) 966-1815, Fax: +1(306) 966-6815
EMail: carla.vipond@usask.ca

International Relations: Leigh-Ellen Keating, Coordinator, Global Relations
Tel: +1(306) 966-2428, Fax: +1(306) 966-4530
EMail: leighellen.keating@usask.ca

Centres
Continuing and Distance Education *(CCDE)* (Adult Education; Agriculture; Business Administration; Chinese; Design; Ecology; Educational Psychology; English; Environmental Studies; Fine Arts; Foreign Languages Education; French; German; Horticulture; Indigenous Studies; Japanese; Leadership; Mathematics; Music; Music Education; Spanish; Special Education)

Colleges
Agriculture and Bioresources (Agricultural Business; Agricultural Economics; Agriculture; Agronomy; Animal Husbandry; Biochemistry; Biotechnology; Botany; Chemistry; Computer Science; Crop Production; Ecology; Environmental Studies; Food Science; Forestry; Genetics; Horticulture; Meat and Poultry; Microbiology; Molecular Biology; Natural Resources; Nutrition; Physics; Physiology; Plant and Crop Protection; Plant Pathology; Social Sciences; Soil Science; Veterinary Science); **Arts and Science** (Amerindian Languages; Anatomy; Ancient Civilizations; Anthropology; Archaeology; Art History; Astronomy and Space Science; Biochemistry; Biology; Biotechnology; Cell Biology; Chemistry; Computer Science; Criminology; Cultural Studies; Economics; English; Environmental Studies; Fine Arts; Food Science; French; Gender Studies; Geography; Geology; Geophysics; German; Greek (Classical); Hebrew; History; Indigenous Studies; International Studies; Latin; Law; Linguistics; Literature; Mathematical Physics; Mathematics; Medieval Studies; Modern History; Modern Languages; Music; Music Education; Native American Studies; Pharmacology; Philosophy; Physical Engineering; Physics; Physiology; Political Sciences; Psychology; Public Administration; Regional Planning; Religion; Religious Studies; Russian; Sanskrit; Slavic Languages; Social Sciences; Sociology; Spanish; Statistics; Theatre; Town Planning; Toxicology; Women's Studies); **Dentistry** (Dentistry); **Education** (Curriculum; Education; Educational Psychology; Educational Technology; Music Education; Natives Education; Physical Education; Primary Education; Secondary Education; Special Education; Teacher Training); **Engineering** (Agricultural Engineering; Bioengineering; Chemical Engineering; Civil Engineering; Computer Engineering; Electrical Engineering; Engineering; Environmental Engineering; Geological Engineering; Mechanical Engineering; Physical Engineering); **Graduate Studies and Research** (Accountancy; Agricultural Economics; Agricultural Engineering; Agriculture; Anaesthesiology; Anatomy; Animal Husbandry; Anthropology; Archaeology; Art History; Biochemistry; Bioengineering; Biology; Biomedicine; Botany; Business Administration; Cell Biology; Chemical Engineering; Chemistry; Civil Engineering; Community Health; Computer Engineering; Computer Science; Cultural Studies; Curriculum; Economics; Education; Educational Administration; Educational Psychology; Electrical Engineering; English; Environmental Engineering; Environmental Management; Environmental Studies; Epidemiology; Finance; Fine Arts; Food Science; Gender Studies; Geography; Geological Engineering; Geology; Gynaecology and Obstetrics; Health Sciences; History; Immunology; Indigenous Studies; International Business; Laboratory Techniques; Law; Linguistics; Management; Mathematics; Meat and Poultry; Mechanical Engineering; Microbiology; Music; Native American Studies; Natural Resources; Neurological Therapy; Nursing; Nutrition; Oncology; Paediatrics; Pathology; Pharmacology; Pharmacy; Philosophy; Physical Engineering; Physical Therapy;

Physics; Physiology; Political Sciences; Psychiatry and Mental Health; Psychology; Public Administration; Public Health; Rehabilitation and Therapy; Religion; Sociology; Soil Science; Special Education; Statistics; Surgery; Theatre; Toxicology; Veterinary Science; Women's Studies; Writing); **Kinesiology** (Nutrition; Physical Education; Physical Therapy; Physiology; Psychology; Sports); **Law** (Law); **Medicine** (Anaesthesiology; Anatomy; Biochemistry; Biomedicine; Cardiology; Cell Biology; Community Health; Epidemiology; Gynaecology and Obstetrics; Health Sciences; Immunology; Information Technology; Laboratory Techniques; Medical Technology; Medicine; Microbiology; Neurosciences; Occupational Therapy; Oncology; Ophthalmology; Paediatrics; Pathology; Pharmacology; Physical Therapy; Physiology; Psychiatry and Mental Health; Public Health; Radiology; Rehabilitation and Therapy; Speech Therapy and Audiology; Surgery); **Nursing** (Nursing); **Pharmacy and Nutrition** (Biotechnology; Economics; Epidemiology; Molecular Biology; Nanotechnology; Nutrition; Pharmacy; Toxicology); **Veterinary Medicine** *(Western)* (Biomedicine; Microbiology; Pathology; Veterinary Science)

Graduate Schools

Public Policy *(Johnson-Shoyama)* (Health Administration; International Business; Public Administration)

Schools

Business *(Edwards)* (Accountancy; Business Administration; Business and Commerce; Finance; Human Resources; International Business; Management; Marketing); **Environment and Sustainability** (Arts and Humanities; Education; Engineering; Environmental Management; Environmental Studies; Law; Natural Resources; Natural Sciences); **Physical Therapy** (Physical Therapy); **Public Health** (Anthropology; Biological and Life Sciences; Biology; Business Administration; Chemistry; Computer Science; Dentistry; Epidemiology; Health Administration; Health Sciences; Immunology; Medicine; Microbiology; Native American Studies; Nursing; Nutrition; Pharmacy; Physical Therapy; Psychology; Public Health; Social Sciences; Sociology; Statistics; Veterinary Science)

Further Information: Teaching Hospital. Study Abroad programmes. For more information on units, centres, divisions, institutes and groups, please see http://www.usask.ca/calendar/faculty&staff/ucdi/

History: Founded 1907.

Governing Bodies: Senate; Board of Governors; University Council

Academic Year: September to June (September-December; January-April; May-June). Also summer session (July-August)

Admission Requirements: Secondary school certificate or recognized equivalent. Proof of English proficiency

Fees: (Canadian Dollar): undergraduate tuition, 471-807 per 3 credit unit class; graduate tuition, 517.50 per 3 credit unit course (some programmes such as Master's degrees in Buisness Adminstration, International Trade, Physical Therapy, Professional Accounting, Public Health, Public Administration, Environment and Sustainability have special tuition rates ranging from 3,045 to 23,950 per programme); Tuition for Dentistry programmes, 32,960 per annum; Tuition for Medicine M.D. programme, 12,276 per annum; Tuition for Veterinary Medicine programme, 7,020 per annum; Certificate Programmes, 450-550 per course.

Main Language(s) of Instruction: English

Degrees and Diplomas: *University Certificate/Diploma; Bachelor's Degree; Master's Degree; Doctoral Degree (PhD).* Also Honours Bachelor of Arts and Science; Combined Bachelor of Education/Bachelor of Music in Music Education, and combined Bachelor of Education/Bachelor of Kinesiology, 5 yrs; Postdoctoral Fellowships Programmes. For more information on academic programmes, please see: http://www.usask.ca/university_secretary/programs/index.php

Student Services: Academic counselling, Canteen, Cultural centre, Employment services, Foreign student adviser, Foreign Studies Centre, Handicapped facilities, Health services, Language programs, Nursery care, Social counselling, Sports facilities

Student Residential Facilities: Yes

Special Facilities: Prime Ministerial Museum, Museum of Natural History, Museum of Antiquities, Art Galleries, Observatory, Planetarium

Libraries: 1,900,379 volumes; 3,573,195 other holdings

Academic Staff 2009-2010	MEN	WOMEN	TOTAL
FULL-TIME	733	386	1,119
STAFF WITH DOCTORATE FULL-TIME	242	543	785

Student Numbers 2010-2011			
All (Foreign Included)	–	–	20,515
FOREIGN ONLY	–	–	1,300

Part-time students, 3,378.
Last Updated: 29/03/11

Canada - Yukon

STRUCTURE OF HIGHER EDUCATION SYSTEM

Description:

The Department of Education has responsibility for post-secondary education in Yukon. It does not have its own university, though the Department contributes financially to students from the Yukon pursuing university studies elsewhere in Canada. In June 1990, Yukon College became a board governed community college. To serve people across the territory, Yukon College has a main campus, Ayamdigut, and twelve community campuses. Yukon College is the only public institution providing post-secondary education and offers first and second year university transfer, vocational, technical, academic upgrading and other programmes usually leading to a certificate or diploma. Most of the university transfer courses offered at Yukon College are articulated through the British Columbia Council on Admissions and Transfer (BCCAT). All colleges and universities in BC participate in BCCAT. Further, the College is negotiating a similar agreement with the Alberta Council on Admissions and Transfer (ACAT).Although Yukon College holds the rights to offer degrees, to date it has not introduced its own degree. The College has full autonomy on admissions and all other academic matters. A permanent board of governors was appointed in 1990. Three Bachelor's degree programmes, accredited by other universities, are offered at Yukon College: the Yukon Native Teacher Education Programme, and a Bachelor of Social Work, both programmes are offered in partnership with the University of Regina, and a Bachelor of Environmental and Conservation Science in partnership with the University of Alberta are a part of the core delivery at Yukon College. In addition, through a partnership with University of Alaska Southeast, Yukon College offers a Master in Public Administration and a Master of Business Administration. The University of Northern British Columbia is currently delivering a Master of Education programme at Yukon College. The College has provided several instructors in the programme as well as additional curricular support in northern and First Nations content. The Department's Advanced Education Branch licenses private trade schools (career colleges) located in Yukon that deliver vocational, business, or professional programmes. Apprenticeship training is administered by the Department's Advanced Education Branch.

Stages of studies:

University level first stage:
University level first–stage studies in the Yukon includes general arts, science and business administration courses offered by Yukon College. Almost all of the courses are articulated through BCCAT. Certificates and diplomas in this area include circumpolar studies, general studies, heritage and culture, liberal arts, northern studies, northern outdoor and environmental studies, northern First Nation studies, northern justice and criminology, northern science, visual arts, and women's and gender studies. In addition, Yukon College has several course specific and block transfers with universities across the country for students completing a certificate or diploma.

University level second stage:
For the second stage university-level (degree programmes), Yukon College offers three degree programmes. The degree programmes include: the Yukon Native Teacher Education Programme, offered in conjunction with the University of Regina, leads to a four year Bachelor of Education degree; the Bachelor of Social Work degree which is also delivered in partnership with University of Regina and leads to a four-year degree; and a Bachelor of Environmental and Conservation Science through a partnership with the University of Alberta (this also leads to a four-year degree). Students may also complete a degree in circumpolar studies through participation in the University of the Arctic. Yukon College offers two master programmes by distance through the University of Alaska Southeast –the Master's of Public Administration and the Bachelor of Business Administration. This year the University of Northern British Columbia offered a Master of Education through Yukon College.

Distance higher education:
Yukon College provides distance education using video conferencing and online course delivery with tutor support in community campuses and through a language centre at Ayamdigut campus. Yukon College has an increasing number of courses available through distributed learning.

ADMISSION TO HIGHER EDUCATION

Admission to university-level studies:

Entrance exam requirements: Secondary School Diploma may not be required.

Other admission requirements: No general entrance exams; however, depending on their level of high school completion, students may need to write the Canadian Achievement Test, the GED or the Language Proficiency Index.

Foreign students admission:

Definition of foreign student: Foreign (international) students must have some status under the Immigration Act, but are generally neither Canadian citizens nor permanent residents of Canada, and are enrolled full-time in a recognized academic, professional or vocational training course at a university, college or other educational institution in Canada.

Entrance exam requirements: Generally, as for domestic students, a high school diploma or equivalent will be required. A lack of proficiency in English or French will be taken into account by the Canadian Immigration Office in the evaluation of the application.

Entry regulations: Before coming to study in Canada, students will need:
i. a "Study Permit" if the program of study that they are admitted to is longer than six months in duration, regardless of the length of stay in Canada;
ii. a letter of acceptance from the school of choice;
iii. proof that the student has enough money to pay for school fees and living expenses;
iv. proof of intention to return home at the completion of studies;
v. the student must pass a medical exam if required; and
vi. the student must qualify as a temporary resident in Canada, including holding a temporary resident visa (required for citizens of many countries). A small number a students do not require a Study Permit by virtue of their status in Canada (e.g. diplomats and their children).

Health requirements: Most education institutions require international students to buy health insurance in addition to their tuition fees; those that do not will require proof of independent health insurance coverage. Medical examinations are not required by institutions but are required by Citizenship and Immigration Canada for students from many countries.

Language requirements: For foreign students coming to Canada from non-English speaking countries, Yukon College requires them to write TOFL, IELTS or CLB.

RECOGNITION OF STUDIES

Quality assurance system:

Yukon College has formal transfer credit arrangements through BCCAT and is in the process of negotiating a similar arrangement with ACAT. In addition, Yukon College has several programme or course specific transfer arrangements with colleges and universities across the country.

Special provisions for recognition:

For exercising a profession: In general none. For each profession, both Canadians and non-Canadians who studied abroad have to meet specified educational and experience requirements, and usually pass registration examinations. Non-Canadians may sometimes also need to pass a language test.

PROVINCIAL BODIES

Department of Education
Minister: Patrick Rouble
PO Box 2703
Whitehorse, Yukon Territory Y1A 2C6
Canada
Tel: +1(867) 667 5141
Fax: +1(867) 393 6254
EMail: contact.education@gov.yk.ca
WWW: http://www.education.gov.yk.ca/

Data for academic year: 2011-2012
Source: IAU from The Canadian Information Centre for International Credentials (CICIC), a unit of the Council of Ministers of Education, Canada (CMEC), on behalf of the Province of Yukon, 2011

Cape Verde

STRUCTURE OF HIGHER EDUCATION SYSTEM

Description:

Higher education is provided by universities (universidades) and polytechnics (institutos superiores) that are public or private.

Stages of studies:

University level first stage: *Bacharelato/Licenciatura*
The first stage leads to the Bacharelato after 3 years or the Licenciatura after 4 years.

University level second stage: *Mestrado*
The second stage leads to the Mestrado after two years' further study beyond the Licenciatura.

University level third stage: *Doutoramento*
The third stage leads to the Doutoramento following four years' further study.

Distance higher education:
The Universidade Aberta in Portugal offers courses in fifteen fields of study including: Management; French; English; History; Mathematics; Social Sciences; Computer Science; etc.

ADMISSION TO HIGHER EDUCATION

Admission to university-level studies:

Name of secondary school credential required: Certificado da Habilitações Literárias

For entry to: Universities and Institutes

Alternatives to credentials: Completion of middle level technician courses may also qualify a student for undergraduate entry.

RECOGNITION OF STUDIES

Bodies dealing with recognition:

Direcção-Geral do Ensino Superior e Ciência
Ministério da Educação e Desporto
Praia

NATIONAL BODIES

Ministério da Educação e Desporto (Ministry of Education and Sport)
Minister: Fernanda Maria de Brito Marques
Palácio do Governo - Várzea
Praía 111
Tel: +238 261 0510
Fax: +238 261 5873
EMail: cci.mees@palgov.gov.cv
WWW: http://www.minedu.gov.cv/

Data for academic year: 2009-2010
Source: IAU from the website of the Ministry of Education and Higher Education, 2009. Bodies updated 2011.

INSTITUTIONS

PUBLIC INSTITUTIONS

INSTITUTE OF EDUCATION
Instituto Superior de Educação
C.P. 279, Praia
Tel: +238(282) 262-112
Fax: +238(282) 262-7655
Website: http://www.ise.cv/

Departments
Information and Communication Technology Director: Joaquim Pombo

Degrees and Diplomas: Licenciatura: 4 yrs
Last Updated: 10/08/09

NATIONAL INSTITUTE OF AGRICULTURAL RESEARCH AND DEVELOPMENT/ AGRICULTURAL TRAINING CENTRE
Instituto Nacional de Investigação e Desenvolvimento Agrário/ Centro de Formação Agrária (INIDA)
São Jorge dos Órgãos, Ilha de Santiago 84
Tel: +238 271-11-47
Fax: +238 271-11-33
EMail: inida@inida.gov.cv
Website: http://www.inida.cv

Presidente: Isildo Gonçalves Gomes EMail: igomes@inida.gov.cv

Departments
Agricultural Business and Rural Sociology (Agricultural Business; Rural Studies; Sociology); **Agriculture, Forestry and Fishery**; **Environmental Studies** (Biological and Life Sciences; Environmental Studies; Soil Science; Water Science)

History: Founded 1979 as Centro de Estudos Agrários. Became Instituto Nacional de investigação Agrária (INIA) 1985. Acquired present title 1992.

Degrees and Diplomas: Professional degrees (Técnicos Profissionais; Técnicos Médios; Bacharéis)
Last Updated: 20/02/09

UNIVERSITY OF CAPE VERDE
Universidade de Cabo Verde (UNI-CV)
Praça Antonio Loreno, Praia, Santiago 379-C Praia
Tel: +238 261-99-04
Fax: +238 261-60-26
Website: http://www.unicv.edu.cv

Rector: António Correia e Silva EMail: antonio.silva@unicv.edu.cv
Administrator General: Bartolomeu Varela
EMail: Bartolomeu.varela@unicv.edu.cv
International Relations: Albino Luciano Silva
EMail: albino.silva@unicv.edu.cv

Departments
Engineering and Marine Sciences (DECM) (Accountancy; Applied Mathematics; Automation and Control Engineering; Civil Engineering; Computer Engineering; Computer Science; Electrical and Electronic Engineering; Environmental Engineering; Fishery; Marine Biology; Marine Science and Oceanography; Marine Transport; Mathematics; Mechanical Engineering; Natural Resources; Surveying and Mapping; Telecommunications Engineering; Transport Management) President: Paulino Monteiro; **Human and Social Sciences** (DCSH) (African Studies; Cultural Studies; Education; Educational Sciences; English; European Studies; French; History; Journalism; Literature; Modern Languages; Philosophy; Physical Education; Portuguese; Social Sciences; Special Education) President: Marcelo Galvão; **Science and Technology** (DCT) President: António Querido

Schools
Business and Government (ENG) (Administration; Business and Commerce; Finance; Management; Public Relations) President: Victor Tavares

History: Founded 2006. Incorporated the Instituto Superior de Educação (ISE), the Instituto Superior de Engenharia e Ciências do Mar (ISEC-MAR) and the Instituto Nacional de Administração e Gestão (INAG) 2008.

Governing Bodies: University Council; Administrative Council
Academic Year: September to June (September-December; January-March; April-June)
Admission Requirements: High school diploma and entrance examination
Fees: (Cape Verde Escudos): 108,000.00 per annum (900,000 per month)
Main Language(s) of Instruction: Portuguese
International Co-operation: With institutions in Portugal; Brazil; France; Canary Islands; Spain
Degrees and Diplomas: Bacharelato: 4 yrs; Mestrado: 2 yrs. Also Professional Degrees (2 yrs)
Student Services: Academic counselling, Canteen, Employment services, Handicapped facilities, Social counselling
Student Residential Facilities: No
Libraries: Yes
Publications: Revista da Uni-CV (Uni-CV Review), Academic papers (biannually)
Press or Publishing House: Edicões Uni-CV (Uni-CV Press)

Academic Staff 2008-2009	MEN	WOMEN	TOTAL
FULL-TIME	93	64	157
PART-TIME	67	52	119
STAFF WITH DOCTORATE			
FULL-TIME	12	4	16
PART-TIME	1	–	1
Student Numbers 2008-2009			
All (Foreign Included)	1,539	1,691	3,230
FOREIGN ONLY	19	15	34

Evening students, 330.
Last Updated: 23/06/09

PRIVATE INSTITUTIONS

HIGHER INSTITUTE OF ECONOMICS AND BUSINESS
Instituto Superior de Ciências Económicas e Empresariais (ISCEE)
Praça José Lopes, Mindelo
Tel: +238 232-40-70
Fax: +238 232-31-07
EMail: iscee@cvtelecom.cv
Website: http://www.iscee.edu.cv

Coordenadora: Helena Rebelo Rodrigues

Programmes
Accountancy (Accountancy); **Management** (Business Administration; Management); **Marketing** (Marketing)
History: Founded 1998.
Degrees and Diplomas: Licenciatura; Mestrado: Tourism; Management
Last Updated: 20/02/09

ISIDORO DA GRAÇA INSTITUTE OF HIGHER EDUCATION
Instituto de Ensino Superior Isidoro da Graça (IESIG)
CP 648, Rua Patrice Lumumba, Mindelo - São Vicente
Tel: +238 232-68-10
Fax: +238 232-51-32
EMail: iesig@sapo.cv
Website: http://www.iesig-cv.org

President: Albertino Graça

Head, Academic and Administrative Services: João Dias

Departments
Languages, Literature and Cultural Studies (Cultural Studies; Literature; Modern Languages); **Law** (Law); **Science and Technology** (Natural Sciences; Technology); **Social Sciences and Education** (Education; Social Sciences)

History: Founded 2003.

Main Language(s) of Instruction: Portuguese

Degrees and Diplomas: *Licenciatura*; *Mestrado*
Last Updated: 03/07/09

JEAN PIAGET UNIVERSITY OF CAPE VERDE
Universidade Jean Piaget de Cabo Verde
Cx Postal 775, Campus Universitário da Cidade da Praía,
Palmarejo Grande, Praia
Tel: +238 262-90-85 +238 260-90-00
Fax: +238 262-90-89 +238 260-90-20
EMail: info@unipiaget.cv
Website: http://www.unipiaget.cv

Reitor: Jorge Sousa Brito EMail: jsb@unipiaget.cv

Administrador Geral: Luis Filipe Lopes Tavares
EMail: eft@unipiaget.cv

Courses
Aerobiological Analysis *(Postgraduate)* (Biology); **Architecture** (Architecture); **Art Education** (Art Education); **Business** **Administration** *(Postgraduate)*; **Business Computing**; **Civil Engineering**; **Clinical Analysis** *(Postgraduate)* (Laboratory Techniques); **Clinical Analysis and Public Health** (Public Health); **Communication Sciences** (Communication Studies); **Computer Engineering** *(Postgraduate)* (Computer Engineering); **Ecology and Development Studies** (Development Studies; Ecology); **Economics and Management** (Economics; Management); **Educational Sciences** (Educational Sciences); **Food Technology** (Food Technology); **Hotel Management and Tourism** (Hotel Management; Tourism); **Law** (Law); **Pharmacotherapeutic Accompanying** (Pharmacology); **Pharmacy** (Pharmacy); **Physiotherapy**; **Portuguese Language Teaching** *(Postgraduate)*; **Psychology** (Psychology); **Public and Autocratic Administration** (Public Administration); **Social Work** (Social Work); **Sociology** (Sociology); **Systems Engineering and Computer Engineering** (Computer Engineering; Computer Science; Systems Analysis)

History: Founded 2001.

Main Language(s) of Instruction: Portuguese

Degrees and Diplomas: *Licenciatura*: Architecture; Pharmacy, 5 yrs; *Licenciatura*: Communication Sciences; Educational Sciences; Economics and Management; Social Work; Nursing; Civil Engineering; Computer Engineering; Physics and Chemistry; Mathematics; English; Portuguese; Hotel Management and Tourism; Business Computing; Psychology; Sociology, 4 yrs; *Mestrado*: 2 yrs following Licenciatura; *Doutoramento*: 4 yrs

Libraries: 4,872 vols

Student Numbers *2008-2009*: Total: c. 1,950
Last Updated: 03/06/09

Central African Republic

STRUCTURE OF HIGHER EDUCATION SYSTEM

Description:

Postsecondary education is offered at the Université de Bangui, which is made up of faculties, institutes and a Higher Teacher Training College (Ecole normale supérieure). The Administrative Council, which is presided over by the Minister of Education, Higher Education and Research implements the University's development plan set out by the government. The University Council, presided over by the Rector of the university, approves proposed official documents to be submitted to higher authorities. It is consulted about the regulations, organization and programme of study.

Stages of studies:

University level first stage: Premier cycle
The first cycle lasts for two years. Admission is based on the Baccalauréat. It leads to a degree which bears the name of the specialization in which it is awarded: Diplôme d'Etudes universitaires générales (DEUG), Diplôme universitaire d'Etudes littéraires (DUEL), Diplôme universitaire d'Etudes scientifiques (DUES), Diplôme universitaire d'Etudes juridiques (DUEJ), Diplôme d'Etudes économiques générales (DEEG).

University level second stage: Deuxième cycle
The second cycle lasts for one year after the Diploma programme and leads to the Licence. In Engineering, the Diplôme d'Ingénieur is conferred after a minimum of four years' study.
A further two years after the Licence leads to the Master I/II.
In Medicine, a Doctorate is awarded after six years. It is the only Doctorate awarded by the University.

ADMISSION TO HIGHER EDUCATION

Admission to university-level studies:

Name of secondary school credential required: Baccalauréat

NATIONAL BODIES

Ministère de l'Enseignement supérieur et à la Recherche scientifique (Ministry of Higher Education and Research)
    Minister: Jean Willybiro Sako
    PO Box 35
    Bangui

Data for academic year: 2009-2010
Source: IAU from World Data on Education 2006/07, International Bureau of Education (IBE); Base Curie, Ministère des Affaires étrangères et européennes, France, and documentation, 2009. Bodies, 2011.

INSTITUTIONS

PUBLIC INSTITUTIONS

NATIONAL SCHOOL FOR ADMINISTRATION AND MAGISTRACY

Ecole nationale d'Administration et de Magistrature
BP 1045, Bangui
Tel: +236(61) 08-94 +236(61) 04-88
Fax: +236(61) 27-77 +236(61) 20-78

Directeur: Jean-Marie Yollot

Programmes
Administration and Magistracy (Administration; Economics; Finance; International Relations; Justice Administration; Law)

History: Founded 1962.
Last Updated: 02/07/09

UNIVERSITY OF BANGUI

Université de Bangui
BP 1450, Avenue des Martyrs, Bangui
Tel: +236(61) 20-05
Fax: +236(61) 78-90
EMail: info@univ-bangui.info
Website: http://www.univ-bangui.org

Recteur: Damienne Nanaré Sessou

Campuses
Distance Education *(EUCLID University)* (Arts and Humanities; Business Administration; Cultural Studies; Ethics; Government; Information Technology; International Relations; Theology) *Head*: Emmanuel Touaboy

Faculties
Arts and Humanities (Anthropology; Arts and Humanities; Education; Educational Sciences; English; Geography (Human); History; Modern Languages; Philosophy; Social Sciences; Spanish) *Dean*: Georgette Deballe; **Health Sciences** (Anaesthesiology; Biomedicine; Community Health; Gynaecology and Obstetrics; Health Education; Health Sciences; Laboratory Techniques; Medicine; Midwifery; Nursing; Paediatrics; Public Health; Surgery) *Dean*: Gérard Grésenguet; **Law and Economics** (Economics; Law; Private Law; Public Law) *Dean*: Bernard Voyemakoa; **Science** (Biology; Chemistry; Geology; Mathematics and Computer Science; Physics) *Dean*: Faustin Touadera

Higher Institutes
Business Management *(IUGE)* (Business Administration); **Technology** *(IST)* (Building Technologies; Technology)

Higher Schools
Teacher Training *(Ecole nationale supérieure (ENS))* (Agricultural Education; Agricultural Engineering; Agriculture; Arts and Humanities; Biological and Life Sciences; Cattle Breeding; Earth Sciences; Educational and Student Counselling; Educational Psychology; English; Forestry; Geography; Geography (Human); History; Mathematics; Mathematics Education; Modern Languages; Pedagogy; Physics; Primary Education; Secondary Education; Teacher Training)

Institutes
Applied Linguistics *(ILA)* (Applied Linguistics); **Rural Development** *(ISDR)* (Cattle Breeding; Forestry; Rural Studies)

Further Information: Also 4 other University and Research Centres (History, Traditional Medicine, Pedagogy)

History: Founded 1969. Formerly Institut d'Etudes juridiques of the Fondation de l'Enseignement supérieur en Afrique centrale. Acquired present status 1985.

Governing Bodies: Conseil d'Administration

Academic Year: September to June (September-December; January-March; April-June)

Admission Requirements: Secondary school certificate (Baccalauréat) or special entrance examination

Main Language(s) of Instruction: French

Degrees and Diplomas: *Capacité en Droit*: Law, 2 yrs; *Diplôme universitaire de Technologie (DUT)*: Computer Science, Mining Engineering and Geology, Civil Engineering, Management, Agriculture, 3 yrs; *Diplôme d'Etudes économiques générales (DEEG)*: Law and Economics, 2 yrs; *Diplôme d'Etudes juridiques générales (DEJG)*: Law and Economics, 2 yrs; *Diplôme d'Etudes universitaires générales (DEUG)*: 2 yrs; *Diplôme universitaire d'Etudes littéraires (DUEL)*: 2 yrs; *Diplôme universitaire d'Etudes scientifiques (DUES)*: Science, 2 yrs; *Certificat d'Aptitude pédagogique à l'Enseignement secondaire*; *Diplôme*: Midwifery; Nursing, 3 yrs; *Diplôme de Technicien supérieur de Santé*: 4 yrs; *Diplôme supérieur de Gestion (DSG)*: Management, 3 yrs; *Licence*: Arts and Humanities; Economics; Law; Mathematics; Natural Sciences; Physics, 3 yrs; *Diplôme d'Ingénieur*: 3-4 yrs; *Doctorat en Médecine*: Medicine, 7 yrs; *Master I/II*: Arts and Humanities; Economics; Law, 1 yr following Licence. Also Bachelor (3-4 yrs), Master (1-3 yrs) and Doctor's (2-5 yrs) Degrees through EUCLID University Programmes

Student Residential Facilities: Yes

Libraries: Central Library, 28,000 vols, 600 periodicals; Health Sciences, 5,200 vols, 170 periodicals

Publications: Annales; Revue d'Histoire et d'Archéologie Centrafricaine

Academic Staff *2007-2008*: Total: c. 160
Student Numbers *2007-2008*: Total: c. 6,500
Last Updated: 12/09/11

Chad

STRUCTURE OF HIGHER EDUCATION SYSTEM

Description:

Higher education in Chad is mainly provided by the Université de N'Djaména (former Université du Tchad). There are also other public and private higher education institutions.

Stages of studies:

University level first stage: Premier cycle
The first cycle lasts for two years and leads to a Diplôme d'Etudes universitaires générales in Arts and Humanities, Law and Management, and to a Diplôme universitaire d'Etudes scientifiques in Science.

University level second stage: Deuxième cycle
The second cycle of higher education leads to a Licence after one year's further study in Arts and Humanities, Law and Management, and Science. The Maîtrise is conferred one or two years after the Licence. The University of N'Djamena awards a Doctorate in Medicine after seven years of study.

ADMISSION TO HIGHER EDUCATION

Admission to university-level studies:

Name of secondary school credential required: Baccalauréat

Alternatives to credentials: Special entrance examination to the university instead of secondary school certificate

Foreign students admission:

Entrance exam requirements: Foreign students should hold the Baccalauréat or an equivalent qualification or pass the special entrance examination to the University.

Entry regulations: Students should have a visa and a residence permit.

Language requirements: Good knowledge of French or Arabic is required.

RECOGNITION OF STUDIES

Bodies dealing with recognition:

Commission d'Admission de l'Université de N'Djaména
Recteur: Koina Rodoumta
Vice-Recteur: Zakaria Fadoul Khidir
PO Box 1117
Avenue Mobutu
N'Djaména
Tel: +235 514444
Fax: +235 514033
EMail: recteur@undt.info

NATIONAL BODIES

Ministère de l'Enseignement supérieur, Recherche et Formation professionnelle (Ministry of Higher Education, Research and Professional Training)
Minister: Ahmet Djidda Mahamat
PO Box 743
N'Djamena

Tel: +235 516158

Fax: +235 519231

Role of national body: The Ministry is responsible for the elaboration, coordination, implementation, follow-up of the Government's higher education policy for the public and the private sectors.

Data for academic year: 2007-2008

Source: IAU from the University of N'Djamena, Chad, 2007. Body, 2011.

INSTITUTIONS

PUBLIC INSTITUTIONS

ADAM BARKA UNIVERSITY OF ABÉCHÉ

Université Adam Barka d'Abéché (UNABA)
BP 1173 Route de N'Djamena, Abéché, Ouaddaï
Tel: +235(6) 200-005
Fax: +235(6) 98078
EMail: unaba@intnet.td

Recteur: Mahamat Ali Moustapha (2008-)

Faculties
Arts and Humanities (Arts and Humanities); **Health Sciences** (Health Sciences); **Law and Economics**; **Science and Techniques** (Natural Sciences; Technology)

History: Founded 2003.

Main Language(s) of Instruction: French

Degrees and Diplomas: *Diplôme d'Etudes universitaires générales (DEUG)*; *Licence*; *Maîtrise*
Last Updated: 28/08/09

HIGHER INSTITUTE OF EDUCATION

Institut supérieur des Sciences de l'Education (ISSED)
BP 60, N'Djaména
Tel: +235(51) 4487
Fax: +235(51) 4550
EMail: Issed@intnet.td

Directeur: Kodi Mahamat Tel: +235(51) 6175

Departments
Teacher Trainers Education *Head*: Hamid Mahamat; **Teacher Training for Primary Education** (Education; Educational Administration; Educational Psychology; Primary Education) *Head*: Dingamyo Djedouboum; **Teacher Training for Secondary Education** (Administration; Arabic; Biology; Chemistry; Curriculum; Education; Educational Technology; English; French; Geography; Geology; History; Mathematics; Physics; Secondary Education) *Head*: Bedoumdje Djarangar; **Teacher Training for Technical and Professional Education** (Accountancy; Administration; Finance; Management) *Head*: Baba Abakoura

History: Founded 1992.

Degrees and Diplomas: *Licence*; *Maîtrise*

Special Facilities: Printing workshop. Computer centre
Last Updated: 21/09/09

NATIONAL SCHOOL OF ADMINISTRATION AND MAGISTRACY

Ecole nationale d'Administration et de Magistrature (ENA)
BP 758, N'Djaména
Tel: +235(251) 4097
Fax: +235(251) 4356
EMail: mandigui@yahoo.fr

Directeur Général: Mandigui Yokabdjim
Secrétaire Général: Ahmed Soungui

Departments
Administration (Administration; Business Administration) *Head*: Saleh Baou; **Diplomacy Studies** (International Relations) *Head*: Moussa Dago; **Finance and Economy** (Economics; Finance; Taxation) *Head*: Mahalmat Saleh Ibrahim; **Justice Administration** *Head*: Mokomra Migyana; **Law** (Law); **Technical Studies** (Technology)

History: Founded 1963.

Governing Bodies: Managing Director; Secretary General, Directors; Accountant

Academic Year: October to July

Admission Requirements: Baccalauréat; DEUG; Licence

Main Language(s) of Instruction: French

Degrees and Diplomas: 1st cycle: Attaché d'administration (2 yrs); 2nd cycle: Administrateur civil de 2ème classe (2yrs); 3rd cycle: Inspecteur d'administration générale (2yrs)

Student Services: Health services, Language programs, Sports facilities

Libraries: Yes

Academic Staff 2008-2009	MEN	WOMEN	TOTAL
FULL-TIME	2	2	4
PART-TIME	35	2	37
STAFF WITH DOCTORATE			
FULL-TIME	–	–	2
PART-TIME	–	–	9
Student Numbers 2008-2009			
All (Foreign Included)	121	15	136

Last Updated: 08/07/09

NATIONAL SCHOOL OF CIVIL ENGINEERING

Ecole nationale des Travaux publics (ENTP)
BP 60, N'Djaména
Tel: +235(252) 3420
EMail: entp@intnet.td

Directeur: Koina Rodoumta

Programmes
Civil Engineering (Civil Engineering; Construction Engineering; Rural Planning; Town Planning)

History: Founded 1966.

Degrees and Diplomas: *Diplôme d'Ingénieur*
Last Updated: 21/09/09

UNIVERSITY INSTITUTE OF AGRONOMY AND ENVIRONMENTAL SCIENCES OF SARH

Institut universitaire des Sciences agronomiques et de l'Environnement de Sarh (IUSAES)
BP 105, Sarh, Moyen Chari
Tel: +235(68) 1097
EMail: nguemadjingaye@yahoo.fr

Directeur général: Hougoto Nguemadjingaye

Programmes
Agronomy (Agronomy); **Environmental Sciences** (Environmental Studies)

History: Founded 1997.

Degrees and Diplomas: *Diplôme d'Ingénieur*
Last Updated: 21/09/09

UNIVERSITY INSTITUTE OF BUSINESS TECHNIQUES OF MOUNDOU

Institut universitaire des Techniques d'Entreprise de Moundou (IUTEM)
BP 206, Moundou, Logone occidental
Website: http://www.td.refer.org/partenaires/IUTEM/index.htm

Directeur Général: Ndoassem ar Doumnelng

Departments
Accountancy and Finance (Accountancy; Finance; Management); **Business Techniques** (Business Administration); **Management Computing** (Management)

History: Founded 2002.

Degrees and Diplomas: *Licence*; *Diplôme d'Ingénieur*. 3 yrs
Last Updated: 03/05/07

UNIVERSITY INSTITUTE OF SCIENCE AND TECHNOLOGY OF ABÉCHÉ

Institut universitaire des Sciences et Techniques d'Abéché (IUSTA)
BP 6077, Abéché, Ouaddaï
Tel: +235(55) 16564
EMail: mahamat.abakar@univ-st-etienne.fr
Website: http://iusta-tchad.org/presentation.html

Directeur Général: Mahamout Youssouf Khayal
EMail: aodt2004@yahoo.fr

Departments
Biomedical and Pharmaceutical Sciences (Biomedicine; Pharmacy); **Electrical and Mechanical Engineering** (Computer Science; Electrical Engineering; Mechanical Engineering); **Industrial Computing and Management** (Computer Science; Industrial Management); **Livestock Techniques** (Cattle Breeding)

History: Founded 1997.

Main Language(s) of Instruction: French

Degrees and Diplomas: *Licence*; *Diplôme d'Ingénieur*. 3 yrs. Also Master 1 and Master 2
Last Updated: 21/05/07

⏛ UNIVERSITY OF N'DJAMENA

Université de N'Djaména (UNDJ/UNDT)
BP 1117, Avenue Mobutu, N'Djaména
Tel: +(235) 22-51-44-44
Fax: +(235) 22-51-40-33
EMail: info@undt.info
Website: http://www.undt.info/

Recteur: Malloum Soultan (2008-)
Tel: +(235) 66-29-05-41, Fax: +(235) 22-51-40-33
EMail: rector@undt.info; malloum.soultan@gmail.com

Chef de Service de Relations publiques et protocole: Mahamat Saleh Ali Tel: +235(251) 8751 EMail: salehgarmoudi@yahoo.fr

International Relations: Gilbert Lawane, Chef du Service des Affaires académiques et de la Coopération internationale
EMail: lawane@undt.info; lawanegilbert@yahoo.fr

Faculties
Arts and Humanities (Arabic; Arts and Humanities; Communication Studies; English; Geography; History; Linguistics; Modern Languages; Philosophy; Social Sciences; Sociology); **Exact and Applied Sciences** (Biology; Chemistry; Computer Science; Geology; Hydraulic Engineering; Mathematics; Paleontology; Physics); **Health Sciences** (Biological and Life Sciences; Gynaecology and Obstetrics; Medicine; Paediatrics; Public Health; Surgery); **Law and Economics** (Economics; Law; Management; Private Law; Public Law)

Institutes
Rural Planning *(Observatoire Foncier du Tchad)* (Natural Resources; Rural Planning; Social Sciences; Soil Management)

History: Founded 1971 as University of Chad. Comprising institutions that were formerly part of the Fondation de l'Enseignement supérieur en Afrique Centrale. Acquired present status and title 1994.

Governing Bodies: Conseil de l'Université, comprising Government representatives and members of the academic staff and student body.

Academic Year: October to June (October-February; March-June).

Admission Requirements: Secondary school certificate (baccalauréat).

Fees: (CFA Francs): 40,000 per annum

Main Language(s) of Instruction: French, Arabic, English (Distance programmes).

International Co-operation: With universities in France, Belgium, Italy

Accrediting Agencies: Ministry of Higher Education, Scientific Research and Professional Training

Degrees and Diplomas: *Diplôme d'Etudes universitaires générales (DEUG):* Arts and Humanities, Science, 2 yrs; *Diplôme universitaire d'Etudes scientifiques (DUES):* Science, 2 yrs; *Licence:* Arts and Humanities; Science; Law, 3 yrs; *Diplôme d'Ingénieur:* Engineering; Technology, 5 yrs; *Doctorat en Médecine:* Medicine, 7 yrs; *Maîtrise:* Arts and Humanities; Science; Law, 4 yrs. Also Licence Professionnelle, Maîtrise Professionnelle and Certificates.

Student Services: Academic counselling, Canteen, Cultural centre, Health services, Nursery care, Sports facilities

Libraries: University Documentation Centre, 43 700 vols

Publications: Annales de l'Universite de N'Djaména, Arts and Humanities; Medicine; Science; Social Sciences; Law; Economics *(biannually)*

Academic Staff 2008-2009	MEN	WOMEN	TOTAL
FULL-TIME	–	–	353
Student Numbers 2008-2009			
All (Foreign Included)	6,039	1,196	7,235
FOREIGN ONLY	–	–	28

Last Updated: 05/06/09

UNIVERSITY POLYTECHNIC INSTITUTE OF MONGO

Institut universitaire polytechnique de Mongo (IUPM)
Route d'Aboudéa, Mongo, Guera
Tel: +235(51) 8064
EMail: iupm@intnet.td
Website: http://iupm-tchad.org/entre.htm

Directeur: Mahamat Barka (2003-)

Departments
Basic Sciences (Natural Sciences); **Chemical Engineering** (Chemical Engineering); **Civil Engineering** (Civil Engineering); **Geology; Industrial Maintenance; Mechanical Engineering** (Mechanical Engineering)

History: Founded 2002.

Degrees and Diplomas: *Licence*; *Diplôme d'Ingénieur*
Last Updated: 21/05/07

PRIVATE INSTITUTIONS

KING FAYÇAL UNIVERSITY

Université Roi Fayçal (URF)
N'Djaména
EMail: info@urfchad.org

Faculties
Computer Engineering and Information Technology; Graduate Studies; Law; Management; Modern Languages (Modern Languages); **Pedagogy** (Pedagogy)

History: Founded 1992.

Main Language(s) of Instruction: Arabic
Last Updated: 21/05/07

Chile

STRUCTURE OF HIGHER EDUCATION SYSTEM

Description:

Higher education is provided by universities, professional institutes and technical training centres. The Higher Education Division of the Ministry of Education is responsible for planning and implementing policies and funds allocation in higher education. The main coordinating bodies are the Council of Rectors of Chilean Universities (Consejo de Rectores de Universidades Chilenas) which coordinates the traditional state and private universities which were created before the 1980's reform and those derived from these, and the Council for Higher Education (Consejo Superior de Educación) which is responsible for the assessment and accreditation of other private universities. The Council of Rectors requires to take the university selection test (prueba de selección universitaria, PSU) for higher education admission.

The test is also used by many other HEIs. Higher education relies on direct (only for the universities under the Council of Rectors), indirect (for public and private universities according to their PSU results), competitive (for outstanding research, innovation, quality and equity results) and student-aid (student loans and fellowships) funds. The 2005 law (No. 20.027) establishes a need- and merit-based government guaranteed student loan system for all accredited institutions.

Stages of studies:

University level first stage: *Técnico, Bachiller*
Some universities offer technical training programmes leading to the title of higher education technician. They usually last for four semesters and give access to a profession. Some universities offer courses leading to the Bachiller academic degree, which is an intermediate academic qualification before following studies leading to a Licenciatura or professional title. They usually last for four semesters and do not give access to a profession.

University level second stage: *Licenciatura, Professional title*
The Licenciatura is an academic degree that is sometimes needed as a prior stage to the Professional title (it applies to courses defined as "university courses" by LOCE). Courses length vary from four to seven years. The Professional title is not an academic degree but entitles its holder to exercise a profession.

University level third stage: *Magister*
Students holding the Licenciatura or the Professional title may be awarded a Magister degree after two years' further study.

University level fourth stage: *Doctorado*
The Doctorado takes between three and five years usually beyond the Magister. Candidates must submit a thesis.

ADMISSION TO HIGHER EDUCATION

Admission to university-level studies:

Name of secondary school credential required: Licencia de Educación Media

Entrance exam requirements: The universities under the Council of Rectors legally require students to take the University Selection Test (prueba de selección universitaria, PSU) to enter higher education. This test has also been adopted by other HEIs, especially private ones.

Other admission requirements: Sometimes, students must take a specific entrance examination, as for example in Psychology, Theatre, Dentistry or Medicine.

Foreign students admission:

Entrance exam requirements: Foreign students must have completed their secondary education to be admitted to university. Each higher education institution is free to set up its entrance requirements for foreign students.

RECOGNITION OF STUDIES

Quality assurance system:

The national system of higher education quality assurance provided by the National Accreditation Committee (CNA) was put into place in 2006. The CNA is responsible for licensing, institutional accreditation, course/program accreditation, and information.

Bodies dealing with recognition:

University of Chile

Av. Bernardo O'Higgins 1058, Oficina N° 123
Santiago
Tel: +56(2) 978 1123
Fax: +56(2) 978 1032
EMail: msaldias@uchile.cl
Services provided and students dealt with: The University of Chile is the body that recognize and validate qualifications obtained abroad, taking into account the provisions of international treaties.

NATIONAL BODIES

Ministerio de Educación (Ministry of Education)

Minister: Felipe Bulnes Serrano
Director, Higher Education: Juan José Ugarte
Alameda 1371
Santiago
Tel: +56(2) 390 4000
EMail: consultas@mineduc.cl
WWW: http://www.mineduc.cl
Role of national body: Development of education at all levels. At higher education level, responsible for policy development and implementation, allocation of higher education public funds, and student financial support.

Consejo Nacional de Educación - CNED (National Council for Education)

Executive Secretary: Daniela Torre Griggs
Marchant Pereira 844,
Providencia
Santiago
Tel: +56(2) 341 3412
Fax: +56(2) 225 4616
WWW: http://www.cned.cl/
Role of national body: Independent public body in charge of the accreditation of higher education institutions.

Comisión Nacional de Acreditación - CNA (National Accreditation Committee)

Executive Secretary: Patricio Basso Gallo
Avenida Ricardo Lyon 1532, Providencia
Santiago
Tel: +56(2) 620 1100
Fax: +56(2) 620 1120
EMail: contacto@cnachile.cl
WWW: http://www.cnachile.cl
Role of national body: Public body established to take over the management and coordination of the quality assurance system whose function is to verify and improve the quality of universities, professional institutes and technical training centres, as well as the courses and programs they offer.

Consejo de Rectores de Universidades Chilenas - CRUCH (Rectors' Conference)

President; Minister of Education: Felipe Bulne Serrano
Secretaria General: María Teresa Marshall Infante
Alameda 1371, piso 4
Santiago

Tel: +56(2) 696 4286
Fax: +56(2) 698 8436
EMail: cruch@consejoderectores.cl
WWW: http://www.consejoderectores.cl
Role of national body: The Rectors' Council is a legal entity created in 1954 as the coordination body for public universities. It is chaired by the Minister of Education.

Data for academic year: 2006-2007
Source: IAU from the Higher Education Division, Ministry of Education, Chile, 2006. Bodies updated in 2011.

INSTITUTIONS

PUBLIC INSTITUTIONS

ARTURO PRAT UNIVERSITY
Universidad Arturo Prat
Avenida Arturo Prat 2120, Iquique
Tel: +56(57) 394-444
Fax: +56(57) 441-009
EMail: admision@unap.cl
Website: http://www.unap.cl

Rector: Gustavo Soto Bringas
Tel: +56(57) 441-208 EMail: carlos.merino@unap.cl

Secretario General: Nelson Martínez Arredondo

Departments
Audit and Information Systems (Accountancy; Computer Science; Information Management; Information Sciences) *Director*: Sergio Echeverry Gutiérrez; **Chemistry** (Chemistry; Pharmacy) *Director*: Elia Soto Sanhueza; **Desert Studies** (Agronomy; Arid Land Studies) *Director*: Álvaro Carevic Rivera; **Economics and Administration** (Administration; Business Administration; Business and Commerce; Economics; Management; Marketing; Tourism) *Director*: Aldo Chipoco Jorquera; **Education and Humanities** (Arts and Humanities; Computer Science; Education; English; Preschool Education; Public Relations; Translation and Interpretation) *Director*: María Verónica Frias Pistono; **Engineering** (Civil Engineering; Computer Engineering; Computer Science; Engineering; Industrial Engineering; Metallurgical Engineering; Mineralogy) *Director*: Jaime Tapia Quezada; **Marine Science** (Aquaculture; Fishery; Marine Biology; Marine Science and Oceanography) *Director*: Rosalindo Fuenzalida Fuenzalida; **Physics and Mathematics** (Mathematics; Physics; Sound Engineering (Acoustics)) *Director*: Carlos Anch Chang; **Social Sciences** *Director*: Juan Podestá Arzubiaga

Institutes
Andine Studies *(Isluga)* (Regional Studies) *Director*: Jorge Iván Vergara del Solar; **Health Studies** *Director*: Julio Brito Richards; **International Studies** (Asian Studies; International Studies; Latin American Studies; Pacific Area Studies) *Executive Director*: Sergio González Miranda

Schools
Architecture (Architecture) *Director*: José María Sobrado; **Law** (Law) *Director*: Jorge Tapia Valdés; **Nursing** *Director*: Ximena Ibarra Mendoza

Units
Physical Education *Director*: Sergio Araya Sierralta

History: Founded 1967. Previously regional branch of University of Chile and Instituto Profesional. A State institution.

Governing Bodies: Junta Directiva (Board of Trustees); Consejo Académico

Academic Year: March to December (March-July; August-December)

Admission Requirements: Secondary school certificate (Licencia de Educación Media) and entrance examination

Main Language(s) of Instruction: Spanish

Degrees and Diplomas: *Técnico de Nivel Superior*; *Licenciatura*: Education, 2 yrs; *Licenciatura*: Marine Sciences; Teaching qualifications, 5 yrs; *Magister*; *Título Profesional*: Accountancy and Auditing; Business Administration, 4 yrs; *Título Profesional*: Biology, 5 yrs; *Título Profesional*: Engineering, 4-6 yrs; *Título Profesional*: Statistics, 5 1/2 yrs

Special Facilities: Museum of Anthropology

Libraries: Central Library, c. 16,000 vols; Marine Sciences, c. 2,000

Publications: Colosos de Iquique *(annually)*; Nuestro Norte *(quarterly)*

Press or Publishing House: University Press

ARICA BRANCH
SEDE ARICA
Avenida Santa María 2998, Arica
Tel: +56(58) 261-520
Fax: +56(58) 261-520

Director: Marcelo Urrutia Aldunate
Tel: +56(58) 247-009, Fax: +56(58) 247-009

Programmes
Business Administration
Main Language(s) of Instruction: Spanish

CALAMA BRANCH
SEDE CALAMA
Esmeralda 1810, Calama
Tel: +56(55) 360-800
Fax: +56(55) 360-800
Website: http://www.unap.cl/calama

Directora: Susana Jopia Aguirre

Departments
Accountancy and Audit; **Basic Education Pedagogy**
Main Language(s) of Instruction: Spanish

SANTIAGO BRANCH
SEDE SANTIAGO
Bandera 620, Santiago
Tel: +56(2) 636-6100
Fax: +56(2) 636-6100
Website: http://www.unap.cl/santiago

Director: Enrique Díaz V.

Programmes
Accountancy (Accountancy); **Basic Education Pedagogy** (Pedagogy); **Bilingual Public Relations** (Public Relations);

Business Administration (Business Administration); **Commercial Engineering** (Business and Commerce); **English-Spanish Translation**; **Industrial Civil Engineering** (Civil Engineering; Industrial Engineering); **Management** (Management); **Optics** (Optics); **Pre-school Education**; **Risk Prevention** (Safety Engineering); **Tourism**

History: Founded 1995.

Main Language(s) of Instruction: Spanish

VICTORIA BRANCH
SEDE VICTORIA

Avenida O'Higgins 0195, Victoria
Tel: +56(45) 841-464
Fax: +56(45) 849-019
Website: http://www.unapvic.cl

Vicerrector: Manuel Sobera Gutiérrez EMail: msobera@unapvic.cl

Programmes
Accountancy; **Basic Education Pedagogy**; **Commercial Engineering**; **Computer Engineering**; **Environmental Management** (Environmental Management); **Forestry Engineering**; **Risk Prevention** (Safety Engineering)

Main Language(s) of Instruction: Spanish

Degrees and Diplomas: *Título Profesional*

METROPOLITAN UNIVERSITY OF EDUCATIONAL SCIENCES
Universidad Metropolitana de Ciencias de la Educación (UMCE)
Avenida José Pedro Alessandri 774 Casilla 1487, Correo Central, Santiago
Tel: +56(2) 241-2725
Fax: +56(2) 241-2723
EMail: prensa@umce.cl
Website: http://www.umce.cl

Rector: Jaime Espinoza Araya
Tel: +56(2) 241-2408, Fax: +56(2) 241-2605
EMail: rector@umce.cl

Rector: Ramiro Aguilar Baldomar
Tel: +56(2) 241-2402, Fax: +56(2) 239-3932

International Relations: José Martínez Armesto
Tel: +56(2) 241-2528

Faculties
Arts and Physical Education (Arts and Humanities; Music Education; Painting and Drawing; Physical Education; Physical Therapy; Sculpture; Sports; Sports Management); **History, Geography, and Letters** (Arts and Humanities; Classical Languages; English; French; Geography; German; History); **Philosophy and Education** (Education; Pedagogy; Philosophy; Preschool Education; Religion; Special Education; Teacher Training); **Science** (Biology; Chemistry; Entomology; Natural Sciences; Physics)

Institutes
Entomology (Entomology)

Further Information: Campuses Rectoría, Defder (Santiago) and Rancagua. Regional Branch in Graneros

History: Founded 1986. Previously Institute of Education of University of Chile (1889) and Academia Superior de Ciencias Pedagógicas (1980). A State institution.

Governing Bodies: Junta Directiva (Board of Trustees); Consejo Académico

Academic Year: March to December (March-July; August-December)

Admission Requirements: Secondary school certificate (Licencia de Educación Media) and entrance examination

Main Language(s) of Instruction: Spanish

Degrees and Diplomas: *Técnico de Nivel Medio*; *Licenciatura*; *Licenciatura*: Teaching qualifications, 4-5 yrs; *Magister*: Curriculum; Educational Administration; Educational Testing and Evaluation, 2 1/2 yrs; *Magister*: Entomology; Physical Education; *Doctorado*

Student Services: Academic counselling, Cultural centre, Employment services, Health services, Nursery care, Social counselling, Sports facilities

Libraries: c. 60,000 vols

Publications: Acta Entomológica Chilena *(annually)*; Dimensión Histórica de Chile *(annually)*; Revista Contextos *(biannually)*; Revista Educación Física Chile *(quarterly)*; Revista Limes *(annually)*

Last Updated: 24/03/10

METROPOLITAN UNIVERSITY OF TECHNOLOGY
Universidad Tecnológica Metropolitana (UTEM)
Dieciocho no 161, Santiago
Tel: +56(2) 787-7500
Fax: +56(2) 696-2946
EMail: rectoria@utem.cl
Website: http://www.utem.cl

Rector: Luis Pinto Faverio
Tel: +56(2) 696-4123, Fax: +56(2) 688-1421

Secretario General: Patricio Bastías Román
Tel: +56(2) 688-4899, Fax: +56(2) 699-4722
EMail: secgral@utem.cl

International Relations: Alejandro Velásquez Soto
Tel: +56(2) 787-7655, Fax: +56(2) 787-7515 EMail: relint@utem.cl

Centres
Public Policy (Government; Political Sciences); **UTEM Virtual** (Distance Education)

Faculties
Administration and Economics (Accountancy; Administration; Agricultural Management; Business Administration; Documentation Techniques; Economic and Finance Policy; Economics; Finance; Human Resources; Industrial Management; International Business; International Economics; Library Science; Management; Tourism); **Construction and Regional Planning** (Architecture and Planning; Civil Engineering; Construction Engineering; Regional Planning; Safety Engineering; Town Planning); **Engineering** (Civil Engineering; Computer Engineering; Computer Science; Electronic Engineering; Engineering; Industrial Engineering; Measurement and Precision Engineering; Mechanical Engineering; Transport Engineering); **Humanities and Social Communication Technology** (Communication Studies; Design; Humanities and Social Science Education; Social Work); **Natural Sciences, Mathematics and Environmental Studies** (Chemistry; Environmental Studies; Industrial Chemistry; Mathematics and Computer Science; Natural Sciences)

Further Information: Also San Fernando, Dieciocho, Almirante Latorre, Macul and Providencia (Santiago) branches

History: Founded 1981 as Professional Institute of Santiago, acquired present status and title 1993.

Governing Bodies: Consejo Superior

Academic Year: March to December

Admission Requirements: Secondary school certificate (Licencia de Educación Média) and entrance examination (Prueba de Selección Universitaria)

Fees: (Chilean Pesos): 120,000 per month

Main Language(s) of Instruction: Spanish

Degrees and Diplomas: *Licenciatura*: 4 yrs; *Magister*: 2 yrs; *Post-títulos/ Diploma*: 1 yr; *Título Profesional*: 5-6 yrs

Student Services: Academic counselling, Canteen, Cultural centre, Employment services, Foreign student adviser, Health services, Language programs, Social counselling, Sports facilities

Special Facilities: Auditorium

Libraries: 3 general libraries. 1 specialized library

Publications: Revista Trilogía *(quarterly)*
Last Updated: 24/03/10

UNIVERSITY OF ANTOFAGASTA

Universidad de Antofagasta (UA)
Avenida Angamos 601, Casilla 170, Antofagasta
Tel: +56(55) 637-149
Fax: +56(55) 637-102
EMail: webmaster@uantof.cl
Website: http://www.uantof.cl

Rector: Luis Alberto Loyola MoralesFax: +56(55) 637-183

Secretaria General: Macarena Silva Boggiano
Tel: +56(55) 637-121

Faculties
Basic Sciences *(Coloso)* (Chemistry; Mathematics; Natural Sciences; Physics) *Dean*: Guillermo Mondaca Ortiz; **Education and Humanities** *(Coloso)* (Arts and Humanities; Business Administration; Education; Educational Sciences; Graphic Arts; Pedagogy; Private Administration; Public Administration; Social Work; Teacher Training; Technology; Welfare and Protective Services) *Dean*: Carlos Wormald Díaz; **Engineering** *(Coloso)* (Chemical Engineering; Chemistry; Electrical and Electronic Engineering; Electrical Engineering; Electronic Engineering; Engineering; Industrial Engineering; Measurement and Precision Engineering; Mechanical Engineering; Mining Engineering; Systems Analysis) *Dean*: Marco Crutchik Norambuena; **Health Sciences** *(Coloso)* (Dentistry; Gynaecology and Obstetrics; Health Sciences; Medical Technology; Medicine; Microbiology; Nursing; Paediatrics; Parasitology; Rehabilitation and Therapy) *Dean*: Marcos Cikutovic Salas; **Judicial Sciences** *(Coloso)* (Law) *Dean*: Patricio Lazo González; **Marine Studies** *(Coloso)* (Agriculture; Aquaculture; Ecology; Environmental Studies; Fishery; Food Science; Marine Science and Oceanography; Natural Sciences) *Dean*: Luis Tapia Méndez; **Medicine and Dentistry** (Dentistry; Medicine) *Dean*: Alex Arroyo Meneses

Institutes
Anthropology *(Coloso)* (Anthropology) *Director*: Alejandro Bustos Cortes; **Oceanology** *(Coloso)* (Ecology; Marine Science and Oceanography; Natural Sciences) *Director*: Marcelo Oliva; **Renewable Natural Resources** *(Coloso)* (Natural Resources) *Director*: Patricio Morales

History: Founded 1981, incorporating previous regional branches at Antofagasta of the University of Chile and the Technical State University .

Governing Bodies: Consejo Académico

Academic Year: March to December (March-July; August-December)

Admission Requirements: Secondary school certificate (Licencia de Educación Media) and entrance examination

Main Language(s) of Instruction: Spanish

Degrees and Diplomas: *Técnico de Nivel Superior*; *Licenciatura*: Health Sciences; Education; Administration; Engineering, 4-7 yrs; *Magister*: Engineering, 2 yrs; *Título Profesional*: 3-7 yrs; *Doctorado*

Student Services: Health services, Social counselling, Sports facilities

Student Residential Facilities: Yes

Libraries: Central Library; Health Sciences Library; Marine Studies Library; Anthropology Library

Publications: Estudios Oceanológicos; Innovación *(biennially)*
Last Updated: 04/03/09

UNIVERSITY OF ATACAMA

Universidad de Atacama (UDA)
Casilla 240, Avenida Copayapu 485, Copiapó
Tel: +56(52) 206-500
Fax: +56(52) 206-504
Website: http://www.uda.cl

Rector: Juan Iglesias Díaz Tel: +56(52) 206-503

Faculties
Engineering (Business and Commerce; Computer Science; Engineering; Geology; Industrial Engineering; Marketing; Metallurgical Engineering; Mining Engineering) *Dean*: Cesar Arias Mora; **Humanities and Education** (Arts and Humanities; Education; English; Physical Education; Preschool Education; Spanish) *Dean*: Oscar Painéan Bustamante; **Law** (Law; Private Law; Public Law) *Dean*:

Rodrigo Pérez Lisicic; **Natural Sciences** (Biology; Chemistry; Earth Sciences; Health Education; Marine Science and Oceanography; Natural Sciences; Nursing; Physics) *Dean*: René Maurelia Gómez.

Institutes
Technology (Automation and Control Engineering; Business Administration; Civil Engineering; Computer Engineering; Computer Networks; Industrial Maintenance; Instrument Making; Metallurgical Engineering; Technology) *Director*: Timur Padilla Bocic

Further Information: Campuses in Caldera, Vallenar, Los Andes and Santiago

History: Founded 1857 as School of Mining and became regional branch of State Technical University 1947. Became independent and acquired present status and title 1981. An autonomous institution financially supported by the State. Teacher education started in the Normal School of Copiapó 1905.

Governing Bodies: Junta Directiva (Board of Trustees)

Academic Year: March to December (March-June; August-December)

Admission Requirements: Secondary school certificate (Licencia de Educación Media) and entrance examination

Main Language(s) of Instruction: Spanish

Degrees and Diplomas: *Licenciatura*: Teaching qualification; *Magister*: a further 2 yrs; *Título Profesional*: Engineering; Geology, 6 yrs; *Título Profesional*: Law, 5 yrs

Student Residential Facilities: For c. 250 male and 80 female students

Special Facilities: Mineralogical Museum of Copiapó

Publications: Revista de Ingeniera *(annually)*

Press or Publishing House: Editorial de la Universidad de Atacama
Last Updated: 05/03/09

UNIVERSITY OF BÍO BÍO

Universidad del Bío Bío (UBB)
Avenida Collao 1202, Casilla 5-C, Concepción
Tel: +56(41) 261-200
Fax: +56(41) 313-897
EMail: postmaster@ubiobio.cl
Website: http://www.ubiobio.cl

Rector: Héctor Gaete Feres
Tel: +56(41) 261-201, Fax: +56(41) 316-737
EMail: hgaete@ubiobio.cl

Prorrectora: Gloria Gómez Vera
Tel: +56(41) 275-127, Fax: +56(41) 275-127
EMail: ggomez@ubiobio.cl

Faculties
Architecture, Construction and Design (Architecture; Building Technologies; Construction Engineering; Design; Graphic Design; Industrial Design; Visual Arts) *Dean*: Iván Cartes Siade; **Business Administration** (Accountancy; Administration; Business Administration; Commercial Law; Computer Engineering; Computer Science; Information Sciences; Marketing; Sanitary Engineering) *Dean*: Héctor Saldía Barahona; **Education and Humanities** (Arts and Humanities; Communication Studies; Education; Educational Sciences; English; Geography; History; Pedagogy; Preschool Education; Primary Education; Social Sciences; Social Work; Spanish; Translation and Interpretation) *Dean*: Marco Aurelio Reyes Coca; **Engineering** (Civil Engineering; Electrical and Electronic Engineering; Engineering; Engineering Management; Forestry; Industrial Engineering; Mechanical Engineering; Wood Technology) *Dean*: Peter Backhouse Erazo; **Health and Food Sciences** *(Chillán)* *Dean*: Nora Plaza Ceballos; **Science** (Chemistry; Computer Science; Mathematics; Natural Sciences; Physics; Statistics) *Dean*: Mauricio Cataldo Monsalves

Schools
Nursing (Nursing) *Director*: Gladys Vásquez

History: Founded 1988 and incorporated Instituto Profesional de Chillán.

Governing Bodies: Junta Directiva, comprising 8 members

Academic Year: March to December (March-July; August-December)

Admission Requirements: Secondary school certificate (Licencia de Enseñanza Media) or recognized equivalent, and entrance examination

Fees: (Chilean Pesos): 800,000-1.1m.

Main Language(s) of Instruction: Spanish

Accrediting Agencies: Consejo de Rectores de Universidades Chilenas

Degrees and Diplomas: *Licenciatura:* Teaching Qualification; *Magister:* Wood Science, a further 1 1/2 yrs; *Post- títulos/ Diploma; Título Profesional:* Accountancy; Business Administration; Engineering; Nutrition, 4 yrs; *Título Profesional:* Architecture; Civil Engineering; Computer Science; Forestry, 6 yrs; *Título Profesional:* Construction and Wood Science; Food Technology; Graphic Design, 5 yrs; *Doctorado*

Student Services: Academic counselling, Cultural centre, Foreign student adviser, Health services, Language programs, Nursery care, Social counselling, Sports facilities

Special Facilities: Music Conservatory

Libraries: Two main libraries

Publications: Maderas: Ciencia y Tecnología, Scientific journal in Wood Science *(biannually)*; Teoría, Scientific journal *(annually)*
Last Updated: 06/03/09

UNIVERSITY OF CHILE
Universidad de Chile
Avenida Bernardo O'Higgins 1058, Casilla 10-D, Santiago
Tel: +56(2) 678-2000
Fax: +56(2) 678-1012
Website: http://www.uchile.cl

Rector: Victor L. Pérez Vera (2006-)

Prorrector: Jorge Las Heras EMail: jlashera@med.uchile.cl

International Relations: Soledad Rodriguez, Directora
EMail: srodrigu@uchile.cl

Faculties
Agriculture (Agricultural Engineering; Agriculture; Agronomy; Animal Husbandry; Aquaculture; Biotechnology; Crop Production; Food Science; Food Technology; Forestry; Fruit Production; Natural Resources; Nutrition; Veterinary Science) *Dean:* Antonio Lizana; **Architecture and Town Planning** (Architecture; Design; Geography; Graphic Design; Industrial Design; Landscape Architecture; Regional Planning; Rural Planning; Social Welfare; Town Planning) *Dean:* Julio Chesta; **Chemistry and Pharmacy** (Biochemistry; Chemistry; Food Science; Pharmacy) *Dean:* Luis Nuñez; **Dentistry** (Dental Technology; Dentistry; Oral Pathology; Periodontics) *Dean:* Julio Ramírez; **Economics and Administration** (Accountancy; Administration; Business Administration; Economics; Finance; Management; Public Administration) *Dean:* Felipe Morandé; **Fine Arts** (Art History; Art Management; Art Therapy; Arts and Humanities; Ceramic Art; Computer Education; Dance; Engraving; Heritage Preservation; Jewelry Art; Multimedia; Music; Music Education; Music Theory and Composition; Musicology; Painting and Drawing; Photography; Restoration of Works of Art; Sculpture; Sound Engineering (Acoustics); Textile Design; Theatre; Visual Arts) *Dean:* Pablo Oyarzún; **Forestry** *Dean:* Javier González; **Law** (Commercial Law; Fiscal Law; International Law; Law; Private Law; Public Law) *Dean:* Roberto Nahum Anuch; **Medicine** (Biochemistry; Biological and Life Sciences; Biology; Biophysics; Child Care and Development; Diabetology; Dietetics; Epidemiology; Ethics; Gerontology; Gynaecology and Obstetrics; Haematology; Health Administration; Medicine; Nursing; Occupational Therapy; Otorhinolaryngology; Paediatrics; Physical Therapy; Psychiatry and Mental Health; Public Health; Social and Preventive Medicine; Speech Therapy and Audiology; Statistics; Urology) *Dean:* Cecilia Sepúlveda; **Philosophy and Humanities** (Arts and Humanities; Cognitive Sciences; English; English Studies; Ethics; Ethnology; History; Latin American Studies; Linguistics; Literature; Media Studies; Metaphysics; Philosophy; Spanish) *Dean:* Jorge Hidalgo; **Physics and Mathematics** (Applied Mathematics; Astronomy and Space Science; Automation and Control Engineering; Biomedical Engineering; Biotechnology; Business Administration; Chemical Engineering; Civil Engineering; Computer Engineering; Construction Engineering; Econometrics; Electrical Engineering; Engineering; Environmental Engineering; Geology; Geophysics; History; Hydraulic Engineering; Industrial Engineering; Materials Engineering; Mathematics; Mechanical

Engineering; Metallurgical Engineering; Mining Engineering; Multimedia; Physics; Structural Architecture; Transport Engineering) *Dean:* Francisco Brieva; **Science** (Biology; Biotechnology; Chemistry; Ecology; Environmental Studies; Mathematics; Molecular Biology; Natural Sciences; Physics) *Dean:* Raúl Morales; **Social Sciences** (Anthropology; Archaeology; Communication Studies; Computer Education; Curriculum; Development Studies; Education; Gerontology; Journalism; Preschool Education; Psychology; Social Sciences; Sociology) *Dean:* Marcelo Arnold; **Veterinary Medicine and Stockraising** (Animal Husbandry; Cattle Breeding; Meat and Poultry; Social and Preventive Medicine; Veterinary Science) *Dean:* Hector Alcaino

Institutes
International Studies (American Studies; International Relations; International Studies) *Director:* José Morandé; **Nutrition and Food Technology** *(Postgraduate (INTA))* (Food Science; Food Technology; Genetics; Nutrition; Public Health) *Director:* Fernando Vio del Río; **Public Affairs** (American Studies; International Relations; Political Sciences; Public Administration) *Dean:* Carlos Miranda

Further Information: Also Clinical Hospital

History: Founded 1738 by Philip V of Spain as Universidad de San Felipe. Replaced by present institution 1839, present title adopted 1842. Acquired present autonomous status 1931.

Governing Bodies: Consejo Universitario, comprising 36 members

Academic Year: March to December (March-July; August-December)

Admission Requirements: Secondary school certificate (Licencia de Educación Media) and entrance examination

Main Language(s) of Instruction: Spanish

International Co-operation: Total of 117 cooperation agreements

Degrees and Diplomas: *Licenciatura:* Accountancy; Agriculture; Anthropology; Architecture; Biochemistry; Biology; Biotechnology Engineering; Business Administration; Chemical Engineering; Chemistry; Chemistry and Pharmacy; Dentistry; Design; Economics; Education; Engineering; Food Science; Forestry; Geography; Geology; Geophysics; History; Industrial Engineering; Language and Literature; Law and Social Sciences; Materials Engineering; Mathematics; Mathematics Engineering; Mechanical Engineering; Medical Technology; Midwifery; Mining Engineering; Music; Music Theory; Musical Instruments; Natural Sciences; Nursing; Nutrition; Obstetrics; Occupational Therapy; Pharmacy; Philosophy; Physical Therapy; Physics; Plastic Arts; Psychology; Public Administration; Science; Social Communication; Sociology; Speech Therapy and Audiology; Stage Design; Theatre; Veterinary Medicine, 4 yrs; *Licenciatura:* Art History; Theory and History of Art, 5 yrs; *Licenciatura:* Fine Arts; Medicine; Performing Arts, 4-5 yrs; *Magister; Post- títulos/ Diploma; Título Profesional:* Accountancy; Acting; Administration; Agronomy; Anthropology; Biology; Biotechnology Engineering; Business Administration; Ceramic Art; Design; Education; Environmental Chemistry; Forestry Engineering; Geography; Graphic Design; Industrial Design; Law; Medical Technology; Midwifery; Nursing; Nutrition; Occupational Therapy; Photography; Physical Therapy; Sculpture; Sociology; Speech Therapy and Audiology; Veterinary Medicine; Wood Technology, 5 yrs; *Título Profesional:* Architecture; Biochemistry; Chemical Engineering; Chemistry; Civil Engineering; Computer Engineering; Electrical Engineering; Food Science; Geology; Industrial Engineering; Materials Engineering; Mathematics Engineering; Mechanical Engineering; Mining Engineering; Pharmacy; Psychology, 6 yrs; *Título Profesional:* Dance, 3 yrs; *Título Profesional:* Dental Surgery; Education, 5 1/2 yrs; *Título Profesional:* Fine Arts, 6-7 yrs; *Título Profesional:* Journalism, 4 1/2 yrs; *Título Profesional:* Medicine; Surgery, 7 yrs; *Título Profesional:* Performing Arts, 5-6 yrs; *Título Profesional:* Stage Design, 4 yrs; *Doctorado:* Biochemistry; Biology; Biomedical Sciences; Chemistry; Engineering Sciences; Geology; Literature; Materials Sciences; Mathematics; Philosophy; Physics; Science

Student Residential Facilities: Yes

Special Facilities: Museum of Popular Art; Museum of Modern Art. Three Observatories. Radio MF

Libraries: Total, c. 1,592,500 vols

Publications: Anales de la Universidad de Chile *(annually)*; Anuario Astronómico *(annually)*; Bizantion Nea Hellas; Boletín Chileno de Parasitología *(quarterly)*; Boletín de Filología *(biannually)*; Boletín

Interamericano de Educación Musical *(annually)*; Comentarios sobre la Situación Económica; Cuadernos de Ciencia Política *(quarterly)*; Cuadernos de Historia *(annually)*; Desarrollo Rural *(biannually)*; Estudios Internacionales *(quarterly)*; Ocupación y Desocupación Encuesta nacional *(biannually)*; Política *(biannually)*; Publicaciones Científicas-INTA *(annually)*; Revista Chilena de Antropología *(annually)*; Revista Chilena de Historia del Derecho; Revista Chilena de Humanidades *(annually)*; Revista de Derecho Económico; Revista de Derecho Público; Revista de Filosofía *(annually)*; Revista Economía y Administración *(quarterly)*; Revista Musical Chilena *(biannually)*; Revista Psiquiátrica Clínica *(annually)*; Taller de Coyuntura; Terra Aridae *(biannually)*; Tralka

Press or Publishing House: Editorial Universitaria

Academic Staff *2007-2008*	TOTAL
FULL-TIME	1,087
PART-TIME	2,272
Student Numbers *2007-2008*	
All (Foreign Included)	23,733

Last Updated: 04/03/09

UNIVERSITY OF LA SERENA
Universidad de La Serena (ULS)
Benavente 980, La Serena
Tel: +56(51) 204-000
Fax: +56(51) 204-310
EMail: mberrios@userena.cl
Website: http://www.userena.cl

Rector: Nibaldo Avilés Pizarro Tel: +56(51) 204-439

Secretario General: Calixto Veas Gaz
Tel: +56(51) 204-334, Fax: +56(51) 204-392

International Relations: Ricardo Nicanor Castillo Bozo
Tel: +56(51) 204-448

Faculties
Economics and Social Sciences *Dean*: Luperfina Rojas Escobar; **Engineering** (Architecture; Civil Engineering; Computer Engineering; Construction Engineering; Engineering; Environmental Engineering; Food Technology; Industrial Engineering; Mechanical Engineering; Mechanics; Mining Engineering; Natural Resources) *Dean*: Alberto Cortés Álvarez; **Humanities** (Business and Commerce; Design; Educational Administration; English; Music Education; Philosophy; Primary Education; Psychology; Spanish; Special Education; Teacher Training; Translation and Interpretation) *Dean*: María Zúñiga Carrasco; **Science** (Agricultural Engineering; Arid Land Studies; Biology; Chemistry; Computer Education; Mathematics; Mathematics and Computer Science; Natural Sciences; Nursing; Physics; Science Education) *Dean*: Gustavo Labbé Morales

Further Information: Also campuses in Coquimbo and Ovalle

History: Founded 1981 from La Serena School of Mines, founded 1887, Normal School of La Serena (1890), University of Chile, and State Technical University, La Serena branches.

Governing Bodies: Junta Directiva (Board of Trustees)

Academic Year: March to December (March-July; August-December)

Admission Requirements: Secondary school certificate (Licenciade Educación Media) and entrance examination: Academic Aptitude Test

Fees: (US Dollars): 2,100-3,200 per annum

Main Language(s) of Instruction: Spanish

Degrees and Diplomas: *Licenciatura*: Education, 8-9 sem; *Licenciatura*: Engineering; Education; Psychology; Journalism; Nursing, 10 sem; *Magister*: Education; Business; Mineral Resources; Latin American Studies; Psychology, 4 sem; *Título Profesional*: Engineering; Architecture; Journalism; Nursing; Education, 8-12 sem; *Doctorado*: Education

Student Services: Academic counselling, Canteen, Cultural centre, Foreign student adviser, Handicapped facilities, Health services, Nursery care, Social counselling, Sports facilities

Student Residential Facilities: Yes

Special Facilities: Mineralogy Museum. Gabriela Mistral Documentation Centre. Latin American Centre for Water Resources

Libraries: Central Library, 69,979 vols

Publications: Actas Colombinas *(annually)*; Geoespacios *(annually)*; Investigación y Desarrollo *(annually)*; Logos *(annually)*; Temas de Educación *(annually)*

Last Updated: 05/03/09

UNIVERSITY OF MAGALLANES
Universidad de Magallanes (UMAG)
Avenida Bulnes 01855, Punta Arenas
Tel: +56(61) 207-000
Fax: +56(61) 207-123
EMail: rr.pp@umag.cl
Website: http://www.umag.cl

Rector: Víctor Fajardo Morales Tel: +56(61) 207-161

Secretario General: Francisco Soto Piffault
Tel: +56(61) 207-173 EMail: fpiffo@ona.fi.umag.cl

International Relations: Mónica Buvinic López
Tel: +56(61) 207-006 EMail: monica.buvinic@umag.cl

Centres
Research and Technology Transfer (Computer Science; Tourism) *Director*: Belen Goic Segaric

Faculties
Economics and Law *Dean*: Luis Poblete Davanzo; **Engineering** (Chemical Engineering; Civil Engineering; Computer Engineering; Construction Engineering; Electrical Engineering; Electronic Engineering; Food Technology; Mechanical Engineering; Safety Engineering) *Dean*: Humberto Oyarzo; **Humanities, Social Sciences and Health** (Humanities and Social Science Education; Nursing; Occupational Therapy; Pedagogy; Physical Therapy; Psychology; Social Work) *Dean*: Juan Carlos Judikis Preller; **Science** (Agricultural Engineering; Aquaculture; Biology; Forestry; Marine Biology; Mathematics; Physics) *Dean*: Octavio Lecaros Palma

Institutes
Patagonia (Archaeology; Botany; Geology; History; Paleontology; Zoology) *Head*: Claudio Venegas Canelo

Further Information: University Campus in Puerto Natales

History: Founded 1961 and attached to the State Technical University, and became its regional branch 1964. Became institute of professional studies 1981 and acquired present status and title 1981. Institute of Patagonia Studies, formerly private research institution, incorporated 1985. An autonomous institution financed by the State.

Governing Bodies: Board of Directors

Academic Year: March to December (March-July; July-December)

Admission Requirements: Secondary school certificate (Licencia de Educación Media) and entrance examination (national selection)

Main Language(s) of Instruction: Spanish

International Co-operation: With universities in Spain, Germany, France, USA.

Degrees and Diplomas: *Técnico de Nivel Superior*: Technician, 5 yrs; *Licenciatura*: Education, 5 yrs; *Post- títulos/ Diploma*; *Título Profesional*: Accountancy, 4 1/2 yrs; *Título Profesional*: Biology, 4 yrs; *Título Profesional*: Economy and Business; Kinesiology; Law; Nursing; Occupational Therapy; Social Service, 5 yrs; *Título Profesional*: Engineering, 4-6 yrs

Student Services: Academic counselling, Canteen, Cultural centre, Employment services, Foreign student adviser, Health services, Language programs, Nursery care, Social counselling, Sports facilities

Publications: Anales del Instituto de la Patagonia, Natural and Social Sciences *(annually)*; Austrouniversitario *(annually)*

Last Updated: 05/03/09

UNIVERSITY OF PLAYA ANCHA
Universidad de Playa Ancha (UPLA)
Avenida Playa Ancha 850, Casilla 34-V, Valparaíso
Tel: +56(32) 250 01 00
Fax: +56(32) 285-041
EMail: postmaster@upa.cl
Website: http://www.upla.cl/

Rector: Patricio Sanhueza Vivanco
Tel: +56(32) 500-109 EMail: mbaxman@upla.cl

Secretario General: Jorge Sánchez Valencia
Tel: +56(32) 285-632 EMail: jsanchez@upla.cl

Faculties

Educational Sciences (Computer Education; Education; Educational Administration; Educational and Student Counselling; Educational Sciences; Educational Testing and Evaluation; Pedagogy; Preschool Education; Special Education; Technology Education; Vocational Education) *Dean*: René Flores Castillo; **Fine Arts** (Art Education; Art History; Computer Graphics; Graphic Design; Music; Music Education; Painting and Drawing; Sculpture; Technology Education; Visual Arts) *Dean*: Alberto Teichelmann S.; **Humanities** (Arts and Humanities; Communication Studies; English; French; Geography; German; History; International Business; Journalism; Library Science; Linguistics; Literature; Philosophy; Social Sciences; Spanish; Translation and Interpretation) *Dean*: Juan Saavedra Ávila; **Natural and Exact Sciences** (Biology; Chemistry; Civil Engineering; Computer Education; Computer Science; Environmental Engineering; Industrial Engineering; Information Management; Mathematics; Mathematics Education; Natural Sciences; Physics; Statistics) *Dean*: Rolando Tiemann Astudillo; **Physical Education** (Occupational Therapy; Physical Education; Physical Therapy; Sports) *Dean*: Elias Marín Valenzuela

Institutes

Adult Education *(Ignacio Domeyko)* (Accountancy; Analytical Chemistry; Computer Science; Law) *General Director*: Carlos González Moráles

Further Information: Also Distance Education. Study abroad programmes. Courses for foreign students. Regional Centre in San Felipe

History: Founded 1948 as Instituto Pedagógico, Valparaíso, became an Institute of the University of Chile 1955. Acquired present status and title 1981.

Governing Bodies: Junta Directiva

Academic Year: March to December (March-July; July-December)

Admission Requirements: Secondary school certificate (Licencia de Educación Media) and entrance examination

Main Language(s) of Instruction: Spanish

Degrees and Diplomas: *Licenciatura*: 5 yrs; *Magister*: a further 3 yrs; *Doctorado*: 3 yrs

Student Services: Academic counselling, Canteen, Cultural centre, Employment services, Foreign student adviser, Health services, Nursery care, Social counselling, Sports facilities

Libraries: 'Oscar Guzman Escobar' Library, 50,000 vols

Publications: Diálogos Educacionales; Nueva Revista del Pacífico; Revista Ciencia de la Actividad Física; Revista Orientación Educacional

Press or Publishing House: Editorial Puntangeles
Last Updated: 05/03/09

UNIVERSITY OF SANTIAGO DE CHILE
Universidad de Santiago de Chile (USACH)
Avenida Libertador Bernardo O'Higgins 3363, Estación Central, Santiago
Tel: +56(2) 718-0068
EMail: rectoria@lauca.usach.cl
Website: http://www.usach.cl

Rector: Juan Manuel Zolezzi Cid (2006-)
Tel: +56(2) 781-0001, Fax: +56(2) 681-2663
EMail: jzolezzi@lauca.usach.cl

Secretario General: Gustavo Robles
Tel: +56(2) 718-0006 EMail: grobles@usach.cl

International Relations: María Fernanda Contreras
Tel: +56(2) 718-0042, Fax: +56(2) 776-6954
EMail: mfcontreras@usach.cl

Faculties

Administration and Economics (Accountancy; Administration; Business Administration; Business and Commerce; Economics; Finance; Human Resources; Management; Management Systems; Public Administration; Taxation) *Dean*: Silvia Ferrada Vergara;

Chemistry and Biology (Biochemistry; Biological and Life Sciences; Biology; Chemistry; Environmental Studies; Microbiology) *Dean*: Juan Luis Gautier; **Engineering** (Automation and Control Engineering; Chemical Engineering; Civil Engineering; Computer Engineering; Construction Engineering; Electrical Engineering; Engineering; Environmental Engineering; Geography; Heating and Refrigeration; Industrial Engineering; Materials Engineering; Measurement and Precision Engineering; Mechanical Engineering; Metallurgical Engineering; Mining Engineering; Telecommunications Engineering) *Dean*: Ramón Blasco Sánchez; **Humanities** (Arts and Humanities; Education; Educational Sciences; English; History; Journalism; Latin American Studies; Linguistics; Literature; Native Language Education; Philosophy; Psychology; Sports; Translation and Interpretation) *Dean*: Carmen Norambuena; **Medical Sciences** (Gynaecology and Obstetrics; Medicine; Nursing) *Dean*: Luis Barrueto; **Science** (Computer Education; Computer Science; Mathematics; Mathematics and Computer Science; Mathematics Education; Natural Sciences; Physics; Statistics) *Dean*: Samuel Navarro; **Technology** (Advertising and Publicity; Agricultural Business; Agricultural Management; Automation and Control Engineering; Construction Engineering; Food Science; Food Technology; Graphic Design; Human Resources; Industrial Design; Industrial Engineering; Industrial Maintenance; Labour and Industrial Relations; Technology) *Dean*: Laura Almendares

Programmes
Bachillerato *Director*: Francisco Javier Gil

Schools
Architecture *Director*: Carlos Richards

History: The University's roots go back to the founding of the School of Arts and Trades in 1849 and the Schools of Mining in Copiapó, La Serena and Antofagasta. Later, Industrial Schools were founded in Southern cities and all these institutions became branches of the Universidad Técnica del Estado (State Technical University), founded in 1947. Acquired present title in 1981. An autonomous institution financed by the State.

Governing Bodies: Board of Directors

Academic Year: March to December (March-July; August-December)

Admission Requirements: Secondary school certificate (Licencia de Educación Media) and national entrance examination (Prueba de selección universitaria (PSU))

Fees: (Chilean Pesos) 1,435,350-2,627,250 according to course

Main Language(s) of Instruction: Spanish

International Co-operation: With universities in Argentina, Bolivia, Brasil, Canada, Colombia, Costa Rica, Cuba, Mexico, Paraguay, Panama, Peru, Germany, Austria, Spain, France, United Kingdom, Italy, Portugal and Romania

Degrees and Diplomas: *Licenciatura*: Applied Physics, Biochemistry, Chemistry; Economics, Education, Engineering, Mathematics,; Food Sciences, Agribusiness, Architecture; Linguistics, Communication Studies, Psychology, Administration, Accountancy, Advertizing and Publicity; Nursing, Obstetrics, 4-6 yrs; *Licenciatura*: Medicine, 7 yrs; *Magister*: Chemistry, Accountancy, Economics, Education, International Studies, Philosophy, Public Management; Engineering Management, Engineering, Environment Studies, History, Human Resources, Business Administration, Gender Studies; Linguistics, Literature, Tax Planning, International Relations, Psychology, Food Technology, Telecommunication Engineering, 2 yrs; *Doctorado*: American Studies; Automatic Control, Chemistry, Engineering, Materials Engineering, Physics, Mathematics; Biotechnology, Microbiology, Food Technology, Computer Engineering, Engineering Management, 4 yrs

Student Services: Academic counselling, Canteen, Cultural centre, Employment services, Foreign student adviser, Handicapped facilities, Health services, Language programs, Social counselling, Sports facilities

Student Residential Facilities: Yes

Special Facilities: Planetarium. Radio Station

Libraries: General central libraries and 19 specialized libraries. Total, 260,706 vols

Publications: Revista Contribuciones *(annually)*

Press or Publishing House: Editorial Universidad de Santiago
Last Updated: 05/03/09

UNIVERSITY OF TALCA
Universidad de Talca (UTALCA)
Dos Norte 685, Talca
Tel: +56(71) 200-101
Fax: +56(71) 200-103
EMail: mgreyes@utalca.cl
Website: http://www.utalca.cl

Rector: Juan Antonio Rock Tarud (2006-)

Secretario General: Ricardo Sánchez Venegas
Tel: +56(71) 200-110, Fax: +56(71) 200-150
EMail: cvillagr@utalca.cl

International Relations: Andrew Philominraj
Tel: +56(71) 201-633, Fax: +56(71) 200-390
EMail: andrew@utalca.cl

Faculties
Agronomy *(Experimental Station Panguilemo)* (Agricultural Business; Agricultural Economics; Agricultural Management; Agriculture; Agronomy; Crop Production; Food Science; Fruit Production; Horticulture; Soil Science; Water Science) *Dean:* Hernán Paillán Legué; **Business** (Accountancy; Business Administration; Business and Commerce; Economics; Human Resources; International Business; Management) *Dean:* Claudio Rojas; **Engineering** *(Curicó)* (Bioengineering; Computer Engineering; Electronic Engineering; Engineering; Industrial Engineering; Mechanical Engineering) *Dean:* Claudio Tenreiro Leiva; **Forestry** (Environmental Studies; Forest Management; Forest Products; Forestry; Wood Technology) *Dean:* Juan Franco de la Jara; **Health Sciences** (Dentistry; Medical Technology; Medicine; Physical Therapy; Speech Therapy and Audiology) *Dean:* Carlos Gigoux; **Law and Social Sciences** (Criminal Law; History of Law; Human Rights; International Law; Justice Administration; Labour Law; Notary Studies; Private Law; Public Law) *Dean:* Jorge del Picó

Institutes
Chemlstry of Natural Resources (Analytical Chemistry; Chemistry; Natural Resources; Organic Chemistry) *Director:* Jorge Villaseñor; **Humanities** *(Abate Juan Ignacio Molina)* (Art Criticism; Art History; Arts and Humanities; Contemporary History; Ethics; Latin American Studies; Literature; Philosophical Schools; Regional Studies; Social Sciences; Women's Studies) *Director:* Pedro Zamorano; **Mathematics and Physics** (Mathematics; Pedagogy; Physics; Statistics) *Director:* María Inés Icaza; **Vegetal Biology and Biotechnology** (Agrobiology; Biochemistry; Biology; Biotechnology; Botany; Entomology; Molecular Biology) *Director:* Peter Caligari

Research Institutes
Educational Development (Curriculum; Educational Administration; Educational Research; Educational Sciences; Higher Education; Staff Development) *Director:* Sebastián Donoso

Schools
Architecture (Architectural and Environmental Design; Architecture; Architecture and Planning; Regional Planning) *Director:* Juan Román; **Design** (Industrial Design) *Director:* Jaime Parra; **Music** *Director:* Mirta Bustamante; **Psychology** (Psychology) *Director:* Emilio Moyano

History: Founded 1981, incorporating regional branches of the University of Chile and University of Santiago de Chile. A State institution.

Governing Bodies: Junta Directiva (Board of Trustees)

Academic Year: March to December (March-July; August-December)

Admission Requirements: Secondary school certificate (Licencia de Educación Media) and entrance examination

Fees: (US Dollars): 2,800

Main Language(s) of Instruction: Spanish

International Co-operation: With universities in the United States, Germany, Netherlands, France, Argentina, Brazil. Also participates in higher education networks: Columbus and OUI (Interamerican Association of Higher Education Institutions)

Degrees and Diplomas: *Licenciatura:* Agricultural Sciences; Architecture; Accountancy; Law; Industrial Engineering; Information Technology; Timber Industries; Medical Technology; Forestry; Psychology; Music; Design, 5 yrs; *Licenciatura:* Dentistry, 6 yrs; *Magister:* Administration of Educational Centres; Constitutional Law; Mathematics, 2 yrs; *Magister:* Business Administration, 18 mths; *Magister:* Educational Administration, 6 trim; *Magister:* Horticulture, 3 trim; *Magister:* International Agribusiness, 4 sem; *Magister:* International Business; Taxation, 18 months; *Post- títulos/ Diploma:* Agribusiness Management, 8 months; *Post- títulos/ Diploma:* Business Administration (MBA), 324 hours; *Post- títulos/ Diploma:* Health Administration; Human Resources Management; *Post- títulos/ Diploma:* Industrial Engineering, 1 yr; *Post- títulos/ Diploma:* Legislation and Taxation, 300 hours; *Post- títulos/ Diploma:* Quality Management and Agriculture Good Pratices, 4 months; *Doctorado:* Plant Genetics Engineering, 4 yrs

Student Services: Academic counselling, Canteen, Cultural centre, Employment services, Foreign student adviser, Foreign Studies Centre, Handicapped facilities, Health services, Language programs, Nursery care, Social counselling, Sports facilities

Student Residential Facilities: No

Special Facilities: Pedro Olmos Cultural Centre, Curicó and Carlos Hojas Cultural Centres, Mobile Art Gallery, University Radio Station and TV Channel

Libraries: 82,563 vols

Publications: Lus et Praxis *(biannually)*; Panorama Socioeconómico *(biannually)*; Revista Acontecer *(monthly)*; Serie "Cuadernos Regionales" *(biannually)*; Universum *(annually)*

Press or Publishing House: Editorial Universidad de Talca
Last Updated: 05/03/09

UNIVERSITY OF TARAPACÁ
Universidad de Tarapacá (UTA)
General Velásquez 1775, Casilla 7-D, Arica
Tel: +56(58) 205-100
Fax: +56(58) 232-135
EMail: rrii@uta.cl
Website: http://www.uta.cl

Rector: Sergio Pulido Roccatagliata (2006-)
Tel: +56(58) 205-302 EMail: rec@uta.cl

Secretario General: Carlos Ruiz
Tel: +56(58) 205-319, Fax: +56(58) 232-135 EMail: ajsec@uta.cl

International Relations: Cecilia Robledo
Tel: +56(58) 257-663, Fax: +56(58) 231-797
EMail: crobledo@uta.cl

Faculties
Agronomy (Agronomy; Crop Production; Water Management) *Dean:* Eugenio Doussoulin; **Education and Humanities** (Applied Linguistics; Archaeology; Arts and Humanities; Communication Studies; Curriculum; Education; Educational Administration; Educational and Student Counselling; English; Geography; History; Physical Education; Preschool Education; Primary Education; Secondary Education; Spanish) *Dean:* Carlos Herrera; **Health Sciences** (Health Sciences) *Dean:* Teresa Reyes Rubilar; **Science** (Biological and Life Sciences; Biology; Chemistry; Environmental Studies; Gynaecology and Obstetrics; Haematology; Mathematics and Computer Science; Medical Technology; Midwifery; Natural Sciences; Nursing; Physical Therapy; Radiology; Rehabilitation and Therapy) *Dean:* Liliana Hernández Villaseca; **Social Sciences And Law** (Accountancy; Administration; Anthropology; Business and Commerce; Economics; Finance; Heritage Preservation; Human Resources; Information Sciences; International Business; Law; Management; Marketing; Psychology; Public Administration; Social Sciences; Tourism) *Dean:* Maria Alburquenque Eliash

Schools
Electrical and Electronic Engineering *Dean:* Tomás Sanz Cantillana; **Industrial and Computing Engineering** *Dean:* Marco Villalobos Abarca; **Mechanical Engineering** (Mechanical Engineering) *Dean:* Jaime Villanueva Aguila

Further Information: Campuses in Velásquez, Saucache and Azapa

History: Founded 1981, incorporating Instituto Profesional de Conandes de Arica, a regional branch of Universidad de Chile and Universidad del Norte. An autonomous institution.

Governing Bodies: Junta Directiva

Academic Year: March to January (March-July; August-January)

Admission Requirements: Secondary school certificate (Licencia de Educación Media) or equivalent, and entrance examination (Prueba de Selección Académica)

Fees: (Chilean Pesos): 874,000-1.5m. per annum

Main Language(s) of Instruction: Spanish

International Co-operation: With universities in Latin, Central, and North America and Europe

Degrees and Diplomas: *Técnico de Nivel Superior*: Administration; Law; Business; Drawing; Design, 2-3 yrs; *Licenciatura*; *Magister*: Education, a further 2 yrs; *Post- títulos/ Diploma*: Business; Administration, 1-2 yrs; *Título Profesional*: Engineering, Pedagogy, Accountancy, Law, Psychology, Nursing, Midwifery, Medical Technology, Agronomy, 4-6 yrs; *Doctorado*: Archaeology, 4-5 yrs

Student Services: Academic counselling, Canteen, Cultural centre, Employment services, Foreign student adviser, Health services, Language programs, Nursery care, Social counselling, Sports facilities

Student Residential Facilities: Yes

Special Facilities: Archaeological Museum

Libraries: Central Library, c. 89,027 vols; specialized libraries

Publications: Chungara *(biennially)*; Dialogo Andino *(biennially)*; Idesia *(biennially)*; Limite *(annually)*; Revista Facultad de Ingeniería *(annually)*

Last Updated: 05/03/09

UNIVERSITY OF THE FRONTIER
Universidad de la Frontera (UFRO)
Avenida Francisco Salazar 01145, Casilla 54-D, Temuco
Tel: +56(45) 325-000
Fax: +56(45) 325-905
EMail: ufro@ufro.cl
Website: http://www.ufro.cl

Rector: Sergio Bravo Escobar Tel: +56(45) 325-090

Secretario General: Ricardo Herrera Lara
Tel: +56(45) 325-060, Fax: +56(45) 325-120

Faculties
Agronomy and Forestry Science (Agricultural Engineering; Agriculture; Agronomy; Biotechnology; Forestry; Natural Resources) *Dean*: Aliro Contreras Novoa; **Education and Humanities** (Arts and Humanities; Civics; Communication Studies; Development Studies; Education; Educational Testing and Evaluation; Geography; History; Journalism; Literature; Mathematics Education; Modern Languages; Physical Education; Psychology; Regional Studies; Science Education; Social and Community Services; Social Sciences; Social Work; Sociology; Sports) *Dean*: Hugo Carrasco Muñoz; **Engineering, Science and Administration** (Accountancy; Administration; Agricultural Engineering; Chemical Engineering; Chemistry; Civil Engineering; Computer Engineering; Construction Engineering; Economics; Electrical Engineering; Electronic Engineering; Engineering; Environmental Engineering; Food Science; Food Technology; Industrial Engineering; Management; Mathematics; Mechanical Engineering; Natural Sciences; Physics; Public Administration; Statistics) *Dean*: Plinio Durán García; **Medicine** *(Edificio de la Salud)* (Dentistry; Dietetics; Epidemiology; Gender Studies; Gynaecology and Obstetrics; Medical Technology; Medicine; Nursing; Nutrition; Paediatrics; Physical Therapy; Psychology; Public Health; Social Work; Speech Therapy and Audiology) *Dean*: Eduardo Hebel Weiss

Institutes
Agro-industry (Agricultural Business; Agronomy; Food Technology; Molecular Biology; Soil Science) *Director*: Maria Teresa Fernandez Cabrera; **Computer Education** (Computer Education; Educational Sciences; Information Technology) *Director*: Enrique Hinostroza Schell; **Environmental Studies** (Environmental Studies) *Director*: Itilier Salazar Quintana; **Local and Regional Development** (Regional Planning) *Director*: Heinrich von Baer von Lochow; **Native Studies** (Native American Studies; Natives Education) *Director*: Alejandro Herrera Aguayo

Further Information: Also Teaching Hospitals. Postgraduate specialization programme for foreign students. 2 university campuses in Temuco: Andrés Bello and Ciencas de La Salud

History: Founded 1981, incorporating the former branches of Universidad de Chile and Universidad Técnica del Estado in Temuco.

Governing Bodies: Junta Directiva, comprising 9 members; Consejo Académico comprising 13 members

Academic Year: March to December (March-July; August-December)

Admission Requirements: Secondary school certificate (Licencia de Educación Media) and entrance examination

Main Language(s) of Instruction: Spanish

Degrees and Diplomas: *Licenciatura*: 4-5 yrs; *Magister*: a further 2 yrs; *Título Profesional*: Civil Engineering, 6 yrs; *Título Profesional*: Engineering, 5 yrs; *Título Profesional*: Medicine, 7 yrs; *Título Profesional*: Performance Engineering, 4 yrs; *Doctorado*: a further 3-5 yrs

Student Services: Academic counselling, Canteen, Cultural centre, Handicapped facilities, Health services, Nursery care, Social counselling, Sports facilities

Student Residential Facilities: For c. 120 students

Libraries: Central Library, 100,479 vols; 195 subscriptions

Publications: Educación y Humanidades *(annually)*; International Journal of Morphology *(quarterly)*; Lengua Literatura Mapuche *(biannually)*; Memoria Institucional *(annually)*; Revista Chilena de Anatomía *(biannually)*; Revista Chilena de Ciencias Médico-Biológicas *(biannually)*; Revista Cubo (Mathematics) *(annually)*; Revista Investigaciones en Educatión *(annually)*; Revista Nuestra Muestra *(biennially)*; Vertientes UFRO *(quarterly)*

Press or Publishing House: Ediciones Universidad de La Frontera
Last Updated: 04/03/09

MALLECO BRANCH
SEDE MALLECO
Avenida Libertador Bernardo O'Higgins 50, Angol
Tel: +56(45) 711-503
Fax: +56(45) 715-480
EMail: sangol@ufro.cl
Website: http://www.ufro.cl/presentacion/smalleco.htm

Director: Marcelo Carrere Ibar

Programmes
Administration (Administration); **Agroindustry**; **Primary Education** (Primary Education)

History: Founded 1994.

Main Language(s) of Instruction: Spanish

Degrees and Diplomas: *Técnico de Nivel Medio*

PUCÓN BRANCH
SEDE PUCÓN
Lincoyán 55, Pucón
Tel: +56(45) 442-638
Fax: +56(45) 442-638
EMail: pucon@ufro.cl
Website: http://www.ufro.cl/presentacion/spucon.htm

Director: Claudio Briceño Olivera

Institutes
Tourism *(EuroChileno)* (Hotel Management; Tourism)

Programmes
Administration (Administration); **Computer Science** (Computer Science); **English**

History: Founded 1995.

Main Language(s) of Instruction: Spanish

Degrees and Diplomas: *Técnico de Nivel Medio*. Also Diplomados

UNIVERSITY OF THE LAKES
Universidad de Los Lagos
Lord Cochrane 1046, Osorno
Tel: +56(64) 230-061
Fax: +56(64) 239-517
EMail: secretariageneral@ulagos.cl
Website: http://www.ulagos.cl

Rector: Raúl Aguilar Gatica (1992-)
Tel: +56(64) 237-116 EMail: rectoria@ulagos.cl

Secretario General: Bruno Cárdenas
Tel: +56(64) 246-020, Fax: +56(64) 205-226

International Relations: Álvaro Poblete L. Tel: +56(64) 205-110

Centres

Computer Science (Computer Science) *Director:* Selín Carrasco; **English Translation** (English; Translation and Interpretation); **Limnology** *(Puyehue)* (Limnology) *Director:* Teresa Donoso Lastra; **University Research** *(CIU, Santiago)*; **University Studies** *(CEU)* *Director:* Daniel López Stefoni

Conservatories

Music (Music)

Departments

Administration and Economics (Accountancy; Administration; Economics; Public Administration; Tourism) *Director:* René Reyes I.; **Aquaculture and Marine Resources** (Aquaculture; Marine Biology) *Director:* Alberto Medina A.; **Architecture and Design** (Architecture; Design) *Director:* Cristián Silva L.; **Basic Sciences** (Natural Sciences) *Director:* Jaime Zapata Barra; **Education** (Communication Studies; Computer Education; Education; Geography; History; Mathematics Education; Media Studies; Preschool Education; Translation and Interpretation) *Director:* Roberto Canales Reyes; **Exact Sciences** (Mathematics; Natural Sciences; Physics) *Director:* Jorge Wevar N.; **Food Science and Technology** (Food Science; Food Technology) *Director:* Arnaldo Caqueo D.; **Government and Business** *(Puerto Montt)* (Administration; Business Administration; Business and Commerce; Government; Political Sciences; Public Administration) *Director:* Marcos Gómez S.; **Humanities and Fine Arts** (Arts and Humanities; Design; Fine Arts) *Directora:* Diana Kiss de Alejandro; **Natural Resources and Environment** *(Puerto Montt)* (Agricultural Engineering; Civil Engineering; Environmental Studies; Natural Resources) *Director:* Jorge Basten C.; **Physical Education** (Physical Education) *Director:* Juan Luis Carter B.; **Social Sciences** (Educational Psychology; Social Sciences; Social Work) *Director:* Claudio Rosales U.

Further Information: Campuses in Puerto Montt and Coyhaique. Regional Centre in Santiago

History: Founded 1964 as Universidad Técnica del Estado. Acquired present status and title 1993.

Governing Bodies: Consejo Superior, comprising 9 members; Consejo universitario, comprising 18 members

Academic Year: March to December (March-July; August-December)

Admission Requirements: Secondary school certificate and entrance examination

Main Language(s) of Instruction: Spanish

Degrees and Diplomas: *Licenciatura:* 4 yrs; *Magister:* a further 1-2 yrs; *Post- títulos/ Diploma*; *Título Profesional:* 4 1/2-5 yrs

Student Services: Academic counselling, Canteen, Cultural centre, Foreign student adviser, Handicapped facilities, Health services, Nursery care, Social counselling, Sports facilities

Student Residential Facilities: For c. 3,200 students

Publications: Alpha *(annually)*; Biota *(annually)*; Cuadernos de Historia y Cultura de Aysén *(annually)*; Francachela *(quarterly)*

Press or Publishing House: Editorial Universidad de Los Lagos
Last Updated: 04/03/09

UNIVERSITY OF VALPARAÍSO

Universidad de Valparaíso (UV)
Avenida Errázuriz 2190, Casilla 123-V, Valparaíso
Tel: +56(32) 507-000
Fax: +56(32) 507-143
EMail: secretaria.rectoria@uv.cl
Website: http://www.uv.cl

Rector: Aldo Valle Acevedo
Tel: +56(32) 507-103 EMail: rector@uv.cl

Secretario General: Osvaldo Corrales Jorquera
EMail: osvaldo.corrales@uv.cl

Faculties

Architecture (Architecture; Civil Engineering; Construction Engineering; Design) *Dean:* Juan Luis Moraga Lacoste; **Dentistry** (Dentistry) *Dean:* Osvaldo Badenier Bustamante; **Economics and Administration** *(Viña del Mar)* (Accountancy; Administration; Economics; Finance; Human Resources; Industrial Engineering; International Business; Management; Marketing; Public Administration) *Dean:* Ricardo Barril Villalobos; **Humanities** (Arts and Humanities; Philosophy) *Dean:* Carlos Martel Llano; **Law and Social Sciences** (Arts and Humanities; Hispanic American Studies; History; Humanities and Social Science Education; Law; Logic; Philosophy; Social Sciences; Social Work) *Dean:* Alberto Balbontin Retamales; **Marine Science** *(Viña del Mar) Dean:* Gerardo Leighton Sotomayor; **Medicine** (Chemistry; Gynaecology and Obstetrics; Medicine; Nursing; Nutrition; Paediatrics; Pharmacy; Psychology; Speech Therapy and Audiology) *Dean:* Luis Maldonado Cortés; **Pharmacy** *Dean:* Soledad Lobos Salvo; **Science** (Biological and Life Sciences; Biomedical Engineering; Biomedicine; Chemistry; Computer Science; Mathematics; Meteorology; Natural Sciences; Neurosciences; Physics; Statistics) *Dean:* Ramiro Villar Maturana

History: Founded 1911 as regional branch of the University of Chile. Became an independent institution 1981.

Governing Bodies: Junta Directiva, comprising 6 members; Consejo Académico, Consejo de Facultad

Academic Year: March to December (March-July; August-December)

Admission Requirements: Secondary school certificate and entrance examination

Fees: (Chilean Pesos): c. 680,000-1.5m. per annum

Main Language(s) of Instruction: Spanish

Degrees and Diplomas: *Licenciatura:* 4-7 yrs; *Magister:* a further 2 yrs; *Post- títulos/ Diploma*; *Título Profesional:* 5-7 yrs; *Doctorado*

Student Services: Academic counselling, Canteen, Cultural centre, Employment services, Foreign student adviser, Health services, Nursery care, Social counselling, Sports facilities

Libraries: Faculty, Institute and School libraries, c. 775,000 vols

Publications: Revista de Biología Marina y Oceanografía *(biannually)*; Revista de Ciencias Económicas y Administrativas *(annually)*; Revista de Ciencias Sociales *(annually)*; Revista de la Facultad de Odontología *(annually)*; Revista Facultad de Arquitectura *(annually)*

Press or Publishing House: Sello Editorial Universidad de Valparaíso. Editorial Escuela de Derecho (EDEVAL)
Last Updated: 06/03/09

PRIVATE INSTITUTIONS

ACUARIO DATA PROFESSIONAL INSTITUTE OF COMPUTER SCIENCE

Instituto Profesional de Ciencias de la Computación Acuario Data (IPCC)
Agustinas 2356, Santiago
Tel: +56(2) 673 28 40
EMail: admision@ipcc.cl
Website: http://www.ipcc.cl

Rector: Patricio Santelices

Programmes

Business Administration (Business Administration); **Computer Engineering** (Computer Engineering); **Industrial Engineering**; **Microcomputer Programming**; **Systems Analysis** (Systems Analysis)

History: Founded 1981.

Main Language(s) of Instruction: Spanish

Degrees and Diplomas: *Post- títulos/ Diploma*; *Título Profesional*
Last Updated: 05/03/09

ADOLFO IBÁÑEZ UNIVERSITY
Universidad Adolfo Ibáñez (UAI)
Balmaceda 1625, Recreo, Casilla 17, Viña del Mar
Tel: +56(32) 503-500
Fax: +56(32) 664-006
EMail: info@uai.cl
Website: http://www.uai.cl

Rector: Andrés Benítez Pereira

Secretario General: Agustin Ántola Tel: +56(32) 503-824

Faculties
Engineering (Civil Engineering; Computer Engineering; Engineering; Industrial Engineering; Mathematics) *Dean*: Luis Seccatore; **Humanities** (Arts and Humanities; Education; Fine Arts; History; Journalism; Literature; Philosophy) *Dean*: Lucía Santa Cruz; **Law** (Commercial Law; Law) *Dean*: Rodrigo P. Correa G.

Institutes
Political Economy (Economics; Political Sciences) *Director*: Lucía Santa Cruz

Schools
Business (Agricultural Business; Business Administration; Business and Commerce; Economics; Engineering Management; Finance; Human Resources; International Business; Management; Marketing) *Director*: Alfonso Gómez; **Government** (Government) *Dean*: Leonidas Montes; **Journalism** (Journalism) *Dean*: Ascanio Cavallo; **Psychology** (Psychology) *Dean*: Jorge Sanhueza

Further Information: Also branches in Santiago

History: Founded 1953 as Business School of Valparaíso, acquired present status and title 1989.

Governing Bodies: Board of Trustees; Board of Chairpersons

Academic Year: March to December (March-July; August-December)

Admission Requirements: Secondary school certificate (Licencia de Educación Media) and entrance examination

Fees: (Chilean Pesos): Registration, 152,000; tuition, 2m. per annum

Main Language(s) of Instruction: Spanish

Degrees and Diplomas: *Bachiller*: Humanities, 2 yrs; *Licenciatura*: Business Administration; Engineering; Humanities; Law, 4-5 yrs; *Magister*: Business; Humanities; Law, 1 yr following Licenciatura; *Título Profesional*: Industrial Engineering, 2 yrs following Licenciatura; *Doctorado*

Student Services: Canteen, Employment services, Foreign student adviser, Language programs, Sports facilities

Special Facilities: TV and Radio Studio

Libraries: 3 Libraries. Total, 36,000 vols

Publications: Notebook on Law *(biannually)*
Last Updated: 03/03/09

ADOLFO MATTHEI PROFESSIONAL INSTITUTE OF AGRARIAN SCIENCES
Instituto Profesional Agrario Adolfo Matthei
Avenida René Soriano N° 2615, Osorno
Tel: +56(64) 211-671
Fax: +56(64) 311-676
EMail: info@matthei.com
Website: http://www.instituto-matthei.cl

Rectora: Sonia Mora Sotomayor Tel: +56(64) 311-672

Programmes
Agricultural Engineering (Agricultural Engineering; Agriculture; Agronomy); **Agricultural Technology**; **Forestry**

Further Information: Also Meteorological Station

History: Founded 1932 as Escuela Superior de Agricultura de Osorno. Acquired present status and title 1981.

Academic Year: February to August (February-March; April-August)

Fees: (US Dollars): 55,000 per annum

Main Language(s) of Instruction: Spanish

Degrees and Diplomas: *Técnico de Nivel Superior*; *Título Profesional*
Last Updated: 03/03/09

ADVENTIST UNIVERSITY OF CHILE
Universidad Adventista de Chile
Campus Las Mariposas, Km. 12 Chillán a Tanilvoro, Casilla 7-D, Chillán
Tel: +56(42) 212-902
Fax: +56(42) 226-400
EMail: universidad@unach.cl
Website: http://www.unachile.cl

Rector: Edgar Araya Bishop
Tel: +56(42) 218-052 EMail: rectoria@unach.cl

Vicerrector académico: Ramón Pérez Soto
EMail: viceacademica@unach.cl

Faculties
Agronomy (Agriculture; Agronomy) *Dean*: Raúl Donoso; **Education and Social Sciences** (Biology; Education; Educational and Student Counselling; Educational Testing and Evaluation; English; Geography; History; Mathematics and Computer Science; Music; Natural Sciences; Primary Education; Religious Education; Secondary Education; Social Work; Spanish; Teacher Training; Technology Education) *Dean*: Nelson Gutiérrez Lagos; **Engineering and Trade** (Accountancy; Agricultural Business; Agricultural Engineering; Agronomy; Business Administration; Civil Engineering; Computer Engineering; Electronic Engineering; Engineering; Food Science; Food Technology; Telecommunications Engineering) *Dean*: Pablo San Martín M.; **Theology** (Bible; Pastoral Studies; Religious Studies; Theology) *Dean*: Ricardo Gonzáles

History: Founded 1965 as a Senior College by the General Conference of the Seventh-day Adventist Church, became Instituto Profesional Adventista 1982 and acquired present status and title 1990.

Governing Bodies: Directory of the Chile Seventh-day Adventist Church; Board of Regents of the General Conference of the Seventh-day Adventists; Ministry of Education

Academic Year: March to December

Admission Requirements: Secondary school certificate (Licencia de Enseñanza Media) and entrance examination

Main Language(s) of Instruction: Spanish

Accrediting Agencies: Higher Education Division, Ministry of Education

Degrees and Diplomas: *Licenciatura*: Teaching qualification, 4-5 yrs; *Magister*: Public Health, a further 2 yrs; *Título Profesional*: Civil Engineering; Agronomy; Commercial Engineering; Accountancy, 3-5 yrs

Student Services: Academic counselling, Canteen, Employment services, Foreign student adviser, Health services, Nursery care, Social counselling, Sports facilities

Student Residential Facilities: For 450 students

Libraries: Mariano Renedo Lucero Library, 34,000 vols.

Press or Publishing House: Ediciones Universidad Adventista de Chile
Last Updated: 03/03/09

AIEP PROFESSIONAL INSTITUTE
Instituto Profesional AIEP
Avenida Providencia 729, Santiago
Tel: +56(2) 570-4000
Website: http://www.aiep.cl

Rector: Jesús Villate Castillo

Schools
Administration and Trade (Accountancy; Administration; Business Administration; International Business; Sales Techniques); **Communication Studies** (Communication Studies; Public Relations; Radio and Television Broadcasting); **Construction** (Architectural and Environmental Design; Construction Engineering; Safety Engineering; Surveying and Mapping); **Design and Advertising**; **Education and Social Development**; **Fashion Design**; **Health Sciences** (Dental Technology; Gynaecology and Obstetrics; Health

Sciences; Nursing); **Information Technology** (Computer Engineering; Computer Networks; Information Technology; Multimedia; Systems Analysis); **Sound Engineering and Television** (Radio and Television Broadcasting; Sound Engineering (Acoustics)); **Sports** (Sports; Sports Management); **Theatre**

Further Information: Also branches in Calama, Antofagasta, La Serena, Viña del Mar, Rancagua, San Fernando, Curicó, Concepción, Puerto Montt

History: Founded 1989.

Degrees and Diplomas: *Técnico de Nivel Superior*; *Título Profesional*

Last Updated: 02/03/09

ALBERTO HURTADO UNIVERSITY
Universidad Alberto Hurtado (UAH)
Almirante Barroso 6, Casilla 14446, Correo 21, Santiago, Región Metropolitana
Tel: +56(2) 692-0200
Fax: +56(1) 692-0216
EMail: uah@uahurtado.cl
Website: http://www.uahurtado.cl

Rector: Fernando Montes Matte, S.J.

Secretario General: Alberto Etchegaray

International Relations: Fernando Verdugo R.S.J., Vicerrector Integracíon

Centres
Educational Research and Development *Head*: Juan Eduardo Garcia Huidobro

Faculties
Economics and Business (Administration; Business Administration; Business and Commerce; Economics; Finance; Leadership) *Head*: Jorge Rodriguez; **Education** (Educational Administration; Primary Education; Secondary Education) *Head*: Juan Eduardo Garcia-Huidobro, **Law** *Head*: Pedro Irureta; **Philosophy and Humanities** (Arts and Humanities; Ethics; Literature; Philosophy; Spanish) *Dean*: Eduardo Silva Arévalo; **Social Sciences** (Communication Studies; Ethics; International Relations; Journalism; Political Sciences; Regional Studies; Social Sciences; Social Work; Sociology; Theology) *Dean*: Pedro Güell

Schools
Psychology *Head*: Mauricio Arteaga Manieu

History: Founded 1997.

Governing Bodies: Consejo Superior

Main Language(s) of Instruction: Spanish

Degrees and Diplomas: *Bachiller*: Philosophy; Arts and Humanities; Mass Communication, 2 yrs; *Licenciatura*: Philosophy; Arts and Humanities; Mass Communication; Business, 5 yrs; *Magister*: Business Administration; Economics; Education; Political Science; Ethics; Law; History, 2 yrs; *Post- títulos/ Diploma*: Philosophy; Arts and Humanities; Mass Communication; Journalism; Literature; Social Sciences; Economics; Law; Education; Psychology, 1 yr; *Título Profesional*: Engineering Management; Primary Education; Secondary Education; Sociology; Psychology; Mass Communication; Journalism; Social Work; Law, 5 yrs; *Doctorado*. Also Diplomados

Student Services: Academic counselling, Employment services, Foreign student adviser, Foreign Studies Centre, Social counselling, Sports facilities

Publications: Ethos *(quarterly)*; Persona y Sociedad *(quarterly)*; Revista de Análisis Económico *(biennially)*
Last Updated: 03/03/09

ANDRÉS BELLO UNIVERSITY
Universidad Andrés Bello
Avenida República 237-252, Santiago
Tel: +56(2) 661-8001
Fax: +56(2) 671-1936
EMail: info@unab.cl
Website: http://www.unab.cl

Rector: Rolando Kelly Jara

Secretario General: Luis Cordero Barrera
International Relations: Alexis Yánez Alvarado

Faculties
Architecture and Design *(Casona de Las Condes)* (Architectural and Environmental Design; Architecture; Construction Engineering; Design) *Dean*: Alberto Sato; **Dentistry** (Dentistry) *Dean*: Felipe Stanke; **Ecology and Natural Resources** (Aquaculture; Ecology; Environmental Engineering; Marine Biology; Marine Science and Oceanography; Natural Resources; Tourism; Veterinary Science) *Dean*: Rolando Kelly Jara; **Economics and Trade** (Accountancy; Administration; Economics; Engineering Management) *Dean*: Francisco Javier Labbé Opazo; **Engineering** (Civil Engineering; Computer Engineering; Construction Engineering; Engineering; Industrial Engineering) *Dean*: Juan Bennett Urrutia; **Health Sciences** (Biochemistry; Chemistry; Health Sciences; Medical Technology; Nursing; Occupational Therapy; Pharmacy; Physical Therapy; Speech Therapy and Audiology) *Dean*: Humberto Chiang Miranda; **Humanities and Education** (Arts and Humanities; Education; History; Journalism; Literature; Philosophy; Psychology; Social Sciences) *Dean*: Joaquín Barceló; **Law** *Dean*: Luis Hermosilla; **Nursing** (Nursing) *Dean*: Luz Angélica Muñoz; **Rehabilitation** (Occupational Therapy; Rehabilitation and Therapy; Speech Therapy and Audiology) *Dean*: Mariano Rocabado

Programmes
Liberal Arts (Arts and Humanities; Fine Arts; Natural Sciences) *Dean*: Gustavo Cataldo Sanguinetti

Further Information: Study Abroad Programmes with the University of Reno, Nevada. Also Casona de las Condes and Viña del Mar campuses

History: Founded 1988. Incorporated Universidad Marítima de Chile 2008.

Academic Year: March to December (March-July; August-December)

Admission Requirements: Secondary school certificate (Licencia de Educación Media) and entrance examination

Main Language(s) of Instruction: Spanish

Degrees and Diplomas: *Bachiller*: 5-6 yrs; *Licenciatura*; *Magister*; *Doctorado*

Student Residential Facilities: For c. 5,850 students

Libraries: Central Library, c. 16,000 vols

Press or Publishing House: Andrés Bello Editorial
Last Updated: 18/05/09

ARCOS PROFESSIONAL INSTITUTE OF ART AND COMMUNICATION
Instituto Profesional de Artes y Comunicación ARCOS
Santo Domingo 789, Barrio Bellas Artes, Santiago
Tel: +56(2) 447-8383
EMail: arcos@arcos.cl
Website: http://www.arcos.cl

Rector: José Sanfuentes

Schools
Cinema and Audiovisual Communication; **Design and Multimedia**; **Photography**; **Sound** (Sound Engineering (Acoustics)); **Theatre** (Theatre)

History: Founded 1981.

Main Language(s) of Instruction: Spanish

Degrees and Diplomas: *Técnico de Nivel Superior*; *Título Profesional*: 3-4 yrs
Last Updated: 02/03/09

AUTONOMOUS UNIVERSITY OF CHILE
Universidad Autónoma de Chile (UAS)
Porvenir 580, Temuco
Tel: +56(45) 240-651
Fax: +56(45) 245-897
EMail: admision@uas.cl
Website: http://www.uas.cl

Rector: Teodoro Ribera Neumann EMail: rector@uas.cl

Director General Académico: Mario Lamas Westmeyer
EMail: mlamas@uas.cl

International Relations: Osvaldo Ramírez Castro
EMail: oramirez@uas.cl

Programmes
Accountancy (Accountancy) *Director.* Carlos Bustos Cuevas; **Architecture** (Architecture; Civil Engineering) *Director.* Paz Serra Freire; **Civil Engineering** (Building Technologies; Civil Engineering) *Director.* Izet Ustovic Kaflik; **Commercial Engineering** (Business and Commerce) *Director.* Rafael Díaz Morelli; **Law** (Law) *Director.* Rodolfo Kaufhold Carrasco; **Preschool Education** (Preschool Education) *Director.* María Isabel Cofré Molinet; **Social Services** (Social and Community Services; Welfare and Protective Services) *Director.* Camila Brito Fábrega; **Technology** (Technology) *Director.* Luis Donaire Herrera

History: Founded 1989. Formerly known as Universidad Autónoma del Sur.

Governing Bodies: Junta Directiva

Main Language(s) of Instruction: Spanish

Degrees and Diplomas: *Técnico de Nivel Superior, Licenciatura; Magister, Título Profesional; Doctorado*

BERNARDO O'HIGGINS UNIVERSITY
Universidad Bernardo O'Higgins (UBO'H)
Casilla 344-V, Correo 21, Avenida Viel 1497, Santiago
Tel: +56(2) 477-4100
Fax: +56(2) 555-3031
EMail: info@ubo.cl
Website: http://www.ubo.cl

Rector: Jorge O'Ryan Balbontin
Tel: +56(2) 477-4114 EMail: rector@ubo.cl

Vicerrector de Administración y Finanzas: Claudio Ruff Escobar

Faculties
Engineering (Civil Engineering; Engineering; Environmental Engineering; Industrial Engineering; Safety Engineering; Surveying and Mapping) *Dean:* Rodrigo Aitken Vilches; **Human Sciences and Education** (Arts and Humanities; English; Geography; History; Pedagogy; Physical Education; Preschool Education; Primary Education; Psychology; Secondary Education; Sports) *Dean:* Carolina Salamé Saldías; **Law and Social Communication** (Journalism; Law; Public Relations) *Dean:* Luz María Reyes Santelices

History: Founded 1990.

Governing Bodies: Junta Directiva, comprising 13 members; Consejo Universitario, comprising 10 members; Consejo Académico, comprising 10 members

Main Language(s) of Instruction: Spanish

Degrees and Diplomas: *Técnico de Nivel Superior, Licenciatura; Título Profesional*
Last Updated: 03/03/09

BOLIVARIANA UNIVERSITY
Universidad Bolivariana
Huérfanos 2917, Santiago, Región Metropolitana
Tel: +56(2) 756-0000
Fax: +56(2) 754-3120
EMail: ub@ubolivariana.cl
Website: http://www.ubolivariana.cl

Rector: Alex Figueroa Muñoz Tel: +56(2) 756-3000

Secretario General: Carlos Gaete Becerra
EMail: secretariageneral@ubolivariana.cl

International Relations: Martín Garate
EMail: mgarate@ubolivariana.cl

Campuses
Sede Iquique UB *(Serves the Southern regions of the country)* (Anthropology; Archaeology; History; Law; Pedagogy; Psychology) *Director.* Orietta Ojeda; **Sede Los Angeles UB** *(Serves the*

Southern regions of the country) (English; History; Law; Occupational Therapy; Pedagogy; Psychology) *Director.* Manuel Fernández

Centres
Sustainable Development *(Santiago Campus) Director.* Mario Gonzalez

Institutes
Education (Education) *Director.* Nancy Luco

Schools
Anthropology (Anthropology; Archaeology) *Director.* Bernardo Arroyo; **Archaeology** *Director.* Victor Lucero; **Choreography, Dance and Performing Arts** (Dance; Performing Arts) *Director.* Magaly Rivano; **Commercial Engineering** (Business Administration; Economics) *Director.* Victoria Barruetos; **Economics** (Business and Commerce; Economics) *Director.* Victoria Barruetos; **Engineering Studies** (Engineering) *Director.* Diego Lois; **Geography** (Geography) *Director.* Oscar Liendo; **History** (History) *Director.* Gabriel Salazar; **Journalism** *(Santiago Campus)* (Journalism) *Director.* Carlos Donoso; **Law** *(Santiago Campus)* (Law) *Director.* Daniel Munizaga; **Library Sciences** *(Santiago Campus)* (Library Science) *Director.* Sergio Rodríguez; **Music** *(Santiago Campus) Director.* Belfort Ruz; **Psychology** *(Santiago Campus)* (Psychology) *Director.* Patricio Vergara; **Social Work** (Social Work) *Director.* Javier Barría; **Theatre** *(Santiago Campus)* (Theatre) *Director.* Elena Muñoz

History: Founded 1988.

Governing Bodies: Board of Directors

Academic Year: March to December

Admission Requirements: Secondary school certificate and university selection test (PSU)

Main Language(s) of Instruction: Spanish

International Co-operation: Participates in the UNESCO Human development co-chair and the Alfa Project

Degrees and Diplomas: *Técnico de Nivel Medio*: Library Science; Journalism, $2\frac{1}{2}$-3 yrs; *Bachiller.* Anthropology; Archeology, 2 yrs; *Licenciatura*: Psychology; Law; Anthropology; Archeology; Commercial Engineering; Geography; Journalism; Theatre; Psychology; Nursing; Occupational Therapy; English; Pedagogy; History; History and Social Sciences, 4-5 yrs; *Título Profesional*: Psychology; Law; Anthropology; Archeology; Commercial Engineering; Geography; Journalism; Theatre; Psychology; Nursing; Occupational Therapy; English; Pedagogy; History; History and Social Sciences, 4-5 yrs

Libraries: Yes

Publications: Polis - www.revistapolis.cl *(quarterly)*
Last Updated: 02/02/07

CARLOS CASANUEVA PROFESSIONAL INSTITUTE
Instituto Profesional Carlos Casanueva (ICC)
Londres 46, Santiago
Tel: +56(2) 222-9207
Fax: +56(2) 634-3672
EMail: instprof.esedu001@chilnet.cl
Website: http://www.carloscasanueva.cl

Rectora: Maria Josefina Bilbao Mendezona

Secretaria General: María del Carmen González Urroz

Schools
Administration; **Education**; **Health** (Physical Therapy); **Human and Social Development** (Development Studies; Family Studies; Social Sciences)

History: Founded 1993, acquired present status and title 1997.

Governing Bodies: Consejo Directivo, comprising 7 members

Main Language(s) of Instruction: Spanish

Degrees and Diplomas: *Técnico de Nivel Superior, Post- títulos/ Diploma; Título Profesional*
Last Updated: 02/03/09

CATHOLIC UNIVERSITY OF CHILE

Pontificia Universidad Católica de Chile (PUC)

Avenida Libertador Bernardo O'Higgins 340, Santiago
Tel: +56(2) 222-4516
Fax: +56(2) 222-5515
EMail: soporte@puc.cl
Website: http://www.puc.cl

Rector: Pedro Pablo Rosso R. (2000-)
Tel: +56(2) 354-2346 EMail: rectoria@puc.cl

Secretario General: Raúl Madrid Ramírez
Tel: +56(2) 354-2370, Fax: +56(2) 222-2349
EMail: rmadrid@puc.cl

Vicerrector Académico: Juan José Ugarte Gurruchaga
Tel: +56(2) 354-2390, Fax: +56(2) 354-2423
EMail: jugarte@puc.cl

International Relations: Nuria Alsina Jara
Tel: +56(2) 686-2416, Fax: +56(2) 222-3116
EMail: nalsina@puc.cl

Centres
Tele-Education

Faculties

Agronomy and Forestry Engineering (Agricultural Economics; Agriculture; Agronomy; Animal Husbandry; Cattle Breeding; Forestry; Fruit Production; Oenology; Plant and Crop Protection; Vegetable Production; Zoology) *Dean:* Luis Barrales Vega; **Architecture, Design and Urban Studies** (Architecture; Design; Environmental Studies; Industrial Design; Rural Planning; Town Planning; Urban Studies) *Dean:* José Rosas Vera; **Arts and Humanities** (Acting; Arts and Humanities; Music; Painting and Drawing; Singing; Theatre) *Dean:* Jaime Donoso Arellano; **Biological Sciences** (Biochemistry; Biological and Life Sciences; Biology; Cell Biology; Ecology; Genetics; Marine Biology; Microbiology; Molecular Biology; Natural Resources; Physiology) *Dean:* J. Rafael Vicuña Errázuriz; **Chemistry** (Chemistry; Natural Sciences; Pharmacy) *Dean:* Luis Hernán Tagle Domínguez; **Communication Studies** (Communication Studies; Journalism; Social Psychology) *Dean:* Silvia Pelligrini Ripamonti; **Economics and Administration** (Administration; Business Administration; Economic and Finance Policy; Economics; Finance; Public Administration) *Dean:* Francisco Rosende Ramírez; **Education** (Computer Education; Curriculum; Education; Educational Administration; Educational Sciences; Educational Technology; Media Studies; Pedagogy; Preschool Education; Special Education; Vocational Counselling; Vocational Education) *Dean:* Erika Himmel König; **Engineering** (Civil Engineering; Construction Engineering; Engineering; Engineering Management; Safety Engineering; Structural Architecture) *Dean:* Hernán Solminihac Tampier; **History, Geography, and Political Science** (Environmental Studies; European Studies; Geography; Hispanic American Studies; History; International Relations; Political Sciences) *Dean:* José Ignacio Gonzáles Leiva; **Law** (Commercial Law; Constitutional Law; Criminology; Law; Public Law) *Dean:* Arturo Yrarrázaval Covarrubias; **Letters** (Arts and Humanities; English; Linguistics; Literature; Philology) *Dean:* José Luis Samaniego Aldázaval; **Mathematics** (Mathematics; Mathematics and Computer Science; Natural Sciences; Statistics) *Dean:* Guillermo Marshall Rivera; **Medicine** (Anaesthesiology; Cardiology; Dermatology; Ethics; Gerontology; Gynaecology and Obstetrics; Medicine; Nephrology; Neurology; Nursing; Nutrition; Oncology; Ophthalmology; Orthopaedics; Paediatrics; Pathology; Public Health; Radiology; Social and Preventive Medicine; Surgery) *Dean:* Gonzalo Grebe; **Philosophy** (Literature; Philosophy) *Dean:* Luis Flores Hernández; **Physics** (Astronomy and Space Science; Astrophysics; Natural Sciences; Physics) *Dean:* María Cristina Depassier Terán; **Social Sciences** (Adult Education; Educational Psychology; Family Studies; Psychology; Psychotherapy; Social Sciences; Social Work; Sociology) *Dean:* Pedro Morandé Court; **Theology** (Theology) *Dean:* Samuel Fernández Eyzaguirre

Further Information: Branch in Villarirca. University Hospitals

History: Founded 1888 by decree of Archbishop of Santiago. Recognized by Pope Leo XIII 1889; became Pontifical University 1930. A private, autonomous institution, with degrees recognized by Chilean Law. Financially supported by State subsidy and tuition fees.

Governing Bodies: Consejo Superior, presided over by the Rector and including the Secretary-General, Vice-Rectors, Deans, a student representative, and 4 representatives of University staff

Academic Year: March to December (March-July; August-December)

Admission Requirements: Secondary school certificate (Licencia de Educación Media) and entrance examination

Main Language(s) of Instruction: Spanish

Accrediting Agencies: AACSB (USA); MEXA (MERCOSUR) RIBA (United Kingdom); ABET (USA); AAMC (USA) ACEJMC (USA)

Degrees and Diplomas: *Bachiller:* Philosophy; Religious Science, 3 yrs; *Bachiller:* Theology, 5 yrs; *Licenciatura:* Aesthetics; Agriculture and Natural Resources; Architecture; Arts; Biochemistry, Biology, Chemistry; Economics and Management Science; Education; Engineering; Geography; History; Law; Letters; Mathematics; Music; Philosophy; Physics; Psychology; Religious Science, 5 yrs; *Licenciatura:* Medicine, 7 yrs; *Magister, Título Profesional:* Biochemistry; Business Administration; Design; Economics; Geography; Journalism; Translation, 5 yrs; *Título Profesional:* Engineering; *Título Profesional:* Law; Nursing; Psychology, 6 yrs; *Título Profesional:* Medicine, 7 yrs; *Título Profesional:* Social Work, 4 yrs; *Doctorado:* Biology; Exact Sciences; History; Theology

Student Services: Academic counselling, Canteen, Cultural centre, Employment services, Foreign student adviser, Foreign Studies Centre, Handicapped facilities, Health services, Language programs, Social counselling, Sports facilities

Libraries: Total, c. 870,000 vols

Publications: Aisthesis *(biannually)*; Anales de Educación *(3 per annum)*; Anales de Teología *(annually)*; Apuntes de Ingeniería *(quarterly)*; Apuntes de Teatro *(3 per annum)*; Arq (Arquitectura) *(annually)*; Biología Pesquera *(biannually)*; Boletín de la Escuela de Medicina *(biannually)*; Ciencia e Investigación Agraria *(biannually)*; Ciencia Política *(annually)*; Cuadernos de Economía *(3 per annum)*; Ediciones Gráficas *(annually)*; Filosofía *(annually)*; Historia *(annually)*; Letras *(annually)*; Monografías Biológicas *(annually)*; Notas Matemáticas *(biannually)*; Revista Chilena de Derecho *(3 per annum)*; Revista Eure *(biannually)*; Revista Geografía *(annually)*; Revista Universitaria *(quarterly)*; Serie de Estudios Sociológicos *(annually)*; Teología y Vida *(quarterly)*; Trabajo Social *(3 per annum)*

Press or Publishing House: Editorial Universidad Católica
Last Updated: 03/03/09

CATHOLIC UNIVERSITY OF MAULE

Universidad Católica del Maule

Avenida San Miguel 3605, Casilla 617, Talca
Tel: +56(71) 203-300
Fax: +56(71) 241-767
EMail: webmaster@hualo.ucm.cl
Website: http://www.ucm.cl

Rector: José Antonio Valdivieso Rodríguez
Tel: +56(71) 203-309, Fax: +56(71) 241-767 EMail: rector@ucm.cl

Secretario General: Claudio Enrique Rodríguez Figueroa
EMail: sgeneral@ucm.cl

Faculties

Agrarian Sciences and Forestry *(Curicó)* (Agriculture; Agronomy; Forestry) *Dean:* Nelson Loyola; **Education** (Computer Education; Curriculum; Development Studies; Education; Educational Administration; Physical Education; Preschool Education; Rehabilitation and Therapy; Social Work; Special Education) *Dean:* Patricio Gatica Mandiola; **Engineering** (Accountancy; Administration; Computer Engineering; Construction Engineering; Engineering; Engineering Management; Management Systems; Transport Management) *Dean:* Juan Francisco Figueroa; **Health Sciences** (Epidemiology; Health Administration; Health Sciences; Nursing; Physical Therapy; Public Health) *Dean:* Sara Herrera Leyton; **Religious and Philosophical Sciences** (Philosophy; Religious Studies; Theology) *Dean:* Cesar Lambert Ortiz

Further Information: Campuses Nuestra Señora del Carmen (Curicó), San Ambrosio (Linares), Nuestra Señora de las Mercedes (Cauquenes), Constitución. Extension Centres Victoria and Villa Cultural Huilquilemu

History: Founded 1991. A private institution financially supported by the State.

Main Language(s) of Instruction: Spanish

Degrees and Diplomas: *Magister; Post- títulos/ Diploma; Título Profesional*

Last Updated: 04/03/09

CATHOLIC UNIVERSITY OF TEMUCO

Universidad Católica de Temuco

Avenida Alemania 0211, Casilla 15-D, Temuco, 4780000 Cautín

Tel: +56(45) 205-205

Fax: +56(45) 205-241

EMail: uctemuco@uctemuco.cl

Website: http://www.uctemuco.cl

Rector: Mónica Jiménez de la Jara

Tel: +56(45) 205-200, Fax: +56(45) 234-126

EMail: mjimenez@uctemuco.cl

Secretario General: Arturo Hernández Sallés

Tel: +56(45) 205-685, Fax: +56(45) 234-126

EMail: secgral@uctemuco.cl

International Relations: Alberto Vásquez Tapia, Prorrector

Tel: +52(45) 205-280, Fax: +56(45) 234-126

EMail: avasquez@uctemuco.cl

Centres

Social and Cultural Studies *(CES, San Francisco)* (Cultural Studies; Social Studies) *Director:* Teresa Durán; **Sustainable Development** *(CDS, Campus San Francisco)* (Development Studies) *Director:* José Luis Saavedra

Faculties

Arts and Humanities *(Campus Menchaca Lira)* (Art Management; Arts and Humanities; Design; Painting and Drawing; Visual Arts) *Dean:* Mario Samaniego Sastre; **Education** *(San Francisco)* (Bilingual and Bicultural Education; Education; Foreign Languages Education; Mathematics Education; Modern Languages; Native Language Education; Preschool Education; Primary Education; Science Education; Secondary Education; Special Education) *Dean:* Carmen Paz Tapia Gutiérrez; **Engineering** *(San Francisco)* (Business and Commerce; Civil Engineering; Computer Engineering; Engineering; Environmental Engineering; Management) *Dean:* Orión Aramayo Baltra; **Natural Resources** *(Campus Norte)* (Agronomy; Animal Husbandry; Biological and Life Sciences; Forestry; Natural Resources; Veterinary Science; Water Science) *Dean:* Jaime Millán Herrera; **Social and Legal Sciences** *(Campus San Francisco) Dean:* Alberto Vásquez Tapia

Institutes

Theology *(San Francisco Campus)* (Catholic Theology; Religious Education; Theology; Vocational Education) *Director:* Juan Leonelli Leonelli

History: Founded 1959 as University Schools of La Frontera. Incorporated to the Pontifical Catholic University in Chile 1974, as a regional branch. Acquired present status and title 1991. A private institution financially supported by the State.

Governing Bodies: Superior Council; Directive Council; Academic Council.

Academic Year: March to January

Admission Requirements: Secondary School Certificate and University Selection Test (PSU)

Main Language(s) of Instruction: Spanish

Accrediting Agencies: National Accreditation Committee (CNA)

Degrees and Diplomas: *Técnico de Nivel Superior:* Forestry; Water Science, 3 yrs; *Licenciatura:* Agronomy; Animal Husbandry; Forestry; Water Science; Veterinary Science; Biological and Life Sciences; Education; Mathematics Education; Foreign Languages Education; Native Language Education; Preschool Education; Primary Education; Secondary Education; Bilingual and Bicultural Education; Social Work; Computer Engineering; Civil Engineering; Vocational Education; Religious Education; Catholoic Theology; Environmental Engineering; Law; Special Education; Natural Resources; Science; Education; Modern Languages; English, 5 yrs; *Magister:* Education; Mathematics Education; Foreign Languages Education; Native Languages Education; Preschool Education; Primary Education; Secondary Education; Bilingual and Bicultural Education; Social Work; Anthropology; Environmental Engineering; *Magister:* Environmental Engineering; Environmental Studies; Law;

Special Education; Educational Administration; Teacher Training, a further 2 yrs; *Post- títulos/ Diploma:* Human Resources; Veterinary Science, Mathematics Education; Special Education; Teacher Training; Law; Religious Education; Social Work; Family Studies; Social Sciences, 1-2 yrs; *Post- títulos/ Diploma:* Management; Environmental Studies; Agriculture; Forestry; Law; Computer Science; Catholic Theology; Native Language; Modern Languages; Social Work; Social Sciences, 1 yr; *Título Profesional:* Agronomy; Animal Husbandry; Forestry; Water Science; Veterinary Science; Biological and Life Sciences; Education; Mathematics Education; Foreign Languages Education; Native Language Education; Preschool Education; Primary Education; Secondary Education; Bilingual and Bicultural Education; Social Work; Sociology; Political Science; Computer Engineering; Civil Engineering; Vocational Education; Religious Education; Catholic Theology; Business and Commerce; Translation and Interpretation; Painting and Drawing (Visual Arts); Art Management; Law; Environmental Engineering; Special Education; Natural Resources; Science; Education; Modern Languages; English, 4 1/2 yrs

Student Services: Academic counselling, Cultural centre, Handicapped facilities, Health services, Language programs, Nursery care, Social counselling, Sports facilities

Special Facilities: Art Gallery

Libraries: Central Library; Library of Legal and Political Sciences; Libray of Arts and Humanities; Library of the Institute of Theological Studies; Library of Forestry and Farming Sciences. 58,976 vols

Academic Staff 2007-2008	MEN	WOMEN	TOTAL
FULL-TIME	142	107	**249**
PART-TIME	136	185	**321**
STAFF WITH DOCTORATE			
FULL-TIME	25	12	**37**
PART-TIME	–	–	**3**
Student Numbers 2007-2008			
All (Foreign Included)	2,498	4,032	**6,530**
FOREIGN ONLY	5	13	**18**

Distance students, 29.

Last Updated: 27/02/08

CATHOLIC UNIVERSITY OF THE HOLY CONCEPTION

Universidad Católica de la Santísima Concepción (UCSC)

Caupolicán 491, Concepción 4070129

Tel: +56(41) 2735-000

Fax: +56(41) 2735-001

EMail: ucsc@ucsc.cl

Website: http://www.ucsc.cl

Rector: Juan Miguel Cancino Cancino

Tel: +56(41) 2735-011, Fax: +56(41) 2735-040

EMail: rectoria@ucsc.cl

Secretaria General: Teresa Lobos del Fierro

Tel: +56(41) 2735-014, Fax: +56(41) 2735-037

EMail: tlobos@ucsc.cl

International Relations: Gonzalo Bordagaray

Tel: +56(41) 2735-011, Fax: +56(41) 2735-040

EMail: gbordagaray@ucsc.cl

Faculties

Communication, History and Social Sciences (Communication Studies; History; Journalism; Social Sciences) *Dean:* Mario Urzúa; **Economics and Administration** (Accountancy; Administration; Business Administration; Economics) *Dean:* Iván Valenzuela Díaz; **Education** (Education) *Dean:* Jaime Constenla Nuñez; **Engineering** (Aquaculture; Biotechnology; Civil Engineering; Computer Engineering; Engineering; Fishery; Industrial Engineering; Marine Engineering; Transport Engineering) *Dean:* Hubert Mennickent; **Law** (Criminal Law; Law) *Dean:* Hernan Varela Valenzuela; **Medicine** (Medicine; Nursing; Nutrition) *Dean:* Marcelo Lagos Subiabre

Institutes

Technology; Theology (Theology) *Director:* Juan Carlos Inostroza Lanas

Further Information: Campuses at San Andres and Santo Domingo

History: Founded 1991. Extends the academic activities of the Pontifical Catholic University of Chile. A private institution financially supported by the State.

Governing Bodies: Consejo Superior

Academic Year: March to December

Admission Requirements: Secondary school leaving certificate. National Selection test. Test of specific knowledge according to speciality

Fees: (US Dollars): 1,300-3,200 per annum (Depends on the undergraduate programme)

Main Language(s) of Instruction: Spanish

International Co-operation: With more than 30 universities and institutes in Argentina, Colombia, Peru, Bolivia, Spain, United Kingdom, Germany, Australia, New Zealand, Usa, China, Italy, etc.

Accrediting Agencies: National Accreditation Committee (CNA); CLAEP(for Journalism)

Degrees and Diplomas: *Licenciatura*: Engineering, Medicine, Law, Science, Business, Journalism, Teacher Training, 4-5 yrs; *Magister*: Education, Public Health, Nutrition, Family Orientation, 2 yrs; *Título Profesional*: All the undergraduate programmes, 5-6 yrs

Student Services: Academic counselling, Cultural centre, Employment services, Foreign student adviser, Health services, Language programs, Nursery care, Social counselling, Sports facilities

Student Residential Facilities: No

Special Facilities: Museum. Theatre. Art Gallery

Libraries: Two libraries (one in each campus)

Publications: Civil Engineering Magazine *(annually)*; Law Magazine *(biennially)*; Legete, Jounalism Magazine *(biennially)*; Philosophy Magazine *(annually)*; Rexe, Education Magazine *(biennially)*; Theology Magazine *(annually)*
Last Updated: 03/03/09

CATHOLIC UNIVERSITY OF THE NORTH
Universidad Católica del Norte (UCN)
Avenida Angamos 0610, Casilla 1280, Antofagasta
Tel: +56(55) 355-000
Fax: +56(55) 355-059
EMail: antofagasta@ucn.cl
Website: http://www.ucn.cl

Rector: Misael Camus Ibacache (2001-)
Tel: +56(55) 355-002, Fax: +56(55) 355-093

Secretaria General: Victoria González Stuardo
Tel: +56(55) 355-065, Fax: +56(55) 355-093
EMail: vgonzale@ucn.cl

International Relations: Pamela Vicelja Yaksic
Tel: +56(2) 222-6216, Fax: +56(2) 222-5961
EMail: pavicel@ucn.cl

Centres
Distance Education (Distance Education) *Director*: Eduardo Rojas González

Faculties
Architecture, Civil Construction and Civil Engineering (Architecture; Civil Engineering; Construction Engineering) *Dean*: Pablo Clemente Reyes Franzani; **Economics and Administration** (Accountancy; Administration; Business and Commerce; Economics; Management) *Dean*: Fernando Vial Valdés; **Engineering and Geological Science** (Chemical Engineering; Civil Engineering; Computer Engineering; Computer Science; Engineering; Environmental Engineering; Geology; Industrial Engineering; Metallurgical Engineering) *Dean*: Teodoro Gabriel Politis Jaramis; **Humanities** (Arts and Humanities; Journalism; Law; Philosophy; Psychology; Religious Studies; Theology) *Dean*: Georgina de las Mercedes Mora Jiménez; **Marine Science** *(Coquimbo)* (Aquaculture; Marine Biology; Marine Science and Oceanography) *Dean*: Juan Enrique Illanes Bücher; **Medicine** (Biomedicine; Medicine; Public Health) *Dean*: Nicolás Velasco Morandé; **Science** (Astronomy and Space Science; Chemistry; Computer Education; Environmental Studies; Mathematics; Mathematics and Computer Science; Mathematics Education; Natural Sciences; Pharmacy; Physics; Statistics) *Dean*: Sara Aguilera Morales

Institutes
Applied Economics *(Regional)*; **Archeological Research** (Anthropology; Archaeology); **Astronomy** (Astronomy and Space Science) *Director*: Luis Barrera Salas

Schools
Commercial Engineering *(Coquimbo)* (Business and Commerce) *Director*: Pablo Pinto Cornejo; **Journalism** (Information Sciences; Journalism; Mass Communication) *Director*: Rubén Gómez Quezada; **Law** (Law) *Director*: Manuel A. Núñez P.; **Law** *(Coquimbo)* *Director*: Carlos Mauricio Del Río Ferretti; **Psychology** (Psychology) *Director*: Alfonso Urzúa Morales; **Theology** *(Coquimbo)* *Director*: Alejandro Silva Contreras

History: Founded 1956 under the control of the Universidad Católica de Valparaíso. Recognized by the State as an independent and autonomous institution 1964. Reorganized 1969.

Governing Bodies: Consejo Superior

Academic Year: March to December (March-July; August-December)

Admission Requirements: Secondary school certificate (Licencia de Educación Media) and entrance examination

Fees: (Chilean Pesos): c. 103,000-1,289,000 per annum

Main Language(s) of Instruction: Spanish

Degrees and Diplomas: *Licenciatura*: Architecture; Computer Sciences; Engineering, 6 yrs; *Licenciatura*: Business Administration; Chemistry; Communication Sciences; Juridical Sciences; Marine Sciences; Mathematics; Physics option Astronomy, 5 yrs; *Licenciatura*: Chemistry, 4 yrs; *Licenciatura*: Psychology, 51/2 yrs; *Licenciatura*: Teaching qualification, secondary level; *Magister*; *Post- títulos/ Diploma*; *Título Profesional*: Accountancy, 4 1/2 yrs; *Título Profesional*: Engineering; Geology; *Doctorado*

Student Residential Facilities: For c. 120 women and c. 130 men

Special Facilities: Archaeological Museum (San Pedro de Atacama), Geological Museum (Antofagasta), Aquarium (Coquimbo), Astronomy Observatory (Cerro Armazones)

Libraries: Central Library, 81,205 vols; Guayacán Library (Coquimbo), 15,668 vols, San Pedro de Atacama Library, 2,639 vols.

Publications: Boletín de Educación; Revista de Derecho; Revista de Matemáticas: Proyecciones; Revista Norte; Revista Vertientes; Tercer Milenio

Press or Publishing House: Imprenta Universidad Católica del Norte
Last Updated: 04/03/09

CATHOLIC UNIVERSITY OF VALPARAÍSO
Pontificia Universidad Católica de Valparaíso (UCV)
Avenida Brasil 2950, Casilla 4059, Valparaíso
Tel: +56(32) 273-000
Fax: +56(32) 273-398
EMail: www@ucv.cl
Website: http://www.ucv.cl

Rector: Alfonso Muga Naredo (1998-)
Tel: +56(32) 273-201, Fax: +56(32) 273-393 EMail: rector@ucv.cl

Secretario General: Alan Bronfman Vargas
Tel: +56(32) 273-221 EMail: secgnral@ucv.cl

Faculties
Agronomy *(Quillota)* (Agronomy); **Architecture and Town Planning** *(Viña del Mar)* (Architecture; Graphic Design; Industrial Design; Town Planning); **Basic Science and Mathematics** (Actuarial Science; Biochemistry; Biology; Chemistry; Industrial Chemistry; Mathematics; Optics; Physical Therapy; Physics; Statistics); **Economics and Administration** (Accountancy; Administration; Business Administration; Business and Commerce; Economics; Finance; Management; Social and Community Services); **Engineering** (Bioengineering; Chemical Engineering; Civil Engineering; Computer Engineering; Computer Networks; Construction Engineering; Electrical Engineering; Electronic Engineering; Engineering; Engineering Management; Industrial Engineering; Marine Engineering; Marine Science and Oceanography; Materials Engineering; Mechanical Engineering; Metallurgical Engineering; Production Engineering; Transport Engineering); **Law and Social Sciences** (Law; Social Sciences); **Natural Resources**

(Aquaculture; Food Science; Geography; Marine Science and Oceanography; Natural Resources) **Philosophy and Education** *(Viña del Mar)* (Applied Linguistics; Computer Education; Curriculum; Education; Education of the Handicapped; Educational Administration; History; Linguistics; Literacy Education; Literature; Music Education; Native Language; Pedagogy; Philosophy; Physical Education; Preschool Education; Psychology; Social Sciences; Spanish; Special Education; Translation and Interpretation; Writing)

Institutes

Journalism *(Viña del Mar)* (Journalism); **Religious Sciences** (Christian Religious Studies; Ethics; Religious Studies; Theology)

Further Information: Also courses for foreign students. Branches in Viña del Mar, Quilpué and Quillota

History: Founded 1928, recognized by official decree 1929. Recognized as Catholic university by the Holy See 1961. A private institution financially supported by the State.

Governing Bodies: Claustro Pleno, Consejo Superior, Capítulo Academico, Consejo de Facultades y Consejo de Unidades Académicas

Academic Year: March to December (March-July; August-December)

Admission Requirements: Secondary school certificate (Licencia de Educación Media) or foreign equivalent, and entrance examination

Fees: (Chilean Pesos): 601,755 per semester, according to field of study; foreign students, US$ 2,000 per semester

Main Language(s) of Instruction: Spanish

Degrees and Diplomas: *Bachiller*: Arts; Science, 2 yrs; *Bachiller*: Religious Sciences, 4 yrs; *Licenciatura*: Agronomy; Biochemistry; Business Administration; Commerce and Economics; Law; Philosophy, 5 yrs; *Licenciatura*: Architecture; Engineering, 6 yrs; *Licenciatura*: Biology; Chemistry; Hispanic Language and Literature; History; Mathematics; Music; Physics, 4 yrs; *Licenciatura*: Religious Sciences, a further 1 yr; *Magister*: Applied Linguistics; Biochemistry; Electrical Engineering; Chemistry; Engineering; Biology; Education; Hispanic Literature; History; Law; Management; Accounting and Finance; Mathematics; Oceanography; Philosophy; Science (Chemistry, Physics, Microbiology); Statistics, a further 2-3 yrs; *Magister*: Business Administration (MBA), a further 1-2 yrs; *Post-títulos/ Diploma*: Business Administration; Corrosion; Educational Administration; Educative Computer Science for Experimental Sciences; Electrical Systems for Power Engineering; Finance; Industrial Engineering; Legislative Administration; Psychopedagogy and Mental Defenciency; Regional and Municipal Administration; Representation Techniques for Educational Purpose; Teaching of Mathematics through Computer Tools; Teaching of Physics; Technical-Scientific English; Transport Engineering; Written Communication Development, a further 2 yrs; *Título Profesional*: Accountancy; Agronomy; Biochemistry; Commercial Engineering; Construction Engineering; Electrical Engineering; Electronic Engineering; Fishing Production Engineering; Food Technology; Geography; History, Geography and Social Sciences; Law; Mechanical Engineering; Oceanography; Physical Therapy; Religious Sciences; Social Work; Transport Engineering, 5 yrs; *Título Profesional*: Architecture; Biochemical Engineering; Chemical Engineering; Civil Engineering in Extractive Metallurgy; Computer Science; Electrical Engineering; Industrial Engineering; Mechanical Engineering, 6 yrs; *Título Profesional*: Bioengineering; Computer Engineering; Graphic Design; Optics; Preschool and Early Elementary Education; Social Work; Statistics, 4 yrs; *Título Profesional*: Biology; Biology and Natural Sciences; Chemistry and Natural Sciences; Education; English; Industrial Chemistry; Industrial Design; Journalism; Mathematics; Music; Philosophy; Physical Education; Physics; Psychology; Spanish and Communication; Special Education; Translation, 4 1/2 yrs; *Doctorado*: Biotechnology; Chemistry; Literature; Philosophy; Physics, a further 4 yrs; *Doctorado*: Linguistics, a further 4 years

Student Residential Facilities: Yes

Libraries: c. 251,000 vols

Publications: Monografías Históricas *(annually)*; Revista de Derecho *(annually)*; Revista de Estudios Histórico-Jurídico *(annually)*; Revista de Investigaciones Marinas *(annually)*; Revista Facultad de Ingeniería *(biannually)*; Revista Filosofica *(annually)*; Revista Geográfica *(annually)*; Revista Perspectiva Educacional *(annually)*; Revista Signos *(annually)*

Press or Publishing House: Ediciones Universitarias de Valparaíso

Last Updated: 03/03/09

CATHOLIC UNIVERSITY SILVA HENRÍQUEZ

Universidad Católica Silva Henríquez (UCSH)
General Jofré 462, Casilla 28, Correo 22, Santiago
Tel: +56(2) 460-1100
Fax: +56(2) 635-4192
EMail: universidad@ucsh.cl
Website: http://www.ucsh.cl

Rector: Sergio Torres Pinto (2000-)
Tel: +56(2) 460-1102, Fax: +56(2) 634-5886
EMail: storres@ucsh.cl

Vicerrector de Administración y Finanzas: Gerardo Barros Pérez
EMail: gbarros@ucsh.cl

Departments

Education (Education) *Director*: Luis Ossandón M.; **Humanities and Intermediate Education** *Director*: José Albuccó Henríquez; **Mathematics Education** *Director*: Jorge Iván Ávila Contreras; **Psychology** *Directora*: Ximena Rojas; **Social Work** (Social Work) *Directora*: Daniela Sánchez Stürmer; **Sociology** (Social Sciences; Social Work; Sociology) *Director*: Justino Gómez de Benito

Institutes

Religious Studies *Directora*: Isabel Margarita Gómez Rojas

Schools

Administration and Economics (Accountancy; Administration; Banking; Business Administration; Business and Commerce; Economics; Finance; Management; Marketing) *Director*: Álvaro Acuña Vercelli; **Initial Education** (Pedagogy; Preschool Education; Special Education) *Directora*: Patricia Barrientos Díaz; **Law** (Law) *Coordinadora Académica*: Fabiola Vergara Cevallos; **Physical Education, Sports and Recreation** (Leisure Studies; Physical Education; Sports) *Director*: Alejandro Loyola Licata

History: Founded 1991 from former Instituto Profesional de Estudios Superiores Blas Cañas, acquired present title 1993.

Governing Bodies: Consejo Universitario

Academic Year: March to December (March-July; July-December)

Admission Requirements: Secondary school certificate (Licencia de Educación Media) and Prueba de Aptitud Académica. Some courses require additional examinations

Fees: (Chilean Pesos): 1,038,400-1,254,000 per annum

Main Language(s) of Instruction: Spanish

Degrees and Diplomas: *Licenciatura*: 5 yrs; *Magister*; *Post- títulos/ Diploma*

Student Services: Canteen, Health services, Social counselling, Sports facilities

Publications: Bulletin of Literature and Linguistics *(annually)*; Bulletin of Philosophy *(annually)*; Educational Forum *(annually)*; Journal of Religious Sciences *(annually)*; OIKOS *(quarterly)*; Research Series *(quarterly)*; Sociological Topics *(biannually)*

Last Updated: 03/03/09

CENTRAL UNIVERSITY OF CHILE

Universidad Central de Chile
Toesca 1783, Casilla 285-V, Correo 21, Santiago, 8370178 Región Metropolitana
Tel: +56(2) 582-6000
Fax: +56(2) 582-6109
EMail: rector@ucentral.cl
Website: http://www.ucentral.cl

Rector: Luis Lucero Alday (2006-) Tel: +56(2) 582-6078

Secretario General: Omar Ahumada Mora
Tel: +56(2) 582-6029, Fax: +56(2) 582-6038
EMail: oahumada@ucentral.cl

International Relations: Eliana Abad, National and International Relations Director EMail: eabad@ucentral.cl

Centres

Accountancy and Audit (Accountancy; Taxation); **Agricultural Business** (Agricultural Business; Agricultural Management; Farm

Management) *Director*: Hugo Ortega; **Architectural Restoration** (Architectural Restoration) *Director*: Patricio Gross; **Architectural Studies of Urban and Landscape** (Architectural and Environmental Design; Architectural Restoration; Architecture; Landscape Architecture; Structural Architecture; Town Planning) *Director*: Alfonso Raposo; **Developmental Environment** (Ecology; Environmental Management; Environmental Studies; Natural Resources) *Director*: Andrés González; **Economic Management** *Director*: Juan Scapini; **Juridicial Law** (Comparative Law; Justice Administration; Law) *Director*: José Bernales; **Knowledge Management for Innovation Enterprise** *Director*: Edith Catalán; **Labour and Social Work** (Human Resources; Labour and Industrial Relations; Social Work) *Director*: María Feres; **Professional Women** *Director*: Patricia Gallardo; **Psychological Assistance** (Educational Psychology; Psychology) *Director*: Jaime Yañez; **Science of Law** (Administrative Law; Civil Law; Commercial Law; Comparative Law; Constitutional Law; Fiscal Law; History of Law; Law; Private Law; Public Law) *Dean*: Angela Cattan; **Small Business** *Director*: Sergio Urrutia; **Studies of Public Opinion** (Social Studies; Sociology) *Director*: Andrés Llanos

Faculties

Architecture, Urban Planning and Architectural Landscape (Architectural Restoration; Architecture; Landscape Architecture; Regional Planning; Rural Planning; Structural Architecture; Town Planning) *Dean*: Eliana Israel Jacard; **Communication Studies** (Advertising and Publicity; Communication Arts; Communication Studies; Information Management; Information Technology; Journalism; Marketing; Mass Communication; Media Studies; Multimedia; Public Relations; Radio and Television Broadcasting) *Dean*: Bernardo De La Maza; **Economics and Administration** (Accountancy; Administration; Agricultural Business; Agricultural Economics; Agricultural Management; Banking; Business Administration; Business and Commerce; Business Computing; Economics; Farm Management; Finance; Human Resources; Industrial Management; International Business; Leadership; Management; Management Systems; Small Business; Taxation) *Dean*: Humberto Vega Fernández; **Educational Sciences** (Bilingual and Bicultural Education; Continuing Education; Curriculum; Educational Administration; Educational and Student Counselling; Educational Research; Educational Sciences; Educational Testing and Evaluation; Foreign Languages Education; Higher Education; Humanities and Social Science Education; Mathematics Education; Pedagogy; Physical Education; Preschool Education; Primary Education; Science Education; Secondary Education; Special Education; Teacher Trainers Education; Teacher Training) *Dean*: Selma Simonstein Fuentes; **Law and Social Sciences** (Administrative Law; Civil Law; Commercial Law; Comparative Law; Constitutional Law; Criminal Law; Fiscal Law; History of Law; Human Rights; International Law; Justice Administration; Labour Law; Law; Private Law; Public Law) *Dean*: Ángela Cattan Atala; **Physics and Mathematics** (Civil Engineering; Computer Engineering; Computer Networks; Construction Engineering; Data Processing; Industrial Engineering; Mathematics; Physics; Software Engineering) *Dean*: Sergio Quezada González; **Political Science and Public Administration** (Comparative Politics; Demography and Population; Development Studies; Economic and Finance Policy; Economic History; Economics; Government; Industrial and Production Economics; International Economics; International Relations; International Studies; Political Sciences; Public Administration; Regional Planning; Rural Studies; Urban Studies) *Dean*: Aldo Cassinelli Capurro; **Social Sciences** (Behavioural Sciences; Clinical Psychology; Cognitive Sciences; Comparative Sociology; Developmental Psychology; Educational Psychology; Family Studies; History of Societies; Psychoanalysis; Psychology; Psychometrics; Social and Community Services; Social Policy; Social Problems; Social Psychology; Social Sciences; Social Studies; Social Welfare; Social Work; Sociology; Vocational Counselling) *Dean*: Luis Gajardo Ibáñez

Institutes

Cognitive Development *(International) Director*: Sonia Fuentes; **Elementary Education** *(International)* (Preschool Education; Teacher Training) *Director*: Maria Peralta; **Public Management** (Administration; Comparative Politics; Government; Institutional Administration; Political Sciences; Private Administration; Public Administration) *Director*: Aldo Cassinelli

Further Information: Also La Reina, Parque Almagro Uno and Parque Almagro Dos Campuses

History: Founded 1983. Became autonomous 1993. Accredited by the National Commission of Accreditation 2005.

Governing Bodies: Direction Board and General Assembly

Academic Year: March to January

Admission Requirements: Secondary school certificate (Licencia de Educación Media); PAA (Academic Aptitude Test) and entrance examination

Fees: (US Dollars): Undergraduate programmes, 3,630-5,680 per annum; Magister, 2,900-6,170 per programme; Doctorado, 4,900-10-000 per programme; Diplomados, 530-1,590 per programme; Post- títulos, 880-7,150 per programme

Main Language(s) of Instruction: Spanish

International Co-operation: With universities in Spain and France

Accrediting Agencies: National Accreditation Committee (CNA)

Degrees and Diplomas: *Licenciatura*; *Magister*: Educational Sciences; Informatics; Criminology and Judicial Law; Public Management and Political Planification; Social Pedagogy; Drug Dependency, 2 yrs; *Post- títulos/ Diploma*: Environment Design; Structural Design; Geotechnics; Design and Construction of Asphaltum Pavements; Drugs Dependency; Marketing and Communication; Education; Social Mediation; Municipal Management, less than 1 yr; *Doctorado*

Student Services: Academic counselling, Canteen, Cultural centre, Employment services, Foreign student adviser, Handicapped facilities, Health services, Language programs, Social counselling, Sports facilities

Student Residential Facilities: None

Libraries: One Library per campus (5); c. 21,000 vols. Also Virtual Library

Publications: Diseño Urbano y Paisaje (Digital Version), Urban and Landscape Design *(3 per annum)*; Ingeniería al Día (Printed Version), Engineering and Physics and Mathematics Sciences *(annually)*; Perspectivas (Printed Version), Preschool Education *(annually)*; Revista Central de Sociología (Printed and Digital Version), Sociology, Social Studies *(annually)*; Revista de Derecho (Printed Version), Law, Society, Culture *(annually)*; Revista de Educación Básica (Printed Version), Elementary Education *(annually)*; Revista Ecoengen (Printed Version), Environmental Studies *(biennially)*; Revista Enfoques (Printed Version), Political Studies, Administration, Social Studies *(biennially)*; Revista Mesa Redonda (Printed Version), General Culture *(annually)*; Revista Motricidad y Persona (Printed Version), Physical Edcuation, Human Motricity *(biennially)*; Revista Sociedad y Conocimiento (Printed Version), Globalization, society, knowledge, economy *(quarterly)*; Rumbos TS (Printed Version), Social Works, Social Studies *(annually)*

Academic Staff 2007-2008	MEN	WOMEN	TOTAL
FULL-TIME	120	78	**198**
PART-TIME	631	276	**907**
STAFF WITH DOCTORATE			
FULL-TIME	32	19	**51**
PART-TIME	91	28	**119**
Student Numbers 2007-2008			
All (Foreign Included)	4,041	4,261	**8,302**
FOREIGN ONLY	97	52	**149**

Evening students, 1,324.
Last Updated: 04/03/09

CHILEAN-BRITISH PROFESSIONAL INSTITUTE OF CULTURE

Instituto Profesional Chileno-Británico de Cultura
Miraflores 123, Santiago
Tel: +56(2) 638-2156
Fax: +56(2) 638-6924
EMail: informaciones@ipbritanico.cl
Website: http://www.britanico.cl

Rector: Anthony Adams Turner

Programmes

English Studies (Cultural Studies; English; English Studies); **Translation and Interpretation** (English; Spanish; Translation and Interpretation)

Further Information: Regional Branches in Providencia, Las Condes and Ñuñoa

History: Founded 1982.

Main Language(s) of Instruction: Spanish

Degrees and Diplomas: *Título Profesional*
Last Updated: 03/03/09

CHILEAN-BRITISH UNIVERSITY OF SANTIAGO

Universidad Chileno-Británica de Cultura
Santa Lucia 124, Santiago
Tel: +56(2) 413-20-00
Fax: +56(2) 632-66-37
EMail: admision@ubritanica.cl
Website: http://www.ubritanica.cl

Rectora: María Cristina Brieba Mercado

Vicerrectora Académica: Adriana Pineda

Programmes
Basic Education in English (Education; English); **English-Spanish Translation** (English; Spanish; Translation and Interpretation); **Teaching of English** (Education; Pedagogy)

History: Founded 2006.

Main Language(s) of Instruction: Spanish

Degrees and Diplomas: *Licenciatura; Magister; Doctorado*
Last Updated: 18/05/09

CIISA PROFESSIONAL INSTITUTE

Instituto Profesional CIISA
Avenida República 20, Santiago
Tel: +56(2) 697-2121
Fax: +56(2) 699-8185
EMail: serveduc@ipciisa.cl
Website: http://www.ipciisa.cl

Director General: Antonio Holgado
Tel: +56(2) 697-2121, Fax: +56(2) 699-8185

Programmes
Computer Science

History: Founded 1979, acquired present status 1990.

Main Language(s) of Instruction: Spanish

Degrees and Diplomas: *Título Profesional*
Last Updated: 04/03/09

DIEGO PORTALES PROFESSIONAL INSTITUTE

Instituto Profesional Diego Portales
Maipú 301, Concepción
Tel: +56(41) 910-252
Fax: +56(41) 910-252
Website: http://www.dportales.cl

Rector: Luis Beltrán Troncoso

Programmes
Accountancy (Accountancy); **Aquaculture** (Aquaculture); **Building Techniques**; **Business Administration** (Business Administration); **Business, Tourism and Hotel Management**; **Computer Engineering** (Computer Engineering); **Construction Engineering** (Construction Engineering); **Forestry** (Forestry); **Gastronomy**; **Marketing**; **Preschool Education**; **Risk Prevention** (Safety Engineering); **Secretarial Studies**; **Social Services** (Social and Community Services)

History: Founded 1988.

Main Language(s) of Instruction: Spanish

Degrees and Diplomas: *Título Profesional:* 4 yrs
Last Updated: 02/03/09

DIEGO PORTALES UNIVERSITY

Universidad Diego Portales (UDP)
Manuel Rodríguez Sur 415, Santiago 8370179
Tel: +56(2) 676-2000
Fax: +56(2) 676-2112
EMail: gabriel.libedinsky@udp.cl
Website: http://www.udp.cl

Rector: Carlos Peña (2006-)
Tel: +56(2) 676-2131, Fax: +56(2) 676-2112
EMail: carlos.pena@udp.cl

Vicerrector Academico: Cristóbal Marín
Tel: +56(2) 676-2116, Fax: +56(2) 676-2141
EMail: cristobal.marin@udp.cl

International Relations: Gabriel Libedinsky
Tel: +56(2) 676-8305, Fax: +56(2) 676-2112

Faculties
Architecture, Design and Fine Arts (Architecture; Design; Fine Arts; Graphic Design; Industrial Design) *Dean:* Mathias Klotz; **Business** (Accountancy; Business Administration; Finance; Human Resources; Marketing) *Dean:* Sergio Olavarrieta; **Communication and Literature** (Advertising and Publicity; Communication Studies; Education; Journalism; Literature) *Dean:* Cecilia García-Huidobro; **Engineering** (Civil Engineering; Computer Engineering; Computer Science; Construction Engineering; E-Business/Commerce; Engineering; Industrial Engineering; Information Technology; Statistics; Telecommunications Engineering) *Dean:* Jose Manuel Robles; **Health Sciences** *Dean:* Fernando Mönckeberg; **Law** (Commercial Law; Justice Administration; Law; Social Sciences) *Dean:* Andres Cuneo; **Social Sciences and Education** (Education; Social Sciences) *Dean:* Juan Pablo Toro; **Social Sciences and History** *Dean:* Manuel Vicuña

Institutes
Social Sciences (Social Sciences) *Director:* Eduardo Sabrovsky

Further Information: Regional Branch in Temuco

History: Founded 1982, acquired autonomous status 1993. A private institution.

Governing Bodies: Consejo Directivo Superior; Consejo Académico; Comité de Rectoría

Academic Year: March to December

Admission Requirements: Secondary school certificate; National university admission test and interviews

Fees: (US Dollars): c. 3,000 per annum (equivalent toc. 1,500,000 Chilean Pesos)

Main Language(s) of Instruction: Spanish

International Co-operation: With universities in the United States; Germany; France; Finland; Spain; Latin America

Accrediting Agencies: Red Latinomericana de Cooperación Universitaria (RLCU)

Degrees and Diplomas: *Licenciatura:* 5-6 yrs; *Magister:* 1-2 yrs following Licenciatura; *Post- títulos/ Diploma:* 1-2 sem

Student Services: Academic counselling, Cultural centre, Employment services, Foreign student adviser, Handicapped facilities, Language programs, Nursery care, Social counselling, Sports facilities

Student Residential Facilities: None

Libraries: Faculty libraries
Last Updated: 06/03/09

DR. VIRGINIO GÓMEZ PROFESSIONAL INSTITUTE

Instituto Profesional Dr. Virginio Gómez (IPVG)
Cochrane 32, Concepción
Tel: +56(41) 403-400
Fax: +56(41) 403-400
EMail: infor@atenea.ipvg.cl
Website: http://www.virginiogomez.cl

Rector: Claudio Sáez Fuentes

Director de Administración y Finanzas: Héctor Pereira Sáez

Schools
Commerce and Administration (Administration; Business Administration; Business and Commerce); **Communication** (Advertising and Publicity; Graphic Design; Public Relations); **Computer Science** (Computer Science); **Construction** (Civil Engineering); **Health and Education** (Dental Hygiene; Laboratory Techniques; Nursing; Rehabilitation and Therapy; Special Education); **Industrial Technology** (Electrical and Electronic Engineering;

Industrial Engineering; Mechanical Engineering; Technology; Telecommunications Engineering)

Further Information: Campuses in Chillán and Los Angeles

History: Founded 1989, belongs to Universidad de Concepción.

Governing Bodies: Consejo Directivo, comprising 5 members

Main Language(s) of Instruction: Spanish

Degrees and Diplomas: *Técnico de Nivel Superior*; *Título Profesional*

Last Updated: 05/03/09

DUOCUC PROFESSIONAL INSTITUTE

Instituto Profesional DuocUC (DUOCUC)
Dario Urzúa 2100, Santiago
Tel: +56(2) 640-6800
EMail: info@duoc.cl
Website: http://www.duoc.cl

Rector: Marcelo von Chrismar Werth

Secretario General: Jorge Fernández P.

Schools

Business Management (Accountancy; Business Administration; International Business; Marketing); **Communication Studies** (Acting; Advertising and Publicity; Communication Studies; Fashion Design; Graphic Design; Hotel Management; Industrial Design; Tourism); **Computer Science and Telecommunications**; **Construction Engineering** (Architectural and Environmental Design; Civil Engineering; Construction Engineering; Safety Engineering; Surveying and Mapping); **Design** (Design); **Engineering** (Automation and Control Engineering; Automotive Engineering; Computer Engineering; Computer Networks; Electrical and Electronic Engineering; Engineering; Industrial Engineering); **Health Studies**; **Natural Resources** (Agronomy; Environmental Engineering; Natural Resources); **Tourism** (Cooking and Catering; Hotel Management; Tourism)

Further Information: Also Valparaíso, Viña del Mar, Concepción, Antonio Varas, Alameda and San Carlos de Apoquindo branches

History: Founded 1983.

Governing Bodies: Consejo

Main Language(s) of Instruction: Spanish

Degrees and Diplomas: *Técnico de Nivel Superior*; *Título Profesional*

Last Updated: 02/03/09

EATRI PROFESSIONAL INSTITUTE

Instituto Profesional EATRI
Avenida Condell 451, Providencia, Santiago
Tel: +56(2) 223-1089
Fax: +56(2) 269-2990
EMail: eatri@eatri.cl
Website: http://www.eatri.cl

Rectora: Violeta Morgado Segura

Programmes

Translation and Interpretation (Translation and Interpretation)

History: Founded 1970.

Main Language(s) of Instruction: Spanish

Degrees and Diplomas: *Título Profesional*

Last Updated: 04/03/09

ENAC PROFESSIONAL INSTITUTE

Instituto Profesional ENAC
Alameda 2182, Santiago
Tel: +56(2) 473-8800
EMail: info@enac.cl
Website: http://www.enac.cl

Directora General: Ana Larraín Undurraga

Programmes

Family Guidance (Family Studies); **Preschool Education** (Preschool Education)

Further Information: Also branch in Concepción

History: Founded 1989.

Main Language(s) of Instruction: Spanish

Degrees and Diplomas: *Título Profesional*: 4 yrs

Last Updated: 03/03/09

ESUCOMEX PROFESSIONAL INSTITUTE

Instituto Profesional ESUCOMEX
Avenida Ejército 27, Providencia, Santiago
Tel: +56(2) 367-9758
EMail: info@esucomex.cl
Website: http://www.esucomex.cl

Rector: Fernando Gallardo Aguirre

Schools

Accountancy; **Administration**; **Commerce**; **Computer Science** (Computer Science; Secretarial Studies; Systems Analysis); **Decoration and Design** (Architectural and Environmental Design; Industrial Design; Interior Design); **Tourism** (Tourism)

History: Founded 1989.

Main Language(s) of Instruction: Spanish

Degrees and Diplomas: *Técnico de Nivel Superior*; *Título Profesional*: 4 yrs

Last Updated: 03/03/09

FEDERICO SANTA MARÍA TECHNICAL UNIVERSITY

Universidad Técnica Federico Santa María
Avenida España 1680, Casilla 110-V, Valparaíso
Tel: +56(32) 654-110
Fax: +56(32) 797-501
EMail: info@utfsm.cl
Website: http://www.utfsm.cl

Rector: José Rodríguez Pérez
Tel: +56(32) 654-140, Fax: +56(32) 797-501
EMail: jose.rodriguez@usm.clnospam

Secretario General: Francisco Ghisolfo Araya
Tel: +56(32) 654-264, Fax: +56(32) 797-445
EMail: francisco.ghisolfo@usm.clnospam

International Relations: José M. Gundelach Lagos
EMail: jose.gundelach@usm.clnospam

Academies

Aeronautics *(Santiago)* (Aeronautical and Aerospace Engineering)

Departments

Architecture (Architecture); **Chemical Engineering** (Chemical Engineering); **Chemistry** (Chemistry; Environmental Engineering; Industrial Chemistry; Natural Sciences); **Civil Engineering** (Civil Engineering; Construction Engineering); **Computer Engineering** (Computer Engineering; Computer Science; Information Management; Software Engineering); **Electrical Engineering** (Civil Engineering; Electrical Engineering); **Electronics** (Automation and Control Engineering; Computer Science; Electronic Engineering; Telecommunications Engineering); **Humanities** (Arts and Humanities); **Industrial Engineering** (Business and Commerce; Industrial Engineering); **Materials Science** (Civil Engineering; Materials Engineering; Metallurgical Engineering); **Mathematics** (Mathematics; Natural Sciences); **Mechanical Engineering** (Industrial Design; Mechanical Engineering; Production Engineering); **Physical Education, Sports and Recreation** (Physical Education; Sports); **Physics** (Physics)

History: Founded 1932 as a private institution, endowed by Federico Santa María Carrera. Recognized by the State as technical university 1935. Mainly financed by the government, but enjoying administrative and academic autonomy.

Governing Bodies: Consejo Superior; Consejo Académico; Consejo Normativo de Sedes

Academic Year: March to January (March-June; July-November; November-January)

Admission Requirements: Secondary education (Licencia Secundaria) and entrance examination

Main Language(s) of Instruction: Spanish

Degrees and Diplomas: *Técnico de Nivel Superior*: Technical Studies, 6 sem; *Licenciatura*: Chemistry; Mathematics; Physics,

9 sem; *Magister*: Engineering; Science, a further 3-4 sem; *Título Profesional*: Architecture; Chemistry; Computer Sciences; Electrical Engineering; Electronics; Mechanical Engineering; Metallurgy, 10 sem; *Título Profesional*: Civil Engineering, 12 sem; *Doctorado*: Biotechnology, a further 3-4 yrs; *Doctorado*: Electrical Engineering; Mechanical Engineering, a further 2-3 yrs. Also MBA a further 2 yrs

Student Residential Facilities: None

Libraries: Central Library, c. 107,815 vols

Publications: Gestión Tecnológica; Scientia

GUAYAQUIL BRANCH

CAMPUS GUAYAQUIL

Avenida C.J. Arosemena Km. 4.5, Vía Duale, Guayaquil
Tel: +593(4) 202-020

Prorrector: Anastasio Gallego EMail: agallego@usm.edu.ec

JOSÉ MIGUEL CARRERA BRANCH OF VIÑA DEL MAR

CAMPUS 'JOSÉ MIGUEL CARRERA', VIÑA DEL MAR

Avenida Federico Santa María 6090, Los Aromos, Casilla 920, Viña del Mar
Tel: +56(32) 277-700
Fax: +56(32) 277-711
Website: http://www.jmc.utfsm.cl

Director: Bruno Dondero Lencioni
EMail: bruno.dondero@jmc.utfsm.cl

Programmes
Analytical Chemistry; **Automotive Mechanics**; **Civil Engineering**; **Computer Science**; **Electrical Engineering**; **Electronic Engineering**; **Environmental Management**; **Food Science**; **Industrial Mechanics**; **Plastic and Materials Sciences**; **Risk Prevention**

History: Founded 1971.

RANCAGUA BRANCH

CAMPUS RANCAGUA

Gamero 212, Rancagua
Tel: +56(72) 232-380
Fax: +56(72) 232-382

Director: Reinaldo Espinoza Ponce
EMail: reinaldo.espinoza@crgua.utfsm.cl

History: Founded 1995.

REY BALDUINO DE BÉLGICA BRANCH OF TALCAHUANO

CAMPUS 'REY BALDUINO DE BÉLGICA'

Alemparte 850, Casilla 457, Talcahuano
Tel: +56(41) 410-484
Fax: +56(32) 418-678
EMail: info.rbb@usm.cl
Website: http://www.rbb.utfsm.cl

Director: Ramón Saavedra Rogel (1997-)
EMail: ramon.saavedra@rbb.utfsm.cl

Programmes
Automotive Mechanics; **Civil Construction**; **Computer Science**; **Electricity**; **Electronic Engineering** (Electronic Engineering); **Food Control**; **Industrial Chemistry**; **Industrial Mechanics**; **Risk Prevention**; **Structural Design**; **Wood Industry**

History: Founded 1972.

SANTIAGO BRANCH

CAMPUS SANTIAGO

Avenida Santa María 6400, Vitacura, Santiago
Tel: +56(2) 353-1200
Fax: +56(2) 353-1313
Website: http://www.utfsmcs.cl

Director: Sergio Horlacher Neumann EMail: ahorla@ind.utfsm.cl

Academies
Aeronautics (Aeronautical and Aerospace Engineering; Engineering; Maintenance Technology)

Divisions
Engineering (Business and Commerce; Engineering; Industrial Engineering; Production Engineering)

History: Founded 1995.

FINISTERRAE UNIVERSITY
Universidad FinisTerrae (UFT)
Avenida Pedro de Valdivia 1509, Providencia, Santiago
Tel: +56(2) 420-7100
Fax: +56(2) 420-7600
EMail: fterrae@finisterrae.cl
Website: http://www.finisterrae.cl

Rector: Roberto Guerrero Del Río EMail: rguerrero@finisterrae.cl

Secretario General: Roberto Salim-Hanna S.
Fax: +56(2) 274-5578

Faculties
Architecture and Design (Architectural and Environmental Design; Architecture; Design) *Dean*: José Gabriel Alemparte R.; **Arts** (Acting; Engraving; Fine Arts; Painting and Drawing; Sculpture) *Dean*: Teresa Gazitúa C.; **Business Administration and Economics** (Business Administration; Economics) *Dean*: Ernesto Illanes L.; **Dentistry** *Dean*: Sergio Sánchez Rojas; **Education and Family Studies** (Education; Family Studies; Preschool Education) *Dean*: Luz María Budge C.; **Law** (Commercial Law; Law; Public Law) *Dean*: Miguel Schweitzer W.; **Medicine**; **Social Sciences** (Communication Studies; History; Journalism; Social Sciences) *Director*: Loreta Serrano

Schools
Family Studies (Family Studies) *Director*: Carmen Gloria Beroíza Williamson

History: Founded 1981, acquired autonomous status 1996.

Governing Bodies: Consejo Superior, comprising 23 members

Academic Year: March to December (March-July; August-December)

Admission Requirements: Secondary school certificate (Licencia de Educación Media), Prueba de Aptitud Académica and interview

Main Language(s) of Instruction: Spanish

Degrees and Diplomas: *Licenciatura*: Acting; Plastic Arts; Teaching, 4 yrs; *Licenciatura*: Business Administration; Economics; History; Juridical Sciences, 5 yrs; *Magister*; Post- títulos/ Diploma; *Título Profesional*: Architecture, 6 yrs; *Título Profesional*: Commercial Engineering; Design; Journalism, 5 yrs

Student Services: Academic counselling, Canteen, Cultural centre, Health services, Language programs, Social counselling, Sports facilities

Libraries: Central Library, c. 13,000 vols

Publications: Alas y Raíces *(annually)*; Finis Terrae Review *(annually)*; Revista de Derecho *(annually)*; Teatrae *(biannually)*
Last Updated: 06/03/09

GABRIELA MISTRAL UNIVERSITY
Universidad Gabriela Mistral (UGM)
Avenida Ricardo Lyon 1177, Santiago
Tel: +56(2) 414-4545
Fax: +56(2) 204-9074
EMail: ugmistra@ugm.cl
Website: http://www.ugm.cl

Rectora: Alicia Romo Román

Vicerrector Académico: Ricardo Riesco Jaramillo

Centres
Virtual Education (Educational Sciences) *Director*: Andrés Singh Cornejo

Departments
Sports (Sports) *Director*: Alejandro Serrano Silva

Faculties

Economics and Administration (Accountancy; Administration; Business and Commerce; Economics) *Dean*: Alfonso Serrano S.; **Education** (Education; Family Studies; Media Studies; Preschool Education) *Dean*: Josefina Aragoneses Alonso; **Engineering** (Civil Engineering; Construction Engineering; Information Management; Information Technology) *Dean*: Rodolfo Martínez Ocáriz; **Law** (Law) *Dean*: Arnaldo Gorziglia Balbi; **Psychology** (Psychology) *Dean*: Hernán Berwart Torrens; **Social Sciences** (History; Journalism; Philosophy; Political Sciences; Social Sciences) *Dean*: Fernando Moreno Valencia

Institutes

Economics (Economics) *Director*: Erik Haindl Rondanelli; **Languages** (Modern Languages) *Director*: Juan José Zéron Domínguez; **Pacific Studies** (Pacific Area Studies) *Director*: Jorge Martínez Busch; **Religious Studies** (Religious Studies) *Director*: Raúl Hasbún Zaror

Further Information: Also branch in Puerto Varas

History: Founded 1981, acquired autonomous status 1992.

Academic Year: March to January

Admission Requirements: Secondary school certificate (Licencia de Educación Media) and entrance examination

Main Language(s) of Instruction: Spanish

Degrees and Diplomas: *Bachiller*: Social Sciences, 2 yrs; *Licenciatura*: Economics and/or Administration; Education; Law and Social Sciences, 5 yrs; *Licenciatura*: Psychology, 6 yrs; *Magister*: Natural Resources Management; Political Philosophy; *Post- títulos/Diploma*; *Título Profesional*: Accountancy; Journalism, 5 yrs

Libraries: c. 10,000 vols

Publications: Revista del Instituto de Estudios del Pacífico *(biannually)*; Temas de Derecho *(quarterly)*

Last Updated: 06/03/09

GAMMA PROFESSIONAL INSTITUTE OF ELECTRONICS
Instituto Superior de Electrónica GAMMA
Avenida Manuel Rodríguez Sur 585, Santiago
Tel: +56(2) 672-3333
Fax: +56(2) 695-2006
EMail: infogamma@institutogamma.cl
Website: http://www.institutogamma.cl

Rector: Arnaldo Gaspar Tapia

Programmes
Electronic Engineering (Electronic Engineering)

History: Founded 1990.

Main Language(s) of Instruction: Spanish

Degrees and Diplomas: *Técnico de Nivel Superior*: 2 yrs; *Título Profesional*: 4 yrs
Last Updated: 03/03/09

GUILLERMO SUBERCASEAUX PROFESSIONAL INSTITUTE OF BANKING STUDIES
Instituto Profesional Instituto de Estudios Bancarios Guillermo Subercaseaux
Agustinas 1476 piso 8, Santiago
Tel: +56(2) 469-4000
Fax: +56(2) 499-4091
EMail: ieb@ieb.cl
Website: http://www.ieb.cl

Rectora: Lucía Pardo Vásquez

Programmes
Banking; **Finance** (Finance)

Further Information: Also branches in La Serena, Rancagua, Concepción, Temuco, Viña del Mar

History: Founded 1929.

Main Language(s) of Instruction: Spanish

Degrees and Diplomas: *Técnico de Nivel Superior*; *Título Profesional*. Also Especialización
Last Updated: 05/03/09

IBERO-AMERICAN UNIVERSITY OF SCIENCE AND TECHNOLOGY
Universidad Iberoamericana de Ciencias y Tecnología
Padre Miguel de Olivares 1620 y 1635 Casilla 13901, Santiago
Tel: +56(2) 389-9000
Fax: +56(2) 389-9016
EMail: informaciones@unicit.cl
Website: http://www.unicit.cl

Rector: Carlos Pereira Albernoz Tel: +56(2) 389-9003

Vicerrector Académico: Marcelo Elgueta Vergara
Tel: +56(2) 389-9005 EMail: melgueta@unicit.cl

International Relations: Sergio Burdiles Pinto
Tel: +56(2) 389-9067 EMail: sburdiles@unicit.cl

Divisions
Basic Sciences *Directora*: Alejandra Opazo Godoy

Faculties
Commerce and Administration (Accountancy; Administration; Business Administration; Business and Commerce) *Dean*: Patricia Pérez Crignola; **Education** (Education) *Dean*: Osvaldo Astudillo Castro; **Engineering** (Biomedical Engineering; Computer Science; Electronic Engineering; Engineering; Food Science; Food Technology) *Dean*: Raúl Smith Fontana; **Veterinary Medicine, Agronomy and Forestry** (Agronomy; Cattle Breeding; Forest Economics; Forest Management; Forestry; Fruit Production; Natural Resources; Oenology; Public Health; Veterinary Science) *Dean*: Frederick Ahumada Mania

Further Information: Campuses in Casa Blanca and Las Vizcachas

History: Founded 1989.

Governing Bodies: Junta Directiva, comprising 11 members; Consejo Superior Académico

Academic Year: March to December (March-July; August-December)

Admission Requirements: Licencia de Educación Media and the PSU

Fees: (Chilean Pesos): Day school, c 1.3m. per annum; evening school, c. 850,000

International Co-operation: With universities in Spain; France and USA

Accrediting Agencies: Ministry of Education

Degrees and Diplomas: *Licenciatura*; *Magister*; *Post- títulos/Diploma*; *Título Profesional*: 5 yrs
Libraries: c. 29,320 vols

Student Numbers *2007-2008*: Total 1,800
Last Updated: 06/03/09

INCACEA PROFESSIONAL INSTITUTE OF ART AND SCIENCE
Instituto Profesional de Ciencias y Artes INCACEA
Avenida Cristóbal Colón 7055, Las Condes, Santiago
Tel: +56(2) 366-9000
Fax: +56(2) 366-9005
EMail: info@incacea.cl
Website: http://www.incacea.cl

Rectora: Amada Solervicens Rebolledo

Schools
Communication Studies (Communication Studies; Media Studies; Multimedia; Public Relations; Radio and Television Broadcasting); **Design** (Architectural and Environmental Design; Design; Fashion Design; Graphic Design); **Gastronomy** (Administration; Cooking and Catering); **Hotel and Tourism Management** (Hotel and Restaurant; Hotel Management; Tourism)

Further Information: Also branch in Viña del Mar

History: Founded 1989.

Main Language(s) of Instruction: Spanish

Degrees and Diplomas: *Título Profesional*: 4 yrs
Last Updated: 02/03/09

INTERNATIONAL UNIVERSITY SEK
Universidad Internacional SEK
Avenida José Arrieta I0000 Peñalolén, Casilla postal 1, Villa La Reina, Santiago
Tel: +56(2) 279-2940
Fax: +56(2) 278-3791
EMail: admision@sekmail.com
Website: http://www.sek.cl

Rector: Alejandro Ormeño Ortiz

Faculties
Cultural Heritage Studies (Archaeology; Art History; Cultural Studies; Fine Arts; Heritage Preservation; Journalism; Tourism); **Economics and Administration** (Administration; Economics); **Law** (Administrative Law; Civil Law; Commercial Law; Criminal Law; International Law; Labour Law; Law); **Psychology**; **Science** (Accountancy; Business and Commerce; Economics; English; Finance; International Business; Law; Mathematics; Natural Sciences)

History: Founded 1892, acquired present status and title 1988.

Governing Bodies: Junta Directiva; Consejo Académico

Academic Year: March to December

Admission Requirements: Secondary school certificate (Licencia de Educación Media)

Main Language(s) of Instruction: Spanish

Degrees and Diplomas: *Licenciatura*: Administration and Economics; Art History; Juridical Sciences; Psychology; Social Communication; Tourism; *Doctorado*: Law; Economics

Publications: Faculty Monographs; Serial Publications

Press or Publishing House: Ediciones de la Universidad Internacional SEK

IPROC GAMMA PROFESSIONAL INSTITUTE
Instituto Profesional IPROC GAMMA
Lincoyan 444, Concepción
Tel: +56(41) 2226-455
Fax: +56(41) 2226-664
Website: http://www.iprocgamma.cl

Rector: Rodolfo Becker Barría EMail: rodolfobecker@iproc.cl

Schools
Business; **Construction** (Construction Engineering; Environmental Engineering; Safety Engineering); **Education** *(Luis Galdames)* (Pedagogy; Psychology); **Electronics**; **Health** (Nursing); **Sports**

Further Information: Also branches in Santiago and Rancagua

History: Founded following merger of Instituto Profesional de Concepción, Instituto Profesional Luis Galdames and Instituto Profesional Gamma.

Main Language(s) of Instruction: Spanish
Last Updated: 05/03/09

LA ARAUCANA PROFESSIONAL INSTITUTE
Instituto Profesional La Araucana
Ejército 171, Santiago
Tel: +56(2) 427-1000
Fax: +56(2) 427-1027
Website: http://www.iplaaraucana.cl/

Rector: Nelson Stevenson

Vicerrector Académico: Manuel Garay Baros

Programmes
Accountancy (Accountancy); **Business Administration**; **Computer Engineering**; **Finance**; **Human Resources Management**; **Marketing**; **Multimedia Studies**; **Safety Engineering** (Safety Engineering); **Secretarial Studies**; **Social Service** (Social and Community Services)

Further Information: Regional Branches in La Serena, Curicó, Concepción, Temuco, Osorno and Puerto Montt

History: Founded 1988.

Main Language(s) of Instruction: Spanish

Degrees and Diplomas: *Licenciatura*; *Título Profesional*
Last Updated: 04/03/09

LATIN AMERICAN PROFESSIONAL INSTITUTE OF FOREIGN TRADE
Instituto Profesional Latinoamericano de Comercio Exterior
Dieciocho 182, Providencia, Santiago
Tel: +56(2) 699-4760
EMail: contacto@iplacex.cl
Website: http://www.iplacex.cl/

Rector: Hugo Fredi Fuentes Tejos

Schools
Administration and Trade (Accountancy; Business Administration; International Business); **Art and Communication**; **Education**; **Health Studies** (Dietetics; Nursing; Nutrition; Physical Therapy); **Social Sciences and Law**; **Technology and Computer Science** (Computer Engineering; Systems Analysis)

Further Information: Also branches in Copiapó, Valparaíso, Talca, Concepción, Temuco and Pta Arenas

History: Founded 1990.

Main Language(s) of Instruction: Spanish

Degrees and Diplomas: *Técnico de Nivel Superior*; *Título Profesional*
Last Updated: 03/03/09

LIBERATOR OF THE ANDES PROFESSIONAL INSTITUTE
Instituto Profesional Libertador de Los Andes
Membrillar 360, Los Andes
Tel: +56(34) 424-954
EMail: ipla@ipla.cl
Website: http://www.ipla.cl

Rectora: Carolina Serey Luengo

Programmes
Accountancy (Accountancy); **Administration** (Administration); **Basic Education Teacher Training** (Teacher Training); **Computer Engineering**; **Early Childhood Education** (Preschool Education); **Psychopedagogy** (Educational Psychology); **Social Services**

Further Information: Also branch in Valparaíso

History: Founded 1981.

Main Language(s) of Instruction: Spanish

Degrees and Diplomas: *Técnico de Nivel Superior*; *Título Profesional*
Last Updated: 03/03/09

LOS LEONES PROFESSIONAL INSTITUTE
Instituto Profesional Los Leones
Arturo Prat 386, Alonzo de Ovalle 1546, Santiago
Tel: +56(2) 632-1573
Fax: +56(2) 632-1698
EMail: ipleones@ctcreuna.cl
Website: http://www.ipleones.cl

Rector: Fernando Vicencio Silva

Programmes
Graphic Design; **Photography** (Photography); **Preschool Education**; **Psychopedagogy**; **Public Relations**; **Social Communication and Marketing**

History: Founded 1990.

Main Language(s) of Instruction: Spanish

Degrees and Diplomas: *Título Profesional*: 4 yrs
Last Updated: 03/03/09

MAYOR UNIVERSITY
Universidad Mayor
Manuel Montt 367 - Providencia, Santiago
Tel: +56(2) 328-1000
Website: http://www.umayor.cl

Rector: Rubén Covarrubias Giordano (1998-)
Tel: 328-1114 EMail: rector@umayor.cl

Vicerrectora: Eugenia Camhi Tel: +56(2) 328-1226

Conservatories

Music *(Vespucio Campus/Santiago)* (Music; Music Education; Musical Instruments) *Director*: Roberto Bravo

Faculties

Agriculture and Forestry *(Huechuraba Campus/Santiago) Dean*: Eduardo Venezian; **Architecture** *(Portugal Campus/Santiago)* (Architecture) *Dean*: Jaime Matas; **Art** *(Portugal Campus, Santo Domingo Campus/Santiago)* (Dance; Film; Fine Arts; Theatre; Visual Arts) *Dean*: Héctor Noguera; **Communication and Design** *(Huechuraba Campus/Santiago) Dean*: Lucia Castellon; **Dentistry** *(Alameda Campus/Santiago)* (Dentistry; Speech Therapy and Audiology) *Dean*: Hernán Barahona; **Economics and Business** *(Manuel Montt Campus/Santiago)* (Accountancy; Business Administration; Business and Commerce; Economics; Finance; Marketing) *Dean*: Verónica González Gil; **Education** *(Manuel Montt Campus/Santiago)* (Education; Educational Psychology; English; Music Education; Parks and Recreation; Pedagogy; Physical Education; Primary Education; Secondary Education; Special Education; Sports) *Dean*: Horacio Marin; **Engineering** *(Manuel Montt Campus/Santiago)* (Civil Engineering; Computer Science; Electronic Engineering; Engineering; Industrial Engineering; Information Technology; Telecommunications Engineering) *Dean*: Roberto Acevedo; **Health Sciences** *(Huechuraba Campus/Santiago)* (Dietetics; Gynaecology and Obstetrics; Health Sciences; Medical Technology; Medicine; Nursing; Nutrition; Occupational Therapy; Physical Therapy) *Dean*: Juan Giaconi; **Law and Social Sciences** *(Temuco Campus)* (Law; Social Sciences) *Dean*: Gustavo Cuevas

Schools

Advertising *(Huechuraba Campus/Santiago)* (Advertising and Publicity) *Director*: Maricarmen Estevez; **Agronomy** *(Huechuraba Campus/Santiago) Director*: Norma Sepúlveda; **Architecture I** *(Portugal Campus/Santiago) Director*: Ignacio Volante; **Architecture II** *(Temuco Campus) Director*: Gonzalo Verdugo; **Business Administration I** *(Manuel Montt Campus/Santiago)* (Business Administration) *Director*: Edmundo Duran; **Business Administration II** *(Temuco Campus) Director*: Hugo Cumsille; **Dance** *(Portugal Campus, Santo Domingo Campus/Santiago) Director*: Vicente Ruiz; **Digital Images** *(Vespucio Campus, Portugal Campus/Santiago)* (Visual Arts) *Director*: Alejandro Rojas; **Electronics Civil Engineering** *(Manuel Montt Campus/Santiago) Director*: Hugo Tirado; **Electronics Civil Engineering, Telecommunications Major** *(Manuel Montt Campus/Santiago) Director*: Hugo Tirado; **Film** *(Portugal Campus, Santo Domingo Campus/Santiago)* (Film) *Director*: Ricardo Larrín; **Forestry** *(Huechuraba Campus/Santiago) Director*: Veronica González Barraza; **Graphic Design I** *(Huechuraba Campus/Santiago) Director*: Luis Moro; **Graphic Design II** *(Temuco Campus)* (Graphic Design) *Director*: Patricio Radovan; **Industrial Civil Engineering** *(Manuel Montt Campus/Santiago) Director*: Juan Carvajal; **Industrial Civil Engineering, Information Technology Major** *(Manuel Montt Campus/Santiago)* (Civil Engineering; Industrial Engineering; Information Technology) *Director*: Juan Carvajal; **Industrial Design** *(Huechuraba Campus/Santiago) Director*: Hugo Rojas; **Interior Design** *(Huechuraba Campus/Santiago) Director*: Mariane Irene Pardow; **Journalism** *(Temuco Campus) Director*: Claudia Vera; **Kinesiology I** *(Huechuraba Campus/Santiago)* (Physical Therapy) *Director*: Fernando Lira; **Kinesiology II** *(Temuco Campus)* (Physical Therapy) *Director*: Domingo Salas; **Law II** *(Vespucio Campus/Santiago) Dean*: Gustavo Cuevas; **Medical Technology** *(Huechuraba Campus/Santiago) Director*: Victor Silva; **Medical Technology II** *(Temuco)* (Medical Technology) *Director*: Jaime Inostroza; **Medicine** *(Huechuraba Campus/Santiago) Director*: Adela Contreras; **Nursing I** *(Huechuraba Campus/Santiago) Director*: Cecilia Latrach; **Nursing II** *(Temuco Campus) Director*: Gina Muñoz; **Nutrition and Dietetics** *(Huechuraba Campus/Santiago) Director*: Betty Avila; **Obstetrics** *(Huechuraba Campus/Santiago)* (Gynaecology and Obstetrics) *Director*: Solange Valenzuela; **Occupational Therapy** *(Huechuraba Campus/Santiago) Director*: Soledad Fernandez; **Odontology I** *(Alameda Campus/Santiago)* (Dentistry) *Director*: Dámaso González; **Odontology II** *(Temuco Campus)* (Dentistry) *Director*: Francisco Pérez; **Operations Engineering in Computer Science and Information Technology I** *(Manuel Montt Campus/Santiago)* (Computer Science; Information Technology) *Director*: Hérnan Moraga; **Operations Engineering in Computer Science and Information Technology II** *(Temuco Campus)* (Computer Science; Information Technology) *Director*: Pedro Manquilef; **Organizational Communication** *(Huechuraba Campus/Santiago)* (Communication Studies) *Director*: Raúl Herrera; **Pedagogy in Education of the Handicapped, Mental Deficiency and Multiple Handicaps Major I** *(Manuel Montt Campus/Santiago)* (Pedagogy; Special Education) *Director*: Veronica Albornoz; **Pedagogy in Education of the Handicapped, Mental Deficiency and Multiple Handicaps Major II** *Director*: Sandra Nome; **Pedagogy in English for Elementary and Secondary School Levels I** *(Temuco Campus) Director*: Marcela Araya; **Pedagogy in English for Elementary and Secondary School Levels I** *(Manuel Montt Campus/Santiago)* (English; Pedagogy; Primary Education; Secondary Education) *Director*: Soledad Campo; **Pedagogy in Infant and First Cycle Elementary School Level Education I** *(Manuel Montt Campus/Santiago) Director*: Soledad Campo; **Pedagogy in Infant and First Cycle Elementary School Level Education II** *(Temuco Campus) Director*: Patricia Guerrero; **Pedagogy in Musical Arts for Elementary and Secondary School Levels** *(Manuel Montt Campus/Santiago)* (Music Education; Pedagogy; Primary Education; Secondary Education) *Director*: Carlos Sánchez; **Pedagogy in Physical Education, Sports and Recreation for Elementary and Secondary School Levels I** *(Manuel Montt Campus/Santiago)* (Parks and Recreation; Pedagogy; Physical Education; Primary Education; Secondary Education; Sports) *Director*: Rodolfo Erdmann; **Pedagogy in Physical Education, Sports and Recreation for Elementary and Secondary School Levels II** *(Temuco Campus) Director*: Alejandro Ducassou; **Phonaudiology** *(Alameda Campus/Santiago) Director*: Manuel Perez, **Psychology I** *(Alameda Campus/Santiago) Director*: Ana María Zlachevsky; **Psychology II** *(Temuco Campus) Director*: Tatiana Gonzalez; **Psychopedagogy** *(Manuel Montt Campus/Santiago) Director*: Carolina Salamé; **Public Accounting and Auditing Business Administration** *(Temuco Campus) Director*: Hugo Cumsille; **Technical Business Administration, Finance and Marketing I** *(Manuel Montt Campus/Santiago)* (Business Administration; Finance; Marketing) *Director*: Edmundo Duran; **Technical Business Administration, Finance and Marketing II** *(Temuco Campus)* (Business Administration; Finance; Marketing) *Director*: Hugo Cumsille; **Theatre I** *(Portugal Campus, Santo Domingo Campus/Santiago) Director*: Rodrigo Pérez; **Theatre II** *(Temuco Campus)* (Theatre) *Director*: Rodrigo Pérez; **Veterinary Medicine I** *(Huechuraba Campus/Santiago) Director*: Macarena Vidal; **Veterinary Medicine II** *(Temuco Campus)* (Veterinary Science) *Director*: Ariel Apaoblaza; **Visual Arts** *(Portugal Campus, Santo Domingo Campus/Santiago)* (Visual Arts) *Director*: Eduardo Pérez; **Visual Communications I** *(Huechuraba Campus/Santiago)* (Visual Arts) *Director*: Carlos Araos; **Visual Communications II** *(Temuco Campus)* (Visual Arts) *Director*: Roberto Obreque

History: Founded 1988, acquired present status 1996. A private institution.

Governing Bodies: Junta Directiva

Academic Year: March to December (March-July; August-December)

Admission Requirements: Secondary school certificate (Licencia de Educación Media), and PSU, national examination test

Main Language(s) of Instruction: Spanish

International Co-operation: 163 cooperation agreements with universities in 35 countries

Accrediting Agencies: National Accreditation Committee (CNA)

Degrees and Diplomas: *Licenciatura*; *Magister*; *Post- títulos/Diploma*; *Título Profesional*; *Doctorado*

Student Services: Canteen, Cultural centre, Employment services, Health services, Language programs, Sports facilities

Student Residential Facilities: None

Special Facilities: Art Galleries; Gymnasium; Theatres; Auditoriums

Libraries: Ten University Libraries

Last Updated: 09/03/09

MIGUEL DE CERVANTES UNIVERSITY

Universidad Miguel de Cervantes
Merced 379 al 385, Santiago
Tel: +56(2) 633-9477
Fax: +56(2) 633-4255
EMail: portal@umcervantes.cl
Website: http://www.umcervantes.cl

Rector: Francisco Cumplido Cereceda

Vicerrector Académico: Héctor Casanueva Ojeda

Centres
Work Studies (Labour and Industrial Relations) *Executive Director*: Guillermo Pérez Vega

Institutes
International Relations *(Latin American)* (International Relations) *Executive Director*: Rodrigo Vega Alarcón; **Religious Studies** (Religious Studies) *Executive Director*: Juan Alberto Rabah

Schools
Journalism (Journalism) *Director*: Antonio Rojas Gómez; **Law** (Law) *Director*: José Luis Zavala; **Psychology** (Psychology) *Director*: Gonzalo Zaror Puentes

History: Founded 1998.

Governing Bodies: Junta Directiva; Consejo Académico

Main Language(s) of Instruction: Spanish

Degrees and Diplomas: *Licenciatura; Título Profesional*

PEDRO DE VALDIVIA UNIVERSITY
Universidad Pedro de Valdivia (UME)
Avenida Tobalaba 1275, Providencia, Santiago
Tel: +56(2) 233-5265
Fax: +56(2) 231-8711
EMail: info@ume.cl
Website: http://www.upv.cl/

Rector: Angel Maulén Ríos Tel: +56(2) 232-3485

Secretario General: Aldo Biagini Alarcón Tel: +56(2) 232-3482

Schools
Economics and Administration (Business Administration; Business and Commerce; Management) *Director*: Alejandro Álvarez Guarategua; **Law** (Law) *Director*: Gastón Salinas Ugarte; **Social Sciences** *Director*: Pablo Marassi Linzi

Further Information: Branch in La Serena

History: Founded 1988. Formerly known as Universidad Mariano Egaña.

Governing Bodies: Junta Directiva, comprising 6 members

Main Language(s) of Instruction: Spanish

Degrees and Diplomas: *Magister; Título Profesional*
Last Updated: 08/08/07

PROFESSIONAL INSTITUTE OF CHILE
Instituto Profesional de Chile
República 285, Santiago
Tel: +56(2) 685-0800
EMail: admision@ipdechile.cl
Website: http://www.ipdechile.cl

Rector: Jorge Narbona Lemus

Programmes
Business Administration (Business Administration; International Business); **Communication**; **Education** (Pedagogy; Preschool Education; Primary Education); **Health and Physical Activities** (Nursing; Nutrition; Occupational Therapy; Physical Education; Speech Therapy and Audiology; Sports); **Technology** (Automation and Control Engineering; Computer Engineering; Computer Networks; Construction Engineering; Electrical and Electronic Engineering; Industrial Engineering; Mechanical Engineering)

Further Information: Also branches in La Serena and Rancagua

History: Founded 1988.

Main Language(s) of Instruction: Spanish

Degrees and Diplomas: *Técnico de Nivel Superior; Título Profesional*
Last Updated: 03/03/09

PROFESSIONAL INSTITUTE OF EDUCATIONAL SCIENCES
Instituto Profesional de Ciencias y Educación Helen Keller
Blanco 1089, Valparaíso
Tel: +56(32) 2254-016
EMail: info@helenkeller.cl
Website: http://www.helenkeller.cl

Representante Legal: Julia Calderón Bordali

Programmes
Differential Education (Education of the Handicapped; Special Education)

History: Founded 1989.

Main Language(s) of Instruction: Spanish

Degrees and Diplomas: *Título Profesional*

PROFESSIONAL INSTITUTE OF THE CENTRAL VALLEY
Instituto Profesional del Valle Central
Barros Arana 321 2° piso, Concepción
Tel: +56(41) 220-656
Website: http://www.vallecentral.cl

Rector: Eduardo Conrado Aedo Inostroza

Schools
Administration and Trade; **Agro-industry** (Agricultural Business); **Art, Design and Communication** (Advertising and Publicity; Graphic Design; Photography; Public Relations; Sound Engineering (Acoustics); Theatre); **Construction**; **Criminology** (Criminology); **Education and Social Sciences** (English; Geography; History; Pedagogy; Preschool Education; Social Work; Sociology; Sports); **Engineering and Computer Science** (Business Computing; Computer Science; Environmental Management; Industrial Engineering; Information Technology; Safety Engineering; Transport Engineering); **Forestry and Wood Science**; **Health Sciences** (Dietetics; Gerontology; Gynaecology and Obstetrics; Nursing; Nutrition; Veterinary Science)

Further Information: Also branches in Constitución, La Serena, Curicó, Ovalle and Santiago

History: Founded 1988.

Main Language(s) of Instruction: Spanish

Degrees and Diplomas: *Técnico de Nivel Superior*: 3 yrs; *Título Profesional*: 41/2 yrs
Last Updated: 02/03/09

PROFESSIONAL INSTITUTE/MODERN SCHOOL OF MUSIC
Instituto Profesional Escuela Moderna de Música
Luis Pasteur 5303, Santiago
Tel: +56(2) 365-1818
Fax: +56(2) 195-393
EMail: info@emoderna.cl
Website: http://www.emoderna.cl

Rector: Vivien Wurman Shapiro

Programmes
Dance (Dance); **Music** (Music; Music Theory and Composition; Musical Instruments)

Further Information: Also branch in Viña del Mar

History: Founded 1988.

Main Language(s) of Instruction: Spanish

Degrees and Diplomas: *Título Profesional*
Last Updated: 05/03/09

PROFESSIONAL INSTITUTE/SCHOOL OF ACCOUNTANCY AND AUDITORS OF SANTIAGO
Instituto Profesional Escuela de Contadores Auditores de Santiago
Avenida Providencia 2640, Santiago
Tel: +56(2) 233-1896
Fax: +56(2) 231-4996
EMail: info@ecas.cl
Website: http://www.ecas.cl

Rector: Germán Cerón López EMail: gceron@ecas.cl

Vicerrector Académico: Luis Alberto Werner-Wildner

Departments
Accountancy and Auditing (Accountancy); **Administration** (Administration); **Computer Science**; **Economics** (Economics);

Finance (Finance); **Law**; **Quantitative Methods** (Statistics); **Social Sciences**; **Statistics**
History: Founded 1982.
Main Language(s) of Instruction: Spanish
Degrees and Diplomas: *Título Profesional*
Last Updated: 04/03/09

PROFESSIONAL INSTITUTE/SCHOOL OF PUBLIC RELATIONS

Instituto Profesional Escuela Nacional de Relaciones Públicas
Avenida Lota 2340, Providencia, Santiago
Tel: +56(2) 232-1906
Fax: +56(2) 251-9084
EMail: informacion@escuelarelacionespublicas.cl

Rector: Horacio Salas Reyes

Programmes
Public Relations (Advertising and Publicity; Business Administration; International Relations; Journalism; Marketing; Public Relations; Social Psychology; Social Studies)
Further Information: Also branch in Viña del Mar
History: Founded 1989.
Main Language(s) of Instruction: Spanish
Degrees and Diplomas: *Técnico de Nivel Superior*, *Título Profesional*: 5 yrs
Last Updated: 05/03/09

PROVIDENCIA PROFESSIONAL INSTITUTE

Instituto Profesional Providencia (IPP)
Padre Mariano 220, Santiago
Tel: +56(2) 328-7600
Fax: +56(2) 236-2296
EMail: info@ipp.cl
Website: http://www.ipp.cl

Rector: Álvaro Muñoz J.
Vicerrector Académico: Felipe Vidal Rojas EMail: f.vidal@ipp.cl

Schools
Administration and Commerce (Accountancy; Administration; Business Administration); **Communication**; **Computer Technology** (Computer Engineering; Computer Networks); **Design**; **Education** (Education; Pedagogy; Preschool Education; Primary Education; Psychology); **Health Studies** (Dietetics; Health Sciences; Medical Auxiliaries; Nursing; Nutrition; Occupational Therapy; Toxicology); **Social Law** (Law; Social and Community Services)
Further Information: Also branch in Concepción
History: Founded 1982.
Main Language(s) of Instruction: Spanish
Degrees and Diplomas: *Título Profesional*
Last Updated: 03/03/09

SAINT THOMAS PROFESSIONAL INSTITUTE

Instituto Profesional Santo Tomás
Zenteno 234, Santiago
Tel: +56(2) 495-7000
Fax: +56(2) 697-1200
EMail: ipst_stgo@santotomas.cl
Website: http://www.santotomas.cl/

Rector: Jaime Vatter Gutiérrez

Programmes
Administration (Administration; Tourism); **Communication and Design**; **Engineering and Technology**; **Natural Resources**; **Social Sciences** (Criminology; Social and Community Services; Social Work)
Further Information: Also branches in Arica, Iquique, Antofagasta, Copiapó, La Serena, Ovalle, Viña del Mar, Santiago, Rancagua, Curicó, Talca, Chillán, Concepción, Los Ángeles, Temuco, Valdivia, Osorno, Puerto Montt y Punta Arenas.
History: Founded 2001.

Main Language(s) of Instruction: Spanish
Degrees and Diplomas: *Técnico de Nivel Superior*, *Título Profesional*
Last Updated: 05/03/09

SAN MARCOS REGIONAL UNIVERSITY

Universidad Regional San Marcos
Tucapel No 3158-Valle Paicavi, Concepción
Tel: +56(41) 917-800
EMail: info@ursm.cl
Website: http://www.ursm.cl

Rector: Samuel Arancibia Lavín

Programmes
Basic Education (Education); **Commercial Engineering**; **Dentistry** (Dentistry); **Law** (Law); **Physical Education and Sports**; **Veterinary Medicine**
History: Founded 2004.
Main Language(s) of Instruction: Spanish
Degrees and Diplomas: *Licenciatura*: 41/2-6 yrs

SAN SEBASTIÁN UNIVERSITY

Universidad San Sebastián (USS)
Calle Cruz 1577, Concepción
Tel: +56(41) 400-000
Fax: +56(41) 400-102
EMail: info@mater.uss.cl
Website: http://www.uss.cl

Rector: José Luis Zabala Ponce EMail: jzabala@uss.cl
Vicerrectora Académica: Carmen Bonnefoy Dibarrart EMail: cbonnefoy@uss.cl
International Relations: Cristián Antoine F. EMail: cantoine@mater.uss.cl

Faculties
Business Administration; **Law**

Institutes
Applied Research and Technology (Technology) *Director*: Guillermo Schaffeld Granifo; **Cultural Studies** (Cultural Studies) *Director*: Nélson Vergara Bórquez

Schools
Business Administration Promotion (Business Administration) *Director*: Mónica Rassé; **Early Childhood Education** (Preschool Education) *Director*: Magdalena Burmeister Campos; **Information Sciences** *Director*: Berta Marín; **Kinesiology**; **Medicine** (Medical Technology; Medicine; Nursing) *Director*: Patricio Manzárraga; **Physiotherapy** *Director*: Fernando Quiroga; **Psychology** (Psychology) *Director*: Carmen Bonnefoy Dibarrat; **Social Work** (Social Work) *Director*: Marta Montory Torres
Further Information: Also Study Abroad programme. Regional Centre in Puerto Montt
History: Founded 1989, acquired autonomous status 2001.
Governing Bodies: Junta Directiva; Consejo Académico
Academic Year: March to December (March-July; August-December)
Admission Requirements: Secondary school certificate (Licencia de Educación Media) or equivalent, Prueba de Aptitud Académica
Fees: (Chilean Pesos): c. 900,000-2.3m.
Main Language(s) of Instruction: Spanish
Degrees and Diplomas: *Licenciatura*; *Título Profesional*
Student Services: Canteen, Sports facilities
Libraries: Central Library, c. 8,500 vols; Medical Library, c. 1,000

SANTO TOMÁS UNIVERSITY

Universidad Santo Tomás (UST)
Avenida Ejército Libertador 146, Santiago
Tel: +56(2) 362-5000
Fax: +56(2) 360-1376
EMail: ust@ust.cl
Website: http://www.ust.cl

Rector: Aníbal Vial Echeverría (2001-)
Tel: +56(2) 362-4905, Fax: +56(2) 360-1386 EMail: avial@ust.cl

Secretario General: Cristián Letelier Aguilar
Tel: +56(2) 362-4950, Fax: +56(2) 360-1386
EMail: cletelier@ust.cl

International Relations: Catalina Errazuriz
Tel: 56(2) 362-4822 EMail: cerrazuriz@ust.cl

Areas

Agriculture (Agriculture; Agronomy; Forestry; Natural Resources; Soil Science; Veterinary Science); **Communication Studies** (Communication Studies; Journalism; Public Relations); **Economics** (Administration; Business and Commerce; Economics; Engineering); **Humanities and Social Sciences** (Arts and Humanities; Humanities and Social Science Education; Psychology; Social Sciences; Social Work); **Law** (Law)

Schools

Accountancy (Accountancy); **Design** (Communication Studies; Design; Graphic Design)

Further Information: Campus in Vergara and Experimental Campus in San Bernardo

History: Founded 1988. A private institution under the supervision of the Corporación Santo Tomás.

Governing Bodies: Board of Directors

Academic Year: March to December

Admission Requirements: Secondary school certificate (Licencia de Educación Media), Prueba de Aptitud Académica, and entrance examination

Fees: (Chilean Pesos): 1.5m. per annum

Main Language(s) of Instruction: Spanish

Accrediting Agencies: ICUSTA (International Council of Universities of Saint Thomas Aquinas)

Degrees and Diplomas: Licenciatura: 5 yrs; Título Profesional: 4 yrs

Student Services: Canteen, Foreign student adviser, Handicapped facilities, Health services, Language programs, Social counselling

Special Facilities: Radio. TV

Libraries: 24,200 vols; 385 specialized journals

Publications: IUS Publicum; Law Faculty Journal (biennially)

SOUTHERN UNIVERSITY OF CHILE

Universidad Austral de Chile (UACH)
Independencia 641, Valdivia, Valdivia
Tel: +56(63) 221-960
Fax: +56(63) 213-589
EMail: difusion@uach.cl
Website: http://www.uach.cl

Rector: Víctor Cubillos
Tel: +56(63) 221-960, Fax: +56(63) 221-766
EMail: rectoria@uach.cl

Vicerrector Académico: Oscar Galindo
Tel: +56(63) 221-257, Fax: +56(63) 221-258
EMail: viceacad@.uach.cl

International Relations: José Escalda
EMail: joseescalda@uach.cl

Conservatories
Music Director: Héctor Escobar

Faculties

Agriculture (Agricultural Management; Agriculture; Animal Husbandry; Dairy; Food Science; Food Technology; Nutrition; Rural Planning; Rural Studies; Vegetable Production) Dean: Ricardo Fuentes Pérez; **Economics and Administration** (Accountancy; Business Administration; Economics; Management; Rural Planning; Tourism) Dean: Juan Carlos Miranda Castillo; **Engineering** (Architecture; Business Computing; Computer Engineering; Construction Engineering; Electronic Engineering; Engineering; Information Technology; Mechanical Engineering; Naval Architecture; Safety Engineering; Sound Engineering (Acoustics); Systems Analysis) Dean: Rogelio Moreno Muñoz; **Forestry** (Forest Management; Forest Products; Forestry; Natural Resources; Wood Technology) Dean: Roberto Juacida; **Law and**

Social Sciences (Administration; Justice Administration; Latin American Studies; Law; Safety Engineering; Social Sciences) Dean: Juan Andrés Varas Braun; **Medicine** (Anatomy; Cell Biology; Community Health; Gynaecology and Obstetrics; Haematology; Immunology; Medical Technology; Medicine; Microbiology; Midwifery; Nephrology; Nursing; Orthopaedics; Paediatrics; Pathology; Psychiatry and Mental Health; Surgery; Urology) Dean: Mario Calvo G.; **Philosophy and Humanities** (Anthropology; Arts and Humanities; Communication Studies; Development Studies; Education; Educational Administration; Family Studies; Hispanic American Studies; Information Technology; Journalism; Linguistics; Literature; Mathematics Education; Philosophy; Physics; Preschool Education) Dean: Gonzalo Portales G.; **Science** (Biochemistry; Biology; Botany; Cell Biology; Chemistry; Ecology; Genetics; Immunology; Limnology; Marine Biology; Microbiology; Molecular Biology; Natural Sciences; Pharmacy; Water Science; Zoology) Dean: Carlos Bertrán Vives; **Veterinary Science** (Anatomy; Animal Husbandry; Food Technology; Pathology; Veterinary Science; Zoology) Dean: Néstor Tadich B.

Further Information: Branch in Puerto Montt

History: Founded 1954. A private institution financed by the government.

Governing Bodies: Consejo Académico; Junta Directiva

Academic Year: March to December (March-July; August-December)

Admission Requirements: Secondary school certificate (Licencia de Educación Media) or recognized equivalent, and entrance examination. Also Certificate of Spanish Language Proficiency

Fees: (Chilean Pesos) 1.39m.-2.4m. per annum

Main Language(s) of Instruction: Spanish

International Co-operation: With universities in Germany; USA; Europe; Eastern Europe; Brazil; Venezuela; Uruguay; Spain; Canada; Denmark; Argentina; Mexico

Degrees and Diplomas: Licenciatura: Accountancy; Acoustic Engineering; Agricultural Engineering; Anthropology; Aquaculture Engineering; Business Administration; Computer Science; Construction Engineering; Electronic Engineering; Food Engineering; Health; Journalism; Law; Marine Biology; Mechanical Engineering; Naval Engineering; Veterinary Medicine, 5 yrs; Licenciatura: Biological Sciences; Midwifery; Teacher in Language and Communication; Tourism Management, 4 yrs; Licenciatura: Civil Engineering; Pharmacy, 6 yrs; Licenciatura: Forestry, 5 1/2 yrs; Licenciatura: Medicine, 7 yrs; Magister: Animal Pathology; Business Administration; Communication; Dairy Science and Technology; Ecology; Botany; Genetics; Limnology; Microbiology; Zoology; Water Resources; Animal Production; Animal Reproduction; Animal Health; Preventive Veterinary Medicine; Forestry Resources; Hispanic Literature; Plant Physiology; Plant Protection; Plant Production; Plant Improvement; Regional Economy and Management; Rural Development, 2 yrs; Magister: English; Immunology; Letters; Linguistics; Medicine; Nursing; Philosophy; Physics; Science; Technological Education; Título Profesional: Music, 12 yrs; Doctorado: Cellular and Molecular Biology; Systems; Ecology; Linguistics; Literature; Veterinary Medicine, 5 yrs

Student Services: Academic counselling, Canteen, Foreign student adviser, Foreign Studies Centre, Handicapped facilities, Health services, Language programs, Nursery care, Social counselling, Sports facilities

Student Residential Facilities: Yes

Special Facilities: History and Archaeology Museum; Botanical Garden. Museum of Modern Art. Arboretum

Libraries: Central Library, c. 209,173 vols

Publications: Agrosur (biannually); Archivos de Medicina Veterinaria (biannually); Bosque (biannually); Cuadernos de Cirugía (annually); Estudios Filológicos (biannually); Estudios Pedagógicos (annually); Medio Ambiente; Revista Austral de Ciencias Sociales (annually); Revista de Derecho (annually)

Last Updated: 03/03/09

TECHNOLOGICAL UNIVERSITY OF CHILE

Universidad Tecnológica de Chile
Brown Norte 290, Santiago
Tel: +56(2) 274-5432
Fax: +56(2) 223-8825
EMail: unitec@uvipro.cl
Website: http://www.uvipro.cl

Rectora: Karin Riedemann Hall (1987-)
Tel: +56(2) 274-8407, Fax: +56(2) 204-6796

Programmes

Arts and Humanities; **Arts, Music, Cinema and Design** (Art Education; Art History; Cinema and Television; Design; Fashion Design; Fine Arts; Music; Theatre; Visual Arts); **Engineering and Science**

History: Founded 1982 as Centre, became Institute 1988 and acquired present status 1992. Formerly known as Universidad Tecnológica Vicente Pérez Rosales.

Governing Bodies: Consejo Superior

Academic Year: March to December

Admission Requirements: Secondary school certificate (Licencia de Educación Media) and entrance examination

Main Language(s) of Instruction: Spanish

Degrees and Diplomas: Bachiller; Licenciatura; Título Profesional: 3-6 yrs

Student Services: Cultural centre, Employment services, Foreign student adviser, Social counselling

Libraries: 4,000 vols

UNIVERSITY ACADEMY OF CHRISTIAN HUMANISM

Universidad Academia de Humanismo Cristiano
Compañia 2015-2075, Plaza Brasil, Santiago
Tel: +56(2) 695-4831
Fax: +56(2) 695-4824
EMail: admision@academia.cl
Website: http://www.academia.cl

Rector: Juan Ruz Ruz EMail: rectoria@academia.cl

Secretaria General: Carmen Espinoza Miranda
EMail: mminue@academia.cl

Schools

Accountancy (Accountancy; Business and Commerce); **Anthropology** (Anthropology); **Commercial Engineering** (Business and Commerce); **Computer Engineering**; **Dance** (Dance; Performing Arts); **Education** (Education; Educational Research); **Journalism** (Journalism); **Law and Social Sciences** (Law; Social Sciences); **Political Science** (Political Sciences); **Pre-school Education** (Preschool Education); **Psychology** (Psychology); **Public Administration** (Management; Management Systems; Public Administration); **Social Work** (Social Work); **Sociology** (Development Studies; Social Studies; Sociology); **Teaching of History and Social Sciences** (History; Social Sciences; Teacher Training)

Further Information: Also branch in Huérfanos

History: Founded 1975 as Academia de Humanismo Cristiano, became autonomous private university 1988.

Academic Year: March to January (March-August; August-January)

Admission Requirements: Secondary school certificate (Licencia de Educación Media) and entrance examination

Main Language(s) of Instruction: Spanish

Degrees and Diplomas: Bachiller; Licenciatura; Magister; Doctorado

Libraries: Total, c. 30,000 vols

UNIVERSITY FOR DEVELOPMENT

Universidad del Desarrollo (UDD)
Av. La Plaza 700, San Carlos de Apoquindo, Las Condes, Santiago
Tel: +56(2) 299-9480
Fax: +56(2) 299-9457
EMail: internacional@udd.cl
Website: http://www.udd.cl

Rector: Ernesto Silva Bafalluy

Graduate Academic Vice-Rector: Sergio Hernández Ollarzú

International Relations: Barbara Stengel, Director of International Relations EMail: bstengel@udd.cl

Schools

Architecture, Art and Design (Architecture; Design; Fine Arts; Graphic Design) Dean: Víctor Lobos del Fierro; **Communications** (Advertising and Publicity; Film; Journalism; Theatre) Dean: Carolina Mardones Figueroa; **Design** (Design; Graphic Design) Dean: Alejandra Amenabar; **Economics and Business** (Business Administration; Business and Commerce; Economics; Management; Marketing) Dean: Cristián Larroulet Vignau; **Education** (Santiago and Concepción) (Education; Pedagogy) Director: Ana María Oyaneder Soto; **Education and Humanities** (Arts and Humanities; Literature; Modern Languages; Pedagogy) Dean: Enrique López Bourasseau; **Engineering** (Civil Engineering; Engineering; Engineering Management; Industrial Engineering) Dean: Lionel Sotomayor Lühr; **Government** (Government; Political Sciences) Dean: Eugenio Guzmán Astete; **Law** (Santiago) (Law) Dean: Pablo Rodríguez Grez; **Law** (Santiago) Dean: Gonzalo Rioseco Martínez; **Medicine** (Clinica Alemana-UDD Santiago) (Dentistry; Dietetics; Medical Technology; Medicine; Nursing; Nutrition; Physical Therapy; Speech Therapy and Audiology) Dean: Pablo Vial Claro; **Odontology** (Concepción) (Dentistry; Dietetics; Nursing; Nutrition; Physical Therapy; Speech Therapy and Audiology) Dean: Luis Vicentela Gutiérrez; **Psychology** (Psychology) Dean: Teresita Serrano Gildemeister

Further Information: Also 5 campuses in Santiago and Concepción.

History: Founded 1990.

Governing Bodies: Consejo Directivo, comprising 10 members

Main Language(s) of Instruction: Spanish

Degrees and Diplomas: Licenciatura: Architecture; Art; Setting and Object Design; Graphic Design; Digital Design; Journalism; Advertising; Drama; Film; Business Administration; Business Management; Law; Education; Language and Literature; Science; Humanities and Social Science; Political Science and Public Policy; Civil Industrial Engineering; Psychology; Medicine; Nursing; Odontology; Kinesiology; Speech Therapy; Nutrition and Diet; Medical Technology; Magister: Business Administration; Applied Finance; Applied Martketing; Administration; Bioethics; Adolescent Psychology; Clinical Psychology; Organizational Development and Human Resources; Dynamic Psychotherapies; Psychodiagnosis; Continuity Psychology; Entrepreneurial Law; Law; Health Management; Health Sciences Teaching; Environmental Management; Health Operations Management; Industrial Engineering and Systems; Humanities; Drama Pedagogy; Quality School Management and Supervision; Post-títulos/ Diploma: General Treatment and Muscle-Skeletal Manipulation in Advanced Temporomandibular Pathology; Humanities; Mathematics; Language and Communication; Psychopedagogy; Psychoanalysis Clinic for Personality Disorders; Strategic Psychoeducational Intervention; Current Family Law; Legal Counsel to Enterprise; Specialisation in Endodontics; Odontological Specialisation in Oral Rehabilitation; Reconstructive Surgery of Pelvis and Hip; Arthroscopic Surgery of Knee and Shoulder; Adult Echocardiography; Neuroradiology; Computerised Tomography and Magnetic Resonance; Specialisation in Aesthetical Odontology; Child and Adolescent Odontology; Health Management; Fixed Prosthetic Rehabilitation; Implantology; Orthodontic Diagnosis and Dentomaxillofacial Orthopedics; Surgery; Internal Medicine; Surgery and Morphology; Pediatrics; Radiology; Gynecology-Obstetrics; Pediatric Intensive Medicine; Adult Intensive Medicine; Vascular Neurology; Reproductive Medicine; Epilepsy and Sleep Disorders

Last Updated: 26/02/08

UNIVERSITY OF ACONCAGUA

Universidad de Aconcagua (UAC)
Prat N° 53, San Felipe
Tel: +56(34) 511-414
Fax: +56(34) 515-296
EMail: sede.sanfelipe@uac.cl
Website: http://www.uaconcagua.cl

Rector: Sergio Sepúlveda EMail: rectoria@uac.cl

Faculties

Administration and Commerce (Accountancy; Administration; Business Administration; Business and Commerce; Engineering; Finance; International Business; Public Administration) Dean: Armando Rosas Celis; **Agronomy** (Agricultural Engineering; Agronomy; Horticulture; Landscape Architecture) Dean: Andrés Silva

Arancibia; **Humanities** *(Viña del Mar)* (Arts and Humanities; Communication Studies; Education; English; Journalism; Translation and Interpretation) *Dean*: Luis Chandía Ruiz

Schools
Computer Science (Computer Science; Systems Analysis) *Director*: Andrés Romero Marchant; **Engineering** *(Viña del Mar)* (Civil Engineering; Engineering; Industrial Engineering) *Director*: Raúl Rojas Gutiérrez; **International Trade** *(Valparaíso)* (Finance; International Business; Service Trades) *Director*: Armando Rosas Celis; **Journalism and Communication** (Communication Studies; Journalism) *Director*: Daniel Lillo Cuadra; **Pedagogy and Educational Sciences** *(Viña del Mar)* (Educational Sciences; Pedagogy) *Director*: Luis Chandía Ruiz; **Translation and Interpretation** *(Viña del Mar)* (Translation and Interpretation) *Director*: Jorge Ramírez Jiménez

Further Information: Regional Branches in Calama, Tocopilla, La Serena, La Ligua, San Felipe, Los Andes, Viña del Mar, Quilpué, Santiago, Rancagua, Linares,Temuco, Valdivia, Puerto Montt, Ancud

History: Founded 1978 as Escuela de Comercio Exterior, reorganized 1981 as Centro de Formación Técnica, and acquired present status and title 1989. Incorporated Universidad de Rancagua 2008.

Main Language(s) of Instruction: Spanish

Degrees and Diplomas: *Técnico de Nivel Superior*; *Licenciatura*; *Título Profesional*
Last Updated: 18/05/09

UNIVERSITY OF ARTS AND SOCIAL SCIENCES ARCIS
Universidad de Arte y Ciencias Sociales ARCIS
Libertad 53, Santiago
Tel: +56(2) 386-66-00
EMail: admision@uarcis.cl
Website: http://www.uarcis.cl

Rector: Carlos Margotta Trincado
Tel: +56(2) 386-67-05 EMail: rectoria@universidadarcis.cl

Secretario General: Andrés Pascal Allende Tel: +56(2) 386-67-02

Schools
Architecture; **Cinema** (Cinema and Television); **Commercial Engineering** (Business and Commerce); **Dance Education** (Dance); **Education**; **Fine Arts** (Art History; Fine Arts; Painting and Drawing; Sculpture); **Graphic Design** (Graphic Design); **History**; **Journalism and Social Communication** (Communication Studies; Journalism); **Law** (Law); **Philosophy**; **Photography**; **Political Science** (Political Sciences); **Psychology** (Psychology); **Social Work**; **Sociology** (Sociology); **Theatre**

History: Founded 1982. Acquired present status 1999.

Governing Bodies: University Council; Executive and Corporative Board

Admission Requirements: Secondary school certificate (Licencia de Educación media) and entrance examination

Fees: (Chilean Pesos): 646,154 per annum

Main Language(s) of Instruction: Spanish

International Co-operation: With universities in Australia; Canada; United Kingdom and France

Degrees and Diplomas: *Magister*; *Post- títulos/ Diploma*; *Doctorado*

Student Services: Academic counselling, Cultural centre, Employment services, Language programs, Social counselling, Sports facilities

CABRERO BRANCH
SEDE CABRERO

Río Claro 1030, Cabrero
Tel: +56(42) 411-427
EMail: sedecabrero@universidadarcis.cl
Website: http://www.universidadarcis.cl/sedes_reg/sedes-secc/cabrero.htm
Directora: Carina Foladori

Programmes
Architecture (Architecture); **Basic Pedagogy**; **Law**
Admission Requirements: Licencia de Educación Media
Main Language(s) of Instruction: Spanish

CAÑETE BRANCH
SEDE CAÑETE

Sector Huillinco Km 3 s/n, Cañete, Arauco
Tel: +56(41) 613-542
EMail: sedearauco@universidadarcis.cl
Website: http://sedearauco.universidadarcis.cl
Coordinadora Ejecutiva: Ester Hernández

Programmes
Basic Pedagogy; **Commercial Engineering** (Business and Commerce); **Law** *(Curanilahue)*; **Psychology** *(Lota)*; **Social Work**; **Teaching of English** *(Curanilahue)* (English; Literature; Translation and Interpretation)

MAGALLENES BRANCH
SEDE MAGALLANES

Bernardo O'Higgins 655, Punta Arenas
Tel: +56(61) 228-800
EMail: sedemagallenes@universidadarcis.cl
Website: http://www.uama.cl
Director: Ricardo Salles

Schools
Architecture (Architecture); **Journalism and Social Communication** (Communication Studies; Journalism); **Political Science** (Political Sciences); **Psychology** (Psychology)

Admission Requirements: Licencia de Educación Media
Main Language(s) of Instruction: Spanish
Degrees and Diplomas: *Licenciatura*: 4 yrs

PATAGONIA BRANCH
SEDE PATAGONIA

Luis Espinoza 348, Castro Chiloé
Tel: +56(65) 532-660
EMail: uapa@uapa.cl
Website: http://www.uapa.cl
Director: Edward Rojas

Schools
Agronomy and Sustainable Rural Development; **Architecture**; **Basic Pedagogy**; **Journalism and Social Communication** (Communication Studies; Journalism); **Social Work** (Social Work)

Admission Requirements: Licencia de Enseñanza Media
Main Language(s) of Instruction: Spanish
Degrees and Diplomas: *Técnico de Nivel Superior*: 6 sem; *Post-títulos/ Diploma*: 10 sem

PORTEZUELO BRANCH
SEDE PORTEZUELO

Basquedano 380, Portezuelo
Tel: +56(42) 571-223
EMail: sedeportezuelo@universidadarcis.cl
Director: Patricio Baeza
Coordinadora Académica: Carolina Aguayo

Programmes
Agronomy and Sustainable Rural Development (Agronomy; Rural Studies); **Basic Pedagogy**; **Law** (Law); **Psychology** (Psychology)
Main Language(s) of Instruction: Spanish

VALPARAÍSO BRANCH

SEDE VALPARAÍSO

Lautaro Rosas 428, Cerro Alegre, Valparaíso
Tel: +56(32) 251-235
EMail: sedevalparaiso@universidadarcis.cl
Website: http://www.arcisvalpo.cl

Director: Carlos Zarricueta

Schools
Anthropology (Anthropology); **Fine Arts**; **Journalism and Social Communication**; **Political Science** (Political Sciences); **Psychology**; **Sociology** (Sociology); **Theatre** (Acting; Theatre)

Admission Requirements: Licencia de Educación Media

Main Language(s) of Instruction: Spanish

Degrees and Diplomas: *Licenciatura*

UNIVERSITY OF ARTS, SCIENCE AND COMMUNICATION

Universidad de Artes, Ciencias y Comunicación (UNIACC)
Avenida Salvador 1200, Providencia, Santiago
Tel: +56(2) 640-6000
Fax: +56(2) 640-6200
EMail: difusion@uniacc.cl
Website: http://www.uniacc.cl

Presidente: Andrés Guiloff Dimitstein

Registrar: Gustavo Cárdenas
Tel: +56(2) 640-6209 EMail: gcardenas@uniacc.cl

International Relations: Mireya Letelier
Tel: +56(2) 640-6044 EMail: mletelier@uniacc.cl

Departments
Continuing Education (Architecture and Planning; Communication Studies; Information Sciences; Social Sciences)

Schools
Advertising; **Architecture** (Architecture and Planning); **Audiovisual Communication**; **Business Administration**; **Corporate Public Relations** *(Bilingual)*; **Design and Multimedia**; **Interior Design**; **Journalism**; **Performing Arts**; **Psychology**; **Style Design**; **Tourism**; **Translation and Interpreting** *(English-Spanish)*; **Visual Arts**

History: Founded 1981 as Institute, acquired present status and title 1989, autonomous since 1999.

Governing Bodies: Consejo Consultivo, comprising 10 members

Academic Year: March to December (March-July; August-December)

Admission Requirements: Secondary school certificate (Licencia de Educación Media)

Fees: (Chilean Pesos): 2,806,000 per annum

Main Language(s) of Instruction: Spanish

International Co-operation: With universities in France, Cuba, Spain, United States, Ecuador, Argentina. Also with the International Advertising Association (IAA); the Federación de Escuelas de la Imagen y el Sonido de Iberoamérica; the University Film and Video Association (UFVA); the Asociación de Televisión Educativa Iberoamericana (ATEI); the Asociación de Universidades Privadas del Mercosur, including Chile y Bolivia (ASUPRIM); the Grupo Europeo de Diseño Publicitario y Marketing de las Comunicaciones (COMEURO); the Society of American Registered Architects

Accrediting Agencies: Consejo Superior de Educación

Degrees and Diplomas: *Bachiller*: Fine Arts; Social Sciences; Business Administration; Arts and Humanities; Information Sciences; Performing Arts, 2 yrs; *Licenciatura*: Architecture and Planning; Fine Arts; Information Sciences; Natural Sciences; Business Administration; Arts and Humanities; Education; Performing Arts; Service Trades, 4-5 yrs; *Magister*: Fine Arts and Technology, one further year; *Post- títulos/ Diploma*: Education; Social Sciences, 1 yr; *Título Profesional*: Architecture and Planning; Fine Arts; Information Sciences; Natural Sciences; Business Administration; Arts and Humanities; Education; Performing Arts; Service Trades, 4-5 yrs

Student Services: Academic counselling, Canteen, Cultural centre, Employment services, Foreign student adviser, Nursery care, Social counselling, Sports facilities

Special Facilities: Museum of Communications. TV Channel. Broadcasting Studio. Psychology Experimental Laboratory. Design and Multimedia Equipment

Libraries: 16,000 vols (specialized library in Communications). 4,000 videos

UNIVERSITY OF COMPUTER SCIENCE

Universidad Ciencias de la Informática (UCINF)
Avenida Pedro de Valdivia 450, Santiago
Tel: +56(2) 393-0300
EMail: informaciones@ucinf.cl
Website: http://www.ucinf.cl

Rector: Patricio Muñoz Navarro

Vicerrector de Administración y Finanzas: Pedro Johansen Bertoglio

Faculties
Education (Education; Pedagogy; Preschool Education; Special Education) *Dean*: Romilio Gutiérrez Pino; **Engineering and Trade** (Business and Commerce; Civil Engineering; Computer Education; Computer Engineering; Computer Graphics; Engineering; Systems Analysis) *Dean*: Peter Aubrey Roberts Vergara; **Law, Political and Social Sciences** *Dean*: Félix Lagreze B.

Institutes
Technology *(Melipilla)* (Accountancy; Law; Podiatry; Sports) *Director*: José Antonio Tapia; **Technology** *(Pedro de Valdivia)* (Computer Networks; Law; Sports; Systems Analysis; Telecommunications Engineering); **Technology** *(Puente Alto)* (Accountancy; Computer Networks; Law; Sports)

Schools
Architecture; **Languages** (Chinese; English; Translation and Interpretation) *Director*: Cristián Fonseca; **Scenic Arts** (Acting)

History: Founded 1989 as a private non-profit organization.

Governing Bodies: Junta Directiva; Consejo Superior

Academic Year: April to December (April-July; August-December)

Admission Requirements: Secondary school certificate (Licencia de Educación Media) and entrance examination

Main Language(s) of Instruction: Spanish

Degrees and Diplomas: *Post- títulos/ Diploma*; *Título Profesional*: 4-6 yrs

Libraries: Jorge Ayala Library, c. 600 vols
Last Updated: 04/03/09

UNIVERSITY OF CONCEPCIÓN

Universidad de Concepción
Victor Lamas No 1290, Casilla 160-C, Correo 3, Concepción 41
Tel: +56(41) 204-246
Fax: +56(41) 227-455
EMail: rector@udec.cl
Website: http://www.udec.cl

Rector: Sergio Lavanchy Merino (1998-) EMail: slavanc@udec.cl

Secretario General: Rodolfo Walter Diaz
Tel: +56(41) 204-297, Fax: +56(41) 212-495
EMail: secretariogeneral@udec.cl

International Relations: Mario Silva Osorio Tel: +56(41) 204-594

Centres
Environmental Sciences *(Eula-Chile)* (Environmental Management; Environmental Studies) *Director*: Oscar Parra B.

Faculties
Agricultural Engineering (Agricultural Engineering; Agricultural Equipment; Irrigation) *Dean*: Eduardo Holzapfel Hoces; **Agronomy** *(Chillán)* (Agronomy; Soil Science; Vegetable Production) *Dean*: Raúl Cerda González; **Arts and Humanities** (Arts and Humanities; Engraving; Ethics; Fine Arts; Hispanic American Studies; History; Linguistics; Marine Science and Oceanography; Modern Languages; Painting and Drawing; Philosophy; Sculpture; Social Sciences; Spanish; Theatre; Translation and Interpretation) *Dean*:

Patricio Oyaneder Jara; **Biological Sciences** (Biochemistry; Biological and Life Sciences; Microbiology; Pharmacology; Physiology) *Dean*: Nelsón Carvajal Baeza; **Chemistry** (Chemistry; Geology) *Dean*: Bernabé Rivas Q.; **Dentistry** (Dentistry) *Dean*: Alex Bustos Leal; **Economics and Administration** (Accountancy; Administration; Business and Commerce; Economics; Environmental Studies; Human Resources; International Business; Natural Resources) *Dean*: Juan Saavedra González; **Education** (Art Education; Biology; Chemistry; Computer Education; Education; Educational Administration; Educational Sciences; Foreign Languages Education; Geography; History; Humanities and Social Science Education; Mathematics Education; Music Education; Philosophy; Physical Education; Physics; Preschool Education; Science Education; Social Work; Spanish; Special Education) *Dean*: Abelardo Castro H.; **Engineering** (Aeronautical and Aerospace Engineering; Chemical Engineering; Civil Engineering; Computer Engineering; Computer Science; Electrical Engineering; Electronic Engineering; Engineering; Environmental Engineering; Hydraulic Engineering; Industrial Engineering; Mechanical Engineering; Metallurgical Engineering; Production Engineering) *Dean*: Joel Zambrano Valencia; **Forestry** (Forestry) *Dean*: Miguel Ángel Espinosa Bancalari; **Law and Social Sciences** (Administration; Law; Political Sciences; Social Sciences) *Dean*: Sergio Carrasco Delgado; **Medicine** (Community Health; Gender Studies; Gerontology; Gynaecology and Obstetrics; Medicine; Nursing; Psychiatry and Mental Health; Psychotherapy; Speech Therapy and Audiology; Surgery) *Dean*: Raúl González Ramos; **Oceanography and Natural Sciences** (Biology; Botany; Fishery; Marine Biology; Marine Science and Oceanography; Natural Sciences; Zoology) *Dean*: Franklin Carrasco Vásquez; **Pharmacy** (Biochemistry; Chemistry; Child Care and Development; Dietetics; Pharmacology; Pharmacy) *Dean*: Carlos Calvo Monfil; **Physics and Mathematics** (Mathematics; Mathematics and Computer Science; Physics; Statistics) *Dean*: Rodolfo Araya Durán; **Social Sciences** (Communication Studies; Educational Psychology; Human Resources; Journalism; Psychology; Social and Community Services; Social Policy; Social Sciences; Social Work; Sociology) *Dean*: Jorge Miguel Rojas Hernández; **Veterinary Medicine** *(Chillán)* (Cattle Breeding; Food Technology; Hygiene; Veterinary Science) *Dean*: Alejandro Santa María

Units

Academic *(Los Angeles)* (Food Science; Food Technology; Forestry; Surveying and Mapping) *Director*: Eliseo Rivera A.

History: Founded 1920 as a private institution and recognized by the State 1980. Financed from State subsidies.

Governing Bodies: Board of Directors, comprising 10 members; Academic Council, comprising the Vice-Rector, the Deans of the Faculties, and a student representative

Academic Year: March to December (March-August; August-December)

Admission Requirements: Secondary school certificate (Licencia de Educación Media) or recognized equivalent, and entrance examination (PAA)

Fees: (Chilean Pesos): 780,000-2 m. per annum

Main Language(s) of Instruction: Spanish

Degrees and Diplomas: *Bachiller*: 4-5 yrs; *Magister*: a further 2 yrs; *Título Profesional*: Accountancy; Education, Nursery and Primary Levels; Forestry; Surveying, 3-4 yrs; *Doctorado*

Student Services: Academic counselling, Canteen, Cultural centre, Employment services, Foreign student adviser, Handicapped facilities, Health services, Language programs, Nursery care, Social counselling, Sports facilities

Student Residential Facilities: Yes

Special Facilities: Museums: Anthropology; Art; Botany; Zoology; Palaeontology; Mineralogy; Anatomy

Libraries: Central Library (Concepción), c. 470,000 vols

Publications: Acta Literaria *(annually)*; Agro-Cienca *(biannually)*; Atenea *(biannually)*; Gayana (4 series) *(quarterly)*; Informe Económico Regional *(quarterly)*; Paidieia *(annually)*; R.L.A. *(annually)*; Revista de Derecho *(biannually)*; Revista de Enfermería *(annually)*; Revista de Historia *(annually)*

Press or Publishing House: Editorial Universidad de Concepción
Last Updated: 04/03/09

UNIVERSITY OF THE AMERICAS
Universidad de Las Américas (UDLA)
Avenida Manuel Montt 948, Providencia, Santiago
Tel: +56(2) 463-6100
Fax: +56(2) 225-8520
EMail: udla@uamericas.cl
Website: http://www.uamericas.cl

Rector: José Pedro Undurraga Izquierdo

Vicerrector Académico: Roberto Hojman Guiñerman
EMail: lfuenzal@uamericas

Faculties
Agriculture (Agriculture; Agronomy; Animal Husbandry; Forestry; Veterinary Science) *Dean*: Olivia Prado Meijer; **Agronomy and Environmental Sciences** (Agronomy; Bioengineering; Environmental Engineering; Oenology; Veterinary Science) *Dean*: Beatríz Palma; **Architecture, Design and Art** (Architecture; Dance; Design; Music; Singing; Theatre) *Dean*: Sergio Muñoz de la Parra; **Economics and Administration** (Accountancy; Administration; Advertising and Publicity; Business Administration; Business and Commerce; Communication Studies; Economics; Finance; Hotel and Restaurant; International Business; Psychology; Public Relations; Tourism) *Dean*: Samuel Arancibia; **Education** (Pedagogy; Physical Education; Preschool Education; Primary Education) *Dean*: Hugo Nervi; **Engineering** (Civil Engineering; Computer Engineering; Construction Engineering; Graphic Design; Industrial Design; Industrial Engineering; Sound Engineering (Acoustics)) *Dean*: Izet Ustovic; **Law** (Law) *Dean*: Patricio Zapata; **Physical Education and Health** *Dean*: Mario Muñoz; **Social Sciences and Humanities** *Dean*: Pablo Marassi

Institutes
Health Sciences (Nursing)

Further Information: Also DATVM, a business enterprise providing short specialized courses and using computer equipment. Experimental Station 'Los Nogales' in Talagante. Also La Florida, Maipú and Santiago Centro Campuses

History: Founded 1988, acquired autonomous status 1997. A private institution sharing a common campus with the Instituto Profesional 'Campus'.

Governing Bodies: Consejo Superior, comprising 8 members; Consejo Académico

Academic Year: March to January (March-August; August-January)

Admission Requirements: Secondary school certificate (Licencia de Educación Media) and entrance examination

Main Language(s) of Instruction: Spanish

Degrees and Diplomas: *Técnico de Nivel Superior*; *Licenciatura*: Advertising; Agricultural Engineering, 5 yrs; *Licenciatura*: Civil Engineering, 6 yrs; *Título Profesional*: Advertising; Business Administration, 5 yrs

Libraries: Central Library, c. 3,000 vols
Last Updated: 04/03/09

UNIVERSITY OF THE ANDES
Universidad de los Andes
Casilla 20106, San Carlos de Apoquindo 2200, Las Condes, Santiago
Tel: +56(2) 412-9222
Fax: +56(2) 214-1749
EMail: info@uandes.cl
Website: http://www.uandes.cl

Rector: Orlando Poblete Iturrate

Secretaria General: Carmen Luz Valenzuela P.

Faculties
Communication (Communication Studies; Journalism; Linguistics; Literature; Media Studies; Philosophy; Social Sciences) *Dean*: María Ignacia Errázuriz; **Economics and Business Administration** (Business Administration; Business and Commerce; Economics; Management; Marketing; Social and Community Services) *Dean*: Carlos A. Díaz; **Engineering** (Construction Engineering; Electrical Engineering; Engineering; Industrial Engineering; Mathematics; Physics; Science Education) *Dean*: Jorge Crempien; **Law**

(Canon Law; Civil Law; Commercial Law; Constitutional Law; International Law; Labour Law; Law) *Dean*: Hernán Corral; **Medicine** (Gynaecology and Obstetrics; Medicine; Ophthalmology; Orthopaedics; Paediatrics; Psychiatry and Mental Health; Surgery) *Dean*: Ricardo Espinoza; **Odontology** (Dental Technology; Oral Pathology; Periodontics; Stomatology) *Dean*: J. Antonio Jiménez

Institutes

Baccalaureate Programmes (Mathematics and Computer Science; Natural Sciences) *Director*: Samuel Vial; **Family Studies** *Director*: Claudia Tarud; **History** (Art History; Education; Heritage Preservation; History) *Director*: Francisco J. González; **Philosophy** (Education; Philosophy) *Director*: Jorge Peña

Schools

Nursing (Health Administration; Health Sciences; Nursing; Philosophy; Public Health) *Director*: Ana Isabel Larraín; **Pedagogy** (Child Care and Development; Educational Sciences; Linguistics; Literature; Mathematics; Natural Sciences; Pedagogy; Primary Education; Social Sciences) *Director*: Anna María Reyes; **Psychology** (Clinical Psychology; Educational Psychology; Psychology; Social Psychology) *Director*: María Elena Larraín; **Service Management** (Arts and Humanities; Business Administration; Science Education; Service Trades) *Director*: María Isabel Jottar

History: Founded 1990. Acquired present status 2001.

Governing Bodies: Junta Directiva. Consejo Superior Universitario. Consejo de Administración. Consejos Directivos de Facultades, Escuelas e Institutos

Admission Requirements: Secondary school certificate (Licencia de Educación Media) and national entrance examination (university selection test, PSU)

Fees: (Chilean Pesos): 3,130,000-5,100,000

Main Language(s) of Instruction: Spanish

International Co-operation: With universities in Argentina; Australia; Austria; Belgium; Bolivia; Brazil; Colombia; Ecuador; France; Germany; Italy; Mexico; Paraguay; Peru; Philippines; Spain and USA

Degrees and Diplomas: *Licenciatura*: Business Administration; Engineering; Dentistry; Psychology, 6 yrs; *Licenciatura*: Education; Service Management; Journalism, 5 yrs; *Licenciatura*: Medicine, 7 yrs; *Magister*: Engineering; Psychology; Communication; Law; Philosophy; History, 2 yrs following Licenciatura; *Post- títulos/ Diploma*: Medicine; Nursing; Family Studies; Philosophy; Services Management; Psychology, 6 mths-2 yrs; *Título Profesional*: 5-7 yrs; *Doctorado*: Law, 3 yrs; *Doctorado*: Philosophy, 4 yrs

Student Services: Academic counselling, Canteen, Cultural centre, Foreign student adviser, Handicapped facilities, Language programs, Social counselling, Sports facilities

Student Residential Facilities: None

Libraries: 62,570 vols
Last Updated: 04/03/09

UNIVERSITY OF THE PACIFIC
Universidad del Pacífico (UPACIFICO)
Avenida Las Condes 11121, Las Condes, Santiago
Tel: +56(2) 366-5300
Fax: +56(2) 366-5384
EMail: info@upacifico.cl
Website: http://www.upacifico.cl

Rector: Julio Ortúzar Prado (1990-)
Tel: +56(2) 366-5302, Fax: +56(2) 366-5384
EMail: recsec@upacifico.cl

Secretaria General: Elena Ortúzar Muñoz
Tel: +56(2) 366-5350, Fax: +56(2) 366-5379
EMail: eortuzar@upacifico.cl

International Relations: John Cowell Girardi
Tel: +56(2) 366-5369 EMail: jcowell@upacifico.cl

Faculties
Agronomy and Health; **Business and Marketing** (Business Administration; Business and Commerce; Marketing) *Dean*: Andrés Blake; **Communication Studies** (Advertising and Publicity; Communication Studies; Journalism; Media Studies; Photography; Public Relations) *Dean*: Manuel Segura Cavia; **Design** (Fashion Design; Graphic Design; Interior Design) *Dean*: Santiago Aranguiz; **Humanities and Education** (Pedagogy; Psychology; Social Work) *Dean*: Violeta Vargas

Further Information: Also Ricardo Lyon branch

History: Founded 1976 as Escuela de Publicidad de Chile, became Instituto Profesional del Pacífico in 1982. Acquired present status 1990.

Governing Bodies: Board of Directors

Academic Year: March to December (March-July; August-December)

Admission Requirements: Secondary School Certificate (Licencia de Educación Media), and entrance examination

Fees: (Chilean Pesos): c. 1,260m. per annum

Main Language(s) of Instruction: Spanish

International Co-operation: With universities in Argentina; Brazil; France; United States; Bolivia

Accrediting Agencies: International Advertising Association (School of Advertising)

Degrees and Diplomas: *Licenciatura*: Journalism; Business Administration; Social Work; Pre-school Education, 5 yrs; *Título Profesional*: Multimedia, Photography, 2 yrs. Also Título Universitario (4 yrs) in Advertising/Graphic Design; Public Relations; Textile and Fashion; Media

Student Services: Academic counselling, Canteen, Cultural centre, Employment services, Foreign student adviser, Foreign Studies Centre, Language programs, Social counselling, Sports facilities

Student Residential Facilities: None

Special Facilities: Multimedia Laboratory. Cinema and Film Production Studio. Photography Laboratory

Libraries: Yes

Publications: Revista de Comunicaciones *(quarterly)*
Last Updated: 06/03/09

UNIVERSITY OF THE REPUBLIC
Universidad La República
Casilla 141-D, Agustinas 1831, Santiago
Tel: +56(2) 421-4800
Fax: +56(2) 671-8457
EMail: contacto@ulare.cl
Website: http://www.ulare.cl

Rector: Jorge Carvajal Muñoz (1995-) EMail: rector@ulare.cl

Secretario General: Manuel Figueroa Santos

International Relations: Claudio Martínez

Schools
Accountancy (Accountancy); **Architecture** (Architecture); **Civil Industrial Engineering** (Civil Engineering; Industrial Engineering); **Commerce** (Business and Commerce); **Design** (Design); **Education**; **Journalism** (Journalism); **Law** (History; Law; Philosophy; Political Sciences); **Library Science and Information Sciences**; **Nursing and Public Health**; **Psychology** (Psychology); **Scenography** (Social Sciences; Sociology)

Further Information: Also branches in Los Angeles, Chillán, San Carlos, San Fernando and Antofagasta

History: Founded 1989, under the patronage of the Chilean Masonic Institution, the Grand Lodge of Chile. A private Corporation recognized by the State.

Governing Bodies: Junta Directiva; Academic Council

Academic Year: March to January

Admission Requirements: Secondary school certificate (Licencia de Educación Media), and entrance examination

Main Language(s) of Instruction: Spanish

Degrees and Diplomas: *Bachiller*: Social Sciences, 2 yrs; *Licenciatura*: Administration; Journalism; Law, 5 yrs; *Licenciatura*: Architecture; Engineering, 6 yrs; *Licenciatura*: Psychology, 5 1/2 yrs

Libraries: Germinación University Library, c. 4,000 vols

UNIVERSITY OF THE SEA

Universidad del Mar

Amunátegui 1838, Recreo, Viña del Mar
Tel: +56(32) 625-544
Fax: +56(32) 621-240
EMail: admision@udelmar.cl
Website: http://www.udelmar.cl

Rector: Hector Zúñiga Salinas EMail: hzuniga@udelmar.cl

Vicerrectora de Administración y Finanzas: María Bruna Figueroa EMail: svera@udelmar.cl

Schools

Agronomy *(Valparaíso)* (Agronomy) *Director.* Enrique Zúñiga Salinas; **Business Administration** (Business Administration) *Director.* Guido Martínez Caro; **Civil Industrial Engineering** (Civil Engineering; Industrial Engineering) *Director.* Jovanka Sapunar Gaete; **Commerce** (Administration; Business and Commerce; Technology) *Director.* Ana María Villegas Cerda; **Fishery and Crop Production** *(Valparaíso)* (Agricultural Engineering; Crop Production; Fishery) *Director.* Siegfried Ziller Vásquez; **International Commerce** (Business and Commerce; International Business) *Director.* Osvaldo Espinoza Ibarra; **Law** *(Valparaíso)* (Law) *Director.* Mario Rossel Contreras; **Preschool Education** *(Valparaíso)* (Preschool Education) *Director.* Silvia Redón Pantoja, **Psychology** *(Valparaíso)* (Psychology) *Director.* Mario Aguirre Montaldo; **Publicity** *(Valparaíso)* (Advertising and Publicity; Public Relations) *Director.* Leopoldo Reyes Canepa; **Teacher Training in English** (English; Teacher Training) *Director.* Patricia Vargas Aracena; **Tourism** (Tourism) *Director.* Carlos Jélvez Martínez; **Transport Engineering and Harbours** *(Valparaíso)* (Transport Engineering) *Director.* Luis Torres Clark

Further Information: Campuses in Iquique, Antofagasta, Calama, La Serena, Valparaíso, Santiago, Talca and Curico. Experimental Station in Olmué

History: Founded 1990.

Governing Bodies: Junta Directiva, comprising 4 members

Main Language(s) of Instruction: Spanish

Degrees and Diplomas: *Licenciatura*
Last Updated: 06/03/09

VIÑA DEL MAR UNIVERSITY

Universidad de Viña del Mar (UVM)

Variante Agua Santa 7055, sector Rodelillo, Viña del Mar
Tel: +56(32)246-2400
Fax: +56(32) 266-2818
EMail: rectoria@uvm.cl
Website: http://www.uvm.cl

Rector: Barham Madain Ayub (1990-)

Secretario General: Francisco Barriga Villarino

Schools

Administration and Accountancy (Accountancy; Administration; Business Administration; Engineering Management; Finance; Human Resources; International Business; Management; Marketing) *Director.* Piero Moltedo; **Architecture** (Architecture) *Director.* Mario Orfali; **Art and Design** (Communication Studies; Design; Graphic Design; Interior Design) *Director.* Ana María Chamy; **Commerce** (Business Administration; Business and Commerce; International Business) *Director.* Piero Moltedo; **Computer and Industrial Engineering** (Computer Engineering; Industrial Engineering; Software Engineering) *Director.* Oscar Contreras; **Construction Engineering** (Construction Engineering) *Director.* María Isabel Cortez; **Environmental Studies** (Environmental Engineering; Environmental Management; Environmental Studies; Natural Resources; Safety Engineering) *Director.* Osvaldo Pacheco; **Journalism and Public Relations** (Journalism; Public Relations) *Director.* Sergio Celedón; **Preschool Education** (Preschool Education) *Director.* Miguel Diaz; **Psychology** (Psychology) *Director.* Arturo Prieto

History: Founded 1989.

Academic Year: March to December (March-July; August-December)

Admission Requirements: Secondary school certificate (Licencia de Educación Media) or foreign equivalent and entrance examination

Fees: (Chilean Pesos): Registration, 78,000-98,000; tuition, 626,000-1,4m. per annum

Main Language(s) of Instruction: Spanish

Degrees and Diplomas: *Técnico de Nivel Superior.* Technical Studies, 3 yrs; *Licenciatura:* Architecture; Business Administration; Construction Engineering; Education; Environmental Engineering, 5 yrs; *Licenciatura:* Civil Engineering, 6 yrs; *Magister; Post- títulos/ Diploma*
Last Updated: 06/03/09

SAN FELIPE BRANCH

SEDE SAN FELIPE

Avenida Yungay 1582, San Felipe
Tel: +56(32) 512-694
Fax: +56(32) 515-033

Director: Alberto Luengo Sepulveda

Schools

Business and Technology (Business and Commerce; Technology); **Education** (Education; Preschool Education)

History: Founded 1990.

Main Language(s) of Instruction: Spanish

WILHELM VON HUMBOLDT GERMAN PROFESSIONAL INSTITUTE

Instituto Profesional Alemán Wilhelm von Humboldt

Nuestra Señora del Rosario 1120 Vitacura, Santiago
Tel: +56(2) 220-3167
Fax: +56(2) 201-6984
EMail: instituto@lbi.cl
Website: http://www.lbi.cl

Rector: Alban Schraut EMail: rector@lbi.cl

Programmes

Education (Education; Pedagogy; Preschool Education; Primary Education)

History: Founded 1988.

Degrees and Diplomas: *Título Profesional*
Last Updated: 19/05/09

China

STRUCTURE OF HIGHER EDUCATION SYSTEM

Description:

The State is responsible for the overall planning of higher education. It establishes higher education institutions with the active participation of society. Higher education consists of regular higher education, adult higher education and technical and vocational education and training. The academic degree system is divided into three levels. Most higher education institutions divide their academic year into two semesters, with the first semester starting in September and the second in February. Since 1992, there have been private universities in China. In the past ten years, China has implemented the 211 Project and the 985 Project aiming at constructing first-class universities.

Stages of studies:

University level first stage: *Undergraduate education*
This stage aims at enabling students to master the basic theory, knowledge, skills and know-how and acquiring the capacity for practical and research work in their field of study. Students following these courses are awarded a Bachelor's degree after normally four years of study.

University level second stage: *Postgraduate education*
This stage aims at enabling students to master firm basic theory, systematic knowledge, skills, techniques and know-how and acquiring the capacity for practical and scientific research work in their field. Students following these courses are awarded a Master's degree after three years' study following a Bachelor's degree and taking the National Entrance Test for MA/MS candidates, and the defence of a thesis.

University level third stage: *Doctoral post graduate education*
This stage aims at enabling students to master firm and broad basic theory, systematic and in-depth knowledge, skills and techniques and acquiring the capacity for independent creative scientific research work in their field. Students following these courses are awarded a Doctor's Degree after two years' study following a Master's Degree and taking of the National Entrance Test for PhD candidates, and the defence of a dissertation.

ADMISSION TO HIGHER EDUCATION

Admission to university-level studies:

Name of secondary school credential required: Senior High School Graduation Diploma

Entrance exam requirements: National Matriculation Test

Foreign students admission:

Entrance exam requirements: Foreign students must abide by Chinese laws and decrees, comply with the rules and regulations of the universities and colleges where they study, and respect Chinese customs. Undergraduate students should possess a degree equivalent to the Chinese high school diploma and be under 30 years of age. Master degree students should possess a degree equivalent to the Chinese Bachelor's degree and be under 35 years of age. The Candidate's diploma needs to be evaluated and accredited. Doctor's degree students should possess a degree equivalent to the Chinese Master degree and be under 40 years of age. They must be recommended by two full or associate professors and approved by the university where they want to study. Some tests administered by the Chinese Embassy in the country of the applicant might have to be taken.

Language requirements: Students must pass the Chinese Proficiency Test.

RECOGNITION OF STUDIES

Quality assurance system:

The Academic Degree Committee of the State Council approves the China Service Centre for Scholarly Exchange being in charge of the accreditation of foreign degrees and diplomas. The Ministry has also established the China Academic Degrees and Graduate Education Development Centre to be in charge of the accreditation of Chinese studies and degrees.

Bodies dealing with recognition:

Academic Degrees Committee of the State Council - ADCSC
Ministry of Education
Beijing

China Academic Degrees and Graduate Education Development Centre - CADGEDC
1 Wang Zhuang Road,
HaiDian District
Beijing 100083

NATIONAL BODIES

Ministry of Education
Minister: Yuan Guiren
No. 37 Damucang Hutong, Xidan
Beijing 100816
Tel: +86(10) 6609 6114
EMail: english@moe.edu.cn
WWW: http://www.moe.edu.cn/
Role of national body: Responsible for the overall planning of education.

Ministry of Science and Technology
Minister: Gang Wan
15B, Fuxing Road
Beijing 100862
WWW: http://www.most.gov.cn/eng/

China Education Association for International Exchange - CEAIE
Secretary-General: Jiang Bo
President: Zhang Xinsheng
Shaw Conference Center Fuxingmen Nei Dajie
Beijing 100031
Tel: +86(10) 6641 6080
Fax: +86(10) 6641 6156
EMail: secretariat@ceaie.edu.cn
WWW: http://www.ceaie.edu.cn/
Role of national body: Non-governmental organization affiliated to the Ministry of Education in charge of international educational exchanges.

China Academic Degrees and Graduate Education Development Center - CDGDC
Director: Wu Boda
18th Floor, Tongfang Keji Building B,No.1,Wangzhuang Road, Haidian District
Beijing 100083
Tel: +86(10) 8237 8812
EMail: bgs@mail.cdgdc.edu.cn
WWW: http://www.cdgdc.edu.cn
Role of national body: Administrative department directly under the Ministry of Education evaluating and appraising the academic degrees and graduate education.

Data for academic year: 2008-2009
Source: IAU from Ministry of Education Website and documentation, 2008. Bodies, 2011.

INSTITUTIONS

AGRICULTURAL UNIVERSITY OF HEBEI (AUH)

38 Lingyusi Sreet, Baoding, Hebei Province 071001
Tel: +86(312) 2091276
Fax: +86(312) 2091217
EMail: fauh@mail.hebau.edu.cn
Website: http://www.hebau.edu.cn

President: Wang Zhigang
Tel: +86(312) 2091286, Fax: +86(312) 2091286

Colleges
Adult Education *Dean*: Changchun Huang; **Agronomy** (Agronomy) *Dean*: Cundong Li; **Animal Science and Technology** (Animal Husbandry; Technology; Zoology) *Dean*: Renlu Huang; **Aquaculture** (Aquaculture) *Dean*: Guojun Yan; **Arts** (Fine Arts) *Dean*: Jiping Wang; **Civil Engineering** (Civil Engineering) *Dean*: Shoujun Du; **Economic Management** (Economics; Management) *Dean*: Yizhen Zhang; **Food Science** (Food Science) *Dean*: Yingmin Jia; **Forestry** (Forestry) *Dean*: Dazhuang Huang; **Gardens, Forestry and Tourism** (Forestry; Landscape Architecture; Tourism) *Dean*: Jianmin Yang; **Horticulture** (Horticulture) *Dean*: Yuxing Zhang; **Humanities** (Arts and Humanities) *Dean*: Xiuyan Liu; **Knowledge and Practice** *Dean*: Wensheng Wu; **Life Science** (Biological and Life Sciences) *Dean*: Jingao Dong; **Mechanical and Electrical Engineering** (Electrical Engineering; Mechanical Engineering) *Dean*: Yuejin Ma; **Plant Protection** (Plant and Crop Protection) *Dean*: Keqian Cao; **Resources and Environment** (Environmental Studies; Natural Resources) *Dean*: Hao Xu; **Science** (Mathematics and Computer Science; Natural Sciences) *Dean*: Ruling Luo; **Traditional Chinese Veterinary Medicine** (Traditional Eastern Medicine; Veterinary Science) *Dean*: Xiuhui Zhong; **Vocational and Technical Education** *Dean*: Changchun Huang

Departments
English Courses (English) *Director*: Qiyou Wang; **Physical Education** (Physical Education) *Director*: Zhensheng Tian

Further Information: Also two campuses in Qinghuangdao City and Dingzhou City.

History: Founded 1902, acquired present status 1921.

Academic Year: September to July

Admission Requirements: Graduation from senior high school and entrance examination

Fees: (Yuan): 3,500-4,500 per annum

Main Language(s) of Instruction: Chinese

International Co-operation: With universities in Japan, Korea, USA, Mongolia, Australia, Pakistan

Accrediting Agencies: Ministry of Education; Hebei Provincial Education Department

Degrees and Diplomas: *Zhuanke Certificate of Graduation*: 3 yrs; *Bachelor's Degree*: 4 yrs; *Master's Degree*: a further 3 yrs; *Doctor's Degree*: Plant Pathology; Pomology; Agricultural Economics and Management; Crop Genetics and Breeding, 3 yrs following Master

Student Services: Academic counselling, Canteen, Cultural centre, Employment services, Foreign student adviser, Health services, Language programs, Nursery care, Social counselling, Sports facilities

Libraries: c. 790,000 vols

Publications: Academic Journal *(quarterly)*; Academic Journal on Forestry *(quarterly)*; Education in Agriculture and Forestry of Hebei *(monthly)*; Hebei Village and Town Construction *(monthly)*; Scientific and Technical Development in Rural Areas *(monthly)*
Last Updated: 17/11/08

ANHUI AGRICULTURAL UNIVERSITY

130 West Changjiang Road, Hefei, Anhui Province 230036
Tel: +86(551) 2823795
Fax: +86(551) 5120833
EMail: ioff@ahau.edu.cn
Website: http://www.ahau.edu.cn

President: Zhengzhi Li (2000-)
Tel: +86(551) 2843266 EMail: president@ahau.edu.cn

Schools
Agricultural Resources and Environment (Agriculture; Ecology; Environmental Engineering; Environmental Studies; Natural Resources); **Agronomy** (Agriculture; Agronomy; Plant and Crop Protection) *Dean*: Danian Yao; **Animal Science** (Animal Husbandry; Fishery; Veterinary Science); **Finance and Business** (Finance; International Business); **Foreign Languages**; **Forestry and Landscape Architecture**; **Horticulture**; **Humanities and Social Sciences** (Law; Social Sciences); **Industry and Technology** *Division Head*: g; **Information Technology** (Business Computing; Computer Science; Technology; Telecommunications Engineering); **Life Science** (Biological and Life Sciences; Biology; Sericulture; Traditional Eastern Medicine); **Light Industry and Textile Design** (Design; Packaging Technology; Textile Design; Textile Technology); **Management**; **Plant Protection** (Agricultural Engineering; Biotechnology; Environmental Engineering; Environmental Studies; Plant and Crop Protection); **Science**; **Senior Vocational Education** (Agricultural Economics; Agricultural Engineering; Bioengineering; English; Sericulture; Social Sciences); **Tea and Food Technology**

History: Founded 1995 as Agricultural College of Anhui National University. Acquired present name 1995.

Academic Year: September to July (September-January; March-July)

Admission Requirements: Local students: admission tests by National Testing Centre; Overseas students: previous diploma or degree

Fees: (Yuan): 4,000 per annum for local students; (US Dollars): 2,600 per annum for overseas students

Main Language(s) of Instruction: Chinese

International Co-operation: With Hampshire College and Michigan University, USA

Accrediting Agencies: Anhui Educational Department

Degrees and Diplomas: *Zhuanke Certificate of Graduation*: 3 yrs; *Bachelor's Degree*: Science; Arts; Engineering; Medicine; Management, 3-4 yrs; *Master's Degree*: Science; Engineering; Medicine; Management, 2 yrs; *Doctor's Degree*: 3 yrs

Student Services: Academic counselling, Canteen, Cultural centre, Employment services, Foreign student adviser, Foreign Studies Centre, Health services, Language programs, Nursery care, Sports facilities

Libraries: c. 1,851,100 vols

Publications: Journal of Agricultural Statistics *(quarterly)*; Journal of Anhui Agricultural University *(quarterly)*; Journal of Biomathematics *(quarterly)*
Last Updated: 05/11/08

ANHUI AGROTECHNICAL TEACHERS COLLEGE

Fengyang, Anhui Province 233100
Tel: +86(550) 6732031
Fax: +86(550) 6727343

Departments
Agriculture (Agriculture; Plant Pathology; Soil Science); **Animal Science** (Animal Husbandry; Veterinary Science); **Biology** (Biology); **Foreign Languages** (Modern Languages); **Processing**; **Social Sciences**; **Trade Economy** (Accountancy; Finance)

History: Founded 1950 as North Anhui Advanced Agriculture and Forestry School. Acquired present title 1985.

Degrees and Diplomas: *Bachelor's Degree*

ANHUI INSTITUTE OF ARCHITECTURE

856 Jinzhai Road, Hefei, Anhui Province 230022
Tel: +86(551) 3323501
Fax: +86(551) 3517457
EMail: tansusan1@aiai.edu.cn
Website: http://www1.aiai.edu.cn/EN/lists/About/index2.jsp?enti-tyid=7341

President: Cheng Hua

International Relations: Zhang Kongliang

Departments
Architecture (Architecture; Design; Town Planning); **Basic Sciences**; **Civil Engineering and Building Materials**; **Environmental Engineering and Electronics** (Electronic Engineering; Environmental Engineering; Information Technology; Irrigation; Natural Resources); **Social Science and Economy** (Economics; Social Sciences)

Schools
Adult Education (Adult Education)

History: Founded 1958.

Degrees and Diplomas: *Bachelor's Degree*; *Master's Degree*
Last Updated: 26/09/08

ANHUI MEDICAL UNIVERSITY

81 Meishan Road, Hefei, Anhui Province 230032
Tel: +86(551) 2813965
Fax: +86(551) 2813965
EMail: wb@ahmu.edu.cn
Website: http://www.ahmu.edu.cn

President: Zhang Xuejun

Colleges
Basic Medicine (Medicine); **Health Administration** (Health Administration); **Humanities and Social Sciences** (Arts and Humanities; Social Sciences); **Nursing** (Nursing); **Pharmacy**; **Public Hygiene** (Hygiene); **Stomatology** (Stomatology)

Departments
Anaesthesiology (Anaesthesiology); **Medical Psychology**; **Rehabilitation** (Rehabilitation and Therapy)

History: Founded 1926 as Shangai Southeast Medical College. Moved to Huaiyuan Country 1949, Anhui Province and moved 1952 to Hefei to become Anhui Medical College. Acquired present title 1985.

Degrees and Diplomas: *Bachelor's Degree*; *Master's Degree*; *Doctor's Degree*

Libraries: Central Library, 160,000 vols; 160,000 periodicals

Publications: Journal of Anhui Medical University; Journal of Clinical Medicine and Pathology; Journal of Clinical Orthopedics; Journal of Disease Control; Journal of Lungs; Journal of Nursing; Journal of Ophthalmology; Journal of Surgery; Rural Health Administration of China
Last Updated: 03/11/08

ANHUI NORMAL UNIVERSITY

1 Renmin Road, Wuhu, Anhui Province 241000
Tel: +86(553) 3869405
Fax: +86(553) 3839452
EMail: president@mail.ahnu.edu.cn
Website: http://www.ahnu.edu.cn

President: Lun Wang

Departments
Administration (Administration); **Biology** (Biology); **Chemistry** (Chemistry); **Chinese Language and Literature** (Chinese); **Computer Science** (Computer Science); **Economics** (Economics); **Education** (Education); **Educational Technology** (Educational Technology); **Electronic and Information Engineering** (Electronic Engineering; Information Technology); **Foreign Languages** (Modern Languages); **Geography** (Geography); **History** (History); **Journalism** (Journalism); **Law** (Law); **Mathematics** (Mathematics); **Music and Fine Arts** (Fine Arts; Music); **Physical Education** (Physical Education); **Physics** (Physics); **Political Science** (Political Sciences); **Sociology** (Sociology); **Tourism** (Tourism)

Research Centres
Analytical Test; **Anatomy**; **Basic Education** (Education); **Environmental Science** (Environmental Studies); **Examination**; **Higher Education** (Higher Education)

Research Institutes
Biology (Biology); **Chinese Language** (Chinese); **Classics**; **Computer Science** (Computer Science); **Educational Sciences** (Educational Sciences); **Geography** (Geography); **Literature** (Literature); **Organic Chemistry** (Organic Chemistry); **Sociology**; **Traditional Culture** (Cultural Studies)

Schools
Adult Education (Adult Education); **Art** (Fine Arts); **Economics, Law and Political Science** (Economics; Law; Political Sciences); **Liberal Arts** (Arts and Humanities); **Physical Education** (Physical Education)

History: Founded 1928 as National Anhui University. Acquired present status 1970 and present title 1972. Under the jurisdiction of the National Education Commission and of the Provincial Government.

Academic Year: September to July (September-January; February-July)

Admission Requirements: Graduation from senior middle school and entrance examination

Main Language(s) of Instruction: Chinese

Degrees and Diplomas: *Bachelor's Degree*: 4 yrs; *Master's Degree*: a further 3 yrs; *Doctor's Degree*

Student Residential Facilities: Yes

Libraries: Central Library, c. 2.1m. vols; Library of Chinese Classical Books and Calligraphic Models, c. 231,000

Publications: Journal of Anhui Normal University; Learning Chinese; Mathematics for Middle School Students; Middle School Chemistry; Moral Education Research
Last Updated: 05/11/08

ANHUI UNIVERSITY

3 Feixi Road, Hefei, Anhui Province 230039
Tel: +86(551) 5107600
Fax: +86(551) 5107999
EMail: Xum@ahu.edu.cn
Website: http://www.ahu.edu.cn

President: Huang Dekuan

International Relations: Xu Ming

Research Institutes
Ancient Books Collation and Publication (Ancient Books); **Applied Chemistry** (Applied Chemistry); **Artificial Intelligence** (Artificial Intelligence); **Automation** (Automation and Control Engineering); **Chinese Language and Sinology** (Chinese; Cultural Studies; South Asian Studies); **Computer Application and Recognition Technology** (Computer Science); **Demography** (Demography and Population); **Economic Development** (Economics); **Electronics and Communication Technologies** (Electronic Engineering; Telecommunications Engineering); **Oceanic Literature** (Literature); **Polymer Material** (Polymer and Plastics Technology); **Russian Studies** (Eastern European Studies)

Schools
Adult Education (Adult Education); **Arts** (Chinese; History; Journalism; Philosophy); **Chemistry and Chemical Engineering** (Applied Chemistry; Chemical Engineering; Chemistry); **Economics** (Accountancy; Business Administration; Economics; Finance; International Business); **Electrical Engineering and Information Science** (Automation and Control Engineering; Computer Science; Electrical Engineering; Information Sciences; Technology); **Foreign Studies** (English; Russian); **Law** (Law; Sociology); **Life Science** (Biological and Life Sciences; Biology); **Management** (Archiving; Library Science; Management; Public Administration); **Mathematics and Physics** (Mathematics; Physics); **Teacher Training** (Computer Science; English; Military Science; Physical Education)

Further Information: Also Hospital; courses for foreign students

History: Founded 1928.

Academic Year: September to July

Admission Requirements: Graduation from senior middle school and entrance examination

Main Language(s) of Instruction: Chinese, English

Degrees and Diplomas: *Bachelor's Degree*: 4 yrs; *Master's Degree*: a further 3 yrs; *Doctor's Degree*

Libraries: Central Library, c. 1.5m. vols

Publications: Ancient Book Studies; Anhui Population; Anhui University Journal; Russian Studies

Press or Publishing House: Anhui University Publishing House

ANHUI UNIVERSITY OF FINANCE AND ECONOMICS

255 Hongye Road, Bengbu, Anhui Province 233041
Tel: +86(552) 3111114
EMail: wsb@aufe.edu.cn
Website: http://www.aufe.edu.cn

President: Shi Xiuhe

International Relations: Sun Xuebin

Departments
Accountancy (Accountancy); **Adult Education**; **Basic Courses Teaching** (English); **Business Management** (Business Administration); **Commodity**; **Cotton Engineering**; **Economics** (Economics); **Economy Information Administration**; **Finance** (Finance); **Financial Tax** (Taxation); **Law** (Law); **Trade Economy**

History: Founded 1959 as Anhui Commercial Institute. Renamed Anhui University of Finance and Trade 1978. Acquired present title 2004.

Degrees and Diplomas: *Bachelor's Degree*; *Master's Degree*

ANHUI UNIVERSITY OF SCIENCE AND TECHNOLOGY (AUST)

Huainan, Anhui Province 232001
Tel: +86(554) 6668836
Fax: +86(554) 6668927
EMail: xiaoban@aust.edu.cn
Website: http://www.aust.edu.cn

President: Yan Shilong

Departments
Chemical Engineering (Chemical Engineering); **Economic Management and Social Sciences** (Economics; Management; Social Sciences); **Electrical Engineering** (Electrical Engineering); **Engineering Management** (Engineering Management); **Management and Social Sciences**; **Materials Engineering** (Materials Engineering); **Mathematics and Physics** (Mathematics; Physics); **Mechanical Engineering** (Mechanical Engineering); **Modern Languages** (Modern Languages); **Natural Resources and Environmental Engineering** (Environmental Engineering; Natural Resources); **Resources Development and Management** (Environmental Management)

Schools
Advanced Professional Technology Education (Technology Education); **Medicine** (Medicine)

History: Founded 2002 as a merger of East China Coal Medical College and Huainan Chemical Engineering College.

Degrees and Diplomas: *Bachelor's Degree*; *Master's Degree*; *Doctor's Degree*
Last Updated: 05/11/08

ANHUI UNIVERSITY OF TECHNOLOGY

39 Hudong Road, Ma'anshan, Anhui Province 240302
Tel: +86(555) 2400691
Fax: +86(555) 2473747
EMail: xiaoban@ahut.edu.cn; foreign@ahut.edu.cn
Website: http://www.ahut.edu.cn

President: Cen Yuwan

Schools
Arts and Law (Law; Literature; Management; Public Administration; Social Sciences); **Chemistry and Chemical Engineering** (Applied Chemistry; Chemical Engineering; Polymer and Plastics Technol-

ogy); **Computer Science** (Computer Networks; Computer Science; Software Engineering); **Construction Engineering** (Civil Engineering; Construction Engineering; Environmental Engineering); **Economics** (Economics; Finance; International Business; Statistics); **Electrical Engineering and Information** (Automation and Control Engineering; Electrical Engineering); **Foreign Languages** (Modern Languages); **Management** (Accountancy; Business Administration; Finance; Marketing); **Management Science and Engineering**; **Material Science and Engineering**; **Mathematics and Physics**; **Mechanical Engineering** (Automotive Engineering; Industrial Design; Mechanical Engineering); **Metallurgy and Resources** (Metallurgical Engineering; Thermal Engineering)

History: Founded 1977 as Ma'anshan School of Iron and Steel Industry. Renamed East China University of Metallurgy 1985. Acquired present title 2000.

Degrees and Diplomas: *Bachelor's Degree*; *Master's Degree*

Libraries: c. 300,000 vols

Publications: Journal, Social Science, Natural Sciences
Last Updated: 05/11/08

ANHUI UNIVERSITY OF TECHNOLOGY AND SCIENCE

Wuhu, Anhui Province 241000
Tel: +86(553) 2871221
Fax: +86(553) 2871091
EMail: office@auts.edu.cn
Website: http://www.auts.edu.cn

President: Wang Xueqian

International Relations: Ma Jian

Departments
Artistic Design (Industrial Design; Interior Design); **Biochemical Engineering** (Bioengineering; Chemical Engineering; Food Science; Food Technology); **Computer Science and Engineering** (Computer Engineering; Computer Science); **Electrical Engineering** (Automation and Control Engineering; Electrical Engineering; Electronic Engineering; Information Technology); **Management Engineering** (Business Administration; Industrial Engineering); **Mechanical Engineering** (Automation and Control Engineering; Engineering Drawing and Design; Engineering Management; Materials Engineering; Mechanical Engineering); **Textile and Clothes** (Textile Technology)

Schools
Adult Education; **Career Technology** (Technology)

History: Founded 1978 as Anhui Institute of Mechanical and Electrical Engineering. Acquired present status and title 2001.

Degrees and Diplomas: *Bachelor's Degree*; *Master's Degree*

ANHUI UNIVERSITY OF TRADITIONAL CHINESE MEDICINE (AHTCM)

103 Meishan Road, Hefei, Anhui Province 230038
Tel: +86(551) 5169289
Fax: +86(551) 2819950
EMail: azywb@yahoo.com.cn
Website: http://www.ahtcm.edu.cn

President: Wang Jian

International Relations: Zhang Si-hong

Departments
Social Sciences (Social Sciences)

Schools
Acupuncture and Osteology (Acupuncture; Alternative Medicine; Osteopathy); **Continuing Education** (Continuing Education); **Integrated Traditional Chinese and Western Medicine**; **Medical Economics and Management** (Economics; Health Administration; Management); **Medical Information Technology**; **Nursing**; **Pharmacy** (Pharmacology; Pharmacy); **Traditional Chinese Medicine** (Traditional Eastern Medicine)

History: Founded 1959 as Anhui Advanced School of Traditional Chinese Medicine. Acquired present title 1976.

Admission Requirements: High school diplomas or certificates. Chinese proficiency test

Fees: (US Dollars): Undergraduate, 2,800 per annum; postgraduate, 3,200 (group fare available)

Main Language(s) of Instruction: Chinese and Chinese Mandarin

International Co-operation: With universities in USA, Canada, Japan Australia, Russian Federation, Republic of Korea, Singapore, Nepal, Poland, Denmark and Jamaica

Degrees and Diplomas: *Bachelor's Degree*: Acupuncture and Moxibusion and Tuina; Traditional Chinese Medicine; Integrated Traditional Chinese Medicine and Western Medicine; Traditional Chinese Rehabilitative Therapy; Nursing; Applied Psychology; International Economics and Trading; Chinese Pharmacy; Pharmacology; Pharmaceutical Engineering; Pharmaceutics; Information Management and System; Computer Science and Technology; *Master's Degree*: Pharmaceutics; Acupuncture and Moxibustion and Tuina; Bases of Integrated Traditional Chinese Medicine and Western Medicine; Integrated Traditional Chinese Medicine and Western Medicine in Clinical Work; Chinese Pharmacy; Pharmacognosy; Traditional Chinese Medicine (Basic Theories; Clinical Bases; Literature and History; Science of Prescriptions; Diagnostics; Internal Medicine; Surgery; Orthopedics; Gynaecology; Paediatrics)

Student Residential Facilities: Yes.

Special Facilities: A Special Clinic of Traditional Chinese Medicine. 5 affiliated hospitals.

Last Updated: 05/11/08

ANQING TEACHERS COLLEGE

192 Linhu South Road, Anqing, Anhui Province 246011
Tel: +86(556) 5500900
Fax: +86(556) 5500057
EMail: waish@aqtc.edu.cn
Website: http://www.aqtc.edu.cn/

President: Wang Qiongsong

Departments
Life Sciences (Biological and Life Sciences)

Schools
Chemistry and Chemical Industry (Chemical Engineering; Chemistry); **Computer and Information** (Computer Science; Information Management); **Economics Management** (Economics; International Business; Marketing); **Education**; **Environmental Resources** (Environmental Studies; Geography); **Foreign Languages**; **Humanities** (Arts and Humanities; Chinese; Journalism); **Humanities and Society** (History; Social Work); **Law and Politics**; **Mathematics** (Applied Mathematics; Mathematics); **Music** (Music; Opera); **Painting** (Design; Painting and Drawing); **Physics and Electronic Engineering** (Electronic Engineering; Physics)

History: Founded 1928 as Former Anhui University. Acquired present title 1980.

Degrees and Diplomas: *Bachelor's Degree*
Last Updated: 05/11/08

ANSHAN NORMAL UNIVERSITY

43 Ping'an Street, Tiedong District, Anshan, Liaoning Province 114005
Tel: +86(412) 5847025
Fax: +86(412) 5847019
EMail: anulxs@hotmail.com
Website: http://www.asnc.edu.cn/

President: Zhang Weihua

International Relations: Li Changjiang

Departments
Arts; **Chemistry** (Chemistry); **Chinese** (Chinese; Literature); **Economics and Law** (Accountancy; Economics; Finance; Law); **English** (English); **Mathematics** (Applied Mathematics; Computer Science; Mathematics; Technology); **Mechanics** (Mechanics); **Physical Education** (Physical Education); **Physics** (Physics); **Politics and History** (History; Political Sciences)

History: Founded 1958 as Anshan Teachers College. Acquired present title 1993.

Degrees and Diplomas: *Bachelor's Degree*
Last Updated: 02/09/08

BAICHENG NORMAL COLLEGE

9 Zhongxing Dong Road, Baicheng, Jilin Province 137000
Tel: +86(436) 3243802
Fax: +86(436) 3223381
EMail: teachinbaicheng@hotmail.com
Website: http://www.bcsfxy.com

President: Bo Zhang

Departments
Biology (Biology); **Chemistry** (Chemistry); **Chinese Languages and Literature**; **Civil Engineering** (Civil Engineering); **Computer Science** (Computer Science); **Economics and Management** (Economics; Management); **Education Sciences** (Education; Educational Sciences); **Fine Arts** (Fine Arts); **Foreign Languages and Literature** (Modern Languages); **History** (History); **Mathematics** (Mathematics); **Mechanical and Electronic Engineering** (Electronic Engineering; Mechanical Engineering); **Music** (Music); **Physical Education** (Physical Education); **Physics** (Physics); **Politics and Law** (Law; Political Sciences)

History: Founded 1958. Acquired present title 2000.

Degrees and Diplomas: *Bachelor's Degree*

Libraries: c. 340,000 vols; c. 1,500 periodical subscriptions.
Last Updated: 28/10/08

BAOJI UNIVERSITY OF ARTS AND SCIENCE

No. 1 Hi-Tech Avenue, Baoji, Shaanxi Province 721007
Tel: +86(917) 3364317
Fax: +86(917) 3364273
EMail: webmaster@bjwlxy.edu.cn
Website: http://www.bjwlxy.cn

President: Yang Yijun

International Relations: Liu Zongjie

Departments
Chinese Language and Literature (Chinese; Literature); **Chemistry and Chemical Engineering** (Chemical Engineering; Chemistry); **Economic Management** (Management); **Education**; **Electronic and Electrical Engineering** (Electrical and Electronic Engineering); **Environmental Economics** (Economics; Environmental Studies); **Fine Arts** (Fine Arts); **Foreign Languages and Literature** (English; Modern Languages); **History** (History); **Mathematics** (Applied Mathematics; Mathematics); **Mechanics**; **Music** (Music); **Physical Education**; **Physics** (Physics); **Politics and Law** (Law; Political Sciences)

History: Founded 1958 as Baoji University. Baoji Teachers College 1978. Acquired present title 1993.

Main Language(s) of Instruction: Chinese

Degrees and Diplomas: *Bachelor's Degree*
Last Updated: 28/10/08

BEIHANG UNIVERSITY (BUAA)

37 Xueyuan Road, Haidian District, Beijing 100083
Tel: +86(10) 82317685
Fax: +86(10) 82317688
EMail: webmaster@buaa.edu.cn
Website: http://www.buaa.edu.cn

President: Wei Li

International Relations: Cui Deyu

Departments
Automobile Engineering (Automotive Engineering); **Biological Engineering** (Bioengineering); **Civil Engineering** (Civil Engineering); **Foreign Languages** (Modern Languages); **Mechanical and Electrical Engineering** (Electrical Engineering; Mechanical Engineering); **Project Systems Engineering** (Computer Engineering)

Institutes
Applied Technology *(Haidan)* (Technology)

Schools
Aeronautical Science and Engineering (Aeronautical and Aerospace Engineering); **Astronautics** (Astronomy and Space Science); **Automation Science and Electrical Engineering** (Automation and Control Engineering; Electrical Engineering);

Computer Science (Computer Engineering; Computer Science; Engineering); **Continuing Education**; **Economics and Management** (Economics; Management); **Electronic Engineering** (Electronic Engineering); **Flying** (Aeronautical and Aerospace Engineering); **Humanities and Social Sciences** (Arts and Humanities; Social Sciences); **Jet Propulsion** (Aeronautical and Aerospace Engineering; Thermal Engineering); **Law** (Law); **Management** (Management); **Materials Science and Engineering** (Materials Engineering); **Mechanical Engineering and Automation** (Automation and Control Engineering; Mechanical Engineering); **Science** (Natural Sciences); **Software** (Software Engineering); **Vocational Education**

History: Founded as Beijing Institute of Aeronautics 1952. Renamed Beijing University of Aeronautics and Astronautics 1988. Acquired present title 2002.

Academic Year: September to July (September-January; February-July)

Admission Requirements: Graduation from senior middle school and entrance examination

Main Language(s) of Instruction: Chinese

Accrediting Agencies: Ministry of Aeronautics and Astronautics

Degrees and Diplomas: *Bachelor's Degree*: 4 yrs; *Master's Degree*: a further 2 1/2 yrs

Student Residential Facilities: Yes

Special Facilities: Beijing Aviation Museum; Yi Fu Science Museum

Libraries: University Library, c. 902,480 vols

Publications: Acta Aeronautica et Astronautica Sinica; Acta Materiae Compositae Sinica; Aerospace Knowledge; China Aeronautical Education; Journal of Aerospace Power; Journal of Beijing University of Aeronautics and Astronautics; Journal of Engineering Graphics; Model World

Press or Publishing House: BUAA Publishing House

Last Updated: 28/10/08

BEIHUA UNIVERSITY

No. 3999 Huashan Road, Jilin, Jilin Province 132013
Tel: +86(432) 4683797
Fax: +86(432) 4602163
EMail: bhoffice@beihua.edu.cn
Website: http://www.beihua.edu.cn

President: Liu Hezhong

Colleges
Basic Medicine (Medical Technology; Medicine; Nursing; Social and Preventive Medicine); **Chemistry and Biology** (Biology; Chemistry); **Education** (Educational Technology; Primary Education; Psychology); **Electrical and Information Engineering** (Automation and Control Engineering; Electrical Engineering; Information Technology); **Fine Arts** (Fine Arts); **Foreign Languages** (English; Japanese); **Forestry** (Civil Engineering; Forestry; Horticulture; Painting and Drawing; Transport Engineering); **History and Culture** (Cultural Studies; History); **Law** (Law; Political Sciences); **Mathematics** (Mathematics); **Mechanical Engineering** (Industrial Design; Mechanical Engineering); **Music** (Music); **Nursing** (Nursing); **Physical Education** (Physical Education); **Physics** (Physics); **Software** (Software Engineering); **Transport and Civil Engineering** (Civil Engineering; Transport Engineering)

Schools
Chinese Language and Culture (Chinese); **Computer Science and Technology** (Computer Science); **Economic Management** (Economics; Management)

History: Founded 1999.

Main Language(s) of Instruction: Chinese

Degrees and Diplomas: *Bachelor's Degree*; *Master's Degree*

Libraries: Central Library, 1.2m. vols

Publications: Beihua University Journal, Social Science, Natural Sciences, Medicine and Pharmacy, Education Research
Last Updated: 28/10/08

BEIJING DANCE ACADEMY

19 Minzuxudaxue Nanlu, Haidian District, Beijing 100081
Tel: +86(10) 68935695
Fax: +86(10) 68411605
EMail: bdainter@public.bta.net.cn
Website: http://www.bda.edu.cn

President: Yu Ping

International Relations: Cui Jixun Tel: +86(10) 68935696

Departments
Ballet (Dance); **Chinese Folk Dance** (Dance; Folklore); **Chinese National Dance Drama** (Dance; Theatre); **Choreography** (Dance; Music Theory and Composition); **Dance Study** (Dance); **Social Education of Music and Dance** (Dance; Music)

History: Founded 1954 as Beijing Dance School. Acquired present title 1978.

Degrees and Diplomas: *Bachelor's Degree*; *Master's Degree*
Last Updated: 28/10/08

BEIJING ELECTRONIC SCIENCE AND TECHNOLOGY INSTITUTE

7 Fufeng Road, Fengtai District, Beijing 100070
Tel: +86(10) 63740588
Fax: +86(10) 63742726

President: Wang Zhongwen

Departments
Communication Engineering (Telecommunications Engineering); **Computer Application** (Computer Science); **Computer Science and Technology** (Computer Science); **Social Science** (Social Sciences)

History: Founded 1981 as Beijing Electronic Science and Technology School. Acquired present title 1992.

Degrees and Diplomas: *Bachelor's Degree*

BEIJING FILM ACADEMY (BFA)

4 Xitucheng Road, Haidian District, Beijing 100088
Tel: +86(10) 62013876
Fax: +86(10) 62012132
EMail: lilunshi@bfa.edu.cn
Website: http://www.bfa.edu.cn

Head: Wang Fensheng

International Relations: Yu Jianhong
Tel: +86(10) 62379512, Fax: +86(10) 62013895

Departments
Art Direction; **Cinematography** (Cinema and Television); **Directing** (Conducting); **Literature** (Literature); **Management**; **Performing Arts**; **Recording**

Schools
Photography

History: Founded 1953 as Beijing Film School. Acquired present title 1956.

Degrees and Diplomas: *Bachelor's Degree*; *Master's Degree*

BEIJING FOREIGN STUDIES UNIVERSITY (BFSU)

2 Xisanhuan Beilu, Haidian District, Beijing 100089
Tel: +86(10) 88816309
Fax: +86(10) 88813144
EMail: bwwscb@bfsu.edu.cn
Website: http://www.bfsu.edu.cn

President: Naifang Chen (1997-) Tel: +86(10) 88816999

Departments
Afro-Asian Languages (African Languages; Oriental Languages) *Dean*: Yupei Feng; **Arabic** (Arabic) *Dean*: Hong Zhang; **East European Languages** (Eastern European Studies); **French** (French) *Dean*: Xingying Tang; **German** (German) *Dean*: Wenjian Jia; **Japanese** (Japanese) *Dean*: Riping Yu; **Russian** (Russian) *Dean*: Tieqing Shi; **Social Sciences**; **Spanish** (Spanish) *Dean*: Jian Liu

Graduate Schools
Interpretation and Translation (Translation and Interpretation) *Dean*: Lidi Wang

Schools
English Language Communication (English; International Relations; Journalism) *Dean*: Sun Youzhong; **International Business** (International Business) *Dean*: Peng Long; **International Exchange** *Dean*: Li Yonghui

History: Founded 1941 as Yan'an School of Foreign Languages, acquired present status and title 1954.

Academic Year: September to July (September-January; February-July)

Admission Requirements: Graduation from senior middle school and entrance examination

Fees: (Yuan): For Chinese students, 6,000 per annum; (US Dollars): for International students, 2,600 per annum

Main Language(s) of Instruction: Chinese, English, German, French, Russian, Arabic

International Co-operation: With Universities in Japan, Korea, Thailand, Singapore, Malaysia, Yemen, Jordan, Saudi Arabia, France, Russian Federation, USA, Canada and Australia

Accrediting Agencies: Ministry of Education

Degrees and Diplomas: *Bachelor's Degree*: Albanian; Arabic; Bulgarian; Burmese; Chinese; Croatian; Czech; Diplomacy; English; Finnish; French; German; Hausa; Hungarian; Indonesian; Information Management; International Economics and Trade; Italian; Japanese; Journalism; Kampuchean; Korean; Laotian; Law; Malay; Portuguese; Romanian; Russian; Serbian; Singhalese; Spanish; Swahili; Thai; Turkish; Vietnamese; *Master's Degree*: Afro-Asian Languages; Arabic; English; European Languages; Foreign Languages Linguistics and Applied Linguistics; French; German; Japanese; Linguistics; Applied Linguistics; Russian; Spanish; *Doctor's Degree*: Arabic (PhD); English; European Languages; German; Japanese; Linguistics and Applied Linguistics in Foreign Languages (English, French); Russian; Spanish

Student Services: Academic counselling, Canteen, Employment services, Foreign Studies Centre, Health services, Language programs, Nursery care, Social counselling, Sports facilities

Student Residential Facilities: Yes

Libraries: Central Library, c. 580,000 vols

Publications: English Learning; Foreign Language Teaching and Research; Foreign Literatures; Russian Art and Literature; Russian Learning
Last Updated: 28/10/08

BEIJING FORESTRY UNIVERSITY
Qinghua East Road 35, Haidian District, Beijing 100083
Tel: +86(10) 62554411
Fax: +86(10) 62555276
EMail: service@bjfu.edu.cn
Website: http://www.bjfu.edu.cn

President: Jinzhao Zhu (1999-)
Tel: +86(10) 62338028, Fax: +86(10) 62310316

Director of the Presidents' Office: Enlai Jiang
Tel: +86(10) 62337756

International Relations: Zhiqiang Zhang
Tel: +86(10) 62338367 EMail: zhqzhang@bjfu.edu.cn

Colleges
Basic Science and Technology (Mathematics and Computer Science; Natural Sciences; Technology) *President*: Mengning Gao; **Biological Science and Technology** (Biology; Technology) *President*: Zhixiang Zhang; **Economic Management** (Economics; Management) *President*: Junchang Liu; **Engineering** (Engineering) *President*: Guosheng Yu; **Foreign Languages** (Modern Languages) *President*: Baohui Shi; **Humanities and Social Sciences** (Arts and Humanities; Social Sciences) *President*: Gen Yan; **Information Sciences** (Information Sciences) *President*: Tieying Song; **Landscape Gardening** (Landscape Architecture) *President*: Qixiang Zhang; **Resources and Environment** (Environmental Studies; Forest Products) *President*: Xingcheng Zhou; **Vocational Training and Adult Education** *President*: Jinmin Yan

Further Information: Also 13 Research Institutes

History: Founded 1952.

Academic Year: February to January (February-July; September-January)

Admission Requirements: Graduation from senior middle school and entrance examination

Fees: (US Dollars): 2,000-4,000 per year

Main Language(s) of Instruction: Chinese

International Co-operation: With universities in USA, United Kingdom, Australia, New Zealand, Germany, Finland, Sweden

Accrediting Agencies: Ministry of Education

Degrees and Diplomas: *Bachelor's Degree*: 4 yrs; *Master's Degree*: a further 3 yrs; *Doctor's Degree (PhD)*: a further 3 yrs

Student Services: Academic counselling, Employment services, Foreign student adviser, Language programs, Nursery care, Social counselling, Sports facilities

Student Residential Facilities: Yes

Special Facilities: Movie studio

Libraries: 2 libraries

Publications: Journal of Beijing Forestry University; Journal of Beijing Forestry University-Social Sciences

BEIJING INFORMATION SCIENCE AND TECHNOLOGY UNIVERSITY
12 East Road, Qinghe Xiaoying, HaiDian District, Beijing 100085
Tel: +86(10) 62939325 +86(10)82426859
Fax: +86(10) 62843757
EMail: ibmfao@public.bta.net.cn
Website: http://www.biti.edu.cn

President: Du Lin

International Relations: Fan Yutao Tel: +86(10) 62939325

Departments
Automation (Automation and Control Engineering); **Foreign Languages** (International Business; Modern Languages); **Humanities and Social Sciences** (Arts and Humanities; Social Sciences); **Mechanical and Electronic Engineering** (Automation and Control Engineering; Electronic Engineering; Instrument Making; Mechanical Engineering); **Mechanical Engineering** (Mechanical Engineering)

Divisions
Basic Courses (Accountancy; Information Management); **Postgraduate Studies**

Schools
Adult Education; **Business** (Business Administration)

History: Founded 1986 as Beijing Institute of Machinery and Technology. Acquired present title 2004.

Degrees and Diplomas: *Bachelor's Degree*; *Master's Degree*
Last Updated: 09/01/07

BEIJING INFORMATION TECHNOLOGY INSTITUTE
35 North Sihuan Zhonglu, Beijing 100101
Tel: +86(10) 64884688
Fax: +86(10) 64879080
EMail: nic@biti.edu.cn
Website: http://www.biti.edu.cn/english.php

President: Gan Shengyu

International Relations: Cui Zhongkai

Departments
Business Administration; **Computer Information Management**; **Computer Science and Engineering** (Computer Engineering; Computer Science); **Economics**; **Information and Communication Engineering** (Communication Studies; Engineering; Information Sciences; Telecommunications Engineering); **Sensor Technology** (Automation and Control Engineering; Technology)

History: Founded 1978 as Second Branch of Beijing University. Acquired present title 1985.

Degrees and Diplomas: *Bachelor's Degree*

BEIJING INSTITUTE OF CIVIL ENGINEERING AND ARCHITECTURE

1 Zhanlan Road, Western-city District, Beijing 100044
Tel: +86(10) 68322234
Fax: +86(10) 68364459
Website: http://www.bicea.edu.cn

President: Ye Shuming

International Relations: Niu Huilan

Departments

Architecture (Architecture); **Civil Engineering** (Civil Engineering); **Construction Management** (Engineering Management); **Mechanical and Electrical Engineering** (Electrical Engineering; Mechanical Engineering); **Urban Construction Engineering** (Construction Engineering)

History: Founded 1936 as Beijing Senior Vocational Industry School-Civil Engineering Section. Acquired present status and title 1977.

Degrees and Diplomas: *Bachelor's Degree; Master's Degree*

BEIJING INSTITUTE OF FASHION TECHNOLOGY

North Heping Street, Chaoyang District, Beijing 100096
Tel: +86(10) 64288257
Fax: +86(10) 64210959
EMail: dyb@bict.edu.cn
Website: http://www.bict.edu.cn

President: Wang Yunqiang

International Relations: Hao Xiaomei

Departments

Arts and Crafts; **Clothing** (Clothing and Sewing; Textile Design); **Industrial Design and Automation** (Automation and Control Engineering; Industrial Design); **International Economics and Trade** (Accountancy; International Economics; Marketing); **Materials Engineering**

History: Founded 1959 as Beijing Institute of Textile Technology. Acquired present title 2008.

Degrees and Diplomas: *Bachelor's Degree; Master's Degree*

BEIJING INSTITUTE OF GRAPHIC COMMUNICATION

25 Xinghua Beilu, Daxing, Beijing 102600
Tel: +86(10) 69243981 +86(10) 69243318
Fax: +86(10) 69243485
EMail: ceec@bigc.edu.cn
Website: http://www.bigc.edu.cn

President: Tian Shengli

International Relations: Chen Yinxiang

Departments

Adult Education; **Art Design** (Design); **Basic Courses**; **Electronic Engineering**; **Foreign Languages** (Modern Languages); **Machinery and Electronic Engineering** (Electronic Engineering); **Management Engineering** (Information Management; Marketing; Systems Analysis); **Printing and Packaging Engineering** (Packaging Technology; Printing and Printmaking); **Publishing** (Publishing and Book Trade); **Social Sciences** (Social Sciences)

History: Founded 1978 as Department of Graphic Arts of Beijing Culture College. Renamed Beijing Institute of Printing 1978.

Degrees and Diplomas: *Bachelor's Degree; Master's Degree*

BEIJING INSTITUTE OF PETROCHEMICAL TECHNOLOGY

Daxing, Beijing 102600
Tel: +86(10) 69244752 +86(10) 69244373
Fax: +86(10) 69241846
EMail: biptweb@bipt.edu.cn
Website: http://www.bipt.edu.cn

President: Guo Wenli

Departments

Foreign Languages; **Mathematics and Physics** (Mathematics; Physics); **Physical Education** (Physical Education)

Faculties

Adult Education (Adult Education); **Economics and Management** (Accountancy; International Economics; Management; Marketing); **Humanities and Social Sciences** (Arts and Humanities; Social Sciences); **Information Engineering** (Automation and Control Engineering; Computer Science; Electrical Engineering); **Materials and Chemical Engineering** (Applied Chemistry; Chemical Engineering; Polymer and Plastics Technology); **Mechanical Engineering** (Automation and Control Engineering; Mechanical Engineering)

History: Founded 1978 as Beijing Petrochemical Junior College. Acquired present title 1992.

Degrees and Diplomas: *Bachelor's Degree*

Last Updated: 28/10/08

BEIJING INSTITUTE OF TECHNOLOGY

5 South Zhongguancun Street, Haidian District, Beijing 100081
Tel: +86(10) 68914247
Fax: +86(10) 68468035
EMail: office@bit.edu.cn
Website: http://english.bit.edu.cn

President: Haiyan Hu (2007-) EMail: president@bit.edu.cn

International Relations: Qinglin Wang
Tel: +86(10) 68912312, Fax: +86(10) 68915023
EMail: wangql@bit.edu.cn

Schools

Aerospace Science and Engineering; **Arts and Design** (Design; Fine Arts); **Chemical Engineering and the Environment** (Applied Chemistry; Chemical Engineering; Environmental Studies); **Computer Science and Technology** (Computer Engineering; Computer Science; Technology); **Foreign Languages** (Modern Languages); **Humanities and Social Sciences** (Arts and Humanities; Modern Languages; Social Sciences); **Information Science and Technology** (Information Technology); **Life Science and Technology** (Biological and Life Sciences; Natural Sciences; Technology); **Management and Economics** (Economics; Management); **Materials Science and Engineering**; **Mechanical Engineering and Automotive Engineering** (Automotive Engineering; Mechanical Engineering); **Science** (Chemistry; Mathematics; Mechanical Engineering; Physics); **Software** (Software Engineering)

History: Founded 1940 as Yan'an Academy of Natural Sciences, acquired present title 1951.

Main Language(s) of Instruction: Chinese, English

Degrees and Diplomas: *Bachelor's Degree*: 4 yrs; *Master's Degree*: a further 2-2 1/2 yrs; *Doctor's Degree (Ph.D.)*: a further 3 yrs

Student Services: Academic counselling, Canteen, Cultural centre, Employment services, Foreign student adviser, Health services, Nursery care, Social counselling, Sports facilities

Student Residential Facilities: For c. 23,000 students

Libraries: Total1,875,000 vols

Publications: Journal Beijing Institute of Technology *(quarterly)*; Optical Engineering

Press or Publishing House: Beijing Institute of Technology Press
Last Updated: 15/09/08

BEIJING INTERNATIONAL STUDIES UNIVERSITY

Ding Fuzhuang, Chaoyang District, Beijing 100024
Tel: +86(10) 65778481
Fax: +86(10) 65762520
EMail: webmaster@bisu.edu.cn
Website: http://www.bisu.edu.cn/english

President: Du Jiang

Departments

Modern Languages (Modern Languages)

Institutes
Transculture Studies (Cultural Studies)

Schools
Continuing Education; **International Communication** (Communication Studies); **International Cultural Exchange** (Chinese; International Relations) *Director*: Xu Zhao; **International Economics and Trade** (Finance; International Business; International Economics; Marketing); **Law and Politics** (Law; Political Sciences); **Tourism Management** (Hotel Management; Marketing; Tourism) *Director*: Hui Zhang

History: Founded 1964 as Beijing Second Foreign Languages Institute. Acquired present title 2002.

Admission Requirements: Graduation from high school and national college entrance examination

Accrediting Agencies: Educational Committee of Beijing

Degrees and Diplomas: *Bachelor's Degree*; *Master's Degree*

Student Services: Academic counselling, Canteen, Employment services, Foreign student adviser, Foreign Studies Centre, Language programs, Social counselling, Sports facilities

Student Residential Facilities: Separate dormitories for Chinese and Foreign students

Libraries: 410,000 vols

Publications: Journal of Beijing Second Foreign Languages Institute
Last Updated: 28/10/08

BEIJING JIAOTONG UNIVERSITY (BJTU)

3 Shangyuancun, Xizhimenwai, Beijing 100044
Tel: +86(10) 51688312
Fax: +86(10) 62255671
EMail: wsc@bjtu.edu.cn
Website: http://www.njtu.edu.cn

President: Ning Bin

International Relations: Yugong Xu, Director
EMail: wsclxsk@bjtu.edu.cn

Schools
Civil Engineering and Architecture (Architecture; Civil Engineering; Construction Engineering; Environmental Engineering; Railway Engineering; Structural Architecture); **Computer and Information Technology**; **Economics and Management** (Accountancy; Business Administration; Economics; Industrial Management; Information Technology; Management); **Electrical Engineering** (Electrical Engineering; Energy Engineering; Power Engineering); **Electronics and Information Engineering** (Automation and Control Engineering; Electronic Engineering; Information Management; Information Sciences); **Humanities and Social Sciences** (Arts and Humanities; English; Foreign Languages Education; Law; Modern Languages; Physical Education; Social Sciences); **Mechanical, Electronic and Control Engineering** (Automation and Control Engineering; Electronic Engineering; Materials Engineering; Measurement and Precision Engineering; Mechanical Engineering; Power Engineering); **Science** (Chemistry; Environmental Engineering; Mathematics; Optical Technology; Physics); **Software Engineering** (Software Engineering); **Traffic and Transportation** (Transport and Communications; Transport Engineering)

History: Founded 1896 as Peking Railway Training School of Postal Ministry of Qing Dynasty. Renamed Northern Jiaotong University 1950. Acquired present title 2003.

Academic Year: September to July (September-February; March-July)

Admission Requirements: Graduation from senior middle school and entrance examination

Main Language(s) of Instruction: Chinese

International Co-operation: With universities in USA, UK, Canada, Australia, Sweden, Belgium, Japan, Netherlands and France

Accrediting Agencies: Ministry of Education

Degrees and Diplomas: *Bachelor's Degree*: 4 yrs; *Master's Degree*: a further 3 yrs; *Doctor's Degree (PhD)*: 2 yrs

Student Residential Facilities: Yes

Libraries: Central Library, c. 950,000 vols

Publications: Higher Education Research; Journal of Beijing Jiatong University *(quarterly)*
Last Updated: 28/10/08

BEIJING LANGUAGE AND CULTURE UNIVERSITY

15 Xueyuan Road, Haidian District, Beijing 100083
Tel: +86(10) 62311348
Fax: +86(10) 62311228
EMail: waisshi2@blcu.edu.cn
Website: http://www.blcu.edu.cn

President: Cui Xiliang

International Relations: Dai Chaofu

Colleges
Foreign Languages; **Intensive Chinese Education**

Institutes
Teacher Training

Schools
Adult Education; **Chinese** *(for foreign students)* (Chinese; Cultural Studies); **Culture**

History: Founded 1962. Acquired present status and title 1996.

Degrees and Diplomas: *Bachelor's Degree*; *Master's Degree*; *Doctor's Degree*

Libraries: c. 170,000 vols

Publications: Chinese Culture Research; Chinese Learning; Chinese Teaching in the World; Higher Education Research BLCU; Language Teaching and Linguistic Studies; Teaching and Research
Last Updated: 28/10/08

BEIJING NORMAL UNIVERSITY (BNU)

19 Xinjiekou Wai Street, Beijing 100875
Tel: +86(10) 62208106
Fax: +86(10) 62200823
EMail: info@bnu.edu.cn
Website: http://www.bnu.edu.cn

President: Binglin Zhong (2002-)
Tel: +86(10) 62207960, Fax: +86(10) 62200074
EMail: po_mjb@bnu.edu.cn

Director, President's Office: Wei Tang Tel: +86(10) 62207956

International Relations: Huaying Bao
Tel: +86(10) 62206998 EMail: hybao@bnu.edu.cn

Academies
Creative and Cultural Industry; **Disaster Reduction and Emergency Management** (Safety Engineering)

Centres
Rural Education *(UNESCO International Research and Training Centre)* (Agricultural Education)

Colleges
Chemistry (Analytical Chemistry; Applied Chemistry; Chemistry; Inorganic Chemistry; Organic Chemistry; Physical Chemistry) *Director*: Naijei Hu; **Chinese Language and Culture** (Chinese; Linguistics) *Director*: Xiangyu Lin; **Global Change and Earth System** (Geography; Geography (Human); Regional Planning; Town Planning); **Information Science and Technology** (Computer Science; Information Management; Information Technology; Software Engineering) *Director*: Fuxing Shen; **Life Sciences** (Biochemistry; Biological and Life Sciences; Biology; Biotechnology; Botany; Cell Biology; Ecology; Genetics; Molecular Biology; Physiology; Soil Conservation; Water Management; Wildlife; Zoology); **Nuclear Science and Technology** (Nuclear Engineering); **Resource Sciences and Technology** (Geography; Geography (Human); Natural Resources; Safety Engineering; Surveying and Mapping) *Vice-President*: Peijun Shi; **Water Science**

Departments
Astronomy (Astronomy and Space Science); **Materials Science and Engineering** (Materials Engineering); **Physics**

Faculties
Education (Adult Education; Curriculum; Educational Research; Educational Technology; Higher Education; Pedagogy; Preschool Education; Special Education; Vocational Education)

Institutes

Ancient Books Studies (Ancient Books); Basic Education *(Capital Institute)* (Education); Beijing Cultural Development Research (Cultural Studies); Chinese Information Processing; Cognitive Neuroscience and Learning (Cognitive Sciences; Neurosciences); Criminal Law (Criminal Law); Economics and Resource Management (Economics); Education Economy *(Capital Institute)*; Higher Education (Higher Education); Marxism Studies; Medicine (Medicine); National Assessment of Education Quality; Proteomics *(Universities' Confederated Institute)*

Schools

Arts and Communication (Cinema and Television; Dance; Design; Film; Fine Arts; Musicology; Radio and Television Broadcasting); Chinese Language and Literature; Continuing Education and Teacher Training (Continuing Education; Teacher Training); Economics and Business Administration; Environment (Environmental Management; Environmental Studies); Foreign Languages and Literatures (English; Japanese; Modern Languages; Russian) *Director:* Qiang Wang; Geography; History (Archaeology; History; Museum Studies) *Director:* Hanguo Zhu; Law (Criminal Law; International Law; Law); Management (Administration; Human Resources; Information Management; Management; Public Administration); Mathematical Sciences (Applied Mathematics; Automation and Control Engineering; Mathematics; Statistics) *Director:* Lue'an Zheng; Philosophy and Sociology; Physical Education and Sports Science (Physical Education; Sports); Political Science and International Studies (International Relations; Political Sciences); Psychology (Psychology); Social Development and Public Policy

Further Information: Also Research Bases and Key Laboratories

History: Founded 1902, acquired present status 1923. In the process of reorganization within the academic divisions.

Governing Bodies: Administrative Committee. Academic Committee. Teaching Committee

Academic Year: September to July (September-January; February-July)

Admission Requirements: Graduation from high school and entrance examination

Fees: (Yuan): 4,800 per annum; foreign students, (US Dollars): 2,900-3,350

Main Language(s) of Instruction: Chinese

Accrediting Agencies: Ministry of Education

Degrees and Diplomas: *Bachelor's Degree:* 4 yrs; *Master's Degree:* a further 3 yrs; *Doctor's Degree*

Student Services: Academic counselling, Canteen, Cultural centre, Employment services, Foreign student adviser, Foreign Studies Centre, Health services, Language programs, Nursery care, Social counselling, Sports facilities

Student Residential Facilities: Yes

Libraries: Central Library, c. 2.7m. vols

Publications: Comparative Education Review *(monthly)*; Foreign Language Teaching in Schools *(monthly)*; Journal of Psychological Development and Education *(monthly)*; Journal of Beijing Normal University, Natural Science *(monthly)*; Journal of Beijing Normal University, Social Science *(monthly)*; Journal of Historiography *(monthly)*; Journal of Subject Education *(monthly)*; Journal of Teacher's Education *(monthly)*; Russian Literature *(monthly)*

Press or Publishing House: BNU Press

Academic Staff *2007-2008*	TOTAL
Student Numbers *2007-2008*	
All (Foreign Included)	19,980
FOREIGN ONLY	3,277

Part-time students, 32,689.
Last Updated: 01/07/09

BEIJING SPORT UNIVERSITY (BSU)

Yuanmingyuan East Road, Haidian District, Beijing 100084
Tel: +86(10) 62989244
Fax: +86(10) 62989297
EMail: isc@bsu.edu.cn
Website: http://www.bsu.edu.cn

President: Yang Hua

International Relations: Yu Xuefeng Tel: +86(10) 62989044

Colleges

Management; Physical Education (Physical Education); Sport Science (Sports); Sports Coaching (Sports); Wushu

Departments

Foreign Languages; Sport Journalism and Communication Department; Sport Performance

Schools

Continuing Education; Graduate

History: Founded 1953 as Central Sports Institute. Renamed Beijing Institute of Physical Education 1956. Acquired present title 1993.

Main Language(s) of Instruction: Chinese

Accrediting Agencies: UMAP

Degrees and Diplomas: *Bachelor's Degree:* Physical Education; Sports Coaching; Mass Sports; Sports Medicine; Traditional Chinese Sports; Applied Psychology; Public Affairs Administration; *Master's Degree:* Physical Education and Sports Coaching; Sports Medicine; Sport Sociology; Traditional Chinese Sports; Applied Psychology; *Doctor's Degree:* Physical Education and Sports Coaching; Sports Medicine; Sport Sociology; Traditional Chinese Sports

Libraries: c. 460,000 vols

Publications: Journal of Beijing Sport University; Physical Education in Chinese School

Last Updated: 02/02/07

BEIJING TECHNOLOGY AND BUSINESS UNIVERSITY

33 Fucheng Road, Beijing 100037
Tel: +86(10) 68904774
Fax: +86(10) 68417834
EMail: fao@btbu.edu.cn
Website: http://www.btbu.edu.cn

President: Su Zhiping

International Relations: Gan Yaping

Colleges

Advanced Professional College; Continuing Education

Departments

Foreign Languages; Law; Media and Communication; Postgraduate Studies

Schools

Accountancy; Business; Chemistry; Economics; Information Technology; Mechanical Automation

History: Founded 1999 following merger of Beijing Institute of Business and Beijing Institute of Light Industry.

Degrees and Diplomas: *Bachelor's Degree*; *Master's Degree*

Publications: Journal of Beijing Institute of Business; Journal of Beijing Institute of Light Industry

BEIJING UNION UNIVERSITY

97 Beisihuan East Road, Chaoyang District, Beijing 100101
Tel: +86(10) 64930069
Fax: +86(10) 64930048
EMail: ldwsc@buu.com.cn
Website: http://www.buu.edu.cn

President: Xiong Jiahua

International Relations: Li Jianzhong

Colleges

Advertising (Advertising and Publicity); Arts and Science; Automation (Automation and Control Engineering); Biochemical Engineering; Business; Information; International Language and Culture; Management (Management); Mechanical and Electrical Engineering; Netcom Software Technology; Oriental Information and Technology; Pinggu; Special Education; Tourism

Schools

Teacher Training *(Vocational-Technical)*; **Traditional Chinese Medicine and Pharmacy**

History: Founded 1985.

Main Language(s) of Instruction: Chinese

Degrees and Diplomas: *Bachelor's Degree*

Libraries: Central Library, c. 1m. vols

Publications: Journal of Beijing Union University

BEIJING UNIVERSITY OF AGRICULTURE

Zhuxinzhuang, Dewai, Beijing 102206
Tel: +86(10) 80799225
Fax: +86(10) 80799004
Website: http://www.bac.edu.cn/

President: Younian Wang

Departments

Animal Science and Technology (Animal Husbandry; Veterinary Science); **Basic Sciences**; **Biotechnology** (Biotechnology); **Computer Science and Engineering** (Computer Engineering; Computer Science); **Economics and Trade** (Business and Commerce; Economics); **Food Science and Engineering** (Food Science; Food Technology); **Foreign Languages**; **Humanities and Social Sciences** (Arts and Humanities; Social Sciences); **Landscape Design and Forestry** (Forestry; Landscape Architecture); **Plant Science and Technology** (Agriculture; Plant Pathology)

Research Institutes

Avian Diseases; **Crop Genetics and Breeding**; **Pomology**; **Rural Economy**; **Urban Agriculture**

History: Founded 1956 as Beijing Agricultural School. Acquired present title 1978.

Degrees and Diplomas: *Bachelor's Degree*; *Master's Degree*
Last Updated: 28/10/08

BEIJING UNIVERSITY OF CHEMICAL TECHNOLOGY

Heping Street, Chaoyang District, Beijing 100029
Tel: +86(10) 64434755
Fax: +86(10) 64423610
EMail: faoffice@mail.buct.edu.cn
Website: http://www.buct.edu.cn

President: Wang Zihao

International Relations: Xue Xinjian

Colleges

Adult Education (Applied Chemistry; Applied Mathematics; Applied Physics; Automation and Control Engineering; Computer Science; Modern Languages; Physical Education; Social Sciences); **Mechanical Engineering** (Mechanical Engineering; Polymer and Plastics Technology)

Schools

Administration; **Chemical Engineering** (Biochemistry; Chemical Engineering); **Management**; **Materials Science and Engineering** (Materials Engineering; Polymer and Plastics Technology); **Technology**

History: Founded 1958 as Beijing Institute of Chemical Technology. Acquired present name 1994 following merger of Beijing Institute of Chemical Technology and Beijing Institute of Administrative Cadres.

Academic Year: September to July (September-January; February-July)

Admission Requirements: Graduation from senior middle school and entrance examination

Fees: (Yuan): c. 800-1,500 per annum

Main Language(s) of Instruction: Chinese

Degrees and Diplomas: *Bachelor's Degree*: 4 yrs; *Master's Degree*: a further 2-3 yrs; *Doctor's Degree (Ph.D.)*: 2-3 yrs

Student Services: Academic counselling, Canteen, Cultural centre, Employment services, Foreign student adviser, Health services, Nursery care, Social counselling, Sports facilities

Special Facilities: Observatory

Libraries: c. 480,000 vols

Publications: Journal; Learned Journal of BUCT, Philosophy and Social Science, Natural Sciences; Research of College Education

BEIJING UNIVERSITY OF CHINESE MEDICINE

11 Beisanhuan Donglu, Beijing 100029
Tel: +86(10) 64218624
Fax: +86(10) 64220858
EMail: fuyanling@bjucmp.edu.cn
Website: http://202.204.32.11/english/newpage1.htm

President: Zheng Shouzeng

International Relations: Fu Yanling

Departments

Humanities and Social Sciences (Arts and Humanities; Social Sciences)

Schools

Acupuncture, Moxibustion and Tuina (Acupuncture); **Administration** (Administration; Business Administration); **Chinese Materia Medica** (Chemistry; Mathematics; Pharmacology; Physics); **Continuing Study**; **Distance Education**; **International** (International and Comparative Education); **Pre-Clinical Medicine** (Medicine; Traditional Eastern Medicine); **Traditional Chinese Nursing** (Nursing)

Further Information: Also 2 Affiliated Hospitals, 4 Teaching Hospitals and 18 Hospitals for externs

History: Founded 1956 as Beijing College of Traditional Chinese Medicine. Acquired present title 1993. Incorporated Beijing College of Acupuncture, Orthopedics and Traumatology 2000.

Academic Year: September to July (September-January; February-July)

Admission Requirements: Graduation from senior middle school and entrance examination

Fees: (Yuan): c. 5,800 per annum; foreign students, c. 30,000 per annum; Hong Kong, Macao, Taiwan students, c. 23,000 per annum

Main Language(s) of Instruction: Chinese

Degrees and Diplomas: *Bachelor's Degree*; *Master's Degree*: a further 3 yrs; *Doctor's Degree (Ph.D.)*: a further 3 yrs; *Doctor's Degree*: Medicine (M.D.), 5 yrs following Bachelor

Student Services: Academic counselling, Cultural centre, Employment services, Health services, Social counselling, Sports facilities

Special Facilities: Museum of the History of Chinese Medicine; Museum of Chinese Materia Medica

Libraries: c. 500,000 vols

Publications: Education of Chinese Medicine; Journal of Beijing University of Chinese Medicine
Last Updated: 29/10/08

BEIJING UNIVERSITY OF POST AND TELECOMMUNICATIONS

10 Xitucheng Road, Haidian District, Beijing 100876
Tel: +86(10) 62282273
Fax: +86(10) 62281774
EMail: faoffice@bupt.edu.cn
Website: http://www.bupt.edu.cn

President: Lin Jintong

International Relations: Meng Xiaomin

Schools

Automation; **Computer Science and Technology**; **Continuing Education**; **Economics and Management**; **Electronic Engineering**; **Humanities, Law and Economics** (Arts and Humanities; Economics; Law); **Information Engineering** (Information Technology); **Languages** (Modern Languages); **Management and Humanities** (Arts and Humanities; Management); **Science** (Natural Sciences); **Telecommunications Engineering** (Telecommunications Engineering)

Further Information: Branch at Fuzhou. Also Chinese courses for foreign students

History: Founded 1955. Renamed 1993.

Governing Bodies: Senate, comprising the President, 8 Vice-Presidents, and representatives of the academic staff and student body

Academic Year: September to July (September-January; March-July)

Admission Requirements: Graduation from senior middle school and national unified entrance examination

Fees: (Yuan): c. 25,000 per annum; graduate, 30,000-45,000

Main Language(s) of Instruction: Chinese

Accrediting Agencies: Ministry of Posts and Telecommunications

Degrees and Diplomas: *Bachelor's Degree*; *Master's Degree*; *Doctor's Degree*

Student Services: Academic counselling, Canteen, Cultural centre, Employment services, Foreign student adviser, Health services, Nursery care, Social counselling, Sports facilities

Student Residential Facilities: For c. 5,500 students

Libraries: Central Library, c. 840,000 vols

Publications: Higher Education Research; Journal of Beijing Universitry of Posts and Telecommunications; Journal of China's Post and Telecommunications Higher Education; Journal of Human Studies

Press or Publishing House: The University Press
Last Updated: 29/10/08

BEIJING UNIVERSITY OF TECHNOLOGY (BPU)

100 Pingleyuan, Chaoyang District, Beijing 100022
Tel: +86(10) 67391465
Fax: +86(10) 67392319
EMail: beijingtech@bjut.edu.cn
Website: http://www.bjut.edu.cn

President: Fan Boyuan Tel: +86(10) 67391536

Colleges
Applied Sciences (Applied Mathematics; Applied Physics; Statistics); **Architecture and Civil Engineering** (Architecture; Bridge Engineering; Civil Engineering; Hydraulic Engineering; Railway Engineering; Road Engineering; Structural Architecture; Transport Engineering); **Architecture and Town Planning** (Architecture; Industrial Design; Town Planning); **Art and Design** (Fashion Design; Industrial Design; Media Studies); **Computer Science** (Artificial Intelligence; Computer Networks; Computer Science; Software Engineering); **Economics and Management** (Economics; Management); **Electronic Information and Control Engineering** (Automation and Control Engineering; Electronic Engineering); **Environmental and Energy Engineering** (Energy Engineering; Environmental Engineering; Heating and Refrigeration); **Foreign Languages** (English; Japanese; Korean; Modern Languages); **Humanities and Social Sciences** (Arts and Humanities; Chinese; Economics; History; Law; Pedagogy; Philosophy; Psychology; Social Sciences; Sociology); **Life Sciences and Bioengineering** (Bioengineering; Biological and Life Sciences); **Materials Science and Engineering** (Automation and Control Engineering; Engineering; Materials Engineering); **Mechanical Engineering and Applied Electronic Technology** (Electronic Engineering; Machine Building; Mechanical Engineering; Technology); **Pilot** (Architectural and Environmental Design; Business Administration; Mechanical Engineering)

Institutes
Laser Engineering (Laser Engineering)

Schools
Software Engineering (Software Engineering)

Further Information: Also Chinese Teaching programme for foreign students

History: Founded 1960. Formerly known as Beijing Polytechnic University. Under the jurisdiction of the Beijing Municipality and financially supported by the Beijing Municipality.

Academic Year: September to July (September-January; February-July)

Admission Requirements: Graduation from senior middle school and National Entrance Examination for Universities and Colleges

Fees: (Yuan): c. 5,000 per annum

Main Language(s) of Instruction: Chinese

International Co-operation: With 100 universities and colleges worldwide

Accrediting Agencies: Beijing Municipality, Beijing Education Commission

Degrees and Diplomas: *Bachelor's Degree*: 4-5 yrs; *Master's Degree*: a further 3 yrs; *Doctor's Degree (Ph.D.)*: a further 3 yrs

Student Services: Academic counselling, Canteen, Cultural centre, Employment services, Foreign student adviser, Foreign Studies Centre, Health services, Language programs, Nursery care, Sports facilities

Student Residential Facilities: For c. 10,000 students

Special Facilities: Movie Studio

Libraries: 1.2m vols

Publications: BPU Journal *(quarterly)*

Press or Publishing House: BPU Press
Last Updated: 29/10/08

BEIJING WUZI UNIVERSITY (BMI)

Tongzhou District, Beijing 101149
Tel: +86(10) 89634412
Fax: +86(10) 89534661
EMail: bwuliuxuesheng@sina.com
Website: http://www.admissions.cn/bwu/index.htm

President: Xiangyong Tan

Departments
Accountancy (Accountancy); **Foreign Languages** (English); **Labour and Personnel** (Human Resources; Labour and Industrial Relations); **Law and Politics** (Law; Political Sciences)

Schools
Economics (Business Administration; Economics; Finance; Management); **Information Technology**; **Logistics** (Marketing; Production Engineering)

History: Founded 1980 as Beijing Materials Institute. Acquired present status and title 2005.

Academic Year: September to July

Fees: (US Dollars): 1,800 per annum

International Co-operation: With universities in Japan, USA, Germany, Canada, Russia, Australia, Singapore

Accrediting Agencies: Beijing Municipal Government

Degrees and Diplomas: *Bachelor's Degree*; *Master's Degree*: Industry Economics; Management Science; Engineering; Business Management

Student Services: Canteen

Student Residential Facilities: Yes.
Last Updated: 11/01/08

BENGBU MEDICAL COLLEGE

801 Zhihuai Road, Bengbu, Anhui Province 233003
Tel: +86(552) 3063243
Fax: +86(552) 3063243
EMail: bengbumed@yahoo.com
Website: http://www.bbmc.edu.cn

President: Zhu Yan

Departments
Clinical Medicine (Medicine); **Medical Laboratory Science** (Laboratory Techniques); **Nursing** (Nursing)

History: Founded 1958. Acquired present title 1974.

Degrees and Diplomas: *Bachelor's Degree*; *Master's Degree*
Last Updated: 29/10/08

BINZHOU MEDICAL UNIVERSITY

522, 3rd Huanghe Road, Binzhou, Shandong Province 256603
Tel: +86(543) 3322752
Fax: +86(543) 3322752
EMail: bz.caoguogang@163.com
Website: http://www.bzmc.edu.cn

President: Li Wuxiu

International Relations: Li Yiming

Departments
Clinical Teaching (Medicine); **Nursing** (Nursing); **Stomatology** (Stomatology)

Schools
Handicapped (Education of the Handicapped; Medicine)
History: Founded 1974 as Beizhen Medical College. Acquired present title 1983.
Degrees and Diplomas: *Bachelor's Degree*

BOHAI UNIVERSITY

27 Jiefang Road, Section 5, Linghe District, Jinzhou, Liaoning Province 121000
Tel: +86(416) 2828074
Fax: +86(416) 2822546
EMail: sfxyjzws@yahoo.com.cn
Website: http://www.jznu.edu.cn/page/index.asp

President: Qin Qiutian

International Relations: Ren Lijuan

Departments
Chemistry (Chemistry); **Chinese Language and Literature** (Chinese; Literature); **Fine Arts** (Fine Arts); **Information Technology** (Information Technology); **Journalism** (Journalism); **Mathematics** (Mathematics); **Physics** (Physics); **Political Science and Law** (Law; Political Sciences); **Tourism** (Tourism)
History: Founded 1958 as Jinzhou Teachers College. Acquired present status and title 2003.
Degrees and Diplomas: *Bachelor's Degree*; *Master's Degree*

CAPITAL COLLEGE OF PHYSICAL EDUCATION

11 Beisanhuan Xilu, Beijing 100088
Tel: +86(10) 62030025
Fax: +86(10) 62012987
EMail: btcpeyb@public.bta.net.cn

Departments
Cultural Sports Therapy (Sports Medicine); **Physical Education** (Physical Education); **Sports** (Sports); **Sports Rehabilitation** (Rehabilitation and Therapy); **Sports Training and Management** (Sports; Sports Management)
History: Founded 1956 as Beijing Sports School, became Beijing Teachers College of Physical Education 1978. Acquired present title 2000.
Degrees and Diplomas: *Bachelor's Degree*; *Master's Degree*
Libraries: c. 300,000 vols
Publications: Journal of Capital College of Physical Education

CAPITAL MEDICAL UNIVERSITY

10 Xitoutiao, Youanmen, Beijing 100054
Tel: +86(10) 83911000
Fax: +86(10) 83911029
EMail: webmaster@cpums.edu.cn
Website: http://www.ccmu.edu.cn/english

President: Lu Zhaofeng

Colleges
Medical *(Yan Jing)* (Medicine)

Schools
Basic Medical Sciences; **Biochemical and Pharmaceutical Sciences** (Biochemistry; Chemistry; Pharmacology); **Biomedical Engineering** (Biomedical Engineering); **Health Administration and Education** (Health Administration; Health Education); **Nursing**; **Public Health and Family Medicine** (Public Health); **Traditional Chinese Medicine** (Medicine)
History: Founded 1960 as Beijing Second Medical College, became Institute 1985, and acquired present title 1994.
Academic Year: September to July (September-January; February-July)
Admission Requirements: Graduation from senior middle school and entrance examination

Main Language(s) of Instruction: Chinese, English
Degrees and Diplomas: *Bachelor's Degree*; *Master's Degree*: a further 3 yrs; *Doctor's Degree*: a further 3 yrs
Student Residential Facilities: For c. 2,600 students
Special Facilities: Human Anatomy Exhibition Hall
Libraries: Central Library, 330,000 vols
Publications: Journal
Press or Publishing House: yes
Last Updated: 29/10/08

CAPITAL NORMAL UNIVERSITY

105 Xisanhuan Beilu, Beijing 100037
Tel: +86(10) 689026512
Fax: +86(10) 68416837
EMail: info@mail.cnu.edu.cn
Website: http://www.cnu.edu.cn

President: Liu Xincheng

Colleges
Adult Education (Adult Education); **Fine Arts** (Fine Arts); **Foreign Languages**; **Information Engineering** (Computer Science); **International Education**; **Life Sciences**; **Music** (Music); **Political Science and Law**; **Primary Education** (Primary Education)

Departments
Chemistry (Chemistry); **Educational Technology** (Educational Technology); **Mathematics** (Mathematics); **Physics**

Research Institutes
Culture of Calligraphy of China (Painting and Drawing)

Schools
Continuing Education; **Educational Sciences** (Education; Pedagogy; Preschool Education; Psychology); **International Education**
History: Founded 1954 as Beijing Teachers College. Merged with Beijing Teachers College of Foreign Languages. Acquired present status and title 1992.
Degrees and Diplomas: *Bachelor's Degree*; *Master's Degree*; *Doctor's Degree*
Publications: Capital Normal University Journal
Last Updated: 29/10/08

CAPITAL UNIVERSITY OF ECONOMICS AND BUSINESS

Flower-Town, Fengtai District, Beijing 100070
Tel: +86(10) 83952828
Fax: +86(10) 83952818
EMail: xcb@cueb.edu.cn
Website: http://www.cueb.edu.cn/English/index.htm

President: Wang Jiaqiong (2010-)

Schools
Accountancy (Accountancy); **Business Administration** (Administration; Advertising and Publicity; Business Administration; Human Resources; Information Management; International Business; Management; Marketing; Public Administration; Tourism); **Engineering** (Engineering; Engineering Management; Environmental Engineering; Industrial Engineering; Safety Engineering); **Humanities** (Arts and Humanities; Social Work); **Labour Economics** (Economics; Natural Resources); **Public Finance** (Banking; Finance)
History: Founded 1956. A merger of the Beijing College of Economics and the Beijing Trade and Finance Institute. Acquired present title 1995.
Degrees and Diplomas: *Bachelor's Degree*; *Master's Degree*; *Doctor's Degree*
Libraries: 960,000 vols
Publications: Beijing Economic Outlook; Journal of Capital University of Economics and Business; Population and Economics; Research on Economics and Management
Last Updated: 29/10/08

CENTRAL ACADEMY OF DRAMA (CCAD)
Dongmianhua Hutong 39, Dongcheng District, Beijing 100710
Tel: +86(10) 640 35626
Fax: +86(10) 640 16479
EMail: zhongxi@zhongxi.cn
Website: http://www.zhongxi.cn

President: Xiang Xu (2003-)
Tel: +86(10) 640 17573, Fax: +86(10) 640 14976

Vice-President: Libin Liu
Tel: +86(10) 640 18301, Fax: +86(10) 640 14976

International Relations: Shaoyu Zhou, Head of Foreign Affairs Office
Tel: +86(10) 640 35626, Fax: +86(10) 640 16479
EMail: wsci@chntheatre.edu.cn

Departments
Directing *Dean*: Ruru Ding; **Drama Literature** *(Playwriting; Drama Studies)* (Ancient Civilizations; History; Literature; Modern History; Writing) *Dean*: Xian Zhang; **Performing** *Vice-President and Dean*: Libing Liu; **Stage Art** (Art Management; Design; Display and Stage Design; Fine Arts; Painting and Drawing; Visual Arts) *Dean*: Kangmei Zhang; **Stage Management** *Dean*: Ergang Shang; **TV Arts** *(production, management, advertisement, direction)* (Cinema and Television; Film; Information Sciences; Mass Communication; Performing Arts; Radio and Television Broadcasting; Video) *Dean*: Haibo Lu

History: Founded 1950 as Lu Xun Art College in Yan' an. Merged with Art Faculty of North China University and Nanking National Academy of Drama.

Academic Year: September to June

Admission Requirements: High school certificate

Fees: (Yuan): Undergraduates, 1,600 per term; post-graduates, 2,000 per term

Main Language(s) of Instruction: Chinese

Degrees and Diplomas: *Bachelor's Degree*: 4 yrs; *Master's Degree*: Theatre (Directing); Performing Arts; Arts and Humanities (Drama, Literature); Cinema and Television; Display and Stage Design, 3 yrs; *Doctor's Degree*: Theatre (Directing); Performing Arts; Arts and Humanities (Drama Literature); Cinema and Television, 3 yrs. Also Continuous Study programmes (1 yr) in all fields of study

Student Services: Academic counselling, Canteen, Employment services, Foreign student adviser, Foreign Studies Centre, Health services, Language programs, Nursery care, Social counselling, Sports facilities

Student Residential Facilities: Yes

Special Facilities: Art Gallery; Theatre; Computer Laboratory

Libraries: Yes

Publications: Drama *(monthly)*

CENTRAL ACADEMY OF FINE ARTS
No.8 Hua Jia Di Nan St, Chaoyang District, Beijing 100015
Tel: +86(10) 64380464
Fax: +86(10) 65134140
EMail: xujia@cafa.edu.cn
Website: http://www.cafa.edu.cn/channel.asp?id=10

President: Pan Gongkai

Schools
Architecture (Architecture); **Chinese Painting**; **City Design**; **Design** (Design); **Fine Art**; **Humanities** (Art Education; Art History; Art Management; Heritage Preservation; Restoration of Works of Art)

History: Founded 1918 as Beijing School of Fine Arts, acquired present title 1950.

Degrees and Diplomas: *Bachelor's Degree*; *Master's Degree*; *Doctor's Degree*

Libraries: c. 240,000 vols

Publications: Art Research; World Art
Last Updated: 29/10/08

CENTRAL CONSERVATORY OF MUSIC
43 Baojia Street, Xicheng District, Beijing 100031
Tel: +86(10) 66412585
Fax: +86(10) 66412138
EMail: contactus@ccom.edu.cn
Website: http://www.ccom.edu.cn

President: Wang Cizhao

International Relations: Jiang Xiaoai

Departments
Chinese Traditional Musical Instrument Performance; **Composition** (Music; Music Theory and Composition); **Conducting** (Conducting); **Electronic Music** (Music); **History of Western Music** (Art History); **Instrument Making and Repairing** (Instrument Making); **Keyboard Instrument Performance** (Musical Instruments); **Music Education** (Music Education); **Musicology** (Musicology); **Voice and Opera** (Opera; Singing); **Wind and String Instrument Performance** (Musical Instruments)

History: Founded 1950.

Degrees and Diplomas: *Bachelor's Degree*; *Master's Degree*; *Doctor's Degree*

Libraries: c. 480,000 vols

Publications: Journal of Central Conservatory of Music
Last Updated: 29/10/08

CENTRAL SOUTH FORESTRY UNIVERSITY
Zhuzhou, Hunan Province 412006
Tel: +86(733) 8703331
Fax: +86(773) 8703331
Website: http://www.csfu.edu.cn

President: Su Xiancai

International Relations: Liu Yuan

Departments
Foreign Languages (Modern Languages); **Law** (Law)

Faculties
Architectural Engineering (Structural Architecture); **Economics and Trade** (Economics); **Industry**; **Resources and Environment** (Environmental Studies); Natural Resources)

History: Founded 1958, acquired present title 1964.

Degrees and Diplomas: *Bachelor's Degree*; *Master's Degree*

Libraries: c. 710,000 vols

Publications: CSFU Journal

CENTRAL SOUTH UNIVERSITY
88 Xiangyalu, Changsha, Hunan Province 410078
Tel: +86(731) 4805210
Fax: +86(731) 4471339
EMail: admis@mail.csu.edu.cn
Website: http://www.csu.edu.cn

Schools
Art (Fine Arts); **Business** (Business Administration); **Chemistry and Chemical Engineering** (Chemical Engineering; Chemistry); **Chinese Language and Literature**; **Civil Engineering and Architecture**; **Energy and Power Engineering** (Energy Engineering; Power Engineering); **Foreign Languages** (Modern Languages); **Fundamental Medicine** (Medicine); **Geoscience and Environmental Engineering**; **Information Science and Engineering**; **Law** (Law); **Material Science and Engineering** (Engineering; Materials Engineering); **Mathematical Sciences and Computer Technology** (Mathematics and Computer Science); **Mechanical and Electrical Engineering**; **Medical Technology** (Medical Technology); **Metallurgical Science and Engineering** (Engineering; Metallurgical Engineering); **Nursing**; **Pharmaceutical Sciences** (Pharmacy); **Physics and Technology**; **Political Science and Executive Administration**; **Public Health** (Public Health); **Resources and Safety Engineering**; **Resources Processing and Bioengineering** (Bioengineering); **Stomatology**; **Traffic and Transport** (Transport and Communications)

History: Founded 1914 as Central South University of Technology, merged with Changsha Railway University and Hunan Medical University 2000.

Academic Year: August to July (August-January; February-July)

Admission Requirements: Graduation from senior middle school and entrance examination

Main Language(s) of Instruction: Chinese, English

Degrees and Diplomas: *Bachelor's Degree*: 5 yrs; *Master's Degree*: a further 3 yrs; *Doctor's Degree*: a further 2-3 yrs following Master

Student Residential Facilities: Yes

Special Facilities: Experimental Animal Centre

CENTRAL UNIVERSITY OF FINANCE AND ECONOMICS (CUFE)

39th South College Road, Haidan District, Beijing 100081
Tel: +86(10) 62288335
Fax: +86(10) 62288982
EMail: lxs@cufe.edu.cn
Website: http://www.cufe.edu.cn

President: Wang Guangqian (2002-) Tel: +86(10) 62288117

International Relations: Cai Caishii

Departments
Banking (Banking; Finance); **Chinese**; **Investments Economics**

Schools
Accountancy (Accountancy; Finance); **Adult Education** (Adult Education); **Applied Mathematics** (Applied Mathematics); **Business** (Business Administration; Human Resources; Management; Marketing); **Culture and Communication** (Cultural Studies); **Economics** (Business Administration; Economics; Marketing; Statistics); **Finance** (Finance); **Foreign Languages** (Modern Languages); **Government Administration** (Government); **Information** (Information Sciences); **Insurance** (Insurance); **Law** (Law); **Management** (Management); **Marxism** (Political Sciences); **Public Finance** (Economic and Finance Policy; Finance; Government; Management; Public Administration); **Social Development** (Social Studies); **Sports Economics and Management** (Sports; Sports Management); **Statistics** (Statistics); **Taxation** (Taxation)

History: Founded 1949 as Central School of Taxation, acquired present title 1996 and status 2000.

Admission Requirements: Graduation from high school and entrance examination

Fees: (Yuan): c. 4,500 per annum

Main Language(s) of Instruction: Chinese

Accrediting Agencies: Ministry of Education

Degrees and Diplomas: *Bachelor's Degree*: Accountancy; Banking; Information; Insurance; Law; Management; Public Finance; Taxation, 4 yrs; *Master's Degree*: Banking; Information; Insurance; Management; Public Finance; Taxation Investment, 3 yrs; *Doctor's Degree*: Accountancy; Banking Management, 3 yrs

Student Services: Academic counselling, Canteen, Cultural centre, Employment services, Foreign student adviser, Foreign Studies Centre, Health services, Language programs, Nursery care, Social counselling, Sports facilities

Student Residential Facilities: For c. 8,000 students

Special Facilities: Museum of School History. Movie Studio

Libraries: 2 libraries, c. 600,000 vols

Publications: Journal of Central University of Finance and Economics *(monthly)*
Last Updated: 30/10/08

CHANG'AN UNIVERSITY

Xi'an, Shaanxi Province 710064
Tel: +86(29) 2338114
Fax: +86(29) 5261532
EMail: president@chd.edu.cn
Website: http://www.xahu.edu.cn

President: Ma Jian

International Relations: Zhang Wei

Colleges
Foreign Languages (English; French; German; Japanese; Russian); **Geological Engineering and Geomatics** (Geological Engineering; Geophysics); **Highway** (Road Engineering); **Science** (Applied Mathematics; Applied Physics; Chemistry; Engineering Drawing and Design; Mechanical Engineering)

Institutes
Environmental Science (Environmental Studies)

Schools
Automotive (Automotive Engineering; Transport Engineering); **Civil Engineering** (Automation and Control Engineering; Civil Engineering; Construction Engineering; Electrical Engineering; Engineering Management); **Economics and Management** (Economics; Management); **Humanities and Social Sciences** (Advertising and Publicity; Art Education; Chinese; Law; Political Sciences; Public Administration); **Information** (Information Sciences)

History: Founded 2000 following merger of Xi'an Highway University (founded 1951), Xi'an Engineering University (founded 1953) and North-western Architecture Engineering Institute.

Degrees and Diplomas: *Bachelor's Degree*; *Master's Degree*; *Doctor's Degree*

Libraries: c. 1.5m vols

Publications: Journal of Chang'an University; Journal of China Highway and Transportation Engineering
Last Updated: 30/10/08

CHANGCHUN INSTITUTE OF TECHNOLOGY

395 Kuanping Road, Changchun, Jilin Province 130012
Tel: +86(431) 5955991
Fax: +86(431) 5955991
EMail: webmaster@ccit.edu.cn
Website: http://www.ccit.edu.cn

Colleges
Software Engineering (Software Engineering)

Departments
Applied Chemistry (Applied Chemistry); **Architecture** (Architecture); **Business Management** (Business Administration; Management); **Civil Engineering** (Civil Engineering); **Continuing Education**; **Electronic Engineering** (Electronic Engineering); **Energy and Power Engineering** (Energy Engineering; Power Engineering); **Environmental Engineering** (Environmental Engineering); **Foreign Languages** (Modern Languages); **Industrial Design** (Industrial Design); **Information Engineering** (Information Technology); **Land Resources** (Natural Resources); **Management Engineering** (Management); **Mechanical Engineering**; **Physical Education** (Physical Education); **Social Science**; **Water Conservation Engineering** (Hydraulic Engineering; Water Management)

History: Founded 2000.

Degrees and Diplomas: *Bachelor's Degree*

Libraries: c. 905,000 vols

CHANGCHUN NORMAL UNIVERSITY

3 Jichang Highway (North), Changchun, Jilin Province 130032
Tel: +86(431) 7915263 Ext 3023
Fax: +86(431) 4711779
EMail: cnuice@163.com
Website: http://www.cncnc.edu.cn

President: Zhao Lixing

International Relations: Tian Chunde Tel: +86(431) 4711779

Departments
Biology (Biology); **Chemistry** (Chemistry); **Chinese** (Chinese; Literature); **Fine Arts** (Fine Arts); **Foreign Languages** (English; Modern Languages); **Geography** (Geography); **History** (History); **Mathematics** (Mathematics); **Music** (Music); **Physical Training** (Physical Education); **Physics** (Physics); **Politics** (Political Sciences)

History: Founded 1978.

Degrees and Diplomas: *Bachelor's Degree*

CHANGCHUN TAXATION COLLEGE

6699 Jingyue Street, Changchun, Jilin Province 130012
Tel: +86(431) 4539201
Fax: +86(431) 4539201
Website: http://www.ctu.cc.jl.cn/english/index.jsp

President: Li Dezhong

International Relations: Li Zhongyang

Departments

Accountancy (Accountancy); **Banking** (Banking); **Business Administration** (Business Administration); **Economics** (Economics); **Information Management** (Information Management); **International Economics** (International Economics); **Law** (Law); **Public Finance** (Finance)

History: Founded 1948 as Northeast Bank College, acquired present title 1992.

Degrees and Diplomas: *Bachelor's Degree*; *Master's Degree*

Libraries: c. 310,000 vols

Publications: Modern Economics Research; Taxation and Economics
Last Updated: 31/10/08

CHANGCHUN UNIVERSITY

6543 Weixing Road, Changchun, Jilin Province 130022
Tel: +86(431) 5387435
Fax: +86(431) 5387435
Website: http://www.ccu-edu.cn/

President: Zhang Deijang

Colleges

Aviation (Aeronautical and Aerospace Engineering; Electrical Engineering); **Biological Sciences and Technology** (Automotive Engineering; Biotechnology; Food Technology; Landscape Architecture); **Computer Science and Technology** (Computer Networks; Computer Science; Software Engineering); **Economics** (Economics; International Business); **Electronic Information and Engineering** (Automation and Control Engineering; Electrical and Electronic Equipment and Maintenance; Electronic Engineering); **Fine Arts** (Design; Painting and Drawing); **Foreign Languages and Literature**; **Humanities** (Administration; Chinese; Cultural Studies; Literature; Political Sciences; Special Education); **International** *(Raffles-CU)*; **Machine Engineering** (Automation and Control Engineering; Industrial Design; Industrial Engineering; Machine Building); **Management**; **Music** (Music); **Science** (Applied Mathematics; Applied Physics; Computer Science; Educational Technology; Mathematics); **Software** (Computer Networks; Software Engineering)

Research Institutes

Applied Technology (Technology); **Biological Engineering** (Bioengineering); **Scientific and Technological Development in Higher Education**

History: Founded 1987. Merged with Jilin University of Science and Technology, Jilin Specialized School of Mechanical and Electrical Engineering, Changchun Specialized School of Foreign Languages and Changchun Vocational University.

Degrees and Diplomas: *Bachelor's Degree*

Libraries: c. 270,000 vols

Publications: Journal of Changchun University
Last Updated: 30/10/08

CHANGCHUN UNIVERSITY OF CHINESE MEDICINE

39 Gongnong Street, Changchun, Jilin Province 130021
Tel: +86(431) 5955911 +86(431) 5956499
Fax: +86(431) 5958760
EMail: liumiao_66@hotmail.com
Website: http://www.ccucm.edu.cn

President: Sui Dianjun

International Relations: Song Bailin Tel: +86(431) 5940940

Departments

Acupuncture, Moxibustion and Osteology Nursing (Acupuncture; Health Sciences; Nursing); **Chinese Medical Science** (Traditional Eastern Medicine); **Traditional Chinese Medicine** (Medicine; Traditional Eastern Medicine)

History: Founded 1958 as Changchun College of Traditional Chinese Medicine.

Degrees and Diplomas: *Bachelor's Degree*; *Master's Degree*; *Doctor's Degree*

CHANGCHUN UNIVERSITY OF SCIENCE AND TECHNOLOGY

7 Weixing Road, Changchun, Jilin Province 130022
Tel: +86(431) 5386407
Fax: +86(431) 5303278
EMail: webmaster@cust.edu.cn
Website: http://www.cust.edu.cn

President: Yu Huadong

International Relations: Zhang Qifang

Schools

Biological and Medical Engineering (Bioengineering; Biomedical Engineering); **Chemistry and Environmental Engineering**; **Chinese Literature** (Chinese; Literature); **Computer Science and Technology** (Computer Science); **Economics and Management** (Economics; Management); **Electronics and Information Engineering** (Computer Engineering; Electronic Engineering); **Foreign Languages** (Modern Languages); **Law** (Law); **Life Sciences and Technology**; **Material and Chemical Industry**; **Mechatronical Engineering**; **Photoelectric Engineering**; **Science** (Applied Chemistry; Applied Mathematics; Applied Physics; Chemical Engineering; Materials Engineering; Optical Technology)

History: Founded 1958 as Changchun Institute of Optics and Precision Instruments. Acquired present title 2002.

Main Language(s) of Instruction: Chinese

Degrees and Diplomas: *Bachelor's Degree*; *Master's Degree*; *Doctor's Degree*

Libraries: c. 375,000 vols

Publications: Journal of Changchun Institute of Optics and Precision Instruments; Research in Higher Education
Last Updated: 31/10/08

CHANGCHUN UNIVERSITY OF TECHNOLOGY

17 Yan'an Road, Changchun, Jilin Province 130012
Tel: +86(431) 5955521
Website: http://www.ccut.edu.cn/

President: Du Lizheng

International Relations: Xiao Ning

Departments

Applied Sciences (Applied Chemistry; Applied Mathematics; Applied Physics); **Automation and Electronic Engineering** (Automation and Control Engineering; Electronic Engineering); **Chemical Engineering** (Chemical Engineering); **Materials Engineering** (Materials Engineering); **Metallurgical Engineering**; **Textile Engineering** (Textile Technology); **Transport Engineering** (Transport Engineering)

Schools

Computer Science and Engineering (Computer Engineering; Computer Science); **Humanities** (Arts and Humanities); **Management** (Management); **Mechanical Engineering** (Mechanical Engineering); **Modern Languages** (Modern Languages); **Rural Planning** (Rural Planning)

History: Founded 1952 as Changchun School of Automotive Technology. Renamed Jilin Institute of Science and Technology 1961 and Jilin Institute of Technology 1962. Acquired present title 2002.

Degrees and Diplomas: *Bachelor's Degree*; *Master's Degree*
Last Updated: 03/11/08

CHANGSHA UNIVERSITY

21 Hongshanmiao, Kaifu District, Changsha, Hunan Province
410003
Tel: +86(731) 425 4372
Fax: +86(731) 425 0583
EMail: wsb@ccsu.cn
Website: http://www.ccsu.cn

Departments
Applied Chemistry and Environmental Science (Applied Chemistry; Environmental Studies); **Applied Physics and Electronic Technology** (Applied Physics; Electronic Engineering); **Arts** (Fine Arts); **Computer Science and Technology** (Computer Science; Technology); **Economics and Management** (Economics; Management); **Engineering** (Engineering); **Foreign Languages** (Modern Languages); **Humanities** (Art Criticism); **Mathematics and Information Science** (Information Sciences; Mathematics); **Physical Education** (Physical Education); **Politics and Law** (Law; Political Sciences)

History: Create 1983.

Degrees and Diplomas: *Bachelor's Degree*
Last Updated: 22/11/10

CHANGSHA UNIVERSITY OF SCIENCE AND TECHNOLOGY

9 Chiling Road, Changsha, Hunan Province 410077
Tel: +86(731) 2617768
EMail: study@csust.edu.cn
Website: http://www.csust.cn

President: Yan Guoliang

International Relations: Tu Heping

Departments
Engineering (Engineering); **Humanities** (Arts and Humanities); **Science** (Natural Sciences); **Social Sciences** (Social Sciences)

History: Founded 2002 following merger of Changsha University of Electric Power (founded 1956) and Changsha Communications University (founded 1956).

Degrees and Diplomas: *Bachelor's Degree; Master's Degree; Doctor's Degree*
Last Updated: 03/11/08

CHANGZHI MEDICAL COLLEGE

46 Yanan Nanku, Changzhi, Shanxi Province 046000

President: Wang Yongjin

Departments
Clinical Medicine (Medicine); **Medical X-ray and Imaging**; **Nursing** (Nursing)

History: Founded 1946 as Changzhi Nursing School. Acquired present title 1986.

Degrees and Diplomas: *Bachelor's Degree*

CHANGZHOU INSTITUTE OF TECHNOLOGY

3 Changcheng Road, Changzhou, Jiangsu Province 213002
Tel: +86(519) 5210282 +86(519) 5210284
Fax: +86(519) 5210282
EMail: bgs@oa.czu.cn
Website: http://www.czu.cn

President: Ma Shushan

International Relations: Yu Xinhuai

Departments
Civil Engineering (Civil Engineering); **Computer Application Engineering** (Computer Engineering); **Economic Management** (Economics; Management); **Electrical Engineering** (Electrical Engineering); **Languages and Literature** (Literature; Modern Languages); **Mechanical Engineering** (Mechanical Engineering); **Quality Technology Engineering**

Divisions
Foundation Studies; **Social Sciences** (Social Sciences)

History: Founded 1978 as Changzhou 721 Industrial College. Changed its title 2003. Previously known as Changzhou College of Industrial Technology.

Degrees and Diplomas: *Bachelor's Degree*

CHENGDE MEDICAL COLLEGE

Chengde, Hebei Province 067000
Tel: +86(314) 2065269
Fax: +86(314) 2064089
Website: http://china786.com/Chendge%20Medical%20College/index.htm

President: Jin Yongde

International Relations: Hu Shidong

Departments
Biomedical Engineering (Biomedical Engineering); **Clinical Medicine** (Medicine); **Nursing** (Nursing); **Psychology** (Psychology); **Traditional Chinese Medicine** (Traditional Eastern Medicine); **Traditional Chinese Pharmacy** (Pharmacy)

History: Founded 1945 as Health School of the Jidong Region. Acquired present status and title 1982.

Degrees and Diplomas: *Bachelor's Degree; Master's Degree*

CHENGDU SPORTS UNIVERSITY

2 Tiyuan Road, Chengdu, Sichuan Province 610041
Tel: +86(28) 5593292
Fax: +86(28) 5582752
EMail: kycswp@263.net
Website: http://www.cdsu.edu.cn/en/indexe.asp

President: Zhou Xikuan

International Relations: Li Guodong

Faculties
Athletic Sports (Sports); **Economics and Management** (Economics; Management; Statistics); **Foreign Languages**; **Journalism**; **Physical Education**; **Sports Medicine**; **Wu Shu**

Further Information: Also Hang Kong Gang Campus

History: Founded 1942 as Sichuan Standing Junior Sports College. Chengdu Sport Polytechnic 1950, Chengdu Institute of Physical Education 1956.

Degrees and Diplomas: *Bachelor's Degree; Master's Degree; Doctor's Degree*
Last Updated: 31/10/08

CHENGDU UNIVERSITY

Shiling Town, Chengdu, Sichuan Province 610081
Tel: +86(28) 3389284
Fax: +86(28) 3337939
EMail: faocdu@cdu.edu.cn
Website: http://www.cdu.edu.cn

President: Zhang Rixin

International Relations: Yang Meijin

Faculties
Art (Art Education); **Bio-industry**; **Continuing Education** (Continuing Education); **Economics, Political Science and Law** (Economics; Law; Political Sciences); **Electronic and Information Engineering** (Computer Engineering; Electronic Engineering); **Fine Arts** (Fine Arts); **Foreign Languages and Culture** (Cultural Studies; Modern Languages); **Industrial Manufacturing**; **Information Science and Technology**; **International Education**; **Literature and Journalism**; **Management** (Management); **Medicine and Nursing**; **Normal Education** (Education); **Preschool Education**; **Software Industry**; **Tourism and Cultural Industry** (Cultural Studies; Tourism); **Urban and Rural Construction** (Construction Engineering)

History: Founded 1978.

Main Language(s) of Instruction: Chinese

Degrees and Diplomas: *Bachelor's Degree*
Last Updated: 31/10/08

CHENGDU UNIVERSITY OF INFORMATION TECHNOLOGY

3 Block, Renminnan Road, Chengdu, Sichuan Province 610041
Tel: +86(28) 5533523
Fax: +86(28) 5553580
EMail: wsb@cuit.edu.cn
Website: http://www.cuit.edu.cn

President: Duan Tingyang

International Relations: Tan Jiansheng

Divisions

Arts (Chinese; English; Literature); **Business** (Accountancy; E-Business/Commerce; Finance; Human Resources; International Business; Marketing; Public Administration); **Engineering** (Automation and Control Engineering; Biomedical Engineering; Computer Engineering; Computer Networks; Electrical Engineering; Electronic Engineering; Environmental Engineering; Microelectronics; Software Engineering; Telecommunications Engineering); **Law** (Law; Social Work); **Science** (Information Technology; Mathematics; Optics; Statistics)

History: Founded 1951. Acquired present title 2000. Previously known as Chengdu Institute of Meteorology.

Main Language(s) of Instruction: Chinese

Degrees and Diplomas: *Bachelor's Degree*; *Master's Degree*
Last Updated: 31/10/08

CHENGDU UNIVERSITY OF TECHNOLOGY

1 Dongsanlu Erxianqiao, Chengdu, Sichuan Province 610059
Tel: +86(28) 84078960 +86(28) 84079488
Fax: +86(28) 84077099
EMail: lsg@cdut.edu.cn; yhd@cdut.edu.cn
Website: http://www.cdut.edu.cn

Colleges

Applied Nuclear Technology and Automation Engineering; **Commerce** (Accountancy; Business Administration; Economics; Finance; Tourism); **Communication Science and Art**; **Continuing Education**; **Earth Sciences** (Earth Sciences; Information Technology; Rural Planning; Tourism; Town Planning); **Energy Resources** (Geology; Petroleum and Gas Engineering); **Environment and Civil Engineering** (Architecture; Civil Engineering; Construction Engineering; Environmental Engineering; Geological Engineering); **Foreign Languages and Cultures** (Cultural Studies; English; Japanese; Modern Languages); **Information Engineering** (Computer Engineering; Electronic Engineering; Geophysics; Information Technology; Physics); **Information Management** (Computer Science; E-Business/Commerce; Information Sciences; Management; Mathematics); **Materials and Bioengineering**; **Network Education**

Institutes

Tourism and Hospitality *(Sino-Australian)*

Schools

Humanities and Law (Administration; Arts and Humanities; Law; Political Sciences; Public Administration; Social Sciences; Teacher Training)

History: Founded 1956 as Chengdu College of Geology. Acquired present title in 1993. Incorporated Sichuan Commercial College and the Training Institute for Staff Members of Non-Ferrous Metal Geological Institutions 2001.

Admission Requirements: Graduation from high school and national university entrance examination

Fees: (Yuan): 4,000-17,000 (tuition fees) according to field of study

Accrediting Agencies: Department of Education of Sichuan Provincial Government

Degrees and Diplomas: *Bachelor's Degree*: Accounting; Acting; Advertising; Applied Chemistry; Artistic Designing; Bioengineering; Business Administration; Chemistry; Civil Engineering; Computer Science and Technology; E-Business; Economics; Electrical Engineering and Automation; Electronic and Information Science and Technology; English; Environmental Engineering; Financial Management; Geochemistry; Geographic Information System; Georaphy; Geology; Geophysics; Human Resource Management; Hydrology and Water Resource Engineering; Industrial Design;

Information and Computing Science; Information Engineering; Information Management and Information System; Information Security; International Economics and Trade; Japanese; Landscape Gardening; Law; Literature of Theatre Film and Television; Machine Design and Manufacturing and their Automation; Marketing; Material Science and Engineering; Mathematics and Applied Mathematics; Measuring and Control Technology and Instrumentations; Natural Resources Prospecting Engineering; Nuclear Engineering and Technology; Petroleum Engineering; Political Science and Public Administration; Project Management; Prospecting Techniques and Engineering; Public Utility Management; Radio and Television Science; Science of Chemical and Pharmaceutical Engineering; Sociology; Surveying and Mapping Engineering; Techniques of Broadcasting and TV program Directing; Tourism Management; Urban and Rural Planning and Resources Management; *Master's Degree*: Analytical Chemistry; Applied Chemistry; Applied Geophysics; Applied Mathematics; Cartography and Geography Information Engineering; Cartography and Geography Information System; Chemical Techniques; Computer Application Technology; Computing Mathematics; Enterprise Manegement (including Financial Management, Marketing, and Human Resource Management); Environmental Engineering; Environmental Geology; Environmental Science; Foreign Languages and Applied Linguistics; Geochemistry; Geodetection and Information Technology; Geological Engineering; Hazard Prevention and Protection Engineering; Management Science and Engineering; Material Sciences; Mineral Material Sciences; Mineral Resources Prospecting and Exploration; Mineralogy, Petrology, Mineral Deposits; Nuclear Resources Prospecting Engineering; Nucelar Technology and Applications; Oil-Gas Field Development Engineering; Paleontology and Stratigraphy (including Paleonanthropology); Philosophy of Science and Technology; Photogrammetry and Remote Sensing; Quarternary Geology; Radiation Prevention and Environmental Protection; Sedimantary; Signals and Information Processing; Software and its theories; Solid Geophysics; Structural Geology; Telecommunication and Information System; Testing Technology and Instruments; *Doctor's Degree*: Environmental Geology; Geochemistry; Geodetection and Information Technology; Geological Engineering; Geophysics; Geotechnical Engineering; Mineral Material Sciences; Mineral Resource Prospecting and Exploration; Mineralogy, Petrology, Mineral Deposits; Nuclear Resources Prospecting Engineering; Oil-Gad Field Development Engineering; Paleontology and Stratigraphy (including Paleonanthropology); Quarternary Geology; Sedimentary; Solid Geophysics; Structural Geology

Student Services: Academic counselling, Canteen, Employment services, Foreign student adviser, Health services, Language programs, Nursery care, Social counselling, Sports facilities

Special Facilities: Natural Museum

Libraries: University Library, c. 1,350,000 vols.; c. 14,000 electronic journals

Publications: Computing Techniques for Geophysical and Geochemical Exploration *(quarterly)*; Journal of Chengdu University of Technology (Natural Science) *(bimonthly)*; Journal of Chengdu University of Technology (Social Science) *(quarterly)*; Journal of Geological Hazards and Environmental Preservation *(quarterly)*; Journal of Mineralogy and Petrology *(quarterly)*; Scientific and Technological Management of Land and Resources *(quarterly)*
Last Updated: 31/10/08

CHENGDU UNIVERSITY OF TRADITIONAL CHINESE MEDICINE

37 Shierqiao Road, Chengdu, Sichuan Province 610075
Tel: +86(28) 7768611
Fax: +86(28) 7763471
EMail: wsc@cdutcm.edu.cn
Website: http://www.cdutcm.edu.cn

President: Li Mingfu

International Relations: Huang Qingxian

Schools

Acupuncture and Moxibustion (Acupuncture; Traditional Eastern Medicine); **Clinical Medicine**; **Continuing Education**; **International Education**; **Medicine** (Medicine); **Pharmacy**

History: Founded 1956 as Chengdu College of Traditional Chinese Medicine, acquired present title 1995.

Degrees and Diplomas: *Bachelor's Degree*; *Master's Degree*; *Doctor's Degree*

Libraries: c. 420,000 vols

Publications: Guide of Chinese Medicine Information; Journal of Chengdu University of Traditional Chinese Medicine; Journal of Educational Science

Last Updated: 31/10/08

CHIFENG UNIVERSITY

Airport Road, Chifeng, Inner Mongolia 024000
Tel: +86(476) 2205811
Fax: +86(476) 8810068

History: Founded 1958. Acquired present title 2003, following merger with Chifeng Teachers Training College for Nationalities, Chifeng College of Education and Chifeng Branch of Inner Mongolian TV University.

Degrees and Diplomas: *Bachelor's Degree*

Libraries: c. 3,488,000 vols.

CHINA ACADEMY OF ART

218 Nanshan Road, Hangzhou, Zhejiang Province 310002
Tel: +86(571) 7038237
Fax: +86(571) 7070039
EMail: caafao@caa.edu.cn
Website: http://www.chinaacademyofart.com/

President: Xu Jiang

Departments

Art History and Theory (Art History); **Environmental Design** (Architectural and Environmental Design); **Fashion and Textile Design** (Fashion Design); **Industrial Design and Ceramics** (Ceramic Art; Design); **Oil Painting** (Painting and Drawing); **Print-Making** (Printing and Printmaking); **Sculpture** (Sculpture); **Traditional Chinese Painting** (Painting and Drawing); **Visual Communication and Design** (Communication Arts; Design)

History: Founded 1928 as National Academy of Art. Renamed China Academy of Art 1993.

Degrees and Diplomas: *Bachelor's Degree*; *Master's Degree*; *Doctor's Degree*

CHINA AGRICULTURAL UNIVERSITY

2 Yuanmingyuan West Road, Haidian District, Beijing 100094
Tel: +86(10) 62892736
Fax: +86(10) 62891055
EMail: cauie@cau.edu.cn
Website: http://www.cau.edu.cn

President: Jiang Shuren

International Relations: Wang Jingguo

Schools

Adult Education (Adult Education); **Agricultural Development** (Agriculture); **Animal Science and Technology** (Technology; Zoology); **Basic Science and Technology** (Natural Sciences; Technology); **Biology** (Biology); **Continuing Education**; **Economics** (Economics); **Electronic and Electrical Power Engineering** (Electrical and Electronic Engineering; Electronic Engineering); **Food Science** (Food Science); **Humanities and Social Sciences** (Arts and Humanities; Social Sciences); **Hydraulic and Civil Engineering** (Civil Engineering; Hydraulic Engineering); **Management** (Management); **Mechanical Engineering** (Mechanical Engineering); **Plant Sciences and Technology** (Agronomy; Botany; Entomology; Pathology; Plant and Crop Protection; Plant Pathology); **Resources and Environment** (Environmental Studies; Natural Resources); **Vehicle Engineering** (Automotive Engineering); **Veterinary Medicine** (Veterinary Science)

History: Founded 1905 as Agricultural Section of Jingshi Daxuetang. Merged with Beijing Agricultural Engineering University. Acquired present title 1995.

Academic Year: September to July (September-January; February-July)

Admission Requirements: Graduation from senior middle school and national entrance examination

Fees: (Yuan): c. 1,600-1,800 per annum

Main Language(s) of Instruction: Chinese

Accrediting Agencies: Ministry of Agriculture

Degrees and Diplomas: *Bachelor's Degree*: 4-5 yrs; *Master's Degree*; *Doctor's Degree*

Student Services: Academic counselling, Canteen, Foreign student adviser, Health services, Nursery care, Sports facilities

Student Residential Facilities: Yes

Special Facilities: Museums of Agricultural Science; University Museum. Botanical Garden

Libraries: c. 1,42m. vols

Publications: Acta Phytopathologica Sinica (in Latin), The Chinese Journal of Plant Pathology *(quarterly)*; Chinese Journal of Animal Sciences *(bimonthly)*; Chinese Journal of Veterinary Medicine *(monthly)*; Journal of Agricultural Biotechnology; Journal of China Agricultural University; Journal of Plant Pathology

Press or Publishing House: Publishing House of CAU

CHINA CRIMINAL POLICE UNIVERSITY (CCPU)

83 Tawan Street, Huanguu District, Shenyang, Liaoning Province 110035
Tel: +86(24) 86982416
Fax: +86(24) 86723000
Website: http://www.ccpc.edu.cn/

President: Wang Siquan

Departments

Criminal Investigation (Criminology); **Economic Crime Investigation**; **Forensic Medicine** (Forensic Medicine and Dentistry); **Forensic Science and Technology** (Forensic Medicine and Dentistry); **Police Physical Training** (Physical Education); **Social Sciences**

History: Founded 1949 as Northeast Public Security Officer School. Acquired present title 1981.

International Co-operation: With universities in USA, Russia, Japan and Hong Kong

Degrees and Diplomas: *Bachelor's Degree*; *Master's Degree*

Student Services: Sports facilities

Special Facilities: Forensic science and technology laboratory centre; forensic medicine laboratory centre. Capillary electrophoresis centre. Language laboratory. Computer centre. Audio-visual centre

Publications: China Criminal Police; China Criminal Police Journal; China Criminal Police Review

Last Updated: 03/11/08

CHINA FOREIGN AFFAIRS UNIVERSITY

24 Zhanlan Road, Xicheng District, Beijing 100037
Tel: +86(10) 68323894
Fax: +86(10) 68348664
EMail: zhuliqu@cfau.edu.cn
Website: http://www.cfau.edu.cn

President: Wu Jianmin

Departments

Basic Education (Education); **Diplomatic Studies** (International Relations); **English and International Studies** (English; International Studies; Modern Languages); **Foreign Languages**; **International Economics** (International Economics); **International Law** (International Law)

History: Founded 1955. Became Institute of International Relations 1958 and Foreign Affairs College 1961. Acquired present title 2000.

Degrees and Diplomas: *Bachelor's Degree*; *Master's Degree*; *Doctor's Degree*

Libraries: c. 220,000 vols

Publications: Journal of Foreign Affairs College
Last Updated: 03/11/08

CHINA JILIANG UNIVERSITY

Xueyuan Street, Xiasha Higher Education Park, Hangzhou,
Zhejiang Province 310034
Tel: +86(571) 86836028
EMail: iecd@cjlu.edu.cn
Website: http://english.cjlu.edu.cn/newslist.php?type=4

President: Zhuang Songling

Colleges

Foreign Languages; **Humanities and Social Sciences**; **Information Engineering**; **Law** (Law); **Life Sciences**; **Management** (Accountancy; Business Administration; Engineering; Information Management; International Business; Management; Marketing); **Mechatronics Engineering**; **Metrological Technology & Engineering** (Measurement and Precision Engineering; Power Engineering; Safety Engineering; Thermal Engineering); **Physical Education and Military Training** (Physical Education); **Science** (Applied Mathematics; Applied Physics; Computer Science; Materials Engineering; Mathematics; Microelectronics)

History: Founded 1978 as China Institute of Metrology.

Degrees and Diplomas: *Bachelor's Degree*; *Master's Degree*
Last Updated: 03/11/08

CHINA MEDICAL UNIVERSITY

92 North Second Road, Heping District, Shenyang, Liaoning
Province 110001
Tel: +86(24) 23875539
Fax: +86(24) 23875539
EMail: mikezxh885@yahoo.com.cn
Website: http://www.cmu.edu.cn

President: Qun Zhao

Colleges

Basic Medical Sciences (Anatomy; Biochemistry; Bioengineering; Biophysics; Cell Biology; Chemistry; Embryology and Reproduction Biology; Genetics; Histology; Immunology; Mathematics; Medicine; Pathology; Pharmacology; Physical Education; Physics; Physiology); **Clinical Medicine I** (Medicine; Nursing); **Clinical Medicine II**; **Clinical Medicine III**

Faculties

Forensic Medicine (Forensic Medicine and Dentistry)

Schools

Adult Education; **Public Health** (Child Care and Development; Nutrition; Occupational Health; Public Health; Statistics; Toxicology); **Stomatology** (Orthodontics; Stomatology)

History: Founded 1931 as Health School of Chinese Workers' and Peasants' Red Army. Merged with National Shenyang Medical College and Liaoning Medical University 1948. Acquired present title 1940. Moved to Shenyang 1948.

Academic Year: September to July (September-January; February-July)

Main Language(s) of Instruction: Chinese

Degrees and Diplomas: *Bachelor's Degree*: 5 yrs; *Master's Degree*: a further 3 yrs; *Doctor's Degree (PhD)*: a further 3 yrs

Student Services: Foreign student adviser, Health services, Sports facilities

Libraries: c. 468,000 vols

Publications: Advance in Anatomy Science; Chinese Journal of Health Statistics *(bimonthly)*; Chinese Journal of Medical Image; Chinese Journal of Practical Ophthalmology; Journal of China Medical University *(bimonthly)*; Journal of Diabetes; Journal of First Aid in Paediatrics; Journal of Practical Rural Medicine; Paediatrics Fascicule Foreign Medicine *(quarterly)*; Progress in Japanese Medicine

Press or Publishing House: China Medical University Press
Last Updated: 03/11/08

CHINA PHARMACEUTICAL UNIVERSITY

24 Tongjiaxiang, Nanjing, Jiangsu Province 210009
Tel: +86(25) 3213611
Fax: +86(25) 3213611
Website: http://www.cpu.edu.cn

President: Wu Xiaoming
International Relations: Lü Qingrong

Schools

Chinese Traditional Pharmacy (Pharmacy; Traditional Eastern Medicine); **Continuing Education**; **International Pharmaceutical Business** (International Business); **Life Science and Technology** (Biochemistry; Biomedical Engineering; Biotechnology; Marine Biology; Microbiology; Molecular Biology; Pharmacology); **Pharmacy** (Pharmacy)

History: Founded 1936 as National Pharmaceutical School. Acquired present title 1986.

Degrees and Diplomas: *Bachelor's Degree*; *Master's Degree*; *Doctor's Degree*

Libraries: c. 380,000 vols

Publications: China Pharmaceutics Yearbook; Journal of China Pharmaceutical University; Pharmaceutical Education Journal on Progress in Pharmaceutical Science
Last Updated: 03/11/08

CHINA THREE GORGES UNIVERSITY (CTGU)

11 Tiyuchang Road, Yichang, Hubei Province 443000
Tel: +86(717) 6461202
Fax: +86(717) 6454495
EMail: dir@ctgu.edu.cn
Website: http://www.ctgu.edu.cn

President: Jianlin Li (2001-)

Colleges

Chemistry and Life Science; **Civil and Hydroelectric Engineering**; **Clinical Medicine** *(Second)* (Medicine); **Clinical Medicine** *(First)*; **Economics and Management**; **Electrical Engineering and Information Technology**; **Foreign Languages** (English; Literature; Modern Languages); **International Communication** (Communication Studies); **Mechanical and Material Engineering**; **Medical Science**; **Nursing Science** (Nursing); **Performing and Fine Arts** (Fine Arts; Performing Arts); **Physical Education and Sports** (Physical Education; Sports); **Political Science and Law** (Law; Political Sciences); **Science**; **Vocational Technology** (Technology)

Laboratories

Construction and Management in Hydroelectric Engineering (Construction Engineering; Electrical Engineering; Hydraulic Engineering; Management)

Research Centres

Biological Engineering (Bioengineering); **Three Gorges Culture and Economic and Social Development** (Cultural Studies; Development Studies; Economics)

History: Founded 2000 following merger of University of Hydraulic & Electric Engineering/Yichang and Hubei Sanxia University.

Admission Requirements: Secondary school certificate or equivalent

Fees: (US Dollars): registration fees, 40; tuition fees, undergraduate, 1,800-2,000 per annum; postgraduate, 1,300-1,800 per annum

International Co-operation: With universities in France, Germany, Ukraine, Netherlands, Sweden, United Kingdom, Russia, Australia, Canada, USA, Japan, Korea, Vietnam

Degrees and Diplomas: *Bachelor's Degree (BA)*; *Master's Degree (MA; MS)*

Student Services: Health services, Sports facilities

Student Residential Facilities: Yes

Libraries: c. 650,000 vols

Publications: Journal of Three Gorges University; Practical Medicine Further Study Notes
Last Updated: 03/11/08

CHINA UNIVERSITY OF GEOSCIENCES

485 Lumo Lu, Hongshan District, Wuhan, Hubei Province 430074
Tel: +86(27) 87482986
Fax: +86(27) 87481364
EMail: ljzhang@cug.edu.cn
Website: http://www.cugb.edu.cn

President: Ganguo Wu

Departments
Foreign Language (English; Modern Languages); **Land Science** (Surveying and Mapping)

Schools
Energy Resources; **Engineering and Technology** (Automation and Control Engineering; Civil Engineering; Machine Building; Safety Engineering); **Gem Studies** (Jewelry Art); **Geophysics and Geoinformation Systems**; **Geosciences and Resources** (Geochemistry; Geology); **Humanities and Economic Management** (Accountancy; Commercial Law; E-Business/Commerce; Industrial Management; Information Management; Law; Marketing; Tourism); **Information Technology**; **Marine Science** (Marine Science and Oceanography); **Materials Science and Technology**; **Water Resources and Environmental Science**

History: Founded 1952 as Wuhan College of Geology, acquired present title 1987.

Degrees and Diplomas: *Bachelor's Degree*; *Master's Degree*; *Doctor's Degree*

Libraries: c. 800,000 vols

Publications: Earth Sciences Journal; Gemstone and Gemmology; Information on Geological Science and Technology; Liberal Arts and Management; Modern Higher Education Research

Last Updated: 03/11/08

CHINA UNIVERSITY OF GEOSCIENCES (BEIJING)

29 Xueyuan Lu, Beijing 100083
Tel: +86(10) 82321080
Fax: +86(10) 82321006
Website: http://www.cugb.edu.cn

President: Wu Ganguo

International Relations: Wan Xiaoqiao

Colleges
Adult Education

Departments
Foreign Languages (English; Modern Languages); **Land Science**; **Physical Education** (Physical Education)

Faculties
Earth Sciences and Resources (Earth Sciences; Natural Resources)

Schools
Energy Resources (Energy Engineering; Petroleum and Gas Engineering); **Engineering and Technology** (Automation and Control Engineering; Civil Engineering; Engineering; Production Engineering; Safety Engineering; Technology); **Gem Studies** (Jewelry Art; Materials Engineering); **Geophysics and Geoinformation Systems** (Automation and Control Engineering; Geophysics; Technology); **Geosciences and Resources** (Geochemistry; Geology); **Humanities and Economic Management** (Accountancy; Arts and Humanities; Business Administration; Commercial Law; E-Business/Commerce; Industrial Management; Information Management; Law; Management; Marketing; Tourism); **Information Technology** (Applied Mathematics; Automation and Control Engineering; Computer Science; Electronic Engineering; Information Technology; Mathematics); **Marine Science** (Marine Science and Oceanography); **Materials Science and Engineering** (Materials Engineering); **Network**; **Software** (Software Engineering); **Water Resources and Environmental Science** (Environmental Engineering; Hydraulic Engineering; Water Science)

History: Founded 1952 as Beijing College of Geology, acquired present title 1987.

Degrees and Diplomas: *Bachelor's Degree*; *Master's Degree*; *Doctor's Degree*

Special Facilities: Laboratories. 10 electronic databases

Libraries: c. 730,000 vols; 30,000 periodical subscriptions

Publications: China Geological Education; Foreign References on Prospecting Engineering; Geological Frontiers; Geological Hazards and Prevention; Modern Geology

Last Updated: 03/11/08

CHINA UNIVERSITY OF MINING AND TECHNOLOGY

Nanhu Campus, Xuzhou, Jiangsu Province 2211116
Tel: +86(516) 8359-0256
Fax: +86(516) 8359-0255
EMail: msca@cumt.edu.cn
Website: http://www.cumt.edu.cn

President: Ge Shirong

International Relations: Zhenkang Zhang
EMail: zhangzk@cumt.edu.cn

Colleges
Adult Education (Accountancy; Business Administration; Civil Engineering; Computer Science; Design; E-Business/Commerce; English; International Business; International Economics; Law; Management; Marketing) *Dean:* Zhiren Zhou; **International Education and Student Exhange** *Dean:* Chuantong Li; **Science and Technology** (Automation and Control Engineering; Chemical Engineering; Civil Engineering; Electrical Engineering; Geological Engineering; Marketing; Mechanical Engineering; Mining Engineering; Safety Engineering; Technology; Tourism) *Dean:* Kaiyong Zhu; **Xuhai College** (Administration; Automation and Control Engineering; Banking; Chinese; Civil Engineering; Computer Science; English; Finance; Fire Science; International Business; International Economics; Literature; Management; Marketing; Materials Engineering; Measurement and Precision Engineering; Mechanical Engineering; Native Language; Power Engineering; Safety Engineering; Technology; Thermal Engineering) *Dean:* Zhongqi Fan

Schools
Architecture and Civil Engineering *Dean:* Guoqing Zhou; **Art and Design**; **Chemical Engineering and Technology** (Applied Chemistry; Bioengineering; Chemical Engineering; Mining Engineering; Technology) *Dean:* Jiongtian Liu; **Computer Science and Technology** (Computer Science; Information Sciences; Information Technology; Technology) *Dean:* Shixiong Xia; **Environmental Science and Spatial Informatics** *Dean:* Baoping Han; **Foreign Studies** (English; German) *Dean:* Shu Yang; **Information and Electrical Engineering** *Dean:* Chonglin Wang; **Literature, Law and Politics** (Administration; Chinese; Law; Literature; Native Language; Radio and Television Broadcasting; Social Work) *Dean:* Zhongjun Chi; **Management** (Accountancy; Banking; Business Administration; E-Business/Commerce; Finance; Human Resources; International Business; International Economics; Management; Marketing) *Dean:* Rui Nie; **Materials Science and Engineering** *Dean:* Yinghuai Qiang; **Mechatronic Engineering** *Dean:* Yimin Li; **Mining and Safety Engineering** (Fire Science; Industrial Engineering; Mining Engineering; Safety Engineering; Transport and Communications) *Dean:* Deming Wang; **Physical Education** (Physical Education; Sports) *Dean:* Chaojun Wang; **Resources and Geosciences** (Biomedical Engineering; Environmental Management; Geological Engineering; Geophysics; Hydraulic Engineering; Rural Planning; Town Planning; Water Science) *Dean:* Wanghua Sui; **Science** (Applied Mathematics; Applied Physics; Computer Science; Information Sciences; Mathematics; Mechanical Engineering; Optical Technology) *Dean:* Gang Tang

History: Founded 1909 as Jiaozuo Institute of Roads and Mines. Merged with Beijing Coal Administration Institute. Ministry of Coal Industry. Acquired present title 1988.

Academic Year: September to July

Admission Requirements: School certificate and entrance examination

Fees: (Yuan): c. 8,000-12,000 per annum

Main Language(s) of Instruction: Chinese, English

Accrediting Agencies: Ministry of Education

Degrees and Diplomas: *Bachelor's Degree*; *Master's Degree*; *Doctor's Degree*

Student Services: Academic counselling, Canteen, Cultural centre, Employment services, Foreign student adviser, Foreign Studies Centre, Handicapped facilities, Health services, Language programs, Nursery care, Social counselling, Sports facilities

Special Facilities: Observatory. Movie studio. Multi-media classroom. Sports facilities

Libraries: Central Library, c. 1.9m. vols

Publications: Coal Mine World *(3 per annum)*; Higher Education Research *(quarterly)*; Meitian Higher Education *(quarterly)*; Mine Pressure and Roof Management *(quarterly)*

Press or Publishing House: CUMT Publishing House
Last Updated: 15/02/07

CHINA UNIVERSITY OF PETROLEUM (CUPB)

271 Bei'er Road, Dongying, Shandong Province 257061
Tel: +86(546) 8392248
Fax: +86(546) 8392253
EMail: netnews@hdpu.edu.cn
Website: http://www.hdpu.edu.cn

President: Shan Honghong
Tel: +86(546) 8392601, Fax: +86(546) 7366374

Centres
Bitumen Technology (Chemistry) *Director:* Yuzhen Zhang; **Chemistry Engineering Technology in Oil Fields** (Chemical Engineering; Petroleum and Gas Engineering) *Director:* Fulin Zhao; **Software Engineering for Petroleum Engineering** (Petroleum and Gas Engineering; Software Engineering) *Director:* Ling Fan

Colleges
Chemistry and Chemical Engineering (Chemical Engineering; Chemistry; Environmental Engineering) *Dean:* Liu Chenguang; **Computer and Communication Engineering** (Computer Science; Mathematics and Computer Science; Telecommunications Engineering; Transport and Communications) *Dean:* Duan Youxiang; **Economics and Management** (Administration; Economics; Management) *Dean:* Zaixu Zhang; **Electrical and Mechanical Engineering** (Electrical and Electronic Engineering; Mechanical Engineering) *Dean:* Mingxia Qi; **Information and Control Engineering** (Automation and Control Engineering; Information Management) *Dean:* Xuemin Tian; **Net-based Education** *Dean:* Gaodai Qi; **Petroleum Engineering** (Petroleum and Gas Engineering) *Dean:* Yao Jun; **Petroleum Resources and Information Sciences** (Geology; Geophysics) *Dean:* Ming Zha; **Storage and Transportation and Construction Engineering** (Architecture and Planning; Construction Engineering; Service Trades; Transport Engineering) *Dean:* Guozhong Zhang

Laboratories
Chemistry Teaching Base for Engineering Courses *(National)* (Chemistry; Teacher Training); **Drilling Engineering** (Production Engineering) *Director:* Ruihe Wang; **Heavy Oil Processing** (Chemistry) *Director:* Guohe Que; **Oil and Oil Well Engineering** (Petroleum and Gas Engineering; Production Engineering) *Director:* Zhichuan Guan; **Oil Reservoir Geology** (Geology) *Director:* Chengyan Lin; **Oil Storage and Transport** (Store Management; Transport Management) *Director:* Shuwen Zhang; **Petroleum Geophysical Exploration** (Geophysics; Petroleum and Gas Engineering) *Director:* Xingyao Yin; **Petroleum Machinery Engineering** (Mechanical Engineering) *Director:* Mingxia Qi; **Petroleum Welllogging** (Geology; Petroleum and Gas Engineering) *Director:* Wenxiao Qiao

Programmes
Accountancy (Accountancy)

Research Centres
Environmental Engineering (Environmental Engineering) *Director:* Chaocheng Zhao; **Non-asbestos Abrasive Materials** (Materials Engineering) *Director:* Yusheng Zhai; **Oil and Gas Catalysis** (Chemistry; Petroleum and Gas Engineering) *Director:* Chenguang Liu; **Oil and Gas Processing Technology** (Petroleum and Gas Engineering) *Director:* Chaohe Yang

Schools
Adult Education *Dean:* Gaodai Qi; **Advanced Vocational** (Vocational Education) *Dean:* Huadong Liu; **Graduate** *Dean:* Zhaomin Li

Units
Chemical Engineering and Technology *(postdoctoral)* (Chemical Engineering; Technology); **Geological Resources and Geological Engineering** *(Postdoctoral)* (Geological Engineering; Geology); **Petroleum and Gas Engineering** *(Postdoctoral)* (Petroleum and Gas Engineering)

Further Information: Also courses for foreign students

History: Founded 1953 as Beijing Petroleum Institute, became East China Petroleum Institute 1969. Acquired present status and title 2005.

Academic Year: September to July (September-January; February-July)

Admission Requirements: Graduation from senior middle school and entrance examination

Fees: (Yuan): 3,800-7,000 per annum according to major

Main Language(s) of Instruction: Chinese

Accrediting Agencies: Ministry of Education

Degrees and Diplomas: *Bachelor's Degree:* Engineering; Science; Literature; Law; Management; Economics, 4 yrs; *Master's Degree:* Engineering; Science; Literature; Law; Management, a further 3 yrs; *Doctor's Degree:* Engineering; Science, 3 yrs

Student Services: Academic counselling, Canteen, Cultural centre, Employment services, Foreign student adviser, Foreign Studies Centre, Handicapped facilities, Health services, Language programs, Nursery care, Social counselling, Sports facilities

Student Residential Facilities: For c. 15,000 students

Special Facilities: Museum for University Development. Movie Studio. Biological Garden

Libraries: Central Library, c. 1.3m. vols

Publications: Higher Education *(quarterly)*; Journal of the University of Petroleum (Natural Sciences and Social Sciences Editions) *(quarterly)*

Press or Publishing House: University of Petroleum Publishing House
Last Updated: 04/11/08

CHINA UNIVERSITY OF PETROLEUM - BEIJING

18 Fuxue Road, Changping, Beijing 102249
Tel: +86(10) 8973 3266
Fax: +86(10) 6970 0644
EMail: overseas@cup.edu.cn
Website: http://www.cup.edu.cn

President: Laibin Zhang (2005-)
Tel: +86(10) 8973 3334 EMail: zhanglb@cup.edu.cn

Director, International Relations: Xudong Sun
Tel: +86(10) 8973 3477 EMail: sxudong@cup.edu.cn

International Relations: Xiaoqing Liu, International Affairs Officer
Tel: +86(10) 8973 1677

Departments
Computer Science (Computer Engineering) *Head:* Hongqi Li; **Foreign Languages** (Linguistics; Modern Languages) *Head:* Wenbin Pei; **Humanities** (Classical Languages; Literature; Philosophy) *Head:* Xinhua Hu; **Mathematics and Physics** (Mathematics; Physics) *Head:* Jingwei Liang; **Physical Education** *Head:* Xialong Zhang

Faculties
Chemical Engineering (Chemical Engineering; Energy Engineering; Environmental Engineering) *Dean:* Chunxi Lu; **Geosciences** *Dean:* Xiaomin Zhu; **Mechanical and Electronic Engineering** (Automation and Control Engineering; Electronic Engineering; Materials Engineering; Mechanical Engineering; Safety Engineering) *Dean:* Deguo Wang; **Petroleum Engineering** (Civil Engineering; Petroleum and Gas Engineering) *Dean:* Mian Chen

Schools
Business Administration (Accountancy; Business Administration; Finance; International Business; Management; Marketing) *Dean:* Zhen Wang

History: Founded 1953 as Beijing Petroleum Institute, acquired present title and status 2005.

Academic Year: September to July

Fees: (Yuan): 20,000, Bachelor; 24,000, Master; 32,000, PhD.

Main Language(s) of Instruction: Chinese

International Co-operation: With universities in United States; United Kingdom; Australia; Canada

Accrediting Agencies: Ministry of Education

Degrees and Diplomas: *Bachelor's Degree*: 4 yrs; *Master's Degree*: 2-3 yrs; *Doctor's Degree*: 3-4 yrs

Student Services: Academic counselling, Canteen, Employment services, Foreign student adviser, Foreign Studies Centre, Handicapped facilities, Health services, Language programs, Nursery care, Social counselling, Sports facilities

Publications: Palaeogeology *(quarterly)*; Petroleum Science *(quarterly)*

Academic Staff *2007-2008*	MEN	WOMEN	TOTAL
FULL-TIME	400	300	700
STAFF WITH DOCTORATE			
FULL-TIME	–	–	420

Student Numbers *2007-2008*			
All (Foreign Included)	–	–	11,000
FOREIGN ONLY	–	–	420

Last Updated: 26/11/08

CHINA UNIVERSITY OF POLITICAL SCIENCE AND LAW

25 Xitucheng Road, Haidian District, Beijing 100088
Tel: +86(10) 62229863
Fax: +86(10) 62228804
EMail: oice@cupl.edu.cn
Website: http://www.cupl.edu.cn

President: Xu Xianming

Institutes
Comparative Law (Comparative Law); **Globalization and Global Issues**

Schools
American and Comparative Law (Comparative Law; Law); **Business** (Business Administration); **Civil, Commercial and Economic Laws**; **Continuing Education**; **Criminal and Judicatory Law** (Criminal Law; Criminology); **Foreign Languages** (English; French; German; Italian; Japanese; Modern Languages; Russian); **German and Comparative Law** (Comparative Law; Law); **Graduate**; **Humanities** (Chinese; Journalism; Literature; Philosophy); **Law** (Law); **Political Science and Public Administration** (Political Sciences; Public Administration); **Sociology** (Sociology)

History: Founded 1952 as Beijing Political Science and Law College. Acquired present title 1983.

Main Language(s) of Instruction: Chinese

Degrees and Diplomas: *Bachelor's Degree*; *Master's Degree*; *Doctor's Degree*

Libraries: c. 1m. vols

Publications: Administrative Law Research; Comparative Law Research; Journal of Central Leadership Institute of Politics and Law; Tribune of Political Science and Law
Last Updated: 04/11/08

CHINA WEST NORMAL UNIVERSITY

1 ShiDa Road, Nanchong, Sichuan Province 637002
Tel: +86(817) 2568017
Fax: +86(817) 2314331
EMail: oice@cwnu.edu.cn
Website: http://www.cwnu.edu.cn

President: Chen Ning **EMail:** cning60@hotmail.com

Colleges
Chemistry and Chemical Engineering (Chemical Engineering; Chemistry); **Chinese Language and Literature** (Chinese; Literature); **Land and Resources** (Environmental Studies; Geography; Rural Planning; Town Planning); **Life Sciences** (Biological and Life Sciences; Biology); **Mathematics and Information** (Applied Mathematics; Information Management; Mathematics); **Physical Education** (Physical Education)

Departments
Fine Arts (Fine Arts); **Music** (Music)

Schools
Business (Business Administration); **Computer Science** (Computer Science); **Educational Science and Technology** (Education; Educational Technology; Pedagogy; Preschool Education; Primary Education); **Foreign Languages** (Modern Languages); **History and Culture** (Cultural Studies; History); **Journalism and Communication** (Communication Studies; Journalism); **Law** (Law); **Management** (Management); **Marxism** (Political Sciences); **Physics and Electrical Information** (Electrical Engineering; Physics); **Politics and Administration** (Administration; Political Sciences)

History: Founded 1946 as Northern Sichuan Agriculture and Industry College, acquired present title 2003.

Degrees and Diplomas: *Bachelor's Degree*; *Master's Degree*
Last Updated: 04/11/08

CHINA YOUTH UNIVERSITY FOR POLITICAL SCIENCES

25 Xisanhuan North Road, Beijing 100089
Tel: +86(10) 68475409
Fax: +86(10) 68475649
EMail: cycp5@263.net
Website: http://cms.cyu.edu.cn

President: Zhou Qiang

International Relations: Zhang Qinghong

Departments
Economic Management (Management); **Journalism** (Journalism); **Law** (Law); **Social Work** (Social Work); **Youth Work**

History: Founded 1985 as Central School of China Youth League. Formerly known as China Youth College for Political Sciences.

Degrees and Diplomas: *Bachelor's Degree*; *Master's Degree*
Last Updated: 02/09/08

CHINESE PEOPLE'S PUBLIC SECURITY UNIVERSITY

Muxudi, Xicheng District, Beijing 100038
Tel: +86(10) 63404433-2126
Fax: +86(10) 63260301

President: Sun Zhongguo

International Relations: Song Qiang

Programmes
Modern Languages (Modern Languages); **Welfare and Protective Services** (Civil Security; Criminology; Police Studies)

History: Founded 1948 as North China Public Security Cadre School. Merged with Chinese People's Police Officers' University and Chinese People's Public Security University. Acquired present title 1984.

Degrees and Diplomas: *Bachelor's Degree*; *Master's Degree*

Libraries: c. 580,000 vols

Publications: Modern World Choice; Public Security Education; Public Security University Journal

CHONGQING INSTITUTE OF TECHNOLOGY

4 Xingsheng Road, Yangjiaping, Jiulongpo District, Chongqing, Sichuan Province 400050
Tel: +86(23) 68777496
Fax: +86(23) 68820848
EMail: wb@cqit.edu.cn
Website: http://www.cqit.com.cn

President: Liu Quanli

Colleges
Business and Information (Business Administration)

Institutes
Automobile *(Chongqing)* (Automotive Engineering)

Schools
Accountancy (Accountancy); **Adult Education** (Adult Education); **Biological Engineering** (Bioengineering); **Business Administration** (Business Administration); **Computer Science and Engineering** (Computer Engineering; Computer Science); **Economics and Trade** (Business Administration; Economics); **Electronic Information and Automation**; **Foreign Languages** (Modern Languages); **Humanities and Social Sciences**; **Material Science and Engineering**; **Mathematics and Science** (Mathematics; Natural Sciences)

History: Founded 1950 as Chongqing Technological University. Acquired present title 1999.

Degrees and Diplomas: *Bachelor's Degree*; *Master's Degree*
Last Updated: 04/11/08

CHONGQING JIAOTONG UNIVERSITY

No. 66 Xuefudadao, Nanan district, Chongqing, Sichuan Province
400074
Tel: +86(23) 62651999
Fax: +86(23) 62650387
EMail: waiban@cquc.edu.cn
Website: http://www.cquc.edu.cn

President: Boming Tang

Departments
Automotive Engineering (Automotive Engineering); **Bridge Engineering** (Bridge Engineering); **Computer and Information Engineering** (Computer Engineering; Information Technology); **Finance and Economics** (Economics; Finance); **Foreign Languages** (Modern Languages); **Highway Engineering** (Civil Engineering; Road Engineering); **Management** (Management); **River and Ocean Engineering** (Marine Engineering; Water Management)

Schools
Adult Education

History: Founded 1951 as Southwest Jiaotong College, acquired present title 1978.

Degrees and Diplomas: *Bachelor's Degree*; *Master's Degree*; *Doctor's Degree*

Libraries: c. 280,000 vols

Publications: Applied Mathematics & Mechanics; Journal
Last Updated: 04/11/08

CHONGQING NORMAL UNIVERSITY

12 Tianchen Road, Shapingba, Chongqing, Sichuan Province
400047
Tel: +86(23) 65362739
Fax: +86(23) 65316566
EMail: interoff@cqnu.edu.cn
Website: http://www.cqnu.edu.cn

President: Qin Zhiren

International Relations: Hu Lang

Departments
Art and Design (Design; Fine Arts); **Biology** (Biology); **Chemistry** (Chemistry); **Chinese Language and Literature** (Chinese); **Economics, Politics and Law** (Economics; Law; Political Sciences); **Foreign Languages** (English); **Geography** (Geography); **History** (History); **Management of Modern Information** (Information Management); **Mathematics and Computer** (Computer Science; Mathematics); **Photographic Engineering**; **Physics and Information Technology** (Information Technology; Physics); **Tourism**

History: Founded 1953 as Chongqing Teachers College. Acquired present status and title 1978.

Degrees and Diplomas: *Bachelor's Degree*; *Master's Degree*

CHONGQING TECHNOLOGY AND BUSINESS UNIVERSITY

Wugongli, Nan'an District, Chongqing, Sichuan Province 400067
Tel: +86(23) 62804306
Fax: +86(23) 62803515
EMail: wshch@ctbu.edu.cn

President: Wang Chongju

International Relations: Chen Quanfu

Departments
Accountancy (Accountancy); **Administration** (Administration); **Commercial Planning** (Business and Commerce); **Computer Engineering**; **Economics** (Economics); **Finance and Investment** (Finance); **Graphic Arts** (Graphic Arts); **Law** (Law); **Tourism Administration** (Tourism)

Further Information: Also campus in Jiangbei

History: Founded 1962 as Chongqing Finance and Commerce School. Acquired present title following merge of two former colleges, Yuzhou University and Chongqing Institute of Commerce.

Degrees and Diplomas: *Bachelor's Degree*; *Master's Degree*
Last Updated: 01/09/08

CHONGQING THREE GORGES UNIVERSITY

780 Shalong Road, Wanzhou, Chongqing, Sichuan Province
404000
Tel: +86(23) 58102298
Fax: +86(23) 58124510
EMail: pxd1998@163.com
Website: http://www.sanxiau.net/english/index.htm

President: Wu Tieqing

International Relations: Ding Jiadi

Departments
Architectural Engineering (Structural Architecture); **Biochemistry** (Biochemistry); **Business Administration** (Business Administration); **Chinese** (Chinese); **Computer Science** (Computer Science); **Economics** (Economics); **Electrical Engineering** (Electrical Engineering); **English** (English); **Fine Arts** (Fine Arts); **Social Sciences** (Social Sciences); **Sports** (Sports)

History: Founded 1994.

Main Language(s) of Instruction: Chinese

Degrees and Diplomas: *Bachelor's Degree*
Last Updated: 04/11/08

CHONGQING UNIVERSITY (CQU)

174 Shazhengjie, Shapingba, Chongqing, Sichuan Province 400044
Tel: +86(23) 65102391
Fax: +86(23) 65106656
EMail: fao101@cqu.edu.cn
Website: http://www.cqu.edu.cn

President: Li Xiaohong
Tel: +86(23) 65102349, Fax: +86(23) 65104905

Academies
Film *(Meishi)* (Film)

Colleges
Architecture and Construction (Architecture; Construction Engineering; Design); **Automation** (Automation and Control Engineering); **Business Administration and Economics** (Accountancy; Business Administration; Economics; Finance; Information Management; Management; Marketing); **Chemistry and Chemical Engineering** (Chemical Engineering; Chemistry); **Computer Science** (Computer Science; Engineering); **Electrical Engineering** (Electrical Engineering) *Dean*: Lichun Shu; **Foreign Languages** (Linguistics; Literature; Modern Languages; Translation and Interpretation) *Dean*: Weishen Yu; **Material Science and Engineering** (Materials Engineering; Metallurgical Engineering) *Dean*: Jiachen Zhang; **Mathematics and Physics** (Mathematics; Physics) *Dean*: Hu Yang; **Mechanical Engineering** (Mechanical Engineering) *Dean*: Datong Qin; **Optical and Electronic Engineering** (Electronic Engineering; Optical Technology) *Dean*: Yingjun Pan; **Resources and Environmental Engineering** (Environmental Engineering; Natural Resources) *Dean*: Guangzhi Yin; **Telecommunications Engineering** (Telecommunications Engineering) *Dean*: Xiaoping Zeng; **Thermal Power Engineering** (Thermal Engineering) *Dean*: Zhuwei He; **Trade and Law** (Commercial Law; Economics) *Dean*: Guoping Zeng

History: Founded 1929. Merged with Chongqing Jianzhu University and Chongqing Architectural College 2000.

Academic Year: September to July

Admission Requirements: Matriculation Examination Score above 550 on average

Fees: (Yuan): 4,500-15,000

Main Language(s) of Instruction: Chinese, English

International Co-operation: With universities in United Kingdom, USA, Canada, Japan, Korea, Thailand

Degrees and Diplomas: *Bachelor's Degree*; *Master's Degree*; *Doctor's Degree*

Student Services: Academic counselling, Canteen, Cultural centre, Employment services, Foreign student adviser, Foreign Studies Centre, Handicapped facilities, Health services, Language programs, Nursery care, Social counselling, Sports facilities

Special Facilities: Museum.

Publications: Chongqing University Journal, Natural Sciences Edition *(bimonthly)*; Chongqing University Journal, Social Sciences Edition *(bimonthly)*

Press or Publishing House: Chongqing University Publishing House

CHONGQING UNIVERSITY OF MEDICAL SCIENCES

1 Yixue Yuan Road, Chongqing, Sichuan Province 400016
Tel: +86(23) 68809229
Fax: +86(23) 68809229
EMail: cqumsfao@mail.cqums.edu.cn

President: Jin Xianqing

International Relations: Tang Haiqig

Departments
Preventive Medicine (Social and Preventive Medicine)

Faculties
Family Planning (Family Studies); **Laboratory Medicine** (Laboratory Techniques; Medicine)

Schools
Adult Education; **Basic Medical Sciences** (Medicine); **Clinical Medicine** (Medicine); **Clinical Medicine II** (Medicine); **Paediatrics** (Paediatrics); **Social Sciences** (Social Sciences)

History: Founded 1956 as Chongqing Medical College, acquired present title 1956.

Degrees and Diplomas: *Bachelor's Degree*; *Master's Degree*; *Doctor's Degree*

Libraries: c. 360,000 vols

Publications: ACTA University Sciences Medicine Chongqing; Journal of Hepatology; Journal of Ultrasonic Medicine
Last Updated: 05/11/08

CHONGQING UNIVERSITY OF POSTS AND TELECOMMUNICATIONS

Huang Jieya, Nan'an District, Chongqing, Sichuan Province 400065
Tel: +86(23) 62461002
Fax: +86(23) 62461882
EMail: gjc@cqupt.edu.cn
Website: http://www.cqupt.edu.cn/

President: Chen Liuting

Departments
Computer Science and Technology (Computer Science); **Information and Computational Science** (Computer Science; Information Sciences); **Management Engineering** (Engineering Management); **Modern Languages** (Modern Languages); **Postal Engineering** (Postal Services; Telecommunications Engineering; Telecommunications Services); **Radio Communications Engineering** (Telecommunications Engineering); **Social Sciences** (Social Sciences); **Telecommunication Engineering** (Telecommunications Engineering)

History: Founded 1959 as Posts and Telecommunications School. Acquired present status 1980.

Degrees and Diplomas: *Bachelor's Degree*; *Master's Degree*
Last Updated: 05/11/08

CIVIL AVIATION FLIGHT UNIVERSITY OF CHINA

Guanghan, Sichuan Province 618307
Tel: +86(838) 5182117
Fax: +86(838) 5191777
EMail: wsb@cafuc.edu.cn
Website: http://www.cafuc.edu.cn/structure/NewWeb/index

President: Zheng Xiaoyong

International Relations: Gong Jianyu

Centres
Aero-Engine Maintenance Training; **Flight Simulator Training**

Departments
Aircraft Oparation; **Airline Transport Communication Services** (Air Transport); **Aviation Engineering**; **English** (English); **Social Sciences**

History: Founded 1956 as CCAC Aviation School. Acquired present title 1987.

Degrees and Diplomas: *Bachelor's Degree*; *Master's Degree*
Last Updated: 18/09/08

CIVIL AVIATION UNIVERSITY OF CHINA

100 Xunhai Road, Dongli District, Tianjin, Tianjin Province 300300
Tel: +86(22) 24960647
Fax: +86(22) 24960647
EMail: cauciad@cauc.edu.cn
Website: http://www.cauc.edu.cn

President: Wu Tongshui

Colleges
Aeronautical Mechanics and Avionics Engineering; **Air Traffic Management** (Air Transport); **Computer Science and Technology** (Computer Science); **Flight**; **Humanities and Social Sciences** (English; Law; Modern Languages; Social Sciences); **Management** (Accountancy; Business Administration; Finance; Industrial Engineering; Management); **Safety Science and Engineering**; **Science** (Chemistry; Computer Science; Physics); **Transport Engineering** (Transport Engineering)

Departments
Physical Education (Physical Education)

History: Founded 1951 as CAAC Training School. Acquired present status and title 1981.

Degrees and Diplomas: *Bachelor's Degree*; *Master's Degree*
Last Updated: 05/11/08

COMMUNICATION UNIVERSITY OF CHINA (CUC)

1 East Street, Dingfuzhuang, Chaoyang District, Beijing 100024
Tel: +86(10) 65779773
Fax: +86(10) 65779138
EMail: jishuqing@cuc.edu.cn
Website: http://www.cuc.edu.cn

President: Jinan Liu

Colleges
Advertising (Advertising and Publicity)

Schools
Animation; **Computer and Software** (Computer Science; Software Engineering); **Information Engineering** (Engineering; Information Sciences); **Literature** (Literature); **Media Management** (Management; Media Studies); **Presentation Art**; **Science** (Natural Sciences); **Social Sciences** (Social Sciences); **Television and Journalism** (Journalism; Radio and Television Broadcasting)

History: Founded 1954. Formerly Beijing Broadcasting University. Acquired present title 2004 following merger with China University of Mining and Technology (Beijing).

Academic Year: March to January (March-July; September-January)

Fees: (US Dollars): 1,900-3,600 per annum

Main Language(s) of Instruction: Chinese

International Co-operation: With universities in USA; Canada; Germany; France; UK; Russian Federation; Japan; South Korea; Singapore; Australia

Degrees and Diplomas: *Bachelor's Degree*: 4 yrs; *Master's Degree*: 2-3 yrs; *Doctor's Degree*: 3 yrs

Student Services: Academic counselling, Canteen, Cultural centre, Employment services, Foreign student adviser, Foreign Studies Centre, Health services, Language programs, Nursery care, Social counselling, Sports facilities

Student Residential Facilities: Yes

Special Facilities: Observatory

Libraries: c. 1m. vols

Publications: Modern Communications *(bimonthly)*

Press or Publishing House: BBU Press

Last Updated: 05/11/08

DALIAN FISHERIES UNIVERSITY

52 Heshijao Street, Dalian, Liaoning Province 116023
Tel: +86(411) 4660163
Fax: +86(411) 4660163
Website: http://www.dlfu.edu.cn

President: Li Hongming

International Relations: Wang Erguang

Departments

Aquaculture (Aquaculture); **Civil Engineering** (Civil Engineering); **Electronic Engineering** (Electronic Engineering); **Management** (Management); **Marine Fisheries** (Fishery); **Mechanical Engineering** (Mechanical Engineering)

History: Founded 1952 as Northeast Fisheries Technical School. Acquired present title 1978.

Degrees and Diplomas: *Bachelor's Degree*; *Master's Degree*

DALIAN JIAOTONG UNIVERSITY

794 Huanghe Road, Dalian, Liaoning Province 116028
Tel: +86(411) 4604323 Ext. 2799
Fax: +86(411) 4629614
EMail: xinxi@djtu.edu.cn
Website: http://www.djtu.edu.cn

President: Ge Jiping

Institutes

International (International Studies); **Software** (Software Engineering)

Schools

Art; **Electronics and Information Engineering** (Electrical Engineering; Electronic Engineering; Information Sciences; Technology); **Environmental and Chemical Engineering**; **Foreign Languages**; **Management** (Management); **Materials Science and Engineering** (Engineering; Materials Engineering); **Mechanical Engineering** (Mechanical Engineering); **Science** (Mathematics and Computer Science; Natural Sciences); **Traffic and Transport** (Architecture; Civil Engineering; Road Engineering; Road Transport; Transport Engineering; Transport Management)

History: Founded 1956 as Dalian Engine Vehicle Production School. Acquired present title 2004.

Degrees and Diplomas: *Bachelor's Degree*; *Master's Degree*; *Doctor's Degree*

Libraries: c. 390,000 vols

Last Updated: 06/11/08

DALIAN MARITIME UNIVERSITY (DMU)

1 Linghai Road, Dalian, Liaoning Province 116026
Tel: +86(411) 84729259
Fax: +86(411) 84727395
EMail: fsodmu@hotmail.com
Website: http://www.dlmu.edu.cn

President: Wang Zuwen (2004-)
Tel: +86(411) 84723311 EMail: wangaw@dlmu.edu.cn

Registrar: Youtao Zhao Tel: +86(411) 84729341

International Relations: Bin Xu, Director, International Cooperation and Communication

Colleges

Automation and Electrical Engineering *Dean*: Xingcheng Wang; **Computer Science and Technology** (Computer Engineering; Computer Science; Software Engineering) *Dean*: Weishi Zhang; **Continuing Education** *Dean*: Yong Ding; **Economics and Management** *Dean*: Yunlong Ding; **Electromechanics and Materials Engineering** (Automation and Control Engineering; Machine Building; Marine Engineering; Materials Engineering) *Dean*: Huichen Zhang; **Environmental Science and Engineering** (Environmental Engineering; Environmental Studies; Nautical Science) *Dean*: Yu Liu; **Foreign Languages** (English; Japanese) *Dean*: Shenglu Li; **Humanities and Social Sciences** *Dean*: Wenhua Feng; **Information Engineering** (Electronic Engineering; Information Sciences; Information Technology; Telecommunications Engineering) *Dean*: Shufang Zhang; **Law** (International Economics; International Law; Labour Law; Law) *Dean*: Guangqing Qu; **Marine Engineering** *Director*: Xinxiang Pan; **Mathematics** (Computer Science; Information Sciences; Mathematics) *Dean*: Yunjie Zhang; **Navigation** (Nautical Science) *Director*: Zhengjiang Liu; **Physics** *Dean*: Haiyang Zhong; **Postgraduate Studies** *Dean*: Hongliang Yu; **Specialised Degree Education** *Dean*: Weiliu; **Transportation and Logistics** *Director*: Nuo Wang

Research Centres

Automation Engineering *Director*: Zi Ma; **Global Navigation Satellite** *Director*: Shufang Zhang; **Globalisation and Foreign Language Teaching** *Director*: Weihua Luo; **IMO Conventions** *Director*: Zhengjiang Liu; **Logistics System Engineering** *Director*: Zhihong Jin

Research Institutes

Antenna *Director*: Shaojun Fang; **Automation and Control Engineering** *Director*: Yongsheng Zhao; **Circuit and System** *Director*: Yisheng Zhu; **Communication Electronics** *Director*: Xiaoming Liu; **Electronic Infomation Technology Education and Application** *Director*: Shuanghe Yu; **Environmental Biology** *Director*: Yeqing Sun; **Environmental Engineering** *Director*: Mindong Bai; **Image Information Processing** *Director*: Dequn Liang; **Information System Engineering** *Director*: Yiwu Xie; **International Shipping Human Resource** *Director*: Zan Yang; **International Trade and Multinational Investment** *Director*: Shuangxi Chen; **Maritime Mobile Communications** *Director*: Fuwen Pang; **Mobile Communications** *Director*: Dianwu Yue; **Nautical Science and Technology** *Director*: Yichen Jin; **Ocean Exploration and Management** *Director*: Weixin Luan; **Optoelectronics Information Engineering** *Director*: Wenhai Xu; **Optoelectronics Technology** *Director*: Wanghe Cao; **Port and Shipping** *Director*: Guangqi Sun; **Road and Bridge Engineering** *Director*: Yinghua Zhao; **Tourism Planning** *Director*: Yuquang Tong; **Transportation Economics** *Director*: Jing Lv; **Transportation Planning** *Director*: Zhongzhen Yang; **Waterway Transportation Acts** *Director*: Lujun Zhao

History: Founded 1953, incorporating Shanghai Nautical College, Northeast Navigation College, and Fujian Navigation School. Became a key maritime university 1960.

Academic Year: March to January (March-July; September-January)

Admission Requirements: Graduation from senior middle school and national college entrance examination

Fees: (US Dollars): 2,500 per annum

Main Language(s) of Instruction: Chinese, English

International Co-operation: With universities in Australia, Japan, Korea, United Kingdom, USA, Sweden, Russian Federation, Belgium, Netherlands, Singapore, Vietnam, Egypt, Hong Kong and Taiwan

Accrediting Agencies: Norwegian Classification Society; China Maritime Safety Administration; Ministry of Communication

Degrees and Diplomas: *Bachelor's Degree*: Science; Technology; Management; Economics; Law, 4 yrs; *Master's Degree*: Technology; Management; Economics; Law (MSc), a further 2 yrs; *Doctor's Degree*: Technology; Law (PhD), 3 yrs. Also Professional Diplomas

Student Services: Academic counselling, Canteen, Cultural centre, Employment services, Foreign student adviser, Foreign Studies

Centre, Handicapped facilities, Health services, Language programs, Nursery care, Social counselling, Sports facilities

Student Residential Facilities: Yes

Special Facilities: Movie Studio. Planetarium. Survival Training Centre

Libraries: DMU Library, c. 1,473,700 vols

Publications: Higher Maritime Education *(quarterly)*; Journal of Dalian Maritime University *(quarterly)*; Nautical Laws of China *(annually)*; World Shipping Journal *(bimonthly)*

Press or Publishing House: Dalian Maritime University Press
Last Updated: 06/11/08

DALIAN MEDICAL UNIVERSITY

465 Zhongshan Road, Shahekou District, Dalian, Liaoning Province 116027
Tel: +86(411) 4672546
Fax: +86(411) 4672546
EMail: admin@dlmedu.edu.cn
Website: http://www.dlmedu.edu.cn

President: Jiang Chao

Colleges
Basic Medical Sciences (Anatomy; Biochemistry; Embryology and Reproduction Biology; Histology; Hygiene; Medicine; Microbiology; Molecular Biology; Parasitology; Pathology; Pharmacology; Physiology); **Cosmetology** (Cosmetology; Plastic Surgery); **Health Administration** (Health Administration); **Stomatology** (Stomatology)

Departments
Clinical Pharmacy (Pharmacy); **Medical Laboratory Tests and Analysis** (Laboratory Techniques; Medical Technology); **Obstetrics and Gynaecology** (Gynaecology and Obstetrics); **Oral Medicine** (Medicine); **Photography** (Photography)

Schools
Adult Education

Further Information: Also 3 Affiliated Teaching Hospitals.

History: Founded 1947 as Guandong Medical college. Became Dalian University Medical College 1949, Dalian Medical College 1950, Zunyi Medical College 1969, and Dalian Medical College 1978. Acquired present title 1994.

Degrees and Diplomas: *Bachelor's Degree*; *Master's Degree*; *Doctor's Degree*

Libraries: c. 200,000 vols

Publications: Journal of Dalian Medical University
Last Updated: 06/11/08

DALIAN NATIONALITIES UNIVERSITY

18 Liaohe Wet Road, Dalian Economic and Technical Development Zone, Dalian, Liaoning Province 116600
Tel: +86(411) 7612616
Fax: +86(411) 7618179
EMail: office@dlnu.edu.cn
Website: http://www.dlnu.edu.cn

Departments
General Studies; **Social Sciences** (Social Sciences)

Faculties
Architecture (Architecture); **Chemical Engineering** (Chemical Engineering); **Electronic and Computer Engineering** (Computer Engineering; Electronic Engineering); **Electronics and Accountancy** (Accountancy; Electronic Engineering); **Industrial Design** (Industrial Design); **International Economics** (International Economics); **Management** (Management); **Mechanical Engineering and Computer Science** (Computer Science; Mechanical Engineering); **Modern Languages** (Modern Languages)

DALIAN POLYTECHNIC UNIVERSITY

1 Qinggongyuan, Dalian, Liaoning Province 116034
Tel: +86(411) 86324486
Fax: +86(411) 86323647
Website: http://www.dlili.edu.cn/

President: Xiao Zhengyang
International Relations: Chen Yang

Departments
Automation (Automation and Control Engineering); **Chemical Engineering** (Chemical Engineering); **Economics**; **Food Engineering and Bioengineering** (Bioengineering; Food Technology); **Materials Science and Engineering** (Materials Engineering); **Mechanical Engineering** (Mechanical Engineering); **Modern Languages**

Schools
Artistic Design (Design); **Textile and Fashion** (Fashion Design; Textile Design)

History: Founded 1958 as Shenyang Institute of Light Industry. Became Dalian Institute of Light Industry 1970. Acquired present title 2007.

Degrees and Diplomas: *Bachelor's Degree*; *Master's Degree*
Last Updated: 06/11/08

DALIAN UNIVERSITY

Dalian Economic and Technology Development Zone, Dalian, Liaoning Province 116622
Tel: +86(411) 87300952
Fax: +86(411) 87403963
EMail: office@dalianu.com
Website: http://202.199.158.1/old/eng/index.htm

President: Xiaopeng Wei

International Relations: Hongtao Wang
Tel: +86(411) 87402135, Fax: +86(411) 87300966

Centres
Advanced Designing Technology (Computer Graphics) *Director*: Xiaopeng Wei; **Gender Studies** (Gender Studies) *Director*: Xiaojiang Li

Colleges
Adult Education (Teacher Training) *Dean*: Shuangqing Wang; **Bioengineering** (Bioengineering; Biological and Life Sciences) *Dean*: Yongqi Wang; **Economics and Administration** (Accountancy; Business Administration; Economics; Management; Marketing) *Dean*: Yanqing Guo; **English Language** *Dean*: Shunde Men; **Fine Arts** (Fine Arts) *Dean*: Peijie Huang; **Humanities** (Arts and Humanities; History; Law; Linguistics; Literature; Philosophy; Psychology; Social Sciences) *Dean*: Shiling Xu; **Information Technology** (Computer Science; Electrical and Electronic Engineering; Information Technology; Library Science; Mathematics) *Dean*: Bingnan Pei; **International Cultural Exchange** (Cultural Studies) *Dean*: Liang Wang; **International studies** *Dean*: Baowen Hou; **Japanese Language and Culture** (Japanese; Linguistics; Teacher Training) *Dean*: Xieyi Song; **Medicine** (Dentistry; Medicine; Nursing; Pharmacy) *Dean*: Yajie Li; **Music** *Dean*: Weitong Zheng; **Physical Education** (Physical Education) *Dean*: Xizhen Chen; **Teacher Training** (Teacher Training) *Dean*: Liping Chen; **Tourism** (Tourism) *Dean*: Xin Li; **Women** (Women's Studies) *Dean*: Yibin Shan

Departments
Chemical Engineering (Chemical Engineering) *Director*: Jirun Xu; **Civil Engineering** (Architecture; Civil Engineering; Industrial Engineering) *Director*: Liedong Wang; **Mechanical Engineering** (Mechanical Engineering) *Director*: Hao Guan; **Physics** (Physics) *Director*: Xuchui Li

History: Founded 1987. Merged with College of Teachers, College of Engineering and Medical College in 1995.

Academic Year: September to February; March to August

Admission Requirements: National Entrance Examination

Fees: (Yuan) 4,000-16,000 per annum

Main Language(s) of Instruction: Chinese

International Co-operation: With universities in Japan; USA; UK; Ireland; Australia; New Zealand; Canada, France; Russia; Macao; Hong Kong

Accrediting Agencies: Ministry of Education

Degrees and Diplomas: *Bachelor's Degree*: 4 yrs; *Master's Degree*: 3 yrs. Also 3 yr University Diploma

Student Services: Academic counselling, Canteen, Cultural centre, Employment services, Foreign student adviser, Foreign Studies Centre, Handicapped facilities, Health services, Language programs, Nursery care, Social counselling, Sports facilities

Student Residential Facilities: Yes

Special Facilities: Museum

Libraries: c. 740,000 vols

Publications: Journal of Dalian University (bimonthly)

Last Updated: 06/11/08

DALIAN UNIVERSITY OF FOREIGN LANGUAGES

94 Yan'an Road, Zhongshan District, Dalian, Liaoning Province
116002
Tel: +86(441) 2801220 +86(441) 2801297
Fax: +86(441) 2639958
Website: http://www.dlufl.edu.cn

President: Sun Yuhua

Departments
French (French); **German** (German); **Korean** (Korean); **Russian Studies** (Russian)

Schools
Chinese Studies (Chinese); **Cultural Communications** (Communication Studies); **English Studies** (English); **International Art and Design** (Design); **International Tourism and Hospitality Management** (Tourism); **Japanese Studies** (Japanese); **Software** (Software Engineering)

History: Founded 1964 as Dalian Japanese Language Institute. Acquired present title 1978.

Degrees and Diplomas: Bachelor's Degree; Master's Degree
Last Updated: 06/11/08

DALIAN UNIVERSITY OF TECHNOLOGY

2 Linggong Road, Ganjingzi District, Dalian, Liaoning Province
116023
Tel: +86(411) 84708702
Fax: +86(411) 84708704
EMail: office@dlut.edu.cn
Website: http://www.dlut.edu.cn

President: Ou Jinping
Tel: +86(411) 84708936, Fax: +86(411) 84671713

Departments
Applied Mathematics (Applied Mathematics) Head: Wei Wu; **Electromagnetic Engineering** (Mechanics); **Materials Engineering** (Materials Engineering) Head: Lai Wang; **Mechanics** (Mechanics) Head: Yuan-Xian Cui; **Physics** (Physics) Head: Dezhen Wang; **Power Engineering** Head: Xigeng Song

Schools
Adult Education Head: Zhihong Tang; **Architecture and Fine Arts** Deputy Head: Yuhang Kong; **Chemical Engineering** (Chemical Engineering; Chemistry; Environmental Engineering; Polymer and Plastics Technology) Head: Fenglin Yang; **Civil and Hydraulic Engineering** (Architecture; Civil Engineering; Hydraulic Engineering) Head: Hongnen Li; **Electronics and Information Engineering** (Automation and Control Engineering; Computer Science; Electronic Engineering; Information Technology) Head: Fuliang Yin; **Environmental and Biological Science and Technology** Head: Xie Quen; **Foreign Languages** (Modern Languages) Head: Fenggang Du; **Humanities and Social Sciences** (Engineering; Law; Linguistics; Media Studies; Philosophy; Political Sciences; Public Administration; Social Sciences); **International Cultural Exchange** (Cultural Studies) Head: Xian Zhang; **Management** (Business Administration; Information Management; Management) Head: Chanyou Wu; **Mechanical Engineering** (Mechanical Engineering) Head: Zhenyuang Fia; **Naval Architectural Engineering** (Marine Engineering; Naval Architecture; Power Engineering) Head: Yujun Lin; **Software Engineering** Head: Hongshn Shen

Further Information: Also 4 national key laboratories; Coastal and Offshore Engineering; Material Surface Modification by Laser, Ionand Electronic beams; Fine Chemical Engineering; Structural Analyses for Industrial Equipment

History: Founded 1949 as School of Engineering of Dalian University, became independent as Dalian Institution of Technology 1950. Acquired present name 1988

Admission Requirements: Score of 565 in National College Entrance Exam

Main Language(s) of Instruction: Chinese

International Co-operation: With institutions in United Kingdom; Australia; Canada; Norway; Japan; South Korea

Accrediting Agencies: Ministry of Education

Degrees and Diplomas: Bachelor's Degree: 4-5 yrs; Master's Degree: 2 1/2 - 3 yrs; Doctor's Degree: 3-4 yrs

Student Services: Academic counselling, Canteen, Cultural centre, Employment services, Foreign student adviser, Handicapped facilities, Health services, Language programs, Nursery care, Social counselling, Sports facilities

Student Residential Facilities: Yes

Special Facilities: Movie Studio

Libraries: c. 1m. vols in Chinese; c. 400,000 in other languages

Publications: Computational Mechanics; Journal, Social Sciences Edition; Journal of Dalian University of Technology; Mathematics Study and Review

Press or Publishing House: Dalian University of Technology Press

Last Updated: 06/11/08

DAQING PETROLEUM INSTITUTE

Daqing 151400
Tel: +86(459) 4653391
Fax: +86(459) 4653380
Website: http://www.dqpi.edu.cn

President: Zheng Guanghan

International Relations: Han Dong

Departments
Architectural Engineering (Structural Architecture); **Automation and Control Engineering** (Automation and Control Engineering); **Computer Science** (Computer Science); **Economics** (Economics); **Electronic Engineering** (Electronic Engineering); **Foreign Languages** (Modern Languages); **Mathematics** (Mathematics); **Petroleum and Gas Engineering** (Chemical Engineering; Mechanical Engineering; Petroleum and Gas Engineering); **Social Sciences** (Social Sciences)

History: Founded 1960 as Northeastern Petroleum Institute.

Degrees and Diplomas: Bachelor's Degree; Master's Degree; Doctor's Degree

Libraries: c. 790,000 vols

Publications: Journal of Daqing Petroleum Institute

DONG HUA UNIVERSITY

1882 Yan-An Road West, Shanghai, Shanghai 200051
Tel: +86(21) 62373678
Fax: +86(21) 62194722
EMail: ices@dhu.edu.cn
Website: http://www.dhu.edu.cn

President: Xu Mingzhi

International Relations: Shen Bai yao

Campuses
Wuxi (Accountancy; Business Administration; Computer Science; E-Business/Commerce; Information Management; Marketing; Technology)

Centres
Modern Education Technology (Educational Technology; Multimedia)

Institutes
Fashion (Fashion Design)

Schools
Adult Education (Adult Education); **Business and Management** (Glorious Sun) (Business Administration; Management); **Business and Management** (Glorious Sun) (Accountancy; Business

Administration; Business and Commerce; E-Business/Commerce; Information Management; International Economics; Management; Marketing); **Chemistry and Chemical Engineering** (Applied Chemistry; Bioengineering; Chemical Engineering; Chemistry; Textile Technology); **Computer Science and Technology** (Computer Science); **Environmental Science and Engineering** (Construction Engineering; Environmental Engineering; Heating and Refrigeration); **Fashion and Art Design** (Fashion Design; Industrial Design); **Foreign Languages** (English; Japanese; Modern Languages); **Humanities** (Administration; Arts and Humanities; Law; Public Administration; Public Relations); **Information Science and Technology** (Computer Science; Electronic Engineering; Information Sciences; Information Technology; Technology; Telecommunications Engineering); **Material Science and Engineering** (Inorganic Chemistry; Materials Engineering; Optical Technology; Optics; Polymer and Plastics Technology); **Mechanical Engineering** (Automation and Control Engineering; Industrial Design; Mechanical Engineering); **Network Education**; **Science** (Applied Mathematics; Applied Physics; Mathematics; Natural Sciences); **Textile** (Information Technology; Textile Technology)

History: Founded 1951 as China Textile University, acquired present title and status 1999.

Academic Year: September to July (September-January; February-July)

Fees: (Yuan): 5,000-10,000 per annum; foreign students, US$ 1,800-4,500

Degrees and Diplomas: *Bachelor's Degree*: 4 yrs; *Master's Degree*: a further 2-3 yrs; *Doctor's Degree (Ph.D)*: a further 3-4 yrs

Special Facilities: Sports Center. Network Centre.

Libraries: Central Library

Publications: Journal of Donghua University *(bimonthly)*; Textile Education *(quarterly)*

Last Updated: 06/11/08

DONGBEI UNIVERSITY OF FINANCE AND ECONOMICS

217 Jianshan Street, Dalian, Liaoning Province 116025
Tel: +86(411) 4691811
Fax: +86(411) 4691811
EMail: dufe@dufe.edu.cn
Website: http://www.dufe.edu.cn

President: Yu Yang

International Relations: Wang Tiejun

Schools
Accountancy (Accountancy); **Chinese Language and Culture** *(International)* (Chinese; Cultural Studies); **Continuing Education** (Banking; Economics; Ethics; Law; Management; Statistics); **Hotel Management** (Hotel Management); **Industrial and Commercial Management** (Industrial Management); **Public Finance and Taxation** (Finance; Taxation)

History: Founded 1952 as Dongbei College of Finance and Economics.

Degrees and Diplomas: *Bachelor's Degree*; *Master's Degree*; *Doctor's Degree*

Libraries: c. 880,000 vols

Publications: Journal of Dongbei University of Finance and Economics; Research in Problems of Finance and Economics

EAST CHINA INSTITUTE OF TECHNOLOGY

14 Xuefu Road, Linchuan, Fuzhou, Fujian Province 344000
Tel: +86(794) 8268345
Fax: +86(794) 8258345
Website: http://www.ecit.edu.cn/

President: Liu Qingcheng

International Relations: Cao Shuanglin

Departments
Applied Chemistry (Applied Chemistry); **Business and Management** (Business Administration; Management); **Engineering** (Engineering); **English** (English); **Geoscience** (Geology); **Information Sciences** (Information Sciences); **Materials Science and Engineering** (Materials Engineering); **Survey Engineering** (Surveying and Mapping)

History: Founded 1956 as Taigu Geological College. Previously known as East China Institute of Geology. Acquired present title and status 2002.

Degrees and Diplomas: *Bachelor's Degree*; *Master's Degree*

EAST CHINA JIAOTONG UNIVERSITY

Changbei Open and Developing District, Nanchang, Jiangxi Province 330013
Tel: +86(791) 7046910
Fax: +86(791) 7046924
EMail: xqb@ecjtu.jx.cn
Website: http://www.ecjtu.jx.cn

President: Lei Xiaoyan
Tel: +86(791) 7046001, Fax: +86(791) 7046924

Centres
Family Education and Female Research (Family Studies; Women's Studies); **Modern Education and Technology** (Education; Technology)

Departments
Foreign Languages (Modern Languages); **Physical Education** (Physical Education); **Social Sciences** (Arts and Humanities; Philosophy; Social Sciences)

Research Centres
Civil Engineering (Civil Engineering); **Mechanical Engineering** (Mechanical Engineering); **Transportation and Economics** (Economics; Transport Management)

Schools
Adult Education (Economics; Engineering; Technology) *Director*: Jingwei Song; **Basic Science** (Applied Chemistry; Applied Physics; Computer Graphics; Software Engineering); **Civil Engineering and Architecture** (Architecture; Bridge Engineering; Civil Engineering; Environmental Engineering; Mechanical Engineering; Railway Engineering; Transport Engineering); **Economics and Management** (Accountancy; Banking; Economics; Finance; International Business; Management); **Electrical and Electronic Engineering** (Automation and Control Engineering; Electrical and Electronic Engineering; Electrical Engineering); **Information Engineering** *Director*: Kefeng Yuan; **Mechanical and Electrical Engineering** (Electrical Engineering; Electronic Engineering; Industrial Management; Mechanical Engineering); **Professional Technology** (Technology) *Director*: Zhilong Huang; **Social Science and Chinese Language** (Chinese; Law; Social Sciences; Social Work) *Director*: Xinhua Wang

Further Information: Also University Hospital

History: Founded 1971.

Academic Year: September to July (September-January; March-July)

Admission Requirements: Graduation from senior middle school and entrance examination

Fees: (Yuan): c. 6,000 per annum

Main Language(s) of Instruction: Chinese

Degrees and Diplomas: *Bachelor's Degree*: Architecture and Environmental Design; Architecture; English; International Business; Accountancy; Human Resources; Automation and Control Engineering; Civil Engineering; Engineering; Economics; Bridge Engineering; Software Engineering (BCE); Electronic Engineering; Environmental Engineering; Industrial Design; Information Management; Mechanical Engineering (BME), 4 yrs; *Master's Degree*: Accountancy; Manufacture; Mechanical Engineering; Structural Engineering; Mechanical Engineering; Labour and Industrial Relations; Road and Railway Engineering; Machine Building; Transport Engineering; Computer Engineering; Statistics; Industrial Management, a further 2 yrs

Student Services: Academic counselling, Employment services, Health services, Language programs, Nursery care, Social counselling, Sports facilities

Student Residential Facilities: Yes

Special Facilities: Movie Studio. Observatory

Libraries: c. 1,000,000 vols

Publications: Journal of East China Jiatong University
Last Updated: 06/11/08

EAST CHINA NORMAL UNIVERSITY

3663 Zhongshan Road North, Shanghai, Shanghai 200062
Tel: +86(21) 62572289
Fax: +86(21) 62570590
EMail: eoffice@admin.ecnu.edu.cn
Website: http://www.ecnu.edu.cn

President: Lizhong Yu Tel: +86(21) 62574476

Schools

Educational Administration (Educational Administration); **Educational Sciences** (Curriculum; Education; Educational Technology; Physical Education; Psychology); **Graduate**; **Humanities** (Advertising and Publicity; Arts and Humanities; Chinese; History; Journalism; Literature; Music; Philosophy; Political Sciences; Radio and Television Broadcasting); **Preschool and Special Education** (Preschool Education; Special Education)

Further Information: Also c. 50 research centres and institutes

History: Founded 1951. Merged with Shanghai Preschool Teacher Junior College, Shanghai Institute of Education and Shanghai Second Institute of Education. Acquired present title 1980.

Academic Year: September to July

Admission Requirements: Graduation from senior middle school and entrance examination

Degrees and Diplomas: *Bachelor's Degree*: 4 yrs; *Master's Degree*: a further 3 yrs; *Doctor's Degree (PhD)*

Libraries: c. 3m. vols

Publications: East Europe and Middle Asia Today; English Teaching and Research in Elementary and Secondary Schools; Journal of East China Normal University, Philosophy; Social Sciences; Educational Technology; Natural Sciences; Psychological Science; Research on Ideology and Politics; Research on Literature and Art Theory; Research on World Geography

Press or Publishing House: University Press
Last Updated: 06/11/08

EAST CHINA UNIVERSITY OF POLITICS AND LAW

1575 Wanghangdu Road, Shanghai, Shanghai 200042
Tel: +86(21) 62512497
Fax: +86(21) 62137121
EMail: ecuplnews@ecupl.edu.cn
Website: http://www.ecupl.edu.cn

President: He Qinhua

Departments
Sociology (Sociology)

Schools

Business; **Criminal Justice** (Criminal Law); **Economic Law** (Commercial Law); **Foreign Languages** (Modern Languages); **Humanities**; **Intellectual Property**; **International Law** (International Law); **Law** (Law); **Politics and Public Administration** (Political Sciences; Public Administration)

History: Founded 1952 as St. John's University, acquired present status 1979.

Degrees and Diplomas: *Bachelor's Degree*; *Master's Degree*; *Doctor's Degree*

Libraries: c. 500,000 vols

Publications: Journal of East China Institute of Politics and Law; Science of Law
Last Updated: 06/11/08

EAST CHINA UNIVERSITY OF SCIENCE AND TECHNOLOGY

China Meilang Road, Shanghai, Shanghai 200237
Tel: +86(21) 64252760
Fax: +86(21) 64250735
EMail: baohua@ecust.edu.cn
Website: http://www.ecust.edu.cn

President: Qian Xuhong

Colleges
Technology *(Sino-German)* (Technology)

Schools

Art, Design and Media; **Bioengineering** (Applied Chemistry; Biochemistry; Bioengineering); **Business** (Accountancy; Business Administration; Business and Commerce; Economics; International Economics; Management); **Chemical Engineering** (Chemical Engineering; Petroleum and Gas Engineering); **Chemistry and Molecular Engineering** (Chemistry; Molecular Biology; Pharmacology; Pharmacy); **Continuing Education**; **Foreign Languages**; **Humanities** (Administration; Arts and Humanities; Industrial Design; Modern Languages; Sociology); **Information Sciences and Engineering** (Automation and Control Engineering; Computer Science; Electronic Engineering; Engineering; Information Sciences; Information Technology); **Law** (Law); **Materials Engineering** (Inorganic Chemistry; Materials Engineering; Polymer and Plastics Technology); **Mechanical and Power Engineering** (Mechanical Engineering; Power Engineering); **Resource and Environmental Engineering** (Environmental Engineering; Natural Resources); **Science** (Mathematics; Physics); **Social and Public Administration**

History: Founded 1952 as East China Institute of Chemical Technology, acquired present title 1980, incorporating previously existing departments of Chiaotung, Tatung, Aurora, Soochow and Kiangnan Universities.

Academic Year: September to July (September-February; February-July)

Admission Requirements: Graduation from senior middle school and entrance examination

Main Language(s) of Instruction: Chinese

Accrediting Agencies: State Education Commission

Degrees and Diplomas: *Bachelor's Degree*: 4 yrs; *Master's Degree*; *Doctor's Degree*

Libraries: Central Library, c. 1.1m. vols

Publications: Journal of Functional Polymers
Last Updated: 06/11/08

FOSHAN UNIVERSITY

18 Jiangwan First Road, Foshan, Guangdong Province 528000
Tel: +86(757) 2713853
Fax: +86(757) 2713853
EMail: ieo@fosu.edu.cn
Website: http://www.fosu.edu.cn

President: Zou Cairong
International Relations: Lin Zhi

Faculties
Physical Education (Physical Education)

Schools

Business; **Educational Sciences**; **Environment and Civil Engineering**; **Life Sciences** (Biological and Life Sciences); **Literature and Arts** (Ceramic Art; Chinese; Design; English; Literature); **Mechanical and Electronic Engineering** (Applied Physics; Automation and Control Engineering; Communication Studies; Mechanical Engineering); **Medical** (Medicine); **Politics and Law** (Law; Political Sciences); **Science**

History: Founded 1955. Acquired present status 2005 after merging with Foshan Medical College and Foshan College of Education.

Degrees and Diplomas: *Bachelor's Degree*
Last Updated: 12/11/08

FUDAN UNIVERSITY

220 Handan Road, Shanghai, Shanghai 200433
Tel: +86(21) 65642260
Fax: +86(21) 65649524
EMail: xjshi@fudan.edu.cn
Website: http://www.fudan.edu.cn

President: Wang Shenghong
International Relations: Shen Dingli

Departments

Chemistry (Chemistry); **Environmental Science and Engineering** (Engineering; Environmental Studies); **Mathematics** (Mathematics); **Physics** (Physics); **Polymer Science** (Polymer and Plastics Technology)

Schools

Economics (Economics; Finance; International Business; International Economics); **Humanities** (Arts and Humanities; Chinese; Cultural Studies; History; Literature; Modern Languages; Philosophy); **Journalism** (Journalism); **Law** (International Law; International Relations; Law; Sociology); **Life Sciences** (Biochemistry; Biological and Life Sciences; Biophysics; Environmental Studies; Genetics; Microbiology; Physiology); **Management** (Accountancy; Finance; International Business; Management; Statistics); **Medicine**; **Nursing** (Nursing); **Pharmacy** (Pharmacy); **Public Health** (Public Health); **Technology** (Computer Science; Materials Engineering; Mechanical Engineering; Technology)

History: Founded 1905 as Fudan College. Merged with Shanghai Medical University 2000.

Academic Year: September to July (two semesters)

Admission Requirements: Graduation from senior middle school and entrance examination

Main Language(s) of Instruction: Chinese, English

Degrees and Diplomas: *Bachelor's Degree*: 4 yrs; *Master's Degree*; *Doctor's Degree*

Student Residential Facilities: Yes

Publications: Chinese Annual of Mathematics; Fudan Natural Sciences Journal; Fudan Social Sciences Journal; Mathematics Annals *(annually)*; Research and Developmental Management; Rhetoric; World Economic Forum

Last Updated: 12/11/08

FUJIAN AGRICULTURE AND FORESTRY UNIVERSITY

Jinshan, Fuzhou, Fujian Province 350002
Tel: +86(591) 3789208
Fax: +86(591) 3741251
EMail: fafufao@126.com
Website: http://www.fjau.edu.cn

President: Zheng Jingui

International Relations: Zhu Pengfei

Departments

Food Science (Food Science); **Fundamental Subjects**; **Horticulture** (Horticulture); **Land and Environmental Science** (Environmental Studies); **Mechanical and Electrical Engineering** (Electrical Engineering; Mechanical Engineering); **Plant Protection** (Plant and Crop Protection)

Schools

Adult Education; **Animal Science** (Zoology); **Crop Science** (Agronomy; Crop Production); **Economics and Trade** (Agriculture; Business and Commerce; Commercial Law; Economics; Finance; Management)

History: Founded 1936 as Private Agricultural College of Fukien Christian University and Fukien Provincial Agricultural College. Renamed Fujian Agricultural University 1994. Acquired present title 2000, following merger with Fujian College of Forestry and Fujian Provincial Agricultural College.

Degrees and Diplomas: *Bachelor's Degree*; *Master's Degree*; *Doctor's Degree*

Libraries: c. 400,000 vols

Publications: Entomological Journal of East China; Journal, Natural Sciences, Social Sciences; Sugarcane; Wuyi Science Journal

FUJIAN MEDICAL UNIVERSITY

88 Jiaotong Road, Fuzhou, Fujian Province 350004
Tel: +86(591) 22862315
EMail: setup@mail.fjmu.edu.cn
Website: http://www.fjmu.edu.cn

President: Chen Liying

International Relations: Xu Huiyuan

Departments

Medicine (Medicine); **Nursing** (Nursing); **Preventive Medicine** (Social and Preventive Medicine); **Stomatology** (Stomatology)

History: Founded 1937 as Fujian Provincial Medical School, acquired present title 1996.

Degrees and Diplomas: *Bachelor's Degree*; *Master's Degree*; *Doctor's Degree*

Libraries: c. 220,000 vols

Publications: Journal of Fujian Medical University; Study of Higher Medical Education

FUJIAN NORMAL UNIVERSITY

8 Shangsan Road, Canshan District, Fuzhou, Fujian Province 350007
Tel: +86(591) 3412820
Fax: +86(591) 3442840
EMail: fjw@fli.com.cn
Website: http://www.fjtu.edu.cn

President: Zeng Minyong (1996-) Tel: +86(591) 3440179

International Relations: Huang Jiahua
Tel: +86(591) 3412820, Fax: +86(591) 3442840

Research Institutes

Polymer (Polymer and Plastics Technology)

Schools

Adult Education; **Arts** (Arts and Humanities; Fine Arts; Music); **Biological Engineering** (Bioengineering; Biology; Microbiology); **Chinese Studies** *(International)* (Administration; Chemistry; Chinese; Computer Science; Education; Educational Technology; Geography; History; Literature; Mathematics; Physical Education; Physics; Sociology; Tourism; Urban Studies); **Foreign Languages** (English; Japanese; Modern Languages; Translation and Interpretation); **Law and Economics** (Economics; Law; Political Sciences)

Further Information: Also Teaching Hospital. Courses for foreign students

History: Founded 1907 as school, acquired present status and title 1972.

Academic Year: September to June (September-February; March-June)

Admission Requirements: Graduation from senior middle school and entrance examination

Degrees and Diplomas: *Bachelor's Degree*: Arts; History; Law, 4 yrs; *Master's Degree*: a further 3 yrs; *Doctor's Degree*: 3 yrs following Master

Libraries: c. 1.5m. Vols

Publications: Chinese and Foreign Education; Chinese World; Chinese World; Education of China and Foreign Countries; Fujian Foreign Language; Fujian Geography; Fujian Secondary School Mathematics; Journal, Philosophy, Social Sciences, Natural Sciences

FUJIAN UNIVERSITY OF TRADITIONAL CHINESE MEDICINE

282 Wusilu, Fuzhou, Fujian Province 350003
Tel: +86(591) 7842528
Fax: +86(591) 7852754
EMail: hwxy@fjtcm.edu.cn
Website: http://www.fjtcm.edu.cn

President: Du Jian

International Relations: Li Candong

Departments

Acupuncture and Massage (Acupuncture); **Medicine** (Medicine); **Nursing** (Nursing); **Postgraduate**; **Social Sciences** (Social Sciences); **Traditional Chinese Medicine** (Orthopaedics; Traditional Eastern Medicine)

Schools

Overseas Education

History: Founded 1953 as Fuzhou Teaching School.

Degrees and Diplomas: *Bachelor's Degree*; *Master's Degree*; *Doctor's Degree*

Libraries: c. 220,000 vols

Publications: Higher Education and Research of TCM; Journal of Fujian TCM University

FUZHOU UNIVERSITY

2 Xue Yuan Road, University Town, Fuzhou, Fujian Province 350002
Tel: +86(591) 22866099
EMail: faomail@fzu.edu.cn
Website: http://www.fzu.edu.cn

President: Wu Minsheng

Colleges

Adult Education (Accountancy; Architecture; Automation and Control Engineering; Banking; Business and Commerce; Chemical Engineering; Computer Science; Electronic Engineering; English; Finance; Secretarial Studies); **Architecture** (Architecture); **Chemistry and Chemical Engineering** (Chemical Engineering; Chemistry); **Civil Engineering** (Civil Engineering; Industrial Engineering; Structural Architecture); **Industrial Arts**; **Management** (Management)

Departments

Accountancy (Accountancy); **Arts and Crafts** (Crafts and Trades; Handicrafts); **Biological and Food Engineering** (Biology; Food Technology); **Chemistry** (Chemistry); **Computer Science and Technology** (Computer Science; Technology); **Electrical Engineering** (Electrical Engineering); **Electronics and Applied Physics** (Applied Physics; Electronic Engineering); **Environmental and Resources Engineering** (Environmental Engineering; Natural Resources); **Finance and Banking** (Banking; Finance); **Humanities and Social Sciences** (Arts and Humanities; Chinese; Cultural Studies; Social Sciences); **Hydraulic Engineering** (Hydraulic Engineering); **Management** (Management); **Materials Science and Engineering** (Materials Engineering); **Mathematics** (Mathematics); **Mechanical Engineering** (Mechanical Engineering); **Radio Engineering** (Telecommunications Engineering); **Trade** (Business and Commerce)

Schools

Adult Education; **Arts and Crafts** (Crafts and Trades; Fine Arts); **Civil Engineering** (Architecture; Civil Engineering); **Foreign Languages** (English; Modern Languages); **Management** (Management); **Materials Science and Engineering** (Engineering; Materials Engineering)

Sections

Bioelectric Chemistry (Chemistry); **Biomedical Engineering** (Biomedical Engineering); **Chemical Engineering** (Chemical Engineering); **Finance Supporting Systems** (Finance); **Geology** (Geology); **Hydraulics** (Hydraulic Engineering); **Industrial Computers and Systems** (Industrial Engineering); **Irrigation and Hydropower** (Hydraulic Engineering; Irrigation); **Microcomputer Applications** (Computer Science)

History: Founded 1958.

Academic Year: September to July (September-January; February-July)

Admission Requirements: Graduation from senior middle school and entrance examination

Main Language(s) of Instruction: Chinese

Degrees and Diplomas: *Bachelor's Degree*: 4 yrs; *Master's Degree*: a further 3 yrs; *Doctor's Degree (Ph.D.)*: 3 yrs

Student Residential Facilities: Yes

Special Facilities: Art Gallery. Movie Studio. Language Laboratory

Libraries: Central Library, c. 1m. vols

Publications: Annals of Differential Equations; Fouzhou University Paper; Journal of Fuzhou University *(quarterly)*; Studies of Higher Education; Yearbook of Differential Equations *(annually)*

Press or Publishing House: Fuzhou University Press
Last Updated: 12/11/08

GANNAN MEDICAL UNIVERSITY

1, Yixueyuan Road, Ganzhou, Jiangxi Province 314000
Tel: +86(797) 8223090
Fax: +86(797) 8223812
Website: http://www.gnmc.net.cn/bumen/gjxy/gmu.html

President: Chen Fangrong

International Relations: Xu Feng

Colleges

International Education (Anaesthesiology; Nursing; Ophthalmology)

Schools

Basic Medicine (Medicine; Pharmacy); **Clinical Medicine** *(Second)*; **Clinical Medicine** *(First)* (Anaesthesiology; Medicine; Nursing); **Social Sciences and Humanities**

Degrees and Diplomas: *Bachelor's Degree*; *Master's Degree*
Last Updated: 12/11/08

GANNAN NORMAL UNIVERSITY

53 Hongqi Road, Ganzhou, Jiangxi Province 341000
Tel: +86(797) 8223690
Fax: +86(797) 8227700
EMail: gnnu1958@yahoo.com.cn
Website: http://www.gntc.net.cn

President: Xiao Dingzhi

International Relations: Liu Ruigui

Departments

Chemistry; **Chinese** (Chinese); **Economics and Law** (Economics; Law); **Fine Arts**; **Information Management** (Information Management); **Mathematics**; **Modern Languages** (Modern Languages); **Physical Education** (Physical Education); **Physics**

Degrees and Diplomas: *Bachelor's Degree*; *Master's Degree*
Last Updated: 12/11/08

GANSU AGRICULTURAL UNIVERSITY (GAU)

N° 1 Yingmen Village, Anning District, Lanzhou, Gansu Province 730070
Tel: +86(931) 7632459
Fax: +86(931) 7631125
EMail: faogau@gsau.edu.cn
Website: http://www.gsau.edu.cn

President: Di Wang Tel: +86(931) 7631140

International Relations: Hui-zhen Qiu
Tel: +86(931) 7631492 EMail: hzqiu@gsau.edu.cn

Chairs

Forestry (Forestry; Landscape Architecture; Soil Conservation; Water Management) *Dean*: Yi Li

Colleges

Agronomy (Agronomy; Crop Production; Farm Management; Horticulture) *Dean*: Ji hua Yu; **Animal Science and Technology** (Animal Husbandry; Aquaculture) *Dean*: Zhao guo Shi; **Economy Management** (Banking; Economics; Finance) *Dean*: Shen lin Wang; **Extended Education** (Education) *Dean*: Zheng sheng Han; **Food Science and Engineering** (Biotechnology; Food Science; Food Technology) *Dean*: Yang Bi; **Foreign Languages** (English) *Division Head*: De-wen Lü; **Grassland Sciences** *Dean*: Shang li Shi; **Humanities** (Arts and Humanities) *Dean*: Zhen hai Shang; **Information Sciences and Technology** (Computer Engineering; Computer Science; Information Sciences; Information Technology) *Dean*: Lian Guo Wang; **Life Science and Technology** (Biotechnology) *Dean*: Wei Li; **Physical Education** (Physical Education) *Dean*: Yong xin Chen; **Resources and Environmental Sciences** (Environmental Engineering; Environmental Management; Natural Resources) *Dean*: Ren zhi Zhang; **Science** (Applied Chemistry; Chemistry; Mathematics; Physics) *Dean*: Xiao ping Zhang; **Technology** (Agricultural Engineering; Agricultural Equipment; Automation and Control Engineering; Hydraulic Engineering; Water Management) *Dean*: Zi yong Cheng; **Veterinary Medicine** (Veterinary Science) *Dean*: Si jiu Yu

History: Founded 1946 as National Veterinary College. Acquired present status 1958.

Academic Year: September to July (two semesters)

Admission Requirements: Graduation from senior middle school and entrance examination

Fees: (Yuan): 3,000-4,000 per annum

Main Language(s) of Instruction: Chinese

International Co-operation: With universities in USA, Australia, France, New Zealand, Germany, Netherlands. Also participates in scientific research cooperation.

Accrediting Agencies: Gansu Province Department of Education

Degrees and Diplomas: *Bachelor's Degree*: Agronomy; Horticulture; Plant Protection; Forestry; Hydrology and Engineering; Agricultural Resources and Environment; Animal Science and Technology; Veterinary Medicine; Economy and Commerce; Agricultural Machinery and Engineering; Food Science and Engineering; Computer Science, 4 yrs; *Master's Degree*: Agronomy; Horticulture; Plant Protection; Animal Husbandry; Grassland; Veterinary Medicine; Forestry, 3 yrs; *Doctor's Degree*: Agronomy; Animal Husbandry; Grassland; Veterinary Medicine (PhD), 2 yrs

Student Services: Canteen, Foreign Studies Centre, Health services, Nursery care, Sports facilities

Student Residential Facilities: Yes

Special Facilities: Movie studio

Libraries: 524,400 vols

Publications: Journal of Gansu Agricultural University *(quarterly)*; Journal of Grassland and Turf *(quarterly)*

GANSU COLLEGE OF TRADITIONAL CHINESE MEDICINE

35 Dinxi Road, Lanzhou, Gansu Province 730000
Tel: +86(931) 8619986
Fax: +86(931) 8627950
EMail: wsc@gszy.edu.cn
Website: http://www.gszy.edu.cn

Dean: Zhang Shiqing

International Relations: Wang Daokun

Departments
Acupuncture and Osteology; **Chinese Botany** (Botany); **Traditional Chinese Medicine** (Traditional Eastern Medicine); **Traditional Tibetan Medicine** (Traditional Eastern Medicine)

Degrees and Diplomas: *Bachelor's Degree*; *Master's Degree*

GANSU INSTITUTE OF POLITICAL SCIENCE AND LAW

2 Annin West Road, Lanzhou, Gansu Province 730070
Tel: +86(931) 7601586
Fax: +86(931) 7678037
EMail: sun@gsli.edu.cn
Website: http://www.gsli.edu.cn

President: Wang Suyuan

Departments
Administration (Administration); **Art** (Fine Arts); **Civil Security** (Civil Security); **Commercial Law** (Commercial Law); **Information Science and Technology** (Information Sciences; Information Technology); **Law** (Law); **Management** (Management)

History: Founded 1984.

Main Language(s) of Instruction: Chinese

Degrees and Diplomas: *Bachelor's Degree*; *Master's Degree*
Last Updated: 02/09/08

GUANGDONG MEDICAL COLLEGE (GDMC)

2 Wenmin East Road, Xiashan, Zhanjiang, Guangdong Province 524023
Tel: +86(759) 2388505
Fax: +86(759) 2284104
EMail: gdmcbgs@gdmc.edu.cn
Website: http://www.gdmc.edu.cn

President: Zhou Keyuan
Tel: +86(759) 2388601 EMail: pres@gdmc.edu.cn

Departments
Clinical Medicine (Medicine); **Laboratory Medicine**

Further Information: Also 3 Affiliated Hospitals

History: Founded 1958 as Zhanjiang Branch of the Sun Yat-sen Medical College, acquired present title 1992.

Main Language(s) of Instruction: Chinese

Degrees and Diplomas: *Bachelor's Degree*; *Master's Degree*

Student Services: Academic counselling, Canteen, Cultural centre, Employment services, Health services, Social counselling, Sports facilities

Student Residential Facilities: Yes

Libraries: c. 220,000 vols

Publications: Journal of Guangdong Medical College
Last Updated: 12/11/08

GUANGDONG OCEAN UNIVERSITY

East Huguangyan, Zhanjiang, Guangdong Province 524088
Tel: +86(759) 2284448
Fax: +86(759) 2284448
EMail: fao@gdou.edu.cn
Website: http://www.gdou.edu.cn/english/index_en.htm

President: He Zhen

Faculties
Agriculture (Agronomy; Animal Husbandry; Biotechnology; Horticulture; Veterinary Science; Zoology); **Art** (Dance; Design; Fine Arts; Music); **Arts** (Arts and Humanities); **Economic Management** (Business Administration; Economics; Finance; International Business; International Economics; Public Administration); **Engineering** (Energy Engineering; Marine Engineering; Mechanical Engineering); **Fishery** (Aquaculture; Bioengineering; Fishery; Food Technology; Marine Science and Oceanography); **Foodstuff Technology** (Food Technology); **Foreign Studies** (International Studies); **Information Technology** (Information Technology); **Law** (Law); **Navigation** (Nautical Science); **Physical Education** (Physical Education); **Politics and Executive Studies** (Political Sciences; Sociology); **Science** (Natural Sciences); **Software** (Software Engineering)

Schools
Engineering (Engineering)

History: Founded 1997 as Zhanjiang Ocean University, acquired present status and title 2005.

Degrees and Diplomas: *Bachelor's Degree*; *Master's Degree*
Last Updated: 12/12/08

GUANGDONG POLYTECHNIC NORMAL UNIVERSITY

293 Zhonghshan Road, Tianhe, Shipai, Guangzhou, Guangdong Province 510633
Tel: +86(20) 38265465
Fax: +86(20) 38256600
EMail: gpnuwsb@163.com
Website: http://www.gdin.edu.cn

President: Wang Lefu

International Relations: Ding Li

Schools
Administration (Administration); **Automatization** (Automation and Control Engineering; Electrical Engineering); **Chinese Language and Literature** (Chinese); **Computer Science** (Computer Science; E-Business/Commerce; Mathematics; Software Engineering); **Economics and Trade**; **Education** (Education); **Educational Technology** (Education; Educational Technology; Vocational Education); **Electronics Information Engineering** (Computer Science; Electronic Engineering; Software Engineering); **Finance and Economics** (Economics; Finance); **Foreign Languages** (Modern Languages); **Mechanics and Electronics** (Electronic Engineering; Mechanical Engineering); **Nationalities** (Social Sciences); **Politics and Law**

History: Founded 1958. Acquired present status 1998.

Main Language(s) of Instruction: Chinese

Degrees and Diplomas: *Bachelor's Degree*; *Master's Degree*
Last Updated: 15/09/08

GUANGDONG UNIVERSITY OF BUSINESS STUDIES

21 Luntou Road, Guangzhou, Guangdong Province 510320
Tel: +86(20) 84096080
Fax: +86(20) 84096140
EMail: guangtuanchen@hotmail.com
Website: http://www.gdcc.edu.cn

Colleges
Accountancy; **Administration**; **Economics and Statistics** (Administration; Economics; Statistics); **Finance** (Finance); **Foreign Languages** (Modern Languages); **Humanities and Communication**; **Information** (Information Management); **Law** (Law); **Taxation and Public Finance** (Taxation); **Tourism and Environment**

Degrees and Diplomas: *Bachelor's Degree*; *Master's Degree*
Last Updated: 13/11/08

GUANGDONG UNIVERSITY OF FOREIGN STUDIES

2 Baiyun Dadaon, Guangzhou, Guangdong Province 510420
Tel: +86(20) 36207007
Fax: +86(20) 86627367
Website: http://www.gdufs.edu.cn

President: Sui Sui Guangjun Guangjun (2008-)
Tel: +86(20) 36207009

Vice-President: Chen Jianping
Tel: +86(20) 36207039 EMail: io@mail.gdufs.edu.cn.

Colleges
Continuing Education *Dean*: Fuqiang Zhou; **Information Science and Technology** (Information Technology; Software Engineering; Statistics) *Dean*: Wanlin Qiao; **International** (International Studies) *Dean*: Linhan Chen

Departments
Chinese for International Students (Chinese) *Head*: Deli He; **Physical Education** *Head*: Xuwu Li

Faculties
Asian Languages and Culture (Cultural Studies; Indonesian; Japanese; Korean; Thai Languages; Vietnamese) *Dean*: Lixin Wei; **English Language and Culture** (American Studies; Cultural Studies; English; English Studies; Linguistics; Tourism; Translation and Interpretation) *Dean*: Weihei Zhong; **European Languages and Culture** (Cultural Studies; French; French Studies; German; Germanic Studies; Italian; Russian; Spanish) *Dean*: Dehua Zhan; **International Communication** (Chinese; English; Foreigners Education; Management; Media Studies; Secretarial Studies) *Dean*: Qing'an Yu

Institutes
English Language Education *Dean*: Hahong Huo

Schools
English for Business *Dean*: Yun Cai; **International Trade and Economics** (Business and Commerce; English; Finance; International Business; International Economics) *Dean*: Xueyan Shao; **Legal Studies** (English; International Business; Law) *Head*: Xingguang Wu; **Management** *Head*: Hua Fang; **Politics and Public Administration** (Administration; Management; Public Administration; Social Sciences) *Dean*: Shuchi Yang

History: Founded 1965 and incorporated the Guangzhou Institute of Foreign Languages and Guangzhou Institute of Foreign Trade 1995.

Academic Year: September to July (September-January; February-July)

Admission Requirements: Graduation from senior middle school and entrance examination

Fees: (Yuan): 4,500 per annum

Main Language(s) of Instruction: Chinese

International Co-operation: With universities in Japan, United Kingdom, Australia, New Zealand, Russian Federation, Indonesia and Thailand

Accrediting Agencies: Department of Education of the Guangdong Provincial Government

Degrees and Diplomas: *Bachelor's Degree*: Foreign Languages and Literature; Economics; Law, 4 yrs; *Master's Degree*: Foreign Languages and Literature; Linguistics and Applied Linguistics, a further 3 yrs; *Doctor's Degree*: Linguistics and Applied Linguistics; French, a further 3 yrs

Student Services: Academic counselling, Canteen, Cultural centre, Employment services, Foreign student adviser, Foreign Studies Centre, Health services, Language programs, Nursery care, Social counselling, Sports facilities

Student Residential Facilities: Yes

Special Facilities: Yunshan Hall

Libraries: c. 1.00,000 vols

Publications: Higher Education Research on Foreign Students *(quarterly)*; International Economics and Trade Research *(bimonthly)*; Modern Foreign Languages *(quarterly)*

Press or Publishing House: University Publishing House
Last Updated: 13/11/08

GUANGDONG UNIVERSITY OF TECHNOLOGY

729 East Dongfeng Road, Guangzhou, Guangdong Province 510080
Tel: +86(20) 87617779
Fax: +86(20) 87302737
EMail: wsc@gdut.edu.cn
Website: http://www.gdut.edu.cn

President: Zhang Xiangwei
International Relations: Wei Guihui

Faculties
Applied Mathematics (Applied Mathematics); **Automation** (Automation and Control Engineering; Electrical Engineering); **Chemical Engineering and Light Industry** (Chemical Engineering); **Computer** (Computer Science); **Construction** (Construction Engineering); **Electro-mechanical Engineering** (Electronic Engineering; Mechanical Engineering); **Environmental Science and Engineering** (Environmental Engineering; Environmental Studies); **Information Engineering** (Information Technology); **Materials and Energy** (Energy Engineering; Materials Engineering); **Physics and Optoelectronic Engineering** (Physics)

Schools
Arts Design (Fashion Design; Fine Arts; Visual Arts); **Business** (Business Administration); **Continuing Education**; **Economics and Management** (Economics; Management); **Foreign Languages** (Modern Languages); **Liberal Arts and Law** (Law; Social Work)

History: Founded 1958. Merged with Guangdong Institute of Technology, Guangdong Mechanical College and East South China Construction College.

Degrees and Diplomas: *Bachelor's Degree*; *Master's Degree*; *Doctor's Degree*

Libraries: c. 660,000 vols

Publications: Industrial Engineering; Journal of Guangdong University of Technology
Last Updated: 13/11/08

GUANGXI ART UNIVERSITY OF CHINA

7 Jiaoyu Road, Nanning, Guangxi Zhuang Province 530022
Tel: +86(711) 5313138
Fax: +86(711) 5312637

President: Huang Gesheng
International Relations: Xuan Si

Departments
Design; **Fine Arts**; **Music**; **Music Education**

Schools
Adult Education

History: Founded 1938 as Guangxi Normal School of Arts, acquired present title 1960.

Degrees and Diplomas: *Bachelor's Degree*; *Master's Degree*

Libraries: c. 20,000 vols

Publications: Exploration in Arts

GUANGXI MEDICAL UNIVERSITY (GMU)

22 Shuangyong Road, Nanning, Guangxi Zhuang Province 530021
Tel: +86(771) 5352512
Fax: +86(771) 5352523
EMail: gxmu1934@263.net
Website: http://www.gxmu.edu.cn

President: Huang Gangwu **Tel:** +86(771) 5350670

Schools

Clinical Sciences (Medicine) *Head*: Tangwei Liu; **Clinical Sciences IV** *(Liuzhou, Guangxi)* (Medicine) *Head*: Aiguo Ding; **Clinical Sciences V** *(Liuzhou, Guangxi)* (Medicine) *Head*: Jianhui Huang; **Clinical Sciences VI** *(Liuzhou, Guangxi)* (Medicine) *Head*: Weimin Wu; **Continuing Education** (Medical Technology) *Head*: Guogiang She; **Dental Sciences** (Dentistry; Stomatology) *Head*: Nur Zhou; **Nursing** (Nursing) *Head*: Weimin Zhu; **Oncology** (Oncology) *Head*: Li Li; **Pre-clinical Sciences** (Health Sciences) *Head*: Guorong Luo; **Public Health and Preventive Medicine** (Public Health; Social and Preventive Medicine) *Head*: Zhang Zhiyong

History: Founded 1934, acquired present status 1996.

Academic Year: September to July

Admission Requirements: Graduation from senior middle school and entrance examination

Fees: (Yuan): 21,250 per annum

Main Language(s) of Instruction: Chinese; English

Accrediting Agencies: Guangxi Education Bureau

Degrees and Diplomas: *Bachelor's Degree*: 5 yrs; *Master's Degree*: a further 3 yrs; *Doctor's Degree*: 3 yrs

Student Services: Academic counselling, Canteen, Cultural centre, Employment services, Foreign student adviser, Foreign Studies Centre, Health services, Language programs, Nursery care, Social counselling, Sports facilities

Libraries: 400,000 vols

Publications: Abstracts of Tumor Diseases *(quarterly)*; Journal of Coloproctocological Surgery *(quarterly)*; Journal of GMU *(bimonthly)*
Last Updated: 13/11/08

GUANGXI NORMAL UNIVERSITY

15 Yucai Road, Guilin, Guangxi Zhuang Province 541001
Tel: +86(773) 2816350
Fax: +86(773) 2825850
EMail: gxnu@public.glptt.gx.cn
Website: http://www.gxnu.edu.cn

President: Huang Jieshan

International Relations: Xu Deqiang

Departments

Arts (Arts and Humanities); **Biology** (Biology); **Chemistry and Chemical Engineering** (Chemical Engineering; Chemistry); **Chinese Language and Literature** (Chinese; Literature); **Foreign Languages and Literature** (Literature; Modern Languages); **History and Information Sciences** (History; Information Sciences); **Mathematics and Computer Science** (Mathematics and Computer Science); **Pedagogy** (Pedagogy); **Physical Education** (Physical Education); **Physics and Electronics** (Electronic Engineering; Physics); **Politics and Economics** (Economics; Political Sciences)

Schools
Continuing Education

History: Founded 1932 as Guangxi Provincial Normal School, acquired present title 1983.

Degrees and Diplomas: *Bachelor's Degree*: 4 yrs; *Master's Degree*: a further 3 yrs

Student Residential Facilities: Yes

Libraries: c. 1m. vols

Publications: Journal of Guangxi Normal University, Natural Sciences and Social Sciences; Oriental Literature Series

Note: Also c. 1,000 Continuing Education Students

GUANGXI TEACHERS EDUCATION UNIVERSITY

19 Mingxiu East Road, Nanning, Guangxi Zhuang Province 530001
Tel: +86(711) 3126960
Fax: +86(711) 3126960
EMail: gxtcwb@public.nn.gx.cn
Website: http://www.gxtc.edu.cn

President: Zhong Haiqing

International Relations: Huang Dou

Departments

Chemistry (Chemistry); **Chinese Language and Literature** (Chinese); **Geography** (Geography); **Mathematics** (Mathematics); **Modern Languages** (Modern Languages); **Physics** (Physics); **Political Science and Economics** (Economics; Political Sciences)

Degrees and Diplomas: *Bachelor's Degree*; *Master's Degree*

GUANGXI TRADITIONAL CHINESE MEDICAL UNIVERSITY

179 Mingxiudong Road, Nanning, Guangxi Zhuang Province 530001
Tel: +86(711) 3137401
Fax: +86(711) 3135812
EMail: FIE@gxtcmu.edu.cn
Website: http://www.gxtcmu.edu.cn/

President: Wang Naiping

International Relations: Huang Cenhan

Departments

Nursing (Nursing); **Pharmacology** (Pharmacology); **Traditional Chinese Medicine** (Traditional Eastern Medicine)

Schools

Clinical Medicine I (Medicine); **Clinical Medicine II** (Medicine)

History: Founded 1956 as Guangxi Traditional Chinese Medical School. Acquired present title 1964.

Degrees and Diplomas: *Bachelor's Degree*; *Master's Degree*
Last Updated: 13/11/08

GUANGXI UNIVERSITY

10 Xixiangtang Road, Nanning, Guangxi Zhuang Province 530004
Tel: +86(771) 3238638 +86(771) 3821264
Fax: +86(771) 3237734
EMail: gjc@gxu.edu.cn
Website: http://www.gxu.edu.cn

President: Tang Jiliang **EMail:** xiaoban@gxu.edu.cn

International Relations: Yang Lin

Schools

Adult Education; **Agriculture** (Agriculture); **Animal Science and Technology** (Animal Husbandry); **Biotechnology and Sugar Engineering** (Agricultural Engineering; Biotechnology); **Business** (Business Administration); **Chemistry and Chemical Engineering** (Chemical Engineering; Chemistry); **Civil Engineering** (Civil Engineering); **Computer Science** (Computer Science); **Culture and Mass Communication** (Cultural Studies; Mass Communication); **Electrical Engineering** (Electrical Engineering); **Foreign Languages** (Modern Languages); **Forestry** (Forestry); **Law** (Law); **Mechanical Engineering** (Mechanical Engineering); **Resource and Environment** (Environmental Studies); **Sciences** (Natural Sciences); **Social Sciences and Administration** (Administration; Social Sciences)

History: Founded 1928. Merged with Guangxi Agricultural University 1997.

Main Language(s) of Instruction: Chinese

Degrees and Diplomas: *Bachelor's Degree*; *Master's Degree*; *Doctor's Degree*

Libraries: c. 1.2m. Vols

Publications: Guangxi Agricultural and Biological Science; Journal of Guangxi University
Last Updated: 13/11/08

GUANGXI UNIVERSITY FOR NATIONALITIES

188, East Daxue Road, Nanning, Guangxi Zhuang Province 530006
Tel: +86(711) 3260111
Fax: +86(711) 3262052
Website: http://www.gxun.edu.cn

President: He Longqun

International Relations: Wei Jinhai

Colleges
Business (Business Administration); **Chemistry and Ecology Engineering** (Chemical Engineering; Chemistry; Ecology; Engineering); **Chinese Language and Literature** (Chinese; Literature); **Ethnology and Sociology** (Ethnology; Sociology); **Foreign Studies** (Modern Languages); **Management** (Management); **Mathematics and Computer Science** (Computer Science; Mathematics); **Music and Fine Arts** (Fine Arts; Music); **Physical Education and Health Sciences** (Health Sciences; Physical Education); **Physics and Electronic Engineering** (Electronic Engineering; Physics); **Political Science and Law** (Economics; Law; Political Sciences)

History: Founded 1952 as Guangxi Institute. Acquired present status and title 2006.

Main Language(s) of Instruction: Chinese

Degrees and Diplomas: *Bachelor's Degree*; *Master's Degree*
Last Updated: 13/11/08

GUANGXI UNIVERSITY OF TECHNOLOGY

268 Donghuan Road, Liuzhou, Guangxi Zhuang Province 5455005
Tel: +86(772) 2615430
Fax: +86(772) 2617698
EMail: gxywsb@public.lsptt.gx.cn
Website: http://www.gxut.edu.cn/english/home/3.htm

President: Li Dewei

Departments
Arts and Design (Design; Fine Arts); **Automobile Engineering** (Automotive Engineering); **Biological and Chemical Engineering** (Bioengineering; Chemical Engineering); **Civil Engineering** (Civil Engineering); **Computer Engineering** (Computer Engineering); **Electronic Information and Control Engineering** (Automation and Control Engineering; Information Technology); **Finance and Economics** (Economics; Finance); **Foreign Languages and Literature** (Literature; Modern Languages); **Information and Computer Science**; **Management Engineering**; **Mechanical Engineering** (Mechanical Engineering); **Social Sciences**

History: Founded 1958. In 1982 Guangxi Light Industry College, Guangxi Mechanical Engineering College and Guangxi Institute of Petroleum and Chemical Engineering merged.

Main Language(s) of Instruction: Chinese

Degrees and Diplomas: *Bachelor's Degree*; *Master's Degree*
Last Updated: 13/11/08

GUANGZHOU ACADEMY OF FINE ARTS

257 East Changgang Road, Guangzhou, Guangdong Province 510261
Tel: +86(20) 84429572
Fax: +86(20) 84497083
Website: http://www.gzarts.edu.cn/english/index.htm

President: Liang Mingcheng
International Relations: Wang Yuesheng

Colleges
Design (Design)

Departments
Art History and Theory (Art History); **Fine Arts Education**; **Fine Arts Teaching** (Art Education); **Painting**; **Printmaking** (Printing and Printmaking); **Sculpture** (Sculpture); **Traditional Chinese Painting**

Degrees and Diplomas: *Bachelor's Degree*; *Master's Degree*
Last Updated: 13/11/08

GUANGZHOU MEDICAL COLLEGE

195, Dongfengxi Road, Guangzhou, Guangdong Province 510182
Tel: +86(20) 81340481
Fax: +86(20) 81340442
Website: http://www.gzhmc.edu.cn

President: Zhong Nanshan

International Relations: Zhou Yuhong

Schools
Clinical Medicine (Medicine; Surgery); **Medical Imaging**; **Medical Technology** (Immunology; Medical Technology; Parasitology)

Degrees and Diplomas: *Bachelor's Degree*; *Master's Degree*

GUANGZHOU SPORT UNIVERSITY (GIPE)

458 Guangzhou North Avenue, Guangzhou, Guangdong Province 510076
Tel: +86(20) 87552071
Fax: +86(20) 87552071
EMail: linw2312@hotmail.com
Website: http://www.gipe.edu.cn

President: Xu Zongxiang

Departments
Graduate Studies; **Adult Education** (Adult Education); **Kinesiology and Science**; **Physical Education** (Physical Education); **Social Sciences**; **Sociology of Sports**; **Sports and Arts**; **Sports Training** (Sports); **Wushu** (Sports)

Research Centres
Sport Science

Further Information: Also Campus in Shenshen.

History: Founded 1958.

International Co-operation: With unversities in USA, Australia, Finland, Maylasia

Accrediting Agencies: Ministry of Education; National Sports Bureau

Degrees and Diplomas: *Bachelor's Degree*; *Master's Degree*

Student Services: Canteen, Sports facilities

Student Residential Facilities: Yes.

Publications: Academic Guangzhou Institute of Physical Education
Last Updated: 13/11/08

GUANGZHOU UNIVERSITY

248 Guangyuan Zhonglu, Guangzhou, Guangdong Province 510405
Tel: +86(20) 86394493
Fax: +86(20) 86370350
EMail: zhaosb@gzhu.edu.cn
Website: http://english.gzhu.edu.cn

President: Jian-she Yu

International Relations: Zhong Xiandong

Schools
Architecture and Urban Planning (Architecture; Environmental Studies; Landscape Architecture; Town Planning); **Art and Design**; **Biology and Chemical Engineering** (Biology; Chemical Engineering; Chemistry; Environmental Engineering); **Civil Engineering** (Building Technologies; Civil Engineering); **Economics and Management**; **Education**; **Foreign Studies**; **Humanities** (Arts and Humanities; Chinese; Communication Studies; History); **Information and Electromechanical Engineering** (Automation and Control Engineering; Computer Science; Electrical Engineering; Electronic Engineering; Mechanical Engineering); **Law** (Ethics; Law; Management; Political Sciences; Social Sciences); **Science** (Geography; Mathematics; Physics; Tourism)

History: Founded 2000, following merger of Guangzhou Normal University, South China Institute of Construction, Guangzhou University, Guangzhou Junior Teachers' College, and Guangzhou Institute of Education.

Degrees and Diplomas: *Bachelor's Degree*; *Master's Degree*; *Doctor's Degree*
Last Updated: 13/11/08

GUANGZHOU UNIVERSITY OF CHINESE MEDICINE

12 Jichang Road, Guangzhou, Guangdong Province 510405
Tel: +86(20) 86593715
Fax: +86(20) 86593715
EMail: xwsc@gzhtcm.edu.cn
Website: http://www.gzhtcm.edu.cn

President: Xu Zhiwei

Departments
Nursing (Nursing); **Social Sciences** (Social Sciences)

Schools
Acupuncture and Massage (Acupuncture; Physical Therapy); **Basic Medicine** (Medicine); **Chinese Pharmacology** (Pharmacology; Traditional Eastern Medicine); **Clinical Medicine** (Medicine); **Continuing Education**; **Management** (Management); **Traditional Chinese Medicine** (Affiliated)

History: Founded 1956 as Guangzhou College of Traditional Chinese Medicine, acquired present title 1995.

Degrees and Diplomas: Bachelor's Degree; Master's Degree; Doctor's Degree

Libraries: c. 630,000 vols

Publications: Education Survey of Traditional Chinese Medicine; Journal of Guangzhou University of Traditional Chinese Medicine; New Journal of Traditional Chinese Medicine; Traditional Chinese Drug Research
Last Updated: 13/11/08

GUILIN MEDICAL UNIVERSITY

109 Huancheng Road, Guilin, Guangxi Zhuang Province 541001
Tel: +86(773) 2822194
Fax: +86(773) 2822194
EMail: cie@glmc.edu.cn
Website: http://www.glmc.edu.cn

President: He Shuilin

International Relations: Luo Fang

Departments
Clinical Medicine (Medicine); **Pharmacy** (Pharmacy)

History: Founded 1935 as Guilin Advanced Nurse Midwives School, renamed Guilin Medical School in 1958, and in 1987 it was promoted Guilin Medical University.

Degrees and Diplomas: Bachelor's Degree; Master's Degree
Last Updated: 02/09/08

GUILIN UNIVERSITY OF ELECTRONIC TECHNOLOGY (GUET)

1 Jinji Road, Guilin, Guangxi Zhuang Province 541004
Tel: +86 (773) 5841372
Fax: +86(773) 5815683
EMail: oic@gliet.edu.cn
Website: http://www.gliet.edu.cn/

President: Mo Wei

International Relations: Yin Zhenhua

Departments
Computer Science and Applied Physics (Applied Physics; Computer Science); **Design** (Design); **Electronic Engineering**; **Electronic Machinery and Transportation Engineering** (Electrical and Electronic Equipment and Maintenance; Transport Engineering); **Management**; **Modern Languages** (Modern Languages); **Social Sciences** (Social Sciences); **Telecommunication and Information Engineering** (Information Sciences; Telecommunications Engineering)

Schools
Continuing Education; **Professional Higher Education**

International Co-operation: With universities in USA, Japan, Australia and European countries

Degrees and Diplomas: Bachelor's Degree; Master's Degree

GUILIN UNIVERSITY OF TECHNOLOGY (GUT)

12 Juangan Road, Guilin, Guangxi Zhuang Province 541004
Tel: +86 (773) 5896078
Fax: +86 (773) 5896078
EMail: fao@glite.edu.cn
Website: http://www.glite.edu.cn

President: Chen Dake

International Relations: Zhu Xiaom

Departments
Art Design (Design); **Civil Engineering** (Civil Engineering); **Computer Science and Technology** (Computer Science; Technology); **Foreign Languages** (Modern Languages); **International Programme**; **Material and Chemistry Engineering**; **Mathematics and Physics** (Mathematics; Physics); **Natural Resources and Environmental Sciences** (Environmental Engineering; Environmental Studies; Natural Resources); **Physical Education**; **Social Sciences** (Social Sciences)

Schools
Continuing Education; **Management**; **Professional Development**; **Tourism** (Tourism)

Further Information: University Clinic

History: Founded 1956 as Guilin College of Technology. Acquired present status and title 1997.

Accrediting Agencies: Ministry of Education

Degrees and Diplomas: Bachelor's Degree; Master's Degree

Special Facilities: Modern Educational Technology Centre. Geological Prospecting Institute; Geophysics Information Centre.

GUIYANG COLLEGE OF TRADITIONAL CHINESE MEDICINE

1 Shidong Road, Guiyang, Guizhou Province 550002
Tel: +86(851) 5928633
Fax: +86(851) 5926551
EMail: zjx@wanfangdata.com.cn

President: Jun Shenfeng

International Relations: Ying Shenghai

Programmes
Traditional Chinese Medicine (Traditional Eastern Medicine)

Degrees and Diplomas: Bachelor's Degree; Master's Degree; Doctor's Degree

GUIYANG MEDICAL UNIVERSITY

4 Beijing Road, Guiyang, Guizhou Province 550004
Tel: +86(851) 6783850
Fax: +86(851) 6783850
EMail: tina@publicl.gy.gz.cn
Website: http://www.gmc.edu.cn

President: Ren Xilin

International Relations: He Keyong

Schools
Clinical Medicine (Medicine); **Medical Laboratory** (Medical Technology); **Pharmacy** (Pharmacy); **Preventive Medicine** (Social and Preventive Medicine); **Social Sciences** (Social Sciences)

Degrees and Diplomas: Bachelor's Degree; Master's Degree

GUIZHOU INSTITUTE FOR NATIONALITIES

Huaxi, Guiyang, Guizhou Province 550025
Tel: +86(851) 3610498
Fax: +86(851) 3610498

President: Pan Shijun

International Relations: Wang Lian

Departments
Administration (Administration); **Chemistry** (Chemistry); **Chinese Language and Literature** (Chinese; Literature); **English** (English); **Fine Arts** (Fine Arts); **History** (History); **Law** (Law); **Management** (Management); **Mathematics** (Mathematics); **Native Language**

(Native Language); **Physical Education** (Physical Education); **Physics** (Physics); **Sociology** (Sociology); **Tourism** (Tourism)

Degrees and Diplomas: *Bachelor's Degree*; *Master's Degree*

GUIZHOU INSTITUTE OF FINANCE AND ECONOMICS

31 South Ruinin Road, Guiyang, Guizhou Province 550003
Tel: +86(851) 5964725
Fax: +86(851) 5970521

President: Zgong Yongxing

International Relations: Li Hua

Departments
Accountancy (Accountancy); **Economics** (Economics); **Finance** (Finance); **Industrial and Commercial Management** (Business Administration; Industrial Management; Management); **Social Sciences** (Social Sciences); **Statistics** (Statistics)

Degrees and Diplomas: *Bachelor's Degree*; *Master's Degree*

GUIZHOU NORMAL UNIVERSITY

270 Waihuandonglu, Guiyang, Guizhou Province 550001
Tel: +86(851) 6766891
Fax: +86(851) 6766891
EMail: gnufa@public.gz.cn
Website: http://www.gznu.edu.cn/english/index.htm

President: He Caihua Tel: +86(851) 6897028

Director: Xiaoming Xi Tel: +86(851) 6897020

International Relations: Linghu Rongfeng Tel: +86(851) 6766891

Departments
Biology (Biology); **Chemistry**; **Chinese** (Chinese); **Education** (Education; Educational Sciences; Psychology); **Foreign Languages** (English; Modern Languages; Russian); **Geology** (Geology); **History** (History); **Mathematics and Computer Science**; **Music**; **Painting** (Painting and Drawing); **Physical Education**; **Physics**; **Politics and Economics** (Economics; Law; Political Sciences); **Teacher Training** (Teacher Training)

History: Founded 1941 as Guiyang Teachers College, acquired present status 1985.

Admission Requirements: Graduation from high school and entrance examination

Main Language(s) of Instruction: Chinese

Accrediting Agencies: Ministry of Education

Degrees and Diplomas: *Bachelor's Degree*: 4 yrs; *Master's Degree*: a further 3 yrs

Student Services: Canteen, Employment services, Health services, Nursery care, Sports facilities

Libraries: c. 200,000 vols

Publications: Journal of Guizhou Normal University, Natural Sciences Edition; Journal of Guizhou Normal University, Social Sciences Edition

GUIZHOU UNIVERSITY

Huaxi, Guiyang, Guizhou Province 550025
Tel: +86(851) 3851187
Fax: +86(851) 3851187
EMail: fa@gzu.edu.cn
Website: http://www.gzu.edu.cn

President: Chen Shuping

International Relations: Jin Kejian

Colleges
Agriculture (Agronomy; Horticulture; Plant and Crop Protection); **Arts** (Dance; Design; Fine Arts; Music; Painting and Drawing; Theatre); **Chemical Engineering** (Bioengineering; Chemical Engineering; Food Science; Materials Engineering; Pharmacology); **Civil Engineering and Building Construction** (Architecture; Civil Engineering; Construction Engineering; Hydraulic Engineering; Industrial Design; Landscape Architecture; Town Planning; Transport Engineering); **Computer Science and Engineering**; **Economics**; **Electrical Engineering**; **Forestry**; **Humanities** (Arts and Humanities; Chinese; Cultural Studies; History; Journalism; Litera-

ture; Modern Languages; Philosophy; Tourism); **Information Engineering**; **International Studies** (English; Japanese; Literature); **Law** (Administration; Law; Political Sciences; Social Work); **Life Sciences** (Agriculture; Biotechnology; Ecology; Environmental Studies; Food Technology; Pharmacy); **Management**; **Mechanical Engineering and Automation** (Agricultural Engineering; Agricultural Equipment; Automation and Control Engineering; Industrial Engineering; Mechanical Engineering); **Mingde**; **Mining** (Construction Engineering; Mineralogy; Mining Engineering; Safety Engineering; Surveying and Mapping); **Resource and Environment Engineering**; **Science** (Applied Chemistry; Applied Mathematics; Chemistry; Computer Science; Information Sciences; Natural Sciences; Physics); **Science and Technology**; **Vocational Education** (Administration; Automation and Control Engineering; Business Administration; Chinese; Civil Engineering; Computer Engineering; E-Business/Commerce; English; Information Technology; Mechanical Engineering; Teacher Training); **Zoology** (Aquaculture; Veterinary Science; Zoology)

History: Founded 1902 as Guizhou Institute of Higher Learning. Merged with Guizhou People's University 1993, Guizhou Agricultural College, Guizhou Institute of Arts and Guizhou Agricultural Cadre-Training School 1997. Acquired present title 2004.

Academic Year: September to June (September-February; March-June)

Admission Requirements: Graduation from senior middle school and entrance examination

Main Language(s) of Instruction: Chinese

Degrees and Diplomas: *Bachelor's Degree*: 4 yrs; *Master's Degree*: a further 2 yrs; *Doctor's Degree*: 3 yrs

Student Residential Facilities: Yes

Special Facilities: Movie Studio

Libraries: 3.81m.vols.

Publications: Journal of Guizhou University, Social Sciences Edition; Journal of Guizhou University, Natural Sciences Edition *(quarterly)*; Journal of Moutain Agriculture and Biology; Social Science Journal *(quarterly)*

Last Updated: 18/09/08

GUIZHOU UNIVERSITY OF TECHNOLOGY

Guigang, Guizhou Province 550003
Tel: +86(851) 4731649
Fax: +86(851) 4731649
EMail: eao@gut.gy.gz.cn

President: Hu Guogen

International Relations: Fan Chaojun

Departments
Adult Education I; **Adult Education II**; **Architecture** (Architecture); **Basic Sciences** (Mathematics; Natural Sciences); **Chemical Engineering** (Chemical Engineering); **Civil Engineering** (Civil Engineering); **Computer Science** (Computer Science); **Electrical Engineering** (Electrical Engineering); **Foreign Languages** (Modern Languages); **Liberal Arts and Social Sciences** (Arts and Humanities; Social Sciences); **Light Industry** (Industrial Engineering); **Management** (Management); **Mechanical Engineering** (Mechanical Engineering); **Metallurgical Engineering** (Metallurgical Engineering); **Mining Engineering** (Mining Engineering); **Physical Education** (Physical Education); **Resources Engineering** (Engineering; Natural Resources); **Science Research**

History: Founded 1958 as Guizhou Institute of Technology, acquired present name 1996. Merged with Guizhou Construction Special School.

Degrees and Diplomas: *Bachelor's Degree*; *Master's Degree*

Libraries: c. 520,000 vols

Publications: Journal of Guizhou University of Technology

HAINAN MEDICAL COLLEGE

Xueyuan Avenue, Longhua Zone, Haikou, Hainan Province 570102
Tel: +86(898) 6772853
Fax: +86(898) 6764351
Website: http://www.hainmc.edu.cn/

President: Jiao Jiege

Faculties

Medicine (Medicine); **Pharmacology** (Pharmacology); **Pharmacy**

Degrees and Diplomas: *Bachelor's Degree*
Last Updated: 14/11/08

HAINAN NORMAL UNIVERSITY

Haikou, Hainan Province 571158
Tel: +86(898) 5884229 +86(898) 5882015
Fax: +86(898) 5883035
EMail: fjm@mail.hainnu.edu.cn
Website: http://www.hainnu.edu.cn

President: Lin Hezhong

International Relations: Feng Naibiao

Departments

Biology (Biology); **Chemistry** (Chemistry); **Chinese Language and Literature** (Chinese; Literature); **English** (English); **Fine Arts** (Fine Arts); **Geography** (Geography); **Mathematics** (Mathematics); **Pedagogy** (Pedagogy); **Physical Education** (Physical Education); **Physics** (Physics); **Political Science and Law** (Law; Political Sciences)

History: Founded 1949 as Hainan Teachers College. Acquired present status 1999.

Degrees and Diplomas: *Bachelor's Degree*
Last Updated: 02/09/08

HAINAN UNIVERSITY

58 Renmin Road, Haikou, Hainan Province 570228
Tel: +86(898) 6259705
Fax: +86(898) 6258369
EMail: cicehn@126.com
Website: http://www.hainu.edu.cn

President: Xu Xiangyuan

International Relations: Liu Jin

Departments

Adult Education; **English** (English); **Physical Education** (Physical Education)

Schools

Agronomy (Agronomy; Animal Husbandry; Veterinary Science); **Arts** (Arts and Humanities; Design; Fine Arts; Music); **Economics** (Accountancy; Economics; Finance; Industrial Management; International Business); **Information Sciences and Technology** (Computer Science; Electronic Engineering; Information Sciences; Technology); **Law** (Civil Law; Commercial Law; International Law; Law; Public Law); **Literature** (Chinese; English; Literature; Tourism); **Science and Technology** (Chemical Engineering; Construction Engineering; Mathematics and Computer Science; Mechanical Engineering; Natural Sciences; Technology)

History: Founded 1983.

Degrees and Diplomas: *Bachelor's Degree*

Libraries: c. 350,000 vols

Publications: School Journal of Hainan University, Social Science Edition; School Journal of Hainan University, Natural Sciences Edition

HANGZHOU DIANZI UNIVERSITY

Hangzhou, Zhejiang Province 310018
Tel: +86(571) 8809198
Fax: +86(571) 8077232
EMail: master@hziee.edu.cn
Website: http://www.hdu.edu.cn/english/

President: Yan Xiaolang

International Relations: Cheng Dexi

Schools

Automation; **Finance and Economics** (Accountancy; Finance; International Business; Management; Statistics); **Information Engineering** (Computer Education; Computer Science; Electronic Engineering; Information Technology; Technology; Telecommunications Engineering); **Mechanical and Electronic Engineering** (Electronic Engineering; Environmental Engineering;

Industrial Design; Mechanical Engineering); **Social Sciences and Arts** (Arts and Humanities; Mathematics Education; Modern Languages; Physical Education; Physics; Social Sciences)

History: Founded 1956 as Hangzhou School of Aviation. Renamed Hangzhou Institute of Electronic Engineering 1980. Acquired present title 2004.

Degrees and Diplomas: *Bachelor's Degree*; *Master's Degree*; *Doctor's Degree*

Libraries: c. 420,000 vols

HANSHAN NORMAL UNIVERSITY

Qiaodong, Chaozhou, Guangdong Province 521041
Tel: +86(768) 2300685
Fax: +86(768) 2312094
EMail: hs_xyb@hstc.edu.cn
Website: http://www.hstc.edu.cn

President: Tang Muzhong

International Relations: Wen Jianhui

Departments

Chemistry and Biology (Biology; Chemistry); **Chinese**; **English**; **Fine Arts** (Fine Arts); **Mathematics**; **Physical Education** (Physical Education); **Physics** (Physics); **Political Science and History** (History; Political Sciences)

History: Founded 1903.

Degrees and Diplomas: *Bachelor's Degree*
Last Updated: 14/11/08

HARBIN ENGINEERING UNIVERSITY

Wenmiao Street, Nangang District, Harbin, Heilongjiang Province
Tel: +86(451) 2519213
Fax: +86(451) 2530010
EMail: weilin@hrbeu.edu.cn
Website: http://www.hrbeu.edu.cn/

President: Liu Zhigang **EMail:** liuzhigang@hrbeu.edu.cn

Colleges

Automation (Automation and Control Engineering); **Civil Engineering** (Civil Engineering); **Computer Science and Technology** (Computer Science; Information Sciences); **Economics and Management** (Economics; Management); **Humanities and Social Sciences**; **Information and Communication Engineering** (Communication Studies; Electronic Engineering; Microelectronics); **Material Science and Chemical Engineering** (Applied Chemistry; Chemical Engineering; Environmental Engineering; Materials Engineering); **Mechanical and Electrical Engineering** (Electrical Engineering; Mechanical Engineering); **Nuclear Science and Technology** (Nuclear Engineering); **Power and Energy Engineering** (Energy Engineering; Power Engineering); **Science** (Applied Mathematics; Computer Science; Mathematics; Optical Technology); **Shipbuilding Engineering** (Marine Engineering; Naval Architecture); **Underwater Acoustics** (Sound Engineering (Acoustics); Water Science)

Departments

Foreign Languages (English; French; German; Japanese; Korean; Modern Languages; Russian)

History: Founded 1953 as Harbin Military Engineering Academy, acquired present title 1994.

Main Language(s) of Instruction: Chinese

Degrees and Diplomas: *Bachelor's Degree*; *Master's Degree*; *Doctor's Degree*

Libraries: c. 600,000 vols

Publications: Applied Science and Technology; Journal of Harbin Engineering University
Last Updated: 17/11/08

HARBIN INSTITUTE OF TECHNOLOGY (HIT)

92 West Dazhi Street, Nangang District, Harbin, Heilongjiang Province 150001
Tel: +86(451) 86413483
EMail: web@hit.edu.cn
Website: http://www.hit.edu.cn

President: Wang Shuguo Tel: +86(451) 6415886

Schools
Astronautics (Aeronautical and Aerospace Engineering; Automation and Control Engineering; Communication Studies; Electronic Engineering; Mechanical Engineering; Telecommunications Engineering); **Automobile Engineering** (Automotive Engineering; Economics; Information Technology; Management; Mechanical Engineering); **Civil Engineering and Architecture** (Architecture; Civil Engineering; Design); **Computer Science and Electrical Engineering** (Computer Science; Electrical Engineering); **Energy Science and Engineering** (Automation and Control Engineering; Automotive Engineering; Energy Engineering; Hydraulic Engineering); **Humanities and Social Sciences** (Arts and Humanities; Economics; Modern Languages; Philosophy; Political Sciences; Social Sciences; Sociology); **Management** (Business Administration; Economics; Finance; International Business; Management); **Materials Science and Engineering** (Materials Engineering; Metal Techniques; Technology); **Mechatronic Engineering** (Automation and Control Engineering; Measurement and Precision Engineering; Mechanical Engineering); **Science** (Applied Chemistry; Applied Physics; Biological and Life Sciences; Engineering; Mathematics; Natural Sciences)

Further Information: Also courses for foreign students

History: Founded 1920, as Sino-Russian Technical School of Harbin. Acquired present title 1938. Harbin University of Civil Engineering and Architecture incorporated 2000.

Academic Year: February to January (February-July; September-January)

Admission Requirements: Graduation from senior middle school and entrance examination

Fees: (Yuan): c. 1,500 per annum

Main Language(s) of Instruction: English, Russian, Japanese

Degrees and Diplomas: *Bachelor's Degree*: 4 yrs; *Master's Degree*: a further 2 yrs; *Doctor's Degree (PhD)*: a further 2-3 yrs

Student Services: Academic counselling, Canteen, Cultural centre, Employment services, Foreign student adviser, Health services, Social counselling, Sports facilities

Libraries: HIT Campus Library, c. 1.05m. vols

Publications: Higher Education Forum; Journal of HIT; Material Science and Technology
Last Updated: 14/11/08

HARBIN MEDICAL UNIVERSITY

157 Baojian Road, Nangang District, Harbin, Heilongjiang Province 150086
Tel: +86(451) 6669485
Fax: +86(451) 6669485
EMail: international@ems.hrbmu.edu.cn
Website: http://www.hrbmu.edu.cn

President: Yang Baofeng

Departments
Bioinformatics; **Humanities and Social Sciences** (Arts and Humanities; Social Sciences); **Sport** (Sports)

Schools
Basic Medicine (Medicine); **Health Management** (Health Administration); **Nursing**; **Pharmacy** (Pharmacy); **Public Health** (Public Health); **Stomatology** (Stomatology)

History: Founded 1926 as Harbin Medical College.

Main Language(s) of Instruction: Chinese

Degrees and Diplomas: *Bachelor's Degree*; *Master's Degree*; *Doctor's Degree*

Libraries: c. 880 vols
Last Updated: 17/11/08

HARBIN NORMAL UNIVERSITY (HNU)

50 Hexinglu, Nangang District, Harbin, Heilongjiang Province 150080
Tel: +86(451) 6315015
Fax: +86(451) 6305382
Website: http://www.hrbnu.edu.cn

President: Shutao Chen
Tel: +86(451) 637-6293, Fax: +86(451) 630-6654
EMail: xb@postoffice.hrbnu.edu.cn

Dean: Baiying Cao
Tel: +86(451) 6320946 EMail: xb@postoffice.hrbnu.edu.cn

International Relations: Dazhu Zhang
Tel: +86(451) 6328706 EMail: Dazhu_Zhang@yahoo.com

Programmes
Administration (Administration); **Biology** (Biology); **Chemistry** (Chemistry); **Chinese Language and Literature** (Chinese); **English Language and Literature** (English); **Fine Arts** (Fine Arts); **Geography** (Geography); **History** (History); **Japanese Language and Literature** (Japanese); **Mathematics** (Mathematics); **Music** (Music); **Physics** (Physics); **Political Education** (Political Sciences); **Russian Language and Literature** (Russian); **Teacher Training** (Preschool Education; Teacher Training)

Research Institutes
Ancient Chinese Books (Ancient Books; Chinese); **Biology** (Biology); **Chemistry** (Chemistry); **Chinese Border Area Economy** (Economics); **Chinese Language and Literature** (Chinese); **Educational Sciences** (Educational Sciences); **Environmental Sciences** (Environmental Studies); **Forestry Engineering** (Forestry); **High and New Technology Exploitation** (Technology); **History** (History); **Ideological and Political Education** (Political Sciences); **Northeast Asian Economics** (Economics); **Physical Education** (Physical Education); **Psychology** (Psychology); **Science Education** (Science Education); **Scientific Philosophy and Social Development** (Philosophy; Social Sciences)

History: Founded 1951, acquired present status 1980.

Admission Requirements: Graduation from senior middle school and entrance examination

Main Language(s) of Instruction: Chinese

International Co-operation: With universities in South Africa, Australia, Japan, Korea, Canada

Accrediting Agencies: Ministry of Education

Degrees and Diplomas: *Bachelor's Degree*: 4 yrs; *Master's Degree*: 3 yrs

Student Services: Academic counselling, Canteen, Cultural centre, Employment services, Foreign student adviser, Foreign Studies Centre, Health services, Language programs, Nursery care, Social counselling, Sports facilities

Special Facilities: Art Gallery, Movie Studio

Libraries: Main Library

Publications: Heilongjiang, Research on Higher Education *(bimonthly)*; Natural Science Journal of Harbin Normal University; The Northern Forum, Educational Scientific Research *(bimonthly)*

HARBIN UNIVERSITY

9 Xufusidaojie, Harbin, Heilongjiang Province 150086
Tel: +86(451) 6688516
Fax: +86(451) 6677510

Departments
Biology (Biology); **Chemistry** (Chemistry); **Chinese** (Chinese); **Computer Science** (Computer Science); **Construction Engineering** (Construction Engineering); **Crafts and Trades** (Crafts and Trades); **Food Technology** (Food Technology); **Geography** (Geography); **History**; **Management**; **Mathematics**; **Mechanics** (Mechanics); **Modern Languages** (Modern Languages); **Music** (Music); **Physical Education** (Physical Education); **Physics**; **Political Science** (Political Sciences); **Secretarial Studies**; **Textile Design**

History: Founded 1997.

HARBIN UNIVERSITY OF COMMERCE

138, Tong Da Street, Harbin, Heilongjiang Province 150076
Tel: +86(451) 84603228
Fax: +86(451) 4601086
EMail: YZS@hrbcu.edu.cn
Website: http://www.hljcu.edu.cn

President: Yan Zesheng

Colleges

Accountancy (Accountancy); **Business Administration** (Business Administration; Human Resources; Marketing); **Civil Engineering and Refrigeration Engineering** (Civil Engineering; Engineering Management; Heating and Refrigeration); **Computer and Information Engineering** (Computer Engineering; Computer Science; Electronic Engineering); **Economics** (E-Business/Commerce; Economics; International Business; Statistics); **Finance**; **Food Engineering** (Bioengineering; Environmental Engineering; Food Science; Food Technology); **Foreign Language** (English; Modern Languages); **Foundation Science** (Journalism); **Law** (Law); **Light Industry** (Automation and Control Engineering; Industrial Engineering; Packaging Technology; Printing and Printmaking); **Medicine**; **Public Finance and Public Administration**; **Tourism and Cuisine** (Cooking and Catering; Tourism)

History: Founded 1952 as Heilongjiang Commercial University. Acquired present title 2000.

Main Language(s) of Instruction: Chinese

Degrees and Diplomas: *Bachelor's Degree*; *Master's Degree*; *Doctor's Degree*
Last Updated: 17/11/08

HARBIN UNIVERSITY OF SCIENCE AND TECHNOLOGY

52 Xuefu Road, Harbin, Heilongjiang Province 150080
Tel: +86(451) 86390081
Fax: +86(451) 86390866
EMail: public@hrbust.edu.cn
Website: http://www.hrbust.edu.cn/

President: Deng Zhongxing

International Relations: Zhao Weihua

Colleges

Management (Accountancy; Business Administration; Economics; International Economics; Management; Marketing)

Schools

Applied Sciences (Applied Chemistry; Applied Physics; Computer Science; Electronic Engineering; Information Technology); **Computer Science and Control Engineering** (Automation and Control Engineering; Computer Science); **Electrical and Electronic Engineering** (Automation and Control Engineering; Electrical and Electronic Engineering; Information Technology); **Humanities and Social Sciences**; **Industrial Technology**; **Instrument and Apparatus** (Measurement and Precision Engineering; Safety Engineering); **Materials Science and Engineering** (Engineering; Inorganic Chemistry; Materials Engineering; Polymer and Plastics Technology); **Mechanical and Power Engineering** (Automation and Control Engineering; Industrial Design; Machine Building; Mechanical Engineering; Power Engineering)

History: Founded 1958, as Heilongjiang Institute of Engineering. Acquired present status and title 1978.

Academic Year: September to July (September-January; February-July)

Admission Requirements: Graduation from senior middle school and entrance examination

Main Language(s) of Instruction: Chinese

Accrediting Agencies: Ministry of Machinery and Electronics

Degrees and Diplomas: *Bachelor's Degree*: 4 yrs; *Master's Degree*: a further 2 1/2-3 yrs; *Doctor's Degree*

Libraries: c. 790,000 vols

Publications: Journal of Electric Motor and Control; Journal of Harbin University of Science and Technology

HEBEI INSTITUTE OF ARCHITECTURE AND CIVIL ENGINEERING

33 Jiangguo Road, Zhangjiakou, Hebei Province 075024
Tel: +86(313) 2050803
Fax: +86(313) 20106I26
EMail: netcenter@hebiace.edu.cn
Website: http://www.hebiace.edu.cn

Departments

Architecture (Architecture); **Civil Engineering** (Civil Engineering); **Computer Science** (Computer Science); **Construction Engineering** (Construction Engineering); **Management**; **Mechanical Engineering** (Automation and Control Engineering; Industrial Engineering; Mechanical Engineering)

History: Founded 1950, acquired present name 1978.

Degrees and Diplomas: *Bachelor's Degree*
Last Updated: 02/09/08

HEBEI INSTITUTE OF PHYSICAL EDUCATION

82 Wuqi Road, Shijiazhuang, Hebei Province 050041
Tel: +86(311) 6839961
Fax: +86(311) 6839726
EMail: intl@mail.hepec.edu.cn
Website: http://www.hepec.edu.cn

President: Sun Banjun

Faculties

English (English); **Human Sports and Exercise Science**; **Physical Education** (Physical Education); **Social Sports**; **Sports Training** (Sports Management; Teacher Training); **Traditional Sport Education** (Natives Education)

Schools

Sports (Sports)

History: Founded 1984.

Degrees and Diplomas: *Bachelor's Degree*
Last Updated: 17/11/08

HEBEI MEDICAL UNIVERSITY

361 Zhongshan East Road, Shijiazhuang, Hebei Province 050017
Tel: +86(311) 6048177
Fax: +86(311) 6048177
EMail: webmaster@hebmu.edu.cn
Website: http://www.hebmu.edu.cn

President: Wen Jinkun

Departments

Foreign Languages (Modern Languages); **Social Sciences and Humanities** (Arts and Humanities; Social Sciences)

Schools

Basic Medical Sciences (Medicine); **Clinical Medicine** *(Second)*; **Clinical Medicine** *(First)*; **Clinical Medicine** *(Third)* (Medicine); **Clinical Medicine** *(Fourth)* (Medicine); **Public Health** (Public Health; Social and Preventive Medicine); **Stomatology** (Stomatology); **Traditional Chinese Clinical Medicine** (Acupuncture; Medicine; Pharmacology; Traditional Eastern Medicine)

History: Founded 1915. Merged with Hebei College of Traditional Chinese Medicine and Shijiazhuang Medical College.

Main Language(s) of Instruction: Chinese

Degrees and Diplomas: *Bachelor's Degree*; *Master's Degree*; *Doctor's Degree*

Libraries: c. 600,000 vols

Publications: Journal of Hebei Medical University
Last Updated: 17/11/08

HEBEI NORMAL UNIVERSITY

113 Yuhua Dong Road, Shijiazhuang, Hebei Province 050016
Tel: +86(311) 6049941
Fax: +86(311) 6049413
EMail: HNUIO@sina.com
Website: http://www.hebtu.edu.cn

President: Wang Lichen

International Relations: Xue Xianlin

Schools

Educational Sciences (Educational Sciences); **Foreign Languages** (Modern Languages); **Physical Education** (Physical Education); **Political Science and Management** (Management; Political Sciences); **Resources and Environmental Science** (Environmental Studies; Natural Resources); **Vocational Education**

History: Founded 1902 as school. Acquired present status and title 1996 following merge of Hebei Teachers University, Hebei Teachers College, Hebei Education Institute established in 1952 and Hebei Vocational and Technological College. Under the jurisdiction of the Provincial Government.

Academic Year: August to July (August-January; February-July)

Admission Requirements: Graduation from high school and entrance examination

Main Language(s) of Instruction: Chinese

Degrees and Diplomas: *Bachelor's Degree*; *Master's Degree*: a further 3 yrs; *Doctor's Degree*

Student Residential Facilities: Yes

Special Facilities: Plant Garden. Art Gallery 'Yihai'

Libraries: c. 2,1m. vols

Publications: Journal of Hebei Normal University, Educational Science, Social Sciences, Natural Sciences *(quarterly)*; Social Sciences Information of Higher Learning Institution; Thought and Wisdom
Last Updated: 17/11/08

HEBEI NORMAL UNIVERSITY OF SCIENCE AND TECHNOLOGY

360 West Hebei Street, Qinhuangdao, Hebei,
Hebei Province 066000
Tel: +86(335) 2039083
Fax: +86(335) 2024487
EMail: sxwcn@sohu.com
Website: http://www.hevttc.edu.cn

Departments
Accounting (Accountancy); **Agronomy**; **Animal Science** (Zoology); **Architecture** (Architecture); **Business Administration** (Business Administration); **Chinese** (Chinese); **Computer Science** (Computer Science); **Economy and Trade** (Business and Commerce; Economics); **Food Engineering** (Food Technology); **Foreign Languages** (Modern Languages); **Horticulture**; **Life Science** (Biological and Life Sciences); **Mathematics and Physics**; **Mechanics and Electronics** (Electronic Engineering; Mechanical Engineering); **Physical Education**; **Social Sciences** (Social Sciences)

History: Founded 1941 as Changli Agro-vocational School. Merged with Qinhuangdao Coal-Industry Management School. Acquired present title 2003.

Degrees and Diplomas: *Bachelor's Degree*

Libraries: c. 535,000 vols.

Publications: Journal of Hebei Normal Normal University of Science and Technology; Journal of Normal University of Science and Technology

HEBEI NORTH UNIVERSITY

14 Changqing Road, Zhangjiakou, Hebei Province 075000
Tel: +86(313) 8032544
Fax: +86(313) 8032544
EMail: gulinu888@yahoo.com.cn
Website: http://www.lieniu.net/hebeinu/homepage.htm

President: Xi Xiaoxian

International Relations: Zhang Mingzhu

Faculties
Agronomy; **Anesthetics** (Anaesthesiology); **Basic Medical Science** (Laboratory Techniques; Medicine); **First Clinical Medicine** (Medicine); **Forensic Medicine** (Forensic Medicine and Dentistry); **Horticulture** (Horticulture); **Veterinary Science** (Veterinary Science)

History: Founded 2003 through merger between Zhangjiakou Medical College (founded 1945), Zhangjiakou Teachers Training College and Zhangjiakou Advanced Postsecondary Agriculture School.

Main Language(s) of Instruction: Chinese

Degrees and Diplomas: *Bachelor's Degree*
Last Updated: 11/09/08

HEBEI POLYTECHNIC UNIVERSITY

46 Xinhua Xidao, Tangshan, Hebei Province 063009
Tel: +86(315) 2592044 +86(315) 2594051
Fax: +86(315) 2592044
EMail: international@heut.edu.cn
Website: http://international.heut.edu.cn/

President: Zhang Yushu

International Relations: Shen Zhiyong

Colleges
Arts (Arts and Humanities; Fine Arts); **Chemical Engineering and Biological Technology** (Biotechnology; Chemical Engineering); **Civil and Architectural Engineering** (Architecture; Civil Engineering); **Computer and Automatic Control** (Automation and Control Engineering; Computer Engineering); **Continuing Education** (Continuing Education); **Economics and Management**; **Foreign Languages** (Modern Languages); **Humanities and Law** (Arts and Humanities; Law); **Information** (Information Sciences); **Light Industry**; **Materials Science and Engineering** (Materials Engineering); **Mechnaical Engineering** (Mechanical Engineering); **Metallurgy and Energy** (Energy Engineering; Metallurgical Engineering); **Physical Education** (Physical Education); **Resources and Environment** (Environmental Studies; Natural Resources); **Science** (Natural Sciences); **Transportation and Mapping** (Surveying and Mapping; Transport and Communications)

Schools
Graduate Studies

History: Founded 1958 as Tangshan Metallurgical College. Changed name 2004.

Degrees and Diplomas: *Bachelor's Degree*; *Master's Degree*
Last Updated: 17/11/08

HEBEI UNIVERSITY

No.180, Wusidong Road, Baoding, Hebei Province 071002
Tel: +86(312) 5079533
Fax: +86(312) 5022648
EMail: webmaster@mail.hbu.edu.cn
Website: http://www.hbu.edu.cn

President: Wang Hongrui

International Relations: Guo Xianting

Schools
Commerce and Business Administration (Business Administration; Business and Commerce); **Computer Science** (Computer Science); **Economics** (Economics); **Electronic Engineering** (Electronic Engineering); **Foreign Languages** (Modern Languages)

Further Information: Also branch in Qinhuangdao City

History: Founded 1921, as University of Industry and Commerce of Tianjin. Acquired present title 1960.

Academic Year: August to July (August-January; March-July)

Admission Requirements: Graduation from senior middle school and entrance examination

Main Language(s) of Instruction: Chinese

Degrees and Diplomas: *Bachelor's Degree*: 4 yrs; *Master's Degree*: a further 2 yrs; *Doctor's Degree*

Student Residential Facilities: Yes

Special Facilities: Chinese Cultural Relics Gallery

Libraries: c. 1,7m. vols

Publications: Bulletin of Physics; Hebei Higher Education Study; Hebei Science and Technology Library Journal; Japanese Study; Journal of Hebei University, Science and Arts

Press or Publishing House: Hebei University Press
Last Updated: 17/11/08

HEBEI UNIVERSITY OF ECONOMICS AND BUSINESS

47 Wuqi Road, Shijiazhuang, Hebei province 050061
Tel: +86(311) 7655607
Fax: +86(311) 6821614
EMail: huebfao@heuet.edu.cn
Website: http://www.heuet.edu.cn

President: Yu Rengang

International Relations: Cheng Jian

Departments

Banking (Banking); **Commerce** (Business and Commerce); **Economics** (Economics); **Finance** (Finance); **Food Engineering**; **Foreign Languages**; **Foreign Trade**; **Industrial and Business Management**; **Labour and Personnel Management**; **Public Relations and Secretarial Studies**; **Statistics**

History: Founded 1995. Merged with Hebei Institute of Economics and Trade, Hebei Institute of Finance and Economics and Hebei Higher Training School of Commerce.

Degrees and Diplomas: *Bachelor's Degree; Master's Degree*

Libraries: c. 700,000 vols

Publications: Economy and Management; Journal of Hebei University of Economics and Trade

HEBEI UNIVERSITY OF ENGINEERING

199 Guangming Nanjie, Handan, Hebei Province 056038
Tel: +86(310) 8579017
EMail: xingyongfang@yahoo.com.cn
Website: http://www.hebeu.edu.cn/en/index.php

President: Zhanzhou Liu

Schools

Agriculture (Agriculture); **Architecture** (Architecture; Town Planning); **Civil Engineering** (Civil Engineering; Transport Engineering); **Economics and Management** (Economics; Management); **Humanities** (Chinese; English; Law; Literature); **Hydraulic Engineering** (Hydraulic Engineering); **Information Sciences and Electronics** (Electronic Engineering; Information Sciences); **Mechanical and Electrical Engineering** (Electrical Engineering; Mechanical Engineering); **Medicine** (Medicine); **Natural Sciences** (Natural Sciences); **Resource Science** (Natural Resources); **Urban Construction** (Building Technologies; Environmental Engineering)

History: Founded 2003 following the amalgamation of Hebei Institute of Architectural Science and Technology, North China Institute of Water Conservancy and Hydro-electric Power, Handan Medicine College and Handan Agriculture College. Acquired present name 2006.

Degrees and Diplomas: *Bachelor's Degree; Master's Degree*
Last Updated: 17/11/08

HEBEI UNIVERSITY OF SCIENCE AND TECHNOLOGY

186 Yuhua East Road, Shijiazhuang, Hebei Province 050018
Tel: +86(311) 8632113
Fax: +86(311) 7882887
EMail: waiban@hebust.edu.cn
Website: http://www.hebust.edu.cn

President: Lu Changfu

International Relations: Yu Shuqiu

Colleges

Architecture Engineering (Architectural and Environmental Design; Civil Engineering); **Art** (Design; Sound Engineering (Acoustics)); **Bioengineering** (Bioengineering; Biotechnology; Food Science); **Chemical Engineering** (Chemical Engineering; Pharmacy); **Economics and Management** *(Huazheng)* (Business Administration; E-Business/Commerce; Finance; Industrial Engineering; Management; Marketing); **Electrical Engineering** (Automation and Control Engineering; Electrical Engineering); **Environmental Engineering** (Environmental Engineering; Safety Engineering; Water Science); **Foreign Languages** (Modern Languages); **Humanities and Social Sciences** (Chinese; Journalism; Law; Literature; Social Work); **Information** (Computer Networks; Computer Science; Software Engineering); **Mechanical Engineering** (Industrial Design; Mechanical Engineering); **Science** (Applied Mathematics; Applied Physics; Engineering; Information Sciences; Mathematics; Mechanical Engineering); **Textile Engineering** (Textile Design)

History: Founded 1996.

Degrees and Diplomas: *Bachelor's Degree*

Libraries: c. 700,000 vols

Publications: Hebei Industrial Science & Technology; Higher Education Study; Journal of Hebei University of Science and Technology
Last Updated: 17/11/08

HEBEI UNIVERSITY OF TECHNOLOGY (HUT)

No 8 Guangrongdao Dingzigu, Hongi Qiao District, Tianjin, Tianjin Province 300130
Tel: +86(22) 26564069
Fax: +86(22) 26545303
EMail: fao@hebut.edu.cn
Website: http://www.hebut.edu.cn

President: Feng Gao (2002-)
Tel: +86(22) 26564072, Fax: +86(22) 26564072
EMail: fengg@hebut.edu.cn

Vice-President: Hexu Sun
Tel: +86(22) 26564060, Fax: +86(22) 26564060

International Relations: Zhen Wei, Director, Foreign Affairs Office
Tel: +86(22) 26564069

Research Centres

Magnetic Technology and Magnetic Materials *(Hebei Provincial)* *Dean*: Weili Yan; **Material Research** *(Hebei Provincial)* *Dean*: Weilian Zhang; **Power Station Equipment** *(Hebei Provincial)* (Power Engineering) *Dean*: Fangquan Yao

Research Institutes

Applied Research Base for Electromagnetic Field and Electrical Engineering Products Reliability *(Hebei Provincial)* (Electrical and Electronic Engineering) *Dean*: Weili Yan; **Electrical Apparatus** *(Hebei Provincial)* (Electrical Engineering; Machine Building) *Dean*: Jianguo Lu; **Electromagnetic Field and Electrical Apparatus Reliability** *(Hebei Provincial)* *Dean*: Qingxin Yang; **Mechatronics Engineering and Technology** *(Hebei Provincial)* (Automation and Control Engineering; Mechanical Engineering; Technology) *Dean*: Runhua Tan

Research Laboratories

Electrical Apparatus *(Hebei Provincial)* *Dean*: Jianguo Lu; **Green Chemical and High Efficiency and Energy Saving Engineering** *(Hebei Provincial)* (Chemical Engineering; Chemistry; Physics) *Dean*: Yanji Wang; **New Function Material** *(Hebei Provincial)* (Chemistry; Physics) *Dean*: Chunxiang Cui

Schools

Architecture and Artistic Design (Architecture; Industrial Design; Town Planning) *Dean*: Yi Xue; **Chemical Engineering** (Applied Chemistry; Bioengineering; Chemical Engineering; Marine Engineering; Polymer and Plastics Technology; Safety Engineering) *Dean*: Yanji Wang; **Civil Engineering** (Bridge Engineering; Civil Engineering; Construction Engineering; Geological Engineering; Road Engineering; Transport Engineering) *Dean*: Yuanming Dou; **Computer Science and Software** (Computer Networks; Computer Science; Software Engineering) *Dean*: Ming Yu; **Continuing Education** *Dean*: Yun Dong; **Electrical Engineering and Automation** (Automation and Control Engineering; Biomedical Engineering; Electrical Engineering) *Dean*: Peng Yang; **Energy and Environmental Engineering** (Energy Engineering; Environmental Engineering; Thermal Engineering) *Dean*: Xiuchun Wang; **Foreign Languages** (English; French; Japanese; Modern Languages) *Dean*: Dayong Liu; **Graduate Studies** *Dean*: Bo Liu; **Humanities and Law** (Arts and Humanities; Labour and Industrial Relations; Law) *Dean*: Tun Bai; **Information** (Communication Studies; Data Processing; Electronic Engineering; Information Management; Information Technology) *Dean*: Ruixia Yang; **Management** (Business Administration; Economics; Finance; Industrial Engineering; Industrial Management; Information Management; International Business; International Economics; Management; Marketing) *Dean*: Yunfeng Wang; **Materials Science and Engineering** (Materials Engineering; Physics) *Dean*: Chunxiang Cui; **Mechanical Engineering** (Automation and Control Engineering; Automotive Engineering; Measurement and Precision Engineering; Mechanical Engineering) *Dean*: Minglu Zhang; **Public Administration** *(City School)* *Dean*: Bing Li; **Science** (Applied Mathematics; Applied Physics; Computer Science; Information Sciences; Mathematics) *Dean*: Guoxin Liu

History: Founded 1903, acquired present status and title 1995.

Admission Requirements: Senior high school certificate and National College entrance examination

Fees: (Yuan): 5,000 per annum

Main Language(s) of Instruction: Chinese

International Co-operation: With universities in Finland; Germany; France; USA; United Kingdom; Russian Federation; Spain; Sweden; Japan

Accrediting Agencies: Ministry of Education; State Education Commission

Degrees and Diplomas: *Bachelor's Degree*: 4 yrs; *Master's Degree*: a further 2 1/2-3 yrs; *Doctor's Degree*: 3 yrs following Master

Student Services: Canteen, Employment services, Foreign student adviser, Foreign Studies Centre, Health services, Sports facilities

Student Residential Facilities: Yes

Libraries: Yes

Publications: Journal of Hebei University of Technology (bimonthly)

Last Updated: 17/11/08

HEFEI UNIVERSITY

37 Huangshan Road, Hefei, Anhui Province 230022
Tel: +86(551) 3634779
Fax: +86(551) 3635969
EMail: yzxx@hfuu.edu.cn
Website: http://www.hfuu.edu.cn/

President: Zhao Liangqing

Departments
Chemical Engineering (Chemical Engineering); **Chinese** (Chinese); **Computer Engineering** (Computer Engineering); **Economics** (Economics); **Foreign Languages and Literature** (Literature; Modern Languages); **Fundamentals; Information Technology** (Information Technology); **Mechanical Engineering** (Mechanical Engineering); **Professional Education; Tourism** (Tourism)

History: Founded 1980. Acquired present title 2002 following merger of Hefei Union University and Hefei Education College.

Degrees and Diplomas: *Bachelor's Degree*

Libraries: c. 130,000 vols

Publications: Hefei Union University Journal
Last Updated: 18/11/08

HEFEI UNIVERSITY OF TECHNOLOGY

193 Tunxi Road, Hefei, Anhui Province 230009
Tel: +86 (551) 4658410
Fax: +86 (551) 4658410
EMail: webmaster@hfut.edu.cn
Website: http://www.hfut.edu.cn

President: Chen Xinzhao
International Relations: Fang Yi

Departments
Architecture (Architecture); **Food Engineering** (Food Science); **Precision Instruments** (Measurement and Precision Engineering)

Schools
Chemical Engineering (Chemical Engineering); **Civil Engineering** (Civil Engineering); **Computer Science and Information Engineering** (Computer Science; Information Technology); **Electrical Engineering** (Electrical Engineering); **Finance and Economics** (Economics; Finance); **Humanities** (Advertising and Publicity; Arts and Humanities; Economics; English; Finance; International Economics; Law; Political Sciences); **Machinery and Automobile Engineering** (Automotive Engineering; Industrial Engineering; Machine Building; Power Engineering); **Management; Materials Science and Engineering** (Materials Engineering); **Resources and Environmental Engineering** (Environmental Engineering; Natural Resources); **Science** (Mathematics and Computer Science; Natural Sciences)

History: Founded 1945 as Bengbu Advanced Industry Vocational School. Acquired present title 1958 and incorporated Anhui Institute of Technology 1997.

Degrees and Diplomas: *Bachelor's Degree*; *Master's Degree*; *Doctor's Degree*

Libraries: c. 1.7m. Vols

Publications: Engineering Mathematics; Forecasting; Journal of Hefei University of Technology, Natural Sciences Edition, Social Sciences Edition; Operation and Management

Last Updated: 18/11/08

HEILONGJIANG BAYI AGRICULTURAL UNIVERSITY

Mishan, Heilongjiang Province 158308
Tel: +86(453) 5070010
Fax: +86(453) 5070015
EMail: skywang2006@yahoo.com.cn
Website: http://www.hlau.cn

President: Xu Mei
International Relations: Liu Fengjun

Schools
Animal Science and Technology (Computer Science; Food Science; Social Sciences; Veterinary Science; Zoology); **Economics and Trade** (Accountancy; Business and Commerce; Economics; Management; Statistics); **Engineering** (Architectural and Environmental Design; Automation and Control Engineering; Engineering); **Plant Science and Technology** (Environmental Engineering; Plant and Crop Protection; Plant Pathology; Technology); **Polytechnic**

History: Founded 1958 as HeiLongJiang August First Land Reclamation University.

Academic Year: March to January (March-July; September-January)

Admission Requirements: Graduation from senior middle school

Main Language(s) of Instruction: Chinese

Accrediting Agencies: Department of Agriculture

Degrees and Diplomas: *Bachelor's Degree*; *Master's Degree*

Libraries: Central Library, c. 260,000 vols

Publications: Journal of Heilongjiang August 1st Land Reclamation University

Press or Publishing House: Nong Da Press

HEILONGJIANG EAST UNIVERSITY

331 Xuefu Road, Nangang District, Harbin, Heilongjiang Province 150086
Tel: +86(451) 6686926
Fax: +86(451) 6684071
EMail: yzbgs@mail.dfxy.net
Website: http://www.dfxy.net

Departments
Accounting (Accountancy); **Applied Arts** (Fine Arts; Technology); **Architectural Design and Engineering** (Architectural and Environmental Design; Structural Architecture); **Arts and Crafts** (Handicrafts); **Business Administration** (Business Administration); **Computer Science and Engineering** (Computer Science; Engineering); **Food Engineering** (Food Science); **Tourism Management** (Tourism)

History: Founded 1993. Acquired present title 1995.

Degrees and Diplomas: *Bachelor's Degree*

Libraries: c. 255,000 vols.

HEILONGJIANG INSTITUTE OF SCIENCE AND TECHNOLOGY

32 Nanxing Street, Jiguan District, Jixi, Heilongjiang Province 158105
Tel: +86(453) 2385022
Fax: +86(453) 2385022
EMail: shuchun@hr.hl.cn
Website: http://www.usth.edu.cn

President: Xing Zhongguang
International Relations: Sun Guoyu

Departments

Automotive Engineering; **Civil Engineering** (Civil Engineering); **Computer Engineering**; **Economics** (Economics); **Natural Resources and Environemental Engineering** (Environmental Engineering; Natural Resources); **Social Sciences** (Social Sciences)

History: Founded 1981 as Heilongjiang Mining Institute. Acquired present status and title 2000.

Degrees and Diplomas: *Bachelor's Degree*

HEILONGJIANG UNIVERSITY

74 Xuefu Road, Harbin, Heilongjiang Province 150080
Tel: +86(451) 6684740
Fax: +86(451) 6665470
EMail: wslb@hlju.edu.cn
Website: http://www.hlju.edu.cn

President: Yi Junqing

International Relations: Zhang Xiaoguang

Schools

Chemistry and Chemical Engineering (Chemical Engineering; Chemistry); **Economics** (Accountancy; Economics; International Economics); **Experimentation**; **Foreign Languages** (English; Modern Languages; Oriental Languages; Russian); **International Cultural Education** (International and Comparative Education); **Law** (Commercial Law; Economics; Law); **Vocational** (Automation and Control Engineering; Bioengineering; Chinese; Computer Science; Electronic Engineering; History; Information Management; Mathematics; Philosophy)

History: Founded 1941 as Russian Military School, acquired present status and title 1958 and incorporated Harbin Institute of Foreign Languages 1972. Under the jurisdiction of the Provincial Government.

Academic Year: September to July (September-January; March-July)

Admission Requirements: Graduation from senior middle school and entrance examination

Main Language(s) of Instruction: Chinese

Degrees and Diplomas: *Bachelor's Degree*; *Master's Degree*; *Doctor's Degree*

Student Residential Facilities: Yes

Libraries: c. 840,000 vols

Publications: Higher Education Studies; Journal of Foreign Languages *(bimonthly)*; Journal of Natural Sciences *(quarterly)*

HEILONGJIANG UNIVERSITY OF CHINESE MEDICINE

24 Heping Road, Harbin, Heilongjiang Province 150040
Tel: +86(451) 2112786
Fax: +86(451) 2112786
EMail: hljutcm@yahoo.com.cn
Website: http://www.admissions.cn/hljucm/index24.htm

President: Kuang Hai

Schools

Acupuncture and Tuina (Acupuncture); **Basic Medicine** (Medicine); **Clinical Medicine** (Orthopaedics; Traditional Eastern Medicine); **Pharmacy** (Pharmacy)

History: Founded 1959 as Heilongjiang Provincial Advanced College for Medical Staff. Acquired present status 1996.

Degrees and Diplomas: *Bachelor's Degree*; *Master's Degree*; *Doctor's Degree*

Libraries: c. 190,000 vols

Publications: Information on Traditional Chinese Medicine; Journal of Acupuncture Clinic; Journal of Traditional Medicine
Last Updated: 18/11/08

HENAN AGRICULTURAL UNIVERSITY

95 Wenhua Road, Zhengzhou, Henan Province 450002
Tel: +86(371) 3943524
Fax: +86(371) 3921072
EMail: 63558627@163.com
Website: http://www.henau.edu.cn

President: Wang Yanling

Schools

Agronomy (Agronomy; Genetics; Plant Pathology; Soil Science); **Animal Husbandry and Veterinary Science** (Animal Husbandry; Veterinary Science; Zoology); **Basic Science** (Chemistry; Physics); **Bioengineering** (Bioengineering; Food Science; Food Technology; Microbiology; Plant Pathology); **Economics** (Economics; Management); **Forestry and Horticulture** (Environmental Management; Forestry; Horticulture; Landscape Architecture); **Humanities and Social Sciences** (Arts and Humanities; Foreign Languages Education; Social Sciences); **Mechanical and Electronic Engineering** (Agricultural Equipment; Electronic Engineering; Information Management; Mechanical Engineering; Rural Planning)

History: Founded 1913 as Henan Agricultural Specialized School. Acquired present title 1984.

Degrees and Diplomas: *Bachelor's Degree*; *Master's Degree*; *Doctor's Degree*

Libraries: c. 660,000 vols

Publications: Acta Agriculturae Universitie Henanensis
Last Updated: 18/11/08

HENAN NORMAL UNIVERSITY

148 Eastern Jianshe Road, Xinxiang, Henan Province 453002
Tel: +86(373) 3383000 Ext. 5269
Fax: +86(373) 3383145
EMail: president@htu.cn
Website: http://www.henannu.edu.cn

President: Liucheng Jiao

Colleges

Chemistry and Environmental Sciences (Chemical Engineering; Chemistry; Environmental Engineering); **Economics and Management** (Economics; Industrial Management; International Business; Marketing); **Life Sciences**; **Literature**; **Mathematics and Information Sciences** (Information Sciences; Mathematics); **Physical Education** (Physical Education); **Physics and Information Engineering** (Educational Technology; Electronic Engineering; Physics); **Politics and Management Science** (Management; Political Sciences); **Social Development**

Departments

Computer Science (Computer Science); **Fine Arts** (Fine Arts); **Law** (Law); **Music** (Music); **Public Relations** (Public Relations); **Secretarial Studies** (Secretarial Studies)

History: Founded 1923 as Zhongzhou University. Acquired present title 1985.

Main Language(s) of Instruction: Chinese

Degrees and Diplomas: *Bachelor's Degree*; *Master's Degree*

Publications: Journal of Hernan Normal University
Last Updated: 18/11/08

HENAN POLYTECHNIC UNIVERSITY

No.2001, Century Avenue, Jiaozuo City, Henan Province 454003
Tel: +86(391) 2930003
Fax: +86(391) 2923353
EMail: President@hpu.edu.cn
Website: http://www.hpu.edu.cn/english/NewsEvents.asp

President: Wang Shao-an

Departments

Foreign Languages (Modern Languages); **Physical Education** (Physical Education); **Physics and Chemistry** (Chemistry; Physics)

Schools

Electrical Engineering and Automation; **Civil Engineering** (Civil Engineering); **Computer Science and Technology**; **Economic Management** (Economics); **Energy Science and Engineering**;

Humanities and Social Sciences (Arts and Humanities; Social Sciences); **Materials Science and Engineering** (Materials Engineering); **Mathematics and Information Science** (Information Sciences; Mathematics); **Mechanics and Power Engineering** (Mechanical Engineering; Power Engineering); **Resources and Environmental Engineering** (Environmental Engineering; Natural Resources); **Safety Science and Engineering**; **Surveying and Land Information Engineering** (Surveying and Mapping)

History: Founded 1909 as Jiaozuo Coal Mining School. Acquired present title 2004.

Main Language(s) of Instruction: Chinese

Degrees and Diplomas: *Bachelor's Degree*; *Master's Degree*; *Doctor's Degree*
Last Updated: 18/11/08

HENAN UNIVERSITY (HNU)

85 Minglun Street, Kaifeng, Henan Province 475001
Tel: +86(378) 2862311 +86(378) 2825161
Fax: +86(378) 8857224 +86(378) 2861029
EMail: hnufao@public.zz.ha.cn
Website: http://www.henu.edu.cn

President: Ai-he Guan (2001-)
Tel: +86(378) 2861125 EMail: gah@henu.edu.cn

International Relations: Fang Wenchang
Tel: +86(378) 2869090, Fax: +86(378) 2857224

Schools
Arts; **Chemical Engineering**; **Chinese Language and Literature** (Chinese; Communication Studies; Literature); **Computer Science**; **Economics and Trade**; **Environment and Planning**; **Foreign Languages** (Modern Languages); **History and Culture** (Cultural Studies; History); **Law** (Law); **Literature** (Literature); **Management** (Management); **Physical Education** (Physical Education; Sports)

History: Founded 1912, acquired present title 1984.

Academic Year: September to July

Admission Requirements: Graduation from senior middle school and entrance examination

Fees: (Yuan): c. 12,000 per annum

Main Language(s) of Instruction: Chinese, English

Accrediting Agencies: Henan Provincial Government

Degrees and Diplomas: *Bachelor's Degree*: 4 yrs; *Master's Degree*: a further 3 yrs

Student Services: Academic counselling, Canteen, Employment services, Foreign student adviser, Foreign Studies Centre, Health services, Language programs, Nursery care, Social counselling, Sports facilities

Special Facilities: Museum of Antiques from the Primitive to the Last Chinese Dynasty

Libraries: c. 1.8m. vols

Publications: Chemistry Study; Foreign Languages and Literature; History Monthly; Journal of Henan; Mathematics Quaterly; Mind World

Press or Publishing House: Henan University Press
Last Updated: 18/11/08

HENAN UNIVERSITY OF FINANCE AND ECONOMICS (HUFE)

80 Wenhua Road, Zhengzhou, Henan Province 450002
Tel: +86(371) 3730583
Fax: +86(371) 3730491
EMail: xjli@hnufe.edu.cn
Website: http://www.hnufe.edu.cn/

President: Xiaojian Li EMail: yaxx@hnife.edu.cn

Departments
Accountancy (Accountancy); **Business Administration** (Business Administration); **Culture** (Chinese; Cultural Studies); **Economics** (Economics); **Foreign Languages** (English; Modern Languages); **International Business** (International Business); **Labour and Human Relations** (Labour and Industrial Relations); **Law** (Law); **Sports** (Sports)

History: Founded 1983.

International Co-operation: With universities in USA, United Kingdom, Japan, Korea, France, Russsia, Australia and New Zealand

Degrees and Diplomas: *Bachelor's Degree*; *Master's Degree*

Student Residential Facilities: Yes.

Special Facilities: Academic exchange centre

Libraries: Total: c. 500,000 vols; over 1,000 titles of Chinese periodicals; 40 titles of foreign periodicals; 9,800 vols of ancient books; 55,000 electronic books; 10 databases
Last Updated: 18/11/08

HENAN UNIVERSITY OF SCIENCE AND TECHNOLOGY (HUST)

48, Xiyuan Road, Luoyang, Henan Province 471003
Tel: +86(379) 64231879
EMail: fao@mail.haust.edu.c
Website: http://www.haust.edu.cn/

President: Wang Jianji

Schools
Architectural Engineering (Architecture); **Chemical Engineering and Pharmaceutics**; **Creative Arts** (Fine Arts); **Electronic Information Engineering** (Automation and Control Engineering; Computer Science; Electronic Engineering; Information Sciences); **Food and Bioengineering** (Bioengineering; Food Science); **Foreign Languages** (Modern Languages); **Forensic Medicine**; **Gardening and Forestry**; **Law and Liberal Arts** (Arts and Humanities); **Livestock Science and Technology** (Agriculture; Animal Husbandry; Technology); **Material Science and Engineering** (Materials Engineering; Metallurgical Engineering); **Medical Technology and Engineering** (Engineering; Medical Technology); **Vehicle and Power Engineering**

History: Founded 1952 as Luoyang Institute of Technology. Acquired present status and title 2002 following merge with Luoyang Medical School and Luoyang Agricultural School.

Fees: (US Dollars): Graduate and postgraduate students, tuition, 1,600 per annum

Main Language(s) of Instruction: Chinese

Degrees and Diplomas: *Bachelor's Degree*; *Master's Degree*
Last Updated: 18/11/08

HENAN UNIVERSITY OF TECHNOLOGY

140 Songshan Road, Zhengzhou, Henan Province 450052
Tel: +86(371) 7447915
EMail: dec@haut.edu.cn
Website: http://www.admissions.cn/haut/

President: Chen Zhaotan

International Relations: Zhao Liuming

Departments
Bioengineering (Bioengineering); **Chemistry and Chemical Engineering**; **Civil Engineering**; **Computer Science and Technology** (Computer Science; Technology); **Economics and Commerce** (Business and Commerce; Economics); **Food Science and Technology**; **Industrial and Commercial Management**; **Mechanical Engineering** (Mechanical Engineering); **Modern Languages** (Modern Languages)

History: Founded 2004 on the basis of the amalgamation of Zhengzhou Institute of Technology and Zhengzhou Polytechnic Institute.

Main Language(s) of Instruction: Chinese

Degrees and Diplomas: *Bachelor's Degree*; *Master's Degree*
Last Updated: 18/11/08

HENAN UNIVERSITY OF TRADITIONAL CHINESE MEDICINE

1 Jinshui Road, Zhengzhou, Henan Province 450003
Tel: +86(371) 5962457
Fax: +86(371) 5955650
EMail: haiwai@hactcm.edu.cn
Website: http://www.henantcm.com/english/intro/default.asp

President: Peng Bo

Departments

Acupuncture-Moxibustion and Massage (Acupuncture); **Chinese Pharmacology** (Pharmacology); **Orthopedics and Traumatology** (Orthopaedics); **Science of the Five Sense Organs** (Health Sciences); **Traditional Chinese Medicine** (Traditional Eastern Medicine)

History: Founded 1954 as Henan School for TCM Continuing Education. Acquired present title 1958.

Main Language(s) of Instruction: Chinese

Degrees and Diplomas: *Bachelor's Degree*; *Master's Degree*; *Doctor's Degree*

Last Updated: 18/11/08

HENGYANG NORMAL UNIVERSITY

167 Huangbai Road, Hengyang, Hunan Province 421008
Tel: +86(734) 8484904
Fax: +86(734) 8485971
EMail: hnkdz@yahoo.com.cn
Website: http://www.hynu.edu.cn/index.jsp

Departments

Art; **Chemistry**; **Chinese**; **Computer Science**; **Foreign Languages**; **Geography**; **History**; **Mathematics**; **Music**; **Physics**; **Political Science**

History: Founded 1958 as Hengyang Teachers College. Merged with Hengyang Educational Training College. Acquired present title 1999.

Degrees and Diplomas: *Bachelor's Degree*

Libraries: c. 15,000 vols

Publications: Journal of Hengyang Normal University; Journal of Wang Chuanshan Studies

HOHAI UNIVERSITY (HHU)

1 Xikang Road, Nanjing, Jiangsu Province 210098
Tel: +86(25) 83723124
Fax: +86(25) 83735375
EMail: hohai@hhu.edu.cn
Website: http://www.hhu.edu.cn

President: Changkuan Zhang Tel: +86(25) 83786807

Dean of President's Office: Weiming Yao Tel: +86(25) 83786169

International Relations: Jichao Guo
Tel: +86(25) 83786001, Fax: +86(25) 83708419
EMail: wbo1@hhu.edu.cn

Colleges

Civil Engineering *Dean*: Zhifang Zhou; **Computer and Information Engineering** *Dean*: Zhijian Wang; **Continuing Education** *Dean*: Guanghua Li; **Electrical Engineering** *Dean*: Yue Yuan; **Environmental Science and Engineering** *Dean*: Chao Wang; **International Languages and Cultures** (English; Literature; Translation and Interpretation) *Dean*: Huaoning Ruan; **Mechanical and Electronic Engineering** *Dean*: Fusheng Ni; **Science** *Dean*: Caisheng Chen; **Traffic and Marine Engineering** *Dean*: Yigang Wang; **Water Conservation and Hydropower Engineering** *Dean*: Hongwu Tang; **Water Resources and Environment** *Dean*: Liliang Ren

Departments

Physical Education *Dean*: Jianmin Wang

Divisions

International Cooperation and Education *Director*: Jichao Guo

Schools

International Business *Dean*: Yang Zhang

History: Founded 1915 as Hohai Civil Engineering School and known as the East China Technical University of Water Resources from 1952 to 1985 when Hohai University was resumed. A key university under the jurisdiction of the Ministry of Education.

Governing Bodies: Academic Council

Academic Year: September to July (September-February; February-July)

Admission Requirements: Graduation from senior middle school or equivalent and entrance examination

Fees: (Dollars) Bachelor: 2,000 per annum; Master: 2,500 per annum; Doctorate: 3,500 per annum; Diploma: 1,600 per annum

Main Language(s) of Instruction: Chinese, English

International Co-operation: With universities in USA; Germany; Netherlands; Australia; Yemen; Japan; France; Ghana; Russian Federation; United Kingdom

Accrediting Agencies: International Cooperation and Education Division, Ministry of Education

Degrees and Diplomas: *Bachelor's Degree*: Engineering; Education; Science; Economics; Management; Law; English, 4 yrs; *Master's Degree*: Engineering; Science; Economics; Management; Law, a further 3 yrs; *Doctor's Degree*: Engineering; Science; Economics; Management, a further 3 yrs

Student Services: Academic counselling, Canteen, Cultural centre, Foreign student adviser, Foreign Studies Centre, Health services, Language programs, Nursery care, Social counselling, Sports facilities

Student Residential Facilities: Yes

Special Facilities: Movie studio

Libraries: 1,080,000 vols

Press or Publishing House: Hohai Publishing House
Last Updated: 18/11/08

HONGHE UNIVERSITY

Mengzi, Yunnan Province 661100
Tel: +86(873) 3694865
Fax: +86(873) 3694865
EMail: kittywangfei@gmail.com; pengjuan1213@hotmail.com
Website: http://www.uoh.edu.cn/

Colleges

Arts (Design; Painting and Drawing); **Business** (Business Administration; International Business; International Economics; Management; Transport Management); **Engineering** (Automotive Engineering; Computer Science; Educational Technology; Electrical Engineering; Mechanical Engineering); **Foreign Languages**; **Humanities** (Administration; Advertising and Publicity; Chinese; History; Journalism; Literature; Native Language; Political Sciences); **International College** (Chinese; Thai Languages; Vietnamese); **Life Sciences and Technology**; **Mathematics** (Applied Mathematics; Computer Science; Information Sciences; Mathematics); **Music**; **Physical Education** (Leisure Studies; Physical Education; Sports); **Science** (Chemistry; Metallurgical Engineering; Physics); **Teacher Education** (Preschool Education; Primary Education; Science Education)

Departments

Social Sciences (Social Sciences)

History: Created in 1978

Degrees and Diplomas: *Bachelor's Degree*
Last Updated: 19/12/08

HUAIBEI COAL INDUSTRY TEACHERS COLLEGE

100 Donghshan Road, Huaibei, Anhui Province 235000
Tel: +86(5611) 3090967
Fax: +86(5611) 3090518
Website: http://www.hbcnc.edu.cn

President: Ma Jian

International Relations: Du Xiansheng

Departments

Biology (Biology); **Chemistry** (Chemistry); **Chinese Language and Literature** (Chinese; Literature); **Computer Science** (Computer Science); **Education**; **Fine Arts** (Fine Arts); **History** (History); **Mathematics** (Mathematics); **Modern Languages** (Modern Languages); **Music** (Music); **Physical Education** (Physical Education); **Physics** (Physics); **Political Science and Law** (Law; Political Sciences)

History: Founded 1974, acquired present name 1978.

Accrediting Agencies: Ministry of Coal Industry

Degrees and Diplomas: *Bachelor's Degree*; *Master's Degree*
Last Updated: 18/11/08

HUAIHAI INSTITUTE OF TECHNOLOGY

Huaguoshan Road, Lianyungang, Jiangsu Province 222005
Tel: +86(518) 5817407
Fax: +86(518) 5806171
EMail: hhit@public.lyg.js.cn
Website: http://www.hhit.edu.cn

President: Jian Liu

Departments
Architecture; Chemical Engineering; Chinese Language and Literature; Electronic Engineering (Electronic Engineering); Food Technology (Food Technology); Management (Management); Mechanical Engineering (Mechanical Engineering); Modern Languages and Literature; Social Sciences (Social Sciences)

Schools
Marine Technology and Aquaculture (Aquaculture; Marine Biology; Marine Science and Oceanography)

History: Founded 1985 as part of Huaihai University, acquired present status and title 1989.

Degrees and Diplomas: *Bachelor's Degree*
Last Updated: 18/11/08

HUAIYIN INSTITUTE OF TECHNOLOGY

1 Mecheng Rd, Huaiyin, Jiangsu Province 223001
Tel: +86(517) 3591010
EMail: faoffice@mail.hyit.edu.cn
Website: http://www.hyit.edu.cn

Departments
Agricultural Engineering and Food Engineering; Architectural Engineering (Structural Architecture); Biological Engineering and Chemical Engineering; Computer Engineering; Computer Sciences (Computer Science); Continuing Education; Economic Management (Economics; Management); Electronic and Information Engineering (Electronic Engineering; Information Technology); Foreign Languages (Modern Languages); Humanity and Social Sciences (Arts and Humanities; Social Sciences); Mechanical Engineering (Mechanical Engineering); Transport Engineering (Transport Engineering)

History: Founded 1958. Acquired present title 2002.

Main Language(s) of Instruction: Chinese

Degrees and Diplomas: *Bachelor's Degree*
Last Updated: 18/11/08

HUAIYIN TEACHERS UNIVERSITY

71 Jiaotong Road, Huaiyin, Jiangsu Province 223001
Tel: +86(517) 3522010
Fax: +86(517) 3942349
EMail: nic@hytc.edu.cn
Website: http://www.hytc.edu.cn

President: Chen Fasong
International Relations: Mao Zonggang

Departments
Biology (Biology); Chemistry (Chemistry); Chinese (Chinese); Computer Science (Computer Science); Education (Education); Educational Technology; English; Fine Arts; Geography; Mathematics; Physical Education; Physics (Physics); Political Science and History; Social Sciences (Social Sciences)

Schools
Educational Administration (Educational Administration)

History: Founded 1958 as Huaiyin Teacher Training College, acquired present name 1997.

Degrees and Diplomas: *Bachelor's Degree*
Last Updated: 09/09/08

HUANGGANG NORMAL UNIVERSITY

10 Shengli Street, Huangzhou, Hubei Province 438000
Tel: +86(713) 8616627
Fax: +86(713) 8616901
EMail: net@hgnu.edu.cn
Website: http://www.hgnc.net

President: Liu Xingmin
International Relations: Zhang Jiying

Departments
Biology; Chemistry (Chemistry); Chinese (Chinese); Computer Science; Fine Arts; Mathematics (Mathematics); Media Studies (Media Studies); Modern Languages; Music (Music); Physical Education; Physics; Political Science and Law

History: Founded 1905 as Huangzhou Teachers Training School, acquired present status 1978 and title 1999.

Degrees and Diplomas: *Bachelor's Degree*; *Master's Degree*

HUAQIAO UNIVERSITY

Quanzhou, Fujian Province 362021
Tel: +86(595) 2680680
Fax: +86(595) 2686969
EMail: sec@hqu.edu.cn
Website: http://www.hqu.edu.cn

President: Wu Chengye EMail: xzbgs@hqu.edu.cn

Colleges
Civil Engineering (Civil Engineering); Foreign Languages (Modern Languages); Humanities and Public Administration; Mechanical Engineering and Automation; Tourism (Tourism)

Departments
Arts (Arts and Humanities) *Dean*: Yaxiong Zeng; Electronic Engineering (Electronic Engineering) *Dean*: Kaiyong Jiang; English *Dean*: Xiqing Pan; Fine Arts *Dean*: Deming Sun; Mathematics (Applied Mathematics; Mathematics); Social Sciences *Dean*: Yaxiong Zeng

Schools
Architecture (Architecture); Business (Business Administration; E-Business/Commerce; Management); Information Science and Technology (Information Sciences; Information Technology); Law (Law)

History: Founded 1960, mainly for students from Hong Kong, Macau, Taiwan, and for Overseas Chinese students in other countries.

Governing Bodies: Board of Directors

Academic Year: February to January (February-July; September-January)

Admission Requirements: Graduation from senior middle school and entrance examination

Main Language(s) of Instruction: Chinese

Degrees and Diplomas: *Bachelor's Degree*: 4-5 yrs; *Master's Degree*: a further 2-3 yrs; *Doctor's Degree*: a further 2-3 yrs

Student Services: Canteen, Cultural centre, Employment services, Foreign student adviser, Health services, Language programs, Sports facilities

Libraries: c. 1,600,000 vols

Publications: Journal of Huaqiao University (quarterly)
Last Updated: 18/11/08

HUAZHONG AGRICULTURAL UNIVERSITY (HAU)

Shizi Shan, Wuhan, Hubei Province 430070
Tel: +86(27) 87282027
Fax: +86(27) 87384670
EMail: fao@hzau.edu.cn
Website: http://www.hzau.edu.cn

President: Duanpin Zhang
Tel: +86(27) 87282031, Fax: +86(27) 87384670
EMail: dpzhang@mail.hzau.edu.cn

International Relations: Youliang Yuan Tel: +86(27) 87282026

Colleges
Adult Education; Animal Husbandry and Veterinary Medicine; Basic Sciences (Applied Chemistry; Computer Science; Information Sciences); Economics and International Trade (Accountancy; Agriculture; Business Administration; Business and Commerce; Economics; Forestry; International Business; Management); Engineering Technology (Automation and Control

Engineering; Engineering; Production Engineering); **Fishery** (Aquaculture; Fishery); **Horticultural and Forestry Sciences**; **Humanities and Social Sciences** (Advertising and Publicity; Arts and Humanities; Human Resources; Law; Marketing; Social Sciences; Social Work; Sociology); **Land Management** (Information Management; Rural Planning); **Life Sciences and Technology**; **Plant Sciences Technology** (Plant and Crop Protection)

Departments

Agronomy (Agronomy; Ecology; Plant and Crop Protection; Rural Planning); **Food Science and Technology** (Food Science; Food Technology); **Foreign Languages** (English; Modern Languages); **Resources, Environment and Agrochemistry** (Agriculture; Crop Production; Environmental Engineering; Environmental Studies)

History: Founded 1898. Acquired present title 1952.

Academic Year: September to June (September-December; February-June)

Main Language(s) of Instruction: Chinese, English

International Co-operation: With universities in Canada. Also cooperates with CIDA and AUCC

Accrediting Agencies: Ministry of Education

Degrees and Diplomas: *Bachelor's Degree*: 4 yrs; *Master's Degree*: a further 3 yrs; *Doctor's Degree*: 3 yrs

Student Services: Academic counselling, Canteen, Cultural centre, Employment services, Foreign student adviser, Foreign Studies Centre, Health services, Language programs, Nursery care, Social counselling, Sports facilities

Publications: Huazhong Agricultural University Journal, Social Science Edition *(monthly)*; Huazhong Agricultural University Journal, Natural Science Edition *(monthly)*

Last Updated: 18/11/08

HUAZHONG NORMAL UNIVERSITY (CCNU)

100 Luoyu Avenue, Wuhan, Hubei Province 430079
Tel: +86(27) 87673048
Fax: +86(27) 87875696
EMail: www@ccnu.edu.cn
Website: http://www.ccnu.edu.cn

President: Ma Ming (1996-)

Departments

Computer Science *Chair*: Debao Xiao; **Physical Education** (Physical Education) *Chair*: Anqing Liu; **Sociology**

Schools

Adult Education; **Chemistry** (Analytical Chemistry; Applied Chemistry; Chemistry; Inorganic Chemistry; Organic Chemistry; Physical Chemistry); **Chinese Language and Literature**; **City and Environmental Science**; **Economics**; **Education** (Education; Preschool Education; Psychology; Special Education); **Fine Arts** (Fine Arts); **Foreign Languages and Literature** (English; Japanese; Linguistics; Literature; Russian); **History and Culture**; **Information Management** (Information Management; Library Science); **Information Technology** (Information Technology); **Life Sciences**; **Literature**; **Management**; **Mathematics and Statistics** (Accountancy; Applied Mathematics; Mathematics; Statistics); **Music** (Music); **Physics and Technology**; **Political Science and Law**; **Tourism**

History: Founded 1903 as Wen-hua University, became Huazhong Institute of Higher Education 1952. Formerly Central China Normal University.

Academic Year: September to July

Admission Requirements: Graduation from senior high school or foreign equivalent, and entrance examination

Main Language(s) of Instruction: Chinese

Accrediting Agencies: Ministry of Education

Degrees and Diplomas: *Bachelor's Degree*: 4 yrs; *Master's Degree*: a further 3 yrs; *Doctor's Degree (PhD)*: a further 3 yrs

Student Services: Academic counselling, Canteen, Cultural centre, Employment services, Foreign student adviser, Foreign Studies Centre, Health services, Language programs, Nursery care, Social counselling, Sports facilities

Student Residential Facilities: Yes

Special Facilities: Museum of Historical Relics. University History Exhibition Hall. Biological Specimen Hall

Libraries: Total, c. 1.8m vols

Publications: Correspondence Studies of Higher Education, Natural Sciences, Social Sciences; Education and Economics; Educational Research and Experiment; Foreign Literature Studies *(quarterly)*; High School Russian; Teaching and Research of Chinese Language

Press or Publishing House: CCNU University Press

Last Updated: 19/11/08

HUAZHONG UNIVERSITY OF SCIENCE AND TECHNOLOGY (HUST)

1037 Luo Yu Road, Wuhan, Hubei Province 430074
Tel: +86(27) 87542157
Fax: +86(27) 87547063
EMail: haoli@hust.edu.cn
Website: http://www.hust.edu.cn

President: Li President Peigen
Tel: +86(27) 87542819, Fax: +86(27) 87545438

Colleges
Medicine *(Tongji)* (Medicine)

Schools
Architecture and Town Planning (Architectural and Environmental Design; Architecture; Urban Studies); **Business and Management** (Business and Commerce; Management); **Civil Engineering and Mechanics** (Civil Engineering; Mechanics); **Computer Science and Technology** (Computer Science; Technology); **Continuing Education** (Continuing Education); **Economics** (Economics); **Electrical and Electronic Engineering** (Automation and Control Engineering; Electrical and Electronic Engineering; Engineering; Power Engineering); **Energy and Power Engineering** (Chemical Engineering; Energy Engineering; Heating and Refrigeration; Mechanical Engineering; Power Engineering; Thermal Engineering); **Environmental Science and Engineering** (Environmental Engineering; Environmental Studies); **Humanities and Social Sciences** (Arts and Humanities; Chinese; History; Modern Languages; Philosophy; Sociology); **Hydropower and Information Engineering** (Hydraulic Engineering; Information Technology); **Journalism and Information Communications** (Communication Studies; Journalism); **Law** (Law); **Life Science and Technology** (Biological and Life Sciences; Biomedical Engineering; Biotechnology; Technology); **Materials Science and Engineering** (Automation and Control Engineering; Engineering; Heating and Refrigeration; Materials Engineering; Metallurgical Engineering); **Mechanical Science and Engineering** (Automation and Control Engineering; Electronic Engineering; Engineering; Industrial Design; Mechanical Engineering; Technology); **Online Education**; **Public Administration** (Public Administration); **Software Engineering** (Software Engineering); **Traffic Science and Engineering** (Engineering; Transport Engineering)

History: Founded 1953 as Huazhong Institute of Technology. Merged with Tongji Medical University (founded 1907), Wuhan Urban Construction Institute (founded 1954) and Wuhan Science and Technology Vocational College (founded 1968) to form the new HUST 2000.

Governing Bodies: University Committee

Admission Requirements: Senior middle school certificate and entrance examination

Fees: (US Dollars): Undergraduate, 2,200 per annum; Master, 3,000; PhD, 4,500 per annum

Main Language(s) of Instruction: Chinese

Accrediting Agencies: Ministry of Education; Ministry of Public Health; Ministry of Construction and Ministry of Science and Technology

Degrees and Diplomas: *Bachelor's Degree*: 4 yrs; *Bachelor's Degree*: Medicine, 5 yrs; *Master's Degree*: a further 3 yrs; *Doctor's Degree (PhD)*: a further 3 yrs or more

Student Services: Academic counselling, Canteen, Cultural centre, Employment services, Foreign student adviser, Foreign Studies Centre, Health services, Language programs, Nursery care, Social counselling, Sports facilities

Student Residential Facilities: Yes

Libraries: Main Library, 3.2 m. vols

Publications: Applied Medicine *(quarterly)*; China Higher Medical Education *(bimonthly)*; China Medical Abstract, (Chinese) *(quarterly)*; Chinese Journal of Clinical Gastroenterology, (Chinese) *(quarterly)*; Chinese Journal Rehabilitation, (Chinese) *(quarterly)*; Deutsche Medizin *(quarterly)*; Journal of Clinical Cardiology, (Chinese) *(quarterly)*; Journal of Clinical Otorhinolaryngology, (Chinese) *(quarterly)*; Journal of Clinical Urology, (Chinese) *(quarterly)*; Journal of Haematology, (Chinese) *(quarterly)*; Journal of Higher Education *(bimonthly)*; Journal of Huazhong University of Science and Technology, Natural Science Edition *(quarterly)*; Journal of Huazhong University of Science and Technology, Social Science Edition *(quarterly)*; Journal of Nursing, (Chinese) *(quarterly)*; Journal of Tongji Medical College, Natural Science Edition; Chinese, English and German version *(quarterly)*; Journal of Wuhan Urban Construction Institute, Social science edition *(quarterly)*; New Architecture *(bimonthly)*; Roentgenpraxis, (German) *(bimonthly)*

Press or Publishing House: Huazhong University of Science & Technology Press

Last Updated: 19/11/08

HUBEI COLLEGE OF TRADITIONAL CHINESE MEDICINE

110 Yunjiaqiao, Wuchang, Wuhan, Hubei Province 430061
Tel: +86(27) 88852621
Fax: +86(27) 88852621
EMail: hbtcmhwjyxy@sina.com
Website: http://www.hbtcm.edu.cn/structure/index.htm

President: Zhang Liutong

International Relations: Lu Gang

Departments
Acupuncture, Moxibustion and Orthopaedics; **Pharmacology** (Pharmacology); **Traditional Chinese Medicine**

Schools
Adult Education

History: Founded 1959 as Hubei Provincial Traditional Chinese Medicine Advanced Training School. Acquired present title 1964.

Degrees and Diplomas: *Bachelor's Degree*; *Master's Degree*; *Doctor's Degree*

Libraries: c. 237,000 vols

Publications: Hepatic Disease Journal of the Combination of TCM and Western Medicine; Hubei Journal of TCM; Journal of Hubei College of TCM

HUBEI INSTITUTE FOR NATIONALITIES

Enshi, Hubei Province 445000
Tel: +86(718) 8430836-3
Fax: +86(718) 8430836-3
EMail: webmaster@hbmy.edu.cn.
Website: http://www.hbmy.edu.cn/html/jxky.htm

President: Peng Zhenkun

International Relations: Hu Yuan

Departments
Chemistry and Chemical Engineering; **Chinese Language and Literature** (Chinese; Literature); **Computer Science and Mathematics**; **Finance and Economics** (Economics; Finance); **Fine Arts**; **Forestry** (Forestry); **Horticulture** (Horticulture); **Modern Languages** (Modern Languages); **Physics and Electrical Engineering** (Electrical Engineering; Physics); **Political Science and Law** (Law; Political Sciences)

History: Founded 1938 as branch of United Rural Teaching School of Hubei Province, acquired present status and title 1989.

Degrees and Diplomas: *Bachelor's Degree*; *Master's Degree*

HUBEI INSTITUTE OF AUTOMOBILE INDUSTRY

Jyaoyukou, Shiyan, Hubei Province 442002
Tel: +86(719) 8238444
Fax: +86(719) 8260748
EMail: wlzx@huat.edu.cn

President: Liu Kaiming

International Relations: Zhang Jingbo

Departments
Automotive Engineering (Automotive Engineering); **Industrial and Electrical Engineering**; **Materials Engineering** (Materials Engineering); **Mechanics** (Mechanics); **Modern Languages** (Modern Languages); **Social Sciences**

History: Founded 1972 as Workers University of Dongfeng Motor Company, acquired present name 1983.

Degrees and Diplomas: *Bachelor's Degree*; *Master's Degree*

HUBEI INSTITUTE OF FINE ARTS

72 Huazhongcun, Wuhan, Hubei Province 430060
Tel: +86(27) 88842566
Fax: +86(27) 88862397
Website: http://www.hifa.edu.cn/

President: Xu Yongmin

Departments
Aesthetics; **Art Education**; **Chinese Painting** (Painting and Drawing); **Design** (Design); **Fashion Design** (Fashion Design); **Oil Painting** (Painting and Drawing); **Printmaking** (Printing and Printmaking); **Sculpture** (Sculpture)

History: Founded 1920 as Wuchang School of Fine Arts, acquired present status and title 1985.

Degrees and Diplomas: *Bachelor's Degree*; *Master's Degree*
Last Updated: 19/11/08

HUBEI NORMAL UNIVERSITY

82 Shenxia Road, Huangchi Gang, Hubei Province 435002
Tel: +86(714) 6525179
Fax: +86(714) 6525179
EMail: zjy7503@tom.com
Website: http://www.hbnu.edu.cn

President: Liu Konggao

International Relations: Zhao Chen

Departments
Arts; Biology; Chemistry; Chinese; Computer Science; Foreign Languages; History; Mathematics; Physics; Political Science; Sports

History: Founded 1973 as Central China Normal University Huangshi Branch, acquired present name 1985.

Main Language(s) of Instruction: Chinese

Degrees and Diplomas: *Bachelor's Degree*; *Master's Degree*

Libraries: c. 640,000 vols

HUBEI UNIVERSITY

11 Xueyuan Road, Wuchang, Wuhan, Hubei Province 430062
Tel: +86(27) 86717841
Fax: +86(27) 86814263
EMail: international@hubu.edu.cn
Website: http://www.hubu.edu.cn

President: An Mingdao

International Relations: Yang Yiping

Departments
Education (Education); **Foreign Languages and Literature** (Literature; Modern Languages); **Physical Education** (Physical Education)

Faculties
Chemistry and Materials Science; Economics; Engineering; Humanities; Life Sciences; Mathematics and Computer

Science; **Physics and Electronic Engineering**; **Political Science and Administration**; **Tourism**

History: Founded 1931 as Hubei Institute of Education. Acquired present status and title 1984.

Governing Bodies: University Council

Academic Year: February to January (February-June; September-January)

Admission Requirements: Graduation from senior middle school and entrance examination

Degrees and Diplomas: *Bachelor's Degree*: 4 yrs; *Master's Degree*: a further 3 yrs

Student Services: Academic counselling, Canteen, Cultural centre, Employment services, Foreign student adviser, Health services, Nursery care, Social counselling, Sports facilities

Student Residential Facilities: For c. 7,000 students

Libraries: c. 1.7m. vols

Publications: Hubei University Journal; Middle-school Chinese Education; Middle-school Mathematics Education

HUBEI UNIVERSITY OF TECHNOLOGY

Nanhu, Wuhan, Hubei Province 430068
Tel: +86(27) 88034023
Fax: +86(27) 88034023
EMail: international@mail.hubpu.edu.cn
Website: http://io.hbut.edu.cn/en/intro.asp

President: Pan Anfu

International Relations: Pan Shaobo

Departments
Bioengineering (Bioengineering); **Civil Engineering**; **Electrical Engineering and Computer Science** (Computer Science; Electrical Engineering); **Industrial and Commercial Management** (Industrial Management; Management); **Mechanical Engineering** (Mechanical Engineering); **Social Sciences** (Social Sciences)

Institutes
Design (Design)

History: Founded 1958 as Hubei Institute of Light Industry, renamed Hubei Polytechnic University. Acquired present title 2004.

Degrees and Diplomas: *Bachelor's Degree*; *Master's Degree*

HULUNBUIR COLLEGE

83 Xuefu Road, Hailar, Hulubuir, Inner Mongolia 021008
Tel: +86(470) 825-9118
Fax: +86(470) 825-9380
EMail: mxh-hlr@163.com
Website: http://www.hlbrc.cn/

Departments
Architecture Engineering (Structural Architecture); **Arts** (Fine Arts); **Biology**; **Chinese**; **Computer Science** (Computer Science); **Continuing Education** (Continuing Education); **Economic Management**; **Education** (Education); **Foreign Language**; **Mathematics** (Mathematics); **Mongolian**; **Music**; **Physical Education** (Physical Education); **Physics**; **Politics and History** (History; Political Sciences); **Public Administration and Law**; **Tourism and Geography** (Geography; Tourism)

History: Founded 1997.

Degrees and Diplomas: *Bachelor's Degree*

Libraries: c. 600,000 vols.
Last Updated: 15/02/07

HUNAN AGRICULTURAL UNIVERSITY

Furong District, Changsha, Hunan Province 410128
Tel: +86(731) 4618060
Fax: +86(731) 4612870
EMail: principal@hunau.edu.cn
Website: http://www.hunau.net/en

President: Zhou Qingming

Colleges
Animal Science and Technology (Animal Husbandry; Aquaculture; Zoology); **Biosafety Science and Technology**; **Bioscience and Biotechnology** (Bioengineering; Biotechnology; Ecology); **Business**; **Economics**; **Engineering**; **Food Science and Technology** (Food Science; Food Technology); **Foreign Languages**; **Horticulture and Landscape** (Horticulture; Landscape Architecture); **Humanities and Social Sciences**; **Science**; **Sport and Art** (Design; Physical Education; Sports); **Vocational Education and Technology**

History: Founded 1951 as Hunan Agricultural College, acquired present title 1994.

Degrees and Diplomas: *Bachelor's Degree*; *Master's Degree*; *Doctor's Degree*

Libraries: c. 600,000 vols

Publications: Crop Research; Journal of Hunan Agricultural University

Last Updated: 19/11/08

HUNAN NORMAL UNIVERSITY

36 Lushan Road, Yuelu Disctrict, Changsha, Hunan Province 410081
Tel: +86(731) 8872245
Fax: +86(731) 8854711
Website: http://www.hunnu.edu.cn

President: Liu Xiangrong

Schools
Chemistry and Chemical Engineering (Chemical Engineering; Chemistry); **Economics** (Economics; Finance; Management; Tourism); **Education** (Education; Educational Technology; Psychology); **Fine Arts** (Arts and Humanities; Design; Fine Arts; Music; Performing Arts); **Foreign Languages** (English; Japanese; Literature; Modern Languages; Russian); **Law** (Law; Philosophy; Political Sciences; Sociology); **Liberal Arts** (Arts and Humanities; Chinese; History; Literature); **Life Sciences** (Biochemistry; Biological and Life Sciences; Biology; Botany; Genetics; Microbiology; Molecular Biology; Zoology); **Physical Education** (Physical Education); **Resource and Environment** (Environmental Studies; Geography; Natural Resources); **Science** (Mathematics and Computer Science; Natural Sciences; Physics); **Vocational Technology** (Clothing and Sewing; Design; Electronic Engineering; Machine Building)

History: Founded 1938 as National Teachers College, acquired present title 1984.

Main Language(s) of Instruction: Chinese

Degrees and Diplomas: *Bachelor's Degree*; *Master's Degree*; *Doctor's Degree*

Libraries: c. 1,6m. vols

Publications: Natural Science Journal of Hunan Normal University; Social Science Journal of Hunan Normal University
Last Updated: 19/11/08

HUNAN UNIVERSITY

Yuelushan, Changsha, Hunan Province 410082
Tel: +86(731) 8822721
Fax: +86(731) 8824287
EMail: clarkzuo@gmail.com
Website: http://www.hunu.edu.cn

President: Zhong Zhihua

Colleges
Accountancy (Accountancy); **Architecture** (Architecture); **Broadcasting, Film and Television Arts**; **Business Administration** (Business Administration; International Business); **Chemistry and Chemical Engineering** (Chemical Engineering; Chemistry); **Civil Engineering** (Civil Engineering); **Computer and Communication Science** (Computer Science); **Design Art** (Design); **Electrical and Information Engineering** (Electrical Engineering); **Environmental Science and Engineering** (Environmental Engineering); **Finance** (Finance); **Foreign Languages** (Literature; Modern Languages); **International Studies** (*Meiya*) (International Studies); **Journalism and Communication**; **Law**; **Marxist Studies** (Political Sciences); **Material Science and Engineering** (Materials Engineering); **Mathematics and Econometrics** (Applied Mathematics;

Econometrics); **Mechanical and Automotive Engineering** (Automotive Engineering; Mechanical Engineering); **Mechanics and Aerospace** (Aeronautical and Aerospace Engineering; Mechanical Engineering); **Physics and Microelectronics**; **Software** (Software Engineering); **Statistics**

History: Founded 1926. Merged with Hunan University of Finance and Economics.

Academic Year: September to July

Admission Requirements: Graduation from senior middle school

Main Language(s) of Instruction: Chinese

Degrees and Diplomas: *Bachelor's Degree*: 4 yrs; *Master's Degree*: a further 3 yrs; *Doctor's Degree (PhD)*

Libraries: c. 1,1m. vols

Publications: Journal of Hunan University, Natural Sciences, Social Sciences; Research of Higher Education for Mechanical Industry

Last Updated: 19/11/08

HUNAN UNIVERSITY OF ARTS AND SCIENCE

170 Dongting Road, Changde, Hunan Province 415000
Tel: +86(736) 7277716
Fax: +86(736) 7283046
EMail: zhangli6161@sina.com
Website: http://www.huas.cn

President: Li Dazhi

Colleges
Chemistry and Chemical Engineering; **Civil Engineering** (Civil Engineering; Construction Engineering); **Economy and Management**; **Fine Arts**; **Foreign Studies**; **History and Culture**; **Law**; **Mathematics and Computer Science** (Applied Mathematics; Mathematics; Mathematics and Computer Science); **Mechanical Engineering** (Automation and Control Engineering; Mechanical Engineering; Mechanics); **Physical Engineering**; **Physics and Electronics** (Electronic Engineering; Physics)

History: Changed its title 2003, previously known as Changde Teachers College.

Degrees and Diplomas: *Bachelor's Degree*
Last Updated: 19/11/08

HUNAN UNIVERSITY OF CHINESE MEDICINE

119 Shaoshan Road, Changsha, Hunan Province 410007
Tel: +86(731) 5537567
Fax: +86(731) 5532948
Website: http://www.hnctcm.com/

President: Chen Dashun

International Relations: Jiang Wenming

Departments
Acupuncture; **Chinese Pharmaceutics**; **Traditional Chinese Medicine** (Traditional Eastern Medicine); **Traditional Chinese Medicine and Western Medicine**

History: Founded 1953 as Hunan Traditional Chinese Medicine Vocational School, acquired present title 1960.

Degrees and Diplomas: *Bachelor's Degree*; *Master's Degree*; *Doctor's Degree*

Libraries: c. 340,000 vols

Publications: Journal of Hunan College of TCM; Medicine Food Research
Last Updated: 19/11/08

HUNAN UNIVERSITY OF COMMERCE

569 Yuelu, Changsha, Hunan Province 410205
Tel: +86(731) 8869018
Fax: +86(731) 8882487
EMail: zsb@hnbc.com.cn
Website: http://www.hnuc.edu.cn

President: Tang Weibing

Schools
Accountancy; **Arts Design**; **Business Administration** (Business Administration; Business and Commerce; Human Resources;

Marketing); **Chinese Language and Literature** (Chinese; Literature); **Computer and Electronic Engineering** (Computer Engineering; Electronic Engineering); **Economy and Trade** (Economics; International Business); **Finance**; **Foreign Languages** (Modern Languages); **Law** (Civil Law; Commercial Law; Criminal Law; Law); **Public Administration**; **Tourism Management**

History: Founded by the merging of Hunan Commercial School and Hunan Business Management School. Formerly known as Hunan College of Commerce.

Main Language(s) of Instruction: Chinese

Degrees and Diplomas: *Bachelor's Degree*
Last Updated: 19/11/08

HUNAN UNIVERSITY OF SCIENCE AND TECHNOLOGY

Shimatou, Yuhu District, Xiangtan, Hunan Province 411201
Tel: +86(732) 8290011 +86(732) 8291452
Fax: +86(732) 8291454
EMail: nic@hnust.edu.cn
Website: http://www.hnust.cn

President: Tian Yinhua

International Relations: Xiong Muqing, Director of Foreign Affairs Office

Schools
Adult Education and Vocational Technology (Adult Education; Vocational Education); **Architecture and Urban Planning**; **Arts**; **Business** (Business Administration); **Chemistry and Chemical Technology**; **Civil Engineering** (Civil Engineering); **Computer Science and Engineering**; **Education**; **Energy and Safety Engineering** (Energy Engineering; Safety Engineering); **Foreign Studies** (Modern Languages); **Human Studies** (Arts and Humanities); **Information and Electrical Engineering** (Electronic Engineering; Information Technology); **Law** (Law); **Life Science**; **Mathematics and Computer Science** (Mathematics and Computer Science); **Physical Education and Sports** (Physical Education; Sports); **Physics**; **Technology**

History: Founded 2003 following merger of Xiangtan Polytechnic University and Xiangtan Normal University.

Degrees and Diplomas: *Bachelor's Degree*; *Master's Degree*

Publications: Forum on Higher Education; Journal of Hunan University of Science and Technology, Social Sciences; Journal of Hunan University of Science and Technology, Natural Sciences; Xiangtan Normal University, Natural Sciences; Xiangtan Normal University, Social Sciences

HUNAN UNIVERSITY OF TECHNOLOGY

Wenhua Road, Zhuzhou, Hunan Province 412008
Tel: +86(733) 8101936
Fax: +86(733) 8100052
EMail: office@zhuzit.edu.cn
Website: http://www.hut.edu.cn

President: Wang Hanqing

International Relations: Wan Youngeng

Departments
Civil Engineering (Civil Engineering); **Commerce and Economics** (Business and Commerce; Economics); **Computer Engineering**; **Electrical Engineering**; **Marketing Engineering**; **Mechanical Engineering** (Mechanical Engineering); **Modern Languages** (Modern Languages); **Packaging Technology** (Packaging Technology); **Physical Education** (Physical Education); **Social Sciences** (Social Sciences)

Schools
Industrial Design (Industrial Design)

History: Founded 1979 as Zhouzhou College. Became Zhuzhou Institute of Technology. Acquired present status 1986 and name 1989.

Degrees and Diplomas: *Bachelor's Degree*
Last Updated: 19/11/08

HUZHOU UNIVERSITY

1 Xueshi Road, Huzhou, Zhejiang Province 313000
Tel: +86(572) 2373422
Fax: +86(572) 2375400
EMail: xcb@hutc.zj.cn
Website: http://pioneer.hutc.zj.cn/new/english
President: Zhangjian Hu

Departments
Art Education; **Chemistry** (Chemistry); **Chinese** (Chinese); **Computer Science** (Computer Science); **English**; **Mathematics** (Mathematics); **Physical Education**; **Physics**; **Political Science and History** (History; Political Sciences); **Primary Education** (Primary Education)

History: Founded 1958 as Huzhou Teachers College. Acquired present title and status 1999.

Degrees and Diplomas: *Bachelor's Degree*
Last Updated: 11/09/08

ILI TEACHERS TRAINING COLLEGE

298 Jiefang Road, Yining, Xinjiang Uygur Province
Tel: +86(999) 8102445
Fax: +86(999) 8124245
EMail: shrek_234@yahoo.com.cn
Website: http://www.ylsy.edu.cn
President: Wu Xiaocheng

International Relations: Liu Jianchang

Departments
Art Education; **Chemistry**; **Chinese**; **Literature** (Literature); **Mathematics** (Mathematics); **Modern Languages** (Modern Languages); **Physical Education** (Physical Education); **Physics** (Physics); **Political Science** (Political Sciences)

History: Founded 1948 as Xinjiang Technical Secondary School, acquired present status and title 1980.

Main Language(s) of Instruction: Chinese

Degrees and Diplomas: *Bachelor's Degree*
Last Updated: 11/09/08

INNER MONGOLIA AGRICULTURAL UNIVERSITY

306 Zhaowu Dalu, Hohhot, Inner Mongolia 010018
Tel: +86(471) 4309294
Fax: +86(471) 4308933
EMail: iecimau@imau.edu.cn
Website: http://www.imau.edu.cn
President: Changyou Li

International Relations: Lin Yubao

Colleges
Agronomy; **Animal Science and Medicine** (Animal Husbandry; Aquaculture; Veterinary Science); **Bioengineering**; **Computer Science and Information Engineering** (Computer Science; Information Management); **Ecology and Environmental Science**; **Economics and Management**; **Food Science and Engineering** (Food Science; Packaging Technology); **Foreign Languages** (English); **Forestry** (Forestry); **Forestry Engineering**; **Mechanical and Electrical Engineering**; **Science** (Applied Chemistry; Statistics); **Social Sciences** (Administration; Law; Social Work)

History: Founded 1952 as Inner Mongolia College of Animal Husbandry and Veterinary Science, acquired present title 1999. Merged with Inner Mongolia Forestry College.

Degrees and Diplomas: *Bachelor's Degree*; *Master's Degree*; *Doctor's Degree*

Libraries: c. 650,000 vols

Publications: Journal of Inner Mongolia Agricultural University; Resources and Environment in Arid Areas
Last Updated: 19/11/08

INNER MONGOLIA FINANCE AND ECONOMICS COLLEGE

47, Hailar Road, Hohhot, Inner Mongolia 010051
Tel: +86(471) 651 2517
Fax: +86(471) 651 2517
EMail: hsyufei@yahoo.com.cn
Website: http://www.imfec.edu.cn
President: Yamin Zhang (2006-)
Tel: +86(471) 366 1193 EMail: zym@imfec.edu.cn
Vice-President: Wenqing Liu
Tel: +86(471) 366 1204 EMail: lwq@imfec.edu.cn
International Relations: Wei Qu
Tel: +86(471) 367 7455 EMail: sinoqsir@163.com

Faculties
Law (Commercial Law; International Law; Law)

Institutes
Accountancy (Accountancy; Finance; Management); **Banking** (Banking; Insurance); **Business** (International Business; International Economics; Management; Marketing); **Business Administration** (Business Administration; Human Resources; Transport Management); **Computer Information Management** (Computer Networks; Computer Science; E-Business/Commerce; Information Management; Information Technology; Software Engineering); **Economics** (Economics); **Finance and Taxation** (Finance; Taxation); **Statistics and Mathematics** (Applied Mathematics; Business Computing; Computer Science; Information Technology; Statistics); **Tourism Management** (Cooking and Catering; Hotel Management; Tourism)

Programmes
Arts (Chinese; Literature; Mongolian)

History: Inner Mongolia Finance and Economics College was founded in 1960. It started undergraduate education in 1979. Authorized to award Master's degrees in 2005.

Governing Bodies: Rectorate

Academic Year: September - December; March - June

Admission Requirements: Ranking in the top 10% of the national college entrance examination.

Fees: (CNY): 3,500 per annum

Main Language(s) of Instruction: Chinese

International Co-operation: with institutions in Australia, Canada, Japan, Mongolia, New Zealand, USA.

Accrediting Agencies: State Education Commission of the People's Republic of China

Degrees and Diplomas: *Bachelor's Degree*: Egineering; Arts; Science, 4 yrs; *Master's Degree*: 3 yrs

Student Services: Academic counselling, Canteen, Cultural centre, Employment services, Foreign student adviser, Foreign Studies Centre, Handicapped facilities, Health services, Language programs, Social counselling, Sports facilities

Special Facilities: Museum, observatory, film studio.

Libraries: 1.2 million vols.

Publications: Journal of Inner Monglia College of Finance and Economics (monthly)

Academic Staff 2010-2011	TOTAL
FULL-TIME	814
PART-TIME	608
STAFF WITH DOCTORATE	
FULL-TIME	160
PART-TIME	0
Student Numbers 2010-2011	
All (Foreign Included)	c. 22,000

Last Updated: 02/12/10

INNER MONGOLIA MEDICAL COLLEGE

Xinhua Street, Huhhot, Inner Mongolia 010059
Tel: +86(471) 6965120 +86(471) 6967406
Fax: +86(471) 6965120
EMail: webmaster@immc.edu.cn
Website: http://www.immc.edu.cn

President: Wang Yanbin
International Relations: Chen Yi

Departments
Medicine (Medicine); **Paediatrics** (Paediatrics); **Pharmacy** (Pharmacy); **Traditional Chinese Medicine** (Traditional Eastern Medicine)

Degrees and Diplomas: *Bachelor's Degree*; *Master's Degree*

INNER MONGOLIA NORMAL UNIVERSITY

Xincheng, Huhhot, Inner Mongolia 010022
Tel: +86(471) 4964444 Ext. 2515
Fax: +86(471) 4964887
EMail: lmast@vip.163.com
Website: http://www.imnu.edu.cn

President: Yang Yijiang

Schools
Foreign Languages and Literature (English; Literature; Modern Languages; Russian); **Modern Art Design** (Chinese; Design; Economics; Education; Fine Arts; History; Literature; Mathematics; Mongolian; Music; Physics; Political Sciences); **Physical Education** (Physical Education)

History: Founded 1952 as Inner Mongolia Teachers College, acquired present title 1982.

Degrees and Diplomas: *Bachelor's Degree*; *Master's Degree*

Libraries: c. 735,000 vols

Publications: Journal of Inner Mongolia Normal University, Natural Sciences, Social Sciences
Last Updated: 19/11/08

INNER MONGOLIA UNIVERSITY

235 West University Road, Huhhot, Inner Mongolia 010021
Tel: +86(471) 4992241 +86(471) 4992278
Fax: +86(471) 4992084
EMail: ndxcb@imu.edu.cn
Website: http://www.imu.edu.cn

President: B. LianJi
Tel: +86(471) 4992238, Fax: +86(471) 4951761

Centres
Biological Engineering; **Experimental Animal Research** (Animal Husbandry; Veterinary Science; Zoology); **Mongolian Studies**

Departments
Accountancy; **Arts**; **Automation** (Automation and Control Engineering); **Biology** (Bioengineering; Biological and Life Sciences; Biology; Biotechnology); **Chemistry**; **Chinese Language and Literature** (Chinese; Literature; Publishing and Book Trade); **Civil Engineering**; **Computer Science**; **Ecology** (Ecology; Environmental Studies); **Economics** (Economics; Industrial Management; International Economics); **Electronic Engineering**; **Engineering Management** (Engineering Management); **Executive Management**; **Finance**; **Foreign Languages and Literatures**; **History** (History); **Journalism** (Journalism; Publishing and Book Trade); **Law**; **Management**; **Mathematics**; **Mechanical Engineering** (Mechanical Engineering); **Mongolian Language and Literature** (Mongolian); **Philosophy**; **Physics** (Physics); **Politics**; **Tourist Management**; **Transportation**

Institutes
High Polymer Science; **Inner Mongolia Natural Resources** (Natural Resources); **Modern and Contemporary History**; **Mongolian Culture**; **Mongolian History**; **Mongolian Language**; **Neighbouring Countries**

Schools
Arts (Dance; Design; Music; Painting and Drawing); **Chemistry and Chemical Industry** (Chemistry; Industrial Chemistry); **Computer Science** (Computer Science); **Continuing Education**; **Economics** (Accountancy; Economics; Finance; Industrial Management; Management); **Foreign Languages**; **Humanities** (Chinese; History; Journalism; Literature; Philosophy; Tourism); **International Education**; **Law**; **Life Sciences**; **Mongolian Studies** (History; Journalism; Literature; Mongolian); **Professional and Vocational Education** (Civil Engineering; Engineering Management; Mechan-

ical Engineering; Transport Engineering); **Public Management** (Management; Political Sciences); **Science and Engineering**

History: Founded 1957.

Governing Bodies: Foreign Affairs Office of Inner Mongolia University

Academic Year: September to July (September-January; February-July)

Admission Requirements: School certificate

Fees: (US Dollars): 1,500-2,500

Main Language(s) of Instruction: Chinese, English, Mongolian

International Co-operation: With universities in Australia , Finland, Japan, Republic of Mongolia, Russian Federation and South Korea.

Degrees and Diplomas: *Bachelor's Degree*: Accounting; Artistic Design; Dance; Choreography; Music; Music Composition and Composition Theory; Music Performance; Painting; Sculptural Arts; Vocal Music; Automation; Biology; Biological Engineering; Biological Technology; Biological Science; Applied Chemistry; Material Chemistry; Chemistry; Chemical Industry; Chemical Engineering and Technology; Chinese Language and Literature; Publishing; Civil Engineering; Computer Science and Technology; Information and Computer Science; Ecology; Environmental Science; Economics; Industrial and Commercial Management; International Economics and Trade; Communication Engineering; Electronic Information Sciences and Technology; Electronic Science and Technology; Information Management and System; Engineering Management; Executive Management; Finance; Financial Management; English, Japanese and Russian Language and Literature; History; Journalism in Chinese; Journalism and Publication in Mongolian; Law; Mathematics; Management; Personnel Resources Management; Public Undertaking Management; Mechanical Engineering; Broadcasting Arts and Management; Mongolian; Nationality Studies; Philosophy; Physics; Politics and Administration; Tourist Management; Transport; *Master's Degree*: Applied Mathematics; Biophysics; Botany; Business and Administration; Chinese Language and Literature; Civil and Economic Laws; Computer Mathematics; Computer Application Technology; Condensed State Physics; Ecology; Economy in Minority Nationality Areas in China; Business Management; Environmental Science; Ethnology; Fundamental Mathematics; Foreign Language and Literature and Applied Linguistics; History of Ancient China; History of Modern and Contemporary China; Inorganic Chemistry; Language and Literature of Minority Nationalities in China; Literature of Ancient China; Marxist Philosphy; Marxist Theory and Political Education; Microbiology; Operation Research and Control Theory; Organic Chemistry; Pattern Recognition and Intelligence System; Physical Chemistry; Physielectronics; Political Economy; Procedural Law; Regional Economics; Scientific and Technological Philosphy; Signal and Information Processing; Software Technology and Theory; Specialized History; Theoretical Physics; World History; Zoology; *Doctor's Degree*: Applied Mathematics; Biochemistry; Biophysics; Botany; Ecology; History of Minority Nationalities in China; Language and Literature of Minority Nationalities in China; Specialized History; Theoretical Physics; Zoology

Student Services: Academic counselling, Cultural centre, Employment services, Foreign student adviser, Foreign Studies Centre, Health services, Nursery care, Sports facilities

Student Residential Facilities: Yes

Special Facilities: Museum. Movie Studio

Libraries:c. 1,500,000 vols

Publications: Journal of Inner Mongolia University
Last Updated: 19/11/08

INNER MONGOLIA UNIVERSITY FOR THE NATIONALITIES

22 Huolinhe Street, Tongliao, Inner Mongolia 028043
Tel: +86(475) 8282292 +86(475) 8282544
Fax: +86(475) 8232937
EMail: nmgxiuquan@126.com
Website: http://www.imun.edu.cn/

President: Jiang Guishi
International Relations: Liu Yunfeng

Departments

Chemistry (Chemistry); **Education** (Education); **Fine Arts** (Fine Arts); **Marxism and Leninism** (Philosophy; Political Sciences); **Mathematics** (Mathematics); **Modern Languages** (Modern Languages); **Mongolian** (Mongolian); **Physical Education** (Physical Education); **Physics** (Physics); **Political Science and History** (History; Political Sciences)

History: Founded 1958 as Inner Mongolia College of Traditional Mongolian Medicine. Acquired present title and status 2000 following merger with Zhelimu Animal Husbandry College.

Degrees and Diplomas: *Bachelor's Degree*; *Master's Degree*

INNER MONGOLIA UNIVERSITY OF SCIENCE AND TECHNOLOGY

7 Aerding Street, Kun District, Baotou, Inner Mongolia 014010
Tel: +86(472) 2107107
Fax: +86(472) 2124408
EMail: webmaster@imust.cn
Website: http://www.imust.cn

President: Li Hanshan

International Relations: Li Menglin
Tel: +86(472) 5961166, Fax: +86(472) 5163797

Departments

Architectural Engineering (Structural Architecture); **Automation and Computer** (Automation and Control Engineering; Computer Engineering); **Basic Courses**; **Economic Management** (Management); **Environmental Engineering** (Environmental Engineering); **Mechanical Engineering** (Mechanical Engineering); **Metallurgical and Chemical Engineering** (Chemical Engineering; Metallurgical Engineering); **Military Sports**; **Resources Engineering**; **Science Material Engineering** (Materials Engineering)

Schools

Graduate Studies

History: Founded 2003 following merger of the Baotou Iron and Steel Colleges, Baotou Medical College and Baotou Teachers College.

Main Language(s) of Instruction: Chinese

Degrees and Diplomas: *Bachelor's Degree*; *Master's Degree*
Last Updated: 20/11/08

INNER MONGOLIA UNIVERSITY OF TECHNOLOGY

221 Aimin Road, Huhhot, Inner Mongolia 010062
Tel: +86(475) 6510939
Fax: +86(475) 6503298
EMail: zsb@imut.edu.cn
Website: http://www.imut.edu.cn

Schools

Continuing Education (Mechanical Engineering); **Electrical Engineering** (Electrical Engineering); **International Business** (Chemical Engineering; Civil Engineering; Electrical Engineering; International Business); **Vocational Engineering Technology** (Power Engineering)

History: Founded 1951 as Suiyuan Provincial Technical School, acquired present title 1993.

Main Language(s) of Instruction: Chinese

Degrees and Diplomas: *Bachelor's Degree*; *Master's Degree*; *Doctor's Degree*

Libraries: c. 450,000 vols

Publications: Journal of Inner Mongolia University of Technology, Natural Sciences, Social Sciences
Last Updated: 20/11/08

JIAMUSI UNIVERSITY

No.188 Xuefu Street, Jiamusi, Heilongjiang Province 154007
Tel: +86(454) 8781844
Fax: +86(454) 8793612
EMail: jmsu_icec@163.com
Website: http://www.jmsu.org/

President: Zhang Shaojie

International Relations: Chen Chun

Schools

Art; **Basic Medicine**; **Chemistry and Pharmacy**; **Clinical Medicine**; **Economics and Management**; **Foreign Languages**; **Humanities**; **Information and Electronic Engineering**; **Materials Engineering**; **Mechanical Engineering**; **Natural Sciences**; **Physical Education**; **Rehabilitation Medicine**; **Stomatology**; **Vocational Technology**

History: Founded 1996, incorporating the former Jiamusi Medical College, Jiamusi Institute of Technology, and Jiamusi Teachers College.

Degrees and Diplomas: *Bachelor's Degree*; *Master's Degree*

Libraries: c. 750,000 vols

Publications: ; Journal of Natural Sciences; Journal of Social Sciences
Last Updated: 20/11/08

JIANGHAN UNIVERSITY

18 Jiangda Road, Wuhan, Hubei Province 430010
Tel: +86(27) 82622241
Fax: +86(27) 82631533
EMail: jdwb@public.wh.hb.cn
Website: http://www.jhun.edu.cn

President: Bai Shengxiang

International Relations: Zhang Yan

Departments

Accountancy and Statistics (Accountancy; Statistics); **Agronomy** (Agronomy); **Applied Physics** (Applied Physics); **Arts and Music** (Fine Arts; Music); **Chinese Language and Literature** (Chinese; Literature); **Foreign Languages and Literature** (Literature; Modern Languages); **Management** (Management); **Mathematics and Computer Science** (Mathematics and Computer Science); **Mechanical and Electrical Engineering** (Electrical Engineering; Mechanical Engineering); **Physical Education** (Physical Education); **Politics and Law** (Law; Political Sciences); **Secretarial Studies** (Secretarial Studies); **Urban Construction and Environmental Protection** (Environmental Studies; Urban Studies)

History: Founded 1980. In 2001, it merged with HUST Hankou branch and Wuhan Worker's Medical College.

Main Language(s) of Instruction: Chinese

Degrees and Diplomas: *Bachelor's Degree*

Publications: Journal of Jianghan University

JIANGNAN UNIVERSITY

1800 Lihu Road, Wuxi, Jiangsu Province 214036
Tel: +86(510) 5806751
Fax: +86(510) 5807976
EMail: xck@jiangnan.edu.cn
Website: http://www.jiangnan.edu.cn

President: Chen Jian

International Relations: Tang Jian

Departments

Architecture (Architecture; Civil Engineering); **Art** (Arts and Humanities; Fine Arts; Music); **International Studies**; **Medical Science** (Nursing)

Schools

Biotechnology; **Business**; **Chemical and Material Engineering** (Applied Chemistry; Biochemistry; Chemical Engineering; Chemistry; Energy Engineering; Materials Engineering; Organic Chemistry; Technology); **Chinese Language and Literature** (Chinese; Literature); **Communication and Control Engineering**; **Design** (Advertising and Publicity; Architecture; Design; Industrial Design); **Education**; **Food Science and Technology** (Food Science; Food Technology; Zoology); **Information Technology** *(Vocational)*; **Law and Politics**; **Mechanical Engineering** (Automation and Control Engineering; Industrial Design; Machine Building; Mechanical Engineering; Packaging Technology; Technology); **Sciences**; **Textile and Garment** (Fashion Design; Textile Design; Textile Technology)

History: Founded 1958 as Sanjiang Normal UNiversity. Renamed Wuxi College of Light Industry 1958 and Wuxi University of Light Industry 1995. Merged with Jiangnan College and Wuxi Teachers College. Acquired present title 2001.

Degrees and Diplomas: *Bachelor's Degree*; *Master's Degree*; *Doctor's Degree*

Libraries: c. 590,000 vols

Publications: Higher Education Research Report; Journal of Wuxi University of Light Industry
Last Updated: 20/11/08

JIANGSU POLYTECHNIC UNIVERSITY

Beiyun Road, Changzhou, Jiangsu Province 213016
Tel: +86(519) 3290140
Fax: +86(519) 3290011
EMail: jlc@jpu.edu.cn
Website: http://eng.jpu.edu.cn

President: Zhigang Chen

Departments
Business Administration (Business Administration); **Chemical Engineering** (Chemical Engineering); **Computer Science and Engineering** (Computer Engineering; Computer Science); **Environmental and Safety Engineering** (Environmental Engineering; Safety Engineering); **Information Sciences** (Information Sciences); **Materials Science and Engineering** (Materials Engineering); **Mechanical Engineering**; **Modern Languages** (Modern Languages)

History: Founded 1978 as Jiangsu Institute of Chemical Technology. Acquired present title 2002. Formerly known as Jiangsu Institute of Petrochemical Technology.

Degrees and Diplomas: *Bachelor's Degree*; *Master's Degree*
Last Updated: 20/11/08

JIANGSU UNIVERSITY

Zhenjiang, Jiangsu Province 212013
Tel: +86(511) 8780035
Fax: +86(511) 8780036
EMail: fying@ujs.edu.cn; waishi@ujs.edu.cn
Website:http: //www.ujs.edu.cn

President: Shouqi Yuan

Colleges
Adult Education; Teacher Training

Schools
Arts; **Automotive and Traffic Engineering** (Automotive Engineering; Road Transport); **Business Administration**; **Chemical Engineering**; **Computer Science and Telecommunications Engineering**; **Electrical and Information Engineering**; **Energy and Power Engineering**; **Environment**; **Food and Biological Engineering**; **Foreign Languages**; **Material Science and Technology** (Materials Engineering; Technology); **Mechanical Engineering**; **Medical Technology**; **Medicine**; **Metallurgical Engineering**; **Pharmacy**; **Science**; **Social Sciences and Humanities**

Further Information: Also College in Jingjiang.

History: Founded 1960. Acquired present status 2001 following merger of Jiangsu University of Science and Technology, Zhenjiang Teacher's College, and Zhenjiang Medical College.

Academic Year: September to June

Admission Requirements: Graduation from High School and HSK Certificate

Fees: (US Dollars): 1,800 per annum

Main Language(s) of Instruction: English, Chinese

International Co-operation: With universities in Germany, USA, Japan, Thailand.

Degrees and Diplomas: *Bachelor's Degree*: Arts; Science; Engineering, 4 yrs; *Master's Degree*: Arts; Science; Engineering, a further 2-3 yrs; *Doctor's Degree*: Science; Engineering, a further 3 yrs. Also Post-Doctor Degree.

Student Services: Academic counselling, Cultural centre, Employment services, Foreign student adviser, Health services, Nursery care, Social counselling, Sports facilities
Publications: Journal of Jiangsu (monthly)
Last Updated: 20/11/08

JIANGSU UNIVERSITY OF SCIENCE AND TECHNOLOGY

2 Huanchen Road, Zhenjiang, Jiangsu Province 212003
Tel: +86(511) 4401002
Fax: +86(511) 4421823
EMail: Office@just.edu.cn
Website: http://www.just.edu.cn/

President: Wu Liren

International Relations: Liu Wenfu

Departments
Electronics and Information Sciences; **Engineering Management**; **Mechanical Engineering** (Mechanical Engineering); **Naval and Civil Architecture**; **Social Sciences**; **Welding and Materials Science** (Materials Engineering)

History: Founded 1953 as Shanghai Shipbuilding School. Also previously known as Eastern China Shipbuilding Institute. Renamed Jiangsu University of Science and Technology 2004.

Degrees and Diplomas: *Bachelor's Degree*; *Master's Degree*; *Doctor's Degree*
Last Updated: 20/11/08

JIANGXI AGRICULTURAL UNIVERSITY

Meiling, Nanchang, Jiangxi Province 330045
Tel: +86(791) 3813351
Fax: +86(791) 3813351
EMail: zhxm889@yahoo.com.cn
Website: http://www.jxau.edu.cn

President: Liu Yibei

International Relations: Wang Jinxiang

Colleges
Agronomy (Agronomy; Horticulture; Plant and Crop Protection); **Animal Science and Techniques**; **Economics and Trade**; **Engineering**; **Forestry**; **Land Resources and Environment**; **Vocational Education**

History: Founded 1969. Acquired present title 1980.

Academic Year: September to July (September-January; February-July)

Admission Requirements: Graduation from senior middle school and entrance examination

Main Language(s) of Instruction: Chinese

Degrees and Diplomas: *Bachelor's Degree*; *Master's Degree*

Libraries: c. 500,000 vols

Publications: Acta Agriculturae Universitatis Jiangxiensis (bimonthly); Jiangxi Plant Protection

JIANGXI NORMAL UNIVERSITY

Nanchang, Jiangxi Province 330027
Tel: +86(791) 8506180
Fax: +86(791) 8502744
EMail: iedept@sina.com
Website: http://www.jxnu.edu.cn

President: You Hai

Departments
Chemistry (Chemistry); **Chinese Language and Literature** (Chinese); **Computer Science** (Computer Science); **Educational Administration** (Educational Administration); **Educational Communication** (Communication Studies); **English** (English; Modern Languages); **Fine Arts** (Fine Arts); **Geography** (Geography); **History** (History); **Mathematics** (Mathematics); **Music** (Music); **Physical Education** (Physical Education); **Physics** (Physics); **Political Education** (Political Sciences); **Teacher Training** (Teacher Training)

Research Institutes

Ancient Books Collation (Ancient Books); **Chemistry** (Chemistry); **China Local History** (History); **Economics** (Economics); **Education** (Education); **History of the Chinese Revolution** (History); **Jiangxi Geography** (Geography); **Language and Literature** (Literature; Modern Languages); **Mathematics** (Mathematics); **Physics** (Physics)

History: Founded 1940 as National Chiang Kai Shek University. Acquired present status and title 1983. Under the jurisdiction of the Provincial Government.

Academic Year: September to July (September-January; March-July)

Admission Requirements: Graduation from senior middle school and entrance examination

Main Language(s) of Instruction: Chinese

Degrees and Diplomas: *Bachelor's Degree*; *Master's Degree*; *Doctor's Degree*

Libraries: Central Library, c. 1.6m. vols

Publications: Study of Higher Education Administration; Study of Middle School Mathematics

Press or Publishing House: University Printing House
Last Updated: 20/11/08

JIANGXI UNIVERSITY OF FINANCE AND ECONOMICS

Lushan Middle Road, Nanchang, Jiangxi Province 330013
Tel: +86(791) 3816418
Fax: +86(791) 3805665
EMail: oec@jxufe.edu.cn
Website: http://www.jxufe.edu.cn

President: Jinqiu Liao

Schools

Accountancy; **Art and Communication**; **Business Administration**; **Economics** (Economics; Engineering Management; Real Estate); **Electronics**; **Finance**; **Foreign Languages**; **Humanities**; **Information Management**; **International Trade and Economics**; **Physical Education** (Physical Education); **Public Administration**; **Resources and Environment Management**; **Software** (Software Engineering); **Statistics**; **Tourism** (Tourism)

History: Founded 1923 as School of Finance and Economics of Jiangxi Province. Merged with Jiangnan Cadres' Institute of Finance and Management. Acquired present title 1996.

Degrees and Diplomas: *Bachelor's Degree*; *Master's Degree*; *Doctor's Degree*

Libraries: c. 600,000 vols

Publications: Contemporary Finance; Journal of Jiangxi University of Finance and Economics
Last Updated: 20/11/08

JIANGXI UNIVERSITY OF SCIENCE AND TECHNOLOGY (JUST)

122 Hongqi Road, Ganzhou, Jiangxi Province 341000
Tel: +86(797) 8312013
Fax: +86(797) 8312107
EMail: posim@mail.sim.jx.cn
Website: http://www.jxust.cn

President: Zhengming Xiong
Tel: +86(797) 8312100, Fax: +86(797) 8312018
EMail: xiongzhengming@mail.jxust.cn

Director: Zaidong Jiang Tel: +86(797) 8312129

International Relations: Qun Yang, Director
EMail: Ynagqun1772@sohu.com

Institutes

Applied Science *(Jinshawan Campus) Dean:* Benxiao Chen

Schools

Environmental and Construction Engineering (Construction Engineering; Environmental Engineering) *Dean:* Mingkang Tang; **Materials and Chemical Engineering** (Chemical Engineering; Materials Engineering) *Dean:* Ruiqing Liu; **Continuing Education** *Dean:* Minshaw Hu; **Economics and Management** *Dean:* Yingliang

Xie; **Foreign Studies** (International Studies; Modern Languages) *Dean:* Zhenghua Ling; **Higher Vocational and Technical Education** *(Nanchang Campus) Dean:* Shanfu Chen; **Information Engineering** *Dean:* Wen Li; **Liberal Arts and Law** (Arts and Humanities; Law) *Dean:* Zhangsheng Lai; **Mechanical and Electronic Engineering** (Automation and Control Engineering; Electronic Engineering; Mechanical Engineering) *Dean:* Yu Lin; **Science** (Natural Sciences) *Dean:* Kuohua Wu

History: Founded 1958 as Jiangxi Metallurgic Institute, acquired present name 2004.

Fees: (Yuan): c. 4,000 per annum

Main Language(s) of Instruction: Chinese

International Co-operation: With universities in USA, United Kingdom, France, Russia, Netherlands, Japan, Iceland, and Thailand

Accrediting Agencies: Jiangxi Provincial Government

Degrees and Diplomas: *Bachelor's Degree:* Arts; Science; Engineering, 4 yrs; *Master's Degree:* Engineering, 3 yrs

Libraries: Campus Library, c. 1,424,000 vols

Publications: Jiangxi University of Science and Technology Academic Periodical
Last Updated: 20/11/08

JIANGXI UNIVERSITY OF TRADITIONAL CHINESE MEDICINE

56 Yangming Road, Nanchang, Jiangxi Province 330006
Tel: +86(791) 6820664
Fax: +86(791) 6820664
EMail: jzied@163.com
Website: http://www.at0086.com/JUTCM/

President: Pi Chiheng

International Relations: Qi Nan

Departments

Acupuncture and Traumatology; **Orthopaedics**; **Pharmacology** (Pharmacology); **Traditional Chinese Medicine** (Traditional Eastern Medicine)

History: Founded 1959.

Degrees and Diplomas: *Bachelor's Degree*; *Master's Degree*
Last Updated: 20/11/08

JIAXING UNIVERSITY

56 Yuexiu Road (South), Jiaxing, Zhejiang Province 314001
Tel: +86(573) 8364 1233
Fax: +86(573) 8364 1210
EMail: yvetyin@126.com
Website: http://www.zjxu.edu.cn

President: Xu Xianmin

Colleges

Accountancy (Accountancy; Finance); **Adult Education**; **Architectural and Civil Engineering** (Architectural and Environmental Design; Civil Engineering; Environmental Engineering); **Biology and Chemical Engineering**; **Economics** (Economics; Finance; International Business); **Electro-mechanics Engineering**; **Foreign Languages**; **Garment and Art Design**; **Information Engineering** (Computer Science; Information Management; Information Sciences; Information Technology); **Liberal Arts and Law** (Chinese; Law; Literature; Native Language); **Management**; **Mathematics and Information Science**; **Medicine** (Medicine; Nursing; Pharmacy)

Programmes

Garment Technology *(Pinghu Campus)*; **Mechanical Design, Manufacturing and Automation** *(Pinghu Campus)* (Automation and Control Engineering; Mechanical Engineering; Production Engineering); **Primary Education** *(Pinghu Campus)*

History: Created 2000. Previously known as Jiaxing Junior College and Zhejiang Junior College of Economics.

Main Language(s) of Instruction: Chinese

Degrees and Diplomas: *Bachelor's Degree:* Business; Modern Languages; Law; Engineering; Computer and Information Science; Primary Teaching; Science; Garment Technology and Design, 4 yrs;

Bachelor's Degree: Medicine, 5 yrs. Also 2-year specialized programmes

Special Facilities: Social Science and Humanities Training Centre; Bio-Chemistry Experimental Centre; Engineering Training Centre; Textiles and Arts laboratory.

Libraries: c. 631,370 vols. incl. periodicals (both Chinese and foreign language)

Academic Staff *2007-2008*: Total: c. 1,200
Student Numbers *2007-2008*: Total: c. 15,000
Last Updated: 24/09/08

JIAYING UNIVERSITY

Meizigang, Eastern District, Meizhou, Guangdong Province 514015
Tel: +86(753) 2357776
Fax: +86(753) 2354276
EMail: fao@jyu.edu.cn
Website: http://www.jyu.edu.cn

President: Cheng Biao

Departments
Architecture (Architecture); **Biology** (Biology); **Chemistry** (Chemistry); **Chinese and Literature** (Chinese); **Computer Science** (Computer Science); **Economics and Finance** (Economics; Finance); **Electronics** (Electronic Engineering); **Fine Arts** (Fine Arts); **Foreign Languages** (Modern Languages); **Geography** (Geography); **Mathematics** (Mathematics); **Physical Education** (Physical Education); **Physics** (Physics); **Politics and Law** (History; Law; Political Sciences)

History: Founded 1913 as Jiaying Teachers College, acquired present title 1988.

Academic Year: September to July

Admission Requirements: Graduation from senior middle school and entrance examination

Main Language(s) of Instruction: Chinese

Degrees and Diplomas: *Zhuanke Certificate of Graduation*: 2-3 yrs; *Bachelor's Degree*

Student Residential Facilities: Yes

Special Facilities: Biological Garden; Movie Studio

Libraries: c. 230,000 vols

Publications: Jiaying University Journal *(quarterly)*
Last Updated: 20/11/08

JILIN AGRICULTURAL UNIVERSITY

Changchun, Jilin Province 130118
Tel: +86(431) 4531646
Fax: +86(431) 4531646
EMail: info@jlau.edu.cn
Website: http://www.jlau.edu.cn

President: Li Yu

International Relations: Zhang Dongming

Faculties
Agricultural Professional Technology; **Agronomy**; **Animal Science and Technology**; **Chinese Traditional Medical Materials**; **Engineering and Technology**; **High Professional Technology**; **Resources and Environment**

History: Founded as college 1948. Acquired present status and title 1959, incorporating previously existing agricultural colleges. Under the jurisdiction of the Provincial Government.

Academic Year: September to July (September-January; March-July)

Admission Requirements: Graduation from senior middle school and entrance examination

Main Language(s) of Instruction: Chinese

Degrees and Diplomas: *Bachelor's Degree*: 4 yrs; *Master's Degree*: a further 3 yrs; *Doctor's Degree*

Libraries: Central Library, c. 450,000 vols

Publications: Higher Education Study; Journal of Jilin Agricultural University *(quarterly)*; Mycology Sinica

Press or Publishing House: JAU Publishing House

JILIN COLLEGE OF ARTS

11 Ziyou Street, Changchun, Jilin Province 130021
Tel: +86(431) 5649101 Ext. 5001
Fax: +86(431) 5643767
EMail: jlart@263.net
Website: http://www.jlart.com.cn

President: Deng Xiemu

International Relations: Xi Chunyou

Departments
Dance (Dance); **Design** (Design); **Fine Arts** (Painting and Drawing; Sculpture); **Music** (Music); **Theatre** (Theatre)

History: Founded 1958 as Jilin Technological Academy of the Arts. Acquired present title 2000.

Degrees and Diplomas: *Bachelor's Degree*; *Master's Degree*

JILIN HUAQIAO FOREIGN LANGUAGES INSTITUTE

3658 Jingyue Street, Changchun, Jilin Province 130117
Tel: +86(431) 4533550 +86(431) 4533627
Fax: +86(431) 4533598
EMail: hqjilin@yahoo.com.cn
Website: http://www.huabridge.com

Departments
German (German); **Japanese** (Japanese); **Vocational Education**

Schools
Applied (Economics; English; Management); **Bilingual** (English; French; Korean; Spanish); **English** (Education; English; Translation and Interpretation)

History: Founded 1995.

Degrees and Diplomas: *Bachelor's Degree*

Libraries: c. 140,000 vols; c. 400 periodical subscriptions.

JILIN INSTITUTE OF ARCHITECTURE AND CIVIL ENGINEERING

27 Hongqi Road, Changchun, Jilin Province 130021
Tel: +86(431) 5935075
Fax: +86(431) 5914478
EMail: faojiae@public.jl.cc.cn
Website: http://www.jliae.edu.cn/newjliae/stylenew111.htm

President: Yin Jun

International Relations: Zhang Wei

Departments
Architecture (Architecture); **Civil Engineering** (Civil Engineering); **Construction Engineering**; **Road and Highway Engineering**; **Town Planning** (Town Planning)

History: Founded 1956.

Degrees and Diplomas: *Bachelor's Degree*; *Master's Degree*
Last Updated: 23/09/08

JILIN INSTITUTE OF CHEMICAL TECHNOLOGY

45 Chengde Street, Jilin, Jilin Province 132022
Tel: +86(432) 3093625
Fax: +86(431) 3093625
EMail: jhxy@public.jl.jl.cn
Website: http://www.jlict.edu.cn

President: Li Gang

International Relations: Zhao Shukui

Departments
Automation Engineering; **Chemical Engineering** (Chemical Engineering); **Chemical Equipment and Machinery** (Machine Building); **Environmental Engineering** (Environmental Engineering); **Fine Chemical Engineering** (Chemical Engineering)

History: Founded 1958 as Jilin Mechanical and Electrical Technological School, acquired present status and title 1978.

Degrees and Diplomas: *Bachelor's Degree*

JILIN NORMAL UNIVERSITY

8 Shida Road, Tiexi District, Siping, Jilin Province 136000
Tel: +86(434) 3290040
Fax: +86(434) 3290363
EMail: wsc@jlnu.edu.cn
Website: http://www.jlnu.edu.cn/english/english/e11.htm
President: Zhang Baijun

Departments
Administration; **Audiovisual Education**; **Biology** (Biology); **Chemistry**; **Chinese Language and Literature** (Chinese; Literature); **Computer Science** (Computer Science; Technology); **Education** (Education; Preschool Education; Psychology; Teacher Training); **Environment Engineering**; **Fine Arts** (Fine Arts); **Foreign Languages and Literature** (English; Japanese; Literature; Modern Languages; Russian); **Geography** (Geography; Information Technology; Tourism); **Information Engineering** (Information Technology; Telecommunications Engineering); **Mathematics**; **Music** (Music); **Physical Education** (Physical Education); **Physics** (Physics); **Politics and Law** (Law; Political Sciences)

History: Founded 1953 as Siping Teachers College. Acquired present title 2002.

Academic Year: September to July (September-February; March-July)

Admission Requirements: Senior High School Graduation Diploma; international students have to pass the Chinese Certificate Examination (HSK); no certificate is required for language training students

Fees: (US Dollar): four years programme, 1,600 per annum; language training, 1,300 per annum; short programme (4 weeks), 200, plus 40 for each extra week

International Co-operation: With universities in USA, Russian Federation, United Kingdom, Canada, Korea, Australia and New Zealand

Degrees and Diplomas: *Bachelor's Degree*; *Master's Degree*

Student Residential Facilities: Dormitories on campus

Libraries: c. 1.25m vol.; 2,400 journals and magazines in Chinese and foreign languages

Last Updated: 20/11/08

JILIN TEACHERS INSTITUTE OF ENGINEERING AND TECHNOLOGY

3050 Kaixuan Road, Changchun, Jilin Province 130052
Tel: +86(431) 2938664
Fax: +86(431) 2938664
EMail: baolong7@126.com
Website: http://www.jltiet.net

Colleges
Business Management (Business Administration); **Continuing Education** (Continuing Education); **Economic Technology** (Economics; Technology); **Fine Arts** (Fine Arts); **Information Engineering** (Information Technology); **Mechatronic Engineering** (Electronic Engineering; Mechanical Engineering)

Departments
Basic Courses (Gender Studies); **Biological Engineering** (Bioengineering); **Foreign Languages** (Modern Languages); **Physical Education** (Physical Education); **Social Science**

History: Founded 1979 as Jilin Teachers College of Technicians. Acquired present title 2002.

Degrees and Diplomas: *Bachelor's Degree*; *Master's Degree*

Libraries: c. 238,000 vols.

JILIN UNIVERSITY

2699 Qianjin Street, Changchun, Jilin Province 130012
Tel: +86(431) 5166571
Fax: +86(431) 5166570
EMail: fsc@jlu.edu.cn
Website: http://www.jlu.edu.cn
President: Zhan Tao

Divisions
Arts and Humanities (Arts and Humanities; Fine Arts; Modern Languages; Philosophy; Physical Education; Sociology); **Engineering** (Agricultural Engineering; Automotive Engineering; Biology; Engineering; Management; Materials Engineering; Mechanical Engineering; Transport and Communications; Transport Engineering); **Geosciences**; **Health Sciences**; **Information Sciences** (Computer Engineering; Computer Science; Electronic Engineering; Information Sciences; Telecommunications Engineering); **Science** (Biological and Life Sciences; Chemistry; Mathematics; Physics); **Social Sciences** (Administration; Business and Commerce; Economics; Law; Social Sciences)

Schools
Business (Accountancy; Business Administration; Business and Commerce; Finance; Human Resources; Information Sciences; Marketing; Tourism); **Economics**; **Law** (Administrative Law; Civil Law; Commercial Law; Constitutional Law; Criminal Law; Environmental Studies; History of Law; International Law; Law)

History: Founded 1946 as Northeast Administration Institute. Merged with Harbin University 1948. Became People's University 1950. Incorporated Jilin University of Technology (founded 1955), Norman Bethune University of Medical Sciences (founded 1939), Changchun University of Science and Technology (founded 1951) and Changchun Institute of Posts and Telecommunications (founded 1947) and acquired present status 2000.

Academic Year: September to July (September-January; February-July)

Admission Requirements: Graduation from senior middle school and entrance examination

Main Language(s) of Instruction: Chinese

Accrediting Agencies: State Education Commission

Degrees and Diplomas: *Bachelor's Degree*: 4 yrs; *Master's Degree*: a further 3 yrs; *Doctor's Degree*: 3 yrs following Master

Student Residential Facilities: Yes

Special Facilities: Historical Relics and Archaeology Exhibition Hall

Libraries: c. 5.3m vols

Publications: Chemical Research in Chinese Universities; Chemistry Journal for Institutions of Higher Learning; Higher Education Research and Practice; Jilin University Natural Science Journal; Journal of Demography; Journal of Historical Studies; Legal System and Social Development; Legality and Social Development; Mathematics of Northeast China; Modern Japanese Economy; Northeast Asia Forum

Press or Publishing House: Jilin University Press
Last Updated: 20/11/08

JIMEI UNIVERSITY (JMU)

Jimei Schools Village, 185 Yinjiang Rd., Jimei District, Xiamen, Fujian Province 361021
Tel: +86(592) 6181097
Fax: +86(592) 6180120
EMail: faojmu@jmu.edu.cn
Website: http://www.jmu.edu.cn

President: Jiande Gu
Tel: +86(592) 6181090, Fax: +86(592) 6180120

International Relations: Guanghuang Ye

Colleges
Arts (Art Education; Design; Fine Arts; Music); **Bioengineering** (Bioengineering; Environmental Engineering; Food Science; Food Technology; Microbiology); **Engineering Technology** (Automotive Engineering; Business Computing; Mechanical Equipment and Maintenance); **Fisheries** (Aquaculture; Fishery); **Information Engineering** (Computer Science; Electronic Engineering; Information Management; Information Technology); **Mechanical Engineering** (Mechanical Engineering; Thermal Engineering); **Physical Education** (Physical Education; Sports); **Science** (Applied Physics; Geography; Information Management; Mathematics); **Teacher Training** (Educational Technology; Pedagogy; Teacher Training)

Institutes
Finance and Economics (Accountancy; Banking; Economics; Finance; Taxation); **Marine Engineering** (Marine Engineering;

Naval Architecture); **Navigation** (Marine Transport; Nautical Science; Transport Engineering)

Schools

Business Administration (Accountancy; Business Administration; Information Management; Marketing; Tourism); **Chinese Language and Literature** (Chinese; Literature); **Computer Science and Engineering**; **Foreign Languages** (English; Japanese); **Political Science and Law** (Law; Political Sciences; Social Work)

History: Founded 1994. Merger between Jimei Navigation Institute, Xiamen Fisheries College, Fujian Physical Education College, Finance and Economics Institute of Fujian and Jimei Teachers College.

Academic Year: September to July

Main Language(s) of Instruction: Chinese

Degrees and Diplomas: *Bachelor's Degree*; *Master's Degree*

Student Services: Canteen, Cultural centre, Health services, Language programs, Sports facilities

Student Residential Facilities: Yes

Libraries: c. 1,130,000 vols

Publications: Journal of Jimei University

Last Updated: 20/11/08

JINAN UNIVERSITY

Shipai, Guangzhou, Guangdong Province 510632
Tel: +86(20) 85220085
Fax: +86(20) 85221395
EMail: owsc@jnu.edu.cn
Website: http://www.jnu.edu.cn

President: Hu Jun

Colleges

Chinese Language and Culture (Chinese; Cultural Studies); **Economics** (Economics; Finance; Information Management; International Business; International Economics; Law; Taxation)

Schools

Education (Education); **Liberal Arts** (Art Education; Chinese; History; International Relations; Journalism; Literature; Modern Languages); **Life Sciences** (Analytical Chemistry; Bioengineering; Biological and Life Sciences; Biomedical Engineering; Chemistry; Environmental Engineering; Food Science; Genetics; Inorganic Chemistry; Zoology); **Management** (Accountancy; Business Administration; Business and Commerce; Human Resources; Management); **Medicine** (Medicine; Nursing; Stomatology; Traditional Eastern Medicine); **Science and Engineering** (Computer Science; Electronic Engineering; Mathematics; Physics; Software Engineering); **Tourism** (Management; Tourism)

Further Information: Also Teaching Hospital

History: Founded 1906 as Jinan School. Became university 1927. Mainly opened to Chinese students coming from abroad, to students from Hong Kong, Macau, Taiwan, and Chinese students of foreign nationality.

Governing Bodies: Board of Trustees

Academic Year: September to July (September-January; February-July)

Admission Requirements: Graduation from senior middle school and entrance examination

Main Language(s) of Instruction: Chinese

Accrediting Agencies: Office of Overseas Chinese Affairs of the State Council; State Education Commission

Degrees and Diplomas: *Bachelor's Degree*; *Master's Degree*: a further 3 yrs; *Doctor's Degree*

Student Residential Facilities: Yes

Libraries: Central Library, c. 1.3m. vols

Publications: Chinese Pathology and Pathophysiology Periodical; Jinan Education; Journal of Jinan University, Philosophy and Social Sciences, Natural Sciences and Medicine *(quarterly)*; Southeast Asian Studies

Last Updated: 20/11/08

JINGDEZHEN CERAMIC INSTITUTE

Eastern Suburb, Jingdezhen, Jiangxi Province 333001
Tel: +86(798) 8449200
Fax: +86(798) 8441837
EMail: jdz_jci@yahoo.cn
Website: http://www.jci.jx.cn/

President: Chou Jianer

Departments

Foreign Languages (Modern Languages); **Physical Education** (Physical Education); **Social Sciences** (Social Sciences); **Thermal Engineering** (Thermal Engineering)

Schools

Art and Design; **Business Administration** (Business Administration; E-Business/Commerce; Finance; Marketing); **Information Engineering**; **Materials Science and Engineering**; **Mechanical and Electronic Engineering** (Automation and Control Engineering; Electronic Engineering; Mechanical Engineering)

History: Founded 1958. Acquired present status and title 1999.

Degrees and Diplomas: *Bachelor's Degree*; *Master's Degree*
Last Updated: 20/11/08

JINING MEDICAL COLLEGE

38 Jianshe Road, Jining, Shandong Province 272013
Tel: +86(537) 2252776
Fax: +86(537) 2252776
EMail: admin@jiningmedicalcollege.com
Website: http://www.jnmc.edu.cn/english/index.asp

President: Jiang Ling
International Relations: Qin Jianzhong

Departments

Clinical Medicine (Medicine); **Nursing** (Nursing); **Preventive Medicine** (Social and Preventive Medicine); **Psychiatry** (Psychiatry and Mental Health); **Social Sciences** (Social Sciences)

History: Founded 1952 as Jining Secondary Medical Practitioner School, acquired present status and name 1987.

Degrees and Diplomas: *Bachelor's Degree*; *Master's Degree*

JINZHOU MEDICAL UNIVERSITY

40 Sanduan, Songpo Road, Linghe District, Jinzhou, Liaoning Province 121000
Tel: +86(416) 4673073
Fax: +86(416) 4673528
EMail: webmaster@jzmu.edu.cn
Website: http://www.jzmu.edu.cn

President: Huanjiu Xi
Administrative Officer: Lizhou Zhang
International Relations: Meng Jie

Departments

Animal Science and Veterinary Science (Veterinary Science; Zoology); **Clinical Medicine**; **Medicine** (Medicine); **Nursing**; **Otorhinolaryngology** (Otorhinolaryngology); **Pharmacy** (Pharmacy)

History: Founded 1946 as Liaoji Military Area Hygiene School, acquired present title 1958.

Admission Requirements: Graduation from senior middle school or recognized equivalent

Fees: (Yuan): 4,800

Main Language(s) of Instruction: Chinese; English

Accrediting Agencies: Ministry of Education

Degrees and Diplomas: *Bachelor's Degree*: Medicine, 4-5 yrs; *Master's Degree*: Medicine, 3 yrs; *Doctor's Degree*: Human Anatomy; History of Embryology (PhD), 3 yrs

Student Services: Academic counselling, Canteen, Cultural centre, Employment services, Foreign student adviser, Foreign Studies Centre, Health services, Language programs, Nursery care, Sports facilities

Libraries: c. 1,100,000 vols

Publications: Jinzhou Medical College Journal

JISHOU UNIVERSITY

Jishou, Hunan Province 416000
Tel: +86(743) 8551001
Fax: +86(743) 8551001
EMail: office@jsu.edu.cn
Website: http://www.jsu.edu.cn

President: Ma Benli **EMail:** president@jsu.edu.cn

International Relations: Liu Xiangsheng

Departments

Arts and Music (Fine Arts; Music); **Biological and Environmental Sciences** (Biological and Life Sciences; Environmental Studies); **Chemistry** (Chemistry); **Chinese Language and Literature** (Chinese; Modern Languages); **Economics** (Economics); **Foreign Languages and Literature** (Literature; Modern Languages); **Mathematics and Computer Science** (Mathematics and Computer Science); **Physics and Electronic Engineering** (Electronic Engineering; Physics); **Politics and Law** (History; Law; Management; Political Sciences); **Sports** (Sports)

Further Information: Also Central Laboratory with 9 Research Institutes. Courses for foreign students

History: Founded 1958, acquired present status 1978.

Academic Year: February to January (February-July; September-January)

Degrees and Diplomas: *Bachelor's Degree*

Libraries: c. 470,000 vols

Publications: Journal of Jishou University

JIUJIANG UNIVERSITY

551 Qianjin Donglu, Jiujiang, Jiangxi Province 332005
Tel: +86(792) 831-4451
Fax: +86(792) 833-7982
EMail: fao@jju.edu.cn; jjuxb@jju.edu.cn
Website: http://www.jju.edu.cn

Colleges

Medicine (Alternative Medicine; Anaesthesiology; Dentistry; Health Administration; Medical Technology; Medicine; Pharmacy)

Faculties

Accounting (Accountancy; Management); **Arts** (Art Education; Design; Fine Arts; Music Education; Musicology); **Business** (Business Administration; E-Business/Commerce; Human Resources; International Business; Marketing; Transport Management); **Chemical Science and Engineering** (Applied Chemistry; Chemical Engineering; Chemistry; Organic Chemistry); **Chinese Literature and Communication** (Chinese; Literature); **Civil Engineering and Urban Construction** (Architecture and Planning; Civil Engineering; Real Estate; Town Planning); **Clinical Medicine** (Medicine); **Electronic Engineering** (Electronic Engineering; Information Sciences; Telecommunications Engineering); **Foreign Languages** (English; Japanese); **Information Science and Technology** (Information Sciences; Information Technology); **Law** (Law); **Life Sciences and Biological Engineering** (Biological and Life Sciences; Biomedical Engineering); **Material Science and Engineering** (Materials Engineering); **Mechanical Engineering** (Mechanical Engineering); **Nursing** (Nursing); **Science and Mathematics** (Applied Mathematics; Applied Physics; Information Sciences; Mathematics; Mathematics Education); **Sports** (Physical Education; Sports); **Tourism** (Hotel Management; Tourism)

History: Created 1981. Acquired current name and status 2000.

Degrees and Diplomas: *Bachelor's Degree*
Last Updated: 24/01/11

KASHGAR TEACHERS COLLEGE

463 Kuonanaizheerbage Road, Kashgar, Xinjiang Uygur Province 844000
Tel: +86(998) 2822996
Fax: +86(998) 2825144
EMail: yixia0110@163.com
Website: http://www.kstc.edu.cn

President: Abdurahman Amad

International Relations: Jiang Jizhao

Departments

Chemistry (Chemistry); **Chinese Language and Literature** (Chinese; Literature); **Fine Arts** (Fine Arts); **Mathematics** (Mathematics); **Modern Languages** (Modern Languages); **Physical Education** (Physical Education); **Physics** (Physics); **Political Science and History** (Political Sciences)

History: Founded 1962 as Kashgar Teachers Training School, acquired present name 1978.

Degrees and Diplomas: *Bachelor's Degree; Master's Degree*

KUNMING MEDICAL UNIVERSITY

191 West Renmin Road, Kunming, Yunnan Province 650031
Tel: +86(871) 5332571
Fax: +86(871) 5332571
EMail: webmaster@kmmc.edu.cn
Website: http://www.kmmc.edu.cn

President: Jiang Runsheng

Institutes
Health Sciences; Neurosciences

Research Centres
Biomedical Engineering (Bioengineering)

Schools

Basic Medical Sciences (Medicine); **Clinical Medicine** (Medicine); **Clinical Oncology** (Oncology); **Forensic Medicine; Humanities and Social Sciences; Nursing** (Nursing); **Pharmaceutical Sciences; Public Health** (Public Health); **Stomatology** (Dentistry; Oral Pathology; Stomatology)

History: Founded 1953 as Medical School of Yunnan University.

Main Language(s) of Instruction: Chinese

Degrees and Diplomas: *Bachelor's Degree; Master's Degree; Doctor's Degree*

Libraries: c. 230,000 vols
Last Updated: 20/11/08

KUNMING UNIVERSITY OF SCIENCE AND TECHNOLOGY (KUST)

68 Wenchang Road, 121 Street, Kunming, Yunnan Province 650093
Tel: +86(871) 5144184
Fax: +86(871) 5198622
EMail: wsc@kmust.edu.cn
Website: http://www.kmust.edu.cn

President: Rong Zhou (2003-)
Tel: +86(871) 5144183, Fax: +86(871) 5192076
EMail: zre@kmust.edu.cn

Chairman of the University Committee: Yulin He
Tel: +86(871) 5192580, Fax: +86(871) 5192580
EMail: ylhe@kmust.edu.cn

International Relations: Gang Deng, Director
Tel: +86(871) 5144212, Fax: +86(871) 5198622
EMail: iep@kmust.edu.cn

Faculties

Applied Technology *Dean:* Cheng Wang; **Applied Technology** *(Chuxiong) Dean:* Delei Zhou; **Arts** (Advertising and Publicity; Design; English; Fine Arts; Publishing and Book Trade) *Dean:* Yi He; **Biological and Chemical Engineering** (Automation and Control Engineering; Biology; Chemical Engineering; Engineering Management; Food Science; Food Technology) *Dean:* Yaming Wang; **Civil and Architectural Engineering** (Architecture; Civil Engineering; Mechanical Engineering; Natural Resources; Town Planning) *Dean:* Heming Cheng; **Continuing Education** (Accountancy; Automation and Control Engineering; Business Administration; Chemical Engineering; Civil Engineering; Computer Engineering; Electrical Engineering; Mining Engineering) *Dean:* Xiping Yuan; **Electrical Engineering** (Automation and Control Engineering; Electrical Engineering; Hydraulic Engineering; Power Engineering; Thermal Engineering; Water Management) *Dean:* Hongchun Shu; **Environmental Science and Engineering** (Environmental Engineering; Natural Resources) *Dean:* Ping Ning; **Information Engineering and Automation** *Dean:* Yunsheng Zhang; **Land Resource Engineering** (Environmental Engineering;

Geography; Mining Engineering; Natural Resources; Rural Planning; Safety Engineering; Surveying and Mapping) *Dean*: Yan-gang Miao; **Law** (Environmental Studies; Law; Political Sciences) *Dean*: Yuehong Han; **Management and Economics** (Accountancy; Business Administration; Economics; Finance; International Business; International Economics; Management; Marketing) *Dean*: Baojian Yang; **Materials and Metallurgical Engineering** (Materials Engineering; Metallurgical Engineering) *Dean*: Zhonghua Liu; **Mechanical and Electrical Engineering** (Automation and Control Engineering; Electrical Engineering; Industrial Design; Industrial Engineering; Mechanical Engineering; Packaging Technology) *Dean*: Yilin Chi; **Modern Agricultural Engineering** (Agricultural Equipment; Water Science) *Dean*: Zhenyang Ge; **Science** (Computer Science; Electronic Engineering; Information Technology) *Dean*: Jinzhu Zhang; **Transport Engineering** (Transport Engineering) *Dean*: Jian Xiong

Schools
Graduate Studies *Director*: Hua Wang

History: Founded 1954 as Kunming Institute of Technology. Changed its name to Kunming University of Science and Technology 1995. Acquired present status following amalgamation with Yunnan Polytechnic University 1999.

Academic Year: March to January (March-July; September-January)

Admission Requirements: National College Entrance Examination or equivalent

Fees: (Yuan): 2,000-10,000 per annum

Main Language(s) of Instruction: Chinese. Some courses in English, French, German

International Co-operation: With universities in France, Germany, Italy, Japan, Canada, USA, United Kingdom, Greece, Sweden, Netherlands, Austria, Portugal, Australia, Malaysia, Thailand, Vietnam, Kazakhstan, Myanmar, Russian Federation

Accrediting Agencies: Ministry of Education

Degrees and Diplomas: *Zhuanke Certificate of Graduation*: 2-3 yrs; *Bachelor's Degree*: 4-5 yrs; *Master's Degree*: 3 yrs; *Doctor's Degree (PhD)*: 3 yrs

Student Services: Academic counselling, Canteen, Employment services, Foreign student adviser, Foreign Studies Centre, Health services, Language programs, Nursery care, Social counselling, Sports facilities

Student Residential Facilities: Yes

Special Facilities: Geo-science Museum. Movie studio

Libraries: 1,014,374 vols in Chinese. 2,640 periodicals in Chinese. 168,623 vols in foreign languages. 658 periodicals in foreign languages

Publications: Journal of KUST *(monthly)*; Newsletter of KUST *(monthly)*

Last Updated: 26/11/08

LANGFANG TEACHERS COLLEGE

100 West Aimin Street, Langfang, Hebei Province 065000
Tel: +86(316) 2115601 +86(316) 2112462
Fax: +86(316) 2112462

Departments
Arts (Fine Arts); **Biology**; **Chemistry** (Chemistry); **Chinese** (Chinese); **Foreign Languages** (Modern Languages); **Mathematics**; **Pedagogy** (Pedagogy); **Physical Education**; **Physics** (Physics); **Politics and History**

History: Founded 1946 as Elementary Teachers School of Anci District. Acquired present title 2000.

Degrees and Diplomas: *Bachelor's Degree*

Libraries: c. 460,000 vols.

Publications: Friends of Chinese Teaching; Hebei Science Teaching Study; Journal of Langfang Teacher's College

LANZHOU JIAOTONG UNIVERSITY

118 West Anning Road, Lanzhou, Gansu Province 730070
Tel: +86(931) 8938030
Fax: +86(931) 7667661
EMail: shunli@mail.lzjtu.cn
Website: http://www.lzjtu.edu.cn/

President: Ren Enen

Schools
Architecture and Urban Planning (Architecture; Architecture and Planning); **Adult Continuing Education** (Adult Education); **Advanced Professional Training and Education** (Education); **Art and Design** (Design; Fine Arts); **Chemical and Biological Engineering** (Biology; Chemical Engineering); **Civil Engineering** (Civil Engineering); **Economics and Management**; **Electronics and Information Engineering** (Electronic Engineering; Information Sciences); **Environmental and Municipal Engineering**; **Foreign Languages** (Modern Languages); **Mathematics, Physics and Software Engineering** (Mathematics; Physics; Software Engineering); **Mechatronic Engineering**; **Traffic and Transportation**

History: Founded 1958 as Lanzhou Railway University. Acquired present status and title 2003.

International Co-operation: With universities in USA, Canada, Australia, Japan, United Kingdom, New Zealand, Netherlands, South Korea, Japan, Russian Federation

Degrees and Diplomas: *Bachelor's Degree*; *Master's Degree*; *Doctor's Degree*

Libraries: Total: c. 930,000 vols; 106,400 foreign books; 2,914 periodicals; 143 foreign periodicals; 6,124 audiovisual periodicals; 3,037 CDs; 439 English electronic periodicals

Last Updated: 26/11/08

LANZHOU MEDICAL COLLEGE

85 Dong Ganxi Road, Chengguan District, Lanzhou, Gansu Province 730000
Tel: +86(931) 8617904
Fax: +86(931) 8617205

President: Wang Jing
International Relations: Sun Long

Departments
Clinical Medicine (Medicine); **Nursing** (Nursing); **Pharmacy** (Pharmacy); **Preventive Medicine** (Social and Preventive Medicine); **Stomatology** (Stomatology)

History: Founded 1954.

Degrees and Diplomas: *Bachelor's Degree*; *Master's Degree*

LANZHOU UNIVERSITY

222, South Tianshui Road, Lanzhou, Gansu Province 730000
Tel: +86(931) 8612850
Fax: +86(931) 8617355
EMail: news@lzu.edu.cn
Website: http://www.lzu.edu.cn

President: Zhou Xuhong

Laboratories
Applied Organic Chemistry (Organic Chemistry) *Head*: Yongqiang Tu; **Arid Agroecology** (Arid Land Studies) *Head*: Jiakuan Chen; **Magnetism and Applied Magnetics Materials** (Applied Physics) *Head*: Desheng Xue; **Western China's Environmental Systems** *Head*: Fahu Chen

Research Centres
Culture of Northwest China *Director*: Jianxin Yang

Research Institutes
Dunhuang Studies *Director*: Binling Zheng

Schools
Art (Music); **Atmospheric Science** (Meteorology); **Chemistry and Chemical Engineering** (Analytical Chemistry; Applied Chemistry; Chemical Engineering; Chemistry; Inorganic Chemistry); **Chinese Language and Literature** (Chinese; Literature); **Economics**; **Education** (Educational Sciences); **Foreign Languages and Literature**; **History and Culture** (Cultural Studies; History) *Director*: Xilong Wang; **Information Science and Engineering** (Computer Science; Electronic Engineering) *Director*: Lian Li; **Journalism and Communication** (Communication Studies; Journalism) *Director*: Wen Li; **Law**; **Life Sciences** (Biochemistry; Bioengineering; Biological and Life Sciences; Botany; Cell Biology; Ecology; Zoology) *Director*: Rui Wang; **Management** (Accountancy; Administration; Advertising and Publicity; Business and Commerce; Information

Management; Library Science; Management; Marketing; Public Relations); **Mathematics and Statistics** *Director:* Heping Zhang; **Pastoral Agriculture and Technology**; **Philosophy and Sociology** (Philosophy; Sociology); **Physics and Technology** (Applied Physics; Materials Engineering; Mechanical Engineering; Microelectronics; Nuclear Physics; Physical Engineering; Solid State Physics; Technology) *Director:* Deyan He; **Politics and Administration** *Director:* Xuejiang Wang

History: Founded 1909 as Gansu School of Law and Politics, acquired present title 1946.

Admission Requirements: Graduation from senior middle school and national entrance examination

Main Language(s) of Instruction: Chinese

Accrediting Agencies: Ministry of Education; Gansu Provincial Education Commission

Degrees and Diplomas: *Bachelor's Degree:* Administration; Atmospheric Science; Biology; Chemistry; Computer Science; Economics; Geography; Geology; History; Journalism; Law; Mathematics; Modern Languages; Philosophy; Physics, 4 yrs; *Master's Degree:* a further 3 yrs; *Doctor's Degree:* a further 3 yrs

Student Services: Academic counselling, Canteen, Cultural centre, Foreign student adviser, Foreign Studies Centre, Health services, Language programs, Nursery care, Social counselling, Sports facilities

Publications: Journal of Lanzhou University (Medical Sciences) *(bimonthly)*; Journal of Lanzhou University (Natural Sciences) *(bimonthly)*; Journal of Lanzhou University (Social Sciences) *(bimonthly)*

Press or Publishing House: Lanzhou University Press
Last Updated: 26/11/08

LANZHOU UNIVERSITY OF FINANCE AND ECONOMICS

418 Duanjiatan Street, Lanzhou, Gansu Province 730020
Tel: +86(931) 8493093
Fax: +86(931) 8660024
EMail: roman@lzcc.edu.cn
Website: http://www.lzcc.edu.cn

President: Lu Zhaoxin

International Relations: Xiao Huaiyun

Schools
Accountancy; **Adult Education**; **Arts** (Design; Fine Arts; Music)

History: Founded 1951 as Gansu Staff Finance and Economics College.Became Lanzhou Commercial College and then Lanzhou University of Finance and Economics.

Degrees and Diplomas: *Bachelor's Degree*; *Master's Degree*
Last Updated: 26/11/08

LANZHOU UNIVERSITY OF TECHNOLOGY

85 Langongping Street, Qilihe District, Lanzhou, Gansu Province 730050
Tel: +86(931) 2404210
Fax: +86(931) 2325630
EMail: www@lut.cn
Website: http://yuanxi.lut.cn/english

Departments
Adult Education; **Basic Sciences** (Mathematics and Computer Science; Natural Sciences); **Civil Engineering**; **Electrical and Information Engineering** (Electrical Engineering; Information Technology); **Fluid Machinery Engineering**; **Foreign Languages** (Modern Languages); **Management** (Management); **Materials Engineering** (Materials Engineering; Metal Techniques); **Mechanical Engineering**; **Physical Education and Art Teaching**; **Social Sciences** (Social Sciences)

Schools
Higher Professional Engineering (Engineering; Technology); **Petrochemical Engineering** (Chemical Engineering; Petrology)

History: Founded 1919 as Lanzhou Technical School. Renamed Lanzhou Polytechnic Institute 1958. Acquired present status and title 2003. Under the jurisdiction of the Ministry of Machine Building Industry and the Provincial Government.

Academic Year: September to July (September-January; March-July)

Admission Requirements: Graduation from senior middle school and entrance examination

Main Language(s) of Instruction: Chinese

Accrediting Agencies: Ministry of Machine Building Industry

Degrees and Diplomas: *Bachelor's Degree*: 4 yrs; *Master's Degree*: a further 2-3 yrs; *Doctor's Degree*

Student Residential Facilities: Yes

Libraries: c. 400,000 vols

Publications: Journal
Last Updated: 26/11/08

LIAOCHENG UNIVERSITY

34 Wenhua Road, Liaocheng, Shandong Province 252059
Tel: +86(635) 8238155
Fax: +86(635) 8238040
EMail: liuxue@lcu.edu.cn
Website: http://www.admissions.cn/lcu/etx.html

President: Song Yiqiao

Colleges
Agricultural Science (Animal Husbandry; Food Science; Horticulture; Plant Pathology; Veterinary Science); **Architectural Engineering** (Civil Engineering); **Arts** (Design; Fine Arts; Music); **Automotive and Mechanical Engineering**; **Business** (Business Administration; Economics; International Business); **Chemistry and Chemical Engineering** (Applied Chemistry; Chemical Engineering; Chemistry); **Computer Science** (Computer Science; E-Business/Commerce; Information Management); **Education**; **Educational Technology and Mass Media**; **Environment and Planning** (Environmental Studies; Geography; Rural Planning; Town Planning); **History and Culture**; **Life Sciences** (Bioengineering; Biological and Life Sciences); **Literature** (Chinese; Journalism; Literature; Media Studies; Secretarial Studies); **Management**; **Material Science and Engineering** (Materials Engineering); **Mathematics**; **Physical Education** (Physical Education; Sports); **Physical Science, Information Technology and Engineering**; **Politics and Law**

Schools
Foreign Languages (English; Japanese; Korean); **International Education** (Chinese)

History: Founded 1974 as Shandong Normal College Liaocheng. Acquired present status and title 2002.

Degrees and Diplomas: *Bachelor's Degree*; *Master's Degree*
Last Updated: 26/11/08

LIAONING INSTITUTE OF TECHNOLOGY

169 Shiying Street, Guta District, Jinzhou, Liaoning Province 121001
Tel: +86(416) 4198745 +86(416) 4199704
Fax: +86(416) 4142701
EMail: iclitjz@mail.jzptt.ln.cn
Website: http://www.lnit.edu.cn/

President: Jianzhong Wang

International Relations: Chen Qingfu

Departments
Architecture; **Chemical Engineering** (Chemical Engineering); **Civil Engineering**; **Design**; **Economics and Administration**; **Information Sciences and Engineering** (Engineering; Information Sciences); **Machine Building and Automotive Engineering** (Automotive Engineering; Machine Building); **Materials Engineering** (Materials Engineering); **Modern Languages**; **Physical Education**; **Political Science** (Political Sciences)

History: Founded 1951 as Technical School, acquired present status 1960 and name 1997.

International Co-operation: With universities in USA, United Kingdom, Germany, Australia, Republic of Korea, Canada, and Japan

Degrees and Diplomas: *Bachelor's Degree*; *Master's Degree*

LIAONING NORMAL UNIVERSITY

850 Huanghe Avenue, Dalian, Liaoning Province 116029
Tel: +86(411) 4121181 Ext. 8366
Fax: +86(411) 4121181 Ext. 8562
EMail: dwhy@dl.cn
Website: http://www.lnnu.edu.cn

President: Qu Qingbiao

Departments
Biology (Biology); **Chemistry** (Chemistry); **Chinese Language and Literature** (Chinese; Literature); **Computer Science** (Computer Science); **Education** (Education); **Educational Technology** (Educational Technology); **Fine Arts** (Fine Arts); **Foreign Languages** (Modern Languages); **Geography** (Geography); **History** (History); **Information Sciences** (Information Sciences); **Mathematics** (Mathematics); **Music** (Music); **Physical Education** (Physical Education); **Physics** (Physics); **Politics and Law** (Law; Political Sciences)

History: Founded 1951 as Luda Teachers Junior School. Acquired present title 1983.

Main Language(s) of Instruction: Chinese

Degrees and Diplomas: *Bachelor's Degree*; *Master's Degree*; *Doctor's Degree*

Libraries: c. 1.3m. vols

Publications: Educational Science; Journal of Liaoning Normal University

Last Updated: 26/11/08

LIAONING TECHNICAL UNIVERSITY

47 Zhonghua Road, Haizhou District, Fuxin, Liaoning Province 123000
Tel: +86(418) 3350184
Fax: +86(418) 2823977
EMail: Lntu@chinatefl.com
Website: http://www.lntu.edu.cn

President: Shi Jinfeng

Departments
Civil Engineering (Civil Engineering); **Electrical Engineering** (Electrical Engineering); **Electronic Engineering** (Electronic Engineering); **Foreign Languages** (Modern Languages); **Social Sciences** (Social Sciences)

Schools
Business Administration; **Mechanical Engineering** (Mechanical Engineering); **Resources and Environment** (Environmental Studies; Natural Resources)

History: Founded 1963 as Fuxin Coalmine Institute. Became Fuxin Mining Institute 1978. Incorporated Fushun Mining Institute, Liaoning Coalmine Teachers Institute and Jixi Mining Institute. Acquired present title 1996.

Degrees and Diplomas: *Bachelor's Degree*; *Master's Degree*; *Doctor's Degree*

Libraries: c. 700,000 vols

Publications: Journal of Liaoning Technical University
Last Updated: 26/11/08

LIAONING UNIVERSITY

66 Chongshan Zhonglu, Huanggu District, Shenyang, Liaoning Province 110036
Tel: +86(24) 86862098
Fax: +86(24) 86862106
EMail: zsk@lnu.edu.cn
Website: http://wwwen.lnu.edu.cn

President: Cheng Wei

International Relations: Ma Xingguo

Colleges
Business *(Asia-Australia)* (Business Administration; Business and Commerce)

Faculties
Chinese Language and Literature (Chinese; Literature); **History** (History); **Korean Studies** (Korean); **Mathematics** (Mathematics); **Philosophy** (Philosophy); **Physics** (Physics)

Schools
Broadcasting and Television (Radio and Television Broadcasting); **Business Administration** (Business Administration); **Chemistry and Engineering** (Chemistry; Engineering); **Economic Administration** (Administration; Economics); **Environment and Life Sciences** (Biological and Life Sciences; Environmental Studies); **Foreign Languages** (Modern Languages); **Higher Professional Techniques**; **Information Sciences and Technology** (Information Sciences; Information Technology; Technology); **International Economics** (International Economics); **Law** (Law)

Further Information: Also University Hospital, 38 laboratories and more than 110 teaching and research sections

History: Founded 1958, incorporating the Northeastern Economy and Accounting College, Shenyang Teachers College, and Shenyang Institute of Russian.

Academic Year: February to January (February-July; August-January)

Admission Requirements: Secondary school certificate and entrance examination

Fees: (Yuan): c. 2,000 per annum

Main Language(s) of Instruction: Chinese

Degrees and Diplomas: *Bachelor's Degree*: Biology; Chemistry; Chinese; Communication; Computer Sciences; Economics; Electronics; Finance and Accountancy; Foreign Languages (English, Japanese, Russian and Korean); History; International Economy; Law; Mathematics; National Economy Administration; Philosophy; Physics, 4 yrs; *Master's Degree*: Accountancy; Ancient Literature; Business Administration; Chinese Ancient History; Chinese Modern Literature; Computer Software; English Language and Literature; Folk Literature; Foreign Economy; History; History of International Communism Movement; Industrial Economy; International Finance; Literature and Art; Marxist Philosophy; Mechanics; Medieval History; Modern History; National Economy Administration; Physics; Political Economics; Russian Language; Science of Socialism; Western Philosophy; World Economy, a further 3 yrs; *Doctor's Degree*: 3 yrs

Student Residential Facilities: Yes

Special Facilities: History Museum

Libraries: Library, 1.8m. vols

Publications: Journal of Japanese Studies; Journal of Korean Studies; Journal of Liaoning University; Journal of Population Research

Press or Publishing House: Liaoning University Press
Last Updated: 26/11/08

LIAONING UNIVERSITY OF PETROLEUM AND CHEMICAL TECHNOLOGY (LUPCT)

1 Dandong Road, Fushun, Liaoning Province 113001
Tel: +86(413) 6690061
Fax: +86(413) 6650866
EMail: liping@lnpu.edu.cn
Website: http://www.lnpu.edu.cn/

President: Li Ping

International Relations: Pei Wenbin

Colleges
Adult Education; **Vocational and Technical Education** (Technology Education)

Schools
Economics and Administration (Administration; Economics); **Foreign Studies** (International Studies); **Humanities** (Arts and Humanities); **Information and Control Engineering** (Automation and Control Engineering; Information Sciences); **Mechanical Engineering** (Mechanical Engineering); **Petrochemical Technology** (Petroleum and Gas Engineering); **Physical Education** (Physical Education); **Science**

History: Founded 1950 as Fushun Petroleum Institute. Acquired present status and title 2002.

Admission Requirements: Secondary school certificate

International Co-operation: With universities in United Kingdom and Russian Federation

Degrees and Diplomas: *Bachelor's Degree*; *Master's Degree*

Student Residential Facilities: Yes.

Libraries: Total: c. 852,000 vols
Last Updated: 23/09/08

LIAONING UNIVERSITY OF TRADITIONAL CHINESE MEDICINE

79 Chongshandong Road, Huanggu District, Shenyang, Liaoning Province 110032
Tel: +86(24) 31207108
EMail: office@lnutcm.edu.cn
Website: http://www.lnutcm.edu.cn

President: Ma Ji

Schools
Traditional Chinese Medicine (Acupuncture; Pharmacology; Traditional Eastern Medicine)

History: Founded 1958. Acquired present title and status 2006.

Main Language(s) of Instruction: Chinese

Degrees and Diplomas: *Bachelor's Degree*; *Master's Degree*; *Doctor's Degree*

Libraries: c. 270,000 vols

Publications: TCM Correspondence Magazine
Last Updated: 26/11/08

LUDONG UNIVERSITY

184 Shixue Road, Zhifu District, Yantai, Shandong Province 264025
Tel: +86(535) 6013012
Fax: +86(535) 6011042
EMail: lxs@ldu.edu.cn
Website: http://www.ytnc.edu.cn

President: Liu Dawen

Departments
Biology (Biology); **Chemistry** (Chemistry); **Chinese Language and Literature**; **Fine Arts**; **Geography**; **History**; **International Studies** (International Studies); **Law, Political Science and Economics** (Economics; Law; Political Sciences); **Mathematics and Computer Sciences** (Computer Science; Mathematics); **Modern Languages** (Modern Languages); **Music** (Music); **Physical Education**; **Physics** (Physics); **Psychology and Education**

History: Founded 1958 as Yantai Normal College, became Yantai Normal University and acquired present status and title 2006.

Main Language(s) of Instruction: Chinese

Degrees and Diplomas: *Bachelor's Degree*; *Master's Degree*
Last Updated: 11/12/08

LUXUN ACADEMY OF FINE ARTS

19 Sanhao Street, Helping District, Shenyang, Liaoning Province 110003
Tel: +86(24) 23892467
Fax: +86(24) 23929750
EMail: lmwsb@lumei.edu.cn
Website: http://www.lumei.edu.cn/dhezuo/hezuo/lxxx-e.htm

President: Wei Ershen

International Relations: Kong Fanping

Departments
Art Education (Art Education); **Chinese Painting** (Painting and Drawing); **Environmental Design** (Design; Environmental Studies); **Fashion and Textile Design** (Fashion Design); **Graphic Design**; **Industrial Design**; **Oil Painting**; **Photography** (Photography); **Printmaking** (Printing and Printmaking); **Sculpture** (Sculpture)

History: Founded 1938 as Luxun College of Arts, acquired present status and title 1958.

Degrees and Diplomas: *Bachelor's Degree*; *Master's Degree*
Last Updated: 26/11/08

LUZHOU MEDICAL COLLEGE

Zhongshan, Luzhou, Sichuan Province 646000
Tel: +86(830) 2394412 Ext. 7630
Fax: +86(830) 2295557
EMail: iceo@lzmc.edu.cn
Website: http://www.lzmc.edu.cn

President: Ma Yuerong

Departments
Clinical Medicine (Medicine); **Dentistry**; **Modern Languages** (Modern Languages); **Social Sciences** (Social Sciences); **Traditional Chinese Medicine** (Traditional Eastern Medicine)

History: Founded 1951as Southern Sichuan Secondary School for Medical Practitioners, acquired present status 1959 and title 1978.

Degrees and Diplomas: *Bachelor's Degree*; *Master's Degree*
Last Updated: 26/11/08

MINZU UINIVERSITY OF CHINA

27 South Zhongguancun Street, Haidian District, Beijing 100081
Tel: +86(10) 68933350 +86(10) 68932847
Fax: +86(10) 68933982
EMail: gjj1@cun.edu.en
Website: http://eng.muc.edu.cn/

President: Chen Li

Colleges
Art (Fine Arts); **Dance** (Dance); **Economics** (Economics; Finance; International Business; International Economics); **Education** (Education); **Ethnology and Sociology** (Archaeology; Ethnology; Law; Museum Studies; Sociology); **Foreign Languages** (English; Italian; Japanese; Korean; Modern Languages; Russian; Translation and Interpretation); **History** (History); **Information Engineering** (Information Technology); **International Education** (Chinese); **Law** (Law); **Life Science and Environmental Sciences** (Alternative Medicine; Biology; Botany; Chemistry; Ecology; Environmental Studies); **Literature and Journalism** (Journalism; Literature); **Management** (Accountancy; Business Administration; Human Resources; Management; Marketing; Public Administration); **Marxism and Leninism** (Political Sciences); **Music** (Music); **Science** (Natural Sciences); **Science**

Departments
Kazakh Language and Literature (Slavic Languages); **Korean Language and Literature** (Korean); **Language and Literature of Chinese Ethnic Minorities** (Asian Studies; Chinese; Literature); **Minority Languages and Literatures** (Literature; Native Language Education); **Mongolian** (Mongolian); **Philosophy and Religion** (Philosophy; Religion); **Uygur Language and Literature** (Asian Studies; Native Language)

Research Institutes
Tibetan Studies

History: Founded 1941 as Yan'an Institute for Nationalities. Became The Central University for Nationalities in 1993. Acquired current title 2008.

Degrees and Diplomas: *Bachelor's Degree*; *Master's Degree*; *Doctor's Degree*

Libraries: c. 1m. vols
Last Updated: 06/03/12

MUDANJIANG TEACHERS COLLEGE

19 Wenhua Street, Xingzhong Road, Mundanjiang, Heilongjiang Province 157422
Tel: +86(453) 6534206
Fax: +86(453) 6511203
EMail: ybz@mail.mdjnu.com
Website: http://www.mdjnu.cn

President: Xiu Pengyue

International Relations: Chen Jingwen

Departments
Biology (Biology); **Chemistry** (Chemistry); **Chinese** (Chinese); **Computer Science** (Computer Science); **Fine Arts**; **History**; **Mathematics** (Mathematics); **Modern Languages**; **Physical**

Education (Physical Education); **Physics** (Physics); **Political Science and Law** (Law; Political Sciences)

History: Founded 1958 as branch school of Northeast Agriculture College, acquired present status and title 1970.

NANCHANG INSTITUTE OF AERONAUTICAL TECHNOLOGY

173 Shanghai Road, Nanchang, Jiangxi Province 330009
Tel: +86(791) 8224596
Fax: +86(791) 8213248

President: Liu Gaohang

International Relations: Luo Liming

Departments
Applied Engineering (Engineering); **Chemical Engineering** (Chemical Engineering); **Computer Science** (Computer Science); **Electronic Engineering** (Electronic Engineering); **Materials Engineering** (Materials Engineering); **Mechanical Engineering** (Mechanical Engineering); **Military Science and Physical Education** (Military Science; Physical Education); **Modern Languages**; **Social Sciences**

History: Founded 1952 as Hankou Aerotechnical School, acquired present status and name 1978.

Degrees and Diplomas: *Bachelor's Degree*; *Master's Degree*

NANCHANG UNIVERSITY

235 Nanjing Donglu, Nanchang, Jiangxi Province 330047
Tel: +86(791) 8305499
Fax: +86(791) 8305835
EMail: newncu@ncu.edu.cn
Website: http://www.ncu.edu.cn

President: Pan Jilun (1993-)
Tel: +86(791) 8305001, Fax: +86(791) 8304888

International Relations: Liu Youwen

Colleges
Gong Qing

Departments
Medical Imaging; **Preventive Medicine**; **Stomatology**

Institutes
Sino-French Business Administration (Business Administration)

Schools
Architecture; **Basic Medical Science** (Medicine); **Chemistry and Materials Science**; **Civil Engineering**; **Computer and Information**; **Economics and Administration** (Accountancy; Administration; Economics; International Economics); **Electric and Automation Engineering**; **Electronic Information Engineering**; **Environmental and Chemical Engineering**; **Foreign Language Studies**; **Humanities**; **Journalism, Culture and Art**; **Life Sciences and Food Engineering** (Aquaculture; Biological and Life Sciences; Biology; Food Science); **Mathematics and Physics**; **Mechanical and Electronic Engineering**; **Paediatrics**; **Physical Education and Military Training** (Military Science; Physical Education); **Politics and Law** (Administration; Law; Political Sciences); **Social Sciences**

Further Information: Also 93 Laboratories

History: Founded 1940 as Zhongzheng University. Acquired present name and status 1993 when the top two universities of Jiangxi Province Jiangxi University and Jiangxi Industrial University merged. NCU entered a new era of development when it merged with Jiangxi Medical College in August 2005

Academic Year: September to July (September-February; March-July)

Admission Requirements: Graduation from senior middle school and entrance examination

Fees: (US Dollars): Foreign students, 1,500-4,500 per annum

Main Language(s) of Instruction: Chinese, English

Accrediting Agencies: Ministry of Education; General Political Department

Degrees and Diplomas: *Bachelor's Degree*; *Master's Degree*; *Doctor's Degree*

Student Services: Academic counselling, Canteen, Cultural centre, Employment services, Foreign student adviser, Foreign Studies Centre, Health services, Language programs, Social counselling, Sports facilities

Student Residential Facilities: Yes

Special Facilities: Audiovisual Education Centre

Libraries: Two libraries, c. 1,720,000 vols.

Publications: Higher Education Reform; Journal of Nanchang University

Press or Publishing House: Nanchang University Editorial Office
Last Updated: 26/11/08

NANJING AGRICULTURAL UNIVERSITY

Nanjing, Jiangsu Province 210095
Tel: +86(25) 4395754
Fax: +86(25) 4396326
EMail: ietc@njau.edu.cn
Website: http://www.njau.edu.cn

President: Zhiming Yan EMail: xb@njau.edu.cn

Academies
Jiling

Colleges
Agriculture (Agronomy; Biological and Life Sciences; Horticulture; Plant and Crop Protection); **Animal Science and Technology** (Animal Husbandry; Fishery; Zoology); **Economics and Management** (Economics; Finance; Management); **Engineering**; **Food Science and Technology** (Food Science; Food Technology); **Foreign Studies**; **Horticulture**; **Humanities and Social Sciences** (Arts and Humanities; English; Japanese; Literature; Political Sciences; Social Sciences); **Information Science and Technology** (Computer Science; Information Management; Software Engineering); **Life Sciences** (Biochemistry; Microbiology; Molecular Biology); **Plant Protection** (Plant and Crop Protection); **Public Administration** (Public Administration); **Resources and Environmental Sciences** (Agriculture; Environmental Studies; Microbiology; Natural Resources; Soil Science); **Science** (Applied Chemistry; Computer Science; Mathematics; Natural Sciences; Physics); **Veterinary Medicine** (Veterinary Science)

History: Founded 1952 as Agricultural College of Nanjing University. Acquired present title 1984.

Degrees and Diplomas: *Bachelor's Degree*; *Master's Degree*; *Doctor's Degree*

Libraries: c. 890,000 vols

Publications: Animal Husbandry and Veterinary Medicine; China Agricultural Education Information; History of China's Agriculture; Journal of Nanjing Agricultural University
Last Updated: 26/11/08

NANJING ARTS INSTITUTE

15 North Huju Road, Nanjing, Jiangsu Province 210013
Tel: +86(25) 3312350
Fax: +86(25) 3733746
EMail: nylxs@njarti.edu.cn
Website: http://www.njarti.edu.cn

President: Feng Jianqin

International Relations: Xia Yanjing

Colleges
Dance; **Design**; **Fine Arts** (Fine Arts); **Humanities** (Literature; Modern Languages; Political Sciences; Sports); **Media** (Media Studies); **Movie and Television**; **Music** (Music); **Pop Music** (Jazz and Popular Music; Music); **Summit**

History: Founded 1912 as Shanghai Art Academy, acquired present title 1958.

Main Language(s) of Instruction: Chinese

Degrees and Diplomas: *Bachelor's Degree*; *Master's Degree*; *Doctor's Degree*

Libraries: c. 240,000 vols

Publications: Garden of Arts, Fine Arts and Music
Last Updated: 26/11/08

NANJING AUDIT UNIVERSITY

77 Beiwei Road, Nanjing, Jiangsu Province 210029
Tel: +86(25) 6618619
Fax: +86(25) 6618619
EMail: nsyb@public1.ptt.js.cn
Website: http://www.nau.edu.cn

President: Wang Jiaxin

International Relations: Yu Su

Departments
Accountancy (Accountancy); **Audit** (Accountancy); **Economics and Commerce** (Business and Commerce; Economics); **Finance** (Finance); **Law**

Schools
Leadership (Leadership)

History: Founded 1983 as Nanjing Finance and Trade College, acquired present status and name 1987. Previously known as Nanjing Audit Institute.

Main Language(s) of Instruction: Chinese

Degrees and Diplomas: *Bachelor's Degree*; *Master's Degree*
Last Updated: 26/11/08

NANJING FORESTRY UNIVERSITY

Lonpan Road, Nanjing, Jiangsu Province 210037
Tel: +86(25) 5412431
Fax: +86(25) 5412589
EMail: nfu@njfu.edu.cn
Website: http://www.njfu.edu.cn

President: Yu Shiyuan

International Relations: Wang Qingyu

Colleges
Chemical Engineering (Chemical Engineering); **Civil Engineering**; **Economics and Management**; **Electronic and Mechanical Engineering**; **Forest Resources and Environment** (Environmental Studies; Forestry); **Humanities and Social Sciences**; **Landscape Architecture**; **Wood Science and Technology** (Wood Technology)

Schools
Vocational Education (Civil Engineering; Forestry)

History: Founded 1952 as Nanjing Institute of Forestry, acquired present status and title 1985.

Academic Year: September to July (September-January; February-July)

Admission Requirements: Graduation from high school and entrance examination

Main Language(s) of Instruction: Chinese

Accrediting Agencies: Ministry of Forestry

Degrees and Diplomas: *Bachelor's Degree*; *Master's Degree*; *Doctor's Degree*

Student Residential Facilities: Yes

Libraries: c. 500,000 vols

Publications: China Forestry Science and Technology; Forestry Energy Conservation Technique; Journal of Nanjing Forestry University *(quarterly)*

Press or Publishing House: Nanjing Forestry University Press
Last Updated: 26/11/08

NANJING INSTITUTE OF PHYSICAL EDUCATION

8 Linggusi Road, Nanjing, Jiangsu Province 210014
Tel: +86(25) 4431317 Ext. 3107
Fax: +86(25) 4431552

President: Hua Hongxing

International Relations: Xin Li

Departments
Athletics (Sports); **Physical Education**; **Sports**

History: Founded 1956 as Nanjing Sports School, acquired present status and name 1958.

Degrees and Diplomas: *Bachelor's Degree*; *Master's Degree*

NANJING INSTITUTE OF TECHNOLOGY

74 West Beijing Road, Nanjing, Jiangsu Province 210013
Tel: +86(25) 3312032
Fax: +86(25) 3702466
EMail: zsb@njit.edu.cn
Website: http://www.njit.edu.cn

President: Chen Xiaohu

Departments
Foreign Languages; **Humanities and Social Sciences** (Arts and Humanities; Social Sciences); **Physical Education**

Schools
Art and Design; **Automation** (Automation and Control Engineering); **Civil Engineering** (Civil Engineering); **Communications Engineering**; **Computer Engineering** (Computer Engineering); **Economics and Management** (Economics; Management); **Energy and Power Engineering** (Electrical Engineering; Energy Engineering; Power Engineering); **Materials Engineering** (Materials Engineering); **Mechanical Engineering** (Mechanical Engineering)

History: Founded 2003.

Degrees and Diplomas: *Bachelor's Degree*

Libraries: c. 667,000 vols; 1,090 periodical subscriptions.
Last Updated: 26/11/08

NANJING MEDICAL UNIVERSITY

140 Hanzhong Road, Nanjing, Jiangsu Province 210029
Tel: +86(25) 6662644
Fax: +86(25) 6508960
EMail: waishi@njmu.edu.cn
Website: http://www.njmu.edu.cn

President: Qi Chen EMail: qchen@njmu.edu.cn

Schools
Basic Medical Sciences (Anatomy; Biochemistry; Medicine; Modern Languages; Molecular Biology; Pharmacology; Pharmacy; Physical Education); **Clinical Medicine**; **Medical Policy and Management**; **Nursing** (Nursing); **Pharmacy** (Pharmacy); **Public Health**; **Stomatology**

History: Founded 1934 as Jiangsu Medical College, became Nanjing Medical College 1957, and acquired present status and title 1993.

Academic Year: September to July (September-January; February-July)

Admission Requirements: Graduation from senior middle school and entrance examination

Main Language(s) of Instruction: Chinese

Degrees and Diplomas: *Bachelor's Degree*: 5 yrs; *Master's Degree*: a further 2-3 yrs; *Doctor's Degree*: a further 3 yrs

Student Residential Facilities: For c. 4,000 students

Libraries: c. 400,000 vols

Publications: Journal Nanjin Medical University
Last Updated: 26/11/08

NANJING NORMAL UNIVERSITY

122 Ninghai Road, Nanjing, Jiangsu Province 210097
Tel: +86(25) 3728418
Fax: +86(25) 3711748
EMail: ydwu@njnu.edu.cn
Website: http://www.njnu.edu.cn

President: Yongzhong Song

Schools
Chinese Language and Literature (Chinese; Literature; Secretarial Studies); **Economics and Law** (Economics; Industrial Management; Law; Political Sciences); **Education** (Education; Preschool Education; Psychology); **Foreign Languages** (English; Japanese; Modern Languages; Russian); **Geography** (Earth Sciences; Geography; Tourism); **International Culture and Education** (Cultural Studies; International Studies); **Jingling** *(For Women)* (Women's Studies); **Mass Communication**

History: Founded 1902 as Sanjinag Normal Academy, acquired present status and title 1984.

Governing Bodies: Board of Directors

Academic Year: February to January (February-June; September-January)

Admission Requirements: Graduation from senior middle school and entrance examination

Fees: (US Dollars): Foreign students, c. 1,800-4,000

Degrees and Diplomas: *Bachelor's Degree*: 4 yrs; *Master's Degree*: a further 3 yrs; *Doctor's Degree (Ph.D.)*: 2-3 yrs

Student Services: Academic counselling, Canteen, Cultural centre, Employment services, Foreign student adviser, Health services, Nursery care, Social counselling, Sports facilities

Libraries: University Library, c. 1.7m. vols

Publications: Fine Arts Education in China; Journal of Nanjing Normal University *(quarterly)*; References for Educational Research

Press or Publishing House: Nanjing Normal University Publishing House
Last Updated: 26/11/08

NANJING UNIVERSITY (NJU)

22 Hankoulu, Nanjing, Jiangsu Province 210093
Tel: +86(25) 3593186
Fax: +86(25) 3302728
EMail: xzbgs@nju.edu.cn
Website: http://www.nju.edu.cn/

President: Chen Jun
Tel: +86(25) 3595219, Fax: +86(25) 3302728

Secretary-General: Xingcheng Hang
Tel: +86(25) 3592503, Fax: +86(25) 3304865
EMail: hangxingo@nju.edu.cn

International Relations: Chenfeng Huang
Tel: +86(25) 3593326, Fax: +86(25) 3307680
EMail: huang@nju.edu.cn

Departments
Astronomy (Astronomy and Space Science) *Director*: Yuhua Tang; **Atmospheric Sciences** (Meteorology) *Director*: Zhemin Tan; **Basic Medicine** (Medicine) *Director*: Xiaodong Han; **Biochemistry** (Biochemistry) *Director*: Genxi Li; **Biology** (Biology) *Director*: Jianqun Cheng; **Chemistry** (Chemistry) *Dean*: Yi Pan; **Chinese Language and Literature** (Chinese) *Director*: Xianzhang Zhao; **Clinical Medical Sciences** (Medicine) *Dean*: Shouniao Gu; **Computer Science** (Computer Science) *Director*: Daoxu Chen; **Decision-Making Policy** (Leadership; Management); **Documentation and Information Sciences** (Documentation Techniques; Information Sciences) *Director*: Guchao Shen; **Earth Sciences** (Earth Sciences) *Director*: Kai Wu; **Economics** (Economics) *Director*: Conglai Fan; **Environmental Sciences** (Environmental Studies) *Dean*: Genfa Lu; **Foreign Languages and Literature** (Literature; Modern Languages) *Dean*: Shouren Wang; **History** (History) *Director*: Yinganan Zhu; **International Business Management** (Business Administration; International Business) *Director*: Ning Mao; **International Economy and Trade** (Economics; International Economics) *Director*: Erzhang Zhang; **Land and Marine Sciences** (Marine Science and Oceanography); **Law** (Law); **Mathematics** (Mathematics) *Director*: Chongain Chen; **Philosophy** (Philosophy) *Director*: Xiaogue Xu; **Physics** (Physics) *Director*: Yi Shi; **Political Science** (Political Sciences) *Director*: Fengyang Zhang; **Sociology** (Sociology) *Director*: Xiaohong Zhou

Research Institutes
Acoustics (Sound Engineering (Acoustics)) *Director*: Jianchun Cheng; **Applied Biotechnology Development** (Biotechnology) *Director*: Pei Gin; **Applied Chemistry** (Applied Chemistry) *Director*: Yanping Yong; **Applied Physics** (Applied Physics) *Director*: Jian Jian Xu; **Classical Chinese Documentation** (Ancient Books) *Director*: Xunchu Zhou; **Computer Applications** (Computer Engineering); **Computer Software** (Software Engineering) *Director*: Jian Lu; **Coordination Chemistry** (Chemistry) *Director*: Qinjin Meng; **Drama, Film and Television** (Cinema and Television; Theatre) *Director*: Jian Dong; **Engineering Exploration** (Engineering); **Environmental Sciences** (Environmental Studies) *Director*: Hongjun Jin; **Foreign Literature** (Literature) *Director*: Yizhong Yu; **Granite, Volcanic Rock and Metal Theory** (Geology) *Director*:

Renmin Hua; **Higher Education** (Higher Education) *Director*: Fang Gong; **History** (History); **International Relations** (History; International Relations) *Director*: Yingauan Zhu; **Materials Science** (Materials Engineering); **Modern and Contemporary Chinese Literature** (Chinese; Literature; Modern Languages) *Director*: Ziming Ye; **Pharmaceutical Development** (Pharmacology) *Director*: Jin Gao; **Population** (Demography and Population) *Director*: Haiyong Xia; **Religion** (Religion) *Director*: Xiaoyue Xu; **Revolutionary Base Areas** (Political Sciences) *Director*: Hongwu Ma; **Sino-American Culture** (Cultural Studies) *Director*: Yongxiang Chen; **Sino-German Economic Law** (Commercial Law) *Director*: Jiandong Shao; **Solid State Physics** (Solid State Physics) *Director*: Dingyu Xing; **Taiwan Studies** (Oriental Studies) *Director*: Zhiaing Cui; **Town Planning and Design** (Town Planning) *Director*: Chadin Gu

History: Founded 1902.

Academic Year: September to July (September-January; February-July)

Admission Requirements: Graduation from senior middle school and entrance examination

Fees: (Yuan): 4,600

Main Language(s) of Instruction: Chinese

Accrediting Agencies: State Education Commission

Degrees and Diplomas: *Bachelor's Degree*: 4 yrs; *Master's Degree*: 3 yrs; *Doctor's Degree*: 3 yrs

Student Services: Academic counselling, Canteen, Cultural centre, Employment services, Foreign student adviser, Foreign Studies Centre, Health services, Nursery care, Sports facilities

Student Residential Facilities: Yes

Special Facilities: Observatory. Movie studio

Libraries: c. 3,000,000 vols

Publications: Approximation Theory and Its Application; Computer Science; Contemporary Foreign Literature; Geology of Higher Education; Humanities and Social Sciences; Inorganic Chemistry; Mathematics of Higher Education; Natural Sciences; Progress in Physics; Research on Higher Education; Review of Mathematics *(biannually)*

Press or Publishing House: Nanjing University Press
Last Updated: 26/11/08

NANJING UNIVERSITY OF AERONAUTICS AND ASTRONAUTICS

29 Yudao Street, Nanjing, Jiangsu Province 210016
Tel: +86(25) 4891458
Fax: +86(25) 4892440
EMail: icedao@nuaa.edu.cn
Website: http://ice.nuaa.edu.cn

President: Wang Fuping

Colleges
Advanced Vocational Education (Automotive Engineering; Computer Engineering; English; Maintenance Technology; Mechanical Equipment and Maintenance; Vocational Education); **Aerospace Engineering**; **Automation Engineering**; **Civil Aviation**; **Economics and Management**; **Energy and Power Engineering** (Automotive Engineering; Energy Engineering; Mechanical Engineering; Power Engineering); **Humanities and Social Sciences** (Arts and Humanities; Economics; English; Japanese; Journalism; Law; Media Studies; Philosophy; Political Sciences; Social Sciences); **Information Science and Technology** (Computer Science; Electronic Engineering; Information Sciences; Information Technology); **Material Science and Engineering** (Applied Chemistry; Engineering; Materials Engineering); **Mechanical Engineering**; **Natural Science** (Applied Physics; Mathematics; Natural Sciences)

History: Founded 1952 as Nanjing Aeronautical Institute, acquired present title 1993.

Degrees and Diplomas: *Bachelor's Degree*; *Master's Degree*; *Doctor's Degree*

Libraries: c. 2,000,000 vols

Publications: Journal of DATA Acquisition and Processing; Journal of NUAA; Journal of Vibration Engineering; Journal of Vibration Measurement and Diagnosis
Last Updated: 27/11/08

NANJING UNIVERSITY OF FINANCE AND ECONOMICS

128 Tielu Bei Jie, Nanjing, Jiangsu Province 210003
Tel: +86(25) 84028966
Fax: +86(25) 84028955
EMail: foreignaffairs@njue.edu.cn
Website: http://www.njue.edu.cn

President: Xu Congcai

International Relations: Hou Lijun

Departments

Accountancy (Accountancy); **Business Administration** (Business Administration); **Computer Science and Technology** (Computer Science; Technology); **Economics** (Economics); **Finance** (Finance); **Food Science and Engineering** (Engineering; Food Science); **International Trade and Economics** (Economics; International Business); **Law** (Law); **Statistics** (Statistics)

History: Founded 1956 as Nanjing University of Economics. Acquired present title 2003.

Degrees and Diplomas: *Bachelor's Degree*

Publications: Journal of Nanjing University of Economics
Last Updated: 27/11/08

NANJING UNIVERSITY OF INFORMATION SCIENCE AND TECHNOLOGY

114 Pancheng New Street, Pukou District, Nanjing, Jiangsu Province 210044
Tel: +86(25) 7010085
Fax: +86(25) 7010085
EMail: qihao@nuist.edu.cn
Website: http://www.nuist.edu.cn

President: Li Lianshui

International Relations: Ye Qihao

Academies
Yue Jian (Political Sciences)

Colleges
Adult Education; Binjiang; Professional Training *(Technical)*

Departments

Applied Meteorology; Atmospheric Sciences (Meteorology); **Chinese Language and Literature; Computer Science and Technology; Economics and Trade** (Business and Commerce; Economics); **Electronic Engineeering** (Computer Engineering; Electronic Engineering); **Environmental Science and Engineering; Foreign Languages; Information Management; Law** (Law); **Mathematics; Physical Education; Physics** (Physics); **Public Administration** (Management; Public Administration); **Resource, Environment and City-rural Planning** (Environmental Studies; Rural Planning; Town Planning); **Spatial Information Science** (Aeronautical and Aerospace Engineering)

History: Founded 1960 as Meteorological College of Nanjing University. Renamed Nanjing Institute of Meteorology 1963. Acquired present title 2004.

Main Language(s) of Instruction: Chinese

Degrees and Diplomas: *Bachelor's Degree*; *Master's Degree*; *Doctor's Degree*

Libraries: 1,350,000 vols
Last Updated: 27/11/08

NANJING UNIVERSITY OF POSTS AND TELECOMMUNICATIONS

66 Xin Mofan Malu, Nanjing, Jiangsu Province 210003
Tel: +86(25) 3492393
Fax: +86(25) 3492349
EMail: wb@njupt.edu.cn
Website: http://www.njupt.edu.cn

President: Zheng Yang

Departments

Applied Mathematics and Physics; Computer Science and Technology; Correspondence; Electronic Engineering; Foreign Languages; Information Engineering; Management; Optical Technology; Physical Education; Social Sciences; Telecommunications Engineering (Telecommunications Engineering)

Institutes
Tong Da

History: Founded 1958 as Nanjing Postal College, acquired present title 2005.

Main Language(s) of Instruction: Chinese

Degrees and Diplomas: *Bachelor's Degree*; *Master's Degree*; *Doctor's Degree*

Libraries: c. 540,000 vols

Publications: Journal of Nanjing University of Posts and Telecommunications
Last Updated: 27/11/08

NANJING UNIVERSITY OF SCIENCE AND TECHNOLOGY (NJUST)

200 Xiaolingwei, Nanjing, Jiangsu Province 210094
Tel: +86(25) 84432727
Fax: +86(25) 84431622
EMail: diec@mail.njust.edu.cn
Website: http://www.njust.edu.cn

President: Xiaofeng Wang
Tel: +86(25) 84315204, Fax: +86(25) 84431339

Departments

Automation (Automation and Control Engineering; Electronic Engineering) *Dean*: Yimin Bo; **Computer Science and Technology** (Computer Science; Engineering; Technology) *Dean*: Zhemmin Tang; **Materials Sciences and Engineering** (Materials Engineering; Metal Techniques) *Dean*: Guang Chen

Schools

Adult Education *Dean*: Xinke Zhang; **Advanced Vocational** *Dean*: Xinke Zhang; **Chemical Engineering** (Chemical Engineering; Energy Engineering; Environmental Engineering; Explosive Engineering; Materials Engineering; Safety Engineering) *Dean*: Liam Jun Wang; **Economics and Management** (Economics; Human Resources; International Business; Management; Management Systems; Marketing) *Dean*: Anping Yu; **Electronic Engineering and Optoelectronic Technology** (Electronic Engineering; Microelectronics; Microwaves; Optical Technology; Telecommunications Engineering) *Dean*: Zhong Liu; **Humanities and Social Sciences** (Arts and Humanities; Human Resources; Labour and Industrial Relations; Law; Modern Languages; Philosophy; Social Work; Sociology) *Dean*: Zaichun Gong; **Mechanical Engineering** (Automotive Engineering; Industrial Design; Machine Building; Measurement and Precision Engineering; Mechanical Engineering; Robotics) *Dean*: Linfang Quian; **Power Engineering** (Laser Engineering; Measurement and Precision Engineering; Mechanics; Power Engineering; Thermal Engineering) *Dean*: Zhongyuan Wang; **Science** (Applied Mathematics; Applied Physics; Civil Engineering; Laser Engineering; Mechanics; Optics) *Dean*: Xiaoping Yang

History: Founded 1953 as Artillery Technology Institute. Acquired present title 1993.

Academic Year: September to July

Admission Requirements: Graduation from senior middle school and national entrance examinations

Fees: (Yuan): 2,700-4,600

Main Language(s) of Instruction: Chinese, English

International Co-operation: 2+2 Undergraduate Programme with University of Central England, UK; 1+1 Graduate Programme with Coventry University, UK

Accrediting Agencies: Jiangsu Education Bureau

Degrees and Diplomas: *Bachelor's Degree*: 4 yrs; *Master's Degree*: a further 2 yrs; *Doctor's Degree*: Engineering, 4 yrs

Student Services: Academic counselling, Canteen, Cultural centre, Employment services, Health services, Sports facilities

Student Residential Facilities: Yes

Special Facilities: Museum.

Libraries: 1.2m. vols

Publications: Journal of Nanjing University of Science and Technology, (Natural Sciences) *(biennially)*; Journal of Nanjing University of Science and Technology, (Philosophical and Social Sciences) *(biennially)*
Last Updated: 27/11/08

NANJING UNIVERSITY OF TECHNOLOGY

5 Xinmofan Road, Nanjing, Jiangsu Province 210009
Tel: +86(25) 3587667
Fax: +86(25) 3211323
EMail: cie@njut.edu.cn
Website: http://www.njut.edu.cn

President: Ouyang Pingkai
International Relations: Han Luping

Colleges
Architecture and Urban Planning; **Artistic Design** (Design); **Automation**; **Chemistry and Chemical Engineering** (Chemical Engineering; Chemistry); **Civil Engineering**; **Continuing Education**; **Economics and Management**; **Foreign Languages and International Exchange** (International Relations; Modern Languages); **Information Science and Engineering**; **Law and Political Science**; **Management Science and Engineering**; **Materials Science and Engineering**; **Mechanical and Power Engineering** (Mechanical Engineering; Power Engineering); **Pharmacology and Life Sciences**; **Pujiang**; **Sciences**; **Techniques**; **Urban Construction and Safety and Environmental Engineering** (Construction Engineering; Environmental Engineering; Safety Engineering; Town Planning)

Departments
Physical Education (Physical Education)

History: Founded 1958. Renamed Nanjing University of Chemical Technology 1995. Acquired present title and status 2001 following merger with Nanjing Institute of Architectural and Civil Engineering.
Main Language(s) of Instruction: Chinese
Degrees and Diplomas: *Bachelor's Degree*; *Master's Degree*; *Doctor's Degree*
Libraries: c. 1.5m. vols.
Publications: Higher Education Research
Last Updated: 27/11/08

NANJING UNIVERSITY OF TRADITIONAL CHINESE MEDICINE

282 Hanzhong Road, Nanjing, Jiangsu Province 210029
Tel: +86(25) 6798078
Fax: +86(25) 6798078
EMail: iec@njutcm.edu.cn
Website: http://www.njutcm.edu.cn

President: Mianhua Wu

Schools
Basic Medical Science (Medicine); **Chinese Medical Equipment**; **Clinical Medicine**; **International Education**; **Medical Administration**

History: Founded 1955 as Jiangsu School for Continuing Study of Traditional Chinese Medicine. Acquired present title 1995.
Degrees and Diplomas: *Bachelor's Degree*; *Master's Degree*; *Doctor's Degree*
Libraries: c. 390,000 vols
Publications: Journal of TCM
Last Updated: 27/11/08

NANJING XIAOZHUANG UNIVERSITY

41 Beiwei Road, Nanjing, Jiangsu Province 210017
Tel: +86(25) 6614926
Fax: +86(25) 6614926
EMail: yuanzhang@njxzc.edu.cn
Website: http://www.njnc.edu.cn

Programmes
Arts and Humanities (Chinese; English; History); **Education** (Education; Physical Education; Preschool Education); **Fine and Performing Arts** (Design; Fine Arts; Music); **Mathematics and Computer Science**; **Natural Sciences** (Biological and Life Sciences; Geography; Physics); **Radio and Television Broadcasting** (Radio and Television Broadcasting); **Social Sciences**; **Welfare and Protective Services** (Environmental Studies; Natural Resources; Social Work)

History: Founded 1927. Acquired present status 2003.
Degrees and Diplomas: *Bachelor's Degree*
Libraries: c. 630,000 vols; c. 1,200 periodical subscriptions.

NANKAI UNIVERSITY

94 Weijin Road, Nankai District, Tianjin, Tianjin Province 300071
Tel: +86(22) 23508229
Fax: +86(22) 23502990
EMail: exchange@nankai.edu.cn
Website: http://www.nankai.edu.cn

President: Gong Ke (2011-)
Tel: +86(22) 23508632 +86(22) 23501631,
Fax: +86(22) 23501631

Vice-President: Naijia Guan EMail: guanj@nankai.edu.cn
International Relations: Haiyan Gao, Director, Office for International Academic Exchanges
EMail: gaohaiyan@nankai.edu.cn; nkexchange@gmail.com

Centres
APEC Studies (International Business; International Economics) *Director:* Zhankui Gong; **Pesticides Engineering** (Chemical Engineering) *Director:* Zhengming Li

Colleges
Arts (Arts and Humanities; Fine Arts) *Dean:* Hong Chen; **Chemistry** (Chemistry) *Dean:* Yu Liu; **Chinese Language and Culture** (Chinese) *Dean:* Feng Shi; **Economics** (Economics) *Dean:* Liqun Zhou; **Environmental Sciences and Engineering** (Environmental Engineering; Environmental Studies) *Dean:* Quxing Zhou; **Foreign Languages** (Japanese) *Dean:* Jianyi Wang; **History** (History) *Dean:* Zhi'an Li; **Information Sciences and Technology** (Information Sciences; Information Technology) *Dean:* Gongyi Wu; **International Business** (International Business) *Dean:* Wei'an Li; **Law and Politics** (Law; Political Sciences) *Dean:* Guanglei Zhu; **Life Sciences** (Biological and Life Sciences) *Dean:* Wenjun Pu; **Mathematical Sciences** (Mathematics) *Dean:* Yongjin Wang; **Mathematics** (Mathematics) *Head:* Yongjin Wang; **Physical Sciences** (Physics) *Dean:* Jingjun Xu; **TEDA** (International Business; International Economics) *Dean:* Guoming Xian; **Zhou En Lai School of Government** *Dean:* Guanglei Zhu

Departments
Accountancy (Accountancy) *Head:* Zhiyuan Liu; **Biochemistry and Molecular Biology** (Biochemistry; Molecular Biology) *Head:* Yong Wang; **Biology** (Entomology) *Head:* Houhun Li; **Chemistry** (Organic Chemistry) *Head:* Yu Liu; **Chinese Language and Literature** (Chinese) *Head:* Yigang Qiao; **Computer Science and Systems** (Mathematics and Computer Science) *Head:* Jingdong Xu; **Economics** (Economics) *Head:* Zili He; **Electronics** (Electronic Engineering) *Head:* Yue Wu; **English** (English; Modern Languages) *Head:* Lichang Su; **Environmental Sciences** (Environmental Studies) *Head:* Hongwen Sun; **Finance** (Finance) *Head:* Junlu Ma; **General Foreign Languages** (Modern Languages) *Head:* Yipu Xue; **History** (History) *Head:* Zhi'an Li; **Information Management and Information Systems** (Information Sciences) *Head:* Jianyuan Yan; **International Economy and Trade** (International Business; International Economics) *Head:* Jiadong Tong; **International Enterprise Management** (International Business; Management) *Head:* Yuli Zhang; **Japanese** (Japanese) *Head:* Jianyi Wang; **Law** (Law) *Head:* Shicheng Fu; **Microbiology** (Microbiology) *Head:* Gang Bai; **Oriental Culture and Art** (Cultural Studies; Fine Arts; Oriental Studies) *Head:* Changli Han; **Philosophy** (Philosophy) *Head:* Nanshi Wang; **Photo Electric Information Science** (Information Sciences) *Head:* Kecheng Lu; **Physics** (Physics) *Head:* Xueqian Li; **Political Science** (Political Sciences) *Head:* Guanglei Zhu; **Risk Management and Insurance** (Insurance) *Head:* Shengzhong Jiang; **Sociology** (Sociology) *Head:* Hongguang Bai; **Tourism** (Tourism) *Head:* Jian Wang; **Western Languages** (Modern Languages; Western European Studies) *Head:* Guodong Yan

Institutes

Ancient Chinese Books and Culture (Ancient Books; Ancient Civilizations) *Director*: Jiaying Ye; **Economics** (Economics) *Director*: Ligun Zhou; **History** (History) *Director*: Bingwen Nan; **International Economic Law** (International Law) *Director*: Xueying Shi; **International Economy** (International Economics) *Director*: Jinping Dai; **International Insurance** (Insurance) *Director*: Shengzhong Jiang; **Machine Intelligence** (Artificial Intelligence; Automation and Control Engineering; Robotics) *Director*: Weihuan Han; **Mathematics** (Mathematics) *Director*: Xingwei Zhou; **Modern Optics** (Optics) *Director*: Guo Guang Mu; **Molecular Biology** (Molecular Biology) *Director*: Ju Zhang; **New Energy Materials Chemistry** (Chemistry; Physical Chemistry) *Director*: Huatang Yuan; **Organic Element Chemistry** (Organic Chemistry) *Director*: Qilin Zhou; **Polymer Chemistry** (Polymer and Plastics Technology) *Head*: Zhi Yuan; **Population and Development** (Demography and Population) *Head*: Jianmin Li; **Taiwan Economy** (Economics) *Director*: Xiaoheng Cao; **Thin Film Devices and Technology** (Film) *Director*: Xinhua Geng; **Transportation Economics** (Transport Economics) *Director*: Zetao Luo

Schools

Medicine (Medicine) *Dean*: Tianhui Zhu; **Modern Distance Education** *Dean*: Honggang Jing

History: Founded 1919. Incorporated the former Tianjin Institute of Foreign Trade 1994.

Academic Year: September to July (September-January; February-July)

Admission Requirements: Graduation from senior middle school and entrance examination

Fees: (Yuan): c. 4,000 per annum

Main Language(s) of Instruction: Chinese

International Co-operation: With over 100 universities in USA, United Kingdom, France, Germany, Japan, Russian Federation, Canada.

Accrediting Agencies: Ministry of Education

Degrees and Diplomas: *Bachelor's Degree*: 4 yrs; *Master's Degree*: a further 3 yrs; *Doctor's Degree*: Arts; Economics; History; Philosophy; Science, a further 2-3 yrs following Master

Student Services: Academic counselling, Canteen, Cultural centre, Employment services, Foreign student adviser, Foreign Studies Centre, Handicapped facilities, Health services, Language programs, Nursery care, Social counselling, Sports facilities

Student Residential Facilities: Yes

Special Facilities: Archives. Exhibition Hall for Historic Relics

Libraries: Central Library, c. 2,8m. vols

Publications: Higher Education *(bimonthly)*; Nankai Business Review *(bimonthly)*; Nankai Economic Research *(bimonthly)*; Nankai Journal (Natural Sciences and Social Sciences Editions) *(bimonthly)*

Press or Publishing House: Nankai University Press
Last Updated: 03/06/11

NANTONG UNIVERSITY

19 Qixiu Road, Nantong, Jiangsu Province 226001
Tel: +86(513) 501-5300
Fax: +86(513) 501-5336
EMail: xiaozhang@ntu.edu.cn
Website: http://english.ntu.edu.cn/index.htm

President: Xiaosong Gu EMail: xsgu@ntu.edu.cn

Schools

Architecture Engineering; **Basic Medical Science**; **Business** (Business Administration; Business and Commerce); **Chemistry and Chemical Engineering** (Chemical Engineering; Chemistry); **Clinical Medicine** (Medicine); **Computer Science and Technology**; **Education** (Education); **Electrical Engineering**; **Electronics and Information Science** (Electronic Engineering; Information Sciences); **Fine Arts and Design** (Design; Fine Arts); **Foreign Studies**; **Further Education**; **Geography** (Geography); **Humanities** (Arts and Humanities); **Law and Politics** (Law; Political Sciences); **Life Sciences**; **Mechanical Engineering** (Mechanical Engineering); **Nursing** (Nursing); **Public Administration**; **Public**

Health (Public Health); **Sciences** (Natural Sciences); **Sports Science** (Sports; Sports Management); **Textile and Clothing**

History: Founded in 1912 as Nantong Medical College. Merged with Nantong Institute of Technology and Nantong Teachers College in 2004, when obtained current title and status.

Admission Requirements: Undergraduate, High School Diploma or equivalent; Postgraduate, Bachelor's degree or equivalent.

Fees: (Yuan): Home students, 160,000 per annum; Foreign students, 16,000 - 25,000 per annum

International Co-operation: With universities in Australia, Canada, Germany, Japan, USA

Accrediting Agencies: Ministry of Education

Degrees and Diplomas: *Bachelor's Degree*; *Master's Degree*; *Doctor's Degree*

Publications: Journals of Nantong University, Natural Sciences; Social Sciences; Medical Sciences; Education Sciences
Last Updated: 27/11/08

NATIONAL ACADEMY OF CHINESE THEATRE ARTS

400 Wanquansi, Fengtai District, Beijing 100073
Tel: +86(10) 6351063
Fax: +86(10) 63351063
Website: http://www.nacta.edu.cn

Departments

Art Education (Art Education); **Chinese Traditional Opera Literature** (Chinese; Cinema and Television; Literature; Theatre); **Directing** (Conducting); **Music** (Music; Opera); **New Media Arts**; **Performance** (Musical Instruments; Performing Arts); **Stage Design** (Display and Stage Design)

History: Founded 1950 as Chinese Traditional Opera School. Acquired present title 1978.

Degrees and Diplomas: *Bachelor's Degree*; *Master's Degree*
Last Updated: 09/09/08

NINGBO UNIVERSITY

Ningbo, Zhejiang Province 315211
Tel: +86(574) 87600249
Fax: +86(574) 87604338
EMail: wsc@nbu.edu.cn
Website: http://www.nbu.edu.cn

President: Yan Luguang Tel: +86(574) 87600255

Vice-President: Nie Qiuhua Tel: +86(574) 87600252

International Relations: Chen Yujuan
Tel: +86(574) 87600271, Fax: +86(574) 87604338
EMail: shelly@nbu.edu.cn

Colleges
Elementary Education

Departments

Arts and Humanities I (Arts and Humanities; Chinese; History; Literature; Modern Languages) *Dean*: Zhou Zhifeng; **Arts and Humanities II** (Arts and Humanities; French; Japanese; Modern Languages) *Dean*: Fan Yi; **Chemistry and Physics** (Analytical Chemistry; Applied Chemistry; Applied Physics; Chemistry; Natural Sciences; Physics) *Dean*: Shen Wenqing; **Economics** (Economics; Social Sciences) *Dean*: Tang Shaoxiang; **Engineering I** *Dean*: Zheng Di; **Engineering II** *Dean*: Xue Yongqi; **Engineering III** (Civil Engineering; Engineering) *Dean*: Cai Zewei; **Fine Arts** (Art Management; Design; Fine Arts) *Dean*: Chen Yueming; **Health Sciences** *Dean*: Hong Guofan; **Information Sciences** (Information Sciences; Mass Communication) *Dean*: Chen Yueming; **Mathematics and Computer Science I** (Computer Science; Mathematics and Computer Science) *Dean*: Xue Yongqi; **Mathematics and Computer Science II** *Dean*: Shen Wenqing

Faculties

Business; **Communication and Arts**; **Education** (Education; Educational Sciences) *Dean*: Hu Chidi; **Foreign Languages** (Modern Languages); **Law**; **Liberal Arts** (Arts and Humanities); **Physical Education**

Further Information: Also courses for foreign students

History: Founded 1986. Incorporated Ningbo Teacher's College and Zhejiang Aquatic Products Institute 1996.

Academic Year: August to July (August-January; February-July)

Admission Requirements: Graduation from senior middle school and entrance examination

Fees: (Yuan): c. 4,400 per annum

Main Language(s) of Instruction: Chinese

International Co-operation: With universities in Germany; Japan; France; Sweden; Canada; Republic of South Korea; South Africa; United Kingdom

Accrediting Agencies: Department of Education of Zhejiang Province

Degrees and Diplomas: *Bachelor's Degree*: 4 yrs; *Master's Degree*: a further 2-3 yrs

Student Services: Academic counselling, Canteen, Cultural centre, Employment services, Foreign student adviser, Foreign Studies Centre, Health services, Language programs, Nursery care, Social counselling, Sports facilities

Student Residential Facilities: For 20,000 students

Libraries: Bao Yugang, Shao Yifu and Bao Yushu Science Libraries

Publications: Journal of Ningbo University *(bimonthly)*
Last Updated: 27/11/08

NINGXIA MEDICAL COLLEGE

692, Shengli Street, Yinchuan, Ningxia Province 750004
Tel: +86(951) 4091732
Fax: +86(951) 4091732
EMail: admission@nxmc.info
Website: http://www.nxmc.info/home.htm

President: Sun Tao

Departments
Clinical Medicine (Medicine); **Preventive Medicine** (Social and Preventive Medicine); **Traditional Chinese Medicine** (Traditional Eastern Medicine)

History: Founded 1958.

Main Language(s) of Instruction: Chinese

Degrees and Diplomas: *Bachelor's Degree*; *Master's Degree*
Last Updated: 27/11/08

NINGXIA UNIVERSITY

Xinshi District, Yinchuan, Ningxia Province 750021
Tel: +86(951) 2061106
Fax: +86(951) 2077740
EMail: dwhjzx@nxu.edu.cn
Website: http://www.nxu.edu.cn

President: Chen Yuning

Schools
Agriculture; **Biological Science**; **Chemistry and Chemical Engineering** (Chemical Engineering; Chemistry); **Civil Engineering and Water Conservation** (Civil Engineering; Water Management); **Economics and Management** (Economics; Management); **Educational Sciences** (Educational Sciences); **Fine Arts** (Fine Arts); **Foreign Languages and Cultures** (Modern Languages); **Humanities** (Arts and Humanities); **Mathematics and Computer** (Computer Science; Mathematics); **Mechanical Engineering** (Mechanical Engineering); **Music** (Music); **Physical Education** (Physical Education); **Physics and Electronic Information Engineering** (Electronic Engineering; Information Technology; Physics); **Politics and Law** (Law; Political Sciences); **Resources and Environment** (Environmental Studies; Natural Resources)

History: Founded 1958. Merged with Ningxia Institute of Engineering and Yinchuan Teachers Training College 1997, and with Ningxia Agricultural College 2002.

Degrees and Diplomas: *Bachelor's Degree*; *Master's Degree*; *Doctor's Degree*

Libraries: c. 940,000 vols

Publications: Higher Education Research of Ningxia University; Journal of Ningxia University
Last Updated: 27/11/08

NORTH CHINA COAL MEDICAL UNIVERSITY

57 Jiangshe South Road, Tangshan, Hebei Province 063000
Tel: +86(315) 3725300
Fax: +86(315) 2823641
Website: http://www.nccmu.com

President: Zhao Boyang
International Relations: Zhu Fangchen

Departments
Bioscience (Biological and Life Sciences); **Clinical Medicine** (Medicine); **Elementary Medicine**; **Foreign Languages** (Modern Languages); **Law** (Law); **Nursing**; **Pharmacology** (Pharmacology); **Physical Education**; **Preventive Medicine** (Social and Preventive Medicine); **Psychology** (Psychology); **Stomatology** (Stomatology); **Traditional Chinese Medicine**

Schools
Sociology and Public Health Management

History: Founded 1926 as North China Coal Medical College. Acquired present status and title 1998.

Degrees and Diplomas: *Bachelor's Degree*; *Master's Degree*
Last Updated: 27/11/08

NORTH CHINA ELECTRIC POWER UNIVERSITY (NCEPU)

204 Qingnian Road, Baoding, Hebei Province 071003
Tel: +86(312) 5016156
Fax: +86(312) 5016156
EMail: dicncepu@heinfo.net; admission@ncepu.edu.cn
Website: http://www.ncepu.net.cn

President: Xu Daping (1995-) Tel: +86(312) 5024951, Ext. 2082
Head: Li Xiaoyun
International Relations: Gao Baoxin

Departments
Accountancy (Accountancy); **Business** (Business and Commerce); **Electric Power Engineering** (Electrical Engineering; Power Engineering); **Electronic Engineering**; **English** (English); **Environmental Engineering** (Environmental Engineering); **Fundamental Science**; **Mechanical Engineering**; **Power Engineering** (Power Engineering) *Head*: Pu Han; **Thermal Power Engineering** (Power Engineering; Thermal Engineering)

Schools
Business Administration (Business Administration); **Management** (Management)

History: Founded 1958 as Beijing School of Electric Power. Merged with North China Institute of Electric Power and Beijing Power Engineering and Economics Institute. Acquired present status 1995. Affiliated with the State Power Corporation of China.

Academic Year: September to July

Admission Requirements: Graduation from high school and entrance examination

Main Language(s) of Instruction: Chinese

Degrees and Diplomas: *Bachelor's Degree*; *Master's Degree*; *Doctor's Degree*

Student Services: Academic counselling, Canteen, Cultural centre, Employment services, Foreign student adviser, Foreign Studies Centre, Health services, Language programs, Nursery care, Social counselling, Sports facilities

Libraries: c. 820,000 vols

Publications: Higher Education of Electric Power; Higher Education Theory and Practice; Journal of North China Electric Power University *(quarterly)*

NORTH CHINA ELECTRIC POWER UNIVERSITY (BEIJING)

Zhuxinzhuang, Dewai, Beijing 102206
Tel: +86(10) 80792683
Fax: +86(10) 80795105
EMail: icd@ncepubj.edu.cn
Website: http://www.ncepubj.edu.cn

President: Liu Jizhen

Departments

Electric Power (Electrical Engineering; Power Engineering); **Information Engineering** (Information Technology); **Social Sciences** (Social Sciences); **Thermal Power Engineering** (Power Engineering; Thermal Engineering)

Schools

Business Administration (Business Administration)

History: Founded 1958 as Beijing Electric Power Institute. Acquired present title 1998.

Degrees and Diplomas: *Bachelor's Degree*; *Master's Degree*; *Doctor's Degree*

Libraries: c. 490,000 vols

Publications: Journal of North China Electric Power University
Last Updated: 27/11/08

NORTH CHINA INSTITUTE OF SCIENCE AND TECHNOLOGY

P.O. Box 206, East Yanjiao, Beijing 101601
Tel: +86(10) 61594928 +86(10) 61595151
Fax: +86(10) 61591963
EMail: office@ncist.edu.cn
Website: http://www.ncist.edu.cn

President: Yang Gengyu

Departments

Architectural Engineering (Civil Engineering; Construction Engineering; Engineering; Heating and Refrigeration; Real Estate); **Basic Curriculum** (Computer Science; Information Sciences); **Computer Science and Technology**; **Electronics and Information Engineering** (Automation and Control Engineering; Electronic Engineering; Industrial Engineering; Information Technology; Telecommunications Engineering); **Environment** (Chemical Engineering; Environmental Engineering; Technology); **Foreign Languages** (Business Administration; English; Modern Languages); **Humanities and Social Sciences**; **Management** (Accountancy; Business Administration; E-Business/Commerce; Economics; Hotel Management; International Economics; Marketing; Tourism); **Mechanical and Electronic Engineering**; **Physical Education** (Physical Education)

Schools

Safety and Engineering (Mining Engineering; Safety Engineering)

History: Founded 1984 as a branch school of Beijing Coal Management Institute in Yanjiao. Became North China Mining College 1994. Acquired present title and status 2002.

Degrees and Diplomas: *Bachelor's Degree*. Also non-degree programs

Libraries: c. 427,000 vols.

Publications: Journal of North China Institute of Science and Technology
Last Updated: 27/11/08

NORTH CHINA UNIVERSITY OF TECHNOLOGY

No.5 Jinyuanzhuang Road, Shijingshan District, Beijing 100041
Tel: +86(10) 68839517
Fax: +86(10) 68875846
EMail: fao@ncut.edu.cn
Website: http://www.ncut.edu.cn

President: Wang Xiaochun Tel: +86(10) 68874420

Schools

Applied Techniques (Technology); **Architecture** (Architecture); **Basic Sciences**; **Continuing Education**; **Economics and Business Administration** (Business Administration; Economics); **Engineering** (Engineering); **Humanities and Social Sciences** (Arts and Humanities; Social Sciences)

History: Founded 1946 as Beijing State Senior Polytechnic High School, became Beijing Metallurgical Institute of Mechanical and Electrical Engineering 1978. Acquired present title 1985.

Academic Year: September to July (September-February; March-July)

Admission Requirements: Graduation from senior middle school and entrance examination

Fees: (Yuan): c. 5,500 per annum

Main Language(s) of Instruction: Chinese

Accrediting Agencies: Central and Beijing Municipal Governments

Degrees and Diplomas: *Bachelor's Degree*: 4 yrs; *Master's Degree*: a further 3 yrs

Student Services: Academic counselling, Canteen, Cultural centre, Employment services, Foreign student adviser, Health services, Nursery care, Social counselling, Sports facilities

Student Residential Facilities: For c. 5,000 students

Special Facilities: Art Gallery

Libraries: c. 440,000 vols

Publications: Journal of North China University of Technology (*quarterly*)

Press or Publishing House: University Printing House
Last Updated: 27/11/08

NORTH CHINA UNIVERSITY OF WATER CONSERVANCY AND ELECTRIC POWER

20 Zhenghua Street, Zhengzhou, Henan Province 450045
Tel: +86(371) 5727655 Ext. 3430
Fax: +86(371) 5729645
EMail: icc@ncwu.edu.cn
Website: http://www.ncwu.edu.cn

President: Lin Jinsong
International Relations: Cui Yunhao

Faculties

Civil Engineering (Civil Engineering); **Environmental Engineering** (Analytical Chemistry; Environmental Engineering; Inorganic Chemistry; Microbiology; Organic Chemistry); **Foreign Languages**; **Geotechnical Engineering** (Geological Engineering; Geology); **Information Engineering** (Artificial Intelligence; Computer Science); **Mathematics and Information Science** (Applied Mathematics; Computer Science; Mathematics; Statistics); **Mechanical Engineering** (Mechanical Engineering); **Power Engineering** (Power Engineering); **Water Conservation Engineering** (Engineering; Water Science)

History: Founded 1951, acquired present name 1978.

Main Language(s) of Instruction: Chinese

Degrees and Diplomas: *Bachelor's Degree*; *Master's Degree*
Last Updated: 27/11/08

NORTH SICHUAN MEDICAL COLLEGE

234# Fujiang Road, Nanchong, Sichuan Province 637007
Tel: +86(817) 2242632
Fax: +86(817) 2242600
EMail: fao@nsmc.edu.cn
Website: http://www.nsmc.edu.cn/en/

President: Li Ren
International Relations: Hu Hongyi

Departments
Clinical Medicine; **Medical Imaging**

History: Founded 1951 as North Sichuan Nursing School, acquired present status and title 1985.

Main Language(s) of Instruction: Chinese

Degrees and Diplomas: *Bachelor's Degree*
Last Updated: 27/11/08

NORTH UNIVERSITY OF CHINA

1 Xueyuan Road, Taiyuan, Shanxi Province 030051
Tel: +86(351) 3922084
Fax: +86(351) 4048163
Website: http://www.nuc.edu.cn

President: Zhang Wen Dong

Schools
Chemical Engineering and Environment (Chemical Engineering; Environmental Engineering; Safety Engineering); **Economics and**

Management (Economics; Management); **Electronic and Computer Science and Engineering** (Computer Networks; Computer Science; Electronic Engineering); **Humanities and Social Sciences**; **Information and Communication Engineering** (Communication Studies; Electrical and Electronic Engineering; Information Sciences); **Materials Science and Engineering** (Materials Engineering); **Mechanical Engineering and Automation** (Automation and Control Engineering; Mechanical Engineering); **Mechatronic Engineering** (Electronic Engineering; Mechanical Engineering); **Science**; **Sports and Arts** (Art Education; Music; Sports)

History: Founded 1940 as Taihang Technical School. Renamed North China Institute of Technology 1993. Acquired present title 2001.

Main Language(s) of Instruction: Chinese

Degrees and Diplomas: *Bachelor's Degree*; *Master's Degree*; *Doctor's Degree*

Libraries: c. 580,000 vols
Last Updated: 27/11/08

NORTHEAST AGRICULTURAL UNIVERSITY

59 Mucai Street, Xiangfang District, Harbin, Heilongjiang Province 150030
Tel: +86(451) 5390588
Fax: +86(451) 5303336
EMail: neauxcb@126.com
Website: http://www.neau.edu.cn

President: Zheng Qiumei

Schools
Administration (Administration); **Agriculture** (Agriculture; Agronomy; Environmental Studies; Horticulture; Natural Resources; Plant and Crop Protection); **Animal Science and Technology** (Animal Husbandry; Technology); **Economics and Trade** (Accountancy; Business and Commerce; Economics; Finance; Management; Rural Planning); **Engineering** (Agricultural Engineering; Civil Engineering; Engineering; Soil Science; Water Science); **Human Development Studies** (Development Studies); **Life Sciences** (Biological and Life Sciences; Biotechnology); **Professional Technology** (Technology); **Town Planning** (Town Planning); **Veterinary Science** (Biological and Life Sciences; Veterinary Science)

Further Information: Also Chinese and Russian Students Exchange programme; courses for foreign students

History: Founded 1948 as Northeast Agricultural College. Merged with Heilongjiang Provincial Agricultural Administrators' Training College. Acquired present title 1994.

Academic Year: September to July (September-January; March-July)

Admission Requirements: Graduation from high school

Main Language(s) of Instruction: Chinese

Degrees and Diplomas: *Bachelor's Degree*: 4-5 yrs; *Master's Degree*: a further 3 yrs; *Doctor's Degree (Ph.D.)*: 3 yrs

Student Services: Academic counselling, Cultural centre, Health services, Nursery care, Social counselling, Sports facilities

Student Residential Facilities: Yes

Libraries: c. 620,000 vols

Publications: Higher Agricultural Education *(annually)*; Journal of Northeast Agricultural University

Press or Publishing House: Northeast Agricultural University Publishing House
Last Updated: 27/11/08

NORTHEAST DINALI UNIVERSITY

169 Changchun Road, Jilin, Jilin Province 132012
Tel: +86(432) 4806412 +86(432) 4806874
Fax: +86(432) 4884186
EMail: dic@mail.nedu.edu.cn
Website: http://www.nedu.edu.cn

President: Mu Gang

Departments
Applied Chemistry (Applied Chemistry); **Automation and Control Engineering** (Automation and Control Engineering); **Civil Engi-**

neering; **Electrical Power Engineering** (Electrical Engineering; Power Engineering); **Engineering Management** (Engineering Management); **Information Technology** (Information Technology); **Mechanical and Electronic Engineering** (Electronic Engineering; Mechanical Engineering); **Modern Languages and Literature** (Literature; Modern Languages); **Thermal Power Engineering** (Power Engineering; Thermal Engineering)

History: Founded 1949. In 1978 name changed to Northeast China Institute of Electric Power Engineering. Acquired present name and status 2005.

Academic Year: September to July (September-January; March-July)

Admission Requirements: Finished 12-year or above education

Fees: (US Dollars): Chinese programme, 1,600 per annum; undergraduate, 1,800; master, 2,000; registration fee, 50

International Co-operation: With universities in USA, Japan, United Kingdom, Russian Federation ,Republic of Korea, Ukraine, Canada, Bulgaria

Degrees and Diplomas: *Bachelor's Degree*: Management Information Engineering; Industrial Analysis; Accounting; Computer Science and Application; Communication Engineering;Japanese Language and Literature Electromechanical Engineering; Applied Electronic Technology; English Language and Literature; Power System and Automation; Relay Protection and Automatic & Telecontrol Technology; Thermal Power Engineering; Dynamic Engineering; Industrial Automation; Civil Engineering; *Master's Degree*: Power System and Automation; Thermal Power Engineering; Engineering Thermodynamic Physics; Applied Chemistry; Technical Economics; Automatic Control; Computer Science and Application; *Doctor's Degree*

Student Services: Employment services

Student Residential Facilities: Yes.
Last Updated: 27/11/08

NORTHEAST FORESTRY UNIVERSITY (NEFU)

26 Hexing Road, Harbin, Heilongjiang Province 150040
Tel: +86(451) 2190337
Fax: +86(451) 2110146
EMail: faob@public.hr.hl.cn
Website: http://www.nefu.edu.cn

President: Yang Chuanping Tel: +86(451) 2190131

Centres
Automobile Testing (Automotive Engineering) *Director*: Guofan Li; **Wild Animal and Plant Testing** (Plant and Crop Protection; Wildlife) *Director*: Song Yan Jing; **Woodworking Machinery Monitoring and Testing** (Wood Technology) *Director*: Zhiren Li

Colleges
Civil Engineering (Civil Engineering; Construction Engineering; Engineering Management; Town Planning); **Engineering and Technique** (Forestry; Industrial Engineering; Packaging Technology) *Director*: Lihai Wang; **Foreign Languages** (Modern Languages) *Director*: Menglan Liu; **Forest Economics and Management** (Accountancy; Economics; Finance; Forestry; Management; Statistics; Taxation); **Forest Resources and Environment** (Bioengineering; Environmental Studies; Food Science; Forest Biology; Forest Products; Zoology) *Director*: Yu Seng Zhao; **Information and Computer Engineering** (Computer Engineering; Computer Science; Information Management) *Director*: Ni Hong Wang; **Landscape Architecture** *Director*: Lihuan Zhuo; **Mechanical and Electrical Engineering** (Computer Engineering; Electrical Engineering; Electronic Engineering; Mechanical Engineering; Transport and Communications) *Director*: Dongsheng Li; **Normal** (Applied Chemistry; Applied Mathematics; Applied Physics; Computer Science; Education; Information Sciences) *Director*: Yie Song; **Social Sciences and Humanities** (Administration; Advertising and Publicity; Arts and Humanities; Law; Political Sciences; Social Sciences) *Director*: Yue Xian Wang; **Transport Engineering** *Director*: Qiang Guan; **Wildlife Resources** (Biological and Life Sciences; Forestry; Tourism; Wildlife) *Director*: Jing Bo Jia

Departments
Physical Education (Physical Education) *Head*: Songshan Mu
History: Founded 1952.

Academic Year: March to February (March-July; September-February)

Admission Requirements: Graduation from senior middle school and entrance examination

Fees: (US Dollars): 1,500-3,000 per annum

Main Language(s) of Instruction: Chinese

Accrediting Agencies: Foreign Affairs Office

Degrees and Diplomas: *Bachelor's Degree*: 4 yrs; *Master's Degree*: a further 3 yrs; *Doctor's Degree (Ph.D.)*: a further 2-3 yrs

Student Services: Academic counselling, Canteen, Cultural centre, Foreign student adviser, Foreign Studies Centre, Health services, Language programs, Nursery care, Sports facilities

Special Facilities: 3 Experimental Forest Stations

Libraries: Northeast Forest Library, 1.09m. vols

Publications: Bulletin of Botanical Research; China Forestry Business; Chinese Wildlife *(bimonthly)*; Forest Engineering; Forest Fire Prevention; Journal of Forestry Research (in English) *(quarterly)*; Journal of Northeast Forestry University

Press or Publishing House: Northeast Forestry University Press
Last Updated: 27/11/08

NORTHEAST NORMAL UNIVERSITY

138 Renmin Street, Changchun, Jilin Province 130024
Tel: +86(431) 5695061
Fax: +86(431) 5684027
EMail: efly@nenu.edu.cn
Website: http://www.nenu.edu.cn

President: Shi Ningzhong

International Relations: Han Yingchang

Institutes
International Relations and Marxism

Schools
Business (Business Administration; International Business); **Chemistry**; **Chinese Language and Literature** (Chinese; Literature); **Computer Science** (Computer Science); **Continuing Education**; **Economics** (Economics); **Education** (Education); **Fine Arts** (Fine Arts); **Foreign Languages** (Literature; Modern Languages); **History and Culture** (Cultural Studies; History); **Life Sciences**; **Mathematics and Statistics** (Mathematics; Statistics); **Media Science**; **Music** (Music); **Physical Education** (Physical Education); **Physics** (Physics); **Politics and Law** (Law; Political Sciences); **Software** (Software Engineering); **Urban and Environmental Science** (Environmental Studies; Urban Studies)

History: Founded 1946. Acquired present title 1980.

Main Language(s) of Instruction: Chinese

Degrees and Diplomas: *Bachelor's Degree*; *Master's Degree*; *Doctor's Degree*

Libraries: c. 1.8m. vols

Publications: Journal of Ancient Civilization; Journal of International Studies; Journal of Molecular Science; Journal of Northeast Normal University
Last Updated: 27/11/08

NORTHEASTERN UNIVERSITY (NEU)

No. 3-11 Wen Hua Road, Heping District, Shenyang, Liaoning Province 110004
Tel: +86(24) 23893000
Fax: +86(24) 23892454
EMail: webmaster@mail.neu.edu.cn
Website: http://www.neu.edu.cn

President: Jicheng He (1998-) EMail: hejc@mail.neu.edu.cn

Vice-President: Liang Zuo
Tel: +86(24) 83687303 EMail: lzuo@mail.neu.edu.cn

International Relations: Yingxue Gao
Tel: +86(24) 23891016, Fax: +86(24) 23891829
EMail: gyx@mail.neu.edu.cn

Centres
Automation Engineering Research *(National)* (Automation and Control Engineering) *Director*: Tianyou Cai; **Computer Software**

Research *(National)* (Computer Science; Software Engineering) *Director*: Jiren Liu

Colleges
Business Administration (Accountancy; Business Administration; Finance; Industrial Engineering; International Business; Management; Marketing) *Dean*: Kai Li; **Foreign Studies** (English; Japanese) *Dean*: Siguo Li; **Humanities and Law** (Administration; Arts and Humanities; International Law; Law) *Dean*: Chengwu Lou; **Information Science and Engineering** (Automation and Control Engineering; Biomedical Engineering; Computer Engineering; Computer Science; Electronic Engineering; Information Management; Information Sciences; Information Technology; Management Systems; Measurement and Precision Engineering) *Dean*: Fuli Wang; **Materials and Metallurgy** (Materials Engineering; Metal Techniques; Metallurgical Engineering; Thermal Engineering) *Dean*: Chunming Liu; **Mechanical Engineering and Automation** (Automation and Control Engineering; Hydraulic Engineering; Mechanical Engineering) *Dean*: Liyang Xie; **Resources and Civil Engineering** (Civil Engineering; Environmental Engineering; Mining Engineering; Natural Resources; Safety Engineering) *Dean*: Baozhi Chen; **Science** (Applied Chemistry; Applied Mathematics; Applied Physics; Mathematics and Computer Science; Natural Resources; Physics) *Dean*: Qingling Zhang

Schools
Distance Education (Business and Commerce; Finance; Software Engineering) *Dean*: Yuehu Duan; **Fine Arts** (Design; Fine Arts; Music) *Dean*: Enpu Gong

History: Founded 1923. Acquired present status and title 1950 and incorporated Shenyang Institute of Gold Technology (founded 1952).

Governing Bodies: University Administration Committee

Academic Year: September to July (September-January March-July)

Admission Requirements: Graduation from high school and entrance examination

Fees: (US Dollars): 2,000-2,500 per annum

Main Language(s) of Instruction: Chinese

Degrees and Diplomas: *Bachelor's Degree*: 4 yrs; *Master's Degree*: 2 1/2 yrs; *Doctor's Degree (PhD)*: 3 yrs

Student Services: Canteen, Employment services, Foreign student adviser, Foreign Studies Centre, Health services, Language programs, Nursery care, Sports facilities

Libraries: 1,1m. vols

Publications: Basic Automation *(bimonthly)*; Control and Decision *(bimonthly)*; Journal of Northeastern University, (Natural Science) *(bimonthly)*; Metallurgical Economy and Management *(quarterly)*; Software Engineers *(bimonthly)*

Press or Publishing House: Northeastern University Press
Last Updated: 27/11/08

NORTHWEST A & F UNIVERSITY (NWSUAF)

3 Taicheng Road, Yangling, Shaanxi Province 712100
Tel: +86(29) 87082857
Fax: +86(29) 87082892
EMail: ipo@nwsuaf.edu.cn
Website: http://www.nwsuaf.edu.cn

President: Wuxue Sun (2001-) Tel: +86(29) 87082812

Vice-President: Xi Hou Tel: +86(29) 7082807

International Relations: Jun Luo, Director
Tel: +86(29) 87082891 EMail: luojun@nwsuaf.edu.cn

Colleges
Agronomy (Agronomy; Botany; Crop Production) *Dean*: Yuncheng Liao; **Animal Science and Technology** (Biology; Horticulture; Veterinary Science; Zoology) *Dean*: Yulin Chen; **Economics and Management** (Accountancy; Agricultural Economics; Agricultural Management; Business and Commerce; Business Computing; Economics; Finance; Forestry; Industrial Management; International Business; Natural Resources) *Dean*: Xuexi Huo; **Food Science and Engineering** *Executive Vice Dean*: Tianli Yue; **Foreign Languages** *Dean*: Qin Dou; **Forestry** (Chemical Engineering; Forestry; Landscape Architecture; Wildlife; Wood Technology) *Dean*: Jianjun Liu;

Horticulture (Agricultural Engineering; Floriculture; Horticulture) *Dean*: Zhirong Zhou; **Humanities** *Vice Dean*: Weidong Lv; **Information Engineering** (Computer Engineering; Computer Science; Information Management; Information Technology; Software Engineering; Systems Analysis) *Dean*: Dongjian He; **Life Science** *Dean*: Zongsuo Liang; **Mechanical and Electronic Engineering** (Agricultural Equipment; Automation and Control Engineering; Electronic Engineering; Industrial Design; Information Technology; Mechanical Engineering; Packaging Technology; Production Engineering) *Vice Dean*: Yougang Yang; **Oenology** (Oenology) *Dean*: Hua Wang; **Plant Protection** (Pharmacology; Plant and Crop Protection) *Dean*: Jinian Feng; **Resources and Environment** (Ecology; Environmental Engineering; Environmental Studies; Hydraulic Engineering; Information Technology; Natural Resources; Rural Planning; Soil Conservation; Town Planning; Water Management) *Dean*: Fenli Zheng; **Science** (Applied Chemistry; Applied Mathematics; Biophysics; Computer Science) *Dean*: Jinming Gao; **Veterinary Science** (Veterinary Science) *Dean*: Yanming Zhang; **Water Resources and Architectural Engineering** *Dean*: Huanjie Cai

History: Founded as school 1934. Merger between Northwest Agricultural University and Northwest Forestry University. Acquired present status and title 1999.

Academic Year: September to July (September-January; February-July)

Admission Requirements: Graduation from senior middle school and entrance examination

Main Language(s) of Instruction: Chinese

International Co-operation: With universities in USA, Germany, France, Netherlands, Finland, Canada, Japan and Thailand

Accrediting Agencies: Ministry of Education

Degrees and Diplomas: *Bachelor's Degree*: Science; Agriculture; Engineering; Economics; Management; Literature; Law; Education, 4 yrs; *Master's Degree*: Science; Agriculture; Engineering; Economics; Management; Literature; Law; Education, a further 3 yrs; *Doctor's Degree*: Science; Agriculture; Engineering; Economics; Management; Literature; Law; Education, 3 yrs following Master

Student Services: Academic counselling, Canteen, Cultural centre, Employment services, Foreign student adviser, Health services, Language programs, Nursery care, Social counselling, Sports facilities

Student Residential Facilities: Yes

Special Facilities: Museum Garden

Libraries: c. 1,93m. Vols

Publications: Agricultural Research in Arid Area *(quarterly)*; Forestry Science and Technology in Shaanxi Province *(quarterly)*; Journal of Insect Classification *(biannually)*; Journal of Northwest Agriculture *(quarterly)*; Journal of Northwest Forestry College *(quarterly)*; Journal of Northwest Plant *(bimonthly)*; Journal of Northwest Sci-University of Agriculture and Forestry, Social Science and Natural Sciences *(bimonthly)*; Journal of Soil and Water Conservation *(quarterly)*; Journal of Wheat Crop *(biannually)*; Livestock Ecology *(quarterly)*; Magazine of Animal Husbandry and Veterinary Medicine *(bimonthly)*; Northwest Water Resource and Irrigation Works *(quarterly)*; Northwest Water Resource and Irrigation Works; Progress of Animal Medicine *(quarterly)*; Soil and Water Conservation Bulletin; Soil and Water Conservation Bulletin *(bimonthly)*; Study of Soil and Water Conservation *(quarterly)*; Village Economy in Shaanxi Province *(monthly)*

Last Updated: 29/09/08

NORTHWEST NORMAL UNIVERSITY

805 East Anning Road, Hanning District, Lanzhou, Gansu Province 730070
Tel: +86(931) 7971274
Fax: +86(931) 7661274
EMail: wlzx@nwnu.edu.cn
Website: http://www.nwnu.edu.cn

President: Wang Limin

Colleges
Biological Science (Biology); **Chemical Engineering** (Chemical Engineering; Chemistry); **Economic Management**; **Education** (Curriculum; Education; Educational Sciences; Educational Technology); **Educational Technology and Communication** (Com-munication Studies; Educational Technology); **Fine Arts**; **Foreign Languages and Literature** (Literature; Modern Languages); **Geography and Environmental Science** (Environmental Studies; Geography); **Mathematics and Information Technology** (Information Technology; Mathematics); **Music**; **Physical Education** (Physical Education); **Physics and Electronic Engineering** (Electronic Engineering; Physics); **Politics and Law** (Economics; Law; Political Sciences); **Teacher Training**; **Tourism** (Tourism)

Schools
Vocational Education

History: Founded 1902 as National Beijing Teachers University. Acquired present title 1998.

Degrees and Diplomas: *Bachelor's Degree*; *Master's Degree*

Libraries: c. 1.1m. vols

Publications: Journal of Northwest Normal University
Last Updated: 27/11/08

NORTHWEST UNIVERSITY

1 Taibai Road, Xi'an, Shaanxi Province 710048
Tel: +86(29) 8302344
Fax: +86(29) 8303511
EMail: OIP@nwu.edu.cn
Website: http://www.nwu.edu.cn

President: Sun Yong

Departments
Applied Social Sciences (Finance; Philosophy; Social Sciences; Social Work); **Chemistry** (Applied Chemistry; Chemistry); **Computer Science**; **Electronic Science** (Electronic Engineering; Information Technology); **Environmental Science** (Environmental Engineering; Environmental Studies); **Geology** (Geochemistry; Geology); **Mathematics** (Applied Mathematics; Information Sciences; Mathematics); **Physics** (Applied Physics; Physics); **Urban Studies and Resource Science** (Environmental Management; Rural Planning; Town Planning; Urban Studies)

Schools
Adult Education; **Arts** (Chinese; Design; Film; Literature; Mass Communication; Radio and Television Broadcasting); **Chemical Engineering**; **Culture and Museology** (Archaeology; Cultural Studies; History; Museum Studies); **Economics and Management** (Accountancy; Business Administration; Business and Commerce; Economics; Management; Tourism); **Foreign Languages** (English; Japanese); **International Cultural Exchange**; **Journalism and Mass Communication** (Advertising and Publicity; Journalism; Mass Communication); **Law** (Law); **Life Sciences** (Biological and Life Sciences; Biotechnology); **Public Administration** (Archiving; Library Science; Public Administration)

History: Founded 1902 as Shaanx iCollege and assumed its present name in 1912. It was renamed National Northwest University in 1923, and called National Xi'an Provisional University after the merger with National Beiping University, Beiping Normal University, Beiyang College of Engineering and other institutions.

Degrees and Diplomas: *Bachelor's Degree*; *Master's Degree*; *Doctor's Degree*

Libraries: c. 1.2m. vols

Publications: Journal of Analytical Chemistry; Journal of Higher Education Studies; Journal of Modern Physics; Journal of the Northwest University; Journal of Theoretical Mathematics and Applied Mathematics
Last Updated: 28/11/08

NORTHWEST UNIVERSITY FOR NATIONALITIES

1 Xibeixincun, Lanzhou, Gansu Province 730030
Tel: +86(931) 2938060
EMail: maqing@xbmu.edu.cn
Website: http://www.xbmu.edu.cn

President: Jin Yasheng

International Relations: Ma Qing

Academies
The Chinese Academy of National Information Technology (Information Technology)

Faculties

Chemical Engineering (Chemical Engineering); **Civil Engineering**; **Computer Science and Information Engineering**; **Continuing and Vocational Education**; **Economics and Management** (Economics; Management); **Electrical Engineering** (Electrical Engineering); **Fine Arts** (Fine Arts); **Foreign Languages** (Modern Languages); **History and Civilization** (History); **Law** (Law); **Life Science and Engineering** (Biological and Life Sciences; Engineering); **Linguistics, Culture and Communication** (Communication Studies; Cultural Studies; Linguistics); **Medicine** (Medicine); **Modern Educational Technology** (Educational Technology); **Mongolian Language & Culture**; **Physical Education** (Physical Education); **Social Anthropology & Folklore** (Anthropology; Folklore)

Institutes

Overseas Ethnic Documents Institute

Research Departments

The Teaching and Research Department of Marxist Theory and Morality

Research Institutes

Islamic Culture; **The Gesar Research Institute** (Philology)

History: Founded 1950. Also know as Northwest Minorities University.

Degrees and Diplomas: *Bachelor's Degree*; *Master's Degree*; *Doctor's Degree*

Libraries: c. 485,000 vols

Publications: Journal of Northwest Minorities University; Northwest Minorities Research

Last Updated: 28/11/08

NORTHWEST UNIVERSITY OF POLITICAL SCIENCE AND LAW

88 South Chang'an Road, Xi'an, Shaanxi Province 710063
Tel: +86(29) 85385410
Fax: +86(29) 85262185
EMail: support@nwupl.edu.cn
Website: http://www.nwupl.edu.cn/index.htm

President: Yu Jia

Departments

Administrative Law (Administrative Law); **Economics and Commerce** (Business and Commerce; International Economics; Marketing); **English and Law**; **Law** (Law); **Media** (Media Studies)

History: Founded 1937 as as Northern Shaanxi School of Politics and Law. Acquired present title 1958.

Main Language(s) of Instruction: Chinese

Degrees and Diplomas: *Bachelor's Degree*; *Master's Degree*
Last Updated: 28/11/08

NORTHWESTERN POLYTECHNICAL UNIVERSITY (NPU)

127 Youyixilu, Xi'an, Shaanxi Province 710072
Tel: +86(29) 8492267
Fax: +86(29) 8491000
EMail: fao@nwpu.edu.cn
Website: http://www.nwpu.edu.cn

President: Jiang Chengyu (2001-) **EMail:** jiangcy@nwpu.edu.cn

Secretary: Ye Jinfu

International Relations: Tang Hong
Tel: +86(29) 8494379, Fax: +86(29) 8491544
EMail: tanghong@nwpu.edu.cn

Schools

Aeronautics (Aeronautical and Aerospace Engineering; Air Transport; Automation and Control Engineering; Mechanical Engineering); **Astronautics** (Aeronautical and Aerospace Engineering; Astronomy and Space Science; Automation and Control Engineering); **Automation** (Automation and Control Engineering; Computer Engineering; Electrical Engineering; Measurement and Precision Engineering); **Computer Science and Engineering** (Business and Commerce; Computer Engineering; Computer Science; E-Business/Commerce; Information Technology; Microelectronics; Software Engineering); **Electronics and Information**; **Humanities, Economics and Law**; **Life Science** (Astronomy and Space Science; Biological and Life Sciences; Biology; Biomedical Engineering; Biotechnology); **Management**; **Marine Engineering** (Automation and Control Engineering; Electronic Engineering; Environmental Engineering; Marine Engineering; Mechanical Engineering; Sound Engineering (Acoustics); Telecommunications Engineering); **Materials Science and Engineering**; **Mechanics, Civil Engineering & Architecture** (Architecture; Civil Engineering; Mechanical Engineering); **Mechatronic Engineering**; **Natural and Applied Sciences** (Applied Chemistry; Applied Mathematics; Applied Physics; Natural Sciences); **Power and Energy** (Aeronautical and Aerospace Engineering; Power Engineering; Thermal Engineering)

History: Founded 1938, incorporating previously existing engineering colleges, institutes and departments.

Academic Year: September to July (September-January; February-July)

Admission Requirements: Graduation from senior middle school and entrance examination

Main Language(s) of Instruction: Chinese

International Co-operation: With universities in USA, United Kingdom, Germany, Russia, Japan, Ukraine, Belgium

Accrediting Agencies: Commission of Science, Technology and Industry

Degrees and Diplomas: *Bachelor's Degree*: 4 yrs; *Master's Degree*: a further 2 1/2 yrs and thesis; *Doctor's Degree*: 3 yrs following Master

Student Services: Canteen, Cultural centre, Foreign student adviser, Foreign Studies Centre, Health services, Language programs, Sports facilities

Special Facilities: Aero-Space Science Museum

Libraries: Central Library, c. 2,6m. vols

Publications: *(quarterly)*; International Journal of Plant Engineering and Management *(quarterly)*; University Journal *(quarterly)*

Press or Publishing House: NPU Press
Last Updated: 28/11/08

OCEAN UNIVERSITY OF CHINA

5 Yushan Road, Qingdao, Shandong Province 266003
Tel: +86(532) 2032173
Fax: +86(532) 2032799
EMail: lpx@ouc.edu.cn
Website: http://www.ouc.edu.cn/english/

President: Dexing Wu

Colleges

Chemistry and Chemical Engineering (Applied Chemistry; Chemical Engineering; Chemistry; Marine Engineering); **Chinese Language and Culture** (Chinese; Cultural Studies; Literature; Native Language); **Continuing Education**; **Economics**; **Engineering** (Civil Engineering; Engineering; Mechanical Engineering); **Environmental Science and Engineering**; **Foreign Languages** (English; Modern Languages; Oriental Languages); **Information Science and Engineering**; **Life Sciences and Technology** (Aquaculture; Ecology; Fishery; Food Science; Food Technology; Marine Biology); **Management** (Accountancy; Business Administration; E-Business/Commerce; Management; Marketing; Tourism); **Marine Geo-Science**; **Materials Science and Engineering** (Materials Engineering); **Physical and Environmental Oceanography** (Applied Physics; Environmental Studies; Marine Science and Oceanography; Meteorology); **Public Administration** (Public Administration); **Vocational and Technical Education**

Departments

Mathematics (Mathematics)

Schools

International Education (Cultural Studies; International Studies; Modern Languages); **Law** (Administration; Law; Political Sciences)

Further Information: Subcampus in Maidao district; research institutes and laboratories

History: Founded 1924 as Private Qingdao University, became Shandong College of Oceanology 1959. Renamed Ocean University of Qingdao 1988. Acquired present title 2002.

Academic Year: September to July (September-January; February-July)

Admission Requirements: Graduation from senior middle school and entrance examination

Fees: (US Dollars): 1,500-3,700 per annum

Main Language(s) of Instruction: Chinese

Accrediting Agencies: Ministry of Education

Degrees and Diplomas: *Bachelor's Degree*: 4 yrs; *Master's Degree*: a further 3 yrs; *Doctor's Degree*: 3 yrs following Master

Student Residential Facilities: Yes

Libraries: c. 800,000 vols

Publications: Journal of Higher Education Studies; Journal of Ocean University

Press or Publishing House: Ocean University of Qingdao Publishing House

Last Updated: 28/11/08

PANZHIHUA UNIVERSITY

Xue Yuan Road, Eastern District, Panzhihua,
Sichuan Province 617000
Tel: +86(812) 3371007
Fax: +86(812) 3371000
EMail: pzhxywsc@163.com
Website: http://www.panzhihua-university.com

President: Liu Guoqin

International Relations: He Yongbing

Departments
Physical Education (Physical Education)

Schools
Art (Fine Arts); **Chemistry and Biology Engineering** (Bioengineering; Chemistry); **Civil Engineering** (Civil Engineering); **Computer Science** (Computer Science); **Economics and Administration** (Administration; Economics); **Electro-mechanical Engineering** (Electrical Engineering; Mechanical Engineering); **Engineering Technology**; **Foreign Languages and Cultures**; **Further Education** (Education); **Humanities and Social Sciences** (Arts and Humanities; Social Sciences); **Information and Electrical Engineering**; **Medical Science** (Medicine)

History: Founded 1984.

Degrees and Diplomas: *Bachelor's Degree*
Last Updated: 28/11/08

PEKING UNION MEDICAL COLLEGE

9 Dongdan Santiao, Beijing 100730
Tel: +86(10) 65253447
Fax: +86(10) 65124876
EMail: gux@cdm.imicams.ac.cn
Website: http://www.pumc.edu.cn

President: Ba Denian

International Relations: Gu Xin

Schools
Basic Medicine; **Clinical Medicine** (Medicine); **Graduate**; **Nursing** (Nursing); **Public Health** (Public Health)

History: Founded 1917.

Degrees and Diplomas: *Bachelor's Degree*; *Master's Degree*; *Doctor's Degree*

Libraries: c. 890,000 vols

Publications: Chinese Medical Sciences Journal

PEKING UNIVERSITY (PKU)

5 Yiheyyuan Road, Haidan District, Beijing 100871
Tel: +86(10) 62751230
Fax: +86(10) 62751233
EMail: oir@pku.edu.cn; study@pku.edu.cn
Website: http://www.pku.edu.cn

President: Zhou Qifeng (2008-) Tel: +86(10) 62751200

Colleges
Chemistry and Molecular Engineering (Analytical Chemistry; Chemistry; Inorganic Chemistry; Physical Chemistry; Polymer and Plastics Technology); **Engineering** (Engineering); **Urban and Environmental Sciences** (Ecology; Environmental Studies; Geography; Geography (Human); Regional Planning; Urban Studies)

Departments
Chinese Language and Literature (Chinese; Linguistics; Literature); **History** (History); **Philosophy** (Logic; Philosophy); **Psychology** (Psychology); **Sociology** (Public Administration; Social Work; Sociology)

Faculties
Humanities; **Information and Engineering Sciences**; **Medicine** (Medicine; Nursing; Pharmacy; Public Health); **Science** (Astronomy and Space Science; Bioengineering; Biological and Life Sciences; Chemistry; Earth Sciences; Environmental Studies; Landscape Architecture; Mathematics; Physics; Psychology; Surveying and Mapping); **Social Sciences** (Anthropology; Chinese; Communication Studies; Demography and Population; Economics; Education; Government; Information Management; International Studies; Journalism; Law; Management; Physical Education; Political Sciences; Social Sciences; Sociology)

Graduate Schools
Education (Education)

Institutes
Computer Science and Technology (Computer Science; Microelectronics; Technology); **Molecular Medicine** (Medicine)

Schools
Archaeology and Museology (Archaeology; Museum Studies); **Arts**; **Earth and Space Sciences** (Aeronautical and Aerospace Engineering; Earth Sciences; Geochemistry; Geology; Mineralogy; Natural Resources); **Economics** (Economics; Finance; Insurance; International Business; International Economics); **Foreign Languages** (Arabic; English Studies; Filipino; French Studies; Germanic Studies; Hebrew; Hindi; Indic Languages; Indonesian; Japanese; Korean; Mongolian; Oriental Languages; Persian; Russian; South and Southeast Asian Languages; Speech Studies; Thai Languages; Vietnamese); **Government** (Government); **International Studies** (Communication Studies; Cultural Studies; International Relations; International Studies); **Journalism and Communication**; **Law** (Civil Law; Commercial Law; Criminal Law; History of Law; International Law; Law); **Life Sciences** (Biological and Life Sciences; Biology; Biotechnology; Ecology); **Management (Guanghua)** (Accountancy; Business Administration; Finance; Management; Marketing); **Marxism** (Political Sciences); **Mathematical Sciences** (Actuarial Science; Computer Engineering; Computer Science; Information Sciences; Mathematics; Statistics); **Physics** (Atomic and Molecular Physics; Nuclear Physics; Optics; Physics; Radiophysics; Solid State Physics; Sound Engineering (Acoustics)); **Software and Microelectronics**

History: Founded 1898 as Metropolitan University. Reorganized 1952. Merged with Beijing Medical University 1999.

Academic Year: September to July (September-February; March-July)

Admission Requirements: Graduation from senior middle school and entrance examination

Main Language(s) of Instruction: Chinese

Degrees and Diplomas: *Bachelor's Degree*: 4-6 yrs; *Master's Degree*: a further 2-3 yrs; *Doctor's Degree (Ph.D.)*: 3-4 yrs

Student Services: Academic counselling, Canteen, Cultural centre, Employment services, Foreign student adviser, Foreign Studies Centre, Handicapped facilities, Health services, Language programs, Nursery care, Social counselling, Sports facilities

Student Residential Facilities: For c. 12,000 students

Special Facilities: Sackler Art and Archaeology Museum

Libraries: c. 4.5m. vols

Publications: Journal of Peking University; Natural Sciences Journal *(bimonthly)*; Peking University Law Journal; Philosophy and Social Sciences Journal *(bimonthly)*

Press or Publishing House: Peking University Press
Last Updated: 28/11/08

QINGDAO AGRICULTURAL UNIVERSITY

65 Wenhua Road, Laiyang, Shandong Province 265200
Tel: +86(535) 7232490
Fax: +86(535) 7215904
EMail: iao@qau.edu.cn
Website: http://en.qau.edu.cn

President: Li Baodu

Colleges

Animal Science and Veterinary Medicine (Animal Husbandry; Veterinary Science); **Architectural Engineering** (Architectural and Environmental Design; Civil Engineering); **Botany Science and Technology** (Agronomy; Botany; Crop Production); **Communication**; **Continuing Education**; **Economics**; **Electro-mechanical Engineering** (Agricultural Engineering; Automation and Control Engineering; Electrical Engineering; Machine Building); **Environmental Arts**; **Fisheries** (Aquaculture; Fishery); **Food Science and Engineering** (Food Science); **Foreign Languages** (English; Japanese; Korean); **Haidu**; **Horticulture** (Horticulture); **Humanities and Social Sciences** (Political Sciences; Public Administration; Social Sciences; Social Studies; Writing); **Information Science and Engineering**; **Life Sciences** (Biochemistry; Biotechnology; Botany; Genetics; Zoology); **Management**; **Physical Education**; **Plant Protection** (Plant and Crop Protection; Plant Pathology); **Resources and Environment**; **Science**

History: Founded 1951 as Laiyang Agricultural School, acquired present status and title 1977.

Main Language(s) of Instruction: Chinese

Degrees and Diplomas: *Bachelor's Degree*; *Master's Degree*

Special Facilities: Audio-visual Education Centre.

Last Updated: 01/12/08

QINGDAO TECHNOLOGICAL UNIVERSITY

11 Fushun Road, Qingdao, Shandong Province 266033
Tel: +86(532) 85071068
Fax: +86(532) 85071098
EMail: wshb@qtech.edu.cn
Website: http://www.qtech.edu.cn

President: Yi Chuijie

International Relations: Liu Xuming

Schools

Architecture (Architecture; Environmental Engineering; Rural Planning; Rural Studies; Town Planning; Urban Studies); **Arts**; **Automotive Engineering**; **Business** (Accountancy; E-Business/Commerce; Finance; International Business; Management; Marketing); **Civil Engineering**; **Communications and Electronic Engineering**; **Computer Engineering**; **Economics and Trade** (Economics; International Economics; Service Trades; Statistics); **Environmental and Municipal Engineering** (Architectural and Environmental Design; Environmental Engineering; Environmental Studies; Water Management); **Foreign Languages**; **Humanities and Social Sciences** (Advertising and Publicity; Social Work); **Management** (Industrial Engineering; Information Management; Information Technology; Management; Natural Resources; Transport Management); **Mechanical Engineering** (Automation and Control Engineering; Computer Graphics; Industrial Design; Instrument Making; Mechanical Engineering; Production Engineering); **Sciences** (Applied Mathematics; Information Sciences; Mathematics); **Vehicle and Traffic Engineering**

History: Founded 1952 as Qingdao Institute of Architecture and Engineering. Acquired present status and title 2004.

Degrees and Diplomas: *Bachelor's Degree*; *Master's Degree*; *Doctor's Degree*

Last Updated: 01/12/08

QINGDAO UNIVERSITY

308 Ningxia Road, Qingdao, Shandong Province 266071
Tel: +86(532) 5896195
Fax: +86(532) 5894822
EMail: xxkhbl@qdu.edu.cn
Website: http://www.qdu.edu.cn

President: Xia Linhua

Colleges

Arts, Music and Performance (Fine Arts; Music; Performing Arts); **Automation Engineering** (Automation and Control Engineering; Electrical Engineering); **Chemical Engineering** (Chemical Engineering; Chemistry); **Chinese Language and Culture**; **Continuing Education**; **Economics** (Economics); **Fine Arts, Painting and Sculpture** (Fine Arts; Painting and Drawing; Sculpture); **Foreign Languages and Literature**; **Haier Software** (Software Engineering); **Information Engineering** (Computer Science; Information Technology); **International Business** (Accountancy; Finance; International Business; Management; Marketing); **Law** (Law); **Literature** (Literature); **Mechanical Engineering** (Electrical Engineering; Mechanical Engineering); **Medicine** (Medicine); **Science** (Chemistry; Environmental Studies; Mathematics; Physics); **Textile and Clothing** (Chemistry; Fashion Design; Fine Arts; Textile Design); **Tourism** (Tourism)

History: Founded 1985. Merged with Shandong Textile Engineering College, Qingdao Medical College and Qingdao Teachers College 1993.

Academic Year: September to July (September-January; February-July)

Admission Requirements: Graduation from senior middle school and entrance examination

Main Language(s) of Instruction: Chinese

Degrees and Diplomas: *Bachelor's Degree*: 4 yrs; *Master's Degree*; *Doctor's Degree*

Student Residential Facilities: Yes

Libraries: Central Library, c. 2.1m. vols

Publications: Journal of Qingdao University

Last Updated: 01/12/08

QINGDAO UNIVERSITY OF SCIENCE AND TECHNOLOGY

69 Songling Road, Laoshan District, Qingdao, Shandong Province 266061
Tel: +86(532) 84023322
Fax: +86(532) 88956566
EMail: ieco@qust.edu.cn
Website: http://www.qust.edu.cn

President: Lianxiang Ma

Colleges

Arts (Fine Arts); **Automation Electrical Engineering** (Automation and Control Engineering; Electrical Engineering); **Chemical Engineering**; **Chemistry and Molecular Engineering**; **Communication and Cartoon**; **Economics and Management** (Economics; Management); **Electromechanical Engineering**; **Environmental and Safety Engineering** (Environmental Engineering; Safety Engineering); **Foreign Languages**; **Information Science and Technology**; **Materials Science and Engineering**; **Mathematical Science and Physics** (Mathematics; Physics); **Physical Education** (Physical Education); **Political Science and Law** (Law; Political Sciences); **Polymer Science and Engineering**

Faculties

Technical (*Chinese-German*)

Schools

Information and Control Engineering (Automation and Control Engineering; Computer Science; Information Technology; Technology)

History: Founded 1950 as Shenyang Senior Vocational School of Light Industry. Renamed Qingdao Institute of Chemical Technology 1984. Acquired present title and status 2002.

Main Language(s) of Instruction: Chinese

Degrees and Diplomas: *Bachelor's Degree*; *Master's Degree*

Last Updated: 01/12/08

QINGHAI NORMAL UNIVERSITY

38 Wusi Xilu, Xining, Qinghai Province 810008
Tel: +86(971) 6107640
Fax: +86(971) 6150977
EMail: webmaster@qhnu.edu.cn
Website: http://www.qhnu.edu.cn

President: Chen Yonggui

International Relations: Cui Wei

Departments
Arts (Arts and Humanities); **Biology** (Biology); **Chemistry** (Chemistry); **Chinese Language and Literature** (Chinese); **Computer Science** (Computer Science); **Education** (Education); **Foreign Languages** (Modern Languages); **Geography**; **History** (History); **Mathematics** (Mathematics); **Physics** (Physics); **Political Studies** (Political Sciences)

Programmes
Physical Education (Physical Education)

History: Founded 1956 as Qinghai Normal School, became college 1958. Acquired present status and title 1984. Under the jurisdiction of the Ministry of Education and the Provincial Government.

Academic Year: August to July (August-January; March-July)

Admission Requirements: Graduation from senior middle school and entrance examination

Main Language(s) of Instruction: Chinese

Accrediting Agencies: Ministry of Education

Degrees and Diplomas: *Bachelor's Degree*; *Master's Degree*

Student Residential Facilities: Yes

Libraries: Central Library, c. 505,460 vols

Publications: Journal of Qinghai Normal University

QINGHAI UNIVERSITY
97 Ningzhang Road, Chengbei District, Xining,
Qinghai Province 810016
Tel: +86(971) 5310410
Fax: +86(971) 5310031
EMail: qhuoffice@qhu.edu.cn; hfq@public.xn.qh.cn
Website: http://www.qhu.edu.cn/

President: Qiang Cheng (2005-) Tel: +86(971) 5310033

International Relations: Yang Hanning, Director, International Relations Tel: +86(971) 5310415

Colleges
Agriculture and Animal Husbandry (Agriculture; Animal Husbandry; Veterinary Science) *Dean*: Gang Cheng; **Finance and Economics** *Dean*: Yongshou Qi; **Medicine** *Dean*: Jianwei Wu

Institutes
Adult Education (Architecture; Economics; Social Sciences; Water Management) *Head*: Cunning Xu; **Chemical Technology** (Applied Chemistry; Chemical Engineering) *Head*: Yingzhi Zhang

History: Founded 1958. Acquired present status 1987. Merged with Qinghai Animal Husbandry and Veterinary Science College 1997, and with Qinghai Medical College 2004.

Academic Year: September to July (September-February, March-July)

Admission Requirements: Graduation from senior middle school and entrance examination

Fees: (Yuan): c. 3,000 per annum

Main Language(s) of Instruction: Chinese

International Co-operation: With universities in Japan and United Kingdom

Degrees and Diplomas: *Bachelor's Degree*: 4 yrs and thesis; *Master's Degree*

Student Services: Academic counselling, Canteen, Cultural centre, Employment services, Health services, Language programs, Nursery care, Social counselling, Sports facilities

Student Residential Facilities: Yes

Special Facilities: Movie Studio; Technology Hall

Libraries: Central Library, 1,010,000 vols

Publications: Journal of Qinghai University (biennially)
Last Updated: 01/12/08

QINGHAI UNIVERSITY FOR NATIONALITIES
3 Bayi Middle Road, Xining, Qinghai Province 810007
Tel: +86(971) 8176888
Fax: +86(971) 8176888
EMail: webmaster@qhmu.edu.cn
Website: http://www.qhmu.edu.cn

President: Wang Zuoquan

Departments
Computer Science and Technology (Computer Science); **Electronic and Information Science and Technology**; **Fine Arts** (Fine Arts); **Foreign Languages** (Modern Languages); **Mongolian** (Mongolian); **Social Sciences**

Faculties
Chemistry and Life Sciences; **Economy and Management** (Economics; Management); **Law**; **Literature**; **Mathematics**; **Tibetology** (Literature; Native Language)

History: Founded 1949 as a class for cadres, acquired present status and title 1956.

Degrees and Diplomas: *Bachelor's Degree*; *Master's Degree*; *Doctor's Degree*
Last Updated: 01/12/08

QIQIHAR MEDICAL UNIVERSITY
No.249, Peace Street, Fularji District, Qiqihar,
Heilongjiang Province 161042
Tel: +86(452) 6731318
EMail: qqhrmcban@126.com
Website: http://english.qqhrmc.net.cn

President: Jicheng Liu

Schools
Medical Technology (Laboratory Techniques; Medical Technology); **Mental Health** (Psychiatry and Mental Health); **Nursing** (Nursing); **Pharmacy**; **Preclinical Medicine** (Physiology); **Public Health** (Public Health)

History: Founded 1946.

Main Language(s) of Instruction: Chinese

Degrees and Diplomas: *Bachelor's Degree*
Last Updated: 01/12/08

QIQIHAR UNIVERSITY
No.42, Wenhua Street, Qiqihar, Heilongjiang Province 161006
Tel: +86(452) 2712809
Fax: +86(452) 2712809
EMail: sss@mail.qqhru.edu.cn
Website: http://www.qqhru.edu.cn

President: Chang Jianghua

Departments
Foreign Languages (Modern Languages); **Light industry and Textile** (Textile Design); **Management** (Management); **Materials Engineering** (Materials Engineering); **Physical Education** (Physical Education)

Schools
Arts (Arts and Humanities); **Chemistry and Chemical Engineering** (Chemical Engineering; Chemistry); **Higher Professional Technology** (Technology); **Information Sciences and Mechanical Engineering** (Automation and Control Engineering; Computer Science; Electrical Engineering; Information Sciences; Mechanical Engineering); **Life Sciences and Engineering** (Biological and Life Sciences; Engineering; Food Science); **Literature and History** (Chinese; History; Literature; Political Sciences); **Science** (Geography; Mathematics; Physics)

History: Founded 1995. Merged with Qiqihar Teachers College and Qiqihar Light Industry Institute.

Degrees and Diplomas: *Bachelor's Degree*; *Master's Degree*

Libraries: c. 610,000 vols

Publications: Journal of Qiqihar University
Last Updated: 01/12/08

QUFU NORMAL UNIVERSITY
Jingxuan West Road, Qufu, Shandong Province 273165
Tel: +86(537) 4412551
Fax: +86(537) 4412551
EMail: lxqsd@mail.qfnu.edu.cn
Website: http://www.qfnu.edu.cn

President: Zhang Youmin

International Relations: Guo Honggui

Schools

Adult Education; **Confucius Culture**; **Educational Sciences** (Education; Educational Sciences); **Mathematics** (Mathematics; Mathematics and Computer Science); **Physics** (Physics); **Vocational Technical Education** (Technology)

History: Founded 1955 as Shanghai Teachers' School, acquired present status and title 1985.

Academic Year: September to July

Admission Requirements: Graduation from senior middle school and entrance examination

Fees: None

Main Language(s) of Instruction: Chinese

Degrees and Diplomas: *Bachelor's Degree*: 4 yrs; *Master's Degree*: a further 3 yrs

Libraries: c. 1.32m. vols

Publications: Journal of Middle School Mathematics; Journal of Qufu Normal University
Last Updated: 01/12/08

RENMIN UNIVERSITY OF CHINA

N° 59 Zhonggucncun Street, Beijing 100872
Tel: +86(10) 82509507
Fax: +86(10) 62515329
EMail: rmdxxb@ruc.edu.cn
Website: http://www.ruc.edu.cn

President: Ji Baocheng

International Relations: Tang Zhong
Tel: +86(10) 62515282, Fax: +86(10) 62515329
EMail: wsc_ies@ruc.edu.cn

Departments
Physical Education

Schools

Agricultural Economics and Rural Development (Agricultural Economics; Real Estate; Regional Planning; Rural Planning; Rural Studies); **Business** (Accountancy; Economics; Management); **Chinese Classics** (Chinese); **Continuing Education**; **Economics** (Economics); **Education and Training** (Education); **Environment and Natural Resources** (Environmental Studies; Natural Resources); **Finance**; **Fine Arts**; **Foreign Languages**; **History** (History); **Information** (Computer Science; Information Management; Mathematics); **Information Resource Management** (Administration; Archiving; Library Science); **International Studies** (Asian Studies; Eastern European Studies; European Studies; International Economics; International Relations; Political Sciences; Social Studies); **Journalism and Communication** (Communication Studies; Journalism); **Labour and Human Resources** (Human Resources; Labour and Industrial Relations); **Law** (Civil Law; Commercial Law; Criminal Law); **Literary Studies** (Arts and Humanities; Comparative Literature; Linguistics; Literature); **Marxism Studies**; **Philosophy** (Ethics; Philosophy; Religious Studies); **Public Administration** (Economics; Education; Finance; Human Resources; Management; Public Administration; Real Estate; Regional Planning; Safety Engineering; Taxation; Urban Studies); **Science**; **Sociology and Demography** (Anthropology; Demography and Population; Development Studies; Gerontology; Social Studies; Sociology); **Statistics**; **Teaching Chinese as a Foreign Language** (Teacher Training)

History: Founded 1937 as Shaan Bei Public School.

Governing Bodies: University Council

Academic Year: September to July

Admission Requirements: Graduation from senior middle school and national entrance examination

Fees: (US Dollars): Foreign students, 2,676-3,920 per annum

Main Language(s) of Instruction: Chinese

Degrees and Diplomas: *Bachelor's Degree*: 4 yrs; *Master's Degree*: 2 yrs; *Doctor's Degree (PhD)*: 3 yrs and thesis. Also postdoctoral programmes

Student Services: Academic counselling, Canteen, Cultural centre, Employment services, Foreign student adviser, Handicapped facilities, Health services, Nursery care, Social counselling, Sports facilities

Student Residential Facilities: Yes

Libraries: c. 2.5m. Vols

Publications: Economic Theory and Business Management; Journal of Renmin University of China; Population Research; Studies in Qing History; Teaching and Research

Press or Publishing House: China Renmin University Press
Last Updated: 01/12/08

SHAANXI COLLEGE OF TRADITIONAL CHINESE MEDICINE

1 Weiyang Road, Xi'anyang, Shaanxi Province 712083
Tel: +86(910) 3212766 Ext.2078
Fax: +86(910) 3216542

President: Jin Zhijia

International Relations: Liu Degui

Departments
Acupuncture and Moxibustion (Acupuncture); **Traditional Chinese Medicine** (Traditional Eastern Medicine); **Treatment Techniques** (Treatment Techniques)

History: Founded 1959.

Degrees and Diplomas: *Bachelor's Degree*; *Master's Degree*

SHAANXI NORMAL UNIVERSITY

199 South Chang'an Road, Xi'an, Shaanxi Province 710062
Tel: +86(29) 85308114
EMail: wsc@snnu.edu.cn
Website: http://www.snnu.edu.cn

President: Fang Yu

Colleges

Arts (Fine Arts); **Chemistry and Materials Science** (Chemistry; Materials Engineering); **Chinese Literature** (Chinese; Literature); **Computer Science** (Computer Science); **Educational Sciences** (Education; Educational Administration; Preschool Education; Psychology); **Food Engineering**; **Foreign Languages** (English; Japanese; Linguistics; Literature; Modern Languages; Russian); **History and Civilization** (History); **International Business** (Commercial Law; Economics; International Business; Management); **Life Sciences** (Biological and Life Sciences); **Mathematics and Information Science** (Information Sciences; Mathematics); **Music** (Music); **News and Media** (Media Studies); **Physics and IT** (Information Technology; Physics); **Political Economy** (Economics; Philosophy; Political Sciences); **Sport** (Physical Education; Sports); **Tourism and Environment** (Environmental Studies; Geography; Tourism)

History: Founded 1944 as Shaanxi Provincial Teachers College, acquired present status and title 1960.

Academic Year: September to July (September-January; March-July)

Admission Requirements: Graduation from senior middle school and entrance examination

Fees: None

Main Language(s) of Instruction: Chinese

International Co-operation: With universities in United Kingdom, Japan, Australia, USA, Canada, Belgium, Malaysia, Singapore, Hong Kong

Accrediting Agencies: State Education Commission

Degrees and Diplomas: *Bachelor's Degree*: 4 yrs; *Master's Degree*: a further 3 yrs; *Doctor's Degree (PhD)*: 3 yrs. Also Certificate, 1-2 yrs

Special Facilities: Audiovisual Centre. Experimental Centre

Libraries: c. 1.92m. vols

Publications: Journal of Shaanxi Normal University; Philosophy and Science (quarterly)

Press or Publishing House: Shaanxi Normal University Press
Last Updated: 01/12/08

SHAANXI UNIVERSITY OF SCIENCE AND TECHNOLOGY

49 People's West Street, Xi'anyang, Shaanxi Province 712081
Tel: +86(910) 3579505
Fax: +86(910) 3579700
EMail: pdshen@sust.edu.cn
Website: http://www.sust.edu.cn/e/

President: Yu Zhaijing

Departments

Automation and Control Engineering (Automation and Control Engineering); **Chemical Engineering** (Chemical Engineering); **Food Technology**; **Industrial and Business Management**; **Industrial Design**; **Leather Techniques** (Leather Techniques); **Light Industry**; **Materials Engineering**; **Mechanical Engineering** (Mechanical Engineering)

History: Founded 1958 as Beijing Institute of Light Industry. Renamed Shaanxi University of Science and Technology 2002.

Degrees and Diplomas: *Bachelor's Degree*; *Master's Degree*

SHAANXI UNIVERSITY OF TECHNOLOGY

Hedongdian, Hanzhong, Shaanxi Province 723003
Tel: +86(916) 2296374 Ext. 2211
Fax: +86(916) 2296407
EMail: gjc@snut.edu.cn
Website: http://www1.snut.edu.cn/english/introduction.asp?id = 1

President: He Ning

International Relations: Wei Shuiyi

Schools

Arts (Design; Fine Arts; Musicology); **Bioscience and Engineering** (Bioengineering; Food Technology); **Chemistry and Environmental Science**; **Economics and Law** (Economics; Human Resources; Law; Management; Political Sciences); **Liberal Arts** (Chinese; Journalism; Radio and Television Broadcasting; Secretarial Studies); **Materials Science and Engineering** (Automation and Control Engineering; Materials Engineering; Metallurgical Engineering); **Mechanical Engineering** (Mechanical Engineering); **Sports Sciences** (Physical Education; Sports)

History: Founded 1978 as Shaanxi Institute of Technology. Acquired present status 2001 following merger of Hanzhong Teacher's College and Shaanxi Institute of Technology.

Degrees and Diplomas: *Bachelor's Degree*; *Master's Degree*
Last Updated: 01/12/08

SHANDONG AGRICULTURAL UNIVERSITY

61 Daizong Street, Tai'an, Shandong Province 271018
Tel: +86(538) 8242297
Fax: +86(538) 8226399
EMail: wugw@sdau.edu.cn
Website: http://www.sdau.edu.cn

President: Fujiang Wen

Colleges

Agronomy (Agronomy; Plant and Crop Protection; Traditional Eastern Medicine); **Animal Science and Technology** (Animal Husbandry; Veterinary Science; Zoology); **Chemistry and Material Science** (Applied Chemistry; Chemistry; Materials Engineering); **Economics and Management** (Accountancy; Agricultural Business; Business and Commerce; Economics; Information Management); **Environmental Science and Resources** (Environmental Management; Environmental Studies; Natural Resources; Soil Science); **Food Science and Engineering**; **Foreign Languages** (English; Japanese); **Forestry**; **Horticulture** (Horticulture); **Humanities and Law** (Administration; Law; Secretarial Studies); **Hydrology and Civil Engineering** (Architectural and Environmental Design; Bridge Engineering; Civil Engineering; Hydraulic Engineering; Road Engineering; Water Management; Wood Technology); **Information Science and Engineering** (Computer Networks; Computer Science); **Life Sciences** (Biochemistry; Bioengineering; Biological and Life Sciences; Biotechnology; Microbiology; Molecular Biology; Plant and Crop Protection); **Mechanical and Electronic Engineering** (Agricultural Engineering; Automation and Control Engineering; Electronic Engineering;

Mechanical Engineering); **Physical Education and Arts** (Physical Education); **Plant Protection** (Forestry; Plant and Crop Protection)

Schools

Engineering and Technology (Agricultural Engineering; Automation and Control Engineering; Engineering; Mechanics; Technology)

Further Information: Also 2 Experimental Farms. Teaching Hospital

History: Founded 1906 as Shandong Agricultural and Forestry School of Higher Learning. Acquired present title 1983, incorporating Shandong Agricultural College, Agricultural College of Shandong University, Agricultural Institute of Qilu University and the Horticulture Departments of Jinling University and Nanjing University.

Degrees and Diplomas: *Bachelor's Degree*; *Master's Degree*; *Doctor's Degree*. Also postgraduate Diplomas

Libraries: Central Library, c. 700,000 vols

Publications: Journal of Shandong Agricultural University; Research of Agricultural Higher Education; Shandong Animal Husbandry and Veterinary Science; Shandong Nongda Bao; Translation Series on New Agricultural Techniques and Methods
Last Updated: 01/12/08

SHANDONG ECONOMIC UNIVERSITY

4 Yanzishan Dinglu, Ji'nan, Shandong Province 250014
Tel: +86(531) 8525287
Fax: +86(531) 8544041
EMail: international@sdie.edu.cn
Website: http://www.sdie.edu.cn

President: Ren Hui

International Relations: Wang Jianbo Tel: +86(531) 8525277

Departments

Accountancy; **Computer Science and Information Management**; **Finance** (Finance); **Industrial and Commercial Management**; **International Business**; **Planning and Statistics** (Statistics)

History: Founded 1958 as Shandong Institute of Finance and Economics, acquired present status 1978.

International Co-operation: With universities in USA, Australia, Germany, Korea and Japan

Degrees and Diplomas: *Bachelor's Degree*; *Master's Degree*

Special Facilities: Technology Centre of Information & Education, network Centre, Computer Laboratory, Language laboratory

Libraries: Total: c. 800,000 vols; 2,000 periodicals
Last Updated: 01/12/08

SHANDONG INSTITUTE OF BUSINESS AND TECHNOLOGY (SDIBT)

191 BinHai Road, Yantai, Shandong Province 264005
Tel: +86(535) 6903730
Fax: +86(535) 6904244
EMail: yzmail@sdibt.edu.cn
Website: http://www.sdibt.edu.cn

President: Qu Jianxin

International Relations: Zhang Yiqiang

Departments

Accountancy (Accountancy); **Computer Science**; **Economics** (Economics; Industrial Management); **Foreign Languages** (Modern Languages); **Law** (Law); **Management**; **Management and Engineering** (Engineering Management; Management; Marketing); **Mathematics and Statistics** (Mathematics; Statistics)

History: Founded 1985. Acquired present title 2003. Previously known as China Coal Economic College.

Main Language(s) of Instruction: Chinese

Degrees and Diplomas: *Bachelor's Degree*

SHANDONG INSTITUTE OF LIGHT INDUSTRY

Daxue Road, Western University Science Park, Jinan,
Shandong Province 250100
Tel: +86(531) 8964221 Ext. 226
Fax: +86(531) 8968485
EMail: Internationaloffice@sdili.edu.cn
Website: http://english.sdili.edu.cn/index.asp

President: Chen Jiachuan

Departments

Food Technology (Food Technology); Industrial Design (Industrial Design); Industrial Economics and Trades; Inorganic Materials (Inorganic Chemistry; Materials Engineering)

Schools

Chemical Engineering; Electronic Information and Control Engineering (Automation and Control Engineering; Electrical and Electronic Engineering); Information Science and Technology (Information Sciences; Information Technology); Light Chemistry and Environmental Engineering (Chemical Engineering; Environmental Engineering; Environmental Studies); Mechanical Engineering (Automation and Control Engineering; Industrial Design; Mechanical Engineering)

History: Founded 1978.

Degrees and Diplomas: *Bachelor's Degree*; *Master's Degree*

SHANDONG JIANZHU UNIVERSITY (SUAE)

106 Jiwei Road, Jinan, Shandong Province 250022
Tel: +86(531) 6952401
Fax: +86(531) 6952404
EMail: international@sdjzu.edu.cn
Website: http://www.sdai.edu.cn

President: Shi Manxing

International Relations: Wen Minliu

Faculties

Computer Science and Technology (Computer Science; Technology); Foreign Languages (Modern Languages); Law and Political Science (Law; Political Sciences); Mathematics and Physics (Mathematics; Physics); Sports Teaching (Education; Sports)

Schools

Civil Engineering (Civil Engineering); Architecture and Urban Planning (Architecture; Architecture and Planning); Art (Fine Arts); Business (Business Administration); Electromechanical Engineering (Electronic Engineering; Mechanical Engineering); Heat Energy Engineering; Information and Electrical Engineering (Electrical Engineering; Information Sciences); Management Engineering; Materials Science and Engineering; Public Works and Environmental Engineering (Environmental Engineering)

History: Founded 1956 as Jinan Urban Construction School. Renamed Shandong Institute of Architecture and Engineering 1978.

International Co-operation: With universities in USA, United Kingdom, New Zealand

Degrees and Diplomas: *Bachelor's Degree*; *Master's Degree*
Last Updated: 02/12/08

SHANDONG NORMAL UNIVERSITY

38 East Wenhua Road, Jinan, Shandong Province 250014
Tel: +86(531) 2966954
Fax: +86(531) 2966954
EMail: sie@sdnu.edu.cn
Website: http://www.sdnu.edu.cn/esdnu/index.htm

President: Zhao Yanxiu

International Relations: Xie Changming

Colleges

Chemistry, Chemical Engineering and Materials Science (Chemical Engineering; Chemistry; Materials Engineering); Chinese Language and Literature (Chinese); Education (Education); English Teaching (English); Fine Arts (Fine Arts); Foreign Languages (English; Japanese; Korean; Literature; Modern Languages; Russian); Historical Culture and Social Development; Information Management; Law (Law; Political Sciences); Life

Sciences (Biological and Life Sciences; Biology); Mathematics (Mathematics); Music (Music); Physical Education; Physics and Electronics (Electronic Engineering; Physics); Population, Resource and Environment

Schools
International Exchanges

History: Founded 1950 as Shandong Teachers College. Acquired present title 1981.

Academic Year: September to July (September-January; March-July)

Admission Requirements: Graduation from senior middle school and entrance examination

Fees: (US Dollars): Foreign students, c. 1,600-2,900 per annum

Main Language(s) of Instruction: Chinese

Degrees and Diplomas: *Bachelor's Degree*: 4 yrs; *Master's Degree*: a further 3 yrs; *Doctor's Degree*

Student Services: Academic counselling, Canteen, Cultural centre, Employment services, Foreign student adviser, Health services, Nursery care, Social counselling, Sports facilities

Special Facilities: Art Gallery. Auditorium. Biological Garden

Libraries: University Library and Libraries of the departments, c. 2m. vols

Publications: China Population, Resources and Environment; Journal of Foreign Languages; Journal of Shandong Normal University

Last Updated: 02/12/08

SHANDONG SPORT UNIVERSITY

10 Wenhua Xilu Road, Jinan, Shandong Province 250063
Tel: +86(531) 2964389
Fax: +86(531) 2964389
EMail: info@sdpei.edu.cn
Website: http://www.sdpei.edu.cn

President: Guo Shaoan

International Relations: Liu Wei

Departments

Physical Education; Social Sciences; Sports; Wushu (Sports)

History: Founded 1958. Formerly known as Shandong Institute of Physical Education.

Degrees and Diplomas: *Bachelor's Degree*; *Master's Degree*
Last Updated: 02/12/08

SHANDONG UNIVERSITY (SDU)

27 South Shanda Road, Jinan, Shandong Province 250100
Tel: +86(531) 8564853
Fax: +86(531) 8565051
EMail: ipo@sdu.edu.cn
Website: http://www.sdu.edu.cn

President: Zhan Tao (2000-)
Tel: +86(531) 8364953, Fax: +86(531) 8565657
EMail: president@sdu.edu.cn

Secretary of President: Wenxi Zhang
Tel: +86(531) 8364972 EMail: zwx@sdu.edu.cn

International Relations: Yongbo Liu, Director
Tel: +86(531) 8364853, Fax: +86(531) 8565051

Schools

Business Administration *Head*: Jinghua Zhao; Chemistry and Chemical Engineering (Analytical Chemistry; Applied Chemistry; Chemical Engineering; Chemistry; Inorganic Chemistry; Organic Chemistry; Physical Chemistry) *Head*: Jianzuang Jiang; Civil Engineering (Architecture; Architecture and Planning; Civil Engineering; Construction Engineering; Geological Engineering; Hydraulic Engineering; Mechanical Engineering; Water Management; Water Science) *Head*: Shengle Cao; Computer Science and Technology *Head*: Xiangxu Meng; Continuing Education *Head*: Ping Zhuang; Control Science and Engineering *Head*: Lei Jia; Dentistry *Head*: Pishan Yang; Electrical Engineering (Automation and Control Engineering; Electrical Engineering; Electronic Engineering) *Head*: Jianguo Zhao; Energy and Power Engineering (Energy Engineering; Heating and Refrigeration; Machine Building;

Mechanical Engineering; Thermal Engineering; Thermal Physics) *Head*: Jihong Pan; **Environmental Science and Engineering** (Environmental Engineering; Environmental Studies) *Head*: Baoyu Gao; **Fine Arts** *Head*: Xiaofeng Li; **Foreign Languages and Literature** (English; French; German; Japanese; Korean; Russian) *Head*: Jide Guo; **History and Culture** (Archaeology; Archiving; History; Tourism) *Head*: Yuji Wang; **Information Science and Engineering** *Head*: Liangmo Mei; **Law** (Civil Law; Commercial Law; International Law; Law) *Head*: Huixing Liang; **Life Sciences** *Head*: Yinbo Qu; **Literature and Journalism** (Chinese; Comparative Literature; Fine Arts; Journalism; Linguistics; Literature; Philology) *Head*: Yan Chen; **Marxist Theory Education** *Head*: Xiangjun Zhou; **Materials Science and Engineering** (Chemistry; Machine Building; Materials Engineering; Mechanics; Physics) *Head*: Minhua Jiang; **Mathematics and System Sciences** (Applied Mathematics; Computer Science; Information Sciences; Mathematics; Operations Research; Statistics; Systems Analysis) *Head*: Jianya Liu; **Mechanical Engineering** (Automation and Control Engineering; Automotive Engineering; Chemical Engineering; Electronic Engineering; Industrial Design; Mechanical Engineering) *Head*: Jianfeng Li; **Medicine** (Medicine) *Head*: Yun Zhang; **Nursing** *Head*: Hongxiang Lou; **Philosophy and Social Development** *Head*: Youde Fu; **Physical Education** *Division Head*: Ruilin Zhang; **Physics and Microelectronics** (Chemistry; Electronic Engineering; Materials Engineering; Microelectronics; Physics) *Head*: Shijie Xie; **Political Science and Public Administration** (Administration; Education; International Studies; Political Sciences; Social Sciences) *Head*: Yu'an Liu; **Public Health** (Child Care and Development; Environmental Studies; Epidemiology; Health Administration; Health Sciences; Hygiene; Laboratory Techniques; Medicine; Nutrition; Occupational Health; Public Health; Social and Preventive Medicine; Statistics; Toxicology) *Head*: Zhongtang Zhao

History: Founded 1901. Merged with Shandong Medical University and Shandong University of Technology (former) 2000.

Academic Year: August to June (August-January; February-June)

Admission Requirements: Graduation from senior middle school and entrance examination

Main Language(s) of Instruction: Chinese and English

International Co-operation: With universities in Italy, USA, Australia, Sweden, Finland, The Netherlands, Germany, France, United Kingdom, Russia, Japan, Malaysia, Korea, Singapore

Accrediting Agencies: Degree Committee of the State Council of China; Ministry of Education

Degrees and Diplomas: *Zhuanke Certificate of Graduation*: vocational 2-3 yrs; *Bachelor's Degree (BA; Bsc.)*: 4 yrs; *Master's Degree (MA; Msc.)*: a further 3 yrs; *Doctor's Degree (Ph.D.)*: 3 yrs following Master

Student Services: Academic counselling, Canteen, Cultural centre, Employment services, Foreign student adviser, Foreign Studies Centre, Health services, Language programs, Nursery care, Social counselling, Sports facilities

Student Residential Facilities: Yes

Special Facilities: Yes

Libraries: Yes

Publications: Issues of Contemporary Socialism *(quarterly)*; Literature, History and Philosophy *(bimonthly)*; Shandong University Journal *(bimonthly)*; Studies of Folklore *(quarterly)*; Studies of Zhouyi *(bimonthly)*; Young Thinker *(quarterly)*

Press or Publishing House: Shandong University Publishing House

Last Updated: 02/12/08

SHANDONG UNIVERSITY OF ARTS

91 East Wenhua Road, Jinan, Shandong Province 250014
Tel: +86(531) 86423601
Fax: +86(531) 86423203
Website: http://www.sdca.edu.cn/

President: Zhang Zhimin (2000-) EMail: sdysxyyb@163.com

International Relations: Shaoli Hu, Director of Foreign Affairs
Tel: +86(531) 86423246, Fax: +86(531) 86990640
EMail: hushaoli@sdca.edu.cn

Colleges
Art and Cultural Management *Director*: Chuanliu Tian

Schools
Dance (Dance) *Director*: Yu Zhao; **Design** (Design) *Director*: Yuquan Liu; **Fine Arts** (Fine Arts) *Director*: Daizong Mao; **International Art Exchange and Creative Design** (Design; Fine Arts; International Relations) *Director*: Shaoli Hu; **Music** (Music) *Director*: Yunping Zhang; **Professional and Adult Education** (Adult Education) *Director*: Guang Liu; **Teachers Training** (Art Education; Teacher Training) *Director*: Janbin Sun; **Theatre** (Theatre) *Director*: Jianjun Ding; **Traditional Chinese Drama** *Director*: Shenglong Gui

History: Founded 1958 as Shandong Arts Training School. Renamed Shandong Arts College 1978. Acquired present status and title 2001, following merger with Shandong Traditional Opera School.

Academic Year: September to July

Admission Requirements: Professional examination

Main Language(s) of Instruction: Chinese

International Co-operation: With universities in Australia, Korea and Russian Federation

Accrediting Agencies: Committee of Academic Degrees of Shandong College of Arts and Shandong Provincial Office of Academic Degrees; Shangdong Provincial Education Department

Degrees and Diplomas: *Bachelor's Degree*: Music; Fine Arts; Art; Drama; Dance (BA), 4 yrs; *Master's Degree*: Music; Fine Arts; Art; Drama; Dance (MA), 3 yrs

Student Services: Academic counselling, Canteen, Cultural centre, Employment services, Foreign student adviser, Foreign Studies Centre, Health services, Language programs, Nursery care, Social counselling, Sports facilities

Student Residential Facilities: Yes

Special Facilities: Art Gallery; Concert Hall; Theatre

Libraries: Yes

Publications: Oilu Realm of Arts, Professional art and academic journal *(bimonthly)*

SHANDONG UNIVERSITY OF ARTS AND DESIGN

23 Qianfu Shan East Road, Jinan, Shandong Province 250014
Tel: +86(531) 2963741 Ext. 379
Fax: +86(531) 2946346
EMail: kangwang59@sdada.edu.cn
Website: http://www.sdada.edu.cn/english/index.php

President: Pan Lusheng

Schools
Applied Design (Design); **Architecture and Landscape Design** (Architecture; Interior Design; Landscape Architecture); **Digital Art and Communication** (Cinema and Television; Film; Photography); **Fashion Design** (Fashion Design); **Fine Arts** (Fine Arts; Painting and Drawing; Sculpture); **Industrial Design** (Industrial Design); **Modern Handicraft Arts** (Handicrafts); **Science of Art**; **Visual Communication Design** (Advertising and Publicity; Graphic Design)

History: Founded 1973 as Shandong School of Arts and Crafts, acquired present status and tile 1994. Formerly known as Shandong Institute of Industrial Arts.

Degrees and Diplomas: *Bachelor's Degree*
Last Updated: 02/12/08

SHANDONG UNIVERSITY OF FINANCE

40 Shungeng Road, Jinan, Shandong Province 250014
Tel: +86(531) 2952520 Ext. 2191 Ext. 2192
Fax: +86(531) 2953447
EMail: info@sdfi.edu.cn
Website: http://www.sdfi.edu.cn

President: Huang Qi

Schools
Business Management (Management); **Computer and Information Engineering**; **Economics**; **Finance** (Banking; Finance); **Finance Taxation and Public Administration**; **Foreign Languages** (Modern Languages); **International Economics**; **Physical Education** (Physical Education); **Statistics and Mathematics** (Mathematics; Statistics)

History: Founded 1986 as Finance College, acquired present status and title 1992.

Admission Requirements: High school certificate or equivalent; Hanyu Shuiping Kaoshi(HSK) 3 grade or equivalent level in chinese language.

Fees: (Yuan): registration fee, 200; undergraduate studies, 13,000 per annum; Master's degree 16,000 per annum; further studies, 12,000 per annum; short-term further studies, 2,500 per 4 weeks or less.

Main Language(s) of Instruction: Chinese

Degrees and Diplomas: *Bachelor's Degree*; *Master's Degree*
Last Updated: 02/12/08

SHANDONG UNIVERSITY OF SCIENCE AND TECHNOLOGY

233 Daizong Street, Tai'an, Shandong Province 271019
Tel: +86(538) 8223311 Ext. 6257
Fax: +86(538) 8210134
EMail: sustfao@sdust.edu.cn
Website: http://www.sdust.edu.cn/english/eindex.htm

President: Wang Chunqiu

Colleges
Arts and Design (Design; Fine Arts); **Chemical and Environmental Engineering** (Chemical Engineering; Environmental Engineering); **Civil Engineering and Architecture** (Architecture; Civil Engineering); **Economics and Management** (Economics; Management); **Foreign Languages** (Modern Languages); **Geomatics** (Geology); **Geoscience and Technology** (Earth Sciences; Geology); **Humanities and Law** (Arts and Humanities; Law); **Information and Electrical Engineering** (Electrical Engineering); **Information Science and Technology** (Information Technology); **Materials Science and Engineering**; **Mechanical and Electronic Engineering** (Electronic Engineering; Mechanical Engineering); **Natural Resources and Environmental Engineering** (Environmental Engineering; Natural Resources); **Science**; **Science and Technology** *(Taishan)* (Natural Sciences; Technology)

History: Founded 1958 as Shandong Technical College of Coal Industry. Merged with Shandong Institute of Mining and Technology 1999.

Main Language(s) of Instruction: Chinese

Degrees and Diplomas: *Bachelor's Degree*; *Master's Degree*; *Doctor's Degree*

Libraries: c. 660,000 vols

Publications: Journal
Last Updated: 02/12/08

SHANDONG UNIVERSITY OF TECHNOLOGY (SDUT)

12 Zhangzhou Road, Zhangdian District, Zibo, Shandong Province 255049
Tel: +86(533) 2782380
Fax: +86(533) 2780944
EMail: international@sdut.edu.cn
Website: http://www.sdut.edu.cn

President: Fusheng Yao

International Relations: Yu Tao

Schools
Architecture Engineering (Civil Engineering; Surveying and Mapping; Town Planning); **Chemical Engineering**; **Computer Science and Technology**; **Economics** (Economics; Finance); **Electrical and Electronic Engineering** (Automation and Control Engineering; Electrical Engineering; Electronic Engineering); **Engineering Technology** (Business Administration; Educational Sciences; Electronic Engineering; Mechanical Engineering); **Fine Arts** (Fine Arts); **Foreign Languages** (English; Japanese; Modern Languages); **Law**; **Life Sciences and Technology** (Biological and Life Sciences); **Light Industry and Agricultural Engineering** (Agricultural Engineering; Automation and Control Engineering; Food Science; Industrial Design); **Literature and Media Dissemination** (Advertising and Publicity; Chinese; History; Literature); **Machinery Engineering** (Machine Building; Mechanical Engineering); **Management** (Accountancy; Business Administration; Indus-

trial Engineering; Information Management; Management); **Materials Science and Engineering** (Materials Engineering); **Mathematics and Information Science** (Information Sciences; Mathematics; Statistics); **Music** (Music); **Physical Education** (Physical Education); **Physics** (Physics); **Resources and Environmental Engineering**; **Traffic and Vehicle Engineering**

History: Founded 1949 as Shandong Provincial Industrial School. Renamed Shandong Institute of Engineering 1951. Acquired present title and status 2001 following merger with Zibo University.

Academic Year: September to July (September-February; March-July)

Admission Requirements: Graduation from senior middle school and entrance examination

Main Language(s) of Instruction: Chinese

International Co-operation: With universities in USA, United Kingdom, France, Pakistan

Degrees and Diplomas: *Bachelor's Degree*: 4 yrs; *Master's Degree*: a further 3 yrs; *Doctor's Degree (PhD)*: a further 2-3 yrs

Student Residential Facilities: Yes

Special Facilities: Movie Studio

Libraries: Central Library, c. 1,080,000 volumes and over 2,650 periodicals both in Chinese and foreign languages.

Publications: Journal of Shandong University of Technology (Edition of Natural Sciences) *(quarterly)*; Journal of Shandong University of Technology (Edition of Social Sciences) *(quarterly)*
Last Updated: 02/12/08

SHANDONG UNIVERSITY OF TRADITIONAL CHINESE MEDICINE

53 Jingshi Road, Jinan, Shandong Province 250014
Tel: +86(531) 2968823
Fax: +86(531) 2968823
EMail: sutcm@public.jn.sd.cn
Website: http://www.sdutcm.edu.cn

President: Wang Xinglu

International Relations: Cui Hongjiang

Departments
Osteotraumatology (Osteopathy)

Schools
Acupuncture and Moxibustion (Acupuncture); **Basic Sciences** (Nursing; Traditional Eastern Medicine); **Traditional Chinese Medicine** (Traditional Eastern Medicine)

History: Founded 1958 as Shandong College of Traditional Chinese Medicine, acquired present title 1996.

Degrees and Diplomas: *Bachelor's Degree*; *Master's Degree*; *Doctor's Degree*

Libraries: c. 300,000 vols

Publications: Shandong Magazine of TCM
Last Updated: 02/12/08

SHANGHAI DIANJI UNIVERSITY

Jiangchuang Road No.690, Minhang District, Shanghai 200240
Tel: +86(21) 64300980
EMail: international@sdju.edu.cn
Website: http://www.sdju.edu.cn

President: Xia Jianguo

Schools
Arts and Science (Cultural Studies; Economics; History; International Economics; Law; Mathematics; Philosophy; Physics; Political Sciences; Writing); **Automotive Engineering** (Automotive Engineering); **Economics and Management** (Economics; Engineering Management; Finance; Industrial Engineering; International Economics; Management; Marketing; Transport Management); **Electrical Engineering** (Automation and Control Engineering; Electrical Engineering; Power Engineering); **Electronic Engineering and Information Science** (Computer Science; Electronic Engineering; Information Technology; Software Engineering; Telecommunications Engineering); **Foreign Languages** (English; German); **Mechanical Engineering** (Electronic Engineering; Industrial Design; Mechanical Engineering)

History: Created 1953
Degrees and Diplomas: *Bachelor's Degree*
Last Updated: 13/12/11

SHANGHAI FINANCE UNIVERSITY

995 Shangchuan Road, Pudong, Shanghai 201209
Tel: +86(21) 58638899 +86(21) 65565443
Fax: +86(21) 35030318
EMail: jzzb@shfc.edu.cn
Website: http://www.shfc.edu.cn

President: Chu Minwei

Departments
Applied Mathematics; **Arts and Humanities**; **Business Management**; **Foreign Languages** (English)

Schools
Accounting (Accountancy); **international Finance and Insurance** (Finance; Insurance); **International Trade and Economics** (International Business; International Economics; International Studies)

History: Founded 1987. Acquired present title 2003.
Main Language(s) of Instruction: Chinese
Degrees and Diplomas: *Bachelor's Degree*
Libraries: c. 578,600 vols; c. 13,000 periodical subscriptions.
Last Updated: 02/12/08

SHANGHAI INSTITUTE OF FOREIGN TRADE (SIFT)

Wenxiang Road 1900, Songjiang, Shanghai, Shanghai 200336
Tel: +86(21) 67703022
EMail: xb@shift.edu.cn
Website: http://www.shift.edu.cn

President: Wang Xinkui
International Relations: Wang Xingsun, Vice-President

Schools
Business; **Finance**; **International Studies** (Chinese; International Studies); **Languages** (English; French; Japanese; Modern Languages); **Law**

History: Founded 1960.
Academic Year: February to September
Fees: (US Dollars): Undergraduate, 1,380 per semester; postgraduate, 1,600
International Co-operation: With universities in USA, Canada, United Kingdom, Australia
Degrees and Diplomas: *Bachelor's Degree*; *Master's Degree*
Last Updated: 02/12/08

SHANGHAI INSTITUTE OF TECHNOLOGY (SIT)

120 Caobao Road, Shanghai, Shanghai 200235
Tel: +86(21) 6494-1159
Fax: +86(21) 3414-1355
EMail: inter@sit.edu.cn
Website: http://www.sit.edu.cn

President: Guanzhong Lu (2004-)
Tel: +86(21) 6494-5020 EMail: pd@sit.edu.cn
Secretary: Xueying Qi
International Relations: Jianyu Zhu, Director, International Relations

Departments
Mathematics and Physics *Director*: Jie Sun

Schools
Art and Design *Dean*: Xiaofu Yu; **Chemical Engineering** (Applied Chemistry; Chemical Engineering; Pharmacology) *Dean*: Xiaozhen Liu; **Computer Science and Information Technology** (Computer Science; Software Engineering) *Director*: Yunxiang Liu; **Construction and Safety Engineering** (Architectural and Environmental Design; Building Technologies; Civil Engineering; Environmental Engineering; Power Engineering; Safety Engineering; Thermal Engineering) *Dean*: Dawen Peng; **Ecological Technology and**

Engineering *Dean*: Zhiguo Zhang; **Economics and Management** *Dean*: Yang Cao; **Foreign Languages** *Director*: Shichang Zhu; **Materials Science and Engineering** (Materials Engineering) *Director*: Jiayue Xu; **Mechanical and Automation Engineering** (Automation and Control Engineering; Automotive Engineering; Electrical Engineering; Mechanical Engineering) *Dean*: Suohuai Zhang; **Perfume and Aroma Technology** (Biotechnology; Chemical Engineering; Food Science) *Dean*: Zuobin Xiao; **Social Sciences** (Labour and Industrial Relations; Social Work) *Director*: Xiaoming Zhong

History: Created in 2000 following a merger between Shanghai College of Metallurgy, Shanghai College of Chemistry and Shanghai College of Light Industry.
Admission Requirements: Undergraduate programmes: National Matriculation Test; Masters programmes: Graduate Candidate Test
Fees: (Yuan): 5,000 - 35,000 per annum
Main Language(s) of Instruction: Chinese
International Co-operation: With institutions in Australia, Canada, France, Germany, New Zealand, Singapore, Sweden, USA, Germany, Spain, Italy, UK, Japan, Republic of Korea, Netherlands
Accrediting Agencies: Ministry of Education
Degrees and Diplomas: *Bachelor's Degree*: Applied Chemistry; Building Environment & Equipment Engineering (BSc); Chemistry; Automation; Mechanical Engineering; Safety Engineering; Pharmaceutical Engineering (BEng); Languages; Art & Design (BA), 4 yrs; *Bachelor's Degree*: Business; Management (BBA / BEc), 4 ys; *Master's Degree*: Applied Chemistry, a further 2.5 yrs
Student Services: Academic counselling, Canteen, Cultural centre, Employment services, Foreign student adviser, Foreign Studies Centre, Handicapped facilities, Health services, Language programs, Nursery care, Social counselling, Sports facilities
Student Residential Facilities: Student dormitories
Special Facilities: Film studio; Art gallery
Libraries: with c. 960,000 vols.
Publications: Journal of Shanghai Institute of Technology, Natural sciences journal. *(quarterly)*
Press or Publishing House: SIT Press

Academic Staff 2007-2008	MEN	WOMEN	TOTAL
FULL-TIME	1,027	733	**1,760**
PART-TIME	132	24	**156**
STAFF WITH DOCTORATE			
FULL-TIME	78	49	**127**
PART-TIME	17	2	**19**
Student Numbers 2007-2008			
All (Foreign Included)	5,796	5,040	**10,836**
FOREIGN ONLY	3	1	**4**

Part-time students, 4,568.
Last Updated: 08/10/08

SHANGHAI INTERNATIONAL STUDIES UNIVERSITY

550 Dalian Road, Shanghai, Shanghai 200083
Tel: +86(21) 65420667
Fax: +86(21) 65420225
EMail: fao@shisu.edu.cn
Website: http://www.shisu.edu.cn

President: Cao Deming

Colleges
English Language and Literature; **Adult Education**; **International Business** (International Business); **International Cultural Exchange** (Cultural Studies; International Studies); **International Finance and Trade** (Business and Commerce; Finance; International Business); **Japanese Economy and Culture**; **Journalism and Communication** (Communication Studies; Journalism; Media Studies); **Oriental Languages and Literature**; **Western Languages** (Modern Languages)

Departments
French; **German** (German); **Russian**

Graduate Institutes
Interpretation and Translation (Translation and Interpretation)

Schools
Graduate; **Law**

History: Founded 1949 as Shanghai Russian College. Acquired present status and title 1994.

Academic Year: September to July (September-February; February-July)

Admission Requirements: Graduation from senior middle school and entrance examination

Main Language(s) of Instruction: Chinese

International Co-operation: With 53 universities worldwide

Accrediting Agencies: State Commission of Education

Degrees and Diplomas: *Bachelor's Degree*: 4 yrs; *Master's Degree*; *Doctor's Degree (Ph.D.)*. Also Advanced Teacher Training qualification

Student Residential Facilities: Yes

Libraries: Central Library, c. 1m. vols

Publications: Arab World; Comparative Literature in China; Foreign Language World; Journal of Foreign Languages; Media in Foreign Language Instruction; Russian Teaching in China

Press or Publishing House: Shanghai Foreign Language Education Press; Shanghai Foreign Language Audio-Visual Publishing House

Last Updated: 02/12/08

SHANGHAI JIAO TONG UNIVERSITY

1954 Huashan Road, Shanghai, Shanghai 200030
Tel: +86(21) 62932414
Fax: +86(21) 62829514
EMail: icae@sjtu.edu.cn
Website: http://www.sjtu.edu.cn/

President: Zhang Jie
Tel: +86(21) 62932448, Fax: +86(21) 62821369

International Relations: Tong Chenjiao

Schools
Agriculture and Biology; **Chemistry and Chemical Engineering** (Applied Chemistry; Chemical Engineering; Chemistry; Materials Engineering; Polymer and Plastics Technology); **Civil Engineering and Mechanics**; **Electronics and Electrical Engineering** (Automation and Control Engineering; Computer Networks; Computer Science; Electronic Engineering; Engineering; Information Technology); **Environmental Sciences and Engineering** (Environmental Engineering; Environmental Studies); **Foreign Languages** (English; Japanese; Modern Languages); **Humanities and Social Sciences**; **Information Security**; **International and Public Affairs** (International Relations); **Law**; **Life Sciences and Technology**; **Management** (Accountancy; Finance; Hotel Management; Industrial Management; Management); **Materials Science and Engineering** (Materials Engineering); **Mechanical and Power Engineering** (Automation and Control Engineering; Mechanical Engineering; Power Engineering); **Media and Design** (Design; Media Studies); **Medicine** (Medicine); **Microelectronics** (Microelectronics); **Naval Architecture and Marine Engineering** (Marine Engineering; Naval Architecture); **Pharmaceutics**; **Science** (Applied Mathematics; Applied Physics; Mathematics); **Software** (Software Engineering)

History: Founded 1896 as Nanyang Public School, became Jiaotong University 1921, and acquired present title 1959.

Degrees and Diplomas: *Bachelor's Degree*; *Master's Degree*; *Doctor's Degree*

Libraries: c. 1.8m. vols

Publications: Academic Journal of Shanghai Jiaotong University; Chinise Journal of Somatic Science; Journal of Shanghai Jiaotong University; Systems Engineering Theory Methodology Applications
Last Updated: 02/12/08

SHANGHAI MARITIME UNIVERSITY

1550 Pudong Dadao, Shanghai, Shanghai 200135
Tel: +86(21) 58218437
Fax: +86(21) 58853909
EMail: smupo@shmtu.edu.cn
Website: http://www.shmtu.edu.cn

President: Sicheng Yu

Schools
Continuing Education; **Engineering**; **Management** (Accountancy; Economics; Finance; International Business; Management; Tourism; Transport Management); **Merchant Navy** (Electrical Engineering; Marine Engineering; Marine Transport)

Further Information: Also courses for foreign students

History: Founded 1909 as Wosong Merchant Marine College, acquired present title and status 1959.

Academic Year: February to January (February-July; September-January)

Main Language(s) of Instruction: Chinese

Degrees and Diplomas: *Bachelor's Degree*: 4 1/2 yrs; *Master's Degree*: a further 2-3 yrs; *Doctor's Degree*

Student Services: Canteen, Cultural centre, Employment services, Foreign student adviser, Health services, Nursery care, Sports facilities

Student Residential Facilities: For c. 5,000 students

Libraries: c. 700,000 vols

Publications: Journal of Shanghai Maritime University; Maritime Transport Information; Ocean Shipping Business; Shipping Management
Last Updated: 02/12/08

SHANGHAI MUSIC CONSERVATORY

20 Fenyang Road, Shanghai, Shanghai 200031
Tel: +86(21) 64370137 +86(21) 64310305
Fax: +86(21) 64330866
EMail: wb@shcmusic.edu.cn
Website: http://www.shcmusic.edu.cn

President: Yang Liqing

International Relations: Zhang Xianping

Centres
International Piano Art; **International String Art**; **Zhou Xiaoyan International Opera**

Departments
Art Management (Art Management); **Chinese Traditional Instruments**; **Composition** (Music Theory and Composition); **Conducting** (Conducting); **Modern Instrumental Music** (Music); **Music Education** (Music Education); **Music Engineering**; **Musical Theater**; **Musicology**; **Orchestral Instruments**; **Piano** (Musical Instruments); **Singing**

Schools
Attached Middle; **Attached Primary**

History: Founded 1927 as National Conservatory of Music, acquired present name 1956.

Degrees and Diplomas: *Bachelor's Degree*; *Master's Degree*; *Doctor's Degree*
Last Updated: 06/10/08

SHANGHAI NORMAL UNIVERSITY

100 Guilin Road, Shanghai, Shanghai 200234
Tel: +86(21) 64322493
Fax: +86(21) 64701661
EMail: xwzx_yy@shtu.edu.cn
Website: http://www.shtu.edu.cn

President: Li Jin

International Relations: Li Meizhen

Schools
Art (Fine Arts; Music); **Assets Management** (Real Estate); **Basic Education** (Education); **Educational Sciences** (Education; Educational Administration; Educational Sciences; Psychology); **Foreign Languages** (English; Japanese; Modern Languages); **Humanities** (Arts and Humanities; Chinese; Cultural Studies; Literature); **Information Sciences and Engineering** (Computer Science; Educational Technology; Engineering; Information Sciences; Physics); **International Cultural Exchange** (International Relations); **Law and Business** (Administration; Business and Commerce; Economics; Education; Law; Management; Political

Sciences); **Life and Environmental Sciences** (Biological and Life Sciences; Biology; Chemistry; Environmental Studies; Geography; Tourism); **Mathematics** (Applied Mathematics; Mathematics; Mathematics and Computer Science); **Physical Education and Hygiene** (Hygiene; Physical Education); **Primary Education** (Natural Sciences; Physical Education; Primary Education; Social Sciences); **Urban and Tourism Management** (Tourism; Urban Studies); **Vocational and Technical Education** (Chemical Engineering; Electronic Engineering; Mechanical Engineering; Structural Architecture; Technology)

History: Founded 1954 as Shangai Teacher Training College. Merged with Shanghai Teachers College of Technology 1994 and with Shangai Higher Normal College 1997. Acquired present title and status 1997.

Degrees and Diplomas: *Bachelor's Degree*; *Master's Degree*; *Doctor's Degree*

Libraries: 1.3m. vols

Publications: Journal of Shanghai Teachers University
Last Updated: 03/12/08

SHANGHAI OCEAN UNIVERSITY

332 Jungong Road, Shanghai, Shanghai 200090
Tel: +86(21) 65710378
Fax: +86(21) 65434287
EMail: xzxx@shfu.edu.cn
Website: http://www.shfu.edu.cn

President: Ying Jie Pan
Tel: +86(21) 65684287, Fax: +86(21) 65710296

Colleges
Aqua-life Science and Technology (Aquaculture; Marine Biology); **Continuing Education** (Technology); **Economic Management** (Economics; Finance; International Business; International Economics; Marketing); **Engineering** (Automation and Control Engineering; Industrial Engineering; Marine Engineering); **Food Science and Technology** (Chemistry; Food Science; Food Technology; Heating and Refrigeration); **Foreign Languages; Humanities; Information Technology** (Applied Mathematics; Computer Science; Information Management; Information Technology); **Marine Science and Technology** (Fishery; Marine Science and Oceanography)

History: Founded 1912 as Fishery School of Jiangsu Province, became college 1952. Became Shanghai Fisheries University and acquired present status and title 2008.

Academic Year: September to July (September-February; February-July)

Admission Requirements: Graduation from senior middle school and entrance examination

Fees: (Yuan): c. 4,000 per annum

Main Language(s) of Instruction: Chinese

International Co-operation: With universities in USA, Japan and Republic of Korea

Accrediting Agencies: Ministry of Agriculture

Degrees and Diplomas: *Bachelor's Degree*: 4 yrs; *Master's Degree*: a further 3 yrs; *Doctor's Degree*

Student Residential Facilities: Yes

Special Facilities: Museum of Ichthyology. Freshwater Fish Research Farm in Nanhui County, Shanghai City and Mariculture Research Farm, Fonghua County, Zhejiang Province. Fishing Fleets

Libraries: Central Library, c. 400,000 vols

Publications: Journal of Fisheries of China Society *(quarterly)*; Journal of Shanghai Fisheries University *(quarterly)*
Last Updated: 02/12/08

SHANGHAI TELEVISION UNIVERSITY

Shanghai, Shanghai
Website: http://www.shtvu.edu.cn
President: Zhan Deming

Programmes
Economics (Business Administration; Finance)

History: Founded 1960.
Degrees and Diplomas: *Bachelor's Degree*
Last Updated: 09/07/09

SHANGHAI THEATRE ACADEMY

630 Huashan Road, Shanghai, Shanghai 200040
Tel: +86(21) 62481866
Fax: +86(21) 62482646
EMail: yzxx@sta.edu.cn
Website: http://members.tripod.com/John_Wang/sta/index.html
President: Rong Guangrun

Departments
Acting (Theatre); **Directing** (Theatre); **Dramatic Literature**; **Stage Design** (Design); **Television Arts** (Cinema and Television)

History: Founded 1945, acquired present title 1956.

Degrees and Diplomas: *Bachelor's Degree*; *Master's Degree*; *Doctor's Degree*

Libraries: c. 290,000 vols

Publications: Theatre Art
Last Updated: 03/12/08

SHANGHAI UNIVERSITY

149 Yanchang Road, Shanghai, Shanghai 200072
Tel: +86(21) 56331830
Fax: +86(21) 56333053
EMail: info@mail.shu.edu.cn
Website: http://www.shu.edu.cn/

President: WeiChang Chien

International Relations: Mao Zhongming

Departments
Civil Engineering (Civil Engineering)

Schools
Communications and Information Engineering (Biomedical Engineering; Communication Studies; Electronic Engineering; Information Technology); **Computer Engineering and Science** (Computer Engineering; Mathematics and Computer Science; Natural Sciences); **Environmental and Architectural Engineering** (Architecture; Chemical Engineering; Civil Engineering; Environmental Engineering; Environmental Studies; Structural Architecture); **Film and Television Technology** (Cinema and Television; Journalism); **Fine Arts** (Fine Arts); **Foreign Languages** (English; Japanese; Modern Languages); **Intellectual Property**; **International Business and Administration** (Administration; Business Administration; Economics; International Business; Management); **International Exchange** (International Relations); **Law** (Law); **Liberal Arts** (Archiving; Arts and Humanities; Chinese; History; Literature; Sociology); **Life Sciences** (Biological and Life Sciences); **Materials Science and Engineering** (Electronic Engineering; Engineering; Materials Engineering; Molecular Biology); **Mechatronic Engineering and Automation** (Automation and Control Engineering; Electronic Engineering; Industrial and Organizational Psychology; Mechanical Engineering); **Science** (Chemistry; Mathematics; Physics); **Social Sciences** (Social Sciences)

History: Founded 1994. Merged with Shanghai University of Technology, Shanghai University of Science and Technology and Shanghai Junior College of Science and Technology.

Academic Year: September to July

Admission Requirements: Graduation from senior middle school and entrance examination

Main Language(s) of Instruction: Chinese

Degrees and Diplomas: *Bachelor's Degree*; *Master's Degree*; *Doctor's Degree*

Libraries: c. 3.2m. vols

Publications: Shanghai University Journal
Last Updated: 03/12/08

SHANGHAI UNIVERSITY OF ELECTRIC POWER

2103 Pingliang Road, Shanghai, Shanghai 200090
Tel: +86(21) 65458500
Fax: +86(21) 65432514
EMail: cieoffice@shiep.edu.com
Website: http://www.shiep.net.cn

President: Cao Jialin

Colleges

Computer and Information Engineering (Computer Science; Telecommunications Engineering); **Electrical Power and Automation Engineering**; **Energy and Environmental Engineering** (Automation and Control Engineering; Chemistry; Environmental Engineering; Mechanical Engineering; Thermal Engineering; Water Science); **Management and Humanities** (Business Administration; Information Management; International Business; Public Administration)

Departments
Mathematics and Physics

History: Founded 1951 as Shanghai Polytecnic Institute. Also known as Shanghai Institute of Electrical Power.

Degrees and Diplomas: Bachelor's Degree; Master's Degree
Last Updated: 03/12/08

SHANGHAI UNIVERSITY OF ENGINEERING SCIENCE

350 Xianxia Road, Shanghai, Shanghai 200336
Tel: +86(21) 62096501
Fax: +86(21) 62758481
EMail: gcd@sues.edu.cn
Website: http://www.sues.edu.cn

President: Wang Hong

Schools

Air Transportation (Air Transport); **Art and Design** (Advertising and Publicity; Design; Fine Arts); **Automotive Engineering** (Automotive Engineering); **Electrical and Electronic Engineering** (Automation and Control Engineering; Computer Science; Electrical Engineering; Electronic Engineering); **Fashion Technology** (Chemical Engineering; Fashion Design; Textile Design); **Management** (Banking; Business Administration; Economics; Finance; Information Management; Management); **Materials Engineering** (Materials Engineering); **Mechanical Engineering** (Automation and Control Engineering; Mechanical Engineering; Thermal Engineering); **Multimedia** (Sino-Korean) (Multimedia); **Urban Rail Transportation** (Transport and Communications; Transport Engineering)

History: Founded 1978, acquired present title 1986.

Academic Year: February to January (February-July; September-January)

Admission Requirements: Graduation from senior middle school and entrance examination

Main Language(s) of Instruction: Chinese

Degrees and Diplomas: Bachelor's Degree: 4 yrs

Libraries: c. 680,000 vols

Publications: Journal of Shanghai University of Engineering Science
Last Updated: 03/12/08

SHANGHAI UNIVERSITY OF FINANCE AND ECONOMICS (SUFE)

777 Guodinglu, Shanghai, Shanghai 200433
Tel: +86(21) 65114738
Fax: +86(21) 65114738
EMail: ieo@mail.shufe.edu.cn
Website: http://www.shufe.edu.cn

President: Min Tan
Tel: +86(21) 65904384, Fax: +86(21) 65100561
EMail: tanmin@mail.shufe.edu.cn

Director of President's Office: Hua Fang
Tel: +86(21) 65904536, Fax: +86(21) 65100561

International Relations: Yamin Jin
Tel: +86(21) 65904899, Fax: +86(21) 65114738
EMail: jinym@mail.shufe.edu.cn

Departments
Foreign Languages (English; Japanese) Chair. Xiaoqun Wang; **Information Management** (Information Management) Chair. Lanjuan Liu; **Mathematics** (Mathematics) Chair. Qihong Chen

Schools
Accountancy (Accountancy) Dean: Xin Yuan Chen; **Economics** (Economics) Dean: Jingbei Hu; **Finance** (Finance) Dean: Guoqiang Dai; **Humanities** (Arts and Humanities; Journalism) Dean: Xiong Zhang; **International Business Management** (Business Administration; International Business) Dean: Haining Sun; **Law** (Fiscal Law; Law) Dean: Bangkai Ding; **Public Economy and Administration** (Economics; Finance; Management; Public Administration) Dean: Hong Jiang; **Statistics** (Statistics) Dean: Xiaoliang Han

History: Founded 1917 as Commerce Department of Nanjing Teachers' College, became Institute 1950, and acquired present status and title 1985.

Academic Year: February to January (February-July; September-January)

Admission Requirements: Graduation from senior middle school and entrance examination

Fees: (US Dollars): 1,100-1,600 per semester

Main Language(s) of Instruction: Chinese

International Co-operation: With institutions in USA; United Kingdom; Japan; Australia; Canada; Netherlands; France; Sweden; Russia; Korea; Finland; New Zealand; Philippines; Vietnam

Accrediting Agencies: Ministry of Education

Degrees and Diplomas: Bachelor's Degree: 4 yrs; Master's Degree: a further 2 1/2 yrs; Doctor's Degree (Ph.D.): a further 3 yrs

Student Services: Academic counselling, Cultural centre, Employment services, Foreign student adviser, Health services, Sports facilities

Libraries: c. 700,000 vols in Chinese; 110,000 in English

Publications: Cai Jing Research; Foreign Economy Management; SUFE Academic Journal (bimonthly)

Press or Publishing House: University Publishing House
Last Updated: 03/12/08

SHANGHAI UNIVERSITY OF SPORT

650 Qing Yuan Huan Road, Shanghai, Shanghai 200438
Tel: +86(21) 65569540
Fax: +86(21) 65568643
EMail: cice@sus.edu.cn
Website: http://www.sus.edu.cn/english/major.htm

President: Yu Jiying

International Relations: Chen Dexin

Departments
Martial Arts (Sports); **Physical Education** (Physical Education; Sports); **Sports Management** (Sports Management)

History: Founded 1952 as East China Institute of Physical Education, acquired present title 1956.

Main Language(s) of Instruction: Chinese

Degrees and Diplomas: Bachelor's Degree; Master's Degree; Doctor's Degree

Libraries: c. 270,000 vols
Last Updated: 03/12/08

SHANGHAI UNIVERSITY OF TRADITIONAL CHINESE MEDICINE

1200 Cailun Road, Zhangjiang Hi-Tech Park, Pudong New District, Shanghai, Shanghai 201203
Tel: +86(21) 64186532
Fax: +86(21) 51322276
EMail: tcmeducation@shtcm.com
Website: http://www.shutcm.edu.cn

President: Yan Shiyun Tel: +86(21) 64037208

International Relations: Li Shang Tel: +86(21) 54231698

Departments

Acupuncture and Moxibustion (Acupuncture); **Chinese Pharmacology** (Pharmacology); **Medical Massage**; **Traditional Chinese Medicine** (Medicine; Pharmacy; Traditional Eastern Medicine)

History: Founded 1956.

Admission Requirements: Graduation from senior middle school and entrance examination

Fees: (Yuan): c. 5,500 per annum

Degrees and Diplomas: *Bachelor's Degree*; *Master's Degree*; *Doctor's Degree*

Student Services: Academic counselling, Canteen, Cultural centre, Employment services, Foreign student adviser, Foreign Studies Centre, Health services, Language programs, Social counselling, Sports facilities

Special Facilities: Museum of Medical History

Libraries: c. 400,000 vols. (including rare hand copied books printed in the Ming or Ch'ing Dynasties, or in Japan)

Publications: ACTA Universitae Traditionis Medicalis Sinensis Pharmacologiae Shanghai *(quarterly)*; ET Academiae Traditionis Medicalis Sinensis Pharmacologiae Shanghai *(quarterly)*; Journal of Shanghai Traditional Chinese Medicine *(monthly)*

Press or Publishing House: University Publishing House
Last Updated: 03/12/08

SHANTOU UNIVERSITY (STU)

Shantou, Guangdong Province 515063
Tel: +86(754) 2902316
Fax: +86(754) 2903520
EMail: icd@stu.edu.cn
Website: http://www.stu.edu.cn

President: Xiao Hu Xu EMail: jcd@stu.edu.cn

Director of President's Office: Miao Xie EMail: o_xzb@stu.edu.cn

International Relations: Xue Quan Liao EMail: xqliao@stu.edu.cn

Centres

Chinese Language Training (Chinese); **Multidisciplinary Research** (Natural Sciences)

Faculties

Engineering (Engineering); **Law** (Law); **Liberal Arts** (Arts and Humanities); **Science** (Mathematics and Computer Science; Natural Sciences)

Institutes

Artificial Intelligence *(Manufacturing Technology Laboratory)* (Artificial Intelligence); **Image Processing** *(Technology Laboratory)* (Higher Education); **Marine Biology** *(Laboratory)* (Marine Biology); **Molecular Pathology** (Molecular Biology; Pathology); **Tumour Pathology** (Oncology)

Schools

Art and Design (Arts and Humanities; Design); **Business** (Business Administration); **Continuing Education** (Continuing Education); **Journalism and Communication** (Communication Arts; Journalism); **Medicine** (Medicine)

Further Information: Also 5 Affiliated Hospitals

History: Founded 1981. Under the jurisdiction of the Provincial authorities.

Governing Bodies: Shantou University Council

Academic Year: September to July (September-January; February-July)

Admission Requirements: Graduation from high school

Fees: (Yuan): c. 5,000-6,000 per annum; foreign students, US Dollars, c. 1,600

Main Language(s) of Instruction: Chinese

Degrees and Diplomas: *Bachelor's Degree*: 4 yrs; *Bachelor's Degree*: Medicine, 5 yrs; *Master's Degree*: 2-3 yrs; *Doctor's Degree* (PhD)

Student Services: Academic counselling, Canteen, Cultural centre, Employment services, Foreign student adviser, Foreign Studies Centre, Handicapped facilities, Health services, Language programs, Nursery care, Social counselling, Sports facilities

Special Facilities: Marine Biology Experimental Base

Libraries: University Library, c. 1m. vols; Medical Library, c. 187,270 vols

Student Numbers *2007-2008*: Total 6,952

Part-time students, 6,054.
Last Updated: 06/10/08

SHANXI AGRICULTURAL UNIVERSITY

Taigu, Shanxi Province 030801
Tel: +86(351) 6288221
Fax: +86(351) 6288303
EMail: info@sxau.edu.cn
Website: http://www.sxau.edu.cn

President: He Yunchun

International Relations: Li Yubling

Colleges

Agriculture (Agriculture; Agronomy; Plant and Crop Protection); **Animal Science and Technology** (Animal Husbandry; Veterinary Science; Zoology); **Art and Science**; **Economics and Trade**; **Engineering** (Engineering); **Food Engineering**; **Forestry** (Forestry); **Horticulture**; **Modern Technology**; **Public Management**; **Resources and Environment** (Environmental Studies; Natural Resources)

History: Founded 1907 as Oberlin Shanxi Memorial School. Acquired present title 1979.

Degrees and Diplomas: *Bachelor's Degree*; *Master's Degree*; *Doctor's Degree*

Libraries: c. 550,000 vols

Publications: Journal of Shanxi Agricultural University
Last Updated: 03/12/08

SHANXI MEDICAL UNIVERSITY

56 Xinjian South Road, Taiyuan, Shanxi Province 030001
Tel: +86(351) 4135479
Fax: +86(351) 2024239
Website: http://www.sxmu.edu.cn

President: Zheng Guo

International Relations: Xiuyun Li

Colleges

Clinical Medicine *(Second)* (Medicine); **Clinical Medicine** *(First)* (Medicine); **Continuing Education**; **Forensic Medicine**; **Humanities and Social Sciences**; **Medicine (Datong)** (Medicine); **Medicine (Fenyang)**; **Medicine (Jinzhong)**; **Medicine (Yuncheng)** (Medicine); **Nursing** (Nursing); **Pharmacy**; **Pre-Clinical Medicine**; **Professional and Technical**; **Public Health**

Departments

Anaesthesiology (Anaesthesiology); **Foreign Languages** (Modern Languages); **Medical Imaging**; **Paediatrics**; **Postgraduate Studies**; **Stomatology** (Stomatology)

History: Founded 1919 as Shanxi Medical College, acquired present title 1996.

Academic Year: September to July

Admission Requirements: National entrance examination

Main Language(s) of Instruction: Chinese

Degrees and Diplomas: *Bachelor's Degree*: Medicine, 5 yrs; *Master's Degree*: Medicine, 3 yrs; *Doctor's Degree*: Medicine, 3 yrs

Student Services: Canteen, Employment services, Health services, Sports facilities

Libraries: c. 13,040,000 vols

Publications: Journal of Shanxi Medical University

SHANXI NORMAL UNIVERSITY

Gongyuan Street., Linfen, Shanxi Province
EMail: waisc2@163.com
Website: http://www.sxnu.edu.cn

President: Wu Haishun

Institutes

Art (Design; Fine Arts; Painting and Drawing); **Biological Technology and Engineering** (Agronomy; Bioengineering; Biotechnology; Civil Engineering; Construction Engineering; Electronic Engineering; Food Science; Horticulture; Zoology); **Chemistry and Materials Science** (Applied Chemistry; Chemistry); **City and Environmental Science** (Environmental Management; Environmental Studies; Geography); **Educational Technology** (Educational Technology); **History**; **Life and Science** (Bioengineering; Biological and Life Sciences; Biotechnology; Botany); **Literature** (Chinese; Literature; Publishing and Book Trade); **Mathematics and Computer Science** (Mathematics and Computer Science); **Music** (Music); **Physical Education** (Physical Education); **Physics and Information Engineering** (Computer Science; Physics); **Politics and Law** (Law; Political Sciences)

Schools

Foreign Languages (Modern Languages)

History: Founded 1958 as Normal Training College of Southern Shanxi. Acquired present title 1984.

Main Language(s) of Instruction: Chinese

Degrees and Diplomas: *Bachelor's Degree*; *Master's Degree*

Libraries: c. 1m. vols

Publications: Journal of Shanxi Teachers University
Last Updated: 03/12/08

SHANXI UNIVERSITY (SXU)

92 Wucheng Rd, Taiyuan, Shanxi Province 030006
Tel: +86(351) 7010255
Fax: +86(351) 7011981
EMail: xiaoban@sxu.edu.cn
Website: http://www.sxu.edu.cn

President: Guichun Guo (2000-)
Tel: +86(351) 7011311 EMail: guoge@sxu.edu.cn

Vice-President: Jiye Liang Tel: +86(351) 7010109

International Relations: Guo-dong Yu, Director of Foreign Office
Tel: +85(351) 7011583, Fax: +86(351) 7011583
EMail: zhj@sxu.edu.cn

Colleges

Fine Arts (Design; Fine Arts; Painting and Drawing); **Music** (Music; Music Theory and Composition); **Physical Education** (Physical Education); **Physics and Electronic Engineering** *Director*: Jiangrui Gao

Departments

Computer Science (Computer Science); **Foreign Language (for Non Majors)**; **History** (History); **Mathematics** (Mathematics)

Schools

Chemistry and Engineering (Chemistry; Engineering); **Chinese Language and Literature** (Chinese; Comparative Literature; Literature); **Economics**; **Education Science** (Educational Sciences); **Environmental Science and Resources** (Environmental Studies; Natural Resources); **Foreign Languages** (English Studies; Linguistics; Literature; Modern Languages; Russian) *Director*: Nie Jianzhong; **Law** (Administrative Law; Commercial Law; Constitutional Law; International Law; Law); **Life Science and Technology** (Biological and Life Sciences; Technology); **Management** (Management); **Philosophy and Sociology** (Philosophy; Sociology); **Political Science and Public Administration** (Political Sciences; Public Administration)

History: Founded 1902. Acquired present status 1949.

Academic Year: August to July

Admission Requirements: Secondary school certificate; entrance examination

Fees: (Yuan): 2,600-6,000 per annum

Main Language(s) of Instruction: Chinese

International Co-operation: With universities in Japan and United Kingdom

Accrediting Agencies: Ministry of Education; Education Commission of Shanxi Province

Degrees and Diplomas: *Bachelor's Degree*: 4 yrs; *Master's Degree*: a further 3 yrs; *Doctor's Degree (PhD)*: A further 3 yrs following Master

Student Services: Academic counselling, Canteen, Cultural centre, Employment services, Foreign student adviser, Foreign Studies Centre, Handicapped facilities, Health services, Language programs, Nursery care, Social counselling, Sports facilities

Student Residential Facilities: 24 flats for students; 46 flats for staff

Libraries: Central Library, c. 1.9m. vols, c. 1.6m. printed documents; 60,800 e-books; 17 national and international documentary databases
Last Updated: 03/12/08

SHANXI UNIVERSITY OF FINANCE AND ECONOMICS

696 Wucheng Road, Taiyuan, Shanxi Province 030012
Tel: +86(351) 7111895
Fax: +86(351) 7111895
EMail: waishiban@sxufe.edu.com
Website: http://www.sxufe.edu.cn/english/index.htm

President: Yuan Meisheng (2005-)

Schools

Accountancy; **Business Administration** (Accountancy; Engineering Management; Hotel Management; Labour and Industrial Relations; Management; Tourism); **Business Foreign Languages** (Modern Languages); **Economics** (Economics; Modern Languages; Statistics); **Finance** (Banking; Finance); **Information Management**; **International Trade**; **Law** (Administrative Law; Law); **Management Science and Engineering** (Management); **Public Management**; **Statistics** (Statistics); **Vocational Skills**

History: Founded 1951, acquired present status and title 1997.

Degrees and Diplomas: *Bachelor's Degree*; *Master's Degree*
Last Updated: 03/12/08

SHANXI UNIVERSITY OF TRADITIONAL CHINESE MEDICINE

89 Jinci Road, Taiyuan, Shanxi Province 030024
Tel: +86(351) 6042281
Fax: +86(351) 6042281
EMail: sxgjzx88@yahoo.com.cn
Website: http://www.sxtcm.com

President: Tao Qongding (1998-)
Tel: +86(351) 2272220, Fax: +86(351) 6042276

Administrative Officer: Sun Wei
Tel: +86(351) 2272258, Fax: +86(351) 6042276

International Relations: Xueli Zhao
Tel: +86(351) 2272240, Fax: +86(351) 2272240
EMail: sxgizx88@yahoo.com.cn

Departments

Acupuncture and Moxibustion (Acupuncture) *Director*: Laixi Ji; **Nursing** (Nursing) *Director*: Zhiying Zhou; **Traditional Chinese Medicine** (Traditional Eastern Medicine) *Director*: Zhonghai Wei; **Traditional Chinese Medicine** (Pharmacology) *Director*: Miaorong Pei

History: Founded 1989.

Admission Requirements: Secondary school certificate, English and Chinese

Fees: (US Dollars): 2,000-16,400

Main Language(s) of Instruction: Chinese and English

Degrees and Diplomas: *Bachelor's Degree*: 5 yrs; *Master's Degree*: 3 yrs; *Doctor's Degree*: 3 yrs

Student Services: Academic counselling, Canteen, Cultural centre, Employment services, Foreign student adviser, Foreign Studies Centre, Handicapped facilities, Health services, Language programs, Nursery care, Social counselling, Sports facilities

Student Residential Facilities: Yes

Libraries: c. 60,000 vols

Publications: Journal of Shanxi College of Traditional Medicine *(quarterly)*
Last Updated: 03/12/08

SHAOGUAN UNIVERSITY

Datand Road, Shaoguan, Guangdong Province 512005
Tel: +86(751) 8120021
Fax: +86(751) 8120025
EMail: sguio@sgu.edu.cn
Website: http://www.sgu.edu.cn

President: He Si'an

Departments
Chemistry (Chemistry); **Chinese Language and Literature** (Chinese); **Computer Science**; **Economics** (Economics); **Fine Arts**; **Foreign Languages** (Modern Languages); **Mathematics**; **Mechanical and Electrical Engineering** (Electrical Engineering; Mechanical Engineering); **Medicine** (Medicine); **Music** (Music); **Physical Education** (Physical Education); **Physics** (Physics); **Political Science and Law**

Schools
Adult Education; **Teacher Training** (Teacher Training)

History: Founded 1989.

Degrees and Diplomas: *Bachelor's Degree*

SHAOXING UNIVERSITY

5 Huancheng West Road, Shaoxing, Zhejiang Province 312000
Tel: +86(575) 8064138
Fax: +86(575) 8067917
EMail: master@zscas.edu.cn
Website: http://www.zscas.edu.cn

President: Fei Junqing

Colleges
Art *(Cai Yuanpei)* (Fine Arts)

Faculties
Economics and Business Administration; **Engineering** (Architectural and Environmental Design; Civil Engineering; Computer Science; Electronic Engineering; Mechanical Engineering; Textile Technology); **Law** (Law); **Mathematics, Physics and Information Science**; **Modern Languages**; **Physical Education** (Physical Education)

History: Founded 1980 as Shaoxing Teachers Training College, acquired present title 1996. Formerly known as Shaoxing College of Arts and Sciences.

Degrees and Diplomas: *Bachelor's Degree*
Last Updated: 03/12/08

SHENYANG AEROSPACE UNIVERSITY

37 Daoyi South Avenue, Shenbei New District, Shenyang, Liaoning Province 110136
Tel: +86(24) 89724298
Fax: +86(24) 89724298
EMail: admission@sau.edu.cn
Website: http://www.sau.edu.cn/

President: Wang Wei

International Relations: Wayne Fu

Departments
Engineering Drawing and Design (Engineering Drawing and Design)

Schools
Aerodynamics and Energy Engineering (Energy Engineering); **Aerospace Engineering** (Aeronautical and Aerospace Engineering); **Airforce Officials Training** (Air and Space Law; Air Transport); **Auto Control** (Automation and Control Engineering); **Civil Aviation and Safety Engineering** (Safety Engineering); **Computer Science** (Computer Science); **Design Art** (Design); **Economics and Management** (Economics; Management); **Electronics Information Engineering** (Computer Engineering; Electronic Engineering); **Foreign Languages** (Modern Languages); **Material Science and Engineering** (Materials Engineering); **Mechanical and Electrical Engineering** (Electrical Engineering; Mechanical Engineering; Mechanics); **Northern Software** (Software Engineering); **Science** (Natural Sciences)

History: Founded 1952 as Shenyang Aeronautical Engineering School. Became Shenyang Institute of Aeronautical Engineering in 1978.

Degrees and Diplomas: *Bachelor's Degree*; *Master's Degree*
Last Updated: 21/07/11

SHENYANG AGRICULTURAL UNIVERSITY

120 Dongling Road, Shenyang, Liaoning Province 110161
Tel: +86(24) 88421031
Fax: +86(24) 88417416
Website: http://www.syau.edu.cn

President: Liu Changjiang

International Relations: Li Yongjian

Schools
Agricultural Engineering (Agricultural Engineering; Water Science); **Agronomy** (Agronomy; Plant and Crop Protection); **Animal Husbandry and Veterinary Medicine** (Animal Husbandry; Aquaculture; Veterinary Science); **Economics and Trade**; **Forestry** (Forestry); **Water Management**

History: Founded 1952, acquired present title 1985.

Degrees and Diplomas: *Bachelor's Degree*; *Master's Degree*; *Doctor's Degree*

Libraries: c. 80,000 vols

Publications: Journal of Shenyang Agricultural University

SHENYANG CONSERVATORY OF MUSIC

61 Sanhao Street, Heping District, Shenyang, Liaoning Province 110003
Tel: +86(24) 23903761
Fax: +86(24) 23903761
EMail: sycm_yb@sohu.com
Website: http://www.sycm.com.cn/web_english.asp

President: Pan Zhaohe

Departments
Chinese Traditional Instruments (Musical Instruments); **Composition** (Music Theory and Composition); **Dance** (Dance); **Musicology**; **Singing** (Singing); **Wind and String Instruments**

History: Founded 1938 as Luxun Academy of Arts, acquired present status and title 1958.

Degrees and Diplomas: *Bachelor's Degree*; *Master's Degree*
Last Updated: 03/12/08

SHENYANG INSTITUTE OF CHEMICAL TECHNOLOGY

11 Aigong South Street, Tiexi District, Shenyang, Liaoning Province 110021
Tel: +86(24) 25858754
Fax: +86(24) 25858754
EMail: syict@syict.edu.cn
Website: http://www.syict.edu.cn

President: Wu Jianhua

International Relations: Hou Yanfeng

Departments
Applied Chemistry (Applied Chemistry); **Automation Engineering** (Automation and Control Engineering); **Chemical Engineering** (Chemical Engineering); **Computer Science and Engineering** (Computer Science); **Engineering Management** (Engineering Management); **Industrial Equipment and Machinery** (Machine Building); **Materials Science and Engineering** (Materials Engineering)

History: Founded 1952 as school of chemical industry, acquired present status and name 1958.

Degrees and Diplomas: *Bachelor's Degree*; *Master's Degree*

SHENYANG INSTITUTE OF ENGINEERING

134 Changjiang Street, Huanggu District, Shenyang, Liaoning Province 110036
Tel: +86(24) 86846531
Website: http://www.sie.edu.cn

Departments

Automation and Control Engineering (Automation and Control Engineering); **Electrical Engineering**; **Energy Engineering** (Energy Engineering); **Information Engineering** (Information Technology); **Management Engineering** (Management)

Sections

Adult Education; **Fundamental Education** (Education); **Sociology and Science**; **Training**

History: Founded 2003 through merger of Shenyang Junior College of Electric Power and Liaoning Vocational College of Commerce.

Degrees and Diplomas: *Bachelor's Degree*

Libraries:c. 280,000 vols.

SHENYANG JIANZHU UNIVERSITY (SJZU)

17 East Wenhua Road, Dongling District, Shenyang, Liaoning Province 110015
Tel: +86(24) 24692693
Fax: +86(24) 24692696
EMail: wb@sjzu.edu.cn
Website: http://www.sjzu.edu.cn/

Director: Liu ChangXin

Deputy Director: Liu XiDong

International Relations: M. Yu EMail: yujin@sjzu.edu.cn

Departments

Communication and Mechanical Engineering; **Engineering Management**; **Modern Languages**; **Physical Education** (Physical Education); **Social Sciences**

Institutes

Technology (Technology)

Schools

Information and Control Engineering; **Material Science and Engineering** (Materials Engineering); **Municipal and Environmental Engineering**; **Urban Construction** (Construction Engineering)

History: Founded 1948 as Shenyang Architectural and Civil Engineering Institute. Acquired present title and status 2004.

Fees: (US Dollars): Tuition, undergraduate, 1,700 per annum, graduate, 2,500

Accrediting Agencies: National Education Department

Degrees and Diplomas: *Bachelor's Degree*; *Master's Degree*
Last Updated: 04/12/08

SHENYANG LIGONG UNIVERSITY

Hunhe New District, Shenyang, Liaoning Province 110168
Tel: +86(24) 24686047
Fax: +86(24) 24686046
EMail: webmaster@mail.sylu.edu.cn
Website: http://www.syit.edu.cn/

President: Jia Chunde

International Relations: Zhou Chenxiao

Departments

Automatic Control (Automation and Control Engineering); **Chemical Engineering**; **Computer Science** (Computer Science); **Electronic Engineering** (Electronic Engineering); **Engineering Management** (Engineering Management); **Materials Engineering** (Materials Engineering); **Mechanical Engineering** (Mechanical Engineering); **Modern Languages** (Modern Languages)

Schools

Automotive Engineering; **Management** (Management)

History: Founded 1953 as Northeast China Industrial School. Acquired present status and title 2004.

Main Language(s) of Instruction: Chinese

Degrees and Diplomas: *Bachelor's Degree*; *Master's Degree*

SHENYANG MEDICAL COLLEGE

146 Huanghe North Street, Shenyang, Liaoning Province 110034
Tel: +86(24) 62215776
Fax: +86(24) 62215656
EMail: shenyiyuanban@symc.edu.cn
Website: http://218.25.15.19/english/

President: Xu Yanhao

International Relations: Li Min

Departments

Basic Medicine (Medicine); **Clinical Medicine**; **Health Administration** (Health Administration); **Nursing** (Nursing); **Preventive Medicine** (Social and Preventive Medicine); **Social Sciences**

Schools

Ophtalmology and Optics (Ophthalmology; Optical Technology; Optics)

History: Founded 1949 as nursing school, acquired present status and title 1987.

Degrees and Diplomas: *Bachelor's Degree*; *Master's Degree*

SHENYANG NORMAL UNIVERSITY

253 Huanghe North Street, Shenyang, Liaoning Province 110031
Tel: +86(24) 86847417
Fax: +86(24) 86230328
Website: http://www.synu.edu.cn/synuen/p1.html

President: Zhao Dayu
Tel: +86(24) 86592023 EMail: zhaodayu@synu.edu.cn

International Relations: Wu Yulun
Tel: +86(24) 86574276, Fax: +86(24) 86574225
EMail: yulunwu@163.com

Colleges

Arts and Design; **Chemistry and Life Sciences** (Biological and Life Sciences; Chemistry); **Drama** (Acting; Theatre); **Educational Sciences** (Educational Sciences); **Educational Technology** (Educational Technology); **Foreign Languages** (English; French; German; Japanese; Literature; Modern Languages; Russian); **International Business** (Economics; International Business); **International Education**; **Law** (Law); **Liberal Arts**; **Management**; **Marxism** (Political Sciences); **Mathematics and Systematic Science** (Computer Science; Mathematics); **Music** (Music); **Physical Science and Technology** (Physics; Technology); **Sociology** (Sociology); **Software**; **Sports**; **Tourism Management**

History: Founded 1951 as Northeastern College of Education, acquired present status 2002.

Academic Year: August-July

Admission Requirements: HSK 4

Main Language(s) of Instruction: Chinese

International Co-operation: With Bloomsburg University; Fort Hays State University

Degrees and Diplomas: *Bachelor's Degree*: 4 yrs; *Master's Degree*: 3 yrs

Student Services: Academic counselling, Canteen, Employment services, Foreign student adviser, Foreign Studies Centre, Health services, Language programs, Nursery care, Sports facilities

Student Residential Facilities: Yes

Special Facilities: Museum; Movie Studio
Last Updated: 04/12/08

SHENYANG PHARMACEUTICAL UNIVERSITY

103 Wenhua Road, Shenhe District, Shenyang, Liaoning Province 110015
Tel: +86(24) 23891685
Fax: +86(24) 23891576
EMail: master@syphu.edu.cn
Website: http://www.syphu.edu.cn

President: Wu Chunfu

Schools

Adult Education; **Business Administration** (Business Administration); **Pharmaceutical Engineering** (Pharmacology);

Pharmacy; **Traditional Chinese Medicine** (Pharmacology; Traditional Eastern Medicine)

History: Founded 1931 as Medical School of the Red Army. Acquired present name 1994.

Degrees and Diplomas: *Bachelor's Degree*; *Master's Degree*; *Doctor's Degree*

Libraries: c. 180,000 vols

Publications: Journal of Shenyang Pharmaceutical University

Last Updated: 04/12/08

SHENYANG SPORT UNIVERSITY

36 Jinqiansong East Road, Sujiatun District, Shenyang, Liaoning Province 110032
Tel: +86(24) 86893492 +86(24) 86891544
Fax: +86(24) 86893614
EMail: zhaoning@163.com
Website: http://www.syty.edu.cn

President: Zhang Guimin

Departments

Chinese Traditional Martial Art (Sports); **Kinesiology** (Physical Therapy); **Management** (Management; Public Administration); **Physical Education** (Physical Education); **Sports Humanities**

History: Founded 1954 as Northeast Institute of Physical Education, acquired present title 1956.

Degrees and Diplomas: *Bachelor's Degree*; *Master's Degree*

Last Updated: 04/12/08

SHENYANG UNIVERSITY

21 Wanghua South Street, Dadong District, Shenyang, Liaoning Province 110044
Tel: +86(24) 88502777-1
Fax: +86(24) 88523363
Website: http://www.syu.edu.cn

President: Cai Qingkui

International Relations: Zhang Yaohua

Schools

Architectural and Environmental Engineering; **Art**; **Economics**; **Foreign Languages**; **Higher Vocational Technology**; **Industrial and Commerce Management**; **Information Engineering**; **Liberal Arts**; **Mechanical Engineering**; **Tourism**

History: Founded 1980.

Degrees and Diplomas: *Bachelor's Degree*

Libraries: c. 6m. vols

Publications: Journal of Shenyang University

SHENYANG UNIVERSITY OF TECHNOLOGY

58 Xinghua South Street, Tiexi District, Shenyang, Liaoning Province 110023
Tel: +86(24) 25415365
Fax: +86(24) 25411629
EMail: webmaster@sut.edu.cn
Website: http://eng.sut.edu.cn

President: Li Rongde
Tel: +86(24) 25415365, Fax: +86(24) 25411629

Departments

Civil Engineering (Civil Engineering); **Foreign Languages** (English; Modern Languages; Russian)

Schools

Business and Commerce (Business and Commerce); **Economic Administration** (Accountancy; Administration; Business Administration; Business and Commerce; Economics; Engineering Management; Finance; International Business; International Economics); **Electrical Engineering** (Automation and Control Engineering; Electrical Engineering; Machine Building); **Information Sciences and Engineering** (Automation and Control Engineering; Computer Science; Electrical and Electronic Equipment and Maintenance; Engineering; Information Sciences; Measurement and Precision Engineering; Telecommunications Engineering); **Literature and Law** (International Relations; Law; Literature);

Materials Science and Engineering (Engineering; Materials Engineering; Metal Techniques); **Mechanical Engineering** (Automation and Control Engineering; Electronic Engineering; Graphic Design; Industrial Design; Industrial Engineering; Mechanical Engineering; Production Engineering); **Science** (Mathematics and Computer Science; Natural Sciences)

History: Founded 1949, acquired present status and title 1985.

Degrees and Diplomas: *Bachelor's Degree*; *Master's Degree*; *Doctor's Degree*

Libraries: c. 600,000 vols

Publications: Academic Journal of Shenyang University of Technology

Last Updated: 01/10/08

SHENZHEN UNIVERSITY

Shenyang University, Shenzhen, Guangdong Province 518060
Tel: +86(755) 26536108.
Fax: +86(755) 26534940
EMail: szufao@szu.edu.cn
Website: http://www.szu.edu.cn

President: Zhang Bigong Tel: +86(755) 26534375

Vice-President: Xing Feng
Tel: +86(755) 26558382 EMail: xingmiao@szu.edu.cn

International Relations: Ruan Shuangchen
Tel: +86(755) 26534794, Fax: +86(755) 26535970

Colleges

Arts (Advertising and Publicity; Chinese; Communication Studies; Japanese; Modern Languages; Tourism) *Dean*: Yuming Wu; **Normal** (Teacher Training)

Schools

Adult Education; **Architecture and Town Planning** (Architectural and Environmental Design; Architecture; Civil Engineering; Town Planning); **Art and Design**; **Chemistry and Chemical Engineering**; **Civil Engineering** (Civil Engineering); **Economics** (Accountancy; Business and Commerce; Economics; Finance; International Business); **Electronic Science and Technology** (Electronic Engineering; Optical Technology); **Foreign Languages** (Modern Languages); **Golf Management** (Sports; Sports Management); **Information Engineering** (Computer Engineering; Electronic Engineering; Information Technology); **Law** (Law; Sociology); **Life Sciences** (Biological and Life Sciences); **Management** (Management; Public Administration); **Mass Communication**; **Material Science** (Materials Engineering); **Mathematics and Computer Science** (Mathematics and Computer Science); **Mechatronics and Control Engineering** (Automation and Control Engineering; Electronic Engineering; Mechanical Engineering); **Medical**; **Optoelectronics Engineering** (Electronic Engineering; Optical Technology)

History: Founded 1983.

Governing Bodies: Administrative Council

Academic Year: September to July (September-February; March-July)

Admission Requirements: Graduation from senior middle school and entrance examination

Fees: (Yuan): c. 5,000

Main Language(s) of Instruction: Chinese

International Co-operation: Queen University of Belfast, Central Lancashire University

Accrediting Agencies: Ministry of Education

Degrees and Diplomas: *Bachelor's Degree*: 4 yrs; *Master's Degree*: 3 yrs; *Doctor's Degree*

Student Services: Canteen, Cultural centre, Employment services, Foreign student adviser, Foreign Studies Centre, Health services, Language programs, Nursery care, Sports facilities

Student Residential Facilities: Yes

Libraries: c. 1,200,000 vols

Publications: Journal of Shenzhen University *(bimonthly)*; World Architecture Review *(quarterly)*

Last Updated: 04/12/08

SHIHEZI UNIVERSITY

Beisi Road, Shihezi, Xinjiang Uygur Province 832003
Tel: +86(993) 2058053
Fax: +86(993) 2017247
EMail: webmaster@shzu.edu.cn
Website: http://www.shzu.edu.cn/structure/index

President: Zheng Guoying

International Relations: Fan Yugang

Colleges

Agriculture; **Economics and Commerce** (Accountancy; Business and Commerce; Economics; Management); **Engineering**; **Humanities** (Bioengineering; History; Law; Physical Education; Political Sciences); **Medicine** (Nursing; Pharmacy); **Teachers Training** (Biology; Chemistry; Chinese; Education; Fine Arts; Geography; Mathematics; Modern Languages; Physics)

History: Founded 1949 as Shihezi Agricultural College. Merged with Shihezi Medical College (founded 1949). Acquired present status and title 1996.

Degrees and Diplomas: *Bachelor's Degree*; *Master's Degree*

SHIJIAZHUANG RAILWAY INSTITUTE

No.17 North 2nd-Ring East Road, Shijiazhuang,
Hebei Province 050043
Tel: +86(311) 87935152
Fax: +86(311) 6832161
EMail: yuanban@sjzri.edu.cn
Website: http://www.sjzri.edu.cn

President: Jiang Zhiqing

International Relations: Dai Yunliang

Departments

Accountancy; **Architecture** (Architecture); **Electronic Engineering** (Electronic Engineering); **Machine Building** (Machine Building); **Management**; **Transport Engineering** (Transport Engineering)

History: Founded 1950 as Railway Engineering College, acquired present status and name 1984.

Degrees and Diplomas: *Bachelor's Degree*; *Master's Degree*
Last Updated: 04/12/08

SHIJIAZHUANG UNIVERSITY OF ECONOMICS

302 Huainan Road, Shijiazhuang, Hebei Province 050031
Tel: +86(311) 5882537
Fax: +86(311) 5882537
EMail: xywmail@sjzue.edu.cn
Website: http://www.sjzue.edu.cn

President: Jia Guiting

International Relations: Lei Shihe

Departments

Accountancy; **Applied Economics** (Economics); **Business Administration**; **Economics** (Economics); **Humanities and Law** (Arts and Humanities; Law); **Information Technology**; **Natural Resources and Environmental Engineering**

History: Founded 1971 as Hebei College of Geology, acquired present title 1996.

Degrees and Diplomas: *Bachelor's Degree*; *Master's Degree*
Last Updated: 09/07/09

SIAS INTERNATIONAL UNIVERSITY

168 Renmin Rd, Xinzheng, Henan Province 451150
Tel: +86(371) 6260-5536
Fax: +86(371) 6260-5536
EMail: sqfang@hotmail.com
Website: http://www.sias.edu.cn/

Chairman: Shawn Chen (1998-) **EMail:** shawn_sias@yahoo.com

International Relations: Fang Wen Chang, Head, International Cooperation and Exchange

Academies
Fine Arts (Fine Arts)

Conservatories
Music (Music)

Schools
Basic Sciences (Natural Sciences); **Business** (Accountancy; Business and Commerce; Economics; Management); **Foreign Languages** (English; Japanese; Translation and Interpretation); **Information Technology** (Information Technology); **International Education** (Business Administration; English; Finance; International Business); **Law** (Law); **Nursing** (Nursing); **Physical Education** (Physical Education)

History: Created 1998.

Degrees and Diplomas: *Bachelor's Degree*

Libraries: 650,000 vols; 1,200 periodical subscriptions; 300,000 e-book holdings.

Academic Staff *2008-2009*: Total 9,000

STAFF WITH DOCTORATE: Total 60

Student Numbers *2008-2009*: Total 21,000
Last Updated: 18/03/10

SICHUAN AGRICULTURAL UNIVERSITY (SAU)

36 Xinkang Road, Ya'an, Sichuan Province 625014
Tel: +86(835) 2242233
Fax: +86(835) 2224766
EMail: aumdwsb@sicau.edu.cn
Website: http://www.sicau.edu.cn

President: Wen Xintian

International Relations: Yin Demo

Schools

Agriculture (Agriculture; Environmental Studies; Genetics; Microbiology; Plant and Crop Protection; Soil Science); **Animal Science and Technology** (Animal Husbandry; Veterinary Science; Zoology); **Economics and Trade** (Business Administration; Business and Commerce; Economics; Finance); **Engineering** (Automation and Control Engineering; Computer Science; Engineering; Food Science; Mechanical Engineering; Physics); **Forestry and Horticulture** (Forestry; Horticulture); **Vocational Technology** (Technology)

History: Founded 1906 as Sichuan Tong Sheng Agricultural School, acquired present title 1985.

Academic Year: September to July

Admission Requirements: Graduation from senior middle school and entrance examination

Main Language(s) of Instruction: Chinese

Degrees and Diplomas: *Bachelor's Degree*; *Master's Degree*: a further 2-3 yrs; *Doctor's Degree*

Libraries: c. 500,000 vols

Publications: Journal of Sichuan Agricultural University
Last Updated: 04/12/08

SICHUAN CONSERVATORY OF MUSIC (SCCM)

6 Xinsheng Road, Chengdu, Sichuan Province 610021
Tel: +86(28) 85430876 +86(28) 85430297
Fax: +86(28) 85430712
EMail: sccmws@126.com
Website: http://www.sccm.cn/

President: Ao Changqun

International Relations: Yang Jianzhong

Departments

Composition (Music Theory and Composition); **Folkloric Music** (Folklore; Music); **Music Education** (Music Education); **Musicology** (Musicology); **Piano** (Musical Instruments); **Singing**; **Wind and String Instruments** (Musical Instruments)

History: Founded 1939 as Sichuan Provincial School of Drama and Music, acquired present status and title 1959.

Fees: (Yuan): Secondary school student, 15,000 per annum; three-year college student and undergraduate, 21,000; master degree, 27,000 or 10,000 per term; general advanced-study student,18,000

Degrees and Diplomas: *Bachelor's Degree*; *Master's Degree*
Last Updated: 04/12/08

SICHUAN FINE ARTS INSTITUTE

108 Huangjiaoping, Jiulongpo District, Chongqing, Sichuan
Province 400053
Tel: +86(23) 86181008
Fax: +86(23) 68514451
EMail: info@scfai.edu.cn
Website: http://www.scfai.edu.cn/

President: Luo Zhongli

International Relations: Chen Zhongying

Departments
Art Education (Art Education); **Art History and Theory** (Art Criticism; Art History); **Chinese Traditional Painting** (Chinese); **Communication Arts**; **Crafts and Design**; **Design** (Design); **Landscape Architecture**; **Oil Painting** (Painting and Drawing); **Printmaking** (Printing and Printmaking); **Sculpture**

Schools
Fashion Design (Fashion Design)

History: Founded 1939 as Chengdu Arts School, acquired present status 1950 and name 1959.

Admission Requirements: Equivalent to Chinese senior high school certificate

Fees: (Yuan): long-term, 10,000 per annum; short-term, 450 per week

International Co-operation: With universities in Germany, France, UK, Republic of Korea

Degrees and Diplomas: *Bachelor's Degree*; *Master's Degree*

Libraries: c. 2,500,000 vols; 1,000 periodicals.

SICHUAN INTERNATIONAL STUDIES UNIVERSITY

Lieshimu, Shapingba, Chongqing, Sichuan Province 400031
Tel: +86(23) 65385218
Fax: +86(23) 65385875
EMail: webmaster@sisu.edu.cn
Website: http://www.sisu.edu.cn

Vice-President: Keyong Li (2001-)
Tel: +86(23) 65385815, Fax: +86(23) 65385207

Assistant President: Xiaochua Li Tel: +86(23) 65385219

International Relations: Chun Zhao Tel: +86(23) 65380010

Centres
Audiovisual Studies (Cinema and Television); **Computer** (Computer Science); **Foreign Language Proficiency Testing**

Colleges
Chengdu (Chinese; English; Journalism); **International Cultural Exchange** *(ICEC)* (Chinese; English; Journalism); **Vocational and Technical Education** (Foreign Languages Education; Home Economics; International Business; Marketing; Secretarial Studies; Tourism)

Departments
English (English; International Relations; Translation and Interpretation); **English Language and Culture** (English Studies); **French** (French); **German** (German; Translation and Interpretation); **Japanese** (Japanese; Translation and Interpretation); **Postgraduate**; **Russian** (Russian; Translation and Interpretation); **Social Sciences** (Social Sciences)

Institutes
Adult Education

Research Institutes
Higher Education (Educational Research; Higher Education); **North American Studies** (American Studies; Canadian Studies); **Sinology Abroad** (Asian Studies; South Asian Studies)

Schools
International Law and Business (Economics; English; International Business; International Law; Law)

History: Founded 1950, acquired present status 1952.

Academic Year: September to July (September-January; February-July)

Admission Requirements: Graduation from high school and entrance examination

Fees: None

Main Language(s) of Instruction: Chinese

International Co-operation: Exchange programmes with more than 20 foreign universities

Degrees and Diplomas: *Zhuanke Certificate of Graduation*: 2-3 yrs; *Bachelor's Degree (BA)*: 4 yrs; *Master's Degree (MA)*: a further 3 yrs. Also Certificates (2 yrs)

Student Services: Academic counselling, Canteen, Cultural centre, Foreign student adviser, Health services, Nursery care, Social counselling, Sports facilities

Student Residential Facilities: For c. 3,000 students

Libraries: c. 500,000 vols

Publications: World Children's Literature *(quarterly)*
Last Updated: 04/12/08

SICHUAN NORMAL UNIVERSITY

Shizishanlu, Chengdu, Sichuan Province 610066
Tel: +86(28) 4770706
Fax: +86(28) 4761103
EMail: scsdxcb@sicnu.edu.cn
Website: http://www.sicnu.edu.cn

President: Zhou Jieming

Colleges
Nanyang

Departments
Accountancy (Accountancy); **Biology** (Biology); **Chemistry** (Chemistry); **Chinese for Foreigners** (Chinese); **Computer Science** (Computer Science); **Education** (Education); **Geography** (Geography); **History** (History); **Law and Politics** (Law; Political Sciences); **Management** (Management); **Mathematics** (Mathematics); **Physical Education** (Physical Education); **Physics** (Physics); **Real Estate** (Real Estate); **Tourism** (Tourism)

Research Institutes
Ancient Chinese Literature (Chinese; Literature); **Chemical Applications New Technology** (Chemical Engineering); **Chinese Language and Literature** (Chinese; Literature); **Marxist Theories** (Philosophy; Political Sciences); **Solid State Physics** (Solid State Physics)

Schools
Biology and Chemistry (Biology; Chemistry); **Chinese Language and Literature** (Chinese; Literature); **Educational Sciences** (Educational Sciences); **Film and Television** (Cinema and Television; Film; Radio and Television Broadcasting); **Foreign Languages** (Modern Languages); **Information Sciences** (Information Sciences); **Music and Painting** (Music; Painting and Drawing)

History: Founded as college 1952, acquired present status and title 1986. Under the jurisdiction of Sichuan Provincial Authorities.

Academic Year: August to June (August-December; January-June)

Admission Requirements: Graduation from senior middle school and entrance examination

Main Language(s) of Instruction: Chinese

Degrees and Diplomas: *Bachelor's Degree*; *Master's Degree*

Student Residential Facilities: Yes

Libraries: SNU Central Library, c. 1.5m. vols

Publications: Journal of Sichuan Normal University; Teaching and Management Research
Last Updated: 01/10/08

SICHUAN UNIVERSITY

Jiuyanqiao, Chengdu, Sichuan Province 610064
Tel: +86(28) 85407199 +86(28) 85405773
Fax: +86(28) 85405773
EMail: wsc@scu.edu.cn
Website: http://www.scu.edu.cn

President: Heping Xie

Colleges
Architecture and Environment (Architecture; Civil Engineering; Environmental Engineering; Environmental Studies; Mechanical

Engineering); **Business**; **Chemical Engineering** (Chemical Engineering); **Chemistry** (Applied Chemistry; Chemistry); **Computer Science** (Computer Science); **Economics** (Economics; Finance; Taxation); **Electrical Engineering and Information Technology**; **Electronics and Information Engineering** (Electronic Engineering; Information Sciences); **Foreign Languages** (Literature; Modern Languages); **History and Culture** (Cultural Studies; History; Tourism); **Hydraulic Engineering**; **Law** (Law); **Life Sciences** (Bioengineering; Biological and Life Sciences; Biology); **Light Industry** (Chemistry; Engineering; Food Science); **Manufacturing Science and Engineering** (Mechanical Engineering; Production Engineering); **Material Science and Engineering** (Materials Engineering; Polymer and Plastics Technology); **Mathematics** (Applied Mathematics; Mathematics); **Medicine**; **Pharmacy** (Pharmacy); **Physics and Technology** (Applied Physics; Physics; Technology); **Politics** (Political Sciences); **Polymer Science and Engineering** (Polymer and Plastics Technology); **Preclinical and Forensic Medicine**; **Public Health**; **Software Engineering**

Further Information: Also Chinese Language Centre for foreign students

History: Founded 1896 as East-West School. Merged with Chengdu University of Science and Technology and West China University of Medical Sciences in 1995 as Sichuan Union University. In 1999 the name of the merged university changed back to Sichuan University.

Admission Requirements: High School Diploma

Fees: (Yuan): 14,500-37,000 per annum depending on faculty and degree

Main Language(s) of Instruction: Chinese

Degrees and Diplomas: *Bachelor's Degree*; *Master's Degree (MBA)*; *Doctor's Degree*

Student Residential Facilities: Yes

Special Facilities: History Museum. Experimental farms

Libraries: c. 4m. vols; c. 30 subscriptions to periodicals

Publications: Journal of Sichuan University
Last Updated: 04/12/08

SICHUAN UNIVERSITY OF SCIENCE AND ENGINEERING

Zigong, Sichuan Province 643033
Tel: +86(813) 5505808
Fax: +86(813) 5505800
Website: http://www.suse.edu.cn

President: Liang Zhiquan

International Relations: Liu Jun

Departments
Bioengineering (Bioengineering); **Economics and Law**; **Electronic Engineering and Information Technology** (Electronic Engineering; Information Technology); **Engineering Management** (Engineering Management); **Materials Science and Chemical Engineering**; **Mechanical and Electrical Engineering** (Electrical Engineering; Mechanical Engineering); **Modern Laguages**; **Physics**

History: Founded 1965 as East China University of Chemical Technology. Acquired present title 2003 following merger of Sichuan Institute of Light Industry and Chemical Technology, Zigong Teachers College, Zigong Polytechnic College and Zigong Institute of Education.

Degrees and Diplomas: *Bachelor's Degree*; *Master's Degree*
Last Updated: 09/07/09

SOOCHOW UNIVERSITY (SU)

1 Shizi Street, Suzhou, Jiangsu Province 215006
Tel: +86(512) 65112308
Fax: +86(512) 65221028
EMail: t_huangxing@suda.edu.cn.
Website: http://www.suda.edu.cn

President: Zhu Xiulin
Tel: +86(512) 65112798, Fax: +86(512) 65231918

Vice-President: Zhang Xueguang
Tel: +86(512) 65113042, Fax: +86(512) 65231918

International Relations: Huang Xing
Tel: +86(512) 65112360 EMail: t_huangxing@suda.edu.cn

Schools
Applied Technology (Accountancy; Computer Science; Electrical Engineering; Electronic Engineering; Fashion Design; Tourism) *Dean*: Shen Meiyuan; **Arts** (Fine Arts; Music; Textile Design) *Dean*: Liao Jun; **Business** (Accountancy; Banking; Economics; Finance; Management) *Dean*: Wang Xieqiu; **Chemistry** *Dean*: Ji Shunjun; **Computer Science and Technology** *Dean*: Zhu Qiaoming; **Electronic Engineering** (Computer Science; Electrical Engineering; Engineering; Industrial Management; Mechanical Engineering) *Dean*: Zhao Heming; **Foreign Languages** (English; French; Japanese; Modern Languages; Russian) *Dean*: Xu Qinggen; **Humanities** (Arts and Humanities; Chinese; Literature; Mass Communication; Secretarial Studies) *Dean*: Luo Shijin; **Law** (Comparative Law; Criminal Law; International Law; Law; Private Law; Public Law) *Dean*: Ai Yongming; **Life Sciences** (Aquaculture; Biology; Chemistry; Sericulture) *Dean*: Zhang Xueguang; **Materials Engineering** (Materials Engineering; Textile Design) *Dean*: Chen Guoqiang; **Mathematics** (Mathematics; Software Engineering; Statistics) *Dean*: Tang Zhongming; **Medicine** (Dentistry; Medicine; Nursing; Pharmacy; Surgery; Traditional Eastern Medicine); **Overseas Education** (Business Administration; Chinese; International Studies; Management) *Dean*: Wang Jiexian; **Physical Education** (Physical Education; Sports) *Dean*: Wang Jiahong; **Physics and Technology** (Energy Engineering; Physics; Technology) *Dean*: Gu Jihua; **Political Science and Public Administration** (Business Administration; Political Sciences; Public Administration; Public Relations; Social Sciences) *Dean*: Zhou Kezhen; **Social Studies** (Archiving; History; Social Studies; Tourism) *Dean*: Wang Weiping

History: Founded 1900. Merged with Suzhou College of Sericulture 1995, Suzhou Institute of Silk Technology 1997 and Suzhou Medical College 2000.

Academic Year: September to July (September-January; February-July)

Admission Requirements: Graduation from senior middle school and entrance examination

Fees: (Yuan): c. 14,000 per annum

Main Language(s) of Instruction: Chinese

International Co-operation: SU-UA Dual Degree programme with Athabasca University, Canada, and Troy State University, USA. Cooperation with universities in Korea; Australia; Japan; Germany; France; UK

Accrediting Agencies: State Commission of Education

Degrees and Diplomas: *Bachelor's Degree*: 4 yrs; *Master's Degree*: a further 2-3 yrs; *Doctor's Degree (PhD)*: a further 2-3 yrs

Student Services: Academic counselling, Canteen, Employment services, Foreign student adviser, Foreign Studies Centre, Health services, Language programs, Nursery care, Social counselling, Sports facilities

Student Residential Facilities: Yes

Libraries: c. 3.78 m. vols

Publications: Journal of Soochow University

Press or Publishing House: Soochow University Press
Last Updated: 04/12/08

SOUTH CENTRAL UNIVERSITY FOR NATIONALITIES

5 Minyuan Road, Wuhan, Hubei Province 430074
Tel: +86(27) 87800443
Fax: +86(27) 87800443
Website: http://www.scuec.edu.cn

President: Peng Yingmin (1996-)

International Relations: Du Zhangwei
Tel: +86(27) 87807805, Fax: +86(27) 87807805

Departments
Biomedical Engineering (Biomedical Engineering); **Chemistry** (Chemistry); **Computer Science** (Computer Science); **Electronic Engineering** (Electronic Engineering); **Foreign Languages** (Modern Languages); **History** (History); **Law** (Law)

Schools

Economics (Economics); **History and Culture** (Cultural Studies; Ethnology; History); **Liberal Arts** (Arts and Humanities; Chinese; Communication Studies; Fine Arts; Journalism; Literature); **Management** (Management); **Tourism** (Tourism)

History: Founded 1951 as Central College for Nationalities, acquired present title 1952.

Fees: (Yuan): c. 3,000

Main Language(s) of Instruction: Chinese

Accrediting Agencies: Commission for Nationalities

Degrees and Diplomas: *Bachelor's Degree*: 4 yrs; *Master's Degree*: a further 3 yrs

Student Services: Academic counselling, Canteen, Cultural centre, Employment services, Foreign student adviser, Foreign Studies Centre, Health services, Language programs, Nursery care, Social counselling, Sports facilities

Special Facilities: Museum. Movie Studio

Libraries: c. 860,000 vols

Publications: Higher Education for Nationalities; Journal of South Central University for Nationalities

Press or Publishing House: University Press

SOUTH CHINA AGRICULTURAL UNIVERSITY

Wushan, Guangzhou, Guangdong Province 510642
Tel: +86(20) 85511299 Ext. 2342
Fax: +86(20) 85511299 Ext. 2344
EMail: xcb@scau.edu.cn
Website: http://www.scau.edu.cn

President: Chen Xiaoyang EMail: sec@scau.edu.cn

Colleges

Agriculture (Agriculture; Agronomy); **Animal Husbandry** (Animal Husbandry); **Economics and Management** (Economics; Management); **Engineering**; **Environment and Natural Resources** (Environmental Studies; Natural Resources); **Food Science** (Food Science); **Foreign Languages**; **Forestry** (Forestry); **Horticulture** (Horticulture); **Humanities** (Arts and Humanities); **Law**; **Life Sciences** (Biological and Life Sciences); **Media** (Media Studies); **Public Administration** (Public Administration); **Science** (Mathematics and Computer Science; Natural Sciences); **Veterinary Medicine** (Veterinary Science); **Water Conservation** (Water Management)

Departments

Sports (Physical Education; Sports)

Schools

Polytechnic

History: Founded 1909 as Lingnan Agricultural School and Guagdong Agricultural School, acquired present status and title 1984. Under the jurisdiction of the Ministry of Agriculture and the Provincial Government.

Academic Year: September to July (September-January; March-July)

Admission Requirements: Graduation from senior middle school and entrance examination

Main Language(s) of Instruction: Chinese

Accrediting Agencies: Ministry of Agriculture

Degrees and Diplomas: *Bachelor's Degree*: 4-5 yrs; *Master's Degree*: a further 3 yrs; *Doctor's Degree*: a further 3 yrs

Student Residential Facilities: Yes

Libraries: Central Library, c. 760,000 vols

Publications: Journal of South China Agricultural University *(quarterly)*
Last Updated: 04/12/08

SOUTH CHINA NORMAL UNIVERSITY

Shipai, Guangzhou, Guangdong Province 510631
Tel: +86(20) 85211062
Fax: +86(20) 85212131
EMail: wsh3@scnu.edu.cn
Website: http://www.scnu.edu.cn

President: Liu Ming

Colleges

Life Sciences (Biological and Life Sciences); **Nanhai** (Administration; Applied Mathematics; Chinese; Computer Science; E-Business/Commerce; Educational Technology; Finance; Information Technology; Law; Political Sciences; Software Engineering)

Research Centres

Audiovisual (Cinema and Television); **Computer and Information** (Computer Science; Information Technology); **Molecular Biological Engineering** (Molecular Biology)

Research Institutes

Ancient Works and Documents (Ancient Books; Documentation Techniques); **Economics** (Economics); **Educational Sciences** (Educational Sciences); **Electronic Technology** (Electronic Engineering); **Environmental Science** (Environmental Studies); **Fine Arts** (Fine Arts); **Philosophical Management** (Philosophy); **Quantum-Electronics** (Physics)

Schools

Chemistry and Environment (Chemistry; Environmental Studies); **Chinese Language and Literature** (Chinese; Literature); **Computer Science** (Computer Science); **Economics and Management** (Economics); **Educational Information Technology** (Information Management; Information Technology); **Educational Sciences** (Education; Educational Sciences; Educational Technology; Psychology); **Fine Arts** (Fine Arts); **Foreign Studies** (English; Japanese; Literature; Modern Languages; Russian); **Geography** (Geography); **History and Culture** (Cultural Studies; History); **Law** (Law); **Mathematics** (Mathematics); **Music** (Music); **Physical Education** (Physical Education); **Physics and Telecommunications Engineering** (Physics; Telecommunications Engineering); **Politics and Administration** (Administration; Political Sciences); **Public Administration** (Public Administration); **Telecommunications Engineering** (Telecommunications Engineering); **Tourism Management** (Management; Tourism)

Further Information: Also Language and Culture Training Centre for foreign students

History: Founded 1933 as Teachers College, Xiangqin University. Acquired present title 1982.

Academic Year: November to June (November-January; February-June)

Admission Requirements: Graduation from senior middle school and entrance examination

Degrees and Diplomas: *Bachelor's Degree*: 4 yrs; *Master's Degree*: a further 3 yrs; *Doctor's Degree*: a further 2-3 yrs. Also Postdoctorate degrees

Libraries: c. 1,7m. Vols

Publications: Chinese Language and Literature *(monthly)*; Journal of South China Normal University; Moral Education for Primary Schools
Last Updated: 05/12/08

SOUTH CHINA UNIVERSITY OF TECHNOLOGY (SCUT)

371 Wushan Road, Guangzhou, Guangdong Province 510641
Tel: +86(20) 87110948
Fax: +86(20) 85516862
EMail: faoc@scut.edu.cn
Website: http://www.scut.edu.cn

President: Yuanyuan Li (2003-)
Tel: +86(20) 8711008, Fax: +86(20) 85516386
EMail: yyli@scut.edu.cn

International Relations: Yiwu Hu
Tel: +86(20) 87110973 EMail: flywhu@scut.edu.cn

Schools

Architecture (Architecture; Civil Engineering; Town Planning); **Arts** (Singing); **Automation Science and Engineering**; **Business Administration** (Business Administration); **Civil Engineering and Transportation** (Civil Engineering; Transport and Communications); **Computer Science and Engineering** (Computer Engineering; Computer Science; Software Engineering); **Electric Power** (Electrical Engineering; Power Engineering); **Electronic and**

Information Engineering (Electronic Engineering); Foreign Languages (English; Japanese; Modern Languages); International Education (International and Comparative Education); Light Chemistry and Food Science; Materials Science and Engineering (Materials Engineering); Mechanical and Automotive Engineering (Automotive Engineering; Mechanical Engineering); Physical Education; Political Science and Public Administration (Political Sciences; Public Administration); Science

History: Founded 1952 as South China Institute of Technology.

Academic Year: September to July (September-February; March-July)

Admission Requirements: High school diploma

Fees: (Yuan): 21,580 per annum

Main Language(s) of Instruction: Chinese

International Co-operation: With universities in USA, Australia, United Kingdom, France

Accrediting Agencies: Ministry of Education

Degrees and Diplomas: Bachelor's Degree: 4 yrs; Master's Degree: 3 yrs; Doctor's Degree: 3 yrs

Student Services: Academic counselling, Canteen, Cultural centre, Employment services, Foreign student adviser, Foreign Studies Centre, Handicapped facilities, Health services, Language programs, Nursery care, Social counselling, Sports facilities

Student Residential Facilities: Yes

Libraries: c. 1.64m. Vols
Last Updated: 05/12/08

SOUTH CHINA UNIVERSITY OF TROPICAL AGRICULTURE

Baodao Xincun, Danzhou, Hainan Province 571737
Tel: +86(890) 3300157
Fax: +86(890) 3300157
EMail: shuji@scuta.org; yuanxiaozhang@scuta.org
Website: http://www.scuta.edu.cn

President: Yu Rangshui

International Relations: Huang Xunjiang

Schools
Agronomy (Agronomy; Crop Production; Environmental Management; Horticulture; Landscape Architecture; Plant and Crop Protection; Tropical Agriculture); Arts and Law (Arts and Humanities; Economics; Law; Public Relations; Secretarial Studies); Economics and Trade (Business and Commerce; Computer Science; Economics; Finance; Mathematics; Technology); Technology (Automotive Engineering; Electrical Engineering; Engineering; Food Science; Materials Engineering; Technology)

History: Founded 1958 as South China College of Tropical Crops, acquired present title 1996.

Degrees and Diplomas: Bachelor's Degree; Master's Degree; Doctor's Degree

Libraries: c. 270,000 vols

Publications: Chinese Journal of Tropical Agriculture; Chinese Journal of Tropical Crops

SOUTHEAST UNIVERSITY

2 Sipailou, Nanjing, Jiangsu Province 210096
Tel: +86(25) 3792412
Fax: +86(25) 3615736
EMail: oic@seu.edu.cn
Website: http://www.seu.edu.cn

President: Hong Yi

Departments
Chinese Literature; Mathematics (Applied Mathematics); Philosophy and Science (Natural Sciences; Philosophy); Physics (Physics); Political Science and Public Administration; Tourism

Schools
Architecture (Architecture; Civil Engineering; Environmental Engineering; Mechanical Engineering; Real Estate); Arts (Fine Arts); Automation (Automation and Control Engineering); Biological Science and Medical Engineering (Biomedical Engineering);

Chemistry and Chemical Engineering (Chemical Engineering; Chemistry); Civil Engineering (Civil Engineering); Computer Science and Engineering (Computer Science; Engineering); Economics and Management (Accountancy; Business Administration; Economics; Finance; Industrial Management; Management); Electrical Engineering (Electrical Engineering); Electronic Science and Engineering (Electronic Engineering); Energy and Environment; Foreign Languages (Modern Languages); Humanities (Arts and Humanities; Chinese; Law; Philosophy; Public Administration; Tourism); Information Science and Engineering (Information Sciences); Instrument Science and Engineering (Measurement and Precision Engineering); Law; Materials Science and Engineering (Materials Engineering); Mechanical Engineering (Mechanical Engineering); Medicine; Public Health; Science (Natural Sciences); Transportation (Civil Engineering; Road Engineering; Road Transport); Vocational Technical Education; Wuxi

History: Founded 1902 as Sanjiang Teachers College, acquired present title 1988. Merged with Nanjing Railway Medical College 2000.

Main Language(s) of Instruction: Chinese

Degrees and Diplomas: Bachelor's Degree; Master's Degree; Doctor's Degree

Libraries: c. 1.4m. vols

Publications: Southeast University Journal of Higher Education
Last Updated: 05/12/08

SOUTHWEST FORESTRY COLLEGE

Kunming, Yunnan Province 650224
Tel: +86(871) 3863211 +86(871) 3862829
Fax: +86(871) 5637217
EMail: oicswfc@swfc.edu.cn
Website: http://www.swfc.edu.cn

President: Liu Huimin

International Relations: Li Maobiao

Departments
Computer and Information Science (Computer Science); Environmental Science and Engineering; Fundamental Courses (Chemistry; Mathematics; Physical Education; Physics); Humanities and Social Sciences (Social Sciences)

Faculties
Continuing Education; Economic Management (Management)

Schools
Conservation Biology; Ecotourism (Ecology; Tourism); Landscape Architecture and Gardening (Landscape Architecture); Natural Resources; Transportation, Machinery and Civil Engineering (Civil Engineering; Machine Building; Transport and Communications); Wood Science and Interior Design

History: Founded 1978 as Yunnan Forestry College, acquired present name 1983.

Degrees and Diplomas: Bachelor's Degree; Master's Degree
Last Updated: 05/12/08

SOUTHWEST JIAOTONG UNIVERSITY (SWJTU)

111, 1st Section, Northern 2nd Ring Road, Chengdu, Sichuan Province 610031
Tel: +86(28) 7600340
Fax: +86(28) 7605147
EMail: fad@home.swjtu.edu.cn
Website: http://www.swjtu.edu.cn

President: Chunyang Chen

Colleges
Professional Training

Schools
Adult Education (Adult Education); Architecture; Arts and Communications (Communication Arts); Biology (Biology); Civil Engineering; Communications and Transport Management (Transport Management); Computer Science and Information Engineering (Computer Science; Engineering; Information Technology); Economics and Business Administration; E-Education; Electrical Engineering (Electrical Engineering); Environmental

Science and Engineering (Environmental Engineering; Environmental Studies); **Foreign Languages** (Modern Languages); **Humanities and Social Sciences**; **Information Science and Technology** (Information Sciences; Information Technology); **Logistics**; **Materials Science and Engineering** (Engineering; Materials Engineering); **Mechanical Engineering** (Mechanical Engineering); **Pharmacy**; **Public Administration** (Public Administration); **Science** (Chemistry; Mathematics; Physics); **Software Engineering** (Software Engineering); **Tourism**; **Traffic and Transportation** (Transport and Communications)

History: Founded 1896 as Imperial Chinese Railway College, acquired present title 1984.

Main Language(s) of Instruction: Chinese, English

International Co-operation: With universities in France; Australia; Canada; USA

Degrees and Diplomas: *Bachelor's Degree*; *Master's Degree*; *Doctor's Degree*

Student Services: Academic counselling, Canteen, Employment services, Foreign student adviser, Foreign Studies Centre, Health services, Language programs, Nursery care, Social counselling, Sports facilities

Libraries: 1,100,000 vols

Publications: Journal of Southwest Jiaotong University; Journal of Transportation Engineering and Information
Last Updated: 05/12/08

SOUTHWEST PETROLEUM UNIVERSITY

Xindu Avenue 8#, Xindu District, Chengdu,
Sichuan Province 637001
Tel: +86(817) 83032308
EMail: swpuaa@swpu.edu.cn
Website: http://www.swpi.edu.cn

President: Du Zhimin

Departments
Foreign Languages (English; Modern Languages); **Physical Education** (Physical Education)

Schools
Chemistry and Chemical Engineering (Chemical Engineering; Chemistry); **Civil Engineering and Architecture** (Architecture; Civil Engineering); **Computer Science** (Computer Science; Information Technology); **Economics and Management** (Economics; Management; Marketing); **Electronics and Information Engineering**; **Humanities and Social Sciences** (Arts and Humanities; Social Sciences); **Law** (Law); **Material Science and Engineering** (Materials Engineering); **Mechanical Engineering** (Machine Building; Management; Mechanical Engineering); **Petroleum Engineering** (Petroleum and Gas Engineering); **Resources and Environmental Engineering** (Environmental Engineering; Natural Resources); **Science** (Natural Sciences)

History: Founded 1958 as Sichuan Petroleum Institute, acquired present title 1970.

Main Language(s) of Instruction: Chinese

Degrees and Diplomas: *Bachelor's Degree*; *Master's Degree*; *Doctor's Degree*

Libraries: c. 930,000 vols

Publications: Journal of Southwest Petroleum Institute
Last Updated: 05/12/08

SOUTHWEST UNIVERSITY

No.2 Tiansheng Road, Beibei District, Chongqing,
Sichuan Province 400715
Tel: +86(23) 68250773
Fax: +86(23) 68863805
EMail: efoffice@swu.cn.edu.cn
Website: http://www.swu.edu.cn/english/index.html

President: Song Naiqing
Tel: +86(23) 68252517, Fax: +86(23) 68866796
EMail: songnq@swnu.edu.cn

International Relations: Wang Jing
Tel: +86(23) 68254388 EMail: Jing67@swnu.edu.cn

Colleges
Agronomy and Biotechnology (Agronomy; Biotechnology); **Animal Science and Technology** (Animal Husbandry); **Computer Science** (Computer Science); **Computer Science and Information Sciences** (Computer Science; Information Sciences; Software Engineering); **Economics and Management** (Economics; Management); **Education** (Education; Educational Sciences); **Engineering and Technology** (Agricultural Engineering; Automation and Control Engineering; Civil Engineering); **Food Science**; **Horticulture and Landscape** (Horticulture; Landscape Architecture); **Journalism and Communication** (Communication Studies; Journalism); **Law**; **Material Science and Engineering** (Materials Engineering); **Music** (Music); **Pharmacy and Chinese Medicine**; **Physical Education** (Physical Education); **Plant Protection**; **Resources and Environment** (Natural Resources; Soil Science; Water Management); **Textile and Garment** (Clothing and Sewing; Textile Design)

Departments
Economics and Trade (Business and Commerce; Economics); **Library and Information Science** (Information Sciences; Library Science)

Schools
Chemistry and Chemical Engineering (Chemical Engineering; Chemistry); **Culture and Social Development** (Cultural Studies; Social Studies); **Fine Arts** (Fine Arts); **Foreign Languages** (Modern Languages); **Geographical Sciences**; **History, Culture and Ethnology** (Cultural Studies; Ethnology; History); **Life Sciences** (Aquaculture; Biological and Life Sciences); **Literature** (Chinese; Literature); **Management** (Management); **Mathematics and Statistics** (Mathematics; Statistics); **Natural Resources and Environment** (Environmental Studies; Natural Resources); **Physics and Technology** (Electronic Engineering; Information Technology; Physics); **Political Science and Public Administration** (Philosophy; Political Sciences; Public Administration); **Psychology** (Psychology)

History: Founded 1950, acquired present name 2005 through the incorporation of former Southwest China Normal University and Southwest Agricultural University

Main Language(s) of Instruction: Chinese and English

International Co-operation: With universities in US; UK; Russian Federation; Japan; South Korea; France; Germany; Canada; Italy; Israel; Austria; New Zealand

Degrees and Diplomas: *Bachelor's Degree*; *Master's Degree*; *Doctor's Degree*

Libraries: c. 1.3m. vols

Publications: Higher Education Research; Journal of Southwest China Normal University
Last Updated: 05/12/08

SOUTHWEST UNIVERSITY FOR NATIONALITIES

16, 4th Section, Yihuan Nanlu, Chengdu, Sichuan Province 610041
Tel: +86(28) 5522042 +86(28) 5522282
Fax: +86(28) 5523220
EMail: jwc@swun.edu.cn
Website: http://211.83.241.165/swun/xxgk/

President: Dayun Chen

Colleges
Arts (Fine Arts); **Chemistry and Environment Protection Engineering** (Chemistry; Environmental Engineering); **Computer Science and Technology** (Computer Engineering; Computer Science); **Economics** (Economics; Finance); **Electric Information Engineering** (Electrical Engineering); **Foreign Languages** (Modern Languages); **International Education**; **Law** (Law; Management); **Life Sciences** (Biological and Life Sciences); **Literature**; **Management** (Management); **Tibetan Studies** (Asian Studies; Native Language); **Tourism and History** (History; Tourism); **Yi Studies** (Native Language)

Departments
Physical Education (Physical Education); **Sociology** (Sociology)

Research Institutes
Nationalities

History: Founded 1951.

Main Language(s) of Instruction: Chinese

Degrees and Diplomas: *Bachelor's Degree*; *Master's Degree*; *Doctor's Degree*

Last Updated: 05/12/08

SOUTHWEST UNIVERSITY OF POLITICAL SCIENCE AND LAW (SUPSL)

Shapingba, Chongqing, Sichuan Province 400031
Tel: +86(23) 65342111
Fax: +86(23) 65316074
Website: http://www.swupl.edu.cn

President: Chen Bin (1998-)

Schools

Administrative Law; **Adult Education**; **Applied Law** (Law); **Civil and Commercial Law** (Civil Law; Commercial Law; Family Studies); **Criminal Investigation Law**; **Economic and Trade Law**; **Economics** (Economics; Finance; International Business); **Foreign Languages**; **Journalism and Communication**; **Law** (Criminal Law; Law); **Management** (Business Administration; Management; Political Sciences); **Poltics and Public Affairs** (Philosophy; Political Sciences; Public Administration); **Postgraduate**

History: Founded 1953 as Southwest University of People's Revolution, acquired present title 1995.

Academic Year: September to July (September-January; February-July)

Admission Requirements: Graduation from senior middle school and entrance examination

Fees: (Yuan): c. 3,500 per annum

Main Language(s) of Instruction: Chinese, English

Accrediting Agencies: Education Committee of Chongqing Municipality Government

Degrees and Diplomas: *Bachelor's Degree*: 4 yrs; *Master's Degree*: a further 3 yrs; *Doctor's Degree (PhD)*: a further 3 yrs

Student Services: Academic counselling, Canteen, Cultural centre, Employment services, Foreign student adviser, Foreign Studies Centre, Health services, Language programs, Nursery care, Social counselling, Sports facilities

Student Residential Facilities: Yes

Special Facilities: Judicial Observatory

Libraries: c. 700,000 vols

Publications: Law Journal of SUPSL *(bimonthly)*; Modern Law Science *(bimonthly)*

Last Updated: 05/12/08

SOUTHWEST UNIVERSITY OF SCIENCE AND TECHNOLOGY (SWUST)

Mianyang, Sichuan Province 621010
Tel: +86(816) 2419114
Fax: +86(816) 2419004
EMail: fao@swust.edu.cn
Website: http://www.swust.edu.cn/

President: Wu Jian

International Relations: Zhong Wenqiao

Departments

Automation Engineering and Mechatronics (Automation and Control Engineering; Mechanics); **Civil Engineering and Architecture**; **Computer Science** (Computer Science); **Construction Engineering** (Construction Engineering); **Economics and Law** (Economics; Law); **Environmental Engineering** (Environmental Engineering); **Information Sciences and Control Engineering** (Automation and Control Engineering; Information Sciences); **Materials Science and Engineering** (Materials Engineering); **Physical Education**; **Social Science**

History: Founded 1952 as Chongqing Civil Engineering School, acquired present status 1978 and name 2000.

Degrees and Diplomas: *Bachelor's Degree*; *Master's Degree*

SOUTHWESTERN UNIVERSITY OF FINANCE AND ECONOMICS

55 Guanghuacun, Chengdu, Sichuan Province 610074
Tel: +86(28) 7352227
Fax: +86(28) 7352040
EMail: ig@swufe.edu.cn
Website: http://www.swufe.edu.cn

President: Wang Yuguo

International Relations: Jing Guang

Departments

Agricultural Economics (Agricultural Economics); **Economic Information Management** (Economics); **Economics** (Economics); **Foreign Languages**; **Law** (Law); **Planning and Statistics** (Statistics); **Political Education** (Political Sciences)

Schools

Accountancy (Accountancy); **Finance** (Finance); **Insurance** (Insurance); **International Business** (International Business; International Economics); **Public Finance and Taxation** (Taxation)

History: Founded 1952 as Sichuan Institute of Finance and Economics. Acquired present status and title 1985.

Main Language(s) of Instruction: Chinese

Degrees and Diplomas: *Bachelor's Degree*; *Master's Degree*; *Doctor's Degree*

Libraries: c. 950,000 vols

Publications: Science of Finance and Economics

Last Updated: 05/12/08

SUN YAT-SEN UNIVERSITY (SYSU)

135 Xingangxilu, Guangzhou, Guangdong Province 510275
Tel: +86(20) 84111085
Fax: +86(20) 84039173
EMail: adpo01@zsu.edu.cn
Website: http://www.sysu.edu.cn

President: Daren Huang (1999-)
Tel: +86(20) 84111683, Fax: +86(20) 84111587
EMail: hdr@sysu.edu.cn

Director, President's Office: Wenbiao Zhang
Tel: +86(20) 84111585, Fax: +86(20) 84111587
EMail: adpoh@sysu.edu.cn

International Relations: Fukang Xie, Director, Office of International Cooperation and Exchange
Tel: +86(20) 84111896, Fax: +86(20) 84036860
EMail: adeao@sysu.edu.cn

Colleges

Lingnan *(Lingnan College)* (Business Administration; Economics; Finance; Insurance; International Business; Taxation) *Dean*: Yuan Shu

Schools

Business (Accountancy; Business Administration; Finance; Hotel Management; Management; Marketing; Tourism) *Dean*: Ming-Hai Wei; **Chemistry and Chemical Engineering** (Applied Chemistry; Chemical Engineering; Chemistry; Materials Engineering; Polymer and Plastics Technology) *Dean*: Xiaoming Chen; **Continuing Education** *Dean*: Guodu Zhao; **Education** *Dean*: Minghua Zhong; **Foreign Languages** (English; French; German; Japanese; Modern Languages) *Dean*: Guowen Huang; **Geographical Science and Planning** (Geography; Geology; Management; Regional Planning; Surveying and Mapping; Tourism; Town Planning) *Dean*: Jigang Bad; **Government** *Dean*: Jiantao Ren; **Graduate Studies** *Dean*: Da-Ren Huang; **Humanities** (Anthropology; Arts and Humanities; Chinese; History; Literature; Philosophy) *Dean*: Chunsheng Chen; **Information Sciences and Technology** (Computer Science; Electronic Engineering; Information Sciences; Telecommunications Engineering) *Dean*: Jiwu Huang; **Law** (Law; Political Sciences; Sociology) *Dean*: Heng Liu; **Life Sciences** (Biochemistry; Biological and Life Sciences; Biology; Biotechnology; Ecology; Pharmacology) *Dean*: Anlong Xu; **Mathematics and Computer Science** (Mathematics and Computer Science) *Dean*: Xi-Ping Zhu; **Nursing** *Dean*: Liming You; **On Line Education** *Dean*: Guodu Zhao; **Overseas Educational Exchange** *Dean*: Ningsheng Xu; **Pharmaceutical Sciences** *Dean*: Xinzi Chen; **Physical Sciences and Engineering**

(Applied Physics; Mechanical Engineering; Mechanics; Physics) *Dean*: Ning-Sheng Xu; **Pre-Clinical Medicine** (Biomedical Engineering; Forensic Medicine and Dentistry; Laboratory Techniques) *Dean*: Fukang Xie; **Public Health** *Dean*: Wenhua Ling; **Software Engineering** *Dean*: Jiwu Huang; **Stomatology** *(Guang Hua) Dean*: Junqi Ling

History: Founded 1924 as Guangdong University. Renamed Zhongshan University 1926. Acquired present title and status 2001, following merger with Sun Yat-Sen University of Medical Sciences.

Academic Year: September to July (September-February; March-July)

Admission Requirements: Graduation from senior middle school and entrance examination

Fees: (Yuan): c. 5,000 per annum

Main Language(s) of Instruction: Chinese

International Co-operation: Yes

Accrediting Agencies: Ministry of Education

Degrees and Diplomas: *Bachelor's Degree*: 4 yrs; *Master's Degree*: a further 2-3 yrs; *Doctor's Degree (PhD)*: 3 yrs following Master

Student Services: Academic counselling, Canteen, Employment services, Foreign student adviser, Foreign Studies Centre, Health services, Language programs, Nursery care, Sports facilities

Student Residential Facilities: Yes

Special Facilities: Anthropology Museum

Libraries: c. 4m. vols

Publications: Journal *(quarterly)*; Journal of Sun Yat-Sen University *(bimonthly)*; Population in the South; Studies of Hong Kong and Macao, The Economy of Pearl River Delta *(biannually)*; Studies on Higher Education

Press or Publishing House: Sun Yat-Sen University Press
Last Updated: 05/12/08

SUZHOU UNIVERSITY OF SCIENCE AND TECHNOLOGY

1701 Binhe Road, New District, Suzhou, Jiangsu Province 215011
Tel: +86(512) 8255226
Fax: +86(512) 8242298
EMail: wsc@mail.usts.edu.cn
Website: http://web.usts.edu.cn/english/index.htm

President: He Ruoquan

Departments
Applied Mathematics; **Applied Physics** (Applied Physics); **Architecture** (Architecture); **Biology**; **Chemistry and Chemical Engineering**; **Chinese**; **Civil Engineering**; **Communication Science**; **Education** (Education); **Electronics and Information Engineering**; **Environmental Science and Engineering** (Environmental Engineering; Environmental Studies); **Fine Arts** (Fine Arts); **Foreign Languages** (Modern Languages); **History and Sociology**; **Music** (Music); **Physical Education** (Physical Education); **Physical Education**; **Political Science and Public Administration**; **Social Sciences**; **Urban and Environmental Science**

Schools
Management (Management)

History: Founded 2001 through the merging of the former Suzhou Institute of Urban Construction and Environmental Protection and the former Suzhou Railway Teachers College.

Main Language(s) of Instruction: Chinese

Degrees and Diplomas: *Bachelor's Degree*; *Master's Degree*
Last Updated: 09/12/08

TAISHAN MEDICAL UNIVERSITY

2 East Yingsheng Road, Tai'an, Shandong Province 271000
Tel: +86(538) 6222034 +86(538) 6229956 +86(538) 6236359
Fax: +86(538) 6222505
EMail: wsb@tsmc.edu.cn; tmcic@public.taptt.sd.cn
Website: http://www.taishanmedicaluniversity.com

President: Jiafu Wang
Tel: +86(538) 6222002 +86(538) 6229902
EMail: jfwang@tsmc.edu.cn

International Relations: Shouliang Wang
EMail: shouliangwang@hotmail.com

Departments
Basic Medicine (Medicine); **Clinical Medicine** (Medicine); **English** (English); **Information Sciences**; **Pharmacy** (Pharmacy); **Postgraduate Studies**; **Practice and Teaching** (Education; Pedagogy); **Radiology**; **Social Sciences**

Faculties
Adult Education (Adult Education; Medicine); **Chemistry and Chemical Engineering** (Chemical Engineering; Chemistry); **Management**; **Nursing** (Nursing); **Population and Family Planning**

History: Founded 1974 as branch of Shangong Medical College, acquired present title 1981.

Fees: (US Dollars): Foreign students, bachelor, 2,000 per annum; master, 3,000

Degrees and Diplomas: *Bachelor's Degree*; *Master's Degree*

TAIYUAN TEACHERS COLLEGE

189, South Neihuan Street, Taiyuan, Shanxi Province 030012
Tel: +86(351) 2279251
Fax: +86(351) 4165215
EMail: abing226@163.com
Website: http://www.tysy.net

Departments
Biology (Biology); **Chemistry** (Chemistry); **Chinese** (Chinese); **Computer Science** (Computer Science); **Dance Studies**; **Economics** (Economics); **Fine Arts** (Fine Arts); **Foreign Language** (Modern Languages); **Geography**; **History**; **Mathematics**; **Musicology**; **Pedagogy**; **Physical Education** (Physical Education); **Physics**; **Politics and Law**

History: Founded 1958. Acquired present title 1999, following merger with Normal College of Shanxi University and Shanxi Educational Institute.

Degrees and Diplomas: *Bachelor's Degree*

Libraries: c. 740,000 vols.

TAIYUAN UNIVERSITY OF SCIENCE AND TECHNOLOGY

138 Waliu Road, Taiyuan, Shanxi Province 030024
Tel: +86(351) 6222521 Ext. 145
Fax: +86(351) 6220233
EMail: fao@tyust.edu.cn
Website: http://www1.tyust.edu.cn/yuanxi/waishiban/englishedition/index.html

President: Guo Yongyi

Departments
Arts (Art Education); **Foreign Languages** (Modern Languages); **Humanities and Social Sciences**; **Law** (Law; Political Sciences); **Physical Education** (Physical Education)

Schools
Applied Sciences (Applied Chemistry; Applied Mathematics; Applied Physics); **Computer Science and Technology**; **Economy and Management** (Economics; Management); **Electronic Information Engineering**; **Materials Science and Engineering** (Materials Engineering); **Mechanical and Electronic Engineering**

History: Founded 1952 as Taiyuan Machine Manufacturing School, acquired present status and name 2004.

Degrees and Diplomas: *Bachelor's Degree*; *Master's Degree*; *Doctor's Degree*
Last Updated: 05/12/08

TAIYUAN UNIVERSITY OF TECHNOLOGY

79 West Yingze Street, Taiyuan, Shanxi Province 030024
Tel: +86(305) 6010360
Fax: +86(305) 6041142
EMail: xiaoban@tyut.edu.cn
Website: http://www.tyut.edu.cn

President: Xie Ke-Chang (1999-)
International Relations: Li Jingbao

Colleges

Architecture and Civil Engineering (Architecture; Civil Engineering; Environmental Engineering; Hydraulic Engineering); **Arts** (Administration; English; Law); **Business Administration** (Accountancy; Business Administration; International Business; Marketing); **Chemistry and Chemical Engineering** (Applied Chemistry; Chemical Engineering; Chemistry); **Computer Engineering and Software** (Computer Engineering; Computer Science; Software Engineering); **Electrical and Power Engineering** (Electrical Engineering; Power Engineering; Thermal Engineering); **Environmental Science and Engineering** (Environmental Engineering; Environmental Studies; Irrigation); **Fiber Textile and Weaving Arts** (Textile Design; Weaving); **Information Engineering** (Automation and Control Engineering; Computer Engineering; Computer Science; Information Technology); **Materials Science and Engineering** (Materials Engineering; Metallurgical Engineering); **Mechanical Engineering** (Mechanical Engineering); **Mining Engineering**; **Science**; **Sports**; **Water Conservation and Engineering** (Water Management; Water Science)

Research Institutes

Applied Mechanics (Mechanical Engineering); **Civil Construction** (Construction Engineering); **Coal Chemical Engineering** (Chemical Engineering); **Fine Chemicals** (Chemistry); **Gear Intensity** (Technology); **Plasma Surface and Heat Treatment**; **Welding Materials**

History: Founded as College of Shanxi University 1902. Became independent institute 1953. Acquired present status and title 1984. Incorporated Shanxi Mining College 1997. Under the jurisdiction of the Provincial Government.

Academic Year: September to July (September-January; February-July)

Admission Requirements: Graduation from senior middle school and entrance examination

Main Language(s) of Instruction: Chinese

Degrees and Diplomas: *Zhuanke Certificate of Graduation*; *Bachelor's Degree*: 4 yrs; *Master's Degree*: a further 3 yrs; *Doctor's Degree*

Student Residential Facilities: Yes

Libraries: Central Library, c. 1.5m. vols

Publications: Journal of Taiyuan University of Technology
Last Updated: 08/12/08

TANGSHAN COLLEGE

38 Huayan North Road, Tangshan, Hebei Province 1063000
Tel: +86(315) 2028301
Fax: +86(315) 2018158
EMail: tsc@tsc.edu.cn
Website: http://www.tsc.edu.cn

President: Hua Yu

Departments

Civil Engineering; **Economics and Management** (Economics; Management); **Environmental Engineering** (Chemical Engineering; Environmental Engineering); **Foreign Languages** (Modern Languages); **Information Engineering** (Information Technology); **Literature and Law** (Law; Literature); **Machinery and Electronic Engineering** (Electronic Engineering; Machine Building)

History: Founded 1956 as Tangshan Adult College of Technology. Acquired present title 2002.

Degrees and Diplomas: *Bachelor's Degree*

Libraries: c. 169,000 vols.
Last Updated: 08/12/08

TANGSHAN TEACHERS COLLEGE

156 Janshebei Road, Tangshan, Hebei Province 063000
Tel: +86(315) 2039727
Fax: +86(315) 2039727
EMail: webmaster@tstc.edu.cn
Website: http://www.tstc.edu.cn

President: Huanzhong Chong

Departments

Art (Fine Arts); **Biology** (Biology); **Chemistry** (Chemistry); **Chinese** (Chinese); **Computer Science and Technology** (Computer Engineering; Computer Science); **Education**; **English**; **Mathematics** (Mathematics); **Music**; **Physics** (Physics); **Politics and History**; **Social Science** (Social Sciences); **Sport**

History: Founded 1956 as Tangshan Speeded-up Teachers Academy College. Acquired present title 2000.

Degrees and Diplomas: *Bachelor's Degree*

Libraries: c. 407,000 vols.

Publications: Journal of Tangshan Teachers College
Last Updated: 08/12/08

TARIM UNIVERSITY

Alar, Xinjiang Uygur Province 843300
Tel: +86(997) 4680609
Fax: +86(997) 4680643
EMail: waheli@taru.edu.cn
Website: http://www.taru.edu.cn/

President: Xinming Li (2002-) Tel: +86(997) 4680601
Vice-President: Heli Wang Tel: +86(997) 4680717
International Relations: Yongzhong Su Tel: +86(997) 4680609

Colleges

Agricultural Engineering (Agricultural Engineering; Agricultural Equipment; Irrigation; Water Management) *Dean*: Hancun Ye; **Animal Science** (Animal Husbandry; Veterinary Science) *Dean*: Cunhui Ma; **Art and Science** (Business and Commerce; Linguistics; Science Education) *Dean*: Xiaoping An; **Economics and Management** (Agricultural Management; Business and Commerce) *Dean*: Xiaoling Yu; **Information Engineering** *Dean*: Xuejin Zhang; **Plant Science and Technology** (Crop Production; Horticulture) *Dean*: Jiangsheng Gao

History: Founded 1958 as Tarim University of Agricultural Reclamation. Acquired present title 2004.

Academic Year: September to July (September-January; March-July)

Admission Requirements: Secondary school certificate and entrance examination

Fees: (Yuan): c. 3,000-4,000 per annum

Main Language(s) of Instruction: Chinese

Accrediting Agencies: Education Bureau of Government of Xingjiang Uygur Autonomous Region; Ministry of Education

Degrees and Diplomas: *Bachelor's Degree (BS)*: 4 yrs; *Master's Degree (MS)*: a further 3 yrs

Student Services: Academic counselling, Canteen, Cultural centre, Employment services, Health services, Language programs, Nursery care, Sports facilities

Student Residential Facilities: Yes

Special Facilities: University Museum

Libraries: c. 520,000 vols

Publications: Journal of Tarim Agricultural University, Academic Journal for Agricultural Science *(quarterly)*

THE CHINA CONSERVATORY

Deshengmenwai Sizhuyuan, Dewai, Chaoyang District, Beijing 100101
Tel: +86(10) 64874884
Fax: +86(10) 64872695
EMail: zyywb@yahoo.com.cn
Website: http://www.ccmusic.edu.cn/

President: Jin Tielin
International Relations: Zhao Wen

Departments

Arts Administration; **Chinese Instruments**; **Composition** (Music); **Music Education** (Music Education); **Musicology**; **Voice and Opera** (Opera; Singing)

History: Founded 1964.

Main Language(s) of Instruction: Chinese

Degrees and Diplomas: *Bachelor's Degree*; *Master's Degree*:
Musicology
Last Updated: 03/11/08

TIANJIN ACADEMY OF FINE ARTS

1 Tianwei Road, Hebei District, Tianjin, Tianjin Province 300341
Tel: +86(22) 26011505
Fax: +86(22) 26011505
EMail: master@tjarts.edu.cn
Website: http://www.tjarts.edu.cn

President: Tang Changjian

Departments
Art Education (Art Education); **Decorative Design** (Design);
Fashion Design, Dyeing and Weaving (Fashion Design; Weaving); **Graphic Arts** (Graphic Arts); **Industrial Design**; **Landscape Architecture** (Landscape Architecture); **Oil Painting** (Painting and Drawing); **Sculpture** (Sculpture); **Traditional Chinese Painting** (Painting and Drawing)

History: Founded 1906 as Normal School, acquired present status and title 1980.

Degrees and Diplomas: *Bachelor's Degree*; *Master's Degree*
Last Updated: 08/12/08

TIANJIN AGRICULTURAL UNIVERSITY

22 Jinjing Road, Xiqing District, Tianjin, Tianjin Province 300384
Tel: +86(22) 23781315
Fax: +86(22) 23792173
EMail: yuanban@tjau.edu.cn
Website: http://www.tjau.edu.cn/

President: Xie Baohua

Departments
Agricultural Engineering (Agricultural Engineering); **Agronomy** (Agronomy); **Animal Husbandry** (Animal Husbandry); **Economics and Management**; **Fishery** (Fishery); **Horticulture** (Horticulture)

History: Founded 1976.

Degrees and Diplomas: *Bachelor's Degree*
Last Updated: 08/12/08

TIANJIN FOREIGN STUDIES UNIVERSITY

117 Machang Road, Hexi District, Tianjin, Tianjin Province 300204
Tel: +86(22) 23280875
Fax: +86(22) 23282410
EMail: foreignexperts@tjfsu.edu.cn
Website: http://www.tjfsu.edu.cn

President: Xiu Gang
International Relations: Zhang Jintong

Departments
Foreign Languages

Schools
English Studies; **International Economics and Law** (International Economics; Law); **Oriental Studies** (Oriental Studies); **Sinology** (Chinese); **Western Languages** (English; French; German)

History: Founded 1964. Acuqired present status and title 1974.
Main Language(s) of Instruction: Chinese
Degrees and Diplomas: *Bachelor's Degree*; *Master's Degree*
Libraries: c. 400,000 vols
Publications: Journal of Tianjin Foreign Studies University; World Culture
Last Updated: 08/12/08

TIANJIN INSTITUTE OF URBAN CONSTRUCTION

Xiqing District, Tianjin, Tianjin Province 300384
Tel: +86(22) 23792015
EMail: zyz@tjuci.edu.cn
Website: http://www.tjuci.edu.cn/

President: Yao Huaide

Departments
Architecture and Town Planning; **Engineering** (Engineering; Engineering Management; Materials Engineering; Petroleum and Gas Engineering); **Heating and Refrigeration**

History: Founded 1978. Acquired present status and title 1987.
Main Language(s) of Instruction: Chinese
Degrees and Diplomas: *Bachelor's Degree*; *Master's Degree*
Last Updated: 08/12/08

TIANJIN MEDICAL UNIVERSITY (TMU)

22 Qixiangtai Road, Heping District, Tianjin, Tianjin Province 300070
Tel: +86(22) 23542757
Fax: +86(22) 23542584
EMail: jwc@tijmu.edu.cn
Website: http://www.tijmu.edu.cn

President: Xishan Hao (1994-)
Tel: +86(22) 23542688, Fax: +86(22) 23542524
EMail: hxs@tijmu.edu.cn

Vice-President: Wenging Zhang
Tel: +86(22) 23542588, Fax: +86(22) 23542524
EMail: zllf@tijmu.edu.cn

International Relations: Fenglin Guo
EMail: fenglin417@hotmail.com

Colleges
Basic Medicine *Head*: Yanxia Liu; **Clinical Medicine** *Head*: Dashi Zhi; **Pharmacology** *Head*: Jianshi Lou; **Public Health** *Head*: Jianhua Wang; **Stomatology** *Head*: Ping Gao

Departments
Biomedical Engineering *Head*: Xin Tian; **Laboratory Sciences** (Laboratory Techniques) *Head*: Yunde Liu; **Medical Imaging** *Head*: Nengshu He; **Medicine** *Head*: Jinzhong Zhang; **Nursing** *Head*: Chunyan Liu; **Traditional Chinese Medicine and Western Medicine** *(International) Head*: Xiaoquan Ji

History: Founded 1951. Incorporated Tianjin Second Medical College. Acquired present title 1993.
Governing Bodies: University Council
Academic Year: September to July
Admission Requirements: Graduation from high School
Fees: (US Dollars): 2,500-4,000 per annum
Main Language(s) of Instruction: Chinese, English, Japanese
International Co-operation: With universities in Japan; USA; France; Australia; Switzerland
Accrediting Agencies: Tianjin Educational Committee
Degrees and Diplomas: *Bachelor's Degree*: 5 yrs; *Master's Degree*: 3 yrs; *Doctor's Degree*
Student Services: Academic counselling, Canteen, Cultural centre, Employment services, Foreign student adviser, Foreign Studies Centre, Health services, Language programs, Nursery care, Social counselling, Sports facilities
Special Facilities: Yes
Libraries: 540,000 vols and 3,000 periodical subscriptions
Publications: Chinese Journal of Clinical Oncology *(bimonthly)*; Foreign Medicine-Endocrinology *(quarterly)*; Journal of Tianjin Medical College *(quarterly)*; Medical Education Research of Foreign Countries *(quarterly)*
Press or Publishing House: Tianjin University Publishing House
Last Updated: 08/12/08

TIANJIN MUSIC CONSERVATORY

57 Eleventh Longitude Road, Hedong District, Tianjin, Tianjin Province 300171
Tel: +86-22-24160049 +86-22-24133176
Fax: +86-22-24319205
EMail: hny@tjcm.edu.cn
Website: http://www.tjcm.edu.cn

President: Yao Shengchang
International Relations: Huina Yang

Colleges
Vocational Studies

Departments
Art Management (Art Management); **Composition** (Music Theory and Composition); **Dance** (Dance); **Drama and Movie** (Film; Theatre); **Keyboard Music** (Musical Instruments); **Music Education**; **Musicology**; **Orchestral Instruments** (Musical Instruments); **Pop Music**; **Traditional Chinese Musical Instruments** (Folklore; Music); **Vocal Music**

Institutes
Adult Education

History: Founded 1958 as Central Conservatory of Music.

Fees: (US Dollars): Tuition, 3,700-5,000 per annum; research and scholar, 600 per month

Degrees and Diplomas: *Bachelor's Degree*; *Master's Degree*

Student Services: Canteen, Health services

Student Residential Facilities: Yes

Libraries: Total: c. 200,000 vols (including AV materials); Books in Chinese: 65,000 vols; Books in foreign languages: 70,000 vols; Periodicals: c. 90 titles; Musical records: 35,000; Cassettes: 28,000; CD/LD: 1,000; Video Tapes: 60

Last Updated: 08/12/08

TIANJIN NORMAL UNIVERSITY (TJNU)

241 Weijin Road, Hexi District, Tianjin, Tianjin Province 300074
Tel: +86(22) 23540221
Fax: +86(22) 23514100
EMail: fatru@public.tpt.tj.cn
Website: http://www.tjnu.edu.cn

President: Gao Ubao (1996-)
Tel: +86(22) 23542443, Fax: +86(22) 23541665
EMail: tigao@mail.tjnu.edu.cn

International Relations: Li Zhenghe Tel: +86(22) 23540221

Colleges
Adult Education; **Arts**; **Chemistry and Life Sciences** (Biological and Life Sciences; Cell Biology; Chemistry; Physical Chemistry); **Chinese Language and Literature** (Chinese; Literature; Modern Languages; Philology); **Computer and Information Engineering** (Computer Science); **Education** (Curriculum; Developmental Psychology; Education; Educational Administration; Educational Psychology; Educational Technology; Pedagogy; Philosophy of Education; Psychology; Secondary Education); **Foreign Languages** (English; French; Grammar; Japanese; Literature; Modern Languages; Phonetics; Russian); **History and Culture**; **Information and Management** *(International)* (Archiving; Business Administration; Information Management; Information Sciences; International Business; Library Science); **Journalism and Media Studies**; **Law** (Law); **Management** (Management); **Mathematics** (Mathematics); **Movie and Television** (Cinema and Television; Film); **Physical Sciences** (Physics); **Physics and Electronic Information** (Electronic Engineering; Physics); **Urban and Environmental Engineering**; **Women's** *(International)* (Radio and Television Broadcasting; Women's Studies)

History: Founded 1958 as Tianjin Teachers' College, acquired present title 1982.

Academic Year: September to July (September-January; March-July)

Admission Requirements: Graduation from senior middle school and entrance examination

Fees: (US Dollars): Foreign students (language learning)c. 1,400

Main Language(s) of Instruction: Chinese

Accrediting Agencies: Education Commission of Tanjin Municipal City

Degrees and Diplomas: *Bachelor's Degree*: 4 yrs; *Master's Degree*: a further 3 yrs; *Doctor's Degree (PhD)*: a further 3 yrs

Libraries: Central Library, c. 1.5m. vols

Publications: High Mathematics *(monthly)*; Journal of Tianjin Normal University, Natural Sciences, Social Sciences *(monthly)*

Last Updated: 08/12/08

TIANJIN POLYTECHNIC UNIVERSITY

63 Chenglin Road, Hedong District, Tianjin, Tianjin Province 300160
Tel: +86(22) 24528077
Fax: +86(22) 24528001
EMail: iotjpu@tjpu.edu.cn
Website: http://www.tjpu.edu.cn

President: Zhang Hongwei

Colleges
Vocational and Technical Education (Technology)

Schools
Business; **Clothing and Art** (Advertising and Publicity; Clothing and Sewing; Design; Fashion Design); **Computer Technology and Automation** (Automation and Control Engineering; Computer Engineering); **Economics** (Economics; International Business; International Economics); **Foreign Languages** (English; Foreign Languages Education; Japanese); **Humanities and Law** (Journalism; Law; Radio and Television Broadcasting); **Management** (Industrial Engineering; Industrial Management; Information Sciences; Management; Public Administration); **Materials Science and Chemical Engineering** (Chemical Engineering; Chemistry; Materials Engineering); **Mechanical and Electronic Engineering** (Automation and Control Engineering; Industrial Design; Mechanical Engineering; Optical Technology); **Science**; **Textiles** (Textile Technology)

History: Founded 1952 as Hebei Textile Industrial School. Renamed Tianjin Institute of Textile Science and Technology 1958. Acquired present title 2000.

Degrees and Diplomas: *Bachelor's Degree*; *Master's Degree*; *Doctor's Degree*

Libraries: c. 640,000 vols

Publications: Journal
Last Updated: 08/12/08

TIANJIN RADIO AND TELEVISION UNIVERSITY

1, Yingshui Road, Tianjin, Tianjin Province 300191
Tel: +86(22) 23679972
EMail: jw@crtvu.edu.cn
Website: http://www.tjrtvu.edu.cn

President: Xuefei Feng

Faculties
Agriculture Management (Agricultural Management); **Arts**; **Economic Management** (Economics; Management); **Engineering** (Engineering); **Science** (Natural Sciences)

Further Information: An open higher education institution. Also 52 Study Centres (18 in communities, 40 in enterprises and institutions, and 4 in forms of organizations).

History: Founded 1979.

Governing Bodies: Municipal Higher Education Committee

Academic Year: September to July

Admission Requirements: Graduation from senior middle school and entrance examination.

Main Language(s) of Instruction: Chinese; English

Degrees and Diplomas: *Zhuanke Certificate of Graduation*: 3 yrs; *Bachelor's Degree*. Also non-certificate training.

Student Residential Facilities: For c. 200 students

Special Facilities: Two Production Centres of Audio-Visual Programs.

Libraries: Centre of Books and Reference Materials, c. 100,000 vols

Last Updated: 08/12/08

TIANJIN UNIVERSITY

92 Weijin Road, Nankai District, Tianjin, Tianjin Province 300072
Tel: +86(22) 27405474 +86(22) 27406146
Fax: +86(22) 27401819
EMail: ies@tju.edu.cn
Website: http://www.tju.edu.cn

President: Gong Ke (2006-)
Tel: +86(22) 27403536, Fax: +86(22) 27401795

International Relations: Fuling Yang, Director, International Cooperation Tel: +86(22) 27405475 EMail: fuling_yang@tju.edu.cn

Centres

Administrators' Higher Education Training *Dean*: Zengwu Li; **Advanced Instrumental Detecting and Analytical**; **Industrial Crystallization** *(State Key Centre for Research and Promotion of Scientific and Technological Achievements)*; **Packing Column and Internal Structure** *(State Key Centre for Research and Promotion of Scientific and Technological Achievements)*

Research Centres

Digital Technology *(Ministerial Engineering Research Centre)*; **Fermentation Technology** *(State Engineering, Tianjin)*; **Medical Crystallization Engineering** *(Ministerial Engineering Research Centre)*; **Modernization of Traditional Chinese Medicine** *(Tianjin Engineering)*; **Motorcycle Technology** *(Ministerial Engineering Research Centre)*; **Optoelectronics Technology** *(Ministerial Engineering Research Centre)*; **Petrochemical Technology** *(Ministerial Engineering Research Centre)*; **Quick Prototype Manufacturing Technology** *(Ministerial Engineering Research Centre)*; **Rectification Technology** *(State Engineering, Tianjin)*; **Shape Memory Materials** *(Ministerial Engineering)*; **Thermoenergy** *(Ministerial Engineering Research Centre)*

Research Institutes

Applied Mathematics *(Nankai-Tianjin University Liuhui)*; **Applied Technology of Electrical Power and Electronics**; **Architectural Design and City Planning** *Dean*: Changming Yang; **Architectural Design and its Theory**; **Architectural History and Theory**; **Architectural Technology**; **Art** *(Wang Xuezhong)*; **Biomedical Engineering**; **Biophotonics**; **Bridge and Tunnel Engineering**; **Ceramics**; **Chemical Engineering**; **Composite Materials**; **Digital Design**; **Digital Manufacturing and Precision Finishing Technology**; **Disaster Prevention and Reduction**; **Electrical Power and Automation**; **Engineering Mechanics and Measurement**; **Environmental Engineering**; **Fine Arts** (Fine Arts; Folklore) *Dean*: Jicai Feng; **Geotechnical Engineering**; **Hydraulic Engineering**; **Hydraulics**; **Illuminating Techniques**; **Information and Control**; **Internal Combustion Engine** *(Tianjin)* *Dean*: Ning Liu; **Laser and Opto-Electronics**; **Management Science**; **Manufacturing Equipment and System**; **Manufacturing Information and Management**; **Marine and Naval Engineering**; **Materials Science and Engineering**; **Mechanic Drive**; **Mechatronic Engineering**; **Military Electronic Materials and Components**; **Modern Education Techniques**; **Modern Materials Physics**; **Modern Optics**; **New Welding Materials**; **Numeric Control and Hydraulic Technology**; **Offshore Marine Environment**; **Opto-Electronic Measuring and Controlling Technology**; **Opto-Electronics and Precision Engineering**; **Polymer Materials and Engineering**; **Power Electronics Technology**; **Product Design and Manufacturing Technology**; **Public Administration**; **Resources and Environment**; **Robot and Automotive Engineering**; **Sensor Engineering**; **Slavdom**; **Solid Waste Disposal Technology**; **Structural Engineering**; **Sustainable Development of Resource, Environmental and Ecological Society**; **Systems Engineering**; **Taiwan**; **Television and Image Information Processing**; **Thermo-energy Engineering**; **Traditional Culture and Humanities**; **Underground Engineering**; **Vehicles and Engines**; **Vocational and Technical Education**; **Water Pollution Control and Reclamation**; **Welding Engineering and Technology**

Schools

Agriculture and Biological Engineering (Food Science; Food Technology) *Dean*: Fuchang Guo; **Architecture** (Architecture; Architecture and Planning; Design; Urban Studies) *Dean*: Jian Zeng; **Chemical Engineering** (Automation and Control Engineering; Bioengineering; Chemical Engineering; Engineering Management; Molecular Biology; Pharmacy; Technology) *Dean*: Yingjing Yuan; **Civil Engineering** (Civil Engineering; Coastal Studies; Electrical Engineering; Hydraulic Engineering; Marine Science and Oceanography) *Dean*: Jijian Lian; **Computer Science and Technology** *Dean*: Jizhou Sun; **Continuing Education** *Dean*: Yongming Jin; **Distance Learning** *Dean*: Zhaopeng Meng; **Electrical Engineering and Automation** *Dean*: Chengshan Wang; **Electronic Information Engineering** (Communication Studies; Computer Engineering; Computer Science; Electronic Engineering; Information Technology) *Dean*: Jufeng Dai; **Environmental Sciences and Engineering** *Dean*: Shuting Zhang; **Film and Television** (Cinema and Television; Film; Performing Arts; Video) *Dean*: Tian Zhou; **International Education** *Dean*: Shujun Zhang; **Management** (Business Administration; Electronic Engineering; Finance; Industrial Engineering; Information Management; Management; Transport Management) *Dean*: Ershi Qi; **Materials Science and Engineering** (Automation and Control Engineering; Materials Engineering) *Dean*: Zhenduo Cui; **Mechanical Engineering** (Energy Engineering; Industrial Design; Machine Building; Mechanics; Production Engineering; Thermal Engineering) *Dean*: Tian Huang; **Pharmaceutical Science and Technology** *Dean*: Kang Zhao; **Precision Instruments and Optoelectronic Engineering** (Automation and Control Engineering; Biomedical Engineering; Electronic Engineering; Information Technology; Measurement and Precision Engineering; Optical Technology) *Dean*: Kexin Xu; **Sciences** (Applied Chemistry; Applied Mathematics; Applied Physics; Mathematics) *Dean*: Haili Bai; **Social Sciences and Foreign Languages** (Chinese; English; Law; Linguistics; Literature; Social Sciences) *Dean*: Xu Li; **Vocational and Technical Education** *Dean*: Zengwu Li

History: Founded 1895 as Peiyang University. Acquired present title 1951.

Academic Year: September to July (September-January; February-July)

Admission Requirements: Graduation from senior middle school and national entrance examination

Fees: (Yuan): 4,200

Main Language(s) of Instruction: Chinese

International Co-operation: With 115 universities in 32 countries, including: USA, Canada, Japan, United Kingdom, France, Germany, Poland, India, Italy, Finland, Sweden, Korea, Australia

Accrediting Agencies: Ministry of Education

Degrees and Diplomas: *Bachelor's Degree*: 4 yrs; *Master's Degree*: a further 2 yrs; *Doctor's Degree*: a further 3 yrs

Student Services: Academic counselling, Canteen, Cultural centre, Employment services, Foreign student adviser, Foreign Studies Centre, Health services, Language programs, Nursery care, Social counselling, Sports facilities

Student Residential Facilities: Yes

Libraries: c. 2m. vols

Publications: Collection of Research Papers; Journal *(quarterly)*

Press or Publishing House: Tianjin University Publishing House

Last Updated: 07/10/08

TIANJIN UNIVERSITY OF COMMERCE

East Entrance of Jinba Road, Beichen District, Tianjin, Tianjin Province 300400
Tel: +86(22) 26653169
Fax: +86(22) 26653169
Website: http://www.tjcu.edu.cn

President: Shuhan Liu

Departments

Accountancy; **Computer Information and Management**; **Economics**; **Food and Bioengineering** (Bioengineering; Food Technology); **Law**; **Modern Languages**; **Packaging Engineering** (Packaging Technology); **Tourism**

Institutes

Freezing and Air Conditioning Technology (Heating and Refrigeration)

History: Founded 1984.

Academic Year: September to July (September-January; February-July)

Admission Requirements: Graduation from high school and entrance examination

Main Language(s) of Instruction: Chinese

Accrediting Agencies: Ministry of Commerce; Provincial Government

Degrees and Diplomas: *Zhuanke Certificate of Graduation*: 2 yrs; *Bachelor's Degree*: 4 yrs; *Master's Degree*: a further 2 yrs

Student Residential Facilities: Yes

Libraries: c. 700,000 vols

Publications: Journal of Tianjin University of Commerce

Press or Publishing House: Tianjin University of Commerce Printing House

Last Updated: 07/10/08

TIANJIN UNIVERSITY OF FINANCE AND ECONOMICS

25 Zhujiang Road, Hexi District, Tianjin, Tianjin Province 300222
Tel: +86(22) 28178279
Fax: +86(22) 28340028
EMail: liuxue@tjufe.edu.cn; network@tjufe.edu.cn
Website: http://www.tjufe.edu.cn

President: Zhang Jiaxing

International Relations: Zhan Min

Departments

Accountancy (Accountancy); **Banking** (Banking); **Economics** (Economics); **International Trade** (International Business); **Law** (Law); **Management** (Management); **Public Finance** (Finance); **Statistics** (Statistics)

History: Founded 1958 as Hebei College of Finance and Economics. Renamed Tianjin College of Finance and Economics 1971. Acquired present title 2004.

Main Language(s) of Instruction: Chinese

Degrees and Diplomas: *Bachelor's Degree*; *Master's Degree*; *Doctor's Degree*

Libraries: c. 670,000 vols

Publications: International Economics and Management; Modern Finance and Economics

Last Updated: 09/12/08

TIANJIN UNIVERSITY OF SCIENCE AND TECHNOLOGY

1038 Dagu Nanlu, Hexi District, Tianjin, Tianjin Province 300222
Tel: +86(22) 28342821
Fax: +86(22)60273235
EMail: gjch@tust.edu.cn
Website: http://www.tust.edu.cn

President: Xiaohong Cao

Schools

Art Design (Design; Fine Arts); **Biological Engineering** (Bioengineering); **Computer Science and Information Engineering**; **Economics and Management** (Economics; International Business; Management); **Electronic Automation** (Automation and Control Engineering; Electronic Engineering); **Food Engineering and Biological Technology** (Biotechnology; Food Science); **Foreign Languages** (Modern Languages); **Law and Politics** (Law; Political Sciences); **Material Science and Chemical Engineering**; **Mechanical Engineering** (Mechanical Engineering); **Ocean Science and Engineering** (Marine Engineering; Marine Science and Oceanography); **Packaging and Printing Engineering** (Packaging Technology; Printing and Printmaking); **Science** (Natural Sciences)

History: Founded 1958 as Tianjin Institute of Light Industry, acquired present title 2002.

Degrees and Diplomas: *Bachelor's Degree*; *Master's Degree*; *Doctor's Degree*

Libraries: c. 90,000 vols

Publications: China Light Industrial Education; Journal of Tianjin Institute of Light Industry

Last Updated: 09/12/08

TIANJIN UNIVERSITY OF SPORT

51 South Weijin Road, Hexi District, Tianjin, Tianjin Province 300381
Tel: +86(22) 23012186
Fax: +86(22) 23383503
EMail: office@tjipe.edu.cn
Website: http://www.tjipe.edu.cn

President: Zong Haoli

International Relations: Li Shunzhang

Departments

Fitness and Recreation (Leisure Studies; Sports); **Physical Education** (Physical Education); **Political Science** (Political Sciences); **Sports** (Sports)

History: Founded 1958.

Main Language(s) of Instruction: Chinese

Degrees and Diplomas: *Bachelor's Degree*; *Master's Degree*

Last Updated: 09/12/08

TIANJIN UNIVERSITY OF TECHNOLOGY

263 Hongqinan Road, Nankai District, Tianjin, Tianjin Province 300191
EMail: cie@tjut.edu.cn
Website: http://www.tjut.edu.cn

President: Jianbiao Ma

Dean: Jingmin Li Tel: +86(22) 23679472, Fax: +86(22) 23360347

International Relations: Hongxiang Cui
Tel: +86(22) 23679458, Fax: +86(22) 23369449
EMail: jgj@tjut.edu.cn

Colleges

Continuing Education; **Foreign Studies** (International Relations); **International Business and Management**; **International Education**

Schools

Art (Arts and Humanities); **Audiology** *(Technical)* (Speech Therapy and Audiology); **Automation and Control Engineering** (Automation and Control Engineering); **Basic Education** (Education); **Basic Science** (Natural Sciences); **Chemistry and Chemical Engineering** (Chemical Engineering); **Computer Science and Technology** (Computer Engineering; Computer Science; Technology); **Electronics Information and Communications Engineering** (Electronic Engineering; Telecommunications Engineering); **Law and Politics** (Law; Political Sciences); **Management** (Management); **Material Science and Engineering** (Materials Engineering); **Mechanical Engineering** (Mechanical Engineering); **Transport and Logistics** (Transport Engineering; Transport Management)

History: Founded 1981 as Branch School of Tianjin University.

Degrees and Diplomas: *Bachelor's Degree*; *Master's Degree*

Libraries: c. 1,420,000 vols

Publications: Academic Journal of Technology; VIP Scientific Journal

Last Updated: 02/02/07

TIANJIN UNIVERSITY OF TRADITIONAL CHINESE MEDICINE

88 Yuquan Road, Nankai District, Tianjin, Tianjin Province 300193
Tel: +86(22) 27373736
Fax: +86(22) 27377931
EMail: wailianb@tjutcm.edu.cn
Website: http://www.tjutcm.edu.cn

President: Zhang Boli

Departments

Acupuncture and Moxibustion (Acupuncture); **Chinese Materia Medica** (Pharmacology); **Traditional Chinese Medicine** (Traditional Eastern Medicine)

History: Founded 1958. Merged with Hebei Medical College 1968.

Main Language(s) of Instruction: Chinese

Degrees and Diplomas: *Bachelor's Degree*; *Master's Degree*; *Doctor's Degree*

Libraries: c. 170,000 vols

Publications: Journal of Tianjin College of TCM

Last Updated: 09/12/08

TIBET INSTITUTE OF TIBETAN MEDICINE

24 Dangre Middle Road, Lhasa, Tibet
Tel: +86(891) 6326272
Fax: +86(891) 6339296

President: Tsoru Tselang

International Relations: Doji Dro Gar

Departments

Tibetan Medicine (Traditional Eastern Medicine); **Training**

History: Founded 1985 as Tibetan Medicine Department of Tibet University. Merged with College of the Temple of God of Tibetan Medicine.

Degrees and Diplomas: *Bachelor's Degree*; *Master's Degree*

Publications: Traditional Tibetan Medicine Studies

TIBET UNIVERSITY

36 Jiangsu Road, Lhasa, Tibet 850000
Tel: +86(891) 6321247
Fax: +86(891) 6334489
EMail: fsd@post.utibet.edu.cn
Website: http://www.utibet.edu.cn

President: Fang Lingmin

Departments

Arts (Arts and Humanities); **Biology and Geography** (Biology; Geography); **Chemistry** (Chemistry); **Foreign Languages** (Modern Languages); **Mathematics and Physics** (Mathematics; Physics); **Politics and History** (History; Political Sciences); **Tibetan Language and Literature** (Literature; Tibetan)

History: Founded 1951 as Tibetan Cadres Training School. Merged with Tibet Institute of Agriculture and Animal Husbandry 2001.

Degrees and Diplomas: *Bachelor's Degree*; *Master's Degree*

Libraries: c. 18,000 vols

Publications: Tibet University Journal

TONGHUA TEACHERS COLLEGE

151 Toudaogou Road, Tonghua, Jilin Province 134002
Tel: +86(435) 3516002
Fax: +86(435) 3516002

President: Hou Lihua

International Relations: Ji Jianye

Departments

Biology; **Chemistry** (Chemistry); **Chinese Language and Literature**; **Computer Science**; **English** (English); **Fine Arts**; **History**; **Mathematics**; **Modern Languages** (Modern Languages); **Physical Education** (Physical Education); **Physics** (Physics); **Political Science and Law**

History: Founded 1958.

Degrees and Diplomas: *Bachelor's Degree*

TONGJI UNIVERSITY

1239 Siping Road, Shanghai, Shanghai 200092
Tel: +86(21) 65981057
Fax: +86(21) 65985216
EMail: wsbgs@mail.tongji.edu.cn
Website: http://www.tongji.edu.cn

President: Gang Pei (2007-)
Tel: +86(21) 65983300, Fax: +86(21) 65188885

International Relations: Qi Dong
Tel: +86(21) 65983057, Fax: +86(21) 65985216

Colleges

Aerospace Engineering and Mechanics (Aeronautical and Aerospace Engineering; Mechanical Engineering); **Architecture and Town Planning** (Architecture; Industrial Design; Landscape Architecture; Tourism; Town Planning); **Automotive Engineering** (Automotive Engineering); **Civil Engineering** (Building Technologies; Civil Engineering; Road Engineering; Surveying and Mapping; Transport Engineering); **Continuing Education**; **Dentistry** (Dentistry; Stomatology); **Economics and Management** (Accountancy; Business Administration; Economics; Finance; Information Management; Management); **Electronics and Information Engineering** (Computer Engineering; Computer Science; Electrical Engineering; Electronic Engineering; Information Technology); **Environmental Science and Engineering** (Environmental Engineering; Environmental Studies); **Foreign Languages** (English; German; Japanese; Modern Languages); **International Education** (International and Comparative Education); **Liberal Arts and Law** (Arts and Humanities; Cultural Studies; Law; Social Sciences); **Life**

Sciences and Technology (Biological and Life Sciences; Natural Sciences); **Materials Science and Engineering** (Inorganic Chemistry; Materials Engineering); **Mechanical Engineering** (Automotive Engineering; Mechanical Engineering; Thermal Engineering); **Medicine** (Medicine; Oncology; Ophthalmology; Otorhinolaryngology; Pathology; Psychiatry and Mental Health); **Ocean and Earth Sciences** (Coastal Studies; Earth Sciences; Marine Science and Oceanography); **Sciences** (Applied Mathematics; Chemistry; Geology; Geophysics; Mechanical Engineering; Natural Sciences; Physics); **Software Engineering**; **Traffic and Transportation Engineering**

Institutes

Sino-German *(Advanced)* (Chinese; German); **Technology** *(Professional)* (Technology); **Technology** (Technology)

Schools

Film (Film); **Graduate**

History: Founded 1907 as Tongji German Medical School. Merged with Shanghai Institute of Urban Construction, Shanghai Institute of Construction Engineering 1996 and Shanghai Tiedao University 2000.

Governing Bodies: University Council

Academic Year: September to July (September-January; February-June; June-July)

Admission Requirements: Graduation from senior middle school and entrance examination

Main Language(s) of Instruction: Chinese

Accrediting Agencies: Ministry of Education; Shanghai Municipality

Degrees and Diplomas: *Bachelor's Degree*: 4-5 yrs; *Master's Degree*: a further 2 1/2 yrs; *Doctor's Degree*: 3-4 yrs following Master. Also Postdoctorate degrees

Student Services: Academic counselling, Canteen, Cultural centre, Employment services, Foreign student adviser, Health services, Nursery care, Social counselling, Sports facilities

Student Residential Facilities: Yes

Libraries: c. 3.49 m. vols

Publications: Higher Education Studies; Journal of Radioimmunology; Journal of Structural Engineering; Shanghai Journal of Mechanics; Study of German; Technical Acoustics; Time and Architecture; Tongji Journal *(monthly)*

Press or Publishing House: Tongji University Press
Last Updated: 22/10/08

TSINGHUA UNIVERSITY

1 Qinghuayuan, Beijing 100084
Tel: +86(10) 62783769
Fax: +86(10) 62789392
EMail: international@tsinghua.edu.cn
Website: http://www.tsinghua.edu.cn

President: Gu Binglin

International Relations: He Kebin

Academies

Arts and Design (Design; Fine Arts)

Departments

Accounting *(School of Economics and Management)*; **Aerospace** *(School of Aerospace)*; **Architecture** *(School of Architecture)* (Architecture); **Art History** *(Academy of Arts and Design)* (Art History); **Arts and Crafts** *(Academy of Arts and Design)* (Crafts and Trades; Fine Arts; Handicrafts); **Automation** *(School of Information Science and Technology)* (Automation and Control Engineering); **Automotive Engineering** *(School of Mechanical Engineering)*; **Biological Sciences and Biotechnology** *(School of Sciences)* (Biological and Life Sciences); **Biomedical Engineering** *(School of Medicine)* (Biomedical Engineering); **Building Science** *(School of Architecture)* (Building Technologies); **Business Strategy and Policy** *(School of Economics and Management)* (Business Administration); **Ceramic Design** *(Academy of Arts and Design)* (Ceramic Art; Ceramics and Glass Technology; Design); **Chemical Engineering** *(School of Information Science and Technology)*; **Chemistry** *(School of Sciences)* (Chemistry); **Chinese Language and Literature** *(School of Humanities and Social Sciences)* (Chinese;

Linguistics; Literature); **Civil Engineering** *(School of Civil Engineering)* (Civil Engineering); **Computer Science and Technology** *(School of Information Science and Technology)*; **Construction Management** *(School of Civil Engineering)* (Construction Engineering); **Decorative Art** *(Academy of Arts and Design)*; **Economics** *(School of Economics and Management)*; **Economics and Management Technology** *(School of Economics and Management)*; **Electrical Engineering** *(School of Information Science and Technology)* (Electrical Engineering); **Electronic Engineering** *(School of Information Science and Technology)*; **Engineering Mechanics** *(School of Aerospace)* (Mechanics); **Engineering Physics** *(School of Information Science and Technology)* (Physical Engineering; Physics); **Environmental Art** *(Academy of Arts and Design)* (Arts and Humanities; Environmental Studies); **Environmental Science and Engineering** *(School of Information Science and Technology)* (Environmental Engineering; Environmental Studies); **Fine Arts** *(Academy of Arts and Design)* (Fine Arts); **Foreign Languages** *(School of Humanities and Social Sciences)* (Modern Languages); **History** *(School of Humanities and Social Sciences)* (History); **Human Resources and Organizational Behavior** *(School of Economics and Management)* (Behavioural Sciences; Human Resources); **Hydraulic Engineering** *(School of Civil Engineering)* (Hydraulic Engineering); **Industrial Design** *(Academy of Arts and Design)*; **Industrial Engineering** *(School of Mechanical Engineering)*; **Information Art and Design** *(Academy of Arts and Design)* (Communication Arts; Design; Fine Arts); **International Trade and Finance** *(School of Economics and Management)* (Finance; International Business); **Landscape Architecture** *(School of Architecture)*; **Management Science and Engineering** *(School of Economics and Management)*; **Marketing** *(School of Economics and Management)*; **Materials Science and Engineering** *(School of Information Science and Technology)* (Materials Engineering); **Mathematical Sciences** *(School of Sciences)* (Mathematics); **Mechanical Engineering** *(School of Mechanical Engineering)*; **Medical Science** *(School of Medicine)*; **Microelectronics and Nanoelectronics**; **Pharmaceutical Science** *(School of Medicine)* (Pharmacy); **Philosophy** *(School of Humanities and Social Sciences)* (Philosophy); **Physics** *(School of Sciences)*; **Political Science** *(School of Humanities and Social Sciences)*; **Precision Instruments and Mechanology** *(School of Mechanical Engineering)*; **Sculpture** *(Academy of Arts and Design)*; **Sociology** *(School of Humanities and Social Sciences)* (Sociology); **Textile and Garment Design** *(Academy of Arts and Design)* (Textile Design); **Thermal Engineering** *(School of Mechanical Engineering)* (Thermal Engineering); **Urban Planning and Design** *(School of Architecture)*

Divisions

Teaching and Reasearch on Physical Education (Physical Education)

Institutes

Microelectronics *(School of Information Science and Technology)*; **Nuclear and New Energy Technology** (Energy Engineering; Nuclear Engineering)

Schools

Aerospace; **Architecture**; **Civil Engineering**; **Economics and Management**; **Environmental Science and Engineering**; **Humanities and Social Sciences**; **Information Science and Technology**; **Journalism and Communication**; **Law**; **Mechanical Engineering**; **Public Policy and Management**; **Sciences**; **Software** *(School of Information Science and Technology)*

History: Founded 1911, became University 1928.

Governing Bodies: University Council

Academic Year: September to June (September-January; February-June)

Degrees and Diplomas: *Bachelor's Degree*: 4 yrs; *Master's Degree*: a further 2-3 yrs; *Doctor's Degree (Ph.D.)*: a further 3-4 yrs

Student Services: Academic counselling, Canteen, Cultural centre, Employment services, Foreign Studies Centre, Health services, Social counselling, Sports facilities

Libraries: c. 3.5m. vols. ; over 0.4m e-books and more than 2,500 seats.

Publications: China Mediatech (Chinese); Computer Education (Chinese); Decorative Arts (Chinese); Journal of Tsinghua University (Chinese); Journal of Tsinghua University (Chinese), Philo-

sophy and Social Sciences; Modern Education Technology (Chinese); Physics and Engineering (Chinese); Tsinghua Journal of Education (Chinese); Tsinghua Science and Technology (English); Word Architecture (Chinese)

Press or Publishing House: Tsinghua University Press

UNIVERSITY OF ELECTRONIC SCIENTE AND TECHNOLOGY OF CHINA (UESTC)

No.4, Section 2, North Jianshe Road, Chengdu,
Sichuan Province 610054
Tel: +86(28) 83202354
Fax: +86(28) 83202365
EMail: oice@uestc.edu.cn
Website: http://www.uestc.edu.cn

President: Shoubin Zou (2001-)
Tel: +86(28) 83203010, Fax: +86(28) 83202365

Chairman of University Executive Committee: Shuxiang Hu
Tel: +86(28) 83202203, Fax: +86(28) 83202365

International Relations: Bin Jiang
Tel: +86(28) 83202353, Fax: +86(28) 83202365

Schools

Applied Mathematics (Applied Mathematics) *Dean*: Tingzhu Huang; **Automation Engineering** (Automation and Control Engineering) *Dean*: Shulin Tian; **Communication and Information Engineering** (Communication Studies; Information Management; Information Technology) *Dean*: Yungjiang Rao; **Computer Science and Engineering** (Computer Engineering; Computer Science; Engineering) *Dean*: Zhiguang Qin; **Electro-mechanical Engineering** (Electrical Engineering; Mechanical Engineering) *Dean*: Hongzhong Huang; **Electronic Engineering** (Electronic Engineering) *Dean*: Yong Fan; **Foreign Languages** (Modern Languages) *Dean*: Wenpeng Zhang; **Life Science and Technology** (Biological and Life Sciences; Technology) *Dean*: Dezhong Yao; **Management** (Management) *Dean*: Yong Zeng; **Microelectronics and Solid State Electronics** (Microelectronics; Solid State Physics) *Dean*: Yanrong Li; **Optoelectronic Information** (Electronic Engineering; Optical Technology) *Dean*: Yadong Jiang; **Physical Education** (Physical Education) *Dean*: Quanhe Yang; **Physical Electronics** (Electronic Engineering) *Dean*: Pukun Liu; **Political Science and Public Administration** (Political Sciences; Public Administration) *Dean*: Xiaoning Zhu

History: Founded 1956 as Chengdu Institute of Radio Engineering.

Governing Bodies: University Executive Committee

Academic Year: September to June

Admission Requirements: Graduation from senior middle school and entrance examination

Fees: (Yuan): 4,900 per annum

Main Language(s) of Instruction: Chinese

International Co-operation: With universities in United Kingdom, USA, France, Japan and Korea

Degrees and Diplomas: *Bachelor's Degree*: 4 yrs; *Master's Degree*: 2-4 yrs; *Doctor's Degree*: 3-6 yrs

Student Services: Academic counselling, Canteen, Cultural centre, Employment services, Foreign student adviser, Health services, Language programs, Nursery care, Sports facilities

Student Residential Facilities: Yes

Libraries: 1.2m. vols

Publications: Journal of Electronic Science and Technology of China *(quarterly)*; Journal of the University of Electronic Science and Technology of China *(bimonthly)*; Journal of the University of Electronic Science and Technology of China (Social Science Additional) *(quarterly)*

Press or Publishing House: UESTC Press
Last Updated: 06/11/08

UNIVERSITY OF INTERNATIONAL BUSINESS AND ECONOMICS

10 Huixin Dongjie, Beijing 100029
Tel: +86(10) 64928099
Fax: +86(10) 64928098
EMail: sie@uibe.edu.cn
Website: http://www.uibe.edu.cn

President: Zhunmin Chen
Tel: +86(10) 64492101, Fax: +86(10) 64493861
EMail: zmchen@uibe.edu.cn

Vice-President: Sudong Chen
Tel: +86(10) 64492119, Fax: +86(10) 64493861
EMail: sdchen@uibe.edu.cn

International Relations: Liqun Jia
Tel: +86(10) 64492132, Fax: +86(10) 64493860

Research Centres
China Trade and Environment (Crafts and Trades; Environmental Management); **South Korea Economy** (Economics); **Taiwan, Hong Kong and Macao Economy** (Economics)

Research Institutes
International Trade (International Business); **Language, Literature and Culture** (Cultural Studies; Linguistics; Literature; Modern Languages)

Schools
Business; **Chinese Language and Literature**; **Finance and Banking** (Banking; Finance); **Foreign Languages and Studies** (Arabic; French; Italian; Japanese; Korean; Modern Languages; Russian; Spanish; Vietnamese); **Humanities and Social Sciences** (Arts and Humanities; International Relations; Social Sciences); **Information Management** (E-Business/Commerce; Information Management; Information Technology); **Insurance** (Insurance); **International Studies** (English; International Business); **International Trade and Economics** (Crafts and Trades; Finance; International Business; International Economics; Transport Management); **Law** (Law) *Dean*: Sibao Shen; **Public Administration**

Further Information: Also Chinese Institute for WTO Studies

History: Founded 1951 as institute. Acquired present status 1984. Merged with the China Institute of Finance and Banking 2000.

Academic Year: September to July (September-January; March-July)

Admission Requirements: Graduation from senior middle school and entrance examination

Fees: (Yuan): 6,000 per annum

Main Language(s) of Instruction: Chinese, English

International Co-operation: With universities in France; United States; Germany; Australia; Japan; Republic of Korea; Finland; United Kingdom; Italy

Accrediting Agencies: Ministry of Foreign Trade and Economic Co-operation; Ministry of Education

Degrees and Diplomas: *Bachelor's Degree*: Economics; Literature, 4 yrs; *Master's Degree*: Business Management; English Language and Literature; French Language and Literature; International Economic Law; International Economics; International Finance; International Trade; Japanese Language and Literature; Science of Law, a further 2-3 yrs; *Doctor's Degree*: International Economic Law; International Trade, 2 yrs

Student Services: Academic counselling, Cultural centre, Employment services, Foreign student adviser, Health services, Social counselling, Sports facilities

Student Residential Facilities: For c. 4,000 students

Special Facilities: Movie Studio

Libraries: c. 460,000 vols

Publications: Issues in Higher Education; Japanese Study; Translation of International Trade Articles; Journal of International Trade *(bimonthly)*; Research on Multinationals; Research on Taiwan, Hong Kong and Macao Economy; UIBE Journal *(bimonthly)*

Press or Publishing House: International Business Educational Press

Academic Staff 2008	TOTAL
FULL-TIME	c. 750

Student Numbers 2008	
All (Foreign Included)	c. 11,000
FOREIGN ONLY	2,600

Last Updated: 09/12/08

UNIVERSITY OF INTERNATIONAL RELATIONS
12 Poshangcun, Haidan District, Beijing 100091
Tel: +86(10) 62861667
Fax: +86(10) 62861660
EMail: uir@chinatefl.com
Website: http://www.uir.edu.cn

International Relations: Liu Pingjie

Departments
Culture and Communication (Administration; Communication Studies); **English** (English); **Information Science Technology** (Information Management; Information Sciences); **International Economics** (International Economics); **International Politics** (International Relations; Political Sciences); **Public Management** (Management; Public Administration); **Sports and Aesthetic Teaching and Research**

Degrees and Diplomas: *Bachelor's Degree*; *Master's Degree*; *Doctor's Degree*
Last Updated: 09/12/08

UNIVERSITY OF JINAN
106 Jiwei Road, Jinan, Shandong Province 250022
Tel: +86(531) 2767683
Fax: +86(531) 7963127
EMail: fao@ujn.edu.cn
Website: http://www.ujn.edu.cn

President: Cheng Xin

Schools
Chemistry and Chemical Engineering (Chemical Engineering; Chemistry); **City Development** (Environmental Studies; Geography; Urban Studies); **Civil and Architectural Engineering** (Civil Engineering); **Control Science and Engineering** (Automation and Control Engineering; Electrical Engineering); **Economics** (Economics); **Foreign Languages**; **Law**; **Literature** (Literature); **Management** (Accountancy; Business Administration; Management); **Materials Science and Engineering** (Materials Engineering); **Science**; **Social Sciences** (Social Sciences); **Tourism** (Tourism)

History: Founded 1948. Acquired present title following merger of Shandong Institute of Building Materials and Jinan United University 2001.

Fees: (US Dollars): 1,800-2,200 per annum

International Co-operation: With universities in USA, Russian Federation, France, United Kingdom, Germany, Canada, Australia, Japan, South Korea, Singapore and Pakistan

Accrediting Agencies: Ministry of Education

Degrees and Diplomas: *Bachelor's Degree*; *Master's Degree*

Libraries: c. 1.7 million vols; 3,200 kinds of journals in Chinese and foreign languages
Last Updated: 09/12/08

UNIVERSITY OF SCIENCE AND TECHNOLOGY BEIJING (USTB)
30 Xueyuan Road, Haidan District, Beijing 100083
Tel: +86(1) 62332541
Fax: +86(1) 62327878
EMail: xiaoban@ustb.edu.cn
Website: http://www.ustb.edu.cn

President: Xu Jinwu Tel: +86(10) 62332318

Centres
Engineering of High-Efficiency Rolling (Engineering)

Laboratories
Corrosion-Erosion and Surface Technology; **Environmental Fracture**

Research Centres
Environmental Protection and Energy Saving; **Metallurgical Strategy Engineering**; **Quality and Reliable Engineering**

Research Institutes
Applied Physics; **Automatic Control**; **Computer Application and System**; **History of Metallurgy and Materials**; **Intelligence Language and Computer Science**; **Logistics**; **Management**

Science; **Mechanical Engineering**; **Metallurgy**; **Mining and Mineral Engineering**; **Robotics**; **Thermal Energy Engineering**

Schools
Applied Sciences (Analytical Chemistry; Applied Chemistry; Applied Mathematics; Applied Physics; Chemical Engineering; Mathematics; Mechanics; Natural Sciences; Solid State Physics; Thermal Physics); **Humanities and Social Sciences** (Arts and Humanities; Commercial Law; Computer Education; Educational Administration; English; History of Law; International Law; Law; Linguistics; Literacy Education; Logic; Modern Languages; Native Language; Philology; Political Sciences; Public Administration; Public Law; Social Sciences); **Information Engineering** (Artificial Intelligence; Automation and Control Engineering; Computer Science; Electronic Engineering; Information Technology; Measurement and Precision Engineering; Software Engineering; Technology); **Management** (Accountancy; Business Administration; Business and Commerce; Commercial Law; Computer Education; Data Processing; Human Resources; Industrial Maintenance; Industrial Management; International Business; International Economics; Management; Marketing); **Materials Science and Engineering** (Industrial Engineering; Materials Engineering; Metallurgical Engineering); **Mechanical Engineering** (Automation and Control Engineering; Electrical Engineering; Energy Engineering; Heating and Refrigeration; Machine Building; Measurement and Precision Engineering; Mechanical Engineering; Power Engineering; Thermal Engineering; Thermal Physics); **Metallurgical Engineering** (Industrial Engineering; Materials Engineering; Metal Techniques; Metallurgical Engineering; Production Engineering); **Resources Engineering** (Automotive Engineering; Civil Engineering; Construction Engineering; Environmental Engineering; Geological Engineering; Mining Engineering; Safety Engineering; Transport Engineering)

Further Information: Also 22 courses for foreign students. University Hospital USTB

History: Founded 1952 as Beijing Institute of Iron and Steel Technology. Acquired present title 1988.

Academic Year: February to January (February-July; September-January)

Admission Requirements: Graduation from senior middle school and entrance examination

Fees: (Yuan): c. 3,200 per annum

Main Language(s) of Instruction: Chinese

Accrediting Agencies: Ministry of Education

Degrees and Diplomas: *Bachelor's Degree*: 4 yrs; *Master's Degree*: a further 2 1/2 yrs; *Doctor's Degree (Ph.D.)*: a further 3 yrs

Student Services: Academic counselling, Cultural centre, Employment services, Foreign student adviser, Health services, Nursery care, Social counselling

Student Residential Facilities: For c. 9,030 students

Libraries: Main Library, c. 790,000 vols

Publications: Higher Education Research; Journal of USTB; Logistic and Material Handling; Metal World
Last Updated: 09/12/08

UNIVERSITY OF SCIENCE AND TECHNOLOGY LIAONING

185 Qianshan Zhong Road, Anshan, Liaoning Province 114051
Tel: +86(412) 5597505
Fax: +86(412) 5564205
EMail: International@ustl.edu.cn
Website: http://www.asust.edu.cn

President: Lu Yang

Departments
Arts (Performing Arts)

Schools
Advanced Professional Technology Education (Technology Education); **Architectural Engineering** (Architecture; Industrial Design); **Business Administration** (Accountancy; Business Administration; E-Business/Commerce; Marketing); **Computer Science and Engineering** (Computer Engineering; Computer Science); **Economics and Law**; **Electronic and Information Engineering**; **Foreign Languages** (English; Modern Languages);

Materials Science and Engineering (Heating and Refrigeration; Materials Engineering; Metallurgical Engineering); **Mechanical Engineering and Automation** (Automation and Control Engineering; Mechanical Engineering); **Medicine** (Medicine); **Resources and Civil Engineering**; **Science** (Applied Mathematics; Information Sciences; Mathematics; Physics)

History: Founded 1948 as Anshan Second College of Steel making. Became Anshan University of Science and Technology 2002 and University of Science and Technology Liaoning 2006.

Main Language(s) of Instruction: Chinese

Degrees and Diplomas: *Bachelor's Degree*; *Master's Degree*
Last Updated: 05/11/08

UNIVERSITY OF SCIENCE AND TECHNOLOGY OF CHINA (USTC)

96 Jinzhai Road, Hefei, Anhui Province 230026
Tel: +86(551) 360-2847 +86(551) 360-2695
Fax: +86(551) 363-2579
EMail: iao@ustc.edu.cn
Website:http://www.ustc.edu.cn

President: Qingshi Zhu
Tel: +86(551) 360-3955, Fax: +86(551) 363-1760
EMail: gszhu@ustc.edu.cn

Secretary-General: Zhongxiao Pan Tel: +86(551) 360-2987

International Relations: Jie Yang EMail: jieyang@ustc.edu.cn

Schools
Business (Business Education; Finance; Management; Statistics) *Head*: Zhaoben Fang; **Chemistry and Materials** (Chemistry; Materials Engineering; Physics; Polymer and Plastics Technology) *Head*: Yitai Qian; **Continuing Education** (Continuing Education) *Head*: Dongpei Zhu; **Earth and Space Science** (Astronomy and Space Science; Earth Sciences) *Head*: Yongfei Zheng; **Engineering** (Energy Engineering; Machine Building; Mechanical Engineering; Thermal Engineering) *Head*: Xiaoping Wu; **Humanities and Social Sciences** (Art Education; Arts and Humanities; History; Modern Languages; Philosophy; Physical Education; Social Sciences) *Head*: Keli Fang; **Information Science and Technology** (Automation and Control Engineering; Computer Science; Electronic Engineering; Information Sciences; Information Technology) *Head*: Xufa Wang; **Life Science** (Biological and Life Sciences; Cell Biology; Molecular Biology; Neurosciences) *Head*: Yunyu Shi; **Science** (Applied Physics; Astronomy and Space Science; Mathematics; Physics) *Head*: Xiaolian Wang

History: Founded 1958. Incorporated Hefei Economic and Technological Institute and acquired present title 1999.

Admission Requirements: Graduation from senior middle school and entrance examination

Main Language(s) of Instruction: Chinese

International Co-operation: With universities in USA, Japan, Republic of Korea, Russian Federation

Degrees and Diplomas: *Bachelor's Degree*: Science, Arts, 4 yrs; *Master's Degree*: Science, Arts, 3 yrs; *Doctor's Degree*: Science (Ph.D.), 3 yrs

Student Services: Academic counselling, Canteen, Cultural centre, Employment services, Foreign student adviser, Health services, Language programs, Nursery care, Social counselling, Sports facilities

Special Facilities: Art Gallery, Movie Studio

Libraries: c. 1,000,036 vols

Publications: USTC Academic Journal

Press or Publishing House: USTC Publishing House
Last Updated: 09/12/08

UNIVERSITY OF SHANGHAI FOR SCIENCE AND TECHNOLOGY

516 Jungong Road, Shanghai, Shanghai 200093
Tel: +86(21) 65681967
Fax: +86(21) 65681967
EMail: usstie@online.sh.cn
Website: http://www.usst.edu.cn

President: Chen Kangmin

International Relations: Li Liren

Schools

Basic Science; **Commerce** (Business and Commerce); **Computer Science** (Computer Science); **Continuing Education**; **Engineering** (Engineering); **Foreign Languages** (Modern Languages); **Instrumentation** (Measurement and Precision Engineering); **Mechanical Engineering** (Mechanical Engineering); **Power Engineering** (Power Engineering); **Systems Engineering** (Computer Engineering); **Urban Construction and Environmental Engineering** (Building Technologies; Environmental Engineering; Town Planning; Urban Studies)

History: Founded 1907 as Tongji German Medical School. Merged with Shanghai Institute of Mechanical Engineering 1972, and acquired present status and title 1979.

Degrees and Diplomas: *Bachelor's Degree*; *Master's Degree*; *Doctor's Degree*

Libraries: c. 800,000 vols

Publications: Journal of Shanghai University of Science and Technology

UNIVERSITY OF SOUTH CHINA

28 Changsheng Road, Hengyang,
Hunan Province 421001
Tel: +86(734) 8280805 +86(734) 8282718
Fax: +86(734) 8280805 +86(734) 8282718
EMail: wdy20012001@yahoo.com
Website: http://www.nhu.edu.cn/

President: Wen Gebo

International Relations: Zhang Zhiying

Schools

Arts and Design (Architecture; Industrial Design); **Chemistry and Chemical Engineering** (Chemical Engineering; Chemistry); **Computer Science and Technology**; **Economics and Management**; **Electrical Engineering** (Automation and Control Engineering; Electronic Engineering; Information Sciences); **Foreign Languages**; **Life Science and Technology** (Medicine; Pharmacy); **Literature and Law**; **Mathematics and Physics**; **Mechanical Engineering**; **Medicine** (Medicine); **Nuclear Engineering Resources and Safety**; **Nuclear Science and Technology** (Nuclear Engineering); **Nursing** (Nursing); **Public Health** (Public Health); **Urban Construction**

History: Founded 1958 as Hengyang Medical College. Acquired present status and title 2002.

Main Language(s) of Instruction: Chinese

Degrees and Diplomas: *Bachelor's Degree*; *Master's Degree*; *Doctor's Degree*

Last Updated: 09/12/08

WANNAN MEDICAL COLLEGE

Weiliu Road, University Park, Wuhu,
Anhui Province 241002
Tel: +86(553) 3832468 Ext. 6306
Fax: +86(553) 3811994
EMail: webmaster@wnmc.edu.cn
Website: http://www.wnmc.edu.cn

President: Song Jianguo

International Relations: Wu Jinyue

Departments

Anaesthesiology (Anaesthesiology); **Clinical Medicine** (Medicine); **Forensic Medicine** (Forensic Medicine and Dentistry); **Medicine**; **Stomatology** (Stomatology)

History: Founded 1958 as Wuhu Medical Vocational School, acquired present status 1971 and title 1974.

Main Language(s) of Instruction: Chinese

Degrees and Diplomas: *Bachelor's Degree*; *Master's Degree*
Last Updated: 09/12/08

WEIFANG MEDICAL UNIVERSITY

288 Shenglidongjie, Kuiwen, Weifang, Shandong Province 261042
Tel: +86(536) 8238243
Fax: +86(536) 8238243
EMail: nic@wfmc.edu.cn
Website: http://www.wfmc.edu.cn

President: Lui Yurui

International Relations: Liu Dianen

Departments

Anaesthesiology (Anaesthesiology); **Clinical Medicine** (Medicine; Ophthalmology; Stomatology); **Health Care Management** (Health Administration)

History: Founded 1951 as Changwei Medical School, acquired present title 1987.

Main Language(s) of Instruction: Chinese

Degrees and Diplomas: *Bachelor's Degree*; *Master's Degree*

Libraries: c. 225,000 vols

Publications: Journal of Weifang Medical College
Last Updated: 09/12/08

WEIFANG UNIVERSITY

149 East Dongfeng Street, Weifang, Shandong Province 261061
Tel: +86(536) 8785119 +86(536) 8785219
Fax: +86(536) 8785256 +86(536) 8785219
EMail: wsb@wfu.edu.cn; wfu@wfu.edu.cn
Website: http://www.wfu.edu.cn/

Departments

Art; **Biology** (Biology); **Chemistry** (Chemistry); **Chinese Language and Literature** (Chinese; Literature; Native Language); **Computer Science** (Computer Science); **Economic Management**; **Electro-Mechanic Engineering** (Electronic Engineering; Mechanical Engineering); **Foreign Languages and Literature**; **Information and Control Engineering** (Automation and Control Engineering; Computer Engineering); **Law** (Law); **Mathematics** (Mathematics); **Music**; **Physical Education**; **Physics** (Physics); **Politics and History** (History; Political Sciences)

History: Created 1960 as Changwei Teachers Training College . Acquired current status and title 2003.

Degrees and Diplomas: *Bachelor's Degree*
Last Updated: 12/10/09

WEINAN TEACHERS UNIVERSITY

24 Zhannan Road, Weinan, Shaanxi Province 714000
Tel: +86(913) 2088766
Fax: +86(913) 2088762
Website: http://www.wntc.edu.cn/index_4/

Departments

Adult Education; **Arts**; **Chemistry**; **Chinese**; **Computer Science** (Computer Science); **English** (English); **History**; **Management Science** (Management); **Mathematics** (Mathematics); **Physical Education** (Physical Education); **Physics** (Physics); **Political Education** (Political Sciences); **Social Sciences**

History: Founded 1978 as Weinan Teachers Training College. Merged with Weinan Educational College. Acquired present title 2000.

Degrees and Diplomas: *Bachelor's Degree*; *Master's Degree*

Libraries: c. 358,000 vols.

WENZHOU MEDICAL COLLEGE

82 Xueyuan Road, Wenzhou, Zhejiang Province 325003
Tel: +86(577) 8833815
Fax: +86(577) 8831041
EMail: io@wzmc.net
Website: http://www.wzmc.edu.cn/en

President: Jia Qui

Departments

Administration; **Arts**; **Engineering** (Biomedical Engineering; Computer Science; Electrical Engineering; Pharmacology); **Medicine** (Anaesthesiology; Laboratory Techniques; Law; Medicine;

Nursing; Ophthalmology; Optometry; Stomatology); **Science** (Biology; Biotechnology; Environmental Studies; Marine Science and Oceanography; Pharmacy; Psychology; Rehabilitation and Therapy); **Sociology**

History: Founded 1958.

Main Language(s) of Instruction: Chinese

Degrees and Diplomas: *Bachelor's Degree*; *Master's Degree*; *Doctor's Degree*
Last Updated: 31/10/08

WENZHOU UNIVERSITY

Chashan University Town, Wenzhou, Zhejiang Province 325035
Tel: +86(577) 8659-6061
Fax: +86(577) 8659-6063
EMail: wzdx@wzu.edu.cn
Website: http://www.wzu.edu.cn

President: Gu Chaohao
Tel: +86(577) 8659-8000, Fax: +86(577) 8659-7000

Colleges
Adult and Further Education; **Architecture and Civil Engineering** (Architecture; Civil Engineering); **Chemistry and Materials Science** (Chemistry; Materials Engineering); **Computer Science and Engineering** (Computer Engineering; Computer Science); **Foreign Languages** (Modern Languages); **Humanities** (Arts and Humanities); **Law and Politics** (Law; Political Sciences); **Life and Environmental Science**; **Mathematics and Information Science** (Mathematics and Computer Science); **Mechanical and Electrical Engineering** (Electrical Engineering; Mechanical Engineering); **Music** (Music); **Physical Education** (Physical Chemistry); **Physics and Electronic Information** (Information Sciences; Physics)

Institutes
Art and Design (Design; Fine Arts); **Fashion** (Fashion Design)

Schools
Business

History: Founded in 1984 when merged with Wenzhou Normal College.

Degrees and Diplomas: *Bachelor's Degree*: Administration; Advertising; Applied Chemistry; Architecture; Artistic Design; Biological Science; Biological Technology; Business Administration; Chemical Engineering and Techniques; Chemistry; Chinese Language and Literature; Civil Engineering; Communication Engineering; Computer Science and Technology; Dress Design; Economics; Educational Techniques; Electronic Information Engineering; Electronic Information Science and Technology; English; Environmental Science; Financial Control; Fine Arts; History; Industrial Engineering; Information and Computation Science; Information Management and Information Systems; International Economy and Trade; Legal Science; Marketing; Materials Science; Mathematics and Applied Mathematics; Mechanical Engineering and Automation; Music; Musicology; Pedagogy; Physics; Political and Moral Education; Primary Education; Social Sports; Social Work; Sports Education; Statistics; *Master's Degree*: Applied Mathematics; Applied Chemistry; Chinese Language; Computer Application and Technology; Curriculum & Teaching Methodology; English Language and Literature; Folk Literature and Art; History; Linguistics and Applied Linguistics; Modern Chinese Literature; Moral and Political Education; Musicology; Organic Chemistry; Physical Chemistry; Physical Education and Training; Physics of Condensed Matter; Theoretical Physics; Traditional Chinese Literature

Academic Staff *2008-2009*: Total: c. 1,300
Student Numbers *2008-2009*: Total: c. 25,000
Last Updated: 03/10/08

WUHAN CONSERVATORY OF MUSIC

255 Jiefang Road, Wuhan, Hubei Province 430060
Tel: +86(27) 88066354
Fax: +86(27) 88069436
EMail: whmusicc@public.wh.hb.cn
Website: http://www.whcm.com.cn

President: Zhao Deyi
International Relations: Yang Danna

Departments
Acoustics (Physics); **Chinese Folk Instruments**; **Composition Technique and Theory** (Music Theory and Composition); **Dance** (Dance); **Keyboard**; **Music Education** (Music Education); **Musicology** (Musicology); **String and Wing Instruments** (Musical Instruments); **Vocal Music**

History: Founded 1920 as Wuchang Art School, acquired present status and title 1985.

Degrees and Diplomas: *Bachelor's Degree*; *Master's Degree*

WUHAN INSTITUTE OF PHYSICAL EDUCATION

46 Luoyu Road, Wuhan, Hubei Province 430079
Tel: +86(27) 87803623 +86(27) 87801226
Fax: +86(27) 87803623
EMail: wipe_fao@yahoo.com.cn
Website: http://www.wipe.edu.cn/international/english/index.html

President: Sun Yiliang

Departments
Physical Education (Physical Education); **Sports Management** (Management; Sports); **Sports Psychology and Recovery**; **Sports Training** (Sports); **Wushu**

History: Founded 1953 as Zhongnan Institute of Physical Education, acquired present name 1956.

Degrees and Diplomas: *Bachelor's Degree*; *Master's Degree*; *Doctor's Degree*
Last Updated: 10/10/08

WUHAN INSTITUTE OF TECHNOLOGY

693 Xiongchu Road, Wuhan, Hubei Province 430073
Tel: +86(27) 87801351
Fax: +86(27) 87801351
Website: http://www.wit.edu.cn/english/

President: Li Jie

Departments
Physical Education (Physical Education)

Schools
Arts (Advertising and Publicity; Industrial Design); **Chemical Engineering and Pharmacy** (Chemical Engineering; Pharmacy); **Computer Science and Engineering**; **Economic Management** (E-Business/Commerce; Information Management; International Economics; Marketing); **Electrical and Electronic Engineering** (Automation and Control Engineering; Electrical and Electronic Engineering; Telecommunications Engineering); **Environment and Civil Engineering** (Civil Engineering; Environmental Engineering; Mineralogy; Town Planning); **Foreign Languages** (English); **Humanities and Management** (Arts and Humanities; Management); **Materials Science and Engineering** (Materials Engineering); **Mechanical and Electrical Engineering** (Automation and Control Engineering; Electrical Engineering; Mechanical Engineering); **Political Science and Law**; **Science** (Computer Science; Heating and Refrigeration; Information Sciences); **Telecommunications and Information Engineering**

History: Founded 1972 as Hubei Institute of Chemical and Petroleum Technology, acquired present name 2006.

Main Language(s) of Instruction: Chinese

Degrees and Diplomas: *Bachelor's Degree*; *Master's Degree*
Last Updated: 09/12/08

WUHAN POLYTECHNIC UNIVERSITY (WHPU)

No 1 West Zhonghuan Road, Changqung Huanyuan, Hankou, Wuhan, Hubei Province 430023
Tel: +86(27) 8391-2601 +86(27) 8395-5620
Fax: +86(27) 8391-2602 +86(27) 8391-1672
EMail: wsb@whpu.edu.cn
Website: http://www.whpu.edu.cn/

President: Jie Li

Head, Educational Administration Department: Xiangyang Sun

International Relations: Shifeng Li, Director, International Office

Colleges

Economics and Management (Accountancy; Business Administration; Finance; International Economics; Marketing; Tourism; Transport Management); **Food Science and Engineering**

Departments

Arts and Design; **Biology and Pharmaceutical Engineering** (Biochemistry; Biomedical Engineering; Pharmacology); **Chemistry and Environmental Engineering**; **Civil Engineering**; **Computer and Information Engineering** (Computer Science; Information Management; Information Sciences; Information Technology; Software Engineering); **Electrical Information Engineering** (Automation and Control Engineering; Electrical Engineering; Electronic Engineering; Telecommunications Engineering); **Food Science and Engineering**; **Foreign Language and Literature** (English); **Health Sciences and Nursing**; **Humanities** (Administration; Advertising and Publicity; Chinese; Human Resources); **Mathematics and Physics** (Mathematics; Physics); **Mechanical Engineering** (Automation and Control Engineering; Automotive Engineering; Industrial Design; Machine Building; Packaging Technology; Production Engineering)

History: Founded 1951 as Wuhan Food Industry College, acquired present title 1999.

Academic Year: September to July (September-January; February-July)

Admission Requirements: Entrance exam

Fees: (Yuan): 4,000-18,000 per annum

Main Language(s) of Instruction: Chinese

International Co-operation: With universities in UK, Australia, Netherlands, Germany

Degrees and Diplomas: *Bachelor's Degree*: all fields (BA), 4-5 yrs; *Master's Degree (MA)*: a further 3 yrs

Student Services: Academic counselling, Canteen, Cultural centre, Health services, Language programs, Nursery care, Social counselling, Sports facilities

Student Residential Facilities: Yes

Special Facilities: Art gallery. Film studio.

Libraries: c. 787,000 vols; E-books c. 280,000

Publications: Journal of Wuhan Polytechnic University, Research papers produced by academic staff *(monthly)*
Last Updated: 09/12/08

WUHAN UNIVERSITY

Luojia Hill, Wuchan District, Wuhan, Hubei Province 430072
Tel: +86(27) 87682810
Fax: +86(27) 87874669
EMail: web@whu.edu.cn
Website: http://www.whu.edu.cn/

President: Liu Jingnan

Colleges

Basic Medicine (Medicine); **Chemistry and Molecular Science**; **Civil Engineering** (Civil Engineering); **Computer Science** (Computer Science; Physics; Software Engineering); **Dynamics and Machinery** (Machine Building; Mechanical Engineering); **Education** (Education; Pedagogy); **Electronic Information** (Electronic Engineering; Information Sciences; Information Technology); **History** (History); **Information Management** (Information Management; Information Sciences); **Journalism and Mass Media** (Advertising and Publicity; Journalism; Media Studies; Radio and Television Broadcasting); **Liberal Studies** (Arts and Humanities); **Life Sciences** (Architecture; Biochemistry; Biological and Life Sciences; Biophysics; Botany; Cell Biology; Genetics; Immunology; Microbiology; Molecular Biology; Pharmacology; Virology); **Materials Science and Engineering** (Materials Engineering); **Mathematics and Statistics** (Mathematics; Statistics); **Pharmacy**; **Physics and Technology**; **Politics and Public Administration** (Political Sciences; Public Administration); **Remote Sensing Information Engineering** (Information Sciences; Surveying and Mapping); **Resources and Environmental Science** (Environmental Engineering; Natural Resources); **Stomatology**; **Water Resources and Hydroelectric Engineering** (Electrical Engineering; Hydraulic Engineering; Natural Resources; Water Science); **WTO**

Departments

Art (Fine Arts)

Schools

Business; **Electrical Engineering**; **Foreign Languages and Literature** (English; French; Literature; Modern Languages); **Geodesy and Geomatics**; **International Software** (Software Engineering); **Law** (International Law; Law); **Medicine** (Medicine); **Public Health** (Hygiene; Public Health); **Urban Studies** (Urban Studies)

History: Founded 1893 as Ziqiang Institute. Acquired present status and title 2000, following merger of Wuhan University, Wuhan University of Hydraulic and Electrical Engineering, Wuhan Technical University of Surveying and Mapping, and Hubei Medical University.

Degrees and Diplomas: *Bachelor's Degree*; *Master's Degree*; *Doctor's Degree*

Libraries: c. 2.7m. vols

Publications: Journal of Wuhan University; Mathematics Journal
Last Updated: 09/12/08

WUHAN UNIVERSITY OF SCIENCE AND ENGINEERING (WUSE)

1 FangZhi Road, Luxiang, Wuhan, Hubei Province 430073
Tel: +86(27) 87801395
EMail: master@wuse.edu.cn
Website: http://www.wuse.edu.cn

President: Zhang Jiangang

Colleges

Art and Design; **Adult Education** (Adult Education); **Apparel Engineering** (Clothing and Sewing; Textile Technology); **Chemical Engineering** (Chemical Engineering); **Computer Science** (Computer Science; Technology); **Economics and Management** (Accountancy; Business and Commerce; Information Sciences; International Economics; Management); **Electromechanical Engineering** (Architectural and Environmental Design; Automation and Control Engineering; Electrical and Electronic Equipment and Maintenance; Electronic Engineering; Industrial Design; Mechanical Engineering); **Electronic Information Engineering** (Electronic Engineering); **Environment and Urban Construction** (Construction Engineering; Environmental Engineering; Urban Studies); **High Vocational Technology** (Technology); **Human and Social Sciences** (Advertising and Publicity; Mathematics; Physics; Social Sciences); **Textile and Material Engineering** (Materials Engineering; Textile Design; Textile Technology)

Departments
Mathematics and Physics

History: Founded 1987 as Hubei Institute of Light Industry, acquired present title 1999.

Degrees and Diplomas: *Bachelor's Degree*; *Master's Degree*
Last Updated: 10/12/08

WUHAN UNIVERSITY OF SCIENCE AND TECHNOLOGY (WUST)

947 Heping Road, Wuhan, Hubei Province 430081
Tel: +86(27) 68862470
Fax: +86(27) 68862860
EMail: webmaster@wust.edu.cn
Website: http://www.wust.edu.cn/wust_en/index.html

President: Kong Jianyi Tel: +86(27) 86841915

Colleges

Art and Design; **Chemical Engineering and Technology** (Chemical Engineering; Environmental Engineering; Safety Engineering; Technology); **Computer Science and Technology** (Computer Science; Software Engineering); **Foreign Languages** (English; Modern Languages); **Information Science and Engineering** (Automation and Control Engineering; Electrical and Electronic Engineering); **Literature, Law and Economics** (Arts and Humanities; Economics; English; Law; Literature; Political Sciences); **Machinery and Automation** (Automation and Control Engineering; Mechanical Engineering); **Management** (Business Administration; Management); **Material and Metallurgical Engineering**; **Medical** (Medicine; Nursing; Pharmacy); **Natural Resources and Environmental Engineering**; **Science** (Applied Physics; Computer

Science; Information Technology); **Urban Construction** (Civil Engineering; Construction Engineering; Urban Studies)

Departments
Physical Education (Physical Education; Sports)

History: Founded 1907 as Wuchang Iron and Steel Industrial School, acquired present title 1999.

Admission Requirements: Graduation from high school and entrance examination

Fees: (Yuan): 5,000 per annum

Main Language(s) of Instruction: Chinese, English

Accrediting Agencies: Hubei Provincial Government

Degrees and Diplomas: *Bachelor's Degree*: 4 yrs; *Master's Degree*: a further 3 yrs; *Doctor's Degree*: a further 3 yrs

Student Services: Academic counselling, Canteen, Cultural centre, Employment services, Foreign student adviser, Foreign Studies Centre, Health services, Language programs, Nursery care, Social counselling, Sports facilities

Student Residential Facilities: Yes

Libraries: c. 1m. vols

Publications: Higher Education Study; Journal of Wuhan University of Science and Technology
Last Updated: 10/12/08

WUHAN UNIVERSITY OF TECHNOLOGY

122 Luoshi Road, Wuhan, Hubei Province 430070
Tel: +86(27) 87658253
Fax: +86(27) 87880253
EMail: randygh@mail.whut.edu.cn
Website: http://www.whut.edu.cn

President: Zhou Zude

Departments
Engineering Structures and Mechanics (Mechanical Engineering); **Foreign Languages** (Modern Languages); **Mathematics and Physics** (Mathematics; Physics)

Schools
Arts and Design (Design; Industrial Design); **Civil Engineering and Architecture** (Architecture; Civil Engineering; Construction Engineering); **Continuing Education**; **Information Technology** (Automation and Control Engineering; Computer Science; Electrical Engineering; Information Technology; Technology); **Literature and Law** (Law; Literature); **Management and Economics** (Accountancy; Economics; Management); **Materials Science and Engineering** (Applied Chemistry; Materials Engineering); **Mechanical Engineering** (Mechanical Engineering); **Resources and Environmental Engineering** (Environmental Engineering; Natural Resources)

History: Founded 2000 on the basis of former Wuhan University of Technology (WUT, founded in 1948) under the Ministry of Education, Wuhan Transportation University (WTU, founded in 1945) under the Ministry of Communications and Wuhan Automotive Polytechnic University (WAPU, founded in 1958) under the China National Automotive Industry Corporation.

Academic Year: September to July (September-January; February-July)

Admission Requirements: Graduation from senior middle school and entrance examination

Fees: (Yuan): c. 3,000 per annum

Main Language(s) of Instruction: Chinese

Degrees and Diplomas: *Bachelor's Degree*: 4 yrs; *Master's Degree*: a further 3 yrs; *Doctor's Degree (Ph.D.)*: 3 yrs

Student Services: Academic counselling, Employment services, Health services, Nursery care, Social counselling, Sports facilities

Student Residential Facilities: Yes

Special Facilities: International Science and Technology Information Retrieval Centre

Libraries: Central Library, c. 860,000 vols

Publications: Journal of Wuhan University of Technology (quarterly)

Press or Publishing House: Wuhan University of Technology Press

WUYI UNIVERSITY

Jiangmen, Guangdong Province 529020
Tel: +86(750) 3296120
Fax: +86(750) 3354323
EMail: xf@wyu.edu.cn
Website: http://www.wyu.edu.cn

President: Jian Lin (1998-)
Tel: +86(750) 3296111 EMail: jianlin@wyu.edu.cn

Administrative Officer: Qiuying Ji
Tel: +86(750) 3296110, Fax: +86(750) 3358395
EMail: op@wyu.cn

International Relations: Changchun Zheng

Colleges
Continuing Education *Dean*: Guoxiong Zhang; **Higher Vocational Technical** (Technology) *Head*: Haizhi Li

Departments
Arts and Social Sciences (Arts and Humanities; Social Sciences) *Director*: Qingxu Luo; **Chemical and Environmental Engineering** (Chemical Engineering; Environmental Engineering) *Dean*: Xueheng Chen; **Chinese Language and Literature** (Chinese; English; Literature) *Dean*: Shaoyu Bai; **Civil Engineering** (Civil Engineering) *Dean*: Zueqin Zeng; **Foreign Languages and Literature** (English; Literature; Modern Languages) *Dean*: Qi'an Song; **Mathematics and Physics** (Mathematics; Physics) *Dean*: Xiangyun Xie; **Mechanical and Electronic Engineering** (Automation and Control Engineering; Computer Graphics; Electronic Engineering; Industrial Design; Mechanical Engineering) *Dean*: Tieniu Yang; **Physical Education** (Physical Education) *Dean*: Bing Pan; **Textile and Clothing** (Clothing and Sewing; Fashion Design; Textile Technology) *Dean*: Jiangfeng Di

Schools
Information *Director*: Zhiyong Liu; **Management** (Business Administration; Economics; Management) *Dean*: Jin Liu

Further Information: Also courses in Chinese Language and Culture; English Language and Literature; Modern China (in English) for foreign students

History: Founded 1985.

Admission Requirements: Entrance examination and achieve minimum score set by the Department of Education of Guangdong Province

Fees: (Yuan): 4,500 per annum

Main Language(s) of Instruction: Chinese and English

Degrees and Diplomas: *Zhuanke Certificate of Graduation*: 3 yrs; *Bachelor's Degree*: 4 yrs; *Master's Degree*: 3 yrs

Student Services: Academic counselling, Canteen, Cultural centre, Employment services, Foreign student adviser, Foreign Studies Centre, Handicapped facilities, Health services, Language programs, Nursery care, Social counselling, Sports facilities

Student Residential Facilities: Yes.

Libraries: 810,000 vols in Chinese; 45,000 vols in foreign languages; 1,277 periodicals in Chinese

Publications: Natural Sciences, Journal of Wuyi University (biennially); Social Sciences, Journal of Wuyi University (quarterly); Wuyi University Newsletter

XI'AN ACADEMY OF FINE ARTS

100 Hanguang South Road, Xi'an, Shaanxi Province 710065
Tel: +86(29) 8821-4243 +86(29) 8214-251
Fax: +86(29) 8825-9909
Website: http://www.xafa.edu.cn/

President: Yang Xiaoyang

International Relations: Wu Shunong, Director, International Cooperation Office EMail: lavender.jasmine@yahoo.com.cn

Departments
Art History and Criticism (Art Criticism; Art History); **Chinese Traditional Painting**; **Design** (Design; Painting and Drawing); **Fashion Design** (Fashion Design); **Oil Painting** (Painting and Drawing); **Printmaking**; **Sculpture** (Sculpture)

Schools
Teacher Training

History: Founded 1948 as Kangri Junzheng Northwest University, acquired present status 1960 and name 1980.

Admission Requirements: Entrance exam and HSK test (Chinese language test)

Main Language(s) of Instruction: Chinese

Degrees and Diplomas: *Bachelor's Degree*: 4 yrs; *Master's Degree*: a further 3 yrs; *Doctor's Degree*: a further 3 yrs

Student Services: Academic counselling, Foreign student adviser, Foreign Studies Centre, Health services, Language programs, Nursery care, Social counselling, Sports facilities

Special Facilities: Museum, Art Gallery
Last Updated: 10/12/08

XI'AN CONSERVATORY OF MUSIC

18 Chang'anzhong Road, Xi'an, Shaanxi Province 710061
Tel: +86(29) 5239738
Website: http://www.xacom.edu.cn

President: Zhai Zhirong

International Relations: Sun Weiguo

Departments
Chinese Traditional Instruments (Folklore; Musical Instruments); **Composition and Theory** (Music Theory and Composition); **Keyboard**; **Music Education** (Music Education); **Musicology** (Musicology); **Vocal Music** (Singing); **Wind and String Instruments** (Musical Instruments)

History: Founded 1949 as Northwest Fine Arts School, acquired present status and name 1960.

Degrees and Diplomas: *Bachelor's Degree*; *Master's Degree*

XI'AN INSTITUTE OF PHYSICAL EDUCATION

38 Hanguang Road, Xi'an, Shaanxi Province 710068
Tel: +86(29) 88409701
Fax: +86(29) 88409703
EMail: webmaster@xaipe.edu.cn
Website: http://www.xaipe.edu.cn

President: Dang Qun

International Relations: Liu Guoyong

Departments
Chinese Martial Arts (Sports); **Economics** (Economics); **Journalism** (Journalism); **Physical Education**; **Physical Sociology** (Sociology); **Sports and Physical Science** (Physical Education; Sports); **Sports Training** (Sports)

History: Founded 1954 as Nortwest Intitute of Physical Education, acquired present name 1956.

International Co-operation: With universities in Japan, USA and Macao

Degrees and Diplomas: *Bachelor's Degree*; *Master's Degree*

Libraries: c. 200,000 vols
Last Updated: 10/12/08

XI'AN INSTITUTE OF TECHNOLOGY

4 Jinhuabeilu, Xi'an, Shaanxi Province 710032
Tel: +86(29) 3244764
Fax: +86(29) 3234896

President: Shu Chaolian

International Relations: Huang Xianshong

Departments
Architecture (Architecture); **Arts and Humanities and Social Sciences** (Arts and Humanities; Social Sciences); **Computer Science and Engineering** (Computer Engineering; Computer Science); **Economic Management** (Management); **Electronic Engineering** (Electronic Engineering); **Instrument Making** (Instrument Making); **Materials Science and Engineering** (Materials Engineering); **Mechanical Engineering** (Mechanical Engineering); **Modern Languages**

History: Founded 1955 as Xi'an Instrument Professional School, acquired present status and name 1965.

Degrees and Diplomas: *Bachelor's Degree*; *Master's Degree*

XI'AN INTERNATIONAL STUDIES UNIVERSITY (XISU)

N°2, South Wenyuan Road, Guodi High-Tech and Education Development ZoneChang'an District, Xi'an, Shaanxi Province 710128
Tel: +86(29) 85309274 +86(29) 8531974
Fax: +86(29) 8531900 +86(29) 85319100
EMail: fao@xisu.edu.cn
Website: http://www.xisu.edu.cn

President: Sishe Hu
Tel: +86(29) 85319002 EMail: hushishe@xisu.edu.cn

Chairman of the CCP Committee: Xiwen Yang

International Relations: Hui Li

Departments
Foreign Languages Education; **French and Spanish** (French; Linguistics; Literature; Spanish; Translation and Interpretation); **German**; **Physical Education** (Physical Education); **Russian**

Schools
Business and Law (Business and Commerce; Finance; International Law; Management); **Chinese Studies**; **Continuing Education** (English; Japanese); **Culture and Communication**; **East Asian Languages and Cultures** (Japanese; Korean); **English Studies** (American Studies; English; English Studies; Linguistics; Literature; Translation and Interpretation); **Graduate** (Geography (Human); Linguistics; Literature; Tourism; Translation and Interpretation); **Language Programmes** *(New Northwest)* (English; French; German; Italian; Japanese; Korean; Russian; Spanish); **Movie and TV Studies**; **Tourism**; **Training** *(New Northwest)*; **Vocational Education** (English; Hotel Management; Tourism)

History: Founded 1952 as Northwest Institute of Russian, acquired present status 1988. Former Xi'an Foreign Languages University. Became Xi'an International Studies University 2002.

Academic Year: September to July

Admission Requirements: National Matriculation Examination

Main Language(s) of Instruction: Chinese

International Co-operation: With over 80 universities worldwide

Accrediting Agencies: Ministry of Education; Education Department of Shaanxi Province

Degrees and Diplomas: *Zhuanke Certificate of Graduation*: 3 yrs; *Bachelor's Degree*: 4 yrs; *Master's Degree*: 3 yrs

Student Services: Academic counselling, Canteen, Cultural centre, Employment services, Foreign student adviser, Foreign Studies Centre, Handicapped facilities, Health services, Language programs, Nursery care, Social counselling, Sports facilities

Special Facilities: Movie Studio. Simultaneous Translation Lab.

Libraries: Yes

Publications: Foreign Language Teaching and Training *(quarterly)*; Journal of Xi'an International Studies University *(quarterly)*

Press or Publishing House: XISU Audio-visual Publishing House
Last Updated: 10/12/08

XI'AN JIAOTONG UNIVERSITY (XJTU)

28 Xianning West Road, Xi'an, Shaanxi Province 710049
Tel: +86(29) 2668830
Fax: +86(29) 3234716
EMail: oic_admin@mail.xjtu.edu.cn
Website: http://www.xjtu.edu.cn

President: Zheng Nanning (2003-)
Tel: +86(29) 2668234, Fax: +86(29) 3234781
EMail: office@mail.xjtu.edu.cn

International Relations: Yu Bingfeng

Departments
Sports (Sports)

Institutes
Vocational, Technical and Continuing Education (Technology Education)

Laboratories
Mechanical Products Quality Assurance and Diagnosis (Mechanical Equipment and Maintenance; Safety Engineering); **Biomedical Engineering** (Biomedical Engineering); **Computer Networks** (Computer Networks); **Electrical Insulation for Power Equipment** (Electrical Engineering; Power Engineering); **Electronic Physics and Devices Research**; **Fine Functional Electronic Materials and Devices**; **Fluid Machinery** (Hydraulic Engineering; Mechanical Engineering); **Intelligent Electrical Apparatus and CAD Software Engineering** (Electrical and Electronic Equipment and Maintenance; Software Engineering); **Manufacturing Systems Engineering** (Computer Engineering; Computer Networks; Engineering Management); **Mechanical Behaviour of Materials** (Materials Engineering); **Mechanical Structural Strength and Vibration** (Mechanical Engineering); **Medical Electronic Technology and Instrumentation**; **Multiphase Flow in Power Engineering** (Power Engineering); **Photonics Technology for Information** (Information Technology; Technology); **Theory of Lubrication and Rotor-Bearing Research**

Research Centres
Engineering (CIMSEC); **Fluid Machinery and Compressor** (Hydraulic Engineering; Mechanical Engineering); **Intelligent Electrical Apparatus and CAD Software Engineering** (Electrical and Electronic Equipment and Maintenance; Software Engineering)

Schools
Aerospace; **Architectural Engineering and Mechanics** (Civil Engineering; Mechanical Engineering; Structural Architecture); **Architecture**; **Chemical Engineering**; **Economics and Finance** (Economics; Finance); **Electrical Engineering** (Computer Engineering; Electrical Engineering; Electronic Engineering); **Electronic and Information Engineering** (Electronic Engineering; Information Sciences); **Energy and Power Engineering** (Automotive Engineering; Energy Engineering; Environmental Engineering; Heating and Refrigeration; Nuclear Engineering; Nuclear Physics; Physics; Power Engineering; Thermal Engineering; Thermal Physics); **Environmental and Chemical Engineering** (Chemical Engineering; Energy Engineering; Environmental Engineering; Materials Engineering; Physical Chemistry; Polymer and Plastics Technology); **Foreign Languages** (Modern Languages); **Humanities and Social Sciences** (Arts and Humanities; Business and Commerce; Chinese; Cultural Studies; Economics; English Studies; Fiscal Law; History; Human Resources; International Economics; International Studies; Japanese; Law; Literature; Management; Marketing; Mathematics and Computer Science; Modern Languages; Natural Sciences; Philosophy; Social Sciences; Sociology; Technology); **Internet Education** (Education); **Life Sciences and Technology**; **Management** (Accountancy; Business Administration; Computer Engineering; Economics; Finance; Industrial Engineering; Information Management; International Business; Management; Tourism); **Materials Science and Engineering** (Materials Engineering); **Mechanical Engineering** (Automation and Control Engineering; Computer Graphics; Design; Electrical and Electronic Engineering; Industrial Design; Machine Building; Materials Engineering; Measurement and Precision Engineering; Mechanical Engineering; Metal Techniques; Thermal Engineering); **Medicine**; **Pharmacy** (Pharmacy); **Software Engineering** (Software Engineering); **Stomatology**

History: Founded 1896 in South Ocean College, moved to Xi'an 1955 and renamed Xi'an Jiaotong University 1959. Acquired present title 2000, following merger of Xi'an Medical University, Shaanxi Institute of Finance and Economics and Xi'an Jiaotong University .

Governing Bodies: University Committee

Academic Year: September to July (September-January; February-July)

Admission Requirements: Graduation from high school and entrance examination

Main Language(s) of Instruction: Chinese

Degrees and Diplomas: *Bachelor's Degree*: 4 yrs; *Master's Degree*: a further 3 yrs; *Doctor's Degree*: 3-4 yrs

Student Services: Academic counselling, Canteen, Cultural centre, Employment services, Foreign student adviser, Foreign Studies Centre, Health services, Language programs, Nursery care, Social counselling, Sports facilities

Student Residential Facilities: Yes

Special Facilities: Concert Hall. Movie Studio

Libraries: Qian Xuesen Library, c. 1.6m. vols

Publications: Journal of Applied Mechanics (*quarterly*); Journal of Engineering Mathematics (*quarterly*); Journal of Xi'an Jiaotong University (*quarterly*)

Press or Publishing House: Publishing House of Xi'an Jiaotong University
Last Updated: 10/12/08

XI'AN POLYTECHNIC UNIVERSITY (XUEST)
19 South Jinhua Road, Xi'an, Shaanxi Province 710048
Tel: +86(29) 82330049
Fax: +86(29) 82330049
EMail: wsb@xaist.edu.cn
Website: http://www.xpu.edu.cn

President: Wang Xianghai

International Relations: Hu Weihua
EMail: hwhfld@mail.china.com

Departments
Automation and Control Engineering; **Chemical Engineering**; **Industrial Management**; **Mechanical Engineering**; **Social Sciences** (Social Sciences); **Textile Technology** (Textile Technology)

History: Founded 1978 as Northwest Institute of Textile Technology. Acquired present status and title 2003.

Fees: (US Dollars): Bachelor, tuition 2,000-2,200 per annum; short course programme, tuition, 250 per month

International Co-operation: With universities in Japan, Germany, USA, UK, Australia

Accrediting Agencies: Ministry of Education

Degrees and Diplomas: *Bachelor's Degree*: Computer Science and Technology; Chinese Knot Weaving; Chinese Culture; Chinese Language; Chinese Gongfu; Chinese Taijiquan; Chinese Traditional Fashion Designing and Sewing; Fashion Design and Engineering; Art Design and Engineering; Environmental Art Design; Applied Chemistry; Human Resources Management; Business Administration; Marketing Promotion; Industrial Design; Testing Techniques and Instruments; Textiles engineering; *Master's Degree*; *Doctor's Degree*

XI'AN SHIYOU UNIVERSITY
2 Dianzi Road, Xi'an, Shaanxi Province 710065
Tel: +86(29) 8234449
Fax: +86(29) 8234449
EMail: waiban@xsyu.edu.cn
Website: http://www.xapi.edu.cn

President: Zhang Zhang Ningsheng Ningsheng

Departments
Modern Languages; **Music** (Music)

Schools
Chemistry and Chemical Engineering; **Computer Science** (Computer Science; Educational Technology; Software Engineering); **Economic Management**; **Electronic Engineering** (Automation and Control Engineering; Electronic Engineering; Instrument Making; Measurement and Precision Engineering; Safety Engineering); **Humanities**; **Petroleum Engineering** (Petroleum and Gas Engineering); **Science** (Applied Physics; Mathematics)

History: Founded 1951 as Xi'an Petroleum School, acquired present status 1958. Renamed Xi'an Shiyou University 2003.

Degrees and Diplomas: *Bachelor's Degree*; *Master's Degree*; *Doctor's Degree*
Last Updated: 10/12/08

XI'AN UNIVERSITY OF ARCHITECTURE AND TECHNOLOGY

13 Yanta Road, Xi'an, Shaanxi Province 710055
Tel: +86(29) 2202169
Fax: +86(29) 2224571
EMail: intl@xauat.edu.cn
Website: http://www.xauat.edu.cn

President: Xu Delong

International Relations: Li Zheng

Schools
Architecture (Architecture; Town Planning); **Civil Engineering** (Civil Engineering; Transport Engineering)

History: Founded 1956 as Xian Institute of Construction Engineering, became Xian Institute of Metallurgy and Construction Engineering 1963. Acquired present status and title 1994.

Academic Year: September to July (September-January; February-July)

Admission Requirements: Graduation from senior middle school and entrance examination

Main Language(s) of Instruction: Chinese

Accrediting Agencies: Ministry of Metallurgy

Degrees and Diplomas: *Bachelor's Degree:* 4 yrs; *Master's Degree:* a further 2 1/2 yrs; *Doctor's Degree (Ph.D.)*

Special Facilities: University Movie Studio

Libraries: Central Library, c. 680,000 vols

Publications: Architecture and Technology; Journal of Xi'an University of Architecture and Technology *(quarterly)*; Study of Higher Education *(quarterly)*

Press or Publishing House: University Press
Last Updated: 10/12/08

XI'AN UNIVERSITY OF FINANCE AND ECONOMICS

81 Xiaozhai East Road, Xi'an, Shaanxi Province 710061
Tel: +86(29) 5228516
Fax: +86(29) 5228510
EMail: yuanzhang@mail.xaufe.edu.cn
Website: http://www.xaufe.edu.cn/English/survey.html

President: Liu Guotai

International Relations: Liu Zongzhao

Schools
Accountancy (Accountancy); **Economics**; **Information**; **Liberal Arts and Law**; **Management**; **Politics and Administration**; **Statistics** (Statistics)

History: Founded 1978 as Shaanxi Business Management Institute. Merged with Shaanxi Institute of Economics and Trade, Xi' an Institute of Statistics and Xi' an Junior College of Finance 2002. Acquired present title the same year. Formerly known as Shaanxi Institute of Economics and Trade.

Main Language(s) of Instruction: Chinese

Degrees and Diplomas: *Bachelor's Degree; Master's Degree*
Last Updated: 10/12/08

XI'AN UNIVERSITY OF POSTS AND TELECOMMUNICATIONS

Changan Road, Xi'an, Shaanxi Province 710121
Tel: +86(29) 88166107
Fax: +86(29) 88166107
EMail: fao@xupt.edu.cn
Website: http://www.xupt.edu.cn/

President: He Suozhu

International Relations: Jia Mingyuan

Departments
Business Management; **Computer Science** (Computer Science); **Economics** (Economics); **Engineering**; **Law**; **Literature** (Literature)

History: Founded 1950 as Northwest School of Post and Telecommunications, acquired present status and name 1959. Formerly known as Xi'an Institute of Posts and Telecommunications.

Degrees and Diplomas: *Bachelor's Degree; Master's Degree*
Last Updated: 28/10/09

XI'AN UNIVERSITY OF SCIENCE AND TECHNOLOGY

14 Yanta Road, Xi'an, Shaanxi Province 710054
Tel: +86(29) 5583033
Fax: +86(29) 5528334
Website: http://www.xust.edu.cn

President: Su Sanqing

International Relations: Xu Xingye

Departments
Chemistry and Chemical Engineering (Chemical Engineering; Chemistry); **Computer Science** (Computer Science); **Foreign Languages and Literature** (Literature; Modern Languages); **Geology and Environmental Engineering**; **Materials Engineering**; **Surveying Engineering**; **Telecommunications Engineering**

Schools
Architecture and Civil Engineering; **Communication Engineering**; **Electrical and Control Engineering**; **Energy and Resources**; **Mechanical Engineering**

History: Founded 1958 as Mining and Geology School of Xi'an Jiatong University. Became Xi'an Mining Institute 1985. Acquired present title 1999.

Main Language(s) of Instruction: Chinese

Degrees and Diplomas: *Bachelor's Degree; Master's Degree; Doctor's Degree*

Libraries: c. 440,000 vols

Publications: Journal of Xi'an University of Science and Technology
Last Updated: 10/12/08

XI'AN UNIVERSITY OF TECHNOLOGY (XUT)

5 South Jinhua Road, Xi'an, Shaanxi Province 710048
Tel: +86(29) 2312558
Fax: +86(29) 2312558
EMail: waiban@xaut.edu.cn
Website: http://www.xaut.edu.cn

President: Liu Ding

International Relations: Tian Jianing Tel: +86(29) 823-12545

Faculties
Automation and Information Engineering (Automation and Control Engineering; Electrical Engineering; Electronic Engineering; Information Technology) *Dean*: Yong Gao; **Business Administration** *Dean*: Xinghua Dang; **Computer Science and Engineering** *Dean*: Yikun Zhang; **Continuing Education** (Automation and Control Engineering; Electronic Engineering; Finance; Information Technology) *Dean*: Longquan Xue; **High Technology** *Dean*: Hui Wang; **Hydraulic and Hydroelectric Enginerering** (Environmental Engineering; Hydraulic Engineering; Power Engineering; Structural Architecture; Water Science) *Dean*: Xingqi Luo; **Material Science and Engineering** (Materials Engineering; Mechanical Engineering) *Dean*: Zhikang Fan; **Mechanical and Precision Instrument Engineering** (Automation and Control Engineering; Industrial Design; Machine Building; Measurement and Precision Engineering; Mechanical Engineering; Robotics) *Dean*: Yan Li; **Printing and Packaging Engineering** (Information Sciences; Packaging Technology; Printing and Printmaking) *Dean*: Jiamin Wang; **Science** *Dean*: Qingxiang He; **Social Sciences and Humanities** *Dean*: Qingming Li

History: Founded 1949 as Beijing Institute of Mechanical Engineering. Merged with Shaanxi Polytechnical University 1972. Acquired present name and title 1994 and merged with Xi'an Instrument Technology School.

Main Language(s) of Instruction: Chinese and English

International Co-operation: With universities in Germany

Degrees and Diplomas: *Bachelor's Degree*; *Master's Degree*; *Doctor's Degree*

Libraries: c. 470,000 vols

Publications: Journal of Xi'an University of Technology

Last Updated: 10/12/08

XIAMEN UNIVERSITY

422 Siming South Road, Xiamen, Fujian Province 361005
Tel: +86(592) 2186237
Fax: +86(592) 2180240
EMail: ws@jingxian.xmu.edu.cn
Website: http://www.xmu.edu.cn

President: Zhu Chongshi

Colleges
Architecture and Civil Engineering; **Art** (Design; Fine Arts; Musicology; Painting and Drawing); **Chemistry and Chemical Engineering**; **Foreign Languages and Cultures**; **Humanities** (Anthropology; Chinese; Ethnology; History; Journalism; Philosophy); **Oceanography and Environment** (Environmental Management; Marine Science and Oceanography)

Schools
Economics (Economics); **Engineering** (Engineering); **Law** (Law); **Life Sciences** (Biological and Life Sciences; Biology; Biotechnology; Ecology); **Management**; **Materials Science**; **Medicine** (Medicine); **Physics and Mechanical and Electrical Engineering** (Automation and Control Engineering; Machine Building; Microelectronics; Physics)

History: Founded 1921, acquired present status 1937.

Academic Year: September to July (September-January; March-July)

Admission Requirements: Graduation from senior middle school and entrance examination

Main Language(s) of Instruction: Chinese

Degrees and Diplomas: *Bachelor's Degree*: 4 yrs; *Master's Degree*: a further 3 yrs; *Doctor's Degree (PhD)*: a further 3 yrs

Student Services: Academic counselling, Canteen, Cultural centre, Employment services, Foreign student adviser, Foreign Studies Centre, Health services, Language programs, Nursery care, Social counselling, Sports facilities

Student Residential Facilities: Yes

Special Facilities: Lu Xun Museum. Tan Kah-Kee Museum. Museum of Anthropology

Libraries: c. 2m. vols

Publications: China Economy *(monthly)*; Higher Education in Foreign Countries *(monthly)*; Mathematics Studies *(monthly)*; Natural Sciences Journal *(monthly)*; Overseas Chinese Education *(monthly)*; Social Sciences Journal *(monthly)*; South-East Asian Studies *(monthly)*

Press or Publishing House: Xiamen University Press

Last Updated: 10/12/08

XIANGFAN UNIVERSITY

7 Longzhong Road, Xiangfang, Hubei Province 441053
Tel: +86(710) 3564876
Fax: +86(710) 3564876

President: Shu Bangxin

International Relations: Wang Weiyi

Centres
Modern Education and Technology

Departments
Administration; **Art**; **Chemistry and Chemical Engineering**; **Chinese Language and Culture**; **Construction Engineering**; **Electrical and Information Engineering**; **Foreign Languages and Culture**; **Geography**; **Mathematics**; **Mechanical Engineering**; **Physical Education**; **Physics**

Degrees and Diplomas: *Bachelor's Degree*

Libraries: c. 330,000 vols

Publications: Journal of Xiangfan University; Research and Administration of Higher Education

XIANGTAN UNIVERSITY

Xiangtan, Hunan Province 411105
Tel: +86(732) 8292130
Fax: +86(732) 8292282
EMail: webmaster@xtu.edu.cn
Website: http://www.xtu.edu.cn

President: Luo He'an

Departments
Physical Education (Physical Education)

Schools
Art (Architecture; Fine Arts); **Chemical Engineering** (Applied Chemistry; Chemical Engineering; Chemistry; Engineering; Environmental Engineering; Food Science); **Chemistry** (Chemistry); **Chinese** (Chinese); **Computer Science** (Computer Science); **Foreign Languages and Literature** (English; French; German; Japanese; Literature; Modern Languages); **Industrial Automation and Electronic Engineering** (Automation and Control Engineering; Electronic Engineering); **Law** (Commercial Law; Law); **Management** (Administration; Information Management; Library Science; Management; Tourism); **Mathematics** (Mathematics); **Mechanical Engineering** (Chemical Engineering; Electrical Engineering; Mechanical Engineering; Metal Techniques; Metallurgical Engineering; Thermal Engineering); **Philosophy and History** (Cultural Studies; History; Philosophy); **Physics** (Physics)

History: Founded 1958.

Degrees and Diplomas: *Bachelor's Degree*; *Master's Degree*; *Doctor's Degree*

Libraries: c. 1.4m. vols

Publications: Journal of Xiangtan University, Natural Sciences, Social Sciences; Research in Higher Education

Last Updated: 10/12/08

XIANNING COLLEGE

3 Guihua Road, Wenqun, Xianning, Hubei Province 437100
Tel: +86(715) 8260538
Fax: +86(715) 8260538

President: Tang Genhua

International Relations: Du Shengfu

Departments
Biomedical Engineering (Biomedical Engineering); **Clinical Medicine** (Medicine); **Clinical Pharmacology** (Pharmacology); **Medical Imaging** (Medical Technology)

History: Founded 1956, acquired present title 1994.

Degrees and Diplomas: *Bachelor's Degree*; *Master's Degree*

Libraries: c. 100,000 vols

Publications: Journal of Xianning Medical College

XIDIAN UNIVERSITY

2 Taibai Road South, Xi'an, Shaanxi Province 710071
Tel: +86(29) 8202221
Fax: +86(29) 8201620
EMail: master@xidian.edu.cn
Website: http://www.xidian.edu.cn

President: Baoyan Duan EMail: byduan@xidian.edu.cn

Schools
Computer Science and Engineering; **Economics and Management**; **Electronic Engineering**; **Humanities and Arts**; **Mechanical and Electronic Engineering**; **Physics**; **Telecommunications Engineering**

History: Founded 1931, acquired present title 1988.

Degrees and Diplomas: *Bachelor's Degree*; *Master's Degree*; *Doctor's Degree*

Libraries: c. 940,000 vols

Publications: China Electronics Education; Journal of Xidian University

Last Updated: 10/12/08

XIHUA UNIVERSITY (XHU)

Chengdu, Sichuan Province 610039
Tel: +86(28) 87720037 +86(28) 87720156
Fax: +86(28) 87720200 +86(28) 87720156
EMail: webmaster@mail.xhu.edu.cn
Website: http://www.xhu.edu.cn

President: Zhongxian Luo (1996-)
Tel: 86(28) 87720002 EMail: xiaoban@mail.xhu.edu.cn

International Relations: Jiachuan Zhang
Tel: +86(28) 87720114, Fax: +86(28) 87725032
EMail: oice@mail.xhu.edu.cn

Schools
Architecture and Civil Engineering *Chairman*: Zeyun Wang; **Arts** (Fine Arts) *Chairman*: Xun Xiao; **Bioengineering** (Bioengineering) *Chairman*: Li Ma; **Computer and Mathematical-Physical Science** (Computer Science; Mathematics; Physics) *Chairman*: Liangzhong Yi; **Economics and Trade** *Chairman*: Zeren Liu; **Electrical and Information Engineering** *Chairman*: Xiucheng Dong; **Energy and Environment** (Energy Engineering; Environmental Engineering) *Chairman*: Xiaobing Liu; **Foreign Languages and Culture** (Cultural Studies; Modern Languages) *Chairman*: Demo Yin; **Humanities** (Humanities and Social Science Education) *Chairman*: Weishu Shi; **Management** (Management) *Chairman*: Daoyun Zhang; **Material Sciences and Engineering** (Materials Engineering) *Chairman*: Daocheng Luan; **Mechanical Engineering and Automation** (Automation and Control Engineering; Mechanical Engineering) *Chairman*: Yuehong Dai; **Transportation and Automotive Engineering** *Chairman*: Haibo Huang

History: Founded 1960 as Sichuan Farm Machine College. Acquired present status and title 2003 following merger of former Sichuan University of Science and Technology and former Teacher's College.

Admission Requirements: Senior high school graduation diploma and entrance examination

Fees: (Yuan): c. 6,000

Main Language(s) of Instruction: Chinese

International Co-operation: With universities in USA, Canada, Germany, Japan

Accrediting Agencies: Ministry of Education

Degrees and Diplomas: *Bachelor's Degree*: Applied Mathemathics; Physics; Chemistry (B.S.); English; Japanese; Fine Arts (B.A.); Human Resources; Management; Accounting; Supply Chain (B.M.); Mechanical Engineering; Automation and Control Engineering; Industrial Engineering; Materials Engineering; Thermal Physics; Architecture; Bioengineering; Electrical Engineering; Computer Science; Technology, 4 yrs; *Bachelor's Degree*: Architecture (Major) (B.E.), 5 yrs; *Master's Degree*: Electronic Engineering; Materials Engineering; Hydraulic Engineering; Power Engineering; Mechanics; Computer Engineering; Software Engineering (M.E.), 3 yrs

Student Services: Academic counselling, Canteen, Cultural centre, Employment services, Foreign student adviser, Foreign Studies Centre, Health services, Language programs, Nursery care, Social counselling, Sports facilities

Libraries: Two Libraries, more than 1,000,000 vols

Publications: Higher Education Research *(quarterly)*; The Journal of Xihua University *(bimonthly)*

XINGTAI UNIVERSITY

3 Shizhuan Street, Xingtai, Hebei Province 054001
Tel: +86(319) 3229963
Fax: +86(319) 7300885
EMail: kickball@sina.com
Website: http://www.xttc.edu.cn

Departments
Arts Education for Primary Schools (Art Education; Primary Education); **Biology and Chemistry**; **Business Administration**; **Chinese** (Chinese); **Computer Science** (Computer Science); **English for Primary Schools** (English; Primary Education); **Financial Accountancy** (Accountancy; Finance); **Fine Arts** (Fine Arts); **Foreign Languages** (English); **Geography** (Geography); **Mathematics**; **Music**; **Physical Education** (Physical Education); **Physics**; **Politics and History** (History; Political Sciences)

History: Founded 1910 as Zhili Fourth Normal School. Acquired present title 2002.

Degrees and Diplomas: *Bachelor's Degree*

Libraries: c. 540,000 vols.

Publications: Journal of Xingtai University
Last Updated: 10/12/08

XINJIANG AGRICULTURAL UNIVERSITY

42 Nanchang Road, Urumqi, Xinjiang Uygur Province 830052
Tel: +86(991) 4523001 Ext. 2577
Fax: +86(991) 4520159
EMail: WEBMASTER@xjau.edu.cn
Website: http://www.xjau.edu.cn

President: Yin Jinzhang

International Relations: Li Baoping

Schools
Agronomy (Agronomy); **Animal Husbandry** (Animal Husbandry; Veterinary Science); **Economics and Trade** (Business and Commerce; Economics); **Forestry** (Forestry); **Hydrology and Civil Engineering** (Civil Engineering; Water Science); **Mechanical Engineering** (Mechanical Engineering)

History: Founded 1952 as Xinjiang August 1st Agricultural College, acquired present title 1995.

Degrees and Diplomas: *Bachelor's Degree*; *Master's Degree*; *Doctor's Degree*

Libraries: c. 420,000 vols

Publications: Journal of Xinjiang Agricultural University

XINJIANG INSTITUTE OF FINANCE AND ECONOMICS

15 North Beijing Road, Urumqi, Xinjiang Uygur Province 830012
Tel: +86(991) 7842017
Fax: +86(991) 3740942
Website: http://www.xjife.edu.cn

President: Yunusi Abulizy

International Relations: Luan Xinrong

Departments
Foreign Languages (Modern Languages); **Accountancy** (Accountancy); **Banking** (Banking); **Business Administration** (Business Administration); **Chinese** (Chinese); **Computer Science** (Computer Science); **Economics** (Economics); **Finance** (Finance); **Industrial and Commercial Management** (Industrial Management); **Law** (Law); **Marketing**; **Marxism and Leninism**; **Physical Education** (Physical Education); **Preparatory Studies**; **Statistics and Information Management** (Information Management; Statistics)

Schools
Adult Education. (Adult Education)

History: Founded 1950 as Xinjiang Province Cadre School, acquired present status and name 1980.

Fees: (US Dollars): Short-term students, 300 for 4 weeks, 50 per additional week); further study students,1,500 per annum (750 per semester); undergraduate, 1,800; postgraduate, 2,400

International Co-operation: With universities in Japan, USA, New Zealand, Kazakhstan

Degrees and Diplomas: *Bachelor's Degree*; *Master's Degree*

Libraries: c. 600,000 vols

XINJIANG MEDICAL UNIVERSITY

8 Xinyi Road, Urumqi, Xinjiang Uygur Province 830054
Tel: +86(991) 4365721
Fax: +86(991) 4361881
EMail: iec.xjmu@yahoo.com.cn
Website: http://www.xjmu.edu.cn

President: Maimaiti Yasin

International Relations: Zhou Hongxia

Schools

Traditional Chinese Medicine (Acupuncture; Traditional Eastern Medicine); **Western Medicine** (Medicine; Nursing; Pharmacology; Public Health; Stomatology)

History: Founded 1956 as Xinjiang Medical College. Merged with Xinjiang Traditional Chinese Medicine College. Acquired present title 1998.

Degrees and Diplomas: *Bachelor's Degree*; *Master's Degree*; *Doctor's Degree*

Libraries: c. 300,000 vols

Publications: Acta Academia Medicine Xinjiang
Last Updated: 10/12/08

XINJIANG NORMAL UNIVERSITY

19 Xinyi Road, Urumqi, Xinjiang Uygur Province 830053
Tel: +86(991) 4841601 Ext. 2535
Fax: +86(991) 4812513
EMail: xsdxbm@mail.wl.xj.cn
Website: http://www.xjnu.edu.cn

President: Ghupur Ismail

International Relations: Anniwar Rozy

Centres
Higher Education *(Xinjiang)*

Departments
Biology (Biology); **Chemistry** (Chemistry); **Chinese Language and Literature** (Chinese; Modern Languages); **Education**; **Fine Arts** (Fine Arts); **Foreign Languages**; **Geography** (Geography); **History** (History); **Law and Economics**; **Mathematics** (Mathematics); **Music** (Music); **Physical Education** (Physical Education); **Physics** (Physics)

History: Founded 1979.

Academic Year: September to July

Admission Requirements: Graduation from senior middle school and entrance examination

Main Language(s) of Instruction: Uygur, Chinese, Mongolian

Degrees and Diplomas: *Bachelor's Degree*: 4 yrs; *Master's Degree*: a further 3 yrs

Student Residential Facilities: Yes

Libraries: c. 600,000 vols

Publications: Journal of Xinjiang Normal University

XINJIANG PETROLEUM INSTITUTE

189 South Friendship Road, Urumqi, Xinjiang Uygur Province 830000
Tel: +86(991) 4521725
Fax: +86(991) 4512026
EMail: syxy@mail.wl.xj.cn

President: Xie Zhiqiang

International Relations: Cheng Zhogjin

Departments
Chemical Engineering (Chemical Engineering); **Computer Science** (Computer Science); **Economic Management**; **Exploration**; **Mechanical Engineering**; **Petroleum Engineering**; **Social Sciences**

History: Founded 1955 as Urumqi Petroleum School, acquired present status and name 1958.

Degrees and Diplomas: *Bachelor's Degree*; *Master's Degree*

XINJIANG UNIVERSITY

14 Shengli Road, Urumqi, Xinjiang Uygur Province 830046
Tel: +86(991) 286753
Fax: +86(991) 286006
EMail: dice@xju.edu.cn
Website: http://www.xju.edu.cn

President: Anwar Amut

International Relations: Jiao Jian

Colleges
Chemistry and Chemical Engineering (Chemical Engineering; Chemistry); **Electrical Engineering**; **Information Sciences and Engineering**; **Liberal Arts** (Arts and Humanities; Chinese; Geography; History); **Mechanical Engineering**; **Science and Technology** (Natural Sciences; Physics; Technology)

Institutes
Life Sciences (Biological and Life Sciences); **Mathematics** (Mathematics); **Resources and Environmental Sciences** (Environmental Studies; Natural Resources)

Schools
Economics and Management (Economics; Finance; Management); **Foreign Languages** (Modern Languages); **Law** (Law); **Politics and Law**

History: Founded 1924 as Xinjiang Russian Political and Law School. Acquired present title 1960. Merged with Xinjiang Institute of Technology 2000.

Main Language(s) of Instruction: Chinese

Degrees and Diplomas: *Bachelor's Degree*; *Master's Degree*; *Doctor's Degree*

Libraries: c. 1.3m. vols

Publications: Journal of Xinjiang University
Last Updated: 11/12/08

XINXIANG MEDICAL UNIVERSITY

Xinyan Road, Xinxiang, Henan Province 453003
Tel: +86(373) 3831919
Fax: +86(373) 3041119
EMail: wzbjben@xxmu.edu.cn
Website: http://www.xxmu.edu.cn/

President: Xing Ying

Departments
Foreign Languages (Modern Languages); **Life Sciences and Technology** (Biological and Life Sciences; Biomedical Engineering); **Medical Tests** (Haematology; Immunology; Microbiology; Molecular Biology); **Medicine** (Medicine); **Psychology** (Psychiatry and Mental Health; Psychology); **Social Sciences**

Institutes
Management; **Nursing**; **Pharmacology** (Pharmacology)

History: Founded 1950 as school of administration, acquired present status title and name 1982.

Main Language(s) of Instruction: Chinese

Degrees and Diplomas: *Bachelor's Degree*; *Master's Degree*
Last Updated: 11/12/08

XINYANG NORMAL UNIVERSITY

237 Changan Road, Xinyang, Henan Province 464000
Tel: +86(376) 6334254
Fax: +86(376) 6334254
EMail: gjc@mail2.xytc.edu.cn
Website: http://210.43.24.4/english/index.htm

President: Qian Yuanyan

International Relations: Zhou Ziliang

Colleges
Huarui (Biotechnology; Chinese; Civil Engineering; Computer Science; English; Fine Arts; Law; Marketing; Mathematics; Music)

Departments
Architectural Engineering; **Computer Science and Technology** (Computer Science); **Fine Arts** (Fine Arts); **Marxism** (Political Sciences); **Music** (Music); **Physical Education** (Physical Education); **Urban and Environmental Science**

Schools
Chemistry and Chemical Engineering (Chemical Engineering; Chemistry); **Economics and Management**; **Educational Sciences** (Education; Educational Technology; Psychology); **Life Sciences** (Biological and Life Sciences; Biology; Biotechnology); **Literature** (Chinese; Literature); **Mathematics and Information Science**;

Physics and Electronic Engineering (Electronic Engineering; Physics); **Political Science and Law** (Law; Political Sciences)

History: Founded 1975 as Xinyang School of Kaifeng Teachers College, acquired present status and title 1978.

Main Language(s) of Instruction: Chinese

Degrees and Diplomas: *Bachelor's Degree; Master's Degree*

Last Updated: 11/12/08

XINZHOU TEACHERS UNIVERSITY

10 Heping Xijie, Xinzhou, Shanxi Province 034000
Tel: +86(350) 3048275
Fax: +86(350) 3031845
EMail: wlzx@xztc.edu.cn
Website: http://www.xztc.edu.cn

President: Li Endian

Departments

Arts; **Chemistry**; **Chinese Language and Literature** (Chinese); **Computer Science** (Computer Science); **Economic Management**; **Educational Technology** (Educational Technology); **Foreign Languages**; **Geography** (Geography); **History** (History); **Law**; **Mathematics** (Mathematics); **Physics** (Physics); **Sports** (Sports)

History: Founded 1958 as Xinxian Teachers Training School. Acquired present status and title 2000 following merger with Xinzhou Teachers School.

Degrees and Diplomas: *Bachelor's Degree*

Special Facilities: Audio-visual labs; physical labs; chemical labs; electronic education centre.

Libraries: c. 400,000 vols; c. 800 periodical subscriptions.
Last Updated: 11/12/08

XUZHOU MEDICAL UNIVERSITY

84 Huaihai West Road, Xuzhou, Jiangsu Province 221002
Tel: +86(516) 5748415
Fax: +86(516) 5748429
EMail: dice@xzmc.edu.cn
Website: http://www.xzmc.edu.cn

President: Wu Yongping
Tel: +86(516) 5748429 EMail: wyp@xzmc.edu.cn

International Relations: Liu Song

Colleges
Medicine

Departments

Clinical Medicine (Medicine); **Continuing Medicine Education** (Medicine); **General Medicine** (Medicine)

Schools

Anaesthesiology (Anaesthesiology); **Basic Medicine**; **Medical Imageology** (Computer Graphics; Radiology); **Nursing** (Nursing); **Pharmacy**; **Public Health** (Public Health); **Stomatology** (Stomatology)

History: Founded 1958 as Xuzhou Branch of Nanjing Medical College, acquired present status 1960.

Main Language(s) of Instruction: Chinese

Degrees and Diplomas: *Bachelor's Degree; Master's Degree*
Last Updated: 11/12/08

XUZHOU NORMAL UNIVERSITY

57 Heping Road, Xuzhou, Jiangsu Province 221009
Tel: +86(516) 83403023
Fax: +86(516) 83403320
EMail: office@xznu.edu.cn
Website: http://www.xznu.edu.cn

President: Zhou Mingru

International Relations: Guan Jidong

Departments

Biology (Biology); **Chemistry** (Chemistry); **Chinese** (Chinese); **Computer Science**; **Educational Technology** (Educational Technology); **Foreign Languages** (Modern Languages); **Geography** (Geography); **History** (History); **Industrial and Commer**-

cial Management; **Mathematics** (Mathematics); **Music**; **Physical Education** (Physical Education); **Physics** (Physics); **Visual Arts**

Schools
Law and Political Science

History: Founded 1957 as Jiangsu Teachers College, acquired present title 1996.

Degrees and Diplomas: *Bachelor's Degree; Master's Degree*

Libraries: c. 1m. vols

Publications: Higher Education Research; Journal of Xuzhou Normal University

YAN'AN UNIVERSITY

Yan'an, Shaanxi Province 716000
Tel: +86(911) 2332015
Fax: +86(911) 2333677
EMail: chunhou2@163.com
Website: http://english.yau.edu.cn/aboutyau/ydgk/ydgk.jsp

President: Lian Zhengmin

Colleges

Arts (*Lu Xun*); **Chemistry and Chemical Engineering** (Chemical Engineering; Chemistry); **Economic Administration**; **Educational Sciences** (Curriculum; Educational Sciences; Educational Technology; Pedagogy); **Humanities and Social Sciences** (History; Public Administration; Social Work); **Life Sciences**; **Literature and Journalism**; **Mathematics and Computer Science** (Computer Science; Economics; Mathematics); **Medicine**; **Physical Education** (Physical Education); **Physics and Electronic Information** (Civil Engineering; Information Technology; Physics; Telecommunications Engineering); **Political Science and Law** (Law; Political Sciences)

Schools
Foreign Languages

History: Founded 1941 through merger of Shanbei Public School with the Woman's University of China, the Zedong School of Young Cadres, the Yanan School of Natural Sciences, the School of Nationalities, the Shanganning Border Region School of Administration and the Xinwenzi Cadre School.

Academic Year: March to January (March-July; September-January)

Admission Requirements: Graduation from senior middle school and entrance examination

Degrees and Diplomas: *Bachelor's Degree*: 4 yrs; *Master's Degree*

Student Services: Academic counselling, Cultural centre, Employment services, Foreign student adviser, Handicapped facilities, Health services, Nursery care, Social counselling, Sports facilities

Student Residential Facilities: Yes

Special Facilities: Museum of Yanan University history

Libraries: Library of Yanan University, c. 800,000 vols

Publications: Journal of Higher Education; Journal of Yanan University
Last Updated: 11/12/08

YANBIAN UNIVERSITY (YBU)

977 Gongyuanlu, Yanji, Jilin Province 133002
Tel: +86(433) 2732052
Fax: +86(433) 2719618
EMail: yinhua229@ybu.edu.cn
Website: http://www.ybu.edu.cn

President: Dongzhi Sun
Tel: +86(433) 2732011 EMail: dzsun@ybu.edu.cn

International Relations: Yongri CuiFax: +86(433) 275759
EMail: yrcui@ybu.edu.cn

Colleges

Adult Education; **Agriculture** (Agriculture); **Art** (Art Education); **Engineering** (Engineering); **Humanities and Social Sciences** (Arts and Humanities; Social Sciences); **Medicine** (Medicine); **Pharmacy** (Pharmacology; Pharmacy); **Physical Education**

(Physical Education); **Science and Technology** (Natural Sciences; Technology); **Teacher Training** (Teacher Training)

Research Centres
Chinese Teaching to Foreigners (Foreigners Education); **Feminine Issues** (Women's Studies); **North and South Korea Studies**

Research Institutes
Agriculture (Agriculture); **Animal Husbandry and Veterinary Science** (Animal Husbandry; Veterinary Science); **Application and Training of Yanbian CAD**; **Basic Mathematics** (Mathematics); **Business Administration** (Business Administration; Management); **Chemistry and Chemical Industry** (Chemical Engineering; Chemistry); **Chinese Literature** (Chinese; Literature); **Chinese Traditional Clinical Medicine** (Traditional Eastern Medicine); **Clinical Medicine** (Medicine); **Comparative Linguistics and Literature** (Linguistics; Literature); **Computer Science** (Computer Science); **Crystal Material**; **Design of Architecture** (Architectural and Environmental Design); **Electromechanical Integration** (Hydraulic Engineering); **English Education** (English); **Environmental Chemistry**; **Epilepsia** (Medicine); **Ethnical Issues** (Ancient Books; Dance; Demography and Population; Ethnology; History; Music; Musical Instruments); **Fine Chemical Industry** (Chemical Engineering; Chemistry); **Korean Medicine** (Traditional Eastern Medicine); **Northeast Asia** (Economics; Geography; International Studies; Korean; Law; Literature; Philosophy); **Preventive Medicine** (Social and Preventive Medicine); **Protection and Exploration of Changbai Mountain Natural Resources** (Natural Resources; Organic Chemistry); **Rice in Northern Cold Region**; **Science of Physical Education** (Physical Education); **Systematic Engineering** (Engineering); **Tumour** (Medicine)

History: Founded 1949, acquired present status 1996.

Admission Requirements: Senior high school certificate

Fees: (Yuan): 3,500 to 5,500 per annum

Main Language(s) of Instruction: Chinese; Korean

International Co-operation: With universities in Republic of Korea, Democratic People's Republic of Korea, Japan

Accrediting Agencies: Ministry of Education; Jilin Province Education Commission

Degrees and Diplomas: *Bachelor's Degree*: Agriculture; Art; Economics; Law; Medicine; Science; *Master's Degree*: Agriculture; Art; Economics; Education; History; Law; Medicine; Philosophy; Science; *Doctor's Degree*: History; Literature; Science

Student Services: Academic counselling, Canteen, Cultural centre, Employment services, Foreign student adviser, Foreign Studies Centre, Health services, Language programs, Nursery care, Social counselling, Sports facilities

Student Residential Facilities: Yes

Special Facilities: Movie Studio, Museum

Libraries: 1,480,000 vols, multimedia room

Publications: Collection of Papers on Korean Issues; Collection of Papers on Korean Nationality; Collection of Papers on North and South Korean Study; Dongjiang, (Eastern Border), Journal; Research on Oriental Philosophy; Study Chinese; Yanbian University Journal of Agricultural Sciences; Yanbian University Journal of Medical Sciences *(quarterly)*; Yanbian University Journal of Sciences and Engineering; Yanbian University Journal of Social Sciences *(quarterly)*

Press or Publishing House: Yanbian University Press

YANCHENG INSTITUTE OF TECHNOLOGY

No. 9 Yingbin Avenue, Yangcheng, Jiangsu Province 224003
Tel: +86(515) 88399183
Fax: +86(515) 88399183
EMail: gjhz@163.net
Website: http://www.ycit.edu.cn

President: Yang Chunseng

Schools
Chemical and Biological Engineering (Applied Chemistry; Bioengineering; Chemical Engineering; Environmental Engineering); **Civil Engineering** (Bridge Engineering; Civil Engineering; Construction Engineering; Engineering Management; Road Engineering); **Economics and Management**; **Electrical and Information Engineering** (Automation and Control Engineering; Computer

Science; Electrical Engineering; Software Engineering); **Humanities** (Chinese; English; Literature; Tourism); **Machinery Engineering**; **Material Engineering** (Materials Engineering; Metal Techniques; Polymer and Plastics Technology); **Textile and Costume Engineering** (Fashion Design; Textile Technology)

History: Founded 1958 as Yancheng College of Technology. Acquired present status and title 1996.

Main Language(s) of Instruction: Chinese

Degrees and Diplomas: *Bachelor's Degree*
Last Updated: 11/12/08

YANCHENG TEACHERS UNIVERSITY

3 South Tongyu Road, Yancheng, Jiangsu Province 224002
Tel: +86(515) 8334240
Fax: +86(515) 8334140
EMail: karenyu1983@yahoo.com
Website: http://www.yctc.edu.cn

President: Chang Bailin

International Relations: Miao Zhihong

Departments
Biology and Geography (Biology; Geography); **Chemistry** (Chemistry); **Chinese** (Chinese); **Computer Science**; **Education** (Education); **Mathematics**; **Modern Languages**; **Music and Fine Arts** (Fine Arts; Music); **Physical Education** (Physical Education); **Physics** (Physics); **Political Science and History**

History: Founded 1958.

Degrees and Diplomas: *Bachelor's Degree*

YANG-EN UNIVERSITY

Majia Town, Quanzhou, Fujian Province 362014
Tel: +86(591) 2082001 Ext. 118
Fax: +86(591) 2082017
EMail: yeu@yeu.qz.fj.cn
Website: http://www.yeu.edu.cn

President: Zhang Guqing

Departments
Banking; **Industrial and Commerce Management**; **International Economics and Trade**

History: Founded 1988 as Yang'en Institute, acquired present title 1994.

Degrees and Diplomas: *Bachelor's Degree*

Libraries: c. 70,000 vols

Publications: Learned Journal of Yang'en University

YANGTZE UNIVERSITY

1 Nanhuan Road, Jingzhou, Hubei Province 434023
Tel: +86(716) 8060236
Fax: +86(716) 8060514
EMail: fao@yangtzeu.edu.cn
Website: http://www.yangtzeu.edu.cn

President: Zhang Changmin

Schools
Agriculture; **Animal Science**; **Arts** (Dance; Design; Fine Arts; Musicology); **Chemistry and Environmental Engineering**; **City Construction** (Architecture; Civil Engineering; Engineering Management; Hydraulic Engineering; Town Planning); **Computer Science**; **Economics** (Economics; Farm Management; Forest Economics; International Business; International Economics); **Electronic Information**; **Foreign Languages** (English; Japanese); **Gardening and Horticulture** (Horticulture); **Geophysics and Oil Resources**; **Geosciences** (Geology); **Information and Mathematics**; **Life Sciences**; **Literature** (Chinese; History; Literature; Radio and Television Broadcasting); **Management** (Accountancy; Business Administration; Human Resources; Information Management; Marketing; Public Administration); **Mechanical Engineering**; **Medicine**; **Petroleum Engineering**; **Physical Education**; **Physics** (Applied Physics; Physics); **Politics and Law** (Law; Political Sciences; Social Work)

History: Founded 2003, following merger of Jianghan Petroleum University, Hubei Agricultural College and Jingzhou Teachers College.

Academic Year: September to July

Admission Requirements: Graduation from senior middle school and entrance examination

Fees: (Yuan): c. 9,950-23,100 per annum

Main Language(s) of Instruction: Chinese, English, Japanese

Accrediting Agencies: China National Petroleum Corporation

Degrees and Diplomas: Bachelor's Degree; Master's Degree; Doctor's Degree

Student Services: Academic counselling, Canteen, Cultural centre, Employment services, Foreign student adviser, Foreign Studies Centre, Handicapped facilities, Health services, Language programs, Nursery care, Social counselling, Sports facilities

Student Residential Facilities: Yes

Special Facilities: Geological Museum. Gallery of Yangtze Three Gorges Rock Samples

Libraries: c. 500,000 vols

Publications: Journal of Natural Sciences; Journal of Social Sciences

Last Updated: 11/12/08

YANGZHOU UNIVERSITY (YZU)

88 University Avenue South, Yangzhou, Jiangsu Province 225009
Tel: +86(514) 7971870
Fax: +86(514) 7352262
EMail: fao@yzu.edu.cn
Website: http://www.yzu.edu.cn

President: Rong Guo (2002-)
Tel: +86(514) 7971858, Fax: +86(514) 7311374
EMail: xiaoban@yzu.edu.cn

Executive Vice-President: Xin'an Jiao
Tel: +86(514) 7971858, Fax: +86(514) 7311374

International Relations: Yongming Tang
EMail: ymtang@yzu.edu.cn

Colleges
Agriculture (Agricultural Economics; Agricultural Management; Agriculture; Agronomy; Environmental Studies; Food Science; Horticulture); Animal Husbandry and Veterinary Science (Animal Husbandry; Veterinary Science; Zoology); Architectural Science and Engineering (Architecture; Civil Engineering; Structural Architecture); Art (Art Management; Design; Fine Arts; Music); Bioscience and Biotechnology (Biological and Life Sciences; Biotechnology); Chemistry and Chemical Engineering (Chemical Engineering; Chemistry); Chinese Language and Literature (Chinese; Literature; Modern Languages) Dean: Wenfang Yao; Economics (Economics; Farm Management; Finance; Forest Management; Forestry; International Business; International Economics) Dean: Naihua Jiang; Educational Science and Technology (Educational Psychology; Educational Technology; Photography; Primary Education) Dean: Yunshan Ye; Engineering (Agricultural Engineering; Agricultural Equipment; Automation and Control Engineering; Automotive Engineering; Industrial Design; Machine Building) Dean: Jiping Zhou; Engineering and Technology (Computer Engineering; Electrical and Electronic Engineering; Engineering; Mechanical Engineering; Technology) Dean: Ling Chen; Engineering, Architecture, Agriculture and Environment (Architecture; Civil Engineering; Environmental Management; Environmental Studies; Structural Architecture; Water Science) Dean: Jiankang Chen; Environmental Science and Engineering (Environmental Engineering; Environmental Management; Environmental Studies) Dean: Ke Feng; Foreign Languages (English; Japanese; Modern Languages) Dean: Hongliang Yu; Information Engineering (Information Technology) Dean: Ling Chen; Law (Law) Dean: Fumin Jiao; Management (Accountancy; Administration; E-Business/Commerce; Finance; Human Resources; Management; Marketing; Public Administration) Dean: Yao Chen; Mathematical Science (Mathematics) Dean: Yao Chen; Medicine (Dermatology; Gynaecology and Obstetrics; Medicine; Nursing; Pharmacology; Traditional Eastern Medicine) Dean: Ping Bo; Physical Education (Physical Education; Sports) Dean: Zhaogang Tong; Physical Science and Technology (Physics; Technology)

Dean: Xiaobing Chen; Social Sciences (History; Library Science; Philosophy; Political Sciences; Social Work) Dean: Jianchao Zhou; Tourism and Culinary Arts (Cooking and Catering; Tourism); Veterinary Medicine (Veterinary Science) Dean: Aijian Qin; Water Conservation and Architectural Engineering (Structural Architecture; Water Management) Dean: Wenqun Yan

Further Information: Also Teaching Hospital. Affiliated Animal Hospital, and Experimental Farm

History: Founded 1992 as a merger of Teachers College of Yangzhou, Agricultural College of Jiangsu, Engineering College of Yangzhou, Medical College of Yangzhou, Water Conservancy Engineering College of Jiangsu and Business School of Jiangsu.

Academic Year: September to July (September-January; February-July)

Admission Requirements: Graduation from senior middle school and entrance examination

Fees: (US Dollars): 1,600-4,500 per annum

Main Language(s) of Instruction: Chinese

International Co-operation: With universities in Canada, USA, Japan, Russian Federation, Belarus, Ireland, Chile, Philippines, Thailand, South Korea, United Kingdom, Australia and Germany

Accrediting Agencies: Jiangsu Education Department

Degrees and Diplomas: Bachelor's Degree: Biotechnology; Clinical Medicine; Traditional Chinese Medicine; Nursing; Economics; Public Finance; International Economy and Trade; Industrial and Commercial Administration; Accountancy; Culinary and Nutrition Education; Chinese Language and Literature; History; Fine Arts; Science of Law; Ideological and Political Education; Administration; English; Mathematics and Applied Mathematics; Physics; Chemistry; Applied Chemistry; Polymer Material and Engineering; Educational Technology; Physical Education; Machinery Design; Manufacture and Automation; Control Engineering; Agricultural Mechanization and Automation; Data Processing; Electrical Engineering and Automation; Computer Science and Technology; Engineering Management; Agriculture; Agricultural Resources and Environmental Studies; Rural Development; Plant Protection; Horticulture; Food Science and Engineering; Farming and Forestry Economics and Management; Zoology; Veterinary Science; Information Management and Information Systems; Hydraulic Engineering; Thermal Power and Dynamic Engineering; Hydrology ; Architecture; Civil Engineering; Built Environment and Equipment Engineering; Water Supply and Drainage Engineering, 4 yrs; Master's Degree: Breeding and Reproduction; Literature and Art; Preventive Veterinary Science; Curriculum and Teaching Methodology; Farming; Water Conservation; Zoology; Nutrition and Food Science; Education; Biochemistry and Molecular Biology; Condensed Matter Physics; Crop Genetics; Ancient Chinese Literature; Crop Cultivation and Farming; Modern and Contemporary Chinese History; Biophysics; Basic Mathematics; Physical Chemistry; Agricultural Entomology and Pest Control; Human Movement Science; Animal Genetics; Machinery Manufacturing and Automation; Computer Engineering; Applied Technology; Clinical Veterinary Science, a further 2-3 yrs; Doctor's Degree: Ancient Chinese Literature; Preventive Veterinary Science; Crop Cultivation and Farming Systems; Crop Genetics; Animal Genetics; Breeding and Reproduction (PhD), a further 1-2 yrs

Student Services: Academic counselling, Canteen, Cultural centre, Employment services, Foreign student adviser, Foreign Studies Centre, Handicapped facilities, Health services, Language programs, Nursery care, Social counselling, Sports facilities

Student Residential Facilities: For 35,000 students

Special Facilities: Biological Garden. Key Laboratories

Libraries: Total, 2.8m. vols

Publications: Research Journal of Yangzhou University (quarterly)
Last Updated: 11/12/08

YANSHAN UNIVERSITY (YSU)

438 Hebei Ave. W., Qinhuangdao, Hebei Province 066004
Tel: +86(335) 8057070
Fax: +86(335) 8061449
EMail: waiban@ysu.edu.cn
Website: http://www.ysu.edu.cn

President: Hong-min Liu
Tel: +86(335) 8051260, Fax: +86(335) 8051148

Colleges

Art and Design (Design; Fine Arts); **Civil Engineering and Mechanics** *Head*: Huijian Li; **Continuing Education** *Head*: Yufeng Liu; **Economic Management** *Head*: Xiaodong Zhao; **Electrical Engineering** *Head*: Xinping Guan; **Environmental and Chemical Engineering** *Head*: Minghua Bai; **Foreign Languages** *Head*: Guosheng Ding; **Graduate Studies** (Applied Mathematics; Automation and Control Engineering; Computer Engineering; Construction Engineering; Electrical Engineering; Electronic Engineering; Machine Building; Management; Materials Engineering; Measurement and Precision Engineering; Mechanics; Political Sciences; Software Engineering; Telecommunications Engineering) *Director*: Bin Liu; **Humanities and Law** *Head*: Yong Wu; **Information Science and Engineering** *Head*: Lingfu Kong; **Material Science and Engineering** *Head*: Yongjun Tian; **Mechanical Engineering** *Head*: Xiangdong Kong; **Science** *Head*: Yiming Chen

History: Founded 1920. Some of the departments of Harbin Institute of Technology moved to Qiqihar, Heilongjan Province, to establish its Heavy Machinery Institute 1958. Completely separated from HIT and renamed Northeast Heavy Machinery Institute 1960. Moved to Hebei Province and acquired present title and status 1997.

Academic Year: September to July

Admission Requirements: Graduation from senior middle school and national college entrance examination

Main Language(s) of Instruction: Chinese

Accrediting Agencies: Educational Department of Hebei Province

Degrees and Diplomas: *Bachelor's Degree*: 4 yrs; *Master's Degree*: a further 2-3 yrs; *Doctor's Degree*: 3 yrs

Student Services: Academic counselling, Canteen, Employment services, Foreign student adviser, Health services, Language programs, Nursery care, Social counselling, Sports facilities

Student Residential Facilities: Yes

Libraries: 330,000 vols. and 2,816 periodicals in Chinese; 58,000 vols and 1,325 periodicals in foreign languages

Publications: Journal of Yanshan University, Research in the fields of Natural and Social Sciences *(quarterly)*; Research in Teaching, Education in China and abroad *(quarterly)*

Last Updated: 11/12/08

YANTAI UNIVERSITY

30 Quingquan Road, Laishan, Yantai, Shandong Province 264005
Tel: +86(535) 6902381
Fax: +86(535) 6901858
EMail: ngelhanchengguo@163.com
Website: http://www.ytu.edu.cn

President: Mingrui Guo Tel: +86(535) 6902060

Secretary-General: Xiangli Han Tel: +86(535) 6902010

International Relations: Shijun Bai

Departments

Architecture (Architectural and Environmental Design; Architecture; Engineering Drawing and Design) *Director*: Shuquang Hao; **Mathematics and Information Science**

Research Institutes

East China Urban and Rural Construction (Rural Studies; South Asian Studies; Urban Studies)

Schools

Chemical and Biological Science and Engineering (Bioengineering; Biology; Chemical Engineering; Chemistry) *Division Head*: Ren; **Civil Engineering** (Civil Engineering); **Computer Science** (Computer Science); **Economics and Business Administration** (Business Administration; Economics); **Electro-mechanical Automobile Engineering**; **Environment and Material Engineering** (Environmental Engineering; Materials Engineering); **Foreign Languages** (Modern Languages); **Humanities**; **Information Technology and Photoelectronics** (Electronic Engineering; Information Technology); **Law** (Law); **Oceanography** (Marine Science and Oceanography); **Pharmacy**; **Physical Education** (Physical Education)

History: Founded 1984.

Academic Year: September to July

Admission Requirements: Entrance Examination

Fees: (Yuan): 6,000 per annum

Main Language(s) of Instruction: Chinese

International Co-operation: With universities in United Kingdom, USA, Germany, Italy, Republic of Korea, Canada, Australia, New Zealand

Accrediting Agencies: Shandong Provincial Education Committee

Degrees and Diplomas: *Bachelor's Degree*; *Master's Degree*

Student Services: Academic counselling, Canteen, Cultural centre, Employment services, Foreign student adviser, Foreign Studies Centre, Health services, Language programs, Nursery care, Social counselling, Sports facilities

Student Residential Facilities: Yes

Libraries: Total, 600,000 vols

Publications: Journal of Yantai University *(monthly)*

Press or Publishing House: Yantai University Press
Last Updated: 11/12/08

YUNNAN AGRICULTURAL UNIVERSITY

Heilongtan, Kunming, Yunnan Province 650201
Tel: +86(871) 5211168 Ext. 2735
Fax: +86(871) 5150303
Website: http://www.ynau.edu.cn

President: Zhu Yuyong

Schools

Agriculture and Biotechnology; **Animal Science and Technology** (Animal Husbandry; Veterinary Science; Zoology); **Continuing Education**; **Economics and Trade**; **Engineering**; **Food Science and Technology** (Food Science; Food Technology); **Foreign Languages**; **Horticulture**; **Humanities and Social Sciences** (Arts and Humanities; Social Sciences); **Physical Education** (Physical Education); **Plant Protection** (Plant and Crop Protection); **Resources and Environment** (Environmental Engineering; Environmental Studies; Natural Resources); **Science and Information** (Information Management; Natural Sciences); **Tobacco Science**; **Water Resources, Hydraulics and Architecture** (Architecture; Hydraulic Engineering; Water Management; Water Science)

History: Founded 1938 as the School of Agricultural at Yunnan University. Renamed Kunming Agriculture and Forestry College (KAFC). The formal title, Yunnan Agricultural University was adopted in 1971 following the merger between KAFC and Yunnan Agriculture Working University (YAWU).

Main Language(s) of Instruction: Chinese

Degrees and Diplomas: *Bachelor's Degree*; *Master's Degree*

Libraries: c. 500,000 vols

Publications: Journal of Yunnan Agricultural University
Last Updated: 12/12/08

YUNNAN ARTS INSTITUTE

9 Mayuan, Kunming, Yunnan Province 650101
Tel: +86(871) 5352026
Fax: +86(871) 5352770
EMail: yaifao@ynart.edu.cn
Website: http://www.admissions.cn/ynart/index01.htm

President: Zhang Jiangzhong

International Relations: Cheng Chunyun

Schools

Art Design; **Dance**; **Drama**; **Fine Arts** (Fine Arts); **Music** (Music)

History: Founded 1959 as department of Kunming Teachers College.

Main Language(s) of Instruction: Chinese

Degrees and Diplomas: *Bachelor's Degree*; *Master's Degree*
Last Updated: 09/09/08

YUNNAN NATIONALITIES UNIVERSITY (YNAU)

Yi'eryi Street, Kunming, Yunnan Province 650031
Tel: +86(871) 5154308
Fax: +86(871) 5154308
Website: http://www.ynni.edu.cn/

President: Li Guowen
International Relations: Yang Hong

Departments
Languages and Literature of Minority Ethnic Groups (Sidai, Dedai, Jingpo, Lahu, Lisu, Wa, Yi) (Literature; Native Language); **Chemistry** (Chemistry); **Chinese Language and Literature** (Chinese); **Economic Management** (Management); **English Language and Literature**; **Ethnic Art** (Dance; Fine Arts; Folklore; Music); **History** (Ethnology; History); **Mathematics and Computer Science** (Applied Mathematics; Computer Science; Mathematics; Technology); **Physical Education** (Physical Education); **Physics** (Physics); **Political Science and Law** (Law; Political Sciences); **Southeast Asian Languages**; **Tourism** (Tourism)

Schools
Continuing Education; **People's Armed Forces** (Law; Secretarial Studies; Tourism); **Preparatory University Education**

Further Information: 8 Graduate Programmes.

History: Founded 1951.

International Co-operation: With universities in USA and Hawaii, Thailand, Japan, Australia, United Kingdom, Myanmar, Republic of Korea.

Degrees and Diplomas: Bachelor's Degree; Master's Degree

Libraries: Total: c. 710,000 vols; over 2,000 journals and magazines

Publications: Ethnological Survey; Journal of Yunnan Nationalities University

Last Updated: 12/12/08

YUNNAN NORMAL UNIVERSITY
Kunming, Yunnan Province 650092
Tel: +86(871) 5516149
Fax: +86(871) 5516804
Website: http://www.ynnu.edu.cn
President: Yi Jidong
International Relations: Wu Yinghui

Departments
Biology (Biology); **Chemistry** (Chemistry); **Chinese**; **History** (History); **Information** (Information Sciences); **Life Sciences**; **Mathematics** (Mathematics); **Natural Resources and Environment** (Development Studies; Environmental Management; Environmental Studies; Natural Resources); **Political Sciences**

Schools
Computer Science and Information Technology; **Continuing Education**; **Education** (Education; Psychology); **Fine Arts**; **Foreign Languages** (Modern Languages); **Physical Education** (Physical Education); **Physics and Electronic Engineering** (Electronic Engineering; Physics); **Tourism and Geography**; **Vocational Education**

Further Information: Also courses for foreign students. Study Abroad programmes

History: Founded 1938 as Teachers' College of the State Southwest Associated University. Acquired present status and title 1984. Under the jurisdiction of the Yunnan Provincial Government.

Academic Year: September to July (September-January; March-July)

Admission Requirements: Graduation from senior middle school and entrance examination

Fees: (Yuan): 2,000-3,000 per annum

Main Language(s) of Instruction: Chinese, English

Degrees and Diplomas: Bachelor's Degree: 4 yrs; Master's Degree

Student Residential Facilities: For c. 4,500 students

Libraries: Central Library, 1.8m. vols; specialized libraries, c. 109,800

Publications: Academic Journal of Yunnan Normal University

YUNNAN UNIVERSITY
2 N. Cuihu Road, Kunming, Yunnan Province 650091
Tel: +86(871) 5034248
Fax: +86(871) 5183424
Website: http://www.ynu.edu.cn
President: He Tianchun

Departments
English Philosophy (General Teaching Department) (English; Philosophy); **Marxist Philosophy** (General Teaching Department) (Philosophy; Political Sciences)

Schools
Art and Design (International) (Design; Fine Arts); **Business Administration and Tourism Management** (Business Administration; Management; Public Relations; Tourism); **Chemical Science and Engineering** (Chemical Engineering; Chemistry; Organic Chemistry); **Economics** (Economics); **Foreign Languages** (Modern Languages); **Humanities and Social Sciences** (Archaeology; Arts and Humanities; Demography and Population; Ethnology; History; Literature; Museum Studies; Philosophy; Sociology); **Information Science and Technology** (Communication Studies; Computer Science; Electronic Engineering; Information Sciences; Information Technology); **Law** (Law); **Life Sciences** (Biological and Life Sciences; Biology; Botany; Zoology); **Mathematics and Statistics** (Applied Mathematics; Mathematics; Statistics); **Physical Education** (Education; Physical Education); **Physical Science and Technology** (Physical Engineering; Physics); **Public Administration** (Public Administration); **Resources, Environment, Natural and Earth Sciences** (Biochemistry; Biophysics; Botany; Cell Biology; Earth Sciences; Ecology; Environmental Studies; Genetics; Meteorology; Microbiology; Molecular Biology; Natural Resources; Physiology); **Software Engineering** (Software Engineering); **Urban Construction and Management** (Construction Engineering; Town Planning); **Vocational and Technical** (Technology)

History: Founded 1923. Renamed Yunnan Provincial University 1938 and Yunnan National University 1938. Acquired present title 1950.

Degrees and Diplomas: Bachelor's Degree; Master's Degree; Doctor's Degree

Student Services: Canteen, Sports facilities

Student Residential Facilities: Yes

Special Facilities: Laboratories

Libraries: 2 public libraries, total 2,694,600 vols, e-books and magazines, 433,400

Publications: Journal of Yunnan University; Yunnan Higher Education; Yunnan Jurisprudence

Academic Staff 2007-2008: Total 1,517
Student Numbers 2007-2008: Total 12,869
Last Updated: 22/11/10

YUNNAN UNIVERSITY OF FINANCE AND ECONOMICS
Longquan Road, Kunming, Yunnan Province 650221
Tel: +86(871) 5151723
Fax: +86(871) 5163384
EMail: YUFE@public.km.yn.cn
Website: http://www.ynufe.edu.cn/english/english.asp
President: Wang Rong
International Relations: Ge Changmin

Schools
Business Administration; **Finance and Accountancy**; **Finance and Banking**; **International Business** (International Business); **Statistics and Information Sciences** (Environmental Studies; Information Management; Natural Resources; Statistics)

History: Founded 1951 as Yunan Finance, Trade and Management School, acquires present status 1999.

Main Language(s) of Instruction: Chinese

Degrees and Diplomas: Bachelor's Degree; Master's Degree
Last Updated: 12/12/08

YUNNAN UNIVERSITY OF TRADITIONAL CHINESE MEDICINE

201 Shuangqiao Road, Guanshang District, Kunming,
Yunnan Province 650200
Tel: +86(871) 7150983
Fax: +86(871) 7150983
EMail: yutcmwu@sina.com
Website: http://www.ynutcm.edu.cn

President: Qingsheng Li (1999-)

International Relations: Ming Li EMail: kmlmlm@sina.com

Departments
Social Sciences (Social Sciences)

Faculties
Acupuncture and Moxibustion *Dean:* Yun Zhang; **Basic Medicine**; **Clinical Medicine** (Medicine) *Dean:* Guozheng Qin; **Pharmacy** (Pharmacy; Traditional Eastern Medicine) *Dean:* Zigang Qian; **Traditional Chinese Pharmacy**

History: Founded 1960 as Yunnan College of Traditional Chinese Medicine.

Admission Requirements: Graduation from senior middle school. Knowledge of Chinese compulsory

Fees: (Yuan): Bachelor's Degree, 20,000; Master's Degree, 30,000

Main Language(s) of Instruction: Chinese

International Co-operation: With Prince of Songkla University (Thailand)

Accrediting Agencies: Ministry of Education; Yunnan Provincial Education Bureau

Degrees and Diplomas: *Bachelor's Degree*; *Master's Degree*: a further 3 yrs; *Doctor's Degree*. Also Certificate (short time training)

Student Services: Cultural centre, Social counselling
Last Updated: 12/12/08

YUNYANG MEDICAL COLLEGE

25 South Peoples' Road, Shiyan, Hubei Province 435002
Tel: +86(719) 8891088
Website: http://www.yymc.edu.cn

President: Yang Guiyan

International Relations: Li Yunxia

Departments
Anaesthesiology; **Clinical Medicine**; **Hygiene**; **Nursing**

History: Founded 1965 as Wuhan Medical College Yunyang Branch, acquired present title 1994.

Main Language(s) of Instruction: Chinese

Degrees and Diplomas: *Bachelor's Degree*; *Master's Degree*

Libraries: c. 340,000 vols

Publications: Journal of Yunyang Medical College
Last Updated: 15/12/08

ZHANGZHOU NORMAL UNIVERSITY

Xianzhi Street, Xiangcheng District, Zhangzhou,
Fujian Province 363000
Tel: +86(596) 2023850
Fax: +86(596) 2026037
EMail: webmaster@fjzs.edu.cn
Website: http://www.fjzs.edu.cn

President: Fu-Xing Wang

Departments
Chemistry (Chemistry); **Chinese**; **English** (English); **History** (History); **Mathematics** (Mathematics); **Physics**; **Political Science** (Political Sciences); **Teacher Training**

History: Founded 1963 as Fujian Second Teachers College, acquired present name 1986.

Main Language(s) of Instruction: Chinese

Degrees and Diplomas: *Bachelor's Degree*; *Master's Degree*

Libraries: c. 736,000 vols
Last Updated: 15/12/08

ZHANJIANG NORMAL UNIVERSITY

29 Cunjin Road, Chikan, Zhanjiang, Guangdong Province 524048
Tel: +86(759) 3183217
Fax: +86(759) 3341440
EMail: waishi@zhjnc.edu.cn
Website: http://www.zhjnc.edu.cn

President: Li Yunsheng

International Relations: Lee Ming

Departments
Art; **Biology**; **Chemistry**; **Chinese** (Chinese); **Educational Administration** (Educational Administration); **English**; **History** (History); **Mathematics** (Mathematics); **Physical Education** (Physical Education); **Physics** (Physics); **Political Science and Law** (Law; Political Sciences)

History: Founded as Leizhou Techers School, acquired present status 1978 and name 1991.

Main Language(s) of Instruction: Chinese

Degrees and Diplomas: *Bachelor's Degree*
Last Updated: 15/12/08

ZHAOQING UNIVERSITY

Donggang, Zhaoqing, Guangdong Province 526061
Tel: +86(758) 2716390
Fax: +86(758) 2716969
EMail: wsc@zqu.edu.cn
Website: http://www.zqu.edu.cn

President: He Fei

International Relations: Xu Zhen Hui

Faculties
Chemistry and Chemical Engineering (Chemical Engineering; Chemistry); **Chinese Language and Literature**; **Computer Science and Software** (Computer Science; Software Engineering); **Economics and Management**; **Education** (Education); **Fine Arts** (Fine Arts); **Foreign Languages** (Modern Languages); **Life Sciences**; **Mathematics and Computer Science** (Computer Science; Mathematics); **Mechanical and Electrical Engineering** (Electrical Engineering; Mechanical Engineering); **Music** (Music); **Physical Education and Health** (Physical Education); **Political Science and Law** (Law; Political Sciences)

History: Founded 1970 as Zhaoqing Teachers College, acquired present status and title 1999 through amalgamation.

Academic Year: September to July

Main Language(s) of Instruction: Chinese

International Co-operation: Exchange programme with Bolton Institute, UK

Degrees and Diplomas: *Bachelor's Degree*
Last Updated: 15/12/08

ZHEJIANG CHINESE MEDICAL UNIVERSITY

548 Bin Wen Road, Bin Jiang District, Hangzhou,
Zhejiang Province 310053
Tel: +86(571) 86613545
Fax: +86(571) 86613522
EMail: zjtcmfao@mail.hz.zj.cn
Website: http://www.zjtcm.net

President: Xiao Luwei

International Relations: Chai Kefu

Centres
International Education (International and Comparative Education)

Departments
Acupuncture and Massage (Acupuncture); **Chinese Pharmacology** (Pharmacology; Traditional Eastern Medicine); **Traditional Chinese Medicine** (Traditional Eastern Medicine)

History: Founded 1953 as Zhejiang Vocational School of Traditional Chinese Medicine. Acquired present status and title 2006.

Main Language(s) of Instruction: Chinese

Degrees and Diplomas: *Bachelor's Degree*; *Master's Degree*; *Doctor's Degree*

Libraries: 1,197,800 vols

Publications: Journal of Zhejiang University of TCM

Last Updated: 12/12/08

ZHEJIANG FORESTRY UNIVERSITY (ZFU)

Lin'an, Zhejiang Province 311300
Tel: +86(571) 63740030
EMail: international@zjfc.edu.cn
Website: http://www.zjfc.edu.cn/

President: Qisheng Zhang
Tel: +86(571) 63732700 +86(571) 6372699

Schools

Agriculture and Food Science; **Art Design**; **Economics and Management** (Economics; Management); **Engineering**; **Environmental Technology** (Environmental Engineering; Environmental Studies; Natural Resources); **Foreign Languages** (Modern Languages); **Forestry and Biotechnology** (Biotechnology; Wood Technology); **Humanities**; **Information Science and Technology** (Information Sciences; Information Technology); **Landscape Architecture** (Landscape Architecture); **Sciences** (Natural Sciences); **Tea Culture**; **Tourism and Health**

History: Founded 1958 as Zhejiang Tianmu Forestry College, acquired present status and name 1996.

Main Language(s) of Instruction: Chinese

Degrees and Diplomas: *Bachelor's Degree*; *Master's Degree*

Student Residential Facilities: The Journal of Zhejiang Forestry University

Last Updated: 12/12/08

ZHEJIANG GONGSHANG UNIVERSITY

149 Jiao Gong Road, Hangzhou, Zhejiang Province 310035
Tel: +86(571) 88055346
Fax: +86(571) 88846798
EMail: international@mail.zjgsu.edu.cn
Website: http://www.hzic.edu.cn

President: Zuguang Hu (1996-)
Tel: +86(571) 88803793, Fax: +86(571) 88053079
EMail: huc2@mail.hz.zj.cn

International Relations: Xingwu Song

Colleges

Accountancy *Dean*: Yongbin Xu; **Art Design** (Design; Media Studies; Painting and Drawing; Sculpture) *Dean*: Jianchun Zhang; **Business Administration** (Business Administration; Economics; Human Resources; Management; Marketing) *Dean*: Fuxin Lu; **Computer Science and Information Technology** (Computer Science; E-Business/Commerce; Information Management; Information Technology) *Dean*: Chunhua Ju; **Economics** *Dean*: Lijun Lu; **Finance** *Dean*: Dezong Han; **Food Science, Biotechnology and Environmental Engineering** (Biochemistry; Bioengineering; Engineering; Environmental Engineering; Food Science; Food Technology) *Dean*: Jiarong Li; **Foreign Languages** (Applied Linguistics; English; Japanese; Modern Languages) *Dean*: Fagong Liu; **Further Education** (Accountancy; Business Administration; Computer Science; Economics; Finance; Fine Arts; Hotel Management; International Business; Law; Marketing) *Dean*: Menglan Cao; **Human Sciences and Public Management** (Advertising and Publicity; Cultural Studies; Management; Public Administration; Religious Studies; Social Studies) *Dean*: Rongfu Chen; **Information and Electronic Engineering** *Dean*: Zhiguo Ren; **International Economics and Trade** (Accountancy; Business Administration; Computer Science; Design; Finance; Information Technology; International Business; International Economics; Law; Marketing; Tourism) *Dean*: Jianchun Zhang; **Law** (Civil Law; Commercial Law; Law; Social Work) *Dean*: Jiexiong Lu; **Statistics and Computer Science** (Computer Science; Statistics) *Dean*: Weihua Su; **Tourism** (Hotel Management; Tourism) *Dean*: Daijian Tang

History: Founded 1911 as business school, renamed Hangzhou University of Commerce 1980. Acquired present title 2004. Under the jurisdiction of the Zhejiang Provincial Government.

Governing Bodies: University Council

Academic Year: September to June (September-January; February-June)

Admission Requirements: Graduation from senior middle school and entrance examination

Fees: (Yuan): 5,000-16,000 per annum

Main Language(s) of Instruction: Chinese, English

International Co-operation: With University of Quebec(Canada)

Accrediting Agencies: Ministry of Education

Degrees and Diplomas: *Bachelor's Degree*: Accountancy Management; Tourism; Law; Social Work; Labour and Social Security System; Food Science and Technology; Food Quality and Safety; Biological Engineering; Environmental Engineering; Electronic Engineering; Telecommunications Engineering; Business Administration; Marketing; Human Resources Management; Project Management; International Economics and Trade; Economics; Finance; Statistics; Information and Computer Science; Accountancy; Mathematics and Applied Mathematics; Computer Science and Technology; Information Systems and Management; E-Commerce; Logistics; Public Management; Administration; Resources Planning and Urban Development; Advertising; Editing and Publishing; Chinese Language and Literature; English; Japanese; Art Design; Cartoon Arts, 4 yrs; *Master's Degree*: Business Administration; Management; Economics; International Trade; Finance; Statistics; Quantitative Economics; Accountancy; Tourism Management; Civil Commercial Law; Procedural Law; Food Science; Biochemistry; Processing and Storage of Aquatic Products; Processing and Storage of Agricultural Products; Signal and Information Processing; Communication and Data Processing; Computer Science and Technology; Management and Engineering; Foreign Languages and Applied Linguistics, a further 2 1/2 yrs; *Doctor's Degree*: Business Administration; Statistics; Food Science, 3 yrs

Student Services: Academic counselling, Canteen, Cultural centre, Employment services, Foreign student adviser, Foreign Studies Centre, Handicapped facilities, Health services, Language programs, Nursery care, Social counselling, Sports facilities

Student Residential Facilities: For 14,000 students

Libraries: Central Library, 1,620,000 vols

Publications: Business Economics and Administration *(monthly)*; Journal of Zhejiang Gongshang University *(monthly)*

Last Updated: 12/12/08

ZHEJIANG NORMAL UNIVERSITY (ZNU)

Beishan Road, Jinhua, Zhejiang Province 321004
Tel: +86(579) 2282380
Fax: +86(579) 2280337
EMail: lgl@mail.zjnu.net.cn
Website: http://www.zjnu.edu.cn

President: Hui Xu
Tel: +86(579) 2282358, Fax: +86(579) 2280322

Secretary-General: Lu Li
Tel: +86(579) 2283887, Fax: +86(579) 2280322
EMail: lilu@mail.zjnu.net.cn

International Relations: Jianxin Gu Tel: +86(579) 2282125

Colleges

Appied Higher Technology (Accountancy; Automotive Engineering; Computer Engineering; Electrical and Electronic Equipment and Maintenance; Electronic Engineering; Finance; Maintenance Technology; Marketing; Mechanical Equipment and Maintenance; Secretarial Studies; Service Trades; Tourism) *Dean*: Xiaomin Liu; **Chemistry & LIfe Science** (Applied Chemistry; Biology; Biotechnology; Chemistry) *Dean*: Ling Yang; **Chuyang Honours** (Cultural Studies; Literature) *Dean*: Jianwen Fang; **Education** *(K.P. Tin)* (Educational Technology; Pedagogy; Psychology) *Dean*: Jianping Zhang; **Foreign Languages and Literature Studies** (English; Japanese) *Dean*: Gang Hong; **Humanities** (Chinese; Literature) *Dean*: Xianliang Zhang; **Law, Political Science & Economics** (International Business; International Economics; Law; Political Sciences; Social Work) *Dean*: Min Wang; **Mathematics & Physics** (Applied Mathematics; Automation and Control Engineering; Computer Science; Information Technology; Mathematics) *Head*: Miaosen Chen; **Physical Education** (Education; Physical Education; Social Psychology) *Dean*: Huiju Pan; **Preschool Teacher Education** *(Hangzhou)* (Preschool Education) *Dean*: Jinliang Qin; **Science and Engineering** (Computer Science; Electronic Engineering; Information Technology) *Dean*: Jianmin Zhao;

Tourism & Resources Management (Geography; Service Trades; Tourism; Town Planning) *Dean*: Gaoyuan Luo; **Xingzhi**

Schools

Business Administration (Accountancy; Business Administration; Finance) *Dean*: Hong'er Chen; **Fine Arts** (Design; Fine Arts) *Dean*: Shaobin Zhou; **Music** (Music; Musicology) *Dean*: Shaohua Guan

History: Founded 1956 as Hangzhou Junior Teacher's College. Evolved into Hangzhou Teacher's College in 1958. In 1962, both Zhejiang Education College and Zhejiang Physical Education College were merged to form Zhejiang Teacher's College, which was moved to Jinhua in 1965. In 1985, the college acquired university status as Zhejiang Normal University. Later, in 2000, 2001, and 2004, three more schools merged into ZJNU, i.e. Zhejiang Financial School, Zhejiang School of Preschool-Teacher Education and Jinhua Railway Engineering School respectively.

Academic Year: September to June (September-January; February-June)

Admission Requirements: Graduation from senior middle school and entrance examination

Main Language(s) of Instruction: Chinese, English

International Co-operation: With universities in Japan, South Korea, Australia

Accrediting Agencies: Provincial Educational Committee

Degrees and Diplomas: *Bachelor's Degree*: Modern Languages; Music; Fine Arts; Tourism; Education; Natural Sciences; Computer Engineering; Computer Science; Information Technology; History; Political Science; Management; Law; Social Work; Business Administration; Finance; Accountancy; Marketing, 4 yrs; *Master's Degree*: Modern Languages; Music; Fine Arts; Tourism; Education; Natural Sciences; Computer Engineering; Computer Science; Information Technology; History; Political Sciences; Management; Law; Social Work; Business Administration; Finance; Accountancy; Marketing

Student Services: Academic counselling, Canteen, Employment services, Foreign student adviser, Health services, Language programs, Nursery care, Social counselling, Sports facilities

Special Facilities: Movie Studio

Libraries: Shao Yifu Library, c. 1,935,000 Vols

Publications: Adult Higher Education; College Teacher Education; Education of Higher Pedagogical Colleges *(biannually)*; Higher Pedagogical Education by Correspondence *(quarterly)*; Teaching and Research of Secondary School Education *(monthly)*; ZNU Journal *(quarterly)*

Last Updated: 12/12/08

ZHEJIANG OCEAN UNIVERSITY (ZOU)

105 Wenhua Road, Dinghai District, Zhoushan,
Zhejiang Province 316004
Tel: +86(580) 2550009
Fax: +86(580) 2551319
EMail: xxbgs@zjou.edu.cn
Website: http://61.153.216.111/zjouenglish

President: Zhenqing Miao
Tel: +86 (580) 255 0004, Fax: +86 (580) 255 1319
EMail: mzq@zjou.net.cn

Secretary-General: Dajun Zhou
Tel: +86 (580) 818 1000, Fax: +86 (580) 255 1319

International Relations: Shuhua Ren, Director of Foreign Affairs Office
Tel: +86 (580) 255 0088, Fax: +86 (580) 255 0088
EMail: rsh@zjou.net.cn

Colleges

Vocational and Technical Training (Hangzhou) *Associate Professor*: Jianxiong Jin

Schools

Economics and Management (Administration; Economics; Marketing; Tourism) *Professor*: Baiqi Li; **Electro-mechanical Engineering** (Architectural and Environmental Design; Automation and Control Engineering; Electrical Engineering; Electronic Engineering; Marine Engineering; Mechanical Engineering; Naval Architecture; Production Engineering); **Food and Pharmacy** (Food Science;

Pharmacy); **Foreign Languages** (English; Foreign Languages Education) *Professor*: Huiping Cai; **Humanities**; **Marine Fishery** (Aquaculture; Fishery; Marine Engineering); **Marine Science**; **Medical** (Medicine; Nursing); **Naval Architecture and Civil Engineering** (Civil Engineering; Naval Architecture); **Petrochemical** (Petroleum and Gas Engineering)

Further Information: Various other academic units

History: Founded 1998 after merger between Zhejiang Fishery University (founded 1958) and Zhoushan Junior Teachers College (founded 1978)

Academic Year: September to July

Admission Requirements: Senior Higher School Graduation Diploma, National Matriculation Test

Fees: (Yuan): 3,000 - 6,000 per annum

Main Language(s) of Instruction: Chinese, English

International Co-operation: With institutions in Japan, New Zealand, Norway

Accrediting Agencies: Ministry of Education

Degrees and Diplomas: *Bachelor's Degree (BA; BSc)*: 4 yrs; *Master's Degree (MA; MSc)*: a further 3 yrs. Also Associated Degree Programme of 3 yrs duration

Student Services: Academic counselling, Canteen, Cultural centre, Employment services, Foreign student adviser, Foreign Studies Centre, Health services, Language programs, Nursery care, Social counselling, Sports facilities

Student Residential Facilities: Dormitories for all students; Teachers' residence

Special Facilities: Museum, Gallery, Observatory, Film Studio, Language Laboratory, Experiment Centre

Libraries: c. 800,000 vols

Publications: Journal of Zhejiang Ocean University *(quarterly)*
Last Updated: 12/12/08

ZHEJIANG UNIVERSITY

866 Yu Hang Road, Hangzhou, Zhejiang Province 310058
Tel: +86(571) 87951583
Fax: +86(571) 87951315
EMail: huzm@zju.edu.cn
Website: http://www.zju.edu.cn

President: Wei Yang
Tel: +86(571) 88981109, Fax: +86(571) 87951315
EMail: yangw@zju.edu.cn

International Relations: Min Li, Deputy, Director, International Relations
Tel: +86(571) 889-81866, Fax: +86(571) 879 51315
EMail: minli@zju.edu.cn

Colleges

Chu Kechen (Biology; Business Administration; Chemistry; Chinese; Computer Engineering; Computer Science; Earth Sciences; Economics; Information Sciences; International Business; International Economics; Journalism; Law; Mass Communication; Mathematics; Philosophy; Physics; Psychology; Sociology)

Faculties

Agriculture, Life and Environment (Agriculture; Agronomy; Animal Husbandry; Apiculture; Aquaculture; Bioengineering; Biological and Life Sciences; Biology; Biotechnology; Crop Production; Environmental Engineering; Environmental Studies; Food Science; Horticulture; Natural Resources; Nutrition; Plant and Crop Protection; Sericulture; Veterinary Science; Zoology); **Engineering** (Aeronautical and Aerospace Engineering; Architecture; Biological and Life Sciences; Chemical Engineering; Civil Engineering; Electrical Engineering; Electronic Engineering; Energy Engineering; Engineering; Marine Engineering; Marine Science and Oceanography; Materials Engineering; Mechanical Engineering; Polymer and Plastics Technology; Regional Planning; Structural Architecture; Town Planning; Water Management; Water Science); **Humanities** (Arts and Humanities; Chinese; Communication Studies; Cultural Studies; English; Film; Heritage Preservation; History; International Studies; Journalism; Linguistics; Literature; Media Studies; Museum Management; Museum Studies; Philosophy; Radio and Television Broadcasting); **Information Technology** (Automation and Control Engineering; Bioengineering; Computer

Engineering; Computer Networks; Computer Science; Electronic Engineering; Industrial Design; Information Sciences; Information Technology; Media Studies; Optical Technology; Software Engineering); **Medicine** (Medicine; Nursing; Pharmacy; Public Health; Stomatology; Traditional Eastern Medicine); **Science** (Behavioural Sciences; Chemistry; Earth Sciences; Mathematics; Physics; Psychology); **Social Sciences** (Accountancy; Agricultural Economics; Agricultural Management; Business Administration; Economics; Education; Finance; Government; Information Management; Information Sciences; International Economics; Law; Management; Management Systems; Natural Resources; Physical Education; Political Sciences; Public Administration; Social Sciences; Social Welfare; Sociology; Tourism)

Schools

Adult Education, Vocational Technical Education and Advanced Studies (Agriculture; Economics; Engineering; History; Law; Literature; Management; Medicine; Natural Sciences; Philosophy); **Distance Education** (Business Administration; Computer Science; English; Management; Medicine); **Graduate** (Agriculture; Economics; Education; Engineering; History; Law; Literature; Management; Medicine; Natural Sciences; Philosophy)

History: Founded 1897. Acquired present status and title 1928. Incorporated Hangzhou University, Zhejiang Agricultural University, and Zhejiang Medical University 1998.

Governing Bodies: University Board

Academic Year: September to June (September-January, February-June)

Admission Requirements: Graduation from senior middle school with satisfactory marks in special entrance examination

Fees: (US Dollars): Foreign students, 1,800-5,800 per annum; short-term, 75-150 per week

Main Language(s) of Instruction: Chinese, English

International Co-operation: With universities in USA; United Kingdom; Germany; Canada; Russian Federation; Belgium; Australia; Japan; Korea; France; Italy; Portugal; Brazil; Singapore; Mexico; Netherlands; Denmark

Accrediting Agencies: Ministry of Education

Degrees and Diplomas: *Bachelor's Degree*: Agriculture; Economics; Education; Engineering; History; Law; Literature; Management; Medicine; Philosophy; Science, 4 yrs; *Bachelor's Degree*: Architecture; Engineering; Medicine, 5 yrs; *Master's Degree*: Agriculture; Economics; Education; Engineering; History; Law; Literature; Management; Medicine; Natural Sciences; Philosophy, a further 2-3 yrs; *Doctor's Degree*: Agriculture; Economics; Education; Engineering; History; Law; Literature; Management; Medicine; Natural Sciences; Philosophy, a further 2-3 yrs. Also postdoctoral research programmes

Student Services: Academic counselling, Canteen, Cultural centre, Employment services, Foreign student adviser, Foreign Studies Centre, Health services, Language programs, Nursery care, Social counselling, Sports facilities

Student Residential Facilities: Yes

Special Facilities: Conference centres

Libraries: 6 libraries: 6.18 m. vols, 20,000 items such as audio-visual tapes, microforms and CDs, databases of abstracts and indexes, such as Chemical Abstracts, BIOSIS (BA), Compendex (EI), INSPEC (SA), SCI, MathSci, ISI-IP, Medline, CAB-CD, AGRICOLA

Publications: Applied Psychology *(biennially)*; China Higher Medical Education *(bimonthly)*; Engineering Design *(quarterly)*; Journals of Zhejiang University, Sciences, in English; Natural Sciences, Medicine, Agricultural and Life Sciences, Humanities and Social Sciences, in Chinese *(bimonthly)*; Management Engineering *(quarterly)*; Materials Science and Engineering *(quarterly)*; Population and Eugenics *(bimonthly)*; Practical Oncology *(bimonthly)*; Spatial Structures *(quarterly)*

Press or Publishing House: Zhejiang University Press

Academic Staff *2009*: Total: c. 7,500

Student Numbers *2009*: Total: c. 41,000
Last Updated: 23/11/10

ZHEJIANG UNIVERSITY OF FINANCE AND ECONOMICS

269 Wenhua Road, Hangzhou, Zhejiang Province 310012
Tel: +86(571) 8853928 Ext. 225
Fax: +86(571) 8851146
EMail: wsb@zufe.edu.cn
Website: http://www.zufe.edu.cn/

President: Tong Benli
International Relations: Jin Minxian

Institutes
Economy and International Business (Economics; International Business)

Schools
Accountancy; **Foreign Languages** (Modern Languages); **Humanities** (Advertising and Publicity; Chinese; English; Finance; Japanese; Journalism; Literature; Philology; Sociology; Tourism)

History: Founded 1974 as Zhejiang Finance and Banking School. Previously known as Zhejian Institute of Finance and Economics. Acquired present status and name 1987.

Degrees and Diplomas: *Bachelor's Degree*
Last Updated: 12/12/08

ZHEJIANG UNIVERSITY OF SCIENCE

88 Wenyi Road, Hangzhou, Zhejiang Province 310033
Tel: +86(571) 8086137
Fax: +86(571) 8074072

President: Huang Shijun

Departments
Fashion Design (Fashion Design); **Textile Technology**

History: Founded 1897 as Zhejiang Sericulture Academy. Became Zhejiang Institute of Silk Textiles 1964. Acquired present title 2004.

Degrees and Diplomas: *Bachelor's Degree*; *Master's Degree*

ZHEJIANG UNIVERSITY OF SCIENCE AND TECHNOLOGY

85 Xueyuan Road, Hangzhou, Zhejiang Province 310012
Tel: +86(571) 5124576
Fax: +86(571) 5121890
EMail: hiat@public.hz.zj.cn
Website: http://www.zust.edu.cn

President: Zhu Shusheng
International Relations: Xu Liqin

Institutes
Chinese-German (German)

Schools
Automation and Electrical Engineering; **Biological and Chemical Engineering** (Biotechnology; Chemical Engineering; Food Science; Materials Engineering); **Civil Engineering and Architecture** (Architecture; Civil Engineering; Town Planning); **Economics and Management** (Industrial Engineering; Information Management; International Business; International Economics; Marketing); **Fashion Design** (Fashion Design; Industrial Design); **Foreign Languages** (English); **Humanities** (Chinese; Literature); **Information and Electronic Engineering** (Computer Science; Educational Technology; Electronic Engineering; Media Studies); **Light Industry**; **Mechanical and Automotive Engineering** (Automation and Control Engineering; Mechanical Engineering); **Science**; **Vocational Training** (Vocational Education)

History: Founded 1980, acquired present title 1992. Acquired present title 2001, formerly known as Hanghzou Institute of Applied Engineering.

Degrees and Diplomas: *Bachelor's Degree*; *Master's Degree*
Last Updated: 12/12/08

ZHEJIANG UNIVERSITY OF TECHNOLOGY (ZUT)

District 6, Zhaohui Xincun, Hangzhou, Zhejiang Province
Tel: +86(571) 88320037 +86(571) 88320451
Fax: +86(571) 88320272 +86(571) 88320667
EMail: wb@zjut.edu.cn
Website: http://www.zjut.edu.cn

President: Zhang Libin

Colleges

Architecture and Civil Engineering (Architecture; Civil Engineering) *Dean*: Jianjun Zheng; **Art**; **Biological and Environmental Engineering** (Bioengineering; Environmental Engineering; Microbiology); **Business Administration** (Business Administration); **Chemical Engineering and Materials Science** (Chemical Engineering; Materials Engineering); **Electro-Mechanical Engineering** (Electrical and Electronic Engineering; Industrial Design; Mechanical Engineering; Power Engineering; Thermal Engineering); **Foreign Languages** (English; Japanese; Linguistics; Literature; Modern Languages); **Information Engineering** (Information Technology); **Pharmaceutical Sciences** (Pharmacology); **Science** *Dean*: Cheng Cheng; **Vocational Education** (Pedagogy; Technology)

Schools

Humanities (Advertising and Publicity; Arts and Humanities; Chinese; Journalism; Radio and Television Broadcasting); **Law** (Civil Law; Criminal Law; International Law; Law) *Dean*: Xu Zhang; **Politics and Public Administration** (Political Sciences; Public Administration)

History: Founded 1953 as Zhejiang Institute of Technology, acquired present title 1991. Merged with Zhejiang Economic Management Cadres College and Zhejiang Institute of Chemical Technology.

Academic Year: September to July (September-January; March-July)

Admission Requirements: High School certificate with minimum NMET score

Fees: (Yuan): General studies, 4,400; attached colleges, 15,000

Main Language(s) of Instruction: Chinese, English

International Co-operation: With universities in Japan, Germany, Belgium, USA, France, United Kingdom, Australia, Canada, Korea

Accrediting Agencies: Ministry of Education; Zhejiang Provincial Education Department

Degrees and Diplomas: *Bachelor's Degree*: Agriculture; Engineering, 4-5 yrs; *Bachelor's Degree*: Arts; Education; International economics, Trade; Law; Management; Medical Sciences; Science, 4 yrs; *Master's Degree*: Agriculture; Engineering, 2 1/2-3 yrs; *Master's Degree*: Economics; Management, 2 1/2-3 yrs; *Doctor's Degree*: Engineering, 3 yrs

Student Services: Academic counselling, Canteen, Cultural centre, Employment services, Foreign student adviser, Foreign Studies Centre, Handicapped facilities, Health services, Language programs, Nursery care, Social counselling, Sports facilities

Student Residential Facilities: Yes

Special Facilities: Art Gallery, Movie Studio, Auditorium

Libraries: c. 1,002,000 vols, 3,800 periodicals. Two new libraries under construction

Publications: Journal of Zhejiang University of Technology, Natural Sciences Edition *(quarterly)*; Journal of Zhejiang University of Technology, Social Sciences Edition *(quarterly)*

Press or Publishing House: Campus News
Last Updated: 12/12/08

ZHEJIANG WANLI UNIVERSITY

No.8, South Qian Hu Road, Ningbo, Zhejiang Province 315101
Tel: +86(574) 88222017
Fax: +86(574) 8411744
EMail: ftr@zwu.edu.cn
Website: http://gjjl.zwu.edu.cn/english

President: Yuanming Wang

Departments
Computer Science (Computer Science)

Faculties
Art and Design; **Biology and Environmental Sciences** (Biology; Environmental Studies); **Culture and Media** (Cultural Studies; Media Studies); **Electronic and Information Engineering** (Electronic Engineering; Information Technology); **Foreign Languages**

Schools
Business (Business Administration; Management); **Law** (Law)

History: Founded 1950 as Ningbo Agricultural College, acquired present status and title 1999.

Degrees and Diplomas: *Bachelor's Degree*
Last Updated: 15/12/08

ZHENGZHOU UNIVERSITY (ZZU)

No.100 Science Road, Zhengzhou, Henan Province 450052
Tel: +86(371) 67780020
Fax: +86(371) 67783222
EMail: fao@zzu.edu.cn
Website: http://www.zzu.edu.cn/

President: Shen Changyu
Tel: +86(371) 7763025, Fax: +86(371) 7973895

Centres
Network (Telecommunications Engineering) *Director*: Zhongyong Wang; **Population Theory** (Demography and Population); **Women's Studies** (Women's Studies)

Departments
Computer Science (Computer Science) *Dean*: Shiqing Wang; **Electronic Engineering** (Electronic Engineering) *Dean*: Fu Yuan Wang; **Foreign Languages** (English; Modern Languages; Russian) *Dean*: Nana Shen; **Ideological Education** (Political Sciences) *Dean*: Youfeng Miao; **Information Management** (Information Management; Library Science) *Dean*: Ping Ke; **Materials Engineering** (Materials Engineering; Packaging Technology; Polymer and Plastics Technology) *Dean*: Jingwu Wang; **Mathematics and System Science** (Computer Science; Information Sciences; Mathematics) *Dean*: Shaochun Chen; **Mechanical and Electrical Engineering** *Dean*: Yuan Zhang

Institutes
Anaesthetics (Anaesthesiology) *Director*: Ning Zhang; **Ancient Books** (Ancient Books); **Applied Chemistry** (Applied Chemistry) *Dean*: Hongmin Liu; **Applied Physics** (Applied Physics); **Basic and Applied Sciences** (Natural Sciences) *Dean*: Yuxiao Li; **Economic Technology Management** (Econometrics); **Electronic, Mechanical and Electrical Technology** (Electrical Engineering; Electronic Engineering; Mechanical Engineering) *Dean*: Jianshe Jiang; **History** (History) *Director*: Jianshe Jiang; **Mathematics** (Mathematics) *Dean*: Guomin Gao; **Microelectronic Technology** (Microelectronics) *Director*: Tiejun Chen; **Yin and Shang Dynasties Culture** (Southeast Asian Studies) *Director*: Kelai Dai

Schools
Architecture (Architecture; Structural Architecture); **Business** (Accountancy; Business and Commerce; Economics; Finance; International Business; Statistics) *Chair*: Tingquan Zan; **Chemistry and Chemical Engineering** (Chemical Engineering; Chemistry; Technology) *Chair*: Yaoting Fan; **Chinese** (Chinese) *Director*: Jihui Chen; **Distance Education** *Head*: Zongmin Wang; **Humanities and Museology** (Archaeology; Archiving; Arts and Humanities; Museum Studies; Tourism) *Chair*: Zhaoxing Yu; **Law** (Law) *Chair*: Shaoqian Zhang; **Medicine** (Medicine) *Dean*: Ying Xing; **Nursing** (Nursing) *Dean*: Fuyou Niu; **Physical Engineering** (Applied Physics; Electronic Engineering; Physical Engineering; Physics) *Chair*: Jingxiao Lu; **Public Management** (Administration; Management; Social Work) *Chair*: Yong Fang He

History: Founded 1956. Acquired present status and title following merger with Henan Medical University and Zhengzhou University of Technology.

Governing Bodies: President Committee

Admission Requirements: Graduation from high school and entrance examination

Fees: (Yuan): 3,000 per annum

Main Language(s) of Instruction: Chinese

International Co-operation: With universities in USA; United Kingdom; France; Japan; Russian Federation; Canada and Australia

Accrediting Agencies: Ministry of Education; Henan Provincial Government

Degrees and Diplomas: *Bachelor's Degree (BA, BSc):* 4 yrs; *Master's Degree:* 2-2 1/2 yrs; *Doctor's Degree:* A further 2-2 1/2 yrs

Student Services: Academic counselling, Canteen, Cultural centre, Employment services, Foreign student adviser, Foreign Studies Centre, Health services, Language programs, Sports facilities

Student Residential Facilities: Yes

Special Facilities: Movie studio

Publications: Journal of Zhengzhou University *(bimonthly)*

Last Updated: 15/12/08

ZHENGZHOU UNIVERSITY OF LIGHT INDUSTRY (ZZULI)

5 Dongfeng Road, Zhengzhou, Henan Province 450002
Tel: +86(371) 3845470
Fax: +86(371) 3813060
EMail: fao@zzuli.edu.cn
Website: http://www.zzuli.edu.cn

President: Zhang Yawei

International Relations: Yang Dongyou

Colleges
Art and Design (Design; Fashion Design); **Eastern International Arts**; **Material and Chemical Engineering** (Chemical Engineering; Materials Engineering)

Departments
Electromechanical Science and Engineering (Electronic Engineering; Engineering; Mechanical Engineering); **Law and Administration** (Law; Public Administration); **Management**; **Computer Science**; **Computer Science and Control Engineering** (Automation and Control Engineering; Computer Science); **Food and Bioengineering** (Bioengineering; Food Technology); **Foreign Languages**; **Physical Education**; **Technical Physics** (Physics)

History: Founded 1977.

Degrees and Diplomas: *Bachelor's Degree*; *Master's Degree*

Libraries: c. 700,000 vols

Last Updated: 15/12/08

ZHONGNAN UNIVERSITY OF ECONOMICS AND LAW

1 South Nanhu Road, Hongshan, Wuhan, Hubei Province 430073
Tel: +86(27) 88386947
Fax: +86(27) 88386240
EMail: wsc@znufe.edu.cn
Website: http://www.znufe.edu.cn

President: Wu Handong

International Relations: Xiao Chongming

Schools
Accountancy (Accountancy; Finance); **Banking and Insurance**; **Business Administration**; **Economics** (Economics); **Finance and Taxation** (Banking; Finance; Taxation); **Foreign Languages**; **Humanities**; **Industrial and Commercial Management**; **Information**; **Journalism and Mass Media** (Journalism; Mass Communication); **Law**; **Public Administration** (Public Administration); **Public Security** (Safety Engineering); **Safety Science and Administration** (Administration; Safety Engineering)

History: Founded 1948 as Zhongyuan University. Renamed Zhongnan University of Finance and Economics 1985. Acquired present status and title 2000, following merger with South Central University of Political Science and Law.

Main Language(s) of Instruction: Chinese

Degrees and Diplomas: *Bachelor's Degree*: English Language; Mass Media; Journalism; International Politics; Economics; Administration of National Economy; Banking; Project Management; Law; Public Security; Criminology; Frontier Management; Industrial and Business Administration; Marketing; Tourism Management; Human Resources Management; Agricultural and Forest Economy Management; International Economy and Trade; Administration; Trade Economics; Finance; Labour and Social Security; Public Service Management; Accounting; Administration; Financial Management; E-commerce; Information Management and System; Statistics; Information and Computer Science; Investment; Insurance; Japanese Language; Logistics and Management; *Master's Degree*: Philosophy; Economics; Laws and JM; Administration and MBA; Foreign Linguistics and Applied Linguistics; History; Engineering; *Doctor's Degree*: Economics, Administration, Law

Libraries: c. 2.79m. Vols

Publications: Journal of Studies in Law and Business; Journal of Zhongnan University of Economics and Law

Last Updated: 15/12/08

ZHONGYUAN UNIVERSITY OF TECHNOLOGY (ZUT)

41 Zhingyuan West Road, Zhengzhou, Henan Province 450007
Tel: +86(371) 7698118 +86(371) 7698802
Fax: +86(371) 7698107
EMail: ieo@zzti.edu.cn; ieo@zut.edu.cn
Website: http://www.zzti.edu.cn

President: Cui Shizhong

International Relations: Sun Wei

Centres
Industrial Engineering and Systems; **Industrial Training**; **Modern Education** (Education); **Textile Engineering and Technology** (Textile Technology)

Colleges
Information and Business; **International Education** (International Studies); **Radio, Movie and Television**; **Software Engineering**

Departments
Computer Science and Technology (Computer Science; Technology); **Foreign Languages**; **Materials and Chemistry** (Chemistry; Materials Engineering); **Mathematics and Physics**; **Physical Education** (Physical Education)

Institutes
Asia-Pacific *(International)*

Schools
Adult Education; **Economics and Management**; **Electronic Information** (Information Technology); **Energy and Environmental Engineering**; **Fashion and Art**; **Humanities and Social Sciences**; **Machinery and Electricity** (Electrical Engineering; Machine Building); **Textile Technology** (Textile Technology)

History: Founded 1955 as Shanxi Jingwei Technical School, acquired present status and name 2000.

International Co-operation: With universities in United Kingdom, Russia, France, Japan, Denmark, Australia, Singapore and Hong Kong

ZUNYI MEDICAL COLLEGE

143 Dalian Road, Zunyi, Guizhou Province 563003
Tel: +86(852) 8623190
Fax: +86(852) 8623729
Website: http://www.zmc.gd.cn/english/index.html

President: Shi Jingshan

Departments
Bioengineering (Bioengineering); **Clinical Medicine**; **Fundamental Medicine** (Medicine); **Nursing** (Nursing); **Stomatology** (Stomatology)

History: Founded 1947 as Dalian Medical College, acquired present name 1969.

Main Language(s) of Instruction: Chinese

Degrees and Diplomas: *Bachelor's Degree*; *Master's Degree*

Last Updated: 15/12/08

China - Hong Kong SAR

STRUCTURE OF HIGHER EDUCATION SYSTEM

Description:

Hong Kong has 15 degree-awarding higher education institutions. 9 are publicly-funded and 6 are self-financing. They may offer undergraduate and postgraduate courses subject to the restraints of their degree awarding power. Sub-degree courses (i.e. Associate degree and Higher diploma) are offered by some of these degree-awarding institutions, the Vocational Training Council and other self-financing post-secondary institutions. Secondary school leavers may apply for admission to both undergraduate and sub-degree courses. While sub-degrees are independent terminal qualifications, meritorious sub-degree graduates may apply for senior year entry to undergraduate programmes or articulation to top-up degree programmes if they wish to pursue further studies Other self-financing degree-awarding and post-secondary institutions offer locally-accredited programmes at degree and/or sub-degree (Associate degree and Higher diploma) level.

Stages of studies:

University level first stage: Bachelor's degree and Honours degree
The first stage of higher education leads to a Bachelor's degree, normally after three years of study (the normative study length will be extended to four years starting from the 2012/13 intake). Some of the Bachelor's degree programmes may take up to six years, depending on the subject areas.

University level second stage: Postgraduate certificate, Postgraduate diploma, Master's degree and Master of Philosophy
Postgraduate diplomas and certificates are offered after one year of full-time postgraduate studies or two years of part-time postgraduate studies. Master's degrees without research training are conferred after one to two years of full-time study following the Bachelor's degree, in general. Masters of Philosophy are conferred usually after two years of research training and on submission of a thesis following the Bachelor's degree.

University level third stage: Doctorate
The third stage leads to the award of a Doctor of Philosophy after a period of research work and on submission of a thesis. Studies generally last for three years.

University level fourth stage: Post-doctorate
The fourth stage leads to a Post-doctorate study diploma after a period of research work and on submission of a thesis. Length of study depends on subject and research work.

Distance higher education:
Distance higher education is offered at the Open University of Hong Kong, founded in 1989. It offers courses in Arts, Business, and Science and Technology. The teaching materials are delivered in various ways including printed texts, television broadcast and multi-media resources on the Internet, etc.

ADMISSION TO HIGHER EDUCATION

Admission to university-level studies:

Name of secondary school credential required: Hong Kong Advanced Level Examination
For entry to: First-year of undergraduate programme.
Name of secondary school credential required: Hong Kong Diploma of Secondary Education
For entry to: First-year of undergraduate programme.

Foreign students admission:

Quotas: Starting from the academic year 2005/2006, the quota for admission of non-local students is relaxed to 10% of the aggregate number of the approved publicly-funded student number targets of full-time programmes at the sub-degree, undergraduate and taught postgraduate levels. For part-time locally accredited and publicly-funded taught postgraduate programmes, the quota for non-local students is 10% of the approved student number target. There is no restriction for the number of non-local students at the research postgraduate level and for part-time self-financing taught programmes. In addition, for full-time self-financing undergraduate and sub-degree programmes, there is no restriction for the number of non-local students coming from places other than Mainland China, Taiwan and Macau. Students from these three countries can be admitted to the full-time self-financing undergraduate and sub-degree programmes only up to 10% of the actual local student enrolment.

Entrance exam requirements: Foreign students must satisfy the entrance requirements of the institution they wish to attend. There may be additional requirements for certain programmes. Application for exemption or credit transfer should be made to individual institutions.

Entry regulations: Foreign students entering Hong Kong for the purpose of education must hold a student visa / entry permit issued by the Director of Immigration.

Language requirements: Students should have a good knowledge of English. Depending on the discipline pursued, proficiency in Chinese may also be required.

RECOGNITION OF STUDIES

Quality assurance system:

The Hong Kong Council for Accreditation of Academic and Vocational Qualifications (HKCAAVQ) is a statutory body responsible for assuring the quality of qualifications awarded by institutions without self-accreditation status. The Joint Quality Review Committee (JQRC) is responsible for the quality assurance of the self-financed sub-degree programmes offered by the University Grants Committee institutions.

Special provisions for recognition:

For exercising a profession: Sub-degree is a worthwhile standalone exit qualification for initial employment at the para-professional level and further studies.

NATIONAL BODIES

Education Bureau - EDB
  Secretary for Education: Michael M.Y. Suen
  Senior Executive Officer: Lucia Lau
  Senior Executive Officer: Conny Y.L. Li Chow
  15/F, Wu Chung House,
  213 Queen's Road East,
  Wan Chai
  Hong Kong
  Tel: +852 2891 0088
  Fax: +852 2893 0858
  EMail: edbinfo@edb.gov.hk
  WWW: http://www.edb.gov.hk/
  Role of national body: The Education Bureau is responsible for formulating, developing and reviewing policies, programmes and legislation in respect of education from pre-primary to tertiary level; and overseeing the effective implementation of educational programmes. The Bureau also monitors the services provided by: the University Grants Committee, the Student Financial Assistance Agency, the Hong Kong Examinations and Assessment Authority, the Hong Kong Council for Accreditation of Academic and Vocational Qualifications and the Vocational Training Council.

University Grants Committee - UGC
  Chairman: Edward Cheng
  Acting Secretary-General: Dorothy Ma
  7/F, Shui On Centre
  6-8 Harbour Road, Wan Chai
  Hong Kong
  Tel: +852 2524 3987

Fax: +852 2845 1596
EMail: ugc@ugc.edu.hk
WWW: http://www.ugc.edu.hk
Role of national body: The University Grants Committee (UGC) advises the Government on the development of the tertiary education sector and the financial needs of UGC-funded institutions. It also administers government grants to UGC-funded institutions.

Hong Kong Council for Accreditation of Academic and Vocational Qualifications - HKCAAVQ

Chairman: York Liao
Executive Director: Yiu-Kwan Fan
10/F (Service Counter) & 23/F, Cambridge House, Taikoo Place, 979 King's Road, Quarry Bay
Hong Kong
Tel: +852 3658 0000
Fax: +852 2845 9910
EMail: info@hkcaavq.edu.hk
WWW: http://www.hkcaa.edu.hk/
Role of national body: The Hong Kong Council for Accreditation of Academic and Vocational Qualifications validates courses and programmes offered by post-secondary institutions that are not self-accrediting.

Data for academic year: 2011-2012
Source: IAU from the Information and Public Relations Section, Education Bureau, Hong Kong, China, 2011

INSTITUTIONS

PUBLIC INSTITUTIONS

CITY UNIVERSITY OF HONG KONG (CITYU)

83 Tat Chee Avenue, Kowloon, Hong Kong, Hong Kong SAR
Tel: +852 3442-7654
Fax: +852 2788-1167
EMail: webmaster@cityu.edu.hk
Website: http://www.cityu.edu.hk

President: Way Kuo (2008-)
Tel: +852 3442-8282, Fax: +852 3442-0328
EMail: way@cityu.edu.hk

International Relations: David Cheng, Associate Vice-President
Tel: +852 3442-7167, Fax: +852 3442-0299
EMail: dxcheng@cityu.edu.hk

Centres
Chinese Civilisation (Architecture; Chinese; Literature; Music; Painting and Drawing; Philosophy; Sculpture; South Asian Studies) *Director*: Pei Kai Cheng; **English Language** (English) *Head (Acting)*: Jane Lockwood

Colleges
Business (Accountancy; Economics; Finance; Information Technology; Management; Marketing) *Dean*: Kwok Kee Wei; **Liberal Arts and Social Sciences** (Chinese; Communication Studies; East Asian Studies; English; Linguistics; Media Studies; Psychology; Public Administration; Social Policy; Social Studies; Social Work; Southeast Asian Studies; Translation and Interpretation) *Dean*: Gregory B. Lee; **Science and Engineering** (Biology; Chemistry; Civil Engineering; Computer Engineering; Computer Science; Electronic Engineering; Engineering Management; Materials Engineering; Mathematics; Physics; Structural Architecture) *Dean*: Jian Lu

Departments
Accountancy (Accountancy; Commercial Law; Information Management) *Head*: Jeong Bon Kim; **Applied Social Studies** (Criminology; Educational and Student Counselling; Psychology; Social Work; Sociology) *Head*: Alex Yui Huen Kwan; **Asian and Interna-tional Studies** (East Asian Studies; International Studies; South and Southeast Asian Languages) *Head (Acting)*: William Case; **Biology and Chemistry** (Applied Chemistry; Biology; Environmental Management; Environmental Studies) *Head*: István T. Horváth; **Chinese, Translation and Linguistics** (Chinese; Cultural Studies; Heritage Preservation; Linguistics; Modern Languages; Translation and Interpretation) *Head*: Jonathan Webster; **Civil and Architectural Engineering** (Architecture; Building Technologies; Civil Engineering; Construction Engineering; Management; Real Estate; Structural Architecture; Surveying and Mapping) *Head*: Sritawat Kitipornchai; **Computer Science** (Computer Education; Computer Science) *Head*: Frances Foong Yao; **Economics and Finance** (Economics; Finance; Insurance) *Head*: Kenneth Shun Yuen Chan; **Electronic Engineering** (Computer Engineering; Electronic Engineering; Information Technology; Telecommunications Engineering) *Head*: Kim Fung Man; **English** (English) *Head*: Kingsley Bolton; **Information Systems** (Business Computing; E-Business/Commerce; Information Management; Marketing) *Head*: Leon L. Zhao; **Management** (Business Administration; Human Resources; International Business; Management) *Head*: Kwok Leung; **Management Sciences** (Business Administration; Management; Statistics) *Head*: Andrew Leong Chye Lim; **Marketing** (Business and Commerce; Marketing) *Head*: Chenting Su; **Mathematics** (Actuarial Science; Applied Mathematics; Finance; Mathematics and Computer Science) *Head*: Dingxuan Zhou; **Media and Communication** (Communication Studies; English; Media Studies) *Head*: Chin Chuan Lee; **Physics and Materials Science** (Applied Physics; Materials Engineering; Nanotechnology; Physics) *Head*: Michel A. van Hove; **Public and Social Administration** (Administration; Environmental Management; Environmental Studies; Management; Public Administration; Social Policy; Social Studies; Town Planning) *Head*: Hon S. Chan; **Systems Engineering and Engineering Management** (Electronic Engineering; Engineering Drawing and Design; Engineering Management; Industrial Engineering; Production Engineering; Safety Engineering) *Head*: Ning Xi

Divisions
Building Science and Technology (Architecture; Building Technologies; Construction Engineering; Engineering Management; Surveying and Mapping) *Head*: Paul H. K. Ho

Research Centres

Applied Computing and Interactive Studies (Computer Science; Media Studies; Multimedia) *Director:* Kim Meow Liew; **Asia-Pacific Climate Impact Centre** (Environmental Studies; Meteorology) *Director:* Johnny Chung Leung Chan; **Chaos and Complex Networks** (Engineering; Mathematics; Physics) *Director:* Guanrong Chen; **Chinese and Comparative Law** (Comparative Law) *Director:* Feng Lin; **Communication Research** (Communication Studies) *Director:* Chin Chuan Lee; **Electronic Packaging and Assemblies, Failure Analysis and Reliability Engineering** (Packaging Technology) *Director:* Archie Yan Cheong Chan; **Functional Photonics** *Director:* Andrey Rogach; **Governance in Asia** (Asian Studies; Government) *Director:* Martin Painter; **Hong Kong Advanced Institute for Cross-Disciplinary Studies** *Director:* Gregory B. Lee; **Innovative Applications of Internet and Multimedia Technologies** (Computer Networks; Multimedia) *Director:* Horace Ho Shing Ip; **Intelligent Applications of Language Studies** *(The Halliday Centre)* (Communication Studies; Linguistics) *Director:* Johnathan Webster; **Maritime and Transportation Law** (Maritime Law) *Director:* Vernon Nase; **Mathematical Sciences** *(Liu Bie Ju)* (Applied Mathematics; Computer Science; Mathematics) *Director:* Roderick Sue Cheun Wong; **Power Electonics** (Electronic Engineering) *Director:* Ron Shu Yuen Hui; **Prognostics and System Health Management** *Director:* Michael Pecht; **Southeast Asia** (Southeast Asian Studies) *Director:* William Case; **State Key Laboratory in Marine Pollution** (Environmental Management; Marine Science and Oceanography) *Director:* Paul Kwan Sing Lam; **State Key Laboratory of Millimeter Waves** *Director:* Kwai Man Luk; **Super-Diamond and Advanced Films** *Director:* Shuit Tong Lee; **Transport, Trade and Financial Studies** *Director:* John Liu

Schools

Creative Media (Cinema and Television; Media Studies; Photography; Writing) *Dean:* Jeffrey Shaw; **Energy and Environment** (Energy Engineering; Environmental Engineering; Environmental Studies) *Dean:* Johnny Chung Leung Chan; **Graduate Studies** *Dean:* Gregory B. Raupp; **Law** (Comparative Law; International Law; Law; Maritime Law) *Dean:* Guiguo Wang

History: Founded 1984 as City Polytechnic, acquired present status and title 1995.

Governing Bodies: University Council

Academic Year: September to May (September-December; January-May), Summer term, June-August

Admission Requirements: Meet general requirement, English and/or Chinese proficiency. Individual programmes may have additional entrance requirements. Consult university for details.

Fees: See University for fee details

Main Language(s) of Instruction: English

International Co-operation: With institutions in Australia; Austria; Belgium; Brazil; Canada; Chile; Croatia; Czech Republic; Denmark; Finland; France; Germany; Hungary; India; Italy; Japan; Latvia; Mainland China; Malaysia; New Zealand; Norway; Poland; Portugal; Romania; Singapore; South Korea; Spain; Sweden; Taiwan; Thailand; The Netherlands; Turkey; United Kingdom and USA

Degrees and Diplomas: *Bachelor's Degree Honours:* Arts; Business Administration; Engineering; Law; Science; Social Science, 3 yrs (4-5 yrs part-time); *Postgraduate Certificate/Diploma:* Laws; Construction Project Management; Information Security; Networking and Information Engineering; Professional Accountancy; Environmental Science and Technology, PCLL: 1 yr (2 yrs part-time); PGC, 3 months-1 yr (1-2 yrs part-time); *Master's Degree:* Arts; Business Administration; Fine Arts ; Law; Science, 1yr (2-5 yrs part-time); *Master of Philosophy:* Advanced Manufacturing Technology and Management; Applied Mathematics; Built Environment; International Economics, Corporate Governance, E-Business & Internet Marketing, Accounting and Finance; Computer Science and Digital Media; Chinese and Comparative Law; Electronic Engineering; Environmental Science; Knowledge and Innovation Management; Linguistics Communication; Materials Science and Engineering, 2 yrs (4 yrs part-time); *Doctor's Degree:* Business Administrative; Juridical Science (Professional), 3-4 yrs; *Doctor's Degree:* Engineering (Building and Construction); Engineering (Engineering Management) (Professional), 4-6 yrs (part-time); *Doctor's Degree:* International Economics; Chinese and Comparative Law; Knowledge and Innovation Management; Communications; Materials Science and Engineering; Corporate Governance and Accountancy; Structural Engineering (PhD), 3-4 yrs (6-8 yrs part-time)

Student Services: Academic counselling, Canteen, Cultural centre, Employment services, Foreign student adviser, Foreign Studies Centre, Handicapped facilities, Health services, Language programs, Social counselling, Sports facilities

Student Residential Facilities: For 3,000 students

Special Facilities: Art Gallery, Bank, Book Store

Libraries: c. 932,500 vols. 2,158,400 vols of electronic books, 199,000 bound periodicals, 2,860 print serial titles

Publications: Research Report *(annually)*

Press or Publishing House: City University of Hong Kong Press

Academic Staff 2010-2011	MEN	WOMEN	TOTAL
FULL-TIME	859	297	1,156
PART-TIME	140	124	264
STAFF WITH DOCTORATE			
FULL-TIME	621	161	782
PART-TIME	23	13	36
Student Numbers 2010-2011			
All (Foreign Included)	9,562	8,480	18,042
FOREIGN ONLY	–	–	2,853

Part-time students, 5,803.
Last Updated: 21/06/11

HONG KONG BAPTIST UNIVERSITY (HKBU)

Kowloon Tong, Kowloon, Hong Kong
Tel: +852 3411-7400
Fax: +852 2338-7644
EMail: cpro@hkbu.edu.hk
Website: http://www.hkbu.edu.hk

President and Vice-Chancellor: Albert Chan (2010-)
Tel: +852 3411-7500, Fax: +852 3411-2123
EMail: pdo@hkbu.edu.hk

International Relations: Peter Li, Director, International Office
Tel: +852 3411-2187, Fax: +852 3411-5563
EMail: intl@hkbu.edu.hk; peterli@hkbu.edu.hk

Academies

Visual Arts (Visual Arts) *Director:* Qingli Wan

Centres

Advanced Luminescence Materials; Advancement of English for Professionals *(Jockey Club Centre)* (English); **Applied Ethics** (Ethics); **Child Development** (Child Care and Development); **China Urban and Regional Studies** (Regional Studies; Urban Studies); **Chinese Cultural Heritage; CIE Wellness Promotion; Corporate Governance and Finance Policy; European Documentation** (European Studies); **Geo-Computation Studies; High Performance Cluster Computing Centre** *(Supported by Dell and Intel (HPCCC))*; **Hong Kong Chinese Medicine Authentication; Hong Kong Energy Studies** (Energy Engineering); **Human Resources Strategy and Development** (Human Resources); **Liberal Studies in Schools** *(Resource Center)*; **Mathematical Imaging and Vision; Nonlinear and Complex Systems** *(Beijing-Hong Kong-Singapore Joint Centre)*; **Non-linear Studies** (Physics); **Olympic Studies; Quantitative Systems Biology; Science Consultancy Services** (Computer Science; Mathematics; Natural Sciences); **Sino-Christian Studies** (Chinese; Christian Religious Studies); **Translation** (Translation and Interpretation)

Divisions

Research and Development Division - School of Chinese Medicine (Traditional Eastern Medicine)

Faculties

Arts (Arts and Humanities; Chinese; English; Music; Philosophy; Religion; Translation and Interpretation) *Dean:* Ling Chung; **Science** (Applied Mathematics; Applied Physics; Biology; Biotechnology; Chemistry; Computer Science; Environmental Studies; Information Technology; Mathematics; Operations Research; Physics; Statistics) *Dean:* Tao Tang; **Social Sciences** (Economics; Education; European Studies; Geography; Geography (Human); Government; History; International Studies; Leisure Studies; Parks and Recreation; Physical Education; Social Sciences; Social Work; Sociology; South Asian Studies) *Dean:* Adrian Bailey

Institutes

Advancement of Chinese Medicine (Traditional Eastern Medicine); **Business Development** *(Wing Lung Bank Institute)* (Business and Commerce); **Computational Mathematics** (Mathematics and Computer Science); **Contemporary China Studies** *(Advanced Institute)*; **Creativity**; **East-West Studies** *(David C. Lam Institute)* (Cultural Studies); **Enterprise Development**; **Environmental Sciences** *(HKBU – RCEES Joint Institute)* (Environmental Studies); **Environmental Sciences** *(Croucher Institute)* (Environmental Studies); **Journalism and Society** (Journalism; Social Studies)

Laboratories

Chemical Testing Services/Advanced Instrumentation Laboratory (Chemistry); **Dioxin Analysis**

Research Centres

Advancement of Social Sciences Research (Social Sciences); **Cancer and Inflammation Research** *(Shum Yiu Foon Shum Bik Chuen Memorial Centre)* (Oncology); **Chinese Businesses Case Research** (Business Administration); **Comparative Governance and Policy Research** (Government); **E-Transformation Technology Research**; **Media and Communication Research** (Communication Studies; Media Studies); **Modern History Research** (History; Modern History); **Pearl River Delta Environment** *(Sino-Forest Applied Research Centre)* (Environmental Studies); **Physical Recreation and Wellness Research** *(Dr Stephen Hui Research Centre)* (Parks and Recreation); **Statistics Research and Consultancy** (Statistics); **Surface Analysis and Research** (Materials Engineering); **Ubiquitous Computing** (Computer Science); **Youth Research and Practice**

Research Institutes

Applied Mathematics *(Peking University-HKBU Joint Research Institute)* (Applied Mathematics)

Schools

Business (Accountancy; Business and Commerce; E-Business/Commerce; Economics; Finance; Human Resources; Information Technology; Marketing) *Dean:* Stephen Cheung; **Chinese Medicine** (Biomedicine; Medicine; Pharmacy; Traditional Eastern Medicine) *Dean (Acting):* Zhaoxiang Bian; **Communication** (Advertising and Publicity; Cinema and Television; Communication Arts; Journalism; Public Relations; Radio and Television Broadcasting) *Dean:* Xinshu Zhao; **Continuing Education** (Business and Commerce; Information Technology; International and Comparative Education; Preschool Education; Teacher Training) *Dean:* Simon C.H. Wong; **Graduate** *Director:* Rick Wong

History: Founded 1956 as Hong Kong Baptist College, became autonomous 1983, and acquired present status and title 1994.

Governing Bodies: Court; Council; Senate

Academic Year: September to June (September-January; January-June). MBA programme: September to May

Admission Requirements: Either Hong Kong Certificate of Education Examination (HKCEE), with Grade E/Level 2 or above in 6 subjects including Chinese Language (or French or German) and English Language with at least 5 subjects in a single sitting; and Hong Kong Advanced Level Examination (HKALE), with Grade E or above in Advanced Supplementary ('AS') subjects of Chinese Language and Culture, and use of English and either 2 advanced Level (AL) subjects or 1 AL subject plus 2 AS subjects obtainable in any two sittings or an acceptable equivalent qualification. Under the new 4-year education system from 2012, the general entrance requirements for applicants with Hong Kong Diploma of Secondary Education (HKDSE) would be: Level 3 for English Language and Chinese Language, and Level 2 for Mathematics, Liberal Studies and One Elective subject. Some programmes have specific minimum entrance requirements, or additions to the above General Entrance Requirements.

Fees: (Hong Kong Dollars): Tuition, 42,100 – 63,000 per annum for local undergraduate students; fees for other levels of study and non-local students vary as approved by the University Council.

Main Language(s) of Instruction: English, Chinese

International Co-operation: With universities in Australia; Austria; Canada; Czech Republic; China; Denmark; Estonia; Finland; France; Germany; Hungary; Indonesia; Italy; Japan; Kazakhstan; Korea; Macau; Mexico; The Netherlands; Norway; Pakistan; The Philippines; Poland; Singapore; Slovenia; Sweden; Switzerland; Taiwan; Thailand; Turkey; United Kingdom; USA

Degrees and Diplomas: *Bachelor's Degree (BA):* 3-5 yrs; *Master's Degree (MA):* a further 2-3 yrs; *Doctor's Degree (PhD):* 2 1/2-4 yrs (3-5 yrs part-time)

Student Services: Academic counselling, Canteen, Cultural centre, Employment services, Foreign student adviser, Foreign Studies Centre, Handicapped facilities, Health services, Language programs, Social counselling, Sports facilities

Student Residential Facilities: For 1,770 students

Special Facilities: Chinese Medicine Clinics

Libraries: Au Shue Hung Memorial Library; Dr. Stephen Riady Chinese Medicine Library, 1,085,854 vols

Publications: Research Report *(annually)*

Student Numbers *2009-2010:* Total 8,262
Note: All (including full and part-time degree programmes offered by the School of Continuing Education): 15,909
Last Updated: 12/07/11

LINGNAN UNIVERSITY (LU)

8, Castle Peak Road, Tuen Mun, Hong Kong
Tel: +852 2616-8888
Fax: +852 2463-8363
EMail: registry@ln.edu.hk
Website: http://www.ln.edu.hk

President: Yuk-Shee Chan (2007-)
Tel: +852 2616-8822, Fax: +852 2462-3361
EMail: yschan@ln.edu.hk

Director of Administration and Registry Services/Secretary to the Council and the Court: Monica Mo-oi Tsang Tai
Tel: +852 2616-8752, Fax: +852 2465-1352
EMail: monicat@ln.edu.hk

International Relations: Joanne Wing-han Lai
Tel: +852 2616-8970, Fax: +852 2465-9660
EMail: joannelai@ln.edu.hk

Divisions

Arts (Chinese; Cultural Studies; English; History; Modern Languages; Philosophy; Translation and Interpretation; Visual Arts) *Academic Dean:* Stephen Ching-kiu Chan; **Business** (Accountancy; Computer Science; Finance; Insurance; International Business; Management; Marketing) *Academic Dean:* William Tjosvold; **Social Sciences** (Economics; Political Sciences; Social Policy; Sociology) *Academic Dean:* William Peter Baehr

Programmes

Hong Kong and South China Historical Research (History; South Asian Studies) *Coordinator:* Chi Pang Lau; **Kwan Fong Cultural Research and Development** (Cultural Studies) *Coordinator:* Meaghan Elizabeth Morris; **Public Governance** (Government) *Director:* Pang Kwong Li

Research Centres

Asian Pacific Studies (Asian Studies; Pacific Area Studies) *Director:* Baohui Zhang; **Humanities Research** (Arts and Humanities) *Director:* Ping Kwan Leung; **Public Policy Studies** *Director:* Lok Sang Ho

Research Institutes

Asia-Pacific Institute of Ageing Studies *Director:* Alfred Cheung Ming Chan; **Hong Kong Institute of Business Studies** *Dean:* William Tjosvold

Schools

Community College and Further Education *Dean:* Edward Pui-wing Fung; **Lingan Institute of Further Education** *Dean:* Edward Pui-wing Fung

History: Founded 1967. A degree-conferring tertiary institution fully funded by Hong Kong Government through the University Grants Committee. Acquired present status and title 1999.

Governing Bodies: Council, Court and Senate

Academic Year: September to May (September-December; January-May)

Admission Requirements: Grade E or above in 2 Advanced Level (AL) subjects (or in 1 AL and 2 Advanced Supplementary (AS) Level subjects other than Use of English (UE) and Chinese Language and Culture (CLC)); and Grade E or above in AS UE and CLC in the Hong Kong Advanced Level Examination. Other equivalent qualifications will be considered on a case-by-case basis.

Fees: (Hong Kong Dollars): Tuition: 42,100 per annum for local students; 100,000 per annum for non-local students

Main Language(s) of Instruction: English

Degrees and Diplomas: *Bachelor's Degree Honours*: Chinese; Translation; Business Administration; Contemporary English Studies; Cultural Studies; History; Philosophy; Visual Studies; Social Sciences (BA), last intake of 3-yr curriculum in 2012-2013, 4-yr curriculum introduced from 2012-2013; *Master of Philosophy*: Business; Chinese; Cultural Studies; Economics; English; History; Philosophy; Social Sciences; Translation; Visual Studies, a further 2 yrs (full-time); *Doctor's Degree*: Business; Chinese; Cultural Studies; Economics; English; History; Philosophy; Social Sciences; Translation; Visual Studies, a further 3 yrs (full-time)

Student Services: Academic counselling, Canteen, Employment services, Foreign student adviser, Handicapped facilities, Health services, Language programs, Social counselling, Sports facilities

Student Residential Facilities: For c. 1,500 students

Special Facilities: Lingnan Education Organization Museum; Art gallery; Studio; Chan Tak Tai Auditorium

Libraries: Fong Sum Wood Library 470,246 vols. and a wide range of electronic information resources

Publications: Alumni Magazine *(biannually)*; Bulletin *(quarterly)*; Chronicle *(biannually)*; E-newsletter *(monthly)*

Academic Staff 2010	MEN	WOMEN	**TOTAL**
FULL-TIME	108	64	**172**
Student Numbers 2010			
All (Foreign Included)	819	1,512	**2,331**

Last Updated: 18/05/11

THE CHINESE UNIVERSITY OF HONG KONG (CUHK)

Shatin, New Territories
Tel: +852 2609-6000
Fax: +852 2603-5544
EMail: oal@cuhk.edu.hk
Website: http://www.cuhk.edu.hk

Vice-Chancellor and President: Joseph J.Y. Sung (2010-)
Tel: +852 2609-8600, Fax: +852 2603-6197
EMail: js_vcoffice@cuhk.edu.hk

Director of Communications and Public Relations: Amy Y.M Tsui
Tel: +852 2609-8894, Fax: +852 2603-5115
EMail: amytsui@cuhk.edu.hk

International Relations: Gordon Cheung, Director, Office of Academic Links
Tel: +852 2609-7778, Fax: +852 2603-5402
EMail: gordonc@cuhk.edu.hk

Faculties
Arts (Anthropology; Chinese; Cultural Studies; English; Fine Arts; History; Japanese; Linguistics; Literature; Modern Languages; Music; Philosophy; Religious Studies; Theology; Translation and Interpretation) *Dean*: Ping-chen Hsiung; **Business Administration** (Accountancy; Economics; Finance; Hotel Management; Management; Marketing; Tourism) *Dean*: Tak-jun Wong; **Education** (Curriculum; Educational Administration; Educational Psychology; Physical Education; Sports) *Dean*: Alvin Seung-ming Leung; **Engineering** (Automation and Control Engineering; Computer Engineering; Computer Science; Electronic Engineering; Engineering Management; Information Technology; Mechanical Engineering) *Dean*: Ching-ping Wong; **Law** (Law) *Dean*: Michael J. McConville; **Medicine** (Anaesthesiology; Anatomy; Biomedicine; Cell Biology; Gynaecology and Obstetrics; Medicine; Microbiology; Nursing; Oncology; Ophthalmology; Orthopaedics; Otorhinolaryngology; Paediatrics; Pathology; Pharmacy; Psychiatry and Mental Health; Public Health; Radiology; Surgery) *Dean*: Tai-Fai Fok; **Science** (Biological and Life Sciences; Chemistry; Mathematics; Physics; Statistics; Traditional Eastern Medicine) *Dean*: Cheuk-yiu Ng; **Social Sciences** (Architecture; Communication Studies; Economics; Geography (Human); Government; Journalism; Psychology; Public Administration; Social Work; Sociology) *Dean*: Paul S.N. Lee

Programmes
International Asian Studies (Asian Studies; International Studies); **Postgraduate - Arts** (Anthropology; Art History; Chinese; Christian Religious Studies; Cultural Studies; English; Fine Arts; History; Japanese; Linguistics; Literacy Education; Literature; Music; Native Language; Native Language Education; Philosophy; Religion; Religious Studies; Theology; Translation and Interpretation; Visual Arts); **PostgraduatE-Business Administration** (Accountancy; Business Administration; Finance; Hotel Management; Leadership; Management; Management Systems; Marketing; Tourism); **Postgraduate - Education** (Chinese; Curriculum; Educational Administration; Educational and Student Counselling; English; Ethics; Foreign Languages Education; Humanities and Social Science Education; Mathematics Education; Native Language; Native Language Education; Physical Education; Preschool Education; Primary Education; Secondary Education; Sports); **Postgraduate - Engineering** (Automation and Control Engineering; Biomedical Engineering; Computer Engineering; Computer Science; E-Business/Commerce; Electronic Engineering; Engineering Management; Information Technology; Mechanical Engineering; Transport Management); **Postgraduate - Law** (Commercial Law; International Law; Law); **Postgraduate - Medicine** (Anaesthesiology; Anatomy; Biochemistry; Biomedical Engineering; Gynaecology and Obstetrics; Microbiology; Nursing; Ophthalmology; Orthopaedics; Otorhinolaryngology; Pathology; Pharmacology; Pharmacy; Physiology; Public Health; Radiology; Surgery); **Postgraduate - Science** (Biochemistry; Biology; Chemistry; Environmental Studies; Food Science; Insurance; Materials Engineering; Mathematics; Molecular Biology; Nutrition; Physics; Statistics; Traditional Eastern Medicine); **Postgraduate - Social Sciences** (Advertising and Publicity; Architecture; Clinical Psychology; Communication Studies; Earth Sciences; Ecology; Economics; Environmental Studies; Family Studies; Gender Studies; Geography; Geology; Government; Industrial and Organizational Psychology; Journalism; Media Studies; Natural Resources; Political Sciences; Psychology; Public Administration; Social and Community Services; Social Policy; Social Sciences; Social Welfare; Social Work; Sociology; Tourism); **Summer Studies** *Director*: Gordon Cheung; **Undergraduate - Art** (Anthropology; Chinese; Cultural Studies; English; Fine Arts; History; Japanese; Linguistics; Literature; Music; Native Language; Philosophy; Religious Studies; Theology; Translation and Interpretation); **UndergraduatE-Business Administration** (Accountancy; Actuarial Science; Business Administration; Commercial Law; Finance; Hotel Management; Insurance; International Business; Tourism); **Undergraduate - Education** (Chinese; English; Foreign Languages Education; Humanities and Social Science Education; Native Language Education; Physical Education; Preschool Education; Sports); **Undergraduate - Engineering** (Automation and Control Engineering; Biomedical Engineering; Computer Engineering; Computer Science; Electronic Engineering; Engineering Management; Information Technology; Mathematics; Mechanical Engineering); **Undergraduate - Law** (Law); **Undergraduate - Medicine** (Medicine; Nursing; Pharmacy; Public Health); **Undergraduate - Science** (Biochemistry; Biology; Biotechnology; Cell Biology; Chemistry; Environmental Studies; Food Science; Information Technology; Mathematics; Molecular Biology; Nutrition; Physics; Statistics; Traditional Eastern Medicine); **Undergraduate - Social Sciences** (Architecture; Communication Studies; Economics; Geography (Human); Government; Human Resources; Journalism; Law; Psychology; Public Administration; Social Work; Sociology)

Research Institutes
Advanced Engineering *(Shun Hing)* (Bioengineering; Biomedical Engineering; Computer Science; Multimedia) *Director*: Ching Pak-chung; **Advanced Integration Technology** *(Shenzhen Institute, Chinese Academy of Sciences) Director*: Fan Jianping; **Asia-Pacific Business** (Air Transport; Asian Studies; Business and Commerce; Finance; Government; Institutional Administration; Management; Marketing; Pacific Area Studies; Real Estate; Tourism) *Executive Director*: Leslie Young; **Asia-Pacific Studies** *(Hong Kong)* (Asian Studies; Pacific Area Studies; South Asian Studies) *Director*: Fanny M.C. Cheung; **Biotechnology** *(Hong Kong)* (Biotechnology) *Direc-

tor: Walter K.K. Ho; **Cancer** *(Hong Kong)* (Oncology) *Director:* Anthony T.C. Chan; **Chinese Medicine** (Traditional Eastern Medicine) *Director:* Fung Kwok-pui; **Chinese Studies** (Ancient Civilizations; Archaeology; Chinese; Cultural Studies; Fine Arts; Museum Studies; Translation and Interpretation) *Director:* Jenny F.S. So; **Diabetes and Obesity** *(Hong Kong)* (Diabetology) *Director:* Juliana C.N. Chan; **Digestive Disease** (Gastroenterology) *Director:* Francis K.L. Chan; **Economics and Finance** *(Co-Director: Zhang Junsen)* (Economics; Finance) *Director:* Joseph P.H. Fan; **Educational Research** *(Hong Kong)* (Education; Educational Administration; Educational Research; Educational Technology; Educational Testing and Evaluation; Information Technology) *Director:* Leslie N.K. Lo; **Global Economics and Finance** (Economics; Finance) *Director:* Liu Pak-wai; **Health Sciences** *(Li Ka Shing)* (Health Sciences) *Director:* Dennis Y.M. Lo; **Human Communicative Research** (Speech Therapy and Audiology) *Director:* Charles A. van Hasselt; **Humanities** (Arts and Humanities; Asian Religious Studies; Comparative Sociology; Cultural Studies; Social Sciences; Urban Studies) *Director:* Laurence K.P. Wong; **Mathematical Sciences** *(Cooperative Centre)* (Mathematics) *Director:* Yau Shing-tung; **Network Coding** *(Co-Director: Raymond W.H. Yeung)* (Computer Networks) *Director:* Robert S.Y. Li; **Optical Science and Technology** (Optical Technology) *Director:* Chan Kam-tai; **Plant Molecular Biology and Agricultural Biotechnology** (Agriculture; Biotechnology; Molecular Biology) *Director:* Samuel S.M. Sun; **Precision Engineering** (Measurement and Precision Engineering) *Director:* Du Ruxu; **Science and Technology** (Bioengineering; Materials Engineering; Sports; Sports Medicine; Technology) *Director:* Wu Chi; **Space and Earth Information Sciences** (Earth Sciences; Environmental Studies; Information Sciences; Surveying and Mapping; Telecommunications Engineering) *Director:* Lin Hui; **Supply Chain Management and Logistics** *(Li and Fung Institute)* (Store Management; Transport Management) *Director:* Cheung Wai-man; **Theoretical Computer Science and Communications** (Communication Studies; Computer Science) *Director:* Andrew C.C. Yao; **Theoretical Physics** (Physics) *Director:* Yang Chen-ning; **Vascular Medicine** *(Director (Clinical Science): Yu Cheuk-man)* (Medicine) *Director (Basic Science):* Huang Yu

Units

Continuing and Professional Studies *(School) Director:* Victor S.K. Lee; **East Asian Studies** *(Center)* (East Asian Studies) *Director:* David Faure; **English Language Teaching** (English; Foreign Languages Education) *Director:* Curtis Andy; **Learning Enhancement and Research** *(Centre)* (Educational Research) *Director:* Carmel McNaught; **New Asia – Yale-in-China Chinese Language** *(Centre)* (Chinese; Linguistics) *Director:* Wu Weiping; **Office of University General Education** (Higher Education) *Director:* Cheung Chan-fai; **Universities Service Center for China Studies** (Chinese) *Director:* Wang Shaoguang

Further Information: Teaching Hospital at Prince of Wales Hospital. Teaching Centre in Central Hong Kong.

History: Founded in 1963. A bilingual, bicultural (Chinese, English) institution of higher learning, consisting of nine Constituent Colleges: New Asia College (founded 1949), Chung Chi College (founded 1951), United College (founded 1956), Shaw College (founded 1986), Morningside College (2006), S.H. College (2006), C.W. Chu College (founded 2007), Wu Yee Sun College (founded 2007) and Lee Woo Sing College (founded 2007), . A self-governing corporation financed from grants made by the HKSAR Government, and fees and donations from private sources.

Governing Bodies: University Council and Senate; University Officers

Academic Year: August to July

Admission Requirements: Local students, Hong Kong Certificate of Education Examination (HKCEE) and Hong Kong Advanced Level Examination (HKALE) or General Certificate of Education Examination (Advanced Level) or other equivalent qualifications. Non-local students, possess a qualification obtained outside Hong Kong which qualifies them for university admission in the country/region where such qualification is obtained.

Fees: (Hong Kong Dollars): 42,100 per annum

Main Language(s) of Instruction: Chinese, English

International Co-operation: With over 200 institutions in Australia, Austria, Belgium, Brazil, Canada, Chile, China, Czech Republic, Denmark, Finland, France, Germany, India, Indonesia, Ireland, Italy,

Japan, Malaysia, Mexico, Netherlands, New Zealand, Norway, Portugal, Russia, Singapore, South Africa, South Korea, Spain, Sweden, Switzerland, Taiwan, Thailand, United Kingdom and United States. Also participates in exchange programmes and linkages through Asia-Pacific Association for International Education (APAIE), Association of International Educators (NAFSA), Association of University Presidents of China (AUPC), European Association for International Education (EAIE), Institute of International Education (IIE), International Student Exchange Program (ISEP), and University Mobility in Asia and the Pacific (UMAP). Linkages in the mainland are promoted through the Association of University Presidents of China (AUCP) of which CUHK is a founding member and serves as its secretariat.

Degrees and Diplomas: *Bachelor's Degree*: Arts, Business Administration, Chinese Medicine; Education; Engineering; Laws; Medicine; Nursing; Pharmacy; Science; Social Science, 3-5 yrs; *Postgraduate Certificate/Diploma*: a further 1-2 yrs; *Master's Degree*: Education; Family Medicine; Laws; Nursing; Nursing Science; Occupational Medicine; Professional Accountancy; Public Health; Science; Social Science; Social Work; Fine Arts; Music; Accountancy; Architecture; Arts; Business Administration; Chinese Medicine; Clinical Pharmacy; Divinity, a further 1-2 yrs; *Master of Philosophy*; *Doctor's Degree*: Music; Philosophy; Education; Nursing; Psychology; Juris Doctor, 3-5 yrs

Student Services: Academic counselling, Canteen, Cultural centre, Employment services, Foreign student adviser, Handicapped facilities, Health services, Language programs, Social counselling, Sports facilities

Student Residential Facilities: For 6,135 students

Special Facilities: Art Museum. Chung Chi College Archive.The Shum Choi Sang United College Archives. Hui Gallery. Yueh Chiao Art Gallery. Sir Run Run Shaw Hall. Shaw College Lecture Theatre. Lee Hysan Concert Hall. Chung Chi College Chapel.

Libraries: 2,451,759 vols; 13,000 periodical subscriptions; 100,000 electronic journals; 580 electronic databases

Publications: Chinese University of Hong Kong Annual Report *(annually)*

Press or Publishing House: The Chinese University Press

Academic Staff 2009-2010	MEN	WOMEN	TOTAL
FULL-TIME	743	233	976
PART-TIME	263	114	377
STAFF WITH DOCTORATE			
FULL-TIME	717	225	942
PART-TIME	120	56	176
Student Numbers 2009-2010			
All (Foreign Included)	–	–	22,639
FOREIGN ONLY	–	–	4,195

Part-time students, 7,343.
Last Updated: 18/05/11

THE HONG KONG ACADEMY FOR PERFORMING ARTS (HKAPA)

1 Gloucester Road, Wan Chai, Hong Kong
Tel: +852 2584-8500
Fax: +852 2802-4722
EMail: aso@hkapa.edu
Website: http://www.hkapa.edu

Director: Kevin Thompson (2004-)
Tel: +852 2584-8588, Fax: +852 2802-8345
EMail: director@hkapa.edu

Registrar: Herbert Huey
Tel: +852 2584-8587, Fax: +852 2584-8725
EMail: herberthuey.dir@hkapa.edu

Centres
Chinese Traditional Theatre Programme (Theatre) *Head:* Herbert Huey

Schools
Dance (Dance) *Dean:* Anita Donaldson; **Drama** (Acting; Theatre) *Dean:* David Jiang; **Film and Television** (Film; Radio and Television Broadcasting; Video) *Dean:* Kenneth Ip; **Music** (Music; Musical

Instruments) *Dean*: Benedict Cruft; **Theatre and Entertainment Arts** (Performing Arts; Theatre) *Dean*: John Williams

History: Founded 1984. Provides professional education, training and research, reflecting the cultural diversity of Hong Kong.

Governing Bodies: Council of the Hong Kong Academy for Performing Arts

Academic Year: September to June.

Admission Requirements: Undergraduate: 5 subject passes, including English and Chinese, in the Hong Kong Certificate of Education Examination (HKCEE), and a Diploma awarded by the Academy. Equivalent certificates are also considered. Master's programmes: Bachelor's Degree in relevant discipline with requisite marks.

Fees: (Hong Kong Dollars): 31,575 per annum (non-degree programme); 42,100 per annum (Bachelor's programme); 75,000 per annum (Master's programme)

Main Language(s) of Instruction: Chinese, English.

Accrediting Agencies: Hong Kong Council for Accreditation of Academic and Vocational Qualifications

Degrees and Diplomas: *Diploma*: Dance; Drama; Music; Chinese Traditional Theatre, 1-2 yrs; *Bachelor's Degree Honours*: Dance; Drama; Film and TV; Theatre and Entertainment Arts; Music (BFA;Bmus), 3 yrs full-time; *Master's Degree*: Dance; Drama; Theatre and Entertainment Arts; Music (MFA; Mmus), 2 yrs full-time / 4 yrs part-time. Also: Advance Diploma (2 yrs); Professional Diploma (1-2 yrs); and Foundation Certificate (1 yr).

Student Services: Academic counselling, Canteen, Health services, Language programs

Special Facilities: Theatres, concert hall, recital hall, TV Studio, dance / rehearsal studios.

Libraries: c. 135,000 items.

Academic Staff 2008-2009	MEN	WOMEN	TOTAL
FULL-TIME	154	154	**308**
PART-TIME	221	160	**381**
STAFF WITH DOCTORATE			
FULL-TIME	8	3	**11**
PART-TIME	7	9	**16**
Student Numbers 2008-2009			
All (Foreign Included)	326	467	**793**
FOREIGN ONLY	48	76	**124**

Part-time students, 81.
Last Updated: 23/10/08

THE HONG KONG INSTITUTE OF EDUCATION (HKIED)

10, Lo Ping Road, Tai Po, New Territories, Hong Kong
Tel: +852 2948-8888
Fax: +852 2948-6000
EMail: info@ied.edu.hk
Website: http://www.ied.edu.hk

President: Anthony B.L. Cheung

International Relations: Fiona Wong, Head, International Office
Tel: +852 2948-7654, Fax: +852 2948-8198
EMail: Fiona@ied.edu.hk

Faculties
Arts and Sciences (Cultural Studies; Environmental Studies; Fine Arts; Health Education; Information Technology; Mathematics; Natural Sciences; Physical Education; Social Sciences); **Education Studies** (Continuing Education; Curriculum; Education; Educational Administration; Educational and Student Counselling; Educational Psychology; Educational Sciences; International and Comparative Education; Preschool Education; Psychology; Special Education); **Languages** (Chinese; English; Native Language)

Research Centres
Asia Pacific Centre for Leadership and Change *(The Joseph Lau Luen Hung Charitable Trust Asia Pacific Centre)*; **Assessment**; **Childhood Research and Innovation** *(Faculty of Education Studies R&D Centre)*; **Chinese Literature and Literacy Culture** (Literacy Education; South Asian Studies); **Development and Research in Small Class Teaching** *(Faculty of Education Studies R&D Centre)*; **Governance and Citizenship**; **Greater China Stu-**

dies *(Faculty of Arts and Sciences R&D Centre)* (South Asian Studies); **Language Education and Acquisition in Multilingual Societies**; **Learning Study** *(Faculty of Education Studies R&D Centre)*; **Lifelong Learning Research and Development** *(Faculty of Education Studies R&D Centre)* (Continuing Education; Educational Research); **Linguistics and Language Information Sciences** (Linguistics); **Popular Culture and Education** *(Faculty of Languages R&D Centre)* (Educational Research; Folklore); **Religious and Spirituality Education** *(Faculty of Education Studies R&D Centre)* (Religious Education); **Research in Interdisciplinary and Liberal Studies** *(Faculty of Arts and Sciences R&D Centre)*; **Special Needs and Studies in Inclusive Education** *(Faculty of Education Studies R&D Centre)* (Special Education)

Schools
Graduate Studies (Chinese; Communication Studies; Education; Educational Administration; Educational Psychology; English; English Studies; Foreign Languages Education; Linguistics; Mathematics; Mathematics Education; Music Education; Native Language; Native Language Education; Pedagogy; Psychology; Science Education; Visual Arts)

History: Established in 1994. A self-accrediting publicly-funded institution.

Degrees and Diplomas: *Bachelor's Degree*; *Bachelor's Degree Honours*: Contemporary Music and Performance Pedagogy; Health Education in School Health or Nursing Studies; Liberal Studies Education; Science Education in Science and Web Technology; Science Education in Sports Science; Social Science Education in Greater China Studies, "Education Plus" Programme; *Bachelor's Degree Honours*: Creative Arts and Culture; Global Environmental Science; Language Studies (Chinese/English Major), Multi-disciplinary programmes; *Bachelor's Degree Honours*: English Language; Chinese Language; Early Childhood Education; Music; Physical Education; Liberal Studies; Visual Arts; General Studies/ Mathematics; *Postgraduate Certificate/Diploma*: Education; English Studies (part-time and full-time); Psychology (Schools and Community Settings); *Master's Degree*: Educational Leadership and Change; Chinese Studies (Language Education); Teaching Chinese as an International Language; Educational Linguistics and Communication Sciences; Teaching English to Speakers of Other Languages; *Master of Philosophy*; *Doctor's Degree*: Education; Philosophy

Last Updated: 20/05/11

THE HONG KONG POLYTECHNIC UNIVERSITY (POLYU)

Hung Hom, Kowloon, Hong Kong
Tel: +852 2766-5111
Fax: +852 2764-3374
EMail: polyu@polyu.edu.hk
Website: http://www.polyu.edu.hk

President: Timothy W. Tong
Tel: +852 2766-5211, Fax: +852 2363-1349

Academic Secretary: Nancy Yuk-Ling Tong Liu
Tel: +852 2766-5544, Fax: +852 2334-3752
EMail: asntong@polyu.edu.hk

International Relations: Winnie Eley
Tel: +852 2766-5118, Fax: +852 2333-9974
EMail: oaweley@polyu.edu.hk

Faculties
Applied Sciences and Textiles (Applied Mathematics; Applied Physics; Biology; Chemical Engineering; Clothing and Sewing; Textile Technology) *Dean*: K.Y. Wong, **Business** (Accountancy; Finance; International Business; Management; Marketing; Transport Management) *Dean (Acting)*: Howard Davies; **Construction and Environment** (Building Technologies; Civil Engineering; Construction Engineering; Environmental Management; Environmental Studies; Real Estate; Regional Planning; Structural Architecture; Surveying and Mapping) *Dean*: Jin-guang Teng; **Engineering** (Computer Engineering; Computer Science; Electrical Engineering; Electronic Engineering; Industrial Engineering; Information Technology; Mechanical Engineering) *Dean (Acting)*: Charles Surya; **Health and Social Sciences** (Health Sciences; Medical Technology; Nursing; Optometry; Rehabilitation and Therapy; Social

Sciences; Social Studies) *Dean*: Maurice Yap; **Humanities** (Asian Studies; Bilingual and Bicultural Education; Chinese; Cultural Studies; English; Modern Languages) *Dean*: Chu-ren Huang

Schools

Design (Design) *Dean*: Lorraine Justice; **Hotel and Tourism Management** (Hotel Management; Tourism) *Dean*: Kaye Chon

History: Founded 1937, acquired present status and title 1994.

Governing Bodies: University Council; Senate

Academic Year: September to June (September-January; January-June). Also Summer Term, June to August

Admission Requirements: Local Student, Hong Kong Diploma of Secondary Education (HKDSE); Non local student, an academic level equivalent to GCE A level standard, or International Baccalaureate (IB) Diploma

Fees: (Hong Kong Dollars): Local student, 42,100 per annum (1,405 per credit); non-local student, 100,000 per annum

Main Language(s) of Instruction: English

International Co-operation: With universities in Australia; Austria; Canada; China; Denmark; Finland; France; Germany; Japan Korea; New Zealand; Singapore; Sweden; Switzerland; Thailand; Netherlands; Philippines; United Kingdom; USA. Also participates in IAESTE; WACE; ASAIHL; AUAP; ISTA; NAFSA; EAIE programmes

Degrees and Diplomas: *Sub-degree*: 2 yrs; *Bachelor's Degree*: 4-5 yrs; *Postgraduate Certificate/Diploma*: 2-3 yrs; *Master's Degree*: 2-3 yrs; *Doctor's Degree*: 3-5 yrs

Student Services: Academic counselling, Canteen, Cultural centre, Employment services, Foreign student adviser, Foreign Studies Centre, Handicapped facilities, Health services, Language programs, Nursery care, Social counselling, Sports facilities

Student Residential Facilities: Yes

Special Facilities: Auditorium

Libraries: Pao Yue-kong Library
Last Updated: 27/04/11

THE HONG KONG UNIVERSITY OF SCIENCE AND TECHNOLOGY (HKUST)

Clear Water Bay, Kowloon, Hong Kong
Tel: +852 2358-6000
Fax: +852 2358-0537
EMail: oudpa@ust.hk
Website: http://www.ust.hk

President: Tony F. Chan (2009-)
Tel: +852 2358-6101, Fax: +852 2358-0029
EMail: preschan@ust.hk

Provost: Wei Shyy
Tel: +852 2358-6122, Fax: +852 2358-0194
EMail: weishyy@ust.hk

Vice-President for Administration and Business: Yuk-Shan Wong
Tel: +852 2358-6151, Fax: +852 2358-0285
EMail: yswong@ust.hk

International Relations: Emily Hui, Director of University Development and Public Affairs
Tel: +852 2358-6302, Fax: +852 2358-0537
EMail: emilyhui@ust.hk

Centres

Advanced Computing and Communication Technologies *(International Centre) Director*: Pascale Fung; **Advanced Microsystem Packaging** (Electronic Engineering) *Director*: Ricky S.W. Lee; **Applied Genomics** (Biotechnology) *Director*: Hong Xue; **Applied Social and Economic Research** (Economics; Social Studies) *Director*: Xiaogang Wu; **Asian Family Business and Entrepreneurship Studies** (Small Business) *Director*: Roger King; **Asian Financial Markets** (Banking; Finance) *Director*: Sudipto Dasgupta; **Atmospheric Research** (Meteorology) *Director*: Alexis Lau; **Bioengineering and Biomedical Devices** (Bioengineering; Biomedical Engineering) *Director*: I-Ming Hsing; **Building Energy Research** *Director*: Christopher Chao; **Business Case Studies** (Business and Commerce) *Director*: Roger King; **Business Strategy and Innovation** (Business and Commerce) *Director*: Jiatao Li; **Cancer Research** (Oncology) *Director*: Randy Poon; **China Business and Management** *(Shui On)* (Business and Commerce; Management) *Director*: Leonard K.H. Cheng; **China's Transnational Relations** *Director*: David Zweig; **Chinese Linguistics** (Linguistics) *Director*: Jingtao Sun; **Chinese Medicine R&D** (Traditional Eastern Medicine) *Director*: Karl Tsim; **Cultural Studies** (Cultural Studies) *Director*: Zongli Lu; **Cyberspace** *Director*: Dit-Yan Yeung; **Digital Life Research** *Director*: Qian Zhang; **Display Research** (Electronic Engineering) *Director*: Hoi Sing Kwok; **Economic Development** (Economic and Finance Policy; Economics) *Director*: Siu Fai Leung; **Electronic Commerce** (E-Business/Commerce) *Director*: Kar Yan Tam; **Engineering Materials and Reliability** (Engineering) *Director*: Jingshen Wu; **Entrepreneurship** (Management) *Director*: Rocky C.S. Law; **Environment, Energy and Resource Policy** (Environmental Management) *Director*: David Zweig; **Experimental Business Research** (Administration; Business Education) *Director*: Soo Hong Chew; **FINETEX R&D** *Principal Investigator*: Jang-Kyo Kim; **Fund Management** (Banking) *Director*: Kalok Chan; **Green Products and Processing Technologies** *Director*: Guuohua Chen; **Hainan** *Director*: John K.C. Wei; **HKUST LED-FPD Technology R&D** *(Foshan) Director*: Ricky S.W. Lee; **Hong Kong-Beijing UST Joint Research** *Director*: Tongyi Zhang; **Huawei-HKUST Innovation Laboratory** *Co-Director*: Vincent Lau; **Marketing and Supply Chain Management** (Marketing) *Director*: Shaohui Zheng; **Molecular Neuroscience** (Neurosciences) *Director*: Nancy Y. Ip; **New Element - HKUST Digital Healthcare Joint Research** *Principal Investigator*: Lionel M. Ni; **Organizational Research** *(Hang Lung) Director*: Jiatao Li; **Photonics Technology** *Principal Investigator*: Kei May Lau; **Polymer Processing and Systems** *Director*: Furong Gao; **Scientific Computation** (Applied Mathematics; Computer Science) *Director*: Xiao Ping Wang; **Semiconductor Product Analysis and Design Enhancement** *Director*: Johnny K.O. Sin; **Smart and Sustainable Infrastructure Research** *Director*: Moe M.S. Cheung; **South China Research** *Director*: Tik Sang Liu; **Space Science Research** *Director*: Kwing-Lam Chan; **Survey Research** *Director*: Raymond S.K. Wong; **Sustainable Energy Technology** *Director*: Tianshou Zhao; **Technology Transfer** *Director*: Claudia Xu; **Visual Computing and Imaging Science at HKUST** *Director*: Long Quan; **Wireless Information Technology** (Information Technology) *Director*: Ross Murch

Departments

Accountancy (Accountancy) *Head*: Kevin C.W. Chen; **Chemical and Biomolecular Engineering** (Bioengineering; Chemical Engineering) *Head (Acting)*: Gordon McKay; **Chemistry** (Chemistry) *Head*: Zhenyang Lin; **Civil and Environmental Engineering** (Civil Engineering; Environmental Engineering) *Head*: Christopher K.Y. Leung; **Computer Science and Engineering** (Computer Engineering; Computer Science) *Head*: Mounir Hamdi; **Economics** (Economics) *Head*: Francis Lui; **Electronic and Computer Engineering** (Computer Engineering; Electronic Engineering) *Head and Chair Professor*: Ross Murch; **Finance** (Finance) *Head and Chair Professor of Finance*: Kalok Chan; **Industrial Engineering and Logistics Management** (Industrial Engineering; Transport Management) *Head*: Fugee Tsung; **Information Systems, Business Statistics and Operations Management** (Information Management; Management Systems) *Head and Chair Professor*: Albert Ha; **Management** (Management) *Head and Chair Professor*: Jiatao Li; **Marketing** (Marketing) *Head and Chair Professor*: Jaideep Sengupta; **Mathematics** (Mathematics) *Head and Chair Professor*: Allen Moy; **Mechanical Engineering** (Mechanical Engineering) *Head*: Matthew M.F. Yuen; **Physics** (Physics) *Head*: Tai Kai Ng

Divisions

Environment (Environmental Studies) *Head*: Chak Keung Chan; **Humanities** (Arts and Humanities) *Head and Chair Professor*: Billy K.L. So; **Life Sciences** (Biological and Life Sciences) *Head (Acting)*: Michael M.T. Loy; **Social Sciences** (Social Sciences) *Head*: Raymond S.K. Wong

Institutes

Advanced Manufacturing (Production Engineering) *Director*: Mitchell Tseng; **Advanced Study** *Director*: Henry Tye; **Biotechnology Research** (Biotechnology) *Director*: Y.H. Wong; **Environment** (Environmental Engineering) *Director*: Chak Keung Chan; **Europe** *Director*: Emily Hui; **Hongkong Telecom Information Technology** (Information Technology; Telecommunications Engineering) *Director*: Khaled Ben Letaief; **Integrated Microsystems** (Microelectronics) *Director*: Qingping Sun; **Logistics and**

Supply Chain Management (Transport Management) *Director*: Chung-Yee Lee; **Nano Science and Technology** *(William Mong Institute)* (Nanotechnology; Physical Engineering) *Director*: Che Ting Chan; **Shenzhen** *Division Head*: Yuk-Shan Wong; **Sino Software Research** (Software Engineering) *Director*: Gary Chan

Laboratories
Molecular Neuroscience *(State Key Laboratory)* (Neurosciences) *Director*: Nancy Y. Ip

Programmes
Atmospheric Environmental Science *(MPhil / PhD Programme)* (Environmental Studies; Meteorology); **Environmental Management and Technology** *(BSc Degree Programme)* (Environmental Management); **Environmental Science and Management** *(Graduate Diploma / MSc Degree Programme)* (Environmental Management; Environmental Studies); **Marine Environmental Science** *(MPhil / PhD Programme)* (Environmental Studies; Marine Science and Oceanography); **Risk Management and Business Intelligence** *(BSc Degree Programme)* (Business and Commerce; Insurance); **Technology and Management** *(Dual Degree Programme (BEng & BBA))* (Management; Technology)

Schools
Business and Management (Accountancy; Business and Commerce; Economics; Finance; Information Management; Management; Marketing) *Dean*: Leonard K. H. Cheng; **Engineering** (Chemical Engineering; Civil Engineering; Computer Science; Electrical and Electronic Engineering; Engineering; Environmental Engineering; Industrial Engineering; Mechanical Engineering) *Dean*: Khaled Ben Letaief; **Humanities and Social Sciences** (Arts and Humanities; Social Sciences) *Dean*: James Lee; **Science** (Applied Physics; Biochemistry; Biology; Chemistry; Mathematics; Natural Sciences; Physics) *Dean*: Nancy Y. Ip

Units
Advanced Engineering Materials *(Central Research Facilities)* (Materials Engineering) *Director*: Jingshen Wu; **Animal and Plant Care** *(Central Research Facilities)* (Animal Husbandry; Horticulture) *Director*: Robert K.M. Ko; **Biosciences Research** *(Central Research Facilities)* (Biological and Life Sciences) *Director*: Randy Y.C. Poon; **CLP Power Wind/Wave Tunnel** *(Central Research Facilities)* *Director*: Yeou-Koung Tung; **Design and Manufacturing Services** *(Central Research Facilities)* (Maintenance Technology) *Director*: Lilong Cai; **Environmental Research** *(Central Research Facilities)* (Environmental Studies) *Director*: Alexis Lau; **Geotechnical Centrifuge Research** *(Central Research Facilities)* (Geological Engineering) *Director*: Charles W. W. Ng; **Materials Characterization and Preparation Research** *(Central Research Facilities)* (Materials Engineering) *Director*: Kwok-Kwong Fung; **Nanoelectronics Fabrication** *(Central Research Facilities)* (Microelectronics; Nanotechnology) *Director*: Johnny K.O. Sin

History: Founded 1988, and opened October 1991 as a technological university devoted to the advancement of learning and scholarship, with special emphasis on research, postgraduate education, and close collaboration with business and industry.

Governing Bodies: Council; Senate

Academic Year: September to May (September-December; February-May)

Admission Requirements: Hong Kong Certificate of Education (HKCEE) and Hong Kong Advanced Level Examination (HKALE), or equivalent

Fees: (Hong Kong Dollars): 42,100 per annum

Main Language(s) of Instruction: English

International Co-operation: With universities in Australia; Austria; Belarus; Belgium; Canada; China; Czech Republic; Denmark; Finland; France; Germany; Hungary; India; Israel; Italy; Japan; Korea (Republic of); Malaysia; Mexico; Netherlands; New Zealand; Norway; Philippines; Poland; Russian Federation; Saudi Arabia; Singapore; South Africa; Spain; Sweden; Switzerland; Thailand; Ukraine; United Kingdom and USA

Degrees and Diplomas: *Bachelor's Degree (BSc)*: 3-5 yrs; *Postgraduate Certificate/Diploma*: a further 1-3 yrs; *Master's Degree (MSc)*: a further 1-5 yrs; *Doctor's Degree (PhD)*: a further 3-8 yrs. Also Executive Master of Business Administration (EMBA) and Master of Technology Management (MTM)

Student Services: Academic counselling, Canteen, Cultural centre, Employment services, Foreign student adviser, Handicapped facilities, Health services, Language programs, Social counselling, Sports facilities

Student Residential Facilities: For 4,522 students (including 212 off- campus)

Libraries: 687,000 vols of printed books and journals; 357,000 units of microforms; 36,000 titles of media resources; 165,000 titles of electronic books; 26,100 titles of electronic journals; 317 databases

Publications: HKUST Newsletter; Research Report *(annually)*; UST Alumni News

Press or Publishing House: Publishing Technology Centre

Last Updated: 10/05/11

THE OPEN UNIVERSITY OF HONG KONG (OUHK)
30, Good Shepherd Street, Homantin, Kowloon, Hong Kong
Tel: +852 2711-2100
Fax: +852 2715-0760
EMail: info@ouhk.edu.hk
Website: http://www.ouhk.edu.hk

President: John Chi-Yan Leong
Tel: +852 2768-6089, Fax: +852 2390-6811
EMail: jcyleong@ouhk.edu.hk

Registrar: Shu-wing Lee
Tel: +852 2768-6651, Fax: +852 2789-2725
EMail: swlee@ouhk.edu.hk

International Relations: Jacqueline Ming-fung Cheng, Head, Public Affairs Department
Tel: +852 2768-6350, Fax: +852 2789-0323
EMail: jmfcheng@ouhk.edu.hk

Institutes
Professional and Continuing Education *(Li Ka Shing)* (Arts and Humanities; Business Administration; Communication Arts; Educational Psychology; Finance; Health Sciences; Law; Management; Marketing; Modern Languages; Tourism) *Director*: Yu-Hon Lui

Schools
Arts and Social Sciences (Arts and Humanities; Chinese; Economics; Film; Law; Literature; Performing Arts; Psychology; Public Administration; Regional Studies; Social Sciences; Translation and Interpretation; Writing) *Dean*: Kwok-kan Tam; **Business and Administration** (Accountancy; Business Administration; E-Business/Commerce; Finance; International Business; Law; Management; Management Systems; Marketing) *Dean*: Yiu-keung Ip; **Education and Languages** (Education; Foreign Languages Education; Pre-school Education) *Dean*: Yvonne Yuk-hang Shi Fung; **Science and Technology** (Applied Chemistry; Computer Engineering; Computer Science; Electronic Engineering; Engineering; Environmental Studies; Industrial Design; Information Technology; Mathematics; Nursing) *Dean*: Kin-Chung Ho

History: Founded 1989 as Open Learning Institute of Hong Kong, acquired present self-accrediting status 1997. Its role is to make higher education available to all, principally through open and flexible learning.

Governing Bodies: Council

Academic Year: Distance-learning programmes: April to March, (April-September; October-March); Full-time face-to-face programmes: September to August

Admission Requirements: Distance-learning programmes: Anyone aged 17 or above. No academic entry requirements, except for postgraduate and professional programmes. Full-time face-to-face programmes: Requirements vary according to different degree programmes: Form-6 school leavers, Associate Degree holders, Hong-Kong Advanced Level Examination (HKALE) and its equivalents

Fees: (Hong Kong Dollars): Distance-learning programmes : 810-1,325 per credit; Full-time-face-to-face programmes: 1,015-1,390 per credit

Main Language(s) of Instruction: English, Chinese

Degrees and Diplomas: *Bachelor's Degree*: Distance learning programmes: 3-8 yrs; Full-time programmes: 3-4 yrs; *Master's Degree*: 2-5 yrs; *Doctor's Degree*: 4-7 yrs

Student Services: Academic counselling, Employment services, Handicapped facilities

Libraries: c. 151,000 vols of printed and multi-media items; 27,400 electronic books

Press or Publishing House: The OUHK Press

Academic Staff *2010-2011*	TOTAL
FULL-TIME	233
PART-TIME	865
STAFF WITH DOCTORATE	
FULL-TIME	90

Student Numbers *2010-2011*	
All (Foreign Included)	17,156

Last Updated: 20/06/11

THE UNIVERSITY OF HONG KONG (HKU)

Pokfulam Road, Hong Kong
Tel: +852 2859-2111
Fax: +852 2858-2549
EMail: cpao@hku.hk
Website: http://www.hku.hk

Vice-Chancellor and President: Lap-Chee Tsui (2002 to present)
Tel: +852 2859-2100, Fax: +852 2858-9435
EMail: vcoffice@hkucc.hku.hk; tsuilc@hkucc.hku.hk

Director of Communications: Katherine Ma (2006 to present)
Tel: +852 2859-2601, Fax: +852 2858-4986
EMail: katherine.ma@hku.hk

International Relations: Henry W.K. Wai, Registrar, International Officer (2002 to present)
Tel: +852 2859-2222, Fax: +852 2546-0456
EMail: henrywai@hkusub.hku.hk

Centres
Enhancement of Teaching and Learning (Pedagogy) *Executive Director:* M. Prosser; **Journalism and Media Studies** (Journalism; Media Studies) *Director:* Y.Y. Chan; **Social Sciences Research** (Social Sciences) *Director:* J.H. Bacon-Shone

Faculties
Architecture (Architecture) *Dean (Acting):* David P.Y. Lung; **Arts** (Arts and Humanities; Modern Languages) *Dean:* K. Louie; **Business and Economics** (Business and Commerce; Economics) *Dean:* E.C. Chang; **Dentistry** (Dentistry) *Dean:* L.P. Samaranayake; **Education** (Education) *Dean:* S.J. Andrews; **Engineering** (Engineering) *Dean:* W.C. Chew; **Law** (Law) *Dean:* J.M.M. Chan; **Medicine** (Medicine) *Dean:* S.P. Lee; **Science** (Natural Sciences) *Dean:* S. Kwok; **Social Sciences** (Social Sciences) *Dean:* I. Holliday

Institutes
E-Business Technology (Business and Commerce; Business Computing; E-Business/Commerce) *Director:* C.J. Tan; **Humanities and Social Sciences** *(Hong Kong Institute for The Humanities and Social Sciences)* (Asian Studies) *Director:* Angela K.C. Leung; **Kadoorie** (Environmental Studies) *Director:* P.R. Hills; **Marine Science** (Marine Science and Oceanography) *Honorary Director:* G.A. Williams

Schools
Chinese Medicine (Traditional Eastern Medicine) *Director:* Y. Tong; **Graduate** *Dean:* Paul K.H. Tan; **Professional and Continuing Education** *Director:* C.F. Lee

Further Information: Also Teaching Hospitals

History: Founded 1911. A self-governing body financed mainly by the HKSAR government.

Governing Bodies: Court and Council

Academic Year: September to June

Admission Requirements: Hong Kong Certificate of Education (HKCEE) or equivalent, and Hong Kong Advanced Level Examination (HKALE) or equivalent, or other qualifications as equivalent

Fees: (Hong Kong Dollars): Undergraduate, local students, 42,100 per annum, overseas students, 100,000; postgraduate, 21,050-363,000 per annum

Main Language(s) of Instruction: English (Department of Chinese, Chinese)

International Co-operation: With universities in Australia, Austria, Canada, China, Denmark, Finland, France, Germany, Italy, Japan, Korea, Malaysia, Mexico, Netherlands, New Zealand, Norway, Singapore, Spain, Sweden, Switzerland, Thailand, United Kingdom, USA

Degrees and Diplomas: *Bachelor's Degree:* 3-5 yrs; *Postgraduate Certificate/Diploma; Master's Degree:* a further 2-4 yrs; *Doctor's Degree:* a further 2-5 yrs

Student Services: Academic counselling, Canteen, Employment services, Foreign student adviser, Health services, Language programs, Social counselling, Sports facilities

Student Residential Facilities: For 4,701 students

Special Facilities: University Museum and Art Gallery

Libraries: Main Library, 2,796,653 vols

Publications: Current Research *(annually)*

Press or Publishing House: University Press

Academic Staff *2010-2011*	MEN	WOMEN	TOTAL
FULL-TIME	721	287	1,008

Student Numbers *2010-2011*			
All (Foreign Included)	10,554	11,523	22,077
FOREIGN ONLY	2,157	2,525	4,682

Last Updated: 18/05/11

PRIVATE INSTITUTIONS

HONG KONG SHUE YAN UNIVERSITY

10 Wai Tsui Crescent, Braemar Hill Road, North Point, Hong Kong
Tel: +852 2570-7110
Fax: +852 2806-8044
EMail: info@hksyu.edu
Website: http://www.hksyu.edu/

President: Henry H.L. Hu

Vice President, Administration: Fai-chung Hu

Departments
Accountancy (Accountancy); **Business Administration** (Business Administration); **Chinese Language and Literature** (Chinese); **Counselling and Psychology** (Educational and Student Counselling; Educational Psychology; Psychology); **Economics and Finance** (Economics; Finance); **English Language and Literature** (English); **History** (History); **Journalism and Communication** (Communication Studies; Journalism; Mass Communication); **Law and Business** (Commercial Law; Law); **Social Work** (Social Work); **Sociology** (Social Sciences; Sociology)

Further Information: Also 9 Research Centres

History: Founded in 1971 as Hong Kong Shue Yan College. Acquired current title and status 2006. Hong Kong's first private university.

Governing Bodies: Board of Governors; University Council.

Admission Requirements: Hong Kong Certificate of Education (or equivalent) in at least six subjects, including English and Chinese.

Fees: (Hong Kong Dollars): 49,000 per annum (degree programme); 38,000 per annum (cooperative degree programme).

Main Language(s) of Instruction: English, Chinese.

International Co-operation: With universities in Australia, UK and USA

Degrees and Diplomas: *Bachelor's Degree Honours; Master's Degree.* Split degrees also offered with overseas institutions. Cooperative Master's degree programmes with overseas institutions.

Last Updated: 26/10/11

China - Macao SAR

STRUCTURE OF HIGHER EDUCATION SYSTEM

Description:

Higher education is offered by public and private institutions. Some of the institutions offer a wide variety of programmes, while others specialize in specific areas.

Stages of studies:

University level first stage: Bacharelato/Licenciatura

The minimum time needed to complete a Bacharelato is three years. Generally, students with Form five or equivalent qualifications can take this degree programme after passing the entrance examinations offered individually by the institutions. The programmes are offered by universities, universty level institutions, and polytechnic/ professional institutes.

The minimum time needed to complete a Licenciatura is four years. Students with Form six or equivalent qualifications can take this degree programme after passing the entrance examinations offered individually by the Institutions. The programmes are offered by universities, university level institutions, and polytechnic/ professional institutes.

University level second stage: Mestrado

Mestrado programmes involve both course work and the writing (and defence) of a dissertation/thesis. The period of course work is between one and two years. Generally, students with a Licenciatura are qualified to apply for the programme which is offered by universities and university level institutions.

University level third stage: Doutoramento

Generally, students with a Mestrado or equivalent qualifications can apply for Doutoramento programmes. The duration of the programmes is between three to five years. The programmes are offered by universities and university level institutions.

Distance higher education:

Distance education is principally offered by the Asia International Open University.

ADMISSION TO HIGHER EDUCATION

Admission to university-level studies:

Name of secondary school credential required: Certificate of Secondary (Form 5) Education

For entry to: Bacharelato programmes

Name of secondary school credential required: Certificate of Senior Secondary Education

For entry to: Associate Degree; Licenciatura programmes

Entrance exam requirements: Entrance examinations operated individually by institutions.

Foreign students admission:

Definition of foreign student: Non-Resident of Macao.

Entrance exam requirements: Depends on requirements imposed by individual institutions.

Entry regulations: Visa

RECOGNITION OF STUDIES

Quality assurance system:

The main decree governing recognition of studies and qualifications is the Decreto-Lei no 11/91/M.

NATIONAL BODIES

Gabinete de Apoio ao Ensino Superior (Tertiary Education Services Office)
Director: Sou Chio Fai
Calçada de St° Agostinho n°19, Edif. Nam Yue, 13° a 15° Andares
Macau
Tel: +853 2834 5403
Fax: +853 2831 8401
EMail: info@gaes.gov.mo
WWW: http://www.gaes.gov.mo
Role of national body: Governmental department in charge of higher education affairs in Macau.

Data for academic year: 2007-2008
Source: IAU from Tertiary Education Services Office, Macao SAR, 2007. Bodies updated in 2009.

INSTITUTIONS

PUBLIC INSTITUTIONS

INSTITUTE FOR TOURISM STUDIES
Instituto de Formação Turística (IFT)
Colina de Mong-Há, Macao
Tel: +853 2856-1252
Fax: +853 2851-9058
EMail: fanny@ift.edu.mo
Website: http://www.ift.edu.mo
President: Fanny Vong (2001-)
Tel: +853 8598-3084, Fax: +853 2852-1694

Administrative Officer: Louisa Lam
Tel: +853 8598-3126 EMail: louisa@ift.edu.mo

International Relations: Louisa Lam
Tel: +853 8598-3126 EMail: louisa@ift.edu.mo

Centres
Advanced Tourism Studies *(Macao-Europe)* (Tourism)

Colleges
Tourism (Tourism)

Schools
Professional and Continuing Education (Tourism)
History: Founded 1995.
Degrees and Diplomas: *Bacharelato*. Also four-year Bachelor Degrees
Last Updated: 03/10/08

MACAO POLYTECHNIC INSTITUTE
Instituto Politécnico de Macau (IPM)
Rua Luís Gonzaga Gomes, Macao
Tel: +853 2857-8722
Fax: +853 2830-8801
EMail: registry@ipm.edu.mo
Website: http://www.ipm.edu.mo
President: Heong-lok Lei (1999-)
Tel: +853 599-6288 EMail: hilei@ipm.edu.mo

Secretary-General: Lai-Ha Ku
Tel: +853 557-275 EMail: wendyku@ipm.edu.mo

International Relations: Ngan-Lin Lei
Tel: +853 599-6132, Fax: +853 560-170
EMail: vivianlei@ipm.edu.mo

Academies
Senior Studies

Centres
Career Development

Schools
Arts (Fine Arts); **Business** (Business Administration; Business and Commerce); **Health Sciences** (Health Sciences); **Language and Translation** (Modern Languages; Translation and Interpretation); **Physical Education and Sports** (Physical Education; Sports); **Public Administration** (Public Administration)

History: Founded 1991.

Degrees and Diplomas: *Bacharelato*; *Licenciatura*. Also joint Master Degree Programme with Hong Kong Polytechnic University
Last Updated: 21/06/07

⚡ UNIVERSITY OF MACAO
Universidade de Macau (UM)
Avenida Padre Tomás Pereira, Taipa, Macao
Tel: +853 2883-1622
Fax: +853 2883-1694
EMail: webmaster@umac.mo
Website: http://www.umac.mo

Rector: Wei Zhao (2008-2013)
Tel: +853 8397-4301, Fax: +853 2883-1964
EMail: weizhao@umac.mo

Head of Information and Public Relations Office: Katrina Cheong
Tel: +853 8397-4336, Fax: +853 2883-1012
EMail: katrinac@umac.mo

Vice-Rector Administration: Iat Long Lai
Tel: +853 3974-303 EMail: alexlai@umac.mo

International Relations: Annie Chan, Functional Head of International Relations
Tel: +853 8397-4301, Fax: +853 8397-4341
EMail: anniec@umac.mo

Centres
Continuing Education *Director*: Hing Wan Cheng; **English Language** (English) *Director*: Kim Hughes Wilhelm; **Pre-University Studies** *Diector*: Teng Lam

Departments
Accounting and Information Management *Head*: Chun Yip Yuen; **Chinese** (Chinese) *Head*: Jie Xu; **Civil and Environmental Engineering** (Civil Engineering; Environmental Engineering) *Head*: Ka Veng Yuen; **Communication** (Communication Studies; Journalism; Multimedia) *Head (Acting)*: Mei Wu; **Computer and Information Sciences** (Computer Science; Information Sciences) *Head*: Zhiguo Gong; **Economics** *Head*: Fung Kwan; **Electrical and Electronic**

Engineering (Electrical and Electronic Engineering) *Head*: Mang I Vai; **Electro-mechanical Engineering** (Electrical Engineering; Mechanical Engineering) *Head*: Lap Mou Tam; **English** (English) *Head*: Glenn Timmermans; **Finance and Business Economics** (Business and Commerce; Economics; Finance) *Head*: Siu Kwan Lam; **Government and Public Administration** *Head*: Ming Ki Lam; **History** *Head*: Chuxiong Wei; **Management and Marketing** (Management; Marketing) *Head*: Long Wai Lam; **Mathematics** (Mathematics) *Head*: Tao Qian; **Portuguese** (Portuguese) *Head*: Alan Norman Baxter; **Psychology** *Head*: Riki Carl D'amato; **Sociology** (Social Sciences; Sociology) *Head*: Zhidong Hao

Faculties

Business Administration (Accountancy; Business Administration; Business and Commerce; Business Computing; Finance; Information Management; Management; Marketing) *Dean (Acting)*: Michael Joseph Gift; **Education** (Chinese; Curriculum; Education; Educational Administration; Educational and Student Counselling; Educational Psychology; English; Physical Education; Preschool Education; Primary Education; Sports) *Dean*: Wen-Jing Shan; **Law** (Comparative Law; European Union Law; International Business; International Law; Law; Political Sciences) *Dean*: Lingliang Zeng; **Science and Technology** (Civil Engineering; E-Business/Commerce; Electrical and Electronic Engineering; Electronic Engineering; Engineering; Environmental Engineering; Health Administration; Hydraulic Engineering; Mathematics; Mechanical Engineering; Medicine; Software Engineering; Structural Architecture) *Dean*: Kai Meng Mok; **Social Sciences and Humanities** (Chinese; Communication Arts; Cultural Studies; Economics; English Studies; Japanese; Journalism; Linguistics; Literature; Mass Communication; Media Studies; Portuguese; Psychology; Public Administration; Social Sciences) *Dean*: Yufan Hao

Institutes

Chinese Medical Sciences (Biomedicine) *Director*: Yitao Wang

Research Centres

Business Research and Training *(Faculty of Business Administration)* (Business and Commerce) *Director*: Peng Chun Vong; **Chinese Culture** (South Asian Studies) *Director*: Dehua Zheng; **Educational** (Education) *Director*: Sou Kuan Vong; **Information and Communication Technology in Education** (Communication Studies; Education; Information Technology) *Director*: Liming Zhang; **Japanese Studies** (Japanese) *Director*: Kazuyoshi Noguchi; **Luso-Asian Studies** *Director*: Isabel Leonor da Silva Diaz de Seabra; **Macau Studies** *Director*: Wang Chong Ieong; **Scientific and Technological Research** *Director*: Zhishi Wang; **Social Science Research on Contemporary China** *Director*: Bolong Liu

Research Institutes

Advanced Legal Studies *Director*: Io Cheng Tong; **Study of Commercial Gaming** *(Faculty of Business Administration) Director*: Ka Chio Fong

History: Founded 1981 as University of East Asia, a private institution. Became public institution 1988. Acquired present status and title 1991. Financially supported by the government, tuition fees and donations.

Governing Bodies: University Council, comprising the University Management Boards, Heads of Academic Units, Senate's representatives, Librarian, representatives from the government and external members appointed by the Chancellor; University Management, comprising the Rector, two Vice-Rectors and the Administrator; Senate, comprising the Rector, Vice-Rectors, Heads of Academic Units, Full Professors, Associate Professors and some elected Assistant-Professors

Academic Year: September to June

Admission Requirements: Completion of secondary school education (Form 6, Grade 12) and UM entrance examination

Fees: (Pataca): for foreign students only, Bacharelato's Degree 28,100, Bachelor's Degree 34,600 per annum, Master's Degree (whole programme): MBA, 85,000 and non-MBA: 76,800, Ph.D (whole programme), 94,500

Main Language(s) of Instruction: Portuguese, English, Chinese

International Co-operation: With universities in Australia, Belgium, Colombia, Denmark, Finland, France, Germany, Japan, China, New Zealand, Norway, Philippines, Portugal, Spain, Sweden, Nether-

lands, United Kingdom, USA. Also participates in APHERN, AULP, CIEE, CRUP, IAU, IAUP, IEEE, IAESTE and UMAP programmes

Degrees and Diplomas: *Bacharelato*: Education; Arts; Social Sciences; Education; Law; Engineering; Business Administration, 4-5 yrs; *Postgraduate Diploma/Certificate*: Education, Law, 1-2 yrs; *Mestrado*: Arts, Social Sciences, Education, Law, Engineering, Science, Business Administration, 2-3 yrs; *Doutoramento*: Arts, Education, Law, Science, Social Sciences, Business Administration, 3-5 yrs

Student Services: Academic counselling, Canteen, Cultural centre, Employment services, Foreign student adviser, Handicapped facilities, Health services, Social counselling, Sports facilities

Student Residential Facilities: Yes

Libraries: 298,000 vols, over 100 electronic databases including c. 42,000 e-books and 35,000 electronic Journals, and over 1,500 Journals in paper format

Publications: Journal of Macau Studies

Academic Staff 2007-2008	MEN	WOMEN	TOTAL
FULL-TIME	250	127	377
PART-TIME	25	5	30
STAFF WITH DOCTORATE			
FULL-TIME	180	76	256
PART-TIME	3	–	3
Student Numbers 2008-2009			
All (Foreign Included)	–	–	c. 6,791
FOREIGN ONLY	–	–	130

Evening students, 1,250.
Last Updated: 22/09/08

PRIVATE INSTITUTIONS

ASIA INTERNATIONAL OPEN UNIVERSITY

Universidade Aberta Internacional da Ásia (AIOU)
3° Andar, Edifício Royal Centre, Avenida do Dr. Rodrigo Rodrigues, Macao
Tel: +853 2878-1698
Fax: +853 2878-1691
EMail: genoffice@aiou.edu
Website: http://www.aiou.edu

Rector: S.Y. Zhuang (2000-)

Executive Director: C.M. Cheung
Tel: +853 2892-2298, Fax: +853 2573-3808
EMail: hkoffice@aiou.edu

International Relations: K.C. Fredrick Tao
Tel: +852 2892-2293, Fax: +852 2573-3808 EMail: ftao@aiou.edu

Schools

Graduate Studies (Business Administration; International Law; Management); **Portuguese Studies**; **Professional Studies** (Business Administration); **Undergraduate Studies** (Business Administration)

History: Founded 1992.

Degrees and Diplomas: *Associate Degree*: 4-8 yrs; *Bacharelato*; *Licenciatura*; *Mestrado*: 15-48 months; *Doutoramento*: 3-5 yrs
Last Updated: 21/06/07

KIANG WU NURSING COLLEGE OF MACAO

Instituto de Enfermagem Kiang Wu de Macau (KWNC)
Est. Repouso No.35, R/C Macao, Macao
Tel: +853 295-6200
Fax: +853 2836-5204
EMail: admin@kwnc.edu.mo
Website: http://www.kwnc.edu.mo/

President: Iat-Kio Van (1999-)
Tel: +853 295-6202, Fax: +853 2836-5244
EMail: van@kwnc.edu.mo

Associate Academic Secretary: Ming-Xia Zhu
Tel: +853 295-6252 EMail: zmx@kwnc.edu.mo

Programmes

Nursing (Nursing)

History: Founded 1923, acquired present status and title 2002.

Degrees and Diplomas: *Bacharelato*. Also Postgraduate Diploma in Advanced Nursing

Last Updated: 21/06/07

ⒾⒶ MACAO UNIVERSITY OF SCIENCE AND TECHNOLOGY

Universidade de Ciência e Tecnologia de Macau (MUST)
Avenida Wai Long, Taipa, Macao
Tel: +853 2888-1122
Fax: +853 2888-0022
EMail: aaxu@must.edu.mo
Website: http://www.must.edu.mo

Rector: Ao Ao Xu (2002-)
Tel: +853 897-2238, Fax: +853 2882-7222

International Relations: Xi Chen, Vice Rector
Tel: +853 8897-2238, Fax: +853 2882 7222
EMail: xichen@must.edu.mo

Faculties

Chinese Medicine (Traditional Eastern Medicine); **Information Technology** (Information Technology); **Law** (Law); **Management and Administration** (Administration; Management)

Institutes

Sustainable Development (Development Studies)

History: Founded 2000.

Degrees and Diplomas: *Bacharelato*; *Mestrado*; *Doutoramento*
Last Updated: 21/06/07

ⒾⒶ UNIVERSITY OF SAINT JOSEPH

Universidade de São José (USJ)
Rua de Londres 16, 3rd Floor, Nape, Macao
Tel: +853 8796-4400
Fax: +853 2872-5517
EMail: pr.officer@usj.edu.mo
Website: http://www.usj.edu.mo

Rector: Ruben Duarte de Freitas Cabral (2004-)
Tel: +853 8796-4507, Fax: +853 2872 5517
EMail: rector@usj.edu.mo; cabral@usj.edu.mo

Director of Rector's Office: Lavena Cheong
Tel: +853 8796-4444 EMail: lavenacheong@usj.edu.mo

International Relations: Ana Paula Mota, Executive Coordinator, International Relations
Tel: +853 8796-4440 EMail: ivo.carneiro@usj.edu.mo

Centres

Language (English; French; Japanese; Portuguese; Russian; Spanish); **Russian** (Russian)

Research Centres

African Research and Development Studies (African Studies; Development Studies); **Arts Research for Human Expression** (Fine Arts); **Economic and Cultural Relations between China and Portuguese-speaking Countries**; **Environmental Sciences** (Environmental Studies); **Global and Strategic Studies** (Political Sciences; Social Sciences); **History and Heritage Studies** (Heritage Preservation; History; Southeast Asian Studies); **Psychological Research and Practice** (Psychology)

Schools

Arts, Letters and Sciences (Arts and Humanities; Education; Philosophy; Psychology; Social Studies); **Christian Studies** (Christian Religious Studies; Religion; Religious Studies); **Intelligent Systems and Technology** (Computer Science; Design; Information Technology; Technology); **Management, Leadership and Government** (Business Administration; Government; International Business; Leadership; Management; Marketing)

Further Information: Also Graduate School, which overseas all postgraduate programmes.

History: Founded 1996. Formerly known as Instituto Inter-Universitário de Macau (Macao Inter-University Institute). Acquired current status and title 2009.

Governing Bodies: Rector, Vice-Rectors, Pro-Rectors, Administrator

Academic Year: September to July

Admission Requirements: Successful completion of Year 12 of secondary studies

Fees: (MOP): 45,000 per annum, Undergraduate; 62,000-80,000 per programme, Master's degree; 50,000 per annum, PhD.

Main Language(s) of Instruction: English

International Co-operation: with institutions in China; Brazil; Portugal; Romania; France; Philippines; Taiwan; Russia; South Korea; Thailand; Australia

Degrees and Diplomas: *Bacharelato (Bachelor's degree)*: 4 yrs; *Licenciatura*; *Mestrado (Master's degree)*: 2 yrs; *Doutoramento*: 3-5 yrs

Student Services: Academic counselling, Canteen, Cultural centre, Employment services, Foreign student adviser, Foreign Studies Centre, Handicapped facilities, Language programs, Social counselling, Sports facilities

Libraries: c. 60,000 vols; 182 periodical subscriptions

Publications: Compass, Semestrial academic and trandsdisciplinary publication focusing on in epistemological new debates and challenges. *(3 per annum)*

Academic Staff 2010-2011	MEN	WOMEN	TOTAL
FULL-TIME	45	26	71
PART-TIME	57	32	89
STAFF WITH DOCTORATE			
FULL-TIME	20	7	27
PART-TIME	23	6	29
Student Numbers 2010-2011			
All (Foreign Included)	787	1,105	1,892
FOREIGN ONLY	73	70	143

Evening students, 156.
Last Updated: 23/11/10

China - Taiwan

STRUCTURE OF HIGHER EDUCATION SYSTEM

Description:

Higher education is provided by universities, colleges, and junior colleges, both public and private.

Stages of studies:

University level first stage: *Bachelor's degree*
Admission to the first stage is based on the results obtained in the Universities and Colleges Joint Entrance Examination. Most Bachelor's degree courses last for four years. The exceptions are Medicine (seven years), Dentistry (six years), Veterinary Medicine (five years). A total of 128 credits is required for a Bachelor's degree. At the Open University, Bachelor's courses last for seven to eight years.

University level second stage: *Master's degree*
Further specialization leads to Master's degrees which require two to four years of study following upon a Bachelor's degree.

University level third stage: *Doctorate*
The third stage leads to the highest university degree, the Doctorate, which requires a minimum of a further two years' study.

Distance higher education:
Distance education courses are offered at Open Universities. There are two types of Open Universities: national and municipality Open Universities. They provide adults with advanced and continuing education through audio-visual media. Open university students can either be officially registered or auditing. Officially registered students, who must be 20 or more, are admitted after passing an entrance examination. There is no pre-requisite educational level for those who are auditing. However, they must be at least 18 years old. Officially registered students who complete the programme requirements are conferred a Bachelor's degree.

ADMISSION TO HIGHER EDUCATION

Admission to university-level studies:

Name of secondary school credential required: Senior High School Leaving Certificate
Name of secondary school credential required: Senior Vocational School Leaving Certificate
Other admission requirements: Pass the university or college entrance examinations.

Foreign students admission:

Entrance exam requirements: Foreign students must be senior secondary school graduates.
Entry regulations: Foreign students must be senior secondary school graduates.
Language requirements: Students must have a reasonable command of the Chinese language, which is the only medium of instruction.

NATIONAL BODIES

Ministry of Education
Minister: Ching-ji Wu
No.5, Zhongshan S. Rd., Zhongzheng Dist
Taipei 10051
Tel: +862(2) 7736 6051
WWW: http://www.moe.gov.tw
Role of national body: Formulates policy and standards for all types of education in both the public and private sectors.

Higher Education Evaluation and Accreditation Council of Taiwan - HEEACT

Chairman of the Board: Cheng Jei-Cheng

President: George J. Jiang

7F., No.179, Sec. 1, Heping E. Rd., Da-an District

Taipei 106

Tel: +886(2) 3343 1200

Fax: +886(2) 3343 1211

EMail: service@heeact.edu.tw

WWW: http://www.heeact.edu.tw/

Role of national body: Responsible for conducting evaluations and accreditations of universities and colleges.

Foundation for International Cooperation in Higher Education of Taiwan - FICHET

CEO: Lily H.M. Chen

Room 202, No. 5, Lane 199, Kinghua Street

Taipei 10650

Tel: +886(2) 2322-2280

Fax: +886(2) 2322-2528

EMail: fichet@fichet.org.tw

WWW: http://www.fichet.org.tw

Data for academic year: 2010-2011
Source: IAU from the website of the Ministry of Education, 2010. Bodies, 2011.

INSTITUTIONS

PUBLIC INSTITUTIONS

NATIONAL CENTRAL UNIVERSITY (NCU)

300, Jhong-da Road, Jhongli, Taoyuan 320
Tel: +886(3) 422-7151
Fax: +886(3) 422-6062
EMail: ncu7010@ncu.edu.tw
Website: http://www.ncu.edu.tw

President: Chuan-Sheng Liu
Tel: +886(3) 425-4822, Fax: +886(3) 425-4842
EMail: preliu@ncu.edu.tw

Secretary-General: Jyh-chen Chen
Tel: +886(3) 425-3650 EMail: jcchen@cc.ncu.edu.tw

International Relations: Shir-Ly Huang
Tel: +886(3) 427-9755, Fax: +886(3) 427-6543
EMail: slhuang@cc.ncu.edu.tw

Colleges
Applied Geology *Chair*: Chia-shyun Chen; **Arts Studies** *Chair*: Ming-ming Lee; **Astronomy** *Chair*: Chung-Ming Ko; **Atmospheric Physics** (Astronomy and Space Science) *Chair*: Neng-Huei Lin; **Atmospheric Sciences** (Astronomy and Space Science) *Chair*: Neng-Huei Lin; **Business Administration** *Chair*: Wen-Hsien Tsai; **Chemical and Materials Engineering** *Chair*: Wen-Yih Chen; **Chemistry** *Chair*: Chung-Kung Lai; **Chinese Literature** (Chinese; Literature) *Chair*: Wei-chu Hung; **Civil Engineering** (Civil Engineering) *Chair*: Ray-Shyan Wu; **Cognitive Neuroscience** *Chair*: Daisy L. Hung; **Communication Engineering** (Computer Engineering) *Chair*: Char-Dir Chung; **Computer Science and Information Engineering** (Computer Engineering; Computer Science) *Chair*: Shing-Tsaan Huang; **Construction Engineering and Management** *Chair*: Chien-Chung John Li; **Earth Sciences** *Chair*: Kuo-Fong Ma; **Economics** *Chair*: Jiunn-Rong Chiou; **Electrical Engineering** (Electrical Engineering) *Chair*: Chin-Long Wey; **English** (English; Literature) *Chair*: Josephine Ho; **Environmental Engineering** (Environmental Engineering) *Chair*: Moo-Been Chang; **Finance** *Chair*: Chung-Da Ho; **French Language and Literature** (French; Literature) *Chair*: Kuang-Neng Liu; **Geophysics** (Geophysics) *Chair*: Kuo-Fong Ma; **Hakka Social and Cultural Studies** *Chair*: Hsueh-Ming Wu; **History** (History) *Chair*: Cheng-Han Wu; **Human Resource Management** (Business Administration; Human Resources) *Chair*: Weng-Jeng Lin; **Hydrology** (Hydraulic Engineering) *Chair*: Wu-ting Tsai; **Industrial Economics** (Business Administration) *Chair*: Jin-Long Liu; **Industrial Management** (Industrial Management) *Chair*: Ying-Chin Ho; **Information Management** *Chair*: Yann-Liang Chen; **Learning and Instruction** (Education; Pedagogy) *Chair*: Hwa-wei Ko; **Life Sciences** (Biological and Life Sciences) *Chair*: Rong-Nan Huang; **Mathematics** (Mathematics and Computer Science) *Chair*: I-Shou Chang; **Mechanical Engineering** *Chair*: Biing Hwa Yan; **Network Learning Technology** *Chair*: Tak-Wai Chan; **Optical Sciences** *Chair*: Chang Jeng-Yang; **Philosophy** *Chair*: Jien-Ming Jue; **Physics** (Physics) *Chair*: Y.H. Chang; **Space Science** (Astronomy and Space Science) *Chair*: Jann-Yenq Liu; **Statistics** *Chair*: Tsai-Hung Fan

History: Founded 1962 incorporating Institute of Geophysics founded 1962, as re-establishment of National Central University, founded in Nanking 1915 and closed 1949. A State institution financed by the government.

Academic Year: August to June (August-January; February-June)

Admission Requirements: Graduation from high school and entrance examination or equivalent

Fees: (New Taiwan Dollars): 25,000-30,000 per semester

Main Language(s) of Instruction: Chinese, English

Degrees and Diplomas: *Bachelor's Degree*: 4 yrs; *Master's Degree*: a further 2 yrs; *Doctorate (PhD)*: 3-7 yrs

Student Services: Academic counselling, Canteen, Cultural centre, Employment services, Foreign student adviser, Handicapped facilities, Health services, Language programs, Nursery care, Sports facilities

Student Residential Facilities: Yes

Libraries: Yes

Publications: Research Summaries

NATIONAL CHANGHUA UNIVERSITY OF EDUCATION (NCUE)

1, Chin-Teh Road, Pai Sha Village, Changhua 50007
Fax: +886(4) 723-2105
EMail: prdnt@cc.ncue.edu.tw
Website: http://www.ncue.edu.tw

President: Tze-Li Kang (1999-)
Tel: +886(4) 721-1030, Fax: +886(4) 726-2739

Secretary-General: Tzy-Yee Liu
Tel: +886(4) 721-1010, Fax: +886(4) 721-1111
EMail: liuty@cc.ncue.edu.tw

International Relations: Wen-Ke Wang, Vice-President
Tel: +886(4) 721-1199 EMail: wkw@cc.ncue.edu.tw

Centres
General Education

Colleges
Arts *Dean*: Shui-Mu Chang; **Education** (Educational and Student Counselling; Special Education) *Dean*: Chong-wen Chen; **Engineering** (Electrical Engineering; Electronic Engineering; Information Technology; Mechanical Engineering); **Management** (Accountancy; Business Administration; Information Management); **Science** *Dean*: Hury-Por Chang; **Technology and Vocational Education** *Dean*: David W.S. Tai

Graduate Institutes
Art Education (Art Education); **Human Resource Management** (Business Administration; Human Resources); **Science Education** (Science Education)

Graduate Schools
Education (Educational Administration; Educational Technology)

History: Founded 1971 as Provincial College, acquired present status and title 1980.

Academic Year: August to July (September-January; February-July)

Admission Requirements: Graduation from high school and entrance examination

Main Language(s) of Instruction: Chinese

Degrees and Diplomas: *Bachelor's Degree*: Education; Science, 4 yrs; *Bachelor's Degree*: Education (Guidance and Special Education), 3 yrs; *Master's Degree*: a further 2-4 yrs; *Doctorate*: 2-4 yrs

Student Residential Facilities: For c. 1,850 students

Libraries: c. 110,000 vols

Publications: Business Education *(quarterly)*; Journal *(annually)*; Journal of Industrial Education *(annually)*; Journal of Special Education *(annually)*; Studies in Language Education *(annually)*

NATIONAL CHENGCHI UNIVERSITY (NCCU)

64, Section 2, Chih Nan Road, Wenshan 116, Taipei 11623
Tel: +886(2) 293-93091
Fax: +886(2) 293-98043
EMail: www@nccu.edu.tw
Website: http://www.nccu.edu.tw

President: Jei-Cheng Cheng (2000-)
Tel: +886(2) 936-8068 EMail: president@nccu.edu.tw

Secretary-General: Shang-Ren Kwan
Tel: +886(2) 939-0169, Fax: +886(2) 937-9611
EMail: secrt@nccu.edu.tw

International Relations: Bih-Jaw Lin, Vice-President
Tel: +886(2) 293-87279, Fax: +886(2) 293-99850
EMail: research@nccu.edu.tw

Colleges
Commerce (Accountancy; Banking; Business Administration; Business and Commerce; Finance; Information Technology; Insurance; International Business; Statistics); **Communication** (Advertising and Publicity; Communication Arts; Journalism; Radio and Television Broadcasting); **Education**; **Foreign Languages** (Arabic; English; Japanese; Korean; Linguistics; Modern Languages; Russian; Turkish); **International Affairs**; **Law** (Civil Law; Constitutional Law; Criminal Law; Law); **Liberal Arts** (Arts and Humanities; Chinese; History; Information Sciences; Library Science; Philosophy; Religious Studies); **Science** (Computer Science; Mathematics; Psychology); **Social Sciences** (Economics; Ethnology; Finance; International Studies; Political Sciences; Public Administration; Social Policy; Social Sciences; Sociology)

Institutes
International Relations (International Relations)

Research Centres
Election Study (Political Sciences)

History: Founded 1927 as Special School for the Training of Administrative Personnel, became Central Institute of Political Science 1929 and University 1946. Closed 1949 and re-established in Taiwan 1954 by the Ministry of Education. A State institution.

Governing Bodies: Executive Council; University Council

Academic Year: August to July (August-January; February-July)

Admission Requirements: Graduation from high school, or recognized foreign equivalent, and entrance examination

Main Language(s) of Instruction: Chinese

International Co-operation: With universities in USA; Korea; Germany; Israel; Saudi Arabia; South Africa; Turkey; Japan; Russia; Austria; Australia; France; Sweden; Belgium; Poland; Canada

Degrees and Diplomas: *Bachelor's Degree*: 4 yrs; *Master's Degree*: a further 2 yrs and thesis; *Doctorate (PhD)*: 4-8 yrs

Student Services: Academic counselling, Cultural centre, Employment services, Foreign student adviser, Foreign Studies Centre, Handicapped facilities, Health services, Language programs, Sports facilities

Student Residential Facilities: For c. 5,000 students

Libraries: Central Library, c. 900,900 vols; Social Science Materials Centre, c. 1,263,075 vols; Institute of International Relations Library, c. 149,332 vols; Centre for Public and Business Administration Education Library, c. 79,344 vols

Publications: America and Europe Monthly *(monthly)*; Bulletin of Library and Information Science *(quarterly)*; Chinese Accounting Review *(quarterly)*; East Asia Quarterly *(quarterly)*; Issues and Studies (in Spanish, Chinese, Japanese, English, and French) *(quarterly)*; Journalistic Studies *(biannually)*; Mainland China Studies *(quarterly)*; Management Review *(quarterly)*; National Chengchi University Legal Essays *(biannually)*

NATIONAL CHENG KUNG UNIVERSITY (NCKU)

1, University Road, Tainan 70101
Tel: +886(6) 275-7575
Fax: +886(6) 236-8660
EMail: em50000@email.ncku.edu.tw
Website: http://www.ncku.edu.tw

President: Michael M.C. Lai
Tel: +886(6) 275-7575, Ext. 50000, Fax: +886(6) 274-3981

Secretary-General: Woei-Shyan Lee
Tel: +886(6) 237-3750, Fax: +886(6) 236-8660
EMail: em50020@email.ncku.edu.tw

Centres
Bioscience and Biotechnology (Biology; Biotechnology) *Dean*: Wen-Chang Chang

Colleges
Electrical Engineering and Computer Science *Dean*: Chin-Ting Lee; **Engineering** *Dean*: Wen-Teng Wu; **Liberal Arts** (Arts and Humanities; Chinese; Fine Arts; History; Literature; Modern Languages; Native Language) *Dean*: Chang-Min Chen; **Management** (Accountancy; Banking; Business Administration; Finance; Health Sciences; Industrial Management; Information Management; International Business; Leisure Studies; Physical Education; Statistics; Telecommunications Engineering; Transport Management) *Dean*: Yu-Hen Chang; **Medicine** (Anaesthesiology; Anatomy; Behavioural Sciences; Biochemistry; Cell Biology; Community Health; Dentistry; Dermatology; Forensic Medicine and Dentistry; Gerontology; Gynaecology and Obstetrics; Immunology; Medical Technology; Medicine; Microbiology; Molecular Biology; Neurology; Nursing; Occupational Health; Occupational Therapy; Ophthalmology; Orthopaedics; Otorhinolaryngology; Paediatrics; Parasitology; Pathology; Pharmacology; Pharmacy; Physical Therapy; Physiology; Psychiatry and Mental Health; Public Health; Radiology;

Rehabilitation and Therapy; Surgery; Urology) *Dean*: Chyi-Her Lin; **Planning and Design** (Architecture; Industrial Design; Town Planning) *Dean*: Min-fu Hsu; **Science** *Dean*: Jyh-Hong Chen; **Social Sciences** (Cognitive Sciences; Economics; Education; Law; Political Sciences; Psychology; Social Sciences) *Dean*: Jenn-Yeu Chen

Divisions
Adult Education

Further Information: Also Affiliated Hospital

History: Founded 1931 as Tainan Higher Technical School. Acquired present status and title 1971.

Governing Bodies: University Affairs Committee

Academic Year: September to June (September-January; February-June)

Admission Requirements: Applicants must be graduates or under-graduates of accredited universities or college or senior high school graduates

Fees: (New Taiwan Dollars): 25,000-45,000 per semester

Main Language(s) of Instruction: Chinese, English

Degrees and Diplomas: *Bachelor's Degree*: 4 yrs; *Master's Degree*: a further 2-4 yrs and thesis; *Doctorate (PhD)*: at least 2 further yrs

Student Services: Academic counselling, Canteen, Cultural centre, Employment services, Handicapped facilities, Health services, Language programs, Nursery care, Social counselling, Sports facilities

Student Residential Facilities: For c. 5,000 students

Special Facilities: Cultural Museum. Theatre and Art Gallery

Libraries: Main Library, c. 1.4m. vols; libraries of colleges and departments

Academic Staff *2007-2008*	TOTAL
FULL-TIME	1,620
PART-TIME	596

Last Updated: 12/12/08

NATIONAL CHI NAN UNIVERSITY (NCNU)

1, University Road, Puli, Nantou Hsien 545
Tel: +886(49) 291-0960
Fax: +886(49) 291-0413
Website: http://www.ncnu.edu.tw

President: Jin-Fu Chang
Tel: +886(49) 291-0272, Fax: +886(49) 291-2569
EMail: presi@ncnu.edu.tw

Secretary-General: Tai-Ping Sun
Tel: +886(49) 291-0890 EMail: tps@ncnu.edu.tw

International Relations: Hsien-Chung Wu
Tel: +886(49) 291-8270, Fax: +886(49) 291-4786
EMail: research@ncnu.edu.tw

Colleges
Humanities; **Management**; **Science and Technology**

Research Centres
Family Education (Family Studies); **Language Teaching**; **South-East Asia**

History: Founded 1995.

Main Language(s) of Instruction: Mandarin Chinese

Degrees and Diplomas: *Bachelor's Degree*: 4 yrs; *Master's Degree*: 2-3 yrs; *Doctorate*: 4-5 yrs

Student Services: Academic counselling, Handicapped facilities, Health services, Nursery care, Sports facilities

Publications: The National Chi Nan University Journal *(biannually)*; The National Chi Nan University News *(monthly)*

NATIONAL CHIAO TUNG UNIVERSITY (NCTU)

1001, Ta Hsueh Road, Hsinchu 30010
Tel: +886(3) 571-2121
Fax: +886(3) 572-1500
EMail: nctuwww@cc.nctu.edu.tw
Website: http://www.nctu.edu.tw/english/index.php

President: Chun-Yu (Peter) Wu (2007-)
Tel: +886(3) 571-8083 EMail: president@mail.nctu.edu.tw

Secretary-General: Jen-Tsai Kuo
Tel: +886(3) 571-0567, Fax: +886(3) 573-1776
EMail: jtkuo@faculty.nctu.edu.tw

Centres
Computer and Network; **Environmental and Safety Studies**; **General Education**

Colleges
Biological Science and Technology; **Computer Science**; **Electrical Engineering and Computer Engineering** (Computer Engineering; Electrical and Electronic Engineering; Telecommunications Engineering); **Engineering**; **Hakka Studies** (Arts and Humanities; Asian Studies; Chinese; Communication Studies; Cultural Studies; Ethnology; Social Sciences; Technology); **Humanities and Social Sciences**; **Management**; **Science**

Groups
Advancement of Fundamental Science Teaching

Research Centres
Biomedical and Biological Engineering; **Brain Research**; **E-learning and E-application**; **Green Energy Technology**; **Information and Communication Technology**; **Interdisciplinary Science**; **Microelectronics and Information Systems**; **Nanoelectronics and Infotronic Systems**; **Nanoscience and Technology** (Nanotechnology); **System on Chip Research**; **Taiwan Information Security**; **Taiwan University System**; **X-photonics Interdisciplinary Studies**

History: Founded 1958 as Institute of Electronics. Undergraduate departments opened 1964. Became College of Engineering 1967. A State institution.

Academic Year: August to July (August-January; February-July)

Admission Requirements: Graduation from high school and entrance examination

Main Language(s) of Instruction: Chinese

Degrees and Diplomas: *Bachelor's Degree*: Business Administration; Engineering, 4 yrs; *Master's Degree*: 2 yrs; *Doctorate (PhD)*: 3-5 yrs

Student Residential Facilities: Yes

Libraries: 1,086,072 vols; current periodicals; 3,216, e-journals, 16,927

Academic Staff *2008*	MEN	WOMEN	TOTAL
FULL-TIME	571	104	675
PART-TIME	345	136	481
STAFF WITH DOCTORATE			
FULL-TIME	537	112	649
PART-TIME	287	64	351
Student Numbers *2008*			
All (Foreign Included)	10,841	3,618	14,459
FOREIGN ONLY	344	156	500

Last Updated: 11/12/08

NATIONAL CHIAYI UNIVERSITY (NCYU)

300, University Road, Chiayi 600
Tel: +886(5) 271-7000
Fax: +886(5) 271-7006
EMail: rdo@ncyu.edu.tw
Website: http://www.ncyu.edu.tw

President: Kuo-Shih Yang (2000-) Tel: +886(5) 271-7006

Administrative Officer: Jin-Mei Kuo
Tel: +886(5) 271-7013 EMail: secretary@adm.ncyu.edu.tw

International Relations: Yuh-Chao Yu
Tel: +886(5) 226-3411, Fax: +886(5) 226-3575
EMail: yuyuhchao@mail.ncyu.edu.tw

Centres
Horticulture Technology (Horticulture)

Colleges
Agriculture (Agriculture; Agronomy; Forest Products; Forestry; Horticulture; Veterinary Science; Zoology) *Head*: Shen Tsai-Mu; **Arts and Humanities** (Arts and Humanities; Chinese; Fine Arts;

Geography; History; Literature; Modern Languages; Music) *Head*: Yuh-Chao Yu; **Business Administration** (Agricultural Business; Business Administration; Econometrics; Economics) *Head*: Wei-shui Tsai; **Education** (Education; Educational and Student Counselling; Educational Technology; Physical Education; Primary Education; Secondary Education; Special Education) *Head*: Rong-Kwey Tsai; **Life Science** (Aquaculture; Biological and Life Sciences; Food Science; Molecular Biology; Natural Resources) *Head*: Ling-Ling Yang; **Science and Engineering** (Applied Chemistry; Applied Mathematics; Applied Physics; Bioengineering; Biotechnology; Civil Engineering; Water Science) *Head*: Chyung Ay

Graduate Schools

Agriculture (Agriculture; Biotechnology; Forestry; Natural Resources); **Education** (Health Education; Leisure Studies; Physical Education); **Life Science** (Biological and Life Sciences; Biomedicine; Marine Science and Oceanography; Pharmacy); **Science and Engineering** (Bioengineering; Chemistry; Civil Engineering; Electronic Engineering; Engineering; Hydraulic Engineering; Mathematics; Physics; Transport Management)

History: Founded 2000, incorporating National Chiayi Institute of Technology and National Chiayi Teachers College

Admission Requirements: Graduation from high school

Fees: (New Taiwan Dollars): c. 20,790-24,320 per annum

Main Language(s) of Instruction: Chinese

Degrees and Diplomas: *Bachelor's Degree*: 4 yrs; *Master's Degree*: a further 2 yrs; *Doctorate (PhD)*: at least 4 yrs

Student Services: Academic counselling, Employment services, Handicapped facilities, Health services, Social counselling, Sports facilities

NATIONAL CHUNG CHENG UNIVERSITY

160, San Hsing, Min-hsiung, Chiayi 621
Tel: +886(5) 272-0411
Fax: +886(5) 272-0408
EMail: www@ccu.edu.tw
Website: http://www.ccu.edu.tw

President: Ren C. Luo (2001-)

Secretary-General: Te-Jui Lin
Tel: +886(5) 272-0402, Fax: +886(5) 272-0402
EMail: secretar@ccu.edu.tw

Colleges

Education; **Engineering** (Chemical Engineering; Computer Science; Electrical Engineering; Engineering; Information Technology; Mechanical Engineering); **Humanities** (Arts and Humanities; Chinese; History; Linguistics; Literature; Modern Languages; Philosophy); **Law**; **Management** (Accountancy; Business Administration; Finance; Information Management; International Economics; Management); **Science** (Applied Mathematics; Chemistry; Natural Sciences; Physics; Seismology); **Social Sciences** (Adult Education; Continuing Education; Labour and Industrial Relations; Labour Law; Law; Political Sciences; Psychology; Social Sciences; Social Welfare; Telecommunications Engineering; Telecommunications Services)

Research Centres

Automation (Automation and Control Engineering); **Cognitive Science** (Cognitive Sciences); **Industry Analysis, Development and Forecasting**; **Innovation and Incubation**; **Language and Literature** (*A critical introduction to 20th century literary criticism*) (Literature; Modern Languages)

History: Founded 1989. A public research-oriented university.

Academic Year: September to June (September-January; February-June)

Admission Requirements: Graduation from high school and entrance examination

Main Language(s) of Instruction: Chinese, English (Institute of Foreign Languages and Literature)

Degrees and Diplomas: *Bachelor's Degree*: 4 yrs; *Master's Degree*: a further 2-4 yrs; *Doctorate*: a further 2-6 yrs

Special Facilities: Audiovisual Centre. Computer Centre

Libraries: National Chung-Cheng University Library, c. 463,400 vols; CD ROM database and other online information services

Publications: Journal of National Chung-Cheng University

NATIONAL CHUNG HSING UNIVERSITY (NCHU)

250, Guo Kuang Road, Taichung 402
Tel: +886(4) 228-73181
Fax: +886(4) 228-70925
EMail: oia@nchu.edu.tw
Website: http://www.nchu.edu.tw/

Head: Shaw Jei-Fu
Tel: +886(04) 228-40201, Fax: +886(04) 228-53813
EMail: presid@nchu.edu.tw

Administrative Officer: Chen Wen Fu
Tel: +886(04) 228-57848, Fax: +886(04) 228-73702

International Relations: Ooi Hong Kean
Tel: +886(04) 228-40550, Fax: +886(04) 228-52787

Colleges

Agriculture and Natural Resources (Agricultural Management; Agriculture; Agronomy; Animal Husbandry; Biotechnology; Economics; Entomology; Food Science; Forestry; Horticulture; Natural Resources; Plant Pathology; Rural Planning; Soil Conservation; Soil Science; Veterinary Science; Water Management); **Engineering**; **Liberal Arts** (Arts and Humanities; Chinese; History; Information Sciences; Library Science; Modern Languages); **Life Science**; **Science** (Applied Mathematics; Chemistry; Computer Science; Natural Sciences; Physics); **Social Science and Management** (Accountancy; Business Administration; Commercial Law; E-Business/Commerce; Finance; International Relations; Management; Marketing; Social Sciences); **Veterinary Medicine** (Veterinary Science)

Research Centres

Agricultural Biotechnology; **Nanotechnology** (Materials Engineering; Microelectronics; Nanotechnology)

History: Founded 1919 as Academy of Agriculture and Forestry, became part of Japanese Taihoku Imperial University 1928, transferred to Taichung as independent institution 1942, re-established as State institution 1945 and became Provincial College of Agriculture 1946 and university 1961. Acquired present title 1971.

Governing Bodies: University Council; Executive Council

Academic Year: August to July (August-January; February-July)

Admission Requirements: Graduation from secondary school or recognized foreign equivalent, and entrance examination

Main Language(s) of Instruction: Chinese, English

Degrees and Diplomas: *Bachelor's Degree*: in all fields, 4-5 yrs; *Master's Degree*: a further 2-4 yrs; *Doctorate (PhD)*: at least 2 further yrs

Student Residential Facilities: For c. 3,600 students

Libraries: Central Library, c. 207,050 vols; Law and Commerce branch library, c. 130,000 vols

Publications: Bulletin of Botanical Research; Bulletin of the Experimental Forest; Economics Studies; Journal of Agriculture and Forestry; Journal of Law and Commerce; Journal of Literature and History; Journal of Science and Engineering

Press or Publishing House: Chung Hsing University Press Division; Taipei College of Law and Commerce Press Division
Last Updated: 12/02/07

NATIONAL DONG HWA UNIVERSITY (NDHU)

1, Section 2, Dahsueh Road, Shou-Feng, Hualien 97401
Tel: +886(3) 863-2013
Fax: +886(3) 863-2010
EMail: minwang@mail.ndhu.edu.tw
Website: http://www.ndhu.edu.tw

President: Wen-Shu Huang (2002-)
Tel: +886(3) 863-2006, Fax: +886(3) 863-2010
EMail: hws@mail.ndhu.edu.tw

International Relations: Chaoshin Chiao, Dean of Research and Development
Tel: +886(3) 863-2501, Fax: +886(3) 863-2500
EMail: cschiao@mail.ndhu.edu.tw

Colleges

Arts (Art Education; Design; Fine Arts; Music; Technology; Visual Arts); **Education** (Child Care and Development; Curriculum; Education; Educational Administration; Physical Education; Preschool Education; Special Education); **Humanities and Social Sciences** (Arts and Humanities; Chinese; Clinical Psychology; Commercial Law; Development Studies; Economics; Education; Educational and Student Counselling; English; Finance; History; International Economics; Law; Leisure Studies; Literature; Native Language; Psychology; Public Administration; Social Sciences; Sports; Writing); **Indigenous Studies** (Communication Studies; Cultural Studies; Ethnology; Indigenous Studies; Native Language Education; Social Work); **Management** (Accountancy; Business Administration; Environmental Management; Environmental Studies; Finance; Information Management; International Business; Leisure Studies; Management; Natural Resources; Parks and Recreation; Tourism; Transport Management); **Marine Sciences**; **Science and Engineering** (Applied Mathematics; Applied Physics; Biological and Life Sciences; Biotechnology; Chemistry; Computer Science; Earth Sciences; Ecology; Educational Technology; Electrical and Electronic Engineering; Engineering; Environmental Studies; Information Technology; Materials Engineering; Natural Sciences; Physics; Science Education)

History: Founded 1994.

Academic Year: August to July

Admission Requirements: High school diploma

Fees: (New Taiwan Dollars): c. 23,000 per semester

Main Language(s) of Instruction: Chinese

Degrees and Diplomas: *Bachelor's Degree*: 4 yrs; *Master's Degree*: 2-4 yrs; *Doctorate*: 2-9 yrs

Student Services: Academic counselling, Canteen, Foreign student adviser, Handicapped facilities, Health services, Language programs, Nursery care, Social counselling, Sports facilities

Student Numbers 2008-2009	MEN	WOMEN	TOTAL
All (Foreign Included)	6,248	4,234	10,482

Last Updated: 11/12/08

NATIONAL FORMOSA UNIVERSITY (NFU)

64, Wen Hua Road, Hu Wei, Yunlin 632
Tel: +886(5) 632-5000
Fax: +886(5) 632-5999
EMail: network@nfu.edu.tw
Website: http://www.nfu.edu.tw

President: Chien-Chang Lin
Tel: +886(5) 632-9642, Fax: +886(5) 633-8302

Dean of Academic Affairs: Yeong-Ley Tsay
Tel: +886(5) 632-9643, Ext. 200, Fax: +886(5) 633-9828

International Relations: Wen-Yuh Jywe
Tel: +886(5) 632-9643, Ext. 150

Departments

Aeronautical Engineering; **Applied Foreign Languages** (Modern Languages); **Automation Engineering**; **Biotechnology** (Biotechnology); **Business Management** (Business Administration; Management); **Computer Science and Information Technology** (Computer Science; Information Technology); **Electrical Engineering** (Electrical Engineering); **Electro-Optical Engineering**; **Finance**; **Industrial Management**; **Information Management** (Information Management); **Leisure Management** (Leisure Studies; Management); **Materials Science and Engineering** (Engineering; Materials Engineering); **Mechanical Design Engineering** (Design; Mechanical Engineering); **Mechanical Manufacturing Engineering** (Mechanical Engineering; Production Engineering); **Multimedia Design**; **Power Mechanical Engineering** (Mechanical Engineering; Power Engineering); **Vehicle Engineering** (Automotive Engineering)

History: Founded 1980, acquired present name and status 2004.

Degrees and Diplomas: *Master's Degree*: Power Mechanical Engineering; Electro-Optical and Materials Science; Industrial Engineering and Management; Information Management

NATIONAL HSINCHU UNIVERSITY OF EDUCATION (NHUE)

521, Nanda Road, Hsinchu 30014
Tel: +886(3) 521-3132
Fax: +886(3) 523-1380
EMail: meich@mail.nhcue.edu.tw
Website: http://www.nhcue.edu.tw/

President: Hsieng-Cheng Tseng (2003-)
Tel: +886(3) 522-6230 EMail: hct@mail.nhcue.edu.tw

Secretary-General: Chunfeng Shey
Tel: +886(3) 521-3132 Ext. 1120
EMail: chunfeng@mail.nhcue.edu.tw

International Relations: Tyan-Show Lin, Vice-President
Tel: +886(3) 521-3132 Ext. 1101, Fax: +886(3) 523-1380
EMail: tslin@mail.nhcue.edu.tw

Colleges

Arts and Humanities (Arts and Humanities; Chinese; Crafts and Trades; Design; English; Fine Arts; Linguistics; Modern Languages; Music; Native Language; Regional Studies; Social Sciences) *Director*: Chung-Ta Yeh; **Education** *Director*: Mei-Yu Chang; **Science** (Applied Chemistry; Applied Mathematics; Applied Physics; Biology; Computer Science) *Director*: Chien-Yu Hunang

Departments

Applied Mathematics (Applied Mathematics; Mathematics; Mathematics Education) *Head*: Wen-Huan Tsai; **Applied Science** (Biological and Life Sciences; Nanotechnology; Science Education) *Head*: Jui-Hsiang Pei; **Arts and Design** (Design; Fine Arts) *Head*: Chuan-Cheng Chang; **Early Childhood Education** *Head*: Tsyr-huey Liou; **Education** (Educational Sciences; Primary Education) *Head*: Kuo-Liang Yen; **Educational Psychology and Counselling** (Educational and Student Counselling; Educational Psychology) *Head*: Yeou-Shann Chyou; **English Instruction** (English) *Head*: T. Sara Tun; **Music** (Music; Music Education; Music Theory and Composition) *Head*: Yu-Li Kao; **Physical Education** *Head*: Chin-Cheng Hsieh; **Regional Studies in Humanities and Social Sciences** *Head*: Tien-Chien Chiang; **Special Education** (Special Education) *Head*: Tsuey-Ling Lee

Graduate Institutes

Arts and Design (Design; Fine Arts) *Director*: Chuan-Cheng Chang; **Computer Science** *Director*: Wernhuar Tarng; **E-Learning Technology** *Director*: Hueyching Janice Jih; **Human Resources Development** (Educational Administration) *Director*: King-Ching Hsieh; **Taiwan Language and Language Education** (Linguistics; Modern Languages; Native Language) *Director*: Ying Cheng

History: Founded 1940 as a three-year normal School. Acquired present status and title 2005.

Academic Year: September to June (September-January; February-June)

Admission Requirements: Graduation from high school and National Joint Examination for the Entrance to Universities and Colleges. Special requirements are subject to the demand of different departments

Fees: (New Taiwan Dollars): 25,000 per semester

Main Language(s) of Instruction: Chinese, English, Taiwanese, Hakka

Accrediting Agencies: Ministry of Education

Degrees and Diplomas: *Bachelor's Degree*: Applied Mathematics; Applied Science (BS); Education; Early Childhood Education; Special Education; Educational Psychology and Counselling; Physical Education (BEd); English Instruction; Languages and Literature Studies; Music; Arts and Design (BA); Regional Studies in Humanities and Social Sciences (BHS), 4 yrs; *Master's Degree*: Applied Mathematics; Applied Science; Computer Science (MS); Applied Science; Music; Languages and Literature Studies; Regional Studies in Humanities and Social Sciences; Arts and Crafts Education; Taiwan Languages and Language Education (MEd); Education; Special Education; Early Childhood Education; Educational Psychology and Counselling; Physical Education; E-Learning Technology; Human Resources Development (MEd); Languages and Literature Studies; Music; Arts and Design (MA); Regional Studies in Humanities and Social Sciences (MHS), a further 1-4 yrs; *Doctorate*: Education; Taiwan Languages and Language Education (DEd), a further 2-7 yrs

Student Services: Academic counselling, Canteen, Cultural centre, Employment services, Handicapped facilities, Health services, Sports facilities

Student Residential Facilities: Yes

Libraries: 297,139 vols; 280,224 microfiches; 21,053 audio-visual materials; 28,000 electronic periodicals; 276,374 electronic books; 1,350 current periodicals

Publications: Educational Journal of NHCUE *(biannually)*; Journal of Humanities and Social Sciences of NHCUE *(biannually)*

Press or Publishing House: Publication Section, Department of Academic Affairs

Academic Staff *2007-2008*	MEN	WOMEN	TOTAL
FULL-TIME	86	86	172
PART-TIME	107	135	242
STAFF WITH DOCTORATE			
FULL-TIME	67	73	140
PART-TIME	29	31	60
Student Numbers *2007-2008*			
All (Foreign Included)	1,050	2,580	3,630

Part-time students, 917.
Last Updated: 11/12/08

NATIONAL HUALIEN UNIVERSITY OF EDUCATION (NHLUE)

123, Hua Hsi, Hualien 970
Tel: +886(3) 822-7106
Fax: +886(3) 822-6664
EMail: web@sparc2.nhltc.edu.tw
Website: http://www.nhlue.edu.tw/

President: His-Chi Liu (2000-)
Tel: +886(3) 822-1006 EMail: sec3@sparc2.nhltc.edu.tw

Administrative Officer: Bor-Chang Hwang Tel: +886(3) 823-7008

International Relations: Chi-Hyong Ku
Tel: +886(3) 822-7106, Ext. 1070, Fax: +886(3) 822-5453
EMail: chku@sparc2.nhltc.edu.tw

Departments
Art Education (Art Education); **Chinese Language and Literature Education** (Chinese; Literature); **Early Childhood Education** (Preschool Education); **Elementary Education** (Primary Education); **English Teaching** (English); **Mathematics Education** (Mathematics); **Music Education** (Music); **Physical Education** (Physical Education); **Psychology Education and Counseling** (Educational and Student Counselling; Educational Psychology); **Science Education** (Science Education); **Social Studies Education** (Social Sciences); **Special Education** (Special Education)

History: Founded 1947, reorganized 1991. Acquired present status 2005.

Degrees and Diplomas: *Bachelor's Degree; Master's Degree; Doctorate*

NATIONAL ILAN UNIVERSITY (NIU)

1, Sec 1, Shennung Road, Ilan 26041
Tel: +886(3) 935-7400
Fax: +886(3) 936-3756
EMail: sec@niu.edu.tw
Website: http://www.niu.edu.tw

President: George L. Jiang (2006-)
Tel: +886(3) 935-7400, Ext.200 EMail: president@niu.edu.tw

Secretary-General: Chi-Hsiang Lo
Tel: +886(3) 935-7400, Ext. 201

Director, Office of Academic Affairs: Hsin Yu
Tel: +886(3) 935-7400, Ext. 300, Fax: +886(3) 936-5239
EMail: acade@niu.edu.tw

International Relations: Po-Ching Wu, Director, Office of Research & Development/International Relations
Tel: +886(3) 935-7400, Ext. 230, Fax: +886(3) 933-3902
EMail: research@niu.edu.tw

Centres
Analysis and Technology Consulting; **E-Life Technology Innovation**; **Humanities and Science Education** (Arts and Humanities; Science Education); **Innovation Incubator**; **Language**; **Leisure Resources and Industry Development**; **Organic Studies**; **Sustainable Development**

Colleges
Bioresources (Biology; Biotechnology; Electronic Engineering; Food Science; Horticulture; Natural Resources; Zoology) *Dean*: Rong-Shinn Lin; **Electrical Engineering and Computer Science** (Computer Science; Electrical Engineering; Electronic Engineering; Information Technology) *Dean*: Han-Chieh Chao; **Engineering** *Dean*: Howard Hwang; **Humanities and Management** (Arts and Humanities; Economics; Literature; Management; Modern Languages; Science Education) *Dean*: Chih-Chin Chang

Graduate Institutes
Architecture and Sustainable Planning (Architecture; Architecture and Planning); **Biotechnology**; **Computer Science and Information Engineering** (Computer Science; Information Technology); **Management**

History: Founded 1926 as Ilan School of Agriculture and Forestry. Formerly known as National Ilan Institute of Technology. Acquired present title and status 2003.

Academic Year: August to July

Main Language(s) of Instruction: Chinese

International Co-operation: With institutions in China; France; Japan; Thaïland and USA

Degrees and Diplomas: *Bachelor's Degree (BA; BS); Master's Degree (MS; MBA; MArch)*

Student Residential Facilities: Yes

Special Facilities: Research Forest; Farm Land

Libraries: Printed materials, 204,300 vols; E-materials, 219,000 vols (including 198,000 e-books, 20,880 e-journals, 57 databases)

Publications: Bulletin of the College of Engineering; Ilan University Journal of Bioresources; Journal of Liberal Arts and Management

Academic Staff *2008*	MEN	WOMEN	TOTAL
FULL-TIME	183	60	243
PART-TIME	56	23	79
STAFF WITH DOCTORATE			
FULL-TIME	140	26	166
PART-TIME	25	8	33
Student Numbers *2008*			
All (Foreign Included)	3,625	1,542	5,167

Last Updated: 11/12/08

NATIONAL KAOHSIUNG FIRST UNIVERSITY OF SCIENCE AND TECHNOLOGY (NKFUST)

2, Juoyue Road, Nantz District, Kaohsiung 811
Tel: +886(7) 601-1000
Fax: +886(7) 601-1011
EMail: cass@ccms.nkfust.edu.tw
Website: http://www.nkfust.edu.tw

President: Chia-hung Ku (1995-)
Tel: +886(7) 601-1000, Ext. 1000 EMail: chku@ccms.nkfust.edu.tw

Secretary-General: Szu-Yuan Sun
Tel: +886(7) 601-1000, Ext. 1010
EMail: sunnyy@ccms.nkfust.edu.tw

International Relations: Roger C.Y. Chen
Tel: +886(7) 601-1000, Ext. 1400, Fax: +886(7) 601-1046
EMail: roger@ccms.nkfust.edu.tw

Colleges
Engineering (Automation and Control Engineering; Computer Engineering; Construction Engineering; Engineering; Environmental Engineering; Health Sciences; Mechanical Engineering; Safety Engineering) *Dean*: I-Chang Jou; **Foreign Languages** (English; German; Japanese; Modern Languages) *Dean*: Shui-Fu Lin; **Management** (Finance; Information Management; Insurance; Management; Marketing; Transport Management) *Dean*: Shyan-Rong Chou

Graduate Institutes
Engineering *(PhD Programme)* (Engineering); **Foreign Languages** (Modern Languages); **Management** *(PhD Programme)* (Management)

History: Founded 1995 as National Institute of Technology at Kaohsiung. Acquired present title and status 1998.

Academic Year: September to June

Main Language(s) of Instruction: Chinese

International Co-operation: With universities in Germany and Japan

Degrees and Diplomas: *Bachelor's Degree*: Business Administration; Arts (BBA, BA), 2-4 yrs; *Bachelor's Degree*: Science (BS), 4 yrs; *Master's Degree*: Science; Business Administration; Arts (M.S., M.B.A, M.A), 2 yrs; *Doctorate*: Engineering and Technology; Management (PhD), 2-7 yrs

Student Services: Academic counselling, Canteen, Employment services, Handicapped facilities, Health services, Language programs, Nursery care, Social counselling, Sports facilities

Student Residential Facilities: Yes

Libraries: Yes

Publications: Journal of Industry Management *(biennially)*

NATIONAL KAOHSIUNG HOSPITALITY COLLEGE

1, Sung-ho Road, Hsiao-kang, Kaohsiung
Tel: +886(7) 806-0505
Fax: +886(7) 806-1473
EMail: hu@mail.nkhc.edu.tw
Website: http://www.nkhc.edu.tw

Departments
Airline Management (Tourism); **Baking and Pastry Arts** (Cooking and Catering); **Chinese Culinary Arts** (Cooking and Catering); **Food and Beverage Management** (Food Science); **Hospitality Marketing Management** (Marketing; Tourism); **Hotel Management** (Hotel Management); **Leisure Recreation and Tourism**; **Travel Management** (Tourism); **Western Culinary Arts** (Cooking and Catering)

Degrees and Diplomas: *Bachelor's Degree*: Business Administration; *Master's Degree*: Hospitality Management; Business Administration

NATIONAL KAOHSIUNG MARINE UNIVERSITY (NKMU)

142, Hai-Chuan Road, Nan Tzu, Kaohsiung 81157
Tel: +886(7) 361-7141
Fax: +886(7) 362-8844
EMail: president@mail.nkmu.edu.tw
Website: http://www.nkmu.edu.tw

President: Chan-Jen Chow (2008-) Tel: +886(7) 363-0061

Secretary-General: Hui-Lung Yu
Tel: +886(7) 363-0063 EMail: hlyu@mail.nkmu.edu.tw

International Relations: Wei-Cheng Lian, Dean, Research & Development Division
Tel: +886(7) 364-8154, Fax: +886(7) 362-9500
EMail: wclian@mail.nkimt.edu.tw

Colleges
Hydrosphere Science (Aquaculture; Biotechnology; Fishery; Food Science; Marine Science and Oceanography; Marine Transport; Production Engineering) *Dean:* Ruy-Chang Chung; **Management** (Information Management; Marine Transport; Nautical Science; Transport Management) *Dean:* T.C. Yu; **Maritime Studies** (Marine Engineering; Nautical Science; Transport Engineering) *Dean:* R.H. Yeh; **Ocean Engineering** (Electronic Engineering; Marine Engineering; Naval Architecture) *Dean:* Jui-Han Lu

History: Founded 1946 as the Kaohsiung branch of the Taiwan Provincial Keelung Fishery Vocational School. Renamed National Kaohsiung Institute of Marine Technology 1982. Acquired present title and status 2004.

Fees: (New Taiwan Dollars): c. 22,000 per semester

Main Language(s) of Instruction: Chinese

Degrees and Diplomas: *Bachelor's Degree*: Marine Science, 2-4 yrs; *Master's Degree*: Marine Science, 2 yrs

Student Services: Academic counselling, Canteen, Employment services, Foreign student adviser, Handicapped facilities, Health services, Language programs, Nursery care, Social counselling, Sports facilities

Academic Staff *2008*	TOTAL
FULL-TIME	189

Student Numbers *2008*	
All (Foreign Included)	5,022
FOREIGN ONLY	14

Evening students, 2,048.
Last Updated: 12/12/08

NATIONAL KAOHSIUNG NORMAL UNIVERSITY

116, Hoping 1st Road, Kaohsiung 802
Tel: +886(7) 717-2930
Fax: +886(7) 711-0315
EMail: wwwadm@ccmail.nknu.edu.tw; r@nknucc.nknu.edu.tw
Website: http://www.nknu.edu.tw

Head: Chi-Nan Tai (2002-)
Tel: +886(7) 722-3971, Fax: +886(7) 711-2909
EMail: t1145@nknucc.nknu.edu.tw

International Relations: Chin-Cheng Yang
Tel: +886(7) 717-2930, Ext. 1001, Fax: +886(7) 722-3972

Centres
Adult Education; **Audiovisual Education** (Educational Technology); **Computer** (Computer Science); **Environmental Education** (Educational Sciences; Environmental Studies); **General Education** (Education); **Research and Development in Humanities Education** (Humanities and Social Science Education); **Science Education** (Science Education); **Special Education**; **Student Counselling** (Educational and Student Counselling); **Teacher Education** (Teacher Training)

Colleges
Continuing and Extension Education; **Education**; **Fine and Applied Arts** (Fine Arts); **Humanities** (Arts and Humanities); **Science** (Natural Sciences); **Technology** (Technology)

Departments
Applied Design (Design); **Chemistry** (Chemistry); **Chinese** (Chinese); **Education**; **English** (English); **Fine Arts** (Fine Arts); **Geography** (Geography); **Industrial Technology Education** (Technology Education); **Information and Communication** (Communication Arts; Communication Studies; Information Management); **Mathematics** (Mathematics); **Music** (Music); **Physical Education** (Physical Education); **Physics** (Physics); **Special Education**

Divisions
Extension Studies

Graduate Institutes
Adult Education; **Classics** (Literature); **Communication Disorders** (Communication Disorders); **Counselling and Guidance** (Educational and Student Counselling); **Environmental Education** (Environmental Management); **Gender Education** (Gender Studies); **Information and Computer Education** (Computer Education); **Life Sciences** (Biological and Life Sciences); **Science Education** (Science Education); **Taiwanese Languages and Language Instruction** (Linguistics); **Teaching Chinese** (Chinese); **Visual Communication and Design** (Communication Arts)

History: Founded 1969 as Provincial College, became National College 1980, and acquired present status 1989.

Academic Year: August to July (August-January; February-July)

Admission Requirements: Graduation from high school and entrance examination or references

Fees: (New Taiwan Dollars): Undergraduates c. 19,800-23,150 per semester

Main Language(s) of Instruction: Chinese

Degrees and Diplomas: *Bachelor's Degree*: 4 yrs; *Master's Degree*: a further 1-4 yrs; *Doctorate*: a further 2-7 yrs

Student Services: Academic counselling, Canteen, Cultural centre, Employment services, Handicapped facilities, Health services, Language programs, Social counselling, Sports facilities

Student Residential Facilities: Yes

Libraries: c. 1,010,110 vols

Publications: University Research Journal *(annually)*

NATIONAL KAOHSIUNG UNIVERSITY OF APPLIED SCIENCES (NKUAS)

415, Jiangung Road, SanMin, Kaohsiung 807
Tel: +886(7) 381-4526
Fax: +886(7) 383-8435
EMail: fdoffice01@cc.kuas.edu.tw; register@cc.kuas.edu.tw
Website: http://www.kuas.edu.tw

President: Ren-Yih Lin (2002-)
Tel: +886(7) 381-4526, Ext. 2202 EMail: lry@cc.kuas.edu.tw

Secretary-General: Hsiou-Hsiang Liu
Tel: +886(7) 381-4526, Ext. 2203 EMail: bachair@cc.kuas.edu.tw

International Relations: Li-Chang Lee
Tel: +886(7) 381-4526, Ext. 2730, Fax: +886(7) 389-9382
EMail: fochair@cc.kuas.edu.tw

Colleges
Commerce; **Engineering** (Chemical Engineering; Civil Engineering; Electrical Engineering; Electronic Engineering; Engineering; Industrial Engineering; Mechanical Engineering); **Humanities and Social Sciences** (Arts and Humanities; Cultural Studies; Education; Human Resources; Modern Languages; Teacher Training); **Management**

Graduate Institutes
Civil Engineering and Disaster Prevention Technology (Civil Engineering; Safety Engineering); **Electrical Energy and Control** (Automation and Control Engineering; Electrical Engineering); **Human Resources** (Human Resources); **Management**; **Mechanical and Precision Engineering**; **Photonics and Communication** (Chemical Engineering; Industrial Engineering; Industrial Management)

History: Founded 1963, acquired present status and title 2000.

Degrees and Diplomas: *Bachelor's Degree*; *Master's Degree*; *Doctorate*

Student Services: Academic counselling, Cultural centre, Employment services, Foreign student adviser, Foreign Studies Centre, Handicapped facilities, Health services, Social counselling, Sports facilities

Student Residential Facilities: Yes

Libraries: Main Library and Departmental Libraries

Publications: Research Papers of the Faculty

NATIONAL OPEN UNIVERSITY (NOU)

172, Chung Cheng Road, Lu Chow 24702
Tel: +886(2) 228-29355
Fax: +886(2) 228-31721
EMail: elec007@mail.nou.edu.tw
Website: http://www.nou.edu.tw

President: Sheng-Shiung Hwang (2001-)
Tel: +886(2) 228-2893, Fax: +886(2) 228-6061
EMail: fukaya@mail.nou.edu.tw

Dean of Academic Affairs: Chia-Shing Yang
Tel: +886(2) 228-6330, Fax: +886(2) 228-0103
EMail: cyang@nou.edu.tw

Departments
General Studies (Chinese; Constitutional Law; History; Modern Languages); **Life Sciences** (Environmental Management; Home Economics; Nursing; Tourism); **Management and Information** (Information Sciences; Management); **Public Administration** (Public Administration); **Social Sciences** (Economics; Education; Law; Political Sciences; Psychology; Public Administration; Social Sciences; Sociology)

Divisions
Research and Development

Further Information: Also Learning Centres in: Kee Lung, Taipei, Lu Chow, Hsin Chu, Tai Chung, Chia Yi, Tai Nan, Kao Hsiun, Ilan, Hua Lien, Tai Tung Peng Hu, Kin Men

History: Founded 1986, acquired present status 1994.

Governing Bodies: Department of Academic Affairs

Academic Year: September to June (September-January; February-June)

Admission Requirements: Application process required for people over the age of 20. Non-Diploma students must be over the age of 18

Main Language(s) of Instruction: Chinese

Degrees and Diplomas: *Bachelor's Degree*: 7-8 yrs

Libraries: Library, c. 67,500 vols

NATIONAL PENGHU UNIVERSITY (NPIT)

300, Liu-He Road, Makung, Penghu 880
Tel: +886(6) 926-4115
Fax: +886(6) 926-5349
EMail: office0@npu.edu.tw
Website: http://www.npu.edu.tw

President: Huei-Jeng Lin
Tel: +886(6) 926-4115, Ext. 1001 EMail: hjlin@npu.edu.tw

Chief-Secretary: Su-Chang Chen Tel: +886(6) 926-7543

International Relations: Tsung-Cheng Yang
Tel: +886(6) 926-4115, Ext. 1701, Fax: +886(6) 926-0043
EMail: yangtsungcheng@yahoo.com.tw

Departments
Applied Foreign Languages and Management; **Aquaculture**; **Computer Science and Information Engineering**; **Electronic Engineering** (Electronic Engineering); **Food Science** (Dietetics; Nutrition); **Hospitality Management**; **Information Management**; **Leisure Management**; **Shipping and Transportation Management**; **Telecommunications Engineering**; **Tourism** (Tourism); **Transportation and Logistics Management** (Transport and Communications; Transport Management)

History: Founded 1995. Acquired present status 2000 and title 2005. Formerly known as National Penghu Institute of Technology.
Last Updated: 08/07/08

NATIONAL PINGTUNG INSTITUTE OF COMMERCE (NPIC)

51, Min Sheng East Road, Pingtung 900
Tel: +886(8) 723-8700
Fax: +886(8) 723-8720
EMail: bcchiou@.npic.edu.tw
Website: http://www.npic.edu.tw

President: Joeng-Feong Duo (1991-) EMail: secretar@npic.edu.tw

International Relations: Kwun-Shen Lin
Tel: +886(8) 723-8700, Ext. 2400, Fax: +886(8) 723-7592
EMail: kslin@npic.edu.tw

Programmes
Business (Accountancy; Banking; Finance; International Business); **Information Technology and Management** (Information Management; Information Technology); **Languages** (Japanese; Modern Languages; Translation and Interpretation); **Management** (Business Administration; Leisure Studies; Management; Marketing; Real Estate; Transport Management)

History: Founded 1991, acquired present status 1998.

Degrees and Diplomas: *Bachelor's Degree*; *Master's Degree*
Last Updated: 08/07/08

NATIONAL PINGTUNG UNIVERSITY OF EDUCATION (NPUE)

4-18, Min Sheng Road, Pingtung 90003
Tel: +886(8) 722-6141
Fax: +886(8) 723-4406
EMail: luyc@linux.npttc.edu.tw
Website: http://www.npue.edu.tw

President: Ching-Chung Liu EMail: lyu@mail.npue.edu.tw

Secretary-General: Lung-Hsi Wang
Tel: +886(8) 722-6141 EMail: mail099@mail.npttc.edu.tw

International Relations: Weigh-Jen Chen
EMail: wchen@mail.npttc.edu.tw

Faculties

Arts and Humanities (Art Education; Arts and Humanities; English; Literacy Education; Modern Languages; Music Education; Social Studies; Visual Arts); **Education** (Educational and Student Counselling; Educational Psychology; Preschool Education; Primary Education; Special Education); **Science** (Computer Science; Earth Sciences; Mathematics Education; Natural Sciences; Physical Education; Physics)

Graduate Institutes

Educational Technology (Educational Technology); **Mathematics and Science Education** (Mathematics; Science Education); **Primary Education**

History: Founded 1940. Acquired present status 2005.

Main Language(s) of Instruction: Mandarin, Chinese

Degrees and Diplomas: *Bachelor's Degree*: Education, 4 yrs; *Master's Degree*: Education, a further 2-3 yrs; *Doctorate*: Primary Education (Ph.D.), a further 2 yrs following Master

Student Services: Academic counselling, Handicapped facilities, Language programs, Sports facilities

Publications: Journal of Pingtung Teachers College *(biannually)*

NATIONAL PINGTUNG UNIVERSITY OF SCIENCE AND TECHNOLOGY

1, Shueh-Fu Road, Nei-Pu, Pingtung 912
Tel: +886(8) 770-3660
Fax: +886(8) 770-2226
EMail: mslin@mail.npust.edu.tw
Website: http://www.npust.edu.tw

President: Chang-Hung Chou (2002-)
EMail: choumasa@mail.npust.edu.tw

Vice-President: Wen-Jinn Liang
Tel: +886(8) 774-0528 EMail: liangwj@mail.npust.edu.tw

International Relations: Po-Yung Lei
Tel: +886(8) 770-3202 Ext. 6216
EMail: international@mail.npust.edu.tw

Colleges

Agriculture (Agriculture; Animal Husbandry; Aquaculture; Botany; Food Science; Forestry; Plant and Crop Protection; Tropical Agriculture; Veterinary Science; Wildlife; Wood Technology) *Director*: C.-T. Chen; **Engineering** *(Graduate)* (Automotive Engineering; Civil Engineering; Engineering; Environmental Engineering; Mechanical Engineering; Soil Conservation; Water Science) *Director*: C.H. Tai; **Humanities and Social Sciences** (Arts and Humanities; Social Sciences) *Director*: L.H. Chiang; **Management** *(Graduate)* (Agricultural Business; Biological and Life Sciences; Child Care and Development; Industrial Management; Information Management; Landscape Architecture; Management; Rural Planning) *Director*: E.J. Wang

History: Founded 1954 as Taiwan Provincial Institute of Agriculture. Acquired present status and title 1997.

Academic Year: September to June (September-December; February-June)

Admission Requirements: Graduation from high school for 4-year Bachelor programmes and Graduation from Junior College for 2-year Bachelor programmes

Fees: (New Taiwan Dollars): c. 30,000 per semester

Main Language(s) of Instruction: Chinese, English

Degrees and Diplomas: *Bachelor's Degree*: Science, 4 yrs; *Master's Degree*: a further 2 yrs; *Doctorate*: a further 4-6 yrs

Student Services: Academic counselling, Canteen, Cultural centre, Employment services, Foreign student adviser, Foreign Studies Centre, Handicapped facilities, Health services, Nursery care, Social counselling, Sports facilities

Student Residential Facilities: For 3,000 students

Special Facilities: Antique Agricultural Machinery Museum. Botanical Garden

Libraries: Yu-Gong Memorial Library, 205,000 vols

Publications: University Journal *(quarterly)*

Press or Publishing House: NPUST Publishing division affiliated to the Office of Academic Affairs

NATIONAL SUN YAT-SEN UNIVERSITY (NSYSU)

70, Lienhai Road, Gushan Chiu, Kaohsiung 80424
Tel: +886(7) 525-2000
Fax: +886(7) 525-2039
EMail: oia@mail.nsysu.edu.tw
Website: http://www.nsysu.edu.tw

President: Hung-Duen Yang (2008-)
Tel: +886(7) 525-2001, Fax: +886(7) 525-2039
EMail: yang@mail.nsysu.edu.tw

Secretary-General: Zin-Huang Liu
Tel: +886(7) 525-2020, Fax: +886(7) 525-2039
EMail: zhliu@mail.nsysu.edu.tw

International Relations: Chi-Cheng Cheng
Tel: +886(7) 525-2633 EMail: chengcc@mail.nsysu.edu.tw

Centres

America *(Sun Yat-Sen)*; **Chinese Language for Foreign Students**; **Ch'ing Dynasty Studies**; **Creativity and Innovation**; **Direct Selling**; **Engineering Technology**; **High Valued Instrument**; **Incubation**; **International NGO Studies**; **Joint Optoelectronic Research and Development** *(NSYSY/ITRI)*; **Management Studies**; **Marine Policy Studies**; **Marine Technology**; **Metropolitan and Environmental Planning**; **Neuroscience**; **Public Opinion Poll Studies**; **Research and Development** *(NSYSU/Sunon)*; **Semiconductor Technology**; **Small and Medium Enterprises**; **Southern Taiwan Optoelectronics**; **Taiwan Computer Emergency Response Team/Coordination**; **Telecom Research Development**; **Urban-Rural and Regional Development**; **Water Resources Studies**

Colleges

Engineering (Computer Engineering; Electrical Engineering; Engineering; Environmental Engineering; Information Technology; Materials Engineering; Mechanical Engineering; Optics); **Liberal Arts** (Arts and Humanities; Chinese; Literature; Modern Languages; Music; Philosophy; Theatre); **Management** (Human Resources; Management); **Marine Sciences** (Marine Science and Oceanography); **Science** (Applied Mathematics; Biological and Life Sciences; Biology; Chemistry; Natural Sciences; Physics); **Social Sciences** (Oriental Studies; Social Sciences)

Research Centres

Advanced Crystal Opto-electronics *(Key Research Centre)*; **Asia-Pacific Ocean Research** *(Key Research Centre)*; **Biotechnology** *(Key Research Centre)*; **E-commerce and Technology Innovation** *(Key Research Centre)*; **Humanities and Social Sciences** *(Key Research Centre)*; **Nano Science and Nanotechnology** *(Key Research Centre)*; **National Policy** *(Key Research Centre)*; **Nonlinear Analysis and Discrete Mathematics** *(Key Research Centre)*; **Wireless Networks and Multimedia** *(Key Research Centre)*

Further Information: Also Chinese Language Centre for foreign students and Research Centres

History: Founded 1980.

Academic Year: September to June (September-January; February-June)

Admission Requirements: Graduation from high school and entrance examination

Main Language(s) of Instruction: Chinese

Degrees and Diplomas: *Bachelor's Degree*: Business Management; Chinese Literature; Foreign Languages and Literature; Music; Theatre Arts; Computer Science and Engineering; Information Management; Finance; Political Economy; Chemistry; Physics; Biological Sciences; Applied Mathematics; Electrical Engineering; Mechanical and Electro-Mechanical Engineering; Materials Science and Optoelectronic Engineering; Photonics; Marine Biotechnology and Resources; Marine Environment and Engineering, 4 yrs; *Master's Degree*: Chinese Literature; Foreign Languages and Literature; Music; Theatre Arts; Philosophy; Chemistry; Physics; Biological Sciences; Applied Mathematics; Biomedical Sciences; Computer Science and Engineering; Materials Science and Engineering; Communications Engineering; Business Management; Information Management; Finance; Public Affairs Management; Human Resource Management; Communications Management; Electrical Engineering; Mechanical and Electro-Mechanical Engineering; Environmental Engineering; Photonics; Health Care Management;

Sociology; Political Science; China and Asia-Pacific Studies; Environmental Engineering; Economics; Education; Marine Biotechnology and Resources; Marine Environment and Engineering; Marine Biology; Marine Geology and Chemistry; Applied Marine Physics and Undersea Technology; Marine Affairs, a further 1-4 yrs; *Doctorate*: Chemistry; Physics; Biological Sciences; Applied Mathematics; Biomedical Science; Electrical Engineering; Mechanical and Electro-Mechanical Engineering; Computer Science and Engineering (PhD); Chinese Literature; China and Asia-Pacific Studies; Foreign Languages and Literature (PhD); Marine Biotechnology and Resources; Marine Environment and Engineering; Marine Biology; Marine Geology and Chemistry (PhD); Materials Science and Engineering; Environmental Engineering; Photonics; Communications Engineering; Business Management; Information Management; Finance; Public Affairs Management; Human Resource Management; Political Science; Economics; Education (PhD), a further 2-7 yrs

Libraries: Library, 364,097 vols in Chinese and other oriental languages; 267,938 vols in English and other western languages

Academic Staff *2007-2008*	MEN	WOMEN	TOTAL
FULL-TIME	368	89	457
Student Numbers *2007-2008*			
All (Foreign Included)	5,950	3,174	**9,124**

Last Updated: 12/12/08

NATIONAL TAICHUNG UNIVERSITY OF EDUCATION (NTCTC)

140, Min Sheng Road, Taichung 403
Tel: +886(4) 222-23793
Fax: +886(4) 222-43450
EMail: cale@ms3.ntctc.edu.tw
Website: http://www.ntctc.edu.tw

President: Ching-Piao Lai (2000-) EMail: cpl@mail.ntctc.edu.tw

Secretary-General: Kai-Cheng Han
EMail: kaicheng@mail.ntctc.edu.tw

Departments

Art Education (Art Education); **Mathematics Education** (Mathematics Education); **Modern Languages** (Modern Languages); **Music Education**; **Physical Education** (Physical Education); **Preschool Education** (Preschool Education); **Science Education**; **Social Studies** (Social Studies); **Special Education**

Graduate Institutes

Counselling and Educational Psychology (Educational and Student Counselling; Educational Psychology); **Educational Measurements Statistics** (Statistics); **Environment Education** (Education; Environmental Studies); **Primary Education**; **Special Educational and Assistive Technology**

History: Founded 1923, acquired present status and title 2005.

NATIONAL TAIPEI COLLEGE OF NURSING (NTCN)

365 Mingte Road, Beitou, Taipei 11257
Tel: +886(2) 282-27101
Fax: +886(2) 282-05680
EMail: kuji@ntcn.edu.tw
Website: http://www.ntcn.edu.tw

President: Ue-Lin Chung

Officer of Academic Affairs: Wei Chen
Tel: +886(2) 282-27101, Ext. 2300, Fax: +886(2) 282-05680
EMail: wei@ntcn.edu.tw

International Relations: Mei-Ling Gau
Tel: +886(2) 282-27101, Ext. 2730, Fax: +886(2) 282-27101
EMail: Meeiling@ntcn.edu.tw

Centres

Education; **Teacher Education**

Departments

Exercise and Health Sciences; **Health Care Management** (Health Administration; Health Sciences; Public Health); **Infant and Child Care** (Child Care and Development); **Information Management** (Information Management); **Nursing** (Nursing)

Graduate Institutes

Allied Health Education; **Health Care Management**; **Integrated Chinese and Western Medicine in Nursing**; **Long-Term Care**; **Midwifery Nursing**; **Nursing**; **Speech and Hearing Disorders and Sciences**

Further Information: Also Teaching Hospital

History: Founded 1947 as Taiwan Provincial Taipei Vocational School of Medicine. Acquired present status and title 1994.

Academic Year: September to July (September-February; March-July)

Admission Requirements: Graduation from high school and entrance examination

Main Language(s) of Instruction: Chinese, English

Degrees and Diplomas: *Bachelor's Degree*: 2-4 yrs

Student Services: Academic counselling, Canteen, Cultural centre, Employment services, Handicapped facilities, Health services, Social counselling, Sports facilities

Student Residential Facilities: Yes

Libraries: Central Library, c. 71,000 vols

Publications: Journal of National Taipei College of Nursing *(annually)*; News of National Taipei College of Nursing *(monthly)*

NATIONAL TAIPEI UNIVERSITY (NTPU)

151, Dashiue Road, Sanshia Jen, Taipei 237
Tel: +886(2) 267-48189 +886(2) 250-24654 +886(2) 250-21520
Fax: +886(2) 267-39331
EMail: yangsf@mail.ntpu.edu.tw
Website: http://www.ntpu.edu.tw

President: Chung-Wen Hou
Tel: +886(2) 250-32763, Fax: +886(2) 250-78708
EMail: president@mail.ntpu.edu.tw

Chief Secretary: Chin-Hua Chen
Tel: +886(2) 251-61351, Ext. 8215, Fax: +886(2) 251-61345
EMail: sfchen@mail.ntpu.edu.tw

Centres

Educational Programme for Secondary School Teachers; **Extension Education**; **General Education**

Colleges

Business; **Humanities**; **Law**; **Public Affairs**; **Social Sciences**

Graduate Institutes

Accountancy; **Business Administration**; **Classical Texts**; **Cooperative Economics**; **Criminology**; **Economics**; **Folk Arts**; **Information Management**; **Land Economics and Administration**; **Law**; **National Resource Management**; **Professional Law**; **Public Administration and Policy**; **Public Finance**; **Social Work**; **Sociology**; **Statistics**; **Urban Planning**

Research Centres

Comparative Law Documentation; **Cooperative Economics and Non-Profit Organizations**; **Electronic Business**; **International Negotiation and Interpretation**; **Land Management and Technology**; **Public Opinion and Election Studies**; **Taiwan Development**

Further Information: Also Taipei Campus

History: Founded 2000.

Degrees and Diplomas: *Bachelor's Degree*; *Master's Degree*; *Doctorate*. Also Executive M.B.A.

NATIONAL TAIPEI UNIVERSITY OF EDUCATION

134, Section 2, Ho Ping East Road, Taipei 10659
Tel: +886(2) 273-21104
Fax: +886(2) 273-30473
EMail: samsheu@tea.ntue.edu.tw
Website: http://english.ntue.edu.tw

President: Yu-Cherng Chang (2001-) Tel: +886(2) 273-31361

Secretary-General: Chung-Chen Cheng
Tel: +886(2) 273-21104 Ext. 2004 EMail: ccc@tea.ntptc.edu.tw

International Relations: Daniel Chan
Tel: +886(2) 273-21104, Ext. 2019, Fax: +886(2) 237-85354
EMail: yuching@tea.ntptc.edu.tw

Departments

Arts and Art Education (Art Education; Handicrafts; Visual Arts) *Head*: Jer-Cherng Lin; **Childrens' English Education**; **Early Childhood Education** (Pedagogy; Preschool Education) *Head*: Ya-Mei Chen; **Educational Psychology and Counseling** (Educational and Student Counselling; Educational Psychology) *Head*: Dwan-Jen Tseng; **Elementary Education** (Curriculum; Pedagogy; Primary Education) *Head*: Yi-Hsiung Tsai; **Language and Literature Education** (Chinese; Literature) *Head*: Hai-Chu Tan; **Mathematics Education** (Computer Science; Mathematics Education) *Head*: Ing-Jye Chang; **Music Education** (Music Education; Musical Instruments; Singing) *Head*: Chung-Shu Liu; **Physical Education** (Physical Education; Sports) *Head*: Jiin-Horng Tang; **Science Education** (Biology; Chemistry; Physics; Science Education) *Head*: Hsiao-Man Ho; **Social Studies Education** (Humanities and Social Science Education; Pacific Area Studies) *Head*: Anthony Tashiou Wang; **Special Education** *Head*: K-Jung Tsai

Graduate Schools

Arts and Art Education; **Children English Education** (English; Foreign Languages Education) *Head*: Shiang-Jiun Chang; **Curriculum and Instruction** (Curriculum; Educational Technology; Pedagogy) *Head*: Ming-Jang Chuang; **Educational Communication and Technology**; **Educational Policy and Management** (Educational Administration) *Head*: Wen-Liuh Lin; **Mathematics and Science Education** (Mathematics Education; Science Education) *Head*: Chao-Ti Hsiung; **Music Education for Traditional Music** *Head*: Chung-Shu Lin; **Taiwan Literature**

History: Founded 1896, became Taiwan Provincial Taipei Teachers College 1987, and acquired present title 2005.

Academic Year: September to July (September-January; February-July)

Admission Requirements: Graduation from high school and entrance examination

Fees: (New Taiwan Dollars): 19,800-32,230 per semester; Graduate, 8,960-10,380 per semester, 1,280 per credit hour

Main Language(s) of Instruction: Mandarin Chinese

Degrees and Diplomas: *Bachelor's Degree*: Education (BEd), 4 yrs; *Master's Degree*: Education (MEd), a further 2-3 yrs

Student Services: Academic counselling, Canteen, Employment services, Health services, Social counselling, Sports facilities

Student Residential Facilities: For 1,400 students

Libraries: c. 240,000 vols; 570,000 items on microfilm

Publications: Elementary Education *(bimonthly)*; Journal of National Taipei Teachers College, Research papers by the teaching staff of the college *(annually)*

NATIONAL TAIPEI UNIVERSITY OF TECHNOLOGY (NTUT)

1, Section 3, Jungshiau East Road, Taipei 106
Tel: +886(2) 277-12171
Fax: +886(2) 275-18845
EMail: npcheng@ntut.edu.tw
Website: http://www.ntut.edu.tw

President: Tsu-Tian Lee (2004-)
Tel: +886(2) 277-14193 EMail: president@ntut.edu.tw

Secretary-General: Chin-Yen Lin
Tel: +886(2) 277-12171, Ext. 1002 EMail: davdl@ntut.edu.tw

International Relations: Jason J.S. SunFax: +886(2) 275-25989
EMail: jssun@ntut.edu.tw

Colleges

Design (Architecture; Design; Industrial Design); **Engineering** (Chemical Engineering; Civil Engineering; Engineering; Materials Engineering; Mineralogy; Mining Engineering; Safety Engineering; Textile Technology); **Humanities and Science** (English; Optics; Physical Education; Teacher Training); **Management** (Business Administration; Industrial Engineering; Management); **Mechanical and Electrical Engineering**

Graduate Colleges
Commerce Automation and Management

Graduate Institutes
Air-conditioning and Refrigeration Engineering; **Architecture and Urban Design**; **Automation Technology**; **Chemical Engineering**; **Civil and Disaster Prevention**; **Computer Science and Information Engineering**; **Computer, Communication and Control Engineering**; **Electrical Engineering**; **Engineering Technology**; **Environment Planning and Management**; **Innovation and Design**; **Manufacturing Technology**; **Materials and Mineral Resources Engineering**; **Mechanical and Electrical Engineering**; **Mechatronic Engineering**; **Opto-Electronic Technology**; **Organic and Polymeric Materials**; **Production System Engineering and Management**; **Technological and Vocational Education**; **Vehicle Engineering**

Research Centres
Electro-Optics; **EMO Materials and Nanotechnology**; **Internet Studies**; **Recycling**; **Silicon Nano Device**; **Water Environment**

History: Founded 1994, acquired present status 1997.

Fees: (US Dollars): Undergraduate, 735-846 per annum; postgraduate, 960-1,020

NATIONAL TAITUNG UNIVERSITY

684, Section 1, Chung-Hua Road, Taitung 950
Tel: +886(89) 318-855
Fax: +886(89) 322-135
Website: http://www.nttu.edu.tw

President: Chorng-Jee Guo (2002-)
Tel: +886(89) 353-100 EMail: president@nttu.edu.tw

Secretary-General: Yung-fa Lin
Tel: +886(89) 353-138 EMail: lyf@nttu.edu.tw

International Relations: Yao-Chung Chang
Tel: +886(89) 318-855, Ext. 1303, Fax: +886(89) 361-480
EMail: ycc@nttu.edu.tw

Centres
Aboriginal Education and Research (Indigenous Studies) *Director*: Chien-Lung Wang; **Child Development** (Child Care and Development) *Director*: Shu-Jane Chien; **Children's Book Research** *Director*: Ming-Cherng Duh; **Computer and Communication** (Computer Science; Information Technology) *Director*: Kun-Lin Hsieh

Colleges
Education; **Humanities and Social Sciences**; **Science and Engineering**

Departments
Arts and Crafts Education (Art Education; Handicrafts) *Chair*: Hsuan Yao; **Chinese and Literature** (Chinese; Literature) *Chair*: Shu-Mei Wu; **Computer Science and Information Engineering** *Chair*: Tah-Yuan Kuo; **Early Chilhood Education** *(MA programme)* *Chair*: She-Chia Sun; **Education** (Education; Primary Education) *Chair*: Tung-Chung Tsia; **English** (English; Literature) *Chair*: Hung-Yueh Wen; **Information Science and Management Systems** (Computer Science; Management) *Chair*: P. Pete Chong; **Language Education** *(MA programme)* (Literature; Modern Languages) *Chair*: Shu-Mei Wu; **Mathematics** (Mathematics; Mathematics Education) *Chair*: Chih-Chen Kao; **Music** *Chair*: Chin-Tsai Lin; **Natural Science Education** *Chair*: Jia-Ching Lin; **Physical Education** (Physical Education) *Chair*: Dah-Feng Lin; **Social Studies Education** (Social Studies) *Chair*: Jwo-Yin Jan; **Special Education** *Chair*: Yung-Yi Wu

Graduate Institutes
Austronesian Studies (Anthropology; Austronesian and Oceanic Languages; Christian Religious Studies; Political Sciences) *Director*: Yuan-Chao Tung; **Children's Literature** *(PhD programme)* (Literature) *Director*: Ming-Cherng Duh; **Life Sciences** (Biological and Life Sciences; Biotechnology; Traditional Eastern Medicine) *Director*: Yen Lee; **Regional Policy and Development** (Regional Planning) *Director*: Yu-Fen Lee

History: Founded 1948 as National Taitung Teachers College. Acquired present status 2003.

Academic Year: September to June (September-January; February-June)

Admission Requirements: Graduation from high school or equivalent, and entrance examination

Fees: (US Dollars): 610-710 per semester; graduate, 350-868 per semester

Main Language(s) of Instruction: Mandarin Chinese, English

Degrees and Diplomas: *Bachelor's Degree*: 4 yrs; *Master's Degree*: 2-4 yrs; *Doctorate*: 5-7 yrs

Student Services: Academic counselling, Canteen, Cultural centre, Employment services, Handicapped facilities, Health services, Social counselling, Sports facilities

Student Residential Facilities: Yes

Special Facilities: Observatory

Libraries: General Library, 805,289 vols

Publications: Journal of NTTU *(biannually)*; NTTU Journal of Literature *(annually)*; NTTU Journal of Physical Education *(annually)*; NTTU Journal of Social Studies Education *(annually)*; NTTU Research Journal of Aboriginal Education *(quarterly)*; NTTU Research Report *(biannually)*

Last Updated: 01/02/07

NATIONAL TAIWAN COLLEGE OF PHYSICAL EDUCATION (NTCPE)

16, Section 1, Shuang-Shih Road, Taichung 404
Tel: +886(4) 222-13108
Fax: +886(4) 222-32463
EMail: ntcpe@alpha3.ntcpe.edu.tw
Website: http://www.ntcpe.edu.tw

President: Chuan-Show Chen (2000-)
Tel: +886(4) 222-36827 EMail: cschen@ntcpe.edu.tw

Secretary-General: Wu-Lon Chang
Tel: +886(4) 222-36827 EMail: 0,092@.ntcpe.edu.tw

International Relations: Miaojin Wang
EMail: miaojin@ms52.hinet.net

Departments
Athletics (Sports) *Head*: Lin Huei-Hsuing; **Dance** (Dance) *Head*: Tsai Li-Hua; **Physical Education** (Physical Education) *Head*: Chen Ding-Shyong; **Recreational Sports** (Parks and Recreation; Sports) *Head*: Lee Ming-Jung; **Sports and Health Science** (Health Sciences; Sports); **Sports Management**

History: Founded 1961. Acquired present status and title 1996.

Academic Year: September to June (September-January; February-June)

Admission Requirements: Graduation from high school and entrance examination

Main Language(s) of Instruction: Mandarin Chinese

Degrees and Diplomas: *Bachelor's Degree*. Also Graduate degrees planned

Student Residential Facilities: For c. 2,000 students

NATIONAL TAIWAN NORMAL UNIVERSITY (NTNU)

162, Section 1, Hoping East Road, Taipei 10610
Tel: +886(2) 236-25101
Fax: +886(2) 239-22607
EMail: webmaster@cc.ntnu.edu.tw
Website: http://www.ntnu.edu.tw

President: Maw-Fa Chien (1999-)
Tel: +886(2) 236-34307, Fax: +886(2) 239-22673

Secretary-General: Hsi-Ping Wang
Tel: +886(2) 236-39607, Fax: +886(2) 239-22673
EMail: e02001@cc.ntnu.edu.tw

International Relations: Chung-Yang Tsai, Vice-President
Tel: 886(2) 236-36804, Fax: 886(2) 236-37025
EMail: mtlai@cc.ntnu.edu.tw

Colleges
Education; **Fine and Applied Arts** (Fine Arts); **Liberal Arts** (Arts and Humanities); **Sciences** (Natural Sciences); **Sports and Recreation** (Leisure Studies; Sports); **Technology** (Technology)

Divisions
Extension for In-service and Continuing Education; **Preparatory Programs for Overseas Chinese Students** *(Lin Kou, Taipei County)* (Agriculture; Arts and Humanities; Business and Commerce; Chinese; Education; Engineering; Fine Arts; Health Sciences; Native Language; Natural Sciences)

Further Information: National University Preparatory School for Overseas Chinese Students (see separate Division entry)

History: Founded 1946 as Taiwan Provincial Teachers' College. Acquired University status 1967 as the first University in Taiwan devoted to the training of secondary school teachers. A State institution responsible to the Ministry of Education.

Governing Bodies: University Council; Executive Council

Academic Year: September to June (September-January; February-June)

Admission Requirements: Graduation from senior high school or recognized foreign equivalent, and entrance examination

Main Language(s) of Instruction: Chinese

Degrees and Diplomas: *Bachelor's Degree*: Fine Arts; Music; Chinese; English; Geography; History; Graphic Arts; Industrial Education; Industrial Technology Education; Physical Education; Life Science; Chemistry; Earth Sciences; Mathematics; Physics, 4 yrs and 1 yr teaching practice (optional); *Master's Degree*: Computer Science and Information Engineering; Earth Sciences; Electro-Optical Science and Technology; Environmental Education; Mathematics; Physics; Science Education; Industrial Technology Education; Mechatronic Technology; International Workforce Education and Development; Applied Electronic Technology; Physical Education; Sports and Leisure Management; Life Science; Chemistry; *Master's Degree*: Fine Arts; Music; Ethnomusic; Design; Performing Arts; Chinese; English; Geography; History; Teaching Chinese as a Second Language; Translation and Interpretation; Taiwan History; Taiwan Culture, Language and Literature; Graphic Arts; Industrial Education, at least a further 2 yrs and thesis; *Doctorate*: Fine Arts; Music; Chinese; English; Geography; History; Industrial Education; Industrial Technology Education; Physical Education; Life Science; Chemistry; Earth Sciences; Mathematics; Physics; Science Education; Teaching Chinese as a Second Language (PhD), a further 2-6 yrs and dissertation

Student Residential Facilities: For c. 7,000 students

Libraries: Central Library and branch libraries, c. 1,056,111 vols

Publications: Abstract of Chinese Educational Literature; Bulletin of Institute of Educational Research; Bulletin of National Taiwan Normal University; Bulletin of Research Institute of Chinese Literature

Last Updated: 07/03/07

NATIONAL TAIWAN OCEAN UNIVERSITY (NTOU)

2, Pei-Ning Road, Keelung 20224
Tel: +886(2) 2462-2192
Fax: +886(2) 2462-0724
EMail: ntou@mail.ntou.edu.tw
Website: http://www.ntou.edu.tw

President: Kuo-Tien Lee (2006-)
Tel: +886(2) 2462-2110, Fax: +886(2) 2462-3563
EMail: po@mail.ntou.edu.tw

Dean of Academic Affairs: Kuo-Kau Lee
Tel: +886(2) 2462-2192, Ext. 1010, Fax: +886(2) 2462-2690
EMail: b0092@mail.ntou.edu.tw

International Relations: Hsuan-Shih Lee
Tel: +886(2) 2462-2192, Ext. 2250, Fax: +886(2) 2463-3744
EMail: hslee@mail.ntou.edu.tw

Colleges
Electrical Engineering and Computer Science (Automation and Control Engineering; Computer Engineering; Computer Science; Electrical Engineering); **Engineering** (Computer Engineering; Electronic Engineering; Engineering; Marine Engineering; Materials

Engineering; Mechanical Engineering; Naval Architecture); **Humanities and Social Sciences**; **Life Sciences** (Aquaculture; Biological and Life Sciences; Biotechnology; Food Science; Marine Biology); **Maritime Science and Management** (Marine Engineering; Marine Science and Oceanography; Marine Transport; Transport Management); **Ocean Science and Resource** (Applied Chemistry; Biology; Chemistry; Ecology; Environmental Studies; Fishery; Marine Biology; Marine Science and Oceanography)

Further Information: Also Research and Extension Centres

History: Founded 1953 as Junior College, became Senior College 1964, and acquired present status and title 1989. Financed by and under the jurisdiction of the Ministry of Education.

Academic Year: August to July (August-January; February-July)

Admission Requirements: Senior high school certificate or recognized equivalent, and entrance examination

Main Language(s) of Instruction: Chinese

Degrees and Diplomas: *Bachelor's Degree*: 4 yrs; *Master's Degree*: a further 2 yrs; *Doctorate (PhD)*: 3 yrs

Student Services: Academic counselling, Canteen, Cultural centre, Employment services, Handicapped facilities, Health services, Language programs, Social counselling, Sports facilities

Student Residential Facilities: Yes

Libraries: Library, 300,237 vols

Publications: Journal of Marine Science and Technology *(biannually)*

Academic Staff 2008	MEN	WOMEN	TOTAL
FULL-TIME	322	47	369
PART-TIME	155	24	179
STAFF WITH DOCTORATE			
FULL-TIME	301	45	346
PART-TIME	110	4	114
Student Numbers 2008			
All (Foreign Included)	5,147	2,006	7,153

Part-time students, 101. **Evening students**, 1,442.
Last Updated: 11/12/08

NATIONAL TAIWAN UNIVERSITY (NTU)

1, Section 4, Roosevelt Road, Taipei 10617
Tel: +886(2) 3366-3366
Fax: +886(2) 2362-7651
EMail: secretor@ntu.edu.tw
Website: http://www.ntu.edu.tw

President: Si-Chen Lee (1993-)
Tel: +886(2) 3366-2000/2001, Fax: +886(2) 2362-1877
EMail: sclee@cc.ee.ntu.edu.tw

Dean of Academic Affairs: Been-Huang Chiang
Tel: +886(2) 2363-1482, Fax: +886(2) 23623-925
EMail: bhchiang@ntu.edu.tw

International Relations: Tung Shen
Tel: +886(2) 3366-2007, Fax: +886(2) 2362-0096
EMail: cfia@ntu.edu.tw

Centres
Biodiversity; **Biotechnology** (Biotechnology) *Director*: Winston T.K. Cheng; **Condensed Matter Sciences**; **Disaster** *Director*: Ming-Kuen Lai; **Humanities**; **Indigenous People**; **Information and Electronics Technology**; **Japanese All-round Research** (Cultural Studies; Law; Political Sciences; Social Sciences) *Director*: Jing-Shown Wu; **Nano Science and Technology** (Nanotechnology) *Director*: Shuo-Hung Chang; **Ocean** (Marine Engineering; Technology) *Director*: Ya-Jung Lee; **Population and Gender Studies** (Demography and Population; Gender Studies) *Director*: Cheng-Tay Hsueh

Colleges
Bio-Resources and Agriculture (Agricultural Economics; Agricultural Education; Agricultural Engineering; Agricultural Equipment; Agriculture; Agronomy; Animal Husbandry; Behavioural Sciences; Biochemistry; Biology; Botany; Crop Production; Ecology; Entomology; Environmental Management; Farm Management; Food Science; Food Technology; Forestry; Genetics; Horticulture; Hydraulic Engineering; Microbiology; Molecular Biology; Natural Resources; Plant and Crop Protection; Plant Pathology; Rural Studies; Soil Science; Statistics; Veterinary Science; Water Science) *Dean*: Bao-Ji Chen; **Electrical Engineering and Computer Science** (Computer Engineering; Computer Networks; Computer Science; Electrical Engineering; Electronic Engineering; Microelectronics; Multimedia; Optical Technology; Power Engineering; Software Engineering; Telecommunications Engineering) *Dean*: Soo-Chang Pei; **Engineering** (Biomedical Engineering; Building Technologies; Chemical Engineering; Engineering; Environmental Engineering; Industrial Engineering; Marine Engineering; Mechanical Engineering; Mechanics; Polymer and Plastics Technology; Town Planning) *Dean*: Huang-Jang Keh; **Law** (Law) *Dean*: Chang-Fa Lo; **Liberal Arts** (Anthropology; Art History; Arts and Humanities; Chinese; History; Information Sciences; Japanese; Library Science; Linguistics; Literature; Modern Languages; Musicology; Philosophy; Theatre) *Dean*: Kuo-Liang Yeh; **Life Science** (Biochemistry; Biological and Life Sciences; Cell Biology; Ecology; Fishery; Microbiology; Molecular Biology; Zoology) *Dean*: Yao-Sung Lin; **Management** (Accountancy; Business Administration; Finance; Human Resources; Information Management; International Business; Management; Marketing; Systems Analysis) *Dean*: Mao-Wei Hung; **Medicine** (Anaesthesiology; Anatomy; Biochemistry; Cardiology; Cell Biology; Dental Hygiene; Dentistry; Dermatology; Endocrinology; Forensic Medicine and Dentistry; Gastroenterology; Gerontology; Gynaecology and Obstetrics; Haematology; Immunology; Medical Technology; Medicine; Microbiology; Molecular Biology; Nephrology; Nursing; Occupational Therapy; Oncology; Ophthalmology; Oral Pathology; Orthodontics; Orthopaedics; Otorhinolaryngology; Paediatrics; Parasitology; Pathology; Periodontics; Pharmacology; Pharmacy; Physical Therapy; Physiology; Plastic Surgery; Psychiatry and Mental Health; Radiology; Rehabilitation and Therapy; Rheumatology; Social and Preventive Medicine; Surgery; Toxicology; Urology) *Dean*: Ding-Shinn Chen; **Public Health** (Behavioural Sciences; Community Health; Environmental Studies; Epidemiology; Health Administration; Hygiene; Management; Occupational Health; Public Health; Social and Preventive Medicine; Statistics; Waste Management) *Dean*: Tung-Liang Chiang; **Science** *(Also Instrumentation Centre)* (Chemistry; Geography; Geology; Instrument Making; Mathematics; Meteorology; Physics; Psychology) *Dean*: Ching-Hua Lo; **Social Sciences** (Economics; Journalism; Political Sciences; Social Sciences; Sociology) *Dean*: Tzong-Ho Bau

Institutes
Astrophysics (Astrophysics); **Industrial Research** *(Yen Tjing Lin)* (Artificial Intelligence; Automation and Control Engineering; Chemical Engineering; Electrical Engineering; Electronic Engineering; Laser Engineering; Materials Engineering; Measurement and Precision Engineering; Metal Techniques; Polymer and Plastics Technology; Telecommunications Engineering) *Director*: Yung-Hsiang Chen; **Marine Science and Oceanography** (Marine Science and Oceanography)

Research Centres
Bio-Resources and Agriculture (Automation and Control Engineering; Biotechnology) *Director*: Winston T.K. Cheng; **Electrical Engineering and Computer Science** (Automation and Control Engineering; Electronic Engineering; Hydraulic Engineering; Industrial Engineering; Mechanical Engineering; Petrology; Polymer and Plastics Technology; Production Engineering; Seismology); **Liberal Arts**; **Medicine**; **Public Health** (Environmental Studies; Health Administration; Occupational Health); **Science** (Instrument Making)

Further Information: Also University Hospital and Veterinary Hospital

History: Founded 1928 as Taihoku Imperial University by the Japanese. Acquired present status and title 1945 following Taiwan's retrocession to Chinese sovereignty. The oldest University in Taiwan.

Academic Year: August to June (September-January; February-June)

Admission Requirements: Graduation from senior high school or foreign equivalent, and entrance examination for local students, direct application for foreign students

Fees: (New Taiwan Dollars): Undergraduate Programmes, 25,230-39,560; Graduate Programmes, 25,640-88,000

Main Language(s) of Instruction: Chinese

International Co-operation: With over 150 universities and colleges in 35 countries. Participation in AEARU, APRU, UMAP, SATU, APAIE programmes

Accrediting Agencies: Ministry of Education

Degrees and Diplomas: *Bachelor's Degree*: Agriculture; Chinese Literature; Foreign Languages and Literatures; History; Law; Business Administration; Veterinary Medicine, 5 yrs; *Bachelor's Degree*: Dentistry, 6 yrs; *Bachelor's Degree*: Engineering; Arts and Humanities; Business Administration; Natural Sciences; Performing Arts, 4 yrs; *Bachelor's Degree*: Medicine, 7 yrs; *Master's Degree*: Social Sciences; Liberal Arts; Engineering; Medicine; Law; Life Science; Management; Science; Public Health; Bio-Resources and Agriculture; Electrical Engineering and Computer Science, 1-4 yrs; *Doctorate*: Social Sciences; Liberal Arts; Engineering; Medicine; Law; Life Science; Management; Science; Public Health; Bio-Resources and Agriculture; Electrical Engineering; Computer Science, 2-7 yrs

Student Services: Academic counselling, Canteen, Cultural centre, Employment services, Foreign student adviser, Handicapped facilities, Health services, Language programs, Nursery care, Social counselling, Sports facilities

Student Residential Facilities: For 9250 Students (dormitories)

Special Facilities: Anthropology Museum, Audiovisual Educational Centre, Tai Herbarium Museum of Ichthylogy

Libraries: Main Library, libraries of Colleges and Departments, total c. 2,894,000 vols

Publications: Acta Botanica Taiwanica; Acta Geologica Taiwanica; Acta Oceanographica Taiwanica *(biannually)*; Acta Zoologica Taiwanica *(1-2 per annum)*; Chinese Paleography; Chungwai Literary Monthly; Civil Engineering Studies; Forum of Women's and Gender Studies *(quarterly)*; History and Chinese Literature Series; Humanitas Taiwanica; Journal of Art History; Journal of Geographical Science *(quarterly)*; Journal of Population Studies *(biannually)*; Journal of Women's and Gender Studies *(biannually)*; Monographs of the College of Agriculture; National Taiwan University Journal of Sociology; National Taiwan University Journalist Forum Journal; National Taiwan University Law Journal; National Taiwan University Library and Information Science Journal; National Taiwan University Philosophical Review; NTU Management Review; NTU Social Work Review *(biannually)*; NTU Studies in Japanese Language and Literature; NTU Studies in Language and Literature; Political Science Review; Studies in Chinese Literature; Taiwan Economic Review; Taiwanese Sociology *(quarterly)*; TAIWANIA, An International Journal of Life Sciences *(quarterly)*; University Library Journal *(biannually)*

Press or Publishing House: National Taiwan University Press

NATIONAL TAIWAN UNIVERSITY OF ARTS

59, Section 1, Tah-Kuan Road, Pan-Chiao, Taipei 22055
Tel: +886(2) 227-22181
Fax: +886(2) 296-87563
EMail: d01@mail.ntua.edu.tw
Website: http://www.ntua.edu.tw

President: Kuang-Nan Huang (2004-)
Tel: +886(2) 227-22181, Ext. 1003

Chief Secretary: Wen-Chih Hsieh
Tel: +886(2) 227-22181, Ext. 1002
EMail: wenchih@mail.ntua.edu.tw

International Relations: Catherine Chan
Tel: +886(2) 227-22181, Ext. 1006
EMail: tsaiyun@mail.ntua.edu.tw

Centres
General Education

Departments
Applied Media Art; **Chinese Calligraphy and Painting** (Painting and Drawing); **Chinese Music**; **Crafts Design**; **Dance**; **Drama**; **Fine Arts** (Fine Arts); **Graphic Communication Arts**; **Motion Picture**; **Music**; **Radio and Television**; **Sculpture**; **Traditional Craft**; **Visual Communication Design**

Graduate Schools
Applied Media Arts; **Art Management and Cultural Policies** *(Postgraduate)* (Art Management; Cultural Studies); **Crafts Design**

(Crafts and Trades; Fine Arts); **Graphic Communication Arts**; **Multimedia and Animation**; **Performing Arts** (Performing Arts); **Plastic Arts**; **Theatre** (Acting; Theatre)

Schools
Art Management and Cultural Policies *(Post-Graduate)* (Art Management; Cultural Studies)

History: Founded 1955, acquired present status 2001.

NATIONAL TAIWAN UNIVERSITY OF SCIENCE AND TECHNOLOGY (NTUST)

43, Section 4, Keelung Road, Taipei 10607
Tel: +886(2) 273-33141
Fax: +886(2) 273-31044
EMail: ntust@mail.ntust.edu.tw
Website: http://www.ntust.edu.tw

President: Shi-Shuenn Chen (2005-)
Tel: +886(2) 273-76101, Fax: +886(2) 273-76107
EMail: president@mail.ntust.edu.tw

Secretary-General: Hong-Chan Chang
Tel: +886(2) 273-76102, Fax: +886(2) 273-71000
EMail: hcchang@mail.ntust.edu.tw

International Relations: Yung-Hui Lee, Dean, Office of International Affairs
Tel: +886(2) 273-01130, Fax: +886(2) 273-01283
EMail: oia@mail.ntust.edu.tw

Centres
Business Incubation; **Innovation and Creativity**; **Technological and Vocational Education** (Technology); **Technology Licensing**; **University-Industry Cooperation**

Colleges
Design (Architecture; Design; Industrial Design) *Dean*: Lin-Lin Chen; **Electrical and Computer Engineering** (Computer Science; Electrical Engineering; Electronic Engineering; Information Technology) *Dean*: Sy-Yen Kuo; **Engineering** (Chemical Engineering; Construction Engineering; Mechanical Engineering; Polymer and Plastics Technology) *Dean*: Chang-Yu Ou; **Liberal Arts and Social Sciences** (Arts and Humanities; Modern Languages; Social Sciences) *Dean*: Mao-Sung Lin; **Management** (Business Administration; Industrial Management; Information Management) *Dean*: Tzong-Chen Wu

Graduate Schools
Design; **Electrical Engineering and Computer Engineering** (Computer Engineering; Electrical Engineering; Optical Technology); **Engineering**; **Finance**; **Management**; **Technological and Vocational Education** (Technology)

Research Centres
Automation and Control (Automation and Control Engineering); **Communication and Electromagnetic Technology**; **Ecological and Hazard Mitigation Engineering** (Ecology); **Expensive Instrument**; **Intelligent Robots** (Robotics); **Material Science and Technology** (Materials Engineering; Technology); **Nanotechnology** (Nanotechnology); **Opto-Mechatronics Technology** (Optical Technology); **Power Electronics Technology**; **Taiwan Building Technology** (Building Technologies); **Taiwan Information Security**; **Teacher Education** (Education; Educational Research; Teacher Training)

History: Founded 1974, acquired present status 1997.

Academic Year: September to June (September-January; February-June)

Admission Requirements: Graduation from senior high school (4-year new undergraduate programme), junior technical college (2-year programme), or vocational senior high school (4-year new undergraduate programme)

Fees: (New Taiwan Dollars): 20,000-28,000 per semester

Main Language(s) of Instruction: Chinese

International Co-operation: With universities in the USA; Costa Rica; United Kingdom; Switzerland; France; Austria; Czech Republic; China; Indonesia; Mongolia; Russian Federation ; Japan; Philippines; Malaysia; Republic of Korea; Thailand and Australia

Degrees and Diplomas: *Bachelor's Degree*: 2-4 yrs; *Master's Degree*: Engineering; Business Administration; Design, a further 2-4 yrs; *Doctorate*: Engineering; Business Administration (PhD), a further 4-6 yrs

Student Services: Academic counselling, Employment services, Handicapped facilities, Health services, Sports facilities

Student Residential Facilities: Yes

Special Facilities: Laboratories and Workshops

Libraries: 343,246 vols

Academic Staff 2007-2008	MEN	WOMEN	TOTAL
FULL-TIME	–	–	425
PART-TIME	–	–	458
STAFF WITH DOCTORATE			
FULL-TIME	–	–	416
PART-TIME	–	–	256

Student Numbers 2007-2008			
All (Foreign Included)	7,237	2,008	9,245

Last Updated: 17/12/08

NATIONAL TSING HUA UNIVERSITY (NTHU)

101, Section 2, Kuang Fu Road, Hsinchu 30013
Tel: +886(3) 571-5131
Fax: +886(3) 572-2467
Website: http://www.nthu.edu.tw

President: Frank S. Shu (2002-)
Tel: +886(3) 571-4155, Fax: +886(3) 571-0582
EMail: presid@my.nthu.edu.tw

Secretary-General: Ming-Chuen Yip
Tel: +886(3) 573-1001, Fax: +886(3) 573-4461
EMail: mcyip@pme.nthu.edu.tw

International Relations: Chung-Min Chen, Chair
Tel: +886(3) 573-1260, Fax: +886(3) 572-4038
EMail: cmichen@mx.nthu.edu.tw

Colleges
Electrical Engineering and Computer Science (Computer Engineering; Computer Science; Electrical Engineering; Electronic Engineering; Physical Engineering; Telecommunications Engineering) *Dean*: Cheng-Wen Wu; **Engineering** (Chemical Engineering; Engineering Management; Industrial Engineering; Materials Engineering; Mechanical Engineering; Microelectronics; Power Engineering) *Dean*: Lih-Jen Chen; **Humanities and Social Sciences** (Anthropology; Chinese; Economics; History; Humanities and Social Science Education; Linguistics; Literature; Modern Languages; Philosophy; Sociology) *Dean*: Yi-Long Huan; **Life Sciences** (Biological and Life Sciences; Biology; Biotechnology; Cell Biology; Medicine; Microbiology; Molecular Biology) *Dean*: Wen-Guey Wu; **Nuclear Science** (Nuclear Engineering; Nuclear Physics) *Dean*: Shiang-Huei Jiang; **Science** (Astronomy and Space Science; Chemistry; Mathematics; Physics; Statistics) *Dean*: Shin-Lin Chang; **Technology Management** (Engineering Management; Finance; Law) *Head*: Shin-Tay Shih

History: Founded in Peking 1911 as College, became University 1925. Closed 1949 and re-established in Hsinchu 1956. A State institution.

Governing Bodies: University Council

Academic Year: August to July (August-January; February-July)

Admission Requirements: Graduation from senior high school and entrance examination

Fees: (New Taiwan Dollars): 28,630 per semester

Main Language(s) of Instruction: Chinese an English

International Co-operation: With universities in USA, Japan, France, China, Canada

Accrediting Agencies: Ministry of Education

Degrees and Diplomas: *Bachelor's Degree*: Humanities and Social Sciences; Science; Engineering; Nuclear Science; Life Science; Electrical Engineering and Computer Science; Technology Management, 4 yrs; *Master's Degree*: Humanities and Social Sciences; Science; Engineering; Nuclear Science; Life Science; Electrical Engineering and Computer Science; Technology Management, a further 2 yrs; *Doctorate*: Science; Engineering; Nuclear Science; Life Science; Electrical Engineering and Computer Science; Technology Management (PhD), a further 2 yrs (minimum) following Master's Degree

Student Services: Academic counselling, Canteen, Cultural centre, Employment services, Foreign student adviser, Foreign Studies Centre, Handicapped facilities, Health services, Language programs, Nursery care, Social counselling, Sports facilities

Student Residential Facilities: Student Dormitory

Special Facilities: Art Gallery

Libraries: Main Library and a branch library of Humanities and Social Science

Publications: Inter-Asia Cultural Studies *(quarterly)*; Tsing Hua Hsiao Yu T'ung Hsur, Alumni Newspaper *(biannually)*; Tsing Hua Journal for General Education *(quarterly)*; Tsing Hua Journal for History Education, History *(biannually)*; Tsing Hua Journal of Chinese Studies, Chinese Literature and Community Science *(quarterly)*; Tsing Hua Shuang Chou K'ar, Review *(other/irregular)*

Press or Publishing House: Tsing Hua University Press

NATIONAL UNITED UNIVERSITY (NUU)

1, Lien-Kung, Kung-Ching Li, Miaoli 360
Tel: +886(37) 381-000
Fax: +886(37) 320-610
Website: http://www.nuu.edu.tw

President: Tsung-Shune Chin (2001-) Tel: +886(37) 381-001

Secretary-General: Chung-Hsiang Wang
Tel: +886(37) 381-188, Fax: +886(37) 331-165

Centres
Education

Colleges
Engineering (Architecture; Chemical Engineering; Civil Engineering; Electrical Engineering; Electronic Engineering; Environmental Engineering; Health Sciences; Industrial Design; Mechanical Engineering; Optical Technology; Optics; Safety Engineering); **Management** (Finance; Industrial Engineering; Industrial Management; Information Management)

History: Founded 1969, acquired present status and title 1999.

NATIONAL UNIVERSITY OF KAOHSIUNG (NUK)

700, Kaohsiung University Road, Nan-Tzu, Kaohsiung 811
Tel: +886(7) 591-9000
Fax: +886(7) 591-9083
Website: http://www.nuk.edu.tw

President: Jen-Huong Wang (2000-)
Tel: +886(7) 591-9022, Fax: +886(7) 591-9029

Secretary-General: Shyh-Nan Kao
Tel: +886(7) 591-9025 EMail: snkao@nuk.edu.tw

International Relations: Michael Sheng-Ti Gau
Tel: +886(7) 591-073422, Fax: +886(7) 591-9294
EMail: mikegau@nuk.edu.tw

Colleges
Asia-Pacific Affairs; **Economics and Management**; **Engineering**; **Humanities and Social Sciences**; **Law**; **Life Sciences**; **Science**

NATIONAL UNIVERSITY OF TAINAN (NUTN)

33, Section 2, Shulin Street, Tainan 70010
Tel: +886(6) 213-3111
Fax: +886(6) 214-4409
EMail: junsam@ipx.ntntc.edu.tw
Website: http://www.nutn.edu.tw

President: Jenq-Jye Hwang (2004-)
Tel: +886(6) 213-2309, Fax: +886(6) 213-0200
EMail: president@mail.nutn.edu.tw

Secretary-General: Chin Tsai Lin
Tel: +886(6) 213-3111, Ext. 110 EMail: tsair@mail.nutn.edu.tw

Colleges
Education (Education; Physical Education; Preschool Education; Special Education); **Humanities** (Arts and Humanities; Fine Arts; Literature; Modern Languages; Music Education; Social Studies);

Science and Engineering (Biological and Life Sciences; Computer Science; Educational Technology; Information Sciences; Information Technology; Mathematics Education; Natural Sciences; Technology)

Graduate Institutes
Education Entrepreneurship and Management; Taiwan Culture; Applied Languages and Literature; Applied Mathematics; Computer Science and Information Education; Counselling Guidance; Elementary Education; Environment and Ecology; Management of Technology; Measurement and Statistics; Sport and Health; Technology Development Communication; Theatre; Visual Arts

History: Founded 1898. Acquired present status 2004.

Academic Year: September to June

Admission Requirements: Graduation from senior high school

Degrees and Diplomas: *Bachelor's Degree*: 4 yrs; *Master's Degree*: a further 2-4 yrs

Student Residential Facilities: For c. 800 students

Libraries: Central Library, c. 132,000 vols

NATIONAL YANG MING UNIVERSITY (NYMU)

155, Section 2, Linong Street, Beitou, Taipei 112
Tel: +886(2) 282-67000
Fax: +886(2) 282-64051
EMail: webmaster@ym.edu.tw
Website: http://www.ym.edu.tw

President: Yan-Hwa Wu Lee
Tel: +886(2) 282-23073, Fax: +886(2) 282-50936
EMail: president@ym.edu.tw

Secretary-General: ray-Yau Wang
Tel: +886(2) 282-64842, Fax: +886(2) 282-39119
EMail: wjsyu@ym.edu.tw

International Relations: Ming-Ta Hsu
Tel: +886(2) 282-67300, Fax: +886(2) 282-37583
EMail: mth@ym.edu.tw

Departments
Biomedical Imaging (Medical Technology; Radiology); **Biotechnology and Laboratory Science in Medicine**; **Dentistry** (Dental Technology; Dentistry; Oral Pathology; Stomatology); **Life Sciences** (Anatomy; Biochemistry; Biological and Life Sciences; Genetics; Immunology; Microbiology; Neurosciences; Parasitology; Pharmacology; Physiology); **Medicine**; **Nursing** (Community Health; Nursing); **Physical Therapy**

Institutes
Anatomy and Cell Biology; Assistant Technology Resources and Popularization; Bioinformatics; Biomedical Engineering; Clinical Dentistry; Clinical Medicine; Clinical Nursing; Community Health Nursing; Emergency and Intensive Care Medicine; Environmental Health Sciences; Genome Sciences; Health and Welfare Policy; Health Informatics and Decision Making; Hospital and Health Care Administration; Microbiology and Immunology; Neuroscience; Oral Biology; Pharmacology; Physical Therapy; Physiology; Public Health; Radiological Sciences; Rehabilitation Sciences and Technology; Traditional Medicine; Tropical Medicine (Tropical Medicine)

Research Centres
AIDS Prevention (Epidemiology); **Bioinformatics** (Computer Science; Health Sciences); **Biomedical Engineering** (Biomedical Engineering); **Biophotonics** *(Interdisciplinary)*; **Cardiovascular Diseases** (Cardiology); **Cellular and Molecular Biology** (Cell Biology; Molecular Biology); **Collaborating** *(Taiwan Joanna Briggs)* (Health Sciences); **Community Medicine** (Community Health; Medicine); **Community Nursing** (Community Health; Nursing); **Exercise and Health Science** (Health Sciences); **Genome** (Genetics); **Health and Welfare Policy**; **Immunology** (Immunology); **Joint Prosthesis Technology**; **Liver Diseases** *(Ti-Wu)* (Hepatology); **Neurosciences** (Neurosciences); **New Drug Development** (Toxicology); **Proteomics** (Genetics); **Urological Science** *(Shu-Tien)* (Urology)

History: Founded 1975 as College, acquired present status 1994.

Academic Year: August to July (August-January; February-July)

Admission Requirements: Graduation from high school and entrance examination

Main Language(s) of Instruction: Chinese, English

Degrees and Diplomas: *Bachelor's Degree*: Dentistry, 6 yrs; *Bachelor's Degree*: Medical Technology, 4 yrs; *Bachelor's Degree*: Medicine, 7 yrs; *Master's Degree*: Science, a further 2 yrs; *Doctorate (PhD)*

Student Residential Facilities: Yes

Libraries: Central Library, c. 100,000 vols

Publications: Scientific Papers
Last Updated: 13/02/07

NATIONAL YUNLIN UNIVERSITY OF SCIENCE AND TECHNOLOGY (NYUST)

123, University Road, Section 3, Douliou, Yunlin 64002
Tel: +886(5) 534-2601, Ext. 2510
Fax: +886(5) 532-1719
EMail: preside@yuntech.edu.tw
Website: http://www.yuntech.edu.tw

President: Tsong-Ming Lin EMail: tmlin@yuntech.edu.tw

Secretary-General: Jung-Chuan Chou
Tel: +886(5) 534-2601, Ext. 2101 EMail: choujc@yuntech.edu.tw

International Relations: Dau-Chung Wang
Tel: +886(5) 534-2601, Ext. 2505, Fax: +886(5) 531-2064
EMail: wangdc@yuntech.edu.tw

Colleges
Design; Engineering; Humanities and Applied Sciences; Management

Further Information: 22 Research Centres

History: Founded 1991. Acquired present status and title 1997.

Academic Year: August to July (August-January; February-July)

Admission Requirements: Graduation from high school and entrance examination

Fees: (New Taiwan Dollars): 60,000 per annum

Main Language(s) of Instruction: Chinese

Degrees and Diplomas: *Bachelor's Degree*: 4-6 yrs; *Master's Degree*: 2-4 yrs; *Doctorate*: 2-7 yrs

Student Services: Academic counselling, Canteen, Employment services, Handicapped facilities, Health services, Language programs, Nursery care, Social counselling, Sports facilities

Student Residential Facilities: Yes

Special Facilities: Art Museum. Computer Centre. Clouds View Pavilion

Libraries: 428,750 vols; 29,961 periodicals; 163,707 data items; 21,245 audio resources and 21,729 e-resources

Publications: Journal of Commerce and Management *(quarterly)*; Journal of Humanities and Sociology *(biannually)*; Journal of Science and Technology *(quarterly)*
Last Updated: 11/12/08

OPEN UNIVERSITY OF KAOHSIUNG (OUK)

436, Daye North Road, Shiaugang, Kaohsiung 812
Tel: +886(7) 801-2008
Fax: +886(7) 806-6720
Website: http://www.ouk.edu.tw

President: Eing-Ming Wu (2008-)
Tel: +886(7) 806-6725 EMail: president@ms1.ouk.edu.tw

Administrative Officer: Chien-Hsiung Lin
Tel: +886(7) 803-4211 EMail: axel@ms1.ouk.edu.tw

International Relations: Tzung-Je Tsai, Chief-Secretary
Tel: +886(7) 801-2008, Ext. 1203 EMail: caijerryy@yahoo.com.tw

Departments
Culture and Art; Foreign Language and Literature; Industry and Business Management; Law and Political Science; Mass Communication; Technology Management (Engineering Management)

History: Founded 1997.

Fees: (New Taiwan Dollars): c. 800 per credit

Main Language(s) of Instruction: Chinese

Degrees and Diplomas: *Bachelor's Degree*: Law; Business

Libraries: 8,000 vols; 150 periodicals

Publications: Campus News of OUK

Last Updated: 12/12/08

TAINAN NATIONAL UNIVERSITY OF THE ARTS (TNUA)

66, Ta-Chi Tsun, Kuan Tien, Tainan 720
Tel: +886(6) 693-0100
Fax: +886(6) 693-0251
EMail: em1102@mail.tnnua.edu.tw
Website: http://www.tnnua.edu.tw

President: Pi-Twan Huang (2000-)
Tel: +886(6) 693-0111, Fax: +886(6) 693-0121

Secretary-General: Charles Chen Tel: +886(6) 693-0120

International Relations: Yu-Tan Chang
Tel: +886(6) 693-0140, Fax: +886(6) 693-0141

Colleges
Arts and Humanities (Art History; Arts and Humanities); **Performing Arts** (Music; Performing Arts); **Sound and Image Studies** (Cinema and Television; Film; Performing Arts); **Visual Arts** (Art Criticism; Fine Arts; History; Museum Studies; Visual Arts)

Graduate Institutes
Animation; **Applied Arts** (Ceramic Art; Graphic Arts); **Art History and Art Criticism**; **Building Arts** (Architecture); **Collaborative Piano**; **Conservation of Cultural Relics**; **Ethnomusicology** (Cultural Studies; Musicology); **Museology** (Cultural Studies; Museum Studies); **Musical Performance and Composition**; **Plastic Arts** (Fine Arts; Painting and Drawing; Sculpture); **Sound and Image Studies in Documentary**; **Sound and Image Studies in Management**

History: Founded 1996. Acquired present name 2004.

Degrees and Diplomas: *Bachelor's Degree*: 4 yrs; *Master's Degree*: a further 3 yrs

Student Services: Cultural centre, Nursery care, Sports facilities

Special Facilities: Museum. Art Gallery. Movie Studio

Publications: Artop

TAIPEI MUNICIPAL UNIVERSITY OF EDUCATION (TMUE)

1, Aiguo West Road, Taipei 10001
Tel: +886(2) 231-13040
Fax: +886(2) 238-14067
Website: http://www.tmue.edu.tw

President (Acting): Kung-chin Lin (2005-)
Tel: +886(2) 231-15585

Administrative Officer: Ming-Yang Hsu

International Relations: Ming-Yang Hsu, Chief Secretary

Departments
Art Education (Art Education); **Early Childhood Education**; **Elementary Education** (Primary Education); **English Instruction**; **Languages and Literature Education** (Literature; Modern Languages); **Mathematics and Computer Science Education** (Mathematics and Computer Science); **Music Education**; **Science Education** (Science Education); **Social Studies Education** (Social Studies); **Special Education** (Special Education)

Graduate Schools
Applied Linguistics and Literature (Linguistics; Literature); **Child Development**; **Creative Thinking and Education of the Gifted** (Education of the Gifted); **Curriculum and Instruction** (Curriculum; Pedagogy); **Elementary Education** (Primary Education); **Environmental Education** (Environmental Studies); **Science Education** (Science Education); **Social Studies** (Social Sciences); **Special Education**; **Visual Arts** (Visual Arts)

History: Founded 1895 as Academy of Language. Acquired present status 2005.

Degrees and Diplomas: *Bachelor's Degree*; *Master's Degree*; *Doctorate*

TAIPEI NATIONAL UNIVERSITY OF THE ARTS (TNUA)

1, Shiueyuan Road, Beitou, Taipei 112
Tel: +886(2) 289-61000
Fax: +886(2) 289-38835
EMail: www@www.tnua.edu.tw
Website: http://www.tnua.edu.tw

President: Tzong-Ching Chiu (2006-)
Tel: +886(2) 289-38704 EMail: president@www.tnua.edu.tw

Administrative Officer: Chung-Shiuan Chang
Tel: +886(2) 289-61000, Ext. 1201

International Relations: Teh-I Chu
Tel: +886(2) 289-61000, Ext. 2601, Fax: +886(2) 289-52913

Centres
Art and Technology (Fine Arts; Technology); **Arts Resources and Educational Outreach**; **Computer** (Computer Science); **Performing Arts** (Performing Arts); **Traditional Arts** (Fine Arts)

Departments
Dance (Dance); **Fine Arts** (Fine Arts); **Music** (Music); **Theatre Arts** (Theatre); **Theatre Design and Technology** (Theatre); **Traditional Music** (Music)

Graduate Institutes
Architecture and Historic Preservation (Architectural Restoration; Architecture); **Art History** (Art History; Fine Arts); **Arts Administration and Management** (Art Management); **Arts and Humanities Education**; **Arts and Technology**; **Dance Choreography** (Dance); **Dance Performance** (Dance); **Dance Theory** (Dance); **Filmmaking** (Cinema and Television; Film); **Fine Arts** (Fine Arts); **Folk Culture and Arts** (Cultural Studies); **Museum Studies** (Museum Studies); **Music** (Music); **Musicology** (Musicology); **Orchestral Instruments** (Musical Instruments); **Plastic Arts** (Sculpture; Visual Arts); **Playwriting**; **Theatre Arts** (Performing Arts; Theatre); **Theatre Design and Technology** (Performing Arts; Theatre); **Theatre Performance** (Performing Arts; Theatre); **Traditional Music**

History: Founded 1982. Acquired present status and title 2004.

Governing Bodies: Executive Council

Academic Year: September to June (September-January; February-June)

Admission Requirements: Graduation from high school and entrance examination

Main Language(s) of Instruction: Chinese

Degrees and Diplomas: *Bachelor's Degree*: Fine Arts, 4 yrs; *Master's Degree*: a further 2-3 yrs; *Doctorate (PhD)*: 4-7 yrs

Student Services: Academic counselling, Canteen, Cultural centre, Employment services, Foreign Studies Centre, Handicapped facilities, Health services, Social counselling, Sports facilities

Student Residential Facilities: For c. 640 students

Libraries: 418,715 vols

Publications: Arts Review *(annually)*

Academic Staff *2008*	MEN	WOMEN	TOTAL
FULL-TIME	75	62	137
PART-TIME	157	111	268
STAFF WITH DOCTORATE			
FULL-TIME	18	24	42
PART-TIME	25	11	36
Student Numbers *2008*			
All (Foreign Included)	786	1,490	2,276
FOREIGN ONLY	1	7	8

Last Updated: 12/12/08

PRIVATE INSTITUTIONS

ALETHEIA UNIVERSITY (AU)

32, Chen-Li Street, Tamsui, Taipei 25103
Tel: +886(2) 262-12121
Fax: +886(2) 262-05236
EMail: cocoliu@email.au.edu.tw
Website: http://www.au.edu.tw

President: Neng-Che Yeh (1971-)
Tel: +886(2) 262-35933, Fax: +886(2) 262-35533
EMail: hchou@email.au.edu.tw

Dean of Studies: Ping-huang Huang
Tel: +886(2) 262-98024, Fax: +886(2) 262-22376
EMail: phhuang@email.au.edu.tw

International Relations: Coco Liu

Colleges

Arts and Humanities (Japanese; Literature; Modern Languages; Music; Religion) *Dean*: Chih-Rong Chen; **Finance and Economics** (Accountancy; Banking; Commercial Law; Economics; Finance; International Business; Taxation) *Dean*: Wen-Ji Lu; **Management** (Business Administration; Industrial Management; Information Management; Management) *Dean*: Chung-Chu Chuang; **Mathematics and Science** (Actuarial Science; Information Sciences; Mathematics; Statistics) *Dean*: Chung-Hsin Wang; **Tourism** (Air Transport; Leisure Studies; Parks and Recreation; Sports Management; Tourism) *Dean*: Chih-Yi Shih

Schools

Graduate *Dean*: Chung-Hsin Wang

History: Founded 1882 as Oxford College. Became Tamsui Oxford College 1965, and Tamsui Oxford University College 1994. Acquired present title and status 1999.

Admission Requirements: Graduation from high school and entrance examination

Fees: (New Taiwan Dollars): Tuition, 90,000-100,000 per annum

Main Language(s) of Instruction: Mandarin Chinese. English in some courses.

International Co-operation: With universities in USA, United Kingdom and Japan

Accrediting Agencies: Ministry of Education

Degrees and Diplomas: *Bachelor's Degree*: Arts; Humanities; Finance; Economics; Tourism; Business Administration; Management; Mathematics and Computer Science, 4 yrs; *Master's Degree*: Religion; Finance; Economics; Business Administration, a further 2-3 yrs

Student Services: Academic counselling, Canteen, Employment services, Foreign student adviser, Foreign Studies Centre, Handicapped facilities, Health services, Language programs, Nursery care, Social counselling, Sports facilities

Student Residential Facilities: For 1300 Students

Special Facilities: Tamsui Oxford Museum

Libraries: Main Library

Press or Publishing House: Aletheia University Press

ASIA UNIVERSITY (AU)

500, Lioufeng Road, Wufeng Shiang, Taichung 413
Tel: +886(4) 233-23456, Ext. 1012
Fax: +886(4) 233-16699
EMail: renee1218@thmu.edu.tw
Website: http://www.asia.edu.tw

President: Horng-jinh Chang
Tel: +886(4) 233-23456, Ext. 1007 EMail: chj@asia.edu.tw

Chief Secretary: Chao-Long Ni
Tel: +886(4) 233-23456, Ext. 1010
EMail: chiefsecretary@thmu.edu.tw

International Relations: Wang-Tran Huang
Tel: +886(4) 233-123456, Ext. 1904 EMail: wthuang@thmu.edu.tw

Departments

Accountancy and Information (Accountancy; Information Sciences); **Applied Foreign Languages** (Modern Languages); **Applied Life Science** (Biological and Life Sciences); **Bioinformatics**; **Biological Science and Technology**; **Business Administration** (Business Administration); **Computer and Communication** (Computer Science; Mass Communication); **Early Childhood Education** (Preschool Education); **Finance**; **Financial Economic Law** (Economic and Finance Policy); **Health Care Administration** (Health Administration; Public Health; Social and Community Services); **Hospital Administration** (Administration; Health Administration); **Information and Communication**; **Information and Design** (Design; Information Sciences); **Information Engineering** (Information Sciences; Information Technology); **Information Sciences and Application** (Information Sciences); **International Business** (International Business); **Leisure and Recreation Management**; **Long-Term Care** (Health Sciences; Social and Community Services); **Multimedia Game Design** (Computer Graphics; Design; Multimedia); **Psychology** (Psychology); **Social Work**

History: Founded 2001 as Taichung Healthcare and Management University. Renamed Asia University 2005.

Degrees and Diplomas: *Bachelor's Degree*: Information and Communication; International Business; Leisure and Recreation Management; Accountancy and Information; Finance; Financial Economic Law; Applied Foreign Languages; Social Work; Hospital Administration; Applied Life Science; Psychology; Early Childhood Education; Information Engineering; Infirmation Sciences and Application; Computer and Communication; Biological Science and Technology; Information and Design; *Master's Degree*: Health Care Administration; Long-Term Care; Social Work; Information Engineering; Information Sciences and Application; Computer and Communication; Bioinformatics; Biological Science and Technology; Multimedia Game Design; Business Administration; International Business; Leisure and Recreation Management

Last Updated: 25/07/08

CENTRAL TAIWAN UNIVERSITY OF SCIENCE AND TECHNOLOGY (CTUST)

No.11, Buzih Lane, Beitun District, Taichung 40601
Tel: +886(4) 223-91647 Ext. 2002
Fax: +886(4) 223-93305
EMail: adsec01@ctust.edu.tw
Website: http://www.ctust.edu.tw

President: Fu-Du Chen (2004-)

Secretary-General: An-Ho Hsu Tel: +886(4) 223-96372

International Relations: Shong-Shei Lin
Tel: +886(4) 223-94072 EMail: adcar01@chtai.ctc.edu.tw

Departments

Applied Foreign Languages; **Dental Technology**; **Early Childhood Caring and Education**; **Food Science**; **Health and Safety and Environmental Engineering** (Environmental Engineering; Health Sciences; Safety Engineering); **Health Care Administration**; **International Business** (International Business); **Management Information Systems**; **Marketing Management** (Management; Marketing); **Medical Technology** (Medical Technology); **Nursing**; **Radiological Technology**

Institutes

Biomedical Engineering and Materials Science; **Health Care Management**; **Medical Biotechnology**; **Nursing**; **Radiological Science**

History: Founded 1996, acquired present name 1998.

Degrees and Diplomas: *Bachelor's Degree*: 4 years. Also 5 year diploma offered.

CHANG GUNG UNIVERSITY (CGU)

259, Wen Hwa 1st Road, Kwei-Shan, Taoyuan 33333
Tel: +886(3) 211-8800
Fax: +886(3) 211-8700
EMail: box@mail.cgu.edu.tw
Website: http://www.cgu.edu.tw

President: Nan-Hung Kuo
Tel: +886(3) 211-8800, Ext. 5011, Fax: +886(3) 211-8900
EMail: president@mail.cgu.edu.tw

Secretary-General: Yih-Her Chen
Tel: +886(3) 211-8800, Ext. 5012 EMail: yoga@mail.cgu.edu.tw

International Relations: Eri-Huei Lu
Tel: +886(3) 211-8800, Ext. 5631 EMail: lueh@mail.cgu.edu.tw

Colleges

Engineering (Chemical Engineering; Electrical and Electronic Engineering; Electronic Engineering; Materials Engineering; Mechanical Engineering); **Management** (Business Administration; Health Administration; Industrial Design; Information Management; Management); **Medicine** (Medical Technology; Medicine; Nursing; Occupational Therapy; Physical Therapy; Respiratory Therapy; Traditional Eastern Medicine)

Schools

Medicine (Medicine); **Traditional Chinese Medicine** (Traditional Eastern Medicine)

Further Information: Also Graduate institutions, Teaching Hospital; Chang Gung Memorial Hospital

History: Founded 1987, acquired present status and title 1997. A private institution under the jurisidiction of the Ministry of Education.

Governing Bodies: Board of Directors

Academic Year: September to June (September-January; February-June)

Admission Requirements: Graduation from high school or recognized equivalent, and entrance examination

Main Language(s) of Instruction: Chinese

Degrees and Diplomas: *Bachelor's Degree*: 4-7 yrs; *Master's Degree*: a further 2 yrs following Bachelor's

Student Residential Facilities: Yes

Libraries: c. 14,000 vols

CHANG JUNG CHRISTIAN UNIVERSITY (CJCU)

396, Section 1, Chang Jung Road, Kawy Jen, Tainan 711
Tel: +886(6) 278-5123
Fax: +886(6) 278-5111
EMail: cweny@mail.cjcu.edu.tw
Website: http://www.cjcu.edu.tw

President: Chin-Seng Chen
Tel: +886(6) 278-5123, Ext. 1011, Fax: +886(6) 278-5787
EMail: cschen@mail.cjcu.edu.tw

Dean of Academic Affairs: Hsing-Chau Tseng
Tel: +886(6) 287-5123, Ext. 1100, Fax: +886(6) 287-5773
EMail: keki@mail.cju.edu.tw

International Relations: Yi-Sen Lin
Tel: +886(6) 278-5123, Ext. 1600, Fax: +886(6) 278-5878

Colleges

Humanities and Social Science (Information Technology; Mass Communication; Media Studies; Modern Languages; Social Work; Translation and Interpretation); **Management** (Accountancy; Business Administration; Finance; Information Management; International Business; Transport Management); **Public Health** (Health Administration; Nursing; Occupational Health; Public Health)

Graduate Schools

Applied Languages for Interpretation and Translation (Modern Languages; Translation and Interpretation); **Business and Operations Management** (Business Administration; Management); **Business Management**; **Health Care Administration** (Health Administration); **Information Management**; **Japan Studies**; **Land Management and Development**; **Medicine**; **Occupational Safety and Hygiene** (Occupational Health); **Visual Arts**

History: Founded 1885 as Middle School by the English Presbyterian Missionaries, acquired present status and title 1993.

Governing Bodies: Board of Trustees

Academic Year: September to June (September-January; February-June)

Admission Requirements: Graduation from high school and entrance examination

Main Language(s) of Instruction: Mandarin Chinese, Taiwanese

Degrees and Diplomas: *Bachelor's Degree*: Business Administration; Science, 4 yrs

Special Facilities: Horticultural Garden

Publications: Chang Jung Hsue Yuan *(quarterly)*
Last Updated: 22/07/08

CHAOYANG UNIVERSITY OF TECHNOLOGY (CYUT)

168, Jifong East Road, Wufeng, Taichung 41349
Tel: +886(4) 233-23000
Fax: +886(4) 233-29898
EMail: secret@mail.cyut.edu.tw
Website: http://www.cyut.edu.tw

President: Chun-Chung Yang (2002-)
Tel: +886(4) 233-20888, Fax: +886(4) 237-42311
EMail: pres@cyut.edu.tw

Dean, Office of R&D: Ching-Fang LiawFax: +886(4) 237-42317
EMail: cfliaw@cyut.edu.tw

International Relations: Shiaofang Sung
Tel: +886(4) 233-23000, Ext. 3121, Fax: +886(4) 237-42317
EMail: sfsung@mail.cyut.edu.tw

Centres
General Education

Colleges

Design (Architecture; Communication Arts; Design; Industrial Design; Landscape Architecture; Town Planning; Visual Arts); **Humanities and Social Sciences** (Child Care and Development; Communication Arts; Modern Languages; Preschool Education; Social Work; Teacher Training); **Management** (Accountancy; Business Administration; Finance; Information Management; Insurance; Leisure Studies; Management; Parks and Recreation; Tourism); **Science and Engineering** (Applied Chemistry; Biotechnology; Computer Networks; Construction Engineering; Engineering; Environmental Engineering; Environmental Management; Industrial Engineering; Industrial Management; Information Technology; Natural Sciences; Telecommunications Engineering)

Graduate Institutes

Accountancy (Accountancy); **Applied Chemistry** (Applied Chemistry); **Applied Foreign Languages** (Modern Languages); **Architecture and Urban Design** (Architecture; Landscape Architecture; Town Planning; Urban Studies); **Biotechnology** (Biotechnology); **Business Administration** (Business Administration); **Computer Science and Information Engineering** (Computer Science; Information Technology); **Construction Engineering** (Construction Engineering); **Design** (Design; Industrial Design; Visual Arts); **Doctoral Programme** (Architecture); **Early Childhood Development and Education** (Preschool Education); **Environmental Engineering and Management** (Environmental Engineering; Environmental Management); **Finance** (Finance); **Industrial Engineering and Management** (Industrial Engineering; Industrial Management); **Information Management** (Information Management); **Insurance** (Insurance; Management); **Leisure, Recreation and Tourism** (Leisure Studies; Tourism); **Networking and Communication Engineering** (Computer Networks; Telecommunications Engineering)

History: Founded 1994. Acquired present status and title 1997.

Academic Year: August to July

Admission Requirements: Graduation from high school and entrance examination

Fees: (US Dollars): Tuition, c. 1,600 per semester

Main Language(s) of Instruction: Chinese (Mandarin)

International Co-operation: Sister School agreements with 29 Schools and Universities in USA, Australia, Japan, Malaysia, Mongolia, Germany, United Kingdom and China

Accrediting Agencies: Ministry of Education

Degrees and Diplomas: *Bachelor's Degree*: 2-4 yrs; *Master's Degree*: a further 2 yrs; *Doctorate*: 2-7 yrs

Student Services: Academic counselling, Canteen, Employment services, Foreign student adviser, Handicapped facilities, Health services, Language programs, Nursery care, Sports facilities

Student Residential Facilities: Yes

Special Facilities: Art Gallery. Movie Studio

Libraries: Multimedia equipment

Publications: Chaoyang Business and Management Review *(biannually)*; Chaoyang Journal of Design *(annually)*; Chaoyang Journal of Humanities and Social Sciences *(biannually)*; International Journal of Applied Science and Engineering *(biannually)*; The Journal of Chaoyang University of Technology *(annually)*

CHENG SHIU UNIVERSITY (CSU)

840, Cheng-Ching Road, Song Shiang, Kaohsiung 833
Tel: +886(7) 731-0606
Fax: +886(7) 731-5367
EMail: present@csu.edu.tw
Website: http://www.csu.edu.tw

President: Jui-Chang Kung
Tel: +886(7) 732-1156, Fax: +886(7) 732-6554

Secretary: Wilson Lee
Tel: +886(7) 731-3945, Fax: +886(7) 733-8946

International Relations: Shuenn-Ren Cheng
Fax: +886(7) 731-5193

Departments
Architecture (Architecture); **Business Management** (Business Administration; Management); **Chemical Engineering** (Chemical Engineering); **Civil Engineering** (Civil Engineering); **Early Childhood Care and Education** (Child Care and Development; Preschool Education; Primary Education); **Electrical Engineering** (Electrical Engineering); **Electronic Engineering** (Electronic Engineering); **Industrial Engineering and Management** (Industrial Engineering; Industrial Management); **Information Management** (Information Management); **International Trade** (International Business); **Mechanical Engineering** (Mechanical Engineering)

History: Founded 1965. Renamed Cheng Shiu Institute of Technology. Acquired present status and title 1999.

CHIA NAN UNIVERSITY OF PHARMACY AND SCIENCE

60, Erh-Jen Road, Section 1, Jen-Te, Tainan 71710
Tel: +886(6) 266-8263
Fax: +886(6) 266-7306
EMail: box195@chna.edu.tw
Website: http://www.chna.edu.tw

President: Chao-Hsiung Wang
Tel: +886(6) 266-2774 EMail: box101@mail.chna.edu.tw

Vice-President: Zong-Shiow Chen
Tel: +886(6) 266-5674, Fax: +886(6) 266-0462
EMail: azschen@mail.chna.edu.tw

International Relations: Jing-Song Chang
Tel: +886(6) 266-4911, Ext. 191, Fax: +886(6) 266-7306
EMail: box190@mail.chna.tw

Centres
General Education; **Teacher Education**

Colleges
Environment; **Human Ecology**; **Pharmacy and Science** (Applied Chemistry; Biotechnology; Food Science; Food Technology; Pharmacy); **Social Sciences and Management** (Cultural Studies; Health Administration; Health Sciences; Information Management; Information Sciences; Modern Languages; Public Health; Social Work; Tourism)

Institutes
Cosmetics (Cosmetology); **Health Information and Management**

Research Centres
Culture and Arts (Arts and Humanities); **Ecological Engineering and Technology**

History: Founded 1966, acquired present status 2000.

CHIEN KUO TECHNOLOGY UNIVERSITY (CTU)

1, Chieh-Shou N. Road, Changhua 500
Tel: +886(4) 722-4676
Fax: +886(4) 725-2774
Website: http://www.ctu.edu.tw

President: Yen Fei Hwang
Tel: +886(4) 717-1166, Fax: +886(4) 711-1172
EMail: yenfei@ctu.edu.tw

Secretary-General: Jeff Lin
Tel: +886(4) 722-4676 Ext. 1213, Fax: +886(4) 711-1171
EMail: jefflin@ctu.edu.tw

International Relations: Yi-Juen Chen, Director
Fax: +886(4) 711-6382 EMail: irischen@ctu.edu.tw

Departments
Applied Foreign Languages Head: Feng-Heng Wei; **Automation Engineering** Head: Jar-Min Laun; **Civil Engineering** Head: Ching-Her Hwang; **Commercial Design** (Design; Fine Arts) Head: Chun-Hung Lin; **Computer and Communication Engineering** Head:

Tai-Ping Hsiung; **Electrical Engineering** Head: Jenn-Gwo Huang; **Electronic Engineering** Head: Chao-Hsing Hsu; **Industrial Engineering and Management** Head: Wen-Feng Tsai; **Information Management** Head: Min-Hsin Chen; **International Business Administration** (Business Administration) Head: Lung-Hsien Chang; **Mechanical Engineering** Head: Hsin-An Hong; **Space Design**

History: Founded 1965, acquired present title 2004.

Academic Year: August to July

Admission Requirements: senior high school certificate with at least 12 years of school education

Fees: (US Dollars): c. 1,560 per semester

Main Language(s) of Instruction: Mandarin

International Co-operation: With universities in Japan, Republic of Korea, USA, United Kingdom, Russian Federation

Accrediting Agencies: Ministry of Education

Degrees and Diplomas: Bachelor's Degree: 4 yrs; Master's Degree: a further 2 yrs

Student Services: Academic counselling, Canteen, Cultural centre, Employment services, Foreign student adviser, Foreign Studies Centre, Handicapped facilities, Health services, Language programs, Nursery care, Social counselling, Sports facilities

Student Residential Facilities: Yes.

Special Facilities: Museum. Art Gallery

Libraries: e-books, video-audio collections, electronic resources

Publications: Chienkuo Monthly, For faculty and students (monthly); Journal of Chienkuo Technology University, Academic journal (quarterly)

Press or Publishing House: Publishing Section, Office of Academic Affairs

CHIHLEE INSTITUTE OF TECHNOLOGY (CIOT)

313, Section 1, Wen-Hua Road, Panchiao, Taipei 220
Tel: +886(2) 225-76167
Fax: +886(2) 225-72764
EMail: l100@chihlee.edu.tw
Website: http://portal.chihlee.edu.tw/front/bin/home.phtml

President: Chi-Tong Yang
Tel: +886(2) 225-83710, Fax: +886(2) 225-83710
EMail: a100@mail.chihlee.edu.tw

Administrative Officer: Chuang-I Juan Lu
Tel: +886(2) 225-89016, Fax: +886(2) 225-88928
EMail: b100@mail.chihlee.edu.tw

International Relations: Shieh-Shun Fu
Tel: +886(2) 225-76167, Fax: +886(2) 225-72764
EMail: ssfu@mail.chihlee.edu.tw

Departments
Accounting Information Systems (Accountancy; Information Technology); **Applied English** (English); **Applied Japanese** (Japanese); **Business Administration and Management** (Business Administration; Management); **Commerce Automation and Management** (Business and Commerce; Information Technology); **Finance** (Finance); **Information Management** (Information Management); **Information Networks Technology** (Information Technology); **Insurance and Finance Management** (Finance; Insurance); **International Trade** (International Business); **Marketing and Logistics Management** (Marketing; Transport Management); **Multimedia Design** (Multimedia)

Further Information: Traditional and Open Learning Institution

History: Founded 1964. Acquired present status 2002.

Degrees and Diplomas: Bachelor's Degree: 4 yrs
Last Updated: 08/07/08

CHINA MEDICAL UNIVERSITY (CMU)

91, Shiuesh Road, Taichung 404
Tel: +886(4) 220-53366
Fax: +886(4) 220-57895
EMail: cc@mail.cmu.edu.tw
Website: http://www.cmu.edu.tw

President: Tsu-Fuh Yeh (2002-)
Tel: +886(4) 220-57153, Fax: +886(4) 220-60248

Secretary-General: Walter Chen

International Relations: Chao-Tien Hsu
Tel: +886(4) 220-63426, Fax: +886(4) 220-30133

Colleges
Biological Science and Technology; **Chinese Medicine**; **Chinese Medicine** *(Post-Baccalaureate)* (Traditional Eastern Medicine); **Cosmetics**; **Dentistry** (Dentistry); **Health Services Management**; **Medical Technology** (Medical Technology); **Medicinal Resources**; **Medicine** (Medicine); **Nursing** (Nursing); **Nutrition** (Nutrition); **Occupational Safety and Health**; **Pharmacy** (Pharmacy); **Public Health** (Public Health); **Rehabilitation** (Rehabilitation and Therapy); **Risk Management**; **Sports Medicine**

Institutes
Chinese Medicine; **Chinese Pharmaceutical Science**; **Environmental Medicine**; **Health Sciences Management**; **Integration of Chinese and Western Medicine**; **Medical Science**; **Nursing**; **Nutrition**; **Pharmaceutical Chemistry**

Further Information: Also Campus at Peikang Town. Two Teaching Hospitals

History: Founded 1958 as China Medical College. Acquired present title 2003. A private institution under the jurisdiction of the Ministry of Education.

Academic Year: August to June (August-January; February-June)

Admission Requirements: Graduation from high school or recognized equivalent, and entrance examination

Main Language(s) of Instruction: Chinese

Degrees and Diplomas: *Bachelor's Degree*; *Master's Degree*; *Doctorate*

Student Residential Facilities: Yes

Special Facilities: Chinese Herbal Museum

Libraries: Chinese Medicine Library, c. 67,080 vols

Publications: Chinese Medicine and Pharmacy Magazine

CHINA UNIVERSITY OF TECHNOLOGY (CUTE)

56, Section 3, Hsing Lung Road, Taipei 116
Tel: +886(2) 293-13416
Fax: +886(2) 293-13992
Website: http://www.cute.edu.tw/eng/

President: Wen-Shen Chou
Tel: +886(2) 293-26560, Fax: +886(2) 893-18847
EMail: secr@mail.ckitc.edu.tw

Dean of Academic Affairs: Ming-Te Liu
Tel: +886(2) 293-03362, Fax: +886(2) 293-12485
EMail: acad@mail.ckitc.edu.tw

International Relations: Hsueh-Cherng Chang
Tel: +886(2) 293-42980, Fax: +886(2) 293-52077
EMail: carr@mail.ckitc.edu.tw

Departments
Accountancy; **Architectural Engineering**; **Business Administration** (Business Administration; Finance; Marketing); **Civil Engineering** (Civil Engineering); **Finance** (Finance); **International Trade** (International Business; International Relations); **Management Information Systems** (Information Management; Management Systems); **Public Finance**

Graduate Schools
Commerce Automation and Management

History: Founded 1965, acquired present status and title 2005.

Degrees and Diplomas: *Master's Degree*: Business Administration

CHINESE CULTURE UNIVERSITY (CCU)

55, Hwa Kang Road, Yang Ming Shan, Taipei 111
Tel: +886(2) 286-10511
Fax: +886(2) 286-15031
Website: http://www.pccu.edu.tw

President: Tien-Rein Lee (1993-)
Tel: +886(2) 286-10511, Ext. 10105, Fax: +886(2) 286-16632
EMail: president@staff.pccu.edu.tw

Provost, Office of Academic Affairs: Tung-Yung Lin
Tel: +886(2) 286-10511, Ext. 11001, Fax: +886(2) 286-11147
EMail: tylin@faculty.pccu.edu.tw

International Relations: Jeffrey Bor Yunchang
Tel: +886(2) 286-10511, Ext. 29325
EMail: byc2@staff.pccu.edu.tw

Colleges
Agriculture (Food Science; Forestry; Horticulture; Natural Resources; Nutrition; Zoology) *Dean*: Carson Kung-Hsien Wu; **Arts** (Dance; Fine Arts; Music; Theatre) *Dean*: Lan-Ku Chen; **Business Administration** (Accountancy; Banking; Business Administration; Finance; Information Management; International Business; Tourism) *Dean*: Tsai-Mei Lin; **Education** (Education; Physical Education; Psychology; Sports) *Dean*: Oscar Jiaw Ouyang; **Engineering** (Chemical Engineering; Computer Science; Electrical Engineering; Mechanical Engineering; Textile Technology) *Dean*: Yih-Young Chen; **Environmental Design** (Architectural and Environmental Design; Environmental Management; Landscape Architecture; Town Planning) *Dean*: Ching-Tzu Chen; **Foreign Languages** (English; French; German; Japanese; Korean; Russian) *Dean*: Chung-kun Yao; **Journalism and Communication** (Advertising and Publicity; Communication Studies; Journalism; Mass Communication) *Dean*: Huei-Sheng Shen; **Law** (Law) *Dean*: Sea-Wain Yau; **Liberal Arts** (History; Literature; Philosophy) *Director*: Chi-lin Wang; **Science** *Dean*: Koung-Ying Liu; **Social Sciences** (Administration; Economics; Human Resources; Political Sciences; Social Welfare) *Dean*: Joseph P.L. Jiang

Schools
Continuing Education

Further Information: Also Extension Education Centre

History: Founded 1962 as a private College, became University 1980.

Governing Bodies: Board of Regents

Academic Year: September to June (September-January; February-June)

Admission Requirements: Graduation from high school or foreign equivalent, and entrance examination

Fees: (New Taiwan Dollars): 40,000 per semester

Main Language(s) of Instruction: Chinese

Degrees and Diplomas: *Bachelor's Degree*: 4 yrs; *Master's Degree*: a further 1-4 yrs; *Doctorate*: a further 2-7 yrs

Student Services: Academic counselling, Foreign student adviser, Foreign Studies Centre, Health services, Social counselling

Student Residential Facilities: For 1598 men and 2253 women students

Special Facilities: Hwa Kang Museum

Libraries: Total, 1,125,452 vols

Publications: Hwa Kang Journal (in Chinese) *(annually)*; Hwa Kang Journal of English Languages and Literature *(annually)*; Hwa Kang Journal of Foreign Languages and Literature (in English) *(annually)*; Hwa Kang Journal of TEFL *(annually)*; Sino-American Relations (in English) *(biannually)*

Press or Publishing House: Chinese Culture University Press

Academic Staff 2008	MEN	WOMEN	TOTAL
FULL-TIME	496	228	**724**
PART-TIME	515	321	**836**
STAFF WITH DOCTORATE			
FULL-TIME	343	156	**499**
PART-TIME	170	54	**224**
Student Numbers 2008			
All (Foreign Included)	–	–	**23,102**
FOREIGN ONLY	–	–	**135**

Last Updated: 11/12/08

CHING-YUN UNIVERSITY (CYU)

229, Chien-Hsin Road, Jungli 320
Tel: +886(3) 458-1196
Fax: +886(3) 459-5684
Website: http://www.cyu.edu.tw

President: Chieh-Hou Yang
Tel: +886(3) 458-1196, Ext. 2200, Fax: +886(3) 457-2400
EMail: president@cyu.edu.tw

Vice-President: Jong-Lan Lin
Tel: +886(3) 458-1196, Ext. 3300, Fax: +886(3) 459-5684

International Relations: Lisa Pan
Tel: +886(3) 458-1196, Ext. 3120

Colleges
Commerce (Banking; Business Administration; Finance; Modern Languages); **Electronic Engineering and Computer Science** (Computer Science; Electrical Engineering; Electronic Engineering; Information Sciences); **Engineering** (Civil Engineering; Mechanical Engineering); **Management** (Industrial Engineering; Industrial Management; Information Management)

Institutes
Central Asian Studies (Asian Studies); **Civil Engineering and Disaster Protection** (Civil Engineering; Safety Engineering); **Electrical Engineering** (Electrical Engineering); **Electronic Engineering** (Electronic Engineering); **International Business Management** (Business Administration; International Business); **Management** (Management); **Mechanical Engineering**

Research Centres
Digital Earth and Disaster Reduction; E-GPS; Euro-Asian; Green Energy; Logistic Management

History: Founded 1996, renamed Ching-Yun Institute of Technology. Acquired present status and title 2003.

Degrees and Diplomas: *Bachelor's Degree*: 2-4 yrs; *Master's Degree*: 1-4 yrs (24 credits). Also Language Specialised Programmes and Professional-Technical Programmes

CHUNG-HUA UNIVERSITY

707, Section 2, WuFu Road, Hsinchu 300
Tel: +886(3) 537-4281
Fax: +886(3) 537-3771
EMail: chnews@chu.edu.tw
Website: http://www.chu.edu.tw

President: Yi-Yu Kuo Tel: +886(3) 518-6115

Secretary-General: Yao-Hsien Lee
Tel: +886(3) 518-6542 EMail: d9003009@chu.edu.tw

International Relations: Hsi-Hsin Chien
Tel: +886(3) 518-6496, Fax: +886(3) 518-6507
EMail: hhchien@chu.edu.tw

Colleges
Architecture and Planning (Architecture); **Engineering** (Aeronautical and Aerospace Engineering; Applied Mathematics; Civil Engineering; Computer Science; Electrical Engineering; Information Technology; Mechanical Engineering); **Humanities and Social Sciences; Management** (Business Administration; Finance; Industrial Engineering; Industrial Management; Information Management; International Business; Management; Transport Management)

Research Centres
Water Ecology Environment

History: Founded 1990, acquired present status and title 1997.

CHUNG SHAN MEDICAL UNIVERSITY (CSMU)

110, Section 1, Chien-Kuo N. Road, Taichung 402
Tel: +886(4) 247-30022
Fax: +886(4) 247-39030
EMail: cs11203a@csmu.edu.tw
Website: http://www.csmu.edu.tw

President: Chung-Sheng Lin (1998-)
Tel: +886(4) 247-59882, Fax: +886(4) 247-59950
EMail: lcs@csmu.edu.tw

Dean of Academic Affairs: Wen-Kang Chen
Tel: +886(4) 247-54392, Fax: +886(4) 247-55372
EMail: cwk@csmu.edu.tw

International Relations: Jeng-Dong Hsu
Tel: +886(4) 247-09318 EMail: dongdong@csmu.edu.tw

Colleges
Health Care and Management; Medical Sciences and Technology; Medicine; Oral Medicine

Institutes
Biochemistry (Biochemistry) *Director*: Chau-Jong Wang; **Dental Materials** (Dental Technology) *Director*: Chii-Chih Hsu; **Immunology** *Director*: Gregory J. Tsai; **Medicine** (Medicine) *Director*: Ruey-Hseng Lin; **Nursing; Nutrition** (Nutrition) *Director*: Chong-Kuei Lii; **Stomatology** (Stomatology) *Director*: Chia-Tze Kao; **Toxicology** (Toxicology) *Director*: Huei Lee

Schools
Applied Chemistry; Clinical Psychology; Dentistry (Dentistry) *Director*: Pao-Hsin Liao; **Diet and Restaurant Management; Health Services Administration** (Health Administration) *Director*: Jar-Yuan Pai; **Laboratory Technology; Life Sciences** *Director*: Ming-Li Hsieh; **Medical Imaging Technology** (Medical Technology; Radiology) *Director*: Kang-Jen Tsai; **Medical Technology; Medicine** (Medicine) *Director*: Ming-Jen Chou; **Nursing** (Nursing) *Director*: Sheuan Lee; **Nutrition** (Nutrition) *Director*: Cheng-Chin Hsu; **Occupational Therapy** (Occupational Therapy) *Director*: Leiu-Ing Bih; **Optometry** (Optometry) *Director*: Keh-Liang Lin; **Physical Therapy** (Physical Therapy) *Director*: Ping-Yen Chiang; **Public Health** (Public Health) *Director*: Tsung-Hsieh Lu; **Speech Language Pathology and Audiology** (Speech Therapy and Audiology) *Director*: Nan-Mai Wang

Further Information: Also Chung Shan Medical University Hospital; Rehabilitation Hospital; Chung Shan Affiliated Clinic, Miao-Li

History: Founded 1960. Acquired present status and title 2001. A private institution under the jurisdiction of the Ministry of Education.

Academic Year: September to June (September-January; February-June)

Admission Requirements: Graduation from high school and entrance examination

Fees: (New Taiwan Dollars): 47,590-60,600 per semester

Main Language(s) of Instruction: Chinese

Degrees and Diplomas: *Bachelor's Degree*: 4 yrs; *Doctorate*: Dental Surgery, 6 yrs; *Doctorate*: Medicine, 7 yrs

Student Services: Academic counselling, Handicapped facilities, Health services, Sports facilities

Libraries: Total, 103,424 vols

Publications: Journal; The Chung Shan Medical Journal

CHUNG YUAN CHRISTIAN UNIVERSITY (CYCU)

22, Pu-Jen, Pu-Chung Li, Jungli, Taoyuan County 320
Tel: +886(3) 265-2010 Ext. 2010
Fax: +886(3) 265-2019
EMail: postmaster@cycu.edu.tw
Website: http://www.cycu.edu.tw

President: Stephen Shen-Kan Hsiung
Tel: +886(3) 265-1000, Fax: +886(3) 265-1099

Secretary-General: Ming Chang
Tel: +886(3) 265-1200, Fax: +886(3) 265-1299
EMail: ming@cycu.edu.tw

International Relations: Chun-Tsung Chin
Tel: +886(3) 265-2530, Fax: +886(3) 265-2535
EMail: chuntsun@cycu.edu.tw

Colleges
Business (Accountancy; Business Administration); **Design** (Design); **Engineering** (Architecture; Engineering); **Humanities and Education** (Arts and Humanities; Education; Social Sciences); **Science** (Mathematics and Computer Science; Natural Sciences; Psychology)

History: Founded 1955 as a private Christian College of Science and Engineering recognized by the Ministry of Education. Acquired present status and title 1980.

Governing Bodies: Board of Trustees

Academic Year: August to July (August-January; February-July)

Admission Requirements: Graduation from high school and entrance examination

Main Language(s) of Instruction: Chinese

Degrees and Diplomas: *Bachelor's Degree*: Architecture, 5 yrs; *Bachelor's Degree*: Business Administration; Science, 4 yrs; *Master's Degree*: a further 2 yrs; *Doctorate (PhD)*: 2-6 yrs

Student Residential Facilities: Yes

Libraries: Central Library, c. 161,000 vols

Publications: Chung Yuan Journal

DA-YEH UNIVERSITY

112, Shan-Jiao Road, Datsuen, Changhua 515
Tel: +886(4) 851-1888
Fax: +886(4) 851-1666
EMail: web@mail.dyu.edu.tw
Website: http://www.dyu.edu.tw

President: Ming-Hsiung Hon
Tel: +886(4) 851-1888, Ext. 1000, Fax: +886(4) 851-1002
EMail: mhhon@mail.dyu.edu.tw

Secretary-General: Tsai-Hsi Wu
Tel: +886(4) 851-1888, Ext. 1005, Fax: +886(4) 851-1002
EMail: taiwu@mail.dyu.edu.tw

Centres
Liberal Arts; **Teacher Education**

Colleges
Biotechnology and Bioresources; **Design and Arts** (Design; Fine Arts; Graphic Arts; Graphic Design; Industrial Design; Visual Arts); **Engineering** (Automotive Engineering; Computer Science; Electrical Engineering; Engineering; Environmental Engineering; Industrial Engineering; Information Technology; Mechanical Engineering; Technology); **Management**; **Modern Languages** (English; European Languages; Japanese; Modern Languages)

Graduate Institutes
Applied Linguistics (Linguistics); **Communication**; **Design** (Design); **Management** (Management); **Mechatronics and Automation Engineering** (Automation and Control Engineering; Electronic Engineering; Mechanical Engineering); **Professional Development in Education** (Education); **Vehicle Engineering** (Automotive Engineering)

Programmes
Honor

Schools
Design; **Engineering** (Engineering); **Foreign Language**; **Management**

History: Founded 1990, acquired present status and title 1997.

Governing Bodies: Board of Trustees

Academic Year: September to June (September-January; February-June)

Admission Requirements: Graduation from high school and/or College entrance examination

Fees: (New Taiwan Dollars): Tuition, c. 41,250-47,500

Main Language(s) of Instruction: Chinese, English

Accrediting Agencies: Ministry of Education

Degrees and Diplomas: *Bachelor's Degree*: 4 yrs; *Master's Degree*: a further 2 yrs. Also College Degree Certificate, 2 yrs

Student Services: Academic counselling, Canteen, Employment services, Health services, Language programs, Nursery care, Sports facilities

Student Residential Facilities: Yes

Special Facilities: Movie Studio

Libraries: c. 154,900 vols; c. 28,800 video tapes; c. 1,400 journals; c. 25 newspapers

Publications: Da-Yeh Communication *(biannually)*; Journal of Da-Yeh University *(biannually)*

Press or Publishing House: Da-Yeh University Press

FAR EAST UNIVERSITY (FEU)

49, Chung Hua Road, Hsin-Shih Town, Tainan Prefecture, Tainan 744
Tel: +886(6) 597-7001
Fax: +886(6) 597-7050
Website: http://www.feu.edu.tw/feu-english/all.htm

President: Nai-Chang Wang
Tel: +886(6) 597-7057, Fax: +886(6) 598-2080

Dean of Academic Affairs: Yen-Zen Wang
Tel: +886(6) 597-7008, Fax: +886(6) 5977010

International Relations: Wang Yen

Departments
Applied English (English); **Business Administration** (Business Administration); **Chemical Engineering** (Chemical Engineering); **Computer Application Engineering** (Computer Engineering); **Computer Science and Engineering** (Computer Engineering; Computer Science); **Control Engineering** (Automation and Control Engineering); **Electrical Engineering** (Electrical Engineering); **Electronic Materials** (Electronic Engineering); **Food And Beverage Management** (Food Science); **Industrial Engineering and Management** (Industrial Engineering; Industrial Management); **Industrial Management** (Industrial Management); **Management Information Systems** (Management Systems); **Mechanical Engineering** (Mechanical Engineering)

History: Founded 1968 as Far East Junior College of Technology. Acquired present status and title 2006.

Degrees and Diplomas: *Bachelor's Degree*; *Master's Degree*
Last Updated: 08/07/08

FENG CHIA UNIVERSITY (FCU)

100, Wen-Hwa Road, Taichung 407
Tel: +886(4) 245-17250, Ext. 2075
Fax: +886(4) 245-10129
EMail: webadmin@fcu.edu.tw
Website: http://www.fcu.edu.tw

President: An-Chi Liu (1998-)
Tel: +886(4) 245-17250, Ext. 2010, Fax: +886(2) 245-14907

Secretary-General: Hai-Ping Hsieh
Tel: +886(4) 245-17250, Ext. 2020, Fax: +886(4) 245-14907
EMail: adm-pr@fcu.edu.tw

International Relations: Shaw-Jyh Shin
Tel: +886(4) 245-17250, Ext. 2070 EMail: sjshin@fcu.edu.tw

Centres
Art (Arts and Humanities); **Chinese** *Director*: Kris Vicca; **General Education** *Director*: Chieh-Ying Chen; **Humanities and Social Studies** (Social Studies); **Leadership Development**; **Teacher Education** *Director*: Shuu-Jane Yang

Colleges
Business (Accountancy; Administration; Business and Commerce; Economics; Finance; Insurance; International Business; Statistics; Taxation) *Dean*: Pao-Long Chang; **Construction and Development** *Dean*: Bing-Jean Lee; **Continuing Education** *Dean*: Yau-Ren Shiau; **Engineering** (Aeronautical and Aerospace Engineering; Chemical Engineering; Engineering; Industrial Engineering; Mechanical Engineering) *Dean*: Tong-Miin Liou; **Humanities and Social Studies** (Arts and Humanities; Chinese; History; Law; Literature; Modern Languages; Social Studies) *Dean*: Yen Chu; **Information and Electrical Engineering** (Automation and Control Engineering; Electrical Engineering; Electronic Engineering; Information Technology) *Dean*: Chuang-Chien Chiu; **Science** (Applied Mathematics; Engineering; Environmental Engineering; Materials Engineering; Mathematics and Computer Science; Natural Sciences) *Dean*: Tai-Lee Hu

Graduate Institutes
Accountancy (Accountancy); **Applied Mathematics** (Applied Mathematics) *Director*: Jiann-Cheng Yang; **Architecture and Town Planning** (Architecture; Town Planning) *Director*: Mei-Jung Lai; **Automatic Control Engineering** (Automation and Control Engineering; Biomedical Engineering) *Director*: Chern-Sheng Lin; **Business Administration** *Director*: Mei-Yane Chung; **Chemical Engineering** (Chemical Engineering) *Director*: Chyi-Tsong Chen; **Chinese Literature** (Chinese; Literature) *Director*: Jiann-Hwa Song; **Civil and Hydraulic Engineering** (Civil Engineering; Hydraulic Engineering) *Director*: Chang-Shian Chen; **Economics** (Economics) *Director*: Chi-Chu Chou; **Electrical and Communications Engineering** (Electrical Engineering; Telecommunications Engineering); **Electrical Engineering** (Electrical Engineering) *Director*: Chang-Chou Hwang; **Electronic Engineering** *Director*: Wen-luh

Yang; **Environmental Engineering and Sciences** *Director*: Jya-jyun Yu; **Fiber and Composite Materials** (Materials Engineering; Textile Technology) *Director*: Tien-wei Shyr; **Finance and Economic Law** (Commercial Law); **History and Cultural Heritage Management** (Heritage Preservation); **Industrial Engineering** (Computer Engineering; Industrial Engineering; Operations Research; Production Engineering) *Director*: Angus Jeang; **Information Engineering** (Information Technology) *Director*: Dan-lin Yang; **Insurance** (Insurance) *Director*: Gow-ning Yuan; **Land Management** (Natural Resources) *Director*: Jing-chzi Hsieh; **Materials Science** (Materials Engineering) *Director*: Hsin-chih Lin; **Mechanical Engineering** (Mechanical Engineering) *Director*: Jin-huang Huang; **Optical Physics** *Director*: Ying-te Lee; **Public Finance** (Finance; Public Administration); **Public Policy** (Political Sciences; Public Administration); **Statistics and Actuarial Sciences** (Actuarial Science; Statistics) *Director*: Woan-shu Chen; **Traffic and Transportation Engineering and Management** *Director*: Ta-yin Hu

Research Centres

Construction and Accident Prevention *Director*: Tse-shan Hsu; **E-Commerce** (E-Business/Commerce); **Geographical Information Systems** (Geography; Information Technology) *Director*: Tien-yin Chou; **Information and Electrical Engineering** *Director*: Chuang-chien Chiu; **Nanotechnology** (Materials Engineering; Microelectronics); **Physics Teaching** *Director*: Ying-te Lee; **Statistical Service and Survey** (Statistics)

Further Information: Also Technical Training Division for overseas Chinese students

History: Founded 1961 as College, acquired present status and title 1980.

Governing Bodies: Board of Trustees

Academic Year: September to June (September-January; February-June)

Admission Requirements: Graduation from high school and entrance examination

Fees: (New Taiwan Dollars): 55,000 per semester

Main Language(s) of Instruction: Chinese

Degrees and Diplomas: *Bachelor's Degree*: Fiber and Composite Materials; Mechanical and Computer-Aided Engineering; Industrial Engineering and Systems Management; Chemical Engineering; Aerospace and System Engineering; Accounting; International Trade; Finance; Insurance; Cooperative Economics; Information Engineering and Computer Science; Electrical Engineering; Electronic Engineering; Automatic Control Engineering; Communications; Civil Engineering; Water Resources Engineering; Architecture; Urban Planning; Public Finance and Taxation; Statistics; Economics; Business Administration; Applied Mathematics; Environmental Engineering and Science; Materials Science and Engineering; Photonics; Chinese Literature; Foreign Languages and Literature; Traffic and Transportation Engineering and Management; Land Management; *Master's Degree*: Applied Mathematics; Environmental Engineering and Science; Materials Science and Engineering; Photonics; Chinese Literature; History and Historical Relics; Fiber and Composite Materials; Mechanical and Computer-Aided Engineering; Industrial Engineering and Systems Management; Chemical Engineering; Aerospace and System Engineering; Mechanical and Aeronautical Engineering; Accounting; International Trade; Finance; Insurance; Public Finance and Taxation; Statistics; Economics; Business Administration; Financial and Economic Law; Management of Technology; Information Engineering and Computer Science; Electrical Engineering; Electronic Engineering; Automatic Control Engineering; Communications; Civil Engineering; Water Resources Engineering; Architecture; Urban Planning; Traffic and Transportation Engineering and Management; Land Management; Landscape and Recreation; Environmental and Spatial Information Science and Technology; *Doctorate*: Electrical and Communication Engineering; Civil and Hydraulic Engineering; Fiber and Composite Materials; Business; Statistics; Economics; Environmental Engineering and Science; Materials Science and Engineering; Chinese Literature; Information Engineering and Computer Science (PhD)

Student Services: Academic counselling, Cultural centre, Employment services, Handicapped facilities, Health services, Social counselling, Sports facilities

Student Residential Facilities: For 1,503 students

Libraries: Main Library, c. 585,000 vols

Publications: Feng Chia Journal

FO GUANG UNIVERSITY (FGU)

160 Linwei Road, Ilan 262
Tel: +886(3) 987-1000
Fax: +886(3) 987-4806
EMail: secretary@mail.fgu.edu.tw
Website: http://www.fgu.edu.tw

President: Peng-Cheng Kung (2000-)
Tel: +886(3) 987-3535 EMail: kung@mail.fgu.edu.tw

Secretary-General: Chung-Feng Lo
Tel: +886(3) 987-1000, Ext. 11500 EMail: cflo@mail.fgu.edu.tw

International Relations: Sally Hsi-Ju Chen
Tel: +886(3) 987-1000, Ext. 11531 EMail: sally@mail.fgu.edu.tw

Departments

Anthropology (Anthropology); **Communication** (Communication Studies); **Economics** (Economics); **Education and Information Sciences**; **Future Studies**; **History** (History); **Informatics** (Computer Science); **Literary Studies**; **Philosophy** (Philosophy); **Political Science** (Political Sciences); **Psychology**; **Public Affairs** (Public Administration); **Religious Studies** (Religious Studies); **Sociology** (Sociology)

Graduate Institutes

Management; **Social Education**

History: Founded 2000 as Fo Guang College of Humanities and Social Sciences. Acquired present title 2006.

Degrees and Diplomas: *Bachelor's Degree*; *Master's Degree*
Last Updated: 08/07/08

FOOYIN UNIVERSITY

151, Ching-Hsueh Road, Ta Liao, Kaohsiung 83101
Tel: +886(7) 781-1151
Fax: +886(7) 782-6146
EMail: so@mail.fy.edu.tw
Website: http://www.fy.edu.tw

President: I-Fan Chang (1995-)
Tel: +886(7) 783-6473, Fax: +886(7) 783-6473
EMail: ifchang@mail.fy.edu.tw

Secretary-General: Chin-lan Chiu
Tel: +886(7) 781-1151, Ext. 485 EMail: Stoob@mail.fy.edu.tw

International Relations: Keshin Chang, Director
Tel: +886(7) 781-1151, Ext. 305, Fax: +886(7) 782-8172
EMail: pr@mail.fy.edu.tw

Schools

Environmental and Life Sciences (Biological and Life Sciences; Environmental Studies) *Dean*: Cheng-Hsien Chang; **Humanities and Social Sciences** (Arts and Humanities; Social Sciences) *Dean*: Huang Ting; **Management and Information Sciences** (Information Sciences; Management) *Dean*: Han-Jung Liu; **Medical and Health Sciences** (Health Sciences; Medicine) *Dean*: Ching-Shan Huang

History: Founded 1958. Acquired present title and status 2002.

Academic Year: August to July

Admission Requirements: Graduation from high school and entrance examination

Fees: (New Taiwan Dollars): c. 55,000 per semester

Main Language(s) of Instruction: Chinese

Degrees and Diplomas: *Bachelor's Degree*: 4 yrs; *Master's Degree*: a further 2 yrs

Student Services: Academic counselling, Canteen, Employment services, Handicapped facilities, Health services, Language programs, Nursery care, Social counselling, Sports facilities

Libraries: Chinese, 145,000 vols; English, 22,850 vols

FU JEN CATHOLIC UNIVERSITY (FJCU)

510, Jungjeng Road, Shinjuang, Taipei 24205
Tel: +886(2) 2905-2000
Fax: +886(2) 2902-6201
EMail: pubwww@mails.fju.edu.tw
Website: http://www.fju.edu.tw

President: John Ning-Yuean Lee (2000-)
Tel: +886(2) 2908-7245, Fax: +886(2) 2901-7391
EMail: president@mails.fju.edu.tw

Secretary-General: John Shiang-Yang Hwang
Tel: +886(2) 2904-1387, Fax: +886(2) 2904-4938
EMail: secret@mails.fju.edu.tw

International Relations: Shu-Fang Chang
Tel: +886(2) 2904-1667 EMail: fjdp1083@mails.fju.edu.tw

Centres
Holistic Education; **Institutum Historiae Ecclesiae**; **Institutum Philosophiae Scholasticae**; **Socio-Cultural Research**; **Teacher Education**

Colleges
Arts (Fine Arts; Landscape Architecture; Music); **Foreign Languages** (Comparative Literature; English; French; German; Italian; Japanese; Linguistics; Modern Languages; Spanish; Translation and Interpretation); **Human Ecology** (Child Care and Development; Clothing and Sewing; Ecology; Family Studies; Food Science; Geography (Human); Hotel and Restaurant; Hotel Management; Museum Studies; Nutrition; Textile Technology); **Law** (Commercial Law; Economic and Finance Policy; Finance; Law); **Liberal Arts** (Advertising and Publicity; Arts and Humanities; Chinese; Communication Arts; Communication Studies; Educational Administration; History; Information Sciences; Journalism; Library Science; Literature; Mass Communication; Philosophy; Physical Education; Public Relations); **Management** (Accountancy; Business Administration; Finance; Information Management; Information Sciences; International Business; Management; Statistics); **Medicine** (Clinical Psychology; Medicine; Nursing; Occupational Therapy; Public Health; Rehabilitation and Therapy; Respiratory Therapy); **Science and Engineering** (Biological and Life Sciences; Chemistry; Electrical Engineering; Electronic Engineering; Engineering; Information Technology; Mathematics and Computer Science; Natural Sciences; Physics; Psychology); **Social Sciences** (Economics; Religious Studies; Social Sciences; Social Work)

Faculties
Theology

Research Institutes
Dialogue for Peace *(John Paul II Institute)*

Schools
Continuing Education

Further Information: Also Study Abroad Programmes for Language Courses in Japan, Germany, France, Spain and Italy. Exchange Programmes for foreign students (courses in Chinese Culture, Chinese Society, and Chinese Economics)

History: Founded 1919 as Fu Jen Academy, became University 1926, and acquired present status 1963.

Governing Bodies: Board of Trustees

Academic Year: September to June (September-January; February-June)

Admission Requirements: Graduation from high school and entrance examination

Main Language(s) of Instruction: Chinese, English

Degrees and Diplomas: *Bachelor's Degree*: Arts; Laws; Science, 4 yrs; *Master's Degree*: Arts; Business Administration; Engineering; Science, a further 2 yrs; *Doctorate (PhD)*

Student Services: Academic counselling, Canteen, Cultural centre, Employment services, Foreign Studies Centre, Handicapped facilities, Health services, Nursery care, Social counselling, Sports facilities

Student Residential Facilities: For c. 20,000 students

Special Facilities: Institutum Documentorum Ecclesiae. School History Office. Textiles and Clothing Culture Centre

Libraries: Liberal Arts; Social Sciences; Natural Sciences, total, c. 673,300 vols

Publications: Economic Journal; Fu Jen Studies; Law Journal; Philosophy Journal; Social Prospective; Theologica Collectanea

Press or Publishing House: Fu Jen Press

HSING KUO UNIVERSITY OF MANAGEMENT (HKU)
89, Yu Ying Street, Annan, Tainan 709
Tel: +886(6) 287-0026
Fax: +886(6) 287-3536
EMail: academic@mail.hku.edu.tw
Website: http://www.hku.edu.tw

President: Haumin Chu

Secretary-General: Fu-Ching Chang
Tel: +886(6) 287-3282, Fax: +886(6) 287-3851
EMail: fcchang@mail.hku.edu.tw

International Relations: Chung-Ming Ku
Tel: +886(6) 287-3527 EMail: jeremiah@mail.hku.edu.tw

Departments
Asset Management Science; **Information Sciences** (Information Sciences); **Applied Internet Science** (Computer Networks); **Business Administration**; **Cultural Educational Management** (Cultural Studies; Educational Administration); **Electronic Commerce** (E-Business/Commerce); **Industrial Engineering and Management** (Industrial Engineering; Industrial Management); **Information Management**; **International Business** (International Business); **Public Finance and Taxation** (Finance; Public Administration; Taxation)

History: Founded 2000.

Degrees and Diplomas: *Bachelor's Degree*: Industrial Engineering and Management; Asset Management Science; Cultural and Educational Administration; Applied English; Applied Japanese; Information Management; Information Science; Electronic Commerce; Applied Internet Science; Finance Administration; Business Administration; Public Finance and Taxation; Accounting Information; International Business

HSUAN CHUANG UNIVERSITY (HCU)
48, Hsuantsang Road, Hsinchu 300
Tel: +886(3) 530-2255
Fax: +886(3) 539-7400
EMail: hcu@hcu.edu.tw
Website: http://www.hcu.edu.tw

President: Chen-Hwa Hsia (2007-)
Tel: +886(3) 539-1206, Fax: +886(3) 539-1208
EMail: president@hcu.edu.tw

Secretary-General: Kuo-Hsiu Tseng
Tel: +886(3) 539-1207, Fax: +886(3) 539-1208
EMail: tgs@hcu.edu.tw

International Relations: Ding-Ming Wang, Vice-President
Tel: +886(3) 530-2255, Ext. 2195, Fax: +886(3) 539-1208
EMail: dmwang@hcu.edu.tw

Centres
Education; General Education

Colleges
Information and Communication (Communication Studies; Information Sciences) *Chairman*: Liang-Wen Kuo; **Liberal Arts** (Arts and Humanities) *Chairman*: Yun-Shi Huang; **Management** (Management) *Chairman*: Shun-Cheng Lee; **Social Sciences** (Social Sciences) *Chairman*: Rueih-Chin Lin

Schools
Law *Chairman*: Lai-Kun Lai

History: Founded 1997 as Hsuan Chuang College of Humanities and Social Sciences. Acquired present status and title 2004.

Governing Bodies: Board of Trustees

Academic Year: August to July

Admission Requirements: Secondary school certificate

Fees: (US Dollars): Tuition, Undergraduate, 1,460-1,665; Graduate, 1,470-1,635

Main Language(s) of Instruction: Chinese

International Co-operation: With universities in USA, Japan, Republic of Korea and China

Accrediting Agencies: Higher Education Evaluation and Accreditation Council of Taiwan

Degrees and Diplomas: *Bachelor's Degree (BA)*: 4 yrs; *Master's Degree (MA)*: 2 yrs; *Doctorate (PhD)*

Student Services: Academic counselling, Canteen, Cultural centre, Employment services, Foreign student adviser, Handicapped facilities, Health services, Language programs, Nursery care, Social counselling, Sports facilities

Student Residential Facilities: Dormitory

Special Facilities: Multimedia studio; virtual/TV broadcast studio; photograph studio; financial simulation classroom, etc.

Publications: Hsuan Chuang - General *(annually)*

Student Numbers *2008*: Total: c. 7,000
Last Updated: 12/12/08

HUAFAN UNIVERSITY

1, Huafan Road, Shihtin Hsiang, Taipei 223
Tel: +886(2) 266-32102
Fax: +886(2) 266-33173
EMail: pr@huafan.hfu.edu.tw
Website: http://www.hfu.edu.tw

President: Sun Ma (1995-)
Tel: +886(2) 266-33098, Fax: +886(2) 266-32142
EMail: sunma@cc.hfu.edu.tw

Secretary-General: Ching-Chao Liao
Tel: +886(2) 266-32102, Ext. 2111, Fax: +886(2) 266-33234

International Relations: Chien-Chi Lu
Tel: +886(2) 266-32102, Ext. 2126, Fax: +886(2) 266-39188
EMail: pr@cc.hfu.edu.tw

Centres
Computer *Director*: Cheng-Yuan Tang; **Extension Education** (Education) *Director*: Sheng-Chai Chi; **Humanities Education Research** *Director*: Chwan-Huei Tsai

Colleges
Arts and Design (Architectural and Environmental Design; Architecture; Fine Arts; Industrial Design) *Dean*: Chen-Ping Chao; **Engineering** (Electronic Engineering; Engineering; Industrial Management; Information Management; Mechanical Engineering) *Dean*: Hung-Yi Li; **Liberal Arts** (Arts and Humanities; Chinese; English; Literature; Modern Languages; Philosophy) *Dean*: Gou-Horng Sheu

Graduate Institutes
Architecture (Architecture) *Chair*: Pai-Hsing Hsiao; **Asian Humanities** *Director*: Yao-Ming Tsai; **Electronic Engineering** *Chair*: Chiang-Ju Chien; **Environmental and Hazard-Resistant Design** (Architectural and Environmental Design; Design) *Chair*: Shiou Chen; **Industrial Design** *Chair*: Chien-Cheng Chang; **Industrial Engineering and Management Information** *Chair*: Jhy-Ping Jhang; **Information Management** *Chair*: Tsung-Yun Tseng; **Mechatronic Engineering** *Chiar*: Sheng-Yih Luo; **Philosophy** (Philosophy) *Chair*: Bau-Ruei Duh

History: Founded 1990 to promote the humanistic spirit of Confucian and Buddhist concepts. Acquired present status and title 1997.

Academic Year: September to June (September-January; February-June)

Admission Requirements: Secondary school certificate and entrance examination

Fees: (New Taiwan Dollars): 50,000 per semester

Main Language(s) of Instruction: Mandarin Chinese

Degrees and Diplomas: *Bachelor's Degree*: Chinese; English; Philosophy; Industrial Management; Information Management (BBA); Mechanical Engineering; Electronic Engineering; Architecture; Industrial Design; Environmental Design (BS), 4 yrs; *Master's Degree*: Asian Humanities; Design Study (MDs); Industrial Management (MBA); Information Management (MIM); Mechatronic Engineering (MS); Philosophy (MA), 2-4 yrs; *Doctorate*: Asian Humanities (PhD); Mechatronic Engineering (PhD), 2-7 yrs

Student Services: Academic counselling, Canteen, Cultural centre, Health services, Sports facilities

Student Residential Facilities: Yes

Special Facilities: Huafan Art Gallery

Libraries: Huafan Library, c. 186,223 vols

Publications: Huafan Journal of Design *(annually)*; Huafan Journal of Humanities

HUNG KUANG UNIVERSITY (HKU)

34, Chung-Chie Road, Sha-Lu, Taichung 43302
Tel: +886(4) 263-18652
Fax: +886(4) 263-10744
EMail: president@sunrise.hk.edu.tw
Website: http://www.hk.edu.tw

President: Guor-Cheng Fang (2001-)
Tel: +886(4) 263-18652, Ext. 1110
EMail: gcfang@sunrise.hk.edu.tw

Chief Secretary: Vicky Wang
Tel: +886(4) 263-18652, Ext. 1130 EMail: vicky@sunrise.hk.edu.tw

International Relations: Jin-Min Sung, Director, Research and Development Affairs
Tel: +886(4) 263-18652, Ext. 2200, Fax: +886(4) 263-15843
EMail: sungjm@sunrise.hk.edu.tw

Departments
Applied Cosmetology; **Applied Foreign Languages**; **Biotechnology** (Biotechnology; Pharmacology); **Child Care and Education**; **Computer Science and Information Engineering**; **Environmental Engineering**; **Food Science and Nutrition**; **Health Administration**; **Hospitality Management**; **Industrial Safety and Health**; **Information Management** (Information Management); **Nursing** (Nursing); **Physical Therapy**

History: Founded 1967 as Hung Kuang Junior College of Nursing. Acquired present title and status 2003.

I-SHOU UNIVERSITY (ISU)

No. 1, Section 1, Syuecheng Road, Dashu Township, Kaohsiung 84008
Tel: +886(7) 657-7711
Fax: +886(7) 657-7056
Website: http://www.isu.edu.tw

President: Shen-Li Fu (1990-)
Tel: +886(7) 657-7001, Fax: +886(7) 657-7051
EMail: slfu@isu.edu.tw

Secretary-General: Jaw-Min Chou
Tel: +886(7) 657-7008 EMail: jmchou@isu.edu.tw

International Relations: Hui-Lan Chao
Tel: +886(7) 657-7711, Ext. 2006 EMail: huilan@isu.edu.tw

Colleges
Electrical Engineering and Information Sciences (Communication Studies; Electrical Engineering; Electronic Engineering; Information Management; Information Technology; Telecommunications Engineering); **Language and Communication** (English; Japanese; Mass Communication); **Management** (Accountancy; Business Administration; English; Finance; Industrial Engineering; Industrial Management; International Business; Public Administration; Social Policy); **Medical Sciences** (Biological and Life Sciences; Biomedical Engineering; Biotechnology; Health Administration; Nursing; Nutrition; Occupational Therapy; Physical Therapy; Radiology); **Science and Engineering** (Applied Mathematics; Automation and Control Engineering; Chemical Engineering; Civil Engineering; Materials Engineering; Mechanical Engineering)

Graduate Schools
Applied Mathematics (Applied Mathematics); **Biological Technology and Chemical Engineering** (Biotechnology; Chemical Engineering); **Biomedical Engineering** (Biomedical Engineering); **Civil and Ecological Engineering** (Civil Engineering; Ecology); **Electrical Engineering** (Electrical Engineering); **Electronic Engineering** (Electronic Engineering); **Healthcare Administration** (Health Administration); **Industrial Engineering and Management** (Industrial Engineering; Industrial Management); **Information Engineering** (Information Sciences; Information Technology); **Information Management** (Automation and Control Engineering; Business Administration; Information Management; Mechanical Engineering); **Management** *(Including MBA, EMBA and Doctoral Programs)*; **Materials Science and Engineering** (Materials Engineering)

History: Founded 1990 as Kaohsiung Polytechnic Institute, acquired present status and title 1997.

Governing Bodies: Board of Trustees

Admission Requirements: Graduation from high school and entrance examination

Main Language(s) of Instruction: Mandarin Chinese

Degrees and Diplomas: *Bachelor's Degree*: 4 yrs; *Master's Degree*: a further 2-3 yrs; *Doctorate (PhD)*

Student Services: Academic counselling, Canteen, Employment services, Handicapped facilities, Health services, Language programs, Nursery care, Social counselling, Sports facilities

Student Residential Facilities: Yes and additional off-campus housing in Nantze, Renwu, Tashe, and Tashu

Special Facilities: Extension Education Centre (EEC); Academic Development Centre (ADC); Centre for Teacher Education, Computer Education, General Education; Learning centres

Libraries: University Library, c. 230,000 vols, c. 1,400 periodicals, c. 6,000 non-book materials and c. 140 CD-ROM databases

Publications: Journal of I-Shou University, Research *(annually)*; Pan Pacific Management Review, Business and Management *(biannually)*

KAINAN UNIVERSITY (KNU)

1, Kainan Road, Shinshing Tsuen, Luchu Shiang, Taoyuan 338
Tel: +886(3) 341-2500
Fax: +886(3) 341-2430
EMail: itc@mail.knu.edu.tw
Website: http://www.knu.edu.tw

President: Michael Tang
Tel: +886(3) 341-2500, Ext. 1302 EMail: minchin@mail.knu.edu.tw

Secretary-General: Chang-Tse Chien
Tel: +886(3) 341-2430, Ext. 1201
EMail: jen45678@mail.knu.edu.tw

Departments
Accountancy (Accountancy); **Air Transportation Management** (Air Transport); **Applied English** (English); **Applied Japanese** (Japanese); **Business Administration** (Business Administration; Management); **Financial Banking** (Banking; Finance); **Information and E-Commerce** (E-Business/Commerce; Information Technology); **International Business** (International Business); **Law** (Law); **Marine Transportation and Logistics Management** (Marine Transport; Transport Management); **Public Administration** (Public Administration); **Risk Management** (Management); **Tourism and Hospitality** (Hotel and Restaurant; Tourism)

Graduate Schools
Business Administration (Business Administration); **Finance and Banking** (Banking; Finance); **Information Management** (Information Management); **International Enterprises** (International Business); **Marine Transportation and Logistics Management** (Marine Transport; Transport Management); **Public Administration** (Public Administration)

Further Information: Traditional and Open Learning Institution

History: Founded 1994, acquired present status and title 2001.

Degrees and Diplomas: *Master's Degree*: Business Administration

KAOHSIUNG MEDICAL UNIVERSITY (KMU)

100, Shih-Chuan 1st Road, Kaohsiung 80780
Tel: +886(7) 312-1101
Fax: +886(7) 321-2062
EMail: kmuinfo@kmu.edu.tw
Website: http://www.kmu.edu.tw

President: Gwo-Jaw Wang (2000-)
Tel: +886(7) 311-7820, Fax: +886(7) 321-2062
EMail: gwojaw@kmu.edu.tw

Chief Secretary: Wen-Shun Hung
Tel: +886(7) 312-1101, Ext. 2107, Fax: +886(7) 321-2062
EMail: sjhwang@kmu.edu.tw

International Relations: Yie Chien
Tel: +886(7) 312-1101, Ext. 2396, Fax: +886(7) 322-3170
EMail: alicelin@kmu.edu.tw

Centres
General Education

Colleges
Health Sciences; **Life Sciences** (Biology; Chemistry); **Medicine** (Medicine); **Nursing** (Nursing); **Oral Medicine** (Dentistry; Oral Pathology); **Pharmacy** (Pharmacy)

Graduate Institutes
Behavioural Sciences; **Biochemistry** (Biochemistry); **Chemistry** (Chemistry); **Dental Sciences** (Dentistry); **Gender Studies** (Gender Studies); **Medicine** (Medicine); **Natural Products** (Natural Resources); **Nursing** (Nursing); **Occupational Safety**; **Oral Health Sciences** (Oral Pathology); **Pharmaceutical Sciences** (Pharmacology; Pharmacy); **Public Health** (Public Health)

Research Centres
Gender Studies (Gender Studies); **Genomics** (Genetics); **Health and Social Services Policy** (Health Sciences; Social and Community Services); **Industrial Hygiene** (Hygiene); **Orthopedics** (Orthopaedics); **Tropical Medicine** (Tropical Medicine)

Further Information: Also Chung-Ho Memorial Teaching Hospital

History: Founded 1954. A private institution under the jurisdiction of the Ministry of Education.

Governing Bodies: Board of Trustees

Academic Year: September to June (September-January; February-June)

Admission Requirements: Graduation from high school or equivalent, and entrance examination

Fees: (New Taiwan Dollars): 50,000-70,000 per semester

Main Language(s) of Instruction: Chinese, English

International Co-operation: With universities in USA

Degrees and Diplomas: *Bachelor's Degree*: Biology; Chemistry; Medical Sciences Technology; Medical Sociology; Nursing; Pharmacy; Psychology; Public Health; Rehabilitation Medicine, 4 yrs; *Bachelor's Degree*: Dentistry, 6 yrs; *Bachelor's Degree*: Medicine, 7 yrs; *Master's Degree*: Science; *Doctorate (PhD)*

Student Services: Academic counselling, Canteen, Employment services, Health services, Language programs, Nursery care, Social counselling, Sports facilities

Student Residential Facilities: For 514 students and 370 teachers

Special Facilities: Audio-visual Centre. Computer Centre. Language Centre

Libraries: c. 158,100 vols

Publications: Abstracts of Theses; Kaohsiung Journal of Medical Sciences *(monthly)*

KUNG SHAN UNIVERSITY (KSU)

949, Da Wan Road, Yung Kang, Tainan Hsien 71003
Tel: +886(6) 272-7175 +886(6) 205-0000
Fax: +886(6) 272-8944
Website: http://www.ksu.edu.tw

President: Yan-Kuin Su
Tel: +886(6) 272-7175, Ext. 201 EMail: rector@mail.ksu.edu.tw

International Relations: Ho-Wen Yang
Tel: +886(6) 205-0659, Fax: +886(6) 205-9422
EMail: rndio@mail.ksu.edu.tw

Departments
Accounting Information (Accountancy); **Applied English** (English); **Computer and Communication** (Communication Studies; Computer Science); **Early Childhood Care and Education** (Child Care and Development); **Electrical Engineering** (Electrical Engineering); **Electronic Engineering** (Electronic Engineering); **Environmental Engineering** (Environmental Engineering); **Finance and Banking** (Banking; Finance); **Information and Communication**; **Information Engineering** (Information Technology); **Information Management** (Information Management); **International Trade** (International Business); **Mechanical Engineering** (Mechanical Engineering); **Motion Picture and Video** (Cinema and Television; Video); **Polymer Materials** (Materials Engineering; Polymer and Plastics Technology); **Public Relations and Advertising** (Advertising and Publicity; Public Relations); **Real Estate Management** (Management; Real Estate); **Spatial Design** (Interior Design); **Visual Communication** (Mass Communication)

History: Founded 1964. Acquired present status 2000.
Last Updated: 24/07/08

LEADER UNIVERSITY (LU)

188, Section 5, An-Chung Road, Tainan 709
Tel: +886(6) 255-2500
Fax: +886(6) 255-1656
EMail: act@mail.leader.edu.tw
Website: http://www.leader.edu.tw

President: Fu-Yih Shih
Tel: +886(6) 255-9899, Fax: +886(6) 255-0885
EMail: fuyih@mail.leader.edu.tw

Vice-President: Maw-Shyong Lee
EMail: leems@mail.leader.edu.tw

International Relations: Ching-Tai Liu
Tel: +886(6) 255-5685, Fax: +886(6) 255-5695
EMail: ching@mail.leader.edu.tw

Departments
Business Management (Business Administration; Management); **Computer Science and Information Engineering** (Computer Science; Information Technology); **Construction and Planning** (Architecture and Planning; Construction Engineering); **English** (English); **Environmental and Resource Studies**; **Financial Management** (Finance); **Food and Drink Management**; **Health Care Management**; **Hotel Management**; **Industrial Management** (Industrial Management); **Information Communication**; **Information Management** (Information Management); **International Business Administration** (International Business); **Japanese** (Japanese); **Leisure Management** (Leisure Studies; Management); **Local Regional Development**; **Logistic Management** (Transport Management); **Real Estate**; **Technology Management**; **Translation**

Graduate Institutes
Applied Information; **Environmental and Resource Studies**; **Foreign Languages**; **Industrial Management**; **International Business**; **Leisure Management**; **Regional Development**; **Technology Management**

History: Founded 1998 as Leader College of Management. Acquired present title 2000.

LUNGHWA UNIVERSITY OF SCIENCE AND TECHNOLOGY

300 Wan-Shou Road, Section 1, Kueishan, Taoyuan 333
Tel: +886(2) 820-93211
Fax: +886(2) 820-94650
EMail: se@mail.lhu.edu.tw
Website: http://www.lhu.edu.tw

President: Wen-Shion Chang (2002-)
Tel: +886(2) 820-90812 EMail: Changws@mail.lhu.edu.tw

Vice-President: Ru-Jen Lin EMail: rjlin@mail.lhu.edu.tw

International Relations: Ta-Lun Sung
Tel: +886(2) 8209-3211, Ext. 3807, Fax: +886(2) 820-94845
EMail: tlsung@mail.lhu.edu.tw

Colleges
Electrical Engineering and Computer Science (Computer Networks; Computer Science; Electrical Engineering; Electronic Engineering; Multimedia); **Engineering** (Chemical Engineering; Instrument Making; Materials Engineering; Mechanical Engineering; Technology); **Liberal Arts and Social Sciences** (Art Education; Cultural Studies; Education; Modern Languages); **Management** (Business Administration; E-Business/Commerce; Finance; Industrial Management; Information Management; International Business)

History: Founded 1969. Acquired present status 2004.

Fees: (New Taiwan Dollars) 44,027-50,615

Main Language(s) of Instruction: Chinese

Student Services: Academic counselling, Canteen, Cultural centre, Employment services, Handicapped facilities, Health services, Language programs, Nursery care, Social counselling, Sports facilities

Special Facilities: Art Centre

MEIHO INSTITUTE OF TECHNOLOGY (MIT)

23, Pung-Kung Road, Nei Pu Hsiang, Pingtung 912
Tel: +886(8) 779-9821
Fax: +886(8) 779-9711
EMail: president@email.meiho.edu.tw
Website: http://www.meiho.edu.tw

President: Shanda Liu
Tel: +886(8) 778-3428, Fax: +886(8) 778-9837

Dean of Academic Affairs: Che-Jen Hsieh
Tel: +886(8) 779-9821, Ext. 180, Fax: +886(8) 779-1550
EMail: cjhsieh@email.meiho.edu.tw

International Relations: Chien-Feng Tai
Tel: +886(8) 779-9821, Ext. 140, Fax: +886(8) 778-9837
EMail: advantech@email.meiho.edu.tw

Deaneries
Finance (Finance)

Departments
Accountancy and Information Systems; **Applied Foreign Languages** (Modern Languages); **Beauty Science** (Cosmetology); **Biological Sciences and Technology** (Biological and Life Sciences; Biotechnology); **Business Administration** (Business Administration); **Business Management** (Graduate School); **Early Childhood Education** (Preschool Education; Primary Education); **Elderly Care Institutions Management**; **Food and Nutrition**; **Health Administration** (Health Administration); **Health Care** (Graduate School) (Health Administration; Health Sciences); **Information Technology** (Information Technology); **Nursing** (Nursing); **Public Finance** (Finance; Public Administration); **Social Work** (Social Work); **Therapeutic Recreation**

History: Founded 1964, acquired present status and title 2000.

Degrees and Diplomas: *Bachelor's Degree*; *Master's Degree*: Business Management

MING CHI UNIVERSITY OF TECHNOLOGY (MIT)

84, Gungjuan Road, Taishan, Taipei 24306
Tel: +886(2) 290-89899
Fax: +886(2) 290-84509
EMail: webmaster@mail.mit.edu.tw
Website: http://www.mit.edu.tw

President: Thu-Hua Liu (2002-)
Tel: +886(2) 290-89899, Ext. 4011 EMail: thliu@mail.mit.edu.tw

Secretary-General: Shen Ming-Hsiung
Tel: +886(2) 290-89899, Ext. 4102 EMail: peter@mail.mit.edu.tw

International Relations: Lee Kuo-Tong
Tel: +886(2) 290-89899, Ext. 4064, Fax: +886(2) 290-41346
EMail: ktlee@mail.mit.edu.tw

Colleges
Engineering (Automotive Engineering; Electrical Engineering; Electronic Engineering; Engineering; Mechanical Engineering); **Environment and Resources** (Biomedical Engineering; Chemical Engineering; Environmental Engineering; Health Sciences; Materials Engineering; Safety Engineering); **Management and Design** (Business Administration; Communication Arts; Design; Engineering; Industrial Design; Industrial Engineering; Industrial Management; Management; Visual Arts)

History: Founded 1964.

Degrees and Diplomas: *Bachelor's Degree*; *Master's Degree*
Last Updated: 02/02/07

MING CHUAN UNIVERSITY (MCU)

250 Chung Shan N. Rd. Sec. 5, Taipei 111
Tel: +886(2) 2881-2549 +886(3) 2881-254 Ext. 2776
Fax: +886(2) 2881-0521
EMail: laeyer@mcu.edu.tw
Website: http://www.mcu.edu.tw

President: Chuan Lee (1998-)
Tel: +886(2) 2881-2549, Fax: +886(2) 2881-0521

General Secretary: Meng-chi Hung
Tel: +886(2) 2881-2549, Fax: +886(2) 2881-0521

International Relations: Curtis Hsu
Tel: +886(3) 3507001Ext. 3703, 3,704, 3,705,
Fax: +886(3) 3593891 +886(3) 3593883 EMail: ihp@mcu.edu.tw

Colleges

International (Gweishan District, Taoyuan; including Graduate School of International Affairs) (Information Management; International Business; International Relations; Mass Communication; Tourism) Dean: Ellen Chen

Schools

Applied Languages (Gweishan District, Taoyuan; including Graduate Schools of Applied Chinese, Applied Japanese and Applied English) (Chinese; English; Foreign Languages Education; Japanese; Modern Languages; Teacher Training) Dean: De-Chao Chen; **Communication** (Including Graduate School of Communication Management) (Advertising and Publicity; Communication Arts; Journalism; Management; Mass Communication; Radio and Television Broadcasting) Dean: Chih-Hung Yang; **Design** (Gweishan, Taoyuan; including Graduate Schools of Creative Design, Design Management, Media and Space Design) (Architecture; Design; Graphic Design; Industrial Design; Management; Town Planning) Dean: Chien-hua Wu; **Health** (Gweishan District, Taoyuan) (Biotechnology; Health Administration; Management); **Information Technology** (Gweishan District; Taoyuan; including Graduate Schools of Information Management, Computer and Communications Engineering, Information Engineering) (Computer Engineering; Electronic Engineering; Information Management; Telecommunications Engineering) Dean: Chong-lin Chia; **Law** (Including Graduate School of Law) (Law) Dean: Yung-Sheng Wu; **Management** (Some programmes at Gweishan District, Taoyuan; including Graduate Schools of Management, Finance, Economics, Accounting, Risk Management, International Business, Applied Statistics and Information Science) (Accountancy; Business Administration; Economics; Finance; Insurance; International Business; Management; Statistics) Dean: Shiuh-Nan Hwang; **Social Sciences** (Some programmes at Gweishan District, Taoyuan; including Graduate Schools of Education and Public Administration) (Comparative Politics; Education; Educational Psychology; Public Administration; Regional Studies) Dean: Chung-Yuan Fan; **Tourism** (Gweishan District, Taoyuan; including Graduate School of Tourism) (Hotel and Restaurant; Leisure Studies; Management; Tourism) Dean: Wu-Chang Wu

History: Founded 1957 as Ming Chuan (Commercial Junior Women's) College. Acquired present status and title 1997.

Academic Year: September to August (September-January; February-June; July-August)

Admission Requirements: Graduation from high school and entrance examination

Fees: (New Taiwan Dollars): c. 38,000-50,000 per semester

Main Language(s) of Instruction: Mandarin Chinese, English, Japanese

International Co-operation: With universities in USA, Australia, UK and Japan

Accrediting Agencies: Ministry of Education

Degrees and Diplomas: Bachelor's Degree: 4 yrs; Master's Degree: 2 yrs; Doctorate (PhD): 3-4 yrs

Student Services: Academic counselling, Canteen, Cultural centre, Employment services, Foreign student adviser, Health services, Language programs, Social counselling, Sports facilities

Student Residential Facilities: For 1,500 students on Taipei Campus and for 3,000 students on Taoyuan Campus.

Special Facilities: Music Theatre; Film Projection Studio; Arts Centre

Libraries: 439,005 vols, 2,226 periodicals, 25 newspapers, 21,845 digitalized periodicals

Publications: Ming Chuan Journal (biannually)

Press or Publishing House: Ming Chuan Publishing Centre

MINGDAO UNIVERSITY (MDU)

369, Wen-hua Road, Peetow, Changhua 52345
Tel: +886(4) 887-6660
Fax: +886(4) 887-6659
EMail: jdcheng@mdu.edu.tw
Website: http://www.mdu.edu.tw

President: Da-Yung Wang (2002-)
Tel: +886(4) 887-6660, Ext. 1020

Secretary-General: Chin-Hsiung Hsieh
Tel: +886(4) 887-6660, Ext. 1600 EMail: hsiehch@mdu.edu.tw

International Relations: J.D. Cheng, Dean, Department of International Affairs Tel: +886(4) 887-6660, Ext. 2000

Colleges

Design; **Humanities**; **Management** (Management); **Science and Engineering** (Engineering)

Departments

Applied English Studies (English Studies; Modern Languages); **Applied Japanese Studies** (Japanese; Modern Languages); **Business Administration** (Business Administration); **Chinese Literature** (Chinese; Literature); **Chinese Studies**; **Computer Science and Information Engineering** (Computer Science; Information Technology); **Digital Design** (Computer Graphics; Design); **Energy Engineering** (Energy Engineering); **Environment and Disaster Management** (Fashion Design; Fine Arts); **Finance** (Finance); **Global Marketing and Logistics**; **Holistic Wellness**; **Hospitality Management**; **Landscape Architecture**; **Life Science** (Biological and Life Sciences); **Materials Science and Engineering** (Materials Engineering; Systems Analysis); **Post-Modern Agriculture**; **Teaching** (Education; Teacher Training)

Institutes

Business Administration (EMBA Programme) (Business Administration; Management); **Electro-optical Engineering** (Electronic Engineering; Optical Technology)

History: Founded 1998 and acquired present status and title 2001.

Academic Year: August to July

Admission Requirements: Graduation from high school

Main Language(s) of Instruction: Chinese

Accrediting Agencies: Ministry of Education

Degrees and Diplomas: Bachelor's Degree (BA): 4 yrs; Master's Degree (MA): 2 yrs

Student Services: Academic counselling, Canteen, Cultural centre, Employment services, Foreign student adviser, Foreign Studies Centre, Handicapped facilities, Health services, Language programs, Nursery care, Social counselling, Sports facilities

Student Residential Facilities: Residence Hall

Libraries: c. 219,000 vols

Publications: MingDao Journal, Articles on Humanities, Engineering, Management and Design Research (biannually)

Academic Staff 2008	MEN	WOMEN	TOTAL
FULL-TIME	212	168	380
STAFF WITH DOCTORATE FULL-TIME	130	41	171
Student Numbers 2008			
All (Foreign Included)	2,617	2,445	5,062
FOREIGN ONLY	1	2	3

Evening students, 1,571.
Last Updated: 12/12/08

MING HSIN UNIVERSITY OF SCIENCE AND TECHNOLOGY (MUST)

1, Hsin-Hsing Road, Hsin Feng, Hsinchu 304
Tel: +886(3) 559-3142
Fax: +886(3) 559-5142
Website: http://www.must.edu.tw

President: Chao-Chen Yang
Tel: +886(3) 559-3142, Ext. 2115, Fax: +886(3) 559-2954
EMail: pre@must.edu.tw

Administrative Officer: Tung-Yuan Pai
Tel: +886(3) 559-3142, Ext. 217

International Relations: Tung-Ming Lee
Tel: +886(3) 559-3142, Ext. 2144

Divisions

Engineering Systems and Management (Engineering; Information Management; Information Technology); **Management Information** (Information Management) Director: Yu-Li Yen

Schools
Service Trades Management (Management; Service Trades)

History: Founded 1966 as Ming Hsin Junior College of Technology. Renamed Ming Hsin Institute of Technology and Commerce 1993. Acquired present status 2002.

Governing Bodies: Board of Directors

Academic Year: September to June (September-January; February-June)

Admission Requirements: Graduation from high school or equivalent, and entrance examination

Fees: (New Taiwan Dollars): c. 200,000 per annum

Main Language(s) of Instruction: Chinese

Accrediting Agencies: Ministry of Education

Degrees and Diplomas: *Bachelor's Degree:* 4 yrs. Diplomas 2-5 yrs

Student Services: Academic counselling, Canteen, Employment services, Handicapped facilities, Health services, Social counselling, Sports facilities

Student Residential Facilities: Yes

Libraries: c. 140,000 vols, 641 journals and periodicals. Internet and audiovisual services

Publications: Collected Research Papers, by School Faculty; Journal of Ming Hsin Institute of Technology *(biannually)*
Last Updated: 25/07/08

NANHUA UNIVERSITY (NHU)
32 Jungkeng Li, Dalin, Chiayi 62248
Tel: +886(5) 272-1001
Fax: +886(5) 272-0170
EMail: wclu@mail.nhu.edu.tw
Website: http://www.nhu.edu.tw

President: Miao Sheng Cheng (1999-)
Tel: +886(5) 272-0168 EMail: mschen@mail.nhu.edu.tw

Secretary-General: Chang-Hsiung Tsai
Tel: +886(5) 242-7101, Fax: +886(5) 242-7147
EMail: chtsai@mail.nhu.edu.tw

Colleges
Humanities (Aesthetics; Art Management; Arts and Humanities; Child Care and Development; Design; Ethnology; Fine Arts; Landscape Architecture; Literature; Modern Languages; Musicology; Preschool Education; Visual Arts); **Management** (Accountancy; Business Administration; Computer Science; E-Business/Commerce; Economics; Finance; Information Management; Information Sciences; Information Technology; Management; Tourism); **Social Sciences** (International Studies; Social Sciences; Sociology)

Graduate Institutes
Asia-Pacific Studies; Economics; Environmental Management (Environmental Management); **European Studies**; **Financial Management** (Finance); **Life-and-Death Studies** (Biological and Life Sciences); **Literature**; **Management** (Management); **Natural Healing Sciences** (Health Sciences); **Non-Profit Organizations Management**; **Philosophy** (Philosophy); **Public Administration and Policy** (Public Administration); **Publishing Organizations Management** (Management); **Religious Studies**; **Tourism Management** (Tourism)

History: Founded 1996 as Nanhua Management College, acquired present title 1999.

Governing Bodies: Board of Trustees

Admission Requirements: Graduation from high school

Fees: (New Taiwan Dollars): c. 60,000 per semester

Main Language(s) of Instruction: Chinese

Accrediting Agencies: Minstry of Education

Degrees and Diplomas: *Bachelor's Degree:* 2-4 yrs; *Master's Degree:* a further 2-3 yrs

Student Services: Academic counselling, Canteen, Cultural centre, Employment services, Foreign student adviser, Handicapped facilities, Health services, Language programs, Social counselling, Sports facilities

Student Residential Facilities: Yes

Special Facilities: TV Studio

Libraries: Books, Journals, Newspapers, Micro Films
Publications: Fu Guang Journal *(annually)*

NAN KAI COLLEGE (NKC)
568, Chung Cheng Road, Tsao Tuen, Nan Tou 542
Tel: +886(49) 256-3489
Website: http://www.nkc.edu.tw

President: Shyh-Chin Huang (2001-)
Tel: +886(49) 256-3489, Ext. 201, Fax: +886(49) 256-3788
EMail: president@bear.nkjc.edu.tw

Vice-President: Tsong-Shin Sheu
Tel: +886(49) 256-3489, Ext. 212, Fax: +886(49) 256-3788
EMail: tsheu@nkjc.edu.tw

International Relations: Sze-Chu Liu
Tel: +886(49) 256-3489, Ext. 581, Fax: +886(49) 255-0846
EMail: scliu@bear.nkjc.edu.tw

Departments
Applied Foreign Languages (Modern Languages); **Electrical Engineering** (Electrical Engineering); **Electronic Engineering** (Electronic Engineering); **Finance** (Finance); **Industrial Engineering and Management** (Industrial Engineering; Industrial Management); **Information Management** (Information Management); **Mechanical Engineering** (Mechanical Engineering); **Real Estate Management** (Real Estate)

History: Founded 1971, acquired present status and title 2001.

Degrees and Diplomas: *Bachelor's Degree*

PROVIDENCE UNIVERSITY (PU)
200, Chungchi Road, Shalu, Taichung 43301
Tel: +886(4) 2632-8001
Fax: +886(4) 2631-1170
EMail: president@pu.edu.tw
Website: http://www.pu.edu.tw

President: Matthew Minh-Teh Yu
Tel: +886(4) 2631-0631 EMail: mtyu@pu.edu.tw

Secretary-General: Chia-Hung Teng
Tel: +886(4) 2652-3292 EMail: chteng@pu.edu.tw

International Relations: Victor Lin
Tel: +886(4) 2664-5073, Fax: +886(4) 2652-6602
EMail: vic@pu.edu.tw

Centres
Chinese Language Education *Director:* Yu Cai; **Foreign Languages** *Director:* Hui-Na Chou; **General Education** (Education) *Director:* Yi-Ren Lin; **Service Learning Development** *Director:* Yi-Pei Hu; **Teacher Education** *Director:* Qing-Qing Zheng

Colleges
Computing and Informatics (Computer Science; Information Management; Information Technology; Telecommunications Engineering) *Dean:* Yao-Ling Lin; **Foreign Languages and Literature** (Chinese; English; Japanese; Linguistics; Literature; Spanish) *Dean:* Kwock-Ping Tse; **Humanities and Social Sciences** (Child Care and Development; Ecology; Law; Literature; Welfare and Protective Services) *Dean:* Zhen-Hui Wang; **Management** (Accountancy; Business Administration; Finance; International Business; Tourism) *Dean:* Cheng-Fong Wu; **Science** (Applied Chemistry; Applied Mathematics; Cosmetology; Food Science; Food Technology; Nutrition) *Dean:* Yong-He Zhang

Departments
Accountancy (Accountancy) *Chairman:* Ying-De Chen; **Applied Chemistry** *Chairman:* Shu-Ping Wang; **Applied Mathematics** (Applied Mathematics) *Chairman:* Ku-Hsing Nien; **Business Administration** (Business Administration) *Chairman:* Chia-Sheng Li; **Chinese Literature** (Chinese; Literature) *Chairman:* Jui-Ching Lu; **Computer Science and Communication Engineering** *Chairman:* Ying-Te Tsai; **Computer Science and Information Engineering** (Computer Science; Information Technology) *Chairman:* Li-Hsing Hsu; **Computer Science and Information Management** *Chairman:* Yung-Ren Chien; **Cosmetic Science** *Chairman:* Zhao-Shun Yang; **Ecology** (Ecology) *Chairman:* Tung-Yao Chen; **English Language, Literature and Linguistics** (English; Linguistics; Literature)

Chairman: Chun-Lin Luo; **Finance** (Finance) *Chairman*: Yu-Sheng Hong; **Food and Nutrition** (Food Science; Food Technology; Nutrition) *Chairman*: Yin-Ching Chan; **International Business** (International Business) *Chairman*: Chiu-Kuei Chan; **Japanese Language and Literature** (Japanese) *Chairman*: Huan-Qi Zen; **Law** (Law) *Chairman*: Ke-Jing Ling; **Mass Communication** (Film; Mass Communication; Radio and Television Broadcasting) *Chairman*: Chih-Yung Chiu; **Spanish Language and Literature** (Spanish) *Chairman*: Shu-Huei Tsai; **Statistics and Information** (Information Sciences; Statistics) *Chairman*: Tai-Fang Chen; **Taiwanese Literature** (Literature) *Chair*: Ming-Ro Chen; **Tourism** *Chairman*: Cheng-Ho Wu; **Youth and Child Welfare** (Child Care and Development; Welfare and Protective Services) *Chairman*: Chin-Shan Chi

History: Founded 1956 as Women's College, acquired present status 1989, present title 1993. A private Catholic University.

Governing Bodies: Board of Trustees, comprising 15 members

Academic Year: August to July (August-January; February-July)

Admission Requirements: Graduation from high school and entrance examination

Fees: (New Taiwan Dollars): c. 50,000 per semester

Main Language(s) of Instruction: Mandarin Chinese, English

Degrees and Diplomas: *Bachelor's Degree*: 4-6 yrs; *Master's Degree*: 1-4 yrs; *Doctorate (PhD)*: 2-7 yrs

Student Services: Academic counselling, Canteen, Cultural centre, Employment services, Foreign student adviser, Foreign Studies Centre, Handicapped facilities, Health services, Language programs, Nursery care, Social counselling, Sports facilities

Student Residential Facilities: Yes. St. Bosco Hall and Schultz Hall

Special Facilities: Art Centre. Audio-visual Centre

Libraries: Luking Library, c. 1,080,000 vols

Academic Staff 2007-2008	MEN	WOMEN	TOTAL
FULL-TIME	298	373	671
PART-TIME	224	193	417
STAFF WITH DOCTORATE			
FULL-TIME	159	98	257
PART-TIME	63	22	85
Student Numbers 2007-2008			
All (Foreign Included)	4,272	6,691	10,963
FOREIGN ONLY	301	214	515

Part-time students, 2,983.
Last Updated: 11/12/08

SHIH CHIEN UNIVERSITY (SCU)

70, Ta-Chih Street, Taipei 104
Tel: +886(2) 253-81111
Fax: +886(2) 250-46293
EMail: ccadm@mail.usc.edu.tw
Website: http://www.usc.edu.tw

President: Mung-Shiung Shieh (1999-)
Tel: +886(2) 253-38411, Fax: +886(2) 253-38213
EMail: presi@mail.usc.edu.tw

Vice-President: Pin-Shou Ting
Tel: +886(2) 667-8000, Fax: +886(2) 667-9551
EMail: ting@mail.usc.edu.tw

International Relations: Hung-Yun Lu
Tel: +886(2) 253-81111, Ext. 1230 EMail: dodo@mail.usc.edu.tw

Centres
General Education

Colleges
Design (Architecture; Communication Studies; Fashion Design; Industrial Design); **Human Ecology** (Gerontology; Music; Nutrition; Social Work); **Management** (Accountancy; Banking; Business Administration; Finance; Information Management; Insurance; International Business; Modern Languages)

Graduate Institutes
Business Administration (Business Administration); **Family Studies and Child Development** (Family Studies); **Fashion Design** (Fashion Design); **Food and Nutrition** (Nutrition); **Industrial Design** (Industrial Design); **Internet Trade Management** (E-Business/Commerce)
Further Information: Kaohsiung Campus

History: Founded 1958 as Home Economics College, acquired present status and title 1997.

Academic Year: September to June (September-January; February-June)

Admission Requirements: Graduation from senior high school

Main Language(s) of Instruction: Mandarin Chinese

Degrees and Diplomas: *Bachelor's Degree*; *Master's Degree*

Special Facilities: Costume Museum

Libraries: c. 100,000 vols

SHIH HSIN UNIVERSITY (SHU)

1, Section 1, Mu-Cha Road, Lane 17, Wen San, Taipei 116
Tel: +886(2) 223-68225
Fax: +886(2) 223-65133
EMail: Pres@cc.shu.edu.tw
Website: http://www.shu.edu.tw

President: Paul Tzung-Tzann Mu
Tel: +886(2) 223-68225, Ext. 2003

Administrative Officer: Chih-Cheng Yeh
Tel: +886(2) 223-68225, Ext. 2008 EMail: sec.@cc.shu.edu.tw

International Relations: Tzu-Hsiang Yu
Tel: +886(2) 223-68225, Ext. 2321 EMail: C15@cc.shu.edu.tw

Colleges
Humanities and Social Sciences (English; Literature; Social Psychology); **Journalism and Communications** (Communication Arts; Journalism; Public Relations; Radio and Television Broadcasting)

Graduate Institutes
Mass Communication (Mass Communication); **Social Transformation Studies** (Social Studies)

Schools
Law (Commercial Law; Law; Private Law); **Management** (Economics; Finance; Information Management; Management; Public Administration; Tourism)

SHU-TE UNIVERSITY (STU)

59, Hun Shan Road, Yen Chau, Kaohsiung 82445
Tel: +886(7) 615-8000
Fax: +886(7) 615-8999
EMail: doc@mail.stu.edu.tw
Website: http://www.stu.edu.tw

President: Ining Yuan-Hsiang Chu
Tel: +886(7) 615-8000, Ext. 1100 EMail: ining@mail.stu.edu.tw

Vice-President: W.S. Hsieh
Tel: +886(7) 615-8000, Ext. 1200 EMail: wshsieh@mail.stu.edu.tw

International Relations: Teresa Ju
Tel: +886(7) 615-8000, Ext. 1700 EMail: tju@mail.stu.edu.tw

Colleges
Design (Design); **Information Technology** (Computer Engineering; Computer Science; Information Technology); **Liberal Education** (Arts and Humanities); **Management** (Business Administration; Finance; Insurance; International Business; Leisure Studies; Management; Tourism; Transport Management); **Social Sciences** (Social Sciences)

History: Founded 1997. Acquired present status 2006.
Last Updated: 01/02/07

SOOCHOW UNIVERSITY (SU)

70 Linshi Road, Shihlin, Taipei 111
Tel: +886(2) 288-19471
Fax: +886(2) 288-29310
EMail: president@scu.edu.tw
Website: http://www.scu.edu.tw

President (Acting): Chun-Mei Ma (2008-)
Tel: +886(2) 288-19184, Fax: +886(2) 288-11468

Dean of Academic Affairs: Wei-Liang Chao
Tel: +886(2) 288-19471, Ext. 6002, Fax: +886(2) 288-32954
EMail: acad@scu.edu.tw

International Relations: Chiung-Feng Ko
Tel: +886(2) 288-19471, Ext 5231, Fax: +886(2) 288-32954
EMail: rae@scu.edu.tw

Schools

Arts and Social Sciences (Chinese; Education; History; Music; Philosophy; Political Sciences; Social Work; Sociology) *Dean*: Li-Li Mo; **Business** (Accountancy; Business and Commerce; Computer Science; Economics; Information Sciences; International Business) *Dean*: Yung-Ho Chiu; **Foreign Languages and Cultures** (English; English Studies; German; Germanic Studies; Japanese) *Dean*: Chin-Chuan Lin; **Law** (Law) *Dean*: Wei-Da Pan; **Science** (Chemistry; Mathematics; Microbiology; Physics; Psychology) *Dean*: Ming-Ren Fuh

History: Founded 1900 in Soochow and received Charter from State of Tennessee. Supported by the Methodist Episcopal Church, South. Closed 1949 and re-established in Taipei 1950. Acquired present status and title 1954. A private institution under the supervision of the Ministry of Education.

Governing Bodies: Board of Trustees

Academic Year: August to July (August-January; February-July)

Admission Requirements: Graduation from high school and entrance examination

Fees: (New Taiwan Dollars): 50,000-64,000 per semester

Main Language(s) of Instruction: Chinese, English

International Co-operation: With universities in USA, Germany, Japan, Netherlands and Sweden

Degrees and Diplomas: *Bachelor's Degree*: Accounting; Business; Administration; International Business; Business Mathematics; Computer and Information Science (B.B.A.); Chinese; History; Philosophy; Political Science; Sociology; Social Work; Music; Education; English Language and Literature; Japanese Language and Culture; German Language and Culture; Economics (B.A.); Law (all fields of law) (LL.B); Mathematics; Physics; Chemistry; Microbiology; Psychology (B.S.), 4 yrs; *Master's Degree*: Accounting; Business; Administration; International Business; Business Mathematics; Computer and Information Science (M.B.A.); Chinese; History; Philosophy; Political Science; Sociology; Social Work; Music; English Language and Literature; Japanese Language and Culture; German Language and Culture; Economics (M.A.); Mathematics; Chemistry; Microbiology; Psychology (M.S.), a further 2-3 yrs; *Doctorate*: Chinese; Political Science; Japanese Language and Culture; Economics (Ph.D.); Law (all fields of law) (LL.D); Microbiology (Ph.D.), a further 3-4 yrs

Student Services: Academic counselling, Canteen, Foreign student adviser, Handicapped facilities, Health services, Language programs, Sports facilities

Student Residential Facilities: For c. 1,400 students

Special Facilities: Language Centre; Computing Centre

Libraries: Central Library 733,782 vols; 166,794 periodicals

Publications: Soochow Journal of Chinese Studies *(annually)*; Soochow Journal of Economics and Business *(quarterly)*; Soochow Journal of Foreign Languages and Cultures *(biennially)*; Soochow Journal of History *(biennially)*; Soochow Journal of Japanese Language Teaching *(annually)*; Soochow Journal of Mathematics *(quarterly)*; Soochow Journal of Philosophical Studies *(quarterly)*; Soochow Journal of Political Science *(biennially)*; Soochow Journal of Social Work *(annually)*; Soochow Journal of Sociology *(biennially)*; Soochow Law Journal *(biennially)*; Soochow Law Review *(3 per annum)*

Academic Staff 2007-2008	MEN	WOMEN	TOTAL
FULL-TIME	279	164	443
PART-TIME	325	209	534
STAFF WITH DOCTORATE			
FULL-TIME	209	9	218
PART-TIME	110	41	151
Student Numbers 2007-2008			
All (Foreign Included)	5,020	7,402	12,422

Evening students, 1,646.
Last Updated: 05/01/09

SOUTHERN TAIWAN UNIVERSITY

1, Nan Tai Street, Yung Kang, Tainan Hsien 710
Tel: +886(6) 253-3131
Fax: +886(6) 254-3031
EMail: coop@mail.stut.edu.tw
Website: http://www.stut.edu.tw

President: Tai Chein
Tel: +886(6) 253-3920 EMail: chang@mail.stut.edu.tw

Secretary-General: Chen-Chang Chuang
Tel: +886(6) 253-3920 EMail: sec@mail.stut.edu.tw

International Relations: Chin-Fa Cheng
Tel: +886(6) 253-1841, Fax: +886(6) 253-7461

Colleges

Business (Accountancy; Finance; Information Management; International Business); **Engineering** (Biotechnology; Chemical Engineering; Computer Science; Electrical and Electronic Engineering; Information Technology; Mechanical Engineering) *Dean*: Deng-Maw Lu; **Humanities and Social Sciences** (Child Care and Development; Education; English; Japanese; Teacher Training); **Management** (Business Administration; Information Management; Information Technology; Leisure Studies; Management; Marketing; Tourism)

History: Founded 1969 as junior college, became Nai Tai College of Industrial Skills 1990. Acquired present status and title 1996.

Governing Bodies: Board of Trustees

Academic Year: August to July (August-January; February-July)

Main Language(s) of Instruction: Mandarin Chinese

Degrees and Diplomas: *Bachelor's Degree*: 2 yrs following junior college study; *Master's Degree*

Student Services: Foreign Studies Centre, Handicapped facilities, Nursery care, Social counselling

Student Residential Facilities: For c. 1,600 students

Libraries: Nan-Tai Library, c. 110,000 vols

TAINAN UNIVERSITY OF TECHNOLOGY (TUT)

529, Chung Cheng Road, Yung Kang, Tainan 710
Tel: +886(6) 253-2106
Fax: +886(6) 254-0702
EMail: twcat@mail.twcat.edu.tw
Website: http://www.tut.edu.tw/

President: Teng-Chi Kuo (1994-)
Tel: +886(6) 253-5641 EMail: kuotc@mail.twcat.edu.tw

Dean of Academic Affairs: Jack Hong-Chu Chen
Tel: +886(6) 242-6028, Fax: +886(6) 254-1309
EMail: emacad@mail.twcat.edu.tw

International Relations: Nai-Nu Yang
Tel: +886(6) 253-1094, Fax: +886(6) 253-1094
EMail: emcoop@mail.twcat.edu.tw

Colleges

Art (Dance; Fine Arts; Music) *Director*: Li-Jen Hou; **Business** (Accountancy; Business Administration; Finance; International Business; Modern Languages) *Director*: Szu-Pi Chao; **Design** (Design; Handicrafts; Interior Design; Visual Arts) *Director*: Tsun-Yu Lee; **Home Economics** (Child Care and Development; Fashion Design; Home Economics) *Director*: Chia-Kai Su

History: Founded 1964 as Tainan Junior College of Home Economics. Acquired present status 1997 and title 2006, with an attached Junior College. The institution is the only Women's University in Taiwan. Formerly known as Tainan Woman's College of Arts and Technology.

Governing Bodies: Board of Directors

Academic Year: September to June (September-January; February-June)

Admission Requirements: Graduation from junior college or high school and college entrance examination

Fees: (New Taiwan Dollars): c. 40,000-50,000

Main Language(s) of Instruction: Chinese

Degrees and Diplomas: *Bachelor's Degree*: 2-4 yrs

Student Services: Academic counselling, Employment services, Health services, Social counselling, Sports facilities

Student Residential Facilities: For c. 1,500 students

Special Facilities: Auditorium. Bookstore. MTV Centre. 4 Audio-visual Rooms. Computer Laboratory. Workshops

Libraries: Main Library, c. 120,000 vols; c. 460 periodical series

Publications: Han-Chia Magazine *(quarterly)*; Journal of Tainan Women's University *(biannually)*; Youth Magazine of Junior College *(annually)*

TAIPEI MEDICAL UNIVERSITY

250, Wushing Street, Taipei 110
Tel: +886(2) 273-61661
Fax: +886(2) 273-87795
EMail: tmu@tmu.edu.tw
Website: http://www.tmu.edu.tw

President: Chung-Yi Hsu EMail: chungyi@tmu.edu.tw

Administrative Officer: Chung-Ye Hong
EMail: hongprof@tmu.edu.tw

International Relations: Jane C-J Chao
Tel: +886(2) 276-1661, Ext. 6548

Centres
Bioinformatics Computing; **General Education**; **Innovation and Incubation** (Embryology and Reproduction Biology; Sports Medicine); **Instrument**; **Laboratory Animal**; **Teaching Resource**

Colleges
Medicine (Biotechnology; Health Administration; Laboratory Techniques; Medical Technology; Medicine; Respiratory Therapy); **Nursing** (Gerontology; Management; Nursing); **Oral Medicine** (Dental Hygiene; Dental Technology; Dentistry); **Pharmacy** (Pharmacology; Pharmacy); **Public Health and Nutrition** (Health Sciences; Nutrition; Public Health)

Graduate Institutes
Biomedical Informatics (Biomedical Engineering; Medical Technology); **Biomedical Technology** (Biomedical Engineering; Medical Technology); **Cell and Molecular Biology** (Cell Biology; Molecular Biology); **Clinical Medicine** (Public Health); **Health Care Administration** (Social and Preventive Medicine); **Humanities in Medicine**; **Medical Laboratory Science and Biothecnlology** (Nursing); **Medical Sciences** (Medical Technology); **Neuroscience**; **Pharmacology** (Pharmacology)

Research Centres
Brain Disease and Aging; **Gastroenterology**; **Herbal Molecular Identification**; **Indigenous Health**; **Obesity Medicine**; **Reproductive Medicine**; **Stem Cell**; **Stroke** *(Doctor Huang Chihsin)*

Further Information: Also Teaching Hospital: Taipei Medical University Hospital (TMUH); TMU-Taipei Municipal Wan Fang Hospital; TMU-Shuangho Hospital, DOH

History: Founded 1960 as Taipei Medical College by Dr. Shui-Wang Hu, Dr Cheng-Tien Hsu and other medical specialists. Acquired present status and title 2000.

Governing Bodies: Board of Trustees, comprising 15 members

Academic Year: August to July (August-January; February-July)

Admission Requirements: Graduation from senior high school or equivalent, or above. Foreign applicants need to submit diploma transcripts and pass basic Chinese language test. For graduate: transcripts, diploma, study plan and might vary for different institutes.

Main Language(s) of Instruction: Chinese, English

Degrees and Diplomas: *Bachelor's Degree*: 4-7 yrs; *Master's Degree*: 2-4 yrs; *Doctorate (PhD)*: 3-7 yrs

Libraries: 183,286 vols

Publications: TMU Today *(monthly)*
Last Updated: 24/01/07

TAJEN UNIVERSITY (TU)

20, Weishin Road, Yanpu Shiang, Pingtung 907
Tel: +886(8) 762-4002~5
Fax: +886(8) 762-3924
EMail: admission@mail.tajen.edu.tw
Website: http://www.tajen.edu.tw

President: Rhei-Long Chen Tel: +886(8) 762-4002, Ext. 102

Chief Secretary: Chu-Chih Huang
Tel: +886(8) 762-4969 EMail: grace@ccsun.tajen.edu.tw

International Relations: Dau-Chang Wei
Tel: +886(8) 762-4509 EMail: dcwei@ccsun.tajen.edu.tw

Departments
Applied Foreign Languages (Modern Languages); **Biotechnology** (Biotechnology); **Computer Science and Information Engineering** (Computer Science; Information Sciences); **Early Childhood Care and Education** (Child Care and Development; Preschool Education; Primary Education); **Environmental Engineering and Science** (Environmental Engineering; Environmental Studies); **Food and Beverage Management** (Food Science); **Food Science and Technology**; **Health Care Administration** (Health Administration); **Hotel and Restaurant Management** (Hotel and Restaurant; Hotel Management); **Management Information Systems** (Information Management; Management Systems); **Nursing** (Nursing); **Occupational Safety and Hygiene** (Hygiene; Occupational Health; Safety Engineering); **Pharmacy** (Pharmacy); **Recreation and Health Business Management** (Health Administration; Management; Parks and Recreation); **Recreation and Sport Management** (Parks and Recreation; Sports Management); **Social Work** (Social Work)

Graduate Institutes
Biotechnology; **Environmental Management** (Environmental Management); **Leisure** (Leisure Studies); **Pharmaceutical Technology**

History: Founded 1966, acquired present status and title 2003.

Fees: (New Taiwan Dollars): International undergraduate, 47,000-53,000 per semester; graduate, 3,000-5,000

Degrees and Diplomas: *Bachelor's Degree*: Pharmacy; Biotechnology; Food and Beverage Management; Hotel and Restaurant Management; Marketing and Distribution Management; *Master's Degree*: Pharmaceutical Technology; Biotechnology

TAMKANG UNIVERSITY (TKU)

151, Ying-Chuan Road, Tamsui, Taipei County 25137
Tel: +886(2) 2621-5656
Fax: +886(2) 2623-7384
EMail: olr@mail.tku.edu.tw
Website: http://foreign.tku.edu.tw/TKUEnglish/

President: Flora Chia I. Chang (2004-)
Tel: +886(2) 2621-6320 EMail: fcic@mail.tku.edu.tw

Vice-President for Academic Affairs: Kan-nan Chen
Tel: +886(2) 2623-5895, Fax: +886(2) 2623-4947
EMail: knchen@mail.tku.edu.tw

Vice-President for Administrative Affairs: Po-yuan Kao
Tel: +886(2) 2623-5965, Fax: +886(2) 2623-5714
EMail: vivid@mail.tku.edu.tw

International Relations: Pei-Wha Chi Lee, Director, Office of Exchange and International Education
Tel: +886(2) 2629-6579, Fax: +886(2) 2629-6582
EMail: pcwl@mail.tku.edu.tw

Centres
Chinese Language (Chinese); **Data Processing** (Information Technology) *Director*: Ming-Dar Hwang; **Extension Education** (Arts and Humanities; Business and Commerce; Continuing Education; Engineering; Natural Sciences) *Dean*: Chin-Tang Lu; **Fine Arts** *(Carrie Chang)* (Fine Arts); **In-service Education**; **Japanese Language** (Japanese); **Teacher Education** (Teacher Training)

Colleges
Business (Banking; Business and Commerce; Economics; Finance; Industrial and Production Economics; Insurance; International Business) *Dean*: Yi-jen Hu; **Community Development** *Dean*: Jyh-horng Lin; **Education** (Curriculum; Education; Educational Administration; Educational and Student Counselling; Educational Psychology; Educational Research; Educational Technology; Higher Education; Teacher Training) *Dean*: Hsun-fung Kao; **Engineering** (Aeronautical and Aerospace Engineering; Architecture; Chemical Engineering; Civil Engineering; Computer Science; Electrical Engineering; Electronic Engineering; Environmental Engineering; Information Technology; Materials Engineering;

Mechanical Engineering; Structural Architecture; Water Science) *Dean*: Gwo-Hsing Yu; **Entrepreneurial Development** *Dean*: Andy Ay-hwa Liou; **Foreign Languages and Literature** (English; French; German; Japanese; Literature; Modern Languages; Russian; Spanish) *Dean*: Mei-hua Sung; **Global Research and Development** (Cultural Studies; Development Studies; Economics; Linguistics; Political Sciences) *Dean*: Jyh-horng Lin; **International Studies** (American Studies; Chinese; Eastern European Studies; European Studies; International Relations; International Studies; Japanese; Latin American Studies; Slavic Languages; Southeast Asian Studies) *Dean*: Wan-chin Tai; **Liberal Arts** (Arts and Humanities; Chinese; Communication Studies; History; Information Sciences; Library Science; Linguistics; Mass Communication) *Dean*: Jeong-Yeou Chiu; **Management** (Accountancy; Business Administration; Information Management; Leadership; Management; Management Systems; Public Administration; Statistics; Transport Management) *Dean*: Chu-ching Wang; **Science** (Biological and Life Sciences; Chemistry; Mathematics; Physics) *Dean*: Bo-Cheng Wang

Divisions
Continuing Education (Chinese; Japanese; Teacher Training) *Dean*: Kuo-Kung Shih

Graduate Institutes
American Studies (American Studies); **China Studies** (Chinese; East Asian Studies); **Chinese Linguistics and Documentation** (Chinese; Linguistics); **Curriculum and Instruction** (Curriculum; Education); **Educational Policy and Leadership** (Educational Administration; Educational Sciences); **Educational Psychology and Counselling**; **European Studies** (European Studies); **Future Studies**; **Higher Education**; **International Affairs and Strategic Studies** (International Relations; Military Science); **Japanese Studies** (Japanese); **Latin American Studies** (Latin American Studies); **Life Sciences**; **Slavic Studies** (Eastern European Studies; Slavic Languages); **Southeast Asian Studies** (Southeast Asian Studies)

Research Centres
Champion Incubator; **China Studies**; **Cross-Strait Financial Research** (Finance); **Energy and Optoelectric Materials Research** (Energy Engineering); **European Union Studies** (European Studies); **Industrial and Financial Research**; **Information Application**; **Life Science Development** (Biological and Life Sciences); **Statistical Survey Research** *(SSRC)* (Statistics); **Study of Globalization and Cultural Differences**; **Tamkang Times**; **Tibetan Studies** (Tibetan); **Water Resources Management and Policy Research** (Water Management; Water Science); **Wind Engineering** *(WERC)* (Engineering)

Further Information: Tamkang University has four campuses: Tamsui, Taipei, Lanyang and Cyber campuses. Also student programmes with Japan, Russia, France, Germany, Spain, USA, Canada, and Belgium

History: Founded 1950 as Junior College of English, became College of Arts and Sciences 1958, and acquired present status and title 1980.

Governing Bodies: Board of Trustees

Academic Year: August to July (August-January; February-July)

Admission Requirements: Graduation from high school and entrance examination

Fees: (New Taiwan Dollars): 46,880-54,720 per semester

Main Language(s) of Instruction: Chinese, English

Degrees and Diplomas: *Bachelor's Degree*: 4-5 yrs; *Master's Degree*: a further 1-4 yrs; *Doctorate*: a further 2-7 yrs by thesis

Student Services: Academic counselling, Cultural centre, Employment services, Foreign student adviser, Handicapped facilities, Health services, Social counselling, Sports facilities

Special Facilities: Maritime Museum. Carrie Chang Fine Arts Centre

Libraries: Chueh-sheng Memorial Library, c. 1m. printed vols; Non-book materials, 140,000 items; subscriptions to periodicals, 60,000 (including electronic journals), electronic databases, 361. All materials are managed by the Library integrated System names Virtua

Publications: International Journal of Information and Management Sciences *(quarterly)*; Journal of Educational Media and Library Sciences *(quarterly)*; Journal of Future Studies *(quarterly)*; Tam-

kang Journal of Humanities and Social Sciences *(quarterly)*; Tamkang Journal of International Affairs *(quarterly)*; Tamkang Journal of Mathematics *(quarterly)*; Tamkang Journal of Science and Engineering *(quarterly)*; Tamkang Review *(biannually)*

Press or Publishing House: Tamkang University Press

Academic Staff 2008-2009	MEN	WOMEN	TOTAL
FULL-TIME	746	748	1,494
PART-TIME	620	288	908
STAFF WITH DOCTORATE			
FULL-TIME	–	–	94
PART-TIME	–	–	184
Student Numbers 2008-2009			
All (Foreign Included)	–	–	27,845
FOREIGN ONLY	–	–	203

Last Updated: 11/12/08

TATUNG UNIVERSITY (TTU)
40, Section 3, Chungshan N. Road, Taipei 104
Tel: +886(2) 259-25252
Fax: +886(2) 259-41371
EMail: postmaster@ttu.edu.tw
Website: http://www.ttu.edu.tw

President: T. S. LinFax: +886(2) 258-53290
EMail: tslin@ttu.edu.tw

Dean of Academic Affairs: C. C. Huang
Tel: +886(2) 259-25252, Ext. 2203 EMail: cchuang@ttu.edu.tw

International Relations: L. M. Tseng
Tel: +886(2) 259-25252, Ext. 2203 EMail: lmtseng@ttu.edu.tw

Colleges
Electrical and Information Engineering (Applied Mathematics; Computer Engineering; Computer Science; Electrical Engineering; Information Technology; Optical Technology); **Engineering** (Bioengineering; Chemical Engineering; Materials Engineering; Mechanical Engineering); **Management and Design** (Business Administration; Industrial Design; Information Management)

History: Founded 1943 as private Vocational School of Industry. Junior college added 1956. Reorganized 1963 as Tatung Institute of Technology, and acquired present status and title 2003.

Governing Bodies: Board of Directors

Academic Year: August to July (August-January; February-July)

Admission Requirements: Graduation from high school and entrance examination

Main Language(s) of Instruction: Chinese, English

Degrees and Diplomas: *Bachelor's Degree*: 4 yrs; *Master's Degree*: a further 2 yrs; *Doctorate (PhD)*: a further 3 yrs

Student Services: Academic counselling, Cultural centre, Employment services, Health services, Sports facilities

Student Residential Facilities: Yes

Special Facilities: Science Museum

Libraries: Institute Library, c. 136,700 vols

Publications: Tatung Journal *(annually)*

Press or Publishing House: Sun-chih Publishing Company

TUNG NAN UNIVERSITY (TNIT)
152, Section 3, Pei Shen Road, Shen Keng, Taipei 22202
Tel: +886(2) 866-25900
Fax: +886(2) 266-43648
Website: http://140.129.140.215/

President: Shen-Tung Huang
Tel: +886(2) 866-25888, Fax: +886(2) 266-22827
EMail: president@mail.tnit.edu.tw

Vice-President: Tai-Ching Chiang
Tel: +886(2) 866-25890, Fax: +886(2) 866-25890
EMail: tcchiang@mail.tnit.edu.tw

International Relations: Yea-Ping Wang
Tel: +886(2) 866-25820 EMail: ypwang@mail.tnit.edu.tw

Departments
Applied Foreign Languages (Modern Languages); **Automation Engineering** (Automation and Control Engineering); **Business**

Administration (Business Administration); **Civil Engineering** (Civil Engineering); **Computer and Communication Engineering** (Information Technology; Telecommunications Engineering); **Computer Science and Information Engineering** (Computer Science; Information Technology); **Construction Management** (Construction Engineering); **Electrical Engineering** (Electrical Engineering); **Electronic Engineering** (Electronic Engineering); **Industrial Management** (Industrial Management); **Information Management** (Information Management); **Mechanical Engineering** (Mechanical Engineering); **Safety Health and Environment Engineering** (Environmental Engineering; Safety Engineering)

History: Founded 1970, acquired present status 2000. Formerly known as Tung Nan Institute of Technology.

Degrees and Diplomas: *Bachelor's Degree*: Electrical Engineering; Mechanical Engineering; Automation Engineering; Industrial Management; Business Management; Information Management; Applied Foreign Languages (BS; BA); Electronic Engineering; Information Engineering; Computer and Communication; Civil Engineering; Construction Management; Environment Engineering and Safety Health Engineering (BA; BS);

TUNGHAI UNIVERSITY (THU)

181, Section 3, Taichung Harbor Road, Taichung 407
Tel: +886(4) 2359-0200
Fax: +886(4) 2359-0361
Website: http://www.thu.edu.tw

President: Haydn Chen (2004-) EMail: president@thu.edu.tw

Secretary-General: Hua-Yuan Tseng
Tel: +886(4) 2359-0523 EMail: huayuan@thu.edu.tw

International Relations: Andrew Wang
Tel: +886(4) 2359-0356, Fax: +886(4) 2359-0884

Centres
Chinese Language (Chinese); **English Language**

Colleges
Agriculture (Agriculture; Biotechnology; Food Science; Hotel Management; Zoology) *Dean*: Yun-Chu Wu; **Arts** (Chinese; Foreign Languages Education; History; Japanese; Literature; Modern Languages; Philosophy; Religious Studies) *Dean*: Eugene Chiu; **Engineering** (Chemical Engineering; Computer Science; Electrical Engineering; Environmental Engineering; Industrial Engineering; Information Technology; Materials Engineering) *Dean*: William Cheng-Chung Chu; **Fine Arts and Creative Design** *Dean*: David Tseng; **Management** (Accountancy; Business Administration; Finance; Information Management; International Business; Statistics) *Dean*: Kai-I Huang; **Science** (Biological and Life Sciences; Chemistry; Physics) *Dean*: Guang-Yuh Hwang; **Social Sciences** (Economics; Law; Political Sciences; Public Administration; Social Work; Sociology) *Dean*: Feng-Wen Wen

Research Centres
Microbiology (Microbiology); **Nano Science and Technology**; **Social and Management Studies in Mainland China**; **Software Engineering** (Software Engineering); **Tropical Ecology and Biodiversity** (Ecology; Tropical Agriculture)

Schools
Extension Education School; **Liberal Arts Education** (Communication Studies; Development Studies; Modern Languages; Regional Studies)

History: Founded 1955 through the efforts of Christian leaders at home and abroad and the active support of the United Board for Christian Higher Education in Asia. The first private university in Taiwan.

Governing Bodies: Board of Directors, comprising 15 members, representing Chinese and Western leaders in Business, Education and Government

Academic Year: September to June (September-January; February-June)

Admission Requirements: Graduation from recognized senior high school or school of equivalent standing, and entrance examination

Fees: (New Taiwan Dollars): 48,217-56,289 per semester

Main Language(s) of Instruction: Chinese, English

International Co-operation: With universities in Japan; USA; China; Republic of Korea; United Kingdom; Australia; Philippines; Argentina; Thailand; Indonesia

Accrediting Agencies: Ministry of Education

Degrees and Diplomas: *Bachelor's Degree (BA, BS)*: 4-5 yrs; *Master's Degree (MA, MS, MBA)*: a further 1-4 yrs; *Doctorate (PhD)*: 2-7 yrs

Student Services: Academic counselling, Canteen, Cultural centre, Employment services, Foreign student adviser, Foreign Studies Centre, Handicapped facilities, Health services, Language programs, Nursery care, Social counselling, Sports facilities

Student Residential Facilities: For 4,500 students

Special Facilities: Auditorium. Experimental Farm

Libraries: 845,798 vols; 41,245 periodical titles; 63,524 non-book materials; 145 electronic databases

Publications: Tunghai Journal

Press or Publishing House: Tunghai University Press

Academic Staff 2007-2008	MEN	WOMEN	TOTAL
FULL-TIME	380	135	515
PART-TIME	21	79	100
STAFF WITH DOCTORATE FULL-TIME	–	–	2,899
Student Numbers 2007-2008			
All (Foreign Included)	5,502	6,681	12,183
FOREIGN ONLY	–	–	34

Evening students, 1,485.
Last Updated: 12/12/08

TZU CHI UNIVERSITY

701, Section 3, Chung Yan Road, Hualien 970
Tel: +886(3) 856-5301
Fax: +886(3) 856-2500
EMail: feedback@mail.tcu.edu.tw
Website: http://www.tcu.edu.tw

President: Jye-Siung Fang (2002-)
Tel: +886(3) 856-5301, Ext. 7001, Fax: +886(3) 857-5228
EMail: jsfang@mail.tcu.edu.tw

Secretary-General: Su-Jen Hung
Tel: +886(3) 857-2084, Ext. 7006, Fax: +886(3) 857-5228
EMail: yun@mail.tcu.edu.tw

Colleges
Education and Communication (Communication Studies; Education); **Humanities** (Arts and Humanities); **Laboratory Medicine and Biotechnology** (Biotechnology; Laboratory Techniques); **Medicine** (Medicine)

Departments
Child Development and Family Learning (Child Care and Development; Family Studies); **Communication Studies** (Communication Studies); **Human Development**; **Life Sciences** (Biological and Life Sciences); **Medical Information Technologies**; **Medicine** (Medicine); **Nursing** (Nursing); **Oriental Literature** (Literature); **Public Health**; **Social Work** (Social Work)

Graduate Institutes
Aboriginal Health (Health Sciences; Indigenous Studies); **Anthropology** (Anthropology); **Education** (Education); **Human Genetics** (Genetics); **Medical Biotechnology** (Biotechnology); **Medical Science** (Medicine); **Molecular Biology and Cell Biology** (Cell Biology; Molecular Biology); **Neurosciences** (Neurosciences); **Nursing Science** (Nursing); **Pharmacology and Toxicology** (Pharmacology; Toxicology); **Public Health** (Public Health); **Religion and Culture** (Cultural Studies; Religious Studies); **Social Work** (Social Work)

History: Founded 1994 as Tzu Chi College of Medicine, expanded to Tzu Chi College of Medicine and Humanities 1998. Acquired present title 2000.

Governing Bodies: Board of Directors

Academic Year: August to July (August-January; February-July)

Admission Requirements: Senior high school certificate and entrance examination. Selection through either a new version of the

Joint University Entrance Examinations or by application and general (SAT II like) examination

Fees: (New Taiwan Dollars): 47,000-59,000 per semester

Main Language(s) of Instruction: Chinese

Accrediting Agencies: Ministry of Education

Degrees and Diplomas: *Bachelor's Degree*: Child Development, Family Learning; Communication Studies, Human Development, Oriental Literature; Life Science, Medical Technology, Nursing, Public Health; Medical Informatics; Social Work, 4 yrs; *Master's Degree*: Aboriginal Health, Human Genetics, Molecular and Cell Biology, Neuroscience, Nursing, Pharmacology, Toxicology; Anthropology, Religious Studies; Education; Medical Science; Social Work, 1-4 yrs; *Doctorate*: Medical Science, 2-7 yrs; *Doctorate*: Medicine, 7 yrs

Student Services: Academic counselling, Canteen, Cultural centre, Employment services, Handicapped facilities, Health services, Language programs, Nursery care, Social counselling, Sports facilities

Student Residential Facilities: Yes

Libraries: 175,240 vols

VANUNG UNIVERSITY (VNU)

1, Van Nung Road, Chungli, Taoyuan 320
Tel: +886(3) 451-5811
Fax: +886(3) 451-3786
EMail: koli1230@msa.vnu.edu.tw
Website: http://www.vnu.edu.tw

President: Shin-Shing Shyu
Tel: +886(3) 451-5811, Ext 327, Fax: +886(3) 453-1300

International Relations: Chien-Seng Wang
Tel: +886(3) 453-1279, Fax: +886(3) 453-2636

Departments
Business Administration (Business Administration); **Chemical Engineering** (Chemical Engineering); **Civil Engineering** (Civil Engineering); **Commercial Design** (Business and Commerce; Design); **Computer Science and Information Engineering** (Computer Science; Information Technology); **Cosmetology** (Cosmetology); **Electronic Engineering** (Electronic Engineering); **Environmental Engineering** (Environmental Engineering); **Finance** (Finance); **Industrial Management** (Industrial Management); **International Trade** (International Business); **Management Information Systems** (Information Technology; Management); **Textile Science** (Textile Technology)

Graduate Schools
Business and Management (Business and Commerce; Management)

History: Founded 1973. Acquired present name and status 2004.

WUFENG INSTITUTE OF TECHNOLOGY (WFC)

117, Section 2, Chian-Kuo Road, Ming-Hsiung, Chiayi 621
Tel: +886(5) 226-7125
Fax: +886(5) 226-0213
EMail: enroll@mail.wfc.edu.tw
Website: http://www.wfc.edu.tw

President: Kuo-Shung Cheng (2000-)
Tel: +886(5) 226-7125, Ext. 21211, Fax: +886(5) 206-3455
EMail: kscheng@mail.wfc.edu.tw

Administrative Officer: Jyun-Jye Liao
Tel: +886(5) 226-7125, Ext. 23101, Fax: +886(5) 226-0213
EMail: jjliao@mail.wfc.edu.tw

International Relations: Yi-Tsern Lin
Tel: +886(5) 206-7125, Ext. 23131
EMail: jacklee@sun5.wfc.edu.tw

Departments
Accountancy Information Systems (Accountancy; Information Technology); **Applied Foreign Languages** (English; Japanese); **Chemical Engineering** (Chemical Engineering); **Computer Science and Information Engineering** (Computer Science; Information Technology); **Early Childhood Care and Education** (Child Care and Development; Preschool Education); **Electrical Engineering** (Electrical Engineering); **Electronic Engineering** (Electronic Engineering); **Fire Science** (Fire Science); **Information Management** (Information Management); **International Trade** (International Business); **Mechanical Engineering** (Mechanical Engineering); **Security Management**

Graduate Schools
Opto-Mechatronics and Materials

History: Founded 1965.

Degrees and Diplomas: *Bachelor's Degree*: Applied English; Applied Japanese; Early Childhood Care and Education (BS); Mechanical Engineering; Electrical Engineering; Electronic Engineering; Chemical Engineering; Computer Science and Information Engineering; Accountancy; Information Management; International Trade; E-Business; Fire Science; Secutity Management (BS), 4 yrs; *Bachelor's Degree*: Electrical Engineering; Electronic Engineering; Information Management; International Trade; Applied English (BS), 2 yrs

YUAN-ZE UNIVERSITY (YZU)

135, Yuan-Tung Road, Chung-Li, Taoyuan 32026
Tel: +886(3) 463-8800
Fax: +886(3) 455-8900
EMail: proffice@saturn.yzu.edu.tw
Website: http://www.yzu.edu.tw

President: Tsong P. Perng (2005-)
Tel: +886(3) 463-6569, Fax: +886(3) 463-6690
EMail: tpperng@saturn.yzu.edu.tw

Secretary-General: Yeh Liang Hsu
Tel: +886(3) 435-6235, Fax: +886(3) 463-6416
EMail: mehsu@saturn.yzu.edu.tw

International Relations: Yi-Ming Sun
Tel: +886(3) 435-2654, Fax: +886(3) 455-9378
EMail: cesunym@saturn.yzu.edu.tw

Centres
Management Studies (Management)

Colleges
Engineering (Chemical Engineering; Electrical Engineering; Electronic Engineering; Environmental Engineering; Industrial Engineering; Management; Mechanical Engineering; Natural Resources; Production Engineering); **Humanities and Social Sciences** (Applied Linguistics; Chinese; Literature; Modern Languages; Sociology); **Information Sciences** (Computer Engineering; Computer Networks; Computer Science; Information Management; Information Sciences); **Management** (Accountancy; Business Administration; Finance; International Business; Management)

Graduate Schools
Biotechnology (Biotechnology); **Electrical and Communication Engineering** (Communication Studies; Electronic Engineering; Optical Technology); **Engineering** (Chemical Engineering; Engineering; Industrial Engineering; Industrial Management; Materials Engineering; Mechanical Engineering); **Humanities and Social Sciences**; **Information Sciences** (Computer Engineering; Computer Science; Information Management; Information Sciences); **Management** (Accountancy; Business Administration; Finance; International Business; Management); **Visual Arts Administration** (Visual Arts)

History: Founded 1989, acquired present status and title 1997.

Academic Year: September to June (September- January; February- June)

Admission Requirements: High school certificate

Fees: (New Taiwan Dollars): 55,000 per semester

Main Language(s) of Instruction: Chinese and English

International Co-operation: With universities in USA, Australia, Canada, Sweden, France, Netherlands, Israel, Kazakhstan

Degrees and Diplomas: *Bachelor's Degree*; *Master's Degree*; *Doctorate*

Student Services: Academic counselling, Foreign student adviser, Handicapped facilities, Health services, Language programs, Sports facilities

Last Updated: 02/02/07

Colombia

STRUCTURE OF HIGHER EDUCATION SYSTEM

Description:

Higher education is provided by university institutions, institutes of technology and technical professional institutions. These three types include both public and private institutions. In university institutions, each faculty is divided into departments. Distance education is provided by universities and regional centres. Higher education comes under the responsibility of the Ministry of National Education. The Instituto Colombiano para el Fomento de la Educación Superior (ICFES) is in charge of the evaluation of the education system. The Consejo Nacional de Educación Superior (CESU) proposes policies for the development of higher education.

Stages of studies:

University level first stage: Pregrado
This stage is characterized by a high level of knowledge and practical experience of the subject and lasts for four or five years. It leads to the Licenciatura or to a professional qualification (Título Profesional). A thesis or monograph and/or preliminary work in the main subjects are sometimes compulsory for the award of the professional qualification. Course work is measured in Unidades de Labor Académica (ULA). A minimum of 3,200 ULAs is required for a Licenciatura.

University level second stage: Postgrado
The entry requirement for Specialist (Especialista) and Magister programmes is the title of Licenciado and, usually, an entrance examination. A Magister is conferred after two years of study. Specialist programmes are usually offered in practical or applied disciplines and vary in length from one to four years. The Doctorado is awarded after two years' postgraduate specialization study and the defence of a thesis. It requires a complete mastery of the specialization and an effective contribution to the advancement of knowledge through extensive research.

Distance higher education:
Institutes of higher education offer distance education programmes. They are also offered by regional centres (CREADS).

ADMISSION TO HIGHER EDUCATION

Admission to university-level studies:

Name of secondary school credential required: Bachillerato

Minimum score/requirement: 50

Entrance exam requirements: Students must sit for an entrance examination.

Other admission requirements: Some universities set their own compulsory examinations.

Foreign students admission:

Entrance exam requirements: Students must hold a secondary school leaving certificate equivalent to the Diploma de Bachiller and must sit for the State examinations.

Entry regulations: Foreign students must hold a visa, a health certificate and warrant financial guarantees.

Language requirements: Students must have a good knowledge of Spanish.

RECOGNITION OF STUDIES

Quality assurance system:

The quality assurance system of higher education comprises 3 interrelated elements: information (SNIES, ECAES, Labor Observatory for Education, SPADIES), evaluation (CNA), and promotion.

NATIONAL BODIES

Ministerio de Educación Nacional (Ministry of National Education)
Minister: María Fernanda Campo
Secretary-General: Nohemy Arias Otero
Vice-Minister, Higher Education: Gabriel Burgos Mantilla
Calle 43 No. 57 – 14
Bogotá
Tel: +57(1) 222 2800
WWW: http://www.mineducacion.gov.co
Role of national body: The Ministry defines the national education policy.

Consejo Nacional de Acreditación - CNA (National Accreditation Council)
Coordinator: Pedro Antonio Prieto Pulido
Secretary-General: Luis Enrique Silva
Calle 19 No. 6-68
Piso 17
Bogota
Tel: +57(1) 341 1050
Fax: +57(1) 341 1052
EMail: cna@cna.gov.co
WWW: http://www.cna.gov.co

Instituto Colombiano para el Fomento de la Educación Superior - ICFES (Colombian Institute for the Development of Higher Education)
Director General: Margarita Peña Borrero
Secretary-General: Gioconda Margarita Piña Elles
Calle 17 No. 3-40
Bogotá
Tel: +57(1) 338 7338
EMail: atencionciudadano@icfes.gov.co
WWW: http://www.icfes.gov.co
Role of national body: Specialized entity offering educational assessment in all educational levels and supporting the Ministry of National Education in the development and administration of state assessments and systematic investigation about the factors that influence the quality of education.

Sistema Nacional de Información de la Educación Superior - SNIES (National Information System on Higher Education)
Calle 43 No. 57
Bogota
WWW: http://www.mineducacion.gov.co/sistemasdeinformacion/1735/channel.html

Asociación Colombiana de Universidades - ASCUN (Association of Colombian Universities)
President: José Fernando Isaza Delgado
Executive Director: Bernardo Rivera Sanchez
Calle 93 No 16 - 43
Bogota
Tel: +57(1) 218 5127
Fax: +57(1) 218 5098
EMail: informa@ascun.org.co; asocolun@uniandes@edu.co
WWW: http://www.ascun.org.co
Role of national body: Not-for-profit and non-governmental association representing public and private universities.

Data for academic year: 2010-2011
Source: IAU from Ministry of National Education (documentation and website), Colombia, 2011.

INSTITUTIONS

PUBLIC INSTITUTIONS

ANTONIO JOSÉ CAMACHO UNIVERSITY INSTITUTION

Institución Universitaria Antonio José Camacho
Avenida Sexta Calle 29A Norte No 5N-01, Cali, Valle del Cauca
Tel: +57(2) 660-9097
Fax: +57(2) 556-9475
EMail: informacion@itmajc.edu.co
Website: http://www.itmajc.edu.co

Rector: Jairo Panneso Tascon EMail: rectoria@itmajc.edu.co

Faculties
Business Studies (Business Administration); **Distance Education** (Health Administration; Occupational Health; Preschool Education); **Engineering** (Electronic Engineering; Mechanical Engineering; Systems Analysis)

History: Founded 1993 as Instituto Tecnológico Municipal Antonio José Camacho. Acquired present title and status 2007.

Main Language(s) of Instruction: Spanish

Degrees and Diplomas: *Tecnólogo*; *Especialización*
Last Updated: 04/11/09

CENTRAL TECHNICAL INSTITUTE

Instituto Técnico Central (ITC)
Calle 13 No. 16-74, Bogotá
Tel: +57(1) 344-3000
Fax: +57(1) 342-0017
EMail: webmaster@itc.edu.co
Website: http://www.itc.edu.co

Rector: Isidro Daniel Cruz Rodríguez EMail: rectoria@itc.edu.co
Secretario General: Javier Polania González

Programmes
Electrical Engineering (Electrical Engineering); **Industrial Processes** (Industrial Engineering); **Machine Design** (Industrial Design); **Mechanical Engineering** (Mechanical Engineering)

Degrees and Diplomas: *Tecnólogo*; *Licenciatura*; *Titulo Profesional*; *Especialización*
Last Updated: 04/11/09

CENTRAL UNIT OF THE VALLEY OF THE CAUCA REGION

Unidad Central del Valle del Cauca (UCEVA)
Carrera 27 A No. 48-144 Kilómetro 1 Salida Sur, Tuluá, Valle del Cauca
Tel: +57(926) 224-2202
Fax: +57(926) 225-9051
EMail: info@uceva.edu.co
Website: http://www.uceva.edu.co/

Rector: Jairo Gutiérrez Obando
EMail: rectoria@uceva.edu.co; rectoria@teletulua.com.co

Faculties
Administration, Economics and Accountancy (Accountancy; Administration; Economics); **Education** (Education; Modern Languages; Social Sciences); **Engineering** (Engineering); **Health Sciences** (Health Sciences; Medicine; Nursing); **Law and Humanities** (Arts and Humanities; Law)

History: Founded 1971.

Main Language(s) of Instruction: Spanish

Degrees and Diplomas: *Tecnólogo*; *Licenciatura*; *Especialización*
Last Updated: 05/11/09

COLOMBIAN COLLEGE OF DENTISTRY

Colegio Odontológico Colombiano
Carrera 9 No. 13-40, Bogotá
Tel: +57(1) 341-5141
Fax: +57(1) 676-0072
Website: http://www.odontologico.edu.co

Rector: Jorge Hernando Arango Mejía
EMail: jarango@odontologico.edu.co

Secretaria General: Rosa Elena Arango Mejía
EMail: rarango@odontologico.edu.co

Faculties
Dentistry (Dental Technology; Dentistry; Health Administration; Oral Pathology; Surgery)

Further Information: Also Branch in Santiago de Cali

History: Founded 1975 as Colegio Odontológico Colombiano. Renamed Colegio Universitario Colombiano 1997. Acquired present title 2003.

Main Language(s) of Instruction: Spanish

Degrees and Diplomas: *Titulo Profesional*; *Especialización*
Last Updated: 28/10/09

DEPARTMENTAL INSTITUTE OF FINE ARTS

Instituto Departamental de Bellas Artes (BELLAS ARTES-CALI)
Avenida 2 Norte 7N -38, Cali, Valle del Cauca
Tel: +57(923) 688-3333
Fax: +57(923) 668-5583
EMail: bellasartes@bellasartes.edu.co
Website: http://www.bellasartes.edu.co

Rector: Henry Caicedo Ospino
Tel: +57(923) 688-3333, Ext. 113
EMail: henrycaicedo@bellasartes.edu.co

Vicerrector Academico y Investigaciones: Oswaldo Alfonso Hernandez Davila
Tel: +57(923) 688-3333, Ext.142 EMail: oshernan@telesat.com.co

International Relations: Luisa Liliana Oviedo Domínguez, Vicerrectora Administrativa
Tel: +57(923) 688-3333, Ext.104
EMail: luisaliliana2000@hotmail.com

Conservatories
Music *(Antonio María Valencia Conservatory)* (Music; Musical Instruments)

Faculties
Theatre (Acting; Theatre); **Visual and Applied Arts** (Engraving; Fine Arts; Graphic Design; Painting and Drawing; Sculpture)

History: Founded 1936, acquired present status 1992.

Governing Bodies: Directive Advice y Academico Advice

Academic Year: February to December (February-June; August-December)

Admission Requirements: Secondary school certificate (Bachillerato) and entrance examination (ICFES test)

Fees: (Pesos): based on family income

Main Language(s) of Instruction: Spanish

Accrediting Agencies: Consejo Nacional de Acreditación; Ministry of Education

Degrees and Diplomas: *Licenciatura*: Theatre, 5 yrs; *Titulo Profesional*: Teaching Qualification, Fine Arts, 5 yrs; *Especialización*: Art Management, 1 yr

Student Services: Academic counselling, Canteen, Sports facilities
Student Residential Facilities: For c. 500 students
Special Facilities: Art Galleries. Auditorium. Theatre. Concert Hall
Libraries: Alvaro Ramírez Sierra Library, c. 7,000 vols. 70,000 diskettes, magazines, films

Publications: Neocomics Magazine, Publications from the comics and visual narrative product of the work of investigation groups *(annually)*; Papel Escena Mazagine, A publication of the theater school with theoretical and critical articles *(annually)*
Last Updated: 04/11/09

DIEGO LUIS CÓRDOBA TECHNOLOGICAL UNIVERSITY OF CHOCÓ

Universidad Tecnológica del Chocó Diego Luis Córdoba
Apartado aéreo 292, Carrera 2 No. 25-22, Quibdó, Chocó
Tel: +57(4) 711-616
Fax: +57(4) 671-0237
EMail: utch@utch.edu.co
Website: http://www.utch.edu.co/

Rector: Eduardo García Vega EMail: rectoria@utch.edu.co

Secretario General: Carlos A. Córdoba Cuesta
EMail: cacocue@hotmail.com

Faculties
Education (Biology; Chemistry; Education; English; Environmental Studies; French; Literature; Mathematics; Natural Sciences; Physical Education; Physics; Primary Education; Social Sciences; Spanish); **Engineering; Humanities and Arts** (Accountancy; Architecture; Arts and Humanities; Business Administration; Fine Arts; Nursing; Social Work); **Law** (Law); **Science** (Biology; Natural Resources)

Institutes
Biodiversity (Ecology); **Pacific Studies** (Pacific Area Studies)

Programmes
Distance Education (Accountancy; Biology; Business Administration; Chemistry; Environmental Studies; Literature; Mathematics; Natural Sciences; Physics; Primary Education; Social Sciences; Social Work; Spanish)

Research Centres
Natural Resources (Natural Resources)

History: Founded 1972 as college, acquired present status and title 1975. A State institution.
Academic Year: February to December (February-July; August-December)
Admission Requirements: Secondary school certificate (bachillerato) and entrance examination
Main Language(s) of Instruction: Spanish
Degrees and Diplomas: *Licenciatura*: 3-4 1/2 yrs; *Titulo Profesional*; *Especialización*
Libraries: c. 5,500 vols
Last Updated: 20/11/09

FRANCISCO JOSÉ DE CALDAS DISTRICT UNIVERSITY

Universidad Distrital Francisco José de Caldas
Apartado aéreo 8668, Carrera 15 No. 57-43, Bogotá
Tel: +57(1) 340-0583
Fax: +57(1) 310-5235
EMail: ynavas@fenixudistrital.co
Website: http://www.udistrital.edu.co

Rector: Carlos Ossa Escobar EMail: rectoria@udistrital.edu.co

Secretario General: Luisa Fernanda Lancheros Parra
EMail: sgral@udistrital.edu.co

Faculties
Arts (Display and Stage Design; Music; Painting and Drawing; Sculpture; Theatre); **Engineering** (Computer Engineering; Electronic Engineering; Engineering; Industrial Engineering; Instrument Making; Surveying and Mapping); **Environmental Sciences** (Environmental Studies; Forestry); **Science and Education**; **Technology** (Civil Engineering; Electronic Engineering; Industrial Engineering; Mechanical Engineering; Technology; Telecommunications Engineering)

History: Founded 1948 under the authority of the municipality of Bogotá. Nationally recognized as an official University 1963.

Governing Bodies: Consejo Superior; Consejo Directivo
Academic Year: February to December (February-June; August-December)
Admission Requirements: Secondary school certificate (bachillerato) and entrance examination
Main Language(s) of Instruction: Spanish
Degrees and Diplomas: *Licenciatura*: 4 yrs; *Especialización*; *Maestría*; *Doctorado*
Libraries: c. 35,000 vols
Last Updated: 13/11/09

GENERAL SANTANDER SCHOOL OF POLICE STUDIES

Escuela Nacional de Policía General Santander (ENPGS)
Apartado aéreo 4670, Calle 44 Sur No. 45 A - 15, Bogotá
Tel: +57(1) 724-6402
EMail: jefat.egsan@policia.gov.co

Rector: Janio León Riaño
Tel: +57(1) 270-4917 EMail: direc.ecsan@policia.gov.co

Faculties
Police Studies I (Police Studies) *Dean*: Henri Camilo Ocampo Herrera; **Police Studies II** (Police Studies) *Dean*: Guillermo Julio Chávez Ocaña

History: Founded 1940.
Governing Bodies: Consejo Superior de Educación Policial
Admission Requirements: Secondary school certificate (bachillerato) and entrance examination
Accrediting Agencies: Asociación Colombiana para el Fomento de la Educación Superior; Consejo Nacional de Acreditación
Degrees and Diplomas: *Licenciatura*: Criminology (ST) (Criminalístico); Police Studies (ST), 4 yrs; *Especialización*
Student Services: Academic counselling, Canteen, Cultural centre, Employment services, Foreign student adviser, Health services, Language programs, Nursery care, Social counselling, Sports facilities
Student Residential Facilities: For c. 1,000 students
Special Facilities: Museum. Theatre. Observatory
Libraries: Main Library: c. 36,000 vols
Publications: *(quarterly)*

HIGHER COLLEGE OF ANTIOQUIA

Colegio Mayor de Antioquia
Calle 65 No 77-126, Medellín, Antioquia
Tel: +57(4) 422-5252
Fax: +57(4) 421-9947
EMail: colmayor@colmayor.edu.co
Website: http://www.colmayor.edu.co

Rectora: Martha Lía Naranjo Jaramillo
EMail: rectoria@colmayor.edu.co

Faculties
Administration (Administration; Business Administration; Secretarial Studies; Tourism); **Architecture**; **Health Sciences** (Health Sciences; Histology; Microbiology); **Social Sciences**

History: Founded 1945 as Colegio Mayor de Cultura Feminina de Antioquia. Acquired present status 1980.
Main Language(s) of Instruction: Spanish
Degrees and Diplomas: *Técnico Profesional*; *Especialización*
Last Updated: 28/10/09

HIGHER COLLEGE OF CAUCA

Colegio Mayor del Cauca
Carrera 5 No 5-40 Barrios El Centro, Popayán, Cauca
Fax: +57(2) 8220022
Website: http://www.colmayorcauca.edu.co

Rectora: Maria Cecilia Vivas De Velasco
EMail: rectoria@colmayor.edu.co
Vicerector Académico: Luis Guillermo Cespedes S.

Faculties

Art and Design (Architecture; Design; Engineering; Fine Arts) *Dean*: Mónica Arboleda Castrillón; **Engineering** (Engineering; Software Engineering) *Dean*: Carolina Andrea Carrascal Reyes; **Social Sciences and Administration**

Degrees and Diplomas: *Técnico Profesional*; *Especialización*

HIGHER COLLEGE OF MUSIC OF TOLIMA
Conservatorio del Tolima
Carrera 1 calle 9 No. 1-18, Ibagué, Tolima
Tel: +57(8) 2618526
Fax: +57(8) 2625378
EMail: info@conservatoriodeltolima.edu.co
Website: http://www.conservatoriodeltolima.edu.co

Rectora: Luz Alba Beltrán Agudelo
EMail: rectoria@conservatoriodeltolima.edu.co

Secretario General: Jairo Bernal Guarnizo
EMail: sec_general@conservatoriodeltolima.edu.co

Colleges
Music (Music)

History: Founded 1909. Acquired present title 1987.

Main Language(s) of Instruction: Spanish

Degrees and Diplomas: *Licenciatura*: 5 yrs; *Titulo Profesional*: 5 yrs
Last Updated: 28/10/09

ICESI UNIVERSITY
Universidad ICESI
Calle 18 No. 122-135, Cali, Valle del Cauca
Tel: +57(2) 555-2334
Fax: +57(2) 555-1706
EMail: webmaster@icesi.edu.co
Website: http://www.icesi.edu.co

Rector: Francisco Piedrahita Plata (1996-)
Tel: +57(2) 321-2022, Fax: +57(2) 555-1528
EMail: frapie@icesi.edu.co

Director: Carlos Gerarado Chaparro
Fax: +57(2) 555-2334, Ext. 300 EMail: chaparro@icesi.edu.co

International Relations: Piedad Gómez
Tel: +57(2) 555-2334, Ext. 425

Centres
Development of Entrepreneurship (Management) *Director*: Rodrigo Varela

Faculties
Administration and Economics (Accountancy; Administration; Business Administration; Economics; Finance; International Business; Marketing); **Engineering** (Engineering; Industrial Design; Industrial Engineering; Systems Analysis; Telecommunications Engineering); **Health Sciences**; **Law and Social Sciences** (Anthropology; Law; Political Sciences; Psychology; Sociology); **Natural Sciences** (Biology; Chemistry; Pharmacology)

History: Founded 1979.

Governing Bodies: Consejo Superior; Junta Directiva

Academic Year: January to December (January-June; August-December)

Admission Requirements: School certificate, test of proficiency in Spanish, national admission test

Fees: (US Dollars): 1,674-3,670 per semester according to field of study

Main Language(s) of Instruction: Spanish

International Co-operation: With universities in Australia; Canada; France; Germany; Italy; Republic of Korea; Netherlands; Spain; Sweden; United Kingdom and USA

Degrees and Diplomas: *Licenciatura*; *Especialización*; *Maestría*

Student Services: Academic counselling, Canteen, Cultural centre, Employment services, Foreign student adviser, Handicapped facilities, Health services, Language programs, Nursery care, Social counselling, Sports facilities

Publications: Estudios Gerenciales *(quarterly)*; Precedente, Law Studies Yearbook *(annually)*; Sistemas y Telemática, Faculty of Engineering *(biannually)*
Last Updated: 16/11/09

INDUSTRIAL UNIVERSITY OF SANTANDER
Universidad Industrial de Santander (UIS)
Cra 27 Calle 9, Ciudad Universitaria, Carrera 27 Calle 9, Bucaramanga, Santander
Tel: +57(7) 634-4000
EMail: rectoria@uis.edu.co
Website: http://www.uis.edu.co

Rector: Jaime Alberto Camacho Pico

Secretaria General: Olga Cecilia González Noriega
EMail: sgeneral@uis.edu.co

International Relations: Alberto Vergara Herrera
Tel: +57(7) 6320615, Fax: +57(7) 6320815
EMail: relext@uis.edu.co; direlext@uis.edu.co

Centres
Academic and Teaching Process *(CEDEDUIS)* (Pedagogy) *Director*: Martha Vitalia Corredor Montagut; **Regionalization** *Director*: Juan Manuel Latorre Carvajal

Faculties
Health Sciences (Anaesthesiology; Dietetics; Gynaecology and Obstetrics; Health Sciences; Medicine; Microbiology; Nursing; Nutrition; Ophthalmology; Orthopaedics; Paediatrics; Pathology; Physical Therapy; Surgery; Virology); **Human Sciences** (Administration; Economics; Education; History; Law; Modern Languages; Music; Philosophy; Physical Education; Political Sciences; Social Work; Sports); **Physics and Chemical Engineering** (Chemical Engineering; Engineering; Geology; Mechanical Engineering; Metallurgical Engineering; Petroleum and Gas Engineering); **Physics and Mechanical Engineering** (Business Administration; Civil Engineering; Computer Engineering; Computer Science; Electrical Engineering; Electronic Engineering; Engineering; Industrial Design; Industrial Engineering; Mechanical Engineering; Production Engineering); **Science** (Biology; Chemistry; Mathematics; Microbiology; Physics)

Institutes
Distance Education

History: Founded 1948.

Governing Bodies: Consejo Superior Universitario; Consejo Académico

Academic Year: February to December (February-June; August-December)

Admission Requirements: Secondary school certificace (bachillerato) and entrance examination

Main Language(s) of Instruction: Spanish

International Co-operation: With universities in Europe, North and South America

Accrediting Agencies: Consejo Nacional de Acreditación

Degrees and Diplomas: *Licenciatura*: Biology; Chemistry; Economy; English; Geology; History; Laboratory Techniques; Law; Mathematics; Middle School; Music; Nursing; Philosophy; Spanish, 10 sem; *Licenciatura*: Medicine, 12 sem; *Licenciatura*: Nutrition; Physiotherapy, 8 sem; *Titulo Profesional*: Civil Engineering; Computer Systems; Electrical, Electronic Engineering; Industrial Engineering; Mechanical Engineering; Petroleum Engineering, 10 sem; *Especialización*; *Maestría*: Education, History; Engineering, Chemical Engineering, Metallurgical Engineering, Electrical Engineering, Computer Science; Science, Chemistry, Microbiology, Physics, Mathematics, Education, 4-6 sem; *Maestría*: Semiology, 4 sem; *Doctorado*: Chemical Engineering; Science, 8 sem. Also Technological Degrees in Distance Education

Student Services: Academic counselling, Cultural centre, Foreign student adviser, Health services, Language programs, Social counselling, Sports facilities

Student Residential Facilities: Yes

Special Facilities: Biology and Natural History Museum. 'Luís A. Calvo' Auditorium. Laboratories

Libraries: Central Library, c. 200,000 vols; faculty libraries, total, c. 49,550 vols; Medical Library, c. 10,500 vols

Publications: Boletín de Geología; Medical UIS; Revista de Humanidades; Revista de Investigaciones; Revista de Medicina; Revista ION

Press or Publishing House: Centro de Publicaciones, UIS
Last Updated: 16/11/09

INSTITUTE OF RURAL EDUCATION
Instituto Superior de Educación Rural (ISER)
Calle 8 No 8-155, Pamplona, Norte de Santander
Tel: +57(975) 682-597
Fax: +57(975) 681-736
Website: http://www.iser.edu.co

Rector: José Gustavo Quintero Guio

Units
Administration and Social Sciences (Agricultural Management; Business Administration; Social and Community Services; Social Work); **Engineering and Computer Science** (Agricultural Engineering; Civil Engineering; Computer Networks; Industrial Engineering; Telecommunications Engineering); **Virtual and Distance Studies**

History: Founded 1956.

Main Language(s) of Instruction: Spanish

Degrees and Diplomas: *Tecnólogo*; *Licenciatura*
Last Updated: 04/11/09

JAIME ISAZA CADAVID COLOMBIAN POLYTECHNIC
Politécnico Colombiano Jaime Isaza Cadavid
Apartado aéro 4932, Carrera 48 No 7-151 El Poblado, Medellín, Antioquia
Tel: +57(94) 319-7933
Fax: +57(94) 266-3635
EMail: admisiones@elpoli.edu.co
Website: http://www.politecnicojic.edu.co

Rector: Efrén Barrera Restrepo EMail: rectoria@elpoli.edu.co

Faculties
Administration (Administration; Information Sciences); **Agriculture** (Agriculture); **Audiovisual Communication** (Radio and Television Broadcasting); **Basic, Social and Human Sciences** (Arts and Humanities; Natural Sciences; Social Sciences; Technology); **Engineering** (Engineering); **Physical Education, Recreation and Sport** (Physical Education; Sports)

Further Information: Also Seccional Oriente (Rionegro), Urabá (Apartadó) and Convenio Bajo Cauca (Caucasia)

History: Founded 1964.

Main Language(s) of Instruction: Spanish

Degrees and Diplomas: *Tecnólogo*; *Licenciatura*; *Especialización*
Last Updated: 05/11/09

LA PAZ UNIVERSITY INSTITUTE
Instituto Universitario de La Paz (UNIPAZ)
Avenida Santander, Calle 9 No. 10-22, Barrancabermeja, Santander
Tel: +57(976) 621-4049
Fax: +57(976) 621-5042
EMail: informacion@unipaz.edu.co
Website: http://www.unipaz.edu.co

Rector: Carlos Augusto Vásquez Rojas
EMail: rectoria@unipaz.edu.co

Schools
Agricultural Engineering (Agricultural Engineering); **Agro-Industrial Engineering** (Industrial Engineering); **Environmental Engineering and Hygiene** (Environmental Engineering; Hygiene); **Health Sciences**; **Production Engineering**; **Science**; **Veterinary Medicine and Zoology**

History: Founded 1987.

Governing Bodies: Consejo Directivo; Consejo Académico; Consejo de Escuela

Main Language(s) of Instruction: Spanish
International Co-operation: Participates in ICD, CDPMM, CIMPA and CEHIPALMA programmes
Accrediting Agencies: ICFES

Degrees and Diplomas: *Licenciatura*; *Titulo Profesional*: 5 yrs
Student Services: Academic counselling, Cultural centre, Health services, Social counselling, Sports facilities

Student Residential Facilities: None

Special Facilities: None

Libraries: Yes

Publications: Educación en Ciencia e Ingenieria *(biennially)*
Last Updated: 05/11/09

METROPOLITAN TECHNOLOGICAL INSTITUTE
Instituto Tecnológico Metropolitano
Calle 73 No. 76A-354, Vía al Volador, Medellín, Antioquia
Tel: +57(4) 440-5100
Fax: +57(4) 440-5103
EMail: itm@itm.edu.co
Website: http://www.itm.edu.co

Rector: José Marduk Sánchez Castañeda (1996-)
Tel: +57(4) 440-5107 EMail: rector@itm.edu.co

International Relations: Claudia Patricia Moreno Botero, Director, National and International Relations
Tel: +57(4) 440-5185 EMail: claudiamoreno@itm.edu.co

Faculties
Arts and Humanities; **Engineering** (Automation and Control Engineering; Business and Commerce; Computer Engineering; Electrical and Electronic Engineering; Engineering; Engineering Drawing and Design; Finance; Industrial Engineering; Mechanical Engineering; Production Engineering); **Technology**

History: Founded 1944 as Instituo Obrero Municipal. Became Universidad Obrera Municipal in the late 1940's and then Instituto de Cultura Popular in the 1960's. Acquired present title in the 1990's. Acquired present status 2005.

Governing Bodies: Consejo Directivo; Consejo Académico; Consejo de Facultad

Academic Year: January to December

Admission Requirements: High school leaving certificate (Diploma de Bachiller), State Higher Education Entrance Examination (ICFES) and Institute's Entrance examination

Fees: (Pesos): 350,000

Main Language(s) of Instruction: Spanish

International Co-operation: With the Universidad del País Vasco (UPV/EHU), Spain

Accrediting Agencies: Consejo Nacional de Acreditación (CNA), attached to the Ministry of Education

Degrees and Diplomas: *Tecnólogo*: Costs and Budget Analysis; Architecture Finish; Quality Management; Industrial Design; Electromechanics; Electronics; Musical Informatics; Maintenance of Biomedical Equipment; Administrative Management; Production Management; Information Systems; Telecommunications Engineering, 3 yrs; *Titulo Profesional*: Industrial Design; Electromechanics; Electronic Engineering; Production Engineering; Finance and Commerce Engineering; Systems Engineering; Telecommunications Engineering (Ingeniero), 5 yrs; *Especialización*: Industrial Energy Management, 1 yr; *Maestría*

Student Services: Academic counselling, Cultural centre, Employment services, Foreign student adviser, Foreign Studies Centre, Handicapped facilities, Health services, Language programs, Social counselling, Sports facilities

Student Residential Facilities: Four apartments for visiting academics

Special Facilities: Planetarium; Interactive Museum of Science and Technology; Conference and Audiovisual Halls; Exposition Halls

Libraries: Library; Newspaper Library; Multimedia Library

Publications: TechnoLógicas, Journal on scientific and technological research outcomes *(biennially)*

Press or Publishing House: Fondo Editorial ITM

Academic Staff *2007-2008*	MEN	WOMEN	**TOTAL**
FULL-TIME	142	97	**239**
PART-TIME	439	154	**593**

Student Numbers *2007-2008*			
All (Foreign Included)	8,193	5,084	**13,277**

Distance students, 168.
Last Updated: 04/11/09

NATIONAL INSTITUTE OF TECHNICAL TRAINING OF CIENAGA

Instituto Nacional de Formación Técnica Profesional de Cienaga
Calle 10 No 12-22 Barrio Centenario, Cienaga, Magdalena
Tel: +57(954) 424-0800
Fax: +57(954) 424-0800
Website: http://www.infotephvg.edu.co

Rector: Reinaldo Rafael Estrada Flórez

Programmes
Accountancy (Accountancy); **Animal Husbandry** (Animal Husbandry); **Basic Education**; **Occupational Health** (Occupational Health); **Pre-school Education** (Preschool Education); **Systems Analysis** (Systems Analysis)

Degrees and Diplomas: *Tecnólogo*; *Licenciatura*: 4-5 yrs
Last Updated: 04/11/09

NATIONAL INSTITUTE OF TECHNICAL TRAINING OF SAN JUAN DEL CÉSAR

Instituto Nacional de Formación Técnica Profesional de San Juan del César
Carrera 13 No 7a-61, Barrio 20 de Julio, San Juan del César, La Guajira
Tel: +57(954) 774-0098
Fax: +57(954) 774-0404
EMail: infotpr@col3.telecom.com.co

Rectora: Mónica Del Carmen Díaz Salinas

Programmes
Accountancy (Accountancy); **Mining Engineering** (Mining Engineering); **Preschool Education** (Preschool Education); **Secretarial Studies** (Secretarial Studies)

Degrees and Diplomas: *Licenciatura*
Last Updated: 04/11/09

NATIONAL OPEN AND DISTANCE UNIVERSITY

Universidad Nacional Abierta y a Distancia (UNAD)
Calle 14 sur No.14-23, Bogotá
Tel: +57(1) 344-3700
Fax: +57(1) 344-3700
EMail: atencionalusuario@unad.edu.co
Website: http://www.unad.edu.co

Rector: Jaime Alberto Leal Afanadro (2004-)
EMail: rectoria@unad.edu.co

General Secretary: Maribel Cordoba Guerrero
Tel: +57(1) 344-3700 Ext. 504, Fax: +57(1) 344-3700 Ext. 507
EMail: sgeneral@unad.edu.co

International Relations: Patricia Illera Pacheco, Interinstitutional Relations Manager
Tel: +57(1) 347-2523
EMail: grelaciones@unad.edu.co; convenios@unad.edu.co

Colleges
Agricultural and Environmental Sciences (Agriculture; Animal Husbandry) *Dean*: M. Priscila Rey Vásquez; **Basic Sciences, Technology and Engineering** (Engineering; Food Technology; Pharmacy; Systems Analysis; Technology) *Dean*: Gustavo Velásquez Quintana; **Educational Sciences** *Dean*: Elizabeth Vidal Arizabaleta; **Management, Accountancy and Business Sciences** (Accountancy; Administration; Business Administration; Management) *Dean*: Edgar Guillermo Rodríguez Díaz; **Social Sciences, Art and Humanities** (Arts and Humanities; Educational Sciences; Philosophy; Psychology; Social Sciences) *Dean*: Patricia Ruiz Perdomo

History: Founded 1981 as Unidad Universitaria del Sur de Bogotá. Acquired status of State institution 1997. Became an autonomous University 2006.

Governing Bodies: Consejo Superior

Academic Year: February to December (February-June; July-December)

Admission Requirements: Secondary school certificate (bachillerato) and entrance examination

Main Language(s) of Instruction: Spanish

Degrees and Diplomas: *Tecnólogo*: 2 yrs; *Licenciatura*: 5 yrs; *Especialización*: 1 yr
Last Updated: 18/11/09

NATIONAL SCHOOL OF SPORTS

Escuela Nacional del Deporte
Calle 9 No 34-01, Cali, Valle del Cauca
Tel: +57(2) 684-0404
Fax: +57(2) 681-5860
EMail: edeporte@emcali.net.co
Website: http://www.endeporte.edu.co

Rector: José Fernando Arroyo Valencia

Programmes
Sports and Physical Education (Physical Education; Physical Therapy; Sports; Sports Management)

History: Founded 1984.

Main Language(s) of Instruction: Spanish

Degrees and Diplomas: *Título Profesional*; *Especialización*
Last Updated: 30/10/09

NATIONAL UNIVERSITY OF COLOMBIA

Universidad Nacional de Colombia
Carrera 45 No 26-85 - Edificio Uriel Gutiérrez, Bogotá
Tel: +57(1) 316-5000, Ext.18220
Fax: +57(1) 316-5000 Ext.18220
EMail: rectoriaun@unal.edu.co
Website: http://www.unal.edu.co

Rector: Moisés Wassermann Lerner (2006-)
Tel: +57(1) 316-5387, Fax: +57(1) 316-5297

Secretario General: Jorge Ernesto Durán P.
Tel: +57(1) 316-5280, Fax: +57(1) 316-5107
EMail: secgener@unal.edu.co

International Relations: Paula Marcela Arias
Tel: +57(1) 316-5650, Fax: +57(1) 316-5423
EMail: ori_bog@unal.edu.co

Faculties
Agronomy (Agricultural Engineering; Agriculture; Agronomy); **Arts** (Architecture; Cinema and Television; Design; Fine Arts; Industrial Design; Music); **Dentistry** (Dentistry; Health Sciences); **Economics** (Accountancy; Administration; Economics); **Engineering** (Agricultural Engineering; Architecture; Chemical Engineering; Civil Engineering; Electrical and Electronic Engineering; Engineering; Industrial Engineering; Mechanical Engineering; Systems Analysis; Urban Studies); **Human Sciences** (Anthropology; Arts and Humanities; English; French; Geography; German; History; Linguistics; Modern Languages; Philology; Philosophy; Psychology; Social Sciences; Social Work; Sociology; Spanish); **Law and Political and Social Sciences** (Law; Political Sciences; Social Sciences); **Medicine** (Dietetics; Health Sciences; Medicine; Nutrition; Occupational Therapy; Physical Therapy; Speech Therapy and Audiology); **Nursing** (Nursing); **Science** (Biology; Chemistry; Geology; Mathematics; Natural Sciences; Physics; Statistics); **Veterinary Medicine and Animal Husbandry** (Agronomy; Animal Husbandry; Veterinary Science)

Institutes
Biotechnology (Biotechnology; Mathematics; Natural Sciences); **Communication and Cultural Studies** *(IECO)* (Communication Studies; Cultural Studies); **Environmental Studies** *(IDEA)* (Environmental

Management); **Food Technology** *(ICTA)* (Food Technology; Health Sciences; Mathematics; Natural Sciences); **Genetics** (Genetics; Mathematics; Natural Sciences); **Political Studies and International Relations** *(IEPRI)* (International Relations; Law; Political Sciences) *Director.* Gabriel Misas Arango; **Research** *(IEI)*; **Urban Studies** (Architecture; Town Planning; Urban Studies)

History: Founded 1867 as Universidad Nacional de los Estados Unidos de Colombia, the university was granted autonomy by the government 1935.

Governing Bodies: Consejo Superior Universitario; Consejo Académico; Consejo de Sede

Academic Year: February to December (February-June; August-December)

Admission Requirements: Secondary school certificate (bachillerato) and entrance examination

Main Language(s) of Instruction: Spanish

Accrediting Agencies: Consejo Nacional de Acreditación

Degrees and Diplomas: *Titulo Profesional*: Engineering; Business Administration; Social Sciences; Architecture; Fine Arts; Natural Sciences; Peforming Arts; Law; Health Sciences; Arts and Humanities; Mathematics; Engineering; Agriculture; Education, 8-12 sem; *Especialización*: Health Sciences, Basic Sciences; Social Sciences; Arts and Humanities; Engineering; Business Administration; Law; Agriculture; Social Sciences; Fine Arts; Mathematics; Fine Arts, 2 -4 sem; *Maestría*: Business Administration; Social Sciences; Architecture and Planning; Fine Arts; Health Science; Natural Sciences; Mathematics; Agriculture; Law; Education; Arts and Humanities; Architecture; Engineering; Performing Arts; Welfare and Protective Services, 4 sem; *Doctorado*: Architecture; Biotechnology; Agriculture Engineering; Chemistry; Biomedicine; Geography; Philosophy, 8 sem; *Doctorado*: Biology; Statistics; Physics; Mathematics; Animal Husbandry; Agriculture; Economics; Pharmacy; Nursing; History; Engineering; Health Sciences, 6 sem

Student Services: Academic counselling, Cultural centre, Employment services, Foreign student adviser, Foreign Studies Centre, Health services, Language programs, Nursery care, Social counselling, Sports facilities

Student Residential Facilities: Yes

Special Facilities: Musical Museum. Museum of Games. Natural Science Museum. Astronomical Obsevatory

Libraries: 18 specialised libraries related to: Natural Sciences; Health Sciences; Human Sciences; Business Administration; Agricultural Engineering; Fine Arts; Law; Political and Social Sciences. 340,330 vols

Publications: Acta Bibliográfica; Agronomía Colombiana; Alimentos (ICTA); Anuario Colombiano de Historia; Anuario del Observatorio Astronómico Nacional; Boletín de Matemáticas; Caldasia (Natural Science); Cuadernos de Economía; Forma y Función (Philology and Languages); Geografía; Geología Colombiana; Ideas y Valores; Ingeniería e Investigación; Lozania (Natural Sciences); Maguaré (Anthropology); Mutisia (Natural Sciences); Revistas (Faculty publications)

Press or Publishing House: Unibiblos

Academic Staff *2007-2008*	MEN	WOMEN	TOTAL
FULL-TIME	1,046	513	1,559
PART-TIME	120	46	166
STAFF WITH DOCTORATE			
FULL-TIME	347	125	472
PART-TIME	6	1	7
Student Numbers *2007-2008*			
All (Foreign Included)	15,190	10,481	25,671

Last Updated: 18/11/09

LETICIA BRANCH

SEDE LETICIA

Kilometro 2 Via Tarapacá, Leticia
Tel: +57(1) 316-5438
Fax: +57(1) 316-5284
EMail: vicgen_nal@unal.edu.co
Website: http://www.imani.unal.edu.co

Director de Sede: Fernando Franco Hernandez
Tel: +57(1) 316-5387, Fax: +57(1) 316-5284
EMail: ffrancoh@unal.edu.co

Programmes
Amazon Studies; **Health Sciences**; **Humanities and Social Sciences** *Director.* Carlos Gilberto Zárate Botia

History: Founded 1989.

Governing Bodies: Consejo Superior Universitario; Consejo Académico; Consejo de Sede

Academic Year: February-June; August-December

Main Language(s) of Instruction: Spanish

Accrediting Agencies: Consejo Nacional de Acreditación

Degrees and Diplomas: *Titulo Profesional*: Linguistics, 10 sem; *Especialización*: Latin American Studies, 2 sem; *Especialización*: Occupational Health, 4 sem; *Maestría*: Latin American Studies, 4 sem

Student Services: Academic counselling, Cultural centre, Employment services, Foreign student adviser, Foreign Studies Centre, Health services, Language programs, Nursery care, Social counselling, Sports facilities

Student Residential Facilities: None

Libraries: A Documentation Centre of 3,778 vols, related to Natural Sciences; Engineering; Arts and Humanities; Health Sciences and Amazonian Studies

Academic Staff *2007-2008*	MEN	WOMEN	TOTAL
FULL-TIME	9	1	10
STAFF WITH DOCTORATE			
FULL-TIME	–	–	2
Student Numbers *2007-2008*			
All (Foreign Included)	24	24	48

MANIZALES BRANCH

SEDE MANIZALES

Manizales
Tel: +57(6) 886-3990
Fax: +57(6) 886-3990
EMail: vicsede_man@unal.edu.co
Website: http://www.manizales.unal.edu.co

Vicerrector: William Ariel Sarache Castro (2006-)

Secretario General: Jorge Ernesto Durán P.
Tel: +57(1) 316-5280, Fax: +57(1) 316-5107
EMail: secgener@unal.edu.co

International Relations: Paula Marcela Arias P.
Tel: +57(1) 316-5650, Fax: +57(1) 316-5423
EMail: ori_bog@unal.edu.co

Faculties
Architecture (Architecture; Chemical Engineering; Civil Engineering; Construction Engineering; Electrical and Electronic Engineering; Industrial Engineering; Town Planning; Urban Studies) *Dean:* Luis Edgar Moreno Montoya; **Business Administration** (Accountancy; Administration; Business Administration; Communication Studies; Cultural Studies; Economics; Mathematics and Computer Science; Natural Sciences; Systems Analysis) *Dean:* Germán Albeiro Castaño Duque; **Engineering and Architecture** (Architecture; Engineering) *Dean:* Gabriel Hernán Bareneche Ramos; **Natural Sciences** *Dean:* Andrés Rosales Rivera

Institutes
Environmental Studies *(IDEA)* (Environmental Studies) *Director.* Fernando Mejía Fernández

History: Founded 1948.

Governing Bodies: Consejo Superior Universitario; Consejo Académico; Consejo de Sede

Academic Year: February-June; August-December

Admission Requirements: Secondary school certificate and entrance examination

Main Language(s) of Instruction: Spanish

International Co-operation: Consejo Nacional de Acreditación

Degrees and Diplomas: *Licenciatura*; *Título Profesional*: Social Sciences; Engineering; Architecture; Mathematics, 10 sem; *Especialización*: Engineering; Social Sciences; Agriculture; Business Administration, 2-3 sem; *Maestría*: Business Administration; Natural Sciences; House Arts and Environment, 4 sem; *Doctorado*: Engineering, 6 sem

Student Services: Academic counselling, Cultural centre, Employment services, Foreign student adviser, Foreign Studies Centre, Health services, Language programs, Nursery care, Social counselling, Sports facilities

Student Residential Facilities: Yes

Libraries: 4 specialised libraries, 27,615 vols, related to Engineering; Social Sciences; Arts and Humanities; Economics; Mathematics and Natural Sciences

Academic Staff *2007-2008*	MEN	WOMEN	TOTAL
FULL-TIME	135	32	167
PART-TIME	–	–	3
STAFF WITH DOCTORATE			
FULL-TIME	21	5	26
PART-TIME	–	–	1
Student Numbers *2007-2008*			
All (Foreign Included)	3,059	1,791	4,850

MEDELLÍN BRANCH
SEDE MEDELLÍN

Calle 59A No 63-20 - Núcleo El Volador, Medellín
Tel: +57(94) 430-9502
Fax: +57(94) 430-9502
EMail: vicmedel@unalmed.edu.co
Website: http://www.unalmed.edu.co

Vicerrector: Oscar Almario Garcia (2006-)

Secretario General: Jorge Ernesto Durán P.
Tel: +57(1) 316-5280, Fax: +57(1) 316-5107
EMail: secgener@unal.edu.co

International Relations: Paula Marcela Arias P.
Tel: +57(1) 316-5650, Fax: +57(1) 316-5423
EMail: ori_bog@unal.edu.co

Faculties
Agriculture (Agricultural Engineering; Agriculture; Agronomy; Animal Husbandry; Forestry; Veterinary Science); **Architecture** (Architecture; Construction Engineering; Engineering; Fine Arts; Urban Studies); **Humanities and Economics** (Accountancy; Administration; Arts and Humanities; Economics; History; Political Sciences; Social Sciences); **Mining** (Architecture; Automation and Control Engineering; Chemical Engineering; Civil Engineering; Computer Engineering; Electrical Engineering; Engineering; Geological Engineering; Industrial Engineering; Mechanical Engineering; Metallurgical Engineering; Mining Engineering; Petroleum and Gas Engineering; Urban Studies); **Science** (Biology; Mathematics; Natural Sciences; Physics; Statistics)

Institutes
Automation and Industrial Processes *Director*: Jesús Antonio Hernández; **Energy Engineering** *Director*: Sergio Hernando Lopera; **Information Systems and Decision Sciences** *Director*: Gloria Patricia Jaramillo; **Infrastructure Studies** (Engineering) *Director*: Fabián Hoyos Patiño; **Materials Engineering** *Director*: Alejandro Octavio Toro Betancur; **Mineralogy** *Director*: Jorge Hernando García Escobar; **Water Science** (Water Science) *Director*: Jaime Ignacio Vélez Upegui

Research Centres
Petroleum and Gas Engineering *Director*: Juan David Pérez Schile; **Seismology** *Director*: Josef Farbiarz

History: Founded 1936.

Governing Bodies: Consejo Superior Universitario. Consejo Académico. Consejo de Sede

Academic Year: February-June; August-December

Admission Requirements: Secondary school certificate and entrance examination

Main Language(s) of Instruction: Spanish

Accrediting Agencies: Consejo Nacional de Acreditacíon

Degrees and Diplomas: *Título Profesional*: Architecture; Fine Arts; Social Sciences; Agriculture; Natural Sciences, 10 sem; *Especialización*: Engineering; Natural Sciences; Social Sciences; Agriculture; Fine Arts; Mathematics; Business Administration, 2-3 sem; *Maestría*: Agriculture; Natural Sciences; Social Sciences; Architecture and Planning; Engineering, 4 sem; *Doctorado*: Mathematics; Engineering; Social Sciences; Agriculture; Arts and Humanities, 6-8 sem

Student Services: Academic counselling, Cultural centre, Employment services, Foreign student adviser, Foreign Studies Centre, Health services, Language programs, Nursery care, Social counselling, Sports facilities

Student Residential Facilities: None

Libraries: Total of 68,006 vols. Three specialised library related to Agriculture; Architecture; Natural Sciences; Economics and Engineering

Academic Staff *2007-2008*	MEN	WOMEN	TOTAL
FULL-TIME	355	116	471
PART-TIME	12	2	14
STAFF WITH DOCTORATE			
FULL-TIME	97	33	130
Student Numbers *2007-2008*			
All (Foreign Included)	6,211	3,854	10,065

ORINOQUIA BRANCH
SEDE ORINOQUIA

Kilómetro 9 vía a Caño Limón, Arauca
Tel: +57(1) 316-5438
Fax: +57(1) 316-5284
EMail: vicgen_nal@unal.edu.co
Website: http://www.arauca.unal.edu.co

Director de Sede: Julian Garcia

Programmes
Environmental Management (Environmental Management); **Management of Projects in Agronomy**; **Occupational Health** (Occupational Health); **Political Science** (Peace and Disarmament; Political Sciences); **Public Law**

History: Founded 1996.

Governing Bodies: Consejo Superior Universitario. Consejo Académico. Consejo de Sede

Academic Year: February-June; August-December

Admission Requirements: Secondary school certificate and entrance examination

Main Language(s) of Instruction: Spanish

Accrediting Agencies: Consejo Nacional de Acreditacíon

Degrees and Diplomas: *Especialización*

Student Services: Academic counselling, Employment services, Foreign student adviser, Foreign Studies Centre, Health services, Language programs, Nursery care, Social counselling, Sports facilities

Student Residential Facilities: None

Libraries: A specialised library, 3,115 vols, related to agriculture, and biology

Academic Staff *2007-2008*	MEN	WOMEN	TOTAL
FULL-TIME	2	1	3
Student Numbers *2007-2008*			
All (Foreign Included)	15	7	22

PALMIRA BRANCH
SEDE PALMIRA

Palmira
Tel: +57(2) 271-7004
Fax: +57(2) 271-7004
EMail: vicerrectoria@palmira.unal.edu.co
Website: http://www.palmira.unal.edu.co

Vicerrector: William Ariel Sarache Castro (2006-)

Secretario General: Jorge Ernesto Durán P.
Tel: +57(1) 316-5280, Fax: +57(1) 316-5107
EMail: secgener@unal.edu.co

International Relations: Paula Marcela Arias P.
Tel: +57(1) 316-5650, Fax: +57(1) 316-5423
EMail: ori_bog@unal.edu.co

Faculties
Agriculture (Agriculture; Agronomy; Animal Husbandry; Biology; Forestry); **Engineering and Administration** (Accountancy; Administration; Agricultural Engineering; Architecture; Business Administration; Economics; Engineering; Environmental Engineering; Industrial Design; Urban Studies)

Research Institutes
Agriculture and Forestry (Agriculture; Forestry); **Rural Studies** (Agricultural Engineering; Agronomy; Rural Studies; Veterinary Science)
History: Founded 1934.

Governing Bodies: Consejo Superior Universitario. Consejo Académico. Consejo de Sede

Academic Year: February-June; August-December

Admission Requirements: Secondary school certificate and entrance examination

Main Language(s) of Instruction: Spanish

Accrediting Agencies: Consejo Nacional de Acreditación

Degrees and Diplomas: *Título Profesional*: Business Administration; Fine Arts; Agriculture, 10 sem; *Especialización*: Agriculture; Natural Sciences, Social Sciences, 3 sem; *Maestría*; *Doctorado*: Agriculture, 6 sem

Student Services: Academic counselling, Cultural centre, Employment services, Foreign student adviser, Foreign Studies Centre, Health services, Language programs, Nursery care, Social counselling, Sports facilities

Student Residential Facilities: None

Libraries: A specialised library, 20,536 vols, related to Agriculture; Engineering; Economics

Academic Staff 2007-2008	MEN	WOMEN	TOTAL
FULL-TIME	63	29	92
PART-TIME	–	–	1
STAFF WITH DOCTORATE			
FULL-TIME	20	10	30
Student Numbers 2007-2008			
All (Foreign Included)	1,243	1,112	2,355

SAN ANDRÉS ISLA BRANCH
SEDE SAN ANDRÉS ISLA

Carretera Circunvalar San Luis, San Andrés Isla
Tel: +57(8) 316-5438
Fax: +57(8) 316-5284
Website: http://www.caribe.unal.edu.co/

Director de Sede: José Ernesto Mancera Pineda (2006-)
Tel: +57(1) 316-5438, Fax: +57(1) 316-5284
EMail: vicgen_nal@unal.edu.co

Secretario General: Jorge Ernesto Durán Pinzón
Tel: +57(1) 316-5280, Fax: +57(1) 316-5107
EMail: secgener@unal.edu.co

International Relations: Paula Marcela Arias P.
Tel: +57(1) 316-5650, Fax: +57(1) 316-5423
EMail: ori_bog@unal.edu.co

Institutes
Caribbean Studies (Caribbean Studies)
History: Founded 1997.

Governing Bodies: Consejo Superior Universitario. Consejo Académico. Consejo de Sede

Academic Year: February-June; August-December

Admission Requirements: Secondary school certificate and entrance examination

Main Language(s) of Instruction: Spanish

Accrediting Agencies: Consejo Nacional de Acreditacíon

Degrees and Diplomas: *Especialización*: 3 sem; *Maestría*: 4 sem

Student Services: Academic counselling, Cultural centre, Employment services, Foreign student adviser, Foreign Studies Centre, Health services, Language programs, Nursery care, Social counselling, Sports facilities

Student Residential Facilities: None

Libraries: A Documentation Centre of 2,611 vols, related to Caribbean Studies; Biology; Law and Human Sciences

Academic Staff 2007-2008	MEN	WOMEN	TOTAL
FULL-TIME	3	4	7
Student Numbers 2007-2008			
All (Foreign Included)	4	10	14

NATIONAL UNIVERSITY OF EDUCATION
Universidad Pedagógica Nacional
Calle 73 No. 11-95, Bogotá
Tel: +57(1) 347-1190
Fax: +57(1) 347-3535
EMail: upn@uni.pedagogica.edu.co
Website: http://www.pedagogica.edu.co

Rector: Oscar Armando Ibarra Russi
Tel: +57(1) 310-1110, Fax: +57(1) 347-3535
EMail: rectoria@uni.pedagogica.edu.co

Vicerrector Académico: Juan Carlos Orozco Cruz

Centres
Educational Research (Educational Research) *Director*: Juan Carlos Orozco

Faculties
Education (Education; Pedagogy; Preschool Education; Psychology; Special Education); **Education**; **Fine Arts**; **Humanities** (Arts and Humanities; Modern Languages; Music; Social Sciences); **Physical Education** (Physical Education); **Science and Technology** (Biology; Chemistry; Design; Mathematics; Natural Sciences; Physics; Technology)

Institutes
Pedagogy *(National)* (Pedagogy) *Director*: Inés Elvira Castaño

History: Founded as School of Education 1936, became university for women 1955 and co-educational 1962. A State institution.

Governing Bodies: Consejo Superior; Consejo Académico

Academic Year: January to December (January-May; August-December)

Admission Requirements: Secondary school certificate (bachillerato) and entrance examination

Fees: According to parents' income

Main Language(s) of Instruction: Spanish, English, French

Degrees and Diplomas: *Licenciatura*: 5 yrs; *Especialización*; *Maestría*: a further 2 yrs; *Doctorado*

Student Services: Academic counselling, Canteen, Employment services, Foreign student adviser, Health services, Social counselling, Sports facilities

Libraries: Central Library, c. 36,000 vols; Documentation Centre, c. 7,000 vols

Publications: Revista Colombiana de Educación
Last Updated: 18/11/09

NUEVA GRANADA MILITARY UNIVERSITY
Universidad Militar Nueva Granada (UMNG)
Carrera 11 No. 101-80, Bogotá
Tel: +57(1) 275-7300
EMail: umng@unimilitar.edu.co
Website: http://www.umng.edu.co

Rector: Eduardo Antonio Herrera
Tel: +57(1) 612-5601 EMail: rectoria@umng.edu.co

Vicerrector Administrativo: Alberto Bravo Silva
Tel: +57(1) 634-3217 EMail: viceadm@umng.edu.co

International Relations: Natalia Currea Dereser, Director, International Relations
Tel: +57(1) 634-3261 EMail: relinter@umng.edu.co

Centres
Language (Modern Languages) *Director*: Libia Martínez; **Research** *Director*: Adriana Rodriguez

Faculties
Economics (Accountancy; Business Administration; Economics); **Engineering** (Civil Engineering; Engineering; Industrial Engineering; Mechanical Engineering; Multimedia; Telecommunications Engineering); **International Relations, Strategy and Security**; **Law** (Law) *Dean*: Jean Carlo Mejía Azuero; **Medicine** (Medicine); **Science** (*Experimental station in Cajica, Bogotá*) (Biology)

Institutes
Distance Studies (Accountancy; Business Administration; Civil Engineering; Distance Education; International Relations; Political Sciences)

History: Founded 1982.

Governing Bodies: Board of Trustees; Academic Board

Admission Requirements: Titulo de Bachiller ; Examen ICFES (State Exam or equivalent)

Fees: (Pesos): 1.91m.-6.53m.

Main Language(s) of Instruction: Spanish

International Co-operation: With universities in USA, Brazil, Spain, Argentina, Canada, Switzerland, Chile

Accrediting Agencies: Consejo Nacional de Accreditación

Degrees and Diplomas: *Titulo Profesional*: Accountancy; Business Administration; Digital Engineering; Art and 3D Design; Economy; Industrial Engineering, 4 1/2 yrs; *Titulo Profesional*: Applied Biology; Civil Engineering; International Relations and Political Studies; Mechatronics Engineering; Telecommunications Engineering, 5 yrs; *Titulo Profesional*: Law; Medicine, 6 yrs; *Especialización*: Administration and Finance; Administrative Development Management; Administrative Law; Administrative Law Management; Aeronautical Administration; Cardiovascular and Thoracic Anesthesia; Constitutional Penal and Military Justice; Fiscal Review and Accountancy; Geomatics; Glaucoma; Hand Surgery; Internal Control; Management; Management in International Commerce; Managing Logistics; Marketing Service; Natural Resources and Environmental Planning; Occuloplasty; Quality Management; Reconstructive Surgery and Replacement of Hip and Knee; Service Trade; University Teaching; Urban Planning Engineering, 1 yr; *Especialización*: Anaesthetics; Biomaterials; Endocrinology; Gynaecology and Obstetics; Haematoloy and Clinical Oncology; Implantology; Internal Medicine; Medicine; Physics and Rehabilitation; Ophthamology; Oral Rehabilitation; Oral Surgery; Orthodontics; Paediatrics; Pathology; Periodontics; Psychiatry; Radiology, 3 yrs; *Especialización*: Cardiology; Cardiovascular Surgery; Coloproctology; Endocrinology; Gastroenterology; Neonatology; Nephrology; Nuclear Medicine; Otology; Pediatric Neurology for Pediatricians; Pneumology; Rhumatology; Surgery; Vascular Surgery and Angiology, 2 yrs; *Especialización*: Child Neurology; Dermatology; Ear; Nose and Throat Disease Studies; Neurology; Neurosurgery; Oral and Maxillofacial Surgery; Orthopaedics and Traumatology; Otolaryngology; Reconstructive and Esthetic Plastic Surgery; Urology, 4 yrs; *Especialización*: High Management of the National Defense; Security Administraiton; Vertebral Column, Pelvis and Acetabulum Surgery; *Especialización*: Integral Management of Projects, 1 1/2 yrs; *Especialización*: Pediatric Surgery, 5 yrs; *Maestría*; *Maestría*: Administrative Law, a further 2 yrs; *Maestría*: Applied Biology

Student Services: Academic counselling, Employment services, Handicapped facilities, Health services, Language programs, Social counselling, Sports facilities

Special Facilities: Engineering Labs; Language Lab; Computer Labs; Museum; Herbarium; Principal Auditorium; Auxiliary Auditorium

Libraries: Main Library, 23,633 vols; 12,141 titles; with virtual library and Magazines, Journals and Newspapers. Medicine Library, 5,815 vols; 3,075 titles.

Publications: Revista de la Facultad de Ciencias Básicas - Revista Latinoamericana de Bioética *(annually)*; Revista de la Facultad de Ciencias Economicas *(biannually)*; Revista de la Facultad de Derecho *(biannually)*; Revista de la Facultad de Ingenería *(biannually)*; Revista de la Facultad de Medicina *(biannually)*; Revista de la Facultad de Relaciones Internacionales, Estrategia y Seguridad *(biannually)*; Revista Latinoamericana de Bioética *(biannually)*

Academic Staff 2007-2008	MEN	WOMEN	TOTAL
FULL-TIME	145	76	221
PART-TIME	33	8	41
STAFF WITH DOCTORATE			
FULL-TIME	–	–	21
PART-TIME	–	–	1
Student Numbers 2007-2008			
All (Foreign Included)	5,072	5,631	10,703

Distance students, 2,044.

Last Updated: 17/11/09

PASCUAL BRAVO TECHNOLOGICAL INSTITUTE
Instituto Tecnológico Pascual Bravo
Calle 73 N° 73A 226, Sector Pilarica, Medellín, Antioquia
Tel: +57(4) 234-0400 +57(4) 234-5082
Fax: +57(4) 264-7577
EMail: rectoria@pascualbravo.edu.co
Website: http://www.pascualbravo.edu.co/

Rectora: María Consuelo Moreno Orrego

Secretaria General: Gloria Elena Cardona
Tel: +57(4) 234-0200 EMail: secretaria@pascualbravo.edu.co

Directora administrativa: Martha Cecilia Yepes
Tel: +57(4) 421-4092, Fax: +57(4) 421-4092
EMail: diradmon@pascualbravo.edu.co

Programmes
Electronic Engineering (Electronic Engineering); **Industrial Engineering** (Industrial Engineering); **Mechanical Engineering** (Mechanical Engineering)

History: Founded 1938. Acquired present status 1982.

Main Language(s) of Instruction: Spanish

Degrees and Diplomas: *Técnico Profesional*; *Tecnólogo*; *Especialización*

Last Updated: 05/11/09

POPULAR UNIVERSITY OF CÉSAR
Universidad Popular del César (UPC)
Apartado aéreo 590, Sede Hurtado, Valledupar, César
Tel: +57(5) 573-6203
Fax: +57(5) 573-4943
EMail: univer@teleupar.net.co
Website: http://www.unicesar.edu.co

Rector: José Guillermo Botero Cotes
Tel: +57(5) 573-5877 EMail: rectoria@unicesar.edu.co

Vicerrector Administrativo: Desiderio Padilla

International Relations: Enrique Meza Tel: +57(5) 573-4870

Faculties
Art and Folklore; **Business Administration, Accountancy and Economics** (Accountancy; Business Administration; Economics; International Business) *Dean*: Elberto Pumarejo; **Education** (Computer Science; Education; English; Environmental Studies; Mathematics; Natural Sciences; Physics; Spanish) *Dean*: Luis Egea; **Engineering and Technology** (Agricultural Engineering; Electronic Engineering; Environmental Engineering; Sanitary Engineering; Systems Analysis) *Dean*: Rodolfo Mejía; **Health Sciences** (Health Sciences; Instrument Making; Medical Technology; Microbiology; Nursing) *Dean*: Nancy Hernández; **Law, Political and Social Sciences** (Law; Political Sciences; Sociology)

Further Information: Also branch in Valledupar

History: Founded 1973 as school of technology, acquired present status 1976.

Governing Bodies: Consejo Superior; Consejo Académico; Consejo de Facultad

Academic Year: February to December (February-July; August-December)

Admission Requirements: Secondary school certificate (bachillerato) and national placement test

Fees: (Pesos) 450,000 per semester

Main Language(s) of Instruction: Spanish

Degrees and Diplomas: *Licenciatura*: Basic Education; Physics; Mathematics, 4 yrs; *Licenciatura*: Business Administration; Nursing, 5 yrs; *Titulo Profesional*: Agro-industrial Engineering; Electrical Engineering; Systems Engineering; Environmental Engineering, 5 yrs; *Especialización*

Student Services: Academic counselling, Canteen, Cultural centre, Health services, Language programs, Social counselling, Sports facilities

Libraries: Central Library; libraries of the faculties

Publications: Perspective *(biennially)*

ROLDANILLO INSTITUTE OF PROFESSIONAL TECHNICAL EDUCATION
Instituto de Educación Técnica Profesional de Roldanillo
Carrera 7 No 10-20, Roldanillo, Valle del Cauca
Tel: +57(92) 229-8586
Fax: +57(92) 229-7226
EMail: secregeneral@intep.edu.co
Website: http://www.intep.edu.co

Rectora: Mandina Quinzza Tomich EMail: rectoria@intep.edu.co

Programmes
Accountancy (Accountancy); **Animal Husbandry**; **Business Administration** (Business Administration); **Computer Science**; **Environmental Studies**; **Secretarial Studies** (Secretarial Studies)

Degrees and Diplomas: *Tecnólogo*; *Titulo Profesional*; *Especialización*

Last Updated: 04/11/09

SCHOOL OF PUBLIC ADMINISTRATION
Escuela Superior de Administración Pública (ESAP)
Apartado aéreo 29745, Diagonal 40 No. 46 A 37, Bogotá
Tel: +57(1) 220-2790
Fax: +57(1) 222-4356
Website: http://www.esap.edu.co

Director: Honorio Miguel Henriquez Pinedo
Tel: +57(1) 222-4315, Fax: +57(1) 222-4053
EMail: direccion.nacional@esap.edu.co

International Relations: Mauricio Ballesteros
EMail: Mauricio.Ballesteros@esap.edu.co

Departments
Administration (Finance; Health Administration; International Relations; Political Sciences; Public Administration); **Advanced Studies**

Research Centres
Public Administration (Public Administration)

Further Information: ESAP sedes: Cundinamarca (Fusagasuga), Atlántico (Baranquilla), Bolívar (Cartagena), Caldas (Manizales), Huila (Neiva), Risaralda (Dosquebradas), Boyacá (Tunja), Santander (Bucaramanga), Antioquia (Medellin), Valle (Cali), Cauca (Popayan), Nariño (Pasto), Norte de Santander (San José de Cúcuta), Tolima (Ibague) and Meta (Villavicencio)

History: Founded 1958, reorganized 2004.

Academic Year: January to December

Admission Requirements: Secondary school certificate (bachillerato) and entrance examination (ICFES test)

Main Language(s) of Instruction: Spanish

Degrees and Diplomas: *Titulo Profesional*: 5-6 yrs; *Especialización*; *Maestría*: 2 yrs

Student Services: Academic counselling, Canteen, Cultural centre, Health services, Language programs, Nursery care, Social counselling, Sports facilities

Libraries: "Luis Oswaldo Beltran Jara" Library, c. 40,000 vols

Publications: Administración y Desarollo *(quarterly)*; Nuevo Municipio *(quarterly)*

Academic Staff *2007-2008*: Total 517
STAFF WITH DOCTORATE: Total 7
Student Numbers *2007-2008*: Total 7,119
Last Updated: 30/10/09

SOUTH COLOMBIAN UNIVERSITY
Universidad Surcolombiana
Apartado aéreo 385, Avenida Pastrana Carrera Borrero 1, Neiva, Huila
Tel: +57(8) 875-4753
Fax: +57(8) 875-8890
EMail: informacion@usco.edu.co
Website: http://www.usco.edu.co

Rector: Luis Alberto Cerquera EMail: rectoria@usco.edu.co

Secretario General: Alberto Polania Puente
EMail: secretariageneral@usco.edu.co

Centres
Scientific Research and Development *(CIDEC)*

Departments
Distance Education (Distance Education); **Extension**

Faculties
Economics and Administration (Accountancy; Administration; Banking; Business Administration; Economics; Finance); **Education** (Art Education; Arts and Humanities; Biology; Chemistry; Education; Educational Administration; Educational Technology; Linguistics; Literature; Mathematics Education; Modern Languages; Music; Nautical Science; Physical Education; Preschool Education; Theatre; Visual Arts); **Engineering** (Agricultural Engineering; Construction Engineering; Electronic Engineering; Engineering; Forestry; Industrial Engineering; Petroleum and Gas Engineering; Systems Analysis); **Exact and Natural Sciences** (Natural Sciences; Science Education); **Health Sciences** (Health Sciences; Medicine; Nursing; Occupational Health; Surgery); **Law** (Law); **Social Sciences and Humanities** (Arts and Humanities; Communication Studies; Documentation Techniques; Journalism; Social Sciences)

Further Information: Also 15 branches

History: Founded 1968 as Instituto Universitario, acquired present status and title 1976. A State institution.

Governing Bodies: Consejo Superior; Consejo Académico

Academic Year: February to December (February-June; July-December)

Admission Requirements: Secondary school certificate (bachillerato) and entrance examination (ICFES test)

Main Language(s) of Instruction: Spanish

Degrees and Diplomas: *Tecnólogo*; *Licenciatura*: 4-5 yrs; *Titulo Profesional*; *Especialización*: 1-2 yrs; *Maestría*: 2-3 yrs

Special Facilities: Geological Museum

Libraries: Central Library, c. 15,000 vols; Health Sciences, c. 2,700 vols

Publications: Crear Empresarial *(annually)*; Cuadernos Surcolombiano *(3 per annum)*; Revista *(3 per annum)*
Last Updated: 20/11/09

TECHNICAL AGRICULTURAL INSTITUTE
Instituto Técnico Agricola (ITA)
Apartado aéreo 185, Carrera 13 Calle 26 C, Buga, Valle
Tel: +57(92) 236-0673
Fax: +57(92) 228-2080
EMail: info@ita.edu.co; instepa@uniweb.net.co
Website: http://www.ita.edu.co

Rector: Héctor Martínez Luna EMail: hectorluna@uniweb.net.co

Programmes
Animal Husbandry (Animal Husbandry); **Business Administration**; **Computer Science**; **Environmental Management** (Environmental Management); **Hotel Management and Tourism** (Hotel Management; Tourism); **Mechanical Engineering**

Degrees and Diplomas: *Técnico Profesional*; *Especialización*
Last Updated: 04/11/09

TECHNOLOGICAL UNITS OF SANTANDER

Unidades Tecnológicas de Santander

Calle de los Estudiantes N° 9-82, Ciudadela Real de Minas,
Bucaramanga, Santander
Tel: +57(7) 641-3000 +57(7) 641-2173 +57(7) 641-3264
Fax: +57(7) 644-7777
EMail: uts@uts.edu.co
Website: http://www.uts.edu.co

Rector: Víctor Raúl Castro Neira
Tel: +57(7) 641-4426, Fax: +57(7) 644-7777
EMail: rectoria@uts.edu.co; vrcn07@yahoo.es

Vicerrector: Alfredo Reyes Serpa

Departments
Basic Sciences (Natural Sciences) *Head*: Zuly Castillo Yeneris; **Humanities**; **Languages** (English; French; Linguistics; Modern Languages)

Faculties
Natural Sciences and Engineering; **Social and Economic Sciences** (Accountancy; Agricultural Management; Banking; Business Administration; Economics; Finance; Marketing; Social Sciences; Sports)

History: Founded 1963. Acquired present title 1986.

Admission Requirements: Secondary school certificate

Main Language(s) of Instruction: Spanish, English

Accrediting Agencies: Ministry of Education

Degrees and Diplomas: *Tecnólogo*: 6 sem; *Licenciatura*; *Especialización*. Also Ingeniero en Control Electrónico e Instrumentación, 5 yrs

Student Services: Academic counselling, Canteen, Cultural centre, Employment services, Health services, Language programs, Social counselling

Libraries: Yes

Publications: Specialized Magazine about Electronics and Informatics Systems, Research works from teachers and students in Telecommunication Area *(annually)*
Last Updated: 05/11/09

TECHNOLOGICAL UNIVERSITY INSTITUTE OF ANTIOQUIA

Institución Universitaria Tecnológico de Antioquia (TDEA)

Calle 78B 72A 220 Robledo, Medellín, Antioquia 011421
Tel: +57(4) 442-4444
Fax: +57(4) 442-2929
EMail: tecnologico@tdea.edu.co
Website: http://www.tdea.edu.co

Rector: Luz Mariela Sorza Zapata (2003-)
Tel: +57(4) 442-7699 EMail: rectoria@tdea.edu.co

Secretary General: Maria Victoria Mejía Orozco
Tel: +57(4) 442-4444, Ext.711
EMail: secretariageneral@tdea.edu.co

Administrative Officer: Juan David Tous Ramirez
Tel: +57(4) 442-4444, Ext.416

Faculties
Administration; **Computer Science**; **Earth Sciences and the Environment**; **Education and Social Sciences**; **Forensic and Health Sciences**

Governing Bodies: Rector; Vice Rector; Secretary General; Directors; Deans

Academic Year: February to November (February-June; July-November)

Admission Requirements: Secondary school certificate, ICFES examination

Fees: (US Dollars): 300

Main Language(s) of Instruction: Spain; English

International Co-operation: With universities in Spain; Mexico; Costa Rica; Panama; Argentina

Accrediting Agencies: Consejo Nacional de Acreditación (CNA)

Degrees and Diplomas: *Técnico Profesional*: 2 yrs; *Tecnólogo*: Tinternational Business; Commerce; Finance; Agriculture and Environment Studies; Gerontology; Water Resource Management; Agricultural Production; Histology; Criminology; Archives; Electronic Engineering; Computer Engineering; Information Systems, 3 yrs; *Licenciatura*: Education; Preschool Education; Primary Education; Spanish; Mathematics Education; Business Administration, 5 yrs; *Titulo Profesional*: International Business, 5 yrs

Student Services: Academic counselling, Employment services, Foreign student adviser, Handicapped facilities, Health services, Social counselling, Sports facilities

Libraries: Yes

Academic Staff 2007-2008	MEN	WOMEN	TOTAL
FULL-TIME	–	–	527
STAFF WITH DOCTORATE			
FULL-TIME	1	1	2
Student Numbers 2007-2008			
All (Foreign Included)	–	–	6,840

Last Updated: 04/11/09

TECHNOLOGICAL UNIVERSITY OF PEREIRA

Universidad Tecnológica de Pereira (UTP)

Hacienda La Julita, Pereira, Risaralda
Tel: +57(6) 323-884 +57(6) 321-4955
Fax: +57(6) 321-5839 +57(6) 321-3292
EMail: rector@utp.edu.co
Website: http://www.utp.edu.co

Rector: Luis Enrique Arango Jiménez

Vicerrector Académico: José Germán López Quintero
EMail: viceac@utp.edu.co

Secretario General: Carlos Alfonso Zuluaga Arango
Tel: +57(6) 216-267 EMail: azuluaga@utp.edu.co

International Relations: María Margarita Lombana
Tel: +57(6) 213-292 EMail: relint@utp.edu.co

Faculties
Arts and Humanities (Arts and Humanities; Fine Arts; Graphic Arts; Music; Philosophy) *Dean*: Cristobal Gómez; **Education** (Education; Pedagogy; Preschool Education); **Engineering** (Computer Science; Electrical Engineering; Electronic Engineering; Physical Engineering); **Environmental Studies** (Environmental Management; Environmental Studies); **Health Sciences** (Medicine; Sports); **Industrial Engineering** (Industrial Engineering); **Mechanical Engineering** (Mechanical Engineering); **Technology** (Technology) *Dean*: Carlos Arturo Botero

History: Founded 1958 as a State institution, supported by the central government and the federal and municipal authorities.

Governing Bodies: Consejo Directivo; Consejo Academico; Consejos de Facultades

Academic Year: January to December (January-May; June-July; August-December)

Admission Requirements: Secondary school certificate (bachillerato) and entrance examination or ICFES (governmental)

Main Language(s) of Instruction: Spanish

Accrediting Agencies: Consejo Nacional de Acreditación

Degrees and Diplomas: *Tecnólogo*: Technical Studies, 3 yrs; *Licenciatura*: Mathematics; Music; Physics, 5 yrs; *Licenciatura*: Medicine, 7 yrs; *Titulo Profesional*: Electrical Engineering; Industrial Engineering; Mechanical Engineering; Systems Engineering, 5 yrs; *Especialización*; *Maestría*; *Doctorado*

Student Services: Health services, Sports facilities

Special Facilities: Planetarium

Libraries: c. 28,620 vols

Publications: Ciencias Humanas *(3 per annum)*; Revista Medica de Risaralda *(biannually)*; Scientia et Technica *(biannually)*
Last Updated: 20/11/09

TOLIMA INSTITUTE OF TECHNICAL TRAINING

Instituto Tolimense de Formación Técnica Profesional (ITFIP)
Calle 18 Carrera 1♀ Barrio/Arkabal, Espinal, Tolima
Tel: +57(982) 248-3503
Fax: +57(982) 248-3502
EMail: info@itfip.edu.co
Website: http://www.itfip.edu.co/

Rectora: Isabel Ortiz Serrano EMail: Itfip2001@yahoo.com

Faculties
Economics, Administration and Accountancy (Accountancy; Business Administration; Economics); **Engineering and Agro-Industrial Sciences** (Civil Engineering; Computer Science; Construction Engineering; Electronic Engineering; Industrial Maintenance); **Social Sciences, Health and Education** (Social Work)

Degrees and Diplomas: *Técnico Profesional*; *Especialización*
Last Updated: 05/11/09

UNIVERSITY COLLEGE OF CUNDINAMARCA

Universidad Colegio Mayor de Cundinamarca
Calle 28 No. 6-02, Bogotá, Cundinamarca
Tel: +57(1) 284-1717 +57(1) 241-8800 Ext. 114115 or 102
Fax: +57(1) 284-1717
Website: http://www.unicolmayor.edu.co

Rector: Miguel Augusto García Bustamante
EMail: rectoria@unicolmayor.edu.co; vice-academ@unicolmayor.edu.co

Secretaria General: Carmen Eliana Caro Nocua
Tel: +57(1) 241-8800 Ext. 104
EMail: secretariageneral@unicolmayor.edu.co

International Relations: José Mauricio Benavides Sandoval, Head, Interinstitutional Promotion and Relations
Tel: +57(1) 241-8800 Ext. 152; +57(1) 336-7788
EMail: promocio@unicolmayor.edu.co

Faculties
Administration and Economics (Administration; Business Administration; Economics); **Engineering and Architecture** (Architecture; Construction Engineering; Engineering); **Health Sciences** (Health Administration; Health Sciences; Laboratory Techniques); **Law** (Law); **Social Sciences** (Occupational Health; Social Sciences; Social Work; Tourism)

History: Founded 1945.

Main Language(s) of Instruction: Spanish

International Co-operation: With UDUAL Network

Accrediting Agencies: Consejo Nacional de Acreditación (CNA)

Degrees and Diplomas: *Tecnólogo*; *Titulo Profesional*; *Especialización*: Laboratory Management; Occupational Health; Health Promotion and Human Development

Student Services: Academic counselling, Canteen, Employment services, Foreign student adviser, Language programs, Social counselling, Sports facilities

Publications: Boletín Institucional Pensamiento Universitario *(biennially)*; Nova, Biomedical Sciences *(biennially)*; Tabula Rasa, Social Sciences and Humanities *(biennially)*

Press or Publishing House: Universidad Colegio Mayor de Cundinamarca

Academic Staff *2007-2008*	TOTAL
FULL-TIME	151
PART-TIME	41
Student Numbers *2007-2008*	
All (Foreign Included)	5,047

Last Updated: 09/11/09

UNIVERSITY FRANCISCO DE PAULA SANTANDER

Universidad Francisco de Paula Santander (UFPS)
Edificio Torre Administrativa, Avenida Gran Colombia 12 E-96, Barrio Colsag, Cúcuta, Norte de Santander
Tel: +57(975) 753-172
Fax: +57(975) 753-893
EMail: rectoria@motilon.ufps.edu.co
Website: http://www.ufps.edu.co

Rector: Hector Miguel Parra López (2002-) Tel: +57(975) 751-906
Secretario General: Julio César Quintero Tel: +57(975)753-196

Departments
Distance Education

Faculties
Administration (Accountancy; Business Administration); **Agricultural and Environmental Sciences** (Agriculture; Environmental Studies); **Education, Arts and Humanities** (Architecture; Arts and Humanities; Biology; Chemistry; Computer Science; Education; Mathematics); **Engineering** (Civil Engineering; Electronic Engineering; Engineering; Mechanical Engineering; Mining Engineering; Production Engineering; Systems Analysis)

Further Information: Branches in Ocaña and Chinácota

History: Founded 1962 as a private institution, recognized by the State 1970. Financed by the national, provincial, and local governments.

Governing Bodies: Consejo Superior; Consejo Académico

Academic Year: February to December (February-June; August-December)

Admission Requirements: Secondary school certificate (bachillerato) and entrance examination

Main Language(s) of Instruction: Spanish

Degrees and Diplomas: *Tecnólogo*: 3 yrs; *Licenciatura*: Accountancy (Contador Público); Biology and Chemistry; Business Administration (Administrador de Empresas); Mathematics and Physics, 5 yrs; *Licenciatura*: Architectural Design (Delineante de Arquitectura); Nursing (Enfermera), 3 yrs; *Titulo Profesional*: Engineering (Ingeniero), 5 yrs; *Especialización*

Libraries: c. 15,000 vols

Publications: Oriente Universitario
Last Updated: 16/11/09

UNIVERSITY INSTITUTE OF FINE ARTS AND SCIENCE OF BOLIVAR

Institución Universitaria Bellas Artes y Ciencias de Bolívar (ESBA)
Centro, San Diego, Kra 9 No. 39, Cartagena de Indias, Bolívar
Tel: +57(5) 660-0391
Fax: +57(5) 660-1336
EMail: info@unibac.edu.co
Website: http://www.esba.edu.co/

Rectora: Sacra Nader David EMail: rectoria@esba.edu.co

Secretaria General: Elzie Torres Anaya
EMail: secgral@esba.edu.co

International Relations: Roben Gonzalez
EMail: info@esba.edu.co

Programmes
Graphic Design (Graphic Design); **Industrial Design**; **Music** (Music); **Plastic Arts** (Fine Arts); **Radio and Television** (Radio and Television Broadcasting); **Scenic Arts** (Theatre)

History: Founded 1899. Acquired present title 2008.

Governing Bodies: Chancellor; Board of Directors

Academic Year: February to November

Admission Requirements: Secondary school certificate and ICFES test

Fees: (US Dollars): 433-700 per semester

Main Language(s) of Instruction: Spanish

Degrees and Diplomas: *Técnico Profesional*; *Titulo Profesional*: 5 yrs

Student Services: Academic counselling, Cultural centre, Employment services, Handicapped facilities, Nursery care, Social counselling

Student Residential Facilities: None

Special Facilities: Art Gallery; Workshops Recording Studio

Libraries: Specialized Arts and Design Library

Publications: Ojo Al Arte, Cultural and Academic Magazine *(biennially)*

Press or Publishing House: Grafikoral
Last Updated: 30/10/09

UNIVERSITY OF ANTIOQUÍA
Universidad de Antioquía
Apartado aéreo 1226, Calle 67 No. 53-108, Ciudad Universitaria, Medellín, Antioquía
Tel: +57(4) 263-0011
Fax: +57(4) 263-8282
EMail: comunicaciones@udea.edu.co
Website: http://www.udea.edu.co

Rector: Alberto Uribe Correa (2006-)
Tel: +57(4) 210-5000, Fax: +57(4) 211-0672

Secretaria General: Ana Lucía Herrera Gómez
Tel: +57(4) 210-5020 EMail: secretar@quimbaya.udea.edu.co

International Relations: Isabel Cristina Arango Calle
Tel: +57(4) 210-5210, Fax: +57(4) 210-5212
EMail: relinter@quimbaya.udea.edu.co

Departments
Distance Education (Distance Education)

Faculties
Agrarian Science (Animal Husbandry; Veterinary Science); **Arts** (Art History; Dance; Music; Theatre; Visual Arts); **Communication** (Communication Studies; Journalism; Philology; Spanish); **Dentistry** (Dentistry); **Economics** (Accountancy; Business Administration; Economics); **Education** (Art Education; Education; Geography; History; Literature; Mathematics; Pedagogy; Physics; Preschool Education; Science Education); **Engineering** (Bioengineering; Chemical Engineering; Computer Science; Electrical Engineering; Electronic Engineering; Engineering; Environmental Engineering; Industrial Engineering; Materials Engineering; Mechanical Engineering; Sanitary Engineering); **Humanities and Social Sciences** (Anthropology; Arts and Humanities; History; Psychology; Social Sciences; Social Work; Sociology); **Law** (Law; Political Sciences); **Medicine** (Medicine); **Natural and Exact Sciences** (Astronomy and Space Science; Biology; Chemistry; Mathematics; Natural Sciences; Physics); **Nursing** (Nursing); **Pharmaceutical Chemistry** (Food Science; Food Technology; Pharmacy); **Public Health** (Health Administration; Public Health)

Institutes
Philosophy (Philosophy) *Director:* Carlos Vásquez Tamayo; **Physical Education** (Physical Education) *Director:* Alain Bustamante Simon; **Political Science** (Political Sciences) *Director:* Manuel Alberto Alonso Espinal; **Regional Studies** (Regional Studies) *Director:* Lucelly Villegas Villegas

Research Centres
Agricultural Research *(CIAG) Director:* Mario Fernando Cerón; **Arts** (Fine Arts) *Director:* Alejandro Tobón; **Bacteriology and Laboratory** (Microbiology) *Director:* María Cristina Acosta Betancur; **Business Administration** *(CICA)* (Behavioural Sciences; Business Administration; Management) *Director:* Fernando Jaramillo Betancur; **Communication** *(CIEC)* (Communication Studies) *Director:* Olga Vallejo; **Dentistry** (Dentistry; Oral Pathology) *Director:* Angela María Franco; **Economics** *(CIE)* (Economics) *Director:* Jorge Alonso Lotero; **Educational Sciences** *(CIEP)* (Educational Sciences; Pedagogy) *Director:* María Alexandra Rendón; **Environment** *(CIA)* (Environmental Engineering) *Director:* John Freddy Duitama; **Humanities and Social Sciences** (Arts and Humanities; History; Social Sciences) *Director:* Victor Álvarez; **Languages** (Educational Testing and Evaluation; Terminology; Translation and Interpretation) *Director:* Adriana González; **Law** (Law) *Director:* María Cristina Gómez; **Library Science** *(CICINF)* (Library Science) *Director:* Martha Valencia; **Medicine** *(CIM)* (Medicine) *Director:* Carlos Alberto Palacio; **Natural and Exact Sciences** *(CIEN)* (Mathematics; Natural Sciences; Physics) *Director:* Nicolás Jaramillo; **Nursing** (Nursing) *Director:* Diva Estela Jaramilla Vélez; **Nutrition** *(CIAN) Director:* Luz María Agudelo; **Pharmacy** *(CIQUIFAR)* (Pharmacy) *Director:* Margarita María Restrepo; **Philosophy** *Director:* Alfonso Monsalve Solórzano; **Political Studies** (Political Sciences) *Director:* Manuel Alberto Alonso; **Public Health** *Director:* Elkin Martínez López; **Regional Studies** *(INER)* (Regional Studies) *Director:* Diego Herrera Gómez; **Sport Science** *(CICIDEP) Director:* Gloria Cecilia Vallejo

Schools
Bacteriology and Clinical Chemistry (Biology; Chemistry; Microbiology; Virology) *Director:* Angela María Arango Rave; **Food and Nutrition** (Food Science; Nutrition) *Director:* Dora Nicolasa Gómez Cifuentes; **Languages** (Modern Languages; Translation and Interpretation) *Director:* Adriana González Moncada; **Library Science** *(Interamerican)* (Library Science) *Director:* María Teresa Múnera Torres

Further Information: Also Teaching Hospital: Hospital Universitario San Vicente de Paúl. Research Groups. Branches: Bajo Cauca, Magdalena Medio, Urabá, Suroeste, Oriente, Occidente, Nordeste, Norte, Envigado and Estación Piscícola

History: Founded 1803 as school by King Charles IV of Spain, became State university 1822.

Governing Bodies: Consejo Superior; Consejo Académico; Consejos de Facultad, Escuela, Instituto y Corporación

Academic Year: February to December (February-June; July-December)

Admission Requirements: Secondary school certificate (bachillerato) and entrance examination

Fees: According to parents'/student's income

Main Language(s) of Instruction: Spanish

Accrediting Agencies: Ministry of Education (Institutional Education Certification for a period of 9 years as from 2003)

Degrees and Diplomas: *Tecnólogo:* 3 yrs; *Licenciatura:* 4-5 yrs; *Especialización:* 1-2 yrs; *Maestría:* 2-3 yrs; *Doctorado:* 3-5 yrs. Also Especialidad Médica 3-5 yrs

Student Services: Academic counselling, Cultural centre, Foreign student adviser, Handicapped facilities, Health services, Language programs, Social counselling, Sports facilities

Special Facilities: Theatre and Museum

Libraries: Central Library; Medicine Library; Public Health Library; Veterinary Medicine, Animal Husbandry and Food and Nutrition Library; Dentistry Library; Nursing Library; Library Science Library. c. 700,000 vols.

Publications: Actualidades Biológicas; Boletín de Antropología; Contaduría; Estudios de Derecho; Estudios de Filosofía; Estudios de Literatura Colombiana; Folios; Iatreia; Investigación y Educación en Enfermería; Lecturas de Economía; Perspectivas en Nutrición Humana; Revista de Contaduría; Revista de la Escuela Interamericana de Bibliotecología; Revista de Linguistica y Literatura; Revista Educación y Pedagogía; Revista Facultad de Ingeniería; Revista Facultad de Odontología; Revista Interamericana de Bibliotecología, Lingüística y Literatura; Tecnológica Administrativa; Temas Microbiológicos; Utopía Siglo XXI; Vitae Revista de Química Farmacéutica

Press or Publishing House: Editorial Universidad de Antioquia
Last Updated: 09/11/09

UNIVERSITY OF CALDAS
Universidad de Caldas
Apartado aéreo 275, Calle 65 No. 26-10, Manizales, Caldas
Tel: +57(6) 878-1500
Fax: +57(6) 878-1507
EMail: ucaldas@ucaldas.edu.co
Website: http://www.ucaldas.edu.co

Rector: Ricardo Gómez Giraldo
Tel: +57(6) 878-1505, Fax: +57(6) 878-1500 Ext. 11150
EMail: rector@ucaldas.edu.co

Secretario General: Fernando Duque García
Tel: +57(6) 878-1595, Fax: +57(6) 878-1500 Ext. 11111
EMail: sgeneral@ucaldas.edu.co

International Relations: Marta Isabel Serna Nieto
Tel: +57(6) 878-1500 Ext. 12169

Faculties

Agriculture (Agricultural Business; Agriculture; Agronomy; Animal Husbandry; Botany; Crop Production; Ecology; Rural Planning; Veterinary Science); **Arts and Humanities** (Arts and Humanities; English; Literature; Modern Languages; Music; Painting and Drawing; Philosophy; Sculpture; Visual Arts); **Engineering** (Computer Engineering; Engineering; Food Technology); **Exact and Natural Sciences** (Biology; Chemistry; Geology; Natural Sciences; Physics); **Health Sciences** (Anaesthesiology; Dermatology; Gynaecology and Obstetrics; Health Sciences; Medicine; Nursing; Ophthalmology; Paediatrics; Physical Education; Psychiatry and Mental Health; Surgery); **Law and Social Sciences** (Anthropology; Family Studies; Law; Social Sciences; Social Work; Sociology)

History: Founded 1937 as Instituto Politécnico de Caldas, became Universidad Popular 1943, and national university 1967. Acquired present status 1993.

Governing Bodies: Consejo Superior; Consejo Directivo

Academic Year: February to December (February-June; July-December)

Admission Requirements: Secondary school certificate (bachillerato) and national entrance examination (ICFES) with a minimum score of 220

Main Language(s) of Instruction: Spanish

Accrediting Agencies: Consejo Nacional de Acreditación (Accreditation for Nursing and Agronomy programmes)

Degrees and Diplomas: Tecnólogo: 3 yrs; Licenciatura: 4 yrs; Especialización: 1 yr; Maestría: a further 2 yrs; Doctorado: 3 yrs

Student Services: Canteen, Cultural centre, Health services, Language programs, Nursery care, Sports facilities

Student Residential Facilities: Yes

Special Facilities: Archaeological Museum. Natural History Museum. Botanical Garden. '8 de Junio' Theatre

Libraries: Central Library. 4 department libraries

Publications: Lumina-Spargo; Revista Cultural Hipsipila (biannually); Revista Universidad de Caldas (biannually); Universidad al Día

Press or Publishing House: Centro Editorial

Academic Staff 2007-2008	TOTAL
FULL-TIME	402
PART-TIME	607
STAFF WITH DOCTORATE	
FULL-TIME	38

Student Numbers 2007-2008
All (Foreign Included) c. **11,000**
Last Updated: 09/11/09

UNIVERSITY OF CARTAGENA
Universidad de Cartagena
Apartado aéreo 1382, Centro Carrera 6 No. 36-100 Calle de la Universidad, Cartagena de Indias, Bolívar
Tel: +57(5) 6600-676
Fax: +57(5) 6600-380
Website: http://www.unicartagena.edu.co

Rector: Germán Sierra Anaya
Tel: +57(5) 6600-380 EMail: rector@unicartagena.edu.co

Secretaria General: Marly Mardini Llamas
Tel: +57(5) 6641-585 EMail: secretariagral@unicartagena.edu.co

International Relations: María Teresa Vélez de López
Tel: +57(5) 6646-304 EMail: postgado@unicartagena.edu.co

Faculties
Dentistry (Dentistry) Dean: Luisa Leonor Arévalo Tovar; **Economics** (Accountancy; Business Administration; Economics; Industrial Management); **Engineering** (Chemical Engineering; Civil Engineering; Food Technology; Systems Analysis); **Exact and Natural Sciences**; **Human Sciences** (Arts and Humanities; Education; History; Linguistics; Literature; Philosophy); **Law and Political Science** (Law; Political Sciences); **Medicine** (Medicine); **Nursing** (Nursing); **Pharmaceutical Sciences** (Chemistry; Pharmacy); **Social Sciences** (Social Sciences; Social Work)

Institutes
Caribbean Studies (Caribbean Studies); **Immunology** (Immunology)

Programmes
Open and Distance Education
Further Information: Also Cartagena University Hospital

History: Founded 1774, became university 1827. A State institution.

Governing Bodies: Consejo Superior; Consejo Académico

Academic Year: February to December (February-June; July-December)

Admission Requirements: Secondary school certificate (Bachillerato) and entrance examination

Fees: According to parents' income

Main Language(s) of Instruction: Spanish

International Co-operation: With Spanish and Cuban universities

Degrees and Diplomas: Licenciatura: Accountancy (Contador público); Business Administration (Administrador de Empresas); Chemistry (Químico); Dentistry (Odontólogo); Economics (Economista); History (Historiador); Industrial Administration (Administrador Industrial); Law (Abogado); Linguistics and Literature; Mathematics (Matemático); Pharmaceutical Chemistry (Químico Farmaceuta); Philosophy (Filósofo), 5 yrs; Licenciatura: Medicine (Médico Cirujano), 7 yrs; Licenciatura: Nursing (Enfermero(a)); Social Work (Trabajador social), 4 yrs; Título Profesional: Civil Engineering (Ingeniero civil); Food Engineering (Ingeniero de Alimentos), 5 yrs; Especialización: Medicine; Economics; Chemical Sciences; Engineering; Law, 2 yrs; Maestría: Immunology; Pharmacology, 2 yrs; Maestría: Microbiology; Doctorado (PhD): 3 yrs

Student Services: Cultural centre, Employment services, Health services, Sports facilities

Libraries: 'Fernández de Madrid' University Library, c. 45,000 vols; Zaragocilla University Library

Publications: History and Culture (annually); Revista de Ciencias Económicas; Revista Jurídica
Last Updated: 10/11/09

UNIVERSITY OF CAUCA
Universidad del Cauca
Apartado Aéreo 1384, Calle 5, No. 4-70, Popayán, Cauca
Tel: +57(2) 820-9900
EMail: viceadm@unicauca.edu.co
Website: http://www.unicauca.edu.co

Rector: Danilo Reinaldo Vivas Ramos
Tel: +57(2) 823-0488, Fax: +57(2) 824-1972
EMail: rectoria@unicauca.edu.co

Secretaria General Encargada: Martha Alejandra Parra Chavarro
Tel: +57(2) 824-3020, Ext. 1107

Centres
Distance Education Director: Henry Maya Andrade

Faculties
Accountancy, Economics and Administration (Accountancy; Administration; Economics); **Animal Husbandry** (Animal Husbandry); **Arts** (Fine Arts); **Civil Engineering** (Civil Engineering); **Electronics and Telecommunications** (Electronic Engineering; Telecommunications Engineering); **Health Sciences** (Health Sciences); **Human and Social Sciences** (Anthropology; Cultural Studies; Geography; History; Modern Languages; Philosophy; Social Sciences); **Law and Political Science** (Law; Political Sciences); **Natural, Exact and Educational Sciences** (Education; Natural Sciences; Science Education)

History: Founded 1827 by decree of General Santander. Title changed to Colegio provincial 1850. Reorganized and became Colegio mayor in 1857. Re-established as university in 1883, became a public autonomous institution 1964.

Governing Bodies: Consejo Superior; Consejo Académico

Academic Year: January to December (January-June; August-December)

Admission Requirements: Secondary school certificate (bachillerato) and entrance examination

Fees: According to parents' income

Main Language(s) of Instruction: Spanish

Degrees and Diplomas: *Licenciatura*: 4 yrs; *Licenciatura*: Law, 5 yrs; *Licenciatura*: Medicine, 7 yrs; *Licenciatura*: Nursing, 3 yrs; *Titulo Profesional*: Engineering, 5 yrs; *Especialización*; *Maestría*: a further 1 1/2 yrs; *Doctorado*

Special Facilities: Natural History Museum

Libraries: Central Library, c. 35,000 vols

Publications: Faculty publications

Press or Publishing House: Editorial de la Universidad del Cauca

Last Updated: 12/11/09

UNIVERSITY OF CÓRDOBA

Universidad de Córdoba (UNICOR)
Apartado aéreo 354, Ciudad Universitaria, Carrera 6 No 76,
Montería, Córdoba
Tel: +57(47) 860-300
Fax: +57(47) 860-054
EMail: webmaster@unicordoba.edu.co
Website: http://www.unicordoba.edu.co

Rector: Claudio Enrique Sánchez Parra (2003-)
EMail: rector@unicordoba.edu.co

Senior Administrative Officer: Luisa Lora

International Relations: Manuel Anniciarico
Tel: +57(47) 860-570, Fax: +57(47) 860-861
EMail: mannichiarico@hotmail.com

Faculties

Agriculture (Agricultural Engineering; Agriculture; Agronomy) *Dean*: Carlos Cardona Ayala; **Education** (Education) *Dean*: Rocío Blanco; **Fishery** (Fishery) *Dean*: Víctor Atencio; **Health Sciences** (Health Sciences; Nursing; Pharmacy) *Dean*: Nilka Brunal Kerguelen; **Science** (Biology; Chemistry; Geography; Industrial Engineering; Natural Sciences; Physics) *Dean*: Havith Barrera Durango; **Veterinary Medicine and Animal Husbandry** *(Berástegui)* (Animal Husbandry; Fishery; Veterinary Science) *Dean*: Lazaro Reza

History: Founded 1966 by the provincial government, incorporating faculties of agriculture and veterinary medicine (founded 1962). The University is autonomous in administrative and academic matters. Financed by the national and provincial governments.

Governing Bodies: Consejo Directivo; Consejo Académico

Academic Year: February to November (February-June; July-November)

Admission Requirements: Secondary school certificate (Bachillerato) and entrance examination

Fees: (Pesos): 109,400-237,000

Main Language(s) of Instruction: Spanish

International Co-operation: With universities in Spain

Degrees and Diplomas: *Licenciatura*: Biology and Chemistry; Mathematics and Physics; Social Sciences; Veterinary Medicine, 5 yrs; *Licenciatura*: Nursing, 4 yrs; *Titulo Profesional*: Agricultural Engineering, 5 yrs; *Especialización*; *Maestría*

Student Services: Canteen, Foreign student adviser, Health services, Language programs, Sports facilities

Special Facilities: Anthropology Museum

Libraries: c. 25,000 vols

Publications: Avance *(quarterly)*; Proyección Investigativa *(biennially)*

UNIVERSITY OF CUNDINAMARCA

Universidad de Cundinamarca (UDEC)
Diagonal 18 No. 20-29, Fusagasuga
Tel: +57(91) 873-2512
Fax: +57(91) 867-7898
EMail: unicundi@unicundi.edu.co
Website: http://www.unicundi.edu.co/

Rector: Adolfo Miguel Polo Solano EMail: rectoria@unicundi.edu.co

Secretario General: Adriano Muñoz Barrera

Faculties

Administration, Economics and Accountancy (Accountancy; Administration; Business Administration; Economics; Environmental Management); **Agriculture** (Agricultural Engineering; Agriculture; Animal Husbandry; Food Science; Zoology); **Education**; **Engineering** (Computer Engineering; Electronic Engineering; Engineering; Industrial Engineering); **Health Sciences** (Health Administration; Health Sciences; Nursing); **Sports and Physical Education** (Parks and Recreation; Physical Education; Sports)

Further Information: Branches in Girardot, Ubaté, Chia, Chocontá, Soacha, Facatativá and Zipaquirá

History: Founded 1969. Acquired present status 1992.

Main Language(s) of Instruction: Spanish

Degrees and Diplomas: *Licenciatura*; *Especialización*

Last Updated: 10/11/09

UNIVERSITY OF EDUCATION AND TECHNOLOGY OF COLOMBIA

Universidad Pedagógica y Tecnológica de Colombia (UPTC)
Tunja, Boyacá 711
Tel: +57(87) 422-175
Fax: +57(87) 436-205
Website: http://www.uptc.edu.co

Rector: Alfonso López Díaz (2007-)
Tel: +57(87) 436-236, Fax: +57(87) 436-236
EMail: rectoria@uptc.edu.co

Director Administrativo y Financiero: John William Rosso Murillo
Tel: +57(87) 436-217, Fax: +57(87) 436-217
EMail: administrativa@uptc.edu.co

International Relations: Miguel Baretto Sánchez, Asesor, Unidad de Relaciones Externas y Convenios
Tel: +57(87) 422-176 Ext. 1880 EMail: relinter@uptc.edu.co

Faculties

Agronomy and Veterinary Science (Agricultural Engineering; Agronomy; Veterinary Science) *Division Head*: Moreno; **Economic and Administrative Sciences**; **Education** (Archiving; Education; Educational Sciences; English; Environmental Studies; Fine Arts; French; Geography; German; History; Mathematics; Modern Languages; Music; Natural Sciences; Pedagogy; Philosophy; Physical Education; Preschool Education; Social Sciences; Spanish); **Engineering** (Civil Engineering; Computer Science; Electronic Engineering; Engineering; Metallurgical Engineering; Mining Engineering); **Health Sciences** (Health Sciences; Medicine; Nursing; Occupational Health; Psychology); **Law and Social Sciences** (Law; Social Sciences); **Science** (Biology; Chemistry; Natural Sciences; Physics); **Technology and Distance Education** (Agricultural Business; Banking; Electrical Engineering; Electronic Engineering; Finance; Health Administration; Information Sciences; Information Technology; Management; Mathematics; Spanish; Technology)

Further Information: Branches in Chinquinquira, Sogamoso and Duitama

History: Founded 1827 as Escuela Normal de Tunja, became Facultad de Pedagogía 1933, Universidad 1953, and acquired present title 1968. A State institution.

Governing Bodies: Consejo Superior Universitario; Consejo Académico; Consejo Directivo

Academic Year: February to December (February-July; August-December)

Admission Requirements: Secondary school certificate (bachillerato) and entrance examination

Fees: According to parents' income

Main Language(s) of Instruction: Spanish

International Co-operation: With universities in Spain; France; USA; Germany; Russian Federation; Argentina; Venezuela; Cuba and Mexico. Also participates in the ALFA programme

Degrees and Diplomas: *Tecnólogo*: 3 yrs; *Licenciatura*: 4 yrs; *Titulo Profesional*: 5 yrs; *Especialización*: 2 yrs; *Especialización*: Medicine, 6 yrs; *Doctorado*: Medicine, 5 yrs

Student Services: Academic counselling, Cultural centre, Employment services, Foreign student adviser, Handicapped facilities, Health services, Language programs, Nursery care, Social counselling, Sports facilities

Student Residential Facilities: Yes

Special Facilities: Museums: Sun; Anthropology

Libraries: Central Library, c. 120,000 vols; Faculty Libraries, c. 20,000 vols

Publications: Pensamiento y Acción *(biennially)*

Academic Staff *2007-2008*	MEN	WOMEN	TOTAL
FULL-TIME	683	376	1,059
PART-TIME	194	160	354
STAFF WITH DOCTORATE			
FULL-TIME	13	40	53
PART-TIME	3	–	3

Student Numbers *2007-2008*			
All (Foreign Included)	8,729	9,540	18,269
FOREIGN ONLY	12	19	31

Distance students, 4,368. **Evening students,** 3,372.

Last Updated: 18/11/09

CHIQUINQUIRÁ BRANCH
SECCIONAL CHIQUINQUIRÁ

Apartado aéreo 16, Calle 14A No. 2-37, Chiquinquirá, Boyacá
Tel: +57(987) 262-598
Fax: +57(987) 262-003
EMail: epostgradoch@latinmail.com

Dean: Francisco Burbano Vásquez (2007-)

Programmes
Agriculture; **Business Administration**

History: Founded 1973.

Main Language(s) of Instruction: Spanish

DUITAMA BRANCH
SECCIONAL DUITAMA

Calle 23 n° 21-55, Duitama, Boyacá
Tel: +57(987) 602-181
Fax: +57(987) 600-076
Website: http://www.uptc.edu.co

Dean: Fabio E. Lozano Suárez

Programmes
Agriculture (Animal Husbandry; Farm Management); **Engineering** (Electrical Engineering; Mechanical Engineering); **Industrial Design** (Industrial Design); **Industrial Management**; **Mathematics and Statistics**; **Tourism and Hotel Management**

History: Founded 1972.

Main Language(s) of Instruction: Spanish

SOGAMOSO BRANCH
SECCIONAL SOGAMOSO

Apartado aéreo 332, Calle 4 Sur No. 15-134, Sogamoso, Boyacá
Tel: +57(987) 770-1693
Fax: +57(987) 770-1693

Dean: Orlando Vergel Portillo (2007-)

Programmes
Business Administration (Accountancy; Management); **Engineering**; **Geology** (Geology)

History: Founded 1972.

Main Language(s) of Instruction: Spanish

UNIVERSITY OF ENVIGADO
Institución Universitaria de Envigado

Carrera 27B N° 34 A sur 57, Envigado, Antioquia
Tel: +57(574) 339-1010
Fax: +57(574) 333-0148
EMail: iue@iue.edu.co
Website: http://www.iue.edu.co

Rector: Jaime Alberto Molina Franco EMail: rectoria@iue.edu.co
Secretaria General: Alejandra Maria Cardenas Nieto

Faculties
Business Studies (Accountancy; Business Administration; International Business); **Engineering** (Electronic Engineering; Engineering; Systems Analysis); **Law and Political Science** (Law; Political Sciences); **Social Sciences** (Arts and Humanities; Psychology; Social Sciences)

History: Founded 1993. Acquired present status 1996.

Main Language(s) of Instruction: Spanish

Degrees and Diplomas: *Técnico Profesional*; *Tecnólogo*; *Licenciatura*: 3-5 1/2 yrs; *Titulo Profesional*

Last Updated: 04/11/09

UNIVERSITY OF LA GUAJIRA
Universidad de La Guajira

Apartado aéro 172, KM 5 salida a Maicao, Ríohacha, La Guajira
Tel: +57(954) 728-5310
Fax: +57(954) 727-1991
Website: http://www.uniguajira.edu.co

Rectora: Maritza del Rosario León Vanegas
EMail: rectoria@uniguajira.edu.co

Faculties
Business Administration (Arts and Humanities; Business Administration; Economics; Industrial and Organizational Psychology; Law; Management; Mathematics; Spanish; Sports; Taxation); **Education** (Education); **Industrial Engineering** (Arts and Humanities; Electrical Engineering; English; Industrial and Organizational Psychology; Industrial Engineering; Labour Law; Marketing; Materials Engineering; Mechanics)

History: Founded 1976. A State institution.

Governing Bodies: Consejo Superior; Consejo Académico

Academic Year: January to December (January-July; August-December)

Admission Requirements: Secondary school certificate (bachillerato) and entrance examination

Main Language(s) of Instruction: Spanish

Degrees and Diplomas: *Licenciatura*: 4 yrs; *Especialización*

Student Residential Facilities: For c. 5,000 students

Libraries: Central Library, c. 45,000 vols. Ethnic Groups, c. 29,000 vols

Press or Publishing House: Centro de Publicaciones Uniguajira
Last Updated: 10/11/09

UNIVERSITY OF MAGDALENA
Universidad del Magdalena

Carrera 32 No. 22-08, Santa Marta, Magdalena
Tel: +57(5) 430-1292
Fax: +57(5) 430-6237
EMail: admin@unimagdalena.edu.co
Website: http://www.unimagdalena.edu.co/

Rector: Carlos Eduardo Caicedo Omar
EMail: rectoria@unimagdalena.edu.co

International Relations: Hans Van Heyl Cleves
EMail: relinternacional@unimagdalena.edu.co

Faculties
Basic Science (Biology; Physics); **Business Administration and Economic Sciences** (Accountancy; Business Administration; Economics; Hotel Management; International Business; Tourism); **Education** (Computer Education; Education; Preschool Education); **Engineering** (Agricultural Engineering; Civil Engineering; Computer Engineering; Electronic Engineering; Environmental Engineering; Industrial Engineering); **Health Sciences** (Dentistry; Medicine; Nursing; Psychology); **Humanities** (Anthropology; Cinema and Television; Law; Visual Arts)

Institutes
Distance Education; **Graduate Studies**; **Tropical Research** (Environmental Studies; Tropical Medicine)

Research Centres

Peace and Conflict Resolution (Peace and Disarmament)

History: Founded 1958. A State institution.

Governing Bodies: Consejo Superior; Consejo Académico

Academic Year: February to December (February-July; August-December)

Admission Requirements: Secondary school certificate (bachillerato) and entrance examination

Fees: (Pesos): 179,000-1.93m. per semester

Main Language(s) of Instruction: Spanish

International Co-operation: With universities in Spain, Mexico, Germany, Canada, Chile, Ecuador and Cuba

Degrees and Diplomas: *Tecnólogo*: Agriculture and Cattle Raising Administration, 3 yrs; *Licenciatura*; *Titulo Profesional*: Agronomy; Agricultural Economics; Biology; Accountancy; International Business; Hotel Management; Tourism; Economics; Education; Preschool Education; Agricultural Engineering; Civil Engineering; Computer Engineering; Electronic Engineering; Environmental Engineering; Industrial Engineering; Dentistry; Medicine; Nursing; Psychology; Law; Cinema and Television; Anthropology, 5 yrs; *Especialización*: Aquaculture; Food Science; Tropical Agriculture; Water Management; Rural Planning; Town Planning; Finance; Education; Social Studies; Food Technology; Environmental Studies; Logistics; Business Administration; University Teaching; Biology; Theory, Methods and Techniques of Social Research; Tropical Fruits, a further 1-3 yrs; *Maestría*: Statistics; Education; Physics; Philosophy; Chemistry; Public Health; Mathematics; Nursing; Agricultural Sciences; Coastal Integrated Management, a further 1-2 yrs following Especialización; *Doctorado*

Student Services: Academic counselling, Cultural centre, Employment services, Foreign student adviser, Health services, Language programs, Social counselling, Sports facilities

Student Residential Facilities: None

Special Facilities: Art Museum; Technology and Sciences Museum; Ethnological Museum; Cultural Centre San Juan Nepomuceno; English Centre

Libraries: c. 55,000 vols

Publications: Clio America, Business Administration Magazine; Duazari, Health Sciences Magazine; Gace, Economics Magazine; Jangwa Panwa, Anthropology Magazine; Praxis, Faculty of Education Magazine; Revista Intropica, Magazine of the Tropical Research Institute

Academic Staff 2007-2008	TOTAL
FULL-TIME	129
PART-TIME	514

Student Numbers 2007-2008	
All (Foreign Included)	8,646

Last Updated: 13/11/09

UNIVERSITY OF NARIÑO
Universidad de Nariño (UDENAR)
Apartado aéro 34185, Torobajo-Carrera 22 No. 18-109, Pasto, Nariño
Tel: +57(927) 235-652
Fax: +57(927) 235-175
EMail: pobando@udenar.edu.co
Website: http://www.udenar.edu.co/

Rector: Silvio Sánchez Fajardo

Secretario General: Jesús Alirio Bastidas Tel: +57(927) 723-5653

Faculties
Agro-industrial Engineering (Agricultural Engineering; Industrial Engineering); **Agronomy** (Agricultural Engineering; Agronomy); **Arts** (Architecture; Fine Arts; Graphic Design; Industrial Design; Music; Visual Arts); **Economics and Administration** (Administration; Business Administration; Economics; Marketing); **Education** (Education); **Engineering** (Civil Engineering; Computer Engineering; Electronic Engineering; Engineering; Systems Analysis); **Health Sciences** (Medicine); **Humanities** (Arts and Humanities; English; French; Literature; Philosophy; Psychology; Social Sciences; Sociology); **Law** (Law); **Natural Sciences and Mathematics** (Biology; Chemistry; Computer Science; Mathematics; Natural

Sciences; Physics); **Stockbreeding** (Animal Husbandry; Veterinary Science; Zoology)

History: Founded 1712 as college, became university 1904.

Governing Bodies: Consejo Superior; Consejo Académico

Academic Year: February to December (February-June; August-December)

Admission Requirements: Secondary school certificate (bachillerato) and entrance examination

Main Language(s) of Instruction: Spanish

Degrees and Diplomas: *Licenciatura*: 4 yrs; *Licenciatura*: Economics, 5-6 yrs; *Titulo Profesional*: Agriculture; Animal Husbandry; Civil Engineering; Teaching Qualification, Plastic Arts, 5 yrs; *Especialización*; *Maestría*: Literature, a further 2 yrs; *Doctorado*: Law and Social Sciences, 5 yrs. Also Certificate in Languages

Student Residential Facilities: Yes

Special Facilities: Arts Museum. Botanical Garden

Libraries: Alberto Quijano Guerrero Library

Publications: Faculty Journals

Press or Publishing House: Centro de Publicaciones Universidad de Nariño

Last Updated: 12/11/09

UNIVERSITY OF PAMPLONA
Universidad de Pamplona (UDEP)
Ciudad Universitaria 'El Buque', Pamplona, Norte de Santander
Tel: +57(7) 568-5303
Fax: +57(7) 562-2750
EMail: admisiones@unipamplona.edu.co
Website: http://www.unipamplona.edu.co

Rectora: Esperanza Paredes Hernández
Tel: +57(7) 568-5303, Ext. 103
EMail: rectoria@unipamplona.edu.co

Secretaria General: Rosalba Omaña Bonilla
Tel: +57(7) 568-5303, Ext. 124

Faculties
Agrarian Sciences (Agriculture; Agronomy; Forestry; Veterinary Science; Zoology); **Architecture and Engineering** (Architecture; Electrical Engineering; Electronic Engineering; Engineering; Environmental Management; Food Technology; Industrial Engineering; Mechanical Engineering; Natural Resources; Telecommunications Engineering); **Arts and Humanities** (Architecture; Arts and Humanities; Communication Arts; Communication Studies; English; Fine Arts; French; Modern Languages; Philosophy; Psychology; Spanish); **Basic Sciences** (Electrical Engineering; Electronic Engineering; Engineering; Environmental Engineering; Environmental Studies; Food Science; Food Technology; Mechanical Engineering; Microbiology; Physics); **Economic and Business Sciences** (Administration; Business Administration; Data Processing; Economics; Management); **Education** *(Includes undergraduate distant and graduate students)* (Art Education; Education; Foreign Languages Education; Literacy Education; Mathematics and Computer Science; Natural Sciences; Pedagogy; Physical Education; Social Sciences); **Health Sciences** (Health Sciences; Parks and Recreation; Physical Education; Physical Therapy; Sports)

History: Founded as a private school 1960. Acquired present status and title 1970. A State institution.

Governing Bodies: Consejo Superior; Consejo Académico; Consejo de Facultad

Academic Year: February to November (February-June; July-November)

Admission Requirements: Secondary school certificate (bachiller) and Certificate of the National Test Service. Entrance examination in some cases (Engineering, Food Science and Microbiology)

Main Language(s) of Instruction: Spanish

International Co-operation: With universities in Argentina; Cuba; Spain; USA

Accrediting Agencies: Consejo Nacional de Acreditación

Degrees and Diplomas: *Tecnólogo*: 3 yrs; *Licenciatura*: Business Administration, Systems Administration; Education; Microbiology, 5 yrs; *Titulo Profesional*: Engineering, 5 yrs; *Especialización*: 3 sem; *Maestría*: 3 yrs

Student Services: Academic counselling, Canteen, Cultural centre, Health services, Language programs, Nursery care, Sports facilities

Special Facilities: TV studio. FM station

Libraries: c. 20,000 vols
Last Updated: 12/11/09

UNIVERSITY OF QUINDÍO
Universidad del Quindío
Avenida Bolívar, Calle 12 Norte, Armenia, Quindío
Tel: +57(6) 746-0112 +57(6) 746-0100
Fax: +57(6) 746-0223
EMail: uq@uniquindio.edu.co
Website: http://www.uniquindio.edu.co

Rector: Alfonso Londoño Orozco
Tel: +57(6) 746-0112, Fax: +57(6) 746-0223
EMail: rector@uniquindio.edu.co

Faculties
Agro-industrial Sciences (Agronomy; Animal Husbandry; Chemistry; Tropical Agriculture; Vegetable Production); **Basic Sciences** (Biological and Life Sciences; Chemistry; Electronic Engineering; Mathematics; Science Education); **Economics and Administration**; **Education** (Biology; Computer Science; Education; Educational and Student Counselling; Educational Technology; Environmental Studies; Mathematics; Modern Languages; Pedagogy; Physical Education; Spanish; Sports); **Engineering** (Civil Engineering; Electronic Engineering; Surveying and Mapping; Systems Analysis); **Health Sciences** (Medicine; Occupational Health); **Human Sciences and Fine Arts** (Communication Studies; Development Studies; Documentation Techniques; Gerontology; Information Sciences; Journalism; Philosophy)

History: Founded 1960 by the Municipality of Armenia with the assistance of the Universidad Nacional de Colombia and with the authorization of the Asociación Colombiana de Universidades. Receives financial support from national and provincial governments.

Governing Bodies: Consejo Superior, including representatives of the national and provincial governments and of the academic staff and students; Consejo Directivo; Consejos Académicos

Academic Year: February to December

Admission Requirements: Secondary school certificate (bachillerato) and entrance examination

Fees: (Pesos): 365,000 per semester (c. 185 US Dollars)

Main Language(s) of Instruction: Spanish

Accrediting Agencies: Consejo Nacional de Acreditación (CNA)

Degrees and Diplomas: *Licenciatura*: 4 yrs; *Titulo Profesional*: 3 yrs; *Maestría*: 1 yr

Student Services: Academic counselling, Canteen, Cultural centre, Health services, Language programs, Social counselling, Sports facilities

Student Residential Facilities: No

Special Facilities: Seismologic Observatory. Television Studio

Libraries: 53,306 vols

Publications: Revista de Investigaciones, Research Magazine *(annually)*; Revista del Quindiio *(annually)*; Revista Faculdad de Educación *(annually)*
Last Updated: 13/11/09

UNIVERSITY OF SUCRE
Universidad de Sucre
Carrera 28# 5-267, Barrio Puerta Roja, Sincelejo, Sucre
Tel: +57(5)282-1240
EMail: rectoria@unisucre.edu.co
Website: http://www.unisucre.edu.co

Rector: Rafael de Jesús Peralta Castro
Tel: +57 (5) 282-1240 ext 220

Secretario General: Jeiny Emiliani Ruiz
Tel: +57 (5) 282-1240 ext 139 EMail: secretaria_gral@hotmail.com

International Relations: Javier Dario Beltran Herrera, Vice-Rector Academic
Tel: +57 (5) 282-1240ext 156 EMail: darbelt2003@yahoo.com

Faculties
Agriculture *(Located in El Perico)*; **Economics and Administration**; **Education and Science** (Applied Mathematics; Biology; Biotechnology; Chemistry; Curriculum; Distance Education; Educational Sciences; Higher Education; Pedagogy) *Division Head*: Jairo Escorcia; **Engineering** (Agricultural Engineering; Civil Engineering; Electronic Engineering; Industrial Engineering)

History: Founded 1978 by State Assembly in order to develop the Sucre State. A State institution.

Governing Bodies: Consejo Superior, Consejo Adademico, Rectoria

Academic Year: January to December (January-July; August-December)

Admission Requirements: National Test of Proficiency (ICFES)

Fees: (Pesos): c. 400,000

Main Language(s) of Instruction: Spanish

International Co-operation: Cooperation programme with Jamaica

Accrediting Agencies: Consejo Nacional de Acreditación (CNA)

Degrees and Diplomas: *Tecnólogo*: Agriculture; Pharmacy; Electronics; Management, 3 yrs; *Licenciatura*: Education; Mathematics, 5 yrs; *Titulo Profesional*: 5 yrs; *Especialización*: Public Management; Project Management; Market Management; Environmental Science; Health Management, 1 yr

Student Services: Academic counselling, Canteen, Cultural centre, Health services, Language programs, Nursery care, Social counselling, Sports facilities

Student Residential Facilities: None

Libraries: c. 20,000 vols; 3 auditoria; study rooms; reference collection; newspaper archives

Publications: Boletin Divulgativo Division de Investigacion, Research Bulletin *(quarterly)*
Last Updated: 12/11/09

UNIVERSITY OF THE AMAZON
Universidad de La Amazonia (UNIAMAZONIA)
Apartado aéro 192, Avenida Circunvalación, Barrio El Porvenir, Florencia, Caquetá
Tel: +57(98) 435-8786 +57(98) 435-2905
Fax: +57(98) 435-8231 +57(98) 435-2434
EMail: relinter@uniamazonia.edu.co
Website: http://www.uniamazonia.edu.co

Rector: Luis Eduardo Torres García (2000-)
Tel: +57(98) 434-0594 EMail: rectoria@uniamazonia.edu.co

Secretario General: Meyer Hurtado Parra
Tel: +57(98) 435-8786, Ext. 165
EMail: sgeneral@uniamazonia.edu.co

International Relations: Mauricio Peña Bermeo
Tel: +57(98) 435-8786, Ext. 129, Fax: +57(98) 435-2434

Faculties
Accountancy, Economics and Administration (Accountancy; Economics; Management; Private Administration; Public Administration; Small Business); **Agriculture** (Agricultural Business; Agricultural Economics; Animal Husbandry; Forestry; Veterinary Science); **Basic Science** (Biology; Botany; Genetics; Microbiology; Molecular Biology; Zoology); **Education** (Bilingual and Bicultural Education; Education; Teacher Training); **Engineering** (Agricultural Engineering; Computer Engineering; Ecology; Engineering; Environmental Engineering; Food Technology); **Law and Political Science** (Comparative Law; Criminal Law; Human Rights; International Law; Justice Administration; Labour Law; Law; Political Sciences; Private Law; Public Law)

History: Founded as the Instituto Tecnológico Universidad Surcolombiana (ITUSCO) in 1971. Acquired present status 1982.

Governing Bodies: Consejo Superior

Admission Requirements: Secondary school leaving certificate and ICFES entrance examination

Fees: (Pesos)c. 150,000 per semester

Main Language(s) of Instruction: Spanish and English

International Co-operation: Exchange programmes with the Conference of Rectors and Principals of Quebec Universities

Accrediting Agencies: Consejo Nacional de Acreditación

Degrees and Diplomas: *Licenciatura*: 5 yrs; *Título Profesional*; *Especialización*; *Maestría*

Student Services: Academic counselling, Canteen, Cultural centre, Health services, Language programs, Social counselling, Sports facilities

Student Residential Facilities: None

Libraries: 22,000 vols

Publications: Teachers and Pedagogy Magazine *(biennially)*
Last Updated: 10/11/09

UNIVERSITY OF THE ATLANTIC
Universidad del Atlántico
Km 7 Antigua Via à Puerto Colombia, Barranquilla, Atlántico
Tel: +57(53) 599-999
EMail: internacionales@uniatlantico.edu.co
Website:http: //www.uniatlantico.edu.co

Rectora: Ana Sofía Mesa de Cuervo
Tel: +57(53) 359-8728, Fax: +57(53) 359-9458
EMail: rector@uniatlantico.edu.co

Faculties
Architecture (Architecture); **Basic Sciences** (Biology; Chemistry; Mathematics; Physics); **Chemistry and Pharmacy** (Chemistry; Pharmacy); **Dietetics and Nutrition** (Dietetics; Nutrition); **Economics** (Accountancy; Business Administration; Economics); **Education** (Education); **Engineering** (Chemical Engineering; Engineering; Industrial Engineering; Mechanical Engineering); **Fine Arts** (Art Education; Fine Arts; Music; Theatre); **Humanities** (Arts and Humanities; History; Philosophy; Sociology); **Law** (Law)

History: Founded 1941 as Museo del Atlántico, acquired present structure and status 1946. A State institution.

Governing Bodies: Consejo Superior; Consejo Académico; Consejo de Facultad

Academic Year: January to December (January-June; July-December)

Admission Requirements: Secondary school certificate (bachillerato) and entrance examination

Main Language(s) of Instruction: Spanish

Degrees and Diplomas: *Licenciatura*: Architecture, Teaching Qualification, Biological and Life Sciences; Chemistry; Physics; Mathematics; Education; Business Administration; Economics; Accountancy; Philosophy; Arts and Humanities; Chemical; Industrial and Mechanical Engineering; Nutrition, 5 yrs; *Licenciatura*: Education; Teacher Education, 6 yrs; *Título Profesional*: Plastic Arts; Drama; Teacher Qualification, 5 yrs; *Especialización*: Arts and Communication; Artistic Education; Natural Sciences Teaching; Clinic Pharmacy; Territorial Finance; Physics; Cultural Management; Chemistry; Quality Engineering; *Maestría*; *Doctorado*

Student Services: Canteen, Cultural centre, Health services, Nursery care, Social counselling, Sports facilities

Special Facilities: Anthropological Museum

Libraries: Central Library, 10,268 vols; Fine Arts, 1,850 vols; Economic Research, 729 vols; Education, 2,402 vols; Engineering, 1,770 vols; Law, 1,442 vols; Architecture, 909 vols; Nutrition, 420 vols; Natural Sciences, 226 vols; Pharmaceutical Chemistry, 633 vols

Press or Publishing House: Fondo de Publicaciones Universidad del Atlántico
Last Updated: 12/11/09

UNIVERSITY OF THE PACIFIC
Universidad del Pacífico
Avenida Simón Bolívar No. 54A-10, Buenaventura
Tel: +57(2) 244-7648
Fax: +57(2) 243-1461
EMail: info@unipacifico.edu.co
Website: http://www.unipacifico.edu.co

Rectora: María Carmela Quiñonez
EMail: mcquinonez@unipacifico.edu.co

Secretario General: José Luis Bernat Fernandez
EMail: jlbernat@unipacifico.edu.co

Programmes
Architecture (Architecture); **Agronomy of the Humid Tropics** (Tropical Agriculture); **Aquaculture**; **Computer Science** (Computer Science); **Sociology** (Sociology)

Further Information: Also branches in Tumaco, Guapi and Bahia Solano

History: Founded 1988.

Main Language(s) of Instruction: Spanish

Degrees and Diplomas: *Tecnólogo*; *Título Profesional*: 5 yrs
Last Updated: 13/11/09

UNIVERSITY OF THE PLAINS
Universidad de Los Llanos (UNILLANOS)
Km. 12 Vía Apiay, Villavicencio, Meta
Tel: +57(8) 669-8600
Fax: +57(8) 669-8602
EMail: oiri@unillanos.edu.co; oiriunillanos@gmail.com
Website: http://www.unillanos.edu.co

Rector: Jairo Iván Frías Carreño
Tel: +57(986) 698-663 EMail: rectoria@unillanos.edu.co

Administrative Officer: Werner Daniel Cardenas de la Cruz
Tel: +57(986) 698-020

Faculties
Agricultural Science and Natural Resources *(Two schools: veterinary and Agronomy)* (Agricultural Engineering; Animal Husbandry; Aquaculture; Natural Resources; Veterinary Science); **Basic Sciences** (Electronic Engineering; Systems Analysis); **Health Sciences**; **Humanities**

History: Founded 1974. Acquired present status 1992. A State institution.

Governing Bodies: Academic Council; Superior Council

Academic Year: February to December (February-June; July-December)

Admission Requirements: Secondary school certificate (bachillerato) and state examination

Fees: Vary according to family income

Main Language(s) of Instruction: Spanish

Accrediting Agencies: Consejo Nacional de Acreditación (CNA)

Degrees and Diplomas: *Licenciatura*: Agricultural Business; Agronomy; Economics; Electronic Engineering; Education; Veterinary Medicine; Animal Husbandry, 5 yrs; *Licenciatura*: Business Administration, 5 1/2 yrs; *Licenciatura*: Children Pedagogy, 6 yrs; *Licenciatura*: Nursing, 4 yrs; *Licenciatura*: Physical Education; Sports; *Título Profesional*: Mathematics; Physics; System Analysis; Electronic Engineering; Agronomy, 5 yrs; *Especialización*; *Maestría*

Student Services: Academic counselling, Cultural centre, Health services, Language programs, Nursery care, Social counselling, Sports facilities

Libraries: c. 10,000 vols

Publications: Cuaderno Pedagogia *(annually)*; Medicina Veterinaria y Zootécnica Juvenil *(annually)*
Last Updated: 12/11/09

UNIVERSITY OF THE VALLEY
Universidad del Valle
Apartado aéreo 25360, Ciudad Universitaria Meléndez, Carrera 100 N°13-00, Cali, Valle del Cauca
Tel: +57(2) 321-2257 +57(2) 321-2100
Fax: +57(2) 331-5111
EMail: ori@univalle.edu.co
Website: http://www.univalle.edu.co

Rector: Iván Enrique Ramos Calderón (2007-)
Tel: +57(2) 331-7745 EMail: rector@univalle.edu.co

Vice-President, Administrative Affairs: Edgar Valera Barrios
EMail: edvarela@univalle.edu.co

International Relations: Patricia Guerrero Zuñiga
Tel: +57(2) 339-3259, Fax: +57(2) 321-2310
EMail: aydeegzu@univalle.edu.co

Institutes

Education and Pedagogy (Biochemistry; Education; Foreign Languages Education; Higher Education; Mathematics; Mathematics Education; Native Language Education; Parks and Recreation; Pedagogy; Physical Education; Physics; Science Education; Sports) *Director*: Stella Valencia Tabares

Schools

Business Administration (Accountancy; Business Administration; Finance; International Business; Management; Marketing; Public Administration) *Dean*: Leonel Leal Cardozo; **Engineering** (Agricultural Engineering; Agricultural Equipment; Automation and Control Engineering; Chemical Engineering; Civil Engineering; Computer Engineering; Computer Networks; Construction Engineering; Ecology; Electrical and Electronic Engineering; Engineering; Environmental Engineering; Environmental Management; Food Technology; Industrial Engineering; Information Management; Materials Engineering; Mechanical Engineering; Power Engineering; Sanitary Engineering; Statistics; Surveying and Mapping; Telecommunications Engineering; Thermal Engineering; Water Science) *Dean*: Juan Manuel Barraza; **Health** (Anaesthesiology; Anatomy; Biochemistry; Biomedicine; Cardiology; Dentistry; Dermatology; Epidemiology; Gynaecology and Obstetrics; Health Administration; Health Sciences; Immunology; Medicine; Microbiology; Nephrology; Neurology; Nursing; Occupational Health; Occupational Therapy; Ophthalmology; Oral Pathology; Orthodontics; Orthopaedics; Otorhinolaryngology; Paediatrics; Pathology; Periodontics; Pharmacology; Physical Therapy; Physiology; Plastic Surgery; Psychiatry and Mental Health; Public Health; Radiology; Rehabilitation and Therapy; Speech Therapy and Audiology; Surgery; Urology; Virology) *Dean*: Aura Liliana Arias Castillo; **Humanities** (Arts and Humanities; Bilingual and Bicultural Education; Development Studies; Family Studies; History; Latin American Studies; Linguistics; Literature; Modern Languages; Native Language; Philosophy; Social Sciences; Social Work; Spanish; Translation and Interpretation) *Dean*: Dario Henao Restrepo; **Integrated Arts** (Architecture; Fine Arts; Graphic Design; Industrial Design; Journalism; Landscape Architecture; Music; Theatre; Visual Arts) *Dean*: Luis Humberto Casas Figueroa; **Psychology** (Psychology) *Director*: Álvaro Enríquez Martinez; **Science** (Biology; Chemistry; Mathematics; Natural Sciences; Physics) *Dean*: Luis Fernando Castro Ramirez; **Social and Economic Sciences** (Economics; Social Sciences; Sociology) *Dean*: Jaime Humberto Escobar Martinez

History: Founded 1945 as Industrial University of the Cauca Valley. Acquired present title in 1954. A State institution.

Governing Bodies: Consejo Superior Universitario; Consejo Académico

Academic Year: August to June (August-December; February-June)

Admission Requirements: Secondary school certificate (bachillerato) and entrance examination (ICFES test)

Fees: According to parents' income

Main Language(s) of Instruction: Spanish

International Co-operation: With universities in USA; Spain; France; Germany; United Kingdom; Mexico; Brazil; Switzerland; Argentina; Australia; Bolivia; Canada; Chile; Costa Rica; Cuba; Ecuador; Netherlands; Honduras; Japan; Nicaragua; Panama; Peru; Puerto Rico; Dominican Republic; Russia and Venezuela

Degrees and Diplomas: *Licenciatura*: Accountancy; Architecture; Business Administration; Chemistry; Dentistry; Education; Nursing; Physics; Physiotherapy; Psychology; Social Communication; Social Work; Speech Therapy; Statistics, 8-11 sem; *Licenciatura*: Agriculture; Mathematics and Physics; Social Sciences, 10 sem; *Licenciatura*: Biology and Chemistry; Drama; History; Languages; Literature; Music; Philosophy; Physical Education; Primary Education, 8 sem; *Licenciatura*: Medicine, 12 sem; *Titulo Profesional*: Arts; Engineering; Music, 8-11 sem; *Titulo Profesional*: Electrical Engineering, 10 sem; *Especialización*: 3 sem; *Maestría*: 4 sem; *Doctorado*: 8 sem

Student Services: Academic counselling, Canteen, Cultural centre, Employment services, Foreign student adviser, Language programs, Social counselling, Sports facilities

Student Residential Facilities: None

Special Facilities: Zoology Museum; Marine Biology Museum; Botanical Museum; Entomology Museum; Prehispanic Museum; Botanical Garden

Libraries: Central Library 'Mario Carvajal', c. 220,000 vols; Health Sciences, 20,000 vols

Publications: Acta Medica del Valle *(monthly)*; Boletín Coyuntura Socio-Económica *(bimonthly)*; Colombia Médica Categoria A2 *(quarterly)*; Cuardernos de Psicología *(bimonthly)*; Diálogos Tecnología apropiada *(bimonthly)*; Estomatologia *(biannually)*; Historia y Espacio *(bimonthly)*; Language *(monthly)*; Neusítica, Ingeniería; Poligramas *(bimonthly)*; Praxis Filosofa *(bimonthly)*; Reflexiones Pedagógicas *(bimonthly)*; Revista de la Universidad del Valle *(monthly)*

Press or Publishing House: Centro Editorial Universidad del Valle

Academic Staff 2007-2008	MEN	WOMEN	TOTAL
FULL-TIME	536	240	776
STAFF WITH DOCTORATE			
FULL-TIME	–	–	655
PART-TIME	–	–	121
Student Numbers 2007-2008			
All (Foreign Included)	–	–	29,039

Distance students, 1,036.
Last Updated: 06/03/08

BUGA BRANCH

SEDE BUGA

Carrera 13 # 5-21, Buga
Tel: +57(2) 237-0000
Fax: +57(2) 228-1077
EMail: uvbugad@uniweb.net.co
Website: http://buga.univalle.edu.co

Directora: Yolanda Domínguez Valverde

Programmes

Business Administration (Business Administration); **Electronics Technology** (Electronic Engineering); **Industrial Engineering** (Industrial Engineering); **Information Systems** (Computer Education; Systems Analysis); **Psychology** (Psychology)

CAICEDONIA BRANCH

SEDE CAICEDONIA

Carrera 14 No 4-48, Caidedonia
Tel: +57(2) 216-0070
Fax: +57(2) 216-0070

Director: Jorge Latorre Montero EMail: jorgelat@univalle.edu.co

Programmes

Business Administration (Business Administration)

CARTAGO BRANCH

SEDE CARTAGO

Calle 10 No 19-05, Cartago
Tel: +57(2) 212-9416, Ext. 109
EMail: cartago@univalle.edu.co
Website: http://cartago.univalle.edu.co

Director: Cecilia Madriñan

Programmes

Public Accountancy (Accountancy); **Technology in Business Administration** (Business Administration); **Technology in Electronics** (Electronic Engineering)

NORTE DEL CAUCA BRANCH

SEDE NORTE DEL CAUCA

Carrera 11 No 5-69, Santander de Quilichao
Tel: +57(2) 829-2013
Fax: +57(2) 829-2013
EMail: nortedelcauca@univalle.edu.co
Website: http://www.nortedelcauca.univalle.edu.co

Director: Nathanael Díaz Saldaña

Programmes
Public Accountancy (Accountancy)

PACÍFICO BRANCH
SEDE PACÍFICO

Autopista Simón Bolívar Km 9 contiguo Colegio ITI, Buenaventura
Tel: +57(2) 244-3609
Fax: +57(2) 244-0852
Website: http://www.univalle-bun.edu.co/programas/index.html
Director: Jesús Glay Mejía Naranjo EMail: jemejia@univalle.edu.co

Programmes
Basic Education (Environmental Studies; Mathematics; Natural Sciences); **Biology** (Biology); **Business Administration; Social Work** (Social Work); **Technology in Informations Systems** (Systems Analysis)

PALMIRA BRANCH
SEDE PALMIRA

Carrera 24 No. 19-00, Coliseo de Ferias, Palmira
Tel: +57(2) 274-6298
Fax: +57(2) 270-4760
EMail: wwwmngr@palmira.univalle.edu.co
Website: http://palmira.univalle.edu.co

Director: Robby Nelson Díaz Vargas
EMail: director@uniweb.net.co

Programmes
Business Administration (Business Administration); **Food Technology; Industrial Engineering** (Industrial Engineering); **Psychology** (Psychology); **Public Accountancy** (Accountancy); **Technology in Electronics; Technology in Information Systems**

TULUÁ BRANCH
SEDE TULUÁ

Calle 43 No 43-33, Tuluá
Tel: +57(2) 224-1816
Website: http://ww.univalletulua.edu.co
Directora: Ana Julia Colmenares de Vélez
EMail: anajulia@univalle.edu.co

Programmes
Business Administration (Business Administration); **Social Work** (Social Work); **Systems Engineering** (Systems Analysis); **Technology in Electronics** (Electronic Engineering)

YUMBO BRANCH
SEDE YUMBO

Calle 2 Norte No 1A-105, Barrio Las Vegas, Yumbo
Tel: +57(2) 669-9323
Fax: +57(2) 669-9324
EMail: yumbo@univalle.edu.co
Website: http://yumbo.univalle.edu.co
Director: Ricaurte Vergara

Programmes
Technology in Electronics (Electronic Engineering); **Technology in Information Systems** (Information Management)

ZARZAL BRANCH
SEDE ZARZAL

Calle 14 Cra.8 Esquina, Zarzal
Tel: +57(2) 220-7051
Fax: +57(2) 220-6971
EMail: univallezarzal@hotmail.com
Website: http://zarzal.univalle.edu.co

Directora: Cecilia Madriñan EMail: cecmadri@univalle.edu.co

Programmes
Business Administration (Business Administration); **Public Accountancy** (Accountancy); **Social Work**

UNIVERSITY OF TOLIMA
Universidad del Tolima (UTOLIMA)
Apartado aéreo 546, Barrio Santa Helena, Ibagué, Tolima
Tel: +57(8) 264-4219
Fax: +57(8) 266-9166
EMail: info@ut.edu.co
Website: http://www.ut.edu.co

Rector: Jesús Ramón Riviera Bulla EMail: jrrivera@ut.edu.co
Secretario General: Francia Helena Betancourth de Betancourth
EMail: sg@ut.edu.co
International Relations: Irma Liliana Vasquez Merchan
EMail: ori@ut.edu.co

Centres
Research *Director:* Juan Pablo Isaza Vargas

Faculties
Agricultural Engineering (Agricultural Business; Agricultural Engineering; Agriculture); **Economics and Administration** (Business Administration; Economics; International Business; Marketing); **Education** (Communication Studies; Education; English; Environmental Studies; International Business; Journalism; Mathematics Education; Natural Sciences; Physical Education; Science Education; Social Sciences; Social Studies; Spanish; Sports); **Forestry** (Agricultural Engineering; Forestry); **Health Sciences** (Health Sciences; Medicine; Nursing); **Human Sciences and Art** (Communication Studies; Cultural Studies; Fine Arts; Human Rights; Journalism; Peace and Disarmament; Social Sciences; Visual Arts); **Science** (Biology; Chemistry; Mathematics; Physics; Statistics); **Technology** (Architecture; Surveying and Mapping; Technology); **Veterinary Medicine and Animal Husbandry** (Animal Husbandry; Veterinary Science; Zoology) *Dean:* Libia Elsy Guzman Osorio

Institutes
Open and Distance Learning *(IDEAD) Director:* Gerardo Montoya
History: Founded 1945, opened 1954. A State institution.
Governing Bodies: Consejo Superior Universitario; Consejo Académico
Academic Year: January to December (January-June; July-December)
Admission Requirements: Secondary school certificate (Bachillerato) and entrance examination
Main Language(s) of Instruction: Spanish
International Co-operation: With universities in Brazil, Canada, Costa Rica, Ecuador, Mexico, UUSA, Australia, Germany, Italy, Spain. Also cooperates with the Agencia Española de Cooperación Internacional (AECI)
Degrees and Diplomas: *Tecnólogo:* Agriculture; Occupational Health; Systems Engineering; Topography, 3 yrs; *Licenciatura:* Biology; Business Administration; Mathematics and Statistics; Nursing; Veterinary Medicine and Zootechnology, 5 yrs; *Licenciatura:* Chemistry and Biology; Education; History and Geography; Mathematics and Physics; Physical Education; Spanish and English, 4 yrs; *Licenciatura:* Human Medicine, 6 yrs; *Título Profesional:* Agro-industry; Agronomy; Forestry, 5 yrs; *Título Profesional:* Architecture and Engineering, 3 yrs; *Especialización:* 1 1/2 yr; *Maestría:* 2 yrs; *Doctorado:* 4 yrs
Student Services: Academic counselling, Canteen, Cultural centre, Foreign Studies Centre, Handicapped facilities, Health services, Nursery care, Social counselling
Student Residential Facilities: Yes
Special Facilities: Anthropology Museum. Botanical Garden. Experimental Centre (Bajo Calima). Experimental farms (Armero-Guayabal, Las Brisas). Laboratories
Libraries: c. 25,000 vols
Publications: Revista de Ciencias de la Universidad del Tolima
Press or Publishing House: University Press
Last Updated: 13/11/09

PRIVATE INSTITUTIONS

ADVANCED CENTRE UNIVERSITY CORPORATION

Corporación Universitaria Centro Superior (CUCES)
Apartado aéreo 5386, Calle 14 Norte No. 8N-35, Barrio Granada, Cali, Valle del Cauca
Tel: +57(2) 667-1111 +57(2) 660-3142
Fax: +57(2) 667-1140
EMail: info@cuces.edu.co
Website: http://www.cuces.edu.co/

Rector: Augusto Narvaez Reyes

Secretaria General: Edilia Diaz de Narvaez

Programmes
Accountancy; **Business Administration**; **Business and Commerce**; **Computer Engineering**; **Electronic Engineering**; **Industrial Engineering**; **Marketing**; **Telecommunications Engineering**

History: Founded 1964.

Main Language(s) of Instruction: Spanish

Degrees and Diplomas: *Titulo Profesional*
Last Updated: 30/10/09

ADVENTIST UNIVERSITY CORPORATION

Corporación Universitaria Adventista (UNAC)
Apartado aéreo 877, Carrera 84 No. 33AA-01, Medellín, Antioquia
Tel: +57(4) 250-8328
Fax: +57(4) 250-7948
Website: http://www.unac.edu.co

Rector: Gamaliel Flórez Gómez (1993-)
EMail: gamaliel@unac.edu.co; rectoria@unac.edu.co

Secretario General: Enoc Iglesias
EMail: eiglesias@hotmail.com

International Relations: Enoc Iglesias, International Relations Director EMail: eiglesias@unac.edu.co

Faculties
Administration (Accountancy; Administration; Business Administration; Business Computing); **Education** (Education; Music; Preschool Education; Primary Education; Theology); **Engineering** (Engineering); **Health Sciences**; **Theology** (Theology)

History: Founded 1937, acquired present status 1983.

Governing Bodies: General Assembly; Council

Academic Year: February to November (February-June; July-November)

Admission Requirements: Secondary school certificate (bachillerato), Grade certificate and State examination (ICFES)

Fees: (Pesos): 1.75m. per semester (US Dollars): 875 per semester

Main Language(s) of Instruction: Spanish

International Co-operation: With universities in USA, Argentina, Chile, Mexico

Accrediting Agencies: Adventist Accrediting Association, Consejo Nacional de Acreditación

Degrees and Diplomas: *Tecnólogo*; *Licenciatura*: 5 yrs; *Especialización*: 1 1/2 yrs; *Maestría*: 4 yrs

Student Services: Academic counselling, Canteen, Employment services, Foreign student adviser, Foreign Studies Centre, Health services, Language programs, Nursery care, Social counselling, Sports facilities

Student Residential Facilities: Yes

Special Facilities: Language Centre; System Laboratory; Music Laboratory; Movie Studio; Broadcasting Studio

Libraries: Main Library

Publications: Review Faculty of Business Adminsitration *(biennially)*; Review Faculty of Theology *(biennially)*
Last Updated: 29/10/09

AGRARIAN UNIVERSITY FOUNDATION OF COLOMBIA

Fundación Universitaria Agraria de Colombia (UNIAGRARIA)
Calle 170 No 54A -10, Bogotá
Tel: +57(1) 677-1515
Fax: +57(1) 672-3773
EMail: rector@uniagraria.edu.co
Website: http://www.uniagraria.edu.co

Rector: Jorge Orlando Gaitan Arciniegas

Faculties
Agronomy (Accountancy; Agronomy; Civil Engineering; Food Technology; Industrial Engineering; Zoology)

History: Founded 1985.

Governing Bodies: Consejo Superior

Admission Requirements: Secondary school certificate; ICFES examination

Fees: Depending on programmes

Main Language(s) of Instruction: Spanish

Degrees and Diplomas: *Licenciatura*; *Especialización*

Student Services: Academic counselling, Canteen, Cultural centre, Employment services, Foreign student adviser, Foreign Studies Centre, Handicapped facilities, Health services, Language programs, Nursery care, Social counselling, Sports facilities

Academic Staff 2007-2008	MEN	WOMEN	TOTAL
FULL-TIME	28	12	40
PART-TIME	7	1	8
STAFF WITH DOCTORATE			
FULL-TIME	–	–	1
Student Numbers 2007-2008			
All (Foreign Included)	446	431	877

Evening students, 672.
Last Updated: 03/11/09

ALEXANDER VON HUMBOLDT BUSINESS UNIVERSITY CORPORATION

Corporación Universitaria Empresarial Alexander von Humboldt (UNIEMPRESARIAL)
Avenida Bolivar No, Armenia, Quindio
Tel: +57(6) 744-1490
Fax: +57(6) 741-0173
EMail: info@cue.edu.co
Website: http://www.cue.edu.co/

Rector: Jose Alejandro Cheyne Garcia
EMail: rector@uniempresarial.edu.c

Programmes
Business Administration (Business Administration; Business and Commerce); **Law**; **Marketing** (Marketing); **Nursing** (Nursing); **Psychology** (Psychology)

History: Founded 2001.

Governing Bodies: Consejo Superior Universitario; Consejo Académico

Main Language(s) of Instruction: Spanish

Degrees and Diplomas: *Titulo Profesional*; *Especialización*
Last Updated: 30/10/09

AMERICAN UNION OF HIGHER EDUCATION

Unión Americana de Educación Superior
Calle 57 No 7-27, Bogotá
Tel: +57(1) 347-8769
Fax: +57(1) 310-3755
EMail: info@unionamericana.edu.co
Website: http://www.unionamericana.edu.co/

Rector: Ricardo Rodríguez Pulido
EMail: ricardo.rodriguezpulido@gmail.com

Programmes
Accountancy (Accountancy); **Advertising and Publicity** (Advertising and Publicity); **Business Administration** (Business

Administration); **Computer Engineering** (Computer Engineering); **Dental Technology** (Dental Technology); **Health Administration** (Health Administration); **Hotel Management** (Hotel Management); **Labour and Industrial Relations** (Labour and Industrial Relations); **Marketing** (Marketing); **Multimedia** (Multimedia); **Natural Resources** (Natural Resources); **Optical Technology** (Optical Technology); **Secretarial Studies** (Secretarial Studies); **Tourism** (Tourism)

Degrees and Diplomas: *Técnico Profesional*; *Tecnólogo*; *Especialización*
Last Updated: 29/08/07

AMERICAN UNIVERSITY CORPORATION

Corporación Universitaria Americana (CORUNIAMERICANA)

Carrerra 53 No. 64-142, Barranquilla, Atlántico
Tel: +57(5) 360-8371
Fax: +57(5) 360-8372
EMail: info@coruniamericana.edu.co
Website: http://www.coruniamericana.edu.co/

Rector: William Corredor Gómez (2006-)
Tel: +57(5) 360-2904
EMail: willcogo@hotmail.com; wcorredor@coruniamericana.edu.co

Vicerrectora Académica: Alba Lucía Corredor Gómez
EMail: acorredor@coruniamericana.edu.co; albasunrise@hotmail.fr

International Relations: Oscar Mauricio Caro Madero, International Relations Officer
EMail: ocaro@coruniamericana.edu.co; ijcvalledupar@gmail.com

Faculties
Administration; **Engineering** (Computer Engineering; Systems Analysis); **Law** (Law)

History: Founded 2006.

Governing Bodies: General Committee; Board of Directors and Academic Council

Admission Requirements: Secondary school certificate and Secondary school certificate (bachillerato) and National test for higher school graduates (ICFES)

Fees: (Pesos): 1,438,500

Main Language(s) of Instruction: Spanish

International Co-operation: With University of Perpignan (France)

Degrees and Diplomas: *Titulo Profesional*: 9 sem.

Student Services: Academic counselling, Canteen, Health services, Language programs, Social counselling, Sports facilities

Student Residential Facilities: None

Special Facilities: Audiovisual Room; Computer Labs

Libraries: Library specialised in Business Administration and Systems Engineering

Publications: Magazine "Pensiamento Americano", Research Projects *(biennially)*

Academic Staff *2007-2008*	MEN	WOMEN	TOTAL
FULL-TIME	1	3	4
PART-TIME	11	9	20
STAFF WITH DOCTORATE			
FULL-TIME	–	–	1
Student Numbers *2007-2008*			
All (Foreign Included)	148	106	254

Evening students, 103.
Last Updated: 29/10/09

ANTONIO DE AREVALO TECHNOLOGICAL FOUNDATION

Fundación Tecnológica Antonio de Arevalo (TECNAR)

Apartado aéreo 3324, Calle del Cuartel No. 36-54, Cartagena de Indias, Bolívar
Tel: +57(5) 660-0671
Fax: +57(5) 664-0253
EMail: tecnar@tecnar.edu.co
Website: http://www.tecnar.edu.co

Rector: Dionisio Vélez White EMail: dioniso@tecnar.edu.co

Director of National and International Relations: Sandra Trofilllo
Tel: +57(5) 660-0645 EMail: sandra.trofillo@tecnar.educ.co

International Relations: Sandra Trofilllo
Tel: +57(5) 660-0645 EMail: sandra.trofillo@tecnar.educ.co

Faculties
Economics; **Engineering** (Electronic Engineering; Fashion Design; Systems Analysis); **Social Sciences**

History: Founded 1984.

Governing Bodies: Rector; Vicerrector; Gerente

Admission Requirements: Secondary school certificate, entrance examination (ICFES)

Fees: (Pesos): c. 1,000

Main Language(s) of Instruction: Spanish

International Co-operation: With University of Valencia (Spain); Florida International University (USA)

Degrees and Diplomas: *Técnico Profesional*: 2 yrs; *Tecnólogo*: 3 yrs; *Titulo Profesional*: 5 yrs. Also Diplomados-Especialidades

Student Services: Academic counselling, Cultural centre, Employment services, Foreign Studies Centre, Health services, Language programs, Nursery care, Social counselling, Sports facilities

Special Facilities: Audiovisual Room

Libraries: Yes, 1,625 titlles; 2,478 vols

Publications: Saberes *(annually)*

Press or Publishing House: Editora Bolivar

Academic Staff *2007-2008*	MEN	WOMEN	TOTAL
FULL-TIME	11	4	15
PART-TIME	84	30	114
STAFF WITH DOCTORATE			
FULL-TIME	–	–	2
Student Numbers *2007-2008*			
All (Foreign Included)	1,388	1,294	2,682

Part-time students, 1,665. **Evening students**, 1,017.
Last Updated: 02/11/09

ANTONIO NARIÑO UNIVERSITY

Universidad Antonio Nariño (UAN)

Calle 58 A No. 37, Bogotá
Tel: +57(1) 315-2980 /7648
EMail: soporte@uan.edu.co
Website: http://www.uan.edu.co

Rectora: Mary Falk de Losada EMail: mariadel@uan.edu.co

Secretaria General: Martha Carvalho Quigua
EMail: martha.carvalho@uan.edu.co

Faculties
Agronomy and Veterinary Science (Veterinary Science; Zoology); **Economics, Administration and Accountancy** (Accountancy; Business Administration; Economics; Hotel Management; International Business; Tourism); **Education; Engineering, Architecture and Town Planning** (Architecture; Automation and Control Engineering; Biomedical Engineering; Civil Engineering; Electrical and Electronic Engineering; Environmental Engineering; Industrial Engineering; Materials Engineering; Mechanical Engineering; Software Engineering; Systems Analysis; Telecommunications Engineering); **Fine Arts** (Fine Arts; Graphic Design; Industrial Design; Music); **Health Sciences** (Dentistry; Medicine; Nursing; Optometry; Psychology); **Mathematics and Natural Sciences** (Mathematics; Physics); **Social and Human Sciences**

Further Information: 36 campuses

History: Founded 1976. Acquired present status 1993.

Governing Bodies: General Assembly; Board of Directors; Academic Committee

Admission Requirements: Secondary school certificate. State examination and interview

Main Language(s) of Instruction: Spanish

Accrediting Agencies: Biomédica-Mexico; Consejo Nacional de Acreditación

Degrees and Diplomas: *Licenciatura*: 5 yrs; *Titulo Profesional*; *Especialización*: 1-1 1/2 yrs

Student Services: Academic counselling, Employment services, Health services, Social counselling, Sports facilities

Last Updated: 05/11/09

AUTONOMOUS TECHNOLOGICAL FOUNDATION OF BOGOTA

Fundación Tecnológica Autónoma de Bogotá (FABA)

Carrera 14, No. 80-35, Bogotá
Tel: +57(1) 691-4004 Ext. 113
Fax: +57(1) 691-4071
EMail: rectoria@faba.edu.co
Website: http://www.faba.edu.co

Rectora: María Fabiola Vargas Mendoza

Programmes

Business Administration; Citohistology; Computer Systems; Marketing and International Business; Radiology

History: Founded 1993.

Governing Bodies: General Assembly; Superior Council; Academic and Administrative Council

Admission Requirements: High School Certificate, National Higher Education Entrance Examination (ICFES), Personal Interview

Main Language(s) of Instruction: Spanish

Accrediting Agencies: Comisión Nacional de Aseguramiento de la Calidad de la Educación Superior (CONACES); Consejo Nacional de Acreditación (CAN)

Degrees and Diplomas: *Tecnólogo*: 3 yrs

Student Services: Academic counselling, Canteen, Health services, Language programs, Social counselling, Sports facilities

Libraries: Library, Newspaper and Magazine Collections - Hemeroteca, Special Editions (CDs, Videos, Films and Acetates); Convenio UNIRECS; Databases (EEBSCO, EBSCO Remoto, HINARI, NOTINET)

Academic Staff 2007-2008	MEN	WOMEN	TOTAL
FULL-TIME	6	22	28
PART-TIME	22	31	53
PART-TIME	2	–	2
Student Numbers 2007-2008			
All (Foreign Included)	110	158	268

Part-time students, 136. **Distance students,** 268. **Evening students,** 132.
Last Updated: 07/03/08

AUTONOMOUS UNIVERSITY CORPORATION OF NARIÑO

Corporación Universitaria Autónoma de Nariño (AUNAR)

alle 19 No. 27-80, Pasto, Nariño
Tel: +57(27) 232-452 +57(27) 291-789
Fax: +57(27) 291-758
Website: http://www.aunar.edu.co

Rector: Tito Jaime Colunge Benavides
EMail: Tj_CB74@hotmail.com

Programmes

Advertising and Publicity (Advertising and Publicity); **Business Administration** (Business Administration); **Communication Studies** (Communication Studies); **Electronic and Telecommunications Engineering** (Electronic Engineering; Telecommunications Engineering); **Fashion Design** (Fashion Design); **Information Management** (Information Management); **International Business** (International Business); **Marketing** (Marketing); **Mechanical Engineering** (Mechanical Engineering)

Degrees and Diplomas: *Tecnólogo*; *Titulo Profesional*
Last Updated: 29/10/09

AUTONOMOUS UNIVERSITY CORPORATION OF THE CAUCA REGION

Corporación Universitaria Autónoma del Cauca

Popayán, Cauca
Tel: +57(2) 821-3000
Fax: +57(2) 821-4000
EMail: uniautonoma@uniautonoma.edu.co
Website: http://www.uniautonoma.edu.co/

Rectora: Martha Elena Segura Sandoval
EMail: rector@uniautonoma.edu.co

Secretaria General: Araminta Sandoval de Belalcazar
EMail: secgeneral@uniautonoma.edu.co

Programmes

Business Administration (Business Administration); **Computer Science** (Computer Science); **Pre-school Education** (Preschool Education); **Sports and Recreation** (Sports); **Systems Analysis** (Systems Analysis); **Topography** (Surveying and Mapping); **Tourism and Hotel Management** (Hotel Management; Tourism)

History: Founded 1979.

Main Language(s) of Instruction: Spanish

Degrees and Diplomas: *Licenciatura*; *Especialización*

AUTONOMOUS UNIVERSITY FOUNDATION OF THE AMERICAS

Fundación Universitaria Autónoma de las Américas

Calle 34A No. 76-35, Medellín, Antioquia
Tel: +57(4) 411-4444
Fax: +57(4) 412-0595
EMail: info@uam.edu.co
Website: http://www.uam.edu.co

Rector: Alvaro Enrique Maestre Rocha
EMail: rector@polinal.edu.co

Programmes

Civil Engineering; Computer Engineering (Computer Engineering); **Dental Technology** (Dental Technology); **Engineering Management** (Engineering Management); **Hotel Management and Tourism** (Hotel Management; Public Relations; Tourism); **International Business** (International Business); **Marketing and Publicity** (Advertising and Publicity; Marketing); **Psychology** (Psychology); **Respiratory Therapy** (Respiratory Therapy); **Veterinary Science and Zoology** (Veterinary Science; Zoology)

Further Information: Also branch in Pereira

History: Founded 1983 as Fundación Tecnológica Politécnico Nacional. Acquired present status and title 2003.

Degrees and Diplomas: *Técnico Profesional*; *Titulo Profesional*; *Especialización*
Last Updated: 03/11/09

AUTONOMOUS UNIVERSITY OF BUCARAMANGA

Universidad Autónoma de Bucaramanga (UNAB)

Apartado aéreo 1642, Calle 48 No. 39-234, Bucaramanga, Santander
Tel: +57(7) 643-6111
Fax: +57(7) 643-3958
Website: http://www.unab.edu.co

Rector: Alberto de Jesús Montoya Puyana
Tel: +57(7) 643-6111, Ext. 102 EMail: rectoria@unab.edu.co

Vicerrectora académica: Eulalia García Beltrán
Tel: +57(7) 643-6111, Ext. 105 EMail: egarcia@unab.edu.co

Vicerrector administrativo y Financiero: Gilberto Ramírez Valbuena
Tel: +57(7) 643-6111, Ext 104 EMail: gramirez5@unab.edu.co

International Relations: María Teresa Camargo Abello
Tel: +57(7) 647-4488, Fax: +57(7) 647-4488
EMail: mcamargoa@unab.edu.co

Departments

Mathematics *Director:* Nhora Najera; **Socio Humanistic Studies** (Arts and Humanities; Social Sciences) *Director:* Angel Barba

Faculties

Administration (Administration; Hotel Management; Tourism); **Economic Sciences and Accountancy** (Accountancy; Economics); **Health Sciences** (Health Sciences; Medicine; Nursing; Psychology); **Law** (Law); **Physical and Mechanical Engineering** (Electronic Engineering; Energy Engineering; Mechanical Engineering); **Social Communication and Audiovisual Arts** (Communication Studies; Journalism; Visual Arts); **System Engineering** (Computer Engineering; Systems Analysis) *Dean*: Wilson Briceno

Institutes

Languages (English; French; Italian; Modern Languages; Spanish) *Director*: Adriana Martinez

Laboratories

Anatomopathology; **Biological Signs**; **Chemical Registration** (Chemistry); **Electric Machines** (Electrical Engineering; Machine Building); **Electronics, Control and Instrumentation** (Automation and Control Engineering; Electronic Engineering; Instrument Making); **Enterprises Incubator**; **Environmental Engineering**; **Finance** *(Specialised)*; **Hardware and Software** (Computer Engineering; Software Engineering); **Hystopathology**; **Industrial Automatisation** (Automation and Control Engineering; Industrial Engineering); **Logistics** (Transport Management); **Manufacture** (Industrial Engineering); **Microbiology - Immunology** (Immunology; Microbiology); **Microscopy**; **Oleoneumatics**; **Physical-chemical Process**; **Physics** (Physics); **Project Development**; **Simulation**; **Telecommunications and Networks** (Computer Networks; Telecommunications Engineering)

Programmes

Virtual and Online Studies (Accountancy; Business Administration; Literature) *Director*: Maria M. Ruiz

Research Centres

Biomedical Sciences (Biomedicine) *Director*: Norma Serrano; **Political Studies** (Political Sciences) *Director*: Lya Fernandez; **Psychosocial projects and programs** *Director*: Edgar Alejo; **Social and Legal Sciences** (Law; Social Sciences) *Director*: Laureano Gómez; **Social Sciences** (Social Sciences) *Director*: Nuria Rodriguez; **Specialized Computer Science** (Computer Science) *Director*: Eduardo Carrillo

Schools

Education (Education) *Dean*: Amparo Galvis; **Music** (Music) *Dean*: Jesus Rey

History: Founded 1952 as Instituto Caldas.

Governing Bodies: Board of Trustees

Academic Year: January to November (January-May; July-November)

Admission Requirements: Secondary school certificate (bachillerato), and State examination (ICFES)

Fees: (Pesos) c. 1,685,000 -3,579,000 per semester depending on field of studies

Main Language(s) of Instruction: Spanish

International Co-operation: With universities in USA, Germany, Belgium, Spain, France, Mexico, Venezuela, Argentina, Uruguay, Chile, Bolivia, Peru, Canada, Brasil, Germany

Accrediting Agencies: CAN; GTZ; CLAEP; SGS

Degrees and Diplomas: *Tecnólogo*: Development of Web Solutions; Logistics and Distribution; Operating Systems and Networks Management; *Titulo Profesional*: Accountancy; Business Administration; Communications; Hotel and Tourism Management; Law; Marketing Engineering; Financial Engineering; Energy Engineering; Systems Engineering; Mechanical and Electronic Engineering; Medicine; Music; Pre-school Education; Basic Education; Psychology, 5 yrs; *Especialización*: Business Administration; Law; Administrative Engineering; Economics and Accountancy; System Engineering; Physical-Mechanical Engineering; Health Sciences; Education; Communication and Visual Arts. Maestria programmes: Computational Sciences with the TEC of Monterrey; E-learning with the Universitat Oberta de Cataluña, Administration with the TEC of Monterrey; Free software with the Universitat de Catluña.

Student Services: Academic counselling, Canteen, Cultural centre, Employment services, Foreign student adviser, Health services, Language programs, Social counselling, Sports facilities

Student Residential Facilities: None

Special Facilities: Art Gallery. Television Production Centre. Recording Centre. Movie Studio. Theatre, Auditoriums, Radio Cabin, Cinema

Libraries: Central Library, 65,664 vols, 50,521 titles, 3,100 journals

Publications: Cuestiones, Publication on Social Commnunciation *(monthly)*; Medunab, Specialized medical journal *(biannually)*; Reflexion Politica, Journal of the Political Sciences Institute *(biennially)*; Revista Colombiana de Computación *(bimonthly)*; Revista Colombiana de Marketing *(biennially)*

Academic Staff 2007-2008	MEN	WOMEN	TOTAL
FULL-TIME	142	93	**235**
PART-TIME	157	62	**219**
STAFF WITH DOCTORATE			
FULL-TIME	11	3	**14**

Student Numbers 2007-2008			
All (Foreign Included)	2,890	3,594	**6,484**
FOREIGN ONLY	8	4	**12**

Last Updated: 27/02/08

AUTONOMOUS UNIVERSITY OF COLOMBIA

Universidad Autónoma de Colombia (FUAC)

Calle 12 No. 4 - 30 y Calle 13 No. 4 - 31, Bogotá
Tel: +57(1) 334-3696
Fax: +57(1) 334-3696
EMail: viceacad@fuac.edu.co
Website: http://www.fuac.edu.co

Rector: Juan Carlos Vergara Silva EMail: rectoria@fuac.edu.co

Secretaria General: Adelsabel Chamorro Ramírez
EMail: secgral@fuac.edu.co

Departments

Humanities (History; Literature; Philosophy); **Natural and Exact Sciences** (Natural Sciences)

Faculties

Economics, Administration and Accountancy (Accountancy; Administration; Economics; International Business); **Engineering** (Electronic Engineering; Engineering; Environmental Engineering; Industrial Design; Industrial Engineering; Mechanical Engineering; Systems Analysis); **Law** (Law)

Institutes

Pedagogy (Pedagogy)

History: Founded 1971 as Fundación Universitaria Autónoma de Colombia.

Governing Bodies: Asamblea General; Consejo Académico; Consejo Directivo

Academic Year: January to December (January-June; July-December)

Admission Requirements: Secondary school certificate (bachillerato) and entrance examination

Main Language(s) of Instruction: Spanish

Degrees and Diplomas: *Licenciatura*; *Especialización*

Libraries: c. 12,000 vols
Last Updated: 09/11/09

AUTONOMOUS UNIVERSITY OF MANIZALES

Universidad Autónoma de Manizales (UAM)

Apartado aéreo 441, Antigua Estación del Ferrocarril, Manizales, Caldas A.A. 441
Tel: +57(6) 881-0450
Fax: +57(6) 881-0290
EMail: uam@manizales.autonoma.edu.co
Website: http://www.autonoma.edu.co

Rector: Gabriel Cadena Gómez
Tel: +57(6) 885-2511, Fax: +57(6) 881-0290
EMail: rector@autonoma.edu.co

Faculties

Engineering (Automation and Control Engineering; Biomedical Engineering; Computer Engineering; Electronic Engineering; Industrial Engineering; Mechanical Engineering; Software Engineering; Systems Analysis); **Health Sciences** (Dentistry; Health

Administration; Medicine; Neurology; Occupational Health; Oral Pathology; Physical Therapy; Public Health; Rehabilitation and Therapy; Sports Medicine; Stomatology); **Social and Business Studies**

Institutes
Languages (Chinese; English; French; German; Italian; Modern Languages)

History: Founded 1979, acquired present status and title 1993.

Governing Bodies: Consejo Superior; Consejo Académico

Academic Year: January to December (January-May; June-July; August-December)

Admission Requirements: Secondary school certificate (bachillerato) and State examination (ICFES)

Main Language(s) of Instruction: Spanish

International Co-operation: With universities in Mexico; Spain; Chile; USA; Australia; Canada; France; New Zealand; Netherlands and Germany

Accrediting Agencies: Consejo Nacional de Acreditación (CNA)

Degrees and Diplomas: *Tecnólogo*: Business Administration, 82 credits; *Tecnólogo*: Industrial Automation, 95 credits; *Tecnólogo*: Management of Agro-industrial Business, 88 credits; *Tecnólogo*: Pre-hospital Emergency Care, 87 credits; *Tecnólogo*: Systems Analysis and Computer Programming, 84 credits; *Titulo Profesional*: Biomedical Engineering; Computer Engineering; Economics (Management), 175 credits; *Titulo Profesional*: Dentistry, 185 credits; *Titulo Profesional*: Electronic Engineering, 181 credits; *Titulo Profesional*: Fashion and Textile Design, 172 credits; *Titulo Profesional*: Industrial Design, 168 credits; *Titulo Profesional*: Industrial Engineering; Mechanical Engineering, 180 credits; *Titulo Profesional*: Physical Therapy, 182 credits; *Titulo Profesional*: Political Science, 161 credits; *Especialización*: Health Auditing; Health Administration; Stomatology; Integral Oral Rehabilitation; Occupational Health; Public Health; Neuro-Rehabilitation; Sports Medicine; Managerial Development; Leadership; Finance Management; Management of Development Projects with Socio-Humanistic Approach; Conflict Mediation; Marketing and Sales; International Business and Marketing; Software Engineering; Control of Industrial Processes; *Maestría*

Student Services: Academic counselling, Canteen, Cultural centre, Employment services, Foreign student adviser, Foreign Studies Centre, Health services, Language programs, Nursery care, Social counselling, Sports facilities

Student Residential Facilities: None

Special Facilities: Radio Station

Libraries: c. 17,500 vols

Publications: Salud UAM Magazine *(biennially)*
Last Updated: 09/11/09

AUTONOMOUS UNIVERSITY OF THE CARIBBEAN
Universidad Autónoma del Caribe
Calle 90 No. 46-112, Barranquilla, Atlántico
Tel: +57(5) 367-1000
Fax: +57(5) 357-5944
EMail: uautonom@3.telecom.com.co
Website: http://www.uac.edu.co

Rectora: Silvia Beatriz Gette Ponce (2003-)
Tel: +57(958) 357-3835 EMail: sgette@uac.edu.co

Vicerrector: Tamid Turbay
Tel: +57(958) 357-5944, Fax: +57(958) 378-0328
EMail: tturbay@uac.edu.co

Centres
Continuing Education *Director*: Gladys Puccini Miranda

Faculties
Architecture, Arts and Design (Architecture; Fashion Design; Graphic Design; Interior Design; Town Planning); **Economics, Administration and Accountancy** (Accountancy; Administration; Economics; Finance; Fiscal Law; Human Resources; Marketing; Tourism); **Engineering** (Computer Engineering; Electronic Engineering; Industrial Engineering; Mechanical Engineering; Systems Analysis; Telecommunications Engineering); **Jurisprudence** (Law);

Social Sciences and Humanities (Communication Studies; Journalism; Psychology; Radio and Television Broadcasting)

History: Founded 1967, formally recognized by the State as a University 1974. A private institution.

Governing Bodies: Consejo Directivo

Academic Year: January to December (January-June; July-December)

Admission Requirements: Secondary school certificate (bachillerato) and entrance examination

Main Language(s) of Instruction: Spanish

Degrees and Diplomas: *Licenciatura*; *Especialización*; *Maestría*

Student Services: Academic counselling, Canteen, Cultural centre, Employment services, Health services, Nursery care, Social counselling, Sports facilities

Special Facilities: Theatre. Radio and TV Programmes

Libraries: 'Benjamin Sarta' Library, 12,000 vols

Press or Publishing House: Taller Litográfico Uniautónoma
Last Updated: 09/11/09

AUTONOMOUS UNIVERSITY OF THE WEST
Universidad Autónoma de Occidente (UAO)
Apartado aéreo 3119, Calle 25 No. 115-85 km.2 vía Cali- Jamundi, Cali, Valle del Cauca
Tel: +57(2) 318-8000
Fax: +57(2) 555-3757
EMail: buzon@uao.edu.co
Website: http://www.uao.edu.co/

Rector: Luís Hernán Pérez Páez
Tel: +57(2) 555-3749 EMail: rector@uao.edu.co

Secretario General: Roberto Navarro Sánchez
Tel: +57(2) 318-8000, Ext. 11590 EMail: sedecuao@uao.edu.co

International Relations: Sandra Toro
Tel: +57(2) 318-8000, Ext. 11210, Fax: +57(2) 555-3755
EMail: sjtoro@uao.edu.co

Faculties
Basic Science (Chemistry; Environmental Management; Mathematics; Natural Resources; Physics); **Economics and Administration** (Accountancy; Business Administration; Economics; Finance; International Business; Marketing); **Engineering** (Computer Science; Electrical Engineering; Electronic Engineering; Industrial Engineering; Information Technology; Mechanical Engineering; Production Engineering); **Humanities and Languages** (Anthropology; Arts and Humanities; Ethics; Government; Modern Languages; Political Sciences); **Social Communication** (Advertising and Publicity; Communication Studies; Graphic Design; Journalism)

Schools
Postgraduate (Automation and Control Engineering; Communication Studies; Economics; Educational Administration; Hygiene; Materials Engineering)

History: Founded 1969. Acquired present status 1970.

Governing Bodies: Consejo superior

Academic Year: January to November

Admission Requirements: Secondary school certificate and National Government examination ICFES

Fees: (Dollars): 1,000 per semester

Main Language(s) of Instruction: Spanish

International Co-operation: With universities in the United States, Cuba. Also participates in ALFA and USA AECI networks

Accrediting Agencies: Consejo Nacional de Acreditación (CNA)

Degrees and Diplomas: *Licenciatura*: Advertising; Graphic Design; Social Communication; Journalism; Marketing and International Trade; International Economics and Finance; Accountancy; Business Administration, 5 yrs; *Titulo Profesional*: Industrial Engineering; Production Engineering; Electrical Engineering; Electronic Engineering; Mechanical Engineering; Mechatronics; Computer Engineering, 5 yrs; *Especialización*: Automation; Hygiene and Industrial Security; Economics; Materials Engineering; Educational Administration, 2 yrs; *Maestría*

Student Services: Academic counselling, Canteen, Cultural centre, Employment services, Foreign student adviser, Foreign Studies Centre, Health services, Language programs, Nursery care, Social counselling, Sports facilities

Special Facilities: Television and Radio Studio

Libraries: Yes

Last Updated: 09/11/09

BUSINESS UNIVERSITY CORPORATION OF SALAMANCA

Corporación Universitaria Empresarial de Salamanca
Carrera 50 No. 79 - 155, Barranquilla, Atlantico
Tel: +57(954) 424-2226
Fax: +57(954) 368-1013
EMail: webmaster@cunivemsa.edu.co
Website: http://www.cunivemsa.edu.co/

Rectora: Maria Carolina Arango Esquivia
EMail: rectoria@cunivemsa.edu.co

Programmes
Accountancy (Accountancy); **Business Administration**

Main Language(s) of Instruction: Spanish

Degrees and Diplomas: *Tecnólogo*; *Titulo Profesional*

Last Updated: 30/10/09

BUSINESS UNIVERSITY FOUNDATION OF THE CHAMBER OF COMMERCE OF BOGOTÁ

Fundación Universitaria Empresarial de la Camara de Comercio de Bogotá
Carrera 33A No. 30-20, Bogotá
Tel: +57(1) 508-2244
EMail: servcliente@uniempresarial.edu.co
Website: http://www.uniempresarial.edu.co

Rector: José Alejandro Cheyne García
EMail: rector@uniempresarial.edu.co

Programmes
Accounting (Accountancy); **Business Administration** (Business Administration; Business and Commerce; Industrial Management); **Environmental Administration** (Environmental Management); **Finance and International Commerce** (Finance; International Business); **Marketing and Logistics** (Marketing; Transport Management); **Tourism** (Tourism)

History: Founded 2001.

Degrees and Diplomas: *Titulo Profesional*; *Especialización*

Last Updated: 20/01/12

CATHOLIC UNIVERSITY FOUNDATION OF THE NORTH

Fundación Universitaria Católica del Norte
Carrera 21 No. 34b-07, Santa Rosa de Osos, Antioquia
Tel: +57(4) 860-9822
EMail: info@ucn.edu.co
Website: http://www.ucn.edu.co

Rector: Orlando de Jesús Gómez Jaramillo
EMail: rectoria@ucn.edu.co

Secretary General: Orlando Ramirez
EMail: qecgeneral@ucn.edu.co

International Relations: Gloria Berrio, Coordinator, International Relations EMail: coordinternal@ucn.edu.co

Higher Institutes
Catechism *(Juan Pablo II)* (Catholic Theology)

Programmes
Basic Education (Primary Education); **Business Administration**; **Computer Engineering**; **Environmental Management** (Environmental Management); **Philosophy and Religious Education** (Philosophy; Religious Education); **Psychology** (Psychology); **Social Communication** (Communication Studies); **Zootechnology**

Further Information: Also Campuses in Medellín, Antioquia and Colombia.

History: Founded 1996. Acquired present status 1997.

Governing Bodies: Consejo diretivo; Rectoria; Administrative Direction; Academic Direction

Admission Requirements: Secondary school leaving (Diploma de Bachiller), Higher Education National Entrance Examination (ICFES)

Fees: (Pesos): 1.56m. per semester

Main Language(s) of Instruction: Spanish

International Co-operation: With universities in Australia, Uruguay and Brazil

Accrediting Agencies: Ministerio Educación Nacional

Degrees and Diplomas: *Técnico Profesional*; *Tecnólogo*; *Titulo Profesional*; *Especialización (Especialista)*: 1 yr

Student Services: Academic counselling, Cultural centre, Language programs, Social counselling

Libraries: Virtual Library

Publications: Revista Fundación Universitaria Catolica Norte, Digital Journal *(3 per annum)*

Academic Staff 2007-2008	MEN	WOMEN	TOTAL
FULL-TIME	15	30	**45**
PART-TIME	30	30	**60**
PART-TIME	–	1	**1**
Student Numbers 2007-2008			
All (Foreign Included)	800	750	**1,550**

Distance students, 1,550.

Last Updated: 03/11/09

CATHOLIC UNIVERSITY OF COLOMBIA

Universidad Católica de Colombia (UCC)
Avenida Caracas No. 46-72, Bogotá
Tel: +57(1) 288-2549
Fax: +57(1) 288-3737
EMail: rectoria@ucatolica.edu.co
Website: http://www.ucatolica.edu.co

Rector: Francisco José Gómez Ortiz
Tel: +57(1) 288-7186, Fax: +57(1) 288-2020

Departments
Basic Sciences; **Humanities**

Institutes
Languages (English; Modern Languages; Spanish)

Programmes
Architecture (Architecture); **Civil Engineering** (Civil Engineering); **Economics** (Economics); **Electronic and Telecommunications Engineering**; **Industrial Engineering** (Industrial Engineering); **Law** (Law); **Psychology**; **Systems Engineering**

Schools
Technology (Administration; Agricultural Engineering; Civil Engineering; Construction Engineering; Electronic Engineering; Engineering Management; Management; Technology; Telecommunications Engineering)

Further Information: Also branches in Ibagué and Neiva

History: Founded 1970. Acquired present status 1974.

Academic Year: January to December (January-May; July-December)

Admission Requirements: Secondary school certificate (bachillerato) or equivalent, and entrance examination

Fees: (US Dollars): Undergraduate, 650-1,450 per semester; Graduate, 800-1,650

Main Language(s) of Instruction: Spanish

Degrees and Diplomas: *Licenciatura*; *Especialización*; *Maestría*

Last Updated: 09/11/09

CATHOLIC UNIVERSITY OF MANIZALES
Universidad Católica de Manizales
Carrera 23 No. 60-63, Manizales, Caldas
Tel: +57(6) 878-2900
Fax: +57(6) 878-2950
EMail: direxco@ucm.edu.co
Website: http://www.ucm.edu.co

Rector: Octavio Marcos Fernando Barrientos Gómez (1996-)
Tel: +57(6) 878-2901, Fax: +57(6) 878-2938
EMail: rec@ucm.edu.co; mpmarin@ucm.edu.co

Secretary-General: Julieta Henao Muñoz
Tel: +57(6) 878-2902 EMail: jhenao@ucm.edu.co

Faculties
Engineering (Engineering); **Humanities, Social Sciences and Education** (Advertising and Publicity; Architecture; Arts and Humanities; Education; Social Sciences; Tourism)

Institutes
Agro-Food Industry Quality (Food Science; Food Technology) *Director*: Paula Andrea Henao Carmona

Programmes
Applied Computer Technology (Computer Engineering) *Director*: José Ferney Pineda Gutierrez; **Architecture** (Architecture) *Director*: José Robert Sánchez Osorio; **Bacteriology** (Microbiology; Virology) *Director*: Martha Gallego de García; **Business Engineering** *Director*: Yesid Forero Paez; **Documentation and Files Technology** *(Virtual Education)* (Documentation Techniques) *Director*: Gloria Esperanza Valencia Loaiza; **Education** (Education) *Director*: Silvio Cardona González; **Environmental Engineering** (Environmental Engineering; Sanitary Engineering) *Director*: Francisco Javier Caicedo Meza; **Health Administration** *(Virtual Education - Postgraduate)* (Health Administration) *Director*: Gloria Esperanza Valencia Loaiza; **Health Sciences** (Health Sciences; Microbiology; Nursing; Virology) *Dean*: Martha Eva Buriticá de Monsalve; **Industrial Engineering** *(Agreement with Pontificia Bolivariana University of Medellín)* (Industrial Engineering) *Director*: Silvio Rosero Otero; **International Business Management** *(Agreement with Jorge Tadeo Lozano of Bogotá - Postgraduate)* (International Business) *Director*: Esperanza Marín; **Mathematics** *(Virtual Education)* (Mathematics; Mathematics Education) *Director*: Gloria Esperanza Valencia Loaiza; **Nursing** (Nursing) *Director*: Alicia Lara Tores; **Pedagogy Evaluation** *(Virtual Education - Postgraduate)* (Educational Testing and Evaluation; Pedagogy) *Director*: Gloria Eseranza Valencia Loaiza; **Pedagogy Management** *(Virtual Education - Postgraduate)* (Pedagogy) *Director*: Gloria Esperanza Valencia Loaiza; **Personal Pedagogy** *(Virtual Education - Postgraduate)* (Pedagogy) *Director*: Gloria Esperanza Valencia Loaiza; **Publicity** (Advertising and Publicity) *Director*: Clara Inés Villegas Bravo; **Publicity Management** *(Agreement with Jorge Tadeo Lozano of Bogotá - Postgraduate)* (Advertising and Publicity) *Director*: Clara Inés Villegas Bravo; **Religious Studies** *(Virtual Education)* (Religious Studies) *Director*: Gloria Esperanza Valencia Loaiza; **Technology and Computer Science** *(Virtual Education)* (Computer Science; Technology) *Director*: Gloria Esperanza Valencia Loaiza; **Telematics Engineering** *Director*: Jaime Alberto Sepúlveda Gómez; **Tourism** (Tourism) *Director*: Diana Lúcia Gaviria Berrio

History: Founded 1954 as Colegio Mayor by the Hermanas de la Caridad Dominicanas de la Presentación, became University 1978 and acquired present status and title 1993.

Governing Bodies: Consejo Superior; Consejo Académico; Consejo de Facultad

Academic Year: February to December (February-June; July-December)

Admission Requirements: Secondary school certificate and State examination (ICFES)

Main Language(s) of Instruction: Spanish

Degrees and Diplomas: *Tecnólogo*: Applied Informatics, 4 yrs; *Licenciatura*: Advertising; Architecture and Town Planning; Bacteriology and Clinical Laboratory Techniques; Nutrition and Dietetics; Respiratory Therapy; Speech Therapy; Tourism Administration, 4-5 yrs; *Licenciatura*: Education and Religious Sciences; Educational Administration; Orientation and Counselling, 4 yrs; *Especialización*

Student Services: Academic counselling, Canteen, Cultural centre, Employment services, Health services, Nursery care, Social counselling, Sports facilities

Libraries: Josefina Nuñez Central Library 20,052 vols, 3,663 theses, 740 periodical publications, 872 videos, 224 CDs-DVDs

Publications: Newspaper "El Obelisco" *(biennially)*; Revista de Investigación *(biennially)*

Press or Publishing House: Centro Editorial Universidad Católica

Academic Staff *2007-2008*: Total: c. 300
Student Numbers *2007-2008*: Total: c. 2,950
Last Updated: 09/11/09

CATHOLIC UNIVERSITY OF RISARALDA
Universidad Católica Popular del Risaralda
Carrera 21 No. 49-95, Avenida de las Américas, Pereira, Risaralda
Tel: +57(96) 312-7722
Fax: +57(96) 312-7613
EMail: comunicaciones@ucpr.edu.co
Website: http://www.ucpr.edu.co

Rector: Rubén Darío Jaramillo Montoya
Vicerrector Académico: Mario Alberto Gaviria Ríos

Faculties
Arts (Architecture; Industrial Design); **Basic Sciences and Engineering** (Engineering; Nautical Science); **Economics and Administration** (Business Administration; Economics; Industrial Management; International Business; Marketing); **Social and Human Sciences** (Communication Studies; Journalism; Psychology; Religious Studies)

History: Founded 1975.

Main Language(s) of Instruction: Spanish

Degrees and Diplomas: *Licenciatura*; *Especialización*
Last Updated: 09/11/09

CATHOLIC UNIVERSITY OF THE EAST
Universidad Católica de Oriente (UCO)
Carrera 46 No. 40B-50, Ríonegro, Antioquia
Tel: +57(94) 531-6666
Fax: +57(94) 531-3972
EMail: uco@uco.edu.co
Website: http://www.uco.edu.co

Rector: Iván Cadavid Ospina Tel: +57(94) 531-6666, Ext. 232

Faculties
Accountancy, Economics and Administration (Accountancy; Administration; Economics); **Agriculture** (Agriculture; Animal Husbandry; Biotechnology; Environmental Engineering; Fruit Production); **Education** (Education; Mathematics; Mathematics Education; Natural Sciences; Pedagogy; Philosophy; Physical Education; Religious Studies; Science Education); **Engineering** (Computer Engineering; Electronic Engineering; Engineering; Environmental Engineering; Human Resources; Industrial Engineering; Software Engineering; Systems Analysis); **Law and Social Sciences** (Law; Social Sciences); **Social Sciences**; **Theology** (Theology)

Further Information: Also five experimental farm centres. Regional distance education centres (CREAD)

History: Founded 1983. Acquired present status 1993.

Governing Bodies: Board of Directors

Academic Year: February to November (February-June; July-November)

Admission Requirements: Secondary school certificate (bachillerato) and State examination (ICFES)

Main Language(s) of Instruction: Spanish

Degrees and Diplomas: *Tecnólogo*; *Licenciatura*: Accountancy; Farming Enterprises Management; International Trade Management, 5 yrs; *Licenciatura*: Philosophy and Religious Sciences, 4 yrs; *Licenciatura*: Psychopedagogy, a further 2 yrs; *Titulo Profesional*: Industrial Engineering; Systems Engineering, 5 yrs; *Especialización*: Pedagogy and Didactics; Finance and Marketing; Human Resources, 1 yr; *Maestría*

Student Services: Academic counselling, Cultural centre, Employment services, Foreign Studies Centre, Social counselling, Sports facilities

Libraries: Yes

Publications: Revista Universidad Católica de Oriente *(quarterly)*

Press or Publishing House: Publicaciones UCO
Last Updated: 09/11/09

CEDESISTEMAS INSTITUTE OF TECHNOLOGY

Institución Tecnológica CEDESISTEMAS (CEDESISTEMAS)
Calle 7 # 45-29, Medellín, Antioquia
Tel: +57(4) 444-0510
Fax: +57(4) 266-1943
EMail: cedesistemas@cedesistemas.edu.co
Website: http://www.cedesistemas.edu.co

Rector: Álvaro Gil Gil EMail: rectoria@cedesistemas.edu.co

Secretario General: Ramón Ramírez Giraldo
EMail: secretario@cedesistemas.edu.co

Programmes
Administration; **Business Administration** (Business Administration); **Computer Engineering**; **Computer Networks**; **Finance**; **Information Technology**; **Marketing**

Degrees and Diplomas: *Tecnólogo*; *Especialización*
Last Updated: 04/11/09

CEIPA UNIVERSITY FOUNDATION

Fundación Universitaria CEIPA
Calle 77 Sur No. 40-165 Via Principal a Sabaneta, Sabaneta, Antioquia
Tel: +57(4) 305-6100
Fax: +57(4) 301-1736
Website: http://www.ceipa.edu.co

Rector: Antonio Mazo Mejía EMail: amazo@ceipa.edu.co

Vicerrector: Diego Mauricio Mazo Cuervo

Schools
Administration (Administration; Business Administration; Finance; International Business; Marketing)

History: Founded 1972. Acquired present status 1992.

Main Language(s) of Instruction: Spanish

Degrees and Diplomas: *Tecnólogo*; *Licenciatura*; *Titulo Profesional*; *Especialización*
Last Updated: 03/11/09

CENTRAL UNIVERSITY

Universidad Central
Carrera 5 No. 21-38, Bogotá
Tel: +57(1) 336-2607
EMail: admision@ucentral.edu.co
Website: http://www.ucentral.edu.co

Rector: Guillermo Páramo Rocha EMail: rectoria@ucentral.edu.co

Vicerrector Administrativo y Financiero: Nelson Gnecco Iglesias

Areas
Social Sciences, Humanities and Arts (Advertising and Publicity; Communication Studies; Fine Arts; Journalism; Music; Social Sciences)

Faculties
Economics, Accountancy and Administration (Accountancy; Business Administration; Economics; Marketing); **Engineering** (Electronic Engineering; Environmental Engineering; Hydraulic Engineering; Industrial Engineering; Mechanical Engineering; Systems Analysis)

History: Founded 1966, formerly Universidad Central de la Nueva Granada (1826).

Governing Bodies: Consejo Superior

Academic Year: February to December (February-June; July-December)

Admission Requirements: Secondary school certificate (bachillerato) and State examination (ICFES test)

Main Language(s) of Instruction: Spanish

Degrees and Diplomas: *Licenciatura*: Accountancy; Advertising; Business Administration; Economics; Journalism; Marketing, 5 yrs; *Titulo Profesional*: Electrical Engineering; Engineering in Hydraulic Resources and Environmental Management; Mechanical Engineering; Music; Systems Engineering, 5 yrs; *Especialización*; *Maestría*

Student Services: Cultural centre, Health services, Language programs, Nursery care, Sports facilities

Special Facilities: Art Gallery. Radio. TV Studios. Theatre

Libraries: c. 26,000 vols

Publications: Colección de publicaciones del Instituto Colombiano de Estudios Latinoamericanos y del Caribe - ICELAC; Nomadas; Temas Humanísticos
Last Updated: 09/11/09

CENTRE OF HIGHER EDUCATION, RESEARCH AND PROFESSIONALIZATION FOUNDATION

Fundación Centro de Educación Superior, Investigación y Profesionalización (CEDINPRO)
Calle 63A No. 16-38, Bogotá
Tel: +57(1) 542-7374 +57(1) 249-8128
Fax: +57(1) 542-8963
EMail: rectoria@cedinpro.edu.co
Website: http://www.cedinpro.edu.co

Rector: Alejandro Rueda Nova

Faculties
Applied Sciences (Computer Networks; Software Engineering); **Business Studies** (Business Administration; Hotel Management; International Business; Marketing; Tourism); **Education** (Education; Preschool Education)

History: Founded 1977.

Main Language(s) of Instruction: Spanish

Degrees and Diplomas: *Técnico Profesional*; *Licenciatura*
Last Updated: 02/11/09

CES UNIVERSITY

Universidad CES
Calle 10 A No. 22-04, Medellín, Antioquia
Tel: +57(4) 444-0555
Fax: +57(4) 266-6046
EMail: osaldarriaga@ces.edu.co
Website: http://www.ces.edu.co

Rector: José María Maya (2000-)
Tel: +57(4) 268-3711 Ext. 151 EMail: jmayam@ces.edu.co

Secretaria General: Patricia Chejne EMail: pchejne@ces.edu.co

International Relations: Oscar Javier Saldarriaga, Head, International RelationsFax: +57(4) 444-0555

Faculties
Dentistry (Dentistry); **Law** (Law); **Medicine** (Medicine; Surgery); **Psychology**; **Veterinary Medicine** (Veterinary Science; Zoology)

Programmes
Biology (Biology); **Biomedical Engineering**; **Physiotherapy** (Physical Therapy)

History: Founded 1977. Previously known as Instituto de Ciencias de la Salud.

Governing Bodies: Board of Founding Fathers; Board of Trustees

Academic Year: January to November

Admission Requirements: Admission Examination, Colombian State Examination (ICFES), Interview

Fees: (US Dollars): 1,500-2,500 per semester

Main Language(s) of Instruction: Spanish

International Co-operation: With universities in USA, Spain, France, Canada, Italy, Mexico, Chile, Argentina, Brazil, Peru, Panama

Degrees and Diplomas: *Titulo Profesional*: 5-6 yrs; *Especialización*: 3-5 yrs; *Maestría*: 2 yrs; *Doctorado*: 4 yrs

Student Services: Academic counselling, Cultural centre, Foreign student adviser, Foreign Studies Centre, Language programs, Sports facilities

Student Residential Facilities: None

Special Facilities: Yes

Libraries: Yes

Publications: Faculties' Journals, Instituional Magazine *(biennially)*

Academic Staff *2007-2008*	MEN	WOMEN	TOTAL
FULL-TIME	–	–	70
PART-TIME	–	–	443
STAFF WITH DOCTORATE			
FULL-TIME	1	1	2
PART-TIME	3	1	4
Student Numbers *2007-2008*			
All (Foreign Included)	–	–	2,500
FOREIGN ONLY	2	3	5

Last Updated: 09/11/09

CHRISTIAN UNIVERSITY CORPORATION OF SAN ANDRÉS, PROVIDENCIA AND SANTA CATALINA

Corporación Cristiana Universitaria de San Andrés, Providencia y Santa Catalina
Km 14 No 2-29 South End, San Andrés, San Andrés
Tel: +57(8) 513-0355
Fax: +57(8) 513-0550

Rector: Bryan Oakley Forbes

Programmes
Bilingual Education (Bilingual and Bicultural Education); **Citizenship**; **Environmental and Coastal Resource Management**; **Food Technology** (Food Technology)

Degrees and Diplomas: *Técnico Profesional*; *Licenciatura*
Last Updated: 30/10/09

COLEGIATURA COLOMBIANA CORPORATION

Corporación Colegiatura Colombiana
Km 7 Vía Las Palmas, Medellín, Antioquia
Tel: +57(4) 354-7120
Fax: +57(4) 354-7120 Ext. 104
EMail: colegiatura@une.net.co
Website: http://www.colegiatura.edu.co

Rector: Humberto de Jesús Palacios Muñoz (1992-)
EMail: rectoria@colegiatura.edu.co

Administrative-Financial Manager: Julio Salleg

International Relations: Luz Gabriela Gomez, Vice-Rector
EMail: vicerrectoria@colegiatura.edu.co

Programmes
Advertising (Advertising and Publicity) *Head*: Lina Puerta; **Communication** *Head*: Ana María Estrada; **Fashion Design** *Head*: Adriana Betancur; **Gastronomy and Cooking** (Cooking and Catering) *Head*: Luz Marina Velez

Further Information: There are three educational cycles in the Gastronomy Programme: technique, technology and professional

History: Founded 1989. Acquired present status 2000.

Governing Bodies: General Assembly; Directive Council; Adminsitrative-Financial and Curriculum Committee.

Admission Requirements: High School certificate and National Examination from the Ministry of Education (ICFES).

Fees: (Pesos): 4.5m.per semester

Main Language(s) of Instruction: Spanish

International Co-operation: With universities in Argentina, France, Italy, Mexico, Spain

Accrediting Agencies: National Office of Design

Degrees and Diplomas: *Técnico Profesional*: Gastronomy, 2 yrs; *Tecnólogo*: Gastronomy, 3 yrs; *Titulo Profesional*: Gastronomy; Graphic Design; Space Design; Advertising and Publicity; Organisational Communication and International Relations, 5 yrs

Student Services: Academic counselling, Canteen, Employment services, Foreign student adviser, Health services, Social counselling

Student Residential Facilities: Off-campus facilities and housing

Libraries: Yes. Subscriptions to international Design and Fashion magazines.

Publications: (Currently untitled publication), Academic Papers, national and local information about design and social projection *(biennially)*

Academic Staff *2007-2008*	MEN	WOMEN	TOTAL
FULL-TIME	7	5	12
PART-TIME	3	–	3
PART-TIME	1	–	1
Student Numbers *2007-2008*			
All (Foreign Included)	200	608	808
FOREIGN ONLY	26	115	141

Last Updated: 06/03/08

COLLEGE OF ADVANCED ADMINISTRATION STUDIES

Colegio de Estudios Superiores de Administración (CESA)
Apartado Aéreo 6528, Calle 35 No. 6-16, Bogotá
Tel: +57(1) 339-5300
Fax: +57(1) 565-7737
Website: http://www.cesa.edu.co

Rector: Manuel Restrepo Abondano

Colleges
Administration (Administration; Finance; Marketing)

History: Founded 1974 with support of INCOLDA (Colombian Business Institute) and ANDI (National Association of Industrials). A private, non-profit oriented institution.

Governing Bodies: Body of Voters; Directory; Rector; Council; Vice-Rector

Admission Requirements: Secondary school cerificate (Bachillerato) or recognized equivalent, entrance examination

Fees: (US Dollars): 3,100 per semester

Main Language(s) of Instruction: Spanish

International Co-operation: With universities in USA, Japan, France and Australia

Accrediting Agencies: Consejo Nacional de Acreditación (CNA)

Degrees and Diplomas: *Licenciatura*: Business Administration, 4 1/2 yrs; *Especialización*: Finance, 13 months; *Especialización*: Marketing, 14 months

Student Services: Academic counselling, Cultural centre, Employment services, Foreign student adviser, Health services, Language programs, Social counselling, Sports facilities

Student Residential Facilities: None

Special Facilities: None

Libraries: Yes

Academic Staff *2007-2008*	MEN	WOMEN	TOTAL
FULL-TIME	12	4	16
PART-TIME	57	21	78
STAFF WITH DOCTORATE			
FULL-TIME	–	–	2
PART-TIME	3	1	4
Student Numbers *2007-2008*			
All (Foreign Included)	471	399	870

Last Updated: 28/10/09

COLOMBIAN SCHOOL OF INDUSTRIAL CAREERS

Escuela Colombiana de Carreras Industriales (ECCI)
Carrera 19 No. 49-20, Bogotá
Tel: +57(1) 353-7171
Fax: +57(1) 353-7171
EMail: centro.informacion@ecci.edu.co
Website: http://www.ecci.edu.co

Principal: Fernando Soler López (1977-)
EMail: rectoria@ecci.edu.co

Secretario General: José Fernando López Quintero
EMail: secretario.general@ecci.edu.co

International Relations: Adriana Matiz, Chief of International Relations EMail: matiz.adriana@ecci.edu.co

Faculties

Economics and Administration (Accountancy; Advertising and Publicity; Business Administration; Business and Commerce; International Business; Marketing; Taxation; Transport Management); **Engineering** (Automation and Control Engineering; Automotive Engineering; Biomedical Engineering; Computer Engineering; Computer Networks; Electronic Engineering; Engineering; Engineering Management; Environmental Engineering; Geological Engineering; Industrial Engineering; Machine Building; Materials Engineering; Mechanical Engineering; Medical Technology; Polymer and Plastics Technology; Software Engineering; Telecommunications Engineering); **Fine Arts** (Arts and Humanities; Fashion Design; Fine Arts; Modern Languages)

History: Founded 1977 as Escuela Colombiana de Carreras Intermedias. Acquired present status 2003.

Governing Bodies: Upper Council; Rector; Vice-Rector for Academic and Management

Admission Requirements: Secondary school certificate (bachillerato), State examination (ICFES) and entrance examination

Fees: (Pesos): 1,160,400 for technical cycle; 1,786,800 for professional cycle; 2,153,600 for specialisation cycle. Subscription fee, 62,900

Main Language(s) of Instruction: English; Spanish

Degrees and Diplomas: *Técnico Profesional*: Automotive Mechanics; Industrial Mechanics; Business Administration; Polymer and Plastics Technology; Telecommunication Engineering; Industrial Electronics; Electromedicine; Environmental Development; Systems Engineering; Foreign Trade and International Business; Taxation and Customs; Marketing; Accountancy; Fashion Design; Modern Languages, 2 1/2 yrs; *Titulo Profesional*: Maintenance; International Production and Logistic; Wireless Telecommunications; Automatisation; Hospital Engineering Management; Software Engineering; *Especialización*: Mechanical Engineering; Industrial Engineering; Plastics Engineering; Electronic Engineering; Biomedical Engineering; Environmental Engineering; Systems Engineering; International Business; Public Accountancy; Fashion Design; Modern Languages;

Student Services: Academic counselling, Employment services, Health services, Language programs, Nursery care, Sports facilities

Special Facilities: Audio Studio

Libraries: 1 library. c. 9,000 vols

Publications: Tecciencia, Publication on Engineering and Economic Sciences *(quarterly)*

Academic Staff *2007-2008*	MEN	WOMEN	TOTAL
FULL-TIME	50	13	63
PART-TIME	292	67	359
STAFF WITH DOCTORATE			
FULL-TIME	–	–	1
Student Numbers *2007-2008*			
All (Foreign Included)	6,950	2,100	9,050
FOREIGN ONLY	7	5	12

Last Updated: 30/10/09

COLOMBIAN SCHOOL OF MARKETING FOUNDATION

Fundación Escuela Colombiana de Mercadotecnia (ESCOLME)
Apartado aéreo 4983, Calle 50 No. 40-39, Medellín, Antioquia
Tel: +57(4) 216-1700
Fax: +57(4) 239-4854
EMail: info@escolme.edu.co
Website: http://www.escolme.edu.co

Rector: Alfonso León Gutiérrez Londoño
EMail: rector@escolme.edu.co

Programmes

Finance (Finance); **International Business** (International Business); **Management Systems** (Management Systems); **Marketing** (Marketing)

Degrees and Diplomas: *Tecnólogo; Especialización*
Last Updated: 02/11/09

COLOMBIAN SCHOOL OF REHABILITATION

Fundación Escuela Colombiana de Rehabilitación (ECR)
Av Carrera 15 No. 151-68, Bogotá
Tel: +57(1) 627-0366
Fax: +57(1) 614-1390
EMail: ecr@ecr.edu.co
Website: http://www.ecr.edu.co

Rector: Gustavo Malagón Londoño EMail: gusmal@ecr.edu.co

International Relations: Luz Juanita Ruiz de Prada

Faculties

Basic Sciences (Biochemistry; Biophysics; Cell Biology; Histology; Molecular Biology; Pathology); **Occupational Therapy** *Dean*: Claudia Andrea Urbina; **Phonology and Audiology** *Dean*: María Helena Medicis; **Physiotherapy** *Dean*: Betty Almanza

History: Founded 1952. Acquired present status 1995.

Governing Bodies: Board, Academic Council

Fees: (Pesos): 2.77m.

Main Language(s) of Instruction: Spanish

Degrees and Diplomas: *Titulo Profesional*: 4 yrs; *Especialización*: 1-2 yrs

Student Services: Academic counselling, Canteen, Handicapped facilities, Health services, Social counselling, Sports facilities

Student Residential Facilities: None

Libraries: Yes

Academic Staff *2007-2008*	MEN	WOMEN	TOTAL
FULL-TIME	7	21	28
Student Numbers *2007-2008*			
All (Foreign Included)	30	270	300

Last Updated: 02/11/09

COLOMBIAN-AMERICAN UNIVERSITY INSTITUTION

Institución Universitaria Colombo-Americana
Avenida 19 No. 2-49, Bogotá
Tel: +57(1) 281-1777
Fax: +57(1) 342-3442
EMail: rectoria@unica.edu.co
Website: http://www.unica.edu.co

Rectora: María Lucía Casas

Programmes

Bilingual Education (Bilingual and Bicultural Education)

History: Founded 1942. Acquired present status 2001.

Main Language(s) of Instruction: Spanish

Degrees and Diplomas: *Licenciatura*. Also Diplomado
Last Updated: 04/11/09

COLOMBIAN TECHNOLOGICAL-INDUSTRIAL CORPORATION

Corporación Tecnológica Industrial Colombiana
Calle 42 No. 16-86, Bogotá
Tel: +57(1) 285-1512
Fax: +57(1) 285-3458
EMail: tinco@col1.telecom.co
Website: http://www.tecnologicaindustrial.edu.co

Rectora: Yolanda Castañeda Ojeda de Ballén
EMail: rectoria@tecnologicaindustrial.edu.co

Programmes

Automation and Control Engineering (Automation and Control Engineering); **Computer Engineering** (Computer Engineering); **Computer Networks** (Computer Networks); **Electronic Engineering** (Electronic Engineering); **Industrial Design** (Industrial Design); **Mechanical Engineering** (Mechanical Engineering)

History: Founded 1987.

Main Language(s) of Instruction: Spanish

Degrees and Diplomas: *Técnico Profesional; Tecnólogo; Titulo Profesional*
Last Updated: 29/10/09

COLOMBO ANDINO POLYTECHNIC CORPORATION

Corporación Politécnico Colombo Andino
Apartado aéreo 27015, Avenida 19 No. 3-16 Piso 2 (Edificio Barichara), Bogotá
Tel: +57(1) 282-7798
Fax: +57(1) 282-6926
Website: http://www.polcolan.edu.co

Rector: Álvaro Jiménez Vélez EMail: alvaro@polcolan.edu.co

Programmes
Business Administration; Computer Systems Analysis and Design; Secretarial Studies

History: Founded 1974.

Main Language(s) of Instruction: Spanish

Degrees and Diplomas: *Técnico Profesional*; *Especialización*
Last Updated: 29/10/09

COMFANORTE FOUNDATION OF ADVANCED STUDIES

Fundación de Estudios Superiores Comfanorte
Av. 4 N° 15-38 Barrio La Playa, Cúcuta, Norte de Santander
Tel: +57(75) 583-3927
Fax: +57(75) 583-3966
Website: http://www.fesc.edu.co/

Rectora: Carmen C. Quero de G.

Programmes
Computer Engineering (Computer Engineering); Fashion Design (Fashion Design); Finance (Finance); International Business (International Business); Marketing (Marketing); Taxation (Taxation)

History: Founded 1993.

Main Language(s) of Instruction: Spanish

Degrees and Diplomas: *Tecnólogo*; *Especialización*
Last Updated: 02/11/09

COMFENALCO TECHNOLOGICAL UNIVERSITY FOUNDATION

Fundación Universitaria Tecnológico Comfenalco (TECNOLOGICO COMFENALCO)
Apartado aéreo 4191, Zaragacilla Calle 30 No. 30B-41 El Cairo, Cartagena de Indias, Bolívar
Tel: +57(5) 669-0754
EMail: tecno@tecnologicocomfenalco.edu.co
Website: http://www.tecnologicocomfenalco.edu.co

Rector: Claudio Aquiles Osorio Lentino
EMail: claudio.osorio@tecnologicocomfenalco.edu.co

Faculties
Accountancy; Environmental Engineering (Environmental Engineering); Finance; Industrial Production; Information Technology; Quality Control (Safety Engineering)

Degrees and Diplomas: *Tecnólogo*; *Titulo Profesional*
Last Updated: 04/11/09

CO-OPERATIVE UNIVERSITY OF COLOMBIA

Universidad Cooperativa de Colombia
Avenida Caracas con 37, Bogotá
Tel: +57(1) 332-3565
Fax: +57(1) 232-0316
EMail: uccbogota@ucc.edu.co; tuttyk@hotmail.com
Website: http://www.universidadcooperativa.org/

Rector: Cesar Pérez García

Faculties
Accountancy; Economics and Administration (Administration; Economics; International Business; Marketing); Education; Engineering; Health Sciences; Law and Political Science

Further Information: Also branches in Apartadó, Arauca, Barrancabermeja, Bogotá, Bucaramanga, Calarcá, Cali, Cartago, Espinal, Girardot, Ibague,Manizales, Medellín, Montería, Neiva, Pasto, Pereira, Popayán, Quibdo, Santa Marta, Villamaría and Villavicencio

History: Founded 1958. A private institution.

Admission Requirements: Secondary school certificate (bachillerato) and entrance examination

Main Language(s) of Instruction: Spanish

Degrees and Diplomas: *Licenciatura*: 4 yrs; *Especialización*

Libraries: Total, c. 25,000 vols
Last Updated: 09/11/09

CORPORATE SCHOOL OF ADMINISTRATION AND TECHNOLOGICAL STUDIES

Corporación Escuela Superior de Administración y Estudios Tecnológicos
Calle 14 No. 49-20, Barrio La Selva, Cali, Valle del Cauca
Tel: +57(2) 326-7000
EMail: info@eae.edu.co
Website: http://www.eae.edu.co

Rectora: Nercyn López De Gómez
EMail: nercynlopez@eae.edu.co

Programmes
Engineering and Technology (Business Administration; Computer Engineering; Criminal Law; Criminology; Electronic Engineering; Finance; Graphic Arts; International Business; Marketing; Mechanical Engineering; Multimedia; Systems Analysis)

History: Founded 1968.

Main Language(s) of Instruction: Spanish

Degrees and Diplomas: *Tecnólogo*; *Titulo Profesional*; *Especialización*
Last Updated: 28/10/09

CORPORATE SCHOOL OF ARTS AND LITERATURE

Corporación Escuela de Artes y Letras
Calle 70 No. 13-39, Barrio Quinta Camacho, Bogotá
Tel: +57(1) 217-5327 +57(1) 217-5367
Fax: +57(1) 543-7601
EMail: Artesyltras@hotmail.com
Website: http://www.artesyletras.com.co

Rector: Edgar Ignacio Díaz Santos

Programmes
Art Techniques (Art Education); Computer Graphics; Fashion Design; Graphic Design; Interior Design; Marketing; Theatre; Tourism; Visual Arts

History: Founded 1969.

Main Language(s) of Instruction: Spanish

Degrees and Diplomas: *Técnico Profesional*; *Especialización*
Last Updated: 28/10/09

CORPORATE TECHNOLOGICAL SCHOOL OF THE EAST

Corporación Escuela Tecnológica del Oriente
Cra 27 No. 19-40, Bucaramanga, Santander
Tel: +57(7) 634-9810
Fax: +57(7) 645-4144
Website: http://www.corporie.edu.co/

Rector: Guillermo Cardozo Correa
EMail: pcorporie@col1.telecom.com.co

Programmes
Business Administration (Business Administration); Civil Engineering (Civil Engineering; Road Engineering); Environmental Management (Environmental Management)

Degrees and Diplomas: *Tecnólogo*; *Titulo Profesional*; *Especialización*
Last Updated: 28/10/09

EAFIT UNIVERSITY
Universidad EAFIT
Carrera 49 - 7 Sur 50, Av. Las Vegas, Medellín, Antioquia
Tel: +57(4) 261-9500
Fax: +57(4) 266-4284
EMail: postmaster@eafit.edu.co
Website: http://www.eafit.edu.co

Rector: Juan Luis Mejía Arango (2004-)
Tel: +57(4) 261-9509, Fax: +57(4) 261-9374
EMail: jlmejia@eafit.edu.co; rectoria@eafit.edu.co

Secretario General: Hugo Alberto Castaño Zapata
Tel: +57(4) 261-9540, Fax: +57(4) 261-9374
EMail: hcastano@eafit.edu.co

International Relations: Marcela Wolff-Lopez, Head of International Relations
Tel: +57(4) 261-9213, Fax: +57(4) 266-4284
EMail: international@eafit.edu.co

Schools
Administration (Accountancy; Administration; Business Administration; Economics; International Business); **Engineering** (Civil Engineering; Engineering; Geology; Mechanical Engineering; Production Engineering; Systems Analysis); **Law** (Law; Private Law); **Science and Humanities** (Arts and Humanities; Mass Communication; Mathematics; Natural Sciences; Physical Engineering; Political Sciences)

Further Information: Also branches in Bogotá, Pereira and Llanogrande

History: Founded 1960 as Business School. A private institution supported by industry and also partly financed by the State. Acquired present status 2003.

Governing Bodies: Consejo Superior; Consejo Directivo; Consejo Académico

Academic Year: January to November (January-June; July-November)

Admission Requirements: Secondary school certificate (bachillerato) and state examination (ICFES). For some courses, proof of proficiency in English

Fees: (Pesos): 171,377 per credit course (a regular course is worth 3 credits)

Main Language(s) of Instruction: Spanish

International Co-operation: With universities in Australia; Belgium; Brazil; Canada; Cuba; France; Italy; Mexico; Netherlands; Peru; Sweden; Switzerland; USA

Accrediting Agencies: Ministry of Education through Consejo Nacional de Acreditación (CNA)

Degrees and Diplomas: *Licenciatura*: 5 1/2 yrs; *Especialización (Especialista)*: 1 1/2 yrs; *Maestría*: a further 2 yrs; *Doctorado*

Student Services: Academic counselling, Canteen, Cultural centre, Foreign student adviser, Handicapped facilities, Health services, Language programs, Sports facilities

Student Residential Facilities: None

Special Facilities: Art gallery

Libraries: c. 68,000 vols, 2,100 periodical subscriptions

Publications: Cuadernos de Investigación *(monthly)*

Press or Publishing House: Fondo Editorial EAFIT
Last Updated: 16/11/09

EAN UNIVERSITY
Universidad EAN
Carrera 11 No 78-47, Bogotá
Tel: +57(1) 593-6160 +57(1) 347-2737
Fax: +57(1) 314-6757 +57(1) 321-2204
EMail: oficinamercadeo@ean.edu.co
Website: http://www.ean.edu.co

Rector: Jorge Enrique Silva Duarte EMail: jsilva@ean.edu.co

Secretario General: Santiago Pinilla Valdivieso
Tel: +57(1) 321-2204, Fax: +57(1) 593-6162
EMail: santiago.pinilla@ean.edu.co·

International Relations: Luz Marina Forero, External Relations Officer

Tel: +57(1) 593-6162, Fax: +57(1) 248-2511
EMail: luzm.forero@ean.edu.co

Faculties
Administration, Finance and Economics (Business Administration; Economics; Finance); **Distance Studies** (Distance Education); **Engineering** (Engineering; Environmental Engineering; Production Engineering; Systems Analysis); **Humanities and Social Sciences** (Arts and Humanities; Cultural Studies; Modern Languages)

History: Founded 1968 as Escuela de Administración de Negocios (EAN).

Degrees and Diplomas: *Licenciatura*; *Especialización*; *Maestría*
Last Updated: 16/11/09

EDUCATIONAL CORPORATION ADMINISTRATION CENTRE OF CALI
Corporación Educativa Centro de Administración de Cali
Apartado aéreo 5386, Avenida 6♀ Norte 21-29, Cali, Valle del Cauca
Tel: +57(2) 668-6025
Fax: +57(2) 661-0227
EMail: secretaria_academica@cenda-cali.edu.co
Website: http://www.cenda-cali.edu.co

Rector: Antonio Salazar Bustamante
EMail: antoniosalazar@cenda-cali.edu.co

Programmes
Art Education (Art Education); **Business Administration** (Business Administration); **International Business** (International Business); **Labour and Industrial Relations** (Labour and Industrial Relations); **Physical Education** (Physical Education); **Preschool Education** (Preschool Education); **Sports** (Sports)

History: Founded 1977.

Main Language(s) of Instruction: Spanish

Degrees and Diplomas: *Licenciatura*: 5 yrs
Last Updated: 21/09/07

EDUCATIONAL CORPORATION OF THE COAST
Corporación Educativa del Litoral
Calle 79 No. 42F-110, Barranquilla, Atlántico
Tel: +57(5) 345-3949 +57(5) 358-8620
Fax: +57(5) 358-8204
EMail: litoral@metrotel.net.co

Rector: Eurípides Guarín Anaya EMail: euripidesg@tutopia.com

Programmes
Accountancy (Accountancy); **Advertising and Publicity** (Advertising and Publicity); **Architectural and Environmental Design** (Architectural and Environmental Design; Environmental Studies); **Business Administration** (Business Administration); **Computer Engineering** (Computer Engineering); **Interior Design** (Interior Design); **International Business** (International Business); **Marine Transport** (Marine Transport); **Marketing** (Marketing); **Occupational Health** (Occupational Health); **Secretarial Studies** (Secretarial Studies); **Software Engineering**; **Tourism**

Degrees and Diplomas: *Técnico Profesional*; *Tecnólogo*; *Maestría*
Last Updated: 02/11/09

EL BOSQUE UNIVERSITY
Universidad El Bosque
Carrera 7 B Bis No. 132 - 11, Bogotá
Tel: 57(1) 274-3096
EMail: unbosque@colomsat.net.co
Website: http://www.unbosque.edu.co

Rector: Jaime Escobar Triana EMail: rectoria@unbosque.edu.co

Vicerrector Administrativo: Carlos Felipe Escobar Roa

International Relations: Jorge Suescún Hernández

Faculties
Administration and Economics (Administration; Economics) *Dean*: Fabio Posada V.; **Arts** (Fine Arts; Music; Painting and Drawing; Theatre); **Engineering and Administration** (Business Administration; Electronic Engineering; Environmental Engineering;

Industrial Engineering; Systems Analysis); **Natural and Health Sciences** (Biology; Dentistry; Medicine; Nursing; Optometry; Psychology; Surgery); **Social and Human Sciences** (Bilingual and Bicultural Education; Philosophy; Preschool Education; Psychology)

History: Founded 1978.

Governing Bodies: Claustro

Main Language(s) of Instruction: Spanish

Degrees and Diplomas: *Licenciatura*; *Especialización*; *Maestría*; *Doctorado*
Last Updated: 16/11/09

ESUMER UNIVERSITY INSTITUTION
Institución Universitaria ESUMER
Calle 76 No. 80-126 Carretera al Mar, Medellín, Antioquia
Tel: +57(4) 264-6011
Fax: +57(4) 264-9855
EMail: esumer@esumer.edu.co
Website: http://www.esumer.edu.co

Rector: John Romeiro Serna Peláez
EMail: jsernap@esumer.edu.co

Programmes
Administration and Finance (Administration; Finance); **Information Management** (Information Management); **International Commerce** (International Business); **Marketing** (Marketing)

History: Founded 1970. Acquired present title and status 1972.

Main Language(s) of Instruction: Spanish

Degrees and Diplomas: *Tecnólogo*; *Especialización*; *Maestría*
Last Updated: 04/11/09

EXTERNADO UNIVERSITY OF COLOMBIA
Universidad Externado de Colombia
Apartado aéreo 34141, Calle 12 No. 1-17 Este, Bogotá
Tel: +57(1) 342-0288 +57(1) 341-9050
Fax: +57(1) 284-3769 +57(1) 341-9050
EMail: sitioweb@uexternado.edu.co
Website: http://www.uexternado.edu.co

Rector: Fernando Hinestrosa
Tel: +57(1) 282-6066 EMail: rectoria@uexternado.edu.co

Secretario General: Hernando Parra Nieto

Centres
Research and Special Projects *(CIPE)*

Faculties
Administration, Tourism and Hotel Management (Administration; Hotel Management; Tourism) *Dean:* Luis Carlos Cruz Cortés; **Business Administration** (Business Administration) *Dean:* Carolina Cabrera de Peñazola; **Conservation and Restoration** (Heritage Preservation) *Dean:* Helena Wiesner; **Economics** (Economics) *Dean:* Mauricio Pérez Salazar; **Education** (Education) *Dean:* Myriam Ochoa Piedrahita; **Finance, Government and International Relations** (Finance; Government; International Relations) *Dean:* Roberto Hinestrosa Rey; **Law** (Law); **Public Accountancy** (Accountancy) *Dean:* Hernando Pérez Durán; **Social Communication and Journalism** (Communication Studies; Journalism); **Social Work** (Social Work)

History: Founded 1886 as Faculty of Law, became university 1958. Privately financed but receives some support from the State.

Governing Bodies: Consejo Directivo

Academic Year: February to December (February-July; July-December)

Admission Requirements: Secondary school certificate (bachillerato) and entrance examination

Main Language(s) of Instruction: Spanish

Degrees and Diplomas: *Licenciatura*: Accountancy; Business Administration; Economics; Finance and International Relations; Hotel Management; Law, 5 yrs; *Licenciatura*: Education; Social Communication (Journalism), 4 1/2 yrs; *Licenciatura*: Social Work, 4 yrs; *Especialización*; *Maestría*; *Doctorado*

Libraries: Central Library, c. 67,000 vols

Publications: Boletín Bibliográfico

Press or Publishing House: Editorial Universidad Externado de Colombia

FINE ARTS UNIVERSITY FOUNDATION
Fundación Universitaria Bellas Artes
Palacio de Bellas Artes, Carrera 42 No 52-33, Medellín, Antioquia
Tel: +57(4) 229-1400
Fax: +57(4) 239-4820
EMail: informacion@bellasartesmed.edu.co
Website: http://www.bellasartesmed.edu.co

Rector: Héctor Guillermo Echeverri Arbeláez
EMail: rector@bellasartesmed.edu.co

International Relations: Carlos Alberto Vélez Escobar
EMail: bellasartes@bellasartesmed.edu.co

Programmes
Fine Arts (Fine Arts); **Graphic Design** (Graphic Arts; Graphic Design); **Music** (Music)

History: Founded 1910 as Escuela de Música, Pintura y Escultura. Acquired present status and title 2006.

Degrees and Diplomas: *Titulo Profesional*: 5 yrs
Last Updated: 03/11/09

FOUNDATION ACADEMY OF PROFESSIONAL DESIGN
Fundación Academia de Dibujo Profesional
Calle 27 Norte No. 6BN-50, Cali, Valle del Cauca
Tel: +57(2) 667-7181 +57(2) 667-7182
Fax: +57(2) 661-0666
EMail: academia@fadp.edu.co
Website: http://www.fadp.edu.co

Rectora: Matha Inés Jaramillo Leiva

Programmes
Advertising and Publicity (Advertising and Publicity); **Architectural and Environmental Design** (Architectural and Environmental Design); **Fashion Design** (Fashion Design); **Graphic Design** (Graphic Design); **Industrial Design** (Industrial Design); **Interior Design** (Interior Design); **Multimedia** (Multimedia)

Degrees and Diplomas: *Técnico Profesional*; *Especialización*
Last Updated: 02/11/09

GARCÍA ROVIRA, NORTE AND GUTIÉRREZ UNIVERSITY FOUNDATION
Fundación Universitaria de García Rovira, Norte y Gutiérrez
Ciudad Universitaria-Málaga, Málaga, Santander
Tel: +57(76) 607-353

Programmes
Animal Husbandry (Animal Husbandry); **Business Administration** (Business Administration); **Forestry** (Forestry); **Zootechnology** (Zoology)

Main Language(s) of Instruction: Spanish

Degrees and Diplomas: *Licenciatura*: 3-5 yrs. Also Professional Title (3-5 yrs)
Last Updated: 23/08/07

GRANCOLOMBIANO POLYTECHNIC
Politécnico Grancolombiano
Apartado aéreo 90853, Calle 57 No. 3-00 Este, Bogotá
Tel: +57(1) 346-8800
Fax: +57(1) 346-9256
EMail: webmast@poligran.edu.co
Website: http://www.poligran.edu.co

Rector: Pablo Michelsen Niño EMail: pmichels@poligran.edu.co

Vicerrector Académico: Jurgen Chiari Escovar

Faculties
Administration and Economics (Accountancy; Banking; Business Administration; Economics; Finance; International Business; Management; Public Administration); **Communication and Arts** (Advertising and Publicity; Graphic Design; Journalism; Marketing;

Media Studies); **Engineering and Basic Sciences**; **Social Sciences** (Law; Psychology)

Degrees and Diplomas: *Tecnólogo*; *Licenciatura*; *Especialización*
Last Updated: 05/11/09

IBEROAMERICAN UNIVERSITY CORPORATION

Corporación Universitaria Iberoamericana
Calle 67 No. 5-27, Bogotá
Tel: +57(1) 348-9292
Fax: +57(1) 210-3553
EMail: contacto@iberoamericana.edu.co
Website: http://www.iberoamericana.edu.co

Rector: Edgar Peña Rodríguez
Tel: +57(1) 3489273 EMail: rectoria@iberoamericana.edu.co

Vice Rector: Luz Angela Alvarez Garcia

Centres
Research (Social Sciences; Social Studies) *Director*: William Rodríguez

Faculties
Accountancy (Accountancy); **Economics and Administration** (Accountancy; Administration; Economics); **Education** (Education; Preschool Education; Special Education); **Kinetics and Physiotherapy**; **Psychology** (Psychology)

History: Founded 1979.

Governing Bodies: Sala General; Consejo Superior; Consejo Administrativo; Consejo Académico

Admission Requirements: Secondary school certificate. ICFES examination

Main Language(s) of Instruction: Spanish

Degrees and Diplomas: *Licenciatura*: 4-5 yrs; *Especialización*: 1 yr

Student Services: Academic counselling, Cultural centre, Employment services, Foreign student adviser, Handicapped facilities, Health services, Language programs, Nursery care, Social counselling, Sports facilities
Last Updated: 30/10/09

IDEAS UNIVERSITY CORPORATION OF COLOMBIA

Corporación Universitaria de Colombia IDEAS
Calle 70 No. 10-75, Bogotá
Tel: +57(1) 255-8321
Fax: +57(1) 217-9073
EMail: ideas@unideas.edu.co
Website: http://www.ideas.edu.co

Rector: Jairo Tapias Ospina

Programmes
Accountancy (Accountancy); **Advertising** (Advertising and Publicity); **Business Administration** (Business Administration); **Marketing** (Marketing); **Simultaneous Interpretation** (Translation and Interpretation); **Telematics Engineering** (Engineering)

History: Founded 1984.

Main Language(s) of Instruction: Spanish

Degrees and Diplomas: *Licenciatura*; *Titulo Profesional*; *Especialización*
Last Updated: 29/10/09

INCCA UNIVERSITY OF COLOMBIA

Universidad INCCA de Colombia
Carrera 13 No. 24-15, Bogotá
Tel: +57(1) 444-2000
EMail: ofinter@unincca.edu.co
Website: http://www.unincca.edu.co

Rector: Enrique Conti Bautista EMail: rectoria@unincca.edu.co

Secretario General: José Gregorio Avellaneda Pulido

International Relations: Alfredo Garcia Molsalve
EMail: vicered1@unincca.edu.co

Faculties
Engineering, Administration and Basic Sciences (Accountancy; Biology; Business Administration; Computer Engineering; Economics; Food Technology; Industrial Engineering; Mechanical Engineering); **Law and Political Science** (Law; Political Sciences); **Pedagogy, Human Sciences and Social Sciences** (English; Modern Languages; Music; Physical Education; Preschool Education; Psychology; Social Sciences; Spanish)

Institutes
Technological (Agronomy; Computer Science; Industrial Engineering; Management; Telecommunications Engineering)

History: Founded 1955 as Institute of Administrative Sciences, recognized as a university by government decree 1970. A private institution.

Governing Bodies: Junta de Gobierno

Academic Year: January to November (January-May; July-November)

Admission Requirements: Secondary school certificate (bachillerato) and entrance examination

Main Language(s) of Instruction: Spanish

Degrees and Diplomas: *Licenciatura*: Accountancy (Contador); Economics (Economista); Education; Law (Abogado); Psychology (Psicólogo); Social Communication (Comunicador Social), 5 yrs; *Titulo Profesional*: Engineering (Ingeniero), 5 yrs; *Especialización*; *Maestría*: a further 2 yrs

Special Facilities: Art Gallery

Libraries: Central Library, c. 40,000 vols

Publications: Revista Científica *(quarterly)*

Press or Publishing House: Unincca Publishing Unit
Last Updated: 16/11/09

INPAHU UNIVERSITY FOUNDATION

Fundación Universitaria INPAHU (INPAHU)
Apartado aéreo 75950, Avenida 39 No. 15-58, Bogotá
Tel: +57(1) 332-0500
Fax: +57(1) 340-0341
EMail: inpahu@inpahu.edu.co
Website: http://www.inpahu.edu.co

Rectora: Myriam Velásquez Bustos
Tel: +57(1) 332-3534, Fax: +57(1) 332-3500, Ext.191
EMail: mvelasquez@inpahu.edu.co

Secretaria General: Maria Angélica Cortés

Faculties
Communication (Journalism; Photography; Radio and Television Broadcasting); **Economics and Administration** (Accountancy; Business Administration; Business and Commerce; Finance; Hotel Management; Marketing; Occupational Health; Tourism); **Engineering and Information Technology**

Governing Bodies: Consejo Superior; Rector; Vicerrectores; Directores; Decanaturas; Directores programas

Admission Requirements: Secondary school certificate. Entrance examination (ICFES)

Fees: (Pesos): 1.4m.

Main Language(s) of Instruction: Spanish

International Co-operation: With universities in Costa Rica and Mexico

Degrees and Diplomas: *Técnico Profesional*: 2 yrs; *Tecnólogo*: 3 yrs

Student Services: Academic counselling, Canteen, Cultural centre, Employment services, Foreign student adviser, Foreign Studies Centre, Handicapped facilities, Health services, Language programs, Nursery care, Social counselling, Sports facilities

Libraries: Yes. Also a virtual library

Publications: Coloquio, Related to Social Communication *(biennially)*; Tahu, Related to Occupational Health *(biennially)*
Last Updated: 03/11/09

INTERAMERICAN TECHNICAL FOUNDATION

Fundación Interamericana Técnica (FIT)
Calle 74 No. 11-74, Bogotá
Tel: +57(91) 235-9385
Fax: +57(91) 210-4671
Website: http://www.fit.edu.co

Rector: Jaime Javier Londoño Gaviria EMail: fitedv@hotmail.com

Programmes
Automotive Engineering (Automotive Engineering); **Commercial Engineering** (Business and Commerce); **Industrial Electronics**; **Thermal Engineering** (Thermal Engineering)

Degrees and Diplomas: *Tecnólogo*; *Especialización*
Last Updated: 02/11/09

INTERNATIONAL COLOMBO UNIVERSITY FOUNDATION

Fundación Universitaria Colombo Internacional
Centro, Calle de la Factoría 36-27, Cartagena de Indias, Bolívar
Tel: +57(5) 660-0098
Fax: +57(5) 660-0415
EMail: info@unicolombo.edu.co
Website: http://www.unicolombo.edu.co

Rector: Mario Ramos Vélez

Programmes
Education (Education; English)

History: Founded 1961 as Centro Colombo Americano de Cartagena. Acquired present status and title 2006.

Degrees and Diplomas: *Licenciatura*: 5 yrs
Last Updated: 03/11/09

INTERNATIONAL CORPORATION FOR EDUCATIONAL DEVELOPMENT

Corporación Internacional para el Desarrollo Educativo (CIDE)
Apartado aéreo 13850, Calle 41 No. 27A-52 La Soledad, Bogotá
Tel: +57(1) 368-9618 +57(1) 268-0530
Fax: +57(1) 368-9616
EMail: contacto@cide.edu.co
Website: http://www.cide.edu.co

Rector: Jairo Orlando Rodríguez Ravelo EMail: rect@cide.edu.co

Vicerrectora Académica: Elizabeth Muñoz Peñuela
EMail: viceacademica@cide.edu.co

International Relations: Elizabeth Muñoz Peñuela, Vicerrectora Académica EMail: viceacademica@cide.edu.co

Programmes
Business Administration (Business Administration); **Business Computing** (Business Computing); **Cinema and Television** (Cinema and Television); **E-Business/Commerce** (E-Business/Commerce); **Electronic Engineering** (Electronic Engineering); **Environmental Technology** (Environmental Studies; Natural Resources); **Food Technology** (Food Technology); **Graphic Design** (Graphic Design); **Industrial Design** (Industrial Design); **Industrial Maintenance** (Industrial Maintenance); **Photography** (Photography); **Preschool Education** (Preschool Education)

Main Language(s) of Instruction: Spanish

Degrees and Diplomas: *Técnico Profesional*: 2 yrs; *Tecnólogo*: 4 yrs; *Licenciatura*: 5 yrs

Student Services: Academic counselling, Nursery care, Social counselling

Publications: Periodico Vozero *(3 per annum)*; Revista Cientifica Silogismo *(biennially)*
Last Updated: 06/11/07

INTERNATIONAL UNIVERSITY FOUNDATION OF THE AMERICAN TROPIC

Fundación Universitaria Internacional del Tropico Américano (UNITROPICO)
Carrera 19 No. 39-40, Yopal, Casanare
Tel: +57(987) 632-0700
Fax: +57(987) 632-0700
EMail: unitropico@unitropico.edu.co
Website: http://www.unitropico.edu.co

Rectora: Silvia Forero de Guerrero
EMail: rectoria@unitropico.edu.co

Programmes
Accountancy; **Architecture** (Architecture); **Biology** (Biology) *Head*: Gilberto Contes Millán; **Civil Engineering** (Civil Engineering); **Economics** (Economics) *Head*: Carlos Alberto Reyes; **Food Technology** (Food Technology); **Forestry** (Forestry); **Genetics**; **International Business** (International Business); **Systems Engineering** (Computer Engineering); **Tourism** (Tourism); **Veterinary Science** (Veterinary Science)

History: Founded 2000.
Governing Bodies: Senate
Fees: (Pesos): 1,432,000
Main Language(s) of Instruction: Spanish
Accrediting Agencies: ICFES
Degrees and Diplomas: *Tecnólogo*; *Especialización*: 1 yr
Student Services: Academic counselling, Cultural centre, Social counselling, Sports facilities
Student Residential Facilities: None
Libraries: Yes
Last Updated: 03/11/09

JOHN F. KENNEDY CORPORATION

Corporación John F. Kennedy
cll 46 No. 13-43, Bogotá
Tel: +57(1) 245-7032
Fax: +57(1) 245-7032
EMail: admisiones@jfk.edu.co
Website: http://www.jfk.edu.co

Rector: Daniel Andrés Murcia Díaz EMail: corpjfk@telesat.com.co

Schools
Education and Human Development; **Logistics**; **Organizations** (Business Administration)

Further Information: Branches in Chia and Ibagué
History: Founded 1993.
Main Language(s) of Instruction: Spanish
Degrees and Diplomas: *Técnico Profesional*; *Tecnólogo*; *Especialización*
Last Updated: 29/10/09

JORGE TADEO LOZANO UNIVERSITY OF BOGOTÁ

Universidad de Bogotá JorgeTadeo Lozano
Carrera 4 No. 22-61, Bogotá
Tel: +57(1) 334-1777
Fax: +57(1) 282-6197
EMail: centro.informacion@utadeo.edu.co
Website: http://www.utadeo.edu.co

Rector: José Fernando Isaza Delgado
Tel: +57(1) 283-4610 EMail: rectoria@utadeo.edu.co

Vicerrector Académico: Diógenes Campos Romero

Centres
Information Technology (Information Technology)

Faculties
Economics and Administration (Accountancy; Business Administration; Economics; Information Management; International Business; Marketing); **Humanities, Arts and Design** (Advertising and Publicity; Communication Studies; Fine Arts; Graphic Design; Industrial Design; Interior Design); **International Relations, Law**

and Political Science (International Relations; Law; Political Sciences); **Natural Sciences and Engineering** (Biology; Chemical Engineering; Food Technology; Industrial Engineering; Marine Biology); **Postgraduate Studies** (Agricultural Economics; Architectural and Environmental Design; Business Administration; Finance; Health Administration; Horticulture; International Business; International Relations; Management; Marketing; Occupational Therapy; Taxation) *Vice-Rector*: Miguel Bermúdez

History: Founded 1954, a private institution partly financed by the State.

Governing Bodies: Board of Trustees

Academic Year: January to November (January-May; August-November)

Admission Requirements: Secondary school certificate (bachillerato) and State examination (ICFES test)

Fees: (Pesos): 1.8m. per semester; postgraduate, 1,6m-2,5m per term

Main Language(s) of Instruction: Spanish

Degrees and Diplomas: *Tecnólogo*; *Licenciatura*: 4 yrs; *Titulo Profesional*; *Especialización*: 3 sem; *Maestría*: a further 2 yrs

Student Services: Canteen, Cultural centre, Foreign student adviser, Health services, Social counselling, Sports facilities

Student Residential Facilities: Yes

Special Facilities: Museum of Marine Sciences

Libraries: Central Library, c. 60,000 vols

Publications: Geotropico *(quarterly)*

Last Updated: 02/11/09

CARTAGENA BRANCH
SECCIONAL CARTAGENA

International Campus Jorge Tadeo Lozano, Cartagena, Bolivar
Tel: +57(95) 655-4000
Fax: +57(95) 655-4090
Website: http://www.utadeo.edu.co

Rector: Max Rodríguez Fadul EMail: haroldo.calvo@utadeo.edu.co

Faculties
Architecture (Architecture); **Foreign Trade** (International Business; International Economics) *Dean*: Max Rodríguez; **Graphic Design** (Graphic Design) *Dean*: Angela Upeguy; **Management** (Management) *Dean*: Max Rodríguez; **Social Communication** (Communication Studies) *Dean*: Angela Upeguy; **Tourism** (Tourism) *Dean*: Max Rodríguez

JUAN DE CASTELLANOS UNIVERSITY FOUNDATION
Fundación Universitaria Juan de Castellanos
Carrera 11 No. 11 - 70, Tunja, Boyocá
Tel: +57(98) 742-3668 +57(98) 743-8138
Fax: +57(98) 740-1541
EMail: info@jdc.edu.co
Website: http://www.jdc.edu.co

Rector: Luis Enrique Pérez Ojeda
Tel: +57 (315) 316-5325, Fax: +57 (98) 740-1541
EMail: rector@jdc.edu.co

Secretaria General: Rosa P. Ayala Becerra
Tel: +57 (98) 744-7115, Fax: +57 (98) 740 1541
EMail: sgeneral@jdc.edu.co

International Relations: Jose Angel Avila Rojas, Director
Tel: +57 (311) 871-3554, Fax: +57 (98) 740-1541
EMail: planeacion@jdc.edu.co

Faculties
Agriculture (Agricultural Management; Agriculture; Ecology; Veterinary Science; Zoology); **Educational Sciences**; **Engineering** (Electrical Engineering; Electronic Engineering; Engineering; Systems Analysis); **International Law**; **Social Sciences and Economics** (Administration; Economics; Finance; Social Work)

History: Founded 1967 as Instituto Catequístico Juan de Castellanos. Acquired present status and title 2002.

Main Language(s) of Instruction: Spanish

Degrees and Diplomas: *Tecnólogo*: 6 sems; *Licenciatura*: 12 sems; *Especialización*: 3 sems. Also Diplomados

Student Services: Academic counselling, Language programs, Social counselling, Sports facilities

Publications: Journal Cientific, Scientific articles *(annually)*; Noticien, Short scientific articles *(monthly)*

Last Updated: 03/11/09

JUAN N. CORPAS UNIVERSITY FOUNDATION
Fundación Universitaria Juan N. Corpas
Apartado aéreo 2787, Avenida Corpas Km. 3 Suba, Bogotá
Tel: +57(1) 681-3637
Fax: +57(1) 683-4481
EMail: info@juanncorpas.edu.co
Website: http://www.juanncorpas.edu.co

Rectora: Ana María Piñeros Ricardo
EMail: ana.pineros@juancorpas.edu.co

Programmes
Medicine (Dentistry; Epidemiology; Health Administration; Medicine; Neurology; Otorhinolaryngology; Plastic Surgery); **Music** (Music)

Degrees and Diplomas: *Titulo Profesional*; *Especialización*
Last Updated: 03/11/09

JULIO GARAVITO COLOMBIAN SCHOOL OF ENGINEERING
Escuela Colombiana de Ingeniería Julio Garavito
Apartado aéreo 14520, Avenida 13 No. 205-59 Autopista Norte Km 13, Bogotá
Tel: +57(1) 676-0236
Fax: +57(1) 676-0479
Website: http://www.escuelaing.edu.co

Rector: Javier Botero Álvarez
Tel: +57(1) 668-3600/210
EMail: rector@escuelaing.edu.co; rquintana@escuelaing.edu.co

Secretary-General: Ricardo Alfredo López Cualla
Tel: +57(1) 668-3600/211 EMail: secreci@escuelaing.edu.co

International Relations: Santiago Restrepo
Tel: +57(1) 668-3600/328 EMail: srestrepo@escuelaing.edu.co

Programmes
Business Administration; **Civil Engineering** (Civil Engineering); **Economics** (Economics); **Electrical Engineering** (Electrical Engineering); **Electronic Engineering** (Electronic Engineering); **Industrial Engineering** (Industrial Engineering); **Mathematics** (Mathematics); **Mechanical Engineering** (Mechanical Engineering); **Systems Engineering** (Computer Engineering)

Governing Bodies: University Council; Rectorate

Academic Year: January to December (January-June; August-December)

Admission Requirements: Bachillerato and State Examination (ICFES)

Fees: (US Dollars): 800-1,600 per semester

Main Language(s) of Instruction: Spanish

International Co-operation: With universities in France, Spain, Germany, Canada, Mexico, Chile

Degrees and Diplomas: *Titulo Profesional*; *Especialización*: 1 yr; *Maestría*

Student Services: Canteen, Employment services, Foreign student adviser, Health services, Language programs, Nursery care, Social counselling, Sports facilities

Libraries: Main Library

Publications: Revista de la Escuela Colombiana de Ingeniería

Press or Publishing House: Editorial Escuela Colombiana de Ingenería
Last Updated: 30/10/09

KONRAD LORENZ UNIVERSITY FOUNDATION

Fundación Universitaria Konrad Lorenz
Apartado aéreo 250724, Calle 73 No. 10-45, Bogotá
Tel: +57(1) 347-2311
Fax: +57(1) 248-0243
EMail: info@fukl.edu
Website: http://www.fukl.edu

Rectora: Sonia Fajardo Forero

Vicerrectora Académica: Graciela Amaya Ochoa
EMail: gamaya@fukl.edu.co

Faculties

Economics and Administration (Business Administration; Economics; International Business); **Mathematics and Engineering** (Industrial Engineering; Mathematics; Systems Analysis); **Psychology** (Psychology)

History: Founded 1981.

Main Language(s) of Instruction: Spanish

Degrees and Diplomas: *Licenciatura*; *Titulo Profesional*; *Especialización*; *Maestría*
Last Updated: 03/11/09

LA GRAN COLOMBIA UNIVERSITY

Universidad La Gran Colombia
Carrera 6 No. 13-12, Bogotá
Tel: +57(1) 243-8047 +57(1) 327-6999
Website: http://www.ugc.edu.co

Rector: José Galat Noumer

Secretario General: Carlos Alberto Pulido Barrantes
EMail: secretariageneral@ulagrancolombia.edu.co

Faculties

Accountancy; **Architecture** (Architecture); **Civil Engineering** (Civil Engineering); **Economics and Administration** (Business Administration; Economics); **Education** (Education); **Law** (Law; Political Sciences)

Further Information: Also branch in Armenia

History: Founded 1953.

Academic Year: February to December

Admission Requirements: Secondary school certificate (bachillerato) and entrance examination

Main Language(s) of Instruction: Spanish

Degrees and Diplomas: *Licenciatura*: 9 sem; *Especialización*

Libraries: c. 26,000 vols

Publications: Revistas
Last Updated: 16/11/09

LA SALLE UNIVERSITY CORPORATION

Corporación Universitaria Lasallista (CUL)
Carrera 51 No. 118 Sur-57, Caldas, Antioquia
Tel: +57(4) 300-0200
Fax: +57(4) 300-0200 Ext. 184
EMail: administrador@lasallista.edu.co
Website: http://www.lasallista.edu.co

Rector: César Augusto Fernández Posada
Tel: +57(4) 300-0200 Ext. 103 EMail: rector@lasallista.edu.co

Director Administrativo: Oscar Aurelio Gómez
Tel: +57(4) 300-0200 Ext. 108 EMail: osgomez@lasallista.edu.co

International Relations: Mónica Alexandra Ríos, Head of International Relations
Tel: +57(4) 3000-200 Ext. 134 EMail: relinter@lasallista.edu.co

Faculties

Administrative and Agricultural Sciences (Agricultural Management; Animal Husbandry; Cattle Breeding; Crop Production; Veterinary Science); **Engineering** (Computer Science; Engineering; Environmental Engineering; Food Technology; Industrial Engineering); **Social Sciences and Education** (Communication Studies; Education; Ethics; Journalism; Preschool Education; Religious Education; Social Sciences)

History: Founded 1982 by ALDEA (Lasallian Association of Exalumni) and the "Brothers'Congregation of Christian Schools of Medellín". Acquired present status 1983.

Governing Bodies: Superior Council; Founders' Assembly

Academic Year: January to December (January-June; August-December)

Admission Requirements: High school certificate, State examination (ICFES) or equivalent and interview

Fees: (US Dollars) 500-1,500 per semester

Main Language(s) of Instruction: Spanish

International Co-operation: With universities in Brazil, Mexico, Spain, France, Italy, Costa Rica, UK, USA, and the Philippines

Accrediting Agencies: Consejo Nacional de Acreditación (CNA)

Degrees and Diplomas: *Licenciatura*: Education; Preschool Education, 5 yrs; *Titulo Profesional*: Agribusiness Management; Animal Husbandry; Veterinary Medicine; Food Engineering; Environmental Engineering; Industrial Engineering; Computer Engineering; Communication Studies; Psychology, 5 yrs; *Especialización*: Agribusiness Management; Agribusiness Marketing; Logistics of Vegetables Harvests; Food Packaging; Ethics; Skills Development from Critical Thinking

Student Services: Academic counselling, Canteen, Foreign student adviser, Handicapped facilities, Health services, Language programs, Nursery care, Social counselling, Sports facilities

Student Residential Facilities: None

Special Facilities: Art Gallery; Radio and TV studios; Computer Room

Libraries: Yes

Publications: Revista Lasallista de Investigación *(biennially)*; Revista Produccíon + Limpia *(biennially)*

Press or Publishing House: Boletín Soy Lasallista

Academic Staff 2007-2008	MEN	WOMEN	TOTAL
FULL-TIME	49	46	95
PART-TIME	71	41	112
STAFF WITH DOCTORATE			
FULL-TIME	–	2	2
PART-TIME	3	2	5
Student Numbers 2007-2008			
All (Foreign Included)	665	576	1,241
FOREIGN ONLY	2	–	2

Last Updated: 30/10/09

LATIN AMERICAN AUTONOMOUS UNIVERSITY

Universidad Autónoma Latinoamericana (UNAULA)
Apartado aéreo 3455, Carrera 55 No. 49-51, Medellín, Antioquia
Tel: +57(4) 511-2199
Fax: +57(4) 512-3418
EMail: info@unaula.edu.co
Website: http://www.unaula.edu.co

Rector: Jairo Uribe Arango EMail: rectoria@unaula.edu.co

Secretario General: Alfonso Tito Mejía Restrepo
EMail: secretariageneral@unaula.edu.co

International Relations: Aníbal Vélez Muñoz, Vicerrector Académico EMail: viceacademico@unaula.edu.co

Faculties

Accountancy (Accountancy); **Economics** (Economics); **Education** (Education; Educational Psychology; Geography; Philosophy; Sociology); **Engineering** (Computer Engineering; Engineering; Industrial Engineering); **Law** (Law); **Postgraduate Studies**

History: Founded 1966 as a private institution. Privately financed but receives some support from the State.

Governing Bodies: Consejo Académico

Academic Year: February to December

Admission Requirements: Secondary school certificate (bachillerato) and entrance examination

Fees: (US Dollars): 1,370 per annum

Main Language(s) of Instruction: Spanish

Degrees and Diplomas: *Licenciatura*: 4-5 yrs; *Especialización*: 1 yr

Student Services: Academic counselling, Canteen, Employment services, Handicapped facilities, Health services, Language programs, Social counselling, Sports facilities

Libraries: Central Library, c. 20,000 vols; Law, c. 2,000 vols

Publications: Ratio Juris, Magazine with speciality in Law (biennially); UNAULA, Institutional Magazine (annually)

Academic Staff 2007-2008	MEN	WOMEN	TOTAL
FULL-TIME	232	38	270
PART-TIME	5	2	c. 7
Student Numbers 2007-2008			
All (Foreign Included)	1,080	1,320	c. 2,400

Evening students, 500.
Last Updated: 09/11/09

LATIN UNION FOUNDATION

Fundación Unión Latina (UNILATINA)
Calle 46 No. 3-05, Bogotá
Tel: +57(1) 287-9421
Fax: +57(1) 573-7488
EMail: informacion@unilatina.edu
Website: http://www.unilatina.edu.co

Rectora: Nelly Teresa Bautista Moller

Programmes
Advertising and Publicity (Advertising and Publicity); **Business Administration** (Business Administration); **Finance** (Finance); **Human Resources** (Human Resources); **International Relations** (International Relations); **Management** (Management); **Marketing** (Marketing); **Music** (Music); **Radio and Television Broadcasting** (Radio and Television Broadcasting); **Transport Management** (Transport Management)

Degrees and Diplomas: Tecnólogo; Especialización

LOS LIBERTADORES UNIVERSITY FOUNDATION

Fundación Universitaria Los Libertadores
Carrera 16 No. 63A-68, Bogotá
Tel: +57(1) 254-4750
Fax: +57(1) 314-5965
EMail: admisio@cit.ulibertadores.edu.co
Website: http://www.ulibertadores.edu.co

Rector: Néstor Cristancho Quintero

Faculties
Administration (Administration; Business Administration; International Relations; Political Sciences); **Communication** (Communication Studies); **Economics and Accountancy** (Accountancy; Economics); **Education** (Education); **Engineering** (Engineering); **Law** (International Relations; Law; Political Sciences); **Psychology** (Psychology)

Schools
Postgraduate Studies

History: Founded 1982.

Main Language(s) of Instruction: Spanish

Degrees and Diplomas: Licenciatura; Titulo Profesional; Especialización
Last Updated: 03/11/09

LUIS AMIGO UNIVERSITY FOUNDATION

Fundación Universitaria Luis Amigó (FUNLAM)
Apartado aéreo 11001, Transversal Fundación Universitaria, Luis Amigó 51A No. 67B-90, Medellín, Antioquia
Tel: +57(4) 260-6666
Fax: +57(4) 230-2181 +57(4) 260-8074
EMail: webmaster@funlam.edu.co
Website: http://www.funlam.edu.co

Rector: José Wílmar Sánchez Duque (2012-)
Tel: +57(4) 260-5092, Fax: +57(4) 260-8074
EMail: jwsanchez@funlam.edu.co

Secretary General: Francisco Acosta Gómez
Tel: +57(4) 260 6666, Ext.167, Fax: +57(4) 260 8074
EMail: facosta@funlam.edu.co

International Relations: Andrés Muñoz Díazgranados
Tel: +57(4) 260-6666, Ext.211, Fax: +57(4) 260-8074
EMail: ocri@funlam.edu.co

Centres
Community Service; **Research Development** (Accountancy; Administration; Economics; Education; Information Technology; Social Sciences)

Departments
Modern Languages (Modern Languages)

Faculties
Business Administration (Accountancy; Business Administration; Economics; International Business); **Computer Engineering**; **Education** (Education; Pedagogy; Preschool Education; Primary Education); **Family Studies** (Family Studies); **Law and Humanities** (Civil Law; Law); **Philosophy and Theology** (Philosophy; Theology); **Psychology** (Psychology; Social Psychology); **Social Communication**

Programmes
Drug Addiction (Postgraduate programme)

History: Founded 1969. Acquired present status 1984.

Governing Bodies: Superior Council; Academic Council; School Council

Academic Year: January to June; July to December

Admission Requirements: Secondary school certificate and ICFES examination

Fees: (Pesos): 764,099 per semester for distance programs; 1,642,031 for full attendance programs

Main Language(s) of Instruction: Spanish

International Co-operation: With universities in Spain, Argentina and Italy

Accrediting Agencies: Instituto Colombiano para el Fomento de la Educación Superior (ICFES); Consejo Nacional de Acreditación (CNA); Ministry of Education

Degrees and Diplomas: Licenciatura: Philosophy; Theology; Pedagogy; Preschool Education; Primary Education;, 6 yrs; Titulo Profesional: Business Administration; International Business; Accounting; Social Studies; Family Studies; Psychology; Law; Economy; Philosophy; Theology; Systems Engineering, 5 yrs; Especialización: Social Studies; Toxicology; Law; Finance; Taxation; Economics, 1-1 1/2 yrs; Maestría: Toxicology; Social Studies, 2 yrs

Student Services: Canteen, Foreign student adviser, Foreign Studies Centre, Health services, Language programs, Nursery care, Social counselling, Sports facilities

Student Residential Facilities: None

Special Facilities: Audiovisual Centre; Internet and computer room service

Libraries: Central Library

Publications: Análisis, Drug addiction related problems magazine (biennially); Theology and Philosophy Faculty Magazine, Articles about Theology and Philosophy fields (annually); Vida Consagrada, Magazine about religion (annually)

Academic Staff 2007-2008	MEN	WOMEN	TOTAL
FULL-TIME	21	23	44
PART-TIME	33	18	51
STAFF WITH DOCTORATE			
FULL-TIME	–	–	1
Student Numbers 2007-2008			
All (Foreign Included)	2,342	5,180	7,522
FOREIGN ONLY	–	–	4

Distance students, 2,588.
Last Updated: 24/01/12

LUMEN GENTIUM CATHOLIC UNIVERSITY FOUNDATION

Fundación Universitaria Católica Lumen Gentium
Carrera 122 No. 12-459, Cali, Valle del Cauca
Tel: +57(2) 555-2767
Fax: +57(2) 555-8767
Website: http://www.unicatolica.edu.co

Rector: Huberto Obando Gil

Departments
Basic Sciences; **Communication and Language** (Modern Languages); **Humanities** (Arts and Humanities; Pedagogy; Philosophy; Social Sciences; Theology)

Faculties
Business Studies; **Education** (Education); **Engineering** (Advertising and Publicity; Automation and Control Engineering; Electronic Engineering; Graphic Design; Marketing; Telecommunications Engineering)

Main Language(s) of Instruction: Spanish

Degrees and Diplomas: *Licenciatura*; *Titulo Profesional*; *Especialización*
Last Updated: 03/11/09

MANUELA BELTRÁN UNIVERSITY

Universidad Manuela Beltrán (UMB)
Apartado aéreo 251046, Avenida Circunvalar No. 60-00, Bogotá
Tel: +57(1) 546-0600
Fax: +57(1) 546-0638 +57(1) 546-0622
EMail: rector@umb.edu.co
Website: http://www.umb.edu.co

Rector: Guido Echeverry Piedrahita

Centres
Language (English)

Departments
Pedagogy (Pedagogy)

Faculties
Arts; **Education, Humanities and Social Sciences**; **Engineering**; **Health Studies**; **Law**

Further Information: Also branch in Bucaramanga

History: Founded 1975. Acquired present status 1992.

Main Language(s) of Instruction: Spanish

Degrees and Diplomas: *Licenciatura*; *Especialización*
Last Updated: 17/11/09

MARÍA CAÑO UNIVERSITY FOUNDATION

Fundación Universitaria María Caño
Apartado aéreo 95748, Carrera 56 No.41-90, Medellín, Antioquia
Tel: +57(4) 291-3575
Fax: +57(4) 254-5957
Website: http://www.fumc.edu.co

Rector: Prospero José Posada Mier **EMail:** rectoria@fumc.edu.co

Faculties
Business Administration (Accountancy; Business Administration; International Business); **Engineering** (Systems Analysis); **Health Sciences**

History: Founded 1987.

Main Language(s) of Instruction: Spanish

Degrees and Diplomas: *Licenciatura*; *Titulo Profesional*; *Especialización*
Last Updated: 03/11/09

MARÍA GORETTI UNIVERSITY INSTITUTE - CENTRE OF HIGHER STUDIES

Institución Universitaria Centro de Estudios Superiores María Goretti (CESMAG)
Carrera 20A No. 14-54, San Juan de Pasto, Nariño
Tel: +57(277) 215-357
Fax: +57(277) 212-314
EMail: goreti@iucesmag.edu.co
Website: http://www.iucesmag.edu.co

Rector: Evaristo Acosta Maestre (1998-)
EMail: pevarist@iucesmag.edu.co

Vice Academic Rector: Gerson Eraso Arciniegas

Faculties
Administration and Accountancy (Accountancy; Business Administration; Finance); **Architecture and Fine Arts** (Architecture; Graphic Design); **Education** (Physical Education; Preschool Education); **Engineering**; **Human and Social Sciences** (Law; Psychology)

History: Founded 1982. Acquired present status and title 2000.

Academic Year: August to June (August-December; January-June)

Main Language(s) of Instruction: Spanish

Degrees and Diplomas: *Tecnólogo*; *Licenciatura*; *Titulo Profesional*; *Especialización*
Last Updated: 04/11/09

MARIANA UNIVERSITY

Universidad Mariana
Apartado aéreo 811, Calle 18 No. 34-104, San Juan de Pasto, Nariño
Tel: +57(927) 313-616
Fax: +57(927) 313-874
EMail: umariana@umariana.edu.co
Website: http://www.umariana.edu.co

Rectora: Martha Estela Santa Castrillon
EMail: rectoria@umariana.edu.co

Secretaria General: Dora Lucy Arce Hidalgo

Faculties
Accountancy, Economics and Administration (Accountancy; Business and Commerce; Economics; Finance; Marketing); **Education**; **Engineering** (Automation and Control Engineering; Environmental Engineering; Sanitary Engineering; Systems Analysis); **Health Sciences**; **Humanities and Social Sciences**

History: Founded 1965.

Main Language(s) of Instruction: Spanish

Degrees and Diplomas: *Licenciatura*: 4 yrs; *Especialización*; *Maestría*: a further 2 yrs; *Doctorado*: 5 yrs

Student Services: Academic counselling, Language programs, Social counselling, Sports facilities

Libraries: 6,300 vols
Last Updated: 17/11/09

METROPOLITAN UNIVERSITY

Universidad Metropolitana
Apartado aéreo 50-576, Calle 76 No. 42-78, Barranquilla, Atlántico
Tel: +57(95) 368-6572
Fax: +57(95) 358-3378
EMail: unimetro@unimetro.edu.co
Website: http://www.unimetro.edu.co

Rector: Eduardo Acosta Bendek **EMail:** rectoria@unimetro.edu.co

Administrative Officer: Sara Silva
Tel: +57(95) 368-6571, Fax: +57(95) 368-6571
EMail: veba13@hotmail.com

International Relations: Olga Lucía Acosta, Treasurer
Tel: +57(95) 360-5738, Fax: +57(95) 368-5443
EMail: olgaacosta@hotmail.com

Programmes
Bacteriology (Biological and Life Sciences); **Dentistry** (Dentistry); **Medicine** (Medicine); **Nursing** (Nursing); **Nutrition and Diet** (Dietetics; Nutrition); **Occupational Therapy** (Occupational Therapy); **Optometry** (Optometry); **Phonology and Audiology** (Speech Therapy and Audiology); **Physiotherapy** (Physical Therapy); **Psychology** (Psychology); **Social Work** (Social Work)

History: Founded 1973.

Governing Bodies: Board

Academic Year: January to December (January-June;July-December)

Admission Requirements: Secondary school certificate and state entrance examination

Fees: (Pesos): Tuition, 1,15m-3,98m per semester

Main Language(s) of Instruction: Spanish

International Co-operation: With universities in Argentina, Brazil, Chile and USA

Degrees and Diplomas: *Licenciatura*: Dentistry; Bacteriology, 5 yrs; *Licenciatura*: Medicine and Surgery, 7 yrs; *Licenciatura*: Nursing; Nutrition; Occupational Therapy; Optometry; Physiotherapy; Psychology; Social Work; Speech Therapy, 4 yrs; *Especialización*: Anesthesiology and Reanimation; Surgery; Gynaecology and Obstetrics; Intern Medicine; Paediatrics; Clinical Nutrition of Adults; Physiotherapy and Orthopedics; Odontopaediatrics; Endodoncy; Periodontics; Haematology; Health Administration; Medical Microbiology; University Teaching; Type Models and Investigation Design; Clinical Psychology; Audiology

Student Services: Academic counselling, Canteen, Cultural centre, Health services

Last Updated: 17/11/09

MINUTO DE DIOS UNIVERSITY CORPORATION

Corporación Universitaria Minuto de Dios (UNIMINUTO)
Calle 81B N° 72 B - 70, Barrio Minuto de Dios, Bogotá
Tel: +57(1) 291-6520
EMail: admisiones@uniminuto.edu
Website: http://academia.uniminuto.edu/uniminuto

Rector: Camilo Eduardo Bernal Hadad
EMail: cbernal@uniminuto.edu.co

Faculties
Computer Science and Telecommunications; Economics and Administration (Administration; Economics); **Education** (Education); **Engineering** (Engineering); **Humanities and Social Sciences** (Arts and Humanities; Social Sciences); **Social Communication** (Communication Studies)

Institutes
Pastoral *(Latin American)* (Pastoral Studies)

History: Founded 1988.

Main Language(s) of Instruction: Spanish

Degrees and Diplomas: *Licenciatura*; *Especialización*
Last Updated: 30/10/09

MONSERRATE UNIVERSITY FOUNDATION

Fundación Universitaria Monserrate (FUM)
Calle 72 No. 11-41, Bogotá
Tel: +57(1) 249-4959
Fax: +57(1) 217-4912
EMail: info@fum.edu.co
Website: http://www.fum.edu.co

Rectora: Berta Revollo Bravo
Tel: +57(1) 2494959, Ext. 121 EMail: rectoria@fum.edu.co

Vicerrectora Administrativa: Josefa Soler Vera
Tel: +57(1) 2494959, Ext. 104

International Relations: Libia Cabra Salinas
Tel: +57(1) 2494959, Ext. 144
EMail: comunicaciones@academia.fum.edu.coco

Faculties
Education (Education; Preschool Education); **Social Sciences and Economics** (Economics; Social Sciences)

History: Founded 1983.

Governing Bodies: Consejo Superior

Academic Year: February to November

Admission Requirements: Secondary school certificate (Bachillerato); entrance examination (ICFES)

Main Language(s) of Instruction: Spanish

International Co-operation: With universities in Chile; Ecuador; Brasil; Haiti; Honduras; Guatemala and other local universities in Colombia

Degrees and Diplomas: *Licenciatura*: Education, 4 yrs; *Titulo Profesional*: Social Sciences and Administration, 4 yrs; *Especialización*: Education, 1 yr

Student Services: Academic counselling, Employment services, Language programs, Nursery care, Social counselling

Publications: Revista Hojas y Hablas *(annually)*; Revista Perspectivas Universitarias *(annually)*

Last Updated: 03/11/09

NATIONAL EDUCATION ADMINISTRATION CORPORATION

Corporación de Educación Nacional de Administración (CENDA)
Avenida Caracas No. 35-18, Bogotá
Tel: +57(1) 232-9084 +57(1) 245-9170
Fax: +57(1) 242-3216
EMail: cenda@cenda.edu.co
Website: http://www.cenda.edu.co

Rectora: Martha Moncada De Rojas EMail: rectoria@cenda.edu.co

Programmes
Art Education (Art Education); **Computer Engineering** (Computer Engineering); **Dance** (Dance); **Finance** (Finance); **Leisure Studies** (Leisure Studies); **Pedagogy** (Pedagogy); **Physical Education** (Physical Education); **Preschool Education** (Preschool Education); **Sports** (Sports)

Degrees and Diplomas: *Técnico Profesional*; *Licenciatura*; *Especialización*
Last Updated: 28/10/09

NEW COLOMBIA UNIVERSITY CORPORATION

Corporación Universitaria Nueva Colombia
Calle 74 No. 11-67, Bogotá
Tel: +57(1) 255-9200
Fax: +57(1) 346-5514
EMail: rector@corunicolombia.edu.co
Website: http://www.corunicolombia.edu.co

Rector: Gabriel Martínez Solano EMail: unicolombia@latinmail.com

Secretary General: Alvaro Suarez Monsalve

Programmes
Accountancy (Accountancy); **Business Administration** (Business Administration); **Cinema and Television** (Cinema and Television); **Marketing** (Marketing); **Public and Institutional Relations** (Public Relations)

History: Founded 1996.

Governing Bodies: Board of Directors

Admission Requirements: Secondary school certificate, ICFES examination

Main Language(s) of Instruction: Spanish

Degrees and Diplomas: *Titulo Profesional*: Accounting; Marketing; Business Administration, 5 yrs

Student Services: Academic counselling, Cultural centre, Employment services, Health services, Language programs, Social counselling, Sports facilities

Libraries: Yes. Also a virtual library

Publications: Academic Magazine *(biennially)*
Last Updated: 30/10/09

PAN-AMERICAN UNIVERSITY FOUNDATION

Fundación Universitaria Panamericana
Avenida 32 No. 17-30, Bogotá
Tel: +57(91) 340-4766
Fax: +57(91) 338-0666
EMail: unipanamericana@unipanamericana.edu.co
Website: http://www.unipanamericana.edu.co

Rector: Francisco Nuñez Lapeira
EMail: rectoria@unipanamericana.edu.co

Director Académico: Héctor Manuel Corte Salazar
EMail: hcortes@unipanamericana.edu.co

Faculties
Administration (Administration); **Communication** (Communication Studies); **Education** (Education; Pedagogy); **Engineering**

(Computer Networks; Computer Science; Software Engineering; Systems Analysis)

Degrees and Diplomas: *Licenciatura*; *Titulo Profesional*; *Especialización*
Last Updated: 03/11/09

PILOT UNIVERSITY OF COLOMBIA
Universidad Piloto de Colombia
Carrera 9 No. 45 A-44, 1er Piso, Bogotá
Tel: +57(1) 245-32-40
EMail: inscripcion@unipiloto.edu.co
Website: http://www.unipiloto.edu.co

Rector: Patricia Piedrahita Castillo
EMail: gppiedrahita@unipiloto.edu.co

Secretaria General: Francina Hernandez Tascon
EMail: fhernandez@unipiloto.edu.co

International Relations: Jorge Sanchez Puyana
Tel: +57(1) 285-3102, Fax: +57(1) 285-8471
EMail: jsanchez@unipiloto.edu.co

Faculties
Accountancy (Accountancy); **Administration** (Administration; Business Administration); **Architecture** (Architecture); **Civil Engineering** (Civil Engineering); **Economics** (Economics); **Environmental Engineering** (Environmental Engineering); **Finance Engineering** (Finance); **Marketing**; **Psychology** (Psychology); **Systems Engineering** (Computer Engineering); **Telecommunications Engineering** (Telecommunications Engineering)

Further Information: Also Seccional del Alto Magdalena, Girardot
History: Founded 1962. A private institution.
Governing Bodies: Conciliatura; Consejo Superior Académico
Academic Year: January to December (January-July; August-December)
Admission Requirements: Secondary school certificate (bachillerato) and entrance examination
Main Language(s) of Instruction: Spanish
Degrees and Diplomas: *Licenciatura*: 5 yrs; *Titulo Profesional*: 5 yrs; *Especialización*; *Maestría*
Student Services: Academic counselling, Canteen, Cultural centre, Employment services, Health services, Nursery care, Social counselling, Sports facilities
Libraries: Biblioteca Alfonso Palacio Rudas
Last Updated: 18/11/09

GIRARDOT BRANCH
SECCIONAL GIRARDOT
Carrera 19 No. 17-33 Barrio Las Quintas, Girardot, Cundinamarca
Tel: +57(183) 32-845
Fax: +57(183) 32-873
EMail: supilo1@col1.telecom.com.co
Website: http://www.unipiloto.edu.co/

Vicerrector: José Ernesto Bermudez Rojas
Tel: +57(183) 32-505 EMail: g-jebermudez@unipiloto.edu.co

Faculties
Accountancy (Accountancy); **Civil Engineering** (Civil Engineering); **Finance** (Finance); **Systems Engineering**
History: Founded 1986.
Main Language(s) of Instruction: Spanish
Degrees and Diplomas: *Licenciatura*; *Especialización*; *Maestría*

POLYTECHNIC CORPORATION OF THE ATLANTIC COAST
Corporación Politécnico de la Costa Atlántica
Apartado aéreo 51312, Carrera 38 No. 79A-67, Barranquilla, Atlántico
Tel: +57(5) 352-0041 +57(5) 356-3338
Fax: +57(5) 358-7200
Website: http://www.pca.edu.co
Rector: Hugo César Santander García EMail: husanta@pca.edu.co

Programmes
Accountancy (Accountancy); **Advertising and Publicity** (Advertising and Publicity); **Computer Engineering** (Computer Engineering); **Construction Engineering** (Construction Engineering); **Electrical Engineering** (Electrical Engineering); **Electronic Engineering** (Electronic Engineering); **Fashion Design** (Fashion Design); **Finance** (Finance); **Industrial Design** (Industrial Design); **Industrial Engineering** (Industrial Engineering); **International Business** (International Business); **Marketing** (Marketing); **Media Studies** (Media Studies); **Medical Technology** (Medical Technology); **Telecommunications Engineering** (Telecommunications Engineering)

Degrees and Diplomas: *Tecnólogo*; *Titulo Profesional*
Last Updated: 29/10/09

PONTIFICAL BOLIVARIANA UNIVERSITY
Universidad Pontificia Bolivariana (UPB)
Apartado Aéreo 56006, Cir. 1a No. 70-01, Medellín, Antioquia
Tel: +57(4) 415-9015
Fax: +57(4) 250-2080
EMail: relinter@logos.upb.edu.co
Website: http://www.upb.edu.co

Rector: Luis Fernando Rodríguez Velásquez (2004-)
Tel: +57(4) 415-9000 EMail: rectoria@logos.upb.edu.co

Secretaria General: Clemencia Restrepo Posada
Tel: +57(4) 415-9004 EMail: clerpo@upb.edu.co

International Relations: Mauricio Molina Molina
Tel: +57(4) 415-9061

Schools
Advanced Studies; **Architecture and Design** (Architecture; Design; Graphic Design; Industrial Design); **Education and Pedagogy** (Computer Science; Education; Modern Languages; Pedagogy); **Engineering** (Agricultural Engineering; Chemical Engineering; Computer Engineering; Electrical Engineering; Electronic Engineering; Engineering; Industrial Engineering; Mechanical Engineering; Textile Technology); **Health Sciences** (Medicine; Nursing); **Law and Political Science** (Law); **Social Sciences** (Advertising and Publicity; Communication Studies; Education; Family Studies; Journalism; Psychology; Social Sciences; Social Work; Visual Arts); **Strategic Sciences** (Accountancy; Business Administration; Development Studies; Economics); **Theology, Philosophy and Humanities** (Arts and Humanities; Ethics; Philosophy; Theology)

History: Founded 1936 by the Archbishop of Medellín, acquired present status and title 1945.
Governing Bodies: Consejo Directivo (Board of Directors)
Academic Year: January to November (January-June; July-November)
Admission Requirements: Secondary school certificate (bachillerato) and state entrance examination. Entrance examination for Graphic and Industrial Design
Main Language(s) of Instruction: Spanish
International Co-operation: Study Abroad Programme. Participates in the International Association for the Exchange of Students for Technical Experience (IAESTE)

Degrees and Diplomas: *Licenciatura*: Architecture; Business Administration; Economy and Development; Law; Psychology; Social Communication; Social Work, 5 yrs; *Licenciatura*: Education; Nursing; Philosophy, 4 yrs; *Licenciatura*: Surgery, 7 yrs; *Licenciatura*: Theology, 3 yrs; *Titulo Profesional*: Chemical Engineering; Computer Engineering; Electrical Engineering; Electronic Engineering; Graphic Design; Industrial Design; Mechanical Engineering; Stockbreeding Engineering; Textile Engineering, 5 yrs; *Especialización*; *Maestría*; *Maestría*: Management Technology; Philosophy with emphasis on Ethics; Political Studies; Private Law; Theology; *Doctorado*: Medical Sciences; Philosophy (PhD); Theology; Thermal Engineering. Also Teaching Qualifications, 5-6 yrs

Student Services: Academic counselling, Cultural centre, Employment services, Foreign student adviser, Health services, Social counselling, Sports facilities
Libraries: Central Library, c. 80,000 vols; Medicine Library, c. 5,500 vols
Publications: Administración de Empresas *(annually)*; Cuestiones Teológicas y Filosóficas *(biannually)*; Escritos *(annually)*; Integral Industrial *(other/irregular)*; Pensamiento Humanista *(annually)*;

Revista Comunicación Social UPB *(annually)*; Revista Faculdad de Derecho y Ciencias Políticas *(other/irregular)*; Revista Facultad de Trabajo Social *(annually)*

Press or Publishing House: Bolivariana
Last Updated: 19/11/09

BUCARAMANGA BRANCH
SECCIONAL BUCARAMANGA

Autopista a Piedecuesta Km. 7, Bucaramanga, Santander
Tel: +57(76) 638-8381
Fax: +57(76) 679-7080
Website: http://www.upb.edu.co

Rector: Néstor Navarro Barrera
EMail: nnavarro@upbbga.edu.co; rectoria@upbbga.edu.co

Secretary-General: Carlos Augusto Mora González
EMail: camora@upbbga.edu.co

International Relations: Sandra Cristina Zapata Agón
Tel: +57(76) 679-6220 Ext. 407, Fax: +57(76) 679-6221
EMail: szapata@upbbga.edu.co

Programmes
Business Administration (Business Administration); **Civil Engineering** (Civil Engineering); **Computer Science** (Computer Science); **Electronic Engineering** (Electronic Engineering); **Environmental Engineering** (Environmental Engineering; Public Health); **Industrial Engineering** (Industrial Engineering); **Mechanical Engineering** (Mechanical Engineering); **Psychology** (Psychology) *Director*: Raúl Jaimes Hernández; **Social Communication and Journalism** (Communication Studies; Journalism)

History: Founded 1990.

Main Language(s) of Instruction: Spanish

Degrees and Diplomas: *Titulo Profesional*; *Especialización*

MONTERÍA BRANCH
SECCIONAL MONTERÍA

Kilómetro 8 vía Cereté-antiguo Colegio de la Presentación, Montería, Córdoba
Website: http://www.upb.edu.co

Rector: José María Hoyos Regino
Tel: +57(4) 782-3622, Fax: +57(4) 786-0912
EMail: rectoria@upbmonteria.edu.co

Secretary-General: Darío Peinado Babilonia
Tel: +57(4) 782-3622 Ext. 173

International Relations: Claudia Gil Salcedo, Director for Communication and Public Relations
Tel: +57(4) 782-0146 Ext. 174
EMail: crelinter@upbmonteria.edu.co

Programmes
Agroindustrial Engineering *Director*: Juan Carlos Palacio; **Architecture** *Director*: Mario Giraldo; **Biotechnology Engineering** (Biotechnology); **Business Management** (Business Administration; Management) *Director*: Alberto Cabrales; **Civil Engineering** (Civil Engineering); **Computer Science and Engineering** *Director*: Carlos Barrios; **Electronic Engineering** *Director*: Jorge Ardila; **Law** (Law) *Dean*: Rafael Figuerosa; **Linguistics and Literature**; **Mechanical Engineering** *Director*: Nelson Escobar; **Psychology** (Psychology) *Director*: Ana Rocío Kerguelen; **Public Health and Environmental Engineering** *Director*: Beatríz Rueda; **Social Communications and Journalism** (Communication Studies; Journalism; Social Studies) *Dean*: Julían Forero Sandoval; **Social Work** (Social Work)

History: Founded 1995.

PALMIRA BRANCH
SECCIONAL PALMIRA

Calle 30 No. 29-79, Palmira, Valle
Tel: +57(2) 272-2545
Fax: +57(2) 272-3121
Website: http://www.upb.edu.co

Rector: Bernardo Escobar Gómez
EMail: upbpalmira@teleset.com.co

Vicerrector académico: Oscar Alirio Millán González
EMail: upbviceacademico@telesat.com.co

Programmes
Advertising; **Economics and Development** (Development Studies; Economics); **Psychology** (Psychology)

History: Founded 1997.

Main Language(s) of Instruction: Spanish

PONTIFICAL XAVIER UNIVERSITY
Pontificia Universidad Javeriana
Apartado aéreo 56710, Carrera 7 a No. 40-62, Bogotá
Tel: +57(1) 320-8320, Ext. 2009
Fax: +57(1) 285-3348
Website: http://www.javeriana.edu.co

Rector: Joaquín Sánchez García Tel: +57(1) 320-8320, Ext.2009
Vicerrector académico: Vicente Durán Casas

Faculties
Economics and Administration; **Architecture and Design** (Architecture; Industrial Design); **Arts** (Music; Performing Arts; Theatre; Visual Arts); **Canon Law** (Canon Law); **Communication and Languages** (Communication Studies; Library Science; Modern Languages); **Dentistry** (Dentistry); **Education** (Education); **Engineering** (Civil Engineering; Computer Engineering; Electronic Engineering; Industrial Engineering); **Environmental and Rural Studies** (Ecology; Environmental Studies; Rural Studies); **Law** (Law); **Medicine** (Medicine); **Nursing** (Nursing); **Philosophy** (Philosophy); **Political Science and International Relations** (International Relations; Political Sciences); **Psychology** (Psychology); **Science** (Agriculture; Biology; Dietetics; Mathematics and Computer Science; Microbiology; Nutrition; Veterinary Science; Virology); **Social Sciences** (Anthropology; History; Literature; Sociology); **Theology** (Theology)

Institutes
Aesthetic Studies *('Carlos Arbelaez Camacho')* (Aesthetics) *Director*: Juan Luís Isaza; **Ageing** (Gerontology) *Director*: Carlos Alberto Cano Guitérrez; **Bioethics** *Director*: Alfonso Llano Escobar; **Development Policies** *(IPD) Director*: Alejandro Vivas Benítez; **Environmental and Rural Studies for Development** *(IDEADE) Director*: Francisco González; **Geophysics** (Geophysics) *Director*: Jorge Alonso Prieto Salazar; **Health Promotion** *Director*: Amelia Fernández Juan; **Housing and Urbanism** *(INJAVIU) Director*: Olga Lucia Ceballos Ramos; **Human Development** *Director*: Rosa Margerita Vargas; **Human Genetics** *Director*: Jaime Eduardo Bernal; **Human Rights and International Relations** *('Alfredo Vasquez Carrizosa') Director*: Augusto Ramirez Ocampo; **Inborn Errors** *Director*: Luis Alejandro Barrera; **Rural Studies** *(IER) Director*: Ricardo Dávila; **Social and Cultural Studies** *(PENSAR)* (Cultural Studies; Social Studies) *Director*: Guillermo Hoyos Vásquez

Further Information: Also Teaching Hospital

History: Founded 1623 as Academia Javeriana by the Society of Jesus. Became university 1704. Formally inaugurated as Pontifical University 1937.

Governing Bodies: Consejo de Regentes; Consejo Directivo

Academic Year: February to November (February-May; August-November)

Admission Requirements: Secondary school certificate (bachillerato), entrance examination and interview

Fees: (US Dollars): 3,500-6,000

Main Language(s) of Instruction: Spanish

International Co-operation: With universities in Argentina; Australia; Bolivia; Brazil; Canada; Republic of Korea; Chile; Costa Rica; Cuba; Ecuador; France; Germany; Guatemala; Honduras; Hungary; Israel; Italy; Japan; Mexico; Netherlands; Nicaragua; Norway; Panama; Peru; Poland; Portugal; Spain; Uruguay and Venezuela

Accrediting Agencies: Comité Nacional de Acreditación (CNA); Ministry of Education

Degrees and Diplomas: *Licenciatura*: Teaching Degree, 4 yrs; *Especialización*: 1-2 yrs; *Maestría (MA; MSc)*: 1-2 yrs; *Doctorado (PhD)*: 4-5 yrs. Also Professional Title, 5 yrs

Student Services: Academic counselling, Canteen, Cultural centre, Foreign student adviser, Health services, Language programs, Social counselling, Sports facilities

Special Facilities: Auditorium

Libraries: Central Library, Philosophy and Theology Library, 304,786 titles and 409,786 vols

Publications: Editorial Pontificia Universidad Javeriana; Revista Alternativa; Revista Cuadernos de Administración; Revista Cuadernos de Desarrollo Rural; Revista Cuadernos de Literatura; Revista Cuadernos de Música, Artes Visuales y Artes Escénicas; Revista Cuadrantephi; Revista Digitario; Revista Directo Bogotá; Revista Fractales; Revista Ingeniera y Universidad; Revista Interlenguajes; Revista Javeriana; Revista Memoria y Sociedad; Revista Nuevas Tecnologías de la Información; Revista Signo y Pensamiento *(biannually)*; Revista Theologica Javeriana; Revista Universitas Humanistica; Revista Universitas Médica *(biannually)*; Revista Universitas Psychologica; Revista Universitas Scientarum

Press or Publishing House: Javegraf. Centro Editorial Javeriano (CEJA)

Last Updated: 05/11/09

CALI BRANCH

SECCIONAL CALI

Apartado aéreo 26239, Calle 18 No.118-250 Av.Cañasgordas, Cali, Valle del Cauca
Tel: +57(2) 321-8365
Fax: +57(2) 555-2180
EMail: internacional@puj.edu.co
Website: http://www.puj.edu.co

Rector Seccional: Jorge Humberto Peláez Piedrahita

Faculties

Economics and Business Administration (Accountancy; Administration; Business Administration; Economics); **Engineering** (Civil Engineering; Computer Engineering; Electronic Engineering; Engineering; Industrial Engineering; Systems Analysis); **Health Sciences** (Medicine; Public Health); **Humanities and Social Sciences** (Arts and Humanities; Communication Studies; Family Studies; Government; Law; Modern Languages; Peace and Disarmament; Political Sciences; Psychology; Social Sciences)

Research Centres

International Affairs Observatory; **Process Automation** (Automation and Control Engineering)

Further Information: Special programme of Spanish as a Foreign Language

History: Founded 1970.

Governing Bodies: Consejo de Regentes; Consejo Directivo

Academic Year: February to November (February-May; August-November)

Admission Requirements: Secondary school certificate (bachillerato) and entrance examination

Fees: (US Dollars): 2,000-3,000

Main Language(s) of Instruction: Spanish

International Co-operation: With universities in USA; Spain; Canada; Austria; Mexico; Australia; France; Germany; Netherlands. Also participates in the Jesuit Universities Network in Latin America (28 universities in 14 Latin American countries, AUSJAL), CINDA, AIESEC and IAESTE programmes

Accrediting Agencies: Comité Nacional de Acreditación (CAN); Colombian Ministry of Education

Degrees and Diplomas: *Licenciatura*: Teaching Degree, 4 yrs; *Especialización*: 1-2 yrs; *Maestría (MA; MSc)*: 1-2 yrs; *Doctorado (PhD)*. Also Professional Title, 5 yrs

Student Services: Academic counselling, Canteen, Cultural centre, Foreign student adviser, Health services, Language programs, Social counselling, Sports facilities

Student Residential Facilities: Yes

Special Facilities: Auditorium

Libraries: Central Library, 46,297 vols; periodical subscriptions, 1,377; on-line subcriptions, 22,000

Publications: Del Lago al Samán, Informativo Electrónico; Periódico Estudiantil El Clavo; Revista Científica Epiciclos; Revista

Criterio Jurídico; Revista Economía, Gestión y Desarrollo; Revista Nuestro Compromiso Social; Revista Pensamiento Psicológico; Revista Perspectivas Internacionales; Revista Universitas Xaveriana; Sello Editorial Javeriano

POPAYÁN UNIVERSITY FOUNDATION
Fundación Universitaria de Popayán
Los Robles Km 8 vía al Sur, Popayán, Cauca
Tel: +57(282) 221-920
Fax: +57(282) 221-920
EMail: info@fup.edu.co
Website: http://www.fup.edu.co

Rector: Mario Alfredo Polo Castellanos EMail: rectoria@fup.edu.co

Secretario General: Orlando Teran Romero
EMail: secretariag@fup.edu.co

Programmes

Architecture (Architecture); **Business Administration** (Business Administration); **Ecology** (Ecology); **Economics**; **Industrial Engineering** (Industrial Engineering); **Psychology** (Psychology); **Systems Engineering** (Systems Analysis)

History: Founded 1980.

Main Language(s) of Instruction: Spanish

Degrees and Diplomas: *Licenciatura*; *Titulo Profesional*; *Especialización*

Last Updated: 03/11/09

PRIVATE UNIVERSITY
Universidad Libre
Calle 8 No. 5-80, Bogotá
Tel: +57(1) 382-1000
Fax: +57(1) 382-1073
Website: http://www.unilibre.edu.co

Rector: Nicolás Enrique Zuleta Hincapié
Tel: +57(1) 282-5843, Fax: +57(1) 243-8973
EMail: nzuleta_rectoria@unilibre.edu.co

Secretario General: Pablo Emilio Cruz Samboni
EMail: secgeneral@unilibre.edu.co

Faculties

Economics (Accountancy; Economics); **Education** (Arts and Humanities; Education; Mathematics; Modern Languages; Natural Sciences; Physical Education); **Engineering** (Engineering; Environmental Engineering; Industrial Engineering; Mechanical Engineering; Systems Analysis); **Law** (Administrative Law; Commercial Law; Constitutional Law; Criminal Law; Labour Law; Law; Public Law); **Philosophy** (Philosophy)

History: Founded 1913. Financed by the student fees.

Academic Year: February to December (February-June; July-December)

Admission Requirements: Secondary school certificate (bachillerato) and entrance examination

Main Language(s) of Instruction: Spanish

Degrees and Diplomas: *Licenciatura*: Accountancy (Contador público); Economics (Economista); Law (Abogado); Law and Social Sciences; Mathematics; Physics; Social Sciences; Surgery (Médico Cirujano), 5 yrs; *Licenciatura*: Biology; Chemistry; Languages, 4 yrs; *Titulo Profesional*: Environmental Engineering (Ingeniero Ambiental); Industrial Engineering (Ingeniero industrial); Mechanical Engineering (Ingeniero Mecánico); Systems Engineering (Ingeniero de Sistemas), 5 yrs; *Especialización*; *Maestría*

Libraries: 67,340 vols (in Bogotá)

Publications: Diálogo de Saberes, Revista
Last Updated: 01/02/07

BARRANQUILLA BRANCH

SECCIONAL BARRANQUILLA

Kilometro 7 Antigua Via a Puerto Colombia, Barranquilla, Atlántico
Tel: +57(958) 568-953
Fax: +57(958) 415-110
Website: http://www.unilibrebaq.edu.co

Rector Seccional: Carlos Tache Zambrano
EMail: ctache@unilibrebaq.edu.co

Faculties

Accountancy (Accountancy); **Health Sciences** (Medicine; Microbiology; Physical Therapy; Surgery); **Industrial Engineering** (Industrial Engineering); **Law** (Law; Social Sciences)

History: Founded 1956.

Main Language(s) of Instruction: Spanish

Degrees and Diplomas: *Título Profesional*; *Especialización*

CALI BRANCH

SECCIONAL CALI

Apartado aéreo 1040, Diagonal 37A No. 3-29, Cali, Valle del Cauca
Tel: +57(23) 524-0007
EMail: unilibre@unilibrecali.edu.co
Website: http://www.unilibrecali.edu.co/

Rector seccional: Jaime Guttiérrez Grisales

Faculties

Economics, Administration and Accountancy (Accountancy; Administration; Economics; Finance; International Business; Marketing); **Engineering** (Industrial Engineering; Systems Analysis); **Health Sciences** (Gynaecology and Obstetrics; Health Administration; Health Sciences; Medicine; Nursing; Occupational Health); **Law, Political Science and Social Sciences** (Administrative Law; Constitutional Law; Criminal Law; Labour Law; Law; Political Sciences; Psychology)

Programmes
Education

Main Language(s) of Instruction: Spanish

Degrees and Diplomas: *Licenciatura*; *Título Profesional*; *Especialización*; *Maestría*

CARTAGENA BRANCH

SECCIONAL CARTAGENA

Pie de la Popa Calle Real No. 20-177, Cartagena
Tel: +57(95) 658-2699
Fax: +57(95) 658-1115
Website: http://www.unilibre.edu.co/cue_cartagena.htm

Rector seccional: Rafael Ballestas Morales

Faculties

Accountancy; **Law and Political Science** (Administrative Law; Criminal Law; Law; Political Sciences)

CÚCUTA BRANCH

SECCIONAL CÚCUTA

Apartado aéreo 180, Avenida Canal Bogotá, Margen Izquierdo, Intersección Benjamín Herrera, Cúcuta, Norte de Santander
Tel: +57(97) 578-1033
Fax: +57(97) 578-1035
Website: http://www.unilibre.edu.co/cucuta.htm

Rector seccional: Luis Emiro Bueno Jaimes

Faculties

Economics, Administration and Accountancy (Accountancy; Administration; Economics); **Engineering** (Industrial Engineering) *Dean*: Rebeca Castellanos Carrillo; **Law** (Law) *Dean*: José Ramón Espinosa

Main Language(s) of Instruction: Spanish

Degrees and Diplomas: *Título Profesional*; *Especialización*

PEREIRA BRANCH

SECCIONAL PEREIRA

Calle 40 No 7-30, Pereira, Risaralda
Tel: +57(96) 329-3330
Fax: +57(96) 336-6024
Website: http://www.unilibrepereira.edu.co/portal

Rectora seccional: Gloria María Atehortúa Rada

Faculties

Economics, Accountancy and Commerce; **Engineering**; **Health Sciences**; **Law** (Law)

Main Language(s) of Instruction: Spanish

Degrees and Diplomas: *Título Profesional*; *Especialización*

SOCORRO BRANCH

SECCIONAL SOCORRO

Campus Universitario Majavita, Calle 16 No 14-08, Socorro, Santander
Tel: +57(97) 727-2639
Fax: +57(97) 727-6262
Website: http://www.unilibre.edu.co

Rectora seccional: Willman Amaya León

Faculties

Accountancy; **Business Administration** (Business Administration); **Education** (Education); **Engineering and Technology** (Engineering; Technology); **Law**

Degrees and Diplomas: *Título Profesional*; *Especialización*

RAFAEL NÚÑEZ UNIVERSITY CORPORATION
Corporación Universitaria Rafael Núñez
Apartado aéreo 1637, Calle Don Sancho No 36-70, Cartagena de Indias, Bolívar
Tel: +57(5) 664-1208
Fax: +57(5) 600-134
EMail: rafaelnunez@curn.edu.co
Website: http://www.curn.edu.co

Rector: Miguel Simón Henriquez Emiliani
EMail: miguelhenriquez@curn.edu.co

Faculties

Accountancy and Administration (Accountancy; Business Administration); **Engineering and Architecture** (Architecture; Systems Analysis); **Health Sciences** (Dentistry; Health Sciences; Medicine; Nursing; Parasitology; Surgery); **Human Sciences** (Law; Preschool Education; Special Education)

History: Founded 1984.

Main Language(s) of Instruction: Spanish

Degrees and Diplomas: *Licenciatura*; *Título Profesional*; *Especialización*

Last Updated: 30/10/09

REFORMED UNIVERSITY CORPORATION
Corporación Universitaria Reformada (CUR)
Carrera 46 No. 48-50, Barranquilla, Atlantico
Tel: +57(5) 349-0943
Fax: +57(5) 349-1955
EMail: sec-general@unireformada.edu.co
Website: http://www.unireformada.edu.co

Rector: James Harley Schutmaat Loew (2004-)
EMail: rector@unireformada.edu.co

Vice-Rector for Administration: Helis Barraza (2004-)

International Relations: Alice Winters, International Relations Officer (2004-)

Programmes

International Business; **Music** (Music; Music Education; Music Theory and Composition) *Director*: Federico Cadena; **Psychology** *Director*: Diana Amaya Jinete; **Theology** (Theology) *Director*: Milciades Púa Gomez

History: Founded 2001. Acquired present status 2003.

Governing Bodies: Consejo Académico; Consejo Administrativo; Consejo de Facultad

Admission Requirements: Diploma de Bachiller, National Examination for Higher Education Entrance (ICFES)

Main Language(s) of Instruction: Spanish

Degrees and Diplomas: *Título Profesional*: Psychology; Theology; Music; International Business, 5 yrs

Student Services: Academic counselling, Cultural centre, Employment services, Handicapped facilities, Health services

Special Facilities: Auditorium; Movie Studio

Libraries: Physical and Virtual Libraries

Publications: La Iguan *(weekly)*; Noticias Virtual Pag. Web *(weekly)*

Academic Staff 2007-2008	MEN	WOMEN	TOTAL
FULL-TIME	2	2	4
PART-TIME	20	9	29
Student Numbers 2007-2008			
All (Foreign Included)	49	56	105

Last Updated: 07/03/08

REGIONAL UNIVERSITY CORPORATION OF THE CARIBBEAN

Corporación Universitaria Regional del Caribe (IAFIC)
Apartado aéreo 4864, Pie Del Cerro, Avenida Pedro Heredia No. 18B-17, Cartagena de Indias, Bolívar
Tel: +57(5) 666-5832 +57(5) 666-4479
Fax: +57(5) 666-6470
EMail: admiafic@iafic.edu.co
Website: http://www.iafic.edu.co

Rectora: Katty Tinoco Tamara **EMail:** kattytinoco@hotmail.com

Programmes
Accountancy; **Agriculture** (Agriculture; Animal Husbandry); **Business Administration**; **Civil Engineering** (Civil Engineering; Environmental Management); **Dental Technology** (Dental Technology); **Electrical and Electronic Engineering**; **Electrical and Electronic Equipment and Maintenance** (Electrical and Electronic Equipment and Maintenance); **Fashion Design**; **Hotel Management** (Hotel Management); **International Business**; **Labour and Industrial Relations** (Labour and Industrial Relations); **Marketing** (Marketing); **Pedagogy**; **Physical Therapy**; **Preschool Education**; **Radio and Television Broadcasting** (Radio and Television Broadcasting); **Software Engineering** (Software Engineering); **Speech Therapy and Audiology**

History: Formerly known as Corporación de Educación Superior Instituto de Administración y Finanzas de Cartagena.

Degrees and Diplomas: *Técnico Profesional*; *Licenciatura*

REMINGTON UNIVERSITY CORPORATION

Corporación Universitaria Remington (UNIREMINGTON)
Ed. Coltabaco, Torre 1, Calle 51-27, Medellín, Antioquia
Tel: +57(4) 511-1000
EMail: info@remington.edu.co
Website: http://www.remington.edu.co

Rector: Jorge Mario Uribe Pardo **EMail:** rectoria@remington.edu.co

Centres
Language

Faculties
Accountancy; **Administration and Economics**; **Architecture**; **Business Management and Finance**; **Fine Arts**; **Law and Political Science**; **Social and Human Sciences**; **Social and Organizational Communication**; **Systems Engineering**

Schools
Health Sciences (Gerontology; Health Sciences; Medicine; Psychology)

History: Founded 1915. Acquired present status 1996.

Main Language(s) of Instruction: Spanish

Degrees and Diplomas: *Licenciatura*; *Especialización*
Last Updated: 30/10/09

REPUBLICAN UNIVERSITY CORPORATION

Corporación Universitaria Republicana
Carrera 7 No. 19-38, Bogotá
Tel: +57(1) 286-2384
Fax: +57(1) 342-2771
EMail: informes@urepublicana.edu.co
Website: http://www.urepublicana.edu.co

Rector: José Miguel Pinilla Malagón

Programmes
Accountancy (Accountancy); **Finance and International Trade** (Finance; International Business); **Industrial Engineering** (Industrial Engineering); **Law and Political Science** (Law; Political Sciences); **Social Work**

Degrees and Diplomas: *Licenciatura*; *Especialización*
Last Updated: 30/10/09

RESEARCH CENTRE ON TEACHING AND ADMINISTRATIVE CONSULTANCY

Centro de Investigación Docencia y Consultoria Administrativa (CIDCA)
Carrera 18 No. 38-19, Bogotá
Tel: +57(1) 337-0770 +57(91) 338-0772
Fax: +57(1) 338-1595
Website: http://www.cidca.edu.co

Rector: Alavaro Cano

Faculties
Economics and Administration; **Engineering** (Electrical Engineering; Electronic Engineering; Industrial Engineering; Mechanical Engineering); **Information and Communication Technology** (Information Technology)

Degrees and Diplomas: *Técnico Profesional*; *Tecnólogo*
Last Updated: 28/10/09

ROSARY UNIVERSITY

Universidad del Rosario
Calle 14 No. 6-25, Bogotá
Tel: +57(1) 297-0200 +57(1) 243-1716
Fax: +57(1) 281-8583
Website: http://www.urosario.edu.co

Rector: Hans Peter Knudsen Quevedo
Tel: +57(1) 297-0210, Fax: +57(1) 243-1716
EMail: crbermud@urosario.edu.co

Secretario General: Luis Enrique Nieto Arango
Tel: +57(1) 297-0213, Fax: +57(1) 341-0208
EMail: lnieto@claustro.urosario.edu.co

International Relations: Jeannette Vélez Ramirez
Tel: +57(1) 297-0279, Fax: +57(1) 341-9060
EMail: cancilleria@urosario.edu.co

Faculties
Administration (Administration; Business Administration; International Business); **Economics** (Economics; Finance; International Business); **Humanities** (Anthropology; History; Journalism; Philosophy; Social Sciences; Sociology); **International Relations**; **Law** (Law); **Political Science and Government** (Government; International Relations; Polish; Urban Studies); **Rehabilitation and Human Development** *Division Head*: Leonardo Palacios

Further Information: Also Teaching Hospital 'San José'

History: Founded 1653 by the Archbishop of Santafé on the model of the Fonseca's Colegio Mayor de Salamanca. Acquired present status 1658.

Governing Bodies: Conciliatory; College

Academic Year: February to December (February-June; July-December)

Admission Requirements: Secondary school certificate (bachillerato), or equivalent, entrance examination, State examination (ICFES), and interview

Fees: (US Dollars): 2,000-3,000 per semester

Main Language(s) of Instruction: Spanish

International Co-operation: Participates in the Intercampus programme

Accrediting Agencies: Consejo Nacional de Acreditación; EUA

Degrees and Diplomas: *Licenciatura*: 5-6 yrs; *Titulo Profesional*; *Especialización*: Business; Law; Economics, 1-1 1/2 yr; *Especialización*: Medicine, 1-4 yrs; *Maestría*: Economics; Law, a further 2 yrs; *Doctorado*

Student Services: Academic counselling, Canteen, Cultural centre, Employment services, Foreign student adviser, Foreign Studies Centre, Health services, Language programs, Social counselling, Sports facilities

Special Facilities: Historical Archives

Libraries: Library 'Antonio Rocha Alvira': 73,382 vols

Publications: Law Collection; Revista Colegio Mayor de Nuestra Señora del Rosario *(quarterly)*

Press or Publishing House: Ediciones Rosaristas
Last Updated: 13/11/09

SALAZAR AND HERRERA UNIVERSITY INSTITUTION
Institución Universitaria Salazar y Herrera
Carrera 70 No 52-49, Barrio los Colores, Medellín, Antioquia
Tel: +57(4) 430-1600
Fax: +57(4) 496-6201
EMail: admisiones@iush.edu.co
Website: http://www.iush.edu.co/

Rector: Gustavo Calle Giraldo

Secretario General: Hernán Rendón Valencia

Faculties
Administration; **Design and Communication** (Fashion Design; Graphic Design); **Engineering**

Degrees and Diplomas: *Titulo Profesional*

SAN ALFONSO UNIVERSITY FOUNDATION
Fundación Universitaria San Alfonso (FUSA)
Calle 37 No. 22-47, Bogotá
Tel: +57(91) 244-5053
Fax: +57(91) 268-3863
EMail: contacto@fusa.edu.co
Website: http://www.fusa.edu.co

Rector: Luis Antonio Rojas López **EMail:** fusa@etb.net.co

Programmes
Philosophy and Theology (Philosophy; Theology); **Psychology** (Psychology); **Social Communication** (Journalism); **Social Work** (Social Work); **Sport Management** (Sports Management); **Theology** (Theology)

Degrees and Diplomas: *Licenciatura*; *Especialización*
Last Updated: 03/11/09

SAN GIL UNIVERSITY FOUNDATION
Fundación Universitaria de San Gil (UNISANGIL)
Carrera 7 No. 14-34, San Gil, Santander
EMail: admisiones@mail.unisangil.edu.co
Website: http://www.unisangil.edu.co

Rector: Lucas Sarmiento Ardila
EMail: rectoria@mail.unisangil.edu.co

Vicerrector Administrativo: José Manuel Camacho Márquez
EMail: vadministrativa@mail.unisangil.edu.co

International Relations: María del Pilar Ortiz Corredor
EMail: dlenguas@mail.unisangil.edu.co

Faculties
Economics and Administration (Accountancy; Business Administration; Economics); **Education and Health Sciences**; **Engineering** (Agricultural Engineering; Environmental Engineering; Health Administration; Industrial Engineering; Systems Analysis); **Social Sciences and Humanities**

History: Founded 1988. Acquired present status 1991.

Governing Bodies: Consejo Superior; Consejo Académico

Admission Requirements: High school diploma

Main Language(s) of Instruction: Spanish

International Co-operation: With universities in Canada; Cuba; Spain

Degrees and Diplomas: *Tecnólogo*; *Licenciatura*; *Titulo Profesional*; *Especialización*

Student Services: Academic counselling, Canteen, Cultural centre, Health services, Language programs, Nursery care, Social counselling, Sports facilities

Student Residential Facilities: None

Special Facilities: Auditorium

Libraries: Yes

Publications: Al Derecho y al Revés *(biennially)*; Unisangil La Revista *(biennially)*
Last Updated: 03/11/09

SAN MARTÍN UNIVERSITY FOUNDATION
Fundación Universitaria San Martín (FUSM)
Carrera 19 # 80-63, Bogotá
Tel: +57(1) 255-5919
Fax: +57(1) 235-8356
EMail: webmaster@sanmartin.edu.co
Website: http://www.sanmartin.edu.co

Rector: Jaime Villamizar Lamus

Secretario General: Jaime Eduardo Mendoza

Faculties
Accountancy (Accountancy); **Advertising and Marketing** (Advertising and Publicity; Marketing); **Business Administration** (Business Administration); **Dentistry** (Dentistry); **Engineering** (Engineering); **Finance and International Studies** (Finance; International Studies); **Law**; **Medicine** (Medicine); **Open and Distance Education**; **Optometry** (Optometry); **Psychology** (Psychology); **Veterinary Science and Zootechnology** (Veterinary Science; Zoology)

History: Founded 1980.

Main Language(s) of Instruction: Spanish

Degrees and Diplomas: *Licenciatura*; *Titulo Profesional*; *Especialización*; *Maestría*; *Doctorado*; *Postdoctorado*
Last Updated: 04/11/09

SANITAS UNIVERSITY FOUNDATION
Fundación Universitaria Sanitas (UNISANITAS)
Avenida Carrera 7 No. 173 - 64, Bogotá
Tel: +57(1) 646-6060
EMail: unisanitas@unisanitas.edu.co
Website: http://www.unisanitas.edu.co/

Rector: Álvaro Caro Mendoza (2005-) **EMail:** aco@colsanitas.com

Vicerrector: Hernando Altahona
Tel: +57(1) 222-1500, Fax: +57(1) 222-1500
EMail: haltahon@unisanitas.edu.co

International Relations: Gustavo Quintero, Director, Education Unit EMail: gaquintero@unisanitas.edu.co

Faculties
Business Administration (Business Administration); **Medicine** (Medicine) *Head*: Juan de Francico; **Nursing** (Nursing); **Psychology** (Psychology)

History: Founded 2001.

Governing Bodies: Consejo Directivo; Rector; Consejo Académico

Academic Year: January to December (January-June; July-December)

Admission Requirements: National Examinstion Score (ICFES) and Interview

Fees: (Pesos): Medicine, 7.9m. per semester; Nursing, 2.9m. per semester

Main Language(s) of Instruction: Spanish

International Co-operation: With Universities in Spain (Universidad de Salamanca, Universidad Castilla La Mancha)

Accrediting Agencies: Ministry of Education

Degrees and Diplomas: *Titulo Profesional*: 5-7 yrs

Student Services: Academic counselling, Canteen, Cultural centre, Employment services, Handicapped facilities, Health services, Language programs, Nursery care, Social counselling, Sports facilities

Special Facilities: Skill Centre (the Multifunctional Advanced Complex for Practices and Simulation - CMAPS)

Libraries: 1 main Library specialised in Problem Based Learning (PBL). Books journals and specific information on Health Sciences. Also Information Centre for Information and Documentation

Press or Publishing House: Editorial Bienestar

Academic Staff 2007-2008	MEN	WOMEN	TOTAL
FULL-TIME	10	28	38
STAFF WITH DOCTORATE FULL-TIME	3	3	6
Student Numbers 2007-2008			
All (Foreign Included)	140	350	490

Distance students, 1,500.
Last Updated: 04/11/09

SANTO TOMÁS UNIVERSITY
Universidad Santo Tomás (USTA)
Carrera 9 No. 51, Bogotá
Tel: +57(1) 313-8360
Fax: +57(1) 217-7749
EMail: usantotomas@correo.usta.edu.co
Website: http://www.usta.edu.co

Rector: José Antonio Balaguera Cepeda, O.P. (2003-)
Tel: +57(1) 310-0387, Fax: +57(1) 574-0383
EMail: rector@usta.edu.co

Secretario General: Alberto Cárdena Patiño
Tel: +57(1) 574-0410, Fax: +57(1) 574-0370
EMail: acardepa@usta.edu.co

International Relations: Orlando Rueda Acevedo, O.P.
Tel: +57(1) 348-3815, Fax: +57(1) 574-0383
EMail: viceacad@usta.edu.co

Programmes
Accountancy (Accountancy); **Civil Engineering** (Civil Engineering); **Economics** (Economics); **Economics and Business Administration** (Administration; Economics); **Electronic Engineering** (Electronic Engineering); **Environmental Engineering; International Business** (International Business); **Law** (Law; Political Sciences); **Mechanical Engineering** (Mechanical Engineering); **Philosophy** (Arts and Humanities; Philosophy; Spanish); **Physical Education, Sports and Recreation; Psychology** (Psychology); **Social Communication** (Communication Studies); **Sociology** (Sociology); **Statistics** (Statistics); **Telecommunications Engineering**

Further Information: Branches in Bucaramanga, Medellin, Tunja and Villavicencio

History: Founded 1580 by Pope Gregorio XIII. Closed 1861 by General Tomás Cipriano de Mosquera. Re-established 1965 and approved by government decree 1966.

Governing Bodies: Consejo de Fundadores; Consejo Superior; Consejo Académico

Academic Year: February to December (February-June; August-December)

Admission Requirements: Secondary school certificate (bachillerato) and entrance examination

Main Language(s) of Instruction: Spanish

Degrees and Diplomas: *Licenciatura:* Accountancy; Architecture; Dentistry; Economics; Electronics; Law; Psychology, 5 yrs; *Licenciatura:* Philosophy; Sociology, 4 yrs; *Titulo Profesional:* Civil Engineering, 5 yrs; *Especialización; Maestría:* Accountancy; Clinical Psychology; Economics and Administration; Latin American Philosophy; Teaching

Student Services: Employment services, Foreign Studies Centre, Health services, Language programs, Nursery care, Sports facilities

Libraries: Central Library, c. 70,000 vols; Bucaramanga, c. 50,000 vols

Publications: Cuaderno de Filosofía; Cuaderno de Sociología; IUSTA, Law Review; Módulos; Revista Análisis; Revista Económica 'Veritatem'

Press or Publishing House: University Press

SCHOOL OF ADMINISTRATION AND MARKETING
Escuela de Administración y Mercadotecnía del Quindio
Carrera 14 No. 3-11, Avenida Bolívar, Armenia, Quindio
Tel: +57(967) 451-101
Fax: +57(967) 465-101
EMail: quindioeam@eam.edu.co
Website: http://www.eam.edu.co

Rector: Francisco Jairo Ramírez Concha

Faculties
Basic Sciences and Engineering (Computer Science; Interior Design; Natural Sciences; Systems Analysis); **Communication and Design** (Advertising and Publicity; Marketing); **Finance and Administration** (Administration; Advertising and Publicity; Business Administration; Hotel Management; International Business; Marketing; Tourism)

Degrees and Diplomas: *Titulo Profesional*

SCHOOL OF BUSINESS STUDIES
Escuela Superior de Ciencias Empresariales
Calle 29 No. 16A-35, Bogotá
Tel: +57(1) 232-3822 +57(1) 232-3825
Fax: +57(1) 323-6685
EMail: escuelasuperior@inteseg.edu.co
Website: http://www.inteseg.edu.co

Rectora: Andrea Milena Silva Cardona
EMail: amsilvac@inteseg.edu.co

Programmes
Environmental Management (Environmental Management); **Human Resources** (Human Resources); **Industrial Hygiene and Security; Insurance** (Insurance); **Security and Prevention of Professional Risks** (Safety Engineering)

History: Founded 1988.

Main Language(s) of Instruction: Spanish

Degrees and Diplomas: *Tecnólogo; Especialización*
Last Updated: 28/10/09

SCHOOL OF ENGINEERING OF ANTIOQUIA
Escuela de Ingeniería de Antioquia (EIA)
Calle 25 Sur No. 42-73, Envigado, Antioquia
Tel: +57(4) 339-3200
Fax: +57(4) 331-7851
EMail: administrador@eia.edu.co
Website: http://www.eia.edu.co

Rector: Carlos Felipe Londoño Alvarez EMail: calon@eia.edu.co

Secretaria general: Olga Lucía Ocampo

International Relations: Luz María Gómez
EMail: relinter@eia.edu.co

Programmes
Administration (Administration); **Biology** (Biology); **Biomedical Engineering; Civil Engineering** (Civil Engineering); **Computer Engineering; Electrical and Electronic Engineering** (Electrical and Electronic Engineering; Mechanical Engineering); **Environmental Engineering; Industrial Engineering**

History: Founded 1978.

Admission Requirements: Bachillerato and ICFES examination

Main Language(s) of Instruction: Spanish

International Co-operation: With universities in Spain; France; Mexico; Germany

Degrees and Diplomas: *Titulo Profesional; Especialización:* 1 1/2 yrs

Student Services: Academic counselling, Canteen, Social counselling, Sports facilities

Libraries: Alberto Quevedo Díaz Library
Publications: Revista EIA *(biennially)*
Last Updated: 30/10/09

SCHOOL OF OPHTHALMOLOGY, BARRAQUER INSTITUTE OF AMERICA

Escuela Superior de Oftalmología, Instituto Barraquer de América
Avenida 100 No. 18A-51, Bogotá
Tel: +57(1) 644-9555
Fax: +57(1) 644-9556
EMail: citas@barraquer.com.co
Website: http://www.barraquer.com.co

Rectora: María Eugenia Salazar De Pieschacón

Programmes
Ophthalmology (Ophthalmology)

Degrees and Diplomas: *Especialización*

SERGIO ARBOLEDA UNIVERSITY

Universidad Sergio Arboleda
Calle 74 No. 14-14, Bogotá
Tel: +57(1) 540-0300
Fax: +57(1) 347-1059
EMail: info@usa.edu.co
Website: http://www.usergioarboleda.edu.co

Rector: Rodrigo Noguera Calderón
EMail: rodrigo.noguera@usa.edu.co

Secretario General: Mario Grosclaude Rojas

Vicerrector Administrativo: Jorge Noguera

Programmes
Music (Music)

Schools
Business Studies (Accountancy; Business Administration; Finance); **Communication and Journalism** (Communication Studies; Journalism) *Dean*: Diana Sofía Giraldo de Melo; **Engineering** (Electronic Engineering; Industrial Engineering; Systems Analysis; Telecommunications Engineering); **Law** (Human Rights; Law; Private Law; Public Law); **Marketing and International Trade**; **Mathematics**; **Philosophy and Humanities** (Arts and Humanities; Philosophy); **Political Science and International Relations**

Further Information: Also branch in Santa Marta

Main Language(s) of Instruction: Spanish

Degrees and Diplomas: *Licenciatura*; *Título Profesional*; *Especialización*; *Maestría*

Libraries: Biblioteca 'Álvaro Gómez Hurtado'
Last Updated: 19/11/09

SIMÓN BOLÍVAR UNIVERSITY

Universidad Simón Bolívar
Apartado aéreo 50595, Carrera 59 N° 59-92, Barranquilla, Atlántico
Tel: +57(5) 368-7759
Fax: +57(5) 368-2892
EMail: webmaster@unisimonbolivar.edu.co
Website: http://www.unisimonbolivar.edu.co

Rector: José Eusebio Consuegra Bolivar
EMail: rectoria@unisimonbolivar.edu.co

Secretario General: Rafael Bolaño Tel: +57(58) 344-4333

International Relations: Sonia Andrea Falla Barrontes
Tel: +57(58) 368-0593, Fax: +57(58) 368-0593
EMail: soniafalla@hotmail.com

Faculties
Basic Education (Education); **Business Administration** *Dean*: Pedro Chiquillo; **Commercial Engineering** *Dean*: Claudia Mora; **Economics** (Economics) *Dean*: Eugenio Bolívar; **Engineering** *Dean*: Fernando Cárdenas; **Industrial Engineering** *Dean*: Claudia Mora; **Law** (Law) *Dean*: Porfirio Bayuelo; **Nursing** *Dean*: Mildred Carroll; **Physiotherapy** *Dean*: Stella Crissien; **Psychology** *Dean*: Luisa Osorio; **Public Accountancy** *Dean*: Pedro Chiquillo; **Social Studies** (Social Studies) *Dean*: Aquiles Escalante; **Social Work**

(Anthropology; Social and Community Services; Social Welfare; Social Work) *Dean*: Ligia Camacho

History: Founded 1972. Formerly known as Corporación Educativa Mayor del Desarrollo Simón Bolívar.

Governing Bodies: Consejo de Gobierno

Academic Year: January to December (January-June; August-December)

Admission Requirements: Secondary school certificate (bachillerato) and entrance examination

Fees: (US Dollars): 600 to 964 per semester

Main Language(s) of Instruction: Spanish

Degrees and Diplomas: *Licenciatura*: Economics, 4-5 yrs; *Licenciatura*: Social Sciences, 4 1/2 yrs; *Licenciatura*: Social Work, 4 yrs; *Licenciatura*: Sociology, 5 yrs; *Especialización*; *Doctorado*: Law, 5 yrs

Student Services: Cultural centre, Health services, Social counselling

Special Facilities: Colombian Bibliographical Museum; Bolivariano Museum; Archaeology Museum

Libraries: 42,481 vols

Publications: Desarrollo Indoamericano *(quarterly)*; Educación y Humanismo *(biannually)*; Encuentro Bolivariano *(biannually)*; Gestión Bolivariána *(biannually)*; Justicia *(biannually)*; Perspectiva Social *(biannually)*; Psicogente *(biannually)*; Salud en Movimiento *(biannually)*

TECHNOLOGICAL CORPORATION OF BOGOTA

Corporación Tecnológica de Bogotá
Apartado aéreo 5189, Carrera 21 No. 54-79, Bogotá
Tel: +57(1) 348-3061
Fax: +57(1) 312-5720
Website: http://www.ctb.edu.co

Rector: Hernán Mauricio Chaves Ardila

Programmes
Chemical Engineering; **Computer Engineering**; **Food Technology**; **Industrial Chemistry** (Industrial Chemistry); **Pharmacy** (Pharmacy); **Physical Chemistry** (Physical Chemistry); **Polymer and Plastics Technology** (Polymer and Plastics Technology); **Telecommunications Engineering**

Degrees and Diplomas: *Tecnólogo*; *Especialización*
Last Updated: 09/08/07

TECHNOLOGICAL UNIVERSITY OF BOLIVAR

Universidad Tecnológica de Bolívar (UTB)
Campus de Ternera, Km 1 vía Turbaco, Cartagena de Indias, Bolívar
Tel: +57(5) 653-5200
Fax: +57(5) 661-9240
Website: http://www.unitecnologica.edu.co

Rectora: Patricia del Pilar Martínez Barrios
Tel: +57(5) 653-5201 EMail: rectora@unitecnologica.edu.co

Secretaria General: Rosario García Gonzalez
Tel: +57(5) 653-5211 EMail: rgarcia@unitecnologica.edu.co

International Relations: María Fernanda Morales
Tel: +57(5) 653-5351 EMail: mmorales@unitecnologica.edu.co

Faculties
Basic Sciences (Natural Sciences); **Economics and Administration** (Accountancy; Administration; Business Administration; Business and Commerce; Economics; Finance; International Business); **Engineering** (Computer Engineering; Construction Engineering; Electrical Engineering; Electronic Engineering; Environmental Engineering; Industrial Engineering; Mechanical Engineering); **Social and Human Sciences** (Communication Studies; Political Sciences; Psychology; Social Sciences)

History: Founded 1970. Acquired present status 2003.

Governing Bodies: Asamblea General; Consejo Superior

Academic Year: January to November (January-May; June- July; August-November)

Admission Requirements: State examination (ICFES test) and interview

Fees: (Pesos) 1.8m.-2.3m. per semester

Main Language(s) of Instruction: Spanish

International Co-operation: With universities in Mexico; Canada; Chile; Spain; Panama; Argentina and Germany

Accrediting Agencies: Instituto Colombiano para el Fomento de la Educación Superior (ICFES)

Degrees and Diplomas: *Licenciatura*: 5 yrs; *Especialización*: 1 1/2 yrs; *Maestría*: 2 yrs

Student Services: Academic counselling, Employment services, Foreign student adviser, Language programs, Social counselling, Sports facilities

Student Residential Facilities: None

Special Facilities: Two auditoriums

Libraries: Two libraries

Publications: Contraste *(bimonthly)*; Economía y Región *(annually)*; Investigación & Desarrollo *(annually)*

Last Updated: 20/11/09

UNIFIED NATIONAL CORPORATION OF HIGHER EDUCATION

Corporación Unificada Nacional de Educación Superior (CUN)

Calle 13 No. 4- 69, Bogotá
Tel: +57(1) 562-8413
Fax: +57(1) 334-3884
EMail: contactenos@cun.edu.c
Website: http://www.cun.edu.co

Rectora: Victoria Eugenia Chávez Montagno
EMail: alvarosanchez@cun.edu.co

Programmes

Accountancy (Accountancy); **Agricultural Management** (Agricultural Management); **Business Administration** (Business Administration); **Computer Engineering** (Computer Engineering); **Electronic Engineering** (Electronic Engineering); **Fashion Design** (Fashion Design); **Finance** (Finance); **Graphic Design** (Graphic Design); **Health Administration** (Health Administration); **Hotel Management** (Hotel Management); **International Business** (International Business); **Public Administration** (Public Administration); **Public Relations** (Public Relations); **Textile Design** (Textile Design); **Tourism** (Tourism)

History: Founded 1983.

Main Language(s) of Instruction: Spanish

Degrees and Diplomas: *Técnico Profesional*; *Titulo Profesional*
Last Updated: 29/10/09

UNITEC UNIVERSITY CORPORATION

Corporación universitaria UNITEC

Calle 76 No. 12-58, Bogotá
Tel: +57(1) 212-9321
Fax: +57(1) 235-1541
EMail: fparra@unitec.edu.co
Website: http://www.unitec.edu.co

Rector: Carlos Fernando Parra Ferro

Secretario General: Gonzalo Murcia Rios
Tel: +57(1) 248-5789 EMail: gmurcia@unitec.edu.co

International Relations: Alcides Muñoz Medina
Tel: +57(1) 248-5789 EMail: almunoz@unitec.edu.co

Areas
English (English)

Schools
Arts and Communication (Advertising and Publicity; Cinema and Television; Graphic Design); **Economics and Administration** (Advertising and Publicity; Business Administration; Finance; Hotel Management; International Business; Marketing; Tourism); **Engineering** (Systems Analysis; Telecommunications Engineering)

Degrees and Diplomas: *Tecnólogo*; *Especialización*
Last Updated: 30/10/09

UNIVERSITY CENTRE OF RURAL WELFARE

Centro Universitario de Bienestar Rural (CUBR)

Apartado aéreo 26170, Puerto Tejada, Cauca
Tel: +57(2) 550-4142
Fax: +57(2) 550-4519
EMail: cubr@cubr.edu.co
Website: http://www.cubr.edu.co

Rector: Taraneh Rezvani Derakhshan EMail: rectoria@cubr.edu.co

Secretaria Académica: Gloria Mina
EMail: secretariacademica@cubr.edu.co

Programmes

Administration of Local Economies (Administration; Economics); **Education and Social Development** *(Postgraduate)* (Development Studies; Education; Social Sciences) *Head*: Roberto Carlos Nahuel; **Rural Studies** (Rural Studies) *Dean*: Carmen Eugenia Pedraza R.

History: Founded 1988.

Academic Year: January to November (January-June; July-November)

Main Language(s) of Instruction: Spanish

Degrees and Diplomas: *Técnico Profesional*: 2 yrs; *Especialización*: 1 1/2 yrs

Student Services: Employment services, Health services, Social counselling, Sports facilities

Special Facilities: Laboratory

Academic Staff 2007-2008	MEN	WOMEN	TOTAL
FULL-TIME	4	10	14
PART-TIME	2	2	4
STAFF WITH DOCTORATE			
FULL-TIME	–	1	1
Student Numbers 2007-2008			
All (Foreign Included)	45	84	129

Last Updated: 28/10/09

UNIVERSITY CORPORATION OF BUSINESS STUDIES, EDUCATION AND HEALTH

Corporación Universitaria de Ciencias Empresariales, Educación y Salud (CORSALUD)

Carrera 53 No. 55-257, Barranquilla, Atlántico
Tel: +57(5) 349-2619 +57(5) 368-2896
Fax: +57(5) 368-2895
EMail: direccion@corsalud.edu.co
Website: http://www.corsalud.edu.co/

Rectora: Lucía Patricia Sánchez Majana

Programmes

Business Administration (Business Administration); **Civil Engineering** (Civil Engineering); **Dental Technology** (Dental Technology); **Food Technology** (Food Technology); **Marketing** (Marketing); **Medical Technology** (Medical Technology); **Occupational Health** (Occupational Health); **Optometry** (Optometry); **Radiology** (Radiology)

Degrees and Diplomas: *Técnico Profesional*; *Licenciatura*
Last Updated: 30/08/07

UNIVERSITY CORPORATION OF RESEARCH AND DEVELOPMENT

Corporación Universitaria de Investigación y Desarrollo UDI

Calle 9 #23-55, Barrio la Universidad, Bucaramanga, Santander
Tel: +57(7) 632-8811 +57(7) 635-2525
Fax: +57(7) 634-5775
EMail: webmaster@udi.edu.co
Website: http://www.udi.edu.co

Rector: Jairo Castro Castro EMail: rector@udi.edu.co

Vicerrector Administrativo: Julio Enrique Anaya Rincón
EMail: vice.administrativa@udi.edu.co

Programmes

Business Administration (Business Administration); **Business Engineering**; **Distance and Continuing Education**; **Electronic**

Engineering (Electronic Engineering); **Graphic Design** (Graphic Design); **Industrial Engineering** (Industrial Engineering); **Metrology** (Measurement and Precision Engineering); **Multimedia**; **Systems Engineering** (Computer Engineering)

History: Founded 1982 as Centro Superior de Sistemas - CENTROSISTEMAS. Acquired present status and title 2003.

Degrees and Diplomas: *Tecnólogo*; *Titulo Profesional*; *Especialización*

Last Updated: 29/10/09

UNIVERSITY CORPORATION OF SANTA ROSA DE CABAL

Corporación Universitaria de Santa Rosa de Cabal (UNISARC)

Apartado aéreo 1371, Km 4 vía Santa Rosa de Cabal - Chinchina, Vereda el Jazmín, Santa Rosa de Cabal, Risaralda
Tel: +57(63) 633-548
Fax: +57(63) 633-700
EMail: unisarc@unisarc.edu.co
Website: http://www.unisarc.edu.co

Rectora: Elizabeth Villamil Castañeda
Tel: +57(63) 633-634 EMail: rectoria@unisarc.edu.co

Secretario General: Carlos Eduardo Castro García
EMail: secgeneral@unisarc.edu.co

International Relations: Isabel Cristina Muñoz Alzate
EMail: viceadministrativa@unisarc.edu.co

Faculties

Administration and Rural Development (Agricultural Business; Agricultural Management; Animal Husbandry; Heritage Preservation; Rural Planning; Tourism; Tropical Agriculture); **Agronomy**; **Basic Sciences**

History: Founded 1982.

Governing Bodies: General Assembly; Higher Council; Academic Council

Admission Requirements: High school certificate

Main Language(s) of Instruction: Spanish

Degrees and Diplomas: *Tecnólogo*: 3 yrs; *Licenciatura*: 5 yrs; *Especialización*: 2 yrs

Student Services: Academic counselling, Cultural centre, Handicapped facilities, Health services, Language programs, Nursery care, Social counselling, Sports facilities

Last Updated: 29/10/09

UNIVERSITY CORPORATION OF SCIENCE AND DEVELOPMENT

Corporación Universitaria de Ciencia y Desarrollo (UNICIENCIA)

Calle 74 No 15-73, Bogotá
Tel: +57(1) 322-0055
Fax: +57(1) 317-0988
EMail: uniciencia@uniciencia.edu.co
Website: http://www.uniciencia.edu.co

Rectora: María Gladys Galindo Lugo
EMail: rectoriabogota@uniciencia.edu.co

Faculties

Arts; **Economics and Administration** (Accountancy; Business Administration; Economics); **Engineering** (Biomedical Engineering; Computer Engineering; Environmental Engineering); **Law** (Law)

Further Information: Also branches in Cali, Medellín, Monteria, Sabaneta and Restrepo

History: Founded 1993. Acquired present status 1996.

Main Language(s) of Instruction: Spanish

Degrees and Diplomas: *Titulo Profesional*
Last Updated: 29/10/09

UNIVERSITY CORPORATION OF THE CARIBBEAN

Corporación Universitaria del Caribe (CECAR)

Apartado aéreo 248, Carretera Troncal Occidente Via Corozal, Sincelejo, Sucre
Tel: +57(5) 280-1060
Fax: +57(5) 280-1554
EMail: jorge.ganem@cecar.edu.co
Website: http://www.cecar.edu.co

Rector: Jorge Ganem Robles

Faculties

Administration and Economics; **Architecture** (Architecture); **Education** (Art Education; Computer Science; Education; English; Environmental Studies; Natural Sciences; Spanish; Technology); **Engineering** (Engineering; Industrial Engineering); **Health Sciences** (Health Sciences); **Humanities** (Arts and Humanities; Psychology; Social Work; Sports); **Law and Social Sciences** (Law)

Main Language(s) of Instruction: Spanish

Degrees and Diplomas: *Licenciatura*; *Titulo Profesional*; *Especialización*

Last Updated: 29/10/09

UNIVERSITY CORPORATION OF THE COAST

Corporación Universitaria de la Costa (CUC)

Calle 58 No. 55-66, Barranquilla, Atlántico
Tel: +57(5) 511-974
Fax: +57(5) 417-678
EMail: info@cuc.edu.co
Website: http://www.cuc.edu.co

Rector: Tito José Crissien Borrero

Faculties

Architecture (Architecture); **Business Administration** (Business Administration); **Engineering** (Civil Engineering; Electrical Engineering; Electronic Engineering; Environmental Engineering; Industrial Engineering; Systems Analysis); **Law** (Law); **Psychology** (Psychology)

History: Founded 1969. A private institution.

Admission Requirements: Secondary school certificate (bachillerato) and entrance examination

Main Language(s) of Instruction: Spanish

Degrees and Diplomas: *Titulo Profesional*; *Especialización*

Libraries: c. 15,000 vols
Last Updated: 29/10/09

UNIVERSITY CORPORATION OF THE REGION OF HUILA

Corporación Universitaria del Huila (CORHUILA)

Calle 21 No. 6-01, Neiva, Huila
Tel: +57(988) 753-046
Fax: +57(988) 754-289
EMail: corhuila@corhuila.edu.co
Website: http://www.corhuila.edu.co

Rector: Virgilio Barrera Castro
Tel: +57(988) 753-852, Fax: +57(988) 754-289
EMail: rectoria@corhuila.edu.co

Vicerrector: Robinson Casallas Montealegre
Tel: +57(988) 753-046, Fax: +57(988) 754-289

Faculties

Economics and Administration (Advertising and Publicity; Banking; Business Administration; Finance; Marketing; Sales Techniques); **Engineering** (Environmental Engineering; Industrial Engineering; Systems Analysis); **Veterinary Science**

History: Founded 1989.

Governing Bodies: Consejo Superior; Rector; Consejo Académico

Fees: (US Dollars): 46,000 per annum

Main Language(s) of Instruction: Spanish

Accrediting Agencies: Ministerio de Educación Nacional

Degrees and Diplomas: *Titulo Profesional*: 10 sem.

Student Services: Academic counselling, Canteen, Cultural centre, Handicapped facilities, Health services, Nursery care, Sports facilities

Student Residential Facilities: None

Special Facilities: None

Libraries: Yes

Publications: Nueva Clase, Radial publication *(biennially)*; Nueva Clase, Periodical publication *(biennially)*

Academic Staff *2007-2008*	MEN	WOMEN	TOTAL
FULL-TIME	7	3	**10**
PART-TIME	176	60	**236**
STAFF WITH DOCTORATE			
FULL-TIME	2	1	**3**

Student Numbers *2007-2008*			
All (Foreign Included)	1,245	1,399	**2,644**

Evening students, 1,019.
Last Updated: 29/10/09

UNIVERSITY CORPORATION OF THE REGION OF META

Corporación Universitaria del Meta (UNIMETA)
Apartado aéreo 3244, Carrera 32 No. 34B-26, Barrio San Fernando, Villavicencio, Meta
Tel: +57(8) 21825
Fax: +57(8) 21827
EMail: unimeta@coll1.telecom.com.co
Website: http://www.unimeta.edu.co

Rector: Rafael Mojica García EMail: rectoria@unimeta.edu.co

Secretaria General: Jenny Andrea Capote Avendaño

International Relations: Rafael Mojica García
EMail: Rectoria@unimeta.edu.co

Faculties
Accountancy (Accountancy; Economics; Finance) *Dean*: María del Carmen Ruíz Sánchez; **Agro-industrial Engineering** (Agricultural Engineering; Computer Science) *Dean*: Manuel González Vacca; **Architecture** (Architecture; Design) *Dean*: Elio Augusto Ramirez Saavedra; **Business Administration** (Accountancy; Agricultural Management; Business Administration; Economics; Finance; Marketing) *Dean*: Guillermo Ariel Villa Mesa; **Civil Engineering** (Civil Engineering; Computer Science; Irrigation; Road Engineering; Soil Science) *Dean*: Yesid Alexander Munar Saavedra; **Economics** (Accountancy; Administration; Economics; Finance) *Dean*: Edilberto Santos Grimaldos; **Electronic Engineering** (Computer Science; Electronic Engineering) *Dean*: César Romero Molano; **Industrial Engineering** (Computer Science; Industrial Engineering) *Dean*: Nancy Esperanza Saray Muñoz; **Law** (Law) *Dean*: Héctor Aguirre Castillo; **Marketing and Publicity** (Accountancy; Advertising and Publicity; Communication Studies; Economics; Finance; Marketing; Psychology) *Dean*: María Deicy Avila Molina; **Social Communication and Journalism** (Communication Studies; Journalism; Theatre) *Dean*: Juan Carlos May Caro; **Systems Engineering** (Systems Analysis) *Dean*: Francine Herrera Cubides; **Tourism and Hotel Management** (Hotel Management; Tourism) *Dean*: Edilberto Santos Grimaldos

History: Founded 1982. Acquired present status 1985.

Governing Bodies: Consejo Superior

Admission Requirements: Secondary school certificate and Prueba del ICFES

Fees: (Pesos): 1,285,000-1,705,000

Main Language(s) of Instruction: Spanish

International Co-operation: With universities in Spain; Mexico; Cuba; Chile; Japan; Thailand; USA

Accrediting Agencies: ICFES; Consejo Nacional de Acreditación (CNA)

Degrees and Diplomas: *Licenciatura*: Business Administration; Accountancy; Marketing and Advertising; Economics; Tourism and Hotel Management; Systems Engineering; Industrial Engineering; Agro-industrial Engineering; Civil Engineering; Electronic Engineering; Social Communication; Law, 5 yrs; *Especialización*

Student Services: Academic counselling, Canteen, Cultural centre, Employment services, Health services, Language programs, Sports facilities

Student Residential Facilities: No

Special Facilities: Museum

Libraries: Biblioteca "Juan Nepomuceno Mojica Angarita"

Publications: Revista Cientifica *(annually)*

Press or Publishing House: Meta Universitaria
Last Updated: 30/10/09

UNIVERSITY FOUNDATION OF ESPINAL

Fundación Universitaria del Espinal
Calle 10 No. 6-67, Espinal, Tolima
Tel: +57(982) 248-3621
Fax: +57(982) 248-5443
EMail: fundes@fundes.edu.co
Website: http://www.fundes.edu.co

Rector: Etilio Aldana Lozano EMail: rectoria@fundes.edu.co

Faculties
Administration (Accountancy; Administration); **Education**

Programmes
Psychology (Psychology)

History: Founded 1997. Acquired present status 2004.

Main Language(s) of Instruction: Spanish

Degrees and Diplomas: *Licenciatura*; *Especialización*
Last Updated: 03/11/09

UNIVERSITY FOUNDATION OF HEALTH SCIENCES

Fundación Universitaria de Ciencias de la Salud
Calle 10 No.8-95, Hospital San José, Bogotá
Tel: +57(1) 599-8977
Website: http://www.fucsalud.edu.co

Rector: Roberto Jaramillo Uricoechea
EMail: rectoria@fucsalud.edu.co

Vicerrector: Esteban Díaz Granados

Faculties
Citohistology (Histology); **Medicine** (Anaesthesiology; Cardiology; Gastroenterology; Gynaecology and Obstetrics; Haematology; Medicine; Surgery); **Nursing** (Neurology; Nursing); **Surgical Instruments** (Instrument Making; Surgery)

History: Founded 1976.

Governing Bodies: Consejo Superior

Main Language(s) of Instruction: Spanish

Degrees and Diplomas: *Titulo Profesional*; *Especialización*
Last Updated: 03/11/09

UNIVERSITY FOUNDATION OF THE ANDEAN REGION

Fundación Universitaria del Area Andina
Apartado aéreo 50814, Calle 71 No. 13-21, Bogotá
Tel: +57(1) 543-0592
Fax: +57(1) 211-5477
EMail: areandina@areandina.edu.co
Website: http://www.areandina.edu.co

Rector: Fernando Laverde Morales

Faculties
Administration; **Engineering**; **Fine Arts** (Fashion Design; Fine Arts; Textile Design; Textile Technology); **Health Sciences**

Further Information: Also branches in Pereira, Ibague, Pasto and Valledupar

Main Language(s) of Instruction: Spanish

Degrees and Diplomas: *Licenciatura*; *Especialización*

UNIVERSITY OF AMERICA
Universidad de América (FUA)
Campus de Los Cerros, Avenida Circunvalar No. 20-53, Bogotá
Tel: +57(1) 337-6680
Fax: +57(1) 336-2941
EMail: payalam@uamerica.edu.co
Website: http://www.uamerica.edu.co

Rector: Jaime Posada Díaz EMail: fua@uamerica.edu.co

Vicerrectora Académica de Posgrados: Ana Josefa Herrera Vargas

Faculties
Architecture and Town Planning (Architecture; Construction Engineering; Regional Planning; Town Planning); **Economics and Finance** (Economics; Finance); **Engineering** (Chemical Engineering; Industrial Engineering; Mechanical Engineering; Petroleum and Gas Engineering; Production Engineering); **Science and Humanities**

History: Founded 1952, reorganized several times, acquired present status 1973.

Governing Bodies: Consejo Superior; Consejo Académico

Academic Year: January to November (January-June; July-November)

Admission Requirements: Secondary school certificate (bachillerato) and entrance examination

Main Language(s) of Instruction: Spanish

Degrees and Diplomas: *Licenciatura*: 5 yrs; *Titulo Profesional*; *Especialización*

Student Services: Academic counselling, Canteen, Cultural centre, Employment services, Health services, Social counselling, Sports facilities

Student Residential Facilities: Yes

Libraries: c. 3,200 vols
Last Updated: 09/11/09

UNIVERSITY OF APPLIED AND ENVIRONMENTAL SCIENCES
Universidad de Ciencias Aplicadas y Ambientales (UDCA)
Calle 222 No. 54-25, Bogotá
Tel: +57(1) 668-4700
Fax: +57(1) 676-1132
EMail: campus@udca.edu.co
Website: http://www.udca.edu.co

Rector: Germán Anzola Montero (1986-)
Tel: +57(1) 676-2402 EMail: ganzola@udca.edu.co

Secretario General: Adalberto Antonio Machado Amador
Tel: +57(1) 668-4700, Ext. 137

International Relations: Ximena Cardoso Arango
Tel: +57(1) 668-4700, Ext. 130 EMail: relint@udca.edu.co

Faculties
Accountancy (Accountancy); **Agricultural Engineering** (Agricultural Engineering; Agriculture); **Business Administration** (Business Administration); **Chemistry** (Chemistry); **Commercial Engineering** (Business and Commerce); **Economics**; **Engineering** (Agricultural Engineering; Environmental Engineering; Geography; Management; Telecommunications Engineering); **Environmental Studies** (Environmental Studies); **Finance** (Finance); **Geographical and Environmental Engineering**; **International Business**; **Marketing** (Marketing); **Medicine** (Medicine); **Nursing**; **Pharmaceutical Chemistry** (Chemistry; Pharmacology); **Science and Technology**; **Sports** (Sports); **Veterinary Science and Zoology** (Veterinary Science; Zoology)

History: Founded 1983 as Corporación Universitaria de Ciencias Agropecuarias.

Governing Bodies: Academic Council; Administrative Council; Planning Council

Academic Year: January-May, August-December

Admission Requirements: High school certificate and ICFES National examination

Main Language(s) of Instruction: Spanish

International Co-operation: With universities in Argentina; Bolivia; Brazil; Canada; Cuba; Chile; Ecuador; Spain; United States; Mexico; Panama; Peru; El Salvador; Uruguay; Venezuela. Participates in IAESTE and PAME-UDUAL programmes

Degrees and Diplomas: *Tecnólogo*: 3 1/2 yrs; *Licenciatura*: 5 yrs; *Titulo Profesional*; *Especialización*; *Maestría*

Student Services: Academic counselling, Canteen, Cultural centre, Foreign student adviser, Health services, Language programs, Social counselling, Sports facilities

Student Residential Facilities: For foreign students

Libraries: c. 13,000 vols

Publications: Actualidad y Divulgación Científica *(biennially)*
Last Updated: 10/11/09

UNIVERSITY OF BOYACÁ
Universidad de Boyacá (UNIBOYACA)
Apartado aéreo 1118, Carrera 2a Este No. 64-169, Tunja, Boyacá
Tel: +57(8) 745-0055
Fax: +57(8) 745-0044
EMail: informa@uniboyaca.edu.co
Website: http://www.uniboyaca.edu.co

Rectora: Rosita Amali Cuervo Payeras
Tel: (57) 8 745 0055, Fax: (57) 8 745 0044
EMail: racuervo@uniboyaca.edu.co

Assistant Rectory: Lillia Maria Alaroon Abella
Tel: (57) 8 745 0055, Fax: (57) 8 745 0044
EMail: lmalarcon@miboyaca.edu.co

International Relations: Boris Orlando Hermandez Bernal, Chief Of International Relations Office
Tel: (57) 8 745 0055, Fax: (57) 8 745 0044

Faculties
Administration and Accountancy; **Architecture and Fine Arts**; **Health Sciences** (Health Sciences); **Human Sciences and Education** (Education); **Law and Social Sciences** (Law; Social Sciences); **Postgraduate Studies**; **Science and Engineering** (Engineering; Natural Sciences)

History: Founded 1979, as a private and non-profit foundation approved by the Colombian Government. Acquired present university status 2004.

Governing Bodies: Consejo de Fundadores; Consejo Directivo; Consejo Académico; Consejo de Faculdad

Academic Year: January to December (January-June; July-December)

Admission Requirements: Secondary school certificate (bachillerato) and entrance examination

Fees: (US Dollars): 450-1,600 per semester

Main Language(s) of Instruction: Spanish

International Co-operation: With universities in Spain; Switzerland; Italy; Mexico; Canada; Argentina and Chile. Also participates in PAME-UDUAL, University Volunteers under UNITeS (UN) programmes

Degrees and Diplomas: *Tecnólogo*: Commercial and Financial Administration; Industrial Administration and Relations; Sales and Marketing, 3 yrs; *Titulo Profesional*; *Especialización*: Architecture; Bacteriology; Business Administration; Computer and Systems Engineering; Graphic Design; Industrial Engineering; Law and Political Science; Mathematics and Statistics; Medicine; Physical Therapy; Public Accountancy; Respiratory Therapy; Sanitation and Environmental Engineering; Social Communication; Surgical Technician, a further 2 yrs; *Especialización*: Computer Science for Teachers; Environmental Management; Epidemiology; Financial Management; Health Care Facility Management; Marketing Management; Tax Law; Telecommunications, postgraduate studies; *Especialización*: Political Science; Probationary Law, 1 1/2 yr. Also 1 1/2 yr postgraduate studies in Projects Management and Urban Development Management; Mass Media Production Management

Student Services: Academic counselling, Canteen, Cultural centre, Foreign student adviser, Health services, Language programs, Social counselling, Sports facilities

Special Facilities: TV Studio. Radio Studio

Libraries: Central Library, 9,000 vols; 12,345 videos; 1,720 monographs

Publications: Proyección Universitaria, Journal Antena Universitaria *(annually)*

Last Updated: 09/11/09

UNIVERSITY OF IBAGUÉ
Universidad de Ibagué (UDI)

Apartado aéreo 487, Carrera 22, Calle 67, Barrio Ambalá, Ibagué, Tolima

Tel: +57(8) 270 9444
EMail: informacion@unibague.edu.co
Website: http://www.unibague.edu.co

Rector: Alfonso Reyes Alvarado
Tel: +57(8) 275-3834, Fax: +57(8) 275-0148
EMail: areyes@unibague.edu.co

Secretaria General: Alejandra López Lozano
Tel: +57(8) 275-3834 EMail: alejandra.lopez@unibague.edu.co

Faculties
Economics and Administration; **Engineering** (Civil Engineering; Electronic Engineering; Industrial Engineering; Mechanical Engineering; Systems Analysis); **Humanities and Social Sciences**; **Integrated Art** (Architecture); **Law and Political Science**; **Natural Sciences and Mathematics** (Mathematics; Natural Sciences)

History: Founded 1980. Previously known as Corporación Universitaria de Ibagué. Acquired present status 2003.

Governing Bodies: Consejo de Fundadores; Consejo Superior; Consejo Académico

Academic Year: January to November (January-May; July-November)

Admission Requirements: Secondary school certificate

Fees: (Pesos): 1.9-2.6m. per semester

Main Language(s) of Instruction: Spanish

International Co-operation: With universities in Spain, Mexico, Brazil, Belgium, Portugal, Poland, Cezch Republic, Italy

Accrediting Agencies: Consejo Nacional de Acreditación

Degrees and Diplomas: *Título Profesional*: Architecture; Financial Administration; Economics; Accountancy; Marketing; Business Administration; Civil Engineering; Electronic Engineering; Industrial Engineering; Systems Engineering; Mechanical Engineering; Psychology; Law (Profesional en...), 5 yrs; *Especialización*: Industrial Automation; Advanced Mathematics; Production Engineering; Material Mechanics; Operation and Technology Management; Computer Science; Law; Political Science; Auditing; Management; Banking; Regional Development; Planification; Finance; Marketing (Especialista), 1 yr; *Maestría*: Industrial Management; Industrial Control studies, 2 yrs

Student Services: Academic counselling, Canteen, Cultural centre, Foreign student adviser, Foreign Studies Centre, Health services, Language programs, Nursery care, Social counselling, Sports facilities

Libraries: Yes

Publications: Actas Pedagógicas, Research Publication *(quarterly)*; Temas y Reflexiones

Academic Staff 2007-2008	MEN	WOMEN	TOTAL
FULL-TIME	93	41	134
PART-TIME	173	99	272
STAFF WITH DOCTORATE			
FULL-TIME	4	4	8
Student Numbers 2007-2008			
All (Foreign Included)	2,812	1,393	4,205

Last Updated: 10/11/09

UNIVERSITY OF LA SABANA
Universidad de La Sabana

Km 21 Autopista Norte de Bogotá, D.C, Chia, Cundinamarca
Tel: +57(1) 861-5555 +57(1) 861-6666
Fax: +57(1) 861-6010
EMail: webmaster@unisabana.edu.co
Website: http://www.unisabana.edu.co

Rector: Obdulio Velásquez PosadaFax: +57(1) 861-4220
EMail: obdulio.velasquez@unisabana.edu.co

Vicerrectora Académica: María Clara Quintero Laverde
EMail: mariac.quintero@unisabana.edu.co

Faculties
Communication (Communication Studies; Journalism; Multimedia); **Education** (Education); **Engineering** (Chemical Engineering; Computer Engineering; Engineering; Industrial Engineering; Production Engineering); **Law** (Law); **Medicine** (Health Sciences; Medicine); **Nursing and Rehabilitation** (Health Sciences; Nursing; Rehabilitation and Therapy); **Psychology** (Health Sciences; Psychology)

Institutes
Family Studies (Family Studies); **Humanities** (Arts and Humanities); **Postgraduate Studies** *Director*: Salomón Frost González

Schools
Administration and Economics *(International)* (Administration; Business Administration; Economics; Finance; International Business)

History: Founded 1971 as Institute for Higher Education. Acquired present status and title 1979.

Academic Year: February to November

Admission Requirements: Secondary school certificate (bachillerato), National Secondary Examination (ICFES) and entrance examination

Fees: (US Dollars): c. 600-2,500 per semester, according to parents' income

Main Language(s) of Instruction: Spanish

International Co-operation: With universities in Canada, Spain, USA, Australia, France, Argentina, Chile and Germany

Accrediting Agencies: Consejo Nacional de Acreditación (CNA)

Degrees and Diplomas: *Licenciatura*: Education, 4-5 yrs; *Título Profesional*; *Especialización*; *Maestría*

Student Services: Academic counselling, Cultural centre, Employment services, Foreign student adviser, Foreign Studies Centre, Handicapped facilities, Health services, Language programs, Sports facilities

Libraries: Central Library, 85,637 vols
Last Updated: 10/11/09

UNIVERSITY OF LA SALLE
Universidad de La Salle (UNISALLE)

Carrera 2 No. 59A-44, Bogotá
Tel: +57(1) 348-8000
Fax: +57(1) 217-0881
EMail: rectoria@lasalle.edu.co
Website: http://www.lasalle.edu.co

Rector: Fabio Gallego Arias, f.s.c. Tel: +57(1) 348-8030

Vicerrector Administrativo: Mauricio Fernández Fernández
Tel: +57(1) 348-8048, Fax: +57(1) 217-0889
EMail: vadministrativa@jupiter.lasalle.edu.co

International Relations: María Victoria Costa López
Tel: +57(1) 348-8032 EMail: jefeori@lasalle.edu.co

Departments
Basic Sciences (Biology; Ecology; Mathematics)

Faculties
Administration and Accountancy (Accountancy; Business Administration); **Agronomy**; **Economics and Social Sciences**; **Education** (English; French; Religious Education; Spanish); **Engineering**; **Habitat** (Architecture); **Health Sciences** (Optometry); **Philosophy and Humanities** (Arts and Humanities; Philosophy)

Institutes
Engineering Projects Management (Engineering Management) *Director*: Gustavo Ramírez Escobar; **Environmental Management** (Environmental Management) *Director*: Clara Inés Pardo; **Finance Management** (Business Administration; Finance) *Director*: Román Leonardo Villareal; **Optometry Research** *(Chapinero)* (Optometry) *Director*: Nelson Leonardo Merchán Bautista; **Social Management** (Social Sciences) *Director*: Elsa de los Angeles Rodríguez Caldas

Further Information: Also Optometry and Veterinary Clinics

History: Founded 1964 as a private institution, recognized by the State 1975.

Governing Bodies: Consejo Superior

Academic Year: February to November (February-June; August-November)

Admission Requirements: Secondary school certificate (bachillerato) and entrance examination (Certificado de Pruebas de Estado del ICFES)

Fees: (Pesos): c. 980,000-4.3m. per semester according to course

Main Language(s) of Instruction: Spanish

International Co-operation: With universities in Australia; Austria; Brazil; Chile; Mexico; Spain; United Kingdom and USA

Accrediting Agencies: Consejo Nacional de Acreditación

Degrees and Diplomas: *Licenciatura*: Agricultural Administration; Animal Sciences; Architecture; Business Administration; Economics; Finance Management; Information Systems; Marketing Management; Mathematics and Computer Science; Modern Languages; Optometry; Philosophy and Letters; Religious Studies; Social Work; Veterinary Medicine, 5 yrs; *Licenciatura*: Education, 10 sem; *Titulo Profesional*: Civil Engineering; Design and Electronic Automation; Electrical Engineering; Food Engineering; Information Systems; Sanitary Engineering, 5 yrs; *Especialización*: Agricultural and Cattle Management; Energy and Environmental Management; Engineering Projects Management; Philosophy of Education; Poultry Medicine and Production; Social Management, a further yr; *Maestría*: Business Administration; Education, a further 2 yrs; *Maestría*: Public Accountancy, 5 yrs

Student Services: Academic counselling, Canteen, Cultural centre, Foreign student adviser, Foreign Studies Centre, Health services, Language programs, Social counselling, Sports facilities

Libraries: Central Library, 138,008 vols

Publications: Actualidades Pedagógicas, Education; Códice, Information Systems and Documentation; Diógenes, Philosophy and Letters; Epsilon, Engineering; Equidad y Desarrollo, Economics and Administration; Journal of Social Work *(quarterly)*; Journal of Veterinary Medicine; Revista Universidad De La Salle *(quarterly)*

Last Updated: 12/11/09

UNIVERSITY OF MANIZALES
Universidad de Manizales
Carrera 9 No. 19-03, Manizales, Caldas 868
Tel: +57(6) 884-1450
Fax: +57(6) 884-1443
EMail: um@um.umanizales.edu.co
Website: http://www.umanizales.edu.co

Rector: Guillermo Orlando Sierra Sierra
Tel: +57(68) 883-3211 EMail: rectoria@um.umanizales.edu.co

Vicerrectora Académica: Ana Gloria Ríos Patiño
Tel: +57(68) 884-2381 EMail: vicacad@um.umanizales.edu.co

Faculties
Accountancy (Accountancy); **Economics** (Business Administration; Economics); **Education** (Education); **Engineering**; **Law** (Law); **Marketing** (Marketing); **Medicine**; **Psychology** (Psychology); **Social Communication and Journalism** (Communication Studies; Journalism)

History: Founded 1972, acquired present status 1992.

Main Language(s) of Instruction: Spanish

Degrees and Diplomas: *Licenciatura*; *Especialización*; *Maestría*; *Doctorado*

Libraries: Yes
Last Updated: 12/11/09

UNIVERSITY OF MEDELLÍN
Universidad de Medellín (UDEM)
Carrera 87 No. 30-65, Belén Los Alpes, Medellín, Antioquia
Tel: +57(4) 340-5555
EMail: udem@guayacan.udem.edu.co
Website: http://www.udem.edu.co

Rector: Néstor Hincapié Vargas (2000-)
Tel: +57(4) 238-3906, Fax: +57(4) 341-4913
EMail: nhincapie@guayacan.udem.edu.co

Secretaria General: Esperanza Restrepo de Isaza
Tel: +57(4) 238-1252, Fax: +57(4) 341-4913

International Relations: Uriel Hernando Sánchez Zuluaga
Tel: +57(4) 345-8143

Departments
Basic Sciences (Chemistry; Mathematics; Mechanics; Physics; Statistics); **Human and Social Sciences** (Social Sciences)

Faculties
Communication (Communication Studies; Information Management); **Economics and Administration** (Administration; Economics); **Engineering** (Civil Engineering; Computer Engineering; Engineering; Environmental Engineering; Telecommunications Engineering); **Law** (Administrative Law; Civil Law; Commercial Law; Criminal Law; History of Law; Human Rights; Labour Law; Law; Notary Studies; Public Law)

History: Founded 1950 as a private institution.

Governing Bodies: Asamblea General; Conciliatura; Consejo Académico

Academic Year: February to December (February-June; August-December)

Admission Requirements: Secondary school certificate (bachillerato) and entrance examination

Fees: (Pesos): c. 1,097,000-3,698,000

Main Language(s) of Instruction: Spanish, English

Accrediting Agencies: Consejo Nacional de Acreditación

Degrees and Diplomas: *Tecnólogo*: Judicial Investigation; Software Development, 3 yrs; *Licenciatura*: 5 yrs; *Licenciatura*: Education; Marketing, 5 yrs; *Especialización*: Law; Economics and International Business; Construction Management; Information Management; Public Government; Marketing; Environmental Studies; Conflict Resolution; Roads and Transport, 2 sem; *Maestría*: Business Administration (MBA); Education; Procedural Law; Urban Engineering, 2 yrs; *Doctorado*. Also Qualified Certificates

Student Services: Academic counselling, Canteen, Cultural centre, Employment services, Foreign student adviser, Health services, Language programs, Nursery care, Social counselling, Sports facilities

Special Facilities: Theatre; TV Production Centre

Libraries: c. 64,403 vols; 833 periodical subscriptions; 16,265 video tapes and DVDs

Publications: Revista Avanzada *(biannually)*

Press or Publishing House: Sello Editorial Universidad de Medellín

Academic Staff *2007-2008*	MEN	WOMEN	TOTAL
FULL-TIME	127	46	**173**
STAFF WITH DOCTORATE			
FULL-TIME	5	2	7
PART-TIME	5	1	6
Student Numbers *2007-2008*			
All (Foreign Included)	3,870	5,146	**9,016**

Last Updated: 12/11/09

UNIVERSITY OF SAN BUENAVENTURA, BOGOTÁ
Universidad de San Buenaventura, Bogotá (U.S.B.)
Cra 8 H # 172 - 20, Bogotá 75010
Tel: +57(1) 677-1090
Fax: +57(1) 677-3003
EMail: informacion@usbbog.edu.co
Website: http://www.usbbog.edu.co

Rector: Fernando Garzón Ramírez (2002-)
EMail: fgarzon@usbbog.edu.co

Senior Administrative Officer: Miguel Roberto Hernández-Saavedra EMail: mhernand@usbbog.edu.co

International Relations: Diana Lucía Patiño-Donoso
EMail: dpatino@usbbog.edu.co

COLOMBIA–Private Institutions

Faculties

Business Administration (Accountancy; Business Administration; Economics); **Education** (Education; English; Preschool Education); **Engineering** (Aeronautical and Aerospace Engineering; Computer Engineering; Electronic Engineering; Engineering; Mechanical Engineering; Sound Engineering (Acoustics); Telecommunications Engineering); **Legal and Political Sciences** (Law; Political Sciences); **Philosophy** (Philosophy); **Psychology** (Psychology); **Theology** (Theology)

History: Founded 1708 by Royal decree. Closed 1861; officially reopened 1961 and recognized by the Ministry of Education 1964. A private institution under the supervision of the Franciscan Order.

Academic Year: February to November

Admission Requirements: Secondary school certificate (bachillerato) and ICFES entrance examination

Fees: (Pesos): 2,272,000-3.5m. per semester

Main Language(s) of Instruction: Spanish

Degrees and Diplomas: *Licenciatura*: Education; Philosophy; Theology, 4-5 yrs; *Especialización*: Education; Pedagogy; University Teaching, 1 yr; *Especialización*: Engineering; Aeronautical Management; Satellite Navigation; Avionics, 1 1/2 yrs. Also Profesional (5 yrs) in Business Administration; Gerontology; Engineering; Psychology; Law; Political Science; and Diplomado (20-64 hours study)

Student Services: Academic counselling, Employment services, Foreign student adviser, Foreign Studies Centre, Handicapped facilities, Social counselling, Sports facilities

Special Facilities: Laboratories of Electronic Engineering; Computer Engineering; Mechanical Engineering; Sound Engineering; Aeronautical Engineering

Libraries: General Collection, 81,006 vols

Publications: Breviloquio *(bimonthly)*; Franciscanum *(3 per annum)*; Ingenium *(biennially)*; Itinerario Educativo *(biennially)*; Management *(biennially)*

Last Updated: 12/11/09

CALI BRANCH
SECCIONAL CALI

Avenida 10 de Mayo, La Umbría, Carretera a Pance, Cali, Valle del Cauca
Tel: +57(2) 318-2201
Fax: +57(2) 555-2006
EMail: informacion@usbcali.edu.co
Website: http://www.usb.edu.co

Rector: Álvaro Cepeda Van Houten
Tel: +57(2) 318-2201 EMail: rectoria@usbcali.edu.co

Secretario General: Hernando Arias Rodríguez
Tel: +57(2) 318-2298 EMail: secretariageneral@usbcali.edu.co

Departments

Continuing Education (Continuing Education) *Director*: Jorge Posada; **Languages** (Modern Languages) *Director*: Georgia Costalas; **Training and Human Development** (Development Studies; Human Resources) *Director*: Rodrígo Rincón

Faculties

Architecture, Art and Design (Architecture; Fashion Design); **Economics** (Accountancy; Business Administration; Economics); **Education**; **Engineering** (Agricultural Engineering; Computer Engineering; Electronic Engineering; Engineering; Industrial Engineering); **Law** (Law) *Dean*: Jorge Luis Romero; **Psychology** (Psychology) *Dean*: Carmen Urrea

Research Centres

Research *Director*: Gloria Valencia

History: Founded 1708 by Royal decree. Closed 1861; officially reopened 1961 and recognized by the Ministry of Education 1964. A private institution under the supervision of the Franciscan Order.

Academic Year: February to November

Admission Requirements: Secondary school certificate (bachillerato) and ICFES entrance examination

Main Language(s) of Instruction: Spanish

Degrees and Diplomas: *Licenciatura*: Law; Business Administration; Education; Engineering; Psychology; Architecture, 4-5 yrs;

Especialización: Law; Business Administration; Education, 1-1 1/2 yrs; *Maestría*: Education; Human Development, 2 yrs

Student Services: Academic counselling, Employment services, Foreign student adviser, Foreign Studies Centre, Handicapped facilities, Health services, Social counselling, Sports facilities

Libraries: 41,763 vols

Publications: Breviloquio *(quarterly)*; Guillermo de Ockham *(biennially)*

CARTAGENA BRANCH
SECCIONAL CARTAGENA

Apartado aéreo 7833, Calle Real de Ternera, Cartagena, Bolivar
Tel: +57(956) 653-9594
Fax: +57(956) 653-9590
EMail: usabuctg@ctgred.net.co
Website: http://www.usbctg.edu.co

Rector: Pablo Castillo Nova

Faculties

Administration and Accountancy (Accountancy; Administration; Business Administration; Business and Commerce); **Architecture** (Architecture); **Education** (Education; Educational Administration); **Engineering** (Engineering); **Health Sciences** (Health Sciences); **Law** (Law); **Psychology** (Psychology)

History: Founded 1992.

Governing Bodies: Board of Directors

Academic Year: February-June; July-December

Main Language(s) of Instruction: Spanish

Degrees and Diplomas: *Licenciatura*; *Especialización*

MEDELLÍN BRANCH
SECCIONAL MEDELLÍN

Calle 45 #61-40 Bello, Medellín, Antioquia
Tel: +57(4) 514-5600
Website: http://www.usbmed.edu.co

Head: Miguel Ángel Builes Uribe (2004-)
Tel: +57(4) 4500-300, Fax: +57(4) 454-2683
EMail: usb@usbmed.edu.co

Administrative Officer: Jose Norberto Agudelo

International Relations: Leon Pelaez
Tel: +57(4) 4500-329, Fax: +57(4) 454-2683
EMail: leon.pelaez@usbmed.edu.co

Faculties

Business Administration (Accountancy; Business Administration; International Business); **Education** (Educational Administration; Physical Education; Preschool Education); **Engineering** (Computer Engineering; Electronic Engineering; Environmental Engineering; Industrial Engineering; Sound Engineering (Acoustics)); **Integrated Arts** (Architecture; Industrial Design); **Law** (Law); **Psychology** (Psychology)

History: Founded 1967. Acquired present status 1975.

Governing Bodies: Board of Directors

Academic Year: February to May and July to November

Admission Requirements: High school Diploma

Main Language(s) of Instruction: Spanish

Accrediting Agencies: National Secretary of Education

Degrees and Diplomas: *Licenciatura*: 5 yrs; *Especialización*: 1 1/2 yr; *Maestría*: a further 2 yrs

Student Services: Cultural centre, Employment services, Foreign student adviser, Handicapped facilities, Health services, Language programs, Nursery care, Social counselling, Sports facilities

Student Residential Facilities: No

Special Facilities: Auditorium

Libraries: c. 36,000 vols

UNIVERSITY OF SANTANDER
Universidad de Santander (UDES)

Carrera 29 No 47-32, Bucaramanga, Santander
Tel: +57(7) 651-6500
Fax: +57(7) 643-6002
Website: http://www.udes.edu.co

Rector: Rafael Serrano Sarmiento
EMail: rserrano@.udes.edu.co; rectoria@udes.edu.co

Secretario General: José Asthul Rangel Chacón
Tel: +57(97) 651-6500, Ext 228, Fax: +57(97) 631-0742

International Relations: Diony Sepúlveda Ramírez F.
Tel: +57(97) 634-977, Fax: +57(97) 436-002
EMail: disepulve@hotmail.com

Faculties

Administration *(Valledupar, Cúcuta and Bogotá)*; **Design** *(Cucúta, Valledupar)*; **Engineering**; **Health Sciences**; **Law** (Law); **Medicine** (Medicine)

History: Founded 1985 as the Corporación Universitaria de Santander offering technical programmes in Administration and Health. Became a university institution in 1996.

Governing Bodies: Board of Trustees

Admission Requirements: High school diploma and National Government Examination (ICFES)

Fees: (Pesos) c; 1.7m.

Main Language(s) of Instruction: Spanish

Accrediting Agencies: ICFES; Consejo Nacional de Acreditación

Degrees and Diplomas: *Licenciatura*: 5 yrs; *Especialización*: 11/2 yrs; *Maestría*

Student Services: Academic counselling, Health services, Language programs, Sports facilities

Student Residential Facilities: None

Special Facilities: No

Libraries: Yes
Last Updated: 12/11/09

UNIVERSITY OF SANTIAGO DE CALI
Universidad Santiago de Cali (USACA)
Calle 5, No. 62-00, Cali, Valle del Cauca 4102
Tel: +57(2) 518-3000
Fax: +57(2) 555-1656
EMail: secretaria@usc.edu.co
Website: http://www.usc.edu.co

Rector: Hebert Celin Navas
Tel: +57(2) 551-6567, Fax: +57(2) 551-6567
EMail: rectoria@usc.edu.co; hcelin@usc.edu.co

Secretario General: Germán Valencia Valencia
Fax: +57(2) 518-3000 EMail: secgeneral@usc.edu.co

Centres
Human Rights (Human Rights)

Faculties
Business Administration and Economics; **Communication and Advertising** (Advertising and Publicity; Communication Studies); **Education** (Chemistry; Computer Science; Education; Mathematics; Preschool Education; Social Sciences); **Engineering**; **Health Sciences**; **Law** (Law)

Institutes
Criminology; **Languages** (English; French; German; Italian)

Further Information: Also branch in Palmira

History: Founded 1958. Acquired present staus 1964.

Main Language(s) of Instruction: Spanish

Degrees and Diplomas: *Licenciatura*: 5 yrs; *Titulo Profesional*; *Especialización*; *Maestría*

Libraries: c. 3,300 vols
Last Updated: 18/11/09

UNIVERSITY OF THE ANDES
Universidad de Los Andes
Apartado aéreo 4976, Carrera 1a No. 18 A 10, Bogotá
Tel: +57(1) 339-4999
Fax: +57(1) 332-4448
EMail: rectoria@uniandes.edu.co
Website: http://www.uniandes.edu.co

Rector: Carlos Angulo Galvis
Tel: +57(1) 332-4370, Fax: +57(1) 332-4369
EMail: cangulo@uniandes.edu.co

Secretaria General: María Teresa Tobón
Tel: +57(1) 332-4376, Fax: +57(1) 332-4369
EMail: secgal@uniandes.edu.co

International Relations: Catalina Rizo
Tel: +57(1) 339-4949, Ext. 3288, Fax: +57(1) 332-4369
EMail: crizo@uniandes.edu.co

Centres
Advanced Computation *(MOX)*; **Bioengineering** *(GIP)*; **Economic Development** *(CEDE)*; **Engineering Research** *(CIFI)*; **Environmental Engineering** *(CIIA)*; **Ethnolinguistic Studies** *(CCELA)* (Ethnology; Indigenous Studies; Linguistics); **Innovation and Technological Development** *(CITEC)*; **Interdisciplinary Regional Studies** *(CIDER)* (Regional Studies); **Journalism** *(CEPER)* (Journalism); **Material and Civil Construction** *(CIMOC)*; **Mechanic Properties and Material Structures** *(CIPEM)*; **Microbiology** *(CIMIC)*; **Microbiology and Tropical Parasitology** *(CIMPAT)*; **Microelectronics** *(CMUA)*; **Polymer Processing** *(CIPP)*; **Research and Development of Informatics in Education** *(LIDIE)*; **Social and International Affairs Studies** *(CESO)*; **Socio-juridical Studies** *(CIJUS)*; **Telecommunications** *(CTUA)*; **Water and Sewage** *(CIACUA)*

Faculties
Administration (Administration); **Architecture and Design** (Architecture; Industrial Design; Textile Design); **Arts and Humanities** (Arts and Humanities; Literature; Music; Painting and Drawing; Sculpture); **Economics** (Economics); **Engineering** (Chemical Engineering; Civil Engineering; Computer Engineering; Electrical Engineering; Electronic Engineering; Engineering; Environmental Engineering; Industrial Engineering; Mechanical Engineering); **Law** (Law); **Medicine** (Medicine); **Science** (Biology; Chemistry; Mathematics; Microbiology; Physics); **Social Sciences** (Anthropology; Cultural Studies; History; Modern Languages; Philosophy; Political Sciences; Psychology; Social Sciences; Social Studies) *Dean*: Carl Langebaeck

Institutes
Genetics *Director*: Mauricio Linares

History: Founded 1948 as an independent private institution. Acquired present status 1949.

Governing Bodies: Consejo Directivo; Consejo Académico; Comité Ejecutivo

Academic Year: January to December (January-May; August-December)

Admission Requirements: Secondary school certificate (bachillerato) and University or State examination (ICFES)

Main Language(s) of Instruction: Spanish

International Co-operation: With universities in France; Germany; Canada; United Kingdom and USA

Accrediting Agencies: EQUIS/AMBA/AACSB/ABET/Consejo Nacional de Acreditación (CNA)

Degrees and Diplomas: *Licenciatura*: 8 sem; *Especialización*: 12-16 months; *Maestría*: 2-3 sem; *Doctorado*: 6-8 sem

Student Services: Academic counselling, Cultural centre, Employment services, Foreign student adviser, Handicapped facilities, Health services, Language programs, Nursery care, Sports facilities

Special Facilities: Astronomy Observatory

Libraries: General Library, 200,907 vols; Law, 21,037 vols; CEDE Library, 35,537 vols; Business Administration, 6,739 vols; Arts, 6,433 vols; Mathematics, 5,596 vols

Publications: Actualidad y Discusiones *(other/irregular)*; Antípoda: Revista de Antropología y Arqueología *(biennially)*; Catedra Corona *(other/irregular)*; Colombia Internacional *(biennially)*; Conversaciones de Arquitectura *(other/irregular)*; Cuadernos Azules *(biennially)*; Cuadernos Grises *(other/irregular)*; Desarrollo y Sociedad *(biennially)*; Documentos CEDE *(other/irregular)*; Documentos CESO *(other/irregular)*; Estudios Ocasionales *(other/irregular)*; Galeras de Administración *(other/irregular)*; Hipotetis: Apuntes Científicos *(biennially)*; Historia Critica *(biennially)*; Mejores Proyectos de Grado *(other/irregular)*; Monografías Meritorias en

Literatura *(other/irregular)*; Monografiías de Administración *(other/irregular)*; Nuevos Estudios Sociojurídicos *(other/irregular)*; Revista de Derecho Privado *(biennially)*; Revista de Derecho, Comunicaciones y Nuevas Tecnologías *(biennially)*; Revista de Ingenieria *(biennially)*; Revista Derecho Público *(biennially)*; Revista Estudios Sociales *(biennially)*; Revista Territorios *(biennially)*; Serie Investigaciones Sociojurídicas *(other/irregular)*

Press or Publishing House: Ediciones Uniandes
Last Updated: 12/11/09

UNIVERSITY OF THE NORTH
Universidad del Norte (UNINORTE)
Kilometro 5 Vía Puerto Colombia, Barranquilla, Atlántico
Tel: +57(5) 350-9509
Fax: +57(5) 350-9548
EMail: webmaster@.uninorte.edu.co
Website: http://www.uninorte.edu.co

Rector: Jesús Ferro Bayona (1980-)
Tel: +57(5) 350-9388, Fax: +57(5) 359-8805
EMail: jferro@uninorte.edu.co

Administrative and Financial Vice-President: Alma Diazgranados
Tel: +57(5) 350-9419, Fax: +57(5) 359-8805
EMail: adiazgra@uninorte.edu.co

International Relations: Carmen de Peña, Rector's Delegate for International Relations
Tel: +57(5) 350-9230 EMail: cpena@uninorte.edu.co

Centres
Continuing Education *Director*: Emelina de Buitrago; **Cultural Studies** *(Cayena)*; **Regional Studies**; **Research and Projects Direction** (Arts and Humanities; Business Administration; Engineering; Law; Medicine; Natural Sciences; Social Sciences)

Divisions
Basic Sciences (Mathematics; Physics); **Engineering**; **Health Sciences** (Biomedicine; Health Sciences; Medicine; Nursing); **Humanities and Social Sciences** (Arts and Humanities; Communication Studies; Development Studies; Economics; Graphic Design; International Relations; Journalism; Mass Communication; Psychology; Social Sciences); **Law** (Government; Law; Political Sciences)

Institutes
Caribbean Economics (Caribbean Studies; Economics); **Education** (Education; Preschool Education); **Languages** (Chinese; English; French; German; Italian; Spanish); **Sustainable Development**

Research Centres
Human Development (Child Care and Development; Development Studies)

Schools
Business Administration (Business Administration; International Business)

Further Information: Also Teaching Hospital and 54 laboratories

History: Founded 1966. A private institution, recognized by the State as a degree granting institution 1973.

Governing Bodies: Board of Trustees

Academic Year: January to December (January-May; July-December)

Admission Requirements: Secondary school certificate (bachillerato) or equivalent, State examination (ICFES), admission test and entrance examination

Fees: (Pesos): 4m. per semester

Main Language(s) of Instruction: Spanish

International Co-operation: With universities in Brazil, Canada, Chile, Dominican Republic, France, Germany, Italy, Jamaica, Mexico, Netherlands, Spain, Sweden, United Kingdom and USA. Also participates in the CINDA, ENIM, PIMA programmes.

Accrediting Agencies: Consejo Nacional de Acreditación; Accreditation Board of Engineering and Technology (ABET) for Industrial and Mechanical undergraduate programmes; SACS; EQUIS

Degrees and Diplomas: *Titulo Profesional*: Child Pedagogy; Economics; International Relations; Political Sciences and Government; Industrial and Graphic Design, 4-5 yrs; *Titulo Profesional*: Law; Engineering; Business Administration; Psychology; Social Communication; International Business, 5 yrs; *Especialización*: Engineering; Humanities and Social Sciences; Medicine; Basic Sciences; Law; Administration, 1 yr; *Especialización*: Surgery, 3-4 yrs; *Maestría*: Biomedical Sciences; Business Administration; Social Development; Engineering; Psychology; Education; Social Communication; Law, 2 yrs; *Doctorado*: Psychology; Mechanical Engineering, 3 yrs

Student Services: Academic counselling, Canteen, Cultural centre, Employment services, Foreign student adviser, Foreign Studies Centre, Handicapped facilities, Health services, Language programs, Social counselling, Sports facilities

Student Residential Facilities: None

Special Facilities: Teaching Hospital; 54 Laboratories; Uninorte FM Cultural Radio Station; Television Studios; Sports and Events Coliseum

Libraries: Central Library, 87,167 vols; 1,032 periodical subscriptions; 40,906 electronic magazines; 364 video titles; 822 CD-Rom titles

Publications: Anuario Científico *(biannually)*; CERES Documentos y Monografías *(annually)*; EIDOS *(biannually)*; Ensayo en Desarrollo Humano *(biannually)*; Huellas *(quarterly)*; Investigación y Desarrollo *(biannually)*; Pensamiento y Gestión *(biannually)*; Psicología desde el Caribe *(biannually)*; Revista de Derecho *(biannually)*; Revista Ingeniería y Desarrollo *(biannually)*; Salud Uninorte *(biannually)*

Press or Publishing House: Ediciones Uninorte (Uninorte Editions)
Last Updated: 13/11/09

UNIVERSITY OF THE SINÚ RIVER
Universidad del Sinú
Calle 38 Cra. 1w barrio Juan XXIII, Montería, Córdoba
Tel: +57(401) 840-340
Fax: +57(401) 841-954
EMail: rector@unisinu.edu.co
Website: http://www.unisinu.edu.co

Rectora: Mara Bechara

Centres
Languages (English; Modern Languages)

Faculties
Economics, Administration and Accountancy (Accountancy; Administration; Advertising and Publicity; Banking; Business Administration; Economics; International Business; Marketing); **Health Sciences** (Dentistry; Medicine; Nursing; Occupational Therapy; Physical Therapy; Psychology; Speech Therapy and Audiology; Surgery); **Human Sciences, Art and Design**; **Law, Social Sciences and Education** (English; Law; Social Work); **Science and Engineering** (Civil Engineering; Electrical Engineering; Industrial Engineering; Mechanical Engineering; Systems Analysis)

Further Information: Also Seccional Cartagena (http://www.unisinucartagena.edu.co/)

History: Founded 1975 as Corporación Universitaria del Sinú.

Main Language(s) of Instruction: Spanish

Degrees and Diplomas: *Tecnólogo*; *Licenciatura*; *Titulo Profesional*; *Especialización*
Last Updated: 13/11/09

URABÁ ANTONIO ROLDÁN BETANCUR FOUNDATION OF ADVANCED UNIVERSITY STUDIES
Fundación de Estudios Superiores Universitarios de Urabá Antonio Roldán Betancur (FESU)
Carrera 111 No 101-64, Barrio Los Pinos, Apartado, Antioquia
Tel: +57(94) 828-3639
Fax: +57(94) 829-0100

Rectora: Edna Margarita Martinez Acosta

Programmes
International Business (International Business)

Degrees and Diplomas: *Titulo Profesional*: 5 yrs
Last Updated: 02/11/09

Congo

STRUCTURE OF HIGHER EDUCATION SYSTEM

Description:

Higher education is mainly provided by the Université Marien Ngouabi and its Instituts and Ecoles. The University is a public institution which is responsible to the Ministère de l'Enseignement supérieur et de la Recherche scientifique. Its resources come from a State subsidy as well as its own funds. Higher education is also provided by a few private higher education institutions. As far as credentials are concerned, the three-tier system (LMD reform) will be introduced from the 2009-2010 academic year.

Stages of studies:

University level first stage: *Premier cycle*
The first stage of studies leads, after two years, to the Diplôme universitaire d'Etudes littéraires (DUEL) in Arts and Humanities and the Diplôme universitaire d'Etudes scientifiques (DUES) in Science. From the 2009-2010 academic year it will lead to the Licence in three years.

University level second stage: *Deuxième cycle*
A further year's study after the DUEL or DUES leads to the Licence, a further year leads to the Maîtrise and a further two years lead to the Diplôme d'Etudes supérieures (DES). The Institut de Développement Rural (IDR) provides training in Agricultural Science. At the Institut supérieur des Sciences de la Santé (INSSA), three years' study are required to become a trained nurse (Licence en Sciences de la Santé pour les Infirmiers). INSSA also awards, after six years' study, the State degree of Doctorat en Médecine.
From the 2009-2010 academic year it will lead to the Master in two years.

University level third stage: *Troisième cycle*
A further year beyond the Maîtrise leads to the Diplôme d'Etudes approfondies in some fields of study. A Doctorat is also offered in some fields.
From the 2009-2010 academic year it will lead to the Doctorat in three to four years following upon a Master.

ADMISSION TO HIGHER EDUCATION

Admission to university-level studies:
Name of secondary school credential required: Baccalauréat
Other admission requirements: Competitive entrance examination for access to the university institutes and portfolio for access to the university faculties.

Foreign students admission:
Quotas: 10% of study places are reserved for foreign students.

NATIONAL BODIES

Ministère de l'Enseignement supérieur et de la Recherche Scientifique (Ministry of Higher Education and Scientific Research)
Minister: Ange-Antoine Abena
B.P. 2078
Brazzaville
Tel: +242 666 3371
Fax: +242 810 815
Role of national body: Supervision of the higher education system and higher education institutions.

Data for academic year: 2009-2010
Source: IAU from the Country Report on the Development of Education prepared for the International Conference on Education 2008, IBE, and documentation, 2009. Minister, 2011.

INSTITUTIONS

MARIEN NGOUABI UNIVERSITY
Université Marien Ngouabi
BP 69, Brazzaville
Tel: +242(81) 01-41 +242(81) 18-28
Fax: +242(81) 01-41
EMail: rectorat@univ-mngb.net
Website: http://www.univ-mngb.net

Recteur: Georges Moyen EMail: georges.moyen@univ-mngb.net

Secrétaire général: Christian Sédar Ndinga

International Relations: Emmanuel Daho

Faculties
Arts and Humanities (African Studies; Arts and Humanities; Communication Studies; English; Geography; History; Linguistics; Literature; Philosophy; Social Sciences; Sociology) *Dean*: Paul Nzete; **Economics** (Economics; Finance) *Dean*: Hervé Diata; **Health Sciences** (Embryology and Reproduction Biology; Haematology; Health Sciences; Histology; Medicine; Microbiology; Midwifery; Physiology; Surgery) *Dean*: Hervé Mayanda; **Law** (Law; Private Law; Public Law) *Dean*: Jean Poaty; **Science** *(Dolisie)* (Biology; Chemistry; Earth Sciences; Mathematics; Natural Sciences; Physics) *Dean*: Jean Maurille Ouamba

Institutes
Management (Justice Administration; Management); **Physical Education and Sport** *(INSSA)* (Physical Education; Sports) *Director*: Richard Oniangue; **Rural Development** *(IDR)* (Agricultural Equipment; Botany; Forestry; Rural Studies; Zoology) *Director*: Paul Yoka

Schools
Administration and Training for the Magistrature *(ENAM)* (Administration; Commercial Law; Educational Sciences; Law; Management; Private Law; Psychology; Public Law) *Director*: José Rigobert Ban Ethat; **Teacher Training** *(ENS)* (Teacher Training) *Director*: Jean-Pierre Mbakidi; **Technical Education** *(ENSET)* (Civil Engineering; Electrical Engineering; Food Technology; Technology Education) *Director*: Bernard Mabiala

Further Information: Also Campus universitaire francophone in Brazzaville, in collaboration with the Agence Universitaire Francophone (AUF)

History: Founded 1959 as Centre d'Etudes administratives et techniques supérieures. Previously formed part of the Fondation de l'Enseignement supérieur en Afrique centrale. Became Université de Brazzaville 1971, acquired present title 1977.

Governing Bodies: Comité de Direction

Academic Year: October to June (October-December; January-March; April-June)

Admission Requirements: Secondary school certificate (baccalauréat) or equivalent. Competitive entrance examination for schools and institutes and the faculty of health sciences

Fees: (CFA Francs): Foreign students: c. 1,500,000

Main Language(s) of Instruction: French

Degrees and Diplomas: *Certificat de Capacité en Droit*: Law; *Certificat d'Aptitude au Professorat dans les Collèges d'Enseignement Géneral*: Education, 3 yrs; *Certificat d'Aptitude au Professorat d'Education Physique et Sportive*: Sports, 5 yrs; *Licence*: Fundamental Sciences, Arts and Humanities, Law, 3 yrs; *Diplôme d'Ingénieur*: Electrical Engineering, Food Technology, 2-5 yrs; *Doctorat en Médecine*: Medicine; *Diplôme d'Etudes supérieures*: Arts and Humanities, 2 yrs following licence; *Diplôme d'Etudes approfondies*: Botany, 1 yr following Maîtrise; *Maîtrise*: Economics; Fundamental Sciences, Arts and Humanities, Law; Geology, 1 yr following Licence. Also Teaching Qualifications

Student Services: Health services, Sports facilities

Libraries: Central Library, c. 70,000 vols

Publications: Revue médicale du Congo
Last Updated: 24/06/09

Congo (Democratic Republic)

STRUCTURE OF HIGHER EDUCATION SYSTEM

Description:

Higher education developed considerably during the 1990s and many new institutions - both public and private - were created. Higher education is mainly provided by universities, higher teacher training institutes and higher technological institutes. It comes under the authority of the Ministry of Higher Education. Each institution has a University or Institute Council, an Administrative Committee, faculties (or sections) and departments. The University or Institute Council is the highest authority. It is composed of the Administration Committee, the deans, a faculty representative, a student representative, a representative of the administrative staff and the head librarian. This body coordinates the academic and scientific policy of the institution. The Administration Committee is appointed by the central authority. The Section or Faculty Council is exclusively concerned with the academic and scientific problems of that faculty or institute. It is made up of full professors and department heads. The Department Council is the source of academic life in the universities and is made up of full professors who elect the department head.

Stages of studies:

University level first stage: *Premier cycle*
The first stage of higher education lasts for three years and leads to the Graduat.

University level second stage: *Deuxième cycle*
The second cycle lasts for two years and grants the Licence, except in Medicine and Veterinary Medicine where this stage lasts for three years and leads to the title of Docteur en Médecine and Docteur en Médecine Vétérinaire.

University level third stage: *Troisième cycle*
The third cycle mainly consists of a programme of higher studies leading to the Diplôme d'Etudes supérieures (DES). This programme lasts for two years and includes a certain number of courses and seminars, as well as the presentation of a dissertation. After obtaining the DES, the candidate can enrol in a doctoral programme and prepare a thesis. The next stage leads to the Doctorate which is conferred after a further four to seven years' further study. At the Faculties of Medicine, doctors devote three or four years to a specialization in one of the medical fields, after which they obtain a Diplôme de Spécialiste. Most Spécialistes become practitioners. Those who prefer to teach prepare an Agrégation. Requirements are the possession of the Diplôme de Spécialiste with "distinction" and three to five years' preparation. The degree conferred is that of Agrégé de l'Enseignement supérieur en Médecine. In Veterinary Medicine, it leads to the Agrégation de l'Enseignement supérieur en Médecine vétérinaire.

ADMISSION TO HIGHER EDUCATION

Admission to university-level studies:

Name of secondary school credential required: Diplôme d'Etat d'Etudes secondaires du Cycle long

For entry to: Universities/Higher education institutions - Minimum Mark: 60%

Entrance exam requirements: Entrance examination for students having less than 60% at the Diplôme d'Etat.

Foreign students admission:

Entrance exam requirements: Students must hold a diploma giving access to higher education in their country of origin.

Entry regulations: Students must ask for a visa at the Embassy of their country.

Language requirements: Students must have a good knowledge of French. Those who wish to improve their knowledge of French may follow courses in learning centres.

RECOGNITION OF STUDIES

Bodies dealing with recognition:

Commisssion d'Enterinnement des Diplômes et des Equivalences (Diploma Recognition Commission)
PO Box 5429
Kinshasa/Gombe

NATIONAL BODIES

Ministère de l'Enseignement supérieur et universitaire (Ministry for Higher and University Education)
Minister: Léonard Mashako Mamba
Kinshasa
WWW: http://www.minesu.gouv.cd

Data for academic year: 2009-2010
Source: IAU from IBE database, 2003, Le système universitaire congolais, Pr. Masiala ma Solo, Ministry of Education, Democratic Republic of the Congo, 2003. School System, Credentials and Admission to university level updated in 2009; Bodies, 2011.

INSTITUTIONS

PUBLIC INSTITUTIONS

ACADEMY OF FINE ARTS
Académie des Beaux-Arts
Avenue du 24 novembre, Kinshasa
Tel: +243(12) 68476

Departments
Ceramics (Ceramic Art); **Interior Architecture** (Architecture; Interior Design); **Metal Work** (Interior Design); **Painting** (Painting and Drawing); **Sculpture** (Sculpture); **Visual Communication** (Communication Disorders)

History: Founded 1943 as Ecole Saint Luc. Acquired present status and title 1957.

Main Language(s) of Instruction: French

Degrees and Diplomas: *Graduat*. Also 2nd cycle studies
Last Updated: 09/05/07

INFORMATION AND COMMUNICATION SCIENCES UNIVERSITY COLLEGE
Institut facultaire des Sciences de l'Information et de la Communication (IFASIC)
BP 14998, Kinshasa I
Tel: +243(12) 25117 +243 810-305-975
EMail: ifasicongo@yahoo.fr

Recteur: Jean Lucien Kithima
Tel: +234(99) 959-934 EMail: jeanlucienkit@yahoo.fr
Secrétaire Académique: Emmanuel Mwangaliwa
International Relations: Vivien Nzikani Tel: +243(99) 8265-845

Faculties
Communication Studies (Communication Disorders) *Dean*: Albert Pombo; **Information and Multimedia** (Information Technology; Multimedia) *Dean*: Bernard Munsoko

Research Centres
Communication Studies *(CECOM)* (Communication Studies) *Director*: Joseph Mbelolo

History: Founded 1973 as Institut supérieur des Techniques de l'Information. Acquired present status and title 1997.

Admission Requirements: (Congolese Francs): 200,000 (US Dollars: 250)
Main Language(s) of Instruction: French
International Co-operation: With universities in France and the Republic of Congo
Degrees and Diplomas: *Graduat*: 3 yrs; *Licence*: 2 yrs; *Diplôme d'Etudes supérieures (DES)*: 2 yrs; *Doctorat*
Student Services: Academic counselling, Canteen, Sports facilities
Special Facilities: Radio and TV studios
Publications: Cahier Congolais de Communication *(biannually)*

Academic Staff 2008-2009	MEN	WOMEN	TOTAL
FULL-TIME	70	6	76
PART-TIME	–	5	5
Student Numbers 2008-2009			
All (Foreign Included)	1,000	2,000	3,000

Last Updated: 17/09/09

INSTITUTE OF AGRONOMY OF YANGAMBI
Institut facultaire des Sciences agronomiques de Yangambi
BP 28, Yangambi
Tel: +243(99) 8539-647

Recteur: Benjamin Dudu Akaibe

Faculties
Agronomy (Agronomy)
History: Founded 1976.
Main Language(s) of Instruction: French
Degrees and Diplomas: *Graduat*: 3 yrs; *Diplôme d'Ingénieur*: 2 yrs; *Diplôme d'Etudes supérieures (DES)*: 2 yrs; *Doctorat*
Last Updated: 03/05/07

INSTITUTE OF APPLIED TECHNIQUES
Institut supérieur des Techniques appliquées (ISTA)
BP 6593, Kinshasa XXXI
Tel: +243(89) 54628
Directeur général: Cabral Beta Mwakatita Moura

Programmes

Civil Aviation (Aeronautical and Aerospace Engineering); **Electronic Engineering** (Electronic Engineering); **Industrial Electrical Engineering** (Electrical Engineering; Industrial Engineering); **Mechanical Engineering** (Mechanical Engineering); **Meteorology** (Meteorology)

Further Information: Branches in Kolwezi; Goma; Ebonda

History: Founded 1971. Acquired present status and title 1981.

Degrees and Diplomas: *Diplôme d'Ingénieur*: 5 yrs

INSTITUTE OF CIVIL AND CONSTRUCTION ENGINEERING

Institut du Bâtiment et des Travaux publics (IBTP)
BP 4731, Kinshasa II

Directeur général: Tshisuaka Ngalula
Tel: +243(99) 9926-821 EMail: tnkz@yahoo.fr

Secrétaire général académique: Mangombi Dei Ilonga
Tel: +243(99) 9959-366 EMail: mangombidei@yahoo.fr

International Relations: Mbolela Ngoie Tel: +243(99) 0167-992

Sections

Architecture (Architecture); **Building Engineering** (Building Technologies; Engineering); **Topography** (Surveying and Mapping); **Town Planning** (Town Planning)

History: Founded 1971 following the merger of the Institut National du Bâtiment et des Travaux Publics, the Institut Supérieur des Géomètres Experts Immobiliers and the Institut Supérieur d'Architecture; Acquired present status 1981.

Main Language(s) of Instruction: French

Degrees and Diplomas: *Diplôme d'Ingénieur*: Civil and Construction Engineering; Topography; Town Planning, 5 yrs. Also Diplôme d'Architecture (5 yrs)

Student Services: Academic counselling, Cultural centre, Employment services, Foreign student adviser, Health services, Social counselling, Sports facilities

Student Residential Facilities: For 500 students.

Libraries: Yes

Publications: Les Annales de l'IBTP, Travaux de recherche des enseignants *(3 per annum)*
Last Updated: 22/05/07

INSTITUTE OF COMMERCE OF KINSHASA

Institut supérieur de Commerce de Kinshasa (ISC)
BP 16596, Kinshasa-Gombe I
Tel: +243(898) 109-143 +243(899) 438-957
Fax: +243(99) 13771

Directeur général: Emmanuel Kanga Matondo

Programmes

Business Computing; **Commerce and Finance** (Accountancy; Business and Commerce; Finance; Marketing); **Management** (Management); **Secretarial Studies** (Secretarial Studies)

Research Centres

Interdisciplinary Research in Management and Development *(Interdisciplinary)*

History: Founded 1964. Acquired present status and title 1981.

Main Language(s) of Instruction: French

Degrees and Diplomas: *Graduat*: 3-4 yrs; *Licence*: 3 yrs (evening classes)
Last Updated: 30/04/07

INSTITUTE OF MEDICAL TECHNIQUES

Institut supérieur des Techniques médicales (ISTM)
BP 774, Kinshasa XI

Directeur général: Kabasele Kabasele

Programmes

Laboratory Techniques (Laboratory Techniques); **Management of Health Institutions** (Health Administration); **Nursing** (Nursing); **Nursing Management**; **Nutrition and Dietetics** (Dietetics; Nutri-

tion); **Physical Therapy** (Physical Therapy); **Radiology Techniques** (Radio and Television Broadcasting)

History: Founded 1970. Acquired present status 1981.

Main Language(s) of Instruction: French

Degrees and Diplomas: *Graduat*: 3 yrs; *Licence*: 2 yrs

INSTITUTE OF RURAL DEVELOPMENT OF TSHIBASHI

Institut supérieur de Développement rural de Tshibashi (ISDR)
BP 720, Kananga

Directeur général: Bukasa Tubadikubub
Tel: +243(81) 604-1298 +243(99) 745-0919
EMail: bukamul@yahoo.fr

Scrétaire général académique: Nkongolo Katende
Tel: +243(81) 603-5456 +243(99) 461-9025

International Relations: Bushabu Ngolo, Secrétaire général administratif

Programmes

Regional Planning (Regional Planning); **Rural Management**; **Social Organizations** (Social Sciences)

History: Founded 1983.

Main Language(s) of Instruction: French

Degrees and Diplomas: *Graduat*: Planning; Social Organizations; Rural Management, 3 yrs; *Licence*: Planning; Social Organizations; Rural Management, 2 yrs

Academic Staff 2008-2009	MEN	WOMEN	TOTAL
FULL-TIME	44	3	47
PART-TIME	16	4	20
STAFF WITH DOCTORATE			
FULL-TIME	2	–	2
PART-TIME	2	–	2
Student Numbers 2008-2009			
All (Foreign Included)	394	81	475

Last Updated: 05/03/10

INSTITUTE OF SOCIAL STUDIES OF LUBUMBASHI

Institut supérieur d'Etudes sociales de Lubumbashi (ISES)
BP 1575, Lubumbashi

Directeur général: Kayamba Badje

Programmes

Community Development (Development Studies); **Human Resources Management**; **Industrial Sociology**; **Social Studies** (Social Studies)

History: Founded 1971. Acquired present status and title 1981.

Main Language(s) of Instruction: French

Degrees and Diplomas: *Graduat*: 3 yrs; *Licence*: 2 yrs

INSTITUTE OF STATISTICS OF KINSHASA

Institut supérieur de Statistique de Kinshasa (ISS)
BP 1757 No 1, Av. Victoire Commune de Kalamu, Cfr. Ecole de Navigation, Kinshasa I
EMail: isskinshasa@yahoo.fr

Directeur général: Osokonda Okenge

Secrétaire général académique: Aloïs Thamba Nkenge
EMail: thambaalois@yahoo.fr

Programmes

Business Computing (Business Computing); **Commerce and Finance** (Business and Commerce; Finance); **Documentation** (Documentation Techniques); **Statistics** (Statistics)

History: Founded 1965.

Main Language(s) of Instruction: French

Degrees and Diplomas: *Graduat*: 3 yrs; *Licence*: 2 yrs

INSTITUTE OF STATISTICS OF LUBUMBASHI
Institut supérieur des Statistiques de Lubumbashi (ISS)
BP 2471, Lubumbashi

Directeur général: Keba Tau

Programmes
Applied Economics; **Business Computing** (Business Computing); **Mathematics for Management** (Applied Mathematics; Mathematics); **Statistics** (Statistics)

History: Founded 1971. Acquired present status and title 1981.

Main Language(s) of Instruction: French

Degrees and Diplomas: *Graduat*: 3 yrs; *Licence*: 2 yrs

NATIONAL INSTITUTE OF THE ARTS
Institut National des Arts (INA)
BP 8332, Kinshasa

Directeur général: Malutama Duma Ngo

Programmes
Leisure Activities; **Music** (Music); **Theatre** (Theatre)

History: Founded 1971. Acquired present status and title 1981.

Degrees and Diplomas: *Graduat*: 3 yrs; *Licence*: 2 yrs

NATIONAL PEDAGOGICAL UNIVERSITY
Université pédagogique nationale
BP 8815, Quartier Binza, Kinshasa I
Tel: +243(98) 204-952

Recteur: Jean-Robert Kasele Laïsi

Schools
Arts and Humanities; **Exact Sciences**; **Teacher Training** (Teacher Training)

History: Founded 1961 as Institut pédagogique national de Léopoldville. Acquired present title and status 2005.

Main Language(s) of Instruction: French

Degrees and Diplomas: *Graduat*: 3-4 yrs; *Licence*: 2-3 yrs; *Diplôme d'Etudes approfondies*

OFFICIAL UNIVERSITY OF BUKAVU
Université officielle de Bukavu
BP 570, Bukavu
Tel: +243(81) 8995-261
Fax: +871(762) 056-981
EMail: unikis-cub@hotmail.com; unikis_cub@yahoo.fr
Website: http://univoffbukavu.org

Recteur: Nyakabwa Mutabana (1994-)
EMail: nyakabwadominique@yahoo.fr
Secrétaire général administratif: Nyabyenda Wa-Tabura

Faculties
Letters; **Sciences and Biomedical Sciences**

History: Founded 1993 as Centre universitaire de Bukavu. Acquired present status 1997.

Governing Bodies: Executive Committee (Rector; Academic Secretary General; Administrative Secretary General; Financial Manager); Deans of Faculties; Heads of Departments

Admission Requirements: Secondary school credential (Diplôme de fin d'études secondaires) or equivalent

Fees: (US Dollars): 185-200 per annum

Main Language(s) of Instruction: French

International Co-operation: with universities in Rwanda; Burundi; Cameroon; Benin; Togo; Belgium and France

Degrees and Diplomas: *Graduat*: 3 yrs; *Licence*: 2 yrs; *Diplôme d'Etudes approfondies (DEA)*

Student Services: Academic counselling, Social counselling

Special Facilities: No
Last Updated: 03/05/07

PEDAGOGICAL INSTITUTE OF BUKAVU
Institut supérieur pédagogique de Bukavu (ESU)
BP 854, Bukavu
EMail: ispcg_ceruki@yahoo.fr

Directeur général: Boniface Kaningini Mwenyimali

Schools
Arts and Humanities; **Exact Sciences** (Biology; Chemistry; Geography; Geology; Health Sciences; Mathematics; Natural Sciences; Physics)

Further Information: Branches in Rutshuru and Kindu

History: Founded 1968. Acquired present status and title 1981.

Main Language(s) of Instruction: French

Degrees and Diplomas: *Graduat*: 3 yrs; *Licence*: 2 yrs

PEDAGOGICAL INSTITUTE OF KANANGA
Institut supérieur pédagogique de Kananga
BP 282, Kananga

Directeur général: Tshimbombo Mudiba

Schools
Arts and Social Sciences (Administration; African Studies; Business and Commerce; English; French; History; Latin; Linguistics; Social Sciences); **Exact Sciences** (Agronomy; Biology; Chemistry; Geography; Mathematics; Natural Sciences; Physics; Technology; Veterinary Science)

History: Founded 1958 as Ecole Normale. Acquired present status and title 1981.

Main Language(s) of Instruction: French

Degrees and Diplomas: *Graduat*: 3 yrs; *Licence*: 2 yrs

PEDAGOGICAL INSTITUTE OF LA GOMBE
Institut supérieur pédagogique de la Gombe (ISP/GOMBE)
BP 3580, Croisement des Avenues Père Boka et Kisangani/Gombe, Kinshasa 3580
Tel: +243(15) 125-331

Directeur général: Maliya Matumele Tel: +243 999-953-935
Secrétaire général: Edumbe Akonga Tel: +243 815-170-299

Departments
Biology and Chemistry (Biology; Chemistry; Teacher Training) *Head*: Aseke Etumangele; **Commerce and Administration** (Administration; Business Administration; Business and Commerce; Business Education; Teacher Training) *Head*: Bongongo Ekina; **English and African Cultures** (African Languages; African Studies; English; Regional Studies; Teacher Training) *Head*: Félix Kabata; **French and African Linguistics** (African Languages; French; Linguistics; Teacher Training) *Head*: Mbo Lefranke; **Geography and Environmental Management** (Environmental Management; Geography; Teacher Training) *Head*: Mansila Fukiau; **History and Patrimonial Management** (Heritage Preservation; History; Teacher Training) *Head*: Kwama Mobwa M.; **Hotel Management** (Hotel Management; Teacher Training) *Head*: Mashiny Manu; **Psychopedagogy** (Educational Psychology; Teacher Training) *Head*: Pindi Mbumba

Sections
Exact Sciences *Head*: Prosper Kuasa Mikandu; **Letters and Human Sciences** (Arts and Humanities; Social Sciences) *Head*: Guidon Manzombi Pibwa; **Technical Sciences** *Head*: Honoré Tukunda Ohanu

History: Founded 1961 by Catholic Sisters to promote women's level of education. Acquired present status and title 1981.

Admission Requirements: Secondary school certificate (state diploma)

Fees: (US Dollars): 150 per annum

Main Language(s) of Instruction: French; English

International Co-operation: With universities in Canada

Degrees and Diplomas: *Graduat (G3)*: 3 yrs; *Licence*: Biology; English; French; Geography; History; Commerce and Administration; Hotel Management (L2), 2 yrs

Student Services: Academic counselling, Employment services, Health services, Sports facilities

Student Residential Facilities: For 335 students

Libraries: Main Library

Publications: Les cahiers de l'ISP/Gombe, Pluridisciplinary *(biennially)*

Academic Staff *2008-2009*: Total: c. 200
Student Numbers *2008-2009*: Total: c. 5,000
Last Updated: 13/08/09

PEDAGOGICAL INSTITUTE OF LUBUMBASHI

Institut supérieur pédagogique de Lubumbashi
BP 1796/L'Shi, Lubumbashi

Directeur général: Irung Tshitambala

Schools

Arts and Humanities (African Studies; English; French; History; Latin; Social Sciences); **Exact Sciences**; **Training**

History: Founded 1959. Acquired present status and title 1981.

Main Language(s) of Instruction: French

Degrees and Diplomas: *Graduat*: 3 yrs; *Licence*: 2 yrs

PEDAGOGICAL INSTITUTE OF MBANZA-NGUNGU

Institut supérieur pédagogique de Mbanza-Ngungu
BP 127, Mbanza-Ngungu, Bas Congo
EMail: ispmbng@yahoo.fr

Directeur général: Nsakala Lengo Tel: +243(81) 5253-609

Secrétaire général académique: Mwaka Lusala
Tel: +243(81) 9050-333

Secrétaire général administratif: Pambu Ntima
Tel: +243(81) 5097-956

Schools

Arts and Social Sciences (African Studies; English; French; History; Latin; Social Sciences); **Exact Sciences** (Biology; Chemistry; Computer Science; Electronic Engineering; Mathematics; Physics; Technology)

History: Founded 1981.

Admission Requirements: Secondary school certificate (state diploma)

Fees: (US Dollars): 500 per annum

Main Language(s) of Instruction: French

Degrees and Diplomas: *Graduat*: Pedagogy, 3 yrs; *Licence*: Pedagogy, 2 yrs

Student Services: Academic counselling, Health services, Sports facilities

Student Residential Facilities: Yes (for male only)

Libraries: Yes

Publications: Scientia - Revue de Sciences, Lettres et Pédagogie appliquée *(biannually)*
Last Updated: 09/05/07

PEDAGOGICAL INSTITUTE OF MBUJI-MAYI

Institut supérieur pédagogique de Mbuji-Mayi (ISP DE MBUJIMAYI)
BP 682, Mbuji-Mayi, Kasai Oriental 682
EMail: sgacispmjm@yahoo.fr

Directeur général: wa Badinga Astrid Nseya (2009-)
Tel: +243(99) 7684 238 EMail: musampanseya@yahoo.fr

Secrétaire général académique: Nzeji Jean Willy Biayi
Tel: +243(81) 5074 575 EMail: jeanwillybiayi@yahoo.fr

Sections

Arts and Humanities (African Studies; Arts and Humanities; Business and Commerce; English; French; History; Latin; Linguistics; Pedagogy; Psychology); **Exact Sciences** (Biology; Chemistry; Geography; Mathematics; Natural Sciences; Physics)

History: Founded 1968. Acquired present status and title 1981.

Governing Bodies: Comité de Gestion; Conseil de l'Institut

Academic Year: October to July

Admission Requirements: High or Secondary School certificate (Diplôme d'Etat)

Fees: (US Dollars): 80.00 per annum

Main Language(s) of Instruction: French

Degrees and Diplomas: *Graduat*: 3 yrs; *Licence*: 2 yrs

Student Services: Academic counselling, Language programs, Nursery care, Social counselling

Special Facilities: Languages, Chemistry, Biology and Physics laboratories

Libraries: Yes

Publications: Annales de l'ISP de Mbujimayi, Applied Research in Pedagogy *(annually)*; Collection Travaux et Recherche *(annually)*

Press or Publishing House: Candip/ISP

Academic Staff *2009-2010*	MEN	WOMEN	TOTAL
FULL-TIME	99	1	100
PART-TIME	8	–	8
Student Numbers *2009-2010*			
All (Foreign Included)	650	328	978
FOREIGN ONLY	152	31	183

Evening students, 72.
Last Updated: 03/05/10

PEDAGOGICAL INSTITUTE OF MUHANGI AT BUTEMBO

Institut supérieur pédagogique de Muhangi à Butembo (ISP/MUHANGI)
BP 380, Butembo, Nord-Kivu
Tel: +243 (99) 7623-482
EMail: ispmuhangi@yahoo.fr

Directeur général: Alphonsine Kakuhi Kaswera
Tel: +243 (99) 7235-239

Secrétaire général académique: Kahavo Sikamango
Tel: +243 (99) 8777-951

International Relations: Kambale Malumalu, Secrétaire général administratif Tel: +243 (99) 7777-002

Schools

Arts and Humanities (African Languages; African Studies; Arts and Humanities; Educational Psychology; English; French; History; Latin; Linguistics); **Business Administration** (Business and Commerce; Business Computing; Information Technology; Management); **Sciences** (Biology; Chemistry; Environmental Studies; Geography; Mathematics; Physics)

History: Founded 1993. Acquired public status 2004.

Admission Requirements: Diplôme d'Etat (after 6 yrs secondary school education)

Fees: (US Dollars): 90 per annum

Main Language(s) of Instruction: French, English

Degrees and Diplomas: *Graduat*: 3 yrs; *Licence*: 2 yrs

Student Services: Sports facilities

Student Residential Facilities: None

Academic Staff *2009-2010*	MEN	WOMEN	TOTAL
FULL-TIME	55	7	62
PART-TIME	36	1	37
STAFF WITH DOCTORATE			
FULL-TIME	4	1	5
PART-TIME	7	–	7
Student Numbers *2009-2010*			
All (Foreign Included)	521	109	630

Last Updated: 04/11/10

PEDAGOGICAL TECHNICAL INSTITUTE OF KINSHASA

Institut supérieur pédagogique technique de Kinshasa (ISPT)
BP 3287, Kinshasa

Directeur général: Jean-Marie Gueben

Programmes
Electrical and Mechanical Engineering (Electrical Engineering; Mechanical Engineering); **Electrical and Technical Studies** (Electrical Engineering; Technology); **Electrical Engineering** (Electrical Engineering); **Electronic Engineering** (Electronic Engineering); **Mechanical Engineering**

History: Founded 1981.

Main Language(s) of Instruction: French

Degrees and Diplomas: *Graduat*: 3 yrs; *Licence*: 2 yrs

UNIVERSITY OF KINSHASA

Université de Kinshasa (UNIKIN)
BP 190, Kinshasa XI
Tel: +243(12) 27793
Fax: +243(12) 21360
EMail: centreinfo@ic.cd
Website: http://www.unikin.cd/

Recteur: Jean Berchmans Labana Lasay' abar
Tel: +243(12) 27793 EMail: rectorat@unikin.cd

Faculties
Agronomy (Agronomy); **Arts**; **Economics** (Economics); **Law** (Law); **Medicine** (Dentistry; Medicine); **Pharmacy** (Pharmacy); **Polytechnic** (Civil Engineering; Engineering; Technology); **Psychology**; **Science** (Mathematics and Computer Science; Natural Sciences); **Social, Political Sciences and Administration**

History: Founded 1949 as Université Lovanium, became a campus of the Université nationale du Zaïre 1971. Acquired present status and title 1981. A State institution.

Governing Bodies: Conseil d'Administration d'Université

Academic Year: October to June (October-February; February-June)

Admission Requirements: Secondary school certificate and entrance examination

Main Language(s) of Instruction: French

Degrees and Diplomas: *Graduat*; *Diplôme d'Ingénieur*: Civil Engineering, 5 yrs; *Docteur en Médecine*: Medicine, 6 yrs; *Licence*: Civil Engineering; Law; Science, 5 yrs; *Licence*: Economics, 4 yrs; *Diplôme d'Etudes supérieures (DES)*: Law; *Diplôme de Spécialiste*: Medicine; *Agrégation de l'Enseignement supérieur en Médecine*: Medicine; *Doctorat*: Economics; Pharmacy; Science

Special Facilities: University museum

Libraries: c. 300,000 vols

Publications: Annales of the Faculties of Science, Polytechnic and Pharmacy; Cahiers économiques et sociaux des Religions africaines *(quarterly)*

Press or Publishing House: Presses universitaires de l'Université de Kinshasa
Last Updated: 09/03/12

UNIVERSITY OF KISANGANI

Université de Kisangani
BP 2012, Kisangani, Haut Zaïre
Tel: +243(21) 1335
Website: http://unikis-ac.cd/index.php

Recteur: Dauly Ngbonda (2005-)

Faculties
Education and Psychology (Education; Psychology); **Medicine** (Dermatology; Gynaecology and Obstetrics; Medicine; Paediatrics; Stomatology); **Science** (Biochemistry; Biology; Ecology; Natural Sciences); **Social Sciences, Administration, and Political Science** (Administration; Political Sciences; Social Sciences; Sociology)

History: Founded 1963 as Université libre du Congo, became a campus of the Université nationale du Zaïre 1971. Acquired present status and title 1981. A State institution.

Governing Bodies: Conseil d'Administration

Academic Year: October to July (October-February; February-July)

Admission Requirements: Secondary school certificate and entrance examination

Main Language(s) of Instruction: French

Degrees and Diplomas: *Graduat*; *Docteur en Médecine*: 6 yrs; *Licence*: Administration; Sociology; *Licence*: Education, 4 yrs; *Licence*: Psychology; Science, 5 yrs; *Diplôme d'Etudes supérieures (DES)*: Pedagogy; Psychology; Science; *Diplôme de Spécialiste*: Medicine; *Agrégation de l'Enseignement supérieur en Médecine*: Medicine; *Doctorat*: Pedagogy; Psychology; Sociology

Student Residential Facilities: Yes

Libraries: c. 46,000 vols

Press or Publishing House: Presses universitaires de Kisangani

UNIVERSITY OF LUBUMBASHI

Université de Lubumbashi (UNILU)
BP 1825, Lubumbashi, Shaba
Tel: +243(22) 5403 +243 (23) 48202
Fax: +243(22) 8099
EMail: unilu@unilu.net
Website: http://www.unilu.ac.cd

Recteur: Chabu Mumba

International Relations: Lubala Toto, Directeur à la Coopération

Faculties
Agronomy (Agronomy); **Arts and Humanities** (Advertising and Publicity; African Languages; African Studies; Ancient Civilizations; Arts and Humanities; Cinema and Television; English; English Studies; French; French Studies; History; Information Sciences; Journalism; Latin; Linguistics; Literature; Performing Arts; Philosophy; Translation and Interpretation); **Economics and Management** (Demography and Population; Economics; Management); **Law** (Commercial Law; Law; Private Law; Public Law); **Medicine** (Biomedicine; Gynaecology and Obstetrics; Medicine; Paediatrics; Pharmacy; Surgery); **Polytechnic** (Electronic Engineering; Industrial Chemistry; Mechanical Engineering; Metallurgical Engineering; Mining Engineering); **Psychology and Educational Sciences** (Educational Sciences; Psychology); **Science** (Chemistry; Geography; Geology; Mathematics; Natural Sciences); **Social, Political, and Administrative Sciences** (Administration; Anthropology; International Relations; Political Sciences; Social Sciences; Sociology); **Veterinary Medicine** (Veterinary Science)

Higher Institutes
Medical Techniques (Health Administration; Laboratory Techniques; Medical Technology; Nursing; Nutrition)

Higher Schools
Commerce (Business and Commerce; Finance; Marketing; Secretarial Studies); **Engineering** (Chemical Engineering; Construction Engineering; Electrical Engineering; Electronic Engineering; Inorganic Chemistry; Laboratory Techniques; Mechanical Engineering; Mining Engineering; Organic Chemistry)

Schools
Cartography; **Criminology** (Criminology); **Public Health** (Public Health)

Further Information: Campuses in Kamina, Likasi, Kolwesi and Kasumbalesa

History: Founded 1955 as Université officielle du Congo, became a campus of the Université nationale du Zaïre 1971, and acquired present status and title 1981. A State institution.

Governing Bodies: Conseil d'Administration

Academic Year: October to June (October-February; February-June)

Admission Requirements: Secondary school certificate and entrance examination

Fees: (Congo Francs): 45,000-105,000

Main Language(s) of Instruction: French

Degrees and Diplomas: *Graduat*; *Diplôme d'Ingénieur*: Civil Engineering, 5 yrs; *Docteur en Médecine*: Medicine; *Docteur en Médecine Vétérinaire*: Veterinary Medicine, 6 yrs; *Licence*: Anthropology; International Relations; Political Science; *Licence*: Engineering; Science, 5 yrs; *Licence*: Letters; Sociology, 4 yrs; *Diplôme d'Etudes approfondies*; *Diplôme de Spécialiste*: Medicine; *Agrégation de l'Enseignement supérieur en Médecine*: Medicine; *Doctorat*; *Doctorat*: Medicine; Pharmacy; Veterinary Medicine; Law; Economics and Management; Agronomy; Educational Sciences; Psychology; Criminology

Student Residential Facilities: For 1,300 students

Libraries: c. 95,000 vols
Last Updated: 10/08/09

PRIVATE INSTITUTIONS

ACQUATORIA UNIVERSITY
Université Acquatoria (UNAEQUA)
BP 400, Gbadolite

Recteur: Ndumba Y'Oole L'Ifefo

Faculties
Agronomy (Agronomy); **Economics** (Economics); **Law**; **Medicine** (Medicine)

Further Information: Branches in Mobayi Mbongo, Lisala and Mbandaka

History: Founded 1991.

Main Language(s) of Instruction: French

ADVENTIST UNIVERSITY OF LUKANGA WALLACE
Université adventiste de Lukanga Wallace
BP 180 Butembo Territoire de Lubero, (à 40 km de Butembo), Lukanga

Faculties
Arts; **Management and Business Administration** (Business Administration; Management); **Psychology and Educational Sciences**; **Theology**

History: Founded 1996.

Main Language(s) of Instruction: French

Degrees and Diplomas: *Graduat*: 3 yrs; *Licence*: 2 yrs

⚡ BEL CAMPUS TECHNOLOGICAL UNIVERSITY
Université technologique Bel Campus (UTBC)
17, 8ème Rue Limete, Quartier Industriel, Kinshasa
Tel: +243 9982 19098
EMail: belcampus@yahoo.fr
Website: http://www.belcampus.org/

Recteur: Albert Essanga Tolongo (2008-)

International Relations: Joseph Nzau Wa Nzau, Chef des Travaux EMail: jose_nzau2003@yahoo.fr

Faculties
Economics and Management (Business Administration; Economics; International Economics; Management); **Information Management** (Computer Networks; Information Management; Information Sciences); **Law** (Law; Private Law; Public Law); **Medicine** (Medicine); **Social, Political and Administrative Sciences** (Administration; Information Sciences; International Relations; Political Sciences; Social Sciences)

Research Centres
Recherche Interdisciplinaire pour le Développement Economique et Sociale *(CRDES)*

History: Founded 1996.

Governing Bodies: Board of Directors

Admission Requirements: State Diploma with at least 60% mark

Fees: (Congo Francs): 137,600 per annum

Main Language(s) of Instruction: French

Degrees and Diplomas: *Licence*: Law; Economics and Management; Information Management; Administrative, Political and Social Sciences, 5 yrs; *Licence*: Medicine, 7 yrs

Student Services: Academic counselling, Cultural centre, Foreign student adviser, Sports facilities

Special Facilities: Observatory, biochemistry laboratory, human anatomy laboratory

Libraries: 1,403 vols.

Academic Staff 2008-2009	TOTAL
FULL-TIME	72
PART-TIME	215
PART-TIME	138

Student Numbers 2008-2009	
All (Foreign Included)	3,428

Last Updated: 11/12/09

CARDINAL MALULA CHRISTIAN UNIVERSITY
Université chrétienne Cardinal Malula (UCCM)
BP 10883, Saio no 2317/bis Q/IEM, Commune de Kasa-Vubu, Kinshasa
Tel: +243(81) 9905-188
Fax: +243(89) 5127-659
EMail: lspluc@yahoo.fr

Recteur: Emmanuel Biangany Gomanu (1984-)
Tel: +243(99) 9905-188

Secrétaire général académique: Robert Neney O' Ter

International Relations: Barnabé Kabaka Makambu, Directeur du Cabinet du Recteur Tel: +243(99) 8219-080

Faculties
Arts (Arts and Humanities); **Economics and Management** (Economics; Management); **International Relations** (International Relations); **Law** (Law); **Philosophy and Humanities** (Arts and Humanities; Philosophy); **Social Sciences** (Social Sciences)

History: Founded 1984 by Biangany Emmanuel. Acquired present status 2006. Formerly known as University Institute of Economics, Philosophy and Humanities (Institut universitaire des Sciences économiques, Philosophie et Lettres - ISPL).

Fees: (US Dollars): 270 per annum

Main Language(s) of Instruction: French; English

International Co-operation: With AUF (Agence Universitaire de la Francophonie)

Degrees and Diplomas: *Graduat*: 3 yrs; *Licence*: 2 yrs

Student Services: Academic counselling, Cultural centre, Employment services, Handicapped facilities, Health services, Language programs, Nursery care, Social counselling, Sports facilities

Libraries: Yes

Publications: Logos, Political, Social and Cultural matters *(biennially)*

Press or Publishing House: ISPL Press

Academic Staff 2008-2009	MEN	WOMEN	TOTAL
FULL-TIME	–	–	2,102

Student Numbers 2008-2009			
All (Foreign Included)	1,090	1,001	2,091

Last Updated: 03/06/09

CARDINAL MALULA UNIVERSITY
Université Cardinal Malula (UCM)
BP 14464, Avenue Kingabwa (Route des poids lourds) no 2973, Kinshasa/Limete, Kinshasa I
EMail: emnkos@yahoo.fr

Recteur: Mazinga Mashin Tel: +243(99) 9944-917

Secrétaire général: Anastase Nzeza
Tel: +243(99) 8303-791 EMail: bilakila@yahoo.fr

International Relations: Jean-Marie Mubaka, Directeur des Services académiques
Tel: +243(99) 9901-165 EMail: efannet1@yahoo.fr

Faculties

Economics; Environmental Sciences; Law; Social Sciences (Social Sciences)

History: Founded 1989. Acquired present status 1996.

Admission Requirements: State diploma

Fees: (US Dollars): 200 per annum

Main Language(s) of Instruction: French

International Co-operation: With universities in Belgium

Degrees and Diplomas: *Graduat (G3)*: 3 yrs; *Licence (L2)*: 2 yrs

Student Services: Cultural centre, Language programs, Sports facilities

Libraries: Yes

CATHOLIC UNIVERSITY INSTITUTE

Institut universitaire catholique (IUC)

BP 10.883, Stade Tata Raphaël, Kalamu, Kinshasa I

Recteur: Carre Adjadoume Omalokenge

Faculties

Administration (Administration); **Economics** (Economics); **Law** (Law)

History: Founded 1994.

Main Language(s) of Instruction: French

Degrees and Diplomas: *Graduat*: 3 yrs; *Licence*: 2 yrs

CATHOLIC UNIVERSITY OF BUKAVU

Université catholique de Bukavu (UCB)

BP 285, Bukavu, Sud-Bukavu
Tel: +243(81) 3180-622
EMail: recteur@ucbukavu.org; recteurucb@yahoo.fr
Website: http://www.ucbukavu.org

Recteur: Joseph Birindwa Gwamuhanya (2002-)
EMail: recteur@ucbukavu.org

Vice-Recteur aux Affaires académiques: Augustin Bashwira
EMail: vracad@ucbukavu.org

Faculties

Agronomy (Agronomy); **Economics** (Economics); **Law** (Law); **Medicine** (Medicine)

History: Founded 1989 by the archbishop of Bukavu.

Governing Bodies: Conseil d'Administration, comprising 23 members; Conseil académique et scientifique, comprising 30 members; Comité de Direction, comprising 4 members

Academic Year: October to July (October-December; January-March; April-July)

Admission Requirements: Secondary school certificate and entrance examination

Fees: (Congo Francs): first three years of studies, 151,000 per annum; 22,500 per annum for the rest

Main Language(s) of Instruction: French

International Co-operation: With universities in Belgium; France; Burundi; Benin and Gabon

Degrees and Diplomas: *Graduat*; *Diplôme d'Ingénieur*: Agronomy, 5 yrs; *Licence*: Economics; Law; Computer Science, 5 yrs; *Doctorat*: Medicine; Surgery; Midwifery, 6 yrs

Student Services: Academic counselling, Health services, Nursery care, Social counselling, Sports facilities

Student Residential Facilities: None

Special Facilities: Internet access

Libraries: 14,048 vols

Publications: Annales de l'U.C.B., Articles by the university faculty *(biennially)*
Last Updated: 18/02/09

CATHOLIC UNIVERSITY OF CONGO

Université catholique du Congo

BP 1534, Avenue de l'Université n° 2, Limete, Kinshasa
Tel: +243(81) 700-7985
Fax: +243(81) 301-6508
EMail: univcac@univcac.org
Website: http://www.univcac.net/

Recteur: Jean-Bosco Matand (2007-)

Centres

African Religions *(CERA)*; **Ecclesiastical Archives** *(Abbé Stephano (CAEK))* (Religious Studies)

Faculties

Canon Law (Canon Law); **Economics and Development**; **Law and Political Sciences** (Law; Political Sciences); **Philosophy**; **Social Communication** (Communication Studies; Social Studies); **Theology** (Christian Religious Studies; Theology)

History: Founded 1957 as Facultés catholiques de Kinshasa. Acquired present status and title 2008 .

Admission Requirements: State Diploma (+60%), and recommendation by a member of the Clergy

Fees: (US Dollars): 375 per annum

Main Language(s) of Instruction: French

Degrees and Diplomas: *Graduat*; *Licence*: Philosophy, Theology, Development Studies, Journalism, 5 yrs; *Diplôme d'Etudes approfondies*; *Doctorat*: Philosophy, Theology

Publications: Journal of African Religions *(quarterly)*; Journal of African Theology *(quarterly)*; Kinshasa Journal of Philosophy *(quarterly)*
Last Updated: 10/08/09

CATHOLIC UNIVERSITY OF THE GRABEN

Université catholique du Graben (UCG)

BP 29, Butembo, Nord-Kivu
Tel: +243(81) 3052-753
Fax: +243(99) 8232-754
EMail: contact@ucg-rdc.org
Website: http://www.ucg-rdc.org

Recteur: Apollinaire Malu Malu

Faculties

Agronomy (Agronomy); **Economics** (Economics); **Human Medicine** (Medicine); **Law** (Law); **Pharmacy** (Pharmacy); **Social and Political Sciences and Administration** (Administration; Political Sciences; Social Sciences); **Veterinary Medicine** (Veterinary Science)

History: Founded 1989.

Main Language(s) of Instruction: French

Degrees and Diplomas: *Graduat*: 3 yrs; *Diplôme d'Ingénieur*; *Docteur en Médecine*: 3 yrs; *Docteur en Médecine Vétérinaire*: 3 yrs; *Licence*: 2 yrs
Last Updated: 18/02/09

CEPROMAD UNIVERSITY

Université du CEPROMAD (UNIC)

BP 768 KIN XI, Av. Mongo no 1, Q. Masina Petro-Congo, Kinshasa I
Tel: +243(81) 6666-769

Recteur: Nsaman O. Lutu (1982-)
Tel: +243(89) 7976-686 EMail: oscarlutu@yahoo.fr

Secrétaire général académique: Payanzo Nsomo
Tel: +243(89) 9924-6871 EMail: ppayanzo@yahoo.fr

International Relations: Maseke Raph, Chargé du Partenariat et de la Coopération internationale Tel: +243(81) 699-402

Faculties

Economics (Economics) *Dean*: Suname Kibwana Mohindo; **International Relations** (International Relations; Peace and Disarmament) *Dean*: Bola Ntotela; **Law I** (Human Rights; Law; Public Law) *Dean*: Citenge Mjanza; **Law II** *(Bukavu; Goma; Lubumbashi; Kolwezi; Butembo; Boma; Matadi; Mbandaka; Kalemi; Isiro; Bunia; Kikwit)* (Human Rights; Law; Public Law) *Dean*: Otshoma Pita; **Social, Political and Administrative Sciences** *(Bukavu; Goma;*

Lubumbashi; Beni; Buytembo; Matadi; Kananga; Mbandaka; Likasi; Kolwezi; Mweka; Isiro; Goma; Bunia) Dean: Utsmumampita; **Technology and Development Studies** (Development Studies; Nursing; Technology) *Dean*: Mukania Buleme

Institutes

Health Sciences *(Institut Facultaire) Head*: Mulamba Ignance

History: Founded 1982 as Institut supérieur de Gestion des Affaires. Acquired present status 1993.

Admission Requirements: Secondary school certificate

Main Language(s) of Instruction: French

International Co-operation: With universities in USA, South Africa, Germany

Degrees and Diplomas: *Graduat*: 3 yrs; *Licence*: 2 yrs; *Diplôme d'Etudes approfondies*: 2 yrs; *Doctorat*: 3-5 yrs

Student Services: Academic counselling, Cultural centre, Language programs, Nursery care, Social counselling, Sports facilities

Publications: CAPM, Revue *(quarterly)*

Academic Staff *2008-2009*	MEN	WOMEN	TOTAL
FULL-TIME	–	–	136
PART-TIME	24	–	24
STAFF WITH DOCTORATE			
FULL-TIME	30	15	45
PART-TIME	24	9	33

Student Numbers *2008-2009*
All (Foreign Included)	–	–	1,534

Part-time students, 134. **Distance students**, 30. **Evening students**, 1,400.
Last Updated: 04/08/09

CHRISTIAN UNIVERSITY OF KINSHASA

Université chrétienne de Kinshasa (UCKIN)
BP 4742, Av. de l'Université no 1 bis, Binza/Ozone-Ngaliema, Kinshasa II

Recteur: Komy Nsilu Diakubikua (2001-)
Tel: +243(81) 8124-642 EMail: komynsilu@yahoo.fr

Faculties
Economics; **Medicine** (Medicine); **Theology** (Theology)

History: Founded 1967.

Governing Bodies: Board of Administration; Administrative Committee

Admission Requirements: Secondary school certificate

Fees: (US Dollars): 250 per annum

Main Language(s) of Instruction: French

International Co-operation: With universities in USA and Canada

Accrediting Agencies: Ministry of Education

Degrees and Diplomas: *Graduat*: Economics; Theology, 3 yrs; *Docteur en Médecine*: Medicine, 7 yrs; *Licence*: Economics; Theology, 2 yrs

Student Services: Health services, Language programs, Social counselling, Sports facilities

Student Residential Facilities: Yes
Last Updated: 09/05/07

DIVINA GLORIA UNIVERSITY

Université Divina Gloria
BP 327, Butembo, Nord-Kivu
Tel: +243(99) 8548-850
Fax: +243(871) 76252-3410
EMail: universitedivinagl@yahoo.fr

Recteur: Kalala Nkudi (2000-)
Tel: +243(99) 8609-333, Fax: +243(871) 76252-3410

Vice-Recteur: Kakule Mumbere Kasindi
Tel: +243(99) 8548-820 EMail: kasindiv@yahoo.fr

International Relations: Wasingya Kalwaghe, Chancelier
Tel: +243(99) 8386-663 EMail: wasingya@yahoo.fr

Faculties
Arts and Humanities (English; French; History); **Management and Computer Science**; **Pharmacy** (Pharmacy); **Psychology and**

Educational Sciences (Educational Sciences; Psychology); **Science** (Biology; Geology); **Social Sciences, Politics and Administration**; **Theology** (Theology)

History: Founded 2000 by agreement with the Government of Democratic Republic of the Congo

Academic Year: October to June (October-February; March-June)

Admission Requirements: Diplôme d'Etat (Secondary school certificate)

Fees: (US Dollars): Graduat, 300; Licence, 200

Main Language(s) of Instruction: French

Degrees and Diplomas: *Graduat*: 3 yrs; *Licence*: 2 yrs; 3 yrs in Pharmacy

Student Services: Academic counselling, Cultural centre, Employment services, Foreign student adviser, Handicapped facilities, Health services, Language programs, Social counselling, Sports facilities

Publications: Revue, Scientific journal

EVANGELICAL UNIVERSITY IN AFRICA

Université évangélique en Afrique (UEA)
BP 3323, Bukavu
Tel: +243(98) 665-052
EMail: ueabukavu@yahoo.fr

Recteur: Gustave Mushagalusa Nachigera (2009-)
Tel: +243(99) 308-4623

Faculties
Agronomy and Environmental Sciences (Agronomy; Environmental Studies); **Economics Applied to Business** (Economics); **Medicine and Community Health** (Community Health; Medicine); **Protestant Theology** (Theology)

History: Founded 1991.

Main Language(s) of Instruction: French

Degrees and Diplomas: *Graduat*; *Diplôme d'Ingénieur*; *Docteur en Médecine*; *Licence*
Last Updated: 02/06/10

FACULTY OF PROTESTANT THEOLOGY OF LUBUMBASHI

Faculté de Théologie protestante de Lubumbashi
BP 2809, Avenue Jason Sendwe, Lubumbashi

Faculties
Medicine (Medicine); **Theology** (Theology)

History: Founded 1970.

Main Language(s) of Instruction: French

Degrees and Diplomas: *Graduat*: 3 yrs; *Licence*: 2 yrs; *Doctorat*: 3 yrs

GELESI UNIVERSITY OF UBANGI

Université Gelesi de l'Ubangi
Ubangi

Président: M. Gelesi

Faculties
Agronomy (Agronomy); **Economics** (Economics); **Humanities** (Arts and Humanities); **Law** (Law); **Medicine** (Medicine); **Polytechnic** (Engineering); **Veterinary Science** (Veterinary Science)

Schools
Languages (Modern Languages)

History: Founded 1997.

Main Language(s) of Instruction: French

Degrees and Diplomas: *Graduat*: 3 yrs; *Licence*: 2 yrs; *Doctorat*: 3 yrs

INSTITUTE OF ADVANCED STUDIES OF COMMERCE
Institut des hautes Etudes commerciales (IHEC)
BP 540, Avenue de la Poste no 1283, Kinshasa-Limete

Schools
Business Administration; **Commercial Engineering** (Business and Commerce); **Office Administration**
History: Founded 1990.
Main Language(s) of Instruction: French
Degrees and Diplomas: *Graduat*: 3 yrs; *Licence*: 2 yrs

INSTITUTE OF COMPUTER SCIENCE, PROGRAMMING AND ANALYSIS
Institut supérieur d'Informatique, Programmation et Analyse (ISIPA)
BP 1895, Avenue Kitega no 238, C/Lingwala, Kinshasa I
Tel: +243(99) 70571
EMail: direction@isipa.net
Website: http://www.isipa.cd/

Président Directeur général: Martin Ekanda Onyangunga
EMail: pdg@isipa.net

Sections
Commerce and Finance (Business Administration; Business and Commerce; Finance; International Business; Taxation); **Computer Science**
History: Founded 1975. Acquired present status 1993.
Main Language(s) of Instruction: French
Degrees and Diplomas: *Graduat*: 3 yrs; *Licence*: 2 yrs
Last Updated: 10/08/09

INSTITUTE OF COOPERATIVE AND TRADE UNION MANAGEMENT
Institut de Gestion coopérative et syndicale (IGECOSY)
Croisement des Avenues Kasa-Vubu/Lac Moero, Kinshasa

Directeur général: Lohekele Kalonda

Schools
Cooperative Management (Management); **Management Computing**; **Trade Union Management** (Management)
History: Founded 1991.
Main Language(s) of Instruction: French
Degrees and Diplomas: *Graduat*: 3 yrs; *Licence*: 2 yrs

INSTITUTE OF DEVELOPMENT AGENTS' TRAINING
Institut facultaire de Développement (IFAD)
BP 1800, Avenue Saio no 2317, Commune de Kasa-Vubu, Kinshasa KIN I
Tel: +243(99) 9939-536

Recteur: Eyenga Liongo On'Asi
Tel: +243(99) 9939-536 EMail: emmanueleyenga@yahoo.fr
Secrétaire général académique: Bonolo Ngilima
Tel: +243(99) 9970-832
International Relations: Itoko Lian'dja, Secrétaire général administratif Tel: +243(99) 8122-503 EMail: itoko_gilles@yahoo.fr

Faculties
Development Science and Techniques; **Health Sciences and Techniques** (Health Administration; Health Sciences; Laboratory Techniques; Medical Technology; Nursing)
History: Founded 1993 as Institut supérieur de Formation des Agents de Développement.
Governing Bodies: Rector; Academic General Secretary and Administrative General Secretary
Academic Year: October to July.

Fees: (US Dollars): 200-300 per annum
Main Language(s) of Instruction: French
Degrees and Diplomas: *Graduat*: Development Science and Techniques; Health Sciences and Techniques, 3 yrs; *Licence*: 2 yrs
Student Services: Language programs
Student Residential Facilities: None
Libraries: c. 4,000 vols.
Publications: Revue "IFAD", Presentation of IFAD *(quarterly)*

Academic Staff *2008-2009*: Total: c. 30
Student Numbers *2008-2009*: Total: c. 600
Note: Also: visiting teaching staff.
Last Updated: 12/10/09

INSTITUTE OF INTEGRATED ACCOUNTANCY
Institut de Comptabilité intégrée (ICI)
BP 104, Croisement des Avenues Kasa-Vubu et Lac Moero, Kinshasa I

Directeur général: N.K. Kinzonzi Mvutukidi

Schools
Accountancy (Accountancy)
History: Founded 1981.
Main Language(s) of Instruction: French
Degrees and Diplomas: *Graduat*: 3 yrs; *Licence*: 2 yrs

INSTITUTE OF MANAGEMENT
Institut facultaire de Gestion (IFAG)
17ème rue Limete, Kinshasa

Recteur: Malembe Tamandiak

Faculties
Advertising and Business Administration (Advertising and Publicity; Business Administration); **Commerce and Finance**; **Computer Science and Humanities**; **Documentation Techniques**; **Economics** (Economics); **Journalism-Communication** (Communication Studies; Journalism)
History: Founded 1994.
Main Language(s) of Instruction: French
Degrees and Diplomas: *Graduat*: 3 yrs; *Licence*: 2 yrs

INSTITUTE OF THEOLOGY AND PASTORAL STUDIES OF MAYIDI
Institut de Théologie et de Pastorale de Mayidi
Mayidi

Schools
Theology (Pastoral Studies; Theology)
History: Founded 1993.
Main Language(s) of Instruction: French
Degrees and Diplomas: *Graduat*: 3 yrs; *Licence*: 2 yrs

INSTITUTE OF THEOLOGY AND PHILOSOPHY - SAINT-AUGUSTIN
Institut supérieur de Théologie et de Philosophie - Saint-Augustin (ISTP-KINSHASA)
BP 241 A, Kindele Monastère, (Près du Prieuré des Chanoines Prémontrés à Kinshasa/Mont-Ngafula), Kinshasa

Schools
Philosophy (Philosophy; Theology)
History: Founded 1993.
Main Language(s) of Instruction: French
Degrees and Diplomas: *Graduat*: 3 yrs; *Licence*: 2 yrs

INTERFACULTY UNIVERSITY OF KINSHASA

Université Interfacultaire de Kinshasa (INTERKIN)
BP 14.130, Av. Irebu n°6/C, Commune de Kasa-Vubu, Kinshasa I
Tel: +243(89) 5090-548
EMail: interkin@yahoo.fr

Recteur: Michel Asumani Kasanga (2005-)
EMail: asumich_michel@yahoo.fr

Secrétaire général académique: Georges Kabaswa Mwana
Babou Tel: +243(81) 3493-678

Faculties
Business Computing (Business Computing); **Economics**; **Social, Political and Administrative Sciences** (Administration; Political Sciences; Social Sciences)

History: Founded 1981 as Institut interuniversitaire de Kinshasa. Acquired present status 1993.

Admission Requirements: State Diploma

Fees: (US Dollars): 50 - 75 per term

Main Language(s) of Instruction: French

Degrees and Diplomas: *Graduat*: 3 yrs; *Licence*: 2 yrs

Student Residential Facilities: None

Libraries: Yes

INTERNATIONAL FRANCOPHONE UNIVERSITY/KANANGA CAMPUS

Université francophone internationale/Campus de Kananga (UFI/KANANGA)
BP 743, Av. Goma no 10, Kananga

Recteur: Mutoke Tujibikile

Faculties
Law (Law); **Management and Communication** (Communication Studies; Management); **Medicine** (Medicine); **Nursing** (Nursing); **Theology, Philosophy and Sociology** (Philosophy; Sociology; Theology)

History: Founded 1993.

Main Language(s) of Instruction: French

Degrees and Diplomas: *Graduat*: 3 yrs; *Licence*: 2 yrs

INTERNATIONAL UNIVERSITY OF THE CONGO

Université internationale du Congo (UIC)
Rue Kwenge no 31C bis, Q/Lumumba, Commune de Matele, Kinshasa

Faculties
Economics and Social Sciences (Economics; Social Sciences); **Law** (Law); **Pharmacy** (Pharmacy); **Polytechnic**; **Science** (Natural Sciences)

History: Founded 2001.

Main Language(s) of Instruction: French

Degrees and Diplomas: *Graduat*: 3 yrs; *Licence*: 2 yrs

KONGO UNIVERSITY

Université Kongo (UK)
BP 202, Mbanza-Ngungu
Tel: +243 9999-39405
EMail: universitekongo@yahoo.fr
Website: http://www.universitekongo.org

Recteur: Kambu Kabangu (2008-)
EMail: kambu_kabangu@yahoo.fr

Secretary-General: Kiyombo Mbela
EMail: guillaume.kiyombo@universitekongo.org

International Relations: Makiese Naoma

Faculties
Agronomy *(Kisantu)* (Agronomy); **Arts and Social Communication** *(Kisantu)* (Arts and Humanities; Communication Studies); **Economics and Management** (Economics; Management); **Law**; **Medicine** *(Kisantu)*; **Polytechnic** (Electrical and Electronic Engineering; Mechanical Engineering)

History: Founded 1990.

Admission Requirements: Diplôme d'Etat

Fees: (US Dollars): 300 per annum

Main Language(s) of Instruction: French

Degrees and Diplomas: *Graduat*; *Diplôme d'Ingénieur*; *Docteur en Médecine*; *Licence*

Student Services: Health services, Social counselling

Libraries: Medical Library; Law and Economics Library

Publications: Racines et Croissance

Academic Staff *2008-2009*	MEN	WOMEN	**TOTAL**
FULL-TIME	2	–	**2**
PART-TIME	114	–	**114**
STAFF WITH DOCTORATE			
FULL-TIME	21	1	**22**
PART-TIME	99	1	**100**
Student Numbers *2008-2009*			
All (Foreign Included)	1,126	398	**1,524**
FOREIGN ONLY	15	7	**22**

Last Updated: 20/07/09

METHODIST UNIVERSITY IN KATANGA

Université méthodiste au Katanga (UMK)
BP 521, Mulungwishi-Likasi

Recteur: Kasap'Owan Tshibang

Faculties
Computer Science (Computer Science); **Educational Sciences** (Educational Sciences); **Theology** (Theology)

History: Founded 1951 as Faculté Méthodiste de Théologie de Mulungwishi. Acquired present status and title 2000.

Main Language(s) of Instruction: French

Degrees and Diplomas: *Graduat*: 2 yrs; *Licence*: 2 yrs; *Diplôme d'Etudes supérieures (DES)*

NATIONAL SCHOOL OF FINANCE AND BANKING ADMINISTRATION

Ecole nationale supérieure de Finance et Administration bancaire (ENSFAB)
BP 14011, Av.Croix-rouge no 141, C/Kinshasa, Kinshasa I

Directeur général: Tshimpamba Tshiteku

Programmes
Business Administration (Business Administration); **Commerce** (Business and Commerce)

History: Founded 1993.

Main Language(s) of Instruction: French

Degrees and Diplomas: *Graduat*: 3 yrs; *Licence*: 2 yrs

NOTRE DAME OF THE KASAYI UNIVERSITY

Université Notre Dame du Kasayi (UKA)
BP 70, Collège Saint Louis, Kananga II
EMail: uka_rectorat@ukardc.org
Website: http://www.ukardc.org

Recteur: Nyeme Tese

Centres
African Cultures; **Modern Languages** (Modern Languages)

Faculties
Agronomy *(Kabinda)* (Agronomy); **Computer Science**; **Economics and Development** *(Kabinda)* (Development Studies; Economics); **Economics and Management** *(Tshumbe)*; **Law** *(Kananga and Kabinda)* (Law); **Medicine** *(Kananga and Tshumbe)*; **Psychology and Educational Sciences** *(Kabinda and Tshumbe)* (Educational Sciences; Psychology)

History: Founded 1996 by the Episcopal Conference of the province of Kananga. Acquired present status 2004.

Degrees and Diplomas: *Graduat*: 3 yrs; *Licence*: 2 yrs; *Doctorat*: 3 yrs

Special Facilities: Experimental farm and botanical garden (medicinal plants)

Student Numbers *2008-2009*: Total 2,073
Last Updated: 10/08/09

PATRICE EMERY LUMUMBA UNIVERSITY OF WEMBO-NYAMA

Université Patrice Emery Lumumba de Wembo-Nyama (UPEL)
BP 560, Wembo-Nyama, Kananga

Président: Djundu Lunge

Faculties
Arts (Arts and Humanities); **Economics** (Economics); **Law** (Law); **Medicine**; **Science** (Natural Sciences); **Social Sciences** (Social Sciences); **Theology** (Theology)

Further Information: Also branch in Kinshasa

History: Founded 1992.

Main Language(s) of Instruction: French

Degrees and Diplomas: *Graduat*: 3 yrs; *Licence*: 2 yrs; *Doctorat*: 3 yrs. Also Doctorat à thèse
Last Updated: 30/04/07

PRESIDENT JOSEPH KASA-VUBU UNIVERSITY

Université Président Joseph Kasa-Vubu (UKV)
BP 314, Boma
Tel: +243(98) 179-706
EMail: josntedika@yahoo.fr; ukvboma@yahoo.fr
Website: http://www.congovision.com/ukv/index.html

Recteur: Joseph Ntedika Konde

Secrétaire Général Administratif: Eddy Maphasi Nuimba

Faculties
Agronomy (Agronomy); **Economics and Management** (Economics; Management); **Law** (Law); **Medicine** (Medicine); **Polytechnic** (Engineering)

History: Founded 1999.

Main Language(s) of Instruction: French

Degrees and Diplomas: *Graduat*: 3 yrs; *Licence*: 2 yrs; *Doctorat*: 3 yrs
Last Updated: 10/05/07

PRIVATE UNIVERSITY COLLEGE OF CONGO

Collège universitaire libre du Congo (CULC)
BP 1908, Avenue Kamayi no. 22, Quartier Kamayi Athénée, Kananga

Recteur: Edmond Mathunda Ngomadiku
Tel: +81 609-14-26 EMail: edmondmatunda@yahoo.fr

Faculties
Clothing and Sewing; **Economics and Management**; **Health Sciences** (Health Sciences; Medical Technology; Nursing); **Law** (Law); **Social Sciences, Political Science and Administration** (Administration; International Relations; Political Sciences; Social Sciences)

History: Founded 1983 as Université de l'Ouest-Congo/University of the West Congo. Renamed Université libre du Congo 2004. Acquired present status and title 2006.

Main Language(s) of Instruction: French

Degrees and Diplomas: *Graduat*: 3 yrs; *Licence*: 2 yrs
Last Updated: 17/10/07

PRIVATE UNIVERSITY OF KINSHASA

Université libre de Kinshasa (ULK)
BP 8321, 15ème Rue Limete no 36, Commune de Limete, Kinshasa

Recteur: Epee Gambwa

Faculties
Economics and Management; **Law** (Law); **Social, Political and Administrative Sciences** (Administration; Political Sciences; Social Sciences)

History: Founded 1988.

Main Language(s) of Instruction: French

Degrees and Diplomas: *Graduat*: 3 yrs; *Licence*: 2 yrs

PRIVATE UNIVERSITY OF LAKE MUKAMBA

Université libre du Lac Mukamba (UNILAM)
BP 1996, Av. Panda no 1, Q. Nkuluse, C/Diulu, Mbuji-Mayi

Recteur: Mwamba T. Wa Kaniki

Faculties
Agronomy (Agronomy); **Economics** (Economics); **Law** (Law); **Medicine** (Medicine); **Polytechnic**; **Science** (Natural Sciences); **Theology** (Theology)

History: Founded 1990.

Main Language(s) of Instruction: French

Degrees and Diplomas: *Graduat*: 3 yrs; *Licence*: 2 yrs; *Doctorat*: 3 yrs

PRIVATE UNIVERSITY OF LUOZI

Université libre de Luozi (ULL)
BP 14, Luozi
Tel: +243(98) 127-885
EMail: univ_lluozi@yahoo.fr
Website: http://www.ne-kongo.net/uni_luozi/

Recteur: Matukanga Mbalu

Faculties
Agronomy (Agronomy); **Business Administration and Computer Science** (Business Administration; Computer Science); **Development and Environmental Studies** (Development Studies; Environmental Studies); **Health Sciences** (Health Sciences); **Polytechnic** (Civil Engineering; Electrical Engineering; Mechanical Engineering)

History: Founded 1975.

Main Language(s) of Instruction: French

Degrees and Diplomas: *Graduat*: 3 yrs; *Licence*: 2 yrs
Last Updated: 04/05/07

PRIVATE UNIVERSITY OF THE GREAT LAKES REGION

Université libre des Pays des Grands Lacs
BP 368, Goma, Nord-Kivu
Tel: +243(81) 3133-066 +243(250) 543-072
Fax: +243(81) 3016-732 +243(250) 0858-1127
EMail: rectorat_ulpgl@yahoo.fr; rectorat@ulpgl.org

Recteur: Samuel Ngayihembako Mutahinga
Tel: +243(81) 3133-066
EMail: sngayihembako@yahoo.fr; ngayihembako@ulplg.org

Secrétaire général: Kabutu Tel: +243(81) 6915-013

Centres
Women's Training

Faculties
Administration and Management (Business Administration; Finance; Management); **Law**; **Protestant Theology** (Missionary Studies; Protestant Theology)

Institutes
Community Health and Development (Community Health; Health Sciences); **Educational Sciences** (Preschool Education; Primary Education; Secondary Education)

Schools
Preschool and Primary School Education *(Kauta)*; **Secondary School Education** *(Metanoia)* (Secondary Education)

History: Founded 1990 as Université Libre des Pays des Grands Lacs on the basis of the Institut Supérieur de Théologie Protestante founded 1985. Acquired present status and title 1996.

Admission Requirements: National Degree; Admission Test ; Financial Support

Main Language(s) of Instruction: French

Degrees and Diplomas: *Graduat*: Protestant Theology; Administration and Management; Law; Community Health and Development; Education Sciences; Technology, 3 yrs; *Licence*: Protestant Theology; Administration and Management; Law; Community Health and Development; Education Sciences; Technology, 3 yrs

Student Services: Academic counselling, Canteen, Employment services, Foreign student adviser, Health services, Language programs, Nursery care, Social counselling, Sports facilities

Publications: Analyse Topique; Annales de la Faculté de Droit; Bulletin de recherches théologiques et sociologiques; Revue de la Faculté de Droit *(biennially)*; Revue de la Faculté de Théologie Protestante *(biennially)*; Revue Interdisciplinaire *(biennially)*

PROTESTANT UNIVERSITY OF CONGO

Université protestante au Congo (UPC)

BP 4745, Croisement des avenues de la Victoire et de libération, Kinshasa / Lingwala, Kinshasa II
Tel: +243(81) 5087-561
EMail: univprocongo@kin.maf.net
Website: http://www.upc-rdc.cd/

Recteur: Daniel Boliya Ngoy (2002-)
EMail: recteur@upc-rdc.cd; ngoyboliya@yahoo.fr

Secrétaire général académique: Roger Masamba Makela
Tel: +243(99) 44467 EMail: sgacad@upc-rdc.cd

Secrétaire général administratif: Léon Nondo Maneng
EMail: sgadm@upc-rdc.cd

International Relations: Daniel Boliya Ngoy, Recteur

Faculties

Business and Economics (Accountancy; Administrative Law; African Studies; Agricultural Economics; Business Administration; Commercial Law; Computer Science; Economics; English; Environmental Studies; Finance; Geography (Human); Industrial Management; Insurance; International Economics; Law; Management; Marketing; Philosophy; Psychology; Small Business; Sociology; Staff Development); **Law**; **Medicine** (African Studies; Anatomy; Biochemistry; Biology; Biophysics; Botany; Chemistry; Community Health; Embryology and Reproduction Biology; English; Entomology; Epidemiology; Ethics; French; Histology; Immunology; Logic; Mathematics; Medicine; Molecular Biology; Nutrition; Organic Chemistry; Parasitology; Pathology; Pharmacology; Philosophy; Physics; Physiology; Public Health; Radiology; Surgery; Urology; Virology; Zoology); **Theology**

History: Founded 1959 in Lubumbashi as a Theology Department. Became Free University of the Congo 1963, Protestant University of Zaire 1990. Acquired present status and title 1994.

Governing Bodies: Board of Trustees, University Council, Executive Committee

Academic Year: October to July

Admission Requirements: State diploma or equivalent

Main Language(s) of Instruction: French

Degrees and Diplomas: *Graduat*; *Licence*: Theology; Law; Business and Economics, 5 yrs; *Diplôme d'Etudes supérieures (DES)*; *Doctorat*: Theology, 5 yrs

Student Services: Academic counselling, Canteen, Employment services, Foreign student adviser, Handicapped facilities, Health services, Language programs, Social counselling, Sports facilities

Libraries: 19,948 vols

Publications: Revue Congolaise de Théologie Protestante *(annually)*; Revue de la Faculté d'Administration des Affaires et Sciences Economiques *(annually)*; Revue de la Faculté de Droit *(annually)*

Press or Publishing House: Editions de l'Université protestante au Congo
Last Updated: 10/08/09

PROTESTANT UNIVERSITY OF KIMPESE

Université protestante de Kimpese

BP 67, Kimpese
EMail: upk_kimpese@yahoo.fr

Recteur: Luyindula Ndiku

Centres
Pastoral Studies

Faculties
Agronomy (Agronomy); **Health Sciences**; **Medicine**; **Theology** (Theology)

History: Founded 1994.

Main Language(s) of Instruction: French

Degrees and Diplomas: *Graduat*: 3 yrs; *Licence*: 2 yrs; *Doctorat*: 4 yrs

SHEPPARD AND LAPSLEY PRESBYTERIAN UNIVERSITY OF THE CONGO

Université presbytérienne Sheppard et Lapsley du Congo (UPRECO)

BP 159, Q. Kamupongo, C/de Ndesha, Kananga
Website: http://upreco.org

Recteur: Mulumba Musumbu

Faculties
Law (Law); **Theology** (History of Religion; Missionary Studies; Theology)

History: Founded 1976. Acquired university status in 1988.

Main Language(s) of Instruction: French

Degrees and Diplomas: *Graduat*: 3 yrs; *Licence*: 2 yrs

Student Numbers 2007-2008	MEN	WOMEN	TOTAL
All (Foreign Included)	100	80	**180**

Last Updated: 10/08/09

SIMON KIMBANGU UNIVERSITY

Université Simon Kimbangu (USK)

BP 1441, 44 avenue Bongolo, Q/ Kauka, Commune de Kalamu, Kinshasa I
Tel: +243(99) 8183-862
EMail: universitsimonkimbangu@yahoo.fr

Recteur: Masamba N'Kazi Angani (2003-)
EMail: smasamba@yahoo.fr

Secrétaire général administratif: Akakiwa Bayago
Tel: +243(99) 9943-107 EMail: akakiwajean@yahoo.fr

International Relations: Munianga Dilenga

Faculties
Agronomy; **Computer Science** (Computer Science); **Economics** (Econometrics; Economics); **Law** (Law; Private Law); **Medicine**; **Theology** (Theology); **Veterinary Science**

History: Founded 1994. Acquired present status 2006.

Governing Bodies: Staff Committee

Admission Requirements: Diplôme d'Etat or equivalent

Fees: (US Dollars): 500.00 per annum

Main Language(s) of Instruction: French

International Co-operation: With Alcala University (Spain)

Degrees and Diplomas: *Graduat*: all disciplines, 3 yrs; *Docteur en Médecine*: 4 yrs; *Docteur en Médecine Vétérinaire*: 3 yrs; *Licence*: all disciplines, 2 yrs

Student Services: Academic counselling, Canteen, Cultural centre, Employment services, Foreign student adviser, Foreign Studies Centre, Health services, Language programs, Social counselling, Sports facilities

Student Residential Facilities: Limited residential facilities at the Faculty of Theology
Last Updated: 19/01/07

TECHNICAL INSTITUTE OF ECONOMIC AND COOPERATIVE STUDIES OF KINSHASA

Institut supérieur technique d'Etudes économiques et coopératives de Kinshasa (ISEC)

BP 825, Av. De l'Université no 99 bis, Commune de Limete Q. Mombele, Kinshasa-Limete

Directeur général: Gaston Kuyu Lubaku
EMail: kuyu_gaston@yahoo.fr

Schools

Economics (Economics); **Electrical and Mechanical Engineering**; **Legal Techniques** (Law)

History: Founded 1994.

Main Language(s) of Instruction: French

Degrees and Diplomas: *Graduat*: 3 yrs; *Licence*: 2 yrs

TECHNICAL SCHOOL OF ADVANCED STUDIES

Ecole technique d'Etudes supérieures (ETES)
BP 4779, Croisement des Avenues Kanda Kanda/Kasa-Vubu,
Kinshasa-Gombe

Directeur général: Mukendi Dikubakuba

Schools

Accountancy (Accountancy); **Business Administration** (Business Administration); **Computer Science** (Computer Science); **Electrical and Electronic Engineering** (Electrical and Electronic Engineering); **Secretarial Studies** (Secretarial Studies)

History: Founded 1981.

Main Language(s) of Instruction: French

Degrees and Diplomas: *Graduat*: 3 yrs; *Licence*: 2 yrs. Also Capacitariat, 2 yrs

THE AMERICAN UNIVERSITY OF KINSHASA

Université franco-américaine de Kinshasa (UAK)
BP 2175, No 3 Avenue de l'Hôpital, Kinshasa-Gombe
EMail: aukuniv@auk-congo.edu
Website: http://www.auk-congo.edu/index.php

Recteur: Basile Osokonda Okenge

Faculties

Computer Science (Computer Science); **Economics** (Economics); **Law** (Law); **Nursing** (Nursing); **Social Sciences** (Social Sciences)

History: Founded 1994.

Main Language(s) of Instruction: French and English

Degrees and Diplomas: *Graduat*: 3 yrs; *Licence*: 2 yrs
Last Updated: 09/05/07

THEOLOGICAL INSTITUTE OF THE ASSEMBLIES OF GOD IN THE CONGO

Institut supérieur théologique des Assemblées de Dieu au Congo (ISTADC)
BP 11758, Av Assossa no 2219, Q. Christ-Roi,
Commune de Kasa-Vubu, Kinshasa I

Directeur général: Belanga Belengeli

Programmes

Evangelical Theology (Theology)

History: Founded 1989.

Main Language(s) of Instruction: French

Degrees and Diplomas: *Graduat*: 3 yrs; *Licence*: 2 yrs

UNIVERSITY COLLEGES OF KINSHASA

Collèges universitaires de Kinshasa (CUK)
BP 1423, Q. Tomba no7/H, Commune de Matete, Kinshasa I

Recteur: Somwe Abamukonkole

Faculties

Economics (Economics); **Law** (Law); **Social, Political and Administrative Sciences** (Administration; Political Sciences; Social Sciences)

Higher Institutes

Medical Sciences *(hospital)* (Medicine)

History: Founded 1989.

Main Language(s) of Instruction: French

Degrees and Diplomas: *Graduat*: 3 yrs; *Licence*: 2 yrs

UNIVERSITY INSTITUTE OF THE CONGO

Institut universitaire du Congo (IUC DE LUBUMBASHI)
BP 4869, Avenue Likasi no 491, Lubumbashi

Recteur: François Kandé

Faculties

Business Administration; **Business Computing** (Business Computing); **Economics**; **Law** (Law); **Social, Political and Administrative Science** (Administration; Political Sciences; Social Sciences); **Theology** (Theology)

Further Information: Also branch in Likasi

History: Founded 1989.

Main Language(s) of Instruction: French

Degrees and Diplomas: *Graduat*: 3 yrs; *Licence*: 2 yrs

UNIVERSITY OF KINSHASA BINZA

Université de Kinshasa Binza (UKB)
BP 3227, Croisement des avenues John Kennedy et du 17 mai,
Commune Ngaliema (Q.IPN), Kinshasa I
Tel: +243(99) 9983-579 +243(81) 0305-870
EMail: ukb_pca@yahoo.fr

Recteur: Munzadi Babole (1999-) Tel: +243(81) 4925-725

Vice-Recteur: Mimbwi Salmoshie Tel: +243(99) 7327-764

International Relations: Kamukenji Lumungulu, International Relations Officer Tel: +243(99) 7343-719

Faculties

Economics (Economics; Finance); **Law** (Commercial Law; Law; Private Law; Public Law); **Medicine** (Biomedicine; Public Health); **Polytechnic** (Air Transport; Computer Science); **Social, Political and Administrative Sciences** (Administration; Political Sciences; Social Sciences)

Institutes

Fine Arts (Fine Arts)

Further Information: Also branches in Lubumbashi: Institut supérieur de Développement et Science économique (ISDSE), Centre d'Etudes commerciales et informatiques (CECI) and in Kalemie

History: Founded 1999. Acquired present status 2001.

Governing Bodies: Governing Council

Admission Requirements: State Diploma

Fees: (US Dollars): 140 per semester

Main Language(s) of Instruction: French

Degrees and Diplomas: *Graduat*: Economics; Law, 3 yrs; *Diplôme d'Ingénieur*: Polytechnics, 5 yrs; *Docteur en Médecine*: 6 yrs; *Licence*: Economics; Law, 2 yrs

Student Services: Academic counselling, Language programs, Sports facilities

Student Residential Facilities: Yes

Special Facilities: National Museum

Libraries: Yes

Publications: PROPEDADI/UKB, Student and teacher publications *(annually)*; YLIS Diary, Information and newspaper *(other/irregular)*

UNIVERSITY OF LUÉLÉ

Université de Luélé
BP 670, Isiro
EMail: gaiseroger@yahoo.fr

Recteur: Roger Gaise

Faculties

Agronomy (Agronomy); **Economics** (Economics); **Law** (Law); **Medicine and Pharmacy** (Medicine; Pharmacy); **Natural Sciences** (Biology; Ecology; Natural Sciences); **Religious Sciences** (Religious Studies); **Social, Political and Administrative Sciences** (Administration; Political Sciences; Social Sciences)

History: Founded 1998.

Main Language(s) of Instruction: French

UNIVERSITY OF MBUJI-MAYI
Université de Mbuji-Mayi (UM)
BP 225, Avenue de l'Université, Campus de Tshikama, Dibindi,
Mbuji-Mayi, Kasaï Oriental
Tel: +243(88) 54890 +243(81) 20905
Fax: +243(88) 54111 +32(2) 7065-818
EMail: univmayi@yahoo.fr

Recteur: Albert Léonard Kabeya
Tel: +243(99) 57314, Fax: +32(2) 7065-818

Secrétaire général: J. Ntumba Tshibambula

International Relations: P. Reyntjens

Faculties
Applied Sciences (Polytechnic) (Engineering); **Economics** (Economics); **Human Medicine** (Biomedicine; Medicine); **Law** (Law; Notary Studies; Private Law; Public Law)

History: Founded 1990. Acquired present status 1992.

Governing Bodies: Council of Founders; Administration Council; University Council; Executive Committee

Academic Year: November to July

Admission Requirements: State diploma (secondary school certificate) or equivalent

Fees: (US Dollars): 280-330 per annum

Main Language(s) of Instruction: French

International Co-operation: With universities in Belgium; Germany; Canada; Japan; Italy and Spain

Degrees and Diplomas: *Graduat*: Biomedical Sciences; Civil Engineering; Mining Engineering; Mechanical Engineering; Law; Economics, 3 yrs; *Licence*: Civil Engineering; Mining Engineering; Mechanical Engineering, a further 2 yrs; *Doctorat*: Medicine, 4 yrs

Student Services: Academic counselling, Canteen, Cultural centre, Health services, Nursery care, Social counselling, Sports facilities

Special Facilities: Research Laboratory; Internet Centre

Libraries: 14,000 vols

Publications: Actes des Journées Scientifiques de l'U.M. *(annually)*

UNIVERSITY OF THE MONGALA
Université de la Mongala (UNIMO)
Lisala

Faculties
Development Sciences; **Economics** (Economics); **Law** (Law); **Medicine** (Medicine)

Further Information: Campus dans le District de la Mongala

History: Founded 2000.

Main Language(s) of Instruction: French

Degrees and Diplomas: *Graduat*: 3 yrs; *Licence*: 2 yrs

WILLIAM BOOTH UNIVERSITY
Université William Booth (UWB)
12 Avenue du Kasai, Kinshasa-Gombe I
Website: http://www.uwbcongo.cd

Recteur: Mpiutu ne Mbodi

Faculties
Economics (Economics); **Law** (Law)

History: Founded 1996.

Main Language(s) of Instruction: French

Degrees and Diplomas: *Graduat*: 3 yrs; *Licence*: 2 yrs; *Diplôme d'Etudes supérieures (DES)*: 2 yrs; *Doctorat*

Costa Rica

STRUCTURE OF HIGHER EDUCATION SYSTEM

Description:

Higher education is provided by public institutions, several private universities, university colleges and various private post-secondary institutions more specifically devoted to commercial studies and regional institutions of higher education which are supervised by the Ministerio de Educación Pública de Costa Rica. State university higher education is coordinated by the Consejo Nacional de Rectores (CONARE) and its technical secretariat, the Oficina de Planificación de la Educación Superior (OPES). Private universities are supervised by the Consejo Nacional de Enseñanza Superior Universitaria Privada (CONESUP).

Stages of studies:

University level first stage: *Diplomado*
The first stage of higher education leads, after two or three years of short-term study, to the award of the title of Diplomado. Holders of this diploma are called diplomados. This diploma does not give the holders professional status. Students may choose whether or not they wish to continue their studies.

University level second stage: *Grado: Bachillerato universitario, Licenciatura*
The second stage of higher education leads to the award of the Bachiller or Bachillerato universitario after four years, and to the Licenciatura after five years.

University level third stage: *Postgrado: Maestría, Especialidad profesional, Doctorado académico*
A Maestría degree requires two years' study after a first degree (Bachiller). The Especialidad Profesional forms part of postgraduate studies centred on specialized practical training in a given professional field. Candidates should hold the Licenciatura and no time limit is imposed. The Doctorado académico is the highest degree. The minimum duration of studies is four years after the Bachillerato universitario.

Distance higher education:
The Universidad Estatal a Distancia, San José, offers formal degree programmes in a number of fields (Education, Administration, Health).

ADMISSION TO HIGHER EDUCATION

Admission to university-level studies:

Name of secondary school credential required: Bachillerato

Entrance exam requirements: Examen de Admisión at the University of Costa Rica and the Technological Institute of Costa Rica. Some private universities have admission tests.

Foreign students admission:

Entrance exam requirements: Students must hold a Bachillerato or a recognized equivalent diploma. They must sit for an entrance examination or have their studies recognized.

Entry regulations: Foreign students must obtain a residence permit and give a financial guarantee.

Language requirements: Students must have a good knowledge of Spanish. The Universidad de Costa Rica, the Universidad Nacional and the Instituto Tecnológico de Costa Rica organize courses for foreign students.

NATIONAL BODIES

Ministerio de Educación Pública (Ministry of Public Education)
Minister: Leonardo Garnier Rímolo
San José 10087-1000
Tel: +506 2258 3745

Fax: +506 2258 3745
WWW: http://www.mep.go.cr
Role of national body: Governing body in charge of the implementation of education policies.

Sistema Nacional de Acreditación de la Educación Superior - SINAES (National System for Higher Education Accreditation)

President: Guillermo Vargas Salazar
Executive Secretary: Rosa Adolio Cascante
San José
Tel: +506 2519-5813
EMail: sinaes@sinaes.ac.cr
WWW: http://www.sinaes.ac.cr/
Role of national body: Official body responsible for the accreditation, on a voluntary basis, of courses of public and private higher education institutions.

Consejo Nacional de Rectores - CONARE (National Council of Rectors)

Edificio "Dr. Franklin Chang Díaz". de la Embajada de los Estados Unidos de América, 1,3 km al Norte. Pavas.
Apdo. 1174-1200
San José
Tel: +506 2519 5700
Fax: +506 2296 5626
EMail: conare@conare.ac.cr
WWW: http://www.conare.ac.cr
Role of national body: Sets the guidelines for the National Plan for Public Higher Education (PLANES); approves PLANES; distributes the lump sum allocated to Public Higher Education among the four public universities; establishes the instruments and coordination procedures for Public Higher Education; designates representatives of Public Higher Education to other public boards; evaluates, creates and closes degree programmes and formulates policy recommendations for public universities.

Data for academic year: 2006-2007
Source: IAU from Consejo Nacional de Rectores, San José, 2005 and documentation, 2007. Bodies updated in 2011.

INSTITUTIONS

PUBLIC INSTITUTIONS

CENTRAL AMERICAN INSTITUTE OF PUBLIC ADMINISTRATION

Instituto Centroamericano de Administración Pública (ICAP)
Apartado 10025-1000, Costado Este de la Heladería Pop's
Curridabat, San José
Tel: +506 234-1011
Fax: +506 225-2049
EMail: info@icap.ac.cr
Website: http://www.icap.ac.cr/

Director: Hugo Zelaya Cálix
Tel: +506 225-4616, Fax: +506 225-2049

Programmes
Development Projects (Development Studies); **Health Management**; **Social Management** (Social and Community Services)
History: Founded 1954, postgraduate programme added 1980.
Governing Bodies: General Board
Academic Year: January to December
Admission Requirements: Graduate certificate at university level
Fees: (US Dollars): 1,500 per annum
Main Language(s) of Instruction: Spanish

International Co-operation: With universities in Central America
Degrees and Diplomas: *Maestría*: Health Management, Public Administration, Management Development Project, 2 yrs
Student Services: Academic counselling, Foreign student adviser, Health services, Language programs
Student Residential Facilities: None
Libraries: Yes
Publications: Revista Centroamericana de Administración Pública *(biennially)*
Press or Publishing House: University Press
Last Updated: 02/12/09

COSTA RICA INSTITUTE OF TECHNOLOGY

Instituto Tecnológico de Costa Rica (ITCR)
Apartado 159-7050, Cártago 159-7050
Tel: +506 552-5333
Fax: +506 551-5348
EMail: archivo@itcr.ac.cr
Website: http://www.tec.cr/Paginas/default.aspx

Rector: Eugenio Trejos
Tel: +506 552-2211, Fax: +506 552-9603 EMail: etrejos@itcr.ac.cr

Administrative Officer: Rafael Hidalgo
Tel: +506 550-2301, Fax: +506 591-5241
EMail: rhidalgo@itcr.accr

International Relations: Carlos Mata
Tel: +506(551) 2216 EMail: camata@itcr.ac.cr

Schools

Agricultural Engineering (Agricultural Engineering); **Agriculture and Livestock Management** (Agriculture; Animal Husbandry); **Agronomy** (Agronomy); **Architecture and Town Planning** (Architecture; Town Planning); **Biology** (Biology; Biotechnology); **Business Administration** (Business Administration); **Chemistry** (Chemistry); **Computer Engineering** (Computer Engineering; Computer Science); **Construction Engineering** (Construction Engineering); **Culture and Sport** (Cultural Studies; Sports); **Electrical and Mechanical Engineering** (Electrical Engineering; Mechanical Engineering); **Electronics** (Electronic Engineering); **Forestry Engineering** (Forestry); **Industrial Design** (Industrial Design); **Language** (Communication Studies; English); **Material Science and Engineering** (Materials Engineering); **Mathematics** (Mathematics); **Occupational Safety and Environmental Health** (Environmental Engineering; Occupational Health; Safety Engineering); **Physics**; **Science and Arts**; **Social Sciences** (Law; Philosophy; Social Sciences)

History: Founded 1971. A State institution financed by the government.

Governing Bodies: Asamblea Institucional; Consejo Institucional comprising the Rector, the Minister of Education, the Minister of Planning and the Economy, 4 members of the administrative sector, a graduate, and 2 student representatives

Academic Year: February to November (February-May; August-November)

Admission Requirements: Secondary school certificate (bachillerato) or equivalent, and entrance examination

Fees: (Colones): 45,000 per semester
Main Language(s) of Instruction: Spanish

Accrediting Agencies: Canadian Engineering Accreditation Board

Degrees and Diplomas: *Bachiller*: 4 yrs; *Licenciatura*: 5 1/2 yrs; *Licenciatura*

Student Services: Academic counselling, Canteen, Employment services, Foreign student adviser, Handicapped facilities, Health services, Language programs, Nursery care, Social counselling, Sports facilities
Student Residential Facilities: Yes

Special Facilities: Experimental Farms
Libraries: Total, 68,526 vols; 450 periodical titles

Publications: Tecnología en Marcha *(quarterly)*
Press or Publishing House: Editorial Tecnológica
Last Updated: 02/12/09

SAN CARLOS CAMPUS
SEDE REGIONAL DE SAN CARLOS

Santa Clara, San Carlos
Tel: +506 475-5033
Fax: +506 475-5395

Director: Bernal Martínez Gutierrez

Faculties
Agronomy (Agronomy); **Business Administration** (Business Administration; Finance; Marketing); **Computer Science** (Computer Science); **Tourism Management**

History: Founded 1976.

Degrees and Diplomas: *Bachiller*. Engineering degree

SAN JOSÉ ACADEMIC CENTRE
CENTRO ACADÉMICO DE SAN JOSÉ

Barrio Amón, Calle 5 y 7, Avenida 9, San José
Tel: +506 223-6398
Fax: +506 223-6894

Director: Jorge Sancho Víquez

Divisions
Architecture and Town Planning (Architecture; Town Planning); **Business Administration** (Accountancy; Business Administration; Human Resources; Management); **Industrial Production** (Industrial Engineering); **Technical Education**

Degrees and Diplomas: *Bachiller*. Engineering diploma

INCAE BUSINESS SCHOOL
Instituto Centroamericano de Administración de Empresas (INCAE)
2 Km Oeste de Vivero Procesa #1, La Garita, Alajuela
Tel: +506 437-2200
Fax: +506 433-9101
EMail: mercadeo@mail.incae.ac.cr
Website: http://www.incae.ac.cr/

Rector: Roberto Artavia Loria
Tel: +506 437-2200, Fax: +506 433-9798
EMail: rectoria@mail.incae.ac.cr

Coordinadora General de la Rectoría: Yolanda Fernández Ochoa
Fax: +506 433-9820 EMail: fernandy@mail.incae.ac.cr

International Relations: Ernesto Ayala Fax: +506 433-9820
EMail: ayalae@mail.incae.ac.cr

Faculties
Business Administration; **Business Economics**

History: Founded 1964.

Governing Bodies: Consejo Directivo, comprising the President, Rector de Oficio, and 9 Directors

Main Language(s) of Instruction: Spanish

Accrediting Agencies: Southern Association of Colleges and Schools, USA

Degrees and Diplomas: *Maestría*
Student Services: Academic counselling
Libraries: Campuses Library, total, 81,000 vols
Publications: Revista INCAE *(biannually)*
Last Updated: 02/11/09

NATIONAL UNIVERSITY
Universidad Nacional (UNA)
Apartado 86-3000, Heredia
Tel: +506 261-0101
Fax: +506 237-7032
EMail: rectoria@una.ac.cr
Website: http://www.una.ac.cr

Rector: Olman Segura Bonilla

Dean: Leiner Vargas Alfaro
Tel: +506 277-3911, Fax: +506 277-3421
EMail: lvargas@una.ac.cr

International Relations: Carlos Álvarez Bogantes
Tel: +506 237-7032 +506 357-7301 EMail: calvarez@una.ac.cr

Centres
General Studies (Arts and Humanities; Fine Arts; Philosophy; Social Sciences; Technology) *Dean*: Mayela Cascante Fonseca; **Research and Teaching in Education** *(CIDE)* (Agricultural Education; Educational and Student Counselling; Educational Research; Educational Sciences; Educational Technology; Pre-school Education; Primary Education; Special Education) *Dean*: Irma Zúñiga León; **Research, Teaching and Outreach in Arts** *(CIDEA)* (Art Education; Communication Arts; Dance; Fine Arts; Music; Music Education; Musical Instruments; Performing Arts; Singing; Visual Arts) *Dean*: Nelly Obando Alvarez

Colleges
Exact and Natural Sciences (Biology; Computer Science; Earth Sciences; Industrial Chemistry; Information Technology; Mathematics; Natural Sciences; Science Education; Surveying and Mapping) *Dean*: Luis Sierra Sierra; **Health Sciences** (Health Sciences; Parks and Recreation; Physical Education; Sports; Sports Medicine; Veterinary Science) *Dean*: Jorge Quirós Arce; **Land and Sea Sciences** (Agricultural Engineering; Earth Sciences; Environmental Management; Forestry; Geography; Marine Science and Oceanography; Surveying and Mapping) *Dean*: Omar Miranda Bonilla; **Philosophy and Letters** (English; French; Gender Studies; Information Sciences; Latin American Studies; Library Science; Philosophy; Publishing and Book Trade; Spanish; Theology) *Dean*: Lucía Chacón Alvarado, **Social Sciences** (Business Education; Economics; History; International Business; International Relations; Leadership; Management; Psychology; Social Policy; Social Sciences; Social Studies; Sociology) *Dean*: Henry Mora Jiménez

Institutes

Forestall Services *(INISEFOR)*; **Interdisciplinary Studies in Childhood and Adolescence** *(INEINA)* (Child Care and Development; Family Studies); **Latin American Studies** *(IDELA)*; **Social Studies in Population** *(IDESPO)*; **Toxic Substances** *(IRET)* (Toxicology); **Vulcanology and Seismology Observatory of Costa Rica** *(OVSICORI)* (Seismology); **Wildlife Conservation and Management** *(ICOMVIS)* (Wildlife); **Women's Studies** *(IEM)*; **Work Studies** *(IESTRA)* (Labour and Industrial Relations)

Research Centres

Economic Policy *(International Centre (CINPE))*; **Tropical Beekeeping** *(CINAT)* (Apiculture)

History: Founded 1973. A State institution.

Governing Bodies: Asamblea Universitaria; Consejo Universitario

Academic Year: February to November (February-June; August-November)

Admission Requirements: Secondary school certificate (bachillerato) and entrance examination

Main Language(s) of Instruction: Spanish

Degrees and Diplomas: *Bachiller*: 4 yrs; *Licenciatura*: 1 yr; *Especialidad Profesional*: Technical Studies (Técnico), 2 yrs; *Maestría*: 2 yrs; *Doctorado Académico*: 2 1/2-3 yrs

Student Services: Canteen, Cultural centre, Sports facilities

Libraries: Total, 245,830 vols

Publications: Revista ABRA *(biennially)*; Revista Ambien-TICO; Revista Educare *(biennially)*; Revista Geográfia de Costa Rica *(biennially)*; Revista Ístmica *(biennially)*; Revista Letras *(biennially)*; Revista Perspectivas *(biennially)*; Revista Relaciones Internacionales *(biennially)*; Revista Uniciencia *(biennially)*

Last Updated: 31/10/07

BRUNCA REGIONAL BRANCH
SEDE REGIONAL BRUNCA (SRB)

Apartado 34-8000, San Isidro del General Pérez Zeledón, San José
Tel: +506 771-3209
Fax: +506 771-3372
EMail: srb@pz.una.ac.cr
Website: http://www.pz.una.ac.cr

Campuses

Coto (Business Administration; Education; Information Management; Pedagogy) *Dean*: Miguel Calderón Fernández; **Pérez Zeledón** (Business Administration; Education; English; French; Information Management; Pedagogy; Teacher Training; Tourism) *Dean*: Miguel Calderón Fernández

CHOROTEGA REGIONAL BRANCH
SEDE REGIONAL CHOROTEGA

Liberia, Guanacaste
Tel: +506 666-0109
Fax: +506 666-0109
Website: http://www.una.ac.cr/chor

Campuses

Liberia (Business Administration; Education; English; Foreign Languages Education; Management; Pedagogy; Tourism) *Dean*: Orlando De la O Castañeda; **Nicoya** (Business Administration; Education; English; Foreign Languages Education; Management; Pedagogy; Tourism) *Dean*: Orlando De la O Castañeda

History: Founded 1973.

STATE UNIVERSITY OF DISTANCE EDUCATION

Universidad Estatal a Distancia (UNED)

Apartado 474-2050, Sabanilla de Montes de Oca, San Pedro de Montes de Oca
Tel: +506 527-2000
Fax: +506 253-4990
EMail: webmaster1@uned.ac.cr
Website: http://www.uned.ac.cr

Rector: Luis Guillermo Carpio Malavassi
Tel: +506 527-2505, Fax: +506 253-4990
EMail: rectoria@uned.ac.cr

Schools

Administration; **Education** (Civics; Education; Educational Psychology; Educational Technology; English; French; Mathematics Education; Preschool Education; Primary Education; Science Education; Secondary Education; Special Education; Teacher Training; Technology Education); **Exact and Natural Sciences** (Agricultural Engineering; Computer Science; Health Administration; Industrial Engineering; Mathematics; Natural Resources; Natural Sciences); **Social Sciences** (Commercial Law; Constitutional Law; Criminology; Family Studies; Human Rights; International Law; Labour Law; Social Work)

History: Founded 1977 to give access to higher education to those who are unable to attend university, particularly those living in rural areas. An autonomous institution financed by the State.

Governing Bodies: Asamblea Universitaria, comprising 66 members; Consejo Universitario, comprising 9 members

Academic Year: January to November (January-April; May-August; September-November)

Admission Requirements: Secondary school certificate (bachillerato) or equivalent

Main Language(s) of Instruction: Spanish

Degrees and Diplomas: *Diploma*: 3 yrs; *Bachiller*: 4 yrs; *Licenciatura*: 5 yrs; *Maestría*; *Doctorado Académico*

Libraries: Central Library, c. 250,000 vols

Publications: Biocenosis; Enlace *(biannually)*; Innovaciones Educativas

Press or Publishing House: Editorial Universidad Estatal a Distancia

Last Updated: 03/12/09

UNIVERSITY OF COSTA RICA

Universidad de Costa Rica (UCR)

Apartado 2060, Ciudad Universitaria Rodrígo Facio, San José
Tel: +506 2511-1257
Fax: +506 234-0452
EMail: ggarcia@rectoria.ucr.ac.cr; imolina@rectoria.ucr.ac.cr
Website: http://www.ucr.ac.cr

Rector: Yamilteh González García (2004-)
Tel: +506 2511-1257 +506 2511-1250, Fax: +506 2234-0452

Director: Lilliana Solis (2008-2012)
Tel: +506 2511-5090, Fax: +506 2511-5152
EMail: lilliana.solis@ucr.ac.cr; odi.prensa@usr.ac.cr

International Relations: Ana Sittenfeld, Director
Tel: +506 2511-5080/+506 2511-4425, Fax: +506 225-5822
EMail: oaice@ucr.ac.cr; seci.oai@ucr.ac.cr

Faculties

Agronomy (Agricultural Economics; Agronomy; Animal Husbandry; Food Technology; Zoology); **Dentistry** (Dentistry); **Economics** (Accountancy; Business Administration; Economics; Health Administration; Public Administration; Taxation); **Education** (Arts and Humanities; Curriculum; Education; Educational Administration; Educational and Student Counselling; Educational Testing and Evaluation; English; French; Higher Education; Information Sciences; Library Science; Literature; Management; Mathematics Education; Music Education; Physical Education; Primary Education; Science Education; Secondary Education; Social Studies; Spanish; Special Education; Sports; Teacher Training); **Engineering** (Agricultural Engineering; Architecture; Chemical Engineering; Civil Engineering; Computer Engineering; Computer Science; Electrical Engineering; Engineering; Industrial Engineering; Mechanical Engineering; Surveying and Mapping); **Fine Arts** (Advertising and Publicity; Fine Arts; Graphic Arts; Music; Painting and Drawing; Sculpture; Theatre); **Humanities** (Arts and Humanities; Literature; Modern Languages; Philology; Philosophy); **Law** (Law); **Medicine** (Anaesthesiology; Biochemistry; Biomedicine; Cardiology; Chemistry; Community Health; Dentistry; Dermatology; Endocrinology; Gastroenterology; Gerontology; Gynaecology and Obstetrics; Haematology; Medicine; Microbiology; Neurological Therapy; Neurology; Nursing; Nutrition; Oncology; Ophthalmology; Paediatrics; Pharmacology; Pharmacy; Physical Therapy; Plastic Surgery; Pneumology; Psychiatry and Mental Health; Public

Health; Radiology; Rehabilitation and Therapy; Respiratory Therapy; Surgery; Urology); **Microbiology** (Haematology; Microbiology; Parasitology); **Pharmacy** (Pharmacy); **Science** (Biology; Chemistry; Computer Science; Geology; Mathematics; Meteorology; Natural Sciences; Physics; Statistics); **Social Sciences** (Anthropology; Communication Studies; Geography; History; Mass Communication; Political Sciences; Psychology; Social Sciences; Social Work; Sociology)

Research Centres
Abnormal Haemoglobin and Related Disorders *(CIHATA)* (Pathology); **Agricultural Economics and Agribusiness** *(CIEDA)* (Agricultural Business); **Agronomy** *(CIA)* (Agronomy); **Animal Nutrition** *(CINA)* (Animal Husbandry); **Atomic, Molecular and Nuclear Sciences** *(CICANUM)* (Atomic and Molecular Physics; Nuclear Physics); **Cellular and Molecular Biology** *(CIBCM)* (Cell Biology; Molecular Biology); **Central American History** *(CIHAC)* (History; Latin American Studies); **Crop Protection** *(CIPROC)* (Crop Production); **Electro-Chemistry and Chemical Energy** *(CELEQ)*; **Environmental Pollution** *(CICA)* (Environmental Studies); **Food Science and Technology** *(CITA)* (Food Science; Food Technology); **Geology** *(CICG)* (Geology); **Geophysics** *(CIGEFI)* (Geophysics; Seismology); **Grains and Seeds** *(CIGRAS)*; **Latin American Identity and Culture** *(CIICLA)* (Cultural Studies; Latin American Studies); **Materials Engineering** *(CICIMA)* (Materials Engineering); **Mathematics and Applied Mathematics** *(CIMPA)* (Applied Mathematics; Mathematics); **Mathematics and Meta-Mathematics** *(CIMM)* (Mathematics); **Microstructures** *(CIEMIC)* (Microelectronics); **Natural Products** *(CIPRONA)* (Natural Resources); **Population Studies** *(Central American, CCP)* (Demography and Population); **Public Administration** *(CICAP)* (Public Administration); **Sea Sciences and Limnology** *(CIMAR)* (Limnology; Marine Science and Oceanography); **Space Studies** *(CINESPA)*; **Tropical Diseases** *(CIET)* (Tropical Medicine); **Women's Studies** *(CIEM)* (Women's Studies)

Research Institutes
Agriculture *(IIA)* (Agriculture); **Clodomiro Picado** *(ICP)*; **Economics** *(IICE)* (Economics); **Education** *(INIE)* (Education); **Engineering** *(INII)*; **Health Sciences** *(INISA)* (Health Sciences); **Law** *(IIJ)*; **Linguistics** *(INIL)*; **Pharmacy** *(INIFAR)* (Pharmacy); **Philosophy** *(IIF)* (Philosophy); **Psychology** *(IIP)* (Psychology); **Social Studies** *(IIS)* (Social Studies)

History: Founded 1940, incorporating former schools of the Universidad de Santo Tomás. An autonomous institution.

Governing Bodies: Consejo Universitario

Academic Year: February to December (February-July; August-December)

Admission Requirements: Secondary school certificate (bachillerato) or foreign equivalent, and entrance examination

Fees: (Colones): Tuition, c. 3,250 per credit

Main Language(s) of Instruction: Spanish

Degrees and Diplomas: *Diploma:* 2-3 yrs; *Bachiller:* 4-5 yrs; *Licenciatura:* 5-6 yrs; *Maestría:* 6-7 yrs; *Doctorado Académico*

Student Services: Academic counselling, Cultural centre, Foreign student adviser, Handicapped facilities, Health services, Nursery care, Sports facilities

Student Residential Facilities: Yes

Special Facilities: Museums: Insects; Zoological. Botanical Garden. San Ramón Forestry Reserve, San Ramón de Tres Ríos Ecological Reserve. Experimental Stations (Agricultural and Breeding Research). Sculpture and Painting Gallery; Audiovisual Exhibition Hall

Libraries: c. 454,000 vols; c. 21,300 audiovisual items; Carlos Monge Alfaro Library (Humanities); Luis Demetrio Tinoco Library (Engineering); Health Library

Publications: Revistas

Press or Publishing House: Editorial Universidad de Costa Rica
Last Updated: 02/12/09

ATLANTIC CAMPUS
SEDE DEL ATLÁNTICO

Turrialba, Cartago
Tel: +506 556-1044
Fax: +506 556-7020

Directora: Elizabeth Castillo Araya

Faculties
Agronomy (Agronomy); **Business Administration** (Business Administration); **Education** (Education); **Social Sciences**

GUANACASTE CAMPUS
SEDE DE GUANACASTE

Liberia y Santa Cruz, Guanacaste
Tel: +506 666-0357
Fax: +506 666-0868

Director: Jorge Moya Montero

Faculties
Agronomy (Agronomy); **Business Administration** (Business Administration); **Education** (Education); **Social Work** (Social Work); **Tourism** (Tourism)

LIMÓN CAMPUS
SEDE DE LIMÓN

Limón
Tel: +506 758-1309
Fax: +506 758-4958

Directora: Ivonne Lepe Jorquera

Faculties
Computer Science (Computer Science); **Education** (Education; Primary Education); **Nursing** (Nursing); **Ports Administration** (Transport Management)

PACIFIC CAMPUS
SEDE DEL PACÍFICO

Puntarenas
Tel: +506 661-1111
Fax: +506 661-2501

Directora: Susan Chen Mok

Faculties
Business Administration (Business Administration); **Education** (Education); **Fishing and Navigation** (Fishery; Nautical Science)

WESTERN CAMPUS
SEDE DE OCCIDENTE

San Ramón y Tacarés de Grecia, Alajuela
Tel: +506 445-5333
Fax: +506 445-6005

Director: José Ángel Vargas Vargas

Faculties
Agronomy (Agronomy); **Business Administration** (Accountancy; Business Administration; Public Administration); **Chemistry**; **Education** (Education; English; French; Mathematics Education; Physical Education; Preschool Education; Primary Education; Social Studies); **Law**; **Social Sciences**; **Social Work** (Social Work)

Further Information: Also Recinto de Golfito

PRIVATE INSTITUTIONS

ADVENTIST UNIVERSITY OF CENTRAL AMERICA

Universidad Adventista de Centroamérica (UNADECA)
Apartado 138-4050, Alajuela 4050
Tel: +506 440-4580
Fax: +506 441-3465
EMail: admisiones@unadeca.org
Website: http://www.unadeca.net

Rectora: Herminia Perla Perla
Tel: +506 440-4580, Ext.108 EMail: herminiaperla@hotmail.com

Administrative Officer: Carlos Martínez Mejía

International Relations: Susy Longa Perla

Schools

Business Administration (Accountancy; Business Administration; Management); **Education** (Computer Education; English Studies; Mathematics Education; Preschool Education; Primary Education; Religious Education; Secretarial Studies; Social Studies); **Nursing** (Nursing); **Psychology**; **Systems Engineering**; **Theology** (Theology)

History: Founded 1986. A private institution authorized by the government.

Governing Bodies: Board of Management

Academic Year: January to November

Admission Requirements: Secondary school certificate (bachillerato)

Main Language(s) of Instruction: Spanish

Accrediting Agencies: Consejo Nacional de Enseñanza Universitaria Privada (CONESUP); Ministerio de Educación Pública

Degrees and Diplomas: *Licenciatura; Maestría*

Student Services: Academic counselling, Handicapped facilities, Health services, Language programs, Sports facilities

Student Residential Facilities: Yes

Libraries: Central Library, c. 41,750 vols

Press or Publishing House: Imprenta Granix

Academic Staff 2007-2008	MEN	WOMEN	TOTAL
FULL-TIME	15	18	**33**
PART-TIME	13	13	**26**
STAFF WITH DOCTORATE			
FULL-TIME	2	1	**3**
PART-TIME	1	1	**2**
Student Numbers 2007-2008			
All (Foreign Included)	680	437	**1,117**
FOREIGN ONLY	303	220	**523**

Last Updated: 02/11/09

ALMA MATER UNIVERSITY
Universidad Fundepos Alma Mater
Edificio San José 2000 tercer piso, contiguo Hotel Irazú, San José
Tel: +506 231-5855
Fax: +506 231-7569
EMail: mbrenes@fundepos.ac.cr
Website: http://www.fundepos.ac.cr

Dean: Wilburg Jiménez Castro

Programmes

Accountancy (Accountancy); **Business Administration** (Business Administration); **Marketing** (Marketing); **Preschool Education** (Preschool Education); **Primary Education** (Primary Education)

History: Founded 2003.

Main Language(s) of Instruction: Spanish

Degrees and Diplomas: *Bachiller; Licenciatura; Maestría*
Last Updated: 03/12/09

AMERICAN UNIVERSITY
Universidad Americana
Apartado 1901-1002, Barrio Los Yoses, frente a Pollos Kentucky, Calle 21, San José
Tel: +506 253-8350
Fax: +506 224-7779
EMail: matricula@uam.ac.cr
Website: http://www.uamcr.com

Rector: Luis Valverde Fallas Tel: +506 258-0985

Administradora Académica: María Luisa González Campos
EMail: mailto:mlgonzalez@uam.ac.cr

Divisions

Administration (Accountancy; Administration; Business Administration; Human Resources); **Communication** (Advertising and Publicity; Graphic Design); **Education** (Accountancy; Computer Science; Education; Educational Administration; Educational Sciences; English; Mathematics Education; Natural Sciences; Preschool Education; Primary Education; Secondary Education; Social Studies; Spanish)

Programmes

Physical Therapy (Physical Therapy); **Systems Engineering** (Industrial Engineering; Systems Analysis)

Further Information: Branches in Cartago and Heredia

History: Founded 1997.

Main Language(s) of Instruction: Spanish

Degrees and Diplomas: *Diploma; Bachiller; Licenciatura; Maestría*
Last Updated: 02/12/09

AUTONOMOUS UNIVERSITY OF CENTRAL AMERICA
Universidad Autónoma de Centro América (UACA)
Apartado 7637-1000, San José
Tel: +506 234-0701
Fax: +506 224-0391
EMail: lauaca@sol.rasca.ca.cr
Website: http://www.uaca.ac.cr

Rector: Guillermo Malavassi Vargas (1997-)
Tel: +506 272-9100, Fax: +506 272-9100
EMail: gmalavassi@uaca.ac.cr

Chancellor: Pablo A. Arce EMail: parce@uaca.ac.cr

Administrative Dean: Mario Granados
Tel: +506 224-0391 EMail: canciller@uaca.ac.cr

Divisions

Business Administration (Business Administration); **Computer Science** (Computer Science); **Economics** (Economics); **Graphic Arts** (Advertising and Publicity; Industrial Design); **International Relations** (International Relations); **Journalism** (Journalism); **Law** (Law); **Medicine** (Medicine); **Nursing** (Nursing); **Physical Therapy** (Physical Therapy); **Psychology** (Psychology); **Tourism** (Tourism)

Institutes

Research and Education *(IEPI)* (Education; Public Law)

History: Founded 1976 as an independent institution authorized by the government. Includes eight independent self-governing Colleges.

Governing Bodies: Senado Académico, comprising the Rector, Deans, and the Minister of Education; Board of Trustees

Academic Year: January to December (January-April; May-August; September-December)

Admission Requirements: Secondary school certificate (bachillerato) or foreign equivalent, and entrance examination

Fees: As authorized by the Ministry of Public Education

Main Language(s) of Instruction: Spanish

Accrediting Agencies: Consejo Nacional de Enseñanza Universitaria Privada (CONESUP)

Degrees and Diplomas: *Bachiller:* 3 yrs; *Bachiller:* Architecture; Civil Engineering; Industrial Engineering; Psychology, 4 yrs; *Licenciatura:* a further 2 yrs; *Maestría:* a further 2 yrs; *Doctorado Académico (PhD); Doctorado Académico:* Law, 2 yrs following Licenciatura or Maestría; *Doctorado Académico:* Medicine, 3 sem following Licenciatura

Student Services: Academic counselling, Canteen, Cultural centre, Foreign student adviser, Health services, Sports facilities

Libraries: 92,000 vols

Publications: Revista Acta Académica *(biannually)*; Revista de Derecho Público *(biannually)*
Last Updated: 04/04/08

ACADEMIC COLLEGE
COLLEGIUM ACADEMICUM

Apartado 1703-1002, San José
Tel: +506 253-0711
Fax: +506 224-0391
EMail: academicum@uaca.ac.cr

Dean: Gastón Certad

Divisions
Business Administration (Business Administration); **Computer Science** (Computer Science); **Economics** (Economics); **International Relations** (International Relations); **Law** (Law)

History: Founded 1976.

ANDRÉS BELLO COLLEGE
COLEGIO ANDRÉS BELLO

Apartado 684-2300, Curridabat
Tel: +506 223-9282
Fax: +506 233-0598
EMail: abello@uaca.ac.cr

Dean: Orelia Chambers

Divisions
Educational Sciences (Educational Sciences); **International Relations** (International Relations); **Nursing** (Nursing); **Psychology** (Psychology); **Public Relations** (Public Relations); **Tourism** (Tourism)

CLORITO PICADO COLLEGE
COLEGIO CLORITO PICADO

Los Cipreses, Intersección Curridabat-Tres Rios, Curridabat
Tel: +506 271-2829
Fax: +506 271-3839
EMail: info@ccp.ac.cr

Dean: Eddy Astorga Sell

Administrative Dean: Eva Cristina Mezas Badilla

Divisions
Medicine (Medicine)

IGNACIO DE LOYOLA COLLEGE
COLEGIO ÍGNACIO DE LOYOLA

Apartado 10528-1000, San José
Tel: +506 225-5413
Fax: +506 257-4332
EMail: loyola@uaca.ac.cr

Dean: Gregorio Contreras Carrillo

Divisions
Business Administration (Business Administration); **Economics** (Accountancy; Economics; International Business; Law; Marketing); **Geological Engineering** (Surveying and Mapping); **Human Resources Administration** (Human Resources); **Industrial Engineering** (Industrial Engineering; Surveying and Mapping); **Psychology** (Psychology); **Transport Administration** (Transport Management)

LEONARDO DA VINCI COLLEGE
COLEGIO LEONARDO DA VINCI

Apartado 7637-1000, San José
Tel: +506 290-2552
Fax: +506 290-2505
EMail: davinci@uaca.ac.cr

Dean: Orlando Saborío

Divisions
Business Administration and Industrial Administration (Business Administration; Industrial Management); **Engineering** (Civil Engineering; Engineering; Industrial Engineering); **Psychology** (Psychology); **Public Relations** (Public Relations)

History: Founded 1978.

STUDIUM GENERALE COSTARRICENSE

Apartado 7651-1000, San José
Tel: +506 271-2100
Fax: +506 271-2015
EMail: info@studium.ac.cr

Dean: Mario Granados-Moreno **EMail:** canciller@uaca.ac.cr

Divisions
Accountancy (Accountancy); **Architecture** (Architecture); **Business Administration** (Business Administration); **Computer Engineering** (Computer Engineering); **Economics** (Economics); **Engineering** (Civil Engineering; Electrical Engineering; Engineering); **History** (History); **Journalism** (Journalism); **Law** (Law); **Music** (Music); **Philology** (Philology); **Philosophy** (Philosophy)

History: Founded 1976.

AUTONOMOUS UNIVERSITY OF MONTERREY
Universidad Autónoma de Monterrey

Apartado 3510-1000, 300 Este y 100 Sur de la Iglesia Sta. Teresita, San José
Tel: +506 283-7853
Fax: +506 223-5615
EMail: info@unam.ac.cr
Website: http://www.unamon.com/

Rector: Gerardo Venegas Solera

Academic Dean: Lourdes Hernández

International Relations: Jaime Barrantes Bermúdez

Programmes
Accountancy; **Banking** (Banking); **Business Administration**; **Finance**; **Human Resources** (Human Resources); **Psychology** (Psychology)

History: Founded 1994.

Main Language(s) of Instruction: Spanish

Degrees and Diplomas: *Bachiller*; *Licenciatura*; *Maestría*
Last Updated: 02/12/09

BRAULIO CARRILLO UNIVERSITY
Universidad Braulio Carrillo

Apartado 1184-2050, Avenida 1, Calle 28/38, San José
Tel: +506 222-6780
Fax: +506 222-6775
EMail: carrillo@racsa.co.cr

Rector: Juan Manuel Gómez Solera **Tel:** +506 223-9717

Administrative Dean: Sonia Villalobos

Divisions
Administration (Administration); **Foreign Trade** (International Business)

History: Founded 1994.

Main Language(s) of Instruction: Spanish

BUSINESS UNIVERSITY OF COSTA RICA
Universidad Empresarial de Costa Rica (UNEM)

San José 62-2050
Tel: +506 2253-4952
Fax: +506 225-5141
EMail: info@unem.edu
Website: http://www.unem.edu/international/

Rector: William Zamora Gonzalez (2003-)
EMail: William.zamora@unem.edu

International Relations: William A. Stack
EMail: wstack@unem.edu

Faculties
Biological Sciences; **Business Administration** (Accountancy; Business Administration; Finance; Human Resources; International

1071

Business; Management; Marketing); **Education and Humanities**; **Post-graduate Studies**; **Psychology and Behavioural Science**; **Social Sciences**

Schools
Languages

History: Founded 1992 as International Postgraduate School. Acquired present status and title 1997.

Governing Bodies: Board of Trustees

Academic Year: January to December

Admission Requirements: Secondary school certificate for all undergraduate programmes. A Bachelor degree for Licenciatura and Master's programmes. A Master's degree for Doctorate programmes

Main Language(s) of Instruction: Spanish. English

Accrediting Agencies: Consejo Nacional de Enseñanza Universitaria Privada (CONESUP)

Degrees and Diplomas: *Licenciatura*: Business (Lic), 1 yr; *Maestría*; *Doctorado Académico*: Administrative Science; Behavioural Science; Biological Science; Education; Humanities; Psychology; Social Sciences, 2-5 yrs following Maestría. Also Bachelor (BA) in Business Administration, Education and Arts (4 yrs). Master (MA) in Administrative Science, Behavioural Sciences, Psychology, Education, Humanities, Social Sciences (a further 2 yrs). Also Diploma of Attendance (issued by the SLI, ELI, FLI)

Student Services: Academic counselling, Canteen, Cultural centre, Employment services, Foreign student adviser, Foreign Studies Centre, Language programs, Social counselling, Sports facilities

Special Facilities: Auditorium. Computer Laboratories

Libraries: c. 120,000 vols including e-libraries

Press or Publishing House: Editorial Universidad Empresarial
Last Updated: 03/12/09

CASTRO CARAZO METROPOLITAN UNIVERSITY
Universidad Metropolitana Castro Carazo (UMCA)
Apartado 325-1005, Calle 7, entre las avenidas Central y segunda, San José
Tel: +506 255-3534
Fax: +506 257-1687
EMail: info@umca.net
Website: http://www.umca.net

Rector: Guillermo Araya Guzmán Tel: +506 258-0174

Administrative Officer: Álvaro Molina

International Relations: Javier Sánchez

Divisions
Accountancy; **Business Administration** (Business Administration); **Computer Science** (Computer Science); **Education** (Education); **Law** (Law); **Secretarial Studies**

History: Founded 1996.

Degrees and Diplomas: *Bachiller*; *Licenciatura*; *Maestría*; *Doctorado Académico*
Last Updated: 03/12/09

CATHOLIC UNIVERSITY OF COSTA RICA
Universidad Católica de Costa Rica
Apartado postal 519-2100, 600 Este, 200 Norte y 100 Este, de la Iglesia de (Antiguo Saint Clare) Moravia, San José
Tel: +506 240-7272; +506 297-0268
Fax: +506 240-2121
EMail: info@ucatolica.ac.cr
Website: http://www.ucatolica.ac.cr

Rector: Arnoldo Montero Martínez (1994-) Tel: +506 240-3290

Administrative Dean: Ligia Cordero

International Relations: Fernando A. Muñoz

Faculties
Business Administration; **Education** (Education); **Law** (Law); **Philosophy** (Philosophy); **Psychology** (Psychology); **Systems Engineering** (Engineering); **Theology** (Theology)

History: Founded 1993 by the Conferencia Episcopal de Costa Rica. Also known as Universidad Católica de Costa Rica Anselmo Llorente y Lafuente.

Governing Bodies: Junta Administrativa; Consejo Universitario

Academic Year: January to December (January-April; May-August; September-December)

Admission Requirements: Secondary school certificate (bachillerato)

Fees: (Colones): 39,500-41,000

Main Language(s) of Instruction: Spanish

Degrees and Diplomas: *Bachiller*: Education;Religion Studies; Educational Counselling; Special Education; Primary School Education; Mathematic Education; Science Education; Social Studies Education; Spanish; English; Psychology; Systems Engineering; Philosophy; Theology, Law (Bach); *Licenciatura*: Education; Theology; Psychology; Philosophy; Systems Engineering, Special Education, Elementary School; English (Lic.); *Maestría*: Business; Educational Administration; Psychology; Educational Psychology; Gerontology; Systems Engineering; Business Administration; Psychotheraphy; *Doctorado Académico*: Education

Student Services: Academic counselling, Canteen, Cultural centre, Employment services, Health services, Sports facilities

Student Residential Facilities: For 2,000 students

Libraries: Central Library, 22,000 vols
Last Updated: 02/12/09

CENTRAL AMERICAN BUSINESS UNIVERSITY
Universidad Centroamericana de Ciencias Empresariales (UCEM)
110 metros norte de la Catedral, Alajuela
Tel: +506 440-2090
Fax: +506 440-0737
EMail: info@ucem.ac.cr
Website: http://www.ucem.ac.cr

Rector: Chester J. Zelaya-Goodman (1998-)
EMail: czelaya@ucem.ac.cr

Divisions
Accountancy (Accountancy); **Bilingual Preschool Education** (Preschool Education); **Bilingual Primary and Secondary Education** (Primary Education; Secondary Education); **Business Administration** (Business Administration); **Industrial Engineering** (Industrial Engineering); **Systems Engineering** (Computer Engineering); **Tourism and Hotel Management** (Hotel Management; Tourism)

History: Founded 1997.

Academic Year: 3 periods starting January, May and September

Admission Requirements: High school diploma

Fees: (Colones): 120,000 per annum

Main Language(s) of Instruction: Spanish

Degrees and Diplomas: *Bachiller*: Accountancy; Business Administration; Systems Engineering; Industrial Engineering; Tourism and Hotel Management; Bilingual Pre-School Education; Bilingual Primary Education (Br), 2 1/2 yrs; *Licenciatura*: Accountancy (Lic.), 3 1/2 yrs

Student Services: Academic counselling, Employment services, Language programs, Social counselling

Student Residential Facilities: None

Libraries: Yes
Last Updated: 02/12/09

CENTRAL AMERICAN SOCIAL SCIENCES UNIVERSITY
Universidad Centroamericana de Ciencias Sociales (UCACIS)
Banco Nacional de San Pedro, 2 cuadras al sur, 5 cuadras al este y 4 cuadras al Sur. Barrio La Granja, San José
Tel: +506 280-5310
EMail: ucacis@racsa.co.cr
Website: http://www.ucacis.com

Rectora: Maribel Soto Arguedas

Programmes
Psychology (Psychology)

Degrees and Diplomas: *Bachiller; Licenciatura; Maestría*
Last Updated: 02/12/09

CENTRAL UNIVERSITY
Universidad Central
Apartado 1788-1002, De la Iglesia Sta. Teresita, 200 Norte y 225
Este, Diagonal Rotonda el Farolito, San José
Tel: +506 224-0551
Fax: +506 224-0531
EMail: info@universidadcentral.com
Website: http://www.universidadcentral.com

Rector: Sergio Mata Navarro
Tel: +506 283-0545, Fax: +506 283-0545
EMail: Rector@universidadcentral.com

Administrative Officer: Armando Mena Villalta
Tel: +506 283-9763

International Relations: Emilio Meléndez Flores

Faculties
Architecture and Planning; **Economics** (Accountancy; Banking;
Business Administration; Business and Commerce; Economics;
Finance; Human Resources; International Business; Management);
Education (Curriculum; Education; Educational Administration;
Educational and Student Counselling; Mathematics Education;
Modern Languages; Preschool Education; Science Education;
Social Studies; Spanish; Teacher Training); **Engineering** (Archi-
tecture; Civil Engineering; Computer Science; Electrical and Elec-
tronic Engineering; Electronic Engineering; Engineering; Hydraulic
Engineering; Industrial Engineering); **Social Sciences** (Journalism;
Law; Psychology; Tourism)

History: Founded 1990.

Main Language(s) of Instruction: Spanish

Degrees and Diplomas: *Bachiller; Licenciatura; Maestría*
Student Services: Language programs, Social counselling
Last Updated: 02/12/09

CONTINENTAL UNIVERSITY OF ARTS AND SCIENCE
Universidad Continental de las Ciencias y el Arte
300 mts este del Museo Nacional, avenida 2°, San José
Fax: +506 256-7944
EMail: info@uccart.com
Website: http://www.uccart.com

Dean: Wilberth Villegas Rodríguez

Programmes
Art Education (Art Education); **Graphic Design** (Graphic Design);
Higher Education (Higher Education); **Music**; **Music Education**
(Music Education); **Preschool Education** (Preschool Education);
Psychology (Psychology)

Degrees and Diplomas: *Bachiller; Maestría*
Last Updated: 02/12/09

COSTA RICAN TECHNOLOGICAL UNIVERSITY
Universidad Tecnológica Costarricense (UTEC)
50 metros del Banco de Costa Rica, Edificio Paz, San José
Tel: +506 223-1124
Fax: +506 223-2461
EMail: unitec@racsa.co.cr

Rector: Carlos Castro Quesada

Programmes
Business Administration; Computer Science

CREATIVE UNIVERSITY
Universidad Creativa
Apartado 1405-2050, Carretera a Sabanilla de la Farmacia la
Paulina 100 Este, 100 Norte y 250 Este Edificio Metálico,
San José
Tel: +506-253-4591
Fax: +506 238-6408
EMail: info@ucreativa.com
Website: http://www.ucreativa.com/

Dean: Luis Montoya Salas

Programmes
Architectural Design (Architectural and Environmental Design);
Architecture (Architecture); **Digital Photography**; **Fashion
Design**; **Graphic Design** (Graphic Design); **Interior Design**
(Interior Design); **Software Engineering** (Software Engineering)

History: Founded 1995.

Main Language(s) of Instruction: Spanish

Degrees and Diplomas: *Bachiller; Licenciatura*
Last Updated: 02/12/09

EARTH UNIVERSITY
Universidad EARTH (EARTH)
Apartado 4442-1000, San José
Tel: +506 713-0000
Fax: +506 713-0001
EMail: jzaglul@earth.ac.cr
Website: http://www.earth.ac.cr/

Rector: José A. Zaglul (1989-)
Tel: +506 713-0224, Fax: +506 713-0002

Vice-President of Administration and Finance: Alex Mata
Tel: +506 713-0012, Fax: +506 713-0383
EMail: a-mata@earth.ac.cr

Administrative Officer: Daniel Sherrard
Tel: +506 713-0000, Ext.3030, Fax: +506 713-0002
EMail: dsherrar@earth.ac.cr

International Relations: Gerardo Mirabelli, Director of External
Relation
Tel: +506 713-0238, Fax: +506 713-0003
EMail: gmirabel@earth.ac.cr

Programmes
Agricultural Sciences (Agriculture)

History: Founded 1990.

Governing Bodies: International Institution governed by International Board of Directors, Students and Faculty from over 25
countries

Academic Year: January to December (3 trimesters)

Admission Requirements: Secondary school certificate

Main Language(s) of Instruction: Spanish

International Co-operation: With universities in Brazil, Colombia,
Ecuador, Uganda, USA, Germany

Accrediting Agencies: Sistema Nacional de Acreditatión de la
Educatión Superior (SINAES)

Degrees and Diplomas: *Licenciatura*: Agricultural Sciences,
4 yrs

Student Services: Language programs, Sports facilities

Student Residential Facilities: Yes

Special Facilities: 3,300 hectare research and commercial farms;
1,000 hectare forest reserve; 1,500 hectare satellite campus on
Pacific Coast; Computer Laboratories

Libraries: W.K. Kellogg Library

Publications: Tierra Tropical, Journal focudes on tropical agriculture, rural development and natural resourses *(biennially)*
Last Updated: 03/12/09

EVANGELICAL UNIVERSITY OF THE AMERICAS

Universidad Evangélica de las Américas (UNELA)
100 Este y 50 al Sur de la Clinica Biblía, San José
Tel: +506 221-7870
Fax: +506 255-0257
EMail: unela@unela.net
Website: http://www.unela.net

Rector: Enrique Guang Tapia
Tel: +506 283-7278 EMail: eguang@unela.net

Administrator: Hernán Fernández Tel: +506 221-7870

International Relations: Paul Bergsma
EMail: pbergsma@unela.net

Schools
Administration of Ecclesiastical Resources; **Applied Sciences and Interdisciplinary Studies** (Cultural Studies; Missionary Studies); **Education** (Education; Educational and Student Counselling); **Theology**

History: Founded 1992 by the Church of Nazarene. Acquired present status and title 1999.

Governing Bodies: UNELA Association

Academic Year: March to November

Admission Requirements: Secondary school certificate (bachillerato)

Fees: (US Dollars): Undergraduate, 50 per semester; Graduate, 80 per semester

Main Language(s) of Instruction: Spanish

International Co-operation: With universities in Mexico and Argentina

Accrediting Agencies: Latin American Association of Institutes of Theological Education (ALIET); Consejo Nacional de Enseñanza Universitaria Privada (CONESUP)

Degrees and Diplomas: *Bachiller*: Theology, Administration of Church Resources, Pastoral Studies, Religions (BT, BARE), 4 yrs; *Licenciatura*: Theology, Administration of Church Resources, Pastoral Studies, Religions (LIC), 5 yrs; *Maestría*: Theology Education, Missiology, Family Counselling (MCR), a further 2 yrs; *Doctorado Académico*

Student Residential Facilities: None

Libraries: Central Library, c. 10,000 vols
Last Updated: 03/12/09

FEDERATED UNIVERSITY OF COSTA RICA

Universidad Federada de Costa Rica
Apartado 250-2120, frente Principal del Museo Nacional, San José
Tel: +506 223-2767 +506 221-5948
Fax: +506 257-0104
EMail: info@ufederada.ac.cr

Rectora: Helia Betancourt
Tel: +506 223-3315, Fax: +506 221-5948

Registrar: Matilde Guevara Lazxo Tel: +506 258-3972

International Relations: Helia Betancourt, Rectora

Colleges
Business Administration (*Santo Tomás*); **Computer Science** (*Santo Tomás*); **Education** (*San Judas*); **Journalism** (*San Judas*); **Law** (*Santo Tomás*); **Medicine** (*San Judas*)

Further Information: Also Spanish Programme for foreign students. Cultural, Political and Latin American History Studies in English

History: Founded 1995.

Academic Year: January to December (January-May; May-August; September-December)

Admission Requirements: Secondary school certificate (bachillerato)

Fees: (Colones): 14,000-35,000 per annum

Main Language(s) of Instruction: Spanish, English

Degrees and Diplomas: *Bachiller*: 2 yrs; *Licenciatura*: 3 yrs; *Maestría*: a further 2 yrs

Student Services: Academic counselling, Canteen, Employment services, Foreign student adviser, Sports facilities

Special Facilities: TV Studio. Radio Studio

Libraries: Main Library, 5,000 vols

Press or Publishing House: Editorial San Judas Tadeo

FIDELITAS UNIVERSITY

Universidad Fidélitas
Apartado 8063-1000, Escuela Santa Marta de Montes de Oca, San José
Tel: +506 253-0262
Fax: +506 253-9576
EMail: informacion@ufidelitas.ac.cr
Website: http://www.ufidelitas.ac.cr

Rector: Gilberto Zeledón Agüero (2008-) Tel: +506 234-8475

Administrative Manager: Indiana Marín Roman
EMail: gerenciaadministrativa@ufidelitas.ac.cr

Divisions
Advertising Design *Director*: Hannia Hoffmann; **Business Administration** (Banking; Business Administration; Finance) *Director*: Marco Villalobos; **Education** (Education; Preschool Education) *Head*: Vitinia Rojas; **Engineering** (Civil Engineering; Computer Engineering; Electrical Engineering; Engineering; Hydraulic Engineering; Industrial Engineering; Information Technology) *Director*: Luis Calvo; **English** *Head*: María José de Briones; **Law** (Law) *Head*: Ana Tereza Vargas; **Psychology** (Psychology) *Head*: Adelita Peralta; **Public Accountancy** (Accountancy) *Head*: Marco Villalobos

History: Founded 1980 as Collegium Fidelitas, acquired present status and title 1995.

Governing Bodies: Consejo Universitario

Academic Year: January to December (January-April; May-August; September-December)

Admission Requirements: Secondary school certificate (bachillerato) or foreign equivalent

Main Language(s) of Instruction: Spanish. Also English for MBA programmes

Degrees and Diplomas: *Bachiller*: 3-5 yrs; *Licenciatura*: a further 1-5 yrs; *Maestría*: 2 yrs

Student Services: Academic counselling, Cultural centre, Employment services, Social counselling

Student Residential Facilities: For 4,000 students

Libraries: c. 7,800 vols

Press or Publishing House: Editorial Fidélitas
Last Updated: 03/12/09

FLORENCIO DEL CASTILLO UNIVERSITY

Universidad Florencio del Castillo
Apartado 653-7050, 100 Metros Sur de la Esquina Sureste de los Tribunales, Cártago
Tel: +506 591-4562
Fax: +506 506-4563
EMail: info@uca.ac.cr
Website: http://www.uca.ac.cr

Rectora: Eva Cristina Meza Castillo

Administrative Officer: Eduardo López

International Relations: Franco Fernández

Divisions
Accountancy; **Administration**; **Business Administration** (Business Administration); **Education** (Education); **Human Resource Management** (Human Resources); **Law**; **Tourism**

History: Founded 1995.

Main Language(s) of Instruction: Spanish

Degrees and Diplomas: *Bachiller*; *Licenciatura*; *Maestría*

FREE SCHOOL OF LAW UNIVERSITY

Universidad Escuela Libre de Derecho

Apartado 296-1002, 75 Oeste del Registro Nacional, Zapote,
San José
Tel: +506 283-3490
Fax: +506 283-8061
EMail: info@uescuelalibre.ac.cr
Website: http://www.uescuelalibre.ac.cr

Rector: Ricardo Guerrero Portilla

Programmes

Administration and Business Law (Administration; Commercial Law); **International Relations** (International Relations); **Law** (Law)

History: Founded 1996.

Main Language(s) of Instruction: Spanish

Degrees and Diplomas: *Bachiller*. 4-5 yrs; *Licenciatura*; *Maestría*: 6-7 yrs; *Doctorado Académico*

Publications: Revistas
Last Updated: 03/12/09

FREE UNIVERSITY OF COSTA RICA

Universidad Libre de Costa Rica (ULICORI)

Apartado 1053-1000, Av. Central y 2, Calle 25, 100 Este de Bomba
La Primavera en Barrio La California, San José
Tel: +506 222-7934
Fax: +506 221-8115
EMail: info@ulicori.ac.cr
Website: http://www.ulicori.com

Rector: Carlos Alberto Paniagua Vargas
Tel: +506 221-1283, Fax: +506 221-8115

International Relations: Willy Soto Tel: +506 222-8196

Faculties

Economics; **Educational Sciences**; **Health Sciences**; **Social Sciences**

History: Founded 1993. A private institution authorized by the government.

Academic Year: January to December

Admission Requirements: Secondary school certficate (bachillerato)

Main Language(s) of Instruction: Spanish

Degrees and Diplomas: *Bachiller*; *Licenciatura*; *Maestría*; *Doctorado Académico*
Last Updated: 03/12/09

HISPANO-AMERICAN UNIVERSITY

Universidad Hispanoamericana

Apartado 408-1002, 100 Oeste y 100 Norte Santa Teresita, Barrio
Aranjuez, San José
Tel: +506 256-8197
Fax: +506 223-2349
EMail: info@uhispanoamericana.ac.cr
Website: http://www.uhispanoamericana.ac.cr

Rector: Ángel Marín Espinoza

Vicerrector: Rafael Garzona Meseguer

Programmes

Administration and Accountancy (Accountancy; Administration); **Advertising** (Advertising and Publicity; Public Relations); **Architecture** (Architecture); **Business Administration** (Business Administration); **Computer Engineering** (Computer Engineering); **Education** (Education; Educational Administration; English; Pre-school Education; Primary Education); **Electronics** (Electronic Engineering); **Industrial Engineering** (Industrial Engineering); **Law** (Law); **Medicine and Surgery** (Medicine; Surgery); **Nursing** (Nursing); **Psychology** (Psychology); **Tourism** (Tourism)

History: Founded 1992. A private institution authorized by the government.

Academic Year: January to December (January-May; May-September; September-December)

Admission Requirements: Secondary school certificate (bachillerato)

Fees: (Colones): c. 23,000 per course per term

Main Language(s) of Instruction: Spanish

Accrediting Agencies: Consejo Nacional de Enseñanza Universitaria Privada (CONESUP)

Degrees and Diplomas: *Bachiller*: 8 sem; *Licenciatura*: 10-12 sem; *Maestría*: a further 4 sem

Student Services: Academic counselling, Employment services, Social counselling, Sports facilities

Student Residential Facilities: Yes

Libraries: University Library, 6,700 vols
Last Updated: 03/12/09

INDEPENDENT UNIVERSITY OF COSTA RICA

Universidad Independiente de Costa Rica (UNICOR)

Apartado 414-2400, Desamparados 50 E. Esquina Noreste del
Cementerio, San José
Tel: +506 219-2781
Fax: +506 259-1038
EMail: info@uindependiente.ac.cr
Website: http://www.uindependiente.ac.cr

Rectora: Sonia Abarca Mora

Dean: María Eugenia Vargas Pinaud

International Relations: Oscar Reyes Padilla

Faculties

Education and Human Sciences; **Social Sciences and Administration** (Accountancy; Administration; Finance; Psychology)

History: Founded 1996.

Admission Requirements: Secondary school certificate (Bachillerato)

Main Language(s) of Instruction: Spanish. Some courses in English

Degrees and Diplomas: *Bachiller*: 3 yrs; *Licenciatura*: 11/2 yrs; *Maestría*

Student Services: Academic counselling, Employment services

Special Facilities: Laboratory

Libraries: Yes
Last Updated: 03/12/09

INTERAMERICAN UNIVERSITY OF COSTA RICA

Universidad Interamericana de Costa Rica (UICR)

Apartado 6495-1000, Contiguo a Pricesmart carretera a Heredia,
Heredia
Tel: +506 261-4242
Fax: +506 261-3212
EMail: infocr@uinteramericana.edu
Website: http://www.uinteramericana.edu

Rector: Henry Rodríguez

Faculties

Administration and Social Sciences; **Engineering and Architecture**

Schools

Hotel Management *(Interamerican)*

History: Founded 1986.

Academic Year: January to December (January-April; May-August; September-December)

Admission Requirements: Secondary school certificate (bachillerato)

Main Language(s) of Instruction: Spanish

Accrediting Agencies: International Consortium for Higher Education (CIDES)

Degrees and Diplomas: *Bachiller*: 31/2 yrs; *Licenciatura*: 1 yr; *Maestría*: a further 1-2 yrs

Student Services: Academic counselling, Employment services, Foreign student adviser, Social counselling, Sports facilities

Special Facilities: Movie Studio
Last Updated: 03/12/09

INTERNATIONAL CHRISTIAN UNIVERSITY

Universidad Cristiana Internacional
200 metros este del Supermercado Hipermás, en San Sebastián,
San José
Tel: +506 22.26.36.84
EMail: informacion@esepa.org
Website: http://www.esepa.org/

Rector: Mark C. Padgett Hobbs

Programmes
Christian Education (Christian Religious Studies); **Pastoral Ministry** (Pastoral Studies); **Transcultural Ministry**

Degrees and Diplomas: *Diploma*; *Bachiller*; *Maestría*
Last Updated: 02/12/09

INTERNATIONAL UNIVERSITY OF THE AMERICAS

Universidad Internacional de las Américas (UIA)
Apartado 1447-1002, San José
Tel: +506 233-4342
Fax: +506 222-3216
EMail: info@uia.ac.cr
Website: http://www.uia.ac.cr

Rector: Álvaro Pazos Baldioceda
Tel: +506 257-4240, Fax: +506 257-6668
EMail: malfaro@uia.ac.cr

Administrative Officer: Armando Córdova
Tel: +506 258-0220 EMail: correo@uia.ac.cr

International Relations: Arcelio Hernández
EMail: ahernandez@uia.ac.cr

Faculties
Economics (Accountancy; Business Administration; Economics; International Business; International Economics); **Engineering and Architecture** (Architecture; Computer Engineering; Electrical Engineering; Engineering; Industrial Engineering; Mechanical Engineering); **Health Sciences** (Medicine; Pharmacy); **Languages** (English; Modern Languages); **Law** (Law); **Social Sciences** (Advertising and Publicity; International Relations; Social Sciences; Tourism)

Further Information: Also Teaching Hospitals; Courses for foreign students

History: Founded 1986 by the International Foundation of the Americas. Acquired present status 1987.

Governing Bodies: Board of Directors

Academic Year: January to December (January-April; May-August; September-December)

Admission Requirements: Secondary school certificate (bachillerato) or foreign equivalent, and entrance examination

Main Language(s) of Instruction: Spanish

Accrediting Agencies: World Association of Universities and Colleges (WAUC)

Degrees and Diplomas: *Bachiller*: 3 yrs; *Licenciatura*: a further 1 yr; *Maestría*: a further 1 1/2 yr

Student Services: Academic counselling, Employment services, Foreign student adviser, Handicapped facilities, Language programs, Sports facilities

Special Facilities: Laboratories (Computer Science, Physics, Chemistry, Anatomy, Histology, Physiology, English); TV Channel

Libraries: c. 10,000 vols

Publications: Law Magazine *(annually)*

Press or Publishing House: International Foundation of the Americas Press
Last Updated: 03/12/09

ISAAC NEWTON UNIVERSITY

Universidad Isaac Newton
125 m este de la rotonda de Betania Sabanilla, San José
Tel: +506 225-9081
Fax: +506 234-1893
EMail: info@unin.ac.cr
Website: http://www.unin.ac.cr

Rector: Gildo Alvardo Gutiérrez

Programmes
Advertising (Advertising and Publicity); **Business Administration** (Administration; Advertising and Publicity; Business Administration; Public Relations); **Civil Engineering**; **Environmental Engineering** (Environmental Engineering); **Industrial Engineering** (Industrial Engineering); **Public Relations** (Public Relations)

History: Founded 1995.

Main Language(s) of Instruction: Spanish

Degrees and Diplomas: *Bachiller*; *Licenciatura*; *Maestría*
Last Updated: 03/12/09

JOHN PAUL II UNIVERSITY

Universidad Juan Pablo II
Apartado 11161Esquina Norteste Iglesia de Curridabat, San José
Tel: +506 272-5909
Fax: +506 272-0311
EMail: admision@ujpii.ac.cr

Rector: Tirza Bustamente Guerrero

International Relations: Claudio M. Solano
Tel: +506 272-5901, Fax: +506 272-5923

Programmes
Family Studies; **Religion**

History: Founded 1996.

Main Language(s) of Instruction: Spanish

LATIN AMERICAN BIBLICAL UNIVERSITY

Universidad Bíblica Latinoamericana (UBL)
100 Este y 25 Sur de la Clínica Bíblica, entre Avenidas 14 y 16,
Calle 3, San José
Tel: +506 283-8848
Fax: +506 283-6826
EMail: ubila@ice.co.cr
Website: http://www.ubila.net/

Rectora: Violeta Rocha
Tel: +506 222-7555 EMail: violeta@ubila.net

Vicerrectora: Nidia Fonseca

Schools
Bible (Bible); **Theology** (Theology)
History: Founded 1997.

Main Language(s) of Instruction: Spanish

Degrees and Diplomas: *Bachiller*; *Licenciatura*; *Maestría*
Last Updated: 02/12/09

LATIN AMERICAN UNIVERSITY OF SCIENCE AND TECHNOLOGY

Universidad Latinoamericana de Ciencia y Tecnología (ULACIT)
Apartado 10235, Barrio Turnón, de la República 150 al Sur,
San José
Tel: +506 523-4000
Fax: +506 223-3283
EMail: info@ulacit.ac.cr
Website: http://www.ulacit.ac.cr

Rector: Alvaro Castro Harrigan

President: Pamela Villalobos

International Relations: Illeana Castillo
Tel: +506 223-3651, Fax: +506 233-9739
EMail: icastillo@ulacit.ac.cr

Faculties
Engineering (Computer Engineering; Electronic Engineering; Industrial Engineering; Occupational Health); **Entrepreurial Sciences**; **Health Sciences** (Dentistry); **Social Sciences** (Educational Administration; English; Foreign Languages Education; Law; Pre-school Education; Psychology; Special Education)

Graduate Schools
Graduate Studies *(Masters Degrees)* (Business Administration; Curriculum; Educational Psychology; English; Foreign Languages

Education; Higher Education Teacher Training; Information Technology; Law; Orthodontics)

Further Information: Also Open University and distance learning (e-learning)

History: Founded 1988. A private institution authorized by the Ministry of Public Education.

Governing Bodies: Board of Trustees, comprising 7 members

Academic Year: January to December

Admission Requirements: Secondary school certficate (bachillerato)

Fees: (Colones): c. 1.2m.-2.4m. per annum

Main Language(s) of Instruction: Spanish

Degrees and Diplomas: *Bachiller*: 4 yrs; *Licenciatura*: a further 2 yrs; *Especialidad Profesional*; *Maestría*: 2 yrs; *Doctorado Académico*. Doctoral Programme in Business Administration

Student Services: Canteen, Cultural centre, Foreign student adviser

Special Facilities: La Marta Biological Reserve

Libraries: Central Library, c. 25,000 vols

Publications: Revista Rhombus, http://www.ulacit.ac.cr/revistarhombus.php

Press or Publishing House: Editorial Técnica Comercial
Last Updated: 03/12/09

LATIN UNIVERSITY OF COSTA RICA
Universidad Latina de Costa Rica (ULATINA)
Apartado 1561-2050, 300 Norte y 150 Este de Muñoz y Nanne, Lourdes, San Pedro de Montes de Oca
Tel: +506 283-2611
Fax: +506 225-2801
EMail: mercadeo@ulatina.ac.cr
Website: http://www.ulatina.ac.cr

Rector: Walter Bolaños Quesada
Tel: +506 224-1920, Fax: +506 225-4161

Faculties
Economics (Accountancy; Administration; Business Administration; Economics; Human Resources; International Relations); **Education** (Education; English; History; Philosophy; Special Education); **Engineering and Architecture** (Architecture; Civil Engineering; Computer Engineering; Engineering; Software Engineering; Telecommunications Engineering); **Health Sciences** (Dentistry; Health Sciences; Nursing; Optometry; Pharmacy; Psychology); **Social Sciences** (Advertising and Publicity; Journalism; Law; Public Relations; Social Sciences); **Tourism and Environmental Management** (Biological and Life Sciences; Hotel and Restaurant; Hotel Management; Tourism)

Further Information: Also Spanish for foreign students. Study Abroad programmes. International programmes

History: Founded as college 1979, acquired present status 1989. Branches in major cities in Costa Rica and Panama.

Governing Bodies: Board of Directors

Academic Year: January to December (January-April; May-August; September-December)

Admission Requirements: Secondary school certificate (bachillerato) or foreign equivalent

Fees: (US Dollars): c. 2,000 per annum

Main Language(s) of Instruction: Spanish

International Co-operation: Member of The Council of Independent Colleges (AUPRICA)

Degrees and Diplomas: *Bachiller*; *Especialidad Profesional*; *Maestría*

Student Services: Academic counselling, Canteen, Cultural centre, Employment services, Foreign student adviser, Health services, Social counselling, Sports facilities

Special Facilities: Audiovisual Centre. Radio Studio. Computer Laboratory

Libraries: Dr. Roberto Podestá Library
Last Updated: 03/12/09

MAGISTER UNIVERSITY
Universidad Magister
Apartado 988-1000, Barrio Dent de la Facultad de Derecho de la U.C.R., 200 metros oeste, San José
Tel: +506 2234-0435
Fax: +506 283-0324
EMail: info@umagister.com
Website: http://www.umagister.com/

Rectora: Vivian González Trejos EMail: rectoria@umagister.com

Programmes
Business Administration (Administration; Business Administration); **Computer Science** (Computer Science); **Education** (Education); **English** (English)

History: Founded 1996.

Main Language(s) of Instruction: Spanish

Degrees and Diplomas: *Bachiller*; *Licenciatura*; *Maestría*
Last Updated: 03/12/09

MEDICAL SCIENCES UNIVERSITY
Universidad de Ciencias Médicas (UCIMED)
Apartado 638-1007, 400 Oeste del Ministerio de Agricultura, Sabana Oeste, San José
Tel: +506 296-3944
Fax: +506 290-2685
EMail: chinchillacm@ucimed.com
Website: http://www.ucimed.com

Rector: Pablo Guzmán Stein
Tel: +506 231-0332, Fax: +506 231-4368

Vicerrectora Académica: Virginia Céspedes Gaitán

Divisions
Medicine (Medicine); **Nutrition** (Nutrition); **Pharmacy** (Pharmacy); **Physiotherapy** (Physical Therapy)

History: Founded 1976.

Governing Bodies: Asamblea General; Junta Administrativa; Vicerrectores; Decanos; Directores de Carrera; Directore de Estudios

Academic Year: January to December (January-June; July-December)

Admission Requirements: Secondary school certificate

Fees: (US Dollars): 5,325 per semester

Main Language(s) of Instruction: Spanish

International Co-operation: With universities in USA and Panama

Accrediting Agencies: SINAES (Costa Rica)

Degrees and Diplomas: *Licenciatura*: Medicine; Surgery, 5 1/2 yrs; *Licenciatura*: Nutrition; Physiotherapy; *Licenciatura*: Pharmacy, 5 yrs; *Especialidad Profesional*; *Maestría*

Student Services: Academic counselling, Foreign student adviser, Handicapped facilities, Health services, Language programs, Nursery care, Social counselling

Special Facilities: Laboratories of practical studies

Libraries: yes
Last Updated: 02/12/09

METHODIST UNIVERSITY OF COSTA RICA
Universidad Metodista de Costa Rica (UNIMET)
Apartado 2148-2050 San Pedro Montes de Oca, San José
Tel: +506 225-0655
Fax: +506 281-3661
EMail: unimet@metodista.ed.cr

Rector: Oscar Aguilar Marín

Vicerrectora Administrativa: Judith Huertas Jiménez

Schools
Business *Director*: Abelardo Delgado Uriarte; **Educational Sciences** (Educational Sciences; Primary Education); **Law** *Director*: Francisco Calderón Castro; **Theology** (Theology)

History: Founded 2000. Acquired present status 2001.

Governing Bodies: Administrative Board; University Council

Admission Requirements: Diploma de Conclusión de Estudios Secundarios

Main Language(s) of Instruction: Spanish

Degrees and Diplomas: *Bachiller*: 3 yrs; *Licenciatura*: 1 yr following Bachillerato; *Maestría*: a further 2 yrs

Student Services: Academic counselling, Handicapped facilities, Sports facilities

Student Residential Facilities: None

Libraries: Yes

PANAMERICAN UNIVERSITY OF SAN JOSÉ

Universidad Panamericana de San José
Del Costado sur del Museo Nacional 50 metros al sur,
mano izquierda, San José
Tel: +506 256-4448
Fax: +506 221-5498
EMail: upanamer@sol.racsa.co.cr

Rectora: Gina Brilla Ramírez
Tel: +506 221-5600, Fax: +506 221-0868

Academic Dean: Marco A. Aguilar
Tel: +506 233-5382, Fax: +506 221-7498

International Relations: Gina Brilla Ramírez Tel: +506 222-6275

Programmes
Administration (Administration); **Architecture** (Architecture); **Graphic Design, Advertising and Publicity** (Advertising and Publicity; Graphic Design); **Nursing** (Nursing)

History: Founded 1988.

Academic Year: January to December (January-April; May-August; September-December)

Admission Requirements: Secondary school certificate (bachillerato) or foreign equivalent, and entrance examination

Main Language(s) of Instruction: Spanish

Degrees and Diplomas: *Bachiller*; *Licenciatura*; *Maestría*

SAINT LUCY UNIVERSITY

Universidad Santa Lucía
100 mts este del Cine Omni, Avenida primera calles 5 y 7, Edificio Rodfon. En los altos de la tienda Chic de Paris, San José
Tel: +506 2257-4552
Fax: +506 223-3779
EMail: info@usantalucia.com
Website: http://www.usantalucia.com

Rectora: Ligia Meneses Sanabria Tel: +506 257-4552

Administrative Officer: Carlos Saborio

International Relations: Ligia Meneses Sanabria

Programmes
Business Administration (Accountancy; Administration; Business Administration); **Education** (Education); **Health Sciences** (Health Administration; Public Health); **Law** (Law); **Nursing** (Nursing)

History: Founded 1996.

Main Language(s) of Instruction: Spanish

Degrees and Diplomas: *Bachiller*; *Licenciatura*; *Maestría*
Last Updated: 04/12/09

SAINT MARK UNIVERSITY FOR ADMINISTRATIVE SCIENCES

Universidad en Ciencias Administrativas San Marcos (USAM)
Apartado 399-1150, 100 Este Parque Morazán, Avenida 3, Calle 11, San José
Tel: +506 257-8715
Fax: +506 221-9024
EMail: info@usam.ac.cr
Website: http://www.usam.ac.cr

Rector: Moisés Daniel Hernández Arias
Tel: +506 256-0394 EMail: jbrizuela@usam.ac.cr

Secretario General: Eduardo Alverez Solano

International Relations: Joaquín Brizuela Rojas

Programmes
Accountancy (Accountancy); **Business Administration**; **Marketing** (Marketing)

History: Founded 1996.

Admission Requirements: Secondary school certificate (bachillerato)

Main Language(s) of Instruction: Spanish

Degrees and Diplomas: *Diploma*; *Bachiller*; *Licenciatura*; *Maestría*
Last Updated: 03/12/09

SAN ISIDRO LABRADOR INTERNATIONAL UNIVERSITY

Universidad Internacional San Isidro Labrador
Apartado 2817-1000, de la Bomba Shell 300 Sur y 150 Oeste,
Antiguo Hospital, Pérez Zeledón
Tel: +506 771-6767
Fax: +506 771-6173
EMail: info@uisil.com
Website: http://www.uisil.com/

Rectora: Miguel Acuña Valerio Tel: +506 771-6173

Programmes
Business Administration (Accountancy; Business Administration; Finance); **Education** (Education); **Engineering** (Systems Analysis); **Law** (Law); **Tourism**

History: Founded 1997.

Main Language(s) of Instruction: Spanish

Degrees and Diplomas: *Bachiller*; *Licenciatura*
Last Updated: 03/12/09

SAN JUAN DE LA CRUZ UNIVERSITY

Universidad San Juan de la Cruz
Apartado 7372-1000, 50 Oeste de la Iglesia La Dolorosa, San José
Tel: +506 255-3461
Fax: +506 257-7933
Website: http://www.sjdlc.cr

Rector: Néstor Chamorro

Schools
Business; **Information Technology** (Computer Science; Information Technology)

History: Founded 1996.

Main Language(s) of Instruction: Spanish

Degrees and Diplomas: *Diploma*; *Licenciatura*; *Maestría*; *Doctorado Académico*
Last Updated: 03/12/09

SCIENCE AND ARTS UNIVERSITY OF COSTA RICA

Universidad de las Ciencias y el Arte de Costa Rica (UNI.C.A. DE COSTA RICA)
Apartado 431-2300, Barrio Luján, 350 Sur de la Corte Suprema de Justicia, San José
Tel: +506 258-1968
Fax: +506 221-1004
EMail: info@udelascienciasyelarte.ac.cr
Website: http://www.udelascienciasyelarte.ac.cr

Rector: Francisco Jiménez Villalobos (1997-)

Academic Dean: Mario Avilés Mata
EMail: maviles@udelascienciasyelarte.ac.cr

International Relations: Álvaro Avilés Mata, Dean
EMail: aaviles@udelascienciasyelarte.ac.cr

Faculties
Business Administration *(Alajuela, Heredia, Cartago, Tibás)* (Accountancy; Administration; Banking; Business Administration; Business and Commerce; Finance; Human Resources; Industrial Management; Management; Marketing); **Health Sciences** *Head*: Flor Chévez Herra

Schools

Architecture and Town Planning *Head*: María Eugenia Vega Aguilar; **Education and Teacher Training** *Head*: Orlando Portilla Fuentes; **Fine and Applied Arts** *Head*: Ana Cecilia Sánchez Rojas; **Information Sciences** *Head*: Ana Cecilia Sánchez Rojas; **Law** *Head*: Mario Cisneros Herrera

History: Founded 1981 as San Agustín College. Acquired present status 1997.

Governing Bodies: University Council; Administrative Board

Academic Year: January to December

Admission Requirements: Secondary School Certificate or equivalent recognized by the Ministry of Education

Fees: (US Dollars): 300-1,500 per quarter

Main Language(s) of Instruction: Spanish

Accrediting Agencies: Consejo Nacional de Enseñanza Superior Privada (CONESUP); Sistema de Acreditación de la Educación Universitaria Privada de Costa Rica-SUPRICORI

Degrees and Diplomas: *Diploma*: Accountancy and Business (Dpl), 2 yrs; *Bachiller*: Business Administration; Accountancy; Administration; Business and Commerce; Finance; Management; Industrial Management; Marketing; Agricultural Business; Nursing; Architecture; Education; Special Education; Art Education; Business Education (Bach.); Native Language Education; Preschool Education; Primary Education; Fine Arts; Graphic Design; Advertising and Publicity; Law; Industrial Arts Education (Bach), 2 yrs and 8 mths; *Licenciatura*: Business Administration; Accountancy; Administration; Business and Commerce; Finance; Human Resources; Management; Industrial Management; Marketing; Agricultural Business; Nursing; Architecture; Town Planning; Education; Curriculum (Lic.); Educational Administration; Educational Research; Educational Testing and Evaluation; Special Education; Education of the Handicapped; Teacher Training; Adult Education; Art Education; Business Education; Health Education; Native Language Education (Lic.); Preschool Education; Primary Education; Technology Education; Fine Arts; Graphic Design; Interior Design; Painting and Drawing; Sculpture; Graphic Arts; Advertising and Publicity; Law (Lic.), 8 mths to 1 yr following Bachillerato; *Maestría*: Accountancy; Administration; Business and Commerce; Finance; Human Resources; Management; Industrial Management; Marketing; Agricultural Business; Health Administration; Architecture; Fine Arts; Graphic Design; Advertising and Publicity; Law; Curriculum; Educational Administration, 1 yr and 4 mths; *Doctorado Académico*: Administration (Dr. (PhD)), 2 yrs and 4 mths following Licenciatura

Student Services: Academic counselling, Canteen, Employment services, Handicapped facilities, Health services, Language programs

Special Facilities: Art gallery

Libraries: Yes

Press or Publishing House: Alexander Gómez Zárate

Last Updated: 13/02/08

SOUTHERN CHRISTIAN UNIVERSITY

Universidad Cristiana del Sur

Apartado 11463-1000, Del liceo Brenes Mesén 325 E., Hatillo 1, San José

Tel: +506 254-3651

EMail: info@scu.ac.cr

Website: http://www.scu.ac.cr

Rector: Fernando Castro R. Tel: +506 382-4480

Centres

Language (Modern Languages)

Schools

Business; **Law** (Law); **Theology** (Bible; Theology)

History: Founded 1998.

Fees: (US dollars): 150-175 per credit

Main Language(s) of Instruction: Spanish

Accrediting Agencies: Consejo Nacional de Enseñanza Superior Privada (CONESUP)

Degrees and Diplomas: *Bachiller*: Business Administration; Theology and Bible Studies; Interior Design; Graphic Design; Accounting; Management; *Licenciatura*: Theology and Bible Studies; *Maestría*: Business Administration (International Management) (MBA); Education; Public Health; Theology; Social Work (with Psychology); *Doctorado Académico*: Management; Psychology; Public Health;

Last Updated: 02/12/09

TROPICAL AGRICULTURE RESEARCH AND HIGHER EDUCATION CENTRE

Centro Agronómico Tropical de Investigación y Enseñanza (CATIE)

Apartado 7170, Escuela de Postgrado, Turrialba

Tel: +506 556-1016

Fax: +506 558-2044

EMail: comunicacion@catie.ac.cr

Website: http://www.catie.ac.cr/

Director: José Joaquín Campos (2008-)
Tel: +506 556-6081, Fax: +506 558-2048

Schools

Graduate (Agriculture; Economics; Forest Management; Forestry; Sociology; Tropical Agriculture)

History: Founded 1946, acquired present status 1973.

Main Language(s) of Instruction: Spanish, English

Degrees and Diplomas: *Maestría*; *Doctorado Académico*

Special Facilities: Botanical Garden

Last Updated: 02/11/09

UNIVERSITY FOR INTERNATIONAL COOPERATION

Universidad para la Cooperación Internacional

Apartado 504-2050, De la Rotonda del Farolito, 200 metros este, 150 norte, San José

Tel: +506 283-6464

Fax: +506 280-8433

EMail: info@uci.ac.cr

Website: http://www.uci.ac.cr

Rector: Eduard Müller Castro
Tel: +506 239-2364, Fax: +506 239-3107
EMail: emuller@uci.ac.cr

Academic Vice Rector: Nolan Guirós EMail: nguiros@uci.ac.cr

General Secretary: Franklin Marin EMail: fmarin@uci.ac.cr

Departments

Administration (Administration); **Agronomy** (Agronomy)

Divisions

Economics (Economics); **Environmental Studies** (Environmental Studies) *Head*: Nolan Quiros; **Human Rights** (Human Rights); **Information Management** (Information Management); **Law** (Law) *Head*: Carlos Manavella; **Project Management** (Management) *Head*: Federico Vargas; **Tourism** (Tourism) *Head*: Amos Bien

History: Founded 1994.

Governing Bodies: Academic Council. Heads Assembly

Academic Year: January to December

Admission Requirements: Bachelorate Degree for Graduate Programmes

Main Language(s) of Instruction: Spanish

International Co-operation: With universities in Mexico, Colombia, Peru, Argentina, Panama, Chile

Accrediting Agencies: Consejo Nacional de Enseñanza Superior Privada (CONESUP)

Degrees and Diplomas: *Maestría*: Commercial Law; Finance (MAF), 2 yrs; *Maestría*: Management, 1 1/2 yrs; *Doctorado Académico*

Student Services: Academic counselling, Employment services

Student Residential Facilities: None

Libraries: Yes

Publications: Ivstitia, Law Journal *(monthly)*

Academic Staff 2007-2008	MEN	WOMEN	TOTAL
FULL-TIME	6	8	**14**
PART-TIME	36	22	**58**
STAFF WITH DOCTORATE			
FULL-TIME	5	1	**6**
PART-TIME	7	4	**11**

Last Updated: 03/12/09

UNIVERSITY FOR PEACE
Universidad para la Paz (UPEACE)
Apartado 138-6100, Ciudad Colón, Cantón de Mora, San José
Tel: +506 205-9000
Fax: +506 249-1929
EMail: info@upeace.org
Website: http://www.upeace.org

Rector: John J. Maresca

Divisions
Gender and Peace Building (Cultural Studies; Development Studies; Economics; Government; Human Rights; International Relations; Peace and Disarmament) *Director:* Dina Rodríguez; **International Law and Conflict Resolution** (Criminal Law; Demography and Population; Economics; Environmental Studies; Human Rights; International Studies; Maritime Law) *Co-Director:* Gundmundur Eiriksson; **International Law and Human Rights** (Human Rights; Peace and Disarmament; Religion) *Co-director:* Juan Amaya-Castro; **International Peace Studies** (Economics; Government; Human Rights; International Relations; Peace and Disarmament) *Director:* Martin Lees; **Natural Resources and Sustainable Development** (Development Studies; Economics; Environmental Studies; International Relations; Peace and Disarmament; Political Sciences) *Director:* Rolain Borel

History: Founded 1980 by the General Assembly of the United Nations.

Governing Bodies: The Council comprising 17 members; the Rector; 2 representatives designated by the Secretary-General and by the Director-General of UNESCO; 2 representatives designated by the host country; the Chancellor of the University for Peace

Academic Year: September to June

Admission Requirements: Bachelor's degree with sufficient average grade, TOEFL and entrance examination (essay)

Fees: (US Dollars): c. 18,000 per annum

Main Language(s) of Instruction: English

International Co-operation: With universities in USA, United Kingdom, Thailand, Japan

Accrediting Agencies: United Nations

Degrees and Diplomas: *Maestría:* Human Rights; International Law; Peace and Disarmament; Environmental Studies (MA); International Peace Studies, 1 yr; *Maestría:* Natural Resources; Development Studies (MA), 2 yrs

Student Services: Academic counselling, Canteen, Foreign student adviser, Handicapped facilities, Language programs, Social counselling, Sports facilities

Student Residential Facilities: Yes

Special Facilities: Audiovisual Centre

Libraries: Yes

Press or Publishing House: Department of Communications and Editorial Services
Last Updated: 03/12/09

UNIVERSITY FOR TOURISM
Universidad del Turismo
Edificio Centro Colón, Paseo Colón, San José
Tel: +506 2258-6290
Fax: +506 2258-7632
EMail: matricula@utur.ac.cr
Website: http://www.utur.ac.cr/

Rector: Ramón Madrigal León Tel: +506 234-6009

Programmes
Ecological Tourism Management (Management; Tourism); **Food and Drinks Management** (Cooking and Catering); **Hotel Management**

History: Founded 1996.
Main Language(s) of Instruction: Spanish
Degrees and Diplomas: *Bachiller, Licenciatura*
Last Updated: 03/12/09

UNIVERSITY OF DESIGN
Universidad del Diseño (INIDIS)
Apartado 1775-2050, Montes de Oca, San José
Tel: +506 234-7290
Fax: +506 234-9308
EMail: info@unidis.ac.cr
Website: http://unidis.ac.cr

Rector: Álvaro Rojas-Quirós (1993-) EMail: arojas@unidis.ac.cr
Registrar: Marysell Mora EMail: mmora@unidis.ac.cr
International Relations: Álvaro Rojas-Quirós

Divisions
Architecture (Architecture; Town Planning); **Interior Design** (Design; Interior Design)
History: Founded 1993.
Academic Year: February to December (February-June; August-December)
Admission Requirements: Secondary school certificate, interview and aptitude test
Fees: (US Dollars): c. 3,000 per annum; foreign students, c. 5,000 per annum
Main Language(s) of Instruction: Spanish
Degrees and Diplomas: *Bachiller:* Interior Design, 4 yrs; *Licenciatura:* Architecture, 5 1/2 yrs
Student Services: Academic counselling
Special Facilities: Computer Laboratory. Photography Laboratory
Libraries: Central Library, c. 2,500 vols
Publications: Glocal, Journal of Architectural Education *(bimonthly)*
Last Updated: 02/12/09

UNIVERSITY OF IBERO-AMERICA
Universidad de Iberoamérica (UNIBE)
Apartado 11870-1000, 600 Suroeste del Colegio Lincoln en Tibás, San José
Tel: +506 240-2941
Fax: +506 236-0426
EMail: info@unibe.ac.cr
Website: http://www.unibe.ac.cr

Rector: Israel Hernández Morales (1995-) Tel: +506 297-2242
Directora Ejecutiva: Ida Gorn Sikora
International Relations: Silvia Muñoz Mata

Faculties
Health Administration (Health Administration); **Medicine** (Medicine); **Nursing** (Nursing); **Pharmacy** (Pharmacy); **Psychology** (Psychology)

Programmes
Health Sciences (Dermatology; Epidemiology; Gastroenterology; Health Administration; Medicine)
Further Information: Also 6 University Hospitals
History: Founded 1995.
Governing Bodies: Academic Council
Academic Year: January to December
Admission Requirements: Secondary school certificate (bachillerato)
Fees: (US Dollars): c. 15,000 per annum
Main Language(s) of Instruction: Spanish
Accrediting Agencies: National Committee on Foreign Medical Education and Accreditation, USA
Degrees and Diplomas: *Bachiller, Licenciatura*
Student Services: Academic counselling, Foreign student adviser
Publications: Infounibe *(monthly)*; Infounibe-Teacher *(monthly)*

UNIVERSITY OF LA SALLE
Universidad de La Salle (ULASALLE)
Apartado 536-1007, Centro Colón, San José
Tel: +506 290-1010
Fax: +506 231-7898
EMail: info@ulasalle.ac.cr
Website: http://www.ulasalle.ac.cr

Rector: Oscar Azmitia

Schools
Administration (Accountancy; Administration; Business Administration; Finance; Marketing); **Education** (Education; Education of the Handicapped; Educational Administration; Educational Psychology; Educational Sciences; English; French; Pedagogy; Preschool Education; Primary Education; Psychology; Secondary Education; Social Studies; Spanish); **Law** (Law); **Psychology** (Psychology)

History: Founded 1994.

Governing Bodies: University Council

Academic Year: January to December (January-April, May-August, September-December)

Admission Requirements: Secondary school certificate

Main Language(s) of Instruction: Spanish

Degrees and Diplomas: *Bachiller*: Education; Business Administration; Law (Bch.); *Licenciatura*: Education; Business Administration; Law (Lic.); *Maestría*: Education (M.Sc.); *Doctorado Académico*: Education (Dr.)

Student Services: Employment services, Social counselling, Sports facilities

Special Facilities: Natural Science Museum

Libraries: Yes
Last Updated: 02/12/09

UNIVERSITY OF SAN JOSÉ
Universidad de San José (USJ)
Apartado 7446-1000, San José 506
Tel: +506 231-5613
Fax: +506 220-3463
EMail: info@usanjose.ac.cr
Website: http://www.usanjose.ac.cr

President: Greivin Arrieta Chacón
Tel: +506 460-444, Fax: +506 460-7375

Rector: Manuel Sandí Murillo

Programmes
Aquaculture (Aquaculture); **Business Administration** (Accountancy; Banking; Business Administration; Finance; Human Resources; International Business); **Education** (Education; Primary Education; Secondary Education); **Food Technology**; **Law** (Law); **Nutrition** (Nutrition)

Further Information: Also campuses in San Carlos, San Ramón, Liberia, Nicoya, Alajuela, Guapiles, Santa Rosa de Pocosol, Guatuso, Sabana Sur.

History: Founded 1978 as Colegio Académico, acquired present title 1992. A private institution authorized by the Government.

Governing Bodies: University Council and Board of Directors

Academic Year: January to December (January-April; May-August; September-December)

Admission Requirements: Secondary school certificate or foreign equivalent, and entrance examination

Main Language(s) of Instruction: Spanish

International Co-operation: With Universidad Abierta de Venezuela and Instituto Politécnico de México

Degrees and Diplomas: *Bachiller*: 4-5 yrs; *Licenciatura*: a further 2 yrs; *Maestría*: a further 2 yrs; *Doctorado Académico*: a further 2 yrs. Also International postgraduate studies, 1-5 yrs

Student Services: Academic counselling, Canteen, Foreign student adviser, Sports facilities

Special Facilities: Computer Centre. University Research Facilities. Experimental Station

Libraries: Central Library: c. 10,000 vols
Publications: Revista Universitaria *(quarterly)*
Press or Publishing House: Editorial Universidad de San José
Last Updated: 04/11/09

UNIVERSITY OF THE VALLEY
Universidad del Valle
Apartado 1994-1002, Costado Norte Apartotel, San José
Tel: +506 280-8308
Fax: +506 280-8448
EMail: info@udelvalle.com
Website: http://www.udelvalle.com

Rector: Miguel Ángel Alfaro Rodríguez

Faculties
Economics; **Education**; **Engineering**; **Social Sciences** (Advertising and Publicity; Law; Social Sciences)

History: Founded 1998.

Main Language(s) of Instruction: Spanish

Degrees and Diplomas: *Bachiller*; *Licenciatura*
Last Updated: 03/12/09

UNIVERSITY SAINT PAULA
Universidad Santa Paula (USP)
Apartado 627, Curridabat, San José 2050
Tel: +506 272-0006
Fax: +506 272-7123
EMail: rvalverde@uspsantapaula.com
Website: http://www.uspsantapaula.com/

Rectora: Rocío Valverde Gallegos
Tel: +506 272-1156 EMail: mquiros@uspsantapaula.com

Schools
Audiology (Speech Therapy and Audiology); **Occupational Therapy** (Occupational Therapy); **Physical Therapy** (Physical Therapy); **Respiratory Therapy** (Respiratory Therapy); **Speech Therapy** (Speech Therapy and Audiology)

Further Information: Also Research Institute IIDCA

History: Founded 1994.

Governing Bodies: Rectory; Academic Committee; Faculty Committee; Legal Committee

Admission Requirements: High school diploma, psychological interview, interview with the programme director

Fees: (Colones): Matricula, 36,000; Subject, 42,000

Main Language(s) of Instruction: Spanish

International Co-operation: With universities in Canada; Chile; Colombia; Cuba; Spain and USA

Degrees and Diplomas: *Bachiller*: Audiology, 4 yrs; *Licenciatura*: Physical Therapy and Rehabilitation; Respiration Therapy; Speech Therapy; Occupational Therapy, 4 yrs; *Maestría*

Student Services: Academic counselling, Cultural centre, Employment services, Foreign student adviser, Foreign Studies Centre, Handicapped facilities, Health services, Language programs, Sports facilities

Student Residential Facilities: Yes, for guest professors

Special Facilities: Laboratory; Room with computers; Wireless connection; Video conference room

Libraries: c. 3,000 vols

Publications: Enterate, Bulletin *(bimonthly)*; Terapeutical Ciencia tecnologia y arte, Magazine *(biennially)*
Last Updated: 04/12/09

VERITAS UNIVERSITY
Universidad Veritas (UVERITAS)
1000 m oeste de Casa Presidencial, Zapote, San José
Tel: +506 283-4747
Fax: +506 225-2907
EMail: info@uveritas.ac.cr
Website: http://www.uveritas.ac.cr

Rector: José Joaquín Seco Aguilar (1994-)

Executive Vice-Rector: Ronald Sasso
EMail: rsasso@uveritas.ac.cr

International Relations: Alejandra Barahona
Tel: +506 283-4747, Ext.132, Fax: +506 253-5355

Faculties

Design (Architecture; Design; Graphic Design; Interior Design);
Image (Advertising and Publicity; Cinema and Television; Computer Graphics; Film; Photography)

History: Founded 1994 as a non-profit private university.

Governing Bodies: Board of Directors

Academic Year: January to December

Fees: (US Dollars): 4,200 per semester

Main Language(s) of Instruction: Spanish

International Co-operation: With universities in USA, Switzerland, Germany, Mexico, Italy, Chile, Spain, Colombia etc.

Accrediting Agencies: Sistema Nacional de Acreditatión de la Educatión Superior (SINAES)

Degrees and Diplomas: *Licenciatura*: Advertising Design; Architecture; Marketing; Photography; *Licenciatura*: Interior Design, 4 yrs; *Maestría*: Design, 2 yrs

Student Services: Academic counselling, Employment services, Foreign student adviser, Foreign Studies Centre, Health services, Language programs, Social counselling

Student Residential Facilities: None

Special Facilities: Two Art Galleries, Film and T.V Studio, Darkrooms, Auditorium

Libraries: Central Library

Publications: Difusion *(biennially)*

Press or Publishing House: Veritas Editorial
Last Updated: 04/12/09

Côte d'Ivoire

STRUCTURE OF HIGHER EDUCATION SYSTEM

Description:

Higher education is offered at universities as well as at centres universitaires and at institutions providing higher professional training. The universities and the teacher college are under the responsibility of the Ministère de l'Enseignement supérieur. There are also some private institutions. The higher education system is undergoing a reform that includes the implementation of the LMD (three-tier) system for credentials and the decentralization of universities.

Stages of studies:

University level first stage: *Premier cycle*
Two years of university study lead to the Diplôme universitaire d'Etudes générales (DEUG). A further year's study after the DEUG leads to the Licence. A Capacité en Droit is conferred after two years' study to candidates who do not hold the Baccalauréat. A Diplôme universitaire de Technologie is awarded after three years' study by the Instituts universitaires de Technologie (IUT).
In engineering schools, studies last for five years and lead to the professional qualification of Ingénieur and the Diplôme d'Ingénieur des Travaux publics. In Agriculture, a Diplôme d'Agronomie générale is conferred after four years and a Diplôme d'Ingénieur agronome is awarded after five years' study with a further year's specialization. In Medicine, a professional Doctorate is awarded after seven years and in Dentistry and Pharmacy after five years.

University level second stage: *Deuxième cycle*
The Maîtrise in Arts and Science subjects requires one year's study after the Licence and includes a mini-thesis.

University level third stage: *Troisième cycle*
The Diplôme d'Etudes supérieures spécialisées (DESS) and the Diplôme d'Etudes approfondies (DEA) are conferred after one year's further study beyond the Maîtrise. After three more years candidates may be awarded the Doctorat. The qualification of Docteur-Ingénieur is conferred after three years' study and the submission of a thesis to holders of a diploma in Engineering.

ADMISSION TO HIGHER EDUCATION

Admission to university-level studies:

Name of secondary school credential required: Baccalauréat

Foreign students admission:

Entrance exam requirements: Foreign students must hold a qualification that is equivalent to the Baccalauréat. Entrance to the Institut national polytechnique Félix Houphouët-Boigny is based on a competitive examination. For universities, students' files are examined.

Entry regulations: They must have a valid passport, a visa and scholarship from their government or an international organization.

Health requirements: Students must be vaccinated against yellow fever.

Language requirements: Knowledge of French is necessary. The University organizes one- to three-year courses for students who are not proficient in French.

NATIONAL BODIES

Ministère de l'Enseignement supérieur et de la Recherche scientifique (Ministry of Higher Education and Scientific Research)
Minister: Ibrahima Cissé Bacongo

Directeur de Cabinet: Alexis Hibault Ogou
Abidjan
WWW: http://www.enseignement.gouv.ci/

Data for academic year: 2009-2010
Source: IAU from the website of the Ministère de l'Enseignement supérieur, Côte d'Ivoire, 2009 (Bodies, 2012)

INSTITUTIONS

PUBLIC INSTITUTIONS

AFRICAN CENTRE FOR MANAGEMENT AND PROFESSIONAL UPGRADING

Centre Africain de Management et de Perfectionnement des Cadres (CAMPC)
08 BP 878, Abidjan 08
Tel: +225(22) 44-49-46 +225(22) 44-49-94
Fax: +225(22) 44-03-78
EMail: info@campc.net; campc_ci@yahoo.fr
Website: http://www.campc.net

Directeur général: Oumarou Amadou Saley
Tel: +225(22) 44-49-46 EMail: asaley@campc.net

Programmes
Management (Management)

History: Founded 1970.

Degrees and Diplomas: *Diplôme d'Etudes supérieures spécialisées:* Human Resources Engineering (DESS-IRH). Also Diplôme de formation et de Perfectionnement in Management (equivalent to Licence); Diplôme supérieur spécialisé in Human Resources (equivalent to Licence) ; Diplôme supérieur de Perfectionnement in Organisations Management, Health Management (equivalent to DESS).
Last Updated: 21/09/09

FÉLIX HOUPHOUËT-BOIGNY NATIONAL POLYTECHNIC INSTITUTE

Institut national polytechnique Félix Houphouët-Boigny (INP-HB)
BP 1093, Yamoussoukro
Tel: +225(30) 64-66-60
Fax: +225(30) 64-04-06
EMail: cic_akpo@aviso.ci
Website: http://www.inphb.edu.ci

Directeur général: Ado Gossan

Secrétaire général: Paul Akpo Bessekon Tel: +225(30) 64-11-36
International Relations: Koffi Kra EMail: karandre@yahoo.fr

Schools
Agriculture (Agriculture); **Civil Engineering** (Civil Engineering); **Commerce and Business Administration** (Business Administration; Business and Commerce); **Industrial Engineering** (Industrial Engineering); **Lifelong Education and Executive Proficiency**; **Mines and Geology** (Geology; Mining Engineering)

History: Founded 1996, incorporating previously existing institutions, including Ecole nationale supérieure d'Agronomie, Ecole nationale supérieure des Travaux Publics, Institut national supérieur de l'Enseignement technique and Institut agricole de Bouaké.

Governing Bodies: Council; Steering Committee; Management Committee

Academic Year: September to June

Admission Requirements: Baccalauréat

Fees: (CFA Francs): c. 3m. per annum

Main Language(s) of Instruction: French

International Co-operation: With universities in France; USA; Canada; China; India; Africa

Degrees and Diplomas: *Brevet de Technicien supérieur; Diplôme d'Ingénieur.* 5 yrs; *Diplôme d'Etudes approfondies:* 5 yrs. Also Master

Student Services: Academic counselling, Canteen, Cultural centre, Foreign student adviser, Health services, Nursery care, Social counselling, Sports facilities

Student Residential Facilities: Yes

Libraries: 3 Libraries

Academic Staff 2008-2009	MEN	WOMEN	TOTAL
FULL-TIME	359	33	392
STAFF WITH DOCTORATE FULL-TIME	80	5	85
Student Numbers 2008-2009			
All (Foreign Included)	2,684	756	3,440
FOREIGN ONLY	37	9	46

Evening students, 285.
Last Updated: 15/06/09

INSTITUTE OF COMMUNICATION SCIENCES AND TECHNOLOGIES

Institut des Sciences et Techniques de la Communication (ISTC)
BP V 205, Boulevard de l'Université, Abidjan
Tel: +225(22) 44-88-58
Fax: +225(22) 44-84-33
EMail: infos@istc.ci
Website: http://www.istc-ci.com

Directeur: Jacques S. Silue Tel: +225(22) 44-88-58

Departments
Advertising and Marketing (Advertising and Publicity; Marketing); **Audiovisual Production** (Film; Video); **Journalism** (Journalism); **Multimedia** (Multimedia); **Science and Technology** (Engineering; Technology)

Degrees and Diplomas: *Diplôme d'Ingénieur.* 4 yrs; *Diplôme d'Etudes supérieures spécialisées:* a further 15 months. Also Diplôme supérieur (DIS-Com), 2 yrs
Last Updated: 21/09/09

NATIONAL SCHOOL OF ADMINISTRATION

Ecole nationale d'Administration (ENA)
BP V 20, Abidjan
Tel: +225(22) 41-40-33
EMail: ena@globeaccess.net

Directeur: Irie Dje Bi
Tel: +225(22) 44-52-25, Fax: +225(22) 41-49-63

Secrétaire général: Mameri Diaby Tel: +225(22) 41-52-31

Centres
Lifelong Education and Executive Retraining

Schools
Administrative and Diplomatic Management (Administration; Political Sciences); **Economics and Financial Management**

(Economics; Management); **Magisterial and Judicial Studies** (Law)

History: Founded 1960.

NATIONAL SCHOOL OF STATISTICS AND APPLIED ECONOMICS
Ecole nationale supérieure de Statistique et d'Economie appliquée (ENSEA)
BP 3, Abidjan 08
Tel: +225(22) 44-08-40
Fax: +225(22) 44-39-88
EMail: ensea@ensea.ed.ci
Website: http://www.ensea.ci

Directeur: Koffi N'guessan (1994-) EMail: nguessan@ensea.ed.ci

Programmes
Statistics and Applied Economics (Economics; Statistics)

History: Founded 1961.

Governing Bodies: Conseil de gestion

Academic Year: October to July

Admission Requirements: Entrance examination

Fees: (CFA Francs): 850,000 per annum

Main Language(s) of Instruction: French

International Co-operation: With universities in France

Accrediting Agencies: Ministère de l'Enseignement supérieur et de la Recherche scientifique

Degrees and Diplomas: *Diplôme d'Ingénieur.* Statistics (ITS); Statistics; Economics (ISE); *Diplôme d'Etudes supérieures spécialisées.* Also Diplomas of Agent Technique (1 yr) and Adjoint Technique (2 yrs)

Student Services: Canteen, Health services, Sports facilities

Student Residential Facilities: Yes

Libraries: Yes

Publications: Etude et Recherche (sur la population et le développement) *(biennially)*

Press or Publishing House: ENSEA Press
Last Updated: 21/09/09

TEACHER TRAINING SCHOOL OF ABIDJAN
Ecole normale supérieure d'Abidjan (ENS)
BP 10, Abidjan 08
Tel: +225(22) 44-31-10
Fax: +225(22) 44-42-32

Directeur: Tapé Goze

Departments
Arts and Humanities (Arts and Humanities); **Educational Sciences** (Educational Sciences; Teacher Training); **History and Geography** (Geography; History); **Languages** (Modern Languages); **Science and Technology** (Natural Sciences; Technology)

Sections
Mathematics (Mathematics)

History: Founded 1964.

Degrees and Diplomas: *Certificat d'Aptitude au Professorat de l'Enseignement secondaire*

UNIVERSITY OF ABOBO-ADJAMÉ
Université d'Abobo-Adjamé
BP 801, Abidjan 02
Tel: +225(20) 30-42-00
Fax: +225(20) 30-43-00
EMail: abobo-adj@abobo.edu.ci
Website: http://www.uabobo.ci

Président: Etienne Ehouan Ehilé (2001-)
Tel: +225(20) 30-42-10, Fax: +225(20) 36-43-50
EMail: ehileeh@uabobo.ci; ehile_eh@yahoo.fr

Secrétaire général: Inza Doumbia
Tel: +225(20) 30-42-27, Fax: +225(20) 20-30-43-02

International Relations: Jocelyne Bosson, Head Manager
Tel: +225(20) 30-42-47 EMail: mamaketci@yahoo.fr

Centres
Advanced Training; **Ecology Research** *(CRE)* (Ecology; Energy Engineering; Environmental Studies) *Director.* Martine Tahou

Institutes
Research; **Research in Renewable Energy** *Director.* Pascal Houenou

Programmes
Natural Sciences (Animal Husbandry; Mathematics and Computer Science; Natural Sciences; Plant and Crop Protection) *Director.* Kouakou Yao

Schools
Health Sciences *(Preparatory)* (Health Sciences) *Director.* Cyrille Dah

Units
Basic Sciences (Chemistry; Computer Science; Mathematics; Natural Sciences) *Director.* Yves-Alain Bekro; **Environmental Science and Management** (Environmental Management; Environmental Studies) *Director.* Issiaka Savané; **Food Technology** (Food Technology) *Director.* Patrice Kouamé; **Higher Education** *(URES Daloa)* (Higher Education)

History: Founded 1995 as University Centre.

Main Language(s) of Instruction: French

Degrees and Diplomas: *Diplôme universitaire d'Etudes générales:* Natural Sciences (DEUG), 2 yrs; *Licence:* 3 yrs; *Maîtrise:* 4 yrs; *Diplôme d'Etudes approfondies:* a further 2 yrs; *Doctorat*

Academic Staff *2008-2009*	MEN	WOMEN	TOTAL
FULL-TIME	122	28	**150**
STAFF WITH DOCTORATE FULL-TIME	121	32	**153**
Student Numbers *2008-2009*			
All (Foreign Included)	5,356	1,326	**6,682**

Last Updated: 03/08/09

UNIVERSITY OF BOUAKÉ
Université de Bouaké
BP V 18, Bouaké 01
Tel: +225(31) 63-32-42
Fax: +225(31) 63-25-13
Website: http://www.ubouake.ci/

Président: Aka Landry Komenan Tel: +225(31) 63-48-57

Secrétaire général: Germain Adja-Diby

Vice-Président: G. Emmanuel Crezoit
Tel: +225(22) 42-47-78 EMail: crezoit@yahoo.fr

Centres
Development Research (Development Studies); **Lifelong Education**

Units
Communication, Environment and Society *(CMS)* (Communication Studies; Environmental Studies); **Economics and Development Studies** *(SED)* (Development Studies; Economics); **Higher Education** *(URES, Korhogo)* (Higher Education); **Law, Administration and Management** (Administration; Law; Management); **Medicine** *(SM)* (Medicine)

History: Founded 1994 as University Centre.

Main Language(s) of Instruction: French

International Co-operation: With universities in France, Usa, Italy, China, Ghana and Georgia

Degrees and Diplomas: *Licence*; *Maîtrise*
Last Updated: 08/09/09

UNIVERSITY OF COCODY
Université de Cocody
01 BP V34, Abidjan 01
Tel: +225(22) 44-08-95
Fax: +225(22) 44-17-07
EMail: sinfuc@univ-cocody.ci
Website: http://www.univ-cocody.ci/

Président: Célestin Téa Gokou Tel: +225(22) 44-08-95

Secrétaire général: Jérôme Toto Baloubi

International Relations: Joseph Aka EMail: jhaka@ucocody.ci

Centres
Economic and Social Research (CIRES) (Economics); **Lifelong Education** (CUFOP)

Institutes
Mathematics (IRMA) (Mathematics)

Units
Bioscience; **Criminology** (Criminology); **Earth Sciences and Mining Resources** (Earth Sciences; Mining Engineering); **Economics and Management** (Economics; Management); **Information, Art and Communication** (Arts and Humanities; Communication Studies; Information Sciences); **Languages, Literature and Civilizations**; **Law, Administration and Political Science** (Administration; Law; Political Sciences); **Mankind and Society** (Social Studies); **Mathematics and Computer Science** (Computer Science; Mathematics); **Medical Sciences** (Medicine); **Odonto-Stomatology** (Dentistry; Stomatology); **Pharmaceutical Sciences** (Pharmacy); **Structure of Matter and Technology** (Technology)

History: Founded 1995 as University Centre. Acquired present status 1996.

Admission Requirements: Baccalauréat or equivalent

Fees: (CFA Francs): c. 6,000-25,000; foreign students, c. 200,000-500,000 (if agreements, foreign students may pay same fees as nationals)

Main Language(s) of Instruction: French

International Co-operation: With universities in France; Germany; Belgium; Brazil; Italy; USA

Degrees and Diplomas: Licence: Science; Humanities; Economics; Law; Arts; Languages, 3 yrs; Diplôme de Docteur: Medicine; Diplôme d'Etudes supérieures spécialisées: Pharmacy, Dentistry; Maîtrise: 4 yrs; Diplôme d'Etudes approfondies: 5 yrs; Doctorat: 3 yrs following DEA

Student Services: Academic counselling, Canteen, Handicapped facilities, Health services, Language programs, Nursery care, Social counselling, Sports facilities

Libraries: Central Library and specialized Libraries per unit (13)

Publications: En-Quête, Letters (biannually); Repères, Letters and Human Sciences (biannually); Revues médicales (quarterly); Revues sociales (biannually)

Press or Publishing House: EDUCI
Last Updated: 09/05/07

PRIVATE INSTITUTIONS

AGITEL - TRAINING INSTITUTE
Agitel - Formation
03 BP 882, Abidjan 03
Tel: +225(20) 22-26-37 +225(22) 47-83-03
Fax: +255(22) 47-20-07
EMail: agitelformation@aviso.ci
Website: http://www.agitel.ci

Directeur Général: Daouda Aidara

Programmes
Accountancy and Finance (Accountancy; Finance); **Computer Science and Information Technology** (Business Administration; Business and Commerce; Business Computing; Computer Networks; Computer Science; Human Resources; Information Technology; Management; Marketing; Transport Management)

Degrees and Diplomas: Brevet de Technicien supérieur; Diplôme d'Ingénieur; Diplôme d'Etudes supérieures spécialisées. Also Master
Last Updated: 08/09/09

CANADIAN UNIVERSITY OF ARTS, SCIENCES AND MANAGEMENT
Université Canadienne des Arts, des Sciences et du Management (UC-ASM)
BP 2875, Abidjan 06
Tel: +225(22) 47-63-16
Fax: +225(22) 47-72-66
EMail: accueil@pucao.org
Website: http://www.pucao.org

Recteur: Hugues Albert EMail: alberthughes@yahoo.ca

Vice-Rectrice à l'Enseignement et à la Recherche: Nicole Laverdure EMail: nicolelaverdure@yahoo.ca

International Relations: Albert Hugues

Programmes
Business Administration (Bachelor) (Business Administration); **Business Administration** (Executive MBA) (Business Administration); **Computer Science** (Computer Science); **Law** (Commercial Law; International Law; Labour Law; Law); **Mining Engineering** (Mining Engineering)

History: Founded 1998 as Université Ivoiro-Canadienne/Ivory-Canadian University (UICA). Acquired present title 2003.

Governing Bodies: Administration Board; Academic Commission

Academic Year: September to July

Admission Requirements: Baccalauréat, Secondary school certificate, Entrance examination

Fees: (CFA Francs): 400,000-4,400,000 per annum (including tuition, textbooks, uniform)

Main Language(s) of Instruction: French

International Co-operation: With universities in Canada

Degrees and Diplomas: Diplôme d'Etudes supérieures spécialisées: Project Management, 2 yrs; Maîtrise: Business Administration; Computer Science; Law; Marketing and Public Relations. Also Bachelor's degree in Business Administration, Computer Science (4 yrs), Law (4,5 yrs), Mining Engineering (5 yrs); Executive MBA (evening courses), 3 yrs; certificates in Administration, Human Resources Management and Marketing, 1yr

Student Services: Academic counselling, Canteen, Employment services, Foreign student adviser, Language programs, Social counselling, Sports facilities

Student Residential Facilities: None

Special Facilities: Internet facilities

Libraries: Yes

Academic Staff 2008-2009	MEN	WOMEN	TOTAL
FULL-TIME	2	2	4
PART-TIME	9	3	12
STAFF WITH DOCTORATE			
FULL-TIME	2	–	2
PART-TIME	6	–	6
Student Numbers 2008-2009			
All (Foreign Included)	50	34	84
FOREIGN ONLY	1	1	2

Evening students, 19.
Last Updated: 22/04/09

CATHOLIC UNIVERSITY OF WEST AFRICA/ UNIVERSITY OF ABIDJAN UNIT
Université Catholique de l'Afrique de l'Ouest/Unité universitaire d'Abidjan (UCAO/UUA)
08 BP 22, Abidjan, 08 Cocody
Tel: +225(22) 40-06-50
Fax: +225(22) 44-15-93
EMail: ucao@aviso.ci
Website: http://www.ucao.fr.fm

Président: Raphaël Tossou Fax: +225(22) 44-15-93

Secrétaire général: Roger Afan

International Relations: Célestin Gnako EMail: aviso@ucao.ci

Faculties
Law (Law); **Philosophy** *Dean*: Frédéric Lot; **Theology** *Dean*: Célestin Gnako

Higher Institutes
Christian Religious Studies *(Institut Supérieur de Catéchèse (ISC)) Director*: Barthélémy Zan; **Communication Studies** *(Institut Supérieur de Communication) Director*: Prosper Akuetey; **Pastoral Studies** *(Institut Supérieur de Pastorale (ISP)) Director*: Cécé Apollinaire Kolie

Schools
Theological Training for the Lay (Theology)

History: Founded 1969 as Institute (ICAO). Acquired present status and title 2000.

Admission Requirements: Baccalauréat or equivalent

Fees: (CFA Francs): 500,000-700,000 per annum

Main Language(s) of Instruction: French

Degrees and Diplomas: *Diplôme universitaire d'Etudes générales*: Christian Religious Studies (DENC); Pastoral Studies; Communication Studies; Philosophy (DEUG), 2 yrs; *Diplôme universitaire d'Etudes générales*: Theology (DUET), 3 yrs; *Licence*: Philosophy; Christian Religious Studies; Communication Studies, a further 1-2 yrs; *Diplôme d'Etudes supérieures spécialisées*; *Maîtrise*: Theology; Philosophy, 1-2 yrs following Licence; *Diplôme d'Etudes approfondies*: Philosophy; Theology, 1 yr following Maîtrise; *Doctorat*: Theology; Philosophy, 3 yrs by thesis

Student Services: Academic counselling, Canteen, Employment services, Health services, Nursery care, Sports facilities

Libraries: Central Library c. 50,000 vols
Last Updated: 09/09/09

HIGHER INTERNATIONAL SCHOOL OF LAW
Ecole supérieure internationale de Droit (ESID)
BP 825, Abidjan 03
Tel: +225(22) 42-88-10
Fax: +225(22) 42-88-10
EMail: esid@aviso.ci

Directrice: Anne-Marie Hortense Assi Esso

Departments
Law (Law)

History: Founded 1999.

NEW SCHOOL OF ADVANCED ENGINEERING AND TECHNOLOGY STUDIES
Ecole nouvelle supérieure d'Ingénieurs et de Technologies (ENSIT)
Bld des Martyrs (Latrille), 01 BP 3427, Rue Farandole K22, Cocody 2 Plateaux, Abidjan 01
Tel: +225(22) 41-65-63
Fax: +225(22) 41-87-24
EMail: scolarite@ensit.ci
Website: http://www.ensit.ci

Directeur: N'Guessan Alain Ahouzi

Departments
Engineering (Computer Science; Information Technology; Software Engineering); **Management and Entrepreneurship** (Accountancy; Finance; International Business; Management; Marketing)

International Co-operation: With Université de Sherbrooke (Canada)

Degrees and Diplomas: *Diplôme d'Ingénieur*; *Diplôme d'Etudes supérieures spécialisées*. Also Bachelor's Degree and Master's Degree
Last Updated: 31/05/07

PIGIER CÔTE D'IVOIRE
01 BP 1585, 23 Boulevard de la République, Abidjan 01
Tel: +225(20) 30-35-00
Fax: +255(20) 22-67-64
EMail: abidjan@pigier.com
Website: http://www.pigierci.com/Index.php

Director: Jeremie N'gouan EMail: pigierci@aviso.com

Programmes
Business and Commerce (Business Administration; Business and Commerce; Communication Studies; Marketing; Secretarial Studies); **Computer and Telecommunications Engineering** (Business and Commerce; Computer Engineering; Software Engineering; Telecommunications Engineering); **Finance and Accountancy** (Accountancy; Business Administration; Commercial Law; Communication Studies; Finance; Fiscal Law; Law; Marketing; Secretarial Studies)

History: Founded 1956.

Accrediting Agencies: Conseil Africain et Malgache pour l'Enseignement Supérieur (CAMES)

Degrees and Diplomas: *Brevet de Technicien supérieur*; *Licence*: Accountancy; *Diplôme d'Ingénieur*; *Diplôme d'Etudes supérieures spécialisées*: Finance, Accountancy. Also Diplôme Supérieur de Spécialité and Master (Business Administration, Accountancy, Fiscal and Commercial Law)
Last Updated: 08/09/09

UNIVERSITY OF THE ATLANTIC
Université de l'Atlantique (UA)
06 BP 6631, 11 rue des Jardins, Abidjan 06
Tel: +225(22) 48-72-55
Fax: +225(22) 44-21-72
EMail: atlantiqueuniversite@ymail.com
Website: http://www.uatlantique.info

Recteur: Antoine Asseypo Hauhouot
Tel: +225(22) 41-08-44 EMail: asseypo@yahoo.fr

International Relations: Enok Okomien Dadié EMail: uatl@aviso.ci

Centres
Art, Theater and Aesthetics

Faculties
Arts and Humanities (Arts and Humanities; Literature; Modern Languages) *Dean*: Bernard Zadi Zahourou; **Economics and Business Administration** (Accountancy; Computer Science; Economics; Finance; Human Resources; Management; Marketing) *Dean*: Léon Naka; **Law and Political Science** *Dean*: Wenceslas Lénissongui-Coulibaly; **Social Sciences**

Institutes
Health Science (Health Sciences; Medical Auxiliaries); **Higher Professional Studies** (Administration; Commercial Law; Communication Studies; Finance; Human Resources; Journalism; Management; Maritime Law; Taxation; Transport Economics); **Journalism and Communication Studies** (Communication Studies; Journalism); **Political Sciences and International Relations** (International Relations; Political Sciences); **Women and Gender Studies**

History: Founded 2000.

Governing Bodies: Scientific Council; University Council; Faculty Council

Admission Requirements: Baccalauréat

Fees: (CFA Francs): 125,000

Main Language(s) of Instruction: French

Degrees and Diplomas: *Licence*: 3 yrs; *Diplôme d'Etudes supérieures spécialisées*: 5 yrs; *Maîtrise*: 4 yrs; *Diplôme d'Etudes approfondies*: 5 yrs

Student Services: Health services

Student Residential Facilities: None

Libraries: Yes
Last Updated: 08/09/09

Croatia

STRUCTURE OF HIGHER EDUCATION SYSTEM

Description:

Croatian higher education is regulated by the Scientific Activity and Higher Education Act which came into force in August of 2003. The Act established a binary system composed of professional education offered at polytechnics (veleučilišta), independent schools of professional higher education (visoke škole) and universities (sveučilišta), and academic education solely conducted in universities. Only universities can offer third-cycle education (postgraduate studies). Private and public higher education institutions are treated equally. Public higher education institutions are those established by the state. Private universities, polytechnics and schools of professional higher education can be established as prescribed in the law and regulations relating to the establishment of institutions. The Act on Academic and Professional Titles and Academic Degrees was passed in September 2007. It established an overarching system of titles for students graduating from Bologna study programmes, as well as a framework for comparison of pre-Bologna and Bologna titles. Higher education is organized according to the system of transferable credits (ECTS) and has three levels: undergraduate, graduate and postgraduate. At the end of each level, a final qualification (certificate or diploma) is awarded together with the Diploma supplement. In 2010, Croatia counts 120 recognized higher education institutions, of which 10 are universities (sveučilišta), 15 are polytechnics (veleučilišta) and 27 are schools of professional higher education/ colleges (visoke škole) and 67 are faculties and academies which are part of universities, but legally recognized as separate entities. While most higher education institutions are publicly owned, 3 universities, 2 polytechnics and 24 schools of professional higher education are private. In 2004, the Agency for Science and Higher Education (ASHE) was created to be in charge of quality assurance and quality improvement in the fields of science and higher education. With the enactment of the Act on Quality Assurance in Science and Higher Education in April 2009, ASHE became an independent public institution responsible for external quality assurance and development in the fields of science and higher education and in charge of carrying out procedures of initial accreditation, re-accreditation, thematic evaluation and audit. The Act on Quality Assurance in Science and Higher Education stipulates that all public and private higher education institutions are subject to re-accreditation in five-year cycles.

With the introduction of the state graduation examination, the Central Applications Office (CAO) was established as a part of ASHE to serve as the national centre for processing applications at higher education institutions and consolidating the related procedures.

Stages of studies:

University level first stage: *Baccalaureaus*
Universities offer 3-4-year courses at undergraduate level leading to a degree of university baccalaureaus after accumulating 180 - 240 ECTS credits. This qualifies students for specialized, artistic or scientific work. They can continue their studies at graduate level studies or enter the labour market.

University level second stage: *Magistar/Magistra*
Universities offer 1-2-year graduate courses leading to the degree of Magistar/Magistra after accumulating a minimum of 300 ECTS credit points. In some fields, integrated 5 or 6 year courses are offered (medical studies, law, pharmacy...) and specific titles are offered (e.g.Doctor in (Dental) Medicine). Graduates can continue their studies at postgraduate level or enter the labour market.

University level third stage: *University Specialist Degree; Doctor of Sciences/Arts*
The University Specialist Degree is awarded after one to two years of postgraduate university studies and 60-120 ECTS credit points. The title of Doctor of Sciences (Dr.Sc.) or the Doctor of Arts (in Arts field) are awarded after three years of doctoral study and upon defence of a doctoral thesis. It is equivalent to a PhD degree.

ADMISSION TO HIGHER EDUCATION

Admission to university-level studies:

Name of secondary school credential required: Svjedodzba o drzavnoj maturi

For entry to: All programmes. Minimum marks: Decided after processing all results of State Graduation Examination. It can differ each year.

Name of secondary school credential required: Potvrda o polozenim ispitima drzavne mature

For entry to: All programmes. Minimum marks: Decided after processing all results of State Graduation Examination. It can differ each year.

Numerus clausus/restrictions: Yes

Other admission requirements: For certain study programmes (e.g. in Arts, ...) additional requirements can be required.

Foreign students admission:

Definition of foreign student: A student with citizenship other than Croatian.

Entrance exam requirements: Foreign students need a certified copy of their school-leaving certificate and any required secondary education documents submitted in their English translation. The certificate must be validated by the Ministry of Science, Education and Sports.

Entry regulations: A student visa is required

Health requirements: Health insurance is required.

Language requirements: Foreign students who do not speak Croatian or do not have a certificate of Croatian language proficiency are requested to complete a 2-semester course in the Croatian language and sit for a final examination.

RECOGNITION OF STUDIES

Quality assurance system:

In Croatia, the areas of higher education and science are closely related. One should point out that the responsibility for the quality of higher education and science lies with HEIs and scientific institutions, whereas external quality assurance of higher education and science is the concern of National Council for Science, National Council for Higher Education and Agency for Higher Education and Science. Quality assurance units were established at all Croatian universities and their faculties. Taking responsibility for quality, for the present level as well as for its constant improvement, should be a concern of all the stakeholders in higher education. Every country develops its own model of evaluating the quality of higher education, and in the Republic of Croatia the evaluation comprises the following processes: accreditation of academic programmes; accreditation of HEIs; evaluation of HEIs; audit of quality assurance systems; evaluation of scientific organizations. The adopted models are constantly improved.

Special provisions for recognition:

Recognition for university level studies: Recognition is based on the Act on Recognition of Foreign Educational Qualifications and is under the authority of Croatian higher education institutions.

For exercising a profession: Recognition is done by Agency for Science and Higher Education (for employment for general purpose) or by the competent authorities (ministries or professional organizations) for employment in certain regulated profession.

NATIONAL BODIES

Ministarstvo znanosti, obrazovanja i športa (Ministry of Science, Education and Sport)
Minister: Radovan Fuchs
Director, International Cooperation and European I: Ivana Puljiz
Donje Svetice 38
Zagreb 10000
Tel: +385(1) 456 9000
Fax: +385(1) 459 4301
EMail: ured@mzos.hr
WWW: http://www.mzos.hr
Role of national body: The highest state body for education issues.

Agencija za znanost i visoko obrazovanje (Agency for Science and Higher Education)
Director: Jasmina Havranek
Head, International Relations: Emita Blagdan

Donje Svetice 38/5
Zagreb 10000
Tel: +385(1) 627 4800
Fax: +385(1) 627 4801
WWW: http://www.azvo.hr/
Role of national body: Specialized institution that carries out professional tasks related to the assessment of scientific activity in higher education, and the recognition of foreign qualifications through the ENIC/NARIC (established within the Agency).

Rektorski zbor (Rectors' Conference)
President: Ivan Pavić
Livanjska 5/II
Split 21000
Tel: +385(2) 155 8259
EMail: rektorat.office@unist.hr
WWW: http://www.unist.hr
Role of national body: Coordinates the activities and participates in the development of higher education.

Nacionalna Zaklada za znanost, visoko školstvo i tehnologijski razvoj (National Foundation for Science, Higher Education and Technological Development)
President, Board of Directors: Pero Lučin
Executive Director: Lovorca Barać Lauc
Head, International Relations: Josipa Bađari
Ilica 24
Zagreb 10000
Tel: +385(5) 122 8692
WWW: http://www.nzz.hr/
Role of national body: Promotion of science, higher education and technological development in the Republic of Croatia with the basic aims of ensuring economic development and stimulate employment.

Data for academic year: 2010-2011
Source: IAU from Agency for Science and Higher Education, Croatia, 2010, Minister's name, 2011

INSTITUTIONS

PUBLIC INSTITUTIONS

COLLEGE OF AGRICULTURE AT KRIŽEVCI
Visoko Gospodarsko Učilište, Križevci
Milislava Demerca 1, 48260 Križevci
Tel: +385(48) 279-180 +385(48) 279-199
Fax: +385(48) 682-790 +385(48) 279-189
EMail: uprava@vguk.hr
Website: http://www.vguk.hr

Dean: Vinko Pintić

Programmes
Agriculture (Agriculture; Animal Husbandry; Cattle Breeding; Crop Production)

Degrees and Diplomas: *Diploma diplomaskog studija*

JOSIP JURAJ STROSSMAYER UNIVERSITY OF OSIJEK
Sveučilište Josipa Jurja Strossmayera u Osijeku
Trg. Sv. Trojstva 3, 31 000 Osijek
Tel: +385(31) 224-102
Fax: +385(31) 207-015
EMail: rektorat@unios.hr
Website: http://www.unios.hr

Rektor: Gordana Kŕalik (1997-) EMail: gordana.kralik@unios.hr
Secretary-General: Dzenka Barišič

Academies
Arts (Arts and Humanities)

Colleges
Teacher Training (Teacher Training)

Departments
Biology (Biology); **Chemistry** (Chemistry); **Mathematics** (Mathematics); **Physics** (Physics)

Faculties
Agriculture (Agriculture; Animal Husbandry); **Civil Engineering** (Civil Engineering); **Economics** (Economics); **Education** (Education); **Electrical Engineering** (Electrical Engineering); **Food Technology** (Food Technology); **Law** (Law); **Mechanical Engineering** *(Slavonski Brod)* (Mechanical Engineering); **Medicine** (Medicine); **Philosophy** (Philosophy); **Theology** (Theology)

Further Information: Also Branch in Slavonski Brod

History: Founded 1975, incorporating Faculty of Economics formerly attached to University of Zagreb. Acquired present title 1990. An independent self-governing institution.

Governing Bodies: Board of Governors; University Senate

Academic Year: October to September (October-February; March-September)

Admission Requirements: Secondary school certificate (Svjedodžba o završenoj srednjoj skoli), or foreign equivalent and Croatian Language examination

Fees: (US Dollars): Foreign students, c. 1,000-1,800 per annum

Main Language(s) of Instruction: Croatian

Degrees and Diplomas: *Svjedodžba preddiplomskog sveucilisnog studija*: 3 yrs; *Diploma poslijediplomskog specijalističkog studija*: 2 yrs; *Doktor znanosti/ Doktor umjetnosti (PhD)*: 3 yrs

Student Services: Canteen

Student Residential Facilities: For c. 750 students

Libraries: Faculty libraries, total, c. 250,000 vols. Central Library-City and University Library, total, c. 307,000 vols

Publications: Ekonomski vjesnik (Economic Courier); Medical Courier; Pravni vjesnik (Law Courier); Research and Practice in Agriculture and Food Technology
Last Updated: 16/09/11

JURAJ DOBRILA UNIVERSITY OF PULA

Sveučilište Jurja Dobrile u Puli
Preradovićeva 1, 52100 Pula
Tel: +385(52) 377-000
Fax: +385(52) 216-416
EMail: ured@unipu.hr
Website: http://www.unipu.hr/

Rektor: Robert Matijašić EMail: rmatija@unipu.hr

Departments
Economics and Tourism (Economics; Tourism); **Education** (Education; Teacher Training); **Humanities** (Arts and Humanities; Classical Languages; History; Native Language; Philology; Romance Languages); **Italian Studies** (Italian); **Music** (Music); **Preschool and Primary Education** (Preschool Education; Primary Education)

History: Founded 2006.

Main Language(s) of Instruction: Croatian

Degrees and Diplomas: *Diploma diplomaskog studija*; *Diploma poslijediplomskog specijalističkog studija*; *Doktor znanosti/ Doktor umjetnosti*

Academic Staff *2007-2008*: Total: c. 250
Student Numbers *2007-2008*: Total: c. 5,000
Last Updated: 27/09/11

KARLOVAC UNIVERSITY OF APPLIED SCIENCES

Veleučilište u Karlovcu
Ivana Meštrovića 10, 47000 Karlovac
Tel: +385(47) 415-455
Fax: +385(47) 415-450
EMail: dekanat@vuka.hr
Website: http://www.vuka.hr

Dean: Branko Wasserbauer

Departments
Business (Economics; Management; Marketing); **Food Technology** (Food Technology); **Gamekeeping and Environmental Protection** (Wildlife); **Mechanical Engineering** (Mechanical Engineering); **Safety and Protection** (Safety Engineering); **Textile Technology** (Textile Technology)
History: Founded 1997.
Degrees and Diplomas: *Diploma diplomaskog studija*; *Diploma diplomaskog studija (Master)*
Last Updated: 26/09/11

UNIVERSITY OF APPLIED HEALTH STUDIES IN ZAGREB

Zdravstveno Veleučilište, Zagreb
Mlinarska Cesta 38, 10000 Zagreb
Tel: +385(1) 4669-750
Fax: +385(1) 4668-080
EMail: dekan@vmskola.hr
Website: http://www.zvu.hr/eng_index.html

Dean: Mladen Havelka Tel: +385(1) 4669-771

Programmes
Environmental Health Engineer (Health Sciences); **Laboratory Techniques** (Laboratory Techniques); **Nursing** (Nursing); **Occupational Therapy** (Occupational Therapy); **Physiotherapy** (Physical Therapy); **Radiological Technology** (Radiology)

History: Founded 1966 as Advanced School of Nursing and Health Technicians.

Degrees and Diplomas: *Diploma diplomaskog studija*; *Diploma poslijediplomskog specijalističkog studija*
Last Updated: 27/09/11

UNIVERSITY OF DUBROVNIK

Sveučilište u Dubrovniku
Ćire Carića 4, 20000 Dubrovnik
Tel: +385(20) 445-700
Fax: +385(20) 435-590
EMail: rektorat@unidu.hr
Website: http://www.unidu.hr

Rektor: Mateo Milković

Departments
Aquaculture (Aquaculture); **Art and Restoration** (Art History; Fine Arts; Heritage Preservation; Restoration of Works of Art); **Economics and Business Economics** (Accountancy; Business Administration; Business Computing; E-Business/Commerce; Economics; Finance; Hotel Management; Human Resources; Marketing); **Electrical Engineering and Computing** (Business Computing; Computer Science); **Maritime** (Engineering; Marine Engineering; Nautical Science); **Mass Communication** (Cultural Studies; Mass Communication; Media Studies); **Tourism** (Tourism)

Programmes
Nursing (Nursing)

History: Founded 2003. Formerly known as Dubrovnik Polytechnic.

Main Language(s) of Instruction: Croatian

Degrees and Diplomas: *Diploma diplomaskog studija*; *Doktor znanosti/ Doktor umjetnosti*
Last Updated: 27/09/11

UNIVERSITY OF RIJEKA

Sveučilište u Rijeci
Trg braće Mažuranića 10, HR 51000 Rijeka
Tel: +385(51) 406-500
Fax: +385(51) 216-671 +385(51) 216-091
EMail: ured@uniri.hr
Website: http://www.uniri.hr

Rektor: Pero Lučin EMail: pero.lucin@uniri.hr

Generalen Sekretar: Roberta Hlača-Mlinar

International Relations: Darko Štefan EMail: darko@uniri.hr

Academies
Applied Arts (Fine Arts)

Faculties
Civil Engineering (Building Technologies; Civil Engineering; Construction Engineering; Geological Engineering; Hydraulic Engineering) *Dean*: Nevenka Ožanić; **Economics** (Accountancy; Banking; Economics; Finance; Information Technology; International Business; Leadership; Management; Marketing); **Engineering** (Electrical Engineering; Engineering; Mechanical Engineering; Naval Architecture); **Law** (Administrative Law; Law); **Maritime Studies** (Electronic Engineering; Information Sciences; Marine Engineering; Marine Science and Oceanography; Marine Transport; Nautical Science; Transport and Communications; Transport Management); **Medicine** (Dentistry; Family Studies; Medicine; Nursing; Psychiatry and Mental Health; Public Health; Radiology; Sanitary Engineering); **Philosophy** *(Rijeka)* (Computer Science; Education; English; Fine Arts; Germanic Languages; History; Mathematics; Pedagogy; Philosophy; Physics; Psychology; Serbocroatian; Slavic Languages; Technology); **Philosophy** *(Pula)* (Comparative Literature; History; Italian; Latin; Literature; Music; Musical Instruments; Philosophy; Serbocroatian; Slavic Languages); **Teacher Education** *(Teacher's School, Gospić)* (Primary Education) *Dean*: Dragica Husanović-

Pejnović; **Tourism and Hospitality Management** *(Opatija)* (Business and Commerce; Hotel Management; Tourism)

History: Founded 1973, incorporating various institutions of higher education which were established during the 17th and 18th centuries.

Governing Bodies: University Council

Academic Year: October to June

Admission Requirements: Secondary school certificate (Svjedodžba o završnom ispitu) or recognized equivalent

Fees: (Kunas): Foreign students, c. 55 per annum

Main Language(s) of Instruction: Croatian. Some courses in Italian, English

International Co-operation: With universities in Europe. Also partcipates in CEEPUS, Tempus, INTERREG and FP6 programmes

Degrees and Diplomas: *Svjedodžba preddiplomskog stručnog studija (DrSc):* by thesis; *Diploma diplomaskog studija (Master)*; *Doktor znanosti/ Doktor umjetnosti*

Student Services: Canteen, Cultural centre, Employment services, Health services, Social counselling

Student Residential Facilities: For 656 students

Special Facilities: Computer Centre

Libraries: University Library, Rijeka, 310,000 vols; University Library, Pula, 250,000 vols
Last Updated: 26/09/11

UNIVERSITY OF SPLIT
Sveučilište u Splitu
Livanjska 5, 21 000 Split
Tel: +385(21) 558-200 +385(21) 348-966
Fax: +385(21) 355-163
EMail: rektorat.office@unist.hr
Website: http://www.unist.hr

Rektor: Ivan Pavic (2006-)

Generalen Sekretar: Josip Alajbeg Tel: +385(21) 558-205

International Relations: Snježana Lisičić
Tel: +385(21) 558-207 EMail: snjezana.lisisic@unist.hr

Academies
Arts (Art Education; Communication Arts; Design; Fine Arts; Music; Music Education; Musical Instruments; Musicology; Painting and Drawing; Restoration of Works of Art; Sculpture; Singing)

Centres
Marine Studies (Biology; Ecology; Fishery; Marine Science and Oceanography); **Mediterranean Agriculture** (Floriculture; Horticulture; Vegetable Production; Viticulture); **Professional Studies**

Faculties
Catholic Theology (Catholic Theology; Religious Studies; Theology); **Chemistry and Technology** (Chemistry; Technology); **Civil Engineering and Architecture** (Architecture; Civil Engineering); **Economics** (Economics; Finance; Marketing); **Electrical Engineering, Mechanical Engineering and Naval Architecture** (Computer Science; Electrical Engineering; Industrial Engineering; Mechanical Engineering; Naval Architecture); **Kinesiology** (Physical Therapy); **Law** (Law); **Maritime** (Electronic Engineering; Information Technology; Management; Marine Engineering; Marine Transport; Nautical Science); **Medicine** (Medicine); **Natural Sciences, Mathematics and Education** (Biology; Chemistry; Computer Science; Mathematics; Mathematics and Computer Science; Physical Education; Physics; Technology; Technology Education); **Philosophy** (Education; English; History; Italian; Philosophy; Pre-school Education; Primary Education; Slavic Languages; Teacher Training)

Further Information: Also Branches in Zadar, Šibenik and Dubrovnik

History: Founded 1974. Formerly College of Philosophy and Theology in Zadar established 1396 by the Dominican Order, incorporating existing faculties in the region and some departments formerly attached to University of Zagreb. An independent self-governing institution financed by the Republic.

Governing Bodies: University Council, comprising 6 members; University Senate, comprising 35 members

Academic Year: October to September (October-February; March-September)

Admission Requirements: Secondary school certificate (Svjedodžba o završnom ispitu) or recognized equivalent, and entrance examination

Fees: None for Croatian citizens. Foreign students: dependent on decision of Ministry of Science and Technology

Main Language(s) of Instruction: Croatian

Degrees and Diplomas: *Svjedodžba preddiplomskog stručnog studija:* 4-6 yrs (second level); *Svjedodžba preddiplomskog sveucilisnog studija:* 2-3 yrs (first level); *Diploma diplomaskog studija (Mr):* 2-3 yrs; *Doktor znanosti/ Doktor umjetnosti (DrSc):* 2-4 yrs

Student Services: Academic counselling, Canteen, Foreign student adviser, Handicapped facilities, Health services, Language programs

Student Residential Facilities: Yes

Special Facilities: Biological Garden

Libraries: Central University Library. Faculty libraries
Last Updated: 26/09/11

UNIVERSITY OF ZADAR
Sveučilište u Zadru (UNIZD)
Ulica Mihovila Pavlinovića bb, 23000 Zadar
Tel: +385(23) 200-555
Fax: +385(23) 316-882
EMail: rektorat@unizd.hr
Website: http://www.unizd.hr

Rector: Ante Uglešic
Tel: +385(23) 200-534, Fax: +385(23) 200-605
EMail: ante.uglesic@unizd.hr

Secretary-General: Antonella Lovric
Tel: +385(23) 200-643 EMail: alovric@unizd.hr

International Relations: Maja Kolega
Tel: +385(23) 200-642 EMail: mkolega@unizd.hr

Departments
Agriculture and Mediterranean Aquaculture (Agriculture; Aquaculture; Crop Production; Ecology); **Archaeology** (Archaeology); **Art History** (Art History); **Classical Philology** (Philology); **Croatian and Slavic Studies** (Slavic Languages) *Division Head*: Mrdeža Antonina; **English Language and Literature** (English; Literature); **Ethnology and Anthropology** (Anthropology; Ethnology); **French and Iberoromance Studies** (French; Literature; Philology; Spanish); **Geography** (Geography); **German Language and Literature** (German); **Health Studies** (Dietetics; Epidemiology; Health Sciences; Nursing; Radiology); **History** (History); **Italian Studies** (Italian); **Library and Information Science** (Information Sciences; Library Science); **Pedagogy** (Pedagogy); **Philosophy** (Philosophy); **Psychology** (Psychology); **Sociology** (Sociology); **Tourism and Communication Studies** (Communication Studies; Tourism); **Traffic and Maritime Studies** (Marine Transport; Nautical Science)

History: Founded 2002, incorporating former Faculty of Philosophy of the University of Split.

Governing Bodies: University Council

Academic Year: October to June

Admission Requirements: High School Certificate

Main Language(s) of Instruction: Croatian

Degrees and Diplomas: *Svjedodžba preddiplomskog stručnog studija (BA):* 3 yrs; *Diploma diplomaskog studija (MA):* a further 2 yrs; *Doktor znanosti/ Doktor umjetnosti (PhD):* 3 yrs

Student Services: Canteen

Libraries: Yes

Publications: Radovi Sveučilišta u Zadru *(annually)*

Press or Publishing House: University Publishing House
Last Updated: 26/09/11

UNIVERSITY OF ZAGREB
Sveučilište u Zagrebu
Trg Maršala Tita 14, HR-10000 Zagreb
Tel: +385(1) 4564-255
Fax: +385(1) 4564-008
EMail: office@unizg.hr
Website: http://www.unizg.hr

Rector: Aleksa Bjeliš
Tel: +385(1) 4564-255, Fax: +385(1) 4564-008
EMail: rector@unizg.hr

International Relations: Ana Ružička
Tel: +385(1) 4698-101, Fax: +385(1) 4698-132
EMail: aruzicka@unizg.hr

Academies
Dramatic Arts (Film; Theatre); **Fine Arts** (Fine Arts); **Music** (Music)

Centres
Croatian Studies *(Studia Croatica)* (Cultural Studies; Philology; Religious Studies; Serbocroatian; Social Studies)

Faculties
Agriculture (Agriculture); **Architecture** (Architectural and Environmental Design; Architecture; Town Planning); **Catholic Theology** (Catholic Theology); **Chemical Engineering and Technology** (Chemical Engineering; Technology); **Civil Engineering** (Civil Engineering); **Education and Rehabilitation** (Rehabilitation and Therapy); **Electrical Engineering and Computer Science** (Computer Science; Electrical Engineering); **Food Technology and Biotechnology** (Biotechnology; Food Technology); **Forestry** (Forestry); **Geodesy** (Earth Sciences; Surveying and Mapping); **Geotechnical Engineering** (Earth Sciences; Geophysics); **Graphic Arts** (Graphic Arts); **Kinesiology** (Physical Education; Sports; Sports Medicine); **Law** (Law); **Mechanical Engineering and Naval Architecture** (Mechanical Engineering; Naval Architecture); **Metallurgy** (Metallurgical Engineering); **Mining, Geology, and Petroleum Engineering** (Geological Engineering; Mining Engineering; Petroleum and Gas Engineering); **Organization and Information Studies** (Business Administration; Information Management; Information Sciences); **Pharmacy and Biochemistry** (Biochemistry; Pharmacy); **Philosophy** (Archaeology; Art History; Comparative Literature; English; Ethnology; French; German; Greek; History; Humanities and Social Science Education; Hungarian; Information Sciences; Italian; Latin; Linguistics; Modern Languages; Philosophy; Phonetics; Polish; Psychology; Scandinavian Languages; Serbocroatian; Slavic Languages; Sociology; Spanish); **Political Science** (Political Sciences); **Science** (Biology; Chemistry; Geography; Geology; Geophysics; Mathematics; Natural Sciences; Physics); **Teacher Education** (Education; Teacher Trainers Education; Teacher Training); **Textile Technology** (Textile Technology); **Transport and Traffic Engineering** (Road Transport; Transport Engineering; Transport Management); **Veterinary Science** (Veterinary Science)

Schools
Dental Medicine (Dentistry); **Medicine** *(Also Graduate School)* (Medicine)

Further Information: Also Centre for Advanced Academic Studies (CAAS) in Dubrovnik; International Centres of Croatian Universities (ICCU) in Istria and Motovun

History: Founded 1669 as Royal Academy of Sciences by edict of Emperor Leopold I granting University status to the existing Jesuit Academy of the Royal Free City of Zagreb. Reorganized 1874 as University of Zagreb, the largest and oldest Croatian university.

Governing Bodies: Senate, comprising the Rector, the Vice-Rectors, Deans and heads of Faculties and University departments, and student representatives

Academic Year: October to June (October-January; February-June)

Admission Requirements: Secondary school certificate (Svjedodžba završene srednje škole) or recognized equivalent, and entrance examination (Razredbeni ispit)

Main Language(s) of Instruction: Croatian

Degrees and Diplomas: *Svjedodžba preddiplomskog stručnog studija*: 4-6 yrs; *Diploma diplomaskog studija*: Arts, a further 4 sem by thesis; *Diploma diplomaskog studija*: Science, a further 4 sem; *Doktor znanosti/ Doktor umjetnosti (DrSc)*: a further 6 sem by thesis. Also Postgraduate Professional/Vocational studies in Arts

Student Services: Canteen, Cultural centre, Health services, Language programs, Sports facilities

Student Residential Facilities: For 7,133 students

Special Facilities: Museums: Mineralogy and Petrography; Geology and Palaeontology; Botanical Gardens; Observatory. SRCE University Computer Centre

Libraries: Croatian National and University Library, also faculty and department libraries

Press or Publishing House: Sveučiliána tiskara; Hrvatska sveučilišna naklada

Last Updated: 26/09/11

PRIVATE INSTITUTIONS

CROATIAN CATHOLIC UNIVERSITY
Hrvatsko katoličko sveučilište
Ilica 242, 10000 Zagreb
Tel: +385(1) 3706 600
EMail: info@unicath.hr
Website: http://www.unicath.hr

Rector: Ivan Šaško

Faculties
History (History); **Psychology** (Psychology); **Sociology** (Sociology)

History: Founded 2006.

Main Language(s) of Instruction: Croat

Accrediting Agencies: Ministry of Science, Education and Sports

Degrees and Diplomas: *Diploma diplomaskog studija*; *Diploma diplomaskog studija (Master)*

Last Updated: 27/02/12

DUBROVNIK INTERNATIONAL UNIVERSITY
DIU - Medunarodno sveučilište
Sv. Dominika 4, Dubrovnik
Tel: +385(20) 414 111
EMail: diu@diu.hr
Website: http://www.diu.hr

Rector: Janice McCormick

Schools
Diplomacy (International Relations); **Health Science** (Embryology and Reproduction Biology; Gynaecology and Obstetrics); **International Business** (Commercial Law; Finance; International Business; International Economics; Management; Marketing); **Visual Arts** (Cinema and Television; Film; Video)

History: Founded 2008.

Fees: (Euros) 3,500 per semester

Accrediting Agencies: Ministry of Science, Education and Sports

Degrees and Diplomas: *Diploma diplomaskog studija*; *Diploma diplomaskog studija (Master)*

Last Updated: 27/02/12

LIBERTAS BUSINESS COLLEGE
Visoka Poslovna Škola "Libertas" u Zagrebu, s Pravom Javnosti
Trg. J.F. Kennedya 6b, 10000 Zagreb
Tel: +385(1) 2323-377
Fax: +385(1) 2315-851
EMail: poslovna.skola@libertas.hr
Website: http://www.vps-libertas.hr

Dean: Duško Pavlovic

Programmes

Economics (Economics); **Finance** (Finance); **Management** (Management)

History: Founded 2004.

Main Language(s) of Instruction: Croatian

Degrees and Diplomas: *Diploma diplomaskog studija*; *Diploma poslijediplomskog specijalističkog studija*

Last Updated: 26/09/11

MEDIA UNIVERSITY, SPLIT

Medijsko sveučilište, Split
Hrvatske mornarice 4, 21000 Split
Tel: +385(21) 352 906
EMail: medijsko_sveuciliste@eph.hr

Rector: Stjepan Oreškovic

Programmes

Journalism (Journalism); **Media Business and Management** (Business Education; Management; Media Studies); **Media Design** (Design; Media Studies)

Accrediting Agencies: Ministry of Science, Education and Sports

Degrees and Diplomas: *Diploma diplomaskog studija*

Last Updated: 28/02/12

UNIVERSITY OF APPLIED SCIENCES VELIKA GORICA

Veleučilište Velika Gorica s Pravom Javnosti
Zagrebačka Cesta 5, 10410 Velika Gorica
Tel: +385(1) 6222-501
Fax: +385(1) 6222-501
EMail: info@vvg.hr
Website: http://www.vvg.hr

Dean: Ivan Toth

Programmes

Aircraft Maintenance (Aeronautical and Aerospace Engineering; Maintenance Technology); **Computer Systems Maintenance** (Computer Engineering; Computer Networks; Maintenance Technology; Software Engineering); **Humanitarian Demining** (Explosive Engineering; Safety Engineering); **Motor Vehicle Maintenance** (Automotive Engineering; Maintenance Technology); **Pyrotechnical Engineering** (Explosive Engineering; Safety Engineering)

History: Founded 2002.

Degrees and Diplomas: *Diploma poslijediplomskog specijalističkog studija*

Libraries: Yes

Last Updated: 13/12/11

VERN POLYTECHNIC

Visoka Škola za Ekonomiju Poduzetništva s Pravom Javnosti, Vern
Tomićeva 5a, 10000 Zagreb
Tel: +385(1) 4816-200
Fax: +385(1) 4831-168
EMail: kristijan.paksec@vern.hr
Website: http://www.vern.hr

Dean: Goran Radman Tel: +385(1) 4825-911

Programmes

Computer Science (Computer Science); **Economics and Entrepreneurship** (Economics; Management); **Tourism and Hotel Management** (Hotel Management; Tourism)

History: Founded 2000.

Main Language(s) of Instruction: Croatian

Degrees and Diplomas: Magistar specijalist računovodstva

Last Updated: 27/09/11

ZAGREB SCHOOL OF ECONOMICS AND MANAGEMENT

Zagrabačka Škola Ekonomije i Managementa
Jordanovac 110, 10000 Zagreb
Tel: +385(1) 2354-242
Fax: +385(1) 2354-243
EMail: dekan@zsem.hr
Website: http://www.zsem.hr

Dean: Djuro Njavro

Departments

Accountancy (Accountancy); **Economics** (Economics); **Finance** (Finance); **Foreign Languages** (Modern Languages); **Information and Communication Technology** (Information Technology); **Law** (Law); **Management** (Management); **Marketing** (Marketing); **Mathematics and Statistics** (Mathematics; Statistics)

Degrees and Diplomas: *Diploma diplomaskog studija*; *Diploma diplomaskog studija (Master)*

Last Updated: 27/09/11

ZAGREB SCHOOL OF MANAGEMENT

Zagrabačka Škola za Menadžment, s Pravom Javnosti
Jurišićea 1 I Mandaličina 17, 10000 Zagreb
Tel: +385(1) 3909-171 +385(1) 3909-170
Fax: +385(1) 3909-177
EMail: marina.fintic@zsm.hr
Website: http://www.zsm.hr

Dean: Zoran Klarić

Programmes

Tourism (Tourism)

Degrees and Diplomas: *Diploma diplomaskog studija (Master)*

Cuba

STRUCTURE OF HIGHER EDUCATION SYSTEM

Description:

Higher education is provided by universities, higher institutes, and university centers. All higher education institutions are public. The Ministerio de Educación Superior (MES) is responsible for policy in matters of undergraduate and postgraduate education. It controls teaching, methodology, courses and programmes and the allocation of student places, as well as the specialization courses offered by centres of higher education which come under the control of other ministries. All institutions have the same status.

Stages of studies:

University level first stage: *Licenciatura/Título Profesional*
The first and main stage of higher education usually lasts for five years. In Medicine, studies last for six years. Courses that are offered to workers usually last longer than traditional courses. At the end of the first stage, students are awarded a Licenciatura or a Título profesional (professional diploma).

University level second stage: *Diplomado, Maestría, Especialista*
Diplomado courses have three levels, each requiring some 200 hours of theoretical instruction, practical work, industrial internship and a final project. Students can gain academic credit towards completion of a Master's degree and are allowed to work on a Master's thesis as they progress through Diplomado studies. The second stage corresponds to a period of in-depth study and research which leads to the Maestría after two years. In Medicine, the first stage is usually followed by a course of professional specialization leading to a specific specialization. Especialista programmes are designed for people in industry.

University level third stage: *Doctor en Ciencias de (+ special field)*
Three to four years' studies and research with a supervisor lead to the Doctor en Ciencias de (+ special field) (for example: Doctor in Mathematics). The research results must have been defended before a jury and published in academic journals.

University level fourth stage: *Doctor en Ciencias*
The Doctor en Ciencias is awarded to Doctors en Ciencias de (+ special field) who, following additional years of scientific research and relevant scientific results, submit and defend a thesis before a jury and publish in academic journals.

ADMISSION TO HIGHER EDUCATION

Admission to university-level studies:

Name of secondary school credential required: Bachillerato

Entrance exam requirements: For access to degree courses, students must sit for the Examen de Ingreso. It is taken in two or three subjects.

Foreign students admission:

Entrance exam requirements: Foreign students must hold a Bachiller or an equivalent degree.

Entry regulations: Students must have a visa.

Health requirements: Students must have a health certificate.

Language requirements: Foreign students arriving from countries whose official language is not Spanish will take an examination to establish the level of the Spanish course they must follow. Spanish and Cuban culture courses are offered in several universities throughout the year.

RECOGNITION OF STUDIES

Quality assurance system:

The National Accreditation Board was created to promote, organize, implement and control the policy of accreditation for higher education in the country. In addition, the Board grants the different categories of accreditation to evaluated programmes and institutions.

Bodies dealing with recognition:

Departamento Jurídico, Ministerio de Educación Superior (Legal Department, Ministry of Education)
Director: Jorge Valdés Asán
Calle 23 esq. F, Vedado
La Havana 10400
Tel: +537 838 2354

NATIONAL BODIES

Ministerio de Educación Superior (Ministry of Higher Education)
Minister: Miguel Díaz Canel Bermúdez
La Habana
WWW: http://www.mes.edu.cu

Junta de Acreditación Nacional - JAN (National Accreditation Committee)
Director: Nora Espi Lacomba
Calle 30 No. 867-1, entre Ave. Kohly y Calle 41, Nuevo Vedado, Plaza de la Revolución Municipality
Lz Havana

Data for academic year: 2010-2011
Source: IAU from the website of the Ministerio de Educación Superior, Cuba, 2010. Bodies, 2011.

INSTITUTIONS

PUBLIC INSTITUTIONS

ART INSTITUTE
Instituto Superior de Arte
Calle 120 No. 1110 e/9na y 13 Cubanacán, Municipio Playa,
La Habana 11600
Tel: +53(7) 210-017
Fax: +53(7) 336-633
EMail: isa@reduniv.edu.cu
Website: http://www.isa.cult.cu

Rectora: Graciela Fernández Mayo Tel: +53(7) 214-257
Secretary-General: Pedro Octavio Ángel González
Tel: +53(7) 212-446

International Relations: Sonia Ortega Bravo Tel: +53(7) 216-075

Departments
Aesthetics and Philosophy (Aesthetics; Philosophy); **Computer Science** (Computer Science); **Cuban Studies**; **Linguistics** (Linguistics); **Pedagogy and Psychology** (Pedagogy; Psychology)

Faculties
Audiovisual Media Communications (Cinema and Television; Media Studies); **Music** (Music); **Plastic Arts** (Fine Arts; Painting and Drawing; Sculpture); **Scenic Arts** (Dance; Display and Stage Design; Theatre)

Degrees and Diplomas: *Licenciatura*; *Diplomado*; *Doctor en Ciencias de (+ special field)*; *Maestría*
Last Updated: 04/11/09

BLAS ROCA CALDERÍO PEDAGOGICAL INSTITUTE OF MANZANILLO
Instituto Superior Pedagógico de Manzanillo Blas Roca Calderío
Avenida Rosales Km 1, Esquina 1, Manzanillo 87510
Tel: +53(23) 545-45 +53(23) 522-068
Fax: +53(23) 575-30
EMail: rector@ispgrm.rimed.Cu

Rector: Oscar Vivero Reyes

Faculties
General Education (Education); **Humanities** (Arts and Humanities); **Pre-School Teacher Training** (Preschool Education); **Science** (Natural Sciences)

Degrees and Diplomas: *Licenciatura*
Last Updated: 08/12/09

CAMILO CIENFUEGOS UNIVERSITY OF MATANZAS
Universidad de Matanzas Camilo Cienfuegos (UMCC)
Km 3 Carretera a Varadero, Matanzas
Fax: +53(45) 262-222
EMail: censeic@umcc.cu
Website: http://www.umcc.cu/

Rector: Miguel Sarraff González EMail: miguel.sarraf@umcc.cu
Vicerrectora: Benita N. García EMail: benita.garcia@umcc.cu

Centres
Anticorrosive and Taut Materials *(CEAT)*; **Combustion Studies and Energy** *(CECYEN)* (Chemical Engineering; Energy Engineering)

Faculties
Agronomy (Agriculture; Agronomy; Biology; Chemistry); **Computer Science**; **Economics and Industrial Engineering** (Accountancy; Computer Science; Economics; Finance; Industrial Engineering; Management); **Mechanical and Chemical Engineering** (Chemical Engineering; Chemistry; Mathematics; Mechanical Engineering; Physics); **Physical Education** (Physical Education; Sports); **Social Sciences and Humanities** (Arts and Humanities; English; Law; Modern Languages; Psychology; Social Sciences; Spanish)

Further Information: Also campus in Panamá.

History: Founded 1972.

Main Language(s) of Instruction: Spanish

Degrees and Diplomas: *Licenciatura*; *Maestría*
Last Updated: 04/12/09

CAPITÁN SILVERIO BLANCO NUÑEZ PEDAGOGICAL INSTITUTE

Instituto Superior Pedagógico Capitán Silverio Blanco Nuñez
Calle Comandante 'Manuel Fajardo', Olivos 1, Sancti Spíritu 60100
Tel: +53(41) 27214
Fax: +53(41) 27214
EMail: rector@ispss.rimed.cu

Rectora: Caridad Cancio López

Centres
Regional Studies (Regional Planning)

Faculties
Humanities (Arts and Humanities); **Pre-School Teacher Training** (Preschool Education); **Science** (Natural Sciences)

History: Founded 1993.

Main Language(s) of Instruction: Spanish

Degrees and Diplomas: *Licenciatura*
Last Updated: 07/12/09

CARLOS MANUEL DE CÉSPEDES PEDAGOGICAL INSTITUTE OF ISLA DE LA JUVENTUD

Instituto Superior Pedagógico Carlos Manuel de Céspedes de la Isla de la Juventud
La Demajagua, Isla de la Juventud 25100
Tel: +53(46) 399-233 +53(46) 399-219
EMail: rector@fpu.gerona.inf.cu

Rectora: Maura Dolores Blanco Hernández

Programmes
Teacher Training (Teacher Training)
History: Founded 1972.
Main Language(s) of Instruction: Spanish
Degrees and Diplomas: *Licenciatura*
Last Updated: 07/12/09

CONRADO BENITEZ GARCÍA PEDAGOGICAL INSTITUTE OF CIENFUEGOS

Instituto Superior Pedagógicao Conrado Benitez García de Cienfuegos
Avenida 20 Reparto Jaredo Punta Gorda, Cienfuegos 55100
Tel: +53(432) 513-612 +53(432) 227-62
Fax: +53(432)
EMail: josecar@jagua.cfg.sld.cu

Rectora: Ángel G. Navarro Otero

Centres
Educational Research

Faculties
Pre-School Teacher Training; **Secondary Teacher Training**
Degrees and Diplomas: *Licenciatura*

DR. ANTONIO NUÑEZ JIMÉNEZ INSTITUTE OF MINING ENGINEERING, MOA

Instituto Superior Minero Metalúrgico de Moa 'Dr Antonio Nuñez Jiménez' (ISMMM)
CP 82329, Las Coloradas s/n, Moa, Holguín
Tel: +53(24) 64214
Fax: +53(24) 62290
EMail: rector@moa.minbas.cu
Website: http://www.ismm.edu.cu

Rector: Dimas Néstor Hernández Gutiérrez

Secretary-General: Manuel Lores Vidal
Tel: +53(24) 66229 EMail: mlores@ismmm.edu.cu

International Relations: Rafael Guardado Lacaba
Tel: +53(24) 66678 EMail: guardado@ismmm.edu.cu

Faculties
Geology and Mining (Geology; Mining Engineering); **Humanities** (Accountancy; Arts and Humanities; Cultural Studies; Finance; Library Science; Social Sciences); **Metallurgy and Electro-mechanics** (Computer Engineering; Electrical Engineering; Mechanical Engineering; Metallurgical Engineering)

History: Founded 1976.

Main Language(s) of Instruction: Spanish

Degrees and Diplomas: *Licenciatura*: 5 yrs; *Título Profesional*: a further 1-2 yrs
Last Updated: 02/11/09

DR. ERNESTO CHÉ GUEVARA DE LA SERNA FACULTY OF MEDICINE OF PINAR DEL RIO

Facultad de Ciencias Médicas de Pinar del Rio Dr. Ernesto Ché Guevara de la Serna
Carretera Central Km 89, Pinar del Río, Pinar del Río 20100
Tel: +53(82) 62889
EMail: decano@guama.dri.sld.cu

Dean: Pedro Alexis Díaz Rodríguez
Tel: +53(82) 63754 +53(82) 62722

Programmes
Medicine (Medicine; Stomatology)
Degrees and Diplomas: *Licenciatura*; *Título Profesional*
Last Updated: 08/12/09

DR. SERAFÍN RUIZ DE ZÁRATE RUIZ INSTITUTE OF MEDICAL SCIENCES OF VILLA CLARA

Instituto Superior de Ciencias Médicas de Villa Clara Dr. Serafín Ruiz de Zárate Ruiz
Carretera del Acueducto Km 2 1/2 y Circunvalación Santa Clara, Villa Clara 50200
Tel: +53(422) 71367
EMail: rector@cunanicay.sld.cu

Rector: Ramiro R. Ramos Ramírez
Tel: +53(422) 72667, Fax: +53(422) 72216

Secretary-General: Jorge Luis López López Tel: +53(422) 71480
International Relations: José Suárez Lorenzo Tel: +53(422) 3011

Faculties
Medical Sciences (Health Sciences; Medicine); **Stomatology** (Stomatology)

History: Founded 1976.

Main Language(s) of Instruction: Spanish

Degrees and Diplomas: *Título Profesional*; *Maestría*
Last Updated: 07/12/09

DR. ZOILO E. MARINELLO VIDAURRETA FACULTY OF MEDICINE OF LAS TUNAS

Facultad de Ciencias Médicinas Dr. Zoilo E. Marinello Vidaurreta de Las Tunas
Avenida de la Juventud s/n, Tunas 75100
Tel: +53(31) 48015
Fax: +53(31) 43325
EMail: decano@cuculambe.ltu.sld.cu

Dean: Ángel Luis Selva Suárez Tel: +53(31) 43325

Programmes
Medicine (Medicine)

Degrees and Diplomas: *Licenciatura*; *Título Profesional*
Last Updated: 08/12/09

ENRIQUE JOSÉ VARONA PEDAGOGICAL INSTITUTE OF HAVANA

Instituto Superior Pedagógico Enrique José Varona de La Habana
Calle 108 No 29, Ciudad Escolar Liberdad, Marianao, La Habana 11400
Tel: +53(7) 260-450 +53(7) 267-1083
Fax: +53(7) 267-1083
EMail: dri@ispejv.rimed.cu

Rector: Alfredo Diaz Fuentes EMail: alfredo@ispejv.rimed.cu

Secretary-General: Mayra Elena Viera González
Tel: +53(7) 201-188

International Relations: María del Carmen Fernández Morales
Tel: +53(7) 200-353

Faculties
Educational Sciences (Education); **Foreign Languages** (Foreign Languages Education); **Humanities** (Arts and Humanities); **Pre-School Teacher Training** (Preschool Education); **Science** (Natural Sciences)

Degrees and Diplomas: *Diplomado*; *Maestría*; *Doctor en Ciencias*
Last Updated: 07/12/09

FACULTY OF MEDICINE OF CIEGO DE AVILA

Facultad de Ciencias Médicas de Ciego de Avila
Circunvalación y carretera de Morón, Ciego de Avila 65100
Tel: +53(33) 24575
EMail: decana@admfcm.cav.slc.cu

Dean: Miladys Castilla Martínez
Tel: +53(33) 25589 EMail: decana@trocha.cav.sld.cu

Faculties
Medicine (Medicine)

Degrees and Diplomas: *Licenciatura*; *Título Profesional*: 6 yrs
Last Updated: 07/12/09

FACULTY OF MEDICINE OF CIENFUEGOS

Facultad de Ciencias Médicas de Cienfuegos
Calle 51 entre 36 y 38, Cienfuegos 55100
Tel: +53(432) 3071
Fax: +53(432) 3852
EMail: dri@infosur.cfg.sld.cu

Dean: José E. Caballero González Tel: +53(432) 3832

Programmes
Medicine

History: Founded 1979.

Main Language(s) of Instruction: Spanish

Degrees and Diplomas: *Licenciatura*; *Título Profesional*: 6 yrs; *Especialista*

FACULTY OF MEDICINE OF GRANMA

Facultad de Ciencias Médicas de Granma
Avenida Camilo Cienfuegos esq. Carretera de Campechuela, Manzanillo 87510
Tel: +53(23) 540-14
EMail: decano@golfo.grm.sld.cu

Dean: Oscar A. Fonseca Capote Tel: +53(23) 53359

Programmes
Medicine (Medicine; Nursing; Stomatology)

History: Founded 1978.

Main Language(s) of Instruction: Spanish

Degrees and Diplomas: *Licenciatura*; *Título Profesional*: 6 yrs

FACULTY OF MEDICINE OF GUANTANAMO

Facultad de Ciencias Médicas de Guantánamo
Calle 5 entre 6 y 9 Norte, Guantánamo 95100
Tel: +53(21) 326-014
EMail: decano@guaso.gtm.sld.cu

Dean: María Inés Jiménez de Castro Tel: +53(21) 326-119

Programmes
Medicine (Medicine; Nursing; Stomatology)

Degrees and Diplomas: *Licenciatura*; *Título Profesional*: 6 yrs
Last Updated: 29/10/09

FACULTY OF MEDICINE OF MATANZAS

Facultad de Ciencias Médicas de Matanzas
Carretera Quintamales Km 101, Matanzas 40100
Tel: +53(52) 5060
EMail: decana@yumuri.mtz.sld.cu

Dean: Víctor Junco Tel: +53(52) 4097

Programmes
Medicine (Medicine; Nursing; Stomatology)

Degrees and Diplomas: *Título Profesional*. Doctor en Medicina, 6 yrs

FACULTY OF MEDICINE OF SANCTI SPIRITU

Facultad de Ciencias Médicas de Sancti Spíritu
Carretera Circunvalación Norte, Placetas, Sancti Spíritu 60100
Tel: +53(41) 24019
EMail: decano@escambray.ssp.sld.cu

Dean: Luis Fernández García Tel: +53(41) 23776

Programmes
Medicine (Medicine)

Degrees and Diplomas: *Licenciatura*; *Título Profesional*

FÉLIX VARELA PEDAGOGICAL INSTITUTE OF VILLA CLARA

Instituto Superior Pedagógico Félix Varela de Villa Clara
Carretera de Circunvalación y Maleza, Apartado 288, Santa Clara, Villa Clara 50100
Tel: +53(42) 206-139 +53(42) 214-050
Fax: +53(42) 208-506

Rector: Ramiro Ramírez García Tel: +53(422) 26139

Centres
Educational Informatics and Video; **Educational Sciences** (Education); **Environmental Sciences** (Environmental Studies)

Faculties
Humanities (Arts and Humanities); **Pre-School Teacher Training** (Preschool Education); **Science** (Natural Sciences); **Technical Sciences** (Technology)

Further Information: Traditional and Open Learning Institution

Degrees and Diplomas: *Licenciatura*
Last Updated: 08/12/09

FRANK PAÍS GARCÍA PEDAGOGICAL UNIVERSITY

Universidad Pedagógica Frank País García
Carretera de la Autopista, Km 3 1/2, Santiago de Cuba 90100
Tel: +53(226) 41298
Fax: +53(226) 43113
EMail: rector@ispscu.rimed.cu
Website: http://www.santiago.cu/hosting/upfrankpais/default.htm

Rectora: Ena Elsa Velásquez Cobiella

Secretary-General: Leonardo Méndez Gil

International Relations: Francisco Pérez Miró

Centres
Educational Sciences (Education)

Faculties
Humanities (Arts and Humanities); **Pre-School Teacher Training** (Preschool Education); **Science** (Natural Sciences); **Technical Sciences** (Technology)

Degrees and Diplomas: *Diplomado*; *Maestría*; *Doctor en Ciencias*
Last Updated: 04/12/09

FRUCTUOSO RODRÍGUEZ PÉREZ AGRICULTURAL UNIVERSITY OF HAVANA

Universidad Agraria de La Habana Fructuoso Rodríguez Pérez (UNAH)
Autopista Nacional y Carretera de Tapaste San José de las Lajas, La Habana
Tel: +53(64) 633-95 +53(64) 62908
Fax: +53(64) 635-28 +53(64) 63513
EMail: febles@main.isch.edu.cu
Website: http://www.isch.edu.cu/

Rector: Ramón González González
Tel: +53(64) 629-08, Fax: +53(64) 633-95
EMail: gilramon@main.isch.edu.cu

Secretaria General: Mercedes Sablón Pérez
Tel: +53(64) 63395, Fax: +53(7) 240-942
EMail: ordes@main.isch.edu.cu

Faculties
Agronomy (Agricultural Business; Agronomy; Biology; Chemistry; Soil Science); **Social Sciences and Humanities** (Arts and Humanities; Social Sciences); **Stockraising** (Animal Husbandry; Cattle Breeding; Mathematics); **Veterinary Science** (Veterinary Science)

Further Information: Traditional and Open Learning Institution
History: Founded 1976.
Main Language(s) of Instruction: Spanish
Last Updated: 04/12/09

GUANTÁNAMO UNIVERSITY CENTRE

Centro Universitario de Guantánamo
Municipio El Salvador, Sabatena, Guantánamo
Tel: +53(21) 325-925 +53(21) 325-375
Fax: +53(21) 324-756
EMail: guibert3@cug.co.cu
Website: http://www.cug.co.cu/

Rector: Idania Núñez de la O
Tel: +53(21) 325-925 EMail: idiana@cug.co.cu
Secretary-General: Máximo Bidot Tel: +53(21) 324-662
International Relations: Eduardo Castillo Corella
Tel: +53(21) 324-589
Faculties
Agro-Forestry (Agriculture; Forest Products); **Economics** (Economics); **Law** (Law); **Social Sciences** (Social Sciences)
Degrees and Diplomas: *Título Profesional*; *Maestría*
Last Updated: 04/12/09

HÉCTOR PINEDA ZALDIVAR PEDAGOGICAL INSTITUTE OF ADVANCED TECHNICAL AND PROFESSIONAL TEACHING

Instituto Superior Pedagógico para la Enseñanza Técnica y Profesional 'Héctor Pineda Zaldivar'
Calle A e/n Calzada de Alday y Calle 100 Reparto Caturla, Boyeros, La Habana 19220
Tel: +53(7) 578-052
Fax: +53(7) 578-508

Rector: Juan Fabián Lastra Herrera Tel: +53(7) 442-571
Faculties
Technical Sciences
History: Founded 1976
Main Language(s) of Instruction: Spanish
Degrees and Diplomas: *Licenciatura*
Last Updated: 10/12/09

HERMANOS SAÍZ MONTES DE OCA UNIVERSITY OF PINAR DEL RÍO

Universidad de Pinar del Río Hermanos Saíz Montes de Oca (UPR)
José Martí #270, esquina a 27 de Noviembre, Pinar del Río, Pinar del Río 20100
Tel: +53(82) 779-353
Fax: +53(82) 779-353
EMail: mfdez@vrect.upr.edu.cu
Website: http://www.upr.edu.cu

Rector: Andrés Erasmo Ares (2004-)
Tel: +53(82) 777-923 EMail: erasmoar@rectoria.upr.edu.cu
Secretaria General: Magalys González
Tel: +53(82) 779354 EMail: magalys@vrect.upr.edu.cu
International Relations: Mariá Elena Fernández

Centres
Development of Cooperatives and Communities Studies *(CEDECOM)* (Agronomy; Development Studies; Forestry; Regional Studies; Rural Studies; Social Studies) *Head*: Claudio Alberto Rivera; **Energy and Sustainable Energy Technologies** *(CETES)* *Head*: Francisco Márquez Montesino; **Environmental and Natural Resources** *(CEMARNA)* (Ecology; Environmental Management; Environmental Studies; Natural Resources) *Head*: Mayra Casas Vilardell; **Forestry Studies** *(CEF)* (Biochemistry; Biotechnology; Forestry) *Head*: Ynocente Betancourt; **Higher Education Sciences** *(CECES)* (Educational Research; Higher Education Teacher Training; Pedagogy) *Head*: Teresa de la C. Díaz; **Management, Development Studies and Tourism** *(GEDELTUR)* (Development Studies; Ecology; Management; Tourism) *Head*: Carlo María Lazo Vento

History: Founded 1972, acquired present status 1994.
Governing Bodies: Council, comprising 27 members
Academic Year: September to July
Admission Requirements: Secondary school certificate
Fees: (US Dollars): First and Second yrs, 4,000; Third yr, 4,500; Fourth yr, 5,000; Fifth yr, 6,000
Main Language(s) of Instruction: Spanish
International Co-operation: With universities in Spain, Germany, Netherlands, Italy, México, Colombia, República Dominicana, Venezuela, Ecuador
Degrees and Diplomas: *Licenciatura*: Accountancy; Finance; Economics; Sociocultural Studies; Law (Lic), 5 yrs; *Título Profesional*: Telecommunications Engineering; Computer Science; Forestry; Agricultural Engineering; Geology; Mechanics Engineering (Ing) (Ingeniero), 5 yrs. Also Diplomas in Spanish as a foreign language, Natural Resources, Business Administration, Tourism, Pedagogy, Cooperativism and Community Work, Agroecology, Forestry, Local Development
Student Services: Canteen, Cultural centre, Foreign student adviser, Health services, Language programs, Nursery care, Sports facilities
Student Residential Facilities: Yes
Special Facilities: Geological Museum, Historical Museum, Theatre
Libraries: Yes
Publications: Educational Sciences Review, Co-supported by the Higher Education Ministry of Cuba *(quarterly)*; Mining and Geology, Co-supported by the Higher Institute of Mining of MOA, Cuba *(quarterly)*; Scientific Year Book *(annually)*

Academic Staff 2007-2008	TOTAL
FULL-TIME	496
PART-TIME	1,538
STAFF WITH DOCTORATE	
FULL-TIME	119
PART-TIME	4
Student Numbers 2007-2008	
All (Foreign Included)	21,271
FOREIGN ONLY	269

Part-time students, 7,485. Distance students, 11,999.
Last Updated: 11/12/07

INSTITUTE OF INDUSTRIAL DESIGN

Instituto Superior de Diseño Industrial
Belascoaín #710 e/ Estrella y Maloja, La Habana
Website: http://www.isdi.co.cu/universidad.html

Rector: José Cuendias Cobrero

Departments
Fashion Design (Fashion Design); **Industrial Design** (Industrial Design); **Theory and Methodology**; **Visual Communication** (Communication Arts; Communication Studies)

History: Founded 1984.

Main Language(s) of Instruction: Spanish

Degrees and Diplomas: *Licenciatura*; *Maestría*
Last Updated: 04/12/09

INSTITUTE OF MEDICAL SCIENCES OF CAMAGUEY

Instituto Superior de Ciencias Médicas de Camagüey
Carretera Central Oeste e/ Madame Curie y 9, Camagüey 70100
Tel: +53 (322) 95241
Fax: +53 (322) 92100
EMail: cpinf@finlay.sld.cu

Rector: Rómulo Rodríguez Ramoz
EMail: romulo@finlay.cmw.sld.cu

Secretary-General: Lucy Caballero García Tel: +53(322) 97775

International Relations: María Luz Fernández González
Tel: +53(322) 82015, Ext. 355

Faculties
Medical Sciences (Health Sciences; Medicine); **Stomatology**

History: Founded 1991.

Main Language(s) of Instruction: Spanish

Degrees and Diplomas: *Título Profesional*
Last Updated: 07/12/09

INSTITUTE OF MEDICAL SCIENCES OF HAVANA

Instituto Superior de Ciencias Médicas de La Habana
146 No. 2504 e/25 y 31, Reparto Cubanacán, Municipio Playa, La Habana 11600
Tel: +53(7) 220-973
Fax: +53(7) 336-257
EMail: lgf@infomed.sld.cu
Website: http://www.ucmh.sld.cu

Rector: Jorge González Pérez
Tel: +53(7) 220-981, Fax: +53(7) 336-258
EMail: rectorch@infomed.sld.cu

Secretary-General: Sandalio Durán Alvarez

International Relations: Eduardo Bascó Fuentes
Tel: +53(7) 220-974 EMail: ebasco@giron.sld.cu

Faculties
Medical Science (Health Sciences; Medicine); **Stomatology** (Stomatology)

Institutes
Basic Science and Pre-Clinical Studies (Natural Sciences)
Main Language(s) of Instruction: Spanish
Degrees and Diplomas: *Título Profesional*
Last Updated: 07/12/09

INSTITUTE OF MEDICAL SCIENCES OF SANTIAGO DE CUBA

Instituto Superior de Ciencias Médicas de Santiago de Cuba
Avenida de las Américas e/calle E y calle I Reparto Sueño, Santiago de Cuba 90100
Tel: +53(226) 26679
Fax: +53(226) 96200
EMail: nayra@sierra.scu.sld.cu

Rector: Mayra I. Pujols Victoria Tel: +53(226) 86200

Secretary-General: Lilliam Leyva Rosales Tel: +53(226) 53011
International Relations: José Suárez Lorens

Faculties
Medical Sciences (Health Sciences; Medicine); **Stomatology** (Stomatology)

Degrees and Diplomas: *Título Profesional*
Last Updated: 07/12/09

INSTITUTE OF NUCLEAR SCIENCE AND TECHNOLOGY

Instituto Superior de Ciencia y Tecnología Nucleares
Avenida Salvador Allende y Luaces, La Habana 10300
Tel: +53(7) 575-662
Fax: +53(7) 785-018
EMail: rectorado@info.isctn.edu.cu
Website: http://www.smf.mx/Catalogo04/CUBA/ISCTN/isctn.html

Rector: Fernando Guzmán Martínez

Secretary-General: Esperanza Marrero Villalonga
Tel: +53(7) 703-913

International Relations: Susana Olivares Reumont
Tel: +53(7) 787-337 EMail: susana@info.isctn.edu.cu

Faculties
Management and Innovation (Management); **Nuclear Technology** (Nuclear Engineering)

Degrees and Diplomas: *Licenciatura*; *Maestría*; *Doctor en Ciencias*
Last Updated: 10/12/09

JOSÉ ANTONIO ECHEVERRÍA POLYTECHNIC INSTITUTE

Instituto Superior Politécnico José Antonio Echeverría
Calle 114, No. 1190, Entre 119 y 129, Cujae, Marianao 15, La Habana
Tel: +53(7) 260-0641
Website: http://www.cujae.edu.cu/

Rector: Alicia Alonso Becerra
Tel: +53(7) 260-8030, Fax: +53(7) 267-7129
EMail: alonso@tesla.cujae.edu.cu

Secretary-General: Ester Michelena Fernández
EMail: maritza@ind.cujae.edu.cu

Faculties
Architecture (Architecture; Design; Technology; Urban Studies); **Chemical Engineering** (Chemical Engineering); **Civil Engineering** (Civil Engineering); **Computer Engineering** (Computer Engineering); **Electrical Engineering** (Electrical Engineering); **Industrial Engineering** (Industrial Engineering); **Mechanical Engineering** (Mechanical Engineering)

History: Founded 1964.

Main Language(s) of Instruction: Spanish

Degrees and Diplomas: *Licenciatura*; *Diplomado*; *Maestría*; *Doctor en Ciencias*
Last Updated: 02/11/09

JOSÉ DE LA LUZ Y CABALLERO PEDAGOGICAL UNIVERSITY

Universidad Pedagógica José de la Luz y Caballero
Calle 5ta e/n Libertad y Maceo, Holguín 80100
Tel: +53(24) 481-217
Fax: +53(24) 481-168

Rector: César Torres Batísta

Secretary-General: Matilde Preston Tel: +53(244) 481-273

International Relations: Fernando Fernández
Tel: +53(244) 481-970

Faculties
Humanities (Arts and Humanities); **Pre-School Teacher Training** (Preschool Education); **Science** (Natural Sciences); **Technical Sciences** (Technology)

Degrees and Diplomas: *Diplomado*; *Doctor en Ciencias*

JOSÉ MARTÍ PEDAGOGICAL INSTITUTE OF CAMAGUEY

Instituto Superior Pedagógico José Martí de Camagüey
Carretera de Circunvalación, Vía Oriente, Camagüey 74100
Tel: +53(32) 262-232
EMail: rector@ispcmw.rimed.cu

Rectora: Ana María Rodríguez Oíz

Secretary-General: Rolando Avila Cisneros

International Relations: Adolfo Nuñez Fernández

Faculties
Humanities (Arts and Humanities); **Pre-School Teacher Training** (Preschool Education); **Science** (Natural Sciences); **Technical Sciences** (Technology)

Further Information: Traditional and Open Learning Institution

History: Founded 1976.

Main Language(s) of Instruction: Spanish

Degrees and Diplomas: *Licenciatura*
Last Updated: 08/12/09

JOSÉ MARTI UNIVERSITY CENTRE OF SANCTI SPIRITUS

Centro Universitario de Sancti Spiritus José Marti
Avenida de los Martines # 360 Esquina Bartolomé Masó Carretera Central, Sancti Spíritu
Website: http://www.suss.co.cu

Rector: Manuel Valle Fasco

Faculties
Accountancy and Finance (Accountancy; Finance); **Engineering** (Computer Engineering; Energy Engineering; Industrial Engineering; Mathematics); **Humanities** (Arts and Humanities); **Stockbreeding** *(Montaña del Escambray)* (Animal Husbandry)

Degrees and Diplomas: *Licenciatura; Maestría*
Last Updated: 04/12/09

JUAN MARINELLO PEDAGOGICAL UNIVERSITY OF MATANZAS

Universidad Pedagógica de Matanzas 'Juan Marinello'
Carretera de Cidra Km 2 1/2, Matanzas 40100
Tel: +53(45) 291-503
Fax: +53(45) 265-514
EMail: rector@ismptz.rimed.cu

Rector: Juan Manuel Gonzáles Castillo

Faculties
Humanities (Arts and Humanities); **Pre-School Teacher Training** (Preschool Education); **Science** (Natural Sciences)

Degrees and Diplomas: *Licenciatura*

MANUEL ASCUNCE DOMENECH PEDOGOGICAL INSTITUTE OF CIEGO DE AVILA

Instituto Superior Pedagógico Manuel Ascunce Domenech de Ciego de Avila
Carretera Ceballos, Km 1 1/2, Ciego de Avila 65100
Tel: +53(33) 227-196 +53(33) 228-952
Fax: +53(33) 227-196 +53(33) 227-713
EMail: oabreu@ispca.rimed.cu

Rector: Omar Abreu Valdivia

Secretary-General: Caridad Torí Ramírez

International Relations: José Luis Sardiñas

Faculties
Humanities (Arts and Humanities); **Pre-School Teacher Training** (Preschool Education); **Secondary Teacher Training** *(PGISB)* (Secondary Education); **Technical Sciences** (Technology)

History: Founded 1996.

Main Language(s) of Instruction: Spanish

Degrees and Diplomas: *Licenciatura*

MANUEL FAJARDO HIGHER INSTITUTE OF PHYSICAL EDUCATION

Instituto Superior de Cultura Física 'Manuel Fajardo'
Santa Catalina 12453, Cerro, La Habana
Tel: +53(7) 813-800
Fax: +53(7) 669-560
EMail: iscf@reduniv.edu.cu

Rector: Rafael Muñoz Silva Tel: +53(7) 577-191

Secretary-General: Luis Torres Farias Tel: +53(7) 577-135

International Relations: Cesar Vega Portilla

Faculties
Physical Education *(Camagüey, Granma, Santiago de Cuba, Villa Clara, Pinar del Río, Holguín)*

Degrees and Diplomas: *Licenciatura*: 5 yrs; *Título Profesional*: 5 yrs; *Doctor en Ciencias de (+ special field)*: a further 3 yrs; *Doctor en Ciencias*

MARIANA GRAJALE FACULTY OF MEDICINE OF HOLGUIN

Facultad de Ciencias Médicas de Holguín 'Mariana Grajales Coello'
Avenida Lenin No.4 esquina Aguilera, Holguín 80100
Tel: +53(24) 422-975
EMail: nancy@bariay.hlg.sld.cu

Dean: Nancy Ríos Hidalgo Tel: +53(24) 462-936

Programmes
Medicine (Medicine; Nursing; Stomatology)

MARTA ABREU CENTRAL UNIVERSITY OF LAS VILLAS

Universidad Central Marta Abreu de Las Villas
Carretera de Camajuaní Km 5.5, Santa Clara, Villa Clara
Tel: +53(42) 281-178
Fax: +53(42) 281-608
EMail: mas@uclv.edu.cu
Website: http://www.uclv.edu.cu/

President: José Ramón Saborido Loidi
EMail: jsaborido@uclv.edu.cu

Registrar General: Ignacio Pérez Elesgaray Tel: +53(42) 281-417

International Relations: Alina Montero Torres
Tel: +53(42) 281-410, Fax: +53(42) 281-608
EMail: amontero@uclv.edu.cu

Centres
Applied Chemistry Studies (Chemistry); **Bioactive Chemistry** *(CBQ)* (Biochemistry; Chemistry); **Business Administration** *(CEDE)* (Business Administration; Business and Commerce; Management); **Community Studies** *(CEC)* (Social Sciences); **Electrical Energy Studies** *(CEE)* (Electronic Engineering); **Farming and Stockbreeding** *(CIAP)* (Cattle Breeding); **Higher Education Studies** *(CEEd)* (Higher Education); **Informatics Studies** *(CEI)* (Computer Science); **Information Technology and Electronic Studies** *(CEETI)* (Electronic Engineering; Information Technology); **Process Analysis** *(CAP)* (Chemistry); **Research and Development of Structures and Materials** *(CIDEM)* (Civil Engineering); **Sugar Thermoenergetic Studies** *(CETA)* (Thermal Engineering); **Tourism Studies** *(CET)*; **Welding Studies** *(CES)* (Metal Techniques)

Faculties
Accountancy and Finance (Accountancy; Finance); **Agricultural and Veterinary Sciences** (Agricultural Equipment; Agriculture; Agronomy; Biology; Veterinary Science); **Chemistry and Pharmacy** (Chemical Engineering; Chemistry; Pharmacy); **Civil Engineering and Architecture** (Architecture; Civil Engineering); **Electrical Engineering** (Automation and Control Engineering; Biomedical Engineering; Electrical Engineering; Telecommunications Engineering); **Humanities** (Arts and Humanities; English; Journalism; Modern Languages; Philology); **Industrial Engineering and Tourism** (Industrial Engineering; Tourism); **Information and Education Sciences** (Information Sciences); **Law** (Law); **Mathematics, Physics and Computer Science** (Computer Science; Mathematics; Physics);

Mechanical Engineering (Mechanical Engineering); **Psychology** (Psychology; Social Psychology); **Social Sciences** (Cultural Studies; Social Sciences; Social Studies)

Institutes
Plant Biotechnology *(IBP)* (Biotechnology; Botany)

History: Founded 1952 and reorganized 1959. Faculty of Medicine and Institute of Education detached 1976 as independent institutions. A State institution financed by the government and under the jurisdiction of the Ministry of Education.

Governing Bodies: Board

Academic Year: September to July (September-January; February-July)

Admission Requirements: Secondary school certificate or Technical school certificate

Main Language(s) of Instruction: Spanish

Degrees and Diplomas: *Licenciatura:* 5 yrs; *Título Profesional:* 5 yrs of postgraduate work and a thesis; *Maestría:* 2 yrs of postgraduate work and a thesis; *Doctor en Ciencias:* by thesis

Student Services: Academic counselling, Canteen, Cultural centre, Health services, Language programs, Nursery care, Social counselling, Sports facilities

Student Residential Facilities: Yes

Special Facilities: University History Museum. Botanical Garden

Libraries: Central Library; Faculty and Department libraries

Publications: Biotecnología Vegetal *(quarterly)*; Centro Agrícola *(quarterly)*; Centro Azúcar *(quarterly)*; Islas *(quarterly)*
Last Updated: 04/12/09

OSCAR LUCERO MOYA UNIVERSITY OF HOLGUÍN

Universidad de Holguín Oscar Lucero Moya (UHOLM)
Gaveta Postal 57, Avenida XX Aniversario, Carretera Vía Guardalavaca, Piedra Blanca, Holguín 80100
Tel: +53(244) 481-851
Fax: +53(244) 481-843
EMail: cordoves@ict.uho.edu.cu

Rector: Segundo Manuel Pacheco Toledo
EMail: spacheco@ict.uho.edu.cu

International Relations: Alexis Cordovés García
Tel: +53(24) 481-690, Fax: +53(24) 468-050

Centres
Business Management *(CEGEM)* (Business Administration); **CAD/CAM and Robotics** (Robotics); **Modern Languages** (Modern Languages)

Faculties
Agricultural Engineering (Agricultural Engineering); **Civil Engineering** (Civil Engineering); **Computer Engineering** (Computer Engineering); **Industrial Engineering** (Accountancy; Economics; Industrial Engineering; Mathematics and Computer Science; Political Sciences); **Mechanical Engineering** (Industrial Maintenance; Mechanical Engineering; Physics; Technology); **Veterinary Medicine** (Veterinary Science)

History: Founded 1973.

Main Language(s) of Instruction: Spanish

PEPITO TEY PEDAGOGICAL INSTITUTE OF LAS TUNAS

Instituto Superior Pedagógico Pepito Tey de Las Tunas
Carretera de Circunvalacion, Vía Las Tunas, Las Tunas 75100
Tel: +53(31) 463-43 +53(31) 437-79
Fax: +53(31) 463-43
EMail: rector@isplt.rimed.cu

Rectora: Zenaida V. Ävila Pérez

Secretary-General: Sonia Méndez Cutiño

International Relations: Rogelio Díaz Castillo Tel: +53(31) 43779

Faculties
Humanities (Arts and Humanities); **Pre-School Teacher Training** (Preschool Education); **Science** (Natural Sciences)

History: Founded 1996.

Main Language(s) of Instruction: Spanish

Degrees and Diplomas: *Licenciatura*; *Maestría*
Last Updated: 08/12/09

RAFAEL MARÍA DE MENDIVE PEDAGOGICAL UNIVERSITY OF PINAR DEL RÍO

Universidad Pedagógica de Pinar del Río 'Rafael María de Mendive'
Calle Los Pinos (final) y Carretera Borrego, Reparto Hermanos Cruz, Pinar del Río, Pinar del Río 2010
Tel: +53(82) 762-259 +53(82) 763-902
Fax: +53(82) 767-046
EMail: rector@isppr.rimed.cu

Rector: Alejandro Collado Piñero Tel: +53(82) 63902

Faculties
Humanities (Arts and Humanities); **Pre-School Teacher Training** (Preschool Education); **Science** (Natural Sciences)

RAÚL GÓMEZ GARCÍA PEDAGOGICAL INSTITUTE OF GUANTANAMO

Instituto Superior Pedagógico de Guantánamo Raúl Gómez García
Carretera de Jamaica, Km 1 1/2, Guantánamo 95100
Tel: +53(21) 325-032 +53(21) 323-41
EMail: rector@ispgt.rimed.cu

Rector: Juan Carlos Gallego Torres
Tel: +53(21) 325-032 EMail: neciped@gtmo.inf.cu

Faculties
Economics and Technical Sciences (Economics; Technology); **Humanities** (Arts and Humanities); **Physical Education** (Physical Education); **Pre-School Teacher Training** (Preschool Education); **Science** (Natural Sciences)

Further Information: Traditional and Open Learning Institution

History: Founded 1980.

Main Language(s) of Instruction: Spanish

Degrees and Diplomas: *Licenciatura*
Last Updated: 08/12/09

RUBÉN MARTÍNEZ VILLENA PEDAGOGICAL INSTITUTE OF HAVANA

Instituto Superior Pedagógico Rubén Martínez Villena de La Habana
Calle 90 Final e/ 103 y 97, Güira de Melena, La Habana
Tel: +53(67) 485-67
Fax: +53(67) 482-28
EMail: rector@ispvillena.rimed.cu

Rector: Eduardo López Núñez

Programmes
Teacher Training (Education; Teacher Training)

Degrees and Diplomas: *Licenciatura*

UNIVERSITY OF CAMAGÜEY

Universidad de Camagüey (UC)
Carretera de Circunvalación, Norte Km 5, Camagüey 74650
Tel: +53(322) 623-36
EMail: vrd@reduc.edu.cu
Website: http://www.reduc.edu.cu

Rector: Carlos Díaz Barranco
Tel: +53(322) 621-29, Fax: +53(322) 621-26
EMail: rector@rec.reduc.edu.cu

International Relations: Alonso Gómez Pérez
Tel: +53(322) 617-76 EMail: dri@reduc.cmw.edu.cu

Centres
Animal Husbandry Development *(CEDEPA)* (Animal Husbandry); **Education** *(CENEDUC)* (Computer Education; Education)

Faculties

Chemical Engineering (Biology; Chemical Engineering; Chemistry; Materials Engineering; Physics); **Construction Engineering** (Applied Mathematics; Civil Engineering; Construction Engineering); **Economics** (Accountancy; Economics; Finance; Management); **Electromechanics** (Computer Science; Electrical Engineering; Machine Building; Mechanical Engineering; Physics); **Law** (Law; Spanish); **Social Sciences** (Social Sciences)

History: Founded 1967 as Centro Universitario de Camagüey, incorporating institutions previously forming part of the Universidad de Las Villas. Acquired present title 1974. A state institution financed by the government and under the jurisdiction of the Ministry of Education.

Governing Bodies: Consejo Universitario

Degrees and Diplomas: *Título Profesional*: 5 yrs; *Título Profesional*: Education, 4 yrs; *Título Profesional*: Medicine, 6 yrs; *Doctor en Ciencias de (+ special field)*: a further 3 yrs; *Doctor en Ciencias*: by thesis

Publications: Revista de Producción Animal

UNIVERSITY OF CIEGO DE AVILA

Universidad de Ciego de Avila (UNICA)
Carretera de Morón Km 9 1/2, Ciego de Avila 69450
Tel: +53(33) 245-44 +53(33) 266-211
Fax: +53(33) 266-365
EMail: rector@rect.unica.cu
Website: http://www.unica.cu/

Rector: Mario Ares Sánchez

International Relations: Oscar Fernández Tel: +53(33) 266-211

Centres
Biotechnology *(CBP)* (Biotechnology; Botany); **Irrigation** (Irrigation)

Faculties
Agronomy (Agronomy; Biology; Cattle Breeding); **Economics** (Economics; Modern Languages; Political Sciences); **Physical Education** (Physical Education); **Stockraising** (Agricultural Equipment; Animal Husbandry; Cattle Breeding)

History: Founded 1978.

Main Language(s) of Instruction: Spanish

UNIVERSITY OF CIENFUEGOS CARLOS RAFAEL RODRÍGUEZ

Universidad de Cienfuegos Carlos Rafael Rodríguez
Carretera a Rodas Km 4, Cuatro Caminos, Cienfuegos 59430
Tel: +53(432) 521-521
Fax: +53(432) 522-762
EMail: reducf@ucf.edu.cu
Website: http://www.ucf.edu.cu

Rector: Juan B. Cogollos Martínez EMail: rector@ucf.edu.cu

Vicerrector Administrativo: Magdiel Chaviano Díaz Tel: +53(43) 522-167 EMail: mchaviano@ucf.edu.cu

International Relations: Julio César Quintero Rodríguez Tel: +53(43) 523-345 EMail: jcquinte@ucf.edu.cu

Centres
Environmental and Energy Studies *(CEEMA)* (Energy Engineering; Environmental Management; Environmental Studies) *Director*: Margarita Lapido Pérez; **Hydraulic Oil and Pneumatic Studies** *(CEDON)* (Hydraulic Engineering) *Director*: Luis Marcos Castellanos Gonzáles; **Pedagogical Studies and Higher Education** *(CEDDES) Division Head*: Silvia Vázquez Cedeño; **Sociocultural** (Cultural Studies; Social Studies) *Director*: Fernando Agüero Contreras; **Sustainable Agriculture** *(CETAS)* (Agriculture) *Director*: Alejandro Socorro Castro

Faculties
Agronomy (Agricultural Engineering; Agronomy; Veterinary Science) *Dean*: José Ramón Mesa Reynaldo; **Computer Engineering**; **Economics and Business** (Accountancy; Economics; Industrial Engineering; Management) *Dean*: Dunia García Lorenzo; **Humanities and Social Sciences** (Cultural Studies; English; History; Law; Psychology; Social Sciences; Social Studies; Sociology;

Spanish) *Dean*: Yailén Monzón Brugueras; **Mechanical Engineering** (Chemistry; Energy Engineering; Environmental Engineering; Hydraulic Engineering; Mechanical Engineering; Physics); **Physical Education** (Physical Education; Sports) *Dean*: Osmany Mena Rodríguez

History: Founded 1979. Acquired present title 1998.

Academic Year: September to July

Admission Requirements: Entrance examination

Main Language(s) of Instruction: Spanish

International Co-operation: With universities in Switzerland and Norway

Degrees and Diplomas: *Licenciatura*: Accountancy; Economics; Law; History; English; Sociocultural Studies; Communication Studies; Sociology; Psychology, 5 yrs; *Título Profesional*: Agricultural Engineering; Computer Engineering, 5 yrs; *Maestría*: Engineering; Education; Accountancy; Agriculture; Mathematics; Accountancy; History, 2 1/2 yrs; *Doctor en Ciencias*: Engineering; Education; Finance, 4 yrs

Student Services: Cultural centre, Foreign student adviser, Foreign Studies Centre, Health services, Language programs, Nursery care, Social counselling, Sports facilities

Student Residential Facilities: For 900 students

Libraries: Yes

Publications: Universidad y Sociedad, Related to Higher Education impacts to society *(quarterly)*

Academic Staff 2007-2008	MEN	WOMEN	TOTAL
FULL-TIME	167	184	351
PART-TIME	575	932	1,507
STAFF WITH DOCTORATE			
FULL-TIME	51	22	73
PART-TIME	–	–	1
Student Numbers 2007-2008			
All (Foreign Included)	957	752	1,709
FOREIGN ONLY	128	57	185

Part-time students, 6,704. **Distance students**, 2,882. **Evening students**, 1,300.
Last Updated: 13/03/08

UNIVERSITY OF COMPUTER SCIENCE

Universidad de las Ciencias Informáticas
Carretera de San, Antonio de los Baños, Km 2 1/2. Torrens, La Habana
Tel: +537 837 2548
EMail: uci@uci.cu
Website: http://www.uci.cu

Rector: Melchor Gil Morell

Programmes
Computer Science (Computer Science)

History: Founded 2002.

Main Language(s) of Instruction: Spanish

Degrees and Diplomas: *Título Profesional*. Also Postgrado

Publications: Revista Cubana de Ciencias Informáticas
Last Updated: 04/12/09

UNIVERSITY OF GRANMA

Universidad de Granma
Apartado 21, Carretera de Manzanillo Km. 17 1/2 Bayamo, Granma, 85100
Tel: +53(23) 921-30
Fax: +53(23) 921-31
EMail: root@udg.granma.inf.cu
Website: http://www.udg.co.cu/

Rectora: Antonia María Castillo Ruiz EMail: antonia@udg.edu.cu

International Relations: Narcys M. Bueno Figueras EMail: isca@ispjam.uo.edu.cu

Centres
Animal Production (Animal Husbandry); **Vegetal Biotechnology** (Biotechnology; Botany)

Faculties

Accountancy (Accountancy; Computer Science; Economics; Political Sciences); **Agriculture** (Agriculture; Biology; Physics; Surveying and Mapping); **Engineering** (Applied Mathematics; Computer Science; Engineering); **Social Sciences and Humanities**; **Veterinary Science** (Veterinary Science)

History: Founded 1967.

Main Language(s) of Instruction: Spanish

Libraries: Yes

UNIVERSITY OF HAVANA
Universidad de La Habana (UH)
Calle San Lázaro y L. Vedado, La Habana 10400
Tel: +53(7) 8783-231
Fax: +53(7) 8735-774
Website: http://www.uh.cu

Rector: Gustavo Cobreiro Suárez
Tel: +53(7) 8783-231 EMail: rector@rect.uh.cu

International Relations: Cristina Díaz Lopez
Tel: +53(7) 8786-200, Fax: +53(7) 8735-774
EMail: cristina@rect.uh.cu

Centres

Biomaterials *(BIOMAT)*; **Cuban Economics** *(CEEC)* (Economics); **Demographic Studies** *(CEDEM)* (Demography and Population); **Environmental Studies** *(CEMA)* (Environmental Studies); **Health and Well-being** *(CESBH)* (Health Sciences; Welfare and Protective Services); **Higher Education Development** *(CEPES)* (Education; Higher Education); **International Economics Research** *(CIEI)* (International Economics); **International Migration** *(CEMI)* (Political Sciences); **Marine Biology** *(CIM)* (Marine Science and Oceanography); **National Botanical Garden**; **Social Sciences** *(Latin American Faculty (FLACSO))*; **Studies of Public Administration** *(CEAP)* (Political Sciences; Public Administration); **United States Studies** *(CESEU)* (American Studies)

Colleges

Preservation and Management of the Cultural Historical Patrimony *(San Gerónimo)*

Faculties

Accountancy and Finance (Accountancy; Finance; Tourism); **Biology** (Biochemistry; Biology; Microbiology); **Chemistry** (Chemistry); **Communication Studies** (Communication Studies; Industrial Management; Journalism; Library Science); **Distance Education** (Accountancy; Cultural Studies; Economics; Finance; History; Information Sciences; Law; Library Science; Social Studies); **Economics** (Economics); **Foreign Languages** (Chinese; English; French; German; Italian; Modern Languages; Portuguese; Russian; Spanish; Speech Therapy and Audiology); **Geography** (Geography); **Law** (Law); **Mathematics and Computer Science** (Computer Science; Mathematics); **Philosophy and History** (History; Philosophy; Political Sciences; Sociology); **Physics** (Physical Engineering; Physics); **Psychology** (Psychology)

Institutes

Pharmacy and Food Technology (Food Technology; Pharmacy); **Science and Technology of Materials** *(IMRE)* (Materials Engineering; Technology)

History: Founded 1728 by the monks of Santa Cruz of the Dominican Order of Preaching Friars following Papal Bull 1721. Approved by the Spanish Royal Council of the Indies 1722. Secularized 1842 and granted autonomy 1933. Reorganized 1959 and university reform law promulgated 1962. A State institution.

Governing Bodies: Consejo Universitario, comprising the members of the Rectoría, the deans of the faculties, the directors of the research centres and of the branches of the University, and representatives of the academic staff and students; Consejo Científico; Comisión Central Metodológica

Academic Year: September to July (September-January; February-July)

Admission Requirements: Secondary school certificate

Main Language(s) of Instruction: Spanish

International Co-operation: With universities in Spain; Brazil; China; Germany; Venezuela

Degrees and Diplomas: *Licenciatura (Lic.)*: 5 yrs; *Título Profesional*: Engineering *(Ing.)* *(Ingeniero)*, 5 yrs; *Doctor en Ciencias de (+ special field)*: a further 3 yrs; *Maestría (MC)*: about 3 yrs postgraduate; *Doctor en Ciencias (Dr.)*: 4-5 yrs postgraduate

Student Residential Facilities: Yes

Special Facilities: Luis Montané Anthropology Museum; Felipe Poey Museum; Fragua Martiana

Libraries: Central Library 'Rubén Martínez Villena', c. 600,000 vols; 20 schools and centre libraries

Publications: Journals of the Faculties and Institutes
Last Updated: 04/12/09

UNIVERSITY OF ORIENTE
Universidad de Oriente (UO)
Avenida Patricio Lumumba s/n, Santiago de Cuba 90500
Tel: +53(22) 633-011 +53(22) 632-042
Fax: +53(22) 632-689
EMail: dri@ri.uo.edu.cu
Website: http://www.uo.edu.cu

Rectora: Zaida Valdés Estrada EMail: zaida@rect.uo.edu.cu

Vicerrector Administrativo: Elio Castellanos Caballeros

International Relations: Roberto Miguel Sagaró Zamora, Director
Tel: +53(22) 641-701, Fax: +53(22) 641-701

Centres

Applied Electromagnetics *(CNEA)*; **Automation**; **Energetics** (Energy Engineering); **Higher Education Studies** *(Manuel F. Gran)* (Curriculum; Educational Sciences); **Industrial Biotechnology** *(CEBI)* (Biotechnology); **Medical Biophysics** *(CBM)* (Biophysics); **Medical Informatics and Equipment** (Medical Technology); **Sugar Research** *(CEIA)*

Faculties

Chemical Engineering (Chemical Engineering); **Construction** (Architecture; Construction Engineering; Hydraulic Engineering; Structural Architecture; Urban Studies); **Distance Education** (Accountancy; Economics; Finance; History; Information Sciences; Law; Library Science); **Economics and Business** (Accountancy; Business Administration; Economics; Finance; Marketing); **Electrical Engineering** (Automation and Control Engineering; Computer Science; Electrical Engineering; Electronic Engineering; Telecommunications Engineering); **Humanities** (Art History; Arts and Humanities; Communication Studies; History; Modern Languages; Philosophy; Physiology; Political Sciences; Psychology; Sociology); **Law** (Civil Law; Constitutional Law; Criminal Law; Labour Law; Law); **Mathematics and Computer Science**; **Mechanical Engineering** (Architecture; Engineering Drawing and Design; Machine Building; Mechanical Engineering; Thermal Engineering; Transport Engineering); **Natural Sciences** (Biology; Chemistry; Natural Sciences; Pharmacy; Physics); **Social Sciences** (Communication Studies; History; Philosophy; Psychology; Social Sciences; Sociology)

History: Founded 1947. Recognized by the State and reorganized 1948. Became an official institution 1949 and reorganized 1959. Under the responsibility of the Ministry of Higher Education.

Governing Bodies: Consejo de Dirección; Asamblea de Dirección y Claustro General de Profesores (General Assembly)

Academic Year: September to July

Admission Requirements: Secondary school certificate or entrance examination

Main Language(s) of Instruction: Spanish

Degrees and Diplomas: *Licenciatura*: 5 yrs; *Título Profesional*: Architecture *(Arquitecto)*; Engineering *(Ingeniero)*, 5 yrs; *Título Profesional*: Education, 4 yrs; *Título Profesional*: Medicine, 6 yrs; *Doctor en Ciencias*: by thesis

Student Services: Academic counselling, Cultural centre, Employment services, Foreign student adviser, Foreign Studies Centre, Health services, Language programs, Nursery care, Social counselling, Sports facilities

Student Residential Facilities: Yes

Special Facilities: Museum of Cuban Archaeology; Zoology Museum

Libraries: c. 175,000 vols

Publications: Revista Cubana de Química *(quarterly)*; Revista Santiago; Revista Tecnologia Química; Taller Literario de la Escuela de Letras
Last Updated: 04/12/09

VLADIMIR ILLICH LENIN UNIVERSITY CENTRE, LAS TUNAS

Centro Universitario Vladimir Illich Lenin, Las Tunas (CULT)
Avenida Carlos J. Finlay s/n, Buenavista, Las Tunas 75200
Tel: +53(31) 47980
Fax: +53(31) 48158
EMail: ebc@ult.edu.cu
Website: http://www.ult.edu.cu

Rector: Maricela Pico García
Tel: +53(31) 465-01, Fax: +53(31) 465-03
EMail: maricela13@ult.edu.cu

Secretary-General: Ana María Piñeiro Hernández

International Relations: Juan Ricardo Botero

Faculties
Agricultural Sciences (Agricultural Engineering; Agronomy); **Economics** (Accountancy; Economics; Finance; Political Sciences); **Physical Education** (Physical Education); **Social Sciences and Humanities**; **Technology**
Degrees and Diplomas: *Licenciatura*; *Maestría*
Last Updated: 04/12/09

Curaçao

STRUCTURE OF HIGHER EDUCATION SYSTEM

Description:

Higher education is provided by the Universiteit van de Nederlandse Antillen. It was founded as a Law School in 1970, became an Institute of Higher Studies in 1973 and acquired its present status and title in 1979, incorporating the School of Engineering. It is an autonomous institution, and its governing bodies are the Board of Trustees and the University Council.

Stages of studies:

University level first stage: Bachelor's degree
Studies last for four years (or two years after Propedeuse in Law).

University level second stage:
A Master's degree is offered two years after the Bachelor's degree in such fields as Business Administration and Accounting.

ADMISSION TO HIGHER EDUCATION

Admission to university-level studies:

Name of secondary school credential required: Voorbereidend Wetenschappelijk Onderwijs Certificate

NATIONAL BODIES

Ministerio di Enseñansa, Siensia, Kultura i Deporte (Ministry of Education, Science, Culture and Sports)

Minister: Lionel Jansen
Secretary-General: Marva Browne
Scharlooweg 102
Willemstad
Tel: +5999 461 5133
Fax: +5999 462 4471

Data for academic year: 2006-2007
Source: IAU from UNESCO Natcom Netherlands Antilles, 2006 (Bodies, 2011)

INSTITUTIONS

PUBLIC INSTITUTIONS

UNIVERSITY OF THE NETHERLANDS ANTILLES

Universiteit van de Nederlandse Antillen
PO Box 3059, Jan Noorduynweg 111, Willemstad
Tel: +599(9) 8442-222 +599(9) 8442-144
Fax: +599(9) 8442-200
EMail: una@una.an
Website: http://www.una.an/

Rector Magnificus: Rupert E. Silberie
Tel: +599(9) 8442-105 EMail: rupert.silberie@una.an

Faculties
Arts (Dutch; English; Foreign Languages Education; Native Language; Spanish; Teacher Training); **Engineering** (Architecture; Civil Engineering; Electrical Engineering; Engineering; Engineering Drawing and Design; Industrial Engineering; Information Technology; Mechanical Engineering); **Law** (Law); **Social and Behavioral Sciences** (Social Work); **Social Sciences and Economics** (Accountancy; Business Administration)

History: Founded 1970 as Law School, became Institute of Higher Studies 1973 and acquired present status and title 1979, incorporating the School of Engineering, founded 1972. The University is responsible to the Ministry of Education.

Governing Bodies: Rector Magnificus supervised by the Supervisory Council

Academic Year: September to June (September-December; January-April)

Admission Requirements: Secondary school certificate or equivalent

Fees: (Antillean Guilders): 1,000

Main Language(s) of Instruction: Dutch

Degrees and Diplomas: *Bachelor's Degree*: Engineering; Business Administration; Accountancy; Education; Law; Social Work, 3-4 yrs;

Master's Degree: Business Administration; Accountancy; Law; Teaching; Engineering; Construction Management, 2 yrs following Bachelor

Student Residential Facilities: Some residential facilities for foreign students and students from other islands in the area

Libraries: c. 110,736 titles

Last Updated: 03/11/11

Cyprus

STRUCTURE OF HIGHER EDUCATION SYSTEM

Description:

The higher education system of Cyprus comprises both public and private institutions. Studies are organized in semesters, and subjects taught are counted in credits.

Stages of studies:

University level first stage: Ptychio
The first stage of university level education lasts for 4 years and leads to the award of a Ptychio (240 ECTS).

University level second stage: Magister Artium/Scientae (Masters)
After completion of the first stage, graduates may follow three to four semesters of full time study (90 to 120 ECTS) leading to a Magister Artium or Magister Scientae degree.

University level third stage: Doctorate
The third cycle lasts between 4 to 8 years and leads to the Didactoriko Diploma. It consists of at least 60 ECTS, a comprehensive examination, the presentation of a research proposal and the defense of an original research thesis.

ADMISSION TO HIGHER EDUCATION

Admission to university-level studies:

Name of secondary school credential required: Apolytirion

Alternatives to credentials: General Certificate of Education Advanced Level

Entrance exam requirements: Admission to State universities is granted upon success in the competitive entrance examinations (Pancyprian Examinations) which are used to rank students. Admission to private universities is granted upon submission of a relevant application and the fulfillment of criteria set by each institution.

Foreign students admission:

Entrance exam requirements: Foreign students should hold a secondary school leaving certificate awarded after six years of secondary education. Entrance examinations are held for the University of Cyprus and all post-secondary non-university institutions. Entrance to private post-secondary non-university institutions requires 12 years of schooling or a secondary school certificate obtained after 6 years of secondary education or its equivalent.

Entry regulations: A visa may be required, depending on the country.

Language requirements: Students should have a good knowledge of Greek for study at the University of Cyprus and some public institutions and English for the other institutions.

RECOGNITION OF STUDIES

Quality assurance system:

The competent authority in the Republic of Cyprus for carrying out programmatic evaluation and accreditation of the private institutions of higher education is the Council of Educational Evaluation–Accreditation (C.E.E.A). The Evaluation Committee of Private Universities is the competent authority in the Republic of Cyprus for the examination of the applications submitted for the establishment and operation of a private university.

Bodies dealing with recognition:

KY.S.A.T.S (Cyprus Council for the Recognition of Higher Education Qualifications)
Chairperson: Constantinos Christou
Executive Director: Marios Antoniades

P.O. Box 12758
Nicosia 2252
Tel: +357 2240 2472
Fax: +357 2240 2481
EMail: info@kysats.ac.cy
WWW: http://www.kysats.ac.cy/

NATIONAL BODIES

Ministry of Education and Culture

Minister: Giorgos Demosthenous
Thoukides and Kimonos Corner
Nicosia 1434
Tel: +357 2280 0600
Fax: +357 2280 0700
EMail: daae@moec.gov.cy
WWW: http://www.moec.gov.cy

SEKAP (Council of Educational Evaluation-Accreditation - CEEA)

P.O. Box 12592 Latsia
Nicosia 2251
Tel: +357 2240 2476
Fax: +357 2240 2466
EMail: sekap@cytanet.com.cy
WWW: http://www.moec.gov.cy/sekap

Role of national body: Independent expert body, appointed by the Council of Ministers upon the recommendation of the Minister of Education and Culture, competent for carrying out the evaluation and accreditation of the private institutions of higher education.

Evaluation Committee of Private Universities - ECPU

Chairperson: George Philokyprou
P.O.Box 12592
Nicosia
Tel: +357 22 402329
Fax: +357 22 402329
EMail: administration@ecpu.ac.cy
WWW: http://www.ecpu.ac.cy/

Data for academic year: 2010-2011
Source: IAU from KYSATS and www.highereducation.ac.cy, 2010, Minister's name, 2011

INSTITUTIONS

PUBLIC INSTITUTIONS

CYPRUS UNIVERSITY OF TECHNOLOGY

P.O. Box 50329, Archbishop Kyprianos 31, Limassol Savings Co-operative Bank Building, 3603 Lemesos
Tel: +357(25) 00-25-00
Fax: +357(25) 00-27-50
EMail: administration@cut.ac.cy
Website: http://www.cut.ac.cy

Chairman: Nicolas Papamichael
EMail: nicolas.papamichael@cut.ac.cy

Vice Chairman Academic Affairs: Tasos Christofides
EMail: tasos.christofides@cut.ac.cy

Centres
Language

Faculties
Applied Arts and Communication (Communication Studies; Fine Arts; Graphic Arts; Multimedia); **Engineering and Technology** (Civil Engineering; Electrical Engineering; Engineering; Information Technology; Materials Engineering; Mechanical Engineering; Technology); **Geotechnical Sciences and Environmental Management** (Agriculture; Biotechnology; Environmental Management;

Food Science); **Health Sciences** (Nursing); **Management and Economics** (Business and Commerce; Economics; Finance; Hotel Management; Management; Marine Transport; Tourism; Transport Management)

History: Founded 2003. Admitted its first students 2007.

Degrees and Diplomas: *Bachelor, Master, Doctorate*
Last Updated: 06/09/10

MEDITERRANEAN INSTITUTE OF MANAGEMENT (MIM)

77 Kallipoleos Avenue, 1679 Nicosia
Tel: +357(22) 80-60-00
Fax: +357(22) 37-68-72
EMail: info@kepa.mlsi.gov.cy
Website: http://www.mlsi.gov.cy/mlsi/kepa/kepa.nsf/DMLmim_en/DMLmim_en?OpenDocument

Departments
Management (Management; Marketing; Public Administration)

History: Founded 1976. A State institution.

Degrees and Diplomas: Postgraduate Diploma in 'Management' and 'Management and Public Administration'.
Last Updated: 09/09/10

OPEN UNIVERSITY OF CYPRUS (OUC)

PO Box 12794, 2252 Latsia
Tel: +357(22) 41-16-00
Fax: +357(22) 41-16-01
EMail: info@ouc.ac.cy
Website: http://www.ouc.ac.cy

President: Panos Razis
Tel: +357(22) 89-28-72, Fax: +357(22) 34-00-66
EMail: razis@ouc.ac.cy

Vice-President: Georgios Filokyprou
EMail: philokyprou@ouc.ac.cy

Faculties
Economics and Management (Banking; Business Administration; Economics; Finance; Management); **Humanities and Social Sciences** (Ancient Civilizations; Arts and Humanities; Education; Greek (Classical); Social Sciences); **Pure and Applied Sciences** (Computer Science; Environmental Management; Information Technology)

History: Founded 2002. An online and distance institution.

Governing Bodies: Governing Board

Degrees and Diplomas: *Bachelor, Master*

Libraries: Yes
Last Updated: 04/01/12

THE CYPRUS INSTITUTE

P.O. Box 27456, 1645 Nicosia
Tel: +357(22) 20-87-00
Fax: +357(22) 44-78-00
EMail: info@cyi.ac.cy
Website: http://www.cyi.ac.cy/

President: Costas N. Papanicolas

Programmes
Computational Sciences (Computer Science; Mathematics and Computer Science); **Digital Cultural Heritage** (Cultural Studies); **Environment and Atmospheric Sciences** (Environmental Management; Environmental Studies)

Research Centres
Computation-based Science and Technology (Computer Science); **Science and Technology in Archaeology** (Archaeology)

History: Created 2005. Programmes commenced 2010-2011. A research institute offering Doctoral programmes.

Degrees and Diplomas: *Doctorate:* Computational Sciences; Digital Cultural Heritage; Environmental and Atmospheric Sciences
Last Updated: 04/01/12

UNIVERSITY OF CYPRUS (UCY)

University House "Anastasios G. Leventis", PO Box 20537, 1678 Nicosia
Tel: +357(22) 89-40-00
Fax: +357(22) 89-21-00
EMail: admin@ucy.ac.cy
Website: http://www.ucy.ac.cy

Rector: Constantinos Christofides (2010-)
Tel: +357(22) 89-40-08, Fax: +357(22) 89-44-69
EMail: ccc@ucy.ac.cy; rector@ucy.ac.cy

Vice-Rector, Academic Affairs: Athanasios Gagatsis
Tel: +357(22) 89-40-03, Fax: +357(22) 89-44-68
EMail: gagatsis@ucy.ac.cy

International Relations: Marios Mavronicolas, Vice-Rector, International Relations, Administration and Finance
Tel: +357(22) 89-94-06, Fax: +357(22) 89-44-67
EMail: mavronic@ucy.ac.cy

Centres
Banking and Financial Research (Banking; Finance); **Economics Research** (Economics); **Intelligent Systems and Networks Research** *(KIOS Research Center)* (Artificial Intelligence; Computer Networks); **Language; Nanotechnology Research** (Nanotechnology); **Oceanography** (Marine Science and Oceanography)

Faculties
Economics and Management (Business Administration; Economics; Management; Public Administration); **Engineering** (Architecture; Civil Engineering; Computer Engineering; Electrical Engineering; Engineering; English; Environmental Engineering; French; Mechanical Engineering; Production Engineering); **Humanities** (Arts and Humanities; English Studies; French Studies; Middle Eastern Studies; Modern Languages; Turkish); **Letters** (Ancient Civilizations; Archaeology; Arts and Humanities; Classical Languages; Greek; History; Philosophy); **Pure and Applied Sciences** (Biological and Life Sciences; Chemistry; Computer Science; Mathematics; Physics; Statistics); **Social Sciences and Education** (Curriculum; Education; Educational Administration; Law; Mathematics Education; Preschool Education; Primary Education; Psychology)

History: Founded 1989. A public Institution. Acquired present status 1992.

Governing Bodies: Council; Senate; Rector's Council

Academic Year: September to June (September-December; January-June)

Admission Requirements: Undergraduate students: General Certificate of Education (GCE) with Ordinary ('O') level in Greek and 3 Advanced ('A') levels, with minimum grades of B or C, or High School Diploma (Apolitirio) and entrance examinations.

Fees: (Cyprus Pounds): Foreign students, 2,000 per semester, students admitted from EU Countries, 1,000. Postgraduate: Master Degree (except MBA), 3,000, Master in Business Administration (MBA), 6,000; PhD, 2,000

Main Language(s) of Instruction: Greek, Turkish

International Co-operation: Participates in LLP Programme

Degrees and Diplomas: *Bachelor:* Electrical Engineering; Mechanical and Manufacturing Engineering; Byzantine and Modern Greek Literature; Classical Studies; Philosophy, History and Archaeology; English Language and Literature; French Language and Literature; Turkish Studies; Biology; Chemistry; Computer Science; Mathematics; Mathematics and Statistics; Physics; Preschool Education; Primary School Education; Psychology; Political Science; Sociology; International Studies; European and Economic Studies; Economics; Accounting; Finance; Management science; Marketing; Achitecture; Civil Engineering; Civil and Environmental Engineering; Computer Engineering, 8 sem; *Master:* Applied Linguistics; Conference Interpreting; English Literature and Comparative Cultural Studies; Turkish Studies; Molecular Biology Research; Chemistry; Advanced Information Technologies; Apllied Mathematics; Pure Mathematics; Statistics; Civil Engineering; Computer Engineering; Mechanical and Manufacturing Engineering; Modern Greek Philology; Classical Studies; Mediterranean Archaeology; Byzantine Studies; Cognitive; Development and Educational Psychology; Economic Analysis; Economics; Monetary and Financial Economics; Business Administration, Finance; Physics; Foundation of Physics; Curriculum Development and Instruction; Didactics and Methodology of Mathematics; Educational Leadership; Learning in Natural Sciences; Mathematics Education; Pedagogical Sciences, minimum 3 sem; *Doctorate*: Applied Linguistics; English Literature and Comparative Cultural Studies; Turkish Studies; Molecular Biology; Chemistry; Computer Science; Applied Mathematics; Pure Mathematics; Applied Statistics; Physics; Curriculum Development and Instruction (PhD); Architecture; Civil Engineering; Computer Engineering; Mechanical and Manufacturing Engineering; Modern Greek Philology; Classical Studies; Mediterranean Archeology; Modern and Contemporary History; Byzantine Studies; Educational Leadership; Learning in Natural Sciences; Mathematics Education; Cognitive; Developmental and Educational Psychology; Political Science; Sociology; Economics; Accounting; Administration; Finance, maximum 8 yrs

Student Services: Academic counselling, Canteen, Cultural centre, Employment services, Foreign student adviser, Foreign Studies Centre, Health services, Sports facilities

Libraries: Central Library, 330,000 vols, 370,000 electronic vols

Academic Staff 2007-2008	MEN	WOMEN	TOTAL
FULL-TIME	196	57	253
Student Numbers 2007-2008			
All (Foreign Included)	1,988	3,358	5,346

Last Updated: 24/01/11

PRIVATE INSTITUTIONS

AMERICAN COLLEGE

P.O.Box 22425, 2 & 3 Omirou Avenue, 1521 Nicosia
Tel: +357(22) 66-11-22
Fax: +357(22) 66-41-18
EMail: college@ac.ac.cy
Website: http://www.ac.ac.cy

Director: Marios Americanos

International Relations: Tasos Anastasiou
EMail: tasos.anastasiou@ac.ac.cy

Programmes
Business Administration (Accountancy; Business Administration; Commercial Law; Finance); **Computer Science** (Computer Science); **Culinary Arts** (Cooking and Catering); **Hotel Management** (Hotel Management); **Human Resource Management** (Human Resources); **International Business** (International Business); **Management Information Systems** (Business Computing; Management Systems); **Marketing** (Marketing); **Travel and Tourism Management** (Tourism)

History: Founded 1975. Previously known as Americanos College.

Degrees and Diplomas: *Diploma*; *Bachelor*: Business Administration; International Business; Marketing; Human Resource Management; Management Information Systems; Computer Science; Hotel Management; Travel and Tourism Management; *Master*: Business Administration

Libraries: American College Library
Last Updated: 04/01/12

COLLEGE OF TOURISM AND HOTEL MANAGEMENT

PO Box 20281, 79 Larnaka Road, Aglangia, 2150 Nicosia
Tel: +357(22) 46-28-46
Fax: +357(22) 33-62-95
EMail: info@cothm.ac.cy
Website: http://www.cothm.ac.cy

Director: Savvas Adamides EMail: adamides@cothm.ac.cy

Programmes
Accounting and Finance (Accountancy; Finance); **Business Administration** (Business Administration); **Business Studies** (Business Administration); **Events Management** (Management); **Hospitality Management** (Hotel Management; Tourism); **Hotel Administration** (Hotel Management); **Information Technology** (Information Technology); **International Business Studies** (International Business); **Leisure Management** (Leisure Studies); **Travel and Tourism Administration** (Tourism)

History: Founded 1987.

Degrees and Diplomas: *Bachelor*: 4 yrs; *Master*. Also Postgraduate Diplomas

Student Residential Facilities: Yes

Libraries: Justin Bugley Library.
Last Updated: 04/01/12

CYPRUS COLLEGE OF ART AND DESIGN

23 Mehmet Ali Street, 6026 Larnaca
Tel: +357 2425 4042
EMail: enquiries@artcyprus.org
Website: http://www.artcyprus.org

Director: Michael Paraskos EMail: michael@artcyprus.org

Divisions
Fine Arts (Art History; Cultural Studies; Fine Arts)
History: Founded 1969.

Degrees and Diplomas: *Bachelor*: Fine Art; *Master*: Fine Art; *Doctorate*. Also: Postgraduate Diploma in Fine Art

Libraries: Herbert Read Library in Larnaca and Norbert Lynton Library in Lempa
Last Updated: 04/01/12

CYPRUS INTERNATIONAL INSTITUTE OF MANAGEMENT (CIIM)

PO Box 20378, 21 Academias Avenue, Aglantzia, 2151 Nicosia
Tel: +357(22) 46-22-46
Fax: +357(22) 33-11-21
EMail: ciim@ciim.ac.cy
Website: http://www.ciim.ac.cy

Director: Theodore Panayotou (2000-)

International Office: Mario Siathas
Tel: +357(22) 46-22-46, Fax: +357(22) 33-11-21
EMail: marios.siathas@ciim.ac.cy

Programmes
Business Administration (Accountancy; Business Administration; Business and Commerce; Commercial Law; Economics; Environmental Management; Finance; Human Resources; Management; Marketing); **Educational Leadership and Management** (Educational Administration; Leadership); **Human Resource Management & Organisational Behaviour** (Human Resources; Management); **Management** (Management); **Public Service Management** (Accountancy; Commercial Law; Economics; Environmental Management; Finance; Human Resources; Management; Marketing; Public Administration)

History: Founded 1990.

Degrees and Diplomas: *Master*

Libraries: Yes
Last Updated: 04/01/12

EUROPEAN UNIVERSITY CYPRUS (EUC)

PO Box 22006, 6, Diogenes Street, Engomi, 22006 Nicosia
Tel: +357(22) 71-30-00
Fax: +357(22) 66-20-51
Website: http://www.euc.ac.cy

President: Andreas Eleftheriades

Schools
Arts and Education Sciences (Advertising and Publicity; Educational Administration; Educational Psychology; Educational Sciences; Graphic Design; Mathematics Education; Music; Music Education; Preschool Education; Primary Education; Special Education); **Business Administration** *(Ioannis Gregoriou)* (Accountancy; Advertising and Publicity; Banking; Business Administration; Business and Commerce; Economics; Finance; Graphic Design; Hotel Management; Human Resources; International Business; Management; Marketing; Public Relations; Sports Management; Tourism); **Humanities and Social Sciences** (Arts and Humanities; Behavioural Sciences; Communication Studies; Comparative Literature; English; European Languages; European Studies;

Journalism; Law; Linguistics; Literature; Psychology; Public Relations; Social Sciences; Social Work; Sociology); **Science** (Computer Engineering; Computer Science; Nursing; Physical Therapy)

History: Founded 1961 as Cyprus College. Acquired present status and title 2007.

Degrees and Diplomas: *Bachelor; Master*

Student Residential Facilities: Yes

Libraries: Yes
Last Updated: 04/01/12

FREDERICK UNIVERSITY

PO Box 24729, 7, Yiannis Frederickou Street, Pallouriotissa,
1303 Nicosia
Tel: +357(22) 43-13-55
Fax: +357(22) 43-82-34
EMail: info@frederick.ac.cy
Website: http://www.frederick.ac.cy

President: Michalis Frederickou

Schools

Architecture, Fine and Applied Arts (Architecture; Fine Arts; Graphic Design; Interior Design); **Economics and Administration** (Accountancy; Business Administration; Economics; Finance; Marine Transport); **Education** (Preschool Education; Primary Education); **Engineering and Applied Sciences** (Automotive Engineering; Civil Engineering; Computer Engineering; Computer Science; Electrical Engineering; Engineering; Mechanical Engineering); **Health Sciences** (Health Administration; Nursing); **Humanities and Social Sciences** (Arts and Humanities; Journalism; Social Sciences; Social Work)

Further Information: Also campus in Limassol

History: Founded 1965 as Frederick Institute of Technology. Acquired present status and title 2007.

Degrees and Diplomas: *Bachelor; Master; Doctorate*: Engineering. Also Postgraduate Diploma

Libraries: Yes
Last Updated: 04/01/12

INTERCOLLEGE (LARNACA)

52, Famagusta Avenue, 6019 Larnaca
Tel: +357(24) 747500
Fax: +357(24) 652213
EMail: info@intercollege.ac.cy
Website: http://www.intercollege.ac.cy/

Executive Director: Stylianos Mavromoustakos

Programmes

Business Administration (Business Administration; Economics; Finance; Marketing); **Business Information Technology** (Business Computing); **Business Studies** (Business and Commerce); **Computer Engineering** (Computer Engineering); **Computing** (Computer Science; Information Technology); **Graphic and Digital Design** (Graphic Design); **Hotel Management** (Hotel Management); **Pre-Primary Education** (Preschool Education); **Sports Science** (Sports; Sports Management)

Further Information: Also campuses in Nicosia and Limassol

Degrees and Diplomas: *Bachelor; Master*
Last Updated: 04/01/12

NEAPOLIS UNIVERSITY PAPHOS

2 Danais Avenue, 8042 Paphos
Tel: +357(26) 84-33-00
Fax: +357(26) 93-19-44
EMail: info@nup.ac.cy
Website: http://www.nup.ac.cy/

Rector: Elias Dinenis

Programmes

Accountancy, Banking, and Finance (Accountancy; Banking; Finance); **Architecture and Environmental Design** *(Undergraduate)* (Architecture; Environmental Studies); **Business Administration** (Business Administration); **Construction Management** *(Postgraduate)* (Construction Engineering; Management);

Educational Psychology (Educational Psychology); **Psychology** *(Postgraduate)* (Psychology); **Real Estate** (Real Estate); **Real Estate, Valuation and Development** *(Undergraduate)* (Real Estate)

History: Created 2007. Programmes commenced 2010-2011.

Fees: (Euros) 9,550 per annum

Degrees and Diplomas: *Bachelor*: Business Administration; Financial Studies; Psychology; Architecture and Environmental Design; Real Estate, Valuation and Development; *Master*: Business Administration; Banking, Investment and Finance; Educational Psychology; Construction Management; Real Estate
Last Updated: 04/01/12

THE C.T.L EUROCOLLEGE

PO Box 51938, 3509 Limassol
Tel: +357(25) 73-65-01
Fax: +357(25) 73-66-29
EMail: college@ctleuro.ac.cy
Website: http://www.ctleuro.ac.cy

Director: Andreas Papathomas

Divisions

Accounting (Accountancy); **Business** (Business Administration); **Computing** (Computer Science; Information Technology); **Hospitality and Tourism** (Hotel Management; Tourism)

History: Created 1966 as CTL Academy. Acquired status and current name 1991.

Degrees and Diplomas: *Bachelor*: Business Administration; Computer Science; Management Information Systems; Hospitality Management; Accounting; *Master*: Business Administration

Libraries: Yes
Last Updated: 04/01/12

THE CYPRUS INSTITUTE OF MARKETING (CIMA)

PO Box 25288, 1308 Nicosia
Tel: +357(22) 77-84-75
Fax: +357(22) 77-93-31
EMail: cima@spidernet.com.cy
Website: http://www.cima.com.cy/

Director: Theophanis Hadjiyiannis (1978-)

Admissions Officer: Alla Pashkova

International Relations: Yangos Hadjiyannis, Deputy Director
EMail: yangos.h@cima.com.cy

Programmes

Banking (Banking); **Business Administration** (Accountancy; Administration; Finance; Human Resources; Insurance; International Business; Marketing); **European Studies** (European Studies); **Financial And Computers Studies** (Business Computing; Finance; Information Sciences); **Insurance** (Insurance); **Shipping** (Marine Transport; Maritime Law); **Tourism Management** (Tourism)

Further Information: Branches in Limassol and British Virgin Isles.

History: Created in 1978. Institution's main aim is to offer specialized programmes to mature and working students.

Governing Bodies: Council

Academic Year: October to June; January to September

Admission Requirements: Secondary School Certificate.

Fees: (Euros): 4,000 per annum

Main Language(s) of Instruction: English

Degrees and Diplomas: *Bachelor*: Business Administration; Shipping; Tourism Management; Financial and Computer Studies; Banking; Insurance; European Studies (BSc), 3 yrs; *Master*: Business Administration (MBA), 1 yrs. Also Postgraduate Diploma in Corporate Management and Strategic Planning.

Student Services: Academic counselling, Canteen, Employment services, Foreign student adviser, Foreign Studies Centre, Handicapped facilities, Health services, Language programs, Social counselling

Libraries: 10,000 vols

Publications: The Global Market, CIMA Journal *(quarterly)*

Academic Staff *2008-2009*	MEN	WOMEN	**TOTAL**
PART-TIME	30	20	**50**

Student Numbers *2008-2009*			
All (Foreign Included)	500	300	**800**

Part-time students, 300. **Distance students**, 100. **Evening students**, 500.
Last Updated: 09/09/10

THE PHILIPS COLLEGE

PO Box 28008, 2090 Nicosia
Tel: +357(22) 44-18-60
Fax: +357(22) 44-18-63
EMail: dina@philips.ac.cy; admissions@philips.ac.cy
Website: http://www.philips.ac.cy

President: Philippos Constantinou

Faculties

Economics and Management (Accountancy; Business Administration; Business and Commerce; Economics; Finance; Real Estate); **Informatics and Telecommunications** (Computer Engineering; Information Technology; Multimedia); **Languages and Communication** (European Languages; Journalism; Public Relations); **Law and Social Studies** (Education; Law; Nursing; Psychology)

History: Created 1978. Acquired status 2000.

Degrees and Diplomas: *Bachelor:* Business Studies; Public Relations; Information Technology; Nursing; Journalism; European Languages; Real Estate Management; Corporate Administration; *Master:* Business Administration; Financial Management; Education
Last Updated: 09/09/10

UNIVERSITY OF NICOSIA

PO Box 24005, 46 Makedonitissas Avenue, 1700 Nicosia
Tel: +357(22) 84-15-00
Fax: +357(22) 35-20-59
EMail: admission-nic@unic.ac.cy
Website: http://www.unic.ac.cy

Rector: Michalis Attalides EMail: attalides.m@unic.ac.cy

Schools

Business (Accountancy; Banking; Business Administration; Business and Commerce; Economics; Finance; Information Management; Management; Marketing; Sports Management; Tourism); **Education** (Dance; Education; Educational Research; Music; Music Education; Preschool Education; Primary Education); **Humanities, Social Sciences and Law** (Architecture; Arts and Humanities; Communication Studies; English; European Studies; Graphic Arts; Graphic Design; International Relations; Law; Marketing; Modern Languages; Multimedia; Psychology; Public Relations; Social Sciences); **Science** (Biology; Computer Engineering; Computer Science; Electronic Engineering; Nursing)

Further Information: Also campuses in Limassol and Larnaca

History: Founded 1980 as Intercollege. Acquired present status and title 2007.

Governing Bodies: Council; Senate

Degrees and Diplomas: *Bachelor (BA/BSc):* 4 yrs; *Master (MA/MSc/MEd):* a further 1-2 yrs; *Doctorate*

Special Facilities: Access to electronic networks

Libraries: 71,000 vols; 1,178 periodical subscriptions
Last Updated: 09/09/10

Czech Republic

STRUCTURE OF HIGHER EDUCATION SYSTEM

Description:

Tertiary professional schools, even though they are not part of higher education, belong to tertiary education and offer professional education leading to a diploma, mostly in economics and health care. Higher education institutions provide accredited study programmes and programmes of lifelong learning. Higher education institutions can be of university and non-university types. The non-university higher education institutions usually offer Bachelor study programmes and, if accredited, Master study programmes. They are not allowed to provide Doctoral study programmes. University-type higher education institutions offer Bachelor, Master and in most case also Doctoral study programmes. Higher education institutions offer courses in the Humanities, Social Sciences, Natural Sciences, Engineering, Medicine and Pharmacy, and Theology, as well as in Economics, Veterinary Medicine, and Agriculture, Teacher Training and Arts. There are public, state or private institutions. Public institutions are financed by the State budget through the Ministry of Education, Youth and Sports. The private institutions can be partially financed by the State. The Czech higher education system also includes 2 other State higher education institutions (the University of Defense and the Police Academy) which are financed by the Ministry of Defense and the Ministry of the Interior. All higher education institutions provide accredited study programmes which are assessed by the Accreditation Commission. The Czech Rectors' Conference and the Council of Higher Education Institutions are two important partners of the Ministry of Education in all decisions concerning higher education.

Stages of studies:

University level first stage: Bachelor studies
The Bachelor study programme usually takes three to four years and covers all the main disciplines, except Medicine, Dentistry, Veterinary Medicine, Pharmacy, Law and some other fields. The programme aims at providing a qualification to both practice a profession and continue studying at the Master level. This cycle leads to the academic degree of "bakalář" (Bc.) or "bakalář umění" (BcA.) in the field of Arts. Students must sit for a state final examination, part of which is usually the defense of a Bachelor thesis.

University level second stage: Master studies (magisterské studium)
The Master programme lasts from one to three years after the Bachelor. In Medicine, Dentistry, Veterinary Medicine, Pharmacy and Law, where there are no Bachelor studies, the Master programme lasts from 4 to 6 years (Medicine, Veterinary Medicine: 6 years; Dentistry, Law, Teacher Training for secondary schools: 5 years; Teacher Training for the first stage of basic school: 4 years). Graduates in the Humanities, Education and Social Sciences, Natural Sciences, Pharmacy, Theology and Law are awarded the academic degree of "magistr" (Mgr.), "magistr umění" (MgA.) in Arts, "inženýr" (Ing.) in Engineering, Economics, Agriculture and Chemistry and Military fields, "inženýr architekt" (Ing.arch.) in Architecture, "doktor medicíny" (MUDr.) in Medicine, "doktor zubního lékařství" (MDDr.) in Dentistry, "doktor veterinární medicíny" (MVDr.) in Veterinary Medicine. At the end of this stage, students must sit for a State final examination, part of which is composed of the defense of a diploma thesis. In Medicine, Dentistry and Veterinary Medicine, they must sit for the "státní rigorózní zkouška (State Rigorosum examination). The holders of the degree of "magistr" can sit for a State Rigorosum examination in the same field and defend a thesis to acquire the academic degree of "doktor práv" (JUDr.) in Law , "doktor filosofie" (PhDr.) in the Humanities, Education and Social Sciences, "doktor přírodních věd" (RNDr.) in Natural Sciences, "doktor farmacie" (PharmDr.) in Pharmacy, "doktor teologie" (ThDr.) or "licenciát teologie" (ThLic.) in Theology. The abbreviations of all the academic degrees mentioned above are written before the name.

University level third stage: Doctoral studies (doktorské studium)
The third and highest level of higher education consists in studies for the Doctorate under the guidance of a tutor. The programme comprises scientific research and independent study. The programme usually lasts between three and four years. Holders of a Master's Degree (Mgr., MgA., Ing., Ing.arch., MUDr., MDDr., MVDr.) may apply. Studies lead to the academic degree of "doktor" (Ph.D.) or "doktor teologie" (Th.D.) in the field of Theology. The abbreviations are written behind the name. Studies end with the State Doctoral examination and the defense of a dissertation.

Distance higher education:

Four distance education centres in Prague, Liberec, Brno and Olomouc have been established. Some non-governmental educational institutions, such as J.A. Comenius and the Open University Fund also offer distance education. The National Centre for Distance Education was established in 1995 as a department of the Centre for Higher Education Studies.

ADMISSION TO HIGHER EDUCATION

Admission to university-level studies:

Name of secondary school credential required: Maturitní zkouška

For entry to: all higher education institutions

Entrance exam requirements: An entrance examination or interview may be required; the form of examination is regulated by the higher education institution (HEI) or the faculty. Forms of entrance examinations are as follows: entrance interview, written exam, oral exam, written + oral exam. There is an increasing number of HEIs accepting students without entrance exams.

Numerus clausus/restrictions: The number of students is limited by the capacity of each institution or faculty.

Other admission requirements: In higher education institutions specialized in Arts study, including Architecture, and in Faculties of Education and Sport, part of the entrance examination is called "talentová zkouška" (talent examination).

Foreign students admission:

Definition of foreign student: A foreign student is a person enrolled at a Czech higher education institution who is not a permanent resident of the Czech Republic.

Quotas: None

Entrance exam requirements: The Secondary School Leaving Certificate must be validated by the Regional School Authorities (školská oddělení krajských úřadů).

Entry regulations: Entry regulations are governed by Act no.326 of 30 November 1999 on Residence of Aliens in the Territory of the Czech Republic. The text of this Act and applications for permission to reside in the Czech Republic can be found at http://www.mvcr.cz/inf_turi/english/index.html.

Health requirements: Health certificate required.

Language requirements: Foreign students who do not have adequate knowledge of the Czech language can follow a basic one-year course. Information is available at http://www.cuni.cz/cuni/ujop. Some faculties teach several courses in English or German.

RECOGNITION OF STUDIES

Quality assurance system:

The study programmes of all higher education institutions are subject to accreditation. Accreditation is conferred by the Ministry of Education, Youth and Sports which decides on the basis of the Accreditation Commission statement.

Bodies dealing with recognition:

Středisko pro ekvivalenci dokladů o vzdělání (Centre for Equivalence of Documents on Education - Czech ENIC/NARIC)

Head: Štěpánka Skuhrová
U Dvou Srpů 2024/2
Praha 5 150 00
Tel: +420 257 011 335
Fax: +420 257 531 672
EMail: naric@csvs.cz
WWW: http://www.naric.cz

Special provisions for recognition:

Recognition for university level studies: Recognition of higher education diplomas obtained abroad is the responsibility of public higher education institutions with similar or equal study programmes. In some special cases, recognition is provided by the Ministry of Education, Youth and Sports.

For access to advanced studies and research: Recognition of higher education diplomas obtained abroad is the responsibility of public higher education institutions with similar or equal study programmes. In some special cases, recognition is provided by the Ministry of Education, Youth and Sports.

For exercising a profession: Recognition of higher education diplomas obtained abroad is the responsibility of public higher education institutions with similar or equal study programmes. In some special cases, recognition is provided by the Ministry of Education, Youth and Sports. The recognition of regulated professions is provided by the competent recognition authority (http://www.msmt.cz/international-cooperation-1/recognition-of-qualifications-and-education).

NATIONAL BODIES

Ministerstvo školství, mládeže a tělovýchovy (Ministry of Education, Youth and Sports)
  Minister: Josef Dobeš
  Deputy Minister, Research and Higher Education: Ivan Wilhelm
  Karmelitská 7
  Praha 1 118 12
  Tel: +420 234 811 111
  Fax: +420 234 811 753
  EMail: info@msmt.cz
  WWW: http://www.msmt.cz
  Role of national body: Responsible for public administration in education, for developing educational, youth and sport policies and international cooperation in these fields.

Rada vysokých škol (Council of Higher Education Institutions)
  Secretary-General: Václav Kuchař
  José Martího 31
  Praha 6, Veleslavín 162 52
  Tel: +420 220 560 221
  Fax: +420 220 560 221
  EMail: arvs@ftvs.cuni.cz
  WWW: http://www.radavs.cz

Akreditační komise (Accreditation Commission)
  Karmelitská 7
  Praha 1 118 12
  Fax: +420 234 811 488
  EMail: smrckaj@msmt.cz
  WWW: http://www.msmt.cz/areas-of-work/akreditacni-komise

Česká konference rektorů (Czech Rectors' Conference)
  President: Václav Hampl
  Secretary-General: Marie Fojtíková
  Masaryk University Nám. Žerotínovo 9
  Brno 601 77
  Tel: +420 549 491 121
  Fax: +420 549 491 122
  EMail: crc@muni.cz
  WWW: http://crc.muni.cz
  Role of national body: Represents the universities in their dealings with the Ministry.

Centrum pro studium vysokého školství (Centre for Higher Education Studies)
  Director: Helena Šebková
  Deputy-Director: Vladimír Roskovec

U dvou srpu 2024/2
Praha 5 150 00
Tel: +420 257 011 311
Fax: +420 257 532 409
WWW: http://www.csvs.cz/

Data for academic year: 2009-2010
Source: IAU from data provided by the Centre for Higher Education Studies, Czech Republic, 2009. Bodies updated in 2011.

INSTITUTIONS

PUBLIC INSTITUTIONS

ACADEMY OF ARTS, ARCHITECTURE AND DESIGN IN PRAGUE

Vysoká škola umělecko-průmyslová v Praze (VŠUP)
Nám. Jana Palacha 80, 116 93 Praha, 1
Tel: +420 251 098 111
Fax: +420 251 098 240
EMail: pr@vsup.cz
Website: http://www.vsup.cz

Rektor: Pavel Liška Tel: +420 251 098 274 EMail: bjirku@vsup.cz

Prorektor: Filip Suchomel
Tel: +420 251 098 295 EMail: suchomel@vsup.cz

Kvestor: Jan Vanda

Departments
Applied Art (Arts and Humanities); **Architecture** (Architecture); **Design** (Design); **Fine Arts** (Fine Arts); **Graphic Arts** (Graphic Arts); **Life Style**

Further Information: Branch in Zlín

History: Founded 1885 as School of Decorative Arts

Governing Bodies: Academic Council; Artistic Council

Academic Year: October to June (October-January; February-June)

Admission Requirements: Secondary school certificate (Maturita) and artistic entrance examination

Fees: None

Main Language(s) of Instruction: Czech

International Co-operation: Participates in the Socrates/Erasmus and Ceepus programmes

Accrediting Agencies: Ministry of Education, Youth and Sports

Degrees and Diplomas: *Magistr:* Arts (MgrA), 6 yrs. Also Postgraduate studies, a further 3 yrs

Student Services: Academic counselling, Foreign student adviser

Student Residential Facilities: Yes

Libraries: Academy Library
Last Updated: 08/10/09

ACADEMY OF FINE ARTS IN PRAGUE

Akademie výtvarných umění v Praze (AVU)
U Akademie 4, 170 22 Praha, 7
Tel: +420 220 408 200
Fax: +420 233 381 662
EMail: a.kratka@avu.cz
Website: http://www.avu.cz

Rector: Jiří Sopko (2003-)
Tel: +420 220 408 211 EMail: budikova@avu.cz

International Relations: Alena Krátká
Tel: +420 220 408 241, Fax: +420 233 381 662

Schools
Fine Arts (Architecture; Fine Arts; Media Studies; Painting and Drawing; Printing and Printmaking; Restoration of Works of Art; Sculpture)

History: Founded 1799, nationalized 1896, and reorganized 1990 as a postgraduate State institution.

Academic Year: October to June (October-February; February-June)

Admission Requirements: Entrance examination

Main Language(s) of Instruction: Czech

International Co-operation: Participates in Erasmus

Degrees and Diplomas: *Magistr umění:* Arts, 6 yrs; *Doktor*

Student Services: Canteen, Foreign student adviser, Language programs, Sports facilities

Special Facilities: Art Studios

Libraries: 60,000 vols
Last Updated: 01/10/09

ACADEMY OF PERFORMING ARTS IN PRAGUE

Akademie múzických umění v Praze (AMU)
Nám. Malostranské 12, 118 00 Praha, 1
Tel: +420 257 534 205
Fax: +420 257 530 405
EMail: info@amu.cz
Website: http://www.amu.cz

Rektor: Ivo Mathé
Tel: +420 234 244 501, Fax: +420 234 244 515
EMail: ivo.mathe@amu.cz

Kvestor: Ladislav Paluska
Tel: +420 234 244 503, Fax: +420 234 244 515
EMail: ladislav.paluska@amu.cz

International Relations: Karel Foustka, Vice-Rector for international and public Relations
Tel: +420 234 244 506, Fax: +420 234 244 515
EMail: karel.foustka@amu.cz

Faculties
Film and Television *(FAMU)* (Cinema and Television; Film; Photography); **Music and Dance** *(HAMU)* (Dance; Music); **Theatre** *(DAMU)* (Theatre)

History: Founded 1945, acquired present status 1946.

Governing Bodies: Academic Council

Academic Year: October to September

Admission Requirements: Secondary school certificate (Maturitní vysvědčeni) and entrance examination

Fees: For non-Czech programmes only

Main Language(s) of Instruction: Czech

International Co-operation: Participates in Socrates-Erasmus and Fullbright programmes.

Degrees and Diplomas: *Bakalář umění (BcA):* 3 yrs; *Magistr umění (MgA):* a further 2 yrs; *Doktor (PhD):* a further 3 yrs

Student Services: Academic counselling, Canteen, Foreign student adviser, Health services, Language programs, Sports facilities

Student Residential Facilities: Yes

Special Facilities: Concert Hall; Theatres; Movie Studio

Libraries: Yes

Last Updated: 29/09/11

BRNO UNIVERSITY OF TECHNOLOGY
Vysoké učení technické v Brně (VUT V BRNĚ)
Antonínská 548/1, 601 90 Brno
Tel: +420 541 141 111
Fax: +420 541 211 309
EMail: prorektor-zahranici@ro.vutbr.cz
Website: http://www.vutbr.cz

Rector: Karel Rais (2006-)
Tel: +420 541 145 201, Fax: +420 541 211 140
EMail: rektor@ro.vutbr.cz

Kvestor: Vladimír Kotek
Tel: +420 541 145 555 EMail: kvestor@ro.vutbr.cz

International Relations: Jaroslav Fiala, Prorektor
Tel: +420 541 235 372, Fax: +420 541 145 115

Centres
Education and Consultancy (Continuing Education; Engineering; Management)

Faculties
Architecture (Architecture; Town Planning); **Business and Management** (Business and Commerce; Computer Science; Economics; Finance; Management); **Chemistry** (Biotechnology; Chemical Engineering; Chemistry; Consumer Studies; Environmental Studies; Food Science); **Civil Engineering** (Architecture; Building Technologies; Chemistry; Civil Engineering; Computer Engineering; Computer Science; Construction Engineering; Geophysics; Landscape Architecture; Mathematics; Mechanical Engineering; Metal Techniques; Physics; Railway Engineering; Road Engineering; Social Sciences; Structural Architecture; Water Management; Water Science; Wood Technology); **Electrical Engineering and Communication** (Automation and Control Engineering; Biomedical Engineering; Electrical and Electronic Engineering; Electrical Engineering; English; German; Mathematics; Microelectronics; Modern Languages; Physics; Power Engineering; Russian; Spanish; Telecommunications Engineering); **Fine Arts** (Design; Environmental Studies; Fashion Design; Fine Arts; Graphic Arts; Graphic Design; Media Studies; Multimedia; Painting and Drawing; Performing Arts; Publishing and Book Trade; Sculpture; Video); **Information Technology** (Applied Mathematics; Artificial Intelligence; Computer Engineering; Computer Graphics; Information Technology; Multimedia); **Mechanical Engineering** (Aeronautical and Aerospace Engineering; Automation and Control Engineering; Automotive Engineering; Computer Science; Electronic Engineering; Energy Engineering; Engineering Management; Environmental Engineering; Heating and Refrigeration; Industrial Design; Materials Engineering; Mathematics; Modern Languages; Physical Engineering; Production Engineering; Robotics; Solid State Physics)

Further Information: Also Branch in Zlín

History: Founded 1849 as Technical School in Brno, a bilingual German-Czech institute. Reorganized 1899 as Czech Technical University of Franz Joseph in Brno. Became the Czech Technical University of Brno 1918 and Technical University of Dr. E. Beneš in Brno 1937. Closed during the German occupation, reopened 1945, and acquired present title 1956. An institution financed by the State. Also derives income from research undertaken for industry.

Governing Bodies: Senate; Scientific Council; Board of Trustees

Academic Year: September to August

Admission Requirements: Secondary school certificate (Maturitní vysvědčeni) and entrance examination

Fees: None for studies taught in Czech

Main Language(s) of Instruction: Czech. Also special programmes in English.

International Co-operation: Participates in Socrates/Erasmus, Leonardo Da Vinci, Grundtvig programmes

Degrees and Diplomas: *Bakalář (Bc)*: 3-4 yrs; *Magistr (Mgr)*: a further 2 yrs; *Doktor (PhD)*: a further 3 yrs by thesis

Student Services: Canteen, Health services, Language programs, Sports facilities

Libraries: Main Library

Publications: Události na VUT v Brně *(monthly)*

Press or Publishing House: Publishing Centre of TU Brno

Student Numbers *2008-2009*: Total: c. 15,000

Last Updated: 08/10/09

CHARLES UNIVERSITY IN PRAGUE
Univerzita Karlova v Praze (UK)
Ovocný trh 3/5, 116 36 Praha, 1
Tel: +420 224 491-301
Fax: +420 224 229-487
EMail: sekretariat@ruk.cuni.cz; zahran@ruk.cuni.cz
Website: http://www.cuni.cz

Rektor: Václav Hampl (2006-)
Tel: +420 224 491-312 4, Fax: +420 224 210-695
EMail: rektor@cuni.cz

Head of Public Relations Department: Vaclav Hajek
Tel: +420 224 491-618 EMail: tiskovy.mluvci@ruk.cuni.cz

Kvestor: Josef Kubiček
Tel: +420 224 491-316, Fax: +420 224 491-750
EMail: josef.kubicek@ruk.cuni.cz

International Relations: Ivana Halaškova, International Relations Officer
Tel: +420 224 491-301, Fax: +420 224 229-487
EMail: ivana.halaskova@ruk.cuni.cz

Centres
Economic Research and Graduate Education (Economics) *Director*: Štěpán Jurajda; **Environmental Questions** (Environmental Management; Environmental Studies) *Director*: Bedřich Moldan; **European Information** (European Studies) *Director*: Jiří Hýbner; **Theoretical Studies** *Director*: Ivan M. Havel

Faculties
Catholic Theology (Bible; Catholic Theology; Ethics; Pastoral Studies; Philosophy; Religious Art) *Dean*: Ludwig Armbruster; **Education** (Art Education; Biology; Chemistry; Czech; Education; Educational Administration; Educational Psychology; English; Environmental Studies; French; German; History; Information Technology; Literature; Mathematics; Mathematics Education; Music Education; Native Language; Native Language Education; Pedagogy; Philosophy; Physical Education; Primary Education; Psychology; Russian; Social Sciences; Special Education; Technology Education) *Dean*: Wildová Radka; **Humanities** *Dean*: Ladislav Benyovszky; **Hussite Theology** (Theology) *Dean*: Ján Lášek; **Law** (Administration; Administrative Law; Civil Law; Commercial Law; Constitutional Law; Criminal Law; Economic and Finance Policy; Environmental Studies; European Union Law; Finance; Forensic Medicine and Dentistry; History of Law; International Law; Labour Law; Law; Modern Languages; Physical Education; Political Sciences; Private Law; Public Law; Sociology; Sports) *Dean*: Aleš Gerloch, **Mathematics and Physics** (Applied Linguistics; Applied Mathematics; Applied Physics; Astronomy and Space Science; Computer Education; Computer Networks; Computer Science; Environmental Management; Geophysics; Logic; Mathematics; Mathematics Education; Meteorology; Nuclear Physics; Optics; Physics; Software Engineering; Statistics) *Dean*: Zdeněk Němeček; **Medicine** *(Hradec Králové)* (Anaesthesiology; Anatomy; Biochemistry; Biology; Biophysics; Cardiology; Dentistry; Dermatology; Embryology and Reproduction Biology; Epidemiology; Family Studies; Forensic Medicine and Dentistry; Genetics; Gerontology; Gynaecology and Obstetrics; Histology; Hygiene; Immunology; Medicine; Microbiology; Modern Languages; Neurology; Nursing; Occupational Health; Oncology; Ophthalmology; Orthopaedics; Otorhinolaryngology; Paediatrics; Pathology; Pedagogy; Pharmacology; Physical Education; Physiology; Pneumology; Psychiatry and Mental Health; Psychology; Radiology; Rehabilitation and Therapy; Social and Preventive Medicine; Social Sciences; Sports Medicine; Surgery; Urology; Venereology) *Dean*: Vladimir Palička; **Medicine** *(Plzeň)* (Anaesthesiology; Anatomy; Applied Chemistry; Biochemistry; Biology; Biophysics; Dentistry; Dermatology; Embryology and Reproduction Biology; Epidemiology; Forensic Medicine and Dentistry; Genetics; Gynaecology and Obstetrics;

Haematology; Histology; Immunology; Medicine; Microbiology; Modern Languages; Neurology; Neurosciences; Occupational Health; Oncology; Ophthalmology; Orthopaedics; Otorhinolaryngology; Paediatrics; Pathology; Pharmacology; Physical Education; Physiology; Psychiatry and Mental Health; Public Health; Radiology; Respiratory Therapy; Social and Preventive Medicine; Sports Medicine; Surgery; Toxicology; Urology; Venereology) *Dean*: Jaroslav Koutenský; **Medicine I** (Anaesthesiology; Anatomy; Biochemistry; Biology; Biophysics; Cardiology; Cell Biology; Computer Science; Dentistry; Dermatology; Embryology and Reproduction Biology; Endocrinology; Epidemiology; Forensic Medicine and Dentistry; Gastroenterology; Genetics; Gerontology; Gynaecology and Obstetrics; Haematology; Hepatology; Histology; Hygiene; Immunology; Medicine; Microbiology; Nephrology; Neurology; Nursing; Occupational Health; Oncology; Ophthalmology; Orthopaedics; Otorhinolaryngology; Paediatrics; Pathology; Pharmacology; Physical Education; Physiology; Plastic Surgery; Pneumology; Psychiatry and Mental Health; Public Health; Radiology; Rehabilitation and Therapy; Rheumatology; Speech Therapy and Audiology; Sports Medicine; Stomatology; Surgery; Toxicology; Urology; Venereology) *Dean*: Tomáš Zima; **Medicine II** (Anaesthesiology; Anatomy; Applied Chemistry; Biochemistry; Biology; Cardiology; Cell Biology; Dermatology; Embryology and Reproduction Biology; Endocrinology; Epidemiology; Ethics; Gynaecology and Obstetrics; Haematology; Histology; Immunology; Medicine; Microbiology; Modern Languages; Neurology; Neurosciences; Nursing; Oncology; Ophthalmology; Orthopaedics; Otorhinolaryngology; Paediatrics; Pathology; Pharmacology; Physical Education; Physical Therapy; Physiology; Pneumology; Psychiatry and Mental Health; Public Health; Radiology; Rehabilitation and Therapy; Social and Preventive Medicine; Stomatology; Surgery; Urology; Venereology) *Dean*: Ondřej Hrušák; **Medicine III** (Anaesthesiology; Anatomy; Applied Chemistry; Biochemistry; Biology; Biomedicine; Biophysics; Cardiology; Cell Biology; Clinical Psychology; Embryology and Reproduction Biology; Epidemiology; Ethics; Forensic Medicine and Dentistry; Genetics; Gynaecology and Obstetrics; Haematology; Histology; Hygiene; Immunology; Medicine; Microbiology; Modern Languages; Molecular Biology; Neurology; Nursing; Nutrition; Occupational Health; Oncology; Orthopaedics; Otorhinolaryngology; Pathology; Pharmacology; Physical Education; Physical Therapy; Physiology; Plastic Surgery; Pneumology; Psychiatry and Mental Health; Radiology; Sports Medicine; Stomatology; Surgery; Urology) *Dean*: Bohuslav Svoboda; **Pharmacy** *(Hradec Králové)* (Analytical Chemistry; Biochemistry; Biological and Life Sciences; Biophysics; Botany; Ecology; Inorganic Chemistry; Modern Languages; Organic Chemistry; Pharmacology; Pharmacy; Physical Chemistry; Physical Education; Sports; Toxicology) *Dean*: Aleksander Hrabálek; **Philosophy and Art** (Adult Education; Aesthetics; African Studies; Ancient Civilizations; Archaeology; Archiving; Art History; Asian Studies; Cinema and Television; Communication Studies; Cultural Studies; Czech; East Asian Studies; Eastern European Studies; Economic History; Education; English; English Studies; Ethnology; Finnish; Gender Studies; Germanic Studies; Greek (Classical); History; Human Resources; Hungarian; Information Sciences; Latin; Latin American Studies; Library Science; Linguistics; Literature; Logic; Middle Eastern Studies; Modern Languages; Musicology; Native Language; Philosophy; Phonetics; Physical Education; Political Sciences; Prehistory; Psychology; Religious Studies; Romance Languages; Slavic Languages; Social Work; Sociology; South Asian Studies; Theatre; Translation and Interpretation) *Dean*: Michal Stehlík; **Physical Education and Sports** (Anatomy; Arts and Humanities; Biochemistry; Biomedicine; English; French; German; Leisure Studies; Military Science; Modern Languages; Parks and Recreation; Pedagogy; Physical Education; Physical Therapy; Physiology; Psychology; Russian; Spanish; Sports; Sports Management; Sports Medicine) *Dean*: Václav Bunc; **Protestant Theology** *(Nové Město)* (Bible; Comparative Religion; Ethics; Foreign Languages Education; History of Religion; New Testament; Philosophy; Protestant Theology; Theology) *Dean*: Martin Prudký; **Science** (Biology; Chemistry; Geography; Geology; Natural Sciences) *Dean*: Bohuslav Gaš; **Social Sciences** (Economics; English; French; German; International Studies; Journalism; Media Studies; Modern Languages; Political Sciences; Russian; Social Sciences; Sociology; Spanish) *Dean*: Jan A'mos Višek

Institutes
Computer Technology (Computer Science) *Director*: Pavel Krbec; **History of Charles University** (History) *Director*: Josef Petráň;

Language and Foundation Studies (Linguistics) *Director*: Jan Podroužek

Further Information: Also Teaching Hospitals. Courses for foreign students

History: Founded 1348 by King Charles IV. Became a State institution 1773 when the Society of Jesus was dissolved. Divided in 1882 into separate Czech and German universities each bearing the title Charles-Ferdinand. Present title adopted 1918. Closed in November 1939 during the German occupation; reopened 1945 at which time the German university was abolished. Acquired present status 1999.

Governing Bodies: University Council

Academic Year: September to June (September-January; February-June)

Admission Requirements: Secondary school certificate (Maturitní vysvědčeni) and entrance examination

Fees: (US Dollars): 4,000-10,500 per annum

Main Language(s) of Instruction: Czech, English, German

International Co-operation: With universities in China-Taiwan; USA; Italy; Germany; Spain; Belgium; Switzerland; Argentina; France; United Kingdom; Japan; Israel; Korea; Canada; Hungary; Mexico; Macedonia; Austria; Poland; Lithuania; Greece; Russian Federation; Portugal; Australia; Bulgaria; Egypt; Ecuador; Finland; Chile; Czech Republic; South Africa; Latvia; Malta; Netherlands; Norway; Peru; Slovenia; Slovak Republic; Serbia; Montenegro; Turkey; Ukraine; Uruguay

Degrees and Diplomas: *Bakalář (BC)*: 3 yrs; *Doktor medicíny*: Medicine (MUDr), 6 yrs; *Magistr (Mgr)*: 4-6 yrs; *Doktor*: 4-5 yrs, by examen rigorosum

Student Services: Academic counselling, Handicapped facilities, Health services, Social counselling, Sports facilities

Student Residential Facilities: For 12,554 students

Special Facilities: Botanical Garden. Czech Pharmaceutical Museum

Libraries: Central and 20 faculty libraries, total, 3,956,683 vols

Publications: Acta Universitatis Carolina: Biologica, Geographica, Geologica, Juridica, Mathematica and Physica, Medica, Oeconomica, Philologica, Philosophica and Historica, Environmentalica, Kinanthropologica; Historia Universitatis Carolinae Pragensis; Ibero-Americana Pragensia *(annually)*; Lékařské Zprávy *(quarterly)*; Novitates Botanicae Univertatis Carolinae *(annually)*; Plzeňský Lékařský Sborník *(annually)*; Prague Bulletin of Mathematical Linguistics; Psychology of Economic Practice *(biannually)*; Recenze Lékařských Monografií; Sborník Lékařský *(quarterly)*

Press or Publishing House: Carolinum (The Charles University Press)

Last Updated: 03/10/11

🏛 CZECH TECHNICAL UNIVERSITY IN PRAGUE

České vysoké učení technické v Praze (ČVUT)
Ul. Zikova 4, 166 36 Praha
Tel: +420(2) 2434-1111
Fax: +420(2) 2431-1042
EMail: pozar@cvut.cz
Website: http://www.cvut.cz

Rector: Václav Havlíček
Tel: +420(2) 2435-3474, Fax: +420(2) 2431-0783
EMail: havlicek@fel.cvut.cz

Kvestor-Bursar: Jan Gazda EMail: gazda@fsv.cvut.cz

Faculties
Architecture (Architecture; Civil Engineering; Town Planning; Urban Studies); **Biomedical Engineering** (Anatomy; Biochemistry; Biomedical Engineering; Physiology); **Civil Engineering** (Building Technologies; Civil Engineering; Construction Engineering; Engineering Management; Environmental Engineering; Surveying and Mapping; Transport Engineering); **Electrical Engineering** (Applied Mathematics; Applied Physics; Artificial Intelligence; Automation and Control Engineering; Biomedical Engineering; Computer Engineering; Electrical and Electronic Equipment and Maintenance; Electrical Engineering; Electronic Engineering; Engineering Management; Mathematics and Computer Science; Power Engineering;

Software Engineering; Systems Analysis; Technology; Telecommunications Engineering); **Information Technology** (Computer Engineering; Computer Science; Information Technology; Multimedia; Software Engineering); **Mechanical Engineering** (Aeronautical and Aerospace Engineering; Automation and Control Engineering; Automotive Engineering; Energy Engineering; Engineering; Engineering Drawing and Design; Engineering Management; Hydraulic Engineering; Machine Building; Materials Engineering; Mechanical Engineering; Metallurgical Engineering; Nuclear Engineering; Production Engineering); **Nuclear Sciences and Physical Engineering** (Mathematics; Nuclear Engineering; Nuclear Physics; Physical Engineering; Physics; Solid State Physics); **Transport Sciences** (Air Transport; Railway Transport; Road Transport; Transport and Communications; Transport Economics; Transport Management)

Institutes

Advanced Studies *(Masaryk)* (Business Administration); **Physical Education and Sport** (Physical Education; Sports)

Further Information: Also Klokner Institute

History: Founded 1707 as Czech State Engineering School, became Polytechnic 1803. Granted university status 1864. Closed 1939 during the German occupation, reopened 1945. A State institution. Acquired present status 1999.

Governing Bodies: Academic Senate

Academic Year: September to June (September-February; February-June)

Admission Requirements: Secondary school certificate (Maturitní vysvědčeni) and entrance examination

Fees: None for Czech students

Main Language(s) of Instruction: Czech. Also English in certain subjects.

Degrees and Diplomas: *Bakalář*: Science (Bc), 3 yrs; *Inženýr*: Engineering (Inž.), a further 2-2 1/2 yrs; *Doktor (PhD)*: at least a further 3 yrs by thesis

Student Services: Canteen, Foreign student adviser, Foreign Studies Centre, Health services, Language programs, Sports facilities

Student Residential Facilities: Yes

Libraries: Faculty libraries, c. 70,000 vols

Publications: Acta Polytechnica *(quarterly)*; Pražská Technika *(quarterly)*

Press or Publishing House: Ediční středisko ČVUT
Last Updated: 30/09/11

CZECH UNIVERSITY OF LIFE SCIENCES IN PRAGUE

Česká zemědělská univerzita v Praze (ČZU/CUA)
Ul. Kamýcká 129, 165 21 Praha, 6-Suchdol
Tel: +420 224 381 076
Fax: +420 220 920 431
EMail: stichova@rektorat.czu.cz
Website: http://www.czu.cz

Rector: Jiří Balík Tel: +420 224 384 082 EMail: balik@af.czu.cz

Kvestor: Josef Vojáček
Tel: +420 224 384 083 EMail: kvestor@rektorat.czu.cz

International Relations: Michal Lošák, Vice-Rector
Tel: +420 224 384 077, Fax: +420 224 382 848 EMail: iro@czu.cz

Faculties

Agrobiology, Food and Natural Resources (Agronomy; Animal Husbandry; Applied Chemistry; Aquaculture; Cattle Breeding; Crop Production; Fishery; Food Science; Fruit Production; Harvest Technology; Horticulture; Natural Resources; Organic Chemistry; Soil Conservation; Soil Management; Soil Science; Vegetable Production; Veterinary Science; Viticulture); **Economics and Management** (Accountancy; Administration; Agricultural Business; Agricultural Economics; Agricultural Equipment; Banking; Business and Commerce; Economics; Finance; Human Resources; Information Technology; Management; Marketing; Statistics; Taxation); **Engineering** (Automation and Control Engineering; Electrical Engineering; Materials Engineering; Mathematics; Mechanical Engineering; Physics); **Environmental Science** (Ecology; Irriga-

tion; Water Management; Water Science); **Forestry, Wildlife and Wood Sciences** (Forestry; Wildlife; Wood Technology)

Institutes

Education and Communication (Agriculture; Communication Studies; Education; Educational Psychology; Forestry; Horticulture; Pedagogy; Veterinary Science); **Tropical and Subtropics** (Tropical Agriculture)

History: The origins go back to 1786 when the Department of Agriculture was established at Charles Ferdinand University. Founded 1906 as Faculty of Agriculture at Prague Polytechnic (now CTU) . Independent University established 1952. Acquired present status 1995. Formerly known as Czech University of Agriculture in Prague.

Governing Bodies: Senate; Board of Trustees

Academic Year: October to September (October-February; March-September)

Admission Requirements: Secondary school certificate (Maturitní vysvědčeni) and entrance examination

Fees: None

Main Language(s) of Instruction: Czech

International Co-operation: Participates in the Socrates and Erasmus programmes and Ceepus

Accrediting Agencies: Ministry of Education, Youth and Sports

Degrees and Diplomas: *Bakalář*: Agricultural Engineering; Forestry Engineering; Economics, 3 yrs; *Magistr*: Agricultural Engineering; Forestry Engineering (Inž.), 5 yrs; *Doktor*: Agricultural and Forestry Sciences; Economics and Management; Natural Resources Sciences (PhD), a further 3 yrs

Student Services: Academic counselling, Canteen, Foreign student adviser, Foreign Studies Centre, Health services, Language programs, Sports facilities

Student Residential Facilities: For 2,200 students in student hostels

Special Facilities: Agricultural Farm in Lány ; University Farms in Kostelec and Černými Lesy

Libraries: Central Library

Publications: Scientia Agriculturae Bohemica *(quarterly)*
Last Updated: 30/09/11

INSTITUTE OF CHEMICAL TECHNOLOGY IN PRAGUE

Vysoká škola chemicko-technologická v Praze (VŠCHT PRAHA)
Technická 5, 166 28 Praha, 6
Tel: +420 220 444 144
Fax: +420 220 445 018
EMail: rektor@vscht.cz
Website: http://www.vscht.cz

Rector: Josef Koubek
Tel: +420 222 044 3824 EMail: Josef.Koubek@vscht.cz

Registrar: Ivana Chválná
Tel: +420 220 443 162, Fax: +420 224 355 113
EMail: Ivana.Chvalna@vscht.cz

International Relations: Tomáš Ruml, Vice-Rector for International Relations Tel: +420 220 443 022 EMail: Tomas.Ruml@vscht.cz

Faculties

Chemical Engineering (Ceramics and Glass Technology; Chemical Engineering; Inorganic Chemistry; Metallurgical Engineering; Organic Chemistry; Physical Chemistry; Polymer and Plastics Technology; Solid State Physics); **Chemical Technology** (Analytical Chemistry; Automation and Control Engineering; Chemical Engineering; Food Science; Food Technology; Mathematics; Physical Chemistry; Physics; Robotics); **Environmental Technology** (Applied Chemistry; Environmental Engineering; Environmental Management; Natural Resources; Petroleum and Gas Engineering; Power Engineering); **Food and Biochemical Technology** (Applied Chemistry; Biochemistry; Chemistry; Dairy; Food Science; Food Technology; Microbiology)

History: Founded 1952. A State institution.

Admission Requirements: Secondary school certificate (Maturitní vysvědčeni)

Fees: (Koruna): 125,000 per annum

Main Language(s) of Instruction: Czech, English

International Co-operation: With more than 100 universities and institutions mostly in Europe, but also in the USA, Canada, Japan and other countries

Degrees and Diplomas: *Bakalář (Bc)*: 3 yrs; *Magistr.* Engineering (Ing.), 2 yrs; *Doktor (PhD)*: a further 3 yrs by thesis

Student Services: Academic counselling, Canteen, Foreign student adviser, Health services, Language programs, Sports facilities

Student Residential Facilities: Yes

Libraries: c. 100,000 vols; c. 300 subscriptions to periodicals

Press or Publishing House: ICT Press

Last Updated: 03/10/11

JAN EVANGELISTA PURKYNĚ UNIVERSITY IN ÚSTÍ NAD LABEM

Univerzita Jana Evangelisty Purkyně v Ústí nad Labem (UJEP)
Hoření 13, 400 96 Ústí nad Labem
Tel: +420 475 282 111
Fax: +420 472 772 982
Website: http://www.ujep.cz

Rector: René Wokoun
Tel: +420 475 282 115 EMail: rektor@ujep.cz

Kvestor: Jana Janáková
Tel: +420 475 282 116 EMail: jana.janakova@ujep.cz

Faculties

Art and Design (Art History; Ceramic Art; Fashion Design; Glass Art; Graphic Design; Interior Design; Media Studies; Painting and Drawing; Photography; Textile Design); **Education** (Education); **Environment** (Ecology; Environmental Management; Environmental Studies; Waste Management; Water Management); **Philosophy** (Philosophy); **Production Technology and Management** (Management; Production Engineering); **Social and Economics Studies** (Accountancy; Business Administration; Development Studies; Economics; Finance; Information Technology; Law; Mathematics; Modern Languages; Political Sciences; Regional Planning; Social Work; Statistics; Town Planning)

Institutes

Health Studies (Ergotherapy; Midwifery; Physical Therapy); **Production Technology and Management** (Design; Economics; Industrial Management; Management; Materials Engineering; Mechanical Engineering; Technology); **Slavonic and Germanic Studies** (Germanic Studies; Slavic Languages)

History: Founded 1954 as Higher Teacher Training College. Acquired present status and title 1991.

Academic Year: September to August (September-January; February-August)

Admission Requirements: Secondary school certificate (Maturitní vysvědčeni ze střední školy)

Fees: (US Dollars): Foreign students, c. 3,100 per annum

Main Language(s) of Instruction: Czech, English

International Co-operation: With universities in Germany, France, United Kingdom, Italy, Sweden, Finland, Austria, Poland, Slovak Republic, Greece

Degrees and Diplomas: *Bakalář.* Environment (Bc); Production Technology and Management (Bc.); Social and Economics Studies (Bc.), 3 yrs; *Bakalář umění*: Art and Design (BcA.), 4 yrs; *Inženýr*: Environment (Ing.); Social and Economics Studies (Ing.), a further 2 yrs; *Magistr*. Teaching, middle secondary level, 4 yrs; *Magistr*. Teaching, secondary level, 5 yrs; *Magistr umění*: Art and Design (MgA.), a further 2 yrs; *Doktor*. Physics; Music Theory; Art Theory (Ph.D;), a further 3 yrs

Student Services: Academic counselling, Canteen, Cultural centre, Employment services, Foreign student adviser, Foreign Studies Centre, Health services, Language programs, Social counselling, Sports facilities

Student Residential Facilities: For c. 1,800 students

Libraries: 253,513 vols

Publications: Acta Universitatis Purkyniana
Last Updated: 03/10/11

JANÁČEK ACADEMY OF MUSIC AND PERFORMING ARTS IN BRNO

Janáčkova akademie múzických umění v Brně (JAMU)
Ul. Beethovenova 2, 662 15 Brno
Tel: +420 542 591 111
Fax: +420 542 591 140
EMail: jamu@jamu.cz; rektor@jamu.cz
Website: http://www.jamu.cz

Rektor: Václav Cejpek (2003-)
Tel: +420 542 591 101, Fax: +420 542 591 140
EMail: rektor@jamu.cz

Kvestor-Bursar: Lenka Valová
Tel: +420 542 591 115 EMail: valova@jamu.cz

International Relations: Leoš Faltus, Prorektor
EMail: faltus@jamu.cz

Faculties

Music (Music; Music Theory and Composition; Musical Instruments; Musicology; Theatre); **Theatre** (Acting; Performing Arts; Theatre)

History: Founded 1881 as Conservatoire of Dramatic Arts, Brno, acquired present status 1945 and title 1947, named after Leoš Janáček. A State institution.

Governing Bodies: Senate

Admission Requirements: Secondary school leaving certificate

Main Language(s) of Instruction: Czech, German, English for lifelong learning courses

Accrediting Agencies: Ministry of Education, Youth and Sports

Degrees and Diplomas: *Bakalář*. Church Music; Composition; Orchestra and Choir ; Voice; Opera Direction; Music Management; Theatre Directing; Dramaturgy; Theatre Management; Drama in Education; Stage Design; Clown Scenic and Film Design; Radio and Television Dramaturgy and Scriptwriting (BcA); Stage Technology; Drama Education for the Deaf; Piano, Organ; Harpsichord; Violin; Viola; Violoncello; Double-Bass; Guitar; Flute; Oboe; Clarinet; Bassoon; French Horn; Trumpet; Trombone; Percussion Instruments (BcA); *Magistr*. Composition; Orchestra and Choir Conducting; Voice; Violin; Viola; Drama; Theatre Directing; Theatre Dramaturgy; Theatre Management; Drama in Education; Musical Acting; Radio and Television Dramaturgy and Scriptwriting; Stage Design; Dance Pedagogy (MgA); *Doktor*. Interpretation and Theory of Interpretation; Composition and Theory of Composition; Theatre Management; Theatre and Education; Dramaturgy and Creative Writing; Dramatic Creation; Author Training; Stage Design (PhD)

Student Services: Academic counselling, Canteen, Foreign student adviser, Foreign Studies Centre, Health services, Language programs

Student Residential Facilities: Yes

Special Facilities: Theatre Studio

Libraries: Yes

Publications: Obcăsník *(biennially)*
Last Updated: 01/10/09

MASARYK UNIVERSITY

Masarykova univerzita (MU)
Žerotínovo nám 9, 601 77 Brno
Tel: +420 549 491 011
Fax: +420 549 491 060
EMail: info@muni.cz; studjni@rect.muni.cz
Website: http://www.muni.cz

Rector: Petr Fiala (2004-)
Tel: +420 549 491 001, Fax: +420 549 491 060
EMail: rektor@muni.cz

Administrative Officer: Simona Brancitora
Tel: +420 54949 5367, Fax: +420 54949 6611
EMail: brancitora@rect.muni.cz

International Relations: Petra Judova, Director Office for International Studies Tel: +420 549 49382, Fax: +420 549 491113

Faculties

Arts (Aesthetics; American Studies; Archaeology; Art History; Baltic Languages; Classical Languages; Czech; Dutch; Education;

English; Ethnology; Film; German; History; Japanese; Linguistics; Museum Studies; Musicology; Philosophy; Psychology; Religion; Romance Languages; Scandinavian Languages; Slavic Languages; Theatre; Visual Arts); **Economics and Administration** (Administration; Applied Mathematics; Business Administration; Communication Studies; Computer Science; Economics; Finance; Information Technology; Law; Public Administration; Regional Studies); **Education** (Art Education; Biology; Chemistry; Civics; Czech; Education; English; Family Studies; French; Geography; German; Health Education; History; Information Sciences; Literature; Mathematics; Modern Languages; Music Education; Native Language; Native Language Education; Physical Education; Physics; Primary Education; Psychology; Russian; Special Education; Technology Education); **Informatics** (Computer Engineering; Computer Graphics; Computer Science; Design; Information Technology); **Law** (Administrative Law; Civil Law; Commercial Law; Constitutional Law; Criminal Law; Economic and Finance Policy; Economics; Environmental Studies; European Union Law; History of Law; International Law; Labour Law; Law; Political Sciences); **Medicine** (Anaesthesiology; Anatomy; Biochemistry; Biology; Biophysics; Cardiology; Dentistry; Dermatology; Embryology and Reproduction Biology; Ethics; Forensic Medicine and Dentistry; Gastroenterology; Gerontology; Gynaecology and Obstetrics; Haematology; Health Administration; Histology; Immunology; Laboratory Techniques; Medicine; Microbiology; Midwifery; Neurology; Nursing; Nutrition; Occupational Health; Oncology; Ophthalmology; Optometry; Orthopaedics; Otorhinolaryngology; Paediatrics; Pathology; Pharmacology; Physiology; Plastic Surgery; Pneumology; Psychiatry and Mental Health; Radiology; Rehabilitation and Therapy; Social and Preventive Medicine; Stomatology; Surgery; Urology; Venereology); **Science** (Anthropology; Astrophysics; Biochemistry; Biology; Biomedical Engineering; Biophysics; Botany; Chemistry; Earth Sciences; Environmental Studies; Geography; Geology; Mathematics; Molecular Biology; Natural Sciences; Physics; Statistics; Toxicology; Zoology); **Social Studies** (Anthropology; Environmental Studies; European Studies; Gender Studies; International Studies; Journalism; Media Studies; Political Sciences; Psychology; Social Work; Sociology) *Dean*: Ladislav Rabušic; **Sports Studies** (Physical Therapy; Social Sciences; Sports; Sports Management; Sports Medicine)

Further Information: Also Summer School of Slavonic Studies, University of the Third Age, Central European Studies Programme, Tesol Te and Faculty Hospital BRNO.

History: Founded 1919 with Faculties of Law and Medicine; Faculty of Science added 1920 and Faculty of Arts 1921. Closed 1939 during the German occupation, reopened 1945. Became Jana Evangelista Purkyně University 1960. Reverted to former name 1989.

Governing Bodies: University Council

Academic Year: September to June (September-January; February-June)

Admission Requirements: Secondary school certificate (Maturitní vysvědčeni) and entrance examination; also working knowledge of the Czech language except for courses in English

Fees: None. Foreign students, (US Dollars): c. 3,000-9,000 per annum

Main Language(s) of Instruction: Czech. Also English in special courses.

International Co-operation: Participates in the Socrates and Leonardo programmes

Degrees and Diplomas: *Bakalář (Bc)*: 3 yrs; *Doktor medicíny*: Medicine (MUDr), 6 yrs; *Magistr (Mgr)*: a further 2 yrs; *Doktor (PhD)*: a further 2-3 yrs by thesis

Student Services: Academic counselling, Canteen, Cultural centre, Employment services, Foreign student adviser, Foreign Studies Centre, Handicapped facilities, Health services, Language programs, Social counselling, Sports facilities

Student Residential Facilities: For 3,800 students

Special Facilities: Botanical Garden. Centre for Cultivation of Medicinal Herbs

Libraries: 9 central libraries, total, 1.6 mi vols.; Faculty libraries

Publications: Special Periodical Publications of the Faculties *(biennially)*; Universitas *(biennially)*

Press or Publishing House: University Press
Last Updated: 03/10/11

MENDEL UNIVERSITY OF AGRICULTURE AND FORESTRY IN BRNO IN BRNO

Mendelova zemědělská a lesnická univerzita v Brně (MZLU)

Zemědělská 1, 613 00 Brno
Tel: +420 545 131 111
Fax: +420 545 211 128
EMail: info@mendelu.cz
Website: http://www.mendelu.cz

Rektor: Jaroslav Hlušek (2006-)
Tel: +420 545 133 098
EMail: rektor@mendelu.cz; jaroslav.hlusek@mendelu.cz

Kvestor-Bursar: Věra Sedlářová
Tel: +420 545 135 009, Fax: +420 545 212 049
EMail: kvestor@mendelu.cz; vera.sedlarova@mendelu.cz

International Relations: Libor Grega, Vice-Rector
Tel: +420 545 132 600 EMail: libor.grega@mendelu.cz

Faculties

Agronomy (Agriculture; Agronomy; Apiculture; Applied Chemistry; Automotive Engineering; Biochemistry; Biology; Cattle Breeding; Chemistry; Crop Production; Ecology; Engineering; Environmental Engineering; Fishery; Food Technology; Meteorology; Microbiology; Molecular Biology; Physical Education; Plant and Crop Protection; Soil Science; Zoology); **Business and Economics** (Accountancy; Business Administration; Business and Commerce; Computer Science; Economics; Finance; Law; Management; Marketing; Operations Research; Social Sciences; Statistics; Taxation); **Forestry and Wood Technology** (Forest Economics; Forest Management; Forest Products; Forestry; Furniture Design; Landscape Architecture; Natural Resources; Tropical Agriculture; Wood Technology); **Horticulture** *(Lednice na Moravě)* (Fruit Production; Horticulture; Landscape Architecture; Vegetable Production; Viticulture); **Regional Development and International Studies** (Development Studies; International Studies; Regional Studies)

Institutes
Lifelong Education

Further Information: Also Institute for Information System (IIS); Institute for Operation of Information Technology and Institute for Scientific Information. 3 Estates (Agricultural, Forestry, Horticultural); 1 School Farm, 1 Forest.

History: Founded 1919, acquired present status and title 1995.

Governing Bodies: Academic Senate

Academic Year: September to August (September-January; February-August)

Admission Requirements: Secondary school certificate (Maturitní vysvědčeni) and entrance examination

Fees: None

Main Language(s) of Instruction: Czech

Degrees and Diplomas: *Bakalář (Bc)*: 3-4 yrs; *Magistr (Mgr)*: a further 2 yrs; *Doktor (PhD)*: a further 3 yrs by thesis following Magistr

Student Services: Academic counselling, Canteen, Foreign student adviser, Foreign Studies Centre, Handicapped facilities, Health services, Language programs, Sports facilities

Student Residential Facilities: For c. 1,800 students

Special Facilities: Botany Garden and Arboretum, Brno. Computing Centre

Libraries: Central Library, c. 400,000 vols

Publications: Acta Universitatis Agriculturae; Silviculturae Mendelianae Brunensis

Press or Publishing House: University Publishing Centre
Last Updated: 03/10/11

PALACKÝ UNIVERSITY IN OLOMOUC

Univerzita Palackého v Olomouci (UP)

Křížkovského 8, 771 47 Olomouc
Tel: +420 585 631 111
Fax: +420 585 232 035
EMail: kancler@upol.cz
Website: http://www.upol.cz

Rektor: Miroslav Mašláň
Tel: +420 585 631 001, Fax: +420 585 222 731
EMail: rektor@upol.cz

Bursar: Tomáš Kopřiva
Tel: +420 585 631 008 EMail: tomas.kopriva@upol.cz

International Relations: Michal Malacka, Vice-Rector for External Relations Tel: +420 585 631 005 EMail: michal.malacka@upol.cz

Centres
Lifelong Education

Faculties
Education (Anthropology; Art Education; Biology; Czech; Education; English; German; Health Education; Information Technology; Literature; Mathematics; Mathematics Education; Music; Music Education; Native Language; Pathology; Primary Education; Psychology; Social Sciences; Special Education; Technology Education); **Law** (Administrative Law; Civil Law; Comparative Law; Constitutional Law; Criminal Law; Economics; European Union Law; Finance; Fiscal Law; History of Law; International Law; Labour Law; Law; Modern Languages; Political Sciences; Private Law; Public Law; Social Sciences; Taxation); **Medicine and Dentistry** (Anaesthesiology; Anatomy; Applied Chemistry; Biochemistry; Biology; Biophysics; Cardiology; Cell Biology; Czech; Dental Technology; Dentistry; Dermatology; Embryology and Reproduction Biology; English; Ethics; Forensic Medicine and Dentistry; Genetics; German; Gynaecology and Obstetrics; Haematology; Health Administration; Histology; Hygiene; Immunology; Laboratory Techniques; Latin; Medicine; Microbiology; Midwifery; Modern Languages; Molecular Biology; Native Language; Neurology; Nursing; Occupational Health; Oncology; Ophthalmology; Oral Pathology; Orthopaedics; Otorhinolaryngology; Paediatrics; Pathology; Pharmacology; Physical Therapy; Physiology; Pneumology; Psychiatry and Mental Health; Radiology; Rehabilitation and Therapy; Social and Preventive Medicine; Sports; Stomatology; Surgery; Urology; Venereology); **Philosophy** (Adult Education; American Studies; Art History; Arts and Humanities; Asian Studies; Chinese; Classical Languages; Czech; Dutch; Economics; English Studies; European Studies; Film; French; German; History; Italian; Japanese; Jewish Studies; Journalism; Linguistics; Literature; Media Studies; Modern Languages; Musicology; Native Language; Philology; Philosophy; Polish; Political Sciences; Portuguese; Psychology; Romance Languages; Russian; Slavic Languages; Social Sciences; Sociology; Spanish; Theatre); **Physical Education** (Anthropology; Leisure Studies; Parks and Recreation; Physical Education; Physical Therapy; Physiology; Social Sciences; Sports); **Science** (Analytical Chemistry; Anthropology; Applied Physics; Biochemistry; Biology; Botany; Cell Biology; Chemistry; Development Studies; Earth Sciences; Ecology; Genetics; Geography; Geology; Inorganic Chemistry; Mathematics and Computer Science; Modern Languages; Optics; Organic Chemistry; Physical Chemistry; Physics; Zoology); **Theology** *(St. Cyril and Methodius Faculty of Theology)* (Religious Education; Religious Studies; Theology)

Further Information: Also Teaching Hospital

History: Founded 1566 and closed 1860. Re-established and acquired present status 1946.

Governing Bodies: University Academic Senate

Academic Year: September to July (September-December; February-July)

Admission Requirements: Secondary school certificate (Maturitní vysvědčení) and entrance examination

Fees: None for those who study in Czech

Main Language(s) of Instruction: Czech, English

International Co-operation: With universities in Europe and USA. Also participates in Erasmus, Comenius, Lingua, Minerva, Leonardo, Ceepus and Aktion programmes

Accrediting Agencies: Ministry of Education, Youth and Sports

Degrees and Diplomas: *Bakalář (Bc)*: 3 yrs; *Doktor medicíny*: Medicine; Dentistry (MUDr), 6 yrs; *Magistr (Mgr)*: a further 2 yrs; *Doktor (PhD)*: a further 3 yrs

Student Services: Academic counselling, Canteen, Cultural centre, Foreign student adviser, Handicapped facilities, Health services, Language programs, Social counselling, Sports facilities

Student Residential Facilities: For 4,052 students

Special Facilities: Art Centre. Botanical Garden. Audiovisual Centre. Teaching Hospital. Archives. Centre for Innovation and Technolgy Transfer

Libraries: Central Library, departmental reference libraries, total, c. 1m. vols

Publications: Acta Universitatis palaskianae *(annually)*

Press or Publishing House: Palacký University Press

Last Updated: 03/10/11

POLICE ACADEMY OF THE CZECH REPUBLIC IN PRAGUE
Policejní akademie České republicky v Praze (PAČR)
PO Box 54, Ul. Lhotecká 559/7, 143 01 Praha, 4
Tel: +420 974 828 140 +420 241 714 809
Fax: +420 974 827 273
EMail: polac@polac.cz
Website: http://www.polac.cz

Rector: Vladimir Plecitý
Tel: +420 974 828 501, Fax: +420 974 827 273
EMail: plecity@polac.cz

Kvestor: František Bašta
Tel: +420 974 828 508 EMail: kvestor@polac.cz

International Relations: Ivana Stachová, Director
Tel: +420 974 828 557 EMail: zs@polac.cz

Faculties
Security and Law (Criminology; Police Studies); **Security Management** (Administrative Law; Information Sciences; Public Administration)

History: Founded 1992. The Police Academy of the Czech Republic is an institution of higher education responsible to the Ministry of Interior. A State institution.

Governing Bodies: Senate

Academic Year: September to June

Admission Requirements: Secondary school certificate (Maturitní vysvědčeni) and entrance examination

Main Language(s) of Instruction: Czech

Degrees and Diplomas: *Bakalář*: Security and Legal Studies; Crisis Management in State Administration and Local Self-Government (Bc), 3 yrs; *Magistr*: Police Management and Criminalistics (Mgr), a further 2 yrs; *Doktor*: Police Management and Criminalistics (Ph.D), 3-4 yrs

Student Services: Academic counselling, Canteen, Cultural centre, Employment services, Health services, Nursery care, Social counselling, Sports facilities

Student Residential Facilities: Yes

Libraries: Study library; Science library; Special library
Last Updated: 03/10/11

SILESIAN UNIVERSITY IN OPAVA
Slezská univerzita v Opavě (SU)
Na Rybníčku 1, 746 01 Opava
Tel: +420 553 684 621
Fax: +420 553 718 019
EMail: rektorat@slu.cz
Website: http://www.slu.cz

Rector: Rudolf Žáček
Tel: +420 553 684 620, Fax: +420 553 718 019
EMail: rudolf.zacek@slu.cz

Centres
Extramural Education

Faculties
Business Administration *(Karviná)* (Business Administration); **Philosophy and Science** (Natural Sciences; Philosophy)

Institutes
Mathematics (Mathematics)

History: Founded 1991, incorporating faculties of Masaryk University, Brno.

Governing Bodies: Academic Senate; Scientific Council; Board of Directors

Academic Year: September to August (September-February; February-August)

Admission Requirements: Secondary school certificate (Maturitní vysvědčeni) or recognized foreign equivalent, and entrance examination

Fees: None for Czech students

Main Language(s) of Instruction: Czech, English

International Co-operation: Participates in Erasmus/Socrates Programmes

Accrediting Agencies: Ministry of Education, Youth and Sports

Degrees and Diplomas: *Bakalář*: Czech Literature (Bc); Economics Policy and Administration; Economics and Management; System Engineering and Computer Science; Hotel and Restaurant; Tourism; Mathematics; Physics; Computer Science; Public Administration; History; Library Science; Linguistics; Photography (Bc), 3 yrs; *Inženýr*: Economics Policy and Administration; Economics and Management; System Engineering and Computer Science (Ing), a further 2 yrs; *Magistr*: Mathematics; Physics; Computer Science; History; Linguistics; Photography (Mgr), a further 2 yrs; *Doktor*: History; Theoretical Physics and Astrophysics; Geometry and Global Analysis; Mathematics; Physics; Business Economics and Management (PhD), following Magistr

Student Services: Canteen, Cultural centre, Foreign student adviser, Language programs, Sports facilities

Student Residential Facilities: Yes

Libraries: Central Library, c. 60,000 vols; English / German / Austrian library

Publications: Differential Geometry and its Applications
Last Updated: 03/10/11

TECHNICAL UNIVERSITY OF LIBEREC
Technická univerzita v Liberci (TUL)
Ul. Hálkova 6, 461 17 Liberec, 1
Tel: +420 485 351 111
Fax: +420 485 105 882
EMail: info@tul.cz
Website: http://www.tul.cz

Rector: Zdeněk Kůs
Tel: +420 485 353 597, Fax: +420 485 105 882
EMail: rektor@tul.cz

Kvestor-Bursar: Vladimír Stach
Tel: +420 485 105 617 EMail: vladimir.stach@tul.cz

International Relations: Oldřich Jirsák, Vice-Rector
Tel: +420 485 353 233, Fax: +420 485 153 113
EMail: oldrich.jirsak@tul.cz

Faculties
Architecture (Architecture); **Economics** (Accountancy; Business Administration; Communication Studies; Computer Science; Economics; Finance; Information Management; Insurance; Law; Modern Languages; Statistics); **Education** (Economics; Education; Geography; Geography (Human); History; Management; Mathematics; Pedagogy; Philology; Philosophy; Physical Education; Physics; Special Education; Sports); **Mechanical Engineering** (Automation and Control Engineering; Engineering; Industrial Engineering; Materials Engineering; Mechanical Engineering; Production Engineering); **Mechatronics and Interdisciplinary Engineering Studies** (Computer Engineering; Computer Science; Electronic Engineering; Engineering; Information Technology); **Textile Engineering** (Textile Design; Textile Technology)

Institutes
Health Studies

History: Founded 1953 as College, acquired present status and title 1995.

Governing Bodies: Senate

Academic Year: September to June (September-January; February-June)

Admission Requirements: Secondary school certificate (Maturitní vysvědčeni)

Main Language(s) of Instruction: Czech

Accrediting Agencies: Ministry of Education, Youth and Sports

Degrees and Diplomas: *Bakalář (Bc)*: 3 yrs; *Bakalář umění (MgA)*: 3 yrs; *Inženýr (Ing.)*: 2-5 yrs; *Inženýr*: Architecture (Ing.arch), 3 yrs; *Magistr (Mgr)*: a further 4-5 yrs; *Doktor (PhD)*: a further 3 yrs by thesis

Student Services: Academic counselling, Canteen, Handicapped facilities, Health services, Sports facilities

Student Residential Facilities: For 3,000 students

Libraries: Central Library, c. 45,000 vols

Publications: Annals of the University *(annually)*
Last Updated: 03/10/11

TECHNICAL UNIVERSITY OF OSTRAVA
Vysoká škola báňská - Technická univerzita Ostrava (VŠB-TUO)
17 Listopadu 15, Poruba, 708 33 Ostrava
Tel: +420(59) 7321 111
Fax: +420(59) 6918 507
EMail: info@vsb.cz; rector@vsb.cz
Website: http://www.vsb.cz

Rektor: Ivo Vondrák (2010-)
Tel: +420(59) 7325 279, Fax: +420(59) 6918 507
EMail: rektor@vsb.cz; ivo.vondrak@vsb.cz

Kvestor: Zdeněk Hodula
Tel: +420(59) 7325 276 +420(59) 7325 279,
Fax: +420(59) 6995 299
EMail: kvestor@vsb.cz; zdenek.hodula@vsb.cz

International Relations: Petr Klement, Vice-Rector
Tel: +420(59) 7321 223, Fax: +420(59) 7321 228
EMail: petr.klement@vsb.cz

Faculties
Civil Engineering (Building Technologies; Civil Engineering; Construction Engineering; Industrial Engineering; Mining Engineering; Transport Engineering); **Economics** (Accountancy; Applied Mathematics; Business Administration; Business Computing; Computer Engineering; Econometrics; Economics; Finance; Information Technology; Law; Management; Marketing; Public Administration); **Electrical Engineering and Computer Science** (Applied Mathematics; Computer Science; Electrical and Electronic Equipment and Maintenance; Electrical Engineering; Measurement and Precision Engineering; Power Engineering; Telecommunications Engineering); **Mechanical Engineering** (Automation and Control Engineering; Energy Engineering; Hydraulic Engineering; Machine Building; Materials Engineering; Mechanical Engineering; Mechanical Equipment and Maintenance; Mechanics; Robotics; Technology; Transport and Communications); **Metallurgy and Materials Engineering** (Analytical Chemistry; Automation and Control Engineering; Chemical Engineering; Chemistry; Environmental Management; Materials Engineering; Metal Techniques; Metallurgical Engineering; Physical Chemistry; Safety Engineering; Thermal Engineering); **Mining and Geology** (Astronomy and Space Science; Environmental Engineering; Geological Engineering; Geology; Mathematics; Mining Engineering; Physics; Safety Engineering; Surveying and Mapping); **Safety Engineering** (Safety Engineering)

Higher Institutes
Analytical Chemistry and Material Testing (Analytical Chemistry; Physics); **European Studies**

Research Centres
Energy (Energy Engineering; Environmental Engineering; Natural Resources); **Nanotechnology** (Nanotechnology)

History: Founded 1716 as School of Mining and Metallurgy at Jáchymov in Bohemia, became part of the Charles University of Prague 1763. Moved to Slovakia 1770 as Mining Academy, Banská Štiavnica, and Příbram, Bohemia 1849. Acquired university status 1904 and moved to present location 1945. A State institution.

Governing Bodies: Academic Council

Academic Year: September to May (September-December; February-May)

Admission Requirements: Secondary school certificate (Maturitní vysvědčeni) and entrance examination

Fees: None

Main Language(s) of Instruction: Czech

Degrees and Diplomas: *Bakalář (Bc)*: 3 yrs; *Inženýr (Ing)*: a further 2 yrs; *Doktor (PhD)*: a further 2-3 yrs by thesis

Student Services: Canteen, Cultural centre, Employment services, Foreign student adviser, Handicapped facilities, Health services, Sports facilities

Student Residential Facilities: Yes

Special Facilities: Mineral Collection.

Libraries: Central Library, c. 560,000 vols

Publications: Proceedings of Scientific Papers

Last Updated: 03/10/11

TOMAS BATA UNIVERSITY IN ZLÍN

Univerzita Tomáše Bati ve Zlíně (UTB)

Mostni 5139, 760 01 Zlin
Tel: +420 576 032 754
Fax: +420 576 032 444
EMail: kancler@utb.cz
Website: http://www.utb.cz

Rektor: Petr Sáha
Tel: +420 576 032 222, Fax: +420 576 032 444
EMail: rektor@utb.cz

Bursar: Alexander Cerný

International Relations: Berenika Hausnerová, Vice-Rector for International Relations

Faculties

Applied Informatics (Automation and Control Engineering; Chemical Engineering; Computer Engineering; Electronic Engineering; Engineering Management; Mathematics; Measurement and Precision Engineering); **Humanities** (American Studies; Business Administration; English Studies; German; Modern Languages; Pedagogy; Philology; Public Health); **Logistics and Crisis Management** (Management); **Management and Economics** (Economics; Management); **Multimedia Communications** (Communication Studies; Fashion Design; Graphic Design; Multimedia; Visual Arts); **Technology** (Chemistry; Food Technology; Materials Engineering; Polymer and Plastics Technology; Production Engineering; Technology)

History: Founded 2000. Acquired present status 2001.

Governing Bodies: Academic Senate; Scientific Board; Board of Governors

Academic Year: September to June

Admission Requirements: High school diploma, entrance examination

Fees: (Koruna): Czech language education, free of charge; admission fee, 250-510

Main Language(s) of Instruction: Czech; English

International Co-operation: Participates in Socrates/ Erasmus programmes; number of research projects with China, India

Accrediting Agencies: Ministry of Education, Youth and Sports

Degrees and Diplomas: *Bakalář (Bc)*: 3 yrs; *Magistr (M.Sc.; M.A.)*: a further 2 yrs; *Doktor (Ph.D.)*: a further 3 yrs. Also Postdoctoral studies (Postdoktorské)

Student Services: Academic counselling, Canteen, Cultural centre, Employment services, Foreign student adviser, Foreign Studies Centre, Handicapped facilities, Language programs, Social counselling, Sports facilities

Student Residential Facilities: For c. 860 students

Libraries: Central Library

Publications: Universalia, bilingual (Czech and English) *(quarterly)*

Last Updated: 03/10/11

UNIVERSITY OF ECONOMICS, PRAGUE

Vysoká škola ekonomická v Praze (VŠE)

Nám. Winstona Churchilla 4, 130 67 Praha, 3
Tel: +420 224 095 111
Fax: +420 224 095 673
EMail: machkova@vse.cz
Website: http://www.vse.cz

Rector: Richard Hindls
Tel: +420 224 095 720, Fax: +420 224 095 699
EMail: hindis@vse.cz

Kvestor: Libor Svoboda

International Relations: Hana Machková, Vice-Rector
Tel: +420 224 095 799, Fax: +420 224 095 695

Centres

European Studies (Cultural Studies; Economics; European Languages; European Studies; European Union Law; History; Law; Modern Languages; Political Sciences)

Faculties

Business Administration (Art Management; Business Administration; Human Resources; Management; Marketing; Psychology; Sociology; Transport Management); **Economics and Public Administration** (Development Studies; Economic History; Economics; Environmental Management; Law; Philosophy; Public Administration; Regional Studies; Social Policy); **Finance and Accounting** (Accountancy; Banking; Economics; Finance; Human Resources; Insurance; Management); **Informatics and Statistics** (Demography and Population; Econometrics; Information Management; Information Technology; Mathematics and Computer Science; Operations Research; Statistics); **International Relations** (Business and Commerce; Commercial Law; English; European Studies; European Union Law; German; International Business; International Economics; International Relations; Political Sciences; Romance Languages; Russian; Tourism); **Management** *(Jindřichův Hradec)* (Business Administration; Health Administration; Information Management; Management; Public Administration; Public Health)

Institutes

Management *(French-Czech Institute)*

Further Information: Also Central and East European Studies Programme

History: Founded 1949 as Prague College of Economic Sciences. Acquired present status and title 1953. A State institution.

Academic Year: September to June (September-January; February-June)

Admission Requirements: Secondary school certificate (Maturitní vysvědčeni) and entrance examination

Main Language(s) of Instruction: Czech

International Co-operation: With more than 70 universities worldwide. Also participates in the Socrates programme

Degrees and Diplomas: *Bakalář (Bc.)*: 3 yrs; *Inženýr (Ing.)*: 5 yrs; *Doktor (PhD)*: 3 yrs

Student Services: Academic counselling, Canteen, Foreign student adviser, Foreign Studies Centre, Handicapped facilities, Language programs, Social counselling, Sports facilities

Student Residential Facilities: For c. 5,400 students

Libraries: c. 460,000 vols

Publications: Acta Economica Pragensia *(biannually)*; Politická Ekonomie; Prague Economic Papers *(quarterly)*

Press or Publishing House: Zpravodaj Uše

Last Updated: 03/10/11

UNIVERSITY OF HRADEC KRÁLOVÉ

Univerzita Hradec Králové (UHK)

Rokitanského 62, 500 03 Hradec Králové, 3
Tel: +420 493 332 508
Fax: +420 495 545 911
EMail: eva.lenderova@uhk.cz
Website: http://www.uhk.cz

Rektor: Josef Hynek
Tel: +420 493-332-286 EMail: josef.hynek@uhk.cz

Kvestor-Bursar: Stanislav Klik
Tel: +420 493 331 511 EMail: stanislav.klik@uhk.cz

International Relations: Antonín Slabý, Prorektor
Tel: +420 493 331 512 EMail: antonin.slaby@uhk.cz

Faculties

Arts (African Studies; Archaeology; Archiving; Arts and Humanities; Czech; History; Latin American Studies; Modern Languages;

Philosophy; Political Sciences; Social Sciences; Sociology); **Education** (Art Education; Biology; Chemistry; Computer Science; Cultural Studies; Czech; Education; Educational Psychology; English; German; Literature; Mathematics; Multimedia; Music; Music Education; Native Language; Pedagogy; Physical Education; Physics; Preschool Education; Primary Education; Psychology; Religious Education; Slavic Languages; Social Studies; Social Work; Sociology; Special Education; Sports; Textile Design); **Informatics and Management** (Computer Science; Economics; English; German; Information Technology; Leisure Studies; Management; Tourism); **Science** (Biology; Chemistry; Computer Science; Mathematics; Physics)

Institutes
Social Work (Social Work)

History: Founded 1959 as Faculty of Education, reorganized 1992 as Higher School of Education and acquired present status and title 2000.

Governing Bodies: Academic Senate

Academic Year: September to June

Admission Requirements: Secondary school certificate (Maturitní vysvědčeni)

Main Language(s) of Instruction: Czech, English

International Co-operation: With universities in United Kingdom, Germany, France, Netherlands, Austria, Spain, Asia, USA, Mexico, Portugal. Also participates in the Socrates and Leonardo programmes.

Accrediting Agencies: Accreditation Commission

Degrees and Diplomas: *Bakalář (Bc)*: 3 yrs; *Magistr (Mgr, Ing)*: a further 2 yrs; *Doktor (PhD)*: by thesis

Student Services: Academic counselling, Employment services, Foreign student adviser, Handicapped facilities, Health services, Language programs, Sports facilities

Student Residential Facilities: Yes

Special Facilities: Art Gallery, Movie Studio

Libraries: Classical and electronic services

Press or Publishing House: GAUDEAMUS
Last Updated: 03/10/11

UNIVERSITY OF OSTRAVA
Ostravská univerzita v Ostravě (OU)
Dvořákova 7, 701 03 Ostrava
Tel: +420 596 160 151
Fax: +420 596 118 219
EMail: info@osu.cz
Website: http://www.osu.cz

Rektor: Jiří Močkoř
Tel: +420 597 091 001 EMail: Jiri.Mockor@osu.cz

Bursar: Jana Poloková
Tel: +420 597 091 004 EMail: Jana.Polokova@osu.cz

International Relations: Igor Fojtík, Vice-Rector for Coordination of Research and External Relations
Tel: +420 597 091 013 EMail: Igor.Fojtik@osu.cz

Faculties
Arts (American Studies; Art History; Czech; English Studies; Germanic Studies; History; Linguistics; Literature; Native Language; Philosophy; Psychology; Regional Studies; Romance Languages; Slavic Languages; Social and Community Services; Social Work); **Fine Arts** (Art History; Graphic Arts; Media Studies; Musical Instruments; Painting and Drawing; Sculpture; Singing); **Health Studies** (Anatomy; Biomedicine; Epidemiology; Forensic Medicine and Dentistry; Midwifery; Nursing; Pathology; Pharmacology; Physiology; Psychiatry and Mental Health; Public Health; Rehabilitation and Therapy; Surgery); **Pedagogical Studies** (Adult Education; Art Education; Communication Studies; Czech; Education; Educational Psychology; Foreign Languages Education; Information Technology; Literature; Mathematics Education; Music Education; Native Language; Native Language Education; Pedagogy; Physical Education; Primary Education; Religious Education; Social Sciences; Special Education; Technology Education); **Science** (Applied Mathematics; Biology; Biophysics; Chemistry; Computer Science; Development Studies; Ecology; Economics; Geography; Geology; Management; Mathematics; Modern Languages; Natural Sciences;

Physics; Regional Studies; Technology); **Social Studies** (Social Studies; Social Work)

Institutes
Research and Application of Fuzzy Modelling (Applied Mathematics); **Social Work** *(European Research Institute)* (Social Work)

History: Founded 1953 as Pedagogical School of Higher Learning at Opava. Became Pedagogical Institute 1959 and moved to Ostrava. Acquired present status and title 1991. A State institution.

Governing Bodies: Board of Trustees; Academic Senate

Academic Year: October to September (October-February; February-July)

Admission Requirements: Secondary school certificate (Maturitní vysvědčeni)

Fees: None

Main Language(s) of Instruction: Czech

International Co-operation: With universities in Austria, United Kingdom, France, Italy, Spain

Degrees and Diplomas: *Bakalář (Bc)*: 3 yrs; *Magistr (Mgr)*: 5 yrs; *Doktor (PhD)*: 3-5 yrs

Student Services: Canteen, Sports facilities

Student Residential Facilities: Yes

Special Facilities: Botanical Gardens. British Council Resource Centre

Libraries: University Library, c. 200,000 vols

Publications: Acta Facultatis Paedagogicae Universitatis Ostraviensis *(annually)*; Acta Facultatis Philosophicae Universitatis Ostraviensis (Studia Slavica, Historica, Psychologia Series) *(annually)*; Acta Facultatis Rerum Naturalium Universitatis Ostraviensis (Biologia-Ecologia, Geographia-Geologia, Physica-Chemia Series) *(annually)*; Acta Mathematica et Informatica Universitatis Ostraviensis *(annually)*

Press or Publishing House: University Publishing House
Last Updated: 03/10/11

UNIVERSITY OF PARDUBICE
Univerzita Pardubice (UPA)
Ul. Studentská 95, 532 10 Pardubice
Tel: +420 466 036 111
Fax: +420 466 036 361
EMail: promotion@upce.cz
Website: http://www.upce.cz

Rektor: Miroslav Ludwig (2010-)
Tel: +420 466 036 553 EMail: rektor@upce.cz

Kvestor-Bursar: Milan Bukač
Tel: +420 466 036 556, Fax: +420 466 036 365
EMail: kvestor@upce.cz

Centres
Ecology *(UEC)*; **Material Science**

Departments
Physical Education and Sports (Physical Education; Sports)

Faculties
Art Restoration (Arts and Humanities; Chemical Engineering; Modern Languages; Painting and Drawing; Restoration of Works of Art); **Arts and Philosophy** *(FHS)* (American Studies; Arts and Humanities; Cultural Studies; English Studies; German; History; Modern Languages; Philosophy; Religious Studies; Social Sciences); **Chemical Technology** *(FCHT)* (Analytical Chemistry; Applied Mathematics; Applied Physics; Biochemistry; Biological and Life Sciences; Chemical Engineering; Chemistry; Environmental Engineering; Food Technology; Graphic Arts; Inorganic Chemistry; Organic Chemistry; Physical Chemistry; Solid State Physics); **Economics and Administration** *(FES)* (Administration; Computer Engineering; Economics; Law; Management; Management Systems; Marketing; Mathematics and Computer Science; Public Administration; Public Law); **Electrical Engineering and Informatics** (Computer Engineering; Electrical Engineering; Information Technology; Software Engineering; Systems Analysis); **Health Studies** (Health Sciences; Midwifery; Nursing; Public Health); **Transport Engineering** *(DFJP, Jan Perner)* (Building Technologies; Civil Engineering; Electrical and Electronic Engineering;

Maintenance Technology; Materials Engineering; Mechanical Engineering; Safety Engineering; Transport and Communications; Transport Economics; Transport Engineering; Transport Management)

Laboratories

Solid State Chemistry *(Joint Laboratory (JLSSC))* (Chemical Engineering; Inorganic Chemistry; Materials Engineering; Solid State Physics)

Research Centres

New Inorganic Compounds and Advanced Materials (Chemical Engineering; Electronic Engineering; Inorganic Chemistry; Materials Engineering)

History: Founded 1950 as the Institute of Chemical Technology in Pardubice, became an independent higher education institution 1953. Reorganized 1991 when the Faculty of Chemical Technology and the Faculty of Economics and Administration became the nucleus of the future University. The Jan Perner Faculty of Transport Engineering was established in 1993 and the Faculty of Humanities in 2001. Acquired present status and title 1994. A public State institution.The university incorporated the Institut restaurování a konzervačnich technik Litomyšl, o.p.s.

Governing Bodies: Academic Senate; Scientific Council; Board of Directors

Academic Year: September to July (September-February; February-July)

Admission Requirements: Secondary school certificate (Maturitní vysvědceni) and entrance examination

Fees: For courses in English

Main Language(s) of Instruction: Czech, English

International Co-operation: Participates in the Tempus, Socrates/ Erasmus, Ceepus, Copernicus and other EU programmes

Degrees and Diplomas: *Bakalář (BC; BSc; BA)*: 3 yrs; *Inženýr (Ing.)*: 5 yrs; *Magistr (Mgr.; MA)*: 5 yrs or a further 2 yrs following BC; *Doktor (PhD)*: 3 yrs following MSc

Student Services: Academic counselling, Canteen, Cultural centre, Employment services, Foreign student adviser, Handicapped facilities, Language programs, Social counselling, Sports facilities

Student Residential Facilities: Student Hall for 1,888 students

Special Facilities: Art Gallery; Computer Centre

Libraries: Central Library, c. 196,000 vols

Publications: Scientific Papers *(annually)*

Last Updated: 03/10/11

UNIVERSITY OF SOUTH BOHEMIA IN ČESKÉ BUDĚJOVICE

Jihočeská univerzita v Českých Budějovicích (JCU)
Branišovská 31, 370 05 České Budějovice
Tel: +420 389 031 111
Fax: +420 385 310 348
EMail: rektorat@jcu.cz
Website: http://www.jcu.cz

Rektor: Tomáš Polívka
Tel: +420 389 032 001 EMail: rektor@jcu.cz

Kvestor-Bursar: Hana Kropáčková
Tel: +420 389 032 002 EMail: hkropack@jcu.cz

International Relations: Jan Zahradník
Tel: +420 389 032 007 EMail: prorektor-zahranici@jcu.cz

Faculties

Agriculture *(ZF)* (Agricultural Equipment; Agriculture; Anatomy; Animal Husbandry; Applied Chemistry; Biological and Life Sciences; Cattle Breeding; Crop Production; Ecology; Fishery; Genetics; Nutrition; Physical Education; Physiology; Veterinary Science); **Economics** (Accountancy; Applied Mathematics; Computer Science; Crafts and Trades; Development Studies; Economics; European Studies; Finance; Law; Management; Rural Planning; Rural Studies; Tourism); **Fisheries and Protection of Waters** (Fishery; Water Management; Water Science); **Health and Social Studies** *(ZSF)* (Economics; Ethics; Health Education; Information Technology; Laboratory Techniques; Law; Management; Medical Technology; Medicine; Nursing; Philosophy; Psychiatry and Mental Health; Psychology; Public Health; Radiology; Social and Preventive Med-

icine; Social Studies; Social Work; Toxicology); **Pedagogy** *(PF)* (Art Therapy; Biology; Chemistry; Czech; Education; English; Fine Arts; Geography; Geography (Human); Germanic Studies; Health Education; History; Information Sciences; Mathematics; Music; Pedagogy; Physics; Primary Education; Psychology; Romance Languages; Russian; Social Sciences; Sports); **Philosophy** *(FF)* (Philosophy); **Science** *(BF)* (Biological and Life Sciences; Biology; Chemistry; Mathematics; Physics); **Theology** *(TF)* (Bible; Canon Law; Civil Law; Education; Ethics; History of Religion; Philosophy; Psychology; Religion; Religious Studies; Sociology; Theology)

Institutes
Physical Biology (Biology)

Research Institutes
Fish Farming and Hydrobiology *(VURH, Vodňany)* (Fishery; Marine Biology)

Further Information: Also Branches in Vodňany and Český Krumlov

History: Founded 1991, incorporating the Faculty of Agronomy (detached part of Prague Agricultural University) with independent Faculty of Education, and recruiting additional staff from several research institutes of the Czechoslovak Academy of Sciences located in the area (Botany, Entomology, Hydrobiology, Landscape Ecology, Microbiology, Molecular Biology of Plants, Parasitology, Soil Science), and from local hospitals and religious institutions. Close extramural collaboration and a high proportion of part-time teachers remain a typical feature of the University, financed by the State.

Governing Bodies: Academic Senate, comprising selected representatives of academic staff and students

Academic Year: October to June (October-January, February-June)

Admission Requirements: Secondary school certificate (Maturitní vysvědceni) with leaving examination, and entrance examinations

Fees: (Euros): Foreign students, c. 3,000-7,000 per annum

Main Language(s) of Instruction: Czech. Also English for PhD students.

International Co-operation: Participates in the Socrates/Erasmus, Leonardo da Vinci, CEEPUS, Aktion, DAAD, Kontakt, Phare Projects programmes.

Degrees and Diplomas: *Bakalář (Bc)*: 3 yrs; *Inženýr (Inž.)*: 2 yrs following Bachelor; *Magistr (Mgr)*: 2 yrs following Bachelor; *Doktor (PhD)*: 3 yrs

Student Services: Canteen, Employment services, Handicapped facilities, Health services, Sports facilities

Student Residential Facilities: For c. 2,270 students

Special Facilities: University Farm (11,000 ha). Centre for Tourism Management; Centre for Transport and Community Management; Centre for Assistance and Care of the Physically and Socially Handicapped; Centre for New Technologies in Education

Libraries: University Library, c. 415,500 vols

Publications: Bulletin of Agricultural Faculty

Press or Publishing House: University Publishing Centre (Pedagogy Faculty)
Last Updated: 03/10/11

UNIVERSITY OF VETERINARY AND PHARMACEUTICAL SCIENCES BRNO

Veterinární a farmaceutická univerzita Brno (VFU)
Palackého 1/3, 612 42 Brno
Tel: +420 541 561 111
Fax: +420 549 250 478
EMail: rektor@vfu.cz
Website: http://www.vfu.cz

Rektor: Vladimír Večerek (2006-)
Tel: +420 541 562 000 +420 541 562 002

Kvestor: Daniela Němcová
Tel: +420 541 562 025 EMail: nemcovad@vfu.cz

International Relations: Alois Nečas, Vice-Rector, Science, reserch and foreign relations
Tel: +420 541 562 020, Fax: +420 541 211 151
EMail: prorektorvvz@vfu.cz

Faculties

Pharmacy (Botany; Pharmacology; Pharmacy; Toxicology); **Veterinary Hygiene and Ecology** (Animal Husbandry; Biochemistry; Biology; Biophysics; Cattle Breeding; Chemistry; Ecology; Environmental Management; Food Technology; Hygiene; Veterinary Science; Wildlife); **Veterinary Medicine** (Anatomy; Embryology and Reproduction Biology; Epidemiology; Histology; Immunology; Microbiology; Parasitology; Pathology; Pharmacology; Physiology; Veterinary Science; Zoology)

Institutes

Foreign Languages and History of Veterinary Medicine (Arts and Humanities; Modern Languages; Philology); **Information Technology** (Information Technology); **Lifelong Education and Informatics** (Computer Science); **Wildlife Ecology** (Ecology; Wildlife)

History: Founded 1918 as Czechoslovak College of Veterinary Medicine, reorganized as University 1969. A State institution.

Governing Bodies: Scientific Council; Academic Senate; Board of Trustees

Academic Year: September to June (September-December; February-June)

Admission Requirements: Secondary school certificate (Maturitní vysvědčení) and entrance examination in Biology, Chemistry and Physics (for Faculty of Pharmacy)

Fees: None for instruction in Czech; (US Dollars): 6,000 per annum for instruction in English (Veterinary Medicine only)

Main Language(s) of Instruction: Czech; English (Veterinary Medicine)

International Co-operation: Participates in Erasmus (Austria, France, Germany, Netherlands) and Ceepus (Hungary, Poland, Slovak Republic, Slovenia)

Degrees and Diplomas: *Bakalář*: Food Hygiene, Technology and Ecology (Bc), 3 yrs; *Doktor veterinární medicíny*: Veterinary Medicine (MVDr), 6 yrs; *Magistr*: Food Hygiene, Technology and Ecology, 2 yrs following Bakalář; *Magistr*: Pharmacy (Mgr), 5 yrs; *Doktor*: Philosophy (PhD), a further 3 yrs by thesis

Student Services: Canteen, Health services, Sports facilities

Student Residential Facilities: For 776 students

Special Facilities: Pathology Museum; Anatomy Museum; Museum of the History of Veterinary Science

Libraries: Central Library, c. 208,000 vols

Publications: Acta Veterinaria Brno *(quarterly)*

Press or Publishing House: Publishing Centre
Last Updated: 03/10/11

UNIVERSITY OF WEST BOHEMIA

Západočeská univerzita v Plzni (ZČU/UWB)
Univerzitní 8, 306 14 Plzeň
Tel: +420 377 631 111
Fax: +420 377 631 112
EMail: info@rek.zcu.cz
Website: http://www.zcu.cz

Rektor: Ilona Mauritzová
Tel: +420 377 631 000, Fax: +420 377 631 002
EMail: rektor@rek.zcu.cz

Centres

European Economic Studies (Economics; European Studies); **Information Technology** (Information Technology); **Japanese Economic Studies** (East Asian Studies; Economics); **Lifelong Learning**; **Regional Development Research** (Development Studies; Regional Studies); **Teaching Practice** (Teacher Trainers Education; Teacher Training)

Faculties

Applied Sciences (Automation and Control Engineering; Business Computing; Computer Engineering; Computer Graphics; Computer Networks; Computer Science; Engineering; Information Technology; Mathematics; Mechanics; Natural Sciences; Physical Engineering; Physics; Software Engineering; Statistics); **Economics** *(Plzeň Cheb)* (Accountancy; Administration; Economic and Finance Policy; Economics; English; Finance; French; German; Information Sciences; Management; Management Systems; Marketing; Modern Languages; Operations Research; Russian; Spanish; Statistics); **Education** (Biology; Chemistry; Computer Science; Cultural Studies; Czech; Education; Educational Technology; English; Fine Arts; French; Geography; Geography (Human); German; History; Literature; Mathematics; Mathematics Education; Music; Music Education; Native Language; Native Language Education; Physical Education; Physics; Psychology; Russian; Sports; Technology Education); **Electrical Engineering** (Computer Science; Ecology; Electrical and Electronic Equipment and Maintenance; Electrical Engineering; Electronic Engineering; Energy Engineering; Multimedia; Power Engineering; Telecommunications Engineering; Transport Engineering); **Health Care Studies** (Nursing; Physical Therapy; Public Health); **Law** (Law; Public Administration); **Mechanical Engineering** (Electrical and Electronic Equipment and Maintenance; Industrial Design; Industrial Engineering; Industrial Management; Maintenance Technology; Materials Engineering; Mechanical Engineering; Metal Techniques; Metallurgical Engineering; Physical Education; Power Engineering; Production Engineering; Sports; Transport Engineering); **Philosophy and Arts** (Anthropology; Archaeology; English; German; Germanic Studies; History; International Relations; Literature; Philosophy; Political Sciences; Romance Languages; Sociology)

Institutes

Applied Language Studies (Dutch; English; Foreign Languages Education; French; German; Portuguese; Russian; Spanish); **Art and Design** (Ceramic Art; Design; Fashion Design; Fine Arts; Graphic Arts; Industrial Design; Jewelry Art; Metal Techniques; Multimedia; Painting and Drawing; Printing and Printmaking; Sculpture)

Further Information: Also Parallel study programmes in English are offered to foreign students. International Summer Language School

History: Founded 1991, incorporating Institute of Technology (founded 1949) and Faculty of Education (founded 1948).

Governing Bodies: Academic Senate

Academic Year: September to June (September-December; February-May)

Admission Requirements: Secondary school certificate (maturitní vysvědčeni) and entrance examination (Přijímací zkoušky)

Fees: None

Main Language(s) of Instruction: Czech

International Co-operation: With universities in Europe, Australia, Belarus, Canada, Japan, Korea, Lithuania, Russian Federation, USA. Also participates to Socrates/Erasmus, Lingua, Comenius, Minerva and Leonardo da Vinci programmes

Degrees and Diplomas: *Bakalář (Bc)*: 3 yrs; *Magistr (Ing.)*: 5 yrs; *Magistr (Mgr)*: 2 yrs; *Magistr (Mgr)*: 4 yrs; *Doktor (PhD)*: 3 yrs

Student Services: Academic counselling, Canteen, Cultural centre, Employment services, Foreign student adviser, Foreign Studies Centre, Health services, Language programs, Sports facilities

Student Residential Facilities: Yes

Special Facilities: University Gallery. Science Park. Audiovisual Centre; West Bohemian Supercomputing Centre

Libraries: Central Library; Specialized departmental libraries and academic libraries

Publications: Sborník ZČU *(annually)*; Výroční zpráva o činnosti Západočeské univerzity v Plzni *(annually)*

Press or Publishing House: University Publishing Centre (Vydavatelství ZČU)
Last Updated: 04/10/11

PRIVATE INSTITUTIONS

BANKING INSTITUTE/COLLEGE OF BANKING IN PRAGUE, INC.

Bankovní institut vysoká škola, a. s. (BIVŠ)
Nárožní 2600/9, 158 00 Praha, 5
Tel: +420(2) 3307-4536
Fax: +420(2) 3307-2083
EMail: info@bivs.cz
Website: http://www.bivs.cz

Rektor: František Jirásek
Tel: +420 251 114 501 EMail: fjirasek@bivs.cz

Vice-Rector: Lubomír Civín

Departments
Banking and Insurance (Banking; Economics; Insurance; Management)

History: Founded 1999.

Main Language(s) of Instruction: Czech

Degrees and Diplomas: *Bakalář*: 3 yrs; *Magistr*: a further 2 yrs

Libraries: Yes
Last Updated: 30/09/11

BRNO INTERNATIONAL BUSINESS SCHOOL (BIBS)
Lidická 81, 602 00 Brno
Tel: +420 545 570 111
Fax: +420 545 570 115
EMail: info@bibs.cz
Website: http://www.bibs.cz

Rektor: Miloslav Keřkovský EMail: kerkovsky@bibs.cz

Director of Academic Development and Quality and Public Relations: Alena Hanzelková EMail: hanzelkova@bibs.cz

Programmes
Business (Business Administration; Commercial Law; Economics; Law; Management)

History: Founded 1998. Acquired present status 2005.

Degrees and Diplomas: *Bakalář*; *Magistr*. Also International Doctorate (PhD) in Business and Administration
Last Updated: 09/11/11

BUSINESS SCHOOL OSTRAVA, PLC.
Vysoká škola podnikání, a.s. (VŠP)
Michálkovická 1810/181, 710 00 Ostrava
Tel: +420(59) 522-8111
Fax: +420(59) 522-8199
EMail: vsp@vsp.cz
Website: http://www.vsp.cz

Rektor: Josef Jünger
Tel: +420(59) 522-8100 EMail: josef.junger@vsp.cz

Prorektor: Renáta Nešporková
Tel: +420(59) 522-8137 EMail: renata.nesporkova@vsp.cz

Departments
Entrepreneurship (Business Administration); **Entrepreneurship and Business Management** (Management); **Entrepreneurship and Environmental Management** (Environmental Management); **Foreign Languages**; **Information Technology and Computer Science**

History: Founded 2000.

Degrees and Diplomas: *Bakalář*; *Magistr*
Last Updated: 30/10/09

COLLEGE OF BUSINESS STUDIES IN PRAGUE, P.B.C.
Vysoká škola obchodní v Praze, o.p.s. (VŠO)
Spálená 76/14, 110 00 Praha, 1
Tel: +420(2) 2405-6011
Fax: +420(2) 2405-6336
EMail: sekretariat@vso-praha.cz
Website: http://www.vso-praha.cz

Rektor: Ivo Straka

Departments
Air Transport; **Computer Science**; **Economics and Finance**; **Foreign Languages**; **Law** (Law); **Management and Marketing** (Management; Marketing); **Mathematics and Statistics**; **Social Sciences** (Social Sciences); **Tourism** (Tourism)

History: Founded 2000.

Degrees and Diplomas: *Bakalář*; *Magistr*
Last Updated: 28/10/09

COLLEGE OF ECONOMICS AND MANAGEMENT, LTD
Vysoká škola ekonomie a managementu, s.r.o. (VŠEM)
Nárožni 2600/9a, 15800 Praha, 5
Tel: +420 841-133-166
Fax: +420 475-600-135
EMail: info@vsem.cz
Website: http://www.vsem.cz

Rector: Milan Žák EMail: rektor@vsem.cz

International Relations: Pavel Marinič, Prorektor
EMail: marinic@vsem.cz

Centres
Economic Studies (Economics)

Departments
Applied Methods (Computer Engineering; Mathematics and Computer Science); **Business & Economics** (Business Administration; Economics); **Economics and Law** (Economics; Law)

History: Founded 2001.

Academic Year: January-April-October

Admission Requirements: "Maturitni zkouška" and "Potvrzeni o praxi"

Fees: (Koruna): for Bachelor level, 30,000 per annum; for Master level, 50,000 per annum

Main Language(s) of Instruction: Czech

Accrediting Agencies: Ministry of Education, Youth and Sports; European Council for Business Administration(ECBE)

Degrees and Diplomas: *Bakalář*. Business Administration (BBA), 31/2 yrs; *Bakalář*. Economics; Management (Bc), 3 1/2 yrs; *Magistr*. Business Administration (MBA)

Student Services: Academic counselling, Sports facilities

Student Residential Facilities: no

Special Facilities: none

Libraries: Yes

Publications: Aktualizace dlouhodobého zóměru *(annually)*

Press or Publishing House: Zpravodaj VŠEM
Last Updated: 03/10/11

COLLEGE OF INTERNATIONAL AND PUBLIC RELATIONS PRAGUE, P.B.C.
Vysoká škola mezinárodních a veřejných vztahů Praha, o.p.s. (VŠMVV)
U Santošky 17, 150 00 Praha, 5
Tel: +420(2) 5156-3158 +420(2) 5156-2124
Fax: +420(2) 5156-1557
EMail: info@vip-vs.cz
Website: http://www.vip-vs.cz

Rektor: Judita Štouračová EMail: stouracova@vip-vs.cz

International Relations: Felix Černoch, Prorektor
EMail: cernoch@vip-vs.cz

Departments
Computer Science (Computer Science); **European Integration** (European Studies); **International Relations** (International Relations); **Languages** (Modern Languages); **Political and Social Sciences** (Political Sciences; Social Sciences); **Public Administration and Law** (Law; Public Administration); **Public Relations and Communication Studies** (Communication Studies; Public Relations)

History: Founded 1999.

Main Language(s) of Instruction: Czech

Degrees and Diplomas: *Bakalář*; *Magistr*
Last Updated: 04/10/11

COLLEGE OF LOGISTICS
Vysoká škola logistiky
Palackého 1381/25, 750 02 Přerov
Tel: +420 581 259 120
Fax: +420 581 259 131
EMail: vslg@vslg.cz
Website: http://www.vslg.cz

Rector: Ivan Barancík EMail: ivan.barancik@vslg.cz

Director: Milena Kolárová EMail: milena.kolarova@vslg.cz

Bursar: Václav Kolár EMail: vaclav.kolar@vslg.cz

Departments
Economic, Legal and Social Sciences (Accountancy; Banking; Commercial Law; Economics; Finance; Industrial and Organizational Psychology; Insurance; International Relations; Law; Management; Social Sciences; Taxation; Tourism); **Logistics and Technical Disciplines** (Air Transport; Information Management; Transport Management); **Natural Sciences and Humanities** (Arts and Humanities; Cultural Studies; Earth Sciences; Engineering; English; Environmental Management; History; Mathematics; Modern Languages; Natural Sciences; Physics; Psychology; Statistics; Surveying and Mapping; Tourism)

History: Founded 2004.

Degrees and Diplomas: *Bakalář, Magistr*
Last Updated: 09/11/11

FILM ACADEMY OF MIROSLAVA ONDŘÍČEK IN PÍSEK, P.B.C.
Filmová Akademie Miroslava Ondříčka v Písku, o.p.s.
Lipová alej 2068, 397 01 Písek
Tel: +420(38) 226-4212
Fax: +420(38) 226-4212
EMail: famo@filmovka.cz
Website: http://www.filmovka.cz/

Rektor: David Jan Novotný

Prorektor: Josef Pecák

Departments
Animated Film (Film); **Cinematography** (Cinema and Television); **Directing and Screenwriting** (Film); **Film and Television Production** (Cinema and Television; Film); **Film Editing** (Film); **Film Sound** (Film; Sound Engineering (Acoustics))

History: Founded 2003 as Film Academy in Písek. Acquired present title 2005.

Main Language(s) of Instruction: Czech

Degrees and Diplomas: *Bakalář, Magistr*
Last Updated: 04/10/11

INSTITUTE OF FINANCE AND ADMINISTRATION, P.B.C.
Vysoká škola finanční a správní, o. p. s. (VŠFS)
Estonská 500, 101 00 Praha, 10
Tel: +420(2) 1008-8800
Fax: +420(2) 7174-1597
EMail: info@vsfs.cz
Website: http://www.vsfs.cz

Rektor: Bohuslava Šenkýřová Tel: +420(2) 1008-8811

International Relations: Petr Budinský, Vice-Rector for Education and External Relations
Tel: +420(2) 1008-8819, Fax: +420(2) 7174-0871
EMail: petr.budinsky@vsfs.cz

Departments
Communication and Management; Company Management and Economy; Foreign Languages; Informatics (Computer Science); **Law** (Law); **Macroeconomics and International Relations; Mathematics and Statistics** (Mathematics; Statistics); **Microeconomics and Public Economy; Public Administration**

History: Founded 1999.

Degrees and Diplomas: *Bakalář, Magistr*
Last Updated: 04/10/11

INSTITUTE OF HOSPITALITY MANAGEMENT, LTD
Vysoká škola hotelová, s.r.o. (VŠH)
Svídnická 506, 181 00 Praha, 8
Tel: +420(2) 8310-1121
Fax: +420(2) 3354-1905
EMail: info@vsh.cz
Website: http://www.vsh.cz

Rektor: Václav Vinš Tel: +420(2) 8310-1122 EMail: rektor@vsh.cz

Vice-Rector for Academic Affairs: Jan Máče
Tel: +420(2) 8310-1120 EMail: mace@vsh.cz

International Relations: Zuzana Roldánová, Prorektor
Tel: +420(2) 8310-1139 EMail: roldanova@vsh.cz

Departments
Economics (Economics); **Hotel Management** (Cooking and Catering; Hotel Management); **Language Studies** (Modern Languages); **Management** (Management); **Marketing and Media Communication** (Marketing; Media Studies)

History: Founded 1999.

Main Language(s) of Instruction: Czech

Degrees and Diplomas: *Bakalář, Magistr*
Last Updated: 04/10/11

JAN AMOS KOMENSKÝ UNIVERSITY PRAGUE
Univerzita Jana Amose Komenského Praha, s.r.o. (VŠJAK)
Roháčova 63, 130 00 Praha, 3
Tel: +420(2) 6719-9015
Fax: +420(2) 6719-9001
EMail: international@ujak.cz
Website: http://www.ujak.cz

Rektor: Luboš Chaloupka
Tel: +420(2) 6719-9001 EMail: rektor@ujak.cz

International Relations: Martina Vošahlíková
Tel: +420(2) 6719-9033

Departments
Adult Education (Adult Education); **Andragogy** (Education; Human Resources); **European Economic and Public Administration Studies** (Economics; Public Administration); **Human Resources Development and the European Union** (European Studies; Human Resources); **Social and Mass Communication** (Communication Studies; Mass Communication); **Special Education** (Special Education)

History: Founded 2001 as Vysoká škola Jana Amose Komenského, s.r.o.

Fees: (Euros): 4,800 per annum

Main Language(s) of Instruction: Czech; English

Degrees and Diplomas: *Bakalář, Magistr, Doktor*
Last Updated: 03/10/11

JOSEF ŠKVORECKÝ WRITERS' ACADEMY
Literární akademie - Soukromá vysoká škola J. Škvoreckého, s.r.o. (LA)
Na Pankráci 54, 140 00 Praha, 4
Tel: +420(2) 2653-9741
EMail: info@literarniakademie.cz
Website: http://www.literarniakademie.cz

Rektor: Martin Štoll
Tel: +420(2) 7277-3045 EMail: rektor@lit-akad.cz

Faculties
Art and Design (Design; Fine Arts); **Arts and Humanities and Philosophy** (German; History; Philosophy; Political Sciences); **Education** (Art Education; Cultural Studies; Education; English; Information Technology; Mathematics; Mathematics Education; Music Education; Pedagogy; Physical Education; Slavic Languages; Sports); **Environmental Studies** (Environmental Management; Environmental Studies; Waste Management); **Production Technology and Management** (Engineering; Engineering Management; Production Engineering; Technology; Technology Education); **Science** (Biology; Chemistry; Computer Engineering; Geography;

Materials Engineering; Mathematics; Natural Sciences; Physics); **Social and Economic Studies** (Economics; Social Studies)

Institutes
Health Studies (Ergotherapy; Health Sciences; Midwifery; Nursing; Physical Therapy)

History: Founded 2000.

Main Language(s) of Instruction: Czech

Degrees and Diplomas: *Bakalář, Magistr, Doktor*
Last Updated: 03/10/11

METROPOLITAN UNIVERSITY PRAGUE

Metropolitni Univerzita Praha (VŠVSMV)
Dubečská 900/10, 100 00 Praha, 10-Strašnice
Tel: +420(2) 7481-5044
Fax: +420(2) 7481-7190
EMail: info@mup.cz
Website: http://www.mup.cz

Rektor: Michal Klíma
Tel: +420(2) 7418-8133 EMail: klima@mup.cz

Prorektor: Jan Bureš EMail: bures@mup.cz

Departments
Anglophone Studies (English); **Asian Studies** (Asian Studies); **Economics** (Economics); **Foreign Languages** (Modern Languages); **Humanities** (Arts and Humanities); **Industrial Property** (Industrial Arts Education); **Information Technologies** (Information Technology); **International Relations and European Studies** (European Studies; International Relations); **International Trade** (International Business); **Law and Public Administration** (Law; Public Administration)

History: Founded 2001 as University of Public Administration and International Relations.

Main Language(s) of Instruction: Czech and English

Degrees and Diplomas: *Bakalář, Magistr, Doktor*
Publications: Journal of International and Security Studies
Last Updated: 03/10/11

PRAGUE COLLEGE OF PSYCHO-SOCIAL STUDIES

Pražská vysoká škola psychosociálních studií, s.r.o. (PVŠPS)
Hekrova 805, 149 00 Praha, 4
Tel: +420(2) 6791-3634
Fax: +420(2) 6791-3634
EMail: viap@viap.cz
Website: http://www.viap.cz

Rektor: Jiří Ružička Tel: +420(2) 6791-0424

International Relations: Jaroslav Kota, Prorektor
Tel: +420(2) 6791-3634 EMail: studijni@viap.cz

Programmes
Psychological and Social Studies (Psychology; Social Policy; Social Studies; Social Work)

History: Founded 2001.

Main Language(s) of Instruction: Czech

Degrees and Diplomas: *Bakalář, Magistr*
Last Updated: 03/10/11

PRIVATE COLLEGE OF ECONOMIC STUDIES, LTD.

Soukromá vysoká škola ekonomických studií, s.r.o. (SVŠES)
Lindnerova 575/1, 180 00 Praha, 8
Tel: +420(2) 8484-1027
Fax: +420(2) 8484-1196
EMail: info@svses.cz
Website: http://www.svses.cz

Rector: Miloslav Marek EMail: rektor@svses.cz

International Relations: Lucie Marková, Prorektor
EMail: lucie.markova@svses.cz

Programmes
Economics and Management (Accountancy; Commercial Law; Economics; International Economics; International Law; Management); **Protection and Safety of Organizations** (Protective Services)

History: Founded 1996. Acquired present status 2001.

Degrees and Diplomas: *Bakalář, Magistr*
Last Updated: 09/01/12

RAŠÍN COLLEGE, LTD.

Rašínova vysoká škola, s.r.o. (RVŠ)
Hudcova 78, 612 00 Brno
Tel: +420 541 632 402
Fax: +420 541 241 624
EMail: info@ravys.cz
Website: http://www.ravys.cz

Rektor: Vladimír Klaban
Kvestor: Miroslav Boršek

Programmes
Law and Economics (Accountancy; Administrative Law; Banking; Civil Law; Commercial Law; Constitutional Law; Criminal Law; Economics; English; Finance; German; Human Resources; Information Technology; Labour Law; Law; Management; Marketing; Psychology; Sociology; Taxation)

History: Founded 2003.

Main Language(s) of Instruction: Czech

Degrees and Diplomas: *Bakalář, Magistr*
Last Updated: 04/10/11

RERUM CIVILIUM ACADEMY, LTD.

Academia Rerum Civilium - Vysoká škola politických a společenských věd, s.r.o. (VŠPSV)
Ovčárecká 312, 280 02 Kolín, V
Tel: +420(32) 173-4711
Fax: +420(32) 173-4720
EMail: arc@vspsv.cz
Website: http://www.vspsv.cz

Rector: Ján Lid'ák EMail: lidak@vspsv.cz

Prorektor: Vladimír Srb EMail: srb@vspsv.cz

Programmes
Political Sciences (Political Sciences)

History: Founded 2001. Acquired present status 2003.

Main Language(s) of Instruction: Czech

Degrees and Diplomas: *Bakalář, Magistr, Doktor*
Last Updated: 29/09/11

ŠKODA AUTO UNIVERSITY

Škoda Auto vysoká škola, a.s. (ŠAVŠ)
Václava Klementa 869, 293 60 Mladá Boleslav
Tel: +420(3) 2682-3029
Fax: +420(3) 2682-3113
EMail: ciam@is.savs.cz
Website: http://www.savs.cz

Rektor: Pavel Nováček EMail: pavel.novacek@skoda-auto.cz

International Relations: Miroslava Nigrinová, Prorektor
EMail: miroslava.nigrinova@skoda-auto.cz

Programmes
Economics and Management (Economics; Management; Marketing)

History: Founded 2000.

Main Language(s) of Instruction: Czech and English

Degrees and Diplomas: *Bakalář, Magistr*
Last Updated: 03/10/11

STING ACADEMY, P.B.C.

Akademie Sting, o.p.s. (AS)
Stromovka 1, 637 00 Brno
Tel: +420(5) 4122-0334
Fax: +420(5) 4122-0334
EMail: akademie@sting.cz
Website: http://www.sting.cz

Rektor: Zdeněk Sadovský

Kvestor: JItka Matějková

Programmes
Administration, Economy and Management (Administration; Economics; Management); **Economic Policy** (Economics)

History: Founded 2000.

Main Language(s) of Instruction: Czech

Degrees and Diplomas: *Bakalář, Magistr*
Last Updated: 29/09/11

THE ANGLO-AMERICAN UNIVERSITY IN PRAGUE, P.B.C.

Anglo-Americká vysoká škola, o.p.s. (AAVŠ)
Lázeňská 4, 118 00 Praha, 1
Tel: +420(2) 5753-0202
Fax: +420(2) 5753-2911
EMail: info@aauni.edu
Website: http://www.aauni.edu

Rektor: Alan Krautstengl EMail: alan.krautstengl@aac.edu

Provost: Milada Polišenská EMail: milada.polisenska@aauni.edu

Schools
Business Administration (Business Administration; Finance; International Business; Law); **Humanities and Social Sciences** (Arts and Humanities; Cultural Studies; Economics; Gender Studies; Political Sciences; Social Sciences); **International Relations and Diplomacy** (Central European Studies; Eastern European Studies; International Relations); **Law** *(John H. Carey II)* (Comparative Law; Law)

History: Founded 1990 as Anglo-American College. Renamed Anglo-American Institute for Liberal Studies 1999. Acquired present status 2001 and title 2003.

Admission Requirements: Secondary School Certificate. for non-native English speakers: TOEFL (min 525 paper-based, 197 computer-based, 71 Internet-based test; DI-CODE of Anglo-americká vysoká škola: 9,734), or FCE (mark A or B), or CAE (mark A or B or C) or Všeobecná státní zkouška, or IELTS (min. 6), or International Baccalaureaute (IB)

Main Language(s) of Instruction: English

Degrees and Diplomas: *Bakalář*: Business Administration; Politics & Society; Humanities, Society & Culture; Comparative Law; International Relations (BA); *Magistr*: Business Administration; Public Policy; Humanities; International Relations & Diplomacy (MA);
Last Updated: 30/09/11

THE COLLEGE OF LOGISTICS, P.B.C.

Vysoká škola logistiky, o.p.s. (VŠL)
Palackého 1380/19, 750 02 Přerov, I - město
Tel: +420(58) 125-9120
Fax: +420(58) 125-9131
EMail: vslg@vslg.cz
Website: http://www.vslg.cz

Rector: Ivan Barančík
Tel: +420(58) 125-9126 EMail: ivan.barancik@vslg.cz

Prorektor: Zdeněk Úředníček
Tel: +420(58) 125-9128 EMail: zdenek.urednicek@vslg.cz

Departments
Economics, Law and Social Studies (Economics; Law; Social Studies); **Humanities and Natural Sciences** (Arts and Humanities; Geography; Natural Sciences; Tourism); **Logistics** (Information Management; Transport Management)

History: Founded 2004.

Main Language(s) of Instruction: Czech

Degrees and Diplomas: *Bakalář, Magistr*
Last Updated: 04/10/11

UNIVERSITY OF NEW YORK IN PRAGUE

Legerova 72, 120 00 Praha
Tel: +420(224) 221-261 +420(224) 221-281
Fax: +420(224) 221-247
EMail: unyp@unyp.cz
Website: http://www.unyp.cz/

President: Elias Foutsis

Departments
Business Administration (Business Administration; Finance; Marketing); **Communications and Mass Media** (Communication Studies; Information Technology; Journalism; Mass Communication; Media Studies); **English Language and Literature** (English; Literature); **International and Commercial Law** (Commercial Law; International Law); **International Economic Relations** (International Economics; International Relations); **Psychology** (Psychology)

History: Created 1998. Acquired status 2001.

Main Language(s) of Instruction: English

Degrees and Diplomas: *Bakalář, Magistr, Doktor.* Both European- and American-style degrees.
Last Updated: 03/10/11

Denmark

STRUCTURE OF HIGHER EDUCATION SYSTEM

Description:

Higher education comprises a university sector and a college sector, i.e. the professionally-oriented higher education sector. The university sector includes 8 universities, most of which are multi-faculty universities. In addition, there are specialist university-level institutions in architecture, design, music, and fine and performing arts. The university sector offers programmes at three levels: Bachelor's Degree (3 years of study), the Candidatus Degree (i.e. Master's Degree, normally 2 years following upon the Bachelor's Degree) and the Ph.D. Degree (normally 3 years' study after the Candidatus Degree). The universities also award the traditional higher Doctoral Degree (dr. phil., dr. scient, etc) after a minimum of 5-8 years' individual and original research. Study programmes of the university sector are research based. The college sector comprises specialized institutions of higher education offering professionally-oriented programmes:

a) The Academy Profession Degree (AP degree) (Danish title: profession + (AK)) is awarded mainly after two years of study (120 ECTS points). The AP programmes are offered by Academies of Professional Higher Education (Erhvervsakademier).

b) The Professional Bachelor's degree is awarded after 3 to 4 1/2 years of study (180-270 ECTS points) at the level corresponding to that of university Bachelor's programmes. The professional bachelor programmes are offered by University Colleges (professionshøjskoler). The Ministry of Science, Technology and Innovation is responsible for university education except for certain higher education programmes which come under the Ministry of Cultural Affairs (e.g. Architecture, Music, Fine Arts, and Librarianship). The Ministry of Education is responsible for short- and medium-cycle higher education. The legislation covers the aims and framework of education, funding and in some cases curricula, examinations and staffing. Higher education institutions are publicly financed and State regulated. Public higher education institutions are publicly financed, and they must follow the national legislation concerning e.g. degree structures, teacher qualifications and examinations, including a system of external examiners. A nationally established – fully independent – accreditation agency assures the quality and the relevance of higher education programmes. Private institutions can operate without any approval. However, if students at private institutions are to be eligible for state study grants, the institutions must abide by a recognition procedure. The use of the European Credit Transfer System (ECTS) became mandatory in all higher education study programmes on 1 September 2001, the use of the Diploma Supplement on 1 September 2002.

Stages of studies:

University level first stage: Bachelorgrad (B.A. or B.Sc.)
Undergraduate study takes 3 years (180 ECTS) and leads to the award of a Bachelor's Degree. The degree is awarded by the universities/specialized higher education institutions upon completion of a research-based study programme concentrating from the first year on the major subject area chosen for the degree. The final year includes a major project. All Bachelor programmes must follow the same national standards and there are no classifications in honours/ordinary programmes. The study programmes do not include components that could be classified as liberal arts. The Bachelor programmes prepare the students for occupational functions and for studies for the candidatus degree. At the universities of Aalborg and Roskilde, the Bachelor programmes begin respectively with a one- and two-year general studies programme (basisuddannelse) in either the humanities or social, technical or natural sciences. In business administration, part of the Bachelor programmes lead to the award of the Handelshøjskolens Afgangsprøve (HA).

University level second stage: Kandidatgrad/Candidatus (cand. + field of study, in English: usually MA or MSc + field)
The Candidatus degree (Master's degree) can be obtained at universities and other research-based institutions of higher education. In most fields of study, admission requires a Bachelor's degree in the same field of study. The degree is normally awarded after a total of 5 years of study: the Bachelor's degree (3 years, 180 ECTS) and a Candidatus programme, which is 2 years (120 ECTS) with the exceptions of medicine (3 years, 180 ECTS) and veterinary medicine (2 1/2 years, 150 ECTS). Independent research activities are an important part of the

Candidatus programme. The candidatus thesis (speciale) is a major requirement and is normally scheduled for 6 months' full-time study (30 ECTS, up to 60 ECTS in the case of experimentally based theses). The Master's degree within fine arts is awarded after 120-180 ECTS, and the programmes are based on research and artistic research. Music academies offer a specialist degree of 2 to 4 years following the Master's degree. Within certain fields of the humanities, the Magister Artium (mag.art.) is awarded on completion of three years' research-oriented study after the Bachelor's degree and public defence of a thesis. The Mag.art. is being phased out, and no new students are admitted.

University level third stage: Ph.d.-grad (PhD)
A Ph.D. degree can be obtained at universities and other research-based institutions of higher education. The typical Ph.D. programme is a 3-year programme following the Candidatus (Master's) degree. The programme must include a scientific project, participation in research programmes and seminars corresponding to six months' work, experience in teaching or other kinds of communication of research results, mobility to ensure experience from working in two or more active research groups (mobility abroad is given high priority) and finally public defence of the PhD thesis.

University level fourth stage: Doktorgrad (dr. + field of study)
The Danish Doctoral degree is an advanced degree usually obtained after five to eight years of original and outstanding research. It is awarded after public defence of a thesis. There is no formal study programme.

Distance higher education:
Some programmes of open education (see Lifelong higher education) are offered as distance education. Students meet with their teachers and co-students for two or three sessions per semester. The educational institution provides the syllabus, exercises and guidance. Distance education may also be Internet-based.

ADMISSION TO HIGHER EDUCATION

Admission to university-level studies:

Name of secondary school credential required: Studentereksamen

Minimum score/requirement: Depending on institution and programme

Name of secondary school credential required: Højere Forberedelseseksamen

Minimum score/requirement: Depending on institution and programme

Name of secondary school credential required: Højere Handelseksamen

Minimum score/requirement: Depending on institution and programme

Name of secondary school credential required: Gymnasialt Indslusningskursus for Fremmedsprogede

For entry to: Depending on institution and programme

Name of secondary school credential required: Højere Teknisk Eksamen

For entry to: Depending on institution and programme

Alternatives to credentials: Individual assessment.

Numerus clausus/restrictions: The Minister of Science, Technology and Innovation may fix a maximum number of student admissions within certain fields of study. Apart from that, individual institutions may have restricted admission for certain fields of study.

Other admission requirements: Depending on what studies the applicant wishes to follow, there may be other requirements concerning the entrance qualification, e.g. subject combinations, levels and minimum marks.

Foreign students admission:

Definition of foreign student: A non-Danish citizen with a foreign entrance qualification.

Quotas: Three quotas are fixed annually for applications for first-cycle programmes. Quota 1 is for applicants who have passed a Danish upper secondary education and who wish to be assessed exclusively on the basis of this. Quota 2 is for applicants who have an international upper secondary education and are EU/EEA citizens, for applicants who do not have an upper secondary education, but who have obtained qualifications comparable to an upper secondary education (exemptees), and for applicants who have a Danish upper secondary education and have subsequently obtained qualifications/experience, e.g. work experience, living abroad, post-secondary courses, extra-curricular activities. Quota 3 is for applicants who apply for an English programme and do not have a Danish upper secondary education and are not EU or EEA citizens and need a student residence permit to study in Denmark.

Entrance exam requirements: The general admission requirement is a qualification that gives access to higher education in the country of origin and which is assessed and found comparable to the Danish entrance qualifications. For many programmes, there are also specific requirements which must be fulfilled. Further information about admission requirements and foreign qualifications accepted for entry to higher education programmes taught in English is available at the Study in Denmark website: http://www.studyindenmark.dk/Default.aspx?ID=4012 .

Entry regulations: Residence permit: You must contact the institution where you have been admitted for detailed information on procedures for obtaining a residence permit. The procedures vary according to nationality. Students from outside the EU/EEA especially should be aware that the residence permit must be applied for from your home country. There are also certain financial requirements. For further information on residence and work permit, please visit the website of the Danish Immigration Service: http://www.nyidanmark.dk/en-us/

Health requirements: Any person staying in Denmark is entitled to free emergency hospital treatment.
1) Persons on temporary stay in Denmark:
a) Nordic countries and UK: same health services as Danes when they need medical treatment;
b) EU and EEA: same health services as Danes when they need medical treatment if they bring their European Health Insurance Card (EHIC);
c) other countries: no free medical care except the emergency hospital treatment mentioned above, a private health insurance is needed.
2) Persons with residence in Denmark and registered at the Municipal civil registration office in Denmark are automatically covered by the Danish health insurance scheme after a period of 6 weeks. Persons from EU/EEA countries and from Macedonia, Morocco, Pakistan, Quebec, Switzerland and Turkey can avoid the waiting period if they are covered by the national health insurance scheme of their home country.

Language requirements: Knowledge of Danish is essential for regular higher education programmes. Non-Danish and non-Nordic applicants have to prove sufficient command of Danish (for programmes in Danish) by passing a test. The same may apply to Danish and other Nordic applicants holding foreign qualifications. For some programmes, there are also English proficiency requirements.
Study programmes taught in English do not have any Danish proficiency requirements. A requirement may then be made for English proficiency at a specific level.

RECOGNITION OF STUDIES

Quality assurance system:

The Accreditation Council, an independent national body, has an overall responsibility for ensuring the quality and relevance of higher education. The council makes the decisions regarding accreditation of all higher education study programmes. Decisions are made on the basis of accreditation reports prepared by accreditation operators: ACE Denmark (university study programmes) and the Danish Evaluation Institute. Publicly financed institutions must follow general regulations concerning teacher qualifications, award structures, study programmes and quality assurance. and the relevant ministries decide which institutions can offer which programmes. Institutions are required to set up their own internal quality assurance procedures. The Universities Act specifies the role of deans, heads of department and study boards in assuring and developing the quality of education and teaching. Self-evaluation, in which students normally participate, is an integral mandatory part of any evaluation.

Bodies dealing with recognition:

ACE Denmark, Akkrediteringsinstitutionen (ACE Denmark, The Danish Accreditation Institution)
Executive Director: Anette Dørge Jessen
Studiestræde 5
Copenhagen 1455
Tel: +45 3392 6900

Fax: +45 3392 6901
EMail: acedenmark@acedenmark.dk
WWW: http://www.acedenmark.dk

Danmarks Evalueringsinstitut - EVA (Danish Evaluation Institute)
Chairman: Ane Arnth Jensen
Executive Director: Agi Csonka
Østbanegade 55
Copenhagen 2100
Tel: +45 3555 0101
Fax: +45 3555 1011
EMail: ttp://www.eva.dk
WWW: eva@eva.dk

Styrelsen for International Uddannelse (Danish Agency for International Education)
Director General: Anders Geertsen
Bredgade 36
Copenhagen 1260
Tel: +45 3395 7000
Fax: +45 3395 7001
EMail: iu@iu.dk
WWW: http://www.iu.dk/

Special provisions for recognition:

Recognition for university level studies: Applicants with foreign credentials should send their application to the relevant institution of higher education before March 15. However, institutions may have different deadlines for applicants who are seeking admission to an English-language programme and need a residence permit for that. Recognition of foreign qualifications and study periods with a view to continuing studies at a Danish higher education institution (admission, credit transfer) falls within the competence of the individual institution. However, if the Danish Agency for International Education (the Danish ENIC/NARIC office) has made an assessment indicating a particular level of education, the educational institution must make its admission decision on the basis of this assessment.

For access to advanced studies and research: Application should be sent to the relevant institution of higher education.

For exercising a profession: Approval of foreign qualifications with a view to practising regulated professions is given by the authority administering the regulated profession in question. The application forms should be sent directly to the relevant competent authority. Information about access to the regulated professions is available at http://en.iu.dk/rp. For non-regulated professions, the Danish Agency for International Education provides assessment of foreign qualifications: http://en.iu.dk/recognition.

NATIONAL BODIES

Ministeriet for Videnskab, Teknologi og Udvikling (Ministry of Science, Technology and Innovation)
Minister: Charlotte Sahl-Madsen
Permanent Secretary: Uffe Toudal Pedersen
Bredgade 43
Copenhagen 1260
Tel: +45 3392 9700
EMail: vtu@vtu.dk
WWW: http://www.vtu.dk
Role of national body: Responsible for university research and education

Undervisningsministeriet (Ministry of Education)
Minister: Troels Lund Poulsen
: Sophus Garfiel
Frederiksholms Kanal 21
Copenhagen 1220

Tel: +45 3392 5000
Fax: +45 3392 5547
EMail: uvm@uvm.dk
WWW: http://www.uvm.dk
Role of national body: Responsible for non-university education, including short- and medium-cycle higher education

Uddannelsesstyrelse (National Education Agency)
Director General: Per Hansen
Frederiksholms Kanal 26
Copenhagen 1220
Tel: +45 3392 5000
EMail: udst@udst.dk
WWW: http://www.udst.dk

Danske Universiteter (Universities Denmark)
Chairman: Jens Oddershede
Secretary-General: Susanne Bjerregaard
Fiolstræde 44, 1. th
Copenhagen 1171
Tel: +45 3392 5405
Fax: +45 3392 5075
EMail: dkuni@dkuni.dk
WWW: http://www.dkuni.dk

Data for academic year: 2011-2012
Source: IAU from the Danish Agency for International Education, 2011

INSTITUTIONS

PUBLIC INSTITUTIONS

AALBORG UNIVERSITY
Aalborg Universitet (AAU)
Postboks 159, Fredrik Bajers vej 5, 9100 Aalborg
Tel: +45 99-40-99-40
Fax: +45 98-15-22-01
EMail: aau@aau.dk
Website: http://www.aau.dk

Rector: Finn Kjærsdam (2005-) EMail: rektor@adm.aau.dk

University Director: Peter Plenge EMail: director@adm.aau.dk

International Relations: Lise Thorup-Pedersen
Tel: +45 99-40-80-89 EMail: hbe@adm.aau.dk

Faculties
Engineering, Science *(Copenhagen Institute of Technology; Esberg Institute of Technology)* (Architecture; Biotechnology; Building Technologies; Chemistry; Civil Engineering; Computer Science; Design; Development Studies; Education; Electrical and Electronic Engineering; Electrical Engineering; Energy Engineering; Engineering; Environmental Engineering; Health Sciences; Industrial Engineering; Mathematics; Mechanical Engineering; Nanotechnology; Natural Sciences; Pedagogy; Physics; Production Engineering; Surveying and Mapping; Technology); **Humanities** (Arts and Humanities; Communication Studies; Cultural Studies; Education; History; International Studies; Modern Languages; Pedagogy; Philosophy; Philosophy of Education; Psychology); **Social Sciences** (Business Administration; Cultural Studies; Education; International Studies; Law; Management; Pedagogy;

Philosophy of Education; Political Sciences; Social Sciences; Social Studies; Social Work; Sociology)

Research Institutes
Building *(Danish)* (Administration; Building Technologies; Communication Studies; Energy Engineering; Environmental Engineering; Management)

History: Founded 1974. A State Institution incorporating previously established Centres of Education in Aalborg and employing new teaching and learning methods based on an 'integrated' approach to higher education, with emphasis on project work in groups. Financed by the State. The University has Departments in Esbjerg and Copenhagen

Governing Bodies: Board; Academic Councils; Departmental Councils; Study Boards

Academic Year: September to June (September-January; February-June)

Admission Requirements: Secondary school certificate (studentereksamen) or Højere-Forberedelseseksamen (HF), Højere, Handelseksamen, (HHX) or Højere Teknisk eksamen (HTX), or recognized equivalent

Fees: None

Main Language(s) of Instruction: Danish, some courses in English

International Co-operation: Participates in the Erasmus and the Leonardo programmes

Degrees and Diplomas: *Bachelorgrad*: Arts; Engineering; Science, 3 yrs; *Mellemlang Videregående Uddannelse/Professionsbachelorgrad*: Business Administration, 4 yrs; *Mellemlang Videregående Uddannelse/Professionsbachelorgrad*: Economics, 3 yrs; *Mellemlang*

Videregående Uddannelse/Professionsbachelorgrad: Social Work, 3 1/2 yrs; *Kandidatgrad*: Administrative Sciences (cand.scient.adm.); Business Administration (cand.merc.); Business Administration and Auditing (cand.merc.aud.); Economics (cand.oecon.); Engineering (cand.polyt.); Humanities (cand.mag.); Mathematics (cand.geom.); Science (cand.scient.), 5 yrs; *Ph.d.-grad*: a further 2-3 yrs; *Doktorgrad*: by thesis. Also Master in Information and Communication Technologies (MICT); and Master in Problem-based Learning (MPBL)

Student Services: Academic counselling, Canteen, Employment services, Foreign student adviser

Student Residential Facilities: Yes

Special Facilities: Nordjyllands Videnpark (NOVI). (Science Park)

Libraries: Aalborg University Library, 700,000 vols

Publications: Årsberetning *(biannually)*; Uglen *(other/irregular)*

Press or Publishing House: Aalborg Universitetsforlag
Last Updated: 19/07/11

AARHUS SCHOOL OF ARCHITECTURE
Arkitektskolen i Aarhus
Nørreport 20, 8000 Aarhus, C
Tel: +45 89-36-00-00
Fax: +45 86-13-06-45
EMail: a@aarch.dk
Website: http://aarch.dk

Rector: Torben Nielsen EMail: torben.nielsen@aarch.dk

Pro-Rector: Charlotte Bundgaard

Departments
Architectural Heritage (Architecture) *Director*: Gert Bech-Nielsen; **Architecture** (Architecture) *Director*: Peter Kjær; **Design** (Design); **Urbanism and Landscape** (Architecture; Landscape Architecture; Town Planning; Urban Studies) *Director*: Niels Albertsen

History: Founded 1965.

Academic Year: September to June (September-January; February-June)

Admission Requirements: Secondary school certificate (Studentereksamen) or recognized equivalent

Main Language(s) of Instruction: Danish

International Co-operation: Participates in the SOCRATES and NORDPLUS programmes

Degrees and Diplomas: *Bachelorgrad*: Architecture (BA), 3 yrs; *Kandidatgrad*; *Ph.d.-grad*: a further 3 yrs. Bachelorgrad equivalent to Bachelor of Arts; Magistergrad equivalent to Master of Arts

Student Services: Academic counselling, Canteen, Foreign student adviser

Student Residential Facilities: Yes

Libraries: Yes
Last Updated: 24/10/11

AARHUS UNIVERSITY
Aarhus Universitet (ASB)
Nordre Ringgade 1, 8000 Aarhus, C
Tel: +45 89-42-11-11
Fax: +45 89-42-11-09
EMail: au@au.dk
Website: http://www.au.dk/en

Rector: Lauritz B. Holm-Nielsen (2005-)
Tel: +45 89-42-11-41 EMail: rektor@au.dk

Pro-Rector: Søren E. Frandsen Tel: +45 89-42-19-59

University Director: Jørgen Jørgensen
Tel: +45 89-42-11-39 EMail: direktor@au.dk

International Relations: Kristian Thorn
Tel: +45 89-42-24-47, Fax: +45 89-42-23-29
EMail: krth@adm.au.dk

Faculties
Art, Music and Design (Accountancy; Aesthetics; Art History; Arts and Humanities; Design; Literature; Music; Theatre); **Arts** (Art History; Art Management; Arts and Humanities; Communication Stu-dies; Cultural Studies; Design; Education; Performing Arts; Visual Arts); **Biology, Chemistry and Nature** (Agriculture; Agrobiology; Biology; Biotechnology; Chemistry; Environmental Studies; Food Science; Geology; Molecular Biology; Natural Sciences; Technology); **Business and Social Sciences** (Administration; Business Administration; Business and Commerce; Business Education; Communication Studies; Computer Education; Cultural Studies; Economics; Humanities and Social Science Education; Law; Psychology; Public Administration; Social Sciences; Technology Education); **Education, Psychology and Teaching** (Education; Psychology; Teacher Training); **Erhversokonomi, handel og ledelse** (Accountancy; Business Administration; Commercial Law; Economics; Finance; International Business; International Economics; Transport Management); **Finance, Business and Management** (Business and Commerce; Commercial Law; Economics; Ethics; Finance; Information Technology; Management; Modern Languages); **Health Sciences** (Biomedicine; Dental Technology; Dentistry; Dermatology; Dietetics; Forensic Medicine and Dentistry; Gynaecology and Obstetrics; Health Sciences; Hygiene; Medical Technology; Medicine; Neurology; Occupational Therapy; Ophthalmology; Paediatrics; Physical Therapy; Plastic Surgery; Psychiatry and Mental Health; Public Health; Rehabilitation and Therapy; Social and Preventive Medicine; Surgery); **Information Technology, Electronics and Programming** (Computer Engineering; Computer Science; Electrical Engineering; Information Technology; Software Engineering; Telecommunications Engineering); **Language, Culture and History** (Anthropology; Arabic; Archaeology; Asian Studies; Classical Languages; Cultural Studies; Eastern European Studies; English; French; French Studies; German; History; Indic Languages; Islamic Studies; Italian; Japanese; Latin American Studies; Linguistics; Literature; Medicine; Modern Languages; Philosophy; Prehistory; Religion; Scandinavian Languages; South Asian Studies; Spanish; Theology); **Media, Communication and Information** (Arabic; Communication Studies; English; European Languages; French; German; Information Sciences; International Business; Journalism; Management; Marketing; Media Studies; Multimedia; Spanish); **Medicine, Health and Care** (Dental Hygiene; Health Sciences; Medicine; Nursing; Physical Education; Public Health; Sports); **Physics, Mathematics and Nanothechnology** (Economics; Mathematics; Nanotechnology; Physics); **Science and Technology** (Astronomy and Space Science; Biological and Life Sciences; Chemistry; Computer Science; Earth Sciences; Ecology; Environmental Studies; Genetics; Mathematics; Molecular Biology; Natural Resources; Natural Sciences; Physics; Wildlife; Zoology); **Social Sciences, Politics and Economics** (Economics; International Business; Law; Management; Political Sciences; Social Sciences); **Technical Science, Construction and Development** (Architectural and Environmental Design; Civil Engineering; Mechanical Engineering; Power Engineering; Structural Architecture)

Further Information: Also University Hospital and Interdisciplinary Research Centres

History: Founded 1928 by municipal authorities, recognized by Parliament 1931, and awarded Government grant. Achieved full University status 1934. Became State Institution 1970 under the supervision of the Ministry of Education.

Governing Bodies: Board, comprising 11 members - six external and five internal

Academic Year: September to June (September-December; February-June)

Admission Requirements: Secondary school certificate (studentereksamen) or equivalent

Main Language(s) of Instruction: Danish (and English at MA-level)

International Co-operation: Participates in Erasmus Mundus and all major EU Framework Programmes. Member of the Coimbra Group and Utrecht-network. Member of EUA, Euroscience, and Columbus. Partner in Sino-Danish Centre in Beijin, China; Member of Nordic Centre Fudan , China, Member of Nordic Centre India; Member of SANORD- South African-Nordic Centre

Degrees and Diplomas: *Kandidatgrad*: Economics (cand.oecon.); Humanities (cand.mag.); Law (cand.jur.); Political Science (cand.scient.polit.); Psychology (cand.psych.); Science (cand.scient.); Theology (cand.theol.), 5-6 yrs; *Kandidatgrad*: Medicine (cand.med.), 6-7 yrs; *Ph.d.-grad*: by thesis

Student Services: Academic counselling, Canteen, Foreign student adviser, Foreign Studies Centre, Sports facilities

Student Residential Facilities: Yes

Special Facilities: Museum of Prehistory. Natural History Museum. Museum at the Psychiatric Hospital. Steno Museum (Danish Museum for the History of Science and Medicine). Collection of Ancient Art

Libraries: State and University Library, c. 3.4m. Vols

Publications: Acta Jutlandica *(annually)*

Press or Publishing House: Aarhus Universitetsforlag

Academic Staff *2010-2011*	TOTAL
FULL-TIME	11,000
Student Numbers *2010-2011*	
All (Foreign Included)	40,500
FOREIGN ONLY	4,000

Last Updated: 20/07/11

AARHUS SCHOOL OF BUSINESS
HANDELSHØJSKOLEN I ÅRHUS

Fuglesangs Allé 4, 8210 Århus, V
Tel: +45 89-48-66-88
Fax: +45 86-15-01-88
EMail: asb@asb.dk
Website: http://www.asb.dk

Rector: Børge Obel
Tel: +45 38-15-20-14, Fax: +45 89-48-66-61 EMail: bo@asb.dk

University Director: Jan Halle
Tel: +45 89-48-62-00, Fax: +45 89-48-66-61 EMail: jh@asb.dk

International Relations: Lene Rehder
Tel: +45 89-48-62-55, Fax: +45 86-15-46-79 EMail: ler@asb.dk

Departments
Business Studies (Business Administration); **Economics**; **Language and Business Communication** (Communication Studies; Modern Languages); **Law** (Law); **Management** (Management); **Marketing and Statistics**

History: Founded 1939, moved to its present location 1963. An independent institution with university status.

Governing Bodies: Board

Academic Year: September to May/June (September-January; January-February-May-June). Also Summer session

Admission Requirements: Secondary school certificate (studentereksamen) or equivalent

Main Language(s) of Instruction: Danish; English

International Co-operation: With universities in Europe, North America, Asia, Australia

Accrediting Agencies: EQUIS (European Quality Improvement System)

Degrees and Diplomas: *Bachelorgrad (BSc; BA)*: 3 yrs; *Kandidatgrad (MSc; MA)*: a further 2 yrs; *Masteruddannelse*: 2 yrs; *Ph.d.-grad*: a further 3 yrs

Student Services: Academic counselling, Canteen, Employment services, Foreign student adviser, Language programs

Libraries: c. 165,000 vols

ENGINEERING COLLEGE OF ÅRHUS
INGENIØRHØJSKOLEN I ÅRHUS

Dalgas Avenue 2, 8000 Århus, C
Tel: +45 87-30-22-00
Fax: +45 87-30-27-31
EMail: iha@iha.dk
Website: http://www.iha.dk

Rector: Ove Poulsen EMail: opo@iha.dk

Programmes
Engineering (Engineering)

Degrees and Diplomas: *Bachelorgrad*; *Kandidatgrad*

INSTITUTE OF BUSINESS AND TECHNOLOGY IN HERNING
HANDELS- OG INGENIØRHØJSKOLEN (HIH)

Birk Centerpark 15, 7400 Herning
Tel: +45 97-20-83-11
Fax: +45 97-20-83-12
EMail: info@hih.au.dk
Website: http://www.hih.au.dk

Director: Erik Ernø-Kjølhede

Programmes
Engineering (Engineering)

SCHOOL OF EDUCATION - UNIVERSITY OF AARHUS
DANISH SCHOOL OF EDUCATION (DPU)
DANMARKS PÆDAGOGISKE UNIVERSITET

Tuborgvej 164, 2400 København, NV
Tel: +45 88-88-90-00
Fax: +45 88-88-90-01
EMail: dpu@dpu.dk
Website: http://www.dpu.dk

Dean: Mette Thunoe
Tel: +45 88-88-90-56, Fax: +45 88-88-97-01
EMail: rektor@dpu.dk

Director of Administration: Per JohansenFax: +45 88-88-97-04
EMail: plj@dpu.dk

Departments
Curriculum Research *Head*: Martin Bayer; **Educational Anthropology** (Anthropology; Education) *Head*: Mie Buhl; **Educational Psychology** *Head*: Niels Egelund; **Educational Sociology** (Education; Sociology) *Head*: Niels Rosendal Jensen; **Philosophy of Education** (Education; Philosophy) *Head*: Ove Korsgaard

Research Centres
Competence Development (Cultural Studies; Education; Educational Research; Pedagogy); **Environmental and Health Education**; **ICT and Media**; **Professional Development and Leadership** (Leadership)

History: Founded 2000 following merger of the Royal Danish School of Educational Studies, the Danish National Institute for Educational Research and the Danish School of Advanced Pedagogy.

Governing Bodies: Board

Academic Year: September to July

Admission Requirements: Bachelor degree (3 years)

Degrees and Diplomas: *Kandidatgrad*: 2 yrs full-time following first degree; *Ph.d.-grad*. Also Master's Degree in Education (MEd), 2 yrs full-time

Student Services: Academic counselling, Canteen, Social counselling

Special Facilities: E-learning access

Libraries: The Danish National Library of Education, c. 1m. vols

Publications: Research periodical, in Danish

COPENHAGEN BUSINESS SCHOOL
Handelshøjskolen i København

Solbjerg Plads 3, 2000 Frederiksberg
Tel: +45 38-15-38-15
Fax: +45 38-15-20-15
EMail: cbs@cbs.dk
Website: http://www.cbs.dk

President: Per Holten-Andersen
Tel: +45 38-15-58-01 EMail: rektor@cbs.dk

University Director: Hakon Iversen
Tel: +45 38-15-20-31 EMail: hi.ls@cbs.dk

Centres
Applied Management Studies (Management; Small Business); **Art and Leadership** (Leadership); **Asian Research** (Asian Studies); **Biotech Business** (Management); **Business Development**

and **Management Technology** (Management); **Business History** (Economic History; Sociology); **Corporate Communication** (Communication Studies); **Corporate Values and Responsibility** (Management; Sociology); **East European Studies** *(Frederiksberg)* (Eastern European Studies); **Electronic Commerce** (E-Business/Commerce); **Financial Law** (Commercial Law; Finance; Law); **Hospital Management and Organization** (Institutional Administration; Management); **Industrial Dynamics** (Business and Commerce); **Innovation and Entrepreneurship** (Small Business); **IT in Policy Organizations** (Information Technology; Public Administration); **Knowledge Governance** (Management); **Law, Economics and Finance** (Economics; Finance; Law); **Management, Organization and Competence** (Management; Small Business); **Market Economics** (Business and Commerce; Economics); **Marketing Communication** (Marketing); **Study of the Americas** (American Studies)

Departments

Accounting and Auditing *(Frederiksberg)* (Accountancy; Finance; Management); **Business and Politics** (Business Administration; International Economics; Political Sciences); **Computer Assisted Linguistics** *(Frederiksberg)* (Computer Science; Linguistics); **Economics** (Economics); **English** *(Frederiksberg)* (English; Linguistics; Modern Languages; Translation and Interpretation); **Finance** *(Frederiksberg)* (Finance; Insurance); **French, German, Italian, Russian and Spanish** *(Frederiksberg)* (French; German; Italian; Linguistics; Russian; Spanish; Translation and Interpretation); **Innovation and Organizational Economics** (Economics; Industrial Management); **Intercultural Communication and Management** *(Frederiksberg)* (Communication Studies; Cultural Studies; Management); **International Culture and Communication Studies** (Communication Studies; Cultural Studies; Modern Languages; Social Sciences); **International Economics and Management** *(Frederiksberg)* (International Economics; Management); **International Languages Studies and Computational Linguistics** (Arts and Humanities; Modern Languages; Translation and Interpretation); **IT Management** (Computer Science; E-Business/Commerce; Information Sciences; Information Technology; Mathematics); **Law** *(International Law related to Business with focus on Law as a Management Tool, Frederiksberg)* (Commercial Law; European Union Law; International Law; Labour Law; Law); **Management, Politics and Philosophy** *(Copenhagen)* (Management; Philosophy; Political Sciences); **Marketing** *(Frederiksberg)* (Marketing); **Operations Management** *(Frederiksberg)* (Industrial Management; Management); **Organization** *(Frederiksberg)* (Human Resources; Industrial Management; Management; Sociology); **Strategic Management and Globalisation** *(Frederiksberg)* (International Business; Management)

Faculties

Economics and Business Administration (Business Administration; Economics); **Languages, Communication and Cultural Studies** *(Frederiksberg)* (Communication Studies; Cultural Studies; Modern Languages)

History: Founded 1917 as a private Institution, integrated into the national system, thus becoming self-governing 1965. Acquired present status 2003.

Governing Bodies: Executive Board of Directors

Academic Year: September to June (September-January; February-June)

Admission Requirements: Secondary school leaving certificate (studentereksamen) or Højere Forberedelseseksamen, Højere Handelseksamen, Højere Teknisk eksamen or recognized equivalent

Main Language(s) of Instruction: Danish, English

Degrees and Diplomas: *Bachelorgrad*: Asian Studies (BSc); Business Administration and Commercial Law (BSc); Business Administration and Computer Science (BSc); Business Administration and Management Science (BSc); Business Administration and Organizational Communication (BSc); Business Administration and Philosophy (BSc); Business Administration and Psychology (BSc); Business Administration and Service Management (BSc); Business, Language and Culture - French or German or Spanish (BSc); Economics and Business Administration (BSc); English and Organisational Communication (BA); International Business Administration (BSc); International Business Commu-

nication - European Studies or American Studies (BA), 3 yrs; *Bachelorgrad*: Business Administration and Sociology; Business, Asian Language and Culture - Japanese or Chinese; Information Management; Intercultural Market Communication - English, French, German, Spanish; International Business and Politics; *Kandidatgrad*: Business Administration and Philosophy; Business Administration and Commercial Law; Business Administration and Organisation Communication; Business Administration and Management; Business Administration and Psychology; Economics; Economics and Business Administration; Business, Language and Culture; International Business and Politics; Business Economics and Auditing; Business Administration and Information Systems, a further 2 yrs; *Kandidatgrad*: Economics; Management of Creative Business Processes; Organisational Innovation and Entrepreneurship; Service Management; Human Resource; Political Communication and Management; International Law, Economics and Management; *Ph.d.-grad*: a further 3 yrs. Also Graduate Certificate and Diploma in Business Administration

Student Services: Academic counselling, Canteen, Employment services, Foreign student adviser, Health services, Language programs, Social counselling

Libraries: c. 309,000 vols, 3,200 periodicals

Press or Publishing House: CBS Publishing Press

Last Updated: 28/03/12

COPENHAGEN UNIVERSITY COLLEGE OF ENGINEERING

Ingeniørhøjskolen i København (IHK)
Lautrupvang 15, 2750 Ballerup
Tel: +45 44-80-50-88
Fax: +45 44-80-50-10
EMail: studadm@ihk.dk
Website: http://www.ihk.dk

Rector: Conni Simonsen EMail: fkr@ihk.dk

Departments

Continuing Education (Engineering; Management; Marketing); **Electronics and Computer Engineering** (Civil Engineering; Computer Engineering; Electronic Engineering); **Information and Communication Technology** (Information Technology; Telecommunications Engineering); **Mechanical Engineering - Design and Industrial** (Industrial Design; Machine Building; Mechanical Engineering; Production Engineering)

History: Created 1881 as Københavns Teknikum. Acquired current title and status 2007.

Governing Bodies: Board of Directors; Rector

Academic Year: September - January (autumn semester); February to June (spring semester); June to July (summer programmes)

Admission Requirements: Minimum 3 years of High School Diploma with Maths level A and Physics and Chemistry. For Bachelor programmes in English, IELTS 6,5 required.

Fees: (Danish Krone): 100,000 per annum

Main Language(s) of Instruction: Danish, English

Accrediting Agencies: CIRIUS

Degrees and Diplomas: *Bachelorgrad (BEng)*: 3 1/2 yrs. Also 'Exportingeniør' in 4 1/2 yrs.

Student Services: Academic counselling, Canteen, Cultural centre, Employment services, Foreign student adviser, Handicapped facilities, Language programs, Social counselling, Sports facilities

Academic Staff 2010-2011	MEN	WOMEN	TOTAL
FULL-TIME	30	20	**50**
PART-TIME	–	10	**10**
STAFF WITH DOCTORATE			
FULL-TIME	–	–	**120**
PART-TIME	–	–	c. **100**
Student Numbers 2010-2011			
All (Foreign Included)	–	–	c. **2,300**
FOREIGN ONLY	–	–	**400**

Evening students, 450.
Last Updated: 24/10/11

FUNEN ART ACADEMY
Det Fynske Kunstakademi
Brandts Passage 43, 5000 Odense, C
Tel: +45 66-11-12-88
Fax: +45 66-19-26-88
EMail: info@detfynskekunstakademi.dk
Website: http://www.detfynskekunstakademi.dk

Rector: Merete Jankowski EMail: mj@detfynskekunstakademi.dk

Programmes
Fine Arts (Fine Arts)

Degrees and Diplomas: *Bachelorgrad*; *Masteruddannelse*

IT UNIVERSITY OF COPENHAGEN
IT-Universitetet i København (ITU)
Rued Langgards Vej 7, 2300 København, S
Tel: +45 72-18-50-00
Fax: +45 72-18-50-01
EMail: itu@itu.dk
Website: http://www.itu.dk

Rector: Mads Tofte EMail: tofte@itu.dk; rektor@itu.dk

International Relations: Leni Schroll, International Coordinator
Tel: +45 72-18-52-30 EMail: leni@itu.dk; interoffice@itu.dk

Programmes
Information Technology (Communication Arts; Computer Graphics; Design; E-Business/Commerce; Information Technology; Media Studies; Software Engineering; Technology)

History: Founded 1999 as faculty hosted by the Copenhagen Business School. Acquired present status 2003.

Governing Bodies: Board of Directors

Academic Year: September to June

Admission Requirements: Bachelor Degree

Fees: (Danish Krone): 50,000 per term: Students from countries outside the European Union (EU) and the European Economic Area (EEA) are charged tuition fees

Main Language(s) of Instruction: Danish and English

International Co-operation: Participates in the Erasmus programme

Degrees and Diplomas: *Diplomuddannelse*: Information Technology, 2 yrs, part-time; *Bachelorgrad*: Information Technology (BSc), 3 yrs; *Kandidatgrad*: Information Technology (MSc), 2 yrs; *Masteruddannelse*: Information Technology, 3 yrs, part-time; *Doktorgrad*: Information Technology (PhD), 3-4 yrs. Kandidatgrad equivalent to Master of Science

Student Services: Academic counselling, Canteen, Foreign student adviser

Academic Staff *2010*: Total: c. 500
Student Numbers *2010*: Total: c. 2,000
Last Updated: 24/10/11

KOLDING SCHOOL OF DESIGN
Designskolen Kolding
Ågade 10, 6000 Kolding
Tel: +45 76-30-11-00
Fax: +45 76-30-11-12
EMail: dk@designskolenkolding.dk
Website: http://www.designskolenkolding.dk

Rector: Elsebeth Gerner Nielsen EMail: egn@dskd.dk

Departments
Ceramics and Glass (Ceramic Art; Glass Art); **Fashion Design** (Fashion Design); **Graphic Design** (Graphic Design); **Illustration Design** (Painting and Drawing); **Industrial Design** (Industrial Design); **Interactive Design** (Design); **Textiles** (Textile Design)

History: Founded 1967 as Kunsthåndværkerskole (Arts and Crafts School). In 1998, the school changed its name to Kolding School of Design. Acquired present status 2010.

Main Language(s) of Instruction: Danish

Degrees and Diplomas: *Bachelorgrad*; *Masteruddannelse*; *Doktorgrad*
Last Updated: 08/03/12

RHYTHMIC MUSIC CONSERVATORY
Rytmisk Musikkonservatorium
Leo Mathisens Vej 1, Holmen, 1437 København, K
Tel: +45 32-68-67-00
Fax: +45 32-68-67-66
EMail: rmc@rmc.dk
Website: http://www.rmc.dk

Principal: Henrik Sveidahl

International Relations: Aage Hagen

Programmes
Music (Music; Music Education; Music Theory and Composition)

Degrees and Diplomas: *Bachelorgrad*; *Kandidatgrad*; *Masteruddannelse*
Last Updated: 24/10/11

ROSKILDE UNIVERSITY
Roskilde Universitet (RUC)
Postbox 260, Universitetsvej 1, 4000 Roskilde
Tel: +45 46-74-20-00
Fax: +45 46-74-30-00
EMail: ruc@ruc.dk
Website: http://www.ruc.dk

Rector: Ib Poulsen
Tel: +45 46-74-20-65, Fax: +45 46-74-30-01 EMail: rektor@ruc.dk
Pro-rector: Hanne Leth Andersen EMail: prorektor@ruc.dk

Departments
Communication, Business and Information Technologies (Business Administration; Communication Studies; Computer Science; Design; Information Technology; Journalism); **Culture and Identity** (Cultural Studies; Danish; English; French; German; History; Philosophy); **Environmental, Social and Spatial Change** (Environmental Studies); **Psychology and Educational Studies** (Educational Sciences; Psychology); **Science, Systems and Models** (Biology; Chemistry; Mathematics; Molecular Biology; Physics); **Society and Globalisation** (Administration; European Studies; Political Sciences; Social Sciences)

History: Founded 1972 by Government decree. A State Institution employing new teaching and learning methods based on an 'integrated' approach to higher education and placing emphasis on group work.

Governing Bodies: Board of Directors, comprising 9 members

Academic Year: September to June (September-January; February-June)

Admission Requirements: Secondary school certificate (studentereksamen), or appropriate educational level reached through formal or non-formal education

Fees: None

Main Language(s) of Instruction: Danish, English

International Co-operation: Participates in the Socrates, Tempus, Nordplus, Crepuq programmes (c. 250 partners)

Degrees and Diplomas: *Bachelorgrad*: Humanities; Natural Sciences; Social Sciences, 3 yrs; *Kandidatgrad*: Humanities; Social Sciences; Natural Sciences, 5 yrs; *Ph.d.-grad*: 8 yrs

Student Services: Academic counselling, Canteen, Foreign student adviser, Handicapped facilities, Language programs, Nursery care, Social counselling, Sports facilities

Libraries: c. 624,594 vols
Last Updated: 05/07/11

ROYAL ACADEMY OF MUSIC, AARHUS
Det Jyske Musikkonservatorium
Skovgaardsgade 2C, 8000 Aarhus, C
Tel: +45 72-26-74-00
Fax: +45 51-17-64-69
EMail: mail@musikkons.dk
Website: http://www.musikkons.dk/

Rector: Thomas Winther
Tel: +45 72-26-74-01 EMail: thw@musikkons.dk

International Relations: Keld Hosbond
Tel: +45 72-26-74-19 EMail: keho@musikkons.dk

Programmes

Music (Music; Music Education; Music Theory and Composition; Musical Instruments; Religious Music)

History: Founded 1927. The Academy of Music, Aalborg, and The Royal Academy of Music, Aarhus, have merged by the 1st of January, 2010.

Main Language(s) of Instruction: Danish

Degrees and Diplomas: *Bachelorgrad*; *Kandidatgrad*
Last Updated: 24/10/11

ROYAL DANISH ACADEMY OF FINE ARTS, SCHOOL OF ARCHITECTURE

Kunstakademiets Arkitektskole
Philip de Langes Allé 10, 1435 København K
Tel: +45 32-68-60-00
Fax: +45 32-68-61-11
EMail: arkitektskolen@karch.dk
Website: http://www.karch.dk

Rector: Sven Felding
Tel: +45 32-68-60-04, Fax: +45 32-68-60-76
EMail: sven.felding@karch.dk

Director: Mette Mejlvang
Tel: +45 32-68-60-15 EMail: mette.mejlvang@karch.dk

International Relations: Rasmus Levy
Tel: +45 32-68-60-26, Fax: +45 32-68-60-76
EMail: rasmus.levy@karch.dk

Departments

Architecture, Building and Realization (Building Technologies); **Architecture, Conurbation and Industrialization** (Architecture; Urban Studies); **Architecture, Design and Industrial Form** (Architecture; Design) *Head*: Anders Brix; **Architecture, Experiment and Technology**; **Architecture, Process and Method** (Architecture); **Architecture, Space and Form**; **Architecture, Space and Habitation** (Architecture); **Architecture, Town and Building** (Architecture; Town Planning); **Architecture, Town and Landscape** (Architecture and Planning; Landscape Architecture)

Institutes

Architectural Technology; **Building Culture (Architectural Theory, History and Restoration)** (Architectural Restoration; Architecture; History); **Design and Communication** (Communication Studies; Design); **Town Planning, Space and Function** (Town Planning)

Research Centres

Design (Design); **Industrial Architecture**; **Information Technology and Architecture**; **Public Space** (Landscape Architecture); **Sports and Architecture** (Architecture; Sports); **Town Planning** (Town Planning)

History: Founded 1754 as the Royal Danish Painting, Sculpture and Building Academy to educate both artists and craftsmen in the three disciplines. Acquired present status and title 1960.

Governing Bodies: School Council

Academic Year: September to June (September-January ; February-June)

Admission Requirements: Secondary school certificate and entrance examination

Fees: None

Main Language(s) of Instruction: Danish; English

International Co-operation: Participates in Erasmus, Nordplus and bilateral agreements (European countries, Japan, Australia, Canada, New Zealand and USA).

Accrediting Agencies: Ministry of Culture

Degrees and Diplomas: *Diplomuddannelse*: Architecture, 5 yrs; *Bachelorgrad*: Architecture (cand.arch), 3 yrs; *Ph.d.-grad*: Architecture, a further 3 yrs following Master

Student Services: Academic counselling, Canteen, Foreign student adviser, Handicapped facilities

Special Facilities: Computer-aided design laboratories

Libraries: c. 150,000 vols
Last Updated: 10/08/11

ROYAL DANISH ACADEMY OF FINE ARTS, SCHOOLS OF ARCHITECTURE, DESIGN AND CONSERVATION

Det Kongelige Danske Kunstakademis Skoler for Arkitektur, Design og Konservering
Philip De Langes Allé 10, 1435 København, K
Tel: +45 3268 6000
EMail: info@kadk.dk
Website: http://www.kadk.dk

Rector: Lene Dammand Lund (2012-)
Tel: +45 33-74-47-03 EMail: rl@kons.dk

International Relations: Christina Lund
Tel: +45 33-74-47-04 EMail: clo@kons.dk

Schools

Fine Arts and Conservation (Fine Arts; Graphic Arts; Heritage Preservation; Sculpture)

History: Founded 1973. Acquired present status following merger between the Royal Danish Academy of Fine Arts, School of Architecture and the Danish Design School.

Governing Bodies: School Council

Academic Year: September to June

Admission Requirements: Upper secondary school leaving certificate (Studentereksamen), Higher preparatory examination (Højere Forberedelseseksamen, HF) or equivalent

Main Language(s) of Instruction: Danish

Degrees and Diplomas: *Bachelorgrad*: Conservation (BSc), 3 yrs; *Kandidatgrad*: Conservation (MSc), a further 2 yrs; *Ph.d.-grad*: Conservation (PhD), a further 3 yrs

Libraries: Central Academic Library
Last Updated: 27/02/12

ROYAL DANISH ACADEMY OF FINE ARTS SCHOOL OF VISUAL ARTS

Det Kongelige Danske Kunstakademi, Billedkunstskolerne
Postboks 9014, Kongens Nytorv 1, 1022 København, K
Tel: +45 33-74-46-00
Fax: +45 33-74-46-66
EMail: bks@kunstakademiet.dk
Website: http://www.kunstakademiet.dk

Rector: Mikkel Bogh (2005-)
Tel: +45 33-74-46-01 EMail: mikkel.bogh@kunstakademiet.dk

Administrator: Kim Gundersen
Tel: +45 33-74-46-08, Fax: +45 33-74-46-64
EMail: kim.gundersen@kunstakademiet.dk

International Relations: Otto Pedersen
Tel: +45 33-74-46-07, Fax: +45 33-74-46-66

Departments

Art Theory (Art Education); **Graphic Arts** (Graphic Arts; Printing and Printmaking; Visual Arts); **Media Arts** (Computer Science; Media Studies; Video); **Painting** (Painting and Drawing); **Sculpture** (Sculpture; Visual Arts); **Visual Arts** (Visual Arts)

Further Information: Also Laboratories/workshops

History: Founded 1754 on the same lines as the Académie des Beaux Arts in France, and later acquired the status of a modern School of Art.

Governing Bodies: Skoleråd

Academic Year: October to June (October-December; January-June)

Admission Requirements: Entrance competition

Fees: None

Main Language(s) of Instruction: Danish; English

International Co-operation: Participates in the Erasmus (with EU-Countries) and Kuno (with Nordic Countries) programmes

Degrees and Diplomas: *Billedkunstner*: Visual Arts (MFA), 6 yrs

Student Services: Academic counselling, Canteen, Foreign student adviser, Social counselling

Special Facilities: Art Gallery

Libraries: Kulturhistorisk Laboratorium, c. 3,000 vols
Press or Publishing House: Billedkunstskolerne Publishers
Last Updated: 24/10/11

ROYAL DANISH ACADEMY OF MUSIC
Det Kongelige Danske Musikkonservatorium (DKDM)
Rosenørns Allé 22, 1970 Frederiksberg C
Tel: +45 72-26-72-26
Fax: +45 72-26-72-72
EMail: dkdm@dkdm.dk
Website: http://www.dkdm.dk

Principal: Bertel Krarup

Head Administrator: Carsten Ruby EMail: cry@dkdm.dk

Departments
Brass, Percussion and Orchestra Conducting (Conducting; Musical Instruments); **Church Music** (Religious Music); **Composition/Theory** (Music Theory and Composition); **Educational Theory** (Music Education); **Piano, Guitar and Accordion** (Musical Instruments); **Recording** (Sound Engineering (Acoustics)); **Singing** (Singing); **Strings** (Musical Instruments); **Woodwind and Harp** (Musical Instruments)

History: Founded 1867 as a private institution. Became a State institution under the jurisdiction of the Ministry of Cultural Affairs 1949.

Governing Bodies: Konservatorierådet (Council, composed of the Rector and Pro-Rector, 11 members of the academic staff, 4 students, and 2 members of the administrative staff)

Academic Year: September to June (September-December; January-June)

Admission Requirements: Entrance examination

Main Language(s) of Instruction: Danish; English

Degrees and Diplomas: *Bachelorgrad*; *Masteruddannelse*. Also Advanced postgraduate diploma

Student Services: Academic counselling, Canteen, Employment services, Social counselling

Special Facilities: Concert Hall; Practice room

Libraries: c. 50,000 vols
Last Updated: 08/06/11

ROYAL SCHOOL OF LIBRARY AND INFORMATION SCIENCE
Informations Videnskabelige Akademi (RSLIS)
Birketinget 6, 2300 København, S
Tel: +45 32-58-60-66
Fax: +45 32-84-02-01
EMail: iva@iva.dk
Website: http://www.iva.dk/english/

Rector: Per Hasle EMail: rektor@iva.dk

Administration Director: Hanne Friis Kaas
Tel: +45 32-58-66-60 EMail: hfk@iva.dk

International Relations: Leif Kajbers EMail: studyabroad@iva.dk

Departments
Culture and Media (Cultural Studies; Media Studies); **Information Studies** (Information Sciences)

Institutes
Library and Information Management (Information Management; Library Science)

Further Information: Also department at Aalborg

History: Founded 1956 as Danmarks Biblioteksskole. Acquired present title ans status 2010.

Main Language(s) of Instruction: Danish

Accrediting Agencies: Danish Evaluation Institute (EVA)

Degrees and Diplomas: *Bachelorgrad*; *Kandidatgrad*; *Ph.d.-grad*

Student Numbers *2010*: Total: c. 1,000
Last Updated: 24/10/11

TECHNICAL UNIVERSITY OF DENMARK
Danmarks Tekniske Universitet
Anker Engelundsvej 1, Bygning 101, 2800 Kgs. Lyngby
Tel: +45 45-25-25-25
Fax: +45 45-88-17-99
EMail: uddannelse@adm.dtu.dk
Website: http://www.dtu.dk

Rector: Lars Pallesen (2001-)
Tel: +45 45-25-10-00, Fax: +45 45-93-40-28
EMail: rektor@adm.dtu.dk

Centres
Communications, Optics and Materials (Communication Studies; Materials Engineering; Optics)

Departments
BioCentrum-DTU *(BIC)* (Biotechnology); **Chemical Engineering** *(KT)* (Chemical Engineering); **Chemistry** *(KI)* (Chemistry); **Civil Engineering** *(BYG)* (Civil Engineering); **Environment and Resources** *(M&R)* (Environmental Studies; Natural Resources); **Informatics and Mathematical Modelling** *(IMM)* (Computer Science); **Manufacturing Engineering and Management** *(IPL)* (Leadership; Management; Production Engineering); **Mathematics** *(MAT)* (Mathematics); **Mechanical Engineering** *(MEK)* (Construction Engineering; Energy Engineering; Mechanical Engineering); **Micro- and Nanotechnology** *(MIC)* (Microelectronics; Nanotechnology); **Ørsted DTU** (Electrical and Electronic Engineering); **Physics** *(FYS)* (Physics); **Traffic and Transport** *(CTT)* (Transport Management)

History: Founded 1829 as a State Institution under the supervision of the Ministry of Education. Departments restructured 1996. Acquired present status 2001.

Governing Bodies: Konsistorium, Board of Governors

Academic Year: September to July (September-January; February-July)

Admission Requirements: Secondary school certificate (studentereksamen) or foreign equivalent with defined levels of education in mathematics, physics and chemistry

Main Language(s) of Instruction: Danish, English

Degrees and Diplomas: *Bachelorgrad*: Engineering (Diplomingeniør), 3 1/2 yrs; *Masteruddannelse*: Engineering (Civilingeniør), 5 yrs; *Ph.d.-grad*: Engineering, 5 yrs (Master Degree) plus 3 yrs of PhD study; *Doktorgrad*: Technical Sciences (dr.tech), by thesis

Student Services: Academic counselling, Canteen, Cultural centre, Foreign student adviser, Foreign Studies Centre, Nursery care, Social counselling, Sports facilities

Libraries: Central Library
Last Updated: 24/10/11

THE ACADEMY OF MUSIC AND DRAMATIC ARTS
Syddansk Musikkonservatorium and Skuespillerskole (SMKS)
Islandsgade 2, 5000 Odense, C
Tel: +45 66-11-99-00
Fax: +45 66-11-99 20
EMail: info@smks.dk
Website: http://www.dfm.dk

Rector: Axel Momme

Vice-Rector: Inger Allan

Departments
Classical/Contemporary Music (Music; Music Theory and Composition); **Film** (Film); **Folk Music** (Music); **Jazz/Rock**; **Music Teaching** (Music Education)

Further Information: Also a branch in Esberg

History: Founded 1929 as a private institution, Det Fynske Musikkonservatorium became a government institution under the supervision of the Ministry of Cultural Affairs 1972. Reoganised and merged with the Academic of Music and Music Communication in Esberg, and the Acting school in Odense, 2010.

Governing Bodies: Council

Academic Year: September to June

Admission Requirements: Audition in the respective major instrument/academic area, plus minors (eartraining, piano, music theory)

Fees: (Euros): 11.000 € per annum for for Bachelor programmes (for students from non EU/EEA countries)

Main Language(s) of Instruction: Danish

Degrees and Diplomas: *Bachelorgrad*: Music; *Kandidatgrad*: Music. Also Advanced Postgraduate diploma

Publications: Yearbook *(annually)*
Last Updated: 24/10/11

THE JUTLAND ART ACADEMY
Det Jyske Kunstakademi
Mejlgade 32-34, 8000 Århus, C
Tel: +45 86-13-69-19
Fax: +45 86-13-69-71
EMail: djk@djk.nu
Website: http://www.djk.nu

Rector: Jesper Rasmussen

Programmes
Fine Arts (Art History; Fine Arts)

Degrees and Diplomas: *Bachelorgrad*; *Masteruddannelse*

UNIVERSITY OF COPENHAGEN
Københavns Universitet
Postboks 2177, Nørregade 10, 1017 København, K
Tel: +45 35-32-26-26
Fax: +45 35-32-26-28
EMail: ku@ku.dk
Website: http://www.ku.dk

Rector: Ralf Hemmingsen (2005-)
Tel: +45 35-32-26-12 EMail: rektor@adm.ku.dk

Pro-Rector: Thomas Bjørnholm
Tel: +45 35-32-26-05 EMail: pro-rektor@adm.ku.dk

Faculties
Health Sciences (Biology; Dentistry; Health Sciences; Medicine); **Humanities** (Arts and Humanities); **Law** (Law); **Life Sciences** (Biological and Life Sciences); **Pharmaceutical Sciences** (Applied Chemistry; Chemistry; Pharmacology; Pharmacy); **Science** (Natural Sciences); **Social Sciences** (Social Sciences); **Theology** (Theology)

History: Founded 1479. Acquired present status 2007 following the merger between the former Den Kgl. Veterinær- og Landbohøjskole (The Royal Veterinary and Agricultural University) and the Danmarks Farmaceutiske Universitet (The Danish University of Pharmaceutical Sciences). Financed by the State.

Governing Bodies: Konsistorium (Senate); Faculty Councils; Institute Boards with representation of academic staff (75%) and members of the technical and administrative staff (25%)

Academic Year: September to July (September-January; February-July)

Admission Requirements: Secondary school certificate (studentereksamen), or foreign equivalent, and entrance examination in Danish language. Foreign exchange and guest students should be enrolled at a University in their home country or elsewhere abroad during their proposed stay at the University of Copenhagen

Fees: None

Main Language(s) of Instruction: Danish (some courses taught in English for foreign exchange students)

International Co-operation: Participates in the Socrates/Erasmus and Nordplus programmes

Degrees and Diplomas: *Bachelorgrad*: Arts (BA); Science (BSc), 3 yrs; *Kandidatgrad (cand. art.)*: 5 yrs; *Kandidatgrad*: Actuarial Science (cand.act.); Dentistry (cand.odont.); Economics (cand.polit.); Economics (cand.scient.oecen.); Humanities (cand.mag.); Law (cand.jur.); Psychology (cand.psyk.); Science (cand.scient.); Sociology (cand.scient.soc.); Statistics (cand.stat.); Theology (cand.theol.), 5 yrs; *Kandidatgrad*: Arts; Social Sciences; *Kandi-*

datgrad: Medicine (cand.med.), 6-7 yrs; *Ph.d.-grad*: a further 3 yrs; *Doktorgrad*: by thesis

Student Services: Academic counselling, Canteen, Foreign student adviser, Language programs, Nursery care, Social counselling, Sports facilities

Student Residential Facilities: For foreign students

Special Facilities: Botanical Museum. Zoological Museum. Medical History Museum. Mineralogy Museum

Libraries: University Libraries (Humanities, Science, Medicine, Social Sciences, Law and Theology), c. 1m. vols
Last Updated: 18/03/11

UNIVERSITY OF SOUTHERN DENMARK
Syddansk Universitet
Campusvej 55, 5230 Odense, M
Tel: +45 65-50-10-00
Fax: +45 66-50-10-90
EMail: sdu@sdu.dk
Website: http://www.sdu.dk

Rector: Jens Oddershede (2001-)
Tel: +45 65-50-10-30 EMail: jod@sdu.dk

International Relations: Lisbeth Pinholt, Director of International Relations
Tel: +45 65-50-31-81, Fax: +45 66-15-75-00 EMail: lp@sdu.dk

Faculties
Engineering (Biotechnology; Engineering; Mechanics; Robotics) *Dean*: Per Michael Johansen; **Health Sciences** (Chiropractic; Health Sciences; Medicine; Sports) *Dean*: Ole Skøtt; **Humanities** (American Studies; Arts and Humanities; Classical Languages; Comparative Literature; Danish; English; French; German; History; Hotel and Restaurant; Marine Science and Oceanography; Mass Communication; Middle Eastern Studies; Nordic Studies; Philosophy; Religion; Spanish; Tourism) *Dean*: Flemming G. Andersen; **Science** (Biology; Chemistry; Computer Science; Marine Science and Oceanography; Mathematics; Natural Sciences; Physics) *Dean*: Henrik Pedersen; **Social Sciences** (Business and Commerce; Economics; European Studies; Journalism; Law; Political Sciences) *Dean*: Jesper Strandskov

History: Founded in 1966 through a merger involving Odense University, the Southern Denmark School of Business and Engineering and South Jutland University Centre.

Governing Bodies: University Board; Faculty Councils; Departmental Councils; Study Boards

Academic Year: September to June (September-January; February-June)

Admission Requirements: Secondary school certificate (studentereksamen) or Højere-Forberedelseseksamen or Handelseksamen, or recognized foreign equivalent

Fees: See website, or contact institution.

Main Language(s) of Instruction: Danish, English

International Co-operation: With 600 universities in Europe, USA, Canada, Asia, Latin America, Australia, New Zealand etc. Also participates in the Socrates and Nordplus progammes.

Degrees and Diplomas: *Diplomuddannelse*: Business Economics; Business Language (HD; ED), 4 yrs; *Bachelorgrad*: Arts (BA); Business Administration and Modern Languages (BA int.); Science in Business Administration (HA); Science in Business Administration and Law (HA (jur.)); Science in Business Administration and Tax Law (HA (jur.) i skat); Science in Physical Education (B.Sc.); Science in Public Health (B. scient. san. publ.); Science or Engineering (B.Sc.), 3 yrs; *Bachelorgrad*: Engineering (diplomingeniør); Journalism (BA), 3 1/2 yrs; *Bachelorgrad*: Physical Education (exam.scient.), 2 yrs; *Kandidatgrad*: Arts and Humanities; *Kandidatgrad*: Arts and Humanities (cand.mag.); Business Administration (cand.-merc.); Business Administration and Auditing (cand.merc.aud.); Business Administration and Law (cand.merc.jur.); Business Administration and Modern Languages (cand.negot.); Clinical Biomechanics (cand.manu.); Economics (cand.oecon.); Engineering (cand.polyt.); International Business Administration (cand.merc.int.); Mathematics and Economics (cand.scient.oecon.); Modern Language and Information Technology (cand.ling.merc.); Physical Education and Health (cand.scient.); Physical Education nad Health (cand.scient.); Political Science (cand.scient.pol.); Political Science (cand.scient.pol.); Science (cand.scient.); Science (cand.scient.), 5 yrs; *Kandidatgrad*: Health Sciences (cand.scient.san.), 2 yrs following a bachelor's degree; *Kandidatgrad*: IT in IT, Communication and Organization (cand.it); IT in Multimedia Design, Technology and Production (cand.it.), 2 yrs following Bachelor's degree; *Kandidatgrad*: Journalism (cand.public.), 5 1/2 yrs; *Kandidatgrad*: Medicine (cand.med.), 6 yrs; *Masteruddannelse*: Business Administration; Language Administration; Public Management; Public Health; Multimedia Design, Technology and Production; IT, Communication and Organization; Culture-historical Informatics; Gender and Culture (MBA; MLA; MPM; MPH), 2 years; *Ph.d.-grad*: Health Sciences (Ph.D.), 8-9 1/2 yrs; *Ph.d.-grad*: Humanities, Social Sciences, Science and Engineering (Ph.D.), 8 yrs

Student Services: Academic counselling, Canteen, Employment services, Foreign student adviser, Foreign Studies Centre, Handicapped facilities, Sports facilities
Libraries: Central Libray (University Library of Southern Denmark), more than 1.2 million vols
Publications: Ny viden, Journal of Education and Research *(monthly)*
Press or Publishing House: Odense University Press

Academic Staff *2008-2009*: Total 2,594
Student Numbers *2008-2009*: Total 19,027
Last Updated: 05/07/11

Dominican Republic

STRUCTURE OF HIGHER EDUCATION SYSTEM

Description:

Higher education is provided by public and private universities and other higher education institutions. All institutions must be authorized by the SEESCYT, which replaced the Consejo Nacional de Educación Superior (CONES) in 2001. The SEESCYT supervises the enforcement of regulations in the field of higher education and provides technical assistance to higher education institutions and advisory services to the executive power.

Stages of studies:

University level first stage: *Licenciatura*
Courses usually last for four years and lead to the Licenciatura. Courses in fields such as Engineering and Architecture take five to six years and lead to a professional title.

University level second stage: *Especialista, Maestría, Doctor*
Studies last between one and three years following the Licenciatura and lead to the title and/or degree of Especialista or Maestría. The only Doctorados conferred are professional qualifications in Law, Medicine, Veterinary Medicine and Dentistry. Studies last for approximately six years and lead to the title of Doctor.

ADMISSION TO HIGHER EDUCATION

Admission to university-level studies:

Name of secondary school credential required: Bachillerato

For entry to: Universidad, Instituto Técnico de Estudios Superiores, Instituto Especializado de Estudios Superiores

Foreign students admission:

Quotas: 33%

Entrance exam requirements: Students must hold the Bachillerato, pass an Examen de Admisión, and hold a copy of their academic record, together with a certification by their home university.

Entry regulations: Foreign students must possess a student visa or a residence permit, depending on their nationality. A good command of Spanish is necessary.

Health requirements: Foreign students must hold a health certificate

Language requirements: Students must have a good command of Spanish.

RECOGNITION OF STUDIES

Quality assurance system:

The SEESCYT authorizes the opening of higher education institutions and the ADAAC is responsible for the evaluation and accreditation, on a voluntary basis, of programmes and institutions.

NATIONAL BODIES

Secretaría de Estado de Educación superior, Ciencia y Tecnología - SEESCyT (Secretariat of State for Higher Education, Science and Technology)
Secretary of State: Ligia Amada Melo de Cardona
Secretary, Higher Education: Isabel Nardelina Datt
Av. Máximo Gómez No. 31, esq Pedro Henriquez Ureña

Santo Domingo
Tel: +1(809) 731 1100
EMail: info@seescyt.gov.do
WWW: http://www.seescyt.gov.do
Role of national body: Responsible for the elaboration of higher education policies, planning, promotion and evaluation.

Asocación Dominicana para el Autoestudio y la Acreditación - ADAAC (Dominican Association for Self-Evaluation and Accreditation)
President: Gustavo Batista Vargas
Executive-Director: Saturnino de los Santos
C/ Máximo Cabral #11, Casi Esq. Canoabo,
Gazcue
Santo Domingo
Tel: +809 686 5264
Fax: +809 688 7562
WWW: http://adaac.org.do/

Asociación Dominicana de Rectores de Universidades - ADRU (Dominican Association of University Rectors)
Executive Director: José Ángel González Hernández
Calle Juan Paradas Bonilla No. 5, Apto. 3, tercer Nivel, Ensanche Naco -
Apartado Postal No.2465
Santo Domingo
Tel: +1(809) 683 0003
Fax: +1(809) 565 4933
EMail: adru@verizon.net.do;adru@cobetel.net
WWW: http://www.adru.org
Role of national body: Encourages inter-university relations to promote academic activities, research and lifelong education, and exchanges with national and international bodies.

Data for academic year: 2008-2009
Source: IAU from National Information System on Higher Education, Science, Technology and Innovation, Santo Domingo, 2008. Bodies updated in 2011.

INSTITUTIONS

APEC UNIVERSITY
Universidad APEC (UNAPEC)
Avenida Máximo Gómez 72, Santo Domingo
Tel: +1 809 686-0021
Fax: +1 809 685-5581
EMail: apec@apec.edu.do
Website: http://www.unapec.edu.do
Rector: Justo Pedro Castellanos (2007-)
International Relations: Inmaculada Madera

Divisions
Post-Baccalaureate and Master's Degrees (Administration; Finance; Industrial and Production Economics; International Law; Management; Marketing)

Schools
Accountancy (Accountancy); **Administration** (Administration) *Dean*: Lourdes Concepción; **Arts** (Advertising and Publicity; Architectural and Environmental Design; Arts and Humanities; Graphic Design; Interior Design); **Computer Science** (Computer Science; Systems Analysis); **Engineering and Technology** (Electrical Engineering; Electronic Engineering; Industrial Engineering; Tech-

nology); **Law** (Law) *Dean*: Alejandro Moscoso; **Marketing** (Marketing); **Tourism** (Hotel Management; Tourism)
History: Founded 1965 as Instituto de Estudios Superiores by the Acción Pro-Educación y Cultura, Inc. (APEC). Acquired present status 1983. A private Institution authorized by the Government to award degrees in 1968.
Governing Bodies: Board of Trustees
Academic Year: January to December (January-April; May-August; September-December)
Admission Requirements: Secondary school certificate (bachillerato) and entrance examination
Main Language(s) of Instruction: Spanish
International Co-operation: With universities in USA, Puerto Rico, Canada, Spain and France.
Accrediting Agencies: Secretariat for Higher Education, Science and Technology of the Dominican Republic
Degrees and Diplomas: *Técnico*: Architectural Drawing, 2 yrs; *Licenciatura*: Accountancy; Advertising; Business Administration; Law; Marketing; Tourism and Hotel Management, 4 yrs; *Professional Title*: Electronics; Industrial Engineering; Interior Design; Systems Analysis and Design, 4 yrs; *Professional Title*: Engineering; Engineering and Architecture Drawing; *Especialista*; *Maestría*:

Business Administration; Executive Management; Marketing Management; Multimedia; Production Management, a further 2 yrs. Also postgraduate Diploma in Finance Management and International Commercial Law, 1 yr

Student Services: Academic counselling, Canteen, Employment services, Health services, Language programs, Sports facilities

Student Residential Facilities: None

Libraries: 39,748 vols

Publications: Coloquios Jurídicos; Investigación y Ciencia; Revista Científica

Press or Publishing House: Imprenta Cenapec
Last Updated: 08/12/09

AUTONOMOUS UNIVERSITY OF SANTO DOMINGO
Universidad Autónoma de Santo Domingo (UASD)
Apartado postal 1355, Ave. Alma Mater, Ciudad Universitaria, Santo Domingo
Tel: +1 809 533-8273
Fax: +1 809 508-7374 +1 809 508-7375
EMail: info@uasd.edu.do
Website: http://www.uasd.edu.do

Rector: Mateo Aquino Febrillet
Tel: +1 809 501-1325 EMail: rectoria@uasd.edu.do
Vicerrector Docente: Jorge Asjana

Colleges
Basic Studies (for 1st yr students)

Faculties
Agronomy and Veterinary Science (Agronomy; Animal Husbandry; Dairy; Veterinary Science); **Arts** (Advertising and Publicity; Cinema and Television; Design; Fine Arts; Music; Theatre); **Economics and Social Sciences** (Accountancy; Administration; Economics; Marketing; Public Administration; Social Work; Sociology; Statistics); **Engineering and Architecture** (Agricultural Engineering; Architecture; Chemical Engineering; Civil Engineering; Electrical Engineering; Engineering; Industrial Engineering; Mechanical Engineering); **Health Sciences** (Medicine; Nursing; Orthodontics; Pharmacology; Pharmacy; Radiology); **Humanities** (Arts and Humanities; Communication Studies; History; Modern Languages; Pedagogy; Philosophy; Psychology; Social Sciences); **Law** (Law; Political Sciences); **Science** (Biology; Chemistry; Computer Science; Mathematics; Microbiology; Natural Sciences; Parasitology; Physics)

History: Founded 1538 by Bull of Pope Paul III. Directed by Dominican Order of Preachers until 1802. Closed during the French occupation. Became a lay institution in 1815 but again closed 1822-44 during Haitian occupation. Again reopened and reorganized 1865, 1914, and 1937. Following Law on University autonomy 1961 adopted new status 1966. Financially supported by the State.

Governing Bodies: Claustro Universitario; Consejo Universitario

Academic Year: January to December (January-May; July-December)

Admission Requirements: Secondary school certificate (bachillerato) or recognized foreign equivalent

Fees: (US Dollars): 300 per semester; foreign students, 900

Main Language(s) of Instruction: Spanish

International Co-operation: With universities in USA, Mexico, Spain, Venezuela, Argentina, Costa Rica and Puerto Rico.

Degrees and Diplomas: *Licenciatura*: Accountancy; Biology; Business Administration; Chemistry; Pharmacy; Philosophy and Letters; Physics; Political Science; Public Administration, 5 yrs; *Licenciatura*: Computer Science; Economics; Education; History; Letters; Psychology; Sociology, 4 yrs; *Licenciatura*: Languages, 4 1/2 yrs; *Licenciatura*: Law, 6 yrs; *Professional Title*: Agriculture (Ingeniero agrónomo); Economics, 5 yrs; *Professional Title*: Architecture (Arquitecto); Chemistry (Ingeniero químico); Mechanical and Electrical Engineering (Ingeniero mecánico electricista), 6 yrs; *Professional Title*: Biology (Técnico biólogo); Physics (Técnico en Ciencias Físicas), 3 yrs; *Professional Title*: Marketing; Medical Technology (Tecnólogo médico), 4 yrs; *Doctor*: Medicine; Odontology, 7 yrs; *Doctor*: Veterinary Medicine, 5 yrs

Student Services: Academic counselling, Canteen, Cultural centre, Handicapped facilities, Health services, Language programs, Social counselling, Sports facilities

Student Residential Facilities: Yes

Special Facilities: Anthropology Museum

Libraries: Central Library, c. 252,470 vols; Agriculture c. 660; Economics and Social Sciences, c. 5,130; Humanities, c. 2,000; Engineering and Architecture, c. 1,170
Last Updated: 21/03/11

CATHOLIC TECHNOLOGICAL UNIVERSITY OF BARAHONA
Universidad Católica Tecnológica de Barahona
Apartado postal 006, Calle 1ra. Barrio Juan Pablo Duarte, Batey Central, Barahona 006
EMail: viceacademica@ucateba.edu.do
Website: http://www.ucateba.edu.do/

Rector: José Angel González Hernández

Schools
Business Studies (Accountancy; Business Administration; Hotel Management; Marketing; Tourism); **Computer Science** (Computer Science); **Education**; **Law**; **Nursing**

History: Founded 1997 as Instituto Católico Tecnológico de Barahona. Acquired present status 2004.

Main Language(s) of Instruction: Spanish

Degrees and Diplomas: *Licenciatura*; *Especialista*; *Maestría*
Last Updated: 10/11/09

CATHOLIC UNIVERSITY OF SANTO DOMINGO
Universidad Católica de Santo Domingo (UCSD)
Apartado postal 2733, Calle Santo Domingo 3, Ens. La Julia, Santo Domingo
Tel: +1 809 544-2812
Fax: +1 809 540-2351
EMail: ucsd@verizon.net.do
Website: http://www.ucsd.edu.do

Rector: Ramón Alonso
Vicerrectora Académica: Rosa Kranwinkel

Faculties
Architecture and Fine Arts (Architecture; Design; Fine Arts; Graphic Design; Handicrafts; Interior Design); **Economics and Administration** (Accountancy; Banking; Business Administration; Economics; Finance; Hotel Management; Marketing; Tourism); **Education** (Education; Education of the Handicapped; English; French; Native Language; Native Language Education; Preschool Education; Primary Education); **Health Sciences** (Health Sciences; Nursing); **Humanities and Education** (Anthropology; Archaeology; Arts and Humanities; Geography; History; Psychology); **Law and Political Science** (Law; Political Sciences); **Science and Technology** (Computer Engineering; Computer Science; Information Sciences; Mathematics; Natural Sciences; Technology); **Social Sciences and Communication** (Advertising and Publicity; Communication Studies; Social Sciences); **Theology** (Theology)

Research Centres
Family Studies and Research (Family Studies)
History: Founded 1982.
Academic Year: January to December (January-May; August-December)
Admission Requirements: Secondary school certificate (bachillerato)
Main Language(s) of Instruction: Spanish
Degrees and Diplomas: *Técnico*: Technical Studies, 2 yrs; *Licenciatura*: 4 yrs; *Especialista*; *Maestría*: a further 2 yrs. Also Postgraduate Diploma, 1 yr
Libraries: Cardenal Octavio Antonio Beras Library
Press or Publishing House: Catholic University Press
Last Updated: 08/12/09

CENTRAL DOMINICAN UNIVERSITY FOR PROFESSIONAL STUDIES

Universidad Central Dominicana de Estudios Profesionales (UCDEP)

Avenida Independencia, Km 9, (Colegio San Gabriel), Apartado Postal 1263, D.N., Santo Domingo
Tel: + 1 809 508-3279
Fax: + 1 809 699-2675
EMail: info@ucdep.edu.do
Website: http://www.ucdep.edu.do

Rector: Dulcilido Vásquez EMail: rector@ucdep.edu.do

Faculties

Health Sciences; **Humanities and Social Sciences** (Education; Law; Library Science; Psychology); **Technology and Natural Resources** (Agricultural Engineering; Agronomy; Computer Science; Electrical Engineering; Forestry; Industrial Engineering; Natural Resources; Technology)

History: Founded 1975.

Main Language(s) of Instruction: Spanish

Degrees and Diplomas: *Técnico*; *Licenciatura*; *Professional Title*
Last Updated: 09/12/09

CENTRAL UNIVERSITY OF THE EAST

Universidad Central del Este (UCE)

Apartado postal 512, Avenida Francisco Alberto Caamaño Deño, San Pedro de Macorís
Tel: + 1 809 520-3562
Fax: + 1 809 246-2266
EMail: info@uce.edu.do
Website: http://www.uce.edu.do

Rector: José E. Hazim-Frappier EMail: jhazim@uce.edu.do

Vicerrector Ejecutivo: Richard Peguero
Tel: + 1 809 529-3562, Ext. 241 EMail: rpeguero@uce.edu.do

International Relations: Kamel Hazim, International Affairs Director
Tel: + 1 809 529-3562, Ext. 280, Fax: + 1 809 246-4341
EMail: khazim@uce.edu.do

Faculties

Architecture (Architecture) *Director*: Vanessa Vélez; **Dentistry** (Dentistry) *Director*: Joanna Nicolas de Diaz; **Economics and Social Sciences** (Accountancy; Business Administration; Hotel Management; Information Sciences; Marketing; Pedagogy; Tourism); **Engineering** (Civil Engineering; Electrical and Electronic Engineering; Industrial Engineering; Mechanical Engineering) *Director*: Maria Cristina Tejada; **Law** (Law) *Director*: Juana Ozuna; **Medicine** (Medicine; Nursing; Pharmacy) *Director*: Jose Wazar

Further Information: Also Teaching Hospitals, Spanish course for foreign students, teaching hotel

History: Founded 1970. A private Institution recognized by the State 1971.

Governing Bodies: Consejo Superior Universitario

Academic Year: January to December (January-April; May-August; September-December)

Admission Requirements: Secondary school certificate (bachillerato) or equivalent, or recognized foreign equivalent

Main Language(s) of Instruction: Spanish

International Co-operation: With universities in USA and Puerto Rico.

Accrediting Agencies: Secretariado de Estado de Educación Superior, Ciencia y Tecnología

Degrees and Diplomas: *Licenciatura*: Accountancy; Business Administration; Education, 3 yrs; *Licenciatura*: Biology; Pharmacy, 4 yrs; *Licenciatura*: Social Communication, 3 1/2 yrs; *Professional Title*: Architecture (Arquitecto); Engineering (Ingeniero), 4 yrs; *Doctor*: Dentistry; Law, 4 yrs; *Doctor*: Medicine, 6 yrs

Student Services: Academic counselling, Foreign student adviser, Social counselling, Sports facilities

Special Facilities: Anthropology Museum

Libraries: Central Library, c. 150,000 vols

Publications: Medical Journal *(monthly)*
Last Updated: 31/01/07

CIBAO TECHNOLOGICAL UNIVERSITY

Universidad Católica Tecnológica del Cibao (UTECI)

Apartado postal 401, Avenida Universitaria esq. Pedro A. Rivera, La Vega
Tel: +1 809 573-1020
Fax: + 1 809 573-6194
Website: http://www.ucateci.edu.do

Rector: Fausto Ramón Mejía Vallejo

Faculties

Administration (Accountancy; Administration; Marketing); **Health Sciences** (Dentistry; Medicine; Nursing; Psychology); **Humanities** (Architecture; Arts and Humanities; Civil Engineering; Education; Law)

Schools

Technology (Agronomy; Computer Science; Industrial Engineering; Technology)

History: Founded 1983 as Instituto Tecnológico del Cibao Acquired present title and status 2002.

Governing Bodies: Asamblea General; Junta Directiva

Academic Year: January to December (January-May; August-December)

Admission Requirements: Secondary school certificate (bachillerato)

Main Language(s) of Instruction: Spanish

Degrees and Diplomas: *Licenciatura*: Accountancy; Business Administration; Education; Law; Nursing, 5 yrs; *Professional Title*: Agricultural Engineering (Ingeniero agrícola); Architecture (Arquitecto); Civil Engineering (Ingeniero civil), 5 yrs; *Professional Title*: Engineering (Ingeniero), 5 1/2 yrs; *Doctor*: Dentistry; Medicine; Veterinary Medicine, 5-6 yrs. Also lower level technical qualifications, 2 1/2 yrs

Libraries: Biblioteca Dr. Rubén Alvarez Valencia, c. 8,000 vols
Last Updated: 10/12/09

DOMINICAN ADVENTIST UNIVERSITY

Universidad Adventista Dominicana (UNAD)

Apartado postal 770, Aut. Duarte, Km 74 1/2, Sonador, Bonao, Monseñor Nouel
Tel: + 1 809 525-7533
Fax: + 1 809 525-4048
EMail: info@unad.edu.do
Website: http://www.unad.edu.do

Rector: Téofilo Pichardo
Tel: + 1 829 257-2969 EMail: teofiloap@hotmail.com

Centres

Research *Head*: Alfa Sueso

Faculties

Administration (Accountancy; Business Administration; Marketing); **Engineering and Technology** (Computer Science; Engineering; Systems Analysis); **Humanities**; **Theology** (Theology)

History: Founded 1982.

Governing Bodies: Administrative Board

Academic Year: September to May (September-December; January-May)

Admission Requirements: Secondary school certificate (bachillerato)

Main Language(s) of Instruction: Spanish

Accrediting Agencies: Adventista Acrediting Association (AAA), Secretaria Educacíon Superior

Degrees and Diplomas: *Licenciatura*: 4 yrs; *Maestría*: Education; Theology, 4 yrs

Student Services: Academic counselling, Canteen, Cultural centre, Employment services, Foreign student adviser, Foreign Studies Centre, Health services, Language programs, Nursery care, Social counselling, Sports facilities

Student Residential Facilities: Yes

Libraries: c. 16,100 vols

Publications: Ciencia y Humanismo *(biennially)*
Last Updated: 10/11/09

DOMINICAN-AMERICAN UNIVERSITY

Universidad Dominico-Americana (ICDA)
Avenida Abraham Lincoln 21, Santo Domingo
Tel: + 1 809 535-0665
Fax: + 1 809 533-8809
EMail: dir.dominicana@codetel.net.do
Website: http://www.dominicoamericano.edu.do

Directora: Elisabeth de Windt

Programmes
Business Administration (Accountancy; Administration; Secretarial Studies); **Computer Engineering** (Computer Engineering); **Education** (Education); **Tourism** (Tourism)

Degrees and Diplomas: *Licenciatura*; *Especialista*
Last Updated: 08/12/09

DOMINICAN O&M UNIVERSITY

Universidad Dominicana O&M
Apartado postal 509, Avenida Independencia 200, Santo Domingo
Tel: + 1 809 533-7733
Fax: + 1 809 535-0084
EMail: rectoria@udoym.edu.do
Website: http://www.udoym.edu.do

Rector: José Rafael Abinader

Centres
Postgraduate and Maestría Studies

Faculties
Economics and Administration (Accountancy; Advertising and Publicity; Banking; Business Administration; Hotel Management; Marketing; Modern Languages; Tourism); **Engineering and Technology** (Architecture; Civil Engineering; Computer Science; Electronic Engineering; Engineering Drawing and Design; Industrial Engineering; Systems Analysis); **Humanities and Science** (Arts and Humanities; Communication Studies; Natural Sciences; Psychology); **Juridical Sciences** (Law)

Units
Continuing Education (Continuing Education)

Further Information: Branches in Moca, Puerto Plata, Romana, San José de Ocoa and Santiago

History: Founded 1966.

Degrees and Diplomas: *Licenciatura*; *Especialista*; *Maestría*
Last Updated: 09/12/09

DOMINICAN UNIVERSITY OF DENTISTRY

Universidad Odontológica Dominicana (UOD)
Avenida 27 de Febrero, esq. Las Palmas, Santo Domingo
Tel: + 1 809 560-7477
Fax: + 1 809 560-7524
EMail: adm@uod.edu.do; kasparov@verizon.net.do
Website: http://www.uod.edu.do

Rectora: Vilma Deschamps De Baez

Schools
Dentistry (Dentistry)
History: Founded 1985.
Main Language(s) of Instruction: Spanish
Degrees and Diplomas: *Professional Title*; *Maestría*
Last Updated: 09/12/09

DOMINICAN UNIVERSITY OF INDUSTRIAL PSYCHOLOGY

Universidad Psicología Industrial Dominicana (UPID)
Apartado postal 2327, Calle 1ra. 27Urb. KG Carr. Sánchez Km. 6 1/2, Santo Domingo
Tel: + 1 809 533-7141
Fax: + 1 809 533-4544
EMail: psicologiadom@codetel.net.do
Website: http://www.upid.edu.do

Rector: Ricardo Winter

Programmes
Administration (Accountancy; Computer Engineering; Human Resources; Industrial and Organizational Psychology; Management; Marketing; Secretarial Studies)

History: Founded 1996 as Instituto Superior de Psicología Industrial Dominicana, acquired present title 2001.

Degrees and Diplomas: *Licenciatura*
Last Updated: 09/12/09

EUGENIO MARÍA DE HOSTOS UNIVERSITY

Universidad Eugenio María de Hostos (UNIREMHOS)
Apartado postal 2694, Avenida Abraham Lincoln 126, Santo Domingo
Tel: + 1 809 532-2495
Fax: + 1 809 535-4636
EMail: uni.eugenio@codetel.net.do
Website: http://www.uniremhos.edu.do/

Rector: José Díaz Vargas

Faculties
Economics and Administration (Administration; Economics); **Health Sciences** (Health Sciences); **Humanities and Social Sciences** (Arts and Humanities; Social Sciences); **Law** (Law); **Science and Technology** (Natural Sciences; Technology)

Schools
Communication and Public Relations

History: Founded 1981. A private institution.

Degrees and Diplomas: *Licenciatura*; *Maestría*
Last Updated: 09/12/09

FEDERICO HENRÍQUEZ Y CARVAJAL UNIVERSITY

Universidad Federico Henríquez y Carvajal (UFHEC)
Avenida Isabel Aguiar 100 casi esq. Guarocuya, Santo Domingo
Tel: + 1 809 531-1000
Fax: + 1 809 531-5288
EMail: info@ufhec.edu.do
Website: http://www.ufhec.edu.do

Rectora: Margarita Cornielle de Fermin
EMail: rectoria@ufhec.edu.do

Faculties
Health Sciences (Dentistry; Health Sciences; Nursing); **Humanities** (Arts and Humanities)

History: Founded 1991.

Main Language(s) of Instruction: Spanish

FELIX ADAM EXPERIMENTAL UNIVERSITY

Universidad Experimental Felix Adam (UNEFA)
Apartado postal 48-2-Feria, Calle Plaza de la Cultura 151, El Millón, Santo Domingo
Tel: + 1 809 683-3121
Fax: + 1 809 683-3425
EMail: unefa@codetel.net.do
Website: http://www.unefa.edu.do

Rector: José Ramón Holguín Brito

Programmes
Business Administration (Business Administration); **Law** (Law); **Marketing**; **Natural Resources and Environment**

History: Founded 1996.

Main Language(s) of Instruction: Spanish

Degrees and Diplomas: *Licenciatura*
Last Updated: 09/12/09

FERNANDO ARTURO DE MERIÑO UNIVERSITY OF AGRICULTURE AND FORESTRY

Universidad Agroforestal Fernando Arturo de Meriño (UAFAM)
Avenida La Confluencia, Jarabacoa
Tel: +1 809 574-6234 +1 809 574-2136
Fax: +1 809 574-6405
EMail: info@uafam.edu.do
Website: http://uafam.edu.do

Rector: Telésforo Gónzalez Mercado

Faculties
Agronomy and Forestry; **Humanities**; **Law and Political Science** (Law; Political Sciences); **Science and Technology**; **Social Sciences and Administration** (Accountancy; Business Administration; Marketing; Social Sciences)

History: Founded 1996.

Main Language(s) of Instruction: Spanish

Degrees and Diplomas: *Licenciatura*; *Professional Title*
Last Updated: 08/12/09

IBERO-AMERICAN UNIVERSITY, SANTO DOMINGO

Universidad Iberomericana (UNIBE)
Apartado postal 22333, Avenida Francia 129, Santo Domingo
Tel: +1 809 689-4111
Fax: +1 809 686-5121
EMail: unibe@codetel.net.do
Website: http://www.unibe.edu.do

Rector: Julio Castaños Guzmán **EMail:** rectoria@unibe.edu.do

Schools
Advertising and Communication (Advertising and Publicity; Communication Arts); **Architecture** (Architecture); **Business Administration** (Business Administration); **Civil Engineering** (Civil Engineering); **Dentistry** (Dentistry); **Early Chilhood Education** (Preschool Education); **Industrial Engineering** (Industrial Engineering); **Information and Communication Technology** (Information Technology); **Interior Design** (Interior Design); **Law** (Law); **Marketing** (Marketing); **Medicine** (Medicine); **Psychology** (Clinical Psychology; Educational Psychology; Psychology); **Religion** (Bible; Religion; Theology); **Tourism and Hotel Management** (Hotel Management; Tourism)

Further Information: Also Teaching Hospital (INDEN); National Centre for Diabetes

History: Founded 1982 as the result of joint efforts of Dominican and Spanish institutions and private citizens interested in the advancement of higher education.

Governing Bodies: Board of Regents

Academic Year: September to August (September-December; January-May; June-August)

Admission Requirements: Secondary school certificate (bachillerato) and entrance exam

Degrees and Diplomas: *Licenciatura*: Arts, 9-11 sem; *Doctor*: Medicine, 11-15 sem; *Especialista*; *Maestría*

Student Services: Academic counselling, Canteen, Handicapped facilities, Social counselling, Sports facilities

Student Residential Facilities: For c. 2,500 students

Special Facilities: computer labs

Libraries: University Library, c. 50,000 vols, c. 1,300 periodicals

Publications: Revista de Ciencia y Cultura
Last Updated: 09/12/09

INSTITUTE OF AGRICULTURE

Instituto Superior de Agricultura (ISA)
Apartado postal 166, Avenida Antonio. Guzmán, Km. 51/2,
la Herradura, Santiago de los Caballeros
Tel: +1 809 247-2000
Fax: +1 809 247-2626
EMail: isa.rectoria@codetel.net.do
Website: http://www.isa.edu.do/isaweb/

Rector: Benito Ferreiras

Programmes
Agricultural Engineering (Agricultural Engineering); **Animal Husbandry** (Animal Husbandry); **Food Technology** (Food Technology); **Forestry Engineering** (Forestry); **Veterinary Science and Zoology** (Veterinary Science; Zoology)

Degrees and Diplomas: *Professional Title*; *Especialista*; *Maestría*
Last Updated: 16/11/09

INTERAMERICAN UNIVERSITY

Universidad Interamericana (UNICA)
Apartado postal 20687, Calle Dr. Báez 2, Gazcue, Santo Domingo
Tel: +1 809 685-6562 +1 809 687-2529
Fax: +1 809 689-8581
EMail: unica@codetel.net.do
Website: http://www.unica.edu.do

Rector: Gabriel Read

Vice-Rector Académico: Raúl Parmenio Díaz

Faculties
Law and Political Science (Law; Political Sciences); **Science and Technology** (Computer Science; Dental Technology; Industrial Engineering); **Social Sciences and Humanities** (Accountancy; Advertising and Publicity; Arts and Humanities; Biology; Business Administration; Chemistry; Communication Studies; Economics; Education; Educational Administration; Educational Psychology; English; French; Human Resources; International Business; Pedagogy; Philosophy; Physical Education; Preschool Education; Primary Education; Psychology; Public Relations; Social Sciences; Sociology; Tourism)

History: Founded 1982.

Degrees and Diplomas: *Licenciatura*; *Professional Title*; *Especialista*; *Maestría*. Also Doctorado
Last Updated: 09/12/09

NATIONAL EVANGELICAL UNIVERSITY, SANTIAGO

Universidad Nacional Evangélica, Santiago
Av. Estrella Sadhalá No. 202, La Terraza, Santiago de los Caballeros
Tel: +1 809 247-3535
Fax: +1 809 583-6700
EMail: miledy_santana@hotmail.com
Website: http://www.unev-rd.edu.do

Rector: Salustiano Bolivar Mojica Rijo

Faculties
Health Sciences (Alternative Medicine; Health Sciences; Nursing; Nutrition; Pharmacology); **Humanities** (Arts and Humanities; Education; Psychology; Theology)

Further Information: Also branches in Santo Domingo and Villa Altagracia

History: Founded 1986 to bring an Evangelical Christian perspective to higher education in the Dominican Republic.

Governing Bodies: Fundación Evangélica Universitaria

Academic Year: January to December

Admission Requirements: High School Diploma and Transcripts (legalized by the Dominican Consulate in country of origin for foreign students)

Main Language(s) of Instruction: Spanish

Degrees and Diplomas: *Licenciatura*: 3-5 yrs; *Maestría*: a further 2 yrs

Student Services: Academic counselling, Canteen, Employment services, Foreign student adviser, Health services, Language programs, Sports facilities

Special Facilities: Experimental Farm

Libraries: Total, c. 50,000 vols

Publications: Homo Novus *(monthly)*

Press or Publishing House: EDUNEV
Last Updated: 10/12/09

NATIONAL TECHNOLOGICAL UNIVERSITY
Universidad Nacional Tecnológica
Dr. Delgado esq. Bolívar, Gazcue
EMail: info@unnatec.edu.do
Website: http://www.insutec.edu.do/portal/index.html
Rector: William Capellan Ferreira

Schools
Business Administration (Accountancy; Business Administration; Marketing; Systems Analysis)
Degrees and Diplomas: *Licenciatura*
Last Updated: 10/12/09

NATIONAL UNIVERSITY-INSTITUTE OF EXACT SCIENCES
Universidad-Instituto Nacional de Ciencias Exactas (INCE)
Apartado postal 1796, Avenida Gustavo Mejía Ricart 211 esq.
Dr. Defilló, Ens. Quisqueya, Santo Domingo
Tel: +1 809 540-7300
Fax: +1 809 567-7424
EMail: ince@tricom.net
Website: http://www.ince.edu.do/
Rector: Manuel Bergés

Departments
Lifelong Education (Accountancy; Architecture; Business Administration; Computer Science; Economics; Engineering; Finance; Fine Arts; Human Resources; Law; Marketing)

Faculties
Economics and Social Sciences; **Engineering, Architecture and Technology**; **Law and Political Science**
Degrees and Diplomas: *Licenciatura*; *Professional Title*. Also post-grados
Last Updated: 10/12/09

NORDESTANA CATHOLIC UNIVERSITY
Universidad Católica Nordestana (UCNE)
Apartado postal 239, Calle 27 de Febrero, Esqo Restauración, San Francisco de Macorís, Duarte 239
Tel: +1 809 588-3239
Fax: +1 809 244-1647
EMail: rectoria@ucne.edu
Website: http://www.ucne.edu
Rector: Ramón Alfredo de la Cruz Baldera Tel: +1 809 588-3505
Vicerrectora Académica: Yany Almanzar De Jiménez
EMail: vicerrectoria.academica@ucne.edu

Faculties
Economics and Social Sciences (Accountancy; Business Administration; Economics; Education; Marketing; Social Sciences); **Engineering** (Architecture; Engineering); **Health Sciences** (Dentistry; Health Sciences; Medicine); **Law** (Law)
History: Founded 1978. A private non-profit institution recognized by the State.
Governing Bodies: Secretaria de Estado de Educatión Ciencia y tecnología (SEESCYT)
Academic Year: January to December (January-April; May-August; September-December)
Admission Requirements: High school degree or official transcript recognised by the University
Main Language(s) of Instruction: Spanish
Accrediting Agencies: ADAAC
Degrees and Diplomas: *Licenciatura*: Education, 3 yrs 8 Month; *Professional Title*: Architecture, 4 yrs 8 moths; *Professional Title*: Engineering, Computer Engineering (Ingeniero); Law, 4 yrs; *Professional Title*: Medicine, 5 yrs 4 mths; *Especialista*; *Maestría*
Student Services: Academic counselling, Canteen, Cultural centre, Employment services, Foreign student adviser, Health services, Language programs, Social counselling, Sports facilities
Libraries: c. 15,000 vols
Publications: Ciencia Humanismo *(annually)*

Academic Staff	MEN	WOMEN	TOTAL
STAFF WITH DOCTORATE			
FULL-TIME	8	6	14
PART-TIME	2	2	4

Last Updated: 08/12/09

OPEN UNIVERSITY FOR ADULTS
Universidad Abierta para Adultos (UAPA)
Apartado postal 1238, Avenida Hispanoamérica, Urb. Thomén, Santiago de los Caballeros, Santiago
Tel: +1 809 724-0266
Fax: +1 809 724-0329
EMail: univ.adultos@uniabierta.edu.do
Website: http://www.uniabierta.edu.do
Rector: Ángel Hernández EMail: angel.hernandez.c@gmail.com
Vicerrectora Administrativa y Financera: Mirian Acosta
EMail: mirianacostap@yahoo.com
International Relations: Magdalena Cruz, Vicerrectora de Relaciones Internacionales y Cooperación
EMail: magdalenacruzb@hotmail.com

Schools
Business (Business Administration; Industrial and Organizational Psychology; Marketing); **Education** (Education; Foreign Languages Education; Mathematics Education; Modern Languages; Physical Education; Science Education; Social Sciences; Spanish; Technology); **Languages** (Modern Languages; Tourism); **Political Science** (Law; Political Sciences); **Postgraduate**; **Psychology** (Clinical Psychology; Psychology); **Science and Technology** (Computer Science; Technology); **Tourism**
History: Founded 1995.
Governing Bodies: Junta de Directores, Consejo Académico, Rectoría
Academic Year: January to December
Admission Requirements: Secondary school certificate (bachillerato)
Main Language(s) of Instruction: Spanish
Accrediting Agencies: Asociación Dominicana de Auto-estudio y Acreditación
Degrees and Diplomas: *Técnico*: Education (TEB), 2 yrs; *Licenciatura*: 4 yrs; *Especialista*; *Maestría*: 2 yrs
Student Services: Academic counselling, Cultural centre, Employment services, Foreign student adviser, Handicapped facilities, Language programs, Nursery care, Sports facilities
Libraries: c. 12,000 vols
Publications: Revista Científica Educación Superior *(biennially)*
Last Updated: 08/12/09

PEDRO HENRÍQUEZ UREÑA NATIONAL UNIVERSITY
Universidad Nacional Pedro Henríquez Ureña (UNPHU)
Apartado postal 1423, Avenida John F. Kennedy, Km. 5 1/2, Santo Domingo
Tel: +1 809 549-6021
Fax: +1 809 566-2206
EMail: info@unphu.edu.do
Website: http://www.unphu.edu.do
Rector: Miguel R. Fiallo
Vicerrectora Académica: Daniela Franco

Faculties
Agriculture and Veterinary Science (Agricultural Economics; Agricultural Equipment; Agriculture; Agronomy; Animal Husbandry; Forestry; Natural Resources; Veterinary Science); **Architecture and Arts** (Advertising and Publicity; Architecture; Arts and Humanities; Graphic Design; Heritage Preservation; Interior Design); **Economics and Social Sciences** (Accountancy; Banking; Business Administration; Economics; Hotel and Restaurant; Social Sciences; Tourism); **Engineering** (Agricultural Engineering; Civil Engineering; Electrical Engineering; Engineering; Environmental Engineering; Industrial Engineering; Sanitary Engineering); **Health**

Sciences (Dentistry; Health Sciences; Medicine; Ophthalmology; Pharmacy; Surgery); **Humanities and Education** (Arts and Humanities; Education; Educational Sciences; Philosophy; Primary Education; Psychology); **Law and Political Science** (International Relations; Law; Political Sciences; Public Administration); **Science and Technology** (Chemistry; Computer Engineering; Natural Sciences)

Institutes
Biomedical Sciences (Biomedicine)

History: Founded 1966.

Academic Year: August to May (August-December; January-May)

Admission Requirements: Secondary school certificate (bachillerato) and entrance examination

Main Language(s) of Instruction: Spanish

Degrees and Diplomas: *Técnico*: 4-6 sem; *Licenciatura*: 10 sem; *Especialista*; *Maestría*: 3-6 sem

Libraries: Central Library

Publications: Cuadernos de Filosofía; Cuadernos Jurídicos

Press or Publishing House: Imprenta UNPHU
Last Updated: 09/12/09

PONTIFICAL CATHOLIC UNIVERSITY MADRE Y MAESTRA
Pontificia Universidad Católica Madre y Maestra (PUCMM)
Apartado postal 822, Autopista Duarte Km 11/2, Santiago de los Caballeros
Tel: +1 809 580-1962
Fax: +1 809 582-4549
EMail: webmaster@pucmm.edu.do
Website: http://www.pucmm.edu.do

Rector: Agripino Núñez Collado (1962-) Fax: +1 809 581-7750 EMail: anunez@pucmmsti.edu.do

Administrative Vice-Rector: Inmaculada Adames
Fax: +1 809 581-8527 EMail: iadames@pucmmsti.edu.do

International Relations: Thelma Román
Tel: +1 809 580-1962, Fax: +1 809 971-3036

Faculties
Engineering (Civil Engineering; Computer Engineering; Electronic Engineering; Industrial Engineering; Systems Analysis; Telecommunications Engineering); **Health Sciences** (Anaesthesiology; Cardiology; Gastroenterology; Gynaecology and Obstetrics; Health Sciences; Medicine; Nephrology; Nursing; Ophthalmology; Orthopaedics; Paediatrics; Pathology; Physical Therapy; Radiology; Stomatology; Surgery; Urology); **Humanities and Social Sciences** (Accountancy; Architecture; Business Administration; Educational Administration; Environmental Management; Finance; Human Resources; Labour Law; Law; Linguistics; Marketing; Mathematics; Primary Education; Psychology)

History: Founded 1962.

Governing Bodies: Conferencia del Episcopado Dominicano

Academic Year: August to July

Admission Requirements: Secondary school certificate

Main Language(s) of Instruction: Spanish

Degrees and Diplomas: *Licenciatura*: 4 1/2-5 yrs; *Professional Title*: Engineering (Ingeniero), 4 1/2-5 yrs; *Maestría*: a further 2 yrs. Also Postgraduate degree 1 1/2 yrs

Student Services: Academic counselling, Canteen, Cultural centre, Employment services, Foreign student adviser, Foreign Studies Centre, Health services, Language programs, Social counselling, Sports facilities

Special Facilities: Herbarium

Libraries: Main Library

Publications: Eme y Eme, Social Sciences and Humanities *(quarterly)*

Press or Publishing House: PUCMM Editorial
Last Updated: 04/04/08

SANTO TOMÁS DE AQUINO BRANCH
CAMPUS RECINTO SANTO TOMÁS DE AQUINO (RSTA)
Apartado postal 2748, Avenida Abraham Lincoln Esquina Rómulo Betancourt, Santo Domingo
Tel: +1 809 535-0111
Fax: +1 809 535-0053
EMail: webmaster@pucmmsti.edu.do
Website: http://rsta.pucmmsti.edu.do

Rector: Agripino Nuñez Collado
Tel: +1 809 580-1962, Fax: +1 809 581-7750
EMail: anunez@pucmmsti.edu.do

Vicerrector Ejecutivo: Radhames Mejia

Faculties
Engineering; **Humanities and Social Sciences** (Accountancy; Business Administration; Development Studies; Economics; Educational Administration; Finance; Hotel Management; Human Resources; Law; Marketing; Mathematics; Philosophy; Primary Education; Public Administration)

Further Information: Also Laboratories

Degrees and Diplomas: *Técnico*: 2 1/2 yrs; *Licenciatura*: 4 yrs

Libraries: Main Library

SALOMÉ UREÑA TEACHER TRAINING INSTITUTE
Instituto Superior de Formacion Docente Salomé Ureña
Calle Manolo Tavárez Justo Esq. Calle Rosario, Urbanización Renacimiento, Sector Mirador Sur, Santo Domingo
EMail: Rectoria@isfodosu.edu.do
Website: http://www.isfodosu.edu.do

Rectora: Ana Dolores Guzmán De Camacho

Programmes
Education (Education; Physical Education)

History: Founded 2003.

Main Language(s) of Instruction: Spanish

Degrees and Diplomas: *Licenciatura*; *Especialista*; *Maestría*
Last Updated: 10/12/09

TECHNOLOGICAL INSTITUTE OF SANTO DOMINGO
Instituto Tecnológico de Santo Domingo (INTEC)
Apartado postal 342-9, Avenida de Los Próceres, Galá, Santo Domingo
Tel: +1 809 567-9271
Fax: +1 809 566-3200
EMail: informacion@intec.edu.do
Website: http://www.intec.edu.do

Rector: Miguel Escala EMail: rectoria@intec.edu.do

Departments
Continuing Education (Continuing Education)

Faculties
Basic and Environmental Sciences (Environmental Studies; Mathematics; Natural Sciences; Statistics); **Business Administration** (Business Administration); **Engineering** (Engineering) *Head*: Indira De Jesús; **Health Sciences** (Health Sciences; Medicine); **Humanities** (Arts and Humanities) *Head*: Migdalia Martínez; **Social Sciences** (Social Sciences)

History: Founded 1972.

Governing Bodies: Board of Regents, Academic Council

Academic Year: August to July (four quarters)

Admission Requirements: Secondary school certificate

Main Language(s) of Instruction: Spanish

Accrediting Agencies: Asociacion Dominicana para el Autoestudio y Acreditacion (ADAAC)

Degrees and Diplomas: *Licenciatura*: Economics, Social Works, Industrial Design, Business Administration, Psychology, Marketing, 3 yrs; *Professional Title*: Civil Engineering, Industrial Engineering, Systems Engineering, Mechanical Engineering, Electrical and Elecronic Engineering (Ingeniero), 3 1/2 yrs; *Doctor*: Medicine, 5 yrs;

Especialista; *Maestría*: Environmental Sciences, Management, Education, Construction Engineering, 2 yrs

Student Services: Academic counselling, Employment services, Health services, Language programs, Sports facilities

Special Facilities: Research and Publication Department

Libraries: Yes

Publications: Ciencia Y Sociedad *(quarterly)*; Genero y Sociedad *(quarterly)*

Last Updated: 10/11/09

TECHNOLOGICAL INSTITUTE OF THE CIBAO ORIENTAL

Instituto Tecnológico del Cibao Oriental (ITECO)
Avenida Universitaria, Km 1, Cotuí
Tel: +1 809 585-2291
Fax: +1 809 240-0603
EMail: iteco@codetel.net.do
Website: http://www.iteco.edu.do

Rectora: Esclarecida Nuñez de Almonte

Faculties
Engineering and Natural Resources (Agriculture; Computer Science; Engineering; Geological Engineering; Mining Engineering; Natural Resources; Zoology); **Humanities** (Accountancy; Administration; Arts and Humanities; Biology; Education; Law; Marketing; Natural Sciences)

History: Founded 1982.

Main Language(s) of Instruction: Spanish

Degrees and Diplomas: *Licenciatura*; *Professional Title*; *Especialista*

Last Updated: 04/12/09

TECHNOLOGICAL UNIVERSITY OF SANTIAGO

Universidad Tecnológica de Santiago (UTESA)
Av. Estrella Sadhalá, Esq. Av. Circunvalación, Santiago de los Caballeros
Tel: +1 809 241-7156
Fax: +1 809 582-7644
EMail: utesa.santiago@verizon.net.do
Website: http://www.utesa.edu

Rector: Priamo Rodríguez Castillo (2000-)
EMail: rectoria@utesa.edu

Vice-Rector Académico: Arnaldo R. Peña V.
EMail: arnaldop@utesa.edu

Faculties
Architecture and Engineering (Architecture; Civil Engineering; Computer Science; Construction Engineering; Electrical Engineering; Electronic Engineering; Interior Design; Mechanical Engineering; Painting and Drawing); **Economics and Social Sciences** (Accountancy; Business Administration; Marketing; Tourism); **Health Sciences** (Biochemistry; Medicine; Nursing; Pharmacology; Veterinary Science; Zoology); **Science and Humanities**; **Secretarial Studies** (Secretarial Studies)

Research Centres
Agriculture, Animal Husbandry and Development (Agriculture; Animal Husbandry; Development Studies); **Bird Study and Development** (Development Studies; Zoology); **Meat Processing and Development** (Development Studies; Food Technology)

Schools
Graduate Studies

Further Information: Also branches in Santo Domingo de Guzmán, Puerto Plata, Mao and Moca and two teaching hospitals

History: Founded 1974.

Governing Bodies: Academic Council

Academic Year: January to December (January-April; May-August; September-December)

Admission Requirements: Secondary school certificate and entrance examination

Main Language(s) of Instruction: Spanish, English for Medicine Students

Degrees and Diplomas: *Técnico*; *Licenciatura*; *Professional Title*; *Doctor*; *Maestría*

Special Facilities: Exhibition Hall

Libraries: Benny Acosta Library, 160,000 vols

Publications: Aves de mi Pais; Codigo Penal Anotado Dominicano; Curso de Trigonometria Plana y Esférica; Desarrollo y Proyección de UTESA; Diálogo Utesiano; Educación para el Medio Ambiente; Epigramas o Voces Folklóricas; Hábitos, Métodos y Técnicas de Estudio; Historia Económica Dominicana; Introduccion a la Medicina Geriátrica; La Educación Superior y sus Aspectos Organizativos; Metodología de la Investigación Aplicada; Neoliberalismo y Globalización; Reflexiones sobre el Sistema Educativo Dominicano; Reflexiones sobre: Educación y Desarrollo; Revistas Universitarias; Una Vida Dedicada a la Ciencia, By Dr. José de Jesus Jiménez Almonte; Versos Escolares; Visión Educativa

Press or Publishing House: Editora Teófilo y Nueva Editora La Información

Last Updated: 09/12/09

UNIVERSITY OF THE CARIBBEAN

Universidad del Caribe
Apartado postal 67-2, Aut. 30 de Mayo Km 7 1/2, Urb. Tropical, Santo Domingo
Tel: +1 809 535-8210
Fax: +1 809 535-0489
EMail: univ.delcaribe@codetel.net.do
Website: http://www.unicaribe.edu.do

Rector: Miguel Rosado

Vicerrector Administrativo: Arturo Mendéz

Programmes
Accountancy (Accountancy); **Advertising**; **Computer Science**; **Education** (Education); **Hotel Management** (Hotel Management); **International Relations** (International Relations); **Law** (Law); **Marketing**; **Social Communication** (Communication Studies)

History: Founded 1995.

Admission Requirements: Bachiller

Main Language(s) of Instruction: Spanish

Degrees and Diplomas: *Licenciatura*
Last Updated: 09/12/09

UNIVERSITY OF THE THIRD AGE

Universidad de la Tercera Edad (UTE)
Calle Camila Henríquez Ureña, Esq. Jesús Maestro, Miarador Norte, Santo Domingo, Distrito Nacional
Tel: +1 809 537-4343
Fax: +1 809 534-0050
EMail: ute@ute.edu.do
Website: http://www.ute.edu.do

Rector: José Nicolás Almanzar García
Tel: +1 809 482-0262 EMail: nalmanzar@codetel.net.do

International Relations: Fanny Victoria Polanco Jorge
Tel: +1 809 531-9651

Departments
Economics and Administration (Accountancy; Business Administration; Marketing); **Health Sciences** (Health Sciences; Optometry); **Humanities** (Arts and Humanities; Design; Education; Journalism; Literature; Psychology; Public Relations); **Law and Political Science** (Law; Political Sciences)

History: Founded 1984. Acquired present status 1992.

Admission Requirements: Secondary school certificate

Main Language(s) of Instruction: Spanish

Degrees and Diplomas: *Técnico*: Education; Design, 3 yrs; *Licenciatura*: Law; Psychology; Administration; Education; Marketing; Social Communication; Public Relations; Political Science; *Especialista*; *Maestría*: International Relations

Student Services: Academic counselling, Canteen, Cultural centre, Employment services, Handicapped facilities, Health services, Language programs, Social counselling, Sports facilities

Libraries: Yes

Publications: Scientific Magazine *(biannually)*
Last Updated: 09/12/09

Ecuador

STRUCTURE OF HIGHER EDUCATION SYSTEM

Description:

Higher education is provided by universities, polytechnics and, at non-university level, institutos pedagógicos and institutos técnicos superiores. All universities, whether public or private, are autonomous. Higher education institutions are controlled by the National Council of Universities and Polytechnics.

Stages of studies:

University level first stage: Licenciatura
Universities offer short three-year courses leading to the qualification of Tecnólogo. The first stage of long-cycle higher education lasts for a period of four to six years. Depending on the subject and the type of institution, it leads to the award of the Licenciatura after four years, a professional qualification after five to six years (Arquitecto, Ingeniero, Profesor, Abogado, etc..) or even, in some universities, to the title of Doctor in such fields as Economics, Architecture and Veterinary Surgery. Studies leading to the title of Doctor in Medicine last for seven years.

University level second stage: Maestría, Especialista, Doctorado
Some institutions offer postgraduate specialized courses leading to the qualification of Maestría/ Magister after two years' further study and the presentation and defence of a thesis. Especialista programmes are offered mainly in Health and Medicine and require one to three years' study. Some universities also offer the Doctorado as a postgraduate degree in such fields as Education, Arts and Humanities, Theology and Law. The Doctorate requires two or three years' study beyond the Licentiatura and the presentation and defence of a thesis.

Distance higher education:
The Faculty of Education of the Universidad Técnica Particular de Loja offers four-year distance education courses in Teacher Training, Social Sciences, Mathematics, Chemistry, Biology, Physics and English Language and Literature.

ADMISSION TO HIGHER EDUCATION

Admission to university-level studies:

Name of secondary school credential required: Bachillerato

Alternatives to credentials: Cursos pre-universitarios and entrance examination.

Entrance exam requirements: Some private institutions require an entrance examination.

Foreign students admission:

Entrance exam requirements: Foreign students must hold the Bachiller or an equivalent title recognized by the Ministry of Education. Candidates applying to some universities must sit for an entrance examination and, in most cases, follow a Curso de Nivelación or a Curso Preuniversitario.

Entry regulations: Foreign students must be in possession of a visa and residence permit.

Language requirements: Foreign students must have a perfect command of Spanish. Some universities offer courses for foreign students to improve their knowledge of Spanish.

RECOGNITION OF STUDIES

Quality assurance system:

The CONESUP evaluates and accredits institutions and programmes.

Special provisions for recognition:

For access to advanced studies and research: For access to post-graduate studies and research, a review of studies completed and qualifications awarded by the foreign country will be undertaken. Recognition will be granted according to the provisions of each one of the universities and polytechnics in accordance with the international agreements and treaties in force. All documents must be provided in Spanish.

For exercising a profession: Those who wish to exercise a profession should apply to the Consejo Nacional de Universidades y Escuelas Politécnicas. They must add the original or the professional qualification recognized by an Ecuadorian university or polytechnic.

NATIONAL BODIES

Ministerio de Educación (Ministry of Education)
Minister: Gloria Vidal Illingworth
Av. Amazonas N34-451 entre Av. Atahualpa y Juan Pablo Sánz
Quito
Tel: +593(02) 396 1300
EMail: info@educacion.gov.ec
WWW: http://www.educacion.gov.ec/

Consejo Nacional de Educación Superior - CONESUP (National Council for Higher Education)
President: Gustavo Vega Delgado
Whimper E7-37 y Alpallana
Quito
Tel: +593(02) 250 5656
Fax: +593(02) 256 3685
EMail: secretariatecnica@conesup.org.ec
WWW: http://www.conesup.net
Role of national body: To define the higher education policy and to structure, plan, lead, regulate, coordinate, control, and evaluate the national higher education system.

Data for academic year: 2006-2007
Source: IAU from Delegacion del Ecuador ante la UNESCO, 2006. Bodies updated in 2011.

INSTITUTIONS

PUBLIC INSTITUTIONS

AGRARIAN UNIVERSITY OF ECUADOR
Universidad Agraria del Ecuador (UAE)
Avenida 25 de Julio y Pio Jaramillo, 09-01-1248 Guayaquil,
Guyagas
Tel: +593(4) 243-9995
Fax: +593(4) 249-3441
EMail: info@uagraria.edu.ec
Website: http://www.uagraria.edu.ec

Rector: Jacobo Bucarám Ortíz
Tel: +593(4) 249-3441, Fax: +593(4) 249-3441
EMail: jbucaram@uagraria.edu.ec

Vicerrector: Ricardo Márquez Ramirez
Tel: +593(4) 243-9037, Fax: +593(4) 243-9037
EMail: rialmara@hotmail.com

International Relations: Carlos Campos Valverde
Tel: +593(4) 243-9283, Fax: +593(4) 243-9283
EMail: convenios@uagraria.edu.ec

Faculties
Agrarian Sciences *(Guayaquil and Milagro Campuses)* (Agriculture; Agronomy; Environmental Engineering; Food Science; Food Technology); **Agricultural Economics** *(Guayaquil and Milagro Campuses)*; **Agricultural Engineering** (Food Science; Food Technology); **Environmental Engineering** (Environmental Engineering); **Veterinary Medicine and Zootechnology** *(Guayaquil Campus)*

Graduate Schools
SIPUAE *(Guayaquil Campus)* (Agricultural Economics; Agriculture; Higher Education Teacher Training; Irrigation; Natural Resources; Plant and Crop Protection)

Schools
Computation and Computer Science *(Guayaquil and Milagro Campuses)* (Computer Engineering; Computer Science)
History: Founded 1992. Created to promote education and research in the farming sector.
Governing Bodies: University Council; Director; Directive Council; Academic Council
Academic Year: April to January
Admission Requirements: Pre-university course, entrance examination; Bachelor's degree for postgraduate courses
Main Language(s) of Instruction: Spanish
International Co-operation: With universities in The Netherlands, France, Spain, Cuba, Colombia, Venezuela
Degrees and Diplomas: *Tecnólogo*: Aquaculture (Tecnólogo en Acuacultura); Computer Technology (Tecnólogo en Computación e Informática); Food Technology (Tecnólogo en Alimentos), 3 yrs; *Professional Title*: Agronomy (Ingeniero Agrónomo); Computer Engineering (Ingeniero en Computación e Informática); Environment Engineering (Ingeniero Ambiental); Food Science (Ingeniero Agrícola - Mención Agroindustrial); Veterinary Science (Médico Veterinario y Zootecnista), 5 yrs; *Professional Title*: Economics (Economista con Mención en Economía Agrícola); Economics (Economista con Mención en Gestión Empresarial);

Economics (Economista con Mención en Gestión de Comercio Exterior), 4 yrs; *Maestría*; *Especialista*

Student Services: Academic counselling, Cultural centre, Employment services, Foreign student adviser, Foreign Studies Centre, Handicapped facilities, Health services, Language programs, Nursery care, Social counselling, Sports facilities

Special Facilities: Laboratories; Multiple use auditorium; Experimental farming centre; Veterinary Clinic

Libraries: On Guayaquil and Milagro campuses

Publications: Labour Activities, Information on academic and administrative activities *(annually)*

Academic Staff 2007-2008	MEN	WOMEN	TOTAL
FULL-TIME	136	38	**174**
PART-TIME	72	46	**118**
Student Numbers 2007-2008			
All (Foreign Included)	1,936	1,291	**3,227**
FOREIGN ONLY	4	2	**6**

Part-time students, 1.
Last Updated: 11/12/09

ARMED FORCES POLYTECHNIC
Escuela Politécnica del Ejército (ESPE)
Campus Politécnico, Avenida El Progreso s/n, Santa Clara,
Sangolqui, Pichincha
Tel: +593(2) 233-4967
Fax: +593(2) 333-4952
EMail: relinter@espe.edu.ec
Website: http://www.espe.edu.ec

Rector: Ruben Navia Loor
Tel: +593(2) 233-4968 EMail: hrnavia@espe.edu.ec

Vicerrector Académico: Carlos Rodríguez Arrieta

Campuses
Latacunga (Administration; Automation and Control Engineering; Business Administration; Computer Science; Electrical Engineering; Electronic Engineering; Engineering; Mathematics and Computer Science; Mechanical Engineering; Modern Languages; Systems Analysis) *Director:* Byron Acosta; **Santo Domingo de los Colorados** (Agriculture; Animal Husbandry) *Director:* Patricio Jaramillo

Faculties
Administration; **Basic Science**; **Biotechnology**; **Business Administration**; **Civil Engineering** (Civil Engineering) *Dean:* Iván Acosta; **Computer Engineering and Systems Analysis** (Computer Engineering; Systems Analysis) *Dean:* Galo Guarderas; **Computer Science** (Computer Science); **Earth Sciences** (Earth Sciences); **Education** (Education); **Educational Sciences** (Educational Sciences) *Dean:* Hugo Nieto; **Electronic Engineering** (Electronic Engineering) *Dean:* Rubén León; **Engineering** (Engineering); **Geography and Environment** (Environmental Studies; Geography) *Dean:* Luis Llerena; **Mechanical Engineering** (Mechanical Engineering) *Dean:* Eddie Novillo; **Military Science** (Military Science) *Dean:* Milton Escobar; **Physical Education** (Physical Education) *Dean:* Luis Verlade

Schools
Distance Education *Director:* Giovanni Granda

History: Founded 1922 by Government Act as Military School; 1937 is changed to Engineering Technical School, and acquires present title 1977.

Governing Bodies: Consejo Politécnico

Academic Year: March to February (March-August; September-February)

Admission Requirements: Secondary school certificate (bachillerato) and entrance examination

Fees: (US Dollars): c. 680 per semester

Main Language(s) of Instruction: Spanish

International Co-operation: With universities in Spain, Mexico, Brazil, Bolivia, USA, Argentina

Degrees and Diplomas: *Tecnólogo:* 3 yrs; *Licenciatura:* Educational Sciences (Lcdo), 4 yrs; *Professional Title (Ing.):* 5 yrs; *Maestría:* Business Aministration (MBA), 2 yrs

Student Services: Academic counselling, Cultural centre, Employment services, Foreign student adviser, Handicapped facilities, Health services, Language programs, Social counselling, Sports facilities

Student Residential Facilities: Yes

Libraries: Main Library, Internet, Video Conferences

Publications: Ciencia *(annually)*; Ingenieria de Estructuras *(3 per annum)*

Last Updated: 11/12/09

CENTRAL UNIVERSITY OF ECUADOR
Universidad Central del Ecuador
Ciudadela Universitaria, Avenida América entre Gilberto Gatto
Sobral y Bolivia, Quito, Pichincha
Tel: +593(2) 223-4722
Fax: +593(2) 223-6367
EMail: rel_int@ac.uce.edu.ec
Website: http://www.uce.edu.ec

Rector: Edgar Gualberto Samaniego Rojas
EMail: esamaniego@ac.uce.edu.ec

Vicerrector Administrativo y Financiero: José Leonardo Villavicencio Rosero
Tel: +593(2) 222-6124, Fax: +593(2) 222-6001
EMail: jvillavicencio@ac.uce.edu.e

Faculties
Administration; **Agriculture** (Agricultural Engineering; Agriculture; Agronomy); **Architecture and Town Planning** (Architecture; Town Planning); **Arts** (Aesthetics; Art History; Ceramic Art; Fine Arts; Painting and Drawing; Photography; Sculpture; Sociology; Theatre); **Chemistry**; **Dentistry** (Dentistry); **Economics** (Economics; Finance; Statistics); **Engineering, Physics and Mathematics**; **Geology, Mining, Petroleum and Environmental Engineering**; **Law, Political and Social Sciences** (Law; Political Sciences; Social Work; Sociology); **Medicine** (Gynaecology and Obstetrics; Medical Technology; Medicine; Nursing; Occupational Therapy; Physical Therapy; Radiology; Speech Therapy and Audiology; Statistics); **Philosophy, Letters and Education** (Biology; Business Administration; Chemistry; Linguistics; Literature; Mathematics; Modern Languages; Philosophy; Physical Education; Psychology; Social Sciences; Teacher Training); **Psychology** (Clinical Psychology; Psychology); **Social Communication**; **Veterinary Science** (Veterinary Science; Zoology)

History: Founded 1586 as Universidad de San Fulgencio and 1622 as Universidad de San Gregorio Magno. Replaced 1786 under Don Carlos III by Real y Pontificia Universidad de Santo Tomás de Aquino. Title changed to Universidad Central 1897. Granted autonomy 1925. Financed by the State.

Governing Bodies: University Council

Academic Year: October to June (October-December; January-March; April-June)

Admission Requirements: Secondary school certificate (bachillerato) or equivalent

Fees: According to parents' income

Main Language(s) of Instruction: Spanish

Degrees and Diplomas: *Licenciatura:* Administration; Arts; Banking; Economics; Education; International Law; Journalism; Nursing; Psychology; Social and Political Sciences; Statistics, 4 yrs; *Professional Title:* Accountancy; Architecture; Commercial Engineering; Economics; Educational Administration; Geology and Mining Engineering; Nursing; Statistics, 5 yrs; *Professional Title:* Agricultural Engineering; Chemical Engineering; Civil Engineering; Law; Midwifery; Veterinary Medicine, 6 yrs; *Professional Title:* Biochemistry; Occupational Therapy, 3 yrs; *Professional Title:* Design; Painting; Sculpture, 4 yrs; *Professional Title:* Surveying, 2 yrs; *Maestría;* *Especialista.* Also posgrados

Student Services: Canteen, Cultural centre, Health services, Language programs, Nursery care, Social counselling, Sports facilities

Student Residential Facilities: Yes

Special Facilities: Ethnography Museum. Natural Science Museum

Libraries: Central Library, c. 29,000 vols. Faculty libraries: Economics, c. 15,000; Agriculture, c. 3,800; Education, c. 2,520; Medicine, c. 1,110; Engineering, c. 320; Dentistry, c. 500; Law, c. 5,000; Pharmacy, c. 410

Publications: Anales; Revistas de: Economía, Derecho, Derecho Internacional, Derecho Comparado, Medicina, Odontología, Bioquímica

Last Updated: 11/12/09

ECOTEC TECHNOLOGICAL UNIVERSITY

Universidad Tecnológica ECOTEC
Av Juan Tanca Marengo Km 2 entre La Llave y Automotores y
Anexos, Guayaquil
Tel: +593(04) 268-1740
EMail: Mguevara@universidadecotec.edu.ec
Website: http://www.universidadecotec.edu.ec

Rector: Fidel Márquez Sánchez
EMail: Fmarquez@universidadecotec.edu.ec

Faculties

Computer Systems and Telecommunications; Economics and Business Administration; Law and Governance; Marketing and Communication; Tourism and Hotel Management

Degrees and Diplomas: *Licenciatura*; *Professional Title*
Last Updated: 16/12/09

INSTITUTE OF ADVANCED NATIONAL STUDIES

Instituto de Altos Estudios Nacionales
Av. Amazonas N37-271 y Villalengua (esq.), Quito
EMail: infoiaen@iaen.edu.ec
Website: http://www.iaen.edu.ec

Director: Carlos Arcos EMail: carcos@iaen.edu.ec

Schools

Culture and Society; Foreign Affairs; Public Administration (Public Administration)

History: Founded 1972. Acquired present status 2008.

Main Language(s) of Instruction: Spanish

Degrees and Diplomas: Diplomado superior
Last Updated: 11/12/09

INSTITUTE OF TECHNOLOGY OF CHIMBORAZO

Escuela Superior Politécnica de Chimborazo
Apartado 06-01-4703, Panamericana Sur Km. 11/2, Riobamba
Tel: +593(3) 296-5269
Fax: +593(3) 961977 +593(3) 961-977
EMail: info@espoch.edu.ec
Website: http://www.espoch.edu.ec

Rector: Romeo Rodríguez Cárdenas
EMail: romeor@live.espoch.edu.ec

Vicerrectora Académica: Rosa Elena Pinos
EMail: rpinos@live.espoch.edu.ec

Faculties

Animal Husbandry (Animal Husbandry; Zoology); **Business Administration** (Administration; Business Administration; Finance; International Business); **Computer Engineering and Electronics** (Computer Engineering; Electronic Engineering; Graphic Design; Systems Analysis); **Mechanical Engineering** (Industrial Engineering; Maintenance Technology; Mechanical Engineering); **Natural Resources** (Agricultural Engineering; Forestry; Natural Resources; Tourism); **Public Health** (Dietetics; Food Technology; Health Education; Nutrition; Public Health); **Science** (Biochemistry; Biophysics; Chemical Engineering; Chemistry; Industrial Chemistry; Mathematics; Natural Sciences; Pharmacy; Physics; Statistics)

History: Founded 1969 as a State institution under the jurisdiction of the Ministry of Education, enjoying some autonomy. Acquired present status as Polytechnic 1973.

Governing Bodies: Asamblea; Consejo

Academic Year: October to July (October-February; March-July)

Admission Requirements: Secondary school certificate (bachillerato)

Main Language(s) of Instruction: Spanish

Degrees and Diplomas: *Certificate*: Technical English, 2 yrs; *Tecnólogo*: 5-6 yrs; *Licenciatura*: Dietetics and Nutrition, 4-5 yrs; *Professional Title*: Engineering (Ingeniero), 5-6 yrs; *Maestría*; *Especialista*

Libraries: Central Library, c. 35,000 vols

Press or Publishing House: Departamento de Publicaciones
Last Updated: 11/12/09

INSTITUTE OF TECHNOLOGY OF THE COAST

Escuela Superior Politécnica del Litoral (ESPOL)
Apartado 09-01-5863, Campus Gustavo Galindo V Km 30.5,
Via Perimetral, Guayaquil
Tel: +593(4) 226-9101
Fax: +593(4) 285-4629
EMail: httpd@espol.edu.ec
Website: http://www.espol.edu.ec

Rector: Moisés Tacle Galárraga (2008-)
EMail: mtacle@goliat.espol.edu.ec

Secretario General: Jaime Véliz Litardo
Tel: +593(4) 226-9135, Fax: +593(4) 285-0508
EMail: jveliz@goliat.espol.edu.ec

International Relations: Pedro Vargas Gordillo
Tel: +593(4) 226-9143, Fax: +593(4) 285-2541
EMail: relex@espol.edu.ec

Faculties

Earth Sciences (Earth Sciences); **Economics and Trade** (Business and Commerce; Economics); **Electrical Engineering and Computer Science** (Computer Science; Electrical Engineering); **Marine Science and Oceanography** (Marine Science and Oceanography); **Mechanical Engineering and Production Engineering** (Mechanical Engineering; Production Engineering)

Institutes

Chemistry and Environmental Sciences (Chemistry; Environmental Studies); **Mathematics** (Mathematics) *Director*: Washington Armas; **Physics** (Physics) *Director*: Carlos Moreno Medina

Research Centres

Biotechnology (Biotechnology) *Director*: Helga Rodriguez; **Economics** *Coordinator*: Manuel González Astudillo; **Educational Services** *Director*: Jaime Vásquez Tito; **Environmental Studies** (Environmental Studies; Welfare and Protective Services) *Coordinator*: Francisco Torres Andrade; **Marine Sciences** (Marine Science and Oceanography) *Director*: Jaime Stern; **Science and Technology** *Director*: Paul Carrión Mero; **Statistics** *Director*: Gaudencio Zurita Herrera

Schools

Design and Visual Communication

History: Founded 1958 as a State institution under the jurisdiction of the Ministry of Education, but enjoys some autonomy.

Governing Bodies: Consejo Politécnico

Academic Year: May to February (May-September; October-February)

Admission Requirements: Secondary school certificate (bachillerato) and entrance examination

Main Language(s) of Instruction: Spanish

Degrees and Diplomas: *Tecnólogo*; *Licenciatura*: 4 yrs; *Professional Title (Ingeniero)*: 6 yrs; *Maestría*: 2-2 1/2 yrs. Also Diplomados and Postgrados

Student Services: Academic counselling, Cultural centre, Employment services, Health services, Language programs, Social counselling, Sports facilities

Libraries: c. 12.000 vols
Last Updated: 11/12/09

LATIN AMERICAN FACULTY OF SOCIAL SCIENCES

Facultad Latinoamericana de Ciencias Sociales
La Pradera E7-174 y Av. Diego de Almagro, Quito
Tel: +593(2) 323-8888
Fax: +593(2) 323-7960
EMail: flacso@flacso.org.ec
Website: http://www.flacso.org.ec

Director: Adrián Bonilla EMail: abonilla@flacso.org.ec

Subdirector Académico: Juan Ponce EMail: jponce@flacso.org.ec

Programmes
Anthropology (Anthropology); **Communication Studies**; **Economics** (Economics); **Environmental Studies** (Environmental Studies); **Gender Studies**; **International Relations**; **Political Science**; **Public Administration and Management**; **Urban Studies** (Urban Studies)

History: Founded 1975. Acquired present status 2000.

Degrees and Diplomas: *Maestría*; *Especialista*; *Doctorado*. Also Diploma Superior
Last Updated: 11/12/09

LUIS VARGAS TORRES DE ESMERALDAS TECHNICAL UNIVERSITY

Universidad Técnica Luis Vargas Torres de Esmeraldas
Apartado 179-619, Avenida Kennedy y Las Palmas, Esmeraldas
Tel: +593 (6) 272-3702
EMail: utelvt@utelvt.edu.ec
Website: http://www.utelvt.edu.ec

Rector: Luis Felipe Pacheco (2009-2013)
Tel: +593(6) 723702, Fax: +593(6) 723700
EMail: rector@utelvt.edu.ec

Faculties
Administration and Economics (Administration; Economics); **Animal Husbandry and Environmental Sciences** (Agriculture; Animal Husbandry; Environmental Studies); **Science, Educational Sciences and Health** (Educational and Student Counselling; Educational Psychology; Educational Sciences; Natural Sciences; Physical Education; Social Sciences)

History: Founded 1970. An autonomous State institution.

Main Language(s) of Instruction: Spanish

Degrees and Diplomas: *Licenciatura*: Chemistry and Biology; History and Geography; Industrial Engineering; Literature; Physical Education; Physics and Mathematics; Political Science and Economics; Psychology; Social Work; Sociology; Vocational Orientation, 4 yrs; *Professional Title*: Animal Husbandry; Business Administration; Commercial Engineering; Forestry Engineering, 5 yrs; *Maestría*; *Especialista*. Also Diplomado Superior
Last Updated: 15/12/09

MILAGRO STATE UNIVERSITY

Universidad Estatal de Milagro (UNEMI)
Km 1, via Milagro km. 26, Milagro, Guayas
Tel: +593 (4) 297-0881
Fax: +593 (5) 297-4317
EMail: rectorado@unemi.edu.ec
Website: http://www.unemi.edu.ec

Rector: Rómulo Minchala Murillo (2001-)

Secretario General: Agustín Arellano Quiroz
EMail: sec_gen@unemi.edu.ec

International Relations: Pedro Silva Anzules
EMail: psilva@unemi.edu.ec

Divisions
Administration and Commercial Sciences (Accountancy; Administration; Business Administration; Business and Commerce; Economics; Marketing; Secretarial Studies; Tourism); **Continuing Education (Distance)** *(Distance)*; **Education and Communication Science** (Communication Studies; Education; Graphic Design; Physical Education; Preschool Education); **Engineering** (Computer Engineering; Computer Science; Industrial Maintenance; Systems Analysis) *Head*: Efraín Sánchez Guevara; **Health Sciences**

History: Founded 2001. Former branch of Guayaquil State University.

Governing Bodies: University Council

Academic Year: May to September; October to March

Admission Requirements: Secondary school certificate (bachillerato) or equivalent

Main Language(s) of Instruction: Spanish

Degrees and Diplomas: *Tecnólogo*: Computer Science; Systems Analysis; Marketing; Graphic Design and Advertising; Tourism; Managerial Bilingual Secretary; Industrial Maintenance; Creation and Business and Management, 3 yrs; *Bachelor*: Physical Education; Social Communication; Tourism; Computer Science and Programming; Nursing; Early Childhood Education; Basic Education; Administration and Educational Supervision; Business Administration; *Licenciatura*: Pre-school Education; Physical Education; Social Communication; Tourism; Business Administration; Nursing; Education, 4 yrs; *Professional Title*: Accountancy; Commerce; Computer Science; Industrial Management; Economics;, 5 yrs; *Maestría*. Also Diplomado Superior

Student Services: Academic counselling, Canteen, Cultural centre, Foreign student adviser, Handicapped facilities, Health services, Language programs, Nursery care, Social counselling, Sports facilities

Libraries: Yes

Publications: Agora *(biennially)*
Last Updated: 14/12/09

NATIONAL POLYTECHNIC SCHOOL

Escuela Politécnica Nacional (EPN)
Apartado 17-12-866, Ladrón de Guevara E11-253, José Rubén Orellana Ricaurte Campus, Quito, Pichincha
Tel: +593(2) 250-7144
Fax: +593(2) 256-7848
EMail: vrector@epn.edu.ec
Website: http://www.epn.edu.ec

Rector: Alfonso Espinosa (2008-2013)
Tel: +593(2) 256-2400 EMail: rector@epn.edu.ec

Vicerrector: Adrián Peña Idrovo

Faculties
Business Sciences (Business Administration; Finance; Health Administration; Higher Education; Human Resources; Management; Marketing) *Director*: Wilson Abad; **Chemical Engineering and Agroindustry** (Agricultural Business; Agricultural Engineering; Biotechnology; Chemical Engineering; Food Science; Industrial Engineering; Metallurgical Engineering; Nuclear Engineering); **Civil and Environmental Engineering** (Civil Engineering; Engineering; Environmental Engineering; Water Management; Water Science); **Electrical and Electronic Engineering** (Automation and Control Engineering; Electrical and Electronic Engineering; Electrical Engineering; Electronic Engineering; Energy Engineering; Telecommunications Engineering); **Geology and Petroleum** (Geology; Petroleum and Gas Engineering); **Mechanical Engineering** (Materials Engineering; Mechanical Engineering); **Science** (Mathematics; Natural Sciences; Physics); **Systems Engineering** (Computer Science; Information Technology)

Schools
Technology (Construction Engineering; Electronic Engineering; Industrial Maintenance; Information Technology; Mechanical Engineering; Production Engineering; Systems Analysis; Technology)

History: Founded 1869 as Esceula Politécnica by President Gabriel García Moreno. Acquired present title 1946.

Governing Bodies: Consejo Politécnico; Consejo Académico; Consejo de Facultad; Consejo de Departamento

Academic Year: October to September (October-March; April-September)

Admission Requirements: Secondary school certificate (bachillerato) and entrance examination

Fees: (US Dollars): pregraduate, 50-600 per semester; postgraduate, 700-1,500 per semester

Main Language(s) of Instruction: Spanish

International Co-operation: With universities in Germany, Switzerland, France and USA.

Degrees and Diplomas: *Tecnólogo*: Electronics and Telecommunications; Systems Analysis; Electromechanics; Industrial Maintenance; Mechanical Production Process; Construction Project Management, 7 sem.; *Professional Title*: Electrical Engineering; Electronic Engineering; Civil Engineering; Environmental Engineering; Infrastructure Engineering; Geological Engineering; Petroleum Engineering; Chemical Engineering; Agroindustrial Engineering; Mechanical Engineering (Ingenerio); Systems Engineering; Physical Engineering; Mathematics; Economics and Finance; Administration (Ingenerio), 10 sem.; *Maestría*: Engineering; Science; Administration, a further 4 sem.; *Especialista*: Engineering; Science; Administration, 4 sem.; *Doctorado*: Physics; Mathematics; Natural Sciences (Phd), a further 8 sem. Also Diplomado Superior in Engineering (Postgraduate), 1 sem.

Student Services: Academic counselling, Canteen, Cultural centre, Foreign student adviser, Health services, Language programs, Social counselling, Sports facilities

Student Residential Facilities: No

Special Facilities: Natural History Museum; Petrographical Museum; Astronomic Observatory; Theatre

Libraries: Central Library, c. 30,300 vols. Also specialised libraries in the following Faculties: Electrical and Electronics Engineering, Chemistry and Agroindustry, Mechanics, Civil and Environmental Engineering, Geology and Petroleum Engineering, Sciences, Systems and other units such as the Astronomic Observatory, the Geophysics Institute, the Biological Sciences Institute, the Food and Biotechnology Department.

Publications: Revista Politécnica *(quarterly)*

Academic Staff 2007-2008	MEN	WOMEN	TOTAL
FULL-TIME	311	34	**345**
PART-TIME	114	6	**120**
STAFF WITH DOCTORATE			
FULL-TIME	42	2	**44**
PART-TIME	7	–	**7**
Student Numbers 2007-2008			
All (Foreign Included)	6,992	2,633	**9,625**

Last Updated: 11/12/09

NATIONAL UNIVERSITY OF CHIMBORAZO

Universidad Nacional de Chimborazo (UNACH)
Avenida Eloy Alfaro y 10 de Agosto, Riobamba
Tel: +593(3) 294-1999
Fax: +593(3) 296-0345
EMail: webmaster@unach.edu.ec
Website: http://www.unach.edu.ec

Rector: Edison Riera RodríguezFax: +593 960343
EMail: rector@unach.edu.ec

Vicerrector Académico: Marcelo Jiménez
EMail: vicerrector@unach.edu.ec

Faculties

Education, Humanities and Technology (Art Education; Bilingual and Bicultural Education; Biology; Business and Commerce; Chemistry; Educational Sciences; Gerontology; Laboratory Techniques; Literature; Modern Languages; Natural Sciences; Physical Education; Primary Education; Psychology; Social Sciences; Spanish; Special Education); **Engineering** (Agricultural Engineering; Civil Engineering; Electrical Engineering; Engineering; Environmental Engineering; Industrial Engineering); **Health Sciences** (Clinical Psychology; Medical Technology; Medicine; Nursing; Physical Education); **Political Science and Administration** (Accountancy; Administration; Communication Studies; Economics; Law)

History: Founded 1995.

Main Language(s) of Instruction: Spanish

Degrees and Diplomas: *Licenciatura*; *Maestría*. Also Diplomado Superior
Last Updated: 14/12/09

NATIONAL UNIVERSITY OF LOJA

Universidad Nacional de Loja
Ciudadela Universitaria 'Guillermo Falconí Espinosa' La Argelia,
11012636 Loja, Loja
Tel: +593(7) 254-7200
Fax: +593(7) 254-6075
EMail: dgb@unl.edu.ec
Website: http://www.unl.edu.ec

Rector: Gustavo Enrique Villacís Rivas EMail: rector@unl.edu.ec

Vicerrector: Ernesto Rafael González Pesantes
Tel: +593(7) 254-6384, Fax: +593(7) 254-6384
EMail: vrector@unl.edu.ec

Areas

Agriculture and Renewable Natural Resources (Agricultural Equipment; Agricultural Management; Agriculture; Agronomy; Animal Husbandry; Aquaculture; Environmental Management; Forestry; Irrigation; Rural Studies; Tropical Agriculture; Veterinary Science); **Education, Arts and Communication Studies** (Aesthetics; Biology; Chemistry; Child Care and Development; Clothing and Sewing; Communication Disorders; Computer Education; Education; Educational Administration; Educational and Student Counselling; Educational Psychology; Educational Research; Educational Technology; English; Higher Education Teacher Training; Information Sciences; Library Science; Literature; Mathematics; Mathematics Education; Music; Physical Education; Physics; Preschool Education; Science Education; Social Sciences; Spanish; Special Education; Teacher Trainers Education; Visual Arts); **Energy, Industry and Non-Renewable Natural Resources** (Automotive Engineering; Computer Science; Construction Engineering; Electrical Engineering; Electronic Engineering; Energy Engineering; Engineering; Environmental Management; Geological Engineering; Geology; Information Technology; Maintenance Technology; Mechanical Engineering; Natural Resources; Video); **Health Sciences** (Anaesthesiology; Clinical Psychology; Community Health; Dentistry; Gynaecology and Obstetrics; Health Administration; Laboratory Techniques; Medical Technology; Medicine; Nursing; Orthopaedics; Paediatrics; Public Health; Radiology; Surgery); **Law, Social Sciences and Administration** (Accountancy; Banking; Business Administration; Development Studies; Economics; Finance; Law; Public Administration; Social Work; Tourism)

History: Founded 1859 as School of Law, acquired present status 1943. An autonomous institution, largely financed by the State.

Governing Bodies: University Assembly; University Board; Academic Administrative Senior Council

Academic Year: October to July

Admission Requirements: Secondary school certificate (bachillerato)

Fees: (US Dollars): First module (Presence Modality): 56-229; (Distance Modality): 200-373

Main Language(s) of Instruction: Spanish

International Co-operation: With universities in Germany; Spain; USA; Cuba; Brazil; Chile; Peru

Accrediting Agencies: Consejo Nacional de Educación Superior (CONESUP); Consejo Nacional de Evaluación y Acreditación (CONEA)

Degrees and Diplomas: *Tecnólogo*: Electrical Engineering; Electronic Engineering; Music; Interior Design; Radiology; Protective Services, 3 yrs; *Doctor*: Dentistry and Odontology; Veterinary Science, 5 yrs; *Doctor*: Medicine, 6 yrs; *Licenciatura*: Chemistry; Biology; Physics; Mathematics; Economics; Public Administration; Education; Educational Psychology; Special Education; Educational Technology; Computer Education; Information Sciences; Literature; Native Language Education; English; Music; Nursing; Laboratory Techniques; Philosophy; Political Sciences; Social Sciences; Communication Studies; Social Work, 4 yrs; *Professional Title*: Accountancy; Banking; Finance; Economics; Engineering; Commercial Engineering; Computer Engineering; Electromechanical Engineering (Ingeniero); Environmental Engineering; Forestry; Agricultural Engineering; Environmental Management; Aquaculture; Agricultural Management; Agronomy; Crop Production; Nursing; (Enfermero(a)); Psychology; Clinical Psychology; Technology (Tecnólogo); Tourism, 5 yrs; *Maestría*: Business Administration; Law; Accountancy; Development Studies; Public Health; Health Sciences; Nursing; Rural Studies; Agriculture and Forestry; Tropical

Engineering; Irrigation; Environmental Management; Animal Husbandry, 1 1/2 yrs; *Maestría*: Electromechanical Engineering, 2 yrs; *Especialista*: Law; Tourism, 1 1/2 yrs; *Especialista*: Natural Resources; Irrigation, 10 months; *Especialista*: Paediatry; Gynaecology; Surgery; Medicine; Orthopaedics; Radiology; Anaesthesiology, 3 yrs. Also Técnico (2 yrs); Auxiliar de Enfermeria (2 yrs), Diplomado (2 months); Diplomado Superior (1 yr) Technical Craft (1 1/2 yrs)

Student Services: Academic counselling, Canteen, Cultural centre, Employment services, Handicapped facilities, Health services, Language programs, Nursery care, Social counselling, Sports facilities

Special Facilities: Music Museum. Art Gallery. Botanical Garden. Movie Studio. Theatre.

Libraries: c. 150,000 vols

Publications: Cigüeña de Papel, Literary Collections: Poetry *(annually)*; El Canto del Llangache, Literary Collection: Music *(annually)*; Estudios Universitarios *(annually)*; Mar de Tinta, Literary Collections: Narrative *(annually)*; Revistas Universitaria *(annually)*

Press or Publishing House: Editorial Universitaria

Academic Staff *2007-2008*	TOTAL
FULL-TIME	1,117
STAFF WITH DOCTORATE	
FULL-TIME	5

Student Numbers *2007-2008*	
All (Foreign Included)	19,446

Part-time students, 13,246. **Distance students**, 6,200.
Last Updated: 14/12/09

POLYTECHNIC STATE UNIVERSITY OF CARCHI
Universidad Politecnica Estatal del Carchi
calle Panamá y Rafael Arellano (Sector Parque Ayora),
Tulcán, Carchi
Tel: +593(6) 298-1009
EMail: info@upec.edu.ec
Website: http://upec.edu.ec

Faculties
Agronomy and Environment (Agronomy; Environmental Studies; Tourism); **International Business, Integration, Business Administration and Economics** (Business Administration; Economics; International Business; Marketing); **Medicine** (Medicine; Nursing)

History: Founded 2008.

Main Language(s) of Instruction: Spanish

Degrees and Diplomas: *Professional Title*
Last Updated: 14/12/09

SIMÓN BOLÍVAR ANDEAN UNIVERSITY ECUADOR
Universidad Andina Simón Bolívar Ecuador (UASB)
Apartado 17-12-569, Toledo 22-80 (Plaza Brasilia), Quito
Tel: +593(2) 250-8150
Fax: +593(2) 250-8156
EMail: uasb@uasb.edu.ec
Website: http://www.uasb.edu.ec

Rector: Enrique Ayala Mora (1997-) EMail: rector@uasb.edu.ec

Vicerrector: Santiago Andrade

Areas
Communication; **Education**; **Health Sciences** (Alternative Medicine; Health Sciences); **History** (History); **International Studies** (International Studies); **Law** (Law); **Letters** (Arts and Humanities; Literature); **Management** (Management)

Programmes
History; Latin American Cultures

Further Information: Also campus in Sucre, Bolivia; and offices in Cali, Colombia and Caracas, Venezuela, support unit for special programmes in Computer Science and Applied Mathematics in the Escuela Politécnica Nacional

History: Founded 1985 by the Parlamento Andino. An international Institution for Andean co-operation and integration, mostly oriented towards Postgraduate studies. Ecuador branch founded in 1992.

Governing Bodies: Consejo Superior; Consejo Académico; Comité de Coordinación Académica

Academic Year: October to September (October-December; January-March; April-June; July-September)

Admission Requirements: Recognized University Degree

Main Language(s) of Instruction: Spanish

Degrees and Diplomas: *Professional Title*: 1 yr; *Maestría*: minimum 1 1/2 yr; *Especialista*. Also Doctorado

Student Services: Academic counselling, Cultural centre, Foreign student adviser

Publications: Kipus (Revista Andina de Letras) *(biannually)*; Procesos (Revista Ecuadoriana de Historia) *(biannually)*
Last Updated: 11/12/09

STATE TECHNICAL UNIVERSITY OF QUEVEDO
Universidad Técnica Estatal de Quevedo (UTEQ)
Km 11/2 de la vía Quevedo-Buena Fe, Quevedo, Los Rios
Tel: +593(5) 275-0320; +593(5) 275-7463
Fax: +593(5) 275-3300; +593(5) 275-3303
EMail: vicerrector@uteq.edu.ec
Website: http://www.uteq.edu.ec

Rector: Manuel Haz Alvarez EMail: rector@uteq.edu.ec

Faculties
Agriculture (Agricultural Engineering; Agricultural Management; Business Administration; Fruit Production; Horticulture); **Business Studies**; **Environmental Science**; **Stockbreeding** (Cattle Breeding; Zoology)

Further Information: Also 2 experimental farms

History: Founded 1976 as branch of University of Esmeraldas, acquired present status and title 1984.

Governing Bodies: Asamblea Universitaria; Consejo Universitario, Consejo Directivo de la Facultad

Academic Year: May to March (May-September; October-March)

Admission Requirements: Secondary school certificate (bachillerato) and entrance examination (curso pre-universitario-tres meses)

Main Language(s) of Instruction: Spanish

International Co-operation: With universities in Japan and Spain. Also participates in the OUI-AUIP programme.

Degrees and Diplomas: *Professional Title (Ing)*: 5 yrs; *Professional Title*: Agronomy; Forestry; Environmental Sciences (Ing); Zootechnology (Ing), 5 yrs; *Maestría*; *Especialista*; *Doctorado*. Also Diplomado Superior

Student Services: Cultural centre, Health services, Language programs, Nursery care, Sports facilities

Student Residential Facilities: None

Libraries: Central Library, 1,500 vols

Publications: Magazine of Agronomy Research *(annually)*
Last Updated: 15/12/09

STATE UNIVERSITY OF BOLÍVAR
Universidad Estatal de Bolívar
Apartado 92, Km. 3 1/2 sector Alpachaca, Guaranda, Bolivar
Tel: +593(3) 298-0121
Fax: +593(3) 298-0123
EMail: info@ueb.edu.ec
Website: http://www.ueb.edu.ec

Rector: Gabriel Galarza López
Tel: +593(3) 298-2819 EMail: rector@ueb.edu.ec

Vicerrector Académico: Pedro Pablo Lucio
EMail: vrector@ueb.edu.ec

International Relations: Joscelito Solano
EMail: relinter@ueb.edu.ec

Faculties
Administration, Business Administration and Computer Science (Administration; Business Administration; Communication Studies; Computer Science; Hotel Management; Secretarial

Studies; Tourism); **Agriculture and Animal Husbandry** (Agricultural Engineering; Agriculture; Agronomy; Animal Husbandry; Ceramics and Glass Technology; Industrial Engineering; Veterinary Science; Zoology); **Educational Sciences** (Educational Administration; Educational Sciences; English; Fashion Design; Fine Arts; Musicology; Physical Education; Primary Education; Spanish; Sports); **Health Sciences** (Health Sciences; Nursing); **Law, Social Sciences and Political Science** (Law; Political Sciences; Sociology)

History: Founded 1989.

Main Language(s) of Instruction: Spanish

Degrees and Diplomas: *Tecnólogo*; *Licenciatura*; *Maestría*; *Especialista*. Also Diplomado Superior
Last Updated: 14/12/09

STATE UNIVERSITY OF THE AMAZON

Universidad Estatal Amazonica
Alvaro Valladares y Cristóbal Colón Puyo, Pastaza
Tel: +593(3) 288-7476
Fax: +593(3) 288-8118
EMail: info@uea.edu.ec

Rector: Gil Vela

Programmes
Agricultural Engineering; **Environmental Engineering**; **Tourism** (Tourism)

History: Founded 2002.

Main Language(s) of Instruction: Spanish

Degrees and Diplomas: *Professional Title*: 5 yrs
Last Updated: 14/12/09

STATE UNIVERSITY OF THE PENINSULA OF SANTA ELENA

Universidad Estatal Península de Santa Elena
Casilla Postal No. 09 - 11 - 16459, Vía La Libertad-Santa Elena, La Libertad
Tel: +593(4) 278-0018
Fax: +593(4) 278-4006
EMail: secretariarectorado@upse.edu.ec
Website: http://www.upse.edu.ec/

Rector: Jimmy Candell Soto

Vicerrector Académico: George Clemente

Faculties
Administration; **Agriculture** (Agriculture); **Industrial Engineering** (Civil Engineering; Industrial Engineering; Petroleum and Gas Engineering); **Marine Sciences** (Marine Biology)

Schools
Education; **Social Sciences** (Law; Nursing; Psychology)

History: Founded 1998.

Main Language(s) of Instruction: Spanish

Degrees and Diplomas: *Licenciatura*; *Professional Title*
Last Updated: 14/12/09

STATE UNIVERSITY OF THE SOUTH OF MANABI

Universidad Estatal del Sur de Manabi (UNESUM)
Calle Santiesteban entre Alejo Lascano y Mejia, Campus Universitario, m 1 vía a Noboa, Jipijapa
Tel: +593(5) 260-0229
EMail: unesum@hotmail.com

Rector: Jorge Climaco Cañarte Murillo
EMail: rectorunesum@aiisat.net

Faculties
Agricultural Administration; **Computer and Systems Engineering** (Computer Engineering; Systems Analysis); **Ecotourism** (Tourism); **Environmental Engineering**; **Forestry Engineering**

History: Founded 2001.

Main Language(s) of Instruction: Spanish

Degrees and Diplomas: *Professional Title*
Last Updated: 14/12/09

TECHNICAL UNIVERSITY OF AMBATO

Universidad Técnica de Ambato (UTA)
Apartado 18-01-334, Avenida Colombia y Chile, Ambato, Tungurahua
Tel: +593(3) 284-3011
Fax: +593(3) 284-9164
EMail: uta@uta.edu.ec
Website: http://www.uta.edu.ec

Rector: Luis Amoroso Mora

Vicerrector Administrativo: Remigio Medina
EMail: saltos@andianet.net

Centres
Postgraduate (Engineering; Management) *Director*: Francisco Fernández

Faculties
Accountancy and Auditing (Accountancy; Economics; Finance); **Administration** (Administration; Marketing; Private Administration; Public Administration); **Agricultural Engineering** (Agricultural Engineering; Agronomy; Veterinary Science; Zoology); **Civil and Mechanical Engineering** (Civil Engineering; Mechanical Engineering); **Food Science and Engineering** (Biochemistry; Food Science; Food Technology); **Health Sciences** (Clinical Psychology; Health Sciences; Medical Technology; Medicine; Nursing; Physical Therapy); **Humanities and Educational Sciences**; **Social Sciences and Law** (Law; Public Law; Social Sciences; Social Work); **Systems Engineering** (Automation and Control Engineering; Computer Engineering; Electronic Engineering; Industrial Engineering; Software Engineering; Systems Analysis)

History: Founded 1959 as an Institute of Accountancy, became an autonomous higher education institution 1963, and acquired University status 1969.

Governing Bodies: Asamblea Universitaria; Consejo Universitario

Academic Year: October to August

Admission Requirements: Secondary school certificate (bachillerato)

Fees: (US Dollars): c. 60-120, depending on field of study

Main Language(s) of Instruction: Spanish

International Co-operation: With universities in Mexico, Colombia, Chile and Spain.

Degrees and Diplomas: *Licenciatura*: Accountancy; Education; Health Sciences, 4 yrs; *Professional Title*: Administration and Management; Agronomy (Ing. Ag); Civil Engineering; Computer Engineering (Ing.Sis); Electrical Engineering (Ing. El); Food Technology (Ing. Al); Industrial Engineering (Ing. Ind); Mechanical Engineering (Ing. Mec), 5 yrs; *Maestría (Mg)*: 2 yrs; *Especialista*. Also Diplomado

Student Services: Academic counselling, Canteen, Cultural centre, Employment services, Social counselling, Sports facilities

Special Facilities: Archeology Museum

Libraries: Central Library, c. 11,780 vols; Administration, c. 5,620; Accountancy and Auditing, c. 5,100, Education, c. 7,220, Civil Engineering, c. 5,000

Publications: Research Publications

Press or Publishing House: Editorial Universitaria
Last Updated: 15/12/09

TECHNICAL UNIVERSITY OF BABAHOYO

Universidad Técnica de Babahoyo
Apartado 730587, Vía Flores, Babahoyo, Los Ríos
Tel: +593 (7) 273-5264
Fax: +593 (7) 273-0646
Website: http://www.utb.edu.ec

Rector: Bolívar Lupera (2008-2013)

Centres
Research

Faculties
Administration, Finance and Computer Studies (Administration; Banking; Computer Science; Finance); **Agriculture** (Agriculture); **Health Sciences** (Health Sciences); **Social Sciences and Education** *(Quevedo)* (Education; Pedagogy; Social Sciences)

Schools

Agronomy (Agronomy); **Clinical Laboratory** (Laboratory Techniques); **Computer Science** (Computer Science); **Finance, Banking and Accountancy** (Accountancy; Banking; Finance); **Management** (Management); **Medical Technology** (Medical Technology); **Natural Sciences** (Natural Sciences); **Nursing** (Nursing); **Psychology** (Psychology); **Social Communication; Technology** (Technology); **Veterinary Medicine and Zoology** (Veterinary Science; Zoology)

History: Founded 1971.

Degrees and Diplomas: *Licenciatura*: Education, 5 yrs; *Professional Title*: Agricultural Engineering (Ingeniero agrónomo), 5 yrs; *Maestría; Especialista*. Also Teaching qualifications, secondary level and Diplomado Superior
Last Updated: 15/12/09

TECHNICAL UNIVERSITY OF COTOPAXI

Universidad Técnica de Cotopaxi (UTC)
Campus Universitario, Av. Simón Rodríguez S/N, Barrio El Ejido, Sector San Felipe, Latacunga, Cotopaxi
Tel: +593(3) 281-0296 +593(3) 281-3157
Fax: +593(3) 281-0295
EMail: webmaster@utc.edu.ec
Website: http://www.utc.edu.ec

Rector: Hernán Yánez

Faculties
Administration, Arts and Humanities; Animal Husbandry, Environmental Sciences and Veterinary Medicine; Engineering and Applied Sciences

History: Founded 1991, acquired present status 1995.

Governing Bodies: University Council; University Assembly

Academic Year: October to March

Admission Requirements: Secondary School Certificate (bachillerato) or equivalent

Fees: (US Dollars): Per term, 39.50 for private high school students and 33.50 for public high school students

Main Language(s) of Instruction: Spanish

International Co-operation: With universities in Argentina; Cuba; Denmark

Accrediting Agencies: CONESUP

Degrees and Diplomas: *Maestría*: Education; Social Studies; Engineering, 2 yrs. Also Diplomado

Student Services: Academic counselling, Canteen, Employment services, Foreign student adviser, Health services, Language programs, Social counselling, Sports facilities

Student Residential Facilities: For guests and advisers only

Libraries: Yes

Publications: Alma Mater, University research *(annually)*

Press or Publishing House: Arcoiris

Academic Staff *2007-2008*	MEN	WOMEN	TOTAL
FULL-TIME	15	4	19
PART-TIME	148	63	211
PART-TIME	–	2	2
Student Numbers *2007-2008*			
All (Foreign Included)	2,266	2,689	4,955

Last Updated: 15/12/09

TECHNICAL UNIVERSITY OF MACHALA

Universidad Técnica de Machala
Ciudadela Universitaria, Av. Panamericana Km. 5 1/2 Via a Pasaje, Machala, El Oro
Tel: +593(7) 298-3362, Ext. 118
Fax: +593(7) 298-3371 Ext. 162
EMail: utm@utmachala.edu.ec
Website: http://www.utmachala.edu.ec

Rector: Alberto Game Solano Tel: +593(7) 298-3364, Ext.102

Vicerrectora Académica: Cecilia Serrano Campain
Tel: +593(7) 298-3365, Ext.103

Faculties

Agriculture (Agricultural Economics; Agronomy; Aquaculture; Veterinary Science) *Division Head*: I; **Business Administration** (Accountancy; Administration; Advertising and Publicity; Banking; Business Administration; Economics; Finance; Hotel Management; International Business; Marketing; Secretarial Studies; Tourism); **Chemistry and Health Sciences** (Biochemistry; Chemical Engineering; Chemistry; Nursing; Pharmacy); **Civil Engineering** (Civil Engineering; Systems Analysis); **Social Sciences** (Chemistry; Communication Studies; Computer Science; Educational Psychology; Educational Sciences; English; Law; Physical Education; Pre-school Education; Social Studies; Social Work; Sociology)

Schools
Medicine

History: Founded 1969.

Admission Requirements: Bachillerato, curso preuniversitario, personal documents

Main Language(s) of Instruction: Spanish

International Co-operation: With universities in Canada and Cuba

Accrediting Agencies: CONEA (Consejo Nacional de Evaluación y Acreditación) (en proceso)

Degrees and Diplomas: *Professional Title*: Administration, Accounting and Auditing Engineering; Agricultural Engineering; Aquaculture Engineering; Civil Engineering; Commerce Engineering; Systems Engineering; Veterinary Medicine and Animal Husbandry, 5 yrs; *Professional Title*: Auditing; Nursing, 4 yrs; *Professional Title*: Biochemistry and Pharmacy; Industrial Engineering; Sociology, 6 yrs. Also diplomas in Food Engineering, Arts and English.

Student Services: Academic counselling, Cultural centre, Health services, Language programs, Nursery care, Social counselling, Sports facilities

Special Facilities: Language Institute, Virtual Room and Laboratories

Libraries: Yes

Publications: Cumbres Magazine *(annually)*
Last Updated: 15/12/09

TECHNICAL UNIVERSITY OF MANABÍ

Universidad Técnica de Manabí
Avenida Universitaria Apdo 82, Portoviejo, Manabí
Tel: +593(5) 263-2677
Fax: +593(5) 265-1569
EMail: bc1@utm.edu.ec
Website: http://www.utm.edu.ec

Rector: José Félix Veliz Briones

Vicerrector: Eliecer David Rodríguez

Faculties
Administration and Economics (Accountancy; Administration; Business and Commerce; Economics); **Agricultural Engineering** (Agricultural Engineering); **Agronomy** (Agronomy); **Computer Science; Health Sciences** (Health Sciences; Medicine; Nursing; Nutrition; Optometry; Surgery); **Humanities** (Arts and Humanities; Secretarial Studies; Social Work); **Mathematics, Physics and Chemistry** (Chemistry; Civil Engineering; Electrical Engineering; Heating and Refrigeration; Industrial Engineering; Mathematics; Mechanical Engineering; Physics); **Philosophy, Literature and Education** (Biology; Chemistry; Education; Geography; History; Linguistics; Literature; Modern Languages; Philosophy; Physical Education; Physics; Spanish); **Veterinary Medicine** (Aquaculture; Veterinary Science); **Zoology** (Zoology) *Dean*: Edgardo Mendoza

History: Founded 1952 as a State Institution.

Governing Bodies: Asamblea General; Consejo Universitario

Academic Year: May to March

Admission Requirements: Secondary school certificate (bachillerato) or foreign equivalent

Main Language(s) of Instruction: Spanish

Degrees and Diplomas: *Licenciatura*: Chemistry and Biology; Languages; Nursing; Physics and Mathematics; Psychology, 4 yrs; *Professional Title*: Agricultural Engineering; Agronomy; Industrial Engineering; Mechanical Engineering; Veterinary Medicine;

Vocational Counselling, 5 yrs; *Professional Title*: Civil Engineering; Economics; Electrical Engineering, 6 yrs; *Maestría*; *Especialista*; *Doctorado*

Libraries: Central Library, c. 4,700 vols; specialized library, c. 1,100
Last Updated: 15/12/09

TECHNICAL UNIVERSITY OF THE NORTH
Universidad Técnica del Norte
Avenida 17 de Julio, Ciudadela Universitaria, Barrio el Olivo, Ibarra
Tel: +593(6) 295-3461
Fax: +593(6) 295-5833
Website: http://www.utn.edu.ec

Rector: Antonio Posso (2007-)

Centres
Research

Faculties
Administration; **Animal Husbandry and Environment**; **Applied Sciences** (Natural Sciences); **Educational Sciences** (Educational Sciences); **Health Sciences**

Institutes
Postgraduate

Schools
Accounting and Auditing; **Agroindustrial Engineering**; **Business Administration** (Business Administration); **Computer Engineering and Systems Analysis**; **Forestry Engineering and Renewable Natural Resources**; **Marketing**; **Nursing** (Nursing); **Nutrition and Dietetics** (Dietetics; Nutrition); **Pedagogy**; **Physical Education** (Physical Education); **Technology**; **Textile Engineering** (Textile Technology)

History: Founded 1986.

Main Language(s) of Instruction: Spanish

Degrees and Diplomas: *Licenciatura*; *Maestría*; *Especialista*. Also Diplomado Superior
Last Updated: 15/12/09

UNIVERSITY OF CUENCA
Universidad de Cuenca
Apartado 01-01-168, Avenida 12 de Abril s/n Ciudadela
Universitaria, Cuenca
Tel: +593(7) 283-1688
Fax: +593(7) 283-5197
EMail: coordaca@ucuenca.edu.ec
Website: http://www.ucuenca.edu.ec

Rector: Fabian Carrasco Castro EMail: rector@ucuenca.edu.ec

Centres
Postgraduate Studies *(CEP) Director*: Fernando Carvajal

Faculties
Agronomy (Agricultural Engineering; Animal Husbandry; Veterinary Science; Zoology); **Architecture** (Architecture); **Arts** (Art Education; Art History; Design); **Chemistry** (Chemistry); **Dentistry** (Dentistry); **Economics** (Economics); **Engineering** (Civil Engineering; Computer Engineering; Electrical Engineering; Electronic Engineering; Engineering; Telecommunications Engineering); **Hospitality**; **Law**; **Medicine** (Medicine) *Dean*: Arturo Qushpe; **Philosophy, Letters and Education** (Arts and Humanities; Education; Literature; Philosophy); **Psychology** (Psychology)

Institutes
Research *(IDIUC)*

Programmes
Water and Soil Management (Soil Management; Water Management)

History: Founded 1867, the University is an autonomous institution, but receives financial support from the State.

Governing Bodies: Consejo Universitario, composed of the Rector, the Vice-Rector, the deans of the Faculties, one representative of the academic staff, one representative of the Ministry of Education, and one student representative for each Faculty

Academic Year: October to July (October-January; April-July)

Admission Requirements: Secondary school certificate (bachillerato) or recognized foreign equivalent

Main Language(s) of Instruction: Spanish

Degrees and Diplomas: *Licenciatura*; *Professional Title*: Accountancy (Contador); Business Administration (Administrador de Empresas); Midwifery (Obstetriz); Nursing (Enfermero(a)), 4 yrs; *Professional Title*: Architecture (Arquitecto); Civil Engineering (Ingeniero civil); Economics (Economista); Electrical Engineering (Ingeniero eléctrico), 5 yrs; *Professional Title*: Surveying (Topógrafo), 2 yrs; *Maestría*; *Especialista*. Also Diplomado Superior

Libraries: Central Library, c. 71,780 vols; Engineering, c. 2,700; Philosophy, c. 6,830; Economics, c. 2,810; Medicine, c. 21,270; Chemistry, c. 1,120; Law, c. 9,850

Publications: Anales de la Universidad de Cuenca *(biannually)*
Last Updated: 21/03/11

UNIVERSITY OF GUAYAQUIL
Universidad de Guayaquil
Apartado postal 471, Ciudadela Universitaria, Salvador Allende y
Malecón del Salado, Guayaquil
Tel: +593(4) 229-6580
Fax: +593(4) 228-1559
EMail: vgeneral@ug.edu.ec
Website: http://www.ug.edu.ec

Rector: Carlos Cedeño Navarrete EMail: ugrector@ug.edu.ec

Vicerrector Administrativo: César Romero Villagrán
Fax: +593(4) 228-7074 EMail: vadminis@ug.edu.ec

Centres
Research

Faculties
Administration (Accountancy; Administration; Business and Commerce; Finance; Marketing); **Agriculture** (Agricultural Economics; Agricultural Engineering; Agricultural Equipment; Biology; Botany; Chemistry; Entomology; Horticulture; Hydraulic Engineering; Meteorology; Microbiology; Plant Pathology; Rural Planning; Soil Conservation; Zoology); **Architecture and Town Planning** (Architecture; Town Planning); **Chemical Engineering** (Chemical Engineering); **Chemistry** (Chemistry); **Dentistry**; **Economics** (Economics); **Industrial Engineering** (Industrial Engineering); **Law, Political and Social Sciences**; **Mathematics and Physics** (Civil Engineering; Mathematics; Physics); **Medicine** (Gynaecology and Obstetrics; Medical Technology; Medicine; Nursing); **Natural Sciences** (Analytical Chemistry; Aquaculture; Biology; Botany; Chemistry; Embryology and Reproduction Biology; Entomology; Forestry; Geology; Hydraulic Engineering; Limnology; Marine Science and Oceanography; Mathematics; Mineralogy; Natural Sciences; Paleontology; Petroleum and Gas Engineering; Tropical Agriculture; Zoology); **Philosophy, Letters and Educational Sciences** (Arts and Humanities; Educational Sciences; Library Science; Linguistics; Philosophy); **Physical Education, Sports and Recreation**; **Psychology** (Clinical Psychology; Psychology); **Social Communication**; **Systems Engineering**; **Veterinary Medicine and Zoology**

Institutes
International Studies and Diplomacy *(Postgraduate)*; **Research and Studies in Mathematics** *(Postgraduate)*

History: Founded 1867 as Junta Universitaria, became Universidad del Guayas, then Universidad de Guayaquil 1897. Became autonomous 1925. Financed mainly by the State, partly by student fees.

Governing Bodies: Asamblea Universitaria; Consejo Universitario

Academic Year: April to January

Admission Requirements: Secondary school certificate (bachillerato) or recognized foreign equivalent, and entrance examination

Main Language(s) of Instruction: Spanish

Degrees and Diplomas: *Tecnólogo*: Médico, Medical Technology, 3 yrs; *Licenciatura*: Education, 5 yrs; *Licenciatura*: Library Science; Nursing; Social and Political Sciences; Social Communication; Sociology, 4 yrs; *Professional Title*: Accountancy; Psychology, 6 yrs; *Professional Title*: Architecture, 5 yrs and thesis; *Professional Title*: Biology; Chemistry; Economics; Geology; Midwifery; Sociology, 5 yrs; *Professional Title*: Engineering, 5-6 yrs; *Professional*

Title: Library Science, 2 yrs; *Professional Title*: Nursing, 4 yrs; *Maestría*; *Especialista*. Also diplomado superior

Libraries: Central Library, c. 15,000 vols; Faculty libraries

Press or Publishing House: Litografía e Imprenta de la Universidad Guayaquil

Last Updated: 14/12/09

PRIVATE INSTITUTIONS

ALFREDO PÉREZ GUERRERO UNIVERSITY
Universidad Alfredo Pérez Guerrero (UNAP)
Avenida de los Shyris 39-33 y el Telegrafo, Quito, Pinchicha
Tel: +593(2) 243-2928
Fax: +593(2) 226-9384 Ext. 104
EMail: info@unap.edu.ec
Website: http://www.unap.edu.ec

Rector: Jorge Enriquez Páez
Tel: +593(2) 243-8846 EMail: rectorado@unap.edu.ec

Coordinador Académica General: Ivan Galarroga
EMail: posgrades@unap.edu.ec

Secretary General: Juan Pablo Martinad
EMail: procurador@gmail.com

International Relations: Frank Enriquez Modena, Coordinador Academica Administrativo
EMail: coordinacionacademica@unap.edu.ec

Programmes
Business Administration (Accountancy; Business Administration; Economics; International Relations; Marketing; Sales Techniques); **Digital Design and Multimedia**; **Education** *(Parvularia)*; **Foreign Trade**; **Law** (Justice Administration; Law); **Marketing** (Marketing); **Social Communication** (Communication Studies); **Systems and Networking** (Computer Networks); **Tourism**

History: Founded 2001.

Governing Bodies: Government Council; Academic Council

Academic Year: Secondary school certificate

Fees: (US Dollars): 1,200 per semester

Main Language(s) of Instruction: Spanish

International Co-operation: With universities in Peru, Costa Rica, Spain, Cuba, Brazil

Accrediting Agencies: AULCPI

Degrees and Diplomas: *Professional Title*: 5 yrs; *Maestría*: 2 yrs; *Especialista*

Student Services: Academic counselling, Cultural centre, Language programs, Social counselling, Sports facilities

Libraries: Yes

Publications: Esquicios *(biennially)*

Academic Staff 2007-2008	MEN	WOMEN	TOTAL
PART-TIME	84	30	114
Student Numbers 2007-2008			
All (Foreign Included)	350	244	594

Part-time students, 284. **Evening students**, 310.
Last Updated: 11/12/09

AMAZON INSTITUTE OF TECHNOLOGY AND ECOLOGY
Escuela Superior Politécnica Ecológica Amazónica (ESPEA)
Tena Km 1 Via Puerto Napo, 17-04-10694 Tena, Napo
Tel: +593(6) 2886901
Fax: +593(6) 2640713 Ext.102
EMail: info@espea.edu.ec; espeam@hotmail.com
Website: http://www.espea.edu.ec/

Rector: Washington Ricardo Estrada Avilés

Vicerrector: Víctor Armando Estrada Avilés
Tel: +593(6) 2640713 EMail: vicerrector@espea.edu.ec

International Relations: Christian Ricardo Estrada Ordóñez
Tel: +593(2) 290-8632, Fax: +593(2) 290-8632
EMail: canciller@espea.edu.ec

Departments
Postgraduate and Distance Education

Faculties
Environmental Sciences and Administration; **Human Ecology** (Civil Law; Ecology; Education; Medicine; Nursing)

History: Founded 1997.

Admission Requirements: Secondary school certificate (bachillerato), or foreign equivalent

Main Language(s) of Instruction: Spanish

Accrediting Agencies: CONESUP

Degrees and Diplomas: *Diploma*: Computer Science, 1 yr; *Doctor*: Medicine, 6 yrs; *Licenciatura*: Nursing, 4 yrs; *Professional Title*: Engineering; Law; Environmental Engineering, 5 yrs; *Maestría*: Environmental Management; Alternative Medicine; Educational Administration (MSc), 2 yrs

Student Services: Academic counselling, Foreign Studies Centre, Health services, Language programs, Social counselling, Sports facilities

Student Residential Facilities: 3 internship residences

Special Facilities: Zoo; 2 Greenhouses; Specialized Eco-Systems Research Facilities in Coastal and Amazon Regions

Libraries: Yes, 11 libraries across the country

Publications: Tierra Adentro, An agricultural magazine about Ecuador's agro-forestry development *(bimonthly)*

Last Updated: 11/12/09

AMERICA TECHNOLOGICAL UNIVERSITY
Universidad Tecnológica América (UNITA)
Oriente 536 y Guayaquil, Quito
Tel: +593(2) 954-528
Fax: +593(2) 581-749
EMail: webmasterunita@unita.edu.ec
Website: http://www.unita.edu.ec

Rector: Pablo Villarroel R

Secretario General: José Martínez

Faculties
Administration and Commerce; **Computer Science and Electronics**; **Graphic Design and Visual Communication**; **Mechanical Engineering**

Institutes
Languages (Modern Languages)

History: Founded 1997.

Main Language(s) of Instruction: Spanish

Degrees and Diplomas: *Professional Title*; *Maestría*; *Especialista*
Last Updated: 15/12/09

AUTONOMOUS REGIONAL UNIVERSITY OF THE ANDES
Universidad Regional Autónoma de los Andes (UNIANDES)
Km. 51/2 Via a Baños, Ambato
Tel: +593(2) 274-8098
Fax: +593(2) 285-1105
EMail: desarrollouniandes@uniandesonline.edu.ec
Website: http://www.uniandes.edu.ec

Rector: Gustavo Alvarez Gavilanes

Vicerrectora: Corona Gómez Armijos

Faculties
Business Administration; **Law** (Law); **Marketing** (Accountancy; Banking; Economics; Finance; Marketing); **Medicine**

History: Founded 1997.

Main Language(s) of Instruction: Spanish

Degrees and Diplomas: *Licenciatura*; *Maestría*; *Especialista.* Also Diplomado Superior
Last Updated: 14/12/09

AUTONOMOUS UNIVERSITY OF QUITO
Universidad Autónoma de Quito (UNAQ)
Calle Mercadillo n°129 entre Paéz y 10 de Agosto, Quito, Pichincha
Tel: +593(2) 222-1457
Fax: +593(2) 222-1458
EMail: info@unaq.net
Website: http://www.unaq.net

Rector: Vicente Rojas A. (1999-) EMail: vrojas@unaq.net

Vicerrector: Freddy Huilca Pinos

Faculties
Computer and Systems Engineering (Computer Engineering) *Dean*: Pablo Jaramillo; **Economics and Administration Science** *Dean*: Jaime Larco; **Educational Sciences** (Educational Administration; Educational Technology; Pedagogy) *Dean*: Ivan Moreno; **Industrial Design Engineering** (Industrial Design) *Dean*: José Revelo; **Law** *Dean*: Xavier Sanchez; **Social Sciences and Theology** *Dean*: Luz Orna, **Visual Communication Engineering** (Communication Studies; Visual Arts) *Dean*: José Revelo

History: Founded 1999.

Governing Bodies: University Council

Academic Year: September to August

Admission Requirements: Secondary school certificate or recognized foreign equivalent

Fees: (US Dollars): 550-600 per semester

Main Language(s) of Instruction: Spanish

International Co-operation: With universities in Taiwan and USA

Degrees and Diplomas: *Tecnólogo*: 3 yrs; *Licenciatura*: 4 yrs; *Professional Title*: Engineering (Ingeniero), 5 yrs

Student Services: Academic counselling, Foreign student adviser, Health services, Language programs, Social counselling, Sports facilities

Student Residential Facilities: None

Libraries: Central Library

CASA GRANDE UNIVERSITY
Universidad Casa Grande (UCG)
Frente a la puerta n°6 del C.C Albán Borja, Guayaquil
Tel: +593(4) 220-2180
Fax: +593(4) 220-2180
EMail: relacionespublicas@casagrande.edu.ec
Website: http://www.casagrande.edu.ec

Rectora: Marcia Gilbert de Babra
EMail: mgilbert@casagrande.edu.ec

Vicerrectora: Leticia Orcés Pareja
EMail: lorces@casagrande.edu.ec

Faculties
Administration and Political Science; **Communication Studies**; **Human Ecology, Education and Development** (Child Care and Development; Development Studies; Education; Human Resources; Special Education)

Units
Postgraduate

History: Founded 1999.

Main Language(s) of Instruction: Spanish

International Co-operation: With universities in Europe, Asia, North and Latin America.

Accrediting Agencies: International Advertising Association (IAA); CONESUP (Consejo Nacional Educacíon Superior)

Degrees and Diplomas: *Licenciatura (BA; BS)*; *Maestría.* Also Técnico superior and Tecnólogos: Associate degrees

Student Services: Academic counselling, Employment services

Special Facilities: WIFI on all campuses

Libraries: Yes
Last Updated: 11/12/09

CATHOLIC UNIVERSITY OF CUENCA
Universidad Católica de Cuenca
Apartado 01-01-1937, PO Box 01, Calle Bolívar 949 entre Benigno Malo y Padre Aguirre, Cuenca
Tel: +593(7) 283-4037
Fax: +593(7) 283-8011
EMail: uccsis@etapa.com.ec
Website: http://www.ucacue.edu.ec

Rector: César Cordero Moscoso (1975-)

Vicerrector Administrativo: Enrique Pozo Cabrera

Departments
Accountancy and Counselling

Faculties
Business Administration; **Chemical Engineering and Industry** (Chemical Engineering; Industrial Engineering); **Civil Engineering and Architecture**; **Commerce, Administration and Accountancy** (Accountancy; Administration; Business and Commerce); **Economics and Finance** (Economics; Finance); **Law, Political and Social Sciences** (Law; Political Sciences; Social Sciences); **Medicine and Health Sciences** (Health Sciences; Medicine); **Mining Engineering and Metallurgical Engineering**; **Psychology, Pedagogy and Education** (Education; Pedagogy; Psychology)

Institutes
Accountancy and Auditing (Accountancy); **Agronomy, Mining Engineering and Veterinary Science** (Agronomy; Mining Engineering; Veterinary Science); **Clinical Psychology** (Clinical Psychology); **Computer Science and Languages** (Computer Science); **Ecology and Forestry**; **Experimental Planning**; **Industrial Engineering**; **Industrial Management** (Industrial Management); **Information Sciences and Social Communication**; **Law and Computer Science**; **Law and Social Assistance**; **Modern Languages** *(elementary level)* (Modern Languages); **Nursing and Obstetrics** (Gynaecology and Obstetrics; Nursing); **Pedagogy and Educational Sciences**; **Physical Education** (Physical Education); **Secretarial Studies** (Secretarial Studies); **Social Work and Community Services** (Social and Community Services); **Systems Analysis** (Systems Analysis); **Theatre and Arts**; **Veterinary Medicine and Zoology**

Research Institutes
Computer Science (Computer Science)

Further Information: Also Veterinary Clinic

History: Founded 1970. A private institution receiving some financial support from the State.

Governing Bodies: Asamblea Universitaria; Consejo Gubernativo; Consejos Académico, Administrativo, de Extensiones

Academic Year: October to July (October-February; March-July)

Admission Requirements: Secondary school certificate (bachillerato) or recognized foreign equivalent

Main Language(s) of Instruction: Spanish

Degrees and Diplomas: *Licenciatura*: Education and Psychology; Languages; Law and Social Sciences; Physical Education; Secretarial Studies; Social Work, 4 yrs; *Professional Title*: Agricultural Engineering; Chemical Engineering; Commercial Engineering; Economics; Industrial Engineering; Psychology; Veterinary Medicine, 5 yrs; *Maestría*: Engineering; *Doctorado*: Education and Psychology; Law and Social Sciences, 6 yrs; *Doctorado*: Medicine. Also teaching qualifications, secondary level

Libraries: Central Library, c. 6,500 vols
Last Updated: 11/12/09

CATHOLIC UNIVERSITY OF SANTIAGO DE GUAYAQUIL
Universidad Católica de Santiago de Guayaquil
Avenida C. J. Arosemena Km 11/2, Via Daule, Guayaquil
Tel: +593(4) 220-9210
Fax: +593(4) 220-0071
EMail: alternativas@ucsg.edu.ec; aaguilar@ucsg.edu.ec
Website: http://www.ucsg.edu.ec

Rector: Michel Doumet Antón

Vicerrector: Joaquín Hernández
Tel: +593(4) 220-2130, Fax: +593(4) 220-6945

Centres
Lifelong Education; Research (SINDE)

Faculties
Architecture (Architecture; Civil Engineering; Interior Design; Landscape Architecture); **Arts and Humanities** (Arts and Humanities; Dance; English; Modern Languages; Multimedia; Music; Theatre); **Business Studies** (Business Administration; Finance; Sales Techniques; Tourism); **Economics** (Accountancy; Administration; Economics; International Business; Management); **Engineering** (Civil Engineering; Engineering; Systems Analysis); **Law** (Law; Political Sciences; Social Sciences); **Medicine** (Dentistry; Dietetics; Medicine; Nursing; Nutrition); **Philosophy, Literature and Education** (Educational Sciences; Literature; Philosophy; Preschool Education; Psychology); **Technology for Development** (Agricultural Economics; Electronic Engineering; Mechanical Engineering; Natural Resources; Rural Planning; Technology; Telecommunications Engineering; Veterinary Science; Zoology)

Institutes
Tropical Molecular Biology (Molecular Biology)

History: Founded 1962 by the Catholic Church in Ecuador. Legally recognized as an autonomous institution.

Governing Bodies: Asamblea Universitaria; Consejo Universitario

Academic Year: May to February (May-September; October-February)

Admission Requirements: Secondary school certificate (bachillerato), or recognized foreign equivalent, and entrance examination

Main Language(s) of Instruction: Spanish

Degrees and Diplomas: *Licenciatura*: Education; Law; Letters; Nursing; Philosophy; Psychology; Social and Political Sciences; Social Work, 4-5 yrs; *Professional Title*: Animal Husbandry; Technical Studies, 2 yrs; *Professional Title*: Architecture; Commercial Engineering; Computer System Engineering; Economics, 5 yrs; *Professional Title*: Design; Nursing; Social Work, 3-4 yrs; *Professional Title*: Law, 6 yrs; *Professional Title*: Psychology; *Maestría*; *Especialista*; *Doctorado*: Education; Law; Medicine; Philosophy; Psychology; Social Service. Also Diplomados superiores

Libraries: Central Library, c. 14,000 vols

Publications: Revista de Historia del Derecho; Revista de Investigación *(biannually)*

Press or Publishing House: Centro de Publicaciones
Last Updated: 11/12/09

COMANDANTE RAFAEL MORÁN VALVERDE NAVAL UNIVERSITY
Universidad Naval Comandante Rafael Morán Valverde
Malecón Sector Chipipe, Base Naval de Salinas, Salinas
Tel: +593(4) 277-3383
EMail: aromerv@hotmail.com

Rector: Carlos Moncayo

Programmes
Nautical Science (Nautical Science); **Naval Logistics**
History: Founded 2006.
Main Language(s) of Instruction: Spanish
Degrees and Diplomas: *Licenciatura*
Last Updated: 14/12/09

ELOY ALFARO LAY UNIVERSITY OF MANABÍ
Universidad Laica Eloy Alfaro de Manabí (ULEAM)
Casilla 13-05-2732, Ciudadela Universitaria Vía Circunvalación, Portoviejo, Manabí
Tel: +593(5) 262-5095
Fax: +593(5) 262-3009
EMail: uleam@uleam.edu.ec
Website: http://www.uleam.edu.ec

Rector: Medardo Mora Solórzano
Tel: +593(4) 625095 EMail: uleamrectorado@yahoo.com
Vicerrector: Vicente González Toala

Departments
Research

Faculties
Administration (Administration; Marketing; Secretarial Studies); **Animal Husbandry** (Animal Husbandry); **Architecture** (Architecture); **Communication Studies** (Communication Studies); **Computer Science** (Administration; Computer Science); **Dentistry** (Dentistry); **Economics** (Economics); **Education** (Education); **Engineering** (Civil Engineering; Electrical Engineering; Engineering; Industrial Engineering); **Foreign Trade**; **Law, Political and Social Sciences** (Law; Political Sciences; Social Sciences); **Medicine**; **Nursing** (Nursing); **Social Work** (Social Work); **Tourism and Hotel Management** (Hotel Management; Tourism)

Schools
Accountancy and Auditing (Accountancy); **Marine Science and Oceanography** (Marine Science and Oceanography; Naval Architecture); **Naval Engineering** (Naval Architecture)

History: Founded 1985.
Academic Year: May to April
Admission Requirements: Secondary school certificate and entrance examination
Main Language(s) of Instruction: Spanish
Degrees and Diplomas: *Licenciatura*; *Professional Title*; *Maestría*; *Especialista*. Also Diplomado Superior
Special Facilities: Museo Antropológico
Last Updated: 14/12/09

EQUATORIALIS UNIVERSITY
Universitas Equatorialis
Noruega 156 y 6 de Diciembre, Quito
Tel: +593(2) 292 0813
EMail: contacto@equatorialis.com
Website: http://www.equatorialis.com

Rector: Rodrigo Crespo Toral

Faculties
Administration (Administration; Finance; Human Resources; Marketing); **Environmental Studies** (Environmental Management; Environmental Studies; Natural Resources)

History: Founded 2002.
Main Language(s) of Instruction: Spanish
Degrees and Diplomas: *Professional Title*
Last Updated: 15/12/09

EQUINOX UNIVERSITY OF TECHNOLOGY
Universidad Tecnológica Equinoccial
Apartado 17-01-2764, Burgeois N34-102 y Rumipamba, Quito
Tel: +593(2) 245-1866
Fax: +593(2) 244-2288
EMail: info@ute.edu.ec
Website: http://www.ute.edu.ec

Rector: Álvaro Trueba Barahona (1993-)
EMail: atrueba@ute.edu.ec
Vicerrector: José Julio Cevallos Gómez

Centres
Research *Director*: Erma Campos

Departments
Modern Languages (English; French; German; Modern Languages) *Director*: Alicia Vanegas

Faculties
Architecture, Arts and Design (Architecture; Fashion Design; Fine Arts; Interior Design; Restoration of Works of Art); **Economics and Trade** (Business Administration; Business and Commerce; Economics; Finance; Marketing); **Engineering** (Computer Engineering; Computer Science; Engineering; Environmental Engineering; Food Technology; Industrial Engineering; Petroleum and Gas Engineering; Textile Technology); **Health Sciences** *(Eugenio Espejo)*; **Social Sciences and Communication**; **Tourism, Hotel Management and Gastronomy**

Further Information: Branches in Santo Domingo de los Colorados, Salinas

History: Founded 1986.

Governing Bodies: University Council

Academic Year: October to July

Admission Requirements: Secondary school certificate (bachillerato) and entrance examination

Main Language(s) of Instruction: Spanish

Degrees and Diplomas: *Tecnólogo*: 3 yrs; *Licenciatura*: 4 yrs; *Professional Title*: Engineering (Ingeniero), 5 yrs; *Maestría*: a further 1-2 yrs; *Especialista*

Student Services: Cultural centre, Sports facilities

Student Residential Facilities: For c. 5,000 students

Special Facilities: Art Centre

Libraries: c. 20,000 vols

Press or Publishing House: Departamento de Publicaciones UTE

Last Updated: 15/12/09

ESPIRITU SANTO UNIVERSITY OF SPECIALIZATIONS

Universidad de Especialides Espíritu Santo (UEES)
Apartado 09-01-4842, Vía La Puntilla, Samborondón, Km 2.5, Guayaquil
Tel: +593(4) 283-5630
Fax: +593(4) 283-5483
EMail: uees@uees.edu.ec
Website: http://www.uees.edu.ec

Rector: Carlos Ortega Maldonado (1993-)
Tel: +593(4) 2835230 EMail: cortega@uees.edu.ec

Vicerrector: David Samaniego Torres
EMail: dsamanie@uees.edu.ec

Faculties
Communication (Arts and Humanities; Communication Studies); **Computing Systems, Telecommunications and Electronics** (Computer Engineering; Electronic Engineering; Systems Analysis; Telecommunications Engineering); **Economics and Business Management** (Business Administration; Business and Commerce; Economics; Finance; Human Resources; International Business; Marketing); **Law, Political Science and Development** (Development Studies; Law; Political Sciences); **Liberal Arts and Education** (Art History; Bilingual and Bicultural Education; Dance; English; Fine Arts; International Business; Music; Public Relations; Special Education; Tourism; Translation and Interpretation); **Medicine**; **Tourism and Hotel Management** (Environmental Management; Hotel Management; Tourism) *Dean:* Sonia Palacios

Schools
Architecture and Design (Architectural and Environmental Design; Architecture; Construction Engineering; Industrial Design; Interior Design; Landscape Architecture; Photography); **Graduate Studies and Continuing Education** *Dean:* Xavier Mármol; **International Studies** (Latin American Studies; Spanish)

History: Founded 1993.

Governing Bodies: Board of Directors

Academic Year: April to December. (Full year study is also possible)

Admission Requirements: Secondary school certificate (bachillerato) or recognized foreign equivalent, and entrance examination, or satisfactory completion of a pre-university programme

Fees: (US Dollars): 1,500 per semester

Main Language(s) of Instruction: Spanish, English

International Co-operation: With universities in Canada, USA, France, United Kingdom, Japan, Philippines and Italy.

Accrediting Agencies: CONESUP

Degrees and Diplomas: *Diploma*: Financial Management; Human Resource Management; Law; Marketing and Sales, 7 mths; *Licenciatura*: Business Science; Communication; Education; Liberal Arts, 4 yrs; *Professional Title*: Economics Engineering, 4 yrs; *Maestría*: Business Administration in Business Strategies; Finance; Marketing; Science, 18-24 mths. Also Diplomado Superior

Student Services: Academic counselling, Canteen, Cultural centre, Employment services, Foreign student adviser, Foreign Studies

Centre, Handicapped facilities, Health services, Language programs, Nursery care, Social counselling, Sports facilities

Student Residential Facilities: For international students

Special Facilities: Computer Laboratories

Libraries: c. 13,000 vols

Publications: Cuadernos
Last Updated: 14/12/09

IBERO-AMERICAN UNIVERSITY OF ECUADOR

Universidad Iberoamericana del Ecuador
9 de Octubre y Colón N25-12, Quito
Tel: +593(2) 254-3142
Fax: +593(2) 223-0377
EMail: info@unibe.edu.ec
Website: http://www.unibe.edu.ec

Rectora: Nohemy Oleas Carrillo

Faculties
Administration (Administration; Business Administration; Finance; Sales Techniques); **Arts and Communications** (Aesthetics; Communication Studies; Cosmetology; Fine Arts; Jewelry Art; Public Relations; Radio and Television Broadcasting); **Law** (Law); **Tourism and Hotel Management** (Hotel and Restaurant; Hotel Management; Tourism)

History: Founded 2005.

Main Language(s) of Instruction: Spanish

Degrees and Diplomas: *Licenciatura*; *Professional Title*
Last Updated: 14/12/09

INDO-AMERICAN TECHNOLOGICAL UNIVERSITY

Universidad Tecnológica Indoamérica (UTI)
Ambato-Bolívar 2035 entre Guayaquil y Quito, Ambato, Tungurahua
Fax: +593(3) 242-1713
EMail: indoamerica@uti.edu.ec
Website: http://www.uti.edu.ec

Rector: Saúl Lara Paredes EMail: slara@indoamerica.net

Faculties
Administration and Economics (Accountancy; Banking; Business Administration; Commercial Law; Economic and Finance Policy; International Business; Management; Marketing; Mathematics; Transport Management); **Architecture and Applied Arts** (Architecture; Fine Arts); **Human and Health Sciences** (Psychology); **Human Sciences, Education and Social Development** (Education; Educational Administration; Preschool Education; Primary Education); **Industrial Engineering** (Accountancy; Business Administration; Chemical Engineering; Economics; English; Finance; Human Resources; Materials Engineering; Mathematics; Physics); **Law** (Constitutional Law; Criminal Law; Ethics; History of Law; Justice Administration; Law; Philosophy; Private Law; Public Law); **Systems Engineering** (Artificial Intelligence; Computer Science; Electrical and Electronic Engineering; English; Mathematics; Systems Analysis)

History: Founded 1998.

Academic Year: October to September (October-March; April-September)

Fees: (US Dollars): c. 120 per semester

Main Language(s) of Instruction: Spanish, English

Degrees and Diplomas: *Tecnólogo*: 3 yrs; *Doctor*: Law, 6 yrs; *Licenciatura*: Law, 4 yrs; *Professional Title*: 5 yrs; *Maestría*

Student Services: Employment services, Sports facilities

Libraries: General library
Last Updated: 15/12/09

INTERAMERICAN UNIVERSITY OF ECUADOR

Universidad Interamericana del Ecuador
Duchicela 17-75 y Princesa Toa, Riobamba
EMail: rectorado@unidec.edu.ec
Website: http://www.unidec.edu.ec

Rector: Luis Coloma Gaibor

Faculties

Architecture (Architecture); **Computer Science**; **Economics and Administration** (Accountancy; Business Administration; Economics; Marketing; Sales Techniques); **Educational Sciences**; **Environment, Production and Development** (Development Studies; Environmental Studies; Production Engineering); **Health Sciences** (Dentistry); **Law and Communication Sciences**

History: Founded 1990 as Instituto Técnico Panamericano. Became Instituto Superior Tecnológico Panaméricano 1992. Acquired present status and title 2006.

Main Language(s) of Instruction: Spanish

Degrees and Diplomas: *Licenciatura*; *Professional Title*
Last Updated: 14/12/09

INTERCULTURAL UNIVERSITY AMAWTAY WASI OF THE INDIGENOUS NATIONALITIES AND PEOPLES

Universidad Intercultural de las Nacionalidades y Pueblos Indigenas Amawtay Wasi
Avenida Gran Colombia N12-30 y Antonio Elizalde, Quito
Tel: +593(2) 258-6919
EMail: informacion@amawtaywasi.edu.ec
Website: http://www.amawtaywasi.edu.ec

Rector: Luis Fernando Sarango
EMail: rector@amawtaywasi.edu.ec

Programmes

Agro-Ecology (Agriculture; Ecology); **Indigenous Studies** (Indigenous Studies); **Intercultural Learning** (Cultural Studies)

History: Founded 2004.

Degrees and Diplomas: *Licenciatura*; *Professional Title*
Last Updated: 10/12/09

INTERNATIONAL UNIVERSITY OF ECUADOR

Universidad Internacional del Ecuador (UIDE)
Km 3 Av. Simon Bolivar, Collacoto, Quito
Tel: +593(2) 2985-600
Fax: +593(2) 2985-666
EMail: informa@internacional.edu.ec
Website: http://www.internacional.edu.ec

Rector: Marcelo Fernández Sánchez (1992-) Tel: +593 266236
Directora Académico: Nohemy Oleas

Faculties

Administration and Science; **Architecture and Design** (Architecture; Interior Design); **Automotive Engineering** (Automotive Engineering); **Basic Sciences**; **Law**; **Medicine and Health Sciences**; **Social Sciences and Communication Studies**

Institutes
Languages

Schools

Applied Science and Technology (Computer Science; Electronic Engineering; Mechanical Engineering; Multimedia; Telecommunications Engineering); **Gastronomy** (Cooking and Catering); **Hotel Management** (Hotel Management); **Tourism and Environmental Studies**

History: Founded 1996.

Governing Bodies: Consejo Consultivo, Consejo Académico, Consejo Administrativo

Admission Requirements: Secondary school certificate (bachillerato) and entrance examination

Main Language(s) of Instruction: Spanish

Accrediting Agencies: Consejo Nacional de Evaluación y Acreditación

Degrees and Diplomas: *Licenciatura*: 4 yrs; *Professional Title*; *Maestría*; *Especialista*. Also Diplomado superior

Student Services: Academic counselling, Cultural centre, Foreign student adviser, Foreign Studies Centre, Health services, Language programs, Sports facilities

Special Facilities: Language Laboratory. Radio

Libraries: Central library
Last Updated: 14/12/09

ISRAEL UNIVERSITY

Universidad Israel (UTECI)
Francisco Pazmiño 256 y Orellana, Quito
Tel: +593(2) 255-741
Fax: +593(2) 255-812
EMail: israel@uio.satnet.net
Website: http://uisrael.ec/portal

Rector: Klein Rodríguez Otañez
Vicerrector: Andrés Chávez

Faculties

Administration and Commerce (Administration; Business and Commerce); **Computer Systems** (Computer Science; Systems Analysis); **Design and Multimedia**; **Electronics and Robotics** (Electronic Engineering; Robotics)

Schools
Languages (English; French; German; Italian; Modern Languages)

History: Founded 1984.

Degrees and Diplomas: *Licenciatura*; *Maestría*

JEFFERSON UNIVERSITY

Universidad Jefferson
Km 6 vía a la Costa, Guayaquil, Guayas
Tel: +593(4) 287-0359
Fax: +593(4) 287-0577
EMail: admissions@jefferson.edu.ec

Rector: Carlos Solorzano Constantine
Presidente: Norberto Nurnberg

Faculties

Business Administration (Banking; Business Administration; Business Computing; Finance; Human Resources; International Business; Marketing); **Design and Communication**; **Tourism**

History: Founded 1999.

Academic Year: May to December (May -August; September-December)

Admission Requirements: Secondary school certificate

Main Language(s) of Instruction: Spanish, English

Degrees and Diplomas: *Licenciatura*: 4 yrs

Libraries: Yes
Last Updated: 04/12/07

JOSÉ PERALTA PRIVATE TECHNICAL UNIVERSITY OF ENVIRONMENTAL SCIENCES

Universidad Técnica Particular de Ciencias Ambientales José Peralta
Ayacucho y Azuay Esq., Azogues
Tel: +593(2) 2244661

Rector: Francisco Zea Zamora

Programmes

Business Administration (Business Administration; Business and Commerce); **Computer Engineering** (Computer Engineering); **Ecology** (Ecology); **Environmental Management** (Environmental Management); **Law, Social and Political Sciences**; **Marketing** (Marketing); **Social Anthropology**; **Tourism**

History: Founded 1998.

Degrees and Diplomas: *Professional Title*
Last Updated: 10/12/09

LATIN AMERICAN CHRISTIAN UNIVERSITY

Universidad Cristiana Latinoamericana (UCL)
Apartado 17-08-8100, Avenida 10 de Agosto N34-38 y Rumipamba, Quito
Tel: +593(2) 226-7152
Fax: +593(2) 226-7154
EMail: ucl@ecuanex.net.ec
Website: http://www.ucl.edu.ec

Rector: Marco Lucio Muñoz Herrería
Vicerrector General: Vinicio Bustos

Schools

Administration (Accountancy; Administration); **Biomedicine**; **Communication Studies**; **Dentistry** (Dentistry; Stomatology); **Design**; **Ecotourism**; **Medicine** (Medicine); **Psychology** (Psychology); **Systems Engineering**; **Theology** (Theology)

History: Founded 1996.

Governing Bodies: Consejo Universitario. Consejo Tutelar

Academic Year: October to July

Admission Requirements: Secondary school certificate

Fees: (US Dollars): 1,100

Main Language(s) of Instruction: Spanish

International Co-operation: With the Council for Christian Colleges and Universities (CCCU) in USA

Accrediting Agencies: CONEA

Degrees and Diplomas: *Licenciatura*: 5 yrs; *Professional Title*: 5 yrs; *Maestría (Master in Systemic Therapy)*: 2 yrs

Student Services: Academic counselling, Cultural centre, Foreign student adviser, Foreign Studies Centre, Health services, Language programs, Nursery care, Social counselling

Student Residential Facilities: None

Special Facilities: Hospital; Clinics

Libraries: A library and 3 virtual libraries

Academic Staff 2007-2008	MEN	WOMEN	TOTAL
FULL-TIME	–	–	62
PART-TIME	–	–	220
STAFF WITH DOCTORATE			
FULL-TIME	–	–	25

Student Numbers 2007-2008			
All (Foreign Included)	915	1,318	2,233
FOREIGN ONLY	–	–	140

Last Updated: 11/12/09

MANUEL FÉLIX LÓPEZ INSTITUTE OF AGRICULTURAL TECHNOLOGY OF MANABI

Escuela Superior Politécnica Agropecuaria de Manabí Manuel Félix López (ESPAM)
10 de Agosto #82 y Granda Centeno, Calceta
Tel: +593(5) 268-5676
Fax: +593(5) 268-5156
EMail: espam@espam.edu.ec
Website: http://www.espam.edu.ec

Rector: Leonardo Félix López EMail: rectorado@espam.edu.ec

Programmes

Agriculture (Agriculture; Cattle Breeding); **Business Administration** (Business Administration; Public Administration); **Computer Engineering**; **Environmental Studies**; **Tourism**; **Veterinary Science**

History: Founded 1999.

Main Language(s) of Instruction: Spanish

Degrees and Diplomas: *Professional Title*
Last Updated: 11/12/09

METROPOLITAN UNIVERSITY

Universidad Metropolitana
Av. 33 Guillermo Cubillo y calle 18i (500 metros atras de la Coca Cola), Guayaquil, Guayas
Tel: +593(2) 227-8346
Fax: +593(2) 227-8344
EMail: jbarrezueta@mail.umetro.edu
Website: http://www.umetro.edu

Rector: Carlos Espinoza Cordero

Areas

Administration and Management (Accountancy; Administration; Agricultural Business; Health Sciences; Human Resources; Leisure Studies; Management; Tourism); **Arts and Humanities** (Arts and Humanities); **Education** (Education); **Engineering** (Engineering); **Exact Sciences and Technology** (Business Computing; Computer Science; Marine Transport; Mathematics and Computer Science; Natural Sciences; Technology); **Health Sciences** (Health Sci-

ences); **Political and Social Sciences** (International Relations; Law; Political Sciences; Social Sciences); **Service Trades**; **Transport and Communications** (Transport and Communications)

Further Information: Branch in Machala

History: Founded 2000.

Main Language(s) of Instruction: Spanish

Degrees and Diplomas: *Licenciatura*; *Professional Title*; *Maestría*

Student Services: Academic counselling, Handicapped facilities, Language programs, Social counselling
Last Updated: 14/12/09

OG MANDINO UNIVERSITY

Universidad Og Mandino
San Francisco 436 y Mariano Echeverría, Sector Quito Tenis, Quito
Tel: +593(2) 246-9457
EMail: info@uom.edu.ec
Website: http://www.uom.edu.ec

Rector: Jesús Vintimilla

Faculties

Administration; **Communication Studies**; **Finance and Insurance** (Finance; Insurance); **Human Resources and Psychology** (Human Resources; Psychology); **Marketing and Sales** (Marketing; Sales Techniques)

History: Founded 2005.

Main Language(s) of Instruction: Spanish

Degrees and Diplomas: *Licenciatura*: Communication Studies; *Professional Title*: Marketing; Commerce; Human Resources; Psychology; Information Technology; Finance; Insurance (Ingenerio)
Last Updated: 14/12/09

PANAMERICAN UNIVERSITY OF CUENCA

Universidad Panamericana de Cuenca
Manuel J. Calle 2-14 y Cornelio Merchán, Cuenca
Tel: +593(7) 288-4047
Fax: +593(7) 281-4625

Rector: Antonio Martínez Borrero

Faculties

Administration (Administration; Advertising and Publicity; Finance; Marketing); **Political Science** (Government; Political Sciences)

History: Founded 2004.

Main Language(s) of Instruction: Spanish

Degrees and Diplomas: *Professional Title*
Last Updated: 10/12/09

PONTIFICAL CATHOLIC UNIVERSITY OF ECUADOR

Pontificia Universidad Católica del Ecuador (PUCE)
Avenida 12 de Octubre n°1076 entre Patria y Veintimilla, 17-01-2184 Quito, Pichincha
Tel: +593(2) 299-1608; +593(2) 299-1700
Fax: +593(2) 299-1609; +593(2) 256-7117
EMail: webmaster@puce.edu.ec
Website: http://www.puce.edu.ec

Rector: Manuel Corrales Pascual (2005-)
EMail: rector@puce.edu.ec; mcorrales@puce.edu.ec

Vicerrector: Pablo Iturralde Ponce

Faculties

Architecture, Design and Fine Arts (Architecture; Design; Fine Arts); **Business Administration and Accountancy**; **Communication, Linguistics and Literature** (Communication Studies; Linguistics; Literature; Modern Languages); **Economics** (Economics); **Education** (Education); **Engineering** (Civil Engineering; Engineering; Systems Analysis); **Human Sciences** (Anthropology; Ecology; Geography; History; Political Sciences; Sociology; Tourism); **Law** (Law); **Medicine** (Medicine); **Natural and Exact Sciences** (Biology; Chemistry; Natural Sciences); **Nursing** (Nursing; Nutrition; Physical Therapy); **Philosophy and Theology**;

Psychology (Clinical Psychology; Educational Psychology; Industrial and Organizational Psychology; Psychology)

Schools

Bioanalysis (Histology; Medical Technology; Microbiology); **Social Work** (Social Work)

History: Founded 1946 under the Cardinal Archbishop of Quito. Legally recognized as an autonomous Institution but partly supported by the State. Other income derived from student fees, from the University's own resources, and from gifts and donations.

Governing Bodies: Consejo Superior; Consejo Académico

Academic Year: September to July (September-February; March-July)

Admission Requirements: Secondary school certificate (bachillerato) or authenticated foreign equivalent, and entrance examination

Fees: (US Dollars): 2,000-3,500 per semester

Main Language(s) of Instruction: Spanish

Degrees and Diplomas: *Doctor:* Surgery, 12 sems; *Licenciatura:* Accountancy; Biology; Chemistry; Business Administration; Communication Studies; Applied Linguistics; Foreign Language Education; Education; Histology; Microbiology; Medical Technology; History; Geography; Tourism; Hotel Management; Political Science; Sociology; Nursing; Nutrition; Physical Therapy; Social Work; Theology, Philosophy; Visual Arts, 8 sems; *Licenciatura:* Law, 10 sems; *Professional Title:* Accountancy; *Professional Title:* Architecture; Civil Engineering; Commercial Engineering; Law, 10 sems; *Professional Title:* Designer; Economics, 8 sems; *Professional Title:* Systems Engineering, 9 sems; *Maestría; Especialista.* Also Diplomado superior

Student Services: Academic counselling, Canteen, Cultural centre, Employment services, Foreign student adviser, Foreign Studies Centre, Handicapped facilities, Health services, Language programs, Nursery care, Social counselling, Sports facilities

Student Residential Facilities: None

Special Facilities: Museo 'Jacinto Jijón y Camaño'; Estación Científica Yasuní; Laboratories; Archivo Histórico Flores

Libraries: Central Library; Philosophy Documentation Centre; Centre for Economic Research; Centre for Anthropological Research

Publications: Revista *(quarterly)*

Press or Publishing House: Centro de Publicaciones

Academic Staff *2007-2008*	MEN	WOMEN	TOTAL
FULL-TIME	–	–	287
PART-TIME	–	–	838
STAFF WITH DOCTORATE			
FULL-TIME	–	–	381
Student Numbers *2007-2008*			
All (Foreign Included)	3,790	4,201	7,991
FOREIGN ONLY	77	53	130

Last Updated: 11/12/09

AMBATO BRANCH
SEDE AMBATO (PUCESA)

Rocafuerte y Lalama Esq., Ambato
Tel: +593(3) 241-6722
Fax: +593(3) 241-1868
EMail: pucesa@puce.edu.ec
Website: http://www.pucesa.edu.ec

Pro-rector: César González Loor

Schools

Business Management *(PYMES)* (Business Administration); **Industrial Design** (Industrial Design); **Languages** (Modern Languages); **Optometry** (Optometry); **Psychology** (Psychology); **Systems Engineering** (Systems Analysis); **Theology** (Theology)

History: Founded 1986.

Main Language(s) of Instruction: Spanish

Degrees and Diplomas: *Licenciatura; Professional Title; Maestría.* Also Diplomado

ESMERALDAS BRANCH
SEDE ESMERALDAS

Apartado 08-01-0065 Calle Espejo y Santa Cruz s/n, Esmeraldas
EMail: pucese@pucese.net
Website: http://www.pucese.net

Pro-rector: Aitor Urbina García de Vicuña

Units

Administration and Accountancy; Educational Sciences; Environmental Management (Environmental Management); **Graphic Design** (Graphic Design); **Health Sciences** (Nursing); **Linguistics**

History: Founded 1981.

Main Language(s) of Instruction: Spanish

Degrees and Diplomas: *Tecnólogo:* 6-7 sem; *Licenciatura:* 9 sem; *Professional Title; Maestría:* 4 sem; *Especialista:* 2 sem

IBARRA BRANCH
SEDE IBARRA

Apartado 10-10-34 Aurelio Pólit, Ciudadela La Victoria, Ibarra
Tel: +593(6) 264-3093
Fax: +593(6) 264-1787
EMail: prorect@pucesi.edu.ec
Website: http://www.pucesi.edu.ec

Pro-rector: María José Rubio

Schools

Agriculture and Environmental Sciences (Agriculture; Environmental Studies); **Architecture** (Architecture); **Business and International Trade** (Accountancy; Business Administration; International Business); **Design; Educational Sciences; Hotel Management and Tourism** (Hotel Management; Tourism); **Law; Social Communication** (Journalism; Radio and Television Broadcasting); **Systems Engineering** (Systems Analysis)

MANABÍ BRANCH
SEDE MANABÍ

Apartado 13-02-100 Ciudadela Primero de Mayo, Calle Eudoro Loor s/n, Portoviejo
Tel: +593(5) 263-7305
Fax: +593(5) 263-7327

Director: Homero Fuentes

Programmes

Agro-industry *(Chone);* **Business Administration** (Business Administration); **Hydrology** *(Bahía)* (Hydraulic Engineering); **Marine Resources** *(Bahía);* **Teacher Training** (Teacher Training); **Tourism**

History: Founded 1993.

Main Language(s) of Instruction: Spanish

Degrees and Diplomas: *Tecnólogo; Licenciatura; Professional Title*

SANTO DOMINGO DE LOS COLORADOS BRANCH
SEDE SANTO DOMINGO DE LOS COLORADOS

Apartado 17-24-377, Av. Chone Km 2 1/2, Santo Domingo de los Colorados
EMail: pucesd@pucesd.edu.ec
Website: http://www.pucesd.edu.ec

Porrectora: Margalida Font Roig

Schools

Administration and Accountancy (Accountancy; Administration; Business and Commerce); **Design** (Graphic Design); **Education** (Education; Educational Administration); **Hotel Management and Tourism; Nursing; Social Communication; Systems Engineering** (Computer Science)

Degrees and Diplomas: *Licenciatura; Professional Title.* Also Diploma superior

PRIVATE TECHNICAL UNIVERSITY OF LOJA

Universidad Técnica Particular de Loja
Casilla Postal 11-01-608, Barrio San Cayetano Alto s/n, Loja
Tel: +593(7) 257-0275
Fax: +593(7) 256-3159
EMail: info@utpl.edu.ec
Website: http://www.utpl.edu.ec

Rector: José Barbosa Corbacho

Vicerrector: Roberto Beltrán EMail: rbeltran@utpl.edu.ec

Centres
Distance Education; **Research** *Dean:* Juan Aranda

Faculties
Animal Husbandry (Animal Husbandry) *Dean:* Jaime Germán Guamán; **Architecture** (Architecture) *Dean:* Juan Flores Cabrera; **Civil Engineering** (Civil Engineering) *Dean:* Jorge Hidalgo Torres; **Economics** (Economics) *Dean:* Fernando Mora J.; **Education** (Education) *Dean:* Felix Rosero G.; **Modern Languages** (Literature; Modern Languages) *Dean:* Jorge Sarmiento R.

Schools
Accountancy and Auditing (Accountancy) *Director:* Elsa Cárdenas Sempértegui; **Bilingual Secretarial Studies** (Secretarial Studies) *Director:* Edith Bravo Luna; **Fine Arts** (Fine Arts) *Director:* Ticiano Cagigal G.; **Geology and Mining Engineering** (Mining Engineering) *Director:* Rudy Valdivieso Lapo

Further Information: Also Campuses in Zamora, Cariamanga, San Cayetano Alto

History: Founded 1971 as School by the Marist Brothers. A private Institution under the jurisdiction of the Comunidad de Misioneros y Misioneras de Cristo Redentor, financed largely by the State.

Governing Bodies: Consejo Gubernativo

Academic Year: October to August (October-March; April-August)

Admission Requirements: Secondary school certificate (bachillerato) or recognized foreign equivalent, and entrance examination

Main Language(s) of Instruction: Spanish

Degrees and Diplomas: *Licenciatura:* Accountancy and Auditing; Education; Secretarial Studies; Tourism, 8 sem; *Licenciatura:* Human and Religious Sciences, 9 sem; *Licenciatura:* Plastic Arts, 6 sem; *Licenciatura:* System Analysis, 10 sem; *Professional Title:* Agricultural Engineering and Animal Husbandry (Ingeniero en Industria Agropecuarias); Architecture (Arquitecto); Civil Engineering (Ingeniero civil); Economics (Economista), 10 sem; *Professional Title:* Chemistry (Químico), 8 sem; *Maestría; Especialista; Doctorado:* Accountancy and Auditing; Jurisprudence. Also teaching qualifications, 10 sem.

Special Facilities: Museo de Arqueología. TV Studio

Libraries: Biblioteca 'Benjamin Carrión', c. 10,000 vols

Publications: Reloj *(monthly)*; Revista *(annually)*; Universidad *(monthly)*

Press or Publishing House: Editorial UTPL

Academic Staff *2008:* Total: c. 650
Last Updated: 04/04/08

SALESIAN POLYTECHNIC UNIVERSITY

Universidad Politécnica Salesiana (UPS)
Turuhuayco No 3-69 y Calle Vieja, 46 Sector 2 Cuenca, Azuay
Tel: +593(7) 286-2529
Fax: +593(7) 286-1750
EMail: srector@ups.edu.ec
Website: http://www.ups.edu.ec

Rector: Javier Herrán Gómez EMail: luciano@ups.edu.ec

Vicerrector: Edgar Loyola Illescas

Faculties
Administration and Economics; Agricultural Engineering and Environmental Sciences; Engineering; Humanities and Educational Sciences

History: Founded 1994.

Governing Bodies: Consejo Superior; Consejo Académico

Academic Year: In Quito and Cuenca: September-July/Octobre-February. In Guayaquil: May-September/October-March

Admission Requirements: Secondary school certificate

Fees: (US Dollars): c. 1,200 per annum

Main Language(s) of Instruction: Spanish; English

International Co-operation: With universities in Spain; Italy; Sweden; Germany; India; Italy; Japan; Brazil; El Salvador; Chile; Honduras; Uruguay; Cuba; Perú; Argentina; Colombia; Bolivia; Venezuela; Mexico. Also participates in IUS; APICE; ODUCAL; OUI; AIESAD; IICA

Degrees and Diplomas: *Licenciatura:* 5 yrs; *Maestría:* Education; Business Administration; Social Studies; Anthropology; Cultural Studies; Design; Development Studies; Psychology; Telecommunication Engineering; Design Engineering, 2 yrs; *Especialista:* Distance Education; Business Administration; Computer Sciences; Development, 1 yr and 6 months. Also Diplomado Superior

Student Services: Academic counselling, Cultural centre, Employment services, Foreign student adviser, Handicapped facilities, Health services, Language programs, Nursery care, Social counselling, Sports facilities

Student Residential Facilities: None

Special Facilities: Museum of Amazon cultures; Laboratories; Multimedia Centre

Libraries: Central Library. Virtual Library and Library for the blind

Publications: Alteritad, Scientific Journal of the Faculty of Administration and Economics *(biennially)*; El Emprendedor, Scientific Journal of the Faculty of Human and Social Sciences *(biennially)*; Ingenius, Journal of the Faculty of Engineering *(annually)*; La Granja, Journal of the Faculty of Agriculture and Environmental Studies *(biennially)*; Sophia, Journal of Philosophy and Pedagogy *(annually)*; Universitas, Scientific Publication *(biennially)*

Academic Staff *2007-2008*	MEN	WOMEN	TOTAL
FULL-TIME	131	89	220
PART-TIME	398	269	667
STAFF WITH DOCTORATE			
FULL-TIME	7	3	10
PART-TIME	59	22	81
Student Numbers *2007-2008*			
All (Foreign Included)	8,249	6,141	14,390
FOREIGN ONLY	–	–	82

Part-time students, 1,136. **Distance students**, 272. **Evening students**, 12,982.

Last Updated: 14/12/09

GUAYAQUIL BRANCH

SEDE GUAYAQUIL (UPS-G)

Casilla 431, Rosa Borja Icaza 115 y Maracaibo, Guayaquil
Tel: +593(4) 580447
Fax: +593(4) 583464

Vicerrector: Andrés Bayolo Garay
Tel: +593(4) 458-0325, Fax: +593(4) 258-3353

Faculties
Administration and Economics (Accountancy; Administration; Business Administration; Economics); **Engineering** (Automation and Control Engineering; Electrical Engineering; Electronic Engineering; Mechanical Engineering; Systems Analysis); **Humanities and Educational Sciences** (Arts and Humanities; Communication Studies; Educational Sciences; Pedagogy; Physical Education; Preschool Education; Primary Education; Psychology; Social Sciences)

History: Founded 1998

Main Language(s) of Instruction: Spanish

Degrees and Diplomas: *Tecnólogo; Licenciatura; Professional Title*

QUITO BRANCH

SEDE QUITO

Apartado 17.12.536, Av. 12 de Octubre N24-22 y Wilson, Quito
Tel: +593(2) 223-6702
Fax: +593(2) 223-6896
EMail: webmaster@ups.edu.ec
Website:http://www.upsq.edu.ec

Vicerrector: Armando Romero Ortega
EMail: vicerrector@upsq.edu.ec

Faculties

Administration and Economics (Accountancy; Administration; Business Administration; Economics) *Dean:* Andrés Bayolo; **Engineering** (Automation and Control Engineering; Electrical Engineering; Electronic Engineering; Mechanical Engineering) *Dean:* Diego Peñaloza; **Human and Social Sciences** (Anthropology; Arts and Humanities; Communication Studies; Social Sciences); **Humanities and Educational Sciences** (Arts and Humanities; Communication Studies; Educational Sciences; Pedagogy; Physical Education; Preschool Education; Primary Education; Psychology; Social Sciences) *Dean:* Armando Romero

History: Founded 1994.

Main Language(s) of Instruction: Spanish

Degrees and Diplomas: *Licenciatura*; *Professional Title*; *Maestría*

SAN ANTONIO TECHNICAL UNIVERSITY OF MACHALA

Universidad Tecnológica San Antonio de Machala
Calle Loja 312, Entre 9 de Octubre y 10 de Agosto, Machala
Tel: +593(72) 296-1201
Fax: +593(72) 296-1200
EMail: utsam@utsam.edu.ec
Website: http://www.utsam.edu.ec

Rector: Manuel Avila Loor

Vicerrector: Jorge Solórzano Noblecilla

Institutes
Languages (English; Modern Languages)

Schools
Computer Engineering (Computer Engineering); **Design** (Design; Graphic Design; Interior Design); **Education** (Clinical Psychology; Education); **Law**

Main Language(s) of Instruction: Spanish

Degrees and Diplomas: *Diploma*; *Maestría*; *Especialista*

SAN FRANCISCO UNIVERSITY OF QUITO

Universidad San Francisco de Quito (USFQ)
Diego de Robles y Vía Interoceánica, Circulo de Cumbayá, Quito, Pichincha
Tel: +593(2) 297-1700
Fax: +593(2) 289-0070
EMail: usfguayaquil@usfq.edu.ec
Website: http://www.usfq.edu.ec

Chancellor: Santiago Gangotena (1988-)
Tel: +593(2) 297-1801 EMail: santiago@usfq.edu.ec

President: Carlos Montúfar F.
Tel: +593(2) 297-1808 EMail: carlosm@usfq.edu.ec

International Relations: Gonzalo Mendieta, Vice President of Academic Affairs
Tel: +593(2) 297-1813 EMail: gonzalom@usfq.edu.ec

Colleges
Administration for Development (Administration; Development Studies; Economics; Finance; Marketing); **Agriculture, Food Sciences and Nutrition** *(CAAN)* (Agricultural Business; Agriculture; Agronomy; Biochemistry; Biology; Botany; Chemistry; Crop Production; Food Technology; Industrial and Production Economics; Laboratory Techniques; Molecular Biology; Nutrition; Packaging Technology; Physics; Physiology; Public Health); **Architecture and Interior Design** *(CARQ)* (Architectural and Environmental Design; Architecture; Interior Design); **Biology and Environmental Sciences**; **Communication and Contemporary Arts** *(COCOA)* (Advertising and Publicity; Communication Studies; Computer Graphics; Cultural Studies; Design; Film; Fine Arts; Journalism; Media Studies; Multimedia; Performing Arts; Photography; Public Relations; Video); **Continuing Education** *(Mayor)* (Continuing Education); **Health Sciences** *(COSCA)* (Dentistry; Health Sciences; Medicine; Nutrition; Optometry; Public Health; Veterinary Science); **Law** *(JUR)* (Law); **Liberal Arts** *(CAL)* (Education; Inter-

national Relations; Psychology); **Science and Engineering** (Aeronautical and Aerospace Engineering; Chemical Engineering; Chemistry; Civil Engineering; Electronic Engineering; Engineering; Industrial Engineering; Mathematics; Mechanical Engineering; Physics; Systems Analysis); **Technology** *(COLTEC)* (Administration; Agriculture; Automotive Engineering; Computer Networks; Electronic Engineering; Fashion Design; Graphic Design; Interior Design; Mechanical Engineering; Preschool Education; Tourism); **Tourism, Hospitality Management and Culinary Arts** (Accountancy; Cooking and Catering; Finance; Food Science; Food Technology; Hotel and Restaurant; Management; Marketing; Tourism) *Dean:* Mauricio Cepeda

Schools
Graduate (Administrative Law; Applied Mathematics; Asian Religious Studies; Business Administration; Chinese; Dentistry; Education; Energy Engineering; Environmental Studies; Food Science; Health Sciences; Information Sciences; Microbiology; Nutrition; Public Health; Real Estate) *Dean:* Victor Viteri B.

History: Founded 1988. Acquired present status 1995.

Governing Bodies: Board; Council of Regents; Council of Deans; Council of Elders

Academic Year: August to May

Admission Requirements: Secondary school certificate and entrance examination, or foreign equivalent

Fees: (US Dollars): Tuition: 3,825; Books: 190; Studies Insurance: 185

Main Language(s) of Instruction: Spanish

International Co-operation: With universities in the United States, Canada, Spain, France, Germany, Netherlands, Switzerland,UK, Poland, Japan, China, Singapore, Korea, Chile and Australia

Degrees and Diplomas: *Tecnólogo*: 3 yrs; *Bachelor (BA; BS)*: 4 yrs; *Doctor*: Medicine; Dentistry and Odontology; Optometry; Clinical Psychology; Nutritionist, 5-6 yrs; *Doctor*: Veterinary, 6 yrs; *Professional Title*: Architecture; Engineering, 5 yrs; *Professional Title*: Law, 6 yrs; *Maestría*: a further 1-2 yrs; *Especialista*; *Doctorado*

Student Services: Academic counselling, Canteen, Employment services, Foreign student adviser, Foreign Studies Centre, Handicapped facilities, Health services, Language programs, Social counselling, Sports facilities

Special Facilities: Theatres; Movie Studio, Sound Production Studio; Photography Studio

Libraries: c. 120,000 vols

Publications: El Periódico *(bimonthly)*

Press or Publishing House: San Francisco University Press

Academic Staff 2007-2008	TOTAL
FULL-TIME	250
PART-TIME	450
STAFF WITH DOCTORATE	
FULL-TIME	100
PART-TIME	c. 30
Student Numbers 2007-2008	
All (Foreign Included)	c. 5,000
FOREIGN ONLY	750

Distance students, 160. Evening students, 750.
Last Updated: 15/12/09

SAN GREGORIO UNIVERSITY OF PORTOVIEJO

Universidad Particular San Gregorio de Portoviejo
Calle Sucre entre García Moreno y Francisco Pacheco, Portoviejo
Tel: +593(5) 2632927
EMail: rectorado@usgp.edu.ec
Website: http://www.sangregorio.edu.ec/index.php

Rector: Marcelo Farfan

Programmes
Accountancy; **Architecture**; **Business Administration** (Business Administration); **Dentistry**; **Economics**; **Education** (Accountancy; Computer Education; Education; Environmental Studies; Geography; History; Literature; Natural Sciences; Secretarial Studies;

Spanish; Tourism); **Graphic Design**; **International Business**; **Journalism** (Journalism); **Law** (Law)

History: Founded 2000.

Main Language(s) of Instruction: Spanish

Degrees and Diplomas: *Professional Title*

Last Updated: 14/12/09

SEK INTERNATIONAL UNIVERSITY
Universidad Internacional SEK
Calle Fray Francisco Compte y Cruz de Piedra, Guápulo, Quito
Tel: +593(2) 248-5104
Fax: +593(2) 248-5105
Website: http://www.uisek.edu.ec

Rector: Rodolfo Ceprián Molina EMail: rc@uisek.edu.ec

Vicerrectora: Katty Coral Carrillo

Faculties
Architecture and Town Planning (Architecture; Town Planning); **Communication** (Communication Studies; Journalism; Mass Communication; Radio and Television Broadcasting); **Computer Systems and Telecommunications** (Computer Networks; Multimedia; Telecommunications Engineering); **Economics and Administration** (Administration; Banking; Economics; Finance; Management; Marketing); **Environmental Studies** (Environmental Studies; Forestry); **Law and Social Sciences** (Comparative Law; International Law; International Relations; Law; Social Sciences); **Mechanical Engineering** (Mechanical Engineering); **Psychology** (Bilingual and Bicultural Education; Clinical Psychology; Preschool Education; Psychology); **Tourism and Cultural Heritage** (Air Transport; Hotel Management; Tourism)

History: Founded 1892 in Madrid, with 15 Schools in 11 countries and 3 Universities in Segovia, Santiago de Chile and Quito (1993).

Governing Bodies: Consejo Universitario; Consejo de Faculdades

Academic Year: October to June

Admission Requirements: Secondary school certificate (bachillerato)

Fees: (US Dollars): 3,000 per annum

Main Language(s) of Instruction: Spanish

Degrees and Diplomas: *Licenciatura*: 4 yrs; *Professional Title*: Architecture; Engineering, 5 yrs; *Maestría*: Business; Finance; Management, a further 18 months

Student Services: Academic counselling, Canteen, Cultural centre, Employment services, Foreign student adviser, Social counselling, Sports facilities

Special Facilities: SEK - Scientific Research Station in the Amazon Jungle (Limoncocha)

Libraries: Biblioteca Central, 28,000 vols

Press or Publishing House: Ediciones de Universidad Internacional SEK

Last Updated: 14/12/09

SERVIO TULIO MONTERO LUDEÑA POLYTECHNIC SCHOOL OF ECOLOGY
Escuela Superior Politécnica Ecológica Servio Tulio Montero Ludeña
Colinas de San Juan, Frente a TVSur, Cariamanga
Tel: +593(7) 2688092
Fax: +593(7) 2688092
EMail: universidad.espec@gmail.com
Website: http://www.espec.edu.ec

Rector: Jorge Montero Rodríguez

Faculties
Social Sciences and Administration; **Technology** (Agricultural Engineering; Automotive Engineering; Computer Engineering; Ecology; Environmental Engineering; Mechanical Engineering)

History: Founded 1998.

Main Language(s) of Instruction: Spanish

Degrees and Diplomas: *Tecnólogo*; *Licenciatura*; *Professional Title*; *Maestría*

Last Updated: 11/12/09

TECHNICAL BUSINESS UNIVERSITY OF GUAYAQUIL
Universidad Tecnológica Empresarial de Guayaquil (UTEG)
Urdesa Central, Guayacanes 399 y la 5ta, Guayaquil, Guayas
Tel: +593(4) 288-6728
Fax: +593(4) 288-4833
EMail: admision@uteg.edu.ec
Website: http://www.uteg.edu.ec

Rector: Galo Cabanilla Guerra EMail: gcabanilla@uteg.edu.ec

Divisions
Foreign Languages (English; French)

Faculties
Business Administration and Economics; **Foreign Trade** (Business and Commerce; International Business; Taxation; Transport Management); **Information Technology** (Computer Networks; Information Technology; Telecommunications Engineering); **Tourism and Environment**

History: Founded 2000.

Academic Year: April to February (April-August; October-February)

Admission Requirements: Secondary school certificate (bachillerato)

Main Language(s) of Instruction: Spanish

Degrees and Diplomas: *Tecnólogo*: 3 yrs; *Licenciatura*; *Professional Title*; *Maestría*: 1 1/2 yr

Student Services: Academic counselling, Employment services, Language programs

Publications: Bitacora Economica *(biennially)*
Last Updated: 15/12/09

TOURISM UNIVERSITY
Universidad de Especialidades Turísticas (UCT)
Avenida Patria E3-67 y 9 Octubre, Edificio UCT, 171292 Quito, Pichincha
Tel: +593(2) 254-4100
Fax: +593(2) 254-4104
EMail: info@uct.edu.ec
Website: http://www.uct.edu.ec

Rectora: María de Lourdes Jarrín (2000-)
EMail: mjarrin@uct.edu.ec

Vicerrector: Gustavo FreireFax: +593(2) 254-4100
EMail: ecabanilla@uct.edu.ec

Colleges
Hotel Management *Director*: Francisco Ortega; **Public Relations** *Director*: Francisco Ortega; **Tourism** (Business Administration; Tourism) *Director*: Pablo Illingworth

History: Founded 2000.

Governing Bodies: University Assembly

Academic Year: October to March; April to September

Admission Requirements: Secondary school certificate (bachillerato) and English language examination

Fees: (US Dollars): 1,650 per semester

Main Language(s) of Instruction: Spanish

Degrees and Diplomas: *Professional Title*; *Maestría*: 2 yrs; *Especialista*. Also Diplomado superior

Student Services: Academic counselling, Employment services, Health services, Language programs, Social counselling

Academic Staff *2007-2008*: Total 110

Student Numbers *2007-2008*: Total 458
Last Updated: 14/12/09

UNIVERSITY OF AZUAY
Universidad del Azuay (UDA)
Apartado 01-01-981, Avenida 24 de Mayo 7-77 y Hernán Malo,
Cuenca, Azuay
Tel: +593(7) 288-1333
Fax: +593(7) 281-5997
EMail: dge@uazuay.edu.ec
Website: http://www.uazuay.edu.ec

Rector: Mario Jaramillo-Paredes (1992-)
Tel: +593(7) 288-1333, Ext. 211 EMail: mjaramil@uazuay.edu.ec

Vicerrector: Joaquín Moreno Aguilar
EMail: jmoreno@uazuay.edu.ec

Faculties
Administration (Accountancy; Business Administration; Computer Science; Economics); **Design** (Fashion Design; Furniture Design; Graphic Design; Textile Design); **Law** (International Studies; Law); **Medicine**; **Philosophy, Letters and Educational Sciences** (Clinical Psychology; Communication Studies; Educational Psychology; Industrial and Organizational Psychology; Preschool Education; Science Education; Special Education; Tourism); **Science and Technology** (Agronomy; Biology; Electronic Engineering; Engineering; Food Science; Mechanical Engineering; Production Engineering); **Theology** (Catholic Theology)

History: Founded 1968. Acquired present status 1990.

Governing Bodies: University Council, Executive Committee, Academic Council

Academic Year: September to July (September-January; March-July)

Admission Requirements: Secondary school certificate (bachillerato) and entrance examination

Main Language(s) of Instruction: Spanish

International Co-operation: With universities in Argentina; Brazil; Chile; Cuba; Peru; Spain; Italy and USA

Degrees and Diplomas: *Tecnólogo*: 2-3 yrs; *Licenciatura*: 4 yrs; *Professional Title*: Engineering, Design, Law, 5 yrs; *Maestría*: a further 2 yrs; *Especialista*. Also Diplomado superior

Student Services: Academic counselling, Cultural centre, Employment services, Foreign student adviser, Health services, Language programs, Social counselling, Sports facilities

Special Facilities: Auditorium, Video Centre

Libraries: Biblioteca 'Hernán Malo', c. 43,000 vols

Publications: Coloquio *(quarterly)*
Last Updated: 14/12/09

UNIVERSITY OF OTAVALO
Universidad de Otavalo
Cdla. Imbaya, Av. De los Sarances s/n y Pendoneros, Otavalo
Tel: +593(6) 2952-0461
EMail: info@uotavalo.edu.ec
Website: http://www.uotavalo.edu.ec

Rectora: Susana Cordero Aguilar

Vicerrectora Académica: Mariana Guzmán Villena

Centres
Languages (Modern Languages)

Faculties
Administration; **Human and Social Sciences**; **Law** (Law); **Tourism** (Management; Marketing; Tourism)

History: Founded 2002.

Governing Bodies: Consejo Universitario, comprinsing the Chancellor, two Vice-Rectors and four Deans.

Academic Year: September to February

Admission Requirements: Secondary School Certificate (bachillerato)

Main Language(s) of Instruction: Spanish and English

Degrees and Diplomas: *Professional Title*: 5 yrs; *Especialista*. Also Diplomado superior

Student Services: Academic counselling, Cultural centre, Health services, Language programs, Social counselling, Sports facilities

Special Facilities: Laboratories and Museum
Libraries: Yes
Publications: Revista Sarance *(biennially)*
Last Updated: 14/12/09

UNIVERSITY OF THE AMERICAS
Universidad de Las Américas
Avenida Colón E9-241 y Avenida 6 de Diciembre, 17-07-9788 Quito
Tel: +593(2) 255-5735
Fax: +593(2) 256-3757
EMail: admision@uamericas.edu.ec
Website: http://www.uamericas.edu.ec

Rector: Carlos Larreátegui Nardi
Tel: +593(2) 255-6263, Fax: +593(2) 255-6263
EMail: clarreategui@uamericas.edu.ec

Vicerrector: Simón Cueva
Tel: +593(2) 255-6263, Fax: +593(2) 255-6263
EMail: scueva@uamericas.edu.ec

International Relations: Alegría Donosso
Tel: +593(2) 290-1200, Fax: +593(2) 290-1200, Ext.117

Faculties
Architecture (Architecture; Interior Design); **Communication Sciences** (Advertising and Publicity; Communication Studies; Graphic Design; Journalism); **Economics and Administration**; **Engineering**; **Health Sciences** (Biotechnology; Dentistry; Medicine; Nursing; Physical Therapy); **Law**, **Tourism and Hospitality** (Cooking and Catering; Hotel Management)

Schools
Social Sciences (Bilingual and Bicultural Education; Clinical Psychology; Industrial and Organizational Psychology; International Relations; Political Sciences); **Technology** (Technology)

History: Founded 1995.

Main Language(s) of Instruction: Spanish

Degrees and Diplomas: *Tecnólogo*; *Licenciatura*; *Professional Title*; *Maestría*
Last Updated: 14/12/09

UNIVERSITY OF THE HEMISPHERES
Universidad de los Hemisferios
Paseo de la Universidad N° 300 y Juan Díaz - Urb. Iñaquito Alto,
Quito
Fax: +593(2) 246-6666
EMail: info@uhemisferios.edu.ec
Website: http://www.uhemisferios.edu.ec

Rector: Alejandro Ribadeneira Espinosa

Secretario General: Sebastián Borja Silva

Vice-Rectora: Maria Graciela Crespo Ponce

Faculties
Arts and Humanities (Arts and Humanities; Cultural Studies; Educational Psychology; Music; Tourism; Translation and Interpretation); **Business Administration and Economics**; **Communication Studies**; **Law and Political Science** (International Relations; Law; Political Sciences); **Technology**

History: Founded 2004.

Main Language(s) of Instruction: Spanish

Degrees and Diplomas: *Licenciatura*
Last Updated: 14/12/09

UNIVERSITY OF THE PACIFIC - SCHOOL OF BUSINESS STUDIES
Universidad del Pacífico - Escuela de Negocios
Apartado 17-08-8229, El Pinar Alto, Calle B N48-177, Quito
Tel: +593(2) 244-4509
Fax: +593(2) 245-9593
EMail: info@upacifico.edu.ec
Website: http://www.upacifico.edu.ec

Canciller: Sonia Roca EMail: sroca@upacifico.edu.ec

Secretario General: José Mario Borja

International Relations: Roberto HouserFax: +593(2) 244-9593
EMail: intrel@upacifico.edu.ec

Centres
Asia-Pacific (Business and Commerce; Development Studies; Pacific Area Studies); **Business Development** (Business Administration; Business and Commerce); **Competitiveness Research**; **Latin American Studies** (Latin American Studies)

Faculties
Languages; Science, Technology and Environment

Schools
Business and Economics; **Graduate**; **Law and International Political Science**

Further Information: Also branches in Guayaquil and Cuenca

History: Founded 1994, legally recognized by the Government of Ecuador 1997.

Governing Bodies: Academic Council, Chancellor

Academic Year: October to August (Quito and Cuenca) and April to February (Guayaquil)

Admission Requirements: Secondary school certificate (bachillerato)

Main Language(s) of Instruction: Spanish, English

Degrees and Diplomas: *Bachelor*: Business Administration (BA); Economics; Technology Administration (BS), 4 yrs; *Diploma*: Banking and Finance; Pacific Area Studies; Stockmarket Studies; *Maestría*: Business Administration (MBA); Economics, Finance and Banking; Human Resource Development (MHRD); Information Technology and Management; International Business (MIM); Political Science, a further $1\frac{1}{2}$ yrs

Student Services: Academic counselling, Cultural centre, Employment services, Foreign student adviser, Language programs
Last Updated: 14/12/09

VICENTE ROCAFUERTE LAY UNIVERSITY OF GUAYAQUIL
Universidad Laica Vicente Rocafuerte de Guayaquil
Avenida de las Américas frente al Cuartel Modelo, Apdo.1133, Guayaquil
Tel: +593(4) 228-7200
EMail: laicared@gye.satnet.net
Website: http://www.ulaicavr.edu.ec

Rector: Elsa Alarcón Soto (1989-)
Vicerrector: J. Alfredo Aguilar Alava

Centres
Postgraduate Studies *(Dr Alfonso Aguilar Ruilova)*; **Research**

Faculties
Administration (Administration); **Architecture** (Architecture); **Civil Engineering** (Civil Engineering); **Economics** (Economics); **Education** (Education); **Journalism** (Journalism); **Law** (Law)

Schools
Accountancy (Accountancy); **Advertising** (Advertising and Publicity); **Commerce**; **Design** (Design); **Marketing** (Marketing); **Modern Languages** (Modern Languages); **Preschool Education** (Preschool Education); **Secretarial Studies** (Secretarial Studies)

History: Founded 1966.

Governing Bodies: Consejo Universitario

Academic Year: April to January (April-August; August-January)

Main Language(s) of Instruction: Spanish

Degrees and Diplomas: *Licenciatura*: Administration; Education; Journalism; Social Service, 5 yrs; *Licenciatura*: Political Science, 4 yrs; *Professional Title*: Architecture; Civil Engineering; Economics; Law, 6 yrs; *Professional Title*: Auditing; Design, 3 yrs; *Professional Title*: Social Work, 4 yrs; *Maestría*; *Especialista*. Also teaching qualifications, secondary level

Special Facilities: Observatory
Last Updated: 14/12/09

XAVIERAN POLYTECHNIC SCHOOL OF ECUADOR
Escuela Politécnica Javeriana del Ecuador (ESPOJ)
Darquea 1553 y 10 de Agosto, Quito, Pichincha
Tel: +593(2) 254-3288
Fax: +593(2) 256-1783
Website: http://www.espoj.edu.ec/

Rector: Pablo Aníbal Yánez Narváez

Faculties
Administration and Economics (Accountancy; Administration; Economics; Finance; Law; Marketing; Mathematics); **Biotechnical and Health Sciences** (Biotechnology; Dental Technology; Food Science; Food Technology; Health Sciences); **Computer and Information Sciences** (Computer Networks; Computer Science; Information Sciences); **Design and Engineering** (Design; Safety Engineering; Transport Engineering); **Electronics and Industrial Science** (Automation and Control Engineering; Electronic Engineering; Mechanical Engineering; Systems Analysis); **Law and Social Sciences** (Law; Social Sciences); **Pedagogy and Educational Sciences** (Education; Educational Administration; Educational Sciences; Educational Technology; Pedagogy; Preschool Education; Primary Education)

History: Founded 1995.

Admission Requirements: Secondary school certificate (bachillerato) and entrance examination

Main Language(s) of Instruction: Spanish

Degrees and Diplomas: *Tecnólogo*; *Licenciatura*; *Professional Title*; *Maestría*; *Especialista*; *Doctorado*

Student Services: Academic counselling, Canteen, Foreign student adviser, Health services, Language programs, Nursery care, Social counselling

Egypt

STRUCTURE OF HIGHER EDUCATION SYSTEM

Description:

Higher education is provided by universities and higher institutes of technical and professional training, both public and private. Responsibility for higher education lies mainly with the Ministry of Higher Education. Organization and administration, as well as academic programmes, are determined by laws, decrees and government regulations. The State universities are under the authority of the Supreme Council of Universities. Universities have full academic and administrative autonomy. They also carry out scientific research. The higher institutes of professional and technical training award qualifications that are equivalent to the first qualification conferred by the universities. Open college education was introduced at the universities of Cairo, Alexandria and Assiut in 1991. Private universities are entitled to implement their own admission criteria and to set fees without intervention from the Ministry.

Stages of studies:

University level first stage:
The first stage of higher education consists of four to six years of multidisciplinary study in basic subjects leading to the award of the Baccalaureos degree. In Medicine, studies last for six years, with one additional year of practical work.

University level second stage:
The second stage is more specialized and comprises two to five years of training in individual research work culminating in the submission of a thesis. The degree awarded is that of Magistr.

University level third stage:
The third stage leads to the Doktora (PhD) after at least two years' study following the Magistr (Master's Degree). Students must have obtained the mark "good" in the Master's Degree. It is awarded for advanced research work culminating in a thesis. In Medicine, a Doktora in Medical Sciences may be prepared concurrently with the professional Doctor of Medicine Degree.

University level fourth stage:
In certain rare cases, after the Doktora, a degree of Doctor of Science is awarded. It is reserved for researchers who have undertaken a substantial body of research work.

Distance higher education:
The Egyptian University for Distance Learning offers distance learning courses.

ADMISSION TO HIGHER EDUCATION

Admission to university-level studies:

Name of secondary school credential required: Thanaweya Am'ma

Minimum score/requirement: 70% or above

For entry to: Universities and higher specialized institutes

Alternatives to credentials: Secondary school students who hold an Advanced Technical Education may enter university Higher Institutes in their speciality if they have obtained scores of at least 75%.

Numerus clausus/restrictions: The Supreme Council of Universities at the Ministry of Higher Education determines the number of students to be admitted by the faculties of each university.

Foreign students admission:

Entrance exam requirements: Foreign students should hold qualifications that are equivalent to the Thanaweya A'amma or a university degree.

Entry regulations: Foreign students must obtain a student visa.

Language requirements: Knowledge of Arabic is essential for regular university studies. English is the language of instruction at the American University in Cairo, some faculties of Helwan University and at the

Faculty of Agriculture of the University of Alexandria. French is the language of instruction at Senghor University.

NATIONAL BODIES

Ministry of Higher Education and Scientific Research

Minister: Ahmed Gamal El-Din Moussa

101, Kasr El-Eini Street

Cairo

Tel: +202 794 7834/ 795 3437

Fax: +202 794 1005

EMail: info@egy-mhe.gov.eg

WWW: http://www.egy-mhe.gov.eg

Role of national body: Coordinates and supervises post-secondary education

Supreme Council of Universities

Chairman: Ahmed Gamal El-Din Moussa

Secretary-General: Salwa El-Gharib

Cairo University Campus,

PO Box 12613

Giza

Tel: +202 3573 8583 +202 3571 6348

Fax: +202 3572-8877 +202 3570-6490

EMail: scu@eun.eg

WWW: http://www.scu.eun.eg

Role of national body: Determines the overall policy of higher education and scientific research in universities and determines the number of students admitted in each faculty.

Bibliotheca Alexandrina

Director: Ismail Serageldin

Director, Centre for Special Studies and Programme: Mohammed El-Faham

P.O. Box 138 - Chatby

Alexandria 21526

Tel: +20(3) 483 9999

EMail: Secretariat@bibalex.org

WWW: http://www.bibalex.org

Data for academic year: 2007-2008

Source: IAU from Ministry of Higher Education and Supreme Council of Universities, Egypt, 2007. Bodies updated in 2011.

INSTITUTIONS

PUBLIC INSTITUTIONS

AIN SHAMS UNIVERSITY

Khalifa El-Maamon st, Abbasiya sq., Cairo 11566

Tel: +20(2) 683-1231 +20(2) 683-1417 +20(2) 683-1474

Fax: +20(2) 684-7824

EMail: info@asunet.shams.edu.eg; ain.shams@frcu.eun.eg

Website: http://net.shams.edu.eg

President: Alaa Fayez

Tel: +20(2) 284-7818, Fax: +20(2) 282-6107

EMail: dralaa_fayez@med.asu.edu.eg

Secretary-General: Hassan Abd Elazeez Ammar

Centres

Genetic Engineering and Biotechnology; **University Education Development** (Higher Education); **Vectors of Diseases** (Epidemiology)

Faculties

Agriculture (Agricultural Economics; Agricultural Equipment; Agriculture; Agronomy; Animal Husbandry; Botany; Food Science; Genetics; Horticulture; Meat and Poultry; Microbiology; Plant Pathology; Soil Science); **Arts** (Ancient Civilizations; Arabic; Arts and Humanities; English; French; Geography; Hebrew; History; Library Science; Literature; Mass Communication; Persian; Philosophy; Psychology; Sociology; Tourism; Turkish; Urdu); **Commerce** (Accountancy; Business Administration; Business and Commerce;

Economics; Insurance; Mathematics; Statistics); **Computer and Information Science**; **Dentistry** (Dentistry; Oral Pathology; Orthodontics; Periodontics); **Education** (Arabic; Biology; Chemistry; Curriculum; Educational Psychology; Educational Sciences; English; French; Geography; Geology; German; History; Islamic Studies; Mathematics; Pedagogy; Philosophy; Physics; Psychiatry and Mental Health; Sociology); **Engineering** (Architecture; Automation and Control Engineering; Civil Engineering; Computer Engineering; Design; Electrical and Electronic Engineering; Engineering; Hydraulic Engineering; Irrigation; Mechanical Engineering; Power Engineering; Production Engineering; Structural Architecture; Systems Analysis; Town Planning); **Languages** *(Al-Alsun)* (African Languages; Arabic; Chinese; Czech; English; French; German; Italian; Japanese; Modern Languages; Persian; Russian; Spanish; Turkish; Urdu); **Law** (Civil Law; Commercial Law; Criminal Law; History of Law; International Law; Islamic Law; Law; Political Sciences; Private Law; Public Law); **Medicine** (Anaesthesiology; Anatomy; Biochemistry; Cardiology; Clinical Psychology; Community Health; Dermatology; Forensic Medicine and Dentistry; Gerontology; Gynaecology and Obstetrics; Histology; Immunology; Medicine; Microbiology; Occupational Health; Ophthalmology; Otorhinolaryngology; Paediatrics; Parasitology; Pathology; Pharmacology; Physiology; Psychiatry and Mental Health; Radiology; Surgery; Toxicology; Tropical Medicine); **Nursing**; **Pharmacy** (Biochemistry; Immunology; Microbiology; Organic Chemistry; Pharmacology; Pharmacy; Toxicology); **Science** (Biochemistry; Botany; Chemistry; Entomology; Geology; Geophysics; Mathematics; Microbiology; Natural Sciences; Physics; Zoology); **Specific Education**; **Women for Arts, Science and Education** (Arabic; Biochemistry; Botany; Chemistry; Curriculum; Education; English; French; Geography; History; Home Economics; Literature; Mathematics; Nutrition; Pedagogy; Philosophy; Physics; Psychology; Social Sciences; Zoology)

Institutes

Environmental Studies and Research (Environmental Studies); **Postgraduate Childhood Studies** (Child Care and Development; Psychology; Sociology)

Research Centres

Middle East (Middle Eastern Studies); **Papyrus Studies** (Ancient Civilizations); **Public Service and Development** (Business Administration; English; French; German; Oriental Languages; Radio and Television Broadcasting; Social and Community Services; Video); **Science Education Development** (Science Education); **Scientific Computing** (Computer Science)

Further Information: Also University Hospitals and specialized Hospital

History: Founded 1950, incorporating Abbassia School of Medicine. Formerly known as Ibrahim Pasha University and also as University of Heliopolis. Faculties of Commerce, Education, Agriculture, and Veterinary Medicine at Zagazig detached 1973 to form new University.

Governing Bodies: University Council, composed of the President, three Vice-Presidents, Deans of the Faculties, a representative of the Ministry of Higher Education, the Secretary-General and three other members

Academic Year: September to May

Admission Requirements: Secondary school certificate or equivalent

Main Language(s) of Instruction: Arabic

Degrees and Diplomas: *Diploma*: Education and Psychology; Home Economics; Law; *Baccalaureos*: Agriculture; Arts; Arts and Education; Civil Engineering; Commerce; Electrical Engineering; Law; Mechanical Engineering; Science; Science and Education, 4-5 yrs; *Magistr*: Agricultural Science; Agriculture; Arts; Arts in Commerce; Education; Engineering; Medicine; Psychology; Science, a further 2-3 yrs; *Doktora*: Architecture; Law; Letters; Medicine; Science, Agriculture, Education, Commerce

Student Residential Facilities: Yes

Libraries: Central Library, c. 90,000 vols; Faculty libraries, c. 3,300 vols

Publications: Al-Ulum Al-Kanounia wal Iktisadia (journal); Annals of Agricultural Science; Annals of the Faculty of Arts; Bulletin of the Faculty of Engineering; Economics and Business Review

Press or Publishing House: Ain Shams University Press
Last Updated: 15/07/09

AL-AZHAR UNIVERSITY

PO Box 11751, Meddina Nasr, Cairo
Tel: +20(2) 262-3274 +20(2) 262-3278
Fax: +20(2) 261-1404
EMail: info@alazhar.org; Azhar@azhar.eun.eg
Website: http://www.azhar.edu.eg

Rector: Ahmed Mohammad El Tayeb (2003-)
Tel: +20(2) 262-3282 EMail: eltayyb@mailer.eun.eg

Secretary-General: Mohammed Mahmoud El-Feshawy
Tel: +20(2) 261-1417

Centres
Heart Diseases and Surgery (Cardiology; Surgery)

Colleges
Islamic Studies *(for Women)* (Arabic; Islamic Studies)

Faculties

Agriculture *(Assiut, Cairo)* (Agricultural Economics; Agricultural Engineering; Agricultural Equipment; Agriculture; Agronomy; Animal Husbandry; Botany; Dairy; Entomology; Fishery; Food Science; Food Technology; Genetics; Horticulture; Meat and Poultry; Microbiology; Plant and Crop Protection; Plant Pathology; Rural Studies; Sericulture; Soil Conservation; Soil Management; Soil Science; Zoology); **Arabic Language** *(Assiut, Mansoura, Menoufia, Behara (Itai Al-Baroud), Sohag, Zagazig)* (Arabic; History; Information Sciences; Journalism; Library Science; Linguistics; Literature); **Commerce** *(for women)* (Accountancy; Business Administration; Business and Commerce; Economics; Statistics); **Commerce** *(Cairo, Tafehna Al-Ashraf)* (Accountancy; Administration; Business Administration; Business and Commerce; Economics; Health Administration; Hotel Management; Insurance; Statistics; Taxation; Tourism); **Education** *(Cairo, Tafehna Al-Ashraf)* (Arabic; Art Education; Chemistry; Educational Psychology; Educational Sciences; Educational Technology; English; French; Geography; History; Islamic Studies; Library Science; Mathematics; Pedagogy; Physical Education; Physics; Psychology); **Engineering** *(Cairo, Kena)* (Architecture; Civil Engineering; Computer Engineering; Electrical Engineering; Electronic Engineering; Engineering; Information Technology; Mechanical Engineering; Mining Engineering; Petroleum and Gas Engineering; Power Engineering; Structural Architecture); **Home Economics** (Biological and Life Sciences; Clothing and Sewing; Food Science; Food Technology; Home Economics; Household Management; Nutrition; Rural Studies; Textile Technology); **Humanities** *(for women)* (Arts and Humanities; Documentation Techniques; Education; English; European Languages; French; Geography (Human); Hebrew; History; Library Science; Literature; Oriental Languages; Persian; Psychology; Social Sciences; Sociology; Translation and Interpretation); **Islamic and Arab Studies** *(Aswan, Beni-Suel, Cairo, Damietta, Kafr-Al-Sheikh)* (Arabic; Islamic Law; Islamic Studies; Islamic Theology); **Islamic and Arab Studies** *(for women, Cairo, Alexandria, Mansoura, Sohag, Zagazig)* (Arabic; Islamic Studies); **Islamic Call** (Islamic Studies; Islamic Theology); **Islamic Fundamentals** *(Cairo, Zagazig)* (Islamic Studies); **Islamic Fundamentals and Call** *(Assiut, Mansoura, Tanta, Shebin El-Kom)* (Islamic Studies); **Islamic Jurisprudence and Law** *(Zagazig, Tanta, Cairo, Assiut, Damanhour, Tafehna Al-Ashraf)* (Comparative Law; Islamic Law; Islamic Studies; Law); **Languages and Translation** (African Languages; Arabic; Classical Languages; French; German; Hebrew; Islamic Studies; Literature; Modern Languages; Persian; Spanish; Translation and Interpretation; Turkish; Urdu); **Medicine** *(for Women)* (Medicine); **Medicine** *(Assiut, Cairo, Damietta)* (Anatomy; Biochemistry; Cardiology; Dermatology; Forensic Medicine and Dentistry; Gynaecology and Obstetrics; Histology; Medicine; Microbiology; Neurology; Parasitology; Pathology; Pharmacology; Physiology; Psychology; Public Health; Radiology; Rheumatology; Surgery; Toxicology; Urology; Venereology); **Pharmacy** *(For women, Tanta)* (Pharmacy); **Pharmacy** *(Cairo, Assiut)* (Applied Chemistry; Biochemistry; Industrial Chemistry; Microbiology; Organic Chemistry; Pharmacology; Pharmacy); **Science** *(Cairo, Assiut)* (Anatomy; Astronomy and Space Science; Botany; Chemistry; Geology; Horticulture; Mathematics; Meteorology; Microbiology; Natural Sciences; Physics; Physiology; Zoology); **Stomatology and Dentistry** *(Cairo, Assiut)* (Dental Hygiene; Dental Technology; Dentistry; Oral Pathology; Stomatology)

Research Centres

Childhood Disabilities (Child Care and Development); **Genetic Engineering** (Genetics); **Islamic Commercial Studies** *(Saleh Kamel)* (Business and Commerce; Islamic Law); **Mycology and Biotechnology**; **Population Studies** *(The International Islamic Centre)* (Demography and Population)

Further Information: Also twenty-five Academic/Research Centres and four University Hospitals

History: Founded 965. Acquired present status 1961.

Governing Bodies: University Council

Academic Year: October to June

Admission Requirements: Secondary certificate of Al-Azhar or equivalent

Main Language(s) of Instruction: Arabic

Degrees and Diplomas: *Baccalaureos*: 4-5 yrs; *Magistr*: 2-3 yrs; *Doktora*: 2-3 yrs following Magistr

Student Services: Academic counselling, Canteen, Cultural centre, Foreign student adviser, Foreign Studies Centre, Handicapped facilities, Health services, Language programs, Nursery care, Social counselling, Sports facilities

Libraries: c. 80,000 vols

Academic Staff 2008-2009	MEN	WOMEN	TOTAL
FULL-TIME	6,572	2,928	**9,500**
STAFF WITH DOCTORATE FULL-TIME	–	–	**9,500**

Student Numbers 2008-2009			
All (Foreign Included)	210,096	112,713	**322,809**
FOREIGN ONLY	12,854	4,121	**16,975**

Last Updated: 30/07/09

ALEXANDRIA UNIVERSITY

Gameat Aliskandaria (AU)
22 Al-Guish Avenue, El Chatby, Alexandria 21526
Tel: +20(3) 591-1152
Fax: +20(3) 596-0720
EMail: v-presstd@alexu.edu.eg
Website: http://www.alexu.edu.eg

President: Osama Ibrahim Sayed Ahmed
Tel: +20(3) 591-1152, Fax: +20(3) 591-0720
EMail: president@alexu.edu.eg

Vice-President for Graduate Studies and Research: Essam Khamis Ibrahim
Tel: +20(3) 591-4285, Fax: +20(3) 590-956
EMail: v-presgradeadmin.alex.edu.eg; hind_hanafy@link.net

Vice-President: Rouchdy Zahran
Tel: +20(3) 591-5848, Fax: +20(3) 590-2715

Faculties

Agriculture *(Saba-Bacha)* (Agricultural Economics; Agriculture; Animal Husbandry; Botany; Crop Production; Fishery; Food Science; Plant and Crop Protection; Soil Science); **Agriculture** *(Alexandria)* (Agricultural Economics; Agriculture; Dairy; Entomology; Forestry; Genetics; Home Economics; Horticulture; Soil Science; Water Science; Wood Technology); **Arts** (Anthropology; Arabic; Archaeology; Arts and Humanities; English; French; Geography (Human); History; Library Science; Linguistics; Literature; Mediterranean Studies; Oriental Languages; Philosophy; Phonetics; Psychology; Social Sciences; Sociology; Theatre); **Commerce** (Accountancy; Business Administration; Business and Commerce; Economics; Finance; Insurance; Management Systems; Mathematics; Political Sciences; Statistics); **Dentistry** (Dental Technology; Dentistry; Oral Pathology; Orthodontics; Surgery); **Education** (Arabic; Biology; Chemistry; Curriculum; Education; Educational Psychology; Foreign Languages Education; Mathematics; Modern Languages; Physics; Social Sciences; Teacher Trainers Education); **Engineering** (Architecture; Building Technologies; Chemical Engineering; Computer Education; Computer Engineering; Electrical Engineering; Electronic Engineering; Engineering; Hydraulic Engineering; Irrigation; Marine Engineering; Mathematics; Mechanical Engineering; Nuclear Engineering; Petroleum and Gas Engineering; Physics; Production Engineering; Sanitary Engineering; Telecommunications Engineering; Textile Technology; Transport Engineering); **Fine Arts**; **Kindergarten** (Educational Sciences;

Preschool Education; Psychology); **Law** (Civil Law; Commercial Law; Criminal Law; History of Law; International Law; Islamic Law; Law; Public Law); **Medicine** (Anaesthesiology; Anatomy; Biochemistry; Cardiology; Community Health; Dermatology; Gynaecology and Obstetrics; Health Sciences; Histology; Medicine; Microbiology; Neurological Therapy; Oncology; Ophthalmology; Orthopaedics; Otorhinolaryngology; Paediatrics; Parasitology; Pathology; Pharmacology; Physiology; Public Health; Surgery; Toxicology; Tropical Medicine; Urology; Venereology); **Nursing** (Nursing); **Pharmacy** (Pharmacology; Pharmacy); **Physical Education for Girls** (Physical Education); **Physical Education for Men** (Physical Education; Sports; Sports Management; Sports Medicine); **Science** (Biochemistry; Botany; Chemistry; Environmental Studies; Geology; Marine Science and Oceanography; Mathematics; Natural Sciences; Physics; Zoology); **Specific Education**; **Tourism and Hotel** (Hotel and Restaurant; Hotel Management; Tourism); **Veterinary Medicine** *(Edfina)* (Biochemistry; Histology; Microbiology; Parasitology; Pathology; Pharmacology; Toxicology; Veterinary Science)

Higher Institutes

Postgraduate Studies (Higher Education); **Public Health** (Behavioural Sciences; Public Health; Statistics; Tropical Medicine)

Institutes

Medical Research (Medicine; Radiology)

History: Founded 1942 as State University, incorporating former branches of the Faculties of Arts, Law, and Engineering of Fouad I University (Cairo), and known as Farouk University until 1953. Faculty of Medicine and Colleges of Education at Tanta detached 1972 to form new University.

Governing Bodies: University Senate

Academic Year: September to June (September-January; February-June)

Admission Requirements: Secondary school certificate or equivalent

Main Language(s) of Instruction: Arabic, English, French

Degrees and Diplomas: *Diploma*: 2 yrs after Baccalaueas; *Baccalaureos*: Commerce, Physical Education, Special Education; Child Care and Development; Science and Education, Agriculture, Nursing, Tourism, Hotel Management, 4 yrs; *Baccalaureos*: Engineering, Dentistry, Medicine, Fine Arts, Pharmacy, 5 yrs; *Baccalaureos*: Medicine, 6 yrs; *Magistr*: All above Disciplines, a further 1-3 yrs and thesis; *Doktora*: 2 yrs after Magistr and dissertation; *Doktora*: All above disciplines, awarded after Doctorate for distinguished contributions to knowledge. Also License Arts and Law (4yrs), Postgraduate Diplomas

Student Services: Academic counselling, Canteen, Employment services, Foreign student adviser, Health services, Language programs, Social counselling, Sports facilities

Student Residential Facilities: For 3446 (males) and 3932 (females)

Special Facilities: Archaeology Museum. Forensic Medical Museum

Libraries: Central Library, c. 28,000 vols; also Faculty and Institute libraries, c. 40,000 vols

Academic Staff 2008-2009	MEN	WOMEN	TOTAL
FULL-TIME	10,647	7,803	**18,450**
PART-TIME	1,204	1,500	**2,704**
STAFF WITH DOCTORATE FULL-TIME	2,354	1,591	**3,945**

Student Numbers 2008-2009			
All (Foreign Included)	79,985	93,533	**173,518**
FOREIGN ONLY	709	473	**1,182**

Last Updated: 22/10/09

DAMANHOUR BRANCH

27 Galal Quretam Sq., Damanhour, Behira
Tel: +20(3) 591-2147 +20(4) 5336-8069
Fax: +20(3) 591-2147 +20(4) 5336-8069
Website: http://www.damanhour.alex.edu.eg

Vice-President: Said Abdou Nafea
Tel: +20(1) 0353-0600, Fax: +20(1) 5336-8069
EMail: v-presdam@admin.alex.edu.eg

Faculties
Agriculture; **Arts** (Fine Arts); **Commerce** (Business and Commerce); **Education** (Education); **Nursing** (Nursing); **Science** (Animal Husbandry; Botany; Chemistry; Geology; Mathematics; Physics); **Veterinary Medicine** (Veterinary Science)

Programmes
Kindergarten; **Pharmacy**

History: Founded 1988.

Degrees and Diplomas: *Baccalaureos*

ASSIUT UNIVERSITY

PO Box 71515, Assiut
Tel: +20(88) 235-7007 +20(88) 235-7557
Fax: +20(88) 235-4130
EMail: saidib@acc.aun.edu.eg
Website: http://www.aun.edu.eg

President: Mostafa Mohamad Kamal (2008-)
EMail: mostafak@aun.edu.eg

Vice-President for Postgraduate Studies & Research: Mohamed Ragab Bayoumi EMail: rbayoumi@aun.edu.eg

Centres
Future Studies *Director:* Mohamed Ibrahim Mansour

Colleges
Education (Curriculum; Education; Psychology)

Faculties
Agriculture (Agricultural Economics; Agriculture; Agronomy; Dairy; Food Science; Food Technology; Genetics; Horticulture; Meat and Poultry; Plant and Crop Protection; Plant Pathology; Rural Studies; Soil Science; Water Science); **Arts** (Arabic; Archaeology; Arts and Humanities; English; French; Geography; History; Information Sciences; Library Science; Media Studies; Philosophy; Psychology; Sociology); **Commerce** (Accountancy; Business Administration; Business and Commerce; Economics; Finance; Insurance; Mathematics; Political Sciences; Public Administration; Statistics); **Computer and Information Science** (Computer Science; Information Sciences; Information Technology); **Education** *(New Valley)* (Curriculum; Education; Educational Psychology; Preschool Education); **Engineering** (Architecture; Civil Engineering; Electrical Engineering; Engineering; Mechanical Engineering; Metallurgical Engineering; Mining Engineering); **Law** (Islamic Law; Law; Private Law; Public Law); **Medicine** (Anaesthesiology; Anatomy; Cardiology; Dermatology; Gastroenterology; Gynaecology and Obstetrics; Medicine; Neurology; Ophthalmology; Otorhinolaryngology; Paediatrics; Pathology; Pharmacology; Psychiatry and Mental Health; Public Health; Radiology; Surgery; Tropical Medicine; Urology; Venereology); **Nursing** (Nursing); **Pharmacy** (Pharmacy); **Physical Education** (Physical Education); **Science** (Botany; Chemistry; Entomology; Geology; Mathematics; Natural Sciences; Physics; Zoology); **Social Work** (Social Work); **Specific Education**; **Veterinary Medicine** (Veterinary Science)

Institutes
Cancer *(South Egypt)* (Medicine; Oncology); **Sugar Technology Research**

Further Information: Also University Teaching Hospital. Traditional and Open Learning Institution

History: Founded 1949 by decree, opened 1957. A State Institution enjoying administrative autonomy. Faculties of Agriculture, Arts and Education at Minya detached 1976 to form new University. Financed by the State. Branches in Sohag, Qena and Aswan merged 1995 to form South Valley University.

Governing Bodies: University Council, comprising the President as Chairman, three Vice-Presidents, the Deans, the Secretary-General, and 4 other members selected by the Council

Academic Year: September to May (September-December; January-May)

Admission Requirements: Secondary school certificate or equivalent

Fees: (Egyptian Pounds): Undergraduate, 100-150; Postgraduate, 200-250; foreign students (Pounds Sterling), Undergraduate, 1,000-1,500; Postgraduate 1,500-2,000

Main Language(s) of Instruction: Arabic, English

Accrediting Agencies: National Authority of Education Accreditation and Quality Assurance

Degrees and Diplomas: *Baccalaureos*: Health Studies, 6 yrs; *Baccalaureos*: Pharmacy; Veterinary Science, 5 yrs; *Baccalaureos*: Science; Agriculture; Commerce; Education; Physical Education; Nursing; Social Work; Special Education; Computer and Information Science, 4 yrs; *Magistr*: All fields, a further 2-3 yrs and thesis; *Doktora*: a further 2-4 yrs by dissertation. Also Diplomas of Specialization, 2 yrs following Baccalaureos, 4-yr Licence in Arts; Law; Education

Student Services: Academic counselling, Canteen, Cultural centre, Employment services, Foreign student adviser, Foreign Studies Centre, Handicapped facilities, Health services, Language programs, Nursery care, Social counselling, Sports facilities

Student Residential Facilities: For 14,850 students

Special Facilities: Geological Museum. Architectural Gallery

Libraries: Central Library and Faculty libraries

Publications: Assiut Bulletin for Environmental Research; Assiut Medical Journal; Journal of Engineering Sciences

Press or Publishing House: Assiut University Publishing and Distributing House

Academic Staff 2008-2009	MEN	WOMEN	TOTAL
FULL-TIME	1,864	645	2,509
STAFF WITH DOCTORATE			
FULL-TIME	867	320	1,187
Student Numbers 2008-2009			
All (Foreign Included)	37,621	32,862	70,483
FOREIGN ONLY	–	–	29

Last Updated: 15/07/09

BENHA UNIVERSITY

Fareed Nada Street, Benha 13511
EMail: president.office@bu.edu.eg
Website: http://www.bu.edu.eg/en/

President: Ali Shams El Din

Faculties
Agriculture (Agricultural Economics; Agricultural Engineering; Agriculture; Agronomy; Animal Husbandry; Biochemistry; Food Science; Genetics; Horticulture; Plant and Crop Protection; Plant Pathology; Soil Science); **Arts** (Arabic; English; French; Geography; History; Library Science; Literature; Mass Communication; Philosophy; Psychology; Sociology); **Commerce** (Accountancy; Economics; Insurance; Management; Statistics); **Computers and Informatics** (Computer Science; Information Technology); **Education** (Education; Educational Administration; Psychiatry and Mental Health; Psychology); **Engineering** (Architecture; Civil Engineering; Electrical Engineering; Industrial Engineering; Mechanical Engineering; Physical Engineering; Surveying and Mapping); **Law** (Civil Law; Commercial Law; Islamic Law; Law; Public Law); **Medicine** (Anatomy; Biochemistry; Cardiology; Dermatology; Forensic Medicine and Dentistry; Gastroenterology; Gynaecology and Obstetrics; Hepatology; Histology; Immunology; Medicine; Microbiology; Neurology; Ophthalmology; Otorhinolaryngology; Paediatrics; Parasitology; Pathology; Pharmacology; Physiology; Rheumatology; Surgery; Toxicology; Urology); **Nursing** (Child Care and Development; Nursing); **Physical Education** (Physical Education; Physical Therapy; Sports; Sports Management); **Science** (Biochemistry; Botany; Entomology; Geology; Mathematics; Physics; Zoology); **Veterinary Science** (Anatomy; Animal Husbandry; Biochemistry; Embryology and Reproduction Biology; Histology; Nutrition; Parasitology; Pathology; Pharmacology; Physiology; Surgery; Veterinary Science; Virology)

Institutes
Technology *(Benha)* (Civil Engineering; Electrical Engineering; Mechanical Engineering; Natural Sciences)

Degrees and Diplomas: *Baccalaureos*; *Magistr*; *Doktora*

Libraries: Yes
Last Updated: 05/03/12

BENI-SUEF UNIVERSITY (BSU)

Salah Salem Street, Beni-Suef
Tel: +20(82) 232-4879
Fax: +20(82) 232-4879
EMail: info@bsu.edu.eg
Website: http://www.bsu.edu.eg/default.aspx

President: Mohamed M. YoussefFax: +20(82) 233-3367
EMail: president@bsu.edu.eg

Secretary-General: Samy Saad Tel: +20(82) 232-4839

International Relations: Hussam El Sheriff, Cultural Affairs
Secretary Tel: +20(82) 235-6841, Fax: +20(82) 235-6841

Faculties

Arts (Arts and Humanities; English; European Studies; Geography; Journalism; Library Science; Mediterranean Studies; Psychology); **Commerce** (Business and Commerce); **Education** (Education); **Engineering** (Engineering); **Industrial Science** (Industrial Engineering); **Law** (Law); **Medicine** (Medicine); **Nursing** (Nursing); **Pharmacy** (Pharmacy); **Physical Education** (Physical Education); **Science**; **Veterinary Medicine** (Veterinary Science)

History: Founded 1983 as Beni-Suef Branch of Cairo University. Acquired present status and title 2005.

Governing Bodies: President and Vice-Presidents

Academic Year: September to June (September to January, February to June

Admission Requirements: High School Certificate or equivalent

Main Language(s) of Instruction: Arabic, English

International Co-operation: Participates in Erasmus programmes

Degrees and Diplomas: *Baccalaureos*: Medicine, 6 yrs; *Baccalaureos*: Pharmacy, Engineering, Veterinary Science, 5 yrs; *Baccalaureos*: Physical Education, Nursing, Industrial Engineering, 4 yrs. Also Licentiate of Law, Arts, Education (4 yrs)

Student Services: Academic counselling, Canteen, Cultural centre, Employment services, Handicapped facilities, Health services, Language programs, Nursery care, Social counselling, Sports facilities

Student Residential Facilities: Yes

Special Facilities: Museum; Art Gallery; Observatory; Theatre; Communication and Technology Centre

Libraries: Library; Digital Library

Academic Staff *2007-2008*: Total 1,314
STAFF WITH DOCTORATE: Total 417
Student Numbers *2007-2008*: Total 42,418
Last Updated: 15/05/09

CAIRO UNIVERSITY

PO Box 12613, Nahdet Misr Street, Giza, Cairo
Tel: +20(2) 572-9584
Fax: +20(2) 568-8884
EMail: scc@cu.edu.eg
Website: http://www.cu.edu.eg

President: Hossam Kamel
Tel: +20(2) 572-7066, Fax: +20(2) 572-8131

Centres
Development and Technology Planning; **Environmental Studies and Research**; **Future Studies and Research**; **Open University E-Learning** (Distance Education)

Faculties
Agriculture; **Archaeology** (Ancient Civilizations; Archaeology; Art History; Museum Studies; Restoration of Works of Art; Tourism); **Arts** (Arabic; Arts and Humanities; English; French; Geography; German; Greek (Classical); History; Japanese; Latin; Library Science; Philosophy; Psychology; Sociology; Spanish); **Commerce** (Accountancy; Banking; Business Administration; Business and Commerce; Health Administration; Hotel Management; Insurance; Marketing; Mathematics; Public Administration; Taxation); **Computer Science and Informatics** (Computer Science; Information Sciences; Information Technology); **Dar el Ulum** (*Dar El-Ulum*) (Arabic; Comparative Literature; Grammar; History; Islamic Law; Islamic Studies; Linguistics; Literature; Oriental Studies; Philoso-

phy); **Dentistry** (Dental Hygiene; Dentistry; Oral Pathology; Orthodontics; Surgery); **Economics and Political Science** (Economics; Political Sciences; Public Administration; Statistics); **Engineering** (Aeronautical and Aerospace Engineering; Architecture; Biomedical Engineering; Civil Engineering; Electrical Engineering; Engineering; Hydraulic Engineering; Irrigation; Mathematics; Mechanical Engineering; Metallurgical Engineering; Petroleum and Gas Engineering; Physics; Telecommunications Engineering); **Kindergarten** (Preschool Education); **Law** (Civil Law; Commercial Law; Criminal Law; Finance; History of Law; International Law; Islamic Law; Labour Law; Law; Public Law); **Mass Communication** (Advertising and Publicity; Journalism; Mass Communication; Radio and Television Broadcasting); **Medicine** (Anaesthesiology; Anatomy; Biochemistry; Cardiology; Dermatology; Forensic Medicine and Dentistry; Gynaecology and Obstetrics; Histology; Hygiene; Medicine; Neurology; Occupational Health; Ophthalmology; Orthopaedics; Paediatrics; Parasitology; Pathology; Physiology; Psychiatry and Mental Health; Radiology; Surgery; Tropical Medicine; Urology; Venereology); **Nursing**; **Pharmacy** (Analytical Chemistry; Biochemistry; Microbiology; Organic Chemistry; Pharmacology; Pharmacy); **Physiotherapy** (Gynaecology and Obstetrics; Neurological Therapy; Orthopaedics; Physical Therapy; Plastic Surgery); **Regional and Urban Planning**; **Science** (Analytical Chemistry; Astronomy and Space Science; Botany; Chemistry; Computer Science; Entomology; Geology; Geophysics; Mathematics; Meteorology; Microbiology; Mineralogy; Natural Sciences; Physics; Statistics; Zoology); **Veterinary Medicine** (Anatomy; Animal Husbandry; Biochemistry; Fishery; Forensic Medicine and Dentistry; Histology; Microbiology; Nutrition; Parasitology; Pharmacology; Physiology; Toxicology; Veterinary Science)

Institutes
Cancer *(National)* (Anaesthesiology; Biology; Epidemiology; Oncology; Pathology; Radiology; Surgery); **Educational Studies and Research** (Curriculum; Educational and Student Counselling; Educational Research; Educational Technology; Pedagogy; Preschool Education; Teacher Training); **Laser Science** *(National)*; **Statistical Studies and Research** (Statistics)

Further Information: Also Qars El Ainy Hospital; Tumour Hospital and Infants Hospital

History: Founded 1908 as National University, became State University 1925. Known as Fouad I University between 1940 and 1953.

Governing Bodies: University Council, composed of the President, Deputies, Heads of the Faculties and Institutes, and four members dealing with university affairs (appointed for two years)

Academic Year: September to June (September-January; January-June)

Admission Requirements: Secondary school certificate or equivalent. University degree for Institutes of Statistical Studies and African Studies

Main Language(s) of Instruction: Arabic, English, French

Degrees and Diplomas: *Diploma*: African Studies; Statistics, 2 yrs; *Baccalaureos*: Chemical Engineering; Civil Engineering; Electrical Engineering; Mechanical Engineering; Mining Engineering; Petroleum Engineering; Pharmaceutical Chemistry, 5 yrs; *Baccalaureos*: Commerce; Journalism; Science in Economics; Science in Political Science; Science in Statistics, 4 yrs; *Baccalaureos*: Dental Surgery, 4 yrs following preparatory yr; *Magistr*: a further 2 yrs; *Magistr*: Dental Surgery; Journalism; Pain Relief; Surgery, a further 2 yrs; *Doktora*: 2 yrs following Magistr; *Doktora*: Anaesthesiology and Pain Relief; Cancer Biology; Clinical Pathology; Dental Medicine; Medical Oncology; Medical Science; Medicine; Oncological Pathology; Paediatric Oncology; Pharmacy; Radiation Oncology; Surgical Oncology; Veterinary Medicine and Surgery, 2 yrs following Magistr

Student Services: Academic counselling, Canteen, Cultural centre, Employment services, Foreign student adviser, Handicapped facilities, Health services, Nursery care, Social counselling, Sports facilities

Student Residential Facilities: For c. 3,150 men students, and c. 7,650 women students

Special Facilities: Egyptology Museum; Islamic Museum; Entomology Museum. Collection of Papyrii and Ancient Coins

Libraries: Central Library, c. 950,000 vols. Fayoum Branch, c. 33,200 vols; Beni Sweif Branch, c. 37,000 vols

Publications: Computer Magazine; Egyptian Journal of Genetics and Psychology; Medical Journal of Cairo University; Population and Family Planning Magazine; Publications of the Faculties; The Egyptian Statistical Magazine

Press or Publishing House: Cairo University Press; Agriculture Faculty Press; Statistical Studies and Research Press; Law Faculty Press; Science Faculty Press
Last Updated: 19/02/09

KHARTOUM BRANCH

Khartoum
Tel: +20(2) 728-841
Fax: +20(2) 728-841

Faculties
Arts; Commerce; Law; Science
History: Founded 1955.

FAYOUM UNIVERSITY (FU)

Said Soliman Street, Fayoum 63514
Tel: +20(84) 633-3274
Fax: +20(84) 637-8666
EMail: sssg00@fayoum.edu.eg; admin@fayoum.edu.eg
Website: http://www.fayoum.edu.eg

President: Abdel Hammed Abdel Tawab
Tel: +20(84) 633-3278, Fax: +20(84) 633-6528
EMail: aas02@fayoum.edu.eg

Vice-President for Postgraduate Studies and Research:
Mohammad Barakat
Tel: +20(84) 637-7064, Fax: +20(84) 637-7064
EMail: mkb00@fayoum.edu.eg

International Relations: Ahmad Abdul Salam
Fax: +20(84) 637-7064 EMail: ama32@fayoum.edu.eg

Faculties
Agriculture (Agriculture; Agronomy; Animal Husbandry; Biochemistry; Botany; Crop Production; Dairy; Food Science; Food Technology; Genetics; Horticulture; Microbiology; Plant and Crop Protection; Soil Science); **Archaeology** (Archaeology; Islamic Studies; Restoration of Works of Art); **Arts** (Arabic; Documentation Techniques; English; French; Geography (Human); History; Information Sciences; Library Science; Philosophy; Psychology; Sociology) *Dean*: Ibrahim Sakr; **Computer and Information Sciences** *Dean*: Kamal Dib; **Dar Al Oloom (Arabic and Islamic Studies)** *Dean*: Khalil Khalil; **Education** (Curriculum; Education; Educational Administration; Educational Psychology; International and Comparative Education) *Dean*: Ragaa Eid; **Engineering** (Civil Engineering; Electrical Engineering; Engineering; Industrial Engineering; Structural Architecture) *Dean*: Hani El Ghazaly; **Kindergarten** (Educational Sciences; Psychology; Science Education) *Dean*: Sanaa Haroon; **Medicine** (Anaesthesiology; Anatomy; Biochemistry; Cardiology; Community Health; Dermatology; Epidemiology; Forensic Medicine and Dentistry; Gynaecology and Obstetrics; Histology; Immunology; Medicine; Microbiology; Neurology; Occupational Health; Oncology; Ophthalmology; Orthopaedics; Otorhinolaryngology; Paediatrics; Parasitology; Pathology; Pharmacology; Physiology; Psychiatry and Mental Health; Public Health; Radiology; Rheumatology; Surgery; Toxicology) *Dean*: Mahmoud Kamal; **Science** (Botany; Chemistry; Geology; Mathematics; Physics; Zoology) *Dean*: Mohammed Yasin; **Social Work** (Social Sciences; Social Work) *Dean*: Hoda Soliman; **Specific Education** (Art Education; Educational Technology; Home Economics Education) *Dean*: Sayed Salah; **Tourism and Hotels** (Hotel and Restaurant; Hotel Management; Tourism) *Dean*: Nashaat Mortada

History: Founded 1976 as Al-Fayoum Branch of Cairo University. Declared independent and acquired present title 2005.

Governing Bodies: President, Vice-Presidents, Deans and Secretary-General

Academic Year: September to May (September-December; February-May)

Admission Requirements: Secondary education certificate or equivalent

Fees: (Egyptian Pounds): 209-229.5

Main Language(s) of Instruction: Arabic

International Co-operation: Participates in the Tempus (Trans-European Mobility Scheme for University Studies), NAQAAE, FP7 (Seventh Framework Programme), Erasmus and JICA (Japan International Cooperation Agency) programmes

Degrees and Diplomas: *Diploma*: Agriculture; Engineering; Social Work; Tourism & Hotels; Arts; *Baccalaureos*: Education; Agriculture; Engineering; Social Work; Dar Al Oloom (Arabic & Islamic Studies); Specific Education; Tourism & Hotels; Science; Archaeology; Medicine; Arts; Computer and Information Sciences; Kindergarten (BSc/BA), 4-6 yrs; *Magistr*: Agriculture; Engineering; Social Work; Dar Al Oloom; Science; Tourism and Hotels; Arts (MSc/MA), 2-5 yrs; *Doktora*: Agriculture; Engineering; Social Work; Dar Al Oloom; Science; Tourism & Hotels; Arts (PhD), 3-5 yrs. Also General/Professional/Special Diploma in Education

Student Services: Academic counselling, Canteen, Cultural centre, Employment services, Foreign student adviser, Foreign Studies Centre, Handicapped facilities, Health services, Language programs, Nursery care, Social counselling, Sports facilities

Student Residential Facilities: 10 student dormitories (4 for males and 6 for females); university hotels

Special Facilities: Theatre and Gymnasium

Libraries: c. 60,530 vols (in Arabic); 25,426 vols (in Foreign Languages); 401 dictionaries; 201 encyclopedias; 7,937 theses and 1,811 subscriptions to periodicals. Also access to 162 electronic books

Publications: Fayoum Journal of Agricultural Research and Development *(biannually)*; Journal of Tourism and Hotels *(biannually)*

Press or Publishing House: Press and Print Unit

Academic Staff 2008-2009	MEN	WOMEN	TOTAL
FULL-TIME	702	232	**934**
STAFF WITH DOCTORATE			
FULL-TIME	493	162	**655**
Student Numbers 2008-2009			
All (Foreign Included)	10,199	13,520	**23,719**

Last Updated: 04/08/09

HELWAN UNIVERSITY

Ein Helwan, Cairo 11795
Tel: +20(2) 556-9064
Fax: +20(2) 555-5023
EMail: helwan@helwan.edu.eg
Website: http://www.helwan.edu.eg

President: Mahmoud Nasser El-Tayeb Nasser
Tel: +20(2) 556-9061, Fax: +20(2) 556-5820
EMail: president@helwan.edu.eg

Centres
Foreign Trade Studies and Research (International Business); **Scientific Computing** (Computer Science); **Scientific Instrument Maintenance** (Instrument Making); **Small Projects Support**; **Social Service** (Social and Community Services); **Technology Development Studies and Research** (Technology); **University Education Development** (Pedagogy); **Youth Studies and Research** (Child Care and Development)

Faculties
Applied Arts; **Art Education**; **Arts** (Ancient Civilizations; Arabic; Arts and Humanities; English; French; Geography; German; Hebrew; History; Information Sciences; Italian; Library Science; Mass Communication; Modern Languages; Persian; Philosophy; Psychology; Sociology; Spanish; Theatre; Turkish); **Commerce and Business Administration** (Accountancy; Business Administration; Business and Commerce; Insurance; International Business; Political Sciences; Statistics); **Computer and Information Sciences** (Computer Science; Information Sciences); **Education** (Curriculum; Education; Educational Psychology; Educational Technology; Pedagogy); **Engineering** (Computer Engineering; Electrical and Electronic Engineering; Engineering; Production Engineering; Telecommunications Engineering); **Engineering** *(Mattaria)* (Architecture; Automation and Control Engineering; Civil Engineering; Engineering; Mechanical Engineering; Power Engineering); **Fine Arts** (Architecture; Fine Arts; Graphic Arts; Interior Design; Painting

and Drawing; Sculpture); **Home Economics** (Food Science; Home Economics; Nutrition; Textile Technology); **Law** (Civil Law; Commercial Law; Criminal Law; History of Law; International Law; Law; Private Law; Public Law); **Music Education** (Music Education; Musical Instruments; Singing); **Pharmacy** (Analytical Chemistry; Biochemistry; Chemistry; Microbiology; Organic Chemistry; Pharmacology; Pharmacy); **Physical Education** *(for men)* (Health Sciences; Parks and Recreation; Physical Education; Physical Therapy; Sports Management); **Physical Education** *(for women)* (Physical Education); **Science** (Astronomy and Space Science; Botany; Chemistry; Geology; Natural Sciences; Physics; Zoology); **Social Work** (Social and Community Services; Social Work); **Tourism and Hotel Management** (Hotel Management; Tourism)

Further Information: Also 46 self-sponsored Research Centres and Units. Traditional and Open Learning Institution

History: Founded 1975, incorporating previously existing Faculties and Institutes of Higher Education. A state Institution under the supervision of the Ministry of Higher Education and financed by the State.

Governing Bodies: University Council, comprising twenty-eight members

Academic Year: September to June

Admission Requirements: Secondary school certificate or equivalent

Main Language(s) of Instruction: Arabic, English

International Co-operation: With universities in Australia, China, Germany, Italy, Romania, Sudan, USA and Yemen.

Degrees and Diplomas: *Diploma:* Education; Science, 1-2 yrs; *Baccalaureos:* Arts (B.A.), 4 yrs; *Baccalaureos:* Science (B.Sc.), 4-5 yrs; *Magistr.* Arts (M.A.); Science (M.Sc.), a further 2 yrs; *Doktora:* Arts; Science (PhD), 3 yrs following Magistr

Student Services: Academic counselling, Canteen, Cultural centre, Employment services, Foreign Studies Centre, Handicapped facilities, Health services, Language programs, Nursery care, Social counselling, Sports facilities

Student Residential Facilities: Yes

Special Facilities: Art Gallery

Libraries: Central Library, 250,000 vols; Faculty libraries, 338,089 vols

Publications: Helwan University Journal

Press or Publishing House: University Press at the Faculty of Applied Arts
Last Updated: 17/08/09

KAFRELSHEIKH UNIVERSITY

El-Geish Street, Kafr Al-Sheikh 33516
Tel: +20(47) 322-4707
Fax: +20(47) 322-3419
EMail: aman485@yahoo.com
Website: http://www.kfs.edu.eg

President: Maged Abdeltawab El Kemary

Secretary General: Samir Amin Sultan Tel: +20(10) 241-4450

Vice-President for Graduate Studies: Ibrahim Mouhamed Aman

Faculties
Agriculture (Agriculture); **Commerce** (Business and Commerce); **Education** (Education; Special Education); **Engineering** (Engineering); **Specific Education** (Art Education; Educational Sciences; Educational Technology; Home Economics; Mass Communication; Music Education; Psychology); **Sports Education** (Sports); **Veterinary Medicine** (Veterinary Science)

History: Founded 1972 as Kafr El-Sheikh Branch of Tanta University. Acquired present status and title 2006.

Governing Bodies: University Council; Faculty Council; Department Council

Academic Year: September to June (2 sems)

Fees: (Egyptian Pounds): Undergraduate, 190; postgraduate, 500-1,000

Main Language(s) of Instruction: English; Arabic

International Co-operation: With Yunnan Agricultural University; East China Normal University (China); Technical University of

Munich; University of Hohenheim (Germany); Zant Shtvan University (Hungary); University of Bologna (Italy); University of Agronomic Science (Romania); Ivanovo State Textile Academy (Russia); Universidad de Castilla (Spain);Teshreen University (Syria)

Accrediting Agencies: Ministry of Higher Education

Degrees and Diplomas: *Baccalaureos:* 4 yrs; *Magistr.* 2 yrs; *Doktora:* 3 yrs

Student Services: Canteen, Health services, Sports facilities

Student Residential Facilities: Student hostels for girls and student hostels for boys

Libraries: Central Library; Digital Library; A library at each Faculty

Publications: Journal of Agricultural Research; Journal of Education Faculty, A scientific journal related to Education, Psychology and Social Sciences; Kafr El Sheikh Veterinary Medical

Academic Staff *2008-2009*	MEN	WOMEN	TOTAL
FULL-TIME	590	269	**859**
PART-TIME	313	84	**397**
Student Numbers *2008-2009*			
All (Foreign Included)	10,482	14,861	**25,343**

Distance students, 5.
Last Updated: 21/04/09

LABOUR UNIVERSITY

Nasr City, Cairo
Tel: +20(2) 275-4601
Fax: +20(2) 275-4604

Sections
Industrial Relations; Technological Development

Further Information: Also branches in Alexandria, Tanta, Zagazig, Assiut, Kafr Al-Sheikh, Ras El-Barr, Mansoura, Ismailia, Aswan and Beni Suef.

History: Founded 1994.

Degrees and Diplomas: *Diploma; Baccalaureos*
Last Updated: 18/02/08

MANSOURA UNIVERSITY

60, El Gomhoria Street, Mansoura, Dakahliya 35516
Tel: +20(50) 239-7054 +20(50) 239-7055 +20(50) 238-3781
Fax: +20(50) 239-7330 +20(50) 239-7900
EMail: mua@mans.edu.eg; hamzaaa@mum.mans.eun.eg
Website: http://www.mans.edu.eg

President: El-Sayed Abdel-Khalek
Tel: +20(50) 239-7387 +20(50) 224-7800
EMail: president@mans.edu.eg; mrayan@mans.edu.eg

Secretary-General: Amira Al-Sorongy
Tel: +20(50) 247-330, Fax: +20(50) 247-330

International Relations: Yehia Hussein Ebeid
Tel: +20(50) 243-587, Fax: +20(50) 243-587

Centres
Urology and Nephrology (Nephrology; Urology)

Faculties
Agriculture (Agricultural Economics; Agricultural Engineering; Agriculture; Agronomy; Animal Husbandry; Botany; Chemistry; Dairy; Floriculture; Food Science; Genetics; Microbiology; Plant Pathology; Soil Science; Vegetable Production; Zoology); **Arts** (Arabic; Archaeology; Arts and Humanities; Documentation Techniques; English Studies; French Studies; Geography; Greek; History; Journalism; Latin; Library Science; Oriental Languages; Philosophy; Psychology; Sociology); **Commerce** (Accountancy; Business Administration; Business and Commerce; Economics; Insurance; Statistics); **Computer and Information Science** (Computer Science; Information Management; Information Sciences); **Dentistry** (Dentistry; Oral Pathology; Orthodontics); **Education** (Arabic; Chemistry; Curriculum; Education; Educational Psychology; Educational Technology; Geography; Geology; History; Islamic Studies; Modern Languages; Primary Education; Teacher Training); **Education** *(Damietta)* (Arabic; Biology; Curriculum; Education; Educational Psychology; Educational Technology; Eng-

lish; French; Geography; Geology; History; Islamic Studies; Modern Languages; Philosophy); **Engineering** (Architectural and Environmental Design; Automation and Control Engineering; Civil Engineering; Computer Engineering; Construction Engineering; Electrical and Electronic Engineering; Engineering; Hydraulic Engineering; Industrial Engineering; Irrigation; Mathematics; Mechanical Engineering; Physics; Power Engineering; Textile Technology); **Law** (Civil Law; Commercial Law; Criminal Law; History of Law; International Law; Islamic Law; Law; Private Law; Public Law); **Medicine** (Anaesthesiology; Anatomy; Biochemistry; Cardiology; Community Health; Dermatology; Forensic Medicine and Dentistry; Gynaecology and Obstetrics; Histology; Medicine; Microbiology; Neurology; Ophthalmology; Orthodontics; Orthopaedics; Paediatrics; Parasitology; Pathology; Pharmacology; Physical Therapy; Physiology; Psychiatry and Mental Health; Radiology; Surgery; Urology); **Nursing** (Community Health; Gerontology; Gynaecology and Obstetrics; Hygiene; Nursing); **Pharmacy** (Analytical Chemistry; Microbiology; Pharmacy); **Science** *(Damietta)* (Botany; Chemistry; Environmental Studies; Geology; Mathematics; Physics; Science Education; Zoology); **Science** (Botany; Chemistry; Geology; Mathematics; Natural Sciences; Physics; Zoology); **Veterinary Science** (Anatomy; Animal Husbandry; Biochemistry; Embryology and Reproduction Biology; Food Science; Forensic Medicine and Dentistry; Histology; Hygiene; Immunology; Nutrition; Parasitology; Pathology; Pharmacology; Physiology; Surgery; Veterinary Science; Virology)

Further Information: Also 2 Teaching Hospitals and 3 Laboratories. Traditional and Open Learning Institution

History: Founded 1972 as East Delta University, incorporating Faculties previously attached to the University of Cairo. Acquired present title 1973. A State Institution under the authority of the Ministry of Higher Education.

Governing Bodies: Board; Boards of the Faculties

Academic Year: September to June (September-January; February-June)

Admission Requirements: Secondary school certificate or equivalent

Main Language(s) of Instruction: Arabic

Degrees and Diplomas: *Baccalaureos*: 4-6 yrs; *Magistr*: a further 2-3 yrs; *Doktora (PhD)*: a further 2-4 yrs

Student Services: Academic counselling, Canteen, Cultural centre, Employment services, Health services, Nursery care, Social counselling, Sports facilities

Student Residential Facilities: For c. 6,000 students

Special Facilities: Midwifery Museum; Anatomy Museum; Forensic Medicine Museum; Pharmacology Museum; Zoology Museum; Botany Museum

Libraries: Central Library; Faculty libraries, total, c. 425,000 vols

Publications: Periodicals of the Community and Environmental Council and the Cultural Affairs and Research Branch; Scientific Journal

Press or Publishing House: University Press
Last Updated: 17/08/09

MENOUFIYA UNIVERSITY

PO Box 32511, Gamal Abdel Nasser Street, Shebin Al-Kom, Menoufia
Tel: +20(48) 2222-170 +20(2) 2575-2777
Fax: +20(48) 2222-170 +20(2) 5752-7779
EMail: menofia@menofia.edu.eg
Website: http://www.menofia.edu.eg

President: Mohamed A. Izzularab
Tel: +20(48) 225-298
EMail: izzularab@menofia.edu.eg; mizzularab@yahoo.com

Secretary-General: Mostafa Khalil
Tel: +20(48) 2220-894, Fax: +20(48) 2220-894
EMail: m.khalil@menofia.edu.eg

International Relations: Thabet Edress, Vice President for Graduate Studies and Research
Tel: +20(48) 2317-540, Fax: +20(48) 2226-454
EMail: HVPresident@menofia.edu.eg

Faculties

Agriculture (Agricultural Engineering; Agriculture; Agronomy; Animal Husbandry; Dairy; Food Technology; Genetics; Horticulture; Meat and Poultry; Soil Science); **Arts** (Arabic; Arts and Humanities; English; French; Geography; German; History; Library Science; Literature; Oriental Languages; Philosophy; Psychology; Sociology); **Commerce** *(Sadat City)* (Accountancy; Business Administration; Business and Commerce; Economics; Insurance; Statistics); **Commerce** (Accountancy; Business Administration; Business and Commerce; Economics; Insurance; Statistics); **Computer Science and Information Technology** (Computer Science; Information Technology); **Education** *(Sadat City)*; **Education** (Curriculum; Education; Educational Psychology; Pedagogy); **Electronic Engineering** (Automation and Control Engineering; Computer Engineering; Computer Science; Electronic Engineering; Telecommunications Engineering); **Engineering** (Civil Engineering; Electrical Engineering; Engineering; Mechanical Engineering; Power Engineering); **Home Economics** (Clothing and Sewing; Food Science; Home Economics; Nutrition; Textile Design); **Law** (Civil Law; Commercial Law; Criminal Law; International Law; Islamic Law; Law; Public Law); **Medicine** (Anaesthesiology; Anatomy; Biochemistry; Cardiology; Forensic Medicine and Dentistry; Histology; Medicine; Microbiology; Oncology; Ophthalmology; Orthopaedics; Otorhinolaryngology; Paediatrics; Parasitology; Pathology; Pharmacology; Physiology; Radiology; Surgery; Toxicology; Tropical Medicine; Urology); **Nursing** (Health Administration; Nursing); **Physical Education** (Physical Education); **Science** (Botany; Chemistry; Geology; Mathematics; Mathematics and Computer Science; Natural Sciences; Physics; Zoology); **Specific Education** (Art Education; Economics; Educational Technology; Media Studies; Music Education; Psychology; Social Sciences); **Tourism and Hotels** *(Sadat City)* (Hotel and Restaurant; Hotel Management; Tourism); **Veterinary Medicine** *(Sadat City)* (Anatomy; Cell Biology; Embryology and Reproduction Biology; Pathology; Veterinary Science)

Institutes

Biotechnology Engineering *(Sadat City)* (Biotechnology; Genetics; Molecular Biology); **Environmental Studies and Research** *(Sadat City)* (Arid Land Studies); **Liver Studies and Research** *(Shebin)* (Hepatology)

History: Founded 1976. A State institution under the authority of the Ministry of Higher Education.

Governing Bodies: University Council

Academic Year: September to May

Admission Requirements: Secondary school certificate or equivalent

Fees: (Egyptian Pounds): 85-100 per annum

Main Language(s) of Instruction: Arabic, English

Accrediting Agencies: Ministry of Higher Education, Supreme Council of Universities

Degrees and Diplomas: *Baccalaureos (BA/BSc)*: 4-5 yrs; *Magistr (MA/MSc)*: a further 2-3 yrs; *Doktora (PhD)*: 3-4 yrs following Magistr

Student Services: Academic counselling, Canteen, Cultural centre, Employment services, Foreign student adviser, Foreign Studies Centre, Handicapped facilities, Health services, Language programs, Nursery care, Social counselling, Sports facilities

Student Residential Facilities: Yes

Libraries: Central Library and faculty libraries, c. 32,500 vols; 6,500 periodicals

Publications: Journal of Psychological and Educational Research; Minufiya Journal of Agricultural Research *(quarterly)*; Minufiya Journal of Electronic Engineering Research *(biennially)*; Minufiya Veterinary Journal *(biennially)*

Academic Staff *2009*	MEN	WOMEN	TOTAL
FULL-TIME	–	–	3,451
STAFF WITH DOCTORATE			
FULL-TIME	–	–	1,615
Student Numbers *2009*			
All (Foreign Included)	–	–	7,261
FOREIGN ONLY	31	9	40

Last Updated: 09/07/09

MINIA UNIVERSITY

PO Box 61519, El-Minia
Tel: +20(86) 321-443
Fax: +20(86) 342-601
EMail: minia@minia.edu.eg
Website: http://www.minia.edu.eg

President: Mohamed Ahmed Shrief
Tel: +20(86) 233-4646 EMail: drmsherif_aly@yahoo.com

Vice-President, Graduate Studies and Research: Gaber Zayed Abdulwanes Bresha
Tel: +20(86) 347-460 EMail: gaberbresha@yahoo.com

Faculties

Agriculture (Agriculture); **Arabic and Islamic Studies** *(Dar El-Uloom)* (Arabic; Islamic Studies); **Dentistry** (Dentistry); **Education** (Education); **Engineering** (Architecture; Automation and Control Engineering; Chemical Engineering; Civil Engineering; Electrical Engineering; Energy Engineering; Engineering; Mechanical Engineering; Production Engineering); **Fine Arts** (Architecture; Fine Arts; Graphic Arts; Interior Design; Painting and Drawing; Sculpture); **Languages** *(Al-Alsun)* (English; French; German; Spanish); **Medicine** (Anatomy; Biochemistry; Community Health; Embryology and Reproduction Biology; Forensic Medicine and Dentistry; Gynaecology and Obstetrics; Histology; Medicine; Ophthalmology; Otorhinolaryngology; Paediatrics; Physiology; Surgery); **Nursing** (Nursing); **Pharmacy** (Analytical Chemistry; Anatomy; Botany; Histology; Organic Chemistry; Pharmacy; Physics; Physiology); **Physical Education** (Physical Education; Sports); **Science** (Biology; Chemistry; Computer Science; Geology; Mathematics; Natural Sciences; Physics); **Special Education** (Special Education); **Tourism and Hotel Management** (Hotel Management; Tourism)

History: Founded 1976, incorporating Faculties of Agriculture, Education, Humanities, Science, and Engineering, previously forming part of the University of Assiut. A State Institution enjoying administrative autonomy. Financed by the Government.

Governing Bodies: University Council; Council for Undergraduate Studies; Council for Graduate Studies and Research

Academic Year: October to May (October-January; February-May)

Admission Requirements: Secondary school certificate or equivalent

Main Language(s) of Instruction: Arabic, English

Degrees and Diplomas: *Diploma*; *Baccalaureos*: Agriculture; Education; Physical Education; Science, 4 yrs; *Baccalaureos*: Engineering, 5 yrs; *Baccalaureos*: Surgery, 6 yrs; *Magistr*: Arts and Education, a further 2 yrs; *Doktora*: 2 yrs following Magistr, by thesis

Student Residential Facilities: For c. 3,000 students

Special Facilities: Art Gallery

Libraries: Central Library, c. 7,200 vols; libraries of the Faculties, c. 130,000 vols

Publications: Educational and Psychological Research Magazine; History and Future Magazine; Journal of Agricultural Research; Minia Medical Magazine; Technical Scientific Magazine

Press or Publishing House: University Press
Last Updated: 23/05/07

NATIONAL TELECOMMUNICATIONS INSTITUTE (NTI)

5 Mahmoud El Miligui St., 6th district, Nasr City, Cairo
Tel: +20 240-23-154
Fax: +20 263-6802
EMail: activity@nti.sci.eg
Website: http://www.nti.sci.eg

Director: Ahmed El-Sherbini EMail: sherbini@mcit.gov.eg

Administrative Officer: Mohamed Atef
Tel: +20 353-42457, Fax: +20 353-42427 EMail: m.atef@nti.sci.eg

Deputy Director: Magdy El-Soudani
Tel: +20 240-23-855, Fax: +20-240-23-855
EMail: melsoudani@nti.sci.eg

Departments

Computer and Systems (Computer Engineering; Computer Networks; Computer Science; Systems Analysis); **Electronics** (Electronic Engineering); **Networks Planning** (Computer Networks);

Switching anf Traffic (Computer Engineering; Computer Networks); **Transmission** (Telecommunications Engineering)

Programmes

Postgraduate (Computer Networks; Information Technology; Telecommunications Engineering)

Further Information: Smart Village: Bldg. B 147- 28th Km. Cairo Alex. Desert Road

History: Founded 1983.

Governing Bodies: Board of Directors headed by Ministers of Communications and Information Technology

Academic Year: October to June (October-January; Februry-June)

Admission Requirements: Bachelor of Science in Electronics or Communication Engineering or Computer Engineering

Fees: (Egyptian pounds): Egyptian students, 2,000 per annum; foreign students, (US Dollars, 2,000)

Main Language(s) of Instruction: English

International Co-operation: Supreme Council of Egyptian Universities

Accrediting Agencies: Ministry of Communications and Information Technology.

Degrees and Diplomas: *Magistr*: Computer Engineering and Communication Networks; Satellite and Mobile Communication, 2 yrs

Student Services: Academic counselling, Canteen, Foreign student adviser, Health services, Sports facilities

Special Facilities: Technical Museum; Audio-Video Studio

Libraries: c. 4,000 recent books and specialized periodicals

Academic Staff *2008-2009*	MEN	WOMEN	TOTAL
FULL-TIME	66	31	**97**

Student Numbers *2008-2009*			
All (Foreign Included)	–	–	**662**

Last Updated: 07/05/09

SOHAG UNIVERSITY

PO Box 82524, Sohag
Tel: +(20) 93457-0001
Fax: +(20) 93460-5745
Website: http://www.sohag-univ.edu.eg

President: Mohammad E. Ibrahim
Tel: +(20) 934611920, Fax: +(20) 934605754
EMail: sohag_uni_president@sohag-univ.edu.eg

Vice-President for Post-Graduate Studies and Research: Lotfy H. Abo-Dahab
Tel: +(20) 93461-2589, Fax: +(20) 93461-0578
EMail: lotfy_hamed@yahoo.com

International Relations: Lotfy H. Abo-Dahab
Tel: +(20) 93461-2589, Fax: +(20) 93461-0578
EMail: lotfy_hamed@yahoo.com

Faculties

Agriculture (Agriculture); **Arts** (Arts and Humanities); **Commerce** (Business and Commerce) *Dean*: Saied M Abdallah; **Commerce** (Business and Commerce) *Dean*: Abd Elhameed A. Mahmoud; **Education** (Education); **Engineering** (Engineering); **Medicine** (Medicine); **Nursing**; **Science** (Mathematics and Computer Science; Natural Sciences); **Veterinary Medicine**

History: Founded 1979 as Sohag Branch of South Valley University. Acquired present status and title 2006.

Degrees and Diplomas: *Baccalaureos*; *Magistr*; *Doktora*

Libraries: 8 Library (6 Digital library)

Publications: Sohag Faculty of Arts Journal *(biannually)*; Sohag Faculty of Medicine Journal *(biannually)*

Academic Staff *2008-2009*	MEN	WOMEN	TOTAL
FULL-TIME	863	400	**1,263**

Student Numbers *2008-2009*			
All (Foreign Included)	15,000	14,600	**29,600**

Distance students, 7,400.
Last Updated: 08/06/09

SOUTH VALLEY UNIVERSITY

Qena 83523
Tel: +20(96) 521-1281 +20(96) 521-1277
Fax: +20(96) 521-1279
EMail: info@svu.edu.eg
Website: http://www.svu.edu.eg

President: Abbas Mohamed Mansour (2006-)
Tel: +20(96) 521-1717, Fax: +20(96) 521-1279
EMail: abbas_mansour@yahoo.com; psvu@svu.edu.eg

Administrative Officer: Hasan Eldewi Muhammad
Tel: +20(96) 521-1280, Fax: +20(96) 521-1280

International Relations: Abdel Fatah M. Hashem, Vice-President
for Graduate Affairs
Tel: +20(96) 521-6128, Fax: +20(96) 521-7213
EMail: vpgrd@svu.edu.eg

Faculties

Agriculture *(Qena)* (Agriculture); **Archaeology** *(Qena)* (Ancient
Civilizations; Archaeology); **Arts** *(Aswan)* (Arts and Humanities);
Arts *(Qena)* (Arts and Humanities); **Commerce** *(Qena)* (Business
Administration; Business and Commerce; Economics); **Education**
(Aswan) (Education); **Education** *(Hurghada)* (Education); **Educa-
tion** *(Qena)* (Education); **Energy** *(Aswan)* (Energy Engineering);
Engineering *(Qena)* (Civil Engineering; Electrical Engineering;
Engineering); **Engineering** *(Aswan)* (Architecture; Civil Engineer-
ing; Electrical Engineering; Mechanical Engineering); **Fine Arts**
(Luxor) (Fine Arts); **Hotels and Tourism** *(Luxor)* (Hotel and Res-
taurant; Tourism); **Law** *(Qena)* (Law); **Medicine** *(Qena)* (Medicine);
Nursing *(Qena)* (Nursing); **Physical Education** *(Qena)* (Education;
Physical Education; Sports); **Science** *(Aswan)* (Computer Science;
Mathematics; Mathematics and Computer Science; Natural Sci-
ences); **Science** *(Qena)* (Mathematics; Mathematics and Computer
Science; Natural Sciences); **Social Work** *(Aswan)* (Social Work);
Special Education *(Qena)* (Education; Special Education); **Veter-
inary Medicine** *(Qena)* (Veterinary Science)

Further Information: Also branches in Luxor, Aswan and Hurghada.

History: Founded as branch of Assiut University 1970. Separated
from Assuit University 1995 to become South Valley University
based in Qena, with campuses in Sohag, Luxor, Aswan and Red
Sea campus. Sohag Campus separated to become Sohag University 2006.

Governing Bodies: Ministry of Higher Education and Scientific
Research, Supreme Council of Universities

Academic Year: September to June

Admission Requirements: General Secondary Certificate

Fees: (Egyptian Pounds): Free of charge for undergraduate programmes; c. 500 for postgraduate programmes

Main Language(s) of Instruction: Arabic and English

International Co-operation: The University signed a number of
MoU and also offers scientific and academic collaboration and
exchange programmes; Participates in the Erasmus Mundus, FP7
and Tempus programmes

Accrediting Agencies: Ministry of Higher Education and Scientific
Research

Degrees and Diplomas: *Diploma*: Education; Natural Sciences, 1-
2 yrs; *Baccalaureos*: Engineering; Pharmacy; Veterinary Medicine,
5 yrs; *Baccalaureos*: Medicine; Surgery, 6 yrs; *Baccalaureos*: Sci-
ence; Agriculture; Commerce; Education; Specific Education; Social
Work, 4 yrs; *Magistr*: Arts and Humanities; Law; Education (M.A.);
Education; Special Education; Physical Education; Medicine;
Veterinary Medicine; Mathematics; Natural Sciences; Computer
Science; Agricultural and Soil Sciences; Business and Commerce;
Economics and Business Administration; Engineering; Social Sci-
ences (M.Sc.), a further 2 yrs; *Doktora*: Arts and Humanities; Law;
Education; Special Education; Physical Education; Medicine;
Veterinary Medicine; Mathematics; Natural Sciences; Computer
Science; Agriculture and Soil Sciences; Commercial Sciences;
Economics and Business Administration (PhD); Engineering; Social
Sciences; Fine Arts; Nursing, a further 2 yrs

Student Services: Academic counselling, Canteen, Health services, Language programs, Nursery care, Social counselling, Sports
facilities

Student Residential Facilities: Student hostels; Campus dorms

Special Facilities: Art Galleries; Laboratories

Libraries: Faculty Libraries; Central Library; Academic Journals;
Periodical subscriptions

Academic Staff *2008-2009*	MEN	WOMEN	TOTAL
FULL-TIME	–	–	636
STAFF WITH DOCTORATE FULL-TIME	–	–	749
Student Numbers *2008-2009*			
All (Foreign Included)	22,000	26,000	48,000
FOREIGN ONLY	4	11	15

Distance students, 51,100. **Evening students**, 3,100.
Last Updated: 06/05/09

SUEZ CANAL UNIVERSITY

45 Km, New Building, Ismaïlia
Tel: +20(64) 3200-125 +20(64) 3223-007
Fax: +20(64) 320-508
EMail: infor@suez.eun.eg
Website: http://www.scuegypt.edu.eg

President: Farouk Mahmoud Abd El Khader Tel: +20-127-962-994

Centres
Education Development (Education)

Faculties

Agriculture (Agricultural Business; Agricultural Engineering; Agriculture; Agronomy; Animal Husbandry; Botany; Crop Production;
Fishery; Food Science; Food Technology; Horticulture; Plant and
Crop Protection; Soil Science); **Arts and Humanities**; **Commerce**
(Accountancy; Advertising and Publicity; Business Administration;
Business and Commerce; Economics; Insurance; Marketing; Political Sciences; Public Relations; Statistics; Taxation); **Computer
and Information Science** (Computer Science; Information Sci-
ences; Mathematics and Computer Science); **Dentistry** (Dentistry);
Education (Curriculum; Education; Educational Psychology; Edu-
cational Sciences; Home Economics; Pedagogy; Social Psychol-
ogy); **Medicine** (Anaesthesiology; Anatomy; Biochemistry;
Cardiology; Community Health; Dermatology; Genetics; Gynaecol-
ogy and Obstetrics; Histology; Medicine; Microbiology; Neurology;
Occupational Health; Ophthalmology; Osteopathy; Paediatrics;
Pathology; Physiology; Psychiatry and Mental Health; Public Health;
Radiology; Speech Therapy and Audiology; Surgery; Tropical
Medicine; Urology); **Nursing** (Nursing); **Pharmacy** (Analytical
Chemistry; Biochemistry; Immunology; Microbiology; Organic
Chemistry; Pharmacology; Pharmacy; Toxicology); **Science** (Bot-
any; Chemistry; Geology; Marine Science and Oceanography;
Mathematics and Computer Science; Natural Sciences; Toxicology;
Zoology); **Tourism and Hotel Management** (Hotel Management;
Tourism); **Veterinary Medicine** (Biochemistry; Forensic Medicine
and Dentistry; Histology; Microbiology; Parasitology; Pathology;
Pharmacology; Physiology; Veterinary Science; Wildlife; Zoology)

Research Institutes
Biotechnology (Biotechnology)

Further Information: Also Teaching Hospital

History: Founded 1976. A State institution under the supervision of
the Ministry of Higher Education.

Governing Bodies: University Council

Academic Year: September to June (September-January; February-June)

Admission Requirements: Secondary school certificate or
equivalent

Main Language(s) of Instruction: Arabic

Degrees and Diplomas: *Baccalaureos*: Arts in Education (BSc);
Commerce (BSc); Science (BSc); Science in Agriculture (BSc);
Science in Education (BSc), 4 yrs; *Baccalaureos*: Engineering
(BSc); Pharmacy, Science in Veterinary Science, Dentistry (BSc), 5
yrs; *Baccalaureos*: Medicine and Surgery (BSc), 6 yrs; *Magistr
(MSc)*: a further 1-5 yrs; *Doktora (PhD)*: a further 4-5 yrs. Also
postgraduate Diplomas

Student Residential Facilities: Yes

Libraries: Central Library, c. 6,500 vols; faculty libraries, c. 190,000

Publications: Scientific Bulletins (Human Sciences, Basic Sciences, Applied Sciences)

Press or Publishing House: Suez Canal University Press

Academic Staff *2008-2009:* Total: c. 700
Student Numbers *2008-2009:* Total: c. 13,000
Last Updated: 20/05/09

NORTH SINAI BRANCH

El-Arish
EMail: webmaster@suez-foe.com

Faculties
Education (Education); **Environmental Agricultural Sciences** (Agriculture; Environmental Studies)

Degrees and Diplomas: *Baccalaureos*; *Magistr*, *Doktora*. Also Postgraduate Diploma

PORT-SAID BRANCH

Port-Said
EMail: webmaster@suez-foe.com
Vice-Chancellor: Hatef Alm El-din (2007-)

Faculties
Commerce (Accountancy; Business Administration; Business and Commerce; Economics; Finance; Insurance; Law; Mathematics and Computer Science; Political Sciences; Public Relations; Statistics); **Education** (Arabic; Chemistry; Education; Educational Psychology; Islamic Studies; Literature; Mathematics; Modern Languages; Physics; Social Sciences); **Engineering** (Engineering); **Kindergarten** (Preschool Education); **Nursing** (Nursing; Paediatrics; Psychiatry and Mental Health; Public Health); **Physical Education** (Physical Education); **Science** (Botany; Chemistry; Geology; Marine Science and Oceanography; Mathematics and Computer Science; Natural Sciences; Toxicology; Zoology); **Special Education** (Special Education)

Higher Institutes
Management and Computer (Computer Engineering; Management)

History: Founded 1989.

SUEZ BRANCH

Suez
EMail: Webmaster@Suez-foe.com
Vice-Chancellor: Fahim Khlefa (2007-)

Faculties
Commerce (Business and Commerce); **Education** (Education); **Industrial Education** (Industrial Arts Education); **Petroleum Engineering and Mining** (Mining Engineering; Petroleum and Gas Engineering); **Science** (Botany; Chemistry; Geology; Marine Science and Oceanography; Mathematics and Computer Science; Natural Sciences; Toxicology; Zoology)

Degrees and Diplomas: *Baccalaureos*; *Magistr*, *Doktora*

TANTA UNIVERSITY

PO Box 31512, El-Geish Street, Tanta, Al-Gharbia
Tel: +20(40) 337-7929
Fax: +20(40) 331-3308
EMail: president@tanta.edu.eg
Website: http://www.tanta.edu.eg

President: AbdelFattah Abdel Mongy Sadakah
Tel: +20(40) 331-7928, Fax: +20(40) 330-2785

Vice-President for Graduate Studies and Research: Mohamed Adel KhalifaFax: +20(40) 332-8004
EMail: makhalifa@tanta.edu.eg; makhalifa@hotmail.com

International Relations: Mohamed Shafik Saied, Vice-President
Tel: +20(40) 330-5978, Fax: +20(40) 330-5978
EMail: mshafeek@dec1.tanta.eun.eg

Faculties
Agriculture (Agricultural Equipment; Agriculture; Agronomy; Animal Husbandry; Botany; Dairy; Economics; Food Science; Food Technology; Genetics; Horticulture; Soil Science); **Arts** (Arabic; Arts and Humanities; French; Geography; History; Philosophy; Psychology; Sociology); **Commerce** (Accountancy; Business Administration; Business and Commerce; Economics; Finance; Insurance; Mathematics; Public Administration; Statistics; Taxation); **Dentistry** (Dentistry); **Education** (Science Education); **Engineering** (Architecture; Design; Electrical Engineering; Electronic Engineering; Engineering; Hydraulic Engineering; Irrigation; Mathematics; Mechanical Engineering; Physical Engineering; Production Engineering; Town Planning); **Law** (Law); **Medicine** (Anaesthesiology; Gynaecology and Obstetrics; Medicine; Paediatrics); **Nursing** (Gynaecology and Obstetrics; Nursing; Paediatrics); **Pharmacy** (Biochemistry; Microbiology; Pharmacy; Toxicology); **Physical Education** (Physical Education); **Science** (Botany; Chemistry; Geology; Mathematics; Natural Sciences; Physics; Zoology); **Specific Education** (Art Education; Educational Technology; Home Economics; Mass Communication; Music Education; Psychology)

Further Information: Also Teaching Hospital and Study Abroad Programmes

History: Founded 1972, incorporating Faculties attached to the University of Alexandria. A State Institution under the supervision of the Ministry of Higher Education.

Governing Bodies: University Council, comprising seventeen members

Academic Year: October to June

Admission Requirements: Secondary school certificate or equivalent

Fees: None

Main Language(s) of Instruction: Arabic, English

International Co-operation: With universities in Hungary, USA, Turkey, Romania, Uzbekistan, Poland, United Kingdom, France, China, Morocco, Jordan, Syria, Saudi Arabia.

Degrees and Diplomas: *Diploma*: Commerce; Education; Law, 2 yrs; *Baccalaureos*: Agriculture; Arts; Arts in Education; Commerce; Law; Science; Science in Education, 4 yrs; *Baccalaureos*: Dentistry; Pharmacy, 5 yrs; *Baccalaureos*: Medicine and Surgery, 6 yrs; *Magistr*: a further 1-6 yrs; *Doktora*: Arts, Dentistry, Law, Medicine, Philosophy, Agriculture, Commerce, Pharmacy, Nursing, Education, a further 2 yrs; *Doktora*: Science, Engineering, Specific Education, Physical Education, Veterinary Medicine, a further 2-3 yrs

Student Residential Facilities: Yes

Libraries: Faculty libraries: c. 135,000 vols in Arabic; c. 85,000 vols in other languages

Publications: Commerce and Finance *(biannually)*
Last Updated: 17/08/09

TIBIN INSTITUTE FOR METALLURGICAL STUDIES

Tibin Iron and Steal St., Helwan, Cairo
Tel: +20(2) 501-1575 +20(2) 501-0176
Fax: +20(2) 501-0171 +20(2) 501-0170
EMail: tins@idsc.gov.eg

Programmes
Chemical Industries (Chemical Engineering); **Metallurgical Engineering**; **Mining Engineering** (Mining Engineering)

Degrees and Diplomas: Diploma of Specialization
Last Updated: 17/08/09

ZAGAZIG UNIVERSITY

Zagazig, Sharkia 44519
Tel: +20(55) 238-470
Fax: +20(55) 238-470
EMail: info@zu.edu.eg
Website: http://www.zu.edu.eg

President: Mohamed Mahmoud Abdelul Aal
Tel: +20(55) 230-2926, Fax: +20(55) 234-5452

Vice-President for Postgraduate Studies: Mohamed Bahgat Awad

International Relations: Ahmed Hashim Basyuny

Faculties

Agriculture (Agriculture; Agronomy; Animal Husbandry; Biochemistry; Fruit Production; Geophysics; Harvest Technology; Nutrition; Plant and Crop Protection); **Arts** (Arabic; Arts and Humanities; English; French; Geography; History; Media Studies; Philosophy; Physiology; Sociology); **Commerce** (Accountancy; Business Administration; Business and Commerce; Mathematics; Statistics); **Computer and Information Science** (Computer Science; Information Sciences; Information Technology); **Education** (Curriculum; Education; Educational Psychology; International and Comparative Education; Pedagogy; Psychiatry and Mental Health); **Engineering** (Civil Engineering; Computer Engineering; Construction Engineering; Electronic Engineering; Engineering; Industrial Engineering; Materials Engineering; Mathematics; Mechanical Engineering; Physical Engineering; Power Engineering; Production Engineering; Structural Architecture); **Law** (Civil Law; Commercial Law; Criminal Law; History of Law; International Law; Islamic Law; Law); **Medicine** (Anaesthesiology; Anatomy; Biochemistry; Cardiology; Community Health; Dermatology; Forensic Medicine and Dentistry; Gynaecology and Obstetrics; Histology; Medicine; Microbiology; Neurology; Ophthalmology; Orthopaedics; Paediatrics; Parasitology; Pathology; Pharmacology; Physiology; Psychiatry and Mental Health; Radiology; Rheumatology; Surgery; Tropical Medicine; Urology); **Nursing** (Gynaecology and Obstetrics; Health Education; Nursing; Surgery); **Pharmacy** (Analytical Chemistry; Biochemistry; Organic Chemistry; Pharmacology; Pharmacy); **Physical Education** (Physical Education); **Physical Education** (for women) (Physical Education); **Science** (Botany; Chemistry; Geology; Mathematics and Computer Science; Natural Sciences; Physics; Zoology); **Special Education** (Art Education; Educational Sciences; Educational Technology; English; Home Economics; Music Education; Preschool Education; Special Education); **Veterinary Medicine**

Higher Institutes

Ancient Near Eastern Studies (Middle Eastern Studies); **Asian Studies and Research** (Asian Studies); **Production Efficiency** (Agriculture; Civil Engineering; Economics; Industrial and Production Economics; Management)

History: Founded 1969 as a branch of Ain-Shams University. Acquired present status 1974.

Academic Year: October to May (October-January; January-May)

Admission Requirements: Secondary school certificate or equivalent

Fees: None

Main Language(s) of Instruction: Arabic, English, French

Degrees and Diplomas: Diploma; Baccalaureos: Arts (BA); Science (BSc), 4-6 yrs; Magistr: Arts (MA); Science (MSc), a further 2-4 yrs; Doktora (PhD): 3 yrs following Magistr

Student Services: Canteen, Cultural centre, Foreign student adviser, Handicapped facilities, Health services, Nursery care, Social counselling, Sports facilities

Student Residential Facilities: Yes

Special Facilities: Tell Basta Museum (Arts)

Libraries: Central Library; libraries of the Faculties

Publications: Scientific Journals
Last Updated: 19/02/09

PRIVATE INSTITUTIONS

AKHBAR AL-YOUM ACADEMY FOR ENGINEERING, PRINTING AND PRESS TECHNOLOGY

Presses Complex, Akhbar Al-Youm Building, Fourth Industrial Zone, 6th of October City, Giza
Tel: +20(11) 334-811

Director: Ahmad Zaki Badr (2000-)

Departments
Administration; **Computer and Information Technology** (Computer Science; Information Technology); **Engineering** (Engineering); **Printing and Press Technology** (Printing and Printmaking)

History: Founded 1999.
Degrees and Diplomas: Baccalaureos: 4 yrs; Baccalaureos: Engineering, 5 yrs
Last Updated: 29/05/07

AL-ABBASYA INSTITUTE FOR COMPUTERS AND COMMERCIAL SCIENCES

Abdu Basha Square, Abbasya

Departments
Computer Science (Computer Science); **Finance**

History: Founded 1958 as "The Management and Secretarial Institute in Al-Abbasya". Acquired present title 1996.

Degrees and Diplomas: Diploma: Finance, 2 yrs; Baccalaureos: Computer Science, 4 yrs
Last Updated: 18/06/07

AL-AHRAM CANADIAN UNIVERSITY

6th of October City, Giza
Tel: +20(2) 833-3078
Fax: +20(2) 833-4379
EMail: info@acu.edu.eg
Website: http://www.acu.edu.eg

President: Farouk Ismail

Faculties
Business Administration (Accountancy; Economics; Finance; Hotel Management; Management; Public Health; Tourism); **Computer Science and Information Technology**; **Mass Communication** (Advertising and Publicity; Communication Arts; Graphic Arts; Journalism; Mass Communication; Public Relations; Radio and Television Broadcasting); **Pharmacy** (Biochemistry; Microbiology; Pharmacology; Pharmacy; Toxicology)

History: Founded 2004.

Degrees and Diplomas: Baccalaureos: 4 yrs
Last Updated: 17/08/09

AL-ALSUN HIGHER INSTITUTE OF TOURISM AND HOTEL MANAGEMENT (AHITH)

Block n° 96, Makram Ebeid Ex., 8th District, Nasr City, Cairo
Tel: +20(2) 287-7522

Director: Nadia Refa'at Abdel-Rahman (2000-)

Departments
Computer Science (Computer Science); **Hotel Management** (Hotel Management); **Tourism Studies** (Tourism); **Tourist Guidance**

History: Founded 1992.

Degrees and Diplomas: Baccalaureos; Magistr. Also Postgraduate Diploma.
Last Updated: 15/06/07

ALEXANDRIA HIGHER INSTITUTE OF ENGINEERING AND TECHNOLOGY

Victor Emanuel Str., Sidi Gaber, Samouha, Alexandria
Tel: +20(3) 425-4942
EMail: info@ait.edu.eg
Website: http://www.ait.edu.eg/index.htm

Dean: El-Sayed Abdel-Moety El-Badawy

Departments
Computer Engineering (Computer Engineering); **Electronics and Communications Engineering** (Electronic Engineering; Telecommunications Engineering); **Industrial Engineering** (Industrial Engineering); **Mechatronics Engineering** (Electronic Engineering; Mechanical Engineering)

History: Founded 1996. Acquired present status 1997.

Degrees and Diplomas: Baccalaureos (BSc): 5 yrs
Last Updated: 23/09/09

AL-MA'AREF HIGHER INSTITUTE FOR LANGUAGES AND TRANSLATION

10, Nasouh Str., Al-Zaytoun
Tel: +20(2) 2257-1324
Fax: +20(2) 2258-005

Director: Mohamed R. Radwan (2005-)
EMail: prfradwan@hotmail.com

Chairman: Micheal Magdy

Institutes

Languages and Translation (Modern Languages; Translation and Interpretation)

History: Founded 1994. Accredited 2006.

Governing Bodies: Board of Directors

Admission Requirements: General Secondary Certificate

Accrediting Agencies: Supreme Council for Universities

Degrees and Diplomas: *Baccalaureos*: 4 yrs

Student Services: Academic counselling, Canteen, Foreign student adviser, Language programs, Nursery care, Social counselling, Sports facilities

Special Facilities: Language laboratories

Libraries: Yes

Academic Staff 2008-2009	MEN	WOMEN	TOTAL
FULL-TIME	5	1	6
STAFF WITH DOCTORATE			
FULL-TIME	5	1	6
PART-TIME	6	–	6

Last Updated: 27/07/09

AL-MADINA HIGHER INSTITUTE FOR INTERNATIONAL LANGUAGES

Shoubra Ment

Director: Ahmad Kamal Mohamed Safwat

Departments

English (English); **French** (French); **German** (German)

Governing Bodies: The Board of Institute managerial directors; Dean of the Institute

Admission Requirements: Secondary school certificate (thanawya amma) or equivalent.

Degrees and Diplomas: *Baccalaureos*

Last Updated: 24/05/07

AL-OBOUR HIGHER INSTITUTE FOR ENGINEERING AND TECHNOLOGY

31 Km Ismailia Desert Road, Cairo
Tel: +20(2) 477-0037
Fax: +20(2) 241-3550

Director: Refa'at Rezq Baseli (2000-)

Programmes

Architectural Engineering (Structural Architecture); **Computer and Control Technology Engineering** (Automation and Control Engineering; Computer Engineering); **Construction Engineering** (Construction Engineering); **Electronics and Communciation Technology Engineering** (Electronic Engineering; Telecommunications Engineering)

History: Founded 1996.

Main Language(s) of Instruction: English

Degrees and Diplomas: *Baccalaureos*: 5 yrs

Last Updated: 29/05/07

AL-OBOUR HIGHER INSTITUTE FOR MANAGEMENT AND INFORMATICS

21, Belbais High Way, Sharquia
Tel: +20(2) 263-6882
Fax: +20(2) 403-0804
EMail: info@ahiedu.com
Website: http://www.ahiedu.com/en/

President: Abd Allah El-Dahshan

Programmes

Business Administration (Accountancy; Business Administration; Management); **Computer Science** (Computer Science); **Management Information System** (Information Management; Information Sciences; Management)

History: Founded 1999.

Degrees and Diplomas: *Baccalaureos*: 4 yrs
Last Updated: 19/02/09

ARAB ACADEMY FOR SCIENCE, TECHNOLOGY AND MARITIME TRANSPORT (AASTMT)

PO Box 1029, Gamal Abdel Nasser Street, Miami, Alexandria
Tel: +20(3) 556-1497 +20(3) 556-5429
Fax: +20(3) 548-7786 +20(3) 550-6042
EMail: admission@aast.edu
Website: http://www.aast.edu

President: Mohamed Farghaly
Tel: +20(3) 548-7785, Fax: +20(3) 548-7786
EMail: mofarghali@aast.edu; mofarghali@yahoo.com

Director, Public Relations: Ayman Ghonem Tel: 2,010 161 06 20

International Relations: Ibrahim El-Mohr, Vice President for Education
Tel: +20(3) 562-4027, Fax: +20(3) 562-4027
EMail: ielmohr@aast.edu; ielmohry@yahoo.com

Centres

Industrial Service Center; **Maritime Research and Consultation**

Colleges

Computing and Information Technology (Computer Science; Information Technology); **Engineering and Technology** (Architectural and Environmental Design; Automation and Control Engineering; Computer Engineering; Construction Engineering; Electrical and Electronic Engineering; Engineering; Industrial Engineering; Marine Engineering; Mechanical Engineering; Natural Sciences; Technology); **International Transport and Logistics** (Transport and Communications; Transport Management); **Management and Technology** (Arts and Humanities; Business Administration; Hotel Management; Management; Modern Languages; Tourism); **Maritime Transport** (Economics; Fishery; Management; Marine Engineering; Marine Science and Oceanography; Marine Transport; Meteorology; Nautical Science; Safety Engineering)

Graduate Schools

Business (Business Administration; Business and Commerce)

Institutes

Advanced Management; **Investment and Finance**; **Language Studies**; **Port Training**; **Productivity and Total Quality** (Production Engineering; Safety Engineering); **Sea Training**

Further Information: Also campus in Syria

History: Founded 1972. A specialized University in Maritime Transport and Building. The majority of national staff members and personnel provided by the Egyptian Government.

Governing Bodies: Board of Directors

Academic Year: September to June

Admission Requirements: High school certificate and admission test

Main Language(s) of Instruction: English; Arabic

International Co-operation: With universities in USA and UK

Degrees and Diplomas: *Baccalaureos*: Engineering; Business; Logistics, 4-5 yrs; *High Diploma*: Engineering; Management; Computer Science, 1 further yr; *Magistr*: Engineering; Computer Science and Management (MSc), a further 2 yrs; *Doktora*: Security Engineering; Business Administration (DSc), a further 3 yrs. Also Master's Degree in Computer Science from George Washington University, USA (off-campus degree)

Student Services: Academic counselling, Canteen, Cultural centre, Employment services, Foreign student adviser, Health services, Language programs, Social counselling, Sports facilities

Libraries: AASTMT Library, c. 36,000 vols, 350 periodicals
Publications: Journal of Arab Maritime Academy *(biannually)*; MRCC Research Magazine *(annually)*

Academic Staff 2008-2009	MEN	WOMEN	TOTAL
FULL-TIME	507	186	**693**
PART-TIME	910	390	**1,300**
STAFF WITH DOCTORATE			
FULL-TIME	197	47	**244**
PART-TIME	500	200	**700**
Student Numbers 2008-2009			
All (Foreign Included)	14,000	6,000	**20,000**
FOREIGN ONLY	1,800	200	**2,000**

Last Updated: 24/07/09

ARAB OPEN UNIVERSITY - EGYPT BRANCH

Intersection of Makram Ebeid Street and Abd Al-Razeq Al-Sanhoury Street, Nasr City, Cairo
Tel: +20(2) 671-1862 +20(2) 671-1865
Fax: +20(2) 671-1868
EMail: info@aou.edu.eg
Website: http://www.aou.edu.eg

Branch Director: Abdel Aziz Khamis

Faculties
Business Administration (Business Administration); **English Language and Literature** (English; Literature)

Programmes
Information Technology and Computer Science (Computer Science; Information Technology)

Degrees and Diplomas: *Baccalaureos*
Last Updated: 19/02/09

CAIRO ACADEMY OF ARTS

Gamal El-Din Al-Afghani Str., Al-Haram Route, Giza
Tel: +20(2) 585-0727
Fax: +20(2) 561-1230
EMail: aoarts@idsc.gov.eg

Director: Madkour Ahmad

Conservatories
Music (Music)

Higher Institutes
Arab Music (Music); **Art Criticism** (Art Criticism); **Ballet**; **Cinema**; **Folklore** (Folklore); **Theatre** (Theatre)

History: Founded 1959. Acquired present status 1969.

Degrees and Diplomas: *Diploma*; *Baccalaureos*; *Magistr*, *Doktora*
Last Updated: 05/06/07

CAIRO HIGHER INSTITUTE FOR COMPUTER, INFORMATION SYSTEMS AND ADMINISTRATION "AL-GOLF"

2, Samir Mokhtar Str., Nabil Al-Waqad Corner, Ard Al-Golf, Heliopolis
Tel: +20(2) 417-6550
Fax: +20(2) 417-6551

Director: Mohamed Abdul-Moneim Hashish (1995-)

Departments
Business Administration and Information System (Business Administration; Information Sciences); **Computer Science** (Computer Science); **Engineering** (Electronic Engineering; Structural Architecture)

History: Founded 1995.

Degrees and Diplomas: *Baccalaureos*: 4 yrs; *Baccalaureos*: Engineering, 5 yrs
Last Updated: 29/05/07

CAIRO HIGHER INSTITUTE FOR LANGUAGES, SIMULTANEOUS TRANSLATION AND ADMINISTRATIVE SCIENCES

Muqatam, Tugaryyan Station, 5 Str. N° 54, off Route 9, In front of Al-Quds Mosque, Cairo
Tel: +20(2) 508-1700
Fax: +20(2) 508-1613

Director: Mohamed Rehan Hussein (2002-)

Departments
Administrative Sciences (Accountancy; Administration; Business Administration; International Business); **Computer Science**; **Languages and Simultaneous Translation**

History: Founded 1995.

Degrees and Diplomas: *Baccalaureos*: 4 yrs
Last Updated: 29/05/07

CAIRO HIGHER INSTITUTE FOR TOURISM AND HOTELS (CHITH)

Muqatam, Tugaryyan Station, 5 St. n° 54, off Route 9, In front of Al-Quds Mosque, Cairo
Tel: +20(2) 508-1600
Fax: +20(2) 508-3303

Director: Mohamed Baher Omar (2002-)

Departments
Hotel Management (Hotel Management); **Tourism Guidance**; **Tourism Studies** (Tourism)

History: Founded 1995.

Main Language(s) of Instruction: Arabic and other Foreign Languages

Degrees and Diplomas: *Baccalaureos*: 4 yrs
Special Facilities: Computer Laboratories
Last Updated: 29/05/07

CANADIAN INTERNATIONAL COLLEGE - CAIRO CAMPUS (CIC)

El Tagamoa El Khames, South of the Police Academy New Cairo City, New Cairo
Tel: +20(10) 288-0288
Fax: +20(2) 617-3110
EMail: admission@cic-cairo.com
Website: http://www.cic-cairo.com/cic/

President: Magdy El Kady
Tel: +20 16242 EMail: magdy_elkady@cic-cairo.com

Academic Vice-President: Roger Winn
Tel: +20 16242 EMail: roger_winn@cic-cairo.com

International Relations: Roger Winn

Schools
Business (Business Administration); **Engineering** (Electrical and Electronic Engineering; Engineering; Industrial Engineering; Technology); **Mass Communication** (Mass Communication)

History: Founded 2004.

Governing Bodies: Ministry of Higher Education of Egypt -Cape Breton University

Academic Year: September to May (September-January; February-May)

Fees: (Egyptian Pounds): 30,000

Main Language(s) of Instruction: English

Degrees and Diplomas: *Baccalaureos*. Canadian Bachelor of Business Administration Degree, with concentrations (majors) available in Marketing, Finance, Accounting and Tourism Management; Canadian Bachelor of Technology in Manufacturing Engineering or Computer Systems Development.

Student Services: Academic counselling, Canteen, Cultural centre, Employment services, Foreign student adviser, Foreign Studies Centre, Handicapped facilities, Health services, Language programs, Nursery care, Social counselling, Sports facilities

Libraries: Yes. Also Audio Visual Material

Academic Staff 2008-2009	TOTAL
FULL-TIME	300
PART-TIME	30

Student Numbers 2008-2009
All (Foreign Included) c. 1,000
Last Updated: 17/08/09

DELTA UNIVERSITY FOR SCIENCE AND TECHNOLOGY

Gamasa Coastal International Road, El Mansourah
EMail: info@deltauniv.edu.eg
Website: http://deltauniv.edu.eg

President: Abbas El-Hefnawy (2000-)
EMail: abbaselhefnawy@yahoo.com

Faculties
Business Administration (Business Administration); **Engineering** (Engineering)

History: Acquired present status 2000. Formerly known as Delta Higher Institute for Computers.

Main Language(s) of Instruction: Arabic; English

Accrediting Agencies: Ministry of Higher Education

Degrees and Diplomas: *Baccalaureos*: 4 yrs

Student Services: Academic counselling, Canteen, Cultural centre, Employment services, Foreign student adviser, Foreign Studies Centre, Health services, Language programs, Nursery care, Social counselling, Sports facilities
Last Updated: 28/09/09

EGYPTIAN HIGHER INSTITUTE FOR TOURISM AND HOTELS (EHITH)

6 Al-Obour St., Off Al-Tahrair St., behind Sheraton Airport Housing, Heliopolis
Tel: +20(2) 266-5951
Fax: +20(2) 266-5950

Director: Ahmad Abdul-Razek Mohamed (2001-)

Departments
Hotel Management (Hotel Management); **Tourism Guidance** (Tourism); **Tourism Studies** (Tourism)

History: Founded 1992.

Main Language(s) of Instruction: Arabic and other Foreign Languages

Degrees and Diplomas: *Baccalaureos*

Special Facilities: Laboratories
Libraries: Yes
Last Updated: 15/06/07

EGYPTIAN HIGHER INSTITUTE OF THE ALEXANDRIA ACADEMY FOR ADMINISTRATION AND ACCOUNTING

Mosque Square, behind Al-Moursa Abu Al-Aabbas Mosque, Alexandria
Tel: +20(3) 484-3384

Director: Adel Abdel-Hamid Ez (2000-)

Departments
Accountancy; **Auditing**; **Finance** (Finance); **Management** (Finance; Management)

History: Founded 1996.

Main Language(s) of Instruction: Arabic; English for programmes offered at the Management Department.

Degrees and Diplomas: *Baccalaureos*: 4 yrs
Last Updated: 29/05/07

EGYPTIAN RUSSIAN UNIVERSITY (ERU)

Badr City, Kilo 42, Suez Road, Cairo
Tel: +20(2) 2864-3342
Fax: +20(2) 2864-3332
EMail: info@eruegypt.com
Website: http://www.eruegypt.com

President: Sherif Helmy (2006-) EMail: president@eruegypt.com
Secretary-General: Ekram Agha

Faculties
Engineering (Aeronautical and Aerospace Engineering; Construction Engineering; Electronic Engineering; Energy Engineering; Engineering; Mechanical Engineering; Nuclear Engineering; Structural Architecture; Telecommunications Engineering); **Pharmacy** (Biochemistry; Chemistry; Microbiology; Pharmacy; Toxicology)

History: Founded 2006.

Admission Requirements: Thanwey Ama or equivalent

Main Language(s) of Instruction: English

International Co-operation: With universities in Russia

Degrees and Diplomas: *Baccalaureos*: 5- 5 1/2 yrs

Student Services: Academic counselling, Canteen, Sports facilities

Student Residential Facilities: Yes

Student Numbers 2008-2009	MEN	WOMEN	TOTAL
All (Foreign Included)	450	400	850

Last Updated: 02/06/09

EL SHOROUK ACADEMY

El Abasya Square El Moltka Towers, Elnakheel Suburb, 6th of October City, Giza Al-Shorouk Academy
Tel: +20(2) 687-0881 +20(2) 687-0882 +20(2) 687-0883
Fax: +20(2) 687-0887
EMail: info@elshoroukacademy.edu.eg
Website: http://www.elshoroukacademy.edu.eg

President: Mohamed Farid Khamis

Higher Institutes
Computer and Information Technology (Computer Engineering; Information Technology); **Engineering** (Computer Engineering; Construction Engineering; Electronic Engineering; Engineering; Industrial Engineering; Information Technology)

History: Founded 1995. Acquired present status 2002.

Admission Requirements: Secondary school certificate (Thanaweya Amma) or equivalent.

Degrees and Diplomas: *Baccalaureos*: 5 yrs
Last Updated: 19/02/09

FRENCH UNIVERSITY IN EGYPT

Université française d'Egypte (UFE)
BP 21, Km 37 Cairo-Ismailia Highway, Shorouk City
Tel: +20(2) 687-34-00 +20(2) 687-52-52
Fax: +20(2) 687-53-53
EMail: info@ufe.eg.org
Website: http://www.ufe.edu.eg/

President: Osman Lotfy El Sayed
EMail: rania.elsebaee@ufe.edu.eg

Vice-Président: Jean-Pierre Faugère

Faculties
Applied Languages (Modern Languages); **Engineering** (Automation and Control Engineering; Information Technology; Production Engineering; Telecommunications Engineering); **Management and Information Technology** (Information Management; Information Technology; Management)

Units
Lifelong Education and Distance Education (Continuing Education; Distance Education)

History: Founded 2002.

Degrees and Diplomas: *Baccalaureos*. Also Licence and Master
Last Updated: 17/08/09

FUTURE UNIVERSITY

Al Tagamoa Al Khames, End of 90th Street, New Cairo
Tel: +20(2) 261-86100 +20(2) 261-86110
Fax: +20(2) 261-86111
EMail: info@fue.edu.eg
Website: http://www.futureuniversity.edu.eg

President: Ebada Sarhan

Faculties
Commerce and Business Administration (Business Administration; Business and Commerce); **Computers and Information Technology** (Computer Networks; Information Technology); **Economics and Political Science** (Economics; Political Sciences); **Engineering and Technology** (Engineering; Technology); **Oral and Dental Medicine** (Dentistry; Oral Pathology); **Pharmaceutical Sciences and Pharmaceutical Industries**

History: Founded 2006.

Degrees and Diplomas: *Baccalaureos*
Last Updated: 17/08/09

HIGHER INSTITUTE FOR ADMINISTRATION AND COMPUTERS

Street 51, Next to the Labour University, Ras Al-Barr, Damietta

Departments
Administration (Administration); **Computer Science** (Computer Science)

Degrees and Diplomas: *Baccalaureos*: 4 yrs
Last Updated: 18/06/07

HIGHER INSTITUTE FOR ADMINISTRATION AND TECHNOLOGY

Sakkara Tourist Road, Shoubra Ment

Departments
Business Administration (Business Administration; Finance; Industrial Management; Marketing); **Computer Sciences** (Computer Science; Information Sciences)

History: Founded 2000.

Degrees and Diplomas: *Baccalaureos*: 4 yrs
Last Updated: 18/06/07

HIGHER INSTITUTE FOR ADMINISTRATION SCIENCES - 6TH OF OCTOBER CITY

Science and Culture City, Central area, Plot 1/1, Central Route, 6th of October City, Giza
Tel: +20(11) 354-271

Director: Mohamed Sayed Hamzawi

Departments
Administration (Administration)
History: Founded 1994.

Degrees and Diplomas: *Baccalaureos*: 4 yrs

HIGHER INSTITUTE FOR ADMINISTRATION SCIENCES - NEW CAIRO

Qatamya, Mahmoudia - Housing Project, Third Complex, New Cairo

Departments
Business Administration; **Information Administration System** (Computer Science; Information Sciences; Information Technology)

Degrees and Diplomas: *Baccalaureos*: 4 yrs
Last Updated: 18/06/07

HIGHER INSTITUTE FOR ADMINISTRATION SCIENCES AND COMPUTERS

Seventh Neighbourhood, First Complex, New Cairo

Departments
Administration; **Computer Science** (Computer Science)

Degrees and Diplomas: *Baccalaureos*: 4 yrs
Last Updated: 18/06/07

HIGHER INSTITUTE FOR ADMINISTRATION SCIENCES AND FOREIGN TRADE

Fifth Urban Complex, third district, fourth zone, New Cairo

Programmes
Administrative Information System (Administration; Information Sciences); **Business Administration** (Accountancy; Business Administration; Economics; International Business)

Degrees and Diplomas: *Baccalaureos*: 4 yrs
Last Updated: 04/06/07

HIGHER INSTITUTE FOR APPLIED ARTS, 6TH OF OCTOBER CITY

First District, 6th of October City, Giza, Cairo
Tel: +20(2) 835-2806
Fax: +20(2) 835-2807
EMail: info@appliedarts.org
Website: http://www.appliedarts.org

Chairman: Moustafa Kamal (1998-)
EMail: profkamal@appliedarts.org

Dean: Mahmoud Ahmad Abdel A'al

Departments
Decoration and Interior Design (Furniture Design; Interior Design); **Fashion** (Fashion Design; Jewelry Art; Textile Design); **Graphics and Advertising**; **Industrial Design**

History: Founded 1994.

Main Language(s) of Instruction: Arabic and English

Degrees and Diplomas: *Baccalaureos*: 5 yrs

Special Facilities: Design halls; Lecture rooms; Laboratories; Workshops
Last Updated: 20/02/09

HIGHER INSTITUTE FOR ARCHITECTURE AND BUSINESS ADMINISTRATION TECHNOLOGY (HIABAT)

Third District, 2nd Zone, 6th of October City, Giza
Tel: +20(23) 835-6496 +20(23) 606-9292
Fax: +20(23) 835-9464
EMail: hi4ab@hiinstitutearch.com
Website: http://www.hiinstitutearch.com

Director: Sawsan El-Toukhy (2007-)
EMail: dr_s_eltoukhy@hotmail.com

International Relations: Basma Sherin, International Relations Office EMail: basma_shr@hotmail.com

Schools
Architectural Engineering (Architectural Restoration; Architecture; Building Technologies; Environmental Engineering; Heritage Preservation); **Business Administration Technology**

History: Founded 1993. Acquired status 1999.

Academic Year: Sept - July

Fees: (Egyptian Pounds): 6,995 per annum for home students; 3,000 first year, 1,500 subsequent years for overseas students (Architecture); 3,520 per annum for home students; 2,000 first year, 1,000 subsequent years for overseas students (Business Administration).

Main Language(s) of Instruction: Arabic, English

International Co-operation: with institutions in Germany, Italy and Romania

Degrees and Diplomas: *Baccalaureos*: Architecture Engineering, 5 yrs; *Baccalaureos*: Business Administration, 4 yrs

Student Services: Canteen, Employment services, Sports facilities

Student Residential Facilities: Student hostel

Libraries: 912 vols; 8 periodical subscriptions

Academic Staff 2008-2009	MEN	WOMEN	**TOTAL**
FULL-TIME	32	29	**61**
PART-TIME	26	10	**36**
STAFF WITH DOCTORATE			
FULL-TIME	14	6	**20**
PART-TIME	22	10	**32**
Student Numbers 2008-2009			
All (Foreign Included)	103	62	**165**

Last Updated: 09/03/10

HIGHER INSTITUTE FOR CIVIL AND ARCHITECTURAL ENGINEERING

15th of May City, Third Neighbourhood, Helwan

Departments
Architectural Engineering (Structural Architecture); **Civil Engineering** (Civil Engineering)

Degrees and Diplomas: *Baccalaureos*: 5 yrs
Last Updated: 19/06/07

HIGHER INSTITUTE FOR COMMERCE AND ECOLOGY

Science and Culture City, Central Area, plot 1/1,
6th of October City, Giza

Departments
Business and Commerce; **Ecology** (Ecology)

Degrees and Diplomas: *Baccalaureos*: 4 yrs
Last Updated: 18/06/07

HIGHER INSTITUTE FOR COMMERCIAL SCIENCES AND COMPUTERS

Army Suburb, behind the Education Directorate, Al-Arish,
North Sinai

Departments
Business and Commerce (Business and Commerce); **Computer Science** (Computer Science)

Degrees and Diplomas: *Baccalaureos*: 4 yrs
Last Updated: 18/06/07

HIGHER INSTITUTE FOR COMPUTER SCIENCES AND INFORMATION SYSTEMS - 6TH OF OCTOBER CITY

Science and Culture City, Central Area, plot 1/1,
6th of October City, Giza
Tel: +20(11) 231-041

Director: Hussein Magdy Zain Al-Din (2001-)

Departments
Computer Science (Computer Science); **Information Systems** (Information Management)

History: Founded 1994.

Degrees and Diplomas: *Baccalaureos*: 4 yrs
Last Updated: 01/06/07

HIGHER INSTITUTE FOR COMPUTER SCIENCES AND INFORMATION SYSTEMS - NEW CAIRO

Fifth Urban Complex, Third District, Fourth Zone, New Cairo

Departments
Computer Science (Computer Science); **Information Systems** (Information Management)

Degrees and Diplomas: *Baccalaureos*: 4 yrs
Last Updated: 18/06/07

HIGHER INSTITUTE FOR COMPUTER SCIENCES AND MANAGEMENT TECHNOLOGY

Al-Kouser district, Sohag
Tel: +20(93) 605-714

Director: Ahmad Abdel A'al Al-Darder (1999-)

Departments
Computer Science (Computer Science); **Management Technology** (Management Systems)

History: Founded 1996.

Degrees and Diplomas: *Baccalaureos*: 4 yrs
Last Updated: 01/06/07

HIGHER INSTITUTE FOR COMPUTER STUDIES

31 Km Al-Kafouri, Cairo Alexandria High Way, King Mariot
Tel: +20(3) 448-3200
EMail: info_king@kinginstitutes.edu.eg;
computer_king@kinginstitutes.edu.eg
Website: http://www.kinginstitutes.edu.eg/general/
computerEng.aspx

Departments
Computer Science (Computer Science)

History: Founded 1996.

Degrees and Diplomas: *Baccalaureos*: 4 yrs
Last Updated: 01/06/07

HIGHER INSTITUTE FOR COMPUTERS AND ADMINISTRATION INFORMATION SYSTEMS

Street 72 off Street 9, across from Al-Quds Mosque,
Higher Elevation, Muqatam

Departments
Computer Science (Computer Science); **Information Management** (Information Management)

Degrees and Diplomas: *Baccalaureos*: 4 yrs
Last Updated: 19/06/07

HIGHER INSTITUTE FOR COMPUTERS AND BUSINESS ADMINISTRATION

High Way, Al-Zarqa City, Damietta
Tel: +20(57) 852-236

Director: Rashed Mokhtar (2002-)

Departments
Business Administration (Business Administration); **Computer Science** (Computer Science)

History: Founded 1999.

Degrees and Diplomas: *Baccalaureos*: 4 yrs
Last Updated: 01/06/07

HIGHER INSTITUTE FOR COMPUTERS AND INFORMATION SYSTEMS

Toson's Land, Abi Qier, Abi Qier

Departments
Computer Science (Computer Science); **Information Systems**

Degrees and Diplomas: *Baccalaureos*: 4 yrs
Last Updated: 19/06/07

HIGHER INSTITUTE FOR COOPERATIVE AND ADMINISTRATIVE STUDIES (HICAS)

Al-Mounira, Sayeda Zainab, Cairo
Tel: +20(2) 795-5135
Fax: +20(2) 795-5686

Programmes
Administration (Administration); **Public Administration** (Public Administration); **Social Services** (Social and Community Services)

Degrees and Diplomas: *Baccalaureos*: 4 yrs

HIGHER INSTITUTE FOR DEVELOPED STUDIES

12 Sherif Str., off Al-Haram Str., besides Al-Farouq School, Haram, Giza
Tel: +20(2) 386-0008 +20(2) 384-4030
Fax: +20(2) 388-5405

Departments
Computer Science; **Trade and Accountancy**
History: Founded 1995.
Degrees and Diplomas: *Baccalaureos*: 4 yrs
Last Updated: 01/06/07

HIGHER INSTITUTE FOR ECONOMICS AND THE ENVIRONMENT

Division 1/1, Central Road, 6th of October City, Giza
Tel: +20(11) 231-161

Programmes
Economics and Environmental Studies (Economics; Environmental Studies)
History: Founded 1994.
Degrees and Diplomas: *Baccalaureos*: 4 yrs

HIGHER INSTITUTE FOR ENGINEERING

Neighbourhood n°13, 10th of Ramadan City
Tel: +20(15) 365-667

Programmes
Engineering (Engineering)
History: Founded 1995.
Degrees and Diplomas: *Baccalaureos*: 5 yrs

HIGHER INSTITUTE FOR HOTEL MANAGEMENT "EGOTH"

31, Mostafa Abou Hief Street, Saba Basha, Alexandria
Tel: +20(2) 583-3924 +20(2) 583-3706
Fax: +20(2) 584-2873
EMail: egoth@dataxprs.com.eg
Website: http://www.egoth.com.eg/en/alex.htm

Programmes
Hotel Management (Hotel Management)
Degrees and Diplomas: *Baccalaureos*: 4 yrs
Last Updated: 01/06/07

HIGHER INSTITUTE FOR HOTEL MANAGEMENT "EGOTH"

10 Ahmed Orabi st., Luxor
Tel: +20(95) 237-4821 +20(95) 236-5351
Fax: +20(95) 237-3357
Website: http://www.egoth.com.eg/en/luxor.htm

Programmes
Hotel Management (Hotel Management)
Degrees and Diplomas: *Baccalaureos*: 4 yrs
Last Updated: 01/06/07

HIGHER INSTITUTE FOR INDUSTRIAL ENGINEERING

Division 1/1, Central Route, 6th of October City, Giza
Tel: +20(11) 355-275

Head: Ali Mohamed Tal'at

Programmes
Industrial Engineering (Industrial Engineering)
History: Founded 1994.
Main Language(s) of Instruction: English and Arabic
Degrees and Diplomas: *Baccalaureos*: 5 yrs

HIGHER INSTITUTE FOR LANGUAGES (HIL)

Terminal of Nozha Metro, Sheraton Housing Project, Heliopolis 17361
Tel: +20(2) 226-72689
Fax: +20(2) 226-72689

Head: Fawzia El Sadr EMail: prof.fawziasadr@yahoo.com
Administrative Officer: Mohamed Abdel Salam
International Relations: Ahmed Al-Kahby Tel: +20(0) 050-63531

Departments
English Language and Literature (English; Literature); **French Language and Literature** (French; Literature); **German Language and Literature** (German; Literature); **Spanish Language and Literature** (Literature; Spanish)
Further Information: A Department of Italian Language and Literature is being established.
History: Founded 1993.
Academic Year: December to May (2 academic terms)
Admission Requirements: General Secondary Education Certificate or IGC
Fees: (Egyptian Pounds): 1st year, 1,970; 2nd year, 2,840; 3rd year, 2,985; 4th year, 2,850
Main Language(s) of Instruction: Arabic, English, German, Spanish, French, Italian
International Co-operation: With Education International Inc. and also participates in E.U. Scholarships programmes
Accrediting Agencies: The Supreme Council of Higher Education for B.A. and Ain-Shams University for Postgraduate Studies
Degrees and Diplomas: *Baccalaureos*: Foreign Languages and Literature (English; French; Spanish; German) (B.A.), 4 yrs
Student Services: Academic counselling, Canteen, Cultural centre, Employment services, Foreign student adviser, Foreign Studies Centre, Health services, Language programs, Social counselling, Sports facilities
Special Facilities: Art Galleries
Libraries: Circulating Library
Publications: El Shabab in Arabic *(annually)*
Press or Publishing House: University Printing House

Academic Staff *2008-2009*	MEN	WOMEN	TOTAL
FULL-TIME	7	9	16
STAFF WITH DOCTORATE			
FULL-TIME	4	6	10
Student Numbers *2008-2009*			
All (Foreign Included)	–	–	1,079
FOREIGN ONLY	–	–	13

Last Updated: 28/04/09

HIGHER INSTITUTE FOR LANGUAGES

Division 1/1, Central Route, 6th of October City, Giza
Tel: +20(11) 231-161
Fax: +20(2) 231-560

Programmes
Modern Languages (Modern Languages)
History: Founded 1994.
Degrees and Diplomas: *Baccalaureos*: 4 yrs

HIGHER INSTITUTE FOR LITERARY STUDIES

Km 31 Alexandria Desert Road, Al-Kafouri, King Mariott, Alexandria
Tel: +20(2) 484-6155

Programmes
Literary Studies (Arts and Humanities; Literature)
Degrees and Diplomas: *Baccalaureos*: 4 yrs
Last Updated: 04/06/07

HIGHER INSTITUTE FOR MANAGEMENT AND COMPUTER

Port-Said

Departments
Administration and Computer Science (Administration; Computer Science; Management)

Degrees and Diplomas: *Baccalaureos*

HIGHER INSTITUTE FOR MASS MEDIA AND COMMUNICATION

Science and Culture City, Central area, Plot 1/1, 6th of October City, Giza
Tel: +20(11) 355-281
Fax: +20(2) 266-4472

Departments
Communication Studies (Communication Studies); **Media Studies** (Media Studies)

History: Founded 1994.

Degrees and Diplomas: *Baccalaureos*: 4 yrs
Last Updated: 04/06/07

HIGHER INSTITUTE FOR OPTICS TECHNOLOGY

6 Al-Obour Str., off Al-Tahrair str., Al-Sheraton blocks, Heliopolis
Tel: +20(2) 2267-2688
Fax: +20(2) 2267-2688
EMail: kmshasan@link.net

Dean: Karam Mahmoud El-Shazly (2008-)
Tel: +20(10) 560-2735, Fax: +20(22) 267-2688

Departments
Information Systems (Information Technology); **Optical Technology** (Optical Technology)

Academic Year: September to June (September-January; February-June)

Admission Requirements: Secondary School Certificate and Diploma from a Medium Institute for Optics

Main Language(s) of Instruction: English and Arabic

Degrees and Diplomas: *Baccalaureos*: 4 yrs

Student Services: Academic counselling, Canteen, Cultural centre, Employment services, Foreign student adviser, Foreign Studies Centre, Health services, Language programs, Nursery care, Social counselling, Sports facilities

Academic Staff 2008-2009	MEN	WOMEN	TOTAL
FULL-TIME	12	8	20
PART-TIME	1	2	3
STAFF WITH DOCTORATE			
FULL-TIME	9	1	10
PART-TIME	14	2	16
Student Numbers 2008-2009			
All (Foreign Included)	780	520	1,300
FOREIGN ONLY	20	20	40

Last Updated: 05/05/09

HIGHER INSTITUTE FOR SOCIAL SERVICES - 6TH OF OCTOBER CITY

Science and Culture City, Central Area, Plot 1/1, 6th of October City, Giza
Tel: +20(11) 355-276

Programmes
Social Services (Social and Community Services)

History: Founded 1994.

Degrees and Diplomas: *Baccalaureos*
Last Updated: 04/06/07

HIGHER INSTITUTE FOR SOCIAL SERVICES - ALEXANDRIA

72, Al-Resafa Street, Moharam Bey, Alexandria
Tel: +20(3) 494-8190
Fax: +20(3) 495-1560

Departments
Community Order; **Community Service** (Social and Community Services); **Fundamental Sciences**; **Individual Services** (Social and Community Services; Social Work); **Social Planning** (Social Welfare)

History: Founded 1934.

Degrees and Diplomas: *Baccalaureos*
Last Updated: 04/06/07

HIGHER INSTITUTE FOR SOCIAL SERVICES - ASWAN

Qisar Al-Hagar Street, Aswan
Tel: +20(97) 314-995

Programmes
Social Services (Social and Community Services)

History: Founded 1974.

Degrees and Diplomas: *Baccalaureos*
Last Updated: 04/06/07

HIGHER INSTITUTE FOR SOCIAL SERVICES - DAMANHOUR

Damanhour
Tel: +20(45) 315-386
Fax: +20(45) 318-420

Departments
Social Services (Social and Community Services)

History: Founded 1980.

Degrees and Diplomas: *Baccalaureos*
Last Updated: 04/06/07

HIGHER INSTITUTE FOR SOCIAL SERVICES - KAFR AL-SHEIKH

Al-Gaish Street, Qisar Al-Malak, Kafr Al-Sheikh
Tel: +20(47) 227-835
Fax: +20(47) 223-184

Departments
Social Services (Social and Community Services)

History: Founded 1971.

Degrees and Diplomas: *Baccalaureos*
Last Updated: 04/06/07

HIGHER INSTITUTE FOR SOCIAL SERVICES - MANSOURA

Abdel-Salam Aref Str., Talkha, Mansoura
Tel: +20(50) 367-077

Programmes
Social Services (Social and Community Services)

History: Founded 1995.

Degrees and Diplomas: *Baccalaureos*
Last Updated: 04/06/07

HIGHER INSTITUTE FOR SOCIAL SERVICES - NEW BANHA

Al-Almal Hospital Str., New Benha
Tel: +20(13) 235-885
Fax: +20(13) 220-554

Programmes
Social Services

History: Founded 1993.

Degrees and Diplomas: *Baccalaureos*
Last Updated: 04/06/07

HIGHER INSTITUTE FOR SOCIAL SERVICES - PORT-SAID

Close to Al-Raswa Port, Port-Said
Tel: +20(66) 324-365

Departments
Social Services (Social and Community Services)
History: Founded 1981.
Degrees and Diplomas: *Baccalaureos*
Last Updated: 04/06/07

HIGHER INSTITUTE FOR SOCIAL SERVICES - QENA

Qena
Tel: +20(96) 334-908

Programmes
Social Services (Social and Community Services)
History: Founded 1997.
Degrees and Diplomas: *Baccalaureos*
Last Updated: 04/06/07

HIGHER INSTITUTE FOR SOCIAL SERVICES - SOHAG

Al Kosar district, Akhmem, Sohag
Tel: +20(93) 640-222

Programmes
Social Services (Social and Community Services)
History: Founded 1993.
Degrees and Diplomas: *Baccalaureos*
Last Updated: 04/06/07

HIGHER INSTITUTE FOR SOCIAL WORK - CAIRO

Nasr City, Abdel Latif Hamza Str., Off Ahmed Fakhari str., Sixth area, Cairo
Tel: +20(2) 2272-0557
Fax: +20(2) 2272-0556
EMail: c.g.c@hisw-cairo.com; cgcp@hisw-cairo.com
Website: http://www.hisw-cairo.com

Dean: Ikbal El-Samaloty (1974-)
Senior Administrative Officer: Amin Gamil

Departments
Community Organization (Social and Community Services) *Head*: Sawsan Osman; **Community Services and Social Planning** *Head*: Ikbal El-Samaloty; **Fundamental Sciences** *Head*: Abdel-Khalik Afify; **Group Work** *Head*: Mohamed Mostafa; **Individual Services and Case Work** (Social and Community Services; Social Work) *Head*: Ali Eldin El-Sayed; **Social Work** *Head*: Mohamed Ewies

History: Founded 1937 through the Egyptian Association of Social Studies.
Academic Year: September to May (September-January; February-May)
Admission Requirements: Secondary school certificate
Fees: (Egyptian Pounds): 1st year, 668; 2nd year, 632; 3rd year, 615; 4th year, 599 per annum
Main Language(s) of Instruction: Arabic
International Co-operation: With Colorado University (USA) and institutions in many Arab countries
Accrediting Agencies: Ministry of Higher Education and Scientific Research
Degrees and Diplomas: *Diploma*: Social Work; Family and Childhood Studies, 2 yrs; *Baccalaureos*: 4 yrs
Student Services: Academic counselling, Canteen, Cultural centre, Employment services, Foreign student adviser, Handicapped facilities, Health services, Language programs, Nursery care, Social counselling, Sports facilities
Special Facilities: Theatre; Data Show; Computer Centre

Libraries: Yes. Vols (Arabic and English) in Social Work and for Master's Degree students
Publications: Cairo Magazine for Social Work, Special researches in Social Work in Egypt and other Arab countries *(annually)*
Press or Publishing House: Dar El-Mohandes Printing Press

Academic Staff 2008-2009	MEN	WOMEN	TOTAL
FULL-TIME	23	14	37
PART-TIME	1	4	5
STAFF WITH DOCTORATE			
FULL-TIME	23	14	37
PART-TIME	1	4	5
Student Numbers 2008-2009			
All (Foreign Included)	8,086	12,129	**20,215**

Note: Also 10 assistant teachers and 13 researchers
Last Updated: 05/08/09

HIGHER INSTITUTE FOR SPECIALIZED TECHNOLOGICAL STUDIES

32 Km. Cairo-Ismaïlia Desert Road, Ismaïlia
Tel: +20(2) 477-2888
Fax: +20(2) 477-1900

Departments
Business Administration (Business Administration); **Computer Science** (Computer Science); **Information Technology** (Information Technology)
History: Founded 1993.
Degrees and Diplomas: *Baccalaureos*: 4 yrs
Last Updated: 04/06/07

HIGHER INSTITUTE FOR SPECIFIC STUDIES (HISS)

General Moh Aly Fahmy street behind Siag Hotel, Haram, Giza, Pyramids
Tel: +20(2) 385-9104
Fax: +20(2) 384-5505 +20(2) 374-26552
EMail: info@tmaegypt.com
Website: http://www.tmaegypt.com.eg

Chairman: Mohamed Elbatran
Tel: +202(358) 50660, Fax: +202(358) 51588
EMail: mbatran@idsc.gov.eg
Dean: Mohse Elbatran Tel: +202(385) 9104
International Relations: May Elbatran Tel: +202(374) 26557-8

Departments
Computer Science; **Economics and Business Administration**; **Languages** (English; French; German; Modern Languages); **TMA Development, Training and Consulting** (Computer Science; Environmental Studies; Industrial Management; Management); **Tourism and Hotel Management**
History: Founded 1994.
Governing Bodies: Board of Directors
Academic Year: September to June
Admission Requirements: Thanaweya Amma, High school diploma
Fees: (Egyptian Pounds): 1,400-1,600 (for Egyptians); 1,000 (for non-Egyptian)
Main Language(s) of Instruction: Arabic; English for the Language Department and some Business Administration courses
Accrediting Agencies: Ministry of Higher Education
Degrees and Diplomas: *Baccalaureos*: 4 yrs. Also Diplomas and certificates for short courses (2days to 9 months)
Student Services: Canteen, Foreign student adviser, Health services, Sports facilities
Special Facilities: Museum
Libraries: c. 12,750 vols (books and publication)

Academic Staff 2008-2009	MEN	WOMEN	TOTAL
FULL-TIME	38	26	**64**
PART-TIME	18	15	**33**
STAFF WITH DOCTORATE			
FULL-TIME	17	9	**26**
PART-TIME	4	7	**11**
Student Numbers 2008-2009			
All (Foreign Included)	6,000	2,745	**8,745**
FOREIGN ONLY	575	80	**655**

Distance students, 40.
Last Updated: 29/07/09

HIGHER INSTITUTE FOR SPECIFIC STUDIES (HISTSH)

154 Al-Hegaz Square, Heliopolis

Departments
Hotel Management (Hotel Management); **Tourism Guidance** (Tourism); **Tourism Studies** (Tourism)

Degrees and Diplomas: *Baccalaureos*: 4 yrs
Last Updated: 18/06/07

HIGHER INSTITUTE FOR TOURISM AND HOTELS - 6TH OF OCTOBER CITY

6th District, 6th of October City, Giza
Tel: +20(11) 330-342
EMail: hith@must.edu.eg
Website: http://hith.must.edu.eg

Dean: Hassan El-Mansoury

Departments
Hotel Management (Hotel Management); **Tourism Studies** (Tourism); **Tourist Guidance** (Tourism)

History: Founded 1990.

Degrees and Diplomas: *Baccalaureos*: 4 yrs

Libraries: Yes
Last Updated: 04/06/07

HIGHER INSTITUTE FOR TOURISM AND HOTELS - ALEXANDRIA (HITHK)

Km 31 Alexandria Desert Road, Al-Kafouri, King Mariout, Alexandria
EMail: info_king@kinginstitutes.edu.eg;
tourism_king@kinginstitutes.edu.eg
Website: http://www.kinginstitutes.edu.eg/general/tourismEng.aspx

Departments
Hotels Studies (Hotel Management); **Tourism Guidance** (Tourism); **Tourism Studies** (Tourism)

History: Founded 1996.

Degrees and Diplomas: *Baccalaureos*
Last Updated: 15/06/07

HIGHER INSTITUTE FOR TOURISM AND HOTELS - HURGHADA

Safaga road, Red Sea, Hurghada
Tel: +20(2) 290-1017 +20 65 3464-801
Fax: +20 65-3464-810
EMail: info@hihtm.com.eg
Website: http://www.hihtmhurghada.com

Dean of Institute: Abd-Elfatah El-Sabahy

Chairman: Kamel Hassan Abo Ali
Tel: +20 65-3464-802 EMail: kamel@pickalbotros.com

Vice-President: Khaled Abd-El-Salam Fax: +20 65 3464-801
EMail: khaled@hihtm.com.eg

Programmes
Hotel Management and Tourism (Hotel Management; Tourism)

History: Founded 2000.

Fees: (Egyptian Pounds): 4,200 per annum

Main Language(s) of Instruction: Arabic

Degrees and Diplomas: *Baccalaureos*: 4 yrs

Student Services: Foreign Studies Centre, Health services, Language programs, Sports facilities

Special Facilities: Museum; Computer Lab

Libraries: Yes
Last Updated: 06/05/09

HIGHER INSTITUTE FOR TOURISM, HOTELS AND COMPUTERS (HITHC)

2, Adel Mostafa Chawki St., Seyouf, Alexandria
Tel: +20(3) 526-1505 +20(3) 526-0377
Fax: +20(3) 526-5254
Website: http://www.seyouf.org/en/main/home

Departments
Business and information Systems Management (Business Administration; Information Sciences; Management); **Hotel Management** (Hotel Management); **Tourism** (Tourism)

History: Founded 1992. Acquired present status 1994.

Main Language(s) of Instruction: Arabic; English; French; German.

Accrediting Agencies: Supreme Council of Universities

Degrees and Diplomas: *Baccalaureos*: 4 yrs

Libraries: Yes
Last Updated: 04/06/07

HIGHER INSTITUTE FOR TOURISM, HOTELS AND MONUMENTS RESTORATION

Toson's Land, Abi Qier

Departments
Hotel Management (Hotel Management); **Monuments Restoration** (Restoration of Works of Art); **Tourism Studies**

Degrees and Diplomas: *Baccalaureos*: 4 yrs
Last Updated: 19/06/07

HIGHER INSTITUTE OF ENGINEERING AT EL SHOROUK CITY

Al-Nakheel district, El-Shourouk 11837
Tel: +20(2) 268-70881
Fax: +20(2) 268-70877
EMail: info@elshoroukacademy.edu.eg
Website: http://www.elshoroukacademy.edu.eg

Dean: Hazem Sakr EMail: sakr2000@hotmail.com

Executive Director: Mahmoud Sharaf

International Relations: Doaa Shoieb
EMail: doaashoieb@yahoo.com

Departments
Architectural Engineering (Structural Architecture); **Bio-Medical Engineering** (Biomedical Engineering; Electronic Engineering; Engineering); **Chemical Engineering**; **Civil Engineering** (Civil Engineering); **Electric Power and Machines Engieering** (Electrical Engineering; Machine Building); **Electronics and Communications Engineering** (Electronic Engineering; Telecommunications Engineering)

History: Founded 1995. Acquired present status 2009. Belongs to El-Shorouk Academy.

Admission Requirements: General secondary school certificate in Mathematics.

Fees: (Egyptian Pounds): 9,000 per annum

Main Language(s) of Instruction: English

International Co-operation: Supreme Council of Universities, Authority of Quality Assurance

Degrees and Diplomas: *Baccalaureos*: 5 yrs

Student Services: Academic counselling, Employment services, Handicapped facilities, Health services, Language programs, Social counselling, Sports facilities

Student Residential Facilities: Yes

Libraries: Yes. Also electronic library

Publications: El-Shorouk Journal of Engineering and Applied Science *(quarterly)*

Academic Staff 2008-2009	MEN	WOMEN	TOTAL
FULL-TIME	102	22	**124**
PART-TIME	2	4	**6**
STAFF WITH DOCTORATE			
FULL-TIME	41	2	**43**
PART-TIME	87	6	**93**

Student Numbers 2008-2009
All (Foreign Included) – – **7,704**
Last Updated: 30/07/09

HIGHER INTERNATIONAL INSTITUTE FOR LANGUAGES AND SIMULTANEOUS INTERPRETATION

Fifth urban complex, New Cairo

Programmes
Languages; **Simultaneous Interpretation** (Translation and Interpretation)
Degrees and Diplomas: *Baccalaureos*: 4 yrs
Last Updated: 04/06/07

HIGHER TECHNOLOGICAL INSTITUTE (HTI)

PO Box 228, Industrial Area 2, Next to Small Industries Complex, 10th of Ramadan City
Tel: +20(15) 363-497
Fax: +20(15) 351-296
Website: http://www.hti.edu.eg

Dean: Mohamed amin Alshaheer

Vice-Dean: Hesham Mostafa Tel: +20(15) 364-732

Departments
Architecture Engineering (Architecture); **Basic Science** (Natural Sciences); **Biomedical Engineering** (Biomedical Engineering); **Civil Engineering** (Civil Engineering); **Electrical Engineering and Computers** (Computer Engineering; Electrical Engineering); **Engineering** (Biomedical Engineering; Chemical Engineering; Civil Engineering; Computer Engineering; Electrical Engineering; Engineering; Environmental Engineering; Mechanical Engineering; Structural Architecture; Textile Technology); **Mechanical Engineering** (Mechanical Engineering); **Technology Management and Information** (Accountancy; Chemical Engineering; Computer Engineering; Economics; Electronic Engineering; Engineering; English; Finance; German; Insurance; Management; Marketing; Mechanical Engineering; Operations Research; Physical Education; Production Engineering; Technology)

Further Information: Also branches in Marsa Matrouh and 6th of October City.
History: Founded 1987.
Governing Bodies: Board of Directors; Board of Trustees
Academic Year: September to July (3 semesters)
Admission Requirements: General Secondary School Certificate (Thanaweya Am'ma); International General Certificate of Secondary Education (IGCSE) or equivalent
Fees: (Egyptian Pounds): 10,000 per annum
Main Language(s) of Instruction: English; Arabic
Accrediting Agencies: Supreme Council of Universities; Ministry of Higher Education
Degrees and Diplomas: *Baccalaureos*: Business and Information Technology (BSc), 4 yrs; *Baccalaureos*: Engineering (BSc (Eng)), 5 yrs
Student Services: Academic counselling, Canteen, Cultural centre, Employment services, Foreign student adviser, Language programs, Social counselling, Sports facilities
Student Residential Facilities: Hostel for male and female students
Libraries: Yes
Last Updated: 18/08/09

INSTITUTE FOR ADMINISTRATION AND SECRETARIAT

2 New Woman St., Misr Al-Qadima

Programmes
Administration (Administration); **Secretarial Studies**
History: Founded 1960 as a vocational institute. Acquired present status 1998.
Degrees and Diplomas: *Diploma*: 2 yrs; *Baccalaureos*: 4 yrs
Last Updated: 18/06/07

INSTITUTE OF ARAB STUDIES

1 Association of Arab Lawyers St., Garden City, Cairo
Tel: +20(2) 795-1648 +20(2) 792-2679
Fax: +20(2) 796-2543
Website: http://www.iars.net

Departments
Economy (Economics); **Education**; **Geography** (Geography); **Heritage Verification**; **History** (History); **Law** (Law); **Literature and Language** (Literature; Modern Languages); **Mass Media** (Mass Communication; Media Studies); **Political Sciences** (Political Sciences); **Sociology** (Sociology)
History: Founded 1952.
Degrees and Diplomas: *Diploma*: 2 yrs; *Magistr.* a further 1-3 yrs; *Doktora (Ph.D.)*: at least 2 yrs
Last Updated: 20/02/08

INTERNATIONAL ACADEMY FOR ENGINEERING AND MEDIA SCIENCE (IAEMS)

Egyptian Media Production City, 6th of October City
Tel: +20(2) 855-5380
Fax: +20(2) 855-5489
EMail: info@iams.edu.eg
Website: http://www.iams.edu.eg

President: Mohamed Safwat El-Sherif

Departments
Media Engineering (Engineering; Media Studies); **Media Science** (Media Studies)
History: Founded 2002.
Degrees and Diplomas: *Baccalaureos*. Also offers specialized technical diplomas and advanced training courses
Last Updated: 19/02/09

MISR INTERNATIONAL UNIVERSITY

Cairo-Ismalia Road, Km 28, Cairo
Tel: +20(2) 4777-1560
EMail: miu@miuegypt.edu.eg
Website: http://www.miuegypt.edu.eg/

President: Mohamed Shebl El Komy

Faculties
Al Alsun (English); **Business Administration** (Accountancy; Business Administration; Economics; Finance; International Business; Marketing); **Computer Science** (Computer Science; Information Technology; Software Engineering; Systems Analysis); **Dentistry** (Anatomy; Biochemistry; Botany; Chemistry; Dentistry; Microbiology; Pathology; Pharmacology; Physics; Physiology; Surgery; Zoology); **Engineering** (Architecture; Electronic Engineering; Engineering); **Mass Communication** (Advertising and Publicity; Journalism; Mass Communication; Public Relations; Radio and Television Broadcasting); **Pharmacy** (Pharmacy)
History: Founded 1996.
Governing Bodies: Board of Trustees; University Council
Degrees and Diplomas: *Baccalaureos*
Last Updated: 20/02/09

MISR UNIVERSITY FOR SCIENCE AND TECHNOLOGY (MUST)

P.O. Box 77, Al Motamayez District, 6th of October City, Giza
Tel: +20(11) 3835-468
Fax: +20(11) 3835-4699
EMail: must@must.edu.eg
Website: http://www.must.edu.eg

President: Mohamed H. El-Azzazi
Tel: +20(11) 354-708, Fax: +20(11) 354-689

Registrar: Mahmoud Abd El Rahman
Tel: +20(11) 354-703, Fax: +20(28) 354-699

International Relations: Mostafa M. Kamel, Vice President for International Co-operation and Quality Assurance

Faculties
Applied Medical Science Dean: Fatma El-Sharkawy; **Biotechnology** (Biotechnology); **Business and Economics** (Accountancy; Business Administration; Business and Commerce; Computer Science; Economic and Finance Policy; Finance; Health Administration; Information Sciences; Political Sciences); **Dental Surgery**; **Engineering** (Biomedical Engineering; Computer Engineering; Construction Engineering; Electronic Engineering; Industrial Engineering; Software Engineering; Structural Architecture; Telecommunications Engineering); **Foreign Languages and Translation** (Modern Languages; Translation and Interpretation); **Information Technology**; **Mass Media and Communication Technology** (Advertising and Publicity; Journalism; Public Relations; Radio and Television Broadcasting); **Medicine** (Medicine); **Pharmacy** (Pharmacy); **Physical Therapy**

History: Founded 1996.

Main Language(s) of Instruction: Arabic and English

Degrees and Diplomas: Baccalaureos; Magistr; Doktora

Student Services: Academic counselling, Canteen, Cultural centre, Employment services, Foreign student adviser, Foreign Studies Centre, Health services, Language programs, Nursery care, Social counselling, Sports facilities
Last Updated: 17/08/09

MODERN ACADEMY

304 Saqr Qureish St, New Maadi
Tel: +20(2)) 72 70 518
EMail: infocs@modern-academy.edu.eg
Website: http://www.modern-academy.edu.eg

Dean: Nabil Deabes

Departments
Computer Science and Management Technology (Accountancy; Computer Science; Economics; Management); **Engineering and Technology** (Architecture; Building Technologies; Computer Engineering; Electronic Engineering; Information Technology; Production Engineering)

History: Founded 1993. Acquired present status 2001.

Degrees and Diplomas: Baccalaureos: Business and Commerce; Administration; Accounting; Management information systems, 4 yrs; Baccalaureos: Computer science; Administration Technology, 5 yrs; Magistr

Libraries: Yes
Last Updated: 20/02/09

MODERN SCIENCES AND ARTS UNIVERSITY (MSA)

11/14 Amer Street, off Mesaha Square, Dokki, Giza
Tel: +20(2) 3837-1517
Fax: +20(2) 3837-1543
EMail: Info@msa.eun.eg; admission@msa.eun.eg
Website: http://www.msa.eun.eg

President: Khayri Abd El Hamied Tel: +20(2) 336-7844

Secretary-General: Omayma Ouf

Faculties
Biotechnology (Analytical Chemistry; Biochemistry; Biology; Biotechnology; Cell Biology; Molecular Biology; Organic Chemistry); **Computer Science** (Computer Science); **Dentistry** (Dentistry);

Engineering (Computer Engineering; Engineering; Industrial Engineering); **Languages** (Arabic; English; Translation and Interpretation); **Management** (Accountancy; Economics; Management; Marketing); **Mass Communication** (Advertising and Publicity; Journalism; Mass Communication; Public Relations; Radio and Television Broadcasting); **Pharmacy** (Pharmacy)

History: Founded 1996.

Degrees and Diplomas: Baccalaureos. A British Bachelor's Degree is also offered.
Last Updated: 20/02/09

MODERN UNIVERSITY FOR TECHNOLOGY AND INFORMATION

Elhadaba Elwosta, Mokatam, 5th District, Cairo
Tel: +20(2) 727-2145
Fax: +20(2) 727-2148
EMail: Info@mti.edu.eg
Website: http://www.mti.edu.eg

President: Olfat Kamel

Faculties
Computer Science (Computer Science); **Engineering** (Civil Engineering; Electrical Engineering; Engineering; Mechanical Engineering; Structural Architecture); **Management** (Accountancy; Economics; Finance; Information Management; Management; Marketing); **Mass Communication** (Advertising and Publicity; Journalism; Mass Communication; Media Studies; Public Relations; Radio and Television Broadcasting)

History: Founded 2004.

Degrees and Diplomas: Baccalaureos; Magistr; Doktora
Last Updated: 03/02/09

NAHDA UNIVERSITY

Nahda University Road, new Bani Sueif City, Beni-Suef
Tel: +20(82) 224-668-011
EMail: nub@nub.edu.eg
Website: http://www.nahdauniversity.org

President: Seddik Afifi

Faculties
Computer Science; **Marketing and Business Administration**; **Mass Communication** (Mass Communication; Media Studies; Printing and Printmaking); **Oral and Dental Medicine**; **Pharmacy** (Analytical Chemistry; Biochemistry; Microbiology; Pharmacology; Pharmacy)

History: Founded 2006. Acquired present status 2007.
Last Updated: 17/07/09

NATIONAL CIVIL AVIATION TRAINING ORGANIZATION (NCATO)

Airport St., Imbaba Airport, Giza
Tel: +20(2) 350-5442 +20(2) 350-5425
Fax: +20(2) 350-5359
EMail: ncato10@hotmail.com
Website: http://www.ncato.org/indexnf-en.asp

Institutes
Air Traffic Control (Air Transport); **Civil Aviation Engineering and Technology** (Transport Engineering); **Egypt Air** (Air Transport); **Space and Aviation information Technology and Computer** (Aeronautical and Aerospace Engineering; Computer Science; Engineering; Information Technology)

History: Founded 1932.

Degrees and Diplomas: Baccalaureos: 5 yrs
Last Updated: 20/02/09

NILE UNIVERSITY

Smart Village - B2 - Km 28, Cairo-Alex Desert Rd, Cairo 12677
Tel: +20(2) 3534 2072
EMail: info@nileuniversity.edu.eg
Website: http://www.nileu.edu.eg

President: Tarek Khalil

Graduate Schools
Management of Technology (Business Administration; Finance; Marketing; Technology)

Schools
Business (Business Administration); **Communications and Information Technology** (Computer Engineering; Electronic Engineering; Information Technology; Radio and Television Broadcasting; Software Engineering); **Engineering and Applied Sciences** (Construction Engineering; Industrial Engineering; Industrial Management; Nanotechnology; Transport and Communications)

History: Founded 2006.

Accrediting Agencies: Ministry of Higher Education

Degrees and Diplomas: *Baccalaureos*; *Magistr*; *Doktora*
Last Updated: 12/03/12

OCTOBER 6 UNIVERSITY (O6U)

Giza-Governerate, Central Axis-Plot 1, 6th of October City, Giza
Tel: +20(2) 835-3942 +20(2) 835-3987
Fax: +20(2) 835-3867 +20(2) 835-3987
EMail: adminoct@o6u.edu.eg
Website: http://www.o6u.edu.eg

President: Ahmed Attia SeidaFax: +20(2) 835-3382
EMail: ahmedseida@hotmail.com

Vice-President for Postgraduate Studies and Research: Talaat Rihan EMail: trihan@o6u.edu.eg

International Relations: Rasha Helmy Omar
Tel: +20(2) 835-3987 EMail: rhelmy@o6u.eg

Faculties
Applied Arts (Advertising and Publicity; Cinema and Television; Design; Furniture Design; Photography); **Applied Medical Sciences** (Laboratory Techniques; Nursing; Radiology); **Dentistry** (Dentistry); **Economics and Management** (Accountancy; Economics; Management; Political Sciences); **Education** (Arabic; Biology; Curriculum; Education; Educational Psychology; Mathematics and Computer Science; Modern Languages; Special Education); **Engineering** (Architecture; Building Technologies; Computer Engineering; Construction Engineering; Electrical Engineering; Electronic Engineering; Industrial Engineering; Mechanical Engineering); **Hotel Management and Tourism** (Hotel Management; Tourism); **Information Systems and Computer Science** (Computer Science; Information Sciences); **Languages and Translation** (Modern Languages; Translation and Interpretation); **Media and Mass Communication** (Mass Communication; Media Studies); **Medicine** (Medicine); **Pharmacy** (Pharmacy); **Physiotherapy** (Physical Therapy); **Social Sciences** (Library Science; Political Sciences; Psychology; Theatre)

Further Information: University Hospital

History: Founded 1996.

Admission Requirements: High school certificate

International Co-operation: With universities in the United Kingdom, Sweden, Denmark, Spain, USA, France, China.

Degrees and Diplomas: *Diploma*; *Baccalaureos*: 4-6 yrs

Student Residential Facilities: Yes

Libraries: Yes
Last Updated: 20/02/09

PHARAOHS HIGHER INSTITUTE FOR COMPUTERS AND INFORMATION ADMINISTRATION

Sakkarra Road, Km 9, Marriott - Haram, Giza

Programmes
Computer Science; Information Management (Information Management)

Degrees and Diplomas: *Baccalaureos*: 4 yrs
Last Updated: 19/06/07

PHARAOHS HIGHER INSTITUTE FOR TOURISM AND HOTELS

Sakkarra Tourism Road, Km 9, Marriott - Haram, Giza

Programmes
Hotel Management and Tourism (Hotel Management; Tourism)
History: Founded 2000.

Degrees and Diplomas: *Baccalaureos*: 4 yrs
Last Updated: 04/06/07

PHAROS UNIVERSITY IN ALEXANDRIA (PUA)

Pharos University, Canal, El Mahmoudia Street, Beside Green Plaza Complex, Alexandria
Tel: +20(3) 387-7210 +20(3) 387-7213
Fax: +20(3) 383-0249
EMail: info@pua.edu.eg
Website: http://www.pua.edu.eg

President: Abd Al Monem Mousa

Faculties
Dentistry (Dentistry); **Engineering** (Engineering); **Financial and Administrative Sciences** (Accountancy; Business Administration; Finance; International Business; Marketing); **Languages and Translation** (Modern Languages; Translation and Interpretation); **Legal Studies and International Relations** (International Relations; Law); **Pharmacy and Drug Manufacturing** (Pharmacology; Pharmacy); **Tourism and Hotel Management** (Hotel Management; Tourism)

History: Founded 2006.

Fees: (Egyptian Pounds): Egyptian students, 7,875-15,750; (US Dollars): Foreign students, 1,730-3,455 per annum.

Accrediting Agencies: Egyptian Supreme Council of Private Universities

Degrees and Diplomas: *Baccalaureos*: 4-5 yrs
Last Updated: 20/02/09

POSTGRADUATE HIGHER INSTITUTE FOR ISLAMIC STUDIES

26, Yolyo Str., Meet Oqba, Giza
Tel: +20(2) 346-8547

Director: Baghat Oteba

Programmes
Islamic Studies (Islamic Studies)
Last Updated: 23/02/09

POSTGRADUATE HIGHER INSTITUTE FOR SOCIAL DEFENCE STUDIES

1, Al-Shahed Ra'af Zaki, Polak Al-Dakrour, Giza
Tel: +20(2) 330-5352

Director: Mohamed Shehata Ali

Programmes
Social Defence Studies (Social and Community Services; Social Policy; Social Problems; Social Welfare)
Last Updated: 23/02/09

RA'AS AL-BAR HIGHER INSTITUTE FOR SPECIFIC STUDIES AND COMPUTER SCIENCE

Domitta Governate, Al-Ara'as City, Street 77, Ras Al-Barr
Website: http://www.rbi.edu.eg/ar/home.aspx

Director: Ahmad Diaa M. Mousa

Programmes
Computer Science (Computer Science)

Degrees and Diplomas: *Baccalaureos*: 4 yrs
Last Updated: 05/06/07

SADAT ACADEMY FOR MANAGEMENT SCIENCES (SAMS)

Cornish E-Nil Road, Maadi Entrance (1), Cairo 2222
Tel: +20(2) 378-7628 +20(2) 378-7629 +20(2) 378-7630
Fax: +20(2) 753-0043 +20(2) 02-3582901
EMail: info@sadatacademy.edu.eg
Website: http://www.sadatacademy.edu.eg

President: Ahmed Mahmoud Youssef (2006-)
EMail: costprof@sadatacademy.edu.eg

Vice-President for Education and Research Affairs: Sherief Hassan Kassem Aly EMail: sh_kassem@sadatacademy.edu.eg

Faculties

Management (Accountancy; Behavioural Sciences; Business Administration; Computer Science; Economics; Insurance; Mathematics; Modern Languages; Public Administration; Staff Development; Statistics)

History: Founded 1981.

Degrees and Diplomas: *Baccalaureos*; *Magistr*, *Doktora*
Last Updated: 20/02/09

SENGHOR UNIVERSITY

Université Senghor/Université internationale de Langue française au Service du Développement africain
BP 21111-415, El Mancheya, 1 Place Ahmed Orabi, Alexandria
Tel: +20(3) 4843-374 +20(3) 4843-504
Fax: +20(3) 4843-479
EMail: info@usenghor-francophonie.org
Website: http://www.usenghor-francophonie.org

Recteur: Albert Lourde
Tel: +20(3) 4843-504 EMail: rectorat@usenghor-francophonie.org

Centres

Distance Education, Information and Communication Technologies *(FAD & TICE)* (Development Studies; Law)

Departments

Administration (Administration; Government; Management; Public Administration); **Cultural Studies** (Communication Studies; Cultural Studies; Heritage Preservation; Media Studies) *Director:* Caroline Gaultier; **Environmental Management** (Environmental Management; Environmental Studies); **Health Studies** (Health Administration; Health Sciences; Nutrition)

History: Founded 1990 following a meeting of Heads of State of Francophone Countries. A private postgraduate institution whose objective is to train and assist professionals and higher level teachers.

Governing Bodies: Haut Conseil de l'Université; Assemblée générale; Conseil d' Administration; Conseil académique

Academic Year: September to May

Admission Requirements: University degree and professional experience

Main Language(s) of Instruction: French

Degrees and Diplomas: *Magistr:* Development Studies, 2 yrs

Student Services: Canteen, Foreign student adviser, Health services, Sports facilities

Libraries: Giovanni Agnelli Library, c. 15,580 vols

Publications: Actes des Conférences; Lettres d'Alexandrie; Patrimoine Culturel Francophone

Student Numbers *2011-2013*	MEN	WOMEN	TOTAL
All (Foreign Included)	142	39	181

Last Updated: 12/03/12

SINAI HIGHER INSTITUTE FOR TOURISM AND HOTELS (SHITH)

14 Al Sadaka St., Ra'as Sedr, South Sinai
Tel: +20(69) 400-871
Fax: +20(2) 402-4977
EMail: sinai_institute@hotmail.com
Website: http://sinai.googoolz.com

Dean: Nervana Mokhtar Harraz (1999-)

Secretary-General: Ra'afat El-Nakhal
International Relations: Emad Eddin Abu El-Enain

Departments

Computer science (Computer Science); **Hotel Management** (Hotel Management); **Tourism** (Tourism)

History: Founded 1993.

Main Language(s) of Instruction: Arabic; English

Degrees and Diplomas: *Baccalaureos:* 4 yrs

Student Services: Academic counselling, Employment services, Foreign student adviser, Health services, Social counselling, Sports facilities

Student Residential Facilities: 50 chalets; 60 rooms

Special Facilities: Museum; IT System including Language Laboratory.

Libraries: Periodical subscriptions and thesis: c. 200 english vols; c. 800 Arabic vols.

Publications: Egyptian Journal of Tourism and Hospitality, Academic and Scientific Research Publication *(biennially)*

Academic Staff	MEN	WOMEN	TOTAL
PART-TIME	10	1	11
STAFF WITH DOCTORATE			
FULL-TIME	6	2	8
PART-TIME	4	1	5

Last Updated: 21/05/07

SINAI UNIVERSITY

Katamia (Sama Tower) 5th Floor, Cairo
EMail: sinai@su.edu.eg
Website: http://www.su.edu.eg

President: Hatem Mostafa El-bolok

Faculties

Business Administration (Business Administration; International Business; Marketing); **Dentistry** (Dentistry); **Engineering Sciences** (Biomedical Engineering; Chemical Engineering; Civil Engineering; Computer Engineering; Electrical Engineering; Electronic Engineering; Engineering; Materials Engineering; Mechanical Engineering; Structural Architecture; Telecommunications Engineering); **Information Technology and Computer Sciences** (Computer Science; Information Technology); **Media Technology** (Communication Studies; Marketing; Mass Communication; Media Studies; Radio and Television Broadcasting); **Pharmacy and Pharmaceutical Industries** (Biochemistry; Immunology; Microbiology; Pharmacology; Pharmacy; Toxicology)

History: Founded 2006.

Degrees and Diplomas: *Baccalaureos*
Last Updated: 17/08/09

TECHNICAL COMMERCIAL INSTITUTE FOR COMPUTERS

Hodh Al-Dars, Port Tawfiq, Suez

Programmes
Computer Science

Degrees and Diplomas: *Diploma*; *Baccalaureos:* 4 yrs
Last Updated: 19/06/07

THE AMERICAN UNIVERSITY IN CAIRO (AUC)

PO Box 74, New Cairo 11835
Tel: +20(2) 794-2964 +1(212) 7308800 (New York Office)
Fax: +20(2) 795-7565 +1(212) 7301600 (New York Office)
EMail: webley@aucegypt.edu
Website: http://www.aucegypt.edu

President: Lisa Anderson (2011-)
Tel: +20(2) 797-5161, Fax: +20(2) 799-1830
EMail: president@aucegypt.edu

Provost: Medhat Haroun EMail: maharoun@aucegypt.edu

Centres

American Studies and Research (*Prince Alwaleed Bin Talal Bin Abdulaziz Alsaud*) (American Studies); **Arabic Study Abroad** (Arabic) *Director:* Nevenka Korica; **Desert Development** (Arid Land Studies; Development Studies); **Journalism** (*Kamal Adham*) (Journalism); **Management** (Management); **Philanthropy and Civic Engagement** (*John Gerhart*) (Civics); **Social Research** (Social Studies)

Institutes

Arabic Language (Arabic); **English Language** (English); **Gender and Women's Studies** (*Cynthia Nelson*) (Gender Studies; Women's Studies)

Research Centres

Economics and Business History (Economic History); **Science and Technology** (*Youssef Jameel*) (Natural Sciences; Technology)

Schools

Business, Economics and Communication (Accountancy; Administration; Business Administration; Business and Commerce; Communication Studies; Economics; Journalism; Management; Mass Communication); **Continuing Education** (Accountancy; Arabic; Computer Science; Education; Finance; Human Resources; Human Rights; Information Technology; International Law; Marketing; Tourism; Translation and Interpretation); **Humanities and Social Sciences** (Anthropology; Arts and Humanities; Comparative Law; Comparative Literature; Demography and Population; English; Film; History; International Relations; Islamic Studies; Middle Eastern Studies; Music; Performing Arts; Political Sciences; Psychology; Social Sciences; Sociology; Theatre; Visual Arts); **Science and Engineering** (Actuarial Science; Analytical Chemistry; Biology; Chemistry; Construction Engineering; Electronic Engineering; Engineering; Mathematics and Computer Science; Mechanical Engineering; Natural Sciences; Organic Chemistry; Physical Chemistry; Physics)

Further Information: Through the Centre of Adult and Continuing Education's Outreach Services programme in English, Computer Education, Arabic and Translation, and/or Business Studies are offered in: The United Arab Emirates (Abu Dhabi and Dubai), Saudi Arabia (Jeddah and Riyadh), and in other cities in Egypt (Alexandria, Damanhour, Ismailia, El Minia, Esna, Heliopolis, Hurgada, Kafr El Sheikh, Mansoura, Tabbin, and Tanta)

History: Founded 1919. A private non-profit Institution located in New Cairo. It operates as a private educational/cultural Institute within the framework of the 1962 Egyptian-American Cultural Co-operation Agreement and in accordance with a protocol with the Government of Egypt through which the University's degrees are recognized as those awarded by the Egyptian national universities. Accredited in the United States by the Middle States Commission on Higher Education, 3624 Market Street, Philadelphia, PA 19104, +1(267) 284-5000, and licensed to grant degrees and incorporated by the State of Delaware.

Governing Bodies: Board of Trustees, comprising primarily American educators and corporate administrators

Academic Year: September to July (September-January; February-June); Winter Session in February and Summer Session in June-July

Admission Requirements: Secondary school certificate (Thanawiya 'Amma) or recognized equivalent

Main Language(s) of Instruction: English

Accrediting Agencies: USA Council for Accreditation of Higher education, the Middle States Association of Colleges and Schools; Protocol with the Egyptian Government

Degrees and Diplomas: *Baccalaureos:* Accountancy; *Baccalaureos:* Actuarial Science; Biology; Chemistry; Computer Science; Construction Engineering; Electronics Engineering; Mathematics; Mechanical Engineering; Physics; Anthropology; Arabic Studies; Art; Economics; Egyptology; English and Comparative Literature; Journalism and Mass Communication; Middle East Studies; Modern History; Philosophy; Political Science; Psychology; Sociology; Theater (BA), 4 yrs; *Baccalaureos:* Business Administration, 4-5 yrs; *Magistr:* Arabic Studies; Economics; Economic/International Development; English and Comparative Literature; Gender and Womens' Studies; International Human Rights Law; Mass Communication; Middle East Studies; Political Science; Sociology and Anthropology; Business Administration; Computer Science; Engi-

neering; Physics; International and Comparative Law (LL.M.); Public Administration; Public Policy and Administration; Teaching Arabic as a Foreign Language; Teaching English as a Foreign Language, a further 2 yrs. Also graduate Diplomas in Computer Science; Economic/International Development; Engineering, European Studies; Middle East Studies; Forced Migration and Refugee Studies; Islamic Studies; Physics; Political Science; Teaching Arabic as a Foreign Language; Teaching English as a Foreign Language; Television Journal

Student Services: Academic counselling, Canteen, Employment services, Foreign student adviser, Health services, Language programs, Nursery care, Social counselling, Sports facilities

Student Residential Facilities: Yes

Libraries: Central Library, 403,482 vols; Cresswell Collection of Islamic Art and Architecture, 2,369 vols and 10,000 photographs and slides.

Publications: ALIF: Journal of Comparative Poetry (*annually*); Cairo Papers in Social Science (*quarterly*); Khamasin; Middle East Management Review (*quarterly*)

Press or Publishing House: American University Press in Cairo
Last Updated: 28/03/11

THE BRITISH UNIVERSITY IN EGYPT

Suez Desert Road, El-Shourouk
Tel: +20(2) 689-0000
Fax: +20(2) 687-5889 +20(2) 687-5897
EMail: info@bue.edu.eg
Website: http://www.bue.edu.eg

President: Ahmed Amin Hamza

Departments
English (English)

Faculties
Business Administration, Economics and Political Science; **Dentistry**; **Engineering** (Automation and Control Engineering; Civil Engineering; Computer Engineering; Electrical and Electronic Engineering; Engineering; Mechanical Engineering; Petroleum and Gas Engineering; Structural Architecture; Technology; Telecommunications Engineering); **Informatics and Computer Science** (Computer Science); **Nursing** (Nursing)

History: Founded 2004.

Fees: (UK Pounds): 3,500 per annum for Business, Economics, Political Science, Informatics and Computer Science Programmes; 4,500 per annum for Engineering, Pharmacy, Dentistry.

Degrees and Diplomas: Honours Degrees
Last Updated: 18/08/09

THE GERMAN UNIVERSITY IN CAIRO (GUC)

Main Entrance Al Tagamoa Al, Khames, New Cairo
Tel: +20(2) 758-1041
Fax: +20(2)758-9990-8
EMail: contact@guc.edu.eg
Website: http://www.guc.edu.eg/

President: Mahmoud H. Abdel-Kader (2002-)

Centres
Languages and Translation; **Lifelong Learning and Distance Education** (Continuing Education)

Faculties
Applied Science and Arts; **Engineering and Materials Science**; **Information Engineering and Technology** (Computer Engineering; Information Technology); **Management Technology** (Management); **Media Engineering and Technology** (Mass Communication; Media Studies); **Pharmacy and Biotechnology** (Biotechnology; Pharmacy); **Postgraduate Studies and Research**

History: Founded 2002.

Degrees and Diplomas: *Baccalaureos*; *Magistr*, *Doktora*. Also German Diploma
Last Updated: 19/08/09

THEBES ACADEMY (ITA)

Maadi Corniche first - behind the Nile Badrawi Hospital, Maadi,
Cairo 11 434
Tel: +20(2) 524-7980
Fax: +20(2) 524-7984
EMail: contact@thebesacademy.org
Website: http://www.thebesacademy.org
President: Seddik Afifi **EMail:** s.afifi@thebesacademy.org

Higher Institutes
Computer and Management Sciences (Maadi Centre) (Accountancy; Business Administration; Computer Science; Information Sciences; Management); **Engineering** (Maadi Centre); **Institute of Management and Information Technology** (Giza Centre)

Further Information: The Academy is composed of two Centres in Maadi and Giza.

History: Founded 1995. Giza Centre established 1995. Maadi Centre established 1999. Received accreditation 2004.

Degrees and Diplomas: Baccalaureos
Last Updated: 19/02/09

WORKERS' UNIVERSITY (WU)

6 Al-Nasr Str., Abbas Al-Aquad, Nasr City, Cairo
Tel: +20(2) 275-4646
Fax: +20(2) 275-4604
EMail: info@workersuniversity.org
President: Hussein Magawer
Vice-President: Mostafa El Sayed
International Relations: Ahmed Abdel Salam, Secretary-General

Academies
Specialized Studies

Programmes
Academic Studies (Labour and Industrial Relations; Safety Engineering; Technology); **Trade Union and Labour Economics Studies** (Labour and Industrial Relations; Management; Protective Services; Social Welfare)

Further Information: Also 11 branches in Egypt

History: Formerly known as Labour University.

Degrees and Diplomas: Baccalaureos: Business Administration; Quality Control, 4 yrs
Last Updated: 21/05/07

El Salvador

STRUCTURE OF HIGHER EDUCATION SYSTEM

Description:

Higher education is provided by universities, both public and private, and specialized institutions. The National University is autonomous and is financed by credits from the State, gifts and student fees. The governing bodies are the General Assembly, the Higher University Council and the Rector. The Ministerio de Educación, through the Dirección Nacional de Educación Superior, is responsible for higher education policy and study programmes. Many private universities have been established. They must submit their programmes to the approval of the Ministry of Education. The specialized institutions include institutos tecnológicos, schools of agriculture, a military school, a school of social work, a school of physical education, a school of telecommunications, a school of French language and computer science schools. Central America's first rural university, Monseñor Oscar Arnulfo Romero University, was founded to serve the rural poor of the country.

Stages of studies:

University level first stage: Técnico
Some universities award the professional qualification of Técnico in clinical laboratory work, Physiotherapy, Anaesthesiology and Maternal and Infant Hygiene after two years' study. The title of Tecnólogo is conferred after four years' study.

University level second stage: Licenciatura, Ingeniero, Arquitecto, Doctor en Cirugía dental.
The title of Ingeniero (Agricultural, Civil, Industrial, Mechanical and Electrical Engineering) requires five years' study, as does that of Arquitecto. The Licenciatura is generally awarded after five years' study in most fields. The title of Doctor en Cirugía Dental is awarded after five years.

University level third stage: Maestría
The Maestría is usually awarded two years after the Licenciatura. Candidates must prepare a short thesis (monograph).

University level fourth stage: Doctorado (Doctor en Medicina and Ph.D.)
There are two kinds of Doctorates in the country. The first is the title of Doctor of Medicine (Doctor en Medicina), awarded after 7 years' study. The second is the title of Doctor of Education and Doctor of Clinical Psychology which can be obtained after having completed a Maestría degree course.

Distance higher education:
The Open University offers courses in Economics, Science, Humanities, Law and Social Sciences.

ADMISSION TO HIGHER EDUCATION

Admission to university-level studies:

Name of secondary school credential required: Bachillerato General

Minimum score/requirement: 5.00 (Scale from 0 to 10)

Entrance exam requirements: Entrance examination for some universities.

Foreign students admission:

Definition of foreign student: A person studying at a Salvadorean educational institution who does not have Salvadorean nationality.

Entrance exam requirements: Foreign students must hold a Título de Bachiller and must sit for an entrance examination. In addition, academic documents must be authenticated by the Ministry of Education and by the Ministry of Foreign Affairs. Students wishing to study in higher education must enrol in the Sistema de Educación Media Salvadoreño before enrolling at university.

Entry regulations: Students must have a residence permit.

Language requirements: Students must have a good knowledge of Spanish.

RECOGNITION OF STUDIES

Quality assurance system:

All higher education training must be recognized by the Ministry of Education of El Salvador.

NATIONAL BODIES

Ministerio de Educación (Ministry of Education)
Minister: Salvador Sánchez Cerén
Director, Higher Education: José Francisco Marroquin
Edificio A-1 Plan Maestro, Alameda Juan Pablo II y Calle Guadalupe, Centro de Gobierno
San Salvador 1175
Tel: +503 2537 2000
EMail: educacion@mined.gob.sv
WWW: http://www.mined.gob.sv

Comisión de Acreditación de la Calidad de la Educación Superior (Committee for the Accreditation of the Quality of Higher Education)
Alameda Juan Pablo II y Calle Guadalupe
Plan Maestro, Centro de Gobierno, Edificio A2
San Salvador
Tel: +503 2281 0282
EMail: cda_dnes@mined.gob.sv
WWW: http://www.mined.gob.sv/cda/acreditacion_institucional.htm

Data for academic year: 2006-2007
Source: IAU from Delegación permanente de El Salvador ante la UNESCO, 2006. Bodies updated in 2011.

INSTITUTIONS

PUBLIC INSTITUTIONS

UNIVERSITY OF EL SALVADOR
Universidad de El Salvador (UES)
Ciudad Universitaria, Final 25 Avenida Norte, San Salvador
Tel: +503 2225-1500
Fax: +503 2225-8826
EMail: mirsalva@sal.gbm.net
Website: http://www.ues.edu.sv

Rector: Rufino Antonio Quezada Sánchez
EMail: rectoria@ues.edu.sv

Vicerrector Académico: Miguel Ángel Pérez Ramos
Tel: +503 225-5415, Fax: +503 225-5415
EMail: viceacad@ues.edu.sv

International Relations: Ada Ruth González de Nieto

Faculties
Agronomy (Agricultural Engineering; Agriculture; Veterinary Science; Zoology); **Chemistry and Pharmacy** (Chemistry; Pharmacy); **Dentistry** (Dentistry; Stomatology); **Economics** (Accountancy; Business Administration; Economics); **Engineering and Architecture** (Architecture; Chemical Engineering; Civil Engineering; Electrical Engineering; Engineering; Food Technology; Industrial Engineering; Mechanical Engineering; Systems Analysis); **Law and Social Sciences** (International Relations; Law; Social Sciences); **Medicine** (Anaesthesiology; Child Care and Development; Clinical Psychology; Medical Technology; Medicine; Nursing; Nutrition; Occupational Therapy; Physical Therapy; Radiology); **Multidisciplinary Studies of the East** (Agronomy; Architecture; Arts and Humanities; Chemistry; Economics; Engineering; Law; Mathe-

matics; Medicine; Natural Sciences; Pharmacy; Social Sciences); **Multidisciplinary Studies of the West** (Biology; Chemistry; Engineering; Law; Literature; Mathematics; Medicine; Philosophy; Physics; Social Sciences); **Natural Sciences and Mathematics** (Biology; Chemistry; Mathematics; Natural Sciences; Physics); **Regional Multidisciplinary Studies** (Agronomy; Computer Science; Economics; Education); **Science and Humanities** (Arts and Humanities; Education; Fine Arts; Journalism; Literature; Modern Languages; Natural Sciences; Philosophy; Psychology; Social Sciences) *Dean*: Pablo de Jesús Castro Hernández

History: Founded 1841, became University 1847. Acquired autonomous status 1950. Also regional centres in Santa Ana, San Miguel and San Vicente.

Governing Bodies: Asamblea General Universitaria, Consejo Superior Universitario

Academic Year: May to March (May-October; October-March)

Admission Requirements: Secondary school certificate (bachillerato) and entrance examination

Main Language(s) of Instruction: Spanish

International Co-operation: With universities in Spain, Mexico, the Netherlands and Central America

Degrees and Diplomas: *Técnico*: Clinical Laboratory Studies; Interior Design; Library science, 3 yrs; *Arquitecto*: 5 yrs; *Doctor en Cirugía Dental*: 5-7 yrs; *Ingeniero*: Agriculture and Animal Husbandry, 5 yrs; *Licenciatura*: Accountancy; Biology; Business Administration; Chemistry; Chemistry and Pharmacy; Dietetics; Economics; Education; Engineering; Health Sciences; International Relations; Journalism; Laboratory Technology; Law and Economics; Letters; Mathematics; Philosophy; Physics; Psychology; Sociology, 5 yrs; *Maestría*; *Doctor en Medicina*: Medicine, 5-7 yrs. Also Diplomados

Student Services: Health services, Language programs, Nursery care, Sports facilities

Libraries: Central library and libraries in every Faculty

Publications: Aquí Odontología *(monthly)*; Búho Dilecto *(bimonthly)*; Cuadernos Didácticos; El Quehacer Científico *(annually)*; El Salvador: Coyuntura Económica *(quarterly)*; El Universitario *(quarterly)*; Enfoque Tecnológico *(biannually)*

Last Updated: 15/12/09

UNIVERSITY OF THE EAST
Universidad de Oriente (UNIVO)
4a. Calle Poniente No. 705, San Miguel
Tel: +503 2661-1180; +503 2661-8287
Fax: +503 2660-0879
EMail: info@univo.edu.sv
Website: http://www.univo.edu.sv

Rector: Rogelio Cisneroz Lazo

Vicerrector: Carlos Alberto Piche Benavides

Faculties
Agronomy; **Economics**; **Engineering and Architecture** (Architecture; Civil Engineering; Engineering; Systems Analysis); **Humanities** (Arts and Humanities; English; Preschool Education; Psychology); **Law** (Law)

History: Founded 1982.

Main Language(s) of Instruction: Spanish

Degrees and Diplomas: *Ingeniero*; *Licenciatura*; *Maestría*
Last Updated: 16/12/09

PRIVATE INSTITUTIONS

ALBERT EINSTEIN UNIVERSITY
Universidad Albert Einstein (UAE)
Urb. Lomas de San Francisco, Antiguo Cuscatlán, La Libertad
Tel: +503 2273-3700; +503 2273-3780
Fax: +503 2273-3783; +503 2273-3784
EMail: infouae@uae.edu.sv
Website: http://www.uae.edu.sv

Rectora: Juana Salazar Alvarenga de Pacheco
EMail: rectoria@einstein.edu.sv

Secretario General: Ivo Osegueda Jiménez

Faculties
Architecture (Architecture); **Business Administration** (Business Administration); **Engineering** (Civil Engineering; Computer Engineering; Electrical Engineering; Engineering; Industrial Engineering; Mechanical Engineering)

History: Founded 1973, first students admitted 1977.

Governing Bodies: Consejo Superior; Rector; Tres Decanos y Secretario General

Admission Requirements: Secondary school certificate (bachillerato) and entrance examination

Fees: (US Dollars): 55-200 per month

Main Language(s) of Instruction: Spanish

International Co-operation: Participates in UNAM and EBSCO

Accrediting Agencies: Asociación de Univesidades Privadas de Centro América (AUPRICA)

Degrees and Diplomas: *Arquitecto*: Urban Planning; Construction; Town Planning, 5 yrs; *Ingeniero*: Civil Engineering; Industrial Engineering;Electrical Engineering; Mechanical Engineering; Computer Engineering, 5 yrs; *Licenciatura*: Business and Commerce; Business Administration; Environmental Design, 5 yrs

Student Services: Academic counselling, Canteen, Cultural centre, Handicapped facilities, Language programs, Social counselling, Sports facilities

Special Facilities: Laboratories

Libraries: Yes
Last Updated: 15/12/09

ALBERTO MASFERRER SALVADOREAN UNIVERSITY
Universidad Salvadoreña Alberto Masferrer (USAM)
19 Avenida Norte, entre 3a. Calle Poniente y Alameda
'Juan Pablo II', San Salvador
Tel: +503 2221-1136
Fax: +503 2222-8006
EMail: usames@telemovil.com
Website: http://www.usam.edu.sv

Rector: Cesar Augusto Calderón

Faculties
Business Studies (Accountancy; Business Administration; Computer Science; Marketing); **Chemistry and Pharmacy** (Chemistry; Pharmacology); **Dental Surgery** (Dentistry; Surgery); **Law and Social Sciences** (Law; Social Sciences); **Medicine** (Medicine; Surgery); **Veterinary Science and Zoology** (Veterinary Science; Zoology)

Institutes
Science and Technological Research (Natural Sciences; Technology)

Further Information: Also 4 hospitals

History: Founded 1979. Received official authorization 1980.

Academic Year: February to December (February-June; July-December)

Admission Requirements: Secondary school certificate (bachillerato) and entrance examination

Main Language(s) of Instruction: Spanish

Accrediting Agencies: Comisión de Acreditación de la Calidad Académica

Degrees and Diplomas: *Doctor en Cirugía Dental*; *Licenciatura*: 5-5 1/2 yrs; *Maestría*; *Doctor en Medicina*. Also Diplomados

Student Residential Facilities: For c. 4,000 students

Special Facilities: Museo de Anatomía Veterinaria

Libraries: Central Library, c. 5,000 vols
Last Updated: 16/12/09

ANDRÉS BELLO UNIVERSITY
Universidad Andrés Bello (UDAB)
1a. Calle Poniente No. 2128, entre 39 y 41 Avenida Norte No 2128, Colonia Flor Blanca, San Salvador
Tel: +503 2260-8533
Fax: +503 2260-8541
EMail: informacion@unab.edu.sv
Website: http://unab.edu.sv

Rector: Marco Tulio Magaña Escalante

Secretary General: Juan Zelaya Jiménez

International Relations: Emy Ponce

Faculties
Economics (Accountancy; Business Administration; Computer Networks; Computer Science; Economics; Marketing; Public Relations); **Health Sciences** (Health Sciences; Nursing; Radiology); **Human Sciences** (Communication Studies; Social Work)

Further Information: Also branches in Sonsonate, Chalatenango and San Miguel

History: Founded 1991.

Main Language(s) of Instruction: Spanish

Degrees and Diplomas: *Licenciatura*; *Maestría*
Last Updated: 16/12/09

AUTONOMOUS UNIVERSITY OF SANTA ANA
Universidad Autónoma de Santa Ana (UNASA)
Autopista Sur Poniente Km 63 1/2, Santa Ana
Tel: +503 2440-0245
EMail: unasarec@sv.intercomnet.net
Website: http://www.unasa.edu.sv/

Rector: Guillermo Martínez Mendoza

Vice-Rector: Sergio Ernesto Carranza
EMail: unasarec@sv.cciglobal.net

Programmes

Dentistry (Dentistry); **Laboratory Techniques**; **Medicine** (Medicine); **Nursing**; **Physiotherapy**

History: Founded 1982.

Governing Bodies: Consejo Superior Universitario

Academic Year: February to January (February-July; August-January)

Admission Requirements: Secondary school certificate (bachillerato) and entrance examination

Main Language(s) of Instruction: Spanish

Degrees and Diplomas: *Doctor en Cirugía Dental*: 6 yrs; *Licenciatura*: Psychology; Social Work, 5 yrs; *Doctor en Medicina*: 7 yrs
Last Updated: 15/12/09

CAPTAIN GENERAL GERARDO BARRIOS UNIVERSITY

Universidad Capitán General Gerardo Barrios (UCGGB)
Calle Las Flores y Avenida Las Magnolias, Colonia Escolan,
San Miguel
Tel: +503 2669-7499
Fax: +503 2669-7489
EMail: nuevoingreso@ugb.edu.sv
Website: http://www.ugb.edu.sv

Rector: Raúl Rivas Quintanilla EMail: rrivas@ugb.edu.sv

Secretary General: Arcadia Sànchez de Alvarado
Fax: +503 2669-7484 EMail: asanchez@ugb.edu.sv

International Relations: Eugenia Gomez
EMail: eugomez@ugb.edu.sv

Faculties

Business Studies; **Engineering and Architecture** (Architecture; Civil Engineering; Engineering); **Law** (Law); **Science and Humanities** (Arts and Humanities; Psychology); **Science and Technology** (Computer Science; Engineering; Software Engineering; Systems Analysis)

History: Founded 1980.

Governing Bodies: Technical-Academic Council; Quality Assurance Committee

Academic Year: January to December (January-June; July-December)

Admission Requirements: Secondary school certificate

Fees: (US Dollars): 65 per month, per course. 45,71: enrolment fee

Main Language(s) of Instruction: Spanish

Degrees and Diplomas: *Tecnólogo*: Accounting; Computer Engineering; Civil Engineering; Secretarial Studies, 2 yrs; *Ingeniero*: Civil Engineering; Computer Engineering; Computer Networks, 5 yrs; *Licenciatura*: Law; Computer Sciences; Psychology; Business Administration, 5 yrs; *Maestría*: International Business (Ms), 2 yrs

Student Services: Academic counselling, Cultural centre, Employment services, Handicapped facilities, Health services, Language programs, Nursery care, Social counselling, Sports facilities

Libraries: Yes, one general and one for law students

Publications: Millenium Magazine, Research results, general articles *(annually)*

Academic Staff *2007-2008*	MEN	WOMEN	**TOTAL**
FULL-TIME	128	31	c. **159**
Student Numbers *2007-2008*			
All (Foreign Included)	1,947	1,547	c. **3,494**

Last Updated: 15/12/09

CATHOLIC UNIVERSITY OF EL SALVADOR

Universidad Católica de El Salvador (UNICO)
Bypass carretera a Metapán y carretera antigua a San Salvador,
Santa Ana
Tel: +503 2484-0600
Fax: +503 2441-2655
EMail: catolica@catolica.edu.sv
Website: http://www.catolica.edu.sv

Rector: Romeo Tovar Astorga (2000-)
Tel: +503 2447-0602 EMail: rector@unico.edu.sv

Secretario General: Cástulo Hernández Robles
Tel: +503 2447-0606 EMail: secretaria@unico.edu.sv

International Relations: Claudia Velásquez de Figueroa, Director, Communication Tel: +503 2447-0621 EMail: ucom@uinco.edu.sv

Faculties

Architecture and Engineering (Architecture; Civil Engineering; Computer Science; Engineering; Industrial Engineering); **Business Studies** (Accountancy; Business Administration; Computer Science; Economics; International Business; Marketing); **Law and Social Sciences** (Law; Social Sciences); **Science and Humanities** (Arts and Humanities; Education; Natural Sciences; Preschool Education; Primary Education; Religious Studies)

History: Founded 1982 as Universidad Católica del Occidente following the Episcopal Conference of El Salvador agreement. Acquired present status and title 2008.

Governing Bodies: Council

Academic Year: January to November (January-June; July-November)

Admission Requirements: Secondary school certificate (bachillerato)

Main Language(s) of Instruction: Spanish

Accrediting Agencies: Comisión de Accreditación de la Calidad Académica

Degrees and Diplomas: *Técnico*: 2 yrs; *Ingeniero*: 5 yrs; *Licenciatura*: 5 yrs; *Maestría*

Student Services: Academic counselling, Language programs, Sports facilities

Libraries: 32,529 vols
Last Updated: 15/12/09

CHRISTIAN UNIVERSITY OF THE ASSEMBLIES OF GOD

Universidad Cristiana de las Asambleas de Dios (UCAD)
27 Calle Oriente No 234, Barrio San Miguelito, San Salvador
Tel: +503 2225-5046
Fax: +503 2235-6264
EMail: informacion@ucad.edu.sv
Website: http://www.ucad.edu.sv

Rector: Fernando Arturo Vásquez Vásquez

Faculties

Economics (Accountancy; Business Administration; Economics); **Law and Social Sciences** (Law; Social Sciences); **Science and Humanities** (Arts and Humanities; Communication Studies; Education; Mathematics; Natural Sciences; Preschool Education); **Theology** (Theology)

History: Founded 1983.

Academic Year: February to November (February-June; August-November)

Admission Requirements: Secondary school certificate (bachillerato)

Main Language(s) of Instruction: Spanish

Degrees and Diplomas: *Ingeniero*; *Licenciatura*: Business Administration; Education; English; Law; Missiology, 5 yrs. Also teaching qualifications

Student Residential Facilities: For c. 1,500 students
Last Updated: 15/12/09

DON BOSCO UNIVERSITY

Universidad Don Bosco (UDB)
Ciudadela Don Bosco, Cantón Venecia, Calle Plan del Pino,
Soyapango 1874
Tel: +503 2251-5030
Fax: +503 2251-5080
EMail: huguet@udb.edu.sv
Website: http://www.udb.edu.sv

Rector: Federico Miguel Huguet Rivera
Tel: +503 2251-5031 EMail: rectoria@udb.edu.sv

Vicerrector: Victor Arnoldo Cornejo Montano

Secretario General: Mario Rafael Olmos Argueta
Tel: +503 2251-5039 EMail: mol@udb.edu.sv

Centres
Research and Transfer (Biomedicine; Communication Studies; Computer Engineering; Electrical and Electronic Engineering; Measurement and Precision Engineering; Mechanical Engineering)
Director: Nélson Quintanilla

Departments
Aeronautics (Aeronautical and Aerospace Engineering)

Faculties
Economics (Economics); Engineering (Biomedical Engineering; Computer Engineering; Computer Science; Electrical and Electronic Engineering; Engineering; Industrial Engineering; Mechanical Engineering); Rehabilitation; Science and Humanities (Communication Studies; Education; Educational Sciences; English; Modern Languages; Preschool Education; Teacher Training; Theology); Technological Studies (Biomedical Engineering; Cinema and Television; Computer Engineering; Electrical and Electronic Engineering; Graphic Design; Mechanical Engineering; Orthopaedics; Technology)

History: Founded 1984. Follows the Salesian tradition and philosophy.

Governing Bodies: Directorio Ejecutivo; Consejo Académico

Academic Year: January to December (January-June; July-December)

Admission Requirements: Secondary school certificate (bachillerato) and entrance examination

Main Language(s) of Instruction: Spanish

Accrediting Agencies: Comisión de Accreditación de la Calidad Académica

Degrees and Diplomas: Técnico: 2-3 yrs; Profesorado; Ingeniero: 5 yrs; Licenciatura: 5 yrs; Maestría: 2 yrs

Student Services: Academic counselling, Canteen, Cultural centre, Employment services, Foreign student adviser, Health services, Language programs, Social counselling, Sports facilities

Libraries: Central Library, 39,764 vols

Publications: Engineering (annually); Revista Científica (biannually); Revista Puntos (biannually); Teoría y Praxis (quarterly)
Last Updated: 16/12/09

DR. JOSÉ MATÍAS DELGADO UNIVERSITY
Universidad Dr. José Matías Delgado (UDJMD)
Apartado postal 1849, Km. 8 1/2 Carretera a Santa Tacla Cuidad Merliot, Antiguo Cuscatlán, La Libertad
Tel: +503 2278-1011
Fax: +203 2289-5314
EMail: informacion@ujmd.edu.sv
Website: http://ujmd.edu.sv/

Rector: David Escobar Galindo
EMail: rectoriacampus@ujmd.edu.sv

Secretario General: Fernando Basilio Castellanos

Vicerrector: Carlos Quintanilla Schmidt

Faculties
Agriculture and Agricultural Research (Agriculture); Economics (Economics); Health Sciences; Law and Social Sciences (Law; Social Sciences); Science and Fine Arts

Schools
Applied Arts (Fine Arts); Architecture; Communication; Industrial Engineering (Engineering; Industrial Engineering); Psychology

History: Founded 1977. Financed by student fees and private and Government grants.

Governing Bodies: Board of Trustees; Consejo de Directores; Consejo Académico

Academic Year: January to December (January-June; July-December)

Admission Requirements: Secondary school certificate (bachillerato) or foreign equivalent, and entrance examination. Presentation of original work for School of Applied Arts

Main Language(s) of Instruction: Spanish

Accrediting Agencies: Comisión de Acreditación de la Calidad Académica

Degrees and Diplomas: Ingeniero; Licenciatura; Maestría; Doctor en Medicina

Student Services: Academic counselling, Canteen, Employment services, Handicapped facilities, Health services, Language programs, Sports facilities

Libraries: Central Library, c. 18,000 vols. Economic, Law and Social Sciences: c. 16,000 vols.
Last Updated: 16/12/09

EVANGELICAL UNIVERSITY OF EL SALVADOR
Universidad Evangélica de El Salvador (UEES)
Prolongación Alameda Juan Pablo II y Calle El Carmen, San Antonio Abad, San Salvador
Tel: +503 2275-4000; +503 2275-4012
Fax: +503 2275-4040
EMail: uevange@uees.edu.sv
Website: http://www.uees.edu.sv

Rector: Víctor Edgardo Segura Lemus
Tel: +503 2262-4000, Fax: +503 2262-4006

Faculties
Business Administration and Economics; Dentistry (Dentistry); Engineering (Computer Networks; Computer Science; Engineering); Law (Law); Medicine (Medicine); Social Sciences (Education; Psychology; Social Sciences; Theology; Translation and Interpretation)

Research Units
Martin Eugenio Rodríguez (Development Studies; Service Trades)

History: Founded 1981. A private, non-profit institution.

Governing Bodies: Directorio Ejecutivo, comprising 11 members; Consejo Académico

Academic Year: February to November (February-June; August-November)

Admission Requirements: Secondary school certificate (bachillerato) and entrance examination

Main Language(s) of Instruction: Spanish

Accrediting Agencies: Comisión de Acreditación de la Calidad Académica; Consorcio de Universidades Cristianas Evangélicas de América Latina (CONDUCE-AL); Asociación de Universidades Privadas (AUPRIDES); Asociación de Universidades Privadas Centroamericanas (AUPRICA)

Degrees and Diplomas: Doctor en Cirugía Dental: 5 yrs; Licenciatura: Education; English Translation and Interpretation; Nutrition and Dietetics; Psychology; Social Work, 4 1/2-5 yrs; Maestría: Education; Health, 2 yrs; Doctor en Medicina: 8 yrs. Also teachinng qualifications

Student Services: Academic counselling, Cultural centre, Employment services, Foreign student adviser, Social counselling, Sports facilities

Student Residential Facilities: For c. 5,000 students

Libraries: Central Library, c. 14,000 vols

Publications: Revista 'Vision Odontológica (biannually)
Last Updated: 16/12/09

FRANCISCO GAVIDIA UNIVERSITY
Universidad Francisco Gavidia (UFG)
Alameda Roosevelt No. 3031, San Salvador
Tel: +503 2209-2810; +503 2209-2800
Fax: +503 2209-2837
EMail: info@ufg.edu.sv
Website: http://www.ufg.edu.sv

Rector: Mario Antonio Ruiz Ramírez (1996-) Fax: +503 2224-2551
EMail: mruiz@ufg.edu.sv

Secretaria General: Teresa de Jesús Gonzáles de Mendoza
Fax: +503 2224-2551 EMail: tmendoza@ufg.edu.sv

Faculties

Architecture and Engineering (Architecture; Engineering; Industrial Engineering; Systems Analysis; Telecommunications Engineering); **Economics** (Accountancy; Advertising and Publicity; Business Administration; Communication Studies; Computer Science; Economics; Marketing; Public Relations); **Law** (Law); **Social Sciences** (Cultural Studies; Psychology)

History: Founded 1981.

Governing Bodies: Board of Directors, comprising 5 members

Academic Year: January to December (January-June; July-December)

Admission Requirements: Secondary school certificate (bachillerato) and entrance examination

Fees: (Colones): 2,430 per semester

Main Language(s) of Instruction: Spanish

Accrediting Agencies: Comisión de Acreditación de la Calidad Académica

Degrees and Diplomas: *Ingeniero*: Computer Engineering; Industrial Engineering, 5 yrs; *Licenciatura*: Business Administration; Economics; Education; Educational Administration; Jurisprudence; Marketing; Psychology; Public Accountancy; Social Work, 5 yrs; *Maestría*: Business Administration (MBA); Education (Med), 2 yrs. Also teaching qualifications

Student Services: Academic counselling, Cultural centre, Employment services, Social counselling, Sports facilities

Special Facilities: Auditorium

Libraries: Central Library, 5,971 vols

Publications: Realidad y Reflexión *(biennially)*; Societatis *(biennially)*; Theorethikos *(biennially)*

Last Updated: 16/12/09

HOLY SPIRIT SPECIALIZED INSTITUTE OF HIGHER EDUCATION

Instituto Especializado de Educación Superior El Espíritu Santo
Urbanización Jardines de Merliot, Av. El Boquerón y Calle Chiltiupán. Lote No. 5 Polígono "O" Cuidad Merliot, La Libertad
Tel: +503 2278-6683
Fax: +503 2278-6683
EMail: info@ieeses.edu.sv
Website: http://www.ieeses.edu.sv/index.php

Rectora: Elsa América Mendoza Mejía

Programmes

Educational Sciences (Educational Sciences; Physical Education; Preschool Education; Primary Education; Sports Management; Teacher Trainers Education)

History: Founded 1995. Acquired present status 1998.

Main Language(s) of Instruction: Spanish

Degrees and Diplomas: *Profesorado*; *Licenciatura*; *Maestría*
Last Updated: 15/12/09

INSTITUTE OF ECONOMICS AND BUSINESS ADMINISTRATION

Instituto Superior de Economía y Administración de Empresas (ISEADE)
Calle El Pedregal y Acceso a Escuela Milar, Antiguo Cuscatlán, La Libertad
Tel: +503 2212-1700
Fax: +503 2212-1736
EMail: maestria@iseade.edu.sv; iseade@telemovil.net
Website: http://www.iseade.edu.sv

Rector: Joaquín Samayoa

Programmes

Business Administration (Business Administration); **Economics** (Economics); **Educational Management**

History: Founded 1997.

Main Language(s) of Instruction: Spanish

Accrediting Agencies: Comisión de Acreditación de la Calidad Académica

Degrees and Diplomas: *Maestría.* Also Diploma de Posgrado
Last Updated: 15/12/09

JOSÉ SIMEÓN CAÑAS CENTRAL AMERICAN UNIVERSITY

Universidad Centroamericana José Simeón Cañas (UCA)
Apartado postal 01-168, Boulevard Los Próceres, San Salvador
Tel: +503 2210-6600
Fax: +503 2210-6655
EMail: correo@www.uca.edu.sv
Website: http://www.uca.edu.sv

Rector: José María Tojeira (1995-)
Tel: +503(2) 210-6620 EMail: rmira@rec.uca.sv

Faculties

Business and Economic Sciences (Accountancy; Administration; Business Administration; Economics; Finance; Marketing; Social Sciences); **Engineering and Architecture** (Architecture; Chemical Engineering; Computer Science; Electrical Engineering; Engineering; Industrial Engineering; Mechanical Engineering; Town Planning); **Social Sciences and Humanities** (Education; English; Philosophy; Preschool Education; Psychology; Special Education; Theology)

History: Founded 1965, first students admitted 1966.

Governing Bodies: Board of Directors

Academic Year: March to December (March-July; August-December)

Admission Requirements: Secondary school certificate (bachillerato) or equivalent, and entrance examination

Fees: (US Dollars): Registration 57; tuition, 44-218 per month

Main Language(s) of Instruction: Spanish

Accrediting Agencies: Comisión de Acreditación de la Calidad Académica

Degrees and Diplomas: *Técnico*: Marketing; Accountancy, 3 yrs; *Arquitecto*: Architecture, 5 yrs; *Ingeniero*: Chemical Engineering; Civil Engineering; Electrical Engineering; Industrial Engineering; Mechanical Engineering, 5 yrs; *Licenciatura*: Accountancy; Business Administration; Computer Sciences; Economics; Law; Philosophy; Psychology; Sociology, 5 yrs; *Maestría*: Business Administration; Finance; Political Science; Educational Policy; Community Psychology; Health Administration; Regional Development; Environmental Management; Constitutional and Penal Law; Iberoamerican Philosophy, 2 1/2 yrs; *Doctorado*: Iberoamerican Philosophy, 5 yrs. Also Teaching qualifications, 2-3 yrs

Student Services: Academic counselling, Cultural centre, Employment services, Language programs, Sports facilities

Special Facilities: Video Centre. Radio YSUGA

Libraries: Central Library, c. 400,000 vols; Theology, c. 35,000 vols

Publications: Carta a los Iglesias; El Salvador Proceso; Estudios Centroamericanos; Realidad; Revista Latinoamericano de Teología

Press or Publishing House: UCA Imprenta
Last Updated: 15/12/09

LATIN AMERICAN TECHNICAL UNIVERSITY

Universidad Técnica Latinoamericana (UTLA)
5a Calle Poniente No. 3-8B, Nueva San salvador, La Libertad
Tel: +503 2228-1917
EMail: registroacademico@utla.edu.sv
Website: http://www.utla.edu.sv

Rector: Mauricio Rosendo Sermeño Palacios
EMail: msermeno@yahoo.com

Secretary General: Francisco Alfredo Carrillo Larreynaga
EMail: utlasg@integra.com

Faculties

Economics (Accountancy; Business Administration; Economics); **Engineering** (Agricultural Engineering; Civil Engineering; Electrical Engineering; Electronic Engineering; Engineering; Industrial Engineering; Mechanical Engineering)

History: Founded 1981.

Academic Year: February to November (February-June; July-November)

Admission Requirements: Secondary school certificate (bachillerato) and entrance examination

Main Language(s) of Instruction: Spanish

Degrees and Diplomas: *Ingeniero*: 5 yrs; *Licenciatura*: 5 yrs; *Maestría*: 2 yrs

Libraries: c. 2,000 vols

Last Updated: 16/12/09

LUTHERAN SALVADOREAN UNIVERSITY
Universidad Luterana Salvadoreña (ULS)
Apdo Postal 3039-3057, Km. 3 1/2 Carretera a los Planes de Renderos, Autopista a Comalapa, San Salvador
Tel: +503 2217-7807
Fax: +503 2217-7814
EMail: uls@uls.edu.sv
Website: http://www.uls.edu.sv

Rector: Fidel Nieto Láinez

Faculties
Human and Natural Sciences (Agriculture; Business Administration; Computer Science; Ecology; Law); **Theology and Humanities** (Preschool Education; Secondary Education; Social Work; Theology)

History: Founded 1991.

Governing Bodies: Junta Directiva

Academic Year: February to June; August to September

Admission Requirements: Secondary school certificate

Main Language(s) of Instruction: Spanish

Accrediting Agencies: Ministry of Education

Degrees and Diplomas: *Ingeniero*: 5 yrs; *Licenciatura*: 5 yrs

Student Services: Academic counselling, Canteen, Employment services, Foreign student adviser, Health services, Language programs

Libraries: 4,107 vols

Last Updated: 16/12/09

MÓNICA HERRERA SCHOOL OF COMMUNICATION STUDIES
Escuela de Comunicación Mónica Herrera
Av. Manuel Gallardo 3-3. Santa Tecla, La Libertad
Tel: +503 2228-1300; +513 2228-8813
Fax: +503 2229-9226; +513 2228-0148
EMail: info@monicaherrera.com
Website: http://www.monicaherrera.com/site/index.php

Directora: Teresa Palacios de Chávez

Programmes
Communication Studies

Main Language(s) of Instruction: Spanish

Accrediting Agencies: Comisión de Acreditación de la Calidad Académica

Degrees and Diplomas: *Técnico*; *Licenciatura*: 5 yrs

MONSEÑOR OSCAR ROMERO UNIVERSITY
Universidad Monseñor Oscar Romero (UMOAR)
Km. 53 1/2, desvio Las Aldeitas Tejutla, Chalatenango
Tel: +503 2309-3914; +503 2309-3915
Fax: +503 2309-3869
EMail: nfo@umoar.edu.sv
Website: http://www.umoar.edu.sv

Rectora: Carmen Navas de Mejía

Faculties
Agriculture and Forestry (Agriculture; Forestry); **Law and Social Sciences** (Law; Social Sciences); **Science and Humanities** (Arts and Humanities; Computer Science; Education; Natural Sciences)

History: Founded 1993.

Main Language(s) of Instruction: Spanish

Degrees and Diplomas: *Técnico*; *Ingeniero*; *Licenciatura*

Last Updated: 16/12/09

NEW UNIVERSITY SAN SALVADOR
Universidad Nueva San Salvador (UNSSA)
Alameda Roosevelt y 41 Av. Sur, San Salvador
Tel: +503 2260-7552; +503 2261-2832
Fax: +503 2261-2693
EMail: unssa@unssa.edu.sv
Website: http://www.unssa.edu.sv

Rector: Rafael Hernán Contreras Rodríguez

Faculties
Economics (Accountancy; Business Administration; Economics); **Health Sciences** (Chemistry; Dentistry; Health Sciences; Medicine; Pharmacy); **Law and Social Sciences** (Advertising and Publicity; Law; Political Sciences; Social Sciences; Social Work)

History: Founded 1981.

Academic Year: January to October (January-May; June-October)

Admission Requirements: Secondary school certificate (bachillerato) and entrance examination

Main Language(s) of Instruction: Spanish

Degrees and Diplomas: *Técnico*: 3 yrs; *Doctor en Cirugía Dental*: 5 yrs; *Licenciatura*: 5 yrs; *Doctor en Medicina*: 5 yrs

Libraries: Central Library, c. 6,000 vols

Publications: Revista Analisis *(monthly)*

Last Updated: 16/12/09

OPEN UNIVERSITY OF SAN SALVADOR
Universidad Modular Abierta (UMA)
1a. Calle Poniente No. 2117, San Salvador
Tel: +503 2222-9805; +503 2223-3408
Fax: +503 2271-4803; +503 2271-4029
EMail: informacion@uma.edu.sv
Website: http://www.uma.edu.sv/

Rector: Judith Virginia Mendoza de Díaz

Faculties
Economics (Accountancy; Business Administration; Economics; Marketing; Software Engineering); **Law and Social Sciences** (Law; Social Sciences); **Science and Humanities** (Arts and Humanities; Education; English; Literature; Natural Sciences; Psychology; Social Sciences)

Further Information: Also campuses in Santa Ana; San Miguel; Sonsonate.

History: Founded 1982.

Main Language(s) of Instruction: Spanish

Degrees and Diplomas: *Técnico*; *Licenciatura*; *Maestría*. Also Diplomado

Last Updated: 16/12/09

PANAMERICAN UNIVERSITY
Universidad Panamericana (UPAN)
Calle Progreso No 234 a 60 Metros de Avenida Bernal, Colonia Miramonte Poniente, San Salvador
Tel: +503 2260-1991
Fax: +503 2260-1991 Ext.122
EMail: upaninfo@upan.edu.sv
Website: http://www.upan.edu.sv

Rector: Oscar Armando Morán Fólgar (1996-)
Tel: +503 2260-1991, Ext.102 EMail: rectoria@upan.edu.sv

Vicerrectora Administrativa: Nubia A. Mendoza Figueroa
Tel: +503 2260-1991, Ext.103 EMail: nmendoza@upan.edu.sv

International Relations: Roberto Molina Castro, Secreterio General Tel: +503 2260-1991, Ext.106 EMail: rmolina@upan.edu.sv

Faculties
Economics (Accountancy; Business Administration; Economics; Marketing) *Dean*: Raúl Antonio Torres; **Humanities and Science** (Arts and Humanities; Educational Sciences; English; Library

Science; Social Work; Teacher Training) *Dean*: Alma Aracely Pozas de Ibarra; **Law** *Dean*: Silvia Colindres de Rosales

Further Information: Also branches in Ahuachapán and San Vicente.

History: Founded 1990.

Governing Bodies: Board of Directors, Academic Council and the Technical Faculty Council

Academic Year: January to December (January-June; July-December)

Admission Requirements: Secondary school certificate

Fees: (US Dollars): 290 per semester

Main Language(s) of Instruction: Spanish

Accrediting Agencies: Ministry of Education

Degrees and Diplomas: *Técnico*: Marketing (Tec.), 3 yrs; *Licenciatura (Lic.; Licdo.; Licda.)*: 5 1/2 yrs

Student Services: Academic counselling, Canteen, Employment services, Language programs, Social counselling, Sports facilities

Student Residential Facilities: None

Libraries: A Central Library and two other libraries in the branches (San Vicente and Ahuachapán)

Last Updated: 16/12/09

PEDAGOGICAL UNIVERSITY OF EL SALVADOR
Universidad Pedagógica de El Salvador (UPED)
25 Avenida Norte, Diagonal Arturo Romero y Primera Diagonal, Colonia Médica
Tel: +503 2226-4065; +503 2226-4059
Fax: +503 2226-4486
EMail: info@pedagogica.edu.sv
Website: http://www.pedagogica.edu.sv

Rector: Luis Alonso Aparicio

Secretario General: Luis Aparicio EMail: luis.aparicio@salnet.net

International Relations: Carmen Aparicio
EMail: carmen.aparicio@salnet.net

Faculties
Economics (Accountancy; Business and Commerce; Marketing); **Education** (Education)

History: Founded 1982.

Governing Bodies: Asamblea General de Miembros Fundadores

Academic Year: January to December (January-July; August-December)

Admission Requirements: Secondary school certificate (bachillerato) and entrance examination

Fees: (Colones): Registration, 275; tuition, 2,100 per semester

Main Language(s) of Instruction: Spanish

Degrees and Diplomas: *Licenciatura*: Education; Business Administration; Accountancy; Marketing; Social Work, 5 yrs; *Maestría*: Educational Administration, 2 yrs. Also Teaching Qualifications, 3 yrs

Student Services: Academic counselling, Social counselling

Student Residential Facilities: For 3,200 students

Libraries: Central Library, c. 8,470 vols
Last Updated: 16/12/09

POLYTECHNIC UNIVERSITY OF EL SALVADOR
Universidad Politécnica de El Salvador (UPES)
Boulevard Tutunichapa y 5ta Avenida Norte, Frente a redondel José Martí (Don Rúa), San Salvador
Tel: +503 2222-7810
EMail: politecnica@upes.edu.sv
Website: http://www.upes.edu.sv

Rector: Roberto López Meyer EMail: lopezmeyer@upes.edu.sv

Secretario General: José Rodolfo Montúfar Argumedo
Tel: +503 2222-2058, Fax: +503 2225-9332
EMail: rodolfo.montufar@upes.edu.sv

International Relations: Mirna Elizabeth Gálvez García
Tel: +503 2226-4176, Fax: +503 2225-7348
EMail: mgalvez@upes.edu.sv

Faculties
Economics and Business (Accountancy; Business Administration; Economics; Marketing); **Engineering and Architecture** (Architecture; Civil Engineering; Computer Engineering; Electrical Engineering; Engineering; Industrial Engineering; Systems Analysis); **Law and Social Sciences** (Law; Social Sciences)

Institutes
Postgraduate; **Research**

History: Founded 1979.

Academic Year: January to December (January-June; July-December)

Admission Requirements: Secondary school certificate (bachillerato)

Main Language(s) of Instruction: Spanish

Accrediting Agencies: Associación de Universidades Privadas de Centro América (AUPRICA)

Degrees and Diplomas: *Técnico*: 2 yrs; *Ingeniero*: 5 yrs; *Licenciatura*: 5 yrs; *Maestría*

Student Services: Academic counselling

Note: 931 students in the 1st cycle in 2007
Last Updated: 16/12/09

SCHOOL OF ECONOMICS AND COMMERCE
Escuela Superior de Economía y Negocios (ESEN)
Km. 12 &/2 Carretera al Puerto de La Libertad, Nueva Calle a Comasagua, La Libertad
Tel: +503 2234-9292
EMail: info@esen.edu.sv
Website: http://www.esen.edu.sv

Rector: Ricardo Poma

Programmes
Business and Commerce (Business and Commerce); **Economics** (Economics); **Law** (Law)

Accrediting Agencies: Comisión de Acreditación de la Calidad Académica

Degrees and Diplomas: *Licenciatura*

UNIVERSITY OF SONSONATE
Universidad de Sonsonate (USO)
29 Calle Oriente y Avenida Central Final Colonia 14 de Diciembre, Sonsonate
Tel: +503 2429-9500
Fax: +503 2429-9503
EMail: informacion@usonsonate.edu.sv
Website: http://www.usonsonate.edu.sv/

Rector: Fernando Rodríguez Villalobos

Faculties
Economics and Social Sciences (Accountancy; Business Administration; Economics; Education; Social Sciences); **Engineering and Natural Sciences** (Agricultural Business; Electrical Engineering; Engineering; Industrial Engineering; Natural Sciences); **Law** (Law)

History: Founded 1982.

Governing Bodies: Consejo de Directores

Academic Year: February to December (February-July; August-December)

Admission Requirements: Secondary school certificate (bachillerato)

Fees: (Colones): c. 3,500 per annum

Main Language(s) of Instruction: Spanish

Degrees and Diplomas: *Profesorado*; *Ingeniero*; *Licenciatura (Lic)*: 5 yrs

Student Services: Academic counselling, Employment services, Sports facilities

Libraries: Yes
Last Updated: 16/12/09

UNIVERSITY OF TECHNOLOGY OF EL SALVADOR

Universidad Tecnológica de El Salvador (UTEC)
Calle Arce No. 1120, San Salvador
Tel: +503 2275-8888
Fax: +503 2271-0765
EMail: infoutec@utec.edu.sv
Website: http://www.utec.edu.sv

Rector: José Mauricio Loucel EMail: mloucel@utec.edu.sv

Faculties

Business (Accountancy; Administration; Finance; Human Resources; Marketing; Sales Techniques); **Computer and Applied Sciences** (Architecture; Computer Science; Graphic Design; Industrial Engineering; Software Engineering); **Law**; **Social Sciences**

History: Founded 1980.

Governing Bodies: Board of Trustees

Academic Year: January to December (January-June; August-December)

Admission Requirements: Secondary school certificate (bachillerato) and entrance examination

Main Language(s) of Instruction: Spanish

Accrediting Agencies: Comisión de Acreditación de la Calidad Académica

Degrees and Diplomas: *Técnico*; *Arquitecto*; *Ingeniero*; *Licenciatura*: Accountancy; Business Administration; Insurance; Marketing; Social Work; *Maestría*

Student Services: Academic counselling, Cultural centre, Health services, Language programs, Nursery care, Social counselling

Special Facilities: TV Channel. Radio Channel

Libraries: c. 22,000 vols
Last Updated: 16/12/09

Equatorial Guinea

STRUCTURE OF HIGHER EDUCATION SYSTEM

Description:

Higher education is mainly provided at the 3 Departments (Environment; Medicine; Arts and Humanities) of the Universidad Nacional de Guinea Ecuatorial (UNGE). The university is in the process of introducing the three-tier degree system.

NATIONAL BODIES

Ministerio de Educación, Ciencia y Deportes (Ministry of Education, Science and Sports)
Minister: Joaquin Nbana Nchama
Malabo

INSTITUTIONS

PUBLIC INSTITUTIONS

UNIVERSITY OF EQUATORIAL GUINEA
Universidad Nacional de Guinea Ecuatorial (UNGE)
Avenida Hassan II s/n, 661, Malabo
Tel: +240 091 644
Fax: +240 094 361
EMail: unge@orange.gq
Website: http://www.unge.gq/unge

Recteur: Carlos Nsé Nsuga EMail: nse_nsuga@yahoo.fr

Vice-Rectrice, Malabo: Trinidad Morgades Besari

Vice-Recteur, Bata: Pedro Ndong Asumu

Secrétaire général: Diosdado Nguema Obono

Faculties
Arts and Humanities *(FLCS)* (Administration; Arts and Humanities; Journalism; Law; Philology; Political Sciences; Social Sciences; Sociology; Spanish); **Environmental Studies** *(FMA)*; **Medicine** *(FM)*

Schools
Administration *(EUA)*; **Agriculture/Fishery/Forestry** *(EUEAPF)* (Agriculture; Fishery; Forestry); **Health and Environment** *(EUSMA)* (Environmental Studies; Health Sciences); **Teacher Training - Bata** *(EUFP)* (Education; Teacher Training); **Teacher Training - Malabo** *(EUFP)* (Education; Teacher Training); **Technology/Engineering** *(EUIT)* (Architecture; Civil Engineering; Electrical Engineering; Electronic Engineering; Energy Engineering; Engineering; Environmental Engineering; Mechanical Engineering; Structural Architecture; Technology)

Further Information: Campuses in Malabo and Bata

Degrees and Diplomas: *Licenciatura*
Last Updated: 07/10/09

Estonia

STRUCTURE OF HIGHER EDUCATION SYSTEM

Description:

The higher education system is binary and consists of universities (ülikool) and professional higher education institutions (rakenduskõrgkool). Since the academic year 2002/2003, the general structure of higher education is divided into two main cycles. The first cycle is the bachelor's level (3 to 4 years: 180240 ECTS credits); the second cycle is the master's level (1 to 2 years: 60120 ECTS credits). For some fields of study, the programmes have been integrated into a single long cycle, following the master's level qualification (5 to 6 years: 300360 ECTS credits). The highest stage at universities is doctoral studies (3 to 4 years: 180240 ECTS credits). Professional higher education programmes are first cycle programmes of higher education and correspond to the bachelor's degree programmes. The duration of studies is 3 to 4.5 years (180270 ECTS credits). Higher education is regulated by Republic of Estonia Education Act, Universities Act, Institutions of Professional Higher Education Act, Private Schools Act, Vocational Education Institutions Act, and Standard of Higher Education.The administration of higher education institutions or their study programmes are the responsibility of the Ministry of Education and Research, Estonian Ministry of the Interior, Estonian Ministry of Defence.

Stages of studies:

University level first stage: *Bakalaureus studies*
Bachelor's programmes are first-cycle higher education programmes. The purpose of bachelor studies is to broaden the scope of general education, to develop the basic knowledge and skills required for a certain field of study necessary for continuing at the master's level or for access to the labour market. The nominal duration of the programmes is generally 3 years (180 ECTS credits), as an exception, it may be up to 4 years (240 ECTS credits). The qualification awarded upon completion of the programme is bakalaureusekraad. The qualification gives access to master's programmes.

University level second stage: *Magister studies*
Master's programmes are second-cycle higher education programmes. The purpose of master's level studies is to develop the knowledge and skills required for a certain field of study and to acquire the necessary competences in order to enter the labour market or to continue studies at the doctoral level. The access requirement is a first-cycle higher education qualification. The nominal duration of the programmes is 1 to 2 years (60-120 ECTS credits), but together with the first-cycle studies it is at least 5 years (300 ECTS credits). The qualification awarded upon completion of a master's degree programme is magistrikraad. The qualification gives access to doctoral programmes. Integrated bachelor's and master's programmes comprise both basic and specialized studies. Such long-cycle programmes are offered in the fields of medicine, dentistry, pharmacy, veterinary medicine, architecture, civil engineering, and class-teacher training. The nominal duration of medical studies and of veterinary studies effective from the 2002/2003 academic year admissions, is 6 years (360 ECTS credits). The nominal duration of other integrated programmes is 5 years (300 ECTS credits). The qualification awarded upon completion of an integrated study programme in the fields of pharmacy, architecture, civil engineering, and class-teacher training is magistrikraad, the other qualifications are arstikraad (in medicine), hambaarstikraad (in dentistry) and loomaarstikraad (in veterinary medicine). The qualifications give access to doctoral programmes.

University level third stage: *Doktor studies*
Doctoral programmes represent higher education of the third cycle, the purpose of which is to acquire knowledge and skills necessary for independent research, development or professional creative work. The access requirement for doctoral studies is a magistrikraad or a corresponding qualification. The nominal period of study is 3 to 4 years (180-240 ECTS credits). The qualification awarded upon completion of doctoral studies is a doktorikraad. Doktorikraad is a research degree obtained after the completion and public defence of a dissertation (doktoritöö) based on independent scientific research or creative work.

Distance higher education:
It is possible to study through distance learning at all higher education cycles.

ADMISSION TO HIGHER EDUCATION

Admission to university-level studies:

Name of secondary school credential required: Gümnaasiumi lõputunnistus

For entry to: Universities, Professional higher education institutions

Name of secondary school credential required: Lõputunnistus kutsekeskhariduse omandamise kohta

For entry to: Universities, Professional higher education institutions

Alternatives to credentials: Tunnistus põhihariduse baasil kutsekeskhariduse omandamise kohta or Tunnistus keskhariduse baasil kutsekeskhariduse omandamise kohta which are certificates conferred on completion of secondary vocational education.

Entrance exam requirements: Since 1997, students must sit for the state entrance examinations (riigiesamid) to have access to higher education institutions. Depending on the speciality, higher education institutions may require some additional entrance examinations.

Numerus clausus/restrictions: There is a numerus clausus for state-commissioned student places.

Other admission requirements: Riigieksamitunnistus (State Examination Certificate)
There is a selection procedure for most higher education institutions and programmes. In general, the results of state examinations (riigieksamid) passed in a general secondary school (gümnaasium) are accepted as the basis of admission, sometimes an interview or a professional aptitude test is required. It may also include a number of entrance examinations.
Entrance examinations are most commonly set by faculties and approved by the boards of higher education institutions. Prevalent subjects are usually those relevant to the course of study. The basis for the admission decision is usually a combination of state examination results of general subjects and entrance examination results in the subject relevant to the course of study.

Foreign students admission:

Definition of foreign student: A student who is studying at an Estonian higher education institution and who is the citizen of a foreign country and does not have a permanent residence permit.

Entrance exam requirements: Applicants must be eligible for higher education in their own country and have a qualification corresponding to Estonian qualification giving access to higher education. Foreign students must usually apply for admission on the same terms as Estonian students. Specific requirements depend on the higher education institution requirements and on the chosen field of study. These can include entrance examinations, an interview, or minimum marks on the secondary-level school leaving certificate.

Entry regulations: Citizens of all third countries need a visa for visits that are 3 to 6 months long.
A temporary residence permit for study is required if a third country student intends to stay in Estonia for more than three months (in some cases only one month).

Language requirements: All the applicants need to provide proof of the proficiency in the language of a respective study programme. Most of the international students apply for the programmes taught in English, but there are also those who prefer to study in Estonian or Russian languages. The documented proof is usually not required from native-speakers or from the applicants who have completed their previous education in a respective language. In most cases, results of internationally accepted foreign language tests are accepted. Some institutions carry out their own language tests and/or interviews.

RECOGNITION OF STUDIES

Quality assurance system:

Since 2009, higher education quality has been assessed by an independent agency Eesti Kõrghariduse Kvaliteediagentuur (The Estonian Higher Education Quality Agency). The responsibility of the agency is to conduct institutional accreditation of higher education institutions and quality assessment of study programme groups. Within the assessment process of study programme groups it is assessed if the programmes correspond with the current legislation and with the national and international standards, including the quality of theoretical and practical training, the qualifications of the teaching and research staff, as well as the availability of the necessary resources. On the basis of external assessment, the Government of the Republic grants the higher education institution the right, for an indefinite or a fixed (1 to 3 years) period of time, to conduct studies according to the programme belonging to the respective study programme group.

Until 01.01.2010, external assessment of study programmes resulted in adopting accreditation decisions. Full accreditation was granted for seven years, conditional accreditation is valid for three years.

Bodies dealing with recognition:

Akadeemilise Tunnustamise Infokeskus (Eesti ENIC/NARIC) (Academic Recognition Information Centre (Estonian ENIC/NARIC))

Head: Gunnar Vaht

L. Koidula 13a

Tallinn 10125

Tel: +372 697 9214

Fax: +372 697 9226

EMail: enic-naric@archimedes.ee

WWW: http://www.archimedes.ee/enic/

Services provided and students dealt with: The main activities of the Estonian ENIC/NARIC are the assessment of foreign educational qualifications (certificates, diplomas, degrees, etc.), their comparison with Estonian qualifications, and making recommendations to employers and higher education institutions for a fair recognition decision

Eesti Kõrghariduse Kvaliteediagentuur (Estonian Higher Education Quality Agency)

Toompuiestee 30

Tallinn 10149

Tel: +372 696 2424

EMail: ekka@archimedes.ee

WWW: http://ekka.archimedes.ee/

Sihtasutus Archimedes (Archimedes Foundation)

L. Koidula 13A

Tallinn 10125

Tel: +372 699 9399

Fax: +372 697 9226

EMail: info@archimedes.ee

WWW: http://www.archimedes.ee

Special provisions for recognition:

Recognition for university level studies: Starting from 2009, educational institutions may provide higher education programmes, award academic degrees and issue diplomas, if, as a result of the assessment of the respective study programme group, the Government of the Republic has granted them such a right. At the same time, until 31.12.2011, official recognition of qualifications is also based upon accreditation decisions. In addition to diplomas issued after accreditation was granted, diplomas issued up to two years before the accreditation decision was adopted, are also recognized. Besides, diplomas issued by public universities, certifying the completion of study programmes entered into the Estonian Education Information System (database) before 01.06.2002, and diplomas issued by state professional higher education institutions, certifying the completion of study programmes entered into the database before 30.06.2003, are officially recognized without accreditation.

For access to advanced studies and research: State recognised diploma is required which will be provided after accreditation.

For exercising a profession: State recognised diploma is required which will be provided after accreditation.

NATIONAL BODIES

Eesti Vabariigi Haridus-ja Teadusminsteerium (Ministry of Education and Research)

Minister: Jaak Aaviksoo

Deputy Secretary General for Higher Education: Andres Koppel

Head, Foreign Relations Division: Katrin Rein

Munga 18
Tartu 50088
Tel: +372 735 0222
Fax: +372 730 1080
EMail: hm@hm.ee
WWW: http://www.hm.ee

Role of national body: The main tasks of the Ministry of Education and Research are to guarantee the expedient and effective development of education, research, youth and language policies and the high level and competitiveness of research and development activities.

Eesti Kõrghariduse Kvaliteediagentuur (Estonian Higher Education Quality Agency)

Chairman, Council: Mati Heidmets
Director: Heli Mattisen
Toompuiestee 30
Tallinn 10149
Tel: +372 696 2424
EMail: ekka@archimedes.ee
WWW: http://ekka.archimedes.ee/

Role of national body: The responsibility of the agency is to conduct institutional accreditation of higher education institutions and quality assessment of study programme groups.

Rektorite Nõukogu (Estonian Rectors' Conference)

Chairman: Signe Kivi
Secretary-General: Kairi Solmann
Ülikooli 18
Tartu 50090
Tel: +372 737 6516
EMail: ern@ern.ee
WWW: http://www.ern.ee/

Role of national body: The aim of the Estonian Rectors' Conference is to contribute to the promotion of the fields of education, research and culture in Estonia through the representation of its members and the opinion formation concerning the issues of common interest.

Data for academic year: 2011-2012
Source: IAU from the Estonian ENIC/NARIC, 2011

INSTITUTIONS

PUBLIC INSTITUTIONS

ESTONIAN ACADEMY OF ARTS

Eesti Kunstiakadeemia (EKA)
Tartu mnt. 1, 10145 Tallinn
Tel: +372 6267-301
Fax: +372 6267-350
EMail: artun@artun.ee
Website: http://www.artun.ee

Rector: Signe Kivi
Tel: +372 6267-309 EMail: karolin.magi@artun.ee
Vice-Rector: Liina Siib EMail: liina.siib@artun.ee
International Relations: Maria Jürisson
Tel: +372 6267-369 EMail: maria.jurisson@artun.ee

Faculties
Architecture (Architecture; Interior Design; Landscape Architecture; Town Planning) *Dean*: Jüri Soolep; **Art and Culture** (Art Education; Art History; Cultural Studies; Folklore; Heritage Preservation); **Design** (Ceramic Art; Fashion Design; Glass Art; Jewelry Art; Leather Techniques; Textile Design) *Dean*: Lennart Mänd; **Fine Arts** (Graphic Arts; Media Studies; Painting and Drawing; Photography; Sculpture) *Dean*: Marko Mäetamm

Institutes
Art History and Aesthetics (Aesthetics; Art History) *Director*: Mart Kalm

Schools
Restoration *Head*: Juhan Maļste
History: Founded 1914 as the Tallinn Industrial Art School of the Estonian Society of Art, became Art University 1989 and acquired present title 1996.
Governing Bodies: University Council
Academic Year: September to May (September-December; January-May)
Admission Requirements: Secondary school certificate (keskkooli lõputunnistus)
Main Language(s) of Instruction: Estonian, English

Degrees and Diplomas: *Bakalaureus*: Arts (BA), 4 yrs; *Rakenduskõrgharidusõppe diplom*: 3 yrs; *Magister*: Arts, a further 2 yrs; *Doktor (PhD)*: 4 yrs

Student Services: Academic counselling, Canteen, Foreign student adviser, Social counselling

Student Residential Facilities: For 260 students

Special Facilities: Art Gallery. E-Media Centre. Photography Centre

Libraries: University Library, c. 50,000 vols
Last Updated: 25/10/11

ESTONIAN ACADEMY OF MUSIC AND THEATRE

Eesti Muusika-ja Teatriakadeemia (EMTA/EAMT)
Rävala pst 16, 10143 Tallinn
Tel: +372 6675-700
Fax: +372 6675-800
EMail: ema@ema.edu.ee
Website: http://www.ema.edu.ee

Rector: Peep Lassmann (1992-)
Tel: +372 6675-701 EMail: peep@ema.edu.ee

Vice-Rector: Margus Pärtlas
Tel: +372 6675-702 EMail: margus@ema.edu.ee

International Relations: Marje Lohuaru
Tel: +372 6675-703 EMail: marje@ema.edu.ee

Centres
Continuing Education *Head*: Ene Kangron; **Humanities** *Head*: Reet Välja

Departments
Brass and Woodwind (Musical Instruments) *Head*: Toomas Vavilov; **Chamber Music** (Music) *Head*: Helin Kapten; **Composition** (Music Theory and Composition) *Head*: Toivo Tulev; **Conducting** (Conducting) *Head*: Tõnu Kaljuste; **Cultural Management and Humanities** *Head*: Kristina Kuznetsova-Bogdanovitš; **Jazz Music** (Jazz and Popular Music; Musical Instruments) *Head*: Jaak Sooäär; **Musicology** (Musicology) *Head*: Urve Lippus; **Piano** (Musical Instruments; Religious Music) *Head*: Ivari Ilja; **Strings** (Musical Instruments) *Head*: Peeter Paemurru; **Voice** (Singing) *Head*: Nadia Kurem

Institutes
Music Education (Music Education) *Head*: Kristi Kiilu; **Musical Performance Teacher Training** (Music Education) *Head*: Tõnu Reimann

Schools
Drama (Theatre) *Head*: Peeter Raudsepp

History: Founded 1919.

Governing Bodies: Board of Trustees, EAMT Council

Academic Year: August to June

Admission Requirements: Secondary school certificate (keskkooli lõputunnistus)

Fees: (Euros): 4,600 per annum. Citizens of the EU can compete for state-commissioned student places
Main Language(s) of Instruction: Estonian
International Co-operation: With institutions in Finland; Germany; Netherlands; United Kingdom. Participates in the Socrates programme

Degrees and Diplomas: *Bakalaureus*: Arts (BA), 3 yrs; *Magister*: Music (MMus); Music Education (MMus Ed), a further 2 yr; *Doktor (PhD)*: a further 4 yrs by thesis following Magister

Student Services: Academic counselling, Foreign student adviser, Handicapped facilities, Language programs, Social counselling, Sports facilities

Student Residential Facilities: Yes

Special Facilities: Electronic Music Studio
Last Updated: 20/05/11

ESTONIAN AVIATION ACADEMY

Eesti Lennuakadeemia (ELA)
Kreutzwaldi 58A, 51014 Tartu
Tel: +372(7) 448-100
Fax: +372(7) 448-101
EMail: eava@eava.ee
Website: http://www.eava.ee

Rector: Jaan Tamm (2009-)
Tel: +372(7) 448-100 EMail: jaan.tamm@eava.ee

Vice-Rector: Ants Aaver
Tel: +372(7) 309-227 EMail: ants.aaver@eava.ee

International Relations: Paul Lääne, Coordinator of Co-operation Programmes Tel: +372(7) 448-106 EMail: paul.laane@eava.ee

Programmes
Air Traffic Management (Air Transport); **Aircraft Piloting** (Air Transport); **Aviation Management** (Air Transport; Transport Management)

History: Founded 1993 as Tartu Lennukolledž. Acquired present status and title 2008. A State institution.

Accrediting Agencies: Ministry of Education and Research

Degrees and Diplomas: *Rakenduskõrgharidusõppe diplom*: 3-5 yrs; *Magister*
Last Updated: 14/09/11

ESTONIAN UNIVERSITY OF LIFE SCIENCES

Eesti Maaülikool (EMÜ)
Kreutzwaldi 64, 51014 Tartu
Tel: +372(7) 313-001
Fax: +372(7) 313-068
EMail: info@emu.ee
Website: http://www.emu.ee

Rector: Mait Klaassen
Tel: +372(7) 313-002 EMail: rektor@emu.ee

Centres
Renewable Energy; **Science Studies** *(Karl Ernst von Baer House)* (Natural Sciences)

Colleges
Technology (Technology)

Institutes
Agricultural and Environmental Sciences (Agriculture; Environmental Studies); **Economics and Social Sciences** (Economics; Social Sciences); **Forestry and Rural Engineering** (Forestry; Rural Studies); **Technology** (Technology); **Veterinary Medicine and Animal Sciences** (Animal Husbandry; Veterinary Science)

Further Information: Also Open Distance Learning courses

History: Founded 1951. Acquired present status and title 1991.

Academic Year: September to August (September-January; January-August)

Admission Requirements: Secondary school certificate (Keskkooli lõputunnistus)

Main Language(s) of Instruction: Estonian

Degrees and Diplomas: *Bakalaureus*: 3 yrs; *Arstikraad; Hambaarstikraad; Loomaarstikraad*: Veterinary Medicine (Dipl.vet.med), 6 yrs; *Magister*: Science (MSc), a further 2 yrs; *Doktor (PhD)*: 4 yrs

Special Facilities: Veterinary Hospital. University Farms. Computer Centre

Libraries: Main Library, 500,000 vols
Last Updated: 25/10/11

TALLINN UNIVERSITY

Tallinna Ülikool (TÜ)
Narva mnt. 25, 10120 Tallinn
Tel: +372 6409-100
Fax: +372 6409-116
EMail: tlu@tlu.ee
Website: http://www.tlu.ee

Rector: Tiit Land (2011-2016) EMail: tiit.land@tlu.ee

Head, Rector's Office: Hille Erik
Tel: +372 6409-121 EMail: hille.erik@tlu.ee

International Relations: Marvi Pulver, Head, International Relations Office
Tel: +372 6409-117, Fax: +372 6409-118
EMail: marvi.pulver@tlu.ee

Centres
Entrepreneurship and Business Studies

Colleges
Catherine's College (Liberal Arts) (Arts and Humanities; Social Sciences); **Haapsalu College** (Computer Science; Handicrafts; Management; Primary Education; Technology); **Rakvere College** (Preschool Education; Social Work)

Institutes
Communication (Advertising and Publicity; Communication Studies; Media Studies); **Confucius Institute** (Chinese); **Ecology** (Ecology); **Educational Sciences** (Adult Education; Educational Sciences; Preschool Education; Primary Education; Secondary Education; Special Education; Teacher Training; Vocational Education); **Estonian Institute for Future Studies**; **Estonian Institute for Humanities** (Anthropology; Arts and Humanities; Cultural Studies; Literature; Modern Languages); **Estonian Language and Culture** (Applied Linguistics; Baltic Languages; Finnish; Linguistics; Literature; Modern Languages; Native Language); **Fine Arts** (Art Therapy; Dance; Fine Arts; Music); **Germanic-Romance Languages and Cultures** (Cultural Studies; Germanic Languages; Romance Languages; Translation and Interpretation); **Health Sciences and Sport** (Leisure Studies; Physical Education; Sports); **History** (Archaeology; History; Medieval Studies); **Informatics** (Information Technology; Multimedia); **Information Studies** (Information Management; Information Sciences); **International and Social Studies** (Gender Studies; International Studies; Social Sciences; Sociology); **Mathematics and Natural Sciences** (Biology; Chemistry; Environmental Management; Geology; Mathematics; Physics); **Political Science and Governance** (Government; Political Sciences; Public Administration); **Population Studies** (Demography and Population); **Psychology** (Behavioural Sciences; Industrial and Organizational Psychology; Psychology); **Slavonic Languages and Culture** (Journalism; Russian; Slavic Languages); **Social Work** (Social Work)

Schools
Film and Media (Baltic School) (Cinema and Television; Film; Journalism; Mass Communication; Public Relations); **Law** (Tallin University Law School formerly University Nord (Akadeemia Nord)) (Advertising and Publicity; Commercial Law; European Union Law; International Law; Law; Marketing; Public Law)

History: Founded 2005 as a merger from several universities and research institutes in Tallinn. Merger with Akadeemia Nord/University Nord 2010.

Governing Bodies: Senate

Academic Year: September to June

Admission Requirements: Secondary school certificate (Gümnaasiumi lõputunnistus) or equivalent.

Fees: (Euros): 900 per semester

Main Language(s) of Instruction: Estonian, Russian, English

International Co-operation: With universities in Finland, United Kingdom, France, Germany, Italy, Spain, Portugal and more

Accrediting Agencies: Estonian Higher Education Quality Agency

Degrees and Diplomas: Bakalaureus: Humanities; Education; Arts; Social Sciences; Natural Sciences; Applied Sciences; Law (Bachelor's Degree), 3 yrs; Magister. Humanities; Education; Arts; Social Sciences; Natural Sciences; Applied Sciences; Law (Master's Degree), a further 2 yrs; Doktor. Humanities; Education; Arts; Social Sciences; Natural Sciences (PhD), a further 4 yrs

Student Services: Academic counselling, Canteen, Cultural centre, Employment services, Foreign student adviser, Foreign Studies Centre, Handicapped facilities, Language programs, Nursery care, Social counselling, Sports facilities

Student Residential Facilities: 3 student dormitories and a guest house for visiting faculty and researchers.

Special Facilities: The Juri Lotman Archive and Memorial Library; Archive-Museum of Estonian Pedagogy; Museum of Estonian Archaeology

Libraries: c. 2,515,385 vols (books, periodicals, electronic- and other publications)

Press or Publishing House: Tallinn University Press

Academic Staff 2010-2011	MEN	WOMEN	TOTAL
FULL-TIME	121	199	**320**
PART-TIME	104	166	**270**
STAFF WITH DOCTORATE			
FULL-TIME	68	85	**153**
PART-TIME	56	68	**124**
Student Numbers 2010-2011			
All (Foreign Included)	2,403	7,234	**9,637**
FOREIGN ONLY	–	–	**357**

Part-time students, 1,268.
Last Updated: 05/07/11

TALLINN UNIVERSITY OF TECHNOLOGY
Tallinna Tehnikaülikool
Ehitajate tee 5, 19086 Tallinn
Tel: +372 6202-002
Fax: +372 6202-020
EMail: ttu@ttu.ee
Website: http://www.ttu.ee

Rector: Andres Keevallik
Tel: +372 6202-003, Fax: +372 6202-004
EMail: peep.surje@ttu.ee

Vice-Rector for Academic Affairs: Kalle Tammemäe
EMail: kalle.tammemae@ttu.ee

Faculties
Chemicals and Materials Technology (Chemical Engineering; Environmental Engineering; Food Technology; Inorganic Chemistry; Materials Engineering; Polymer and Plastics Technology); **Civil Engineering** (Building Technologies; Civil Engineering; Construction Engineering; Environmental Engineering; Transport Engineering); **Information Technology** (Computer Engineering; Electronic Engineering; Information Technology; Telecommunications Engineering); **Mechanical Engineering** (Automotive Engineering; Mechanical Engineering; Metal Techniques; Power Engineering; Production Engineering; Thermal Engineering; Transport Engineering); **Power Engineering** (Electrical Engineering; Geological Engineering; Mining Engineering; Power Engineering); **Science** (Applied Physics; Genetics; Mathematics; Molecular Biology; Organic Chemistry; Physics); **Social Sciences** (Law; Psychology; Public Administration; Social Sciences)

Schools
Economics and Business Administration (Accountancy; Administration; Banking; Business and Commerce; Economics; International Relations; Law; Marketing)

History: Founded 1918 as Engineering College, acquired University status 1936. Name changed to Tallinn Polytechnical Institute 1989. Under the supervision of the Ministry of Education.

Governing Bodies: Council; Board of Governance; Advisory Board

Academic Year: September to June

Admission Requirements: State examination and secondary school certificate (Keskkooli lõputunnistus)

Fees: (Kroons): For EU students: Bachelor, 18,800 per semester; Master, 21,000. For students outside of the EU: Bachelor, 23,500; Master, 27,000.

Main Language(s) of Instruction: Estonian

International Co-operation: With universities in Finland; Sweden; Germany; Denmark; Italy; France; Ireland; United Kingdom; Greece; Portugal

Accrediting Agencies: Estonian Higher Education Accreditation Centre

Degrees and Diplomas: Bakalaureus: Engineering; Natural Sciences; Social Sciences; Humanities (BSc, BA), 3 yrs; Magister. Engineering; Natural Sciences; Social Sciences; Humanities; Business Administration; Public Administration (MSc, MA), a further 2 yrs; Doktor. Engineering; Natural Sciences; Social Sciences; Humanities; Business Administration; Public Administration (Ph, DPA, DEng, DBA), a further 4 yrs

Student Services: Academic counselling, Cultural centre, Employment services, Foreign student adviser, Language programs, Social counselling, Sports facilities

Student Residential Facilities: Yes

Special Facilities: Observatory

Libraries: 750,000 vols

Publications: Proceedings of the Tallinn Technical University and the Estonian Academy of Sciences, Engineering (quarterly)

Press or Publishing House: Tallinn Technical University Press

Last Updated: 25/10/11

TARTU ART COLLEGE
Tartu Kõrgem Kunstikool
Tähe 38b, 50103 Tartu
Tel: +372(7) 309-822
Fax: +372(7) 309-810
EMail: artcol@artcol.ee
Website: http://www.artcol.ee/

Rector: Vallo Nuust Tel: +372(7) 309-822

Departments
Furniture; **General Subjects**; **Leather Design** (Leather Techniques); **Media and Advertisement Design** (Advertising and Publicity; Design; Media Studies); **Painting** (Painting and Drawing); **Photography** (Photography); **Sculpture** (Sculpture); **Textiles** (Textile Technology)

Degrees and Diplomas: Rakenduskõrgharidusõppe diplom: 4 yrs
Last Updated: 14/09/11

UNIVERSITY OF APPLIED SCIENCES
Tallinna Tehnikakõrgkool (TTK)
Pärnu mnt. 62, 10135 Tallinn
Tel: +372 6664-500
Fax: +372 6664-510
EMail: tktk@tktk.ee
Website: http://www.tktk.ee/

Rector: Arvi Altmäe Tel: +372 6664-501

Vice-Rector: Lauri Peetrimägi Tel: +372 6664-502

International Relations: Anne Kraav, Vice-Rector
Tel: +372 6664-503 EMail: anne@tktk.ee

Faculties
Architecture and Enviromental Engineering (Architecture; Ecology; Environmental Engineering); **Clothing and Textile** (Textile Design; Textile Technology); **Construction Engineering** (Civil Engineering; Construction Engineering; Road Engineering); **Mechanical Engineering** (Machine Building; Materials Engineering; Mechanical Engineering); **Transport Logistics** (Automotive Engineering; Railway Engineering; Transport and Communications)

History: Created 1962, acquired present status 1992.

Degrees and Diplomas: Rakenduskõrgharidusõppe diplom: Engineering, 4 yrs
Last Updated: 20/05/11

UNIVERSITY OF TARTU
Tartu Ülikool (TÜ)
Ülikooli 18, 50090 Tartu
Tel: +372(7) 375-100
Fax: +372(7) 375-440
EMail: info@ut.ee
Website: http://www.ut.ee

Rector: Alar Karis Tel: +372(7) 375-600 EMail: rektor@ut.ee

Academies
Culture (Viljandi) Director: Anzori Barkalaja

Colleges
Eurocollege (European Studies); **Narva** (Modern Languages); **Pärnu** (Business Administration; Economics; Environmental Management; Hotel Management; Social Work; Tourism); **Türi**

Faculties
Economics and Business Administration (Business Administration; Economics); **Exercise and Sport Sciences** (Physical Therapy; Sports); **Law** (Law); **Mathematics and Computer Science** (Computer Science; Mathematics); **Medicine** (Dentistry; Medicine; Nursing; Pharmacy); **Philosophy** (Educational Sciences; History; Modern Languages; Painting and Drawing; Philosophy); **Science and Technology**; **Social Sciences and Education** (Cultural Studies; Journal-

ism; Linguistics; Political Sciences; Psychology; Public Administration; Public Relations; Social Sciences; Social Work; Sociology; Special Education; Teacher Training); **Thelology** (Theology)

Institutes
Law (Tallinn) (Law) Director: Heiki Lindpere

Schools
Teacher Education (Teacher Training) Director: Toomas Kink

History: Founded 1802 as Universitas Dorpantensis by Alexander I, with German as the language of instruction but tracing its origins to the Academy founded by Gustav II Adolphus of Sweden in 1632. German was replaced by Russian in 1893, when the University was renamed Universitas Iurievensis. Acquired present title 1919. Has incorporated the Institute of Law, Tallinn, and Tartu Teacher Training College.

Governing Bodies: Advisory Board; Academic Council; Faculty Councils

Academic Year: September to July (September-January; February-July)

Admission Requirements: Secondary school certificate (Keskkooli lõputunnistus) and entrance examination (Sisseastumiseksamid)

Fees: None

Main Language(s) of Instruction: Estonian, Russian, English, German

Degrees and Diplomas: Bakalaureus: 3-4 yrs; Rakenduskõrgharidusõppe diplom: Higher Education, 3-4 yrs; Arstikraad; Hambaarstikraad; Loomaarstikraad: Basic Medical Study, 4-6 yrs; Magister: a further 2 yrs; Doktor (PhD): by thesis after a further 3-5 yrs of research

Student Services: Foreign student adviser

Student Residential Facilities: For c. 3,200 students

Special Facilities: Zoology and Geology Museum; History of Tartu University Museum; Art Museum; Botanical garden

Libraries: c. 4 m. vols

Publications: Acta et Commentationes Universitatis Tartuensis (44 series)

Press or Publishing House: University Press
Last Updated: 25/10/11

PRIVATE INSTITUTIONS
ESTONIAN BUSINESS SCHOOL (EBS)
Lauteri 3, 10114 Tallinn
Tel: +372 6651-300
Fax: +372 6313-959
EMail: ebs@ebs.ee
Website: http://www.ebs.ee

Rector: Peeter Kross
Tel: +372 6651-300 EMail: peeter.kross@ebs.ee

Centres
EBS Executive Training; **Entrepreneurship** (Business Administration); **Ethics** (Ethics)

Departments
Accounting and Finance (Accountancy; Finance); **Behaviour Sciences** (Behavioural Sciences); **Economics** (Economics); **Entrepreneurship** (Business Administration); **Information Technology** (Information Technology); **Management** (Management); **Marketing** (Marketing)

Higher Schools
EBS High School

Institutes
Foreign Languages (Modern Languages) Director: Aet Toots; **Management** (Accountancy; Ethics; Finance; Leadership; Management) Director: Tõnu Kaarelson; **Social Sciences** (Administrative Law; Behavioural Sciences; Economics; Information Technology; Public Administration) Director: Alari Purju

Programmes
Business Administration (Full-time and Master Studies) (Business Administration; Information Technology; International Busi-

1221

ness; Leadership; Management; Modern Languages; Public Administration) *Director*: Kadri Osula

Further Information: Also an Open University Structure Unit

History: Founded 1988, acquired University status 1995, and accredited by the Estonian Government 1997.

Governing Bodies: Senate

Academic Year: September to June (September-December; January-June)

Admission Requirements: Secondary school certificate (Keskkooli lõputunnistus) or equivalent

Fees: (Euros): For EU citizens : 3,304 per annum (Bachelor's level), 3,500 per annum (Master's level), 2,700 per annum (Doctoral level)

Main Language(s) of Instruction: Estonian, English, Russian

International Co-operation: With 70 universities worldwide

Accrediting Agencies: Council of Higher Education in Estonia; Central and East European Management Development Association (CEEMAN)

Degrees and Diplomas: *Bakalaureus*: Social Sciences (BA); *Magister*: Business Administration; Social Sciences; *Doktor*: Management

Student Services: Academic counselling, Foreign student adviser, Sports facilities

Libraries: c. 30,000 vols (8,000 items)

Publications: EBS Review, Scientific University Journal *(biannually)*; Publications of Estonian Business School *(biannually)*
Last Updated: 14/09/11

ESTONIAN-AMERICAN BUSINESS ACADEMY

Eesti-Ameerika Äriakadeemia (EABC)
Punane 29, 13611 Tallinn
Tel: +372 6054-100
Fax: +372 6334-719
EMail: info@eaba.ee
Website: http://www.eaba.ee

Vice-Rector: Helena Gussarova
Tel: +372 6054-114 EMail: helena.gussarova@eaba.ee

Secretary of academic council: Dzaneta Slepak
EMail: dzaneta.slepak@eaba.ee

International Relations: Julia Skoljar, +372 6054-113
EMail: julia.skoljar@eaba.ee

Programmes
Business Administration (Business Administration; Economics; International Business; International Economics; Management; Marketing; Public Administration; Public Relations); **International Tourism Management** (Accountancy; Cultural Studies; English; Finance; History; Law; Management; Social Sciences; Tourism)

History: Founded 1989.

Degrees and Diplomas: *Rakenduskõrghariduōppe diplom*: Higher Education, 4 yrs
Last Updated: 25/10/11

ESTONIAN ENTREPRENEURSHIP UNIVERSITY OF APPLIED SCIENCES

Eesti Ettevõtluskõrgkool Mainor (EUAS)
Suur-Sõjamäe 10A, 11415 Tallinn
Tel: +372 6057-222
Fax: +372 6207-533
EMail: eek@eek.ee
Website: http://www.eek.ee/

Rector: Krista Tuulik (2010-)
Tel: +372 7387-404 EMail: krista.tuulik@eek.ee

Administrative Officer: Tauno Õunapuu
EMail: tauno.ounapuu@eek.ee

Institutes
Design (Graphic Design; Interior Design; Textile Design); **Entrepreneurship**; **Information Technology**; **Management**

History: Founded 1992 as Mainori Majanduskool. Became Mainori Kõrgkool (Mainori Business School) 2003.

Degrees and Diplomas: *Bakalaureus*; *Magister*

Academic Staff *2010*	TOTAL
FULL-TIME	70
PART-TIME	c. 300

Student Numbers *2010*	
All (Foreign Included)	c. 3,000

Last Updated: 25/10/11

EUROACADEMY

Euroakadeemia
Mustamäe tee 4, 10621 Tallinn
Tel: +372 6115-801
Fax: +372 6115-811
EMail: euro@euroakadeemia.ee
Website: http://www.eurouniv.ee

Rector: Jüri Martin
Tel: +372 6115-804 EMail: jmartin@euroakadeemia.ee

Vice-rector: Peeter Karing
Tel: +372 6115-809 EMail: peeter.karing@euroakadeemia.ee

International Relations: Toomas Alatalu
EMail: toomas.alatalu@euroakadeemia.ee

Faculties
Business Administration (Business Administration); **Design** (Design); **Environmental Protection** (Environmental Studies); **International Relations** (International Relations); **Translation and Interpretation** (Translation and Interpretation)

History: Founded as Euro University 1997. Acquired present title 2009.

International Co-operation: Participates in the Erasmus and DoRa Programmes

Degrees and Diplomas: *Bakalaureus*; *Magister*
Last Updated: 25/10/11

Ethiopia

STRUCTURE OF HIGHER EDUCATION SYSTEM

Description:

Higher education is provided by universities, university colleges and specialized institutions. They are under the responsibility of the Ministry of Education. There are also Junior colleges and colleges offering diploma programmes that are under the responsibility of regional governments and private providers.

Stages of studies:

University level first stage: Bachelor's degree
The first stage of university level education leads to the Bachelor's degree after three to four years' study. Examinations are organized at the end of each semester. In Medicine and Veterinary Medicine, the professional qualification of Doctor is conferred after five years' study.

University level second stage: Master's degree; Specialization
The second stage leads to a Master's degree after a minimum of two years' further study (not compulsory). In Medicine and Veterinary Medicine the specialization degree is obtained after a minimum of three years' further study beyond the MD and DVM degrees.

University level third stage: Doctor of Philosophy
The Doctor of Philosophy is conferred after some three years' study (not compulsory) beyond the Master's degree.

Distance higher education:
Distance learning in MBA is offered by Addis Ababa University. Diploma level training is offered by several institutions.

ADMISSION TO HIGHER EDUCATION

Admission to university-level studies:

Name of secondary school credential required: Ethiopian Higher Education Entrance Examination

Minimum score/requirement: Preparatory school transcript 50% and Ethiopian Higher Education Examination score 50% will be considered when students are placed in their field of study.

Other admission requirements: Special privileges for female students and students from disadvantaged/remote regions.

Foreign students admission:

Definition of foreign student: A person enrolled at an institution of higher education in a country of which he/she is not permanently resident.

Quotas: The School of Information Studies for Africa (SISA) admits students from the Eastern and Southern African Region on a quota basis.

Entrance exam requirements: Foreign students must provide the academic certificates required by the institution concerned. Foreign qualifications recognized as equivalent to the Ethiopian school-leaving certificate are: the General Certificate of Education of the University of London; the Cambridge Overseas Examination; the West African School Certificate and the Oxford Examination. The Higher Education Department may grant equivalence to other secondary school-leaving certificates in individual cases. All foreign students must cover their living expenses.

Entry regulations: Visas; financial guarantee. In addition, all foreign students, including ECOWAS citizens, are required to secure resident permits for the period of their stay.

Health requirements: Students must present a health certificate.

Language requirements: Students must be proficient in English at TOEFL level.

RECOGNITION OF STUDIES

Quality assurance system:

The University Senate awards credentials which are recognized by the country. The Ministry of Education is mandated to accredit private and public higher education institutions according to whether they fulfil the required standards.

Bodies dealing with recognition:

Higher Education Sector, Ministry of Education

PO Box 1367
Addis Ababa
Tel: +251(1) 553133/ 560063
Fax: +251(1) 550877/ 550299
Deals with credential recognition for entry to institution: yes
Deals with credential recognition for entry to profession: yes

Special provisions for recognition:

Recognition for university level studies: It applies to nationals who wish to enter medical schools.

NATIONAL BODIES

Ministry of Education

Minister: Mekonnen Demeke
PO Box 1367
Addis Ababa
Tel: +251(111) 553133/ 560063
Fax: +251(111) 550877/ 565565
EMail: heardmoe@telecom.net.et
WWW: http://www.moe.gov.et

Data for academic year: 2007-2008
Source: IAU from UNESCO Delegation for Ethiopia, 2007. Bodies updated in 2011.

INSTITUTIONS

PUBLIC INSTITUTIONS

ADAMA UNIVERSITY (ADU)

PO Box 1888, Nazareth, Oromia
Tel: +251(22) 111-0400
Fax: +251(22) 111-0480
EMail: internationaloffice@adama-university.net
Website: http://www.adama-university.net/

President: Jang Gyu Lee
Tel: +251(22) 111-0494 EMail: PSecretary@adama-university.net

Vice-President for Business and Development: Abdu Abagibie

Vice-President for Administration: Tola Berisso
Tel: +251(22) 111-0511

Faculties
Business Teacher Education; **Computer and Information Technology** (Computer Education; Computer Science; Geology; Information Technology); **Languages and Social Sciences** (Civics; Educational Psychology; English; Ethics); **Natural Sciences** (Applied Chemistry; Applied Mathematics; Applied Physics; Chemistry; Health Education; Health Sciences; Mathematics; Natural Sciences; Physical Education; Physics); **Technical Teacher Education** (Automation and Control Engineering; Construction Engineering; Electrical Engineering; Industrial Engineering; Painting and Drawing; Surveying and Mapping; Technology Education; Wood Technology)

History: Founded 1993 as Nazareth Technical College (NTC). Became Nazareth College of Technical Teacher Education (NCTTE) 2000. Acquired present title 2005.

Degrees and Diplomas: *Bachelor's Degree*; *Master's Degree*. Also Manufacturing Technology programmes: degree programme for Technical Education majors, 3yrs and degree programme for Technicians, 4yrs; programme in Electrical and Electronic Engineering , 4 yrs. Also technology programmes in Automotive Engineering; Construction Engineering; Design and Drafting; Surveying; Electrical and Electronic Engineering; Wood Technology. Also programmes in Accounting; Business Management; Marketing and Sales; Purchasing and Supplies Management; Banking and Insurance.
Last Updated: 30/07/09

ADDIS ABABA UNIVERSITY (AAU)

PO Box 1176, Addis Ababa
Tel: +251(11) 123-9800
Fax: +251(11) 123-9768
EMail: infolib@lib.aau.edu.et; parmilia@yahoo.com
Website: http://www.aau.edu.et

President: Admasu Tsegaye
Tel: +251(11) 123-9752, Fax: +251(11) 123-9768
EMail: poffice@aau.edu.et; commoffice@aau.edu.et

Vice-President for Business and Development: Estifanos G. Hawariat
Tel: +251(11) 123-9783, Fax: +251(11) 123-9729
EMail: hawariat7@yahoo.com

International Relations: Abye Tasse, Associate Vice-President for International Affairs
Tel: +251(11) 123-1084, Fax: +251(11) 123-9766
EMail: abyetas@aau.edu.et

Academies
Ethiopian Languages and Cultures (African Languages; Cultural Studies)

Centres
Research Training and Information for Women Development

Colleges
Commerce (Human Resources); **Education and Behavioural Studies** (Curriculum; Education; Educational Administration; Educational and Student Counselling; Educational Psychology; Educational Research; Educational Sciences; Educational Testing and Evaluation; Geography; Higher Education; Natural Sciences; Physics; Social Psychology; Special Education); **Social Sciences and Humanities** (African Languages; Anthropology; Archaeology; Geography; History; International Relations; Philosophy; Political Sciences; Sociology)

Faculties
Business and Economics (Accountancy; Business Administration; Economics; Finance; Management; Public Administration); **Informatics** (Computer Science; Information Sciences); **Journalism and Communication** (Communication Studies; Journalism); **Law** (Law); **Medicine** (Anaesthesiology; Anatomy; Biochemistry; Community Health; Dental Hygiene; Dermatology; Gynaecology and Obstetrics; Medical Technology; Medicine; Microbiology; Midwifery; Neurology; Nursing; Ophthalmology; Orthopaedics; Otorhinolaryngology; Paediatrics; Parasitology; Pathology; Pharmacology; Physiology; Plastic Surgery; Psychiatry and Mental Health; Radiology; Surgery; Venereology); **Science** (Biology; Biotechnology; Chemistry; Computer Science; Earth Sciences; Environmental Studies; Food Science; Geology; Geophysics; Mathematics; Physics; Statistics); **Technology** (Architecture and Planning; Chemical Engineering; Civil Engineering; Computer Engineering; Construction Engineering; Electrical Engineering; Energy Engineering; Environmental Engineering; Food Technology; Materials Engineering; Mechanical Engineering; Power Engineering; Technology); **Veterinary Medicine** ((Debre Zeit)) (Anatomy; Embryology and Reproduction Biology; Epidemiology; Gynaecology and Obstetrics; Microbiology; Parasitology; Pathology; Physiology; Public Health; Tropical Medicine; Veterinary Science)

Institutes
Language Studies (African Languages; Foreign Languages Education; Linguistics; Literature; Modern Languages; Philology; Theatre)

Programmes
Academic; **Distance and Continuing Education**; **Graduate Studies and Research**

Research Institutes
African Studies (African Studies); **Development** (Demography and Population; Development Studies; Environmental Studies; Gender Studies; Water Science); **Ethiopian Studies**; **Federal Studies**; **Pathobiology** (Pathology); **Peace and Security**

Schools
Fine Arts and Design; **Music** (Music); **Pharmacy** (Pharmacology; Pharmacy)

History: Founded 1961 as Haile Sellassie I University, incorporating University College of Addis Ababa, founded 1950; Imperial College of Engineering, 1953; Ethio-Swedish Institute of Building Technology, 1954; Imperial Ethiopian College of Agricultural and Mechanical Arts, 1951; Public Health College, 1954; and Theological College of the Holy Trinity, 1960. Acquired present title 1975.

Governing Bodies: Board of Governors, Senate

Academic Year: September to July (September-February; February-July). Also Summer programme (July-August)

Admission Requirements: Preparatory Programme certificate, or foreign equivalent

Fees: (US Dollars): 125 - 150 per credit per semester for Master, extra 600 per semester for supervison fee; Research fee, 1,035 - 1,425; for Medicine, 4,658 per annum. Application fee, 10. Registration fee, 10 per semester. Entrance exam fee, 20. Graduation fee, 25.

Main Language(s) of Instruction: English

Degrees and Diplomas: *Bachelor's Degree*: Humanities (BA); Natural and Physical Sciences; Engineering (BSc), 3-4 yrs; *Doctor*: Medicine (MD); Veterinary Medicine (DVM), 5 yrs; *Master's Degree*: Humanities (MA); Natural and Physical Sciences; Engineering (MSc), a further 2 yrs; *Specialization Diploma*: Medicine, a further 2 yrs following MD; *Doctorate*: History; Languages; Chemistry; Biology (PhD), a further 3-4 yrs following MA/MSc

Student Services: Academic counselling, Canteen, Cultural centre, Foreign student adviser, Health services, Social counselling, Sports facilities

Special Facilities: Archives Museum; Natural Museum. Geophysical Observatory. Cultural Centre. Herbarium. Audio-Visual Centre

Libraries: Total, c. 493,000 vols. One main library and other 8 branch libraries.

Publications: Development Forum Bulletin *(quarterly)*; Ethiopian Journal of Development Research *(biannually)*; Ethiopian Journal of Education *(biannually)*; Ethiopian Journal of Science (SINET) *(biannually)*; Ethiopian Medical Journal *(quarterly)*; IGS Informs *(biannually)*; Register of Current Research on Ethiopia and Horn of Africa *(biannually)*

Press or Publishing House: Addis Ababa University Press

Academic Staff 2008-2009	MEN	WOMEN	TOTAL
FULL-TIME	1,512	183	1,695
STAFF WITH DOCTORATE			
FULL-TIME	371	34	405
PART-TIME	84	6	90
Student Numbers 2008-2009			
All (Foreign Included)	20,915	7,311	28,226

Evening students, 16,620.
Note: Evening students are not included in total
Last Updated: 20/05/11

ARBA MINCH UNIVERSITY (AMU)
PO Box 21, Arba Minch, Debub
Tel: +251(46) 881-0097
Fax: +251(46) 881-0279
EMail: president@arbaminch-univ.com
Website: http://www.arbaminch-univ.com/

President: Tarekegn Tadesse
Tel: +251(46) 881-0071 EMail: Tarekegn.tadess@amu.edu.et

Vice-President for Administration and Development: Alemayehu Cufamo EMail: AVP@arbaminch-univ.com

International Relations: Getu Lema
Tel: +251(46) 881-4986 EMail: shewareged2000@yahoo.com

Faculties
Applied Sciences (Applied Chemistry; Applied Mathematics; Applied Physics; Biology); **Business and Economics** (Accountancy; Economics; Finance; Management); **Education** (Education); **Engineering** (Architecture; Civil Engineering; Computer Engineering; Electrical Engineering; Information Technology; Mechanical Engineering)

Institutes
Water Technology (Hydraulic Engineering; Irrigation; Meteorology; Water Management; Water Science)

Schools
Postgraduate Studies (Analytical Chemistry; Biotechnology; Botany; Economics; Environmental Engineering; Hydraulic Engineering; Irrigation; Mathematics; Meteorology; Power Engineering; Water Management; Water Science)

History: Founded 1986 as Arba Minch Water Technology Institute. Acquired present status and title 2004.

Governing Bodies: University Board

Academic Year: September to June

Admission Requirements: High School certificate, National General School Leaving Certificate

Fees: (Ethiopian Birr): Engineering and Technology: 3,011.80; Teacher Education and Social Sciences: 3,011.76; Business and Economics: 2,970.32; Applied Science: 2,971.22 (per Annum)

Main Language(s) of Instruction: English

Accrediting Agencies: Ministry of Education; Higher Education Relevance and Quality Agency of Ethiopia

Degrees and Diplomas: *Bachelor's Degree*: Social Science; Natural and Computational Science; Engineering and Technology; Teacher Education (BSc), 4 yrs; *Master's Degree*: Hydraulic and Water Resource Engineering; Irrigation; Hydrology; Water Resource Development; Meteorology; Water Supply and Environmental Engineering; Botany; Biotechnology; Analytical Chemistry; Power Engineering; Mathematics; Economics (MSc), 2 yrs. Also advanced diploma programmes.

Student Services: Academic counselling, Canteen, Handicapped facilities, Health services, Language programs, Nursery care, Social counselling, Sports facilities

Student Residential Facilities: Student Dormitories, Staff Residence

Libraries: Yes

Publications: Sustainable Water Resources Development in Ethiopia *(annually)*

Academic Staff 2007-2008	MEN	WOMEN	TOTAL
FULL-TIME	310	26	336
STAFF WITH DOCTORATE FULL-TIME	23	–	23
Student Numbers 2007-2008			
All (Foreign Included)	6,657	3,363	10,020

Last Updated: 21/03/11

BAHIR DAR UNIVERSITY (BDU)

PO Box 79, Bahir Dar, Amhara
Tel: +251(58) 220-0137
Fax: +251(58) 220-2025
EMail: infobdu@gmail.com
Website: http://www.bdu.edu.et

President: Baylie Damtie
Tel: +251(58) 220-0143 EMail: bayliedamtie@yahoo.com

Vice-President for Business and Development: G. Egziabher Kahsay Tel: +251(58) 220-0698, Fax: +251(58) 220-2239

Colleges

Agriculture and Environmental Sciences (Agricultural Management; Agriculture; Botany; Development Studies; Environmental Management; Fishery; Natural Resources; Rural Planning; Water Management; Water Science; Wildlife; Zoology); **Business and Economics** (Accountancy; Business Administration; Business and Commerce; Economics; Information Technology; Management; Marketing; Transport Management); **Medical and Health Sciences** (Health Sciences); **Science** (Biology; Chemistry; Industrial Chemistry; Mathematics; Physics; Sports; Statistics)

History: Founded 2000 following merger of Bahir Dar Teachers College and Bahir Dar Polytechnic Institute (Bahir Dar Teachers College, initially known as College of Pedagogy founded 1972 following a tripartite agreement signed between the Ethiopian Government, UNESCO and UNDP; Bahir Dar Polytechnic Institute created 1963 based on an agreement between the former USSR and the Imperial Government of Ethiopia).

Governing Bodies: Board

Academic Year: September to June (September-December; January-March; April-June)

Admission Requirements: Ethiopian School Leaving Certificate (ESLCE) or equivalent

Fees: Cost sharing arrangement

Main Language(s) of Instruction: English

International Co-operation: With universities in United Kingdom and USA.

Accrediting Agencies: Ministry of Education

Degrees and Diplomas: *Bachelor's Degree*: Education (B.Ed.), 3-4 yrs; *Bachelor's Degree*: Engineering (B.Sc.), 4-5 yrs; *Doctor*: Medicine (M.D.), 6 yrs; *Master's Degree*: Education; Science; Social Sciences (M.Ed.), 2-3 yrs

Student Services: Academic counselling, Canteen, Cultural centre, Health services, Sports facilities

Student Residential Facilities: Yes

Libraries: Yes

Publications: Education Bulletin, Research articles *(biannually)*

Academic Staff 2009	MEN	WOMEN	TOTAL
FULL-TIME	893	139	1,032
STAFF WITH DOCTORATE FULL-TIME	40	2	42
Student Numbers 2009			
All (Foreign Included)	19,299	8,454	27,753

Distance students, 9,437. Evening students, 6,585.

Last Updated: 04/08/09

DILLA UNIVERSITY

P.O. Box 419, Dilla
Tel: +251(46) 331-2097
Fax: +251(46) 331-2674
EMail: Dillauniversity@yahoo.com
Website: http://www.dillauniversity.edu.et

President (Acting): Ato Tariku Berasso

Faculties

Agriculture and Rural Development (Agriculture); **Applied Natural Sciences**; **Applied Social Sciences and Humanities** (Anthropology; Journalism; Law; Sociology); **Business and Economics**; **Health Sciences** (Health Sciences); **Teacher Education** (African Languages; Biology; Chemistry; Civics; Educational Administration; English; Environmental Studies; Geography; History; Mathematics; Pedagogy; Physics; Sports)

History: Founded 1996 as Dilla College of Teachers' Education and Health Sciences. Acquired present status 2007.

Degrees and Diplomas: *Bachelor's Degree*

Last Updated: 08/06/07

ETHIOPIAN CIVIL SERVICE COLLEGE (ECSC)

PO Box 5648, Addis Ababa
EMail: ecscpro@ecsc.edu.et
Website: http://www.ecsc.edu.et

President: Haile Michael Aberra (1996-)
EMail: hailemichael.aberra@ecsc.edu.et

Associate Vice-President for Business and Development: Solomon Fisseha EMail: solomonfis@hotmail.com

Academic Vice-President: Abebe Haile-Gabriel
EMail: abebehg@excite.com

Institutes

Distance Education *(IDE)*; **Federalism and Legal Studies**; **Public Management and Development Studies**; **Tax and Customs Administration** (Management; Public Administration; Taxation); **Urban Planning and Management** (Town Planning)

History: Founded 1995.

Governing Bodies: Board; Senate

Academic Year: September to August

Admission Requirements: Ethiopian School Leaving Certificate and pass in entrance examination

Fees: Cost sharing scheme adopted, students pay 25% of net salary to the College

Main Language(s) of Instruction: English

Accrediting Agencies: Ministry of Education

Degrees and Diplomas: *Bachelor's Degree:* Accountancy (BAcc); Development Administration (BDA); Economics (BEc), 3 yrs; *Bachelor's Degree:* Law (LLB); Urban Planning (BSc), 4 yrs; *Master's Degree:* Law; Development Economics; Leadership; Public Financial Management; Urban Management; Federalism; Comparative Public Law and Good Governance; Institutional Law (LLM). Also Advanced Diploma in Urban Engineering, 3 yrs

Student Services: Academic counselling, Canteen, Health services, Language programs, Social counselling, Sports facilities

Student Residential Facilities: Yes

Special Facilities: Interactive video conferencing centre

Libraries: Three libraries in three campuses

Publications: Ethiopian Law Review *(biannually)*; Interaction *(quarterly)*

Last Updated: 28/07/09

HARAMAYA UNIVERSITY (HU)

PO Box 138, Dire Dawa, Harrar
Tel: +251(25) 553-0319
Fax: +251(25) 553-0325
EMail: haramaya@haramaya.edu.et
Website: http://www.haramaya.edu.et

President: Belay Kassa
Tel: +251(25) 661-0707, Fax: +251(25) 553-0335
EMail: belayk@hotmail.com

Vice-President for Academic Affairs and Research: Tena Alamirew
Tel: +251(25) 553-0320, Fax: +251(25) 553-0331
EMail: talamirew@haramaya.edu.et

Vice-President for Administration and Development: Belaineh Legesse
Tel: +251(25) 553-0323 EMail: belaineh_legesse@yahoo.com

Colleges

Agriculture (Agricultural Economics; Agricultural Engineering; Agriculture; Animal Husbandry; Botany; Development Studies; Food Science; Harvest Technology; Rural Planning)

Faculties

Business and Economics; **Computing and Information Technology**; **Continuing and Distance Education**; **Education** (Biology; Chemistry; Education; English; History; Mathematics; Physics); **Health Sciences** (Health Sciences; Laboratory Techniques; Midwifery; Nursing; Public Health); **Law** (Law); **Natural Sciences**; **Social Sciences and Humanities** (Arts and Humanities; English; Geography; History; Native Language; Social Sciences; Sociology); **Technology**

Schools

Medical Sciences (Anatomy; Biochemistry; Medicine; Microbiology; Pathology; Pharmacology; Physiology)

Further Information: Also international Research Centres

History: Founded 1954 as College of Agriculture. A State institution. Acquired present status 1985. Formerly known as Alemaya University.

Governing Bodies: University Board; Senate

Academic Year: September to July (September-February; February-July)

Admission Requirements: Secondary school certificate or equivalent

Main Language(s) of Instruction: English

Degrees and Diplomas: *Diploma:* Accounting; Management; Law; School Principalship; *Bachelor's Degree:* Accounting; Cooperatives (Accounting and Auditing); Cooperatives (Business and Management); Economics; Management (B.A.); Afan Oromo; Biology; Chemistry; English; Geography and Environmental Studies; History; Mathematics; Physics; Sports and Physical Education (B.Ed); Computer Science and IT; Environmental Health; Health Officer - Accelerated Training Program; Medical Laboratory Technology; Public Health; Nursing (B.Sc.); Electrical Engineering; Civil Engineering; Livestock Production and Rangeland Management (B.Sc.); Food Sciences and Postharvest Technology; Natural Resource Management; Plant Sciences; Rural Development and Agricultural Extension; Soil and Water Engineering and Management (B.Sc.); Law (LLB);

Bachelor's Degree: Agribusiness Management; Agricultural Economics; Animal Production and Health; Animal Sciences; Crop Production and Protection (B.Sc), 4-5 yrs; *Doctor:* Veterinary Medicine (MVD); *Master's Degree:* Agricultural Economics; Agricultural Entomology; Agricultural Machinery; Agriculture and Food Marketing; Agronomy; Animal Genetics and Breeding; Animal Production; Food Engineering; Food Science and Technology; Horticulture; Integrated Pest Management (MSc); Irrigation Engineering; Plant Breeding; Plant Pathology; Postharvest Technology; Range Ecology and Management; Rural Development and Agricultural Extension (Rural Development Stream and Agricultural Communication and Innovation Stream) (MSc); Seed Science and Technology; Soil and Water Conservation Engineering; Soil Science; Weed Science; Irrigation; Agronomy; Biology; Physics; Chemistry (MSc), a further 2-3 yrs; *Master's Degree:* Biology; Chemistry; English; Physics (M.Ed.); *Doctorate:* Agricultural Economics; Agronomy/Crop Physiology; Plant Breeding; Plant Pathology; Soil Science; Agricultural Entomology; Animal Genetics and Breeding; Animal Nutrition; Soil and Water Engineering (PhD). Also Certificate Programmes. Also summer and distance learning programmes.

Student Services: Academic counselling, Cultural centre, Health services, Nursery care, Social counselling, Sports facilities

Student Residential Facilities: For c. 1,700 students

Special Facilities: Arboretum. Greenhouse

Libraries: 45,759 vols, 103 periodical subscriptions

Publications: Annual Research Reports *(annually)*; East African Journal of Sciences, Journal *(biannually)*

Academic Staff *2008-2009*	MEN	WOMEN	TOTAL
FULL-TIME	451	58	**509**
PART-TIME	30	–	**30**
STAFF WITH DOCTORATE			
FULL-TIME	61	10	**71**
PART-TIME	20	–	**20**

Student Numbers *2008-2009*			
All (Foreign Included)	22,000	8,000	**30,000**

Part-time students, 6,591. **Distance students**, 6,700. **Evening students**, 3,333.

Last Updated: 27/04/09

HAWASSA UNIVERSITY (HU)

PO Box 05, Hawassa
Tel: +251(46) 220-9676 +251(46) 220-9677
Fax: +251(46) 220-5421
EMail: info@hu.edu.et
Website: http://www.hu.edu.et

President: Yosef Mamo
Tel: +251(46) 220-4627, Fax: +251(46) 220-4975

Vice-President for Administration and Development: Bekele Bulado
Tel: +251(46) 220-4628, Fax: +251(46) 220-4975
EMail: bekelebulado@yahoo.com

International Relations: Seyuom Hameso
Tel: +251(46) 220-5168, Fax: +251(46) 220-4975
EMail: hameso@gmail.com

Colleges

Agriculture *(Awassa)* (Agriculture); **Forestry and Natural Resources** *(Wondogenet)* (Forest Products; Forestry; Natural Resources); **Health Sciences** (Health Sciences); **Public Health** (Public Health)

Faculties

Business and Economics (Accountancy; Business Administration; Economics); **Education** (Biology; Chemistry; Education; English; Geography; History; Mathematics; Native Language; Physics; Teacher Training); **Hotel Management and Tourism** (Hotel Management; Tourism); **Law** (Law); **Medicine** (Medicine); **Natural Sciences** (Applied Chemistry; Applied Mathematics; Applied Physics; Biology; Computer Science; Statistics); **Social Sciences** (Anthropology; Civics; Development Studies; English; Ethics; Geography; Government; Psychology; Social Sciences; Sociology); **Technology** (Agricultural Engineering; Civil Engineering; Electrical Engineering; Soil Management; Technology; Water Management); **Veterinary Science** (Veterinary Science)

History: Founded 2000 following merger of Awassa College of Agriculture (ACA), Dilla College of Teachers Education and Health Sciences (DCTEHS) and Wondo Genet College of Forestry (WGCF). Previously known as Debub University. Acquired present title 2006.

Governing Bodies: Board of Directors

Academic Year: September to June

Admission Requirements: Secondary school leaving certificate

Fees: (US Dollars): 100 per credit hour for foreign students

Main Language(s) of Instruction: English

Accrediting Agencies: Ministry of Education

Degrees and Diplomas: *Diploma*: 2 yrs; *Bachelor's Degree*: Agricultural Engineering (BSc), 5 yrs; *Bachelor's Degree*: Science; Education; Arts, 4 yrs; *Master's Degree*: Plant Sciences; Animal Sciences; Production Forestry (MSc), a further 2 yrs

Student Services: Academic counselling, Canteen, Foreign student adviser, Health services, Language programs, Social counselling, Sports facilities

Student Residential Facilities: Yes (for all regular students)

Libraries: Central Library

Academic Staff 2008-2009	MEN	WOMEN	TOTAL
FULL-TIME	831	102	**933**
STAFF WITH DOCTORATE FULL-TIME	44	2	**46**
Student Numbers 2008-2009			
All (Foreign Included)	–	–	**13,755**

Part-time students, 5,590.
Last Updated: 25/05/09

JIMMA UNIVERSITY (JU)

PO Box 378, Jimma, Oromia
Tel: +251(47) 111-2202 +251(47) 111-1458
Fax: +251(47) 111-1450 +251(47) 111-2040
EMail: eroq@ju.edu.et
Website: http://www.ju.edu.et

President: Fikre Lemessa
Tel: +251(47) 111-1457
EMail: kaba.urgessa@ju.edu.et; urgessak2001@yahoo.co.in

Vice-President for Administration and Development: Kora Tushune
Tel: +251(47) 111-1095, Fax: +251(47) 111-6874
EMail: korat@ju.edu.et; ktushune@yahoo.com

International Relations: Melkamu Dumessa, Director for Public Relations and Communications
Tel: +251(47) 111-2202, Fax: +251(47) 111-0122
EMail: ero@ju.edu.et

Colleges
Agriculture and Veterinary Medicine (Agricultural Economics; Animal Husbandry; Aquaculture; Crop Production; Fishery; Forestry; Horticulture; Natural Resources; Plant and Crop Protection; Soil Science); **Business and Economics** (Business Administration; Economics); **Natural Sciences** (Biology; Chemistry; Mathematics; Physical Education; Physics; Sports; Statistics); **Public Health and Medical Sciences** (Medicine; Public Health); **Social Sciences and Law** (African Languages; English; Environmental Studies; Folklore; Geography; Government; History; Law; Psychology; Sociology)

Institutes
Technology (Biomedical Engineering; Chemical Engineering; Civil Engineering; Computer Engineering; Computer Science; Electrical Engineering; Information Technology; Mechanical Engineering; Water Science)

Programmes
Continuing and Distance Education (Accountancy; African Languages; Banking; Biology; Chemistry; Civil Engineering; Economics; Electrical Engineering; English; Geography; History; Horticulture; Information Technology; Insurance; Law; Management; Marketing; Mathematics; Native Language; Nursing; Pharmacy; Physics; Secretarial Studies)

Schools
Graduate Studies (Entomology; Epidemiology; Gynaecology and Obstetrics; Horticulture; Medicine; Natural Resources; Paediatrics; Plant Pathology; Public Health; Surgery)

History: Founded 1999 through amalgamation of Jimma College of Agriculture (founded 1952) and Jimma Institute of Health Sciences (founded 1983)

Governing Bodies: Board of Governors; University Senate

Academic Year: September to June

Admission Requirements: Ethiopian General Secondary School examination

Fees: None

Main Language(s) of Instruction: English

Accrediting Agencies: HERQA

Degrees and Diplomas: *Bachelor's Degree*: Accounting; Afaan Oromo; Amharic; Banking and Finance; Economics; English; Geography; Governance; History; Law; Management; Oromo Folklore; Psychology; Sociology (BA); Agro Economics; Anaesthesia; Animal Sciences; Biology; Chemistry; Environmental Health; Health Education; Health Service Management; Horticulture and Plant Sciences; Information Sciences (BSc); Information Technology; Mathematics; Medical Laboratory; Natural Resources Management; Pharmacy; Physical Education and Sports; Physics; Population and Family Health; Statistics (BSc), 3 yrs; *Bachelor's Degree*: Engineering: (Civil, Mechanical, Biomedical, Computer, Electrical, Water Resource) (BSc), 5 yrs; *Doctor*: Medicine (MD), 6 yrs

Student Services: Academic counselling, Canteen, Cultural centre, Health services, Sports facilities

Student Residential Facilities: Yes

Special Facilities: Computer Centre; Audio-Visual Service

Libraries: University Library

Publications: Ethiopian Journal of Health Science (*biennially*)
Last Updated: 10/08/09

MEKELLE UNIVERSITY (MU)

PO Box 231, Mekelle, Tigrai
Tel: +251(34) 440-7500 +251(34) 440-0512
Fax: +251(34) 440-9304
EMail: muccm@mu.edu.et
Website: http://www.mu.edu.et

President: Joachim Herzig Tel: +251(34) 440-9228

Vice-President for Support Services: Yassin Ibrahim
Tel: +251(344) 440-5529
EMail: yassinibrahim2006@yahoo.com; yasin.ibrahim@mu.edu.et

International Relations: Fredu Nega, Director, Corporate Communication and Marketing
Tel: +251(34) 440-404005
EMail: fredu.nega@mu.edu.et; tfredu@yahoo.com

Colleges
Business and Economics (Business and Commerce; Economics); **Dry Land Agriculture and Natural Resources** *(FDAR)* (Agricultural Economics; Agricultural Management; Agriculture; Animal Husbandry; Arid Land Studies; Crop Production; Development Studies; Environmental Studies; Horticulture; Natural Resources; Pastoral Studies; Rural Planning; Soil Management; Tropical Agriculture; Wildlife); **Engineering** (Architecture; Computer Engineering; Computer Science; Electrical Engineering; Engineering; Industrial Engineering; Information Sciences; Mechanical Engineering; Town Planning); **Health Sciences** (Health Sciences); **Law and Governance** (Civics; Ethics; Law); **Natural and Computational Science** (Biology; Chemistry; Earth Sciences; Geological Engineering; Geology; Mathematics; Mathematics and Computer Science; Natural Sciences; Physics; Water Science); **Social Sciences and Languages** (Communication Studies; Environmental Studies; Geography; History; Journalism; Modern Languages; Native Language; Psychology; Social Sciences); **Veterinary Medicine** (Veterinary Science)

Institutes
Pale Environment and Heritage Conservation (Heritage Preservation); **Pedagogical Sciences** (Pedagogy)

History: Founded 2000 following merger of Mekelle Business College and Mekelle University College.

Governing Bodies: Mekelle University Board

Academic Year: September to June (September-January; February-June)

Main Language(s) of Instruction: English

International Co-operation: With universities in Belgium and Norway

Degrees and Diplomas: *Bachelor's Degree*: Applied Geology; Petroleum Engineering (B.Sc.); Economics; Physics; Chemistry; Mathematics; Biology; Sport Science; Natural Resource Economic Management; Land Resource Management and Environmental Protection; Animal and Wild Life Sciences; Crop and Horticulture; Heritage Conservation (B.Sc.); Journalism and Communication; Geography and Environmental Sciences; History; Amharic; Tigrina; Foreign Languages; Psychology; Accounting and Finance; Cooperative Studies; Business Management; Public Development and Management; Civics and Ethics (B.A.); Nursing; Public Health (B.A.), 3 yrs; *Bachelor's Degree*: Law (LL.B.), 5 yrs; *Bachelor's Degree*: Pharmacy (B.Pharm), 4 yrs; *Doctor*: Medicine (MD); Veterinary Medicine (DVM), 6 yrs; *Master's Degree*: Dry Land Agronomy; Tropical Land Resource Management; Livestock Production and Pastoral Development; Engineering Geology; Hydrogeology; Economic Geology; Rural Development; Physics; Development Policy and Natural Resource Economics (M.Sc.); Finance and Development; Cooperative Marketing; Development Studies; Business Administration (M.Sc.); Public Health (MPH), 2 yrs; *Master's Degree*: Integrated Emergency Obstetric and Surgery, 3 yrs

Student Services: Academic counselling, Canteen, Cultural centre, Health services, Sports facilities

Student Residential Facilities: For staff and regular students

Libraries: Six libraries (reading room; Periodical Subscriptions and Documentation; Book Store; Catalogue; Internet)

Publications: Journal of Drylands, An interdisciplinary journal for dryland research and sustainable development *(1-2 per annum)*; Momona Ethiopian Journal of Science, A peer reviewed journal that focuses on research related to Earth, Physical, Chemistry, Biological and Computational Sciences *(1-2 per annum)*; Profile of Research Projects *(annually)*; Tigray Livelihood Working Paper

Academic Staff 2008-2009	MEN	WOMEN	TOTAL
FULL-TIME	1,011	108	1,119
STAFF WITH DOCTORATE FULL-TIME	36	2	38
Student Numbers 2008-2009			
All (Foreign Included)	11,526	4,944	16,470

Last Updated: 27/04/09

UNIVERSITY OF GONDAR (UGR)

PO Box 196, Gondar, Amhara
Tel: +251(58) 111-0174
Fax: +251(58) 114-1240
EMail: uogmail@uog.edu.et
Website: http://www.ugondar.edu.et

President (Acting): Mengesha Admasu
Tel: +251(58) 114-1231 EMail: kal_meng@yahoo.com

International Relations: Ephrem Melaku Mamo
EMail: ephmelk@yahoo.com

Colleges
Medicine and Health Sciences (Anaesthesiology; Health Sciences; Laboratory Techniques; Medicine; Midwifery; Nursing; Nutrition; Occupational Health; Ophthalmology; Optometry; Pharmacy; Public Health)

Faculties
Engineering; **Law** (Law); **Management and Economics**; **Natural Sciences** (Biology; Chemistry; Computer Science; Mathematics; Physics; Statistics); **Social Sciences and Humanities** (Anthropology; English; Environmental Management; Environmental Studies; Geography; History; Modern Languages; Psychology; Sociology; Zoology); **Veterinary Science** (Veterinary Science; Zoology)

Further Information: Campuses: Maraki, Science Amba, Tewodros
History: Founded 1954 as Gondar Public Health College and Training Centre. Acquired present status 2004.

Governing Bodies: Board of Directors

Admission Requirements: Ministry of Education decides

Fees: (Ethiopian Birr): 2,937.43-3,829.15

Main Language(s) of Instruction: English

Degrees and Diplomas: *Bachelor's Degree*: 3-4 yrs; *Doctor*: 6 yrs; *Master's Degree*: 2 yrs; *Doctorate*: 3 yrs. Also satellite Training Programmes (diploma level degrees offered in junior colleges outside Gondar); Semi-distance Training (students need to be present only 10-12 weeks per annum).

Student Services: Academic counselling, Canteen, Health services, Nursery care, Social counselling, Sports facilities

Publications: Ethipian Journal of Health and Biomedical Sciences *(annually)*

Academic Staff 2008-2009	MEN	WOMEN	TOTAL
FULL-TIME	578	87	665
STAFF WITH DOCTORATE FULL-TIME	6	–	6
Student Numbers 2008-2009			
All (Foreign Included)	9,654	4,143	13,797

Evening students, 2,812.
Last Updated: 04/06/09

WOLLEGA UNIVERSITY (WU)

PO Box 395, Nekemte, Oromia
Tel: +251(57) 661-7981
Fax: +251(57) 661-7980
EMail: wu@ethionet.et
Website: http://www.wuni.edu.et

President: Fekadu Beyene
Tel: +257(57) 661-7979, Fax: +257(57) 661-7890
EMail: fekadu.beyene@yahoo.com

Vice-President for Administration and Development: Abera Fite

International Relations: Getu Abebe, Public and External Relation Officer

Colleges
Agriculture and Rural Development (Agriculture; Animal Husbandry; Food Science; Food Technology; Irrigation; Natural Resources; Plant and Crop Protection; Rural Studies; Soil Management; Veterinary Science; Water Management); **Education**; **Health Sciences** (Environmental Studies; Health Sciences; Laboratory Techniques; Nursing; Pharmacy; Public Health)

Faculties
Business and Economics; **Engineering and Technology** (Architecture; Civil Engineering; Computer Science; Electrical Engineering; Engineering; Information Technology; Mechanical Engineering); **Natural sciences and Mathmatics** (Biology; Chemistry; Earth Sciences; Mathematics; Physics; Statistics); **Social Sciences and Language**

Schools
Law (Law)

History: Founded 2007.

Governing Bodies: Board; Senate; Academic Commission and Department Council

Academic Year: October to June: (October-January; March-June)

Admission Requirements: General Secondary School Completion Certificate Examination; Completion of Preparatory Program (10+2), pass mark in Entrance Examination

Main Language(s) of Instruction: English

International Co-operation: Ethiopian Higher Education Relevance and Quality Assurance Agency

Degrees and Diplomas: *Bachelor's Degree*: Law (LLB); Technology; Veterinary Medicine, 5 yrs; *Bachelor's Degree*: Natural Sciences; Social Sciences (BSc; BA), 3 yrs; *Master's Degree*

Student Services: Academic counselling, Canteen, Cultural centre, Employment services, Foreign student adviser, Health services, Language programs, Social counselling, Sports facilities

Student Residential Facilities: For 7,000 students

Libraries: Two library: For Business and Economics and Social Science; and for Natural Sciences, Techonology, Agriculture and Health Sciences

Publications: Research Report, Research activities and Guidelines *(annually)*; WU Info Sciences *(quarterly)*

Academic Staff *2008-2009*	MEN	WOMEN	TOTAL
FULL-TIME	352	15	**367**
PART-TIME	–	–	**12**
STAFF WITH DOCTORATE			
FULL-TIME	–	–	**15**
PART-TIME	–	–	**10**
Student Numbers *2008-2009*			
All (Foreign Included)	3,250	755	**4,005**
FOREIGN ONLY	–	–	**4**

Part-time students, 28. **Distance students**, 960. **Evening students**, 1,890.

Last Updated: 06/05/09

UNITY UNIVERSITY

Gerji
Website: http://www.uu.edu.et

President: Arega Yirdaw

Faculties

Architecture and Urban Planning (Architecture; Town Planning); **Business and Economics** (Business and Commerce; Economics); **Humanities and Social Sciences** (Modern Languages; Philosophy; Psychology); **Information Technology and Computer Science** (Computer Science; Information Technology; Mathematics; Statistics)

Schools

Distance and Continuing Education (Continuing Education; Distance Education); **Health Sciences** (Health Sciences); **Journalism and Communication** (Communication Studies; Journalism); **Law and International Studies** (International Studies; Law)

History: Founded 1991 as Unity College. Became Unity University College 2002. Acquired present status 2008.

Degrees and Diplomas: *Bachelor's Degree*; *Master's Degree*
Last Updated: 18/07/11

Fiji

STRUCTURE OF HIGHER EDUCATION SYSTEM

Description:

Higher education is mainly provided by the University of the South Pacific and institutions of higher education. The University serves eleven English-speaking territories in the South Pacific. It is financed by fees, funds from the Fiji government and other territories and aids from Australia, New Zealand, Canada and the United Kingdom.

Stages of studies:

University level first stage: *Bachelor's degree*
The first stage of higher education leads, after three years' study, to the Bachelor's degree. A Diploma in Tropical Agriculture is conferred by the Fiji College of Agriculture after three years. In Medicine, the first degree takes six years at the Fiji School of Medicine.

University level second stage: *Master's degree*
The Master's degree is conferred after one-and-a-half years' full-time or two-and-a-half years' part-time study beyond the Bachelor's degree. It is awarded either after the submission of a thesis following research in an approved topic or after course work, examination and thesis.

University level third stage: *Doctor of Philosophy*
The third stage leads to the award of a Doctor of Philosophy Degree. Studies last for two years' full-time or four years' part-time after the Master's degree.

Distance higher education:
The University Extension Service offers distance education throughout the area served by the University. There are Extension Centres in most countries in the area. Courses are provided by correspondence or satellite. The University has a network of terminals which provides a wide range of educational facilities to most regional centres. No formal qualifications are required for entry to non-credit courses. The University may award Certificates, Diplomas or Degrees to students who have satisfactorily completed such programmes of credit study organized by extension services.

ADMISSION TO HIGHER EDUCATION

Admission to university-level studies:

Name of secondary school credential required: Seventh Form Examination

Alternatives to credentials: One-year foundation course at the University.

Foreign students admission:

Entrance exam requirements: Foreign students must hold qualifications equivalent to the university's foundation programme, e.g. the General Certificate of Education, Advanced Level, the New Zealand Form 7 or successful completion of the final year in Australian secondary education.

NATIONAL BODIES

Ministry for Education
Minister: Filipe Bole
Director, Higher Education: Salote Rabuka
Marela House
Suva
Tel: +679 331 4477
Fax: +679 330 3511
WWW: http://www.education.gov.fj/
Role of national body: The Ministry is concerned with broad policy issues on all aspects of education.

Data for academic year: 2006-2007
Source: IAU from documentation and International Comparisons website, UK Naric, 2007 (Laws, 2008; Bodies, 2011)

INSTITUTIONS

FIJI NATIONAL UNIVERSITY

Private Mail Bag, Hoodless House, CWM Hospital Campus, Suva
EMail: ian.rouse@fnu.ac.fj
Website: http://www.fsm.ac.fj

Dean: Ian Rouse

Departments
Health Science (Anatomy; Biochemistry; Medical Technology; Microbiology; Pharmacology; Pharmacy; Physical Therapy; Physiology; Radiology); **Medical Sciences** (Anaesthesiology; Gynaecology and Obstetrics; Medicine; Paediatrics; Surgery); **Oral Health** (Dentistry; Epidemiology); **Public Health** (Dietetics; Epidemiology; Health Administration; Nutrition; Public Health)

History: Founded 1855. Acquired present status and title 2010 following merger of the Fiji School of Medicine and the Fiji School of Nursing.

Degrees and Diplomas: *Diploma*: Physiotherapy; Radiography; Medical Laboratory Technology; Pharmacy Technician; Public Health; Public Health Nutrition; Dietetics; Environmental Health; Applied Epidemiology; Health promotion; Health Service Management; Dental Therapy; Dental Technology; *Bachelor's Degree*: Dental Surgery (BDS), 5 yrs; *Bachelor's Degree*: Environmental Health (BEH); Public Health (BPH), 3 yrs; *Bachelor's Degree*: Medicine and Surgery (MBBS), 6 yrs; *Bachelor's Degree*: Pharmacy (Bpharm), 4 yrs; *Master's Degree*: Obstetrics and Gynaecology; Paediatrics; Internal Medicine; Surgery; Anaesthesia
Last Updated: 21/03/11

UNIVERSITY OF THE SOUTH PACIFIC (USP)

Laucala Campus, Suva
Tel: +679 323-1000
Fax: +679 323-1531
EMail: studentinfo@usp.ac.fj
Website: http://www.usp.ac.fj

Vice-Chancellor: Rajesh Chandra
Tel: +679 323-2312, Fax: +679 323-1550
EMail: chandra_r@usp.ac.fj

Registrar: Walter Fraser
Tel: +679 323-2292, Fax: +679 323-1521
EMail: fraser_w@usp.ac.fj

Faculties
Arts and Law (Arts and Humanities; Development Studies; Education; Educational Psychology; Government; History; Law; Linguistics; Literacy Education; Literature; Pacific Area Studies; Political Sciences; Social Sciences; Sociology; Teacher Training) *Dean*: Robert Hughes; **Business and Economics** (Accountancy; Business Administration; Business and Commerce; Economics; Finance; Management; Public Administration) *Dean*: Jeffery Born; **Islands and Oceans** (Agricultural Education; Agricultural Engineering; Agriculture; Animal Husbandry; Crop Production; Cultural Studies; Environmental Studies; Fine Arts; Food Technology; Geography; Marine Science and Oceanography; Natural Resources; Soil Science; Tourism) *Dean*: Pa'olelei Luteru; **Science and Technology** (Biology; Chemistry; Computer Science; Electrical Engineering; Environmental Studies; Information Sciences; Mathematics; Mechanical Engineering; Physics; Statistics) *Dean*: Derek Gardiner

Further Information: Campuses in Fiji (Laucala Campus), Samoa (Alafua Campus) and Vanuatu (Emalus Campus). Also Centres in Cook Islands, Fiji, Kiribati, Nauru, Niue, Marshall Islands, Samoa, Solomon Islands, Tokelau, Tonga, Tuvalu and Vanuatu. Also Analytical Laboratory. Courses in Pacific Culture and English bridging programmes for foreign students

History: Founded 1968. Acquired present status 1970.

Governing Bodies: University Council

Academic Year: February to November (February-June; July-November)

Admission Requirements: Secondary school certificate and successful completion of the Foundation programme

Fees: Varies according to campus

Main Language(s) of Instruction: English

Degrees and Diplomas: *Diploma*: Accountancy; Banking; Community Development; Computing; Early Childhood Education; Economics; Educational Evaluation; Fisheries Economics and Management; Geographic Information Systems (GIS); Industrial Relations; Information Systems; Land Use Planning; Library and Information Studies; Management; Ocean Resources Management and Policy; Pacific Journalism; Pacific Language Studies; Police Management; Population Studies and Demography; Real Estate; Social Services; Special and Diverse Educational Needs; Tropical Agriculture; Vernacular Languages : Fijian and Hindi; Youth in Development Work, 1 yr; *Bachelor's Degree*: Agriculture (Bagr); Arts; Education (Bed); Engineering Technology (BETech); Science (BSc), 3 yrs; *Bachelor's Degree*: Law (LLB), 4 yrs; *Master's Degree*: Arts (MA), a further 11/2 yrs; *Master's Degree*: Education (Med), a further 2 yrs; *Master's Degree*: Law (LLM); *Postgraduate Certificate/Diploma*: Accountancy and Finacial Management; Applied Psychology; Banking and Finance; Biology; Business Administration; Chemistry; Computer Science; Development Studies; Earth Sciences; Economics; Education; Engineering; Geography; Governance; History; Politics; Graduate : Education; Public Sector Management; Tertiary Teaching; Postgraduate : Business Administration; Climate Change; Tertiary Teaching; Literature; Linguistics; Pacific Media Studies; Management and Public Administration; Marine Affairs; Marine Science; Physics; Population Studies and Demography; Real Estate; Social Policy and Administration; Sociology; Tourism, a further 1 yr; *Doctor of Philosophy (PhD)*: a further 3 yrs. Also 1 to 2 yr certificates

Student Services: Academic counselling, Cultural centre, Foreign student adviser, Health services, Nursery care, Social counselling, Sports facilities

Student Residential Facilities: For 675 students

Special Facilities: South Pacific Regional Herbarium. Oceania Centre for Arts and Culture

Libraries: c. 980,000 vols; Pacific Collection, c. 56,000 vols

Publications: Report of the Higher Education Mission to the South Pacific (the Morris Report); USP Strategic Plan/Planning for the Fourth Decade
Last Updated: 23/03/09

Finland

STRUCTURE OF HIGHER EDUCATION SYSTEM

Description:

Finland has a binary system of higher education which comprises universities and polytechnics. The Finnish higher education system comprises universities (yliopisto/universitet) and polytechnics (ammattikorkeakoulu, AMK/yrkeshögskola, YH). Some universities are multi-faculty universities and others are specialized institutions. All universities engage in both education and research and have the right to award doctorates. The polytechnics are multi-field institutions of professional higher education. They are specialized in applied research and development. Universities award first cycle university degrees (Kandidaatti/Kandidat), second cycle university degrees (Maisteri/Magister) and third cycle scientific post-graduate degrees (Lisensiaatti/Licentiat and Tohtori/Doktor). Polytechnics award first cycle polytechnic degrees (ammattikorkeakoulututkinto - AMK/yrkehögskoleexamen - YH) and second cycle polytechnic degrees (ylempi ammattikorkeakoulututkinto - ylempi AMK/högre yrkeshögskoleexamen - högre YH).

Stages of studies:

University level first stage: Universities: kandidaatti/kandidat (first cycle)
First-cycle university degrees consist of at least 180 credits (3 years of full-time study). They are called kandidaatti/kandidat in all fields except in Law (oikeusnotaari/rättsnotarie) and Pharmacy (farmaseutti/farmaceut). Studies leading to the degree provide the student with: (1) knowledge of the fundamentals of the major and minor subjects or corresponding study entities or studies included in the degree programme and the prerequisites for following developments in the field; (2) knowledge and skills needed for scientific thinking and the use of scientific methods or knowledge and skills needed for artistic work; 3) knowledge and skills needed for studies leading to a higher university degree and for continuous learning; (4) a capacity for applying the acquired knowledge and skills to work; and (5) adequate language and communication skills. Studies may include: basic and intermediate studies; language and communication studies; interdisciplinary programmes; other studies and work practice for professionnal development. The degree includes a Bachelor's thesis (6-10 credits).

University level second stage: Universities: maisteri/magister (second cycle)
The second-cycle university degree consists of at least 120 credits (two years of full-time study). The degree is usually called maisteri/magister. Other second-cycle degrees are diplomi-insinööri/diplomingenjör (Technology); arkkitehti/arkitekt (Architecture); and proviisori/provisor (Pharmacy). The admission requirement to second cycle university courses is a first cycle degree. The second cycle university degree title in the fields of medicine, dentistry and veterinary medicine is lisensiaatti/licentiate. In the field of medicine and dentistry, the university may arrange the education leading to the second cycle university degree without including a lower university degree. In medicine, the degrees consists of 360 credits (6 years of full-time study) and in dentistry the degree consists of 300 credits (5 years of full-time study). Studies leading to the second cycle university degree provide the student with: (1) good overall knowledge of the major subject or a corresponding entity and conversant with the fundamentals of the minor subject or good knowledge of the advanced studies included in the degree programme; (2) knowledge and skills needed to apply scientific knowledge and methods or knowledge and skills needed for independent and demanding artistic work; (3) knowledge and skills needed for operating independently as an expert and developer of the field; (4) knowledge and skills needed for scientific or artistic postgraduate education; and (5) good language and communication skills. Studies leading to the second cycle university degree may include: basic, intermediate and advanced studies, language and communication studies; interdisciplinary study programme; other studies; and internship improving expertise. The degree includes a Master's thesis (20-40 credits). The reformed university degree structure was adopted August 1, 2005. The reform created a two-tier degree structure with an obligatory first cycle degree in all fields except for medicine, dentistry and veterinary medicine. Before, students were able to pursue one-cycle Masters in five years. The degrees from the former structure are fully comparable to the new degrees and they give the same academic and professional rights.

University level third stage: Universities: lisensiaati/licenciat; tohtori/doktor (third cycle)
Students can apply for doctoral programmes after the completion of a relevant second-cycle degree. The aim of doctoral studies is to provide the student with in-depth knowledge of his/her field of research and capabilities to

produce new scientific knowledge independently. A pre-doctoral degree (lisensiaati/licenciat) in two years may be taken before the Doctor's Degree programme. Studies for the Doctor's degree take approximately four years of full-time study beyond a second-cycle degree or two years of full-time study beyond a pre-doctoral degree. Students admitted to doctoral studies must complete a certain number of courses, show independent and critical thinking in their field of research and write a doctoral dissertation to be defended in public.

Distance higher education:
Open university and open polytechnic education is organized according to university syllabi by Universities and Polytechnic Centres for Continuing Education. There are no formal education pre-requisites for entering. Although open universities and open polytechnics do not award degrees, students may have their studies recognized as part of degree studies upon admission at a higher education institution.

ADMISSION TO HIGHER EDUCATION

Admission to university-level studies:

Name of secondary school credential required: Ammatillinen perustutkintotodistus/ Betyg över yrkesinriktad grundexamen

For entry to: Universities

Name of secondary school credential required: Ylioppilastutkintotodistus/Studentexamensbetyg

For entry to: Universities

Alternatives to credentials: Lukion päättödistus/Avgångsbetyg från gymnasiet; Certificate for the International Baccalaureate; European Baccalaureate, Reifeprüfung; Vocational (3 years) Qualification Certificate (Ammatillinen perustutkintotodistus/Betyg over yrkesinriktad grundexamen). Foreign equivalents.

Entrance exam requirements: Various types of entrance examinations.

Numerus clausus/restrictions: Restricted entry in all fields of study.

Foreign students admission:

Definition of foreign student: The term foreign student usually applies to students, regardless of nationality or native language, who have completed their secondary education in any country other than Finland.

Entrance exam requirements: Students must have completed secondary education. Foreign qualifications equivalent to the Finnish qualifications that give eligibility to apply for higher education in the country of origin. Higher education institutions select their students independently. Entrance examinations are applied and there is a numerus clausus in all fields of study.

Entry regulations: Depending on the nationality and the length of stay in Finland, a visa or a residence permit may be required by immigration authorities.

Language requirements: In most cases, students must have good working knowledge of Finnish or Swedish. In international degree programmes, the teaching language can be English or some other foreign language in which case the applicants must show proof of their good knowledge of the foreign language.

RECOGNITION OF STUDIES

Quality assurance system:

The Finnish degrees of higher education are listed in the Decree on the structure of higher education degrees. The field-specific national decrees on university degrees define the objectives, length and overall structure of university degrees. The national decree on polytechnics defines the objectives, length and overall structure of polytechnic degrees. The Ministry of Education confirms the degree programmes of the polytechnics. Universities and polytechnics are obliged by legislation to evaluate their activities systematically. The Finnish Higher Education Evaluation Council is an independent expert body assisting universities, polytechnics and the Ministry of Education in matters relating to evaluation. The Finnish Higher Education Evaluation Council (FINHEEC) has been conducting audits of the quality assurance (QA) systems of higher education institutes (HEIs) since autumn 2005, with the aim of auditing all Finnish HEIs by the end of 2011. Auditing assesses the comprehensiveness, performance and effectiveness of the QA system and focuses on two levels: the HEI's QA system as a whole and the quality assurance related to the HEI's basic mission (education, research/R&D,

interaction with and impact on society and regional development).

In 2003, the five Nordic ENIC/NARIC offices (Denmark, Finland, Iceland, Norway and Sweden) established a regional network named Nordic National Recognition Information Centres (NORRIC) to initiate joint Nordic projects to learn from each other and reduce barriers to the recognition of foreign qualifications in the Nordic region (www.norric.org).

The academic recognition of qualifications is the responsibility of the higher education institution to which the holder of a foreign qualification is applying for admission. The institutions decide independently on matters related to student selection and the recognition of previous studies.

Special provisions for recognition:

For exercising a profession: The National Board of Education decides on the competence for civil service posts conferred by qualifications taken abroad. -Decisions on the right to practise a profession are made by the competent authority in the respective field. The right to practice a profession in Finland is required from, e.g. health-care professionals and seafarers.

The recognition of professional competence of citizens of EU/EEA countries, who have gained their professional competence in another EU/EEA country, is regulated by law (1093/2007). Recognition decisions concerning other foreign qualifications are made in accordance with law (531/1986) on the professional competence foreign qualifications confer.

Further information from the National Board of Education, www.oph.fi/recognition.

Recognition for university level studies: Universities make the decisions concerning admissions and credit transfer independently. The Finnish National Board of Education (ENIC/NARIC) supports the work of universities.

For access to advanced studies and research: Recognition decisions concerning studies and research for access into Finnish higher education are passed in the higher education institutions. The Finnish National Board of Education supports the work of the higher education institutions.

Further information from the National Board of Education, www.oph.fi/recognition - or directly from the higher education institution in question.

NATIONAL BODIES

Opetus- ja kulttuuriministeriö (Ministry of Education and Culture)
Minister, Education and Science: Jukka Gustafsson
Director General, Education and Science Policy: Sakari Karjalainen
PO Box 29
Helsinki 00023
Tel: +358(0)9 160 04
Fax: +358(0)9 135 9335
EMail: kirjaamo@minedu.fi
WWW: http://www.minedu.fi
Role of national body: Responsible for the development of educational, science, cultural, sport and youth policies as well as international cooperation in these fields.

Opetushallitus (Finnish National Board of Education - FNBE)
Director General: Timo Lankinen
PO Box 380
Helsinki 00531
Tel: +358 40 348 7555
Fax: +358 40 348 7865
EMail: opetushallitus@oph.fi
WWW: http://www.oph.fi/
Role of national body: Development, evaluation and information services related to education; Finnish ENIC-NARIC; competent authority for the professional recognition of foreign higher education qualifications.

Korkeakoulujen arviointineuvosto - KKA (Finnish Higher Education Evaluation Council - FINHEEC)
Chairperson: Riitta Pyykkö
Secretary-General: Helka Kekäläinen
P.O. Box 133
Helsinki 00171

Tel: +358(9) 1607 6913
Fax: +358(9) 1607 7608
EMail: finheec@minedu.fi
WWW: http://www.kka.fi/
Role of national body: Independent expert body assisting universities, polytechnics and the Ministry of Education in matters relating to evaluation.

Kansainvälisen henkilövaihdon keskus (Centre for International Mobility - CIMO)
PO Box 343
Helsinki 00531
Tel: +358 207 868 500
Fax: +358 207 868 601
WWW: http://www.cimo.fi
Role of national body: Services and expertise in cross-cultural communication; promotion and administration of scholarship and exchange programmes; implementation of EU education, training, culture and youth programmes at national level.

Suomen yliopistot - UNIFI (Universities Finland)
Chairperson: Lauri Lajunen
Secretary-General: Liisa Savunen
Pohjoinen Makasiinikatu 7 a 2
Helsinki 00130
Tel: +358 50 5229 421
EMail: rectors-council@helsinki.fi
WWW: http://www.rectors-council.helsinki.fi/
Role of national body: Development of the university sector of higher education; a common forum for universities.

Ammattikorkeakoulujen Rehtorineuvosto - ARENE (Rectors' Conference of Finnish Universities of Applied Sciences)
President: Vesa Saarikoski
Secretary-General: Timo Luopajärvi
Pohjoinen Makasiinikatu 7 A 2
Helsinki 00130
WWW: http://www.arene.fi
Role of national body: ARENE is the Rectors' Conference of Finnish Universities of Applied Sciences. Its main functions are: influencing on the development of the Finnish higher education system and promoting closer cooperation between the universities of applied sciences.

Data for academic year: 2009-2010
Source: IAU from Opetushallitus, National Board of Education, 2009. Bodies updated in 2011.

INSTITUTIONS

PUBLIC INSTITUTIONS

AALTO UNIVERSITY
Aalto-universitetet
PO Box 11000, Lämpömiehenkuja 2, FI-02015 Espoo
Tel: +358(9) 47001
EMail: reception@aaltouniversity.fi
Website: http://www.aalto.fi/fi/
President: Tuula Teeri
Tel: +358(50) 512-4194 EMail: president@aaltouniversity.fi
Vice-President, Academic Affairs (Research and Education): Heikki Mannila
Tel: +358(50) 511-2913 EMail: heikki.mannila@aaltouniversity.fi

Vice-President, Knowledge Networks: Hannu Seristö
Tel: +358(50) 383-2478 EMail: hannu.seristo@aaltouniversity.fi

Institutes
Information Technology *(Helsinki)* (Information Technology); **Physics** *(Helsinki)* (Physics)

Schools
Art and Design (Art Education; Art History; Business and Commerce; Ceramics and Glass Technology; Cinema and Television; Design; Display and Stage Design; Fashion Design; Film; Fine Arts; Furniture Design; Graphic Design; Industrial Design; Interior Design; Media Studies; Painting and Drawing; Photography; Sculpture; Textile Design); **Chemical Technology** (Applied Physics; Biotechnology; Building Technologies; Chemical Engineering; Chemistry; Computer Science; Engineering; English; Forest Products;

French; Geophysics; German; Industrial Management; Japanese; Materials Engineering; Mathematics; Mechanics; Modern Languages; Physics; Real Estate; Regional Studies; Russian; Spanish; Swedish; Systems Analysis; Technology; Urban Studies); **Economics** *(http://www.hse.fi)* (Accountancy; Commercial Law; Communication Studies; Economics; English; Finance; French; Geography (Human); German; Information Sciences; Information Technology; International Business; International Economics; Italian; Japanese; Labour Law; Leadership; Management; Management Systems; Marketing; Modern Languages; Philosophy; Regional Studies; Russian; Small Business; Spanish; Swedish; Transport Management); **Electrical Engineering** (Automation and Control Engineering; Computer Networks; Electrical Engineering; Electronic Engineering; Nanotechnology; Radio and Television Broadcasting; Sound Engineering (Acoustics)); **Engineering** (Architecture; Civil Engineering; Construction Engineering; Energy Engineering; Engineering Drawing and Design; Environmental Engineering; Mechanical Engineering; Surveying and Mapping); **Science** (Applied Physics; Biomedical Engineering; Computer Engineering; Computer Science; Industrial Engineering; Industrial Management; Mathematics; Media Studies; Systems Analysis)

History: Founded 2010 following the merger of Helsingin kauppakorkeakoulu (Helsinki School of Economics and Business Administration - HSE) founded 1911; Taideteollinen korkeakoulu - Konstindustriella högskolan (University of Art and Design, Helsinki - TaiK) founded 1871 and Teknillinen korkeakoulu-Tekniska högskolan (Helsinki University of Technology - TKK) founded 1849.

Governing Bodies: Council

Admission Requirements: Secondary school certificate (ylioppilastutkinto) or equivalent and entrance examination

Main Language(s) of Instruction: Finnish, Swedish, English

Degrees and Diplomas: *Kandidaatti/Kandidat*; *Arkkitehti/Arkitekt*; *Diplomi-insinööri/Diplomingenjör*; *Lisensiaatti/Licentiat*; *Maisteri/Magister*; *Tohtori/Doktor*
Last Updated: 27/09/11

ÅBO AKADEMI UNIVERSITY
Åbo Akademi
Tuomiokirkontori 3, FI-20500 Turku
Tel: +358(2) 215-31
Fax: +358(2) 251-7553
EMail: international@abo.fi
Website: http://www.abo.fi

Rector: Jorma Mattinen (2003-)
Tel: +358(2) 215-4100 EMail: jorma.mattinen@abo.fi

Förvaltningsdirektör (Administrative Director): Roger Broo
Tel: +358(2) 215-4101, Fax: +358(2) 215-7553
EMail: forvaltningsdirektor@abo.fi; roger.broo@abo.fi

International Relations: Harriet Klåvus
Tel: +358(2) 215-4510, Fax: +358(2) 215-3230
EMail: harriet.klavus@abo.fi

Centres
Biotechnology *(Turku/Åbo)* (Biotechnology); **British Studies** (English Studies); **Computer** (Computer Science); **Computer Science** *(Turku/Åbo)* (Computer Science); **Continuing Education** *(Turku/Vasa)*; **Language** (Linguistics; Modern Languages); **Process Analytical Chemistry and Sensor Technology** (Chemistry; Technology); **Process Chemistry** (Chemical Engineering)

Faculties
Arts (Art History; Arts and Humanities; Comparative Literature; Comparative Religion; Cultural Studies; English; Ethnology; Finnish; Folklore; French; German; History; Modern Languages; Musicology; Philosophy; Psychology; Russian; Scandinavian Languages; Speech Therapy and Audiology; Swedish); **Economics and Social Sciences** (Accountancy; Business Administration; Civil Law; Commercial Law; Economics; Information Sciences; International Business; International Economics; International Law; International Relations; Law; Management; Maritime Law; Political Sciences; Private Law; Public Administration; Social Policy; Social Sciences; Sociology; Statistics; Women's Studies); **Education** *(Vasa)* (Child Care and Development; Education; Foreign Languages Education; Home Economics; Home Economics Education; Humanities and Social Science Education; Mathematics Education; Pedagogy; Preschool Education; Science Education; Special Education;

Sports); **Mathematics and Natural Sciences** (Analytical Chemistry; Biochemistry; Biology; Cell Biology; Chemistry; Computer Science; Environmental Studies; Geology; Inorganic Chemistry; Marine Biology; Mathematics; Mineralogy; Natural Sciences; Organic Chemistry; Pharmacy; Physical Chemistry; Physics; Statistics); **Social and Caring Sciences** *(Vasa)* (Developmental Psychology; Political Sciences; Social Policy; Social Studies); **Technology** (Analytical Chemistry; Chemical Engineering; Computer Engineering; Computer Science; Engineering Drawing and Design; Industrial Engineering; Industrial Management; Information Technology; Inorganic Chemistry; Organic Chemistry; Paper Technology; Polymer and Plastics Technology; Software Engineering; Thermal Engineering; Wood Technology); **Theology** (Comparative Religion; Ethics; History of Religion; Jewish Studies; New Testament; Religious Practice; Theology)

Institutes
Advanced Management Systems Research (Management Systems); **Ecumenics and Social Ethics** (Ethics; Religion); **Folklore** (Folklore); **Human Rights** (Human Rights); **Judaism** (Judaic Religious Studies); **Maritime and Commercial Law** (Commercial Law; Maritime Law); **Medieval Studies** (Medieval Studies); **Parasitology** (Parasitology); **Religious and Cultural History** (History of Religion; History of Societies); **Social Research on Swedish Finland** (Social Studies); **Women's Studies** (Women's Studies)

Schools
Teacher Training *(Vasa)* (Teacher Training)

Further Information: Also Graduate Schools, Centres of Excellence and National Centres of Excellence. Branch in Vaasa

History: Founded 1918 as Centre of Research and Higher Education for the Swedish-speaking minority in Finland. First University established at Åbo 1640, and transferred to Helsingfors (Helsinki) 1828. Incorporated Swedish School of Economics, Åbo 1980. Under supervision of the Ministry of Education.

Governing Bodies: Senate (Styrelsen)

Academic Year: August to July

Admission Requirements: Secondary school certificate (ylioppi lastutkinto/studentexamen) or equivalent, and in some cases entrance examination

Fees: None

Main Language(s) of Instruction: Swedish. Several courses in English

International Co-operation: Member of the Santander and Coimbra Groups. Also participates in Nordplus, Erasmus, Tempus, FIRST and ISEP programmes.

Degrees and Diplomas: *Farmaseutti/Farmaceut*: Pharmacy, 3 yrs; *Kandidaatti/Kandidat*: Arts; Economics; Education; Law; Political Science; Science; Theology, 3 yrs; *Maisteri/Magister*: Arts; Economics; Education; Health Care; Political Science; Science; Theology, a further 2 yrs; *Maisteri/Magister*: Chemical Engineering; Psychology, 6 yrs; *Tohtori/Doktor (PhD)*: a further 2-3 yrs

Student Services: Academic counselling, Canteen, Cultural centre, Employment services, Foreign student adviser, Health services, Nursery care, Social counselling, Sports facilities

Special Facilities: Maritime Museum; Sibelius Museum; Museum 'Ett hem'. Biological Collections; Collection of Coins and Medals. Swedish Textiles Archives. Ecclesiastical Archives

Libraries: Åbo Akademi Library, 2.5 m. vols; Steiner Memorial Library, c. 37,000 vols

Publications: Acta Academiae Aboensis, matematik, naturvetenskaper, teknik; Meddelanden från Åbo Akademi *(bimonthly)*

Press or Publishing House: Åbo Akademi University Press
Last Updated: 03/12/09

ARCADA UNIVERSITY OF APPLIED LIFE
ARCADA
Jan-Magnus Janssonin aukio 1, FI-00550 Helsinki
Tel: +358(9) 0207-699 699
Fax: +358(9) 0207-699-622
EMail: information@arcada.fi
Website: http://www.arcada.fi

Rector: Henrik Wolff
Tel: +358(9) 5253-2200 EMail: henrik.wolff@arcada.fi

International Relations: Ann Karkulahti
Tel: +358(9) 5253-2525, Fax: +358(9) 5253-2555
EMail: ann.karkulahti@arcada.fi

Departments

Business, Information Technology and Media (Business Administration; Cinema and Television; Film; Information Technology; International Business; Media Studies); Energy and Materials Technology (Energy Engineering; Industrial Management; Polymer and Plastics Technology); Health and Welfare (Nursing; Social and Community Services; Sports)

History: Founded 1996. Acquired present status 1998.

Main Language(s) of Instruction: Finnish

Degrees and Diplomas: Ammattikorkeakoulututkinto (AMK)/ Yrkeshögskoleexamen (YH); Ylempi ammattikorkeakoulututinto (ylempi AMK)/ Högre yrkeshögskoleexamen (högre YH)
Last Updated: 03/12/09

CENTRAL OSTROBOTHNIA UNIVERSITY OF APPLIED SCIENCES

Keski-Pohjanmaan ammattikorkeakoulu - Mellersta Österbottens yrkeshögskola

Talonpojankatu 2, FI-67100 Kokkola
Tel: +358(6) 825-0000
Fax: +358(6) 825-2000 +358(6) 825-2074
EMail: info@cou.fi
Website: http://www.cou.fi

Rector: Marja-Liisa Tenhunen (1994-)
Tel: +358(6) 825-2010 EMail: marja-liisa.tenhunen@cou.fi

International Relations: Peter Finell
Tel: +358(6) 825-2012 EMail: peter.finell@cop.fi

Departments

Culture; Humanities and Education; Natural Resources and the Environment (Environmental Studies; Natural Resources); Natural sciences (Natural Sciences); Social Sciences, Business and Administration; Social Services, Health and Sport (Health Administration; Public Health; Social Welfare; Sports); Technology, Communication and Transport (Technology; Transport and Communications); Tourism, Catering and Domestic Services

History: Founded 1991, acquired present status and title 1998.

Main Language(s) of Instruction: Finnish, Swedish, English

Degrees and Diplomas: Ammattikorkeakoulututkinto (AMK)/ Yrkeshögskoleexamen (YH); Maisteri/Magister
Last Updated: 21/12/09

DIACONIA UNIVERSITY OF APPLIED SCIENCES

Diakonia-ammattikorkeakoulu (DIAK)

Sturenkatu 2, FI-00510 Helsinki
Tel: +358(20) 160-6201
Fax: +358(20) 160-6222
EMail: info.ypy@mail.diak.fi
Website: http://www.diak.fi

Rector: Jorma Niemelä
Tel: +358(20) 160-6209 EMail: jorma.niemela@diak.fi

International Relations: Riikka Hälikkä
Tel: +358(20) 160-6221 EMail: riikka.halikka@diak.fi

Programmes

Communications and Media (Communication Studies; Media Studies); Sign Language Interpretation (Special Education); Social Welfare, Health Care and Education (Nursing; Public Health; Social Welfare)

History: Founded 2000.

Main Language(s) of Instruction: Finnish and English

Degrees and Diplomas: Ammattikorkeakoulututkinto (AMK)/ Yrkeshögskoleexamen (YH); Ylempi ammattikorkeakoulututinto (ylempi AMK)/ Högre yrkeshögskoleexamen (högre YH)

Libraries: Diak Library
Last Updated: 27/09/11

FINNISH ACADEMY OF FINE ARTS

Kuvataideakatemia - Bildkunstakademin

Kaikukatu 4, FI-00530 Helsinki
Tel: +358(9) 680-3320
Fax: +358(9) 6803-3260
EMail: kanslia@kuva.fi; office@kuva.fi
Website: http://www.kuva.fi

Rector: Markus Kontinnen EMail: markus.konttinen@kuva.fi

Departments

Painting (Painting and Drawing); Printmaking (Printing and Printmaking); Sculpture (Sculpture); Time and Space Based Arts (Media-Arts) (Cinema and Television; Fine Arts; Media Studies; Photography)

History: Founded 1848 as the Finnish Fine Arts Association School of Drawing, acquired present status and title 1998.

Governing Bodies: Board of Directors

Academic Year: September to May (September-December; January-May)

Admission Requirements: Artistic talent

Main Language(s) of Instruction: Finnish

International Co-operation: Participates in the Erasmus and Nordplus programmes

Degrees and Diplomas: Kandidaatti/Kandidat: Arts, 4 yrs; Maisteri/ Magister: Arts, a further 1-2 yrs; Tohtori/Doktor: Arts, 2-3 yrs

Special Facilities: Art Gallery

Libraries: c. 5,000 vols

Academic Staff 2009-2010: Total: c. 50
Student Numbers 2009-2010: Total: c. 260
Last Updated: 28/09/11

HAAGA-HELIA UNIVERSITY OF APPLIED SCIENCES

HAAGA-HELIA ammattikorkeakoulu - HAAGA-HELIA yrkeshögskolan (HAAGA-HELIA)

Ratapihantie 13, FI-00520 Helsinki
Tel: +358(9) 2296-11
Fax: +358(9) 2296-5310
EMail: viestinta@haaga-helia.fi
Website: http://www.haaga-helia.fi

Managing Director, President: Ritva Laakso-Manninen
Tel: +358(9) 2296-5455, Fax: +358(9) 2296-5346
EMail: ritva.laakso-manninen@haaga-helia.fi

Financial Director: Jorma Alkula
Tel: +358(9) 2296-5345, Fax: +358(9) 2296-5346
EMail: jorma.alkula@haaga-helia.fi

International Relations: Tarja Hoyer, Head of International Relations
Tel: +358(9) 2296-5426, Fax: +358(9) 2296-5310
EMail: tarja.hoyer@haaga-helia.fi

Departments

Business (Business Administration; Business and Commerce; Finance; International Business); Hotel, Restaurant and Tourism (Cooking and Catering; Hotel Management; Leisure Studies; Tourism); Information Technology (Business Administration; Business Computing; Information Management; Information Sciences; Information Technology; Management Systems); Management Assistant and Journalism (Journalism; Modern Languages; Secretarial Studies); Sports (Vierumäki) (Leisure Studies; Sports; Sports Management); Tourism (Porvoo) (Business and Commerce; International Business; Tourism); Vocational Teacher Education (Teacher Training)

History: Founded 1992. Acquired present title 2007, following merger with Haaga ammattikorkeakoulu (Haaga Polytechnic). Formerly known as Helsingin liiketalouden ammattikorkeakoulu Helsingfors yrkeshögskola för företagsekonomi (Helsinki Business Polytechnic).

Governing Bodies: Board

Academic Year: August to December; January to May

Admission Requirements: Bachelor level:lukion päättötodistus / ylioppilastutkintotodistus = Upper secondary education and Matriculation examination completed in Finland;opistoasteen / ammatillisen korkea-asteen tutkinto = a vocational college diploma or higher vocational diploma completed in Finland (ex. insinööri, merkonomi);ammatillinen perustutkinto = Vocational upper secondary diploma/higher vocational diploma/vocational qualification in adult education completed in Finland (ex. liiketalouden perustutkinto, tietojenkäsittelyn perustutkinto, matkailualan perustutkinto); ammattitutkinto = further vocational qualification completed in Finland;erikoisammattitutkinto = specialist vocational qualification completed in Finland;Foreign degree or qualification which gives eligibility for higher education in the awarding country.Entrance examination. In English-language programmes, applicants who are not a citizen of an EU/EEA country must provide proof of his/her English language skills (example IELTS, TOEFL).Master level:alempi ammattikorkeakoulututkinto = Bachelor's degree completed in Finland in University of Applied Sciences (ex. tradenomi, restonomi (AMK), medianomi (AMK));kandidaatin tutkinto = Bachelor's degree completed in Finland in University;maisterin tutkinto = Master's degree completed in Finland in University;Foreign Bachelor or Master's degree ;Minimum requirements: Entrance examination. Degree must be completed from the corresponding field. Three years of working experience after the degree from the same field.

Fees: None for EU / EEA students; Master students from outwith EU / EEA, 3,750 Euro per semester.

Main Language(s) of Instruction: Finnish, English, Swedish

International Co-operation: Participates in Erasmus, Nordplus; exchange programmes with institutions in Canada, China, France, Japan, Malaysia, Mexico, Peru, Puerto Rico, Russia, Switzerland, Thailand, United Arab Emirates, USA.

Degrees and Diplomas: *Ammattikorkeakoulututkinto (AMK)/ Yrkeshögskoleexamen (YH)*: Culture and Arts; Hospitality Management; Tourism; Sports and Leisure; Business Administration; Information Technology (Bachelor's Degree), 3 1/2 - 4 yrs; *Ylempi ammattikorkeakoulututinto (ylempi AMK)/ Högre yrkeshögskoleexamen (högre YH)*: Business Administration; Tourism; Sports and Leisure (Master's Degree), 1 1/2 yrs. Also MBA

Student Services: Academic counselling, Canteen, Employment services, Foreign student adviser, Foreign Studies Centre, Handicapped facilities, Health services, Language programs, Nursery care, Social counselling, Sports facilities

Student Residential Facilities: none

Libraries: 133,136 print monographs, 849 print journal titles and 20 823 electronic journals. Seven campus libraries; group study rooms; special reading room; newspaper/periodical reading rooms; computer classroom; private study desks with computer workstations.

Last Updated: 27/09/11

HAMK UNIVERSITY OF APPLIED SCIENCES

Hämeen ammattikorkeakoulu HAMK
PO Box 230, FI-13100 Hämeenlinna
Tel: +358(3) 6461
Fax: +358(3) 646-4200
EMail: hamk@hamk.fi
Website: http://www.hamk.fi

Rector: Veijo Hintsanen
Tel: +358(3) 646-4210 EMail: veijo.hintsanen@hamk.fi

Administrative Officer: Mirja Pöhö
Tel: +358(3) 646-4810 EMail: mirja.poho@hamk.fi

International Relations: Pertti Puusaari
Tel: +358(3) 646-4220 EMail: pertti.puusaari@hamk.fi

Programmes
Business Administration (Business Administration); **Engineering** (Automation and Control Engineering; Construction Engineering; Mechanical Engineering; Production Engineering); **Health Care and Social Services** (Health Education; Social and Community Services); **Natural Resources** (Agriculture; Forestry; Horticulture; Natural Resources); **Technology and Transport** (Technology; Transport and Communications); **Tourism, Catering and Institutional Management** (Cooking and Catering; Tourism)

History: Founded 1996.

Main Language(s) of Instruction: Finnish and English

Degrees and Diplomas: *Ammattikorkeakoulututkinto (AMK)/ Yrkeshögskoleexamen (YH)*; *Ylempi ammattikorkeakoulututinto (ylempi AMK)/ Högre yrkeshögskoleexamen (högre YH)*. Also international degree programmes

Last Updated: 27/09/11

HANKEN SCHOOL OF ECONOMICS

Hanken Svenska handelshögskolan
PO Box 479, Arkadiankatu 22, FI-00101 Helsinki
Tel: +358(9) 431-331
Fax: +358(9) 4313-33404
EMail: info@hanken.fi
Website: http://www.hanken.fi

Rector: Eva Liljeblom (2010-2015)
Tel: +358(9) 4313-32221, Fax: +358(9) 4313-3404
EMail: eva.liljeblom@hanken.fi

Director of External relations and communication: Camilla Sagbom
Tel: +358-40-3521-213, Fax: +358-9-431-33404
EMail: camilla.sagbom@hanken.fi

International Relations: Maj-Britt Hedvall, Research Director
Tel: +358(9) 4313-3346, Fax: +358(9) 4313-3409
EMail: maj-britt.hedvall@hanken.fi

Centres
Financial Research (Finance); **International Economic Law** (Commercial Law; International Law); **Languages and Intercultural Communication** (Communication Studies; Modern Languages); **Real Estate Investment and Finance** (Finance; Real Estate); **Relationship Marketing and Service Management** (Management; Marketing)

Departments
Accountancy (Accountancy; Business Administration; Economics; Finance); **Commercial Law** (Accountancy; Commercial Law; Finance; Labour Law; Law; Management; Taxation); **Economics** (Economics); **Finance and Statistics** (Finance; Real Estate; Statistics); **Languages and Communication** (Communication Studies; Modern Languages); **Management and Organization** (Human Resources; Information Technology; International Business; Leadership; Management; Political Sciences); **Marketing** (Consumer Studies; Geography (Human); Marketing; Transport Management)

Research Groups
Gender Relations in Organisations, Management and Society; **Intellectual Capital/Knowledge Management research**

Further Information: Also Campus in Vaasa

History: Founded 1909. Authorized to grant Master of Science (Econ.) 1927, Doctor 1944, and Licentiate 1953. Unit in Vaasa established 1980. Under the supervision of and entirely financed by the Ministry of Education since 1975. Previously known as Svenska handelshögskolan Hanken (Hanken Swedish School of Economics and Business Administration)

Governing Bodies: Board; Teaching and Research Council

Academic Year: September to July (September-December; January-July)

Admission Requirements: Secondary school certificate (studentexamen) or equivalent and entrance examination

Fees: None

Main Language(s) of Instruction: Swedish, English

International Co-operation: With universities in Scandinavia, Europe, USA, East and Southeast Asia, Australia. Also participates in Socrate/Erasmus and Nordplus programmes, and the EU Framework for Research and Development.

Accrediting Agencies: EQUIS (European Quality Improvement System)

Degrees and Diplomas: *Kandidaatti/Kandidat*: Economics (EK; BSc(Econ)), 3 yrs; *Lisensiaatti/Licentiat*: Economics (EL; LSc(Econ)), a further 2 yrs; *Maisteri/Magister*: Economics (EM; MSc(Econ)), 4-5 yrs; *Tohtori/Doktor*: Economics (ED; DSc(Econ)), by thesis. Also Bachelors, Masters and Doctorates

Student Services: Academic counselling, Canteen, Employment services, Foreign student adviser, Foreign Studies Centre, Handicapped facilities, Language programs

Libraries: c. 99,000 books; 250 print periodicals; 3,600 online periodicals

Publications: Economics and Society; Research Catalogue *(biennially)*

Last Updated: 27/09/11

HELSINKI METROPOLIA UNIVERSITY OF APPLIED SCIENCES

Metropolia-ammattikorkeakoululsinki
Bulevardi 31, FI-01800 Helsinki
Tel: +358(20) 783-5000
Fax: +358(9) 3108-3001
EMail: hakutoimisto@metropolia.fi
Website: http://www.metropolia.fi

President: Riitta Konkola EMail: riitta.konkola@metropolia.fi

Faculties

Culture and Creative Industries (Cinema and Television; Design; Fashion Design; Heritage Preservation; Jazz and Popular Music; Media Studies; Music; Performing Arts); **Health Care and Nursing** (Biomedicine; Nursing; Oral Pathology; Radiology; Social and Community Services); **Welfare and Human Functioning** (Dental Technology; Gerontology; Occupational Therapy; Optometry; Osteopathy; Physical Therapy; Rehabilitation and Therapy; Social and Community Services)

Schools

Business (Business Administration; Business Computing; International Business; Management); **Civil Engineering and Building Services** (Building Technologies; Civil Engineering; Construction Engineering; Real Estate; Surveying and Mapping); **ICT** (Industrial Management; Information Technology); **Industrial Engineering** (Automation and Control Engineering; Automotive Engineering; Biotechnology; Chemical Engineering; Electrical Engineering; Food Technology; Materials Engineering; Mechanical Engineering; Transport Engineering)

History: Founded 2008 following merger of EVTEK University of Applied Sciences and Helsinki Polytechnic Stadia.

Main Language(s) of Instruction: Finnish

Degrees and Diplomas: *Ammattikorkeakoulututkinto (AMK)/ Yrkeshögskoleexamen (YH); Ylempi ammattikorkeakoulututinto (ylempi AMK)/ Högre yrkeshögskoleexamen (högre YH)*

Libraries: Yes
Last Updated: 29/09/11

HUMAK UNIVERSITY OF APPLIED SCIENCES

Humanistinen ammattikorkeakoulu (HUMAK)
Annankatu 12 A 17, FI-00120 Helsinki
Tel: +358(9) 5404-2428
Fax: +358(9) 5404-2444
EMail: humak@humak.edu
Website: http://www.humak.edu

Rector: Eeva-Liisa Antikainen
Tel: +358(9) 6818-2460 EMail: eeva-liisa.antikainen@humak.edu

International Relations: Timo Sorvoja
Tel: +358(20) 7621-352, Fax: +358(20) 7621-391
EMail: timo.sorvoja@akatemia.org

Faculties

Cultural Management (Cultural Studies); **NGO and Youth Work** (Humanities and Social Science Education); **Sign Language Interpretation** (Special Education)

History: Founded 1998.

Degrees and Diplomas: *Ammattikorkeakoulututkinto (AMK)/ Yrkeshögskoleexamen (YH); Kandidaatti/Kandidat; Ylempi ammattikorkeakoulututinto (ylempi AMK)/ Högre yrkeshögskoleexamen (högre YH); Maisteri/Magister*
Last Updated: 19/08/08

JYVÄSKYLÄ UNIVERSITY OF APPLIED SCIENCES

Jyväskylän ammattikorkeakoulu
PO Box 207, Rajakatu 35, FI-40101 Jyväskylä
Tel: +358(20) 743-8100
Fax: +358(14) 449-9700
EMail: jamk@jamk.fi
Website: http://www.jamk.fi

Rector: Jussi Halttunen EMail: Jussi.Halttunen@jamk.fi

Director of Administration: Pekka Jääskö

International Relations: Nina Björn EMail: international@jamk.fi

Colleges

Teacher Education *(Professional training)* (Teacher Training)

Schools

Business and Services Management (Business and Commerce; Management); **Health and Social Studies** (Health Sciences; Social Studies); **Technology** (Civil Engineering; Information Technology; Mechanical Engineering; Natural Resources)

History: Founded 1992, acquired present status and title 1997.

Main Language(s) of Instruction: Finnish

Degrees and Diplomas: *Ammattikorkeakoulututkinto (AMK)/ Yrkeshögskoleexamen (YH); Ylempi ammattikorkeakoulututinto (ylempi AMK)/ Högre yrkeshögskoleexamen (högre YH)*
Last Updated: 28/09/11

KAJAANI UNIVERSITY OF APPLIED SCIENCES

Kajaanin ammattikorkeakoulu
PO Box 52, Ketunpolku 3, FI-87101 Kajaani
Tel: +358(8) 618-991
Fax: +358(8) 6189-9620
EMail: kajaanin.amk@kajak.fi
Website: http://www.kajak.fi

President: Turo Kilpeläinen
Tel: +358(8) 6189-9600, Fax: +358(8) 6189-9603
EMail: etunimi.sukunimi@kajak.fi

Management Assistant: Anne Väätäinen Tel: +358(8) 6189-9602

Schools

Business (Business Administration); **Engineering** (Construction Engineering; Information Technology; Mechanical Engineering; Production Engineering); **Health and Sports** (Leisure Studies; Nursing; Sports; Sports Management); **Tourism** (Tourism)

History: Founded 1992. Acquired present status 1996.

Main Language(s) of Instruction: Finnish and English

Degrees and Diplomas: *Ammattikorkeakoulututkinto (AMK)/ Yrkeshögskoleexamen (YH); Ylempi ammattikorkeakoulututinto (ylempi AMK)/ Högre yrkeshögskoleexamen (högre YH)*
Last Updated: 28/09/11

KEMI-TORNIO UNIVERSITY OF APPLIED SCIENCES

Kemi-Tornion ammattikorkeakoulu
PO Box 505, Sauvosaarenkatu 4, FI-94101 Kemi
Tel: +358(10) 383-50
Fax: +358(16) 251-120
EMail: ktamk@tokem.fi
Website: http://www.tokem.fi

Rector: Riitta Käyhkö
Tel: +358(16) 258-402 EMail: riitta.kayhko@tokem.fi

Vice-Rector, Education and Study Affairs: Markku Tarvainen

International Relations: Annikki Pulkkinen
Tel: +358(16) 258-580, Fax: +358(16) 258-584
EMail: annikki.pulkkinen@tokem.fi

Departments

Business and Culture (Administration; Business and Commerce; Data Processing; Economics; Finance; Information Technology; Management; Marketing); **Health Care and Social Services** (Health Education; Nursing; Public Health; Social and Community Services; Social and Preventive Medicine); **Technology** (Electrical Engineering; Engineering; Industrial Management; Information

Technology; Mechanical Engineering; Production Engineering; Technology)

History: Founded 1992, acquired present status and title 1997.

Degrees and Diplomas: *Ammattikorkeakoulututkinto (AMK)/ Yrkeshögskoleexamen (YH):* Business Information Technology; Business Management; Information Technology; Nursing; Social Services, 3.5-4 yrs; *Ylempi ammattikorkeakoulututinto (ylempi AMK)/ Högre yrkeshögskoleexamen (högre YH):* International Business Management, a further 1 1/2 yrs
Last Updated: 22/12/09

KYMENLAAKSO UNIVERSITY OF APPLIED SCIENCES
Kymenlaakson ammattikorkeakoulu
PO Box 9, FI-48401 Kotka
Tel: +358(5) 220-8111
Fax: +358(5) 220-8209
EMail: registry@kyamk.fi
Website: http://www.kyamk.fi

President/Rector: Ragnar Lundqvist
Tel: +358(5) 220-8200 EMail: ragnar.lundqvist@kyamk.fi

Vice President/Vice Rector: Pirkko Rautaniemi

International Relations: Henrik Luikko
Tel: +358(5) 220-8231 EMail: henrik.luikko@kyamk.fi

Programmes
Culture (Design; Media Studies; Restoration of Works of Art); **Social Sciences, Business and Administration** (Administration; Business and Commerce; Social Sciences); **Social Services and Health Care** (Public Health; Social and Community Services); **Technology, Communications and Transport** (Technology; Telecommunications Engineering; Transport Engineering; Transport Management)

History: Founded 1996.

Main Language(s) of Instruction: Finnish and English

Degrees and Diplomas: *Ammattikorkeakoulututkinto (AMK)/ Yrkeshögskoleexamen (YH); Ylempi ammattikorkeakoulututinto (ylempi AMK)/ Högre yrkeshögskoleexamen (högre YH)*
Last Updated: 28/09/11

LAHTI UNIVERSITY OF APPLIED SCIENCES
Lahden ammattikorkeakoulu
PO Box 214, Teinintie 4, FI-15101 Lahti
Tel: +358(3) 828-18
Fax: +358(3) 828-2066
EMail: lamk@lamk.fi
Website: http://www.lamk.fi

President: Risto Ilomäki
Tel: +358(3) 828-2050 EMail: risto.ilomaki@lamk.fi

Vice-President: Helena Karento Tel: +358(3) 828-2052

Vice-President: Juhani Nieminen Tel: +358(3) 828-2051

International Relations: Timo Ahonen, Head of International Relations
Tel: +358(3) 828-2062 EMail: intoffice@lamk.fi; timo.ahonen@lpt.fi

Faculties
Business Studies *(Heinola)* (Business Administration; Business and Commerce; Business Computing; Finance; Information Technology; International Business; Management; Marketing); **Music** (Music; Performing Arts; Theatre); **Social and Health Care** (Nursing); **Technology** (Biotechnology; Environmental Engineering; Environmental Management; Information Technology; Materials Engineering; Mechanical Engineering; Polymer and Plastics Technology; Production Engineering; Software Engineering; Telecommunications Engineering; Textile Technology; Wood Technology); **Tourism and Hospitality** *(Fellmanni Institute)* (Hotel and Restaurant; Hotel Management; Tourism)

Institutes
Design (Art Education; Design; Fashion Design; Film; Furniture Design; Graphic Design; Industrial Design; Interior Design; Jewelry Art; Multimedia; Photography; Radio and Television Broadcasting); **Fine Arts** (Fine Arts; Media Studies; Painting and Drawing; Printing and Printmaking; Sculpture)

History: Founded 1991, acquired present status and title 1996.
Main Language(s) of Instruction: Finnish and English
Degrees and Diplomas: *Ammattikorkeakoulututkinto (AMK)/ Yrkeshögskoleexamen (YH); Ylempi ammattikorkeakoulututinto (ylempi AMK)/ Högre yrkeshögskoleexamen (högre YH)*
Last Updated: 28/09/11

LAPPEENRANTA UNIVERSITY OF TECHNOLOGY
Lappeenrannan teknillinen yliopisto
PO Box 20, Skinnarilankatu 34, FI-53851 Lappeenranta
Tel: +358(5) 621-11
Fax: +358(5) 621-2350
EMail: info@lut.fi
Website: http://www.lut.fi

Rector: Ilkka Pöyhönen (2008-)
Tel: +358(5) 621-2000, Fax: +358(5) 621-2350
EMail: ilkka.poyhonen@lut.fi

Hallintojohtaja (Administrative Director): Juha-Matti Saksa
Tel: +358(5) 621-2003, Fax: +358(5) 621-2350

International Relations: Minna Martikainen
Tel: +358(5) 621-6080, Fax: +358(5) 621-6099

Faculties
Technology (Chemical Engineering; Electrical Engineering; Energy Engineering; Environmental Engineering; Mathematics; Mechanical Engineering; Physics); **Technology Management** (Industrial Management; Information Technology)

Research Centres
Carelian Drives and Motor *(CDMC)* (Electrical Engineering); **Computational Engineering and Integrated Design** *(CEID)* (Computer Engineering); **Northern Dimension** *(NORDI)* (Central European Studies; Eastern European Studies; Russian); **Separation Technology** *(CST)* (Environmental Engineering; Environmental Management); **Technology Business Research** (Business and Commerce; Technology)

Research Institutes
South Karelian (Arts and Humanities; Development Studies; Regional Studies; Social Sciences)

Schools
Business (Finance; Marketing)

Further Information: Also International Business and Technology, International Study programme (in English) and International Master's Programme in Information Technology (in English). Mikkeli, Savonlinna, Ruokolahti, Joensuu, Kouvola and Lahti Regional Units

History: Founded 1969. A State institution under the supervision of the Ministry of Education.

Governing Bodies: University Council; Teaching and Research Council; Department Councils

Academic Year: September to May (September-December; January-May)

Admission Requirements: Secondary school certificate (ylioppilastutkinto) or equivalent

Fees: None

Main Language(s) of Instruction: Finnish

International Co-operation: With universities in Russian Federation; Asia; Oceania; North and South America. Participates in the Erasmus/Socrates, Tempus, Nordplus, Leonardo and International Student Exchange programmes.

Degrees and Diplomas: *Kandidaatti/Kandidat:* Science, 3 yrs; *Diplomi-insinööri/Diplomingenjör:* Science in Engineering (DI), 5 yrs; *Lisensiaatti/Licentiat:* Economics and Business Administration; Technology, 2 yrs following Maisteri; *Maisteri/Magister:* Science in Economics and Business Administration (KTM), 5 yrs; *Tohtori/ Doktor:* Economics and Business Administration; Philosophy; Technology, 4 yrs following Maisteri

Student Services: Academic counselling, Canteen, Cultural centre, Employment services, Foreign student adviser, Health services, Language programs, Sports facilities

Libraries: University Library, c. 140,000 vols

Publications: Kuulumisia *(quarterly)*; Lappeenranta University of Technology Research Papers *(other/irregular)*

Last Updated: 28/09/11

LAUREA UNIVERSITY OF APPLIED SCIENCES
Laurea-ammattikorkeakoulu
Ratatie 22, FI-01300 Vantaa
Tel: +358(9) 8868-7300
Fax: +358(9) 8868-7301
EMail: intl.info@laurea.fi
Website: http://www.laurea.fi

President: Pentti Rauhala
Tel: +358(9) 8868-7210 EMail: pentti.rauhala@laurea.fi

Director, Administration and Finance: Kimmo Hannonen
Tel: +358(9) 8868-7219 EMail: kimmo.hannonen@laurea.fi

International Relations: Arja Majakulma, Director of International Affairs Tel: +358(9) 8868-7215 EMail: arja.majakulma@laurea.fi

Programmes
Beauty and Cosmetics (Cosmetology); **Business Information Technology** (Business Computing); **Business Management** (Business Administration); **Correctional Services**; **Facility Management** (Cooking and Catering; Hotel Management; Human Resources; Tourism); **Health Promotion** *(Master's Programme)* (Health Sciences); **Hospitality Management** *(Master's Programme)* (Social and Community Services; Tourism); **Hotel and Restaurant Management** (Hotel and Restaurant; Hotel Management); **Nursing** (Nursing; Public Health; Social Welfare); **Physiotherapy** (Physical Therapy); **Security Management** (Protective Services); **Service Innovation and Design** *(Master's Programme)* (Business Administration; Leadership); **Service Management** (Social and Community Services; Tourism); **Social Sciences, Business and Administration** *(Master's Programme)* (Business Administration; Business and Commerce; Information Management; Information Technology; Management; Social Sciences); **Social Services** (Social and Community Services; Social Work); **Social Services, Health and Sports** *(Master's Programme)* (Development Studies; Health Education; Public Health; Regional Studies; Social and Community Services; Social and Preventive Medicine; Social Welfare; Social Work; Sports); **Tourism** (Tourism)

History: Founded 2001.

Degrees and Diplomas: *Ammattikorkeakoulututkinto (AMK)/ Yrkeshögskoleexamen (YH)*; *Ylempi ammattikorkeakoulututinto (ylempi AMK)/ Högre yrkeshögskoleexamen (högre YH)*

Student Numbers *2008-2009*: Total: c. 8,000
Last Updated: 22/12/09

MIKKELI UNIVERSITY OF APPLIED SCIENCES
Mikkelin ammattikorkeakoulu
PO Box 181, Tarkkampujankuja 1, FI-50101 Mikkeli
Tel: +358(15) 355-61
Fax: +358(15) 355-6377 +358(15) 355-6464
EMail: mamk@mamk.fi
Website: http://www.mikkeliamk.fi

Rector: Heikki Saastamoinen
Tel: +358(15) 355-6300 EMail: heikki.saastamoinen@mamk.fi

International Relations: Henrik Luikko Tel: +358(44) 702-8232

Programmes
Business Operations in Forestry *(Master's degree)* (Forest Management; Forestry; Natural Resources); **Culture - Cultural Management** (Cultural Studies); **Development and Management in Health Care and Social Services** *(Master's degree)* (Health Administration); **Entrepreneurship and Business Operations** *(Master's degree)* (Business Administration; Management); **Environmental Technology** *(Master's degree)* (Environmental Engineering); **e-Services and Digital Archiving** *(Master's degree)* (Archiving); **Hospitality Management** *(Master's degree)* (Tourism); **Humanities and Education - Civic Activities and Youth Work** (Civics; Social Work); **Natural Resources and the Environment - Forestry** (Environmental Management; Environmental Studies; Forestry; Natural Resources); **Natural Sciences - Business Information Technology** (Business Computing; Information Technology); **NGO and Youth Work** *(Master's degree)*; **Social Sciences, Business and Administration**

(Business Administration; Social Sciences); **Social Services, Health and Sports** (Nursing; Physical Therapy; Public Health; Social and Community Services; Social Work; Sports); **Technology, Communication and Transport** (Electrical Engineering; Environmental Engineering; Information Technology; Materials Engineering; Transport and Communications); **Tourism, Catering and Domestic Services** (Cooking and Catering; Tourism)

Further Information: Also Nikkarila and Savonniemi campuses

History: Founded 1997.

Main Language(s) of Instruction: Finnish and English

Degrees and Diplomas: *Ammattikorkeakoulututkinto (AMK)/ Yrkeshögskoleexamen (YH)*; *Ylempi ammattikorkeakoulututinto (ylempi AMK)/ Högre yrkeshögskoleexamen (högre YH)*
Last Updated: 29/09/11

NORTH KARELIA UNIVERSITY OF APPLIED SCIENCES
Pohjois-Karjalan ammattikorkeakoulu
Tikkarinne 9, FI-80200 Joensuu
Tel: +358(13) 260-6412 +358(13) 260-6402
Fax: +358(13) 260-6411 +358(13) 260-6401
EMail: info@pkamk.fi; international@pkam.fi
Website: http://www.ncp.fi

President: Vesa Saarikoski EMail: Vesa.Saarikoski@pkamk.fi

International Relations: Harri Mikkonen
Tel: +358(13) 260-6729, Fax: +358(13) 260-6721
EMail: international@pkamk.fi

Programmes
Culture (Communication Studies; Design; Fine Arts; Media Studies; Music); **Natural Resources and the Environment** (Environmental Studies; Forest Products; Forestry; Natural Resources; Rural Studies); **Natural Sciences** (Natural Sciences); **Social Sciences, Business and Administration** (Administration; Business and Commerce; Economics; Information Technology; International Business); **Social services, Health and Sports** (Biomedicine; Nursing; Physical Therapy; Social Sciences; Social Welfare; Social Work); **Technology, Communication and Transport** (Civil Engineering; Environmental Engineering; Information Technology; Mechanical Engineering; Production Engineering; Wood Technology); **Tourism, Catering and Domestic Services** (Cooking and Catering; Tourism)

History: Founded 1992, acquired present status and title 1996.

Main Language(s) of Instruction: Finnish and English

Degrees and Diplomas: *Ammattikorkeakoulututkinto (AMK)/ Yrkeshögskoleexamen (YH)*; *Ylempi ammattikorkeakoulututinto (ylempi AMK)/ Högre yrkeshögskoleexamen (högre YH)*: Technology Competence Management and Development; Environmental Technology; Management in Social Welfare Work and Health Care;
Last Updated: 29/09/11

NOVIA UNIVERSITY OF APPLIED SCIENCES
Yrkeshögskolan Novia
PO Box 6, Fabriksgatan 1, FI-65201 Vaasa
Tel: +358(6) 328-5000
Fax: +358(6) 328-5110
EMail: info@novia.fi; fornamn.efternamn@novia.fi
Website: http://www.novia.fi

Rector: Örjan Andersson (2007-)
Tel: +358(6) 328-5100 EMail: orjan.andersson@novia.fi

Förvaltningschef: Kjell Heir EMail: kjell.heir@novia.fi

Programmes
Culture (Cultural Studies; Design; Fine Arts; Media Studies; Music; Painting and Drawing; Performing Arts; Sculpture; Theatre); **Humanities and Education** (Civics; Social Work); **Natural Resources and the Environment** (Agricultural Engineering; Architectural and Environmental Design; Coastal Studies; Environmental Management; Environmental Studies; Forestry; Horticulture; Landscape Architecture; Natural Resources; Rural Studies); **Natural Sciences - Business Information Systems**; **Social Sciences, Business and Administration** (Business Administration); **Social Services, Health and Sports** (Biomedicine; Cosmetology; Midwifery; Nursing; Public Health; Radiology; Social and Community Services); **Technology, Communications and Transport** (Automation and Control

Engineering; Construction Engineering; Electrical Engineering; Electronic Engineering; Information Technology; Laboratory Techniques; Marine Engineering; Mechanical Engineering; Production Engineering; Surveying and Mapping; Technology; Telecommunications Engineering); **Tourism, Catering and Domestic Services** (Cooking and Catering; Tourism)

History: Founded 2008 following the merger of Yrkeshögskolan Sydväst (Sydväst University of Applied Sciences) and Svenska yrkeshögskolan (Swedish Polytechnic, Finland).

Main Language(s) of Instruction: Finnish and English

Degrees and Diplomas: *Ammattikorkeakoulututkinto (AMK)/ Yrkeshögskoleexamen (YH)*; *Ylempi ammattikorkeakoulututinto (ylempi AMK)/ Högre yrkeshögskoleexamen (högre YH)*: Engineering
Last Updated: 30/09/11

OULU UNIVERSITY OF APPLIED SCIENCES
Oulun seudun ammattikorkeakoulu
PO Box 222, Albertinkuja 20, FI-90101 Oulu
Tel: +358(10) 272-1030
Fax: +358(10) 272-1371
EMail: international@oamk.fi
Website: http://www.oamk.fi

Rector: Jouko Paaso (1996-)
Tel: +358(10) 272-3819 EMail: jouko.paaso@oamk.fi

Schools
Business and Information Management (Administration; Business and Commerce; Information Management); **Engineering** (Automation and Control Engineering; Biomedical Engineering; Civil Engineering; Engineering; Information Technology; Laboratory Techniques; Mechanical Engineering; Production Engineering); **Enginering and Business** *(Raahe)* (Business Computing; Economics; Information Technology; Mechanical Engineering; Production Engineering); **Health and Social Care** (Public Health; Social and Community Services); **Music, Dance and Media** (Cultural Studies; Dance; Journalism; Media Studies; Music); **Renewable Natural Resources** (Agriculture; Forestry; Horticulture; Natural Resources); **Vocational Teacher Education** (Teacher Training)

History: Founded 1992, acquired present status and title 1996.

Main Language(s) of Instruction: Finnish and English

Degrees and Diplomas: *Ammattikorkeakoulututkinto (AMK)/ Yrkeshögskoleexamen (YH)*; *Ylempi ammattikorkeakoulututinto (ylempi AMK)/ Högre yrkeshögskoleexamen (högre YH)*

Libraries: Yes
Last Updated: 29/09/11

POLICE COLLEGE OF FINLAND
Poliisiammattikorkeakoulu - Polisyrkeshögskolan (POLIISI/POLISEN/POLICE)
PO Box 123, Vaajakatu 2, FI-33721 Tampere
Tel: +358(3) 285-0111
Fax: +358(3) 285-0297
EMail: viestinta.polamk@poliisi.fi
Website: http://www.poliisiammattikorkeakoulu.fi

Director: Seppo Kolehmainen

Programmes
Police Command; **Police Studies** (Police Studies)

History: Founded 1998.

Degrees and Diplomas: *Ammattikorkeakoulututkinto (AMK)/ Yrkeshögskoleexamen (YH)*; *Ylempi ammattikorkeakoulututinto (ylempi AMK)/ Högre yrkeshögskoleexamen (högre YH)*. Also Diploma in Police Studies

Libraries: Yes
Last Updated: 29/09/11

ROVANIEMI UNIVERSITY OF APPLIED SCIENCES
Rovaniemen ammattikorkeakoulu (RAMK)
Jokiväylä 11C, FI-96300 Rovaniemi
Tel: +358(20) 798-4000
Fax: +358(20) 798-5499
EMail: international@ramk.fi
Website: http://www.ramk.fi

Rector: Pentti Tieranta (1996-)
Tel: +358(20) 798-5311, Fax: +358(20) 798-5491
EMail: pentti.tieranta@ramk.fi

Head of Quality Management: Martti Lampela
Tel: +358(20) 798-5471

International Relations: Pasi Kokko, Information and Communications Officer Tel: +358(16) 798-5315

Schools
Business and Administration (Business Administration; Economics; Information Technology; International Business); **Forestry and Rural Industries** (Agricultural Engineering; Agricultural Equipment; Forestry); **Health Care and Social Services** (Health Administration; Nursing; Physical Therapy; Public Health; Social and Community Services; Social Welfare); **Sports and Leisure** (Leisure Studies; Sports); **Technology** (Construction Engineering; Information Technology; Mechanical Engineering; Production Engineering; Software Engineering; Surveying and Mapping; Technology); **Tourism and Hospitality Management** (Cooking and Catering; Hotel and Restaurant; Hotel Management; Tourism)

Further Information: Also Open University of Applied Sciences

History: Founded 1996, acquired present status and title 1998.

Main Language(s) of Instruction: Finnish and English

Degrees and Diplomas: *Ammattikorkeakoulututkinto (AMK)/ Yrkeshögskoleexamen (YH)*; *Ylempi ammattikorkeakoulututinto (ylempi AMK)/ Högre yrkeshögskoleexamen (högre YH)*
Last Updated: 23/12/09

SAIMAA UNIVERSITY OF APPLIED SCIENCES
Saimaan ammattikorkeakoulu
PO Box 303, Pohjolankatu 23, FI-53101 Lappeenranta
Tel: +358(20) 496-6411
Fax: +358(20) 496-6505
EMail: info@saimia.fi
Website: http://www.saimia.fi/fi-FI/

Rector: Anneli Pirttilä
Tel: +358(20) 496-6411 EMail: anneli.pirttila@saimia.fi

Secretary to the Management: Eeva Hyvönen
EMail: eeva.hyvonen@saimia.fi

International Relations: Seppo Pellinen
Tel: +358(20) 496-6755, Fax: +358(20) 496-6750
EMail: seppo.pellinen@saimia.fi

Faculties
Business and Culture (Business Administration; Fine Arts; International Business); **Health Care and Social Services** (Nursing; Occupational Therapy; Physical Therapy; Public Health; Social and Community Services); **Technology** (Chemical Engineering; Civil Engineering; Construction Engineering; Electrical Engineering; Industrial Engineering; Industrial Management; Information Technology; Mechanical Engineering; Paper Technology; Technology; Transport Management)

Units
Tourism and Hospitality (Cooking and Catering; Hotel and Restaurant; Tourism); **Visual Arts** (Design; Fine Arts; Visual Arts)

History: Founded 1992. Acquired present title 2009. Formerly known as Etelä-Karjalan ammattikorkeakoulu (South-Karelia University of Applied Sciences).

Main Language(s) of Instruction: Finnish and English

Degrees and Diplomas: *Ammattikorkeakoulututkinto (AMK)/ Yrkeshögskoleexamen (YH)*; *Ylempi ammattikorkeakoulututinto (ylempi AMK)/ Högre yrkeshögskoleexamen (högre YH)*
Last Updated: 29/09/11

SATAKUNTA UNIVERSITY OF APPLIED SCIENCES
Satakunnan ammattikorkeakoulu
Tiedepuisto 3, FI-28600 Pori
Tel: +358(2) 620-3000
Fax: +358(2) 620-3030
EMail: info@samk.fi; int.office@samk.fi
Website: http://www.samk.fi

Rector: Seppo Pynnä (1997-)
Tel: +358(2) 620-3010 EMail: seppo.pynna@samk.fi

Opintosihteeri: Matti Isokallio
Tel: +358(2) 620-3012 EMail: matti.isokallio@samk.fi

International Relations: Jari Heiniluoma, Head of International
Relations Tel: +358(2) 620-3013 EMail: jari.heiniluoma@samk.fi

Faculties

Business and Culture (Business Administration; Business and Commerce; Cultural Studies; Fine Arts; International Business; Management; Marketing; Tourism); **Health Care and Social Services** (Nursing; Physical Therapy; Public Health; Rehabilitation and Therapy; Social and Community Services; Social Welfare); **Technology and Maritime Management** (Automation and Control Engineering; Chemical Engineering; Construction Engineering; Electrical Engineering; Energy Engineering; Environmental Engineering; Industrial Engineering; Information Technology; Marine Transport; Mechanical Engineering; Production Engineering; Technology; Transport Management)

Further Information: Also campuses in Pori, Rauma, Huittinen, Kankaanpää and Harjavalta

History: Founded 1997.

Main Language(s) of Instruction: Finnish and English

Degrees and Diplomas: *Ammattikorkeakoulututkinto (AMK)/ Yrkeshögskoleexamen (YH); Ylempi ammattikorkeakoulututinto (ylempi AMK)/ Högre yrkeshögskoleexamen (högre YH)*
Last Updated: 29/09/11

SAVONIA UNIVERSITY OF APPLIED SCIENCES

Savonia-ammattikorkeakoulu
PO Box 6, Microkatu 1, FI-70201 Kuopio
Tel: +358(17) 255-6000
Fax: +358(17) 255-5014
EMail: savonia@savonia.fi
Website: http://www.savonia.fi

Rector: Veli-Matti Tolppi
EMail: veli-matti.tolppi@pelastusopisto.fi

International Relations: Ilkka Toroi, Head of International
Affairs Tel: +358(17) 255-5061 EMail: Ilkka.Toroi@savonia.fi

Academies

Design *(Kuopio)* (Ceramic Art; Fashion Design; Furniture Design; Glass Art; Graphic Design; Industrial Design; Interior Design; Jewelry Art; Textile Design); **Music and Dance** *(Kuopio)* (Dance; Music)

Programmes

Business and Administration *(Iisalmi, Kuopio and Varkaus)* (Administration; Business and Commerce; International Business); **Engineering and Technology** *(Kuopio and Varkaus)* (Engineering; Industrial Management); **Natural Resources** *(Peltosalmi)* (Agriculture; Natural Resources; Rural Planning; Rural Studies); **Social and Health Care** *(Kuopio and Iisalmi)* (Nursing; Public Health; Social and Community Services); **Tourism and Catering** *(Kuopio)* (Cooking and Catering; Hotel and Restaurant; Hotel Management; Tourism)

History: Founded 1992, acquired present status and title 1998.

Main Language(s) of Instruction: Finnish and English

Degrees and Diplomas: *Ammattikorkeakoulututkinto (AMK)/ Yrkeshögskoleexamen (YH); Ylempi ammattikorkeakoulututinto (ylempi AMK)/ Högre yrkeshögskoleexamen (högre YH)*: Industrial Management

Libraries: Libraries on all campuses

Academic Staff *2009-2010*	TOTAL
FULL-TIME	350

Student Numbers *2009-2010*	
All (Foreign Included)	7,000
FOREIGN ONLY	240

Last Updated: 30/09/11

SEINÄJOKI UNIVERSITY OF APPLIED SCIENCES

Seinäjoen ammattikorkeakoulu
PO Box 412, Keskuskatu 34, FI-60101 Seinäjoki
Tel: +358(20) 124-5000
Fax: +358(20) 124-5001
EMail: seamk@seamk.fi
Website: http://www.seamk.fi

Rector: Tapio Varmola
Tel: +358 201-245-002 EMail: tapio.varmola@seamk.fi

Sihteeri (Secretary General): Leena Löfhjelm
Tel: +358 201-245-012 EMail: leena.lofhjelm@seamk.fi

International Relations: Helli Kitinoja
Tel: +358 201-245-004 EMail: helli.kitinoja@seamk.fi

Schools

Agriculture and Forestry (Agricultural Engineering; Agriculture; Forest Products; Forestry; Natural Resources); **Business** (Administration; Business and Commerce; International Business; Management; Tourism); **Culture and Design** (Cultural Studies; Design; Fine Arts; Furniture Design; Graphic Design; Heritage Preservation; Industrial Design; Information Sciences; Library Science; Media Studies); **Health Care and Social Work** (Gerontology; Nursing; Physical Therapy; Public Health; Social and Community Services; Social Work); **Technology** (Automation and Control Engineering; Automotive Engineering; Biotechnology; Computer Networks; Construction Engineering; Food Technology; Information Technology; Mechanical Engineering; Production Engineering; Software Engineering; Technology; Wood Technology)

History: Founded 1996.

Academic Year: September to June (September-December; January-June)

Main Language(s) of Instruction: Finnish and English

Degrees and Diplomas: *Ammattikorkeakoulututkinto (AMK)/ Yrkeshögskoleexamen (YH); Ylempi ammattikorkeakoulututinto (ylempi AMK)/ Högre yrkeshögskoleexamen (högre YH)*
Libraries: Yes
Last Updated: 30/09/11

SIBELIUS ACADEMY

Sibelius-Akatemia - Sibelius-Akademin
PO Box 86, Pohjoinen Rautatiekatu 9, FIN-00251 Helsinki
Tel: +358(20) 753-90
Fax: +358(20) 753-9600
EMail: info@siba.fi
Website: http://www.siba.fi

Rector: Gustav Djupsjöbacka (2004-)
Tel: +358(20) 753-9620 EMail: gustav.djupsjobacka@siba.fi

Hallintojohtaja (Administrative Director): Seppo Suihko
Tel: +358(20) 753-9617 EMail: suihko@siba.fi

International Relations: Tuovi Martinsen
Tel: +358(20) 753-9489 EMail: tuovi.martinsen@siba.fi

Centres
Continuing Education

Departments

Art Management (Art Management); **Church Music** *(Helsinki and Kuopio campuses)* (Religious Music); **Composition and Music Theory** (Music Theory and Composition); **Folk Music** (Folklore; Music); **Jazz Music** (Jazz and Popular Music); **Music Education** (Music Education); **Music Performance and Research** *(Doctoral programme)* (Music; Music Theory and Composition; Religious Music); **Music Technology** (Music); **Orchestral Instruments** (Music; Musical Instruments); **Piano Music** (Music; Musical Instruments); **Vocal Music** (Opera; Singing)

Programmes

Music, Theatre and Dance *(Doctoral Programme)* (Dance; Music; Theatre)

History: Founded 1882 as Helsinki College of Music, a private Institution, became Conservatory 1924. Reorganized and present title adopted 1939. Status as State Institution 1980, acquired present status as University 1998.

Governing Bodies: Hallitus; Opetus- ja tutkimusneuvosto

Academic Year: September to May (September-December; January-May)

Admission Requirements: Secondary school certificate (ylioppilastutkinto)

Fees: None

Main Language(s) of Instruction: Finnish, Swedish, English

International Co-operation: Participates in the Erasmus and Nordplus programmes, and several bilateral agreements.

Degrees and Diplomas: *Kandidaatti/Kandidat*: Music, 3 yrs; *Lisensiaatti/Licentiat*: Music, a further 2 yrs; *Maisteri/Magister*: Music, a further 2 1/2 yrs; *Tohtori/Doktor*: Music, a further 3 yrs

Student Services: Academic counselling, Canteen, Employment services, Foreign student adviser, Social counselling

Student Residential Facilities: No

Libraries: c. 79,000 vols; c. 21,000 gramophone records. Kuopio, 26,000 vols; c. 2,000 grammophone records

Last Updated: 30/09/11

TAMPERE UNIVERSITY OF APPLIED SCIENCES

Tampereen ammattikorkeakoulu (TAMK)
Kuntokatu 4, FI-33520 Tampere
Tel: +358(3) 245-2111 +358(3) 565-47111
Fax: +358(3) 245-2351
EMail: international.office@tamk.fi; international.office@piramk.fi
Website: http://www.tamk.fi

President: Markku Lahtinen (2010-)
Tel: +358(3) 245-2350 EMail: markku.lahtinen@tamk.fi

Programmes
Bachelor's Degree - in English (Environmental Engineering; International Business; Media Studies; Nursing; Social and Community Services; Tourism); **Bachelor's Degree - in Finnish** (Automotive Engineering; Biomedical Engineering; Building Technologies; Business Administration; Chemical Engineering; Computer Engineering; Construction Engineering; Electrical Engineering; Film; Fine Arts; Forestry; Information Technology; Laboratory Techniques; Mechanical Engineering; Media Studies; Music; Nursing; Paper Technology; Physical Therapy; Production Engineering; Public Health; Radio and Television Broadcasting; Radiology; Textile Technology; Tourism; Transport Engineering); **Master's Degree - in English**; **Master's Degree - in Finnish**

Further Information: Also campuses in Ikaalinen, Mänttä-Vilppula and Virrat

History: Founded 2010 following the merger of Pirkanmaan ammattikorkeakoulu (PIRAMK University of Applied Sciences) and Tampereen ammattikorkeakoulu (TAMK University of Applied Sciences).

Main Language(s) of Instruction: Finnish and English

Degrees and Diplomas: *Ammattikorkeakoulututkinto (AMK)/ Yrkeshögskoleexamen (YH)*; *Ylempi ammattikorkeakoulututinto (ylempi AMK)/ Högre yrkeshögskoleexamen (högre YH)*
Last Updated: 30/09/11

TAMPERE UNIVERSITY OF TECHNOLOGY

Tampereen teknillinen yliopisto (TUT)
PO Box 527, Korkeakoulunkatu 10, FI-33101 Tampere
Tel: +358(3) 3115-11
Fax: +358(3) 3115-2640
EMail: interoff@tut.fi
Website: http://www.tut.fi

Rector: Markku Kivikoski
Tel: +358(3) 3115-2011, Fax: +358(3) 3115-3790
EMail: markku.kivikoski@tut.fi

Hallintojohtaja (Administrative Director): Tiina Äijälä
Tel: +358(3) 3115-2013, Fax: +358(3) 3115-2170
EMail: tiina.aijala@tut.fi

International Relations: Eila Hirvonen
Tel: +358(3) 3115-2447 EMail: eila.hirvonen@tut.fi

Centres
Continuing Education (EDUTECH); **Language** (Linguistics; Modern Languages)

Faculties
Automation, Mechanical and Materials Engineering *(The Faculty consists of five departments)* (Automation and Control Engineering; Hydraulic Engineering; Industrial Design; Materials Engineering; Mechanical Engineering; Production Engineering); **Built Environment** *(The Faculty consists of two Departments)* (Architecture; Architecture and Planning; Civil Engineering; Town Planning); **Business and Technology Management** *(The Faculty consists of three departments)* (Business Administration; Economics; Industrial Management; Information Management; Information Technology; Media Studies; Multimedia; Transport Management); **Computing and Electrical Engineering** *(The Faculty consists of six departments)* (Computer Engineering; Electrical Engineering; Electronic Engineering; Energy Engineering; Software Engineering; Telecommunications Engineering); **Science and Environmental Engineering** *(The Faculty consists of five departments)* (Bioengineering; Biomedical Engineering; Chemical Engineering; Energy Engineering; Engineering Management; Mathematics; Physics)

Further Information: Also courses for foreign exchange students in Information Technology, Materials Science, Biomedical Engineering (in English), Architecture, Industrial Management and Engineering

History: Founded 1965 and attached to the Helsinki University of Technology. Acquired independent status 1972. An autonomous State institution under the supervision of the Ministry of Education.

Governing Bodies: University Board; Education and Research Council

Academic Year: September to May (September-January; February-May)

Admission Requirements: Secondary school certificate (lukion päästötodistus) or equivalent, and entrance examination

Main Language(s) of Instruction: Finnish, some courses in English

International Co-operation: Participates in Socrates/Erasmus, Leonardo, Nordplus/Nordtek and the International Student Exchange Programme and Global Engineering GE3

Degrees and Diplomas: *Arkkitehti/Arkitekt*: Bachelor of Science in Architecture, 3 yrs; *Diplomi-insinööri/Diplomingenjör (DI)*; *Lisensiaatti/Licentiat*: Technology (tekn.lis.), at least a further 2 yrs; *Maisteri/Magister*: 2 yrs; *Tohtori/Doktor*: Technology (PhD, tekn.tri.), a further 2 yrs and thesis. Also Bachelor and Master degrees

Student Services: Academic counselling, Canteen, Employment services, Foreign student adviser, Health services, Social counselling, Sports facilities

Student Residential Facilities: Yes

Libraries: 8,000 electronic journals; 20,000 digital handbooks and dictionaries and encyclopaedias

Academic Staff *2009*	TOTAL
FULL-TIME	c. 1,600

Student Numbers *2009*	
All (Foreign Included)	c. 11,600
FOREIGN ONLY	1,000

Last Updated: 30/09/11

THEATRE ACADEMY HELSINKI

Teatterikorkeakoulu - Teaterhögskolan
PO Box 163, Haapaniemenkatu 6, FI-00531 Helsinki
Tel: +358(9) 431-361
Fax: +358(9) 4313-6200
EMail: international@teak.fi
Website: http://www.teak.fi

Rector: Paula Tuovinen
Tel: +358(9) 4313-6215 EMail: paula.tuovinen@teak.fi

Hallintojohtaja (Administrative Director): Maarit Hildén
Tel: +358(9) 4313-6211 EMail: maarit.hilden@teak.fi

International Relations: Jonna Sundberg, International Relations Coordinator
Tel: +358(4) 0079-2170 EMail: jonna.sundberg@teak.fi

Centres

Continuing Education (Dance; Display and Stage Design; Theatre); **Development of Theatre Technology** *(Tampere)* (Theatre)

Departments

Acting in Swedish *(Also in Swedish)* (Acting); **Dance** (Dance; Performing Arts); **Dance and Theatre Pedagogy** (Dance; Performing Arts; Theatre); **Sound and Lighting Design** *(Tampere)* (Display and Stage Design; Theatre)

Institutes

The Training Theatre (Performing Arts; Theatre)

History: Founded 1979, integrating the Svenska teaterskolan (1908) and Suomen teatterikoulu (1948). An autonomous State institution under the supervision of the Ministry of Education.

Governing Bodies: Board

Academic Year: August to May (August-December; January-May)

Admission Requirements: Secondary school certificate (ylioppilastutkinto) or equivalent, and entrance examination

Fees: None

Main Language(s) of Instruction: Finnish, Swedish

International Co-operation: With universities in the Baltic and Nordic countries; Europe; Russian Federation.

Degrees and Diplomas: *Kandidaatti/Kandidat*: Theatre; Dance, 120 credits; *Lisensiaatti/Licentiat*: Theatre; Dance, a further 2 yrs following Maisteri; *Maisteri/Magister*: Theatre; Dance, 4-5 1/2 yrs (160-180 credits); *Tohtori/Doktor*: Theatre; Dance, a further 4 yrs

Student Services: Academic counselling, Canteen, Employment services, Foreign student adviser, Health services, Social counselling

Libraries: Central Library of Theatre and Dance, 35,000 vols

Publications: Teatterikorkeakoulun tiedotuslehti *(biennially)*
Last Updated: 30/09/11

TURKU UNIVERSITY OF APPLIED SCIENCES

Turun ammattikorkeakoulu - Åbo yrkeshögskola
Joukahaisenkatu 3 A, FI-20520 Turku
Tel: +358(2) 263-350
Fax: +358(2) 2633-5791
EMail: ammattikorkeakoulu@turkuamk.fi
Website: http://www.turkuamk.fi

Rector: Juha Kettunen
Tel: +358(10) 553-5612 EMail: juha.kettunen@turkuamk.fi

Vice-Rector: Saara Lampelo

Vice-Rector: Olli Mertanen Tel: +358(2) 2633-5684

International Relations: Kirsti Virtanen
Tel: +358(10) 553-5681 EMail: kirsti.virtanen@turkuamk.fi

Academies

Arts (Design; Fine Arts; Media Studies; Music; Performing Arts)

Faculties

Health Care (Dental Hygiene; Laboratory Techniques; Midwifery; Nursing; Public Health; Radiology; Social and Community Services); **Life Sciences and Business** (Biological and Life Sciences; Biotechnology; Business Administration; Business and Commerce; Food Technology; Information Technology; International Business; Laboratory Techniques); **Technology, Environment and Business** (Automotive Engineering; Business Administration; Civil Engineering; Construction Engineering; Cultural Studies; Design; Engineering; Environmental Engineering; Environmental Management; Fine Arts; Fishery; Handicrafts; Industrial Management; Mechanical Engineering; Restoration of Works of Art; Transport Engineering); **Telecommunication and E-Business** (Business Administration; E-Business/Commerce; Electronic Engineering; Information Technology; Library Science; Media Studies); **Wellbeing Services** (Business Administration; Cooking and Catering; Cosmetology; Hotel and Restaurant; Hotel Management; Occupational Therapy; Physical Therapy; Rehabilitation and Therapy; Social and Community Services; Sports; Tourism)

History: Founded 1997.

Main Language(s) of Instruction: Finnish and English

Degrees and Diplomas: *Ammattikorkeakoulututkinto (AMK)/ Yrkeshögskoleexamen (YH)*; *Ylempi ammattikorkeakoulututinto (ylempi AMK)/ Högre yrkeshögskoleexamen (högre YH)*
Last Updated: 30/09/11

UNIVERSITY OF EASTERN FINLAND

Itä-Suomen Yliopisto
PO Box 111, FI-80101 Joensuu
Tel: +358(13) 251-111
Fax: +358(13) 251-2050
EMail: intnl@uef.fi
Website: http://www.uef.fi/

Rector: Perttu Vartiainen (2009-2014)
Tel: +358(13) 251-2001 EMail: perttu.vartiainen@uef.fi

Director, Communications: Liisa Hakola
Tel: +358(40) 355-3274, Fax: +358(17) 162-131
EMail: liisa.hakoka@uef.fi

International Relations: Outi Savonlahti, Director, International Relations EMail: savonla@uef.fi

Faculties

Health Sciences (Biotechnology; Health Sciences; Medicine; Molecular Biology; Neurosciences; Nursing; Pharmacy); **Philosophy** (Philosophy); **Science and Forestry** (Biology; Chemistry; Computer Science; Environmental Studies; Forestry; Mathematics; Natural Sciences; Physics; Statistics); **Social Sciences and Business** (Business Administration; Business and Commerce; Criminology; Economics; Geography; Health Administration; History; Law; Management; Social Sciences; Social Work; Sociology)

History: Created January 2010 from merger between Joensuun yliopisto (University of Joensuu, created 1969) and Kuopion yliopisto (University of Kuopio, created 1966).

Governing Bodies: University Senate

Academic Year: August to May (September-December; January-May)

Admission Requirements: Secondary school certificate (ylioppilastutkinto) or equivalent. Knowledge of Finnish or English. TOEFL test for non-Finnish speaking degree students

Fees: (Euros): None for degree/exchange students; visiting non-degree students, 1,750 per semester; 3,500 per annum

Main Language(s) of Instruction: Finnish, English

International Co-operation: With universities in Bosnia Herzegovina, Canada, China, Cyprus, Czech Republic, Estonia, France, Germany, Hong Kong, Japan, Kazakhstan, Latvia, Lithuania, Malaysia, Morocco, Namibia, Norway, Philippines, Russian Federation, South Africa, South Korea, Sweden, Tanzania, Thailand, Venezuela and USA. Also participates in Erasmus and exchange programmes.

Degrees and Diplomas: *Kandidaatti/Kandidat*: Administrative Sciences; Arts; Arts (Education); Arts (Psychology); Economics and Business; Administration; Health Sciences; Science (Bachelor's degree); Science (Agriculture and Forestry); Science (Economics and Business Administration); Science (Pharmacy); Social Sciences; Theology (Bachelor's degree), 3 yrs; *Lisensiaatti/Licentiat*: Administrative Sciences; Psychology; Health Sciences; Philosophy; Philosophy (Education); Economics and Business Administration; Pharmacy; Social Sciences; Theology, a further 2 yrs; *Lisensiaatti/ Licentiat*: Dentistry, 5 yrs; *Lisensiaatti/Licentiat*: Medicine, 6 yrs; *Maisteri/Magister*: Administrative Sciences; Arts; Arts Education; Psychology; Economics and Business Administration; Health Sciences; Science; Agriculture and Forestry; Pharmacy; Social Sciences; Theology, a further 2 yrs; *Tohtori/Doktor*: Administrative Sciences; Dental Science; Health Sciences; Medical Science; Philosophy (Education); Philosophy (Psychology); Social Sciences; Agriculture and Forestry; Economics and Business Administration; Pharmacy; Theology, 4 yrs following Master's

Student Services: Academic counselling, Canteen, Employment services, Foreign student adviser, Health services, Language programs, Social counselling

Special Facilities: A.I. Virtanen Research Institute for Molecular Medicine; Biocenter Kuopio; Clinical Research Centre; Drug Research and Development Centre; Food and Health Research Centre; InFotonics Centre Joensuu; Karelian Institute; Kuopio Welfare Research Centre; Kuopio Research Institute of Exercise

Medicine; Kuopio University Centre for Environment, Health and Society; Mekrijärvi Research Station; Neuroscience Centre; Research Institute for Public Health; Special Materials Research Centre, SMARC

Libraries: University Library, c. 1,435,000 vols; 32,000 periodical subscriptions.

Publications: Acta Universitatis Finlandiae Orientalis A. Paedagogica et Humaniora; Acta Universitatis Finlandiae Orientalis B. Naturalia et Silvestria; Acta Universitatis Finlandiae Orientalis C. Sanitaria; Acta Universitatis Finlandiae Orientalis D. Socialia et Commercialia
Last Updated: 28/09/11

UNIVERSITY OF HELSINKI

Helsingin yliopisto - Helsingfors Universitet
PO Box 33, Yliopistonkatu 4, FI-00014 University of
Helsinki Helsinki
Tel: +358(9) 1911
Fax: +358(9) 1912-3008
Website: http://www.helsinki.fi/yliopisto

Rector: Thomas Wilhelmsson (2008-2014)
Tel: +358(9) 191-22211, Fax: +358(9) 191-3008
EMail: thomas.wilhelmsson@helsinki.fi

Communications Directors: Kirsti Lehumusto
Tel: +358(9) 191-23225, Fax: +358(9) 191-23010
EMail: kirsti.lehmusto@helsinki.fi

International Relations: Markus Laitinen, Head of International affairs
Tel: +358(9) 191-22605, Fax: +358(9) 191-23008
EMail: matti.j.tikkanen@helsinki.fi

Centres
Continuing Education (Palmenia Centre); **Economic Research** (HECER, Helsinki); **Genome**; **Language**; **Neurosciences**

Colleges
Advanced Studies (Helsinki Collegium)

Faculties
Agriculture and Forestry Dean: Jukka Kola; **Arts** (Aesthetics; African Studies; Archaeology; Art History; Asian Studies; Baltic Languages; Cinema and Television; Comparative Literature; Comparative Religion; Cultural Studies; English; Ethnology; Film; Finnish; Folklore; German; History; Hungarian; Linguistics; Literature; Marine Science and Oceanography; Museum Studies; Musicology; Philology; Philosophy; Romance Languages; Scandinavian Languages; Slavic Languages; Theatre; Translation and Interpretation; Women's Studies) Dean: Ulla-Maija Forsberg; **Behavioural Sciences** (Cognitive Sciences; Education; Educational Testing and Evaluation; Handicrafts; Higher Education; Home Economics; Psychology; Speech Studies) Dean: Patrik Scheinin; **Biosciences** (Biological and Life Sciences; Ecology; Environmental Studies) Dean: Jari Niemelä; **Law** (Commercial Law; Criminal Law; Human Rights; International Economics; International Law; Justice Administration; Private Law; Public Law) Dean: Jukka Kekkonen; **Medicine** (Biomedicine; Dentistry; Forensic Medicine and Dentistry; Medicine; Public Health) Dean: Kimmo Kontula; **Pharmacy** Dean: Raimo Hiltunen; **Science** (Astronomy and Space Science; Chemistry; Computer Science; Geography; Geology; Mathematics; Physics) Dean: Jukka Paakki; **Social Sciences** (Anthropology; Communication Studies; Development Studies; Economics; Mathematics; Philosophy; Political Sciences; Social Policy; Social Psychology; Social Sciences; Social Work; Sociology; Statistics) Dean: Hannu Niemi; **Theology** (Bible; Comparative Religion; History of Religion; Orthodox Theology; Theology) Dean: Aila Lauha; **Veterinary Medicine** (Environmental Studies; Food Science; Hygiene; Veterinary Science) Dean: Antti Sukura

Institutes
Biotechnology (Biotechnology); **Information Technology** (Helsinki Institute); **Molecular Medicine - Finland** (FIMM); **Physics** (HIP, Helsinki); **Ruralia** (Mikkeli and Seinäjoki units); **Russian and East European Studies** (Aleksanteri Institute); **Seismology**; **Verification of the Chemical Weapons Convention** (VERIFIN)

Further Information: Traditional and Open Higher Education Institution

History: Founded as Royal Academy of Turku 1640. Transferred to Helsinki 1828. The first and only one university in the country until 1919.

Governing Bodies: University Senate

Academic Year: September to May (September-December; January-May)

Admission Requirements: Secondary school certificate (ylioppilastutkinto/studentexamen) or foreign equivalent

Fees: None

Main Language(s) of Instruction: Finnish, Swedish, English

International Co-operation: Participates in the Socrates, Nordplus-Tempus, Jean Monnet and other international student exchange programmes. Actively participates in European research programmes and other forms of international research collaboration. Also 80 bilateral agreements with universities in North America, Latin America, Asia and Africa.

Degrees and Diplomas: Eläinlääketieteen lisensiaatti/Veterinärmedicine licentiat: 3 yrs; Hammaslääketieteen lisensiaatti/Odontologie licentiat: Dentistry, 5 yrs; Lääketieteen lisensiaatti/Medicine licentiat: 6 yrs; Lisensiaatti/Licentiat: Theology; Law; Veterinary Medicine; Arts; Education; Psychology; Science; Pharmacy; Agriculture and Forestry; Social Sciences, 3 yrs; Maisteri/Magister: Theology; Law; Arts; Education; Science; Pharmacy; Agriculture and Forestry; Social Sciences, 2 yrs; Tohtori/Doktor: Theology; Law; Veterinary Medicine; Arts; Education; Philosophy; Psychology; Science; Pharmacy; Agriculture and Forestry; Social Sciences, 4 yrs

Student Services: Academic counselling, Canteen, Employment services, Foreign student adviser, Foreign Studies Centre, Handicapped facilities, Health services, Language programs, Social counselling, Sports facilities

Student Residential Facilities: Yes

Special Facilities: Finnish Museum of Natural History; Helsinki University Museum (University History, Medical History, Collections of Craft Science, Mineral Cabinet); Agriculture Museum, Bird and Mammal Collection; Botanical Gardens; Observatory

Libraries: Helsinki University Library; Undergraduate Library; National Library of Health Sciences; Learning Centre Alexandria

Publications: Universitas Helsingiensis (quarterly)

Press or Publishing House: Helsinki University Press

Academic Staff 2008-2009: Total: c. 7,900
Student Numbers 2008-2009: Total: c. 35,000
Last Updated: 23/12/09

UNIVERSITY OF JYVÄSKYLÄ

Jyväskylän yliopisto (JY)
PO Box 35, Seminaarinmäki, FI-40014 Jyväskylä
Tel: +358(14) 260-1211
Fax: +358(14) 260-1021
EMail: tiedotus@jyu.fi
Website: http://www.jyu.fi

Rector: Aino Sallinen (1992-)
Tel: +358(14) 260-1007, Fax: +358(14) 260-1011
EMail: aino.sallinen@adm.jyu.fi

Hallintojohtaja (Director of Administration): Kirsi Moisander
Tel: +358(14) 260-1009, Fax: +358(14) 260-1389
EMail: marjo.havila@adm.jyu.fi

Vice-Rector: Jaakko Pehkonen EMail: jaakko.k.pehkonen@jyu.fi

Vice-Rector: Helena Rasku-Puttonen
EMail: helena.rasku-puttonen@jyu.fi

International Relations: Tuija Koponen, Head of the International Office
Tel: +358(14) 260-1086, Fax: +358(14) 260-1061
EMail: intl@jyu.fi

Centres
Computing (Computer Science); **Continuing Education**; **Environmental Research** (Environmental Studies); **Human Technologies** (Agora) (Computer Science; Information Technology; Psychology); **Language** (Communication Studies; Linguistics; Modern Languages)

Faculties

Business and Economics (Business and Commerce; Economics; Environmental Management); **Education** (Adult Education; Curriculum; Education; Educational Administration; Educational and Student Counselling; Preschool Education; Primary Education; Special Education; Teacher Training); **Humanities** (Applied Linguistics; Art Education; Art History; Arts and Humanities; Communication Studies; Cultural Studies; English; Ethnology; Finnish; French; German; History; Hungarian; Journalism; Linguistics; Literature; Modern Languages; Museum Studies; Music; Music Education; Musicology; Public Relations; Romance Languages; Russian; Speech Studies; Swedish; Teacher Training); **Information Technology** (Applied Mathematics; Cognitive Sciences; Information Technology; Mathematics and Computer Science); **Mathematics and Science** (Biological and Life Sciences; Biology; Cell Biology; Chemistry; Ecology; Environmental Management; Environmental Studies; Marine Science and Oceanography; Mathematics; Mathematics Education; Molecular Biology; Natural Resources; Natural Sciences; Nuclear Physics; Physics; Science Education; Statistics); **Social Sciences** (Philosophy; Political Sciences; Psychology; Social Policy; Social Sciences; Social Work; Sociology); **Sports and Health Sciences** (Biology; Gerontology; Health Education; Health Sciences; Physical Education; Physical Therapy; Physiology; Public Health; Social Sciences; Sociology; Sports Management; Sports Medicine)

Institutes

Chydenius *(Kokkola)* (Education; Information Technology; Teacher Training); **Educational Research** (Educational Research); **Open University**

History: Founded 1863 as a Teacher Training College, became College of Education 1934 and acquired present status and title 1966. An autonomous State institution under the supervision of the Ministry of Education.

Governing Bodies: University Senate

Academic Year: August to July (September-December; January-May; June-July)

Admission Requirements: Secondary school certificate (ylioppilastutkinto) or foreign equivalent, and entrance examination

Fees: None

Main Language(s) of Instruction: Finnish, English

International Co-operation: With universities in the USA, Russian Federation, Japan, Canada, Germany, Estonia, Spain, Italy, Chile, Hungary, South Africa, China, Poland, Zambia, Australia, South Korea, Taiwan, India. Also participates in the Socrates, Leonardo, Tempus, Nordplus, ISEP, EU-Canada and Jean Monnet programmes.

Degrees and Diplomas: *Kandidaatti/Kandidat:* Arts; Economics and Business Administration; Education; Health Sciences; Psychology; Science; Social Sciences; Sports Science, 3-4 yrs; *Lisensiaatti/Licentiat:* Arts; Economics and Business Administration; Education; Health Sciences; Psychology; Science; Social Sciences; Sports Science, 7-8 yrs; *Maisteri/Magister:* Arts; Economics and Business Administration; Education; Health Sciences; Psychology; Science; Social Sciences; Sports Science, 5-6 yrs; *Tohtori/Doktor:* Arts; Economics and Business Administration; Health Sciences; Science; Sports Science, 2-3 yrs following upon Lisensiaatti; *Tohtori/Doktor:* Education; Psychology; Social Sciences, by thesis

Student Services: Academic counselling, Canteen, Cultural centre, Employment services, Foreign student adviser, Handicapped facilities, Health services, Nursery care, Social counselling, Sports facilities

Student Residential Facilities: Yes

Special Facilities: University Museum. University Botanical Garden. Konnevesi Biological Research Station

Libraries: Central Library, 1.5m vols

Publications: Jyväskylä Studies in Arts; Jyväskylä Studies in Biological and Environmental Science; Jyväskylä Studies in Business and Economics; Jyväskylä Studies in Communication; Jyväskylä Studies in Computing; Jyväskylä Studies in Education, Psychology and Social Research; Jyväskylä Studies in Sport, Physical Education and Health; Kasvatus (Finnish Journal of Education); Studia Historica Jyväskyläensia; Studia Philologica Jyväskyläensia

Press or Publishing House: University Printing House
Last Updated: 07/03/12

UNIVERSITY OF LAPLAND
Lapin yliopisto
Box 122, Yliopistonkatu 8, FI-96101 Rovaniemi
Tel: +358(16) 341-341
Fax: +358(16) 362 936
EMail: international.relations@ulapland.fi
Website: http://www.ulapland.fi

Rector: Mauri Ylä-Kotola (2006-2014)
Tel: +358 400 276 288, Fax: +358(16) 362 936
EMail: mauri.yla-kotola@ulapland.fi

Director of Communication and Pr: Olli Tiwaniemi
Tel: +358 400 695 418 EMail: olli.tiwaniemi@ulapland.fi

International Relations: Outi Snellman, Director of International Relations
Tel: +358 40 201 0209, Fax: +358(16) 362 941
EMail: outi.snellman@ulapland.fi

Centres

Arctic (Arctic Studies; Data Processing; Environmental Studies; Natural Sciences) *Director:* Paula Kankaanpää; **Language** (Linguistics; Modern Languages) *Director:* Jukka Mäkelä

Faculties

Art and Design (Art Education; Clothing and Sewing; Fine Arts; Graphic Design; Industrial Design; Media Studies; Textile Design); **Education** (Adult Education; Education; Teacher Training); **Law** (Law); **Social Sciences** (Administration; International Relations; Management; Political Sciences; Psychology; Public Law; Rehabilitation and Therapy; Social Sciences; Social Work; Sociology; Tourism); **Tourism and Business** (Accountancy; Management; Marketing; Tourism) *Dean:* Markku Vieru

Schools

Teacher Training (Teacher Training) *Principal:* Eija Valanne

History: Founded 1979. A State institution.

Governing Bodies: Board of Directors; Advisory Council

Academic Year: August to May (August-December; January-May)

Admission Requirements: Secondary school certificate (ylioppilastutkinto) or equivalent

Main Language(s) of Instruction: Finnish, English

International Co-operation: Participates in the Socrates/Erasmus and Nordplus programmes, FIRST (Finnish Russian Student Exchange), North2North (Circumpolar pilot mobility programme coordinated by University of the Artic).

Degrees and Diplomas: *Kandidaatti/Kandidat:* Administrative Sciences (BA); Arts (BA); Laws (BA); Social Sciences (BA), 3 yrs; *Lisensiaatti/Licentiat:* Administrative Sciences; Education; Laws; Social Sciences; *Maisteri/Magister:* Administrative Sciences (MA/MSC); Arts (MA); Education (MA); Law; Social Sciences (MA/MSC), a further 2 yrs; *Tohtori/Doktor:* Administrative Sciences (PhD); Arts (PhD); Education (PhD); Laws (PhD); Philosophy (PhD); Social Sciences (PhD). Certificate, Diploma in Arctic Studies, 1 1/2 yrs

Student Services: Academic counselling, Canteen, Cultural centre, Employment services, Foreign student adviser, Foreign Studies Centre, Health services, Language programs, Nursery care, Social counselling, Sports facilities

Student Residential Facilities: Yes

Special Facilities: Faculty of Art and Design has galleries and library. Student Theatre.

Libraries: University of Lapland Library, 155,000 vols

Publications: Acta Universitatis Lapponiensis; Faculty Publications
Last Updated: 28/09/11

UNIVERSITY OF OULU
Oulun yliopisto (OY)
PO Box 8000, Pentti Kaiteran katu 1, 90014 Oulu
Tel: +358(8) 553-4011
Fax: +358(8) 554-4551
EMail: international.office@oulu.fi
Website: http://www.oulu.fi/yliopisto

Rector: Lauri Lajunen (1993-)
Tel: +358(8) 553-4071, Fax: +358(8) 554-4557
EMail: lauri.lajunen@oulu.fi

International Relations: Kimmo Kuortti, Head of International Relations (2003-)
Tel: +358(8) 553-4022, Fax: +358(8) 553-4040
EMail: kimo.kuortti@oulu.fi

Centres
Biocentre (Biological and Life Sciences; Cell Biology; Molecular Biology); **Brain and Sensory Research** (Neurosciences); **Computer Services** (Computer Engineering); **Human Reproduction Research** (Biology; Embryology and Reproduction Biology); **Infotech** (Information Technology); **Languages** (Applied Linguistics; English; Finnish; French; German; Italian; Japanese; Modern Languages; Russian; Spanish; Swedish); **Learning and Research Services** (Education; Pedagogy; Regional Planning); **Research and Development** *(Kajaani)* (Biotechnology; Continuing Education; Measurement and Precision Engineering)

Faculties
Education (Education; Educational Psychology; Educational Sciences; Music Education; Preschool Education; Primary Education; Teacher Training; Technology Education) *Dean:* Pauli Siljander; **Humanities** (Anthropology; Archaeology; Art History; Arts and Humanities; Cultural Studies; East Asian Studies; English; Environmental Studies; Ethics; European Studies; Film; Finnish; French; German; History; Information Sciences; Japanese; Linguistics; Literature; Museum Studies; Nordic Studies; Philology; Philosophy; Phonetics; Political Sciences; Scandinavian Languages; South Asian Studies; Speech Therapy and Audiology; Theology) *Dean:* Matti Lehtihalmes; **Medicine** (Anaesthesiology; Anatomy; Biochemistry; Cell Biology; Chemistry; Dentistry; Dermatology; Forensic Medicine and Dentistry; Genetics; Gynaecology and Obstetrics; Health Administration; Medical Technology; Medicine; Microbiology; Molecular Biology; Neurology; Nursing; Ophthalmology; Otorhinolaryngology; Paediatrics; Pathology; Pharmacology; Physical Therapy; Physiology; Psychiatry and Mental Health; Public Health; Radiology; Rehabilitation and Therapy; Surgery; Toxicology; Venereology) *Dean:* Heikki Ruskoaho; **Science** (Astronomy and Space Science; Biochemistry; Biology; Biophysics; Botany; Chemistry; Genetics; Geography; Geology; Geophysics; Information Technology; Mathematics; Natural Sciences; Physics; Zoology) *Dean:* Jouni Pursiainen; **Technology** (Architecture; Automation and Control Engineering; Chemical Engineering; Computer Networks; Electrical Engineering; Electronic Engineering; Engineering Management; Environmental Engineering; Industrial Engineering; Industrial Management; Information Technology; Mechanical Engineering; Technology) *Dean:* Vilho Lantto

Institutes
Geophysical *(Sodankyla)* (Geophysics); **Meri-Lappi** (Design; Environmental Engineering; Microelectronics; Production Engineering; Regional Studies); **Thule** (Arctic Studies; Nordic Studies)

Programmes
Master of Education *(in English)* (Education; International and Comparative Education); **Modern Nordic Architecture** *(in English)* (Architecture); **Nordic Design** *(in English)* (Industrial Design; Interior Design); **Northern Cultures and Societies** *(in English)* (Nordic Studies); **Northern Nature and Environment Studies** *(in English)* (Environmental Studies; Natural Resources); **Scandinavian Studies** *(in English)* (Nordic Studies); **Software Business** *(in English)* (Business Education; Marketing; Software Engineering)

Research Groups
Northern Environmental (Environmental Engineering; Environmental Studies)

Schools
Business *(Oulu)* (Accountancy; Business Administration; Economics; Management; Marketing)

Further Information: Also University Central Hospital and Teacher Training School

History: Founded 1958. An autonomous State institution financed by the Government.

Governing Bodies: Oulun yliopiston hallitus (Senate)

Academic Year: September to July (September-December; January-May)

Admission Requirements: Secondary school certificate (ylioppilastutkinto), or equivalent, and selection according to entrance examination results

Fees: None

Main Language(s) of Instruction: Finnish, some English

International Co-operation: With universities in Australia, New Zealand, USA, Japan, China. Also participates in Nordplus,Tempus, Socrates Erasmus, Leonardo, International Student Exchange Programme (ISEP) and Multilateral ISEP, UNC-EP.

Degrees and Diplomas: *Kandidaatti/Kandidat:* Arts (Huk); Economics; Education (KK); Science (LuK), 3-4 yrs; *Arkkitehti/Arkitekt:* Science in Architecture, 3 yrs following Maisteri; *Diplomi-insinööri/ Diplomingenjör:* Science in Technology (DI), a further 2 yrs; *Hammaslääketieteen lisensiaatti/Odontologie licentiat:* Dentistry (HLL), 6 yrs; *Lääketieteen lisensiaatti/Medicine licentiat:* Medicine (LL), 6 yrs; *Lisensiaatti/Licentiat:* 3 yrs following Maisteri; *Maisteri/Magister:* Arts (FM); Economics; Education (KM); Health Care (THK); Science, a further 2 yrs; *Tohtori/Doktor:* a further 2 yrs

Student Services: Academic counselling, Canteen, Employment services, Foreign student adviser, Handicapped facilities, Health services, Language programs, Sports facilities

Student Residential Facilities: For 3,400 students

Special Facilities: Zoology Museum; Geology Museum. Botanical Garden. Field stations in Biology and Geography. Video Conference facilities/studio

Libraries: Central Library, c. 663,000 vols; department libraries, c. 621,300

Publications: Acta Universitatis Ouluensis

Student Numbers *2011-2012:* Total 18,000
Last Updated: 29/09/11

UNIVERSITY OF TAMPERE
Tampereen yliopisto
Kalevantie 4, FIN-33014 Tampere
Tel: +358(3) 355-111
Fax: +358(3) 213-4473
EMail: intoffice@uta.fi
Website: http://www.uta.fi

Rector: Kaija Holli (2009-2014)
Tel: +358(3) 3551-6200, Fax: +358(3) 3213 4473
EMail: kaija.holli@uta.fi

Administrative Director: Petri Lintunen

International Relations: Mikko Markkola, Head of Department Academic and International Affairs
Tel: +358(3) 3551-6830, Fax: +358(3) 3551-8600
EMail: mikko.markkol@uta.fi

Centres
Computer (Computer Science)

Institutes
Biomedical Technology (Biological and Life Sciences; Biomedical Engineering; Biomedicine; Biotechnology)

Research Institutes
Regenerative Medicine; **Social Sciences** (Social Sciences)

Schools
Communication, Media and Theatre (Journalism; Mass Communication; Media Studies; Speech Studies; Theatre); **Education** (Adult Education; Education; Preschool Education); **Health Sciences** (Nursing; Public Health); **Information Sciences** (Computer Science; Mathematics; Statistics); **Language, Translation and Literary Studies** (Cultural Studies; Finnish; Literature; Modern Languages; Swedish; Translation and Interpretation); **Management** (Business Administration; Economics; European Studies); **Medicine** (Health Sciences; Medicine; Nursing; Public Health); **Social Sciences and Humanities** (Ethnology; History; Information Sciences; International Relations; Journalism; Mass Communication; Musicology; Pedagogy; Philosophy; Political Sciences; Psychology; Social Policy; Social Psychology; Social Sciences; Social Work; Sociology; Women's Studies)

Further Information: Also Hämeenlinna and Seinäjoki Centres for Extension Studies; International School of Social Sciences; Hämeenlinna Teacher Training Department

History: Founded 1925 as private Civic College in Helsinki, became School of Social Sciences 1930 and transferred to Tampere 1960. Formerly known as Yhteiskunnallinen korkeakoulu. Acquired present status and title 1966. An autonomous institution until August 1974, financed by the State 75%, by the city of Tampere 20%, and by students' fees 5%. Subsequently under the supervision of the Ministry of Education and entirely financed by the State.

Governing Bodies: Hallitus (University Council)

Academic Year: September to May (September-December; January-May)

Admission Requirements: Secondary school certificate (ylioppilastutkinto) or foreign equivalent, and entrance examination

Fees: None

Main Language(s) of Instruction: Finnish, English

International Co-operation: Participates in the Nordplus, Socrates/Erasmus, Socrates/Lingua,Tempus and International Student Exchange Programmes

Degrees and Diplomas: *Kandidaatti/Kandidat*: 3 yrs; *Lääketieteen lisensiaatti/Medicine licentiat*: Medicine, 6 yrs; *Lisensiaatti/Licentiat*: Administrative Sciences; Education; Health Care; Philosophy; Psychology; Social Sciences; Theatre Arts, a further 2-3 yrs following Maisteri; *Maisteri/Magister*: Administrative Sciences; Sciences (Economics/Business); Social Sciences, a further yr following Kandidaatti; *Maisteri/Magister*: Arts; Education; Psychology; Theatre Arts, a further 2 yrs following Kandidaatti; *Maisteri/Magister*: Health Sciences, a further 3 yrs following Kandidaatti or equivalent; *Tohtori/Doktor*: 1-2 yrs following Lisensiatti or 4 yrs

Student Services: Academic counselling, Canteen, Employment services, Foreign student adviser, Foreign Studies Centre, Handicapped facilities, Health services, Language programs, Nursery care, Sports facilities

Student Residential Facilities: For 5,000 students

Special Facilities: Folk music instruments; tv studio

Libraries: Main Library and department libraries, c. 1m. vols; European Documentation Centre

Publications: Acta Universitatis Tamperensis (Tampereen yliopiston julkaisusarja)

Press or Publishing House: Tampere University Press
Last Updated: 30/09/11

UNIVERSITY OF TURKU

Turun yliopisto
FI-20014 Turku
Tel: +358(2) 333-51
Fax: +358(2) 333-6363
EMail: international@utu.fi
Website: http://www.utu.fi

Rector: Keijo Virtanen (1999-)
Tel: +358(2) 333-6101, Fax: +358(2) 333-6440
EMail: rector@utu.fi

Director of Communications and Publics Affairs: Maija Palonheimo Tel: +(358) 2 333 6129, Fax: +(358) 2 333 6310

International Relations: Irinja Paakkanen, Head of International Affairs Tel: +358(2) 333-6142, Fax: +385(2) 333-6370

Centres
Biotechnology (Biotechnology); **Computer Science** (Computer Science); **Extension Studies**; **Functional Foods Forum**; **Language**; **Maritime Studies**; **Turku PET Centre**

Faculties
Education (Adult Education; Education; Educational Sciences; Preschool Education; Special Education; Teacher Training; Technology Education) *Dean*: Marja Vauras, **Humanities** (American Studies; Anthropology; Archaeology; Art History; Baltic Languages; Classical Languages; Comparative Literature; Comparative Religion; Cultural Studies; English; Ethnology; Finnish; Folklore; Foreign Languages Education; French; German; History; Hungarian; Italian; Linguistics; Literature; Media Studies; Museum Studies; Musicology; Phonetics; Romanian; Russian; Scandinavian Languages;

Spanish; Swedish; Translation and Interpretation; Women's Studies; Writing) *Dean*: Kaisa Häkkinen; **Law** (Law) *Dean*: Heikki Kulla; **Mathematics and Natural Sciences** (Mathematics; Natural Sciences) *Dean*: Jarmo Hietarinta; **Medicine** (Dentistry; Health Sciences; Medicine; Nursing) *Dean*: Tapani Rönnemaa; **Social Sciences** (Asian Studies; Contemporary History; Economics; Philosophy; Political Sciences; Psychology; Social Policy; Social Work; Sociology; Statistics) *Dean*: Veli-Matti Ritakallio

Institutes
Archipelago Research (*in Nauvo, Seili Island*); **Kevo Subarctic Research** (*in Utsjoki*); **Satakunta Environmental Research** (*in Pori*)

Schools
Cultural Production and Landscape Studies (*Rauma and Pori*) (Cultural Studies; Landscape Architecture); **Economics** (*Turku*) (Economics)

Further Information: Also Turku University Central Hospital. Master programmes and non-degree programmes in English in various fields. For information http://www.utu.fi/en/studying/

History: Founded 1920 as a private institution on the initiative of the Finnish University Society. Inaugurated 1922. Became State institution 1974 under the supervision of the Ministry of Education. Merged with Turku School of Economics 2010.

Governing Bodies: Board (Hallitus)

Academic Year: August to July (August-December; January-July)

Admission Requirements: Secondary school certificate (Ylioppilastutkinto) or foreign equivalent, and entrance examination. Applicants not fluent in Finnish are required to hold a lower university degree (BA, BSc) and TOEFL test

Fees: None

Main Language(s) of Instruction: Finnish; Master's programmes available in English

International Co-operation: Participates in Erasmus, Nordplus and other international student exchange programmes; coordinator and partner in Edulink and Lingua projects; member of the Coimbra Group, the Southern African-Nordic Centre,the University of the Arctic and the Baltic Sea Region University Network

Degrees and Diplomas: *Kandidaatti/Kandidat*: Arts; Science; Social Sciences; Psychology; Education; Health Sciences (Bachelor's Degree), 3-4 yrs; *Diplomi-insinööri/Diplomingenjör*: Science in Technology (Master of Science in Technology), a further 2 yrs; *Hammaslääketieteen lisensiaatti/Odontologie licentiat*: Dentistry, 5 yrs; *Lääketieteen lisensiaatti/Medicine licentiat*: Medicine, 6 yrs; *Lisensiaatti/Licentiat*: Education; Health Care; Law; Philosophy; Science inTechnology; Psychology; Social Sciences, 3 yrs following Maisteri; *Maisteri/Magister*: Arts; Education; Health Sciences; Law; Psychology; Science; Social Sciences (Master's Degree), a further 2 yrs; *Tohtori/Doktor*: Dentistry; Education; Health Care; Law; Medicine; Philosophy; Science in Technology; Psychology; Social Sciences, a further 2-3 yrs following lisensiaatti

Student Services: Academic counselling, Canteen, Cultural centre, Employment services, Foreign student adviser, Handicapped facilities, Health services, Language programs, Social counselling, Sports facilities

Student Residential Facilities: Yes

Special Facilities: Zoological Museum. Vanhalinna Museum (Archaeological and Ethnological Collections). Syntax Archives. Botanical Garden. Herbarium. Learning Disability Clinic. Tuorla Observatory (in Piikkiö)

Libraries: Central Library, total c. 2.8 m. vols

Publications: Turun yliopiston julkaisuja - Annales Universitatis Turkuensis, University journals in various fields
Last Updated: 30/09/11

UNIVERSITY OF VAASA

Vaasan yliopisto
PO Box 700, Wolffintie 34, FI-65101 Vaasa
Tel: +358(6) 324-8111
Fax: +358(6) 324-8208 +358(6) 324-8187
EMail: international.affairs@uwasa.fi
Website: http://www.uwasa.fi

Rector: Matti Jakobsson (1998-2013)
Tel: +358(6) 324-8202
EMail: matti.jakobsson@uwasa.fi; rehtori@uwasa.fi

Hallintojohtaja (Director of Administration): Anja Britschgi
Tel: +358(6) 324-8204

Faculties

Business Studies (Accountancy; Commercial Law; Economics; Finance; Management; Marketing); **Philosophy** (Arts and Humanities; Communication Arts; Communication Studies; English; Finnish; French; German; Health Administration; Information Sciences; Philosophy; Public Administration; Public Law; Regional Studies; Russian; Scandinavian Languages; Sociology; Swedish; Terminology; Translation and Interpretation); **Technology** (Automation and Control Engineering; Computer Science; Electrical Engineering; Mathematics; Production Engineering; Statistics)

History: Founded 1968 as private School of Economics and Business Administration. Became state institution 1977. Acquired present status and title 1991.

Governing Bodies: University Senate

Academic Year: September to May (September-December; January-May)

Admission Requirements: Secondary school certificate (ylioppilastutkinto) or certificate of secondary vocational education (opistoasteen tutkinto) or Bachelor degree.

Main Language(s) of Instruction: Finnish, English, Swedish

International Co-operation: Participates in Erasmus, Nordplus and bilateral programmes

Degrees and Diplomas: *Kandidaatti/Kandidat*: Administration; Economics and Business Administration; Humanities; Science in Technology, 3 yrs; *Diplomi-insinööri/Diplomingenjör*: Technology, a further 2 yrs; *Lisensiaatti/Licentiat*: Administration; Economics and Business Administration; Humanities; Science in Technology, a further 3 yrs; *Maisteri/Magister*: Administration; Arts; Economics and Business Administration; Science in Technology, a further 2 yrs; *Tohtori/Doktor*: Administrative Sciences; Economics and Business Administration; Humanities; Science in Technology, a further 3 yrs

Student Services: Academic counselling, Canteen, Cultural centre, Employment services, Foreign student adviser, Handicapped facilities, Health services, Social counselling, Sports facilities

Student Residential Facilities: Yes

Libraries:c. 300,000 vols

Publications: Acta Wasaensia; Proceedings of the University of Vaasa

Press or Publishing House: University of Vaasa Publishing House
Last Updated: 30/09/11

VAASA UNIVERSITY OF APPLIED SCIENCES
Vaasan ammattikorkeakoulu - Vaasa yrkeshögskola (VAMK)
Raastuvankatu 29, FI-65100 Vaasa, Pohjanmaa
Tel: +358(207) 663-300
Fax: +358(6) 326-3002
EMail: info@puv.fi
Website: http://www.puv.fi

President: Tauno Kekäle Tel: +358(207) 663-400

Director of Administration: Minna Laatu
Tel: +358(207) 663-359, Fax: +358(6) 326-3002
EMail: minna.laatu@puv.fi

International Relations: Tuija Tammi, International Relations Officer
Tel: +358(207) 663-427, Fax: +358(6) 326-3112
EMail: tuija.tammi@puv.fi

Faculties

Business Economics and Tourism (Accountancy; Business Administration; Business and Commerce; Finance; Information Sciences; International Business; Marketing; Tourism); **Health Care and Social Services** (Community Health; Health Sciences; Nursing; Public Health; Social and Preventive Medicine; Social Welfare; Social Work); **Technology and Communications** (Civil Engineering; Computer Engineering; Electrical and Electronic Engineering; Environmental Engineering; Mechanical Engineering; Production Engineering)

History: Founded 1996, acquired present status and title 2006.

Governing Bodies: Ministry of Education; City Council of Vaasa; Board of Directors; Advisory Boards; Management Group; Rector; Deans

Academic Year: August to July

Admission Requirements: Completed Finnish Matriculation Examination or Upper Secondary Examination, European or International Baccalaureate or Reifeprufung examination or vocational qualification of 3 years or more or other non-Finnish equivalents.

Fees: None

Main Language(s) of Instruction: Finnish, English, Swedish

International Co-operation: With institutions in Austria, Belgium, Cyprus, Czech Republic, Denmark, Estonia, France, Germany, Greece, Hungary, Iceland, Italy, Latvia, Liechtenstein, Lithuania, Netherlands, Norway, Poland, Portugal, Spain, Sweden, Turkey, United Kingdom.

Degrees and Diplomas: *Kandidaatti/Kandidat*: Business Administration; Hospitality Management; Health Care and Social Services (Bachelor's Degree), 3.5 yrs; *Kandidaatti/Kandidat*: Engineering (Bachelor's Degree), 4 yrs; *Ylempi ammattikorkeakoulututinto (ylempi AMK)/ Högre yrkeshögskoleexamen (högre YH)*; *Maisteri/Magister*: Engineering; Business Administration; Health Care and Social Services; Technology; Business (Master's Degree), 5 yrs

Student Services: Academic counselling, Canteen, Employment services, Foreign student adviser, Foreign Studies Centre, Health services, Language programs, Nursery care, Social counselling

Special Facilities: Technology laboratory.

Libraries: Yes.
Last Updated: 30/09/11

France

STRUCTURE OF HIGHER EDUCATION SYSTEM

Description:

Higher education in France is characterized by a dual system : it is provided in universities (including Instituts nationaux polytechniques) opened to a large number of students, whose programmes are generally geared towards research and its applications and in "Grandes Ecoles" and other professional higher education institutions which have more selective admission policies. Lycées also offer non-university higher education courses leading to the Brevet de Technicien supérieur (BTS). Whereas most institutions come under the responsibility of the Ministry of Higher Education and Research, some "Grandes Ecoles" come under the responsibility of other Ministries. Universities are made up of units offering curricula in academic fields and of various institutes and schools, such as IUTs (Instituts universitaires de Technologie) which offer courses in Engineering and Technology and special programmes in Management, Political Science, Languages and Physical Education and IUPs (Instituts universitaires professionalisés) which offer technological courses and practical training with an introduction to research and foreign languages. The "Grandes Ecoles" offer a high standard of professional education in three or more years after two years of "classes préparatoires" and the passing of a very selective competitive entrance examination. They offer scientific training, teacher training or advanced business studies. Five Catholic higher education institutions (Etablissements d'Enseignement supérieur catholique) prepare for either national and professional diplomas or for church diplomas. National diplomas are awarded by universities.

Stages of studies:

University level first stage: Premier Cycle
Three years' study after the Baccalauréat leads to the Licence degree which confers 180 ECTS.
Prior to the Bologna reform, the Diplôme d'Etudes universitaires générales (DEUG) was awarded after two years' study. It has been maintained in the new system as an intermediate diploma corresponding to 120 ECTS that can be awarded upon request. It gives access to the third and final year of the Licence.
Two years in Classes préparatoires aux Grandes Ecoles (CPGE) are generally required to enter a Grande Ecole. No diploma is awarded but, since 2007, this carries 120 ECTS.

University level second stage: Deuxième Cycle
The second cycle leads to the Grade de Master which corresponds to 120 ECTS after the Licence and gives access to third cycle study. It replaced the former Diplôme d'Etudes approfondies (DEA) and Diplôme d'Etudes supérieures spécialisées (DESS) which also represented a total of five years higher education study. The Grade de Master has however also been awarded since 1999 to holders of DEA, DESS and Engineering degrees (titres d'ingénieur). Today it is also awarded to select Ecoles de Commerce degrees (diplômes visés).
In the Grandes Ecoles, a Diploma is awarded in Engineering or Commerce, generally three years after two years at university or at CPGE. The Titre d'Ingénieur is conferred upon successful completion of five years of study beyond the Baccalauréat. Some Ecoles d'Ingénieur accept students on the basis of a competitive examination generally taken two years after the Baccalauréat (in this case, studies last three years at most) or according to the Baccalauréat results, followed by aptitude tests and an interview (in this case, studies last four or five years).
In the old system, there was also the Maîtrise awarded one year after the Licence. The Maîtrise has been maintained as an intermediate diploma and can be awarded upon request of the student. In professional fields, the following Maîtrises can still be awarded : Maîtrise des Sciences et Techniques (MST), Maîtrise des Sciences de Gestion (MSG), Maîtrise des Méthodes informatiques appliquées à la gestion (MIAGE). The Magistère was awarded three years directly after the DEUG (or the DUT). It is not a national diploma, but rather a "diplôme d'université" (DU) accredited in the past by the Ministry of Education. In Medicine, DCEM consists of five years of study and hospital internship. In Dentistry and Pharmacy, it leads to the Diplôme d'Etat de Docteur en Chirurgie Dentaire and to the Diplôme d'Etat de Docteur en Pharmacie after a total of six years.

University level third stage: Troisième Cycle
In the post-Bologna system, the third cycle corresponds to Doctoral studies. A Doctorate is usually obtained after at least three years of extensive research under the supervision of a thesis director and the writing and successful defence of a thesis.

In the pre-Bologna system, the Doctorat was obtained three or four years after the DEA and after extensive research, either individual or as part of a group, supervised by a Directeur de Thèses (thesis director) and the writing and successful defence of a thesis.

In general Medicine, the third cycle culminates in the Diplôme d'Etat de Docteur en Médecine after three years' further study following DCEM. In specialised Medicine, it leads to the Diplôme d'Etudes spécialisées (DES) after two years' further study.

University level fourth stage: *Post-doctorat*

The Doctorat may be followed by a post-doctoral qualification, the Habilitation à Diriger les Recherches, which constitutes the highest national award and is offered to academics who display the ability to carry out high level scientific research and to supervise theses. It allows them to become university professors.

Distance higher education:

Télé-enseignement universitaire is offered to students who are unable to attend regular courses. At least 42 universities cooperate in this. The Centre national d'Enseignement à Distance (CNED) provides training leading to a large variety of diplomas, to adult education courses and to competitive examinations for civil service positions. Formasup (http://www.formasup.fr/) presents the major institutions involved in distance education.

ADMISSION TO HIGHER EDUCATION

Admission to university-level studies:

Name of secondary school credential required: Baccalauréat

Minimum score/requirement: 10/20

Alternatives to credentials: Diplomas or titles accepted in place of Baccalauréat. Diplôme d'Accès aux Etudes universitaires (DAEU). Capacité en Droit for Law studies only.

Other admission requirements: Competitive entrance examination to some Grandes Ecoles and other institutions following two years of preparatory courses given in lycées or integrated in the institution itself.

Foreign students admission:

Definition of foreign student: Foreign student holding a foreign Secondary School-Leaving Certificate.

Entrance exam requirements: Students must hold the Baccalauréat or a diploma giving access to higher education in their country. For more information, visit: http://www.enseignementsup-recherche.gouv.fr/cid24144/-dossier-blanc-demande-prealable-a-une-inscription-en-premier-cycle.html

Entry regulations: Student visa issued by French consulates abroad (long-stay visa: more than 3 months) except for EU, Andorra, Holy See, Liechtenstein, Monaco, San Marino and Swiss students who must present a valid passport. Students must ask for a "carte de séjour" (except for EU citizens). For other documents to be presented, see: http://www.cnous.fr

Language requirements: Foreign students (except EEA students) must hold either the DELF (diplôme d'études en langue française), the DALF (diplôme approfondi de langue française), or pass the TCF DAP (test de connaissance du français pour une demande d'admission préalable) to register for a 1st university cycle, or another test of French as a foreign language for other higher education institutions or registration to higher university levels.

RECOGNITION OF STUDIES

Quality assurance system:

The Agence d'évaluation de la recherche et de l'enseignement supérieur (AERES), created in 2007, is the agency for the evaluation of higher education in France.

Bodies dealing with recognition:

Agence d'Evaluation de la Recherche et de l'Enseignement supérieur - AERES (Evaluation Agency for Research and Higher Education)

20, rue Vivienne
Paris 75002
Tel: +33(1) 5555 6000
WWW: http://www.aeres-evaluation.fr/

Commission des Titres d'Ingénieur - CTI

President: Bernard Remaud
34 avenue Charles de Gaulle
Neuilly sur Seine 92200
Tel: +33 1 4192 3619
WWW: http://www.cti commission.fr

Services provided and students dealt with: Allows graduate schools to deliver the title of engineer.

Conférence des Directeurs des Ecoles françaises d'Ingénieurs - CDEFI

151 boulevard de l'Hopital
Paris 75013
Tel: +33(1) 4424 6449
Fax: +33(1) 4424 6451
EMail: cdefi@cdefi.fr
WWW: http://www.cdefi.fr

Conférence des Grandes Ecoles - CGE

60, boulevard Saint-Michel
Paris Cedex 06 75272
Tel: +33 1 4326 2557
Fax: +33 1 4634 5670
EMail: info@cge.asso.fr
WWW: http://www.cge.asso.fr/

Conférence des Présidents d'Université - CPU (Conference of University Presidents)

103 boulevard Saint Michel
Paris 75005
Tel: +33 1 4432 9000
Fax: +33 1 4432 9158
EMail: cpu@cpu.fr
WWW: http://www.cpu.fr

ENIC-NARIC, Centre International d'Etudes Pédagogiques - CIEP

Head: Myriam Leroux
1 avenue Léon Journault
Sèvres 92318
Tel: +33 1 4507 6321
Fax: +33 1 4507 6302
EMail: enic-naric@ciep.fr
WWW: http://www.ciep.fr/enic-naricfr/

Union des Etablissements d'Enseignement supérieur catholique - UDESCA (Union of Catholic Higher Education Institutions)

Institut catholique de Toulouse
31 rue de la Fonderie – BP 7012
Toulouse cedex 7 31068
WWW: http://www.udesca.fr/

Special provisions for recognition:

Recognition for university level studies: The applicant should first get in touch with the HEI as they are autonomous in their admission policies and decisions. Should the institution require a recognition document, the French ENIC-NARIC can issue a comparability statement ("attestation de comparabilité") for foreign qualifications upon request of the applicant.

For access to advanced studies and research: The applicant should first get in touch with the HEI as they are autonomous in their admission policies and decisions. Should the institution require a recognition document, the French ENIC-NARIC can issue a comparability statement ("attestation de comparabilité") for foreign qualifications upon request of the applicant.

For exercising a profession: For non-regulated professions, the applicant should directly ask the employer. The employer decides if the foreign diploma corresponds to the competencies required. The French ENIC-NARIC can award a comparability statement ("attestation de comparabilité") upon request of the applicant. For each regulated profession, there is a designated competent authority responsible for the assessment of qualifications in order to give authorization to exercise the relevant profession.

NATIONAL BODIES

Ministère de l'Enseignement supérieur et de la Recherche (Ministry of Higher Education and Research)
Minister: Laurent Wauquiez
Director-General, Higher Education: Patrick Hetzel
1 rue Descartes
Paris Cedex 05 75231
Tel: +33(1) 5555 9090
WWW: http://www.enseignementsup-recherche.gouv.fr
Role of national body: Prepares and implements the Government's policy relative to higher education development.

Agence d'Evaluation de la Recherche et de l'Enseignement supérieur - AERES (Evaluation Agency for Research and Higher Education)
President: Didier Houssin
20, rue Vivienne
Paris 75002
Tel: +33(1) 5555 6000
WWW: http://www.aeres-evaluation.fr/

Conférence des Directeurs des Ecoles françaises d'Ingénieurs - CDEFI
President: Paul Jacquet
Executive Director: Antoine Rigal
151 boulevard de l'Hopital
Paris 75013
Tel: +33(1) 4424 6449
Fax: +33(1) 4424 6451
EMail: cdefi@cdefi.fr
WWW: http://www.cdefi.fr
Role of national body: Public consultative body responsible for the study of the profession and training of engineers.

Conférence des Grandes Ecoles - CGE
President: Pierre Tapie
Secrétaire: Eric Maurincomme
60, boulevard Saint-Michel
Paris Cedex 06 75272
Tel: +33 1 4326 2557
Fax: +33 1 4634 5670
EMail: info@cge.asso.fr
WWW: http://www.cge.asso.fr/
Role of national body: The Conférence des Grandes Ecoles is a non-profit association founded in 1973. Its role is to develop information and solidarity between its members ; to promote the Grandes Ecoles system both on a national and international scale ; to encourage innovations in engineering and management education, to develop continuing education and research activities ; to act as a voice with government policy-makers and the research community.

Conférence des Présidents d'Université - CPU (Conference of University Presidents)
President: Louis Vogel
103 boulevard Saint Michel
Paris 75005
Tel: +33 1 4432 9000
Fax: +33 1 4432 9158
EMail: cpu@cpu.fr

WWW: http://www.cpu.fr
Role of national body: Exchange and stopping place between the academic community and civil society.

Union des Etablissements d'Enseignement supérieur catholique - UDESCA (Union of Catholic Higher Education Institutions)

President: Pierre Debergé
Institut catholique de Toulouse
31 rue de la Fonderie – BP 7012
Toulouse cedex 7 31068
WWW: http://www.udesca.fr/
Role of national body: Regroups the five French Catholic universities.

Data for academic year: 2011-2012
Source: IAU from the ENIC-NARIC Centre, CIEP, France, 2011

INSTITUTIONS

PUBLIC INSTITUTIONS

AERONAUTICAL AND SPACE INSTITUTE

Institut supérieur de l'Aéronautique et de l'Espace (ISAE)
BP 54032, 10, avenue Edouard Belin, 31055 Toulouse, Cedex 4
Tel: +33(5) 62-17-80-80
Fax: +33(5) 62-17-83-30
EMail: isae@isae.fr
Website: http://www.isae.fr

Directeur: Olivier Fourure
Tel: +33(5) 62-17-80-01 EMail: Olivier.Fourure@isae.fr

Secretaire Général: Jean-Sébastien Guyere
Tel: +33(5) 62-17-82-02 EMail: jean-sebastien.guyere@isae.fr

International Relations: Bénédicte Escudier
Tel: +33(5) 61-33-80-91 EMail: Benedicte.Escudier@isae.fr

Schools
Aeronautical and Space Engineering *(SUPAERO)* (Aeronautical and Aerospace Engineering); **Aeronautical Construction** *(ENSICA)* (Aeronautical and Aerospace Engineering; Applied Mathematics; Mechanical Engineering)

History: The Institute was created in 2007 through the merger of two "Grandes Ecoles": ENSICA and SUPAERO.

Governing Bodies: Director; Administrative Council; Ministère de la Défense

Academic Year: September to June

Admission Requirements: Competitive entrance examination (1st year); on application (2nd year)

Fees: (Euros): 1,100 per annum

Main Language(s) of Instruction: French

International Co-operation: With 80 universities in 25 countries

Accrediting Agencies: Commission des titres d'ingénieur, Conférence des Grandes Ecoles

Degrees and Diplomas: *Diplôme d'Ingénieur*: Fluid Dynamics, Microelectronics, Telecommunication Engineering, Electrical Engineering, Electronical Engineering, Applied Mathematics, Transport Economics, Astrophysics, Astronomy & Space Science; *Mastère spécialisé*: Aeronautics, Astronautics, Management, Engineering etc. , 1yr; *Diplôme national de Master*; *Doctorat*: Aeronautics, Electrical Engineering, Electronic Engineering, Telecommunications, Mechanics, Energy Engineering, Civil Engineering, Processes, Science of the Universe, the Environment and Space. Also Research Masters

Student Services: Canteen, Employment services, Foreign student adviser, Health services, Language programs, Social counselling, Sports facilities
Student Residential Facilities: Yes
Libraries: Central Library
Publications: Reseach Reports and Publications
Last Updated: 17/05/11

AGROCAMPUS WEST

AGROCAMPUS OUEST
65, rue de Saint-Brieuc, 35042 Rennes
Tel: +33(2) 23-48-50-00
Fax: +33 ()2 23-48-55-10
EMail: direction.generale@agrocampus-ouest.fr
Website: http://www.agrocampus-ouest.fr

Directeur général: Grégoire Thomas

Departments
Agriculture, Rural Environments and the Environment *(AGRERE)* (Agriculture; Ecology; Plant and Crop Protection; Soil Science); **Animal Science** (Animal Husbandry; Biochemistry; Genetics); **Biology** (Biology; Crop Production; Plant Pathology); **Economics, Data Processing and Communication** *(Angers)* (Economics; English; French; German; Management; Social Sciences; Spanish); **Engineering** (Applied Mathematics; Computer Science; Physics); **Food Science** (Food Science; Food Technology; Microbiology); **Horticulture** *(Angers)* (Fruit Production; Horticulture; Vegetable Production); **Landscape** *(Angers)* (Ecology; Geography; Landscape Architecture); **Languages** (English; German; Italian; Spanish); **Rural Economics and Management** (Agricultural Economics; Management; Rural Planning)

History: Founded 1999. A merger between Ecole nationale supérieure agronomique de Rennes (ENSAR) and Institut national supérieur de Formation agro-alimentaire (INSFA). Acquired present title and status following merger in 2008 between Agrocampus Rennes and the Institut national d'Horticulture d'Angers.

Main Language(s) of Instruction: French

Degrees and Diplomas: *Licence professionnelle*; *Diplôme d'Ingénieur*; *Diplôme national de Master*; *Doctorat*
Last Updated: 27/06/11

AGROPARISTECH

19, avenue du Maine, 75732 Paris, Cedex 15
Tel: +33(1) 45-49-88-00
Fax: +33(1) 45-49-88-27
EMail: ri@agroparistech.fr
Website: http://www.agroparistech.fr

Directeur général: Gilles Trystram (2011-)
Tel: +33(1) 45-49-89-88

International Relations: Christophe Sodore

Departments

Agronomy, Forestry, Water and Environmental Science and Technology (Agronomy; Environmental Studies; Forestry; Soil Science; Water Management; Water Science); **Economics, Social Sciences and Management** (Agricultural Business; Business Administration; Economics; Management; Rural Planning; Sociology); **Life Science and Health** (Biochemistry; Biological and Life Sciences; Biology; Demography and Population; Genetics; Microbiology; Nutrition; Plant and Crop Protection; Plant Pathology); **Modeling: Mathematics, Informatics and Physic** (Computer Science; Mathematics; Physical Engineering); **Science and Engineering for Food and Bioproducts** (Analytical Chemistry; Food Science; Food Technology; Wood Technology)

Schools

Rural Engineering, Water and Forest Sciences *(ENGREF)* (Agricultural Engineering; Forestry; Rural Planning; Water Science)

History: Founded 2007 following merger of the Ecole nationale du génie rural, des eaux et des forêts; ENSIA, Ecole nationale supérieure des industries agricoles et alimentaires and INA P-G, Institut national agronomique Paris-Grignon.

Academic Year: September to July

Admission Requirements: Competitive entrance examination following 2-3 yrs further study after secondary school certificate (baccalauréat) or following first university qualification (DEUG, DUT or BTS), or equivalent

Main Language(s) of Instruction: French

International Co-operation: Erasmus, Cooperation programmes with Anglo-Saxon Universities

Degrees and Diplomas: *Diplôme d'Ingénieur*: 4 yrs; *Mastère spécialisé*: 6 yrs; *Diplôme national de Master*: Environemental Sciences, 5 yrs; *Doctorat*: Environmental Engineering (PhD); Forestry (PhD); Water Sciences (PhD). Masters recherche

Student Services: Academic counselling, Canteen, Employment services, Foreign student adviser, Social counselling, Sports facilities
Last Updated: 27/06/11

AIX-MARSEILLE UNIVERSITY

Aix-Marseille Université
58 bd Charles Livon, 13284 Marseille
Tel: +33(4) 91-39-65-17/18
EMail: suio-pharo@univmed.fr
Website: http://www.aix-marseille.fr

Président: Yvon Berland

Areas

Arts, Literature, Languages and Human Sciences (Ancient Civilizations; Anthropology; Arts and Humanities; Behavioural Sciences; Cinema and Television; Cognitive Sciences; Communication Studies; Cultural Studies; Education; English; Geography; German; Jewish Studies; Journalism; Linguistics; Literature; Modern Languages; Mountain Studies; Music Education; Oriental Languages; Psychology; Regional Planning; Romance Languages; Slavic Languages; Social Sciences; Teacher Training); **Economics and Management** (Accountancy; Administration; Banking; Economics; Finance; Human Resources; International Business; Management); **Health** (Biological and Life Sciences; Dentistry; Medicine; Midwifery; Nutrition; Oncology; Pharmacy; Physical Education; Physical Therapy; Sanitary Engineering; Sports); **Law and Political Science** (Commercial Law; Criminology; Fiscal Law; Law; Maritime Law; Political Sciences; Public Administration; Regional Planning); **Science and Technology** (Aeronautical and Aerospace Engineering; Applied Mathematics; Astronomy and Space Science; Atomic and Molecular Physics; Bioengineering; Chemistry; Civil Engineering; Earth Sciences; Ecology; Energy Engineering; Environmental Engineering; Hydraulic Engineering; Industrial Engineering; Information Technology; Marine Biology; Marine Science and Oceanography; Materials Engineering; Mathematics and Computer Science; Mechanical Engineering; Microbiology; Microelectronics; Multimedia; Neurosciences; Oenology; Physical Chemistry; Physics; Software Engineering; Sound Engineering (Acoustics); Technology; Thermal Engineering; Water Science)

Further Information: Also campuses in Aix-en-Provence, Arles, Aubagne, Avignon, Digne-les-Bains, Gap, La Ciotat, Lambesc and Salon de Provence

History: Founded 1409 as University of Provence. Re-organized into 3 institutions in 1968. Acquired present status 2012 following merger of Université de Provence, Université Paul Cézanne and Université de la Méditerranée.

Governing Bodies: Conseil d'Administration

Main Language(s) of Instruction: French

Degrees and Diplomas: *Diplôme universitaire de Technologie*; *Licence*; *Licence professionnelle*; *Magistère*; *Diplôme national de Master*; *Doctorat*

Libraries: Yes
Last Updated: 25/01/12

AMIENS SCHOOL OF ART AND DESIGN

Ecole supérieure d'Art et de Design d'Amiens
40 rue des Teinturiers, Amiens
Tel: +33(3) 22-66-49-90
EMail: esad@amiens-metropole.com
Website: http://www.esad-amiens.fr

Directrice: Barbara Dennys

Departments
Waide Somme (Graphic Arts)

Programmes
Graphic Design (Graphic Design; Painting and Drawing; Photography; Sculpture); **Visual Communication** (Multimedia)

History: Founded 1990. Acquired present status 2011.

Admission Requirements: Secondary school certificate. Competitive entrance examination

Fees: French

Accrediting Agencies: Ministère de la culture et de la communication

Degrees and Diplomas: DNAP Design graphique(3 ans)DNSEP Design graphique (+2 ans), homologué au grade de Master
Last Updated: 11/07/11

ART SCHOOL OF THE AGGLOMERATION OF ANNECY

Ecole supérieure d'Art de l'Agglomération d'Annecy
52 bis, rue des Marquisats, 74000 Annecy
Tel: +33(4) 50-33-65-50
Fax: +33(4) 50-33-65-55
EMail: contact@esaaa.fr
Website: http://www.esaaa.fr

Directeur: Stéphane Sauzedde

Programmes
Art (Fine Arts; Painting and Drawing; Photography; Video); **Design** (Design)

Admission Requirements: Secondary school certificate and competitive entrance examination

Main Language(s) of Instruction: French

Accrediting Agencies: Ministry of Culture

Degrees and Diplomas: *Diplôme national de Master*. Diplôme national d'arts plastiques (DNAP) 3 yrs; Diplôme national d'arts et techniques (DNAT) 3 yrs; Diplôme national supérieur d'expression plastique (DNSEP) a further 2 yrs; Diplôme Supérieur de Recherche en Art

Libraries: Yes
Last Updated: 18/07/11

AVIGNON ART SCHOOL

Ecole supérieure d'Art d'Avignon
7 Rue Violette, 84000 Avignon
Tel: +33(4) 90-27-04-23
Fax: +33(4) 90-86-46-10
EMail: secretariat.ecole-beaux-arts@mairie-avignon.com
Website: http://www.esa-avignon.org

Directeur: Jean-Marc Ferrari

Programmes

Fine Arts (Fine Arts; Restoration of Works of Art)

History: Founded 1801. Acquired present status 1979.

Main Language(s) of Instruction: French

International Co-operation: Participates in ERASMUS

Degrees and Diplomas: Diplôme national d'arts plastiques (DNAP) 3 yrs; Diplôme national supérieur d'expression plastique (DNESP) a further 2 yrs

Last Updated: 08/07/11

BESANÇON REGIONAL SCHOOL OF ART

Ecole régionale des Beaux-Arts de Besançon

12 rue Denis Papin, 25000 Besançon
Tel: +33(3) 81-87-81-30
Fax: +33(3) 81-88-60-94
EMail: christelle.botton@besancon.fr
Website: http://www.erba.besancon.com/

Directeur: Laurent Deveze

Programmes

Visual Arts (Communication Arts; Design; Visual Arts)

History: Founded 1756.

Admission Requirements: Baccalauréat or equivalent secondary school exam. Entrance exam with a selection jury.

Fees: (Euros): 477 per annum

Main Language(s) of Instruction: French

Accrediting Agencies: Ministry of Culture and Communication

Degrees and Diplomas: Diplôme national d'arts plastiques (DNAP) 3 yrs; Diplôme national d'arts et techniques (DNAT) 3 yrs; Diplôme national supérieur d'expression plastique (DNSEP in Design) a further 2 yrs

Last Updated: 07/06/11

BORDEAUX I UNIVERSITY

Université Bordeaux I

351, cours de la Libération, 33405 Talence, Cedex
Tel: +33(5) 56-84-60-00
Fax: +33(5) 56-80-08-37
EMail: communication@presidence-bx1.u-bordeaux.fr
Website: http://www.u-bordeaux1.fr/

Président: Alain Boudou
Tel: +33(5) 56-84-60-44
EMail: a.boudou@presidence.u-bordeaux1.fr

Directeur général des Services: Eric Dutil
EMail: sgal@u-bordeaux1.fr

International Relations: Martine Lenglet, Vice-Président
Tel: +33(5) 56-84-60-45, Fax: +33(5) 40-00-31-01
EMail: dai@u-bordeaux1.fr

Centres

Lifelong Education (Continuing Education)

Departments

Science *(DUSA)* (Agricultural Engineering; Computer Science; Earth Sciences; International Business; Materials Engineering; Mathematics)

Graduate Schools

Chemical Sciences *(EDSC)* (Chemistry); **Environmental Sciences** *(ED SE)*; **Mathematics and Computer Sciences** (Mathematics and Computer Science); **Physics and Technology** (Astrophysics; Laser Engineering; Mechanical Engineering; Microelectronics; Wood Technology)

Institutes

Civil Engineering, Construction Engineering *(IUP)* (Civil Engineering; Construction Engineering); **Data Processing for Management** *(I.U.P.)* (Data Processing); **Electrical Engineering and Industrial Computer Science** *(IUP GEII)* (Computer Science; Electrical Engineering); **Food Technology** *(ISTAB)* (Food Technology); **Industrial Systems Engineering and Aeronautical Maintenance** *(IUP IMA)* (Aeronautical and Aerospace Engineering; Industrial Engineering); **Mechanical Engineering** *(IUP)* (Mechanical Engineering); **Teacher Training** *(IUFM has five sites located throughout the Aquitaine Province)* (Teacher Training); **Technology** *(IUT)* (Biology; Business Administration; Civil Engineering; Computer Science; Mechanical Engineering; Production Engineering; Technology)

Research Laboratories

Astronomy and Space Sciences *(Observatoire Aquitain des Sciences de l'Univers OASU)* (Astrophysics; Marine Science and Oceanography)

Schools

Chemical and Physical Engineering *(ENSCPB)* (Chemical Engineering; Physical Engineering); **Electronics and Radioelectrical Engineering** *(ENSEIRB)* (Electrical and Electronic Engineering); **Mathematical Modelling and Mechanics** *(MATMECA)*

Units

Biological Sciences (Biological and Life Sciences); **Chemistry** (Chemistry); **Earth and Marine Sciences** (Earth Sciences; Marine Science and Oceanography); **Mathematics and Computer Science** (Mathematics and Computer Science); **Physics** (Physics)

History: Founded 1970 under the 1968 law reforming higher education as one of the four Universities replacing the former Université de Bordeaux - founded 1441 by Papal Bull with Faculties of Theology; Canon Law; Civil Law; Medicine; and Arts. The University was suppressed by the Revolution and replaced by Faculties of Theology; Letters; and Science of the Université de France. Reconstituted as university 1896. A State institution enjoying academic and financial autonomy, operating under the jurisdiction of the Minister of Education and financed by the State.

Governing Bodies: Conseil de l'Université, including elected representatives of teaching staff, research workers, students, and administrative and technical staff, as well as non-university members drawn from the public and private sectors; Conseil of each Unit, comprising representatives of its teaching staff, research workers, students, and administrative and technical staff; and Conseil scientifique, competent in matters of research. The President is elected by the Conseil de l'Université. The Chancelier, who represents the Minister of Education, is the Recteur of the Académie de Bordeaux

Academic Year: October to June (October-February; February-June)

Admission Requirements: Secondary school certificate (baccalauréat) or equivalent, or special entrance examination

Main Language(s) of Instruction: French

Degrees and Diplomas: *Diplôme universitaire de Technologie*: Civil Engineering, 2 yrs; *Licence*: 3 yrs; *Licence professionnelle*; *Diplôme de Recherche technologique*; *Diplôme national de Master*; *Doctorat*: 2-4 yrs following Masters

Student Residential Facilities: Yes

Special Facilities: Observatory

Libraries: Bibliothèque interuniversitaire; specialized libraries

Publications: Bordeaux 1 recherche
Last Updated: 27/07/07

BORDEAUX II UNIVERSITY

Université Bordeaux Segalen

146, rue Léo Saignat, 33076 Bordeaux, Cedex
Tel: +33(5) 57-57-10-10
Fax: +33(5) 56-99-03-80
EMail: info@u-bordeaux2.fr
Website: http://www.univ-bordeauxsegalen.fr

Président: Manuel Tunon de Lara (2008-)
EMail: president@u-bordeaux2.fr

Directrice générale des Services: Corinne Duffau
Tel: +33(5) 57-57-14-91, Fax: +33(5) 56-99-03-80
EMail: secretariat.general@u-bordeaux2.fr

Centres

Applied Social Sciences (Social Policy; Social Sciences); **Lifelong Education** (Continuing Education)

Departments

Languages *(DLVP)* (Modern Languages)

Faculties
Medicine I (Medicine); **Medicine II** (Medicine); **Medicine III** (Medicine)

Graduate Schools
Health and Life Sciences *(In partnership with University of Bordeaux I)* (Biomedicine; Pharmacy; Public Health); **Human and Social Studies** *(SHS)* (Social Sciences)

Institutes
Cognitive Sciences (Cognitive Sciences); **Public Health, Epidemiology and Development** *(ISPED)* (Epidemiology; Public Health); **Teacher Training** *(IUFM has five sites located throughout the Aquitaine Province)* (Teacher Training); **Thermalism Studies**

Schools
Biomolecular Technology *(ESTBB)* (Biomedical Engineering)

Units
Dentistry (Dentistry); **Human Sciences** (Demography and Population; Educational Sciences; Ethnology; Psychology; Social Sciences; Sociology); **Life Sciences** (Biological and Life Sciences); **Oenology** *(Talence)* (Oenology); **Pharmacy** (Pharmacy); **Physical Education and Sports** *(STAPS)* (Physical Education; Sports); **Science and Modelling** (Cognitive Sciences; Computer Science; Mathematics; Social Sciences; Statistics)

History: Founded 1970 under the 1968 law reforming higher education as one of four Universities replacing the former Université de Bordeaux - founded 1441 by Papal Bull with Faculties of Theology; Canon Law; Civil Law; Medicine; and Arts. The University was suppressed by the Revolution and replaced by Faculties of Theology; Letters; and Science of the Université de France. Reconstituted as University 1896. A State institution enjoying academic and financial autonomy, operating under the jurisdiction of the Minister of Education and financed by the State.

Governing Bodies: Conseil de l'Université, 60 members including elected representatives of teaching staff, research workers, students, and administrative and technical staff, as well as non-university members drawn from the public and private sectors; Conseil of each Unit, comprising representatives of its teaching staff, research workers, students, and administrative and technical staff; and Conseil scientifique, competent in matters of research. The President is elected by the Conseil de l'Université. The Chancelier, who represents the Minister of Education, is the Recteur of the Académie de Bordeaux

Academic Year: September to June (September-January; February-June)

Admission Requirements: Secondary school certificate (baccalauréat) or equivalent or special entrance examination

Main Language(s) of Instruction: French

Degrees and Diplomas: *Licence*: 3 yrs; *Licence professionnelle*; *Diplôme d'Etat*: Dental Surgery; Pharmacy, 6 yrs; *Diplôme d'Etat*: Medicine, 6 yrs and 2 yrs hospital practice and thesis; *Diplôme national de Master*: 5 yrs; *Doctorat*: 3 yrs following Masters; *Doctorat*: Pharmacy, by thesis following Diplôme d'Etat; *Certificat de Spécialité*: Medicine, a further 2 yrs

Student Residential Facilities: Yes

Special Facilities: Museum of Ethnography

Libraries: Bibliothèque interuniversitaire
Last Updated: 22/12/08

BORDEAUX III UNIVERSITY
Université Michel de Montaigne (Bordeaux 3)
Domaine Universitaire, 33607 Pessac, Cedex
Tel: +33(5) 57-12-44-44
Fax: +33(5) 57-12-44-90
EMail: relations.internationales@u-bordeaux3.fr
Website: http://www.u-bordeaux3.fr/fr/index.html

Président: Patrice Brun (2009-)
EMail: presidence@u-bordeaux3.fr

Secrétaire générale: Thomas Rambaud
Tel: +33(5) 57-12-46-46
EMail: secretariat.general@u-bordeaux3.fr

International Relations: Patricia Budo
Tel: +33(5) 57-12-21-08, Fax: +33(5) 57-12-45-70

Departments
French as a Foreign Language *(DEFLE)* (French); **Lifelong Education** *Director*: Didier Paquelin; **Sports and Physical Education** (Physical Education; Sports)

Institutes
Environment, Geo-Engineering and Development *(EGID)* (Earth Sciences; Ecology; Environmental Engineering; Geology; Geophysics; Hydraulic Engineering; Surveying and Mapping); **Journalism** *(IJBA Bordeaux Aquitaine)* (Journalism); **Technology** *(IUT Michel de Montaigne)* (Communication Studies; Documentation Techniques; Information Sciences; Library Science; Publishing and Book Trade; Technology)

Units
Humanities (Archaeology; Art History; Arts and Humanities; Fine Arts; History; Literature; Philosophy); **Languages and Civilisations** (English; Germanic Studies; Latin American Studies; Linguistics; Mediterranean Studies; Modern Languages; Oriental Languages; Slavic Languages; Spanish); **Regional Studies and Communication** (Communication Studies; Geography; Regional Planning; Regional Studies; Tourism; Town Planning)

Further Information: Also numerous research centres

History: Founded 1970 under the 1968 law reforming higher education as one of four Universities replacing the former Université de Bordeaux - founded 1441 by Papal Bull with Faculties of Theology; Canon Law; Civil Law; Medicine; and Arts. The University was suppressed by the Revolution and replaced by Faculties of Theology; Letters; and Science of the Université de France. Reconstituted as university 1896. A State institution enjoying academic and financial autonomy, operating under the jurisdiction of the Minister of Education and financed by the State.

Governing Bodies: Conseil de l'Université, including elected representatives of teaching staff, research workers, students, and administrative and technical staff, as well as non-university members drawn from the public and private sectors; Conseil of each Unit, comprising representatives ofits teaching staff, research workers, students, and administrative and technical staff; and Conseil scientifique, competent in matters of research. The President is elected by the Conseil de l'Université. The Chancelier, who represents the Minister of Education, is the Recteur de l'Académie de Bordeaux

Academic Year: September to June (September-January; January-June)

Admission Requirements: Secondary school certificate (baccalauréat) or equivalent

Fees: (Euros): c. 180-225 per annum

Main Language(s) of Instruction: French

Degrees and Diplomas: *Diplôme universitaire de Technologie*: 2 yrs; *Licence*: Arts and Humanities, 3 yrs; *Licence professionnelle*: Arts and Humanities, 3 yrs of specialised licence; *Diplôme national de Master*: Arts and Humanities, 2 yrs following Licence; *Diplôme national de Master*: Environmental Engineering; *Doctorat*: Arts and Humanities, 4 yrs following Master. 'Certificat d'études françaises' (for foreign students), Masters recherche, Masters professionnel

Student Services: Academic counselling, Canteen, Cultural centre, Foreign student adviser, Handicapped facilities, Social counselling, Sports facilities

Student Residential Facilities: Yes

Libraries: Bibliothèque universitaire de Lettres, c. 382,000 vols

Publications: Bulletin hispanique; Cahiers d'Outre-Mer; Les annales du Midi - Revue géographique des Pyrénées et du Sud Ouest *(annually)*; Revue des études anciennes

Press or Publishing House: Presses Universitaires de Bordeaux
Last Updated: 19/07/11

BORDEAUX IV UNIVERSITY
Université Montesquieu-Bordeaux IV
Avenue Léon Duguit, 33608 Pessac
Tel: +33(5) 56-84-85-86
Fax: +33(5) 56-37-00-25
EMail: dri@u-bordeaux4.fr
Website: http://www.u-bordeaux4.fr

Président: Yannick Lung (2011-)
Tel: +33(5) 56-84-29-34, Fax: +33(5) 56-84-29-20
EMail: president@u-bordeaux.fr

International Relations: Véronique Lacorre
Tel: +33(5) 56-84-29-40, Fax: +33(5) 56-84-29-02

Departments
Juridical Studies *(D.E.J.A., Agen)* (Economics; Law; Social Sciences) *Director:* Jean-François Brisson

Faculties
Economics and Management (Demography and Population; Economic History; Economics; Environmental Studies; Finance; Management); **Law and Political Science** (Law; Political Sciences)

Institutes
Business Administration *(I.A.E.)* (Business Administration; Management); **Political Science** *(I.E.P.)* (Political Sciences); **Teacher Training** *(IUFM Aquitaine)* (Teacher Trainers Education; Teacher Training); **Technology** *(Bordeaux-Montesquieu)* (Business Administration; Sales Techniques; Transport Management); **Technology** *(I.U.T., Périgueux Bordeaux IV)* (Bioengineering; Business and Commerce; Chemical Engineering; Tourism)

Research Centres
African Studies (African Studies; Economics; International Relations; Political Sciences; Public Administration); **Agroalimentary Research of Perigord** (Food Science); **Aquitania Group of Research and Logistic Analysis; Comparative Law of Labour and Social Welfare** (Comparative Law; European Union Law; International Law; Labour Law); **Comparative Politics Analysis, Geostrategy and International Relations** (Comparative Politics; International Relations; Political Sciences); **Computing and Immaterial Creations** (Computer Science); **Economic and Commercial Research** *(Interuniversity)* (Economics); **Economic Dynamics** *(Federative)* (Economic History; Economics; Industrial and Production Economics); **Economic History** (Development Studies; Economic History; Economics); **Economics of Development** (Development Studies; Economics); **European Research and Documentation** (European Studies); **Family and Persons Law** *(European)* (Family Studies; Law); **Industries, Innovation and Institutions** (Economics; Industrial and Production Economics); **International Control and Accountancy** (Accountancy; Management); **Philosophy of Law** (Law; Political Sciences); **Power, Public Action and Territories; Studies and Research on Contract Law** (Civil Law; Private Law) *Director:* Bernard Saintourens; **Studies and Research on Family and Personal Law** *(European Centre)* (Human Rights) *Director:* Jean Hauser; **Studies and Research on Regional and Institutional History** (History of Law; Social Studies) *Director:* Gérard Aubin; **Studies and Research on Social Sciences in Canada and Quebec** (Canadian Studies; Political Sciences; Social Sciences) *Director:* Jacques Palard; **Studies and Research on Spain and the Iberian World** *(Comparative Legal Research) Director:* Ferdinand Melin-Soucramanien; **Studies and Research on the Balkans** (Central European Studies); **Studies and Research on the European Law of Health; Studies on African Rights and Institutional Development of Developing Countries** (Comparative Law; Private Law; Public Law); **Studies on Business Management** (Finance; Management; Marketing); **Studies on the European Constitution and Freedoms; Vine and Wine** *(Montesquieu)* (Oenology)

Research Groups
Economic Analysis and Politics (Applied Mathematics; Econometrics; Economics; Environmental Studies; Finance)

Research Institutes
Business Management *(Federative)* (Economics; Human Resources; Management; Marketing); **Criminal Sciences** (Criminal Law); **Demography Studies** (Demography and Population); **Insurance; Labour Studies** (Labour and Industrial Relations); **Legal Studies** (Law); **Public Law** (Administrative Law; Finance); **Regional Economics of the South West Region** (Ecology; Economics; Environmental Studies)

Research Laboratories
International Economics and Finance

Further Information: Two sites: Agen and PérigueuxCreated in 2006, the University Centre of Management Studies houses the IAE, IUP Commerce and Trade, Dept of Specialised Training in Economics and Management and two IUT depts.

History: Founded 1870. Incorporated former departments of the University of Bordeaux I 1995.

Academic Year: October to June (October-February; February-June)

Admission Requirements: Secondary school certificate (baccalauréat) or equivalent, or special entrance examination

Fees: (Euros): c. 161-330 per annum

Main Language(s) of Instruction: French

International Co-operation: With universities in Europe, North America, Latin America, Caribbean, Indian Ocean, Near and Middle East, Africa and Asia. Participates in various programmes: Erasmus (Europe) and CREPUQ (Quebec)

Degrees and Diplomas: *Capacité en Droit:* Law, 2 yrs; *Diplôme universitaire de Technologie:* Business, Management, Transport, 2 yrs following 2 yrs; *Licence:* Law, Social and Political Science, Economics and Management, Economics and Social Administration, Econometrics, 3 yrs; *Magistère:* International Management, Finance (Magefi), 3 yrs following DEUG; *Diplôme national de Master:* Law; Political Science; Economics; Social Sciences; Management, 2 yrs following Licence; *Doctorat:* Law, Social and Political Science, Economics and Management, 2-4 yrs following Masters. Masters recherche, Masters professionnel

Student Services: Academic counselling, Canteen, Cultural centre, Employment services, Foreign student adviser, Handicapped facilities, Health services, Social counselling, Sports facilities

Student Residential Facilities: Yes

Libraries: Library: c. 12,500 vols, 2,000 periodical subscriptions, 30,000 theses and mémoires
Last Updated: 19/07/11

BORDEAUX INSTITUTE OF TECHNOLOGY
Institut polytechnique de Bordeaux
1 avenue du Dr Albert Schweitzer, 33402 Talence
Tel: +33(5) 40-00-37-26
EMail: direction@ipb.fr
Website: http://www.ipb.fr

Directeur général: François Cansell

Schools
Biomolecule Technology *(ENSTBB)* (Biotechnology; Microbiology); **Chemistry, Biology and Physics** *(ENSCBP)* (Biology; Chemical Engineering; Food Science; Food Technology; Physics); **Cognitive Sciences** *(National)* (Artificial Intelligence; Computer Science; Neurosciences); **Electronics, Computer Science, Telecommunications, Mathematics and Mechanics** *(ENSEIRB-MATMECA)* (Computer Science; Electronic Engineering; Mathematics; Mechanical Engineering; Telecommunications Engineering); **Environment, Georesources, and Sustainable Development** *(ENSEGID)* (Environmental Management; Environmental Studies; Geology; Hydraulic Engineering; Natural Resources)

History: Founded 2009.

Main Language(s) of Instruction: French

Degrees and Diplomas: *Diplôme d'Ingénieur; Mastère spécialisé*
Last Updated: 02/01/12

BORDEAUX SCHOOL OF ARCHITECTURE AND LANDSCAPE
Ecole nationale supérieure d'Architecture et de Paysage de Bordeaux (ENSAPBX)
740 cours de la Libération - BP 70109, 33405 Talence, Cedex
Tel: +33(5) 57-35-11-00
Fax: +33(5) 56-37-03-23
EMail: eapbx@bordeaux.archi.fr
Website: http://www.bordeaux.archi.fr

Directeur: Pierre Culand
Tel: +33(5) 57-35-11-11 EMail: pierre.culand@bordeaux.archi.fr

Administrative Officer: Philippe Cougrand
Tel: +33(5) 57-35-11-11
EMail: philippe.cougrand@bordeaux.archi.fr

International Relations: Michèle Michel
Tel: +33(5) 57-35-11-08 EMail: michele.michel@bordeaux.archi.fr

Programmes
Architecture (Architecture); **Landscape Architecture** (Landscape Architecture)

History: Founded 1968.

Admission Requirements: Competitive entrance examination for students at baccalauréat + 2 years

Main Language(s) of Instruction: French

Degrees and Diplomas: *Licence*: 3 yrs; *Diplôme national de Master*: 2 yrs; *Doctorat*. Habilitation à l'exercice de la maîtrise d'oeuvre en son nom propre (HMONP).Diplôme de Paysagiste DPLG

Special Facilities: Multimedia and Audio-Visual Centre

Libraries: 19,000 vols, subscriptions to 150 periodicals, 1,000 maps

Last Updated: 28/06/11

BURGUNDY SCHOOL OF BUSINESS
Groupe ESC Dijon-Bourgogne (GROUPE ESC DIJON-BOURGOGNE)
29, rue Sambin, BP 50608, 21000 Dijon
Tel: +33(3) 80-72-59-00
Fax: +33(3) 80-72-59-99
EMail: escdijon@escdijon.com
Website: http://www.escdijon.eu

Directeur général: Stéphan Bourcieu Tel: +33(3) 80-72-59-08

Directeur académique: Alexandre Asselineau
Tel: +33(3) 80-72-59-15

International Relations: Marie-José Albert-Batt
Tel: +33(3) 80-72-59-67, Fax: +33(3) 80-72-59-88
EMail: malbert-batt@escdijon.com

Departments
Finance and Law (Accountancy; Finance; Law) *Director*: Joël Ernult; **Foreign Languages and Cultures** (Cultural Studies; Modern Languages) *Director*: Peter Dunn; **Management and Human Organization** (Labour and Industrial Relations; Management) *Director*: Sophie Reboud; **Marketing** (Marketing) *Director*: Patrice Piccardi

Further Information: Also Study Abroad programmes and US Study programme

History: Founded 1900. A public 'Grande Ecole', now under the jurisdiction of the Chamber of Commerce.

Governing Bodies: Conseil d'Orientation et de Gestion

Academic Year: September to May

Admission Requirements: Competitive written and oral examination for the ESC and ACI programmes and written application and interview for the other programmes.

Fees: (Euros): 6,000-12,000 per annum

Main Language(s) of Instruction: French and English.

International Co-operation: With universities in Argentina, Australia, Canada, China, Mexico, Morocco, Russian Federation and USA. Also participates in Erasmus programme.

Accrediting Agencies: Conférence des Grandes Ecoles

Degrees and Diplomas: *Licence professionnelle*: Business and Commerce (ACI), 3 yrs; *Diplôme d'Etudes d'Ecole de Commerce et Gestion*: Business Administration, 3 yrs; *Mastère spécialisé*: International Wine and Spirits Trade (M/S CIVS); Management of Cultural Organizations (M/S MEC); Management of Health Food Industry (M/S MAS); Management of Pharmaceutical Industry (M/S MIP), 1 yr; *Diplôme national de Master*: Business (MiB); European Business Administration (MSc EBA); International Management, 16 months

Student Services: Academic counselling, Canteen, Employment services, Foreign student adviser, Foreign Studies Centre, Handicapped facilities, Language programs, Social counselling, Sports facilities

Libraries: c. 17,000 vols; 250 subscriptions to the French and international press; 2,800 online periodicals; 1,000 annual company reports and research works, dissertations, case studies, CD-ROMs, etc

Last Updated: 05/07/11

CAEN/CHERBOURG SCHOOL OF ARTS AND MEDIA
Ecole supérieure d'Arts et Médias de Caen/Cherbourg
17 cours Caffarelli, 14000 Caen
Tel: +33(2) 14-37-25-00
Fax: +33(2) 14-37-25-01
EMail: info@esam-c2.fr
Website: http://www.esamcaen.fr

Directeur: Eric Lengereau

Programmes
Art and Communication (Communication Arts; Design; Graphic Design; Visual Arts)

History: Founded in 2011 following the merger of the Ecole supérieure d'arts & média de Caen and the Ecole supérieure des beaux-arts de Cherbourg-Octeville.

Admission Requirements: Baccalauréat or equivalent secondary school exam. Entrance exam with a selection jury.

Main Language(s) of Instruction: French

International Co-operation: Has exchanges with Mannheim, Bremen, Dessau (Germany) along with several UK, Irish and Canadian universities.

Accrediting Agencies: Ministry of Culture and Communication

Degrees and Diplomas: Diplôme national des Arts et Techniques (DNAT in Graphic Design); Diplôme national d'arts plastiques (DNAP in Communication and Art) 3 yrs; Diplôme national supérieur d'expression plastique (DNSEP in Communication and Art) a further 2 yrs

Last Updated: 25/05/11

CAMBRAI REGIONAL ART SCHOOL
Ecole supérieure d'Art de Cambrai
7 rue du Paon, BP 361, 59407 Cambrai
Tel: +33(3) 27-72-78-78
Fax: +33(3) 27-72-78-79
EMail: cambrai@esa-npdc.net
Website: http://cambrai.esa-npdc.net

Programmes
Communication and Design (Communication Arts; Design; Graphic Design; Multimedia)

History: Founded 1780.

Admission Requirements: Baccalauréat or equivalent secondary school exam. Entrance exam with a selection jury.

Main Language(s) of Instruction: French

Accrediting Agencies: Ministry of Culture and Communication

Degrees and Diplomas: Diplôme national d'arts plastiques (DNAP) 3 yrs; Diplôme national supérieur d'expression plastique (DNSEP in Communication) a further 2 yrs

Last Updated: 01/07/11

CENTRAL SCHOOL OF LILLE
Ecole centrale de Lille (EC LILLE)
BP 48, Cité scientifique, 59851 Villeneuve d'Ascq, Cedex
Tel: +33(3) 20-33-53-53
Fax: +33(3) 20-33-54-99
EMail: etienne.craye@ec-lille.fr
Website: http://www.ec-lille.fr

Directeur: Etienne Craye (2005-) Tel: +33(3) 20-33-50-97

Departments
Automation and Industrial Engineering (Automation and Control Engineering; Computer Science); **Civil Engineering** (Civil Engineering); **Electronical and Electrical Engineering** (Electrical and Electronic Engineering; Power Engineering); **General Mathematics and Computer Engineering** (Computer Engineering; Mathematics); **Material Engineering** (Materials Engineering); **Mechanics** (Materials Engineering; Mechanical Engineering); **Systems Engineering** (Computer Engineering; Industrial Engineering; Systems Analysis)

Institutes

Computer Technology and Industrial Engineering *(IG21)* (Computer Engineering; Engineering; Industrial Engineering; Technology) *Division Head*: Arnaud Toguyeni

History: Founded 1872. A public 'Grande Ecole'.

Academic Year: September to June (September-December; January-June)

Admission Requirements: Competitive entrance examination following 2-3 yrs further study after secondary school certificate (baccalauréat) or equivalent

Fees: (Euros): 379 per annum

Main Language(s) of Instruction: French

Degrees and Diplomas: *Diplôme d'Ingénieur*: 3 yrs; *Mastère spécialisé*: Advanced Computer Sciences, a further yr; *Doctorat*

Student Services: Academic counselling, Cultural centre, Employment services, Foreign student adviser, Nursery care, Sports facilities

Student Residential Facilities: For c. 600 students

Libraries: c. 10,000 vols
Last Updated: 23/06/11

CENTRAL SCHOOL OF LYON

Ecole centrale de Lyon (ECL)

BP 163, 36, avenue Guy de Collongue, 69131 Ecully
Tel: +33(4) 72-18-60-00
Fax: +33(4) 78-43-39-62
EMail: brigitte.pavone@ec-lyon.fr
Website: http://www.ec-lyon.fr

Directeur: Frank Debouck (2011-)
Tel: +33(4) 72-18-63-39, Fax: +33(4) 78-33-07-29

Secrétaire Général: Jean-Pierre Bertoglio

Departments

Communication, Languages, Business, Sport (Arts and Humanities; Economics; Management; Modern Languages; Sports); **Electronics and Automation** (Automation and Control Engineering; Electrical Engineering; Electronic Engineering); **Fluid Mechanics, Acoustics and Energy** (Energy Engineering; Mechanical Engineering; Sound Engineering (Acoustics)); **Materials and Surfaces Science and Techniques of** (Chemistry; Materials Engineering; Physical Engineering; Physics); **Mathematics and Computer Science** (Mathematics and Computer Science); **Solid Mechanics, Mechanical Engineering and Civil Engineering** (Civil Engineering; Mechanical Engineering)

Further Information: Has 6 research laboratories

History: Founded 1857, became public 1947, and acquired present status 1992. A public 'Grande Ecole'.

Governing Bodies: Board of Trustees

Academic Year: September to July

Admission Requirements: Competitive entrance examination following 2-3 yrs further study after secondary school certificate (baccalauréat) or equivalent

Main Language(s) of Instruction: French

Degrees and Diplomas: *Diplôme d'Ingénieur*: 3 yrs; *Mastère spécialisé*; *Diplôme national de Master*; *Doctorat (PhD)*: a further 3 yrs

Student Services: Canteen, Foreign student adviser, Health services, Sports facilities

Student Residential Facilities: For c. 640 students

Libraries: 15,000 vols
Last Updated: 23/06/11

CENTRAL SCHOOL OF MARSEILLES

Ecole centrale Marseille (EC-MARSEILLE)

Technopôle de Château Gombert, 38, rue Frédéric Joliot Curie,
13451 Marseille, Cedex 20
Tel: +33 (0)4 91-05-45-45
Fax: +33 (0)4 91-05-43-80
EMail: info@centrale-marseille.fr
Website: http://www.centrale-marseille.fr/

Directeur: Frédéric Fotiadu

Directeur général des Services: Laurent Barbieri
Tel: +33(4) 91-05-47-98

Research Institutes

Optical Science and Technology *(Fresnel)* (Computer Graphics; Microwaves; Optics; Physics; Surveying and Mapping)

Schools

Applied Physics (Applied Physics; Engineering; Physics); **Engineering** (Engineering)

History: Founded 1891 as École Supérieure d'Ingénieurs de Marseille. Acquired present status 2004 following the merger of three engineering schools (ENSPM, ENSSPICAM and ESM2) and title 2006.

Academic Year: September to June (September-February; March-June)

Admission Requirements: 2 yrs study following secondary school certificate (baccalauréat)

Fees: (Euros): 450 per annum

Main Language(s) of Instruction: French

International Co-operation: With universities in Germany, United Kingdom, Finland, Sweden, Italy, Spain, Canada and USA. Also participates in the Socrates programme.

Degrees and Diplomas: *Diplôme d'Ingénieur*: 3 yrs; *Mastère spécialisé*; *Diplôme national de Master*; *Doctorat*: Natural Sciences (PhD), a further 2-3 yrs

Student Services: Academic counselling, Canteen, Employment services, Foreign student adviser, Language programs, Social counselling, Sports facilities
Last Updated: 23/06/11

CENTRAL SCHOOL OF NANTES

Ecole centrale de Nantes (ECN)

BP 92101, 1, rue de la Noë, 44321 Nantes, Cedex 03
Tel: +33(2) 40-37-16-00
Fax: +33(2) 40-74-74-06
EMail: international@ec-nantes.fr
Website: http://www.ec-nantes.fr

Directeur: Patrick Chedmail (2002-)
Tel: +33(2) 40-37-25-15, Fax: +33(2) 40-14-00-28
EMail: Patrick.Chedmail@ec-nantes.fr

Secrétaire générale: Dominique Allemandou
Tel: +33(2) 40-37-16-01
EMail: Dominique.Allemandou@ec-nantes.fr

International Relations: Foaud Bennis
Tel: +33(2) 40-37-25-24, Fax: +33(2) 40-37-25-78
EMail: fouad.bennis@ec-nantes.fr

Departments

Automation and Robotics (Automation and Control Engineering; Robotics); **Civil Engineering** (Civil Engineering); **Communication and Language of Business and Sports** (Business Education; Physical Education); **Computer Engineering and Mathematics** (Computer Engineering; Mathematics); **Fluid Dynamics** (Energy Engineering; Hydraulic Engineering); **Material and Mechanical Engineering** (Materials Engineering; Mechanical Engineering); **Production and Systems Engineering** (Mechanics; Production Engineering)

Further Information: Has 5 research laboratories

History: Founded 1919 as Institut polytechnique de l'Ouest by the Chambre de Commerce de Nantes, became Ecole nationale supérieure de Mécanique de Nantes 1947. Acquired present status and title 1991. A public 'Grande Ecole'.

Academic Year: September to June

Admission Requirements: National competitive entrance examination following 2-3 yrs further study after secondary school certificate (baccalauréat) or equivalent

Fees: (Euros): c. 245 per annum

Main Language(s) of Instruction: French

International Co-operation: Participates in the Time network for double degree

Degrees and Diplomas: *Diplôme d'Ingénieur*: 3 yrs following preparatory studies; *Mastère spécialisé*; *Diplôme national de Master*;

Doctorat: Civil Engineering (PhD); Control Automatism (PhD); Fluid Dynamics (PhD); Mechanical Engineering (PhD), a further 2-3 yrs

Student Services: Foreign student adviser, Foreign Studies Centre

Student Residential Facilities: For c. 170 students

Libraries:c. 16,000 vols

Last Updated: 23/06/11

CENTRAL SCHOOL PARIS
Ecole centrale Paris (ECP)
Grande Voie des Vignes, 92295 Châtenay-Malabry, Cedex
Tel: +33(1) 41-13-10-00
Fax: +33(1) 41-13-10-10
EMail: communication@ecp.fr
Website: http://www.ecp.fr

Directeur: Hervé Biaussier
Tel: +33(1) 41-13-12-54 EMail: direction@ecp.fr

Secrétaire Générale: Martine Beurton
Tel: +33(1) 41-13-14-45 EMail: martine.beurton@ecp.fr

International Relations: Dominique Depevre
Tel: +33(1) 41-13-12-54-46 EMail: dominique.depeyre@ecp.fr

Departments
Business Studies (Business Administration; Business Education); **Energy Engineering** (Energy Engineering); **Humanities and Social Sciences** (Arts and Humanities; Social Sciences); **Information Technology** (Information Technology); **Languages and Cultures** (Cultural Studies; Modern Languages); **Leadership and Engineering Professions** (Engineering; Leadership); **Mathematics** (Mathematics); **Mechanical and Civil Engineering** (Civil Engineering; Mechanical Engineering); **Physics** (Physics); **Processes** (Production Engineering); **Sports** (Sports)

Further Information: Also 13 Research Laboratories. Institut Centralien des Technologies et du Management (ICTM)

History: Founded 1829 as the first 'Grande Ecole' to train engineers, became State Institution 1857. Transferred from Paris to Châtenay-Malabry 1969. Acquired present status 1991. Under the jurisdiction of the Ministry of Education. A public 'Grande Ecole'.

Governing Bodies: Board, comprising 32 members

Academic Year: September to June

Admission Requirements: Competitive entrance examination following 2-3 yrs further study after secondary school certificate (baccalauréat scientifique) or equivalent

Fees: (Euros): diplôme d'ingénieur, 686; mastère spécialisé, c. 12,500.

Main Language(s) of Instruction: French

International Co-operation: Participates in Time (Top Industrial Managers for Europe)

Degrees and Diplomas: *Diplôme d'Ingénieur*: 3 yrs; *Mastère spécialisé*: a further yr; *Diplôme national de Master*; *Doctorat*: 3 yrs following DEA

Student Services: Academic counselling, Canteen, Cultural centre, Employment services, Foreign student adviser, Handicapped facilities, Health services, Social counselling, Sports facilities

Student Residential Facilities: For c. 1,150 students

Libraries: Centre de Documentation, c. 60,000 vols. Historical Collection; CD-ROM Collection

Publications: Echos de Centrale Paris, (quarterly).

Last Updated: 23/06/11

CERGY-PONTOISE UNIVERSITY
Université de Cergy-Pontoise (UCP)
33, boulevard du Port, 95011 Cergy-Pontoise, Cedex
Tel: +33(1) 34-25-60-00
EMail: communication@ml.u-cergy.fr
Website: http://www.u-cergy.fr

Présidente: Françoise Moulin Civil (2008-)
Tel: +33(1) 34-25-61-25, Fax: +33(1) 34-25-61-27
EMail: francoise.moulin-civil@u-cergy.fr

International Relations: Catherine Mayaux
Tel: +33(1) 34-25-60-03, Fax: +33(1) 34-25-60-93
EMail: catherine.mayaux@u-cergy.fr

Graduate Schools
Economics, Management and Mathematics (Economics; Management; Mathematics); **Law and Humanities** (Arts and Humanities; Law); **Science and Engineering** (Information Sciences; Physics)

Institutes
Preparatory Administrative Studies *(IPAG)* (Administration); **Teacher Training** *(IUFM with 5 sites)* (Teacher Trainers Education; Teacher Training); **Technology** *(IUT Neuville-sur-Oise, Cergy-Saint-Christophe, Saint-Martin, Sarcelles and Argenteuil)* (Business and Commerce; Civil Engineering; Computer Engineering; Electrical Engineering; Marketing; Multimedia; Production Engineering; Transport Management)

Units
Arts and Humanities (Arts and Humanities; Geography; History; Literature); **Economics and Management** (Economics; Management); **Languages** (Chinese; English; German; Japanese; Literature; Modern Languages; Spanish); **Law** (Law); **Science and Technology** (Biology; Chemistry; Civil Engineering; Computer Science; Earth Sciences; Electrical Engineering; Environmental Studies; Mathematics; Natural Sciences; Physics; Technology)

History: Founded 1991.

Academic Year: September to June

Admission Requirements: Secondary school certificate (baccalauréat) or foreign equivalent, or special entrance examination

Main Language(s) of Instruction: French, English

International Co-operation: With universities in the United Kingdom, Brazil, Korea, Germany, Spain, Italy, Canada, Poland, Denmark, Belgium, Bulgaria, Lithuania, Finland, Ireland, Mexico, Sweden, Japan, China, Australia and Africa

Degrees and Diplomas: *Diplôme universitaire de Technologie*: Shipping and Logistics Management; Business Techniques; Civil Engineering; Electrical Engineering and Industrial Data Processing; Industrial Logistics Quality and Organization; Communication Networks and Services, 2 yrs; *Licence*: 3 yrs; *Licence professionnelle (LP)*: 3 yrs; *Diplôme national de Master*: 2 yrs following Licence; *Doctorat*. Masters recherche, Masters professionnel, Preparation for CAPES, Agrégation, Judicial and Administrative exams

Student Services: Academic counselling, Canteen, Foreign student adviser, Handicapped facilities, Health services, Language programs, Social counselling, Sports facilities

Last Updated: 12/07/11

CLERMONT-FERRAND II UNIVERSITY
Université Blaise Pascal (Clermont-II) (UBP)
BP 185, 34, avenue Carnot, 63006 Clermont-Ferrand, Cedex 01
Tel: +33(4) 73-40-63-63
Fax: +33(4) 73-40-64-31
EMail: Secretaire.General@univ-bpclermont.fr
Website: http://www.univ-bpclermont.fr

Président: Nadine Lavignotte
Tel: +33(4) 73-40-63-01
EMail: Nadine.LAVIGNOTTE@univ-bpclermont.fr;
president@univ-bpclermont.fr

Directeur général des Services: Hervé Combaz
Tel: +33(4) 73-40-63-03

Divisions
French for Foreign Students (French) *Director*: Anne-Laure Foucher

Graduate Schools
Arts and Humanities (Arts and Humanities) *Director*: Jean-Pierre Dubost; **Chemistry and Chemical Engineering** *(ENSCCF)* (Chemical Engineering; Chemistry; Inorganic Chemistry; Organic Chemistry) *Head*: Jacques Lacoste; **Engineering** *(EDSPI works with University of Clermint-Ferrand I)* (Automation and Control Engineering; Civil Engineering; Mechanical Engineering; Microelectronics) *Director*: Philippe Mahay; **Fundamental Sciences** (Astronomy and Space Science; Chemistry; Mathematics; Physics) *Director*: Pierre Henrard; **Life and Health Sciences** *(In cooperation with University of Clermont-Ferrand I)* (Biological and Life Sciences; Health Sciences) *Director*: Georges Picard

Higher Institutes
Engineering and Computer Science *(ISIMA)* (Computer Science; Engineering) *Director*: Alain Quilliot

Institutes
Industrial Systems Engineering *(IUP GSI)* (Industrial Engineering) *Director*: Christophe Guicheney; **Information and Communication Studies** *(IUP Infocom)* (Communication Studies); **International Commerce** *(IUP CI)* (Business and Commerce; International Business) *Director*: Geoffrey Heels; **Print and Electonic Publishing** *(IUP)* (Publishing and Book Trade) *Director*: Françoise Le Borgne; **Science and Technology** *(CUST, Aubière)* (Natural Sciences; Technology) *Director*: Claude-Gilles Dussap; **Teacher Training** *(IUFM has four sites in the Province of Auvergne)* *Director*: Paul Busuttil; **Technology** *(IUT Montlucon with two additional sites at Moulins and Vichy-Lardy)* (Business and Commerce; Mechanics; Multimedia; Technology; Transport Management) *Director*: Bernard Guillemet; **Tourism** *(IUP Tourisme)* (Tourism) *Director*: Anne Gaugue

Units
Arts and Humanities (Art History; Arts and Humanities; Geography; History; Literature; Modern Languages; Philosophy; Tourism) *Director*: Mathias Bernard; **Exact and Natural Sciences** *(Aubière)* (Biology; Chemistry; Electronic Engineering; Geology; Mathematics; Natural Sciences; Physics) *Director*: Gilles Bourdier; **Languages, Commerce and Communication** *(LACC)* (Applied Linguistics; Business and Commerce; Modern Languages) *Director*: Susan Goutet; **Physical Education and Sport** *(STAPS, Aubière)* (Physical Education; Sports) *Director*: Pascale Duché; **Psychology, Social Sciences, and Education** (Education; Educational Sciences; Psychology; Social Sciences) *Director*: Sylvie Droit-Volet; **Science and Technology** (Biology; Computer Science; Ecology; Mathematics; Meteorology; Physics; Seismology) *Director*: Gilles Petel

History: Founded 1970 under the 1968 law reforming higher education and replacing former Université de Clermont-Ferrand, founded 1854 as Faculty of Letters and Faculty of Science. Became University 1896 and acquired present title 1987. The University, which until 1976 formed a single institution with the University of Clermont-Ferrand I, is a State Institution enjoying academic and financial autonomy, operating under the jurisdiction of the Minister of Education and financed by the State.

Governing Bodies: Conseil d'Administration, including representatives of teaching staff, research workers, students, and administrative and technical staff, as well as non-university members drawn from the public and private sectors; Conseil scientifique, competent in matters of research; Conseil des Etudes et de la Vie universitaire; and Conseil of each Unit, comprising representatives of its teaching staff, research workers, students, and administrative and technical staff. The President is elected by the first three bodies. The Chancelier, who represents the Minister of Education, is the Recteur of the Académie de Clermont-Ferrand

Academic Year: September to June (September-January; February-June)

Admission Requirements: Secondary school certificate (baccalauréat) or brevet supérieur, or recognized foreign equivalent, or special entrance examination

Fees: (Euros): Registration, 145-395 per annum

Main Language(s) of Instruction: French

International Co-operation: With universities in Algeria, Germany, Argentina, Australia, Belgium, Benin, Brazil, Bulgaria, Canada, Chili, China, Congo, Côte d'Ivoire, Denmark, Spain, USA, Finland, Greece, Hungary, Ireland, Italy, Laos, Lebanon, Madagascar, Mali, Morocco, Mexico, Moldova, Norway, Netherlands, Peru, Poland, Portugal, Czech Republic, Romania, United Kingdom, Russian Federation, Slovak Republic, Sweden, Switzerland, Tunisia, Turkey and Ukraine.

Degrees and Diplomas: *Diplôme universitaire de Technologie*: Technology; Business and Commerce; Transport Management; Multimedia, 2 yrs; *Licence*: Letters; Languages; Social Sciences; Natural Sciences; Mathematics and Computer Science; Sports; Physical Education, 3 yrs; *Licence professionnelle*; *Diplôme d'Ingénieur*. 3 yrs following DUT; *Diplôme de Recherche technologique*; *Diplôme national de Master*. Letters; Languages; Social Sciences; Natural Sciences; Mathematics and Computer Science; Sports; Physical Education, a further 2 yrs following Licence; *Doc-torat*: Arts and Humanities; Natural Sciences; Mathematics and Computer Science; Sports, 3-4 yrs following Master. Diplome université; Diplomes nationaux

Student Services: Academic counselling, Canteen, Cultural centre, Foreign student adviser, Foreign Studies Centre, Handicapped facilities, Health services, Social counselling, Sports facilities

Student Residential Facilities: Yes

Special Facilities: Museums and movie studios

Libraries: Central Library, c. 1m. vols; Letters, c. 124,700 vols; Science, c. 35,000 vols

Last Updated: 07/06/11

CLERMONT-FERRAND SCHOOL OF ARCHITECTURE
Ecole nationale supérieure d'Architecture de Clermont-Ferrand (EACF)
71, boulevard Côte-Blatin, 63000 Clermont-Ferrand
Tel: +33(4) 73-34-71-50
Fax: +33(4) 73-34-71-69
EMail: ensacf@clermont-fd.archi.fr
Website: http://www.clermont-fd.archi.fr

Directeur: Paul Leandri EMail: pleandri@clermont-fd.archi.fr

Secrétaire Général: Alain Fayard
EMail: afayard@clermont-fd.archi.fr

International Relations: Philippe Bucherer
EMail: pbucherer@clermont-fd.archi.fr

Programmes
Architecture (Architecture)

History: Founded 1968.

Main Language(s) of Instruction: French

Degrees and Diplomas: *Licence*; *Mastère spécialisé*; *Diplôme national de Master*; *Doctorat*. Also HEMONP - Habilitation d'Exercer la Maîtrise d'Oeuvre en son Nom Propre
Last Updated: 12/04/11

CLERMONT GRADUATE SCHOOL OF MANAGEMENT
Groupe ESC Clermont
4, boulevard Trudaine, 63037 Clermont-Ferrand, Cedex 1
Tel: +33(4) 73-98-24-24
Fax: +33(4) 73-98-24-49
EMail: info@esc-clermont.fr
Website: http://www.esc-clermont.fr

Directeur général: Thierry Robin

International Relations: Mike Bryant
EMail: mike.bryant@esc-clermont.fr

Programmes
Bachelor Studies (International Business; International Economics); **Graduate Studies** (Accountancy; Banking; International Business; International Economics; Management; Marketing)

History: Founded 1919. A public 'Grande Ecole'.

Governing Bodies: Department Chamber of Commerce.

Academic Year: September to May

Admission Requirements: Competitive entrance examination following 2 yrs further study after secondary school certificate (baccalauréat) or equivalent

Fees: (Euros):bachelor 4,950 per annum, master 7,000, executive MS-MSC 11,000

Main Language(s) of Instruction: French. English for international programmes

International Co-operation: Universities worldwide

Accrediting Agencies: AACSB, Ministère, Conférence des Grandes Ecoles, Edufrance

Degrees and Diplomas: *Mastère spécialisé*; *Diplôme national de Master*. Bachelor, postgraduate degrees

Student Services: Academic counselling, Foreign student adviser, Language programs, Sports facilities

Special Facilities: Movie Studio/Theatre

Libraries: Central Library
Last Updated: 13/04/11

CLERMONT METROPOLE GRADUATE SCHOOL OF ART

Ecole supérieure d'Art de Clermont Métropole (ESACM)
25, rue Kessler, 63000 Clermont-Ferrand
Tel: +33(4) 73-17-36-10
Fax: +33(4) 73-17-36-11
EMail: esa@esacm.fr
Website: http://www.esacm.fr

Directrice: Muriel Lepage

Administrative Officer: Frédérique Rutyna

Programmes
Visual Arts (Design; Graphic Arts; Visual Arts)

History: Founded 2005 as Ecole supérieure d'Art de Clermont-Communauté. Acquired present title and status 2010.

Admission Requirements: Baccalauréat or equivalent secondary school exam. Entrance exam with a selection jury.

Fees: (Euros): 450-500 per annum

Main Language(s) of Instruction: French

International Co-operation: Participates in Socrates/Erasmus and has an exchange programme with Thessalonican art schools.

Accrediting Agencies: Ministry of Culture and Communication

Degrees and Diplomas: Diplôme national d'arts plastiques (DNAP in visual arts) 3yrs; Diplôme national supérieur d'expression plastique (DNSEP in visual arts) a further 2 yrs. Also Certificates (CEAP) after 2 yrs and (CESAP) for 4th yr.
Last Updated: 11/04/11

CNAM - PARIS

Conservatoire National des Arts et Métiers (CNAM)
292, rue Saint-Martin, 75141 Paris, Cedex 03
Tel: +33(1) 40-27-20-00
Fax: +33(1) 42-71-93-29
EMail: secretariat.general@cnam.fr
Website: http://www.cnam.fr

Administrateur général: Christian Forestier (2008-)
Tel: +33(1) 40-27-23-06, Fax: +33(1) 40-27-26-25
EMail: administrateur.general@cnam.fr

Directrice générale des Services: Astrid Krechner
Tel: +33(1) 40-27-23-08, Fax: +33(1) 42-71-93-29

International Relations: Laurent Perez
Tel: +33(1) 40-27-21-21, Fax: +33(1) 40-27-20-70
EMail: laurent.perez@cnam.fr

Divisions
Industrial Sciences and Communication Technology (Agricultural Engineering; Automation and Control Engineering; Biochemistry; Biological and Life Sciences; Biology; Chemistry; Civil Engineering; Computer Science; Construction Engineering; Economics; Electrical Engineering; Electronic Engineering; Energy Engineering; Engineering; Geological Engineering; Geology; Heating and Refrigeration; Hygiene; Industrial Engineering; Instrument Making; Laser Engineering; Law; Machine Building; Maintenance Technology; Management; Marine Science and Oceanography; Materials Engineering; Measurement and Precision Engineering; Mechanical Engineering; Mechanics; Nuclear Engineering; Nuclear Physics; Organic Chemistry; Physics; Polymer and Plastics Technology; Real Estate; Safety Engineering; Sound Engineering (Acoustics); Technology; Telecommunications Services; Water Management); **Management and Society** (Accountancy; Banking; Commercial Law; Communication Studies; Cultural Studies; Economics; Fashion Design; Health Administration; Health Sciences; Insurance; International Business; International Relations; Management; Marketing; Real Estate; Sales Techniques; Social Work; Technology; Technology Education; Tourism; Town Planning; Transport and Communications; Transport Management)

Schools
Engineering School *(EICnam)* (Surveying and Mapping)

Further Information: Has 28 regional institutes

History: Founded 1794 as an Institute of Adult Education, reorganized as College of Applied Sciences 1819. The Conservatoire offers Professional Training courses outside normal working hours in a wide variety of fields. Courses are also given in associated Centres in all parts of the country and some are offered through distance learning technology.

Governing Bodies: Conseil d'Administration, including elected members of academic staff, and members drawn from industry, the trade unions, scholarly and learned bodies, Parliament, and the City of Paris; Conseil de perfectionnement, including elected members of academic staff and students

Academic Year: October to June

Admission Requirements: High school certificate (Baccalauréat). Open to people at any stage of their working life. Foreign students admitted in the third cycle only, except for those working in France

Fees: (Euros): Basis, 125 per annum; plus 80 (1st and 2nd cycle)-100 (3rd cycle) per UV and 40 (1st and 2nd cycle)-50 per 1/2 UV

Main Language(s) of Instruction: French; some MBA courses offered by the International Institute of Management are in English

International Co-operation: With universities in Germany, Denmark, United Kingdom, Spain, Italy, Portugal, Greece, Romania, Hungary, Maghreb countries, Benin

Degrees and Diplomas: *Diplôme universitaire de Technologie*: 2 yrs; *Licence (Bachelor)*: 3 yrs; *Licence professionnelle*: Economics (DESE), a further 3-4 yrs (evening study); *Licence professionnelle*: Social Studies (DPC), 3-4 yrs (evening studies); *Licence professionnelle*: Technical Studies (DPCT), 3-4 yrs (evening study); *Diplôme d'Ingénieur*: 1-2 yrs following DEST or DESE or DESA; *Diplôme d'Ingénieur*; *Mastère spécialisé*; *Diplôme national de Master*: 2 yrs following Licence; *Doctorat*: 3-4 yrs following DEA or Master Degree. Also IIM MBA in Economics and Management, 1 yr (full-time)-3 yrs (part-time); Certificate of Competence

Student Services: Academic counselling, Canteen, Employment services, Foreign student adviser, Language programs, Social counselling

Student Residential Facilities: No

Special Facilities: Musée des Arts et Métiers

Libraries: c. 250,000 vols; 1,500 on-line subsciptions; E-library (www.cnum.cnam.fr)
Last Updated: 22/06/11

COLLÈGE DE FRANCE

11, place Marcelin Berthelot, 75231 Paris, Cedex 05
Tel: +33(1) 44-27-12-11
Fax: +33(1) 44-27-11-09
Website: http://www.college-de-france.fr

Administrateur: Pierre Corvol Tel: +33(1) 44-27-11-00

Administrative Officer: Marylène Meston de Ren
Tel: +33(1) 44-27-11-02

International Relations: Florence Terrasse-Riou
Tel: +33(1) 44-27-11-01
EMail: f.terrasse-riou@college-de-france.fr

Programmes
History, Philology and Archaeology (Archaeology; History; Philology); **Mathematics** (Mathematics); **Natural Sciences** (Biology; Chemistry; Genetics; Immunology; Medicine; Meteorology; Microbiology; Natural Sciences; Paleontology; Physiology; Psychology); **Philosophy and Sociology** (Anthropology; Comparative Law; Contemporary History; Cultural Studies; Economics; European Studies; History; International Law; Law; Middle Eastern Studies; Modern History; North African Studies; Philosophy; Political Sciences; Social Sciences); **Physics** (Physics)

History: Founded 1530 by François I, a Centre of Adult Education and Research at the highest level. The institution has 52 professorial chairs, 33 in Human Sciences and 19 in Exact Sciences, each held by a scholar of exceptional distinction.

Governing Bodies: Assemblée des Professeurs which elects the academic head of the institution, the Administrateur

Academic Year: September to July

Admission Requirements: None. Courses are open to the public

Fees: None

Main Language(s) of Instruction: French

Degrees and Diplomas: No Degrees and Diplomas awarded

Libraries: Library of the Collège (for professors only), c. 125,000 vols

Publications: Annuaire du Collège de France - Recueil de travaux *(annually)*

Last Updated: 13/04/11

EIVP - PARIS

Ecole des Ingénieurs de la Ville de Paris (EIVP)
15, rue Fénelon, 75010 Paris
Tel: +33(1) 56-02-61-00
Fax: +33(1) 44-41-11-06
EMail: eivp@eivp-paris.fr
Website: http://www.eivp-paris.fr

Directeur: Régis Vallée EMail: regis.vallee@eivp-paris.fr

Secrétaire général: Marc Gayda EMail: marc.gayda@eivp-paris.fr

Departments
Computer Science (Computer Science); **Construction and Environment** (Civil Engineering; Construction Engineering; Waste Management; Water Management); **Languages** (Chinese; English; German; Italian; Spanish); **Management** (Law; Management); **Public Space Management** (Town Planning; Transport and Communications; Transport Management)

History: A public 'Grande Ecole'.

Fees: (Euros): 1,036 per annum

Main Language(s) of Instruction: French (English compulsory)

Degrees and Diplomas: *Diplôme d'Ingénieur*; *Diplôme national de Master*

Student Services: Canteen

Libraries: Yes

Publications: Les Carrefours du Génie urbain

Last Updated: 24/06/11

EMA - ALES

Ecole des Mines d'Alès (EMA)
6, avenue de Clavières, 30319 Alès
Tel: +33(4) 66-78-50-00
Fax: +33(4) 66-78-50-34
EMail: contact@ema.fr
Website: http://www.ema.fr

Directeur: Alain Dorison (2003-)
Tel: +33(4) 66-78-50-23 EMail: alain.dorison@mines-ales.fr

Secrétaire général: André Moulin EMail: Andre.Moulin@ema.fr

Programmes
Mining Engineering (Mining Engineering)

Research Centres
Computer Engineering and Automation (Artificial Intelligence; Automation and Control Engineering; Computer Engineering; Electrical Engineering; Electronic Engineering; Software Engineering; Telecommunications Engineering) *Director (Acting)*: Yannick Vimont; **Industrial Environment and Risk Management** (Chemical Engineering; Environmental Engineering; Safety Engineering; Surveying and Mapping; Waste Management) *Director (Acting)*: Catherine Gonzalez; **Mass Materials** (Automation and Control Engineering; Civil Engineering; Construction Engineering; Geological Engineering; Industrial Engineering; Materials Engineering; Mechanical Engineering; Mining Engineering; Production Engineering) *Director*: Mireille Fouletier

Further Information: Campuses in Nîmes and Pau.

History: Founded 1843.

Academic Year: September to June

Admission Requirements: Competitive entrance examination following 1 or 2 yrs university studies after secondary school certificate (baccalauréat)

Fees: (Euros): For postgraduate diploma of 'Ingénieur diplômé' 450 per annum, 1,530-3,800 per annum for specialization courses

Main Language(s) of Instruction: French. English for specialization course on' Risk Management and Social Impact Assessment'

International Co-operation: With over 30 universities in Europe and worldwide. Also participates in the Socrates-Erasmus programme

Accrediting Agencies: Commission des Titres d'Ingénieur

Degrees and Diplomas: *Diplôme d'Ingénieur*: 4 yrs at school; *Mastère spécialisé*: 9 mths to 2 yrs; *Diplôme national de Master*; *Doctorat*: 3 yrs. Also Ingénieur de spécialisation in Computer Science and Digital Communication

Student Services: Canteen, Cultural centre, Foreign student adviser, Foreign Studies Centre, Language programs, Social counselling, Sports facilities

Student Residential Facilities: For c. 500 students

Special Facilities: Mineralogy Museum

Libraries: Centre de Documentation, 13,000 vols

Last Updated: 24/06/11

EMAC - ALBI

Ecole des Mines d'Albi-Carmaux (EMAC)
Campus Jarlard, 81013 Albi, Cedex 09
Tel: +33(5) 63-49-30-00
Fax: +33(5) 63-49-30-99
EMail: ecole@enstimac.fr
Website: http://www.enstimac.fr

Directeur: Bruno Verlon
Tel: +33(5) 63-49-30-10 EMail: bruno.verlon@enstimac.fr

Secrétaire général: Guy Ferreira

Divisions
Chemical Engineering (Chemical Engineering); **Environmental and Energy Engineering** (Energy Engineering; Environmental Engineering); **Materials Engineering** (Materials Engineering); **Process Engineering** (Engineering)

History: Founded 1992 under the authority of the Ministry of Industry.

Academic Year: September to July (September-January; February-July)

Admission Requirements: Entrance examination

Fees: (Euros): Registration 349 per annum

International Co-operation: Socrates and other bilateral agreements

Degrees and Diplomas: *Diplôme d'Ingénieur*: 4 yrs; *Mastère spécialisé*; *Diplôme national de Master*; *Doctorat*

Student Services: Canteen, Cultural centre, Employment services, Foreign student adviser, Health services, Social counselling, Sports facilities

Student Residential Facilities: Yes

Special Facilities: Toulouse Lautrec Museum

Last Updated: 24/06/11

EMD - DOUAI

Ecole des Mines de Douai (EMD)
BP 838, 941, rue Charles Bourseul, 59508 Douai
Tel: +33(3) 27-71-22-22
Fax: +33(3) 27-71-25-25
EMail: mines@ensm-douai.fr
Website: http://www.ensm-douai.fr

Directeur: Jean-Claude Duriez
Tel: +33(3) 27-71-22-01 EMail: jean-claude.duriez@mines-douai.fr

Secrétaire général: Kader Amara
Tel: +33(3) 27-71-20-25, Fax: +33(3) 27-71-26-45
EMail: amara@mines-douai.fr

International Relations: Marc Bonpain
Tel: +33(3) 27-71-20-50 EMail: marc.bonpain@mines-douai.fr

Departments
Chemistry and Environment (Chemistry; Environmental Management; Environmental Studies; Waste Management; Water Management); **Civil and Environmental Engineering** (Civil Engineering; Environmental Engineering); **Computer Science and**

Automation (Automation and Control Engineering; Computer Science; Information Technology; Systems Analysis); **Industrial Energy** (Energy Engineering; Heating and Refrigeration; Industrial Engineering); **Polymer Technology and Mechanical Engineering** (Materials Engineering; Mechanical Engineering; Polymer and Plastics Technology)

History: Founded 1878. A public 'Grande Ecole'.

Admission Requirements: Competitive entrance examination following 2 yrs further study after secondary school certificate (baccalauréat) or following first university qualification (DEUG, DUT or BTS), or equivalent

Fees: (Euros): 400 per annum

Main Language(s) of Instruction: French and English

International Co-operation: With institutions in UK; Germany; Finland; Spain; China; India; South America; USA; Canada

Accrediting Agencies: Commission des Titres d'Ingénieurs

Degrees and Diplomas: *Diplôme d'Ingénieur*; *Mastère spécialisé*; *Diplôme national de Master*; *Doctorat*

Student Services: Academic counselling, Canteen, Employment services, Foreign student adviser, Foreign Studies Centre, Language programs, Social counselling, Sports facilities

Student Residential Facilities: Yes

Libraries: Yes
Last Updated: 24/06/11

EMNANTES SCHOOL OF ENGINEERING
Ecole des Mines de Nantes (EMN)
BP 20722, La Chanterie 4, rue Alfred Kastler, 44307 Nantes, Cedex 03
Tel: +33(2) 51-85-81-00
Fax: +33(2) 51-85-81-99
EMail: concours@mines-nantes.fr
Website: http://www.mines-nantes.fr

Directrice: Anne Beauval
Tel: +33(2) 51-85-81-10 EMail: anne.beauval@mines-nantes.fr

Secrétaire général: Serge Wattelier
EMail: serge.wattelier@mines-nantes.fr

International Relations: John Miller Jones
Tel: +33(2) 51-85-85-30 EMail: mjones@mines-nantes.fr

Departments
Automation and Industrial Engineering (Automation and Control Engineering; Industrial Engineering; Production Engineering; Robotics); **Computer Science** (Computer Science; Systems Analysis); **Energetics and Environment** (Energy Engineering; Environmental Engineering; Environmental Management); **Human and Social Sciences** (Development Studies; Industrial Design; Industrial Management; Social Sciences); **Subatomic Physics and Associated Technologies** (Nuclear Physics; Physics; Technology; Waste Management)

History: Founded 1990. A public 'Grande Ecole'.

Governing Bodies: Conseil d'Administration

Academic Year: September to July

Admission Requirements: Competitive entrance examination following 2 yrs higher education after secondary school certificate (baccalauréat) or equivalent

Fees: (Euros): Engineer diploma (Master in Engineering), 800 per annum; master of science and technology 15,000 for the 2-year programme

Main Language(s) of Instruction: French (Diplôle d'Ingénieur); English (Master of Science and Technology)

International Co-operation: Socrates, Erasmus, bilateral agreements

Accrediting Agencies: Commission des Titres d'Ingénieur

Degrees and Diplomas: *Diplôme d'Ingénieur*: Quality and Reliability Engineering; Operations Management in Production and logistics; Computer Science, Information and Production Systems; Information Technology for Decision Making; Information Systems Engineering; Control Engineering and Industrial Information Technology Organisation and Management of Information Technology; Environment, Energy and Nuclear Engineering: Environmental Engineering Energy Systems Engineering Nuclear Engineering:

Technologies, Safety Environment Systems and Technologies Applies to nuclear Reactors, 5 yrs. Master of Science and Technology (in English): Project Management in Environmental and Energy Engineering; Management of Logistics and Production Systems; Sustainable Nuclear Engineering and Waste Management; Evolving Complex Software Systems

Student Services: Academic counselling, Canteen, Employment services, Foreign student adviser, Handicapped facilities, Health services, Language programs, Sports facilities

Student Residential Facilities: Yes. Individual fully-equipped studios

Publications: Talents des Mines, Magazine on innovation and developments in science and technology *(other/irregular)*
Last Updated: 26/01/12

ENPC - MARNE-LA-VALLÉE
Ecole des Ponts ParisTech (ENPC)
6 et 8, avenue Blaise Pascal, Cité Descartes, Champs sur Marne, 77455 Marne-la-Vallée, Cedex 2
Tel: +33(1) 64-15-30-00
Fax: +33(1) 64-15-34-09
EMail: Elisabeth.vitou@mail.enpc.fr
Website: http://www.enpc.fr

Directeur: Philippe Courtier (2004-) Tel: +33(1) 64-15-34-01
Secrétaire général: Xavier Guérin Tel: +33(1) 64-15-34-29
International Relations: Pierre Michaux Tel: +33(1) 64-15-36-69

Departments
Civil and Construction Engineering (Civil Engineering; Construction Engineering); **Economics, Management and Finance** (Economics; Finance; Management); **Humanities and Social Sciences** (Arts and Humanities; Philosophy; Social Sciences; Sociology); **Industrial Engineering** (Industrial Engineering); **Mathematics and Computer Science** (Mathematics and Computer Science); **Mechanical Engineering and Material Science** (Materials Engineering; Mechanical Engineering); **Town, Environment and Transport** (Environmental Engineering; Transport Engineering; Urban Studies)

History: Founded 1747, acquired present status 1994. A public 'Grande Ecole'.

Academic Year: September to June (2 semesters)

Admission Requirements: Maîtrise or foreign equivalent (Master's Degree)

Fees: (Euros): 300 per annum

Main Language(s) of Instruction: French

International Co-operation: With universities in Spain, Italy, Germany, Hungaria, Romania, China, Brazil, Morocco, Lebanon, Canada, Netherlands, Portugal and Vietnam.

Accrediting Agencies: Ministère de l'Écologie, de l'Énergie, du Développement durable et de la Mer

Degrees and Diplomas: *Diplôme d'Ingénieur*; *Mastère spécialisé*; *Diplôme national de Master*. 3 yrs; *Doctorat (PhD)*: 3 yrs following Master

Student Services: Academic counselling, Canteen, Employment services, Foreign student adviser, Health services, Language programs, Social counselling, Sports facilities

Student Residential Facilities: Yes

Libraries: Yes

Press or Publishing House: Les Presses de l'École nationale des ponts et chaussées
Last Updated: 27/06/11

ENS - CACHAN
Ecole normale supérieure de Cachan (ENS CACHAN)
61, avenue du Président-Wilson, 94235 Cachan
Tel: +33(1) 47-40-20-00
Fax: +33(1) 47-40-20-74
EMail: ri@.ens-cachan.fr
Website: http://www.ens-cachan.fr

Président: Jean-Yves Merindol
Tel: +33(1) 47-40-53-02, Fax: +33(1) 47-40-28-88
EMail: presidence@ens-cachan.fr

Directrice des services: Gwenaëlle Verscheure
EMail: dgs@ens-cachan.fr

International Relations: Bogdana Neuville
Tel: +33(1) 47-40-21-71, Fax: +33(1) 47-40-23-79

Departments
Biochemistry and Bioengineering (Biochemistry; Bioengineering); **Chemistry** (Chemistry); **Civil Engineering** (Civil Engineering); **Computer Science** (Computer Science); **Computer Science and Telecommunications** *(Ker Lann campus)* (Computer Science; Telecommunications Engineering); **Design** (Design); **Economics and Management** (Accountancy; Economics; Finance; Management; Marketing); **Economics, Law and Management** *(Ker Lann campus)* (Economics; Law; Management); **Electrical Engineering and Applied Physics** *Head*: Cécile Durieu; **Electronics, Electronic Techniques and Automation** (Applied Physics; Automation and Control Engineering; Electronic Engineering; Nanotechnology; Systems Analysis; Telecommunications Engineering); **English** (English); **Mathematics** *(Ker Lann campus)* (Mathematics); **Mathematics** (Mathematics); **Mechanical Engineering** (Mechanical Engineering); **Mechatronics** *(Ker Lann campus)* (Electronic Engineering; Mechanical Engineering); **Physical and Sport Education** *(Ker Lann campus)* (Physical Education; Sports); **Physics** (Physics); **Social Sciences** (Social Sciences) *Head*: Patrice Duran

Laboratories
Automated Production Research (Automation and Control Engineering) *Head*: Jean-Jacques Lesage; **Biotechnology and Applied Genetic Pharmacology** *Head*: Christian Auclair; **Centre for Mathematical Studies and their Applications** (Mathematics) *Head*: Frédéric Pascal; **Institutions and Historical Dynamics of Economics** (Economics) *Head*: Claude Didry; **Mathematical Research** *(Rennes)* (Mathematics) *Division Head*: Nicolas Lerner; **Mechanics of Materials and Structures** (Materials Engineering; Mechanical Engineering) *Head*: Pierre Ladevèze; **Public Policy Analysis Group** (Political Sciences) *Head*: Jean-Charles Szurek; **Quantum and Molecular Photonics** (Physics) *Head*: Isabelle Ledoux; **Science, Techniques, Education, Training** *Head*: Joël Lebeaume; **Specifications and Verification** *Head*: Philippe Schnoebelen; **Supramolecular and Macromolecular Photophysics and Photochemistry** (Chemistry; Physics) *Head*: Jacques Delaire; **Systems and Applications of Information Technology and Energy** (Energy Engineering; Information Technology) *Head*: Pascal Larzabal

Further Information: Branch in Bruz

History: Founded 1912. A public 'Grande Ecole'.

Governing Bodies: Ministry of Education and Research

Admission Requirements: BA. Specific requirements for each department and laboratory

Main Language(s) of Instruction: French

International Co-operation: With universities in Algeria; Australia; Belgium; Brazil; Canada; Chile; China; Czech Republic; Germany; Greece; Ireland; Italy; Japan; Lebanon; Madagascar; Norway; Portugal; Romania; South Africa; Spain; Switzerland; Netherlands; Tunisia; United Kingdom; Uruguay; USA

Degrees and Diplomas: *Diplôme national de Master*: 2 yrs; *Doctorat*: 3 yrs. Preparation for Agrégation examination; Diplôme d'Université

Student Services: Academic counselling, Canteen, Foreign student adviser, Foreign Studies Centre, Health services, Language programs, Social counselling, Sports facilities

Libraries: Yes
Last Updated: 30/06/11

ENS - LYONS
Ecole normale supérieure de Lyon (ENS LYON)
15 Parvis René Descartes, 69364 Lyon, Cedex 07
Tel: +33(4) 72-72-60-00
EMail: directeur@ens-lyon.fr
Website: http://www.ens-lyon.fr

Président (p.i.): Jacques Samarut (2010-)
Tel: +33(4) 72-72-80-17, Fax: +33(4) 72-72-86-81

Departments
Arts (Arts and Humanities; Music; Musicology; Theatre); **Biology** (Biology); **Chemistry** (Chemistry); **Computer Science** (Computer Science); **Earth Sciences** (Earth Sciences); **Foreign Languages, Literature and Civilizations** (Cultural Studies; Literature; Modern Languages); **Humanities** (Arts and Humanities; Philosophy); **Letters** (French; Greek (Classical)); **Mathematics** (Computer Science; Mathematics); **Physics** (Physics); **Social Sciences** (Geography; History; Social Sciences); **Transversal Studies** (Documentation Techniques; English; Sports)

Institutes
Education *(Français)* (Education)

History: Founded 1987. A public 'Grande Ecole'. Acquired present status following merge with Ecole normale supérieure Lettres et sciences humaines.

Governing Bodies: Ministry of Research and Education

Academic Year: September to July

Admission Requirements: Competitive entrance examination following two years of studies after secondary school certificate (baccalauréat). Admission via application following undergraduate studies

Main Language(s) of Instruction: French (with some courses in English)

International Co-operation: With universities in Canada, Romania, China, India, Japan, Singapore. Also participates in Erasmus and Erasmus Mundus programmes (with universities in Sweden, Germany, Italy, United Kingdom, Spain, Netherlands).

Accrediting Agencies: Ministry of Higher Education and Research

Degrees and Diplomas: *Licence*; *Diplôme national de Master*: Arts and Humanities; Languages; Social Sciences; *Diplôme national de Master*: Biology; Computer Science; Earth Sciences; Mathematics; Physics and Chemistry, 2 yrs following BS; *Doctorat*: Biology; Computer Science; Earth Sciences; Mathematics; Physics and Chemistry, 3 yrs following Master

Student Services: Academic counselling, Canteen, Foreign student adviser, Foreign Studies Centre, Health services, Language programs, Sports facilities

Student Residential Facilities: Yes

Libraries: Main Library; Department Libraries
Last Updated: 01/07/11

ENS - PARIS
Ecole normale supérieure Paris (ENS)
45, rue d'Ulm, 75230 Paris, Cedex 05
Tel: +33(1) 44-32-30-00
Fax: +33(1) 44-32-20-99
EMail: communication@ens.fr
Website: http://www.ens.fr

Directrice: Monique Canto-Sperber (2005-)
Tel: +33(1) 44-32-31-57

Departments
Ancient Civilizations (Archaeology; Greek (Classical); Latin; Oriental Languages); **Art History and Theories** (Aesthetics; Art History; Cinema and Television; Musicology; Theatre); **Biology** (Biology); **Chemistry** (Chemistry); **Cognitive Studies** (Cognitive Sciences; Neurosciences); **Geography** (Geography); **Geosciences** (Geology; Marine Science and Oceanography; Meteorology); **History** (History); **Languages and Literature** (English; German; Literature; Modern Languages; Russian; Spanish); **Mathematics and Applications** (Applied Mathematics; Mathematics); **Philosophy** (Philosophy); **Social Sciences** (Anthropology; Economics; Law; Political Sciences; Social Sciences; Sociology)

History: Founded 1794. Acquired present status following merger of the Ecole normale supérieure de la rue d'Ulm and the Ecole normale supérieure de jeunes filles (Sèvres). A public 'Grande Ecole'.

Governing Bodies: Conseil d'Administration

Academic Year: September to July

Admission Requirements: Competitive entrance examination following 2-3 yrs further study after secondary school certificate (baccalauréat) or following first university qualification, or equivalent

Main Language(s) of Instruction: French

Degrees and Diplomas: *Diplôme national de Master*; *Doctorat*. Preparation d'Agrégation exam; Diplôme d'Université

Student Residential Facilities: For c. 800 students

Libraries: c. 800,000 vols
Last Updated: 30/06/11

ENSA DIJON ART & DESIGN

Ecole nationale supérieure d'Art de Dijon (ENSA DIJON)
3, rue Michelet, 21000 Dijon
Tel: +33(3) 80-30-21-27
Fax: +33(3) 80-58-90-65
EMail: estelle.desreux@ensa-dijon.fr
Website: http://www.ensa-dijon.fr

Directrice: Anne Dallant EMail: anne.dallant@ensa-dijon.fr

Secrétaire général: Jean-Louis Villemin
EMail: jeanlouis.villemin@ensa-dijon.fr

Programmes
Fine Arts and Design (Design; Fine Arts)

History: Founded 1766.

Admission Requirements: Baccalauréat or equivalent secondary school exam. Exam and jury selection

International Co-operation: Cooperation with Universities in Belgium, Bulgaria, Czech Republic, Estonia, Finland, Germany, Italy, Norway, Spain, The Netherlands, UK, Turkey, Argentina, Australia, Brazil, China, Gabon, Israel, Japan, South Korea, USA and Tunisia

Accrediting Agencies: Ministry of Culture

Degrees and Diplomas: Diplôme national d'arts plastiques (DNAP Art and DNAP Design) 3 yrs; Diplôme national supérieur d'expression plastique (DNSEP Art and DNSEP Design) a further 2 yrs equivalent to a Master's as from June 2012.
Last Updated: 25/05/11

ENSAIT-ROUBAIX

Ecole nationale supérieure des Arts et Industries textiles (ENSAIT)
BP 30329, 2 Allée Louise et Victor Champier, 59100 Roubaix, Cedex 1
Tel: +33(3) 20-25-64-64
Fax: +33(3) 20-24-84-06
EMail: contact@ensait.fr
Website: http://www.ensait.fr

Directeur: Xavier Flambard (2005-) Tel: +33(3) 20-25-64-51

Secrétaire général: Michel Vancapelle
Tel: +33(3) 20-25-64-51 EMail: michel.vancapelle@ensait.fr

International Relations: Marie-Pierre Delespierre
Tel: +33(3) 20-25-64-87, Fax: +33(3) 20-25-64-72
EMail: marie-pierre.delespierre@ensait.fr

Divisions
Economics and Social Sciences (Economics; Social Sciences); Science for Engineering (Applied Mathematics; Automation and Control Engineering; Computer Engineering; Electronic Engineering; Engineering; Mechanical Engineering); Specialisation (Textile Design; Textile Technology)

History: Founded 1889, acquired present status 1945. A public 'Grande Ecole'.

Admission Requirements: Competitive entrance examination following 2-3 yrs further study after secondary school certificate (baccalauréat) or following first university qualification (DEUG, DUT or BTS), or equivalent

Fees: (Euros): c. 300 per annum

Main Language(s) of Instruction: French

Degrees and Diplomas: *Diplôme d'Ingénieur*: Engineering, a further 3 yrs; *Mastère spécialisé*: Commerce and Fashion Innovation, a further 1 yr; *Diplôme national de Master*: Création d'Entreprise et Entrepreneuriat, a further 1 yr

Student Services: Academic counselling, Foreign student adviser, Handicapped facilities, Health services, Language programs, Sports facilities

Student Residential Facilities: Yes

Libraries: School Library: c. 6,000 current references; c. 25,000 ancient documents on textiles as far back as 17th century

Publications: Fil d'Ariane, Innovating aspects of textile industry *(quarterly)*
Last Updated: 06/06/11

ENSAM - PARIS

Ecole nationale supérieure d'Arts et Métiers - Paris Tech (ENSAM)
147, boulevard de l'Hôpital, 75013 Paris
Tel: +33(1) 44-24-63-20
Fax: +33(1) 45-24-63-26
EMail: direction.generale@ensam.fr
Website: http://www.ensam.fr

Directeur général: Laurent Carraro
Tel: +33(1) 44-24-63-20, Fax: +33(1) 44-24-63-26
EMail: directeur.general@ensam.eu

Directeur général adjoint: Marc Le Coq

International Relations: Jean-Marie Castelain, Directeur des Relations internationales
Tel: +33(1) 44 24 63 99 EMail: jean.marie.castelain@ensam.eu

Centres
Mechanical Engineering and Industrial Engineering *(Paris, Aix-en-Provence, Angers, Bordeaux-Talence, Châlons-en-Champagne, Cluny, Lille, Metz)* (Industrial Engineering; Management; Mechanical Engineering)

Institutes
Image Processing *(Chalon-sur-Saône)*; Mechanics and Environmental Sciences *(Le Bourget-du-Lac/Chambéry)* (Environmental Studies; Mechanical Engineering)

Laboratories
Advanced Instrumentation and Robotics *(Angers)* (Robotics); Automatic Control (Automation and Control Engineering); Biomechanics (Mechanical Engineering); Design of New Products (Design); Energetics and Internal Fluid Mechanics (Energy Engineering; Mechanics); Energetics and Transfer Phenomena *(Bordeaux)* (Energy Engineering); Manufacturing Processes and Production Techniques (Production Engineering); Materials and Processes *(Cluny)* (Materials Engineering); Materials, Biomechanics, Solids Dynamics *(MECASURF, Aix-en-Provence)* (Materials Engineering); Materials, Damage, Reliability *(Bordeaux)* (Materials Engineering); Mechanics *(Lille)* (Mechanical Engineering); Microstructure and Mechanics of Materials (Materials Engineering; Mechanical Engineering); Numerical Simulation in Fluid Mechanics (Mechanics); Polymers Processing, Transformation and Ageing (Polymer and Plastics Technology); Production Engineering *(Bordeaux)* (Production Engineering); Structural Mechanics (Mechanics); Surface Physico-Chemistry *(Angers)* (Chemistry; Physical Chemistry); Systems and Machine Engineering *(Aix-en-Provence)* (Machine Building)

Further Information: Also Teaching and Research Centres in Aix-en-Provence, Angers, Bordeaux, Châlons-en-Champagne, Chalon-sur-Saône, Chambéry, Cluny, Lille and Metz. ENSAM institutes in Bastia and Chambéry

History: Founded 1780, became Ecole nationale supérieure 1963, Grande Ecole 1966, reorganized 1990. Acquired present title 2007.

Academic Year: September to June (September-February; March-June)

Admission Requirements: Competitive entrance examination following 2 yrs further study after secondary school certificate (baccalauréat) or following first university qualification (DUT, BTS, Maîtrise), or equivalent

Main Language(s) of Instruction: French

International Co-operation: With institutions in China; Canada; Brazil; Mexico; Morocco. Also participates in Erasmus. Is a member of the ParisTech graduate and research programme.

Degrees and Diplomas: *Diplôme d'Ingénieur*: Applied Arts and Trades, 3 yrs; *Mastère spécialisé*: 1 yr following Diplôme; *Diplôme national de Master*; *Doctorat (PhD)*: 2-4 yrs following Master. Masters recherche

Student Services: Academic counselling, Canteen, Employment services, Foreign student adviser, Language programs, Social counselling, Sports facilities

Student Residential Facilities: For c. 3,500 students

Special Facilities: Multimedia Centre in Cluny (Chalon-sur-Saône)

Libraries: Paris, 15,000 vols; Aix-en-Provence, 6,000; Angers, 20,000; Bordeaux, 3,100; Châlons-en-Champagne, 2,500; Cluny, 4,500; Lille, 5,000; Metz, 1,000

Last Updated: 23/02/12

ENSBA - PARIS

Ecole nationale supérieure des Beaux-Arts (ENSBA)
14, rue Bonaparte, 75272 Paris, Cedex 06
Tel: +33(1) 47-03-50-00
Fax: +33(1) 47-03-50-80
EMail: info@ensba.fr
Website: http://www.ensba.fr

Directeur: Nicolas Bourriaud (2011-)

Schools

Fine Arts (Design; Fine Arts; Graphic Arts; Graphic Design; Printing and Printmaking) *Directeur:* Henry-Claude Cousseau

History: Founded 1648 as Academy. Acquired present name 1816 and status 1984. A public 'Grande Ecole'.

Governing Bodies: Conseil d'Administration

Academic Year: October to June

Admission Requirements: School jury selection and entrance exam.

Fees: (Euros): 252 per annum

Main Language(s) of Instruction: French

International Co-operation: With universities in the USA, Canada, Australia, Bosnia-Herzegovine, Brazil, Korea, Cuba, Ghana, India, Israel, Japan, Lebanon, Switzerland, Thailand. Also participates in the Erasmus/Socrates Programmes.

Accrediting Agencies: Ministry of Culture

Degrees and Diplomas: *Licence*; *Diplôme national de Master*. Diplôme national supérieur d'artsplastiques (Dnsap)

Student Services: Employment services, Foreign student adviser, Foreign Studies Centre, Health services, Language programs, Social counselling, Sports facilities

Publications: Journal des Beaux-Arts *(monthly)*
Last Updated: 30/06/11

ENSEA

Ecole nationale supérieure de l'Electronique et de ses Applications (ENSEA)
6, avenue du Ponceau, 95014 Cergy-Pontoise, Cedex
Tel: +33(1) 30-73-66-66
Fax: +33(1) 30-73-66-67
EMail: directeur@ensea.fr
Website: http://www.ensea.fr

Directeur: Pierre Pouvil (1993-)
Tel: +33(1) 30-73-62-15 EMail: pouvil@ensea.fr

International Relations: Christian Faye
Tel: +33(1) 30-73-62-34 EMail: faye@ensea.fr

Departments

Automation (Automation and Control Engineering); **Computer Science and Digital Technology** (Computer Science); **Electronics and Physics** (Electronic Engineering; Physics); **Humanities** (Communication Studies; Economics; English; German; Spanish); **Signals and Telecommunications** (Mathematics; Telecommunications Engineering)

History: Founded 1952. Moved to Cergy-Pontoise 1977.

Academic Year: September to June (September- January; February-June)

Admission Requirements: Competitive entrance examination following 2-3 yrs further study after secondary school certificate (baccalauréat) or following first university qualification (DUT or BTS), or equivalent

Fees: (Euros): Engineer course, 750 per annum

Main Language(s) of Instruction: French
International Co-operation: With institutions in 35 countries

Degrees and Diplomas: *Diplôme d'Ingénieur.* Electronics, 3 yrs; *Mastère spécialisé*; *Diplôme national de Master.* Electronics; Image and Signal Processing, a further yr
Last Updated: 30/06/11

ENSM-SAINT ETIENNE

Ecole nationale supérieure des Mines de Saint-Etienne (ENSM SAINT-ETIENNE)
158, cours Fauriel, 42023 Saint-Etienne, Cedex 02
Tel: +33(4) 77-42-01-23
Fax: +33(4) 77-42-00-00
EMail: inform@emse.fr
Website: http://www.emse.fr

Directeur: Philippe Jamet (2008-2013) EMail: begon@emse.fr

International Relations: Michel Cournil
Tel: +33(4) 77-49-97-28 EMail: cournil@emse.fr

Institutes

Henri Fayol (Computer Science; Environmental Engineering; Industrial Engineering)

Programmes

Electronical Engineering (*Georges Charpak Centre in Provence*) (Electronic Engineering; Microelectronics); **Engineering Sciences for Health** (Engineering); **Materials Science and Mechanical Engineering** (Materials Engineering; Mechanical Engineering)

Schools

Applied Microelectronics (*ISMEA*); **Industrial Techniques** (Computer Science; Electronic Engineering; Industrial Engineering); **Microelectronics Engineering** (Microelectronics); **Software Engineering** (Software Engineering)

History: Founded 1816. Acquired present status 1991.

Admission Requirements: Competitive entrance examination following 2 yrs further study after secondary school certificate (baccalauréat)

Fees: (Euros): Civil Engineering course, 400 per annum, Mastère spécialisé, 6,000-10,000 depending on course; Doctoral programme, 190

Main Language(s) of Instruction: French

International Co-operation: With universities in USA, Canada, Germany, United Kingdom, Spain, Italy, China, Russian Federation, Brazil and Chile.

Degrees and Diplomas: *Diplôme d'Ingénieur.* 3 yrs; *Mastère spécialisé*: 1 further yr; *Doctorat*: 3 yrs

Student Services: Academic counselling, Cultural centre, Employment services, Foreign student adviser, Handicapped facilities, Health services, Language programs, Social counselling, Sports facilities

Special Facilities: Science and Technology Centre

Libraries: c. 40,000 vols
Last Updated: 12/05/11

ENSTA - BRETAGNE

Ecole nationale supérieure de Techniques Avancées Bretagne
2, rue François Verny, 29806 Brest, Cedex 9
Tel: +33(2) 98-34-88-00
Fax: +33(2) 98-34-88-46
EMail: ingrid.le_toutouze@ensta-bretagne.fr
Website: http://www.ensta-bretagne.fr

Directeur: Francis Jouanjean
Tel: +33(2) 98-34-88-34 EMail: directeur@ensta-bretagne.fr

Departments

Electronics, Automatics, Computer Science (Automation and Control Engineering; Computer Engineering; Computer Science; Electronic Engineering; Power Engineering); **Mechanics** (Mechanical Engineering)

Programmes

Detection and Information Systems (Electronic Engineering; Information Technology; Marine Engineering; Nautical Science); **Energy Materials** (Energy Engineering); **Hydrographic and Cartographic Engineering**; **Mechanics, Automatics** (Mechanical Engineering); **Naval Architecture** (Naval Architecture)

History: Founded 1971as ENSIETA. Acquired present status and title 2010. A public 'Grande Ecole'.

Governing Bodies: Conseil d'Administration

Academic Year: September to June

Admission Requirements: Competitive entrance examination following 2-3 yrs further study after secondary school certificate (baccalauréat) or equivalent

Fees: (Euros): Engineer course 398 per annum, master 6,500-7,500 per course

Main Language(s) of Instruction: French

Accrediting Agencies: Commission des Titres d'Ingénieurs (Engineer Course); Conférence des Grandes Ecoles (Master Courses)

Degrees and Diplomas: *Diplôme d'Ingénieur*: 3 yrs; *Mastère spécialisé*: Pyrotechnics and Propulsion; Automotive Engineering, 1 yr; *Diplôme national de Master*: Naval Architecture; Hydrography, 1 1/2 yr

Student Services: Academic counselling, Canteen, Employment services, Foreign student adviser, Language programs, Sports facilities

Student Residential Facilities: For c. 360 students

Special Facilities: Language Multimedia Laboratory

Libraries: Médiathèque, c. 10,000 vols
Last Updated: 30/06/11

ENSTA-PARIS TECH

Ecole nationale supérieure de Techniques avancées (ENSTA PARIS TECH)
32, Boulevard Victor, 75739 Paris
Tel: +33(1) 45-52-54-01
Fax: +33(1) 45-52-55-87
EMail: communication@ensta.fr
Website: http://www.ensta-paristech.fr

Directeur: Yves Demay
Tel: +33(1) 45-52-44-01, Fax: +33(1) 45-52-59-54

Secrétaire générale: Lise Guénot Tel: +33(1) 45-52-54-03

International Relations: Christophe de Beauvais
Tel: +33(1) 45-52-54-07 EMail: International@ensta.fr

Departments

Applied Economics (Economics); **Applied Mathematics** *(UMA-Unité d'Enseignement et de Recherche en Mathématiques Appliquées)* (Applied Mathematics; Automation and Control Engineering; Mathematics); **Chemical Engineering** *(UCP- Unité d'Enseignement et de Recherche en Chimie et Procédés)* (Chemical Engineering; Organic Chemistry); **Electronics and Computer Science** *(UEI-Unité d'Enseignement et de Recherche en Electronique et Informatique)* (Computer Science; Electronic Engineering; Telecommunications Engineering); **Mechanics** *(UME- Unité d'Enseignement et de Recherche en Mécanique)* (Marine Science and Oceanography; Materials Engineering; Mechanical Engineering; Naval Architecture; Nuclear Engineering)

Laboratories

Applied Optics *(LOA)* (Optical Technology)

History: Founded 1741 as École du Génie Maritime. Changed name to ENSTA 1970.

Governing Bodies: Director; Administrative Board

Academic Year: September to June

Admission Requirements: Competitive entrance examination following 2 yrs further study after secondary school certificate (baccalauréat). Also French Maitrise (4yrs higher education) or foreign equivalent (BSc)

Fees: (Euros): Diplôme d'Ingénieur, 430 per annum; Master, 11,000; Mastère spécialisé, 9,200

Main Language(s) of Instruction: French

International Co-operation: With universities in Spain, Italy, Germany, Sweden, Norway, USA, Finland; Canada; Hungary; Czech Republic; Russian Federation; China; Romania; Austria; Portugal; Australia; Brazil

Degrees and Diplomas: *Diplôme d'Ingénieur*: General Engineering, 3 yrs; *Mastère spécialisé*: Naval Engineering, Information Systems; Naval Architecture and Offshore; Information Systems, a further 1 yr; *Diplôme national de Master*: Advanced Technologies in Materials and Structures, 2 yrs; *Doctorat (PhD)*: 3 yrs

Student Services: Academic counselling, Canteen, Employment services, Foreign student adviser, Foreign Studies Centre, Handicapped facilities, Language programs, Social counselling, Sports facilities

Student Residential Facilities: Yes

Libraries: Centre de Documentation, 28,000 vols

Press or Publishing House: Service Edition de l'ENSTA
Last Updated: 30/06/11

ENTPE - VAULX-EN-VELIN

Ecole nationale des Travaux publics de l'Etat (ENTPE)
Rue Maurice Audin, BP 2, 69518 Vaulx-en-Velin
Tel: +33(4) 72-04-70-70
Fax: +33(4) 72-04-62-54
EMail: jean-pierre.rajot@entpe.fr
Website: http://www.entpe.fr

Directeur: Jean-Baptiste Lesort (2010-)
EMail: jean-baptiste.lesort@entpe.fr

Departments

Civil and Construction Engineering (Civil Engineering; Construction Engineering; Materials Engineering); **Town and Environment** (Biological and Life Sciences; Ecology; Urban Studies); **Transport** (Transport Engineering; Transport Management)

History: Founded 1953.

Governing Bodies: Conseil de Perfectionnement; Conseil scientifique

Academic Year: September to June (September-December; January-March; April-June)

Admission Requirements: Competitive entrance examination following 3 yrs further study after secondary school certificate (baccalauréat). Direct entrance to second and third yr following appropriate university degree (Maîtrise)

Fees: (Euros): 379 per annum

Main Language(s) of Instruction: French

Accrediting Agencies: ministre de l'Ecologie, de l'Energie du Développement durable et de la Mer (MEEDDM), habilité depuis 1972 par la Commission du Titre d'Ingénieur (CTI)

Degrees and Diplomas: *Diplôme d'Ingénieur*: 3 yrs; *Diplôme national de Master*: 1 yr following Ingénieur; *Doctorat*: 3-4 yrs following DEA. Masters recherche, Masters professionnel

Student Services: Academic counselling, Canteen, Employment services, Foreign student adviser, Handicapped facilities, Health services, Social counselling, Sports facilities

Student Residential Facilities: For c. 30 students
Last Updated: 27/06/11

EP - PALAISEAU

Ecole polytechnique (EP/X)
Route de Saclay, 91128 Palaiseau, Cedex
Tel: +33 (1) 69-33-33-33
Fax: +33 (1) 69-33-30-40
EMail: dre@polytechnique.edu
Website: http://www.polytechnique.edu

Directeur général: Xavier Michel
Tel: +33 (1) 69-33-40-01 EMail: xavier.michel@polytechnique.edu

Secretary-General: Marcel Belloc
Tel: +33 (1) 69-33-40-04 EMail: marcel.belloc@polytechnique.edu

International Relations: Elisabeth Crepon
Tel: +33(1) 69-33-39-40
EMail: Elisabeth.crepon@polytechnique.edu

Departments

Applied Mathematics (Applied Mathematics); **Biology** (Biology; Cell Biology; Molecular Biology); **Chemistry** (Chemistry) *Head*: Sam Zard; **Computer Science** (Computer Science) *Head*: Jean-Marc Steyaert; **Economics** (Economics); **Foreign Languages, Cultures and Communication** (Communication Studies; Cultural Studies; Modern Languages); **Humanities and Social Sciences** (Anthropology; Arts and Humanities; Demography and Population; Economics; Law; Linguistics; Management; Social Sciences; Sociology); **Mathematics** (Mathematics); **Mechanical Engineering** (Mechanical Engineering); **Physics** (Physics)

Research Laboratories

Applied Epistemology (Philosophy); **Applied Mathematics** (Applied Mathematics); **Applied Optics** (Optics); **Biochemistry**; **Computer Science** (Computer Science); **Condensed Matter Physics** (Physics); **Economics and Management Research** (Economics; Management); **Hydrodynamics** (Hydraulic Engineering); **Irradiated Solids**; **Leprince-Ringuet** (Nuclear Physics); **Mathematics** (*Laurent Schwartz*) (Mathematics); **Meteorology** (Meteorology); **Optics and Biosciences** (Biology; Optics); **Organic Synthesis**; **Particle Physics and Astrophysics** (Astrophysics; Physics); **Physics of Interfaces and Thin Films** (Physics); **Plasma Physics** (Physics); **Solids Mechanics** (Physics); **Use of Intense Lasers** (Laser Engineering)

History: Founded 1794 during the French Revolution. Its main missions are: to prepare students to assume positions of responsibility and leadership in industry, business, government and research; and, to develop the most advanced research. It recruits prestigious and diverse faculty from the academic, research, government and industrial world.

Governing Bodies: Conseil d'administration

Academic Year: September to July

Admission Requirements: Ingénieur Polytechnicien curriculum: Competitive entrance examination following 2-3 yrs university level studies in Sciences after secondary school certificate (baccalauréat), or equivalent. Master of Science: Students must hold a Bachelor's degree; PhD programme: students must hold a Master of Science by Research degree and obtain prior approval of a thesis director and of the director of host laboratory

Fees: (Euros): Ph.D. programme, c. 220 per annum; Master programme, 440-11,000 depending on the duration of the programme; Ingénieur Polytechnicien, 22,000 per annum

Main Language(s) of Instruction: French

International Co-operation: With universities in Brazil, Chile, Japan, Italy, Spain, Sweden, United Kingdom, Norway, Canada, Germany, Singapore, USA.

Degrees and Diplomas: *Diplôme national de Master*: 2 yrs; *Doctorat*: 3-4 yrs of research. Diplôme de l'Ecole Polytechnique: Engineering, 6 yrs (2 yrs of preparatory classes and 4 yrs at Ecole Polytechnique)

Student Services: Academic counselling, Canteen, Cultural centre, Employment services, Foreign student adviser, Foreign Studies Centre, Handicapped facilities, Health services, Language programs, Social counselling, Sports facilities

Student Residential Facilities: Yes

Libraries: Bibliothèque centrale, 300,000 vols

Publications: La Jaune et la Rouge *(monthly)*; X-Passion *(3 per annum)*

Last Updated: 01/07/11

EPHE - PARIS

Ecole pratique des Hautes Etudes (EPHE)
46, rue de Lille, 75007 Paris
Tel: +33(1) 53-63-61-20
Fax: +33(1) 53-63-61-94
EMail: presidence.ephe@ephe.sorbonne.fr
Website: http://www.ephe.sorbonne.fr

Président: Jean-Claude Waquet
Tel: +33(1) 53-63-61-63, Fax: +33(1) 53-63-61-94
EMail: beatrice.argant@ephe.sorbonne.fr

Directrice générale des services: Nicole Dairé
Tel: +33(1) 53-63-61-75, Fax: +33(1) 53-63-61-92
EMail: nicole.daire@ephe.sorbonne.fr

International Relations: Laurence Fabrolot
Tel: +33(1) 53-63-61-80, Fax: +33(1) 53-63-61-97

Institutes

Ageing *(Transdisciplinary)* (Gerontology); **Pacific Coral Reefs** (Coastal Studies); **Religious Sciences** *(European, Institut Européen en Sciences des Religions (IESR))* (Religious Studies)

Sections

History and Philology (Ancient Civilizations; Archaeology; Art History; Asian Studies; History; Linguistics; Middle Eastern Studies; Philology); **Life and Earth Sciences** (Biological and Life Sciences; Cell Biology; Earth Sciences; Ecology; Environmental Studies; Molecular Biology; Neurosciences); **Religious Sciences** (Asian Religious Studies; Christian Religious Studies; Islamic Theology; Judaic Religious Studies; Religious Studies)

History: Founded 1868 by Victor Duruy, a centre of postgraduate education and research at the highest level.

Governing Bodies: Scientific Board; Board of Administration

Academic Year: October to September

Admission Requirements: University degree

Fees: (Euros): c. 460 per annum

Main Language(s) of Instruction: French

International Co-operation: With universities in Europe and North America; China. Japan; India; Central Asia; Mediterranean countries. Also participates in Erasmus

Degrees and Diplomas: *Diplôme national de Master; Doctorat*: 4 yrs; *Habilitation à Diriger les Recherches*. Also Diplômes de l'EPHE

Student Services: Academic counselling, Foreign student adviser, Handicapped facilities, Language programs

Libraries: Two libraries, one for the History and Philology sections and one for the Religious Sciences section

Publications: Hautes Etudes du Monde Gréco-Romain; Hautes Etudes Médiévales et Modernes; Hautes Etudes Orientales; Histoire et Civilisation du Livre; Publications of the Sections
Last Updated: 01/07/11

ESIGETEL

Ecole supérieure d'Ingénieurs en Informatique et Génie des Télécommunications (ESIGETEL)
1, rue des Port de Valvins, 77215 Avon, Cedex
Tel: +33(1) 60-72-70-51
Fax: +33(1) 60-72-11-32
EMail: info@esigetel.fr
Website: http://www.esigetel.fr

Directeur: Eric Parlebas EMail: eric.parlebas@esigetel.fr

Programmes

Telecommunications and Computer Engineering (Computer Engineering; Electronic Engineering; Telecommunications Engineering)

Main Language(s) of Instruction: French

Degrees and Diplomas: *Brevet de Technicien supérieur; Licence; Diplôme d'Ingénieur*. Also Master
Last Updated: 04/07/11

ESM-SAINT-CYR

Ecole spéciale militaire de St Cyr (ESM SAINT-CYR)
56381 Coëtquidan, Cedex
Tel: +33(2) 97-70-72-99
Fax: +33(2) 97-79-75-87
EMail: dircom@st-cyr.terre.defense.gouv.fr
Website: http://www.st-cyr.terre.defense.gouv.fr

Directeur: Eric Bonnemaison

Programmes

Engineering (Engineering); **International Relations and Strategy** (International Relations); **Military Studies** (Military Science)

History: Founded 1802. Moved to Britanny 1945.

Admission Requirements: Competitive entrance examination following 2-3 yrs further study after secondary school certificate (baccalauréat) or following first university qualification (DEUG, DUT or BTS), or equivalent

Main Language(s) of Instruction: French

Degrees and Diplomas: *Diplôme d'Etat*; *Diplôme national de Master*

Last Updated: 01/07/11

ESPCI PARISTECH

Ecole supérieure de Physique et de Chimie industrielles de la Ville de Paris (ESPCI PARISTECH)
10, rue Vauquelin, 75005 Paris, Cedex 05
Tel: +33(1) 40-79-44-00
Fax: +33(1) 40-79-44-25
EMail: contact@espci.fr
Website: http://www.espci.fr

Directeur: Jacques Prost (2003-)
Tel: +33(1) 40-79-45-00, Fax: +33(1) 45-35-14-74
EMail: Jacques.Prost@espci.fr

Secrétaire Général: François Fuseau
Tel: +33(1) 40-79-44-04, Fax: +33(1) 43-31-42-22

Laboratories

Applied Statistics (Statistics) *Head*: Léon Personnaz; **Biology** (Neurosciences) *Head*: Jean Rossier; **Colloids and Divided Materials** *Head*: Jérome Bibette; **Electromagnetism and General Electronics** (Electrical and Electronic Engineering) *Head*: Jacques Lewiner; **Electronics** (Applied Mathematics; Electronic Engineering) *Head*: Gerard Dreyfus; **Environment and Analytical Chemistry** (Chemistry); **Hydrodynamics and Physical Mechanics** (Hydraulic Engineering; Physical Engineering); **Microfluids, MEMS and Nanostructures**; **Organic Chemistry** (Chemistry); **Physical Chemistry of Macromolecules** (Organic Chemistry; Physical Chemistry); **Physical Optics** (Optics; Physical Engineering); **Polymer Physical Chemistry and Spectroscopy** (Physical Chemistry); **Quantum Physics** (Mathematical Physics); **Soft Matter and Chemistry** (Chemistry); **Solid State Physics** (Solid State Physics); **Theoretical Chemical Physics** (Chemical Engineering); **Thermal Physics** (Thermal Physics); **Waves and Acoustics** (Microwaves; Sound Engineering (Acoustics))

History: Founded 1882. A 'Grande Ecole'.

Academic Year: September to June

Admission Requirements: Competitive entrance examination following 2 yrs preparatory classes

Fees: (Euros): 150 per annum

Main Language(s) of Instruction: French

International Co-operation: United Kingdom, Spain, Norway, Belgium, Netherlands and China. Also participates in Erasmus

Accrediting Agencies: Commission des Titres de l'Ingénieur (CTI)

Degrees and Diplomas: *Diplôme d'Ingénieur*: Physics; Chemistry; Biology, 4 yrs; *Diplôme national de Master*: Bio-engineering; *Doctorat*. Masters professionnel

Student Services: Canteen, Language programs

Student Residential Facilities: Yes

Libraries: Yes
Last Updated: 04/07/11

EUROPEAN ART SCHOOLS OF BRITANNY

Ecole européenne supérieure d'art de Bretagne
8, esplanade François Mitterrand, 29000 Quimper
Tel: +33(2) 98-55-61-57
Fax: +33(2) 98-55-70-51
EMail: contact@esa-quimper.fr
Website: http://www.esa-quimper.fr

Directrice: Danièle Yvergniaux

Programmes

Visual Arts and Communication (Communication Arts; Design; Painting and Drawing; Visual Arts)

History: Founded 2011 following the merger of the art schools in Brest, Lorient, Quimper and Rennes.

Academic Year: September-May

Admission Requirements: Baccalauréat or equivalent secondary school exam. Entrance exam with a selection jury.

Main Language(s) of Instruction: French

Accrediting Agencies: Ministry of Culture and Communication

Degrees and Diplomas: Diplôme national d'arts plastiques (DNAP) 3 yrs; Diplôme national supérieur d'expression plastique (DNSEP) a further 2 yrs both in fields of Art and Communication.
Last Updated: 04/07/11

EUROPEAN SCHOOL OF VISUAL ARTS

Ecole européenne supérieure de l'Image (EESI)
134 rue de Bordeaux, 16000 Angoulême
Tel: +33(5) 45-92-66-02
EMail: direction.generale@eesi.eu
Website: http://www.eesi.eu

Directrice générale: Sabrina Grassi-Fossier (2005-)

Programmes

Design and Art (Design; Fine Arts; Visual Arts)

Further Information: Has a second site in Poitiers.

History: Founded 1995.

Admission Requirements: Baccalauréat or equivalent secondary school exam. Entrance exam with a selection jury.

Main Language(s) of Instruction: French

Accrediting Agencies: Ministry of Culture and Communication

Degrees and Diplomas: *Diplôme national de Master*: Digital Art, 2 yrs following DNAP; *Doctorat*: Digital Art. Diplome national d'arts plastiques (DNAP) 3 yrs; Diplome national supérieur d'expression plastique (DNSEP, speciality in digital art) a further 2 yrs; Masters recherche (digital art)
Last Updated: 30/10/07

FÉLIX CICCOLINI ART SCHOOL OF AIX EN PROVENCE

Ecole supérieure d'Art Félix Ciccolini d'Aix-en-Provence
1 rue Émile Tavan, 13100 Aix-en-Provence
Tel: +33(4) 42-91-88-70
Fax: +33(4) 42-91-88-69
EMail: secretariat@ecole-art-aix.fr
Website: http://www.ecole-art-aix.fr

Directeur: Jean-Paul Ponthot

International Relations: Julie Karsenty
EMail: karsenty@ecole-art-aix.fr

Programmes

Visual Arts (Visual Arts); **Visual Arts and Design** (Design; Graphic Design; Visual Arts)

Admission Requirements: Baccalauréat or equivalent secondary school exam. Entrance exam with a selection jury.

Fees: (Euros): 260 for local residents; 360 for EU citizens; 390 for other citizens.

Main Language(s) of Instruction: French

Accrediting Agencies: Ministry of Culture and Communication

Degrees and Diplomas: Diplome national d'arts plastiques (DNAP) 3 yrs; Diplome national supérieur d'expression plastique (DNSEP) a further 2 yrs, i.e. Master's Degree in Fine Arts
Last Updated: 17/05/11

FRENCH ARMY ENGINEERING SCHOOL

Ecole du Génie (ESAG)
BP 34125, 106, rue Eblé, 49041 Angers
Tel: +33(2) 41-24-82-99
Fax: +33(2) 41-24-83-39
EMail: oci@esag.terre.defense.gouv.fr
Website: http://www.genie-militaire.com/index_gen.html

Commandant: Francis Autran (2011-)
Tel: +33(2) 41-24-82-00
EMail: cabinet@esag.terre.defense.gouv.fr

Divisions

Military Engineering (Engineering; Military Science)

History: Founded 1771 as Ecole royale du génie de Mézières. Acquired present status and title 2009.

Admission Requirements: 2 yrs university science studies plus service as army officer

Fees: None

Main Language(s) of Instruction: French

Accrediting Agencies: C.T.I., Ministry of Defence

Degrees and Diplomas: *Diplôme d'Ingénieur*: Army Engineering (BTP), 2 yrs; *Mastère spécialisé*: Infrastructure Engineering

Special Facilities: Laboratories
Last Updated: 26/01/12

FRENCH INSTITUTE FOR ADVANCED MECHANICS

Institut français de Mécanique avancée (IFMA)
BP 265, Campus de Clermont-Ferrand/Les Cézeaux,
63175 Aubière
Tel: +33(4) 73-28-80-00
Fax: +33(4) 73-28-81-00
EMail: direction@ifma.fr
Website: http://www.ifma.fr

Directeur: Pascal Ray
Tel: +33(4) 73-28-80-01 EMail: Pascal.Ray@ifma.fr

Secrétaire Général: Frantz Hurtebise
Tel: +33(4) 73-28-80-09 EMail: Frantz.Hurtebise@ifma.fr

International Relations: Christophe Caux
Tel: +33(4) 73-28-80-08 EMail: Christophe.Caux@ifma.fr

Divisions
Advanced Mechanical Engineering (Civil Engineering; Mechanical Engineering)

History: Founded 1993.

Governing Bodies: Conseil d'Administration

Admission Requirements: Competitive entrance examination following 2 yrs further study after secondary school certificate (baccalauréat) or equivalent

Fees: (Euros): Engineer diploma course none, Mastère, 7,200 per annum

Main Language(s) of Instruction: French

International Co-operation: With universities in Brazil; Japan. Also participates in Erasmus

Accrediting Agencies: Ministry of Higher Education, Commission des Titres d'Ingénieur

Degrees and Diplomas: *Diplôme d'Ingénieur*: 3 yrs + 1 yr abroad; *Mastère spécialisé*; *Diplôme national de Master*

Student Services: Academic counselling, Canteen, Cultural centre, Employment services, Foreign student adviser, Foreign Studies Centre, Handicapped facilities, Health services, Language programs, Social counselling, Sports facilities

Student Residential Facilities: Yes

Special Facilities: Movie Studio. Multimedia Facilities. Television Satellite Network

Libraries: Campus Main Library; Institute Library
Last Updated: 05/07/11

FRENCH NAVAL ACADEMY

Ecole navale (EN)
Lanvéoc Poulmic, BP 600, 29240 Brest
Tel: +33(2) 98-23-40-00
Fax: +33(2) 98-23-40-49
EMail: econav@ecole-navale.fr
Website: http://www.ecole-navale.fr

Commandant: Marc de Briançon (2009-)
Tel: +33(2) 98-23-40-01 EMail: amiral@ecole-navale.fr

International Relations: François Ceccaldi
Tel: +33(2) 98-23-42-62, Fax: +33(2) 98-23-39-51
EMail: dir-com@ecole-navale.fr

Divisions
Humanities and Management (Arts and Humanities; Management); **Maritime Studies** (Marine Transport); **Naval Studies** (Nautical Science)

Further Information: Has a research laboratory, IRENav

History: Founded 1830.

Admission Requirements: Competitive entrance examination following 2-3 yrs further study after secondary school certificate (baccalauréat)

Fees: (Euros): engineer courses, none, mastère 9,147 per annum

Main Language(s) of Instruction: French (English obligatory)

Accrediting Agencies: Commission des titres d'Ingénieurs

Degrees and Diplomas: *Diplôme d'Ingénieur*; *Mastère spécialisé*; *Diplôme national de Master*. Masters professionnel

Student Services: Canteen, Foreign student adviser
Last Updated: 30/06/11

GRADUATE ENGINEERING SCHOOL FOR INFORMATION AND COMMUNICATION TECHNOLOGIES - TELECOM PARIS TECH

Télécom Paris Tech
46, rue Barrault, 75634 Paris, Cedex 13
Tel: +33(1) 45-81-77-77
Fax: +33(1) 45-89-79-06
EMail: communication@telecom-paristech.fr
Website: http://www.telecom-paristech.fr

Directeur: Yves Poilane
Tel: +33(1) 45-81-73-99, Fax: +33(1) 45-89-54-42
EMail: yves.poilane@telecom-paristech.fr

International Relations: Jean-François Naviner
Tel: +33(1) 45-81-78-38
EMail: jean-francois.naviner@telecom-paristech.fr

Departments
Computer Science and Networks (Computer Networks; Computer Science); **Economics and Social Sciences** (Economics; Social Sciences); **Signal and Image Processing** (Electrical and Electronic Engineering; Telecommunications Engineering)

History: Founded 1878. Acquired present status 2007.

Academic Year: September to July

Admission Requirements: Competitive entrance examination following 2-3 yrs further study after secondary school certificate (baccalauréat) or following first university qualification (Licence/Master)

Fees: (Euros): Diplôme d'Ingénieur, 1,144 per annum; Advanced Master, 7,500-16,000; Master of Science, 10,000

Main Language(s) of Instruction: French or English (Sophia Antipolis)

Accrediting Agencies: Commission des Titres d'Ingénieur

Degrees and Diplomas: *Diplôme d'Ingénieur*: 3 yrs; *Mastère spécialisé*; *Diplôme national de Master*; *Doctorat*: 3 yrs

Student Services: Academic counselling, Canteen, Employment services, Foreign student adviser, Foreign Studies Centre, Handicapped facilities, Language programs, Social counselling, Sports facilities

Student Residential Facilities: For 527 students.

Libraries: Centre de Documentation
Last Updated: 17/06/11

GRENOBLE I UNIVERSITY

Université Joseph Fourier (Grenoble I) (UJF)
BP 53, Domaine universitaire St Martin d'Hères, 621, Avenue Centrale, 38041 Grenoble, Cedex 09
Tel: +33(4) 76-51-46-00
Fax: +33(4) 76-51-48-48
EMail: dgs@ujf-grenoble.fr
Website: http://www.ujf-grenoble.fr

Président: Farid Ouabdesselam (2007-)
Tel: +33(4) 76-51-47-02, Fax: +33(4) 76-51-44-10
EMail: presidence@ujf-grenoble.fr; christine.chaubet@ujf-grenoble.fr

Directeur général des Services: Jean-Luc Argentier
Tel: +33(4) 76-51-48-20

International Relations: Eric Beaugnon
Tel: +33(4) 76-51-45-13, Fax: +33(4) 76-51-42-52
EMail: relations.internationales@ujf-grenoble.fr;
Eric.Beaugnon@grenoble.cnrs.fr

Centres
Drôme-Ardèche *(Valence)* (Natural Sciences; Physical Education; Tourism) *Director*: Isabelle Colomb de Daunant

Departments
Science and Technology *(DLST Offers undergraduate degrees)* (Applied Mathematics; Biological and Life Sciences; Chemistry; Earth Sciences; Physics)

Graduate Schools
Chemistry and Life Sciences (Biological and Life Sciences; Chemistry; Microbiology); **Computer Science** *(MSTII in collaboration with Institut National Polytechnique de Grenoble)* (Mathematics and Computer Science); **Earth, Astronomy and Environment** *(In collaboration with Institut National Polytechnique de Grenoble)* (Earth Sciences; Geography; Marine Science and Oceanography; Meteorology); **Electrical and Electronic Engineering** *(EEATS In collaboration with Institut National Polytechnique de Grenoble)* (Automation and Control Engineering; Electrical and Electronic Engineering; Microelectronics; Telecommunications Engineering); **Health Engineering** *(EDISCE)* (Biomedicine; Cognitive Sciences; Health Sciences); **Humanities and Political Science** *(In collaboration with University Pierre Mendes-France)*; **Physics** *(In collaboration with Institut National Polytechnique de Grenoble)* (Astrophysics; Atomic and Molecular Physics; Physics)

Institutes
Engineering *(IUT Grenoble I with a second site at Isle d'Abeau)* (Chemical Engineering; Civil Engineering; Computer Engineering; Computer Networks; Electrical Engineering; Energy Engineering; Mechanical Engineering; Physical Engineering; Production Engineering; Technology; Telecommunications Engineering) *Director*: Jean-Michel Terriez; **Industrial, Materials, Mechanical and Process Engineering** *(I-MEP2 in collaboration with Institut National Polytechnique de Grenoble)* (Industrial Engineering; Materials Engineering; Mechanical Engineering; Production Engineering); **Teacher Training** *(IUFM in partnership with Grenoble I)* (Teacher Trainers Education; Teacher Training); **Technological** *(IUT Grenoble I)* (Chemical Engineering; Civil Engineering; Computer Engineering; Computer Networks; Electrical Engineering; Energy Engineering; Mechanical Engineering; Physical Engineering; Production Engineering; Technology; Telecommunications Engineering)

Schools
Engineering *(Polytech' Grenoble)* (Computer Networks; Geological Engineering; Industrial Engineering; Information Technology; Materials Engineering; Multimedia)

Units
Biology (Biochemistry; Biology; Botany; Cell Biology; Ecology; Genetics; Microbiology; Molecular Biology; Neurosciences; Physiology); **Chemistry** (Analytical Chemistry; Chemistry; Inorganic Chemistry; Organic Chemistry; Physical Chemistry); **Computer Science, Mathematics and Applied Mathematics** *(IMAG)* (Applied Mathematics; Artificial Intelligence; Computer Science; Operations Research; Systems Analysis); **Earth and Space Sciences** *(OSUG)* (Astronomy and Space Science; Geology; Geophysics; Seismology); **Geography** (Geography; Mountain Studies; Regional Planning); **Medicine** *(La Tronche)* (Medicine; Surgery); **Pharmacy** *(La Tronche)* (Pharmacology; Pharmacy); **Physical Education and Sport** *(APS)* (Physical Education; Sports; Sports Management); **Physics, Engineering, Earth and Environmental Sciences, Mechanics** *(PHITEM)* (Applied Physics; Atomic and Molecular Physics; Civil Engineering; Geological Engineering; Mechanical Engineering; Nuclear Physics; Optics; Physics; Solid State Physics)

History: Founded 1970 under the 1968 law reforming higher education as one of three Universities replacing former Université de Grenoble. Founded 1339 and confirmed by Papal Bull. Suppressed by the Revolution, replaced by Faculties of Law; Letters; and Science. Reconstituted as University 1896. A State institution enjoying academic and financial autonomy, operated under the jurisdiction of the Minister of Education and financed by the State.

Governing Bodies: Conseil d'administration, including elected representatives of teaching staff, research workers, students and administrative and technical staff, as well as non-university members drawn from the public and private sectors; Conseil of each Unit, comprising representatives of its teaching staff, research workers, students, and administrative and technical staff; and Conseil scientifique, competent in matters of research. The President is elected by the Conseil d'Administration for one non-renewable five-year term

Academic Year: September to June (September-December; January-June)

Admission Requirements: 1st year: Secondary school certificate (baccalauréat) or foreign equivalent, or special entrance examination. For later years by individual application examined by validation committee

Fees: (Euros): Undergraduates, c. 195 per annum; graduates, c. 255 per annum; Engineering, 575 per annum

Main Language(s) of Instruction: French

International Co-operation: With universities in Europe; North America; Asia. Also participates in ERASMUS coordinates one Master ERASMUS MUNDUS and participates in two others; Ontario-Rhône-Alpes Programme; CREPUQ Programme 8 (Japan); TASSEP (USA and Canada); EAP (California)

Degrees and Diplomas: *Diplôme universitaire de Technologie*: Chemistry, Civil Engineering, Communications and Networks, Electrical Engineering, Mechanical and Production Engineering, Physical Engineering, Telecommunications, Thermal and Energy Engineering, 2 yrs; *Licence*: Physical Education and Sports, Geography; Science and Technology, Biology, Chemistry, Computer Science, Earth Sciences, Mathematics, Mechanical Engineering, Electrical Engineering, Physics, 3 yrs; *Licence professionnelle*: Regional Planning, Environment, Food-processing Industries, Animal Biotechnology, Health, Networks and Telecommunications, Electricity and Electronics, Industrial Production, Energy and Thermal Engineering, Building and Construction, 1 yr (selection after first two years of higher education); *Diplôme d'Etat*: Medicine; Pharmacy, 6 yrs; *Diplôme d'Ingénieur*: Electrical and Electronical Engineering; Telecommunications Engineering, 3 yrs following successful completion of 2 yrs of higher education; *Diplôme d'Ingénieur*: Geotechnical Engineering; Materials Engineering; Safety Engineering, 3 years following successful completion of 2 yrs of higher education; *Diplôme national de Master*: Science; Technology; Health; Sports; Mathematics; Computer Science, 2 yrs following Licence; *Doctorat*: Chemistry and Life Sciences; Health Engineering; Cognitive Sciences; Environmental Studies; Mathematics; Computer Science; Physics; Earth and Space Sciences; Electronics; Telecommunications; Materials and Process Engineering; Mechanics; Geography, 3 yrs following Master. Numerous Certificates of Specialization in Medicine

Student Services: Academic counselling, Canteen, Foreign student adviser, Handicapped facilities, Health services, Social counselling, Sports facilities

Student Residential Facilities: Cité universitaire

Special Facilities: Observatory.60 research laboratories

Libraries: c. 355,000 vols, 1,500 periodicals, 5,600 electronic periodicals and 40,000 theses, and specialized resource libraries in departments
Last Updated: 10/06/11

GRENOBLE II UNIVERSITY
Université Pierre-Mendès-France (Grenoble II)
BP 47, 151, rue des Universités, 38040 Cédex 9 Grenoble
Tel: +33(4) 76-82-54-00
Fax: +33(4) 76-82-56-54
EMail: communication@upmf-grenoble.fr;
accueil@upmf-grenoble.fr
Website: http://www.upmf-grenoble.fr

Président: Alain Spalanzani (2002-)
Tel: +33(4) 76-82-55-74, Fax: +33(4) 76-82-58-54
EMail: presidence@upmf-grenoble.fr

Secrétaire Général: Franck Lenoir
EMail: Franck.Lenoir@upmf-grenoble.fr

International Relations: Jacques Fontanel
Tel: +33(4) 76-82-59-60, Fax: +33(4) 38-49-84-51
EMail: Jacques.Fontanel@upmf-grenoble.fr

Centres
Library, Documentation and Books *(Médiat is an interuniversity centre providing services to partner Universities Grenoble III, Lyon I, II and III)*

Faculties
Economics *(Grenoble)* (Business and Commerce; Economics; International Business; Management; Regional Planning; Social

Policy); **Law** *(Also in Valence)* (Commercial Law; European Union Law; Human Rights; International Law; Law; Private Law; Public Law)

Graduate Schools

Economics (Economics); **Health, Cognitive and Environmental Engineering** *(In collaboration with Universities Grenoble I and Savoie and Institut National Polytechnique de Grenoble)* (Cognitive Sciences; Environmental Engineering; Health Sciences; Psychology); **Humanities and Political Science** *(In collaboration with University Grenoble I)* (Political Sciences; Social Sciences); **Industrial Organisation and System Production** *(In partnership with Institut National Polytechnique de Grenoble)*; **Judical Studies** (Human Rights; Law; Public Administration); **Management** (Management); **Mathematics, Information Technology and Computer Science** *(ED MSTII in collaboration with Grenoble I and Savoie Universities and Institut National Polytechnique de Grenoble)* (Applied Mathematics; Mathematics; Mathematics and Computer Science); **Philosophy** *(In partnership with University Lyon I)*

Institutes

Business Administration *(IAE also in Valence)* (Business Administration); **Juridical Studies** *(IEJ)* (Law) *Director:* Michel Farge; **Mediat Rhône-Alpes** (Library Science); **Political Science** *(IEPG Science Po)* (Econometrics; Finance; Political Sciences; Public Administration; Social Studies); **Technology** *(IUT de Grenoble 2: second site at Vienne)* (Business Administration; Computer Science; Information Management; Sales Techniques; Technology); **Technology** *(IUT Valence)* (Administration; Business Administration; Computer Networks; Computer Science; Technology; Telecommunications Engineering); **Town Planning** *(UFR IUG)* (Town Planning; Urban Studies)

Units

Human and Social Sciences *(UFR SHS)* (Cognitive Sciences; Educational Sciences; Information Sciences; Psychology; Social Sciences; Sociology); **Humanities** *(UFR SH)* (Art History; Arts and Humanities; Geography (Human); History; Music; Philosophy)

History: Founded 1970 under the 1968 law reforming higher education as one of three Universities replacing former Université de Grenoble - founded 1339 and confirmed by Papal Bull. Suppressed by the Revolution, replaced by Faculties of Law; Letters; and Science. Reconstituted as University 1896. A State Institution enjoying academic and financial autonomy, operating under the jurisdiction of the Minister of Education and financed by the State.

Governing Bodies: Conseil d'Administration, including representatives of teaching staff, research workers, students, and administrative and technical staff, as well as non-university members drawn from the public and private sectors; Conseil scientifique, competent in matters of research; Conseil des Etudes et de la Vie universitaire; and Conseil of each Unit, comprising representatives of its teaching staff, research workers, students, and administrative and technical staff. The President is elected by the first three bodies. The Chancelier, who represents the Minister of Education, is the Recteur of the Académie de Grenoble

Academic Year: October to June (October-December; December-April; April-June)

Admission Requirements: Secondary school certificate (baccalauréat) or foreign equivalent, or special entrance examination

Main Language(s) of Instruction: French

Degrees and Diplomas: *Capacité en Droit; Diplôme universitaire de Technologie:* Computer Science, Statistics, Business Administration, Communication, Computer Science, Telecommunications, 2 yrs; *Licence:* Economics, Management, Educational Sciences, History of Art, History, Law, Music, Philosophy, Applied Mathematics, Psychology, Public Administration, Sociology, 3 yrs; *Licence professionnelle:* Biostatistics; Human Resources Management; Management; Information Systems, Health, Communication, Tourism, Economics, Documentation Techniques, 3 yrs; *Diplôme d'Etat:* Social Assistant, Educational Assistant, Accountancy; *Diplôme national de Master:* History, Art History, Psychology, Sociology, Educational Sciences, Urban Planning, Cognitive Sciences; Private Law, Public Law, International Law, European Law, International and Globalisation of Economics, Finance, Management, Marketing, Information Management; *Doctorat:* Clinical and Pathological Psychology, Cognitive Psychology, Cognitive Sciences, Computer Science Applied to Social Sciences, Economocs, Educational Sciences, Experimental Social Psychology, History, Human Rights,

Industrial Engineering; International Security and Defence, International Law, European Law, Criminal Law, Public Law, Private Law, Management, Mathematics Applied to Social Sciences, Philosophy, Political Science, Public Administration, Sociology, Town and Regional Planning, 2-4 yrs following Masters; *Certificat de Spécialité:* Management Psychology, Economics and Energy Policies. Masters de Recherche, Masters professionnel, Certificat d'université, Diplome de l'IEP

Student Services: Academic counselling, Canteen, Cultural centre, Foreign student adviser, Foreign Studies Centre, Handicapped facilities, Health services, Language programs, Social counselling, Sports facilities

Student Residential Facilities: Yes

Libraries: Central Library, c. 6,780 vols; specialized libraries, c. 110,000 vols

Publications: ARES-Sécurité Défense Internationale; Bulletin du Centre de Documentation départemental du Travail; Cahiers de l'Institut de Recherche Economique et de Planification; Cahiers de Philo; Cahiers de Sciences Economiques; Economie Appliquée; Les Cahiers de l'Espace Europe
Last Updated: 22/07/11

GRENOBLE III UNIVERSITY

Université Stendhal (Grenoble III)
BP 25, Domaine universitaire St. Martin d'Hyères, 38040 Grenoble, Cedex 09
Tel: +33(4) 76-82-43-00
Fax: +33(4) 76-82-41-85
EMail: nadia.samba@u-grenoble3.fr
Website: http://www.u-grenoble3.fr

Présidente: Lise Dumasy
Tel: +33(4) 76-82-43-01, Fax: +33(4) 76-82-43-84
EMail: presidence@u-grenoble3.fr

Directrice générale des Services: Martine Pevet
Tel: +33(4) 76-82-43-46 EMail: martine.pevet@u-grenoble3.fr

International Relations: François Mangenot
Tel: +33(4) 76-82-43-10, Fax: +33(4) 76-82-41-73
EMail: francois.mangenot@u-grenoble3.fr

Centres
French Studies *(CUEF)* (French) *Director:* Dominique Abry; **Stendhal** (English; German; Library Science; Literature; Spanish; Theatre)

Departments
Language Studies for Specialists in Other Disciplines *(LANSAD)* (Foreign Languages Education; Teacher Trainers Education)

Graduate Schools
Cultural Studies and Letters

Units
Anglophone Studies (English); **Arts and Letters** (Literature; Performing Arts); **Communication** (Communication Studies); **Language Sciences** (Linguistics); **Languages, Literatures and Foreign Civilisations** (German; Italian; Literature; Modern Languages; Oriental Languages; Russian; Spanish)

History: Founded 1970 under the 1968 law reforming higher education as one of three Universities replacing former Université de Grenoble - founded 1339 and confirmed by Papal Bull. Suppressed by the Revolution, replaced by Faculties of Law; Letters; and Science. Reconstituted as University 1896. A State institution enjoying academic and financial autonomy, operating under the jurisdiction of the Minister of Education and financed by the State.

Governing Bodies: Conseil de l'Université, including elected representatives of teaching staff, research workers, students, and administrative and technical staff, as well as non-university members drawn from the public and private sectors; Conseil of each Unit, comprising representatives of its teaching staff, research workers, students, and administrative and technical staff; and Conseil scientifique, competent in matters of research. The President is elected by the Conseil de l'Université. The Chancelier, who represents the Minister of Education, is the Recteur de l'Académie de Grenoble

Academic Year: October to June (October-February; February-June)

Admission Requirements: Secondary school certificate (baccalauréat) or equivalent, or special entrance examination

Main Language(s) of Instruction: French

Degrees and Diplomas: *Diplôme d' Accès aux Etudes universitaires*; *Licence*: Foreign Languages, Art History, Information and Communication, Modern and Classical Letters, 3 yrs; *Licence professionnelle*: Communication (webmaster); *Diplôme de Recherche technologique*: Computer and Information Engineering; *Diplôme national de Master*: Arts and Letters, French, Linguistics, Englsih Studies, Germanic Studies, Slavic Studies, Mediterranean Studies, Information and Communication, Journalism, 2 yrs following Licence; *Doctorat*: Modern Languages, Arts and Humanities, Information and Communication, 2-4 yrs following Masters. Masters recherche, Masters professionnel

Student Residential Facilities: Cité universitaire

Libraries: Bibliothèque interuniversitaire

Last Updated: 22/07/11

GRENOBLE INSTITUTE OF TECHNOLOGY

Institut polytechnique de Grenoble (INP GRENOBLE)
46, avenue Félix Viallet, 38031 Grenoble, Cedex 1
Tel: +33(4) 76-57-45-00
Fax: +33(4) 76-57-45-01
EMail: communication@grenoble-inp.fr
Website: http://www.grenoble-inp.fr

President: Paul Jacquet (2002-)
Tel: +33(4) 76-57-45-05, Fax: +33 (4) 56-52-89-00
EMail: presidence@grenoble-inp.fr

Directeur général des Services: Xavier Fauveau
Tel: +33(4) 76-57-45-06, Fax: +33(4) 56-52-89-00
EMail: xavier.fauveau@grenoble-inp.fr

International Relations: Jean-Luc Koning
Tel: +33(4) 76-57-47-51, Fax: +33(4) 76-57-48-03
EMail: international.vp@grenoble-inp.fr

Colleges
Doctoral (Applied Mathematics; Automation and Control Engineering; Cognitive Sciences; Computer Science; Earth Sciences; Electronic Engineering; Engineering; Environmental Engineering; Environmental Studies; Health Sciences; Materials Engineering; Mathematics; Mechanical Engineering; Physics; Power Engineering)

Departments
Advanced Systems and Networks *(ESISAR)* (Computer Networks; Systems Analysis); **Applied Mathematics and Computer Science** *(ENSIMAG)* (Applied Mathematics; Computer Science); **Energy, Water and Environmental Science** *(Ense 3)* (Energy Engineering; Environmental Studies; Water Science); **Industrial Engineering** *(ENSGI)* (Industrial Engineering); **Lifelong Education** *(CUEFA, two sites)*; **Paper Science, Print Media and Biomaterials** *(Pagora)* (Materials Engineering; Media Studies; Paper Technology; Printing and Printmaking); **Physics, Applied Physics, Electronics and Materials Science** *(Phelma)* (Applied Physics; Electronic Engineering; Materials Engineering; Physics)

Programmes
Preparatory Class *(Prépa INP - CPP)* (Mathematics; Physics)

Further Information: 30 laboratories

History: Founded 1971 under the 1968 law reforming higher education and incorporating various Ecoles nationales supérieures, the first of which was founded in 1901. Acquired Grand Etablissement status 2007.

Governing Bodies: Board, Scientific Council, Studies and Students' Life Council

Academic Year: September to June (September-February; February-June)

Admission Requirements: Competitive entrance examination following 2-3 yrs further study after secondary school certificate (baccalauréat) or equivalent

Fees: (Euros): Bachelor and Engineering, 568,57; Master of Science, 241,57; PhD, 563.57

Main Language(s) of Instruction: French, English (10 international degrees)

International Co-operation: With universities worldwide; CLUSTER network; ERASMUS Mundus; Brazil; India

Accrediting Agencies: Commission des Titres d'Ingénieurs (CTI); EURACE

Degrees and Diplomas: *Licence professionnelle*; *Diplôme d'Ingénieur*: Electrical Engineering; Automation and Control Engineering; Applied Mathematics; Computer Science; Electrical Engineering; Industrial Engineering; Telecommunications Engineering; Physical Engineering; Energy Engineering; Nuclear Engineering; Paper Technology; Graphic Arts; Industrial Engineering; Hydraulic Engineering; Electronic Engineering; Chemistry; Chemical Engineering; Metallurgical Engineering, 5 yrs; *Diplôme de Recherche technologique*: Electronics; Electrical Engineering; Automation and Control Engineering; Environmental Engineering; Materials Engineering; Process Engineering; Systems Engineering; Industrial Engineering; Computer Engineering; Mechanical and Production Engineering, 1 further yr following Engineer's diploma; *Diplôme national de Master*: Electronic Engineering; Electric Engineering; Automation and Control Engineering; Information Sciences; Cognitive Sciences; Materials Engineering; Process Engineering; Mechanical Engineering; Energy Engineering; Strategic Management; Organizations Engineering; Chemistry; Sanitary Engineering; Mathematics and Computer Science; Physics; Physical Engineering; Earth Sciences; Environmental Sciences, a further 2 yrs; *Diplôme national de Master*: Pulp and Paper Science and Engineering (International), 1 yr following Master's Degree; *Doctorat*: Electronics; Electrical Engineering; Automation and Signal Processing; Materials and Process Engineering; Mechanics and Energy Engineering; Industrial Management and Production Engineering; Sanitary Engineering; Cognitive Sciences; Environmental Sciences; Mathematics; Information Science; Information Technology; Computer Science; Physics; Earth Sciences; Environmental Studies, 2 yrs following Master's Degree. International Masters

Student Services: Academic counselling, Canteen, Employment services, Foreign student adviser, Health services, Language programs, Social counselling, Sports facilities

Student Residential Facilities: Yes

Libraries: Interuniversity library; specialized libraries of the schools

Publications: Ingénieur INPG, Sciencetific topics *(quarterly)*

Press or Publishing House: Presses universitaires de Grenoble (PUG)

Last Updated: 17/05/11

GRENOBLE SCHOOL OF ARCHITECTURE

Ecole nationale supérieure d'Architecture de Grenoble (EAG)
BP 2636, 60, avenue de Constantine, 38036 Grenoble, Cedex 02
Tel: +33(4) 76-69-83-00
Fax: +33(4) 76-69-83-38
EMail: lucie.scotet@grenoble.archi.fr
Website: http://www.grenoble.archi.fr

Directeur: Jean-Michel Knop
EMail: jean-michel.knop@grenoble.archi.fr

Programmes
Architecture (Architecture)

History: Founded 1927. Acquired present status 1968.

Main Language(s) of Instruction: French

Degrees and Diplomas: *Licence*; *Diplôme national de Master*; *Doctorat*. Also DSA : diplôme de spécialisation et d'approfondissement; DPEA : diplôme propre aux écoles d'architecture

Last Updated: 30/05/11

GRENOBLE-VALENCE SCHOOL OF ART AND DESIGN

Ecole supérieure d'Art et Design Grenoble-Valence
Place des Beaux-Arts, 26000 Valence
Tel: +33(4) 75-79-24-00
Fax: +33(4) 75-79-24-00
EMail: erba@erba-valence.fr
Website: http://www.erba-valence.fr

Directeur: Jacques Norigeon

Programmes
Visual Arts and Graphic Design

History: Founded 2011 following merger of the l'École supérieure d'art de Grenoble and the École régionale des beaux-arts de Valence.

Admission Requirements: Baccalauréat or equivalent secondary school exam. Entrance exam with a selection jury.

Main Language(s) of Instruction: French

Accrediting Agencies: Ministry of Culture and Communication

Degrees and Diplomas: Diplome national d'arts plastiques (DNAP) 3 yrs; Diplome national d'arts et techniques (DNAT) 3 yrs; Diplome national supérieur d'expression plastique (DNSEP) a further 2 yrs
Last Updated: 18/04/11

HAINAUT-CAMBRÉSIS INSTITUTE OF TECHNOLOGY
Institut polytechnique du Hainaut-Cambrésis (IPHC)
Site de TECH 3000 - Chemin des Bourgeois, 59301 Aulnoy les Valenciennes
Tel: +33(3) 27-28-49-79
Fax: +33(3) 27-28-42-01
EMail: iphc@ndf.cci.fr
Website: http://www.iphc.fr

Directeur: Frédéric Daumont

Programmes
Industrial Production Management (Industrial Management)

Admission Requirements: 2 yrs undergraduate studies

Main Language(s) of Instruction: French

International Co-operation: Partnership programme with Ecole de Mines de Douai.

Accrediting Agencies: Commission du Titre d'Ingénieur

Degrees and Diplomas: Diplôme d'Ingénieur. Industrial Production Management, 3 yrs. in cooperation with Ecoles des Mines de Douai
Last Updated: 07/07/11

IFP SCHOOL
228-232, Avenue Napoléon Bonaparte, 92852 Rueil-Malmaison
Tel: +33(1) 47-52-64-57
Fax: +33(1) 47-52-67-65
EMail: info-ifpschool@ifp.fr
Website: http://www.ifp-school.com

Directeur: Jean-Luc Karnik Tel: +33(1) 47-52-64-92

Secrétaire général: Pierre Duclos Tel: +33(1) 47-52-64-77

International Relations: Jean-Christophe Fleche
Tel: +33(1) 47-52-64-41, Fax: +33(1) 47-52-70-36

Centres
Economics and Management (Economics; Finance; Management) Director: Jean-Pierre Favennec; **Exploration-Production** (Earth Sciences; Petroleum and Gas Engineering; Production Engineering) Director: Gilles Gabolde; **Internal Combustion Engines and Hydrocarbon Utilizations** (Automotive Engineering; Energy Engineering; Environmental Studies) Director: Pierre Duret; **Refining, Petrochemicals, Gas** (Chemical Engineering; Construction Engineering; Engineering; Petroleum and Gas Engineering; Polymer and Plastics Technology; Technology) Director: Jean-Bernard Sigaud

History: Founded 1924, IFP School is an integral part of "Institut Français du Petrole".

Academic Year: September to July

Admission Requirements: University Degree or Diplôme d'Ingénieur or equivalent

Fees: (Euros): Registration for Undergraduate, 400 per annum

Main Language(s) of Instruction: French, English

Accrediting Agencies: Ministry of Education

Degrees and Diplomas: Diplôme d'Ingénieur. 11-16 months; Diplôme national de Master. Science (MSc), 11-16 months. Master recherche

Student Services: Academic counselling, Canteen, Cultural centre, Employment services, Foreign student adviser, Handicapped facil-

ities, Health services, Language programs, Social counselling, Sports facilities

Student Residential Facilities: Yes

Libraries: Centre d'Information de l'IFP

Publications: Revue de l'Institut français du Pétrole

Press or Publishing House: Editions TECHNIP
Last Updated: 24/06/11

INSA - LYONS
Institut national des Sciences appliquées de Lyon (INSA LYON)
20, avenue Albert Einstein, 69621 Villeurbanne
Tel: +33(4) 72-43-83-83
Fax: +33(4) 72-43-85-00
EMail: info@insa-lyon.fr
Website: http://www.insa-lyon.fr

Directeur: Eric Maurincomme (2011-)
Tel: +33(4) 72-43-81-14, Fax: +33(4) 72-43-85-07
EMail: dir@insa-lyon.fr

Secrétaire Général: Georges Roqueplan
Tel: +33(4) 72-43-81-17 EMail: dgs@insa-lyon.fr

International Relations: Marie-Pierre Favre
Tel: +33(4) 72-43-79-34, Fax: +33(4) 78-94-61-40
EMail: dri@insa-lyon.fr

Schools
Applied Sciences (Bioengineering; Civil Engineering; Energy Engineering; Engineering; Environmental Engineering; Materials Engineering; Mechanical Engineering; Telecommunications Engineering; Town Planning)

Further Information: 20 research laboratories

History: Founded 1957.

Governing Bodies: Ministry of Education

Academic Year: Mid-September to June

Admission Requirements: Competitive entrance examination, secondary school certificate (baccalauréat) or equivalent

Fees: (Euros): Engineer diploma course none, Mastère 4,000 - 9,500 per annum

Main Language(s) of Instruction: French

International Co-operation: With 250 partner universities worldwide (Germany, United Kingdom, Spain, Sweden, Italy, Japan, Brazil, Mexico, Morocco, China)

Degrees and Diplomas: Diplôme d'Ingénieur. 5 yrs; Mastère spécialisé (SM): a further 2 yrs; Diplôme national de Master; Doctorat. Masters recherche

Student Services: Academic counselling, Canteen, Foreign student adviser, Foreign Studies Centre, Health services, Language programs, Sports facilities

Student Residential Facilities: Yes

Libraries: Yes
Last Updated: 24/05/11

INSA - RENNES
Institut national des Sciences appliquées de Rennes (INSA RENNES)
20, avenue des Buttes de Coësmes, CS 14315, 35043 Rennes
Tel: +33(2) 23-23-82-00
Fax: +33(2) 23-23-83-96
EMail: direction@insa-rennes.fr
Website: http://www.insa-rennes.fr

Directeur: M'Hamed Drissi
Tel: +33(2) 23-23-83-26 EMail: Mhamed.Drissi@insa-rennes.fr

International Relations: Mireille Ducasse, Director, European and International Relations
Tel: +33(2) 23-23-82-82, Fax: +33(2) 23-23-87-20
EMail: international@insa-rennes.fr

Departments
Civil Engineering and Urban Planning (Architecture; Business Administration; Construction Engineering; Geology; Hydraulic Engineering; Labour Law; Materials Engineering; Mechanics;

Statistics; Surveying and Mapping); **Computer Science** (Computer Science; Software Engineering; Systems Analysis); **Electronic and Computer Engineering** (Computer Engineering; Electronic Engineering; Mathematics); **Electronics and Communication Systems** (Computer Science; Electronic Engineering; Telecommunications Engineering); **Materials Science and Nanotechnology** (Materials Engineering; Nanotechnology); **Mechanical and Control System Engineering** (Automation and Control Engineering; Mechanical Engineering; Mechanics; Production Engineering); **Science and Technology for Engineers** (Engineering; Technology)

History: Founded 1966.

Governing Bodies: Management Committee

Academic Year: September - June

Admission Requirements: Baccalauréat plus Selection Committee

Fees: (Euros): Undergraduate, 512 per annum; Master's Programme, 215; Doctorate, 326

Main Language(s) of Instruction: French

International Co-operation: With universities in Brazil, Vietnam, Mexico, Bulgaria, United States, Canada. Also participate in Socrates-Erasmus.

Accrediting Agencies: Commission des Titres d'Ingénieurs; Agence d'Evaluation de la Recherche et de l'Enseignement Supérieur

Degrees and Diplomas: *Diplôme d'Ingénieur*: Electronics and Computer Engineering; Electronics and Communications Systems; Civil Engineering and Urban Planning; Mechanical and Control Systems Engineering; Computer Science; Materials Science and Nanotechnology, 5 yrs; *Diplôme national de Master*: Research: Chemistry; Physics; Electronic; Computer Science; Mechanics; Mathematics, a further 2 yrs; *Doctorat*: Mathematics; Computer Science; Signal, Electronics and Telecommunications; Physics; Universe and Earth Sciences; Chemistry; Engineering Sciences; Materials; Optical Functions for Telecommunications, 3-4 yrs

Student Services: Academic counselling, Canteen, Cultural centre, Employment services, Foreign student adviser, Foreign Studies Centre, Handicapped facilities, Health services, Language programs, Nursery care, Social counselling, Sports facilities

Student Residential Facilities: Yes

Special Facilities: Multimedia Centre.

Libraries: Bibliothèque centrale
Last Updated: 09/05/11

INSA - ROUEN

Institut national des Sciences appliquées de Rouen (INSA ROUEN)
Avenue de l'Université, 76801 Saint-Étienne-du-Rouvray
Tel: +33(2) 32-95-97-00
Fax: +33(2) 32-95-98-60
EMail: insa@insa-rouen.fr
Website: http://www.insa-rouen.fr

Directeur: Jean-Louis Billoët (2007-)
Tel: +33(2) 35-52-83-11, Fax: +33(2) 32-52-83-60

Directrice générale des Services: Marie France Detalminil
Tel: +33(2) 35-52-83-13

International Relations: Eduardo Souza
Tel: +33(2) 35-52-83-65, Fax: +33(2) 35 -52-83-60

Departments
Chemistry and Engineering (Chemical Engineering; Chemistry; Polymer and Plastics Technology); **Civil and Construction Engineering** (Civil Engineering; Construction Engineering); **Energy Engineering and Propulsion** (Energy Engineering); **Information Systems Design** (Computer Science; Data Processing; Electronic Engineering); **Mathematical and Software Engineering** (Mathematics and Computer Science; Software Engineering); **Mechanical Engineering** (Mechanical Engineering); **Risk Management** (Environmental Management)

History: Founded 1985. Moved to Saint-Étienne-du-Rouvray 2009.

Academic Year: September to June (September-January; February-June)

Admission Requirements: According to baccalauréat results and academic record

Fees: (Euros): c. 300 per annum

Main Language(s) of Instruction: French

International Co-operation: With universities in Europe, Canada, Brazil, Far East

Accrediting Agencies: CTI

Degrees and Diplomas: *Diplôme d'Ingénieur*: Engineering, 5 yrs; *Diplôme national de Master*: a further yr; *Doctorat*

Student Services: Academic counselling, Canteen, Foreign student adviser, Foreign Studies Centre, Health services, Language programs, Sports facilities

Student Residential Facilities: Yes

Special Facilities: Theatre. Music. Sport Centres.

Libraries: Yes
Last Updated: 07/07/11

INSA - STRASBOURG

Institut national des Sciences appliquées de Strasbourg (INSA STRASBOURG)
24, boulevard de la Victoire, 67084 Strasbourg, Cedex
Tel: +33(3) 88-14-47-00
Fax: +33(3) 88-24-14-90
EMail: secretariat.direction@insa-strasbourg.fr
Website: http://www.insa-strasbourg.fr

Directeur: Marc Renner
Tel: +33(3) 88-14-47-01, Fax: +33(3) 88-24-14-90

Secrétaire général: Roger Cervantès
Tel: +33(3) 88-14-47-08
EMail: secretariat.general@insa-strasbourg.fr

International Relations: Angelika Hammann-Uribe
Tel: +33(3) 88-14-47-80 +33(3) 88-14-47-02
EMail: relations.internationales@insa-strasbourg.fr

Departments
Architecture (Architecture); **Civil Engineering and Topography** (Civil Engineering; Surveying and Mapping); **Electrical Engineering and Climate** (Electrical Engineering); **Fluids and Solids Mechanics** (Physics); **Mechanical Engineering** (Mechanical Engineering); **Technology and Humanities** (Arts and Humanities; Technology)

History: Founded 1875.

Admission Requirements: Competitive entrance examination following 2-3 yrs further study after secondary school certificate (baccalauréat) or following first university qualification (DEUG, DUT or BTS) or equivalent.

Fees: (Euros): 418 per annum

Main Language(s) of Instruction: French

International Co-operation: Participates in the Erasmus and CREPUQ (Quebec) programmes

Accrediting Agencies: Ministère de l'enseignement supérieur et de la recherche

Degrees and Diplomas: *Diplôme d'Ingénieur*: Civil Engineering, Topography, Mechanical Engineering, Plastics Engineering, Mechatronics, Electrical and Electronic Engineering, Building Services and Energy Conservation Engineering, 5 yrs; *Mastère spécialisé*; *Diplôme national de Master*

Student Services: Employment services, Foreign student adviser, Health services, Sports facilities

Student Residential Facilities: Yes

Libraries: Yes
Last Updated: 07/07/11

INSA - TOULOUSE

Institut national des Sciences appliquées de Toulouse (INSA TOULOUSE)
135, avenue de Rangueil, 31077 Toulouse, Cedex 4
Tel: +33(5) 61-55-95-13
Fax: +33(5) 61-55-95-00
EMail: servicecom@insa-toulouse.fr
Website: http://www.insa-toulouse.fr/

Directeur: Didier Marquis
Tel: +33(5) 61-55-95-01, Fax: +33(5) 61-55-92-80
EMail: direct@insa-toulouse.fr

Secrétaire général: Pierre Stoecklin,
Tel: +33(5) 61-55-95-12 EMail: Sec_gene@insa-toulouse.fr

International Relations: Lucien Baldas
Tel: +33(5) 61-55-95-45, Fax: +33(5) 61-55-95-40
EMail: direction-ri@insa-toulouse.fr

Departments

Automation and Electronic Engineering (Automation and Control Engineering; Computer Engineering; Electrical and Electronic Engineering; Telecommunications Engineering); **Biochemichal Engineering** (Biochemistry; Bioengineering; Biological and Life Sciences; Biotechnology; Chemistry; Microbiology; Molecular Biology); **Civil Engineering** (Building Technologies; Civil Engineering); **Computer and Network Engineering** (Computer Engineering; Computer Networks); **Industrial Process Engineering** (Industrial Engineering); **Mathematical Engineering** (Engineering; Mathematics); **Mechanical Engineering** (Mechanical Engineering); **Physical Engineering** (Physical Engineering)

Sections

Dance (Dance); **Music** (Music); **Sports** (Sports)

History: Founded 1963.

Academic Year: September to June

Admission Requirements: Competitive entrance examination following secondary school certificate (baccalauréat) or equivalent. Selection on grades

Fees: (Euros): 512 per annum

Main Language(s) of Instruction: French

Accrediting Agencies: Conférence des Grandes Ecoles

Degrees and Diplomas: *Diplôme d'Ingénieur*: Engineering, 5 yrs; *Mastère spécialisé*: Applied Mathematics, Networks and Tele-communications Engineering, Micro and Nano Systems, Automatic, Information and Decision Systems, Mechanical Engineering, Civil Engineering, Materials Engineering, Structures, Chemical Engineering, Physics; Risk Engineering; Industrial Engineering; *Diplôme national de Master*: Biochemical Engineering, Civil Engineering, Automatic Control and Electronics, Comptuer Engineering, Neworks and Telecommunications Engineering, Machanical Engineering, Systems Engineering, Physics Engineering, Chemical Engineering, 5 yrs; *Doctorat*: Automatic Systems, Industrial Systems, Information Systems, Computer Networks, Telecommunicaions Engineering, Computer Engineering, Industrial Microbiology, Biocatalysis, Civil Engineering, Fluid Dynamics, Chemical Engineering (PhD), a further 3-4 yrs; *Doctorat*: Mechanical and Material Engineering, Electronics and Plasma Engineering, Applied Mathematics, Nanophysics, Energy Engineering, Microwave and Optical Fibre Telecommunications, Microbe and Enzyme Engineering, Computer Graphics, Computer Film. Also Master of Science programmes for non-French speaking students.

Student Services: Academic counselling, Canteen, Foreign student adviser, Foreign Studies Centre, Handicapped facilities, Health services, Language programs, Social counselling, Sports facilities

Student Residential Facilities: Yes

Libraries: Central library
Last Updated: 07/07/11

INSTITUTE OF ADVANCED INDUSTRIAL TECHNOLOGIES

Ecole supérieure des Technologies industrielles avancées (ESTIA)
Technopole Izarbel, 64210 Bidart
Tel: +33(5) 59-43-84-00
Fax: +33(5) 59-43-84-01
EMail: estia@estia.fr
Website: http://www.estia.fr

Head: Jean-Roch Guiresse
Tel: +33(5) 59-43-84-12 EMail: j.guiresse@estia.fr

International Relations: Olivier Patrouix
Tel: +33(5) 59-43-84-10 EMail: o.patrouix@estia.fr

Programmes
Information Technology

Admission Requirements: Preparatory classes degree, 2-3 yrs undergraduate studies in sciences or technology

Fees: (Euros): 4,500 per annum

Main Language(s) of Instruction: French

International Co-operation: Cooperation with local Universities and Universities of Bilboa (Spain), Cranfield, Wolverhampton, and Salford-Manchester (UK) to continue with a Masters

Degrees and Diplomas: *Diplôme d'Ingénieur*: 3 yrs; *Mastère spécialisé*
Last Updated: 04/07/11

INSTITUTE OF EARTH PHYSICS OF PARIS

Institut de Physique du Globe de Paris
4, place Jussieu - Case 89, 75252 Paris, Cedex 05
Tel: +33(1) 44-27-24-30
Fax: +33(1) 44-27-33-73
EMail: secretdir@ipgp.fr
Website: http://www.ipgp.fr

Directeur: Claude Jaupart
Tel: +33(1) 44-27-36-12 EMail: laude@ipgp.fr

Directrice générale des Services: Lydia Zerbib
EMail: zerbib@ipgp.fr

International Relations: Jean-Paul Montagnier
Tel: +33(1) 44-27-28-28

Programmes
Physics of the Globe (Earth Sciences; Geochemistry; Physics; Seismology)

History: Founded 1921; became a 'Grand Etablissement' 1991.

Governing Bodies: Conseil d'administration; Conseil scientifique

Academic Year: October to June

Admission Requirements: University degree of Maîtrise or foreign equivalent

Main Language(s) of Instruction: French

Accrediting Agencies: Centre national de la Recherche scientifique (CNRS)

Degrees and Diplomas: *Licence*; *Diplôme national de Master*; *Doctorat*: a further 3 yrs

Special Facilities: Volcanic Observatories in Réunion, Guadeloupe, Martinique and Djibouti

Publications: Rapport d'Activité scientifique *(biannually)*
Last Updated: 05/07/11

INSTITUTE OF MECHANICAL ENGINEERING OF PARIS

Institut supérieur de Mécanique de Paris (SUPMECA)
3, rue Fernand Hainaut, 93407 Saint-Ouen, Cedex
Tel: +33(1) 49-45-29-00
Fax: +33(1) 49-45-29-91
EMail: informations@supmeca.fr
Website: http://www.supmeca.fr

Directeur général: Alain Rivière
Tel: +33(1) 49-45-29-99 EMail: alain.riviere@supmeca.fr

International Relations: Marie-Sophie Pawlak
Tel: +33(1) 49-45-29-73 EMail: marie-sophie.pawlak@supmeca.fr

Departments
Automated Systems and Industrial Processes (Automation and Control Engineering) *Head*: Samir Lamouri; **Materials Engineering and Processes** (Materials Engineering) *Head*: René Gras; **Mecatronics** *(St Ouen; Toulon)* (Mechanical Engineering; Systems Analysis) *Head*: Jean-Yves Cholley

Divisions
Engineering (Automation and Control Engineering; Industrial Engineering; Materials Engineering; Production Engineering) *Head*: Alain Rivière

Further Information: Branch in Toulon

History: Founded 1956. The ISMCM (Institut Supérieur des Matériaux et de la Construction Mécanique) was created 1948 jointly by the Federation of Mechanical Industries and by the Ministry of Education : it is an autonomous State Institution of Training and

Research in Mechanical Engineering, placed under the Ministry of Education. Since 1956 in Paris and 1994 in Toulon, the Institute has launched the CESTI (Centre d'Etudes supérieures des Techniques Industrielles) Engineering curriculum. In 2004, ISMCM-CESTI changed its name to Supméca.

Academic Year: September to July

Admission Requirements: French students : Secondary school certificate (baccalauréat) and "Classes préparatoires" (intensive selective scientific curriculum preparing to the national competitive exam to Enginnering Schools), or selective entrance exam for holders of a French university degree. For foreign students : Bachelor's degree and profiency in French and selection of the applicants.

Fees: (Euros): Minimum, 700 per annum; Maximum, 2,500 for 2 yrs in the frame of the n + I programme.

Main Language(s) of Instruction: French

International Co-operation: Participates in Erasmus/Socrates programmes (United Kingdom, Germany, Belgium, Portugal, Italy, Spain), Crepuq Scheme (Québec), n + I Programme (more than 120 universities in 28 countries).

Accrediting Agencies: Commission des Titres d'Ingénieurs

Degrees and Diplomas: *Diplôme d'Ingénieur:* Mechanical Engineering, 5 yrs; *Diplôme national de Master*

Student Services: Canteen, Foreign student adviser, Sports facilities

Student Residential Facilities: Yes

Last Updated: 08/07/11

INSTITUTE OF POLITICAL STUDIES PARIS- 'SCIENCES PO'

Institut d'Etudes politiques de Paris-'Sciences Po' (IEP PARIS)

27, rue Saint-Guillaume, 75337 Paris, Cedex 07
Tel: +33(1) 45-49-50-50
Fax: +33(1) 42-22-31-26
EMail: admission@sciences-po.fr
Website: http://www.sciences-po.fr

Directeur: Richard Descoings (1996-)
Tel: +33(1) 45-49-50-51 EMail: richard.descoings@sciences-po.fr

Secrétaire général: Guillaume Piketty
Tel: +33(1) 45-49-50-68 EMail: guillaume.piketty@sciences-po.fr

International Relations: Francis Vérillaud
Tel: +33(1) 45-49-50-48, Fax: +33(1) 45-44-12-52
EMail: info@international.sciences-po.fr;
nadia.nazet@sciences-po.fr

Divisions
Lifelong Education (Business and Commerce; Communication Studies; Finance; Human Resources; Law; Management)

Institutes
Journalism (Journalism)

Programmes
Masters Programme (Administrative Law; Commercial Law; Communication Studies; Finance; Human Resources; International Business; International Economics; International Studies; Marketing; Public Administration; Regional Planning; Urban Studies)

Research Centres
20th Century European History; **Administrative Research** (Administration); **Economic Activity** (Economics); **French Economic Conditions** (Economics); **French Politics** (Political Sciences); **International Studies** (International Studies); **Inter-regional Politics** (Political Sciences); **Sociological Change** (Sociology)

Sections
Business and Finance (Business and Commerce; Economics; Finance); **Communication and Human Resources** (Communication Studies; Human Resources); **International Affairs** (European Studies; International Relations; International Studies; Political Sciences); **Public Administration** (Public Administration); **Sociology** (History; Sociology)

Further Information: Also branches in Aix, Lille, Lyon, Rennes, Strasbourg, Grenoble, Toulouse and Bordeaux. Special programmes for foreign students: one-year undergraduate programme;

one year graduate programme (CIEP), postgraduate research project programme; European Union Summer Programme. A variety of Study Abroad programmes for 200 students

History: Founded 1871 as Ecole libre des Sciences politiques; became institute attached to the Université de Paris 1945, independent autonomous institution 1969 and 'Grand Etablissement' 1984. Under the supervision of and financially supported by the Fondation nationale des Sciences politiques.

Governing Bodies: Conseil de Direction, comprising 24 members; Commission paritaire, comprising 16 members; Conseil d'Administration de la FNSP, comprising 36 members

Academic Year: October to June (October-December; January-April; April-June)

Admission Requirements: Entrance by competition following 1 undergraduate programmes study after secondary school certificate (baccalauréat) or two university years (foreigners). Direct entrance to graduate programme (master degree) by competition following appropriate university degree

Fees: (Euros): c. 900 per annum

Main Language(s) of Instruction: French

Degrees and Diplomas: *Diplôme national de Master; Doctorat:* Political Science, 2-4 yrs following DEA. Certificat for foreign Students, Masters recherche

Student Services: Academic counselling, Employment services, Foreign student adviser, Health services, Sports facilities

Special Facilities: Research Observatory

Libraries: Bibliothèque générale de la Fondation nationale des Sciences politiques, c. 700,000 vols

Press or Publishing House: Presses de Sciences Po
Last Updated: 05/07/11

ISMANS - LE MANS

Institut supérieur des Matériaux et Mécaniques avancées du Mans (ISMANS)

44, avenue Frédéric Auguste Bartholdi, 72000 Le Mans
Tel: +33(2) 43-21-40-00
Fax: +33(2) 43-21-40-39
EMail: ismans@ismans.fr
Website: http://www.ismans.fr

Directeur général: Mouad Lamrani EMail: alm@ismans.fr

Divisions
Engineering (Engineering; Materials Engineering; Mechanical Engineering); **Management** (Business Administration; Economics; Management)

History: One of the youngest 'Grandes Ecoles', it is modelled after Quebec Universities, being created in 1987 by the Chamber of Commerce and Industry of Le Mans and Sarthe.

Admission Requirements: Entrance exam with 2 yrs undergraduate studies or preparatory classes.

Fees: (Euros): 4,200 per annum

Main Language(s) of Instruction: French, English

International Co-operation: Has cooperation accords with South Africa, Germany, Cameroon, Canada, Denmark, Spain, Poland and Russia.

Accrediting Agencies: Ministry of Economy, Finance and Industry, Commission des Titres d'Ingénieur

Degrees and Diplomas: *Diplôme d'Ingénieur:* Management, Mechanical and Material Engineering, 3 yrs following 2 yrs undergraduate; *Mastère spécialisé.* Masters professional in Project Management
Last Updated: 08/07/11

JEAN-FRANÇOIS CHAMPOLLION UNIVERSITY CENTRE FOR STUDY AND RESEARCH - ALBI

Centre universitaire de Formation et de Recherche Jean-François Champollion

Place de Verdun, 81012 Albi
Tel: +33(5) 63-48-17-17
Fax: +33(5) 63-48-17-19
EMail: contact.albi@univ-jfc.fr
Website: http://www.univ-jfc.fr

Directeur: Hervé Pingaud
Tel: +33(5) 63-48-64-28 EMail: herve.pingaud@univ-jfc.fr

Administrative Officer: Pascal Guerrin Tel: +33(5) 63-48-19-68

International Relations: Elyn Monatin
Tel: +33(5) 63-48-19-66 EMail: elyn.monatin@univ-jfc.fr

Departments

Human and Social Sciences (Geography; History; Psychology; Rural Planning; Sociology; Town Planning); **Languages and Literature** *(Rodez campus)* (English; Literature; Modern Languages; Spanish); **Law and Social Sciences** *(Rodez campus)* (Administration; Economics; Law); **Physical Education and Sports** *(Rodez campus)* (Physical Education; Sports); **Science, Technology and Health** (Chemical Engineering; Computer Engineering; Physics)

Schools

Engineering *(Castres campus)* (Engineering; Information Technology)

Further Information: Also campuses in Castres, Figeac and Rodez

History: Founded 2002.

Main Language(s) of Instruction: French

Degrees and Diplomas: *Licence*; *Licence professionnelle*; *Diplôme national de Master*
Last Updated: 15/04/11

JEAN MONNET UNIVERSITY - SAINT-ETIENNE

Université Jean Monnet Saint-Etienne (UJM)
Maison de l'Université, 10 rue Tréfilerie - CS 82301,
42023 Saint-Etienne, Cedex 02
Tel: +33(4) 77-42-17-00
Fax: +33(4) 77-42-17-99
EMail: secgen@univ-st-etienne.fr
Website: http://www.univ-st-etienne.fr

Président: Khaled Bouabdalla (2002-)
Tel: +33(4) 77-42-17-04, Fax: +33(4) 77-42-17-99
EMail: president@univ-st-etienne.fr

Secrétaire générale: Evelyne Sarmejeanne
Tel: +33(4) 77-42-17-09
EMail: evelyne.sarmejeanne@univ-st-etienne.fr

International Relations: Serge Riffard
Tel: +33(4) 77-42-17-53, Fax: +33(4) 77-42-17-88
EMail: serge.riffard@univ-st-etienne.fr

Centres

Language and Civilization *(CILEC, for foreign students)* (French); **Lifelong Education** *(SUFC)* (Continuing Education)

Departments

Physical Education and Sports *(STAPS)* (Physical Education; Sports)

Faculties

Arts, Letters, Languages and Philology *(ALL)* (Arts and Humanities; Modern Languages; Philology); **Human and Social Sciences** *(SHS)* (Arts and Humanities; Geography; History; Social Sciences; Sociology); **Law** (History of Law; Law; Political Sciences; Private Law; Public Law); **Medicine** (Medicine; Sports); **Science and Technology** (Biology; Chemistry; Computer Science; Geology; Mathematics; Natural Sciences; Physics; Technology)

Graduate Schools

Interdisciplinary Studies *(ED SE in cooperation with ENSM and ENI of St. Etienne)*

Higher Institutes

Advanced Techniques *(ISTASE)* (Electronic Engineering; Engineering; Optical Technology; Telecommunications Engineering); **Economics, Business Administration, Management** *(ISEAG (IAE))* (Business Administration; Economics; Management; Public Administration)

Institutes

Technology *(IUT de Saint-Etienne)* (Biology; Computer Engineering; Electrical Engineering; Industrial Management; Marketing; Measurement and Precision Engineering; Mechanical Engineering; Production Engineering; Public Administration; Technology); **Tech-**

nology *(IUT Roanne)* (Industrial Management; Marketing; Technology)

Further Information: Centre Universitaire Roannais (CUR-facultés) is a decentralised centre offering Licence, Masters and professional courses.

History: Founded 1970 under the 1968 law reforming higher education and incorporating Colleges previously attached to the former Université de Lyon. The University is a State institution enjoying academic and financial autonomy, operating under the jurisdiction of the Minister of Education and financed by the State.

Governing Bodies: Conseil d'Administration, including representatives of teaching staff, research workers, students, and administrative and technical staff, as well as non-university members drawn from the public and private sectors; Conseil scientifique, competent in matters of research; Conseil des Etudes et de la Vie universitaire; and Conseil of each Unit, comprising representatives of its teaching staff, research workers, students, and administrative and technical staff. The President is elected by the first three bodies. The Chancelier, who represents the Minister of Education, is the Recteur of the Académie de Lyon

Academic Year: September to June (September-January; February-June) and Summer University

Admission Requirements: Secondary school certificate (baccalauréat) or foreign equivalent, or special entrance examination

Fees: (Euros): c. 220 per annum

Main Language(s) of Instruction: French

International Co-operation: With universities in Germany; Austria; Belgium; Bulgaria; Denmark; Spain; Finland; Ireland; Italy; Finland; Romania; United Kingdom; Russian Federation; Slovak Republic; Sweden; Switzerland; Czech Republic; Algeria, Australia; Canada: China; Ecuador; USA; Lebanon; Morocco; Tunisia

Accrediting Agencies: Ministère de l'Education/Conseil national d'Evaluation (CNE)

Degrees and Diplomas: *Capacité en Droit*; *Diplôme d' Accès aux Etudes universitaires*; *Diplôme universitaire de Technologie*: Maintenance Technology, Business Administration, 2 yrs; *Licence*: Arts and Humanities, Languages, Literature, Economics, Management, Science and Technology, Biology, Medicine, Social Sciences, 3 yrs; *Licence professionnelle*: Technology, Administration, Management, Social Work, Urban Planning, Computer Education, 3 yrs; *Diplôme d'Etat*: Medicine, 6 yrs plus 1 yr hospital practice and thesis; *Diplôme d'Ingénieur*: Optical Technology, Telecommunications, Electronics, 3 yrs following Licence; *Diplôme national de Master*: Arts and Humanities, Languages, Literature, Economics, Management, Science and Technology, Biology, Medicine, Social Sciences, 2 yrs after Licence; *Doctorat*: Earth Sciences, Educational Sciences, History, Ancient Languages, Modern Lnaguages, Mathematics and Computer Science, Medicine, 2 yrs following Master Recherche; *Certificat de Spécialité*: Medicine, at least 2 yrs following Diplôme d'Etat; *Habilitation à Diriger les Recherches*. Masters recherche, Masters professionnel, Preparation for CAPES and Agrégation exams

Student Services: Academic counselling, Canteen, Cultural centre, Foreign student adviser, Foreign Studies Centre, Handicapped facilities, Health services, Social counselling, Sports facilities

Student Residential Facilities: Yes

Libraries: c. 280,000 vols; Periodicals 2,250/4,087 (digital)

Press or Publishing House: Presses Universitaires de Saint Etienne
Last Updated: 22/04/11

LE HAVRE-ROUEN SCHOOL OF ART AND DESIGN

École supérieure d'Art et Design Le Havre-Rouen
65 rue Demidoff, 76600 Le Havre
Tel: +33(2) 35-53-30-31
Fax: +33(2) 35-24-04-38
EMail: esadhar@esadhar.fr
Website: http://www.esadhar.fr/lh

Directeur: Thierry Heynen

Departments

Art (Fine Arts); **Design** (Design; Graphic Design)

History: Founded 1800. Acquired present status and title following merger of the Ecole Régionale des Beaux-Arts de Rouen and the Ecole Supérieure d'Art du Havre.

Admission Requirements: Baccalauréat or equivalent secondary school exam. Entrance exam with a selection jury.

Main Language(s) of Instruction: French

Accrediting Agencies: Ministry of Culture and Communication

Degrees and Diplomas: Diplôme national d'arts plastiques (DNAP) 3 yrs; Diplôme national supérieur d'expression plastique (DNSEP) a further 2 yrs
Last Updated: 01/07/11

LES ATELIERS-PARIS DESIGN INSTITUTE
Ecole nationale supérieure de Création industrielle (ENSCI)
48, rue Saint-Sabin, 75011 Paris
Tel: +33(1) 49-23-12-12
Fax: +33(1) 43-38-51-36
EMail: davis@ensci.com
Website: http://www.ensci.com

Directeur: Alain Cadix
Tel: +33(1) 49-23-12-01, Fax: +33(1) 49-23-12-03
EMail: directeur@ensci.com

International Relations: Elisabeth Davis Tel: +33(1) 49-23-12-30

Programmes
Industrial Design (Industrial Design); **New Media** (Media Studies); **Textile Design** (Textile Design)

History: Founded in 1982, ENSCI is the first French public institute specialising in advanced studies in design. In 1985 ENSCI extended its activities to include the ANAT, National Textile Art Studio.

Main Language(s) of Instruction: French

Degrees and Diplomas: *Mastère spécialisé.* 3-year Diploma in Textile Design
Last Updated: 30/06/11

LILLE I UNIVERSITY
Université des Sciences et Technologies de Lille (Lille I)
Cité scientifique, 59655 Villeneuve d'Ascq, Cedex
Tel: +33(3) 20-43-43-43
Fax: +33(3) 20-43-49-95
EMail: communication@univ-lille1.fr
Website: http://www.univ-lille1.fr

Président: Philippe Rollet (2007-) EMail: president@univ-lille1.fr

Secrétaire général: Patrice Serniclay
Tel: +33(3) 20-43-42-95 EMail: sec-general-lille@univ-lille1.fr

International Relations: Jacques Brocard
Tel: +33(3) 20-43-65-01 EMail: international@univ-lille1.fr

Centres
Educational Sciences *(CUEEP)* (Adult Education; Educational Sciences)

Departments
Marine and Regional Biology *(Wimereux)* (Coastal Studies; Marine Biology; Marine Science and Oceanography)

Graduate Schools
Biomedicine *(In cooperation with University Lille II)* (Biomedicine; Genetics; Neurosciences); **Economics and Social Sciences** (Economics; Social Sciences); **Matter, Laser and Environment** (Biochemistry; Ecology; Environmental Engineering; Environmental Studies; Microbiology); **Sciences for Engineers** *(In cooperation with Universities of Artois, Lille III, Littoral and Valenciennes)* (Automation and Control Engineering; Business Computing; Civil Engineering; Electrical and Electronic Engineering; Mathematics; Mechanical Engineering) *Director:* Max Dauchet

Institutes
Business Administration *(IAE)* (Business Administration; Business and Commerce; Management; Marketing); **Teacher Training** *(IUFM du Nord - Pas de Calais with seven sites) Director:* Dominique Guy Brassart; **Technology** *(IUT 'A')* (Bioengineering; Business Administration; Chemistry; Computer Science; Electrical Engineer-

ing; Mechanical Engineering; Production Engineering; Technology); **Telecommunications Engineering** *(TELECOM Lille I)* (Telecommunications Engineering) *Director:* Bertrand Bonte

Schools
Chemistry *(ENSCL)* (Chemical Engineering; Chemistry); **Engineering** *(Ecole Polytechnique Universitaire de Lille)* (Civil Engineering; Computer Engineering; Engineering; Food Technology; Materials Engineering; Mechanical Engineering; Microelectronics; Production Engineering; Statistics; Water Management)

Units
Biology (Biochemistry; Biology; Cell Biology; Microbiology; Physiology); **Chemistry** (Chemistry); **Computer Science, Electronics and Automation** *(IEEA)* (Automation and Control Engineering; Computer Science; Electronic Engineering); **Earth Sciences** (Earth Sciences; Geology; Paleontology; Soil Science; Water Science); **Economics and Social Sciences** *(Groups two institutions: Economics and Management Institute and Sociology and Anthropology Institute)* (Anthropology; Banking; Business Administration; E-Business/Commerce; Economics; Ethnology; Finance; Insurance; Public Administration; Social Sciences; Sociology); **Geography and Regional Planning** (Geography; Regional Planning); **Mathematics** (Applied Mathematics); **Physics** (Physics) *Director:* Michel Foulon

History: Founded 1970 under the 1968 law reforming higher education as one of three Universities replacing the former Université de Lille - founded 1560 at Douai and authorized by Papal Bull. The University was suppressed by the Revolution and replaced by Faculties in Lille and Douai, the latter being subsequently transferred to Lille in 1887. Reconstituted as University 1896. A State institution enjoying academic and financial autonomy, operating under the jurisdiction of the Ministry of Education and financed by the State.

Governing Bodies: Conseil d'Administration, including representatives of teaching staff, research workers, students, and administrative and technical staff, as well as non-university members drawn from the public and private sectors; the Conseil scientifique, competent in matters of research; the Conseil des Etudes et de la Vie universitaire; and the Conseil of each Unit, comprising representatives of its teaching staff, research workers, students, and administrative and technical staff. The President is elected by the first three bodies

Academic Year: October to June (October-February; February-June)

Admission Requirements: Secondary school certificate (baccalauréat) or recognized foreign equivalent, or special entrance examination

Main Language(s) of Instruction: French

Degrees and Diplomas: *Diplôme universitaire de Technologie:* 2 yrs; *Licence:* Science and Technology, Economics, Administration, Social Sciences, Arts and Humanities, 3 yrs; *Licence professionnelle:* Science and Technology, Economics, Administration, Social Sciences, Arts and Humanities; *Diplôme d'Ingénieur:* Engineering, 5 yrs; *Diplôme national de Master:* Science and Technology, Economics, Administration, Social Sciences, Arts and Humanities; *Doctorat:* Science and Technology, Economics, Administration, 2-4 yrs following Masters. Also Certificates and Diplomas, Masters recherche and Masters profesionnel

Libraries: Bibliothèque universitaire, c. 120,000 vols

Publications: Espace, populations, sociétés; Hommes et Terres du Nord; Le Bulletin de l'Institut de Recherche dans l'Enseignement des Mathématiques; Les Cahiers de Géographie physique; Les Cahiers de l'Institut d'administration des entreprises; Les Cahiers de l'Institut de Recherches sur les mathématiques avancées; Les Cahiers lillois d'Economie et de Sociologie; Les Nouvelles d'Archimède *(bimonthly)*; Sphères d'échanges *(bimonthly)*
Last Updated: 18/07/11

LILLE II UNIVERSITY OF LAW AND HEALTH
Université Lille 2 Droit et Santé
42, rue Paul Duez, 59000 Lille
Tel: +33(3) 20-96-43-43
Fax: +33(3) 20-88-24-32
EMail: administration@univ-lille2.fr
Website: http://www.univ-lille2.fr

Président: Christian Sergheraert (2004-)
Tel: +33(3) 20-96-43-01, Fax: +33(3) 20-96-45-95
EMail: christian.sergheraert@univ-lille2.fr

Directeur général des Services: Pierre-Marie Robert
Tel: +33(3) 20-96-43-48 EMail: pierre-marie.robert@univ-lille2.fr

International Relations: Salem Kacet
Tel: +33(3) 20-96-43-21, Fax: +33(3) 20-96-43-86
EMail: salem.kacet@univ-lille2.fr

Faculties

Dentistry (Dentistry); **Finance, Banking and Accountancy** *(FFBC)* (Accountancy; Banking; Finance); **Law, Political and Social Sciences** (Law; Political Sciences; Social Sciences); **Medicine** (Medicine); **Pharmacy** (Pharmacy); **Physical Education and Sports Sciences** *(Ronchin)* (Physical Education; Sports)

Graduate Schools

Health and Biology *(Offered by Universities of Lille I and II)* (Biology; Health Sciences); **Law, Political Science and Administration** (Administration; Law; Political Sciences)

Institutes

Criminal Law *(IEJ)* (Criminal Law; Law); **Criminology** (Criminology); **Forensic and Social Medicine** *(IML)* (Forensic Medicine and Dentistry; Social and Preventive Medicine); **Health Engineering** *(ILIS)* (Public Health); **Labour Relations** *(IST)* (Labour and Industrial Relations); **Marketing Retail Management** *(IMMD)* (Management; Marketing; Retailing and Wholesaling); **Pharmaceutical Chemistry** *(ICPAL)* (Pharmacology); **Political Science** *(IEP Sciences Po Lille)* (Political Sciences); **Preparatory Administrative Studies** *(IPAG)* (Administration); **Speech Therapy** *(Institut d'Orthophonie Gabriel Decroix)* (Speech Therapy and Audiology); **Technology** *(IUT C, Roubaix)* (Business and Commerce; Justice Administration; Statistics; Technology)

History: Founded 1970 under the 1968 law reforming higher education as one of three Universities replacing the former Université de Lille - founded 1559 at Douai and authorized by Papal Bull. The University was suppressed by the Revolution and replaced by Faculties in Lille and Douai, the latter being subsequently transferred to Lille in 1887. Reconstituted as university 1896. A State institution enjoying academic and financial autonomy, operating under the jurisdiction of the Minister of Education and financed by the State.

Governing Bodies: Conseil de l'Université, including elected representatives of teaching staff, research workers, students, and administrative and technical staff, as well as non-university members drawn from the public and private sectors; Conseil of each unit, comprising representatives of its teaching staff, research workers, students, and administrative and technical staff; and Conseil scientifique, competent in matters of research. The President is elected by the Conseil de l'Université. The Chancelier, who represents the Minister of Education, is the Recteur of the Académie de Lille

Academic Year: September to June

Admission Requirements: Secondary school certificate (baccalauréat) or recognized foreign equivalent, or special entrance examination

Fees: (Euros): 180-780 per annum

Main Language(s) of Instruction: French

International Co-operation: Participates in LLP Erasmus (159 Universities), Crepuq (Canada-Québec), Utrecht Network, RPB (Peru), Erasmus Mundus Section 2, Bilateral agreements (106 universities)

Degrees and Diplomas: *Licence*: Economics, Public Administration, Law, Law Administration, Sports, Business and Commerce, Banking, 3 yrs; *Licence professionnelle*: Health, Environment, Business Administration, Real estate; *Diplôme d'Etat*: Dentistry, Medicine, Pharmacy; Midwifery, Rehabilitation Medicine and Therapy; *Diplôme national de Master*: Business Administration, International Business, Biomedical Engineering, Sports Management, 2 yrs following Licence; *Diplôme national de Master*: Law, Public Law, Commercial Law, Political Science, International Business, Accountancy, Business Administration, Human Resources, Sports, Sanitary Engineering, 2 yrs; *Diplôme national de Master*: Medicine, Pharmacy, Sports, 1 yr; *Doctorat*: Pharmacy, Law, by thesis following Diplôme d'Etat; *Certificat de Spécialité*: Medicine, Pharmacy,

at least 2 yrs following Diplôme d'Etat. Capacity of Speech Therapy, Masters recherche, Masters professionnel

Student Services: Academic counselling, Canteen, Cultural centre, Employment services, Foreign student adviser, Handicapped facilities, Health services, Language programs, Social counselling, Sports facilities

Libraries: Law/Management and Medicine/Health Libraries
Last Updated: 10/06/11

LILLE III UNIVERSITY
Université Charles de Gaulle (Lille III)
BP 60149, Domaine universitaire du "Pont de Bois", rue du Barreau -, 59653 Villeneuve d'Ascq, Cedex
Tel: +33(3) 20-41-60-00
Fax: +33(3) 20-91-91-71
EMail: ri.direction@univ-lille3.fr
Website: http://www.univ-lille3.fr

Président: Jean-Claude Dupas (2005-)
Tel: +33(3) 20-41-65-97, Fax: +33(3) 20-41-65-97
EMail: presidence@univ-lille3.fr; jean-claude.dupas@univ-lille3.fr

Secrétaire général: Emmanuel Parisis
Tel: +33(3) 20-41-62-33, Fax: +33(3) 20-41-62-02

International Relations: Norah Dei Cas
Tel: +33(3) 20-41-66-79, Fax: +33(3) 20-41-63-90

Centres
Lifelong Education *Director*: Julien Deceuninick; **Music Teacher Training** *(CFMI)* *Administrator*: Jacqueline Bruckert

Departments
Books and Documentation *(DFMLD MédiaLille)* (Documentation Techniques; Library Science; Publishing and Book Trade)

Graduate Schools
Human Sciences and Society *(Works in collaboration with the University of Littoral Cote d'Opal (ULCO))* (Aesthetics; Archaeology; Arts and Humanities; Automation and Control Engineering; Cognitive Sciences; Computer Engineering; Cultural Studies; History; Information Sciences; Linguistics; Neurosciences; Psychology; Social Sciences)

Institutes
Technology *(IUT B, Tourcoing)* (Information Technology; Technology; Transport Management)

Units
Ancient Languages and Cultures (Ancient Civilizations; Ancient Languages); **Applied Foreign Languages** *(UFR LEA)* (International Business; Modern Languages); **Arts and Culture** (Communication Studies; Cultural Studies; Dance; Fine Arts; Media Studies; Music; Theatre); **Educational Sciences** (Educational Sciences); **Germanic and Scandinavian Studies** (Danish; Dutch; German; Icelandic; Scandinavian Languages; Swedish); **History, Arts, and Political Science** (Arts and Humanities; History; Political Sciences) *Director*: René Grevet; **Information and Communication Studies** *(Infocom, Roubaix)* (Communication Studies; Information Sciences; Mass Communication); **Language, Literatures and Civilizations of English-speaking Countries** *(UFR Angellier)* (English Studies; Linguistics; Literature; Modern Languages); **Mathematics, Economics, and Social Sciences** *(UFR MSES)* (Economics; Mathematics; Social Sciences); **Modern Literature** (Linguistics; Literature); **Philosophy** (Philosophy); **Psychology** (Psychology); **Romance, Slavonic and Oriental Studies** (Arabic; Chinese; Hebrew; Italian; Japanese; Oriental Languages; Oriental Studies; Polish; Portuguese; Romance Languages; Russian; Slavic Languages; Spanish) *Director*: Constantin Bobas; **Scientific and Information Techniques and Documentation** *(UFR IDIST)* (Documentation Techniques; Information Sciences; Information Technology)

Further Information: Also 29 Research Centres and Institutes

History: Founded 1970 under the 1968 law reforming higher education as one of three Universities replacing the former Université de Lille - founded 1560 at Douai and authorized by Papal Bull. The University was suppressed by the Revolution and replaced by Faculties in Lille and Douai, the latter being subsequently transferred to Lille in 1887. Reconstituted as university 1896. A State institution enjoying academic and Financial autonomy, operating under the jurisdiction of the Ministry of Education and financed by the State.

Governing Bodies: Conseil de l'Université, including elected representatives of teaching staff, research workers, students, and administrative and technical staff, as well as non-university members drawn from the public and private sectors; Conseil of each Unit, comprising representatives of its teaching staff, research workers, students, and administrative and technical staff; Conseil scientifique, competent in matters of research. The President is elected by the Conseil de l'Université. The Chancelier, who represents the Minister of Education, is the Recteur of the Académie de Lille

Academic Year: October to June (October-December; January-March; April-June)

Admission Requirements: Secondary school certificate (baccalauréat) or recognized foreign equivalent, or special entrance examination

Main Language(s) of Instruction: French

Degrees and Diplomas: *Diplôme universitaire de Technologie*: Information and Communication, Logistics, Transport Management, Social Work, Publishing and Book Trade, 2 yrs; *Licence*: Social Sciences, Arts and Humanities, Information and Communication, Modern Languages, Administration, 3 yrs; *Licence professionnelle*: Documentation Techniques, Communication, Administration; *Diplôme d'Etat*: Educational and Student Counselling, School Psychologist; *Diplôme national de Master*: Arts and Humanities, Documentation Techniques, Information and Communication, Cultural Studies, Linguistics, Modern Languages, Applied Mathematics, Computer Science, Economics, Administration, History, Educational Sciences, Philosophy, Psychology; Social Work in Behavioural Disorders; *Doctorat*: Modern Languages, Social Sciences, Arts and Humanities, 2-4 yrs following Masters. Masters Recherche, Masters professionnel, Diplôme Universitaire - Proficiency in Modern Languages, Preparation for CAPES, Agrégation and IEP

Student Services: Academic counselling, Canteen, Cultural centre, Employment services, Foreign student adviser, Handicapped facilities, Health services, Nursery care, Social counselling, Sports facilities

Student Residential Facilities: Yes

Special Facilities: Museum of Egyptology

Libraries: Bibliothèque interuniversitaire

Publications: Revue des Sciences humaines *(quarterly)*; Revue du Centre de Recherches sur l'Histoire de l'Europe du Nord-Ouest; Revue du Nord *(quarterly)*

Press or Publishing House: Presses Universitaires du Septentrion
Last Updated: 11/07/11

LILLE SCHOOL OF ARCHITECTURE AND LANDSCAPE

Ecole nationale supérieure d'Architecture et de Paysage de Lille (ENSAPL)
2 rue Verte, 59650 Villeneuve d'Ascq
Tel: +33(3) 20-61-95-50
Fax: +33(3) 20-61-95-51
EMail: ensap@lille.archi.fr
Website: http://www.lille.archi.fr

Directeur: Jean-Marc Zuretti (2006-)

International Relations: Virginie Perotti
EMail: v-perotti@lille.archi.fr

Programmes
Architecture (Architecture); **Landscape Architecture** (Landscape Architecture)

History: Founded 1979.

Main Language(s) of Instruction: French

Accrediting Agencies: Ministère de la Culture

Degrees and Diplomas: *Licence*; *Diplôme national de Master*. diplôme d'Architecte Diplômé d'Etat; Habilitation à exercer la maîtrise d'oeuvre en son nom propre
Last Updated: 28/06/11

LIMOGES-AUBUSSON NATIONAL ART SCHOOL

Ecole nationale supérieure d'Art de Limoges-Aubusson
19 avenue Martin Luther King, 87000 Limoges
Tel: +33(5) 55-43-14-00
Fax: +33(5) 55-43-14-01
EMail: accueillimoges@ensa-l-a.fr
Website: http://www.ensa-limoges-aubusson.fr

Directeur: Benoit Bavouset (2008-)

Programmes
Visual Arts (Ceramic Art; Design; Textile Design; Visual Arts)

Further Information: Has studio in Jingdezhen (China).

History: Acquired present status in 2003.

Admission Requirements: Baccalauréat or equivalent secondary school exam. Entrance exam with a selection jury.

Main Language(s) of Instruction: French

Accrediting Agencies: Ministry of Culture and Communication

Degrees and Diplomas: Diplome national d'arts plastiques (DNAP) 3 yrs; Diplome national supérieur d'expression plastique (DNSEP) a further 2 yrs
Last Updated: 07/07/11

LORRAINE SCHOOL OF ART

Ecole supérieure d'Art de Lorraine
1 rue de la Citadelle, 57000 Metz
Tel: +33(3) 87-39-61-30
EMail: beauxarts@metzmetropole.fr
Website: http://esam.metzmetropole.fr

Directrice: Nathalie Filser

Administrative Officer: Béatrice Chirre

International Relations: Blandine Wolff

Programmes
Visual Arts (Communication Arts; Multimedia; Visual Arts)

Further Information: Also branch in Epinal

History: Founded 1950.

Academic Year: October-May

Admission Requirements: Baccalauréat or equivalent secondary school exam. Entrance exam with a selection jury.

Main Language(s) of Instruction: French

Accrediting Agencies: Ministry of Culture and Communication

Degrees and Diplomas: Diplôme national d'arts plastiques (DNAP) 3 yrs; Diplôme national d'arts et techniques (DNAT) 3 yrs; Diplôme national supérieur d'expression plastique (DNSEP) a further 2 yrs
Last Updated: 18/05/11

LOUVRE SCHOOL

Ecole du Louvre
Palais du Louvre, Place du Carroussel, porte Jaujard, 75038 Paris, Cedex 01
Tel: +33(1) 55-35-18-35
Fax: +33(1) 55-35-18-64
EMail: international@ecoledulouvre.fr
Website: http://www.ecoledulouvre.fr

Directeur: Philippe Durey

International Relations: Sophie Mouquin
Tel: +33(1) 55-35-18-02 EMail: sophie.mouquin@ecoledulouvre.fr

Programmes
History of Art and Museum Studies (Archaeology; Art History; Museum Studies)

History: Established in 1882.

Academic Year: September-May

Admission Requirements: Baccalauréat or equivalent Secondary School Degree; competitive entrance exam

Fees: (Euros): 360 p.a. for undergraduate studies; 520 p.a. for graduate studies

Main Language(s) of Instruction: French, English, Italian, Greman

International Co-operation: With University of Montreal, Venice Institution, University of Neuchâtel, University of Maryland, etc.

Accrediting Agencies: Ministry of Culture

Degrees and Diplomas: Undergraduate Degree in History of Arts (3yrs); Diplôme de deuxième cycle de l'Ecole du Louvre (Masters-level Degree, a further 2 yrs); Diplôme de recherche approfondie de l'Ecole du Louvre

Last Updated: 27/06/11

LYONS I UNIVERSITY

Université Claude Bernard (Lyon I)

43, boulevard du 11 novembre 1918, 69622 Villeurbanne, Cedex
Tel: +33(4) 72-44-80-00
Fax: +33(4) 72-43-10-20
EMail: secretaire.general@adm.univ-lyon1.fr
Website: http://www.univ-lyon1.fr

Président: Alain Bonmartin (2011-)
Tel: +33(4) 72-44-80-16, Fax: +33(4) 72-43-12-36
EMail: Secretariat.presidence@adm.univ-lyon1.fr;
presidence@adm.univ-lyon1.fr

Directeur général des services: Gilles Gay
Tel: +33(4) 72-44-80-28, Fax: +33(4) 72-43-12-36

International Relations: Dominique Marcel-Chatelain, Vice-Présidente
Tel: +33(4) 72-43-26-03, Fax: +33(4) 72-43-12-13
EMail: Dominique.Marcel-Chatelain@adm.univ-lyon1.fr

Centres
Astronomy (OAL) (Astronomy and Space Science; Astrophysics)

Departments
Research in Human Biology (Biological and Life Sciences; Biology)

Graduate Schools
Chemistry, Processes and Environment (In collaboration with INSA Lyon, ENS Lyon, IFP School and partner with ENTPE) (Chemistry; Environmental Studies); **Computer Science and Mathematics** (ED InfoMaths in collaboration with INSA, ENS, ECL and University Lyon II) (Computer Science; Mathematics); **Economics and Management Sciences** (ED SEG in collaboration with University Lyon III, Lyon II and Jean Monnet University of Saint-Etienne) (Economics; Management); **Education, Psychology, Information and Communication** (ED EPIC in collaboration with University Lyon II, University Lyon III, Jean Monnet University of Saint-Etienne, IEP of Lyon, INSA of Lyon, ENS of Lyon) (Communication Studies; Education; Information Sciences; Psychology); **Electronics, Electro Techniques and Automation of Lyon** (ED EEA In collaboration with INSA and ECL of Lyon) (Electrical Engineering; Electronic Engineering; Production Engineering); **Evolution, Ecosystems and Microbiology Modelling** (E2MR In collaboration with INSA of Lyon and partner with VetAgro Sup of Lyon) (Ecology; Microbiology); **Interdisplinary Basic and Health Sciences** (EDISS in collaboration with INSA and partner with VetAgro Sup of Lyon) (Biochemistry; Biotechnology); **Materials Sciences and Engineering** (In collaboration with INSA, ECL and ENS) (Materials Engineering; Mathematics; Nanotechnology); **Mechanics, Energy, Civil and Acoustics Engineering** (ED MEGA in collaboration with INSA and ECL) (Civil Engineering; Energy Engineering; Mechanical Engineering; Sound Engineering (Acoustics)); **Molecular, Integrative and Cellular Biology** (ED BMIC in collaboration with ENS Lyon) (Biology; Cell Biology; Molecular Biology); **Neurosciences and Cognition** (ED NSCo in collaboration with University Lyon II) (Cognitive Sciences; Neurosciences); **Physics and Astrophysics** (ED PHAST in collaboration with ENS Lyon) (Astrophysics; Physics)

Institutes
Applied Mathematics, Management and Economics (Applied Mathematics; Economics; Finance; Management); **Engineering Science and Techniques** (EPUL) (Engineering; Technology); **Finance and Insurance** (ISFA) (Finance; Insurance); **Pharmacy and Biology** (ISPB) (Biology; Pharmacy); **Readaptation Techniques** (ISTR) (Medical Technology; Rehabilitation and Therapy); **Teacher Training** (IUFM Lyon with 5 centres: Bourg en Bresse, Lyon, Saint-Etienne, Venissieux and Villeurbanne) (Teacher Trainers Education; Teacher Training); **Technology** (IUT Lyon 1, two sites: Bourg en Bresse and Lyon-Villeurbanne) (Biotechnology; Computer Engineering; Technology; Thermal Engineering)

Units
Biology (Biology); **Chemistry and Biochemistry** (Biochemistry; Chemistry); **Computer Science** (Computer Science); **Dentistry** (Dentistry); **Earth Sciences** (Earth Sciences); **Electrical Engineering** (UFR GEP) (Electrical Engineering); **Mathematics** (Mathematics); **Mechanical Engineering** (Mechanical Engineering); **Medicine** (Lyon Est) (Medicine); **Medicine** (Lyon Sud) (Medicine); **Physical Education and Sports** (STAPS) (Physical Education; Sports); **Physics** (Physics)

History: Founded 1970 under the 1968 law reforming higher education as one of two universities replacing the former Université de Lyon, founded 1809 as Faculties of Letters, Science, and Theology, although the origin of higher education in Lyon may be traced back to a Papal Bull of 1245. Constituted as university 1896. A State institution enjoying academic and financial autonomy, operating under the jurisdiction of the Minister of Education and financed by the State.

Governing Bodies: Conseil d'Administration, including representatives of teaching staff, research workers, students, and administrative and technical staff, as well as non-university members drawn from the public and private sectors; Conseil scientifique, competent in matters of research; Conseil des Etudes et de la Vie universitaire; Conseil of each Unit, comprising representatives of its teaching staff, research workers, students, and administrative and technical staff. President is elected by the first three bodies. The Chancelier, who represents the Minister of Education, is the Recteur of the Académie de Lyon

Academic Year: September to June (September-February; February-June)

Admission Requirements: Secondary school certificate (baccalauréat) or equivalent, or special entrance examination

Fees: (Euros): Licence, 174 per annum; Master, 237; Engineering 564, Doctorate 359, Health Insurance 200

Main Language(s) of Instruction: French

Degrees and Diplomas: Diplôme universitaire de Technologie: Electrical Engineering; Industrial Engineering; Mechanical Engineering; Business and Commerce; Bioengineering; Chemistry; Civil Engineering; Chemical Engineering; Engineering Management; Computer Science; Business Administration; Thermal and Energy Engineering, 2 yrs; Licence: Biochemistry; Biology; Chemistry; Computer Science; Mathematics; Apllied Mathematics and Social Sciences; Physics; Earth Sciences; Engineering; Physical Education and Sport, 6 sem; Licence professionnelle: 2 sem after the 2 first yrs; Diplôme d'Etat: Dental Surgery, 6 yrs; Diplôme d'Etat: Medicine, 6 yrs plus 1 yr thesis; Diplôme d'Etat: Pharmacy, 4 yrs and 1 yr practical work; Diplôme d'Ingénieur: Engineering, 3 yrs following 1st 2 yrs; Diplôme national de Master: 4 sem.; Doctorat: 2-4 yrs following Master or DEA; Doctorat: Human Biology, 2-4 yrs following Master or DEA; Doctorat: Pharmacy, 2 yrs following Diplome d'Etat; Certificat de Spécialité: Medicine, at least 3 yrs following Diplôme d'Etat. Also various professional qualifications for health personnel

Student Services: Cultural centre, Foreign Studies Centre, Handicapped facilities, Health services, Sports facilities

Special Facilities: History of Medicine Museum. Mineral Museum. Herbarium. Observatory

Libraries: Bibliothèque universitaire: Science, c. 331,500 vols; Health, c. 350,000

Publications: Isotopes (quarterly)

Academic Staff 2009-2010	MEN	WOMEN	TOTAL
FULL-TIME	1,647	983	**2,630**
Student Numbers 2009-2010			
All (Foreign Included)	16,276	18,135	**34,411**

Last Updated: 06/06/11

LYONS II UNIVERSITY

Université Lumière (Lyon II)

86, rue Pasteur, 69365 Lyon, Cedex 07
Tel: +33(4) 78-69-70-00
Fax: +33(4) 78-69-56-01
EMail: dri@univ-lyon2.fr
Website: http://www.univ-lyon2.fr

Président: André Tiran
Tel: +33(4) 78-69-71-52, Fax: +33(4) 78-58-91-77
EMail: president@univ-lyon2.fr

Secrétaire général: Alain Helleu
Tel: +33 (4) 78-69-56-01 EMail: alain.helleu@univ-lyon2.fr

International Relations: Christian Montès
Tel: +33(4) 78-69-71-82, Fax: +33(4) 37-28-92-80

Centres
French Studies (CIEF for foreign students) (French) Director: François Nsuka-Nkutsi; **Lifelong Education; Modern Languages** (Lyon) (Modern Languages) Director: Isabel Pradat-Paz; **Preparatory Administrative Studies** (CPAG) (Public Administration); **Training of Music Teachers** (CFMI) (Music Education) Director: Alain Dessigne

Faculties
Anthropology and Sociology (Bron campus) (Anthropology; Sociology); **Economics and Management** (Lyon) (Economics; Management) Dean: André Tiran; **Geography, History, Art History and Tourism** (Bron) (Ancient Civilizations; Archaeology; Art History; Geography; History; Rural Studies; Urban Studies); **Languages** (Arabic; English; German; Portuguese; Spanish; Translation and Interpretation); **Law and Political Science** (Bron) (Administration; Economics; Law); **Letters, Language Sciences and Arts** (LESLA Lyon) (Arts and Humanities; Cinema and Television; Gender Studies; Linguistics; Literature; Music; Musicology; Theatre; Visual Arts)

Graduate Schools
Arts and Humanities (ED HSH In cooperation with ENS) (Arabic; Arts and Humanities; English Studies; Germanic Studies; Hispanic American Studies; Information Sciences; Linguistics; Literature; Mediterranean Studies; Psychology; Translation and Interpretation); **Civilisations and Law** (ED SSD In cooperation with ENS) (Ancient Civilizations; Ancient Languages; Anthropology; Demography and Population; Educational Sciences; History; Law; Political Sciences; Sociology); **Cognitive Sciences** (ED CS In cooperation with ENS Lyon) (Cognitive Sciences; Neurosciences; Psychology); **Computer Science and Information for Societies** (ED ISS In partnership with INSA, ECL and University Lyon I) (Computer Science); **Economics and Administration** (ED ECOGEST In cooperation with ENS) (Administration; Economics)

Institutes
Communication (Bron) (Communication Studies); **Educational Sciences** (Educational Sciences); **Fashion** (Fashion Design); **Labour Studies** (Lyon) (Labour and Industrial Relations; Labour Law); **Political Studies** (IEP) (Political Sciences); **Psychology** (Bron) (Psychology); **Technology** (IUT Bron) (Business Administration; Hygiene; Safety Engineering; Technology; Transport Management); **Union Training** (IFS Lyon) (Labour and Industrial Relations)

Further Information: Two sites: Central campus located in Lyon and 2nd campus located at Bron

History: Founded 1970 under the 1968 law reforming higher education as one of three Universities replacing the former Université de Lyon, founded 1809 as Faculties of Letters; Science; and Theology, although the origin of higher education in Lyons may be traced back to a Papal Bull of 1245. Constituted as University 1896. A State institution enjoying academic and financial autonomy, operating under the jurisdiction of the Minister of Education and financed by the State.

Governing Bodies: Conseil d'Administration, including representatives of teaching staff, research workers, students, and administrative and technical staff, as well as non-university members drawn from the public and private sectors; Conseil scientifique, competent in matters of research; Conseil des Etudes et de la Vie universitaire; and Conseil of each Unit, comprising representatives of its teaching staff, research workers, students, and administrative and technical staff. The President is elected by the first three bodies. The Chancelier, who represents the Minister of Education, is the Recteur of the Académie de Lyon

Academic Year: October to June (October-February; February-June)

Admission Requirements: Secondary school certificate (baccalauréat) or equivalent, or special entrance examination

Main Language(s) of Instruction: French

Degrees and Diplomas: Capacité en Droit: Law, 2 yrs; Diplôme d' Accès aux Etudes universitaires; Diplôme universitaire de Technologie: Industrial Management; Licence: Arts and Humanities, Modern Languages, Classical Languages, Social Sciences, Law, Economics, Administration, French, 3 years; Licence professionnelle: Administration, Banking, Human Resources, Industrial Management, Textile Technology, 3 years; Diplôme national de Master: Arts and Humanities, Modern Languages, Classical Languages, Social Sciences, Law, Economics, Administration, French, 2 years following Licence; Doctorat: Demography, Law, Social Law, English Studies, Germanic Studies, Mediterranean Studies, Geography, History, Computer Sciences, Ancient Civilisations, Translation, Neurosciences, Psychology, Cognitive Sciences, Economics, Political Science, 2-4 yrs following Masters; Doctorat: Educational Sciences, Modern Languages and Literature, Sociology, Anthropolgy, Administration, 2-4 years following Masters. Masters de recherche, Masters professionnel, Diplome de l'IEP

Special Facilities: Musée des Moulages

Libraries: Bibliothèque interuniversitaire

Publications: Textes et documents (monthly)

Press or Publishing House: Presses universitaires de Lyon
Last Updated: 19/07/11

LYONS III UNIVERSITY
Université Jean Moulin (Lyon III)
Manufacture des Tabacs, 6 cours Albert Thomas, 69355 Lyon, Cedex 08
Tel: +33(4) 78-78-78-78
Fax: +33(4) 78-78-79-79
EMail: ri@univ-lyon3.fr
Website: http://www.univ-lyon3.fr

Président: Hugues Fulchiron (2007-)
Tel: +33(4) 26-31-85-12, Fax: +33(4) 26-31-86-13
EMail: presid@univ-lyon3.fr

Secrétaire général: Bernard Pascal
Tel: +33(4) 78-78-70-05 EMail: dgs@univ-lyon3.fr

International Relations: Jean-Jacques Wunenburger
Tel: +33(4) 78-78-73-93, Fax: +33(4) 26-31-85-97

Centres
Law, Letters and Languages (CEUBA, Antenne Bourg-en-Bresse) (Arts and Humanities; Law; Modern Languages)

Faculties
Humanities (Arts and Humanities; Classical Languages; Communication Studies; Geography; Information Technology; Literature; Modern Languages); **Languages** (Cultural Studies; Linguistics; Modern Languages); **Law** (European Union Law; International Law; Law; Notary Studies; Political Sciences); **Philosophy** (Aesthetics; Ethics; Philosophy)

Graduate Schools
Law (Law) Director: Blandine Mallet-Bricout; **Management, Information, Finance** (ED MIF in cooperation with University Lyon I) (Finance; Management; Mass Communication) Director: Bernard Wuilleme; **Systems, Images and Languages** Director: Pierre Servet

Institutes
Business Administration (IAE) (Business Administration; Management) Director: Gilles Guyot; **French Studies and Globalisation** (FRAMOND) (French Studies) Director: Michel Guillou; **Health Services Management** (IFROSS) (Health Administration) Director: Jean-Pierre Claveranne; **Information Sciences and Communication Studies** (IUP INFOCOM) (Communication Studies; Information Sciences); **Law in Art and Culture** (IUP) (Law); **Technology** (IUT) (Information Technology; Justice Administration; Management; Technology)

Programmes
Law in Art and Culture (IUP) (Law) Director: Gérard Sousi

Schools
Business Studies (IAE) (Accountancy; Economics; Finance; Human Resources; Information Technology; Management)

History: Founded 1973, formerly part of Université de Lyon II and tracing its origins to the former Université de Lyon, founded 1809 as Faculties of Letters; Science and Theology, although the origin of higher education in Lyon may be traced back to a Papal Bull of 1245. Constituted as University 1896. A State institution enjoying academic and financial autonomy, operating under the jurisdiction of the Minister of Education and financed by the State.

Governing Bodies: Conseil de l'Université, including elected representatives of teaching staff, research workers, students, and administrative and technical staff, as well as non-university members drawn from the public and private sectors; Conseil of each Unit, comprising representatives of its teaching staff, research workers, students, and administrative and technical staff; Conseil scientifique, competent in matters of research. The President is elected by the Conseil de l'Université. The Chancelier, who represents the Minister of Education, is the Recteur de l'Académie de Lyon

Academic Year: September to May (September-December/January; January- April/May)

Admission Requirements: Secondary school certificate (baccalauréat) or equivalent, or special entrance examination

Main Language(s) of Instruction: French

International Co-operation: With universities in the European Union; Central Europe; North America; China; Japan; Australia

Degrees and Diplomas: *Licence*: Business Administration, Languages, Law, Arts and Humanities, 3 years; *Licence professionnelle*: Human Resources, Management, Business Administration, 3 yrs; *Diplôme national de Master*; *Doctorat*: Modern Languages and Literature, Law, Management, Communication, Finance, Geography, History, Philosophy, 3 yrs following Masters

Libraries: 4 libraries

Publications: Annales de la Faculté de Droit *(annually)*; Revue d'Etudes indo-européennes *(quarterly)*
Last Updated: 24/06/11

LYONS SCHOOL OF ARCHITECTURE
Ecole nationale supérieure d'Architecture de Lyon (EAL)
BP 170, 3, rue Maurice Audin, 69512 Vaulx-en-Velin
Tel: +33(4) 78-79-50-50
Fax: +33(4) 78-80-40-68
EMail: ensal@lyon.archi.fr
Website: http://www.lyon.archi.fr

Directrice: Nathalie Mezureux
EMail: nathalie.mezureux@lyon.archi.fr

Programmes
Architecture (Architecture)
History: Founded 1906 as École d'Architecture de Lyon.
Admission Requirements: Baccalauréat or equivalent
Main Language(s) of Instruction: French
Degrees and Diplomas: *Licence*; *Diplôme national de Master*; *Doctorat*. Habilitation de l'architecte diplômé d'état à l'exercicede la Maîtrise d'ouvre en son Nom Propre (HMONP)
Last Updated: 27/06/11

MARSEILLES-MEDITERRANEAN SCHOOL OF ART AND DESIGN
École supérieure d'Art et de Design Marseille-Méditerranée (ESADMM)
184 avenue de Luminy, 13288 Marseille, Cedex 9
Tel: +33(4) 91-82-83-10
Fax: +33(4) 91-82-83-11
EMail: contact.web.esbam@free.fr
Website: http://www.esbam.fr

Directeur: Jean-Louis Connan EMail: mray@mairie-marseille.fr

Programmes
Design; **Fine Arts** (Fine Arts)
History: Founded 1752 as École des beaux-arts de Marseille. Acquired present title 2011.
Admission Requirements: Baccalauréat or equivalent secondary school exam. Entrance exam with a selection jury.

Main Language(s) of Instruction: French
Accrediting Agencies: Ministry of Culture and Communication
Degrees and Diplomas: Diplôme national d'arts plastiques (DNAP in design) 3 yrs; Diplôme national d'arts et techniques (DNAT in interior design) 3 yrs; Diplôme national supérieur d'expression plastique (DNSEP) a further 2 yrs
Last Updated: 03/11/11

MARSEILLES SCHOOL OF ARCHITECTURE
Ecole nationale supérieure d'Architecture de Marseille (ENSA-MARSEILLE)
184, avenue de Luminy, 13288 Marseille, Cedex 09
Tel: +33(4) 91-82-71-00
Fax: +33(4) 91-82-71-80
EMail: contact@marseille.archi.fr
Website: http://www.marseille.archi.fr

Directrice: Marielle Riche (2009-)
EMail: directeur@marseille.archi.fr

Secrétaire Général: Noël Fornari
EMail: noël.fornari@marseille.archi.fr

Programmes
Architecture (Architecture)
History: Founded 1752.
Main Language(s) of Instruction: French
Degrees and Diplomas: *Licence*; *Diplôme national de Master*; *Doctorat*. Also master professionnel; Diplôme Propre aux Écoles d'Architecture; Habilitation de l'architecte diplômé d'État à exercer la Maîtrise d'Oeuvre en son Nom Propre
Libraries: Yes
Last Updated: 27/06/11

MINES PARIS TECH GRADUATE SCHOOL
Mines Paris Tech
60, boulevard Saint-Michel, 75272 Paris, Cedex 06
Tel: +33(1) 40-51-90-00
Fax: +33(1) 43-54-18-98
EMail: contact@mines-paristech.fr
Website: http://www.mines-paristech.fr

Directeur: Benoît Legait
Tel: +33(1) 40-51-90-14, Fax: +33(1) 43-25-94-95

Secrétaire générale: Patricia Fournier
Tel: +33(1) 40-51-90-53, Fax: +33(1) 40-51-92-50
EMail: patricia.fournier@ensmp.fr

International Relations: Julien Bohdanowicz
Tel: +33(1) 40-51-91-46, Fax: +33(1) 40-51-93-10
EMail: julien.bohdanowicz@mines-paristech.fr

Departments
Earth Sciences and Environment (Earth Sciences; Environmental Management; Geology; Geophysics); **Economics, Management and Society** (Economics; Management; Sociology); **Energy and Process Engineering** (Energy Engineering; Materials Engineering; Thermal Engineering); **Mathematics and Systems** (Applied Mathematics; Automation and Control Engineering; Computer Science; Mathematics; Robotics); **Mechanical and Material Engineering** (Materials Engineering; Mechanical Engineering); **Physical Sciences and Engineering** (Biotechnology; Energy Engineering; Materials Engineering; Mechanical Engineering; Physics)

Laboratories
Applied Mathematics *(Sophia Antipolis)* (Applied Mathematics) *Director*: Nadia Maïzi; **Computational Biology** *(Fontainebleau)* *Head*: Jean-Philippe Vert; **Computer Science** *(Fontainebleau)* (Computer Science) *Director*: Robert Mahl; **Energy and Processes** (Energy Engineering) *Director*: Jérôme Gosset; **Geosciences** *(Fontainebleau)* (Geology; Geophysics; Mining Engineering) *Director*: Damien Goetz; **Industrial Economics** (Industrial Management) *Director*: Gilles Le Blanc; **Materials Engineering** *(Evry)* (Materials Engineering) *Director*: Esteban Busso; **Materials Forming** *(Sophia Antipolis)* (Materials Engineering) *Director*: Jean-Loup Chenot; **Mathematical Morphology** *(Fontainebleau)* (Mathematics) *Director*: Fernand Meyer; **Robotics** (Automation and Control Engineering) *Director*: Claude Laurgeau; **Scientific Management**

(Management) *Director*: Daniel Fixari; **Sociology of Innovation** (Sociology) *Director*: Madeleine Akrich; **Solids Mechanics** *(Palaiseau)* (Mechanics; Solid State Physics) *Director*: Bernard Halphen; **Systems and Control** *(Fontainebleau)* (Automation and Control Engineering) *Director*: Philippe Martin

Programmes
Economic Evaluation of Mining Projects *(CESPROMIN, Fontainebleau)* *Head*: Michel Duchene; **Environmental Engineering and Management** (Environmental Engineering; Environmental Management) *Head*: Frédérique Vincent; **Environmental Management** (Environmental Management) *Head*: Frédérique Vincent; **Gas Engineering and Management** (Engineering Management; Petroleum and Gas Engineering) *Head*: Dominique Marchio; **Geostatics** *(CSFG, Fontainebleau)* *Head*: Gaëlle Le Loc'h; **Industrial Management and Logistics Systems** (Production Engineering) *Head*: Hugues Molet; **Information and Technology Systems Management** (Information Management; Systems Analysis) *Head*: Robert Mahl; **Materials and Shaping** (Polymer and Plastics Technology) *Head*: Jean-Marc Haudin; **Materials Behaviour and Structural Design** (Materials Engineering; Structural Architecture) *Head*: Jacques Renard; **Multimedia Network Applications Engineering** (Computer Networks; Multimedia) *Head*: Robert Mahl; **Numerical Mechanics** (Mechanical Engineering) *Head*: François Bay; **Opencast Mining Quarries** *(CESECO)* (Mining Engineering) *Head*: Jean-Alain Fleurisson; **Production Engineering** (Production Engineering) *Head*: Hugues Molet; **Public Administration of Mines** *(CESAM, Fontainebleau)* (Administration; Mining Engineering) *Head*: Hugues Accarie

History: Founded 1783, moved to its present location 1816, expanded to Fontainebleau and Evry 1969, and to Sophia Antipolis, near Nice, 1976.

Academic Year: September to June

Admission Requirements: Competitive entrance examination following 2-3 yrs further study after secondary school certificate (baccalauréat) or following first university qualification (maîtrise es-science), Ecole Polytechnique alumni, or B.Sc level.

Main Language(s) of Instruction: French

International Co-operation: With universities in USA, Canada, Mexico, Brazil, Japan, Singapore, Russian Federation, Norway, Sweden, Finland, United Kingdom, Belgium, Germany, Switzerland, Italy, Spain, Portugal, Greece, Israel, Tunisia, Morocco, Niger, Côte d'Ivoire

Degrees and Diplomas: *Diplôme d'Ingénieur*; *Mastère spécialisé*: 1 yr; *Diplôme national de Master*: Engineering, 3 yrs; *Doctorat (PhD)*: a further 3 yrs

Student Services: Academic counselling, Cultural centre, Health services

Special Facilities: Mineralogy Museum

Libraries: c. 30,000 vols; 10,000 maps

Press or Publishing House: Presses de l'Ecole des Mines de Paris

Last Updated: 30/06/11

MONTPELLIER 1 UNIVERSITY
Université Montpellier 1
BP 1017, 5, boulevard Henri IV, 34006 Montpellier, Cedex 1
Tel: +33(4) 67-41-74-00
Fax: +33(4) 67-41-74-56
EMail: sri@univ-montp1.fr
Website: http://www.univ-montp1.fr

Président: Philippe Augé (2009-)
EMail: presidence@sc.univ-montp1.fr

Secrétaire général: Pascal Beauregard Tel: +33(4) 67-41-74-10

International Relations: Bernard Durand
Tel: +33(4) 67-82-12-56, Fax: +33(4) 67-82-12-58

Centres
Lifelong Education *(DIDERIS)* *Director*: Jean-Louis Monino

Graduate Schools
Economics and Management *(EDEG in cooperation with Montpellier II and ENSA)* (Economics; Management) *Director*: Jean-Marie Boisson; **Law and Social Sciences** *(In cooperation with Universities of Toulon, Avignon and Perpignan)* *Director*: Bernard

Durand; **Physical Therapy** *(In cooperation with Universities of Nice, Aix-Marseilles II, Toulon and Avignon)* (Health Sciences; Physiology) *Director*: Reinaud Bootsma

Institutes
Business *(ISEM)* (Business and Commerce) *Director*: Monique Lacroix; **Juridical Studies** *(IEJ UFR Law)* *Director*: Philippe Petel; **Law and Safety Engineering** *(ICH UFR Law)* (Law; Safety Engineering) *Director*: Marie-Elisabeth André; **Preparatory Administrative Studies** *(IPAG)* (Administration) *Director*: Eric De Mari; **Teacher Training** *(IUFM with 5 sites throughout Montpellier Department)* (Teacher Trainers Education; Teacher Training) *Director*: Patrick Demougin

Units
Dentistry (Dentistry); **Economic and Social Administration** *(UFR AES)* (Business Administration; Marketing; Public Administration); **Economics** (Economics); **Law and Political Science** (Law; Political Sciences); **Medicine** (Medicine); **Pharmaceutical and Biological Sciences** (Biological and Life Sciences; Pharmacy); **Physical Education and Sports** *(STAPS)* (Physical Education; Sports)

History: Founded 1970 under the 1968 law reforming higher education as one of three Universities replacing the former Université de Montpellier, founded 1220 by promulgation of statutes by Cardinal Conrad and confirmed by Papal Bull 1289. The university was suppressed by the Revolution and replaced by Faculties of Medicine; Pharmacy; Science; and Letters of the Université de France. Reconstituted as University 1896. A State institution enjoying academic and financial autonomy, operating under the jurisdiction of the Minister of Education and financed by the State.

Governing Bodies: Conseil de l'Université, including representatives of teaching staff, research workers, students, and administrative and technical staff, as well as non-university members drawn from the public and private sectors; Conseil of each Unit, comprising representatives of its teaching staff, research workers, students, and administrative and technical staff; and Conseil scientifique, competent in matters of research. The President is elected by the Conseil de l'Université. The Chancelier, who represents the Minister of Education, is the Recteur de l'Académie de Montpellier

Academic Year: October to June

Admission Requirements: Secondary school certificate (baccalauréat) or equivalent, or special entrance examination

Fees: (Euros): 83.85 per annum

Main Language(s) of Instruction: French

Degrees and Diplomas: *Capacité en Droit*: Law, 2 yrs; *Licence*: Law, Political Science, Economics, Administration, Management, Sports, Health, 3 yrs; *Licence professionnelle*: Law, Administration, Management, Sports, Biology, Pharmacy, 3 yrs; *Diplôme d'Etat*: Dental Surgery, Pharmacy, 6 yrs; *Diplôme d'Etat*: Medicine, 8 yrs; *Diplôme national de Master*: Law, Political Science, Economics, Management, Health, Medicine, 2 ys following Licence; *Doctorat*: Chemistry, Life Science, Social Sciences, Physical Education and Sports (PhD), at least 3 yrs following Masters; *Certificat de Spécialité*: Medicine, at least 2 yrs following Diplôme d'Etat. Masters recherche, Masters professionnel, Preparation for CAPES and Agrégation

Student Services: Canteen, Handicapped facilities, Health services, Sports facilities

Student Residential Facilities: Yes

Special Facilities: Musée d'Anatomie. Musée Atger

Libraries: Specialized libraries: Law; Economics; Medicine; Pharmacy; Dentistry

Publications: La Revue de l'Economie méridionale; LUS : Littérature ultrasonore / Faculté de Médecine Nîmes
Last Updated: 19/07/11

MONTPELLIER 2 UNIVERSITY
Université Montpellier 2 Sciences et Techniques
Place Eugène Bataillon, 34095 Montpellier, Cedex 05
Tel: +33(4) 67-14-30-30
Fax: +33(4) 67-14-30-31
EMail: presidence@univ-montp2.fr
Website: http://www.univ-montp2.fr

Présidente: Danièle Hérin
Tel: +33(4) 67-14-30-15, Fax: +33(4) 67-14-48-08

Directeur général des Services: Philippe Paillet
Tel: +33(4) 67-14-30-13 EMail: dgs@univ-montp2.fr

International Relations: Jean-Michel Portefaix
Tel: +33(4) 67-14-49-71, Fax: +33(4) 67-14-93-25
EMail: Jean-Michel.Portefaix@univ-montp2.fr

Centres
Lifelong Education (Continuing Education); **Structural Biochemistry** (Biochemistry; Biophysics); **Studies of Pathological Agents and Biotechnologies for Health** *(CPBS)* (Biophysics; Cell Biology; Microbiology; Virology)

Faculties
Science (Automation and Control Engineering; Biology; Chemistry; Computer Science; Earth Sciences; Electrical Engineering; Electronic Engineering; Environmental Studies; History; Mathematics; Mechanical Engineering; Natural Sciences; Pedagogy; Philosophy; Physics; Technology)

Graduate Schools
Chemistry *(ED Sciences Chimiques in collaboration with Montpellier I)* (Chemistry); **Health-related Chemical and Biological Processes** *(CBS2 in collaboration with Montpellier I)* (Biology; Chemistry; Health Sciences)

Institutes
Biomolecules *(Max Mousseron (IBMM))* (Molecular Biology; Pharmacology); **Business Administration** *(IAE)* (Business Administration); **Functional Genetics** *(IGF)* (Cell Biology; Genetics; Neurology; Oncology); **Human Genetics** *(IGH)* (Genetics; Molecular Biology; Pathology); **Membrane** *(European)*; **Molecular and Materials Chemistry** *(Charles Gerhardt)* (Chemistry); **Molecular Genetics** *(Montpellier)* (Cell Biology; Genetics; Oncology; Virology); **Neurosciences** *(Montpellier)* (Cell Biology; Physiology); **Separative Chemistry** *(Marcoule)* (Chemistry); **Teacher Training** *(IUFM with 5 sites throughout Montpellier Department)* (Teacher Trainers Education; Teacher Training); **Technology** *(IUT Montpellier)* (Applied Physics; Bioengineering; Biotechnology; Business Computing; Chemistry; Data Processing; Electrical Engineering; Environmental Management; Information Technology; Management; Technology); **Technology** *(IUT Nîmes)* (Business Administration; Civil Engineering; Construction Engineering; Electrical Engineering; Electronic Engineering; Management; Materials Engineering; Mechanical Engineering; Metallurgical Engineering; Technology); **Technology** *(IUT Béziers)* (Business Education; Communication Studies; Computer Networks; Marketing; Telecommunications Engineering)

Laboratories
Biology and Health Sciences *(MMDN)* (Molecular Biology); **Dynamics of Normal and Pathogenic Membrane Interactions** *(DIMNP)* (Cell Biology; Parasitology); **Physiology and Experimental Medicine of the Heart and Muscles** (Physiology)

Research Centres
Macromolecular Biochemistry *(CRBM)* (Biochemistry; Cell Biology)

Schools
Engineering *(Polytech Montpellier)* (Computer Science; Food Technology; Management; Materials Engineering; Mechanical Engineering; Robotics; Water Science)

History: Founded 1970 under the 1968 law reforming higher education as one of three Universities replacing the former Université de Montpellier, founded 1220 by promulgation of statutes by Cardinal Conrad and confirmed by Papal Bull 1242. The University was suppressed by the Revolution and replaced by Faculties of Medicine; Pharmacy; Science; and Letters of the Université de France. Reconstituted as University 1896. A State institution enjoying academic and financial autonomy, operating under the jurisdiction of the Minister of Education and financed by the State.

Governing Bodies: Conseil de l'Université, including elected representatives of teaching staff, research workers, students, and administrative and technical staff, as well as non-university members drawn from the public and private sectors; Conseil of each Unit, comprising representatives of its teaching staff, research workers, students, and administrative and technical staff; and Conseil scientifique, competent in matters of research. The President is elected

by the Conseils de l'Université. The Chancelier, who represents the Minister of Education, is the Recteur of the Académie de Montpellier

Academic Year: September to June (September-December; January-March; April-June)

Admission Requirements: Secondary school certificate (baccalauréat) or equivalent

Fees: (Euros): c. 200 per annum

Main Language(s) of Instruction: French

International Co-operation: With universities in the United Kingdom; Spain; Germany; Italy; Belgium; Netherlands; Greece; Poland; Portugal; Romania; North and Latin America; Africa

Degrees and Diplomas: *Diplôme d' Accès aux Etudes universitaires*; *Diplôme universitaire de Technologie*: Chemisty, Civil Engineering, Business Administration, Management, Telecommunications, 2 yrs; *Licence*: Mathematics and Computer Science, Erath Sciences, Environmental Studies, Physics, Chemistry, Biology, 3 yrs; *Diplôme d'Ingénieur*; *Diplôme de Recherche technologique*; *Diplôme national de Master*: Management, Science, Technology, 2 yrs following Licence; *Doctorat*: Chemistry, Physics, Biology, Agronomy, Environmental Studies, Economics, Management, Food Technology, 2-4 yrs following Masters. Preparation for Agrégation in Economics, Mathematics and Management

Student Services: Academic counselling, Foreign student adviser, Handicapped facilities, Health services, Nursery care, Social counselling, Sports facilities

Student Residential Facilities: Yes

Special Facilities: Natural History Museum

Libraries: Bibliothèque universitaire (section sciences)

Publications: Cahiers de Mathématiques; Naturalia Monopelianesa; Palaeovertebra
Last Updated: 28/07/11

MONTPELLIER III UNIVERSITY
Université Paul Valéry (Montpellier 3)
Route de Mende, 34199 Montpellier, Cedex 05
Tel: +33(4) 67-14-20-00
Fax: +33(4) 67-14-20-52
EMail: burghart.schmidt@univ-montp3.fr
Website: http://www.univ-montp3.fr

Présidente: Anne Fraïsse (2008-)
EMail: secretariat.presidence@univ-montp3.fr

Secrétaire général: Yves Chaimbault Tel: +33(4) 67-14-20-49

Departments
Applied Languages *(LEA) Director*: Pablo Nerin; **Lifelong Education** *(SUFCO) Director*: Patrick Gilli

Institutes
French Studies for Foreign Students *(IEFE)* (French); **Information and Communication Technosciences** (Communication Studies; Documentation Techniques; Information Sciences; Linguistics); **Teacher Training** *(IUFM has 5 sites throughout Montpellier)* (Teacher Trainers Education; Teacher Training) *Director*: Patrick Demougin

Units
Economics, Mathematics and Social Sciences (Administration; Applied Mathematics; Computer Science; Economics; Educational Sciences; Sanitary Engineering; Social Policy; Social Sciences); **Foreign and Regional Languages** (Arabic; Catalan; Chinese; English; German; Greek; Hebrew; Italian; Polish; Portuguese; Regional Studies; Romanian; Russian; Slavic Languages; Spanish); **Human and Environmental Sciences** (Archaeology; Art History; Biology; Ecology; Environmental Studies; History; Regional Planning); **Letters, Arts, Philosophy, and Psychoanalysis** (Arts and Humanities; Cinema and Television; Classical Languages; Fine Arts; Linguistics; Literature; Music; Performing Arts; Philosophy; Psychoanalysis; Theatre); **Man and Society** (Ethnology; Information Sciences; Psychology; Social Sciences; Sociology)

History: Founded 1970 under the 1968 law reforming higher education as one of three Universities replacing the former Université de Montpellier, founded 1220 by promulgation of statutes by Cardinal Conrad and confirmed by Papal Bull 1242. The University was suppressed by the Revolution and replaced by Faculties of

Medicine; Pharmacy; Science; and Letters of the Université de France. Reconstituted as University 1896. A State institution enjoying academic and financial autonomy, operating under the jurisdiction of the Minister of Education and financed by the State.

Governing Bodies: Conseil d'Administration, including representatives of teaching staff, research workers, students, and administrative and technical staff, as well as non-university members drawn from the public and private sectors; Conseil scientifique, competent in matters of research; Conseil des Etudes et de la Vie universitaire; and Conseil of each Unit, comprising representatives of its teaching staff, research workers, students, and administrative and technical staff. The President is elected by the first three bodies. The Chancelier, who represents the Minister of Education, is the Recteur of the Académie de Montpellier

Academic Year: October to June (October-December; January-March; April-June)

Admission Requirements: Secondary school certificate (baccalauréat) or equivalent, or special entrance examination

Main Language(s) of Instruction: French

Degrees and Diplomas: *Licence*: Literature, Modern Languages, Social Sciences, Arts and Humanities, 3 yrs; *Licence professionnelle*: Agronomy, Documentation Techniques, Social Work, Environmental Studies, 3 yrs; *Diplôme national de Master*: Literature, Arts and Humanities, Social Sciences, Modern Languages, 2 yrs following Licence; *Doctorat*: 2-4 yrs following Masters. Masters recherche, Masters professionnel, Preparation for Agrégation exams

Student Residential Facilities: Yes

Special Facilities: Musée des Moulages

Libraries: Bibliothèque interuniversitaire (Section Lettres)
Last Updated: 21/07/11

MONTPELLIER ART SCHOOL
Ecole supérieure des Beaux-Arts Montpellier Agglomération (ESBAMA)
130 rue Yéhudi Menuhin, 34000 Montpellier
Tel: +33(4) 99-58-32-85
Fax: +33(4) 99-58-32-86
EMail: esbama@montpellier-agglo.com
Website: http://esbama.free.fr/

Directeur: Philippe Reitz (2011-)

Programmes
Visual Arts (Fine Arts)

Further Information: Branch in Nîmes

Admission Requirements: Baccalauréat or equivalent secondary school exam. Entrance exam with a selection jury.

Fees: (Euros): 266 p.a.; non-residents, 594

Main Language(s) of Instruction: French

Accrediting Agencies: Ministry of Culture and Communication

Degrees and Diplomas: Diplôme national d'arts plastiques (DNAP) 3 yrs; Diplôme national supérieur d'expression plastique (DNSEP) a further 2 yrs
Last Updated: 04/07/11

MONTPELLIER SCHOOL OF ARCHITECTURE
Ecole nationale supérieure d'Architecture de Montpellier (EALR)
179, rue de l'Espérou, 34093 Montpellier, Cedex 05
Tel: +33(4) 67-91-89-89
Fax: +33(4) 67-41-35-07
EMail: christine.beauvallet@montpellier.archi.fr
Website: http://www.montpellier.archi.fr

Directeur: Laurent Heulot
EMail: laurent.heulot@montpellier.archi.fr

Programmes
Architecture (Architecture)

Further Information: Ecole d'architecture de l'île de la Réunion

History: Founded 1903 as Ecole Régionale d'Architecture.

Main Language(s) of Instruction: French

Degrees and Diplomas: *Licence*; *Diplôme national de Master*. Habilitation de l'architecte diplômé d'Etat à l'exercice de la maîtrise d'oeuvre en son nom propre
Last Updated: 27/06/11

MONTPELLIER SUPAGRO
Montpellier SupAgro
2, place Pierre Viala, 34060 Montpellier, Cedex 01
Tel: +33(4) 99-61-22-00
Fax: +33(4) 99-61-25-80
EMail: robinius@supagro.inra.fr
Website: http://www.supagro.fr

Directeur général: Etienne Landais (2001-)
Tel: +33(4) 99-61-21-42 EMail: landais@supagro.inra.fr

Directrice Adjointe: Isabelle Touzard Tel: +33(4) 99-61-24-58

International Relations: Jean-Luc Bosio Tel: +33(4) 99-61-25-69

Departments
Agro-Bio-Process Science (Biochemistry; Computer Science; Mathematics; Microbiology; Physics; Production Engineering; Statistics); **Ecology and Plant Health** (Agronomy; Biology; Ecology; Genetics; Plant and Crop Protection); **Economics, Social Sciences and Management** (Agricultural Economics; Business Administration; Environmental Management; Food Science; Management; Natural Resources; Rural Planning; Water Management); **Media, Productions, Resources and Systems** (Agronomy; Animal Husbandry; Irrigation; Soil Science); **Plant Sciences** (Botany; Ecology; Genetics; Physiology; Plant and Crop Protection; Viticulture)

Institutes
Tropical Agrofood Industries and Rural Development *(IRC)* (Agriculture; Agronomy; Food Science; Rural Planning; Rural Studies; Tropical Agriculture); **Vine and Wine Advanced Studies** *(IHEV)* (Oenology; Viticulture)

History: Founded 1872. Acquired present status 2007 following merger of Montpellier National School of Agronomy, The National Centre for Tropical and Sub-tropical Environments, The National School of Agro-Food Industry.

Governing Bodies: Conseil Général; Conseil des Enseignants; Conseil Scientifique; Conseils de Départements

Academic Year: Organized on a semester and modular basis

Admission Requirements: Competitive entrance examination following 2 yrs further study after secondary school certificate (baccalauréat) or specific examination after a Bachelor of Science in Agricultural Sciences for foreign students

Fees: (Euros): Engineer course, 900 per annum, Mastère, 4,500; Post- Master, 7,000-9,000

Main Language(s) of Instruction: French

International Co-operation: Participates in Erasmus (Spain; Germany; Belgium; Netherlands; Czech Republic; Italy; Sweden), Morocco, Algeria, Tunisia, Latin America, Thailand, Cambodia Senegal

Accrediting Agencies: Commission des Titres d'Ingenieurs (CTI); Conférence des Grandes Ecoles (CGE)

Degrees and Diplomas: *Licence professionnelle*; *Diplôme d'Ingénieur*; *Mastère spécialisé (MIAL)*: 1 yr; *Diplôme national de Master*. Agriculture Economics; Management (MSc); Animal Husbandry; Breeding Systems (MSc); Crop protection (MSc); Crops; Tropical Agriculture (MSc); Ecology; Biodiversity; Plant Pathology; Biological Interaction (MSc); Ecosystems; Soil Science; Agronomy (MSc); Food Science; Food Technology (MSc); Food Science; Quality Management; Tropical productions (MSc); Microbiology; Symbiosis (MSc); Molecular Biology (MSc); Oenology; Viticulture (MSc); Vegetal Biotechnology (MSc), 2 yrs(possibility of 1 yr according to previous schooling); *Doctorat*: Biology; Agronomy (PhD); Economics and Management (PhD); Food Sciences (PhD); Soil and Water Sciences (PhD), 3 yrs

Student Services: Academic counselling, Canteen, Employment services, Foreign student adviser, Handicapped facilities, Language programs, Sports facilities

Student Residential Facilities: Yes

Libraries: Central Library
Last Updated: 30/05/11

NANCY NATIONAL ART SCHOOL

Ecole nationale supérieure d'Arts de Nancy (ENSAN)

BP 3129, 1, avenue Boffrand, 54013 Nancy, Cedex

Tel: +33(3) 83-41-61-61
Fax: +33(3) 83-28-78-60
EMail: ecole.art@ensa-nancy.fr
Website: http://www.ensa-nancy.fr

Directeur: Christian Debize EMail: direction@ensa-nancy.fr

International Relations: Susan Mollon
Tel: +33(3) 82-27-23-04 EMail: susan.mollon@ensa-nancy.fr

Departments
Communication (Communication Arts; Communication Studies); **Design** (Design); **Fine Arts** (Fine Arts)

History: Founded 1702 as Académie de peinture et de sculpture. Acquired present status 2003.

Fees: (Euros) 360 per annum

Main Language(s) of Instruction: French

Accrediting Agencies: Ministère de la culture et de la communication

Degrees and Diplomas: *Diplôme national de Master.* Diplome national d'arts plastiques (DNAP) 3 yrs; Diplome national supérieur d'expression plastique (DNSEP) a further 2 yrs
Last Updated: 30/06/11

NANCY SCHOOL OF ARCHITECTURE

Ecole nationale supérieure d'Architecture de Nancy (EAN)

BP 40435, 2, rue Bastien Lépage, 54001 Nancy, Cedex

Tel: +33(3) 83-30-81-00
Fax: +33(3) 83-30-81-30
EMail: ean@nancy.archi.fr
Website: http://www.nancy.archi.fr

Directeur: Lorenzo Diez
Tel: +33(3) 83-30-81-25 EMail: lorenzo.diez@nancy.archi.fr

Secrétaire générale: Bernadette Clavel
Tel: +33(3) 83-30-81-24 EMail: bernadette.clavel@nancy.archi.fr

International Relations: Fabrice Picquet
Tel: +33(3) 83-30-81-05 EMail: fabrice.picquet@nancy.archi.fr

Schools
Architecture (Architecture)

History: Founded 1970. Under the responsibility of the Ministry of Culture and Communication.

Academic Year: October to June

Admission Requirements: Secondary school certificate (baccalauréat)

Fees: (Euros): First cycle, 180; 2nd and 3rd cycles, 330

Main Language(s) of Instruction: French

International Co-operation: With universities in Germany, Belgium, Spain, Finland, United Kingdom, Greece, Italy, Netherlands, Hungary, Poland, Portugal, Czech Republic and China.

Degrees and Diplomas: *Licence*; *Diplôme national de Master*; *Doctorat*

Student Services: Canteen

Libraries: Mediathèque
Last Updated: 12/05/11

NANTES SCHOOL OF ARCHITECTURE

Ecole nationale supérieure d'Architecture de Nantes (ENSA-NANTES)

BP 16202, 6 quai François Mitterrand, BP 81931, 44262 Nantes, Cedex 2

Tel: +33(2) 40-16-01-21
Fax: +33(2) 40-59-16-70
EMail: ensa@nantes.archi.fr
Website: http://www.nantes.archi.fr

Directeur: Philippe Bataille

International Relations: Nathalie Aknin
Tel: +33(2) 40-16-02-33 EMail: nathalie.aknin@nantes.archi.fr

Programmes
Architecture (Architecture)

History: Founded 1945.

Main Language(s) of Instruction: French

Degrees and Diplomas: *Licence*: 3 yrs; *Mastère spécialisé*; *Diplôme national de Master*: 2 yrs. Also DPEA Naval Architecture (13 mths), Scenography (3 yrs), Habilitation à exercer la maîtrise d'oeuvre en son nom propre for graduate architects
Last Updated: 06/06/11

NANTES SCHOOL OF FINE ARTS

Ecole supérieure des Beaux-Arts de Nantes Métropole (ESBA NANTES)

Place Dulcie September, BP 20119, 44000 Nantes, Cedex 01

Tel: +33(2) 40-35-90-20
Fax: +33(2) 40-35-90-69
EMail: contact@esba-nantes.fr
Website: http://www.esba-nantes.fr/

Directeur: Pierre-Jean Galdin
EMail: pierre-jean.galdin@]esba-nantes.fr

Programmes
Art (Fine Arts)

Further Information: Engaged in a research project, Abstraction.

History: Founded 1904. Acquired present status 2010.

Admission Requirements: Baccalauréat or equivalent secondary school exam. Entrance exam with a selection jury.

Fees: (Euros): 509

Main Language(s) of Instruction: French

International Co-operation: With schools in China, Japan, Germany, Austria, Denmark, Finland, UK, Ireland, Italy, Norway, Netherlands, Canada

Accrediting Agencies: Ministry of Culture and Communication

Degrees and Diplomas: Diplôme national d'arts plastiques (DNAP) 3 yrs; Diplôme national supérieur d'expression plastique (DNSEP) a further 2 yrs equivalent to Master level
Last Updated: 30/05/11

NANTES-ATLANTIQUE NATIONAL SCHOOL OF VETERINARY SCIENCE, FOOD PROCESSING AND FOOD STUDIES

Ecole nationale vétérinaire, agroalimentaire et de l'alimentation, Nantes-Atlantique (ONIRIS)

BP 82225, Rue de la Géraudière, 44322 Nantes, Cedex 03

Tel: +33(2) 51-78-54-54
Fax: +33(2) 51-78-54-55
EMail: contact@oniris-nantes.fr
Website: http://www.oniris-nantes.fr

Directeur général: Pierre Saï EMail: direction@vet-nantes.fr

International Relations: Dominique Colin

Areas
Engineering (Biotechnology; Engineering; Pharmacology); **Food and Food Processing** (Food Science; Food Technology); **Veterinary Science** (Veterinary Science)

History: Founded 2009 following merger of the École nationale d'ingénieurs des techniques des industries agricoles et agroalimentaires (ENITIAA) and the École nationale vétérinaire de Nantes (ENVN).

Academic Year: October to June

Admission Requirements: Competitive entrance examination following 2-3 yrs further study after secondary school certificate (baccalauréat) or following first university qualification (DEUG, DUT, BTS), or equivalent

Fees: (Euros): 838 per annum

Main Language(s) of Instruction: French

International Co-operation: Socrates, Tempus, Cooperation programmes with Canada, USA and Mexico

Accrediting Agencies: Ministry of Agriculture

Degrees and Diplomas: *Brevet de Technicien supérieur*; *Licence professionnelle*: 3 yrs; *Diplôme d'Ingénieur*: 5 yrs; *Diplôme national de Master*. Masters recherche, Masters professionnel

Student Services: Academic counselling, Canteen, Employment services, Foreign student adviser, Handicapped facilities, Language programs, Sports facilities

Special Facilities: Hall of Industrial Food Technology

Libraries: Central Library

Last Updated: 27/06/11

NATIONAL ART SCHOOL OF BOURGES

Ecole nationale des Beaux-Arts de Bourges (ENBA BOURGES)

BP 297, 7, rue Edouard Branly, 18006 Bourges, Cedex
Tel: +33(2) 48-69-78-78
Fax: +33(2) 48-69-78-84
EMail: informations@ensa-bourges.fr
Website: http://www.ensa-bourges.fr

Directeur: Stéphane Doré EMail: direction@ensa-bourges.fr

Departments
Fine Arts (Art History; Fine Arts; Sound Engineering (Acoustics); Video; Visual Arts)

History: Founded 1824.

Admission Requirements: Baccalauréat or equivalent secondary school exam. Entrance exam and selection jury.

Fees: (Euros): 350 per annum

Main Language(s) of Instruction: French

Accrediting Agencies: Ministry of Culture and Communication

Degrees and Diplomas: Diplôme national d'arts plastiques (DNAP) 3 yrs; Diplôme national supérieur d'expression plastique (DNSEP) a further 2 yrs

Libraries: Yes

Last Updated: 23/05/11

NATIONAL ART SCHOOL OF LYON

Ecole nationale des Beaux-Arts de Lyon (ENBA LYON)

8bis quai St Vincent, 69001 Lyon
Tel: +33(4) 72-00-11-71
Fax: +33(4) 72-00-11-70
EMail: infos@enba-lyon.fr
Website: http://www.ensba-lyon.fr

Directeur: Emmanuel Tibloux (2011-)

International Relations: Estelle Nabeyrat
Tel: +33(4) 78-28-13-67 EMail: estelle.nabeyrat@enba-lyon.net

Departments
Fine Arts (Design; Fine Arts; Industrial Design; Interior Design; Textile Design); **Urban Design**

History: Founded 1756 as Ecole Royale Académique de Dessin et Géométrie. Became the Ecole Nationale des Beaux-Arts 1848.

Admission Requirements: Baccalauréat or equivalent secondary school exam. Entrance exam and selection jury.

Fees: (Euros): 300 per annum

Main Language(s) of Instruction: French

International Co-operation: With institutions in Canada, China, Mexico, Israel, Lebanon. Also participates in Erasmus

Accrediting Agencies: Ministry of Culture

Degrees and Diplomas: Diplôme national d'arts plastiques (DNAP) 3 yrs; Diplôme national d'arts et techniques (DNAT) 3 yrs; Diplôme national supérieur d'expression plastique (DNSEP) a further 2 yrs

Last Updated: 27/06/11

NATIONAL FILM, PHOTOGRAPHY AND SOUND ENGINEERING SCHOOL

Ecole nationale supérieure Louis Lumière (ENS LOUIS LUMIÈRE)

7, allée du Promontoire, 93161 Noisy-le-Grand
Tel: +33(1) 48-15-40-10
EMail: sg@ens-louis-lumiere.fr
Website: http://www.ens-louis-lumiere.fr/

Directrice: Francine Lévy (2007-)
EMail: direction@ens-louis-lumiere.fr

Sécretaire générale: Danielle Lapert

Departments
Cinema; **Photography** (Photography; Visual Arts); **Sound Engineering**

History: Founded in 1926.

Admission Requirements: Baccalauréat or equivalent Secondary School Degree and two years of higher education and competitive entrance exam

Fees: (Euros): 250 per annum

Main Language(s) of Instruction: French

Accrediting Agencies: Ministry of Education

Degrees and Diplomas: *Diplôme national de Master*. Diplôme d'Université

Last Updated: 23/06/11

NATIONAL INSTITUTE FOR NUCLEAR SCIENCE AND TECHNOLOGY

Institut national des Sciences et Techniques nucléaires (INSTN)

CEA Saclay, 91191 Gif-sur-Yvette, Cedex
Tel: +33(1) 69-08-88-99
Fax: +33(1) 69-08-79-93
EMail: m3nuclear@cea.fr
Website: http://www-instn.cea.fr

Directeur: Laurent Turpin

Programmes
Applied Physics (Applied Physics); **Nuclear Engineering** (Applied Physics; Nuclear Engineering); **Radiology** (Radiology)

Further Information: Also four branches set up in CEA's centres at Grenoble, Cadarache and Valrhô-Marcoule, and campus of Cherbourg-Octeville.

History: Founded in 1956.

Fees: (Euros): Engineering Degree, 400 per annum; BTS, 250

Main Language(s) of Instruction: French

Accrediting Agencies: French Atomic Energy Commission, both Ministries of Education and Industry

Degrees and Diplomas: *Brevet de Technicien supérieur*. Radiology Protection, 2 yrs; *Diplôme d'Ingénieur*. Nuclear Engineering; *Diplôme national de Master*. Sciences, Technology and Health, further 2 yrs; *Doctorat*

Last Updated: 16/12/11

NATIONAL INSTITUTE OF ORIENTAL LANGUAGES AND CIVILIZATIONS - PARIS

Institut national des Langues et Civilisations orientales (INALCO)

65 rue des Grands Moulins, CS21351, 75013 Paris
Tel: +33(1) 81-70-10-00
EMail: communication@inalco.fr
Website: http://www.inalco.fr

Président: Jacques Legrand (2005-2013) Tel: +33(1) 81-70-10-30

Directeur général des Services: Jean Bayle
Tel: +33(1) 81-70-10-30 EMail: dsg@inalco.fr

International Relations: Martine Montoya
Tel: +33(1) 81-70-11-74 EMail: martine.montoya@inalco.fr

Departments
African Studies (African Languages; African Studies; Anthropology; Art History; Development Studies; Economics; Geography; History; Literature; Political Sciences; Religion; Swahili); **Arab Studies** (Anthropology; Arabic; Art History; Arts and Humanities; Cultural Studies; Development Studies; Economics; Geography; History; Literature; Political Sciences; Religion); **Central and Eastern European Studies** (Albanian; Anthropology; Art History; Baltic Languages; Central European Studies; Czech; Development Studies; Eastern European Studies; Economics; Finnish; Geography; Greek; History; Hungarian; Literature; Polish; Political Sciences; Religion; Romance Languages; Romanian; Slavic

Languages); **Chinese Studies** (Anthropology; Art History; Chinese; Development Studies; Economics; Geography; History; International Relations; Literature; Political Sciences; Religion; Translation and Interpretation); **Civilizations of the Americas** (American Studies; Amerindian Languages; Anthropology; Art History; Development Studies; Economics; Geography; History; Indigenous Studies; Political Sciences; Religion); **French as a Foreign Language** (French); **Hebrew and Jewish Languages and Civilizations** (Anthropology; Art History; Development Studies; Economics; Geography; Hebrew; History; Jewish Studies; Political Sciences; Religion); **International Business** (International Business; International Economics); **International Studies** *(HEI)* (International Relations; International Studies); **Japanese Studies** (Anthropology; Art History; Development Studies; Economics; Geography; History; International Relations; Literature; Political Sciences; Religion); **Russian Studies** (Anthropology; Armenian; Art History; Development Studies; Economics; Geography; History; Literature; Mongolian; Oriental Languages; Political Sciences; Religion; Russian; Slavic Languages); **South Asian Studies** (Anthropology; Art History; Development Studies; Economics; Geography; Hindi; History; Indic Languages; Literature; Political Sciences; Religion; South and Southeast Asian Languages; South Asian Studies; Urdu); **South East Asian, Upper Asian and Pacific Studies** (Anthropology; Art History; Development Studies; Economics; Filipino; Geography; History; Literature; Malay; Political Sciences; Religion; South and Southeast Asian Languages; Tibetan; Vietnamese)

Research Centres
ASIEs (Austronesian and Oceanic Languages; Chinese; Korean; Literature; South and Southeast Asian Languages); **Automatic Language Processing** (Linguistics; Modern Languages); **Central Europe-Eurasia** (Central European Studies; Russian); **History, Societies and World Territories** (History; Social Sciences); **Iranian and Indian Worlds** (Asian Studies; Middle Eastern Studies); **Japanese Studies** (History; Japanese; Literature; Southeast Asian Studies); **Languages and Cultures of Black Africa** (African Languages; Cultural Studies); **Languages and Cultures of North Africa and Diasporas** (Arabic; Cultural Studies; Jewish Studies; North African Studies); **Linguistic Research on East Asia** (East Asian Studies; Linguistics); **Middle Eastern and Mediterranean Studies** (Hebrew; Jewish Studies; Mediterranean Studies; Middle Eastern Studies); **Plurality of Languages and Identities in Teaching** (Applied Linguistics)
History: Founded 1699 as Royal School, reorganized 1795 and 1866. Became Ecole nationale 1870, Centre universitaire 1969, and acquired present status and title 1991. Since 1985, INALCO has been recognized as a 'Grand établissement à caractère scientifique, culturel et professionnel'.
Governing Bodies: Conseil d'administration, comprising 40 members; Conseil scientifique;Commission des études
Academic Year: October to June
Admission Requirements: Secondary school certificate (baccalauréat) or foreign equivalent, or entrance examination
Main Language(s) of Instruction: French
International Co-operation: Participates in the Tempus and Erasmus programmes
Degrees and Diplomas: *Licence*: Languages and Civilization, 3 yrs; *Diplôme national de Master*: Languages and Civilization, Asian Studies, Automatic Language Techniques, International Exertise, Modern Languages, Social Language and Translation, Computer Science, Literature, 2 yrs following Licence; *Doctorat*: 2-4 yrs following Masters. Degrees in Teaching French as a Foreign Language, Masters recherche, Masters professionnel
Libraries: Central Library, c. 521,000 vols
Publications: Cahiers Balkaniques *(biannually)*; Cahiers de Littérature Orale *(biannually)*; Cipango *(annually)*; Comptes rendus du Groupe Linguistique d'études chamito-sémitiques *(annually)*; Etudes de l'Océan Indien *(biannually)*; Slovo *(biannually)*; Yod *(annually)*
Last Updated: 18/10/11

NATIONAL INSTITUTE OF SPORTS, EXPERTISE AND PERFORMANCE
Institut national du Sport, de l'Expertise et de la Performance (INSEP)
11, avenue du Tremblay, 75012 Paris
Tel: +33(1) 41-74-41-00
Fax: +33(1) 41-74-45-30
EMail: communication@insep.fr
Website: http://www.insep.fr

Directeur: Thierry Maudet (2007-) EMail: thierry.maudet@insep.fr
Programmes
Sports and Physical Activity *(STAPS)* (Physical Education; Sports; Sports Medicine); **Sports Management**; **Sports Trainer** (Physical Education; Sports)
History: Founded in 2009 on the basis of the Institut National du Sport et de l'Éducation Physique (INSEP).
Governing Bodies: Conseil d'Administration
Main Language(s) of Instruction: French
Accrediting Agencies: Ministry of Youth and Sports
Degrees and Diplomas: *Brevet de Technicien supérieur*: Sports Trainer, 2 yrs; *Licence*: Sports, 3 yrs; *Diplôme national de Master*: Sports, Sports Management, 2 yrs following Licence. Preparation for CAPEPS exam.
Last Updated: 13/11/07

NATIONAL MARITIME SCHOOL
Ecole nationale supérieure maritime (ENMM)
Antenne Voltaire - 1 place des degrés, 92 055 Paris la Défense
Tel: +33(1) 40-81-87-88
Website: http://www.supmaritime.fr

Directeur général: Henri Poisson
History: Founded 2010 following merger of the 4 Merchant Navy Schools of Le Havre, Marseilles, Nantes and St Malo.
Main Language(s) of Instruction: French
Last Updated: 25/07/11

NATIONAL MARITIME SCHOOL - LE HAVRE CENTRE
ECOLE NATIONALE SUPÉRIEURE MARITIME - CENTRE DU HAVRE
66 rue du cap, BP 41, 76310 Sainte Adresse
Tel: +33(2) 35-54-78-00
Fax: +33(2) 35-46-12-81
EMail: centre.le-havre@supmaritime.fr

Programmes
Nautical Studies (Nautical Science)
Main Language(s) of Instruction: French
Degrees and Diplomas: Diplôme d'élève officier de 1ère classe de la marine marchande (DEO1MM); Diplôme d'études supérieures de la marine marchande (DESMM); Brevet de capitaine de 1ère classe de la navigation maritime

NATIONAL MARITIME SCHOOL - MARSEILLE CENTRE
ECOLE NATIONALE SUPÉRIEURE MARITIME - CENTRE DE MARSEILLE
39, avenue du Corail, 13285 Marseille, Cedex 08
Tel: +33(4) 91-76-82-82
Fax: +33(4) 91-73-88-64
EMail: centre.marseille@supmaritime.fr

Directeur: M. Ledouec
Departments
Energy (Energy Engineering); **Naval Architecture** (Naval Architecture); **Navigation** (Marine Engineering)
History: Founded 1761 as Ecole d'Hydrographie de Marseille. Acquired present status 2010.
Main Language(s) of Instruction: French
Degrees and Diplomas: *Mastère spécialisé*

NATIONAL MARITIME SCHOOL - NANTES CENTRE
ECOLE NATIONALE SUPÉRIEURE MARITIME - CENTRE DE NANTES
rue Gabriel Peri BP 90303, 44103 Nantes
Tel: +33(2) 40-71-01-80
EMail: centre.nantes@supmaritime.fr

Programmes
Nautical Studies (Engineering; Nautical Science)
History: Founded 1672. Acquired present status 2010.
Main Language(s) of Instruction: French

NATIONAL MARITIME SCHOOL - ST MALO CENTRE

ECOLE NATIONALE SUPÉRIEURE MARITIME - CENTRE DE SAINT MALO

BP 109, 4, rue de la Victoire, 35412 Saint-Malo, Cedex
Tel: +33(2) 99-40-68-80
Fax: +33(2) 99-40-57-63
EMail: centre.st-malo@supmaritime.fr

Directeur des Etudes: Jean-Pierre Legendre

Programmes
Marine Engineering

History: Founded 1669. Acquired present status 2010.
Main Language(s) of Instruction: French

NATIONAL SCHOOL OF ADVANCED AGRONOMY STUDIES - DIJON

AgroSup Dijon
26, boulevard Petitjean, BP 87999, 21079 Dijon, Cedex
Tel: +33(3) 80-77-25-25
Fax: +33(3) 80-77-25-00
EMail: international.agrosupdijon@agrosupdijon.fr
Website: http://www.agrosupdijon.fr

Directeur général: Claude Bernhard
Tel: +33(3) 80-77-25-01, Fax: +33(3) 80-77-28-48

Directrice des Services généraux: Pascale Seyssel
Tel: +33(3) 80-77-25-04, Fax: +33(3) 80-77-28-48
EMail: p.seyssel@agrosupdijon.fr

International Relations: Catherine Constant
Tel: +33(3) 80-77-26-09

Departments
Agronomy, Agricultural Equipment, Animal Husbandry and Environment (Agricultural Equipment; Agronomy; Animal Husbandry; Environmental Studies); **Engineering and Processing Sciences** (Engineering); **Food Sciences and Nutrition** (Food Science; Nutrition); **Human and Social Sciences** (Humanities and Social Science Education)

Institutes
Eduter (Computer Engineering; Engineering; Rural Planning)

History: Founded 2009 following merger of the Établissement National d'Enseignement Supérieur Agronomique de Dijon (ENESAD - formation d'ingénieurs agronomes) andthe École Nationale Supérieure de Biologie Appliquée à la Nutrition et à l'Alimentation (ENSBANA - formation d'ingénieurs en agroaliment)

Admission Requirements: Competitive entrance examination following 2 yrs further study after secondary school certificate (baccalauréat) or equivalent

Fees: (Euros): 900 per annum

International Co-operation: With universities in Belgium, Greece, Italy, Spain, Slovenia, Czech Republic, United Kingdom and Switzerland

Accrediting Agencies: Ministry of Agriculture

Degrees and Diplomas: *Licence professionnelle*: Teacher Training; Agricultural Equipments; *Diplôme d'Ingénieur*: Agriculture, 3 yrs; *Diplôme national de Master*: Humanities and Social Sciences; Sciences, Technology and Health; Technical and Economic Management of Agricultural Equipments; *Doctorat*

Student Services: Handicapped facilities

Student Residential Facilities: 2 Student Hostels

Libraries: Mediadoc
Last Updated: 05/07/11

NATIONAL SCHOOL OF ADVANCED STUDIES IN NATURE AND LANDSCAPE ARCHITECTURE, BLOIS

Ecole nationale supérieure de la Nature et du Paysage (ENSNP)
9 rue de La Chocolaterie, cs 2902, 41029 Blois
Tel: +33(2) 54-78-37-00
Fax: +33(2) 54-78-40-70
EMail: ensnp@ensnp.fr
Website: http://www.ensnp.fr/

Directrice: Marie Pruvost EMail: pruvost@ensnp.fr

Programmes
Nature and Landscape Architecture (Biology; Botany; Ecology; Geography; Geology; Landscape Architecture; Photography)

History: Founded 1993.

Academic Year: September-June

Admission Requirements: Secondary School certificate (baccalauréat) or equivalent, entrance exam or professional experience

Main Language(s) of Instruction: French

Degrees and Diplomas: *Diplôme national de Master*
Last Updated: 28/09/07

NATIONAL SCHOOL OF AGRICULTURAL ENGINEERING OF BORDEAUX AQUITAINE

Ecole Nationale Supérieure des Sciences Agronomiques de Bordeaux Aquitaine
1, cours du Général de Gaulle, CS40201, 33175 Gradignan
Tel: +33(5) 57-35-07-07
Fax: +33(5) 57-35-07-09
EMail: direction@enitab.fr
Website: http://www.enitab.fr

Directeur: Olivier Lavialle Tel: +33(5) 57-35-07-01

International Relations: Tanya Froute-Pardo
Tel: +33(5) 57-35-07-04, Fax: +33(5) 57-35-07-49
EMail: t-pardo@]enitab.fr

Departments
Agriculture and Biotechnology (Agriculture; Biological and Life Sciences; Crop Production; Environmental Engineering; Forestry; Oenology; Soil Science); **Continuing Education** (Agriculture; Fishery; Forestry); **Economics, Rural Development and Engineering** (Agricultural Economics; Business Administration; Computer Science; Engineering; Farm Management; Rural Planning)

History: Founded 1963 as École Nationale d'Ingénieurs des Travaux Agricoles. Acquired present title 2011.

Governing Bodies: Conseil Général including professionals, government representatives, professors, students and staff

Academic Year: September to June

Admission Requirements: Two years of preparatory studies after baccalauréat and competitive entrance examination

Main Language(s) of Instruction: French

International Co-operation: With universities in Europe and Canada. Also participates in Erasmus and Crepuq programmes

Accrediting Agencies: Commission des titres d'ingénieurs; Ministère de l'agriculture et de la pêche.

Degrees and Diplomas: *Licence professionnelle*: 3 yrs; *Diplôme d'Ingénieur*: Agricultural Sciences, 5 yrs following 2 yrs of preparatory studies; *Diplôme national de Master*: Forestry; Agronomy; Viticulture; Oenology, 2 yrs; *Diplôme national de Master*: Wineries Management, 1 yr, includes 6 months Internship

Student Services: Canteen, Foreign student adviser, Handicapped facilities, Health services, Language programs, Social counselling, Sports facilities

Student Residential Facilities: Yes

Libraries: Central Library
Last Updated: 22/04/11

NATIONAL SCHOOL OF AGRICULTURE STUDIES OF TOULOUSE-AUZEVILLE

Ecole nationale de Formation agronomique de Toulouse-Auzeville (ENFA)
BP 87, 2, route de Narbonne, 31326 Castanet Tolosan, Cedex
Tel: +33(5) 61-75-32-32
Fax: +33(5) 61-75-03-09
EMail: secretariat-direction.enfa@educagri.fr
Website: http://www.enfa.fr

Directeur: Michel Bascle (2011-)

Programmes
Agricultural Education (Agricultural Education; Agricultural Equipment; Management; Rural Planning)

History: Founded 1963.

Main Language(s) of Instruction: French

International Co-operation: With institutions in Germany and Spain. Also participates in the AUF programme

Degrees and Diplomas: *Licence*; *Licence professionnelle*; *Diplôme national de Master*. Masters recherche, Masters professionnel
Last Updated: 02/11/11

NATIONAL SCHOOL OF APPLIED ARTS

Ecole nationale supérieure des Arts appliqués et des Métiers d'Art (ENSAAMA)
63-65, rue Olivier-de-Serres, 75015 Paris
Tel: +33(1) 53-68-16-90
Fax: +33(1) 53-68-16-99
EMail: info@ensaama.net; relations-internationales@ensaama.net
Website: http://www.ensaama.net

Directeur: Marie-José Mascioni

Programmes
Applied Arts (Ceramic Art; Design; Fine Arts; Industrial Design; Textile Design; Visual Arts)

History: Established in 1922, ENSAAMA was later created in 1969 with the merger of two schools: École des Arts Appliqués à l'industrie and École des Métiers d'Art

Academic Year: September – May

Admission Requirements: Baccalauréat or equivalent secondary school exam. Entrance exam and selection jury.

Fees: (Euros): 500 p.a.

Main Language(s) of Instruction: French

International Co-operation: With institutes in Suzhou, China, UQUAM (Quebec) and Emily Carr Institute (Canada). Also participates in the EU exchange programmes Erasmus and Leonardi di Vinci.

Accrediting Agencies: Ministry of Culture and Communication

Degrees and Diplomas: *Brevet de Technicien supérieur*. Diplôme des métiers d'art (DMA) 3 yrs; Diplôme supérieur d'arts appliqués créateur-concepteur (DSAA) 4 yrs
Last Updated: 30/06/11

NATIONAL SCHOOL OF ARCHIVAL STUDIES PARIS

Ecole nationale des Chartes
19, rue de la Sorbonne, 75005 Paris
Tel: +33(1) 55-42-75-00
Fax: +33(1) 55-42-75-09
EMail: secretariat@enc.sorbonne.fr
Website: http://www.enc.sorbonne.fr

Directeur: Jean-Michel Leniaud

International Relations: Séverine Blenner-Michel
Tel: +33(1) 55-42-75-19 EMail: ri@enc.sorbonne.fr

Programmes
Art History and Archaeology (Archaeology; Art History); **Books and Media**; **History of Books and Bibliography** (Ancient Books; Library Science); **History of Civil and Canon Law** (Canon Law; Civil Law; Law); **History of French Institutions, Archives and Diplomatic Studies** (Archiving; Documentation Techniques; History); **Mediaeval Literature and Codicology** (Literature; Medieval Studies); **Palaeography**; **Roman Philology** (Philology; Romance Languages)

History: Founded 1821, reorganized 1846. An autonomous institution.

Governing Bodies: Conseil d'administration; Conseil scientifique

Academic Year: October to June (October-February; February-June)

Admission Requirements: Competitive entrance examination following 2-3 yrs further study after secondary school certificate (baccalauréat) or equivalent

Fees: None

Main Language(s) of Instruction: French

Degrees and Diplomas: *Diplôme national de Master*. Diplôme d'archiviste paléographe; doctorats conjoints, avec les universités Paris I-Panthéon-Sorbonne et Paris-Sorbonne Paris-IV.

Libraries: c. 150,000 vols

Publications: Positions des thèses *(annually)*
Last Updated: 27/06/11

NATIONAL SCHOOL OF CIVIL AVIATION

Ecole nationale de l'Aviation civile (ENAC)
BP 4005, 7, avenue Edouard Belin, 31055 Toulouse
Tel: +33(5) 62-17-40-00
Fax: +33(5) 62-17-40-23
EMail: jean.louis.latieule@enac.fr
Website: http://www.enac.fr

Directeur: Marc Houalla
Tel: +33(5) 62-17-40-01, Fax: +33(5) 62-17-40-37
EMail: marc.houalla@enac.fr

Secrétaire général: G. Le Breton

International Relations: Guy Lagarrigue
Tel: +33(5) 62-17-40-05, Fax: +33(5) 62-17-40-24
EMail: guy.lagarrigue@enac.fr

Schools
Civil Aviation (Aeronautical and Aerospace Engineering; Air Transport; Transport Management)

History: Founded 1948.

Admission Requirements: Baccalauréat and competitive entrance examination

Fees: (Euros): Engineering diploma courses, none; Mastère 9,590 per annum

Main Language(s) of Instruction: French

International Co-operation: Participates in Erasmus, Pegasus, GE4

Accrediting Agencies: Ministry of Transport

Degrees and Diplomas: *Diplôme d'Ingénieur*; *Mastère spécialisé*; *Diplôme national de Master*
Last Updated: 27/06/11

NATIONAL SCHOOL OF DECORATIVE ARTS

Ecole nationale supérieure des Arts décoratifs (ENSAD)
31, rue d'Ulm, 75240 Paris, cedex 05
Tel: +33(1) 42-34-97-00
Fax: +33(1) 42-34-97-85
EMail: info@ensad.fr
Website: http://www.ensad.fr

Directrice: Geneviève Gallot

Directrice adjointe: Mireille Delbeque

Schools
Fine Arts (Fine Arts; Furniture Design; Industrial Design; Photography; Video; Visual Arts)

History: ENSAD has its roots in the Royal Free School of 1766 to develop crafts relating to the arts in order to improve the quality of manufactured goods. After several name changes, in 1877 the school became the National School of Decorative Arts (l'Ecole nationale des arts décoratifs) before taking its present name of ENSAD (l'Ecole nationale supérieure des arts décoratifs) in 1927.

Academic Year: September-June

Admission Requirements: By entrance exam and Jury selection. Candidates can only apply up to three times.

Fees: (Euros): 290

Main Language(s) of Instruction: French

International Co-operation: Participates in Ersamus/Socrates with 34 other art schools and has several bilateral agreements with Universities in the USA, India, Canada, Japan, China and Korea.

Accrediting Agencies: Ministry of Culture.

Degrees and Diplomas: Diplôme de l'ENSAD (4yrs)
Last Updated: 30/06/11

NATIONAL SCHOOL OF ENGINEERING - SAINT-ETIENNE

Ecole nationale d'Ingénieurs de Saint-Etienne (ENISE)
58, rue Jean Parot, 42023 Saint-Etienne, Cedex 2
Tel: +33(4) 77-43-84-84
Fax: +33(4) 77-43-84-99
EMail: direction@enise.fr
Website: http://www.enise.fr

Directeur: Roland Fortunier
International Relations: Hélène Hennion
Tel: +33(4) 77-43-84-44 EMail: helene.hennion@enise.fr
Programmes
Engineering (Civil Engineering; Engineering; Mechanical Engineering)

History: Founded 1961.

Admission Requirements: Competitive entrance examination following 2-3 yrs further study after secondary school certificate (baccalauréat) or following first university qualification (DEUG, DUT or BTS), or equivalent

Fees: (Euros): 533

Main Language(s) of Instruction: French

Degrees and Diplomas: *Diplôme d'Ingénieur*, *Diplôme national de Master*
Last Updated: 27/06/11

NATIONAL SCHOOL OF GEOGRAPHIC SCIENCES

Ecole nationale des Sciences géographiques (ENSG-GÉO)
6 et 8, avenue Blaise Pascal, Cité Descartes, Champs-sur-Marne, 77455 Marne-la-Vallée, Cedex 2
Tel: +33(1) 64-15-30-01
Fax: +33(1) 64-15-31-07
EMail: info@ensg.ign.fr
Website: http://www.ensg.ign.fr
Directeur: Michel Kasser
Tel: +33(1) 64-15-31-00 EMail: michel.kasser@ensg.ign.fr
Secrétaire Général: Didier Maillard
Tel: +33(1) 64-15-32-41 EMail: didier.maillard@ensg.eu
International Relations: Patricia Bordin
Tel: +33(1) 64-15-31-48 EMail: Patricia.bordin@ensg.ign.fr

Divisions
Cartography (Arts and Humanities; Computer Science; Geography; Surveying and Mapping)
History: Founded 1941.

Main Language(s) of Instruction: French
International Co-operation: Cooperation programmes with Universities in Canada, Spain, Germany, Italy, Morocco and Switzerland. Also participates in Erasmus
Accrediting Agencies: Ministry of Ecology and Sustainable Development; Ministry of Higher Education
Degrees and Diplomas: *Licence professionnelle*: Géomatique (with Université Paris I); *Diplôme d'Ingénieur*: Information System Management and Spacial Applications (MSIAG), 1 1/2 yrs; *Diplôme d'Ingénieur*: Surveying and Mapping (IT), 3 yrs; *Mastère spécialisé*: 1 yr; *Diplôme national de Master*: Geomatics (with ESTP, ESGT, INSA-Strasbourg); Cathageo (with Université Paris I); Sustainable Development, Environmental Management and Geomatics (with Université Paris I); Informatique et Architecture des Systèmes d'Informations Géographiques; Information Géographique (with Université Paris Est Marne la Vallée)
Student Services: Cultural centre, Sports facilities
Last Updated: 08/04/11

NATIONAL SCHOOL OF INSURANCE

Ecole nationale d'Assurances (ENASS)
Paris La Défense 8, 20 bis Jardins Boieldieu, 92071 la Défense cedex Paris
Tel: +33(1) 44-63-58-47
Fax: +33(1) 44-63-58-37
EMail: info@enass.fr
Website: http://www.enass.fr
Directeur: François Ewald

International Relations: Laurence Winthrop
Tel: +33(1) 44-63-58-24 EMail: lwinthrop@enass.fr
Programmes
Insurance (Insurance)
History: Founded 1946.
Governing Bodies: Conseil d'administration
Fees: (Euros): Licence professionnelle, 3,000 p.a.; ENASS Diploma, 5,000 p.a.
Degrees and Diplomas: *Brevet de Technicien supérieur*: Insurance; *Licence professionnelle*: Insurance, 1 yr; *Diplôme national de Master*. MBA; Certificat assurance des risques internationaux
Last Updated: 13/05/11

NATIONAL SCHOOL OF LANDSCAPE ARCHITECTURE OF VERSAILLES-MARSEILLES

Ecole nationale supérieure du Paysage de Versailles-Marseille
1 rue Maréchal Joffre, 78000 Versailles
Tel: +33(1) 39-24-62-00
EMail: a.decastelnau@versailles.ecole-paysage.fr
Website: http://www.ecole-paysage.fr
Directeur: Vincent Piveteau
EMail: v.piveteau@versailles.ecole-paysage.fr
Secrétaire général: Gilles Beslay
Tel: +33(1) 39-24-62-04
EMail: g.beslay@versailles.ecole-paysage.fr

Programmes
Landscape Architecture (Landscape Architecture)
Further Information: Branch in Marseilles
History: Founded 1976.
Admission Requirements: Competitive entrance examination for students following baccalauréat + 2 years' study
Fees: (Euros): 900
Main Language(s) of Instruction: French
Degrees and Diplomas: Diplôme de Paysagiste diplômé par le gouvernement (DPLG); certificat d'études supérieures paysagères (CESP); Masters recherche in Theory and Methods in Landscaping
Last Updated: 30/06/11

NATIONAL SCHOOL OF LIBRARY AND INFORMATION SCIENCES

Ecole nationale supérieure des Sciences de l'Information et des Bibliothèques (ENSSIB)
17-21, boulevard du 11 Novembre 1918, 69623 Villeurbanne, Cedex
Tel: +33(4) 72-44-43-43
Fax: +33(4) 72-44-43-44
EMail: com@enssib.fr
Website: http://www.enssib.fr
Directrice: Anne-Marie Bertrand (2005-)
Tel: +33(4) 72-44-43-07 EMail: anne-marie.bertrand@enssib.fr
Secrétaire générale: Odile Jeannin
Tel: +33(4) 72-44-43-10 EMail: odile.jeannin@enssib.fr
International Relations: Raphaëlle Bats
Tel: +33(4) 72-44-43-18, Fax: +33(4) 72-44-43-43
EMail: raphaelle.bats@enssib.fr

Divisions
Information and Documentation Sciences Research (Documentation Techniques; Information Sciences); **Library Science** (Library Science)
History: Founded 1964. Acquired present status 1992.
Admission Requirements: Licence and competitive entrance examination for civil servants preparing the DCB, licence for students preparing the master degree
Main Language(s) of Instruction: French
International Co-operation: Participates in the Socrates programme and in other bilateral agreements with Africa and North America

Degrees and Diplomas: *Diplôme d'Etat:* Head Librarian, 1 1/2 yr; *Diplôme national de Master:* Library and Information Science; Cultures of the written word and image; Library and Documentation Policy; Digital Publishing; Digital Archiving, 2 yrs following Licence; *Doctorat:* Information and Communication Sciences

Student Services: Canteen, Health services, Sports facilities

Libraries: 26,000 vols; periodicals; e-books

Publications: Bulletin des Bibliothèques de France *(bimonthly)*

Press or Publishing House: Enssib

Last Updated: 14/06/11

NATIONAL SCHOOL OF MAGISTRACY STUDIES

Ecole nationale de la Magistrature
10, rue des Frères-Bonie, 33000 Bordeaux
Tel: +33(5) 56-00-10-10
Fax: +33(5) 56-00-10-99
EMail: samuel.vuelta-simon@justice.fr
Website: http://www.enm.justice.fr

Directeur: Jean-François Thony (2007-)
Tel: +33(5) 56-00-10-02 EMail: Jean-Francois.Thony@justice.fr

International Relations: Samuel Vuelta Simon
Tel: +33(1) 44-41-88-23

Departments

Languages and Civilizations (Cultural Studies; Modern Languages)

Programmes

Judicial Studies (Criminal Law; Justice Administration; Law)

Further Information: Has a second site in Paris focusing on in-service and non-professional training and international relations.

History: Created in 1958 to train future judges and public prosecutors.

Governing Bodies: Conseil d'administration and presided by the President of the Supreme Court.

Admission Requirements: Entrance exam, 4 yrs of University studies or a degree from an Institute of Political Science. Also possible with a minimum of 4 yrs professional experience.

Main Language(s) of Instruction: French

International Co-operation: Twinning programmes or call for tenders on multilateral funding by the European Union or international organizations: member of EJTN, IOJT, EAJTN, Lisbon ntework

Accrediting Agencies: Ministry of Justice

Degrees and Diplomas: Studies cover a continuous 31-month period with internships. The third year is devoted to a specialisation in a field.

Last Updated: 10/05/11

NATIONAL SCHOOL OF METEOROLOGICAL STUDIES - TOULOUSE

Ecole nationale de la Météorologie (ENM)
42 Avenue Gaspard Coriolis, BP 45712, 31057 Toulouse, Cedex 1
Tel: +33(5) 61-07-80-80
Fax: +33(5) 61-07-96-30
EMail: enm.fr@meteo.fr
Website: http://www.enm.meteo.fr

Directeur: François Lalaurette
Tel: +33(5) 61-07-94-17 EMail: Francois.Lalaurette@meteo.fr

Secrétaire général: Jean Claude Camoin Tel: +33(5) 61-07-94-19

Programmes

Meteorology (Meteorology)

History: Founded 1922, acquired present status 1969.

Academic Year: September to July

Admission Requirements: Competitive entrance examination following 2-3 yrs' further study after secondary school certificate (baccalauréat)

Main Language(s) of Instruction: French

Accrediting Agencies: Ministry of Transport

Degrees and Diplomas: *Diplôme d'Ingénieur:* Meteorology (IENM), 3 yrs

Student Services: Academic counselling, Canteen, Cultural centre, Foreign student adviser, Handicapped facilities, Health services, Nursery care, Social counselling, Sports facilities

Student Residential Facilities: For c. 300 students

Special Facilities: Movie studio

Last Updated: 27/06/11

NATIONAL SCHOOL OF PHOTOGRAPHY, ARLES

Ecole nationale supérieure de la Photographie (ENSP)
16, rue des Arènes, BP 1014, 13631 Arles
Tel: +33(4) 90-99-33-33
Fax: +33(4) 90-99-33-59
EMail: communication@ensp-arles.com
Website: http://www.ensp-arles.com

Directeur: Rémy Fenzy (2010-)

International Relations: Laurence Canaux
EMail: laurence.canaux@ensp-arles.com

Boards Of Study

Photography (Photography)

Admission Requirements: Competitive examination two years after the Baccalauréat

Fees: (Euros) 342 per annum

Main Language(s) of Instruction: French

Accrediting Agencies: Ministère de la Culture.

Degrees and Diplomas: Diplôme de l'École Nationale Supérieure de la Photographie

Libraries: Yes

Last Updated: 30/06/11

NATIONAL SCHOOL OF PUBLIC ADMINISTRATION

Ecole nationale d'Administration (ENA)
1, rue Sainte Marguerite, 67080 Strasbourg, Cedex
Tel: +33(3) 88-21-44-44
Fax: +33(3) 88-21-44-59
EMail: presentation@ena.fr
Website: http://www.ena.fr

Directeur: Bernard Boucault (2007-)

Secrétaire général: François Ambroggiani

International Relations: Maxime Lefèvre
Tel: +33(1) 49-26-44-55 +33(1) 44-41-85-90,
Fax: +33(1) 44-41-85-19

Programmes

Administration (Administration; Public Administration); **European Studies** (European Studies); **Territorial Administration** (Public Administration)

Further Information: Also 2 branches in Paris

History: Founded 1945. Incorporated the Institut international d'Administration publique, Paris, 2002.

Admission Requirements: University or engineer school diploma or competitive entrance examination for active civil servants

Main Language(s) of Instruction: French

Degrees and Diplomas: *Diplôme d'Etat; Mastère spécialisé.* Masters

Last Updated: 09/06/11

NATIONAL SCHOOL OF STATISTICS AND INFORMATION ANALYSIS

Ecole nationale de la Statistique et de l'Analyse de l'Information (ENSAI)
Campus de Ker-Lann, Rue Blaise Pascal, BP 37203, 35172 Bruz
Tel: +33(2) 99-05-32-32
Fax: +33(2) 99-05-32-05
EMail: communication@ensai.fr
Website: http://www.ensai.com

Directeur: Pascal Chevalier (2011-) Tel: +33(2) 99-05-32-83

International Relations: Esther Lalau Keraly
Tel: +33(2) 99-05-32-43 EMail: international@ensai.fr

Schools
Statistics (Arts and Humanities; Computer Science; Economics; Management; Marketing; Statistics)

History: Founded 1942 (see ENSAE).

Governing Bodies: Conseil d'Ecole

Academic Year: September to June

Admission Requirements: Competitive entrance examination following 2-3 yrs study after secondary school certificate (baccalauréat) or transfer following first university qualification or equivalent

Fees: (Euros): 550 per annum

Main Language(s) of Instruction: French

International Co-operation: With Humboldt University and University of Mannheim, Iowa Northern University and Colorado State University(USA). Also participates in Erasmus, Socrates

Accrediting Agencies: Ministry of Finance, Commission des Titres d'Ingénieur

Degrees and Diplomas: *Diplôme d'Etat*: 3 yrs; *Diplôme d'Ingénieur*: Statistics, 3 yrs; *Diplôme national de Master*

Student Services: Academic counselling, Canteen, Handicapped facilities, Language programs, Sports facilities

Student Residential Facilities: Yes

Libraries: Yes

Academic Staff *2010-2011*	MEN	WOMEN	TOTAL
FULL-TIME	12	8	20
Student Numbers *2010-2011*			
All (Foreign Included)	200	120	320

Last Updated: 14/06/11

NATIONAL SCHOOL OF THEATRE ARTS AND TECHNIQUES

Ecole nationale supérieure des Arts et Techniques du Théâtre (ENSATT)
4, rue Soeur Bouvier, 69005 Lyon
Tel: +33(4) 78-15-05-05
Fax: +33(4) 78-15-05-39
EMail: administration@ensatt.fr
Website: http://www.ensatt.fr

Directeur: Thierry Pariente (2009-)

Sécrétaire générale: Antonietta Mendez

Programmes
Theatre Studies (Performing Arts; Theatre)

History: Founded 1941 in Paris. Moved to Lyon 1997.

Admission Requirements: Minimum age of 25 and must pass the Institute's own exam, specific for each department

Main Language(s) of Instruction: French

Degrees and Diplomas: Diplôme d'Université
Last Updated: 30/06/11

NATIONAL SCHOOL OF WATER AND ENVIRONMENTAL ENGINEERING - STRASBOURG

Ecole nationale du Génie de l'Eau et de l'Environnement de Strasbourg (ENGEES)
BP 61039, 1, quai Koch, 67070 Strasbourg, Cedex
Tel: +33(3) 88-24-82-82
Fax: +33(3) 88-37-04-97
EMail: contact@engees.unistra.fr
Website: http://engees.unistra.fr

Directeur: Claude Bernhard

Secrétaire générale: Danielle Stanek Tel: +33(3) 88-24-82-10

International Relations: Didier Bellefleur
Tel: +33(3) 88-24-82-16, Fax: +33(3) 88-37-04-97
EMail: didier.bellefleur@engees.unistra.fr

Research Laboratories
Plant Ecology and Hydrology (Ecology; Hydraulic Engineering); **Public Utilities Management** *(GSP)* (Management; Social and Community Services); **Urban Hydraulic Systems** *(IMFS-HU)* (Water Science)

Units
Continuing Education (Civil Engineering; Construction Engineering; Environmental Studies; Human Resources; Public Administration; Public Law; Waste Management); **Engineering** (Biotechnology; Environmental Engineering; Environmental Management; Hydraulic Engineering; Irrigation; Waste Management; Water Management); **Research** (Biotechnology; Environmental Engineering; Environmental Management; Hydraulic Engineering; Public Administration; Social and Community Services; Water Science)

History: Founded 1952. Acquired present status and title 1992.

Academic Year: September to June

Admission Requirements: From 2 to 5 years following secondary school certificate (baccalauréat) in accordance with the degree

Fees: (Euros): Engineer course 1,350 per annum, MS and higher education certificates 5,800-8,300 per annum; licence 174 per annum

Main Language(s) of Instruction: French

International Co-operation: With universities in United States; Canada; Morocco; Burkina Faso, Germany, Spain, UK, Netherlands. Participates in the Erasmus programme

Accrediting Agencies: Commission des Titres d'Ingénieur, Conférence des Grandes Ecoles

Degrees and Diplomas: *Licence professionnelle*: 1 yrs; *Diplôme d'Ingénieur*: Environmental Engineering, 2-3 yrs; *Diplôme national de Master*: 2 yrs

Student Services: Academic counselling, Canteen, Employment services, Foreign student adviser, Handicapped facilities, Health services, Social counselling, Sports facilities

Libraries: 13,000 vols

Academic Staff *2010-2011*	MEN	WOMEN	TOTAL
FULL-TIME	37	37	74
PART-TIME	–	–	400
Student Numbers *2010-2011*			
All (Foreign Included)	185	134	319
FOREIGN ONLY	19	15	34

Last Updated: 17/06/11

NATIONAL VETERINARY SCHOOL - MAISONS-ALFORT

Ecole nationale vétérinaire d'Alfort (ENVA)
7, avenue du Général de Gaulle, 94704 Maisons-Alfort
Tel: +33(1) 43-96-71-00
Fax: +33(1) 43-96-71-25
EMail: communication@vet-alfort.fr
Website: http://www.vet-alfort.fr

Directeur: Jean-Pierre Mialot Tel: +33(1) 43-96-71-80

Programmes
Veterinary Science (Veterinary Science)

Further Information: Has 8 research laboratories

History: Founded 1765.

Governing Bodies: Conseil d'administration

Academic Year: September to July

Admission Requirements: Competitive entrance examination following a preparatory class after secondary school certificate (baccalauréat) or (DEUG) or equivalent

Fees: (Euros): 2,000 per annum

Main Language(s) of Instruction: French

Accrediting Agencies: Ministry of Agriculture

Degrees and Diplomas: *Diplôme d'Etat*: Veterinary Medicine, 6 yrs; *Diplôme national de Master*: Masters professionnel, Masters recherche, CEAV (certificat d'études approfondies vétérinaires)

Student Services: Cultural centre, Sports facilities

Student Residential Facilities: Yes

Special Facilities: Fragonard d'Alfort Museum

Libraries: 160,000 vols

Publications: Recueil de Médecine vétérinaire
Last Updated: 13/04/11

NATIONAL VETERINARY SCHOOL - TOULOUSE

Ecole nationale vétérinaire de Toulouse (ENVT)
23, chemin des Capelles, 31076 Toulouse, cedex 3
Tel: +33(5) 61-19-38-00
Fax: +33(5) 61-19-39-93
EMail: direction@envt.fr
Website: http://www.envt.fr

Directeur: Alain Milon (2005-)

International Relations: Françoise Artero
Tel: +33(5) 61-19-32-09 EMail: international@envt.fr

Programmes
Veterinary Medicine (Veterinary Science)

History: Founded 1828. New campus 1964. Academic link to Institut National Polytechnique de Toulouse 2010.

Admission Requirements: Competitive entrance examination following 2-3 yrs further study after secondary school certificate (baccalauréat) or following first university qualification (DEUG, DUT or BTS), or equivalent

Fees: (Euros): 2,000 per annum

Main Language(s) of Instruction: French

Degrees and Diplomas: *Licence professionnelle*; *Diplôme d'Etat*: Veterinary Medicine
Last Updated: 24/05/11

NICE NATIONAL ART SCHOOL - VILLA ARSON

Ecole nationale supérieure d'Art de Nice
20 avenue Stéphen Liégeard, 06105 Nice, Cedex 2
Tel: +33(4) 92-07-73-73
Fax: +33(4) 93-84-41-55
EMail: verchere@villa-arson.org
Website: http://www.villa-arson.org

Directeur: Yves Robert

International Relations: Catherine Verchère

Programmes
Design (Design; Graphic Arts; Photography; Sculpture; Visual Arts)
History: Founded in 1973.

Admission Requirements: Baccalauréat or equivalent secondary school exam. Entrance exam with a selection jury.

Main Language(s) of Instruction: French

International Co-operation: Has partnerships with several European Universities, including cooperation programmes with other Anglo-Saxon countries and China.

Accrediting Agencies: Ministry of Culture and Communication

Degrees and Diplomas: Diplôme national d'arts plastiques (DNAP) 3 yrs; Diplôme national supérieur d'expression plastique (DNSEP) a further 2 yrs
Last Updated: 18/05/11

NORD-PAS-DE CALAIS ART SCHOOL

École supérieure d'Art du Nord-Pas-de Calais, Dunkerque/Tourcoing
36 bis, rue des Ursulines, Tourcoing
EMail: ersep@ville-tourcoing.fr
Website: http://www.tourcoing.fr/presentation, 40,951,fr.html

Directeur: Roland Decaudin

Programmes
Fine Arts (Aesthetics; Art History; Painting and Drawing; Photography; Video)

History: Founded 2010 following merger of the Ecole régionale des beaux arts de Dunkerque and the Ecole régionale supérieure d'expression plastique de Tourcoing.

Main Language(s) of Instruction: French

Degrees and Diplomas: DNAP Diplôme National d'art plastique (3 ans) and DNSEP Diplôme National Supérieur d'Expression Plastique (5 ans)
Last Updated: 07/07/11

NORMANDY NATIONAL SCHOOL OF ARCHITECTURE

Ecole nationale supérieure d'Architecture de Normandie
27 rue Lucien Fromage, BP 04, 76161 Darnétal
Tel: +33(2) 32-83-42-00
Fax: +33(2) 32-83-42-10
EMail: ecole@rouen.archi.fr
Website: http://www.rouen.archi.fr

Directrice: Fabienne Fendrich
Tel: +33(2) 32-83-42-01 EMail: fabienne.fendrich@rouen.archi.fr

Programmes
Architecture (Architecture; Urban Studies)

History: Founded 1904.

Main Language(s) of Instruction: French

Degrees and Diplomas: *Licence*; *Diplôme national de Master*; *Doctorat*
Last Updated: 07/04/11

ORLEANS SCHOOL OF HIGHER EDUCATION IN ART AND DESIGN

Ecole supérieure d'Art et de Design d'Orléans (ESAD)
14 rue Dupanloup, 45000 Orléans
Tel: +33(2) 38-79-24-67
Fax: +33(2) 38-79-21-16
EMail: esad@ville-orleans.fr
Website: http://www.esad-orleans.com

Directrice: Jacqueline Febvre

International Relations: Doris Géraud

Programmes
3D Design (Design; Furniture Design; Interior Design; Production Engineering); **Visual Design** (Design; Graphic Design; Multimedia; Photography; Video)

History: Originally known as the Ecole gratuite de dessin de la Ville d'Orléans, in 1991 it changed its focus to design and applied arts, becoming L'École supérieure d'Art et de Design d'Orléans in 2011.

Admission Requirements: Baccalauréat or equivalent secondary school exam. Entrance exam with a selection jury.

Fees: (Euros): 488

Main Language(s) of Instruction: French, sometimes English

Accrediting Agencies: Ministry of Culture and Communication

Degrees and Diplomas: Diplome national d'arts et techniques (DNAT) 3 yrs; Diplome national supérieur d'expression plastique (DNSEP) a further 2 yrs (MA level)
Last Updated: 09/05/11

PARIS 1 PANTHÉON-SORBONNE UNIVERSITY

Université Paris 1 Panthéon Sorbonne
12, place du Panthéon, 75231 Paris, Cedex 05
Tel: +33(1) 44-07-80-00
Fax: +33(1) 46-34-20-56
EMail: secom@univ-paris1.fr
Website: http://www.univ-paris1.fr

Président: Jean-Claude Colliard (2009-)
Tel: +33(1) 44-07-77-03, Fax: +33(1) 46-34-20-56
EMail: cabpresi@univ-paris1.fr

Directeur général des Services: François Riou
Tel: +33(1) 47-07-77-05, Fax: +33(1) 44-07-76-96
EMail: secretg@univ-paris1.fr

International Relations: Christiane Prigent
Tel: +33(1) 44-07-76-71, Fax: +33(1) 44-07-76-76
EMail: relinter@univ-paris1.fr

Centres
Advanced Studies in Tourism *(CEP)* (Tourism)

Departments
Public and Private Sector Management and Social Law (Management; Social Policy); **Business Law** (Commercial Law); **Business Management** (Business Administration); **Economics** (Economics); **Economics and Social Administration, Labour and Social Studies** (Business Administration; Economics; Labour Law; Social Studies) *Director:* Grégoire Loiseau; **General Law** (Law); **Geography** (Environmental Studies; Geography; Rural Planning); **History** (Ancient Civilizations; History; Medieval Studies; Modern History); **History of Art and Archaeology** (Archaeology; Art History); **International and European Studies** (European Studies; International Studies); **Law, Administration and Public Sector Studies** (Administration; Law; Public Administration); **Management and Business Administration** (Business Administration; Management) *Director:* Hubert de la Bruslerie; **Mathematics and Computer Science** (Applied Mathematics; Mathematics and Computer Science); **Philosophy** (Philosophy); **Plastic Arts and Arts Sciences** (Aesthetics; Cinema and Television; Design; Fine Arts; Media Studies; Multimedia; Painting and Drawing; Sculpture); **Political Science** (Political Sciences)

Graduate Schools
Doctoral Studies *(College des Ecoles Doctorales)* (Archaeology; Art History; Economics; Fine Arts; Geography; History; Law; Management; Philosophy; Political Sciences; Regional Planning) *Director:* Claude Gauvard

Institutes
Business Administration *(IAE)* (Business Administration) *Director:* Jérôme Caby; **Communication** *(IFC)* (Communication Studies; Journalism); **Demography** *(IDUP)* (Demography and Population); **Economic and Social Development Studies** *(IEDES)* (Development Studies; Economics; Social Studies); **Insurance** *(IAP)* (Insurance); **Juridical Studies** *(Jean-Domat, IEJ)* (Law); **Labour Studies** *(ISST)* (Labour Law; Social Policy; Social Sciences)

Schools
Law *(Sorbonne)*

Further Information: Also Research Centres and Laboratories

History: Founded 1970 under the 1968 law reforming higher education as one of the new Universities replacing the former Université de Paris - founded in the 12th century, constituted as Universitas Magistrorum et Scholarium Parisiensium and confirmed by Papal Bull 1215; suppressed by the Revolution in 1793; replaced 1808 by an Academy of the Université impériale; reconstituted as University 1890. A State institution enjoying academic and financial autonomy, operating under the jurisdiction of the Minister of Education and financed by the State.

Governing Bodies: Conseil d'administration, comprising elected representatives of teaching staff, research workers, students, and administrative and technical staff, as well as non-university members drawn from the public and private sectors; Conseil scientifique, competent in matters of research; Conseil des Etudes et de la Vie universitaire; Conseil of each Unit, comprising representatives of its teaching staff, research workers, students, and administrative and and technical staff. The President is elected by the first three bodies. The Chancelier, who represents the Minister of Education, is the Recteur of the Académie de Paris

Academic Year: September to July (September-December; January-March; April-June)

Admission Requirements: Secondary school certificate (baccalauréat) or equivalent, or special entrance examination

Main Language(s) of Instruction: French

International Co-operation: Participates in the Erasmus/Socrates programmes

Accrediting Agencies: Ministère de l'Education nationale

Degrees and Diplomas: *Capacité en Droit:* 2 yrs; *Licence:* Law, Political Science, Social Sciences, Economics, Management, Fine Arts, Mathematics and Computer Sciences, Applied Mathematics, Arts and Humanities, Fine Arts, 3 yrs; *Licence professionnelle:* Law, Political Science, Social Sciences, Economics, Management, Fine Arts, Mathematics and Computer Sciences, Applied Mathematics, Arts and Humanities, Fine Arts, 1 yr following 2 yrs university studies; *Diplôme d'Etat:* Archaeology, Art History, Geography, History,

Philosophy, 2 yrs; *Magistère:* Law, 3 yrs; *Diplôme national de Master:* Law, Political Science, Social Sciences, Economics, Management, Fine Arts, Mathematics and Computer Sciences, Applied Mathematics, Arts and Humanities, Fine Arts, Labour and Development Studies, 2 yrs following Licence; *Doctorat:* Accountancy, Administration, Demography, Economics, European Institutions, Labour Studies, Law, Management, Public Finance, Rural Social Science, Sociology, 2-4 yrs by thesis following Masters. Masters recherche, Masters professionnel

Student Services: Canteen, Foreign student adviser, Health services, Sports facilities

Libraries: Bibliothèque Cujas; Bibliothèque de la Sorbonne; Centre de documentation de la maison des sciences économiques; Centre de documentation de l'Institut André TUNC; Bibliothèque de Géographie; Bibliothèques d'art et d'archéologie Michelet ; Maison d'archéologie et d'ethnologie René Ginouvès; Bibliothèque du centre d'histoire sociale du XXe siècle; Bibliothèque de l'institut d'histoire de la révolution française; Bibliothèque du centre de recherche en histoire du XIXe siècle

Press or Publishing House: Publications de la Sorbonne
Last Updated: 20/07/11

PARIS 2 UNIVERSITY
Université Panthéon-Assas (Paris 2)
12, place du Panthéon, 75231 Paris, Cedex 05
Tel: +33(1) 44-41-57-00
Fax: +33(1) 44-41-55-13
EMail: presidence@u-paris2.fr
Website: http://www.u-paris2.fr

Président: Louis Vogel (2006-)
Tel: +33(1) 44-41-55-01, Fax: +33(1) 44-41-47-15

Directrice générale des Services: Sylvie Toraille
Tel: +33(1) 44-41-55-12, Fax: +33(1) 44-41-55-13
EMail: secretariat-general@u-paris2.fr

International Relations: Georgia Schneider
Tel: +33(1) 44-41-55-07, Fax: +33(1) 44-41-56-86
EMail: georgia.schneider@u-paris2.fr

Centres
Building and Housing Studies *(CERCOL)* (Construction Engineering; Town Planning) *Director:* Hugues Périnet-Marquet; **Lifelong Education** *Director:* Pierre-Louis Dubois

Colleges
European *(Paris)* (European Union Law)

Departments
Economics and Management (Economics; Management); **Information and Communication Sciences** (Communication Studies; Information Sciences); **Languages** *Director:* Claude Brenner; **Private Law and Criminology** (Criminology; Private Law); **Public Law and Political Science** (Political Sciences; Public Law); **Roman Law and History of Law** (History of Law; Law)

Institutes
Advanced International Studies (International Studies); **Business Law** *(IDA)* (Commercial Law); **Comparative Law** (Comparative Law); **Criminology** (Criminology); **Journalism** *(IFP)* (Journalism); **Juridical Studies** *(Pierre Raynau IEJ)* (Law); **Law and Economics** *(Melun)* (Economics; Law); **Preparatory Administrative Studies** *(IPAG)* (Administration)

Schools
Law and Management *(Paris)* (Law; Management); **Marketing** *(Sorbonne-Assas)* (Marketing)

Units
Law and Political Science *(Capacité and 1st cycle)* (Law; Political Sciences); **Law and Political Science** *(2nd and 3rd cycle)* (Law; Political Sciences) *Director:* Laurent Leveneur; **Private and Public Management** (Management)

History: Founded 1970 under the 1968 law reforming higher education as one of the new Universities replacing the former Université de Paris, founded in 12th century, constituted as Universitas Magistrorum and confirmed by Papal Bull 1215; suppressed by the Revolution in 1793; replaced 1808 by an Academy of the Université Impériale; reconstituted as University 1890. A State institution enjoying academic and financial autonomy, operating under the jurisdiction of the Minister of Education and financed by the State.

Governing Bodies: Conseil de l'Université, including elected representatives of teaching staff, research workers, students, and administrative and technical staff, as well as non-University members drawn from the public and private sectors; the Conseil of each Unit, comprising representatives of its teaching staff, research workers, students, and administrative and technical staff; the Conseil scientifique, competent in matters of research. The President is elected by the Conseil de l'Université. The Chancelier, who represents the Minister of Education, is the Recteur de l'Académie de Paris

Academic Year: October to May (October-February; February-May)

Admission Requirements: Secondary school certificate (Baccalauréat) or equivalent, or special entrance examination

Main Language(s) of Instruction: French

Degrees and Diplomas: *Capacité en Droit*: 2 yrs; *Licence*: Information and Communication Science, Law, Economics, Management, Social and Business Administration, 3 yrs; *Licence professionnelle*; *Magistère*: 3 yrs following 1 yr; *Diplôme national de Master*: Law, Political Science, Social Sciences, Management, Economics, 2 yrs following Licence; *Doctorat*: Law, Political Science, Social Sciences, Management, Economics, Information, 2-4 yrs following Masters. Masters recherche, Masters professionnel

Student Services: Academic counselling, Canteen, Cultural centre, Employment services, Foreign student adviser, Handicapped facilities, Health services, Social counselling, Sports facilities

Student Residential Facilities: For c. 20,000 students

Libraries: Bibliothèques interuniversitaires
Last Updated: 20/07/11

PARIS 3 UNIVERSITY
Université Sorbonne Nouvelle (Paris 3)
17, rue de la Sorbonne, 75230 Paris, Cedex 05
Tel: +33(1) 40-46-28-97
Fax: +33(1) 43-25-74-71
EMail: presidence@univ-paris3.fr
Website: http://www.univ-paris3.fr

Présidente: Marie-Christine Lemardeley (2008-)
Tel: +33(1) 40-46-28-84, Fax: +33(1) 40-46-29-36

Directeur général des Services: Vincent Gaillot
Tel: +33(1) 40-46-28-97 +33(1) 40-46-28-99,
Fax: +33(1) 40-46-28-77 EMail: secretaire.general@univ-paris3.fr

International Relations: Philippe Dubois
Tel: +33(1) 45-87-48-48, Fax: +33(1) 45-87-48-01
EMail: rel.int@univ-paris3.fr

Centres
Lifelong Education *(FCP3) Director*: Jean-Claude Sergeant

Graduate Schools
Contemporary European Studies (European Studies); **English, German and European Studies** (Canadian Studies; English Studies; European Studies; Germanic Studies; History; Irish; Linguistics; Media Studies; Political Sciences; Translation and Interpretation); **Languages** (Linguistics); **Latin America/Europe** (European Studies; Latin American Studies; Romance Languages); **Performing Arts and Communication** *(ASSIC)* (Communication Arts; Information Sciences; Performing Arts) *Director*: Catherine Naugrette

Institutes
Latin American Studies *(IHEAL)* (Latin American Studies)

Schools
Interpreters and Translators *(ESIT)* (Translation and Interpretation)

Units
Arts and Media (Cinema and Television; Communication Studies; Media Studies; Theatre); **Foreign Languages, Literature, Cultures and Societies** (Arabic; English Studies; European Studies; Germanic Languages; Hebrew; Indic Languages; Italian; Latin American Studies; Middle Eastern Studies; Modern Languages;

Romanian; Spanish); **Literature, Linguistics, Didactics** (Comparative Literature; Linguistics; Literature; Pedagogy; Phonetics)

History: Founded 1970 under the 1968 law reforming higher education as one of the Universities replacing the former Université de Paris, founded in the 12th century, constituted as Universitas Magistrorum and confirmed by Papal Bull 1215; suppressed by the Revolution in 1793; replaced 1808 by an Academy of the Université impériale; reconstituted as university 1890. A State institution enjoying academic and financial autonomy, operating under the jurisdiction of the Minister of Education and financed by the State.

Governing Bodies: Conseil d'Administration, including representatives of teaching staff, research workers, students, and administrative and technical staff, as well as non-university members drawn from the public and private sectors; Conseil scientifique, competent in matters of research; Conseil des Etudes et de la Vie universitaire; and Conseil of each Unit, comprising representatives of its teaching staff, research workers, students, and administrative and technical staff. The President is elected by the first three bodies. The Chancelier, who represents the Minister of Education, is the Recteur de l'Académie de Paris

Academic Year: October to June (October-December; January-March; April-June)

Admission Requirements: Secondary school certificate (baccalauréat) or equivalent, or special entrance examination

Main Language(s) of Instruction: French

International Co-operation: With universities in Europe, USA, Australia, Canada, Middle East, South East Asia, Japan, Korea, Eastern Europe, Latin America (PECO).

Degrees and Diplomas: *Licence*: Arts, Fine Arts, Languages, Literature, Contemporary Cultural Studies, 3 yrs; *Diplôme national de Master*: Arts, Fine Arts, Languages, Literature, Contemporary Cultural Studies, 2 yrs following Licence; *Doctorat*: 2-4 yrs following Masters. Masters recherche, Masters professionnel

Student Services: Foreign student adviser, Nursery care, Social counselling, Sports facilities

Libraries: 3 Bibliothèques interuniversitaires; Bibliothèques des Unités, c. 233,200 vols

Publications: Cahiers de la Bibliothèque Gaston Baty; Cahiers de l'Ut. des Etudes Ibériques *(annually)*; Italique *(annually)*; Lalies *(annually)*; Publication du Centre de la Renaissance *(annually)*; Publication du Centre Interuniversitaire de Recherche des Etudes Roumaines; Trema *(annually)*

Press or Publishing House: Service des Publications de la Sorbonne Nouvelle
Last Updated: 22/07/11

PARIS 5 UNIVERSITY
Université Paris Descartes (Paris 5)
12, rue de l'Ecole de Médecine, 75270 Paris, Cedex 06
Tel: +33(1) 76-53-16-16
Fax: +33(1) 76-53-16-15
EMail: secretaire.general@parisdescartes.fr
Website: http://www.parisdescartes.fr

Président: Frédéric Dardel (2011-)
Tel: +33(1) 76-53-16-01, Fax: +33(1) 76-53-16-43
EMail: president@parisdescartes.fr

Secrétaire général: François Paquis
Tel: +33(1) 76-53-16-98
EMail: secretariat.general@parisdescartes.fr

International Relations: Michèle Cambra
Tel: +33(1) 76-53-16-10, Fax: +33(1) 76-53-16-91
EMail: sri@parisdescartes.fr

Centres
Lifelong Education *Director*: Jean-Pierre Hazemann

Colleges
Doctoral Schools Paris Descartes

Faculties
Biomedical Studies (Biomedicine); **Dentistry** (Dentistry); **Humanities and Social Sciences** (Arts and Humanities; Social Sciences); **Law** (Law); **Mathematics and Computer Science** (Mathematics and Computer Science); **Medicine** (Medicine);

Pharmacy (Biology; Pharmacy); **Physical Education and Sports** *(STAPS)* (Physical Education; Sports); **Psychology** (Psychology)

Graduate Schools
Cultures, Citizens, Societies *(ED SHS)* (Cultural Studies; Social Sciences); **Frontiers in Life Sciences** (Biological and Life Sciences); **Genetic, Cell, Contagious Diseases Studies** *(GC2ID)* (Cell Biology; Genetics); **Human Behaviour** (Behavioural Sciences); **International Relations** (International Law; International Relations); **Molecular Biology** (Biochemistry; Molecular Biology)

Institutes
Technology *(IUT Paris 5)* (Business Administration; Communication Studies; Computer Science; Information Sciences; Marketing; Social Work; Statistics; Technology)

History: Founded 1970 under the 1968 law reforming higher education as one of the Universities replacing the former Université de Paris - founded 12th century, constituted as Universitas Magistrorum and confirmed by Papal Bull 1215; suppressed by the Revolution in 1793; replaced 1808 by an Academy of the Université impériale; reconstituted as University 1890. A State institution enjoying academic and financial autonomy, operating under the jurisdiction of the Minister of Education and financed by the State.

Governing Bodies: Conseil d'Administration, comprising 30 members, including elected representatives of teaching staff, research workers, students, and administrative and technical staff, as well as non-university members drawn from the public and private sectors; Conseil scientifique, competent in matters of research; Conseil des Etudes et de la Vie universitaire; Conseil of each Unit, comprising representatives of its teaching staff, research workers, students, and administrative and technical staff. The President is elected by the Conseil d'administration. The Chancelier, who represents the Minister of Education, is the Recteur de l'Académie de Paris

Academic Year: September to June (September-January; February-June)

Admission Requirements: Secondary school certificate (baccalauréat) or equivalent, or special entrance examination

Fees: (Euros): 150-300 per annum

Main Language(s) of Instruction: French

International Co-operation: With institutions in North and Sub-Saharan Africa, Canada, Asia, Latin America. Also participates in Erasmus

Degrees and Diplomas: *Diplôme universitaire de Technologie (DUT)*: 2 yrs; *Licence*: 3 yrs; *Licence professionnelle*: 3 yrs; *Diplôme d'Etat*: Dental Surgery, 6 yrs; *Diplôme d'Etat*: Medicine, 6 yrs plus 2 yrs or 4 yrs (Internat) hospital practice and thesis; *Diplôme d'Etat*: Pharmacy, 5 yrs and 1 yr practical work or 4 yrs (Internat); *Diplôme national de Master*: 2 years following Licence; *Doctorat*: 3 yrs following Masters. Two types for Masters recherche, Masters professionnel

Student Services: Academic counselling, Foreign student adviser, Handicapped facilities, Health services, Social counselling, Sports facilities

Student Residential Facilities: Yes

Special Facilities: History of Medicine Museum

Libraries: Library of the University; common library for Medicine and Pharmacy

Publications: Dialogues de Descartes *(quarterly)*
Last Updated: 26/01/12

PARIS 6 UNIVERSITY PIERRE AND MARIE CURIE

Université Pierre et Marie Curie (Paris 6) (UPMC)
4, place Jussieu, 75252 Paris, Cedex 05
Tel: +33(1) 44-27-44-27
Fax: +33(1) 44-27-38-29
EMail: relations.internationales@upmc.fr
Website: http://www.upmc.fr

Président: Maurice Renard (2011-)
Tel: +33(1) 44-27-70-11 +33(1) 44-27-33-50,
Fax: +33(1) 44-27-38-29

Directrice générale des Services: Martine Ramond
Tel: +33(1) 44-27-33-26 EMail: martine.ramond@upmc.fr

International Relations: Sabine Lopez
Tel: +33(1) 44-27-26-74 +33(1) 44-27-32-06,
Fax: +33(1) 44-27-51-40

Centres
Marine Station *(Villefranche-sur-Mer)* (Marine Science and Oceanography); **Marine Station** *(Roscoff)* (Marine Science and Oceanography); **Marine Station** *(Banyuls sur Mer)* (Marine Science and Oceanography)

Faculties
Chemistry (Chemistry); **Earth, Environment and Biodiversity** (Earth Sciences; Environmental Studies); **Engineering** (Engineering); **Life Sciences** (Biological and Life Sciences); **Mathematics** (Mathematics); **Medicine** *(Site Pierre and Marie Curie)* (Medicine); **Theoretical and Applied Physics** (Applied Physics; Physics)

Institutes
Astrophysics *(Paris)* (Astrophysics); **Doctorate Studies**; **Mathematics** *(Henri Poincaré)* (Mathematics); **Statistics** (Statistics); **Teacher Training** *(IUFM 2 sites) Director*: Claudette Lapersonne

Research Centres
Biomedicine *(CRC)* (Biomedicine)

Research Units
Energy, Matter and the Universe (Energy Engineering; Physics); **Life and Health** (Health Sciences); **Living Earth and Environment** (Earth Sciences; Environmental Studies); **Modelling and Engineering** (Engineering)

Schools
Chemistry *(ENSCP)* (Chemistry); **Engineering** *(Polytech' Paris-UPMC)* (Engineering)

History: Founded 1970 under the 1968 law reforming higher education as one of the Universities replacing the former Université de Paris - founded in the 12th century, constituted as Universitas Magistrorum and confirmed by Papal Bull 1215; suppressed by the Revolution in 1793; replaced 1808 by an Academy of the Université impériale; reconstituted as University 1890.

Governing Bodies: Conseil d'Administration, comprising 29 members, including elected representatives of teaching staff, research workers, students, and administrative and technical staff, as well as non-university members drawn from the public and private sectors; Conseil scientifique, comprising 41 members, competent in matters of research; Conseil des Etudes et de la Vie universitaires; and the Conseil of each Unit, comprising representatives of its teaching staff, research workers, students, and administrative and technical staff. The President is elected by the first three bodies. The Chancelier, who represents the Minister of Education, is the Recteur de l'Académie de Paris

Academic Year: September to June (September-December; January-March; April-June)

Admission Requirements: Secondary school certificate (baccalauréat)or equivalent, or special entrance examination

Main Language(s) of Instruction: French

International Co-operation: Co-operates with 550 universities. Participates in over 100 European exchange programmes, Socrates.

Degrees and Diplomas: *Licence*: Mathematics; Mathematics and Computer; Computer Science; Physics; Mechanics; Electronics; Earth Sciences; Chemistry; Life Sciences; Basic, Natural and Experimental Sciences; *Licence professionnelle*; *Diplôme d'Ingénieur*: Electronics and Computing; Industrial Computing; Computer Science; Agribusiness; Materials Engineering; Earth Sciences; *Diplôme national de Master*: Medicine; Paramedical Studies; *Doctorat*: Medicine; Paramedical Studies; Modeling and Engineering; Physical Sciences and New Materials; Space, Environment, Ecology; Genomics, Cellular Communications Systems New Therapeutic Approaches. Also Certificates and Diplomas in Statistics and Programming

Student Services: Academic counselling, Canteen, Cultural centre, Foreign student adviser, Handicapped facilities, Health services, Social counselling, Sports facilities

Special Facilities: Mineral Collection; paleontology collection. Map reference library; Charcot Library. Dupuytren Museum (Medicine).

Libraries: Medical libraries. Science libraries (research and teaching)

Publications: Futur(e)s *(quarterly)*

Last Updated: 26/01/12

PARIS 7 UNIVERSITY

Université Denis Diderot (Paris 7)
2, place Jussieu, 75251 Paris, Cedex 05
Tel: +33(1) 57-27-57-27
EMail: communic@univ-paris-diderot.fr
Website: http://www.univ-paris-diderot.fr/

Président: Vincent Berger (2009-)
Tel: +33(1) 57-27-55-10
EMail: president@univ-paris-diderot.fr;
secretariat.president@paris7.jussieu.fr

Secrétaire général: Denis Guillaumin
Tel: +33(1) 57-27-57-00 EMail: secretariat.sg@univ-paris-diderot.fr

International Relations: Frédéric Ogée
Tel: +33(1) 57-27-55-08 +33(1) 57-27-58-80,
Fax: +33(1) 57-27-57-07
EMail: vice.presidentbri@univ-paris-diderot.fr

Departments

Arts and Humanities (Arts and Humanities; Cinema and Television; Economics; Geography; History; Literature; Social Sciences; Sociology); **Exact Sciences** (Chemistry; Mathematics; Physics; Psychology; Social Sciences); **Lifelong Education** *(DEPAES)* *Director:* Elisabeth Gaudin; **Natural and Life Sciences** (Biological and Life Sciences; Chemistry; Computer Science; Earth Sciences; Environmental Studies; Linguistics; Mathematics; Modern Languages; Physics); **Philosophy** (Philosophy) *Director:* Jean-Jacques Szczeciniarz

Graduate Schools

Science, Health and Applications *(Houses 4 Doctoral Schools and offers several other graduate studies in partnership with other Paris institutes)* (Biological and Life Sciences; Earth Sciences; Health Sciences; Physics; Public Health); **Social Sciences, Languages, Arts and Humanities** *(Houses 5 Doctoral Schools and offers several other graduate studies in partnership with other Paris institutes)* (Arts and Humanities; English Studies; French Studies; Linguistics; Literature; Modern Languages; Psychoanalysis; Social Sciences; Town Planning)

Institutes

Contemporary Thought *(IPC)* (Philosophy); **Haematology** *(IUH)* (Haematology); **Mathematics Education Research** *(IREM)* (Mathematics Education); **Technology** *(IUT Paris 7)* (Measurement and Precision Engineering; Safety Engineering; Technology)

Schools

Engineering *(Denis Diderot)* (Computer Engineering; Engineering; Nanotechnology)

Units

Biology, Life and Natural Sciences (Biology; Natural Sciences) *Director:* Marc Maier; **Chemistry** (Chemistry); **Computer Science** (Computer Science); **Dentistry** (Dentistry); **Earth, Environmental and Planet Sciences** *(STEP)* (Earth Sciences; Environmental Studies); **East Asian Studies** *(LCAO)* (Chinese; Cultural Studies; East Asian Studies; Japanese; Korean; Vietnamese); **English Studies** (English); **Geography, History, Social Sciences** *(GHSS)* (Economics; Geography; History; History of Societies; Law; Social Sciences); **Human Clinical Sciences** *(SHC)* (Clinical Psychology); **Intercultural Studies on Applied Languages** *(EILA)* (Cultural Studies; English; German; Linguistics; Spanish); **Life Sciences** (Biological and Life Sciences); **Linguistics** (Linguistics); **Literature, Arts and Cinema** *(LAC)* (Aesthetics; Cinema and Television; Comparative Literature; Literature); **Mathematics** (Mathematics); **Medicine** *(2 sites: Xavier Bichat, Villemin)* (Medicine); **Physics** (Physics); **Social Sciences** (Anthropology; Social Sciences; Sociology)

History: Founded 1970 under the 1968 law reforming higher education as one of the Universities replacing the former Université de Paris, founded in 12th century, constituted as Universitas Magistrorum and confirmed by Papal Bull 1215; suppressed by the Revolution in 1793; replaced by an Academy of the Université

impériale; reconstituted as University 1890. A State Institution enjoying academic and financial autonomy, operating under the jurisdiction of the Minister of Education and financed by the State.

Governing Bodies: Conseil d'Administration, including representatives of teaching staff, research workers, students, and administrative and technical staff, as well as non-university members drawn from the public and private sectors; Conseil scientifique, competent in matters of research; Conseil des Etudes et de la Vie universitaire; and Conseil of each Unit, comprising representatives of its teaching staff, research workers, students, and administrative and technical staff. The President is elected by the first three bodies. The Chancelier, who represents the Minister of Education, is the Recteur of the Académie de Paris

Academic Year: October to June (October-February; February-June)

Admission Requirements: Secondary school certificate (baccalauréat) or equivalent, or special entrance examination

Main Language(s) of Instruction: French

Degrees and Diplomas: *Diplôme d' Accès aux Etudes universitaires*; *Licence*: Science, Social Sciences, Arts and Humanities, Modern Languages, 3 yrs; *Diplôme d'Etat*: Dental Surgery, 5 yrs; *Diplôme d'Etat*: Medicine, 6 yrs and a further 2 yrs medical practice and thesis; *Magistère*: Genetics, Physics, 3 yrs following 1st yr or DUT; *Diplôme national de Master*: 2 yrs following Licence; *Doctorat*: Science, Social Sciences, Arts and Humanities, 2-4 yrs following Masters; *Habilitation à Diriger les Recherches*. Masters recherche, Masters professionnel, Preparation for CAPES, Agrégation exams

Student Residential Facilities: Yes

Libraries: Interuniversity library; specialized libraries (Letters and Human Sciences; Sciences; Medicine), total, 67,000 vols

Last Updated: 26/07/11

PARIS 8 UNIVERSITY OF VINCENNES-SAINT DENIS

Université Vincennes-Saint-Denis (Paris 8)
2, rue de la Liberté, 93526 Saint-Denis, Cedex 02
Tel: +33(1) 49-40-67-89
Fax: +33(1) 48-21-04-46
EMail: sgen@univ-paris8.fr
Website: http://www.univ-paris8.fr

Président: Pascal Binczak (2006-)
Tel: +33(1) 49-40-67-00, Fax: +33(1) 49-40-67-12
EMail: pre@univ-paris8.fr

International Relations: David Constans-Martigny
Tel: +33(1) 49-40-65-25/26, Fax: +33(1) 49-40-65-16
EMail: inter@univ-paris8.fr

Graduate Schools

Aesthetics, Science and Technologies of the Arts *(EDESTA)* (Fine Arts; Performing Arts); **Applied and Theoritical Linguistics** (Applied Linguistics; Literature; Modern Languages); **Cognition, Language, Interaction** *(ED SIIC)* (Linguistics; Psycholinguistics; Psychology); **Humanities** (Arts and Humanities)

Institutes

Distance Education *(IED)* (Clinical Psychology; Educational Sciences; Social Psychology); **European Studies** *(IEE)* (European Studies; International Business); **Geopolitics** (International Studies; Political Sciences); **Teacher Training** *(IUFM with 7 sites throughout Créteil)* (Teacher Trainers Education; Teacher Training); **Technology** *(IUT, Tremblay-en-France)* (Industrial Maintenance; Technology; Transport Management); **Technology** *(IUT, Montreuil)* (Computer Engineering; Production Engineering; Technology)

Units

Administration, Economics and Management Studies *(AES-EG)* (Business Administration; Institutional Administration; Public Administration); **Arts, Philosophy, and Aesthetics** *(APE)* (Arts and Humanities; Cinema and Television; Dance; Fine Arts; Graphic Arts; Music; Performing Arts; Philosophy; Photography; Theatre); **Communication, Computer and Technology** *(MITSIC)* (Information Sciences; Mathematics and Computer Science) *Director:* Jacqueline Signorin; **Culture and Communication** *(CC)* (Communication Studies; Education; Psychoanalysis; Social Sciences); **Educational Sciences, Psychoanalysis and French as Foreign Language** (Educational Sciences; French;

Psychoanalysis); **Foreign Languages and Culture** *(LLCE-LEA)* (Arabic; English; German; Italian; Modern Languages; Portuguese; Russian; Spanish); **Law** (Civil Law; Commercial Law; Comparative Law; European Union Law; International Law; Law; Public Law); **Linguistics** (French Studies; Linguistics); **Psychology** *(PPCS)* (Clinical Psychology; Psychology); **Territorial, Environmental and Social Studies** (Anthropology; Environmental Studies; European Studies; Geography; History of Societies; North African Studies; Social Studies); **Texts and Societies** (Comparative Literature; History; Literature; Political Sciences; Sociology)

History: Founded as experimental academic centre 1969. Moved to Saint Denis 1980.

Governing Bodies: Conseil d'Administration, including representatives of teaching staff, research workers, students, and administrative and technical staff, as well as non-university members drawn from the public and private sectors; Conseil scientifique, competent in matters of research; Conseil des Etudes et de la Vie universitaire; and Conseil of each Unit, comprising representatives of its teaching staff, research workers, students, and administrative and technical staff. The President is elected by the first three bodies. The Chancelier, who represents the Minister of Education, is the Recteur of the Académie de Paris

Academic Year: October to June (October-February; February-June)

Admission Requirements: Secondary school certificate (baccalauréat) or equivalent, or special entrance examination

Main Language(s) of Instruction: French

Degrees and Diplomas: *Diplôme universitaire de Technologie*: Technology, Administration (DUT); *Licence*: Fine Arts, Mathematics and Computer Sciences, Technology, Social Sciences, Arts and Humanities, Modern Languages, Law, 3 yrs; *Licence professionnelle*: Mathematics and Computer Science, Technology, Social Work; *Diplôme national de Master*: Fine Arts, Mathematics and Computer Sciences, Technology, Social Sciences, Arts and Humanities, Modern Languages, Law, Cultural Studies, Communication, 2 yrs following Licence; *Doctorat*: 2-4 yrs following Masters. Masters recherche, Masters professionnel

Student Services: Academic counselling, Canteen, Cultural centre, Handicapped facilities, Health services, Nursery care, Social counselling, Sports facilities

Libraries: Total, c. 600,000 vols

Publications: Extrême-Orient/Extrême-Occident, Comparative Research *(annually)*; Histoire, Epistémologie, Langage *(biannually)*; 'Le fil d'Ariane' (IEE), Essays on Contemporary Art, Historic issues *(biannually)*; Médiévales; Pratiques de Formation; Recherches linguistiques de Vincennes *(annually)*; Théorie Littérature Enseignement *(annually)*

Press or Publishing House: Presses Universitaires de Vincennes (PUV)

Last Updated: 10/06/11

PARIS 13 UNIVERSITY

Université Paris Nord- Paris 13 (UP13)
Avenue Jean-Baptiste Clément, 93430 Villetaneuse
Tel: +33(1) 49-40-30-00
Fax: +33(1) 49-40-33-33
EMail: secretaire.gen@univ-paris13.fr
Website: http://www.univ-paris13.fr

Président: Jean-Loup Salzmann
Tel: +33(1) 49-40-30-07, Fax: +33(1) 49-40-32-52
EMail: cab-pres@univ-paris13.fr

Directeur général des Services: Rémy Gicquel
Tel: +33(1) 49-40-30-09, Fax: +33(1) 49-40-30-04

Graduate Schools
Life and Societies (Communication Studies; Linguistics; Psychology) *Director*: Robert Muchembled; **Science, Technology and Health** *(Institut Galilé)* (Engineering; Health Sciences; Information Sciences; Mathematics) *Director*: Alain Grigis

Institutes
Galilée (Chemistry; Computer Science; Electrical Engineering; Laser Engineering; Materials Engineering; Mathematics; Physics; Statistics; Systems Analysis; Telecommunications Engineering); **Technology** *(IUT, Saint-Denis)* (Business Administration; Business

and Commerce; Civil Security; Industrial Maintenance; Measurement and Precision Engineering; Mechanical Engineering; Production Engineering; Public Administration; Technology); **Technology** *(IUT Bobigny)* (Bioengineering; Business Administration; Business Computing; Computer Networks; Computer Science; Social Work; Technology; Telecommunications Engineering); **Technology** *(IUT Villetaneuse)* (Accountancy; Banking; Business Administration; Computer Science; Electronic Engineering; Finance; Human Resources; Insurance; Law; Technology; Telecommunications Engineering)

Units
Arts, Human Sciences and Social Sciences (Arts and Humanities; Educational Sciences; English; Geography; History; History of Societies; Literature; Psychology; Spanish); **Communication Sciences** (Communication Studies); **Economics and Management** (Economics; Management); **Health, Medicine and Human Biology** *(Léonard de Vinci, Bobigny)* (Biology; Health Sciences; Medicine); **Law, Social and Political Science** (Law; Political Sciences; Social Sciences)

Further Information: Also 46 Research Laboratories and Centres and offers 4 higher education professional programmes (IUP).

History: Founded 1970 under the 1968 law reforming higher education as one of the Universities replacing the former Université de Paris - founded in 12th century, constituted as Universitas Magistrorum and confirmed by Papal Bull 1215; suppressed by the Revolution in 1793; replaced 1808 by an Academy of the Université impériale; reconstituted as University 1890. A State institution enjoying academic and financial autonomy, operating under the jurisdiction of the Minister of Education and financed by the State.

Governing Bodies: Conseil de l'Université, including elected representatives of teaching staff, research workers, students, and administrative and technical staff, as well as non-university members drawn from the public and private sectors; Conseil of each Unit, comprising representatives of its teaching staff, research workers, students, and administrative and technical staff; and Conseil scientifique, competent in matters of research. The President is elected by the Conseil de l'Université. The Chancelier, who represents the Minister of Education, is the Recteur of the Académie de Créteil

Academic Year: October to June (October-January; February-June)

Admission Requirements: Secondary school certificate (baccalauréat) or equivalent, or special entrance examination

Main Language(s) of Instruction: French

International Co-operation: Participates in Tempus and Erasmus programmes

Degrees and Diplomas: *Capacité en Droit*; *Diplôme universitaire de Technologie*: 2 yrs; *Licence*: 3 yrs; *Licence professionnelle*: 3 yrs; *Diplôme d'Etat*: Medicine, 6 yrs plus 1 yr hospital practice and thesis; *Diplôme d'Ingénieur*: 2-3 yrs following 2 yrs; *Diplôme national de Master*: 2 yrs following Licence; *Doctorat*: 2-4 yrs following Masters. Also Diplômes d'Université, Masters recherche, Masters professionnel, Preparation for CAPES, Agrégation and Administrative exams

Student Services: Academic counselling, Canteen, Cultural centre, Employment services, Foreign student adviser, Foreign Studies Centre, Handicapped facilities, Health services, Language programs, Social counselling, Sports facilities

Student Residential Facilities: Yes

Libraries: University libraries; Scientific Library
Last Updated: 20/07/11

PARIS EAST CRÉTEIL VAL DE MARNE UNIVERSITY

Université Paris-Est Créteil Val de Marne (UPVM)
61, avenue du Général de Gaulle, 94010 Créteil
Tel: +33(1) 45-17-10-00 +33(1) 45-17-12-61
Fax: +33(1) 42-07-70-12 +33(1) 45-17-12-52
EMail: webmaster@univ-paris12.fr; ri@univ-paris12.fr
Website: http://www.univ-paris12.fr

Présidente: Simone Bonnafous (2006-)
Tel: +33(1) 45-17-10-11, Fax: +33(1) 48-99-27-31
EMail: bonnafous@univ-paris12.fr; president@univ-paris12.fr

Directrice générale des Services: Pascale Saint-Cyr
Tel: +33(1) 45-17-10-14 EMail: Sgp12@univ-paris12.fr

International Relations: Patricia Pol
Tel: +33(1) 45-17-12-57, Fax: +33(1) 45-17-12-52
EMail: ri@univ-paris12.fr; pol@univ-paris12.fr

Departments
Lifelong Education *Director:* Micheline Barthout

Faculties
Administration and International Exchanges (Administration; Business Administration; Human Resources; International Business; Public Administration); **Economics and Management** *(La Varenne-St. Hilaire)* (Business Administration; Economics; Management); **Law** *(La Varenne-St.-Hilaire)* (Civil Law; Constitutional Law; Criminal Law; Economic and Finance Policy; Economic History; European Union Law; Finance; History of Law; International Relations; Law; Political Sciences; Private Law); **Letters, Languages and Humanities** (Arts and Humanities; Communication Studies; Cultural Studies; English; Geography; German; History; Literature; Philosophy; Romance Languages); **Medicine** (Medicine); **Physical Education, Sports, Social and Educational Sciences** (Educational Sciences; Physical Education; Sports); **Science and Technology** (Biological and Life Sciences; Biology; Chemistry; Computer Science; Earth Sciences; Engineering; Mathematics; Physics)

Institutes
Data Processing for Management *(ISIAG-IUP MIAGE, Saint Simon Créteil)* (Data Processing); **Ergotherapy** (Rehabilitation and Therapy); **Preparatory Administrative Studies** *(IPAG)* (Administration); **Teacher Training** *(IUFM Académie de Créteil)* (Teacher Training); **Technology** *(IUT Créteil / Vitry)* (Bioengineering; Biology; Chemistry; Computer Engineering; Electrical Engineering; Marketing; Measurement and Precision Engineering; Technology; Telecommunications Engineering); **Technology** *(IUT Sénart-Fontainebleau)* (Business Administration; Business and Commerce; Computer Engineering; Electrical Engineering; Industrial Maintenance; Sales Techniques; Technology); **Town Planning** (Town Planning; Urban Studies)

Programmes
French Language for Foreigners *(DELCIFE)* (French)

Schools
Health Administration *(Ecole Supérieure Montsouris)* (Health Administration; Sanitary Engineering)

Units
Science and Technology (Biology; Ecology; Mathematics; Medicine; Natural Sciences; Technology)

Further Information: Also numerous research centres within the units

History: Founded 1970 under the 1968 law reforming higher education as one of the Universities replacing the former Université de Paris - founded in 12th century, constituted as Universitas Magistrorum and confirmed by Papal Bull 1215; suppressed by the Revolution in 1793; replaced 1808 by an Academy of the Université impériale; reconstituted as University 1890. A State institution enjoying academic and financial autonomy, operating under the jurisdiction of the Minister of Education and financed by the State. Previously known as Université Paris-Val-de-Marne (Paris 12) (University of Paris 12).

Governing Bodies: Conseil de l'Université, including elected representatives of teaching staff, research workers, students, and administrative and technical staff, as well as non-university members drawn from the public and private sectors; Conseil of each Unit, comprising representatives of its teaching staff, research workers, students, and administrative and technical staff; Conseil scientifique, competent in matters of research. The President is elected by the Conseil de l'Université. The Chancelier, who represents the Minister of Education, is the Recteur de l'Académie de Créteil

Academic Year: October to June (October-February; February-June)

Admission Requirements: Secondary school certificate (baccalauréat) or equivalent, or special entrance examination

Fees: (Euros): c. 170-400 per annum

Main Language(s) of Instruction: French

International Co-operation: With Universities in Africa, Latin America, Asia, Eastern Europe. Also participates in Erasmus, Tempus, Leonardo Da Vinci, Crepuq, Micefa.

Degrees and Diplomas: *Capacité en Droit*; *Diplôme d' Accès aux Etudes universitaires (DAEU)*; *Diplôme universitaire de Technologie*: 2 yrs; *Licence*: Economics, Administration, Arts and Humanities, Law, Science, Physical Education, Sports, 3 yrs; *Licence professionnelle*: Economics, Administration, Languages, Social Sciences, Science and Technology, 3 yrs; *Diplôme d'Etat*: Animal Biology and Pathology; Ergotherapy; Veterinary Sciences; *Diplôme d'Etat*: Medicine, 6 yrs plus 1 yr hospital practice and thesis; *Diplôme national de Master*: Economics, Administration, Arts and Humanities, Law, Science, Town Planning, Health, Education, Sports, Languages, 2 yrs following Licence; *Doctorat*: Economics, Humanities, Law, Letters, Management, Science, a further 2-4 yrs following Masters. Masters recherche, Masters professionnels, Préparation for CAPES, Agrégation, Judicial and Administrative exams

Student Services: Academic counselling, Canteen, Cultural centre, Employment services, Foreign student adviser, Handicapped facilities, Health services, Language programs, Social counselling, Sports facilities

Student Residential Facilities: Yes

Libraries: Central Library, c. 274,000 vols; c. 3,550 periodical titles

Student Numbers *2009*: Total: c. 31,000
Last Updated: 20/07/11

PARIS EAST MARNE-LA-VALLÉE UNIVERSITY
Université Paris-Est Marne-la-Vallée (UMLV)
Cité Descartes, 5, boulevard Descartes, Champs-sur-Marne, 77454 Cedex 2 Marne-la-Vallée
Tel: +33(1) 60-95-75-00
Fax: +33(1) 60-95-75-75
EMail: presidence@univ-mlv.fr
Website: http://www.univ-mlv.fr

Président: Gilles Roussel
Tel: +33(1) 60-95-70-02, Fax: +33(1) 60-95-70-70

Directrice générale des Services: Sophie Julien
Tel: +33(1) 60-95-70-03, Fax: +33(1) 60-95-70-70
EMail: sophie.julien@univ-mlv.fr

International Relations: Thierry Berkover
Tel: +33(1) 60-95-70-24 +33(1) 60-95-70-19,
Fax: +33(1) 60-95-70-90 EMail: thierry.berkover@univ-mlv.fr

Institutes
Applied Sciences *(Institut Francilien (ISFA))* (Computer Science; Electronic Engineering; Engineering; Mechanical Engineering; Technology; Town Planning); **Electronics and Computer Science** *(Gaspard Monge)* (Electronic Engineering; Mathematics and Computer Science; Telecommunications Engineering); **Services Engineering** *(Institut Francilien d'Ingénierie des Services)* (Engineering; Management; Real Estate; Service Trades; Technology; Tourism); **Technology** *(IUT Marne-la-Vallée)* (Business Administration; Civil Engineering; Energy Engineering; Industrial Engineering; Marketing; Public Administration; Technology); **Town Planning** *(IFU)* (Town Planning)

Schools
School of Engineering *(Ingénieurs 2000)* (Computer Engineering; Mechanical Engineering; Production Engineering)

Units
Economics and Management (Economics; Management); **Human and Social Sciences** (Geography; History; Social Sciences); **Languages and Civilizations** (American Studies; English Studies; Germanic Languages; Hispanic American Studies; Modern Languages; Spanish); **Literature, Arts and Communication** (Arts and Humanities; Communication Studies; Literature); **Mathematics** (Mathematics); **Physical Education and Sports** *(STAPS)* (Physical Education; Sports; Sports Management)

History: Founded 1991.

Academic Year: September to June (September-January; February-June)

Admission Requirements: Secondary school certificate (baccalauréat)

Fees: (Euros): Undergraduate 170 per annum; Graduate 250 per annum

Main Language(s) of Instruction: French

International Co-operation: Participates in the Socrates programme, also Crepuq agreement with all Quebec universities; ERASMUS; MICEFA with United States; CODFIL with Louisiana. Agreements with universities worldwide

Degrees and Diplomas: *Diplôme universitaire de Technologie*: 2 yrs; *Licence*: Science,Technology, Health, Human and Social Sciences, Law, Economics, Management, Physical Education and Sports, Arts, Literature, Languages, 3 yrs; *Licence professionnelle*: Science and Technology, Human and Social Sciences, 1 yr following 2 yrs' undergraduate studies; *Diplôme d'Ingénieur*: 3 yrs following 2 yrs' undergraduate studies; *Diplôme national de Master*: Science,Technology, Health, Human and Social Sciences, Law, Economics, Management, Physical Education and Sport, Arts, Literature, Languages, 2 yrs following Licence; *Doctorat*. Preparation for CERPE and CAPES exams; Doctoral Schools: Cultures and Societies, City, Transport and Territories, Mathematics and ICST, Organizations, Markets, Institutions, Science, Engineering and Environment

Student Services: Canteen, Foreign student adviser, Handicapped facilities, Health services, Language programs, Social counselling

Last Updated: 26/01/12

PARIS NATIONAL CONSERVATORY OF MUSIC AND DANSE

Conservatoire national supérieur de Musique et de Danse de Paris (CNSMDP)
Parc de la Villette, 209, avenue Jean Jaurès, 75019 Paris
Tel: +33(1) 40-40-45-45
Fax: +33(1) 40-40-45-00
EMail: cnsmdp@cnsdmp.fr
Website: http://www.cnsmdp.fr

Directeur: Bruno Mantovani (2010-) Tel: +33(1) 40-40-45-00

Administrative Officer: Jean Garnero EMail: jgarnero@cnsdmp.fr

International Relations: Gretchen Amussen
Tel: +33(1) 40-40-46-51 EMail: gamussen@cnsdmp.fr

Programmes
Performing Arts (Dance; Jazz and Popular Music; Music; Music Education; Sound Engineering (Acoustics))
History: Founded in 1795.
Admission Requirements: Competitive entrance examination
Degrees and Diplomas: *Diplôme national de Master*; *Doctorat*. Diplôme national supérieur professionnel de musicien
Last Updated: 14/12/11

PARIS SORBONNE UNIVERSITY (PARIS 4)

Université Paris Sorbonne (Paris 4)
1, rue Victor Cousin, 75230 Paris, Cedex 05
Tel: +33(1) 40-46-22-11
Fax: +33(1) 40-46-25-12
EMail: president@paris-sorbonne.fr
Website: http://www.paris-sorbonne.fr

Président: Georges Molinié (2008-)
Tel: +33(1) 40-46-33-79, Fax: +33(1) 40-46-25-12

Directrice générale des services: Sylvie Nguyen

Departments
Arabic and Islamic Studies (Islamic Studies; Middle Eastern Studies; North African Studies)

Graduate Schools
Ancient and Medieval Civilisations (Ancient Civilizations; Medieval Studies); **Art History and Archaeology** (Archaeology; Art History); **Concepts and Languages** (Applied Linguistics; Applied Mathematics; Communication Studies; Social Sciences); **Cultural and Literature Studies** (Cultural Studies; Literature); **French Literature** (Comparative Literature; French Studies); **Geography** (Geography); **Modern and Contemporary History** (Contemporary History; Modern History)

Institutes
Applied Humanities *(ISHA)* (Arts and Humanities); **Modern Western Civilizations** *(IRCOM)* (Western European Studies); **Religious Studies** *(IREL)* (Anthropology; History of Religion; Jewish Studies; Religious Studies); **Teacher Training** *(IUFM 2 sites)* (Teacher Trainers Education; Teacher Training); **Town Planning** *(IUAS)* (Town Planning)

Schools
Information and Communication Sciences *(CELSA)* (Communication Studies; Human Resources; Information Sciences; Journalism; Marketing; Public Relations) *Director*: Véronique Richard

Units
Applied Foreign Languages *(LEA)* (Modern Languages); **Art History and Archaeology** (Archaeology; Fine Arts; History); **Comparative Literature** (Comparative Literature; Literature); **English and North American Studies** (American Studies; English Studies); **French Studies** (French; French Studies); **Geography** (Geography; Regional Planning); **Germanic Studies** (German; Germanic Studies); **Greek** (Greek); **History** (History); **Iberian and Latin American Studies** (Latin American Studies; Spanish); **Italian and Romanian Studies** (Italian; Romanian); **Latin** (Latin); **Music and Musicology** (Music; Musicology); **Philosophy and Sociology** (Philosophy; Sociology); **Slavonic Studies** (Slavic Languages)

History: Founded 1970 under the 1968 law reforming higher education as one of the new Universities replacing the former Université de Paris - founded in 12th century, constituted as Universitas Magistrorum and confirmed by Papal Bull 1215; suppressed by the Revolution in 1793; replaced 1808 by an Academy of the Université impériale; reconstituted as university 1890. A State institution enjoying academic and financial autonomy, operating under the jurisdiction of the Minister of Education and financed by the State.

Governing Bodies: Conseil d'Administration including elected representatives of teaching staff, research workers, students, and administrative and technical staff, as well as non-university members drawn from the public and private sectors; Conseil scientifique, competent in matters of research; Conseil des Etudes et de la Vie universitaire; Conseil of each Unit, comprising representatives of its teaching staff, research workers, students, and administrative and technical staff. The President is elected by the first three bodies. The Chancelier, who represents the Minister of Education, is the Recteur of the Académie de Paris

Academic Year: October to June (October-February; February-June)

Admission Requirements: Secondary school certificate (baccalauréat) or equivalent, or special entrance examination

Fees: (Euros): c. 150 per annum

Main Language(s) of Instruction: French

International Co-operation: Participates in the Erasmus programme

Degrees and Diplomas: *Licence*: Arts and Humanities, 3 yrs; *Diplôme national de Master*: Arts and Humanities, 2 yrs following Licence; *Doctorat*: 2-4 yrs following Masters; *Habilitation à Diriger les Recherches*. Masters recherche, Masters professionnel, National Diplomas for French and French Studies

Student Services: Academic counselling, Canteen, Cultural centre, Employment services, Foreign student adviser, Foreign Studies Centre, Language programs, Social counselling, Sports facilities

Libraries: Specialized libraries, 470,000 vols

Publications: Actes des différents colloques publiés aux Presses de l'Université de Paris-Sorbonne

Press or Publishing House: Presses de l'Université Paris-Sorbonne

Last Updated: 16/05/11

PARIS WEST NANTERRE LA DÉFENSE UNIVERSITY

Université Paris Ouest Nanterre La Défense
200, avenue de la République, 92001 Nanterre, Cedex
Tel: +33(1) 40-97-72-00
Fax: +33(1) 40-97-75-71
EMail: presidence@u-paris10.fr
Website: http://www.u-paris10.fr

Présidente: Bernadette Madeuf (2008-)
Tel: +33(1) 40-97-74-32, Fax: +33(1) 40-97-71-70

Directeur général des Services: Didier Ramond
Tel: +33(1) 40-97-74-39, Fax: +33(1) 40-97-47-09
EMail: didier.ramond@u-paris10.fr

International Relations: Jacqueline Domenach
Tel: +33(1) 40-97-74-95, Fax: +33(1) 40-97-71-14

Centres
Lifelong Education (Computer Science; Labour Law; Social Psychology) *Director:* Bruno Lefebvre

Departments
Publishing *(IUP Site Saint Cloud) Director:* Michel Bruillon

Faculties
Arts, Letters and Languages (Cinema and Television; English; German; Information Sciences; Italian; Linguistics; Literature; Performing Arts; Philosophy; Portuguese; Russian; Spanish; Theatre); **Economics and Management** (Economics; Management); **Human and Social Sciences** (Archaeology; Art History; Educational Sciences; Ethnology; Geography; History; Psychology; Sociology); **Law and Political Science** (European Union Law; Law; Political Sciences); **Physical Education and Sports** *(STAPS)* (Physical Education; Sports); **Science, Tecnology and Health** (Construction Engineering; Electrical and Electronic Engineering; Energy Engineering; Industrial Engineering; Mechanical Engineering)

Institutes
Preparatory Administrative Studies *(IPAG)* (Administration); **Teacher Training** *(IUFM Versailles with 5 sites)* (Teacher Trainers Education; Teacher Training); **Technology** *(IUT, Ville-d'Avray)* (Computer Engineering; Electrical Engineering; Electronic Engineering; Mechanical Engineering; Production Engineering; Technology; Thermal Engineering)

Research Institutes
Archaeology and Ethnology *(René Ginouvès House, MAE)* (Archaeology; Ethnology); **Economics, Sociology, Political Science and Geography** *(Max Weber House)*; **International and Contemporary Documentation** *(BDIC, Member of IALHI Network)* (Library Science); **Law Studies** *(IEJ/Henri Motulsky)*

History: Founded 1970 under the 1968 law reforming higher education as one of the Universities replacing the former Université de Paris - founded in 12th century, constituted as Universitas Magistrorum and confirmed by Papal Bull 1215; suppressed by the Revolution in 1793; replaced 1808 by an Academy of the Université impériale; reconstituted as university 1890. A State institution enjoying academic and financial autonomy, operated under the jurisdiction of the Minister of Education and financed by the State. Acquired present title 2010.

Governing Bodies: Conseil d'Administration (CA), comprising 80 members, including elected representatives of teaching staff, research workers, students, and administrative and technical staff, as well as non-university members drawn from the public and private sectors; Conseil des Etudes et de la Vie Universitaire (CEVU), competent in matters of studies and student life; Conseil scientifique (CS), competent in matters of research; Conseil of each Unit, comprising representatives of teaching staff, research workers, students and administrative and technical staff. The President is elected by the three Conseils (CA, CEVU, CS). The Chancelier, who represents the Minister of Education, is the Recteur of the Académie de Versailles

Academic Year: October to June (October-January; February-June)

Admission Requirements: Secondary school certificate (baccalauréat) or equivalent, or special entrance examination

Fees: (Euros): c. 200 per annum

Main Language(s) of Instruction: French

International Co-operation: With universities in Europe; USA; Canada; China; Japan; South America; Thailand; Tunisia; Jordan

Degrees and Diplomas: *Capacité en Droit; Diplôme d' Accès aux Etudes universitaires; Diplôme universitaire de Technologie*: 2 yrs; *Licence*: Law, Political Science, Social Sciences, Economics, Management, Arts and humanities, Performing Arts, Publishing and Book Trade, Information and Communication Studies, 3 yrs; *Diplôme national de Master*: Law, Political Science, Social Sci-

ences, Economics, Management, Arts and humanities, Performing Arts, Publishing and Book Trade, Information and Communication Studies, Classical Languages, Sciences of Education , Physical Education and Sports, 2 yrs following Licence; *Doctorat*: Law, Political Science, Social Sciences, Economics, Management, Arts and humanities, Performing Arts, Publishing and Book Trade, Information and Communication Studies, Classical Languages, Sciences of Education, Physical Education and Sports. Masters recherche, Masters professionnel

Student Services: Academic counselling, Canteen, Cultural centre, Employment services, Foreign student adviser, Foreign Studies Centre, Handicapped facilities, Health services, Language programs, Social counselling, Sports facilities

Student Residential Facilities: Yes

Special Facilities: Art Gallery; Theatre

Libraries: Bibliothèque universitaire, c. 1m. vols

Publications: Cahiers de Recherche Freudienne; Cahiers de RITM, Studies on Modernity; Cahiers de Sémiotique Textuelle; Cinéma et Sciences humaines; Confluences, Modernity in English-speaking Countries; CRISOL, Spanish, Portuguese, and Latin American Studies; Culture/Cultures, Anglo-American Culture; Droit et Cultures, Law, Anthropology, History and Culture *(biannually)*; Etudes Lawrenciennes; Ibériques; Italian Studies; Italie Années 90; LINX; Litérales; Musique et Sciences Humaines; Narrativa; Parcours J., Jewish Studies; Temps philosophique; Tropismes

Press or Publishing House: Publidix
Last Updated: 20/07/11

PARIS-BELLEVILLE SCHOOL OF ARCHITECTURE

Ecole nationale supérieure d'Architecture de Paris-Belleville (ENSAPB)
6O bld de la Villette, 75019 Paris
Tel: +33(1) 53-38-50-00
Fax: +33(1) 53-38-50-01
EMail: ensa-pb@paris-belleville.archi.fr
Website: http://www.paris-belleville.archi.fr

Directeur: Jean-Pierre Bobenriether

Programmes
Architecture (Architecture)

History: Founded 1969. Acquired present status 1986.

Main Language(s) of Instruction: French

Degrees and Diplomas: *Licence; Diplôme national de Master; Doctorat.* Graduate degrees in Architecture: DSA and DPEA; Habilitation de l'architecte diplômé d'Etat à l'exercice de la maîtrise d'oeuvre en son nom propre
Last Updated: 27/06/11

PARIS-CERGY NATIONAL ART SCHOOL

Ecole nationale supérieure d'Arts Cergy-Pontoise (ENSA PARIS-CERGY)
2 rue des Italiens, Parvis de la Préfecture, 95000 Cergy-Pontoise
Tel: +33(1) 30-30-54-44
Fax: +33(1) 30-38-38-09
EMail: accueil@ensapc.fr
Website: http://www.ensapc.fr/

Directeur: Sylvain Lizon

International Relations: Geraldine Longueville
EMail: geraldine.longueville@ensapc.fr

Programmes
Fine Arts (Fine Arts)

History: Founded in 1975.

Admission Requirements: Baccalauréat or equivalent secondary school exam. Entrance exam with a selection jury.

Main Language(s) of Instruction: French

International Co-operation: Has partnerships with University of Maine (USA), Concordia (Canada) and Universities in Turkey and South Korea.

Accrediting Agencies: Ministry of Culture and Communication

Degrees and Diplomas: Diplome national d'arts plastiques (DNAP) 3 yrs; Diplome national supérieur d'expression plastique (DNSEP) a further 2 yrs
Last Updated: 30/06/11

PARIS-DAUPHINE UNIVERSITY
Université Paris Dauphine
Place du Maréchal de Lattre de Tassigny, 75775 Paris, Cedex 16
Tel: +33(1) 44-05-44-05
Fax: +33(1) 44-05-49-49
EMail: service.communication@dauphine.fr
Website: http://www.dauphine.fr

Président: Laurent Batsch (2007-)
Tel: +33(1) 44-05-42-18 +33(1) 44-05-43-64,
Fax: +33(1) 44-05-45-98 EMail: Laurent.Batsch@dauphine.fr

Secrétaire général: Gérard Broussois
Tel: +33(1) 44-05-40-15 +33(1) 44-05-43-11/12,
Fax: +33(1) 44-05-41-41
EMail: gerard.broussois@dauphine.fr; secretariatgeneral@dauphine.fr

International Relations: Martine Beroud
Tel: +33(1) 44-05-41-50, Fax: +33(1) 44-05-48-04
EMail: martine.beroud@dauphine.fr

Centres
Lifelong Education (Business Administration; Economics; Finance; Management)

Graduate Schools
Management *(EDOGEST)* (Economics; Management); **Science of Organisations** *(EDOCIF)*; **Sciences of Decision-Making** *(EDDIMO)* (Economic and Finance Policy; Mathematics and Computer Science); **Social Sciences** *(EDOSSOC)*

Institutes
Finance *(IFD)* (Finance); **Research and Innovation Management** *(IMRI)* (Economics; Management)

Research Centres
Business Management *(CEREG)* (Accountancy; Business Administration; Business and Commerce; Finance; Management); **Economics and Applied Economics** *(CREPA)* (Economics); **Economics and Management of Health Organizations** *(CERESA-LEGOS)* (Economics; Health Administration; Management); **Energy and Raw Materials Geopolitics** *(IRI-CGEMP)* (Comparative Politics); **European Finance and Management** *(CREFIGE)* (Accountancy; Finance; Management); **Finance and Management** *(IRI-GRES)* (Finance; Management; Media Studies); **Identities and Cultural Interactions on Applied Linguistics in Languages for Special Purpose** *(CICLaS)* (Applied Linguistics); **Institutional Management** *(EURISCO)* (Economics; Institutional Administration); **Law** *(I2D)* (Law); **Management and Sociology of Organizations** *(CERSO)* (Management; Sociology); **Mathematics of Decision-Making** *(CEREMADE)* (Mathematics); **Prospective Marketing Strategy** *(DMSP)* (Marketing); **Rationalization of Systems Design for Decision-Making** *(LAMSADE)*; **Sociology, Economics, Political Science** *(IRISES)* (Economics; Political Sciences; Sociology)

Units
Applied Economics *(LSO 1st cycle)* (Business Administration; Economics; Management); **Applied Economics** *(MSO 2nd cycle)* (Business Administration; Economics; Law; Management; Political Sciences); **Mathematics and Computer Science of Decision-Making and Applied Economics** *(MIDO 1st, 2nd, 3d cycles)* (Computer Science; Economics; Management; Mathematics)

History: Founded 1970 under the 1968 Law reforming higher education as one of the Universities replacing the former Université de Paris - founded in 12th century, constituted as Universitas Magistrorum and confirmed by Papal Bull 1215; suppressed by the Revolution in 1793; replaced 1808 by an Academy of the Université impériale; reconstituted as university 1890. A State institution enjoying academic and financial autonomy, operating under the jurisdiction of the Minister of Education and financed by the State. Its structure is based on a series of Unités d'enseignement et de recherche (teaching and research Units) with emphasis on studies in Management Sciences. Each Unit enjoys academic and administrative independence. Becomes grand établissement 2004.

Governing Bodies: Conseil d'administration de l'Université, including elected representatives of teaching staff, research workers, students, and administrative and technical staff, as well as non-university members drawn from the public and private sectors; Conseil of each Unit, comprising representatives of its teaching staff, research workers, students, and administrative and technical staff; and Conseil scientifique, competent in matters of research. The President is elected by the Conseils de l'Université. The Chancelier, who represents the Minister of Education, is the Recteur of the Académie de Paris

Academic Year: September to July (September-February; February-June)

Admission Requirements: Secondary school certificate (baccalauréat) or equivalent, or special entrance examination

Fees: (Euros): 177 per annum

Main Language(s) of Instruction: French

International Co-operation: Participates in the Erasmus programme

Degrees and Diplomas: *Licence*: Law and Management, Mathematics and Computer Science, Applied Economics, Business Administration, 3 yrs; *Licence professionnelle*: Hotel and Tourism, 3 yrs; *Magistère*: Business Management, 3 yrs follwing 2 yrs study; *Diplôme national de Master*: Accountancy and Finance, Management, Economics, Mathematics and Computer Science, Applied Economics, Political Science, Sociology, 3 yrs following Licence; *Doctorat*: Economics, Applied Mathematics, Sociology, Poltical Science, Law, Management, 2-4 yrs following Masters. Masters recherche, Masters professionnel

Student Services: Academic counselling, Canteen, Cultural centre, Employment services, Handicapped facilities, Health services, Language programs, Nursery care, Social counselling, Sports facilities

Libraries: Centre d'acquisition et de diffusion de l'information scientifique et technique (CADIST), c. 190,000 vols
Last Updated: 11/09/07

PARIS-LA-VILLETTE SCHOOL OF ARCHITECTURE
Ecole nationale supérieure d'Architecture de Paris-la-Villette (EAPLV)
144, avenue de Flandre, 75019 Paris
Tel: +33(1) 44-65-23-00
Fax: +33(1) 44-65-23-01
EMail: directeur@paris-lavillette.archi.fr/
Website: http://www.paris-lavillette.archi.fr/

Directeur: Guy Ansellem

International Relations: Danielle Hugues
EMail: danielle.hugues@paris-lavillette.archi.fr

Programmes
Architecture (Architecture)

History: Founded 1969 as Unité Pédagogique d'Architecture n° 6 (UPA n°6).

Main Language(s) of Instruction: French

Degrees and Diplomas: *Licence*; *Diplôme national de Master*; *Doctorat*. Diplômes propres aux écoles d'architecture (DPEA), diplômes de spécialisation et d'approfondissement en architecture; Habilitation à exercer la maîtrise d'uvre en son nom propre (HMONP)
Last Updated: 27/06/11

PARIS-MALAQUAIS SCHOOL OF ARCHITECTURE
Ecole nationale supérieure d'Architecture Paris-Malaquais (ENSA DE PARIS-MALAQUAIS)
14 rue Bonaparte, 75272 Paris, Cedex 06
Tel: +33(1) 55-04-56-50
Fax: +33(1) 55-04-56-97
EMail: info@paris-malaquais.archi.fr
Website: http://www.paris-malaquais.archi.fr

Directrice: Nasrine Seraji
EMail: directeur@paris-malaquais.archi.fr

Departments

Art, Architecture, Politics (Architecture)

Degrees and Diplomas: *Licence*; *Diplôme national de Master*
Last Updated: 02/10/07

PARIS-SOUTH 11 UNIVERSITY

Université Paris-Sud 11 (UPS)
15, rue Georges Clémenceau, 91405 Orsay, Cedex
Tel: +33(1) 69-15-67-50
Fax: +33(1) 69-15-61-03
EMail: christine.Arnulf-Koechlin@u-psud.fr
Website: http://www.u-psud.fr

Président: Guy Couarraze (2008-)
Tel: +33(1) 69-15-74-06, Fax: +33(1) 69-15-61-03
EMail: presidence@.u-psud.fr

Directrice générale des Services: Christine Arnulf-Koechlin
Tel: +33(1) 69-15-70-41, Fax: +33(1) 69-15-43-50

International Relations: Grégory Maggion
Tel: +33(1) 69-15-30-84 +33(1) 69-15-77-50,
Fax: +33(1) 69-15-30-92 EMail: gregory.maggion@u-psud.fr

Faculties

Law, Economics and Management *(Jean Monnet)* (Accountancy; Business Administration; Economics; Law; Management); **Medicine** *(Kremlin-Bicêtre)* (Medicine); **Pharmacy** *(Châtenay-Malabry)* (Pharmacy); **Science** *(Orsay)* (Biology; Chemistry; Computer Science; Earth Sciences; Mathematics; Natural Sciences); **Sports** *(Orsay - STAPS)* (Sports; Sports Management)

Graduate Schools

Doctoral Schools (Ecology; Environmental Engineering; Genetics; Law; Mathematics; Medicine; Molecular Biology; Neurosciences; Physical Chemistry; Public Health; Sports; Telecommunications Engineering)

Institutes

Technology *(IUT Sceaux)* (Business and Commerce) *Director:* R. Milkoff; **Technology** *(IUT Cachan)* (Automation and Control Engineering; Computer Engineering; Electrical Engineering; Mechanical Engineering; Production Engineering; Robotics; Technology; Telecommunications Engineering)

Schools

Engineering *(Polytech Paris-Sud)* (Computer Engineering; Electronic Engineering; Engineering; Materials Engineering; Optical Technology)

History: Founded 1970 under the 1968 law reforming higher education as one of the Universities replacing the former Université de Paris - founded 12th century, constituted as Universitas Magistrorum and confirmed by Papal Bull 1215; suppressed by the Revolution in 1793; replaced 1808 by an Academy of the Université impériale; reconstituted as University 1890. A State institution enjoying academic and financial autonomy, operating under the jurisdiction of the Minister of Education and financed by the State.

Governing Bodies: Conseil d'Administration, including elected representatives of teaching staff, research workers, students, and administrative and technical staff as well as non-university members drawn from the public and private sectors; Conseil scientifique, competent in matters of research; Conseil des Etudes et de la Vie Universitaire, competent in matters of degrees; Conseil of each Unit, comprising representatives of its teaching staff, research workers, students, and administrative and technical staff. The President is elected by the Conseil de l'Université. The Chancelier, who represents the Minister of Education, is the Recteur de l'Académie de Versailles

Academic Year: September to June (September-January; February-June)

Admission Requirements: Secondary school certificate (baccalauréat) or equivalent, or special entrance examination. Admissions at various levels is possible, subject to recognition of previous degrees.

International Co-operation: With universities in Afghanistan, Cameroon, Canada, China, Colombia, Cuba, Italy, Lebanon, Morocco, Nigeria, New Zealand, Uzbekistan, Palestine, Peru, Senegal, Singapore, Syria and Vietnam

Degrees and Diplomas: *Diplôme universitaire de Technologie*: 2 yrs; *Licence*: Law; Natural Sciences; Mathematics and Computer Sciences; Sports (STAPS); Economics, 3 yrs; *Diplôme d'Etat*: Medicine, 6 yrs and 1further yr hospital practice and thesis; *Diplôme d'Etat*: Pharmacy, 4 yrs and 1 yr practical work; *Diplôme d'Ingénieur (IFIPS)*: 5 yrs; *Doctorat*: Human Biology; Law; Science, 3-4 yrs following Research Master; *Doctorat*: Pharmacy, by thesis following Diplôme d'Etat; *Certificat de Spécialité*: Medicine, at least 2 yrs following Diplôme d'Etat. Masters recherche, Masters professionnel

Student Residential Facilities: Cité universitaire

Libraries: University Library: c. 250,000 vols, c. 67,000 thesis vols, c. 9,400 periodical subscriptions; Laboratories and IUT libraries: 140,000 vols, 12,000 thesis vols, 4,600 periodical subscriptions
Last Updated: 20/07/11

PARIS-VAL-DE-SEINE SCHOOL OF ARCHITECTURE

Ecole nationale supérieure d'Architecture Paris-Val-de-Seine (ENSAPVS)
3 quai Panhard et Levassor, 75013 Paris
Tel: +33(1) 72-69-63-00
Fax: +33(1) 72-69-63-81
EMail: evelyne.berger@paris-valdeseine.archi.fr
Website: http://www.paris-valdeseine.archi.fr

Directeur: Jean-Claude Moreno

Directrice adjointe: Evelyne Berger Tel: 33(1) 72-69-63-02

International Relations: Cécile Mauras
Tel: +33(1) 72-69-63-36
EMail: cecile.mauras@paris-valdeseine.archi.fr

Programmes

Architecture (Architecture)

History: Founded 2001.

Academic Year: September-February; February-July

Admission Requirements: Secondary school certificate (Baccalauréat)

Fees: (Euros) c. 500 per annum

Main Language(s) of Instruction: French

International Co-operation: With schools in Germany, Austria, Belgium, Finland, Spain, Portugal, Greece, Italy, Romania, Czech Republic, Sweden

Degrees and Diplomas: Diplôme d'études en architecture (3 yrs); Diplôme d'Etat en architecture (5 yrs); Habilitation à exercer la maîtrise d'oeuvre en son nom propre (HMONP) (6 yrs)

Publications: Laboratoire Architecture Ville Urbanisme Environnement (LAVUE)

Academic Staff *2010-2011*: Total 220
Student Numbers *2010-2011*: Total 1,850
Last Updated: 22/06/11

PERPIGNAN ART SCHOOL

Haute Ecole d'ART de Perpignan (HEART)
3, rue du Maréchal Foch, 66000 Perpignan
Tel: +33(4) 68-66-31-84
Fax: +33(4) 68-35-68-51
EMail: heart@mairie-perpignan.com
Website: http://www.heart-bloc.eu

Directeur: Jordi Vidal

Programmes

Art (Fine Arts; Painting and Drawing; Photography)

Admission Requirements: Secondary school certificate and competitive entrance examination

Main Language(s) of Instruction: French

Accrediting Agencies: Ministère de la culture

Degrees and Diplomas: Diplôme National d'Art Plastique (3 yrs), Diplôme National Supérieur d'Expression Plastique (5 yrs)
Last Updated: 19/07/11

PYRENEES ART SCHOOL

Ecole supérieure d'Art des Pyrénées

Villa Formose 74 allées de Morlaas, 64000 Pau

Tel: +33(5) 59-02-20-06

Fax: +33(5) 59-90-34-85

EMail: administration@esac-pau.fr

Website: http://www.esac-pau.fr/

Directrice: Odile Biec EMail: directeur@esac-pau.fr

Programmes

Applied Arts *(Pau and Tarbes)* (Design; Furniture Design); **Ceramic Art** *(Tarbes)* (Ceramic Art); **Graphic Arts** *(Pau and Tarbes)* (Graphic Arts); **Plastic Arts** *(Pau and Tarbes)* (Engraving; Fine Arts; Painting and Drawing; Sculpture); **Visual Communication** *(Pau and Tarbes)* (Advertising and Publicity; Photography)

History: Founded 2011 following merger of the Ecole supérieure des Arts et de la Communication de Pau and the Ecole supérieure d'arts et céramique de Tarbes.

Admission Requirements: Baccalauréat or equivalent secondary school exam. Entrance exam with a selection jury.

Main Language(s) of Instruction: French

Accrediting Agencies: Ministry of Culture and Communication and Ministère de l'Enseignement Supérieur et dela Recherche

Degrees and Diplomas: Diplome national d'arts plastiques (DNAP in graphic design and multimedia, art) 3yrs; Diplome national supérieur d'expression plastique (DNSEP in graphic design and multimedia) a further 2 yrs.

Last Updated: 04/07/11

REIMS SCHOOL OF ART AND DESIGN

Ecole supérieure d'Art et de Design de Reims

12 rue Libergier, 51100 Reims

Tel: +33(3) 26-84-69-90

EMail: contact@esad-reims.fr

Website: http://www.esad-reims.fr/

Directrice: Claire Peillod (2005-)

Programmes

Visual Arts and Design (Design; Fine Arts; Furniture Design; Graphic Design)

History: Created in 1748, acquiring its current status in 2000.

Admission Requirements: Baccalauréat or equivalent secondary school exam. Entrance exam with a selection jury.

Main Language(s) of Instruction: French

Accrediting Agencies: Ministry of Culture and Communication

Degrees and Diplomas: Diplôme national d'arts plastiques (DNAP) 3 yrs; Diplôme national supérieur d'expression plastique (DNSEP in Design) a further 2 yrs. Prepares for the teaching exams: Visual Arts CAPES and Applied Arts CAPET.

Last Updated: 30/10/07

RENNES I UNIVERSITY

Université de Rennes I

2, rue du Thabor, CS 46510, 35065 Rennes, Cedex

Tel: +33(2) 23-23-35-35

Fax: +33(2) 23-23-36-00

EMail: webur1@listes.univ-rennes1.fr

Website: http://www.univ-rennes1.fr

Président: Guy Cathelineau Tel: +33(2) 23-23-36-61

Directrice générale des Services: Martine Ruaud
Tel: +33(2) 23-23-36-41 +33(2) 23-23-36-83
EMail: martine.ruaud@univ-rennes1.fr

International Relations: C. Réminiac
Tel: +33(2) 23-23-36-01, Fax: +33(2) 99-38-22-92

Faculties

Dental Surgery (Dentistry); **Economics** (Banking; Business Administration; Economics; Finance; Public Administration; Public Health; Statistics); **Law and Political Science** (Law; Political Sciences); **Medicine** (Health Sciences; Medicine); **Pharmaceutical and Biological Sciences** (Biological and Life Sciences; Biology; Biomedicine; Pharmacology; Pharmacy)

Institutes

Management *(IGR)* (Management); **Preparatory Administrative Studies** *(IPAG)* (Administration); **Teacher Training** *(IUFM Bretagne with 5 sites throughout region)* (Teacher Trainers Education; Teacher Training) *Director:* Norbert Fleury; **Technology** *(IUT, Rennes)* (Administration; Chemistry; Civil Engineering; Computer Engineering; Electrical Engineering; Industrial Maintenance; Mechanical Engineering; Production Engineering; Technology); **Technology** *(IUT, Lannion)* (Computer Engineering; Computer Science; Journalism; Measurement and Precision Engineering; Technology; Telecommunications Engineering); **Technology** *(IUT, St Malo)* (Administration; Business Administration; Industrial Maintenance; Law; Telecommunications Engineering); **Technology** *(IUT, St Brieuc)* (Bioengineering; Business Education; Civil Engineering; Materials Engineering; Polymer and Plastics Technology; Real Estate; Sales Techniques; Technology)

Schools

Applied Sciences and Technology *(ENSSAT, Lannion)* (Computer Science; Electronic Engineering; Software Engineering; Telecommunications Engineering); **Chemistry** *(ENSCR)* (Chemistry) *Director:* Daniel Plusquellec; **Engineering** *(ESIR, Rennes)* (Bioengineering; Computer Science; Materials Engineering; Telecommunications Engineering)

Units

Life and Environmental Sciences *(SVE)* (Biochemistry; Biological and Life Sciences; Biology; Ecology; Environmental Studies; Food Science; Genetics; Microbiology; Physiology); **Mathematics** *(IMR)* (Mathematics); **Philosophy** (Philosophy); **Structure and Properties of Matter** *(SPM)* (Archaeology; Chemistry; Earth Sciences; Materials Engineering; Mechanical Engineering; Physics)

History: Founded 1970 under the 1968 law reforming higher education as one of the Universities replacing the former Université de Rennes, established in 1461 as University of Nantes with Colleges and Faculties in Nantes and Rennes; suppressed by the Revolution, reconstituted 1896. A State institution enjoying academic and financial autonomy, operating under the jurisdiction of the Minister of Education and financed by the State.

Governing Bodies: Conseil d'administration de l'Université, comprising 80 members, including elected representatives of teaching staff, research workers, students, and administrative and technical staff, as well as non-university members drawn from the public and private sectors; Conseil of each Unit, comprising representatives of its teaching staff; and Conseil scientifique, competent in matters of research. The President is elected by the three Conseils de l'Université, the Conseil d'administration, the Conseil scientifique, the Conseil des études et de la vie universitaire. The Chancelier, who represents the Minister of Education, is the Recteur de l'Académie de Rennes

Academic Year: September to June (September-January; February-June)

Admission Requirements: Secondary school certificate (baccalauréat) or equivalent, or special entrance examination

Fees: (Euros): 305-600 per annum

Main Language(s) of Instruction: French

International Co-operation: With universities in Europe and USA. At the doctoral level, works in close cooperation with Rennes University II, Agrocampus and other higher institutes.

Accrediting Agencies: Ministère de l'Education Nationale

Degrees and Diplomas: *Capacité en Droit:* Law, 2 yrs; *Diplôme universitaire de Technologie (DUT)*; *Licence:* Humanities, Law, Economics, Science, 3 yrs; *Diplôme d'Etat:* Dental Surgery, 5 yrs; *Diplôme d'Etat:* Medicine, 6 yrs and 1 yr hospital practice and thesis; *Diplôme d'Etat:* Pharmacy, 4 yrs and 1 yr practical work; *Diplôme d'Ingénieur.* 5 yrs; *Magistère:* Town Planning, 3 yrs following initial yr or DUT; *Diplôme de Recherche technologique:* Telecommunications, Business Computing (DRT); *Diplôme national de Master:* Humanities, Law, Economics, Science, 2 yrs following Licence; *Doctorat:* Humanities, Law, Economics, Science, 2-4 yrs following Master; *Doctorat:* Pharmacy, by thesis following Diplôme d'Etat; *Certificat de Spécialité:* Medicine, at least 2 yrs after Diplôme d'Etat; *Habilitation à Diriger les Recherches.* Masters recherche, Masters professionnel, Preparation for CAPES, CAPET and Administrative exams

Student Services: Academic counselling, Canteen, Cultural centre, Foreign student adviser, Foreign Studies Centre, Handicapped facilities, Health services, Language programs, Social counselling, Sports facilities

Special Facilities: Musée préhistorique Armoricain de Penmarc'h (Finistère). Geology Museum. Collection Mathurin Méheut

Libraries: Documentation Interfaculty Centre (Centre Commun de Documentation)

Publications: Bulletin de la Société Scientifique de Bretagne

Press or Publishing House: Université de Rennes I Publishing House

Last Updated: 18/07/11

RENNES 2 UNIVERSITY

Université Rennes 2

Place du Recteur Henri le Moal CS 24307, 35043 Rennes, Cedex
Tel: +33(2) 99-14-10-00
Fax: +33(2) 99-14-10-17
EMail: presidence@univ-rennes2.fr
Website: http://www.univ-rennes2.fr

Président: Jean-Emile Gombert (2011-)
Tel: +33(2) 99-14-10-12 EMail: president@univ-rennes2.fr

Directeur général des Services: Amine Amar
Tel: +33(2) 99-14-10-26/25 EMail: amine.amar@univ-rennes2.fr

International Relations: Roselyne Lefrançois
Tel: +33(2) 99-14-10-05
EMail: roselyne.lefrancois@univ-rennes2.fr

Centres
Distance Education *(SUED)* (Distance Education); **French for Foreign Students** *(CIREFE)* (French); **Lifelong Education** (Continuing Education); **Music Teacher Training** *(CFMI)* (Music; Teacher Training)

Departments
Business Administration *(AES)* (Business Administration)

Graduate Schools
Humanities (Applied Linguistics; Cultural Studies; Linguistics); **Social Sciences** (Social Sciences)

Institutes
Criminology *(ICSH)* (Criminology; Psychology); **Labour Studies in the West** *(ISSTO)* (Labour and Industrial Relations); **Teacher Training** *(IUFM Bretagne with 5 sites in the region)* (Teacher Trainers Education; Teacher Training)

Units
Arts, Letters and Communication (Art History; Fine Arts; Information Sciences; Literature; Music; Performing Arts); **Human Sciences** (Educational Sciences; Linguistics; Psychology; Sociology); **Languages** (Arabic; Celtic Languages and Studies; Chinese; English; German; Italian; Portuguese; Russian; Spanish); **Physical Education and Sports** *(STAPS)* (Physical Education; Sports); **Social Sciences** (Administration; Applied Mathematics; Geography; History; Regional Planning; Social Sciences)

Further Information: Also 19 research units

History: Founded 1970 under the 1968 law reforming higher education as one of the Universities replacing the former Université de Rennes, established in 1461 as University of Nantes with Colleges and Faculties in Nantes and Rennes; suppressed by the Revolution, reconstituted 1896. A State institution enjoying academic and financial autonomy, operating under the jurisdiction of the Minister of Education and financed by the State.

Governing Bodies: Conseil de l'Université, comprising 27 members, including elected representatives of teaching staff, research workers, students, and administrative and technical staff, as well as non-university members drawn from the public and private sectors; Conseil of each unit, comprising representatives of its teaching staff; and the Conseil scientifique, comprising 30 members, competent in matters of research. The President is elected by the Conseil de l'Université. The Chancelier, who represents the Minister of Education, is the Recteur of the Académie de Rennes

Academic Year: September to June

Admission Requirements: Secondary school certificate (baccalauréat) or equivalent, or special entrance examination

Main Language(s) of Instruction: French

International Co-operation: Participates in the Socrates programme, and the International Student Exchange Programme (ISEP). At the doctoral level, works closely with other universities in Britanny in the framework of the European University of Britanny.

Degrees and Diplomas: *Licence*: Arts and Humanities, Languages, 3 yrs; *Licence professionnelle*; *Diplôme national de Master*: Arts and Humanities, Languages, 2 yrs following Licence; *Doctorat*: Arts and Humanities, 4 yrs

Student Services: Academic counselling, Canteen, Cultural centre, Employment services, Foreign student adviser, Handicapped facilities, Health services, Language programs, Nursery care, Social counselling, Sports facilities

Student Residential Facilities: For c. 5,000 students

Special Facilities: Art Gallery, Galerie Art et Essai

Libraries: Bibliothèque de l'Université Rennes II (S.C.D.: Service commun de Documentaion), c. 200,000 vols; 10 specialized libraries (English, History, Geography, etc.)

Press or Publishing House: Presses Universitaires de Rennes
Last Updated: 01/06/11

SAINT-ETIENNE SCHOOL OF ARCHITECTURE

Ecole nationale supérieure d'Architecture de Saint-Étienne (EASE)

1, rue Buisson, BP 94, 42003 Saint-Etienne, Cedex 1
Tel: +33(4) 77-42-35-42
Fax: +33(4) 77-42-35-40
EMail: ensase@st-etienne.archi.fr
Website: http://www.st-etienne.archi.fr

Directeur: Martin Chénot

Programmes
Architecture (Architecture)

History: Founded 1971.

Main Language(s) of Instruction: French

Accrediting Agencies: Ministère de la Culture et de la Communication

Degrees and Diplomas: *Licence*; *Diplôme national de Master*. Habilitation à exercer la maîtrise d'uvre en son nom propre (HMONP)

Libraries: Yes
Last Updated: 27/06/11

SAINT-ETIENNE SCHOOL OF ART AND DESIGN

École supérieure d'Art et Design de Saint Etienne (ESADSE)

3, rue Javelin Pagnon, Saint-Etienne, Cedex 1
Tel: +33(4) 77-47-88-00
Fax: +33(4) 77-47-88-01
EMail: infos@esadse.fr
Website: http://www.esadse.fr

Directeur: Emmanuel Tibloux

Programmes
Art (Graphic Arts; Painting and Drawing; Photography; Video; Visual Arts); **Design** (Design)

History: Founded 1857 as École régionale des Beaux-arts de Saint-Etienne. Acquired present status and title 2006.

Admission Requirements: Baccalauréat or equivalent secondary school exam. Entrance exam with a selection jury.

Main Language(s) of Instruction: French

International Co-operation: Participates in Socrates/Erasmus programmes

Accrediting Agencies: Ministry of Culture and Communication

Degrees and Diplomas: Diplome national d'arts plastiques (DNAP) 3 yrs; Diplome national supérieur d'expression plastique (DNSEP) a

further 2 yrs. Also has a Post-graduate Certificate in design and research: Certificat d'Études d'Arts Plastiques
Last Updated: 01/07/11

SCHOOL OF ADVANCED STUDIES IN PUBLIC HEALTH

Ecole des Hautes Etudes en Santé Publique (EHESP)
Avenue du Professeur Léon Bernard, CS 74312, 35043 Rennes, Cedex
Tel: +33(2) 99-02-22-00
Fax: +33(2) 99-02-26-25
EMail: christian.queyroux@ehesp.fr
Website: http://www.ehesp.fr/

Directeur: Antoine Flahault EMail: antoine.flahault@ehesp.fr

Secrétaire général: Christian Queyroux Tel: +33(2) 99-02-27-51

Departments
Environmental Health and Health at Work (Health Sciences); **Epidemiology and Clinical Research** (Epidemiology); **Human and Social Sciences and Health Behaviour** (Civil Law; Economics; Ethics; Health Administration; Health Education; Public Law; Sociology); **Information Sciences and Biostatistics** (Computer Science; Statistics); **Nursing and Paramedical Sciences** (Nursing; Paramedical Sciences)

Institutes
Management (Health Administration; Management)

History: Founded 1945. Previously known as Ecole nationale de la Santé Publique. Acquired current title and status 2008.

Main Language(s) of Instruction: French

Degrees and Diplomas: *Diplôme d'Ingénieur*: Public Health; *Diplôme national de Master*; *Doctorat*. Preparation for national exams for Medical and Health Administrative Positions
Last Updated: 24/06/11

SCHOOL OF ADVANCED STUDIES IN SOCIAL SCIENCES (EHESS) - PARIS

Ecole des Hautes Etudes en Sciences Sociales (EHESS)
190-198 avenue de France, 75244 Paris cedex 13
Tel: +33(1) 49-54-25-25
Fax: +33(1) 45-44-93-11
EMail: dinah.ribard@ehess.fr
Website: http://www.ehess.fr

Président: François Weil (2009-)
Tel: +33(1) 49-54-25-01, Fax: +33(1) 49-54-24-96
EMail: preside@ehess.fr

Directrice des Services: Hélène Moulin-Rodarie

Departments
Cultural Affairs (Cultural Studies); **Economics** (Economics); **History** (History); **Sociology, Social Anthropology and Psychology** (Anthropology; Psychology; Sociology)

Further Information: Has Centres in Marseilles, Lyon and Toulouse

History: Founded 1975, as the VIth Section of the Ecole pratique des hautes Etudes, founded 1868 by Victor Duruy. A centre of postgraduate education and research at the highest level. Financially supported by the Ministry of Education.

Governing Bodies: Conseil d'Administration, comprising 33 members; Conseil scientifique, comprising 20 members

Academic Year: November to June

Admission Requirements: None. Courses are open to the public

Main Language(s) of Instruction: French

Degrees and Diplomas: *Diplôme national de Master*; *Doctorat*: 2-4 yrs following Masters; *Habilitation à Diriger les Recherches*

Libraries: Libraries of the research centres, c. 65,000 vols

Publications: Bulletins des centres de recherches; Revues

Press or Publishing House: Editions de l'Ecole des Hautes Etudes en Sciences Sociales
Last Updated: 16/05/11

SCHOOL OF AERONAUTICS - SALON DE PROVENCE

Ecole de l'Air de Salon de Provence (EA)
Base Aérienne 701, 13661 Salon-de-Provence
Tel: +33(4) 90-17-80-00
Fax: +33(4) 90-17-61-77
EMail: cab.ea-ema@inet.air.defense.gouv.fr
Website: http://ecole-air.fr/

Général de brigade aérienne: Gilles Modéré
Tel: +33(4) 90-17-82-10

International Relations: Isabelle Ménager
Tel: 33 (4) 90-17-81-24
EMail: isabelle.menager@inet.air.defense.gouv.fr

Schools
Aeronautical and Aerospace Engineering (Aeronautical and Aerospace Engineering)

Further Information: Has a research centre and several labs

History: Founded 1935.

Academic Year: September to July

Admission Requirements: Competitive entrance examination following 2 yrs further study after secondary school certificate (baccalauréat) or following first university qualification (Bachelor degree) or competitive political science examination

Main Language(s) of Instruction: French

Accrediting Agencies: Ministry of Defence, Commission des Titres d'Ingénieur

Degrees and Diplomas: *Diplôme national de Master*: Engineering, 3 yrs
Last Updated: 08/06/11

SCHOOL OF ARCHITECTURE OF THE CITY AND TERRITORIES OF MARNE-LA-VALLÉE

Ecole d'Architecture de la Ville et des Territoires à Marne-la-Vallée (EAVT)
10-12 avenue Blaise-Pascal, 77447 Champs-sur-Marne, Cedex 02
Tel: +33(1) 60-95-84-00
Fax: +33(1) 60-95-84-47
EMail: vt@marnelavallee.archi.fr
Website: http://www.marnelavallee.archi.fr

Directeur: Alain Derey (2010-)

Secrétaire générale: Sophie Perdrial

Programmes
Architecture

History: Founded 1998.

Main Language(s) of Instruction: French

Degrees and Diplomas: *Licence*; *Diplôme national de Master*. diplôme d'études en architecture, conférant grade de licence; diplôme d'Etat d'architecte, conférant grade de master; diplôme de spécialisation et d'approfondissement en architecture (DSA) d'architecte-urbaniste; habilitation à la maîtrise d'uvre en son nom propre
Last Updated: 22/06/11

SCHOOL OF STATISTICS AND ECONOMIC ADMINISTRATION PARIS TECH

Ecole nationale de la Statistique et de l'Administration économique (ENSEA Paris Tech)
3, avenue Pierre Larousse, 92245 Malakoff, Cedex
Tel: +33(1) 41-17-65-25
Fax: +33(1) 41-17-64-80
EMail: info@ensae.fr
Website: http://www.ensae.fr

Directeur: Julien Pouget

Divisions
Finance, Insurance, Economics and Statistics (Economics; Finance; Insurance; Statistics)

History: Founded 1942. Founding member of the Paris Institute of Technology (Paris Tech)30/05/2011

Admission Requirements: Competitive entrance examination following 2 yrs further study after secondary school certificate (baccalauréat) or equivalent. On the basis of their academic qualification. Graduates in economics and/or mathematics or graduates of Grandes Ecoles

Fees: (Euros): statistician course, 550 per annum; mastère spécialisé 5,000

Degrees and Diplomas: *Diplôme d'Etat*; *Mastère spécialisé*; *Certificat de Spécialité*
Last Updated: 30/05/11

STRASBOURG CONSERVATORY

Conservatoire de Strasbourg

1 Place Dauphine, 67076 Strasbourg Cedex
Tel: +33(3) 88 43 68 00
Fax: +33 (3) 88 43 68 01
EMail: marie-claude.segard@strasbourg.eu
Website: http://www.conservatoire.strasbourg.eu

Directrice: Marie-Claude Ségard

Programmes
Dance (Dance); **Music** (Music; Music Theory and Composition; Musical Instruments; Singing); **Theatre** (Acting; Theatre)

History: Founded 1855.

Main Language(s) of Instruction: French

Degrees and Diplomas: *Licence*; *Diplôme national de Master*. Diplôme national supérieur professionnel de musicien, diplôme supérieur d'interprète ou de compositeur, certificat d'études théâtrales, Diplôme d'études chorégraphiques

Libraries: Yes

Press or Publishing House: Éditions du Conservatoire de Strasbourg
Last Updated: 30/01/12

STRASBOURG SCHOOL OF ARCHITECTURE

Ecole nationale supérieure d'Architecture de Strasbourg (ENSAS)

BP 37, 8, boulevard Wilson, 67068 Strasbourg
Tel: +33(3) 88-32-25-35
Fax: +33(3) 88-32-82-41
EMail: ecole@strasbourg.archi.fr
Website: http://www.strasbourg.archi.fr

Directeur: Philippe Bach EMail: direction@strasbourg.archi.fr

Programmes
Architecture (Architecture)

History: Founded 1922 as École d'Architecture de Strasbourg. Acquired present title 2005.

Main Language(s) of Instruction: French

International Co-operation: Germany, Austria, Belgium, Bulgaria, Spain, Greece, Hungary, Italy, Latvia, Lithuania, Poland, Portugal, Romania, United Kingdom, Slovakia, Switzerland, Turkey, Australia, Canada, Peru and Lebanon

Accrediting Agencies: Ministère de la Culture et de la Communication

Degrees and Diplomas: *Licence*; *Licence professionnelle*; *Diplôme national de Master*. Habilitation à l'exercice de la maîtrise d'uvre en son nom propre (HMONP); Master de recherche EST; DPEA

Libraries: Yes
Last Updated: 27/06/11

STRASBOURG SCHOOL OF DECORATIVE ARTS

Ecole supérieure des Arts décoratifs de Strasbourg (ESAD STRASBOURG)

1, rue de l'Académie, 67000 Strasbourg
Tel: +33(3) 69-06-37-77
Fax: +33(3) 69-06-37-60
EMail: esad@esad-stg.org
Website: http://www.esad-stg.org

Directeur: Otto Teichert (2008-)
Administrative Officer: Ella Gilger
International Relations: Edwige Toffoli
EMail: international@esad-stg.org

Programmes
Communication (Graphic Design; Media Studies); **Design** (Design); **Visual Arts** (Ceramic Art; Glass Art; Jewelry Art)

Admission Requirements: Baccalauréat or equivalent secondary school exam. Entrance exam with a selection jury.

Main Language(s) of Instruction: French

International Co-operation: Participates in Socrates/Erasmus

Accrediting Agencies: Ministry of Culture and Communication

Degrees and Diplomas: Diplôme national d'arts plastiques (DNAP) 3 yrs; Diplôme national supérieur d'expression plastique (DNSEP) a further 2 yrs
Last Updated: 04/07/11

TELECOM BRETAGNE

Télécom Bretagne

CS 83818, Technopôle de Brest Iroise, 29238 Brest, Cedex 03
Tel: +33(2) 29-00-11-11
Fax: +33(2) 29-00-10-00
EMail: anne.pierre-duplessix@telecom-bretagne.eu
Website: http://www.telecom-bretagne.eu

Directeur: Paul Friedel Tel: +33(2) 29-00-11-00

Secrétaire général: Jean-Pierre Belleudy
Tel: +33(2) 29-00-12-00, Fax: +33(2) 29-00-11-08
EMail: jean-pierre.belleudy@telecom.eu

International Relations: Anne Pierre-Duplexis
Tel: +33(2) 29-00-14-80

Departments
Computer Engineering (Computer Engineering; Computer Science); **Electronics** (Electronic Engineering); **Image and Data Processing** (Computer Graphics; Data Processing); **Languages and International Culture** (Cultural Studies; Linguistics; Modern Languages); **Logics in Uses, Social Science and Information Science** (Artificial Intelligence; Arts and Humanities; Cognitive Sciences; Economics; Social Sciences); **Microwaves** (Microwaves); **Multimedia Networks and Systems** (Computer Networks; Computer Science; Data Processing; Multimedia); **Optics** (Optics); **Signal and Telecommunications Engineering** (Computer Engineering; Telecommunications Engineering)

Further Information: Also campuses in Rennes and Toulouse.

History: Founded 1977. Acquired present title 2008.

Academic Year: September to June

Admission Requirements: Competitive entrance examination following 2-3 yrs further study after secondary school certificate (baccalauréat) or following first university qualification in Science subjects (DEUG, DUT or BTS)

Fees: (Euros): 1,122 per annum

Main Language(s) of Instruction: French

International Co-operation: With universities in Denmark, Germany, Poland, Spain, Sweden, United Kingdom, Ireland, Finland, Norway, Hungary, Italy, Belgium

Degrees and Diplomas: *Diplôme d'Ingénieur*. Telecommunications, 3 yrs; *Mastère spécialisé*; *Diplôme national de Master*. Computer Networks; Telecommunciations Engineering, 13 months; *Diplôme national de Master*. Telecommunications, 18 months; *Doctorat*

Student Services: Academic counselling, Canteen, Employment services, Foreign student adviser, Language programs, Social counselling, Sports facilities

Student Residential Facilities: Yes

Libraries: Centre de Documentation, c. 24,350 vols (scientific); c. 12,000 vols (general). CD ROM databases
Last Updated: 07/07/11

TÉLÉCOM SUDPARIS

9, rue Charles Fourier, 91011 Evry, Cedex
Tel: +33(1) 60-76-40-40
Fax: +33(1) 60-76-43-37
EMail: webmaster@it-sudparis.eu
Website: http://www.telecom-sudparis.eu/

Directeur: Pierre Rolin
Tel: +33(1) 60-76-42-01, Fax: +33(1) 60-76-43-30

International Relations: Roisin Donohoe

Research Centres
Business Administration (Business Administration; Economics; Human Resources; Law; Management; Marketing; Production Engineering); **Computer Science** (Computer Science; Human Resources); **Electronics and Physics** (Electronic Engineering; Optics; Physics); **Foreign Languages and Humanities** (Arabic; Chinese; English; German; Italian; Japanese; Modern Languages; Russian; Spanish); **Information Systems** (Computer Networks; Computer Science; Design; Information Technology; Systems Analysis); **Signal and Image Processing** (Computer Engineering; Electronic Engineering); **Software Networks** (Computer Networks; Software Engineering); **Telecommunications Networks and Services** (Computer Networks; Telecommunications Engineering)

Schools
Continuing Education; **Management** (Business Administration; Management); **Telecommunications**

History: Founded 1979. Became Institut national des Télécommunications (INT) 1996. Acquired present title and status 2010.

Admission Requirements: Competitive entrance examination following 2 yrs further study after secondary school certificate (baccalauréat) or equivalent

Fees: (Euros): Engineer diploma course 1,080 per annum, Mastère 5,336 per annum

Main Language(s) of Instruction: French, English

Accrediting Agencies: C.T.I., Ministry of Education

Degrees and Diplomas: *Licence*: Telecommunications Management, 3 yrs; *Diplôme d'Etudes d'Ecole de Commerce et Gestion*; *Diplôme d'Ingénieur*: 3 yrs; *Mastère spécialisé*: Telephone Networks and Management, a further yr; *Diplôme national de Master*: International Management

Student Services: Academic counselling, Canteen, Cultural centre, Employment services, Foreign student adviser, Foreign Studies Centre, Handicapped facilities, Health services, Language programs, Nursery care, Social counselling, Sports facilities

Student Residential Facilities: For c. 510 students

Special Facilities: Video Conference

Libraries: Central Library, 13,500 vols, 550 periodicals, CD Rom
Last Updated: 11/07/11

THE BRITANNY NATIONAL COLLEGE OF ARCHITECTURE

Ecole nationale supérieure d'Architecture de Bretagne (ENSA BRETAGNE)
44, boulevard de Chézy - CS 16427, 35064 Rennes, Cedex
Tel: +33(2) 99-29-68-00
Fax: +33(2) 99-30-42-49
EMail: ensab@rennes.archi.fr
Website: http://www.rennes.archi.fr

Directrice: Marie Minier

Programmes
Architecture (Architecture; Real Estate; Urban Studies)

History: Founded 1905 as École Régionale d'Architecture de Rennes. Became Britanny School of Architecture 1984. Acquired present title 2005.

Admission Requirements: Baccalauréat (www.admission-post-bac.fr)

Main Language(s) of Instruction: French

Degrees and Diplomas: *Licence*: 3 yrs; *Diplôme national de Master*. diplôme d'études" in architecture; diplôme d'Etat d'architecte" equivalent to the Master's degree; Habilitation de l'architecte

diplômé d'Etat à l'exercice de la maîtrise d'oeuvre en son nom propre
Last Updated: 31/05/11

THE QUAI, ART SCHOOL OF MULHOUSE

Le Quai, Ecole supérieure d'Art de Mulhouse
3 quai des Pêcheurs, 68200 Mulhouse
Tel: +33(3) 89-32-12-92
Fax: +33(3) 89-59-40-43
EMail: esa@lequai.fr
Website: http://www.lequai.fr

Directeur: David Cascaro EMail: dcascaro@lequai.fr

Programmes
Visual Arts (Art History; Design; Graphic Arts; Painting and Drawing; Textile Design; Visual Arts)

History: Having its origins in 1834, the school hosted drawing classes. It became officially governed by the city of Mulhouse in 1945 to offer advanced studies both in the fine arts and in industrialised textiles. In 1986, it was inaugurated by the Ministry of Culture in its current location and re-baptised as Le Quai in 1990.

Academic Year: October-June

Admission Requirements: Baccalauréat or equivalent secondary school exam. Selection jury.

Main Language(s) of Instruction: French

Accrediting Agencies: Ministry of Culture and Communication

Degrees and Diplomas: Diplôme national d'arts plastiques (DNAP) 3 yrs; Diplôme national supérieur d'expression plastique (DNSEP) a further 2 yrs
Last Updated: 08/07/11

TOULON PROVENCE MEDITERRANEAN ART SCHOOL

Ecole supérieure d'Art de Toulon Provence Méditerranée
168 boulevard du Commandant Nicolas, 83000 Toulon
Tel: +33(4) 94-62-01-48
EMail: pmoiteaux@tpmed.org
Website: http://www.esart-tpm.fr

Directeur: Jean-Marc Réol

Programmes
Art (Fine Arts); **Design** (Design)

History: Founded in 1899. Acquired present status 2010.

Main Language(s) of Instruction: French

Degrees and Diplomas: Diplôme National d'Art Plastique; Diplôme National d'Art et Technique; Diplôme National Supérieur d'Expression Plastique
Last Updated: 08/07/11

TOULOUSE ART SCHOOL

Ecole supérieure des Beaux-Arts de Toulouse
5, quai de la Daurade, 31000 Toulouse
Tel: +33(5) 61-22-21-95
Fax: +33(5) 61-22-24-21
EMail: ecole.beaux.arts@mairie-toulouse.fr
Website: http://www.esba-toulouse.org

Directeur: Michel Métayer

Programmes
Fine Arts (Cinema and Television; Communication Arts; Design; Engraving; Fine Arts; Painting and Drawing; Photography; Video)

Main Language(s) of Instruction: French

International Co-operation: Participates in Socrates/Erasmus

Accrediting Agencies: Ministère de la Culture

Degrees and Diplomas: Diplôme national d'arts et techniques (3 yrs) and Diplôme national supérieur d'expression plastique (5 yrs)
Last Updated: 07/07/11

TOULOUSE I UNIVERSITY
Université Toulouse I Capitole
2 rue du Doyen-Gabriel-Marty, 31042 Toulouse, Cedex 9
Tel: +33(5) 61-63-35-00
Fax: +33(5) 61-63-37-98
EMail: direction.generale@univ-tlse1.fr
Website: http://www.univ-tlse1.fr

Président: Bruno Sire
Tel: +33(5) 61-63-35-25, Fax: +33(5) 61-63-38-02
EMail: cabinet.president@univ-tlse1.fr;
Henry.Roussillon@univ-tlse1.fr

Directrice générale des Services: Cécile Chicoye
Tel: +33(5) 61-63-35-23

International Relations: Laurent Grosclaude
Tel: +33(5) 61-63-36-45, Fax: +33(5) 61-63-36-39
EMail: relinter@univ.tlse1.fr; Jean-Pierre.Theron@univ-tlse1.fr

Centres
Preparatory Administrative Studies *(CPAG)* (Administration)

Departments
Languages and Civilizations; **Mathematics**; **Physical Education and Sports** *(DAPS)* (Physical Education; Sports; Sports Management)

Faculties
Computer Science (Computer Science); **Economic and Social Administration** (Economics; Public Administration); **Economics** (Economics); **Law** (Law)

Graduate Schools
Economics; **Management** (Management); **Political Science and Law** (Law; Political Sciences)

Institutes
Business Administration *(IAE)* (Business Administration; Management); **Juridical Studies** *(IEJ)* (Law); **Political Studies** *(IEP)* (Political Sciences); **Teacher Training** *(IUFM Midi-Pyrénées with 9 sites throughout region)* (Teacher Training); **Technology** *(IUT, Rodez)* (Business Administration; Data Processing; Management; Mechanical Engineering; Production Engineering; Technology)

Laboratories
Economic, Political and Social Structures Research *(LEREPS)*; **Environmental Economics and Natural Resources** *(LERNA)*; **Social Sciences of Policy-Making** *(LaSSP (IEP))* (European Union Law; Journalism; Political Sciences)

Programmes
Organizational Management and Development (Management); **Social Sciences, Computer Research and Studies** *(IUP)* (Data Processing; Social Sciences)

Research Centres
Business Law *(CDA)* (Commercial Law); **Constitutional and Political Studies** *(CERCP)* (Constitutional Law; Political Sciences); **European Research on Economic Law** *(IRDEIC)* (Commercial Law); **History of Law of Institutions and Political Ideas** *(CTHDIP)* (History of Law; Political Sciences); **Human Resources and Employment** *(LIRHE)* (Human Resources; Law); **Management** *(CRG)* (Management); **Mathematical and Quantitative Economics** *(GREMAQ)* (Econometrics; Mathematics); **Mathematics** *(IMT-CEREMATH)* (Mathematics); **Military Studies** *(CMJ Morris Janowitz)* (Military Science); **Police Studies** *(CERP)* (Police Studies); **Private Law** *(CDA)* (Law; Private Law); **Quantitative Methods Applied for Economic Development** *(ARQADE)* (Econometrics); **Security and Governance** *(GRSG)* (Leadership; Military Science; Political Sciences); **Space, Territories and Communication Law** *(IDETCOM)* (Communication Studies; Law); **Theory of Public Institutions Control** *(TACIP)* (Law; Public Administration); **Town Planning and Construction Laws** *(IEJUC)* (Law; Town Planning)

History: Founded 1970 under the 1968 law reforming higher education as one of three Universities replacing the former Université de Toulouse, founded 1229. Suppressed by the Revolution and replaced by Faculties of Law; Theology; Science; Letters; and Medicine 1808. Reconstituted as University 1896. A State institution enjoying academic and financial autonomy, operating under the jurisdiction of the Minister of Education and financed by the State. Acquired present title 2010.

Governing Bodies: Conseil d'Administration, comprising 60 members, including elected representatives of teaching staff, research workers, students, and administrative and technical staff, as well as non-university members drawn from the public and private sectors; Conseil scientifique, comprising 40 members, competent in matters of research; Conseil des Etudes et de la Vie universitaire; and Conseil of each Unit, comprising representatives of its teaching staff, research workers, students, and administrative and technical staff. The President is elected by the first three bodies. The Chancelier, who represents the Minister of Education, is the Recteur of the Académie de Toulouse

Academic Year: October to June (October-February; February-June)

Admission Requirements: Secondary school certificate (baccalauréat) or equivalent

Main Language(s) of Instruction: French

International Co-operation: Participates in Socrates/Erasmus, Tempus and Enter programmes.

Degrees and Diplomas: *Capacité en Droit*: Law, 2 yrs; *Licence*: Administration; Economics; Law, 3 yrs; *Magistère*: Economics, 3 yrs following 2 first yrs at university; *Diplôme national de Master*: Law, Economics, Administration, a further 2 yrs following Licence; *Doctorat*: Economics, Law, 2-4 yrs following Masters. Masters recherche, Masters professionnel

Student Services: Academic counselling, Canteen, Cultural centre, Foreign student adviser, Foreign Studies Centre, Handicapped facilities, Health services, Language programs, Social counselling, Sports facilities

Student Residential Facilities: Yes

Libraries: Central Library, c. 37,700 vols; Interuniversity Library, 1m. vols

Publications: Annales *(annually)*; Civilisations *(annually)*; Livret de la Recherche; Publications de Sciences Politiques; Working Papers (Cahier de Publications de l'U.E.R. Sciences économiques)
Last Updated: 22/12/08

TOULOUSE II UNIVERSITY
Université de Toulouse-le-Mirail (Toulouse II)
5, allée Antonio Machado, 31058 Toulouse, Cedex 9
Tel: +33(5) 61-50-42-50
Fax: +33(5) 61-50-42-09
EMail: presidence@univ-tlse2.fr
Website: http://www.univ-tlse2.fr

Président: Daniel Filatre
Tel: +33(5) 61-50-44-99/98, Fax: +33(5) 61-50-43-50

Secrétaire général: Christophe Giraud
Tel: +33(5) 61-50-43-65, Fax: +33(5) 61-50-43-73
EMail: secretariat.general@univ-tlse2.fr

International Relations: Daniel Weissberg
Tel: +33(5) 61-50-45-99 +33(5) 61-50-38-48,
Fax: +33(5) 61-50-35-20 EMail: rintutm@univ-tlse2.fr

Centres
University Centre *(Rodez)*; **University Centre** *(Albi)*

Graduate Schools
Doctoral Schools (Arts and Humanities; Behavioural Sciences; Cognitive Sciences; Education; Modern Languages; Social Sciences)

Institutes
Archival and Library Sciences *(IUP)* (Archiving; Library Science); **Arts and Culture, Applied Arts** (Cultural Studies; Fine Arts); **Latin American Studies** *(IPEALT)* (Latin American Studies); **Maintenance, Reliability, Quality Control, Ergonomy; Regional Development and Management** (Management; Regional Planning); **Regional Labour Institute** *(IRT)* (Labour and Industrial Relations); **Sociology, Management and Business Administration** (Business Administration; Management; Sociology); **Teacher Training** *(IUFM Midi-Pyrénées with 9 sites in the region)* (Teacher Trainers Education; Teacher Training) *Division Head*: Bru; **Technology** *(IUT Figeac)* (Technology); **Technology** *(IUT Blagnac)* (Technology); **Tourism, Hotel Management and Transport** (Hotel

Management; Tourism; Transport and Communications); **Tourism, Hotel Management and Transport** *(IUP, Site de Foix)* (Hotel Management; Tourism; Transport and Communications); **Training of Music Teachers** *(IFMI)* (Music Education)

Schools
Audiovisual Studies *(ESAV)* (Media Studies)

Units
Foreign Languages, Literatures and Civilizations (Cultural Studies; Literature; Modern Languages); **History, Arts and Archaeology** (Archaeology; Arts and Humanities; History); **Letters, Philosophy and Music** (Arts and Humanities; Music; Philosophy); **Psychology** (Psychology); **Science, Geography and Civilisations** (Economics; Educational Sciences; Geography; Mathematics and Computer Science; Social Sciences; Sociology)

History: Founded 1970 under the 1968 law reforming higher education as one of three Universities replacing the former Université de Toulouse, founded 1229. Suppressed by the Revolution and replaced by Faculties of Law; Theology; Science; Letters; and Medicine 1808. Reconstituted as University 1896. A State institution enjoying academic and financial autonomy, operating under the jurisdiction of the Minister of Education and financed by the State.

Governing Bodies: Conseil d'administration, including representatives of teaching staff, research workers, students, and administrative and technical staff, as well as non-university members drawn from the public and private sectors; Conseil scientifique, competent in matters of research; Conseil des Etudes et de la Vie universitaire; and Conseil of each Unit, comprising representatives of its teaching staff, research workers, students, and administrative and technical staff. The President is elected by the three bodies. The Chancelier, who represents the Minister of Education, is the Recteur of the Académie de Toulouse

Academic Year: October to June (October-December; January-April; April-June)

Admission Requirements: Secondary school certificate (baccalauréat) or equivalent, or Diplôme d'Accès aux Etudes Universitaires (DAEU)

Main Language(s) of Instruction: French

International Co-operation: Participates in the Erasmus, Lingua and Tempus programmes

Degrees and Diplomas: *Diplôme universitaire de Technologie*: Technology, Social Work, Commerce, 2 yrs; *Licence*: Arts and Humanities, Modern Languages, Science, Technology, Health, Social Sciences, 3 yrs; *Licence professionnelle*: Arts and Humanities, Modern Languages, Science, Technology, Health, Social Sciences, 1 yr following initial 2 yrs; *Diplôme national de Master*: Arts and Humanities, Modern Languages, Science, Technology, Health, Social Sciences, 2 yrs following Licence; *Doctorat*: 2-4 yrs following Masters. Diplomas for Languages, French, and Teaching French as a Foreign Language; Masters recherche, Masters professionnel

Libraries: Bibliothèque interuniversitaire, c. 250,000 vols. Also specialized libraries (German, English, Hispano-American, History, Art History, Mediterranean Languages, Modern Languages, Philosophy, Mediterranean Studies, Geography, Portuguese, Behavioural and Educational Sciences, Social and Economic Sciences, Psychology, Classical Languages and Letters)

Publications: Correspondances

Press or Publishing House: Presses universitaires du Mirail (PUM)

Last Updated: 26/05/11

TOULOUSE III UNIVERSITY
Université Toulouse III Paul Sabatier
118, route de Narbonne, 31062 Toulouse, Cedex 09
Tel: +33(5) 61-55-66-11
Fax: +33(5) 61-55-64-70
EMail: contact-ups@adm.ups-tlse.fr
Website: http://www.ups-tlse.fr

Président: Gilles Fourtanier EMail: srpups@adm.ups-tlse.fr

Directeur général des Services: Claude Debat
Tel: +33(5) 61-55-66-13 EMail: secgen@adm.ups-tlse.fr

Centres
Lifelong Education *Director*: Jean-François Sautereau

Departments
Engineering (Engineering) *Director*: Michel Barrioulet

Faculties
Dentistry (Dentistry); **Medicine** *(Purpan)* (Medicine); **Medicine** *(Rangueil)* (Medicine); **Pharmacy** (Pharmacy)

Graduate Schools
Doctoral Schools *(Houses 6 Doctoral Schools and works in partnership with other regional universities to offer other graduate programmes)* (Agronomy; Biology; Chemistry; Earth Sciences; Ecology; Health Sciences; Information Sciences; Medicine)

Institutes
Observatory Midi-Pyrénées *(OMP) (Acting) Director*: Bernard Dupré; **Teacher Training** *(IUFM Midi-Pyreenes with 9 sites throughout region) Director*: Marc Bru; **Technology** *(IUT Paul Sabatier: sites at Toulouse, Auch, Castres)* (Business Administration; Business and Commerce; Chemical Engineering; Civil Engineering; Computer Science; Management; Measurement and Precision Engineering; Mechanical Engineering; Production Engineering; Sales Techniques; Technology); **Technology** *(IUT, Site de Tarbes)* (Business Administration; Business and Commerce; Computer Engineering; Electrical Engineering; Management; Production Engineering; Sales Techniques; Technology; Telecommunications Engineering)

Schools
Engineering *(UPSSITECH)* (Civil Engineering; Energy Engineering; Environmental Engineering; Instrument Making; Systems Analysis; Telecommunications Engineering); **Midwifery** (Midwifery)

Units
Life Sciences and Earth Sciences *(STV)* (Biochemistry; Biological and Life Sciences; Biology; Biotechnology; Chemistry; Earth Sciences; Ecology; Health Sciences); **Mathematics, Computer Science and Management** (Health Administration; Management; Mathematics and Computer Science; Mechanical Engineering); **Modern Languages** (English; German; Modern Languages; Russian; Spanish); **Physical Education and Sports** *(STAPS)* (Physical Education; Sports); **Physics, Chemistry, and Automation** *(PCA)* (Automation and Control Engineering; Chemistry; Physics)

History: Founded 1970 under the 1968 law reforming higher education as one of three Universities replacing the former Université de Toulouse, founded 1229. Suppressed by the Revolution and replaced by Faculties of Law; Theology; Science; Letters; and Medicine 1808. Reconstituted as University 1896. A State Institution enjoying academic and financial autonomy, operating under the jurisdiction of the Minister of Education and financed by the State. Its structure is based on a series of Unités de formation et de recherche (training and research Units). Each Unit enjoys academic and administrative independence.

Governing Bodies: Conseil d'Administration, including representatives of teaching staff, research workers, students, and administrative and technical staff, as well as non-university members drawn from the public and private sectors; Conseil scientifique, competent in matters of research; Conseil des Etudes et de la Vie universitaire; and Conseil of each Unit, comprising representatives of its teaching staff, research workers, students, and administrative and technical staff. The President is elected by the first three bodies. The Chancelier, who represents the Minister of Education, is the Recteur of the Académie de Toulouse

Academic Year: September to June (September-January; February-June)

Admission Requirements: Secondary school certificate (Baccalauréat) or equivalent, or special entrance examination

Main Language(s) of Instruction: French

Degrees and Diplomas: *Diplôme universitaire de Technologie*: 2 yrs; *Licence*: Science, Technology, Sports, 3 yrs; *Licence professionnelle*: Science, Technology, Sports, 1 yr after initial 2 yrs; *Diplôme d'Etat*: Dental Surgery, Midwifery, 5 yrs; *Diplôme d'Etat*: Medicine, 6 yrs plus 1 yr hospital practice and thesis; *Diplôme d'Etat*: Pharmacy, 4 yrs and 1 yr practical work; *Diplôme de Recherche technologique*; *Diplôme national de Master*: Science, Technology and Sports, 2 yrs following Licence; *Doctorat*:

Pharmacy, by thesis following Diplôme d'Etat; *Doctorat*: Science, 2-4 yrs following Masters; *Certificat de Spécialité*: Medicine, at least 2 yrs following Diplôme d'Etat. Masters recherche, Masters professionnel

Student Services: Academic counselling, Canteen, Cultural centre, Handicapped facilities, Health services, Social counselling, Sports facilities

Student Residential Facilities: Yes

Libraries: Science library; Medical library
Last Updated: 21/07/11

TOULOUSE INSTITUTE OF TECHNOLOGY
Institut national polytechnique de Toulouse (INP TOULOUSE)
BP 34038, 6, Allée Emile Monso, 31029 Toulouse, Cedex 4
Tel: +33(5) 34-32-30-00
Fax: +33(5) 62-24-21-03
EMail: inp@inp-toulouse.fr
Website: http://www.inp-toulouse.fr

Président: Gilbert Casamatta (2005-)
Tel: +33(5) 34-32-30-03, Fax: +33(5) 34-32-30-06
EMail: president@inp-toulouse.fr

Secrétaire général: Gilles Boucher
Tel: +33(5) 34-32-30-04 EMail: gilles.boucher@inp-toulouse.fr

International Relations: Joëlle Courbières
Tel: +33(5) 34-32-31-80, Fax: +33(5) 34-32-31-83
EMail: courbieres@inp-toulouse.fr

Centres
Continuing Education

Departments
Polytechnic Preparatory School (Engineering; Technology)

Graduate Schools
Energy, Civil and Mechanical Engineering *(ED MEGeP)* (Civil Engineering; Energy Engineering; Hydraulic Engineering; Mechanical Engineering)

Schools
Agriculture *(INP-EI PURPAN)* (Agriculture; Agronomy; Animal Husbandry; Arts and Humanities; Biological and Life Sciences; Computer Science; Cultural Studies; Engineering; Management); **Agronomy** *(INP-ENSAT)* (Agriculture; Agronomy; Crop Production; Food Science; Meat and Poultry; Oenology); **Chemical Engineering and Technology** *(INP-ENSIACET)* (Analytical Chemistry; Applied Chemistry; Bioengineering; Biomedical Engineering; Chemical Engineering; Chemistry; Industrial Chemistry; Inorganic Chemistry; Organic Chemistry; Physical Chemistry; Technology); **Electrical Engineering, Electronics, Computer Science and Hydraulics** *(INP-ENSEEIHT)* (Automation and Control Engineering; Automotive Engineering; Computer Science; Electrical Engineering; Electronic Engineering; Engineering Management; Hydraulic Engineering; Physical Engineering; Telecommunications Engineering); **Engineering School** *(INP-ENIT)* (Engineering); **Meteorology** (Meteorology); **Veterinary Science** (Veterinary Science)

History: Founded 1970 under the 1968 law reforming higher education and incorporating various Ecoles nationales supérieures. Acquired present status and title 1984.

Governing Bodies: Board of Administrration; Scientific Council and Academic Council

Academic Year: September to September

Admission Requirements: Competitive entrance examination following 2 yrs further study after secondary school certificate (baccalauréat)

Fees: (Euros):800 per annum; Masters,450; HDR, 560; PhD, 555

Main Language(s) of Instruction: French and 4 Master's degrees in English

International Co-operation: With 200 universities worldwide.

Accrediting Agencies: Commission des Titres d'Ingénieurs

Degrees and Diplomas: *Diplôme d'Ingénieur*. 5 yrs; *Diplôme national de Master*. 5 yrs; *Doctorat*: 8 yrs. Also Diplôme national d'Oenologue

Student Services: Academic counselling, Canteen, Employment services, Foreign student adviser, Handicapped facilities, Health services, Language programs, Social counselling, Sports facilities

Student Residential Facilities: Yes

Libraries: Libraries of the 7 schools, total, c. 20,000 vols. Also online library and publications

Publications: Les Activités de Recherche; Polytech.
Last Updated: 27/05/11

TOULOUSE SCHOOL OF ARCHITECTURE
Ecole nationale supérieure d'Architecture de Toulouse (EAT)
83 rue Aristide Maillol, BP 10629, 31106 Toulouse, Cedex 01
Tel: +33(5) 62-11-50-50
Fax: +33(5) 62-11-50-99
EMail: ensa@toulouse.archi.fr
Website: http://www.toulouse.archi.fr

Directrice: Nicole Roux-Loupiac
Tel: +33(5) 62-11-50-61 EMail: directrice@toulouse.archi.fr

Programmes
Architecture (Architecture)

Degrees and Diplomas: *Licence*: 3 yrs; *Diplôme national de Master*. 2 yrs; *Doctorat*. Diplôme propre aux écoles d'architecture (DPEA); Habilitation de l'architecte diplômé d'Etat à l'exercice de la maîtrise d'oeuvre en son nom propre
Last Updated: 01/06/11

TOURS - ANGERS - LE MANS ART SCHOOL
Ecole supérieure des Beaux-Arts Tours - Angers - Le Mans
Hôtel d'Ollone, 72 rue Bressigny, 37011 Angers
Tel: +33(2) 41-24-13-50
Fax: +33(2) 41-87-26-49
EMail: contact@esba-angers.eu
Website: http://www.esba-angers.eu

Directeur: Christian Dautel EMail: christian.dautel@ville.angers.fr

Departments
Art (Sculpture; Visual Arts); **Conservation** (Restoration of Works of Art)

History: Founded in 1760. Acquired present status 2010.

Admission Requirements: Baccalauréat or equivalent secondary school exam. Entrance exam with a selection jury.

Fees: (Euros): 207 p.a.

Main Language(s) of Instruction: French

Accrediting Agencies: Ministry of Culture and Communication

Degrees and Diplomas: Diplôme national d'arts plastiques (DNAP) 3 yrs; Diplôme national d'arts et techniques (DNAT) 3 yrs; Diplôme national supérieur d'expression plastique (DNSEP) a further 2 yrs; Diplôme de Conservateur-Restaurateur des oeuvres sculptées (Masters level)
Last Updated: 03/11/11

UNIVERSITY FRANÇOIS RABELAIS - TOURS
Université François Rabelais de Tours
BP 4103, 3, rue des Tanneurs, 37041 Tours, Cedex 01
Tel: +33(2) 47-36-66-00
Fax: +33(2) 47-36-64-10
EMail: secretariat.general@univ-tours.fr
Website: http://www.univ-tours.fr

Président: Loïc Vaillant (2008-)
Tel: +33(2) 47-36-64-00 EMail: president@univ-tours.fr

Secrétaire général: Pierre Gabette Tel: +33(2) 47-36-64-01

International Relations: Arnaud Giacometti

Centres
Renaissance Studies *(CESR)* (Medieval Studies)

Faculties
Arts and Humanities (Archaeology; Art History; Educational Sciences; History; Music; Musicology; Psychology; Sociology); **Law, Economics and Social Sciences** (Economics; Geography; Law;

Management; Public Administration; Social Sciences); **Letters and Languages** (English; Linguistics; Literature; Modern Languages; Portuguese; Spanish); **Medicine** (Medicine); **Pharmacy** (Pharmacy); **Science and Technology** (Behavioural Sciences; Biochemistry; Biology; Chemistry; Computer Science; English; Environmental Studies; Geology; Mathematics; Microbiology; Natural Sciences; Physics; Physiology; Technology)

Graduate Schools
Health, Science, Technology *Director*: Michel Isingrini; **Social Sciences** *Director*: Jean Rossetto

Institutes
Lifelong Education (Continuing Education) *Director*: René Clarisse; **Technology** *(IUT Blois)* (Materials Engineering; Technology; Telecommunications Engineering); **Technology** *(IUT Tours)* (Bioengineering; Business Administration; Communication Studies; Electrical Engineering; Sales Techniques; Social Work; Technology)

Programmes
Environmental, Water and River Engineering *(IUP IMACOF, Chinon)* (Environmental Engineering; Water Management) *Director*: Jean-Pierre Berton

Schools
Engineering *(Polytech' Tours)* (Computer Engineering; Computer Science; Engineering; Industrial Engineering) *DIrector*: Christian Proust; **Engineering** *(ENIVL Blois)* (Engineering) *(Acting) Director*: Romaumd Boné

Further Information: Also 'Antenne universitaire' at Blois (Law, Economics, Economic and Social Administration, Science and Techniques)

History: Founded 1970 under the 1968 law reforming higher education as one of two Universities replacing the Université d'Orléans-Tours, re-established 1962, but tracing its history to the original Université d'Orléans, 1306-1793. A State institution enjoying academic and financial autonomy, operating under the jurisdiction of the Minister of Education and financed by the State.

Governing Bodies: Conseil d'Administration, including representatives of teaching staff, research workers, students, and administrative and technical staff, as well as non-university members drawn from public and private sectors; Conseil scientifique, competent in matters of research; Conseil des Etudes et de la Vie universitaire; Conseil of each Unit, comprising representatives of teaching staff, research workers, students, and administrative and technical staff. President is elected by first three bodies. The Chancellor, who represents the Minister of Education, is the Rector of the Académie d'Orléans

Academic Year: October to June (October-December; January-March; April-June)

Admission Requirements: Secondary school certificate (baccalauréat) or equivalent, or special entrance examination

Main Language(s) of Instruction: French

Degrees and Diplomas: *Capacité en Droit*: Law, 2 yrs; *Diplôme universitaire de Technologie*: 2 yrs; *Licence*: Arts, Human and Social Sciences, Law, Economics and Management, Letters and Languages, Science and Technology, 3 yrs; *Licence professionnelle*: Arts, Human and Social Sciences, Law, Economics and Management, Science and Technology, Health, 3 yrs; *Diplôme d'Etat*: Medicine, 6 yrs plus 1 yr hospital practice and thesis; *Diplôme d'Etat*: Midwifery, 3 yrs; *Diplôme d'Etat*: Pharmacy, 4 yrs and 1 yr practical work; *Diplôme national de Master*: Arts, Human and Social Sciences, Law, Economics and Management, Letters and Languages, Science and Technology, 2 yrs; *Doctorat*: Health, Science and Technology; Human and Social Sciences, 3 yrs following Master; *Doctorat*: Pharmacy, by thesis following Diplôme d'Etat; *Certificat de Spécialité*: Medicine, at least 2 yrs following Diplôme d'Etat. Certificats and Diplômes d'Etudes françaises (for foreign students), Masters recherche, Masters professionnel

Student Services: Cultural centre, Foreign Studies Centre, Health services, Social counselling, Sports facilities

Student Residential Facilities: Yes

Libraries: Libraries of Letters and Law, 91,538 vols; MedicalLibrary, 17,496 vols; Science Library, 12,427 vols
Last Updated: 19/07/11

UNIVERSITY OF ANGERS
Université d'Angers
BP 73532, 40, rue de Rennes, 49035 Angers, Cedex 01
Tel: +33(2) 41-96-23-23
Fax: +33(2) 41-23-23-00
EMail: relations.internationales@univ-angers.fr
Website: http://www.univ-angers.fr

Président: Daniel Martina (2007-)
Tel: 33(2) 41-23-23-63 EMail: presidence@univ-angers.fr

Directeur général des Services: Henri-Marc Papavoine
Tel: +33(2) 41-96-23-05
EMail: henri-marc.papavoine@univ-angers.fr

International Relations: Lydie Jouis
Tel: +33(2) 41-96-21-38 +33(2) 41-96-23-02
EMail: lydie.jouis@univ-angers.fr

Faculties
Tourism and Hospitality Management *(ITBS)* (Cooking and Catering; Heritage Preservation; Hotel and Restaurant; Hotel Management; Protective Services; Service Trades; Tourism)

Institutes
Technology *(IUT Angers 2 sites: Angers, Cholet)* (Biotechnology; Business Computing; Electrical Engineering; Mechanical Engineering; Social Work; Technology) *Director*: Yves Meignen

Units
Industrial Systems Engineering *(ISTIA IUP)* (Automation and Control Engineering; Computer Engineering; Industrial Engineering); **Languages, Humanities and Social Sciences** (Arts and Humanities; Geography; History; Modern Languages; Psychology); **Law, Economics, and Business Studies** (Business Education; Economics; Law); **Medicine** (Medicine); **Pharmacology and Health Engineering** (Pharmacology; Sanitary Engineering); **Science** (Biology; Chemistry; Computer Science; Environmental Studies; Geology; Materials Engineering; Natural Sciences; Physics; Plant and Crop Protection)

Further Information: 3 campuses at Cholet Antenna and Saumur site

History: Founded 1971 as Centre universitaire d'Angers under the 1968 law reforming higher education and incorporating Institutions previously attached to the Ministry of Health and Université de Nantes and Université de Rennes. Acquired full University status 1972. A state Institution enjoying academic and financial autonomy operating under the jurisdiction of the Minister of Higher Education and Research and financed by the State.

Governing Bodies: Conseil de l'Université, comprising 30 members, including elected representatives of teaching staff, research workers, students, and administrative and technical staff, as well as non-university members drawn from the public and private sectors; Conseil scientifique, competent in matters of research; Conseil of each Unit, comprising representatives of its teaching staff, research workers, students and administrative and technical staff; Conseil scientifique, competent in matters of research. The President is elected by the Conseil de l'Université

Academic Year: October to June (October-December; January-March; April-June)

Admission Requirements: Secondary school certificate (baccalauréat) or equivalent, or special entrance examination

Main Language(s) of Instruction: French

Degrees and Diplomas: *Capacité en Droit*: 2 yrs; *Diplôme universitaire de Technologie (DUT)*: 2 yrs; *Licence*: 3 yrs; *Licence professionnelle*: 1 yr; *Diplôme d'Etat*: Dental Surgery, 5 yrs; *Diplôme d'Etat*: Medicine, 6 yrs plus 1 yr hospital practice and thesis; *Diplôme d'Etat*: Pharmacy, 4 yrs and 1 yr practical work; *Diplôme d'Ingénieur*; *Magistère*; *Diplôme national de Master*; *Doctorat*: 2-4 yrs following Masters; *Certificat de Spécialité*: Medicine, at least 2 years after Diplôme d'Etat

Student Residential Facilities: Yes

Libraries: Bibliothèque universitaire, 500,000 vols
Last Updated: 10/06/11

UNIVERSITY OF ARTOIS
Université d'Artois
BP 10665, 9, rue du Temple, 62030 Arras, Cedex
Tel: +33(3) 21-60-37-00
Fax: +33(3) 21-60-37-37
EMail: sri@univ-artois.fr
Website: http://www.univ-artois.fr

Président: Christian Morzewski
Tel: +33(3) 21-60-37-16 EMail: christian.morzewski@univ-artois.fr

Directrice générale des Services: Laurence Deloffre
Tel: +33(3) 21-60-37-71

International Relations: Yannis Karamanos
Tel: +33(3) 21-60-38-96, Fax: +33(3) 21-60-49-31

Faculties
Applied Sciences *(Béthune campus)* (Civil Engineering; Construction Engineering; Electrical Engineering; Industrial Engineering; Industrial Maintenance); **Economics, Administration and Social Sciences** *(Arras campus)* (Administration; Banking; Economics; Finance; Health Administration; Human Resources; Management); **History and Geography** *(Arras campus)* (Geography; History); **Law** *(Alexis de Toqueville, Douai campus)* (Law); **Science** *(Jean Perrin, Lens campus)* (Biology; Chemistry; Computer Science; Food Technology; Natural Sciences; Physics; Waste Management); **Sports and Physical Education** *(STAPS, Liévin campus)* (Physical Education; Sports)

Graduate Schools
Administration, Political Science and Law *(ED SJPG)* (Ethics; Heritage Preservation; Justice Administration; Law; Public Administration) *Director:* Arnaud De Raulin; **Human Sciences and Societies** *(ED SHS)* (Arts and Humanities; Comparative Literature; French; History; Linguistics; Translation and Interpretation); **Matter, Laser and Environment** *(ED SMRE)* (Chemistry); **Sciences for Engineering** *(ED SPI)* (Automation and Control Engineering; Civil Engineering; Computer Engineering; Environmental Engineering; Mathematics)

Institutes
Confucius (Chinese); **Study of Religious Facts** (Religious Studies); **Teacher Training** *(IUFM for Nord-Pas de Calais with seven sites)* (Teacher Trainers Education; Teacher Training); **Technology** *(IUT, Lens)* (Business Administration; Business and Commerce; Computer Science; Management; Technology); **Technology** *(IUT, Béthune)* (Chemistry; Civil Engineering; Computer Engineering; Electrical Engineering; Management; Mechanical Engineering; Production Engineering; Technology; Telecommunications Engineering)

Laboratories
Blood-Brain Barrier *(Lens, LBHE)* (Biochemistry; Cell Biology; Molecular Biology; Physiology); **Electronic Systems and Environment** *(Bethune, LSEE)* (Electronic Engineering; Energy Engineering)

Research Centres
Computer Science *(Lens, CRIL)* (Computer Science) *Division Head:* Grégoire; **Economic Environment, Modernization, European Integration** *(Arras, CRHEC)* (Economics; European Studies); **Electronic Literary Texts** *(CERTEL, Arras)* (Comparative Literature; Computer Science; Linguistics); **Ethics and Procedures** *(Douai campus)* (Ethics; Law); **Grammar** *(Arras, GRAMATICA)* (Grammar; Linguistics); **History and Societies** *(CRHES)* (Ancient Civilizations; Education; History; Political Sciences; Religious Studies; Social Studies)

Units
Economic and Social Administration *(AES, Arras)* (Administration; Economics; Social Policy) *Director:* Philippe Duez; **Foreign Languages and Civilizations** *(Arras campus)* (English; German; Literature; Modern Languages; Spanish); **Letters and Arts** *(Arras campus)* (Comparative Literature; Linguistics; Literature); **Social Economics, Regional Planning and Management** *(ED SESAM)* (Agricultural Management; Development Studies; Economics; Environmental Studies; Regional Planning; Regional Studies) *Director:* Jean-Pierre Renard

History: Founded 1991.

Academic Year: September to June (September-February; February-June)

Admission Requirements: Secondary school certificate (baccalauréat) or equivalent

Main Language(s) of Instruction: French

International Co-operation: With universities in USA, Canada and Brazil. Also participates in the Tempus, Socrates and Leonardo da Vinci programmes

Degrees and Diplomas: *Diplôme universitaire de Technologie*: Business Administration, Chemistry, Commerce, Civil Engineering, Computer Science, Industrial Organisation, Telecommunication; *Licence*: Modern Languages, French Literature, History, Geography, Law, Economics, Administration, Mathematics and Computer Science, Life Sciences, Physical Education and Sports, 3 yrs; *Licence professionnelle*: Justice Administration, Banking, Insurance, Commerce, Human Resources, Robotics, Electrical and Electronic Engineering, Mechanical Engineering, Food Technology, Building Technology, Transport Management, Waste Management; *Diplôme national de Master*: Arts and Humanities, French, Modern Languages, History, Heritage Preservation, Public Administration, Law, Economic Management, Human Resources, Trade, Mathematics and Computer Science, Food Technology, Physical Education and Sports, Engineering; *Doctorat*: Arts and Humanities, Law, Economics, Engineering, Biomedicine, Environmental Studies, Adminstration, 3 yrs following Masters. Master recherche, Master professionnel

Student Services: Academic counselling, Canteen, Cultural centre, Employment services, Handicapped facilities, Health services, Social counselling, Sports facilities

Libraries: Library on each campus

Press or Publishing House: Artois Presse Université (A.P.U.)
Last Updated: 11/07/11

UNIVERSITY OF AVIGNON AND THE VAUCLUSE
Université d'Avignon et des Pays de Vaucluse
74, rue Louis-Pasteur, 84029 Avignon, Cedex 01
Tel: +33(4) 90-16-25-00
Fax: +33(4) 90-16-25-10
EMail: uapv@univ-avignon.fr
Website: http://www.univ-avignon.fr

Président: Emmanuel Ethis (2007-)

Directeur général des Services: Fathie Boubertekh
Tel: +33(4) 90-16-25-11, Fax: +33(4) 90-16-25-20

International Relations: Carole Guéret
Tel: +33(4) 90-16-25-61, Fax: +33(4) 90-16-25-60
EMail: carole.gueret@univ-avignon.fr

Faculties
Applied Sciences and Languages *Dean:* Pierre-Louis Suet; **Arts and Humanities** *Dean:* Jacques Maby; **Exact and Natural Sciences** *Dean:* Yvan Cotta; **Law, Political and Economic Sciences** *Dean:* Pierre Fressoz

Institutes
Computer Science *Director:* Philippe Gilles; **Technology** *(IUT)* *Director:* Hélène Dominguez

Research Laboratories
Avignon Research Laboratory for Computer Science (Computer Science) *Director:* Marc El-Bèze; **Bees and Environment** (Environmental Studies) *Director:* Luc Belzunces; **Cardiovascular Adaptations to Exercise** *Director:* Philippe Odert; **Chemistry: Vectorial Molecular Systems and Bioorganic Chemistry, Chemistry Applied to Art and Archaeology** (Chemistry) *Director:* Bernard Pucci; **Cultural Identity, Texts and Theatricality** (Cultural Studies) *Director:* Patrice Brasseur; **Culture and Communication: Cultural Institutions and Audiences** *Director:* Jean Davallon; **Fruit and Vegetable Physiology** (Fruit Production; Vegetable Production) *Director:* Huguette Sallanon; **Geography** (Geography) *Director:* Loic Grasland; **History: Territories, Powers and Identities** *Director:* Guy Lobrichon; **Law: Possessions, Norms, Contracts** (Law) *Director:* Delphine Costa; **Mediterranean Institute of Ecology and Paleoecology** *Director:* Thierry Dutoit; **Modelling of Agricultural and Hydrological Systems** *Director:* Yves Travi;

Nonlinear Analysis and Geometry *Director*: Philippe Bolle; **Safety and Quality of Plant Products** *Director*: Olivier Dangles

Further Information: French Language Study Centre (CUEFA) offers French as a foreign language and French teacher training courses.

History: Founded in 1303 under the Pope. Closed during the French Revolution. Founded in 1972 as Centre universitaire. Formerly the Unit of Arts and Humanities of the Université de Provence. Acquired present status and title 1984. The Head of the Institution is its elected President. The Chancelier, who represents the Minister of Education, is the Recteur of the Académie d'Aix-Marseille.

Governing Bodies: Conseil d'Administration, comprising 40 members; Conseil scientifique, comprising 24 members; Conseil des Etudes et de la Vie étudiante, 20 members

Academic Year: September to June

Admission Requirements: Secondary school certificate (baccalauréat) or equivalent, or special entrance examination.

Main Language(s) of Instruction: French

International Co-operation: Participates in the Erasmus programme; ALFA (Europe-Latin America); Tempus; Comenius; Leonardo; IP. Scholarships with AUF (Agence Universitaire de la Francophonie).

Degrees and Diplomas: *Diplôme universitaire de Technologie*: Commercialisation Techniques; Biological Engineering; Packaging Engineering; Statistics & Data Processing, 2 yrs; *Licence*: Foreign Languages; French; Applied Foreign Languages; Law; Economic and Social Administration; Business Management & Economics; Public Administration; Geography; History; Communication Sciences; Physics & Chemistry; Earth & Life Sciences; Mathematics; Computer Science; Sports Science, 3 yrs; *Licence professionnelle*: Banking; International Commercialisation of Agrofood Products; Human Resource Management; Tourism & Hotel Industry; Risk Management & Security; Tourism & Solidarity Economics; Agrofood Production Management; Occupational & Technological Risk Management; Medical Information Management & Engineering; Distribution Information Systems, 1 yr; *Diplôme national de Master*: Arts & Languages; Law; Management & International Trade; Social Policy; Geography; History; Cultural Development Strategy; Chemistry; Agrosciences; Computer Science; Sports Science, 2 yrs; *Doctorat*: Biology; Chemistry; Hydrology; Computer Science; Mathematics; Mechanics; Agronomy; Earth Sciences; Life Sciences; Sports Science; Foreign Languages & Literature; French Language & Literature; Comparative Literature; Langauge Science; Law; Management Sciences; Communication; Geography; History

Student Services: Academic counselling, Canteen, Cultural centre, Foreign Studies Centre, Handicapped facilities, Health services, Sports facilities

Student Residential Facilities: Yes.

Special Facilities: Digital work environment.

Libraries: c. 133,000 vols; 1,327 periodicals; 3,342 video documents

Publications: Culture et Musées; Etudes vauclusiennes; Glossalalia; Mythes, Croyances et Religions; Théâtres du Monde

Student Numbers 2007-2008	MEN	WOMEN	TOTAL
All (Foreign Included)	2,822	4,438	**7,260**

Last Updated: 11/07/11

UNIVERSITY OF BURGUNDY, DIJON
Université de Bourgogne

BP 27877, Maison de l'Université, Esplanade Erasme, 21078 Dijon, Cedex
Tel: +33(3) 80-39-50-00
Fax: +33(3) 80-39-50-69
EMail: president@u-bourgogne.fr
Website: http://www.u-bourgogne.fr

Présidente: Sophie Béjean (2007-) Tel: +33(3) 80-39-50-11

Directeur général des Services: Jean Nervaez
Tel: +33(3) 80-39-50-13 EMail: catherine.petit@u-bourgogne.fr

International Relations: Fabrice Mériaudeau
Tel: +33(3) 80-39-39-44
EMail: fabrice.meriaudeau@u-bourgogne.fr

Centres
University Centre *(Condorcet Centre) Director*: Bernard Lamalle

Higher Institutes
Automobile and Transport *(ISAT)* (Automotive Engineering; Transport and Communications)

Institutes
Business Administration *(IAE)* (Accountancy; Agricultural Business; Business Administration; Finance; Management; Marketing); **Denis Diderot** (Cultural Studies; Education; Management); **Engineering in Business Documentation, Networks and Image** (Computer Networks; Documentation Techniques); **Management and Business Administration** *(IUP)* (Business Administration; Management) *Director*: Claude Patriat; **Preparatory Administrative Studies** *(IPAG)* (Administration); **Technology** *(IUT Dijon-Auxerre)* (Archiving; Bioengineering; Biotechnology; Communication Studies; Computer Networks; Computer Science; Information Technology; Management); **Technology** *(IUT Auxerre)* (Marketing; Production Engineering) *Director*: André Bernard; **Technology** *(IUT Chalon-sur-Saône)* (Materials Engineering; Transport Management); **Technology** *(IUT Le Creusot)* (Aeronautical and Aerospace Engineering; Automation and Control Engineering; Electrical Engineering; Electronic Engineering; Laser Engineering; Measurement and Precision Engineering; Mechanical Engineering; Production Engineering; Technology); **Wine Studies** *(IUVV Jules Guyot)* (Oenology)

Schools
Materials Research *(ESIREM)* (Materials Engineering)

Units
Earth Sciences (Earth Sciences) *Director*: Jean-Pierre Garcia; **Economics and Management** (Administration; Economics; Management); **Human Sciences** (Archaeology; Art History; Educational Sciences; English; Geography; History; Musicology; Psychology; Social Sciences; Sociology); **Law and Political Science** (Law; Political Sciences); **Letters and Philosophy** (Arts and Humanities; Classical Languages; Literature; Philosophy); **Life Sciences, Earth Sciences and Environment** (Biological and Life Sciences; Earth Sciences; Environmental Studies); **Medicine** (Dentistry; Medicine; Midwifery; Physical Therapy); **Modern Languages and Communication** (Communication Studies; Modern Languages); **Pharmaceutical and Biological Sciences** (Biological and Life Sciences; Pharmacology); **Physical Education and Sports** (Physical Education; Sports); **Science and Technology** (Applied Linguistics; Chemistry; Computer Science; Mathematics; Natural Sciences; Physics; Technology)

History: Founded 1970 under the 1968 law reforming higher education and replacing former Université de Dijon, founded 1722. The University was suppressed by the Revolution and replaced by Faculties of Law; Science; and Letters. Reconstituted as University 1896. A State Institution enjoying academic and financial autonomy, operating under the jurisdiction of the Minister of Education and financed by the State.

Governing Bodies: Conseil d'Administration, including representatives of teaching staff, research workers, students, and administrative and technical staff, as well as non-university members drawn from the public and private sectors; Conseil scientifique, competent in matters of research; Conseil des Etudes et de la Vie universitaire; Conseil of each Unit, comprising representatives of its teaching staff, research workers, students, and administrative and technical staff. The President is elected by the first three bodies. The Chancelier, who represents the Minister of Education, is the Recteur of the Académie de Dijon

Academic Year: October to June (October-January; January-June)

Admission Requirements: Secondary school certificate (baccalauréat) or equivalent, or special entrance examination

Main Language(s) of Instruction: French

Degrees and Diplomas: *Diplôme universitaire de Technologie*; *Licence*: 3 yrs; *Licence professionnelle*; *Diplôme national de Master*: 2 yrs following Licence; *Doctorat*

Student Services: Academic counselling, Canteen, Cultural centre, Foreign student adviser, Handicapped facilities, Health services, Nursery care, Social counselling, Sports facilities

Student Residential Facilities: Cité Universitaire and student hostels

Special Facilities: Radio Station; Theatre

Libraries: Central Library

Publications: La Recherche à l'Université de Bourgogne *(biannually)*

Last Updated: 12/07/11

UNIVERSITY OF CAEN-BASSE-NORMANDIE

Université de Caen Basse-Normandie
Esplanade de la Paix, B.P. 5186, 14032 Caen, Cedex
Tel: +33(2) 31-56-55-00
Fax: +33(2) 31-56-56-00
EMail: relations.internationales@unicaen.fr
Website: http://www.unicaen.fr

Présidente: Josette Travert (2006-)
Tel: +33(2) 31-56-55-70, Fax: +33(2) 31-56-58-00
EMail: presidence@unicaen.fr

Directrice générale des Services: Hélène Brochet-Toutiri
Tel: +33(2) 31-56-53-15 EMail: secretariat.general@unicaen.fr

International Relations: Isabelle Triniac
Tel: +33(2) 31-56-60-76, Fax: +33(2) 31-56-60-78

Centres
French for Foreign Students *(CEUIE)* (French)

Graduate Schools
Chemistry and Biology *(In collaboration with Universities of Rouen and Havre)* (Medical Technology; Sanitary Engineering); **Economics Management** *(In collaboration with Universities of Rouen and Havre)* (Economics); **Law** *(In collaboration with Universities of Rouen and Havre)* (Law); **Literature, Cultures and Social Sciences** (Arts and Humanities; Cultural Studies; Literature; Social Sciences); **Materials Engineering** *(In collaboration with ENSI-CAEN)*

Institutes
Banking, Insurance *(IUP)* (Banking; Insurance); **Basic and Applied Biology** *(IBFA)* (Biology); **Business Administration and Management** *(IAE)* (Business Administration; Management); **Food Technology** *(IUP)* (Food Technology); **Preparatory Administrative Studies** *(IPAG)* (Administration); **Teacher Training** (Teacher Training); **Technology** *(IUT Caen)* (Biology; Business Administration; Management; Physics; Technology); **Technology** *(IUT, Cherbourg Manche)* (Business Administration; Energy Engineering; Human Resources; Industrial Maintenance; Management; Technology); **Technology** *(IUT, Alençon)* (Mechanical Engineering; Production Engineering; Social and Community Services; Technology; Transport Management)

Research Centres
Coastal Environment *(CREC)* (Coastal Studies)

Schools
Engineering *(ESIX-Cherbourg, Caen, St Lô)* (Cooking and Catering; Dairy; Engineering; Food Technology; Industrial Engineering)

Units
Economics and Management (Business Administration; Economics; Management); **Geography** (Development Studies; Environmental Studies; Geography; Regional Studies); **History** (History); **Human Sciences** (Ancient Civilizations; Comparative Literature; Educational Sciences; Linguistics; Literature; Performing Arts; Philosophy; Sociology); **Law and Political Science** (Administration; Law; Political Sciences); **Medicine** (Medicine); **Modern Languages** *(LVE)* (English Studies; German; Italian; Latin American Studies; Modern Languages; Romance Languages; Scandinavian Languages; Slavic Languages); **Pharmacy** (Pharmacy); **Physical Education and Sports** *(STAPS)* (Physical Education; Sports); **Psychology** (Psychology); **Sciences** (Automation and Control Engineering; Chemistry; Computer Science; Electronic Engineering; Environmental Studies; Mathematics; Mechanical Engineering; Natural Sciences; Physics)

Further Information: Six antenna sites: four IUT sites are located at Ifs, Lisieux, Vire, and Saint Lo. Cherbourg and Alencon have sites for Sciences, Law and LVE Units.

History: Founded 1970 under the 1968 law reforming higher education and replacing former Université de Caen, founded 1432 by Henry VI of England and granted Papal recognition 1437. The university was suppressed by the Revolution. Reconstituted 1896. A State institution enjoying academic and financial autonomy, operating under the jurisdiction of the Minister of Education and financed by the State.

Governing Bodies: Conseil d'Administration, including representatives of teaching staff, research workers, students, and administrative and technical staff, as well as non-university members drawn from the public and private sectors; Conseil scientifique, competent in matters of research; Conseil des Etudes et de la Vie universitaire; and Conseil of each Unit, comprising representatives of its teaching staff, research workers, students, and administrative and technical staff. The President is elected by the first three bodies. The Chancelier, who represents the Minister of Education, is the Recteur of the Académie de Caen

Academic Year: October to June

Admission Requirements: Secondary school certificate (baccalauréat) or equivalent, or special entrance examination

Fees: (Euros): 156 per annum

Main Language(s) of Instruction: French

International Co-operation: With universities in Africa, Europe, Canada, USA, Mexico, Venezuela, Argentina, Australia, Thailand, Vietnam, Russian Federation, Japan, Korea

Degrees and Diplomas: *Capacité en Droit*: 2 yrs; *Diplôme universitaire de Technologie*; *Licence*: a further y3 yrs; *Licence professionnelle*; *Diplôme d'Etat*: Medicine, 6 yrs plus 1 yr hospital practice and thesis; *Diplôme d'Etat*: Pharmacy, 4 yrs and 1 yr practical work; *Diplôme d'Ingénieur*: Industrial Engineering; *Diplôme de Recherche technologique*: Food Technology; Industrial Engineering; *Diplôme national de Master*: 2 yrs following Licence; *Doctorat*: 2-4 yrs following Masters; *Certificat de Spécialité*: Medicine, at least 2 yrs after Diplôme d'Etat. Certificat and Diplôme d'études françaises (for foreign students), Masters recherche, Masters professionnel

Student Services: Academic counselling, Canteen, Foreign student adviser, Foreign Studies Centre, Handicapped facilities, Health services, Language programs, Social counselling, Sports facilities

Student Residential Facilities: Yes

Libraries: Total, c. 600,000 vols

Last Updated: 12/07/11

UNIVERSITY OF CORSICA PASCAL PAOLI

Université de Corse Pascal Paoli
BP 52, Campus Caraman, 7, avenue Jean Nicoli, 20250 Corte, Cedex
Tel: +33(4) 95-45-00-00
EMail: presidence@univ-corse.fr
Website: http://www.univ-corse.fr

Président: Antoine Aiello (2002-)
Tel: +33(4) 95-45-01-37, Fax: +33(4) 95-45-00-88

Secrétaire générale: Fabienne Palmaro
Tel: +33(4) 95-45-06-62, Fax: +33(4) 95-45-06-39
EMail: palmaro@univ-corse.fr

International Relations: Amiel Buisset-Orsoni
Tel: +33(4) 95-45-02-23, Fax: +33(4) 95-45-02-38
EMail: buisset-orsini@univ-corse.fr

Graduate Schools
Environment and Society (Environmental Studies) *Division Head*: Kathy Guglielmi

Institutes
Business Administration *(IAE)* (Business Administration; Management); **Health Studies** (Health Sciences; Nursing); **Teacher Training** *(IUFM with two sites: Ajaccio and Bastia)* (Teacher Trainers Education; Teacher Training); **Technology** *(IUT Corte)* (Biology; Management; Sales Techniques; Technology)

Units
Law, Economics and Management (Economics; Law; Management); **Letters, Languages, Humanities and Social Sciences** (Arts and Humanities; Literature; Modern Languages; Social Sciences); **Science and Techniques** *(FST)* (Natural Sciences; Technology)

Further Information: Two Sites: Ajaccio and Bastia Centres

History: Founded 1765 as Université de Corte. Reopened 1981.

Academic Year: September to June

Admission Requirements: DAFL-DEFL

Main Language(s) of Instruction: French

International Co-operation: With universities in UK; Spain; Italy; Poland; Finland; Sweden; Ireland; Romania; Greece; Quebec

Degrees and Diplomas: *Capacité en Droit*; *Diplôme universitaire de Technologie*; *Licence*: Arts and Humanities, Science and Technology, Languages, Social Sciences, Law, Economics, Management, 3 yrs; *Diplôme national de Master*: Arts and Humanities, Science and Technology, Languages, Social Sciences, Law, Economics, Management, 2 yrs; *Diplôme national de Master*: Environmental Engineering, New Technologies; *Doctorat*

Student Services: Canteen, Cultural centre, Foreign student adviser, Handicapped facilities, Health services, Language programs, Social counselling, Sports facilities

Last Updated: 12/07/11

UNIVERSITY OF EVRY-VAL D' ESSONNE

Université d'Evry-Val d'Essonne

Boulevard François Mitterrand, Bât. Ile-de-France, 91025 Evry, Cedex

Tel: +33(1) 69-47-70-00
Fax: +33(1) 64-97-27-34
EMail: rel.int@univ-evry.fr
Website: http://www.univ-evry.fr

Président: Philippe Houdy (2011-) Tel: +33(1) 69-47-70-29

Directeur général des Services: Hakim Khellaf
Tel: +33(1) 69-47-70-15, Fax: +33(1) 69-47-70-07

Graduate Schools
Genetics (Genetics) *Director*: Francis Quetier; **Sitevry** (Information Sciences; Mathematics) *Director*: Pascale Le Gall

Institutes
Teacher Training *(IUFM Versailles with 5 sites) Director*: Serge Goursaud; **Technology** *(IUT Evry)* (Business and Commerce; Computer Engineering; E-Business/Commerce; Electrical Engineering; Information Technology; Mechanical Engineering; Production Engineering; Technology; Transport Management) *Director*: Paul Demarez

Laboratories
Analysis and Environment *Director*: Pierre Toulhoat; **Analysis and Probabilities** (Mathematics) *Director*: François Hirsch; **Data Processing** (Data Processing) *Director*: Michel Israel; **Genetics of Hereditary Skin Diseases** (Dermatology; Genetics) *Director*: Gilles Waksman; **Polymer Interfaces** (Polymer and Plastics Technology) *Director*: Hervé Cheradame

Programmes
Arts and Culture *(IUP ASAC)* (Arts and Humanities; Cultural Studies) *Director*: Patrick Tafforeau; **Biotechnology** *(IUP GBI)* (Bioengineering; Biotechnology) *Director*: Flavio Toma; **Business Administration - Business Law** *(IUP)* (Business Administration; Commercial Law; Management) *Director*: Claude Ferry; **Business Administration - Economics and Statistics** *(IUP)* (Banking; Business Administration; Finance; Insurance; Statistics) *Director*: Ferhat Mihoubi; **Business Administration - Management** *(IUP)* (Business Administration; Management) *Director*: Eric Paget-Blanc; **Business and Commerce** *(IUP)* (Business and Commerce; Sales Techniques) *Director*: Sophie Campoy; **Data Processing for Management** *(IUP MIAGE)* (Data Processing) *Director*: Alain Kavenoky; **Industrial Engineering** *(IUP)* (Aeronautical and Aerospace Engineering; Electrical Engineering; Industrial Design; Mechanical Engineering; Production Engineering; Thermal Engineering) *Director*: Francis Artigue; **Materials Engineering** *(IUP)* (Materials Engineering) *Director*: Richard Messina; **Regional Planning** *(IUP)* (Regional Planning; Sports Management; Town Planning) *Director*: Alain Le Guyader

Schools
Computer Science for Industry anf Business *(ENSIIE)* (Business Computing; Computer Engineering; Engineering) *Director*: Florent Chavand

Units
Basic and Applied Sciences (Applied Mathematics; Biology; Biotechnology; Chemistry; Computer Science; Physical Education; Physics; Sports); **Languages, Arts and Music** (Fine Arts; Modern Languages; Music; Performing Arts); **Law** (Law); **Science and Technology** (Automation and Control Engineering; Chemistry; Electrical Engineering; Engineering; Mechanical Engineering; Natural Sciences; Physics; Robotics; Technology; Telecommunications Engineering); **Social Sciences and Management** (Economics; History; Management; Social Sciences; Sociology)

History: Founded 1993, acquired present status 1997.

Academic Year: September to June (September-January; February-June)

Admission Requirements: Secondary school certificate (baccalauréat)

Main Language(s) of Instruction: French

Degrees and Diplomas: *Diplôme universitaire de Technologie*: Mechanical Engineering, Electrical Engineering, 2 yrs; *Licence*: Economics, Law, Management, Social Sciences, Arts and Humanities, Science and Technology, 3 yrs; *Licence professionnelle*; *Diplôme de Recherche technologique*: Material Engineering, Industrial Engineering (DRT); *Diplôme national de Master*: Economics, Law, Management, Social Sciences, Arts and Humanities, Science and Technology, 2 yrs following Licence; *Doctorat*: Economics, Law, 2-4 yrs following Masters. Masters recherche, Masters professionnel, Preparation for CAPES and Law Administration exams

Student Services: Academic counselling, Canteen, Employment services, Foreign student adviser, Handicapped facilities, Health services, Social counselling, Sports facilities

Publications: Les cahiers d'Evry
Last Updated: 26/01/12

UNIVERSITY OF FRANCHE-COMTÉ, BESANÇON

Université de Franche-Comté

1, rue Claude-Goudimel, 25030 Besançon
Tel: +33(3) 81-66-66-66
Fax: +33(3) 81-66-50-09
EMail: dri@univ-fcomte.fr
Website: http://www.univ-fcomte.fr

Président: Claude CondéFax: +33(3) 81-66-50-25

Directeur général des Services: Louis Bérion
EMail: louis.berion@univ-fcomte.fr

International Relations: Rudy Chaulet
Tel: +33(3) 81-66-50-34 EMail: rudy.chaulet@univ-fcomte.fr

Centres
Applied Linguistics *(CLA)* (Applied Linguistics); **Distance Education** *(CTU)* (Administration; Economics; History; Mathematics; Social Sciences)

Graduate Schools
Engineering and Microtechnology *(ED SPIM In collaboration with University of Technology - Belfort-Montbéliard and National School of Mechanics and Microelectronics)* (Automation and Control Engineering; Electronic Engineering; Materials Engineering; Mechanical Engineering; Microelectronics; Optical Technology); **Language, Space, Time and Society** *(ED LETS)* (Arts and Humanities; Law; Linguistics; Literature; Management; Social Sciences); **Louis Pasteur** (Chemistry; Economic and Finance Policy; Mathematics; Physics); **Man, Environment and Health** *(ED HES)* (Biology; Cell Biology; Environmental Studies; Health Sciences)

Institutes
Business Administration *(IAE) Director*: Benoît Pigé; **Engineering** *(ISIFC Franche-Comté)* (Biological and Life Sciences; Biomedical Engineering; Engineering); **Engineering** *(IUP)*; **Preparatory Administrative Studies** *(IPAG)* (Administration) *Director*: Jean-Louis Doney; **Teacher Training** *(IUFM has 5 sites in Belfort; Lons le Saunier, Fort Griffon, Vesoul and Montjoux)* (Teacher Trainers Education; Teacher Training); **Technology** *(IUT Besançon-Vesoul)* (Business Administration; Chemistry; Hygiene; Industrial Engineering; Industrial Maintenance; Information Technology; Mechanical Engineering; Production Engineering; Technology; Transport and Communications); **Technology** *(IUT Belfort-Montbéliard)* (Business

and Commerce; Computer Engineering; Electrical Engineering; Energy Engineering; Mechanical Engineering; Social Studies; Technology; Telecommunications Engineering; Thermal Engineering)

Laboratories

Astronomy and Space (Astronomy and Space Science; Astrophysics) *Director*: François Vernotte

Schools

Engineering (ENSMM) *Director*: Jean-Claude Gelin

Units

Languages, Human and Social Sciences (Archaeology; Art History; Arts and Humanities; Geography; History; Linguistics; Modern Languages; Musicology; Performing Arts; Philosophy; Psychology; Social Sciences; Sociology; Theatre) *Dean*: Antonio Gonzales; **Law, Economics and Political Science, Management** *(SJEPG, Besançon)* (Administration; Economics; Law; Management; Political Sciences; Social Sciences); **Medicine and Pharmacy** *(SMP, Besançon)* (Medicine; Pharmacy); **Physical Education and Sports** *(STAPS, Besançon)* (Physical Education; Sports); **Science and Technology** (Biology; Chemistry; Computer Science; Earth Sciences; Engineering; Geology; Mathematics; Natural Sciences; Neurosciences; Physics; Technology; Waste Management); **Science, Technology and Industrial Administration** *(STGI Belfort)* (Administration; Economics; Electrical Engineering; Energy Engineering; Industrial Engineering; Industrial Management; Water Science)

Further Information: The University is spread across 5 campuses, located in Belfort, Montbéliard, Lons le Saunier and Vesoul.

History: Established 1971 under the 1968 law reforming higher education as one of the new Universities and replacing the former Université de Besançon founded 1422 at Dôle and transferred to Besançon 1691. The University was suppressed by the Revolution and replaced by Faculties of Science and Letters and School of Medicine. Reconstituted as university 1896. A State institution enjoying academic and financial autonomy, operating under the jurisdiction of Minister of Education and financed by the State.

Governing Bodies: Conseil de l'Université, including elected representatives of teaching staff, research workers, students and administrative and technical staff, as well non-university members drawn from the public and private sectors; Conseil of each Unit, comprising representatives of its teaching staff, research workers, students, and administrative and technical staff; and Conseil scientifique, competent in matters of research. The President is elected by Conseil de l'Université. Chancelier, who represents Minister of Education, is Recteur of Académie de Besançon

Academic Year: October to June (October-January; February-June)

Admission Requirements: Secondary school certificate (baccalauréat) or equivalent, or special entrance examination

Main Language(s) of Instruction: French

Degrees and Diplomas: *Capacité en Droit*: 2 yrs; *Diplôme universitaire de Technologie*: 2 yrs; *Licence*: Law, Economics, Letters, Science, 3 yrs; *Licence professionnelle*; *Diplôme d'Etat*: Dental Surgery, 5 yrs; *Diplôme d'Etat*: Medicine, 6 yrs plus 1 yr hospital practice and thesis; *Diplôme d'Etat*: Pharmacy, 4 yrs and 1 yr practical work; *Diplôme national de Master*: Law and Economics, Letters, Science, 2 yrs following Licence; *Doctorat*: Law and Economics, Letters, Pharmacy, Science, 2-4 yrs following Masters; *Certificat de Spécialité*: Medicine, at least 2 yrs after Diplôme d'Etat. Masters recherche, Masters professionnel

Student Services: Canteen, Cultural centre, Employment services, Foreign student adviser, Handicapped facilities, Health services, Social counselling, Sports facilities

Student Residential Facilities: Yes

Libraries: Central Library, c. 300,000 vols; Scientific library

Press or Publishing House: Presses Universitaires Franc-comtoises
Last Updated: 13/07/11

UNIVERSITY OF HAUTE ALSACE

Université de Haute-Alsace
2, rue des Frères Lumière, 68093 Mulhouse, Cedex
Tel: +33(3) 89-33-60-00
Fax: +33(3) 89-33-63-19
EMail: international@uha.fr
Website: http://www.uha.fr

Président: Alain Brillard
Tel: +33(3) 89-33-63-10 EMail: presidence@uha.fr

Directeur général des services: Samuel Bitsch
Tel: +33(3) 89-33-63-11 EMail: samuel.bitsch@uha.fr

Centres

Foreign Languages (Modern Languages); **Lifelong Education** *(SERFA)*; **Sports** (Sports)

Faculties

Agricultural Production (Agriculture); **Arts and Humanities** *(FLSH)* (Arts and Humanities); **Commerce and Marketing** *(PEPS)* (Business and Commerce; Marketing); **Economics, Social Sciences and Law** *(FSES)* (Economics; Law; Social Sciences); **Science and Techniques** *(FST)* (Natural Sciences; Technology)

Institutes

Technology *(IUT)* (Business Administration; Business and Commerce; Electrical Engineering; Mechanical Engineering; Technology; Transport Management); **Technology** *(IUT, Colmar)* (Biology; Business and Commerce; Hygiene; Law; Technology; Telecommunications Engineering)

Schools

Applied Sciences for Engineering *(ESSAIM)* (Applied Chemistry; Applied Mathematics; Applied Physics; Computer Science; Engineering) *Director*: François-Marie Schmitt; **Chemistry** *(ENSCMu)* (Chemistry) *Director*: Claude Le Drian; **Textile Engineering** *(ENSITM)* (Textile Technology) *Director*: Marc Renner

History: Founded 1970 as Centre Universitaire under the 1968 law reforming higher education and incorporating Institutions previously attached to former Université de Strasbourg. Became Université du Haut-Rhin with full University status 1975. Acquired present title 1977. The Head of the Institution is its elected President. The Chancelier, who represents the Minister of Education, is the Recteur of the Académie de Strasbourg.

Governing Bodies: Board of Trustees

Academic Year: September to June (September-December; January-March; April-June)

Admission Requirements: Secondary school certificate (baccalauréat) or recognized equivalent, or special entrance examination

Main Language(s) of Instruction: French

Degrees and Diplomas: *Diplôme universitaire de Technologie*: 2 yrs; *Licence*: 3 yrs; *Licence professionnelle*: 3 yrs; *Diplôme national de Master*: 2 yrs following Licence; *Doctorat*: 3-4 yrs following Masters

Student Services: Academic counselling, Canteen, Cultural centre, Employment services, Handicapped facilities, Health services, Social counselling, Sports facilities

Student Residential Facilities: For c. 460 students

Libraries: Science, 70,000 vols; Letters, 62,000
Last Updated: 13/04/11

UNIVERSITY OF LA ROCHELLE

Université de La Rochelle
23, avenue Albert Einstein, 17071 La Rochelle, Cedex 9
Tel: +33(5) 46-45-91-14
Fax: +33(5) 46-44-93-76
EMail: vp-ri@univ-lr.fr
Website: http://www.univ-larochelle.fr

Président: Gérard Blanchard
Tel: +33(5) 46-45-87-09, Fax: +33(5) 46-45-72-26
EMail: presidentlarochelle@univ-lr.fr; michel.pouyllau@univ-lr.fr

Directeur général des Services: Philippe Bezagu
Tel: +33(5) 46-45-87-45 EMail: sgu@univ-lr.fr

International Relations: Fernando Pedraza Diaz
Tel: +33(5) 46-51-39-61 +33(5) 46-45-87-19

Centres
Preparatory Administrative Studies (Administration)

Graduate Schools
Doctoral School

Institutes

Technology *(IUT)* (Bioengineering; Business and Commerce; Civil Engineering; Data Processing; Sales Techniques; Technology; Telecommunications Engineering)

Units

Exact Sciences and Engineering (Biochemistry; Biology; Chemistry; Civil Engineering; Computer Science; Earth Sciences; Mathematics; Natural Sciences; Physics); **Law, Political Science and Management** (Law; Management; Political Sciences; Private Law; Public Administration; Public Law); **Letters, Languages, Arts and Humanities** *(FLASH)* (Economics; Geography; History; International Relations; Literature; Modern Languages)

History: Founded 1993.

Academic Year: September to June

Main Language(s) of Instruction: French

Degrees and Diplomas: *Diplôme universitaire de Technologie (DUT)*; *Licence*: Law, Administration, Languages, Arts and Humanities, Science and Technology, Environmental Studies, 3 yrs; *Licence professionnelle*: Languages, Arts and Humanities, Science and Technology, 1 yr following initial 2 yrs; *Diplôme national de Master*: Law, Administration, Languages, Arts and Humanities, Science and Technology, Environmental Studies, 2 yrs following Licence; *Doctorat*. Masters recherche, Masters professionnel, Preparation for Teaching, Administrative and Judicial Exams

Student Services: Canteen, Handicapped facilities, Health services, Language programs, Social counselling, Sports facilities
Last Updated: 13/07/11

UNIVERSITY OF LE HAVRE
Université du Havre
BP 1123, 25, rue Philippe Lebon, 76063 Le Havre, Cedex
Tel: +33(2) 32-74-40-00
Fax: +33(2) 35-21-49-59
EMail: sri@univ-lehavre.fr
Website: http://www.univ-lehavre.fr

Président: Camille Galap (2005-)
Tel: +33(2) 32-74-40-54 EMail: presidence@univ-lehavre.fr

Secrétaire général: Jean Clarisse
Tel: +33(2) 35-74-40-02 EMail: jean.clarisse@univ-lehavre.fr

International Relations: Cristian Nichita Tel: +33(2) 32-74-42-25

Centres
Lifelong Education

Departments
Commerce Engineering and Sales Techniques *(IUP)* (Sales Techniques)

Faculties
International Affairs (Cultural Studies; English; German; History; International Business; International Economics; Law; Management; Marketing; Modern Languages; Oriental Languages; Romance Languages)

Higher Institutes
Logistic Studies *(ISEL)* (Arts and Humanities; Engineering; Management; Natural Sciences; Technology)

Institutes
Technology *(IUT Le Havre)* (Business Administration; Civil Engineering; Communication Studies; Computer Science; Electrical Engineering; Human Resources; Mechanical Engineering; Sales Techniques; Technology; Transport and Communications)

Units
Arts and Humanities (Geography; History; Literature; Sociology); **Science and Techniques** (Biology; Chemistry; Civil Engineering; Computer Science; Cosmetology; Electronic Engineering; Industrial Engineering; Mathematics; Mechanical Engineering; Physics; Technology)

History: Founded 1984.

Governing Bodies: Conseil d'administration; Conseil scientifique; Conseil de la vie de l'étudiant

Academic Year: October to June (October-December;January-March; April-June)

Admission Requirements: Secondary school certificate (baccalauréat) or brevet supérieur, or recognized foreign equivalent, or specialized entrance examination

Main Language(s) of Instruction: French

Degrees and Diplomas: *Diplôme universitaire de Technologie (DUT)*; *Licence*: Law, Economics, Management, Commerce, Science, Social Sciences, Arts and Humanities, 3 yrs; *Licence professionnelle*: Social Work, Science, Commerce, Management, 3 yrs; *Diplôme d'Ingénieur*. Logistical Engineering; *Diplôme national de Master*. Law, Economics, Management, Commerce, Science, Social Sciences, Arts and Humanities, 2 yrs following Licence; *Doctorat*: 6-7 yrs. Masters recherche, Masters professionnel

Libraries: The libraries of the city and of the university are connected within a network
Last Updated: 18/07/11

UNIVERSITY OF LIMOGES
Université de Limoges
BP 23204, 33, rue François-Mitterrand, 87032 Limoges, Cedex 1
Tel: +33(5) 55-14-91-00
Fax: +33(5) 55-14-91-01
EMail: ri@unilim.fr
Website: http://www.unilim.fr

Président: Jacques Fontanille (2004-)
Tel: +33(5) 55-14-91-11
EMail: presidence@unilim.fr; jacques.fontanille@unilim.fr

Directeur général des Services: Vincent Jolys
Tel: +33(5) 55-14-91-13 EMail: vincent.jolys@unilim.fr

International Relations: Hélène Déjoux
Tel: +33(5) 55-14-90-96 +33(5) 55-45-73-25,
Fax: +33(5) 55-14-91-06

Centres
Lifelong Education *(CFASup) Director*. Paulette Dolhan

Faculties
Arts and Humanities (Arts and Humanities; Comparative Literature; Educational Sciences; English; Geography; German; Greek; Heritage Preservation; Hispanic American Studies; History; Latin; Library Science; Linguistics; Literature; Sociology; Spanish); **Law and Economics** *(FDSE)* (Administration; Economics; Law); **Medicine** (Medicine); **Pharmacy** (Pharmacy); **Science and Technology** (Biological and Life Sciences; Chemistry; Civil Engineering; Computer Science; English; Information Technology; Mathematics; Natural Sciences; Physical Education; Physics; Sports)

Graduate Schools
Man and Society (Economics; European Union Law; Finance; French Studies; Law; Linguistics; Modern Languages; Social Sciences) *Director*. Bertrand Westphal; **Science, Technology and Health** (Applied Chemistry; Biomedicine; Ceramics and Glass Technology; Chemistry; Civil Engineering; Computer Engineering; Ecology; Mathematics) *Director*. Abbas Chazad Movahhedi

Institutes
Business Administration *(IUP, formerly known as IAE)* (Business Administration); **Preparatory Administrative Studies** *(IPAG)* (Administration; Public Administration); **Teacher Training** *(IUFM Limousin with 3 sites: Guéret, Tulle, Limoges)* (Teacher Trainers Education; Teacher Training) *Director*. Bernard Valadas; **Technology** *(IUT Limoges with 4 sites: Brive, Egletons, Limoges and Tulle)* (Biology; Civil Engineering; Computer Science; Electrical Engineering; Industrial Engineering; Maintenance Technology; Management; Marketing; Measurement and Precision Engineering; Mechanical Engineering; Production Engineering; Safety Engineering; Technology)

Schools
Engineering *(ENSIL)* (Electronic Engineering; Engineering; Environmental Engineering; Materials Engineering; Mechanical Engineering; Telecommunications Engineering; Water Science); **Industrial Ceramics Studies** *(ENSCI)* (Ceramic Art)

Further Information: Also 4 research institutes

History: Founded 1970 under the 1968 law reforming higher education and incorporating former Université de Limoges with School of Law, founded 1909, and School of Medicine tracing its history to

1626. A State institution enjoying academic and financial autonomy, operating under the jurisdiction of the Minister of Education and financed by the State.

Governing Bodies: Conseil d'Administration, including representatives of teaching staff, research workers, students, and administrative and technical staff, as well as non-university members drawn from the public and private sectors; Conseil scientifique, competent in matters of research; Conseil des Etudes et de la Vie universitaire; and Conseil of each Unit, comprising representatives of its teaching staff, research workers, students, and administrative and technical staff. The President is elected by the first three bodies. The Chancelier, who represents the Minister of Education, is the Recteur of the Académie de Limoges

Academic Year: October to June

Admission Requirements: Secondary school certificate (baccalauréat) or equivalent or foreign equivalent, or special entrance examination

Main Language(s) of Instruction: French

International Co-operation: Participates in the Erasmus, Lingua, and Comett programmes

Degrees and Diplomas: *Capacité en Droit*: Law, 2 yrs; *Diplôme universitaire de Technologie*: Technology, 2 yrs; *Licence*: Law, Economics, Administration, Management, Modern Languages, Science and Technology, Health, 3 yrs; *Licence professionnelle*: Real Estate, Accountancy, Business Management; *Diplôme d'Etat*: Medicine; *Diplôme d'Etat*: Pharmacy, 6 yrs; *Diplôme d'Ingénieur*: 3 yrs; *Diplôme de Recherche technologique*: Ceramics and Glass Technology, Information Technology, Environmental Engineering; *Diplôme national de Master*: Biomedicine, Medicine, Neurosciences, Law, European Law, Economics, Finance, Environmental Studies, Regional Studies, Chemistry, Health, Life Sciences, Applied Languages, Cultural Studies, Science and Technology; *Doctorat*: Pharmacy, By thesis following Diplôme d'Etat; *Doctorat*: Science and Technology, Health, Humanities, Social Sciences, 2-4 yrs following Masters

Student Residential Facilities: Yes

Libraries: c. 181,810 vols

Press or Publishing House: Pulin

Last Updated: 13/07/11

UNIVERSITY OF LORRAINE
Université de Lorraine
34 cours Léopold, CS 25233, 54 052 Nancy
Tel: +33(3) 54-50-54-00
Fax: +33(3) 54-50-54-01
EMail: administrateur.provisoire@univ-lorraine.fr
Website: http://www.univ-lorraine.fr

Administrateur provisoire: Jean-Pierre Finance

Areas
Arts, Letters and Languages (Arts and Humanities; Cinema and Television; English; European Studies; Fine Arts; Geography; German; History; Linguistics; Literature; Mathematics and Computer Science; Music; Musicology; Philosophy; Spanish; Teacher Training; Theology); **Humanities and Social Sciences** (Arts and Humanities; Psychology; Regional Planning; Social Sciences; Sociology); **Law, Economics and Management** (Banking; Business Administration; Economics; Finance; Hotel Management; Insurance; Labour and Industrial Relations; Labour Law; Law; Management; Marketing; Political Sciences); **Science, Technology and Health** (Agronomy; Applied Chemistry; Applied Mathematics; Applied Physics; Aquaculture; Automation and Control Engineering; Biological and Life Sciences; Chemical Engineering; Civil Engineering; Computer Engineering; Computer Science; Dentistry; Earth Sciences; Ecology; Electrical Engineering; Electronic Engineering; Energy Engineering; Engineering; Food Science; Geology; Industrial Engineering; Materials Engineering; Mathematics and Computer Science; Mechanical Engineering; Medical Technology; Medicine; Mining Engineering; Optics; Pharmacy; Physical Chemistry; Physical Education; Sports; Technology; Telecommunications Engineering)

History: Founded 2012 following merger of Université Henri Poincaré, Université Nancy 2, Institut national polytechnique de Lorraine and Université Paul Verlaine-Metz

Main Language(s) of Instruction: French

Degrees and Diplomas: *Diplôme universitaire de Technologie*; *Licence*; *Licence professionnelle*; *Diplôme d'Ingénieur*; *Diplôme national de Master*; *Doctorat*

Libraries: Yes
Last Updated: 25/01/12

UNIVERSITY OF MAINE
Université du Maine
Avenue Olivier Messiaen, 72085 Le Mans, Cedex 9
Tel: +33(2) 43-83-30-00
Fax: +33(2) 43-83-30-77
EMail: ri@univ-lemans.fr
Website: http://www.univ-lemans.fr

Président: Yves Guillotin (2007-)
Tel: +33(2) 43-83-30-01, Fax: +33(2) 43-83-30-77
EMail: president@univ-lemans.fr; Yves.Guillotin@univ-lemans.fr

International Relations: Philippe Daniel
Tel: +33(2) 43-83-30-05 +33(2) 43-83-37-34,
Fax: +33(2) 43-83-35-30

Centres
Law and Economics *(CESDEML)* (Economics; Law) *Director*: Yves Brard; **Lifelong Education**

Faculties
Law *(Laval-Mayenne)* (Commercial Law; Law); **Law, Economics and Management** (Economics; Law; Management); **Letters, Languages and Humanities** (Arts and Humanities; English; French; Geography; German; History; Literature; Modern Languages; Spanish); **Science and Techniques** (Biology; Chemistry; Computer Science; Earth Sciences; Mathematics; Mechanical Engineering; Natural Sciences; Physical Education; Physics; Physiology; Sound Engineering (Acoustics); Sports; Technology)

Institutes
Technology *(IUT Le Mans)* (Business and Commerce; Chemistry; Mechanical Engineering; Public Administration; Technology); **Technology** *(IUT Laval)* (Biology; Biotechnology; Business and Commerce; Computer Engineering; Multimedia; Technology)

Schools
Engineering *(ENSIM)* (Computer Engineering; Engineering; Sound Engineering (Acoustics))

History: Founded 1969 as Centre Universitaire under the 1968 law reforming higher education and replacing Institutions attached to former Université de Caen. Acquired full University status 1976. The University is a State institution enjoying academic and financial autonomy, operating under the jurisdiction of the Minister of Education and financed by the State.

Governing Bodies: Conseil d'Administration, including representatives of teaching staff, research workers, students, and administrative and technical staff, as well as non-university members drawn from the public and private sectors; Conseil scientifique, competent in matters of research; Conseil des Etudes et de la Vie universitaire; Conseil of each Unit, comprising representatives of its teaching staff, research workers, students, and administrative and technical staff. The President is elected by the first three bodies. The Chancelier, who represents the Minister of Education, is the Recteur of the Académie of Nantes

Academic Year: October to June (October-December; January-April; May-June)

Admission Requirements: Baccalauréat or foreign equivalent, or ESAEU (Examen spécial d'accès aux études universitaires)

Main Language(s) of Instruction: French

International Co-operation: With universities in the United Kingdom; Germany; Spain; Lithuania; Poland; Czech Republic; Denmark

Degrees and Diplomas: *Capacité en Droit*: 2 yrs; *Diplôme universitaire de Technologie*: Economics, Administration, Science and Technology, 2 yrs; *Licence*: Law, Social Sciences, Arts and Humanities, Sports, Languages, Science and Technology, Administration, Economics, 3 yrs; *Licence professionnelle*: Law, Social Sciences, Arts and Humanities, Sports, Languages, Science and Technology, Administration, Economics, 1 yr following 2 yrs university studies; *Diplôme national de Master*: Law, Social Sciences, Arts and Humanities, Languages, Science and Technology, Management, Economics; *Doctorat*: Economics, Law, Arts and

Humanities, 2-4 yrs following Masters. Certificat and Diplômes d'Etudes françaises (for foreign students), Masters recherche, Masters professionnel

Student Services: Foreign student adviser, Handicapped facilities, Health services, Language programs, Social counselling, Sports facilities

Student Residential Facilities: Yes

Libraries: Bibliothèque interuniversitaire: Science, 70,000 vols
Last Updated: 18/07/11

🎓 UNIVERSITY OF NANTES
Université de Nantes
BP 13522, 1, quai de Tourville, 44035 Nantes, Cedex 01
Tel: +33(2) 40-99-83-83
Fax: +33(2) 40-99-83-00
EMail: international@univ-nantes.fr
Website: http://www.univ-nantes.fr

Président: Yves Lecointe (2007-)
Tel: +33(2) 40-99-83-20
EMail: president@univ-nantes.fr; Yves.Lecointe@univ-nantes.fr

Secrétaire général: Philippe Diaz
Tel: +33(2) 40-99-83-31 +33(2) 40-99-83-33
EMail: sg@univ-nantes.fr

International Relations: Françoise Le Jeune, Vice Présidente, Relations Internationales
Tel: +33(2) 40-99-83-24, Fax: +33(2) 40-99-84-22
EMail: vpri@univ-nantes.fr

Centres
Lifelong Education (Continuing Education)

Faculties
Dental Surgery (Dentistry; Surgery); **Law and Political Science** (Law; Political Sciences); **Psychology** (Psychology)

Graduate Schools
Chemistry Biology (Agronomy; Biology; Chemistry; Ecology); **Information and Material Engineering** *(STIM in cooperation with Ecole Centrale Nantes)* (Applied Mathematics; Information Technology); **Knowledge, Language, Culture** (Cognitive Sciences; Cultural Studies; Modern Languages); **Law, Social Sciences** (Law; Social Sciences)

Institutes
Economics and Management *(IAE)* (Accountancy; Banking; Business Administration; Economics; Finance; Insurance; Management); **French for Foreigners** *(IRRFLE)* (French; French Studies); **Geography and Regional Development** *(IGARUN)* (Geography; Regional Planning); **Juridical Studies** *(IEJ)* (Law); **Preparatory Administrative Studies** *(IPAG)* (Administration); **Teacher Training** *(IUFM)* (Teacher Trainers Education; Teacher Training); **Technology** *(IUT Nantes)* (Business Administration; Data Processing; Electrical Engineering; Energy Engineering; Materials Engineering; Mechanical Engineering; Public Administration; Technology; Thermal Engineering); **Technology** *(IUT, Saint-Nazaire)* (Business and Commerce; Chemical Engineering; Civil Engineering; Industrial Engineering; Sales Techniques; Technology); **Technology** *(IUT, La Roche-sur-Yon)* (Bioengineering; Business Administration; Information Technology; Mass Communication; Public Administration; Telecommunications Engineering)

Schools
Engineering *(Polytech' Nantes)* (Computer Engineering; Electrical Engineering; Electronic Engineering; Energy Engineering; Materials Engineering; Thermal Engineering)

Units
Foreign Languages *(International Language Centre (CIL))* (English; German; Italian; Modern Languages; Spanish); **History, History of Art and Archaeology** (Archaeology; Art History; History); **Languages** (Arabic; Chinese; English; German; Italian; Japanese; Modern Languages; Portuguese; Russian; Slavic Languages; Spanish); **Medicine** *(4 sites)* (Medicine; Speech Therapy and Audiology); **Pharmacy and Biology** (Biology; Pharmacy); **Physical Education and Sports** *(STAPS)* (Physical Education; Sports); **Science and Techniques** (Chemistry; Earth Sciences; Mathe-

matics and Computer Science; Natural Sciences; Physics); **Sociology** (Sociology)

History: Founded 1970 under the 1968 law reforming higher education and replacing former Université de Nantes, founded 1962, incorporating previously existing faculties, but tracing its history to the original Universities of Nantes, founded by Papal Bull in 1460, and of Angers, recognized and authorized by Charles V in 1364. A State institution enjoying academic and financial autonomy, operating under the jurisdiction of the Minister of Education and financed by the State.

Governing Bodies: Conseil de l'Université, including elected representatives of teaching staff, research workers, students, and administrative and technical staff, as well as non-university members drawn from the public and private sectors; Conseil of each Unit, comprising representatives of its teaching staff, research workers, students, and administrative and technical staff; and Conseil scientifique, competent in matters of research. The President is elected by the Conseil de l'Université. The Chancelier, who represents the Minister of Education, is the Recteur of the Académie de Nantes

Academic Year: October to June (October-February; February-June)

Admission Requirements: Secondary school certificate (baccalauréat) or equivalent, or special entrance examination

Fees: (Euros): 159.60 per annum

Main Language(s) of Instruction: French

International Co-operation: With universities in Spain, Germany, United Kingdom, Italy, Côte d'Ivoire, Senegal, South Korea, USA, Canada

Degrees and Diplomas: *Capacité en Droit*: Law, 2 yrs; *Diplôme universitaire de Technologie*: 2 yrs; *Licence*: Economics, Law, Management, Arts and Humanities, Science, Technology, Health, Mass Communication, Social Sciences, 3 yrs; *Licence professionnelle*: Economics, Law, Management, Arts and Humanities, Science, Technology, Health, Mass Communication, Social Sciences, 3 yrs; *Diplôme d'Etat*: Dental Surgery, 6 yrs; *Diplôme d'Etat*: Medicine, 6 yrs and a further 2 yrs hospital practice and thesis; *Diplôme d'Etat*: Pharmacy, 5 yrs and 1 yr practical work; *Diplôme d'Ingénieur*: Engineering, 3 yrs following 1st year or DUT; *Diplôme national de Master*: Economics, Law, Management, Arts and Humanities, Science, Technology, Health, Mass Communication, Social Sciences, 2 yrs following Licence; *Doctorat*: Law, Arts and Humanities, Pharmacy, Science, 2-4 yrs following Master; *Certificat de Spécialité*: Medicine, at least 2 yrs after Diplôme d'Etat. Masters recherche, Masters professionnel

Student Services: Academic counselling, Canteen, Cultural centre, Foreign student adviser, Handicapped facilities, Health services, Language programs, Social counselling, Sports facilities

Special Facilities: International Language Centre (CIL)

Libraries: University Library, c. 166,000 vols; specialized libraries
Last Updated: 13/07/11

UNIVERSITY OF NICE-SOPHIA ANTIPOLIS
Université de Nice-Sophia Antipolis (UNSA)
BP 2135, Grand Château, 28 avenue de Valrose, 06103 Nice, Cedex 02
Tel: +33(4) 92-07-60-60
Fax: +33(4) 92-07-66-00
EMail: com@unice.fr
Website: http://unice.fr

Président: Albert Marouani (2004-)
Tel: +33(4) 92-07-66-01 EMail: Albert.MAROUANI@unice.fr

Directeur général des Services (p.i.): Éric Djamakorzian
Tel: +33(4) 92-07-60-65, Fax: +33(4) 92-07-60-40

International Relations: Michel Cassac
Tel: +33(4) 92-07-61-28, Fax: +33(4) 92-07-66-11

Centres
Juridical Studies *(IEJ)* (Law); **Lifelong Education** *(ASURE)* (Continuing Education)

Faculties
Arts and Humanities (Arts and Humanities); **Dentistry** (Dentistry); **Geography and Culture** *(UFR Espaces et Cultures)* (Cultural Studies; Geography (Human)); **Law and Political Science**

(Development Studies; Economics; Law; Management; Peace and Disarmament; Political Sciences); **Medicine** (Medicine); **Physical Education and Sports** *(STAPS)* (Physical Education; Sports); **Sciences** (Natural Sciences)

Graduate Schools

Arts and Humanities (Arts and Humanities); **Basic and Applied Sciences** *(Applied Physics; Physics)*; **Economies and Organisations** *(ED MODEG)*; **Information Sciences** *(EDSTIC)* (Information Sciences); **Medicine** (Medicine); **National, European and International Relations** *(ED INEI)* (International Law); **Physical Therapy** *(Works in cooperation with Universities of Aix-Marseiles II, Montpellier I, Toulon and Avignon) Director:* Reinaud Bootsma

Higher Institutes

Economics and Management (Economics; Management)

Higher Schools

Computer Science *(PolyTech)* (Computer Engineering; Computer Science; Engineering; Software Engineering)

Institutes

Business Administration *(IAE)* (Business Administration); **Law and Development** *(IDPD)* (Development Studies; Law); **Teacher Training** *(IUFM with 4 sites throughout Nice)* (Teacher Trainers Education; Teacher Training); **Technology** *(IUT Nice with 4 sites: Nice, Menton, Cannes, Sophia-Antipolis)* (Business Administration; Business and Commerce; Business Computing; Data Processing; Electrical Engineering; Management; Technology; Telecommunications Engineering)

Programmes

Business Administration *(IUP)* (Business Administration; Econometrics); **Data Processing for Management** *(IUP MIAGE)* (Data Processing); **Tourism and Hotel Management** *(IUP Tourisme)* (Hotel Management; Tourism)

History: Founded 1971 under the 1968 law reforming higher education and replacing former Université de Nice, founded 1965. A State institution enjoying academic and financial autonomy, operating under the jurisdiction of the Minister of Education and financed by the State.

Governing Bodies: Conseils de l'Université, consisting of the Conseil d'administration, comprising 60 members, Conseil scientifique, comprising 40 members, and Conseil d'études et de la vie universitaire, comprising 40 members

Academic Year: October to June (October-February;February-June)

Admission Requirements: Secondary school certificate (baccalauréat) or equivalent, or special entrance examination

Main Language(s) of Instruction: French

International Co-operation: With OCA, INRIA, IRD and many foreign universities.

Degrees and Diplomas: *Capacité en Droit:* Law, 2 yrs; *Diplôme universitaire de Technologie:* 2 yrs; *Licence:* Law, Political Science, Economics, Management, Business Administration, Arts and Humanities, Social Sciences, Science, Technology, Health, Sports, 3 yrs; *Diplôme d'Etat:* Dental Surgery, 6 yrs; *Diplôme d'Etat:* Medicine, 6 yrs and 1 further yr hospital practice and thesis; *Diplôme d'Etat:* Pharmacy, 4 yrs and 1 yr practical work; *Diplôme d'Ingénieur; Diplôme national de Master:* Law, Political Science, Economics, Management, Business Administration, Arts and Humanities, Languages, Social Sciences, Science, Technology, Health, 2 yrs following Licence; *Doctorat:* Law, Science, 2-4 yrs following Masters; *Certificat de Spécialité:* Medicine, at least 2 yrs following Diplôme d'Etat de Docteur. Masters recherche, Masters professionnel

Student Services: Academic counselling, Canteen, Cultural centre, Foreign student adviser, Foreign Studies Centre, Handicapped facilities, Health services, Language programs, Social counselling, Sports facilities

Student Residential Facilities: Yes

Libraries: Central Library, c. 172,000 vols

Publications: Annales de la Faculté de Droit; Annales de la Faculté des Lettres; Revue d'Odonto-stomatologie tropicale; Specialized scientific reviews

Last Updated: 10/06/11

UNIVERSITY OF NÎMES

Université de Nîmes (UNÎMES)

Rue du Docteur Georges Salan, 30021 Nîmes, Cedex 01
Fax: 33(4) 66-36-45-87
EMail: contact@unimes.fr
Website: http://www.unimes.fr

Président: Jacques Marignan Tel: +33 (0)4.66.36.46.18

Laboratories

Geochemistry (GIS) (Geochemistry)

Units

Arts (Fine Arts; Textile Design); **Arts and Humanities** (Arts and Humanities; English; History; Literature; Spanish); **Law and Economy** (Criminal Law; Economics; Law; Private Law; Public Law); **Linguistics** (English; Linguistics; Literature; Spanish); **Psychology**; **Science**

Further Information: Also Carmes Site

History: Previously known as the University Centre for Study and Training, the University of Nimes was created in 2007. It becomes the first French University solely dedicated to professional training.

Main Language(s) of Instruction: French

Degrees and Diplomas: *Licence; Licence professionnelle; Diplôme national de Master*
Last Updated: 11/04/11

UNIVERSITY OF ORLÉANS

Université d'Orléans

BP 6749, Château de la Source, 45067 Orléans, Cedex 02
Tel: +33(2) 38-41-71-71
Fax: +33(2) 38-41-70-69
EMail: international@univ-orleans.fr
Website: http://www.univ-orleans.fr

Président: Youssoufi Touré
Tel: +33(2) 38-41-71-86 +33(2) 38-49-47-48,
Fax: +33(2) 38-41-70-69 EMail: president@univ-orleans.fr

Directeur général des Services: André Pillot
Tel: +33(2) 38-41-71-96, Fax: +33(2) 38-49-47-91
EMail: secretaire.general@univ-orleans.fr

Faculties

Law, Economics and Management (Business Administration; Economics; Law; Management) *Division Head:* Onne; **Letters, Humanities, and Languages** (Arts and Humanities; English; Geography; History; Modern Languages; Spanish); **Physical Education and Sports** *(STAPS)* (Physical Education; Sports); **Science** (Biochemistry; Biology; Chemistry; Computer Science; Earth Sciences; Environmental Studies; Mathematics; Natural Sciences; Physics)

Graduate Schools

Science and Technology (Chemistry; Information Sciences; Mathematics; Physics) *Director:* Luc Morin-Allory; **Social Sciences** *Director:* Jean-Paul Pollin

Institutes

Teacher Training *(IUFM Orléans, Blois, Chartres, Tours, Bourges, Châteauroux)* (Teacher Trainers Education; Teacher Training); **Technology** *(IUT Indre)* (Business Administration; Chemistry; Computer Science; Mechanical Engineering; Production Engineering; Technology); **Technology** *(IUT, Bourges)* (Business Administration; Civil Engineering; Mechanical Engineering; Production Engineering; Technology); **Technology** *(IUT, Châteauroux)* (Business Administration; Computer Engineering; Electrical Engineering; Management; Technology); **Technology** *(IUT, Chartres)* (Business Computing; Electrical Engineering; Maintenance Technology; Technology; Transport Engineering)

Schools

Engineering *(ENSI de Bourges) Director:* Joël Allain; **Engineering** *(Polytech' Orléans)* (Civil Engineering; Electronic Engineering; Energy Engineering; Environmental Engineering; Mechanical Engineering; Optics; Production Engineering)

Further Information: University Centres: Bourges, Châteauroux

History: Founded 1970 under the 1968 law reforming higher education as one of two Universities replacing the Université d'Orléans-Tours, re-established 1962, but tracing its history to the original Université d'Orléans, 1306-1793. A State Institution enjoying academic and financial autonomy, operating under the jurisdiction of the Minister of Education and financed by the State.

Governing Bodies: Conseil de l'Université, including elected representatives of teaching staff, research workers, students, and administrative and technical staff, as well as non-university members drawn from the public and private sectors; Conseil of each Unit, comprising representatives of its teaching staff, research workers, students, and administrative and technical staff; Conseil scientifique, competent in matters of research. The President is elected by the Conseil de l'Université. The Chancelier, who represents the Minister of Education, is the Recteur of the Académie d'Orléans

Academic Year: October-June (October-December; January-March; April-June)

Admission Requirements: Secondary school certificate (baccalauréat) or equivalent, or special entrance examination

Main Language(s) of Instruction: French

Degrees and Diplomas: *Diplôme universitaire de Technologie*; *Licence*: Law, Economics, Administration, Arts and Humanities, Sports, Earth Sciences, Health, Social Sciences, Science, 3 yrs; *Licence professionnelle*: Law, Economics, Administration, Arts and Humanities, Sports, Earth Sciences, Health, Social Sciences, Science; *Diplôme d'Ingénieur*; *Diplôme national de Master*: Law, Modern Languages, Economics, Administration, Arts and Humanities, Sports, Earth Sciences, Health, Social Sciences, Science, 2 yrs following Licence; *Doctorat*: Law, Modern Languages, Economics, Administration, Arts and Humanities, Sports, Social Sciences, Science, 2-4 yrs following Masters. Preparation for Agrégation exam

Student Residential Facilities: Yes

Libraries: Central Library, c. 60,000 vols; specialized libraries

Publications: Revue 'Symbioses' Biologie *(quarterly)*
Last Updated: 11/07/11

UNIVERSITY OF PAU AND THE ADOUR REGION

Université de Pau et des Pays de l'Adour (UPPA)
BP 576, avenue de l'Université, 64012 Pau, Cedex
Tel: +33(5) 59-40-70-00
Fax: +33(5) 59-40-70-01
EMail: communication@univ-pau.fr
Website: http://www.univ-pau.fr

President: Jean-Louis Gout
Tel: +33(5) 59-40-70-20/21 EMail: president@univ-pau.fr

Departments
Lifelong Education *(FORCO)*

Faculties
Scientific Research *(University Centre)*

Graduate Schools
Applied Sciences (Applied Chemistry; Applied Physics; Biology);
Social Sciences (Arts and Humanities)

Institutes
Building Technologies *(ISA-BTP)* (Building Technologies); **Business Administration** *(IAE)* (Business Administration); **Industrial Systems Engineering** *(IUT Pays de l'Ardour, Pau site)*; **Teacher Training** *(IUFM has five sites located throughout the Aquitaine Province)* (Teacher Trainers Education; Teacher Training); **Technology** *(IUT Pays de l'Ardour, Mont de Marsan site)* (Biology; Computer Science; Statistics; Technology; Telecommunications Engineering); **Technology** *(IUT, Bayonne)* (Business Administration; Computer Science; Marketing; Technology)

Schools
Industrial Technology Engineering *(ENSGTI)* (Industrial Engineering)

Units
Law, Economics and Management *(Pau)* (Economics; International Business; Law; Management; Marketing); **Letters, Languages and Humanities** *(Pau, Tarbes)* (Arts and Humanities; Modern Languages); **Multidisciplinary** *(Bayonne)* (Accountancy;

Economics; International Law; Law; Modern Languages); **Science and Technology** *(Pau)* (Mathematics and Computer Science; Natural Sciences); **Science and Technology** *(Anglet)* (Biology; Chemistry; Civil Engineering; Computer Science; Physics)

Further Information: The University is spread across five sites: Pau (central institution), Bayonne, Anglet, Tarbes and Mont-de-Marsan

History: Founded 1970, The Université de Pau et des Pays de l'Ardour is a network of 4 campuses (Pau, Bayonne/Anglet, Mont de Marsan and Tarbes). It is supported by the state and regional authorities.

Governing Bodies: Conseil de l'Université, including elected representatives of teaching staff, research workers, students, and administrative and technical staff, as well non-university members drawn from the public and private sectors; Conseil of each Unit, comprising representatives of its teaching staff, research workers, students, and administrative and technical staff; and Conseil scientifique, competent in matters of research. The President is elected by the Conseil de l'Université. The Chancelier, who represents the Minister of Education, is the Recteur of the Académie de Bordeaux

Academic Year: October to June

Admission Requirements: Secondary school certificate (baccalauréat) or equivalent, or special entrance examination

Fees: (Euros): Licence, 128 per annum; Master, 191; Doctorat, 310

Main Language(s) of Instruction: French

International Co-operation: Participates in the Santander Group and Crepuq (Canada) network

Accrediting Agencies: Ministry of National Education

Degrees and Diplomas: *Diplôme universitaire de Technologie*: 2 yrs; *Licence*: 3 yrs; *Diplôme national de Master*: a further 2 yrs; *Doctorat*: a further 3 yrs

Student Services: Canteen, Cultural centre, Foreign student adviser, Foreign Studies Centre, Handicapped facilities, Health services, Language programs, Social counselling, Sports facilities

Student Residential Facilities: 11 residences managed by the CLOUS (Centre Local University Works)

Libraries: University library

Press or Publishing House: Presses Universitaires de Pau et des Pays de l'Adour (PUPPA)
Last Updated: 16/06/11

UNIVERSITY OF PERPIGNAN VIA DOMITIA

Université de Perpignan Via Domitia
52, avenue Paul Alduy, 66860 Perpignan, Cedex
Tel: +33(4) 68-66-20-00
Fax: +33(4) 68-66-20-19
EMail: sec-dir@univ-perp.fr
Website: http://www.univ-perp.fr

Président: Jean Benkhelil (2007-)
Tel: +33(4) 68-66-20-02 +33(4) 68-66-21-67
EMail: president@univ-perp.fr; benkhelil@univ-perp.fr

Secrétaire général: Paul Taverner
Tel: +33(4) 68-66-20-03 EMail: sec-gen@univ-perp.fr

International Relations: Patrick Bellegarde
Tel: +33(4) 68-66-17-22 +33(4) 68-66-17-38,
Fax: +33(4) 68-66-17-49 EMail: bellegarde@univ-perp.fr

Centres
Lifelong Education *(CREUFOP)*

Faculties
Arts and Humanities *(LSH)* (Archaeology; Art History; Arts and Humanities; Catalan; Classical Languages; English; Geography; History; Literature; Modern Languages; Sociology; Spanish); **Exact and Experimental Sciences** *(SEE)* (Applied Mathematics; Biological and Life Sciences; Earth Sciences; Geology; Heating and Refrigeration; Marine Science and Oceanography; Mathematics; Mathematics and Computer Science; Physical Engineering; Physics; Social Sciences); **Law and Economics** *(SJE)* (Economics; Law); **Legal Systems in Francophone African Countries** *(FIDAF)* (Law); **Sports, International Hotel Management and Tourism** *(STHI)* (Hotel Management; International Business; Sports; Tourism; Transport and Communications)

Graduate Schools
Energy and Environment

Institutes
Business Administration *(IAE)* (Business Administration; Management); **Franco-Catalan Studies** *(Trans Frontier Institute IFCT)* (Catalan; French); **Preparatory Administrative Studies** (Administration); **Technology** *(IUT Perpignan with 2 other sites at Carcassone and Narbonne)* (Administrative Law; Biotechnology; Business Administration; Data Processing; Industrial Maintenance; Technology; Transport Engineering); **Urban and Real Estate Law** (Law; Real Estate)

History: Founded 1970 as Centre Universitaire de Perpignan under the 1968 law reforming higher education and incorporating institutions previously attached to the former Université de Montpellier. Acquired present status and title 1979. A State Institution enjoying academic and financial autonomy, operating under the jurisdiction of the Minister of Education and financed by the State.

Governing Bodies: Conseil de l'Université, including elected representatives of teaching staff, research workers, students, and administrative and technical staff, as well as non-university members drawn from the public and private sectors; Conseil of each Unit, comprising representatives of its teaching staff, research workers, students and administrative and technical staff; and Conseil scientifique, competent in matters of research. The President is elected by the Conseil de l'Université. The Chancelier, who represents the Minister of Education, is the Recteur of the Académie de Montpellier

Academic Year: October to June

Admission Requirements: Secondary school certificate (baccalauréat) or foreign equivalent, or special entrance examination

Main Language(s) of Instruction: French

Degrees and Diplomas: *Diplôme universitaire de Technologie*: 2 yrs; *Licence*: Science, Technology, Health, Social Sciences, Law, Economics, Business Administration, 3 yrs; *Licence professionnelle*; *Diplôme national de Master*: Science, Technology, Health, Social Sciences, Law, Economics, Management, 2 yrs following Licence; *Doctorat*: Energy Engineering, Environmental Sciences, 2-4 yrs following Master 2 recherche. Also Master 2 recherche 1 yr following Master 1; Master 2 professionnel 1 yr following Master 1

Libraries: Central Library; Law library; Science library
Last Updated: 13/07/11

UNIVERSITY OF PICARDIE JULES VERNE (AMIENS)

Université de Picardie Jules Verne (Amiens) (UPJV)
Chemin du Thil, Campus, 80025 Amiens, Cedex 01
Tel: +33(3) 22-82-72-72
Fax: +33(3) 22-82-75-00
EMail: katarina.kilani@u-picardie.fr
Website: http://www.u-picardie.fr

Président: Georges Fauré (2006-)
Tel: +33 (3)22-82-72-63 EMail: georges.faure@u-picardie.fr

Directeur général des Services: Laurent Anne
Tel: +33(3) 22-82-72-65 EMail: laurent.anne@u-picardie.fr

International Relations: Katarina Kilani
Tel: +33(3) 22-82-72-45, Fax: +33(3) 22-82-72-47

Faculties
Arts (Art History; Fine Arts; Performing Arts); **Economics and Management** *(Pôle Université Cathédrale)* (Economics; Management); **Foreign Languages and Cultures** *(Pôle Campus)* (Communication Studies; Dutch; English; German; Italian; Russian; Spanish); **History and Geography** *(Pôle Campus)* (Geography; History); **Law and Political Sciences** *(Pôle Université Cathédrale)* (Law; Political Sciences); **Letters** *(Pôle Campus)* (Arts and Humanities; Communication Studies; Library Science; Literature; Media Studies); **Medicine** *(Pôle Santé)* (Medicine) *Division Head*: Némitz; **Pharmacy** *(Pôle Santé)* (Pharmacy); **Philosophy, Human and Social Sciences** *(Pôle Campus)* (Arts and Humanities; Educational Sciences; Philosophy; Psychology; Social Sciences; Sociology); **Science** *(Pôle Science)* (Automation and Control Engineering; Biological and Life Sciences; Biology; Chemistry; Computer Science; Earth Sciences; Electronic Engineering; Mathematics; Physics); **Sport Sciences** *(Pôle Campus)* (Sports)

Graduate Schools
Health Sciences (Neurosciences); **Social Sciences** (Social Sciences)

Institutes
Business Administration *(IAE de Picardie)* (Accountancy; Business Administration); **Preparatory Administration Studies** *(IPAG)* (Administration); **Science and Technology** *(INSSET, Saint Quentin)* (Education; Engineering; Management; Software Engineering; Technology); **Teacher Training** *(IUFM: Training is also provided at INSSET and the Technology University of Compiegne)* (Teacher Trainers Education; Teacher Training); **Technology** *(IUT, Amiens)* (Bioengineering; Business Administration; Civil Engineering; Computer Science; Mechanical Engineering; Sales Techniques; Technology); **Technology** *(IUT, Site de Creil)* (Technology); **Technology** *(IUT, Site de Saint-Quentin)* (Technology); **Technology** *(IUT, Aisne)* (Technology)

History: Founded 1970 under the 1968 law reforming higher education as one of the new Universities and replacing former Université d'Amiens founded 1964 as Centre Universitaire de Picardie and incorporating previously existing Institutions of higher education. A State institution enjoying academic and financial autonomy, operating under the jurisdiction of the Minister of Education and financed by the State.

Governing Bodies: Conseil de l'Université, including elected representatives of teaching staff, research workers, students, and administrative and technical staff, as well as non-university members drawn from the public and private sectors; Conseil scientifique, competent in matters of research; Conseil des Etudes et de la Vie universitaire; Conseil of each Unit, comprising representatives of its teaching staff, research workers, students and administrative and technical staff. The President is elected by the first three bodies. The Chancelier, who represents the Minister of Education, is the Recteur of the Académie d'Amiens

Academic Year: October to June (October-February; February-June)

Admission Requirements: Secondary school certificate (baccalauréat) or equivalent

Main Language(s) of Instruction: French

Degrees and Diplomas: *Capacité en Droit*: 2 yrs; *Diplôme universitaire de Technologie*: 2 yrs; *Licence*: 3 yrs; *Licence professionnelle*; *Diplôme d'Etat*: Dental Surgery, 5 yrs; *Diplôme d'Etat*: Medicine, 6 yrs plus 1 yr hospital practice and thesis; *Diplôme d'Etat*: Pharmacy, 4 yrs and 1 yr practical work; *Diplôme national de Master*; *Doctorat*: 2-4 yrs following Masters; *Certificat de Spécialité*: Medicine, at least 2 yrs after Diplome d'Etat. Masters recherche, Masters professionnel

Student Residential Facilities: Yes

Libraries: Central Library; faculty libraries

Publications: Bouillon de Culture *(monthly)*; Bulletin de l'Ecole doctorale en sciences humaines et sociales
Last Updated: 15/07/11

UNIVERSITY OF POITIERS

Université de Poitiers
15, rue de l'Hôtel-Dieu, 86034 Poitiers, Cedex
Tel: +33(5) 49-45-30-00
Fax: +33(5) 49-45-30-50
EMail: communication@univ-poitiers.fr.
Website: http://www.univ-poitiers.fr

Président: Jean-Pierre Gesson (2003-)
Tel: +33(5) 49-45-30-33 EMail: president@univ-poitiers.fr

Directeur général des Services: Bernard Contal
Tel: +33(5) 49-45-30-40 EMail: sg@univ-poitiers.fr

International Relations: Hervé Sabourin
Tel: +33(1) 49-45-42-64 +33(1) 49-36-62-71,
Fax: +33(1) 49-45-30-39
EMail: ri@univ-poitiers.fr; herve.sabourin@univ-poitiers.fr

Centres
French as a Foreign Language *(CFLE)* (Foreign Languages Education; French) *Director*: Patricia Bouhier; **Training for Music Teachers** *(CFMI)* (Music Education) *Director*: Christophe Vuillemin

Faculties
Sports *(STAPS)* (Physical Education; Sports)

Graduate Schools
Doctoral Studies (Aeronautical and Aerospace Engineering; Arts and Humanities; Bioengineering; Chemical Engineering; Geological Engineering; Law)

Institutes
Business Administration *(IAE)* (Business Administration); **Industrial, Insurance and Financial Risks Studies** *(IRIAF)* (Finance; Insurance); **Preparatory Administrative Studies** *(IPAG)* (Administration); **Teacher Training** *(IUFM with sites in Angoulême, La Rochelle, Niort)* (Teacher Trainers Education; Teacher Training) *Director*: Daniele Houpert; **Technology** *(IUT Poitiers)* (Business Administration; Chemistry; Computer Engineering; Data Processing; Electrical Engineering; Energy Engineering; Mechanical Engineering; Production Engineering; Sanitary Engineering; Technology; Telecommunications Engineering); **Technology** *(IUT, Angoulême)* (Business and Commerce; Computer Engineering; Electrical Engineering; Management; Mechanical Engineering; Production Engineering; Technology)

Schools
Engineering *(ESIP)* (Automation and Control Engineering; Chemistry; Civil Engineering; Electrical Engineering; Engineering; Environmental Engineering; Materials Engineering; Sound Engineering (Acoustics); Water Management); **Mechanical and Aeronautical Engineering** *(ENSMA)* (Aeronautical and Aerospace Engineering; Mechanical Engineering) *Director*: Jean Brillaud

Units
Basic and Applied Sciences *(SFA)* (Applied Chemistry; Applied Mathematics; Applied Physics; Biological and Life Sciences; Chemistry; Computer Science; Mathematics; Natural Sciences) *Director*: Gilles Raby; **Economics** (Economics); **Humanities and Arts** (Arts and Humanities; Classical Languages; Cognitive Sciences; Geography; History; Medieval Studies; Music; Philosophy; Psychology; Sociology); **Languages and Literature** (Cinema and Television; Classical Languages; Latin American Studies; Linguistics; Literature; Medieval Studies; Modern Languages; Theatre); **Law and Social Sciences** (Criminal Law; Law; Private Law; Public Law; Social Sciences); **Medicine and Pharmacy** (Health Sciences; Medicine; Pharmacy)

History: Founded 1970 under the 1968 law reforming higher education and replacing the former Université de Poitiers, founded 1431 by Bull of Pope Eugene IV, and confirmed by letters patent granted by Charles VII, 1432. The University was suppressed by the Revolution and replaced by Faculties of Law; Letters; and Science and a School of Medicine of the Université de France. Reconstituted as University 1896. A State institution enjoying academic and financial autonomy, operating under the jurisdiction of the Ministry of Education and financed by the State.

Governing Bodies: Conseil d'Administration, including representatives of teaching staff, research workers, students, and administrative and technical staff, as well as non-university members drawn from the public and private sectors; Conseil scientifique, competent in matters of research; Conseil des Etudes et de la Vie universitaire; and Conseil of Unit, comprising representatives of its teaching staff, research workers, students, and administrative and technical staff. The President is elected by the first three bodies. The Chancelier, who represents the Minister of Education, is the Recteur of the Académie de Poitiers

Academic Year: October to June (October-February; February-June)

Admission Requirements: Secondary school certificate (baccalauréat) or foreign equivalent, or special entrance examination

Main Language(s) of Instruction: French

International Co-operation: Participates in the Erasmus and Lingua Programmes (28 exchange programmes), and in the Coimbra Group with 23 European universities

Degrees and Diplomas: *Capacité en Droit*: Law, 2 yrs; *Diplôme d' Accès aux Etudes universitaires (DAEU)*; *Diplôme universitaire de Technologie*: Science and Technology, Economics, Administration (DUT), 2 yrs; *Licence*: Law, Economics, Administration, Science and Technology, Arts and Humanities, Literature, Modern Languages, Sports and Health, 3 yrs; *Licence professionnelle*: Science and Technology, Economics, Administration, Sports; *Diplôme d'Etat*: Medicine, 6 yrs and 1 yr hospital practice and thesis; *Diplôme d'Etat*: Pharmacy, 4 yrs and 1 yr practical work; *Diplôme d'Ingénieur*: Industrial Techniques and Management Systems, 3 yrs following 1st yr; *Diplôme national de Master*: Law, Economics, Administration, Science and Technology, Arts and Humanities, Literature, Modern Languages, Sports and Health; *Doctorat*; *Certificat de Spécialité*: Medicine, at least 2 yrs after Diplôme d'Etat. Masters recherche, Masters professionnel

Student Services: Canteen, Cultural centre, Foreign student adviser, Health services, Language programs, Social counselling, Sports facilities

Student Residential Facilities: Yes

Libraries: Total, 500,000 vols
Last Updated: 15/07/11

UNIVERSITY OF REIMS CHAMPAGNE-ARDENNE
Université de Reims Champagne-Ardenne (URCA)
Villa Douce, 9, boulevard de la Paix, 51097 Reims, Cedex
Tel: +33(3) 26-91-30-00
Fax: +33(3) 26-91-30-98
EMail: presidence@univ-reims.fr
Website: http://www.univ-reims.fr

Président: Richard Vistelle (2007-)
Tel: +33(3) 26-91-39-55, Fax: +33(3) 26-91-30-98
EMail: richard.vistelle@univ-reims.fr

Directrice générale des Services: Isabelle Terrail
Tel: +33(3) 26-91-39-55, Fax: +33(3) 26-91-30-98
EMail: isabelle.terrail@univ-reims.fr

International Relations: Laure Castin
Tel: +33(3) 26-91-39-39, Fax: +33(3) 26-91-30-63
EMail: sri@univ-reims.fr; laure.castin@univ-reims.fr

Centres
French Studies *(International)*; **Distance Education**; **Lifelong Education** (Continuing Education)

Graduate Schools
Human Sciences and Societies; **Science, Technology and Health** (Biology; Health Sciences; Medicine)

Institutes
Juridical Studies *(IEJ)* (Law); **Preparatory Administrative Studies** *(IPAG)*; **Rural Planning, Environmental Studies and Town Planning** *(IATEUR)* (Environmental Studies; Rural Planning; Town Planning); **Teacher Training** *(IUFM Champagne Ardenne with 5 sites throughout region)* (Teacher Trainers Education; Teacher Training) *Director*: Gilles Baillat; **Technical Training** *(IFTS, Charleville-Mézières)* (Materials Engineering; Metallurgical Engineering; Polymer and Plastics Technology; Technology Education); **Technology** *(IUT Reims with sites: Châlonsand Charleville)* (Business Administration; Business and Commerce; Civil Engineering; Data Processing; Mechanical Engineering; Physics; Technology; Transport Management) *Director*: Yves Delmas; **Technology** *(IUT, Troyes)* (Business Administration; Business and Commerce; Computer Engineering; Electrical Engineering; Mechanical Engineering; Production Engineering; Technology)

Research Centres
Decentralization *(C.R.D.T.)* *Director*: Jean-Claude Némery

Schools
Engineering *(ESIReims)* (Energy Engineering; Packaging Technology; Thermal Engineering)

Units
Physical Education and Sports Science and Techniques *(STAPS)* (Physical Education; Sports); **Arts and Humanities** (Arts and Humanities; English; Geography; German; History; Literature; Musicology; Philosophy; Psychology; Romance Languages); **Dentistry** (Dentistry); **Economics, Social Sciences and Management** (Economics; Management; Social Work); **Exact and Natural Sciences** (Automation and Control Engineering; Biochemistry; Biology; Chemistry; Civil Engineering; Earth Sciences; Electronic Engineering; Energy Engineering; Environmental Studies; Mathematics and Computer Science; Mechanical Engineering; Natural Sciences;

Physics; Thermal Engineering); **Law and Political Science** (Law; Political Sciences; Public Administration); **Medicine** (Medicine); **Pharmacy** (Pharmacy)

History: Founded 1970 under the 1968 law reforming higher education and replacing the former Université de Reims, founded 1967, which incorporated previously existing Faculties and re-established the original University created by Papal Bull in 1548 and suppressed by the Revolution. A State Institution enjoying academic and financial autonomy operating under the jurisdiction of the Minister of Education and financed by the State.

Governing Bodies: Conseil d'Administration, including representatives of teaching staff, research workers, students, and administrative and technical staff, as well as non-university members drawn from the public and private sectors; Conseil scientifique, competent in matters of research; Conseil des Etudes et de la Vieuniversitaire; and the Conseil of each Unit, comprising representatives of its teaching staff, research workers, students, and administrative and technical staff. The President is elected by the first three bodies. The Chancelier, who represents the Minister of Education, is the Recteur of the Académie de Reims

Academic Year: September to June (September-December; January-March; April-June)

Admission Requirements: Secondary school certificate (baccalauréat) or equivalent, or special entrance examination

Main Language(s) of Instruction: French

Degrees and Diplomas: *Diplôme universitaire de Technologie*: Economics, Management; Science and Technology (DUT), 2 yrs; *Licence*: Law and Economics, Languages, Letters, Management, Political Science, Social Sciences, Sports, Science and Technology, 3 yrs; *Licence professionnelle*: Economics and Management, Science and Technology, 1 yr following 2 initial yrs; *Diplôme d'Etat*: Dental Surgery, 5 yrs; *Diplôme d'Etat*: Medicine, 6 yrs and 1 yr hospital practice and thesis; *Diplôme d'Etat*: Oenology, 2 yrs; *Diplôme d'Etat*: Pharmacy, 4 yrs and 1 yr practical work; *Diplôme d'Ingénieur*; *Diplôme national de Master*: Law and Economics, Languages, Letters, Management, Political Science, Social Sciences, Sports, Science and Technology, 2 yrs following Licence; *Doctorat*: Pharmacy, by thesis following Diplôme d'Etat; *Doctorat*: Science, Law, Economics, Letters, 2-4 yrs following Masters; *Certificat de Spécialité*: Medicine, at least 2 yrs following Diplôme d'Etat. Masters recherche, Masters professionnel, Preparation for Teaching exams

Student Residential Facilities: Yes

Libraries: Service de Documentation et Bibliothèque de l'Université, c. 240,000 vols

Press or Publishing House: Presses Universitaires de Reims
Last Updated: 26/07/11

UNIVERSITY OF ROUEN
Université de Rouen
1, rue Thomas Becket, 76821 Mont-Saint-Aignan, Cedex
Tel: +33(2) 35-14-60-00
Fax: +33(2) 35-14-63-48
EMail: communication@univ-rouen.fr
Website: http://www.univ-rouen.fr

Président: Cafer Ozkul (2007-)
Tel: +33(2) 35-14-63-32, Fax: +33(2) 35-14-63-33
EMail: presidence@univ-rouen.fr

Directeur général des Services: Frédéric Forest
Tel: +33(2) 35-14-60-90/91, Fax: +33(2) 35-14-63-48
EMail: dgs@univ-rouen.fr

International Relations: Sylvain Lamourette
Tel: +33(2) 35-14-61-34 +33(2) 35-14-63-40,
Fax: +33(2) 35-14-61-36
EMail: service.international@univ-rouen.fr

Centres
Lifelong Education *(CFC)*

Faculties
Law, Economics and Management (Economics; Law; Management); **Physical Education and Sports** *(STAPS)* (Physical Education; Sports)

Graduate Schools
Biology, Health and Environment (Biology; Environmental Studies; Health Sciences); **Chemistry** *(Normandy)* (Chemistry); **Knowledge, Critique, and Expertise** (Arts and Humanities); **Law** *(Normandy)* (Law)

Institutes
Business Administration *(IAE)* (Business Administration) *Director*: Gérald Orange; **Juridical Studies** *(IEJ)* (Administrative Law; Law) *Division Head*: Christian Pigache; **Preparatory Administrative Studies** *(IPAG)* (Administration) *Director*: Philippe Lagrange; **Teacher Training** *(Haute Normandie)* (Teacher Training); **Technology** *(IUT Rouen with sites at Elbeuf, Mont St. Aignan and Pasteur)* (Business and Commerce; Chemistry; Computer Networks; Electrical Engineering; Energy Engineering; Law; Measurement and Precision Engineering; Physical Engineering; Technology; Telecommunications Engineering; Telecommunications Services); **Technology** *(IUT, Evreux)* (Biology; Business Administration; Business and Commerce; Measurement and Precision Engineering; Packaging Technology; Sales Techniques; Technology)

Units
Human and Social Sciences (Education; Psychology; Sociology); **Letters and Humanities** (Arts and Humanities; English; Geography; German; History; Literature; Musicology; Philosophy; Spanish); **Medicine and Pharmacy** (Medicine; Pharmacy) *Dean*: Christian Thuillez; **Science and Technology** (Biology; Chemistry; Communication Studies; Computer Science; Geology; Mathematics; Natural Sciences; Physics; Technology)

History: Founded 1970 under the 1968 law reforming higher education and replacing the former Université de Rouen, founded 1966 and incorporating previously existing facilities. A State institution enjoying academic and financial autonomy, operating under the jurisdiction of the Minister of Education and financed by the State.

Governing Bodies: Conseil de l'Université, comprising 80 members, including elected representatives of teaching staff, research workers, students, and administrative and technical staff, as well as non-university members drawn from the public and private sectors; Conseil of each Unit, comprising representatives of its teaching staff, research workers, students, and administrative and technical staff; and Conseil scientifique, comprising 40 members, competent in matters of research. The President is elected by the Conseil de l'Université. The Chancelier, who represents the Minister of Education, is the Recteur of the Académie de Rouen

Academic Year: October to June (October-February; February-June)

Admission Requirements: Secondary school certificate (baccalauréat) or equivalent, or special entrance examination

Main Language(s) of Instruction: French

International Co-operation: Participates in Erasmus, Leonardo, Tempus, Crepuq programmes

Degrees and Diplomas: *Capacité en Droit*: Law, 2 yrs; *Diplôme universitaire de Technologie*: 2 yrs; *Licence*: Arts and Humanities; Modern Languages and Literatures; Cultural Studies; Musicology; Philosophy; History; Geography; German; French (Foreign Language and Native Language Education); Economics Management; Economics; Accountancy; Finance; Education; Psychology; Sociology; Sports; Sports Management; Law; Public Administration; Mathematics; Computer Science; Mechanics; Physics; Electronics; Electronic Engineering; Automation and Control Engineering; Biological and Life Sciences; Chemistry, 3 yrs; *Licence professionnelle*: Law, Science and Technology, Business Management, Commerce; *Diplôme d'Etat*: Dental Surgery, 5 yrs; *Diplôme d'Etat*: Medicine, 6 yrs plus 1 yr hospital practice and thesis; *Diplôme d'Etat*: Pharmacy, 4 yrs and 1 yr practical work; *Diplôme national de Master*: Arts and Humanities; Modern Languages and Literatures; Cultural Studies; Musicology; Philosophy; History; Geography; German; French (Foreign Language and Native Language Education); Education; Psychology; Sociology; Sports; Sports Management; Mathematics; Computer Science; Mechanics; Physics; Electronics; Electronic Engineering; Automation and Control Engineering; Biological and Life Sciences; Chemistry, 2 yrs following Licence; *Doctorat*: Pharmacy, by thesis following Diplôme d'Etat; *Doctorat*: Science, Economics, 2-4 yrs following Masters

Student Services: Foreign student adviser, Health services, Sports facilities

Student Residential Facilities: Yes

Libraries: c. 141,000 vols; 16,000 microfiches

Last Updated: 18/07/11

UNIVERSITY OF SOUTHERN BRITTANY

Université de Bretagne Sud

BP 92116, Rue Armand Guillemot, 56321 Lorient, Cedex

Tel: +33(2) 97-87-66-66

Fax: +33(2) 97-87-66-00

EMail: arlette.eveno@univ-ubs.fr

Website: http://www.univ-ubs.fr

Président: Olivier Sire (2010-) EMail: president@univ-ubs.fr

Secrétaire général: Christian Bily
Tel: +33(2) 97-68-16-45 +33(2) 97-01-70-89,
Fax: +33(2) 97-68-31-96 +33(2) 97-01-70-98
EMail: christian.bily@univ-ubs.fr

International Relations: Jean Peeters
Tel: +33(2) 97-87-11-24 +33(2) 97-87-11-27,
Fax: +33(2) 97-87-11-29
EMail: Jean.Peeters@univ-ubs.fr; sai@univ-ubs.fr

Faculties

Law, Economics and Management (Economics; Law; Management); **Letters, Languages, Humanities and Social Sciences** (Arts and Humanities; Documentation Techniques; English; Heritage Preservation; History; Literature; Publishing and Book Trade; Social Sciences; Social Work; Spanish); **Science and Engineering** (Biology; Biotechnology; Chemistry; Civil Engineering; Computer Science; Cosmetology; Electronic Engineering; Energy Engineering; Engineering; Environmental Studies; Health Sciences; Mathematics; Mechanical Engineering; Natural Sciences; Physics; Polymer and Plastics Technology; Statistics)

Graduate Schools

Doctoral School *Director:* Nathalie Bourgougnon

Institutes

Technology *(IUT Lorient with antenna at Pontivy)* (Energy Engineering; Industrial Maintenance; Management; Safety Engineering; Technology); **Technology** *(IUT, Vannes)* (Business Administration; Business and Commerce; Data Processing; Statistics; Technology)

Schools

Engineering *(ENSIBS)* (Computer Engineering; Electrical Engineering; Engineering; Industrial Engineering; Mechanical Engineering)

Further Information: Also branches in Vannes and Pontivy

History: Founded 1995.

Academic Year: October to June (October-February; February-June)

Admission Requirements: Secondary school certificate (baccalauréat) or equivalent, or special entrance examination

Main Language(s) of Instruction: French

Degrees and Diplomas: *Diplôme universitaire de Technologie; Licence:* 3 yrs; *Licence professionnelle; Diplôme national de Master.* 2 yrs following Licence; *Doctorat.* Masters recherche, Masters professionnel, Preparation for CAPES, Agrégation exams

Last Updated: 12/07/11

UNIVERSITY OF STRASBOURG

Université de Strasbourg

4, rue Blaise Pascal, 90032 Strasbourg, Cedex

Tel: +33(3) 68-85-00-00

EMail: president@unistra.fr

Website: http://www.unistra.fr

Président: Alain Beretz

Directeur général des Services: Frédéric Dehan

International Relations: Roya Naddaf

Centres

Intellectual Proprerty *(International)*; **Journalism** (Journalism)

Faculties

Catholic Theology (Catholic Theology); **Chemistry** (Chemistry); **Dental Surgery** (Dentistry; Surgery); **Economics and Management** (Economics; Management); **Educational Sciences**; **Geography and Regional Planning** (Geography; Regional Planning); **Law, Political Science and Management** (Law; Management; Political Sciences); **Life Sciences** (Biological and Life Sciences); **Medicine**; **Pharmacy**; **Protestant Theology** (Protestant Theology); **Psychology** (Psychology); **Sports** (Sports)

Institutes

European Studies (European Studies); **Labour**; **Political Science** (Political Sciences); **Preparation for General Administration** (Administration); **Teacher Training**; **Technology** *(Robert Schuman)*; **Technology** *(Hagueneau)* (Technology); **Technology** *(Louis Pasteur)* (Bioengineering; Business Administration; Industrial Engineering)

Schools

Biotechnology *(Strasbourg)*; **Chemistry, Polymers and Materials** *(European)* (Chemistry; Materials Engineering; Polymer and Plastics Technology); **Management** *(Strasbourg)* (Management); **Observatory and Earth Sciences**; **Physics** *(National)*

Units

Applied Languages and Human Sciences (Modern Languages; Regional Planning; Translation and Interpretation); **Arts** (Music; Performing Arts; Visual Arts); **History** (History); **Letters** (Greek; Latin; Literature; Phonetics); **Mathematics and Computer Science** (Computer Science; Mathematics); **Modern Languages**; **Philosophy, Linguistics andc Education**; **Physics and Engineering**; **Social Sciences, Social Practices and Development** (Development Studies; Social Sciences; Sociology)

History: Founded 1970 under the 1968 law reforming higher education as one of three Universities replacing the former Université de Strasbourg, founded 1537 as School. Became Academy 1566 and University 1621, suppressed by the Revolution, replaced by German university 1872-1918, evacuated to Clermont-Ferrand 1939-1945. A State institution enjoying academic and financial autonomy, operating under the jurisdiction of the Minister of Education and financed by the State. Acquired present status 2009 following the merge of the Université Louis Pasteur, Marc Bloch and Robert Schuman.

Governing Bodies: Conseil d'Administration, including representatives of teaching staff, research workers, students, and administrative and technical staff, as well as non-university members drawn from the public and private sectors; Conseil scientifique, competent in matters of research; Conseil des Etudes et de la Vie universitaire; Conseil of each Unit, comprising representatives of its teaching staff, research workers, students, and administrative and technical staff. The President is elected by the first three bodies. The Chancelier, who represents the Minister of Education, is the Recteur of the Académie de Strasbourg

Academic Year: September to June (September-February; February-June)

Admission Requirements: Secondary school certificate (baccalauréat) or recognized equivalent, or special entrance examination

Fees: (Euros): 174 per annum for Bachelor's degree; 273 for Master's and 359 for a Doctorate

Main Language(s) of Instruction: French

International Co-operation: With universities in Japan; Poland; Hungary; Italy; Germany; Russian Federation; Israel; Tunisia; Ghana; Madagascar; Azerbaidjan; Iran; USA; Canada; Australia

Degrees and Diplomas: *Diplôme universitaire de Technologie; Licence:* 3 yrs; *Diplôme national de Master.* 2 yrs following Licence; *Doctorat:* 2-4 yrs following Masters

Student Services: Academic counselling, Canteen, Cultural centre, Handicapped facilities, Language programs, Social counselling, Sports facilities

Student Residential Facilities: Yes

Libraries: National University Library; specialized libraries

Last Updated: 20/05/11

UNIVERSITY OF TECHNOLOGY - BELFORT-MONTBELIARD

Université de Technologie de Belfort-Montbéliard (UTBM)
90010 Belfort, Cedex
Tel: +33(3) 84-58-30-00
Fax: +33(3) 84-58-30-30
EMail: contact@utbm.fr
Website: http://www.utbm.fr

Administrateur provisoire: Chrsitian Coddet

International Relations: Frédéric Holweck
Tel: +33(3) 84-58-32-92 EMail: relations.internationales@utbm

Departments
Computer Science (Computer Science); **Electrical Engineering** (Electrical Engineering); **Engineeering and Processing** (Production Engineering); **Ergonomy, Design and Mechanical Engineering** (Industrial Design; Mechanical Engineering); **Mechanical Engineering** (Mechanical Engineering)

Graduate Schools
Engineering and Microtechnology (ED SPIM In collaboration with University of France-Comté and National School of Mechanics and Microelectronics); **Language, Space, Time and Society** (In collaboration with University of France-Comté) (Arts and Humanities; Law; Management)

Further Information: 2 other campuses at Severans and Montbéliard

History: Founded 1962 as Ecole nationale d'Ingénieurs de Belfort and 1985 as Polytechnic Institute of Sévenans. Acquired present status and title 1998 after merging with IPSé and Ecole nationale d'Ingénieurs de Belfort.

Main Language(s) of Instruction: French

Degrees and Diplomas: *Diplôme d'Ingénieur*; *Diplôme de Recherche technologique*; *Diplôme national de Master*; *Doctorat*. Also Diplôme d'Etudes universitaires de Technologie (DEUTEC)
Last Updated: 18/07/11

UNIVERSITY OF TECHNOLOGY - COMPIEGNE

Université de Technologie de Compiègne (UTC)
BP 60319, Université de Technologie de Compiègne Centre Pierre Guillaumat, Cedex 60203 Compiègne
Tel: +33(3) 44-23-44-23
Fax: +33(3) 44-20-43-00
EMail: utc@utc.fr
Website: http://www.utc.fr

Président: Alain Storck
Tel: +33(3) 44-23-43-39, Fax: +33(3) 44-23-46-74
EMail: presidence@utc.fr

International Relations: Cornélia Marin
Tel: +33(3) 44-23-73-96, Fax: +33(3) 44-23-73-88
EMail: cornelia.marin@utc.fr

Departments
Biological Engineering (Biotechnology; Engineering); **Computer Science**; **Industrial Process Engineering** (Industrial Engineering); **Mechanical Engineering**; **Mechanical Systems Engineering**; **Technology and Humanities**; **Urban Systems Engineering**

Graduate Schools
Engineering Sciences (Engineering)

Institutes
Teacher Training (IUFM: Studies are also provided at Jules Verne University) (Teacher Trainers Education; Teacher Training) *Director*: Jeannine Caplet

Schools
Graduate (Engineering)
History: A public 'Grande Ecole', and University.

Governing Bodies: Conseil d'administration, comprising 28 members; Directoire, comprising 12 members

Academic Year: September to June (September-January; February-June)

Admission Requirements: Secondary school certificate (baccalauréat) or equivalent/or 2 years after the baccalauréat

Main Language(s) of Instruction: French

International Co-operation: Participates in 120 programmes worldwide

Accrediting Agencies: Comité national d'Evaluation; Commission du Titre d'Ingénieur

Degrees and Diplomas: *Diplôme d'Ingénieur*: 5 yrs; *Mastère spécialisé*: a further yr; *Diplôme national de Master*: Science and Technology, 2 yrs; *Doctorat*: a further 3 yrs following Ingénieur or Master

Student Services: Academic counselling, Canteen, Cultural centre, Foreign student adviser, Foreign Studies Centre, Health services, Language programs, Sports facilities

Student Residential Facilities: Yes

Libraries: 2 Libraries
Last Updated: 25/01/12

UNIVERSITY OF TECHNOLOGY - TROYES

Université de Technologie de Troyes (UTT)
BP 2060, 12, rue Marie Curie, 10010 Troyes, Cedex
Tel: +33(3) 25-71-76-00
Fax: +33(3) 25-71-76-76
EMail: infos.utt@utt.fr
Website: http://www.utt.fr

Président: Christian Lerminiaux (2004-) EMail: president@utt.fr

Units
Aleatory Systems and Decision Methods; **Knowledge Management and Communication** (SIM2C) (Communication Studies; Information Management); **Languages** (Modern Languages); **Logistics and Operational Research** (LRO); **Mechanical and Materials Engineering** (Materials Engineering; Mechanical Engineering); **Networks and Telecommunications** (RT) (Computer Networks; Telecommunications Engineering); **Physics, Materials and Nanotechnology** (PMN) (Materials Engineering; Nanotechnology; Physics); **Sustainable Development** (DD) (Development Studies; Environmental Studies)

History: Founded 1994 as State University, cooperating with University of Technology of Compiègne and University of Belfort-Montbéliard.

Governing Bodies: Executive Board; Ministry of Higher Education and Research

Academic Year: September to June (September-January; March-June)

Admission Requirements: Competitive entrance examination after secondary school certificate (baccalauréat) or after 1st cycle (engineering degree), or after 2nd cycle (master's degree). Adequate knowledge of French required.

Main Language(s) of Instruction: French

International Co-operation: With more than 140 partner universities worldwide. Also participates in Erasmus, GE4, Crepuq and CSC programmes.

Accrediting Agencies: Ministry of Higher Education and Research. Commission des Titres d'Ingénieur

Degrees and Diplomas: *Diplôme d'Ingénieur*: Mechanical Systems; Information and Telecommunications Systems; Industrial Systems; Materials; Technology; Economics, 5 yrs; *Diplôme national de Master*: Mechanics and Physics; Information and Communication Science and Technologies; Engineering and Management, 2 yrs following Licence; *Doctorat*: Systems Optimisation; Optics and Nanotechnologies; Networks-Knowledge-Organizations; Materials and Mechanical Systems; Sustainable Development, 3 yrs

Student Services: Academic counselling, Canteen, Cultural centre, Employment services, Foreign student adviser, Foreign Studies Centre, Handicapped facilities, Health services, Language programs, Social counselling, Sports facilities

Student Residential Facilities: Students' Residences close to the campus

Libraries: Yes.
Last Updated: 19/04/11

UNIVERSITY OF THE AUVERGNE
Université d'Auvergne
BP 32, 49, boulevard François Mitterrand, 63001 Clermont-Ferrand, Cedex 01
Tel: +33(4) 73-17-79-79
Fax: +33(4) 73-17-72-01
EMail: mathonnatj@wanadoo.fr
Website: http://www.u-clermont1.fr

Président: Philippe Dulbecco (2007-)
Tel: +33(4) 73-17-74-24 EMail: philippe.dulbecco@u-clermont1.fr

International Relations: Jacky Mathonnat
Tel: +33(4) 73-17-72-71, Fax: +33(4) 73-17-72-05

Centres
Lifelong Education *Vice-Président*: Jean-Pierre Vedrine

Faculties
Dental Surgery (Dentistry; Surgery); **Economics and Management** (Economics; Management); **Law and Political Science** (Law; Notary Studies; Political Sciences); **Medicine** (Medicine); **Pharmacy** (Pharmacy)

Graduate Schools
Economics, Law and Management (Economics; Law; Management) *Director*: Florent Garnier; **Health and Life Sciences** *(In cooperation with University of Clermont-Ferrand II)* (Health Sciences) *Director*: George Picard

Institutes
Management and Business Administration *(IUP)* (Business Administration; Management); **Preparatory Administrative Studies** *(IPAG)* (Administration); **Technology** (Biology; Computer Engineering; Industrial Engineering; Technology); **Technology** *(IUT, Aurillac)* (Biotechnology; Multimedia; Technology); **Technology** *(IUT, Puy-en-Velay)* (Biology; Computer Science; Multimedia; Technology; Telecommunications Engineering)

Research Centres
International Development *(CERDI) Director*: Patrick Guillamont

History: Founded 1970 under the 1968 law reforming higher education and replacing former Université de Clermont-Ferrand, founded 1854 as Faculty of Letters and Faculty of Science. Became University 1896. The University, which until 1976 formed a single institution with the University of Clermont-Ferrand II, is a State institution enjoying academic and financial autonomy, operating under the jurisdiction of the Minister of Education and financed by the State.

Governing Bodies: Conseil de l'Université, including elected representatives of teaching staff, research workers, students, and administrative and technical staff, as well as non-university members drawn from the public and private sectors; Conseil of each Unit, comprising representatives of its teaching staff, research workers, students, and administrative and technical staff; Conseil scientifique, competent in matters of research. The President is elected by the Conseil de l'Université. The Chancelier, who represents the Minister of Education, is the Recteur de l'Académie de Clermont-Ferrand

Academic Year: October to June (October-December; January-March; April-June)

Admission Requirements: Secondary school certificate (baccalauréat) or brevet supérieur, or recognized foreign equivalent, or special entrance examination

Main Language(s) of Instruction: French

International Co-operation: Participates in Erasmus, Tempus, Lingua

Degrees and Diplomas: *Diplôme universitaire de Technologie*; *Licence*: Law; Economics and Administration; Management; Medicine; Pharmacy; Odontology; Technology; *Licence professionnelle*: Management, Health; *Diplôme de Recherche technologique*: Management; *Diplôme national de Master*: Law; Economics and Administration; Management; Medicine; Pharmacy; Odontology; *Doctorat*: Law; Economics and Administration; Management; Medicine; Pharmacy; Odontology; Technology. Diplome universitaire: 2 yrs

Student Services: Canteen, Cultural centre, Health services, Sports facilities

Student Residential Facilities: Yes

Libraries: Central Library, 400,000 vols; Medicine and Pharmacy, 37,000; Law, 70,000
Last Updated: 11/07/11

UNIVERSITY OF THE LITTORAL CÔTE D'OPALE
Université du Littoral Côte d'Opale (ULCO)
BP 1022, 1, place de l'Yser, 59375 Dunkerque, Cedex 1
Tel: +33(3) 28-23-73-73
Fax: +33(3) 28-23-73-13
EMail: relinter@univ-littoral.fr
Website: http://www.univ-littoral.fr

Président: Roger Durand
Tel: +33(3) 28-23-73-00 EMail: president@univ-littoral.fr

Secrétaire générale: Catherine Sion Tel: +33(3) 28-23-73-18

International Relations: Faustin Aissi
Tel: +33(3) 28-23-73-28; +33(3) 28-65-82-49
EMail: faustin.aissi@univ-littoral.fr

Centres
Lifelong Education *(CUEEP) Director*: Jean-Claude Fiers

Divisions
Arts, Letters and Languages *(Boulogne and Dunkirk)* (Cultural Studies; English; German; Literature; Media Studies; Spanish); **Human and Social Sciences** *(Dunkirk, Boulogne)* (Geography; History); **Law, Economics and Management** *(Dunkirk, Boulogne, Saint Omer)* (Economics; Health Administration; Hotel Management; Human Resources; Law; Management; Marketing; Public Administration; Sales Techniques; Tourism; Transport Management); **Science, Technology and Health** *(Calais, Boulogne, Dunkirk, Saint-Omer)* (Biology; Chemistry; Computer Science; Electrical and Electronic Engineering; Food Technology; Industrial Engineering; Mathematics; Metallurgical Engineering; Physical Education; Physics; Sports; Telecommunications Engineering)

Institutes
Technology *(IUT Saint Omer-Dunkerque: two sites)* (Technology); **Technology** *(IUT Calais-Boulogne: two sites)* (Biotechnology; Business Administration; Computer Engineering; Electrical Engineering)

Schools
Engineering *(Littoral)* (Computer Engineering; Engineering; Industrial Engineering)

History: Founded 1991.

Admission Requirements: Secondary school certificate (baccalauréat) or equivalent

Fees: (Euros): 150-300

Main Language(s) of Instruction: French

Degrees and Diplomas: *Diplôme universitaire de Technologie*: Biotechnology, Electrical Engineering, Computer Science, Energy and Thermal Engineering, Industrial Engineering, Maintenance Technology, Business Administration; *Licence*: Science and Technology, Economics, Administration, Law, Modern Languages, Social Sciences, Arts and Humanities; *Licence professionnelle*: Electrical and Electronic Engineering, Telecommunications, Industrial Engineering, Safety Engineering, Human Resources, Marketing, International Business, Management, Law Administration; *Diplôme d'Etudes d'Ecole de Commerce et Gestion*: 3 years following 2 years of university studies; *Diplôme national de Master*: Science and Technology, Economics, Administration, Law, Modern Languages, Social Sciences, Arts and Humanities; *Doctorat*: Environment, Sustainable Development, Mathematics, Engineering, Modern Languages, Cultural Studies, History. Preparation for CAPES and Agrégation, Masters professionnel, Masters recherche

Student Services: Academic counselling, Canteen, Cultural centre, Foreign student adviser, Health services, Social counselling, Sports facilities

Student Residential Facilities: None

Libraries: 4 libraries

Publications: L'Esprit de la Côte *(quarterly)*
Last Updated: 18/07/11

UNIVERSITY OF THE SAVOIE, CHAMBÉRY
Université de Savoie
BP 1104, 27, rue Marcoz, 73011 Chambéry, Cedex
Tel: +33(4) 79-75-85-85
Fax: +33(4) 79-75-84-44
EMail: dri@univ-savoie.fr
Website: http://www.univ-savoie.fr

Président: Gilbert Angénieux
Tel: +33(4) 79-75-84-22, Fax: +33(4) 79-75-83-51
EMail: Presidence@univ-savoie.fr

Directeur général des Services: Gilles Stoll
Tel: +33(4) 79-75-84-20 EMail: gilles.stoll@univ-savoie.fr

International Relations: Claire Lucarelli
Tel: +33(4) 79-75-83-50, Fax: +33(4) 79-75-85-65
EMail: international@univ-savoie.fr

Centres
Mountain Research *(Interdisciplinary, CISM Le Bourget du Lac)* (Mountain Studies)

Faculties
Fundamental and Applied Sciences *(SFA, Le Bourget-du-Lac)* (Chemistry; Information Technology; Mathematics; Physics); **Law and Economics** *(FDE Chambéry)* (Economics; Law); **Literature, Languages and Human Sciences** *(LLSH)* (Arts and Humanities; Cultural Studies; History; Literature; Modern Languages; Philosophy; Psychology; Social Sciences; Sociology)

Institutes
Business Administration *(IAE Savoie Mont-Blanc, Annecy-le-Vieux with a second site at Chambéry)* (Business Administration; Finance; Hotel Management; International Business; Management; Marketing; Tourism); **Environmental Engineering for Mountainous Regions** (Environmental Studies; Mountain Studies); **French Studies** *(for foreign students, AGISEFE)* (French; French Studies) *Director*: Jean-Paul Gaillard; **Technology** *(IUT Annecy-le-Vieux)* (Administration; Computer Engineering; Electrical Engineering; Management; Marketing; Mechanical Engineering; Production Engineering; Technology; Telecommunications Engineering); **Technology** *(IUT, Chambéry)* (Administration; Business and Commerce; Materials Engineering; Packaging Technology; Technology); **Transport Management, Tourism and Hotel Management** *(IUP THTL)* (Hotel Management; Tourism; Transport Management) *Director*: Paul Constable

Schools
Engineering *(Polytech in partnership with ITII of Savoies. Second site at Annecy)* (Automation and Control Engineering; Civil Engineering; Energy Engineering; Environmental Engineering; Mechanical Engineering) *Director*: Thierry Foulley

Further Information: Science Campus at Le Bourget du Lac site. Annecy-le-Vieux is the second site.

History: Founded 1970 as Centre Universitaire de Savoie under the 1968 law reforming higher education and replacing institutions attached to former Université de Grenoble. Acquired present status and title 1979. A State institution enjoying academic and financial autonomy, operating under the jurisdiction of the Minister of Education and financed by the State.

Governing Bodies: Conseil de l'Université, including elected representatives of teaching staff, research workers, students, and administrative and technical staff, as well as non-university members drawn from the public and private sectors; Conseil of each Unit, comprising representatives of its teaching staff, research workers, students, and administrative and technical staff; and Conseil scientifique, competent in matters of research. The President is elected by the Conseil de l'Université. The Chancelier, who represents the Minister of Education, is the Recteur of the Académie de Grenoble

Academic Year: September to June

Admission Requirements: Secondary school certificate (baccalauréat) or foreign equivalent, or special entrance examination

Main Language(s) of Instruction: French

Degrees and Diplomas: *Diplôme universitaire de Technologie*: 2 yrs; *Licence*: 3 yrs; *Licence professionnelle*: 3 yrs; *Diplôme d'Ingénieur*. 5 yrs; *Diplôme national de Master*. 2 yrs following Licence; *Doctorat*: 2-4 yrs following Masters. Certificat and Diplômes

d'études françaises (for foreign students), Masters recherche, Masters professionnel

Student Residential Facilities: Yes

Libraries: c. 200,000 vols
Last Updated: 01/06/11

UNIVERSITY OF THE SOUTH TOULON-VAR
Université du Sud Toulon-Var
BP 132, Avenue de l'Université, 83957 La Garde, Cedex
Tel: +33(4) 94-14-20-00
Fax: +33(4) 94-14-21-57
EMail: sri@univ-tln.fr
Website: http://www.univ-tln.fr

Président: Marc Saillard
Tel: +33(4) 94-14-23-69 +33(4) 94-14-22-61,
Fax: +33(4) 94-14-21-23 EMail: president@univ-tln.fr

Secrétaire générale: Françoise Villeval
Tel: +33(4) 94-14-22-62, Fax: +33(4) 94-14-25-04
EMail: francoise.villeval@univ-tln.fr

International Relations: Pierre Sanz de Alba
Tel: +33(4) 94-14-21-37, Fax: +33(4) 94-14-21-26
EMail: pierre.sanz-de-alba@univ-tln.fr

Centres
Lifelong Education *Director*: Martine Hardy

Faculties
Arts and Humanities (Arts and Humanities; Cultural Studies; English; Literature; Spanish; Tourism); **Economics and Management** (Economics; Management); **Law** (Law); **Physical Education and Sports** *(STAPS)* (Physical Education; Sports); **Science and Techniques** (Biology; Chemistry; Computer Science; Electronic Engineering; Marine Science and Oceanography; Mathematics; Physics; Telecommunications Engineering)

Graduate Schools
Euro-Mediterranean Comparative Civilizations and Societies (Mediterranean Studies)

Institutes
Business Administration (Business Administration; Management); **Engineering Sciences** *(ISITV)* (Engineering; Marine Engineering; Materials Engineering; Telecommunications Engineering); **Information and Communication** *(Ingémédia)* (Communication Studies; Media Studies; Sound Engineering (Acoustics)); **Technology** *(IUT Toulon)* (Bioengineering; Business Administration; Electrical Engineering; Industrial Engineering; Management; Sales Techniques; Technology; Telecommunications Engineering)

History: Founded 1970 as Centre universitaire under the 1968 law reforming higher education. Acquired present status and title 1979. A State institution enjoying academic and financial autonomy, operating under the jurisdiction of the Minister of Education and financed by the State.

Governing Bodies: Conseil de l'Université, including 37 elected representatives of teaching staff, research workers, students, and administrative and technical staff, as well as non-university members drawn from the public and private sectors; Conseil of each Unit, comprising representatives of its teaching staff, research workers, students, and administrative and technical staff; Conseil scientifique, competent in matters of research. The President is elected by the Conseil de l'Université. The Chancellor, who represents the Minister of Education, is the Recteur of the Académie de Nice

Academic Year: September to July (September-December; January-March; April-July)

Admission Requirements: Secondary school certificate (baccalauréat) or equivalent, or special entrance examination

Main Language(s) of Instruction: French

International Co-operation: With universities in United Kingdom; Germany; Italy; Spain; Ireland; Morocco; Australia; United States; China

Degrees and Diplomas: *Capacité en Droit*; *Diplôme universitaire de Technologie*: 2 yrs; *Licence*: Science, Sports, Law, Economics, Business Administration, Arts and Humanities, 3 yrs; *Licence professionnelle*: Tourism, Multimedia, Law, Sports, Technology, 3 yrs; *Diplôme d'Ingénieur*: 3 yrs following 2 yrs university studies;

Diplôme national de Master: Science, Sports, Law, Economics, Business Administration, Arts and Humanities, Multimedia, 2 yrs following Licence; *Doctorat*: 2-4 yrs following Masters. Also Certificat d'Aptitude à la Profession d'Avocat, 5 yrs, Masters recherche, Masters professionnel

Student Services: Academic counselling, Canteen, Cultural centre, Employment services, Foreign student adviser, Handicapped facilities, Health services, Language programs, Social counselling, Sports facilities

Student Residential Facilities: Yes

Libraries: Central Library, c. 55,000 vols and periodicals
Last Updated: 19/07/11

UNIVERSITY OF VALENCIENNES AND HAINAUT-CAMBRÉSIS

Université de Valenciennes et du Hainaut-Cambrésis (UVHC)

Le Mont-Houy, 59313 Valenciennes, Cedex 9
Tel: +33(3) 27-51-12-34
Fax: +33(3) 27-51-11-00
EMail: uvhc@univ-valenciennes.fr
Website: http://www.univ-valenciennes.fr

Président: Mohamed Ourak
Tel: +33(3) 27-51-16-76 +33(3) 27-51-16-97,
Fax: +33(3) 27-51-16-75

International Relations: Fabrice Guizard
Tel: +33(3) 27-51-77-36, Fax: +33(3) 27-51-77-30
EMail: int.relations@univ-valenciennes.fr;
sylvie.merviel@univ-valenciennes.fr

Centres
Continuing Education *Director*: Gérard Déchy

Faculties
Law, Economics and Management *(FDEG)* (Economics; Law; Private Law; Public Law); **Letters, Languages, Arts and Humanities** *(FLLASH)* (Arts and Humanities; English; Fine Arts; French; German; History; Information Sciences; Literature; Modern Languages; Multimedia; Performing Arts; Spanish; Theatre; Visual Arts); **Sports Sciences** *(FSMS)* (Sports; Sports Management; Welfare and Protective Services)

Higher Institutes
Industrial Engineering *(ISIV)* (Electrical Engineering; Industrial Engineering; Mechanical Engineering) *Director*: François Verheyde

Institutes
Business Administration *(IAE)* (Accountancy; Administration; Business Administration; Finance; Human Resources; Management; Marketing; Real Estate); **Public Administration** *(IPAG)* (Administration; Institutional Administration; Public Administration); **Science and Technology** *(ISTV)* (Business Computing; Chemistry; Food Technology; Materials Engineering; Mathematics and Computer Science; Mechanics; Multimedia; Telecommunications Engineering); **Technology** *(IUT de Valenciennes with 3 sites: Valenciennes, Cambrai and Maubeuge)* (Computer Science; Electrical Engineering; Maintenance Technology; Management; Marketing; Physical Engineering; Production Engineering)

Schools
Engineering *(ENSIAME)* (Automation and Control Engineering; Computer Engineering; Electronic Engineering; Energy Engineering; Mechanical Engineering)

Further Information: Also courses of French as a foreign language for foreign students. Has 9 research labs. Campuses in Cambrai and Maubeuge

History: Founded 1970 as Centre Universitaire de Valenciennes under the 1968 law reforming higher education and incorporating institutions previously attached to the former Université de Lille. Acquired present status and title 1979. A State institution enjoying academic and financial autonomy, operating under the jurisdiction of the Minister of Education and financed by the State.

Governing Bodies: Conseil de l'Université (Council of University) including elected representatives of teaching staff, research workers, students, and administrative and technical staff, as well as non-university members drawn from the public and private sectors; Council of each teaching and research unit, comprising representatives of its teaching staff, research workers, students, and administrative and technical staff; and the Conseil scientifique, competent in matters of research. The President is elected by the Conseil de l'Université. The Chancelier, who represents the Minister of Education, is the Recteur of the Académie de Lille

Academic Year: September to June (September-Januaryr; February-June)

Admission Requirements: Secondary school certificate (baccalauréat) or foreign equivalent

Fees: (Euros): 164-441 per annum

Main Language(s) of Instruction: French

International Co-operation: Participates in the Erasmus/Socrates, Leaonardo, Tempus, Alfa and Interreg programmes; also with univesities in Canada, Chile, China, Morocco, Mexico, Russian Federation, Switzerland and USA

Accrediting Agencies: National Ministry of Education

Degrees and Diplomas: *Diplôme universitaire de Technologie*: Management; Marketing; Maintenance Technology; Production Engineering; Electrical Engineering; Computer Science; Physical Engineering, 2 yrs; *Licence*: Fine Arts; Management; Mechanical Engineering; Electrical Engineering; Civil Engineering; Materials Engineering; Food Technology; History; French Literature; Modern Languages; Law; Public Administration; Physics; Mathematics; Computer Science; Economics, 3 yrs; *Licence professionnelle*: Management; Accountancy; Marketing; Maintenance Technology; Production Engineering; Industrial Engineering; Civil Engineering; Electronic Engineering; Computer Science, 1 further yr following DUT or DEUST; *Diplôme d'Ingénieur*: 5 yrs; *Maîtrise de Sciences et Techniques*: Management; Accountancy; Finance; Mechanical Engineering; Electrical Engineering; Civil Engineering; Food Technology; Mathematics; Computer Science, 4 yrs; *Diplôme de Recherche technologique*: Mechanical Engineering, Energy and Matter Engineering, Electrical and Electronic Engineering, 1 year following Masters; *Diplôme national de Master*: Automation and Control Engineering; Electronical Engineering; History; French Literature; Linguistics; German; Mathematics; Information Technology; Sports; Fine Arts, Performing Arts, Finance, Accountancy, Food Technology; Law; Real Estate; Computer Science; Radio and Broadcasting; Sports; Multimedia; Management; International Business; Accountancy; Finance; Mechanical Engineering; Measurement and Precision Engineering; Railway Transport; Civil Engineering; Materials Engineering, a further 2 yrs; *Doctorat*: Transport, Material Engineering, Electronic Engineering, Food Technology, Construction Engineering, Service Trades, Multimedia, Economics. Masters recherche, Masters professionnel

Student Services: Academic counselling, Canteen, Cultural centre, Employment services, Foreign student adviser, Handicapped facilities, Health services, Language programs, Social counselling, Sports facilities

Student Residential Facilities: Yes

Libraries: University Library, c. 30,000 vols

Press or Publishing House: Presses Universitaires de Valenciennes (PUV); Septentrion
Last Updated: 18/07/11

UNIVERSITY OF VERSAILLES SAINT-QUENTIN-EN-YVELINES

Université de Versailles Saint-Quentin-en-Yvelines (UVSQ)

55 avenue de Paris, 78035 Versailles, Cedex
Tel: +33(1) 39-25-78-00
Fax: +33(1) 39-25-78-01
EMail: relations.internationales@uvsq.fr
Website: http://www.uvsq.fr

Présidente: Sylvie Faucheux (2002-)
Tel: +33(1) 39-25-78-03, Fax: +33(1) 39-25-79-24
EMail: presidente@admin.uvsq.fr

Directeur général des Services: Nicolas Mignan
Tel: +33(1) 39-25-78-13 EMail: nicolas.mignan@uvsq.fr

International Relations: Patricia Orduy-Rey, Directrice des Relations internationales
Tel: +33(1) 39-25-51-32, Fax: +33(1) 39-25-51-35

EMail: relations.internationales@admin.uvsq.fr; Diana.cooper-richet@uvsq.fr

Faculties
Law and Political Science (Law; Political Sciences)

Graduate Schools
Cultures, Organisations, Legislation (Cultural Studies; Public Law)

Institutes
Cultural Studies (Arts and Humanities; Cultural Studies); **Languages and International Studies** (International Studies; Modern Languages); **Management** (Management); **Teacher Training** *(IUFM Versailles with 5 sites)* (Education; Teacher Trainers Education; Teacher Training); **Technology** *(IUT Vélizy with Antenne de Rambouillet)* (Business Administration; Business and Commerce; Chemical Engineering; Communication Studies; Computer Engineering; Electrical Engineering; Technology; Telecommunications Engineering); **Technology** *(IUT Mantes-en-Yvelines)* (Business Administration; Business and Commerce; Civil Engineering; Hygiene; Industrial Engineering; Mechanical Engineering; Sales Techniques; Technology)

Units
Health Sciences *(Garches, Hopital Raymond Poincaré)* (Anatomy; Biochemistry; Biology; Biophysics; Biotechnology; Chemistry; Embryology and Reproduction Biology; Genetics; Haematology; Health Administration; Health Sciences; Histology; Immunology; Medicine; Midwifery; Oncology; Pathology; Physics; Physiology; Public Health; Radiology; Virology); **Science** (Applied Mathematics; Biology; Biotechnology; Chemistry; Computer Science; Earth Sciences; Engineering; Environmental Studies; Industrial Chemistry; Mathematics; Molecular Biology; Natural Sciences; Optics; Physics; Robotics); **Social Sciences** *(Saint-Quentin-en-Yvelines)* (Banking; Business Administration; Demography and Population; Economics; Environmental Management; Finance; Geography (Human); Hotel and Restaurant; Human Resources; Insurance; Law; Management; Social Sciences; Sociology; Tourism)

History: Founded 1991, incorporating divisions of University Paris VI and University Paris X.

Fees: (Euros): c. 180-400 per annum

International Co-operation: With universities in Canada; United States; Brazil; Chile; Peru; Argentina; Colombia; Mexico; Uruguay; Syria; Jordan; Algeria; Tunisia; Russian Federation; Spain; Belgium; Georgia; Côte d'Ivoire; Cameroon; Madagascar; Vietnam; China; Australia. Also participates in Erasmus

Degrees and Diplomas: *Diplôme universitaire de Technologie (DUT)*: 2 yrs; *Licence*: Science; Law and Political Science; Humanities and Social Sciences, 3 yrs; *Licence professionnelle*; *Diplôme d'Etat*: Medicine, 9 yrs; *Diplôme d'Ingénieur*: Engineering; *Diplôme national de Master*: Science; Law and Political Science; Humanities and Social Sciences, 2 yrs following Licence; *Doctorat*: 3 yrs following Master. Several Diplomes universitaires in Medicine. Preparation for CAPES, Agrégation, Administrative and Judicial exams

Student Services: Academic counselling, Canteen, Foreign student adviser, Health services, Social counselling, Sports facilities

Libraries: c. 27,000 vols
Last Updated: 18/07/11

UNIVERSITY OF WESTERN BRITTANY, BREST
Université de Bretagne Occidentale
CS 93837, 3, rue des Archives, 29238 Cedex 3 Brest
Tel: +33(2) 98-01-60-00
Fax: +33(2) 98-01-60-01
EMail: drh@univ-brest.fr
Website: http://www.univ-brest.fr

Président: Pascal Olivard (2007-)
Tel: +33(2) 98-01-65-76 EMail: president@univ-brest.fr

Directeur général des Services: Stéphane Charpentier
Tel: +33(2) 98-01-60-04, Fax: +33(2) 98-01-60-01
EMail: Stephane.Charpentier@univ-brest.fr

International Relations: Anne-Marie Galliou Scanvion
Tel: +33(2) 98-01-81-56 +33(2) 98-01-82-51,
Fax: +33(2) 98-01-60-01

EMail: Anne-Marie.Galliou-Scanvion@univ-brest.fr; scuee@univ-brest.fr

Graduate Schools
Health, Information-Communication, Mathematics, Matter (Analytical Chemistry; Biology; Health Sciences; Mathematics; Physics); **Human and Social Sciences** (Celtic Languages and Studies; Cognitive Sciences; Communication Studies; Education; Ethics; Psychology; Sociology); **Languages, Literature and Societies** (Arts and Humanities; Management; Modern Languages; Social Sciences); **Marine Studies** (Marine Science and Oceanography)

Institutes
Art and Culture Professions (Art Education; Cultural Studies; Heritage Preservation); **Business Administration** (Banking; Business Administration; Finance; Management); **Computer Engineering** *(Brest)* (Computer Engineering); **Euro Actuarial Studies** *(EURIA)* (Actuarial Science); **Food Industries** *(IUP IIA, Quimper)* (Food Science); **Marine Studies** *(IUEM)* (Marine Science and Oceanography); **Mechanical and Production Engineering** (Mechanical Engineering; Production Engineering); **Preparatory Administrative Studies** *(IPAG)* (Administration); **Teacher Training** *(IUFM Bretagne with campuses in BrestQuimperRennesSaintBrieucVanne)* (Teacher Trainers Education; Teacher Training); **Technology** *(IUT Brest with 2nd site at Morlaix)* (Biology; Business Administration; Civil Engineering; Computer Engineering; Electrical Engineering; Mechanical Engineering; Production Engineering; Technology) *Director*: Yvan Leray; **Technology** *(IUT, Quimper)* (Biology; Business Administration; Business and Commerce; Technology; Transport Management); **Telecommunications and Networks** *(Brest)* (Computer Networks; Telecommunications Engineering)

Research Centres
Rural Food Science and Production Sciences *(ISAMOR, Brest)* (Food Science) *Director*: Adrien Binet

Schools
Engineering (Engineering); **Microbiology and Food Security** *(ESMISAB)* (Food Technology; Microbiology); **Midwifery** (Midwifery)

Units
Arts and Humanities (Archaeology; Art History; Arts and Humanities; Ethnology; Geography; Gerontology; History; Literature; Modern Languages; Philosophy; Psychology; Social Sciences; Tourism); **Dentistry** (Dentistry); **Law, Economics and Management** (Economics; Law; Management); **Medicine** (Medicine) *Dean*: Yves Bizais; **Physical Education and Sports** (Physical Education; Sports); **Science and Technology** (Biology; Chemistry; Computer Science; Earth Sciences; Electronic Engineering; Mathematics; Modern Languages; Natural Sciences; Physics; Technology; Town Planning)

Further Information: Has 3 sites: Quimper, Brest, Morlaix

History: Founded 1970 under the 1968 law reforming higher education as one of two Universities replacing the former Université de Rennes, established in 1461 as University of Nantes with Colleges and Faculties in Nantes and Rennes; suppressed by the Revolution, reconstituted 1896. A State Institution enjoying academic and financial autonomy, operating under the jurisdiction of the Minister of Education and financed by the State.

Governing Bodies: Conseil d'Administration, including representatives of teaching staff, research workers, students, and administrative and technical staff, as well as non-university members drawn from the public and private sectors; Conseil scientifique, competent in matters of research; Conseil des Etudes et de la Vie universitaire; and Conseil of each Unit, comprising representatives of its teaching staff, research workers, students, and administrative and technical staff. The President is elected by the first three bodies. The Chancelier, who represents the Minister of Education, is the Recteur of the Académie de Rennes

Academic Year: October to June (October-December; January-March; April-June)

Admission Requirements: Secondary school certificate (baccalauréat) or equivalent, or special entrance examination

Main Language(s) of Instruction: French

Degrees and Diplomas: *Capacité en Droit*: Law, 2 yrs; *Diplôme universitaire de Technologie*: 2 yrs; *Licence*: 3 yrs; *Licence professionnelle*; *Diplôme d'Etat*: Dental Surgery, 5 yrs; *Diplôme d'Etat*: Medicine, 6 yrs plus 1 yr hospital practice and thesis; *Diplôme d'Etat*: Midwifery, 3 yrs; *Diplôme d'Ingénieur*; *Diplôme national de Master*: 2 yrs following a licence; *Doctorat*: 2-4 yrs following a Master Research; *Certificat de Spécialité*: Medicine, at least 2 yrs following Diplôme d'Etat. Masters recherche, Masters professionnel

Student Residential Facilities: Yes

Libraries: Bibliothèque universitaire, c. 90,000 vols; Research Centre for Breton and Celtic Studies, c. 18,000
Last Updated: 12/07/11

VALENCIENNES ART SCHOOL

Ecole supérieure des Beaux-Arts de Valenciennes
132 Avenue du Faubourg de Cambrai, 59300 Valenciennes
Tel: +33(3) 27-22-57-59
Fax: +33(3) 27-22-57-60
EMail: info@ecoledesbeauxarts.valenciennes.fr
Website: http://ecoledesbeauxarts.valenciennes.fr

Directrice: Sonia Criton

Programmes
Art (Engraving; Multimedia; Painting and Drawing; Photography; Sculpture; Video); **Design** (Design)

History: Founded 1782.

Main Language(s) of Instruction: French

Degrees and Diplomas: Diplôme national d'arts et techniques (3 yrs) and Diplôme national supérieur d'expression plastique (5 yrs)
Last Updated: 07/07/11

VERSAILLES SCHOOL OF ARCHITECTURE

Ecole nationale supérieure d'Architecture de Versailles (ENSA-V)
5 avenue de Sceaux, BP 674, 78006 Versailles, Cedex
Tel: +33(1) 39-07-40-00
Fax: +33(1) 39-07-40-99
EMail: ensav@versailles.archi.fr
Website: http://www.versailles.archi.fr

Directeur: Vincent Michel EMail: vincent.michel@versailles.archi.fr

Directrice adjointe: Suzanne Kalé
Tel: +33(1) 39-07-40-35 EMail: suzanne.kale@versailles.archi.fr

Programmes
Architecture (Architecture)

History: Founded 1969.

Main Language(s) of Instruction: French

Accrediting Agencies: Ministère de la Culture et de la Communication

Degrees and Diplomas: *Licence*; *Mastère spécialisé*; *Diplôme national de Master*; *Doctorat*. Habilitation à exercer la maîtrise d'oeuvre en son nom propre (HMONP)
Last Updated: 28/06/11

VETAGRO SUP SCHOOL

VetAgro Sup
1, avenue Bourgelat, 69280 Marcy l'Etoile
Tel: +33(4) 78-87-25-25
Fax: +33(4) 78-87-82-62
EMail: s.martinot@vetagro-sup.fr
Website: http://www.vetagro-sup.fr

Directeur: Stéphane Martinot (2009-2014)
Tel: +33(4) 78-87-25-00, Fax: +33(4) 78-87-26-18

International Relations: Gabriella Sonohat-Sinoquet

Campuses
Agronomy *(Clermont)* (Agricultural Engineering; Biology; Environmental Studies; Food Science; Nutrition; Rural Planning); **Veterinary Medicine** (Animal Husbandry; Microbiology; Pathology; Physiology; Veterinary Science)

Schools
Veterinary Services (Veterinary Science)

History: Founded 2010 following merger of the École nationale vétérinaire de Lyon, the École nationale d'ingénieurs des travaux agricoles de Clermont-Ferrand and the École nationale des services vétérinaires. Veterinary campus founded 1762.

Governing Bodies: Conseil d'administration

Academic Year: September to June (September-January; February-June)

Admission Requirements: Competitive entrance examination following 2-3 yrs further study after secondary school certificate (baccalauréat) or following first university qualification (DEUG, DUT or BTS), or equivalent

Fees: (Euros): 2,000 per annum

Main Language(s) of Instruction: French

Degrees and Diplomas: *Licence professionnelle*; *Diplôme d'Etat*: Veterinary Science; *Diplôme d'Ingénieur*; *Mastère spécialisé*: Quality Animal Breeding; *Diplôme national de Master*; *Doctorat*

Student Services: Canteen, Cultural centre, Health services, Sports facilities

Student Residential Facilities: For c. 600 students

Special Facilities: Anatomy Museum. Ancient Works Collection

Libraries: c. 10,500 vols
Last Updated: 23/02/12

PRIVATE INSTITUTIONS

3IL ENGINEERING SCHOOL

Institut d'Ingénierie informatique de Limoges (3IL)
BP 834, 43, rue Saint Anne, 87015 Limoges, Cedex
Tel: +33(5) 55-31-67-29
Fax: +33(5) 55-51-06-30-16
EMail: e3il@3il.fr
Website: http://www.3il.org

Directeur: Ali Mankar-Bennis EMail: mankar@3il.fr

International Relations: Annabelle Dumontheil
Tel: +33(5) 55-31-67-07 EMail: Dumontheil@3il.fr

Programmes
Computer Engineering (Computer Engineering)

History: Founded in 1987, acquiring present status in 1995.

Admission Requirements: Competitive entrance exam, DUT or BTS Degree

Fees: (Euros): Engineering Programme, 4,400 per annum; Preparatory Studies, 2,472

Main Language(s) of Instruction: French

International Co-operation: Has partnership programmes with University of Shanghai, Athens University and two institutions in Burkina Faso.

Accrediting Agencies: Commission des Titres d'Ingénieur

Degrees and Diplomas: *Diplôme d'Ingénieur*: Computer Engineering, 3 yrs
Last Updated: 05/07/11

ACADEMY OF WOOD SCIENCE AND TECHNOLOGY

Ecole supérieure du Bois (ESB NANTES)
BP 10605, Atlanpole, Rue Christian Pauc, 44306 Nantes, Cedex 03
Tel: +33(2) 40-18-12-12
Fax: +33(2) 40-18-12-00
EMail: contact@ecoledubois.fr
Website: http://www.ecoledubois.fr

Directeur: Arnaud Godevin EMail: direction@ecoledubois.fr

International Relations: Antoine Lebeau
Tel: +33(2) 40-18-12-12 EMail: antoine.lebeau@ecoledubois.fr

Divisions
Forestry (Forestry); **Wood Technology** (Wood Technology)

Further Information: Also French language courses for foreign students

History: Founded 1934 in Paris. Moved to Nantes 1994.

Governing Bodies: Conseil de surveillance comprising 31 members

Academic Year: September to June (September-February; March-June)

Admission Requirements: Competitive entrance examination following 2 yrs further study after secondary school certificate (baccalauréat) or equivalent

Fees: (Euros): 3,900 per annum

Main Language(s) of Instruction: French, English

Accrediting Agencies: Commission des Titres d'Ingénieurs (CTI)

Degrees and Diplomas: *Licence professionnelle*; *Diplôme d'Ingénieur*; *Diplôme national de Master*

Student Services: Academic counselling, Canteen, Employment services, Foreign student adviser, Handicapped facilities, Language programs, Social counselling

Special Facilities: Media Laboratory

Libraries: 5,000 references

Publications: Research publications
Last Updated: 04/07/11

ANGERS SCHOOL OF COMPUTER AND PRODUCTION ENGINEERING
Ecole supérieure angevine d'Informatique et de Productique (ESAIP)
BP 80022, 18, rue du 8 Mai 1945, 49180 Saint Barthélémy d'Anjou, Cedex
Tel: +33(2) 41-96-65-10
Fax: +33(2) 41-96-65-11
EMail: info@esaip.org
Website: http://www.esaip.org/

Directeur: Jacky Lépicier EMail: jlepicier@esaip.org

International Relations: Anne Cordier
Tel: +33(2) 41-96-65-22 EMail: acordier@esaip.org

Departments
IT and Networks (Computer Science; Environmental Engineering; Safety Engineering); **Safety and Risk Management** (Safety Engineering)

Further Information: Other campuses in Grasse, Rennes, Nantes, Dijon, La Roche sur Yon, Lyon and Toulouse

History: Founded 1988.

Admission Requirements: 2 yrs of university studies in science and technology

Fees: (Euros): 4,950 per annum

Main Language(s) of Instruction: French, English, German, Spanish, Italian

International Co-operation: With universities in United Kingdom, Germany, Spain, Poland, Finland, Belgium, Sweden, Hungary, Romania, Portugal, Italy, Greece, Denmark, The Netherland, Norway

Accrediting Agencies: Commission des Titres d'Ingénieurs

Degrees and Diplomas: *Diplôme d'Ingénieur*. IT and Networks, Environmental Engineering, Risk Management, 5 yrs. International Master in Computer Science (5 yrs)

Student Services: Academic counselling, Employment services, Foreign student adviser, Foreign Studies Centre, Handicapped facilities, Language programs, Sports facilities

Libraries: Yes

Academic Staff 2011	MEN	WOMEN	TOTAL
FULL-TIME	13	17	30
PART-TIME	3	5	8
STAFF WITH DOCTORATE			
FULL-TIME	3	1	4
PART-TIME	1	–	1
Student Numbers 2011			
All (Foreign Included)	272	88	360
FOREIGN ONLY	–	–	32

Last Updated: 16/05/11

ANGERS SCHOOL OF NOTARY STUDIES
Institut des Métiers du Notariat d' Angers
35 bd. Pierre de Coubertin, Angers
Tel: +33(2) 41-86-09-17
EMail: imn.angers@orange.fr
Website: http://www.imn-angers.fr

Directrice: Marie Bart

Programmes
Notary Studies (Notary Studies)

Main Language(s) of Instruction: French

Degrees and Diplomas: *Brevet de Technicien supérieur*; *Licence professionnelle*. Diplôme de L'IMN (4 yrs)
Last Updated: 27/07/11

AUDENCIA NANTES SCHOOL OF MANAGEMENT
Audencia Group (AUDENCIA-NANTES)
BP 31222, 8, route de la Jonelière, 44312 Nantes, Cedex 3
Tel: +33(2) 40-37-34-34
Fax: +33(2) 40-37-34-07
Website: http://www.audencia.com

Directeur général: Frank Vidal

Schools
Commerce *(Atlantique)* (Business and Commerce; Marketing); **Communication and Media** *(Sciences Com)* (Communication Studies; Journalism; Media Studies); **Management** (Business Administration; Business and Commerce; Management; Sales Techniques)

Further Information: Also Summer School for foreign students

History: Founded 1900 as l'École Supérieure de Commerce de Nantes. Acquired present title 2011 following merger of Audencia Nantes, the Ecole atlantique de Commerce and Sciences Com.

Governing Bodies: Board of Directors, comprising representatives of the Chamber of Commerce and Industry of Nantes, City of Nantes, and the Council of Loire Atlantique

Academic Year: September to June (September-December; January-March; March-June)

Admission Requirements: Competitive entrance examination following 1-2 yrs further study after secondary school certificate (baccalauréat) or following first 3-yr university qualification (Licence or Maîtrise), or equivalent

Fees: (Euros): Management diploma course, 5,183 per annum; Master 9,147

Main Language(s) of Instruction: French, English (Summer School)

Degrees and Diplomas: *Diplôme d'Etudes d'Ecole de Commerce et Gestion*: 3 yrs; *Mastère spécialisé*; *Diplôme national de Master*

Student Services: Academic counselling, Canteen, Cultural centre, Employment services, Foreign student adviser, Handicapped facilities, Health services, Social counselling, Sports facilities

Libraries: Médiathèque, 13,000 vols
Last Updated: 29/09/11

AUVERGNE SCHOOL OF NOTARY STUDIES
Institut des Métiers du Notariat d'Auvergne
26 avenue Léon Blum, BP 283, 63000 Clermont-Ferrand, Cedex
Tel: +33(4) 73-17-77-60
Fax: +33(4) 73-17-77-61
EMail: institut.notariat@laposte.net
Website: http://www.institut-des-metiers-du-notariat-auvergne.fr

Directeur: Didier Laurent-Bonne

Programmes
Notary Studies (Notary Studies)

History: Founded 1913.

Main Language(s) of Instruction: French

Accrediting Agencies: Ministry of Justice, Centre National de l'Enseignement Professionnel Notarial

Degrees and Diplomas: *Brevet de Technicien supérieur, Licence professionnelle.* Diplôme des instituts des métiers du notariat 1 yr after Licence professionnelle
Last Updated: 15/10/07

BEM - BORDEAUX

BEM - Bordeaux Management School
680, cours de la Libération, 33405 Talence, Cedex
Tel: +33(5) 56-84-55-55
Fax: +33(5) 56-84-55-00
EMail: info@bem.edu
Website: http://www.bem.edu

Directeur: Philip McLaughlin

International Relations: Anne-Claire Charpentier
Tel: +33(5) 56-84-55-54 EMail: anne-claire.charpentier@bem.edu

Programmes
Commerce and Finance (Business and Commerce; Finance); **Commerce and Finance Bachelor Programme** *(SUP'TG) Division Head:* Dominique Billon; **Industrial Logistics** *(ISLI)* (Transport Management); **Industrial Purchasing Management** *(MAI)* (Management); **International Business** *(MACI)* (International Business; Management); **International Business** *(EBP International)* (International Business; Management); **International Management** *(EBP International)* (International Business; Management); **International Purchasing** *(MAI)* (Management); **Management** *(ESC Bordeaux Grande Ecole)* (Business Administration; Management); **Quality Management** *(ISMQ)* (Management; Safety Engineering); **Real Estate and Asset Management** *(IMPI)* (Management; Notary Studies; Real Estate); **Risk Management** *(IMR)* (Insurance; Management); **Supply Chain Management** *(ISLI)* (Management; Transport Management); **Wine and Spirits Management** (Management; Viticulture)

History: Founded 1874 as Ecole Supérieure de Commerce . Acquired present title 2007.

Admission Requirements: After secondary school certificate (baccalauréat) or equivalent or following two years' further study after the Baccalauréat or Baccalauréat and five years of higher education

Fees: (Euros): depending on the programme

Main Language(s) of Instruction: French, English

Degrees and Diplomas: *Diplôme d'Etudes d'Ecole de Commerce et Gestion:* 3 yrs; *Mastère spécialisé; Diplôme national de Master.* MSc, MBA and Master Grande Ecole

Student Residential Facilities: For c. 160 students

Libraries: Informathèque, 26,000 vols, 400 press and journal subscriptions; 20 databases

Publications: Logistique & Management; Supply Chain Forum
Last Updated: 06/06/11

BORDEAUX SCHOOL OF NOTARY STUDIES

Institut des Métiers du Notariat de Bordeaux
7, rue Mably, 33000 Bordeaux
Tel: +33(5) 56-48-69-60
Fax: +33(5) 56-48-69-68
EMail: imn-cfpnbx@orange.fr

Directrice: Delphine Feigna

Programmes
Notary Studies (Notary Studies)

Admission Requirements: Baccalauréat or equivalent Secondary School degree; Capacité en droit for the 2nd year; 2 yrs undergraduate studies in Law or DUT in Law

Main Language(s) of Instruction: French

Accrediting Agencies: Ministry of Justice, Centre National de l'Enseignement Professionnel Notarial

Degrees and Diplomas: *Brevet de Technicien supérieur, Licence professionnelle.* Diplôme de l'institut des métiers du notariat 1 yr after Licence
Last Updated: 15/10/07

BRITANNY SCHOOL OF MANAGEMENT

Ecole supérieure de Commerce Bretagne Brest (ESC BRETAGNE, BREST)
2 avenue de Provence CS 23812, 29238 Brest, Cedex 3
Tel: +33(2) 98-34-44-44
Fax: +33(2) 98-34-44-69
EMail: communication@esc-bretagne-brest.com
Website: http://www.esc-bretagne-brest.com

Directeur: Philippe Le Glas (2010-)
Tel: +33(2) 98-34-44-41
EMail: philippe.leglas@esc-bretagne-brest.com

International Relations: Gilles Gueguery
Tel: +33(2) 98-34-45-07
EMail: gilles.gueguer@esc-bretagne-brest.com

Graduate Colleges
Management (Management)

History: Founded 1962.

Governing Bodies: Chamber of Commerce and Industry of Brest

Admission Requirements: Competitive entrance examination following 2 yrs further study after secondary school certificate (baccalauréat) or equivalent

Fees: (Euros): 5,000-8,000 per annum

Main Language(s) of Instruction: French, English

International Co-operation: With universities and schools worldwide

Accrediting Agencies: Conférences des grandes Ecoles(France), Ministry of Higher Education

Degrees and Diplomas: *Diplôme d'Etudes d'Ecole de Commerce et Gestion:* Management, 3 yrs; *Mastère spécialisé:* Finance; Management; Logistics; Management Control, 1 yr; *Diplôme national de Master:* International Business (MSC), 1 yr. Also Bachelor in Management (3 yrs)

Student Services: Academic counselling, Canteen, Employment services, Foreign student adviser, Handicapped facilities, Language programs, Social counselling, Sports facilities

Student Residential Facilities: None

Libraries: Yes
Last Updated: 31/05/11

BUSINESS INSTITUTE OF MARKETING AND COMMERCE

Institut supérieur de Commerce et de Marketing (ISTEC)
12, rue Alexandre Parodi, 75010 Paris
Tel: +33(1) 40-03-15-68
Fax: +33(1) 40-03-15-89
EMail: istec@istec.fr
Website: http://www.istec.fr

Directeur général: Benoît Herbert EMail: b.herbert@istec.fr

Programmes
Marketing (Business and Commerce; Marketing)

History: Founded 1961.

Admission Requirements: Baccalauréat or equivalent Secondary School leaving certificate

Fees: (Euros): 6,850 p.a.

Main Language(s) of Instruction: French

Accrediting Agencies: Ministry of Education

Degrees and Diplomas: *Licence:* Marketing, Management, 3 yrs; *Diplôme national de Master:* Luxury Brands, Event Management and Marketing, 2 yrs following Licence
Last Updated: 07/07/11

BUSINESS MANAGEMENT SCHOOL

Institut de Formation aux Affaires et à la Gestion (IFAG)
25, rue Claude Tiller, 75012 Paris
Tel: +33(1) 46-59-20-76
Fax: +33(1) 46-59-25-05
EMail: paris@ifag.com
Website: http://www.ifag.com

Directeur: Dominique Lemaire

Programmes

Management (Business Administration; International Business; Management; Marketing)

Further Information: Also schools in: Paris, Lyon, Toulouse. Montluçon, Auxerre, Angers, Nîmes and Caen

History: Founded in 1986.

Academic Year: October-May with a summer internship at an enterprise

Admission Requirements: 2 yrs undergraduate studies and entrance exam

Fees: (Euros): 6,400

Main Language(s) of Instruction: French, English

Degrees and Diplomas: *Diplôme national de Master.* Also MSc International Business & Management
Last Updated: 16/12/11

CATHOLIC INSTITUTE OF ADVANCED STUDIES
Institut catholique d'Etudes supérieures (ICES)
17, boulevard des Belges, BP 691, 85017 La Roche-sur-Yon, Cedex
Tel: +33(2) 51-46-12-13
Fax: +33(2) 51-46-15-17
EMail: info@ices.fr
Website: http://www.ices.fr

Président: Hervé Magnouloux EMail: hmagnouloux@ices.fr

Departments

Biology (Biological and Life Sciences; Biology; Biotechnology; Genetics; Molecular Biology; Pharmacology; Physiology); **History** (Ancient Civilizations; Contemporary History; History; Medieval Studies); **Languages** (Modern Languages); **Law** (Law); **Letters** (Arts and Humanities; Literature); **Mathematics** (Mathematics; Physics); **Physics and Chemistry** (Chemistry; Physics); **Political Science** (Economics; International Relations; Political Sciences)

History: Founded 1990.

Academic Year: September to July

Admission Requirements: Baccalauréat or equivalent Secondary School degree, entrance exams and interview

Fees: (Euros): Licence/Master 1,2,995 per annum; Master 23,150

Main Language(s) of Instruction: French, some courses in English

International Co-operation: With 53 universities in over 40 countries

Degrees and Diplomas: *Licence:* Biology; Law; History; Arts and Humanities; Modern Languages; Political Science; Mathematics; Physics, 3 yrs; *Diplôme national de Master:* Private Law; International Relations; History

Student Services: Academic counselling, Foreign student adviser, Foreign Studies Centre, Handicapped facilities, Language programs, Social counselling, Sports facilities

Student Residential Facilities: Yes.

Libraries: c. 90,000 vols; 400 periodicals
Last Updated: 23/05/11

CATHOLIC INSTITUTE OF TOULOUSE
Institut catholique de Toulouse
BP 7012, 31, rue de la Fonderie, 31068 Toulouse, Cedex 7
Tel: +33(5) 61-36-81-00
Fax: +33(5) 61-36-81-08
EMail: secr.univ@ict-toulouse.asso.fr
Website:http: //www.ict-toulouse.asso.fr

Recteur: Pierre Debergé (2004-)
Tel: +33(5) 61-36-81-27, Fax: +33(5) 61-53-97-91

Secrétaire général: Monique Delcroix Tel: +33(5) 61-36-81-36

International Relations: Annie Despatureaux
Tel: +33(5) 61-36-81-27 EMail: ri@ict-toulouse.asso.fr

Centres

African Studies *(CEA)* (African Studies) *Division Head:* Robert Chuquet; **Hygiene and Social Studies** *(CEPRESS)* (Social Sciences);** Religious Training** *(AFP)* (Religious Education) *Division Head:* Jean Joseph; **Teacher Training** *(CFP)* (Teacher Training)

Colleges

Occitan Studies *(by correspondence)* (Regional Studies) *Director:* Georges Passerat

Faculties

Arts and Humanities (Arts and Humanities; Communication Studies; History; Literature; Modern Languages; Psychology); **Canon Law** (Canon Law); **Law** (Law); **Philosophy** (Philosophy); **Theology** (Theology)

Institutes

Communication *(ISCAM)* (Communication Studies; Multimedia); **French Studies for Foreigners** *(IULCF)* (French; French Studies); **Preschool and Health Education** *(IFRASS)* (Health Education; Preschool Education; Special Education); **Religions and Pastoral Studies** *(IERP)* (Pastoral Studies; Religion); **Religious Art and Sacred Music** *(IAMS)* (Religious Art; Religious Music); **Religious Training** *(AFP)* (Religious Education; Religious Studies); **Sciences and Theology of Religions** *(ISTR)* (Religious Studies; Theology); **Teacher Training** *(ISFEC)* (Teacher Training)

Schools

Agriculture *(ESAP, Purpan)* (Agriculture); **Journalism** *(EJT)* (Journalism)

Further Information: Has sites in Bayonne, Bordeaux, Perpignan and Rodez.

History: Founded 1877 but traces its history to the original University of Toulouse founded 1229.

Governing Bodies: Assembly of the Archbishops and Bishops of the 18 dioceses of the region; Administrative Council; Academic Council. In civil matters the institution is subject to the jurisdiction of the Minister of Education

Academic Year: October to June (October-February; February-June)

Admission Requirements: Secondary school certificate (baccalauréat) or equivalent; competitive examination for certain schools

Fees: (Euros): Faculties, c. 950 per annum; Schools or Institutes, c. 3,000

Main Language(s) of Instruction: French

International Co-operation: University of Valencia; University of Vigo; University of Granada; University of Navarra; Eichstadt-Ingostadt University; University of Ljubljana; Ostfold University College; University of Stockholm; University of Lublin; University of Messina; Universidade Catolica de Lisboa

Degrees and Diplomas: *Licence:* canonique; *Diplôme national de Master; Doctorat:* canonique. Under French law Catholic institutions are not entitled to award official degrees and diplomas. Students prepare for State degrees and diplomas at the same time. However, the Faculties of Theology, Canon Law, and Philosophy award a Baccalauréat canonique, Licence canonique and Doctorat canonique and the various schools award their own diplomas

Student Residential Facilities: Yes

Special Facilities: Georges Baccrabère Museum

Libraries: c. 250,000 vols; School of Agriculture (Purpan), 12,000

Publications: Bulletin de Littérature Ecclésiastique *(quarterly)*; Les Cahiers de la Faculté de Théologie; Les Cahiers de l'ISTR; Recherches philosophiques
Last Updated: 24/05/11

CATHOLIC UNIVERSITY OF LILLE
Université catholique de Lille
BP 109, 60, boulevard Vauban, 59016 Lille, Cedex
Tel: +33(3) 20-13-40-00
Fax: +33(3) 20-13-40-01
EMail: saio@fupl.asso.fr
Website: http://www.univ-catholille.fr/

Recteur: Thérèse Lebrun-Cardon (2003-)
Tel: +33(3) 20-13-40-86, Fax: +33(3) 20-13-40-95
EMail: therese.lebrun@icl-lille.fr

Secrétaire général: Jean-Marc Assié
Tel: +33(3) 20-13-40-82, Fax: +33(3) 20-13-40-95
EMail: jean-marc.assie@icl-lille.fr

International Relations: Anne-Marie Michel
Tel: +33(3) 59-56-69-97, Fax: +33(3) 59-56-69-99
EMail: anne-marie.michel@univ-catholille.fr

Departments
Ethics (Ethics)

Faculties
Arts and Humanities (Arts and Humanities; Communication Studies; Cultural Studies; History; Literature; Marketing; Media Studies; Modern Languages; Psychology; Social Sciences); **Economics** (Economics); **Law** (Commercial Law; Criminal Law; Law; Private Law; Public Law); **Medicine** (Medicine); **Science** (Natural Sciences); **Theology** (Theology)

Institutes
Agricultural Studies *(ISA)* (Agriculture); **Catechism** *(IiFAC)* (Religious Education); **Civil and Mechanical Engineering** *(ICAM)* (Civil Engineering; Mechanical Engineering); **Electronics** *(ISEN)* (Electronic Engineering); **Medical Communication; Nursing and Child Welfare** *(IFSanté)* (Child Care and Development; Nursing); **Physiotherapy and Chiropody** (Chiropractic; Physical Therapy); **Scientific Economics and Management** *(IESEG)* (Economics; Management); **Social Work** *(ISL)* (Social Work); **Strategy and Communication Techniques** *(ISTC)* (Communication Studies); **Teacher Training** *(IFP Lille/Arras)* (Primary Education; Teacher Training)

Research Laboratories
Economics and Social Sciences *(LEM)* (Economics; Social Sciences); **Medicine** (Medicine); **Science** (Natural Sciences)

Schools
Applied Sciences *(ESPAS)* (Applied Chemistry; Applied Mathematics; Applied Physics; Natural Sciences); **Business Management** *(ESPEME Lille)* (Accountancy; Finance; Law; Marketing); **Business Management** *(ESPEME Nice)* (Accountancy; Finance; Law; Management; Marketing); **Commercial Studies** *(EDHEC)* (Business and Commerce); **Industrial Studies** *(HEI)* (Industrial Management); **Midwifery** *(ESF)* (Midwifery); **Translators, Interpreters and International Commerce** *(ESTICE)* (Translation and Interpretation)

Further Information: Also French courses for foreign students

History: Founded 1875 as a Catholic Faculty of Law; Letters and Science added 1876; Medicine and Pharmacy, and Theology added 1877. Reorganised and acquired present title 1974. In civil matters the Institution is subject to the jurisdiction of the Ministry of Education.

Governing Bodies: Conseil supérieur, comprising 20 members; Conseil d'administration; Conseil de la Fédération

Academic Year: September or October to June

Admission Requirements: Secondary school certificate (baccalauréat) or recognized foreign equivalent, and entrance examination

Fees: (Euros): 1,000-2,500 per annum in a faculty; 2,300-4,500 per annum in a school or institute

Main Language(s) of Instruction: French. Some courses in English

International Co-operation: With universities in the United States; Canada; Mexico; Chile; Australia. Also participates in Erasmus

Accrediting Agencies: EQUIS

Degrees and Diplomas: *Licence*: 3 yrs; *Diplôme d'Etat*: Nursing; Midwifery; Social Work; Medicine; Physiotherapy; Podology; *Diplôme d'Ingénieur*: Electronics; Engineering; Landscape Engineering; Textile Engineering; Environmental Engineering; Agricultural Engineering, 5 yrs; *Diplôme national de Master; Doctorat*: Theology

Student Services: Academic counselling, Canteen, Cultural centre, Foreign student adviser, Foreign Studies Centre, Handicapped facilities, Health services, Language programs, Nursery care, Social counselling, Sports facilities

Student Residential Facilities: Yes

Special Facilities: Zoology Museum; Botany Museum; Geology Museum; Pathology Museum; Anatomy Museum

Libraries: Central Library, c. 550,000 vols; specialized libraries

Publications: Catho-International *(annually)*; Encyclopédie catholicisme; Journal des Sciences médicales *(monthly)*; Mélanges de Science Religieuse *(quarterly)*; Mémoires et Travaux (63 vols); Vie et Foi *(quarterly)*

Last Updated: 26/07/11

CATHOLIC UNIVERSITY OF LYONS
Université catholique de Lyon
25, rue du Plat, 69288 Lyon, Cedex 2
Tel: +33(4) 72-32-50-12
EMail: riucl@univ-catholyon.fr
Website: http://www.univ-catholyon.fr

Recteur: Thierry Magnin (2011-) Tel: +33(2) 72-32-50-01

Secrétaire générale: Claudine Dargent
Tel: +33(4) 72-32-50-70, Fax: +33(4) 72-32-51-48

International Relations: Nicole Ughetto Tel: +33(4) 72-32-50-03

Faculties
Law, Economics, and Social Sciences *(FDSES)* (Development Studies; Economics; Family Studies; Human Rights; Law; Management; Social Sciences); **Letters and Languages** (Arts and Humanities; French; Modern Languages; Regional Studies; Translation and Interpretation); **Philosophy and Human Sciences** (Educational and Student Counselling; Philosophy; Psychology); **Science** (Biochemistry; Biology; Biotechnology; Health Education; Laboratory Techniques; Natural Sciences); **Theology and Religious Studies** (Judaic Religious Studies; Pastoral Studies; Religious Studies; Theology)

History: Founded 1875.

Governing Bodies: Assembly of Archbishops and Bishops of the 29 dioceses of the region; Conseil supérieur. In civil matters the Institution is subject to the jurisdiction of the Ministry of Education

Academic Year: October to June (October-February; February-June)

Admission Requirements: Secondary school certificate (baccalauréat) or recognized foreign equivalent

Main Language(s) of Instruction: French

International Co-operation: Over 80 partnerships. Also participates in Erasmus and Leonardo

Degrees and Diplomas: *Licence*: Arts; Philosophy; Law; Psychology; ESTBB; ESTRI, 3 yrs; *Diplôme national de Master*: Canon Law; Philosophy; Theology, 5 yrs; *Doctorat*: Theology; Philosophy; Science (EPHESS), 8 yrs

Student Services: Canteen, Language programs, Sports facilities

Student Residential Facilities: Yes

Libraries: University Library, 210,000 vols; Faculty of Science library; Institute of Pedagogy library; Institut Pierre Gardette library

Publications: Cahiers *(biennially)*
Last Updated: 16/12/11

CATHOLIC UNIVERSITY OF PARIS
Institut catholique de Paris
21, rue d'Assas, 75006 Paris
Tel: +33(1) 44-39-52-02
Fax: +33(1) 42-84-25-78
EMail: recteur@icp.fr
Website: http://www.icp.fr

Recteur: Philippe Bordeyne (2011-)

International Relations: Muriel Cordier, Directrice du développement international Tel: +33(1) 44 39 84 76 EMail: m.cordier@icp.fr

Faculties
Canon Law (Canon Law); **Economics and Social Sciences** *(FASSE)* (Economics; Social Sciences); **Education** *(ISP)* (Education); **Letters** (Arts and Humanities); **Philosophy** (Philosophy); **Theology** *(FTSR)* (Religious Studies; Theology)

Institutes
French Language and Culture *(ILCF, for foreign students)* (Cultural Studies; French); **Physical Education** *(ILEPS)* (Physical Education); **Religious Studies** *(IER)* (Religious Studies)

Schools

Library Science *(EBD)* (Library Science); **Psychology** *(EPP)* (Psychology); **Psycho-pedagogical Training** *(EFPP)* (Education; Psychology)

History: Founded 1875.

Governing Bodies: General Assembly of Bishops of the dioceses of the region; Conseil d'Etablissement, including the Rector, Deans and elected representatives of academic staff and students. In civil matters the Institution is subject to the jurisdiction of the Minister of Education

Academic Year: October to June (October-February; February-June)

Admission Requirements: Secondary school certificate (baccalauréat) or recognized equivalent

Fees: (Euros): 2,000-3,500 for Licences.

Main Language(s) of Instruction: French

International Co-operation: Participates in Erasmus, MICEFA and CIEP exchange programmes and has signed bilateral parternership agreements with Universities situated worldwide.

Degrees and Diplomas: *Licence*: Letters, Languages, Educational Sciences, Science of Religion, Social Sciences, 3 yrs; *Diplôme national de Master*: Philology, Philosophy, Theology, Social Sciences; *Doctorat*: Philology, Theology, Philosophy, Educational Sciences. Under French law, Catholic Institutions are not entitled to award official degrees and diplomas. Students prepare for State degrees and diplomas at the same time. The Faculties of Theology, Canon Law, and Philosophy award a Baccalauréat canonique, Licence canonique and Doctorat canonique recognized by the Holy See, and the various institutes and schools award their own specialised diplomas. The Faculty of Theology also awards an MBA.

Student Services: Cultural centre, Foreign student adviser, Health services, Social counselling, Sports facilities

Student Residential Facilities: Yes

Special Facilities: Collection géologique de l'Institut géologique Albert-de-Lapparent. Musée Branly; Musée d'Archéologie biblique

Libraries: University Library, 700,000 vols

Publications: Eduquer et Former; Transversalités. Revue de l'Institut Catholoique de Paris *(quarterly)*

Last Updated: 25/01/12

CATHOLIC UNIVERSITY OF THE WEST, ANGERS

Université catholique de l'Ouest (UCO)
BP 10808, 3, place André Leroy, 49008 Angers, Cedex 01
Tel: +33(2) 41-81-66-00
Fax: +33(2) 41-81-66-09
EMail: comm@uco.fr
Website: http://www.uco.fr

Recteur: Guy Bedouelle (2008-)
Tel: +33(2) 41-81-66-01 EMail: rectorat@uco.fr

Secrétaire général: Patrice Lecomte Tel: +33(2) 41-81-66-07

Centres

International French Studies (International Studies) *Director*: Marc Melin; **Lifelong Education** *Director*: Catherine Nafti-Malherbe

Faculties

Theology (Theology)

Institutes

Applied Mathematics *(IMA)* (Applied Mathematics; Computer Science); **Applied Psychology and Sociology** *(IPSA)* (Clinical Psychology; Psychology; Sociology); **Arts and Humanities** *(IALH)* (Arts and Humanities; Cultural Studies; Fine Arts; History; Literature; Music; Musicology); **Biology and Applied Ecology** *(IBEA)* (Biology; Ecology; Environmental Studies); **Communication and Educational Sciences** (Communication Studies; Education; Educational Sciences; Teacher Training); **Modern Languages** *(IPVL)* (Arabic; Chinese; Dutch; English; German; Hungarian; Italian; Japanese; Modern Languages; Portuguese; Russian; Spanish; Translation and Interpretation); **Physical Education and Sports** *(IFEPSA)* (Physical Education; Sports); **Pure Mathematics** *(DMP)* (Mathematics) *Director*: Ahmed Guergueb; **Teacher Training** *(IFUCOME)* (Teacher Training) *Director*: Marie-Dominique Pacteau

Schools

Chemistry *(ETSCO)* (Chemistry) *Directeur*: Bernard David; **Commercial Sciences** *(ESSCA)* (Business and Commerce) *Director*: Michel Poté; **Computer Science and Production** *(ESAIP)*

Units

Catholic Studies *(North Brittany)* (Christian Religious Studies) *Director*: Michel Dorveaux; **Catholic Studies** *(South Brittany)* (Christian Religious Studies) *Director*: Sylvie Murzeau

Further Information: Campuses in Guingamp and Arradon

History: Founded between 1875 and 1879 when higher education institutions in France became fully secular. Reorganized 1970 following establishment of a State university in Angers.

Governing Bodies: Council of Bishops of the diocese of the region, represented by the Chancelier, who is the Bishop of Angers; Conseil Rectoral. Financed by student fees, subventions by the Ministry, the local authorities and the dioceses, gifts, and donations. In civil matters the institution is subject to the jurisdiction of the Minister of Education

Academic Year: October to June (October-January; February-June). Centre of French Studies: October (1st semester); February (2nd semester)

Admission Requirements: Secondary school certificate (baccalauréat) or equivalent

Fees: (Euros): c. 2,500 per annum

Main Language(s) of Instruction: French

International Co-operation: Participates in Cidef (Centre international d'Etudes Françaises), Tempus, Socrates, Lingua, Comenius and Crepuq programmes

Degrees and Diplomas: *Licence*: 3 yrs; *Diplôme national de Master*: 2 yrs after Licence; *Doctorat*. Under French law, Catholic faculties are not entitled to award official degrees and diplomas without State University agreement. Students prepare for State degrees and diplomas under convention with several French State Universities. Professional titles of Ingénieur are officially recognized. The University awards specific professional titles

Student Services: Cultural centre, Employment services, Foreign student adviser, Foreign Studies Centre, Handicapped facilities, Health services, Language programs, Social counselling

Special Facilities: Art Gallery. Movie Studio. Commission Présence des Arts.

Libraries: Bibliothèque Lamoricière, c. 350,000 vols; Bibliothèque du Moreanum

Publications: Cahiers du C.R.E.O. *(quarterly)*; Impacts (revue de l'Université Catholique de l'Ouest) *(quarterly)*; Les Cahiers de l'I.M.A. *(quarterly)*; Les Cahiers de l'I.P.S.A. (Institut de Psychologie) *(quarterly)*; Moreana *(quarterly)*

Last Updated: 11/07/11

CENTRAL SCHOOL OF ELECTRONICS

Ecole centrale d'Electronique (ECE)
Immeuble POLLUX, 37, Quai de Grenelle, CS 71520, 75007 Paris
Tel: +33(1) 44-39-06-00
Fax: +33(1) 42-22-59-02
EMail: contact@ece.fr
Website: http://www.ece.fr

Directeur: Pascal Brouaye

Programmes

Electronic Engineering (Electronic Engineering)

History: Founded 1919 as l'Ecole Centrale de TSF.

Main Language(s) of Instruction: French

Degrees and Diplomas: *Diplôme d'Ingénieur*; *Mastère spécialisé*; *Diplôme national de Master*

Last Updated: 23/06/11

CENTRE FOR JOURNALISM STUDIES

Centre de Formation des Journalistes (CFJ)
35, rue du Louvre, 75002 Paris
Tel: +33(1) 44-82-20-00
Fax: +33(1) 44-82-20-09
EMail: cfpj@cfpj.com
Website: http://www.cfpj.com

Directeur: Christophe Deloire EMail: cdeloire@cfpj.com

Programmes

Journalism (Journalism; Modern Languages; Radio and Television Broadcasting)

Further Information: Is part of the CFPJ Groupe which also includes a Centre for Continuing Education in Journalism.

History: Founded 1946.

Academic Year: October-May

Admission Requirements: 3-year degree course. Under 26 years of age

Fees: (Euros): 2-year Journalism course 3,500 per annum. Students on special grants 1,900

Main Language(s) of Instruction: French

Accrediting Agencies: Commission Nationale Paritaire pour l'Emploi des Journalistes (CNPEJ); Ministère de l'Enseignement supérieur et de la Recherche

Degrees and Diplomas: CFJ diploma (2 yrs after degree course) Masters-level degree in Journalism (2 yrs with internship) in partnership with Université de Paris I Panthéon Sorbonne

Last Updated: 10/06/11

CENTRE OF ADVANCED INDUSTRIAL STUDIES

Groupe CESI
30 rue Cambronne, 75015 Paris, Cedex
Tel: +33(1) 44-19-23-45
Fax: +33(1) 42-50-25-06
EMail: contact@cesi.fr
Website: http://www.cesi.fr/

Directeur général: Hilaire de Chergé (2011-)
Tel: +33(1) 44-19-23-45 EMail: jbahry@cesi.fr

Centres

Apprenticeship Centre *(CESFA Bagneux)* (Construction Engineering); **Industrial Training in Alternance** *(CEFIPA Bagneux)*

Divisions

Continuing Education (Construction Engineering; Human Resources; Industrial Management; Information Technology; Management; Marketing; Real Estate)

Schools

Computer Science *(EXIA)* (Computer Science; Information Technology); **Engineering** *(EI CESI)* (Civil Engineering; Construction Engineering; Human Resources; Industrial Management; Management; Safety Engineering)

Further Information: Branches in Lyon; Arras; Nantes; Toulouse; Strasbourg; Aix-en-Provence; Le Mans; Bordeaux; Grenoble; Rouen; Orléans; Nancy; CESI Iberia - Montpellier; Reims; Angoulême; Saint Nazaire; Pau; CESI Algérie; Rennes; Nice

History: Founded 1958.

Admission Requirements: Secondary school certificate and a 2 yr university diploma (DUT, BTS or equivalent), tests, interview and portfolio

Fees: (Euros): Diplôme d'Ingénieur, 84 per annum; Mastère, 11,400

Main Language(s) of Instruction: French

International Co-operation: Partnerships with Northumbria and Oxford Brookes (UK), Laval and Montreal Universities (Quebec) and Coblence Technology University in Germany. Participates in Force, Tempus, Leonardo programmes.

Accrediting Agencies: Commission des Titres d'Ingénieur, Conférence des Grandes Ecoles

Degrees and Diplomas: *Diplôme d'Ingénieur*: Industrial Engineering, 2-3 yrs; *Mastère spécialisé*: Industrial Management, Quality Management, HR Management, Project Management, 1 yr following Diplôme d'Ingénieur

Last Updated: 23/06/11

CHAMBERY GRADUATE SCHOOL OF BUSINESS

Groupe ESC Chambéry Savoie
Savoie Technolac, 73381 Le Bourget du Lac, Cedex
Tel: +33(4) 79-25-32-54
Fax: +33(4) 79-25-33-54
EMail: supdeco@esc-chambery.fr
Website: http://www.esc-chambery.fr

Directeur: Bernard Pinat

International Relations: Michel Guilmault

Programmes

Management (Business and Commerce; International Business; Management; Marketing; Sports Management)

History: Founded 1992.

Academic Year: October-May with an internship in an International Company

Admission Requirements: Preparatory Classes Diploma in Economics and Business or Literature; 3-4 yrs undergraduate studies and entrance exam

Fees: (Euros): 6,690

Main Language(s) of Instruction: French, English

International Co-operation: Possible to do a 6-9 months. exchange with selected Institutions in Australia, UK, Ireland and Hungry. Includes a MBA in Sports Management partnership programme with Savoie University.

Accrediting Agencies: Association des Chambres Française de Commerce et d'Industrie (ACFCI), Répertoire Nationale des Certifications Professionnelles (RNCP), Ministry of Education

Degrees and Diplomas: *Brevet de Technicien supérieur*; *Diplôme universitaire de Technologie*; *Licence professionnelle*: Products sales and financial services; *Diplôme national de Master*. Also Bachelor's degrees. Grande Ecole programme

Last Updated: 05/07/11

CHAMPAGNE SCHOOL OF MANAGEMENT

Groupe ESC Troyes (ESC TROYES)
BP 710, 217, avenue Pierre Brossolette, 10002 Troyes, Cedex
Tel: +33(3) 25-71-22-22
Fax: +33(3) 25-49-22-17
EMail: infos@groupe-esc-troyes.com
Website: http://www.groupe-esc-troyes.com

Directeur: Francis Bécard
Tel: +33(3) 25-71-22-46
EMail: francis.becard@groupe-esc-troyes.com

International Relations: Jean-Louis Chaperon
Tel: +33(3) 25-71-22-39, Fax: +33(3) 25-71-22-63
EMail: jean.louis.chaperon@groupe-esc-troyes.com

Programmes

ESC Troyes Grande Ecole (Business Administration; Finance; Human Resources; Management; Marketing)

Schools

Graphic Arts and Design *(ESAA)* (Design; Graphic Arts); **Management** *(International INBA)* (International Business; Management); **Tourism** *(International EMVOL)* (Management; Regional Planning; Tourism)

History: ESC Troyes founded in 1992, acquiring current title and status in 1999.

Admission Requirements: ESC Troyes 2 years undergraduate studies and entrance exam; INBA, EMVOL and ESAA high school certificate or equivalent and entrance examination

Main Language(s) of Instruction: French

Degrees and Diplomas: Bachelors; Master's

Last Updated: 10/06/11

DIJON SCHOOL OF NOTARY STUDIES

Institut des Métiers du Notariat de Dijon
2 Avenue de Marbotte, 21000 Dijon
Tel: +33(3) 80-67-15-71
Fax: +33(3) 80-66-89-95
Website: http://www.imn-dijon.com

Directrice: Isabelle Di Giovanni

Programmes
Notary Studies (Notary Studies)

History: Founded 1908.

Academic Year: October-June

Admission Requirements: Baccalauréat or equivalent Secondary School degree; Capacité en droit for the 2nd year; 2 yrs undergraduate studies in Law or DUT in Law

Accrediting Agencies: Ministry of Justice, Centre National de l'Enseignement Professionnel Notarial

Degrees and Diplomas: *Brevet de Technicien supérieur; Licence professionnelle.* Diplôme de l'Institut des Métiers du Notariat 1 yr after Licence Professionnelle

Last Updated: 15/10/07

ECAM LYON GRADUATE SCHOOL OF ENGINEERING
Ecole catholique d'Arts et Métiers (ECAM)
40, montée Saint-Barthélemy, 69321 Lyon, Cedex 05
Tel: +33(4) 72-77-06-00
Fax: +33(4) 72-77-06-11
EMail: info@ecam.fr
Website: http://www.ecam.fr

Directeur général: Didier Desplanche
Tel: +33(4) 72-77-06-10 EMail: direction@ecam.fr

Directeur des Etudes: Patrice Couvrat
Tel: +33(4) 72-77-06-54, Fax: +33(4) 72-77-06-12
EMail: patrice.couvrat@ecam.fr

Departments
Computer Engineering (Computer Engineering); **Electrical and Electronic Engineering and Automation** (Automation and Control Engineering; Electrical and Electronic Engineering); **Industrial Engineering** (Industrial Engineering); **Materials Science** (Materials Engineering); **Mechanical Engineering** (Mechanical Engineering)

Further Information: Forms the Groupe ECAM which includes ECAM Rennes- Louis de Broglie, ECAM Strasbourg and EPMI Cergy

History: Founded 1900.

Governing Bodies: Fondation ECAM

Admission Requirements: Scientific high school certificate (baccalauréat S)

Fees: (Euros): 1,316-2,054 per annum (1-2 yrs); 4,750 (3-5 yrs)

Main Language(s) of Instruction: French

International Co-operation: With universities in South Africa, United Kingdom, USA, Australia, Germany, Canada, China, Italy, Mexico, Poland, Peru, Netherlands.

Accrediting Agencies: Commission des Titres d'Ingénieur (CTI)

Degrees and Diplomas: *Mastère spécialisé.* ECAM Masters of Engineering (3 yrs part-time, 5 yrs full-time)

Student Services: Academic counselling, Employment services, Foreign student adviser, Language programs, Social counselling, Sports facilities

Student Residential Facilities: Yes

Libraries: Main Library

Publications: Journal de l'Association des Ingénieurs ECAM *(quarterly)*; Revue des Ingénieurs ECAM/ICAM *(annually)*

Last Updated: 31/05/11

ECAM RENNES -LOUIS DE BROGLIE
ECAM Rennes- Louis de Broglie
Campus de Ker Lann-Bruz, 35091 Rennes, Cedex 9
Tel: +33(2) 99-05-84-00
Fax: +33(2) 99-05-84-19
EMail: contact@ecam-rennes.fr
Website: http://www.ecam-rennes.fr

Directeur: Jean Vimal du Monteil (2008-)
EMail: vimal@ecole-debroglie.fr

Departments
Communications Engineering (Telecommunications Engineering); **Industrial Engineering** (Automation and Control Engineering; Energy Engineering; Industrial Engineering; Mechanical Engineering; Robotics); **Materials Engineering** (Materials Engineering); **Software Engineering and Information Technology** (Information Technology; Software Engineering)

History: Founded 1990.

Main Language(s) of Instruction: French

Accrediting Agencies: CTI (Commission des Titres d'ingénieur)

Degrees and Diplomas: *Diplôme d'Ingénieur*

Last Updated: 27/06/11

EDHEC BUSINESS SCHOOL
24, avenue Gustave Delory, CS 50411, 59057 Roubaix, Cedex 1
Tel: +33(3) 20-15-45-00
Fax: +33(3) 20-15-45-01
EMail: sergine.gallot@edhec.edu
Website: http://www.edhec.com

Directeur général: Olivier Oger
Tel: +33(3) 20-15-45-07 EMail: oger.ol@edhec.edu

International Relations: Anne Zuccarelli Tel: +33(3) 20-15-44-54

Programmes
Commerce (Business and Commerce; Finance; Management)

Further Information: Also campus in Nice, Paris, London, Singapore.

History: Founded 1906. A private 'Grande Ecole'.

Admission Requirements: Competitive entrance examination following 2 yrs further study after secondary school certificate (baccalauréat) or following first university qualification (DEUG, DUT), or equivalent

Fees: (Euros): 7,500-22,000 per annum

Main Language(s) of Instruction: French

Degrees and Diplomas: *Mastère spécialisé; Diplôme national de Master; Doctorat.* Also Bachelor

Last Updated: 04/07/11

EFAP, SCHOOL OF COMMUNICATION PROFESSIONALS
EFAP, Ecole des Métiers de la Communication
61, rue Pierre-Charron, 75008 Paris
Tel: +33(1) 53-76-88-00
Fax: +33(1) 53-76-88-45
Website: http://www.efap.com

Directeur général: Serge Lestrat

International Relations: Sophie-Caroline De Koning
Tel: +33(1) 53-76-88-37 EMail: sc.dekoning@groupe-edh.com

Programmes
Public Relations (Communication Studies; Marketing; Media Studies; Public Relations)

Further Information: Has schools in Paris, Bordeaux, Lille and Lyon. Also in New York, Lisbon, Tokyo, Abidjan and Algiers

History: Founded in 1961, acquiring its present status in 1993.

Academic Year: September to following October for Masters

Admission Requirements: Baccalauréat or equivalent Secondary School Degree for Undergraduate Studies

Fees: (Euros): 6,950

Main Language(s) of Instruction: French, English

Degrees and Diplomas: *Diplôme national de Master.* Media Management, Communication and Marketing, Events Management (Paris), Corporate Communication (Lille), Communication and Sustainable Development (Bordeaux). Diplôme d'Université

Last Updated: 12/05/11

EIGSI LA ROCHELLE ENGINEERING SCHOOL
Ecole d'Ingénieurs généralistes La Rochelle (EIGSI)
26, rue Vaux de Foletier, 17041 La Rochelle, Cedex 1
Tel: +33(5) 46-45-80-05
Fax: +33(5) 46-45-80-10
EMail: info@eigsi.fr
Website: http://www.eigsi.fr

Directeur: Sylvain Orsat
Tel: +33(5) 46-45-80-01 EMail: direction-generale@eigsi.fr

International Relations: Hannelore Guerrand
Tel: +33(5) 46-45-80-17 EMail: international@eigsi.fr

Programmes
Industrial Engineering (Industrial Engineering)

Further Information: Also branch in Casablanca

History: Founded 1901as École d'Électricité et de Mécanique Industrielle (EEMI). Acquired present status and title 1990.

Admission Requirements: Baccalauréat S or STI

Main Language(s) of Instruction: French

Accrediting Agencies: CTI (Ministry of Education)

Degrees and Diplomas: *Diplôme d'Ingénieur*; *Mastère spécialisé*: Urban Sustainable Development, 5 yrs. 3ème Cycle Management Industriel
Last Updated: 24/06/11

EISTI - CERGY-PONTOISE
Ecole internationale des Sciences du Traitement de l'Information (EISTI)
Avenue du Parc, 95011 Cergy-Pontoise, Cedex
Tel: +33(1) 34-25-10-10
Fax: +33(1) 34-25-10-00
EMail: administration@eisti.fr
Website: http://www.eisti.fr

Directeur Général: Nesim Fintz
Tel: +33(1) 34-25-10-11 EMail: fintz@eisti.fr

International Relations: Marie-Josée Lamerre
Tel: +33(1) 34-25-10-03 EMail: mjl@eisti.fr

Programmes
Computer Science (Computer Science; Information Sciences)

Further Information: Also campus in Pau.

History: Founded 1983.

Academic Year: September to June

Admission Requirements: Baccalauréat

Fees: (Euros): 3,100-5,300 per annum

Main Language(s) of Instruction: French

International Co-operation: Participates in Erasmus

Degrees and Diplomas: *Diplôme d'Ingénieur*: 5 yrs; *Mastère spécialisé*; *Diplôme national de Master*: 5 yrs

Student Services: Academic counselling, Canteen, Employment services, Handicapped facilities, Social counselling, Sports facilities

Student Residential Facilities: Yes

Libraries: Yes
Last Updated: 27/06/11

EM LYON BUSINESS SCHOOL
Ecole de Management de Lyon (EM LYON)
BP 174, 23, avenue Guy de Collongue, 69132 Ecully, Cedex
Tel: +33(4) 78-33-78-00
Fax: +33(4) 78-33-61-69
EMail: info@em-lyon.com
Website: http://www.em-lyon.com

Président: Patrick Molle (1996-)
Tel: +33(4) 78-33-78-14, Fax: +33(4) 78-33-78-55
EMail: molle@em-lyon.com

International Relations: Damien Roux
Tel: +33(4) 78-33-78-29 EMail: roux@em-lyon.com

Graduate Schools
Business Administration and Management (Business Administration; Finance; International Business; Management; Marketing)

Research Centres
Management (Management) *Division Head*: David Courpasson

Further Information: Campus in Shanghai

History: Founded 1872.

Governing Bodies: Board of Directors

Academic Year: September to June

Admission Requirements: University level Degree

Fees: (Euros): mastère, 6,350-13,004 per annum; MBA, 18,150

Main Language(s) of Instruction: French, English

Degrees and Diplomas: *Mastère spécialisé*: Marketing, a further yr; *Diplôme national de Master*: Business Administration; Management, a further yr

Student Services: Academic counselling, Canteen, Cultural centre, Employment services, Foreign student adviser, Health services, Social counselling, Sports facilities

Student Residential Facilities: For c. 340 students in 2 residences

Libraries: 16,110 vols
Last Updated: 24/06/11

EPF SCHOOL OF ENGINEERING
EPF Ecole d'Ingénieurs (EPF)
3 bis, rue Lakanal, 92330 Sceaux
Tel: +33(1) 41-13-01-51
Fax: +33(1) 46-60-39-94
EMail: webmaster@epf.fr
Website: http://www.epf.fr

Directeur: Jean-Michel Nicolle Tel: +33(1) 41-13-01-62

International Relations: Gisela Bouzon
Tel: +33(1) 41-13-01-65 EMail: gisela.bouzon@epf.fr

Departments
General Engineering (Engineering); **Industrial Engineering**; **Information Sciences**

Further Information: Also branch in Troyes and Montpellier

History: Founded 1925 as Institut électromécanique féminin, became École polytechnique féminine (EPF) 1933. Acquired present title 1994.

Governing Bodies: Board of Directors

Academic Year: September to June

Admission Requirements: Secondary school certificate (baccalauréat 'S') or equivalent and competitive entrance examination

Fees: (Euros): 6,690 per annum

Main Language(s) of Instruction: French

International Co-operation: With universities in USA, Canada, Mexico, Singapore, Finland, Sweden, Switzerland, Turkey, Germany, Spain.

Degrees and Diplomas: *Diplôme d'Ingénieur*: 5 yrs; *Diplôme national de Master*: General Engineering. Alsqo Master professionnel in Business Engineering

Student Services: Academic counselling, Canteen, Employment services, Foreign student adviser, Foreign Studies Centre, Handicapped facilities, Health services, Language programs, Social counselling, Sports facilities

Student Residential Facilities: Yes

Libraries: Yes

Publications: Interfaces *(biennially)*
Last Updated: 04/07/11

ESA GROUP - GRADUATE SCHOOL OF FOOD, AGRONOMY AND AGRIBUSINESS, ANGERS
Groupe Ecole supérieure d'Agriculture d'Angers (ESA)
55, rue Rabelais, BP 30748, 49007 Angers, Cedex 01
Tel: +33(2) 41-23-55-15
Fax: +33(2) 41-23-55-32
EMail: s.brochier@groupe-esa.com
Website: http://www.groupe-esa.com

Directeur général: Hervé Salkin (2011-)
Tel: +33(2) 41-23-55-02, Fax: +33(2) 41-23-55-00

International Relations: Stéphane Brochier
Tel: +33(2) 41-23-55-06, Fax: +33(2) 41-23-55-32

Departments

Agriculture (Animal Husbandry; Crop Production; Vegetable Production); **Commerce** (Agricultural Business; Business and Commerce; Management; Marketing); **Environment** (Environmental Management; Environmental Studies); **Food Processing** (Agricultural Business; Food Science); **Horticulture** (Horticulture; Vegetable Production); **Landscape Architecture** (Landscape Architecture); **Management and Counselling** (Management); **Viticulture and Oenology** (Oenology; Viticulture)

Graduate Schools

Graduate School *Director*: Alain Bourgeois

Higher Vocational Schools

Agritec (Agricultural Business; Agriculture; Farm Management; Horticulture) *Head*: Marie-Laure Jeuland

Laboratories

Plant Eco-physiology and Agro-ecology (Agriculture; Ecology; Plant and Crop Protection); **Social Sciences** *(LARESS)*

Programmes

Adult Continuing Education (Agriculture; Business and Commerce; Horticulture) *Director*: Luc Albert

Research Groups

Agro-industries specializing in Products and Processes (Agricultural Business)

History: Founded 1898. Acquired present status 2004. Became a non-profit organization 1970.

Academic Year: September to June

Admission Requirements: Competitive entrance examination after secondary school certificate (baccalauréat). Foreign students integrate ESA with a Bachelor or Master of Science (or equivalnet). Selection on C.V., university marks and referees' recommendation and interview. Good knowledge of English and French

Fees: (Euros): Engineer course 4,980 per annum; MSc International Vintage, 9,000.14,000 for foreign students; MSc International Agribusiness, 15,750; MS Juturna (Environment), 7,650; Agricadre (4 yrs course), 3,480 per annum for 2 yrs; European Engineer Degree, 2,235; Licence professionnelle (3 yrs advanced vocational diploma), 3,060; advanced vocational diploma (BTS), 1,104 per annum

Main Language(s) of Instruction: French, English

International Co-operation: Participates in Erasmus, Erasmus-Mundus, Leonardo programmes. Also bilateral agreements with institutions in Europe, USA, Canada, Latin America, Asia

Accrediting Agencies: Ministry of Agriculture; Ministry of Education

Degrees and Diplomas: *Brevet de Technicien supérieur*: Agriculture; Horticulture; Business and Commerce, 2 yrs; *Licence professionnelle*: Management; Crop Production, 1 yr; *Diplôme d'Ingénieur*: Agriculture; Agribusiness; Economy; Environment; Social Sciences, 2-5 yrs; *Mastère spécialisé*: Environmental Studies, 1 yr; *Diplôme national de Master*: Vine, Wine and Territory Management, 2 yrs. Agricadre Diploma, Management and Trade 2 yrs (Diploma level: 4 years of higher education); BSc Honours - European Engineer Degree (EED) in Biotechnology, Seeds and Horticulture/ or Animal Husbandry/ or International Agribusiness, 1 1/2 yr; Master of Science 2 yrs

Student Services: Academic counselling, Canteen, Cultural centre, Employment services, Foreign student adviser, Foreign Studies Centre, Handicapped facilities, Health services, Language programs, Nursery care, Social counselling, Sports facilities

Student Residential Facilities: For c. 650 students

Libraries: Médiathèque, 35,000 vols; 300 periodical subscriptions; specialised databases

Publications: Mag'ESA, Magazine presenting ESA strategy of development, educational methods, international cooperation, relations with companies *(quarterly)*

Press or Publishing House: None
Last Updated: 16/12/11

ESC - AMIENS PICARDIE
Ecole supérieure de Commerce d'Amiens Picardie
(ESC AMIENS PICARDIE)
18, place Saint-Michel, 80038 Amiens, Cedex 1
Tel: +33(3) 22-82-23-00
Fax: +33(3) 22-82-23-01
EMail: information@supco-amiens.fr
Website: http://www.supco-amiens.fr

Directeur général: Jean-Louis Mutte

International Relations: Christophe Crabot, Responsable des Relations internationales
Tel: +33(3) 22-82-24-15
EMail: christophe.crabot@supco-amiens.fr

Programmes
Bachelor *(ISAM)* (Administration; Management); **Master's** *(ESC)*

Further Information: Institut supérieur d'Administration et de Management (ISAM)

History: Founded 1942.

Governing Bodies: Conseil d'Administration

Academic Year: September to June

Admission Requirements: Secondary school certificate (or equivalent) for bachelor's programme; Secondary school certificate and 2 yrs preparatory classes or first university degree for master's programme

Fees: (Euros): Bachelor's programme, 4,590 per annum (no fees in first and second year for students from Picardie); Master's programme, 6,640 per annum

Main Language(s) of Instruction: French, English

International Co-operation: Participates in the Erasmus programme

Degrees and Diplomas: *Licence*: Administration and Management, 3 yrs; *Diplôme d'Etudes d'Ecole de Commerce et Gestion*: 2 yrs after licence

Student Services: Academic counselling, Employment services, Foreign student adviser, Foreign Studies Centre, Language programs, Sports facilities

Student Residential Facilities: Yes

Libraries: Yes
Last Updated: 04/07/11

ESC - PAU
Groupe ESC Pau
3, rue Saint John Perse, 64000 Pau
Tel: +33(5) 59-92-64-64
Fax: +33(5) 59-92-64-55
EMail: info@esc-pau.fr
Website: http://www.esc-pau.fr

Directeur: Jean-Pierre Lahille
Tel: +33(5) 59-92-64-58 EMail: jean-pierre.lahille@esc-pau.fr

International Relations: Francine Maubourguet
Tel: +33(5) 59-92-64-63 EMail: francine.maubourguet@esc-pau.fr

Programmes
Management (Management)

History: Founded 1969.

Admission Requirements: Competitive entrance examination following 2 yrs further study after secondary school certificate (baccalauréat) or equivalent

Fees: (Euros): Commercial diploma course, 5,700 per annum; Mastère 5,946-6,880; MBA, 9,000

Degrees and Diplomas: *Diplôme d'Etudes d'Ecole de Commerce et Gestion*; *Mastère spécialisé*: Auditing, Managing Family Business and Heritage
Last Updated: 04/07/11

ESC RENNES SCHOOL OF BUSINESS
2, rue Robert d'Abrissel, 35065 Rennes
Tel: +33(2) 99-54-63-63
Fax: +33(2) 99-33-08-24
EMail: webmaster@esc-rennes.fr
Website: http://www.esc-rennes.fr

Directeur général-Doyen: Olivier Aptel (2001-)
EMail: olivier.aptel@esc-rennes.fr

International Relations: Laurence Lambert
EMail: laurence.lambert@esc-rennes.fr

Divisions
Finance and Operations; **Management and Organization** (Management); **Strategy and Marketing** (Marketing; Sales Techniques)

Further Information: Also campus in Rabat

History: Founded 1990 by a group of company managers to train global managers.

Governing Bodies: Association with an Advisory Board of companies

Academic Year: September to June

Admission Requirements: Bachelor degree with or without work experience and good level of English (TOEFL: 213 and computer based).

Fees: (Euros): 5,850-25,000 per annum

Main Language(s) of Instruction: English

International Co-operation: With 150 partner universities in Argentina, Austria, Australia, Belgium, Canada, China, Cyprus, Denmark, Egypt, Eire, England, Ecuador, Finland Germany,Greece, Hong Kong, Japan, India, Italy, Lithuania, Mexico, Netherlands, Norway, Peru, Poland, Czech Republic, Russian Federation, USA, South Africa, Spain, Sweden

Accrediting Agencies: Ministry of Higher Education (France); Open University (UK); European Foundation for Management Development (EFMD); EPAS

Degrees and Diplomas: *Diplôme national de Master*: International Business; International Marketing; International Negotiation; (MA); Sports, Leisure and Tourism Management; International Finance; Innovation Management; International Human Resource Management; Management of non-profit Organizations; Managing Diversity; Services Marketing Management (MSc); *Doctorat (PhD)*. Bachelor Degree (IBPM) Master Programme Grande Ecole; Master of Arts in International Business; Executive MBA; PhD

Student Services: Academic counselling, Canteen, Employment services, Foreign student adviser, Foreign Studies Centre, Health services, Language programs, Social counselling, Sports facilities

Student Residential Facilities: Yes.

Libraries: c. 55,000 vols and magazines

ESCEM SCHOOL OF BUSINESS AND MANAGEMENT - POITIERS

Ecole supérieure de Commerce et de Management Paris-Tours-Poitiers (ESCEM)
BP 5, 11, rue de l'Ancienne Comédie, 86001 Poitiers, Cedex
Tel: +33(5) 49-60-58-00
Fax: +33(5) 49-60-58-30
EMail: info@escem.fr
Website: http://www.escem.fr

Président: François Duvergné
Tel: +33(2) 47-71-71-44, Fax: +33(2) 47-71-71-05
EMail: fduverge@escem.fr

Secrétaire Générale: Mireille Lefebvre
Tel: +33(2) 47-71-71-01, Fax: +33(2) 47-71-72-50

International Relations: Véronique Bourdin
Tel: +33(5) 49-60-58-04 EMail: vbourdin@escem.fr

Programmes
Marketing and Management (Human Resources; Management; Marketing)

Further Information: Also campuses in Prague and Athens

History: Founded 1961, merged 1998 with ESCEM Tours, acquired present status and title same year.

Academic Year: September to May

Admission Requirements: National competitive entrance examination

Fees: (Euros): Commerce diploma course, 6,900 per annum

Main Language(s) of Instruction: French, English

Degrees and Diplomas: *Diplôme d'Etudes d'Ecole de Commerce et Gestion*: 3 yrs; *Mastère spécialisé*. Also Bachelor

Student Services: Academic counselling, Canteen, Employment services, Foreign student adviser, Handicapped facilities, Language programs, Sports facilities

Special Facilities: Multimedia Centre

Libraries: Libraries in each campus
Last Updated: 05/07/11

ESCP-EUROPE - PARIS (ESCP-EAP)

79, avenue de la République, 75543 Paris, Cedex 11
Tel: +33(1) 49-23-20-00
Fax: +33(1) 43-55-99-63
EMail: info@escp-eap.net
Website: http://www.escp-eap.eu/campus/paris/

Directeur général: Pascal Morand (2006-)
Tel: +33(1) 49-23-20-05, Fax: +33(1) 49-23-22-12

Secrétaire général: Daniel Julien Tel: +33(1) 49-23-21-75

International Relations: Kenneth Casler
Tel: +33(1) 49-23-27-90, Fax: +33(1) 49-23-22-25
EMail: kcasler@escp-eap.net

Programmes
Business Administration *(MBA programmes)* (Management) *Director*: François Kolb; **Executive Education** *Director*: Anne Gazengel; **Postgraduate Studies** (Management) *Director*: Jérôme Bon

Further Information: Also branches in London, Madrid, Berlin and Turin

History: Founded 1819. Previously known as ESCP-EAP European School of Management. Acquired current name 2009.

Academic Year: September to July

Admission Requirements: First university degree or equivalent (BSc)

Accrediting Agencies: European Advisory Council

Degrees and Diplomas: *Diplôme d'Etudes d'Ecole de Commerce et Gestion*: Business Management, 3 yrs; *Mastère spécialisé (MS)*: a further yr; *Diplôme national de Master*: Business Administration (MBA); European Business (MEB); Management (MiM), a further yr; *Doctorat (PhD)*

Student Services: Academic counselling, Canteen, Employment services, Foreign student adviser, Handicapped facilities, Health services, Social counselling, Sports facilities

Publications: ESCP-EAP News *(quarterly)*; ESCP-EAP Sector News *(biennially)*; European Management Journal *(biennially)*; International Journal of Cross-Cultural Management *(quarterly)*
Last Updated: 04/07/11

ESEO-ANGERS

Ecole supérieure d'Electronique de l'Ouest (ESEO)
BP 926, 4, rue Merlet-de-la-Boulaye, 49009 Angers, Cedex 01
Tel: +33(2) 41-86-67-67
Fax: +33(2) 41-87-99-27
EMail: information@eseo.fr
Website: http://www.eseo.fr

Directeur général: Jacky Charrault
EMail: jacky.charruault@eseo.fr

International Relations: Pierre-Yves Paques

Programmes
Engineering and Mathematics (Automation and Control Engineering; Data Processing; Electronic Engineering; Mathematics); **Management** (Management)

Further Information: Also campuses in Paris, Dijon and Shanghai.

History: Founded 1956.

Academic Year: September to June

Admission Requirements: Competitive entrance examination following 2-3 yrs further study after secondary school certificate (baccalauréat) or following first university qualification (DEUG, DUT or BTS), or equivalent

Fees: (Euros): 2,140 - 4,590 per annum

Main Language(s) of Instruction: French

International Co-operation: With universities in United Kingdom, Germany, Argentina, Australia, New-Zealand and Canada

Degrees and Diplomas: *Diplôme d'Ingénieur*: Electrical Engineering, Computer Engineering, Telecommunications, For Bachelor 2-3 yrs; for Baccalauréat 5 yrs; *Mastère spécialisé*: Management and Technology. Also joint degrees

Student Services: Academic counselling, Cultural centre, Employment services, Health services, Social counselling, Sports facilities

Student Residential Facilities: Yes
Last Updated: 01/07/11

ESG MANAGEMENT SCHOOL

25, rue Saint-Ambroise, 75011 Paris
Tel: +33(1) 53-36-44-00
Fax: +33(1) 43-55-15-23
EMail: esg@esg.fr
Website: http://www.esg.fr

Directeur: Armand Derhy EMail: aderhy@esg.fr

Administrative Officer: Cyril Blondet
Tel: +33(1) 53-36-44-42 EMail: cblondet@esg.fr

International Relations: Servane Gandais
Tel: +33(1) 55-25-46-99, Fax: +33(1) 55-25-69-55

Programmes
Commerce and Management (Business and Commerce; Management)

History: Founded 1974, acquired present status 1984.

Governing Bodies: Board of Directors

Academic Year: October to June

Admission Requirements: Competitive entrance examination following 2 yrs further study after secondary school certificate (baccalauréat) or 2-3 yr university degree and interview

Fees: (Euros) 7,250-7,980

Main Language(s) of Instruction: French; English

International Co-operation: With universities in Algeria, Argentina, Australia, Austria, Brazil, Chile, China, Colombia, Croatia, Cyprus, Denmark, Germany, Iceland, India, Ireland, Israel, Italy, Greece, Hungary, Finland, Ghana, Kuwait, Côte d'Ivoire, Mali, Malaysia, Mexico, Morocco, Nigeria, Peru, Poland, Singapore, Spain, Portugal, Latvia, Liechtenstein, Russia, Taiwan, United Kingdom, UAE and USA. Also participates in Erasmus.

Accrediting Agencies: Ministry of Education

Degrees and Diplomas: *Licence*: Business Administration (BBA); Finance; Auditing; Accounting; Human Resources; Marketing and Advertising; Tourism Management; Sports Management; Luxury Brands Management; IT Management; International Business, 4 yrs; *Diplôme national de Master (MBA)*: 2 futher yrs; *Diplôme national de Master*: Finance; Auditing; Accounting; Human Resources; Marketing and Advertising; Tourism Management; Sports Management; Luxury Brands Management; IT Management; International Business, 2 further yrs

Student Services: Academic counselling, Canteen, Employment services, Foreign student adviser, Foreign Studies Centre, Handicapped facilities, Language programs, Sports facilities

Student Residential Facilities: Yes

Special Facilities: Radio Studio

Libraries: Cyberlibris; Thomson NET-G; Crossknowledge

Publications: Annuaire de la Recherche de l'ESG Management School *(quarterly)*

Academic Staff *2010-2011*	MEN	WOMEN	TOTAL
FULL-TIME	36	31	**67**
PART-TIME	73	68	**141**
STAFF WITH DOCTORATE			
FULL-TIME	32	18	**50**
PART-TIME	45	25	**70**
Student Numbers *2010-2011*			
All (Foreign Included)	1,308	930	**2,238**
FOREIGN ONLY	50	37	**87**

Last Updated: 19/05/11

ESIEA SCHOOL OF ENGINEERING
Ecole supérieure d'Informatique, Electronique et Automatique (ESIEA)

9, rue Vésale, 75005 Paris
Tel: +33(1) 43-90-21-21
Fax: +33(1) 43-90-21-33
EMail: accueil@esiea.fr
Website: http://www.esiea.fr

Directeur: Mohammed Lambarki
Tel: +33(1) 43-90-21-05, Fax: +33(1) 43-90-21-33

International Relations: Susan Loubet
Tel: +33(2) 43-59-46-11 EMail: loubet@esiea-ouest.fr

Divisions
Computer Engineering (Computer Engineering); **Control Engineering and Automation** (Automation and Control Engineering); **Electronic Engineering** *(ESIEA Ouest, Laval)* (Electronic Engineering); **Electronic Engineering** (Electronic Engineering)

Further Information: Also campus in Laval

History: Founded 1958 by Maurice Lafargue, became property of the Association des anciens Elèves et des Amis de l'ESIEA 1975; diplomas officially recognized 1985.

Governing Bodies: Board of Governors

Academic Year: September to June

Admission Requirements: Competitive entrance examination after secondary school certificate (baccalauréat) or following 2-3 years further study after secondary school certifictae or first university qualification (DEUG, DUT or BTS), or equivalent

Fees: (Euros): c. 7,600

Main Language(s) of Instruction: French

International Co-operation: With institutions in United Kingdom, Germany, Italy, Spain, Hungary, Finland, Japan, Australia, United States, Canada

Accrediting Agencies: Commission des Titres d'Ingénieur

Degrees and Diplomas: *Diplôme d'Ingénieur*: 5 yrs; *Mastère spécialisé*: Information Security System (in French), Network and Information Security (in English), a further year; *Diplôme national de Master*

Student Services: Academic counselling, Canteen, Employment services, Foreign student adviser, Language programs

Libraries: Main Library, 11,000 vols
Last Updated: 23/05/11

ESIEE AMIENS

14 Quai de la Somme, BP 100, 80082 Amiens, Cedex 2
Tel: +33(3) 22-66-20-00
Fax: +33(3) 22-66-20-10
EMail: koutani@esiee-amiens.fr
Website: http://www.esiee-amiens.fr

Directeur: Pierre Loonis
Tel: +33(3) 22-66-20-05 EMail: loonis@esiee-amiens.fr

Programmes
Engineering (Electrical Engineering; Energy Engineering; Engineering; Production Engineering; Telecommunications Engineering)

Admission Requirements: Entrance exam after a secondary school degree in Science or 1st university studies in Science

Accrediting Agencies: Commission des Titres d'Ingénieur, Ministry of Industry

Degrees and Diplomas: *Diplôme d'Ingénieur*: 3 yrs; *Mastère spécialisé*; *Diplôme national de Master*
Last Updated: 01/07/11

ESIEE PARIS

2 boulevard Blaise Pascal, 93162 Noisy-le-Grand
Tel: +33(1) 45-92-65-00
Fax: +33(1) 45-92-66-99
EMail: communication@esiee.fr
Website: http://www.esiee-paris.fr

Directeur Général: Dominique Perrin
Tel: +33(1) 45-92-60-00 EMail: d.perrin@esiee.fr

International Relations: Derek Mainwaring
Tel: +33(1) 45-92-66-14 EMail: mainwade@istm.fr

Schools

Engineering (Computer Networks; Computer Science; Electronic Engineering; Information Technology; Microelectronics; Telecommunications Engineering); Management (Management)

History: Founded 1904 as Ecole Breguet.

Admission Requirements: 2-3 yrs of University Studies in Science and Technology

Fees: (Euros): 4,800 per annum

Main Language(s) of Instruction: French

Accrediting Agencies: Chambre de Commerce et d'Industrie de Paris

Degrees and Diplomas: Mastère spécialisé; Diplôme national de Master

Libraries: Yes
Last Updated: 08/07/11

ESME-SUDRIA ENGINEERING SCHOOL
ESME SUDRIA
38 rue Molière, 94200 Ivry-sur-Seine
Tel: +33(1) 56-20-62-00
Fax: +33(1) 56-20-62-62
EMail: contact@esme.fr
Website: http://www.esme.fr

Président: Marc Sellam

Programmes

Computer Engineering and Information Sciences (Computer Engineering; Information Sciences); Electrical Engineering (Automation and Control Engineering; Electrical Engineering; Electronic Engineering; Energy Engineering); Electronics, Telecommunications, Signal Processing and Networks (Computer Networks; Electronic Engineering; Telecommunications Engineering); Systems and Energy (Computer Science; Energy Engineering; Industrial Engineering)

History: Founded 1905. State-accredited since 1922. Under supervision of the Ministry of Education.

Admission Requirements: Foreign Students: TEF: 500 or DELF

Fees: (Euros): 6,700-8,100 per annum according to level

Main Language(s) of Instruction: French

International Co-operation: With universities in Denmark, Hungary, Switzerland, United Kingdom, Ireland, USA, Canada, Lebanon, China and South Africa

Accrediting Agencies: Campus France, Commission des Titres d'Ingénieur, Conférence des Grandes Ecoles, N+I

Degrees and Diplomas: Diplôme d'Ingénieur. 5 yrs

Student Services: Academic counselling, Canteen, Foreign student adviser, Language programs, Sports facilities
Last Updated: 26/05/11

ESSCA BUSINESS SCHOOL - ANGERS
Ecole supérieure des Sciences commerciales d'Anger (ESSCA)
BP 40348, 1, rue Lakanal, 49003 Angers, Cedex 01
Tel: +33(2) 41-73-47-47
Fax: +33(2) 41-73-47-48
EMail: info@essca.asso.fr
Website: http://www.essca.fr

Directrice générale: Catherine Leblanc
Tel: +33(2) 41-73-47-20 EMail: catherine.leblanc@essca.asso.fr

International Relations: Carol Chaplais
Tel: +33(2) 41-73-57-17, Fax: +33(2) 41-73-47-90
EMail: carol.chaplais@essca.fr

Programmes
Management (Management)

Further Information: Has schools in Paris, Shanghai and Budapest.

History: Founded 1909.

Admission Requirements: Competitive entrance examination following secondary school certificate (baccalauréat). Entrance in 3rd year following DEUG, DUT, BTS or equivalent

Fees: (Euros): 7,400 per annum

Main Language(s) of Instruction: French

Accrediting Agencies: EPAS

Degrees and Diplomas: Diplôme d'Etudes d'Ecole de Commerce et Gestion; Diplôme national de Master. Management, International Business, Corporate Finance
Last Updated: 14/04/11

ESSEC BUSINESS SCHOOL
Ecole supérieure des Sciences économiques et commerciales (ESSEC)
BP 50105, 1, avenue Bernard Hirsch, 95021 Cergy-Pontoise
Tel: +33(1) 34-43-30-00
Fax: +33(1) 34-43-30-01
Website: http://www.essec.fr

Directeur général: Pierre Tapie
Tel: +33(1) 34-43-31-35, Fax: +33(1) 34-43-31-11

International Relations: Michèle Pekar Lempereur
Tel: +33(1) 34-43-31-43

Institutes
Health Management (Economics; Health Administration; Management) Chair: Gregory Katz; International Agro-Business Management (Agricultural Business; Management) Chair: Francis Declerck; International Hotel Management (IMHI) (Hotel and Restaurant; Management; Tourism) Director: Jeanine Picard; Research of Negotiation in Europe (IRENE) (Business and Commerce) Director: Alain Pekar Lempereur; Service Innovation and Strategy (ISIS) (Business and Commerce; Management; Service Trades) Director: Hervé Mathe; Urban and Regional Management (Management; Real Estate; Regional Planning; Urban Studies) Director: Franck Vallerugo

Programmes
International Management (EPSCI) (Economics; Finance; Management) Dean: Martine Bronner; Luxury Brand Management (MBA Luxe) (Consumer Studies; Management; Marketing) Executive Director: Denis Morisset; Management (ESSEC MBA) (Accountancy; Business and Commerce; Economics; Finance; Management) Dean: Laurent Bibard

Further Information: Also French Language courses for foreign students and a school in Singapore.

History: Founded 1907. Accredited by the International Association for Management Education 1997 for all the programmes. Associated with the Institut catholique de Paris.

Governing Bodies: Conseil de surveillance, comprising 31 members; the Directoire

Academic Year: September to June (September-December; January-March; April-June)

Admission Requirements: Secondary school certificate (baccalauréat), or equivalent, preparatory courses for 'Grandes Ecoles', and entrance examination

Fees: (Euros): ESSEC MBA 7,400 for 1st yr, 9,000 2nd yr; Mastère 14,600 for French students, 19,800 for EU students and 34,000 for non EU-students, International or Luxe MBA 14,000 or 27,000 for 2 yrs

Main Language(s) of Instruction: French, English

Accrediting Agencies: International Association for Management Education

Degrees and Diplomas: Diplôme d'Etudes d'Ecole de Commerce et Gestion; Mastère spécialisé: Insurance, Finance, Human Resources, International Business, Sports Management, Agronomical Management, Public Services and Health Management; Doctorat

Student Services: Academic counselling, Canteen, Cultural centre, Employment services, Foreign student adviser, Handicapped facilities, Social counselling, Sports facilities

Student Residential Facilities: For c. 600 students

Special Facilities: Medialab

Libraries: Groupe ESSEC Library, c. 45,000 vols

Publications: Research Publications
Last Updated: 24/01/12

ESTA - BELFORT
Ecole supérieure des Technologies et des Affaires (ESTA)
BP 199, 3, rue du Docteur Fréry, 90004 Belfort, Cedex
Tel: +33(3) 84-54-53-53
Fax: +33(3) 84-54-53-84
EMail: esta@esta-belfort.fr
Website: http://www.esta-belfort.fr

Directeur: Jean Grenier Godard

International Relations: Janet Laine
Tel: +33(3) 84-54-53-60 EMail: jlaine@esta-belfot.fr

Programmes
Business and Commerce (Business and Commerce)

History: Founded 1986.

Admission Requirements: Baccalauréat or equivalent Secondary School degree

Main Language(s) of Instruction: French

Accrediting Agencies: Ministry of Education

Degrees and Diplomas: *Diplôme d'Etudes d'Ecole de Commerce et Gestion*: 4 yrs; *Diplôme national de Master*
Last Updated: 04/07/11

ESTACA - LEVALLOIS-PERRET
Ecole supérieure des Techniques aéronautiques et de Construction automobile (ESTACA)
34, rue Victor Hugo, 92300 Levallois-Perret
Tel: +33(1) 41-27-37-00
Fax: +33(1) 47-37-50-83
EMail: infos@estaca.fr
Website: http://www.estaca.fr

Directrice: Pascale Ribon Tel: +33(1) 41-27-37-02

Programmes
Enginering (Aeronautical and Aerospace Engineering; Automotive Engineering; Railway Engineering; Transport Engineering)

Further Information: Also campus in Laval

History: Founded 1925.

Academic Year: September to June

Admission Requirements: Competitive entrance examination following 2 yrs further study after secondary school certificate (baccalauréat) or equivalent

Fees: (Euros): 5,490 per annum for first four years; 5,250 for fifth year

Main Language(s) of Instruction: French

International Co-operation: With institutions in Germany; Italy; Sweden; Spain; United Kingdom; Canada; USA; Mexico; Brazil; China; Thailand. Also participates in Erasmus, Crepuq

Accrediting Agencies: Commission des Titres d'Ingénieur

Degrees and Diplomas: *Diplôme d'Ingénieur*: 5 yrs; *Diplôme national de Master*: 16 months. Also European Master in Design and Technology of Advanced Vehicle Systems; Aeronautical and Aerospace Engineering; Marine Engineering; Automotive Engineering 18 mths

Student Services: Academic counselling, Employment services, Foreign student adviser
Last Updated: 04/07/11

ESTP - PARIS
Ecole spéciale des Travaux publics, du Bâtiment et de l'Industrie (ESTP)
57, boulevard Saint-Germain, 75240 Paris, Cedex 05
Tel: +33(1) 44-41-11-18
Fax: +33(1) 44-41-11-12
EMail: estp@adm.estp.fr
Website: http://www.estp.fr

Directrice: Florence Darmon (2008-)
Tel: +33(1) 44-41-11-21, Fax: +33(1) 44-41-11-05
EMail: cmauguin@adm.estp.fr

Secrétaire général: Pierre-Yves Suard
Tel: +33(1) 44-41-11-10 EMail: edeoliveira@adm.estp.fr

International Relations: Marie-Jo Goedert
Tel: +33(1) 44-41-11-26
EMail: information@adm.estp.fr; mjgoeder@adm.estp.fr

Programmes
Engineering (Civil Engineering; Construction Engineering; Electrical Engineering; Mechanical Engineering; Surveying and Mapping)

Further Information: Has been annexed to National School of Applied Arts (ENSAM).

History: Founded 1891.

Governing Bodies: Conseil d'administration

Academic Year: September to June, practical training periods in July and August

Admission Requirements: Baccalauréat, Bachelor degree, Master's degree

Fees: (Euros): Bachelor, 4,000; Master, 5,139; Professional specializations, 7,000 per annum

Main Language(s) of Instruction: French

International Co-operation: With universities in Germany, Denmark, Spain, Great Britain, Greece, Hungary, Italy, Norway, Sweden, Romania, Switzerland, Ukraine, Australia, Brazil, Canada, China, India, Morocco, Mexico, Panama, USA

Accrediting Agencies: Commission des Titres d'Ingénieurs, Conférence des Grandes Ecoles

Degrees and Diplomas: *Licence professionnelle*; *Diplôme d'Ingénieur*: Civil Engineering, Building Engineering, Mechanical-Electrical Engineering, Topography Surveying, 3 yrs following 2 yrs; *Mastère spécialisé*: 12 months; *Diplôme national de Master*; *Doctorat*

Student Services: Academic counselling, Canteen, Employment services, Foreign student adviser, Foreign Studies Centre, Language programs, Social counselling, Sports facilities

Student Residential Facilities: Yes

Libraries: c. 10,000 vols

Press or Publishing House: Editions Eyrolles
Last Updated: 01/07/11

EUROMED MANAGEMENT
Euromed Management
BP 921, Domaine de Luminy, 13288 Marseille, Cedex 9
Tel: +33(4) 91-82-78-00
Fax: +33(4) 91-82-79-01
EMail: zoubir@euromed-management.com
Website: http://www.euromed-management.com

Directeur général: Bernard Belletante

International Relations: Cynthia Zoubir Tel: +33(4) 91-82-78-10

Programmes
Management (Management; Town Planning)

Further Information: Also campus in Toulon, La Joliette; Euromed Management Maroc; campus in Suzhou

History: Founded 1872. A private 'Grande Ecole'.

Admission Requirements: Depending on programmes: competitive entrance examination following 2 yrs further study after the secondary school certificate or application with interview

Fees: (Euros): Depending on programme from 5,000 to 20,000

Degrees and Diplomas: *Diplôme d'Etudes d'Ecole de Commerce et Gestion*; *Mastère spécialisé*; *Diplôme national de Master*. Bachelor EGC-PMF-CESEMED; Diplômes PMG and MBA (Executive Education)
Last Updated: 21/06/11

EUROPEAN BUSINESS SCHOOL
Ecole européenne de Gestion (EBS)
37-39 boulevard Murat, 75016 Paris
Tel: +33(1) 40-71-37-37
Fax: +33(1) 40-71-37-04
EMail: contact@ebs-paris.com
Website: http://www.ebs-paris.com

Directeur général: Bruno Neil

Programmes

Management (Finance; International Business; Management; Marketing)

Further Information: Has 8 centres in Europe, New York and Shanghai.

History: Founded in 1967.

Admission Requirements: Competitive entrance exam, fluent in two languages

Fees: (Euros): 7,400 p.a.

Main Language(s) of Instruction: French, English

Accrediting Agencies: Ministry of Education

Degrees and Diplomas: *Licence*: Business, Management, 3 yrs; *Diplôme national de Master*: Marketing, International Business, Management, Finance, 2 yrs following Bachelors
Last Updated: 24/06/11

GRADUATE SCHOOL OF FASHION
Institut francais de la mode (IFM)
36 quai d'Austerlitz, 75013 Paris
Tel: +33(1) 70-38-89-89
Fax: +33(1) 70-38-89-00
EMail: ifm@ifm-paris.com
Website: http://www.ifm-paris.com

Directeur général: Dominique Jacomet
Tel: +33(1) 56-59-22-11 EMail: direction@ifm-paris.com

Programmes
International Fashion Management Executive MBA (International Business); **Management** (Management); **Postgraduate Fashion Design** (Fashion Design)

History: Founded in 1986.

Fees: (Euros)10,000 per year

Main Language(s) of Instruction: French, English

Accrediting Agencies: Ministry of Industry
Last Updated: 10/05/11

GRENOBLE SCHOOL OF MANAGEMENT
Grenoble Ecole de Management
Grenoble Ecole de Management, 12, rue Pierre Sémard, BP 127, 38003 Grenoble, Cedex 01
Tel: +33(4) 76-70-60-60
Fax: +33(4) 76-70-60-99
EMail: info@grenoble-em.com
Website: http://www.grenoble-em.com

Directeur: Thierry Grange (2002-)
Tel: +33(4) 76-70-60-60 EMail: thierry.grange@grenoble-em.com

Directeur adjoint: Loïck Roche Tel: +33(4) 76-70-64-22

Schools
ESC Grenoble *(ESC Grenoble)* (Business Administration; Management); **Grenoble Graduate School of Business** *(GGSB)* (Business Administration; International Business; Marketing); **Information Systems Management** *(EMSI)* (Management; Systems Analysis)

History: Founded 1984. Previously known as Ecole supérieure de Commerce de Grenoble (Grenoble Graduate School of Business). Acquired current title 2003.

Governing Bodies: Board of executive representatives, under the auspices of the Grenoble Chamber of Commerce and Industry

Admission Requirements: Competitive entrance examination following 2 yrs further study after secondary school certificate (baccalauréat) or equivalent

Fees: Depends on the programme

Main Language(s) of Instruction: French; English

International Co-operation: With more than 100 partner universities worldwide

Accrediting Agencies: AACSB, EQUIS and AMBA

Degrees and Diplomas: *Diplôme d'Etudes d'Ecole de Commerce et Gestion*; *Mastère spécialisé*: Technology Management; E-Business; Industrial Management; Management; Business Computing;, 1yr Part-time; *Diplôme national de Master*: Global Management; Technology Management; Management Consulting; Business Computing, 2 yrs; *Diplôme national de Master*: International Business, 1 yr; *Diplôme national de Master*: Project Management; Global Management; Technology Management; Business Intelligence; Managing the Digital Enterprise; Finance; International Accounting and Auditing; Management Consulting, 1yr Full-time; *Doctorat*

Student Services: Academic counselling, Canteen, Cultural centre, Employment services, Foreign student adviser, Foreign Studies Centre, Handicapped facilities, Language programs, Social counselling, Sports facilities

Student Residential Facilities: Yes

Libraries: Dieter Schmidt Library

Publications: Les Cahiers du Management Technologique, Technology Management and its evolution *(3 per annum)*
Last Updated: 05/07/11

HEC SCHOOL OF MANAGEMENT
Ecole des Hautes Etudes Commerciales (GROUPE HEC)
1, rue de la Libération, 78351 Jouy-en-Josas, Cedex
Tel: +33(1) 39-67-70-00
Fax: +33(1) 39-67-74-40
EMail: hecinfo@hec.fr
Website: http://www.hec.fr

Directeur Général: Bernard Ramanantsoa
Tel: +33(1) 39-67-71-62, Fax: +33(1) 39-67-74-88
EMail: ramanantsoa@hec.fr

Secrétaire Général: Jean-Luc Neyraut
Tel: +33(1) 39-67-72-30, Fax: +33(1) 39-67-71-42
EMail: neyraut@hec.fr

International Relations: Jean-Paul Larçon
Tel: +33(1) 39-67-72-46, Fax: +33(1) 39-67-94-90
EMail: larcon@hec.fr

Faculties
Doctoral Studies (Management); **Executive Development**

Graduate Schools
Higher Management (Management); **MBA Programme** (Management); **Specialized Studies in Higher Management** (Management)

History: Founded 1881. HEC became one of the academic partners in Europe with the American Association AIMR for the preparation of the CFA (Chartered Financial Analysts) diploma.

Governing Bodies: Chamber of Commerce and Industry of Paris

Academic Year: September to July (September-January; January-July)

Admission Requirements: Competitive entrance examination following further study after secondary school certificate (baccalauréat)

Fees: (Euros): Diplôme 7,500 per annum (6,950-7,500, varies according to year); mastère 13,300; MBA, 38,000

Main Language(s) of Instruction: French, English, 9 other languages

International Co-operation: With universities in Germany, Austria, Belgium, Denmark, Spain, Finland, United Kingdom, Hungary, Ireland, Italy, Lithuania, Norway, Poland, Czech Republic, Russian Federation, Sweden, Switzerland, Canada, USA, Argentina, Brazil, Chile, Mexico, Venezuela, China, India, Japan, Kazakhstan, Philippines, Singapore, Thailand, Australia, New Zealand, Israel, South Africa.

Degrees and Diplomas: *Mastère spécialisé*: 1 yr; *Diplôme national de Master*: Business and Administration (MBA), a further 16 months; *Doctorat*: Management (PhD), a further 5 yrs

Student Services: Academic counselling, Canteen, Cultural centre, Employment services, Foreign student adviser, Handicapped facilities, Health services, Language programs, Social counselling, Sports facilities

Student Residential Facilities: For c. 1,140 students

Special Facilities: Theatre.

Libraries: c. 60,000 vols; 736 periodicals, various internal/external data bases

Publications: Les Cahiers de recherche
Last Updated: 24/06/11

HEI-HEP
HEI-HEP
54 Avenue Marceau, 75008 Paris
Tel: +33(1) 47-20-57-47
Fax: +33(1) 47-20-57-30
EMail: contact@hei-hep.com
Website: http://www.hei-hep.com

Directeur: Bruno Neil

Schools
International Studies (Communication Studies; Economics; English; International Relations; Law; Political Sciences); **Political Sciences** (Communication Studies; Economics; English; Law; Political Sciences; Social Sciences)

History: Founded 1899.

Admission Requirements: Secondary school certificate

Main Language(s) of Instruction: French

Degrees and Diplomas: Bachelor; Mastère
Last Updated: 24/06/11

ICAM SCHOOL OF ENGINEERING
Groupe ICAM - Institut catholique d'Arts et Métiers (ICAM)
35, rue de la Bienfaisance, 75008 Paris
Tel: +33(1) 53-77-22-40
Fax: +33(1) 53-77-22-23
EMail: beatrice.ducroux@icam.fr
Website: http://www.icam.fr

Directeur général: Jean-Michel Viot

International Relations: Jean-Philippe Pernet
EMail: jean-philippe.pernet@icam-toulouse.fr

Programmes
Engineering (Engineering)

Further Information: The ICAM Group is composed of 3 main ICAM Campuses and 4 Technology Institutes (IST) in Lille, Vannes, La Roche-sur-Yon and Toulouse and 2 in Central Africa (Pointe Noire and Douala).

History: Founded 1898.

Academic Year: September-June

Admission Requirements: Competitive entrance examination following 2 yrs further study after secondary school certificate (baccalauréat) or equivalent.

Fees: (Euros): preparatory classes, 1,785; engineering programme, 4,000 per annum

Main Language(s) of Instruction: French

International Co-operation: Master's degrees exchange programmes with Ecole Polytechnique of Montreal and Leuven University (Belgium).

Degrees and Diplomas: Diplôme d'Ingénieur. 3-5 yrs; Mastère spécialisé: Railway Engineering; Diplôme national de Master. Industrial Management. Offers Preparatory Classes (2 yrs) to take entrance exam for the Engineering Schools.
Last Updated: 05/07/11

ICAM LILLE SCHOOL OF ENGINEERING
ICAM LILLE - INSTITUT CATHOLIQUE D'ARTS ET MÉTIERS (ICAM LILLE)

6, rue Auber, 59046 Lille
Tel: +33(3) 20-22-61-61
Fax: +33(3) 20-93-14-89
EMail: contact.lille@icam.fr
Website: http://www.icam.fr

Directeur: Bernard-Gilles Flipo EMail: bernard-gilles.flipo@icam.fr

Programmes
Engineering (Engineering; Railway Engineering)

Degrees and Diplomas: Diplôme d'Ingénieur; Mastère spécialisé: Railway Engineering; Diplôme national de Master

ICAM NANTES SCHOOL OF ENGINEERING
ICAM NANTES - INSTITUT CATHOLIQUE D'ARTS ET MÉTIERS (ICAM NANTES)

35, avenue du Champ de Manoeuvres, 44470 Carquefou
Tel: +33(2) 40-52-40-52
Fax: +33(2) 40-52-40-99
EMail: icam.nantes@groupe-icam.fr
Website: http://www.groupe-icam.fr

Directeur: Jean-Louis Bigotte (2000-)

International Relations: Nicolas Gary
EMail: nicolas.gary@groupe-icam.fr

Departments
Automation and Electrical Engineering (Automation and Control Engineering; Electrical Engineering); **Computer Science** (Computer Science); **Engineering** (Engineering); **Human Sciences and Languages** (Arts and Humanities; Human Resources; Management; Modern Languages); **Materials Science** (Materials Engineering; Polymer and Plastics Technology); **Mechanics** (Mechanical Engineering)

Main Language(s) of Instruction: French

Degrees and Diplomas: Diplôme d'Ingénieur. 3 yrs; Mastère spécialisé

Student Services: Academic counselling, Canteen, Cultural centre, Employment services, Foreign student adviser, Handicapped facilities, Sports facilities

Student Residential Facilities: For c. 300 students

Libraries: c. 5,000 vols

ICAM TOULOUSE SCHOOL OF ENGINEERING
ICAM TOULOUSE - INSTITUT CATHOLIQUE D'ARTS ET MÉTIERS DE TOULOUSE (ICAM TOULOUSE)

75, avenue de Grande Bretagne, 31300 Toulouse
Tel: +33(5) 34-50-50-50
Fax: +33(5) 34-50-50-51
EMail: toulouse@icam.fr
Website: http://www.groupe-icam.fr

Directeur: Louis de Montety
Tel: +33(5) 34-50-50-53 EMail: louis.demontety@groupe-icam.fr

International Relations: Jean-Philippe Pernet
Tel: +33(5) 34-50-50-53

Departments
Computer Science (Computer Science); **Electrical Engineering** (Electrical Engineering); **Energy Engineering** (Energy Engineering); **Humanities** (Arts and Humanities); **Industrial Management** (Industrial Management); **Materials Engineering** (Materials Engineering); **Mechanical Engineering** (Mechanical Engineering)

History: Founded 1993.

Main Language(s) of Instruction: French

Degrees and Diplomas: Diplôme d'Ingénieur. 3 yrs; Mastère spécialisé; Diplôme national de Master

ICD INTERNATIONAL BUSINESS SCHOOL
Institut international de Commerce et de Distribution (IDC PARIS)
12 rue Alexandre Parodi, 75010 Paris
Tel: +33(1) 40-03-15-52
Fax: +33(1) 40-03-15-45
EMail: info@icdparis.com
Website: http://www.icdparis.com

Directeur général: Erwan Poiraud

International Relations: Patricia Giordano
Tel: +33(1) 40-03-15-23 EMail: pgiordano@groupe-igs.asso.fr

Programmes
Management (Business Administration; Business and Commerce; International Business; Management)

Further Information: Also campus in Toulouse and Dublin

History: Founded 1980.

Main Language(s) of Instruction: French, English

International Co-operation: Exchange programme with University of Fudan, China

Accrediting Agencies: Ministry of Education
Last Updated: 15/10/07

IGS GROUP
Groupe IGS
B.P 752, 1, rue Jacques Bingen, 75827 Paris, Cedex 17
Tel: +33(1) 56-79-69-69
EMail: kgrivot@groupe-igs.fr
Website: http://www.groupe-igs.asso.fr

Directeur Général: Roger Serre

Institutes
American Business (ABS Paris) (Business Administration); **Human Resources Management** (IGS Paris, Lyon and Toulouse) (Human Resources; Management; Marketing; Service Trades); **International Commerce and Distribution** (ICD Paris and Toulouse) (Business and Commerce; International Business; Management; Marketing); **Marketing and Management of Health Services** (IMIS Lyon) (Health Administration; Management; Marketing); **Media** (ISCPA Paris, Lyon); **Operations Management** (ESAM Paris, Lyon, Toulouse in partnership with Lille II) (Business Administration; Finance; Management; Real Estate; Service Trades); **Real Estate** (IMSI Paris) (Real Estate)

Schools
Decision (Economics; International Relations; Law; Marketing; Modern History; Political Sciences; Sales Techniques; Taxation)

Further Information: Has three sites: Paris, Lyon and Toulouse.

History: Founded in 1975 as the Ecole of Gestion Sociale, expanding to integrate new business schools and training centres over the last 30 years.

Main Language(s) of Instruction: French

Accrediting Agencies: Ministry of Education

Degrees and Diplomas: Brevet de Technicien supérieur: Management, 2 yrs; Licence: Business, Management, 3 yrs. Masters professionnel
Last Updated: 13/11/07

INSEAD
INSEAD
Boulevard de Constance, 77305 Fontainebleau, Cedex
Tel: +33(1) 60-72-40-00
Fax: +33(1) 60-74-55-00
EMail: communications.fb@insead.fr
Website: http://www.insead.edu

Dean: Dipak C. Jain (2010-) Tel: +33(1) 60-71-26-22

Secrétaire générale: Claire Pike
Tel: +33(1) 60-72-90-38 EMail: claire.pike@insead.edu

International Relations: Melissa Joelson
Tel: +33(1) 60-71-26-62, Fax: +33(1) 60-71-26-90
EMail: communications.fb@insead.edu

Programmes
Accounting and Control (Accountancy); **Decision Sciences**; **Economics and Political Science** (Economics; Political Sciences); **Entrepreneurship and Family Enterprise** (Management); **Finance** (Finance); **Marketing** (Marketing); **Organizational Behaviour**; **Strategy** (Management); **Technology and Operations Management**

Further Information: Also campuses in Singapore and Abu Dhabi
History: Founded 1957.
Governing Bodies: INSEAD Board
Academic Year: September to August and January to December

Admission Requirements: Secondary school certificate, Entrance Examination (TOEFL, Essay, Interview)

Fees: (Euros): MBA, 45,000; EMBA, 85,000

Main Language(s) of Instruction: English

International Co-operation: With universities in Europe, USA, Hong Kong, Japan, Turkey.

Accrediting Agencies: Association of Advanced Collegiate Schools of Business (AACSB); EQUIS

Degrees and Diplomas: Diplôme national de Master: Business Administration (MBA), 10 months; Doctorat: Business Administration (PhD), 4 yrs. Also Executive MBA, 14 months (EMBA)

Student Services: Academic counselling, Canteen, Employment services, Foreign student adviser, Handicapped facilities, Health services, Language programs, Social counselling, Sports facilities

Libraries: c. 200,000 vols
Last Updated: 05/07/11

INSEEC BUSINESS SCHOOL
Institut des hautes Etudes économiques et commerciales (INSEEC)
26 rue Raze, 33300 Bordeaux, Cedex
Tel: +33(5) 56-00-73-73
Fax: +33(5) 57-87-58-95
EMail: heig@inseec.com
Website: http://www.inseec-france.com

Directrice générale: Catherine Lespine
EMail: clespine@groupeinseec.com

International Relations: Christa Vauguin
EMail: cvauguin@groupeinseec.com

Institutes
Bordeaux International Wine Institute (BIWI) (Business and Commerce; Viticulture) Division Head: Laurant Bergeruc; **MBA Institute** (MBA Paris) (Business and Commerce) Division Head: Clive Gallery

Programmes
Business Administration; **Communication** (Sup de Pub Paris) (Business and Commerce; Communication Studies; Marketing)

Schools
Business (INSEEC Bordeaux, INSEEC Paris); **European School of Commerce** (ECE Bordeaux Lyon) (Business and Commerce; International Business)

Further Information: Has a campus in Paris, Lyon, London and Monaco.

History: Founded in 1975.

Admission Requirements: INSEEC entrance exam, Undergraduate Degree

Main Language(s) of Instruction: French

International Co-operation: Works in cooperation with over 53 Higher Education Institutions and Universities worldwide to offer a double degree in MBA and Masters of Science

Degrees and Diplomas: MBA
Last Updated: 08/07/11

INSTITUTE OF INTERCULTURAL MANAGEMENT AND COMMUNICATION
Institut de Management et de Communication interculturels
21 rue d'Assas, 75006 Paris
Tel: +33(1) 42-22-33-16
Fax: +33(1) 45-44-17-67
EMail: direction@isit-paris.fr
Website: http://www.isit-paris.fr

Directrice: Marie Mériaud-Brischoux

Programmes
International Law (International Law); **Interpreting** (Translation and Interpretation); **Management, Communication and Translation** (Communication Studies; Management; Translation and Interpretation)

History: Founded 1957 as Institut Supérieur d'Interprétation et de Traduction within the Institut catholique de Paris. Acquires present title 2008. Becomes associate of the Institut catholique de Paris.

Main Language(s) of Instruction: French

Degrees and Diplomas: Diplôme national de Master
Last Updated: 24/01/12

INSTITUTE OF OPTICS GRADUATE SCHOOL

Institut d'Optique Graduate School (IO)

Campus Polytechnique RD 128, 91127 Palaiseau
Tel: +33(1) 64-53-31-00
Fax: +33(1) 64-53-31-01
EMail: accueil@institutoptique.fr
Website: http://www.institutoptique.fr/

Directeur Général: Jean-Louis Miartin (2006-)
Tel: +33(1) 64-53-31-02, Fax: +33(1) 64-53-31-19
EMail: dg@institutoptique.fr

Secrétaire générale: Annie Montagnac
EMail: daf@institutoptique.fr

International Relations: Alan Swan, International Coordinator
Tel: +33(1) 69-35-88-83 EMail: international@institutoptique.fr

Graduate Schools
Optical Science *(Joint programme - Ecole Polytechnique)* (Optical Technology)

Research Laboratories
Charles Fabry (Optics)

Schools
Optical Science and Engineering *(Also Saint-Etienne Campus)* (Electrical Engineering; Laboratory Techniques; Optics; Physics; Technology; Telecommunications Engineering)

Further Information: Also sites in Palaiseau, Saint-Etienne and Bordeaux

History: Founded 1920.

Governing Bodies: Ministère de l'Education Nationale et de la Recherche, CNRS, Industry leaders, Université de Paris Sud 11 board.

Academic Year: September to June

Admission Requirements: Competitive entrance examination following 2 yrs further study after secondary school certificate (baccalauréat) or equivalent

Fees: (Euros): 1,340 per annum; non-EU students, 5,000. Fellowships from the French Government can be obtained

Main Language(s) of Instruction: French

International Co-operation: With universities in Belgium, Hungary, Italy, Netherlands, Romania, Finland, United Kingdom, Germany, Switzerland, USA, Canada and Singapore.

Accrediting Agencies: Ministry of Education and Commission des Titres d'Ingénieur

Degrees and Diplomas: *Diplôme d'Ingénieur*: Optical Science and Engineering, 3 yrs; *Mastère spécialisé*; *Diplôme national de Master*: Optical Science; Optical Science and Engineering. Master Erasmus Mundus "Optics in Science and Technology"

Student Services: Academic counselling, Canteen, Cultural centre, Employment services, Foreign student adviser, Handicapped facilities, Health services, Language programs, Sports facilities

Student Residential Facilities: Yes.

Libraries: Yes.

Publications: Fiat Lux *(monthly)*; Opto *(quarterly)*
Last Updated: 05/07/11

INSTITUTE OF PERFUME, COSMETICS AND FLAVOURING INDUSTRIES

Institut supérieur international du Parfum, de la Cosmétique et de l'Aromatique alimentaire (ISIPCA)

36, rue du Parc de Clagny, 78000 Versailles
Tel: +33(1) 39-23-70-00
Fax: +33(1) 39-54-43-84
EMail: info@isipca.fr
Website: http://www.isipca.fr

Directrice: Isabelle Dufour

Programmes
Perfume and Cosmetology (Cosmetology; Food Technology; Management)

History: Founded in 1970 by Jean-Jacques Guerlain, becoming backed by the Versailles Val d'Oise-Yvelines Chamber of Commerce and Industry in 1984.

Academic Year: September to May with internship

Admission Requirements: Baccalauréat or equivalent for BTS, Undergraduate Studies in Chemistry or Biology for Masters programme

Fees: (Euros): 300 per annum for Masters, 800 for Masters Professionnel, 700 for Licence; 10,500 for foreign students

Main Language(s) of Instruction: French, English

Accrediting Agencies: Versailles Val d'Oise-Yvelines Chamber of Commerce and Industry

Degrees and Diplomas: *Brevet de Technicien supérieur*: 2 yrs; *Licence professionnelle*: 1 yr following 2 yrs undergraduate studies; *Diplôme national de Master*: International Management, 15 mos. following Licence. Masters professionnel
Last Updated: 08/07/11

INTERNATIONAL BUSINESS SCHOOL

Ecole supérieure du Commerce extérieur (ESCE)

Pôle universitaire Léonard de Vinci, 12, rue Léonard de Vinci, 92916 Paris La Defense, Cedex
Tel: +33(1) 41-16-73-76
Fax: +33(1) 41-16-73-80
EMail: esce@esce.fr
Website: http://www.esce.fr

Directeur général: Jean Audouard EMail: jean.audouard@esce.fr

International Relations: Yves Marmiesse
Tel: +33(1) 41-16-70-57 EMail: yves.marmiesse@esce.fr

Programmes
International Business

Further Information: Has schools in Lyon, Beijing, Mexico and Sao Paulo.

History: Founded in 1968.

Admission Requirements: SESAME national exam

Main Language(s) of Instruction: French, English

International Co-operation: Participates in Erasmus and has signed 21 agreements to offer Double-Degrees with other Universities outside France.

Accrediting Agencies: Ministry of Education

Degrees and Diplomas: *Diplôme d'Etudes d'Ecole de Commerce et Gestion*: International Business, 5 yrs; *Diplôme national de Master*
Last Updated: 26/05/11

INTERNATIONAL SPACE UNIVERSITY (ISU)

1 rue Jean-Dominique Cassini, 67400 Illkirch-Graffenstaden
Tel: +33(3) 88-65-54-30
Fax: +33(3) 88-65-54-47
EMail: info@isu.isunet.edu
Website: http://www.isunet.edu/

Président: Walter Peeters Tel: +33(3) 88-65-54-62

Programmes
Master of Space Management (Aeronautical and Aerospace Engineering; Air and Space Law; Architecture; Astronomy and Space Science; Astrophysics; Biological and Life Sciences; Business Administration; Information Management; International Economics; International Studies; Telecommunications Services) *Acting Director*: Nikolai Tolyarenko; **Master of Space Studies** (Aeronautical and Aerospace Engineering; Air and Space Law; Architecture; Astronomy and Space Science; Astrophysics; Biological and Life Sciences; Business Administration; Information Management; International Business; International Studies; Telecommunications Services) *Director*: Nikolai Tolyarenko; **Space Studies Programme** *(9-week certificate programme)* (Aeronautical and Aerospace Engineering; Air and Space Law; Architecture; Astronomy and Space Science; Astrophysics; Biological and Life Sciences; Business Administration; Information Management; International Economics; International Studies; Telecommunications Services) *Director*: Joe Conley

History: Founded in 1987 and first Space Studies Programme held in MIT, Massachusetts, USA in 1988. Moved to Strasbourg in 1994. Acquired current title and status 2004.

Governing Bodies: General Assembly; Board of Trustees

Academic Year: September to August

Admission Requirements: Bachelor's degree or equivalent. (BAC+4 in French system)

Fees: (Euros): 25,000

Main Language(s) of Instruction: English

Accrediting Agencies: Ministry of Education and Research

Degrees and Diplomas: MSc: Space Studies; Space Management (1 yr). Also 9-week Space Studies Programme Certificate (held around the world every year)

Student Services: Academic counselling, Employment services, Foreign student adviser, Foreign Studies Centre, Handicapped facilities, Language programs, Social counselling

Student Residential Facilities: No

Special Facilities: Tele-education facilities; Show-case of space objects and equipment; Canteen and sports facilities available by agreement with neighbouring universities.

Libraries: Yes

Publications: The Universe, Recent events and alumni news *(3 per annum)*

Academic Staff	MEN	WOMEN	**TOTAL**
STAFF WITH DOCTORATE FULL-TIME	7	2	**9**

Last Updated: 16/12/11

IPAG BUSINESS SCHOOL

Institut de Préparation à l'Administration et à la Gestion (GROUPE IPAG)
184, bd Saint-Germain, 75006 Paris
Tel: +33(1) 53-63-36-00
Fax: +33(1) 45-44-40-46
EMail: international@ipag.fr
Website: http://www.ipag.fr

Directeur général: Guillaume Bigot

International Relations: Bernard Terrany

Programmes

Management (Advertising and Publicity; E-Business/Commerce; International Business; Management; Marketing; Public Relations)

Further Information: Has a school in Nice.

History: Founded in 1965, having its origins in the Collège des sciences sociales et économiques.

Governing Bodies: Conseil d'Administration

Admission Requirements: Baccalauréat or equivalent Secondary School degree and entrance exam.

Fees: (Euros): 6,600 p.a.

Main Language(s) of Instruction: French, English

International Co-operation: Participates in Socrates/Erasmus programmes and has exchange programmes with universities in China, Russia, Canada, Australia, USA, and Mexico.

Accrediting Agencies: Ministry of Education

Degrees and Diplomas: *Mastère spécialisé*; *Diplôme national de Master*. Also MBA
Last Updated: 05/07/11

ISARA LYONS

Institut supérieur d'Agriculture et d'Agro-alimentaire Rhône-Alpes (ISARA)
23, rue Jean Baldassini, 69364 Lyon, Cedex 07
Tel: +33(4) 27-85-85-85
Fax: +33(4) 27-85-85-86
EMail: contact@isara.fr
Website: http://www.isara.fr

Directeur: Pascal Désamais (2009-) Tel: +33(4) 27-85-85-32

International Relations: Christophe David EMail: relint@isara.fr

Departments

Agrosystem Environment Production (Aquaculture; Biotechnology; Ecology; Farm Management; Natural Resources); **Food Processing and Quality** (Food Technology); **Social Science and Management** (Agricultural Economics; Development Studies; Marketing; Rural Studies)

History: Founded 1968.

Governing Bodies: Administrative Council

Academic Year: September to June

Admission Requirements: Secondary school certificate (baccalauréat)

Fees: (Euros): 4,500 per annum

Main Language(s) of Instruction: French

International Co-operation: With universities in Eastern and Western Europe (Socrates- Leonardo); South Africa (Alfa)

Accrediting Agencies: Commission des titres d'ingérieur; Ministère de l'Agriculture

Degrees and Diplomas: *Licence professionnelle*: Fruit and Vegetables Quality Management; Food Industry Management; *Diplôme d'Ingénieur*: Quality in Animal Production; Food Industry Development; Agriculture; Economic Development; From Conception to Industrialization Food Production, 5 yrs or 3 yrs by apprenticeship; *Mastère spécialisé*: Agroecology; Organic Agriculture; Animal Management; Supply Chain in Food Industry; Food Markets Management in China (QUAPA), a further 1 1/2 yr. Also doubles diplômes: Pharmacist/Engineer; Engineer/ Master Entrepreneurship and Management of SMOs; Engineer/Master of Science

Student Services: Employment services, Foreign student adviser, Language programs, Sports facilities

Libraries: Central Library
Last Updated: 21/04/11

ISC PARIS SCHOOL OF MANAGEMENT

Institut supérieur du Commerce de Paris (ISC PARIS)
22 boulevard du Fort de Vaux, 75848 Paris, Cedex 17
Tel: +33(1) 40-53-99-99
Fax: +33(1) 40-53-98-98
EMail: contact@groupeisc.com
Website: http://www.iscparis.com

Directeur général: Andrés Atenza

International Relations: Michael Dolan
EMail: midolan@iscparis.com

Programmes

Management (Finance; International Business; Management; Marketing)

History: Founded 1963.

Admission Requirements: National entrance exam (CPGE) or 2 yrs undergraduate studies in Economics and Technology followed by an entrance exam

Fees: (Euros): 9,900 p.a.

Main Language(s) of Instruction: French, English

Accrediting Agencies: Ministry of Education

Degrees and Diplomas: *Diplôme d'Etudes d'Ecole de Commerce et Gestion*; *Mastère spécialisé*; *Diplôme national de Master*. Also MBA
Last Updated: 08/07/11

LA ROCHELLE BUSINESS SCHOOL

Groupe Sup de Co La Rochelle (ESC LA ROCHELLE)
102, rue de Coureilles - Les Minimes, 17023 La Rochelle
Tel: +33(5) 46-51-77-00
Fax: +33(5) 46-51-79-08
EMail: com@esc-larochelle.fr
Website: http://www.esc-larochelle.fr

Directeur général: Daniel Peyron
Tel: +33(5) 46-51-77-06 EMail: peyrond@esc-larochelle.fr

Directeur général adjoint: Gérard Gimenez
Tel: +33(5) 46-51-77-77 EMail: gimenezg@esc-larochelle.fr

International Relations: David Evan
Tel: +33(5) 46-51-77-19 EMail: evansd@esc-larochelle.fr

Programmes
Management

Schools
Tourism (Tourism)

Governing Bodies: Chambre de commerce et d'industrie de La Rochelle; Ministère de l'Enseignement supérieur et de la Recherche

Academic Year: September to September

Admission Requirements: Entrance exam

Fees: (Euros) 5,000-10,000

Main Language(s) of Instruction: French and English

International Co-operation: With institutions in Europe, US, Asia. 96 partner universities worldwide

Degrees and Diplomas: *Diplôme d'Etudes d'Ecole de Commerce et Gestion*: 3 yrs. Bachelor, 3 yrs; Masters professionnel: Environmental Management, Tourism Management; Programme Grande Ecole 3 yrs; 3ème cycle 1-2 yrs

Student Services: Academic counselling, Canteen, Cultural centre, Employment services, Foreign student adviser, Foreign Studies Centre, Handicapped facilities, Health services, Language programs, Nursery care, Social counselling, Sports facilities

Libraries: Main library; Business School Library

Student Numbers 2010-2011	MEN	WOMEN	TOTAL
All (Foreign Included)	900	1,400	2,300
FOREIGN ONLY	–	–	300

Part-time students, 160.
Last Updated: 31/05/11

LASALLE BEAUVAIS POLYTECHNIC INSTITUTE

Institut polytechnique LaSalle Beauvais
19, rue Pierre Waguet - BP 30313, 60026 Beauvais Cedex
Tel: +33(3) 44-06-25-25
EMail: contact@lasalle-beauvais.fr
Website: http://www.lasalle-beauvais.fr

Président: Gérard Friès

International Relations: Philippe Caron
EMail: philippe.caron@lasalle-beauvais.fr

Departments
Agro-Industrial Science and Technology (Analytical Chemistry; Biochemistry; Biotechnology; Food Science; Industrial Management; Microbiology; Nanotechnology; Organic Chemistry; Physics; Production Engineering; Statistics); **Agronomy and Animal Science** (Agronomy; Analytical Chemistry; Animal Husbandry; Biotechnology; Cell Biology; Crop Production; Ecology; Forestry; Microbiology; Molecular Biology; Plant Pathology; Soil Science); **Geoscience** (Geology; Geophysics; Marine Science and Oceanography; Mining Engineering; Petroleum and Gas Engineering); **Nutrition and Health** (Analytical Chemistry; Biotechnology; Epidemiology; Immunology; Microbiology; Molecular Biology; Nutrition; Pharmacology; Physiology; Toxicology); **Transversal Engineering Science and Management** (Accountancy; Communication Studies; Economics; Engineering; Management; Marketing; Sociology)

History: Founded 1854 as Institut Normal Agricole. Acquired present title and status 2006 following merger of the Institut Géologique Albert-de-Lapparent and the Institut Supérieur d'Agriculture de Beauvais. Associated with the Institut catholique de Paris.

Main Language(s) of Instruction: French

Degrees and Diplomas: *Brevet de Technicien supérieur; Diplôme d'Ingénieur; Mastère spécialisé*
Last Updated: 26/01/12

LEONARDO DA VINCI UNIVERSITY POLE

Pôle Universitaire Léonard De Vinci
92916 Paris La Défense
Tel: +33(1) 41-16-70-00
Fax: +33(1) 41-16-70-79
EMail: contact@devinci.fr
Website: http://www.devinci.fr

Directeur Général: Michel Bera (2006-)

Secrétaire Général: Max De Grandi
International Relations: Marie Josèphe Gridel

Centres
Continuing Education *(CFA)* (Computer Networks; Information Management; Mechanical Equipment and Maintenance; Sales Techniques) *Director*: Colette Lucien

Institutes
Internet and Multimedia *(IIM)* (Computer Engineering; Computer Graphics; Multimedia; Software Engineering)

Schools
Engineering *(ESILV)* (Business Computing; Computer Engineering; Engineering); **Management** *(EMLV)* (Accountancy; Banking; Business and Commerce; Communication Studies; Finance; Human Resources; Management; Marketing)

History: Created in 1995 by the Conseil Général des Hauts-de-Seine, it aimed to address a gap between Universities and the Grandes Ecoles.

Academic Year: September-May

Admission Requirements: Baccalauréat or equivalent Secondary School Degree, entrance exam, written English exam and interview.

Fees: (Euros): IIM, 4,900 per annum; ESILV, 5,400; EMLV, 6,000, and a 60% reduction for local residents.

Main Language(s) of Instruction: French, English

International Co-operation: MBA exchange programmes with universities in Boston and New York (USA) and agreements with several universities in Europe, Canada, including China, Mexico and Russia.

Accrediting Agencies: Ministry of Education, Commission des Titres d'Ingénieur

Degrees and Diplomas: *Licence*; *Diplôme d'Ingénieur*; *Mastère spécialisé*. équivalent Master
Last Updated: 08/07/11

LILLE NOTARY SCHOOL

Ecole de Notariat de Lille
7, rue de Puebla, 59900 Lille
Tel: +33(3) 20-54-54-52
Fax: +33(3) 20-54-54-52
EMail: ecolenotariat@orange.fr
Website: http://ednl.free.fr/

Directeur: Serge Bordzakian

Programmes
Notary Studies (Notary Studies)

Admission Requirements: Baccalauréat or equivalent Secondary School degree; Capacité en droit for the 2nd year; 2 yrs undergraduate studies in Law or DUT in Law

Main Language(s) of Instruction: French

Accrediting Agencies: Ministry of Justice, Centre National de l'Enseignement Professionnel Notarial

Degrees and Diplomas: Diplôme de clerc de notaire (2 yrs) Diplôme de 1er clerc (further 2 yrs) Diplôme de Notaire (6 yrs)
Last Updated: 15/10/07

LYON SCHOOL OF CHEMISTRY, PHYSICS AND ELECTRONICS

Ecole supérieure de Chimie Physique Electronique de Lyon (CPE LYON)
BP 2077, 43, boulevard du 11 Novembre 1918, 69616 Villeurbanne, Cedex
Tel: +33(4) 72-43-17-00
Fax: +33(4) 72-43-16-88
EMail: tizon@cpe.fr
Website: http://www.cpe.fr

Directeur: Gérard Pignault (2004-)
Tel: +33(4) 72-43-17-02, Fax: +33(4) 72-43-16-84
EMail: pignault@cpe.fr

Secrétaire général: Thierry Tizon Tel: +33(4) 72-43-17-38

International Relations: Anthony K. Smith
Tel: +33(4) 72-43-17-39 EMail: smith@cpe.fr

Departments

Chemistry and Chemical Engineering (Chemical Engineering; Chemistry); **Computer Science and Telecommunications** *(IRC)* (Computer Science; Telecommunications Engineering); **Electronics, Telecommunications, Computer Science** (Computer Engineering; Computer Science; Electronic Engineering)

Further Information: Also 16 Research Laboratories

History: Founded 1994 incorporating Lyons School of Industrial Chemistry (1883) and Industrial Chemistry and Physics Institute (1919).

Governing Bodies: Board of governors (Conseil d' Administration)

Academic Year: September to June

Admission Requirements: Competitive entrance examination following 2-3 yrs further study after secondary school certificate (baccalauréat) in Science.

Fees: (Euros): c. 5,150 per annum

Main Language(s) of Instruction: French

International Co-operation: With universities in Australia, Canada and USA. Also participates in Erasmus, TASSEP, CREPUQ Programmes.

Accrediting Agencies: Commission des Titres d'Ingénieur

Degrees and Diplomas: *Diplôme d'Ingénieur:* Chemistry and Chemical Engineering; Electronics, Telecommunications, Computer Science, 3 yrs; *Diplôme national de Master*

Student Services: Academic counselling, Canteen, Employment services, Foreign student adviser, Handicapped facilities, Health services, Language programs, Nursery care, Social counselling, Sports facilities

Libraries: Yes.
Last Updated: 12/05/11

LYON TEXTILE AND CHEMICAL INSTITUTE

Institut textile et chimique de Lyon (ITECH LYON)

87, chemin des Mouilles, 69134 Ecully, Cedex
Tel: +33(4) 72-18-04-80
Fax: +33(4) 77-18-95-45
EMail: info@itech.fr
Website: http://www.itech.fr

Directeur: Jérôme Marcilloux (2012-)

Secrétaire générale: Estelle Vlieghe EMail: e.vlieghe@itech.fr

International Relations: Nathalie Pinton
Tel: +33(4) 72-18-01-72 EMail: n.pinton@itech.fr

Departments

Textiles and Chemical Engineering (Chemical Engineering; Leather Techniques; Textile Technology)

History: Founded 1988 following merger of the Ecole supérieure des Industries Textiles de Lyon, founded in 1840 and the Ecole Française de Tannerie, founded in 1899.

Academic Year: September to June

Admission Requirements: Competitive entrance examination following 2 yrs further study after secondary school certificate (bac + 2)

Fees: (Euros): c. 4,600 per annum

Main Language(s) of Instruction: French

Degrees and Diplomas: *Brevet de Technicien supérieur:* Paint, Inks, Adhesives / Leather Technology, 2 yrs; *Licence professionnelle*; *Diplôme d'Ingénieur:* Leather; Paint and Inks / Adhesives / Chemistry Formulation; Plastics; Textile, 3 yrs; *Mastère spécialisé*: Cosmetics; Materials and Coatings; Technical Textile, a further yr; *Diplôme national de Master:* Leather; Plastics; Science in Chemistry; Science in Chemistry Formulation; Science in Textile, a further 18 months following Bachelor

Student Services: Academic counselling, Employment services, Social counselling
Last Updated: 30/01/12

MANAGEMENT AND BUSINESS SCHOOL NETWORK

Ecole de gestion et de commerce (RÉSEAU EGC)

46 avenue de la Grande Armée, 75016 Paris
Tel: +33(1) 40-69-38-61
Fax: +33(1) 53-57-18-61
EMail: reseauegc@6tm.com
Website: http://www.bachelor-egc.fr

Président: Pascal Crépin (2007-)

Programmes

Business and Commerce (Business Administration; Business and Commerce; Marketing)

Further Information: EGC consists of a network of 25 schools throughout France

Admission Requirements: Baccalauréat, Equivalent Secondary School Degree, and entrance exam

Fees: (Euros): 3,580

Main Language(s) of Instruction: French

International Co-operation: Possible to do a 6-9 months exchange with selected Institutions in Australia, UK, Ireland and Hungary.

Accrediting Agencies: Association des Chambres Française de Commerce et d'Industrie (ACFCI), Répertoire Nationale des Certifications Professionnelles (RNCP), Ministry of Education

Degrees and Diplomas: *Licence*: Marketing, Management and Business, 3 yrs; *Diplôme d'Etudes d'Ecole de Commerce et Gestion*: 3 yrs. Business-Marketing and Sales Manager Diploma (Diplome EGC)
Last Updated: 15/10/07

MONTPELLIER BUSINESS SCHOOL

Groupe Sup de Co Montpellier (ESC MONTPELLIER)

2300, avenue des Moulins, 34185 Montpellier, Cedex 4
Tel: +33(4) 67-10-25-00
Fax: +33(4) 67-45-13-56
EMail: lmaire@supco-montpellier.fr
Website: http://www.supdeco-montpellier.com

Directeur: Didier Jourdan
Tel: +33(4) 67-10-25-33, Fax: +33(4) 67-40-56-50

International Relations: Laurence Maire Tel: +33(4) 67-10-26-56

Institutes

International Commerce (International Business; Management)

Schools

Business Administration and Management (Business Administration; Management)

History: Founded 1897 by the Chambre de Commerce et d'Industrie de Montpellier.

Academic Year: September to June

Admission Requirements: Competitive entrance examination following 2 yrs further study after secondary school certificate (baccalauréat) or equivalent

Fees: (Euros): Commercial diploma course, 5,869 per annum; MBA, 12,200

Main Language(s) of Instruction: French

Degrees and Diplomas: *Diplôme d'Etudes d'Ecole de Commerce et Gestion*: 3 yrs; *Diplôme national de Master.* Bachelor's degree in International Business
Last Updated: 04/07/11

MONTPELLIER SCHOOL OF NOTARY STUDIES

Institut des Métiers du Notariat de Montpellier

565, avenue des Apothicaires, Parc Euromédecine, 34196 Montpellier, Cedex 05
Tel: +33(4) 67-54-16-38
Fax: +33(4) 67-41-00-82
EMail: ecole-notaire-34@wanadoo.fr
Website: http://www.ecole-notariat.fr

Directeur: M. Campels

Programmes

Notary Studies (Law; Notary Studies)

Admission Requirements: Baccalauréat or equivalent Secondary School degree and entrance examination; Capacité en droit for the 2nd year; 2 yrs undergraduate studies in Law or DUT in Law

Main Language(s) of Instruction: French

Accrediting Agencies: Ministry of Justice, Centre National de l'Enseignement Professionnel Notarial

Degrees and Diplomas: *Brevet de Technicien supérieur*; *Licence*; *Diplôme national de Master.* Diplôme supérieur du Notariat
Last Updated: 15/10/07

NANTES ATLANTIC SCHOOL OF DESIGN

Ecole de Design Nantes Atlantique
Atlanpole La Chantrerie, Rue Christian-Pauc - BP30607,
44306 Nantes, Cedex 03
Tel: +33(2) 51-13-50-70
Fax: +33(2) 51-13-50-65
EMail: info@lecolededesign.com
Website: http://www.lecolededesign.com

Directeur général: Christian Guellerin

International Relations: Katrin Dierks

Programmes
Design (Design)

Further Information: Has a school in China

History: Founded 1988.

Admission Requirements: September-May

Fees: (Euros): 1st yr, 4,000; following yrs, 4,900

Main Language(s) of Instruction: French

International Co-operation: Cumulus Association. All fourth year students spend a semester abroad.

Accrediting Agencies: Ministry of Education

Degrees and Diplomas: *Brevet de Technicien supérieur*; *Licence professionnelle*; *Mastère spécialisé.* Diplôme de design de L'École de design Nantes Atlantique est visé par le ministère en charge de l'Enseignement supérieur au niveau I (bac + 5 équivalent master universitaire).
Last Updated: 24/06/11

NANTES SCHOOL OF NOTARY STUDIES

Institut des Métiers du Notariat de Nantes
119, rue de Coulmiers, 44000 Nantes, Cedex
Tel: +33(2) 40-74-08-76
Fax: +33(2) 40-37-02-40
EMail: econota@wanadoo.fr
Website: http://www.ecole-notariat.com

Directeur: Benoist Boussion

Programmes
Notary Studies (Law; Notary Studies)

History: Founded 1905 as Ecole de Notariat de Nantes. Acquired present title 2008.

Admission Requirements: Baccalauréat or equivalent Secondary School degree; Capacité en droit for the 2nd year; 2 yrs undergraduate studies in Law or DUT in Law

Fees: (Euros) 3,240 per annum

Main Language(s) of Instruction: French

Accrediting Agencies: Ministry of Justice, Centre National de l'Enseignement Professionnel Notarial

Degrees and Diplomas: *Brevet de Technicien supérieur*; *Licence professionnelle.* Diplôme des métiers du notariat
Last Updated: 21/07/11

NEW SCHOOL OF ECONOMIC AND SOCIAL ORGANISATION

Ecole nouvelle d'Organisation économique et sociale (ENOES)
62, rue de Miromesnil, 75008 Paris
Tel: +33(1) 45-62-80-59
Fax: +33(2) 53-75-33-80
EMail: thierry.carlier@enoes.com
Website: http://www.enoes.com

Président: Gilles de Courcel

Centres
Accountancy *(CECS)* (Accountancy)

Schools
Human Resources *(ERH)* (Human Resources; Management);
Transport *(EST)* (Transport Economics; Transport Management)

History: Founded in 1937 with the creation of the Accounting Centre, the Ecole Nationale d'Organisation Economique et Sociale was goverened directly by the Ministry of Economy until gaining its autonomy in 1949.

Admission Requirements: Competitive entrance exam following 2 yrs of undergraduate studies or min. 5 yrs of validated professional experience

Fees: (Euros): 4,800 p.a.

Main Language(s) of Instruction: French

Accrediting Agencies: Ministry of Economy, Finance and Industry.

Degrees and Diplomas: *Diplôme d'Etat*: Accountancy (DESCF, DECF, DPECF or DEC), 1-2 yrs following 2 yrs of University studies. Masters 1 (2 yrs) in Transport and Logistics; Human Resources
Last Updated: 25/05/11

NÎMES SCHOOL OF NOTARY STUDIES

Institut des Métiers du Notariat de Nîmes
26-28, quai de la Fontaine, 30900 Nîmes
Tel: +33(4) 66-67-85-40
Fax: +33(4) 66-67-86-99
EMail: imn.nimes@notaires.fr
Website: http://www.imn-nimes.notaires.fr

Directeur: Michel Milian

Programmes
Notary Studies (Notary Studies)

Academic Year: October-June

Admission Requirements: Baccalauréat or equivalent Secondary School degree; Capacité en droit for the 2nd year; 2 yrs under-graduate studies in Law or DUT in Law

Fees: (Euros) 2,416 for the First cycle; 1,377 for the Second cycle (per year)

Main Language(s) of Instruction: French

Accrediting Agencies: Ministry of Justice, Centre National de l'Enseignement Professionnel Notarial

Degrees and Diplomas: *Brevet de Technicien supérieur*; *Licence professionnelle.* Diplôme de l'Institut des Métiers du Notariat (D.I.M.).
Last Updated: 15/10/07

NORMANDY BUSINESS SCHOOL

Ecole de Management de Normandie
30, rue Richelieu, 76087 Le Havre, Cedex 4
Tel: +33(2) 32-92-59-99
Fax: +33(2) 35-42-11-16
EMail: info@em-normandie.fr
Website: http://www.ecole-management-normandie.fr

Directeur Général: Jean Guy Bernard
Tel: +33(2) 31-46-94-49, Fax: +33(2) 31-43-81-01
EMail: jg.bernard@em-normandie.fr

Directeur des affaires administratives: Daniel Choplet
Tel: +33(2) 32-92-59-95 EMail: d.choplet@em-normandie.fr

International Relations: Alain Ouvrieu
Tel: +33(2) 31-45-35-02 EMail: a.ouvrieu@em-normandie.fr

Programmes
Graduate and Professional Studies (IPER, Le Havre); **Graduate Studies in Management** (Management); **Undergraduate Studies** (Accountancy; International Business; Management; Marketing)

History: Founded 1871 as Ecole supérieure de Commerce du Havre. Became Ecole de Management de Normandie 2004 with campuses in Le Havre and Caen.

Governing Bodies: Chambers of Commerce and Industry of Le Havre and Caen; Association Ecole de Management de Normandie

Admission Requirements: ESC Le Havre, competitive entrance examination following first university degree (DEUG); SUP EUROPE CESEC, Baccalauréat or equivalent; IPER, first university degree-postgraduate level and English test.

Fees: (Euros): 7,095 -7,525 per annum

Main Language(s) of Instruction: French, English

International Co-operation: With universities in Australia, Austria, Belgium, Brazil, Canada, Chile, China, Colombia, Cyprus, Czech Republic, Germany, Denmark, Korea, Egypt, Spain, Finland, Italy, Netherlands, Hungary, India, Japan, Latvia, Lithuania, Morocco, New Zealand, Poland, Portugal, Sweden, United Kingdom, USA, UAE, Mexico, Russia

Degrees and Diplomas: Licence (BHs): 4 yrs; Mastère spécialisé; Diplôme national de Master. Global Logistics and International Transports; Value Chain and Logistics Management, 1 yr; Diplôme national de Master. Management, 5 yrs. Also Bachelor's

Student Services: Academic counselling, Canteen, Employment services, Foreign student adviser, Language programs, Social counselling, Sports facilities

Publications: Cahiers de Recherche (quarterly)
Last Updated: 01/06/11

NOVANCIA BUSINESS SCHOOL
Novancia
8, avenue de la Porte de Champerret, 75017 Paris
Tel: +33(1) 55-65-50-00
EMail: information@novancia.fr
Website: http://www.novancia.fr

Directrice: Anne Stéfanini

Programmes
Entrepreneurship (Business and Commerce; Economics; Finance; Human Resources; Management; Marketing)

Further Information: Two sites in Paris

History: Founded 2011 following merger of Advancia and Négocia.

Academic Year: September-June

Admission Requirements: National exam 'Atout +3'

Main Language(s) of Instruction: French

Degrees and Diplomas: Diplôme national de Master. Entrepreneurship, Management, 2 yrs following Licence. Bachelor in Entrepreneurship and Management; Programmes are organised either as full-time studies or in alternating between studies and internships.
Last Updated: 14/12/11

PARIS SCHOOL OF NOTARY STUDIES
Institut des Métiers du Notariat de Paris
10 rue Traversière, 75012 Paris
Website: http://www.imn-paris.com/fr

Directeur: Christian Boutry

Programmes
Notary Studies (Notary Studies)
History: Founded 1830. Acquired present status 2007.

Main Language(s) of Instruction: French

Degrees and Diplomas: Brevet de Technicien supérieur; Licence professionnelle. Diplôme de l'Institut des Métiers du Notariat
Last Updated: 23/01/12

PENNINGHEN SCHOOL OF DESIGN, GRAPHIC ART AND INTERIOR DESIGN
Ecole supérieure de Design, d'Art graphique et d'Architecture intérieure Penninghen
31 rue du Dragon, 75006 Paris
Tel: +33(1) 42-22-55-07
Fax: +33(1) 42-22-61-98
EMail: esag@penninghen.fr
Website: http://www.penninghen.fr

Programmes
Graphic Arts (Design; Graphic Arts); **Interior Architecture and Design** (Architecture; Interior Design)

History: Finds its origins in the Académie Julian. Founded 1953.

Main Language(s) of Instruction: French

Degrees and Diplomas: Licence; Diplôme national de Master
Last Updated: 22/06/11

PRIVATE FACULTY OF LAW, ECONOMICS AND MANAGEMENT
Faculté libre de Droit, d'Economie et de Gestion
115-117 rue Notre Dame des Champs, 75006 Paris
Tel: +33(1) 53 10 24 70
EMail: faco@facoparis.org
Website: http://www.facoparis.com/

Doyen: J. P. Audoyer

Programmes
Economics and Management (Chinese; Economics; English; German; Italian; Management; Spanish); **Law and Political Science** (Law; Political Sciences)

History: Created 1967.

Governing Bodies: Conseil d'Administration; Conseil de Faculté

Academic Year: September to July (Sept - Dec; Jan - May)

Admission Requirements: Baccalauréat or equivalent

Fees: (Euros): 4,900 per annum

Degrees and Diplomas: Licence: Law; Economics; Management, 3 yrs; Diplôme national de Master. Law, 4 yrs

Academic Staff 2010-2011: Total 116
Student Numbers 2010-2011: Total 380
Last Updated: 20/05/11

REIMS MANAGEMENT SCHOOL (ESC REIMS)
BP 302, 59 rue Pierre Taittinger, 51061 Reims, Cedex
Tel: +33(3) 26-77-47-47
Fax: +33(3) 26-04-69-63
EMail: contact@reims-ms.fr; service.com@reims-ms.fr
Website: http://www.reims-ms.fr

Directeur: Hervé Colas
Tel: +33(3) 26-77-47-21, Fax: +33(3) 26-08-03-56

International Relations: Brigitte Panciera
Tel: +33(3) 26-77-46-12, Fax: +33(3) 26-04-69-63
EMail: brigitte.panciera@reims-ms.fr

Departments
Executive Education (Finance; Human Resources; Management; Marketing)

Laboratories
Service Marketing and Customer Satisfaction (Management; Marketing)

Programmes
Business Administration and Management (Business Administration; Business and Commerce; Management); **International Management** (International Business); **Management** (Management); **Technology and Management**

Further Information: Also International Management and Summer programmes for foreign students

History: Founded 1928 as Ecole Supérieure de Commerce de Reims. Acquired present title 2000.

Academic Year: September to June (September-January; February-June), with flexibility for specialization programmes

Admission Requirements: Competitive entrance examination following 2 yrs further study after secondary school certificate (baccalauréat) or equivalent

Fees: (Euros): 6,500 per annum

Main Language(s) of Instruction: French, English

Degrees and Diplomas: *Diplôme d'Etudes d'Ecole de Commerce et Gestion*; *Mastère spécialisé*: International Financial Analysis, Management in Distribution, Services, Large Accounts, Buying Strategies; *Diplôme national de Master*. MBA in International Industrial Management; PhD Universa

Student Services: Academic counselling, Canteen, Employment services, Foreign student adviser, Sports facilities

Student Residential Facilities: For c. 220 students

Libraries: Centre de documentation

Publications: Chorus (*quarterly*)

Last Updated: 08/07/11

RENNES SCHOOL OF NOTARY STUDIES

Institut des Métiers de Notariat de Rennes
2, mail Anne-Catherine, 35000 Rennes
Tel: +33(2) 99-65-00-21
Fax: +33(2) 99-63-53-6
EMail: contact@imnrennes.fr
Website: http://www.imnrennes.fr

Directrice: Anne-Sophie Lamé

Programmes
Notary Studies (Justice Administration; Law; Notary Studies)

History: Founded 1892.

Admission Requirements: Competitive entrance exam and 4yrs of Law Studies (Master I or Maîtrise).

Fees: (Euros): 3,450-6,040

Main Language(s) of Instruction: French

Accrediting Agencies: Ministère de la Justice

Degrees and Diplomas: *Brevet de Technicien supérieur*; *Licence professionnelle*. Diplome supérieur du notariat (2 yrs following licence professionnelle with internship).

Last Updated: 24/06/11

ROUEN BUSINESS SCHOOL

BP 188, 1 Rue du Maréchal Juin, 76825 Mont-Saint-Aignan, Cedex
Tel: +33(2) 32-82-57-00
Fax: +33(2) 32-82-57-01
EMail: info@rouenbs.fr
Website: http://www.rouenbs.fr

Directeur Général: Arnaud Langlois-Meurinne (2002-)
Tel: +33(2) 32-82-57-05, Fax: +33(2) 32-82-57-03

Directeur administratif et financier: Isabelle Geneste
Tel: +33(2) 32-82-57-35
EMail: Isabelle.Geneste@groupe-esc-rouen.fr

International Relations: Stephen Murdoch
Tel: +33(2) 32-82-57-19, Fax: +33(2) 32-81-58-36
EMail: international@groupe-esc-rouen.fr

Departments
Accounting, Law, Operations and Information Management (Accountancy; Information Management; Law); **Finance and Economics** (Economics; Finance); **Languages, Culture and Societies** (Cultural Studies; Modern Languages); **Management and Strategy** (Business Administration; Management); **Marketing** (Advertising and Publicity; Marketing; Retailing and Wholesaling; Sales Techniques)

History: Founded 1871. Formerly known as Groupe ESC Rouen. Acquired present title 2009.

Academic Year: September to June

Admission Requirements: Competitive entrance examination and interview

Fees: (Euros): c. 6,300-10,000 per annum

Main Language(s) of Instruction: French, English

Accrediting Agencies: Ministry of Education; Conférence des Grandes Ecoles; Chamber of Commerce and Industry of Rouen

Degrees and Diplomas: *Diplôme d'Etudes d'Ecole de Commerce et Gestion*: General Management, a further 3 yrs; *Diplôme d'Etudes d'Ecole de Commerce et Gestion*: General Management, 3 yrs; *Diplôme d'Etudes d'Ecole de Commerce et Gestion*: International Business, 4 yrs; *Mastère spécialisé*: Childhood and Teen Marketing (MS), a further yr; *Mastère spécialisé*: Corporate Communication (MS); European Management (MS); International Finance Management (MS); International Management Strategies (MS); Marketing and Management Research (MS); Retail Network Management (MS), a further 1 yr; *Diplôme national de Master*. Also International MBA a further yr

Student Services: Academic counselling, Canteen, Cultural centre, Employment services, Foreign student adviser, Foreign Studies Centre, Handicapped facilities, Health services, Language programs, Social counselling, Sports facilities

Student Residential Facilities: Yes

Special Facilities: Movie Studio

Libraries: Central Library

Last Updated: 08/07/11

ROUEN SCHOOL OF NOTARY STUDIES

Institut des Métiers du Notariat de Rouen
BP 248, 39, rue du Champ-aux-Oiseaux, 76003 Rouen, Cedex 2
Tel: +33(2) 35-70-50-41
Fax: +33(2) 35-89-61-28
EMail: ecoledenotariat@fr.oleane.com
Website: http://www.ecolenotariat-rouen.com/

Directeur: F. Maurer

Programmes
Notary Studies (Notary Studies)

History: Founded 1893.

Main Language(s) of Instruction: French

Degrees and Diplomas: Diplôme de l'Institut des Métiers du Notariat (4 yrs)

Last Updated: 05/07/11

SAINT ETIENNE SCHOOL OF MANAGEMENT

Ecole supérieure de Commerce de Saint-Etienne (ESC SAINT-ETIENNE/SESOM)
BP 29, 51-53, cours Fauriel, 42009 Saint-Etienne, Cedex 2
Tel: +33(4) 77-49-24-50
Fax: +33(4) 77-49-24-51
EMail: info@esc-saint-etienne.fr
Website: http://www.esc-saint-etienne.fr

Directeur: Michel Rollin
Tel: +33(4) 77-49-24-52, Fax: +33(4) 77-49-24-53
EMail: michel_rollin@esc-saint-etienne.fr

Administrative Officer: Jean-Christophe Prost
EMail: jc_prost@esc-saint-etienne.fr

International Relations: Vincent Beausejour
Tel: +33(4) 77-49-24-50, Fax: +33(4) 77-49-24-51
EMail: vincent_beausejour@esc-saint-etienne.fr

Programmes
Management (Business and Commerce; International Business; Management)

History: A private 'Grande Ecole'.

Governing Bodies: Conseil de Gouvernance

Academic Year: September-May

Admission Requirements: 2-3 yrs undergraduate studies and entrance exam

Main Language(s) of Instruction: French

Degrees and Diplomas: *Mastère spécialisé*: Purchasing Management, Supply Chain Management; *Diplôme national de Master*. Bachelor EGC, Bachelor Centre du Management International, Bachelor IFC, Master ESC Grande Ecole

Last Updated: 16/06/11

SCHOOL OF ADVANCED ENGINEERING STUDIES

HEI - Hautes Etudes d'Ingénieur (HEI)
13, rue de Toul, 59046 Lille
Tel: +33(3) 28-38-48-58
Fax: +33(3) 28-38-48-59
EMail: jean-marc.idoux@hei.fr
Website: http://www.hei.fr

Directeur Général: Jean-Marc Idoux

Secrétaire Générale: Agnès Gucker EMail: agnes.gucker@hei.fr

International Relations: Grant DouglasFax: +33(3) 28-38-48-04
EMail: grant.douglas@hei.fr

Departments
Chemistry and Chemical Engineering (Chemical Engineering; Chemistry); **Construction and Civil Engineering** (Civil Engineering; Construction Engineering); **Energy Engineering, Electrical Engineering and Automation** (Automation and Control Engineering; Electrical Engineering; Energy Engineering); **Mechanical Engineering** (Mechanical Engineering); **Systems Management/Computer Science** (Computer Science; Systems Analysis); **Textile** (Textile Technology)

History: Founded 1885. Acquired present title 2004.

Academic Year: September to June

Admission Requirements: Secondary school certificate (baccalauréat) or equivalent

Fees: (Euros): Diplôme d'ingénieur, 1,625-4,000 per annum

Main Language(s) of Instruction: French

International Co-operation: Participates in cooperation programmes with local Universities to offer a Masters recherche. Exchange programmes with universities in Anglo-Saxon countries, several EU and Eastern European countries, Mexico, Brazil and Argentina.

Accrediting Agencies: Commission des Titres d'Ingénieur, Conférence des Grandes Ecoles

Degrees and Diplomas: *Licence professionnelle*: Textile Production and Management; *Diplôme d'Ingénieur*: Civil Engineering, Mechanics, Chemistry, Electrical Engineering, Computer Science, Industrial Management and Textile Production and Management., 5 yrs; *Diplôme national de Master*: Innovative Technologies in Transportation Systems, a further yr; *Doctorat*: Science and Technology, a further 2-3 yrs

Student Services: Academic counselling, Canteen, Cultural centre, Employment services, Foreign student adviser, Language programs, Sports facilities

Libraries: Bibliothèque scientifique, 10,000 vols
Last Updated: 05/07/11

SCHOOL OF AGRICULTURAL ENGINEERING

Ecole d'Ingénieurs en Agriculture (ESITPA)
3 rue du Tronquet, CS 40118, 76134 Mont-Saint-Aignan
Tel: +33(2) 32-82-92-00
Fax: +33(2) 35-05-27-40
EMail: contact@esitpa.org
Website: http://www.esitpa.org/

Directeur: Daniel Roche (2009-)

International Relations: Nathalie Roguez

Departments
Agronomy (Agronomy; Animal Husbandry; Biotechnology; Environmental Studies; Vegetable Production); **Biometrics and Computer Science** (Computer Science; Mathematics; Statistics); **Economics and Management** (Economics; Management); **Food Processing** (Agricultural Business; Biotechnology; Chemistry; Food Science); **Humanities** (Arts and Humanities; Communication Studies; English; German; Spanish)

History: Founded 1919 as Institut technique de pratique agricole. Becomes Ecole supérieure d'ingénieurs et de techniciens pour l'agriculture 1970. Acquired present title 2007.

Admission Requirements: Baccalauréat, Equivalent Secondary School Degree

Fees: (Euros): 3,500 per year

Main Language(s) of Instruction: French

International Co-operation: With Madagascar Universities. Also participates in Erasmus, Socrates programmes

Accrediting Agencies: Commission des titres d'ingénieur (CTI). Ministry of Agriculture

Degrees and Diplomas: *Diplôme d'Ingénieur*. 5 yrs; *Mastère spécialisé*
Last Updated: 04/07/11

SCHOOL OF BUSINESS - SUP DE CO COMPIÈGNE

Ecole supérieure de Commerce de Compiègne (ESC COMPIÈGNE)
32 rue Hippolyte Bottier, 60200 Compiègne
Tel: +33(3) 44-38-55-00
Fax: +33(3) 44-38-55-09
EMail: esc@wanadoo.fr
Website: http://www.esc-compiegne.com

Directrice: Odile Gonzalez de Peredo

Departments
Economics (Economics); **Finance** (Finance); **Languages** (Modern Languages); **Law** (Law); **Management** (Management); **Marketing** (Marketing); **Sales Techniques** (Sales Techniques)

History: Founded 1985.

Admission Requirements: Baccalauréat or equivalent Secondary School Degree to enter Preparatory Classes (2 yr programme); National exam or ESCC entrance exam for the Second cycle programme

Main Language(s) of Instruction: French

Degrees and Diplomas: *Licence professionnelle*: Human Resources, Marketing (ESTER), 1 yr; *Diplôme d'Etudes d'Ecole de Commerce et Gestion*: 3 yrs
Last Updated: 04/07/11

SCHOOL OF ELECTRICAL ENGINEERING

Ecole supérieure d'Ingénieurs en Génie électrique (ESIGELEC)
B.P. 10024 Technopôle du Madrillet, 76801 St Etienne du Rouvray, Cedex
Tel: +33(2) 32-91-58-58
Fax: +33(2) 32-91-58-59
EMail: com@esigelec.fr
Website: http://www.esigelec.fr

Directeur général: Eric Durieux (2011-)

Secrétaire Générale: Virginie Le Clec'h
EMail: virginie.leclech@esigelec.fr

International Relations: Cyril Marteaux
EMail: cyril.marteaux@esigelec.fr

Departments
Communication and Information Technologies (Information Technology); **Electrical Engineering and Energies** (Electrical Engineering; Energy Engineering); **Electronics and Telecommunications** (Electronic Engineering; Telecommunications Engineering); **Embedded System and Instrumentation** (Computer Science; Electronic Engineering; Instrument Making); **Humanties, Languages and Management** (Accountancy; Economics; Ethics; Law; Management; Modern Languages; Music)

Graduate Schools
Electrical Engineering (Electrical Engineering)

Laboratories
Data Processing (Computer Engineering; Data Processing); **Industrial Automation** (Automation and Control Engineering; Electrical Engineering; Industrial Engineering); **Networks Architecture** (Computer Networks); **Optical Telecommunications** (Telecommunications Engineering)

History: Founded 1901 as Ecole Pratique d'Electricité Industrielle. Acquired present status and title 1980.

Governing Bodies: Chamber of Commerce of Rouen

Academic Year: September to June (September-January; February-June)

Admission Requirements: Competitive entrance examination following 2-3 yrs further study after secondary school certificate (baccalauréat) or following first university qualification (DEUG, DUT or BTS), or equivalent

Fees: (Euros): c. 5,380 per annum

Main Language(s) of Instruction: French, English

Degrees and Diplomas: *Diplôme d'Ingénieur*; *Diplôme national de Master*; *Doctorat*

Student Services: Canteen, Employment services, Foreign student adviser, Handicapped facilities

Libraries: c. 6,000 technical vols

Last Updated: 04/07/11

SCHOOL OF ELECTRONICS - PARIS

Institut Supérieur d'Electronique de Paris
28, rue Notre Dame des Champs, 75006 Paris
Tel: +33(1) 49-54-52-43
EMail: info@isep.fr
Website: http://www.isep.fr/

Directeur général: Michel Ciazynski
EMail: michel.ciazynski@isep.fr

International Relations: Catherine Miannay
EMail: catherine.miannay@isep.fr

Programmes
Engineering (Computer Engineering; Electronic Engineering; Engineering; Information Technology; Telecommunications Engineering)

History: Founded 1955. Affiliated to the Institut catholique de Paris.

Main Language(s) of Instruction: French

Degrees and Diplomas: *Diplôme d'Ingénieur*; *Mastère spécialisé*; *Diplôme national de Master*
Last Updated: 16/02/12

SCHOOL OF ENGINEERS IN ELECTRICAL ENGINEERING, PRODUCTION AND INDUSTRIAL MANAGEMENT

Ecole supérieure d'Ingénieurs en Génie Electrique, Productique et Management Industriel
13 Boulevard de l'Hautil, 95092 Cergy-Pontoise
Tel: +33(1) 30-75-60-40
Website: http://www.epmi.fr

Directeur général: Moumen Darchérif

Programmes
Engineering (Electrical Engineering; Production Engineering); **Industrial Management** (Industrial Management)

History: Founded 1992. Associated with the Institut catholique de Paris.

Main Language(s) of Instruction: French

Degrees and Diplomas: *Diplôme d'Ingénieur*; *Mastère spécialisé*
Last Updated: 24/01/12

SCHOOL OF ENTERPRENEURS AND BUSINESS EXECUTIVES

Ecole des Dirigeants et des Créateurs d'Entreprise (EDC PARIS)
70, galerie des Damiers, La Défense 1, 92415 Courbevoie
Tel: +33(1) 46-93-02-70
Fax: +33(1) 46-93-02-74
EMail: informations@edcparis.edu
Website: http://www.edcparis.edu

Président: Alain Dominique Perrin

Institutes
Luxury Brand Marketing (Marketing)

Programmes
Management (Business and Commerce; Finance; International Business; Management; Marketing)

Further Information: Also Observatory and Research Entrepreneurship Centre (OCRE)

History: Founded 1950. Recognized by the State 1967. In 1995, it was bought by the EDC Alumni and transformed into a specialized business school.

Admission Requirements: Baccalauréat or equivalent Secondary School degree, entrance exam

Main Language(s) of Instruction: French, English

International Co-operation: Erasmus, Socrates and has set up school partnerships with Universities in Quebec, San Diego University (USA), and TEC de Monterrey (Mexico).

Accrediting Agencies: Ministère de l'Enseignement supérieur et de la Recherche, Conférence des Grandes Ecoles

Degrees and Diplomas: *Diplôme national de Master*. MBA specialised in Luxury Brand Marketing
Last Updated: 30/06/11

SCHOOL OF INFORMATION AND COMMUNICATIONS ENGINEERING TECHNOLOGIES

Ecole d'Ingénieur des Technologies de l'Information et de la Communication (EFREI)
30-32, av. de la République, 94815 cedex Villejuif
Tel: +33(1) 46-77-64-67
Fax: +33(1) 43-37-65-77
EMail: informations@efrei.fr
Website: http://www.efrei.fr

Directeur: Eric Parlebas

Programmes
Information and Communications Technologies

History: Founded 1936. Acquired present status 1956.

Admission Requirements: Secondary school certificate (Baccalauréat) and competitive oral examination

Fees: (Euros): 7,500 per annum

Main Language(s) of Instruction: French

International Co-operation: With universities in Europe, USA, Canada, Mexico, Singapore, China

Accrediting Agencies: CTI (Ministry of Education)

Degrees and Diplomas: *Diplôme universitaire de Technologie*; *Licence*: 3 yrs; *Diplôme d'Ingénieur*: Information Technology, 5 yrs; *Diplôme national de Master*: 2 yrs

Student Residential Facilities: 2 sudents hostels
Last Updated: 23/06/11

SCHOOL OF ORGANIC AND MINERAL CHEMISTRY

Ecole supérieure de Chimie organique et minérale
1 allée du réseau Jean-Marie Buckmaster, 60200 Compiègne
Tel: +33(3) 44-23-88-00
Fax: +33(3) 44-97-15-91
EMail: s.jourdain@escom.fr
Website: http://www.escom.fr

Président: François Darrort

Programmes
Chemistry (Analytical Chemistry; Chemical Engineering; Chemistry; Inorganic Chemistry; Organic Chemistry)

History: Founded 1957. Associate status with Institut catholique de Paris.

Main Language(s) of Instruction: French

Degrees and Diplomas: *Diplôme d'Ingénieur*; *Mastère spécialisé*; *Diplôme national de Master*
Last Updated: 24/01/12

SCHOOL OF REAL ESTATE STUDIES

Ecole supérieure des Professions immobilières (ESPI)
20-22 rue du Théâtre, 75015 Paris
Tel: +33(1) 45-67-20-82
Fax: +33(1) 42-73-19-85
EMail: accueil@espi.asso.fr
Website: http://www.espi.asso.fr

Directeur: Xavier Boulet
Tel: +33(1) 45-67-20-56 EMail: x.boulet@espi.asso.fr

Programmes
Real Estate (Real Estate)

Further Information: Also site in Nantes.

History: Founded 1972.

Governing Bodies: Conseil d'administration

Admission Requirements: Baccalauréat or equivalent Secondary School degree

Fees: (Euros): Undergraduate studies, 6,000 per annum; Masters, 6,000-7,100

Main Language(s) of Instruction: French

International Co-operation: Participates in EUREDUC programme.

Accrediting Agencies: Ministry of Education

Degrees and Diplomas: *Diplôme national de Master.* Real Estate, 2 yrs. Diploma ESPI (undergraduate studies in 3 yrs).
Last Updated: 11/04/11

SCHOOL OF WELDING AND ITS APPLICATIONS
Ecole supérieure du Soudage et de ses Applications (ESSA)
Espace Cormontaigne, 4, Bd Henri Becquerel, 57970 Yutz
Tel: +33(1) 82-59-86-35
Fax: +33(1) 82-59-86-40
EMail: ec@institutdesoudure.com
Website: http://www.essa-isgroupe.com

Directeur: Michel Dijols
Tel: +33(1) 82-59-86-20 EMail: m.dijols@institutdesoudure.com

Directeur des Etudes: Philippe Roguin
Tel: +33(1) 82-59-86-36 EMail: p.roguin@institutdesoudure.com

International Relations: Philippe Roguin
Tel: +33(1) 82-59-86-36 EMail: p.roguin@institutdesoudure.com

Programmes
Welding (Construction Engineering; Materials Engineering; Metal Techniques)

History: Founded 1930, acquired present status and title 1931.

Academic Year: September to June

Admission Requirements: Diplôme d'Ingénieur or equivalent

Fees: (Euros): Members of EU, 2,745 per annum; others, 6,099

Main Language(s) of Instruction: French

International Co-operation: Participates in European and International cooperation programmes.

Accrediting Agencies: Ministry of Education. Industries

Degrees and Diplomas: *Diplôme d'Ingénieur.* Welding, 1 yr

Student Residential Facilities: For 15 students

Libraries: Central Library of the Institut de Soudure

Publications: Soudage et techniques connexes *(bimonthly)*; Souder *(bimonthly)*

Press or Publishing House: PSA (Publications du Soudage et de ses Applications)
Last Updated: 08/06/11

SKEMA BUSINESS SCHOOL
60 Rue Dostoïevski, 06902 Sophia Antipolis
Tel: +33(4) 93-95-44-44
Fax: +33(4) 93-65-45-24
EMail: regis.brandinelli@skema.edu
Website: http://www.skema-bs.fr

Directrice générale: Alice Guilhon

Schools
Commerce (Business and Commerce; Finance; Management; Marketing; Technology); **Management** (Aeronautical and Aerospace Engineering; Law; Management; Marine Science and Oceanography)

Further Information: Also campuses in Paris, Lille, Suzhou (China), Raleigh (US)

History: Founded 1963 as CERAM Business School. Acquired present status following merger with ESC Lille in 2009.

Academic Year: September to June

Admission Requirements: Competitive entrance examination following secondary school certificate (baccalauréat) and 2 yrs preparatory class. Also admissions following first university qualification

Fees: (Euros): 8,842 per annum

Main Language(s) of Instruction: French, English

Degrees and Diplomas: *Mastère spécialisé*; *Diplôme national de Master.* 3 yrs; *Doctorat.* Also Bachelor

Student Services: Academic counselling, Canteen, Employment services, Foreign student adviser, Health services, Language programs, Social counselling, Sports facilities

Student Residential Facilities: Yes

Special Facilities: Multimedia Laboratory; TV studio
Last Updated: 08/07/11

SPECIAL SCHOOL OF ARCHITECTURE
Ecole spéciale d'Architecture
254 boulevard Raspail, 75014 Paris
Tel: +33(1) 40-47-40-47
Fax: +33(1) 43-22-81-16
EMail: info@esa-paris.fr
Website: http://www.esa-paris.fr

Directeur général: Odile Decq

Programmes
Architecture (Architecture)

Degrees and Diplomas: 1er cycle (3 ans): Diplôme de l'ESA Grade 1, valant grade de Licence.2ème cycle (2 ans): Diplôme de l'ESA Grade 2, valant grade de Master.Habilitation à exercer la maîtrise d'oeuvre en son nom propre : Architecte DESA (hmonp).3ème cycle : Environnementaliste DESA, Urbaniste DESA
Last Updated: 12/04/11

STRASBOURG SCHOOL OF NOTARY STUDIES
Institut des Métiers du Notariat - Strasbourg
2, rue des Juifs, 67000 Strasbourg
Tel: +33(3) 88-32-10-55
Fax: +33(3) 88-75-65-11
EMail: nicole.muller@notaires.fr

Directeur: Jean-Marie Ohnet EMail: jeanmarie.ohnet@unistra.fr

Programmes
Notary Studies (Notary Studies)

Main Language(s) of Instruction: French

Degrees and Diplomas: *Brevet de Technicien supérieur*; *Licence professionnelle.* Diplôme de l'institut des métiers du notariat 1 yr after Licence professionnelle
Last Updated: 11/04/11

SUPÉLEC
Ecole supérieure d'Electricité (SUPELEC)
Plateau de Moulon, 3 rue Joliot-Curie, 91192 Gif-sur-Yvette, Cedex
Tel: +33(1) 69-85-12-12
Fax: +33(1) 69-85-12-34
EMail: catherine.luce@supelec.fr
Website: http://www.supelec.fr

Directeur général: Alain Bravo
Tel: +33(1) 69-85-12-41 EMail: alain.bravo@supelec.fr

Secrétaire générale: Nadine Brière Tel: +33(1) 69-85-12-71

International Relations: Claude Lhermitte
Tel: +33(1) 69-85-12-43, Fax: +33(1) 69-85-12-48
EMail: claude.lhermitte@supelec.fr

Departments

Automatic Control Systems (Automation and Control Engineering); **Computer Science** (Artificial Intelligence; Computer Engineering; Computer Science); **Electromagnetism** (Applied Physics; Telecommunications Engineering); **Electronics and Signal Processing** (Electronic Engineering); **Languages and Culture** (Cultural Studies; Modern Languages); **Power Systems and Power Electronics** (Electrical Engineering; Power Engineering); **Telecommunications** (Radio and Television Broadcasting; Telecommunications Engineering)

Laboratories

Electrical Engineering (LGEP) (Electrical Engineering); **Electromagnetism and Radars** (SONDRA: Singapore cooperation project) (Applied Physics); **Optics and Solids Electronics** (LMOPS) (Optics; Solid State Physics); **Signals and Systems** (L2S) (Automation and Control Engineering; Statistics; Systems Analysis; Telecommunications Engineering)

Further Information: Also campuses in Metz and Rennes

History: Founded 1894. Managed by the Société des Electriciens et des Electroniciens (SEE); Electricité de France; Fédération des Industries électriques, électroniques et de Communication.

Academic Year: September to June

Admission Requirements: Competitive entrance examination following secondary school certificate (baccalauréat) or equivalent

Fees: (Euros): French/EU students, 1,185-3,050; foreign students: 3,655; Mastère, 6,000-12,000 H.T

Main Language(s) of Instruction: French

International Co-operation: With institutions in Australia; Austria; Belgium; Canada; Germany; Italia; Romania; Spain; Sweden; United Kingdom; USA

Accrediting Agencies: Commission du Titre d'Ingénieur

Degrees and Diplomas: Diplôme d'Ingénieur. 3 yrs; Mastère spécialisé; Doctorat (PhD). Also Masters Recherche

Student Services: Academic counselling, Canteen, Cultural centre, Foreign student adviser, Handicapped facilities, Language programs, Sports facilities

Student Residential Facilities: For 1,200 students

Libraries: Yes

Last Updated: 01/07/11

SUPINFO INSTITUTE OF INFORMATION TECHNOLOGY

SUPINFO International University
23 rue du Château Landon, 75010 Paris
Tel: +33(1) 53-35-97-00
Fax: +33(1) 53-35-97-01
EMail: info@supinfo.com
Website: http://www.supinfo.com/

Président: Alick Mouriesse

Directrice académique: Marianne Belis
EMail: marianne.belis@supinfo.com

Programmes

Computer Science (Computer Science; Information Technology; Software Engineering); **Management** (Management)

History: Created 1965. Previously known as Ecole Supérieure d'Informatique de Paris (ESI).

Fees: (Euro): 5,000 per annum

Main Language(s) of Instruction: French

Degrees and Diplomas: Mastère spécialisé: Computer Science;
Last Updated: 17/11/10

THE ISG INTERNATIONAL SCHOOL OF BUSINESS

Institut supérieur de Gestion (ISG)
8, rue de Lota, 75116 Paris
Tel: +33(1) 56-26-26-26
Fax: +33(1) 56-26-26-00
EMail: isg@isg.fr
Website: http://www.isg.fr

Président: Marc Sallem

International Relations: Juliette Leroy
Tel: +33(1)56-26-26-28 EMail: international@isg.fr

Programmes

Management (Business Administration; Finance; International Business; Management; Marketing; Sports Management)

Research Centres

Applied Research in Management (IRSAM in collaboration with Paris XII)

Further Information: Has schools in New York and Tokyo.

History: Founded in 1967.

Admission Requirements: Baccalaureate or equivalent high school diploma for Preparatory Classes; 2 yrs undergraduate studies and entrance exam

Fees: (Euros): Bachelor's degrees, 6,000 per annum; International MBA, 12,900

Main Language(s) of Instruction: French, English

International Co-operation: Partnership agreements with schools worldwide

Accrediting Agencies: Association of Collegiate Business Schools and Programs, International Assembly for Collegiate Business Education

Degrees and Diplomas: Diplôme national de Master. Bachelors in Business Administration, International MBA in English (offered in French or English), MBA spécialisé.
Last Updated: 13/11/07

TOULOUSE BUSINESS SCHOOL

Groupe ESCToulouse
(ESC TOULOUSE)
20, boulevard Lascrosses, 31068 Toulouse, Cedex 7
Tel: +33(5) 61-29-49-49
Fax: +33(5) 61-29-49-94
EMail: info.esc@esc-toulouse.fr
Website: http://www.esc-toulouse.fr

Directeur général: Hervé Passeron

International Relations: Marie-Hélène Richard
Tel: +33(5) 61-29-49-29 EMail: mh.richard@esc-toulouse.fr

Centres

Business Studies (Business and Commerce); **Research and Engineering** (Engineering)

Institutes

European Negotiation (Business Administration)

Programmes

European MBA (Business Administration)

Schools

Business Administration and Management (Business Administration; Management)

Further Information: Also campuses in Barcelona and Casablanca

History: Founded 1903 by the Chambre de Commerce et d'Industrie de Toulouse.

Academic Year: September to June (September-December; January-March; April-June)

Admission Requirements: Competitive entrance examination following 2 yrs further study after secondary school certificate (baccalauréat) or equivalent

Fees: (Euros): Commercial diploma course, 6,022 per annum; Mastère, 9,200

Main Language(s) of Instruction: French

Accrediting Agencies: Association des Chambres Française de Commerce et d'Industrie (ACFCI), Répertoire Nationale des Certifications Professionnelles (RNCP), Ministry of Education

Degrees and Diplomas: Licence professionnelle; Diplôme d'Etudes d'Ecole de Commerce et Gestion: 3 yrs; Mastère spécialisé: a further 2 yrs. Also MBA, DBA

Student Residential Facilities: For c. 160 students

Libraries: Médiathèque, 10,000 vols
Publications: Les Cahiers de Recherche *(biannually)*
Last Updated: 04/07/11

TOURS SCHOOL OF NOTARY STUDIES

Institut des Métiers du Notariat de Tours
32, rue Richelieu, 37000 Tours
Tel: +33(2) 47-05-52-84
EMail: info@imn-tours.fr
Website: http://www.imn-tours.fr

Directrice: Manuela Leduc

Programmes
Notary Studies (Accountancy; Law; Notary Studies; Taxation)
Admission Requirements: Bac général, Bac technologique STG, Bac professionnel.
Fees: (Euros) 3.240 per annum
Degrees and Diplomas: *Brevet de Technicien supérieur; Licence professionnelle.* Diplôme des Instituts des Métiers du Notariat (4 yrs)
Last Updated: 21/07/11

TRAINING CENTRE FOR BANKING

Centre de formation de la profession bancaire (CFPB)
Immeuble le Carillon, 5 esplanade Charles de Gaulle, 92739 Nanterre
Tel: +33(1) 41-02-55-00
Fax: +33(1) 41-02-55-55
EMail: contact@cfpb.fr
Website: http://www.cfpb.fr

Directeur général: Olivier Robert de Massy
International Relations: François-Xavier Noir

Institutes
Banking *(ITB)* (Banking; Management) *Director:* Gérard Delrue;
Markets *(ITM)* (Banking; Finance; Management) *Director:* Olivier Plaisant

International Co-operation: Has partnerships with Morocco and countries in Sub-sahara Africa.

Degrees and Diplomas: *Brevet de Technicien supérieur.* Banking; *Licence professionnelle:* Banking; *Diplôme national de Master.* Masters professionnel
Last Updated: 13/11/07

France - French Guyana

INSTITUTIONS

PUBLIC INSTITUTIONS

UNIVERSITY OF THE FRENCH ANTILLES AND GUYANA

Université des Antilles et de la Guyane
Avenue Bois Chaudat, BP 725, Kourou 97157
Tel: +594-32-12-40
Fax: +594 32-10-64
EMail: charge.communication@guyane.univ-ag.fr
Website: http://www.univ-ag.fr

Président: Pascal Saffache

Secrétaire Général: Angèle Ferrus
Tel: +590 48-35-40 EMail: angele.ferus@+univ-ag.fr

International Relations: Fred Reno
Tel: +590 48-35-44
EMail: bri@univ-ag.fr; maryvonne.charlery@univ-ag.fr

Institutes
Higher Education *(Guyane)* (Arts and Humanities; Biochemistry; Biological and Life Sciences; Economics; English; Geology; Health Sciences; Law; Literature; Mathematics and Computer Science; Musicology; Portuguese; Waste Management; Water Management); **Teacher Training** (Teacher Training); **Technology** *(IUT Guyana)* (Bioengineering; Biotechnology; Business Administration; Business Computing; Electrical Engineering; Hygiene; Management; Safety Engineering; Sales Techniques; Technology; Telecommunications Engineering; Transport Engineering)

Further Information: Has seven campuses in Guadeloupe, Martinique and Guyana along with ten Research Units.

History: Established by the Bordeaux Law Faculty in 1883 as a Centre of Law Studies in Antilles-Guyane. It was expanded to include a Literature and Science Unit in 1963 and by 1971, it had gained its independent status with the addition of the Basic and Natural Science Unit. In 1982, the Ministry of Education awarded its full title of University.

Governing Bodies: General Administration Committee

Academic Year: September-June

Admission Requirements: Baccalauréat or equivalent Secondary School Diploma

Main Language(s) of Instruction: French

International Co-operation: Is a member of AUF, CREPUQ (Quebec) and UNICA (Caribbean) and cooperation agreements with several European and South American Universities, including Brook University, Earlham College and JMU in the USA.

Accrediting Agencies: Ministry of Education

Degrees and Diplomas: *Capacité en Droit*; *Diplôme universitaire de Technologie*; *Licence*: Sports, Physical Education, Mathematics, Sciences for Engineering, Economics, Social Sciences, Modern Languages, Educational Sciences, 3 yrs; *Diplôme national de Master*: Political Science, Economics, History, French, Modern languages, Educational Sciences, 2 yrs. Prepares for Teaching Certificate

Last Updated: 21/07/11

France - French Polynesia

INSTITUTIONS

PUBLIC INSTITUTIONS

UNIVERSITY OF FRENCH POLYNESIA
Université de la Polynésie française
BP 6570-98 702 FAA'A Tahiti, 98702 Papeete, Tahiti
Tel: +689 80-38-03
Fax: +689 80-38-04
EMail: courrier@upf.pf
Website: http://www.upf.pf
Présidente: Eric Conte (2011-) **Tel:** +689 80-38-14

Departments
Arts, Languages and Humanities (Arts and Humanities; Communication Studies; Development Studies; English; French; Geography; History; Island Studies; Literature; Spanish; Translation and Interpretation); **Law, Economics and Accountancy** (Accountancy; Economics; Law); **Science** (Biological and Life Sciences; Biology; Cell Biology; Chemistry; Computer Science; Earth Sciences; Marine Science and Oceanography; Mathematics; Mathematics and Computer Science; Natural Sciences; Physical Engineering; Physics; Technology)

Institutes
Teacher Training *(IUFM)* (Teacher Trainers Education; Teacher Training)

History: Founded 1987. Acquired present status 1999.

Academic Year: September to June (September-December; January-June)

Admission Requirements: Secondary school certificate (baccalauréat) and entrance examination

Main Language(s) of Instruction: French

International Co-operation: With universities in Italy, Australia, New Zealand, Canada, Chile and Fiji. Also participates in Erasmus and AUF programmes.

Degrees and Diplomas: *Diplôme d' Accès aux Etudes universitaires*; *Licence*: Science, Medical Sciences and Technologies, Law, Economics and Management, Arts and Humanities and Social Sciences, 3 yrs; *Diplôme national de Master*: Arts and Humanities, Social Sciences, Law and Management, 2 yrs following Licence. Also Continuing Education Degrees; Diplôme d'Université

Student Services: Academic counselling, Canteen, Foreign student adviser, Handicapped facilities, Health services, Social counselling, Sports facilities

Student Residential Facilities: Yes.

Libraries: University Library, c. 16,200 vols

Publications: Revue juridique polynésienne
Last Updated: 21/07/11

France - Guadeloupe

INSTITUTIONS

PUBLIC INSTITUTIONS

UNIVERSITY OF THE ANTILLES AND GUYANA
Université des Antilles et de la Guyane
BP 250, Campus de Fouillole, 97157 Pointe-à-Pitre, Cedex
Tel: +590-48-90-00
Fax: +590-91-06-57
Website: http://www.univ-ag.fr

Président: Pascal Saffache (2009-)

Secrétaire général: Jean-Pierre Darras
Tel: +590 48-35-40 EMail: Jean-Pierre.Darras@univ-ag.fr

Faculties
Basic and Natural Sciences (Biology; Chemistry; Computer Science; Geology; Mathematics; Physics); **Law and Economics** (Economics; Law); **Medical Sciences** (Medicine)

Institutes
Teacher Training *(IUFM)* (Teacher Trainers Education; Teacher Training); **Technology** (Biotechnology; Business Administration; Business Computing; Electrical Engineering; Management; Technology; Transport Management)

Units
Sports (Physical Education; Sports; Sports Management)

History: Founded 1970 as Centre Universitaire, incorporating previously existing University centres in Guadeloupe and Martinique.

Became University 1982. Attached to the Académie de Bordeaux. Financially supported by the Ministry of Education.

Governing Bodies: Conseil d'Administration

Academic Year: October to June (October-December; January-March; April-June)

Admission Requirements: Secondary school certificate (baccalauréat) or foreign equivalent or special entrance examination

Main Language(s) of Instruction: French

International Co-operation: Is a member of AUF, CREPUQ (Quebec) and UNICA (Caribbean) and has cooperation agreements with several European and South American Universities, including Brook University, Earlham College and JMU in the USA.

Accrediting Agencies: Ministry of Education

Degrees and Diplomas: *Capacité en Droit*: 2 yrs; *Diplôme universitaire de Technologie*; *Licence*: Sports, Physical Education, Mathematics, Sciences for Engineering, Economics, Social Sciences, Modern Languages, Educational Sciences, 3 yrs; *Diplôme national de Master*: Political Science, Economics, History, French, Modern languages, Educational Sciences, a further 2 yrs. Also prepares for Teaching Certificate

Student Residential Facilities: Yes

Libraries: c. 9,500 vols

Publications: Bulletin de liaison des chercheurs
Last Updated: 31/03/09

France - Martinique

INSTITUTIONS

UNIVERSITY OF THE ANTILLES AND GUYANA
Université des Antilles et de la Guyane
Campus de Schoelcher, 97200 Fort-de-France, Cedex
Website: http://www.univ-ag.fr/

Président: Pascal Saffache (2009-)

Secrétaire général: Angèle Ferus
Tel: +590 48-34-14 EMail: angele.ferus@+univ-ag.fr

Institutes
Higher Education (Arts and Humanities; Civil Engineering; Computer Science; Economics; English; Law; Literature; Materials Engineering; Mathematics; Musicology; Portuguese)
History: Founded 1850 as School of Law, became Centre universitaire des Antilles-Guyane 1949 and Université 1982. Attached to the Académie de Bordeaux. Financially supported by the Ministry of Education.

Governing Bodies: General Administration Committee

Academic Year: October to June (October-December; January-March; April-June)

Admission Requirements: Secondary school certificate (baccalauréat) or foreign equivalent, or special entrance examination

Fees: (Euros): c. 362

Main Language(s) of Instruction: French

International Co-operation: With universities in United Kingdom, Germany, Spain, Italy, USA, Canada, West Indies (UWI)

Degrees and Diplomas: *Capacité en Droit*: 2 yrs; *Diplôme universitaire de Technologie*: 2 yrs; *Licence*: 3 yrs; *Diplôme national de Master*: 2 yrs

Student Services: Academic counselling, Canteen, Foreign student adviser, Foreign Studies Centre, Handicapped facilities, Health services, Language programs, Social counselling, Sports facilities

Student Residential Facilities: Yes

Libraries: c. 30,000 vols
Last Updated: 21/07/11

France - New Caledonia

INSTITUTIONS

PUBLIC INSTITUTIONS

CENTRE RÉGIONAL ASSOCIÉ DU C.N.A.M. (CONSERVATOIRE NATIONAL DES ARTS ET MÉTIERS)

15 bis, rue de Verdun, BP 3562, 98846 Nouméa, Cedex
Tel: +687 28-37-07
Fax: +687 27-79-96
EMail: noucnam@lagoon.nc
Website: http://cnam.nc/index.php
Head: Bernard Schall EMail: noucnam@offratel.nc

UNIVERSITY OF NEW CALEDONIA

Université de la Nouvelle Calédonie
BPR4, 98851 Nouméa, CEDEX
Tel: +687 29-02-90
Fax: +687 25-48-29
EMail: international@univ-nc.nc
Website: http://www.univ-nc.nc

Président: Jean-Marc Boyer (2007-)
EMail: jean-marc.boyer@univ-nc.nc

Directrice générale des Services: Odile Boyer
EMail: sg@univ-nc.nc

International Relations: Pierre Chaillan
Tel: +687 26-58-77 EMail: pierre.chaillan@univ-nc.nc

Departments
Continuing Education (Continuing Education); **Law, Economics and Management** (Business Administration; Economics; Law; Private Law; Public Law); **Literature, Languages and Humanities** *(Magenta)* (Ancient Civilizations; Comparative Literature; English; French; Geography (Human); History; Literature; Medieval Studies; Modern Languages; Pacific Area Studies); **Science and Technology** *(Nouville)* (Biochemistry; Biology; Cell Biology; Chemistry; Computer Science; Geology; Marine Biology; Mathematics; Metallurgical Engineering; Microbiology; Molecular Biology; Physics; Physiology)

Graduate Schools
Multidisciplinary *(in cooperation with the University of French Polynesia)*

Institutes
Teacher Training *(IUFM)* (Teacher Training)

History: Founded 1987. A Centre of the Université française du Pacifique.

Academic Year: February to November

Admission Requirements: Secondary school certificate (baccalauréat) and entrance examination

Main Language(s) of Instruction: French

International Co-operation: Participates in Erasmus and AUF programmes and has exchange programmes with Australian Universities, University of Auckland (NZ), USP (Fiji), Japan and Vietnam.

Accrediting Agencies: Ministry of Education

Degrees and Diplomas: *Licence*; *Diplôme national de Master*; *Doctorat*

Libraries: University Library, c. 70,000 vols
Last Updated: 25/05/11

France - Réunion

INSTITUTIONS

PUBLIC INSTITUTIONS

UNIVERSITY OF LA RÉUNION

Université de La Réunion

15, avenue René Cassin, BP 7151, 97715 Saint-Denis Messag, Cedex 9

Tel: +262(93) 80-80
Fax: +262(93) 81-34
EMail: cabinet@univ-reunion.fr
Website: http://www.univ-reunion.fr

Président: Mohamed Rochdi (2008-)

Secrétaire générale: Jean Claude Mire
EMail: jean-claude.mire@univ-reunion.fr

Faculties

Arts and Humanities (Arts and Humanities; Communication Studies; Educational Sciences; English; Ethnology; Geography; Germanic Studies; History; Literature); **Environment and Social Sciences** *(Campus SUD)* (Cultural Studies; French; Sports; Town Planning); **Health** (Dentistry; Medicine; Midwifery; Occupational Therapy; Pharmacy); **Law, Economics, and Political Science** (Economics; Law; Political Sciences); **Science and Technology** (Biochemistry; Biology; Chemistry; Computer Science; Earth Sciences; Food Technology; Mathematics; Molecular Biology; Natural Sciences; Physics; Technology)

Institutes

Business Administration *(IAE)* (Business Administration); **Teacher Training** *(IUFM, at both campuses)* (Educational Research; Educational Sciences; Teacher Trainers Education; Teacher Training); **Technology** *(IUT Saint-Pierre)* (Banking; Business Administration; Civil Engineering; E-Business/Commerce; Management; Technology; Telecommunications Engineering)

Schools

Engineering (Engineering; Food Technology; Information Technology)

Further Information: Has a second campus at Le Tampon

History: Founded 1982 as Ecole de Jurisprudence, became Ecole de Droit 1926, Institut d'Etudes juridiques, politiques et économiques1950, and Centre Universitaire 1971. Acquired present status and title as a full-functioning French University and title 1982.

Governing Bodies: Conseil

Academic Year: September to June (September-December; February-June)

Admission Requirements: Secondary school certificate (Baccalauréat) or equivalent and entrance examination

Main Language(s) of Instruction: French

International Co-operation: Participates in the Erasmus and the CREPUQ and ISEP programmes

Degrees and Diplomas: *Licence*: Law, Economics, Business Administration, Social Sciences, Arts and Humanities, Science, Technology and Health, 3 yrs; *Diplôme national de Master*: Law, Economics, Business Administration, Social Sciences, Arts and Humanities, Science, Technology and Health, 2 yrs following Licence; *Doctorat*: a further 3 yrs. Masters recherche, Masters professionnel. Also prepares for Teaching Certificate and French as a Foreign Language Certificates (DELF, DALF).

Student Residential Facilities: Yes

Libraries: Service commun de la documentation, c. 10,000 vols
Last Updated: 01/06/11

Gabon

STRUCTURE OF HIGHER EDUCATION SYSTEM

Description:

Higher education is provided by 3 public universities as well as by various independent institutions, both public and private.

Stages of studies:

University level first stage: *Premier cycle*
The first stage leads after three years' study to the Licence.

University level second stage: *Deuxième cycle*
A further year of study leads to the Maîtrise. The Ecole nationale de la Magistrature trains Magistrates in four years after the Baccalauréat and in two years for holders of the Licence in Law. The title of Ingénieur is awarded on completion of five years' study.
This stage is progressively being replaced by the Master as part of the implementation of the three-tier (LMD) reform in the country.

University level third stage: *Troisième cycle*
Doctorates are awarded after a minimum of three years' study and research after the Maitrise or Master.
The Ecole nationale d'Administration (advanced cycle) offers two-year training to holders of a Maîtrise following a competitive examination. Candidates are then awarded the Diplôme d'Administrateur civil (General Administration, Diplomacy, Factory Inspectorate). The Doctorat d'Etat in Medicine is awarded after six years' study. It leads to three post-doctoral specializations: Paediatrics, Surgery, and Gynaecology.

ADMISSION TO HIGHER EDUCATION

Admission to university-level studies:

Name of secondary school credential required: Baccalauréat

For entry to: University

Alternatives to credentials: Capacité en Droit (for studies in Law)

Foreign students admission:

Entrance exam requirements: For access to university-level studies, foreign students must hold a secondary school leaving Certificate (Baccalauréat) or its equivalent and/or obtain the approval of the teachers' Commission of the department where they wish to be admitted. For access to postgraduate study and research, they must hold a Maîtrise/Master or its equivalent.

Entry regulations: Foreign students must hold a visa and have financial guarantees.

Language requirements: Students must have a good command of French.

NATIONAL BODIES

Ministère de l'Education nationale, de l'Enseignement supérieur et technique (Ministry of National, Higher and Technical Education)
Minister: Séraphin Moundounga
B.P. 2217
Libreville
Tel: +241 760784
Fax: +241 763909
WWW: http://educasup-recherche-gabon.org/

Data for academic year: 2008-2009
Source: IAU from documentation and the Country Report on the Development of Education prepared by Gabon for the International Conference on Education, 2008. Bodies updated in 2012.

INSTITUTIONS

AFRICAN INSTITUTE OF COMPUTER SCIENCE

Institut africain d'Informatique (IAI)
BP 2263, Libreville
Tel: +241 72-00-05
Fax: +241 72-00-11
Website: http://iaisiege.net/index.php?printpage=2tmplt=1
Directeur général: Souleymane Koussoube

Departments
Computer Networks (Computer Networks); **Economics/Management and Communication** (Communication Studies; Economics; Management); **Information Systems Engineering** (Information Technology); **Mathematics** (Mathematics); **Software Engineering**

Further Information: Also branches in other African countries

History: Inter-states school founded in 1971.

Main Language(s) of Instruction: French

Degrees and Diplomas: *Brevet de Technicien supérieur*; *Diplôme d'Ingénieur*; *Maîtrise*

Special Facilities: Research laboratories
Last Updated: 02/07/09

INTERNATIONAL CENTRE FOR MEDICAL RESEARCH OF FRANCEVILLE

Centre international de Recherches médicales de Franceville (CIRMF)
BP 769, Franceville
Tel: +241 67-70-92
Fax: +241 67-72-95
EMail: faxcirmf@yahoo.com
Website: http://www.cirmf.org
Directeur général: Jean-Paul Gonzalez

Departments
Parasitology; **Primatology**; **Tropical Ecosystems**; **Virology** (Virology)

History: Founded 1979.

Governing Bodies: Administrative Board; Scientific Committee; Committee of Ethics

Admission Requirements: Master's Degree

Main Language(s) of Instruction: French

Degrees and Diplomas: Postgraduate training at MSc and PhD levels
Last Updated: 02/07/09

NATIONAL SCHOOL OF FORESTRY AND WATER MANAGEMENT

Ecole nationale des Eaux et Forêts (ENEF)
BP 3960, Libreville
Tel: +241 48-02-12
Fax: +241 48-02-11

Directeur général: Athanase Boussengue
Tel: +241 07-61-78-75 EMail: bousseng1@yahoo.fr

Director of Studies: David Désiré Allogo Obague
Tel: 241 06-97-33-33 EMail: davidallogo@yahoo.fr

International Relations: Jean Paul Obame Engone, Department Manager Tel: 241 07 11 99 17 EMail: jpobame@hotmail.com

Departments
Basic Sciences (Natural Sciences); **Continuing and Distance Education** (Civil Security; Environmental Studies; Hygiene); **Fauna and Hunting**; **Fishing and Aquaculture**; **Forest and Environmental Management**; **Forest Exploitation and Wood Technology**

History: Founded 1953. Acquired present status 1975.

Governing Bodies: 27 members from various sectors.

Academic Year: September to April: (September-April; April-July)

Main Language(s) of Instruction: French

International Co-operation: Network of Institutions of Forest and Environmental Formation of Central Africa. (RIFFEAC: www.riffeac.org)

Degrees and Diplomas: *Diplôme de Technicien supérieur*; *Diplôme d'Ingénieur*. A level +5. Also Diplôme d'Etudes Supérieures Spécialisées; Technician (Water and Forest) 2yrs

Student Services: Academic counselling, Canteen, Foreign student adviser, Health services, Sports facilities

Student Residential Facilities: 110 rooms (90 of which are single rooms)

Special Facilities: Laboratories; Protected Forest

Libraries: c. 1,300 books; perodicals

Academic Staff 2008-2009	MEN	WOMEN	TOTAL
FULL-TIME	22	3	25
PART-TIME	40	6	46
STAFF WITH DOCTORATE			
FULL-TIME	–	–	3
PART-TIME	9	2	11
Student Numbers 2008-2009			
All (Foreign Included)	91	47	138
FOREIGN ONLY	–	–	5

Evening students, 10.
Last Updated: 08/06/09

NATIONAL SCHOOL OF MAGISTRACY

Ecole nationale de la Magistrature (ENM)
BP 46, Libreville
Tel: +241 72-00-06

Departments
Administrative Law (Administrative Law); **Civil Law** (Civil Law); **Commercial Law**; **Justice**; **Law** (Law); **Magistracy** (Justice Administration); **Penal Law** (Criminal Law)

History: Founded 1971.

NATIONAL SCHOOL OF PUBLIC ADMINISTRATION

Ecole nationale d'Administration (ENA)
BP 86, Libreville
Tel: +241 72-49-89 +241 74-56-37
Fax: +241 72-91-48 +241 72-49-89

Directeur Général: Dieudonné Egnina-Ndombi

Departments
Administration (Administration); **Diplomacy**; **School Administration**; **University Administration** (Educational Administration)

History: Founded 1962.

Accrediting Agencies: Ministère de la fonction publique et de la réforme administrative

Degrees and Diplomas: *Diplôme d'Administrateur civil*; *Diplôme d'Administration de l'Economie et des Finances*
Last Updated: 02/07/09

OMAR BONGO UNIVERSITY
Université Omar Bongo (UOB)
BP 13131, Libreville, Estuaire
Tel: +241 73-20-33
Fax: +241 73-45-30
Website: http://www.uob.ga

Recteur: Pierre Nzinzi
Tel: +241 73-20-33 EMail: pierre.nzinzi@gmail.com

Administrative Officer: Michel Mboumi

International Relations: Lucie Mba
EMail: relations.internationales@yahoo.fr

Faculties
Arts and Humanities (African Studies; Anthropology; Archaeology; Arts and Humanities; English; Geography; History; Latin American Studies; Literature; Modern Languages; Philosophy; Psychology; Social Sciences; Sociology; Spanish); **Law and Economics** (Economics; Law; Private Law; Public Law)

Institutes
Management (INSG)

Schools
Organization Studies (ENSS) (Management; Secretarial Studies); **Teacher Training** (ENS); **Technical Teacher Training** (ENSET) (Automotive Engineering; Civil Engineering; Construction Engineering; Metal Techniques; Teacher Training; Wood Technology)

History: Founded 1970 incorporating institutions which were previously part of the Fondation de l'Enseignement supérieur en Afrique Centrale (FESAC) as Université nationale du Gabon (UNG). Renamed 1978 as Université Omar Bongo (UOB). Acquired present status 2002.

Academic Year: October to July (October- March; April-July)

Admission Requirements: Secondary school certificate (baccalauréat) or equivalent or entrance examination

Main Language(s) of Instruction: French

Accrediting Agencies: MESRSDT

Degrees and Diplomas: *Licence*: 3 yrs; *Maîtrise*: 1 yr following Licence; *Master*; *Doctorat*

Student Services: Academic counselling, Employment services, Foreign student adviser, Health services, Social counselling, Sports facilities

Student Residential Facilities: Yes

Libraries: 24,356 vols
Last Updated: 04/06/09

UNIVERSITY OF HEALTH SCIENCES
Université des Sciences de la Santé
BP 18231, Owendo, Libreville
Tel: +241 70-20-28
Fax: +241 70-28-19
Website: http://www.labogabon.net/uss/index.html

Recteur: André Moussavou-Mouyama

Secrétaire général: Lucien Nzong

Faculties
Medicine

History: Founded 2002.

Accrediting Agencies: MESRIT

Degrees and Diplomas: *Docteur en Médecine*: Medicine. Also Certificat d'Etudes spécialisées, Diplôme d'Etat de Sage-Femme
Last Updated: 24/06/09

UNIVERSITY OF SCIENCE AND TECHNIQUES OF MASUKU
Université des Sciences et Techniques de Masuku (USTM)
BP 901, Franceville
Tel: +241 67-77-25
Fax: +241 67-75-20
EMail: ustm.libreville@inet.ga
Website: http://www.labogabon.net/ustm

Recteur: Jacques Lebibi

Secrétaire général: Léon Ngadi

Faculties
Science (Biology; Chemistry; Geology; Mathematics; Physics)

Institutes
Agronomy and Biotechnology (National)

Schools
Polytechnic

History: Founded 1987, incorporating faculty of sciences of UOB and ENSIL.

Accrediting Agencies: MESRIT

Degrees and Diplomas: *Diplôme de Technicien supérieur*: Agricultural Engineering; Civil Engineering; Electrical Engineering; Industrial Engineering; *Licence*; *Diplôme d'Ingénieur*: Engineering; *Maîtrise*: Science
Last Updated: 23/02/09

Gambia (The)

STRUCTURE OF HIGHER EDUCATION SYSTEM

Description:

Higher education in the Gambia is provided by the University of The Gambia, created in 1999, which comprises four faculties, and a College (Gambia College) which includes four schools: Agriculture, Science, Education, Nursing and Midwifery and Public Health.

Stages of studies:

University level first stage: *Bachelor's degree*
The first stage of university education leads to a Bachelor's degree after four years of study in Humanities and Social Studies, Economics and Management Science and Nursing and Public Health and seven years in Medicine and Surgery.

ADMISSION TO HIGHER EDUCATION

Admission to university-level studies:

Name of secondary school credential required: West African Examinations Council Senior Secondary School Leaving Certificate

Minimum score/requirement: Minimum qualification is 5 credits.

Alternatives to credentials: Varying credentials for mature students

Foreign students admission:

Entry regulations: A visa is required for non-Commonwealth citizens as well as study or residential permits for all non-Gambians.

Language requirements: Proficiency in English is required.

NATIONAL BODIES

Department of State for Higher Education, Research, Science and Technology
Secretary of State: Mariama Sarr-Ceesay
GRTS Building
MDI Road, Kanifing
Serrekunda
Tel: +220 4378715
Fax: +220 4392996
WWW: http://www.edugambia.gm

Data for academic year: 2007-2008
Source: IAU from Department of State for Higher Education, Research, Science and Technology, The Gambia, 2007. Bodies updated in 2011.

INSTITUTIONS

PUBLIC INSTITUTIONS

UNIVERSITY OF THE GAMBIA (UTG)

PO Box 3530, Administrative Building, Kanifing, Serekunda, Greater Banjul
Tel: +220 4372-213
Fax: +220 4395-064
EMail: unigambia@qanet.gm
Website: http://www.unigambia.gm/

Vice-Chancellor/President: Muhammadou M.O. Kah (2009-)
EMail: mkah@utg.edu.gm
Registrar: Lamin S. Jaiteh Tel: +220 4393-291

Departments
Agriculture and Biological Sciences (Agriculture; Biology; Farm Management; Plant and Crop Protection); **Arts, Languages and Humanities** (Arabic; English; French; Islamic Studies; Literature); **Economics and Management Sciences** (Economics; Finance;

Human Resources; Information Technology; Management; Marketing); **Education**; **Law** (Law); **Science and Technology** (Chemistry; Mathematics; Physics; Statistics; Technology); **Social Sciences** (Development Studies; History; Social Sciences)

Schools

Medicine and Allied Health Sciences

History: Founded 1999. Established by an Act of the National Assembly. Introduction of a 2-year Higher National Diploma (HND) programme in Construction Management in the Gambia Technical Training Institute, GTTI, under a franchise from South Bank University, London. With assistance from the Ministry of Health of Cuba, the pre-medical programme began September 1999.

Governing Bodies: University Council; Senate

Academic Year: October to July (October-February; March-July)

Admission Requirements: West African Senior School Certificate with five credits; General Certificate of Education with five credits

Fees: (Dalasis): Other than Science, c. 14,000; Science, c. 16,000; Medicine, c. 18,000; (US Dollars): Foreign Student, Humanities, 2,000; Science and Agriculture, 2,500; Medicine, 3,000.

Main Language(s) of Instruction: English

International Co-operation: With universities in Canada.

Degrees and Diplomas: *Bachelor of Arts*: Development Studies; History; French; English (BA), 4 yrs; *Bachelor of Arts*: Education (B.Ed.); *Bachelor of Science*: Agriculture; Biology; Chemistry; Physics (BSc, BA); Nursing; Public Health (BsC), 4 yrs; *Bachelor of Medicine*: Medicine; Surgery (MB/CHB), 7 yrs

Student Services: Academic counselling, Health services, Social counselling, Sports facilities

Special Facilities: Computer Laboratory

Libraries: Technical Training Institute Library, University of The Gambia Library

Last Updated: 11/08/09

Georgia

STRUCTURE OF HIGHER EDUCATION SYSTEM

Description:

Higher Education system of Georgia consists of three cycles: first cycle – Bachelor's degree (240 credits); second cycle – Master's degree (120 credits); third cycle – Doctor's degree (180 credits).

Stages of studies:

University level first stage: *Bakalavriati, Diplomirebuli specialisti*
The duration of the first stage is usually four years. Students are awarded a Bakalavris Xarisxi (Bachelor's degree). Students with excellent marks are awarded a Diplomi Tsarchinebis (Diploma with Honour). The Diplomirebuli Specialisti is awarded in a field of specialization after 5-6 years' study (6 years in Medicine).

University level second stage: *Magistratura*
The second stage leads to the award of a Magistris Xarisxi (Master's degree) after two years' study. Students with excellent marks are awarded a Diplomi Tsarchinebis (Diploma with Honour).

University level third stage: *Doktorantura*
Students awarded a Magistris Xarisxi or its equivalent (Certified Specialist's Academic Degree) may continue their studies at the third stage. Doctorandura comprises three years' study and ends with the presentation and defence of a dissertation that leads to the Doctoris Akademiuri Xaraisxi (Doctor's academic degree).

ADMISSION TO HIGHER EDUCATION

Admission to university-level studies:

Name of secondary school credential required: Zogadi Sashualo Ganatlebis Atestati

For entry to: All institutions

Name of secondary school credential required: Dackebiti Prophesiuli Ganatlebis Diplomi

For entry to: All universities

Numerus clausus/restrictions: The enrolment is limited by accreditation requirements: an institution shall have at least 1000 square meters and not less than 4 square meters per student; it must have a computer for 15 students and one handbook for 10 students in the library.

Other admission requirements: Entrance exam.
For less demanded specialties, candidates may enroll on the basis of document submission, graded according to academic record.

Foreign students admission:

Definition of foreign student: Foreign students are those who are not citizens of Georgia.

Quotas: The quotas are established each year following upon the agreement of the Council of Ministers of the proposal of the Minister of Education, Youth and Science on the grounds of proposals of state higher education schools in conformity with the capacity of the higher school, of the professional branches; and of the specialties from the regulated professions in it.

Entrance exam requirements: Foreign students are admitted to higher education institutions on the basis of an interview.

Entry regulations: Visas

Language requirements: Students must have a good knowledge of Georgian, Russian or English.

RECOGNITION OF STUDIES

Quality assurance system:

Quality assurance (QA) system in Georgia consists of internal and external QA mechanisms. Internal self-evaluation is carried out by educational institutions commensurate with the procedure of evaluation of own performance and shall be summarised in an annual self-evaluation report. External QA is implemented through authorization and accreditation. Authorization grants a right to educational institutions to operate and is based on similar criteria as institutional accreditation. Accreditation looks more at the programme level and is linked with the state funding. All programmes in regulated professions have to pass accreditation. The national agency implementing external QA is the National Centre for Educational Quality Enhancement (NCEQE). Authorisation and accreditation have to be renewed in every 5 years.

Bodies dealing with recognition:

National Center for Educational Quality Enhacement

1 Aleksidze st
Tbilisi 0193
Tel: +995(32) 365 792
EMail: info@eqe.ge
WWW: http://www.eqe.ge/

NATIONAL BODIES

SaqarTvelos ganaTlebisa da mecnierebis saministro (Ministry of Education and Science)
Minister: Dimitri Shashkin
52, D. Uznadze Street
Tbilisi 0102
Tel: +995(32) 200 220
Fax: +995(32) 910 447
EMail: pr@mes.gov.ge
WWW: http://www.mes.gov.ge
Role of national body: Provides the unified educational policy of the country.

National Center for Educational Quality Enhacement

1 Aleksidze st
Tbilisi 0193
Tel: +995(32) 365 792
EMail: info@eqe.ge
WWW: http://www.eqe.ge/

Data for academic year: 2011-2012
Source: IAU from the website of the Ministry of Education and Science of Georgia, 2011

INSTITUTIONS

PUBLIC INSTITUTIONS

AKAKI TSERETELI STATE UNIVERSITY
Akaki Čeretlis Sakhelobis Sakhelmtsipo Universiteti (KSU)
55 Tamar Mepe Street, 4600 Kutaisi, Imereti
Tel: +995(331) 45784
Fax: +995(331) 43833
EMail: atsu@atsu.edu.ge
Website: http://www.atsu.edu.ge/eng/

Rector: George Gavtadze
Tel: +995(331) 42173, Fax: +995(331) 43833
EMail: rector@atsu.edu.ge

Deputy Rector: Shalva Kirtadze
Tel: +995(331) 45667 EMail: sh.kirtadze@atsu.edu.ge

Faculties
Arts (American Studies; Ancient Civilizations; Archaeology; English; French; German; Literature; Modern Languages; Native Language; Oriental Studies; Philology; Slavic Languages; Western European Studies); **Exact and Natural Sciences** (Biology; Chemistry; Computer Science; Geography; Mathematics; Physics); **Maritime**

Transport (Marine Transport); **Medicine** (Medicine); **Pedagogy** (Pedagogy); **Social Sciences** (Business Administration; Economics; History; Journalism; Law; Philosophy; Political Sciences; Psychology); **Technical Engineering** (Civil Engineering; Electrical Engineering; Engineering; Machine Building; Mechanical Engineering; Mechanics; Safety Engineering; Transport Engineering); **Technological Engineering** (Chemical Engineering; Food Technology; Industrial Engineering; Textile Design; Textile Technology)

History: Founded 1933 as State Pedagogical Institute, Tbilisi. Acquired present status and title 2006 following merger of Kutiasi Akaki Tsereteli State University and Kutaisi N. Muskhelishvili State Technical University.

Governing Bodies: Scientific Board

Academic Year: September to June

Admission Requirements: Secondary school certificate (Sashualo Skolis Atestati)

Main Language(s) of Instruction: Georgian

Degrees and Diplomas: *Bakalavris Diplomi*: 4 yrs; *Diplomirebuli Specialistis Diplomi*: 5 yrs; *Magistris Diplomi*: 2 yrs; *Doktoris Diplomi*

Student Services: Academic counselling, Canteen, Cultural centre, Foreign student adviser, Foreign Studies Centre, Health services, Language programs, Social counselling, Sports facilities

Special Facilities: Museum

Libraries: Scientific Library

Publications: Kutaisi University Moambe *(quarterly)*; Kutaisi University Papers *(annually)*
Last Updated: 08/02/12

BATUMI ART TEACHING UNIVERSITY

Pirosmani Street N16, Batumi
Tel: +995(422) 24-43-59
EMail: gelodi26@mail.ru
Website: http://www.batu.edu.ge

Rector: Ermile Meskhia EMail: ermile_mesxia@mail.ru

Head of Administration: Gela Beridze

Faculties
Education, Humanities and Social Sciences (Art Criticism; Art History; Cultural Studies); **Music** (Conducting; Musical Instruments; Singing); **Visual, Theatre and Film-TV Arts** (Acting; Architecture; Cinema and Television; Fashion Design; Interior Design; Painting and Drawing; Textile Design; Wood Technology)

History: Founded 1995 as State Institute of Art . Acquired present status 2009.

Main Language(s) of Instruction: Georgian

Degrees and Diplomas: *Bakalavris Diplomi*; *Magistris Diplomi*

Libraries: Yes
Last Updated: 17/02/12

BATUMI STATE MARITIME ACADEMY

Batumis Sakhelmtsipo Sazghvao Akademia
53, Rustaveli Street, 6010 Batumi, Adjara
Tel: +995(222) 75388 +995(222) 74957
Fax: +995(222) 74850
EMail: info@bma.edu.ge
Website: http://www.bma.edu.ge

Rector: Nadim Varshanidze EMail: n.varshanidze@gmail.com

Faculties
Maritime Training (Marine Science and Oceanography); **Navigational and Marine Engineering** (Marine Engineering; Nautical Science); **Ship Management** (Marine Transport)

History: Founded 1992.

Main Language(s) of Instruction: Georgian, Russian

Degrees and Diplomas: *Bakalavris Diplomi*; *Diplomirebuli Specialistis Diplomi*; *Magistris Diplomi*
Last Updated: 15/02/12

GEORGIAN STATE AGRARIAN UNIVERSITY

Saqartvelos Sakhelmtsipo Agraruli Universiteti
13km, David Agmašenebeli Alley, 0131 Tbilisi
Tel: +995(32) 533-806
Fax: +995(32) 534-395
EMail: inter@gsau.edu.ge

Rector: Gela Javakhishvili
Tel: +995(32) 533-806 EMail: rector@gsau.edu.ge

Chancellor: Irakli Kruashvili Tel: +995(32) 594-903

International Relations: Nanuli Tedeeva Tel: +995(93) 164-164

Faculties
Agricultural Business (Agricultural Business); **Agricultural Economics and Humanities** (Accountancy; Agricultural Economics; Agricultural Management; Economics; International Economics; International Relations; Law; Management); **Agricultural Engineering** (Agricultural Engineering; Agricultural Equipment; Water Management); **Agricultural Technology** (Agricultural Engineering); **Animal Science** (Zoology); **Food Technology** (Food Technology); **Forestry** (Forest Products; Forestry); **Veterinary Medicine** (Veterinary Science)

Further Information: Also branches in Batumi, Telavi and Marneuli

History: Founded 1919 as faculty of Tbilisi State University, became Georgian Agricultural Institute 1929, and acquired present status and title 1991.

Governing Bodies: Representative Council; Academic Council

Academic Year: September to June (September-January; February-June)

Main Language(s) of Instruction: Georgian

Degrees and Diplomas: *Bakalavris Diplomi*: 4 yrs; *Magistris Diplomi*: 2 yrs; *Doktoris Diplomi (PhD)*: a further 3 yrs following Magistris

Special Facilities: Sericulture Museum; Museum of Soil Science; Dendrological Museum

Libraries: Scientific Library, c. 1,248,006 vols

Publications: Annals of Agrarian Sciences; Practical Veterinary Medicine; Scientific Works
Last Updated: 16/02/12

GEORGIAN STATE UNIVERSITY OF SUBTROPICAL AGRICULTURE

Saqartvelos Subtropikul Meurneobis Sakhelmtsipo Universiteti
21, Chavchavadze Street, 4616 Kutaisi, Imereti
Tel: +995(231) 21146
Fax: +995(231) 20614
EMail: qualityi@ssmsu.edu.ge

Rector: Roland Kopaliani Tel: +995(899) 10-09-91

Faculties
Mechanization, Subtropical Agriculture and Technology (Agricultural Engineering; Biotechnology; Food Technology; Tropical Agriculture); **Subtropical Agriculture, Economics and Tourism** (Agricultural Business; Agricultural Economics; Agricultural Engineering; Agricultural Management; Agriculture; Botany; Forestry; Plant and Crop Protection; Tourism)

History: Founded 1952 as Agricultural Institute and acquired present title 2002.

Admission Requirements: At least 2 competitive entrance examinations following secondary school certificate

Fees: None for home students

Main Language(s) of Instruction: Georgian

Degrees and Diplomas: *Bakalavris Diplomi*: 4 yrs; *Diplomirebuli Specialistis Diplomi*: 4 yrs; *Magistris Diplomi*: a further 2 yrs; *Doktoris Diplomi*: 3 yrs

Student Services: Academic counselling, Canteen, Cultural centre, Handicapped facilities, Health services, Language programs, Social counselling, Sports facilities

Libraries: Central Library

Publications: Collection of Scientific Works
Last Updated: 13/02/12

GEORGIAN TECHNICAL UNIVERSITY

Saqartvelos Teqnikuri Universiteti (STU)
77, Kostava Street, 0175 Tbilisi
Tel: +995(32) 365-429 +995(32) 365-173
Fax: +995(32) 987-027
EMail: pr@gtu.ge; kanc@gtu.ge
Website: http://www.gtu.ge/

Rector: Archil Prangishvili (2009-)
Tel: +995(32) 441-161 EMail: rectoroffice@gtu.ge

Deputy-Rector for Research: Zurab Gasitashvili

Deputy-Rector for Education: Levan Klimiashvili
Tel: +995(32) 365-152

International Relations: Otar Zumburidze
EMail: o_zumburidze@gtu.ge

Faculties
Architecture, Urban Planning and Design (Architecture; Town Planning); **Business-Engineering** (Business Administration; Communication Studies; Economics; German; Law; Modern Languages); **Chemical Technology and Metallurgy** (Biotechnology; Chemical Engineering; Metal Techniques; Metallurgical Engineering); **Civil Engineering** (Civil Engineering; Hydraulic Engineering; Industrial Engineering; Mechanical Engineering); **Computer and Control Systems** (Computer Engineering; Instrument Making; Mathematics; Physics); **Mining and Geology** (Geological Engineering; Geology; Mining Engineering; Petroleum and Gas Engineering); **Power Engineering and Telecommunications** (Electrical and Electronic Engineering; Hydraulic Engineering; Mechanical Engineering; Power Engineering; Telecommunications Engineering; Thermal Engineering); **Transportation and Machine Building** (Machine Building; Road Engineering; Transport and Communications; Transport Engineering)

Institutes
Construction, Special Systems and Engineering Maintenance (Construction Engineering)

Research Centres
Technical Diagnosis and Expertise (Technology) *Head*: Anzor Kvaratskhelia

Schools
Architecture (Architecture; Landscape Architecture; Town Planning); **Aviation** (Air Transport); **Polytechnic** *(Batumi)*

Further Information: Also Health Care Polyclinic.

History: Founded 1922 as Polytechnic Faculty of Tbilisi State University. Became Polytechnic Institute 1936 and acquired present title 2007.

Governing Bodies: Representative Board. Academic Council

Academic Year: September to June (September-January; February-June)

Admission Requirements: Competitive entrance examination following general or special secondary school certificate

Fees: (US Dollars): Foreign students, c. 1,000-3,000 per annum

Main Language(s) of Instruction: Georgian, Russian, English, French, German

Degrees and Diplomas: *Bakalavris Diplomi*: 4 yrs; *Diplomirebuli Specialistis Diplomi*: 5 yrs; *Magistris Diplomi*: a further 1-2 yrs; *Doktoris Diplomi*: 2-3 yrs following Master

Student Services: Canteen, Cultural centre, Foreign student adviser, Foreign Studies Centre, Health services, Sports facilities

Special Facilities: Museum

Libraries: Central Scientific Library, 1m. vols

Publications: Technical Essays

Press or Publishing House: GTU Publishing House
Last Updated: 13/02/12

GORI SULKHAN TINTSADE MUSICAL COLLEGE
Gori
Website: http://www.gorimuscollege.edu.ge/eng/index.php?cat=10

Director: Aleksandre Kacharava

Programmes
Music (Music; Singing)

History: Founded 1963 as Gori Sulkhan Tsintsadze Art College. Acquired present title and status 2009.

Main Language(s) of Instruction: Georgian

Degrees and Diplomas: *Bakalavris Diplomi*; *Magistris Diplomi*
Last Updated: 22/02/12

IAKOB GOGEBASHVILI TELAVI STATE UNIVERSITY

Telavis Iakob Gogebashvilis' Sakhelobis Sakhelmtsipo Universiteti (TESAU)
1, Kartuli Universiteti Street, 2200 Telavi, Kakheti
Tel: +995(350) 72401
Fax: +995(350) 73264
EMail: info@tesau.edu.ge
Website: http://www.tesau.edu.ge

Rector: Tinatin Javakhishvili
Tel: +995(350) 73264 EMail: rectortesau@gmail.com

Vice-Rector: Davit Makhashvili
Tel: +995(350) 73551 EMail: davit_makhashvili@posta.ge

International Relations: Marina Javakhishvili
Tel: +995(350) 71533 EMail: office@tesau.edu.ge

Faculties
Agriculture and Food Production (Agriculture; Chemistry; Food Technology); **Exact and Natural Sciences** (Biology; Data Processing; Ecology; Geography; Information Technology; Mathematics; Natural Sciences; Physics); **Humanities** (English; French; German; History; International Relations; Law; Literature; Native Language; Russian); **Medicine** (Dentistry; Genetics; Medicine; Pharmacology; Pharmacy; Physical Therapy; Rehabilitation and Therapy); **Pedagogy** (Pedagogy; Physical Education; Primary Education; Sports); **Social Sciences, Business and Law** (Accountancy; Business Administration; Journalism; Law; Social Sciences; Sociology; Taxation)

History: Founded 1939 as Pedagogical Institute, acquired present status 2001.

Academic Year: September to July

Admission Requirements: Secondary school certificate (Atestati) and national examination

Fees: (GEL): c. 200-1,500 per annum

Main Language(s) of Instruction: Georgian

International Co-operation: Participates in Tempus

Accrediting Agencies: Ministry of Education and Science

Degrees and Diplomas: *Bakalavris Diplomi*: 4 yrs; *Diplomirebuli Specialistis Diplomi*: 5 yrs; *Magistris Diplomi*: 2 yrs; *Doktoris Diplomi*: 3 yrs

Student Services: Academic counselling, Canteen, Cultural centre, Health services, Language programs, Nursery care, Sports facilities

Student Residential Facilities: Yes

Libraries: c. 200,000 vols

Publications: University Scientific Works *(biennially)*
Last Updated: 14/02/12

ILIA STATE UNIVERSITY

Ilia Sakhelmtsipo Universiteti
3/5, Kakutsa Cholokashvili Avenue, 0162 Tbilisi
Tel: +995(32) 231-026
Fax: +995(32) 294-197
EMail: uni@iliauni.edu.ge
Website: http://www.iliauni.edu.ge

Rector: Gigi Tevzadze (2006-)
EMail: gigi@iliauni.edu.ge; rector@lingua.edu.ge

Head of University Administration: Sergo Ratiani
EMail: sergo_ratiani@iliauni.edu.ge

International Relations: Nino Dvalidze, Head, Office of Development and Foreign Relations EMail: development@iliauni.edu.ge

Colleges

Arts and Science (Arts and Humanities; History; Modern Languages; Music; Natural Sciences; Political Sciences; Social Sciences; Theatre); **Business** (Banking; Business Administration; Finance; Management; Sports Management; Tourism); **Engineering** (Architecture; Computer Science; Construction Engineering); **Law** (Law)

Faculties

Sport Sciences (Physical Therapy; Physiology; Sports; Sports Management; Sports Medicine)

Schools

Graduate (Archaeology; Christian Religious Studies; Earth Sciences; Ecology; Educational Administration; Educational Psychology; Journalism; Mathematics; Medieval Studies; Neurosciences; Philology; Physics; Public Administration; Regional Studies; Social Work; Sociology)

Further Information: Also Tsageri and Marneuli branches

History: Created 2006 following the merger between 'Tbilisi 'Ilia Čavčavadze' State University of Languages and Culture' (Tbilisis 'Ilia Čavčavadzis' Sakhelobis Enata da Kulturata Sakhelmtsipo Universiteti, founded 1948) and Tbilisi Sulkhan-Saba Orbeliani State Pedagogical University (Tbilisis Sulkhan-Saba Orbelianis Sakhelobis Sakhelmtsipo Pedagogiuri Universiteti, founded 1935). Previously known as Ilia Čavčavadze Sakhelmtsipo Universiteti (Ilia Čavčavadze State University). Acquired present title 2010.

Academic Year: September to June

Admission Requirements: Unified National Exam

Fees: (GEL): c. 500-2,000 per annum, depending on entrance examination (c. 50% study free)

Main Language(s) of Instruction: Georgian

International Co-operation: With universities in Germany, France and United Kingdom. Also participates in the Tasis and Tempus programmes

Degrees and Diplomas: *Bakalavris Diplomi*: 4 yrs; *Diplomirebuli Specialistis Diplomi*: 5 yrs; *Magistris Diplomi*: a further 2 yrs; *Doktoris Diplomi*: a futher 3-5 yrs

Student Services: Academic counselling, Canteen, Health services, Language programs, Sports facilities

Special Facilities: Movie studio

Libraries: University Library

Last Updated: 15/02/12

IVANE JAVAHIŠVILI TBILISI STATE UNIVERSITY

Ivane Javahišvilis Sakhelobis Tbilisis Sakhelmtsipo Universiteti (TSU)
1, Čavčavadze Avenue, 0128 Tbilisi
Tel: +995(32) 221-103
Fax: +995(32) 221-103
EMail: tea.gergedava@tsu.ge
Website: http://www.tsu.edu.ge/

Acting Rector: Alexander Kvitashvili (2010-)
Tel: +995(32) 220-241 EMail: sandro.kvitashvili@tsu.ge

Vice-Rector: Teimuraz Khurodze
Tel: +995(32) 252-348, Fax: +995(32) 222-392

International Relations: Tea Gergedava, Head, Department of Foreign Relations

Departments

Applied Mathematics and Computer Science (Applied Mathematics; Computer Science); **Biology** (Biology); **Business Administration** (Business Administration); **Chemistry** (Chemistry); **Commerce and Marketing** (Business and Commerce; Marketing); **Economics** (Economics); **Fine and Liberal Arts** (Fine Arts); **Geography** (Geography); **Geology** (Geology); **History** (History); **International Law and International Relations** (International Law; International Relations); **Journalism** (Journalism); **Law** (International Relations; Law); **Management and Micro Economics** (Business Administration; Management); **Mathematics** (Mathematics); **Medicine** (Medicine); **Oriental Studies** (Asian Studies; Middle Eastern Studies; Oriental Languages); **Philology** (Philology); **Philosophy and Sociology** (Philosophy; Sociology); **Physics**

(Physics); **Psychology** (Psychology); **Western European Languages and Literature** (European Languages)

Institutes

European Studies (European Studies)

Research Institutes

Applied Mathematics (Applied Mathematics); **High Energy Physics** (Physics)

Further Information: Also 6 Research and Educational Centres. 80 Research Laboratories. Branches in Akhaltsine, Ozurgeti, Signani, Sokhumi and Zugdidi

History: Founded 1918.

Governing Bodies: Scientific Council

Academic Year: September to June (September-February; February-June)

Admission Requirements: Competitive entrance examination following general or special secondary school certificate

Fees: (US Dollars): c. 1,000-1,500 per annum

Main Language(s) of Instruction: Georgian, Russian, English, French

International Co-operation: With universities in France, Germany, United Kingdom, USA, Turkey, Greece, Italy, Spain; Iran; Poland; Russian Federation; Armenia; Azerbaijan; Czech Republic

Degrees and Diplomas: *Bakalavris Diplomi*: 4-5 yrs; *Magistris Diplomi*: a further 2 yrs; *Doktoris Diplomi (PhD)*

Student Services: Sports facilities

Student Residential Facilities: For c. 2,500 students

Special Facilities: Museums: History of the University; Palaeontology; Mineralogy; Zoology; Botany

Libraries: Central Scientific Library, c. 2.5m. vols; 9 faculty libraries

Publications: Proceedings of Tbilisi University

Student Numbers 2009-2010: Total 18,000
Last Updated: 08/02/12

IVERIA TEACHING UNIVERSITY

Zedazeni Str. #4, 3200 Tbilisi
Tel: +995(322) 667 703
EMail: univ.iveria@gmail.com
Website: http://www.iveria.edu.ge

Programmes

Nursing (Nursing)

History: Founded 1991.

Main Language(s) of Instruction: Georgian

Degrees and Diplomas: *Bakalavris Diplomi*; *Magistris Diplomi*
Last Updated: 17/02/12

'SHOTA RUSTAVELI' GEORGIAN STATE UNIVERSITY OF THEATRE AND CINEMA

Saqartvelos 'Šota Rustavelis' Sakhelobis Teatrisa da Kinos Sakhelmtsipo Universiteti
19, Rustavili Avenue, 0118 Tbilisi
Tel: +995(32) 999-411 +995(32) 931-074
Fax: +995(32) 990-575
EMail: info@tafu.edu.ge
Website: http://www.tafu.edu.ge

Rector: Giorgi Margvelashvili

Faculties

Art and Social Science (Art Education; Film; Journalism; Management; Radio and Television Broadcasting; Theatre; Tourism); **Drama** (Acting; Dance; Display and Stage Design; Film; Music; Theatre); **Film and TV Media** (Cinema and Television; Film)

History: Founded 1923, acquired present status 1992.

Main Language(s) of Instruction: Georgian

Degrees and Diplomas: *Bakalavris Diplomi*; *Magistris Diplomi*; *Doktoris Diplomi*
Last Updated: 08/02/12

'SHOTA RUSTAVELI' STATE UNIVERSITY
Šota Rustavelis Sakhelobis Sakhelmtsipo Universiteti (BSU)
35, Ninošvili Street, 6010 Batumi, Adjara
Tel: +995(222) 71780
Fax: +995(222) 71787
EMail: info@bsu.edu.ge
Website: http://www.bsu.ge

Rector: Aliosha Bakuridze (2008-)
Tel: +995(222) 71780, Fax: +995(222) 71780

Head of Administration: Edisher Chavleishvili
EMail: e.chavleishvili@bsu.edu.ge

Faculties
Agrarian Technologies and Ecology (Agricultural Business; Agricultural Engineering; Agriculture; Ecology; Forestry); **Education and Sciences** (Education; Natural Sciences; Pedagogy); **Engineering and Technology** (Civil Engineering; Industrial Engineering; Mining Engineering; Petroleum and Gas Engineering; Technology; Telecommunications Engineering; Transport and Communications); **Social Sciences, Business and Law** (Accountancy; Banking; Business Administration; European Studies; Finance; Law; Management; Marketing; Psychology); **Tourism** (Tourism)

History: Founded 1935. Acquired present status 2010.

Admission Requirements: Secondary school certificate, entrance examination

Fees: (US Dollars): c. 350 per annum for local students; c. 1,000 for foreign students

Main Language(s) of Instruction: Georgian

International Co-operation: With universities in Greece, Russian Federation and Turkey

Degrees and Diplomas: *Bakalavris Diplomi*: 4 yrs; *Diplomirebuli Specialistis Diplomi*: 5 yrs; *Magistris Diplomi*: a further 2 yrs; *Doktoris Diplomi*

Student Services: Academic counselling, Canteen, Cultural centre, Foreign student adviser, Health services, Language programs, Social counselling, Sports facilities

Student Residential Facilities: University students Hostel

Special Facilities: Yes

Libraries: 300,000 vols.

Publications: "Collection of works", Journal of Scientific research centre of Western region Georgia *(3 per annum)*; "Historical Herald" *(monthly)*; Scientific Works of Shota Rustaveli Batumi State University *(biennially)*; Series of Natural Sciences *(biennially)*; The Humanities *(quarterly)*

Press or Publishing House: University Publishing House
Last Updated: 14/02/12

SOKHUMI STATE UNIVERSITY
Sokhumis Sakhelmtsipo Universiteti
9, Jikia Street, Sukhumi, Abkhazeti
Tel: +995(32) 541-406
EMail: info@sou.edu.ge
Website: http://www.sou.edu.ge

Rector: J. Apakidze (2009-)

Faculties
Economics and Business (Business Administration; Business and Commerce; Economics; Management); **Education** (Education); **Humanities** (Arts and Humanities; English; German; History; Law; Literature; Native Language; Oriental Languages; Philology; Turkish); **Law** (Law); **Mathematics and Computer Science** (Mathematics and Computer Science; Statistics); **Natural Sciences and Health Care** (Health Education; Natural Sciences); **Social and Political Sciences** (International Relations; Oriental Studies; Political Sciences; Psychology; Social Sciences; Sociology)

History: Founded 1932 as Sokhumi Pedagogical Institute. Reorganized 1979 into Abkhazian State University. Acquired present status and title 2008. Under the jurisdiction of the Ministry of People's Education of Georgia.

Governing Bodies: Rector's Council; University Council; University Academic Council; Faculty Academic Councils

Academic Year: September to July (September-December; February-July)

Admission Requirements: Competitive entrance examination following general or special secondary school certificate

Main Language(s) of Instruction: Abkhazian, Georgian, Russian

Degrees and Diplomas: *Bakalavris Diplomi*; *Diplomirebuli Specialistis Diplomi*: 5 yrs; *Magistris Diplomi*; *Doktoris Diplomi*

Student Services: Health services

Student Residential Facilities: Yes

Special Facilities: Experimental Biological Garden

Libraries: Main Library, c. 600,000 vols

Publications: Staff Research Works *(annually)*
Last Updated: 14/02/12

SULKHAN SABA ORBELIANI TEACHING UNIVERSITY
4a Gia Abesadze, 0105 Tbilisi
Tel: +995(32) 2 98-95-16
EMail: info@sabauni.edu.ge
Website: http://www.sabauni.edu.ge

Rector: Vaja Vardidze EMail: v.vardidze@sabauni.edu.ge

Pro-rector: Nukri Gelashvili EMail: n.gelashvili@sabauni.edu.ge

Faculties
Humanities (Bible; Ethics; Modern Languages; Religious Art; Religious Practice; Theology); **Law** (Law)

History: Founded 2002 as Sulkhan Saba Orbeliani Institute of Philosophy, Theology, History and Culture. Acquired present title and status 2009.

Degrees and Diplomas: *Bakalavris Diplomi*; *Magistris Diplomi*
Libraries: Yes
Last Updated: 17/02/12

TBILISI STATE ACADEMY OF ARTS
Tbilisis Apolon Qutateladzis Sakhelobis Sakhelmtsipo Samkhatvro Akademia
22, Griboedov Street, 0108 Tbilisi
Tel: +995(32) 932-972 +995(32) 995-425
Fax: +995(32) 920-164
EMail: info@art.edu.ge
Website: http://www.art.edu.ge

Rector: Giorgi Bugadze
Tel: +995(32) 963-959, Fax: +995(32) 920-164

Faculties
Architecture (Architectural and Environmental Design; Architecture; Civil Engineering; Interior Design; Landscape Architecture); **Design** (Ceramic Art; Design; Fashion Design; Glass Art; Industrial Design; Interior Design; Jewelry Art; Textile Design); **Media Arts** (Media Studies); **Restoration and Art History** (Architecture; Art History; Cultural Studies; Fine Arts; Heritage Preservation; Restoration of Works of Art); **Visual Arts** (Visual Arts)

History: Founded 1922 as Georgian Academy of Arts.

Governing Bodies: Scientific Council

Admission Requirements: Secondary School Certificate

Main Language(s) of Instruction: Georgian

International Co-operation: With universities in Germany

Degrees and Diplomas: *Bakalavris Diplomi*: 4 yrs; *Magistris Diplomi*: a further 2 yrs; *Doktoris Diplomi*

Student Services: Academic counselling, Canteen, Handicapped facilities, Health services, Language programs, Sports facilities

Special Facilities: Museum. Art Gallery. Concert Hall

Libraries: 4 Libraries
Last Updated: 26/11/09

TBILISI STATE MEDICAL UNIVERSITY

Tbilisis Sakhelmtsipo Samedicino Universiteti (TSMU)
33, Vazha-Pšavela Avenue, 0177 Tbilisi
Tel: +995(32) 391-567 +995(32) 392-613
Fax: +995(32) 942-519
EMail: info@tsmu.edu; iad@tsmu.edu
Website: http://www.tsmu.edu

Rector: Zurab Vadachkoria
Tel: +995(32) 395-432, Fax: +995(32) 942-516

Deputy-Rector: Rima Beriashvili

Vice-Rector: Davit Chavchanidze

Centres
Clinical Anatomy and Skills (Anatomy); **Family Medicine** (Medicine); **Interventional Radiology** (Radiology); **Language Teaching** (Modern Languages); **Strategic Development and Research in Medical Education**

Faculties
Dentistry (Dental Technology; Dentistry; Orthodontics; Stomatology; Surgery); **Medicine** (Anatomy; Biology; Biophysics; Cell Biology; Embryology and Reproduction Biology; Genetics; Histology; Immunology; Medicine; Microbiology; Molecular Biology; Parasitology; Pathology; Physics; Physiology; Surgery); **Pharmacy** (Applied Chemistry; Cosmetology; Pharmacy; Toxicology); **Physical Medicine and Rehabilitation** (Biological and Life Sciences; Biology; Cardiology; Gerontology; Neurosciences; Oncology; Pathology; Physical Therapy; Rehabilitation and Therapy; Respiratory Therapy; Sports Medicine; Urology); **Public Health** (Anatomy; Behavioural Sciences; Biochemistry; Biology; Biophysics; Cell Biology; Chemistry; Community Health; Dermatology; Embryology and Reproduction Biology; Epidemiology; Forensic Medicine and Dentistry; Genetics; Health Administration; Histology; Hygiene; Immunology; Mathematics; Modern Languages; Nutrition; Ophthalmology; Otorhinolaryngology; Parasitology; Pathology; Pharmacology; Philosophy; Physical Education; Physics; Physiology; Public Health; Radiology; Rehabilitation and Therapy; Social and Preventive Medicine; Sociology; Sports Medicine; Surgery; Toxicology; Venereology)

Higher Schools
Nursing (Nursing)

Institutes
Postgraduate Medical Studies and Continuous Medical Education (Anaesthesiology; Anatomy; Cardiology; Forensic Medicine and Dentistry; Gynaecology and Obstetrics; Medicine; Neurology; Oncology; Ophthalmology; Orthopaedics; Otorhinolaryngology; Paediatrics; Parasitology; Pathology; Psychiatry and Mental Health; Radiology; Stomatology; Surgery; Urology)

Further Information: Also preparatory courses for foreign students

History: Founded 1918, acquired present status 1992.

Governing Bodies: Scientific Council

Academic Year: September to July

Main Language(s) of Instruction: Georgian, Russian, English, French

International Co-operation: With universities in Austria; France; Germany; USA

Degrees and Diplomas: *Diplomirebuli Specialistis Diplomi*: 5-7 yrs; *Magistris Diplomi*; *Doktoris Diplomi*

Student Services: Sports facilities

Special Facilities: Pathological Anatomy Museum; History of Medicine Museum; Biology Museum. Sport and Art Centre

Libraries: Central Library, c. 600,000 vols

Publications: Georgian Medical News; Proceedings of Scientific Societies (*annually*)
Last Updated: 14/02/12

TBILISI VANO SARAJIŠVILI STATE CONSERVATORY

Tbilisis Vano Sarajišvilis Sakhelobis Sakhelmtsipo Konservatoria
8-10, Griboedov Street, 0108 Tbilisi
Tel: +995(32) 987-186
Fax: +995(32) 987-187
EMail: info@conservatoire.edu.ge
Website: http://www.conservatoire.edu.ge

Rector: Rezo Kiknadze
Tel: +995(32) 987-187 EMail: rector@conservatoire.edu.ge

Head of Administration: Tamar Djandieri
Tel: +995(32) 999-147 EMail: admin@conservatoire.edu.ge

Faculties
Composition and Music Theory (Folklore; Music Theory and Composition; Religious Music); **Performing** (Conducting; Musical Instruments; Opera; Singing)

History: Founded 1917.

Main Language(s) of Instruction: Georgian

Degrees and Diplomas: *Bakalavris Diplomi*; *Magistris Diplomi*; *Doktoris Diplomi*

Special Facilities: Museum; Opera Studio; Concert halls

Libraries: Yes
Last Updated: 14/02/12

PRIVATE INSTITUTIONS

AKHALTSIKHE STATE TEACHING UNIVERSITY

Akhaltsikhe Sakhelmtsipo Sastsavlo Universiteti
106, Rustaveli Street, Akhaltsikhe
Tel: +995(265) 21990
EMail: contact@akhaltsikhe.edu.ge
Website: http://www.tsu-meskheti.edu.ge

Rector: Tina Gelashvili EMail: tinikogel@rambler.ru

Chancellor: Nodar Gorokhovi EMail: nodargoroxovi@rambler.ru

Faculties
Business Administration (Accountancy; Administration; Agricultural Business; Banking; Business Administration; Finance; Insurance; Management; Real Estate; Taxation); **Education, Social Sciences and Humanities** (Education; English; Ethnology; French; German; Greek; History; Linguistics; Literature; Philology; Russian; Slavic Languages; Turkish); **Engineering, Agriculture and Exact Sciences** (Applied Mathematics; Astronomy and Space Science; Ecology; Information Technology); **Law** (Criminal Law; Law)

History: Established 1990 as Meskheti Branch of Ivane Javakhishvili State University of Tbilisi.

Main Language(s) of Instruction: Georgian

Degrees and Diplomas: *Bakalavris Diplomi*; *Diplomirebuli Specialistis Diplomi*; *Magistris Diplomi*

Libraries: Yes
Last Updated: 08/02/12

AMERICAN UNIVERSITY FOR HUMANITIES - TBILISI COLLEGE CAMPUS

Amerikuli Humanitaruli Universiteti Tbilisis Filiali Koleji
2 Tornike Eristavi Str., 0192 Tbilisi
Tel: +995(32) 660-091
Fax: +995(32) 660-094
EMail: info@auhtc.edu
Website: http://www.auhtc.edu/

Rector: Alexander Rondeli
Tel: +995(95) 333-322 EMail: arondeli@gfsis.org

Director: Zurab Abashidze EMail: zabashidze@auhtc.edu

International Relations: Revaz Aslamazishvili, Head of International Relations Department
Tel: +995(98) 115-377 EMail: rezoasl@yahoo.com

Divisions

Business Administration (Business Administration; Management); **Law and Diplomacy** (International Relations; International Studies; Law)

History: Created 2004. Acquired status 2007

Academic Year: October to January; February to May

Admission Requirements: School leaving certificate, English language proficiency

Fees: (GEL): 6,400 per annum

Main Language(s) of Instruction: English

Accrediting Agencies: Ministry of Education and Science

Degrees and Diplomas: *Bakalavris Diplomi*: Business Administration; International Relations; International Law (Bachelor); *Magistris Diplomi*: International Business; International Management (Master's), 2 yrs

Student Services: Academic counselling, Canteen, Employment services, Foreign student adviser, Health services, Language programs, Social counselling, Sports facilities

Last Updated: 08/02/12

BATUMI NAVIGATION TEACHING UNIVERSITY

Batumis Navigaciis Sastsavlo Universiteti

26, Tbilisi Avenue, Batumi, Adjara
Tel: +995(222) 92525
Fax: +995(222) 74840
EMail: info@bntu.edu.ge
Website: http://www.bntu.edu.ge/

Rector: Parmen Khvedelidze

Centres

International Maritime Training (Marine Engineering; Marine Science and Oceanography)

Faculties

Maritime Engineering (Electrical Engineering; Marine Engineering; Transport Engineering; Transport Management)

History: Founded 1999 as Batumi Maritime College. Acquired present status and title 2009.

Main Language(s) of Instruction: Georgian

Degrees and Diplomas: *Bakalavris Diplomi*; *Magistris Diplomi*
Last Updated: 08/02/12

CAUCASUS ACADEMIC CENTRE

Kavkasiis Akademiuri Centri (CAC)

28 Pekiniave. V floor, Tbilisi
Tel: +995(32) 251-730
EMail: cac@cac.edu.ge
Website: http://www.cac.edu.ge

Executive Manager: David Tsetskhladze

Programmes

Business Administration (Business Administration)

History: Founded 1999.

Main Language(s) of Instruction: Georgian

Degrees and Diplomas: *Bakalavris Diplomi*; *Magistris Diplomi*
Last Updated: 15/02/12

CAUCASUS INTERNATIONAL UNIVERSITY

Kavkasiis Saertašoriso Universiteti

73, Chargali street, Tbilisi
Tel: +995(32) 308-641 +995(32) 105-203
Fax: +995(32) 611-298
EMail: ciu@caucasus.net
Website: http://www.ciu.edu.ge

Rector: Kakhaber Kordzaia **EMail:** rector@ciu.edu.ge

Faculties

Business (Business Administration); **Humanities and Social Sciences** (Arts and Humanities; Economics; English; German; History; International Relations; Native Language; Oriental Studies; Philology; Political Sciences; Psychology; Social Sciences; Sociology); **Law** (Commercial Law; Law); **Medicine** (Medicine)

History: Founded 1995.

Main Language(s) of Instruction: Georgian; Russian

Degrees and Diplomas: *Bakalavris Diplomi*; *Magistris Diplomi*; *Doktoris Diplomi*

Libraries: Yes
Last Updated: 08/02/12

⫍⫎ CAUCASUS UNIVERSITY

Kavkasiis Universiteti (CU)

77, Kostava Street, 0175 Tbilisi
Tel: +995(32) 941-691 +995(32) 313-225
Fax: +995(32) 313-226
EMail: info@cu.edu.ge
Website: http://www.cu.edu.ge/

President: Kakha Shengelia (2004-)
Tel: +995(32) 941-691, Ext. 101 EMail: president@cu.edu.ge

Vice-President for Academic Affairs: Nugzar Skhirtladze
EMail: nskhirtladze@cu.edu.ge

International Relations: Tea Tevdorashvili, Director, International Relations Department
Tel: + 995(32) 313-225, Ext. 1131 EMail: ttevdorashvili@cu.edu.ge

Schools

Business (Accountancy; Business Administration; Finance; Health Administration; Management; Marketing); **Governance** (International Relations; Public Administration); **Humanities** (Arts and Humanities); **Law** (Law); **Media Studies** (Journalism; Media Studies); **Technology** (Computer Science; Information Technology); **Tourism** (International Business; Tourism)

History: Created in 1998 as Caucasus School of Business in partnership with Georgia State University, USA. Acquired current title and status 2004.

Governing Bodies: Board of Directors

Admission Requirements: High School Certifiate; sufficient scores in the Unified National Exam.

Fees: (Euros): Bachelor's programme, 3,000 per annum; Master's programme, (US Dollars): 6,000-8,000

Main Language(s) of Instruction: Georgian; English

International Co-operation: With institutions in Canada; France; Japan; Korea; Latvia; Portugal; USA

Accrediting Agencies: Ministry of Education and Science

Degrees and Diplomas: *Bakalavris Diplomi*: Business Administration; Law; Media; Technology, 4 yrs; *Magistris Diplomi*: Global Management; Management Consulting; Business Intelligence (EMBA/MBA), 1 1/2 yrs; *Magistris Diplomi*: Marketing; Management; Finance; Health Management; Hospitality (MBA), 2-3 yrs; *Doktoris Diplomi*: 4-5 yrs. Also double degrees with overseas institutions.

Student Services: Academic counselling, Canteen, Employment services, Foreign student adviser, Foreign Studies Centre, Language programs, Social counselling

Libraries: yes
Last Updated: 08/02/12

DAVID AGHMASHENEBELI UNIVERSITY OF GEORGIA

Saqartvelos Davit Agmašeneblis Sakhelobis Universiteti (SDASU/DAUG)

25, Ilya Chavchavadze Avenue, 0179 Tbilisi
Tel: +995(32) 989-445
Fax: +995(32) 252-788
EMail: info@sdasu.ge
Website: http://www.sdasu.edu.ge

Rector: Nino Chalaganidze Tel: +995(32) 253-677

Faculties

Economics and Business (Business Administration; Economics); **Health Care** (Anatomy; Biology; Chemistry; Dentistry; Dermatology; Forensic Medicine and Dentistry; Gynaecology and Obstetrics; Hygiene; Medicine; Microbiology; Neurology; Ophthalmology; Paediatrics; Physiology; Rehabilitation and Therapy; Stomatology; Surgery; Urology; Venereology); **Humanities** (Arts and Humanities;

English; Journalism; Philology); **Law** (Law); **Social Studies** (Social Studies)

History: Founded 1992.

Main Language(s) of Instruction: Georgian

International Co-operation: With universities in USA, United Kingdom, Germany, Israel

Degrees and Diplomas: *Bakalavris Diplomi*; *Magistris Diplomi*; *Doktoris Diplomi*

Last Updated: 13/02/12

DAVID TVILDIANI MEDICAL UNIVERSITY

Umaghlesi Sameditsino Skola AIETI (AIETI)

2/6 Lubliana Street, 0159 Tbilisi
Tel: +995(32) 516-898
Fax: +995(32) 527-196
EMail: aieti@aieti.edu.ge
Website: http://www.aieti.edu.ge

President: Levan Tvildiani EMail: rector@dtmu.edu.ge

Faculties
General Medicine (Medicine)

Schools
Public Health (Public Health)

History: Founded 1991 as AIETI Medical School, acquired present title 2011.

Governing Bodies: Academic Council

Academic Year: September to July

Admission Requirements: Sašualo Skolis Atestati. Unified Entrance Examinations. For foreign citizens: permission of Ministry of Education and Science of Georgia

Fees: (GEL): 2,450 per annum

Main Language(s) of Instruction: Georgian, English

Accrediting Agencies: National Education Accreditation Centre of Ministry of Education and Science

Degrees and Diplomas: *Diplomirebuli Specialistis Diplomi*: Medicine (MD), 6 yrs; *Magistris Diplomi*; *Doktoris Diplomi*

Student Services: Employment services, Health services, Language programs

Special Facilities: PC equipped classroom

Libraries: Medical Library with audiovisual aids

Publications: Transactions of Scientific Conference *(annually)*

Last Updated: 14/02/12

EUROPEAN INTERNATIONAL EDUCATIONAL UNIVERSITY

95 Agmashenibeli Ave, 380178 Tbilisi
Tel: +995(32) 308-661

Chairman: John Eapen

Faculties
Medicine (Medicine)

Programmes
Health Care Management (Health Administration); **Nursing** (Nursing); **Sports Medicine and Rehabilitation** (Rehabilitation and Therapy; Sports Medicine)

History: Founded 1992.

Main Language(s) of Instruction: Georgian and English

Degrees and Diplomas: *Bakalavris Diplomi*; *Diplomirebuli Specialistis Diplomi*; *Magistris Diplomi*

Last Updated: 22/02/12

FREE UNIVERSITY OF TBILISI

Tbilisis Tavisufali Universiteti

Bedia Street, Nutsubidze Plateau, I Mirco District, 0182 Tbilisi
Tel: +995(32) 220-0901
Fax: +995(32) 220-0902
EMail: info@freeuni.edu.ge
Website: http://www.freeuni.edu.ge/

Rector: Guram Chikovani (2009-)
Tel: +995(599) 55-32-23 EMail: g.chikovani@freeuni.edu.ge

Chancellor: George Meladze
Tel: +995(577) 20-10-22 EMail: g.meladze@freeuni.edu.ge

International Relations: Douglas Osborne, Head of International Programs
Tel: +995(595) 33-50-04 EMail: d.osborne@freeuni.edu.ge

Institutes
Asia and Africa (African Studies; Asian Studies; East Asian Studies; International Relations; Middle Eastern Studies; Oriental Languages; Oriental Studies; South Asian Studies)

Schools
Business *(ESM)* (Business Administration); **Computer Science and Mathematics** (Applied Mathematics; Mathematics and Computer Science; Software Engineering); **Governance and Social Sciences** (Government; Social Sciences); **Law** (Law); **Physics** (Physics)

History: Established 2007 through the merger of two higher education schools, the European School of Management (ESM-Tbilisi) and the Tbilisi Institute of Asia and Africa (TIAA).

Governing Bodies: Board of Trustees

Academic Year: September-January; March -June

Admission Requirements: Unifies State Exam

Fees: (GEL): 6,900.00 per annum

Main Language(s) of Instruction: Georgian

International Co-operation: with institutions in Czech Republic, China

Degrees and Diplomas: *Bakalavris Diplomi*; *Diplomirebuli Specialistis Diplomi*; *Magistris Diplomi*

Student Services: Academic counselling, Canteen, Employment services, Foreign student adviser, Foreign Studies Centre, Handicapped facilities, Language programs, Nursery care, Sports facilities

Libraries: 14,531 vols; 9 periodical subscriptions; access to electronic networks: JSTOR, EBSCO, E-LIBRARY

Academic Staff *2011-2012*	MEN	WOMEN	TOTAL
FULL-TIME	51	35	86
STAFF WITH DOCTORATE FULL-TIME	30	10	40
Student Numbers *2011-2012* All (Foreign Included)	452	301	753

Evening students, 35.

Last Updated: 26/03/12

GEOMEDI UNIVERSITY

3 Krtsanisi Street, Tbilisi
Tel: +995(32) 293-789
Fax: +995(32) 292-306
EMail: info@geosis.ge
Website: http://www.geosis.ge/

Rector: Marina Pirtskhalava EMail: geosis@edu.ge

Faculties
Dentistry (Dentistry); **Physical Medicine and Rehabilitation** (Medicine; Rehabilitation and Therapy); **Public Health Economics and Management** (Health Administration; Medicine; Public Health)

History: Founded 1998.

Degrees and Diplomas: *Bakalavris Diplomi*; *Magistris Diplomi*

Libraries: Yes

Last Updated: 15/02/12

GEORGIA ECONOMY AND LAW TEACHING UNIVERSITY

Saqartvelos Ekonomikisa da Samartlis Instituti

42-44, Vazha Pshavela Avenue, Tbilisi
Fax: +995(32) 398-725 +995(32) 391-803
EMail: sesi2008@gmail.com; ge.econlawinst@yahoo.com
Website: http://www.sesi.edu.ge

Faculties

Economics and Business (Banking; Business Administration; Business and Commerce; Economics; Finance; Insurance); **Health Protection** (Dentistry; Health Sciences; Public Health; Stomatology); **Humanities** (American Studies; Arts and Humanities; English; Literature; Modern Languages); **Jurisprudence** (Law)

Main Language(s) of Instruction: Georgian

Degrees and Diplomas: *Bakalavris Diplomi*: 4 yrs; *Magistris Diplomi*: 2 yrs
Last Updated: 27/11/09

GEORGIAN-AMERICAN UNIVERSITY

SH.P.S. Qartul-Amerikuli Universiteti (GAU)
Chavchavadze ave. 2nd cul de sac, #5, 0179 Tbilisi
Tel: +995(32) 915-003 +995(32) 915-004
Fax: +995(32) 915-044
EMail: info@gau.ge
Website: http://www.gau.ge

President: R. Michael Cowgill EMail: rmichaelcowgill@yahoo.com

Chancellor: Nino Toronjadze EMail: ntoronjadze@taobamk.ge

International Relations: Kenneth A. Cutshaw, Vice-President, Global Affairs EMail: kcutshaw@churchs.com

Departments

Languages (English; French; German; Native Language)

Schools

Business (Business Administration; English; Finance; Management; Marketing); **Law** (Administrative Law; Civics; Constitutional Law; Criminal Law; International Law; Law)

History: Created 2005. Western-style education system designed for the Georgian environment.
Governing Bodies: Partners, Chancellor, President, Deans, Council of Representatives, Academic Council
Academic Year: September to February; February to June; June to August
Admission Requirements: Secondary school certificate; UNE exam for Georgian students; university entrance exam for non-Georgian and transfer students.
Fees: (GEL): Undergraduate, 7,500 per annum; Master and PhD programmes, 5,000
Main Language(s) of Instruction: Georgian, English
International Co-operation: With institutions in Australia; France; India; Italy; UK; USA
Accrediting Agencies: Ministry of Education and Science

Degrees and Diplomas: *Bakalavris Diplomi*: Business Administration (BBA); Civil Law; Administrative Law; Criminal Law; Institutional Law; Constitutional Law (LLB), 4 yrs; *Magistris Diplomi*: Business Administration (MBA); Civil Law; Administrative Law; Criminal Law; Institutional Law; Constitutional Law (LLM), a further 2 yrs; *Doktoris Diplomi*: Business Administration (DBA); Civil Law; Administrative Law; Criminal Law; Institutional Law; Constitutional Law (PhD), 3 yrs
Student Services: Academic counselling, Canteen, Employment services, Foreign student adviser, Handicapped facilities, Health services, Language programs, Social counselling, Sports facilities

Special Facilities: Forensic laboratory, fencing academy

Libraries: Yes

Academic Staff 2009-2010	MEN	WOMEN	TOTAL
FULL-TIME	34	30	64

Student Numbers 2009-2010			
All (Foreign Included)	–	–	731

Note: Also visiting staff of approximately 40.
Last Updated: 14/02/12

GEORGIAN AVIATION UNIVERSITY

Saqartvelos Saaviatsio Universiteti
16, Ketevan Tsamebuli Street, 0103 Tbilisi
Tel: +995(32) 776-571
Fax: +995(32) 776-572
EMail: rector.gau@gmail.com; mail@ssu.edu.ge
Website: http://www.ssu.edu.ge/

Rector: Sergo Tepnadz

Faculties

Air Transport Flight Exploitation (Transport Management); **Business and Management** (Air Transport; Business Administration; International Economics; Management; Transport Management); **Engineering** (Aeronautical and Aerospace Engineering); **Law** (International Law; Law)

History: Founded 1992 as Aviation Institute of Georgian Technical University (GTU).

Main Language(s) of Instruction: Georgian

Degrees and Diplomas: *Bakalavris Diplomi*; *Diplomirebuli Specialistis Diplomi*; *Magistris Diplomi*; *Doktoris Diplomi*

Libraries: Yes
Last Updated: 09/02/12

GEORGIAN-BRITISH UNIVERSITY OF INTERNATIONAL LAW AND MANAGEMENT

SH.P.S. 'Saertašoriso Samartlisa da Martvis Kartul-Britanuli' Universiteti
32/34 Al. Khazbegi Bystreet Floor II, 0177 Tbilisi
Tel: +995(32) 397-610
Fax: +995(32) 242-466
EMail: info@ssmu.edu.ge

Rector: Zurab Gvišaini

Divisions

International Journalism (Journalism); **International Law** (International Law; Law); **Management** (Administration; Management)

History: Founded 2004.

Degrees and Diplomas: *Bakalavris Diplomi*; *Magistris Diplomi*; *Doktoris Diplomi*
Last Updated: 16/12/09

GEORGIAN INSTITUTE OF PUBLIC AFFAIRS

Saqartvelos Sazogadoebriv Sakmeta Instituti (GIPA)
2, Maria Brosset Street, 0108 Tbilisi
Tel: +995(32) 931-466 +995(32) 932-201
Fax: +995(32) 931-466
EMail: admin@gipa.ge
Website: http://www.gipa.ge

Rector: Giorgi Margvelashvili EMail: margvel@gipa.ge

Schools

Government (Government; International Relations; Law; Public Administration); **Journalism and Media Management** *(Caucasus)* (Journalism; Media Studies); **Law and Politics** (International Relations; Law; Political Sciences)

History: Founded 1994 as Institute of Public Administration. Acquired present title 2001.

Main Language(s) of Instruction: Georgian and English

Degrees and Diplomas: *Bakalavris Diplomi*; *Magistris Diplomi*
Last Updated: 16/02/12

GORGASALI - TBILISI INDEPENDENT UNIVERSITY

Tbilisis Damoukidebeli Universiteti 'Gorgasali'
64, Guramishvili Avenue, 0104 Tbilisi
Tel: +995(32) 453-865
EMail: Gorgasali1@rambler.ru
Website: http://www.gorgasali.edu.ge

Faculties

Health Care (Health Education); **Humanities and Social Sciences** (Arts and Humanities; Civil Law; Criminal Law; Economics; English; Finance; German; International Economics; International Relations; Law; Social Sciences)

Degrees and Diplomas: *Bakalavris Diplomi*; *Magistris Diplomi*; *Doktoris Diplomi*
Last Updated: 16/02/12

GORI TEACHING UNIVERSITY

53, Chavchavadze Street, Gori, Shida Kartli
Tel: +995(270) 72413
Fax: +995(270) 73554
EMail: contact@gu.edu.ge
Website: http://www.gu.edu.ge

Rector: Giorgi Sosiashvili EMail: giorgisosiashvili@gmail.com

Faculties

Education, Exact and Natural Sciences (Biology; Chemistry; Computer Science; Education; Geography; Mathematics; Natural Sciences); **Humanities** (English; German; History; Literature; Philology; Russian); **Social Sciences, Business and Law** (Business Administration; Business and Commerce; Law; Social Sciences)

History: Established 2007 following merger of Gori State University and Tskhinvali State University.

Main Language(s) of Instruction: Georgian

Degrees and Diplomas: *Bakalavris Diplomi*; *Magistris Diplomi*

Libraries: Yes
Last Updated: 08/02/12

GRIGOL ROBAKIDZE UNIVERSITY

Grigol Robakidzis Sakhelobis Universiteti 'Alma Mater' (GRU)
6, Jano Bagrationi Street, 0160 Tbilisi
Tel: +995(32) 385-849 +995(32) 384-406
Fax: +995(32) 252-981
EMail: info@gruni.edu.ge
Website: http://www.gruni.edu.ge

Rector: Mamuka Tavkelidze (1992-)
Tel: +995(32) 385-849, Fax: +995(32) 252-981
EMail: gr_uni@posta.ge; m.tavkhelidze@gruni.edu.ge

Vice-Rector: Nino Kemertelidze Tel: +995(32) 382-706

Schools

Business and Management (Business Administration; Management); **Humanities and Social Sciences** (Arts and Humanities; Philosophy; Social Sciences); **Law** (Civil Law; European Union Law; Government; Labour Law; Law); **Medicine** (Dentistry; Medicine)

Further Information: Also 3 Dentistry clinics; Centre of Thrombosis Research; Institute of Clinical Psychology; Anti-terrorism Research Centre; Linguaphone Centre; Computer Centre; Different Laboratories

History: Founded 1992.

Governing Bodies: Academic Council

Academic Year: September to July

Admission Requirements: Secondary school certificate

Main Language(s) of Instruction: Georgian, English, German

International Co-operation: With universities UK and USA. Also participates in Tacis

Degrees and Diplomas: *Bakalavris Diplomi*: 4 yrs; *Diplomirebuli Specialistis Diplomi*: 5 yrs; *Magistris Diplomi*: a further 2 yrs following Bakalavris Diplomi; *Doktoris Diplomi*

Student Services: Academic counselling, Canteen, Cultural centre, Employment services, Foreign student adviser, Foreign Studies Centre, Health services, Language programs, Social counselling, Sports facilities

Special Facilities: TV-Studio. Dental Clinic

Libraries: Main Library; Electronic Library

Publications: Collective Works of Lecturers of the University *(annually)*

Last Updated: 08/02/12

HIPPOCRATES MEDICAL EDUCATION UNIVERSITY TBILISI

Tbilisis Samedicino Instituti 'Hipokrate'
8, Gogol Street, 0164 Tbilisi
Tel: +995(32) 963-496
EMail: medicina@hippokrates.edu.ge
Website: http://www.hippocrates.edu.ge

Rector: David Kiteishvili EMail: hippocrates2003@yandex.ru

Departments

Dentistry (Dentistry); **Medicine** (Medicine); **Pharmacy** (Pharmacy)

History: Founded 2003.

Admission Requirements: Secondary school certificate

Fees: (GEL): 2,000 per annum

Main Language(s) of Instruction: Georgian, Russian, English

International Co-operation: With institutions in Russia

Accrediting Agencies: Ministry of Education and Science

Degrees and Diplomas: *Bakalavris Diplomi*: Medicine, 6 yrs; *Bakalavris Diplomi*: Stomatology; Pharmacy, 5 yrs; *Magistris Diplomi*

Student Services: Academic counselling, Canteen, Foreign student adviser, Health services, Language programs, Social counselling, Sports facilities

Press or Publishing House: Tbilisi State University Press
Last Updated: 14/02/12

HOLY APOSTLE ST ANDREW THE FIRST-CALLED GEORGIAN UNIVERSITY OF GEORGIAN PATRIARCHATE

Saqartvelos Sapatriarqos Tsmida Andria Pirveltsodebulis Sakhelobis Qartuli Universiteti
53a, Chavchavadze Avenue, 0162 Tbilisi
Tel: +995(32) 258-246
Fax: +995(32) 258-247
EMail: sanguadmin@gmail.com
Website: http://www.sangu.ge/

Programmes

Biology (Biology); **Business Administration** (Business Administration; Business and Commerce); **Chemistry** (Chemistry); **Computer Technology** (Computer Engineering; Computer Science); **History** (History); **Mathematics** (Mathematics); **Philology** (Philology); **Physics** (Physics)

History: Founded 2008.

Main Language(s) of Instruction: Georgian

Degrees and Diplomas: *Bakalavris Diplomi*; *Magistris Diplomi*; *Doktoris Diplomi*
Last Updated: 16/02/12

IB EURO-CAUCASIAN UNIVERSITY

Aibi Evro-Kavkasiuri Universiteti
34, Pekin Street, Tbilisi
Tel: +995(99) 907-991
EMail: info@ibeku-tbilisi.edu.ge
Website: http://www.ibeku-tbilisi.edu.ge

Faculties

Business and Applied Sciences (Business Administration; Business and Commerce; Economics); **Health and Rehabilitation** (Health Sciences; Rehabilitation and Therapy); **Psychology** (Psychology); **Social Sciences** (Social Sciences)

Degrees and Diplomas: *Bakalavris Diplomi*; *Magistris Diplomi*; *Doktoris Diplomi*

Libraries: Yes
Last Updated: 15/02/12

INTERNATIONAL BLACK SEA UNIVERSITY

Šavi Zgvis Saertašoriso Universiteti (IBSU)
David Agmashenebeli Alley 13km, 2, 0131 Tbilisi
Tel: +995(32) 595-005
Fax: +995(32) 595-008
EMail: contact@ibsu.edu.ge
Website: http://www.ibsu.edu.ge

Rector: Ş. Ercan Tunç EMail: rector@ibsu.edu.ge

Faculties

Business Administration (Accountancy; Business Administration; Finance; Management; Marketing); **Computer Technologies and Engineering** (Computer Engineering; Computer Graphics; Computer Networks; Industrial Engineering; Software Engineering; Technology); **Education** (Education; Educational Administration;

Pedagogy; Philology); **Humanities** (American Studies; Literature; Turkish); **Social Sciences** (Economics; International Relations; Law; Social Sciences)

Schools
Languages (English; French; Russian; Spanish; Turkish)
History: Founded 1995. A joint Georgian-Turkish Educational Establishment.
Governing Bodies: Board of Trustees
Academic Year: September to July
Admission Requirements: Competitive entrance examination following general or special secondary school certificate
Main Language(s) of Instruction: English
Accrediting Agencies: Ministry of Education and Science
Degrees and Diplomas: *Bakalavris Diplomi*: 4 yrs; *Magistris Diplomi*: 2 yrs; *Doktoris Diplomi*
Student Services: Academic counselling, Canteen, Cultural centre, Employment services, Foreign student adviser, Health services, Language programs, Nursery care, Social counselling, Sports facilities
Student Residential Facilities: For c. 100 students
Libraries: Yes
Publications: Academic Journal of IBSU, Scientific Journal in English *(biennially)*
Last Updated: 13/02/12

INTERPHARM PLUS UNIVERSITY
Universiteti 'Interpharmi Plus'
8, Tetelashvili St, 0179 Tbilisi
Tel: +995(32) 294-140
EMail: University@interpharrm.edu.ge
Website: http://www.interpharm.ge

Faculties
Health Care (Analytical Chemistry; Applied Mathematics; Applied Physics; Biochemistry; Biology; Business Administration; Chemistry; Computer Science; Hygiene; Inorganic Chemistry; Medicine; Microbiology; Nursing; Organic Chemistry; Pathology; Pharmacology; Pharmacy; Physiology; Public Health; Toxicology)
History: Founded 2004.
Degrees and Diplomas: *Bakalavris Diplomi*; *Magistris Diplomi*
Last Updated: 14/02/12

KUTAISI COLLEGE OF MUSIC
Kutaisis Samusiko Koleji
43a, K. Gamsakhurdia Street, 4600 Kutaisi, Imereti
Tel: +995(231) 70911
EMail: admin@kutmuscollege.edu.ge
Website: http://www.kutmuscollege.edu.ge

Programmes
Music
Degrees and Diplomas: *Diplomirebuli Specialistis Diplomi*
Last Updated: 17/12/09

KUTAISI MEDICAL INSTITUTE
Kutaisis Samedicino Instituti (KSI)
13, Dvališvili Street, 4600 Kutaisi, Imereti
Tel: +995(231) 48989
Fax: +995(231) 48085
EMail: info@mik.edu.ge
Rector: Nugzar Maghlakelidze

Faculties
Dentistry (Dentistry); **Medicine** (Medicine); **Pharmacy** (Pharmacy)
History: Founded 1992.
Admission Requirements: Secondary school certificate and national examination
Fees: (GEL): 1,500 per annum
Main Language(s) of Instruction: Georgian, English

Accrediting Agencies: Ministry of Education and Science
Degrees and Diplomas: *Bakalavris Diplomi*; *Diplomirebuli Specialistis Diplomi*: 5-6 yrs; *Magistris Diplomi*
Student Services: Academic counselling, Canteen, Cultural centre, Foreign Studies Centre, Health services, Language programs, Nursery care, Social counselling
Student Residential Facilities: None
Libraries: Yes
Press or Publishing House: Kulaisi Publishing House
Last Updated: 08/02/12

KUTAISI UNIVERSITY
Kutaisis Universiteti
13, Tsereteli Street, 4601 Kutaisi, Imereti
Tel: +995(331) 45297
Fax: +995(331) 45772
EMail: info@unik.edu.ge
Website: http://www.unik.edu.ge/
Rector: Lela Kelbakiani (2002-)
Tel: +995(99) 505956 EMail: rector@unik.edu.ge

Departments
Mathematics and Information Technology (Information Technology; Mathematics); **Economics** (Banking; Business Administration; Economics; Finance; International Economics; Law; Management; Taxation)

Faculties
Humanities (Arts and Humanities; English; French; German; History; Modern Languages; Philosophy; Religious Studies)
History: Founded 1991 as Kutaisi Institute of Law and Economics. Acquired present title 2010.
Academic Year: September to June
Admission Requirements: Examination held by National Assessment and Examination Centre
Main Language(s) of Instruction: Georgian
Accrediting Agencies: Ministry of Education and Science
Degrees and Diplomas: *Bakalavris Diplomi*: 4 yrs; *Magistris Diplomi*: 2 yrs; *Doktoris Diplomi*
Student Services: Academic counselling, Canteen, Cultural centre, Employment services, Health services, Language programs, Sports facilities
Student Residential Facilities: None
Libraries: Yes
Publications: Economic Profile *(quarterly)*
Last Updated: 08/02/12

PETRE SHOTADZE TBILISI MEDICAL ACADEMY
Petre Šotadzis Sakhelobis Tbilisis Samedicino Akademia (TMA)
Ketevan Tsamebuli Ave., 51/2, 0179 Tbilisi
Tel: +995(32) 291-2484
Fax: +995(32) 274-7134
EMail: tmac@caucasus.net
Website: http://www.tma.edu.ge
Head: Michael Tsverava

Faculties
Medicine (Anatomy; Cardiology; Dermatology; Ethics; Gynaecology and Obstetrics; Medicine; Physiology; Radiology; Rehabilitation and Therapy; Sports Medicine; Surgery; Virology); **Stomatology** (Dentistry; Stomatology)
History: Founded 1992. Acquired present title 1999.
Main Language(s) of Instruction: Georgian
Degrees and Diplomas: *Bakalavris Diplomi*; *Diplomirebuli Specialistis Diplomi*: 5 yrs; *Magistris Diplomi*; *Doktoris Diplomi*
Last Updated: 08/02/12

RVALI TEACHING UNIVERSITY
Saqartvelos Sastsavlo Universiteti 'Rvali'
3, Machabeli street, 3700 Rustavi, Kvemo Kartli
Tel: +995(34) 178-054
Fax: +995(34) 122-297
EMail: rvali@rvali.edu.ge
Website: http://www.rvali.edu.ge/

Rector: Gulkan Tsitskhvaia

Departments
Humanities (English; Literature)

Faculties
Social Sciences (Banking; Business Administration; Economics; Finance; Insurance; Law; Primary Education)
History: Founded 1995.
Main Language(s) of Instruction: Georgian
Degrees and Diplomas: *Bakalavris Diplomi; Magistris Diplomi*
Libraries: Yes
Last Updated: 13/02/12

SAKARTVELO UNIVERSITY
Universiteti Sakartvelo
1b, Guram Panjikidze Street, 0160 Tbilisi
Tel: +995(32) 374-098
Fax: +995(32) 384-072
EMail: unisak@internet.ge
Website: http://www.unisak.edu.ge

Rector: Irakly Gagoidze
Executive Director: Apziauri Nazi Tel: +995(32) 376-744

Departments
Business and Management *Head*: Antia Vkhtang; **Law** (Law) *Head*: Giorgi Amashukeli; **Medicine** *Head*: David Zhgenti
History: Founded 1992. Acquired present status 2000.
Academic Year: September to July
Fees: (US Dollars): 7,500-8,000 per annum
Main Language(s) of Instruction: Georgian and English
Accrediting Agencies: State Accreditation Service of Educational Institutions of Georgia
Degrees and Diplomas: *Bakalavris Diplomi; Magistris Diplomi.* Also Diploma 5-6 yrs. Diplomas awarded by this Institution are valid only if they were issued before the 2007-2008 academic year
Student Services: Academic counselling, Canteen, Cultural centre, Health services, Sports facilities
Libraries: Yes

SHOTA MESKHIA ZUGDIDI STATE TEACHING UNIVERSITY
Šota Meskia Zugdidis Sakhelmtsipo Sastsavlo Universiteti
Janašia 14, Zugdidi
Tel: +995(77) 419-041
EMail: zssuedu@gmail.com
Website: http://www.zssu.ge

Programmes
Business Administration (Business Administration; Management); **Law** (Law); **Pharmacy** (Pharmacy)
Main Language(s) of Instruction: Georgian
Degrees and Diplomas: *Bakalavris Diplomi; Magistris Diplomi; Doktoris Diplomi*
Last Updated: 17/12/09

ST. GRIGOL PERADZE TBILISI UNIVERSITY
Tsminda Grigol Peradzis Sakhelobis Tbilisis Universiteti
4, Jikia Street, Tbilisi
Tel: +995(321) 87107
EMail: p-tato@mail.ru
Website: http://www.gpstu.com

Programmes
Banking and Finance (Banking; Finance; Insurance); **Business and Management** (Business Administration; Business and Commerce; Management); **Journalism** (Journalism; Radio and Television Broadcasting); **Law**; **Modern Languages** (English; German; Modern Languages; Native Language); **Pedagogy**; **Pharmacy** (Pharmacy)
History: Founded 1991. Acquired present status 2002.
Degrees and Diplomas: *Bakalavris Diplomi; Magistris Diplomi; Doktoris Diplomi*
Last Updated: 16/12/09

SUKHISHVILI TEACHING UNIVERSITY
Sukhishvilis Universiteti
9, Tskinvali Highway, 1400 Gori, Shida Kartli
Tel: +995(270) 70557
Fax: +995(270) 72408
EMail: info@sukhishvilebi.edu.ge; sukhishvilebi@mail.ru
Website: http://www.sukhishvilebi.edu.ge

Rector: Valeri Z. Sukhishvili EMail: sukhishvilebi@mail.ru
International Relations: Zurab Chkhikvadze

Faculties
Business Administration and Management (Accountancy; Administration; Banking; Business Administration; Economics; Finance; Hotel Management; Information Technology; Insurance; Management; Marketing; Taxation; Tourism); **Law** (Law); **Public Health Care** (Agricultural Engineering; Analytical Chemistry; Biochemistry; Ecology; Forestry; Medicine; Oncology; Pathology; Pharmacology; Pharmacy; Physiology; Public Health; Toxicology)
History: Founded 1995 as a branch of the Georgian Agrarian Science Academy. Acquired present status and title 2003.
Main Language(s) of Instruction: Georgian
Degrees and Diplomas: *Bakalavris Diplomi; Magistris Diplomi; Doktoris Diplomi*
Last Updated: 16/02/12

TBILISI DAVID AGMASHENEBELI UNIVERSITY
Tbilisis Davit Agmašeneblis Sakhelobis Universiteti (TDASU)
38a, Saburtalo Street, 0194 Tbilisi
Tel: +995(32) 987-878 +995(32) 378-866
Fax: +995(32) 385-566 +995(32) 932-288
EMail: tdasutdasu@yahoo.com; tdasu@posta.ge
Website: http://www.tdasu.edu.ge

Rector: Anzor Šarašenidze (1992-) Tel: +995(99) 206-363
Quality Manager: Anzor Benidze
International Relations: Nino Patsatsia

Colleges
Tbilisi David Agmashenebeli College *Director*: Anna Mamatsašvili
History: Founded 1992.
Governing Bodies: Academic Council
Academic Year: September-June
Admission Requirements: Entrance Examination
Fees: (GEL): 2,500-2,800 per annum
Main Language(s) of Instruction: Georgian
International Co-operation: With universities in Vietnam; Russia; Armenia; Azerbaijan; Lithuania
Accrediting Agencies: State Accrediting Agency
Degrees and Diplomas: *Bakalavris Diplomi*: Stomatology, Pharmacy, Biological Medicine, Economics, Tax Law, Customs Law, Accounting, International Relations, 4 yrs; *Magistris Diplomi*: a further 2 yrs; *Doktoris Diplomi*
Student Services: Academic counselling, Canteen, Cultural centre, Language programs, Nursery care, Sports facilities
Student Residential Facilities: none
Special Facilities: Radio station
Libraries: c. 20,000 volumes

Academic Staff 2008-2009	MEN	WOMEN	TOTAL
FULL-TIME	24	48	72
STAFF WITH DOCTORATE			
FULL-TIME	24	48	72

Student Numbers 2008-2009			
All (Foreign Included)	165	516	681

Last Updated: 17/12/09

TBILISI HUMANITARIAN TEACHING UNIVERSITY

Tbilisis Humanitaruli Universiteti (THU)
3, Sandro Euli Street, 0186 Tbilisi
Tel: +995(32) 545-908
EMail: rector@thu.edu.ge
Website: http://www.thu.edu.ge

Rector: Valentina Sakvarlize

Faculties
Economics, Business and Administration (Business Administration; Economics; Management; Marketing); **Health Care** (Dentistry); **Humanities** (European Studies; History; Literature; Modern Languages; Philology; Slavic Languages); **Law** (Law; Private Law; Public Law)

History: Founded 1992.

Main Language(s) of Instruction: Georgian, Russian

Degrees and Diplomas: *Bakalavris Diplomi*; *Magistris Diplomi*; *Doktoris Diplomi*

Libraries: Yes
Last Updated: 16/02/12

TBILISI TEACHING UNIVERSITY

Tblilisis Universiteti
10, Jikia Street, 0156 Tbilisi
Tel: +995(32) 188-134
Fax: +995(32) 186-792
EMail: info@tbuniver.edu.ge
Website: http://www.tbuniver.edu.ge

Faculties
Economics and Law (Banking; Economics; Finance; Insurance; Law); **Health Care** (Public Health; Stomatology); **Humanities**

Main Language(s) of Instruction: Georgian

Degrees and Diplomas: *Bakalavris Diplomi*; *Magistris Diplomi*; *Doktoris Diplomi*
Last Updated: 26/11/09

TBILISI TEACHING UNIVERSITY OF INTERNATIONAL RELATIONS

Tbilisis Saertašoriso Urtiertobebis Universiteti
4, Jikia Street, 0177 Tbilisi
Tel: +995(32) 369-160
Fax: +995(32) 366-165
EMail: contact@tsuu.edu.ge
Website: http://tsuu.edu.ge

Faculties
Business and Management (Banking; Business Administration; Business and Commerce; Finance; Insurance; Management); **Humanities** (English; Literature); **Law** (Criminal Law; Law; Private Law)

History: Founded 19911 from the Academy of Science of Georgia and the Institute of Law Psychology. Acquired present title 1999.

Main Language(s) of Instruction: Georgian

Degrees and Diplomas: *Bakalavris Diplomi*; *Magistris Diplomi*; *Doktoris Diplomi*
Last Updated: 14/02/12

TBILISI UNIVERSITY METEKHI

Tbilisis Saero Universiteti 'Metekhi'
23, Bochorma Street, 0144 Tbilisi
Tel: +995(32) 748-595 +995(32) 748-610
Fax: +995(32) 748-595
EMail: int@metekhiuni.edu.ge
Website: http://metekhiuni.edu.ge/

Rector: Manon Kirtbaia
Tel: +995(32) 223-504 **EMail:** manon@metekhiuni.edu.ge
International Relations: Maka Khvedelidze, International Programmes Manager **EMail:** maka@metekhiuni.edu.ge

Faculties
Business and Management (Banking; Business Administration; Finance; International Business; International Economics; Taxation; Tourism); **Health Care** (Dentistry; Medicine; Pharmacy); **Humanities and Social Sciences** (English; German; Journalism; Native Language; Primary Education); **Law** (Criminal Law; Law; Private Law; Public Law)

History: Founded 2002.

Main Language(s) of Instruction: Georgian

Degrees and Diplomas: *Bakalavris Diplomi*: 4 yrs; *Magistris Diplomi*: a further 2 yrs; *Doktoris Diplomi*

Libraries: Yes.
Last Updated: 14/02/12

TEACHING UNIVERSITY OF INTERNATIONAL RELATIONS OF GEORGIA

Saqartvelos Sagadasaskhado Sabazho Akademia
20, Rustavi Highway, Tbilisi
Tel: +995(32) 402-947
EMail: ssuu_university@yahoo.com
Website: http://ssuu.edu.ge/indexe.html

Faculties
Law (Law); **Social Sciences and Business** (Accountancy; Business Administration; Business and Commerce; Economics; International Economics; International Relations; Taxation)

History: Established 2002 as Customs Academy of Georgia. Acquired present title 2003.

Main Language(s) of Instruction: Georgian

Degrees and Diplomas: *Bakalavris Diplomi*; *Magistris Diplomi*; *Doktoris Diplomi*
Last Updated: 09/02/12

THE UNIVERSITY OF GEORGIA

M. Kostava str. 77, 0161 Tbilisi
Tel: +995(32) 364-665
EMail: ug@ug.edu.ge
Website: http://www.ug.edu.ge

Rector: Manana Sanadze **EMail:** msanadze@ug.edu.ge

Schools
Business and Economics (Business Administration; Business and Commerce; Economics); **Humanities** (Anthropology; Art History; English; German; History; Italian); **Law** (Criminology; Law); **Mathematics and Informatics** (Mathematics and Computer Science; Statistics); **Public Health** (Health Administration; Public Health); **Social Sciences** (Advertising and Publicity; International Relations; Journalism; Media Studies; Political Sciences; Public Relations)

History: Founded 2004 as Georgian University of Social Sciences.

Main Language(s) of Instruction: Georgian

Degrees and Diplomas: *Bakalavris Diplomi*; *Magistris Diplomi*; *Doktoris Diplomi*

Libraries: Yes
Last Updated: 14/02/12

ZUGDIDI TEACHING UNIVERSITY

Zugdidis Damoukidebeli Universiteti
1, University Street, 2100 Zugdidi
Tel: +995(821) 552-012
Fax: +995(821) 552-011
EMail: zdu@gol.ge
Website: http://www.zdu.edu.ge

Faculties
Business Administration (Business Administration); **Dentistry** (Dentistry); **Tourism** (Tourism)

Main Language(s) of Instruction: Georgian, German

Degrees and Diplomas: *Bakalavris Diplomi*; *Magistris Diplomi*
Last Updated: 14/02/12

Germany

STRUCTURE OF HIGHER EDUCATION SYSTEM

Description:

There are public and private state-recognized institutions of higher education categorized as: 1. universities (Universitäten) and equivalent higher education institutions (Technische Hochschulen/Technische Universitäten, Pädagogische Hochschulen); 2. colleges of art and music (Kunsthochschulen and Musikhochschulen); 3. Fachhochschulen (universities of applied sciences) and Verwaltungsfachhochschulen. Since the early 1990s, the structure of higher education study courses and the internal organization have been the subject of reform. This has involved a review of the standard periods of study and examination requirements and improvements in teaching and a separation of study aimed at preparing students for the practice of a profession and the qualification of a new generation of academics and scientists. One priority is to expand Fachhochschulen and consolidate applied research and technology transfer. With the amendments of the Framework Act for Higher Education of the Federal Government of 1998 and 2002, the Länder dispose of greater scope for their own decisions and have already carried out reforms accordingly by amending their laws on higher education. Higher education institutions are to be made more efficient by granting them further autonomy, allowing them to build an individual profile in a particular area and encouraging more competition. Further reforms concerning the staff structure and recruitment requirements for professors were introduced through the Act's amendment in 2002.

An alternative to HE institutions is provided by Berufsakademien. These professional academies have taken the principle of the dual system of vocational education and training and applied it to the tertiary sector. The qualifications they award are recognized as tertiary sector qualifications that fall under the EU directive on higher education degrees by a resolution of the Standing Conference of the Ministers of Education and Cultural Affairs of the Länder of 29 September 1995, provided that they satisfy certain criteria (entrance requirements, qualifications of the teaching staff, institutional requirements).

Stages of studies:

University level first stage:
Fachhochschulen (universities of applied sciences): offer application-oriented study courses mainly in engineering, economics, social work, public and legal administration and health and therapy. A Diplomgrad (Diplom degree) is awarded after the Diplomprüfung (Diploma examination), e.g. Diplom-Ingenieur (FH). The initials "FH" are added to the Diplom degrees of the Fachhochschulen. According to the Regelstudienzeit (standard period defined for each period of study), a degree programme at Fachhochschulen should be completed in 8 semesters (2 semesters = 1 academic year), including one or two practical semesters. Success in the final academic examination usually qualifies the candidate for a particular profession. Some Fachhochschulen have adopted a similar approach to the Berufsakademien, particularly in engineering and business management and have introduced courses that combine academic studies with on-the-job training, along the lines of a dual system. These courses are called dual courses of study (duale Studiengänge). The students have training or employment contracts. Fachhochschulen also confer Bachelor's and Master's degrees. The new graduation system introduced in 1998 supplements the traditional Diplomgrad conferred by the Fachhochschulen. For courses with a more theoretical orientation the Bachelor/Master of Arts or Bachelor/Master of Science is awarded. In the case of study courses that are more application oriented the actual degree has a subject-related supplement (e.g. Bachelor/Master of Engineering).

Universities: Stage I, or basic studies (Grundstudium), usually lasting four semesters (2 academic years) at universities culminate in an intermediate examination (Diplom-Vorprüfung, Zwischenprüfung). This examination gives the right to continue in Stage II (Hauptstudium). A degree is not awarded. Since 1998, a basic higher education degree within the new graduation system of consecutive study courses, the Bachelor (or Baccalaureus) has also been introduced in universities requiring a minimum of three years' study (maximum four years). It normally leads to a career.

University level second stage: Hauptstudium
Stage II consists of more advanced studies (Hauptstudium) leading to the final degree examination. The Hauptstudium usually lasts for five more semesters and leads to the award of the Diplom. The Magister is awarded by universities, predominantly in the arts, on the basis of the Magister examination. The course of study

comprises either two equally weighted major subjects or a combination of one major and two minor subjects. As a first degree, the Magister is usually awarded as a Magister Artium/MA without specifying individual subjects. The Magistergrad can also be awarded at the end of one or two years' postgraduate studies following upon the acquisition of a first degree. Within the new graduation system of consecutive courses leading to a BA/BSc after three to four years, a Master of Arts/Science may be acquired after another one to two years.

University level third stage: *Promotion*

Doctoral studies are only pursued in universities (Universitäten). There are several procedures for admitting particularly qualified holders of a degree obtained at a Fachhochschule to doctoral studies at universities. The period of doctoral studies, known as the Promotion, consists of two to four years' independent research and the submission of a thesis following the award of the Diplom/Erstes Staatsexamen/Magister Artium/Master of Arts/ Science. The title of Doktor is conferred following upon a written thesis and either an oral examination or the defence of a thesis. The Habilitation is a post-doctoral qualification proving ability to teach and engage in research in an academic subject. It is awarded by the departments of universities and equivalent higher education institutions, usually on the basis of a post-doctoral thesis and a public lecture followed by a discussion. Following the amendment of the Framework Act for Higher Education in 2002, the Habilitation will be phased out as a recruitment requirement for professors.

Distance higher education:

Courses leading to a Diplom and Magister, as well as to Bachelor's and Master's degrees are offered by the Fernuniversität Hagen, distance Fachhochschulen and a number of institutions. Distance learning associations have been set up at Fachhochschulen in a number of regions. In addition, an association of private, state-recognized institutions offer first degree and post-graduate courses at university level to employed persons (Hochschulen für Berufstätige) in several study locations. The courses offered by the "AKAD. Die Privat-Hochschulen" are mainly in the field of business/economics and languages/translating.

ADMISSION TO HIGHER EDUCATION

Admission to university-level studies:

Name of secondary school credential required: Hochschulreife/Abitur

For entry to: All programmes.

Name of secondary school credential required: Fachgebundene Hochschulreife

For entry to: Subject-restricted programmes.

Name of secondary school credential required: Fachhochschulreife

For entry to: All types of programmes at Fachhochschulen.

Alternatives to credentials: Interview, test grades, aptitude test, temporary registration for a trial study period. Completion of evening courses by employed adults or day school courses for pupils with work experience at Kollegs who hold a Nichtschülerprüfung (school examination for external candidates) or a Begabtenprüfung (examination for gifted working applicants).

Numerus clausus/restrictions: There is a numerus clausus in certain subjects: e.g. medicine, veterinary medicine, dentistry, biology, psychology and pharmacy. Such courses may differ from one semester to the nExt. Places for these courses are allocated through a central selection procedure (see www.zvs.de). Courses outside the national selection procedure may be subject to local selection procedures at certain higher education institutions on criteria such as average mark in the higher education entrance examination, the waiting period and social criteria.

Foreign students admission:

Entrance exam requirements: Access to higher education programmes in Germany is granted to holders of foreign higher education entrance qualifications regarded as comparable to the German Abitur.

Entry regulations: Students from non-EU countries must apply for a residence permit (Aufenthaltsgenehmigung) before the applicant/student visa (usually granted for three months) expires. A residence permit for the purpose of studying is initially issued for a period of two years, but can be extended by a further two years, subject to appropriate academic progress.

Health requirements: Students need to have proof of health insurance recognized in Germany before they begin studying. Students are eligible for health insurance at a discounted student rate.

Language requirements: Good knowledge of German is essential. Students have to demonstrate a satisfactory knowledge of German as evidenced by the Deutsche Sprachdiplom Stufe II (DSD II) or equivalent. Most universities offer German courses for foreign students. Some universities offer international study programmes in English.

RECOGNITION OF STUDIES

Quality assurance system:

In order to guarantee the equivalence of academic degrees and enable students to move freely between higher education institutions, the Association of Universities and other Higher Education Institutions in Germany and the Standing Conference of Ministers of Education and Cultural Affairs of the Länder agree on general conditions for academic examinations (Diplom exams at universities and Fachhochschulen and Magister exams). For individual courses these are then complemented by framework examination regulations (Diplom exams) or by conditions specific to the subject (Magister exams).

Courses leading to Bachelor's or Master's degrees are regulated by the Standing Conference's agreement on Structural Requirements. Depending on the Land law, these courses may be or have to be accredited by an accreditation agency that must be accredited by the national accreditation council (Akkreditierungsrat) founded in 1998. The objective of the accreditation is to guarantee minimum standards in terms of academic content and to check the vocational relevance of the degrees.

HEIs are competent for the academic recognition of foreign degrees/certificates/diplomas for academic purposes (i.e. further studies). Public authorities (i.e. DG for non-compulsory education and scientific research) are competent for the academic recognition of foreign degrees/certificates/diplomas for professional purposes (i.e. use of the academic degree on the labor market).

Bodies dealing with recognition:

Zentralstelle für ausländisches Bildungswesen (ENIC/NARIC) (Central Office for Foreign Education (ENIC/NARIC Centre))

> Head: Barbara Buchal-Hoever
> PO Box 2240
> Bonn 53012
> Tel: +49 228 501 264
> Fax: +49 228 501 229
> EMail: zab@kmk.org
> WWW: http://www.kmk.org/zab/unsere-aufgaben/enic-naric.html

NATIONAL BODIES

Bundesministerium für Bildung und Forschung - Bonn (Federal Ministry of Education and Research - Bonn Office)

> Minister: Annette Schavan
> Head, Science System: Ulrich Schüller
> Heinemannstrasse 2
> Bonn 53175
> Tel: +49 22899 57-0
> Fax: +49 28899 57-83601
> EMail: bmbf@bmbf.bund.de
> WWW: http://www.bmbf.de

Bundesministerium für Bildung und Forschung - Berlin (Federal Ministry of Education and Research - Berlin Office)

> Hannoversche Strasse 30
> Berlin 10115
> Tel: +49 3018 57-0
> Fax: +49 3018 57-83601
> EMail: bmbf@bmbf.bund.de
> WWW: http://www.bmbf.de

Kultusministerkonferenz - Bonn (Standing Conference of the Ministers of Education and Cultural Affairs of the Länder)
President: Bernd Althusmann
Secretary-General: Udo Michallik
Graurheindorfer Str. 157
Postfach 2240
Bonn 53012
Tel: +49 228 501-0
Fax: +49 228 501 777
WWW: http://www.kmk.org
Role of national body: To unite the ministers and senators of the Länder responsible for school education, higher education, research and cultural affairs in order to present a common viewpoint and a common will as representing common interests. It is based on an agreement between the Länder.

Kultusministerkonferenz - Berlin (Standing Conference of Ministers of Education and Cultural Affairs of the Länder)
Taubenstraße 10
Berlin 10117
Tel: +49 30 25418-3
Fax: +49 30 25418-450

Hochschulrektorenkonferenz - HRK (German Rectors' Conference)
President: Margret Wintermantel
Secretary-General: Thomas Kathöfer
Ahrstrasse 39
Bonn 53175
Tel: +49 228 887-0
Fax: +49 228 887-110
WWW: http://www.hrk.de
Role of national body: To deal with questions relating to research, teaching and extension; to represent public and private state-recognized higher education institutions in Germany.

Gemeinsame Wissenschaftskonferenz (Joint Science Conference)
Secretary-General: Hans-Gerhard Husung
Friedrich-Ebert-Allee 38
Bonn 53113
Tel: +49 228 54020
Fax: +49 228 5402150
EMail: gwk@gwk-bonn.de
WWW: http://www.gwk-bonn.de
Role of national body: Deals with research funding and research policy strategies.

Deutscher Akademischer Austauschdienst - DAAD (German Academic Exchange Service)
President: Margret Wintermantel
Secretary-General: Dorothea Rüland
Kennedyallee 50
Bonn 53175
Tel: +49 228 882-0
Fax: +49 228 882-444
EMail: postmaster@daad.de
WWW: http://www.daad.de
Role of national body: Funding organisation supporting the international exchange of students and scholars.

Deutscher Hochschulverband - DHV (German Association of University Professors and Lecturers)
President: Bernhard Kempen
Rheinallee 18
Bonn 53173

Tel: +49 228 902 66-17
Fax: +49 228 902 66-80
EMail: dhv@hochschulverband.de
WWW: http://www.hochschulverband.de/cms/

Akkreditierungsrat (Accreditation Council)

Chairman: Reinhold R Grimm
Managing Director: Achim Hopbach
Adenauerallee 73
Bonn 53113
Tel: +49 228 338 306-0
Fax: +49 228 338 306-79
EMail: akr@akkreditierungsrat.de
WWW: http://www.akkreditierungsrat.de

Role of national body: The Association of Universities and other Higher Education Institutions in Germany (HRK) and the Standing Conference of Ministers of Education and Cultural Affairs of the Länder in the Federal Republic of Germany (KMK) established the Akkreditierungsrat for the purpose of providing accreditation services. The Akkreditierungsrat is responsible for the establishment of comparable quality standards for Bachelor's and Master's degree courses in an essential decentralised accreditation process which will be carried out by accreditation agencies. The Akkreditierungsrat performs these responsibilities by accrediting, coordinating and monitoring these agencies.

Universität Bayern e.V. (Association of Bavarian Universities)

Chairman: Godehard Ruppert
CEO: Ines Young
Seitzstrasse 5
München 80538
Tel: +49 89 2101 9940
Fax: +49 89 2101 9941
EMail: info@unibayern.de
WWW: http://www.unibayern.de

Role of national body: This regional association of institutions has for its mission to provide support to the state and the community by using its member institutions to further develop the Bavarian research landscape.

Data for academic year: 2008-2009
Source: IAU from Leiterin der Zentralstelle für ausländisches Bildungswesen Kultusministerkonferenz, 2008 (Bodies and Quality assurance, 2011)

INSTITUTIONS

AACHEN UNIVERSITY OF APPLIED SCIENCES

Fachhochschule Aachen (ACUAS)
Kalverbenden 6, 52066 Aachen
Tel: +49(241) 6009-51001
Fax: +49(241) 6009-51090
EMail: info@fh-aachen.de
Website: http://www.fh-aachen.de

Rektor: Marcus Baumann
Tel: +49(241) 6009-51000, Fax: +49(241) 6009-51065
EMail: rektor@fh-aachen.de

Kanzler: Reiner Smeetz
Tel: +49(241) 6009-51005, Fax: +49(241) 6009-51012
EMail: kanzler@fh-aachen.de

Departments

Aerospace Technology (Aeronautical and Aerospace Engineering; Astronomy and Space Science; Automotive Engineering; Electronic Engineering; Mechanical Engineering); **Architecture** (Architecture; Regional Planning; Town Planning); **Business** (Business and Commerce; International Business); **Chemistry and Biotechnology** (Applied Chemistry; Biotechnology; Chemistry; Polymer and Plastics Technology); **Civil Engineering** (Civil Engineering; Construction Engineering; Structural Architecture; Transport Engineering; Waste Management; Water Management); **Design** (Communication Arts; Design; Industrial Design; Interior Design; Media Studies; Visual Arts); **Electrical Engineering and Information Technology** (Computer Science; Electrical Engineering; Electronic Engineering; Information Technology; Multimedia; Telecommunications Engineering); **Energy Technology** (Electrical Engineering; Energy Engineering; Environmental Engineering; Mechanical Engineering; Physical Engineering); **Mechanical Engineering and Mechatronics** (Business Administration; Electronic Engineering; Machine Building; Mechanical Engineering); **Medical Technology and Technomathemacis** (Biomedical Engineering; Computer Science; Mathematics and Computer Science; Medical Technology)

History: Founded as University of Applied Science in 1971 out of four colleges dating back to the beginning of the 20th century. Acquired university status in 1976.

Governing Bodies: Rectorate; Senate

Academic Year: September-February; March-July

Admission Requirements: Allgemeine Hochschulreife (Abitur), Fachhochschulreife (Fachabitur). Basic three-month internship for most courses. Language certificate for international degree courses and artistic qualification for Design

Fees: None for first degree courses

Main Language(s) of Instruction: German, English

International Co-operation: Participates in most EU programmes

Accrediting Agencies: Ministry of Science and Research North-Rhine Westphalia. Special accreditation agencies for the BEng and MSc courses

Degrees and Diplomas: *Bachelor/Bakkalaureus*: Applied Chemistry; Architecture; Civil Engineering; Biomedical Engineering; Biotechnology; Communication and Multimedia Design; Electrical Engineering; Electrical Egineering; Automotive Integration/Body Technology; Informatics; Business Studies; Business Studies/Anglophone Countries; Business Studies/German-French; European Business Studies; Communication Design; Aircraft and Aerospace Technology; Mechanical Engineering; Mechatronics; Physical Engineering; Process Technology; Product Design; Scientific Programming, 3-3 1/2 yrs; *Master/Magister*: Aerospace Engineering; Applied Polymer Science; Automotive Vehicle Integration; Biomedical Engineering.; Civil Engineering.; Energy Systems; Entrepreneurship; Facility-Management; International Business Management;, 2 yrs following upon Bachelor; *Master/Magister*: Mechatronics; Nuclear Applications; Service-Management

Student Services: Academic counselling, Canteen, Employment services, Foreign student adviser, Foreign Studies Centre, Handicapped facilities, Language programs, Social counselling, Sports facilities

Special Facilities: Solar Research Centre

Libraries: One central library and four department libraries
Last Updated: 06/02/12

AALEN UNIVERSITY
Hochschule Aalen
PO Box 1728, Beethovenstrasse 1, 73430 Aalen
Tel: +49(7361) 576-0
Fax: +49(7361) 576-2250
EMail: info@htw-aalen.de
Website: http://www.fh-aalen.de

Rektor: Gerhard Schneider
Tel: +49(7361) 576-101, Fax: +49(7361) 576-329
EMail: Gerhard.Schneider@fh-aalen.de

Verwaltungsdirektor: Heinz Kistner
Tel: +49(7361) 576-2120, Fax: +49(7361) 576-2297
EMail: Kistner@vw.htw-aalen.de

International Relations: Pascal Cromm, Head, Office of International Affairs
Tel: +49(7361) 576-2125, Fax: +49(7361) 576-2136
EMail: Pascal.Cromm@htw-aalen.de

Faculties
Business Administration (Business Administration; Engineering; Health Administration; International Business; Management; Small Business); **Chemistry** (Analytical Chemistry; Chemistry; Molecular Biology); **Electronics and Informatics** (Automation and Control Engineering; Computer Science; Electronic Engineering; Information Technology); **Machine Building and Materials Engineering** (Machine Building; Materials Engineering); **Optics and Mechatronics** (Optics)

History: Founded 1962.

Main Language(s) of Instruction: German

Degrees and Diplomas: *Bachelor/Bakkalaureus*; *Master/Magister*
Last Updated: 01/02/12

ACADEMY OF FINE ARTS DRESDEN
Hochschule für Bildende Künste Dresden
Postfach 160 153, 01287 Dresden
Tel: +49(351) 440-20
Fax: +49(351) 459-0025
EMail: post@serv1.hfbk-dresden.de
Website: http://www.hfbk-dresden.de

Rektor: Christian Sery
Tel: +49(351) 492-6715, Fax: +49(351) 495-2023
EMail: rektor@serv1.hfbk-dresden.de

Kanzler: Hans-Jürgen Schönemann
Tel: +49(351) 440-2146 EMail: kanzler@serv1.hfbk-dresden.de

Programmes
Acting and Theatre Costumes (Theatre); **Art Therapy** (Art Therapy); **Fine Arts and Visual Arts** (Fine Arts; Visual Arts); **Restoration and Conservation** (Heritage Preservation; Restoration of Works of Art); **Theatre Equipment** (Theatre)

History: Founded 1764.

Academic Year: October to April; April to September

Admission Requirements: Portfolio and entrance examination

Main Language(s) of Instruction: German

Degrees and Diplomas: *Diplom*: 5 yrs; *Diplom*: Art Therapy, 2 yrs; *Diplom*: Theatre Décor, 4 yrs

Special Facilities: Art Gallery
Last Updated: 01/02/12

ACADEMY OF FINE ARTS MUNICH
Akademie der Bildenden Künste München
Akademiestrasse 2, 80799 München
Tel: +49(89) 3852-0
Fax: +49(89) 3852-206
EMail: post@adbk.mhn.de
Website: http://www.adbk.mhn.de

Präsident: Nikolaus Gerhart
Tel: +49(89) 3852-104, Fax: +49(89) 3852-203
EMail: rektorat@adbk.mhn.de

Kanzlerin: Corinna Deschauer
Tel: +49(89) 3852-102 EMail: sekretariat@adbk.mhn.de

International Relations: Herta Grill

Courses
Fine Arts (Architecture; Art Education; Art Therapy; Ceramic Art; Fine Arts; Glass Art; Graphic Arts; Interior Design; Painting and Drawing; Photography; Sculpture)

History: Founded 1808.

Degrees and Diplomas: *Diplom*; *Lehramt*. Also Postgraduate Degree (Aufbaustudiengang)
Last Updated: 06/02/12

ACADEMY OF FINE ARTS MÜNSTER
Kunstakademie Münster - Hochschule für Bildende Künste
Leonardo-Campus 2, 48149 Münster
Tel: +49(251) 83-61330
EMail: kunstakademie@muenster.de
Website: http://www.kunstakademie-muenster.de

Rektor: Maik Löbbert (2005-)
Tel: +49(251) 8361-330, Fax: +49(251) 8361-430
EMail: rektorat@kunstakademie-muenster.de

Kanzler: Frank Bartsch
EMail: bartsch@kunstakademie-muenster.de

Programmes
Fine Arts (Art Education; Fine Arts; Media Studies; Painting and Drawing; Performing Arts; Photography; Sculpture; Video); **Teachers Training** (Art Education; Teacher Training)

History: Founded 1972. Acquired present status 1987.

Admission Requirements: Abitur and artistic aptitude test

Main Language(s) of Instruction: German

International Co-operation: Participates in Erasmus

Degrees and Diplomas: *Diplom*: 4 1/2 yrs; *Staatsprüfung*; *Promotion*; *Doktorgrad*

Student Services: Academic counselling, Canteen, Cultural centre, Foreign student adviser, Language programs, Social counselling, Sports facilities

Special Facilities: Exhibition halls. Movie studio. Workshops

Libraries: Yes

Last Updated: 21/01/10

ACADEMY OF MEDIA ARTS COLOGNE
Kunsthochschule für Medien Köln
Peter-Welter-Platz 2, 50676 Köln, Nordrhein-Westfalen
Tel: +49(221) 20189-0
Fax: +49(221) 20189-17
EMail: studoffice@khm.de
Website: http://www.khm.de

Rektor: Klaus Jung
Tel: +49(221) 20189-111 EMail: rektor@khm.de

Kanzlerin: Sabine Schulz
Tel: +49(221) 20189-116 EMail: kanzlerin@khm.de

International Relations: Andreas Altenhoff
Tel: +49(221) 20189-126 EMail: andreas@khm.de

Divisions
Artistic and Media Studies (Film; Painting and Drawing; Performing Arts; Photography; Video); Film (Display and Stage Design; Film); Media Design (Design; Media Studies); Media Studies (Aesthetics; Art Education; Computer Science; Information Sciences; Mass Communication; Media Studies; Music)

History: Founded 1990.

Main Language(s) of Instruction: German

Degrees and Diplomas: *Diplom*; *Promotion*. Also Postgraduate programmes, 4 yrs
Last Updated: 21/01/10

ACADEMY OF MUSIC HANNS EISLER BERLIN
Hochschule für Musik Hanns Eisler Berlin
Charlottenstrasse 55, 10117 Berlin
Tel: +49(30) 688305-700
Fax: +49(30) 688305-701
EMail: rektorat.hfm@berlin.de
Website: http://www.hfm-berlin.de

Rektor: Jörg-Peter Weigle (2008-)
Tel: +49(30) 688305-800, Fax: +49(30) 688305-801
EMail: rektorat@hfm.in-berlin.de

Kanzler: Hans-Joachim Völz
Tel: +49(30) 688305-802, Fax: +49(30) 688305-701
EMail: fischer_waltraud@hfm.in-berlin.de

International Relations: Ute Schmidt, International Affairs Officer
Tel: +49(30) 688305-831, Fax: +49(30) 688305-730
EMail: auslandsinfo.hfm@berlin.de; schmidt_ute@hfm.in-berlin.de

Centres
Continuing Education

Departments
Brass and Woodwind, Percussion, Conducting, Piano Accompaniment and Coaching (Conducting; Musical Instruments); Piano, Accordion, Composition, Harmony and Musicology (Music Theory and Composition; Musical Instruments; Musicology); Strings, Harp and Guitar (Musical Instruments); Voice, Music Theatre and Stage Direction (Music; Singing; Theatre)

Institutes
Jazz *(Berlin)* (Jazz and Popular Music); Musicians' Health *(Kurt Singer)* (Health Sciences; Music; Physiology); New Music *(klangzeitort)* (Music)

History: Founded 1950. Acquired present title 1964.

Governing Bodies: Senate

Academic Year: October to july (October-February; April-July)

Admission Requirements: Entrance examination and special entrance qualification for each course

Fees: (Euros): c. 90 per semester

Main Language(s) of Instruction: German

International Co-operation: With universities in Austria; Denmark; Finland; France; United Kingdom; Hungary; Canada; Sweden; Norway; USA.

Degrees and Diplomas: *Zertifikat*: 2-2 1/2 yrs; *Diplom*: 8-12 sem.; *Diplom*: 4-6 yrs; *Master/Magister*

Student Services: Academic counselling, Canteen, Employment services, Foreign student adviser, Language programs, Social counselling, Sports facilities

Special Facilities: Electro acoustic music Studio, Recording Studio, Video Studio

Libraries: Music Library
Last Updated: 19/01/10

ACADEMY OF MUSIC, DETMOLD
Hochschule für Musik Detmold
Willi-Hofmann-Straße 5, 32756 Detmold
Tel: +49(5231) 975-5
Fax: +49(5231) 975-972
EMail: info@hfm-detmold.de
Website: http://www.hfm-detmold.de

Rektor: Martin Christian Vogel
Tel: +49(5231) 975-601, Fax: +49(5231) 975-604
EMail: rektor@hfm-detmold.de

Kanzler: Hans Bertels
Tel: +49(5231) 975-700 EMail: kanzler@hfm-detmold.de

International Relations: Rainer Peters, Head, International Office
Tel: +49(5231) 975-773, Fax: +49(5231) 975-754
EMail: peters@hfm-detmold.de

Programmes
Chamber Music (Music); Choir and Orchestra Conducting (Conducting; Singing); Church Music (Religious Music); Composition (Music Theory and Composition); Conducting (Conducting); Free-Lance Musician (Music); Music (Music); Music and Sound Recording (Music; Sound Engineering (Acoustics)); Music Education (Music Education); Music Teaching *(Lehramt)* (Music Education); Music Teaching and Musical Instruments and Singing (Music Education; Musical Instruments; Singing); Musical Instruments and Singing (Musical Instruments; Singing); Musical Instruments and Singing Education (Music Education; Musical Instruments; Singing); Musical Mediation/Concert Pedagogy (Conducting; Music; Music Theory and Composition); Musical Theater and Opera (Music; Opera; Theatre); Musical Theory (Music Theory and Composition); New Music (Music); Opera/Concert (Music; Opera); Orchestra (Conducting; Music); Orchestral Musician (Music); Piano Chamber Music and Accompanying (Music)

History: Founded 1947.

Admission Requirements: Secondary school certificate and qualification examination

Main Language(s) of Instruction: German

International Co-operation: Participates in Socrates-Erasmus programme

Degrees and Diplomas: *Bachelor/Bakkalaureus*; *Diplom*; *Staatsprüfung*; *Master/Magister*; *Promotion*. Also Certificate
Last Updated: 19/01/10

ACADEMY OF VISUAL ARTS LEIPZIG
Hochschule für Grafik und Buchkunst Leipzig
Wächerstrasse 11, 04107 Leipzig
Tel: +49(341) 2135-0
Fax: +49(341) 2135-166
EMail: hgb@hgb-leipzig.de
Website: http://www.hgb-leipzig.de

Rektor: Joachim Brohm
Tel: +49(341) 2135-155, Fax: +49(341) 9604-331
EMail: rektor@hgb-leipzig.de

Kanzlerin: Maria-Cornelia Ziesch
Tel: +49(341) 2135-159 EMail: kanzler@hgb-leipzig.de

International Relations: Frances Kind EMail: aaa@hgb-leipzig.de

Institutes
Book Design/Graphic Design (Graphic Design; Printing and Printmaking)

Programmes
Media Art (Media Studies); **Painting/Graphic Art** (Graphic Arts; Painting and Drawing); **Photography** (Photography)

History: Founded 1763.

Main Language(s) of Instruction: German

Degrees and Diplomas: *Diplom*. Postgraduate "Meisterschüler" programme
Last Updated: 03/02/10

ACCADIS BAD HOMBURG UNIVERSITY OF APPLIED SCIENCE
Accadis Hochschule Bad Homburg
Du Pont-Straße 4, 61352 Bad Homburg, Hesse
Tel: +49(6172) 9842-0
Fax: +49(6172) 9842-20
EMail: info@accadis.com
Website: http://www.accadis.com

President: Werner Meissner (2004-)
EMail: w.meissner@accadis.com

Managing Partner: Gerda Meinl-Kexel
EMail: g.meinl@accadis.com

International Relations: Britta Laudon-Reece, Head of International Programmes

Programmes
International Business Administration (Business Administration; Communication Studies; Health Administration; International Business; Marketing; Media Studies; Sales Techniques; Sports Management; Tourism; Transport Management); **Management** (Management; Tourism)

History: Created 1990 as International Business School Bad Homburg; 2001 added cooperative programmes with local businesses. Acquired current title and status 2004.

Governing Bodies: University Senate

Academic Year: October to August

Admission Requirements: Abitur or equivalent university entry qualification; proficiency in German and English; personality and intelligence structure test.

Fees: (Euro): Undergraduate, 22,000 (total cost); Postgraduate, 17,500 (total cost)

Main Language(s) of Instruction: German, English

International Co-operation: With institutions in UK; USA; France; Netherlands; Spain; South Africa

Accrediting Agencies: Foundation for International Business Administration Accreditation, Germany (FIBAA)

Degrees and Diplomas: *Bachelor/Bakkalaureus*: Business Communication (Bachelor of Arts); International Business Administration: (Business Consulting; China Management; Health Care Management; Logistics Management; Marketing – Media & Communication; Tourism Management) (Bachelor of Arts); International Sports Management (Bachelor of Arts), 3 yrs; *Master/Magister*: International Management; Business Administration, a further 1.5-2 yrs

Student Services: Academic counselling, Employment services, Foreign student adviser, Language programs, Social counselling

Libraries: c. 1,700 vols; Online access in library to "MegaWorld" and "LexisNexis" as well as e-book and e-journal database of the Frankfurt Goethe University; residential use of the Frankfurt Universitätsbibliothek and Deutsche Bibliothek Frankfurt.
Last Updated: 06/02/12

AKAD UNIVERSITY OF APPLIED SCIENCES LAHR
Wissenschaftliche Hochschule Lahr (WHL)
Hohbergweg 15-17, 77933 Lahr
Tel: +49(7821) 9238-50
Fax: +49(7821) 9238-52
EMail: info@whl-lahr.de
Website: http://www.whl-lahr.de

Rektor: Martin Reckenfelderbäumer
EMail: martin.reckenfelderbaeumer@whl-lahr.de

Programmes
Business Administration; **Clinical Research Management** (Management); **Finance and Banking** (Banking; Finance); **Management** (Management)

Main Language(s) of Instruction: German

Degrees and Diplomas: *Bachelor/Bakkalaureus*; *Diplom (FH)*; *Master/Magister*
Last Updated: 03/02/10

AKAD UNIVERSITY OF APPLIED SCIENCES LEIPZIG
AKAD Fachhochschule Leipzig
Gutenbergplatz 1E, 04103 Leipzig
Tel: +49(341) 226193-0
Fax: +49(341) 226193-9
EMail: akad-leipzig@akad.de
Website: http://www.akad.de/Hochschule-Leipzig.156.0.html

Rektor: Hans-Christian Brauweiler

Programmes
Business Administration (Business Administration); **Business Computing**; **Business Engineering**; **Business Translation** (Business Administration; Translation and Interpretation); **Finance and Banking**; **International Business Communication**; **Machine Building** (Machine Building); **Management** (Management)

History: Founded 1992.

Degrees and Diplomas: *Bachelor/Bakkalaureus*; *Diplom (FH)*; *Master/Magister*
Last Updated: 22/03/11

AKAD UNIVERSITY OF APPLIED SCIENCES PINNEBERG
AKAD Hochschule Pinneberg
Am Rathaus 10, 25421 Pinneberg
Tel: +49(4101) 8558-0
Fax: +49(4101) 8558-55
EMail: akad-pinneberg@akad.de
Website: http://www.akad.de/Hochschule-Pinneberg.154.0.html

Rektor: Lukas Beyer

Prorektor: Wolfgang Bohlen

Programmes
Business Administration; **Business Computing** (Business Computing); **Business Engineering**; **Business Translation** (Business Administration; Translation and Interpretation); **Finance and Banking** (Banking; Finance); **International Business Communication** (Communication Studies; International Business); **Machine Building**

Degrees and Diplomas: *Bachelor/Bakkalaureus*; *Diplom (FH)*; *Master/Magister*
Last Updated: 22/03/11

AKAD UNIVERSITY OF APPLIED SCIENCES STUTTGART
AKAD Hochschule Stuttgart
Maybachstraße 18-20, 70469 Stuttgart
Tel: +49(711) 81495-222
Fax: +49(711) 81495-999
EMail: beratung@akad.de
Website: http://www.akad.de/Hochschule-Stuttgart.155.0.html

Rektorin: Eva Schwinghammer

Programmes

Business Administration (Business Administration); **Business Computing** (Business Computing); **Business Engineering** (Business Administration; Engineering); **Business Translation** (Business Administration; Translation and Interpretation); **International Business Communication** (Communication Studies; International Business); **Machine Building** (Machine Building)

Degrees and Diplomas: *Bachelor/Bakkalaureus*; *Diplom (FH)*; *Master/Magister*. Also College Certificate (Hochschulzertifikat) and Postgraduate diploma (Uni-Aufbaustudiengänge)

Last Updated: 06/02/12

APOLLON UNIVERSITY OF HEALTH MANAGEMENT

APOLLON Hochschule der Gesundheitswirtschaft
Universitätsallee 18, 28359 Bremen
Tel: +49(421) 378266-0
Fax: +49(421) 378266-190
EMail: info@apollon-hochschule.de
Website: http://www.apollon-hochschule.de

Präsident: Bernd Kümmel

Kanzler: Michael Timm

Programmes

Health Economics (Economics; Health Administration; Health Sciences); **Health Management**

History: Founded 2005.

Main Language(s) of Instruction: German

Degrees and Diplomas: *Bachelor/Bakkalaureus*; *Master/Magister*. Also Hochschulzertifikatskurse, 1 week-8 Months depending on Field of Studies.

Last Updated: 06/02/12

ALANUS UNIVERSITY OF ARTS AND SOCIAL SCIENCES

Alanus Hochschule für Kunst und Gesellschaft
Johannishof, 53347 Alfter bei Bonn
Tel: +49 (2222) 93210
Fax: +49(2222) 932121
EMail: info@alanus.edu
Website: http://www.alanus.edu

Rektor: Marcelo da Veiga
Tel: +49(2222) 9321-28 EMail: marcelo.daveiga@alanus.edu

Kanzler: Werner Zidek
Tel: +49(2222) 9321-11 EMail: werner.zidek@alanus.edu

Institutes

Arts in Dialogue (Art Management; Art Therapy; Fine Arts)

Programmes

Architecture; **Art Teacher Qualification** (Art Education; Teacher Training); **Art Therapy** (Art Therapy); **Business Administration**; **Education** (Education); **Eurythmics**; **Painting** (Painting and Drawing); **Palliative Care**; **Sculpture** (Sculpture) *Head:* Andreas Kienlin; **Studium Generale**; **Voice/Drama** (Singing; Theatre) *Head:* Michael Schwarzmann

History: Founded 1973. Acquired present status 2002.

Admission Requirements: Allgemeine Hochschulreife (Abitur)

Fees: (Euros): 260 per month

Main Language(s) of Instruction: German

International Co-operation: With institutions in Senegal; Sudan; Japan

Degrees and Diplomas: *Bachelor/Bakkalaureus*: Painting; Sculpture; Eurythmy (Dance); Business Administration; Studium Generale; *Diplom*: Theatre; *Master/Magister*: Painting; Sculpture; Eurythmy (Dance); Art Therapy; Education; Palliative Care; Studium Generale. Also Diplom Ingenieur in Architecture 5 yrs

Student Residential Facilities: Yes
Last Updated: 06/02/12

ALBERT LUDWIG UNIVERSITY FREIBURG IM BREISGAU

Albert-Ludwigs-Universität Freiburg im Breisgau
Fahnenbergplatz, 79085 Freiburg im Breisgau
Tel: +49(761) 203-0
Fax: +49(761) 203-8866
EMail: info@verwaltung.uni-freiburg.de
Website: http://www.uni-freiburg.de

Rektor: Hans-Jochen Schiewer (2008-)
Tel: +49(761) 203-4315, Fax: +49(761) 203-4390
EMail: rektor@uni-freiburg.de

Kanzler: Matthias Schenek
Tel: +49(761) 203-4321 EMail: kanzler@uni-freiburg.de

International Relations: Katharina Aly, Director, International Office
Tel: +49(761) 203-4376, Fax: +49(761) 203-8857
EMail: katharina.aly@io.uni-freiburg.de

Faculties

Biology (Biology); **Chemistry, Pharmacy and Earth Sciences** (Analytical Chemistry; Biochemistry; Chemical Engineering; Chemistry; Crystallography; Geology; Inorganic Chemistry; Mineralogy; Organic Chemistry; Pharmacy); **Economics and Behavioural Sciences** (Business Administration; Cognitive Sciences; Economics; Education; Finance; Psychology; Sports); **Forest and Environmental Sciences** (Botany; Environmental Studies; Forest Biology; Forest Economics; Forest Management; Forest Products; Forestry; Geography; Hydraulic Engineering; Landscape Architecture; Meteorology; Soil Science); **Humanities** (Anthropology; Archaeology; Art History; Asian Studies; Ethnology; History; Musicology; Philosophy; Political Sciences; Prehistory; Sociology); **Law** (Civil Law; Commercial Law; Criminal Law; Criminology; International Law; Law; Private Law); **Mathematics and Physics** (Mathematics; Physics); **Medicine** (Biochemistry; Dentistry; Forensic Medicine and Dentistry; Gynaecology and Obstetrics; Medicine; Molecular Biology; Ophthalmology; Paediatrics; Pathology); **Philology** (English; Linguistics; Modern Languages; Philology; Romance Languages; Slavic Languages); **Theology** (Bible; Theology)

Research Centres

Anthropology and Gender Studies *(ZAG)* (Anthropology; Gender Studies); **Applied Biosciences** *(ZAB)*; **Biological Signalling Studies** *(Bioss)* (Biological and Life Sciences); **Business and Law** (Business Administration; Law); **Computational Neuroscience** *(Bernstein)* (Computer Science; Neurosciences); **Data Analysis and Modelling** *(Freiburg - FDM)*; **Interdisciplinary Ethics** *(Freiburg)* (Ethics); **Interdisciplinary Studies and Research on Contemporary France** (French Studies); **Linguistics** *(Hermann Paul)*; **Materials** *(Freiburg - FMF)* (Materials Engineering); **Medieval Studies** (Medieval Studies); **Neurosciences** *(ZfN)* (Neurosciences); **Renewable Energy** *(ZEE)* (Energy Engineering); **Water** *(ZWF)*

Research Institutes

Computer Science and Society (Computer Science) *Director (Acting):* Gerhard Strube

History: Founded 1457 by Archduke Albrecht of Austria and confirmed by the Emperor and the Pope. Brought into strongly dependent relationship to the State in the 18th century. The City of Friburg and University became part of the Grand Duchy of Baden in 1806. Now academically autonomous but financially supported by the State of Baden-Württemberg and under the jurisdiction of its Ministry of Science and Research. Teaching staff employed by the State (Land), independent in teaching and research, responsible to the above mentioned Ministry. The status of the University is guaranteed by the Constitution of the State (Land).

Governing Bodies: Grosser Senat; Senat; Unirat

Academic Year: October to July (October-February; April-July)

Admission Requirements: Secondary school certificate (Reifezeugnis) or equivalent. For international students, good command of the German language

Main Language(s) of Instruction: German, English

International Co-operation: Member of EUCOR (European Confederation of Upper Rhine Universities)

Degrees and Diplomas: *Bachelor/Bakkalaureus*; *Diplom*: Biology; Chemistry (Dipl.Chem); Economics; Geology (Dipl.Geol); Mathematics (Dipl.Math); Mineralogy (Dipl.Min); Physics (Dipl.Phys); Psychology (Dipl.Psych); *Lehramt*: Teaching Qualification, Secondary level; *Magister Artium (MA)*: 8 sem; *Staatsprüfung*: Dentistry; Law; Pharmacy; *Staatsprüfung*: Medicine, 11 sem; *Master/ Magister*: Applied Computer Science (MA); Sustainable Forestry and Land Use Management (MA), 2 yrs; *Doktorgrad*: in all fields (Dr), 10-12 sem; *Doktorgrad*: Medicine (Dr.med.), 11 sem; *Habilitation*: at least 3 yrs following Doktor. Also post-doctoral studies

Student Services: Canteen, Cultural centre, Foreign student adviser, Handicapped facilities, Nursery care, Social counselling, Sports facilities

Student Residential Facilities: For c. 3,760 students

Special Facilities: Botanical Garden

Libraries: University Library, 3.38 m. vols
Last Updated: 06/02/12

ALBSTADT-SIGMARINGEN UNIVERSITY

Hochschule Albstadt-Sigmaringen
PO Box 1254, Anton-Günter-Strasse 51, 72481 Sigmaringen
Tel: +49(7571) 732-0
Fax: +49(7571) 732-229
EMail: info@hs-albsig.de
Website: http://www.fh-albsig.de

Rektor: Günter Rexer (2001-)
Tel: +49(7571) 732-221 EMail: rexer@hs-albsig.de

Verwaltungsleiterin: Bernadette Boden
Tel: +49(7571) 732-400 EMail: boden@hs-albsig.de

Departments
Business and Computer Science (Business Administration; Business Computing; Computer Science; Management); **Engineering** (Business Administration; Clothing and Sewing; Communication Studies; Industrial Engineering; Machine Building; Mechanical Engineering; Software Engineering; Textile Technology); **Life Sciences** (Biological and Life Sciences; Biomedical Engineering; Food Technology; Hygiene; Management; Nutrition; Pharmacology)

Further Information: Also campus in Albstadt.

History: Founded 1971.

Main Language(s) of Instruction: German

Degrees and Diplomas: *Bachelor/Bakkalaureus*; *Master/Magister*: Clothing Technology; Machine Building; Systems Engineering; Business Engineering; Business Administration; Business Computing; Biomedical Engineering; Design and Management
Last Updated: 08/01/10

ALICE-SALOMON UNIVERSITY OF APPLIED SCIENCES BERLIN

Alice-Salomon Hochschule Berlin (ASH)
Alice-Salomon-Platz 5, 12627 Berlin
Tel: +49(30) 99245-0
Fax: +49(30) 99245-245
EMail: ash@ash-berlin.de
Website: http://www.ash-berlin.eu/

Rektorin: Theda Borde
Tel: +49(30) 99245-309, Fax: +49(30) 99245-594

Kanzler: Andreas Flegl
Tel: +49(30) 99245-305, Fax: +49(30) 99245-594
EMail: Flegl@verwaltung.asfh-berlin.de

International Relations: Jens Beiderwieden, International Relations Officer
Tel: +49(30) 99245-306, Fax: +49(30) 99245-245
EMail: ausland@asfh-berlin.de

Programmes
Biographical and Creative Writing (Writing); **Clinical Social Work** *(Postgraduate)* (Social Work); **Community Development, Neighbourhood Management and Local Economy** *(Postgraduate)* (Development Studies; Economics; Management); **Comparative European Social Studies** *(MA CESS)* (European Studies; Social Studies); **Early Childhood Education** (Education);

European Master in Social Policy and Social Work in Urban Areas *(Postgraduate)* (Social Policy; Social Work); **Health and Social Care Management** (Health Administration; Welfare and Protective Services); **Intercultural Conflict Management** *(Postgraduate)*; **Management and Quality Development in the Health Sector** *(Consecutive Master)*; **Nursing** (Nursing); **Physiotherapy/ Occupational Therapy** (Occupational Therapy; Physical Therapy); **Research in Social Work and Pedagogy** *(Consecutive Master)*; **Russian-German Double-Master Intercultural Social Work** *(Postgraduate)*; **Social Care Management** *(Postgraduate)*; **Social Work** *(Sozialarbeit/Sozialpädagogik)* (Social Work) *Division Head*: Brigitte Geißler-Piltz; **Social Work as a Human Rights Profession** *(Postgraduate)* (Human Rights; Social Work)

History: Founded 1908 as Women School of Social Work. Acquired present status and title 1971.

Governing Bodies: Kuratorium; Rector

Academic Year: April to February (April-July; October-February)

Admission Requirements: Final secondary school examination

Main Language(s) of Instruction: German and English

International Co-operation: With 23 European countries, USA and Japan. Also participates in Erasmus and Leonardo da Vinci programmes.

Accrediting Agencies: German Accreditation Council

Degrees and Diplomas: *Bachelor/Bakkalaureus*: Social Work; Health and Social Care Management; Early Childhood Education; Physiotherapy/Occupational Therapy (BA, BSc), $3\frac{1}{2}$ yrs; *Diplom (FH)*: Social Work; Management (s.a), 4 yrs; *Master/Magister*: Community Development, Neighbourhood Management and Local Economy; Comparative European Social Studies – MA CESS; European Master in Social Policy and Social Work in Urban Areas; Intercultural Conflict Management; Biographical and Creative Writing; Clinical Social Work; Social Care Management; Russian-German Double-Master Intercultural Social Work; Social Work as a Human Rights Profession; Nursing; (MA, MSW, MSc); Research in Social Work and Pedagogy; Management and Quality Development in the Health Sector

Student Services: Academic counselling, Canteen, Employment services, Foreign student adviser, Foreign Studies Centre, Handicapped facilities, Language programs, Nursery care, Social counselling, Sports facilities

Special Facilities: Computer Centre; Music Studio; Art Studio

Libraries: Yes

Publications: Alice-Wissenschaft, Special issues on science *(biennially)*
Last Updated: 22/03/11

AMBERG-WEIDEN UNIVERSITY OF APPLIED SCIENCES

Hochschule Amberg Weiden
Kaiser-Wilhelm-Ring 23, 92224 Amberg
Tel: +49(9621) 482-0
Fax: +49(9621) 482-110
EMail: amberg@haw-aw.de
Website: http://www.haw-aw.de

Präsident: Eric Bauer (2003-)
Tel: +49(9621) 482-100, Fax: +49(9621) 482-118
EMail: praesident@haw-aw.de

Kanzler: Ludwig von Stern
Tel: +49(9621) 482-102 EMail: kanzler@haw-aw.de

International Relations: Wolfgang Weber, Head, International Relations Tel: +49(9621) 482-197 EMail: w.weber@haw-aw.de

Faculties
Business Studies *(Weiden)* (Business Administration; Engineering); **Electrical Engineering and Information Technology** *(Amberg)* (Computer Engineering; Electronic Engineering; Information Technology; Media Studies); **Industrial Engineering** *(Weiden)* (Biomedical Engineering; Industrial Engineering); **Mechanical Engineering/Environmental Engineering** *(Amberg)* (Energy Engineering; Engineering; Environmental Engineering; Management; Mechanical Engineering; Polymer and Plastics Technology)

History: Began first academic year October 1995.

Governing Bodies: Senate, Board of Advisers

Academic Year: September-September

Admission Requirements: Hochschulreife

Fees: (Euros): 35 per semester

Main Language(s) of Instruction: German

International Co-operation: With institutions in USA; Spain; France; Czech Republic; Poland. Also participates in Erasmus/ Leonardo and international programmes outside Europe

Accrediting Agencies: Ministry of Science, Research and Arts (Bavaria)

Degrees and Diplomas: *Bachelor/Bakkalaureus*: 3-4 yrs; *Diplom (FH)*: Engineering, 4 yrs; *Master/Magister*: Environmental Engineering; Innovation Focused Engineering and Management; Industrial Information Technology; Media Technology and Media Production; Human Resource Management; Intercultural Business and Technology Management; Marketing Management; Bus. Law

Student Services: Academic counselling, Canteen, Foreign student adviser, Handicapped facilities, Language programs, Social counselling, Sports facilities

Student Residential Facilities: Yes

Libraries: 2 libraries
Last Updated: 01/02/12

ANHALT UNIVERSITY OF APPLIED SCIENCES
Hochschule Anhalt
PO Box 1458, Bernburger Strasse 55, 06354 Köthen
Tel: +49(3496) 67-1000
Fax: +49(3496) 67-1099
EMail: praesident@hs-anhalt.de
Website: http://www.hs-anhalt.de

Präsident: Dieter Orzessek (1996-)
Tel: +49(3496) 67-1000, Fax: +49(3496) 67-1099

International Relations: Klaus Mehner, Head, International Office
Tel: +49 (3496) 67-5101, Fax: +49 (3496) 67-5199
EMail: k.mehner@aaa.hs-anhalt.de

Centres
Life Sciences

Departments
Agriculture, Ecotrophology and Landscape Development *(Bernburg)* (Agronomy; Environmental Studies; Landscape Architecture; Rural Planning); **Applied Biosciences and Process Engineering** *(Köthen)*; **Architecture, Facility Management and Geoinformation** *(Dessau)* (Architecture; Management); **Computer Science** *(Köthen)* (Computer Networks; Computer Science; Information Management; Media Studies); **Design** *(Deassau)* (Design); **Economics** *(Bernburg)* (Business Administration; Commercial Law; Economics; International Business; Real Estate); **Electrical and Electronic Engineering, Mechanical Engineering and Industrial Engineering** *(Köthen)* (Electrical Engineering; Industrial Engineering; Mechanical Engineering)

Institutes
Wine

Further Information: Also campuses in Dieter and Orzessek

History: Founded 1991.

Main Language(s) of Instruction: German

Degrees and Diplomas: *Bachelor/Bakkalaureus*; *Diplom (FH)*: Computer Networks (E-Learning); *Master/Magister*
Last Updated: 18/01/10

ANSBACH UNIVERSITY OF APPLIED SCIENCES
Fachhochschule Ansbach
Residenzstr. 8, 91522 Ansbach, Bavaria
Tel: +49(981) 4877-0
Fax: +49(981) 4877-188
EMail: poststelle@fh-ansbach.de
Website: http://www.fh-ansbach.de

Präsidentin: Doris Seifert
Tel: +49(981) 4877-100, Fax: +49(981) 4877-102
EMail: doris.seifert@fh-ansbach.de

Kanzlerin: Michaela Ringler
Tel: +49(981) 4877-150, Fax: +49(981) 4877-102
EMail: mringler@hs-ansbach.de

Faculties
Economic and General Sciences (Business Administration; Business Computing; Communication Studies; International Business; Journalism; Management; Multimedia); **Engineering** (Biomedical Engineering; Biotechnology; Energy Engineering; Engineering; Environmental Engineering; Industrial Engineering)

History: Founded 1996.

Admission Requirements: Secondary school certificate

Fees: (Euros): 28 per semester

Main Language(s) of Instruction: German

International Co-operation: With universities in China, Russian Federation, Uzbekistan, Spain Austria, USA.

Degrees and Diplomas: *Bachelor/Bakkalaureus*; *Diplom (FH)*: Engineering, 4 yrs; *Master/Magister*: International Product and Service Management

Student Services: Academic counselling, Canteen, Foreign student adviser, Handicapped facilities, Health services, Language programs, Social counselling

Student Residential Facilities: Yes

Special Facilities: TV studio. Computer centre. Multimedia, language, computer and technical laboratories

Libraries: Main Library

Publications: Wirtschaft und Technik für die Praxis
Last Updated: 31/01/12

ART ACADEMY OF KARLSRUHE
Staatliche Akademie der Bildenden Künste Karlsruhe
PO Box 111209, Reinhold-Frank-Strasse 67, 76062 Karlsruhe
Tel: +49(721) 926-5205
Fax: +49(721) 926-5206
EMail: rektorat@kunstakademie-karlsruhe.de
Website: http://www.kunstakademie-karlsruhe.de

Rektor: Erwin Gross (2000-)

Kanzler: Rüdiger Weis
Tel: +49(721) 85018-14 EMail: vd@kunstakademie-karlsruhe.de

International Relations: Ilona Günthner

Divisions
Fine Arts (Art History; Fine Arts; Painting and Drawing)
History: Founded 1854.

Main Language(s) of Instruction: German

Degrees and Diplomas: *Diplom*; *Staatsprüfung*
Last Updated: 26/01/10

ART ACADEMY OF NÜRNBERG
Akademie der Bildenden Künste in Nürnberg
Bingstrasse 60, 90480 Nürnberg
Tel: +49(911) 9404-0
Fax: +49(911) 9404-150
EMail: info@adbk-nuernberg.de
Website: http://www.adbk-nuernberg.de

Präsident: Ottmar Hörl
Tel: +49(911) 9404-113 EMail: praesident@adbk-nuernberg.de

Kanzler: Peter Ochs

Courses
Architecture / Architecture and Urban Studies *(Post-graduate)* (Architecture; Interior Design); **Art and Public Places** *(Post-graduate)*

Programmes
Artistic Concepts; **Artistry** (Film; Fine Arts; Video); **Fine Art and Art Pedagogy**; **General Principles of Creativity and Visual Arts** (Visual Arts); **Gold and Silversmith**; **Graphic Design (Visual Communication)**; **Painting** (Painting and Drawing); **Painting and Art Education** (Art Education; Painting and Drawing); **Sculpture** (Sculpture); **Visual Arts (Sculpture)** (Sculpture; Visual Arts)

History: Founded 1662.

Main Language(s) of Instruction: German

Degrees and Diplomas: *Diplom*: Graphic Design; Art and Public Places; *Master/Magister*: Architecture; Arts. Also Staatsexamen in Art Education

Last Updated: 06/02/12

AUGSBURG UNIVERSITY OF APPLIED SCIENCES

Hochschule Augsburg

An der Fachhochschule 1, 86161 Augsburg
Tel: +49(821) 5586-0
Fax: +49(821) 5586-3222
EMail: info@hs-augsburg.de
Website: http://www.fh-augsburg.de

Präsident: Hans-Eberhard Schurk
Tel: +49(821) 5586-3213, Fax: +49(821) 5586-3253
EMail: hans.e.schurk@hs-augsburg.de

Kanzlerin: Tatjana Dörfler
Tel: +49(821) 5586-3217, Fax: +49(821) 5586-3222
EMail: kanzlerin@fh-augsburg.de

International Relations: Ingrid Hahn-Eisenhardt
Tel: +49(821) 5586-204, Fax: +49(821) 5586-207
EMail: ausland@fh-augsburg.de

Faculties

Architecture and Civil Engineering (Architecture; Civil Engineering); **Business Administration** (Accountancy; Business Administration; Finance; International Business; Management; Taxation); **Computer Science** (Computer Science; Information Technology); **Design** (Communication Arts; Design; Media Studies; Multimedia); **Electrical Engineering** (Computer Engineering; Electrical and Electronic Engineering; Electronic Engineering; Mechanical Engineering); **General Studies** (Mathematics; Natural Sciences); **Mechanical and Process Engineering** (Mechanical Engineering; Production Engineering)

History: Founded 1971.

Main Language(s) of Instruction: German

Degrees and Diplomas: *Zertifikat*; *Bachelor/Bakkalaureus*; *Diplom (FH)*; *Master/Magister*

Last Updated: 01/02/12

AUGUSTANA COLLEGE OF NEUENDETTELSAU

Augustana-Hochschule Neuendettelsau (AHS)

PO Box 20, Waldstrasse 11, 91564 Neuendettelsau
Tel: +49(9874) 509-0
Fax: +49(9874) 509-555
EMail: hochschule@augustana.de
Website: http://www.augustana.de

Rektorin: Renate Jost
Tel: +49(9874) 509-111 EMail: rektorat-lydia.wolf@augustana.de

Director, Administration: Helene Gress
Tel: +49(9874) 509-222 EMail: helene.gress@augustana.de

Institutes

Evangelical Aesthetics and Evangelical Religiousness Research (Religion); **Feminist Research in Theology and Religion** *(International)*; **Personality and Ethics**

Programmes

Divinity (Bible; Hebrew; History of Religion; Music Education; Philology; Philosophy; Religious Music; Singing; Theology)

History: Founded 1947 as a Divinity School of the Evangelical-Lutheran Church in Bavaria.

Main Language(s) of Instruction: German

Degrees and Diplomas: *Bachelor/Bakkalaureus*; *Doktorgrad*
Last Updated: 06/02/12

BALTIC COLLEGE

Plauer Straße 81, D - 18273 Güstrow
Tel: +49 (3843) 4642-0
Fax: +49 (3843) 4642-11
EMail: info@baltic-college.de
Website: http://www.baltic-college.de

Präsident: Jens Engelke EMail: engelke@baltic-college.de

Programmes

Business Administration (Business Administration); **Ergotherapy** (Ergotherapy); **Hotel and Tourism Management** (Hotel Management; Management; Tourism); **Management in Health Tourism** (Health Administration; Management; Tourism); **Physiotherapy** (Physical Therapy)

History: Founded 2001.

Main Language(s) of Instruction: German

Degrees and Diplomas: *Bachelor/Bakkalaureus*; *Master/Magister*
Last Updated: 06/02/12

BERLIN IB UNIVERSITY

IB-Hochschule Berlin

Gerichtstr. 27, 13347 Berlin - Wedding
EMail: info@ib-hochschule.de
Website: http://www.ib-hochschule.de

Rektor: Uli Rothfuss

Departments

Cultural Studies (Communication Studies; Cultural Studies; Design); **Economic Science** *(Stuttgart)* (Art Management; Economics; Health Administration; Management; Marketing; Social Problems); **Educational Sciences** (Educational Sciences; Pedagogy); **Health Sciences** (Ergotherapy; Health Sciences; Physical Therapy; Speech Therapy and Audiology)

Further Information: Also sites in Stuttgart and Köln.

History: Founded 2006.

Main Language(s) of Instruction: German

Degrees and Diplomas: *Bachelor/Bakkalaureus*; *Master/Magister*
Last Updated: 20/01/10

BERLIN PROTESTANT UNIVERSITY OF APPLIED SCIENCES

Evangelische Hochschule Berlin

Postfach 37 02 55, Teltower Damm 118-122, 14132 Berlin
Tel: +49(30) 84582-0
Fax: +49(30) 84582-450
EMail: info@evfh-berlin.de
Website: http://www.evfh-berlin.de

Rektorin: Angelika Thol-Hauke
Tel: +49(30) 84582-101, Fax: +49(30) 84582-122
EMail: thol-hauke@eh-berlin.de

Kanzler: Helmut Sankowski
Tel: +49(30) 84582-400, Fax: +49(30) 84582-445
EMail: sankowski@eh-berlin.de

Programmes

Elementary Education (Education; Pedagogy; Preschool Education); **Evangelical Religion Pedagogy** (Pedagogy; Protestant Theology; Religious Education); **Health Care and Care Management** (Health Administration; Health Sciences); **Nursing** (Nursing); **Social Work** *(Master)* (Social Work); **Social Work and Pedagogy** (Pedagogy; Social Work)

History: Founded 1971. Acquired present title 2010.

Main Language(s) of Instruction: German

Degrees and Diplomas: *Diplom-Vorprüfung*; *Bachelor/Bakkalaureus*; *Diplom (FH)*; *Master/Magister*
Last Updated: 22/03/11

BERLIN SCHOOL OF ECONOMICS AND LAW

Hochschule für Wirtschaft und Recht Berlin

Alt-Friedrichsfelde 60, 10315 Berlin
Tel: +49(30) 9021-4005
Fax: +49(30) 9021-4013
EMail: info@fhv-berlin.de
Website: http://www.fhvr-berlin.de

Präsident: Bernd Reissert
Tel: +49(30) 9021-4000, Fax: +49(30) 9021-4006
EMail: praesident@fhvr-berlin.de

Departments
Business and Economics (Business Administration; Economics)

Faculties
Cooperative Studies (Banking; Civil Engineering; Computer Science; Insurance; Mechanical Engineering; Real Estate; Retailing and Wholesaling; Taxation; Tourism); **Legal Studies** (Law); **Police and Security Management** (Police Studies); **Public Administration** (Public Administration)

History: Founded 2009 following merger of University of Applied Sciences for Administration and Law (FHVR) and Berlin School of Economics

Admission Requirements: Abitur, Fachgebundene Hoschschulreife, Fachhochschulereife, pre-study internship

Fees: None

Main Language(s) of Instruction: German

Degrees and Diplomas: *Bachelor/Bakkalaureus*; *Diplom (FH)*: Consulate Secretary Studies; Police Studies; Jurisprudence; *Master/Magister*: European Administration Management; Public Administration

Student Services: Academic counselling, Canteen, Employment services, Foreign student adviser, Handicapped facilities, Sports facilities
Last Updated: 22/03/11

BERLIN UNIVERSITY FOR PROFESSIONAL STUDIES
Deutsche Universität für Weiterbildung
P.O. Box 33 20 02, 14180 Berlin
EMail: ada.pellert@duw-berlin.de
Website: http://www.duw-berlin.de
Präsidentin: Ada Pellert

Departments
Business and Management (Business Administration; Management); **Communication** (European Studies; Management; Media Studies); **Education** (Education); **Health Care** (Health Education)

History: Founded 2008.
Main Language(s) of Instruction: German
Degrees and Diplomas: *Master/Magister*
Last Updated: 06/02/12

BERLIN UNIVERSITY OF TECHNOLOGY
Technische Universität Berlin
Strasse des 17. Juni 135, 10623 Berlin
Tel: +49(30) 3140
Fax: +49(30) 3142-3222
EMail: k@tu-berlin.de; pressestelle@tu-berlin.de
Website: http://www.tu-berlin.de
Präsident: Jörg Steinbach (2010-)
Tel: +49(30) 3142-2200, Fax: +49(30) 3142-6760
Kanzlerin: Ulrike Gutheil
Tel: +49(30) 3142-2500, Fax: +49(30) 3142-1118

Faculties
Economics and Management (Business Administration; Economics; Energy Engineering; Health Sciences; Law; Management; Technology; Transport Management); **Electrical Engineering and Computer Science** (Automation and Control Engineering; Computer Engineering; Computer Science; Electrical Engineering; Energy Engineering; Microelectronics; Software Engineering; Telecommunications Engineering); **Humanities** (Communication Arts; French; Gender Studies; History; Literature; Pedagogy; Philosophy; Social Sciences; Vocational Education); **Mathematics and Natural Sciences** (Astronomy and Space Science; Chemistry; Mathematics and Computer Science; Optics; Physics; Solid State Physics); **Mechanical Engineering and Transport System** (Aeronautical and Aerospace Engineering; Astronomy and Space Science; Engineering Drawing and Design; Management; Mechanics; Psychology; Transport and Communications); **Planning, Building, Environment** (Architectural and Environmental Design; Ecology; Environmental Management; Heritage Preservation; Landscape Architecture; Regional Planning; Sociology; Town Planning; Urban Studies); **Process Sciences** (Biotechnology; Energy Engineering;

Environmental Engineering; Food Science; Food Technology; Materials Engineering; Sound Engineering (Acoustics))

History: Founded 1799 as Bauakademie (Building Academy), became Technische Hoschschule 1879. The Bergakademie (Mining Academy), founded 1770, was incorporated in 1916. Reopened as Technische Universität in 1946. Reorganized 1969 and faculties replaced by series of Fachbereiche (departments). The structural reform decided by the Berlin University of Technology came into force officially in October 1993. As part of this reform, the number of departments was reduced from 22 to 15, and again reformed, reducing the number of faculties to 8.

Governing Bodies: Kuratorium; Senat; Konzil
Academic Year: October to September (October-March; April-September)
Admission Requirements: Secondary school certificate (Reifezeugnis) or equivalent
Fees: Tuition, none
Main Language(s) of Instruction: German
International Co-operation: With universities worldwide

Degrees and Diplomas: *Bachelor/Bakkalaureus*; *Diplom*: Architecture; Biotechnology; Chemistry; Civil Engineering; Computer Sciences; Educational Sciences; Electrotechnics; Energy and Systems Techniques; Environmental Technology; Food Technology; Landscape Planning; Management; Mathematics; Mechanics; Physics; Psychology; Town and Regional Planning; *Lehramt*: Teaching qualification; *Magister Artium*; *Master/Magister*; *Promotion*; *Doktorgrad*: Engineering (Dr.Ing.); *Habilitation*: at least 3 yrs following Doktor

Student Services: Academic counselling, Canteen, Cultural centre, Foreign student adviser, Handicapped facilities, Health services, Nursery care, Social counselling, Sports facilities
Libraries: University Library, c. 2.6m vols
Publications: Vorlesungsverzeichnis der Technischen Universität Berlin *(biennially)*
Last Updated: 22/03/11

BERLIN UNIVERSITY OF THE ARTS
Universität der Künste Berlin
PO Box 120544, 10595 Berlin
Tel: +49(30) 3185-0
Fax: +49(30) 3185-2758
EMail: beratung@udk-berlin.de
Website: http://www.udk-berlin.de
Präsident: Martin Rennert
Tel: +49(30) 3185-2447, Fax: +49(30) 3185-2870
EMail: p1@intra.udk-berlin.de
Kanzler: Wolfgang Abramowski
Tel: +49(30) 3185-2445, Fax: +49(30) 3185-2496
EMail: wolfgang.abramowski@intra.udk-berlin.de

Colleges
Architecture, Media and Design (Architecture; Design; E-Business/Commerce; Industrial Design; Visual Arts); **Fine Arts** (Fine Arts); **Music** (Art Education; Art Therapy; Conducting; Instrument Making; Music; Music Education; Music Theory and Composition; Religious Music; Sound Engineering (Acoustics)); **Performing Arts** (Performing Arts)

History: Founded 1975. Consists of the Hochschule für Bildende Künste, dating back to the Prussian Academy of Fine Arts, founded in 1696, and the Hochschule für Musik, established in 1869.
Main Language(s) of Instruction: German
Degrees and Diplomas: *Bachelor/Bakkalaureus*; *Master/Magister*; *Doktorgrad*
Libraries: Yes
Last Updated: 28/01/10

BERLIN-WEISSENSEE SCHOOL OF ART
Kunsthochschule Berlin-Weissensee
Bühringstrasse 20, 13086 Berlin
Tel: +49(30) 47705-0
Fax: +49(30) 47705-290
EMail: rektor@kh-berlin.de
Website: http://www.kh-berlin.de

Rektor: Leonie Baumann
Tel: +49(30) 47705-220, Fax: +49(30) 47705-289

Kanzlerin: Silvia Durin
Tel: +49(30) 47705-316 EMail: kanzlerin@kh-berlin.de

International Relations: Leoni Adams
Tel: +49(30) 47705-342 EMail: studienberatung@kh-berlin.de

Departments
Art Theory and History (Art History); **Art Therapy** (Art Therapy); **Fashion Design** (Fashion Design); **Painting** (Painting and Drawing); **Sculpture** (Sculpture); **Space Strategies** (Display and Stage Design); **Stage/ Costume Design**; **Textile and Surface Design** (Design; Textile Design); **Visual Communication** (Advertising and Publicity)

History: Founded 1946.

Main Language(s) of Instruction: German

Degrees and Diplomas: *Bachelor/Bakkalaureus*; *Master/Magister*. Art Therapy
Last Updated: 03/02/12

BEUTH UNIVERSITY OF APPLIED SCIENCES BERLIN

Beuth Hochschule für Technik Berlin
Luxemburger Strasse 10, 13353 Berlin
Tel: +49(30) 4504-1
Fax: +49(30) 4504-2705
EMail: praesident@tfh-berlin.de
Website: http://www.tfh-berlin.de

Präsident: Monika Gross (2011-) Tel: +49(30) 4504-2335

International Relations: Michael Kramp
Tel: +49(30) 4504-2950, Fax: +49(30) 4504-2959
EMail: ausland@tfh-berlin.de

Departments
Architecture (Architecture); **Civil Engineering**; **Computer Science and Media** (Computer Science; Media Studies); **Economics and Business Administration** (Business Administration; Economics); **Electronic Engineering** (Automation and Control Engineering; Electronic Engineering; Telecommunications Engineering); **Life Sciences and Technology** (Biological and Life Sciences; Biotechnology; Landscape Architecture); **Mathematics, Physics and Chemistry** (Chemistry; Mathematics; Physics); **Mechanical Engineering** (Environmental Management; Mechanical Engineering)

History: Founded 1971 as Technische Fachhochschule Berlin.

Academic Year: October to July (October-February; April-July)

Admission Requirements: Secondary school certificate

Fees: (Euros): Registration fees, 130 per semester

Main Language(s) of Instruction: German

International Co-operation: Erasmus,Global Engineering 4

Degrees and Diplomas: *Bachelor/Bakkalaureus*; *Master/Magister*

Student Services: Academic counselling, Canteen, Foreign student adviser, Language programs, Sports facilities

Libraries: Main Library
Last Updated: 31/01/12

BIBERACH UNIVERSITY OF APPLIED SCIENCES

Hochschule Biberach
Karlstraße 11, 88400 Biberach
Tel: +49(7351) 582-0
Fax: +49(7351) 582-119
EMail: Info@hochschule-bc.de
Website: http://www.hochschule-biberach.de

Rektor: Thomas Vogel (2003-)
Tel: +49(7351) 582-100, Fax: +49(7351) 582-109
EMail: rektor@hochschule-bc.de

Kanzler: Wolfram Bürster
Tel: +49(7351) 582-110 EMail: burster@hochschule-bc.de

International Relations: Sinje Miebach
Tel: +49(7351) 582-103 EMail: aaa@fh-biberach.de

Departments
Architecture (Architecture); **Business Administration** (Business Administration); **Civil Engineering** (Civil Engineering); **Energy and Climate** (Building Technologies; Energy Engineering; Heating and Refrigeration); **General Studies** (English; French; Italian; Japanese; Modern Languages; Spanish; Writing); **Pharmaceutical Biotechnology** (Biology; Biotechnology; Cell Biology; Chemistry; Mathematics; Microbiology; Pharmacy; Physics); **Project Management** (Building Technologies; Management)

History: Founded 1964.

Main Language(s) of Instruction: German

Degrees and Diplomas: *Bachelor/Bakkalaureus*; *Master/Magister*
Last Updated: 18/01/10

BIELEFELD UNIVERSITY OF APPLIED SCIENCES

Fachhochschule Bielefeld (FH BIELEFELD)
PO Box 101113, Kurt-Schumacher-Strasse 6, 33511 Bielefeld
Tel: +49(521) 106-01
Fax: +49(521) 106-7790
EMail: info@fh-bielefeld.de
Website: http://www.fh-bielefeld.de

Präsidentin: Beate Rennen-Allhoff (2001-)
Tel: +49(521) 106-7738/39, Fax: +49(521) 106-7791
EMail: präsidentin@fh-bielefeld.de

Kanzlerin: Gehsa Schnier
Tel: +49(521) 106-7736/37, Fax: +49(521) 106-7792
EMail: gehsa.schnier@fh-bielefeld.de

International Relations: Dorit Hekel
Tel: +49(521) 106-7710, Fax: +49(521) 106-7790
EMail: aaa@fh-bielefeld.de; marie_elisabeth.mueller@fh-bielefeld.de

Departments
Architecture and Civil Engineering (Architecture; Civil Engineering); **Business Administration and Health Sciences** (Business Administration; Business Computing; Commercial Law; Health Sciences; Industrial and Organizational Psychology; International Studies; Law; Management; Nursing); **Design** (Design; Fashion Design; Graphic Design; Media Studies; Multimedia; Photography); **Engineering and Mathematics** (Applied Mathematics; Biotechnology; Business Administration; Computer Engineering; Electronic Engineering; Energy Engineering; Engineering; Machine Building; Mathematics; Mechanical Engineering; Production Engineering); **Social Studies** (Management; Pedagogy; Social Sciences; Social Studies; Social Work)

History: Founded 1971.

Admission Requirements: Fachhochschulreife

Main Language(s) of Instruction: German

International Co-operation: Participates in Erasmus; Socrates; Tempus

Degrees and Diplomas: *Bachelor/Bakkalaureus*: 3 yrs; *Master/ Magister*. 2 yrs

Student Services: Academic counselling, Canteen, Employment services, Foreign student adviser, Foreign Studies Centre, Handicapped facilities, Language programs, Nursery care, Social counselling, Sports facilities

Student Residential Facilities: Yes

Libraries: Yes
Last Updated: 06/02/12

BOCHUM UNIVERSITY OF APPLIED SCIENCES

Hochschule Bochum
Postfach 100741, Lennershofstr. 140, 44707 Bochum
Tel: +49(234) 32-202
Fax: +49(234) 32-14312
EMail: hochschulverwaltung@fh-bochum.de
Website: http://www.hochschule-bochum.de

Rektor: Martin Sternberg
Tel: +49(234) 32-10000, Fax: +49(234) 32-14780
EMail: martin.sternberg@hs-bochum.de

Vizepräsident Wirtschafts- und Personalverwaltung: Christina Reinhardt

Tel: +49(234) 32-10001, Fax: +49(234) 32-14126
EMail: christina.reinhardt@hs-bochum.de

International Relations: Siegfried Engesser-Paris
Tel: +49(234) 32-10081, Fax: +49(234) 32-14660
EMail: engesser-paris@hv.fh-bochum.de

Centres
Geothermal Engineering *(Bochum)* (Geological Engineering; Thermal Engineering); **Mechatronics** *(NRW)* (Electronic Engineering; Mechanical Engineering)

Departments
Architecture (Architecture; Media Studies); **Civil Engineering** (Civil Engineering); **Economics** (Accountancy; Business Administration; Business Computing; Economics; Finance; Human Resources; International Economics; Marketing; Taxation); **Electrical Engineering and Computer Science** (Computer Science; Electrical Engineering); **Land Surveying and Geo-Computer Science** (Computer Science; Surveying and Mapping); **Mechatronics and Mechanical Engineering** (Mechanical Engineering)

History: Founded 1972. Formerly known as Fachhoschschule-bochum.

Main Language(s) of Instruction: German

International Co-operation: With universities in France, United Kingdom, Spain, Italy

Degrees and Diplomas: *Bachelor/Bakkalaureus*: Architecture, 8 sem.; *Bachelor/Bakkalaureus*: Economics; Engineering (Measurement and precision, Telecommunications, Geology, Electrical and Electronic, Construction); Machine Building; Computer Science; Information Technology; Mechatronics; Business and Commerce; Robotics; International Business, 7-10 sem.; *Bachelor/Bakkalaureus*: Mechanical Engineering; Electrical and Electronic Engineering; Automation and Control Engineering; Machine Building; Economics; Information Science; Mechatronics, 6 sem.; *Master/Magister*: Architecture, 2 1/2 sem.; *Master/Magister*: Architecture and Media Management, 2 1/2; *Master/Magister*: International Management; Machine Building; Mechatronics; Engineering, 4 sem.

Student Services: Academic counselling, Canteen, Cultural centre, Employment services, Foreign student adviser, Language programs, Sports facilities

Publications: FHBO Journal *(biennially)*
Last Updated: 01/02/12

BONN-RHEIN-SIEG UNIVERSITY OF APPLIED SCIENCES
Hochschule Bonn-Rhein-Sieg
Grantham-Allee 20, 53757 Sankt Augustin
Tel: +49(2241) 865-0
Fax: +49(2241) 865-609
EMail: vera.schneider@fh-bonn-rhein-sieg.de
Website: http://www.fh-bonn-rhein-sieg.de

Präsident: Hartmut Ihne
Tel: +49(2241) 865-600, Fax: +49(2241) 865-8600
EMail: praesident@hochschule-bonn-rhein-sieg.de

Kanzler: Hans Stender
Tel: +49(2241) 865-606, Fax: +49(2241) 865-8606
EMail: kanzler@hochschule-bonn-rhein-sieg.de

International Relations: Vera Schneider
Tel: +49(2241) 865-628, Fax: +49(2241) 865-8628

Departments
Business Administration *(Rheinbach)* (Business Administration); **Business Administration** *(Sankt Augustin)* (Business Administration); **Computer Science** (Computer Science); **Electrical Engineering, Mechanical Engineering and Technical Journalism** (Electrical Engineering; Journalism; Mechanical Engineering) *Dean*: Volker Sommer; **Natural Sciences** *(Rheinbach)* (Applied Chemistry; Applied Physics; Biology; Chemistry; Natural Sciences); **Social Security Management**

History: Founded 1995, acquired present status 2006.

Admission Requirements: Secondary school certificate or equivalent

Fees: (Euros): 500 per semester

Main Language(s) of Instruction: German

International Co-operation: With universities in United Kingdom, USA, France, Japan, Bulgaria, Spain, Australia.

Accrediting Agencies: FIBAA; ASIIN

Degrees and Diplomas: *Bachelor/Bakkalaureus*; *Master/Magister*: Autonomous Systems; Biology with Biomedical Sciences; Business Administration; Computer Science

Student Services: Academic counselling, Canteen, Handicapped facilities, Language programs, Nursery care, Social counselling, Sports facilities

Special Facilities: Radio and movie studio

Libraries: Main Libraries
Last Updated: 01/02/12

BRANDENBURG UNIVERSITY OF APPLIED SCIENCES
Fachhochschule Brandenburg
Magdeburger Strasse 50, D-14770 Brandenburg
Tel: +49(3381) 355-0
Fax: +49(3381) 355-199
EMail: info@fh-brandenburg.de
Website: http://www.fh-brandenburg.de

Präsident: Hans Georg Helmstädter
Tel: +49(3381) 355-101 EMail: praesident@fh-brandenburg.de

Kanzle: Walter Kühme
Tel: +49(3381) 355-150 EMail: kanzler@fh-brandenburg.de

International Relations: Heike Wolff
EMail: auslandsamt@fh-brandenburg.de

Departments
Business and Management (Business Administration; Business Computing; Information Management; International Business; Management; Safety Engineering; Technology); **Engineering** (Automation and Control Engineering; Electronic Engineering; Information Technology; Machine Building; Mechanical Engineering; Optical Technology; Physical Engineering); **Informatics and Media** (Computer Science; Media Studies)

History: Founded 1992.

Main Language(s) of Instruction: German

Degrees and Diplomas: *Bachelor/Bakkalaureus*; *Diplom (FH)*: Business Administration; *Master/Magister*
Last Updated: 06/02/12

BRANDENBURG UNIVERSITY OF TECHNOLOGY COTTBUS
Brandenburgische Technische Universität Cottbus
PO Box 101344, Konrad-Wachsmann-Allee 1, 03046 Cottbus
Tel: +49(355) 69-0
Fax: +49(355) 69-2721
EMail: webmaster@tu-cottbus.de
Website: http://www.tu-cottbus.de

Präsident: Walther Ch. Zimmerli (2007-)
Tel: +49(355) 69-2292, Fax: +49(355) 69-2156
EMail: praesident@tu-cottbus.de

Kanzler: Wolfgang Schröder
Tel: +49(355) 69-3311, Fax: +49(355) 69-2274
EMail: kanzler@.tu-cottbus.de

International Relations: Beate Körner
Tel: +49(355) 69-3305, Fax: +49(355) 69-2108

Faculties
Architecture, Civil Engineering and Town Planning (Architecture; Civil Engineering; Structural Architecture; Town Planning); **Environmental Science and Process Engineering** (Automation and Control Engineering; Environmental Engineering); **Mathematics, Natural Sciences and Computer Science** (Applied Mathematics; Chemistry; Computer Science; Information Technology; Mathematics; Media Studies; Natural Sciences; Physics; Technology); **Mechanical, Electrical and Industrial Engineering** (Electrical Engineering; Electronic Engineering; Industrial Engineering; Mechanical Engineering)

Research Centres

Energy Technology *(Brandenburg)* (Energy Engineering); **Lightweight Construction** *(Panta Rhei)* (Civil Engineering); **Logistic, Planning System and Information Systems** *(Fraunhofer)*; **Technology** *(UTC)*

Research Institutes

Business Setting and Small/Medium-Sized Business Promotion *(HöZ)* (Anthropology)

History: Founded 1991.

Governing Bodies: Senat

Academic Year: October to July (October-February; April-July)

Admission Requirements: Secondary school certificate (Abitur) or equivalent. German Language Admission Test (DSH or TestDaF min. 16 points), and for programmes taught in English TOEFL 550, 213 Computer based or IELTS 6,5

Fees: None

Main Language(s) of Instruction: German (several degree programmes taught in English)

International Co-operation: Participates in the Erasmus programme. Bilateral agreements wiith some 40 non-European universities. Member of GE3 network of Engineering schools worldwide

Degrees and Diplomas: *Bachelor/Bakkalaureus*: 3 yrs; *Diplom*; *Master/Magister*: 2 yrs

Student Services: Academic counselling, Canteen, Cultural centre, Foreign student adviser, Language programs, Social counselling, Sports facilities

Student Residential Facilities: Yes

Libraries: 837,171 Media units

Publications: Forum der Forschung *(annually)*
Last Updated: 06/02/12

BRAUNSCHWEIG UNIVERSITY OF ART

Hochschule für Bildende Künste Braunschweig (HBK BRAUNSCHWEIG)

PO Box 2538, Johannes-Selenka-Platz 1, 38118 Braunschweig, Lower Saxony
Tel: +49(531) 3919-122
Fax: +49(531) 3919-307
EMail: studienberatung@hbk-bs.de
Website: http://www.hbk-bs.de

Präsident: Hubertus von Amelunxen
Tel: +49(531) 3919-120, Fax: +49(531) 3919-215
EMail: praesident@hbk-bs.de

Programmes

Aesthetics and Art History (Aesthetics; Art History); **Art Education** (Art Education); **Art Mediation** (Art Management); **Communication Design** (Graphic Design); **Fine Arts** (Art Education; Fine Arts; Performing Arts; Visual Arts); **Industrial Design** (Industrial Design); **Media Studies** (Media Studies); **Performing Arts** (Performing Arts); **Representing Game** (Art Management; Display and Stage Design; Fine Arts)

History: Founded 1963.

Governing Bodies: Präsidium

Academic Year: October to September

Admission Requirements: School leaving certificate or equivalent and entrance examination

Fees: According to programme

Main Language(s) of Instruction: German

International Co-operation: With institutions in United Kingdom; France; Spain; Italy; Netherlands; Poland; Lithuania; Indonesia; Mexico

Accrediting Agencies: ZEVA

Degrees and Diplomas: *Bachelor/Bakkalaureus*: 3-4 yrs; *Diplom*: 5 yrs; *Lehramt*; *Master/Magister*: 2 yrs; *Promotion*

Student Services: Academic counselling, Canteen, Cultural centre, Foreign student adviser, Foreign Studies Centre

Special Facilities: Art Gallery. Studios. Workshops

Libraries: Yes
Last Updated: 21/03/11

BREMEN UNIVERSITY OF APPLIED SCIENCES

Hochschule Bremen

Neustadtwall 30, 28199 Bremen
Tel: +49(421) 5905-0
Fax: +49(421) 5905-2292
EMail: info@hs-bremen.de
Website: http://www.hs-bremen.de

Rektorin: Karin Luckey
Tel: +49(421) 5905-2221, Fax: +49(421) 5905-2150
EMail: Karin.Luckey@hs-bremen.de
Kanzler: Jens Andreas Meinen
Tel: +49(421) 5905 2224 EMail: Kanzler@hs-bremen.de
International Relations: Heike Tauerschmidt, Head of International Office
Tel: +49(421) 5905-2640
EMail: Heike.Tauerschmidt@hs-bremen.de

Areas

Economic Sciences (Business Administration; Economics); **Engineering and Natural Sciences** (Aeronautical and Aerospace Engineering; Architecture; Biology; Civil Engineering; Computer Engineering; Electrical Engineering; Electronic Engineering; Energy Engineering; Engineering; Environmental Engineering; Industrial Engineering; Industrial Management; International Studies; Management; Marine Engineering; Mechanical Engineering; Media Studies; Natural Sciences; Physics); **Social Sciences** (Communication Studies; European Studies; Health Administration; Health Sciences; International Studies; Journalism; Leisure Studies; Management; Political Sciences; Social Sciences; Social Work; Tourism)

History: Founded 1982.

Degrees and Diplomas: *Bachelor/Bakkalaureus*; *Master/Magister*
Last Updated: 01/02/12

BREMERHAVEN UNIVERSITY OF APPLIED SCIENCES

Hochschule Bremerhaven

An der Karlstadt 8, 27568 Bremerhaven
Tel: +49(471) 4823-0
Fax: +49(471) 4823-555
EMail: info@hs-bremerhaven.de
Website: http://www.hs-bremerhaven.de

Rektor: Josef Stockemer (2001-)
Tel: +49(471) 4823-100, Fax: +49(471) 4823-199
EMail: rektorat@hs-bremerhaven.de
Kanzler: Karsten Gerlof
Tel: +49(471) 4823-136, Fax: +49(471) 4823-159
EMail: kanzler@hs-bremerhaven.de

International Relations: Kerstin Groscurth
Tel: +49(471) 4823-103, Fax: +49(471) 4823-115
EMail: kgroscurth@hs-bremerhaven.de

Faculties

Business Administration, Media and Transport (Business Administration; Media Studies; Transport and Communications); **Engineering** (Energy Engineering; Food Technology; Industrial Engineering; Marine Engineering; Medical Technology; Nautical Science; Production Engineering)

History: Founded 1975.

Admission Requirements: University Entry Qualification or equivalent

Fees: None

Main Language(s) of Instruction: German, English (Partly)

International Co-operation: With universities in Finland, Ireland, Netherlands, Spain, Poland.

Degrees and Diplomas: *Bachelor/Bakkalaureus*: 3 yrs; *Master/ Magister*: a further 2 yrs
Last Updated: 01/02/12

BUCERIUS LAW SCHOOL

Bucerius Law School, Hochschule für Rechtswissenschaft

P.O. Box 301030, Jungiusstrasse 6, 20304 Hamburg
Tel: +49(40) 30706-0
Fax: +49(40) 30706-145
EMail: info@law-school.de
Website: http://www.law-school.de/

President: Karsten Schmidt (2005-)
Tel: +49(40) 30706-100, Fax: +49(40) 30706-106
EMail: praesident@law-school.de

CEO: Hariolf Wenzler
Tel: +49(40) 30706-100, Fax: +49(40) 30706-105
EMail: hariolf.wenzler@law-school.de

International Relations: Kasia Kwietniewska, Director, International Exchange
Tel: +49(40) 30706-109, Fax: +49(40) 30706-293
EMail: kasia.kwietniewska@law-school.de

Institutes
Corporate and Capital Markets Law (Commercial Law; Law); **Foundation Law and Law of Non-Profit Organizations** (Law)

History: Founded 2000.

Governing Bodies: Supervisory Council

Academic Year: October to July. Only the Fall semester is open for international students

Admission Requirements: Secondary school certificate (Abitur)

Fees: (Euros): 9,000 per annum (only for German students)

Main Language(s) of Instruction: German; English (international and comparative Business Law programme)

International Co-operation: With partner American Law schools (all approved by the American Bar Association)

Degrees and Diplomas: *Bachelor/Bakkalaureus*: Law (LLB), 3 1/2 yrs; *Staatsprüfung*: Law, 4 yrs; *Master/Magister*: Law and Business

Student Services: Academic counselling, Canteen, Employment services, Foreign student adviser, Foreign Studies Centre, Handicapped facilities, Language programs, Sports facilities

Libraries: c. 45,000 vols; Law databases

Publications: Law Yearbook; Schriftenreihe der Bucerius Law School; Schriftenreihe des Instituts für Stiftungsrechts; Schriftenreihe zu Kunst und Recht

Last Updated: 31/01/12

BURG GIEBICHENSTEIN UNIVERSITY OF ART AND DESIGN HALLE

Burg Giebichenstein Kunsthochschule Halle
PO Box 200252, 06003 Halle
Tel: +49(345) 7751-510
Fax: +49(345) 7751-522
EMail: burgpost@halle.de
Website: http://www.burg-halle.de

Rektor: Axel Müller-Schöll (2010-)
Tel: +49(345) 7751-510, Fax: +49(345) 7751-522
EMail: rektorat@burg-halle.de

Kanzler: Wolfgang Stockert
Tel: +49(345) 7751-520 EMail: stockert@burg-halle.de

International Relations: Stefanie Schaaf
EMail: international@burg-halle.de

Departments
Design (Communication Studies; Design; Fashion Design; Industrial Design; Interior Design; Multimedia; Textile Design); **Fine Arts** (Ceramic Art; Fine Arts; Glass Art; Graphic Arts; Jewelry Art; Metal Techniques; Painting and Drawing; Printing and Printmaking; Sculpture; Textile Design)

History: Founded 1915. Acquired present status 1952.

Governing Bodies: Academic Senate

Academic Year: October to March; April to September

Admission Requirements: Allgemeine Hochschulreife and entrance examination (artistic abilities)

Fees: (Euros): 70 per semester

Main Language(s) of Instruction: German

International Co-operation: Participates in Erasmus

Degrees and Diplomas: *Bachelor/Bakkalaureus*: Design; *Diplom*: Fine Arts, 5 yrs; *Master/Magister*: Design

Student Services: Academic counselling, Canteen, Foreign student adviser, Language programs, Sports facilities

Student Residential Facilities: None

Special Facilities: Art Gallery
Libraries: Yes
Last Updated: 22/03/11

BUSINESS AND INFORMATION TECHNOLOGY SCHOOL ISERLOHN (BITS)

Reiterweg 26b, 58636 Iserlohn
Tel: +49(2371) 776-500
Fax: +49(2371) 776-503
EMail: info@bits-iserlohn.de
Website: http://www.bits-iserlohn.de

Präsident: Thorsten Bagschik
Tel: +49(2371) 909-350, Fax: +49(2371) 909-390
EMail: thorsten.bagschik@bits-iserlohn.de

Director: Ulrich Freitag
Tel: +49(2371) 776-140, Fax: +49(2371) 776-596
EMail: ulrich.freitag@bits-iserlohn.de

International Relations: Christine Müller
Tel: +49(2371) 776-511, Fax: +49(2371) 776-503
EMail: Christine.Mueller@bits-iserlohn.de

Faculties
Business and Management (Business Administration; Finance; Management; Marketing); **Business Psychology** (Business Administration; Human Resources; Management; Marketing; Psychology; Staff Development) *Dean*: Martina Stangel-Meseke; **Communication and Media Management** (Journalism; Management; Media Studies); **International Service Industries** (Management; Sports Management); **Media and Communication** (Communication Studies; Journalism; Management; Media Studies)

History: Founded 2000.

Academic Year: March to July; October to February

Admission Requirements: Abitur, Fachabitur

Fees: (Euros): 3,600 per semester; Business Journalism: 3,900

Main Language(s) of Instruction: German, English

International Co-operation: With universities in Australia; New Zealand; Argentina; Canada; Spain; United Kingdom; Sweden

Degrees and Diplomas: *Bachelor/Bakkalaureus*: Business and Management Studies; Business Psychology; Communication and Media Management; Sport and Event Management; Business Journalism; Green Business Management, 3 yrs; *Master/Magister*: Corporate Management

Student Services: Academic counselling, Canteen, Foreign student adviser, Handicapped facilities, Language programs, Sports facilities
Last Updated: 31/01/12

CARL MARIA VON WEBER UNIVERSITY OF MUSIC, DRESDEN

Hochschule für Musik Carl Maria von Weber Dresden
PO Box 120039, Wettiner Platz 13, 01001 Dresden
Tel: +49(351) 4923-600
Fax: +49(351) 4923-657
EMail: rektorat@hfmdd.de
Website: http://www.hfmdd.de

Rektor: Ekkehard Klemm
Tel: +49(351) 4923-641, Fax: +49(351) 4923-604

Kanzler: Peter Neuner
Tel: +49(351) 4923-627 EMail: kanzler@hfmdd.de

International Relations: Gerda Werner
Tel: +49(351) 4923-638 EMail: ausland@hfmdd.de

Departments
Department 1 (Conducting; Music; Musical Instruments; Singing); **Department 2** (Jazz and Popular Music; Music Education; Music Theory and Composition; Pedagogy)

History: Founded 1952.

Main Language(s) of Instruction: German

Degrees and Diplomas: *Bachelor/Bakkalaureus*; *Diplom*; *Konzertexamen*; *Staatsprüfung*; *Master/Magister*
Last Updated: 02/02/12

CARL VON OSSIETZKY UNIVERSITY OLDENBURG

Carl von Ossietzky Universität Oldenburg
Ammerländer Heerstr. 114-118, 26129 Oldenburg
Tel: +49(441) 798-0
Fax: +49(441) 798-3000
EMail: praesidium@uni-oldenburg.de
Website: http://www.uni-oldenburg.de

Präsidentin: Babette Simon (2010-)
Tel: +49(441) 798-5452 / -5464, Fax: +49(441) 798-2399
EMail: praesidentin@uni-oldenburg.de

Faculties

Mathematics and Science (Applied Chemistry; Biology; Chemistry; Environmental Studies; Marine Biology; Marine Science and Oceanography; Mathematics; Physics)

Schools

Computing Science, Business Administration, Economics, and Law (Business Administration; Computer Science; Economics; Education; Law; Technology Education); **Educational and Social Sciences** (Education; Social Sciences; Special Education); **Humanities and Social Sciences** (History; Philosophy; Political Sciences; Psychology; Religious Education; Sociology; Sports; Theology); **Linguistics and Cultural Studies** (Cultural Studies; Fashion Design; German; Media Studies; Modern Languages; Music; Textile Design)

Further Information: Also Special Research Field 517 of the German Research Authority 'Human Brain's Cognitive Processes'

History: Founded 1973. Teaching started 1974 with incorporation of the Oldenburg branch of the College of Education, Niedersachsen. An autonomous institution financially supported by the State of Lower Saxony and under the jurisdiction of its Ministry of Education.

Governing Bodies: Senate

Academic Year: October to September (October-March; April-September)

Admission Requirements: Secondary school certificate (Abitur) or recognized equivalent. Technical secondary education (Fachhochschulreife) for certain courses. Examination for Master craftman's diploma (Meisterprüfung); and special course of studies (Zalassungsprüfung)

Fees: (Euros): 700 per semester

Main Language(s) of Instruction: German; English

International Co-operation: With universities in Netherlands, USA, Russian Federation, France, Czech Republic, Israel, Japan, Kazakhstan, Poland, South Africa, Turkey, United Kingdom, Finland, Spain, Italy, Canada, Australia, New Zealand, Lithuania, Hungary. Participates in the Socrates/ Erasmus programmes

Degrees and Diplomas: *Bachelor/Bakkalaureus*: English; Biology; Chemistry; Mathematics; Theology; Religious Education; German; History; Computer Science; Cultural Studies; Arts; Media; Fashion; Music; Dutch; Economic; Philosophy (B.Sc); Law (LL.B.); Physical Engineering (B.Eng); Social Sciences; Special Education; Sport; Technology Education; Slavic Studies (B.A.), 3 yrs; *Diplom*: Economics; Biology; Chemistry; Computer Science; Intercultural Education; Education; Physics; Mathematics; Marine Environment, 4-5 yrs; *Master/Magister*: Museum and Exhibition (M.A.); Physical Engineering; Computer Science; Integrated Coastal Zone Management; Microelectronics and Robotics; Audiology; Renewable Energy (M.Sc.), 2-3 yrs; *Doktorgrad*: Neurosensory Science and Systems (PhD). Also Double-Major Bachelor's degrees.

Student Services: Academic counselling, Canteen, Cultural centre, Foreign student adviser, Foreign Studies Centre, Handicapped facilities, Health services, Language programs, Nursery care, Social counselling, Sports facilities

Student Residential Facilities: For 1,341 students

Special Facilities: Botanical Garden

Libraries: Bibliotheks- und Informationssystem, c. 1m. vols. Mediothek with 15,000 video cassettes, 3,500 films, 20,000 LPs, 6,500 CDs

Publications: Einblicke, Research Magazine *(biennially)*
Last Updated: 22/03/11

CATHOLIC UNIVERSITY FOR APPLIED SCIENCES BERLIN (KHSB)

Katholischen Hochschule für Sozialwesen Berlin
Köpenicker Allee 39-57, 10318 Berlin
Tel: +49(30) 5010100
Fax: +49(30) 501010-88
EMail: rektorat@kfb-berlin.de
Website: http://www.khsb-berlin.de

Rektorin: Monika Treber
Tel: +49(30) 501010-13, Fax: +49(30) 501010-94
EMail: monika.treber@khsb-berlin.de

Verwaltungsleiter: Martin Wrzesinski
Tel: +49(30) 501010-14
EMail: verwaltung@khsb-berlin.de; wrzesinski@khsb-berlin.de

International Relations: Elvira Stachovic

Programmes

Education (Education); **Health Education** (Health Education); **Religious Education** (Religious Education); **Social Work** (Social Work)

History: Founded 1991.

Main Language(s) of Instruction: German

Degrees and Diplomas: *Bachelor/Bakkalaureus*; *Master/Magister*
Last Updated: 03/02/12

CATHOLIC UNIVERSITY OF APPLIED SCIENCES IN FREIBURG

Katholische Hochschule Freiburg
Karlstrasse 63, 79104 Freiburg
Tel: +49(761) 200-476
Fax: +49(761) 200-444
EMail: rektorat@kfh-freiburg.de
Website: http://www.kh-freiburg.de

Rektorin: Barbara Herr
Tel: +49(761) 200-476 EMail: rektorat@kh-freiburg.de

Kanzler: Martin Kraft
Tel: +49(761) 200-488 EMail: kanzler@kh-freiburg.de

Programmes

Health Care Management; **Inclusive Education**; **Management of Education Institutions** (Educational Administration); **Nursing**; **Nursing Education** (Health Education; Nursing); **Physiotherapy** (Physical Therapy); **Social Work** *(Master)*

History: Founded 1918, acquired present status 1971.

Governing Bodies: Board; Senate

Academic Year: September to August

Admission Requirements: Academic Standard required for University Entrance

Fees: None

Main Language(s) of Instruction: German

International Co-operation: With Universities in France, Italy, Spain

Degrees and Diplomas: *Bachelor/Bakkalaureus*: 3 yrs; *Master/Magister*: a further 2 yrs

Student Services: Nursery care
Last Updated: 22/03/11

CATHOLIC UNIVERSITY OF APPLIED SCIENCES IN MAINZ

Katholische Fachhochschule Mainz
PO Box 2340, 55013 Mainz
Tel: +49(6131) 28944-0
Fax: +49(6131) 28944-50
EMail: e-mail@kfh-mainz.de
Website: http://www.kfh-mainz.de

Rektor: Peter Orth
Tel: +49(6131) 28944-45
EMail: rektorat@kfh-mainz.de; orth@kfh-mainz.de

Prorektorin: Ruth Remmel-Fassbender EMail: re-fa@kfh.mainz.de

Departments
Health Sciences and Nursing (Gerontology; Health Administration; Health Sciences; Nursing); **Social Work** (Social Work); **Theology** (Theology)

History: Founded 1972.

Main Language(s) of Instruction: German

Degrees and Diplomas: *Bachelor/Bakkalaureus*; *Diplom (FH)*; *Master/Magister*
Last Updated: 21/01/10

CATHOLIC UNIVERSITY OF APPLIED SCIENCES MUNICH
Katholische Stiftungsfachhochschule München
Preysingstrasse 83, 81667 München
Tel: +49(89) 480-92271
Fax: +49(89) 480-1907
EMail: ksfh.muc@ksfh.de
Website: http://www.ksfh.de

Präsident: Egon Endres
Tel: +49(89) 48092-1272, Fax: 0
EMail: praesident@ksfh.de; egon.endres@ksfh.de

Verwaltungsleiterin: Cordula Schön
Tel: +49(89) 48092-1277 EMail: verwaltungsleitung@ksfh.de

Departments
Care Management and Nursing Education (Health Administration; Nursing); **Child Education** (Child Care and Development); **Health Management** (Health Administration); **Social Work** (Social Work); **Social Work** *(Benediktbeuern)* (Social Work)

Programmes
Nursing *(Dual)* (Nursing); **Science in Addiction Prevention and Treatment** *(Master)*

Further Information: Also Theology Additional Programme in Munich and Benediktbeuern; E-Learning programme offered by the KSFH München and the Virtuellen Hochschule Bayern.

History: Founded 1971.

Main Language(s) of Instruction: German

Degrees and Diplomas: *Bachelor/Bakkalaureus*; *Master/Magister*
Last Updated: 21/01/10

CATHOLIC UNIVERSITY OF APPLIED SCIENCES NORTH RHINE-WESTPHALIA
Katholische Hochschule Nordrhein-Westfalen (KFH NW)
Robert-Schuman Str. 25, 52066 Aachen
Tel: +49(241) 600 03-0
Fax: +49(241) 600 03-88
EMail: postmaster@kfhnw.de
Website: http://www.katho-nrw.de

Rektor: Peter Berker
Tel: +49(221) 973147-15 EMail: rektor@kfhnw.de

Kanzler: Bernward Robrecht (2009-)
Tel: +49(221) 973147-10 EMail: kanzler@katho-nrw.de

Departments
Health Management (Health Administration; Nursing); **Social Work** (Social Work; Special Education); **Theology** (Theology)
Further Information: Campuses in Köln, Münster and Paderborn
History: Founded 1971.

Main Language(s) of Instruction: German

Degrees and Diplomas: *Bachelor/Bakkalaureus*; *Diplom*; *Master/Magister*
Last Updated: 22/03/11

CENTRAL HESSE TECHNICAL UNIVERSITY OF APPLIED SCIENCE
Technische Hochschule Mittelhessen
Wiesenstrasse 14, 35390 Giessen, Hessen
Tel: +49(641) 309-0
Fax: +49(641) 309-2901
EMail: info@thm.de
Website: http://www.thm.de

Präsident: Günther Grabatin (2006-)
Tel: +49(641) 309-1000, Fax: +49(641) 309-2900
EMail: praesident@thm.de

Departments
Business Engineering *(Friedberg)* (Engineering); **Construction** *(Gießen)* (Construction Engineering); **Economics** *(Gießen)* (Economics); **Electronic Engineering and Information Technology** *(Gießen)* (Electrical Engineering; Information Technology); **Hospital and Medical Technology, Environmental and Bioengineering** *(Gießen)* (Bioengineering; Environmental Engineering; Health Sciences; Medical Technology); **Information Technology, Electronic Engineering, Mechatronics** *(Friedberg)* (Electronic Engineering; Information Technology; Mechanical Engineering); **Machine Building, Mechatronics, Materials Engineering** *(Friedberg)* (Machine Building; Materials Engineering); **Machine Building, Microengineering, Energy and Heating Engineering** *(Gießen)* (Energy Engineering; Engineering; Heating and Refrigeration; Machine Building; Mechanical Engineering); **Mathematics, Natural Sciences and Computer Science** *(Gießen)* (Computer Science; Mathematics; Natural Sciences); **Mathematics, Natural Sciences and Data Processing** *(Friedberg)* (Data Processing; Mathematics; Natural Sciences); **Social and Cultural Studies** *(Gießen, Friedberg)* (Cultural Studies; Social Sciences; Social Studies; Transport Management)

Faculties
Scientific Centre for Dual University Studies, Studium Plus *(Wetzlar)* (Business Administration; Engineering; Engineering Management)

History: Founded 1971. Previously known as Fachhochschule Giessen-Friedberg (University of Applied Sciences Giessen-Friedberg).

Academic Year: October to July

Admission Requirements: Secondary School Certificate (Fachhochschulreife or Abitur)

Fees: None

Main Language(s) of Instruction: German

International Co-operation: With universities in South Africa, USA, Cuba, Ukraine, Australia. Participates in Erasmus, Leonardo, DAAD

Accrediting Agencies: ZEVA; ASIIN; AQUIN

Degrees and Diplomas: *Bachelor/Bakkalaureus*: Clinical Engineering; Business Administration; Computer Science; Microsystems; Multimedia Engineering; Computer Science in Economics, 3 yrs; *Diplom (FH)*: Engineering; Business Administration; Computer Science, 4 yrs; *Master/Magister*: Business Administration; Computer Science, 2 yrs; *Master/Magister*: Business Administration; Marketing, 1-2 yrs; *Master/Magister*: Information and Communication Engineering; Technical Editing and Multimedia Documentation, 11/2 yrs; *Master/Magister*: Multimedia Engineering; Computer Science in Economics

Student Services: Academic counselling, Canteen, Foreign student adviser, Handicapped facilities, Language programs, Social counselling, Sports facilities

Student Residential Facilities: Yes
Last Updated: 03/11/11

CHEMNITZ UNIVERSITY OF TECHNOLOGY
Technische Universität Chemnitz
Strasse der Nationen 62, 09107 Chemnitz
Tel: +49(371) 531-0
EMail: iuz@tu-chemnitz.de
Website: http://www.tu-chemnitz.de

Rektor: Cornelia Zanger
Tel: +49(371) 531-10000, Fax: +49(371) 531-10009
EMail: rektor@tu-chemnitz.de

Kanzler: Eberhard Alles
Tel: +49(371) 531-12000, Fax: +49(371) 531-12009
EMail: kanzler@tu-chemnitz.de

International Relations: Esther Smykalla
Tel: +49(371) 531-13500, Fax: +49(371) 531-13509

Faculties
Computer Science (Computer Science); **Economics and Business Administration** (Business Administration; Economics;

Finance; Management; Marketing); **Electrical Engineering and Information Technology** (Electrical Engineering; Information Technology; Microelectronics); **Humanities and Social Sciences** (Adult Education; American Studies; Arts and Humanities; Communication Studies; Economics; Educational Sciences; English Studies; European Studies; Geography; Germanic Studies; History; International Studies; Linguistics; Literature; Media Studies; Philosophy; Political Sciences; Psychology; Romance Languages; Sociology; Sports); **Mathematics** (Finance; Mathematics); **Mechanical Engineering** (Construction Engineering; Industrial Engineering; Mechanical Engineering; Natural Sciences; Production Engineering); **Natural Sciences** (Chemistry; Computer Science; Materials Engineering; Natural Sciences; Physics)

History: Founded 1836 as Royal Trade School of Chemnitz, became College of Mechanical Engineering 1953, and College of Technology 1963. Acquired present title 1986. Responsible to the Ministry of Science and Culture.

Governing Bodies: Konzil; Kuratorium; Senat

Academic Year: October to September (October-March; April-September)

Admission Requirements: Secondary school certificate (Reifezeugnis) or equivalent

Fees: None

Main Language(s) of Instruction: German

International Co-operation: With universities in UK; Finland; France; Spain; Czech Republic; Japan; USA

Degrees and Diplomas: *Bachelor/Bakkalaureus (BA)*: 3-4 yrs; *Diplom (Dipl.)*: 4-5 yrs; *Master/Magister*: 1-2 yrs; *Doktorgrad (Dr.)*: first level, a further 4 yrs; *Habilitation (Habil.)*: second level, 4-5 yrs after first level, by thesis. Also Combined Degrees

Student Services: Academic counselling, Canteen, Employment services, Foreign student adviser, Handicapped facilities, Health services, Nursery care, Social counselling, Sports facilities

Student Residential Facilities: Yes

Libraries: Universitätsbibliotek, c. 1,200,000 vols
Last Updated: 06/02/12

CHRISTIAN ALBRECHT UNIVERSITY OF KIEL

Christian-Albrechts-Universität zu Kiel
Christian-Albrechts-Platz 4, 24118 Kiel
Tel: +49(431) 880-00
Fax: +49(431) 880-2072
EMail: mail@uni-kiel.de
Website: http://www.uni-kiel.de

President: Gerhard Fouquet (2008-)
Tel: +49(431) 880-3000, Fax: +49(431) 880-7333
EMail: rektor@rektorat.uni-kiel.de

Kanzler: Oliver Herrmann
Tel: +49(431) 880-3003, Fax: +49(431) 880-7333
EMail: kanzler@praesidium.uni-kiel.de

International Relations: Martina Schmode, Director
Tel: +49(431) 880-3715, Fax: +49(431) 880-1666
EMail: mschmode@uv.uni-kiel.de

Faculties
Agriculture and Nutritional Sciences (Agricultural Economics; Agricultural Engineering; Agriculture; Animal Husbandry; Crop Production; Food Science; Nutrition; Soil Science); **Arts and Humanities** (Archaeology; Art History; Arts and Humanities; History; Linguistics; Musicology; Pedagogy; Philology; Philosophy; Phonetics; Psychology); **Business, Economics and Social Sciences** (Business Administration; Economics; Social Sciences; Statistics); **Engineering** (Computer Science; Electronic Engineering; Materials Engineering; Technology); **Law** (Criminology; European Union Law; Law); **Mathematics and Natural Sciences** (Biology; Chemistry; Marine Science and Oceanography; Mathematics; Natural Sciences; Pharmacy; Physics); **Medicine** (Health Sciences; Medicine); **Theology** (Theology)

History: Founded 1665 by Christian Albrecht, Duke of Holstein-Gottorf. Became Landes-Universität (provincial University) for the State of Schleswig-Holstein 1773. Incorporated as Prussian University 1867 and re-established as Landes-Universität 1945.

Autonomous institution financially supported by the State of Schleswig-Holstein.

Governing Bodies: Senat; Konsistorium

Academic Year: October to September (October-March; April-September)

Admission Requirements: Secondary school certificate (Abitur) or equivalent

Fees: None

Main Language(s) of Instruction: German

International Co-operation: With universities in France; Italy; Spain; Sweden; United Kingdom; Finland; Poland. Also participates in Socrates/Erasmus

Degrees and Diplomas: *Bachelor/Bakkalaureus*: Agricultural Science, Computer Science, Materials Science, 3 yrs; *Diplom*: Agricultural Economics, Protestant Theology; Psychology, 4.5 yrs; *Diplom*: Biology, Biochemistry and Molecular Biology, 5 yrs; *Diplom*: Business Administration, Pedagogics; Geography; Geology/Palaeontology; Mathematics; Mineralogy, 4-5 yrs; *Diplom*: Chemistry; Computer Science, Computer Engineering, Electrical Engineering and Information Technology, Materials Science; Meterology; Oceanography; Physics, Geophysics; *Diplom*: Economics, 4 yrs; *Lehramt*: Teaching Qualifications, Secondary level, 4 yrs; *Staatsprüfung*: Dentistry, 5.5 yrs; *Staatsprüfung*: Law; Pharmacy, 4 yrs; *Staatsprüfung*: Medicine, 2-4.25 yrs; *Master/Magister*: Agricultural Science, Electrical Engineering and Information Technology, Materials Science, Geostal Geosciences and Engineering, 2 yrs; *Master/Magister*: Political Science, Art History, Musicology, Pedagogics, Philosophy, Psychology, Sport Sciences, Geography, 4-5 yrs; *Doktorgrad*: a further 3-5 yrs; *Habilitation*: at least 3 yrs following Doktor. Also Kirchlich-Theologisches Examen

Student Services: Academic counselling, Canteen, Cultural centre, Employment services, Foreign student adviser, Foreign Studies Centre, Handicapped facilities, Health services, Language programs, Nursery care, Social counselling, Sports facilities

Student Residential Facilities: Yes

Special Facilities: Zoologisches Museum; Mineralogisch-Petrographisches Museum; Geologische-Paläontologisches Museum; Wanderndes Museum; Archäologisches Landesmuseum und Wikinger-Museum Haithabu. Kunsthalle. Botanischer Garten. Theatergeschichtliche Sammlung und Hebbelsammlung; Antiken Sammlung; Medizin-Historische Sammlung

Libraries: University Library, c. 4m. vols; Institute of World Economics Library, c. 2.4m

Publications: Forschungsbericht Christiana Albertina; Vorlesungsverzeichnis
Last Updated: 06/02/12

CLAUSTHAL UNIVERSITY OF TECHNOLOGY

Technische Universität Clausthal
Adolph-Roemer-Strasse 2A, 38678 Clausthal-Zellerfeld
Tel: +49(5323) 72-0
Fax: +49(5323) 72-3500
EMail: international@tu-clausthal.de
Website: http://www.tu-clausthal.de

Präsident: Thomas Hanschke
Tel: +49(5323) 72-3018 EMail: praesident@tu-clausthal.de

Faculties
Energy and Management (Chemistry; Economics; Electrical Engineering; Energy Engineering; Environmental Studies; Geology; Management; Mechanical Engineering; Mineralogy; Paleontology); **Mathematics, Computer Science and Mechanical Engineering** (Computer Science; Machine Building; Mathematics; Mechanical Engineering; Production Engineering; Thermal Engineering); **Natural and Material Sciences** (Inorganic Chemistry; Laser Engineering; Metallurgical Engineering; Organic Chemistry; Physical Chemistry; Physics; Polymer and Plastics Technology)

History: Founded 1775, became 'Bergakademie Clausthal' 1864, acquired University status 1920. Present title conferred 1968. An autonomous institution under the jurisdiction of and financially supported by the State of Lower Saxony.

Governing Bodies: Hochschulrat; Senat; Präsidium

Academic Year: October to September (October-March; April-September)

Admission Requirements: Secondary school certificate (Reifezeugnis/Abitur) or equivalent

Fees: (Euros): 500 per semester

Main Language(s) of Instruction: German

International Co-operation: With universities in France; Italy; Spain; UK; Poland; Romania.

Degrees and Diplomas: *Bachelor/Bakkalaureus*: 4 1/2 yrs; *Diplom*: Chemical Engineering; Environmental Engineering; Information Engineering; Mechanical Engineering; Power Systems Engineering; Process Engineering, 4 1/2 yrs; *Master/Magister*: 4 1/2 yrs

Student Services: Academic counselling, Canteen, Foreign student adviser, Language programs, Social counselling, Sports facilities

Student Residential Facilities: For c. 1,000 students

Special Facilities: Mineralogy Museum

Libraries: University Library, c. 400,000 vols; Calvörsche Bibliothek, 4,400 vols
Last Updated: 27/01/10

COBURG UNIVERSITY OF APPLIED SCIENCES

Hochschule Coburg (FH COBURG)
Friedrich-Streib-Strasse 2, 96450 Coburg
Tel: +49(9561) 317-0
Fax: +49(9561) 317-275
EMail: poststelle@fh-coburg.de
Website: http://www.fh-coburg.de

Präsident: Michael Pötzl
Tel: +49(9561) 317-112, Fax: +49(9561) 317-109
EMail: poetzl @ hs-coburg.de

Kanzlerin: Maria Knott-Lutze
Tel: +49(9561) 317-140 EMail: knott-lutze@fh-coburg.de

International Relations: Annette Stegemann
Tel: +49(9561) 317-140, Fax: +49(9561) 317-109
EMail: stegeman@fh-coburg.de

Departments
Electrical Engineering and Computer Science (Civil Engineering; Computer Engineering; Construction Engineering; Electrical and Electronic Engineering; Information Sciences; Information Technology; Machine Building; Mechanical Engineering; Physical Engineering); **Mechanical Engineering** (Mechanical Engineering)

Faculties
Business Studies (Accountancy; Banking; Data Processing; Human Resources; Insurance; International Business; Management; Marketing; Sales Techniques); **Design** (Architecture; Civil Engineering; Industrial Design; Interior Design); **Science** (Technology); **Social Work and Health Sciences** (Health Sciences; Social Work)

History: Founded 1971.

Academic Year: October to September (October-March; March-September)

Admission Requirements: Secondary school certificate (Fachhochschulreife)

Fees: None

Main Language(s) of Instruction: German

International Co-operation: With universities in Mexico, USA, Spain, France, United Kingdom, Netherlands, Italy, Poland, Czech Republic, Hungary, Lithuania, Latvia, Iceland, Austria.

Degrees and Diplomas: *Bachelor/Bakkalaureus*: Automotive Engineering and Management; Computer Science; Electronic Engineering; Business Administration; Insurance; Social Work; Integrative Health Promotion; Architecture; Civil Engineering; Interior Architecture; Integrated Product Design; *Diplom (FH)*: Machine Building; Physical Engineering; *Master/Magister*: Information Technology and Enterprise Applications; Electronic Engineering and Information Technology; Strategic Innovation; Financial Management; Insurance Management; Management in Health Sciences; Social Work; Interior Architecture

Student Services: Academic counselling, Canteen, Foreign student adviser, Foreign Studies Centre, Handicapped facilities, Language programs, Social counselling

Student Residential Facilities: For 450 Students

Libraries: 70,000 vols, 330 newspaper subscriptions
Last Updated: 22/03/11

COLLEGE OF APPLIED LANGUAGES MUNICH

Hochschule für Angewandte Sprachen München - Fachhochschule des SDI
Sprachen und Dolmetscher Institut München, Amalienstraße 73, 80799 München
Tel: +49(89) 288102-0
Fax: +49(89) 288440
EMail: kontakt@sdi-muenchen.de
Website: http://www.sdi-muenchen.de

Präsident: Felix Mayer
Tel: +49(89) 288102-16 EMail: Felix.Mayer@sdi-muenchen.de

Geschäftsführer: Stefan Broschwitz
EMail: Stefan.Broschwitz@sdi-muenchen.de

Programmes
Chinese Corporate Communication; **Chinese Translation** (Chinese; Translation and Interpretation); **Conference Interpretation** *(Master)* (Modern Languages; Translation and Interpretation); **Intercultural Moderation and Multilingual Communication** *(Master)* (Communication Studies; Cultural Studies; Modern Languages); **International Corporate Communication** (Communication Studies; Modern Languages); **Multlingual Technical Redaction** (Communication Studies; Modern Languages; Technology); **Technico-scientific Communication** *(Master)* (Communication Studies; Engineering; English; Modern Languages; Technology)

History: Founded 2007.

Main Language(s) of Instruction: German

Degrees and Diplomas: *Bachelor/Bakkalaureus*; *Master/Magister*
Last Updated: 18/01/10

COLLEGE OF DESIGN, KARLSRUHE

Staatliche Hochschule für Gestaltung Karlsruhe
Lorenzstrasse 15, 76135 Karlsruhe
Tel: +49(721) 8203-0
Fax: +49(721) 8203-2159
EMail: hochschule@hfg-karlsruhe.de
Website: http://www.hfg-karlsruhe.de

Rektor: Peter Sloterdijk (2001-)
Tel: +49(721) 8203-2306 EMail: r.nolte@mh-freiburg.de

Leitender Verwaltungsbeamter: Manfred Erlewein
Tel: +49(721) 8203-2365
EMail: manfred.erlewein@verwaltung.hfg-karlsruhe.de

International Relations: Michael Schuster

Departments
Graphic Design (Graphic Design); **Media Arts** (Media Studies); **Philosophy and Aesthetics** (Aesthetics; Philosophy); **Production Design** (Design); **Scenography** (Display and Stage Design)

History: Founded 1992.

Main Language(s) of Instruction: German

Degrees and Diplomas: *Diplom*; *Magister Artium*
Last Updated: 26/01/10

COLLEGE OF JEWISH STUDIES, HEIDELBERG

Hochschule für Jüdische Studien Heidelberg (HJS)
Landfriedstr. 12, 69117 Heidelberg
Tel: +49(6221) 54 19 200
EMail: info@hfjs.eu
Website: http://www.hfjs.eu

Rektor: Johannes Heil (2008-) EMail: rektor@hfjs.eu

Head of Administration: Michael Göckel
Tel: +49(6221) 1631-31, Fax: +49(6221) 43851-29
EMail: michael.goeckel@hfjs.eu

International Relations: Irene Kaufmann
Tel: +49(6221) 43851-12
EMail: aaa@zuv.uni-heidelberg.de; irene.kaufmann@hfjs.eu

Programmes

Community Work (Social Work); **Jewish Studies** (Jewish Studies); **Medieval Studies** (Medieval Studies); **Rabbinics** (Jewish Studies)

History: Founded 1979, recognized by the State of Baden-Württemberg 1981. An institution of the Zentralrat der Juden in Deutschland and associated with the University of Heidelberg.

Governing Bodies: Kuratorium; Senat

Academic Year: October to July (October-February; April-July)

Admission Requirements: Secondary school certificate (Abitur)

Main Language(s) of Instruction: German

Degrees and Diplomas: *Bachelor/Bakkalaureus*: Community Work; Jewish Studies; *Magister Artium*; *Staatsprüfung*: Jewish Studies, 10 sem; *Master/Magister*: Jewish Culture and History (Joint degree); Jewish Studies; Rabbinat; *Promotion*: Jewish Studies (PhD)

Student Services: Canteen

Libraries: 40,000 vols

Publications: Trumah *(annually)*
Last Updated: 19/01/10

COLLEGE OF THE SPARKASSEN-FINANCIAL GROUP - UNIVERSITY OF APPLIED SCIENCES BONN

Hochschule der Sparkassen-Finanzgruppe, University of Applied Sciences, Bonn GmbH
Simrockstraße 4, 53113 Bonn
Tel: +49(228) 204-900
Fax: +49(228) 204-903
EMail: s-hochschule@dsgv.de
Website: http://www.s-hochschule.de/home/index.html

Rektor: Eberhard Stickel (2006-) EMail: eberhard.stickel@dsgv.de

Kanzler: Andreas Brunold
Tel: +49(228) 204-910 EMail: andreas.brunold@dsgv.de

Programmes

Corporate Banking (Banking; Business Administration; Economics; Finance; Law; Mathematics); **Finance** (Banking; Business Administration; Economics; Finance; Law; Mathematics); **Financial Information Systems** *(Bachelor programme)* (Banking; Business Administration; Communication Studies; Computer Science; E-Business/Commerce; Finance; Law; Management; Mathematics; Software Engineering)

Academic Year: September to August (September-January;February-August)

Admission Requirements: Applicants must hold a Secondary School Leaving Certificate or equivalent or have a working/training contract with a finance service company or have had one year of relevant work experience; additionally, applicants to the "Corporate Banking" programme must pass TOEFL exam (with at least 250 points for the computerised version and 600 points for the paper version)

Fees: (Euros): tuition fee, 12,600-13,100; registation fee, 600-1,100

Degrees and Diplomas: *Bachelor/Bakkalaureus*; *Master/Magister*
Last Updated: 12/02/09

COLOGNE UNIVERSITY OF APPLIED SCIENCES

Fachhochschule Köln
Claudiusstrasse 1, 50678 Köln, Nordrhein-Westfalen
Tel: +49(221) 8275-1
Fax: +49(221) 8275-3131
EMail: kerstin.keller@fh-koeln.de
Website: http://www.fh-koeln.de

Rektor: Joachim Metzner (1989-)
Tel: +49(221) 8275-3100, Fax: +49(221) 8275-3136
EMail: rektorat@zv.fh-koeln.de

Kanzlerin: Gisela Nagel
Tel: +49(221) 8275-3104, Fax: +49(221) 93179-001
EMail: kanzlerin@fh-koeln.de

International Relations: Elisabeth Holuscha, Head, International Office
Tel: +49(221) 8275-3110, Fax: +49(221) 8275-3369
EMail: elisabeth.holuscha@fh-koeln.de

Faculties

Applied Social Sciences (Child Care and Development; Family Studies; Gender Studies; Media Studies; Social Sciences; Social Work); **Architecture** (Architecture; Architecture and Planning); **Automotive Systems and Production Engineering** (Automotive Engineering; Production Engineering); **Civil Engineering and Environmental Technology** (Construction Engineering; Hydraulic Engineering; Transport Engineering); **Computer and Engineering Science** (Business Computing; Computer Science; Engineering; Information Technology); **Cultural Sciences** (Cultural Studies); **Economic Sciences** (Banking; Business Administration; Commercial Law; Economics; Finance); **Information Science and Communication Studies** (Information Sciences; Telecommunications Services); **Information, Media and Electrical Engineering** (Automation and Control Engineering; Electrical Engineering; Information Technology; Telecommunications Engineering); **Process Engineering, Energy and Mechanical Systems** (Energy Engineering; Industrial Engineering; Mechanical Engineering)

Institutes
Tropical Technology (Technology)

History: Founded 1971.

Fees: (Euros): 110-750

Main Language(s) of Instruction: German

International Co-operation: Egypt, Argentina, Australia, Belgium, Brazil, Chile, China, France, United Kingdom, Italy, Cuba, Colombia, Mexico, Nepal, Netherlands, Poland, Russian Federation, Slovenia, Spain, USA and Vietnam. Also participates in Erasmus and Socrates programmes.

Degrees and Diplomas: *Bachelor/Bakkalaureus*; *Master/Magister*

Student Services: Academic counselling, Canteen, Foreign student adviser, Foreign Studies Centre, Handicapped facilities, Language programs, Sports facilities

Student Residential Facilities: Yes

Libraries: Yes
Last Updated: 06/02/12

CONSTANCE UNIVERSITY OF APPLIED SCIENCES

Hochschule Konstanz Technik, Wirtschaft und Gestaltung (FHK)
Brauneggerstrasse 55, 78405 Konstanz, Baden-Württemberg
Tel: +49(7531) 206-0
Fax: +49(7531) 206-400
EMail: kontakt@htwg-konstanz.de
Website: http://www.fh-konstanz.de

Präsident: Kai Handel
Tel: +49(7531) 206-110, Fax: +49(7531) 206-117
EMail: handel@htwg-konstanz.de

Kanzlerin: Margit Plahl
Tel: +49(7531) 206-118 EMail: plahl@htwg-konstanz.de

International Relations: Klemens Blass, Head, Office of International Affairs
Tel: +49(7531) 206-297, Fax: +49(7531) 206-253
EMail: blass@htwg-konstanz.de

Departments

Architecture and Design (Architecture; Graphic Design); **Civil Engineering** (Civil Engineering; Industrial Engineering); **Computer Science** (Business Computing; Computer Science; Information Technology; Software Engineering; Systems Analysis); **Economics and Social Sciences** (Accountancy; Business Administration; Economics; Finance; Human Resources; International Business); **Electrical Engineering and Information Technology** (Automation and Control Engineering; Communication Studies; Electrical Engineering; Information Technology; Power Engineering); **Mechanical Engineering** (Environmental Engineering; Industrial Engineering;

Industrial Management; Mechanical Engineering; Sales Techniques)

History: Founded 1906 as Higher Technical Training Institute for Mechanical, Electrical and Civil Engineering. Acquired present status 1971.

Governing Bodies: Board of Governors (Hochschulrat); Senate

Academic Year: October to July (October-February; March-July)

Admission Requirements: Abitur or equivalent qualification

Main Language(s) of Instruction: German

International Co-operation: With universities in Belgium; Denmark; Finland; France; United Kingdom; Austria; Portugal; Romania; Russian Federation; Spain; Sweden; South Africa; Brazil; Canada; Mexico; USA; India; Indonesia; Thailand; China

Degrees and Diplomas: *Bachelor/Bakkalaureus*; *Master/Magister*. Architecture; Asian-European Relations and Management; Automotive Systems Engineering; Civil Engineering; Business Computing; Electrical Systems; Computer Science; Communication Design; Mechanical Engineering and International Sales Management; Mechatronics; Environmental and Process Engineering; Business Engineering

Student Services: Academic counselling, Canteen, Cultural centre, Employment services, Foreign student adviser, Foreign Studies Centre, Handicapped facilities, Language programs, Nursery care, Social counselling, Sports facilities

Student Residential Facilities: Yes

Libraries: Yes

Publications: FHK - Forum, Research *(1-2 per annum)*
Last Updated: 12/01/10

DARMSTADT UNIVERSITY OF APPLIED SCIENCES
Hochschule Darmstadt (FHD)
Haardtring 100, 64295 Darmstadt, Hessen
Tel: +49(6151) 16-0
Fax: +49(6151) 16-8949
EMail: info@h-da.de
Website: http://www.h-da.de

Präsidentin: Maria Overbeck-Larisch (2004-)
Tel: +49(6151) 16-8002, Fax: +49(6151) 16-8949
EMail: praesident@fh-darmstadt.de

Kanzlerin: Ellen Göbel
Tel: +49(6151) 16-8006 EMail: goebel@fh-darmstadt.de

International Relations: Lucia Koch
Tel: +49(6151) 16-8016, Fax: +49(6151) 16-8028
EMail: lucia.koch@h-da.de

Departments
Architecture (Architecture; Interior Design); **Chemical Engineering** (Biotechnology; Chemical Engineering); **Civil Engineering** (Civil Engineering); **Computer Science** (Computer Science); **Design** (Graphic Design; Industrial Design); **Economics** (Business Administration; Economics); **Electrical Engineering and Information Technology** (Electrical Engineering; Electronic Engineering; Microelectronics); **Electrical Engineering/ Telecommunication** (Electrical Engineering; Telecommunications Engineering); **Information and Knowledge Management** (Information Management); **Mathematics and Science** (Mathematics; Optical Technology); **Mechanical Engineering** (Mechanical Engineering); **Media** (Media Studies); **Plastics Engineering** (Polymer and Plastics Technology); **Social and Cultural Studies** (Cultural Studies; Journalism; Social Studies); **Social Education** (Humanities and Social Science Education)

History: Founded 1971, merged in 2000 with Telekom FH Dieburg, now site of second campus.

Governing Bodies: Senate

Academic Year: September to August (September-February; March-August)

Admission Requirements: Secondary school certificate (Abitur; Fachabitur)

Fees: (Euros): 174.50 per semester

Main Language(s) of Instruction: German; some courses are in English

International Co-operation: With universities in Europe, USA, Brazil, India, Australia, Russian Federation, China. Also participates in Erasmus, Leonardo, Tempus, DAAD

Accrediting Agencies: ASIIN; ZEVA; AHPGS

Degrees and Diplomas: *Bachelor/Bakkalaureus*: 3 yrs; *Diplom (FH)*: Industrial Design; Information Rights; Communication Design; Online Journalism; *Master/Magister*. Also Engineering Diploma in cooperation with CNAM, Paris and Strasbourg

Student Services: Academic counselling, Canteen, Employment services, Foreign student adviser, Foreign Studies Centre, Handicapped facilities, Language programs, Social counselling, Sports facilities

Student Residential Facilities: Yes

Libraries: Central Library; Department Libraries
Last Updated: 01/02/12

DARMSTADT UNIVERSITY OF TECHNOLOGY
Technische Universität Darmstadt (TUD)
Karolinenplatz 5, 64289 Darmstadt, Hessen
Tel: +49(615) 116-1
Fax: +49(615) 116-5489
EMail: praesident@tu-darmstadt.de;
woerner@pvw.tu-darmstadt.de
Website: http://www.tu-darmstadt.de

Präsident: Hans Jürgen Prömel Tel: +49(615)116-2120

Kanzler: Manfred Efinger
Tel: +49(615) 116-3630 EMail: kanzler@tu-darmstadt.de

Departments
Applied Mechanics (Mechanical Engineering); **Architecture** (Architecture); **Biology** (Biology); **Chemistry** (Chemistry); **Civil Engineering and Geodesy** (Civil Engineering; Surveying and Mapping); **Computer Science** (Computer Science); **Electrical Engineering and Information Technology** (Electrical Engineering; Energy Engineering; Information Technology); **Humanities** (Educational Sciences; Psychology; Sports); **Law and Economics** (Economics; Law); **Material and Earth Sciences** (Geography; Geology; Materials Engineering); **Mathematics** (Mathematics); **Physics** (Physics); **Social Sciences and History** (History; Social Sciences)

History: Founded 1836 as Höhere Gewerbeschule, became Technische Hochschule in 1877 and acquired University status in 1895. Faculties replaced by departments 1971. An autonomous institution under the jurisdiction of the State of Hesse.

Governing Bodies: Senat; Hochschulversammlung; Hochschulrat

Academic Year: October to July (November-February; April-July)

Admission Requirements: Secondary school certificate (Reifezeugnis) or equivalent

Fees: (Euros): 50 per semester

Main Language(s) of Instruction: German

Accrediting Agencies: AVI e.U.

Degrees and Diplomas: *Bachelor/Bakkalaureus*: Computer Engineering; Mechanical and Process Engineering; Mathematics with Computer Science; Applied Mechanics; Information and Communication Technology; Political Science; *Diplom*: Biology; Chemistry; Computer Sciences; Engineering; Geology; Mathematics; Mineralogy; Physics; Psychology; Sociology; Sports; *Diplom*: Industrial Engineering, 11-14 sem; *Lehramt*; *Magister Artium*: Educational Theory; Geography; History; Literature and Language (German Studies); Political Science; Sports Studies, 9-12 sem; *Staatsprüfung*: 4 yrs; *Master/Magister*: Computer Engineering; Mechanical and Process Engineering; Paper Science and Technology; Information-and Communication Technology; Political Science; Information and Communication Engineering; *Doktorgrad*: Engineering (Dr.Ing.), a further 2-3 yrs; *Habilitation*: at least 3 yrs following Doktor

Student Services: Academic counselling, Canteen, Cultural centre, Employment services, Foreign student adviser, Foreign Studies Centre, Handicapped facilities, Language programs, Social counselling, Sports facilities

Student Residential Facilities: For c. 2,350 students

Special Facilities: Botanical Garden

Libraries: State and University Library, c. 1,297,000 vols

Publications: Thema Forschung (*biannually*)
Last Updated: 27/01/10

DEGGENDORF UNIVERSITY OF APPLIED SCIENCES

Fachhochschule Deggendorf (FHD)
Edlmairstrasse 6 + 8, 94469 Deggendorf, Bavaria
Tel: +49(991) 3615-0
Fax: +49(991) 3615-297
EMail: auslandsamst@fh-deggendorf.de
Website: http://www.fh-deggendorf.de

Präsident: Reinhard Höpfl (1996-)
Tel: +49(991) 3615-201, Fax: +49(991) 3615-299
EMail: praesident@fh-deggendorf.de

Kanzler: Gregor Biletzki
Tel: +49(991) 3615-210, Fax: +49(991) 3615-81210
EMail: gregor.biletzki@fh-deggendorf.de

International Relations: Elise von Randow
Tel: +49(991) 3615-202, Fax: +49(991) 3615-292
EMail: EvR@fh-deggendorf.de

Faculties

Business Administration and Business Computing (Business Administration; Business and Commerce; Business Computing; Management; Tourism); **Civil Engineering** (Civil Engineering; Construction Engineering; Environmental Management); **Electrical Engineering and Media Engineering** (Electrical Engineering; Electronic Engineering; Information Technology; Media Studies) *Dean*: Johann Plankl; **Machine Building and Mechatronics** (Business Administration; Electronic Engineering; Engineering; Machine Building; Mechanical Engineering)

History: Founded 1994.

Academic Year: October-July (October-February; March-July)

Admission Requirements: Abitur or equivalent qualification

Fees: (Euros): 80 per semester

Main Language(s) of Instruction: German. Also English for International Management programme

International Co-operation: With universities in Belgium; Finland; Ireland; Spain; Poland; Czech Republic; Korea; Australia; Brazil. Also participates in Erasmus

Degrees and Diplomas: *Bachelor/Bakkalaureus*; *Diplom*: Bauingenieurwesen; *Master/Magister*: Construction and Project Management; Strategic and International Management; Human Ressource Management; Business Computing; Business Creation, Management and Following

Student Services: Academic counselling, Canteen, Employment services, Foreign student adviser, Foreign Studies Centre, Handicapped facilities, Language programs, Sports facilities

Student Residential Facilities: Yes

Libraries: Yes
Last Updated: 06/02/12

DESIGN ACADEMY - UNIVERSITY OF COMMUNICATION AND DESIGN, BERLIN (UNIVERSITY OF APPLIED SCIENCES)

Design Akademie Berlin - Hochschule für Kommunikation und Design (FH)
Paul-Lincke-Ufer 8e, 10999 Berlin
Tel: +49 (30) 6165-480 +49 (30) 6953-5160
Fax: +49 (30) 6165-4819 +49 (30) 6953-5188
EMail: kd@design-akademie-berlin.de;
mk@design-akademie-berlin.de
Website: http://www.design-akademie-berlin.de

Rektor: Dieter von Froreich

Departments
Communication Design (Communication Studies; Design); **Marketing Communication** (Communication Studies; Marketing)

History: Founded 2007 on the basis of the of the Design Akademie Berlin (created in 1995).

Degrees and Diplomas: *Bachelor/Bakkalaureus*: Communication Design; Marketing Communication; *Master/Magister*: Creative Direction; Marketing Communication; Corporate Communication
Last Updated: 06/02/12

DEUTSCHE TELEKOM UNIVERSITY OF APPLIED SCIENCES LEIPZIG

Hochschule für Telekommunikation Leipzig
Gustav-Freytag-Strasse 43/45, 04277 Leipzig
Tel: +49(341) 3062-100
Fax: +49(341) 3015-069
EMail: pr@hft-leipzig.de
Website: http://www.hft-leipzig.de

Präsident: Michael Messolen (2007-)
Tel: +49(341) 3062-100, Fax: +49(341) 3062-278
EMail: messollen@hft-leipzig.de

Kanzlerin: Eva Hornung
Tel: +49(341) 3062-300, Fax: +49(341) 3062-309
EMail: eva.hornung@telekom.de

International Relations: Birgit Graf
Tel: +49(341) 3062-250, Fax: +49(341) 3062-285
EMail: graf.b@fh-telekom-leipzig.de

Programmes

Communications and Information Technology (*Cooperative*) (Information Technology; Telecommunications Engineering); **Information and Communication Engineering** (*Postgraduate*) (Information Technology; Telecommunications Engineering); **Information Technology** (Information Technology); **Telecommunications and Informatics** (Computer Science; Telecommunications Engineering)

History: Founded 1991. Previously known as Deutsche Telekom Fachhochschule Leipzig.

Main Language(s) of Instruction: German

Degrees and Diplomas: *Bachelor/Bakkalaureus*; *Diplom (FH)*; *Master/Magister*
Last Updated: 08/01/10

DIU - DRESDEN INTERNATIONAL UNIVERSITY

Chemnitzer Str. 46b, 01187 Dresden
Tel: +49(351) 463-323-26
Fax: +49(351) 463-339-56
EMail: info@di-uni.de
Website: http://www.di-uni.de

Rektor: Hans Wiesmeth

Centres
Health Science and Medicine (Health Sciences; Information Management; Medicine; Physical Therapy; Traditional Eastern Medicine)

Departments
Economic and Social Sciences (Economics; Social Sciences); **Jurisprudence** (Law); **Natural Sciences and Engineering** (Electronic Engineering; Engineering; Hydraulic Engineering; Natural Sciences)

History: Founded 2003.

Main Language(s) of Instruction: German

Degrees and Diplomas: *Zertifikat*: Healt Administration; *Bachelor/Bakkalaureus*; *Master/Magister*
Last Updated: 06/02/12

DORTMUND UNIVERSITY OF APPLIED SCIENCES AND ARTS

Fachhochschule Dortmund
PO Box 105018, Sonnenstrasse 96, 44047 Dortmund
Tel: +49(231) 9112-0
Fax: +49(231) 9112-313
EMail: rektor@fh-dortmund.de
Website: http://www.fh-dortmund.de

Rektor: Wilhelm Schwick
Tel: +49(231) 9112-100, Fax: +49(231) 9112-335

Kanzler: Rolf Pohlhausen
Tel: +49(231) 9112-104, Fax: +49(231) 9112-710
EMail: rolf.pohlhausen@h-dortmund.de

International Relations: Gisela Moser
Tel: +49(231) 9112-345, Fax: +49(231) 9112-273
EMail: moser@fh-dortmund.de

Faculties

Applied Social Studies (Social Studies; Social Work); **Architecture** (Architecture); **Business Studies** (Business Education; International Business); **Computer Science** (Computer Engineering; Computer Science; Medical Technology); **Design** (Communication Arts; Design; Film; Graphic Design); **Information and Electronics** (Communication Studies; Electronic Engineering; Information Technology; Multimedia; Telecommunications Engineering); **Mechanical Engineering** (Energy Engineering; Environmental Engineering; Mechanical Engineering; Production Engineering)

History: Founded 1971.

Academic Year: September to August

Admission Requirements: Secondary school certificate (Abitur, Fachhochschulreife)

Fees: (Euros): 110 per semester

Main Language(s) of Instruction: German

International Co-operation: With universities in Netherlands, France, Spain, Italy, Greece, Portugal, Sweden, Austria, Finland, Norway, United Kingdom, Ireland, Poland, Hungary, Slovenia, Belarus, Latvia, USA, South Africa, China. Also participates in Sokrates, Erasmus.

Degrees and Diplomas: *Bachelor/Bakkalaureus*; *Master/Magister*

Student Services: Academic counselling, Canteen, Foreign student adviser, Foreign Studies Centre, Language programs, Social counselling

Last Updated: 06/02/12

DORTMUND UNIVERSITY OF TECHNOLOGY
Technische Universität Dortmund
PO Box 500500, August-Schmidt-Strasse 4, 44221 Dortmund
Tel: +49(231) 755-1
Fax: +49(231) 755-4664
EMail: kanzler@tu-dortmund.de
Website: http://www.uni-dortmund.de

Rektorin: Ursula Gather
Tel: +49(231) 755-2200, Fax: +49(231) 755-5145
EMail: rektorin@tu-dortmund.de

Kanzler: Albrecht Ehlers

Centres
Continuing Education (Continuing Education); **Higher Education Research and Instructional Development** (Educational Research); **Multimedia** (Information Technology; Multimedia)

Faculties
Architecture and Civil Engineering (Architecture; Civil Engineering; Construction Engineering); **Art and Sport** (Art Education; Music; Musicology; Sports; Textile Design); **Biochemical and Chemical Engineering** (Bioengineering; Chemical Engineering); **Chemistry** (Chemistry); **Computer Science** (Computer Science); **Cultural Studies** (Cultural Studies); **Economics and Social Sciences** (Economics; Social Sciences); **Education and Sociology** (Education; Sociology); **Electrical Engineering and Information Technology** (Electrical Engineering; Information Technology); **Human Sciences and Theology** (Arts and Humanities; Philosophy; Social Sciences; Theology); **Mathematics** (Chemistry; Mathematics; Physics; Statistics); **Mechanical Engineering** (Mechanical Engineering); **Physics** (Physics); **Rehabilitation Sciences** (Rehabilitation and Therapy); **Spatial Planning**; **Statistics** (Statistics)

Institutes
Environmental Studies *(INFU)* (Environmental Studies); **Gerontology** (Gerontology); **Materials Flow and Logistics**; **Occupa-**

---

tional Physiology (Occupational Health); **Robotics Research** (Robotics); **Spectrochemistry and Applied Spectroscopy** (Applied Chemistry)

Further Information: Also language courses and several tutorials for foreign students

History: Founded 1965, opened 1968. College of Education of the Ruhr incorporated 1980. An autonomous institution financially supported by the State of North Rhine-Westphalia and under the jurisdiction of its Ministry of Science and Research.

Governing Bodies: Senat; Kuratorium

Academic Year: October to July (October-February; April-July)

Admission Requirements: Secondary school certificate (Reifezeugnis) or equivalent

Fees: None

Main Language(s) of Instruction: German

Degrees and Diplomas: *Bachelor/Bakkalaureus*; *Diplom*: Chemiker, Chemistry; Economics; Informatiker, Computing; Mathematics; Physics; Statistics, 4-5 yrs; *Lehramt*: Teaching Qualification, Secondary level, 3-4 yrs; *Master/Magister*, *Doktorgrad*: Economics (Dr.oec.); Economics (Dr.rer.pol.); Engineering (Dr.Ing.); Natural Sciences (Dr.rer.nat.); Philosophy (Dr.phil.), 3-4 yrs following Diplom; *Doktorgrad*: Education (Dr.paed.), 3-4 yrs following Diplom; *Habilitation*: at least 3 yrs following Doktor

Student Services: Academic counselling, Canteen, Employment services, Foreign student adviser, Handicapped facilities, Health services, Nursery care, Social counselling, Sports facilities

Student Residential Facilities: Yes

Special Facilities: Radio Station 'Eldoradio'

Libraries: University Library, c. 1.6 m. vols; libraries of the departments and institutes, c. 468,000 vols

Publications: Amtliche Mitteilungen; Forschungsbericht; Uni-Report *(biannually)*; Uniwelt *(biannually)*; Vorlesungsverzeichnis

Press or Publishing House: Presse-und Informationsstelle der Universität Dortmund
Last Updated: 27/01/10

DRESDEN UNIVERSITY OF APPLIED SCIENCES
Hochschule für Technik und Wirtschaft Dresden (FH)
Friedrich-List-Platz 1, 01069 Dresden
Tel: +57(351) 462-3101
Fax: +57(351) 462-2185
EMail: rektor@htw-dresden.de
Website: http://www.htw-dresden.de

Rektor: Roland Stenzel (2010-) Tel: +49(351) 462-3101

Kanzlerin: Monika Niehues
Tel: +57(351) 462-3103, Fax: +57(351) 462-2194
EMail: kanzler@htw-dresden.de

International Relations: Steffi Söhnel
Tel: +57(351) 462-3177, Fax: +57(351) 462-2174
EMail: soehnel@verwaltung.htw-dresden.de

Faculties
Agriculture/Landscape Management (Agricultural Economics; Horticulture; Landscape Architecture); **Business Administration** (Business Administration; Modern Languages); **Civil Engineering/Architecture** (Architecture; Civil Engineering); **Design** (Design); **Electrical Engineering** (Electrical Engineering); **Information Technology/Mathematics** (Information Technology; Mathematics); **Mechanical Engineering/Process Engineering** (Chemical Engineering; Mechanical Engineering; Physics); **Spatial Information** (Real Estate; Surveying and Mapping)

History: Founded 1992.

Main Language(s) of Instruction: German

Degrees and Diplomas: *Bachelor/Bakkalaureus*; *Diplom*; *Master/Magister*: Civil Engineering; *Promotion*
Last Updated: 22/03/11

DRESDEN UNIVERSITY OF TECHNOLOGY
Technische Universität Dresden
Mommsenstrasse 7, 01069 Dresden
Tel: +49(351) 463-0
Fax: +49(351) 463-37165
EMail: pressestelle@tu-dresden.de
Website: http://www.tu-dresden.de

Rektor: Hans Müller-Steinhagen (2010-)
Tel: +49(351) 463-34312, Fax: +49(351) 463-37121
EMail: rektor@tu-dresden.de

Kanzler: Wolf-Eckhard Wormser
Tel: +49(351) 463-34717, Fax: +49(351) 463-37101
EMail: Kanzler@tu-dresden.de

International Relations: Marion Helemann, Head, International Office
Tel: +49(351) 463-35358, Fax: +49(351) 463-37738
EMail: auslandsamt@tu-dresden.de

Faculties
Architecture (Architecture; Landscape Architecture; Urban Studies); **Civil Engineering** (Civil Engineering); **Computer Science** (Computer Science); **Economics and Business Management** (Business Administration; Computer Science; Economic and Finance Policy; Economics; Engineering; Industrial Management); **Education Science** (Education; Educational Sciences); **Electrical Engineering** (Electrical Engineering); **Forestry, Hydrology and Geosciences** (Earth Sciences; Forestry; Water Science); **Law** (Law); **Literature and Linguistics** (Linguistics; Literature); **Mathematics and Natural Sciences** (Biology; Chemistry; Mathematics; Natural Sciences; Physics; Psychology); **Mechanical Engineering** (Chemical Engineering; Energy Engineering; Materials Engineering; Mechanical Engineering; Production Engineering); **Medicine** *(Carl Gustav Carus)* (Medicine; Public Health); **Philosophy** (Art History; Communication Studies; History; Music; Philosophy; Political Sciences; Sociology; Theology); **Transport and Traffic Engineering** (Road Transport; Transport Engineering)

Schools
Applied Languages and Cultural Studies (Ancient Languages; Arabic; Chinese; Czech; English; Finnish; French; Italian; Japanese; Latin; Modern Languages; Polish; Portuguese; Russian; Spanish; Swedish)

Further Information: Also Teaching Hospital. 50 European Mobility Programmes. German language courses (in August and September)

History: Founded 1828 as a technical college and renamed Polytechnische Schule in 1851. Became Technische Hochschule 1890, renamed Technische Universität 1961. Responsible to the Ministry of Science and Art.

Governing Bodies: Konzil; Senat

Academic Year: October to September (October-March; April-September)

Admission Requirements: Secondary school certificate (Reifezeugnis) or equivalent

Fees: None

Main Language(s) of Instruction: German

International Co-operation: With universities in Central and Eastern Europe, North America, Latin America and Asia. Also participates in the Tempus programme.

Accrediting Agencies: Saxon Ministry of Science and Art

Degrees and Diplomas: *Bachelor/Bakkalaureus*: 3-3 1/2 yrs; *Diplom*; *Staatsprüfung*: Food Technology; Medicine; Dentistry, 4-5 yrs; *Master/Magister*: a further 1-2 yrs; *Promotion*; *Habilitation*

Student Services: Foreign student adviser, Language programs

Student Residential Facilities: For 12,000 students

Special Facilities: Botanical Garden (Dresden and Tharandt). Geological Collection

Libraries: Saxon State-Library and University Library, total, c. 3.2m. vols

Publications: Vorlesungsverzeichnis der TUD *(biennially)*; Wissenschaftliche Zeitschrift der Technischen Universität Dresden *(biennially)*

Last Updated: 22/03/11

DÜSSELDORF ART ACADEMY
Kunstakademie Düsseldorf
Eiskellerstrasse 1, 40213 Düsseldorf
Tel: +49(211) 1396-0
Fax: +49(211) 1396-225
EMail: postmaster@kunstakademie-duesseldorf.de
Website: http://www.kunstakademie-duesseldorf.de

Rektor: Anthony Cragg (2010-)
Kanzler: Peter Michael

Faculties
Fine Arts (Architecture; Fine Arts; Painting and Drawing; Photography; Sculpture; Visual Arts)

History: Founded 1773.

Main Language(s) of Instruction: German

Degrees and Diplomas: *Diplom*; *Lehramt*. Also Postgraduate Certificate (Aufbaustudiengang)

Last Updated: 10/02/10

EBERHARD-KARLS UNIVERSITY TÜBINGEN
Eberhard-Karls-Universität Tübingen
Wilhelmstrasse 7, 72074 Tübingen
Tel: +49(7071) 29-0
Fax: +49(7071) 29-5990
EMail: info@uni-tuebingen.de
Website: http://www.uni-tuebingen.de

Rektor: Bernd Engler (2006-)
Tel: +49(7071) 29-72512, Fax: +49(7071) 29-5300
EMail: bernd.engler@uni-tuebingen.de

Kanzler: Andreas Rothfuss
Tel: +49(7071) 29-72515
EMail: andreas.rothfuss@kanzler.uni-tuebingen.de

International Relations: Wolfgang Mekle
Tel: +49(7071) 29-72938, Fax: +49(7071) 29-5404
EMail: intrel@uni-tuebingen.de

Faculties
Catholic Theology (Catholic Theology); **Cultural Studies** (Ancient Civilizations; Ancient Languages; Archaeology; Art History; Asian Studies; Chinese; Cultural Studies; Ethnology; Greek (Classical); Japanese; Korean; Latin; Music; Musicology; Oriental Studies; Philology; Prehistory; Religion; South Asian Studies); **Economics and Social Sciences** (Accountancy; Business Administration; Econometrics; Economics; Finance; International Business; International Economics; Management; Statistics); **Humanities** (American Studies; Archaeology; Art History; Chinese; English; Ethnology; German; Greek; History; Japanese; Jewish Studies; Korean; Latin; Linguistics; Literature; Media Studies; Middle Eastern Studies; Music; Oriental Studies; Philology; Romance Languages; Russian; Scandinavian Languages; Slavic Languages); **Law** (Law); **Medicine** (Behavioural Sciences; Cell Biology; Dentistry; Medicine; Molecular Biology; Neurology; Neurosciences); **Protestant Theology** (Judaic Religious Studies; Protestant Theology); **Science** (Biochemistry; Biology; Chemistry; Computer Science; Earth Sciences; Mathematics; Pharmacy; Physics; Psychology)

Further Information: 17 Teaching Hospitals

History: Founded 1477 by Count Eberhard the Bearded, 1863 the first German University to establish a faculty of Natural Sciences. An autonomous institution financially supported by the State of Baden-Württemberg and under the jurisdiction of its Ministry of Arts and Sciences.

Governing Bodies: Universitätsrat; Senat

Academic Year: October to September (October-March; April-September)

Admission Requirements: Secondary school certificate (Reifezeugnis) or equivalent

Fees: (Euros): 500 per semester

Main Language(s) of Instruction: German

International Co-operation: With universities in Argentina; Australia; Belgium; Brazil; Chile; China; Denmark; Finland; France; United Kingdom; Ireland; Italy; Japan; Jordan; Cambodia; Canada; Morocco; Mexico; New Zealand; Poland; Norway; Romania; Russian Federation; Sweden; Switzerland; Slovenia; Turkey; Hungary; United States

Accrediting Agencies: Accreditation, Certification and Quality Assurance Institute (ACQUIN)

Degrees and Diplomas: *Bachelor/Bakkalaureus*: Arts in Philosophy; History; Sports Science; Computer Linguistics; German; Japanese Studies; Sinology; Geosciences (BA), 4 yrs; *Diplom*: Protestant Theology; Catholic Theology; Economics; Business Administration; Pedagogy; Psychology; Sports Science; Media Studies; Mathematics; Physics; Chemistry; Biochemistry; Biology; Geography; Geosciences; Geo Ecology; Informatics; Bioinformatics (Dipl.), 4-4 1/2 yrs; *Lehramt*: Teaching qualification: Mathematics; Physics; Chemistry; Biology; Geography; Teaching qualification: Protestant Theology; Catholic Theology; Philosophy; History; Pedagogy; Political Science; Sports Science; German; English; French; Italian; Russian; Spanish; Greek; Latin, 4 yrs; *Magister Artium*: American Studies; German; Roman Languages; Slavic Languages; Cultural Studies (all subjects); Geography; Prehistory (MA); Protestant Theology; Catholic Theology; Law; Philosophy; History; Empirical Cultural Studies; Pedagogy; Political Science; Sociology; Sports Science; Rhetorics; Linguistics; Latin; English (MA), 4 yrs; *Staatsprüfung*: Law; Medicine; Dentistry; Pharmacy, 4-6 yrs; *Master/Magister*: Arts in Neuro- and Behavioural Sciences; European Studies; Computer Linguistics; Japanese Studies; Tropical Hydrogeology; Applied Environmental Geoscience (MA), a further 2 yrs; *Promotion*; *Doktorgrad*: Cognitive Neurobiology; Biology of Infections; Chemistry and Interphase; Knowledge Acquisition and Exchange with new Media; Business Administration and Development Studies; Astrophysics; Global Ethics; Cell Biology; Bioethics; Molecular Medicine (Dr.), c. 8-10 sem; *Habilitation (Prof. or Habil.)*: at least 3 yrs following Doktor

Student Services: Academic counselling, Canteen, Employment services, Foreign student adviser, Handicapped facilities, Health services, Language programs, Nursery care, Social counselling, Sports facilities

Student Residential Facilities: For c. 3,500 students

Special Facilities: Schloss Hohentübingen Museum; Archaeology Museum; Egyptology Museum; Geology and Palaeontology Museum; Zoology Museum; Numismatics Museum. Botanical Gardens

Libraries: University Library, c. 3m. vols; 100 institute libraries, c. 3m vols

Last Updated: 31/01/12

EICHSTÄTT CATHOLIC UNIVERSITY

Katholische Universität Eichstätt-Ingolstadt

Ostenstrasse 26, 85071 Eichstätt
Tel: +49(8421) 93-0
Fax: +49(8421) 93-1796
EMail: info@ku-eichstaett.de
Website: http://www.ku-eichstaett.de

Präsident: Richard Schenk
Tel: +49(8421) 93-1230, Fax: +49(8421) 93-2121
EMail: president@ku.de

Faculties

Business Administration and Economics (Business Administration; Economics; Ethics; Law; Statistics); **Education and Philosophy** (Art History; Education; Fine Arts; Music; Philosophy; Psychology; Sports); **History and Social Sciences** (Folklore; History; Political Sciences; Social Sciences; Sociology); **Languages and Literature** (American Studies; Archaeology; English; German; Journalism; Latin; Philosophy; Romance Languages); **Mathematics and Geography** (Biology; Chemistry; Computer Science; Geography; Mathematics; Pedagogy); **Religious Education and Ecclesiastical Educational Work** (Ethics; Religious Education); **Social Work** (Social Work); **Theology** (Bible; Catholic Theology; Philosophy)

Institutes

Central and East European Studies (Central European Studies; Eastern European Studies); **Entrepreneursh!p**; **Latin American Studies** (Latin American Studies); **Marriage and Family in Society** *(The Central)* (Family Studies)

Research Institutes

Comparative History of Religious Orders (History)

History: Founded 1972 as Gesamthochschule, incorporating College of Education, founded 1958 and College of Philosophy and Theology, established 1924 and tracing its origins to the Collegium Willibaldinum, founded 1564. Became University 1980. An autonomous institution financially supported by the State of Bavaria 80% and the seven Bavarian Dioceses (20%).

Governing Bodies: Senat; Hochschulleitung. Hochschulrat

Academic Year: October to September

Admission Requirements: Secondary school certificate (Reifezeugnis)

Fees: None for most degrees

Main Language(s) of Instruction: German

International Co-operation: With universities in Brazil, Mexico, Philippines, Colombia, Argentina

Degrees and Diplomas: *Bachelor/Bakkalaureus*: European Studies; Business Administration; Political science; Sociology, 3 yrs; *Diplom*: Education; Journalism; Mathematics; Psychology, 4 1/2 yrs; *Diplom*: Geography; *Diplom*: Religion; Social Education, 4 yrs; *Lehramt*: Teaching Qualification, Secondary level; *Lizentiat*: Theology; *Master/Magister*; *Promotion*: Natural Sciences (Dr.rer.nat); Philosophy (Dr.phil.); Theology (Dr. theol.); Theology (Dr.theol.); *Habilitation*: at least 3 yrs following Doktor

Student Residential Facilities: Yes

Special Facilities: T.V. and Broadcasting Studio; Computer Centre; German Language Training Centre

Libraries: Central Library, c. 1.8m. vols

Publications: Eichstätter Beiträge; Eichstätter Hochschulreden; Eichstätter Materialien; Eichstätter Theologische Studien; Forum für osteuropäische Ideen- und Zeitgeschichte; Mesa Redonda

Last Updated: 03/02/12

ERFURT UNIVERSITY OF APPLIED SCIENCES

Fachhochschule Erfurt

Post Box 450155, Altonaer Strasse 25, 99051 Erfurt
Tel: +49(361) 6700-700
Fax: +49(361) 6700-703
EMail: information@fh-erfurt.de
Website: http://www.fh-erfurt.de

Rektor: Heinrich H. Kill (2005-) EMail: rektorat@fh-erfurt.de

Kanzlerin: Heike Klemme EMail: unbehau@fh-erfurt.de

International Relations: Cornelia Witter
Tel: 49(361) 6700-707 EMail: witter@fh-erfurt.de

Faculties

Architecture and Urban Planning (Architecture; Town Planning); **Business, Logistics and Transport** (Business Administration; Transport and Communications); **Civil Engineering and Conservation/Restoration** (Archaeology; Civil Engineering); **Engineering in Building and Computer Science** (Computer Science; Construction Engineering; Energy Engineering); **Landscape Architecture, Horticulture and Forestry** (Forestry; Horticulture; Landscape Architecture)

History: Founded 1991.

Governing Bodies: Senate

Academic Year: September to August

Admission Requirements: Abitur or Fachhochschulreife or Fachgebundene

Fees: None

Main Language(s) of Instruction: German

International Co-operation: With universities in France; United Kingdom; Lithuania; Slovenia; Italy; Spain; Belgium; Poland; Switzerland; Hungary

Degrees and Diplomas: *Bachelor/Bakkalaureus (BSc)*; *Diplom (FH)*: Horticulture and Gardening; *Master/Magister*. Also postgraduate Diplom in Civil Engineering, Construction and Energy Engineering

Student Services: Academic counselling, Canteen, Cultural centre, Employment services, Foreign student adviser, Foreign Studies Centre, Handicapped facilities, Language programs, Nursery care, Social counselling, Sports facilities

Student Residential Facilities: Yes

Libraries: Yes

Last Updated: 31/01/12

ERNST-MORITZ-ARNDT UNIVERSITY GREIFSWALD

Ernst-Moritz-Arndt-Universität Greifswald
Domstraße 11 / Eingang II, 17487 Greifswald
Tel: +49(3834) 86-0
Fax: +49(3834) 86-1248
EMail: rektor@uni-greifswald.de; pressestelle@uni-greifswald.de
Website: http://www.uni-greifswald.de

Rektor: Rainer Westerman
Tel: +49(3834) 86-1100, Fax: +49(3834) 86-1105
EMail: rektor@uni-greifswald.de

Centres
Computer (Computer Science)

Faculties
Law and Economics (Economics; Law); **Mathematics and Natural Science** (Biochemistry; Biology; Chemistry; Computer Science; Genetics; Geography; Geology; Mathematics; Microbiology; Natural Sciences; Pharmacy; Physics); **Medicine** (Dentistry; Medicine); **Philosophy** (American Studies; Baltic Languages; English Studies; Music; Philology; Philosophy; Religious Music); **Theology** (Theology)

Units
Foreign Languages (Modern Languages) *Head*: Heidrun Peters

History: Founded 1456 and confirmed by Papal Bull of Calixtus III. The University came under the control of Sweden in 1648, becoming a Prussian University in 1815. Reorganized 1946 and 1990.

Governing Bodies: Senat

Academic Year: October to July

Admission Requirements: Secondary school certificate (Reifezeugnis) or equivalent

Fees: None

Main Language(s) of Instruction: German

Degrees and Diplomas: *Bachelor/Bakkalaureus*: Arts; Law; Science, 3 yrs; *Diplom*: Business Administration; Biochemistry; Biology; Biomathematics; Evangelistic Religious Education; Geography; Human Biology; Church Music; Landscapes Ecology and Nature Preservation; Mathematics; Physics; Psychology, 4-5 yrs; *Lehramt*: Teacher Training; *Staatsprüfung*: Medicine; Pharmacy; Law; Dentistry; *Master/Magister*: Arts; Law; Science, 2 yrs

Student Services: Academic counselling, Canteen, Foreign student adviser, Handicapped facilities, Health services, Social counselling, Sports facilities

Student Residential Facilities: For c. 17,500 students

Special Facilities: Anatomy Museum; Zoological Museum. Geological Collection. Exhibition Centre. Arboretum. Botanical Garden. Observatory

Libraries: University Library, c. 2.3 m. vols; Institute libraries, c. 700,000 vols

Publications: Greifswalder Universitätsreden

Press or Publishing House: University Press

Last Updated: 31/01/12

ESCP-EUROPE - BERLIN

Heubnerweg 6, 14059 Berlin
Tel: +49(30) 32007-100
Fax: +49(30) 32007-111
EMail: info.de@escp-eap.net
Website: http://www.escp-eap.de

Direktor: Ayad Al-Ani EMail: ayad.al-ani@escpeurope.de

Prorektor: Ulrich Pape EMail: ulrich.pape@escpeurope.de

Programmes
Central European MBA *(CEMBA)* (Business Administration; International Business; Management); **European Executive MBA** *(EEMBA)* (Accountancy; Business Administration; Commercial Law; Economics; Finance; International Business; Management; Marketing); **Executive Specialized Masters** (Banking; Business Administration; Communication Studies; Energy Engineering; Finance; Health Administration; Management; Marketing; Safety Engineering); **Full-time Specialized Masters** (Business Administration; Communication Studies; Finance; Management; Marketing); **General Management Programme** *(GMP)* (Accountancy; Business Administration; Commercial Law; Finance; International Business; Management; Marketing); **Management** *(MIM)* (Business Administration; Management; Modern Languages); **Master in European Business** *(MEB)*; **Ph. D.** (Business Administration)

History: Founded 1819 by Parisian entrepreneurs and scientists, the ESCP is one of the oldest Business Schools in Europe. In 1973 the Chambre de Commerce et d'Industrie de Paris decided to set up the first European Business School (EAP) in four countries. Both French Grandes Ecoles merged in 1999 to form ESCP-EAP European School of Management. Previously known as ESCP-EAP Europäische Wirtschaftshochschule Acquired current name 2009.

Academic Year: Starts September (two and three terms)

Admission Requirements: At least 2 years' university studies in business administration or work experience

Fees: (Euros): 3,900-32,000 per annum, depending on the programme

Main Language(s) of Instruction: German; English

International Co-operation: With universities in Estonia; Czech Republic; Hungary; Poland; Slovak Republic; Ukraine

Accrediting Agencies: AACSB; EQUIS; AMBA; DFH/UFA

Degrees and Diplomas: *Master/Magister*: Business Administration (MBA), 2 yrs; *Promotion*: International Business Administration (PhD). Also Diplôme de Grande Ecole

Student Services: Academic counselling, Cultural centre, Employment services, Foreign student adviser, Foreign Studies Centre, Handicapped facilities, Language programs, Nursery care, Social counselling, Sports facilities

Libraries: c. 15,000 vols

Last Updated: 31/01/12

ESMT - EUROPEAN SCHOOL OF MANAGEMENT AND TECHNOLOGY - BERLIN

Schlossplatz 1, 10178 Berlin
Tel: +49 30) 212 31-0
EMail: info@esmt.org
Website: http://www.esmt.org

Präsident: Jörg Rocholl

Programmes
Business Administration (Business Administration); **Executive Education** (Business Education)

History: Founded 2002.

Degrees and Diplomas: *Master/Magister*
Last Updated: 31/01/12

ESSLINGEN UNIVERSITY OF APPLIED SCIENCES

Hochschule Esslingen (HE)
Kanalstrasse 33, 73728 Esslingen
Tel: +49(711) 397-49
Fax: +49(711) 397-3100
EMail: info@hs-esslingen.de
Website: http://www.hs-esslingen.de

Rektor: Bernhard Schwarz
Tel: +49(711) 397-3000
EMail: Bernhard.Schwarz@hs-esslingen.de

Kanzler: Lothar Übele
Tel: +49(711) 397-3010, Fax: +49(711) 397-3012
EMail: Lothar.Uebele@hs-esslingen.de

International Relations: Beate Maleska
Tel: +49(711) 397-3082, Fax: +49(711) 397-3081
EMail: Beate.Maleska@hs-esslingen.de

Faculties
Automotive Engineering (Automotive Engineering; Engineering; Engineering Drawing and Design); **Basic Sciences**; **Building**

Services, **Energy and Environmental Engineering**; **Information Technology** (Automotive Engineering; Computer Engineering; Information Technology; Media Studies; Software Engineering; Telecommunications Engineering); **Management** (Engineering Management; Industrial Engineering); **Mechanical Engineering** (Design; Development Studies; Mechanical Engineering; Production Engineering); **Mechatronics and Elecrical Engineering**; **Natural Sciences** (Biotechnology; Chemical Engineering; Environmental Studies; Materials Engineering; Natural Sciences); **Social Work, Health and Nursing** (Health Sciences; Nursing; Social Work)

Graduate Schools
Automotive Engineering (Automotive Engineering); **Design and Development in Automotive and Mechanical Engineering** (Automation and Control Engineering; Design; Information Technology); **International Industrial Management** (Automotive Engineering; Industrial Management; Information Technology)

History: Founded 1971. Acquired present status through merger between Fachhochschulen in Esslingen - Hochschule für Technik (FHTE) and Hochschule für Sozialwesen (HfS) 2006.

Governing Bodies: Senate

Academic Year: September to July (September-February; March-July)

Admission Requirements: Abitur and German Language Test for International Applicants (DSH or Test DGF)

Fees: None

Main Language(s) of Instruction: German; English

International Co-operation: With universities in Argentina, Czech Republic, Finland, France, United Kingdom, Hungary, Ireland, Italy, Japan, Mexico, Poland, Romania, Russia, Singapore, Spain, Sweden, USA

Accrediting Agencies: FIBAA, DQS

Degrees and Diplomas: *Bachelor/Bakkalaureus*; *Master/Magister*: Energy and Construction Engineering; Innovations Management; International Industrial Management; Surface and Materials Sciences; Environmental Engineering; Automotive Systems; Design and Development in Automotive and Mechanical Engineering; Automotive Systems; Social Work; Nursing

Student Services: Academic counselling, Canteen, Foreign student adviser, Foreign Studies Centre, Language programs, Sports facilities

Student Residential Facilities: Yes

Libraries: Main Library

Publications: Spektrum, Science and Technology, FHTE International, FHTE Internal *(biennially)*
Last Updated: 18/01/10

EURO BUSINESS COLLEGE HAMBURG

Esplanade 6, Hamburg
Tel: +49(40) 323-3700
EMail: hamburg@ebc-hochschule.de
Website: http://www.ebc-hochschule.de
Dekan: Johann Stooss EMail: stooss.johannebc-hochschule.de

Programmes
Business Psychology (Business Education; Psychology); **International Business Economics and Politics** (Economics; International Business; Political Sciences); **International Business Management** (Business Administration; International Business); **International Business Management China**; **Tourism and Event Management** (Management; Tourism); **Tourism and Event Management China** (Management; Tourism)

Main Language(s) of Instruction: German

Degrees and Diplomas: *Bachelor/Bakkalaureus*; *Master/Magister*
Last Updated: 31/01/12

EUROPEAN BUSINESS SCHOOL (EBS)

Rheingaustraße 1, 65375 Oestrich-Winkel
Tel: +49(6723) 69-0
Fax: +49(6723) 69-133
EMail: info@ebs.de
Website: http://www.ebs.de
Präsident: Rolf D. Cremer

Geschäftsführer: Rolf Tilmes

Centres
Economic Languages (Arabic; Chinese; English; French; German; International Business; Japanese; Management; Modern Languages; Portuguese; Russian; Spanish)

Schools
Business (Finance; Health Administration; International Business; Management; Marketing; Real Estate); **Law** (Law)

History: Founded 1971. A private institution authorized by the government to award degrees.

Academic Year: September to April

Admission Requirements: Secondary school certificate (Abitur) and entrance examination

Fees: (Euros): 4,950 per semester

Main Language(s) of Instruction: English

Degrees and Diplomas: *Bachelor/Bakkalaureus*: General Management; Aviation Management; *Master/Magister*: Management; Business and Law; Finance; Real Estate; Logistic and Supply Chain Management; *Promotion*; *Doktorgrad*; *Habilitation*

Libraries: c. 22,000 media items
Last Updated: 31/01/12

EUROPEAN DISTANCE EDUCATION UNIVERSITY OF APPLIED SCIENCES HAMBURG

Europäische Fernhochschule Hamburg (EURO-FH)
Doberaner Weg 20, 22143 Hamburg
Tel: +49(40) 6757-0700
Fax: +49(40) 6757-0710
EMail: Information@euro-fh.com
Website: http://www.euro-fh.com

Präsident: Jens-Mogens Holm
EMail: jens-mogens.holm@euro-fh.de

Kanzler: Martin Hendrik Kurz EMail: martin.kurz@euro-fh.de

Programmes
Continuing Education

Schools
Business (Business Administration; International Business; Management; Marketing); **Law** (Law); **Logistics**

Fees: (Euros): undergraduate, 280 per month; postgraduate, 11,760 (24 months at 490 per month); the monthly rate for a reduced period of study is 590 (18 months)/ 690 (14 months), i.e a minimum fee of 9.660.

Main Language(s) of Instruction: German; some courses in English.

Degrees and Diplomas: *Bachelor/Bakkalaureus*: Business Administration; Commercial Law; Logistics, 3-4 yrs; *Diplom (FH)*: Business Administration, 3-4 yrs; *Master/Magister*: Business Administration, a further 1-2 yrs
Last Updated: 06/02/12

EUROPEAN UNIVERSITY OF APPLIED SCIENCES

Europäische Fachhochschule
Kaiserstraße 6, 50321 Brühl
Tel: +49(2232) 5673-0
Fax: +49(2232) 5673-219
EMail: info@eufh.de
Website: http://www.eufh.de
Präsident: Birger Lang EMail: b.lang@eufh.de

Departments
Building Industry (Construction Engineering); **Business Administration** (Business Administration); **General Management** (Management); **Industrial Management** (Industrial Management); **Investment Management** (Finance; Management); **Logistics Management** (Transport Management)

Schools
Business *(Cologne)* (Business Administration)

History: Founded 2001.

Main Language(s) of Instruction: German

Degrees and Diplomas: *Bachelor/Bakkalaureus (B.Sc.)*; *Bachelor/Bakkalaureus (B.A.)*; *Master/Magister*

Last Updated: 22/03/11

EUROPEAN UNIVERSITY OF APPLIED SCIENCES BERLIN - INTERNATIONAL BUSINESS SCHOOL BERLIN

EBC Hochschule Berlin (EBC)
Alexanderplatz 1, 10178 Berlin
Tel: +49(30) 3151-935-0
Fax: +49(30) 3151-935-20
EMail: berlin@bc-hochschule.de
Website: http://www.ebc-hochschule.de/de/standorte/campus-berlin/kontakt-anfahrt.html

Director: Felix Philipp Lutz EMail: felix-philipp.lutz@ibsberlin.com

Director of Studies: Iris Peinl EMail: iris.peinl@ibsberlin.com

International Relations: Marion Müller, Career Center and International Office EMail: marion.mueller@ibsberlin.com

Departments
Communication and Media Management (Communication Studies; Labour Law; Marketing; Media Studies; Private Law); **International Management** (Economics; Finance; International Business; Labour Law; Management; Private Law; Public Relations; Taxation); **International Tourism and Event Management** (Tourism)

History: Formerly know as International Business School Berlin - University of Applied Sciences.

Main Language(s) of Instruction: German

Degrees and Diplomas: *Bachelor/Bakkalaureus*; *Master/Magister*
Last Updated: 18/11/11

EUROPEAN UNIVERSITY VIADRINA FRANKFURT (ODER)

Europa-Universität Viadrina Frankfurt (Oder)
PO Box 1786, Grosse Scharrnstrasse 59, 15207 Frankfurt (Oder), Brandenburg
Tel: +49(335) 5534-0
Fax: +49(335) 5534-4305
EMail: presidents.office@euv-frankfurt-o.de
Website: http://www.euv-frankfurt-o.de

Präsident: Gunter Pleuger (2008-)
Tel: +49(335) 5534-4274, Fax: +49(335) 5534-4305
EMail: president@euv-frankfurt-o.de

Kanzler: Christian Zens
Tel: +49(335) 5534-4334 EMail: kanzler@euv-frankfurt-o.de

International Relations: Petra Weber, Head, Department of International Affairs
Tel: +49(335) 5534-2486, Fax: +49(335) 5534-2535
EMail: head-office@euv-frankfurt-o.de; pweber@euv-frankfurt-o.de

Centres
Language (Foreign Languages Education; Linguistics; Modern Languages)

Faculties
Cultural and Social Studies *(Interdisciplinary)* (Arts and Humanities; Cultural Studies; Linguistics; Literature; Modern Languages); **Economics and Business Administration** (Accountancy; Business Administration; Economics; Finance; International Business; Marketing); **Law** (Criminal Law; International Law; Law; Public Law)

Institutes
Ethics *(Interdisciplinary, for graduates)* (Ethics); **Literature and Politics** *(Heinrich von Kleist for Graduate)* (Literature; Political Sciences); **Transformation Studies** *(Interdisciplinary, for graduates)* (Econometrics)

History: Founded 1991. Reviving the tradition of the first Brandenburg University, the Alma Mater Viadrina (1506-1811), the new Viadrina is an international and innovative University, bridging the gap between Eastern and Western Europe. The Collegium Poloni-

cum, a teaching and research centre, is jointly managed by the Viadrina and the University of Poznan.

Governing Bodies: Senat

Academic Year: October to September (October-March; April-September)

Admission Requirements: Secondary school certificate (Reifezeugnis)

Main Language(s) of Instruction: German, English, Polish

Degrees and Diplomas: *Bachelor/Bakkalaureus*: International Business Administration (in German and English); Business Administration; Economics; Cultural Studies; German and Polish Law, 3 yrs; *Master/Magister*: Cultural History of Europe; Culture and History of Central and Eastern Europe; Socio-Cultural Studies; Intercultural Communication Studies; Cultural Management and Tourism; Mediation; European Cultural Heritage; Management for Central and Eastern Europe; European Studies; International Business Administration; Management for Central and Eastern Europe; Business Informatics (International), 2 yrs; *Master/Magister*: German and Polish Law, 1 further yr; *Master/Magister*: Law (LLM), for foreign students who have Law degree, 1 yr; *Promotion*: Arts (PhD (Dr.phil)); Economics (PhD (Dr.rer.pol)); Law (PhD (Dr.jur.))

Student Services: Academic counselling, Canteen, Foreign student adviser, Foreign Studies Centre, Handicapped facilities, Language programs, Sports facilities

Student Residential Facilities: For c. 2,400 students

Special Facilities: Self-directed study centre. Data banks. Interactive computer-assisted learning programmes

Libraries: University Library, 370,000 vols, 2,100 journals, 133,000 other media
Last Updated: 31/01/12

EVANGELICAL UNIVERSITY OF APPLIED SCIENCES FOR CHURCH MUSIC

Evangelische Hochschule für Kirchenmusik Halle an der Saale
Kleine Ulrichstrasse 35, 06108 Halle
Tel: +49(345) 21969-0
Fax: +49(345) 21969-29
EMail: sekretariat@ehk-halle.de
Website: http://www.ehk-halle.de

Rektor: Wolfgang Kupke (2000-)
Tel: +49(345) 21969-19, Fax: +49(345) 21969-19
EMail: Kupke@ehk-halle.de

Prorektorin: Franziska Seils
Tel: +49(345) 21969-30 EMail: seils@ehk-halle.de

Programmes
Choir and Conducting (Conducting); **Music Education** (Music Education); **Religious Music** (Religious Music); **Singing** (Singing)

History: Founded 1926.

Main Language(s) of Instruction: German

Degrees and Diplomas: *Bachelor/Bakkalaureus*; *Diplom*; *Master/Magister*
Last Updated: 31/01/12

EVANGELICAL UNIVERSITY OF APPLIED SCIENCES FOR SOCIAL WORK, EDUCATION AND CARE, DRESDEN

Evangelische Hochschule für Sozialarbeit Dresden
PO Box 200143, Semperstrasse 2A, 01191 Dresden
Tel: +49(351) 46902-0
Fax: +49(351) 4715-993
EMail: info@ehs-dresden.de
Website: http://www.ehs-dresden.de

Rektor: Ralf Evers (2004-)
Tel: +49(351) 46902-10
EMail: rektorat@ehs-dresden.de; ralf.evers@ehs-dresden.de

Verwaltungsleiter: Peter Schiller
Tel: +49(351) 46902-18 EMail: peter.schiller@ehs-dresden.de

International Relations: Uta Heinrich-Barth
Tel: +49(351) 46902-33 EMail: auslandsamt@ehs-dresden.de

Programmes

Child Care and Development (Child Care and Development);
Elementary and Preschool Education (Preschool Education);
Nursing/Care Management (Health Administration; Nursing);
Social Work (Social Work)

History: Founded 1991.

Main Language(s) of Instruction: German

Degrees and Diplomas: *Bachelor/Bakkalaureus*; *Master/Magister*
Last Updated: 06/02/12

FACULTY OF THEOLOGY IN PADERBORN

Theologische Fakultät Paderborn
Kamp 6, 33098 Paderborn
Tel: +49(5251) 121-0
Fax: +49(5251) 121-700
EMail: theol-fakultaet-paderborn@t-online.de
Website: http://www.theol-fakultaet-pb.de

Rektorin: Maria Neubrand Tel: +49(5251) 121-701

Quästor: Anton Schäfers Tel: +49(5251) 121-704

Programmes

Philosophy (Philosophy); **Theology** (Theology)

History: Founded 1614.

Main Language(s) of Instruction: German

Degrees and Diplomas: *Diplom*; *Lizentiat*; *Doktorgrad*; *Habilitation*
Last Updated: 27/01/10

FILM AND TELEVISION UNIVERSITY 'KONRAD WOLF'

Hochschule für Film und Fernsehen 'Konrad Wolf' Potsdam-Babelsberg
Marlene-Dietrich-Allee 11, 14482 Potsdam-Babelsberg
Tel: +49(331) 6202-130
Fax: +49(331) 6202-199
EMail: info@hff-potsdam.de
Website: http://www.hff-potsdam.de/

Präsident: Dieter Wiedemann (2000-)
Tel: +49(331) 6202-100, Fax: +49(331) 6202-199
EMail: d.wiedemann@hff-potsdam.de

Kanzlerin: Brigitte Klotz
Tel: +49(331) 6202-120 EMail: kanzlerin@hff-potsdam.de

International Relations: Martin Steyer, Vizepräsident für künstlerische Praxis und internationale Beziehungen
Tel: +49(331) 6202-385 EMail: m.steyer@hff-potsdam.de

Programmes

Animation (Film); **Camera Techniques** (Cinema and Television; Film); **Editing**; **Film and Television Direction** (Cinema and Television); **Film and Television Production** (Cinema and Television; Film); **Film Music** (Film); **Media Studies: Analysis, Aesthetics, Public** (Media Studies); **Scenography** (Theatre); **Screenplay/Dramaturgy** (Cinema and Television; Writing); **Sound** (Sound Engineering (Acoustics)); **Theatre** (Theatre)

History: Founded 1954.

Main Language(s) of Instruction: German

Degrees and Diplomas: *Bachelor/Bakkalaureus*: Theatre; *Diplom*; *Master/Magister*: Media Studies; *Promotion*: Media Studies
Last Updated: 24/01/09

FLENSBURG UNIVERSITY OF APPLIED SCIENCES

Fachhochschule Flensburg
P.O. Box 1561, Kanzleistrasse 91-93, 24905 Flensburg
Tel: +49(461) 805-01
Fax: +49(461) 805-1300
EMail: presse@fh-flensburg.de
Website: http://www.fh-flensburg.de

Präsident: Herbert Zickfeld
Tel: +49(461) 805-1200, Fax: 151
EMail: praesidium@fh-flensburg.de

Kanzlerin: Sabine Christiansen
Tel: +49(461) 805-1202, Fax: +49(461) 805-1511

Faculties

Business Administration (Business Administration); **Engineering** (Applied Mathematics; Biotechnology; Computer Science; Electrical Engineering; Energy Engineering; Engineering Management; Environmental Management; Industrial Engineering; Marine Engineering; Marine Transport; Mechanical Engineering; Technology; Transport and Communications)

History: Founded 1969.

Degrees and Diplomas: *Bachelor/Bakkalaureus*; *Diplom (FH)*; *Master/Magister*
Last Updated: 06/02/12

FOLKWANG UNIVERSITY OF THE ARTS

Folkwang Universität der Künste
PO Box 164428, Klemensborn 39, 45224 Essen
Tel: +49(201) 4903-0
Fax: +49(201) 4903-288
EMail: info@folkwang-hochschule.de
Website: http://www.folkwang-uni.de

Rektor: Kurt Mehnert
Tel: +49(201) 183-3,355; +49(201) 4903-100,
Fax: +49(201) 4903-332
EMail: kurt.mehnert@folkwang-hochschule.de

Kanzler: Michael Fricke
Tel: +49(201) 4903-201, Fax: +49(201) 4903-203
EMail: fricke@folkwang-hochschule.de

International Relations: Christa Nolte
Tel: +49(201) 183-3,349; +49(201) 4903-307,
Fax: +49(201) 183-4226
EMail: christa.nolte@folkwang-hochschule.de

Faculties

Faculty 1 (Conducting; Jazz and Popular Music; Music; Music Theory and Composition; Musical Instruments); **Faculty 2** (Music; Pedagogy; Religious Music); **Faculty 3** (Acting; Dance; Singing; Theatre); **Faculty 4** (Communication Studies; Industrial Design; Photography)

History: Founded 1927 as Folkwang Hochschule. Acquired present status and title 2010.

Academic Year: October to September (October-February; April-September)

Admission Requirements: Secondary school certificate (Abitur); aptitude test

Fees: (Euros): tuition fee, 650 per semester

Degrees and Diplomas: *Bachelor/Bakkalaureus*; *Diplom*; *Lehramt*; *Promotion*: Musicology and Music Education (Ph.D.), 4 sem.

Libraries: c. 118,000 vols
Last Updated: 01/02/12

FRANKFURT SCHOOL OF FINANCE AND MANAGEMENT

PO Box 100341, Sonnemannstraße 9-11, 60314 Frankfurt am Main
Tel: +49(69) 154008-0
Fax: +49(69) 154008-728
EMail: info@frankfurt-school.de
Website: http://www.frankfurt-school.de

President: Udo Steffens (1996-)
Tel: +49(69) 154008-136 EMail: steffens@hfb.de

Dekan: Thomas Heimer
Tel: +49(69) 154008-725 EMail: heimer@hfb.de

International Relations: Brigitte Gebhart
Tel: +49(69) 154008-738, Fax: +49(69) 154008-4738
EMail: b.gebhart@frankfurt-school.de

Programmes

Accounting and Taxation *(Master)* (Accountancy; Taxation); **Banking** *(Master)* (Banking); **Business Administration** (Business Administration); **Business Computing** (Business Computing);

Development Finance *(Master)* (Development Studies; Finance); **Finance** *(Master)* (Finance); **Finance and Management** *(Doctorate)* (Finance; Management); **International Business Administration** (Business Administration; International Business); **International Business and Tax Law** *(Master)* (Fiscal Law; International Business); **International Hospital and Healthcare Management** *(Master)* (Health Administration); **Management and Financial Markets** (Finance; Management); **Management, Philosophy and Economics** (Economics; Management; Philosophy); **Mergers and Acquisitions** *(Master)* (Business Administration; Commercial Law); **Quantitative Finance** *(Master)* (Finance)

History: Founded 1990. Bankakademie and the Hochschule für Bankwirtschaft Frankfurt am Main (HfB) (Business School of Finance and Management, Frankfurt am Main).

Governing Bodies: Supervisory Body; Board of Trustees

Admission Requirements: Graduation from high school and selection process

Fees: (Euros): 4,700 per semester

Main Language(s) of Instruction: German, English

International Co-operation: With universities in Australia, United Kingdom, USA, Spain, Ireland, France and Italy.

Accrediting Agencies: FIBAA

Degrees and Diplomas: *Bachelor/Bakkalaureus*: Business Administration; International Business Administration; Business Computing; Management, Philosophy and Economics; Management and Financial Markets, 3-4 yrs; *Master/Magister*: Accounting and Taxation; Banking; Development Finance; Finance; Quantitative Finance (M.Sc.), 1-2 yrs; *Master/Magister*: International Business (M.A.); International Business and Tax Law; Mergers and Acquisitions (LL.M.); International Hospital and Healthcare Management; Finance (MBA); *Doktorgrad*: Finance and Management. Also Frankfurt Evening MBA, 1-2 yrs

Student Services: Canteen, Employment services, Foreign student adviser, Foreign Studies Centre, Language programs

Student Residential Facilities: None

Libraries: Yes

Press or Publishing House: Bankakademie Verloj
Last Updated: 14/01/10

FRANKFURT UNIVERSITY OF MUSIC AND PERFORMING ARTS

Hochschule für Musik und Darstellende Kunst Frankfurt am Main
Eschersheimer Landstrasse 29-39, 60322 Frankfurt am Main
Tel: +49(69) 154007-0
Fax: +49(69) 154007-108
EMail: praesident@hfmdk-frankfurt.de
Website: http://www.hfmdk-frankfurt.de

Präsident: Thomas Rietschel

Kanzlerin: Angelika Gartner
Tel: +49(69) 154007-321, Fax: +49(69) 154007-322
EMail: angelika.gartner@hfmdk-frankfurt.de

International Relations: Albrecht Eitz
Tel: +49(69) 154007-256, Fax: +49(69) 154007-125
EMail: albrecht.eitz@hfmdk-frankfurt.de

Departments
I (Conducting; Music; Music Education; Musical Instruments; Musicology; Religious Music; Singing); **II** (Music; Music Education; Music Theory and Composition; Secondary Education; Teacher Training); **III** (Dance; Opera; Theatre)

History: Founded 1878.

Main Language(s) of Instruction: German

Degrees and Diplomas: *Bachelor/Bakkalaureus*; *Lehramt*; *Master/ Magister*

Student Services: Canteen

Libraries: c. 100 000 Media Units (65,000 Sheet Music, 20,000 vols, 7,000 CDs)
Last Updated: 19/01/10

FRANKFURT AM MAIN COLLEGE OF FINE ARTS

Staatliche Hochschule für Bildende Künste (Städelschule) Frankfurt
Dürerstrasse 10, 60596 Frankfurt
Tel: +49(69) 605008-0
Fax: +49(69) 605008-66
Website: http://www.staedelschule.de

Rektor: Nikolaus Hirsch
Tel: +49(69) 605008-29, Fax: +49(69) 605008-50
EMail: rektor@staedelschule.de

Institutes
Art Criticism (Art Criticism)

Programmes
Architecture (Architecture); **Fine Arts** (Fine Arts)

History: Founded 1942.

Main Language(s) of Instruction: German

Degrees and Diplomas: *Master/Magister*
Last Updated: 13/02/09

FRANKFURT AM MAIN UNIVERSITY OF APPLIED SCIENCES

Fachhochschule Frankfurt am Main
Nibelungenplatz 1, 60318 Frankfurt am Main
Tel: +49(69) 1533-0
Fax: +49(69) 1533-2400
EMail: post@fh-frankfurt.de
Website: http://www.fh-frankfurt.de

Präsident: Detlev Buchholz
Tel: +49(69) 1533-2415 EMail: praesident@fh-frankfurt.de

Kanzler: Reiner Frey
Tel: +49(69) 1533-2412 EMail: kanzler@fh-frankfurt.de

International Relations: Günter Kleinkauf, Head, International Affairs
Tel: +49(69) 1533-2735, Fax: +49(69) 1533-2748
EMail: kuf@aa.fh-frankfurt.de

Faculties
Architecture (Architecture; Civil Engineering; Construction Engineering; Geological Engineering; Information Technology; Surveying and Mapping; Town Planning); **Computer Science and Engineering** (Automation and Control Engineering; Automotive Engineering; Bioengineering; Business Computing; Computer Engineering; Computer Science; Electronic Engineering; Energy Engineering; Engineering; Machine Building; Materials Engineering; Mechanical Engineering); **Economics and Law** (Air Transport; Business Administration; Commercial Law; Economics; Engineering; Finance; Information Management; International Business; Law; Leadership; Management; Public Administration); **Social Work and Health** (Health Sciences; Nursing; Pedagogy; Rehabilitation and Therapy; Social Work; Welfare and Protective Services)

History: Founded 1971.

Main Language(s) of Instruction: German

Degrees and Diplomas: *Bachelor/Bakkalaureus*; *Master/Magister*
Last Updated: 06/02/12

FREE UNIVERSITY OF BERLIN

Freie Universität Berlin (FUB)
Kaiserswerther Str. 16-18, 14195 Berlin
Tel: +49(30) 838-1
Fax: +49(30) 838-73187
EMail: info-service@fu-berlin.de
Website: http://www.fu-berlin.de

Präsident: Peter-André Alt
Tel: +49(30) 838-73,100; +49(30) 838-73104,
Fax: +49(30) 838-73107 EMail: praesident@fu-berlin.de

Kanzler: Peter Lange
Tel: +49(30) 838-73211, Fax: +49(30) 838-73217
EMail: kanzler@fu-berlin.de

International Relations: Elke Löschhorn
Tel: +49(30) 838-73400, Fax: +49(30) 838-73444
EMail: international-office@fu-berlin.de

Centres
French Studies (French); **Italian Studies**

Departments
Biology, Chemistry and Pharmacy (Biology; Chemistry; Pharmacy); **Earth Sciences** (Earth Sciences; Geology; Meteorology); **Education and Psychology** (Educational Sciences; Primary Education; Psychology; Sports); **History and Cultural Studies** (History; Philosophy; Social Sciences); **Law** (Law); **Mathematics and Computer Science** (Mathematics and Computer Science); **Philosophy and Humanities** (Film; German; Music; Philosophy; Theatre); **Physics**; **Political and Social Sciences** (Advertising and Publicity; Communication Studies; Ethnology; Political Sciences; Sociology); **Veterinary Science** (Veterinary Science)

Institutes
Eastern Europe Studies (Eastern European Studies); **Latin American Studies** (Latin American Studies); **North American Studies** *(John F. Kenney)* (American Studies)

Schools
Business and Economics (Business Administration; Economics); **Medicine** *(Charité)* (Medicine)

History: Founded 1948 in response to the demand for the creation of a University in West Berlin. Reorganized and faculty structure replaced 1970. An independent body financially supported by the State of Berlin.

Governing Bodies: Kuratorium; Konzil; Akademischer Senat

Academic Year: October to July (October-February; April-July)

Admission Requirements: Secondary school certificate (Reifezeugnis). Certificate of excellent knowledge of German

Fees: None

Main Language(s) of Instruction: German

International Co-operation: With 120 countries worldwide. Also participates in Erasmus Programme.

Degrees and Diplomas: *Bachelor/Bakkalaureus*; *Diplom*: Biochemistry; Political Science, 4-6 yrs; *Lehramt*: 4-6 yrs; *Staatsprüfung*: Medicine: Pharmacy; Dentistry; Law, 4-6 yrs; *Master/Magister*: 4-6 yrs; *Promotion*

Student Services: Academic counselling, Canteen, Foreign student adviser, Language programs, Social counselling, Sports facilities

Special Facilities: Botanical Garden and Museum

Libraries: Central Library, 1.55m. vols; libraries of the departments and Central Institutes
Last Updated: 22/03/11

FREIBERG UNIVERSITY OF MINING AND TECHNOLOGY

Technische Universität Bergakademie Freiberg
Akademiestrasse 6, 09596 Freiberg
Tel: +49(3731) 39-0
Fax: +49(3731) 2-2195
EMail: rektorat@zuv.tu-freiberg.de
Website: http://www.tu-freiberg.de

Rektor: Bernd Meyer
Tel: +49(3731) 39-2550, Fax: +49(3731) 39-3323
EMail: Rektor@zuv.tu-freiberg.de

Kanzler: Andreas Handschuh
Tel: +49(3731) 39-2700, Fax: +49(3731) 39-3634
EMail: kanzler@zuv.tu-freiberg.de

Centres
Interdisciplinary Ecology (Ecology)

Faculties
Business Administration (Business Administration; Economics); **Chemistry and Physics** (Analytical Chemistry; Chemical Engineering; Chemistry; Inorganic Chemistry; Natural Sciences; Physical Chemistry; Physics); **Geosciences, Geo-Engineering and Mining** (Earth Sciences; Geochemistry; Geology; Geophysics; Mineralogy; Mining Engineering; Petroleum and Gas Engineering; Surveying and Mapping); **Materials Science and Technology** (Materials Engineering; Metallurgical Engineering; Physical Engineering); **Mathematics and Computer Science** (Computer Science; Mathematics); **Mechanical, Energy and Process Engineering** (Chemical Engineering; Energy Engineering; Engineering Management; Environmental Engineering; Mechanical Engineering)

Further Information: Also preparatory courses and German language courses

History: Founded 1765, acquired University status 1905. Became Technical University 1991.

Governing Bodies: Konzil; Senat; Kuratorium

Academic Year: October to July (October-February; April-July)

Admission Requirements: Secondary school certificate (Reifezeugnis) or equivalent, and German language certificate (DSH) for international students

Fees: None

Main Language(s) of Instruction: German, English

International Co-operation: With universities in France, Italy, Norway, Poland, Spain, the Czech Republic, Hungary, Russian Federation, Ukraine and USA. Also participates in Erasmus, Tempus, Alpha

Degrees and Diplomas: *Bachelor/Bakkalaureus*: Business Mathematics; Chemistry; Geo-Ecology; Geology, Paleontology; Geophysics; Network Computing, 3 yrs; *Bachelor/Bakkalaureus*: Materials Technology, Foundry Technology, $3\frac{1}{2}$ yrs; *Diplom*: Applied Mathematics; Applied Natural Sciences; Archaeometry (Engineering Archaeology); Geo-Ecology; Geo-Engineering and Mining; Geo-Informatics; Geological Surveying and Geodesy; Mineralogy, $4\frac{1}{2}$ yrs; *Diplom*: Automotives: Materials and Components; *Diplom*: Business Administration, 4 yrs; *Diplom*: Ceramic, Glass, and Building; Chemistry; Electronic and Sensor Materials; Engineering Management; Environmental Engineering; Geology/ Paleontology; Geophysics; Management and Technology; Materials Science and Technology; Mechanical Engineering; Process Engineering, 5 yrs; *Master/Magister*. Also Dual Degree Programmes

Student Services: Academic counselling, Canteen, Cultural centre, Employment services, Foreign student adviser, Foreign Studies Centre, Handicapped facilities, Health services, Language programs, Nursery care, Social counselling, Sports facilities

Student Residential Facilities: Yes

Special Facilities: Mineralogical Collection

Libraries: 685,256 vols

Publications: Freiberger Forschungshefte; Report *(biennially)*
Last Updated: 27/01/10

FREIBURG UNIVERSITY OF MUSIC

Staatliche Hochschule für Musik Freiburg im Breisgau
Schwarzwaldstrasse 141, 79095 Freiburg
Tel: +49(761) 31915-0
Fax: +49(761) 31915-42
EMail: info@mh-freiburg.de
Website: http://www.mh-freiburg.de

Rektor: Rüdiger Nolte
Tel: +49(761) 31915-49 EMail: r.nolte@mh-freiburg.de

Kanzler: Manfred Klimanski
Tel: +49(761) 31915-44 EMail: m.klimanski@mh-freiburg.de

Institutes
Music Medicine (Art Therapy; Music)

Programmes
Music (Conducting; Music; Music Education; Music Theory and Composition; Musical Instruments; Musicology; Opera; Religious Music; Singing)

History: Founded 1946.

Main Language(s) of Instruction: German

Degrees and Diplomas: *Bachelor/Bakkalaureus*; *Master/Magister*; *Promotion*: Musicology and Music Education. Also postgraduate diplomas

Last Updated: 26/01/10

FRESENIUS UNIVERSITY OF APPLIED SCIENCES

Hochschule Fresenius (HSF)

Limburger Strasse 2, 65510 Idstein
Tel: +49(6126) 9352-0
Fax: +49(6126) 9352-10
EMail: idstein@hs-fresenius.de
Website: http://www.fh-fresenius.de

Präsident: Botho von Portatius EMail: service@fh-fresenius.de

International Relations: Leo Gros, Vizepräsident (International Relations) EMail: auslandsamt@fh-fresenius.de

Faculties

Chemistry and Biology (Biology; Chemistry); **Economics and Media Studies** (Administration; Commercial Law; Media Studies; Psychology); **Health Sciences** (Health Sciences; Occupational Therapy; Osteopathy; Physical Therapy; Speech Therapy and Audiology)

Further Information: Also branches in Köln, Hamburg, Darmstadt, Munich, Zwickau and Vienna.

History: Founded 1848.

Main Language(s) of Instruction: German

Degrees and Diplomas: *Bachelor/Bakkalaureus*; *Diplom (FH)*: 8-9 sem; *Master/Magister*
Last Updated: 18/01/10

FRIEDENSAU ADVENTIST UNIVERSITY

Theologische Hochschule Friedensau

An der Ihle 19, 39291 Friedensau
Tel: +49(3921) 916-0
Fax: +49(3921) 916-120
EMail: hochschule@thh-friedensau.de
Website: http://www.thh-friedensau.de/

Rektor: Johann Gerhard Tel: +49(3921) 916-131

Kanzler: Roland Nickel
Tel: +49(3921) 916-107 EMail: roland.nickel@thh-friedensau.de

International Relations: Lilli Unrau
Tel: +49(3921) 916-134 EMail: zulassung@thh-friedensau.de

Departments
German as a Foreign Language (German)

Institutes
Church Music (Music)

Schools
Social Sciences (Social Sciences; Social Work); **Theology** (Hebrew; Missionary Studies; Music; Pastoral Studies; Theology)
History: Founded 1899.

Main Language(s) of Instruction: German

Degrees and Diplomas: *Bachelor/Bakkalaureus*; *Master/Magister*
Last Updated: 22/03/11

FRIEDRICH-ALEXANDER UNIVERSITY OF ERLANGEN-NUREMBERG

Friedrich-Alexander-Universität Erlangen-Nürnberg

PO Box 3520, Schlossplatz 4, 91023 Erlangen, Bavaria
Tel: +49(9131) 85-0
Fax: +49(9131) 85-22131
EMail: rektorat@zuv.uni-erlangen.de
Website: http://www.uni-erlangen.de

Präsident: Karl-Dieter Grüske
Tel: +49(9131) 852-6605, Fax: +49(9131) 852-2188
EMail: president@fau.de

Kanzler: Thomas A.H. Schöck
Tel: +49(9131) 852-6603, Fax: +49(9131) 852-6712
EMail: kanzler@fau.de

International Relations: Christoph Korbmacher
Tel: +49(9131) 852-4801, Fax: +49(9131) 852-6335
EMail: Christoph.Korbmacher@fau.de

Centres
Astrophysics *(Bamberg)* (Astrophysics); **Computer** *(Regional)* (Computer Science); **Social Sciences Research** (Social Sciences); **Sports** (Sports)

Faculties
Business, Economics and Law (Business Administration; Business Computing; Civil Law; Criminal Law; Criminology; Economics; International Law; Labour Law; Law; Private Law); **Engineering** (Bioengineering; Chemical Engineering; Computer Engineering; Computer Science; Electrical Engineering; Electronic Engineering; Engineering; Information Technology; Machine Building; Materials Engineering; Mechanical Engineering; Production Engineering; Technology); **Humanities and Theology** (American Studies; Archaeology; Art History; Chinese; Cultural Studies; Economics; Education; English Studies; Germanic Languages; Gerontology; History; History of Religion; Japanese; Media Studies; Modern Languages; Music; Musicology; Oriental Languages; Pedagogy; Philosophy; Political Sciences; Psychology; Romance Languages; Social Sciences; Sociology; Sports; Teacher Training; Theology); **Medicine** (Anatomy; Biochemistry; Biomedicine; Computer Science; Epidemiology; Ethics; Medical Technology; Medicine; Molecular Biology; Occupational Health; Orthopaedics; Pathology; Pharmacology; Physiology; Social and Preventive Medicine; Toxicology); **Sciences** (Astronomy and Space Science; Biochemistry; Biological and Life Sciences; Biology; Biotechnology; Chemistry; Genetics; Geography; Geology; Information Technology; Mathematics; Microbiology; Optics; Pharmacy; Physics; Physiology; Plant Pathology)

Institutes
Biomedical Engineering (Biomedical Engineering); **Philosophy and History of Science** (Philosophy); **Regional Studies** (Regional Studies)

History: Founded 1743 by Friedrich of Bayreuth. In the 19th century the University occupied the Palace of Erlangen. The former Hochschule für Wirtschafts-und Sozialwissenschaften (Business Administration), Nürnberg, was formally incorporated as a faculty of the University 1961, and the name Nürnberg was added to its title. College of Education, Nürnberg incorporated 1972. Reorganized 1974. An autonomous institution, financially supported by the State of Bavaria and under the jurisdiction of its Ministry of Education.

Governing Bodies: Senat

Academic Year: October to September (October-March; April-September)

Admission Requirements: Secondary school certificate (Reifezeugnis) or equivalent. Knowledge of German

Fees: (Euros): 50

Main Language(s) of Instruction: German

Degrees and Diplomas: *Bachelor/Bakkalaureus*; *Lehramt*; *Kirchliche Abschlussprüfung*: Evangelical Theology; *Staatsprüfung*: Dentistry, 5 yrs; *Staatsprüfung*: Law, 6 yrs; *Staatsprüfung*: Medicine; Pharmacy, 4 yrs; *Master/Magister*: 4 yrs; *Promotion*. Habilitation awarded in the same fields of studies as Doktor

Student Services: Academic counselling, Canteen, Cultural centre, Employment services, Foreign student adviser, Foreign Studies Centre, Language programs, Social counselling, Sports facilities

Student Residential Facilities: Yes

Special Facilities: School Museum. Botanical Garden. Art Collection. Geological Collection

Libraries: University Library, c. 4m. vols, including 3 branch libraries (Economics and Social Sciences, Engineering, and Education), c. 1,687,500 vols

Publications: Erlangen Forschungen; Erlangen Universitätsreden; Forschungsbericht; Jahrbuch der Fränkischen Landesforschung *(annually)*
Last Updated: 01/02/12

FRIEDRICH SCHILLER UNIVERSITY JENA

Friedrich-Schiller-Universität Jena
Fürstengraben 1, 07743 Jena
Tel: +49(3641) 9300
Fax: +49(3641) 93-1682
Website: http://www.uni-jena.de

Rektor: Klaus Dicke
Tel: +49(3641) 93-1000, Fax: +49(3641) 93-1002
EMail: rektor@uni-jena.de

Kanzler: Klaus Bartholmé
Tel: +49(3641) 93-1050, Fax: +49(3641) 93-1052
EMail: kanzler@uni-jena.de

International Relations: Jürgen Hendrich, Head, International Relations
Tel: +49(3641) 93-1160, Fax: +49(3641) 93-1162
EMail: aaa@uni-jena.de; juergen.hendrich@uni-jena.de

Faculties

Behavioural and Social Sciences (Behavioural Sciences; Educational Sciences; Political Sciences; Psychology; Social Sciences; Sociology; Sports); **Biology and Pharmacy** (Biology; Pharmacy); **Chemistry and Earth Sciences** (Chemistry; Earth Sciences; Geography; Geology; Geophysics; Mineralogy); **Economics and Business Administration** (Business Administration; Economics); **Law** (Law); **Mathematics and Computer Science** (Computer Science; Mathematics); **Medicine** (Dentistry; Medicine); **Philosophy** (Archaeology; Art History; Classical Languages; History; Linguistics; Literature; Modern Languages; Musicology; Philosophy); **Physics and Astronomy** (Astronomy and Space Science; Physics); **Theology** (Protestant Theology)

History: Founded 1548 as academy by Kurfürst Johann Friedrich von Sachsen, became University 1558. Recognized after German unification, the University is under the jurisdiction of the Thuringian Ministry of Science and Arts.

Governing Bodies: Senat; Konzil

Academic Year: October to September (October-March; April-September)

Admission Requirements: Secondary school certificate (Reifezeugnis) or equivalent

Fees: None

Main Language(s) of Instruction: German

International Co-operation: With universities in Europe, Canada, USA, Japan, Brazil, Chile, Vietnam. Also participates in Socrates, Tempus and Coimbra Group.

Accrediting Agencies: Ministry of Science, Research and Arts, State of Thuringia

Degrees and Diplomas: *Zertifikat*; *Bachelor/Bakkalaureus*: Business Mathematics; Geography; Mathematics; Physics, 3 yrs; *Diplom*: Biochemistry; Biology; Business Administration; Business Mathematics; Chemistry; Computer Science; Engineering Physics; Environmental Chemistry; Geography; Geology; Geophysics; Intercultural Management; Materials Science; Mathematics; Mineralogy; National Economy; Nutritional Science; Physics; Protestant Theology; Psychology; Sports Science; Teaching of Economics, 4-5 yrs; *Lehramt*: Teaching qualification, secondary level; *Magister Artium*; *Staatsprüfung*: Dentistry; Law; Medicine; Pharmacy, 4-6 yrs; *Master/Magister*: German as a Foreign Language; Political Science; Law; Private and Public Commercial Law, 1-2 yrs; *Promotion*; *Doktorgrad*: Medicine (Dr.Med.), 6 yrs; *Habilitation*: at least 3 yrs following Doktor

Student Services: Canteen, Cultural centre, Social counselling, Sports facilities

Student Residential Facilities: For 2,800 students

Special Facilities: Phylogenetic Museum. Ernst-Haeckel-Haus (History of Medicine and Natural Science). Botanical Garden. Observatory. Herbarium

Libraries: Thüringer Universitäts-und Landesbibliothek, 3.8m. items

Publications: Bibliographische Mitteilungen der Universitätsbibliothek, Jena; Forschungsmagazin *(biannually)*; Jenaer Reden und Schriften; Jenaer Universitätsreden

Press or Publishing House: Uni-Journal
Last Updated: 18/01/10

FULDA UNIVERSITY OF APPLIED SCIENCES

Hochschule Fulda
Marquardstrasse 35, 36039 Fulda
Tel: +49(661) 9640-0
Fax: +49(661) 9640-199
EMail: info@verw.hs-fulda.de
Website: http://www.fh-fulda.de

Präsident: Karim Khakzar
Tel: +49(661) 9640-111, Fax: +49(661) 9640-182
EMail: praesident@bitte-loeschen.hs-fulda.de

International Relations: Winnie Rosatis
Tel: +49(661) 9640-147, Fax: +49(661) 9640-189
EMail: winnie.rosatis@hs-fulda.de

Faculties

Applied Computer Science (Business Computing; Computer Science); **Business Administration** (Business Administration; Management); **Electrical Engineering and Information Technology** (Electrical Engineering; Information Technology); **Food Technology** (Food Technology); **Nursing and Health Sciences** (Health Administration; Nursing; Physical Therapy); **Nutritional, Food and Consumer Sciences** (Food Science; Food Technology; Nutrition); **Social and Cultural Studies** (Cultural Studies; European Studies; International Relations; Social Sciences; Social Studies); **Social Work** (Social Work)

History: Founded 1974 as Fachhochschule Fulda. Acquired present title 2006.

Admission Requirements: General higher education entrance qualification (HEEQ)

Fees: (Euros): 120 per semester; Master tuition, 500

Main Language(s) of Instruction: German

International Co-operation: With universities in Bulgaria, Czech Republic, Finland, France, Greece, Hungary, Ireland, Italy, United Kingdom, Latvia, Netherlands, Norway, Poland, Romania, Slovak Republic, Spain, Sweden, USA, Australia. Also participates in Erasmus.

Degrees and Diplomas: *Bachelor/Bakkalaureus*: Applied Computer Science; Business Administration and Electrical Engineering; Process Engineering; Electrical Engineering and Information Technology; Health Care Management; Social Sciences for Intercultural Relations; Social Work (BA), 3-31/2 yrs; *Bachelor/Bakkalaureus*: Electrical Engineering and Information Technology; International Management; Food Technology; Nutritional, Food and Consumer Sciences, 3-31/2 yrs; *Bachelor/Bakkalaureus*: Social Insurance and Welfare Law, 4 yrs; *Master/Magister (MA)*: 1 1/2-2 yrs. Also Distance Learning Bachelor in Social Work, 4 yrs; Distance Learning Master; 21/2 yrs

Student Services: Academic counselling, Canteen, Foreign student adviser, Foreign Studies Centre, Handicapped facilities, Language programs, Social counselling, Sports facilities

Student Residential Facilities: Yes

Libraries: University and Hessian State Library

Publications: Thema *(quarterly)*
Last Updated: 01/02/12

FURTWANGEN UNIVERSITY

Hochschule Furtwangen - Informatik, Technik, Wirtschaft, Medien (HFU)
Robert-Gerwig-Platz 1, 78120 Furtwangen
Tel: +49(7723) 920-0
Fax: +49(7723) 920-1109
EMail: info@hs-furtwangen.de
Website: http://www.hs-furtwangen.de

Rektor: Rolf Schofer
Tel: +49(7723) 920-1110, Fax: +49(7723) 920-1119
EMail: rk@hs-furtwangen.de

Kanzler: Gerd Kusserow
Tel: +49(7723) 920-1113 EMail: kus@hs-furtwangen.de

International Relations: Brigitte Minderlein, Head, International Office
Tel: +49(7723) 920-1310, Fax: +49(7723) 920-1109
EMail: international@hs-furtwangen.de; min@hs-furtwangen.de

Departments

Business Administation (Business Administration; International Business; Management); **Business Computing** (Business Administration; Business Computing; E-Business/Commerce); **Computer and Electrical Engineering** (Computer Engineering; Electrical Engineering; Safety Engineering); **Computer Science** (Computer Networks; Computer Science); **Digital Media** (Computer Science; Media Studies); **Industrial Technologies** (Industrial Engineering); **Mechanical and Process Engineering** (Bioengineering; Biomedical Engineering; Biotechnology; Machine Building; Mechanical Engineering; Medical Technology; Production Engineering); **Product Engineering/Engineering with Business Studies** (Design; Documentation Techniques; Marketing; Production Engineering; Sales Techniques)

History: Founded 1971. Formerly known as Fachhochschule Furtwangen - Hochschule für Technik und Wirtschaft.

Admission Requirements: Secondary school certificate (Fachhochschulreife)

Fees: None for undergaduate courses

Main Language(s) of Instruction: German. English in some courses.

International Co-operation: With universities in United Kingdom, France, Spain, Denmark, Netherlands, USA, China, Hungary.

Degrees and Diplomas: *Bachelor/Bakkalaureus*: 3 yrs; *Master/Magister*: a further 3 sem

Student Services: Academic counselling, Canteen, Foreign student adviser, Language programs, Social counselling

Student Residential Facilities: Yes

Special Facilities: Museum

Libraries: Main Library
Last Updated: 19/01/10

GELSENKIRCHEN UNIVERSITY OF APPLIED SCIENCES

Fachhochschule Gelsenkirchen
Neidenburger Strasse 43, 45877 Gelsenkirchen
Tel: +49(209) 9596-0
Fax: +49(209) 9596-445
EMail: praesident@fh-gelsenkirchen.de
Website: http://www.fh-gelsenkirchen.eu

Präsident: Bernd Kriegesmann (2008-)
Tel: +49(209) 9596-461, Fax: +49(209) 9596-562

Departments

Business Administration (Business Administration); **Computer Science** (Computer Science); **Electrical Engineering and Technology** (Electrical Engineering); **Journalism and Public Relations** (Journalism; Public Relations); **Physics** (Physics)

Further Information: Also branches in Bocholt and Recklinghausen

History: Founded 1992.

Main Language(s) of Instruction: German

Degrees and Diplomas: *Bachelor/Bakkalaureus*; *Master/Magister*
Last Updated: 06/02/12

GEORG AGRICOLA UNIVERSITY OF APPLIED SCIENCES

Technische Fachhochschule 'Georg Agricola' zu Bochum
Herner Strasse 45, 44787 Bochum
Tel: +49(234) 968-02
Fax: +49(234) 968-3359
EMail: info@tfh-bochum.de
Website: http://www.tfh-bochum.de

Rektor: Jürgen Kretschmann Tel: +49(234) 968-3381

Sections

Electronical Engineering and Information Technology (Electronic Engineering; Information Technology); **Geological and Mining Engineering** (Geological Engineering; Mining Engineering); **Machine Building and Process Engineering** (Engineering Management; Machine Building)

History: Founded 1816 as Bochumer Bergschule. Acquired present name 1995. Acquired present title 1998.

Governing Bodies: Rectorate; Senate

Academic Year: March to February (March-August; September-February)

Admission Requirements: Secondary school certificate (Abitur) or recognized equivalent

Fees: (Euros): c. 80 per semester

Main Language(s) of Instruction: German

International Co-operation: Yes

Degrees and Diplomas: *Bachelor/Bakkalaureus*: Business Economics and Electrotechnology (Technical); Business Economics and Machine Building (Technical); Business Economics and Natural Resources (Technical); Machine Building; Machine Building and Computer Science; *Master/Magister*: Business Economics (Technical); Machine Building; Machine Building and Computer Science
Last Updated: 26/01/10

GEORG AUGUST UNIVERSITY GÖTTINGEN

Georg-August-Universität Göttingen
Wilhelmsplatz 1, 37073 Göttingen
Tel: +49(551) 39-0
Fax: +49(551) 39-9612
EMail: poststelle@uni-goettingen.de
Website: http://www.uni-goettingen.de

Präsidentin: Ulrike Beisiegel
Tel: +49(551) 39-4311, Fax: +49(551) 39-4135
EMail: praesidentin@uni-goettingen.de

Vice-President: Markus Hoppe
Tel: +49(551) 39-4202, Fax: +49(551) 39-4135
EMail: markus.hoppe@zvw.uni-goettingen.de

International Relations: Uwe Muuss, Head, International Office
Tel: +49(551) 39-13585, Fax: +49(551) 39-14254
EMail: uwe.muuss@zvw.uni-goettingen.de;
international.office@zvw.uni-goettingen

Faculties

Agricultural Sciences (Agriculture); **Biology** (Biology); **Chemistry** (Chemistry); **Economics** (Accountancy; Business Administration; Economics; Finance; Human Resources; Management; Marketing; Taxation); **Forest Science and Forest Ecology** (Ecology; Forestry); **Geoscience and Geography** (Environmental Management; Geography; Geology); **Humanities** (Ancient Civilizations; Arabic; Archaeology; Art History; Arts and Humanities; Classical Languages; East Asian Studies; Finnish; History; Musicology; Philology; Philosophy; Romance Languages; Scandinavian Languages; Slavic Languages); **Law** (Law); **Mathematics and Computer Science** (Mathematics); **Physics** (Physics); **Social Sciences** (Ethnology; Gender Studies; Indic Languages; Political Sciences; Social Sciences; Sociology); **Theology** (Bible; Ethics; Jewish Studies; New Testament; Religious Studies; Theology)

Schools

Medicine (Dentistry; Medicine)

History: Founded 1737 by George II, Prince Elector of Hanover and King of England, the first modern University founded in Germany. Measures to guarantee quality and to promote excellence in research and teaching, reforms to strengthen autonomy and responsibility at all levels of the University, and the internationalization of the University have been implemented within the past few years. 2003, the University of Göttingen was the first full university in Germany to be converted into a publicly endowed university.

Governing Bodies: Senate; STIFTUNGSRAT

Academic Year: April to March (April-September; October-March)

Admission Requirements: Secondary school certificate (Reifezeugnis) or equivalent

Fees: (Euros): 165.70 per semester

Main Language(s) of Instruction: German and English

International Co-operation: With institutions of higher education worldwide. Also participates in the Erasmus programme

Accrediting Agencies: Zentrale Evaluations und Akkreditierungsagentur (ZevA)

Degrees and Diplomas: *Bachelor/Bakkalaureus*: 3 yrs; *Staatsprüfung*; *Master/Magister*: Agricultural Sciences; Applied Computer Science; Computer Sciences; Forestry; International Economics; Mathematics, a further 2 yrs; *Master/Magister*: Educational Sciences; Information Systems; International Studies, a further 1 yr; *Master/Magister*: Molecular Biology; Neurosciences; Physics, a further 1-2 yrs; *Promotion*: Agricultural Sciences (PhD); Applied Statistics (PhD); Forestry and Wood Modification Technologies (PhD); Medieval Studies (PhD); Molecular Biology (PhD); Neurosciences (PhD); Physics (PhD), a further 3 yrs; *Doktorgrad (PhD)*: a further 2-4 yrs; *Habilitation*: at least 3 yrs following Doktor

Student Services: Academic counselling, Canteen, Cultural centre, Employment services, Foreign student adviser, Handicapped facilities, Health services, Language programs, Social counselling, Sports facilities

Student Residential Facilities: Yes

Special Facilities: Art Gallery. Ethnological Museum; Zoological Museum; Chemical Museum; Archaeological Museum; Musical Instruments Museum; Physical Instruments Museum; Geological Museum. Biological Garden. Movie Studio

Libraries: University and State Library of Lower Saxony, c. 3m. vols

Publications: Georgia Augusta Wissenschaftmagazin der Georg-August-Universität Göttingen, Magazine of Science *(1-2 per annum)*
Last Updated: 01/02/12

GEORG-SIMON-OHM UNIVERSITY OF APPLIED SCIENCES NUREMBERG

Georg-Simon-Ohm-Hochschule Nürnberg (GSO-FHN)
Kesslerplatz 12, 90489 Nürnberg
Tel: +49(911) 5880-0
Fax: +49(911) 5880-8309
EMail: presse@ohm-hochschule.de
Website: http://www.fh-nuernberg.de

Präsident: Michael Braun (2006-)
Tel: +49(911) 5880-4225, Fax: +49(911) 5880-8269
EMail: rektor@fh-nuernberg.de

Kanzler: Achim Hoffmann
Tel: +49(911) 5880-4241, Fax: +49(911) 5880-8241
EMail: kanzler@fh-nuernberg.de

International Relations: Nikolaus Hackl
Tel: +49(911) 5880-4,136; +49(911) 5880-4298,
Fax: +49(911) 5880-8804
EMail: International.Office@ohm-hochschule.de;
nikolaus.hackl@fh-nuenberg.de

Departments
Applied Chemistry (Applied Chemistry); **Architecture** (Architecture); **Business Administration** (Business Administration); **Civil Engineering** (Civil Engineering); **Computer Science** (Business Computing; Computer Science); **Design** (Design); **Electrical Engineering, Precision Engineering and Information Technology** (Electrical Engineering; Information Technology); **General Studies** (Journalism); **Materials Engineering** (Materials Engineering); **Mechanical Engineering and Building Services Engineering** (Engineering; Mechanical Engineering); **Process Engineering** (Engineering Management); **Social Sciences** (Social Work)

History: Founded 1823. Acquired present status 1971.

Governing Bodies: University Board; Senate

Academic Year: October to September

Admission Requirements: German Abitur or equivalent (plus language test for foreign students), pre-practicals

Main Language(s) of Instruction: German, English

International Co-operation: With universities in Europe, America, Asia, Australia, Africa. Also participates in Erasmus.

Degrees and Diplomas: *Bachelor/Bakkalaureus*: Applied Chemistry; Architecture; Building Services Engineering; Business Administration; Economics; Civil Engineering; Electrical Engineering; Information Technology; Information Systems and Management; International Business; Mechanical Engineering; Media Design; Media Technology; Material Technology; Precision Engineering/Mechatronics; Process Engineering; Social Work; Visual Communication Design, at least 4 yrs; *Bachelor/Bakkalaureus*:

Architecture; Building Services Engineering; Business Administration; Computer Science; Economics; Civil Engineering; Information Technology; Information Systems and Management; International Business; Mechanical Engineering; Material Technology; (BSc; BBA), 3 yrs; *Bachelor/Bakkalaureus*: Process Engineering; Social Work, 31/2 yrs; *Diplom (FH)*; *Master/Magister*: Building Engineering; Business Administration; Computer Science; Counseling; Facility Management; Mechanical Engineering; Information Systems and Management; International Business; Software Engineering and Information Technology (MSc; MBA), a further 1 term-2 yrs

Student Services: Academic counselling, Canteen, Foreign student adviser, Foreign Studies Centre, Handicapped facilities, Language programs, Nursery care, Social counselling, Sports facilities

Publications: Schriftenreihe *(other/irregular)*
Last Updated: 01/02/12

GERMAN GRADUATE SCHOOL OF MANAGEMENT AND LAW, HEILBRONN

Bahnhofstraße 1, 74072 Heilbronn
Tel: +49(7131) 6456-36-0
EMail: info@ggs.de
Website: http://www.ggs.de

Präsident: Dirk Zupancic Tel: +49(7131) 645636-15

Programmes
Business Law (Commercial Law); **Business Management** (Business Administration)

History: Founded 2005 as Heilbronn Business School. Acquired present status and title 2009.

Fees: (Euros): 18,000-24,000

Main Language(s) of Instruction: German

Degrees and Diplomas: *Master/Magister (M.B.A.; LL.M.; M.Sc.)*
Last Updated: 01/02/12

GERMAN SPORT UNIVERSITY COLOGNE

Deutsche Sporthochschule Köln
Am Sportpark Müngersdorf 6, NRW 50933 Köln,
Nordrhein-Westfalen
Tel: +49(221) 4982-0
Fax: +49(221) 4982-8330
EMail: info@dshs-koeln.de
Website: http://www.dshs-koeln.de

Rektor: Walter Tokarski
Tel: +49(221) 4982-2000, Fax: +49(221) 4982-8500
EMail: tokarski@dshs-koeln.de

Kanzler: Johannes Horst
Tel: +49(221) 4982-3000, Fax: +49(221) 4982-8000
EMail: horst@dshs-koeln.de

International Relations: Werner Sonnenschein
Tel: +49(221) 4982-2160, Fax: +49(221) 4982-8120
EMail: auslandsamt@dshs-koeln.de

Chairs
Professorship of Music and Dance Education (Art Education; Dance; Music; Music Education)

Divisions
Basketball and Handball (Sports)

Faculties
Applied Movement Sciences (Pedagogy; Sports); **Education, Humanities and Social Sciences** (Arts and Humanities; Education; Social Sciences); **Medicine and Natural Sciences** (Medicine; Natural Sciences)

Institutes
Biochemistry (Biochemistry); **Biomechanics and Orthopedics** (Biotechnology; Orthopaedics); **Cardiology and Sports Medicine** (Cardiology; Sports Medicine); **Coaching Science and Sport Informatics**; **Communication and Media Research** (Communication Studies; Media Studies; Sports); **Dance and Movement Culture** (Dance); **Environmental Sport and Ecology** (Ecology; Sports); **European Sport Development and Leisure Studies** (Leisure Studies); **Motor Control and Movement Techniques**; **Movement and Sport Gerontology**; **Movement Science in Sport**

Games (Sports); **Pedagogy and Philosophy**; **Physiology and Anatomy** (Anatomy; Physiology); **Psychology** (Psychology); **Rehabilitation and Sports for the Disabled** (Rehabilitation and Therapy); **School Sport and School Development** (Pedagogy; Sports); **Sport Economy and Management**; **Sport History** (Sports); **Sport Sociology** (Sports)

History: Founded 1947 and tracing its origins to the former Berliner Hochschule für Leibesübungen, founded 1920. Acquired University status 1970. Under the jurisdiction of and financially supported by the State of North Rhine-Westphalia.

Governing Bodies: Konvent; Senat

Academic Year: April to March (April-September; October-March)

Admission Requirements: Secondary school certificate (Abitur) and Athletic aptitude test. German Language Proficiency Certificate (DSH level 2 or TESTDAF level 4)

Fees: (Euros): 500 per semester

Main Language(s) of Instruction: German

International Co-operation: With universities in 21 European countries and 11 non-European countries

Degrees and Diplomas: *Bachelor/Bakkalaureus*; *Diplom*: Physical Education, Sport Science, 8 sem; *Lehramt*: Teaching Qualification, 6-8 sem; *Master/Magister*; *Promotion*; *Doktorgrad*: Sports Science (PhD)

Student Services: Academic counselling, Canteen, Foreign student adviser, Foreign Studies Centre, Handicapped facilities, Health services, Language programs, Sports facilities

Student Residential Facilities: Yes

Libraries: c. 377,000 vols

Publications: F.I.T. - Das Wissenschaftsmagazin der DSHS Köln (*biennially*)

Last Updated: 06/02/12

GERMAN UNIVERSITY OF ADMINISTRATIVE SCIENCES SPEYER

Deutsche Hochschule für Verwaltungswissenschaften
Freiherr-vom-Stein-Strasse 2, Post Box 1409, 67346 Speyer
Tel: +49(6232) 654-0
Fax: +49(6232) 654-208
EMail: dhv@dhv-speyer.de; rektor@dhv-speyer.de
Website: http://www.dhv-speyer.de

Rektor: Joachim Wieland
Tel: +49(6232) 654-212 EMail: rektor@dhv-speyer.de

Head Administrative Officer: Christiane Müller
Tel: +49(6232) 654-214 EMail: mueller@dhv-speyer.de

International Relations: Klauspeter Strohm
Tel: +49(6232) 654-225, Fax: +49(6232) 654-446
EMail: strohm@dhv-speyer.de

Departments
Administration (Administration; Computer Science; Economics; History; Law; Political Sciences; Psychology; Sociology)

Institutes
Research

Further Information: Also International Studies Programme and Continuing education programme in Knowledge Management

History: Founded 1947 as Staatliche Akademie, acquired present status and title 1997.

Governing Bodies: Senat; Verwaltungsrat

Academic Year: October to September

Admission Requirements: Staatsexamen, Diplom, or Magister Artium (corresponding to University degree of Master in Law, Economics, Political or Social Sciences). Certified knowledge of the German language (PNDS or DSH of a German University or Zentrale Mittelstufenprüfung (ZMP) of the Goethe Institute)

Fees: None

Main Language(s) of Instruction: German

Degrees and Diplomas: *Master/Magister*: Administrative Sciences, 1-1 1/2 yrs; *Doktorgrad*: Administrative Sciences, 2-3 yrs; *Habilitation*

Student Services: Academic counselling, Canteen, Foreign student adviser, Foreign Studies Centre, Handicapped facilities, Language programs, Social counselling, Sports facilities

Student Residential Facilities: For c. 190 students

Libraries: Central Library, 250,000 vols

Publications: Schriftenreihe der Hochschule Speyer; Speyer Forschungsberichte; Speyerer Arbeitshefte
Last Updated: 31/01/12

GERMAN UNIVERSITY OF APPLIED SCIENCES FOR PREVENTION AND HEALTH MANAGEMENT

Deutsche Hochschule für Prävention und Gesundheitsmanagement
Hermann Neuberger Sportschule, D-66123 Saarbrücken
Tel: +49(681) 6855-150
Fax: +49(681) 6855-190
EMail: info@dhpg.org
Website: http://www.dhfpg.de

Rektor: D. Luppa

Programmes
Fitness and Economics (Business Administration; Economics; Marketing; Medicine; Nutrition; Pedagogy; Psychology; Sports); **Fitness Training** (Business Administration; Marketing; Medicine; Nutrition; Pedagogy; Psychology; Service Trades; Sports); **Health Care Management**; **Nutritional Consulting** (Nutrition)

History: Founded 2001 Occupational Academy (Berufsakademie). Acquired present status and title 2008.

Main Language(s) of Instruction: German

Degrees and Diplomas: *Bachelor/Bakkalaureus*; *Master/Magister*: Health Care Management
Last Updated: 06/02/12

GOETHE UNIVERSITY FRANKFURT AM MAIN

Goethe-Universität Frankfurt am Main
PO Box 111932, Senckenberganlage 31, 60054 Frankfurt am Main
Tel: +49(69) 798-0
Fax: +49(69) 798-28383
EMail: praesident@uni-frankfurt.de
Website: http://www.uni-frankfurt.de

Präsident: Werner Müller-Esterl
Tel: +49(69) 7982-2231, Fax: +49(69) 7982-8793

International Relations: Martin Bickl
Tel: +49(69) 7982-2263, Fax: +49(69) 7982-3983
EMail: bickl@em.uni-frankfurt.de

Centres
Environmental Research (Environmental Studies); **North American Studies** (American Studies; Gender Studies; Geography; History; Literature; Political Sciences; Sociology); **Teachers' Education** (Teacher Training)

Faculties
Biochemistry, Pharmacy and Chemistry (Biochemistry; Chemistry; Food Technology; Inorganic Chemistry; Organic Chemistry; Pharmacy; Physical Chemistry); **Biology** (Apiculture; Biology; Botany; Computer Science; Genetics; Microbiology; Zoology); **Computer Sciences and Mathematics** (Mathematics and Computer Science); **Economics and Business Administration** (Accountancy; Business Administration; Development Studies; Economics; Finance; Marketing; Statistics); **Educational Sciences** (Adult Education; Educational Sciences; International and Comparative Education; Primary Education; Special Education); **Geosciencs and Geography** (Earth Sciences; Economics; Geochemistry; Geography; Geography (Human); Geology; Geophysics; Meteorology; Mineralogy; Petrology); **Law** (Commercial Law; Criminal Law; History of Law; International Law; Labour Law; Law; Public Law); **Linguistics, Cultural and Civilization Studies, Art Studies** (African Languages; Anthropology; Archaeology; Art Education; Art History; Chinese; Classical Languages; Cultural Studies; Ethnology; Fine Arts; Japanese; Latin; Music; Music Education; Oriental Languages; Philology; Phonetics; Slavic Languages; South and Southeast Asian Languages); **Mathematics and Computer Science** (Mathematics; Mathematics and Computer Science); **Medi-**

cine (Dentistry; Medicine); **Philology** (English; French; German; Italian; Modern History; Philology; Portuguese; Scandinavian Languages; Spanish; Theatre); **Philosophy and History** (History; Philosophy); **Physics** (Applied Physics; Biophysics; History; Nuclear Physics; Physics); **Protestant Theology** (Protestant Theology); **Psychology and Sports** (Educational Psychology; Labour and Industrial Relations; Physical Education; Psychoanalysis; Psychology; Sports); **Roman Catholic Theology** (Catholic Theology); **Social Sciences** (Political Sciences; Social Sciences; Sociology)

Further Information: Also German language courses for advanced students

History: Founded 1914 by public subscription and with the support of the City of Frankfurt. As a result of the Krach in the 1920s the University lost most of its capital. Financial responsibility accepted by the Prussian State and City of Frankfurt 1923. Title of Johann Wolfgang Goethe adopted 1932. An autonomous institution financed by the State of Hesse.

Governing Bodies: Presidium; Senat

Academic Year: October to September (October-March; April-September)

Admission Requirements: Secondary school certificate (Reifezeugnis) or equivalent

Fees: None for basic study programmes

Main Language(s) of Instruction: German

International Co-operation: With universities in USA; China; Russian Federation; Latin America; South Africa. Also participates in Erasmus, Fulbright, DAAD programmes

Accrediting Agencies: ZEVA

Degrees and Diplomas: *Bachelor/Bakkalaureus*: Biology; Business Administration; Business Administration; Economics; Catholic Theology; Chemistry; Commercial Teaching Qualification; Computer Science; Economics; Education; Geography; Geology; Geophysics; Mathematics; Meteorology; Mineralogy; Physical Education; Physics; Psychology; Sociology; *Diplom*: Biochemistry; Evangelical Theology; Pedagogy; *Diplom (FH)*: Pedagogy; *Lehramt*: Teaching Qualifications; *Magister Artium*: 8 sem; *Staatsprüfung*: Dentistry; Medicine, 10 sem; *Staatsprüfung*: Food Chemistry; Law; Pharmacy; *Promotion*; *Doktorgrad*: Dentistry (Dr.Med.Dent.), 10 sem; *Habilitation*

Student Services: Academic counselling, Canteen, Cultural centre, Foreign student adviser, Handicapped facilities, Health services, Language programs, Nursery care, Social counselling, Sports facilities

Student Residential Facilities: For 2,600 students

Special Facilities: Senckenberg Museum; Biological Garden

Libraries: Municipal and University Library, c. 2.4m. vols; Senckenberg Library, c. 930,000 vols; libraries of the departments and institutes, c. 2m. vols

Publications: Forschungsbericht *(biennially)*; Jahresbibliographie *(3 per annum)*; Rechenschaftsbericht *(annually)*; Vorlesungsverzeichnis *(biannually)*
Last Updated: 01/02/12

GOTTFRIED WILHELM LEIBNIZ UNIVERSITY OF HANOVER

Gottfried Wilhelm Leibniz Universität Hannover
PO Box 6009, 30060 Hannover
Tel: +49(511) 762-0
Fax: +49(511) 762-3456
EMail: info@pressestelle.uni-hannover.de
Website: http://www.uni-hannover.de

Präsident: Erich Barke (2005-)
Tel: +49 511.762 - 5110, Fax: +49(511) 762-4004
EMail: praesident@zuv.uni-hannover.de

International Relations: Birgit Barden
Tel: +49(511) 762-5110, Fax: +49(511) 762-4004
EMail: birgit.bardenzuv.uni-hannover.de

Centres
Biomedical Engineering (Biomedical Engineering); **Business Accountancy** (Accountancy); **Computer-aided Engineering Sciences** *(International)* (Computer Science; Engineering); **Educa-**

tional Technology (Educational Technology); **Life Sciences** (Biological and Life Sciences); **Mechatronics** (Electronic Engineering; Mechanical Engineering); **Nano- and Quantenengineering** (Engineering; Nanotechnology); **Nanoelectronics** (Nanotechnology); **Organic Chemistry/Biologically Active Natural Materials** (Organic Chemistry); **Solid State Chemistry and New Materials** (Chemistry; Materials Engineering)

Faculties
Architecture and Landscape Sciences (Architectural and Environmental Design; Architecture; Architecture and Planning; Biology; Chemistry; Geology; Horticulture; Plant and Crop Protection); **Civil Engineering and Geodesic Science** (Civil Engineering; Surveying and Mapping); **Economics and Management** (Business Administration; Economics; Management); **Electrical Engineering and Computer Science** (Computer Science; Electrical Engineering; Electronic Engineering; Information Technology); **Humanities** (Adult Education; American Studies; Educational Sciences; English Studies; French Studies; Germanic Studies; History; Italian; Linguistics; Literature; Philosophy; Political Sciences; Psychology; Religious Education; Religious Studies; Social Sciences; Sociology; Special Education; Teacher Training; Theology; Vocational Education); **Law** (European Union Law; Law); **Mathematics and Physics** (Mathematics; Mathematics and Computer Science; Physics); **Mechanical Engineering** (Electronic Engineering; Mechanical Engineering; Metal Techniques; Production Engineering; Transport Management); **Natural Sciences** (Biology; Chemistry; Geography; Geology; Horticulture; Surveying and Mapping)

Further Information: Also Collaborative Research Centres

History: Founded 1831 as Höhere Gewerbeschule (secondary vocational school), became "Königliche Technische Hochschule" 1879. Reorganized 1921 and became "Technische Universität" 1968 and "Universität" 1978. Acquired present title 2006. An autonomous institution under the jurisdiction of and financed by the State of Lower Saxony.

Governing Bodies: Senat

Academic Year: October to September (October-March; April-September)

Admission Requirements: Secondary school certificate (Reifezeugnis) or foreign equivalent

Fees: None for regular students. Fees for Continuing Education

Main Language(s) of Instruction: German, in some fields, English

International Co-operation: With universities in Australia, Egypt, Belgium, Brazil, China, Taiwan, France, United Kingdom, Japan, Poland, Russian Federation, Syria, Thailand, Hungary, USA, Vietnam.

Degrees and Diplomas: *Bachelor/Bakkalaureus*: Biology; Chemistry; Civil Engineering; Computer Engineering; Electrical Engineering; Earth Science; History; Horticulture; Information Technology; Multidisciplinary Studies; Life Science; Mathematics; Computer Sciences; Mechatronics; Catholic Theology; Computer Science; Electrical Engineering and Information Technology; English Studies/American Studies; Economics and Business Administration; Food Science; Geodesy and Geoinformatics; Geography; German Studies;Horticulture; Industrial Engineering; Landscape Architecture and Environmental Planning; Metals Technology; Mechanical Engineering; Biotechnology; Production and Logistics; Protestant Theology and Religious Studies; Religious Studies; Role Play; Site Engineering; Social Sciences; Special Needs Education/Social Education and Community Work; Special Needs Education; Technical Education; *Diplom*: Adult Education/Extra-Curricular Youth Education; Architecture; Civil Engineering; Electrical Engineering; Geography; Mathematics/Computer Science; Mechanical Engineering; School; Special Needs Education; *Staatsprüfung*: Law; *Master/Magister*: Analytics; English Studies/American Studies; Biomedical Engineering; Catholic Theology; Chemistry; European Integration/European Studies; Geography; Geotechnical Engineering; German Studies; History; International Horticulture; Legal Informatics; Civil Engineering; Computer Engineering; Electrical Engineering; Earth Sciences; Horticulture; Law; Electronic Engineering; Mechanical Engineering; Biotechnology; Production and Transport Management; Vocational Education; Life Sciences; Materials Chemistry and Nanochemistry; Mathematics; Mechanical Engineering; Mechatronics; Medicinal and Natural Product Chemistry; Metals Technology; Philosophy; Physics; Plant Biotechnology; Political Science; Production and Logistics; Protestant Theology and

Religious Studies; Religious Studies; Special Needs Education/ Social Education and Community Work; Sport; Technical Education; Technical Physics. Also Postgraduate Course in Industrial Science; Rubber Technology

Student Services: Academic counselling, Cultural centre, Employment services, Foreign student adviser, Handicapped facilities, Health services, Language programs, Nursery care, Social counselling, Sports facilities

Student Residential Facilities: Yes

Special Facilities: IT Centre

Libraries: University Library; Library of Lower Saxony

Publications: Research Report (Forschungsbericht)
Last Updated: 01/02/12

GUSTAV-SIEWERTH ACADEMY

Gustav-Siewerth-Akademie
Oberbierbronnen 1, 79809 Weilheim-Bierbronnen
Tel: +49(7755) 364
Fax: +49(7755) 80109
EMail: sekretariat@siewerth-akademie.de
Website: http://www.siewerth-akademie.de

Rektor: Albrecht Graf von Brandenstein-Zeppelin (1999-)
Tel: +49(7755) 6616, Fax: +49(7755) 12933

Kanzler: August Weh Tel: +49(7755) 3081, Fax: +49(7755) 7559

International Relations: Alma von Stockhausen

Programmes
Family Studies (Family Studies; Pedagogy; Theology); **Journalism** (Journalism); **Natural Sciences Philosophy** (Natural Sciences; Philosophy); **Philosophy** (Philosophy); **Sociology** (Sociology)

History: Founded 1985, acquired present status 1993.

Admission Requirements: Abitur

Fees: (Euros): 1,640 per annum

Main Language(s) of Instruction: German

Accrediting Agencies: Volksbank Hochrhein Waldshut

Degrees and Diplomas: *Master/Magister*. 4 yrs

Student Services: Academic counselling, Employment services, Foreign student adviser, Social counselling

Libraries: Yes
Last Updated: 18/01/10

HAWK UNIVERSITY OF APPLIED SCIENCES AND ARTS

Hochschule für Angewandte Wissenschaft und Kunst, Hildesheim/Holzminden/Göttingen
Hohnsen 4, 31134 Hildesheim
Tel: +49(5121) 881-0
Fax: +49(5121) 881-125
Website: http://www.hawk-hhg.de

Präsidentin: Christiane Dienel (2011-)
Tel: +49(5121) 881-100, Fax: +49(5121) 881-132
EMail: praesident@fh-hildesheim.de

Kanzler: Marc Hudy
Tel: +49(5121) 881-101 EMail: iris.linke@fh-hildesheim.de

International Relations: Sylvia Korz
Tel: +49(5121) 881-147 EMail: auslandsamt@hawk-hhg.de

Faculties
Architecture, Engineering and Management (Architecture; Architecture and Planning; Construction Engineering; Wood Technology); **Design** (Advertising and Publicity; Design; Graphic Design; Interior Design); **Natural Sciences and Technology** (Electrical Engineering; Information Technology; Mechanical Engineering; Optical Technology); **Preservation of Cultural Heritage** (Heritage Preservation; Restoration of Works of Art); **Resource Management** (Computer Science; Environmental Management; Forestry; Regional Planning); **Social Work and Health Sciences** (Health Administration; Health Sciences; Preschool Education; Social Work)

History: Founded 1971 as Fachhochschule Hildesheim. Became Fachhochschule Hildesheim/Holzminden/Göttingen 2000. Acquired present title 2003.

Main Language(s) of Instruction: German

Degrees and Diplomas: *Bachelor/Bakkalaureus*; *Master/Magister*
Last Updated: 22/03/11

HAFENCITY UNIVERSITY HAMBURG

HafenCity Universität Hamburg
Hebebrandstraße 1, 22297 Hamburg
Tel: +49 (40) 42827-2727
Fax: +49 (40) 42827-2728
EMail: info@hcu-hamburg.de
Website: http://www.hcu-hamburg.de

Präsident: Walter Pelka (2010-)
Tel: +49 (40) 42827-2726, Fax: +49 (40) 42827-2728

Kanzler: Niels Helle-Meyer
Tel: +49 (40) 42827-2732, Fax: +49 (40) 42827-2728
EMail: niels.helle-meyer@hcu-hamburg.de

International Relations: Christiane Brück, Head, International Office
Tel: +49 (40) 42827-4360, Fax: +49 (40) 42827-4309
EMail: christiane.brueck@hcu-hamburg.de

Departments
Architecture (Architecture); **Civil Engineering** (Civil Engineering); **Geomatics**; **Metropolitan Culture** (Cultural Studies); **Town Planning** (Town Planning)

History: Founded 2006 as "HafenCity Universität Hamburg – Universität für Baukunst und Raumentwicklung" through unification of four Departments from three Colleges in Hamburg. Reorganised 2008.

Main Language(s) of Instruction: German

Degrees and Diplomas: *Bachelor/Bakkalaureus*; *Master/Magister*
Last Updated: 18/01/10

HAMBURG DISTANCE TEACHING UNIVERSITY OF APPLIED SCIENCES

Hamburger Fern-Hochschule
Alter Teichweg 19, 22081 Hamburg
Tel: +49(40) 35094-360
Fax: +49(40) 35094-335
EMail: info@hamburger-fh.de
Website: http://www.hamburger-fh.de

Präsident: Michael Bosch
Tel: +49(40) 35094-333 EMail: michael.bosch@hamburger-fh.de

International Relations: Uwe Ploch, Kanzler
Tel: +49(40) 35094-334 EMail: uwe.ploch@hamburger-fh.de

Programmes
Business Administration (Business Administration); **Business Engineering** (Business and Commerce); **Health/Care Management** (Health Administration; Health Sciences)

Degrees and Diplomas: *Bachelor/Bakkalaureus*; *Diplom*: Care Management; *Master/Magister*: Global Business (MBA); Management
Last Updated: 18/01/10

HAMBURG PROTESTANT UNIVERSITY OF APPLIED SCIENCES FOR SOCIAL AND COMMUNITY WORK

Evangelische Hochschule für Soziale Arbeit und Diakonie
Horner Weg 170, 2111 Hamburg
Tel: +49(40) 65591-180
Fax: +49(40) 65591-228
EMail: ev-fhs-hh@rauheshaus.de
Website: http://www.ev-hochschule-hh.de

Rektor: Andreas Theurich (2011-)
Tel: +49(40) 65591-182 EMail: atheurich@rauheshaus.de

International Relations: Timm Kunstreich
Tel: +49(40) 65591-186 EMail: timmkunstreich@aol.com

Centres
Deaconry Education (Theology)

Programmes
Social Work *(Part-time)* (Social Work); **Social Work and Deaconry** (Law; Protestant Theology; Social Sciences; Social Studies; Social Work)

History: Founded 1834, acquired present status 1971. Formerly known as Evangelische Fachhochschule für Sozialpädagogik - Diakonenanstalt des Rauhen Hauses Hamburg.

Admission Requirements: Secondary school certificate (Abitur) or equivalent

Fees: (Euros): 93 per semester

Main Language(s) of Instruction: German

Degrees and Diplomas: *Bachelor/Bakkalaureus*: 4 yrs; *Master/ Magister*: Planning and Administration

Student Services: Academic counselling, Canteen, Foreign student adviser, Social counselling

Student Residential Facilities: Yes

Libraries: Main Library
Last Updated: 31/01/12

HAMBURG SCHOOL OF BUSINESS ADMINISTRATION
Adolphsplatz 1, 20457 Hamburg
Tel: +49(40) 36138-714
Fax: +49(40) 36138-751
EMail: info@hsba.de
Website: http://www.hsba.de
Präsident: Hans-Jörg Schmidt-Trenz Tel: +49(40) 36138-736

Programmes
Business Administration; **Business Administration and Honourable Leadership** *(MBA)* (Business Administration; Leadership); **Global Management and Governance** *(Postgraduate)* (Government; Management); **Logistics Management** (Management); **Media Management** (Business Administration; Information Technology; Media Studies); **Shipping and Ship Finance** (Business Administration; Finance; Marine Transport; Taxation; Transport and Communications)

Main Language(s) of Instruction: German

Degrees and Diplomas: *Bachelor/Bakkalaureus*; *Master/Magister*
Last Updated: 03/02/12

HAMBURG UNIVERSITY OF APPLIED SCIENCES
Hochschule für Angewandte Wissenschaften Hamburg (HAW Hamburg)
Berliner Tor 5, 20099 Hamburg
Tel: +49(40) 42875-0
Fax: +49(40) 42875-9149
EMail: info@haw-hamburg.de
Website: http://www.haw-hamburg.de
Präsident: Michael Stawicki (2005-)
Tel: +49(40) 42875-9000 EMail: praesident@haw-hamburg.de

Kanzler: Bernd Klöver
Tel: +49(40) 42875-9003 EMail: kanzler@haw-hamburg.de

International Relations: Manja Bartlog, Head, International Office
Tel: +49(40) 42875-9180, Fax: +49(40) 42875-9189
EMail: international@haw-hamburg.de

Faculties
Business and Social Sciences (Business Administration; Economics; Health Administration; Nursing; Public Administration; Social Sciences; Social Work); **Design, Media and Information** (Design; Information Sciences; Information Technology; Media Studies); **Engineering and Computer Science** (Aeronautical and Aerospace Engineering; Automotive Engineering; Computer Science; Electrical Engineering; Mechanical Engineering; Production Engineering); **Life Sciences** (Biological and Life Sciences; Biomedical Engineering; Biotechnology; Environmental Engineering; Health Sciences; Home Economics; Industrial Engineering; Nutrition)

History: Founded 1970. Acquired present status 2001.

Degrees and Diplomas: *Bachelor/Bakkalaureus*; *Diplom*: Nursing; Communication Design; Illustration; Fashion Design; Costume Design; Textile Product Design; Textile Engineering; *Master/Magister*
Last Updated: 01/02/12

HAMBURG UNIVERSITY OF MUSIC AND THEATRE
Hochschule für Musik und Theater Hamburg
Harvestehuder Weg 12, 20148 Hamburg
Tel: +49(40) 42848-2586
Fax: +49(40) 42848-2666
EMail: info@hfmt.hamburg.de
Website: http://www.hfmt-hamburg.de

Präsident: Elmar Lampson (1978-)
Tel: +49(40) 42848-2582, Fax: +49(40) 42848-2648
EMail: elmar.lampson@hfmt.hamburg.de

Kanzler: Bernhard Lange
Tel: +49(40) 42848-2581 EMail: bernd.lange@hfmt.hamburg.de

International Relations: Svenja Tiedt, International Coordinator
Tel: +49(40) 428482-415, Fax: +49(40) 428482-666
EMail: international@hfmt.hamburg.de

Faculties
I (Conducting; Jazz and Popular Music; Music Theory and Composition; Musical Instruments; Religious Music); **II** (Opera; Singing; Theatre); **III** (Art Therapy; Cultural Studies; Management; Media Studies; Music Education)

History: Founded 1950.

Main Language(s) of Instruction: German

Degrees and Diplomas: *Zertifikat*; *Bachelor/Bakkalaureus*; *Konzertexamen*; *Master/Magister*; *Promotion*. Distance Programme in Cultural and Media Management
Last Updated: 12/02/09

HAMBURG UNIVERSITY OF TECHNOLOGY
Technische Universität Hamburg-Harburg (TUHH)
Schwarzenbergstrasse 95, 21071 Hamburg
Tel: +49(40) 42878-0
Fax: +49(40) 42878-2040
EMail: wilberg@tu-harburg.de
Website: http://www.tu-harburg.de

Präsident: Garabed Antranikian Tel: +49(40) 42878-3001

International Relations: Elvira Wilberg
Tel: +49(40) 42878-3158, Fax: +49(40) 42878-4081

Departments
Civil Engineering and Marine Technology Research (Civil Engineering; Marine Engineering); **Environment and Technology Research** (Environmental Studies; Technology; Urban Studies); **Information and Communication Technologies Research** (Information Technology); **Materials, Design and Manufacturing Research** (Design; Materials Engineering; Production Engineering); **Processing Technology and Energy Systems Research** (Energy Engineering; Engineering Management); **Systems Engineering Research** (Computer Engineering); **Vocational and Technology Education** (Civil Engineering; Electrical Engineering; Mechanical Engineering; Technology Education)

Schools
Civil Engineering (Civil Engineering; Environmental Engineering; Water Science); **Electrical and Electronic Engineering** (Electrical and Electronic Engineering); **Mechanical Engineering** (Industrial Engineering; Industrial Management; Mechanical Engineering; Naval Architecture); **Processing Technology and Chemical Engineering** (Biotechnology; Engineering; Engineering Management; Environmental Engineering; Technology)

History: Founded 1978. Admitted first students 1982. Under the jurisdiction of the State of Hamburg.

Governing Bodies: Präsidium (President, 2 Vice-Presidents, Chancellor)

Academic Year: October to September (October-March; April-September)

Admission Requirements: Secondary school certificate (Abitur) or equivalent. Sufficient knowledge of German

Fees: (Euros): Tuition: 500; social/administrative fees: 242

Main Language(s) of Instruction: German, English

International Co-operation: With universities in Europe, India, Singapore, USA, Canada, Latin America, Thailand. Also participates in the Socrates programme.

Degrees and Diplomas: *Bachelor/Bakkalaureus*: 3 yrs; *Master/ Magister*: a further 2 yrs; *Doktorgrad (Ingenieur)*: 3 yrs

Student Services: Academic counselling, Canteen, Foreign student adviser, Social counselling, Sports facilities

Student Residential Facilities: Yes

Libraries: University Library, c. 400,000 vols
Last Updated: 06/02/12

HANOVER MEDICAL SCHOOL

Medizinischen Hochschule Hannover
Carl-Neuberg Strasse 1, 30625 Hannover
Tel: +49(511) 532-0
Fax: +49(511) 532-5550
Website: http://www.mh-hannover.de

Rektor: Dieter Bitter-Suermann (2004-)
Tel: +49(511) 532-6000, Fax: +49(511) 532-6003
EMail: bitter-suerman@mh-hannover.de

Vorstand: Holger Bauman
Tel: +49(511) 532-6034, Fax: +49(511) 532-6032
EMail: bauman.holger@mh-hannover.de

International Relations: Sigurd Lenzen
Tel: +49(511) 532-6026, Fax: +49(511) 532-6027
EMail: lenzen.sigurd@mh-hannover.de

Centres
Anatomy (Anatomy; Cell Biology; Microbiology; Neurosciences); **Biochemistry** (Biochemistry; Biophysics; Cell Biology; Chemistry; Physiology); **Biometry, Medical Informatics and Medical Technology** (Biomedicine; Computer Science; Medical Technology); **Laboratory Medicine**; **Pathology** (Cell Biology; Genetics; Law; Molecular Biology; Pathology); **Pharmacology and Toxicology** (Pharmacology; Toxicology); **Physiology** (Cell Biology; Molecular Biology; Neurosciences; Physiology; Sports Medicine); **Public Health** (Epidemiology; Ethics; Health Sciences; History; Medicine; Philosophy; Psychology; Public Health; Rehabilitation and Therapy; Social and Preventive Medicine; Sociology); **Radiology** *(Institute)* (Neurological Therapy; Oncology; Radiology)

Institutes
Sports Medicine (Medicine; Sports); **Standardised and Applied Hospital Management** (Health Administration)

History: Founded 1963. Admitted first students 1965. An autonomous institution under the jurisdiction of and financially supported by the State of Lower Saxony.

Governing Bodies: Senat; Hochschulrat

Academic Year: October to September (October-March; April-September)

Admission Requirements: Secondary school certificate (Allgemeine Hochschulreife) or equivalent

Fees: (Euros): 500 per semester

Main Language(s) of Instruction: German, English

International Co-operation: With universities in France, Japan, Russian Federation. Participates in the Erasmus programme

Degrees and Diplomas: *Diplom*; *Staatsprüfung*: Dentistry; Medicine, 6 yrs; *Master/Magister*: Public Health; Biomedicine (MSP; MSc), 3 yrs; *Promotion*: Dentistry (Dr.Med.Dent.); Medicine (Dr.med.); *Promotion*: Human Biology (Dr.biol.hum.), 3 yrs; *Habilitation*: at least 3 yrs following Doktor

Student Services: Academic counselling, Canteen, Employment services, Foreign student adviser, Foreign Studies Centre, Handicapped facilities, Health services, Language programs, Nursery care, Social counselling, Sports facilities

Student Residential Facilities: Yes

Libraries: c. 212,000 vols

Student Numbers *2008-2009*	TOTAL
All (Foreign Included)	2,808
FOREIGN ONLY	220

Last Updated: 13/02/09

HANOVER UNIVERSITY OF APPLIED SCIENCES FOR ECONOMICS

Fachhochschule für die Wirtschaft Hannover (FHDW)
Freundallee 15, 30173 Hannover
Tel: +49(511) 28483-70
Fax: +49(511) 28483-72
EMail: info-ha@fhdw.de
Website: http://www.fhdw-hannover.de

Präsident: Karl-Wilhelm Müller-Siebers (1999-)
Tel: +49(511) 284-8371 EMail: mueller-siebers@ha.bib.de

Programmes
Business Administration (Business Administration); **Business Computing** (Business Computing); **Business Process Administration**; **Business Process Engineering** (Business Administration; Engineering); **Computer Science** (Computer Science)

History: Founded 1996.

Main Language(s) of Instruction: German

Degrees and Diplomas: *Bachelor/Bakkalaureus*: Business Administration; Computer Science; Business Computing; *Master/ Magister*: Business Process Administration; Business Process Engineering
Last Updated: 06/02/12

HANOVER UNIVERSITY OF MUSIC, DRAMA AND MEDIA

Hochschule für Musik, Theater und Medien Hannover
Emmichplatz 1, 30175 Hannover
Tel: +49(511) 3100-1
Fax: +49(511) 3100-200
EMail: hmt@hmt-hannover.de
Website: http://www.hmt-hannover.de

Präsidentin: Susanne Rode-Breymann
Tel: +49(511) 3100-231, Fax: +49(511) 3100-300
EMail: praesidentin@hmtm-hannover.de

Centres
Jewish Music *(European)* (Music); **World Music** (Music)

Faculties
Jazz Rock Pop (Jazz and Popular Music; Music; Music Education; Musical Instruments)

Institutes
Journalism and Communication Research (Communication Studies; Journalism); **Music Physiology and Music Medicine** (Art Therapy; Music); **Musical Education Research** (Music Education); **New Music** (Music); **Popular Music** *(Hannover)* (Jazz and Popular Music; Music; Sound Engineering (Acoustics))

Research Centres
Music and Gender (Gender Studies; Music)

History: Founded 1950.

Main Language(s) of Instruction: German

Degrees and Diplomas: *Bachelor/Bakkalaureus*; *Master/Magister*: Chamber Music; Choir Conducting; Music Education (Secondary); Media Management; Media and Music; Music Research and Musical Mediation; Music Theory, 4 sem.
Last Updated: 19/01/10

HARZ UNIVERSITY OF APPLIED SCIENCES

Hochschule Harz
Friedrichstrasse 57-59, 38855 Wernigerode
Tel: +49(3943) 659-0
Fax: +49(3943) 659-109
EMail: info@hs-harz.de
Website: http://www.hs-harz.de/

Rektor: Armin Willingman (2003-)
Tel: +49(3943) 659-100 EMail: rektor@hs-harz.de

Kanzler: Michael Schilling
Tel: +49(3943) 659-102 EMail: kanzler@hs-harz.de

International Relations: Birgit Apfelbaum
Tel: +49(3943) 659-435, Fax: +49(3943) 659-499
EMail: bapfelbaum@hs-harz.de

Departments
Automation and Computer Science (Automation and Control Engineering; Industrial Engineering; Information Technology); **Business Studies**; **Public Administration** (Administration; Economics; Government; Public Administration)

History: Founded 1991.

Governing Bodies: Senate; Council

Admission Requirements: Abitur or equivalent

Main Language(s) of Instruction: German and English

International Co-operation: With more than 60 universities worldwide. Participates in Erasmus; Integrated Studies Abroad; GoEast

Accrediting Agencies: ASIIN, AQUIN

Degrees and Diplomas: *Bachelor/Bakkalaureus*: 3-3 1/2 yrs; *Master/Magister*: Computer Science / Mobile Systems; Tourism and Destination Development; Business Consulting

Student Services: Academic counselling, Canteen, Foreign student adviser, Handicapped facilities, Language programs, Social counselling, Sports facilities

Student Residential Facilities: Yes

Libraries: 100,261 vols.

Publications: Forschungsbericht *(annually)*
Last Updated: 20/01/10

HEIDELBERG UNIVERSITY
Ruprecht-Karls-Universität Heidelberg
PO Box 105760, Grabengasse 1, 69047 Heidelberg
Tel: +49(6221) 54-0
Fax: +49(6221) 54-2147
EMail: rektor@rektorat.uni-heidelberg.de
Website: http://www.uni-heidelberg.de

Rektor: Bernhard Eitel (2007-2013)
Tel: +49(6221) 54-2315, Fax: +49(6221) 54-2147

Kanzlerin: Marina Frost
Tel: +49(6221) 54-2100 EMail: kanzlerin@zuv.uni-heidelberg.de

International Relations: H.Joachim Gerke, Head of International Relations (1998-)
Tel: +49(6221) 54-2335, Fax: +49(6221) 54-2332
EMail: gerke@zu.uni-heidelberg.de

Centres
Biochemistry (Biochemistry); **Molecular Biology** (Molecular Biology); **Scientific Computing** *(Interdisciplinary)* (Computer Science)

Faculties
Behavioural and Cuturall Studies (Behavioural Sciences; Classical Languages; Ethnology; Gerontology; Psychology; Sports); **Biosciences** (Biology; Molecular Biology; Neurology; Pharmacy; Zoology); **Chemistry and Earth Sciences** (Chemistry; Earth Sciences; Geography; Geology; Inorganic Chemistry; Mineralogy; Organic Chemistry; Paleontology; Physical Chemistry); **Economics and Social Studies** (Asian Studies; Economics; Political Sciences; Sociology); **Law** (Law); **Mathematics and Computer Science** (Computer Science; Mathematics); **Medicine** *(Heidelberg)* (Medicine); **Medicine** *(Mannheim)* (Medicine); **Modern Languages** (English; Modern Languages; Philology; Slavic Languages; Translation and Interpretation); **Philosophy** (History; Philosophy); **Physics and Astronomy** (Astronomy and Space Science; Physics); **Theology** (Protestant Theology)

Institutes
South Asian Studies (South Asian Studies)

History: Founded 1386 by Rupert I, Elector of the Palatinate. The character of the University was profoundly affected by the Renaissance and the Reformation. It was reorganized as an independent institution by the Grand Duke Charles Frederick of Baden in 1803 and is now an autonomous University financially supported by the State of Baden-Württemberg, and under the jurisdiction of its Ministry of Science and Art.

Governing Bodies: Grosser Senat; University Council

Academic Year: October to September (October-March; April-September)

Admission Requirements: Secondary school certificate (Reifezeugnis) or equivalent

Fees: None

Main Language(s) of Instruction: German. English in selected programmes.

International Co-operation: Participates in the Socrates, Leonardo and Tempus programmes

Degrees and Diplomas: *Bachelor/Bakkalaureus*: Science in Application Oriented Computer Science; Molecular Biotechnology (BSc); *Diplom*: Biology; Chemistry; Economics; Geology; Interpretation; Mathematics; Mineralogy; Physics; Psychology; Translation; *Lehramt*: Teaching qualification, secondary level, 4 yrs; *Magister Artium*: Humanities and Social Sciences, 4 yrs; *Staatsprüfung*: Law; Medicine; Pharmacy; Dentistry, 4 yrs; *Master/Magister*: Science in Application Oriented Computer Science; Community Health and Health Management in Developing Countries; Molecular and Cellular Biology; Molecular Biotechnology; Physics (MSc); *Doktorgrad*: a further 2-4 yrs; *Habilitation*: at least 3 yrs following Doktor

Student Services: Academic counselling, Canteen, Employment services, Foreign student adviser, Foreign Studies Centre, Handicapped facilities, Language programs, Nursery care, Social counselling, Sports facilities

Student Residential Facilities: For c. 3,600 students

Special Facilities: Museum of Antiquities; Museum of Egyptology; Zoology Museum; Geology and Palaeontology Museum. Botanical Garden. Mineralogy Collection; Prehistory Collection; Archaeological Collection of Plaster Casts; Collection of Historical Instruments

Libraries: University Library, c. 2.6m. vols; libraries of the institutes and seminars

Publications: Ruperto Carola Forschungsmagazin
Last Updated: 22/01/10

HEIDELBERG UNIVERSITY OF EDUCATION
Pädagogische Hochschule Heidelberg
Keplerstrasse 87, 69120 Heidelberg
Tel: +49(6221) 477-0
Fax: +49(6221) 477-432
EMail: ph@vw.ph-heidelberg.de
Website: http://www.ph-heidelberg.de

Rektorin: Anneliese Wellensiek
Tel: +49(6221) 477-112, Fax: +49(6221) 477-444

Kanzler: Christoph Glaser
Tel: +49(6221) 477-113, Fax: +49(6221) 477-432
EMail: kanzler@vw.ph-heidelberg.de

International Relations: Henrike Schön
Tel: +49(6221) 477-543, Fax: +49(6221) 477-495
EMail: akad@vw.ph-heidelberg.de

Faculties
Cultural Studies (Catholic Theology; Cultural Studies; English; Ethics; Fine Arts; Foreign Languages Education; French; German; Media Studies; Music; Native Language Education; Philosophy; Religious Education; Social Sciences; Theatre; Theology); **Education and Social Sciences** (Education; Social Sciences); **Natural and Social Sciences** (Natural Sciences; Social Sciences)

History: Founded 1904, acquired present status 1971.

Governing Bodies: Senat

Academic Year: October to September (October-March; April-September)

Admission Requirements: Secondary school certificate (Reifezeugnis)

Main Language(s) of Instruction: German

International Co-operation: Participates in the Socrates/Erasmus programmes

Degrees and Diplomas: *Bachelor/Bakkalaureus*: 4 sem; *Lehramt*: Teaching Qualifications; *Magister Artium*; *Master/Magister*; *Promotion*: Education (Dr.päd.)

Libraries: c. 140,000 vols

Publications: Schriftenreihe *(other/irregular)*
Last Updated: 22/01/10

HEILBRONN UNIVERSITY

Hochschule Heilbronn

Max-Planck-Strasse 39, 74081 Heilbronn
Tel: +49(7131) 504-0
Fax: +49(7131) 252-470
EMail: info@hs-heilbronn.de; poststelle@hs-heilbronn.de
Website: http://www.hs-heilbronn.de

Rektor: Jürgen Schröder
Tel: +49(7131) 504-200, Fax: +49(7131) 504-14200
EMail: rektor@hs-heilbronn.de

Kanzler: Lars Kulke
Tel: +49(7131) 504-202, Fax: +49(7131) 504-14-2021
EMail: kanzler@hs-heilbronn.de

Faculties

Business *(W2)* (Business Administration; International Business; Management; Tourism); **Business and Transport** (Business Administration; E-Business/Commerce; Management; Transport and Communications; Transport Management); **Computer Science** *(IT)* (Computer Science; Management; Medical Technology; Software Engineering); **Engineering** *(T2)* (Engineering; Engineering Management; Environmental Engineering; Production Engineering; Transport Management); **Engineering and Business Künzelsau** *(TW)* (Business Administration; Electronic Engineering; Energy Engineering; Engineering; Engineering Management; Industrial Engineering; Leisure Studies; Marketing; Mechanical Engineering; Sports Management); **Mechanical and Electronical Engineering** *(T1)* (Automation and Control Engineering; Automotive Engineering; Electronic Engineering; Engineering; Information Technology; Machine Building; Mechanical Engineering; Robotics)

Further Information: Also Schwäbisch Hall and Künzelsau Campuses.

History: Founded 1961 as a School of Engineering. Acquired present status 1971.

Main Language(s) of Instruction: German

Degrees and Diplomas: *Bachelor/Bakkalaureus*; *Master/Magister*
Last Updated: 20/01/10

HEINRICH-HEINE-UNIVERSITY DUSSELDORF

Heinrich-Heine-Universität Düsseldorf (HHUD)

Universitaetsstrasse 1, 40225 Duesseldorf, North Rhine-Westfalia
Tel: +49(211) 81-00
EMail: aaa@zuv.uni-duesseldorf.de
Website: http://www.uni-duesseldorf.de

Rektor: Hans Michael Piper (2009-)
Tel: +49(211) 811-0000, Fax: +49(211) 811-5193
EMail: rektor@uni-duesseldorf.de

Director, Communication office: Joachim Tomesch
Tel: +49(211) 811-0898, Fax: +49(211) 811-5279
EMail: tomesch@zuv.uniduesseldorf.de

International Relations: Anne Gellert, Director, International Office
Tel: +49(211) 811-4107, Fax: +49(211) 811-1334
EMail: gellert@zuv.uni-duesseldorf.de

Faculties

Arts and Humanities (Arts and Humanities; Cultural Studies; History; Linguistics; Literature; Philosophy; Social Sciences); **Economics** (Economics); **Law** (Law); **Mathematics and Natural Sciences** (Mathematics; Natural Sciences); **Medicine** (Medicine)

History: Founded 1907 as an Academy for practical medicine. Became a university 1965 and acquired present title 1988. Under the jurisdiction of and financially supported by the State of North Rhine-Westphalia.

Governing Bodies: Senat, University Council

Academic Year: October to September (Oct - Mar; Apr - Sept).

Admission Requirements: School leaving certificate (Hochschulzugangsberechtigung) or equivalent

Fees: (Euros): 500 per semester

Main Language(s) of Instruction: German

International Co-operation: With universities in Italy; Japan; Netherlands; Poland; Portugal; Sweden; Slovak Republic; Slovenia; Spain; Czech Republic; Hungary; USA; United Kingdom; Denmark; Finland; Belgium; France; Greece; Austria; Ireland; Israel

Degrees and Diplomas: *Bachelor/Bakkalaureus (Bachelor's degree):* 3-4 yrs; *Staatsprüfung; Master/Magister (Master' degree):* 1-2 yrs; *Doktorgrad*

Student Services: Academic counselling, Canteen, Employment services, Foreign student adviser, Handicapped facilities, Health services, Language programs, Nursery care, Social counselling, Sports facilities

Student Residential Facilities: For c. 3,500 students

Special Facilities: Botanical Institute; Botanical Garden

Libraries: Central Library, c. 2.5m. vols; specialized libraries, c. 610,000 vols.

Academic Staff *2008-2009*	MEN	WOMEN	TOTAL
FULL-TIME	342	510	852
STAFF WITH DOCTORATE FULL-TIME	1,115	621	1,736
Student Numbers *2008-2009*			
All (Foreign Included)	6,741	9,758	16,499
FOREIGN ONLY	1,025	1,690	2,715

Evening students, 85.
Last Updated: 01/02/12

HELMUT SCHMIDT UNIVERSITY - UNIVERSITY OF THE FEDERAL ARMED FORCES OF HAMBURG

Helmut Schmidt Universität - Universität der Bundeswehr Hamburg

PO Box 700822, Holstenhofweg 85, 22043 Hamburg
Tel: +49(40) 6541-1
Fax: +49(40) 6541-2869
EMail: pressestelle@hsu-hh.de
Website: http://www.hsu-hh.de

Präsident: Wilfried Seidel
Tel: +49(40) 6541-2700 EMail: praesident@hsu-hh.de

Kanzler: Volker Stempel
Tel: +49(40) 6541-2701, Fax: +49(40) 6541-2869
EMail: kanzler@unibw-hamburg.de

International Relations: Martin Nassua, Head, International Office
EMail: martin.nassua@hsu-hh.de

Centres

Computer (Computer Science); **Didactics** (Pedagogy); **Language** (Linguistics; Modern Languages)

Departments

Economics and Social Sciences (Administration; Economics; Social Sciences); **Electrical Engineering** (Electrical Engineering); **Humanities and Social Sciences** (History; Pedagogy; Psychology; Social Sciences; Sociology; Theology); **Mechanical Engineering** (Mechanical Engineering)

History: Founded 1972. Teaching started 1973. Under the authority of the Hamburg Ministry of Science and Research and the Ministry of Defence.

Governing Bodies: Senat

Academic Year: October to September (October-December; January-March; April-September)

Admission Requirements: Secondary school certificate (Abitur). Students must have passed the Armed Forces Officer examination

Main Language(s) of Instruction: German

Degrees and Diplomas: *Bachelor/Bakkalaureus:* Business Administration (Kaufmann); Economics (Volkswirt); Education (Pädagoge); Engineering (Ingenieur); Industrial Engineering (Wirstchaftsingenieur); Political Science (Politologe); *Magister Artium:* Historical Science (Geschichtswissenschaftler), 10 trimesters; *Master/Magister*

Student Services: Canteen, Handicapped facilities, Health services, Language programs, Sports facilities

Student Residential Facilities: Yes

Special Facilities: Sound and Vision Centre; Sports Centre

Libraries: c. 750,000 vols

Publications: Uniforschung *(annually)*
Last Updated: 01/02/12

HERTIE SCHOOL OF GOVERNANCE

Quartier 110 - Friedrichstraße 180, 10117 Berlin
Tel: +49 (30) 259-219 -0
Fax: +49 (30) 259-219-111
EMail: info@hertie-school.org
Website: http://hertie-school.org

Dean: Helmut K. Anheier (2009-) **EMail:** anheier@hertie-school.org

Programmes

Public Management *(Executive Master)*; **Public Policy** (Government; Public Administration)

History: Founded 2003.

Main Language(s) of Instruction: German

Degrees and Diplomas: *Master/Magister*
Last Updated: 18/01/10

HOF UNIVERSITY OF APPLIED SCIENCES

Hochschule für Angewandte Wissenschaften -
Fachhochschule Hof
Alfons-Goppel-Platz 1, 95028 Hof
Tel: +49(9281) 409-300
Fax: +49(9281) 409-400
EMail: mail@fh-hof.de
Website: http://www.fh-hof.de

Präsident: Jürgen Lehmann (2002-)
Tel: +49(9281) 409-301, Fax: +49(9281) 409-399
EMail: praesident@fh-hof.de; juergen.lehmann@fh-hof.de

Kanzlerin: Dagmar Pechstein
Tel: +49(9281) 409-316 EMail: dagmar.pechstein@fh-hof.de

International Relations: Susanne Krause
Tel: +49(9281) 409-307, Fax: +49(9281) 409-55-307
EMail: susanne.krause@fh-hof.de

Faculties

Business (Business Administration; Commercial Law; International Business; Management; Marketing; Transport Management); **Engineering** (Environmental Engineering; Industrial Engineering; Materials Engineering; Mechanical Engineering; Textile Design); **Information Technology** (Business and Commerce; Business Computing; Computer Science; Media Studies)

History: Founded 1994.

Academic Year: October to September (October-March; March-September)

Admission Requirements: Secondary school certificate (Hochschulreife) together with a placement of 6 weeks related to study programme, entrance examination

Fees: (Euros): administration fee, 50 per semester; Master of Engineering, 2,000 per semester

Main Language(s) of Instruction: German; English (in selected classes and Master of Engineering)

International Co-operation: With universities in Europe, Canada, USA, Australia, Asia and South America. Also participates in Socrates/Erasmus, Leonardo.

Degrees and Diplomas: *Bachelor/Bakkalaureus*; *Master/Magister*: Industrial Information Technology; Software Engineering; Logistics; Marketing Management; Composite Materials; Supply Chain Management (MBE), a further 2 yrs

Student Services: Academic counselling, Canteen, Employment services, Foreign student adviser, Foreign Studies Centre, Handicapped facilities, Language programs, Sports facilities

Student Residential Facilities: Student Residence in town

Special Facilities: Language and Technical Labs

Libraries: 2 libraries on Campus
Last Updated: 01/02/12

HUMBOLDT UNIVERSITY OF BERLIN

Humboldt-Universität zu Berlin
Unter den Linden 6, 10099 Berlin
Tel: +49(30) 2093-0
Fax: +49(30) 2093-2770
EMail: press@pr.hu-berlin.de
Website: http://www.hu-berlin.de

Präsident: Jan-Hendrik Olbertz (2010-)
Tel: +49(30) 2093-2100, Fax: +49(30) 2093-2729
EMail: praesident@uv.hu-berlin.de

Vizepräsident: Frank Eveslage
Tel: +49(30) 2043-2101, Fax: +49(30)2093-2490
EMail: frank.eveslage@uv.hu-berlin.de

International Relations: Michael Kämper-van den Boogaart, Director, International Office
Tel: +49(302) 093-2738, Fax: +49(302) 093-2780
EMail: vpsi@uv.hu-berlin.de

Faculties

Agriculture and Horticulture (Agriculture; Horticulture); **Arts and Humanities I** (Ethnology; European Studies; History; Library Science; Philosophy); **Arts and Humanities II** (American Studies; English Studies; Linguistics; Philology; Romance Languages; Slavic Languages); **Arts and Humanities III** (African Studies; Archaeology; Art History; Asian Studies; Cultural Studies; Gender Studies; Media Studies; Musicology; Social Sciences); **Arts and Humanities IV** (Educational Sciences; Rehabilitation and Therapy; Sports); **Economics and Business Administration** (Business Administration; Economics); **Law** (Law); **Mathematics and Natural Sciences I** (Biology; Chemistry; Mathematics; Natural Sciences; Physics); **Mathematics and Natural Sciences II** (Computer Science; Geography; Mathematics; Natural Sciences; Psychology); **Theology** (Theology)

Graduate Schools

Humboldt (Safety Engineering; Service Trades); **International Humboldt** (Electronic Engineering; Materials Engineering; Mathematics; Natural Sciences); **Mathematics** *(Berlin)*; **Mind and Brain** *(Berlin)* (Behavioural Sciences; Neurosciences); **Social Sciences** *(Berlin)*

Further Information: Also German language courses for foreign students; Natural History Museum; Great Britain Central Institute - Centre.

History: Founded 1810 as Friedrich-Wilhelms-Universität. Reorganized 1946 and renamed 1948 Humboldt-Universität zu Berlin. Faculty structure replaced under 1968 reform by series of subject sections, and replaced following reunification 1990. An independent institution financially supported by the 'Land' of Berlin.

Governing Bodies: Kuratorium; Konzil; Senat

Academic Year: October to September (October-March; April-September)

Admission Requirements: Secondary school certificate (Abitur)

Fees: None

Main Language(s) of Instruction: German

International Co-operation: With institutions worldwide. A full listing may be obtained from the University

Degrees and Diplomas: *Bachelor/Bakkalaureus*; *Diplom*: Chemistry; Evangelical Theology; Computer Science; Mathematics; Psychology; Rehabilitation Pedagogy; *Staatsprüfung*: Law, 8- 9 sem; *Master/Magister*; *Promotion*: in all fields, a further 2-4 yrs; *Habilitation*: in all fields, a further 2-4 yrs following Doktor. Staatsprüfung and Diplom are starting on Winter semesters only

Student Services: Academic counselling, Canteen, Employment services, Foreign student adviser, Foreign Studies Centre, Handicapped facilities, Language programs, Nursery care, Social counselling, Sports facilities

Special Facilities: Natural History Museum

Libraries: University Library, c. 4.1 m. vols; 25 specialized libraries, c. 1.7 m

Publications: Humboldt spektrum *(quarterly)*
Last Updated: 03/02/12

ILMENAU UNIVERSITY OF TECHNOLOGY

Technische Universität Ilmenau
PO Box 100565, 98684 Ilmenau
Tel: +49(3677) 69-0
Fax: +49(3677) 69-1701
EMail: webmaster@tu-ilmenau.de
Website: http://www.tu-ilmenau.de

Rektor: Peter Scharff (2004-)
Tel: +49(3677) 69-5001, Fax: +49(3677) 69-5009
EMail: rektor@tu-ilmenau.de

Kanzlerin: Margot Bock
Tel: +49(3677) 69-5030, Fax: +49(3677) 69-5039
EMail: kanzler@tu-ilmenau.de

Faculties
Computer Science and Automation (Automation and Control Engineering; Biotechnology; Computer Engineering; Computer Science; Electronic Engineering; Mathematics; Mechanical Engineering; Telecommunications Engineering); **Economic Sciences** (Automation and Control Engineering; Data Processing; Economics; Electrical Engineering; Information Management; Mechanical Engineering); **Electrical Engineering and Information Technology** (Automation and Control Engineering; Biotechnology; Computer Science; Electrical Engineering; Electronic Engineering; Information Technology; Materials Engineering; Microelectronics); **Mathematics and Natural Sciences** (Mathematics; Natural Sciences; Physical Engineering); **Mechanical Engineering** (Electronic Engineering; Materials Engineering; Measurement and Precision Engineering; Mechanical Engineering)

History: Founded 1884 as a private school. Became Hochschule für Elektrotechnik 1953. Became Technische Hochschule 1963. Acquired present status 1992.
Governing Bodies: Konzil; Senat; Rat (Council) for each section
Academic Year: October to September (October-March; April-September)
Admission Requirements: Secondary school certificate (Reifezeugnis) or equivalent
Fees: (Euros): c. 65 per semester
Main Language(s) of Instruction: German; partly English
International Co-operation: With universities in Armenia, Brazil, Bulgaria, China, Czech Republic, Denmark, Finland, France, Georgia, Greece, Italy, Latvia, Uniteg Kingdom, Serbia and Montenegro, Austria, Peru, Poland, Portugal, Romania, Russian Federation, Slovak Republic, Spain, Sweden, Ukraine, Hungary, USA, Vietnam, Belarus
Degrees and Diplomas: *Bachelor/Bakkalaureus*; *Diplom*: Applied Media Sciences; Computer Science in Economics; Materials Science; Mathematics; Media Economics, 4 1/2 yrs; *Diplom*: Computer Engineering; Computer Science; Electrical Engineering and Information Technology; Engineering Physics; Industrial Engineering; Mechanical Engineering; Mechatronics; Media Technology, 5 yrs; *Lehramt*: Teaching Qualification, Vocational School, 4 1/2 yrs; *Master/Magister*; *Doktorgrad*: Applied Media Science (Dr.phil.); Economic Science (Dr.rer.pol.); Engineering (Dr.Ing.); Mathematics and Natural Sciences (Dr.rer.nat.), a further 3-4 yrs by thesis; *Habilitation*: 4-5 yrs following Doktor, first level
Student Services: Academic counselling, Canteen, Cultural centre, Employment services, Foreign student adviser, Foreign Studies Centre, Handicapped facilities, Language programs, Nursery care, Social counselling, Sports facilities
Student Residential Facilities: For 30% of the students
Special Facilities: Audio and Video Studios; Campus Radio and TV
Libraries: Central Library and Section libraries, 514,000 vols
Publications: Summaries of the International Scientific Colloquium *(annually)*; Wissenschaftlicher Veranstaltungskalender *(annually)*
Last Updated: 27/01/10

INGOLSTADT UNIVERSITY OF APPLIED SCIENCES

Hochschule für Angewandte Wissenschaften FH Ingolstadt
PO Box 210454, Esplanade 10, 85019 Ingolstadt
Tel: +49(841) 9348-0
Fax: +49(841) 9348-200
EMail: info@fh-ingolstadt.de
Website: http://www.fh-ingolstadt.de

Präsident: Gunter Schweiger (1998-)
Tel: +49(841) 9348-100
EMail: praesident@fh-ingolstadt.de; gunter.schweiger@fh-ingolstadt.de

Kanzlerin: Barbara Rehr
Tel: +49(841) 9348-120, Fax: +49(841) 9348-177
EMail: kanzler@fh-ingolstadt.de

International Relations: Birgit Mölder, Birgit Mölder
Tel: +49(841) 9348-121, Fax: +49(841) 9348-474
EMail: auslandsamt@fh-ingolstadt.de

Faculties
Business Administration (Accountancy; Business Administration; Business Computing; Commercial Law; Data Processing; E-Business/Commerce; International Business; Management; Marketing; Taxation; Transport Management); **Electrical Engineering and Computer Science** (Automotive Engineering; Computer Engineering; Computer Science; Electrical Engineering; Electronic Engineering; Information Technology; Mechanical Engineering)

Programmes
Mechanical Engineering (Automotive Engineering; Construction Engineering; Electronic Engineering; Environmental Engineering; Geological Engineering; Industrial Engineering; Machine Building; Materials Engineering; Mathematics and Computer Science; Mechanical Engineering; Operations Research; Production Engineering; Safety Engineering; Thermal Engineering)

History: Founded 1994.
Admission Requirements: Secondary school certificate
Fees: None
Main Language(s) of Instruction: German
International Co-operation: Participates in the Erasmus/Socrates programme
Degrees and Diplomas: *Bachelor/Bakkalaureus*: Business Administration; Electro- and Information Engineering; Automotive Engineering; Computer Science; International Business; Machine Building and Professional Training; Mechatronics; Machine Construction; Business Engineering; *Master/Magister*: Applied Computational Mechanics; Compliance and Corporate Governance; Health Management; Information Technology Management; Staff and organisation De Development; Business Consulting; Computer Science; International Automotive Engineering; Technological Development
Student Services: Academic counselling, Canteen, Foreign student adviser, Handicapped facilities, Language programs, Social counselling, Sports facilities
Last Updated: 12/01/10

INSTITUTE OF HEALTH AND SPORT

Hochschule für Gesundheit und Sport (H:G)
Vulkanstraße 1, 10367 Berlin
Tel: +49 (030) 577 97 37 0
Fax: +49 (030) 577 97 37 999
EMail: info@my-campus-berlin.com
Website: http://www.my-campus-berlin.com

Präsident: Christian Werner
EMail: christian.werner@my-campus-berlin.com

Campus Director: Martin Elbe
EMail: martin.elbe@my-campus-berlin.com

Departments
Applied Health Care (Health Sciences); **Complementary Medicine** (Alternative Medicine; Biology; History; Natural Sciences; Psychology; Statistics; Terminology; Traditional Eastern Medicine); **Health Management** (Accountancy; Data Processing; Economics; Health Administration; Health Sciences; Human Resources; Safety Engineering; Welfare and Protective Services); **Psychology and Mental Health** (Clinical Psychology; Psychiatry and Mental Health; Psychology); **Sports** (Sports); **Sports and Leisure Management**

History: Founded 2007.
Main Language(s) of Instruction: German
Degrees and Diplomas: *Bachelor/Bakkalaureus*: Health Management; Psychology and Mental Health; Complementary Medicine and Natural Treatments; Applied Health Care; Sports and Leisure

Management; Sports and Applied Traning Education; *Master/Magister*. Health Management; Psychology and Mental Health; Complementary Medicine and Natural Treatments; Elder Care and Gerontology; Sports and Leisure Management; Sports and Applied Training Education; Sports Performance; Sports Psychology
Last Updated: 19/01/10

INTERNATIONAL GRADUATE SCHOOL (IHI) ZITTAU

Internationales Hochschulinstitut Zittau (IHI)
Markt 23, 02763 Zittau
Tel: +49(3583) 7715-0
Fax: +49(3583) 7715-34
EMail: info@ihi-zittau.de
Website: http://www.ihi-zittau.de

Rektor: Albert Löhr (2003-)
Tel: +49(3583) 7715-78 EMail: loehr@ihi-zittau.de

Kanzlerin: Karin Hollstein
Tel: +49(3583) 61-2700/ 1407 EMail: hollstein@ihi-zittau.de

International Relations: Rosemarie Konschak
EMail: konschak@ihi-zittau-de

Chairs
Environmental Engineering; **General Business Administration - Controlling and Environmental Management** (Business Administration; Environmental Management; International Business); **International Management** (International Business; Management); **Production Economy and Information Technology** (Human Resources; Information Management; Information Technology; International Business; Management; Production Engineering; Social Sciences; Transport Management); **Social Sciences** (Communication Studies; Ethics; Human Resources; International Business; Management; Social Sciences)

Institutes
Environmental Biotechnology (Biotechnology); **Innovation Management and Middle Size Business** (Business Administration; Management; Public Administration; Small Business)
History: Founded 1993.
Governing Bodies: Board of Governors
Academic Year: October to July
Admission Requirements: Secondary school certificate (Abitur) and furst degree (Vordiplom/Bachelor)
Fees: None
Main Language(s) of Instruction: German
International Co-operation: With universities in Poland, Czech Republic
Degrees and Diplomas: *Diplom*: Business Management; Environmental Engineering; Administration and Industrial Engineering; Social Sciences (Dipl.), 3 yrs following 2 yrs of preparatory studies; *Master/Magister*; *Doktorgrad*; *Habilitation*
Student Services: Academic counselling, Foreign student adviser, Language programs
Student Residential Facilities: Student Hostel
Last Updated: 20/01/10

INTERNATIONAL PSYCHOANALYTIC UNIVERSITY BERLIN

Stromstr. 3, 10555 Berlin
Tel: +49(30) 300-117
EMail: info@ipu-berlin.de
Website: http://www.ipu-berlin.de

Präsident: Jürgen Körner EMail: juergen.koerner@ipu-berlin.de

Programmes
Child Protection (Child Care and Development); **Clinical Psychology/Psychoanalysis** (Clinical Psychology; Psychoanalysis); **Juvenile Delinquency** (Social Problems)
History: Founded 2009.
Main Language(s) of Instruction: German

Degrees and Diplomas: *Master/Magister*
Last Updated: 22/01/10

INTERNATIONAL SCHOOL OF MANAGEMENT (ISM)

Otto-Hahn-Strasse 19, 44227 Dortmund
Tel: +49(231) 975-1390
Fax: +49(231) 975-13939
EMail: ism@ism-dortmund.de
Website: http://www.ism.de

Präsident: Bert Rürup

Vizepräsident: Ingo Böckenholt EMail: ingo.boeckenholt@ism.de

Programmes
Communications and Marketing *(BA)* (Communication Studies; Marketing); **Corporate Finance** (Finance); **Energy Management** (Management); **General Management** (Management); **International Management** *(MA)* (Management); **Psychology and Management** (Management; Psychology); **Strategic Marketing Management** (Management; Marketing); **Strategic Tourism Management** (Tourism); **Tourism and Event Management** *(BA)* (Hotel Management; Tourism)

Further Information: Also campuses in Frankfurt and München
History: Founded 1991.
Fees: (Euros): 3,500 per semester
Main Language(s) of Instruction: German, English
International Co-operation: Participates in Erasmus
Degrees and Diplomas: *Bachelor/Bakkalaureus*; *Master/Magister*
Libraries: Yes
Last Updated: 13/02/09

INTERNATIONAL UNIVERSITY OF APPLIED SCIENCES BAD HONNEF - BONN

Internationale Fachhochschule Bad Honnef - Bonn
Mühlheimer Strasse 38, 53604 Bad Honnef
Tel: +49(2224) 9605-102
Fax: +49(2224) 9605-500
EMail: info@iubh.de
Website: http://www.iubh.de

Rektor: Kurt Jeschke (2011-)
Tel: +49(2224) 9605-200, Fax: +49(2224) 9605-119
EMail: k.jeschke@iubh.de

Kanzler: Georg Ummenhofer
Tel: +49(2224) 9605-222, Fax: +49(2224) 9605-500
EMail: g.ummenhofer@fh-bad-honnef.de

International Relations: Ulrike von Aswegen, Head, International Office
Tel: +49(2224) 9605-114, Fax: +49(2224) 9605-116
EMail: u.von-aswegen@fh-bad-honnef.de

Departments
Audit and Taxation (Taxation); **Aviation Management** (Air Transport); **Business Administration and Economics** (Business Administration; Economics); **Event Management** (Management); **Hospitality Management** (Hotel Management); **Languages** (Modern Languages); **Tourism Management** (Tourism); **Transport Management** (Management; Transport and Communications)
History: Founded 1999.
Admission Requirements: Secondary school certificate (Abitur, Fachhochschulreife) and entrance examination, TOEFL (minimum score 80) or IELTS (minimum score 6.0)
Fees: (Euros): c. 8,200 per annum
Main Language(s) of Instruction: English
International Co-operation: With universities in USA, Latin America, Europe, Australia, Asia
Degrees and Diplomas: *Zertifikat*: Aviation Certificate; Hospitality Real Estate Professional; *Bachelor/Bakkalaureus*: 3 yrs; *Master/Magister*: International Management; Transport Management (MBA), $1\frac{1}{2}$ yrs

Student Services: Academic counselling, Canteen, Employment services, Foreign student adviser, Foreign Studies Centre, Language programs, Social counselling, Sports facilities

Student Residential Facilities: Yes

Special Facilities: Computer laboratory

Libraries: Yes

Last Updated: 03/02/12

ISS INTERNATIONAL BUSINESS SCHOOL OF SERVICE MANAGEMENT

Hans–Henny–Jahnn–Weg 9, 22085 Hamburg
Tel: +49 (40) 536991-30
Fax: +49 (40) 536991-66
EMail: nitsche@iss-hamburg.de
Website: http://www.iss-hamburg.de

Präsident: Odd Gisholt
Tel: +49 (40) 536991-13 EMail: gisholt iss-hamburg de

Programmes

Business Administration (with Specialisation in Service Management *(MBA)* (Business Administration; Finance; Human Resources; Management; Marketing; Service Trades); **Service Management** (Business Administration; Information Technology; Insurance; Management; Service Trades)

Degrees and Diplomas: *Bachelor/Bakkalaureus*; *Master/Magister*. Business Administration (Service Management)
Last Updated: 03/02/12

JACOBS UNIVERSITY

PO Box 750561, 28725 Bremen
Tel: +49(421) 2004-0
Fax: +49(421) 2004-113
EMail: info@jacobs-university.de
Website: http://www.jacobs-university.de/

Präsident: Joachim Treusch (2006-)

Schools

Engineering and Science (Astronomy and Space Science; Biochemistry; Biology; Biotechnology; Chemistry; Computer Science; Earth Sciences; Electrical Engineering; Mathematics; Neurosciences; Physics); **Humanities and Social Sciences**

History: Founded 1999. Acquired present title 2007. Formerly known as International University Bremen.

Governing Bodies: Board of Governors

Academic Year: September to May

Admission Requirements: Secondary school certificate (Reifezeugniss) or equivalent. SAT and TOEFL test

Fees: (Euros): Undergraduate, 15,000; graduate, 20,000

Main Language(s) of Instruction: English

International Co-operation: With Rice University and Washington State University USA.

Accrediting Agencies: City-State of Bremen, Wissenschaftsrat

Degrees and Diplomas: *Bachelor/Bakkalaureus (BA / BS)*: 3 yrs; *Master/Magister (MA)*: a further 2 yrs; *Doktorgrad (PhD)*: 5 yrs

Student Services: Academic counselling, Canteen, Foreign student adviser, Foreign Studies Centre, Language programs, Social counselling, Sports facilities

Libraries: c. 10,000 vols, 8,000 periodicals
Last Updated: 20/01/10

JADE UNIVERSITY OF APPLIED SCIENCES

Jade Hochschule

Fachhochschule Wilhelmshaven/Oldenburg/Elsfleth, Friedrich-Paffrath-Straße 101, 26389 Wilhelmshaven
Tel: +49(4421) 985-0
Fax: +49(4421) 985-2304
EMail: info@jade-hs.de
Website: http://www.jade-hs.de

Präsident: Elmar Schreiber
Tel: +49(4421) 985-2200, Fax: +49(4421) 985-2656
EMail: praesident@hs-woe.de

Areas

Architecture *(Oldenburg, Elsfleth)* (Architecture); **Construction and Geo-information Engineering** *(Oldenburg, Elsfleth)* (Civil Engineering; Construction Engineering; Engineering; Rehabilitation and Therapy; Speech Therapy and Audiology; Surveying and Mapping); **Economic Engineering** *(Wilhelmshaven)* (Business Computing; Economics; Engineering; Journalism; Media Studies); **Economics** *(Wilhelmshaven)* (Economics; Tourism); **Engineering** *(Wilhelmshaven)* (Computer Science; Electronic Engineering; Engineering; Machine Building; Mechanical Engineering; Medical Technology; Multimedia); **Marine Transport** *(Elsfleth)* (Marine Transport; Transport and Communications)

History: Founded 2009 through the splitting of the Fachhochschule Oldenburg/Ostfriesland/Wilhelmshaven into Fachhochschule Emden/Leer and Jade Hochschule.

Main Language(s) of Instruction: German

Degrees and Diplomas: *Bachelor/Bakkalaureus*; *Master/Magister*. Architecture; Facility Management and Real Estate; Management and Construction Engineering; Hearing Technology and Audiology; Machine Building; Maritime Management; Economic Engineering
Last Updated: 20/01/10

JOHANNES GUTENBERG UNIVERSITY MAINZ

Johannes Gutenberg-Universität Mainz

Saarstrasse 21D, 55099 Mainz
Tel: +49(6131) 39-0
Fax: +49(6131) 39-22919
EMail: postmaster@verwaltung.uni-mainz.de
Website: http://www.uni-mainz.de

Präsident: Georg Krausch (2007-) Tel: +49(6131) 39-22301
Kanzler: Götz Scholz Tel: +49(6131) 39-22201

Academies

Arts *(Mainz)* (Film; Media Studies; Metal Techniques; Painting and Drawing; Photography)

Faculties

Biology (Biology); **Catholic Theology** (Catholic Theology); **Chemistry, Pharmacy and Geoscience** (Chemistry; Crystallography; Earth Sciences; Geography; Geology; Mineralogy; Paleontology; Pharmacy); **History and Cultural Studies** (Cultural Studies; History); **Law, Management and Economics** (Economics; Law; Management); **Medicine** (Medicine); **Philosophy and Philology** (American Studies; Ancient Civilizations; Archaeology; Art History; Asian Studies; Classical Languages; English; German; Indic Languages; Linguistics; Literature; Middle Eastern Studies; Oriental Languages; Philology; Philosophy; Romance Languages; Slavic Languages); **Physics, Mathematics and Computer Science** (Computer Science; Mathematics; Physics); **Protestant Theology** (Protestant Theology); **Social Sciences, Media and Sports** (African Studies; Communication Studies; Ethnology; Journalism; Political Sciences; Psychology; Social Sciences; Sociology; Sports); **Translation Studies, Linguistics and Cultural Studies** *(Germersheim)* (Cultural Studies; English; French; Italian; Linguistics; Polish; Russian; Spanish; Translation and Interpretation)

Research Centres

Environmental Studies (Environmental Studies); **Materials Sciences** (Materials Engineering); **Natural Sciences and Medicine** (Medicine; Natural Sciences)

Schools

Music (Jazz and Popular Music; Music; Musical Instruments; Religious Music; Singing)

Further Information: Also integrated Master's Programme (leading to a German-French academic double degree Magister/Maître). International Summer School 'The Federal Republic of Germany': Language, Literature, Economy, 'Politics and Art' (end of July to end of August of each year) designed for advanced students and teachers of German to improve their knowledge of German and Germany

History: Founded 1477 by the Archbishop of Mainz. Closed 1816 although the Faculty of Catholic Theology continued as a seminary. Re-established 1946. An autonomous institution financially supported by the State of Rhineland-Palatinate, and under the jurisdiction of its Ministry of Education, Science and Continuing Education.

Governing Bodies: Versammlung; Senat

Academic Year: October to September (October-March; April-September)

Admission Requirements: Secondary school certificate (Reifezeugnis) or equivalent

Main Language(s) of Instruction: German

Degrees and Diplomas: *Bachelor/Bakkalaureus*; *Diplom*: 5 yrs; *Lehramt*; *Magister Artium*: 5 yrs; *Staatsprüfung*: 5 yrs; *Lizentiat*; *Master/Magister*; *Doktorgrad*: 2-5 yrs; *Habilitation*

Student Services: Academic counselling, Canteen, Employment services, Foreign student adviser, Handicapped facilities, Health services, Nursery care, Social counselling, Sports facilities

Student Residential Facilities: For c. 3,930 students

Special Facilities: Botanical Garden

Libraries: Central library, c. 3m. vols. Additional department libraries

Publications: Scientific Reports

Last Updated: 20/01/10

JULIUS-MAXIMILIAN UNIVERSITY OF WÜRZBURG

Julius-Maximilians-Universität Würzburg
Sanderring 2, D 97070 Würzburg
Tel: +49(931) 31-0
Fax: +49(931) 31-2600
EMail: universitaet@zv.uni-wuerzburg.de
Website: http://www.uni-wuerzburg.de

Präsident: Alfred Forschel
Tel: +49(931) 31-2240 EMail: praesident@uni-wuerzburg.de

Kanzler: Uwe Klug
Tel: +49(931) 31-2231, Fax: +49(931) 31-2100
EMail: kanzler@uni-wuerzburg.de

Faculties

Arts I (American Studies; Ancient Civilizations; Archaeology; Art History; Arts and Humanities; Asian Studies; Cultural Studies; East Asian Studies; Ethnology; French; Geography; German; Germanic Languages; Greek (Classical); History; Indic Languages; Japanese; Latin; Literature; Modern Languages; Music Education; Musicology; Philology; Slavic Languages); **Arts II** (Arts and Humanities; Pedagogy; Philosophy; Political Sciences; Psychology; Religion; Social Studies; Sports; Theology); **Biology** (Biology; Biotechnology; Botany; Genetics; Microbiology; Pharmacology; Zoology); **Catholic Theology** (Catholic Theology); **Chemistry and Pharmacy** (Biochemistry; Food Technology; Inorganic Chemistry; Organic Chemistry; Pharmacy; Physical Chemistry); **Economics** (Business Administration; Economics); **Law** (Law); **Mathematics and Computer Science** (Computer Science; Mathematics; Statistics); **Medicine** (Anaesthesiology; Dentistry; Hygiene; Immunology; Medicine; Nursing; Otorhinolaryngology; Pharmacology; Surgery; Toxicology; Virology); **Physics and Astronomy** (Astronomy and Space Science; Astrophysics; Physics)

History: Founded 1402 by the Prince Bishop Johann von Egloffstein, refounded 1582 by Julius Echter von Mespelbrunn, Duke of Franconia, the University is an autonomous institution financially supported by the State of Bavaria and under the jurisdiction of its Ministry of Science, Research and Art.

Governing Bodies: Senat; Erweiterter Senat; Hochschulrat; Präsidialkollegium

Academic Year: October to July (October-February; April-July)

Admission Requirements: Secondary school certificate (Reifezeugnis) or equivalent

Main Language(s) of Instruction: German

International Co-operation: With universities in France; United Kingdom; Ireland; Italy; Japan; Korea; Spain; Sweden; USA. Also participates in Erasmus and bilateral programmes

Degrees and Diplomas: *Bachelor/Bakkalaureus*: Arts and Humanities (MA); Biology; Business Administration; Catholic Theology; Chemistry; Computer Science; Computer Science; Technology; Economics; Education; Geography; Mathematical; Financial Economics; Mathematics; Mineralogy; Nanostructure Technologies (Dipl.Ing.); Physics; Psychology; Sport Science, 4-5 yrs; *Bachelor/Bakkalaureus*: Arts and Humanities (BA); Biology (BSc); Biomedi-

cine (B.Sc); Business Computing (B.Sc); Modern China (B.A.); Technology of Advanced Materials (B.Sc.), 3 yrs; *Bachelor/Bakkalaureus*: Theology; *Lehramt*: Teaching Qualification, 4-6 yrs; *Staatsprüfung*: Dentistry; Food chemistry; Law; Medicine; Pharmacy, 4-6 yrs; *Master/Magister*: Biomedicine (MSc), 3 yrs; *Master/Magister*: Business Integration (MBA); Chinese Studies (MA); Focus Physics (MSc); Space Science and Technology (MSc), 2 yrs; *Master/Magister*: European Law (MLLeur), a further 2 yrs; *Master/Magister*: Law (MLL), a further yr; *Promotion*: Arts and Humanities (Dr.phil); Dentistry (Dr.med.dent); Economics and Business Administration (Dr.rer.pol); Law (Dr.iur); Science (Dr.rer.nat); Theology (Dr.theol), 2-5 yrs; *Promotion*: Medicine (Dr.med), 6 yrs; *Doktorgrad*; *Habilitation*: at least 3 yrs following Doktor

Student Services: Academic counselling, Canteen, Foreign student adviser, Foreign Studies Centre, Handicapped facilities, Language programs, Nursery care, Sports facilities

Student Residential Facilities: Yes

Special Facilities: Martin-von-Wagner Museum; Mineralogy Museum

Libraries: c. 3.5 m. vols

Publications: Blick, Research, Teaching, Services, Report *(3 per annum)*

Last Updated: 22/03/11

JUSTUS LIEBIG UNIVERSITY GIESSEN

Justus-Liebig-Universität Giessen (JLU)
Ludwigstrasse 23, D-35390 Giessen, Hessen
Tel: +49(641) 99-0
Fax: +49(641) 99-12259
EMail: poststelle@admin.uni-giessen.de
Website: http://www.uni-giessen.de

Präsident: Joybrato Mukherjee
Tel: +49(641) 99-12000, Fax: +49(641) 99-12009
EMail: joybrato.mukherjee@uni-giessen.de

Kanzler: Michael Breitbach
Tel: +49(641) 99-12030, Fax: +49(641) 99-12039
EMail: Breitbach@admin.uni-geissen.de

International Relations: Julia Voltz
Tel: +49(641) 99-12130, Fax: +49(641) 99-12149
EMail: julia.volz@admin.uni-giessen.de

Faculties

Agriculture, Nutrition and Environment Management (Agriculture; Environmental Management; Nutrition); **Biology and Chemistry** (Biology; Chemistry); **Economics and Business Studies** (Business Administration; Economics); **History and Cultural Studies** (Catholic Theology; Classical Languages; History; Philology; Protestant Theology; Theology); **Languages, Literature, and Culture** (English; German; Philology; Romance Languages; Slavic Languages; Theatre); **Law** (Law); **Mathematics and Computer Science, Physics and Geography** (Computer Science; Geography; Mathematics; Physics); **Medicine** (Medicine); **Psychology and Sports** (Psychology; Sports); **Social Sciences and Cultural Studies** (Art Education; Music; Music Education; Pedagogy; Social Sciences); **Veterinary Medicine** (Veterinary Science)

History: Founded 1607 as University. Became the Justus Liebig-Hochschule (academy) in 1946. Full University status restored 1957. An autonomous institution financially supported by the State of Hesse, and under the jurisdiction of its Ministry of Education.

Governing Bodies: Präsidium

Academic Year: October to July (October-February; April-July)

Admission Requirements: Secondary school certificate (Reifezeugnis) or equivalent

Fees: None

Main Language(s) of Instruction: German

International Co-operation: With universities in France; United Kingdom; Spain; Italy; Poland; Sweden; Hungary; Australia; Uzbekistan; Russian Federation; Spain; Italy; USA

Accrediting Agencies: Federal Government State of Hesse

Degrees and Diplomas: *Bachelor/Bakkalaureus*: Agricultural Sciences; Nutrition; Biology; Chemistry; Physics; *Diplom*: Drama; Economics; Geography; Mathematics; Modern Languages; Pedagogy; Psychology; Social Sciences; *Lehramt*; *Staatsprüfung*:

Medicine; Law; Teaching; *Master/Magister*: Agrobiology; Language Technology GFL, 4 sem; *Promotion*: 8-14 sem; *Doktorgrad*; *Habilitation*: at least 3 yrs following Doktor

Student Services: Academic counselling, Canteen, Cultural centre, Foreign student adviser, Foreign Studies Centre, Handicapped facilities, Language programs, Social counselling, Sports facilities

Student Residential Facilities: Yes

Libraries: University Library, c. 3.8 m vols

Publications: Spiegel der Forschung *(biennially)*
Last Updated: 20/01/10

KAISERSLAUTERN UNIVERSITY OF APPLIED SCIENCES

Fachhochschule Kaiserslautern

Morlauterer Str. 31, 67657 Kaiserslautern, Rheinland-Pfaltz
Tel: +49(631) 3724-0
Fax: +49(631) 3724-105
EMail: presse@fh-kl.de
Website: http://www.fh-kl.de

Präsident: Konrad Wolf
Tel: +49(631) 3724-100, Fax: +49(631) 3724-129
EMail: praesident@fh-kl.de

Kanzler: Rudolf Becker
Tel: +49(631) 3724-110 EMail: becker@fh-kl.de

International Relations: Silvia Czerwinski
Tel: +49(631) 3724-133, Fax: +49(631) 3724-133
EMail: auslandsamt@verw-kl.fh-kl.de; silvia.czerwinski@fh-kl.de

Faculties

Applied Logistics and Polymer Science (Polymer and Plastics Technology; Transport Management); **Business Administration** (Business Administration; Business Computing; Engineering; Finance; Information Management; Small Business); **Construction and Design** (Architecture; Construction Engineering; Design; Interior Design); **Engineering** (Business Administration; Computer Engineering; Electronic Engineering; Engineering; Information Technology; Machine Building; Mechanical Engineering); **Informatics and Microsystem Engineering** (Automation and Control Engineering; Computer Engineering; Electrical Engineering; Electronic Engineering; Information Technology; Systems Analysis; Telecommunications Engineering)

Further Information: Also branches in Pirmasens and Zweibrücken

History: Founded 1959. Acquired present status 1996.

Governing Bodies: Senat; Versammlung; Kuratorium

Admission Requirements: Fachhochschulreife, allgemeine Hochschulreife

Fees: (Euros): 55-110 with term ticket

Main Language(s) of Instruction: German

International Co-operation: Participates in Socrates

Degrees and Diplomas: *Bachelor/Bakkalaureus*; *Master/Magister*

Student Services: Academic counselling, Canteen, Foreign student adviser, Foreign Studies Centre, Handicapped facilities, Language programs, Sports facilities

Student Residential Facilities: Yes

Libraries: Yes

Publications: Forschungsbericht *(biannually)*; Rundschau *(biennially)*
Last Updated: 06/02/12

KARLSHOCHSCHULE INTERNATIONAL UNIVERSITY

Karlstraße 36-38, 76133 Karlsruhe
Tel: 721 1303-500
Fax: 721 1303-300
EMail: info@karlshochschule.de
Website: http://www.karlshochschule.de

Präsident: Michael Zerr

Head of Administration: Gérard Massé

International Relations: Elisabeth Hunkel

Programmes

Cultural Management (Accountancy; Cultural Studies; Finance; Human Resources; Law; Management); **Energy Management** (Energy Engineering; Management); **Intercultural Management and Communication** (Accountancy; Communication Studies; Human Resources; Management; Marketing); **International Business** (International Business); **International Marketing** (Accountancy; E-Business/Commerce; Finance; Human Resources; International Business; Management; Marketing); **International Tourism Management** (Accountancy; Finance; Human Resources; International Business; Management; Tourism); **Management of Meetings, Expositions, Events and Conventions** (Management); **Media and Communication Management** (Communication Studies; Management; Media Studies)

History: Founded as Merkur Internationale FH Karlsruhe.

Main Language(s) of Instruction: German

Degrees and Diplomas: *Bachelor/Bakkalaureus*; *Master/Magister*
Last Updated: 21/01/10

KARLSRUHE INSTITUTE OF TECHNOLOGY

Karlsruher Institut für Technologie

Kaiserstrasse 12, D-76131 Karlsruhe
Tel: +49(721) 6080
Fax: +49(721) 608-4290
Website: http://www.kit.edu

Rektor: Horst Hippler (2002-)
Tel: +49(721) 608-2000, Fax: +49(721) 608-6122
EMail: horst.hippler@kit.edu

Centres

Computer (Computer Science); **Environmental Sciences** (Environmental Studies)

Faculties

Architecture (Architecture); **Chemical and Process Engineering** (Chemical Engineering); **Chemistry and Bio-Sciences** (Biology; Botany; Chemistry; Genetics; Inorganic Chemistry; Microbiology; Organic Chemistry; Physical Chemistry; Polymer and Plastics Technology; Toxicology; Zoology); **Civil Engineering, Geo- and Environmental Sciences** (Civil Engineering; Environmental Engineering; Geography; Mechanical Engineering; Mineralogy; Regional Planning); **Computer Science** (Computer Science); **Electrical Engineering and Information Technology** (Electrical Engineering; Information Technology); **Mathematics** (Mathematics); **Mechanical Engineering** (Mechanical Engineering); **Physics** (Meteorology; Physics); **Social Sciences and Humanities** (Arts and Humanities; Philosophy; Social Sciences; Sports)

Schools

Economics and Business Engineering (Economics; Finance; Management)

Further Information: Also International Seminar for Science and Teaching in Chemical Engineering, Technical and Physical Chemistry

History: Founded 1825 as Polytechnische Schule on the model of the Ecole polytechnique, Paris. Acquired University status 1865. Became Technische Hochschule Fridericiana 1885, acquired present title 2009 following merger with merged with the Forschungszentrum Karlsruhe. An autonomous institution under the jurisdiction of and financed by the State of Baden-Württemberg.

Governing Bodies: Senate, Board of Governors (Universitätsrat)

Academic Year: October to September (October-February; April-July)

Admission Requirements: Secondary school certificate (Abitur) or equivalent

Fees: Tuition, none

Main Language(s) of Instruction: German

International Co-operation: With universities in France, Spain, Italy, Switzerland, China, Sweden, Norway.

Degrees and Diplomas: *Bachelor/Bakkalaureus (BA, BSc)*; *Diplom*: Architecture; Biology; Chemical Engineering; Chemistry; Civil Construction Engineering; Computer Science; Economics; Economics Mathematics; Electronic Engineering; Engineering; Geological Ecology; Geophysics; Mathematics; Mechanical Engineering; Meteorology; Mineralogy; Physics; Surveying and Mapping

Engineering; Technical Mathematics; *Magister Artium*: 4 yrs; *Staatsprüfung*: Chemistry; Food Chemistry; Geography; German Language; Mathematics; Physics; Sports/Sport Sciences; *Lizentiat*: a further 2 yrs; *Master/Magister*. Electrical Engineering; Civil Engineering (MSc), a further 2 yrs; *Doktorgrad*: Economic Science (Dr.rer.pol.); Engineering (Dr.Ing.); Natural Sciences (Dr.rer.nat.); Philosophy (Dr.phil.), 2-4 yrs; *Habilitation*: at least 3 yrs following Doktor

Student Services: Academic counselling, Canteen, Cultural centre, Foreign student adviser, Foreign Studies Centre, Handicapped facilities, Language programs, Nursery care, Social counselling, Sports facilities

Student Residential Facilities: For c. 1,700 students

Libraries: University Library, c. 850,000 vols; faculty and institute libraries
Last Updated: 28/01/10

KARLSRUHE UNIVERSITY OF APPLIED SCIENCES

Hochschule Karlsruhe -Technik und Wirtschaft
PO Box 2440, 76012 Karlsruhe
Tel: +49(721) 925-0
Fax: +49(721) 925-2000
EMail: mailbox@fh-karlsruhe.de
Website: http://www.hs-karlsruhe.de

Rektor: Karl-Heinz Meisel
Tel: 49(721) 925-1000, Fax: 49(721) 925-1005
EMail: rektor@hs-karlsruhe.de

Kanzlerin: Daniela Schweitzer
Tel: 49(721) 925-1020 EMail: daniela.schweitzer@fh-karlsruhe.de

International Relations: Joachim Lembach
EMail: joachim.lembach@hs-karlsruhe.de

Faculties
Architecture and Construction Engineering (Architecture; Civil Engineering; Construction Engineering); **Computer Science and Business Information Systems** (Business Computing; Computer Science; Multimedia); **Electrical Engineering and Information Technology** (Automation and Control Engineering; Electrical Engineering; Electronic Engineering; Information Technology; Telecommunications Engineering); **Geomatics** (Surveying and Mapping); **Management and Engineering** (Business Administration; Communication Studies; Engineering; Management; Sales Techniques); **Mechanical Engineering and Mechatronics** (Electronic Engineering; Machine Building; Mechanical Engineering)

History: Founded 1878. Acquired present status 2005.

Main Language(s) of Instruction: German

Degrees and Diplomas: *Bachelor/Bakkalaureus*; *Master/Magister*
Last Updated: 20/01/10

KARLSRUHE UNIVERSITY OF EDUCATION

Pädagogische Hochschule Karlsruhe
Bismarckstrasse 10, 76133 Karlsruhe
Tel: +49(721) 925-3
Fax: +49(721) 925-4000
EMail: info@ph-karlsruhe.de
Website: http://www.ph-karlsruhe.de/cms/

Rektorin: Christine Boeckelmann
Tel: +49(721) 925-4011, Fax: +49(721) 925-4010
EMail: christine.boeckelmann@ph-karlsruhe.de

Institutes
Art and Music (Fine Arts; Music); **Education** (Education); **European Studies and Bilingualism** (Bilingual and Bicultural Education; European Studies); **Foreign Languages** (Modern Languages); **German Language and Literature** (German; Literature; Pedagogy); **Integrative Media Education** (Media Studies); **Mathematics and Computer Science** (Mathematics and Computer Science); **Movement Education and Sports** (Sports); **Natural Sciences** (Biology; Chemistry; Physics); **Philosophy and Theology** (Catholic Theology; Ethics; Philosophy; Religious Education; Theology); **Psychology** (Psychology); **Social Sciences** (Economics; European Studies; Geography; History; Political Sciences; Social Sciences; Sociology); **Sports** (Sports); **Technical and**

Household Education (Household Management; Technology Education; Textile Technology); **Test Development and Evaluation** (Safety Engineering)

History: Founded 1768 as Schul-Seminarium. Acquired present status 1962.

Academic Year: October to July

Admission Requirements: Secondary school certificate (Reifezeugnis)

Fees: (Euros): 500

Main Language(s) of Instruction: German

Degrees and Diplomas: *Bachelor/Bakkalaureus*; *Diplom*: Educational Sciences, 5-6 yrs; *Lehramt*: Teaching qualifications, 3-4 yrs; *Master/Magister*; *Promotion*: Educational Sciences; *Habilitation*: Educational Sciences

Student Services: Canteen, Foreign student adviser, Sports facilities

Special Facilities: Audiovisual Centre; Computer Centre; Computer Supported Language Learning Centre

Libraries: c. 380,000 vols

Publications: Karlsruher Pädagogische Beiträge *(3 per annum)*
Last Updated: 03/02/12

KARLSRUHE UNIVERSITY OF MUSIC

Hochschule für Musik Karlsruhe
PO Box 6040, Am Schloss Gottesaue 7, 76040 Karlsruhe
Tel: +49(721) 6629-0
Fax: +49(721) 6629-266
EMail: hartmut.hoell@hfm-karlsruhe.de
Website: http://www.hfm-karlsruhe.de/

Rektor: Hartmut Höll
Tel: +49(721) 6629-270
EMail: josefine.beinhauer@hfm-karlsruhe.de

Kanzler: Wolfram Scherer
Tel: +49(721) 6629-260 EMail: wolfram.scherer@hfm-karlsruhe.de

International Relations: Isabel Eisenmann, International Relations Coordinator Tel: +49(721) 6629-285 EMail: eisenmann@hfm.eu

Faculties
Chamber Music (Piano); **Chamber Music (String Instruments)** (Musical Instruments); **Chamber Music (Wind Instruments)** (Musical Instruments); **Composition** (Music Theory and Composition); **Direction** (Music); **Musical Instruments** (Musical Instruments); **Singing/Opera** (Opera; Singing); **Song Design** (Music Theory and Composition)

Institutes
LernRadio (Journalism; Media Studies; Multimedia; Radio and Television Broadcasting); **Musical Theatre** (Music; Theatre); **Musicology/Music Informatics** (Computer Science; Music; Musicology); **New Music and Media** (Media Studies; Music)

History: Founded 1929.

Governing Bodies: Ministerium für Wissenschaft und Kunst Baden-Würtemberg

Admission Requirements: Entrance Examination

Fees: (Euros): Summer semester, 1,600; Winter semester, 2,000.

Main Language(s) of Instruction: German, English

International Co-operation: With universities in Netherlands, Portugal, Czech Republic, Belgium, Hungary, United Kingdom, Sweden, Austria, Finland, Denmark, Poland, France, Spain, Italy, Switzerland

Accrediting Agencies: Examination Office

Degrees and Diplomas: *Zertifikat*: Chamber Music; *Bachelor/Bakkalaureus*: Musicology; Music Informatics; Opera; Music Journalism for Radio and Multimedia; Musical Instruments; *Diplom*; *Lehramt*; *Staatsprüfung*: 9 sem; *Master/Magister*: Musicology; Music Informatics; Opera; Music Journalism for Radio and Multimedia; Musical Instruments

Student Services: Canteen, Cultural centre, Foreign student adviser, Language programs

Special Facilities: Radio Station

Libraries: Yes
Last Updated: 19/01/10

KEMPTEN UNIVERSITY OF APPLIED SCIENCES

Hochschule für Angewandte Wissenschaften - Fachhochschule Kempten
Bahnhofstrasse 61, 87406 Kempten
Tel: +49(831) 2523-0
Fax: +49(831) 2523-104
EMail: post@fh-kempten.de
Website: http://www.hochschule-kempten.de

Präsident: Robert F. Schmidt
Tel: +49(831) 2523-102 EMail: praesident@fh-kempten.de

Kanzler: Christian Herrmann
Tel: +49(831) 2523-110, Fax: +49(831) 2523-305
EMail: kanzler@fh-kempten.de

International Relations: Donata Santüns
Tel: +49(831) 2523-117
EMail: auslandsamt@fh-kempten.de; donata.santuens@fh-kempten.de

Faculties
Business Administration and Tourism Management (Business Administration; Management; Tourism); **Engineering** (Electrical Engineering; Energy Engineering; Engineering; Environmental Engineering; Industrial Engineering; Information Technology); **Informatics and Multimedia** (Computer Science; Multimedia); **Social and Health Sciences** (Economics; Health Administration; Social Sciences)

History: Founded 1978.

Main Language(s) of Instruction: German

Degrees and Diplomas: *Bachelor/Bakkalaureus*; *Diplom (FH)*; *Master/Magister*: Applied Informatics
Last Updated: 01/02/12

KIEL UNIVERSITY OF APPLIED SCIENCES

Fachhochschule Kiel
Sokratesplatz 1, 24149 Kiel
Tel: +49(431) 210-0
Fax: +49(431) 210-1900
EMail: info@fh-kiel.de; presse@fh-kiel.de
Website: http://www.fh-kiel.de

Rektor: Udo Beer
Tel: +49(431) 210-1000, Fax: +49(431) 210-61000
EMail: udo.beer@fh-kiel.de

Kanzler: Klaus-Michael Heinze
Tel: +49(431) 210-1300, Fax: +49(431) 210-61300
EMail: klaus.heinze@fh-kiel.de

International Relations: Christine Boudin
Tel: +49(431) 210-1800, Fax: +49(431) 210-1810
EMail: aaa@fh-kiel.de

Departments
Mechanical Engineering (Mechanical Engineering)

Faculties
Agriculture (Agriculture); **Business Administration** (Business Administration); **Computer Science and Electrical Engineering** (Computer Science; Electrical and Electronic Engineering; Energy Engineering; Information Technology; Mechanical Engineering); **Media** (Media Studies; Multimedia); **Social Work and Health** (Physical Therapy; Social Work)

History: Founded 1969.

Main Language(s) of Instruction: German

Degrees and Diplomas: *Bachelor/Bakkalaureus*; *Master/Magister*
Last Updated: 06/02/12

KOBLENZ UNIVERSITY OF APPLIED SCIENCES

Fachhochschule Koblenz (FH KOBLENZ)
Rheinau 3-4, 56075 Koblenz-Oberwerth
Tel: +49(261) 9528-0
Fax: +49(261) 9528-567
EMail: infos@fh-koblenz.de
Website: http://www.fh-koblenz.de

Präsident: Kristian Bosselmann-Cyran
Tel: +49(261) 9528-110, Fax: +49(261) 9528-113
EMail: praesident@fh-koblenz.de

Kanzlerin: Heidi Mikoteit-Olsen
Tel: +49(261) 9528-202, Fax: +49(261) 9528-113
EMail: kanzlerin@fh-koblenz.de

International Relations: Anne Dommershausen
Tel: +49(261) 9528-243, Fax: +49(261) 9528-225
EMail: dommersh@fh-koblenz.de; international@fh-koblenz.de

Departments
Business Administration (Business Administration); **Business Administration and Social Management** *(Remagen)* (Business Administration; Child Care and Development; E-Business/Commerce; Educational Administration; Health Administration; Management; Marketing; Social and Community Services; Social Sciences; Sports Management; Tourism; Transport Management); **Civil Engineering** (Architecture; Civil Engineering; Town Planning); **Engineering** (Ceramic Art; Ceramics and Glass Technology; Computer Engineering; Design; Electrical Engineering; Electronic Engineering; Information Technology; Machine Building; Materials Engineering; Mechanical Engineering; Production Engineering); **Mathematics and Technology** *(Remagen)* (Mathematics; Technology); **Social Sciences** (European Union Law; Social Sciences; Social Work)

History: Founded 1996.

Governing Bodies: Senat; Hochschulrat

Academic Year: October-January; March-July

Admission Requirements: Hochschulreife, Practical Training, Language Competence

Fees: (Euros): 101.20 per semester (social contribution)

Main Language(s) of Instruction: German

International Co-operation: Participates in Erasmus and Leonardo

Degrees and Diplomas: *Bachelor/Bakkalaureus*: 3 yrs; *Master/Magister*: 2 yrs

Student Services: Academic counselling, Canteen, Foreign student adviser, Foreign Studies Centre, Language programs, Social counselling

Libraries: Yes
Last Updated: 31/01/12

LANDSHUT UNIVERSITY OF APPLIED SCIENCES

Hochschule Landshut
Am Lurzenhof 1, 84036 Landshut
Tel: +49(871) 506-0
Fax: +49(871) 506-506
EMail: fh-landshut@fh-landshut.de
Website: http://www.fh-landshut.de

Präsident: Karl Stoffel
Tel: +49(871) 506-101 EMail: praesident@fh-landshut.de

Departments
Computer Science (Computer Science); **Economics** (Banking; Business Computing; Economics; Finance; Marketing); **Electrical and Commercial Engineering** (Automation and Control Engineering; Electrical Engineering; Microelectronics); **Mechanical Engineering** (Construction Engineering; Mechanical Engineering; Production Engineering); **Social Work** (Social Work)

History: Founded 1978. Formerly Fachhochschule Landshut.

Main Language(s) of Instruction: German

Degrees and Diplomas: *Bachelor/Bakkalaureus*; *Master/Magister*
Last Updated: 02/02/12

LAUSITZ UNIVERSITY OF APPLIED SCIENCES

Hochschule Lausitz
Grossenhainer Strasse 57, 01968 Senftenberg
Tel: +49(3573) 85-0
Fax: +49(3573) 85-209
EMail: praesident@fh-lausitz.de
Website: http://www.fh-lausitz.de

Präsident: Günter H. Schulz
Tel: +49(3573) 85-200, Fax: +49(3573) 85-209

Administrative Officer: Volker Schiffer
Tel: +49(3573) 85-210, Fax: +49(3573) 85-219
EMail: kanzler@fh-lausitz.de

International Relations: Thomas Reif, Head, Office of International
Affairs Tel: +49(3573) 85-287

Faculties
**Business Administration and Social Sciences, Music Educa-
tion** *(Cottbus)* (Business Administration; Music Education; Musical
Instruments; Singing; Social Work); **Construction** *(Cottbus)*
(Architecture; Civil Engineering; Construction Engineering); **Engi-
neering and Computer Science** (Biomedical Engineering; Com-
puter Science; Electrical Engineering; Industrial Engineering;
Mechanical Engineering; Physical Therapy); **Natural Sciences**
(Biotechnology; Chemistry)

History: Founded 1991.

Degrees and Diplomas: *Bachelor/Bakkalaureus*; *Diplom
(FH)*: Music Education; *Master/Magister*: Biotechnology; Computer
Science; Communication and Electronic Engineering; Machine
Building; Natural Substance Chemistry; Architecture; Computa-
tional Mechanics; Gerontology; Climate-friendly Building; Social
Work
Last Updated: 02/02/12

LEIPZIG GRADUATE SCHOOL OF MANAGEMENT

Handelshochschule Leipzig
Jahnallee 59, 04109 Leipzig
Tel: +49(341) 985-160
Fax: +49(341) 477-3243
EMail: info@hhl.de
Website: http://www.hhl.de

Rektor: Andreas Pinkwart EMail: rektor@hhl.de

Kanzler: Axel Baisch EMail: kanzler@hhl.de

International Relations: Frank Hoffmann
Tel: +49(341) 985-1626, Fax: +49(341) 985-1810
EMail: hoffmann@hhl.de

Deaneries
Sustainability and Global Ethics (Ethics)

Departments
Accounting and Auditing; **Applied Economic Theory** (Economics); **Economics and Information Systems** (Economics; Information Sciences; Information Technology); **Finance** (Finance); **IT-
based Logistics**; **Macroeconomics** (Economics); **Marketing
Management** (Marketing); **Microeconomics** (Economics); **Strategic Management** (Management)

Programmes
International Entrepreneurship (International Business)

Further Information: Also preparatory courses for foreign students;
one semester abroad compulsory for all students

History: Founded 1898, acquired present status 1996.

Academic Year: September to August (September-December;-
January-March; April-June; July-August)

Admission Requirements: Equivalence to BA; practical experience; TOEFL; GMAT; entrance examination

Fees: (Euros) 8,000-12,000 per semester depending on programme

Main Language(s) of Instruction: English

International Co-operation: With 86 universities worldwide

Accrediting Agencies: AACSB, German Government

Degrees and Diplomas: *Master/Magister (MBA)*: 15 months (2 yrs
part-time); *Doktorgrad (Dr.rer.oec; Dr.habil.oec)*

Student Services: Academic counselling, Canteen, Employment
services, Foreign student adviser, Foreign Studies Centre, Language programs, Social counselling, Sports facilities
Last Updated: 01/02/12

LEIPZIG UNIVERSITY OF APPLIED SCIENCES

**Hochschule für Technik, Wirtschaft und Kultur Leipzig
(FH)**
PO Box 30 11 66, 04251 Leipzig
Tel: +49(341) 307-60
Fax: +49(341) 307-6456
EMail: studinf@k.htwk-leipzig.de
Website: http://www.htwk-leipzig.de

Rektorin: Renate Lieckfeldt (2011-)
Tel: +49(341) 307-6305, Fax: +49(341) 307-6380
EMail: rektor@htwk-leipzig.de; milke@fbb.htwk-leipzig.de

Kanzler: Ulrich Ziegler
Tel: +49(341) 307-6307, Fax: +49(341) 307-6320
EMail: kanzler@htwk-leipzig.de

International Relations: Christiane Hinrichs, Head, International
Office
Tel: +49(341) 307-6243, Fax: +49(341) 307-6507
EMail: internationales@htwk-leipzig.de; hinrichs@r.htwk-leipzig.de

Faculties
Applied Social Sciences (Preschool Education; Social Work);
Business Administration (Business Administration; Manage-
ment); **Civil Engineering and Architecture** (Architecture; Civil
Engineering; **Computer Science, Mathematics and Natural
Sciences** (Computer Science; Mathematics; Natural Sciences);
Electrical Engineering and Information Technology (Electrical
Engineering; Information Technology; Management); **Mechanical
and Energy Engineering** (Energy Engineering; Mechanical Engi-
neering); **Media Studies** (Multimedia; Packaging Technology;
Printing and Printmaking)

History: Founded 1992 in succession to Technische Hochschule
Leipzig, Fachschule für wissenschaftliches Bibliothekswesen and
Institute für Museologie. Under the jurisdiction of and financially
supported by the State of Saxony.

Governing Bodies: State of Saxony

Academic Year: September to August (September-February;
March-August)

Admission Requirements: Secondary school certificate (Abitur)
and certificate of German language proficiency

Fees: None

Main Language(s) of Instruction: German

International Co-operation: With universities in China; Denmark;
Finland; France; Greece; United Kingdom; Iceland; Italy; Lithuania;
Poland; Russian Federation; Switzerland; Spain; Ukraine; Hungary;
USA

Degrees and Diplomas: *Bachelor/Bakkalaureus*: 3-4 yrs; *Master/
Magister*: 1-2 yrs. Also Podtgraduate Diploma in Civil Engineering

Student Services: Academic counselling, Canteen, Foreign student adviser, Foreign Studies Centre, Language programs, Nursery
care, Social counselling, Sports facilities

Libraries: 320,000 vols
Last Updated: 02/02/12

LEUPHANA UNIVERSITY OF LÜNEBURG

Leuphana Universität Lüneburg (LU)
Scharnhorststrasse 1, 21335 Lüneburg, Lower Saxony
Tel: +49(4131) 677-0000
Fax: +49(4131) 677-1090
EMail: info@leuphana.de
Website: http://www.leuphana.de/

Präsident: Sascha Spoun (2006-)
Tel: +49(4131) 677-1000, Fax: +49(4131) 677-1090
EMail: sascha.spoun@leuphana.de

Vice-President: Holm Keller
Tel: +49(4131) 677-1005 EMail: holm.keller@leuphana.de

International Relations: Sabine Busse, Director, International
Office
Tel: +49(4131) 677-1071, Fax: +49(4131) 677-1075
EMail: sbusse@uni.leuphana.de

Faculties
Business and Economics (Accountancy; Banking; Business
Computing; Commercial Law; Economics; Finance; Human

Resources; Management; Marketing; Taxation; Tourism); **Education** (Communication Studies; Cultural Studies; Education; English Studies; Leisure Studies; Mathematics; Media Studies; Philology; Physical Education; Political Sciences; Psychology; Religious Education; Social Studies; Sociology; Visual Arts); **Sustainability** (Ecology; Environmental Studies; Ethics)

Further Information: Also Leuphana Professional School, for continuing education, Executive and Leadership Training.

History: Founded in 1946 as a teacher training college and awarded university status in the late 1970s. Today, it integrates two formerly independent institutions of higher education – the University of Lüneburg and the University of Applied Sciences – at four different locations. In 1993 the University of Lüneburg was among the first universities in Germany to become a foundation under public law – the highest degree of autonomy awarded to state universities.

Governing Bodies: Foundation board, Academic Senate (or Council) and Executive committee.

Academic Year: October to July (October-February; April-July)

Admission Requirements: Secondary school leaving certificate (Abitur) or equivalent.

Fees: (Euros): 500 per semester

Main Language(s) of Instruction: German

International Co-operation: Australia, Belgium, Chile, China, Cyprus, Czech Republic, Denmark, Ecuador, Estonia, Finland, France, Greece, Hungary, Iceland, India, Ireland, Italy, Japan, Latvia, Netherlands, Norway, Peru, Poland, Portugal, Russian Federation, Slovenia, South Korea, Spain, Sweden, Switzerland, Turkey, United Kingdom, USA. Also participates in Erasmus, Tempus and Leonardo programmes.

Degrees and Diplomas: *Bachelor/Bakkalaureus*: Business Law (LLB); Cultural Studies; Business Administration; Business Law; Teacher Education for Primary and for Lower Secondary Schools; Teacher Education for Vocational Schools. (BA); Economics; Business Psychology; Environmental Sciences; Information Sciences. (BSc); Industrial Engineering. (BEng), 3 yrs; *Master/Magister*: Management & Human Resources; Management & Marketing; Management & Information; Public Economics; Law and Politics; Educational Sciences. (MA); Management & Tax/Audit (LLM); Sustainability Sciences; Management & Engineering. (MSc); Teacher Education (MEd), 2 yrs; *Master/Magister*: Medical Practice Management. (MBA), 2 yrs (part time); *Master/Magister*: Performance Management; Manufacturing Management; Sales and Distribution Management. (MBA), 1.5 yrs (part time); *Master/Magister*: Public Health (Prevention and Health Promotion). (MPH), 2 yrs (part time programme); *Master/Magister*: Social Management. (MSH), 2.5 yrs (part time programme); *Master/Magister*: Strategic Management. (MBA), 2 yrs (part time corporate programme); *Master/Magister*: Sustainability Management. (MBA), 1 yr (full time); 2 yrs (part time); *Promotion*

Student Services: Academic counselling, Canteen, Cultural centre, Employment services, Foreign student adviser, Foreign Studies Centre, Handicapped facilities, Language programs, Social counselling, Sports facilities

Student Residential Facilities: 10 residential facilities for 770 students.

Special Facilities: Biological Garden. Radio and Movie Studios. Kunstraum (Art Gallery)

Libraries: Four libraries with c. 718,000 vols.

Press or Publishing House: Leuphana University Press
Last Updated: 21/01/10

LUDWIG-MAXIMILIAN-UNIVERSITY OF MUNICH

Ludwig-Maximilians Universität München (LMU)
Geschwister-Scholl-Platz 1, 80539 München
Tel: +49(89) 2180-0
Fax: +49(89) 2180-2322
EMail: rektorat@lmu.de
Website: http://www.uni-muenchen.de

Präsident: Bernd Huber (2002-)
Tel: +49(89) 2180-2412, Fax: +49(89) 2180-3656
EMail: praesidium@lmu.de

Kanzler: Christoph Mülke
Tel: +49(89) 2180-3269, Fax: +49(89) 2180-6324
EMail: kanzler@lmu.de

International Relations: Stephan Fuchs
Tel: +49(89) 2180-2823, Fax: +49(89) 2180-3136
EMail: international@lmu.de

Centres

Applied Policy Research *(CAP)*; **Bioimaging** *(BIZ)* (Biotechnology); **Digital Technology and Management** *(CDTM)*; **Gene** (Genetics) *Head*: Patrick Cramer; **Geobiology and Biodiversity Research** *(Geobio)*; **Human Science** *(HWZ)*; **Information and Language Processing** *(CIS)* (Computer Science) *Head*: Franz Guenthner; **Internet Research and Media Integration** *(ZIM)* (Information Technology; Media Studies); **Japan** (Japanese) *Head*: Peter Pörtner; **Nanoscience** *(CeNS)*; **Teacher Education** (Teacher Training) *Head*: Kristina Reiss; **Theoretical Physics** *(Anold-Sommerfeld (ASC))*

Faculties

Biology (Biology; Botany; Genetics; Zoology); **Business Administration** (Business Administration); **Catholic Theology** (Catholic Theology); **Chemistry and Pharmacy** (Biochemistry; Chemistry; Nutrition; Pharmacy); **Cultural Sciences** (Cultural Studies); **Economics** (Economics); **Geosciences** (Earth Sciences); **History and the Arts** (Art History; Fine Arts); **Languages and Literatures** (Classical Languages; Comparative Literature; English; German; Indic Languages; Nordic Studies; Phonetics; Romance Languages; Slavic Languages); **Law** (Law); **Mathematics, Computer Science and Statistics** (Computer Science; Mathematics; Science Education; Statistics); **Medicine** (Dentistry; Medicine); **Philosophy, Philosophy of Science and Religious Science** (Philosophy; Religious Studies); **Physics** (Astronomy and Space Science; Meteorology; Physics); **Protestant Theology** (Protestant Theology); **Psychology and Educational Sciences** (Educational Sciences; Pedagogy; Psychology); **Social Sciences** (American Studies; Behavioural Sciences; Mass Communication; Media Studies; Political Sciences; Social Sciences; Sociology); **Veterinary Science** (Veterinary Science)

Laboratories

Nuclear Physics-High Energy Physics (Natural Sciences; Nuclear Physics)

History: Founded 1472 at Ingolstadt by Duke Ludwig, the Wealthy, transferred to Landshut 1800 by Elector Max IV Joseph, later King Maximilian I, and to Munich 1826 by King Ludwig I. An autonomous institution financially supported by the State of Bavaria, and under the jurisdiction of its Ministry for Sciences, Research and Arts.

Governing Bodies: Senat; Rektoratskollegium

Academic Year: October to July (October to February; April to July)

Admission Requirements: Secondary school certificate (Reifezeugnis) or equivalent

Fees: (Euros): 1,000 per annum; Administrative fee 100 and student welfare union 70 per annum

Main Language(s) of Instruction: German and English

International Co-operation: Participates in the Erasmus programme. With some 100 universities outside Europe

Degrees and Diplomas: *Bachelor/Bakkalaureus*: 3 yrs; *Diplom*: Bioinformatics, 41/2 yrs; *Diplom*: Biology; Business Teaching Qualification; Computer Science; Economics; Mathematics; Media Informatics; Psychology; Publishing Studies; Orthodox Theology; Sociology; Statistics; Theatre Studies, 4 1/2 yrs; *Diplom*: Catholic Theology, 5 yrs; *Lehramt*: Teaching Qualification; *Magister Artium*: Humanities, 4 1/2 years; *Staatsprüfung*: Dentistry, 5 yrs; *Staatsprüfung*: Law, 4 1/2 yrs; *Staatsprüfung*: Medicine, 6 yrs; *Staatsprüfung*: Pharmacy, 4 yrs; *Staatsprüfung*: Veterinary Medicine, 5 1/2 yrs; *Lizentiat*: Theology, 3 yrs; *Master/Magister*: 1-2 yrs; *Promotion*: Canon Law (Dr.jur.can.); Dentistry (Dr.med.dent.); Economic Sciences (Dr.rer.pol.); Human Biology (Dr.rer.biol.hum.); Law (Dr.jur.); Medicine (Dr.med.); Natural Sciences (Dr.rer.nat); Philosophy (Dr.phil.); Public Economics (Dr.oec.publ.); Theology (Cath. and Prot.) (Dr.theol.); Veterinary Medicine (Dr.med.vet.); *Habilitation*: 3 yrs or more following Doktor

Student Services: Academic counselling, Canteen, Employment services, Foreign student adviser, Handicapped facilities, Nursery care, Social counselling, Sports facilities

Student Residential Facilities: Yes

Special Facilities: Observatories. Botanical garden

Libraries: University Library, c. 2.4m. vols; faculty libraries, c. 4.2m vols

Publications: Münchener Universitätsschriften (Monograph Series) *(monthly)*

Press or Publishing House: Pressereferat

Last Updated: 21/01/10

LUDWIGSHAFEN UNIVERSITY OF APPLIED SCIENCES

Fachhochschule Ludwigshafen am Rhein

Ernst-Boehe-Str. 4, 67059 Ludwigshafen am Rhein
Tel: +49(621) 5203-0
Fax: +49(621) 6224-67
EMail: verw@fh-ludwigshafen.de
Website: http://www.fh-ludwigshafen.de

Präsident: Hans-Ulrich Dallmann
Tel: +49(621) 5203-144, Fax: +49(621) 5203-200
EMail: praesident@fh-lu.de

Kanzler: Norbert Reichert
Tel: +49(621) 5203-142 EMail: kanzler@fh-lu.de

Faculties

Management, Controlling and Health Care *(Fachbereich I)* (Business Computing; Health Sciences; Information Technology; Management); Marketing and Human Resources *(Fachbereich II)* (Human Resources; International Business; Marketing); Services and Consulting *(Fachbereich III)*; Social Work and Social Welfare *(Fachbereich IV)*

History: Founded 1996. Integrated the Ludwigshafen Protestant University of Applied Sciences (Evangelische Fachhochschule Ludwigshafen) as Faculty of Social work and Social Welfare 2008.

Main Language(s) of Instruction: German

Degrees and Diplomas: *Bachelor/Bakkalaureus*; *Diplom (FH)*; *Master/Magister*

Last Updated: 06/02/12

LÜBECK UNIVERSITY OF APPLIED SCIENCES

Fachhochschule Lübeck

Mönkhofer Weg 239, 23562 Lübeck
Tel: +49(451) 300-6
Fax: +49(451) 300-5100
EMail: praesidium@fh-luebeck.de
Website: http://www.fh-luebeck.de

Rektor: Stefan Bartels
Tel: +49(451) 300-5300, Fax: +49(451) 300-5082
EMail: bartels@fh-luebeck.de

Kanzler: André Bösch
Tel: +49(451) 300-5002 EMail: boesch@fh-luebeck.de

International Relations: Dagmar Diehl, Head, Office of International Affairs Tel: +49(451) 300-5098 EMail: diehl@fh-luebeck.de

Departments

Applied Natural Sciences (Biomedical Engineering; Chemical Engineering; Environmental Engineering; Physical Engineering); Construction Engineering; Electronic Engineering and Computer Science (Automation and Control Engineering; Energy Engineering; Information Technology; Media Studies); Mechanical Engineering and Economics (Economics; Machine Building; Mechanical Engineering)

History: Founded 1969.

Main Language(s) of Instruction: German

International Co-operation: With institutions in China; Denmark; Finland; France; Ghana; Ireland; Latvia; Sweden; Spain; USA

Degrees and Diplomas: *Bachelor/Bakkalaureus*; *Diplom (FH)*: Electronic Engineering, Energy Systems and Automation; Information Technology and Design; Communication Engineering, Information and Media Technology; *Master/Magister*: Media Informatics Online; Applied Information Technology

Last Updated: 06/02/12

LUTHERAN UNIVERSITY OF APPLIED SCIENCES IN NUREMBERG

Evangelische Fachhochschule Nürnberg

Bärenschanzstrasse 4, 90429 Nürnberg
Tel: +49(911) 27253-6
Fax: +49(911) 27253-799
EMail: zentrale@evfh-nuernberg.de
Website: http://www.evfh-nuernberg.de/

Präsident: Hans-Joachim Puch
Tel: +49(911) 27253-700
EMail: hans-joachim.puch@evfh-nuernberg.de

Kanzler: Kurt Füglein
Tel: +49(911) 27253-777 EMail: kurt.fueglein@evfh-nuernberg.de

International Relations: Dorothea Guethner, Vizepräsidentin
Tel: +49(911) 27253-834
EMail: dorothea.geuthner@evfh-nuernberg.de

Faculties

Health and Care (Health Administration; Health Education; Nursing; Rehabilitation and Therapy); Religious Education (Adult Education; Religious Education); Social Sciences (Business Administration; Social Work; Special Education)

History: Founded 1971.

Main Language(s) of Instruction: German

Degrees and Diplomas: *Bachelor/Bakkalaureus*; *Master/Magister*: Adult Education; Social Management

Last Updated: 31/01/12

MACROMEDIA UNIVERSITY FOR MEDIA AND COMMUNICATION

Macromedia Hochschule für Medien und Kommunikation

Gollierstraße 4, 80339 München
Tel: +49(89) 544-151-0
Fax: +49(89) 544-151-15
EMail: info.muc@macromedia.de
Website: http://www.macromedia.de

Präsident: Herbert Schmid-Eickhoff EMail: hse@macromedia.de

Kanzler: Joachim Scheurer EMail: j.scheurer@macromedia.de

Programmes

Digital Media Production (Computer Science; Design; Information Technology; Media Studies; Software Engineering); Film and Television (Film; Radio and Television Broadcasting); Journalism (Cultural Studies; Economics; Journalism; Sports); Media Management (Communication Studies; Management; Media Studies; Music; Radio and Television Broadcasting; Sports Management)

Further Information: Also campuses in Stuttgart, Cologne, Hamburg, Berlin, Osnabruck.

History: Founded 2006.

Main Language(s) of Instruction: German

Degrees and Diplomas: *Bachelor/Bakkalaureus*; *Master/Magister*
Last Updated: 21/01/10

MAGDEBURG-STENDAL UNIVERSITY OF APPLIED SCIENCES

Hochschule Magdeburg-Stendal

Postfach 3655, 39011 Magdeburg, Sachsen-Anhalt
Tel: +49(391) 8864-01
Fax: +49(391) 8864-04
EMail: poststelle@hs-magdeburg.de
Website: http://www.hs-magdeburg.de

Rektor: Andreas Geiger (1998-)
Tel: +49(391) 886-4100, Fax: +49(391) 886-4104
EMail: rektor@hs-magdeburg.de

Kanzler: Frank Richter
Tel: +49(391) 8864-103, Fax: +49(391) 8864-104
EMail: kanzler@hs-magdeburg.de

International Relations: Marita Sand
Tel: +49(391) 8864-252, Fax: +49(391) 8864-253
EMail: marita.sand@hs-magdeburg.de

Departments

Engineering and Industrial Design *(Magdeburg)* (Design; Engineering; Industrial Design); **Applied Human Sciences** *(Stendal)* (Child Care and Development; Psychology; Rehabilitation and Therapy); **Civil Engineering** *(Magdeburg)* (Civil Engineering); **Communication and Media** *(Magdeburg)* (Communication Studies; Media Studies; Translation and Interpretation); **Economics** *(Stendal)* (Business Administration; Economics; Health Administration); **Social and Health Studies** *(Magdeburg)* (Public Health; Rehabilitation and Therapy; Social Sciences; Social Work; Special Education); **Water and Waste Management** *(Magdeburg)* (Waste Management; Water Management)

History: Founded 1991. Fachhoschule Magdeburg unites different schools of former GDR in Magdeburg. Renamed Hochschule Magdeburg-Stendal 2000.

Governing Bodies: Senate; Commissions

Academic Year: October to July

Admission Requirements: Secondary school certificate (Abitur) or equivalent.

Fees: (Euros): 53.11

Main Language(s) of Instruction: German

International Co-operation: With universities in Spain, United Kingdom, USA, Argentina, Poland, China, Finland, Cuba, Ghana, Peru, Jordan. Also participates in Erasmus-Socrates programmes.

Degrees and Diplomas: *Bachelor/Bakkalaureus*: Applied Health Science (BSc), 3 1/2 yrs (part-time distance); *Bachelor/Bakkalaureus*: Business Administration, 3 yrs, 31/2 yrs (distance course); *Bachelor/Bakkalaureus*: Business Engineering; Mechanical Engineering (Beng), 31/2 yrs; *Bachelor/Bakkalaureus*: Civil Engineering; Electrical Engineering; Systems Engineering (Beng); Court Interpreting; Sign Language Interpreting; Translation, Business and Languages (BA); Safety and Hazard Defence; Statistics (BSc); Social Insurance Management, 3 1/2 yrs; *Bachelor/Bakkalaureus*: Health Promotion and Management; Journalism; Industrial Design; Social Work (BA); Rehabilitation Psychology, 3 yrs; *Master/Magister*: Ecological Engineering; Regenerative Engineering; Safety Engineering; Water Management (MSc), 1 1/2 yrs; *Master/Magister*: European Perspectives on Social Inclusion; Media Management; Rehabilitation and Theraphy; Social Security Management, a further 2 yrs; *Master/Magister*: Health Business Administration (MSc), 2 yrs (distance course); *Master/Magister*: Health Promotion; Social work (MA), 2 yrs

Student Services: Academic counselling, Canteen, Foreign student adviser, Foreign Studies Centre, Handicapped facilities, Language programs, Social counselling, Sports facilities

Student Residential Facilities: Yes

Libraries: Yes

Publications: Treffpunkt Campus *(quarterly)*
Last Updated: 20/01/10

MANNHEIM UNIVERSITY OF APPLIED SCIENCES

Hochschule Mannheim

Windeckstrasse 110, 68163 Mannheim, Baden-Württemberg
Tel: +49(621) 2926-111
Fax: +49(621) 2926-420
EMail: info@hs-mannheim.de
Website: http://www.hs-mannheim.de

Rektor: Dieter Leonhard
Tel: +49(621) 2926-401, Fax: +49(621) 2926-425
EMail: rektor@hs-mannheim.de

Kanzlerin: Birgitt Schulz
Tel: +49(621) 292-6378, Fax: +49(621) 292-6410
EMail: kanzlerin@hs-mannheim.de

International Relations: Annette Flach, Head, International Office
Tel: +49(621) 2926-6447 EMail: a.flach@hs-mannheim.de

Departments

Biotechnology (Biotechnology); **Chemical Process Engineering** (Chemical Engineering); **Computer Science** (Computer Science); **Design** (Design); **Electrical Engineering** (Automation and Control Engineering; Computer Science; Electrical Engineering; Electronic Engineering; Energy Engineering; Information Technology); **Engi-**

neering and Management (Engineering; Management); **Information Engineering** (Information Technology); **Mechanical Engineering** (Mechanical Engineering); **Social Work** (Social Sciences; Social Work)

History: Founded 1898. Merged with the Mannheim University of Applied Sciences for Social Studies (Fachhochschule Mannheim - Hochschule für Sozialwesen) 2006.

Main Language(s) of Instruction: German

Degrees and Diplomas: *Bachelor/Bakkalaureus*; *Master/Magister*
Last Updated: 20/01/10

MANNHEIM UNIVERSITY OF MUSIC AND PERFORMING ARTS

Staatliche Hochschule für Musik und Darstellende Kunst Mannheim

68161 Mannheim, Baden-Württemberg
Tel: +49(621) 292-3512
Fax: +49(621) 292-2072
EMail: rektorat@muho-mannheim.de
Website: http://www.muho-mannheim.de

Rektor: Rudolf Meister (1997-)
Tel: +49(621) 292-3511 EMail: praesidium@muho-mannheim.de

Kanzler: Thilo Fischer
Tel: +49(621) 292-3510 EMail: fischer@muho-mannheim.de

International Relations: Thilo Fischer

Divisions

Music and Dance (Conducting; Dance; Jazz and Popular Music; Music; Music Education; Music Theory and Composition; Musical Instruments; Musicology; Opera; Singing; Teacher Training)

History: Founded 1762. Acquired present status 1971

Governing Bodies: Hochschulrat, Senat, Rektorat

Academic Year: October to July

Admission Requirements: Secondary school certificate (Abitur) and entrance examination

Fees: (Euros): 84 per semester

Main Language(s) of Instruction: German

International Co-operation: With universities in European Countries, USA, China, Republic Korea, Russian Federation

Degrees and Diplomas: *Bachelor/Bakkalaureus*; *Master/Magister*. Also Diplom Aufbaustudiengang in Music and Dance, 1/2 yrs

Student Services: Academic counselling, Canteen, Cultural centre, Foreign student adviser, Foreign Studies Centre, Nursery care, Social counselling, Sports facilities

Student Residential Facilities: Yes

Special Facilities: 2 Recording Studios

Libraries: Yes

Publications: Mannheim Hochschulschriften *(other/irregular)*

Press or Publishing House: Palatium Verlag
Last Updated: 26/01/10

MARTIN LUTHER UNIVERSITY HALLE-WITTENBERG

Martin-Luther-Universität Halle-Wittenberg

Universitätsplatz 10, 06099 Halle, Saale
Tel: +49(345) 552-0
Fax: +49(345) 552-7075
EMail: nr2@verwaltung.uni-halle.de
Website: http://www.uni-halle.de

Rektor: Udo Sträter (2010-) EMail: rektor@uni-halle.de

Kanzler: Martin Hecht
Tel: +49(345) 552-1011, Fax: +49(345) 552-7076
EMail: kanzler@uni-halle.de

International Relations: Manfred Pichler
Tel: +49(345) 552-1313, Fax: +49(345) 552-7052
EMail: auslandsamt@uni-halle.de

Centres

European Enlightenment International Research (European Studies)

Faculties

Arts and Humanities I (Ethnology; Japanese; Oriental Studies; Philosophy; Political Sciences; Psychology; Sociology); **Arts and Humanities II** (American Studies; Arts and Humanities; Communication Studies; English; English Studies; Media Studies; Music; Philology; Phonetics; Romance Languages; Slavic Languages; Sports); **Arts and Humanities III** (Arts and Humanities; Education; Educational Sciences; Pedagogy; Teacher Training); **Engineering** (Engineering); **Law and Economics** (Business Computing; Economics; Law); **Medicine** (Anatomy; Dentistry; Genetics; Hygiene; Medicine; Occupational Therapy; Pathology; Pharmacology; Physiology; Toxicology); **Natural Sciences I** (Biochemistry; Biology; Biotechnology; Natural Sciences; Pharmacy); **Natural Sciences II** (Chemistry; Mathematics; Physics); **Natural Sciences III** (Agriculture; Computer Science; Food Science; Geology; Mathematics; Natural Sciences); **Theology** (Archaeology; Bible; Religious Art; Religious Studies; Theology)

Further Information: Also International College Summer Course: Institute of German Language and Culture

History: Universität Wittenberg founded 1502, Universität Halle founded 1694. Merged 1817. Title changed to Martin-Luther-Universität 1933. Responsible to the Ministry of Education and Culture of the Federal State of Saxony-Anhalt.

Governing Bodies: Konzil, Senate

Academic Year: October to September (October-March; April-September)

Admission Requirements: Secondary school certificate (Reifezeugnis) or equivalent

Fees: None

Main Language(s) of Instruction: German

International Co-operation: With universities in the USA, Russian Federation and Japan. Also participates in Erasmus.

Degrees and Diplomas: *Bachelor/Bakkalaureus*: Science in Economics, 3 yrs; *Diplom*: 4-5 yrs; *Konzertexamen*; *Staatsprüfung*: Dentistry; Medicine, 6 yrs; *Master/Magister*: 4 1/2 yrs; *Promotion*; *Habilitation*

Student Services: Academic counselling, Canteen, Foreign student adviser, Handicapped facilities, Language programs, Social counselling, Sports facilities

Student Residential Facilities: For c. 2,500 students

Special Facilities: Archaeological Museum; Museum für mitteldeutsche Erdgeschichte mit Geiseltalsammlung. Zoological Collections. Botanical Garden. Julius-Kühn Collection

Libraries: University and State Library c. 5m. vols; Bibliothek der Deutschen-Morgenländischen-Gesellschaft, c. 53,000 vols; Institute libraries, c. 2,3m. vols

Last Updated: 03/02/12

MEDIADESIGN UNIVERSITY OF APPLIED SCIENCES

Mediadesign Hochschule für Design und Informatik (MD.H)
Lindenstrasse 20-25, 10969 Berlin
Tel: +49(30) 399-2660
Fax: +49(30) 399-26615
EMail: info-ber@mediadesign-fh.de
Website: http://www.mediadesign.de

Rektor: Hartmut Bode

Kanzler: Arnim Zubke

Programmes

Digital Film Design - Animation (Film; Visual Arts); **Fashion Design** (Fashion Design); **Gamedesign** (Computer Graphics; Mathematics); **Media Design** (Communication Arts; Design; Visual Arts); **Media Management** (Communication Studies; Journalism; Marketing; Mathematics; Media Studies)

Further Information: Also sites in München und Düsseldorf.

Governing Bodies: University Board (Hochschulsrat)

Fees: (Euros): 349-799 per month; registration fee, 350.

Degrees and Diplomas: *Bachelor/Bakkalaureus*: Mode Design; Media Design; Media Management; Game Design; Media Infor-

matics; *Master/Magister*: Media Design; Media Management; Game Design

Last Updated: 21/01/10

MERSEBURG UNIVERSITY OF APPLIED SCIENCES

Hochschule Merseburg
Geusaer Strasse, 06217 Merseburg
Tel: +49(3461) 46-2902
Fax: +49(3461) 46-2906
EMail: rektorat@hs-merseburg.de
Website: http://www.hs-merseburg.de

Rektor: Heinz W. Zwanziger (2000-)
Tel: +49(3461) 46-2902, Fax: +49(3461) 46-2906

Kanzler: Bernd Janson
Tel: +49(3461) 46-2901 EMail: kanzler@hs-merseburg.de

International Relations: Uwe Schiffke
Tel: +49(3461) 46-2294 EMail: uwe.schiffke@hs-merseburg.de

Departments

Computer Science and Communication Systems (Automation and Control Engineering; Communication Studies; Computer Networks; Computer Science; Media Studies); **Economics** (Business Administration; Economics; Management); **Engineering and Natural Sciences** (Business Administration; Chemical Engineering; Electronic Engineering; Engineering; Environmental Engineering; Industrial Engineering; Mechanical Engineering; Physics); **Social Work, Media and Culture** (Cultural Studies; Media Studies; Social Work)

History: Founded 1992.

Admission Requirements: Secondary school certificate (Fachhochschulreifezeugnis)

Fees: None

Main Language(s) of Instruction: German

International Co-operation: With universities in Belgium; Ireland; United Kingdom; France; Portugal; China; Poland; Romania; Russian Federation; Czech Republic and USA. Also participates in Erasmus, Leonardo and Tempus

Degrees and Diplomas: *Bachelor/Bakkalaureus (BSc)*: 6 sem; *Master/Magister*: a further 4 sem. Also Certificates 2-4 sem

Student Services: Academic counselling, Canteen, Cultural centre, Foreign student adviser, Foreign Studies Centre, Handicapped facilities, Language programs, Social counselling, Sports facilities

Student Residential Facilities: Yes

Special Facilities: German Chemistry Museum. Movie studio

Libraries: Main Library
Last Updated: 20/01/10

MERZ ACADEMY - UNIVERSITY OF APPLIED ARTS STUTTGART

Merz Akademie
Teckstrasse 58, 70190 Stuttgart
Tel: +49(771) 26866-0
Fax: +49(771) 26866-21
EMail: info@merz-akademie.de
Website: http://www.merz-akademie.de

Rektor: Markus Merz (1981-)
Tel: +49(771) 26866-20 EMail: markus.merz@merz-akademie.de

Verwaltungsleiter: Stefan Grünenwald
Tel: +49(771) 26866-28
EMail: stefan.gruenenwald@merz-akademie.de

Programmes

Design, Art and Media (Design; Film; Graphic Design; Media Studies; Video)

History: Founded 1918. Acquired present status 1985.

Academic Year: October to February; March to July

Admission Requirements: Fachhochschulreife

Fees: (Euros): 330 per semester

Main Language(s) of Instruction: German

Degrees and Diplomas: *Bachelor/Bakkalaureus*: 4 yrs; *Master/Magister*: Media Design (EMMA), 1 1/2 yrs

Student Services: Academic counselling, Canteen, Foreign student adviser, Social counselling

Student Residential Facilities: None

Libraries: Yes
Last Updated: 23/02/09

MITTWEIDA UNIVERSITY OF APPLIED SCIENCES

Hochschule Mittweida
Technikumplatz 17, 09644 Mittweida
Tel: +49(3727) 58-0
Fax: +49(3727) 58-1379
EMail: kontakt@htwm.de
Website: http://www.htwm.de

Rektor: Lothar Otto
Tel: +49(3727) 58-1202, Fax: +49(3727) 58-1217
EMail: rektor@hs-mittweida.de

Kanzlerin: Sylvia Bässler
Tel: +49(3727) 58-1206, Fax: +49(3727) 58-1433
EMail: kanzler@hs-mittweida.de

International Relations: Saskia Langhammer
Tel: +49(3727) 948 -137, Fax: +49(3727) 948 -143
EMail: langhamm@htwm.de

Faculties
Economics (Business Administration; Economics); **Information Technology and Electrical Engineering** (Automation and Control Engineering; Electrical Engineering; Electronic Engineering; Energy Engineering; Industrial Engineering; Information Technology; Microelectronics; Multimedia; Power Engineering; Telecommunications Engineering); **Mathematics, Physics and Computer Science** (Applied Mathematics; Biomedical Engineering; Computer Engineering; Computer Networks; Environmental Engineering; Laser Engineering; Mathematics; Physics; Software Engineering; Sound Engineering (Acoustics)); **Mechanical Engineering** (Mechanical Engineering); **Media Studies** (Media Studies); **Social Work** (Social Work)

History: Founded 1867.

Academic Year: September to July (September-January; March-July)

Admission Requirements: Secondary school certificate (Reifezeugnis)

Fees: None

Main Language(s) of Instruction: German

International Co-operation: With universities in Africa, Asia and America. Also participates in Socrates/ Erasmus.

Degrees and Diplomas: *Zertifikat*; *Bachelor/Bakkalaureus*: Business; Engineering; Media; Social Work; Heath Sciences; Film and Television, 3 yrs; *Diplom (FH)*: Business Engineering; Information Technology; Mechanical Engineering;, 4 yrs; *Master/Magister*: Mathematics; Electronic Engineering; Industrial Management; Computer Science; Information and Communication Science; Mechanical Engineering; Physical Engineering; Social Work; Social Management, A further 2 yrs

Student Services: Canteen, Foreign student adviser, Language programs, Sports facilities

Student Residential Facilities: Yes

Special Facilities: Laser Application Centre, TV and Radio Studio, Centre for Biokinetic Medical Engineering

Libraries: 90,000 vols
Last Updated: 20/01/10

MUNICH BUSINESS SCHOOL

Elsenheimerstrasse 61, 80687 München
Tel: +49(89) 54 76 78 0
Fax: +49(89) 54 76 78 26
EMail: info@munich-business-school.debusiness-school.de
Website: http://www.munich-business-school.de

Präsident: Rudolf Gröger

Programmes
Health Care Management (Health Administration; Management); **International Business** (International Business); **Management** (Management)

History: Founded 1991.

Main Language(s) of Instruction: German

Degrees and Diplomas: *Bachelor/Bakkalaureus*; *Master/Magister*
Last Updated: 13/02/09

MUNICH SCHOOL OF PHILOSOPHY

Hochschule für Philosophie München
Kaulbachstrasse 31, 80539 München
Tel: +49(89) 2386-2300
Fax: +49(89) 2386-2302
EMail: admin@hfph.mwn.de
Website: http://www.hfph.mwn.de

Rektor: Johannes Wallacher
Tel: +49(89) 2386-2310 EMail: rektor@hfph.mwn.de

Institutes
Communications and Media Research *(IKE)* (Communication Studies; Media Studies); **Philosophy of Religion** *(IRP)* (Philosophy; Religion); **Scientific Issues related to Philosophy and Theology** *(ING)* (Philosophy; Theology); **Social and Development Studies** *(IGP)* (Development Studies; Social Studies)

History: Founded 1925. Acquired present status 1971.

Governing Bodies: Hochschulrat

Main Language(s) of Instruction: German

Degrees and Diplomas: *Bachelor/Bakkalaureus*: Philosophy, 2 yrs; *Master/Magister*: Philosophy, a further 2- 2 1/2 yrs; *Promotion*: Philosophy, 4-5 yrs

Publications: Theologie und Philosophie *(biennially)*
Last Updated: 19/01/10

MUNICH UNIVERSITY OF APPLIED SCIENCES

Hochschule München
Lothstrasse 34, 80335 München
Tel: +49(89) 1265-0
Fax: +49(89) 1265-3000
EMail: verw@hm.edu
Website: http://www.fh-muenchen.de

Präsident: Michael Kortstock
Tel: +49(89) 1265-1133, Fax: +49(89) 1265-2000
EMail: praesident@hm.edu; monika.wildenhain@hm.edu

Kanzler: Kai Wülbern
Tel: +49(89) 1265-1294, Fax: +49(89) 1265-1300
EMail: kanzler@hm.edu

Departments
Applied Social Sciences (Educational and Student Counselling; Management; Nursing; Social Sciences; Social Work); **Architecture** (Architecture); **Business Administration** (Business Administration); **Civil Engineering** (Civil Engineering; Construction Engineering; Structural Architecture); **Computer Science and Mathematics** (Business Computing; Computer Science; Mathematics and Computer Science); **Design** (Communication Arts; Industrial Design; Photography); **Electrical Engineering and Information Technology** (Electrical Engineering; Information Technology; Systems Analysis); **General Studies** (English; Foreign Languages Education; German; Modern Languages; Music); **Geoinformatics** (Surveying and Mapping); **Mechanical, Automotive and Aeronautical Engineering** (Aeronautical and Aerospace Engineering; Automation and Control Engineering; Mechanical Engineering); **Precision-and-Micro-Engineering, Physical Engineering; Supply Engineering, Process Engineering, Printing and Media Technology** (Chemical Engineering; Media Studies; Packaging Technology; Paper Technology; Printing and Printmaking; Waste Management); **Tourism** (Hotel Management; Tourism)

History: Founded 1971.

Degrees and Diplomas: *Bachelor/Bakkalaureus*; *Diplom (FH)*; *Master/Magister*
Last Updated: 02/02/12

MUNICH UNIVERSITY OF TECHNOLOGY
Technische Universität München
Arcisstrasse 21, 80333 München
Tel: +49(89) 289-01
Fax: +49(89) 2892-2000
EMail: postmaster@tu-muenchen.de
Website: http://www.tum.de

Präsident: Wolfgang A. Herrmann (1999-)
Tel: +49(89) 2892-2200, Fax: +49(89) 2892-3399
EMail: Praesident@tum.de

Kanzler: Albert Berger
Tel: +49(89) 2892-2203, Fax: +49(89) 2892-8300
EMail: kanzler@tum.de

International Relations: Edmund Cmiel
Tel: +49(89) 2892-5330, Fax: +49(89) 2892-5331
EMail: cmiel@zv.tum.de

Faculties
Architecture (Architecture); **Business Administration** (Business Administration); **Chemistry** *(Garching)* (Biochemistry; Chemistry); **Civil Engineering and Surveying** (Civil Engineering; Surveying and Mapping); **Electrical Engineering and Information Technology** (Automation and Control Engineering; Electrical Engineering; Information Technology; Power Engineering); **Informatics** (Computer Science); **Life and Food Sciences** (Biological and Life Sciences; Food Science); **Mathematics** (Mathematical Physics; Mathematics; Mathematics and Computer Science; Statistics); **Mechanical Engineering** (Mechanical Engineering); **Medicine** (Medicine); **Physics** *(Garching)* (Biophysics; Physics); **Sports Science** (Sports)

Further Information: Also Teaching Hospital

History: Founded 1827 as Polytechnische Zentralschule, became Polytechnische Schule 1868, Technische Hochschule 1877 and University 1970. An autonomous institution under the jurisdiction of the State of Bavaria.

Governing Bodies: Board of Directors; Extended Board of Directors; Executive Supervisory Board

Academic Year: October to September (October-March; April-September)

Admission Requirements: Secondary school certificate (Reifezeugnis) or equivalent

Fees: (Euros): 500

Main Language(s) of Instruction: German

International Co-operation: With universities in Europe; Asia; Latin America; United States. Participates in Socrates, Tempus, Laotse, Innovative Multi-Cultural Curricula (IMCC), American European Engineering Exchange Program (AE3), Latin American European Engineering Exchange Program (LAE3)

Degrees and Diplomas: *Bachelor/Bakkalaureus (BSc)*: 3 yrs; *Diplom (Dipl.-ing.agr.)*: 4 1/2 yrs; *Staatsprüfung*: Teaching qualification, secondary level, 3 1/2 - 4 1/2 yrs; *Master/Magister (MSc)*: a further 1 1/2-2 yrs; *Doktorgrad (Dr.agr.)*: at least 2 yrs after end of studies; *Habilitation (Habil.)*: at least 2 yrs of scientific research following Doktor. Also Double Degrees

Student Services: Academic counselling, Canteen, Cultural centre, Employment services, Foreign student adviser, Foreign Studies Centre, Handicapped facilities, Health services, Language programs, Nursery care, Social counselling, Sports facilities

Libraries: University Library, c. 1.7m. vols., 3,600 print journal subscriptions; 3,500 e-journal subscriptions; 37,000 electronic media
Last Updated: 18/01/07

MÜNSTER UNIVERSITY OF APPLIED SCIENCES
Fachhochschule Münster
Hüfferstrasse 27, 48149 Münster
Tel: +49(251) 83-0
Fax: +49(251) 8364-060
EMail: verwaltung@fh-muenster.de
Website: http://www.fh-muenster.de

Präsidentin: Ute von Lojewski
Tel: +49(251) 8364-64050, Fax: +49(251) 8364-64060
EMail: praesidium@fh-muenster.de

Kanzler: Werner Jubelius
Tel: +49(251) 8364-000, Fax: +49(251) 8364-001
EMail: jubelius@fh-muenster.de

International Relations: Nicole Strate-Speidel
Tel: +49(251) 8364-102, Fax: +49(251) 8364-104
EMail: internationaloffice@fh-muenster.de; strate@fh-muenster.de

Faculties
Architecture (Architecture); **Business Administration**; **Chemical Engineering** (Chemical Engineering; Industrial Engineering); **Civil Engineering** (Civil Engineering); **Design** (Design); **Electrical Engineering and Computer Science** (Computer Science; Electrical Engineering); **Energy, Building and Environmental Engineering**; **Home Economics and Nutrition** (Home Economics; Nutrition); **Mechanical Engineering** (Mechanical Engineering); **Nursing and Health** (Health Sciences; Nursing); **Physical Engineering** (Physical Engineering); **Social Studies** (Social Studies)

Institutes
Logistics and Facility Management (Management; Transport Management); **Professional Teacher's Education**; **Technical Business Administration**

History: Founded 1971.

Admission Requirements: Fachhochschulreife, Abitur

Main Language(s) of Instruction: German, English

International Co-operation: Participates in Socrates/Erasmus, Deutsch-Französische Hochschulen, European Business Programme

Degrees and Diplomas: *Bachelor/Bakkalaureus*; *Master/Magister*

Student Services: Academic counselling, Canteen, Cultural centre, Employment services, Foreign student adviser, Foreign Studies Centre, Language programs, Nursery care

Publications: F(h)orum *(quarterly)*
Last Updated: 06/02/12

MUTHESIUS ACADEMY OF FINE ARTS AND DESIGN
Muthesius Kunsthochschule
Lorentzendamm 6-8, 24103 Kiel
Tel: +49(431) 5198-400
Fax: +49(431) 5198-408
EMail: presse@muthesius.de
Website: http://www.muthesius.de

Präsident: Rainer W. Ernst
Tel: +49(431) 5198-401 EMail: rwernst@muthesius.de

Kanzler: Dirk Mirow
Tel: +49(431) 5198-409, Fax: +49(431) 5198-459
EMail: mirow@muthesius.de

International Relations: Maud Zieschang, International Relations Officer
Tel: +49(431) 5198-501, Fax: +49(431) 5198-408
EMail: fernweh@muthesius.de

Centres
Media (Media Studies)

Programmes
Art Education (Art Education); **Design** (Industrial Design); **Fine Arts** (Ceramic Art; Fine Arts; Graphic Arts; Painting and Drawing; Sculpture); **Spatial Structuring/Interior Design** (Architecture; Interior Design)

History: Founded 1907 as Werkkunstschule. Acquired present status 2005.

Governing Bodies: Konsistorium; Senat

Main Language(s) of Instruction: German

International Co-operation: With universities in Japan; China; Spain; Netherlands; France; Norway; Sweden; Portugal; Slovak Republic

Degrees and Diplomas: *Bachelor/Bakkalaureus*; *Diplom*; *Diplom*: 5 yrs; *Master/Magister*; *Promotion*: Communciation Studies

Student Services: Academic counselling, Canteen, Foreign student adviser, Foreign Studies Centre

Libraries: Yes
Last Updated: 21/01/10

NEUBRANDENBURG UNIVERSITY OF APPLIED SCIENCES

Hochschule Neubrandenburg

PO Box 110121, Brodaer Strasse 2, 17041 Neubrandenburg
Tel: +49(395) 5693-0
Fax: +49(395) 5693-199
EMail: presse@fhs-nb.de
Website: http://www.hs-nb.de

Rektor: Micha Teuscher
Tel: +49(395) 5693-101, Fax: +49(395) 5693-105
EMail: rektor@hs-nb.de

Kanzler: Rudolf Zimmer
Tel: +49(395) 5693-107, Fax: +49(395) 5693-109
EMail: kanzler@hs-nb.de

International Relations: Dorina Mackedanz, Head
Tel: +49(395) 5693-126, Fax: +49(395) 5693-125
EMail: aaa@hs.nb.de

Departments

Agriculture and Food Technology (Agriculture; Food Technology); **Health, Nursing, Management** (Health Administration; Health Sciences; Nursing); **Landscape Architecture, Geodesy, Geoinformatics and Civil Engineering** (Building Technologies; Civil Engineering; Construction Engineering; Environmental Management; Landscape Architecture; Surveying and Mapping); **Social Work and Education** (Preschool Education; Social Work)

History: Founded 1991. Acquired present status 2005.

Governing Bodies: Senate; Council

Admission Requirements: High school diploma or equivalent, knowledge of German (DSH, Test Daf)

Fees: (Euros): 3,850 per semester

Main Language(s) of Instruction: German

International Co-operation: Participates in Socrates, Erasmus, Tempus and other bilateral cooperation programmes

Accrediting Agencies: Ministry of Education, Sciences and Culture, Mecklenburg-West Pomerania

Degrees and Diplomas: *Bachelor/Bakkalaureus (BA)*: 3 yrs; *Diplom*: Social Work; *Master/Magister (MA)*: a further 2 yrs

Student Services: Academic counselling, Canteen, Employment services, Foreign student adviser, Foreign Studies Centre, Handicapped facilities, Health services, Social counselling, Sports facilities

Student Residential Facilities: Yes

Special Facilities: Multimedia Centre. Radio, Cinema, Language Centre. Computer Centre. Business Start-up Advice Office. Psychological Counselling Offices.

Libraries: University Library
Last Updated: 20/01/10

NEU-ULM UNIVERSITY OF APPLIED SCIENCES

Hochschule für Angewandte Wissenschaften Neu-Ulm

Wileystraße 1, 89231 Neu-Ulm, Bavaria
Tel: +49(731) 9762-0
Fax: +49(731) 9762-299
EMail: info@hs-neu-ulm.de
Website: http://www.hs-neu-ulm.de

Präsidentin: Uta M. Feser
Tel: +49(731) 9762-1000, Fax: +49(731) 9762-1099
EMail: uta.feser@hs-neu-ulm.de

Kanzlerin: Anke Jaeger EMail: anke.jaeger@hs-neu-ulm.de

Faculties

Business Administration and Business Engineering (Business Administration); **Information Management** (Information Management)

History: Founded 1994. Acquired present status 1998.

Academic Year: October to September (October-March; March-September)

Main Language(s) of Instruction: German

International Co-operation: With universities in USA, France, Ireland, Denmark, Spain, Switzerland, China and Portugal.

Degrees and Diplomas: *Bachelor/Bakkalaureus*; *Master/Magister*
Student Services: Canteen, Foreign student adviser
Libraries: Main Library
Last Updated: 12/01/10

NIEDERRHEIN UNIVERSITY OF APPLIED SCIENCES

Hochschule Niederrhein (HN)

PO Box 100762, Reinarzstrasse 49, 47707 Krefeld
Tel: +49(2151) 822-0
Fax: +49(2151) 822-555
EMail: rektor@hs-niederrhein.de
Website: http://www.hs-niederrhein.de

Rektor: Hans-Hennig von Grünberg
Tel: +49(2151) 822-1500, Fax: +49(2151) 822-1507

Kanzler: Kurt Kühr
Tel: +49(2151) 822-2110, Fax: +49(2151) 822-2111
EMail: kanzler@hs-niederrhein.de

International Relations: Margot Timmer
Tel: +49(2151) 822-691, Fax: +49(2151) 822-699
EMail: margot.timmer@hs-niederrhein.de

Faculties

Applied Social Sciences (Cultural Studies; Education; Management; Social Work); **Business Administration and Economics** (Business Administration; Commercial Law; Economics; Management; Taxation); **Chemistry** (Biotechnology; Chemical Engineering; Chemistry); **Design** (Design); **Electrical Engineering and Computer Science** (Computer Science; Electrical Engineering; Information Technology); **Food, Nutrition and Hospitality Sciences** (Cooking and Catering; Food Science; Nutrition); **Health Care Management** (Health Administration); **Industrial Engineering** (Industrial Engineering); **Mechanical and Process Engineering** (Electronic Engineering; Mechanical Engineering); **Textile and Clothing Technology** (Textile Technology)

History: Founded 1971.

Governing Bodies: Rektorat; Senat

Academic Year: September to August (September-February; March-August)

Admission Requirements: Secondary school certificate (Fachhochschulreife) and 3 months practical in subject of study

Fees: (Euros): 105.11 per semester

Main Language(s) of Instruction: German. Also English in BA in Textile and Clothing Management.

International Co-operation: With universities in China, Finland, France, United Kingdom, Ireland, Netherlands, Russian Federation, Spain and USA.

Degrees and Diplomas: *Bachelor/Bakkalaureus*: Business Informatics (Dipl.-Wirt.Inform.FH); Business Management Engineering, Logistics Management (Dipl.-Wirt.Ing.FH); Chemistry, Electrical and Computer Engineering, Mechanical and Process Engineering, Textile and Clothing Technology, Mechatronics (Dipl.-Ing.(FH)); Design (Dipl.-Des.(FH)); Health Care (Dipl.-Ges.Ök.(FH)); Social Management (Dipl.-Sozialw.(FH)); Social Work (Dipl.-Soz.Arb/Soz.Päd.(FH)), 4 yrs; *Bachelor/Bakkalaureus*: Business Management and Business Law (Dipl.-Betriebsw.FH), 5 yrs; *Bachelor/Bakkalaureus*: Business Studies, International Marketing (Dipl.-Kfm (FH)); Nutrition and Home Economics, Nutrition and Dietics (Dipl.-Oecotroph.(FH)), 3 1/2-4 yrs; *Bachelor/Bakkalaureus*: Chemistry and Biotechnology, Computer Engineering, Mechanical Engineering, Process Engineering, Mechatronics, Textile and Clothing Management, Cultural Studies, 3-4 yrs; *Master/Magister*: Instrumental Analysis and Laboratory Management; Information and Communication Engineering; Computer Sciences; Computer Aided Process Engineering; Textile and Clothing Management; Commercial Law; Business Engineering (MSc), 2 yrs. Also Double Degree Programmes with The Netherlands and France

Student Services: Academic counselling, Canteen, Employment services, Foreign student adviser, Handicapped facilities, Language programs, Social counselling, Sports facilities

Student Residential Facilities: Yes
Libraries: University Libraries
Publications: Report Research and Development *(biennially)*
Last Updated: 23/03/11

NORDHAUSEN UNIVERSITY OF APPLIED SCIENCES

Fachhochschule Nordhausen (FHN)
Weinberghof 4, 99734 Nordhausen
Tel: +49(3631) 420-0
Fax: +49(3631) 420-810
EMail: info@fh-nordhausen.de
Website: http://www.fh-nordhausen.de

Präsident: Jörg Wagner
Tel: +49(3631) 420-100, Fax: +49(3631) 420-812
EMail: praesident@fh-nordhausen.de

Kanzler: Hans-Wolfgang Köllmann
Tel: +49(3631) 420-200, Fax: +49(3631) 420-812
EMail: kanzler@fh-nordhausen.de

International Relations: Thomas Hoffmann
Tel: +49(3631) 420-135, Fax: +49(3631) 420-823
EMail: international@fh-nordhausen.de

Faculties

Business and Social Sciences (Business Administration; Business Education; Public Administration; Public Health; Social Sciences); **Engineering** (Energy Engineering; Environmental Engineering; Materials Engineering)

History: Founded 1997, acquired present status 1998.

Governing Bodies: Thüringer Ministerium für Wissenschaft, Forschung und Kunst (TMWFK)

Academic Year: September to August

Admission Requirements: Secondary school certificate (Abitur)

Fees: None

Main Language(s) of Instruction: German

International Co-operation: Participates in Erasmus

Degrees and Diplomas: *Bachelor/Bakkalaureus*; *Master/Magister*: Systems Engineering; Business Engineering; Innovation and Change-Management; Public Management and Governance; *Promotion*: 6 Sem.

Student Services: Academic counselling, Canteen, Cultural centre, Foreign student adviser, Foreign Studies Centre, Language programs, Sports facilities

Student Residential Facilities: Yes

Special Facilities: Language Laboratory

Libraries: c. 60,000 vols
Last Updated: 06/02/12

NORDHESSEN UNIVERSITY OF APPLIED SCIENCES, BAD SOODEN-ALLENDORF

DIPLOMA - Fachhochschule Nordhessen
Am Hegeberg 2, 37242 Bad Sooden-Allendorf
Tel: +49(5652) 9170-83
Fax: +49(5652) 9170-81
EMail: sg@diploma.de; info@diploma.de
Website: http://diploma.de

Präsident: Hans F.W. Hübner (1997-)
Tel: +49(5722) 950-526, Fax: +49(5722) 950-513

Kanzler: Bernd Blindow
Tel: +49(5722) 950-50 EMail: drg@diploma.de

International Relations: Hans F.W. Hübner

Departments

Business Administration (Business Administration; Management); **Business Law** (Business Administration; Commercial Law; Finance; Human Resources; Insurance; Law; Taxation); **Health and Social Sciences** (Ergotherapy; Gerontology; Health Sciences; Occupational Therapy; Physical Therapy; Social Sciences; Speech Therapy and Audiology)

Further Information: Also campuses in Berlin-Treptow, Bonn, Friedrichshafen, Heilbronn, Kassel, Mannheim, Nürnberg, Plauen, Schwentinental, Baden-Baden, Bochum, Bückeburg, Hannover, Kaiserslautern, Leipzig, München, Oldenburg, Regenstauf.

History: Founded 1997.

Main Language(s) of Instruction: German

Degrees and Diplomas: *Bachelor/Bakkalaureus*: Business Administration; Commercial Law; Health Sciences; *Diplom (FH)*: Ergotherapy; Physical Therapy; *Master/Magister*: Business Administration; Commercial Law; Management; *Doktorgrad*: Health Sciences; Business Administration; Law; Pedagogy
Last Updated: 06/02/12

NUREMBERG SCHOOL OF MUSIC

Hochschule für Musik Nürnberg
Veilhofstraße 34, 90489 Nürnberg
Tel: +49(911) 231-8443
Fax: +49(911) 231-7697
EMail: hfm-rektorat@stadt.nuernberg.de
Website: http://hfm-n-a.de

Präsident: Martin Ullrich (2009-)

Kanzler: Hans-Werner Ittmann
Tel: +49(911) 231-8442 EMail: hfm-kanzler@nuernberg.de

Departments

Music (Jazz and Popular Music; Music Education; Musical Instruments; Religious Music; Singing)

History: Founded 1999 following merging of the Meistersinger-Konservatoriums in Nuremberg and the Leopold-Mozart-Konservatorium in Augsburg

Main Language(s) of Instruction: German

Degrees and Diplomas: *Diplom*. Also Postgraduate Studies Programme
Last Updated: 19/01/10

NÜRTINGEN-GEISLINGEN UNIVERSITY

Hochschule für Wirtschaft und Umwelt Nürtingen-Geislingen
Neckarsteige 6-10, 72603 Nürtingen
Tel: +49(7022) 201-0
Fax: +49(7022) 201-303
EMail: info@hfwu.de
Website:http: //www.hfwu.de

Rektor: Werner Ziegler (2007-)
Tel: +49(7022) 201-364, Fax: +49(7022) 201-365
EMail: werner.ziegler@hfwu.de

Kanzler: Roland Bosch
Tel: +49(7022) 201-362 EMail: boschr@hfwu.de

International Relations: Gerhard Schmücker, Head, International Office
Tel: +49(7022) 719-4026 EMail: gerhard.schmuecker@hfwu.de

Faculties

Agriculture, Economics and Management *(Nürtingen)* (Agriculture; Animal Husbandry; Economics; Management); **Business Administration and International Finance** *(Nürtingen)* (Accountancy; Business Administration; Finance; Taxation); **Business and Law** *(Geislingen)* (Automotive Engineering; Commercial Law; Health Administration; Leadership; Management; Real Estate); **Landscape Architecture, Environmental and Urban Planning** (Environmental Studies; Landscape Architecture; Town Planning)

History: Founded 1949 as Institute of Higher Education in Agriculture. Acquired present status 1971.

Governing Bodies: Hochschulrat; Senat

Academic Year: October to August (October to February; March to August)

Admission Requirements: Fachhochschulreife

Main Language(s) of Instruction: German

International Co-operation: With universities in United Kingdom; Ireland; Sweden; Finland; France; Netherlands; Italy; Spain; Slovak Republic; USA, Lithuania, Korea, South Africa, Ukraine and Japan.

Degrees and Diplomas: *Bachelor/Bakkalaureus*; *Master/Magister*

Student Services: Academic counselling, Canteen, Cultural centre, Employment services, Foreign student adviser, Handicapped facilities, Language programs, Social counselling, Sports facilities

Student Residential Facilities: Yes

Libraries: Yes

Publications: FH Journal *(biennially)*
Last Updated: 19/01/10

NÜRTINGEN UNIVERSITY OF APPLIED SCIENCES FOR ART THERAPY

Hochschule für Kunsttherapie Nürtingen (HKT)
Sigmaringer Strasse 15, 72622 Nürtingen
Tel: +49(7022) 93336-0
Fax: +49(7022) 93336-23
EMail: info@hkt-nuertingen.de
Website: http://www.hkt-nuertingen.de

Rektor: Johannes Junker
Tel: +49(7022) 93336-13 EMail: j.junker@hkt-nuertingen.de

Kanzlerin: Roswitha Bader
Tel: +49(7022) 93336-12 EMail: r.bader@fhkt.de

Programmes

Art Therapy (Art Therapy; Fine Arts; Psychotherapy; Rehabilitation and Therapy)

History: Founded 1987. Formerly known as Fachhochschule für Kunsttherapie Nürtingen.

Main Language(s) of Instruction: German

Degrees and Diplomas: *Bachelor/Bakkalaureus*: Art Therapy, 8 Sem.; *Diplom*: 8 Sem; *Master/Magister*

Student Services: Cultural centre, Foreign student adviser, Health services

Special Facilities: Art Gallery

Libraries: Yes
Last Updated: 02/02/12

OFFENBACH UNIVERSITY OF ART AND DESIGN

Hochschule für Gestaltung Offenbach am Main
PO Box 100823, Schlossstrasse 31, 63008 Offenbach
Tel: +49(69) 80059-0
Fax: +49(69) 80059-109
EMail: praesidium@hfg-offenbach.de
Website: http://www.hfg-offenbach.de

Präsident: Bernd Kracke Tel: +49(69) 80059-102

Kanzlerin: Vera Sponheimer-Bram
Tel: +49(69) 80059-101 EMail: pokojewski@hfg-offenbach.de

Programmes

Communication Design (Design); **Fine Arts** (Fine Arts); **Media Studies** (Media Studies); **Product Design** (Design; Industrial Design); **Visual Communication** (Visual Arts)

History: Founded 1970.

Main Language(s) of Instruction: German

Degrees and Diplomas: *Diplom*; *Promotion*
Last Updated: 05/02/10

OSNABRÜCK UNIVERSITY OF APPLIED SCIENCES

Hochschule Osnabrück
PO Box 1940, D-49009 Osnabrück
Tel: +49(541) 969-2104
Fax: +49(541) 969-2066
EMail: pressestelle@hs-osnabrueck.de
Website: http://www.hs-osnabrueck.de

Präsident: Andreas Bertram
Tel: +49(541) 969-2100 EMail: praesident@hs-osnabrueck.de

Departments

Communications and Society *(Lingen/Ems Campus)* (Communication Studies; Theatre); **Management and Technology** *(Lingen/ Ems Campus)* (Business Administration; Business Computing; Engineering; Machine Building; Management; Technology)

Faculties

Agricultural Sciences and Landscape Architecture (Agriculture; Landscape Architecture); **Business Management and Social Sciences** (Business Administration; Commercial Law; International Studies; Management; Public Administration; Social Sciences);

Engineering and Computer Science (Chemical Engineering; Computer Science; Electrical Engineering; Materials Engineering; Mechanical Engineering)

Institutes
Music

History: Founded 1971. Acquired present status 2003.

Governing Bodies: Stiftungsrat; Präsidium

Admission Requirements: Higher education entry qualification, knowledge of German

Fees: (Euros): Tuition 500 per semester plus approximately 170 per semester

Main Language(s) of Instruction: German

Degrees and Diplomas: *Bachelor/Bakkalaureus*: 3 yrs; *Master/ Magister*: 2 yrs

Student Services: Academic counselling, Canteen, Employment services, Foreign student adviser, Foreign Studies Centre, Handicapped facilities, Language programs, Nursery care, Social counselling, Sports facilities

Student Residential Facilities: Yes

Libraries: Yes
Last Updated: 23/03/11

OSTFALIA UNIVERSITY OF APPLIED SCIENCES

Ostfalia Hochschule für angewandte Wissenschaften (FH BS/WF)
Salzdahlumer Strasse 46-48, 38302 Wolfenbüttel, Lower Saxony
Tel: +49(5331) 939-0
Fax: +49(5331) 939-1072
EMail: m.blaesing@fh-wolfenbuettel.de
Website: http://www.ostfalia.de/cms/de

Präsident: Wolf-Rüdiger Umbach
Tel: +49(5331) 939-1000, Fax: +49(5331) 939-1002
EMail: praesident@fh-wolfenbuettel.de

Hauptamtlicher Vizepräsident: Volker Küch
Tel: +49(5331) 939-1010, Fax: +49(5331) 939-1012
EMail: hvp@fh-wolfenbuettel.de

International Relations: Holger Zimpel
Tel: +49(5331) 939-1650, Fax: +49(5331) 939-1702
EMail: h.zimpel@fh-wolfenbuettel.de

Faculties

Automotive Engineering *(Wolfsburg Campus)* (Automotive Engineering; Machine Building; Materials Engineering; Polymer and Plastics Technology; Production Engineering); **Business Administration** *(Wolfsburg Campus)* (Banking; Business Computing; Industrial Management; Insurance); **Computer Science/IT** *(Wolfenbüttel Campus)* (Computer Engineering; Computer Networks; Computer Science; Information Technology; Media Studies; Software Engineering); **Construction, Water and Soil** (Construction Engineering; Soil Science; Water Science); **Electrical Engineering** *(Wolfenbüttel Campus)* (Electrical and Electronic Engineering; Microelectronics; Power Engineering; Telecommunications Engineering); **Law** *(Wolfenbüttel Campus)* (Commercial Law; Law; Private Law); **Mechanical Engineering** *(Wolfenbüttel)* (Automation and Control Engineering; Mechanical Engineering; Production Engineering); **Public Health Services** *(Wolfsburg Campus)* (Health Administration; Health Sciences; Optometry; Public Health); **Social Work** *(Wolfenbütte Campus)* (Social and Community Services; Social Welfare; Social Work); **Supply Engineering** *(Suderburg Campus)*; **Transport, Media, Sports and Tourism Management** *(Salzgitter Campus - Karl-Scharfenberg-Fakultät)* (Leisure Studies; Media Studies; Sports; Sports Management; Tourism)

History: Founded 1928. Acquired present status 1971.

Governing Bodies: Government of Lower Saxony

Academic Year: September to August (September-February; March-August)

Admission Requirements: Secondary school certificate (Abitur, Fachhochschulreife)

Fees: None

Main Language(s) of Instruction: German

International Co-operation: With universities in France, United Kingdom, Finland, Poland, Mexico, Brazil, Argentina, India and

China. Also participates in Erasmus, Leonardo and Tempus programmes.

Degrees and Diplomas: *Zertifikat*: Pedagogy; *Bachelor/Bakkalaureus*; *Master/Magister*

Student Services: Academic counselling, Cultural centre, Employment services, Foreign student adviser, Handicapped facilities, Language programs, Nursery care, Social counselling, Sports facilities

Student Residential Facilities: Yes

Libraries: Main Library
Last Updated: 22/01/10

OSTWESTFALEN-LIPPE UNIVERSITY OF APPLIED SCIENCES

Hochschule Ostwestfalen-Lippe (FH LUH)
Liebigstrasse 87, 32657 Lemgo, Northrhine-Westphalia
Tel: +49(5261) 702-0
Fax: +49(5261) 702-222
EMail: rektorat@fh-luh.de
Website: http://www.hs-owl.de

Rektor: Oliver Herrmann
Tel: +49(5261) 702-211, Fax: +49(5261) 702-223
EMail: tilmann.fischer@fh-luh.de

Kanzler: Helmuth Hoffstetter
Tel: +49(5261) 702-200, Fax: +49(5261) 702-221
EMail: helmuth.hoffstetter@fh-luh.de

International Relations: Stefanie Heissenberg, Head, International Office
Tel: +49(5261) 702-335 EMail: stefanie.heissenberg@hs-owl.de

Departments
Civil Engineering *(Detmold Campus)* (Civil Engineering; Construction Engineering); **Electrical Engineering and Computer Science** *(Lemgo Campus)* (Computer Science; Electrical Engineering); **Environmental Engineering and Applied Computer Science** *(Höxter Campus)* (Computer Science; Environmental Engineering); **Landscape Architecture and Environment Planning** *(Höxter Campus)* (Environmental Management; Landscape Architecture); **Life Science Technologies** *(Lemgo Campus)* (Biological and Life Sciences; Biotechnology; Cosmetology; Food Technology; Pharmacology); **Mechanical Engineering and Mechatronics** *(Lemgo Campus)*; **Media Production** *(Lemgo Campus)* (Media Studies); **Production and Economics** *(Lemgo Campus)* (Economics; Production Engineering)

Schools
Architecture and Interior Design *(Detmold)* (Architecture; Interior Design)

Further Information: Also campuses in Detmold and Höxter.

History: Founded 1971, acquired present name and status 2002. Formerly known as Fachhochschule Lippe und Höxter (University of Applied Sciences of Lippe and Höxter).

Governing Bodies: Board of Directors (Rektorat)

Academic Year: September to July (September-February; March-July)

Admission Requirements: Secondary school certificate (Abitur) or equivalent; German language test for foreign students

Fees: (Euros): 60 per semester

Main Language(s) of Instruction: German. Also English in some courses and degree programmes

International Co-operation: With universities in USA, China, Singapore, Brazil. Also participates in Erasmus

Degrees and Diplomas: *Bachelor/Bakkalaureus*; *Master/Magister*. Also Dual Study Programmes

Student Services: Academic counselling, Canteen, Foreign student adviser, Foreign Studies Centre, Language programs, Social counselling

Student Residential Facilities: Yes

Special Facilities: Observatory

Libraries: Campus Libraries
Last Updated: 02/02/12

OTTERSBERG UNIVERSITY OF APPLIED SCIENCES FOR ART THERAPY AND ART

Fachhochschule Ottersberg
PO Box 1251, Am Wiestebruch 68, 28870 Ottersberg
Tel: +49(4205) 3949-0
Fax: +49(4205) 3949-79
EMail: info@fh-ottersberg.de; verwaltung@fh-ottersberg.de
Website: http://www.fh-ottersberg.de

Rektor: Peer de Smit (1997-)
Tel: +49(4205) 3949-15 EMail: rektor@fh-ottersberg.de

Administrative Officer: Nicole Woelk
Tel: +49(4205) 3949-10 EMail: nicole.woelk@fh-ottersberg.de

International Relations: Albrecht Lampe, Curator/Managing Director Tel: +49(4205) 3949-18 EMail: kurator@fh-ottersberg.de

Programmes
Art Therapy (Art Therapy); **Drama** (Art Therapy; Pedagogy; Theatre); **Fine Arts** (Fine Arts)

History: Founded 1967. Acquired present status 1984. Formerly known as Freie Kunst-Studienstätte Ottersberg - Fachhochschule für Kunsttherapie und Kunst.

Governing Bodies: Executive Committee; General Assembly

Admission Requirements: Secondary school certificate (Fachhochschulreife)

Fees: (Euros): Fine Arts, 207 per month; Drama, 233 per month

Main Language(s) of Instruction: German

Degrees and Diplomas: *Bachelor/Bakkalaureus*: 4 yrs; *Master/Magister*

Student Services: Academic counselling, Canteen, Cultural centre, Employment services, Social counselling
Last Updated: 31/01/12

OTTO BEISHEIM SCHOOL OF MANAGEMENT

Wissenschaftliche Hochschule für Unternehmensführung - Otto-Beisheim - Hochschule (WHU KOBLENZ)
Burgplatz 2, 56179 Vallendar
Tel: +49(261) 650-90
Fax: +49(261) 650-9509
EMail: info@whu.edu
Website: http://www.whu.edu/

Rektor/Dean: Michael Frenkel
Tel: +49(261) 650-9150, Fax: +49(261) 650-9159
EMail: rektorat@whu.edu

Centres
Asia (International Business); **Collaborative Commerce**; **Consumer Goods** *(Henkel)*; **European Studies**; **Logistics Management** *(Kuehne)*; **Management** *(Biopharma)*; **Market-oriented Corporate Management** (Business Administration); **Private Banking** (Banking)

Institutes
Management, Accounting and Control (Accountancy; Management)

Programmes
Business Administration/Management (Business Administration; Commercial Law; Economics; Management)

History: Founded 1984 under the auspices of the Chamber of Industry and Commerce. A private institution recognized by the Ministry of Education.

Governing Bodies: Senat

Academic Year: September to May (September-December; January-May)

Admission Requirements: Secondary school certificate (Reifezeugnis), practical experience and proficiency in German, good knowledge of English, and working knowledge of French, Spanish, Italian, Japanese, Russian, Chinese or Portuguese

Fees: (Euros): 3,579 per semester

Main Language(s) of Instruction: German, English

International Co-operation: With universities in France, Spain, United Kingdom, USA, Australia, Canada, Japan.

Accrediting Agencies: Foundation for International Business Administration Accreditation (FIBAA)

Degrees and Diplomas: *Diplom-Vorprüfung*: 3 sem; *Bachelor/ Bakkalaureus*; *Diplom*: Business Administration, 8 sem; *Master/ Magister*: Business Administration, 4 sem; *Doktorgrad*: Economic Science (Dr.rer.pol.), 2 yrs following Master

Student Services: Academic counselling, Canteen, Employment services, Foreign student adviser, Handicapped facilities, Language programs, Sports facilities

Student Residential Facilities: Yes

Libraries: c. 33,000 vols
Last Updated: 03/02/10

OTTO-FRIEDRICH UNIVERSITY BAMBERG

Otto-Friedrich-Universität Bamberg
Kapuzinerstrasse 16, 96047 Bamberg
Tel: +49(951) 863-1001
Fax: +49(951) 863-1005
EMail: post@uni-bamberg.de
Website: http://www.uni-bamberg.de

Präsident: Godehard Ruppert
Tel: +49(951) 863-1011 EMail: rektorat@uni-bamberg.de

Kanzlerin: Dagmar Steuer-Flieser
EMail: kanzlerin@uni-bamberg.de

International Relations: Andreas Weihe
Tel: +49(951) 863-1048, Fax: +49(951) 863-1054
EMail: auslandsamt@uni.bamberg.de

Centres
Bamberg Centre for European Studies (BACES); Didactic Research and Teaching; Interreligious Studies *(ZIS)* (Religious Studies); Medieval Studies *(ZEMAS)*; Physical Education (Physical Education)

Faculties
Catholic Theology (Bible; Catholic Theology); Education, Philosophy and Psychology (Art Education; Education; Mathematics; Music; Musicology; Natural Sciences; Philosophy; Protestant Theology; Psychology; Sports); History and Geography (Archaeology; Art History; Ethnology; Geography; Heritage Preservation; History); Information Systems and Applied Computer Science (Business Computing; Computer Science; Information Sciences; Systems Analysis); Languages and Literature (English; Germanic Studies; Oriental Studies; Philology; Romance Languages; Slavic Languages); Social Sciences and Economics (Business Administration; Economics; Political Sciences; Social Sciences; Sociology)

Graduate Colleges
Anthropological Foundations and Developments of Christianity and Islam (Anthropology; Christian Religious Studies; Islamic Studies); Generation Awareness and Generation Gap in the Ancient World and in Medieval Times; Markets and Social Systems in Europe (European Studies; Social Sciences; Social Studies)

Institutes
European Forum for Migration Studies (efms) (Demography and Population); State Institute for Family Research (ifb) (Family Studies)

Research Groups
Clinical Psychology (Clinical Psychology); Government and Growth *(Bamberg Economic)* (Government); History of the European Expansion in Early Modern Times (European Studies; History); Intercultural Philosophy and Comenius Research (Philosophy); Rural Jewry (Jewish Studies); School Development and School Management (Educational Administration); Turkish Law (Law)

Further Information: Also Language Courses for foreign students

History: Founded 1647. Incorporated School of Theology, formerly part of 18th century University of Bamberg, and a College of Education established in 1958. An autonomous institution under the jurisdiction of and financially supported by the State of Bavaria. Acquired present title 1979.

Governing Bodies: Senat

Academic Year: October to September (October-February; April-July)

Admission Requirements: Secondary school certificate (Reifezeugnis)

Fees: (Euros): c. 500 per semester

Main Language(s) of Instruction: German

International Co-operation: With universities in Spain, France, United Kingdom, USA, Italy, Scandinavia (and more)

Degrees and Diplomas: *Bachelor/Bakkalaureus*: 3; *Lehramt*: 4-5 yrs; *Master/Magister (MA)*: 5 yrs; *Promotion (Dr.theol.)*: a further 3 yrs

Student Services: Academic counselling, Canteen, Foreign student adviser, Handicapped facilities, Nursery care, Social counselling, Sports facilities

Student Residential Facilities: Yes

Special Facilities: Natural History Museum

Libraries: Central Library, c. 1.6m. Vols

Publications: Forschungsbericht *(other/irregular)*
Last Updated: 22/01/10

OTTO-VON-GUERICKE UNIVERSITY MAGDEBURG

Otto-von-Guericke-Universität Magdeburg
Universitätsplatz 2, 39016 Magdeburg, Sachsen-Anhalt
Tel: +49(391) 67-01
Fax: +49(391) 671-1156
EMail: rektor@uni-magdeburg.de
Website: http://www.uni-magdeburg.de

Rektor: Klaus Erich Pollmann (1998-)
Tel: +49(391) 671-8543, Fax: +49(391) 671-1157

Kanzler: Volker Zehle
Tel: +49(391) 671-8503, Fax: +49(391) 671-1154
EMail: kanzler@uni-magdeburg.de

Centres
Audiovisual Media (Media Studies); Computer (Computer Science); Languages *(Multimedia and Methods in Teaching a Foreign Language)* (English; French; German; Italian; Latin; Modern Languages; Phonetics; Russian; Spanish)

Faculties
Computer Science (Computer Science; Information Management; Systems Analysis; Telecommunications Engineering); Economics and Management (Accountancy; Economic and Finance Policy; Economics; Finance; International Economics; Management; Marketing; Operations Research; Taxation); Electrical Engineering and Information Technology (Automation and Control Engineering; Electrical Engineering; Energy Engineering); Engineering (Artificial Intelligence; Automation and Control Engineering; Building Technologies; Materials Engineering; Measurement and Precision Engineering; Mechanical Engineering); Humanities, Social Sciences and Education (Business Education; Educational Sciences; Germanic Studies; History; History of Societies; Literature; Philology; Political Sciences; Psychology; Sociology; Sports; Vocational Education); Mathematics (Applied Mathematics; Mathematics; Statistics); Medicine (Medicine); Natural Sciences (Biology; Experimental Psychology; Natural Sciences; Physics); Process and Systems Engineering (Chemical Engineering; Chemistry; Environmental Engineering; Thermal Engineering)

Further Information: Also Hospitals (Krankenhaus Altstadt Magdeburg, Krankenhaus Olvenstedt Magdeburg, Krankenhaus Halberstadt). German language courses for foreign students

History: Founded 1953 as College of Heavy Mechanical Engineering, became Technical University (Technische Hochschule) 1961. Renamed Technische Universität 1987. Acquired present status and title 1993 after the merging of 3 Universities of Magdeburg (Technische Universität Otto von Guericke, Pädagogische Hochschule, Medizinische Akademie Magdeburg).

Governing Bodies: Konzil, Senate

Academic Year: October to September (October-March; April-September)

Admission Requirements: Secondary school certificate (Reifezeugnis)

Fees: None

Main Language(s) of Instruction: German. Also English in Faculty of Economics and some Master.

International Co-operation: With universities in Russian Federation; Ukraine; Italy; Slovakia; Czech Republic; Poland; USA

Degrees and Diplomas: *Zertifikat*; *Bachelor/Bakkalaureus*: 3-4 yrs in English language; *Diplom*; *Lehramt*; *Staatsprüfung*: Medicine; *Staatsprüfung*: Teaching of Chemistry, 4 to 4 1/2 yrs; *Master/Magister*: Arts in European Studies, Management and Economics; Science in Computer Science, Computer Graphics and Electrical Energy Systems, 1 1/2 yrs; *Master/Magister*: Science in Chemical, Mechanical and Process and Engineering, 2 yrs; *Master/Magister*: Science in Quality, Safety and Environment, 1 yr; *Promotion*; *Habilitation*

Student Services: Academic counselling, Canteen, Cultural centre, Employment services, Foreign student adviser, Handicapped facilities, Health services, Language programs, Social counselling, Sports facilities

Student Residential Facilities: For 2,000 students

Special Facilities: Audiovisual Centre

Libraries: University Library, c. 993,000 vols

Publications: Umweltbericht *(annually)*; Universitätsschriften und Preprint *(annually)*

Last Updated: 22/01/10

PADERBORN UNIVERSITY OF APPLIED SCIENCES FOR ECONOMICS
Fachhochschule für die Wirtschaft Paderborn
Fürstenalle 3-5, 33102 Paderborn
Tel: +49(5251) 301-02
Fax: +49(5251) 301-188
EMail: info-pb@fhdw.de
Website: http://www.fhdw.de

Präsident: Franz Wagner EMail: franz.wagner@fhdw.de

International Relations: Karin Carroll-Scott
Tel: +49(5251) 301-183, Fax: +49(5251) 301-188
EMail: karin.carroll-scott@fhdw.de

Programmes
Business Administration (Business Administration); **Business Computing**; **Business Management** *(Master)* (Business Administration; Management); **Commercial Law**; **General Management** *(MBA)* (Management); **Information Technology Management and Information Systems** *(Master)*; **International Business** (International Business); **Management** (Management)

History: Founded 1993.

Main Language(s) of Instruction: German

Degrees and Diplomas: *Bachelor/Bakkalaureus*; *Master/Magister*
Last Updated: 06/02/12

PALUCCA UNIVERSITY OF DANCE DRESDEN
Palucca Hochschule für Tanz Dresden
Basteiplatz 4, D-01277 Dresden
Tel: +49(351) 25906-0
Fax: +49(351) 25906-11
EMail: Info@palucca.eu
Website: http://www.palucca-schule-dresden.de

Rektor: Jason Beechey
Tel: +49(351) 25906-40 EMail: Rektor@palucca.eu

International Relations: Martina Preissler
Tel: +49(351) 25906-21
EMail: martina.preissler@palucca.smwk.sachsen.de

Programmes
Choreography (Dance); **Dance** (Dance; Theatre); **Elevenprogramm** *(with the Dresden SemperOper Ballett)*; **Teaching of Dancing (extension course)** (Dance); **Teaching of Dancing (foundation course)** (Dance)

History: Founded 1925. Acquired present status 1999.

Admission Requirements: School-leaving certificate qualifying for university entrance, aptitude tests and entrance examination

Fees: (Euros): 159.50 per semester

Main Language(s) of Instruction: German

International Co-operation: With institutions in France; Japan; USA; Netherlands; United Kingdom; Russian Federation

Degrees and Diplomas: *Bachelor/Bakkalaureus*; *Master/Magister*

Student Services: Academic counselling, Canteen, Foreign student adviser, Foreign Studies Centre, Health services, Social counselling, Sports facilities

Student Residential Facilities: Yes

Libraries: Yes
Last Updated: 22/01/10

PFORZHEIM UNIVERSITY
Hochschule Pforzheim
Tiefenbronner Strasse 65, 75175 Pforzheim
Tel: +49(7231) 28-5
Fax: +49(7231) 28-6666
EMail: info@hs-pforzheim.de
Website: http://www.hochschule-pforzheim.de

Rektor: Martin Erhardt
Tel: +49(7231) 28-6000, Fax: +49(7231) 28-6006
EMail: martin.erhardt@hs-pforzheim.de

Kanzler: Wolfgang Hohl
Tel: +49(7231) 28-6021, Fax: +49(7231) 28-7021
EMail: wolfgang.hohl@hs-pforzheim.de

International Relations: Wolfgang Schöllhammer, Head, International Office
Tel: +49(7231) 28-6145, Fax: +49(7231) 28-6140
EMail: aaa@hs-pforzheim.de; schoellhammer@hs-pforzheim.de

Schools
Business (Accountancy; Advertising and Publicity; Business Administration; Commercial Law; Economics; Finance; Human Resources; International Business; Marketing; Taxation); **Design** (Design; Fashion Design; Jewelry Art); **Engineering** (Engineering; Industrial Engineering; Machine Building; Mechanical Engineering)

History: Design School founded 1877, Business School founded 1966, Engineering School founded 1992. Acquired present status 1992.

Governing Bodies: State of Baden-Wuerttemberg

Academic Year: October to July (October-February; March-July)

Admission Requirements: Abitur or Fachhochschulreife

Main Language(s) of Instruction: German and English

Accrediting Agencies: Department of Education and Science of the Land of Baden-Wuerttemberg

Degrees and Diplomas: *Bachelor/Bakkalaureus*; *Master/Magister*

Student Services: Academic counselling, Canteen, Cultural centre, Employment services, Foreign student adviser, Foreign Studies Centre, Handicapped facilities, Language programs, Social counselling, Sports facilities

Student Residential Facilities: Yes

Libraries: Two libraries

Publications: Konturen *(annually)*
Last Updated: 20/01/10

PHILIPPS-UNIVERSITY OF MARBURG
Philipps-Universität Marburg
Biegenstrasse 10, 35032 Marburg/Lahn
Tel: +49(6421) 282-0
Fax: +49(6421) 282-2500
EMail: Seip@verwaltung.uni-marburg.de
Website: http://www.uni-marburg.de

Präsidentin: Katharina Krause
Tel: +49(6421) 282-6000, Fax: +49(6421) 282-8910
EMail: praesidentin@uni-marburg.de

Kanzler: Friedhelm Nonne
Tel: +49(6421) 282-6100, Fax: +49(6421) 282-8949
EMail: kanzler@verwaltung.uni-marburg.de

International Relations: Thomas Komm
Tel: +49(6421) 282-6176, Fax: +49(6421) 282-8998
EMail: komm@verwaltung.uni-marburg.de

Centres

Canadian Studies (Canadian Studies); Conflict Studies (Peace and Disarmament); Gender Studies and Feminist Futurology; Japanese Studies

Faculties

Biology (Biology; Cell Biology; Ecology; Genetics; Microbiology; Molecular Biology; Parasitology; Plant Pathology); Business Administration and Economics (Business Administration; Economics); Chemistry (Analytical Chemistry; Biochemistry; Chemistry; Inorganic Chemistry; Organic Chemistry); Education (Education; Pedagogy; Sports); Foreign Languages and Cultures (Classical Languages; English; Latin; Oriental Languages; Romance Languages; Slavic Languages); Geography (Geography; Geology); German Studies and History of the Arts (Art History; German; Germanic Studies; Graphic Arts; Media Studies; Musicology; Painting and Drawing; Phonetics); History and Cultural Studies (Ancient Civilizations; Archaeology; Chinese; History; Japanese; Modern History; Prehistory); Law (Law); Mathematics and Computer Science (Computer Science; Mathematics); Medicine (Anatomy; Cell Biology; Dentistry; Dermatology; Genetics; Gynaecology and Obstetrics; Haematology; Hygiene; Medicine; Neurosciences; Ophthalmology; Otorhinolaryngology; Pathology; Surgery); Pharmacy (Pharmacology; Pharmacy; Toxicology); Physics (Physics); Protestant Theology (Archaeology; Bible; Ethics; Protestant Theology); Psychology (Clinical Psychology; Psychology); Social Sciences and Philosophy (Anthropology; Ethnology; Peace and Disarmament; Political Sciences; Sociology)

History: Founded 1527 by Philip the Generous of Hesse as a Protestant State University. An autonomous institution financially supported by the State of Hesse under the jurisdiction of its Ministry of Science and Art.

Governing Bodies: Konvent

Academic Year: October to July (October-February; April-July)

Admission Requirements: Secondary school certificate (Reifezeugnis) or equivalent

Fees: None

Main Language(s) of Instruction: German

Degrees and Diplomas: Bachelor/Bakkalaureus; Diplom: Chemistry (Chemiker); Economics (Volkswirt); Geology; Mathematics; Physics; Psychology; Lehramt: Teaching Qualification, Secondary Level; Magister Artium; Staatsprüfung: Dentistry, 10 sem; Staatsprüfung: Law; Pharmacy, 7 sem; Staatsprüfung: Medicine, 12 sem; Master/Magister; Promotion: c. 8 sem; Promotion: Dentistry (Dr.med.dent.), 10 sem; Habilitation: at least 3 yrs following Doktor

Student Residential Facilities: Yes

Special Facilities: Museum of Art and Cultural History; Mineralogy Museum. Collection of Religious Art and Ceremonial Utensils

Libraries: University Library, c. 1m. vols; libraries of the institutes and departments

Publications: Forschungsbericht; Vorlesungsverzeichnis (biannually)

Last Updated: 03/02/12

PRIVATE DISTANCE LEARNING UNIVERSITY OF APPLIED SCIENCES SAXONY

Private Fernfachhochschule Sachsen
Rathausstr. 7, 09111 Chemnitz
Tel: +49(372) 09 687-80
Fax: +49(372) 09 687-79
EMail: info@ffh-sachsen.com
Website: http://www.fh-studiengang.de/index.html

Rektor: Steffen Rössler

Kanzler: Axel Brückom

Courses

Preparatory Studies (Business Administration; Economics; Mathematics)

Programmes

Business Engineering and Administration (Business Administration; Engineering)

Degrees and Diplomas: Bachelor/Bakkalaureus
Last Updated: 26/01/09

PRIVATE HANSEATIC UNIVERSITY ROSTOCK

Private Hanseuniversität Rostock
Friedrich-Barnewitz-Straße 7, D-18119 Rostock
Tel: +49(381) 5196-4600
Fax: +49(381) 5196-4601
EMail: info@hanseuni.de

President: Wolf Schäfer EMail: wschaefer@hanseuni.de

Chancellor / CFO: Knut Einfeldt EMail: keinfeldt@hanseuni.de

Programmes

Business Administration (Business Administration; Leadership; Management); Business Information Technology (Business Administration; Business Computing; Economics; Information Technology); Global Management (Master) (Cultural Studies; Economics; Law; Management; Political Sciences); Law; Preparations of the First Examination in Law (Erste juristische Prüfung) (Law)

History: Founded 2007.

Degrees and Diplomas: Bachelor/Bakkalaureus; Master/Magister. Also First Examination in Law (Erste juristische Prüfung)
Last Updated: 27/01/09

PRIVATE UNIVERSITY OF APPLIED SCIENCES FOR ECONOMIC AND TECHNICAL STUDIES VECHTA/DIEPHOLZ/OLDENBURG

Private Fachhochschule für Wirtschaft und Technik Vechta-Diepholz-Oldenburg
Rombergstrasse 40, 49377 Vechta
Tel: +49(4441) 915-0
Fax: +49(4441) 915-109
EMail: info@fhwt.de
Website: http://www.fhwt.de

Rektor: Jons T. Kersten (1998-)
Tel: +49(4441) 915-111 EMail: kersten@fhwt.de

Full time Vice-President and Head of Administration: Anne-Katrin Reich
Tel: +49(4441) 915-401, Fax: +49(4441) 915-401
EMail: reich@fhwt.de

Programmes

Business Administration (Accountancy; Agricultural Business; Business Administration; Finance; Human Resources; Information Technology; Marketing; Transport and Communications); Business Engineering (Accountancy; Business Administration; English; Finance; Marketing; Production Engineering; Safety Engineering; Transport Management); Electronic Engineering (Business Administration; Communication Studies; Electronic Engineering; English; Information Technology; Mathematics; Software Engineering); Machine Building (Machine Building; Mechanical Engineering); Mechatronics (Electronic Engineering; Information Technology; Mathematics; Mechanical Engineering)

Degrees and Diplomas: Bachelor/Bakkalaureus; Diplom (FH); Master/Magister
Last Updated: 25/01/09

PRIVATE UNIVERSITY OF APPLIED SCIENCES GÖTTINGEN

Private Fachhochschule Göttingen
Weender Landstrasse 3-7, 37073 Göttingen
Tel: +49(551) 54700-0
Fax: +49(551) 54700-190
EMail: studieninfo@pfh-goettingen.de
Website: http://www.pfh-goettingen.de

Präsident: Bernt R.A. Sierke (1999-)

Kanzler: Benno Fleer

International Relations: Peggy Repenning, Vizekanzlerin

Programmes

Business Information Systems; Composite Materials; General Management (Management)

History: Founded 1995.

Main Language(s) of Instruction: German

Degrees and Diplomas: Bachelor/Bakkalaureus; Master/Magister
Last Updated: 22/01/10

PROTESTANT UNIVERSITY OF APPLIED SCIENCES DARMSTAD

Evangelische Fachhochschule Darmstadt (EFHD)
Zweifalltorweg 12, 64293 Darmstadt, Hessen
Tel: +49(6151) 8798-0
Fax: +49(6151) 8798-58
EMail: efhd@efh-darmstadt.de
Website: http://www.efh-darmstadt.de

Präsidentin: Alexa Köhler-Offierski (1994-)
Tel: +49(6151) 8798-11 EMail: köhler-offierski@efh-darmstadt.de

Kanzler: Gustav Fetzer
Tel: +49(6151) 8798-13 EMail: fetzer@efh-darmstadt.de

International Relations: Heide Remmele
Tel: +49(6151) 8798-33 EMail: remmele@efh-darmstadt.de

Programmes
Child Education and Development (Child Care and Development); **Inclusive Education** (Education); **Nursing** (Nursing); **Postgraduate Studies** (Education; Management; Nursing; Psychology; Social Work; Theology); **Social Work** (Social Work)
History: Founded 1971.
Governing Bodies: Steering Committee
Academic Year: September to August

Admission Requirements: Fachhochschulreife/Abitur

Fees: None

Main Language(s) of Instruction: German

International Co-operation: With universities in Bulgaria; Finland; France; Poland; Romania; Russian Federation; Sweden

Accrediting Agencies: Akkreditierungsagentur für Studiengänge im Bereich Heilpädagogik, Pflege, Gesundheit und Soziale Arbeit
Degrees and Diplomas: *Bachelor/Bakkalaureus*: 4 yrs; *Diplom (FH)*: Social Work; Social Pedagogy, 4 yrs; *Master/Magister*: 1 yr
Student Services: Academic counselling, Employment services, Foreign student adviser, Language programs, Social counselling
Special Facilities: Multimedia Centre
Libraries: Yes
Last Updated: 06/02/12

PROTESTANT UNIVERSITY OF APPLIED SCIENCES FREIBURG

Evangelische Fachhochschule Freiburg
Bugginger Strasse 38, 79114 Freiburg
Tel: +49(761) 47812-0
Fax: +49(761) 47812-30
EMail: mail@efh-freiburg.de
Website: http://www.efh-freiburg.de

Rektor: Reiner Marquard (2007-)
Tel: +49(761) 47812-10 EMail: rektor@efh-freiburg.de

Verwaltungsdirektor: Ulrich Rolf
Tel: +49(761) 47812-15
EMail: verwaltungsdirektor@eh-freiburg.de

International Relations: Markus Breuer
Tel: +49(761) 47812-433 EMail: internationaloffice@eh-freiburg.de

Departments
Pedagogy and Supervision (Pedagogy); **Social Work** (Social Work); **Theological Education and Diaconia Studies** *(Protestant)* (Religious Education; Theology)
History: Founded 1972.
Main Language(s) of Instruction: German

Degrees and Diplomas: *Bachelor/Bakkalaureus*; *Master/Magister*
Last Updated: 06/02/12

PROTESTANT UNIVERSITY OF APPLIED SCIENCES RHINELAND-WESTPHALIA-LIPPE IN BOCHUM

Evangelische Fachhochschule Rheinland-Westfalen-Lippe Bochum
Immanuel-Kant-Str. 18, 44803 Bochum
Tel: +49(234) 36901-0
Fax: +49(234) 36901-100
EMail: efh@efh-bochum.de
Website: http://www.efh-bochum.de

Rektor: Gerhard K. Schäfer
Tel: +49(234) 36901-133, Fax: +49(234) 36901-111
EMail: rektor@efh-bochum.de

Kanzlerin: Heike Schmidtchen
Tel: +49(234) 36901-131 EMail: rektorat@efh-bochum.de

International Relations: Helen Ahlert, Referentin des Rektorates
Tel: +49(234) 36901-144, Fax: +49(234) 36901-111
EMail: ahlert@efh-bochum.de

Departments
Community Education and Deaconry (Education; Theology); **Religious Education** (Religious Education); **Social Work** (Social Work)
History: Founded 1971.
Main Language(s) of Instruction: German

International Co-operation: With institutions in USA; Turkey; Russian Federation; Netherlands. Also participates in Socrates/Eramus programmes

Degrees and Diplomas: *Bachelor/Bakkalaureus*; *Diplom (FH)*: 4 yrs; *Master/Magister*
Student Services: Academic counselling, Canteen, Foreign student adviser, Handicapped facilities, Social counselling
Student Residential Facilities: None
Special Facilities: Movie Studio; Art Gallery
Libraries: Yes
Last Updated: 06/02/12

PROTESTANT UNIVERSITY OF APPLIED SCIENCES OF REUTLINGEN-LUDWIGSBURG

Evangelische Fachhochschule Reutlingen-Ludwigsburg
Paulusweg 6, 71638 Ludwigsburg
Tel: +49(7141) 9745-200
Fax: +49(7141) 9745-400
EMail: u.hafner@efh-ludwigsburg.de
Website: http://www.efh-reutlingen-ludwigsburg.de

Rektor: Norbert Collmar
Tel: +49(7141) 9745-201, Fax: +49(7141) 9745-400
EMail: n.collmar@efh-ludwigsburg.de

Verwaltungsdirektorin: Beate Käser
Tel: +49(7141) 9745-205, Fax: +49(7141) 99745-405
EMail: b.kaeser@efh-ludwigsburg.de

Programmes
Religious Education and Social Work (Bible; Humanities and Social Science Education; Religion; Religious Education; Social Work; Theology); **Social Work** (Social Work); **Social Work and Diaconical Studies** (Religion; Social Work)
History: Founded 1954.

Degrees and Diplomas: *Bachelor/Bakkalaureus*: 6-7 sem.; *Master/Magister*: Social Work; Deaconry; Organisations Development; Religious Education
Last Updated: 06/02/12

PROVADIS SCHOOL OF INTERNATIONAL MANAGEMENT AND TECHNOLOGY

Industriepark Höchst, Geb. B845, 65926 Frankfurt am Main
Tel: +49(69) 305-41880
Fax: +49(69) 305-16277
EMail: info@provadis-hochschule.de
Website: http://www.provadis-hochschule.de

Präsident: Uwe Faust
Tel: +49(69) 305-418-80, Fax: +49(69) 305-162-77
EMail: uwe.faust@provadis-hochschule.de

Departments
Business Administration (Business Administration; Industrial Management); **Business Computing** (Business Computing; Information Management); **Chemical Engineering** (Chemical Engineering)
Main Language(s) of Instruction: German

Degrees and Diplomas: *Bachelor/Bakkalaureus*; *Master/Magister*. Also dual Bachelors programme in Business Administration in cooperation with Deutsche Telekom
Last Updated: 03/02/12

RAVENSBURG-WEINGARTEN UNIVERSITY OF APPLIED SCIENCES

Hochschule Ravensburg-Weingarten - Technik, Wirtschaft, Sozialwesen
Doggenriedstrasse, 88241 Weingarten
Tel: +49(751) 501-0
Fax: +49(751) 501-9876
EMail: info@hs-weingarten.de
Website: http://www.hs-weingarten.de

Rektor: Thomas Spägele
Tel: +49(751) 501-9540, Fax: +49(751) 501-9873
EMail: spaegele@fh-weingarten.de

Kanzler/Verwaltungsdirektor: Henning Rudewig
Tel: +49(751) 501-9543, Fax: +49(751) 501-9873
EMail: rudewig@fh-weingarten.de

International Relations: Christine Lauer
Tel: +49(751) 501-9659 EMail: lauer@fh-weingarten.de

Faculties
Electrical Engineering and Computer Science (Business Computing; Computer Science; E-Business/Commerce; Electrical Engineering; Electronic Engineering; Engineering; Information Technology; Mechanical Engineering); **Mechanical Engineering** (Mechanical Engineering); **Social Work, Health and Management** (Health Administration; Nursing; Social Work); **Technology and Management** (Management; Technology)

History: Founded 1964. Acquired present status 1971.

Governing Bodies: Senate

Academic Year: September to August (September-February; March-August)

Fees: (Euros): 500 per semester

Main Language(s) of Instruction: German, English

International Co-operation: With universities in Eastern and Western Europe, North America, Asia

Accrediting Agencies: ASIIN

Degrees and Diplomas: *Bachelor/Bakkalaureus*; *Master/Magister*

Student Services: Academic counselling, Canteen, Employment services, Foreign student adviser, Language programs, Sports facilities

Student Residential Facilities: Yes

Libraries: Central Library
Last Updated: 20/01/10

REGENSBURG UNIVERSITY OF APPLIED SCIENCES

Hochschule Regensburg
PO Box 120327, Prüfeningerstrasse 58, 93025 Regensburg
Tel: +49(941) 943-02
Fax: +49(941) 943-1422
EMail: poststelle@fh-regensburg.de
Website: http://www.fh-regensburg.de

Präsident: Josef Eckstein
Tel: +49(941) 943-1001, Fax: +49(941) 943-1419
EMail: josef.eckstein@fh-regensburg.de

Kanzler: Peter Endres
Tel: +49(941) 943-1005, Fax: +49(941) 943-1420
EMail: kanzler@fh-regensburg.de

International Relations: Wilhelm Bomke
Tel: +49(941) 943-1068, Fax: +49(941) 943-1427
EMail: auslandsamt@fh-regensburg.de

Departments
Architecture (Architecture); **Business Administration** (Business Administration); **Civil Engineering** (Civil Engineering); **Electrical Engineering** (Electrical Engineering); **General Sciences and Microsystem Engineering** (Computer Engineering; Electronic Engineering; Engineering; Measurement and Precision Engineering;

Natural Sciences); **Mathematics and Computer Science** (Mathematics and Computer Science); **Mechanical Engineering** (Mechanical Engineering); **Social Work** (Social Sciences; Social Work)

History: Founded 1971.

Governing Bodies: Senate

Academic Year: October to July (October-February; March- July)

Admission Requirements: Secondary school certificate (Abitur, Fachhochschulreife)

Main Language(s) of Instruction: German

International Co-operation: With universities in France, Finland, Denmark, Czech Republic, Romania, USA, Italy.

Degrees and Diplomas: *Bachelor/Bakkalaureus*; *Diplom (FH)*: European Business Administration; *Master/Magister*: Automotive Electronics; Business Administration; Leadership and Communications Management

Student Services: Academic counselling, Canteen, Foreign student adviser, Foreign Studies Centre, Handicapped facilities, Language programs, Sports facilities

Libraries: c. 127,000 vols

Publications: Spectrum, Magazine *(biennially)*
Last Updated: 13/01/10

REUTLINGEN UNIVERSITY

Hochschule Reutlingen
Alteburgstrasse 150, 72762 Reutlingen, Baden-Württemberg
Tel: +49(7121) 271-457
Fax: +49(7121) 271-688
EMail: Paula.Mattes@fh-reutlingen.de
Website: http://www.fh-reutlingen.de

Rektor: Peter Niess
Tel: +49(7121) 271-1001, Fax: +49(7121) 271-1002
EMail: evi.zeisel@reutlingen-university.de

Kanzlerin: Paula Mattes Tel: +49(7121) 271-454

International Relations: Baldur Veit
Tel: +49(7121) 271-1004, Fax: +49(7121) 271-498
EMail: Baldur.Veit@fh-reutlingen.de

Faculties
Applied Chemistry (Applied Chemistry); **Informatics** (Computer Science); **Technology** (Electronic Engineering; Engineering; Machine Building; Mechanical Engineering); **Textile and Design** (Design; Textile Design)

Schools
Business (Business Administration; Business and Commerce)

History: Founded 1971.

Admission Requirements: Secondary school certificate (Abitur, Fachhochschulreifezeugnis)

Main Language(s) of Instruction: German

International Co-operation: With universities in Belgium, Denmark, Spain, France, Hungary, Ireland, Netherlands, Portugal, Romania, Sweden, Finland, United Kingdom

Degrees and Diplomas: *Bachelor/Bakkalaureus*: 3 yrs; *Master/Magister*: a further 2 yrs

Student Services: Academic counselling, Canteen, Foreign student adviser, Foreign Studies Centre, Handicapped facilities, Language programs, Social counselling, Sports facilities

Student Residential Facilities: Yes
Last Updated: 20/01/10

RHEIN-MAIN UNIVERSITY OF APPLIED SCIENCES

Hochschule Rhein-Main
Kurt-Schumacher-Ring 18, 65197 Wiesbaden
Tel: +49(611) 9495-01
Fax: +49(611) 444696
EMail: kanzler@hs-rm.de
Website: http://www.hs-rm.de

Präsident: Detlev Reymann
Tel: +49(611) 9495-1100, Fax: +49(611) 9495-106
EMail: praesident@hs-rm.de

Kanzler: Wilfried Friedl
Tel: +49(611) 9495-1102, Fax: +49(611) 9495-1108

Faculties

Applied Social Sciences *(Wiesbaden)* (Social Work); **Architecture and Civil Engineering** *(Wiesbaden)* (Architecture; Civil Engineering); **Design, Informatics, Media** *(Wiesbaden)* (Computer Science; Design; Interior Design; Media Studies); **Engineering** *(Rüsselsheim)* (Electrical Engineering; Engineering; Environmental Engineering; Industrial Engineering; Information Technology; Management); **Geisenheim** (Horticulture; Landscape Architecture; Oenology; Viticulture)

Schools

Business Studies *(Wiesbaden)* (Business Administration; Economics)

History: Founded 1971 as Fachhochschule Wiesbaden. Acquired present title 2009.

Main Language(s) of Instruction: German

Degrees and Diplomas: *Bachelor/Bakkalaureus*; *Diplom (FH)*: Engineering; *Master/Magister*
Last Updated: 02/02/12

RHENISH FRIEDRICH-WILHELM UNIVERSITY BONN

Rheinische Friedrich-Wilhelms-Universität Bonn
PO Box 2220, Regina-Pacis-Weg 3, 53012 Bonn
Tel: +49(228) 730
Fax: +49(228) 73-1780
Website: http://www.uni-bonn.de

Rektor: Jürgen Fohrmann
Tel: +49(228) 73-7297, Fax: +49(228) 73-7262
EMail: rektor@uni-bonn.de

Kanzler: Reinhard Lutz
Tel: +49(228) 73-7636, Fax: +49(228) 73-9046
EMail: kanzler@uni-bonn.de

Centres

Development Research (Development Studies); **European Integration** (European Studies); **Teacher Training** *(Bonner Ausbildungszentrum für Lehrerinnen und Lehrer) Director:* K. Priem

Faculties

Agriculture (Agriculture; Economics; Food Science; Food Technology; Nutrition; Surveying and Mapping); **Arts** (Archaeology; Art History; Classical Languages; Comparative Religion; Educational Sciences; History; Linguistics; Literature; Modern Languages; Musicology; Philosophy; Political Sciences; Psychology; Sociology; Sports); **Catholic Theology** (Catholic Theology; Pastoral Studies; Religious Studies); **Law and Economics** (Economics; Law); **Mathematics and Natural Sciences** (Astronomy and Space Science; Biology; Chemistry; Computer Science; Geography; Geology; Meteorology; Mineralogy; Physics); **Medicine** (Dentistry; Medicine); **Protestant Theology** (Protestant Theology)

Institutes

Old Catholic Theology Seminary (Theology)

Research Institutes

Discrete Mathematics (Mathematics); **Late Classical Antiquity** *(Franz Joseph Dölger)*

History: Founded 1777 by the Electoral Archbishop of Cologne, raised to University rank 1786, dissolved 1794. Refounded 1818 by William III of Prussia. Academy of Agriculture incorporated 1934. An autonomous institution financially supported by the State of North Rhine-Westphalia, and under the jurisdiction of its Ministry of Education.

Governing Bodies: Senat; Konvent

Academic Year: October to September (October-February; April-July)

Admission Requirements: Secondary school certificate (Reifezeugnis) or equivalent

Fees: None

Main Language(s) of Instruction: German

International Co-operation: Arrangements for co-operation at faculty level and about 1,200 international research projects. The University of Bonn is also member of the European network (University of Bologna; University of Leiden; University of Geneva; University of Oxford; University of Paris)

Degrees and Diplomas: *Bachelor/Bakkalaureus*; *Diplom*: Agriculture; Economics; Mathematics and Computer Sciences; Natural Sciences; Nutrition and Household Management; Oriental Languages; Psychology; Translation, 4-5 yrs; *Lehramt*: Teaching qualification, secondary schools; *Magister Artium*: Arts, 4-5 yrs; *Staatsprüfung*: Dentistry; Food Technology; Law; Medicine; Pharmacy; *Master/Magister*: Arts; *Doktorgrad*; *Habilitation*: at least 3 yrs following Doktor

Student Services: Academic counselling, Canteen, Handicapped facilities, Health services, Nursery care, Social counselling, Sports facilities

Student Residential Facilities: For c. 5,000 students

Special Facilities: König Museum; Akademisches Kunstmuseum (Classical Art). Collection of Mineralogy. Botanical Garden

Libraries: University Library, c. 5.8m. vols

Publications: Bonner Akademische Reden
Last Updated: 22/01/10

RHENISH UNIVERSITY OF APPLIED SCIENCES, COLOGNE

Rheinische Fachhochschule Köln
Hohenstaufenring 16-18, 50674 Köln, Nordrhein-Westfalen
Tel: +49(221) 20302-0
Fax: +49(221) 20302-49
EMail: verw@rfh-koeln.de
Website: http://www.rfh-koeln.de

Rektor: Gunter Cox
Tel: +49(221) 20302-15, Fax: +49(221) 20302-45
EMail: rektorat@rfh-koeln.de

Faculties

Business and Law (Business and Commerce; Business Computing; Law; Media Studies); **Engineering** (Electronic Engineering; Engineering; Mechanical Engineering)

History: Founded 1958. Acquired present status 1971.

Main Language(s) of Instruction: German

International Co-operation: With universities in the United Kingdom and Africa.

Degrees and Diplomas: *Bachelor/Bakkalaureus*; *Diplom (FH) (Dipl.-Ing. (FH)) (Diplomingenieur (FH))*: 3 1/2 yrs; *Master/Magister*

Student Services: Academic counselling, Employment services, Foreign student adviser, Foreign Studies Centre, Language programs, Social counselling, Sports facilities

Special Facilities: Computer centre

Libraries: Main Library
Last Updated: 12/02/09

RHINE-WAAL UNIVERSITY OF APPLIED SCIENCES

Hochschule Rhein-Waal
Landwehr 4, D-47533 Kleve
EMail: info@hochschule-rhein-waal.de
Website: http://www.hochschule-rhein-waal.de

Präsidentin: Marie Louise Klotz

Departments

Communication and Environmental Studies (Communication Studies; Computer Science; Energy Engineering; Environmental Studies; Industrial Engineering; International Business; Media Studies; Psychology; Social Sciences); **Life Sciences** (Agricultural Business; Agriculture; Bioengineering; Biological and Life Sciences; Health Sciences); **Society and Economics** (Economics; Finance; Gender Studies; International Business; Preschool Education; Social Sciences; Taxation; Tourism); **Technology and Bionics** (Biotechnology; Electronic Engineering; Industrial Engineering; Materials Engineering)

History: Founded 2009.

Main Language(s) of Instruction: German

Degrees and Diplomas: *Bachelor/Bakkalaureus*; *Master/Magister*
Last Updated: 04/02/10

RIEDLINGEN UNIVERSITY

SRH FernHochschule Riedlingen

Robert-Bosch-Str. 23, 88499 Riedlingen
Tel: +49(7371) 9315-0
Fax: +49(7371) 9315-15
EMail: info@fh-riedlingen.srh.de
Website: http://www.fh-riedlingen.de/

Rektorin: Julia S. Sander
Tel: +49(7371) 9315-18 EMail: julia.sander@fh-riedlingen.srh.de

Kanzlerin: Sabine Sarrazin
Tel: +49(7371) 9315-17 EMail: sabine.sarrazin@fh-riedlingen.de

International Relations: Thomas Schempf

Departments

Business Administration (Business Administration); **Business Psychology** (Psychology); **Health Sciences and Social Work** (Health Administration; Health Sciences; Social Work)

History: Founded 1996.

Main Language(s) of Instruction: German

Degrees and Diplomas: *Bachelor/Bakkalaureus*; *Master/Magister*
Last Updated: 26/01/10

ROBERT SCHUMANN SCHOOL OF MUSIC AND MEDIA

Robert-Schumann-Hochschule Düsseldorf

Fischerstrasse 110, 40476 Düsseldorf
Tel: +49(211) 4918-0
Fax: +49(211) 4911-618
EMail: kontakt@rsh-duesseldorf.de
Website: http://www.rsh-duesseldorf.de/de/index.php

Rektor: Raimund Wippermann (2004-) Tel: +49(211) 4918-109

Kanzlerin: Cathrin Muller
Tel: +49(211) 4918-108, Fax: +49(211) 4911-618

Institutes

Music (Music; Musical Instruments; Singing); **Music and Media** (Media Studies; Music); **Music Education** (Conducting; Music Theory and Composition; Religious Music)

History: Founded 1935.

Main Language(s) of Instruction: German

Degrees and Diplomas: *Bachelor/Bakkalaureus*; *Master/Magister*
Last Updated: 22/01/10

ROSENHEIM UNIVERSITY OF APPLIED SCIENCES

Hochschule Rosenheim

Hochschulstraße 1, 83024 Rosenheim
Tel: +49(8031) 805-0
Fax: +49(8031) 805-105
EMail: info@fh-rosenheim.de
Website: http://www.hs-rosenheim.de

Präsident: Heinrich Köster
Tel: +49(8031) 805-110, Fax: +49(8031) 805-111
EMail: koester@fh-rosenheim.de

Kanzler: Oliver Heller
Tel: +49(8031) 805-130, Fax: +49(8031) 805-132
EMail: heller@fh-rosenheim.de

International Relations: Barbara Fest
Tel: +49(8031) 805-118, Fax: +49(8031) 805-127
EMail: auslandsamt@fh-rosenheim.de

Faculties

Applied Sciences and Humanities (Chemistry; Computer Science; Cultural Studies; Data Processing; Economics; Environmental Studies; Industrial Management; Mathematics; Modern Languages; Natural Sciences; Operations Research; Physics; Public Administration; Safety Engineering; Social Sciences; Statistics; Transport

Management); **Business Administration** (Business Administration; Business and Commerce; Business Computing); **Engineering** (Business Administration; Engineering); **Engineering and Management** *(KPE)* (Electronic Engineering; Information Technology; Management; Materials Engineering; Production Engineering); **Informatics** (Business Computing; Computer Science); **Interior Architecture** (Interior Design); **Wood Technology and Industrial Engineering** (Industrial Engineering; Wood Technology)

History: Founded 1971. Formerly known as Fachhochschule Rosenheim - Hochschule für Technik und Wirtschaft.

Governing Bodies: Leitungsgremium

Academic Year: October to July (October- February; March-July)

Admission Requirements: Secondary school certificate

Main Language(s) of Instruction: German. Also English in Master courses

International Co-operation: Participates in Erasmus

Degrees and Diplomas: *Bachelor/Bakkalaureus*: Electrical Engineering and Information Technology; Informatics; Interior Architecture; Interior Engineering; Wood Construction; Wood Technology, 31/2 yrs; *Diplom (FH)*: Business Administration, 4 yrs; *Master/Magister*: Electrical Engineering and Information Technology; Wood Engineering; Production Engineering; Industrial Engineering, 1 1/2 yrs

Student Services: Academic counselling, Canteen, Foreign student adviser, Language programs, Social counselling, Sports facilities

Student Residential Facilities: Yes
Last Updated: 20/01/10

ROSTOCK UNIVERSITY OF MUSIC AND DRAMA

Hochschule für Musik und Theater Rostock

Beim St.-Katharinenstift 8, 18055 Rostock
Tel: +49(381) 5108-0
Fax: +49(381) 5108-101 +49(381) 5108-233
EMail: hmt@hmt-rostock.de
Website: http://www.hmt-rostock.de

Rektorin: Christfried Göckeritz
Tel: +49(381) 5108-100, Fax: +49(381) 5108-101
EMail: rektor@hmt-rostock.de

Kanzler: Frank Ivemeyer
Tel: +49 (381) 5108-200 EMail: Kanzler@hmt-rostock.de

International Relations: Philippe Olivier, international Relations
Tel: +33(1) 429-33958 EMail: philippe.olivier@berlin.de

Institutes

Drama (Acting; Theatre); **Music** (Music); **Musicology and Music Education** (Music Education; Musicology)

History: Founded 1994.

Main Language(s) of Instruction: German

Degrees and Diplomas: *Bachelor/Bakkalaureus*; *Lehramt*; *Master/Magister*: Artistic Education
Last Updated: 19/01/10

ROTTENBURG UNIVERSITY OF APPLIED FOREST SCIENCES

Hochschule für Forstwirtschaft Rottenburg (HFR)

Schadenweilerhof, 72108 Rottenburg am Neckar
Tel: +49(7472) 951-0
Fax: +49(7472) 951-200
EMail: hfr@hs-rottenburg.de
Website: http://www.fh-rottenburg.de

Rektor: Bastian Kaiser
Tel: +49(7472) 951-204 EMail: BKaiser@hs-rottenburg.de

Kanzler: Dieter Kienzle
Tel: +49(7472) 951-201 EMail: Kienzle@hs-rottenburg.de

International Relations: Stefan Ruge, Head, International Office
Tel: +49(7472) 951-233, Fax: +49(7472) 951-200
EMail: Ruge@hs-rottenburg.de

Programmes

Bioenergy (Biological and Life Sciences; Energy Engineering); **Forestry** (Forestry); **Sustainable Energy Competence** *(SENCE)* (Energy Engineering); **Water Management**

History: Founded 1954, acquired present status 1979. Formerly known as Fachhochschule Rottenburg - Hochschule für Fortswirtschaft.

Academic Year: October to July

Admission Requirements: Secondary school certificate (Hochschulreife) or equivalent

Fees: None

Main Language(s) of Instruction: German, English

International Co-operation: With universities in the Netherlands, Finland, France, Sweden, United Kingdom, Spain, Czech Republic, Brazil.

Degrees and Diplomas: *Bachelor/Bakkalaureus*: Forestry; Bioenergy; Water Management; *Master/Magister*: Sustainable Energy Competence (SENCE). Double Degree: Dipl.-Ing.FH/BSc in Tropical Forestry, 4 1/2 yrs

Student Services: Academic counselling, Canteen, Foreign student adviser, Language programs, Social counselling, Sports facilities

Student Residential Facilities: Yes

Libraries: c. 28,000 items
Last Updated: 19/01/10

RUHR-WEST UNIVERSITY OF APPLIED SCIENCES

Hochschule Ruhr-West
Brunshofstraße 12, 45470 Mülheim an der Ruhr
Tel: +49(208) 302 46-0
Fax: +49(208) 302 46-102
EMail: info@hs-ruhrwest.de
Website: http://www.hochschule-ruhr-west.de

Präsident: Eberhard Menzel
EMail: menzel.eberhard@hs-ruhrwest.de

Programmes

Business Administration (Business Administration); **Computer Science** (Computer Science); **Electrical Engineering** (Electrical Engineering); **Industrial Engineering and Energy Systems** (Energy Engineering; Industrial Engineering); **Mechanical Engineering** (Machine Building; Mechanical Engineering)

History: Founded 2009.

Main Language(s) of Instruction: German

Degrees and Diplomas: *Bachelor/Bakkalaureus*; *Master/Magister*
Last Updated: 08/02/10

RWTH - AACHEN UNIVERSITY

Rheinisch-Westfälische Technische Hochschule Aachen
Templergraben 55, 52056 Aachen
Tel: +49(241) 80-1
Fax: +49(241) 80-92312
EMail: international@rwth-aachen.de
Website: http://www.rwth-aachen.de

Rektor: Ernst M. Schmachtenberg (2008-)
Tel: +49(241) 80-94000, Fax: +49(241) 80-92102
EMail: rektor@rwth-aachen.de

Kanzler: Manfred Nettekoven
Tel: +49(241) 80-94010, Fax: +49(241) 80-92101
EMail: kanzler@zhv.rwth-aachen.de

International Relations: Heide Naderer
Tel: +49(241) 80-90,660; +49(241) 80-90663,
Fax: +49(241) 80-92662
EMail: heide.naderer@zhv.rwth-aachen.de

Faculties

Architecture (Architectural and Environmental Design; Architecture; Art History; Design; Fine Arts; Landscape Architecture; Painting and Drawing; Regional Planning; Structural Architecture; Town Planning); **Arts and Humanities** (Educational Sciences; English; German; History; Linguistics; Literature; Philosophy; Political Sciences; Psychology; Romance Languages; Sociology; Theology; **Business and Economics** (Accountancy; Banking; Business Administration; Commercial Law; E-Business/Commerce; Economics; Finance; Industrial Management; Information Sciences; International Business; Management; Operations Research; Taxation; Technology; Transport Management); **Civil Engineering** (Business Administration; Civil Engineering; Construction Engineering; Environmental Engineering; Geological Engineering; Hydraulic Engineering; Management; Mechanical Engineering; Town Planning; Transport Engineering; Waste Management; Water Management); **Electrical Engineering and Information Technology** (Biomedical Engineering; Computer Science; Electrical Engineering; Electronic Engineering; Engineering; Information Technology; Measurement and Precision Engineering; Petroleum and Gas Engineering; Power Engineering; Sound Engineering (Acoustics); Telecommunications Engineering); **Georesources and Materials Engineering** (Geology; Materials Engineering; Metallurgical Engineering; Mining Engineering; Waste Management); **Mathematics, Computer Science and Natural Sciences** (Biology; Chemistry; Computer Science; Mathematics; Natural Sciences; Physics); **Mechanical Engineering** (Aeronautical and Aerospace Engineering; Automation and Control Engineering; Automotive Engineering; Biochemistry; Ceramics and Glass Technology; Chemical Engineering; Computer Engineering; Computer Science; Heating and Refrigeration; Industrial Engineering; Laser Engineering; Materials Engineering; Mechanical Engineering; Mechanics; Medical Technology; Metal Techniques; Nuclear Engineering; Operations Research; Optical Technology; Physical Engineering; Polymer and Plastics Technology; Power Engineering; Production Engineering; Railway Engineering; Textile Technology; Thermal Engineering); **Medicine** (Anaesthesiology; Cardiology; Dentistry; Gynaecology and Obstetrics; Medicine; Neurology; Ophthalmology; Orthodontics; Orthopaedics; Plastic Surgery; Psychiatry and Mental Health; Radiology; Surgery; Urology)

Further Information: Language courses and MSc programmes for international students. International Study programmes

History: Founded 1870 as Polytechnikum, became Technische Hochschule in 1880 and acquired present title 1948, reorganized 1970. Under the jurisdiction of and financed by the State of North Rhine-Westphalia.

Governing Bodies: Rektorat; Senat

Academic Year: October to September (October-March; April-September)

Admission Requirements: Secondary school certificate (Reifezeugnis) or equivalent

Fees: (Euros): c. 1,300 per annum

Main Language(s) of Instruction: German

International Co-operation: With institutions worldwide

Degrees and Diplomas: *Bachelor/Bakkalaureus*: Arts and Humanities (B.A.); Natural Sciences; Economics; Engineering (B.Sc.), 3-4 yrs; *Staatsprüfung*: Medicine, 6 yrs; *Master/Magister*: Arts and Humanities; Natural Sciences, Engineering and Economics, 1-2 yrs; *Doktorgrad*: 3-5 yrs; *Habilitation*: at least 3 yrs after Doctorate

Student Services: Canteen, Foreign student adviser, Social counselling, Sports facilities

Student Residential Facilities: Yes

Libraries: Central Library, 1,200,000 vols; institute libraries

Publications: Alma Mater Aquensis *(annually)*; RWTH-Themen
Last Updated: 22/01/10

SAAR COLLEGE OF FINE ARTS

Hochschule der Bildenden Künste Saar
Keplerstraße 3-5, 66117 Saarbrücken
Tel: +49(681) 92652-101
Fax: +49(681) 92652-149
EMail: info@hbks.uni-sb.de
Website: http://www.hbks.uni-sb.de

Rektor: Ivica Maksimovic
Tel: +49(681) 92652-126, Fax: +49(681) 92652-149
EMail: i.maksimovic@hbks.uni-sb.de

Kanzler: Heinz Scherber EMail: h.scherber@hbks.uni-sb.de

International Relations: Sabine Rauber, Officer, International Academic Affairs
Tel: +49(681) 92652-115, Fax: +49(681) 92652-112
EMail: s.rauber@hbks.uni-sb.de

Departments
Design (Design); **Fine Arts** (Fine Arts)
History: Founded 1989.

Degrees and Diplomas: *Diplom-Vorprüfung*; *Diplom*: Design; Fine Arts, 5 yrs
Last Updated: 11/02/09

SAARLAND UNIVERSITY
Universität des Saarlandes
PO Box 151150, Im Stadtwald, 66041 Saarbrücken
Tel: +49(681) 302-0
Fax: +49(681) 302-2609
EMail: postzentrale@univw.uni-saarland.de
Website: http://www.uni-saarland.de

Präsident: Volker Linneweber (2006-)
Tel: +49(681) 302-2000, Fax: +49(681) 302-3001
EMail: praesident@uni-saarland.de

International Relations: Stefan Lauterbach
Tel: +49(681) 302-4487, Fax: +49(681) 302-4489
EMail: s.lauterbach@io.uni-saarland.de

Faculties
Humanities I (Art History; Catholic Theology; History; Music; Theology); **Humanities II** (American Studies; English; German; Linguistics; Modern Languages; Romance Languages; Slavic Languages); **Humanities III** (Geography; Psychology; Sociology; Sports); **Law and Economics** (Business Administration; Economics; Law; Statistics); **Medicine** *(Homburg Campus)* (Health Sciences; Medicine); **Natural Sciences and Technology I** (Mathematics and Computer Science); **Natural Sciences and Technology II** (Mechanical Engineering; Physics); **Natural Sciences and Technology III** (Biotechnology; Chemistry; Materials Engineering; Pharmacy)

History: Founded 1948 with the help of France, the University became a member of the Western German Rectors' Conference (WRK; today Hochschulrektorenkonferenz-HRK) 1957. Financially supported by the State of the Saar, and under the jurisdiction of its Ministry of Education and Science.
Governing Bodies: Senat; Universitätsrat
Academic Year: October to September (October-March; April-September)
Admission Requirements: Secondary school certificate (Abitur) or equivalent
Fees: (Euros): Tuition in some postgraduate programmes; normal course per semester 300 first year, 1,000 each following year
Main Language(s) of Instruction: German, English, French in some programmes.
International Co-operation: With some 280 universities worldwide
Degrees and Diplomas: *Bachelor/Bakkalaureus*; *Diplom*; *Lehramt*; *Staatsprüfung*; *Master/Magister*; *Promotion*
Student Services: Academic counselling, Canteen, Employment services, Foreign student adviser, Handicapped facilities, Language programs, Nursery care, Social counselling, Sports facilities
Student Residential Facilities: Yes
Libraries: University Library, c. 1.7m. vols; c. 4,000 CD-Rom Databases; Medicine (Homburg), 250,000; Institute libraries, c. 1.8m. Vols
Last Updated: 28/01/10

SALESIAN DON BOSCO COLLEGE OF PHILOSOPHY AND THEOLOGY, BENEDIKTBEUERN
Philosophisch-Theologische Hochschule der Salesianer Don Boscos Benediktbeuern (PTH)
Don-Bosco-Strasse 1, 83671 Benediktbeuern
Tel: +49(8857) 882-01
Fax: +49(8857) 882-49
EMail: sekretariat@pth-bb.de
Website: http://www.pth-bb.de

Rektor: Lothar Bily Tel: +49(8857) 882-00

Faculties
Philosophy (Philosophy); **Theology** *(Catholic)* (Theology)
History: Founded 1931.
Main Language(s) of Instruction: German
Degrees and Diplomas: *Bachelor/Bakkalaureus*; *Diplom*; *Lizentiat*; *Master/Magister*; *Promotion*; *Habilitation*
Last Updated: 22/01/10

SANKT GEORGEN GRADUATE SCHOOL OF PHILOSOPHY AND THEOLOGY, FRANKFURT AM MAIN
Philosophisch-Theologische Hochschule Sankt Georgen Frankfurt am Main
Offenbacher Landstrasse 224, D-60599 Frankfurt am Main
Tel: +49(69) 6061-0
Fax: +49(69) 6061-307
EMail: rektorat@sankt-georgen.de
Website: http://www.sankt-georgen.de

Rektor: Heinrich Watzka Tel: +49(69) 6061-219

Institutes
Economic and Societal Ethics *(Oswald von Nell-Breuning)* (Ethics); **History of Dogma and Liturgy** (Religious Studies); **Pastoral Psychology and Spirituality** (Psychology); **Philosophy** (Philosophy); **Study of the Middle Ages** *(Hugo von Sankt Viktor)* (Medieval Studies)

Programmes
Theology (Catholic Theology; Theology)
History: Founded 1926.
Academic Year: October to September
Admission Requirements: Hochschulzugangsberechtigung, Abitur, Matura
Fees: (Euros): 80 per semester
Main Language(s) of Instruction: German
International Co-operation: With universities in Europe, Mexico; USA. Also participates in Erasmus
Degrees and Diplomas: *Bachelor/Bakkalaureus*; *Diplom*: 5 yrs; *Lizentiat*: 2 yrs; *Doktorgrad*: 3-4 yrs; *Habilitation*
Student Services: Academic counselling, Canteen, Cultural centre, Foreign student adviser, Foreign Studies Centre, Handicapped facilities, Language programs, Social counselling, Sports facilities
Student Residential Facilities: Yes
Libraries: Yes
Publications: Theologie und Philosophie *(quarterly)*
Last Updated: 03/02/12

SCHWÄBISCH GMÜND UNIVERSITY OF APPLIED SCIENCES FOR DESIGN
Hochschule für Gestaltung Schwäbisch Gmünd
Postfach 1308, Rektor-Klaus-Straße 100, 73503 Schwäbisch Gmünd
Tel: +49(7171) 602-600
Fax: +49(7171) 692-59
EMail: info@hfg-gmuend.de
Website: http://www.hfg-gmuend.de

Rektorin: Cristina Salerno (2003-)
Tel: +49(7171) 6026-03 EMail: cristina.salerno@hfg-gmuend.de

Kanzler: Wolfgang Neumann
Tel: +49(7171) 6026-02
EMail: wolfgang.neumann@hfg-gmuend.de

International Relations: George Burden
EMail: international@hfg-gmuend.de

Programmes
Communication Design (Graphic Design); **Communication Planning and Design** *(Master)* (Design); **Interaction Design** (Design); **Product Design** (Industrial Design); **Production Planning and Design** *(Master)* (Design)
History: Founded 1907. Acquired present status 1971.

Admission Requirements: Fachhochschulreife and entrance examination

Fees: None

Main Language(s) of Instruction: German and English

International Co-operation: Participates in the Erasmus, Unibral, Leonardo and Cumulus programmes

Degrees and Diplomas: *Bachelor/Bakkalaureus*: Interaction Design; Communication Design; Product Design, 3 1/2 yrs; *Master/ Magister*: Communication Planning and Design; Product Planning and Design, 1 1/2 yrs

Student Services: Academic counselling, Canteen, Foreign student adviser

Special Facilities: Media Centre

Last Updated: 19/01/10

SOUTH WESTPHALIA UNIVERSITY OF APPLIED SCIENCES

Fachhochschule Südwestfalen

PO Box 2061, Frauenstuhlweg 31, 58644 Iserlohn
Tel: +49(2371) 566-0
Fax: +49(2371) 566-274
EMail: aaa@fh-swf.de
Website: http://www.fh-swf.de

Präsident: Claus Schuster
Tel: +49(2371) 566-110 EMail: schuster@fh-swf.de

Vizepräsident für Wirtschafts- und Personalverwaltung: Heinz-Joachim Henkemeier
Tel: +49(2371) 566-121 EMail: Henkemeier@fh-swf.de

International Relations: Dagmar Perizonius
Tel: +49(2371) 566-210 EMail: perizonius@fh-swf.de

Courses

Agriculture *(Soest)*; **Applied Computer Science**; **Automotive**; **Business Administration** *(Meschede)* (Business Administration); **Business Administration and Computer Science** *(Hagen)*; **Business Administration and Engineering** *(Hagen)*; **Business Administration with Informatics** *(Soest)* (Business Administration; Computer Science); **Business Administration with Mechanical Engineering** *(Meschede)* (Business Administration; Mechanical Engineering); **Computer Engineering** *(Hagen)* (Computer Engineering); **Computer Vision and Computational Intelligence**; **Corrosion Protection Technology**; **Engineering** *(Soest)* (Engineering); **Management** *(Meschede)* (Engineering; Management); **Mechatronics** (Electronic Engineering; Mechanical Engineering); **Natural Sciences**; **Production Engineering** (Production Engineering)

Departments

Electrical Engineering *(Soest, Hagen, Meschede)* (Electrical Engineering); **Mechanical and Automation Engineering** *(Soest)*; **Mechanical Engineering** *(Meschede, Soest)*

Institutes

Integrated Campus and Distance Learning *(IfV NRW)*

History: Founded 2002, after merger with Märkischen Fachhochschulen Hagen and Iserlohn and Fachhochschulabteilungen Meschede and Soest of the Gesamthochschule-Universität Paderborn.

Main Language(s) of Instruction: German

Degrees and Diplomas: *Bachelor/Bakkalaureus*; *Master/Magister*: Technical Business Administration; Commercial Law

Last Updated: 06/02/12

SRH UNIVERSITY BERLIN

SRH Hochschule Berlin

Ernst-Reuter-Platz 10, 10587 Berlin
Tel: +49(309) 225-3531
Fax: +49(309) 225-3557
EMail: info@srh-hochschule-berlin.de
Website: http://www.www-srh-hochschule-berlin.de

Präsident: Peter Eichhorn
EMail: eugenia.keim@srh-hochschule-berlin.de

Departments

Business Administration (Business Administration); **Information and Communication** (Communication Studies; Information Management; Mass Communication)

History: Founded 2002 as OTA Hochschule (OTA Private University of Applied Sciences). Acquired current title 2008.

Governing Bodies: Academic Senat; Student Parliament; Examination Board

Academic Year: October to August

Admission Requirements: For Bachelor programs: Abitur/Fachabitur (University entrance diploma) or equivalent; TOEFL iBT score of 79 to 80 required for programmes in English. For Master's programme: Bachelor's or advanced academic degree (Diploma) in the related subject.

Fees: (Euros): 700 per month for Bachelor's and Master's Programmes.

Main Language(s) of Instruction: German; English

International Co-operation: Erasmus exchanges with institutions in France, Ireland and Turkey

Accrediting Agencies: FIBAA; AHPGS

Degrees and Diplomas: *Bachelor/Bakkalaureus*: Business Administration; Information and Communication Management (BA); *Master/Magister*: International Strategic Management (MA), 2 yrs

Student Services: Academic counselling, Canteen, Employment services, Foreign student adviser, Handicapped facilities, Language programs, Social counselling, Sports facilities

Student Residential Facilities: Yes - at Technical University Berlin.

Libraries: Own in-house library; Access to library of Technical University Berlin.

Academic Staff 2008-2009	MEN	WOMEN	TOTAL
FULL-TIME	8	7	15
PART-TIME	19	7	26
STAFF WITH DOCTORATE			
FULL-TIME	2	4	6
PART-TIME	9	3	12
Student Numbers 2008-2009			
All (Foreign Included)	110	64	174
FOREIGN ONLY	28	13	41

Last Updated: 26/01/10

SRH UNIVERSITY HEIDELBERG

SRH Hochschule Heidelberg

PO Box 101409, 69004 Heidelberg
Tel: +49(6221) 88-1000
Fax: +49(6221) 88-4122
EMail: info@fh-heidelberg.de
Website: http://www.fh-heidelberg.de

Rektor: Jörg M. Winterberg Tel: +49(6221) 88-2258

Schools

Applied Psychology (Psychology); **Business** (Business Administration; Sports Management); **Computer Science** (Business Computing; Computer Science; Health Administration; Multimedia); **Engineering and Architecture** (Architecture; Construction Engineering; Electrical Engineering; Engineering; Industrial Engineering; Information Technology; Mechanical Engineering; Production Engineering); **Social and Legal Sciences** (Law; Leadership; Management; Social Sciences); **Therapy** (Art Therapy; Music; Physical Therapy)

History: Founded 1969. Formerly known as Fachhochschule Heidelberg.

Main Language(s) of Instruction: German

Degrees and Diplomas: *Bachelor/Bakkalaureus*; *Master/Magister*
Last Updated: 26/01/10

SRH UNIVERSITY OF APPLIED SCIENCES CALW

SRH Hochschule Calw

Badstr. 27, 75365 Calw
Tel: +49(7051) 9203-0
Fax: +49(7051) 9203-59
EMail: info@hs-calw.de
Website: http://www.hochschule-calw.de

Rektor: Jörg M. Winterberg

Programmes

Media and Communication Management in Businesses (Communication Studies; Media Studies); **Taxation and Auditing** (Finance; Taxation)

Main Language(s) of Instruction: German

Degrees and Diplomas: *Bachelor/Bakkalaureus*; *Master/Magister*
Last Updated: 03/02/12

SRH UNIVERSITY OF APPLIED SCIENCES GERA

SRH Fachhochschule für Gesundheit Gera

Villa Hirsch, Hermann-Drechsler-Str. 2, 07548 Gera
Tel: +49(365) 773-407-0
Fax: +49(365) 773-407-77
EMail: info@gesundheitshochschule.de
Website: http://www.gesundheitshochschule.de

Rektor: Thomas Körner

Head of Administration: Ilona Renken-Olthoff

Programmes

Health Psychology; **Interdisciplinary Early Learning** (Law; Medicine; Pedagogy; Psychology); **Logotherapy**; **Nursing** (Nursing); **Occupational Therapy** (Occupational Therapy); **Physiotherapy** (Physical Therapy); **Theory and Practice of Medical Education** (Medicine)

Main Language(s) of Instruction: German

Degrees and Diplomas: *Bachelor/Bakkalaureus*; *Master/Magister*
Last Updated: 22/01/10

SRH UNIVERSITY OF APPLIED SCIENCES FOR LOGISTICS AND ECONOMICS

SRH Hochschule für Logistik und Wirtschaft

Sachsenweg 12, 59073 Hamm
Tel: +49(23) 818710-732
Fax: +49(23) 818710-739
EMail: info@fh-hamm.srh.de
Website: http://www.fh-hamm.srh.de

Rektor: Heinz Joachim Opitz (2012-)

Programmes

Dental Technology (Anatomy; Biology; Dental Technology; Hygiene; Medicine; Physiology; Transport Management); **Facility Management** (Business Administration; Finance; Management); **Logistic Management** *(Postgraduate)* (Management; Transport Management); **Logistics** (Transport Management)

Main Language(s) of Instruction: German

Degrees and Diplomas: *Bachelor/Bakkalaureus*; *Master/Magister*. Logistics Management, 2 yrs
Last Updated: 03/02/12

STATE UNIVERSITY OF MUSIC AND PERFORMING ARTS STUTTGART

Staatliche Hochschule für Musik und Darstellende Kunst Stuttgart

Urbanstrasse 25, 70182 Stuttgart
Tel: +49(711) 212-0
Fax: +49(711) 21246-39
EMail: post@mh-stuttgart.de
Website: http://www.mh-stuttgart.de

Rektor: Werner Heinrichs
Tel: +49(711) 21246-31, Fax: +49(711) 21246-32
EMail: rektor@mh-stuttgart.de

Kanzler: Albrecht Lang
Tel: +49(711) 21246-37 EMail: albrecht.lang@mh-stuttgart.de

International Relations: Shoshana Rudiakov
Tel: +49(711) 21246-60
EMail: shoshana.rudiakov@mh-stuttgart.de

Faculties

I (Music; Music Education; Music Theory and Composition; Musicology); **II** (Jazz and Popular Music; Music; Musical Instruments); **III** (Conducting; Music; Musical Instruments); **IV** (Communication Arts; Opera; Pedagogy; Singing; Theatre)

History: Founded 1857 as Stuttgarter Musikschule.

Academic Year: October to March; April to September

Admission Requirements: Graduation diploma, entrance examination, language examination

Main Language(s) of Instruction: German

International Co-operation: Participates in Erasmus/Socrates and DAAD

Degrees and Diplomas: *Bachelor/Bakkalaureus*; *Diplom*: 4 yrs; *Lehramt*; *Master/Magister*, *Promotion*; *Doktorgrad*

Student Services: Canteen

Special Facilities: Recording studio

Libraries: Yes

Publications: Vorlesungsverzeichnis *(biannually)*
Last Updated: 26/01/10

STEINBEIS UNIVERSITY BERLIN

Steinbeis-Hochschule-Berlin

Gürtelstrasse 29A/30, 10247 Berlin
Tel: +49(30) 293309-0
Fax: +49(30) 293309-20
EMail: shb@stw.de
Website: http://www.steinbeis-hochschule.de

Präsident: Johann Löhn (1998-) EMail: loehn@stw.de

Academies

Business (Business Administration)

Institutes

Management and Technology *(Stuttgart)* (Management; Technology)

Schools

Dental and Oral Medicine Alliance (Dentistry); **Executive Management** *(IBR)* (Management); **Governance, Risk and Compliance** (Government); **International Business and Entrepreneurship** (Business Administration); **Management and Innovation** (Management); **Management and Technology** (Management; Technology)

History: Founded 1998.

Main Language(s) of Instruction: German

Degrees and Diplomas: *Bachelor/Bakkalaureus*; *Master/Magister*; *Promotion*; *Doktorgrad*
Last Updated: 26/01/10

STRALSUND UNIVERSITY OF APPLIED SCIENCES

Fachhochschule Stralsund

Zur Schwedenschanze 15, 18435 Stralsund
Tel: +49(3831) 45-5
Fax: +49(3831) 456-680
EMail: rektor@fh-stralsund.de
Website: http://www.fh-stralsund.de

Rektor: Joachim Venghaus
Tel: +49(3831) 456-500, Fax: +49(3831) 456-658

Kanzlerin: Susanne Wilcken
Tel: +49(3831) 456-503, Fax: +49(3831) 456-655
EMail: kanzler@fh-stralsund.de

Schools

Business Studies (Business Administration; Business Computing; Management; Tourism); **Electrical Engineering and Computer Science** (Biomedical Engineering; Computer Engineering; Electrical

Engineering; Medical Technology); **Mechanical Engineering** (Mechanical Engineering)

History: Founded 1991.

Governing Bodies: Rectorate

Academic Year: September to August (September-February; March-August)

Admission Requirements: Secondary school certificate (Abitur) or foreign equivalent

Fees: None

Main Language(s) of Instruction: German; English (2 courses)

International Co-operation: Participates in the Erasmus programme

Accrediting Agencies: Foundation for International Business Administration Accreditation (FIBAA) - Stiftung der Deutschen, Österreichischen und Schweizerischen Wirtschaft; Akkreditierungsagentur für Studiengänge der Ingenieurwissenschaften, der Informatik, der Naturwissenschaften und der Mathematik (ASIIN)

Degrees and Diplomas: *Bachelor/Bakkalaureus*; *Diplom (FH)*: Business Engineering; *Master/Magister*: Business Computing; Electronic Engineering; Computer Science; Medicine Computing; Machine Building - Automotive Engineering; Machine Building - Developemtn and Production

Student Services: Academic counselling, Canteen, Employment services, Foreign student adviser, Handicapped facilities, Language programs, Social counselling, Sports facilities

Student Residential Facilities: For 308 students

Special Facilities: Planetarium

Libraries: c. 80,000 vols; c. 250 periodical subscriptions

Publications: Wissenschaftliche Schriftenreihe *(annually)*

Last Updated: 06/02/12

STUTTGART MEDIA UNIVERSITY

Hochschule der Medien
Nobelstrasse 10, 70569 Stuttgart
Tel: +49(711) 8923-10
Fax: +49(711) 8923-11
EMail: info@hdm-stuttgart.de
Website: http://www.hdm-stuttgart.de

Rektor: Alexander W. Roos
Tel: +49(711) 8923-2004 EMail: roos@hdm-stuttgart.de

International Relations: Gottfried Ohnmacht-Neugebauer
Tel: +49(711) 8923-2031 EMail: ohnmacht@hdm-stuttgart.de

Faculties
Electronic Media (Advertising and Publicity; Media Studies); **Information and Communication** (Information Management; Library Science); **Print and Media** (Media Studies; Packaging Technology; Printing and Printmaking)

History: Founded 2001 through the merger of the Fachhochschule Stuttgart – Hochschule fuer Bibliotheks- und Informationswesen (HBI) University of Applied Sciences and the Fachhochschule Stuttgart – Hochschule fuer Druck und Medien (HDM) University of Applied Sciences.

Main Language(s) of Instruction: German

Degrees and Diplomas: *Bachelor/Bakkalaureus*; *Master/Magister*
Last Updated: 01/02/12

STUTTGART STATE ACADEMY OF ART AND DESIGN

Staatliche Akademie der Bildenden Künste Stuttgart
Am Weissenhof 1, 70191 Stuttgart
Tel: +49(711) 28440-0
Fax: +49(711) 28440-225
EMail: info@abk-stuttgart.de
Website: http://www.abk-stuttgart.de

Rektorin: Petra von Olschowski
Tel: +49(711) 28440-101, Fax: +49(711) 28440-102
EMail: rektorat@abk-stuttgart.de

Kanzler: Matthias Knapp
Tel: +49(711) 28440-114, Fax: +49(711) 28440-102
EMail: m.knapp@abk-stuttgart.de

Departments
Architecture and Design (Architecture; Design; Textile Design); **Art Education** (Art Education); **Fine Arts** (Ceramic Art; Glass Art; Graphic Arts; Painting and Drawing; Sculpture); **Restoration** (Restoration of Works of Art)

Institutes
Book Design and Media Development (Media Studies; Publishing and Book Trade); **Museology** (Museum Studies); **Weissenhof** (Architecture)

History: Founded 1902 from the Académie des Arts founded in 1761 and the Württemberg State School of Arts and Crafts founded in 1869 which were both amalgamated with the Royal teaching and Experimental Workshops in 1902.

Main Language(s) of Instruction: German

Degrees and Diplomas: *Bachelor/Bakkalaureus*; *Diplom (FH)*; *Master/Magister*; *Promotion*
Last Updated: 03/02/12

STUTTGART UNIVERSITY OF APPLIED SCIENCES

Hochschule für Technik Stuttgart
PO Box 101452, Schellingstrasse 24, 70013 Stuttgart
Tel: +49(711) 8926-2660
Fax: +49(711) 8926-2666
EMail: studsek.vw@hft-stuttgart.de
Website: http://www.fht-stuttgart.de

Rektor: Rainer Franke
Tel: +49(711) 121-2664 EMail: rainer.franke@hft-stuttgart.de

Kanzler: Gerhard Blöchle
Tel: +49(711) 121-2661 EMail: gerhard.bloechle@hft-stuttgart.de

International Relations: Michael Geiger
Tel: +49(711) 121-2868, Fax: +49(711) 121-2682
EMail: michael.geiger@hft-stuttgart.de

Faculties
Architecture and Design (Architecture; Interior Design; Town Planning); **Building Physics** (Construction Engineering; Physical Engineering); **Civil Engineering** (Business Administration; Civil Engineering; Structural Architecture; Town Planning); **Computer Science** (Computer Science; Software Engineering; Surveying and Mapping); **Economics** (Business Administration; Economics; Management); **Mathematics** (Mathematics); **Surveying** (Surveying and Mapping; Town Planning)

History: Founded 1971.

Academic Year: September to August

Main Language(s) of Instruction: German, English

Accrediting Agencies: ASIIN (Akkreditierungsagentur für Studiengänge der Ingenieurwissenschaften, der Informatik, der Naturwissenschaften und der Mathematik e.V.)

Degrees and Diplomas: *Bachelor/Bakkalaureus*: All other fields, 3 1/2 yrs; *Bachelor/Bakkalaureus*: Architecture; Interior Architecture; Business Administration, 3 yrs; *Master/Magister*: All other fields, 1 1/2 yrs; *Master/Magister*: Architecture; IMIAD; Urban Planning; SENCE, 2 yrs

Student Services: Academic counselling, Canteen, Foreign student adviser, Foreign Studies Centre, Handicapped facilities, Language programs, Sports facilities
Last Updated: 19/01/10

SVD SAINT AUGUSTIN UNIVERSITY OF PHILOSOPHY AND THEOLOGY

Philosophisch-Theologische Hochschule Sankt Augustin
Arnold-Janssen-Strasse 30, 53754 Sankt Augustin
Tel: +49(2241) 237-222
Fax: +49(2241) 237-204
EMail: pth@steyler.de
Website: http://www.philtheol-augustin.de

Rektor: Joachim Piepke (1998-)
Tel: +49(2241) 237-314 EMail: pth.rektor@steyler.de

Programmes

Philosophy (Philosophy); **Theology** (Theology)

History: Founded 1965.

Main Language(s) of Instruction: German

Degrees and Diplomas: *Diplom*; *Lizentiat*; *Doktorgrad*

Last Updated: 22/01/10

TECHNICAL UNIVERSITY OF BRAUNSCHWEIG

Technische Universität Carolo-Wilhelmina zu Braunschweig (TU BS)

PO Box 3329, Pockelsstrasse 14, 38023 Braunschweig,
Lower Saxony

Tel: +49(531) 391-4331
Fax: +49(531) 391-4332
EMail: international@tu-braunschweig.de
Website: http://www.tu-braunschweig.de

Präsident: Jürgen Hesselbach (1999-)
Tel: +49(531) 391-4111, Fax: +49(531) 391-4575
EMail: president@tu-braunschweig.de

International Relations: Astrid Sebastian Tel: +49(531) 391-4331

Centres

Languages (Modern Languages) *Director*: Peter Nübold

Faculties

Architecture, Civil Engineering, and Environmental Sciences (Architecture; Civil Engineering; Environmental Studies; Geophysics; Industrial Engineering; Water Management); **Business Administration, Economics and Social Sciences** (Business Administration; Economics; Media Studies; Social Sciences); **Electrical Engineering and Information Technology** (Electrical and Electronic Engineering; Industrial Engineering; Information Technology); **Humanities and Educational Sciences** (Educational Sciences; English; German; History; Literature; Philosophy; Primary Education; Protestant Theology; Religious Education; Secondary Education); **Life Sciences** (Bioengineering; Biology; Biotechnology; Chemical Engineering; Chemistry; Food Science; Pharmacy; Psychology); **Mathematics and Computer Science** (Business Computing; Computer Science; Mathematics; Mathematics Education); **Mechanical Engineering** (Mechanical Engineering); **Physics** (Physics)

Units

Instructional Development in Higher Education (Higher Education)

History: Founded 1745 as Collegium Carolinum and divided into Faculties of Arts, Commerce, and Technology 1835. Reorganized 1862, became Technische Hochschule 1877, and Technische Universität 1968. The Braunschweig branch of the College of Education, Lower Saxony, incorporated 1978. An autonomous institution under the jurisdiction of and financed by the State of Lower Saxony.

Governing Bodies: University Council, University Senate

Academic Year: October to September (October-March; April-September)

Admission Requirements: Secondary school certificate (Abitur) or equivalent

Fees: (Euros): 500 per semester

Main Language(s) of Instruction: German

International Co-operation: With universities in USA, Canada, South America, China, Japan, Indonesia. Also participates in Socrates/Erasmus programme

Degrees and Diplomas: *Bachelor/Bakkalaureus (BSc)*: 6 sem; *Diplom*: Architecture, Engineering, Biology, Biotechnology, Chemistry, Educational Sciences, Computer Sciences, Mathematics, Physics, Psychology, 10 sem; *Lehramt*: Teaching Qualification, 10 sem; *Magister Artium*: Media Studies (MA), 10 sem; *Staatsprüfung*: Food Chemistry, Pharmacy, 10 sem; *Master/Magister*: Chemistry, Engineering, Computer Science (MSc), a further 4 sem; *Doktorgrad*: Engineering (DrIng); Humanities (DrPhil); Natural Sciences (DrRerNat); Political Science (DrRerPol), 3-4 yrs

Student Services: Academic counselling, Canteen, Cultural centre, Employment services, Foreign student adviser, Foreign Studies Centre, Handicapped facilities, Language programs, Nursery care, Social counselling, Sports facilities

Student Residential Facilities: For 1,860 students

Libraries: University Library, c. 1.60m. Vols

Last Updated: 27/01/10

TECHNICAL UNIVERSITY OF KAISERSLAUTERN

Technische Universität Kaiserslautern

Gottlieb-Daimler-Strasse, 67663 Kaiserslautern, Rheinland-Pfalz

Tel: +49(631) 205-0
Fax: +49(631) 205-3200
EMail: info@uni-kl.de
Website: http://www.uni-kl.de

Präsident: Helmut J. Schmidt (2002-)
Tel: +49(631) 205-2201, Fax: +49(631) 205-4365
EMail: president@uni.kl.de

Kanzler: Stefan Lorenz
Tel: +49(631) 205-2204, Fax: +49(613) 205-4366
EMail: kanzler@verw.uni-kl.de

International Relations: Marc Frey
Tel: +49(631) 205-2050, Fax: +49(631) 205-3599
EMail: auslandsamt@uni-kl.de

Centres

Analysis of Materials and Surfaces *(IFOS)* (Physics)

Faculties

Architecture (Architecture); **Biology** (Biology); **Business Studies and Economics** (Business Administration; Economics; Industrial Management); **Chemistry** (Biochemistry; Chemistry; Organic Chemistry; Toxicology); **Civil Engineering** (Civil Engineering); **Computer Science** (Computer Science); **Electrical and Computer Engineering** (Computer Engineering; Electrical Engineering; Information Technology); **Mathematics** (Mathematics); **Mechanical and Process Engineering** (Mechanical Engineering; Production Engineering); **Physics** (Physics); **Social Sciences** (Social Sciences); **Town and Environmental Planning** (Environmental Management; Town Planning)

Institutes

Biotechnology and Drug Research *(ibwf)*; **Composite Materials** (Materials Engineering); **Experimental Software Engineering** *(Frauenhofer, IESE)* (Software Engineering); **Max Planck**; **Physical Measurement** *(Fraunhofer)* (Measurement and Precision Engineering); **Technical and Industrial Mathematics** *(Fraunhofer, ITWM)* (Mathematics)

Research Centres

Artificial Intelligence *(DFKI)* (Artificial Intelligence)

Further Information: Also courses in "German as a Foreign Language" and in technical English, French and Spanish. Regional Computing Centre (RHRK)

History: Founded 1970 with divisions in Kaiserslautern and Trier which were detached 1975 to form separate Universities. An autonomous institution under the jurisdiction of and financially supported by the State of Rheinland-Pfalz.

Governing Bodies: Senat

Academic Year: October to September (October-March; April-September)

Admission Requirements: Secondary school certificate (Reifezeugnis)

Fees: None

Main Language(s) of Instruction: German

International Co-operation: With universities in France, Italy, Austria, Poland, Czech Republic, Hungary, Russian Federation, Australia, Vietnam, Israel, China, Japan, USA, Colombia. Also participates in the Socrates programme

Degrees and Diplomas: *Bachelor/Bakkalaureus*: Mathematics, Mechanical and Process Engineering, Computer Science; *Diplom*: Biology; Business and Engineering; Chemistry; Computer Sciences; Engineering (Mechanical/Electrical Engineering); Mathematics; Physics, 4-6 yrs; *Lehramt*: Teaching qualification, secondary level, 4-6 yrs; *Magister Artium*; *Master/Magister*: Mathematics, Electrical Engineering, Mechanical Engineering; *Doktorgrad*: Economics (Dr.rer.pol.); Engineering (Dr.Ing.); Natural Sciences (Dr.rer.nat.);

Philosophy (Dr.phil.); *Habilitation*: Teaching qualification, university level, at least 3 yrs following Doktor

Student Services: Academic counselling, Canteen, Cultural centre, Employment services, Foreign student adviser, Foreign Studies Centre, Health services, Language programs, Nursery care, Social counselling, Sports facilities

Student Residential Facilities: Yes

Libraries: 898,613 vols
Last Updated: 27/01/10

THE COLOGNE UNIVERSITY OF MUSIC AND DANCE

Hochschule für Musik und Tanz Köln
Dagobertstrasse 38, 50668 Köln, Nordrhein-Westfalen
Tel: +49(221) 912818-0
Fax: +49(221) 131-204
EMail: joachim.ullrich@hfmt-koeln.de
Website: http://www.mhs-koeln.de

Rektor: Reiner Schuhenn
Tel: +49(221) 912818-100 EMail: rektor@hfmt-koeln.de

Kanzlerin: Ursula Wirtz-Knapstein
Tel: 49(221) 912818-111 EMail: kanzler@hfm-koeln.de

International Relations: Birgit Kirstein, International, Academic and Student Affairs Officer EMail: kirstein@mhs-koeln.de

Programmes
Dance (Dance); **Music** (Conducting; Jazz and Popular Music; Music; Music Theory and Composition; Musical Instruments; Religious Music; Singing); **Music Education** (Music Education)

History: Founded 1925. Acquired present title 2009.

Main Language(s) of Instruction: German

Degrees and Diplomas: *Bachelor/Bakkalaureus*; *Master/Magister*: Music

Libraries: Yes
Last Updated: 02/02/12

THE LISZT SCHOOL OF MUSIC WEIMAR

Hochschule für Musik Franz Liszt Weimar
Postfach 2552, 99406 Weimar
Tel: +49(3643) 555-0
Fax: +49(3643) 555-188
EMail: presse@hfm-weimar.de
Website: http://www.hfm-weimar.de

Präsident: Christoph Stölzl
Tel: +49(3643) 555-115, Fax: +49(3643) 555-117
EMail: praesident@hfm-weimar.de

Kanzlerin: Christine Gurk
Tel: +49(3643) 555-161, Fax: +49(3643) 555-188
EMail: kanzler@hfm-weimar.de

Centres
Chamber Music (Music); **Franz-Liszt** (Music); **Music Theory** (Music Theory and Composition)

Faculties
I (Conducting; Musical Instruments; Opera; Singing); II (Jazz and Popular Music; Music; Music Education; Musical Instruments; Pedagogy); III *(Church Music; School Music)* (Art Management; Musicology)

History: Founded 1872 as one of the first German Orchestra Schools. Acquired present status 1930. Named after Franz Liszt 1956.

Governing Bodies: Board of Trustees

Academic Year: October to July

Admission Requirements: Successful audition; German Language Proficiency Test (proof); A-level for Musicology and School Music

Fees: None

Main Language(s) of Instruction: German

International Co-operation: Participates in Erasmus Programme (Austria, Belgium, Czech Republic, Estonia, United Kingdom, Fin-

land, France, Hungary, Italy, Netherlands, Norway, Poland, Slovak Republic, Spain, Switzerland, Romania, Russian Federation).

Degrees and Diplomas: *Bachelor/Bakkalaureus*; *Master/Magister*: Music Education; Cultural Management, a further 2 yrs

Student Services: Academic counselling, Canteen, Foreign student adviser, Foreign Studies Centre, Handicapped facilities, Health services, Language programs, Nursery care, Social counselling, Sports facilities

Student Residential Facilities: 1,120 single apartments for students (92-213 Euros per month)

Special Facilities: Music Archive with handwritten manuscripts

Libraries: Books, 35,860; printed music, 61,533; journals, 103; records/CDs, 18,825

Publications: Resonanz, Reports on the Academic Life and Projects *(biennially)*
Last Updated: 23/03/11

THE NORDAKADEMIE

NORDAKADEMIE
Köllner Chaussee 11, 25337 Elmshorn
Tel: +49(4121) 4090-0
Fax: +49(4121) 4090-40
EMail: fh@nordakademie.de
Website: http://www.nordakademie.de

Rektor: Georg Plate (1993-)
Tel: +49(4121) 4090-15 EMail: g.plate@nordakademie.de

Kanzler: Jörg Meier
Tel: +49(4121) 4090-13, Fax: +49(4121) 4090-17
EMail: j.meier@nordakademie.de

International Relations: Kirsten Andersen, Head, International Office
Tel: +49(4121) 4090-63
EMail: auslandsamt@nordakademie.de;
kirsten.andersen@nordakademie.de

Departments
Business Administration (Business Administration); **Computer Science and Business Administration** (Business Administration; Business Computing; Computer Science); **Industrial Engineering and Business Administration** (Business Administration; Industrial Engineering)

History: Founded 1992.

Admission Requirements: Secondary school certificate (Abitur or Fachhochschulreife)

Fees: (Euros): c. 2,040-2,180 per semester; MBA, 3,750 per semester

Main Language(s) of Instruction: German

International Co-operation: Participates in the Erasmus programme

Degrees and Diplomas: *Bachelor/Bakkalaureus*; *Master/Magister* (MBA)

Student Services: Academic counselling, Canteen, Employment services, Foreign student adviser, Language programs, Sports facilities

Student Residential Facilities: Yes

Libraries: Yes
Last Updated: 12/01/10

THEOLOGICAL FACULTY TRIER

Theologische Fakultät Trier
Universitätsring 19, 54296 Trier, Rhineland Palatinate
Tel: +49(651) 201-3520
Fax: +49(651) 201-3951
EMail: theofak@uni-trier.de
Website: http://www.uni-trier.de/uni/theo/aktuelles.php

Rektor: Klaus Peter Dannecker (2011-)
EMail: dannecker@liturgie.de

Courses
Classical Languages (Classical Languages; Greek (Classical); Latin)

Programmes
Theology

Academic Year: October to September (October-March; April-September)

Degrees and Diplomas: *Diplom-Vorprüfung*; *Bachelor/Bakkalaureus*; *Diplom (Dipl.-Theol.))*; *Lizentiat*; *Master/Magister*; *Doktorgrad*; *Habilitation*
Last Updated: 23/03/11

TOURO COLLEGE BERLIN

Am Rupenhorn 5, 14055 Berlin
Tel: +49(30) 3006-860
Fax: +49(30) 3006-8639
EMail: info@touroberlin.de
Website: http://www.touroberlin.de

Vice President/Director: Sara Nachama

Departments
Holocaust Studies (Jewish Studies); **Management** (Business Administration; Management)

History: Founded 2003.

Degrees and Diplomas: *Bachelor/Bakkalaureus*: Management and International Business; *Master/Magister*: Holocaust Communication
Last Updated: 27/01/10

TRIER UNIVERSITY OF APPLIED SCIENCES

Fachhochschule Trier - Hochschule für Wirtschaft, Technik und Gestaltung
PO Box 1826, 54208 Trier, Rhineland Palatinate
Tel: +49(651) 8103-0
Fax: +49(651) 8103-333
EMail: info@fh-trier.de
Website: http://www.fh-trier.de

Präsident: Jörg Wallmeier
Tel: +49(651) 8103-445, Fax: +49(651) 8103-557
EMail: Praesident@fh-trier.de

Kanzler: Detlef Jahn
Tel: +49(651) 8103-492, Fax: +49(651) 8103-566
EMail: kanzler@fh-trier.de

International Relations: Georg Schneider, Head, International Office
Tel: +49(651) 8103-378, Fax: +49(651) 8103-547
EMail: aaa@fh-trier.de

Departments
Computer Science (Computer Science); **Design** (Design); **Engineering and Technology** (Business Administration; Electrical Engineering; Engineering; Industrial Engineering; Machine Building; Management; Mechanical Engineering); **Environmental Planning/ Environmental Technology** *(Birkenfeld Campus)* (Bioengineering; Business Administration; Commercial Law; Computer Science; Energy Engineering; Engineering; Environmental Engineering; Environmental Management; Environmental Studies; European Union Law; Mechanical Engineering; Media Studies; Physical Engineering; Transport Management)

Schools
Business (Business Administration; Business Computing; Industrial Engineering; International Business; Management)

History: Founded 1971, acquired present status 1996.

Governing Bodies: President, Senate, Board of Trustees, Department Councils

Academic Year: September to August

Admission Requirements: Upper Secondary school certificate (Allgemeine Hochschul- or Fachhochschulreife)

Fees: None

Main Language(s) of Instruction: German

International Co-operation: With universities on 4 continents. Also participates in c. 120 Socrates agreements and international degree programmes

Accrediting Agencies: Agentur für Qualitätssicherung durch Akkreditierung von Studiengängen (AQAS) and others for the accreditation of individual courses

Degrees and Diplomas: *Bachelor/Bakkalaureus*; *Master/Magister*
Student Services: Academic counselling, Canteen, Foreign student adviser, Language programs, Social counselling, Sports facilities

Student Residential Facilities: Yes

Libraries: Main Library
Last Updated: 06/02/12

TROSSINGEN UNIVERSITY OF MUSIC

Staatliche Hochschule für Musik Trossingen
Schultheiss-Koch-Platz 3, 78647 Trossingen
Tel: +49(7425) 9491-0
Fax: +49(7425) 9491-48
EMail: rektorat@mh-trossingen.de
Website: http://www.mh-trossingen.de

Rektorin: Elisabeth Gutjahr Tel: +49(7425) 9491-12

Kanzlerin: Margit Mosbacher
Tel: +49(7425) 9491-13 EMail: mosbacher@mh-trossingen.de

International Relations: Birgit Hermle-Marquart
Tel: +49(7425) 9491-17
EMail: hermle-marquart@mh-trossingen.de

Programmes
Church Music (Music Theory and Composition; Musical Instruments; Religious Music); **Music** (Conducting; Music; Music Theory and Composition; Musical Instruments; Singing); **Music Education** (Conducting; Music Education; Music Theory and Composition; Musical Instruments; Singing); **Music Education (Secondary School)** *(Lehramt)* (Jazz and Popular Music; Music; Music Education); **Musicology and Music Education** *(Promotion)* (Music Education; Musicology)

Degrees and Diplomas: *Diplom*; *Lehramt*; *Master/Magister*; *Promotion*
Last Updated: 26/01/10

ULM UNIVERSITY OF APPLIED SCIENCES

Hochschule Ulm Technik, Informatik und Medien (FHU)
Prittwitzstrasse 10, 89028 Ulm
Tel: +49(731) 5020-8
Fax: +49(731) 5028-270
EMail: info@hs-ulm.de
Website: http://www.hs-ulm.de

Rektor/Präsident: Achim Bubenzer (2001-)
Tel: +49(731) 5028-104, Fax: +49(731) 5028-483
EMail: bubenzerhs-ulm.de

Kanzler: Herbert Jarosch
Tel: +49(731) 5028-108 EMail: jarosch@fh-ulm.de

International Relations: Klaus Peter Kratzer
Tel: +49(731) 5028-272, Fax: +49(731) 5028-269
EMail: kratzerhs-ulm.de

Faculties
Computer Science (Business Computing; Computer Science); **Electrical Engineering and Information Technology** (Electrical Engineering; Information Technology); **Mechanical and Automotive Engineering** (Automotive Engineering; Mechanical Engineering); **Mechatronics and Medical Engineering** (Biomedical Engineering; Mechanical Engineering); **Production Engineering and Production Economics** (Economics; Production Engineering); **Science and Economics** (Chemistry; Economics; Mathematics; Modern Languages; Physics; Social Sciences)

History: Founded 1960. Formerly known as Fachhochschule Ulm - Hochschule für Technik.

Admission Requirements: Secondary school certificate (Abitur, Fachhochschulreife)

Main Language(s) of Instruction: German

Degrees and Diplomas: *Bachelor/Bakkalaureus*; *Master/Magister*. Also Dual Study Programmes

Student Services: Academic counselling, Canteen, Cultural centre, Employment services, Foreign student adviser, Foreign Studies Centre, Handicapped facilities, Health services, Language programs, Nursery care, Social counselling, Sports facilities
Last Updated: 20/01/10

UMC POTSDAM - UNIVERSITY OF MANAGEMENT AND COMMUNICATION (FH)

Palais am Stadtkanal, Am Kanal 16-18, D-14467 Potsdam
Tel: +49(331) 5856-559-00
Fax: +49(331) 5856-559-09
EMail: kontakt@umc-potsdam.de
Website: http://www.umc-potsdam.de

Rektor: Werner Siebel

Kanzler: Jonas F. Müller

Departments
Communication (Communication Studies; Management; Media Studies); **Economics and Society** (Communication Studies; Economics; Environmental Studies; European Studies; Health Administration; Political Sciences; Social Studies); **Industrial Psychology; Management; Marketing** (International Business; Law; Marketing; Media Studies); **Personnel and Organisation**

Further Information: Also Campus in Berlin (Tietzhöfe). Also Independent Institutes.

Degrees and Diplomas: *Bachelor/Bakkalaureus*: Communication Management; Industrial Psychology; Mid-size Business Administration; *Master/Magister*: Corporate Communication; Energy and Infrastructure; Sustainability Management. Also Evening and Distance Programmes in Communication and Media Management.
Last Updated: 27/01/09

UNIVERSITY 21

Hochschule 21
Harburger Str. 6, 21614 Buxtehude
Tel: +49(4161) 648-0
Fax: +49(4161) 648-123
EMail: info@hs21.de
Website: http://www.hs21.de

Präsident: Martin Betzler Tel: +49(4161) 648-148

Manager: Susanne Russell Tel: +49(4161) 648-240

International Relations: Anja Schuback, International Officer
Tel: +49(4161) 648-128

Courses
Architecture (Architecture); **Civil Engineering** (Civil Engineering); **Construction and Real Estate Management** (Management; Real Estate); **Physiotherapy** (Physical Therapy)

History: Founded 2004.

Main Language(s) of Instruction: German

Degrees and Diplomas: *Bachelor/Bakkalaureus*; *Master/Magister*
Last Updated: 01/02/12

UNIVERSITY LÜBECK

Universität zu Lübeck
Ratzeburger Allee 160, 23538 Lübeck
Tel: +49(451) 500-0
Fax: +49(451) 500-3016
EMail: rektorat@zuv.uni-luebeck.de
Website: http://www.uni-luebeck.de

Rektor: Peter Dominiak
Tel: +49(451) 500-3000 EMail: dominiak@uni-luebeck.de

Kanzler: Oliver Grundei Tel: +49(451) 500-3003

Areas
Computer Science and Technology (Cognitive Sciences; Computer Science; Mathematics; Medical Technology; Multimedia; Robotics; Software Engineering); **Medicine** (Anatomy; Dermatology; Medicine; Otorhinolaryngology; Psychiatry and Mental Health; Rheumatology; Surgery); **Natural Sciences** (Biochemistry; Biology; Chemistry; Mathematics; Medical Technology; Molecular Biology; Physics)

History: Founded 1964 as academy and faculty of Christian Albrecht University of Kiel. Became independent 1973 and acquired present status 1985.

Governing Bodies: Konsistorium; Senat

Academic Year: October to September (October-March; April-September)

Admission Requirements: Secondary school certificate (Reifezeugnis) or equivalent

Fees: None

Main Language(s) of Instruction: German

International Co-operation: With Universities in Estonia; China; Spain; Austria; Netherlands; Romania; Italy; Belgium; Poland; Finland; Sweden; France; Norway

Accrediting Agencies: ANSII

Degrees and Diplomas: *Bachelor/Bakkalaureus*; *Diplom*; *Staatsprüfung*: 8 yrs; *Master/Magister*; *Doktorgrad (Dr.med.dent.)*; Habilitation

Student Services: Academic counselling, Canteen, Cultural centre, Foreign student adviser, Foreign Studies Centre, Handicapped facilities, Social counselling, Sports facilities

Student Residential Facilities: Yes

Libraries:c. 166,500 vols

Publications: FOCUS MUL *(quarterly)*; Sonderheft Forschung *(annually)*
Last Updated: 07/02/12

UNIVERSITY FOR CHURCH MUSIC OF THE DIOCESE OF ROTTENBURG-STUTTGART

Hochschule für Kirchenmusik Rottenburg
Sankt-Meinrad-Weg 6, 72108 Rottenburg am Neckar
Tel: +49(7472) 9363-0
Fax: +49(7472) 936363
EMail: info@hfk-rottenburg.de
Website: http://www.hfk-rottenburg.de

Rektor: Bernhard Schmid (1997-)

Prorektor: Wolfram Rehfeldt

Programmes
Church Music (Religious Music); **Postgraduate Studies** (Music Education; Musical Instruments; Singing)

History: Founded 1949. Acquired present status 1997.

Degrees and Diplomas: *Diplom*. Also Postgraduate Degree (Aufbaustudiengänge); Part-time programmes in Church Music, 1-2 yrs
Last Updated: 25/01/09

UNIVERSITY FOR PROTESTANT CHURCH MUSIC OF THE PROTESTANT LUTHERAN CHURCH IN BAVARIA

Hochschule für Evangelische Kirchenmusik Bayreuth
Wilhelminenstrasse 9, 95444 Bayreuth, Bavaria
Tel: +49(921) 75934-17
Fax: +49(921) 75934-36
EMail: info@hfk-bayreuth.de
Website: http://www.hfk-bayreuth.de

Rektor: Thomas Albus EMail: rektor@hfk-bayreuth.de

Prorektor: Karl Rathgeber EMail: rathgeber@hfk-bayreuth.de

Programmes
Church Music (Musical Instruments; Religious Music)

History: Founded 2000.

Main Language(s) of Instruction: German

Degrees and Diplomas: *Diplom*. Also Postgraduate Degree (Aufbaustudiengang)

Libraries: Yes
Last Updated: 01/02/12

UNIVERSITY OF APPLIED MANAGEMENT

Fachhochschule für Angewandtes Management
Am Bahnhof 2, 85435 Erding
Tel: +49 (8122) 955-948-0
Fax: +49 (8122) 955-948-49
EMail: info@my-fham.de
Website: http://www.myfham.de

Präsident: Christian Werner
Tel: +49 (8122) 955-948-22 EMail: christian.werner@myfham.de

Kanzlerin: Isabella Müller
Tel: +49 (8122) 955-948-21 EMail: isabella.mueller@myfham.de

Faculties
Business Administration (Business Administration; Health Administration; Media Studies; Real Estate); **Industrial Psychology** (Accountancy; Business Administration; Communication Studies; Data Processing; English; Management; Marketing; Psychology; Statistics); **Sports Management** (Business Administration; Law; Psychology; Sociology; Sports Management)

History: Founded 2004.

Main Language(s) of Instruction: German

Degrees and Diplomas: *Bachelor/Bakkalaureus*; *Master/Magister*
Last Updated: 06/02/12

UNIVERSITY OF APPLIED SCIENCES ASCHAFFENBURG

Hochschule Aschaffenburg
Würzburger Strasse 45, 63743 Aschaffenburg, Bavaria
Tel: +49(6021) 314-5
Fax: +49(6021) 314-600
EMail: info@h.ab.de
Website: http://www.fh-aschaffenburg.de

Präsident: Wilfried Diwischek (2001-)
Tel: +49(6021) 314-602, Fax: +49(6021) 314-601
EMail: wilfried.diwischek@fh-aschaffenburg.de

Kanzler: Gerhard Sarich
Tel: +49(6021) 314-605, Fax: +49(6021) 314-601
EMail: gerhard.sarich@fh-aschaffenburg.de

International Relations: Bettina Huhn
Tel: +49(6021) 314-604 EMail: bettina.huhnfh-aschaffenburg.de

Faculties
Business and Law (Business Administration; Finance; Insurance; Law; Management; Marketing; Real Estate); **Engineering** (Business Administration; Electrical and Electronic Engineering; Electronic Engineering; Energy Engineering; Industrial Engineering; Mechanical Engineering) *Division Head*: Hinrich Mewes

History: Founded 1995, acquired present status 2000.

Fees: None

Main Language(s) of Instruction: German

International Co-operation: Participates in Socrates and Erasmus

Degrees and Diplomas: *Bachelor/Bakkalaureus*; *Diplom (FH)*; *Master/Magister*

Student Services: Academic counselling, Canteen, Employment services, Foreign student adviser, Handicapped facilities, Language programs, Sports facilities

Student Residential Facilities: Yes

Libraries: University Library
Last Updated: 08/01/10

UNIVERSITY OF APPLIED SCIENCES BINGEN

Fachhochschule Bingen
Berlinstrasse 109, 55411 Bingen am Rhein
Tel: +49(6721) 409-0
Fax: +49(6721) 409-100
EMail: poststelle@fh-bingen.de; info@fh-bingen.de
Website: http://www.fh-bingen.de

Präsident: Klaus Becker (2003-)
Tel: +49(6721) 409-400, Fax: +49(6721) 409-400
EMail: praesident@fh-bingen.de

Kanzlerin: Astrid Clesius
Tel: +49(6721) 409-404 EMail: clesius@fh-bingen.de

Faculties
Faculty 1 (Agriculture; Biotechnology; Computer Engineering; Energy Engineering; Environmental Studies; Farm Management; Production Engineering); **Faculty 2** (Automation and Control Engineering; Automotive Engineering; Computer Engineering; Computer Science; Electronic Engineering; Engineering; Machine Building)

History: Founded 1897.

Admission Requirements: Fachhochschulreife or equivalent diploma

Main Language(s) of Instruction: German

International Co-operation: With institutions in USA

Degrees and Diplomas: *Bachelor/Bakkalaureus*; *Diplom (FH)*: 4 yrs; *Master/Magister*

Student Services: Canteen, Cultural centre, Social counselling, Sports facilities

Libraries: Yes
Last Updated: 06/02/12

UNIVERSITY OF APPLIED SCIENCES DÜSSELDORF

Fachhochschule Düsseldorf
Universitätsstrasse, Gebäude 23.31/32, 40225 Düsseldorf
Tel: +49(211) 4351-0 +49(211) 811-4915
Fax: +49(211) 811-5049
EMail: vizepraesidentin@fh-duesseldorf.de
Website: http://www.fh-duesseldorf.de

Präsidentin: Brigitte Grass EMail: brigitte.grass@fh-duesseldorf.de

Faculties
Business Studies; **Design** (Design); **Electrical Engineering** (Electrical Engineering); **Mechanical Engineering** (Mechanical Engineering; Production Engineering); **Media Studies** (Media Studies); **Social Science and Cultural Studies** (Cultural Studies; Pedagogy; Social Sciences; Social Studies)

Schools
Architecture *(Peter Behrens)* (Architecture)

History: Founded 1971.

Academic Year: September to August

Admission Requirements: Abitur, Fachhochschulreife, Praktikum

Fees: (Euros): 115 per semester

Main Language(s) of Instruction: German

International Co-operation: With universities in the United Kingdom; France; Spain; Belgium; Ireland; Netherlands; Australia

Degrees and Diplomas: *Bachelor/Bakkalaureus*: Architecture; Design; Electronic Engineering; Communication and Information Technology; Mechanical Engineering; Business Studies; Media Studies, 3 yrs; *Diplom*: Architecture; Design; Business Studies; Media Studies, 3-4 yrs; *Master/Magister*: Architecture; Design; Electronic Engineering; Communication and Information Technology; Mechanical Engineering; Business Studies; Media Studies

Student Services: Academic counselling, Canteen, Foreign student adviser, Language programs, Sports facilities

Student Residential Facilities: Yes

Libraries: Yes
Last Updated: 06/02/12

UNIVERSITY OF APPLIED SCIENCES EMDEN/LEER

Fachhochschule Emden/Leer
Constantiaplatz 4, 26723 Emden
Tel: +49(4921) 807-0
Fax: +49(4921) 807-1000
EMail: info@fh-oow.de
Website: http://www.fh-emden-leer.de

Präsident: Gerhard Kreutz
Tel: +49(4921) 807-1001, Fax: +49(4921) 807-1003

International Relations: Iris Wilters EMail: iris.wilters@fh-oow.de

Faculties
Economics (Business Administration; Business and Commerce; Economics; International Business; Management); **Social Work and Health Sciences** (Health Sciences; Social Work); **Technology** (Automation and Control Engineering; Biological and Life Sciences; Biotechnology; Chemical Engineering; Computer Science; Electronic Engineering; Energy Engineering; Engineering; Engineering Management; Environmental Engineering; Environmental Management; Industrial Design; Information Technology; Machine Building; Physical Engineering; Physics; Technology)

Institutes
Marine Transport *(Leer)* (Transport and Communications)

Further Information: See also: www.fho-emden.de and www.fh-wilhelmshaven.de

History: Founded 1971. Oldenburg, Ostfriesland and Wilhelmshaven merged in 2000. Splitted into Fachhochschule Emden/Leer and Jade Hochschule 2009.

Governing Bodies: Board of Trustees; Presidency; Senate

Academic Year: September to July

Admission Requirements: Secondary school certificate or equivalent. DaF or DSH Test for foreign students

Fees: (Euros): 106.32 per semester

Main Language(s) of Instruction: German

International Co-operation: With universities in 9 countries worldwide. Also participates in Erasmus (22 European countries)

Accrediting Agencies: ZEVA; ASII

Degrees and Diplomas: *Bachelor/Bakkalaureus*; *Bachelor/Bakkalaureus*: Marine Transport; *Master/Magister*: Applied Life Science; Business Management; Engineering Physics; Environmental Technology and Management; Industrial Informatics; Management Consulting; Public Health; Media Computing (Online Programme); Media Computing (Part-time Programme); Social Work and Health Sicences in the context of Social Cohesion; Technical Management. Medieninformatik (Online-Studiengang)

Student Services: Academic counselling, Canteen, Foreign student adviser, Foreign Studies Centre, Handicapped facilities, Language programs, Social counselling, Sports facilities

Student Residential Facilities: Yes

Special Facilities: Multi-media laboratories. Distance learning facilities

Libraries: Main Library

Publications: Blickpunkt *(biennially)*
Last Updated: 31/01/12

UNIVERSITY OF APPLIED SCIENCES JENA
Fachhochschule Jena
PO Box 100314, Carl-Zeiss-Promenade 2, 07745 Jena
Tel: +49(3641) 205-100
Fax: +49(3641) 205-101
EMail: info@fh-jena.de
Website: http://www.fh-jena.de

Rektorin: Gabriele Beibst (2011-)
EMail: Rektorat@fh-jena.de; gabriele.beibst@fh-jena.de

Kanzler: Theodor Peschke
Tel: +49(3641) 205-200, Fax: +49(3641) 205-201
EMail: Kanzler@fh-jena.de

International Relations: Angelika Förster, Leiterin Akademisches Auslandsamt
Tel: +49(3641) 205-135, Fax: +49(3641) 205-136
EMail: auslandsamt@fh-jena.de

Departments
Business Administration (Business Administration; Management); **Business Engineering** (Business Administration; Engineering; Marketing; Transport Management); **Electrical Engineering and Information Technology** (Automation and Control Engineering; Computer Engineering; Design; Electrical Engineering; Electronic Engineering; Information Technology; Mechanical Engineering; Media Studies; Telecommunications Engineering); **Fundamental Sciences**; **Mechanical Engineering**; **Medical Technology and Biotechnology** (Biomedical Engineering; Biotechnology; Medical Technology; Pharmacology); **Social Work**

Faculties
SciTec - Precision - Optics - Materials - Environment (Environmental Engineering; Laser Engineering; Materials Engineering; Natural Sciences; Optical Technology; Physical Engineering; Technology)

History: Founded 1991.

Main Language(s) of Instruction: German

Degrees and Diplomas: *Bachelor/Bakkalaureus*; *Master/Magister*
Last Updated: 06/02/12

UNIVERSITY OF APPLIED SCIENCES MAINZ
Fachhochschule Mainz
PO Box 1967, Seppel-Glückert-Passage 10, 55009 Mainz
Tel: +49(6131) 2859-0
Fax: +49(6131) 2859-712
EMail: zentrale@fh-mainz.de
Website: http://www.fh-mainz.de

Präsident: Gerhard Muth (2007-)
Tel: +49(6131) 2859-710
EMail: praesident@fh-mainz.de; muth@fh-mainz

Kanzler: Franz Pfadt
Tel: +49(6131) 2859-733, Fax: +49(6131) 2859-722
EMail: kanzler@fh-mainz.de; pfadt@fh-mainz.de

International Relations: Ursula Plate, Head, International Office
Tel: +49(6131) 2859-717 EMail: ulla.plate@fh-mainz.de

Schools
Business Studies *(Bruchspitze)* (Business Administration; Commercial Law; Economics; Health Administration; International Business); **Design** *(Holzstraße)* (Communication Arts; Design; Interior Design; Media Studies); **Technology** *(Holzstraße)* (Architecture; Architecture and Planning; Civil Engineering; Information Sciences; Surveying and Mapping)

Further Information: Also 7 Research Institutes

History: Founded 1996.

Governing Bodies: Senate; Council

Academic Year: October to July (October-February; March-July)

Admission Requirements: Secondary school certificate (Abitur or Fachhochschulreife), 12 weeks of work in relevant field

Fees: None

Main Language(s) of Instruction: German

International Co-operation: With universities in United Kingdom, France, Spain, Sweden, Finland, Italy, Netherlands, Greece, Czech Republic, Poland, Estonia, USA, Australia and Thailand

Accrediting Agencies: German Accreditation Agency

Degrees and Diplomas: *Bachelor/Bakkalaureus (B.Eng)*: 3 yrs; *Diplom (FH) (Dipl.-des.FH)*: 4 yrs; *Master/Magister (MSc)*: a further 1 1/2 yrs

Student Services: Academic counselling, Canteen, Foreign student adviser, Handicapped facilities, Language programs, Social counselling, Sports facilities

Libraries: Main Library

Publications: FH Mainz-Forum *(biennially)*
Last Updated: 06/02/12

UNIVERSITY OF APPLIED SCIENCES OFFENBURG
Hochschule Offenburg
Badstrasse 24, 77652 Offenburg
Tel: +49(781) 205-0
Fax: +49(781) 205-214
EMail: info@fh-offenburg.de
Website: http://www.fh-offenburg.de

Rektor: Winfried Lieber (1997-)
Tel: +49(781) 205-200, Fax: +49(781) 205-333
EMail: lieber@fh-offenburg.de

Kanzler: Thomas Wiedemer
Tel: +49(781) 205-211 EMail: wiedemer@fh-offenburg.de

International Relations: Birgit Teubner
Tel: +49(781) 205-218, Fax: +49(781) 205-237
EMail: teubner@fh-offenburg.de

Departments
Business Administration and Industrial Engineering *(Gengenbach)* (Business and Commerce; Industrial Engineering; Industrial Management; International Business); **Electrical and Information Engineering** (Automation and Control Engineering; Telecommunications Engineering); **Mechanical and Process Engineering** (Automotive Engineering; Biotechnology; Computer Engineering; Energy Engineering; Engineering Management; Environmental Engineering; Mechanical Engineering); **Media and Information Engineering** (Information Technology; Media Studies)

Graduate Schools

Automotive Engineering *(AME)* (Automotive Engineering); **Communication and Media Engineering** *(CME)* (Communication Studies; Media Studies); **Energy Conversion and Management** *(ECM)* (Energy Engineering; Management); **International Business Consulting** *(IBC)* (International Business)

Further Information: CME and IBC entirely taught in English, ECM taught partly in English, partly in German. Systems Engineering (Génie des Systèmes), German-French bilingual study programme at University of Applied Sciences Offenburg and Université Louis Pasteur, Strasbourg

History: Founded 1964, acquired present status 1971. Formerly known as Fachhochschule Offenburg - Hochschule für Technik, Wirtschaft und Medien.

Governing Bodies: Senate; Rector's Office; Board of Trustees

Academic Year: September to August

Admission Requirements: Secondary school certificate (Hochschulreife) or equivalent

Fees: None, except 'International Business Consulting': 5,300 Euros for 3 semesters

Main Language(s) of Instruction: German. Also English in some Master Programmes

International Co-operation: With universities in France, Finland, Poland, Ireland, Spain; Netherlands; Mexico; Brazil; Chile

Accrediting Agencies: Akkreditierungsagentur für Studiengänge der Ingenieurwissenschaften und Informatik (ASII); Foundation of International Business Administration Accreditation (FIBAA)

Degrees and Diplomas: *Bachelor/Bakkalaureus*: Business Administration (Dipl.-Betriebswirt (FH)); Electrical Engineering, Mechanical Engineering, Process- and Environmental Engineering, Media and Information Engineering (Dipl.-Ing.(FH)); Industrial Engineering (Dipl.-wirt.Ing. (FH)), 4 yrs; *Bachelor/Bakkalaureus*: Mechanical Engineering (BEng), 3 yrs; *Bachelor/Bakkalaureus*: Systems Engineering (French-German programme) (BSc), 3 1/2 yrs; *Master/Magister*: Automotive Engineering, Communication and Media Engineering, Energy Conversion and Management (MSc), 2 yrs; *Master/Magister*: International Business Consulting (MBA), 1 1/2 yrs and part-time programme

Student Services: Academic counselling, Canteen, Foreign student adviser, Foreign Studies Centre, Language programs, Social counselling, Sports facilities

Student Residential Facilities: Yes

Special Facilities: Movie and audio studio

Libraries: Main Library

Publications: IAF-Bericht, Report on research activities *(annually)*
Last Updated: 20/01/10

UNIVERSITY OF APPLIED SCIENCES POTSDAM

Fachhochschule Potsdam
PO Box 600608, 14406 Potsdam
Tel: +49(331) 580-00
Fax: +49(331) 580-2999
EMail: rektor@fh-potsdam.de
Website: http://www.fh-potsdam.de

Rektor: Johannes Vielhaber
Tel: +49(331) 580-1000, Fax: +49(331) 580-1009

Kanzler: Rainald Wurzer
Tel: +49(331) 580-1040, Fax: +49(331) 580-1009
EMail: kanzler@fh-potsdam.de

International Relations: Uta Kotulla
Tel: +49(331) 580-2010, Fax: +49(331) 580-2019
EMail: kotulla@fh-potsdam.de

Faculties
Architecture and Town Planning (Architectural Restoration; Architecture; Town Planning); **Civil Engineering** (Civil Engineering; Construction Engineering); **Design** (Design; Graphic Design; Industrial Design); **Information Science** (Archiving; Documentation Techniques; Library Science); **Social Work** (Social Work)

Further Information: Also European Media Studies programme jointly offered with the Potsdam University.

History: Founded 1992.

Admission Requirements: Abitur; Fachabitur

Fees: (Euros): c. 200

Main Language(s) of Instruction: German

International Co-operation: With universities in Cuba, USA, Lithuania, Czech Republic, Austria, Singapore and Estonia. Also participates in Socrates (Denmark, Finland, France, United Kingdom, Israel, Italy, Netherlands, Poland, Russian Federation, Spain),

Degrees and Diplomas: *Bachelor/Bakkalaureus*; *Diplom*: Conservation and Restoration; Culture Management; Civil Engineering; *Master/Magister*: Architecture and Urban Design; Social Work; Building Research; Building Preservation; Design; European Media Studies

Student Services: Academic counselling, Foreign student adviser

Part-time students, 75. Distance students, 0.
Last Updated: 06/02/12

UNIVERSITY OF APPLIED SCIENCES AND ARTS IN HANOVER

Fachhochschule Hannover
PO Box 920251, Ricklinger Stadtweg 118, 30441 Hannover
Tel: +49(511) 9296-0
Fax: +49(511) 9296-1010
EMail: praesidium@fh-hannover.de
Website: http://www.fh-hannover.de

Präsidentin: Rosemarie Kerkow-Weil (2011-)
Tel: +49(511) 9296-1003 EMail: praesidentin@fh-hannover.de

Vice-President: Henning Ahlers

Faculties
Architecture (Architecture; Building Technologies; Construction Engineering; Design; Management; Town Planning); **Economics and Informatics** *(Fakultät IV)* (Banking; Business Administration; Business and Commerce; Business Computing; Industrial Management; Information Management; Insurance; Marketing); **Electrical Engineering and Information Technology** *(Fakultät I)* (Automation and Control Engineering; Computer Science; Data Processing; Electrical Engineering; Energy Engineering; Information Technology; Mechanical Engineering; Microwaves; Power Engineering; Telecommunications Engineering); **Mechanical and Bioengineering** *(Fakultät II)* (Bioengineering; Construction Engineering; Data Processing; Electronic Engineering; Energy Engineering; Environmental Engineering; Machine Building; Mechanical Engineering; Packaging Technology; Production Engineering; Technology); **Media, Information and Design** *(Fakultät III)* (Communication Arts; Communication Studies; Design; Documentation Techniques; Fashion Design; Industrial Design; Information Management; Interior Design; Journalism; Media Studies; Public Relations); **Social Welfare, Health and Social Sciences** *(Fakultät V)* (Health Administration; Health Education; Health Sciences; Psychotherapy; Religious Education; Social Sciences; Social Work)

History: Founded 1971. Integrated the Hanover Protestant University of Applied Sciences (Evangelische Fachhochschule Hannover), which was renamed as Fakultät V – Diakonie, Gesundheit und Soziales 2007.

Academic Year: March to February (March-August; September-February)

Admission Requirements: Secondary school certificate (Abitur, Fachhochschulreife), Vorpraktikum

Fees: (Euros): 7.50-90 per semester

Main Language(s) of Instruction: German

International Co-operation: With universities in China, Japan, Italy, Spain, Greece, Hungary, Australia, USA, Belgium, Denmark, Finland, Estonia, France, United Kingdom, Ireland, Iceland, Lithuania, Mongolia, Netherlands, Poland, Slovak Republic. Also participates in Erasmus, Leonardo

Degrees and Diplomas: *Bachelor/Bakkalaureus*: 3-4 yrs; *Diplom (FH)*: Bio Process Engineering; *Diplom (FH)*: Business Administration; Computer Science; Engineering; Information and Communication, 4 yrs; *Diplom (FH)*: Design and Media, Interior Design, 4 1/2 yrs; *Diplom (FH)*: Fine Arts, 5 yrs; *Master/Magister*: Automatisation and Control Engineering; Technical Redaction; Machine Construction; Bioengineering; Design; Information and Knowledge

Management; Journalism; Communication; Applied Informatics; Business Administration; Health Administration; Social Work

Student Services: Academic counselling, Canteen, Foreign student adviser, Handicapped facilities, Language programs, Social counselling, Sports facilities

Student Residential Facilities: Yes

Libraries: 1 Central and 3 Extensive Libraries
Last Updated: 31/01/12

UNIVERSITY OF APPLIED SCIENCES FOR ECONOMICS AND MANAGEMENT ESSEN

Fachhochschule für Oekonomie und Management Essen
PO Box Rolandstrasse 5-9, 45128 Essen
Tel: +49(201) 81004-25
Fax: +49(201) 81004-310
EMail: fom@fh-essen.de
Website: http://www.fom.de

Rektor: Burghard Hermeier (2000-)
Tel: +49(201) 81004-350, Fax: +49(201) 81004-410
EMail: burghard.hermeier@bildungscentrum.de

Kanzler: Harald Beschorner
Tel: +49(201) 81004-27
EMail: harald.beschorner@bildungscentrum.de

International Relations: Carola Hirsch
Tel: +49(201) 81004-442 EMail: carola.hirsch@fom.de

Programmes
Banking and Finance (Banking; Finance); **Business Administration** (Business Administration); **Business Computing** (Business Computing); **Business Computing (Web Engineering)** (Business Computing); **Commercial Law** (Commercial Law); **Human Resources** *(Master)* (Human Resources); **Information Technology Management** *(Master)* (Information Management; Information Technology); **International Management** (Business Administration; International Business; Management); **Marketing and Communications** (Communication Studies; Marketing); **Marketing and Sales** (Marketing; Sales Techniques); **Mechanical Engineering** (Mechanical Engineering); **Taxation** (Taxation)

Further Information: Campuses in Aachen, Berlin, Bochum, Bonn, Bremen, Cologne, Dortmund, Duisburg, Düsseldorf, Essen, Frankfurt a. M., Gütersloh, Hamburg, Kassel, Leipzig, Marl, Munich, Neuss, Nürnberg, Siegen, Stuttgart and Luxemburg.

History: Founded 1993.

Fees: (Euros): c. 1,620-1,800 per semester

Main Language(s) of Instruction: German, English

Degrees and Diplomas: *Bachelor/Bakkalaureus*: Business Administration; International Management; Taxation; Commercial Law; Business Computing; Business Computing (Web Engineering); Engineering, 3 1/2 yrs; *Diplom*: Business Computing; Business Law, 3 1/2 yrs; *Master/Magister*: Accountancy; Human Resources; Information Technology Management; Marketing and Communications; Marketing and Sales; Commercial Law; Business Administration, 2 yrs

Student Services: Academic counselling, Canteen, Foreign student adviser

Libraries: Yes
Last Updated: 06/02/12

UNIVERSITY OF APPLIED SCIENCES FOR TECHNOLOGY AND ECONOMICS BERLIN

Fachhochschule für Technik und Wirtschaft Berlin
Treskowallee 8, 10313 Berlin
Tel: +49(30) 5019-0
Fax: +49(30) 5090-134
EMail: fhtw@fhtw-berlin.de
Website: http://www.htw-berlin.de

Präsident: Michael Heine
Tel: +49(30) 5019-2607, Fax: +49(30) 5019-2805
EMail: m.heine@fhtw-berlin.de

Kanzler: Stephan Becker
Tel: +49(30) 5019-2810, Fax: +49(30) 5019-2805
EMail: kanzler@fhtw-berlin.de

International Relations: Jochen Hönow, Head, International Affairs
Tel: +49(30) 5019-2622, Fax: +49(30) 5019-2210
EMail: Jochen.Hoenow@HTW-Berlin.de

Faculties
Design (Archaeology; Communication Arts; Design; Fashion Design; Museum Studies; Restoration of Works of Art; Textile Design); **Economics I** *(Treskowallee)* (Accountancy; Business Administration; Economics; Finance; Management; Real Estate; Taxation); **Economics II** *(Wilhelminenhof)* (Business Administration; Business Computing; Computer Science; Media Studies); **Engineering I** *(Wilhelminenhof)* (Automotive Engineering; Bioengineering; Business Computing; Construction Engineering; Engineering; Environmental Engineering; Information Technology; Machine Building; Mechanical Engineering; Real Estate); **Engineering II** *(Wilhelminenhof)* (Building Technologies; Computer Engineering; Electronic Engineering; Energy Engineering; Engineering; Environmental Engineering; Information Technology; Telecommunications Engineering)

History: Founded 1991.

Main Language(s) of Instruction: German

Degrees and Diplomas: *Bachelor/Bakkalaureus*; *Diplom*; *Master/Magister*
Last Updated: 06/02/12

UNIVERSITY OF APPLIED SCIENCES FOR THE MIDDLE CLASSES BIELEFELD

Fachhochschule des Mittelstandes (FHM) Bielefeld
Ravensberger Strasse 10G, 33602 Bielefeld
Tel: +49(521) 96655-222
Fax: +49(521) 96655-11
EMail: info@hm-mittelstand.de
Website: http://www.fhm-mittelstand.de/

Rektor: Gerhard Klippstein EMail: klippstein@fhm-mittelstand.de

Faculties
Economics (Banking; Business Administration; Economics; Finance; Management); **Media Studies** (Communication Arts; Communication Studies; Design; Journalism; Media Studies)

History: Founded 2000.

Main Language(s) of Instruction: German

Degrees and Diplomas: *Bachelor/Bakkalaureus*; *Master/Magister*
Last Updated: 06/02/12

UNIVERSITY OF APPLIED SCIENCES IN EBERSWALDE

Hochschule für nachhaltige Entwicklung Eberswalde
Friedrich-Ebert-Strasse 28, 16225 Eberswalde
Tel: +49(3334) 657- 0
Fax: +49(3334) 657-142
EMail: rektorat@fh-eberswalde.de
Website: http://www.fh-eberswalde.de/

Rektor: Wilhelm-Günther Vahrson (1998-)
Tel: +49(3334) 657-142, Fax: +49(3334) 657-151
EMail: president@fh-eberswalde.de

Kanzler: Claas Cordes
Tel: +49(3334) 657-152, Fax: +49(3334) 657-139
EMail: ccordes@fh-eberswalde.de

International Relations: Lilianne C. Meier
Tel: +49(3334) 657-137, Fax: +49(3334) 657-136
EMail: lmeier@fh-eberswalde.de

Faculties
Business Administration (Business Administration; Finance; Management; Marketing; Tourism); **Forestry and Environment** (Ecology; Environmental Studies; Forest Management; Forestry; Information Technology); **Landscape Management and Nature Protection** (Ecology; Environmental Management; Landscape Architecture; Regional Planning; Tourism); **Wood Science and Technology** (Engineering; Wood Technology)

History: Founded 1992.

Admission Requirements: Hochschulzugangsberechtigung, DSH

Fees: (Euros): 106 per semester

Main Language(s) of Instruction: German and English

International Co-operation: With institutions in Finland; Netherlands; France; Spain; United Kingdom; Sweden; Hungary; Poland; Norway; Canada; USA

Degrees and Diplomas: *Bachelor/Bakkalaureus*: 3 yrs; *Diplom (FH)*: Wood Technology, 4; *Master/Magister*: Forest Information Technology; Global Change Management; Regional Development and Nature Protection; Ecological Agricultural Management; Sustainable Tourism Management; Wood Technology; Marketing and Management, 2 yrs

Student Services: Academic counselling, Canteen, Employment services, Foreign student adviser, Language programs, Social counselling

Student Residential Facilities: Yes

Libraries: Yes
Last Updated: 12/01/10

UNIVERSITY OF APPLIED SCIENCES IN SAARBRÜCKEN

Hochschule für Technik und Wirtschaft des Saarlandes Saarbrücken
Goebenstrasse 40, 66117 Saarbrücken
Tel: +49(681) 5867-0
Fax: +49(681) 5867-122
EMail: info@htw-saarland.de
Website: http://www.htw-saarland.de

Rektor: Wolfgang Cornetz (2001-)
Tel: +49(681) 5867-100, Fax: +49(681) 5867-123
EMail: rektor@htw-saarland.de

Head of Administration: Norbert Hudlet
Tel: +49(681) 5867-110 EMail: vd@htw-saarland.de

International Relations: Doris Kollmann
Tel: +49(681) 5867-609, Fax: +49(681) 5867-608
EMail: auslandsamt@htw-saarland.de; kollmann@htw-saarland.de

Faculties
Architecture and Construction Engineering *(Waldhausweg)* (Architecture; Construction Engineering); **Business Administration** *(Waldhausweg)* (Aeronautical and Aerospace Engineering; Business Administration; International Business; Management); **Engineering** (Computer Engineering; Electronic Engineering; Machine Building; Mechanical Engineering); **Social Work** (Social Work)

History: Founded 1971.

Main Language(s) of Instruction: German

Degrees and Diplomas: *Bachelor/Bakkalaureus*; *Master/Magister*
Last Updated: 19/01/10

UNIVERSITY OF APPLIED SCIENCES OF ZWICKAU

Westsächsische Hochschule Zwickau
PO Box 201037, Dr.-Friedrichs-Ring 2a, 08012 Zwickau
Tel: +49(375) 536-0
Fax: +49(375) 536-1127
EMail: rektorat@fh-zwickau.de
Website: http://www.fh-zwickau.de/

Rektor: Gunter Krautheim
Tel: +49(375) 536-1000, Fax: +49(375) 536-1011
EMail: gunter.krautheim@fh-zwickau.de

Kanzler: Joachim Körner
Tel: +49(375) 536-1100, Fax: +49(375) 536-1103
EMail: joachim.koerner@fh-zwickau.de

International Relations: Lothar Wolf
Tel: +49(375) 536-1161, Fax: +49(375) 536-1033
EMail: akademisches.auslandsamt@fh-zwickau.de

Faculties
Applied Arts *(Schneeberg)* (Fine Arts); **Architecture** (Architecture; Landscape Architecture; Town Planning); **Economics** (Economics);

Electrical Engineering (Electrical Engineering); **Health and Health Care** (Health Administration; Health Sciences); **Languages** (Chinese; English; French; Modern Languages; Spanish); **Mechanical and Automotive Engineering** (Automotive Engineering; Mechanical Engineering); **Physical Engineering and Computer Science** (Computer Science; Physical Engineering); **Textile and Leather Technology** (Leather Techniques; Textile Technology)

History: Founded 1969.

Governing Bodies: Gesellschaftliche Rat (Social Council); Wissenschaftliche Rat (Academic Council)

Academic Year: September to July (September-January; February-July)

Admission Requirements: Technical training and secondary school certificate (Reifezeugnis)

Fees: None

Main Language(s) of Instruction: German

Degrees and Diplomas: *Bachelor/Bakkalaureus*; *Diplom*: 4 yrs; *Master/Magister*

Student Residential Facilities: Residential facilities for 1,300 students

Libraries: c. 105,000 vols
Last Updated: 07/02/12

UNIVERSITY OF APPLIED SCIENCES SCHMALKALDEN

Fachhochschule Schmalkalden - Hochschule für Technik und Wirtschaft
PO Box 100452, Blechhammer, 98564 Schmalkalden
Tel: +49(3683) 688-0
Fax: +49(3683) 688-1920
EMail: info@fh-schmalkalden.de
Website: http://www.fh-schmalkalden.de

Rektor: Elmar Heinemann (2007-)
Tel: +49(3683) 688-1000, Fax: +49(3683) 688-1920
EMail: rektor@fh-schmalkalden.de

Kanzler: Thomas Losse
Tel: +49(3683) 688-1002 EMail: kanzler@fh-schmalkalden.de

International Relations: Joachim Bach, Head, International Affairs
Tel: +49(3683) 688-1010, Fax: +49(3683) 688-1999
EMail: j.bach@fh-sm.de; auslandsamt@fh-schmalkalden.de

Faculties
Business and Economics (Business Administration; Economics); **Business Law** (Commercial Law; Law); **Computer Science** (Computer Science); **Electrical Engineering** (Electrical Engineering; Information Technology); **Mechanical Engineering** (Machine Building; Mechanical Engineering)

History: Founded 1992.

Main Language(s) of Instruction: German

Degrees and Diplomas: *Bachelor/Bakkalaureus*; *Diplom*; *Master/Magister*
Last Updated: 06/02/12

UNIVERSITY OF AUGSBURG

Universität Augsburg
Universitätsstrasse 2, 86159 Augsburg
Tel: +49(821) 598-1
Fax: +49(821) 598-5505
EMail: wwwadm@uni-augsburg.de
Website: http://www.uni-augsburg.de

Präsidentin: Sabine Doering-Manteuffel (2011-)
Tel: +49(821) 598-5100, Fax: +49(821) 598-5116
EMail: praesidentin@praesidium.uni-augsburg.de; rektor@rektor-at.uni-augsburg.de

Kanzler: Alois Zimmermann
Tel: +49(821) 598-5200 EMail: kanzler@zv.uni-augsburg.de

International Relations: Sabine Tamm
Tel: +49(821) 598-5135, Fax: +49(821) 598-5142
EMail: sabine.tamm@aaa.uni-augsburg.de

Centres

Informatics (Computer Science); **Computer Science (RZ)** (Computer Science); **Continuing Education and Knowledge Transfer (ZWW)** (Continuing Education); **Educational and Instructional Research** (Education; Educational Sciences; Pedagogy); **Environmental Sciences (WZU)** (Environmental Studies); **Languages (SZ)** (Arts and Humanities; Modern Languages)

Departments

Sports (Sports; Welfare and Protective Services)

Faculties

Applied Computer Science (Computer Science; Software Engineering); **Business Administration and Economics** (Business Administration; Economics; Marketing); **History and Philology** (Arts and Humanities; History; Modern Languages; Philology; Philosophy); **Law** (Law); **Mathematics and Natural Sciences** (Mathematics; Natural Sciences); **Philosophy and Social Sciences** (Education; Philosophy; Social Sciences); **Theology** (Catholic Theology)

History: Founded 1970. An autonomous institution financially supported by the State of Bavaria.

Governing Bodies: Senat; Erweiterter Senat; Rektorat

Academic Year: October to September (October-March; April-September)

Admission Requirements: Secondary school certificate (Reifezeugnis) or equivalent

Fees: None

Main Language(s) of Instruction: German

International Co-operation: Participates in the Erasmus/Socrates Programmes and with over 50 universities worldwide

Degrees and Diplomas: *Bachelor/Bakkalaureus*: Business Administration; European Cultural Studies; Computer Science and Electronic Commerce; Computer Science and Multimedia; Materials Science; Media and Communication; Economics; Business Mathematics (BA; BSc); *Diplom*: Catholic Theology, 5 yrs; *Lehramt*: Teaching qualifications, primary and secondary levels, in all fields; *Staatsprüfung*: Law; *Master/Magister*: Financial Management and E-Commerce; Computer Science and E-Commerce; Computer Science and Multimedia; Intellectual Property Law; Materials Science; Media and Communication; Management (MSc; MA; MBA; LLM); *Doktorgrad*: in all fields; *Habilitation*

Student Services: Academic counselling, Canteen, Employment services, Foreign student adviser, Foreign Studies Centre, Handicapped facilities, Language programs, Nursery care, Social counselling, Sports facilities

Student Residential Facilities: Yes

Libraries: Central Library, c. 1,960,000 vols

Publications: Forschungsbericht *(other/irregular)*
Last Updated: 06/02/12

UNIVERSITY OF BAYREUTH

Universität Bayreuth (UBT)
95440 Bayreuth, Bavaria
Tel: +49(921) 55-0
Fax: +49(921) 55-5290
EMail: poststelle@uvw.uni-bayreuth.de
Website: http://www.uni-bayreuth.de

Präsident: Rüdiger Bormann
Tel: +49(921) 55-5200, Fax: +49(921) 55-5213
EMail: praesident@uni-bayreuth.de

Kanzler: Markus Zanner
Tel: +49(921) 55-5210, Fax: +49(921) 55-5214
EMail: kanzler@uvw.uni-bayreuth.de

International Relations: Heinz Pöhlmann
Tel: +49(921) 55-5240, Fax: +49(921) 55-5248
EMail: heinz.poehlmann@uni-bayreuth.de

Centres

Colloids and Interfaces *(Bayreuther Zentrum für Kolloide und Grenzflächen BZKG)* (Physical Chemistry); **Computer** (Computer Science); **Languages** (Linguistics; Modern Languages); **Molecular Life Sciences** *(Bayreuther Zentrum für Molekulare Biowissenschaften BZMB)* (Biochemistry; Biomedicine; Biophysics; Cell Biology; Molecular Biology)

Faculties

Applied Sciences (Applied Chemistry; Applied Mathematics; Applied Physics; Bioengineering; Engineering; Environmental Engineering; Materials Engineering; Natural Sciences); **Biology, Chemistry and Earth Sciences** (Biochemistry; Biology; Chemistry; Geography; Regional Planning; Soil Science; Town Planning; Water Science); **Cultural Studies** (Cultural Studies; Economics; Education; Ethnology; History; Modern History; Music; Philosophy; Political Sciences; Religious Studies; Sociology; Sports; Theology); **Law and Economics** (Banking; Business Administration; Business and Commerce; Civil Law; Economics; Finance; Health Administration; International Law; Labour Law; Law; Management; Public Law); **Linguistics and Literature** (African Languages; Arabic; English; English Studies; French Studies; German; Islamic Studies; Literature; Modern Languages; Romance Languages; Slavic Languages; Swahili; Theatre); **Mathematics, Physics and Computer Science** (Applied Mathematics; Applied Physics; Atomic and Molecular Physics; Computer Science; Mathematics; Physics; Statistics; Systems Analysis; Thermal Physics)

Institutes

African Studies (African Studies); **Earth Eco-Systems Research** *(Bayreuther Institut für Terrestrische Ökosystemforschung BITÖK)* (Earth Sciences; Forest Biology; Forestry; Soil Science; Water Science); **Experimental Geochemistry and Geophysics Research** *(Bayerisches Forschungsinstitut für experimentelle Geochemie und Geophysik BGI)* (Crystallography; Geochemistry; Geology; Geophysics; Mineralogy; Petrology; Seismology); **Macromolecular Research** *(Bayreuther Institut für Makromolekülforschung BIMF)* (Molecular Biology); **Materials Science** (Materials Engineering); **Music and Drama Research** *(Schloß Thurnau)* (Music; Theatre)

History: Founded 1972. Formally opened 1975. An autonomous institution financially supported by the State of Bavaria, and under the jurisdiction of its Ministry of Science, Research and Arts.

Governing Bodies: Versammlung; Konzil; Senat

Academic Year: October to September (October-March; April-September)

Admission Requirements: Secondary school certificate (Reifezeugnis)

Fees: (Euros): None for initial studies; additional study, 500 per semester

Main Language(s) of Instruction: German

International Co-operation: With universities in the USA, several African countries, Japan and China. Also participates in Erasmus programme

Accrediting Agencies: ACQUIN

Degrees and Diplomas: *Bachelor/Bakkalaureus*: Linguistics; Literature; Languages; Cultural Studies; African Studies; Mathematics; Applied Informatics (BA), 3 yrs; *Diplom*: Biology; Chemistry; Biochemistry; Geography; Geo-ecology; Business Administration; Economics; Sports Management; Health Management; Technical Physics; Physics; Statistics; Mathematics, 4 1/2-5 yrs; *Diplom*: Materials Science; Environmental and Bio-Engineering, 5 yrs; *Diplom*: Sports Science and Management, 4 yrs; *Lehramt*: Teaching qualification, secondary level, 4 1/2 yrs; *Lehramt*: Teaching qualification, primary level, 3 1/2 yrs; *Magister Artium*: Law; Linguistics; Literature; Languages; Cultural Studies, 4 1/2 yrs; *Staatsprüfung*: Law, 4 1/2 yrs; *Master/Magister*: Law; Linguistics; Literature; Languages; Cultural Studies (MA), 2 yrs following BA; *Doktorgrad*; *Habilitation*: at least 3 yrs following Doktor. Also Certificates of postgraduate studies: African Sciences, 2 yrs

Student Services: Academic counselling, Canteen, Employment services, Foreign student adviser, Handicapped facilities, Language programs, Social counselling, Sports facilities

Student Residential Facilities: Yes

Special Facilities: Ecological Garden; IWALEWA-Haus (Cultural Centre for African Arts, Theatre and Literature); Rossmann Paleobotanic Collection; BGI (Large Scale Facility of the EU)

Libraries: Total, 1,330,644 vols; computerized information and loan system

Publications: Arbeitsmaterialien zur Raumordnung und Raumplanung; Bayreuther African Studies Series; Bayreuther Beiträge zur Dialektologie; Bayreuther Beiträge zur Literaturwissenschaft; Bayreuther Bodenkundliche Berichte; Bayreuther Forum Ökologie; Bayreuther Frankofonie Studien; Bayreuther Geowissenschaftliche Arbeiten; Bayreuther Historische Kolloquien; Bayreuther Mathematische Schriften; Beiträge zur Stadt- und Regionalplanung; Betriebswirtschaftliche Forschungsbeiträge; Forschungsbericht; Kolloquium Mathematik-Didaktik; Materialien zur Stadt- und Regionalplanung; Schriften zur Gesundheitsökonomie; Thurnauer Schriften zum Musiktheater; Universität Bayreuth: Fachgruppe Geowissenschaften: Forschungsmaterialien
Last Updated: 28/01/10

UNIVERSITY OF BIELEFELD
Universität Bielefeld
PO Box 100131, Universitätsstrasse 25, 33501 Bielefeld
Tel: +49(521) 106-00
EMail: post@uni-bielefeld.de
Website: http://www.uni-bielefeld.de

Rektor: Gerhard Sagerer
Tel: +49(521) 106-2000, Fax: +49(521) 106-6464
EMail: rektor@uni-bielefeld.de

Kanzler: Hans-Jürgen Simm
Tel: +49(521) 106-3000
EMail: hans-juergen.simm@uni-bielefeld.de

International Relations: Thomas Lüttenberg
Tel: +49(521) 106-4088, Fax: +49(521) 106-4079
EMail: thomas.luettenberg@uni-bielefeld.de

Centres
Biotechnology (Biophysics; Biotechnology; Genetics; Nanotechnology); **Interdisciplinary Research**; **Interdisciplinary Women's Research** (Women's Studies); **Research and Development in Higher Education** (Higher Education); **Teacher Training** (Teacher Training); **Transfer of Technology**

Faculties
Biology (Biology); **Chemistry** (Chemistry); **Economics** (Economics); **Educational Sciences** (Educational Sciences); **History, Philosophy and Theology** (History; Philosophy; Theology); **Law** (Law); **Linguistics and Literary Studies** (Linguistics; Literature); **Mathematics** (Mathematics); **Physics** (Physics); **Psychology and Sport Sciences** (Psychology; Sports); **Public Health** (Public Health); **Sociology** (Sociology); **Technology** (Biological and Life Sciences; Information Technology; Technology)

Graduate Schools
Bioinformatics and Genome Research (International NRW) (Biotechnology; Genetics); **Chemistry and Biochemistry Bielefield** (International) (Biochemistry; Chemistry); **Economics and Management** (Bielefeld) (Economics; Management); **History** (Bielefeld International) (History); **Sociology** (International) (Sociology)

Institutes
Conflict and Violence Research (Interdisciplinary) (Peace and Disarmament); **Mathematical Economics Research** (Economics); **Science and Technology Studies** (Natural Sciences; Technology); **Simulation of Complex Systems** (Systems Analysis)

History: Founded in 1969 in response to the demand for the creation of a University in East Westphalia. An autonomous institution financially supported by the State of North Rhine-Westphalia and under the jurisdiction of its Ministry of Science and Research.

Governing Bodies: Rektorat; Senat

Academic Year: October to September (October-March; April-September)

Admission Requirements: Secondary school certificate (Reifezeugnis) or equivalent

Fees: (Euros): Tuition fees: 100-500 plus 150.60 social fees

Main Language(s) of Instruction: German

International Co-operation: With universities in France, Japan, Poland and Russian Federation. Also participates in Erasmus

Degrees and Diplomas: Bachelor/Bakkalaureus; Master/Magister; Doktorgrad: Biology, Business, Chemistry, Economics, Education,

Language and Literature, History, Law, Linguistics, Mathematics, Philosophy, Physics, Psychology, Sociology, Theology (Ph.D);

Student Services: Academic counselling, Canteen, Cultural centre, Employment services, Foreign student adviser, Foreign Studies Centre, Handicapped facilities, Health services, Language programs, Nursery care, Social counselling, Sports facilities

Student Residential Facilities: Yes

Special Facilities: Pedagogical Museum; Art Gallery; Media Centre

Libraries: c. 2m. vols

Publications: Bielefelder Forschungsmagazin (biannually); Vorlesungsverzeichnis (biannually)
Last Updated: 28/01/10

UNIVERSITY OF BREMEN
Universität Bremen
PO Box 330440, Bibliotheksstrasse 1, 28334 Bremen
Tel: +49(421) 218-1
Fax: +49(421) 218-4259
EMail: info@uni-bremen.de
Website: http://www.uni-bremen.de

Rektor: Wilfried Müller
Tel: +49(421) 218-2708 EMail: rektor@uni-bremen.de

Kanzler: Gerd-Rüdiger Kück
Tel: +49(421) 218-2712 EMail: sekrkanz@uni-bremen.de

International Relations: Anne Renate Schönhagen

Centres
European Law Policy (ZERP); **Marine Tropical Ecology** (ZMT); **Medical Diagnosis Systems and Visualization** (MeVis)

Faculties
Biology and Chemistry (Aquaculture; Biology; Chemistry); **Cultural Studies** (Art Education; Cultural Studies; Music; Philosophy; Religious Studies; Sports); **Economics** (Economics; International Relations; Management); **Geosciences** (Geology; Geophysics; Mineralogy; Paleontology); **Human and Health Sciences** (Nursing; Psychology; Public Health; Social Sciences; Social Studies); **Law** (European Union Law; International Law; Law); **Linguistics and Literature** (American Studies; English; English Studies; French; Germanic Studies; Linguistics; Romance Languages; Spanish); **Mathematics and Computer Science** (Mathematics and Computer Science); **Physical and Electrical Engineering** (Electrical Engineering; Physical Engineering); **Production Technology**; **Social and Educational Sciences** (Education; Education of the Handicapped; Educational Sciences; Social Sciences); **Social Sciences** (Eastern European Studies; Geography; History; Polish; Political Sciences; Social Studies; Sociology)

Institutes
Advanced Study (Hanse); **Applied Materials Research** (Fraunhofer IFAM); **Applied Radiation Technology** (Bremen BIAS); **Applied System Technology** (Bremen ATB); **Energy** (Bremen BEI); **Fibre** (FIBRE); **Industrial Technology and Applied Work Science** (Bremen BIBA); **Marine Microbiology** (Max Planck); **Marine Transport and Logistics** (ISL) (Marine Transport; Transport and Communications); **Materials Technology** (IWT) (Materials Engineering); **Polar Research and Oceanography** (Alfred Wegener AWI) (Marine Science and Oceanography); **Preventive Research and Social Medicine** (Bremen BIPS) (Medicine); **Technology Transfer by Scientific Continuing Education** (IfW) (Technology)

Research Centres
Cognitive Studies (Cognitive Sciences); **Computing Technology** (TZI) (Computer Science); **Environmental Research and Technology** (UTF) (Environmental Studies); **Gender Studies** (Gender Studies); **Human Genetics** (Genetics); **Neuronal Basis of Cognitive Performances** (Neurosciences); **Philosophical Foundations of the Sciences** (Public Health); **Safety Engineering** (Safety Engineering); **Social Policy** (Social Policy); **Solid State Physics** (Solid State Physics); **Technology and Education** (ITB) (Education; Technology); **The South Atlantic in the Late Quaternary: Reconstruction of Materials Budget and Current Systems** (Geochemistry; Geophysics; Marine Biology; Marine Science and Oceanography; Paleontology); **Work-Environment-Technology**

Research Institutes
Independent Literature and Social Movements in Eastern Europe (Eastern European Studies)

History: Founded 1971 as an autonomous institution under the jurisdiction of and financed by the State of Bremen. Previously existing College of Education (1947) incorporated 1973.

Governing Bodies: Senat

Academic Year: October to September (October-March; April-September)

Admission Requirements: Secondary school certificate (Reifezeugnis) or equivalent

Fees: None

Main Language(s) of Instruction: German

Degrees and Diplomas: *Bachelor/Bakkalaureus*; *Lehramt*: Teaching Qualification, Secondary level, 4 1/2 yrs; *Staatsprüfung*: Law, 4 1/2 yrs; *Master/Magister*: Biology; Computer Science; Economics; Geoscience; Physics; Production Engineering; *Doktorgrad*: Economics (DrRerPol); Engineering (DrIng); Law (DrJur); Natural Sciences (DrRerNat); Philosophy (DrPhil), 3 yrs

Student Services: Academic counselling, Employment services, Foreign student adviser, Handicapped facilities, Health services, Social counselling, Sports facilities

Student Residential Facilities: For c. 1,515 students

Libraries: University Library, c. 3m. vols

Publications: Impulse aus der Forschung; Research Reports and Papers

Last Updated: 28/01/10

UNIVERSITY OF CATHOLIC CHURCH MUSIC AND MUSIC EDUCATION
Hochschule für Katholische Kirchenmusik und Musikpädagogik Regensburg
Andreasstrasse 9, 93059 Regensburg
Tel: +49(941) 83009-0
Fax: +49(941) 83009-46
EMail: info@hfkm-regensburg.de
Website: http://www.hfkm-regensburg.de

Rektor: Stefan Baier
Tel: +49(941) 83009-10 EMail: s.baier@hfkm-regensburg.de

Geschäftsführer: Johannes Lederer
Tel: +49(941) 83009-13, Fax: +49(941) 83009-46
EMail: j.lederer@hfkm-regensburg.de

Programmes
Church Music (Conducting; Music Education; Musical Instruments; Religious Music; Singing)

History: Founded 2001.

Main Language(s) of Instruction: German

Degrees and Diplomas: *Bachelor/Bakkalaureus*: 8 sem.; *Lehramt*; *Master/Magister*: 4 sem. Also Postgraduate Diploma
Last Updated: 02/02/12

UNIVERSITY OF CHURCH MUSIC OF THE PROTESTANT CHURCH OF WESTPHALIA
Hochschule für Kirchenmusik der Evangelischen Kirche von Westfalen
Parkstrasse 6, 32049 Herford
Tel: +49(5221) 991-450
Fax: +49(5221) 830-809
EMail: info@hochschule-herford.de
Website: http://www.hochschule-herford.de

Rektor: Helmut Fleinghaus
Tel: +49(5221) 5731-94720
EMail: Fleinghaus@hochschule-herford.de

Programmes
Church Music (Music; Musical Instruments; Religious Music)

History: Founded 1947.

Main Language(s) of Instruction: German

Degrees and Diplomas: *Bachelor/Bakkalaureus*: 8 sem.; *Künstlerische Abschlussprüfung*: 4 sem.; *Master/Magister*: 4 sem.
Last Updated: 19/01/10

UNIVERSITY OF CHURCH MUSIC OF THE PROTESTANT LUTHERAN REGIONAL CHURCH IN SAXONY
Hochschule für Kirchenmusik Dresden
Käthe-Kollwitz-Ufer 97, 01309 Dresden
Tel: +49(351) 31864-0
Fax: +49(351) 31864-22
EMail: hfkimudd@t-online.de
Website: http://www.kirchenmusik-dresden.de/

Rektor: Christfried Brödel (1992-)
Prorektor: Martin Strohhäcker

Programmes
Church Music (Conducting; Music Education; Religious Music)

History: Founded 1949.

Degrees and Diplomas: *Bachelor/Bakkalaureus*. 4-year Diplom Also Postgraduate Degree (Aufbaustudiengang)
Last Updated: 02/02/10

UNIVERSITY OF CHURCH MUSIC OF THE PROTESTANT REGIONAL CHURCH IN BADEN
Hochschule für Kirchenmusik der Evangelischen Landeskirche in Baden - Heidelberg
Hildastrasse 8, 69115 Heidelberg
Tel: +49(6221) 270-62
Fax: +49(6221) 218-76
EMail: sekretariat@hfk-heidelberg.de
Website: http://www.hfk-heidelberg.de

Rektor: Bernd Stegmann EMail: rektor@hfk-heidelberg.de

Programmes
Artistic Education (Musical Instruments; Religious Music; Singing); **Church Music** (Religious Music); **Soloist Class** (Musical Instruments; Religious Music); **Special courses** (Religious Music; Theology)

History: Founded 1931.

Degrees and Diplomas: *Diplom*. Also Postgraduate Diploma (Aufbaustudium)
Last Updated: 19/01/10

UNIVERSITY OF CHURCH MUSIC OF THE PROTESTANT REGIONAL CHURCH IN WÜRTTEMBERG
Hochschule für Kirchenmusik der Evangelischen Landeskirche in Württemberg - Tübingen
Gartenstrasse 12, 72074 Tübingen
Tel: +49(7071) 925-997
Fax: +49(7071) 925-998
EMail: info@kirchenmusikhochschule.de
Website: http://www.kirchenmusikhochschule.de

Rektor: Christian Fischer
Tel: +49(7072) 922-148, Fax: +49(7072) 915-617
EMail: rektorat@kirchenmusikhochschule.de

Prorektor: Bernhard Leube
Tel: +49(711) 76515-50, Fax: +49(711) 76515-90

Programmes
Religious Music (Musical Instruments; Religious Music; Singing)

History: Founded 1945 in Esslingen. Acquired university status 1989. Moved to Tübingen 1998.

Admission Requirements: Abitur and entrance examination

Main Language(s) of Instruction: German

Degrees and Diplomas: *Bachelor/Bakkalaureus*; *Diplom*; *Master/Magister*
Last Updated: 25/01/09

UNIVERSITY OF COLOGNE
Universität zu Köln
Albertus-Magnus-Platz, 50923 Köln, Nordrhein-Westfalen
Tel: +49(221) 470-0
Fax: +49(221) 470-5151
EMail: pressestelle@uni-koeln.de
Website: http://www.uni-koeln.de

Rektor: Axel Freimuth
Tel: +49(221) 470-2201, Fax: +49(221) 470-4893
EMail: rektor@uni-koeln.de

Kanzler: Johannes Neyses
Tel: +49(221) 470-2236, Fax: +49(221) 470-5134
EMail: kanzler@verw.uni-koeln.de

International Relations: Stefan Bildhauer
Tel: +49(221) 470-2382, Fax: +49(221) 470-5016
EMail: s.bildhauer@verw.uni-koeln.de

Faculties
Arts and Humanities (Ethnology; History; Media Studies; Modern Languages; Musicology; Philosophy; Psychology; Theology); **Human Sciences**; **Law** (Law); **Management, Economics, and Social Sciences** (Business Administration; Economics; Management; Social Sciences); **Mathematics and Natural Sciences** (Biology; Chemistry; Earth Sciences; Mathematics; Natural Sciences; Physics); **Medicine** (Dentistry; Medicine; Neurosciences; Surgery)

History: Founded 1388 as a Municipal University. Closed 1798. At the beginning of the 20th century a College of Commerce, a Medical Academy and a College of Social Administration were estabished. These formed the basis for the re-establishment of the University 1919. Rheinland College of Education incorporated 1980. An autonomous institution financially supported by the State of North Rhine-Westphalia and under the jurisdiction of its Ministry of Education since 1953. Since 1970 under the jurisdiction of its Ministry of Science and Research.

Governing Bodies: Senat; Kuratorium

Academic Year: October to September (October-March; April-September)

Admission Requirements: Secondary school certificate (Reifezeugnis) or equivalent

Fees: None

Main Language(s) of Instruction: German

Degrees and Diplomas: *Bachelor/Bakkalaureus*; *Diplom*: Economics; Education; *Staatsprüfung*: Dentistry; Law; Medicine; *Master/Magister*; *Doktorgrad*; *Doktorgrad*: Dentistry (Dr.med.dent); Law (Dr.jur.); Political Science (Dr.rer.pol.); *Habilitation*

Special Facilities: Theatermuseum; Papyrus Museum; Musical Instruments Museum; Biology Museum

Libraries: University and City Library, c. 2.2m. vols; Library of Medicine, c. 600,000 vols

Publications: Research Report *(biennially)*; Universitätsreden; Veröffentlichungen einzelner Institute; Vorlesungsverzeichnis
Last Updated: 02/02/10

UNIVERSITY OF DUISBURG-ESSEN, DUISBURG CAMPUS
Universität Duisburg-Essen, Standort Duisburg
Lotharstrasse 65, 47048 Duisburg
Tel: +49(203) 379-0
Fax: +49(203) 379-3333
EMail: webmaster@uni-duisburg-essen.de
Website: http://www.uni-duisburg-essen.de/

Rektor: Ulrich Radtke
Tel: +49(203) 379-2465, Fax: +49(203) 379-3500
EMail: rektor@uni-due.de

Kanzler: Rainer Ambrosy EMail: kanzler@uni-due.de

International Relations: Petra Günther
Tel: +49(203) 379-2459, Fax: +49(203) 379-3705
EMail: petra.guenther@uni-due.de

Centres
Higher Education and Quality Development *(ZfH)*; **Interdisciplinary Studies** *(ZIS)*; **Logistics and Transport** *(ZLV)* (Transport and Communications; Transport Management)

Departments
Economics (Accountancy; Banking; Business Administration; Civil Law; Economics; Finance; Information Management; International Relations; Management; Marketing; Taxation) *Dean*: Peter Chamoni; **Humanities** (American Studies; Cultural Studies; English; Germanic Studies; Greek; History; Japanese; Latin; Linguistics; Literature; Philology; Philosophy; Theology; Turkish) *Dean*: Erhard Reckwitz; **Mathematics** (Mathematics) *Dean*: Werner Haussmann; **Physics** (Applied Physics; Physics) *Dean*: Rolf Möller; **Social Sciences** (Cognitive Sciences; Communication Studies; Development Studies; Education; Geography; Peace and Disarmament; Political Sciences; Social Sciences; Sociology) *Dean*: Gerhard Bäcker

Faculties
Engineering (Computer Science; Electrical Engineering; Engineering; Information Technology; Materials Engineering; Mechanical Engineering; Multimedia; Software Engineering) *Dean*: Andrés Kecskeméthy

Institutes
Automation and Robotics *(German-French Institute, IAR)* (Automation and Control Engineering; Robotics) *Head*: Steven X. Ding; **Cultural History and Regional Development of the Lower Rhine Region** *(InKuR)*; **Development and Peace** *(INEF)* (Development Studies; Peace and Disarmament; Political Sciences) *Head*: Franz Nuscheler; **East Asian Studies** *(INEAST)*

Further Information: Also international summer courses

History: Founded 2003 following merger between the University of Duisburg and the University of Essen (independent universities founded 1972).

Governing Bodies: Senate/Rectorate

Academic Year: October to September (October-March; April-September)

Admission Requirements: Secondary school certificate (Reifezeugnis)

Fees: None

Main Language(s) of Instruction: German. Also English in some courses

International Co-operation: With universities in Afghanistan; Austria; Brazil; Egypt; Australia; Belarus; Belgium; China; Denmark; Estonia; Finland; France; Greece; Iceland; Ireland; Italy; Japan; Republic of Korea; The Netherlands; Norway; Poland; Portugal; Romania; Russian Federation; Sweden; Switzerland; Spain; Slovenia; Slovak Republic; South Africa; Czech Republic; Turkey; Hungary; United Kingdom; USA

Accrediting Agencies: AQAS; ASIIN; ZEvA

Degrees and Diplomas: *Bachelor/Bakkalaureus*: 6 sem; *Lehramt*: Teaching qualification, secondary level, 9 sem; *Master/Magister*: a further 4 sem; *Promotion*

Student Services: Academic counselling, Canteen, Cultural centre, Employment services, Foreign student adviser, Handicapped facilities, Language programs, Nursery care, Social counselling, Sports facilities

Student Residential Facilities: For 1,030 students; International Guest House

Libraries: University Library, c. 1,1 m vols; department libraries

Publications: Forum Forschung; Universitätsreden

Press or Publishing House: Pressestelle der Universität Duisburg-Essen
Last Updated: 13/02/09

UNIVERSITY OF DUISBURG-ESSEN, ESSEN CAMPUS

Universität Duisburg-Essen, Standort Essen
Universitätsstrasse 2, 45117 Essen
Tel: +49(201) 183-1
Fax: +49(201) 183-2151
EMail: webmaster@uni-duisburg-essen.de
Website: http://www.uni-duisburg-essen.de/

Rektor: Ulrich Radtke EMail: rektor@uni-duisburg-essen.de

International Relations: Petra Günther
Tel: +49(201) 183-2068, Fax: +49(201) 183-2257
EMail: petra.guenther@uni-due.de

Centres
Medical Biotechnology *(ZMB)*; **Microscale Ecosystems** *(ZMU)*; **Teacher Education** *(ZLB)*

Departments
Art and Design (Art Education; Communication Arts; Design; Fine Arts; Industrial Design; Music Education) *Dean*: Kurt Mehnert; **Biology and Geography** (Biology; Geography) *Dean*: Ulrich Schreiber; **Building Sciences** *Dean*: Renatus Widmann; **Chemistry** (Applied Chemistry; Chemistry; Inorganic Chemistry; Organic Chemistry; Physical Chemistry) *Dean*: Elke Sumfleth; **Economics** (Business Computing; Computer Engineering; Economics; Health Administration; Law) *Dean*: Hendrik Schröder; **Educational Sciences** (Education; Educational Psychology; Physical Education; Physical Therapy; Psychology; Social Sciences; Sports; Women's Studies) *Dean*: Horst Bossong; **Humanities** (Cultural Studies; English; German; Germanic Studies; History; Linguistics; Literature; Philosophy; Theology) *Dean*: Erhard Reckwitz; **Mathematics** (Mathematics; Mathematics and Computer Science) *Dean*: Werner Haussmann

Faculties
Engineering (Automation and Control Engineering; Civil Engineering; Computer Engineering; Electrical and Electronic Engineering; Energy Engineering; Engineering; Information Technology; Materials Engineering; Microelectronics; Production Engineering; Telecommunications Engineering) *Dean*: Gerd Bacher; **Medicine and University Clinic** (Medicine; Pharmacy; Psychiatry and Mental Health) *Dean*: Karl-Heinz Jöckel

Institutes
Experimental Mathematics *(IEM)* (Mathematics)

Research Colleges
Gender Studies *(Essen Kollegium, EKfG)*

Further Information: Also international summer courses for foreign students

History: Founded 2003 following merger between the University of Duisburg and the University of Essen (independent universities founded 1972).

Governing Bodies: Senate/Rectorate

Academic Year: October to September (October-March; April-September)

Admission Requirements: Secondary school certificate (Reifezeugnis)

Fees: None

Main Language(s) of Instruction: German. Also English in some courses

International Co-operation: With universities in Afghanistan; Austria; Brazil; Egypt; Australia; Belarus; Belgium; China; Denmark; Estonia; Finland; France; Greece; Iceland; Ireland; Italy; Japan; Republic of Korea; Netherlands; Norway; Poland; Portugal; Romania; Russian Federation; Sweden; Switzerland; Spain; Slovenia; Slovak Republic; South Africa; Czech Republic; Turkey; Hungary; United Kingdom; USA

Accrediting Agencies: AQAS; ASIIN; ZEvA

Degrees and Diplomas: *Bachelor/Bakkalaureus*: Arts; Science; Engineering; Business Administration, 6 sem; *Diplom*: 8-9 sem; *Lehramt*: Teaching qualification, secondary level, 9 sem; *Master/ Magister*: Arts; Science; Engineering; Business Administration, 4 sem; *Doktorgrad*; *Habilitation*: following Doktor

Student Services: Academic counselling, Canteen, Cultural centre, Employment services, Foreign student adviser, Handicapped facilities, Language programs, Nursery care, Social counselling, Sports facilities

Student Residential Facilities: For c. 1,420 students. International Guest House

Libraries: University Library, c. 1,5 m vols; department libraries

Publications: Forum Forschung; Universitätsreden

Press or Publishing House: Pressestelle der Universität Duisburg-Essen

Last Updated: 04/04/08

UNIVERSITY OF EDUCATION OF FREIBURG

Pädagogische Hochschule Freiburg
Kunzenweg 21, 79117 Freiburg
Tel: +49(761) 682-0
Fax: +49(761) 682-402
EMail: postmaster@ph-freiburg.de
Website: http://www.ph-freiburg.de

Rektor: Ulrich Druwe
Tel: +49(761) 682-261, Fax: +49(761) 682-180
EMail: Druwe@ph-freiburg.de

Verwaltungsleiter: Peter Mollus
Tel: +49(761) 682-263, Fax: +49(761) 682-603
EMail: kanzler@ph-freiburg.de

International Relations: Johannes Lebfrom
Tel: +49(761) 682-578, Fax: +49(761) 682-575
EMail: aaa@ph-freiburg.de

Faculties
Arts (Music; Visual Arts); **Education** (Education); **Languages** (English; French; German; Modern Languages); **Mathematics and Computer Science** (Mathematics and Computer Science); **Natural Sciences** (Health Sciences; Mathematics; Natural Sciences); **Protestant and Catholic Theology**; **Social Sciences** (Social Sciences); **Sports** (Sports); **Technology** (Technology; Textile Technology)

History: Founded 1962. Acquired present status 1971. Under the jurisdiction of and financially supported by the State of Baden-Württemberg.

Governing Bodies: Senat; Hochschulrat

Academic Year: April to March (April-September; October-March)

Admission Requirements: Secondary school certificate (Reifezeugnis) or equivalent

Fees: None

Main Language(s) of Instruction: German, English, French

International Co-operation: With institutions in New Zealand; Australia; France; United Kingdom; Canada; USA

Degrees and Diplomas: *Diplom*: Education (Diplompädagoge), 4 yrs; *Lehramt*: Teaching qualification, 3 yrs; *Magister Artium*; *Master/ Magister*; *Promotion*

Student Residential Facilities: Yes

Libraries: c. 120,000 vols

Publications: PH-FR, Zeitschrift der Pädagogischen Hochschule Freiburg *(biannually)*
Last Updated: 13/02/09

UNIVERSITY OF EDUCATION OF LUDWIGSBURG

Pädagogische Hochschule Ludwigsburg
PO Box 220, Reuteallee 46, 71602 Ludwigsburg
Tel: +49(7141) 1400
Fax: +49(7141) 140-434
EMail: rektorat@vw.ph-ludwigsburg.de
Website: http://www.ph-ludwigsburg.de

Rektor: Martin Fix
Tel: +49(7141) 140-450 EMail: martin.fix@vw.ph-ludwigsburg.de

Kanzlerin: Vera Brüggemann
Tel: +49(7141) 140-204
EMail: vera.brueggemann@ph-ludwigsburg.de

Departments
Further Education (Greek; Italian; Romance Languages; Turkish)

Faculties
Cultural and Natural Sciences (Biological and Life Sciences; Chemistry; Computer Science; Cultural Studies; English; Fine Arts; French; German; Handicrafts; Linguistics; Literature; Mathematics; Music; Natural Sciences; Physics; Sports; Technology); **Education and Social Sciences** (Economics; Education; Educational Sciences; Geography; History; Philosophy; Political Sciences; Psychology; Sociology; Theology); **Special Education** *(Reutlingen)* (Special Education)

History: Founded 1962 in Stuttgart, transferred to present site 1966. Acquired present status 1971. External Department Reutlingen (Special Education) founded 1987. Under the jurisdiction of and financially supported by the State of Baden-Württemberg.

Governing Bodies: Senat, Hochschulrat

Academic Year: October to September (October- March; April-September)

Admission Requirements: Secondary school certificate (Reifezeugnis)

Fees: None

Main Language(s) of Instruction: German. Also English in Faculty of Economics and some Master programmes.

Degrees and Diplomas: *Bachelor/Bakkalaureus*; *Diplom*: Education, 3-5 yrs; *Lehramt*: Teaching degree, 3-4 yrs; *Magister Artium*: Cultural Administration, Theory of Subject Teaching, 2 yrs following Diplom, 5 yrs following Staatsprüfung; *Master/Magister*, *Doktorgrad*: Education (Dr.päd.), 2 yrs following Diplom; *Habilitation*: Teaching qualification, University level, at least 3 yrs following Doktor

Student Services: Academic counselling, Canteen, Cultural centre, Employment services, Foreign student adviser, Foreign Studies Centre, Language programs, Nursery care, Social counselling, Sports facilities

Student Residential Facilities: For c. 480 students

Libraries: Total, c. 400,000 vols

Publications: Hochschulschriften, Publication of symposium proceedings, outstanding theses, etc.
Last Updated: 22/01/10

UNIVERSITY OF EDUCATION OF SCHWÄBISCH GMÜND

Pädagogische Hochschule Schwäbisch Gmünd
Oberbettringer Strasse 200, 73525 Schwäbisch Gmünd
Tel: +49(7171) 983-0
Fax: +49(7171) 983-212
EMail: info@ph-gmuend.de
Website: http://www.ph-gmuend.de

Rektorin: Astrid Beckmann
Tel: +49(7171) 983-346, Fax: +49(7171) 983-388
EMail: rektorin@ph-gmuend.de

Kanzler: Edgar Buhl
Tel: +49(7171) 983-237, Fax: +49(7171) 983-361
EMail: wolfgang.goihl@ph-gmuend.de

International Relations: Monika Becker Tel: +49(7171) 983-225

Faculties
Faculty II *(Fakultät II)* (Biology; Chemistry; Civics; Computer Science; Economics; English; Fine Arts; Geography; German; History; Household Management; Literature; Mathematics; Music; Physics; Political Sciences; Social Studies; Sports; Technology; Textile Technology); **I** (Educational Sciences; Pedagogy; Philosophy; Political Sciences; Psychology; Religion; Religious Education; Sociology; Theology)

Institutes
Education Development *(Fakultätsübergreifendes)* (Continuing Education; Educational Research; Media Studies)
Further Information: Continuing Education for Senior Citizens

History: Founded 1825 as University College with the right to award Doctorates since 1977. Became institute 1947 and college 1962. Under the jurisdiction of and financially supported by the State of Baden-Württemberg.

Governing Bodies: Senat; Hochshulsrat
Academic Year: October to September (October-March; April-September)

Admission Requirements: Secondary school certificate (Allgemeine Hochschulreife) or foreign equivalent

Fees: (Euros): Tuition, none; administration fee, 75 per term

Main Language(s) of Instruction: German

International Co-operation: With universities in United Kingdom, Denmark, Netherlands, Austria, Ukraine, Hungary, Israel, Italy, Turkey, Finland, New Zealand

Accrediting Agencies: EVALAG

Degrees and Diplomas: *Bachelor/Bakkalaureus*; *Diplom*: Computer Education; Educational Counselling; Educational Sciences; Media Education; Multicultural Education, 4 yrs; *Lehramt*: Teaching qualifications, 3-4 yrs; *Master/Magister*; *Promotion*: Education (Dr.päd.), 2 yrs following Diploma

Student Services: Academic counselling, Canteen, Foreign student adviser, Foreign Studies Centre, Social counselling, Sports facilities

Student Residential Facilities: Yes

Special Facilities: Multimedia Centre

Libraries: c. 250,000 vols

Press or Publishing House: Gmünder Press
Last Updated: 03/02/12

UNIVERSITY OF EDUCATION OF WEINGARTEN

Pädagogische Hochschule Weingarten
Kirchplatz 2, 88250 Weingarten
Tel: +49(751) 501-0
Fax: +49(751) 501-8200
EMail: poststelle@ph-weingarten.de
Website: http://www.ph-weingarten.de

Rektor: Werner Knapp (2011-)
Tel: +49(751) 501-8240, Fax: +49(751) 501-8250
EMail: rektor@ph-weingarten.de

Centres
Basic Education (Education; Primary Education; Teacher Training)

Faculties
I (Catholic Theology; Economics; Educational Psychology; Educational Sciences; Ethics; Geography; History; Home Economics; Philosophy; Political Sciences; Protestant Theology; Sociology; Sports; Textile Technology); **II** (Biology; Chemistry; Computer Science; English; Fine Arts; French; Mathematics; Media Studies; Music; Physics; Technology)

History: Founded 1949 as institute, became college 1962. Acquired present status 1971. Under the jurisdiction of and financially supported by the State of Baden-Württemberg.

Governing Bodies: Hochschulrat; Senat

Academic Year: April to February (April-July; October-February)

Admission Requirements: Secondary school certificate (Reifezeugnis) or aptitude test

Fees: None

Main Language(s) of Instruction: German

International Co-operation: With institutions in France, United Kingdom, China, Russian Federation, USA. Participates in the Erasmus programme

Degrees and Diplomas: *Bachelor/Bakkalaureus*: Automotive Engineering (B.Eng.), 7 sem.; *Diplom*: Education, 2 yrs; *Lehramt*: Primary Education, Secondary Education, 3-4 yrs; *Master/Magister*: Automotive Engineering, 3 sem.; *Promotion*: Education (Dr. päd.), 2 yrs following Teaching qualification

Student Services: Academic counselling, Canteen, Foreign student adviser, Sports facilities

Student Residential Facilities: Yes

Libraries: Total, c. 270,000 vols
Last Updated: 03/02/12

UNIVERSITY OF ERFURT

Universität Erfurt
PO Box 900221, Nordhäuser Strasse 63, 99105 Erfurt
Tel: +49(361) 737-0
Fax: +49(361) 737-5009
EMail: poststelle@uni-erfurt.de
Website: http://www.uni-erfurt.de

Rektor: Kai Brodersen (2008-)
Tel: +49(361) 737-5000, Fax: +49(361) 737-5009
EMail: praesident@uni-erfurt.de

Kanzler: Michael Hinz
Tel: +49(361) 737-5010, Fax: +49(361) 737-5019
EMail: kanzler@uni-erfurt.de

Centres
Language (Linguistics; Modern Languages)

Colleges
Cultural and Social Sciences *(Max Weber)* (Fine Arts; Geography; History; Music; Philosophy; Political Sciences; Sociology; Theology)

Faculties
Catholic Theology (Catholic Theology; Theology); **Education** (Business Education; Education; Physical Education; Psychology; Special Education); **Law and Economics** (Economics; Law); **Philosophy** (Communication Studies; Geography; History; Literature; Modern Languages; Philosophy; Religion)

History: First founded 1372. Closed 1816. Acquired present status and title 1994. Incorporated the Katholisch-Theologische Fakultät 2001. Responsible to the Ministry of Science and Culture of Thuringia.

Governing Bodies: Senat; Konzil

Academic Year: October to July (October-February; April-July)

Admission Requirements: Secondary school certificate (Abitur)

Main Language(s) of Instruction: German

International Co-operation: Participates in the Erasmus programme

Degrees and Diplomas: *Bachelor/Bakkalaureus*; *Lehramt*: Teaching qualification, primary, intermediate, vocational levels, 7-9 sem; *Magister Artium*; *Master/Magister*

Libraries: Central Library, 171,000 vols

Press or Publishing House: Druckerei Jaecklein, Erfurt
Last Updated: 28/01/10

UNIVERSITY OF FINE ARTS OF HAMBURG

Hochschule für Bildende Künste Hamburg
Lerchenfeld 2, 22081 Hamburg
Tel: +49(40) 428989
Fax: +49(40) 428989-271
EMail: presse@kunsthochschule.uni-hamburg.de
Website: http://www.hfbk-hamburg.de

Präsident: Martin Köttering
Tel: +49(40) 428989-201 / 202, Fax: +49(40) 428989-208
EMail: martin.koettering@hfbk.hamburg.de

Kanzlerin: Anna Neubauer
Tel: +49(40) 428989-203, Fax: +49(40) 428989-390
EMail: kanzlerin@hfbk.hamburg.de

International Relations: Andrea Klier
Tel: +49(40) 428989-207, Fax: +49(40) 428989-206
EMail: andrea.klier@hfbk.hamburg.de; internationaloffice@hfbk.hamburg.de

Departments
Design (Design); **Film** (Film); **Graphic Art, Typography, Photography** (Graphic Arts; Graphic Design; Photography); **Painting and Drawing** (Painting and Drawing); **Sculpture** (Sculpture); **Stage Design** (Fine Arts; Theatre); **Time-based Media** (Media Studies)

Programmes
Theory and History (Art History; Fine Arts)

History: Founded 1972.

Main Language(s) of Instruction: German

Degrees and Diplomas: *Bachelor/Bakkalaureus*: Fine Arts; *Lehramt*: Fine Arts; *Master/Magister*
Last Updated: 01/02/12

UNIVERSITY OF FLENSBURG

Universität Flensburg
Auf dem Campus 1, 24943 Flensburg
Tel: +49(461) 805-02
Fax: +49(461) 2144
EMail: rektorat@uni-flensburg.de
Website: http://www.uni-flensburg.de

Präsidentin: Waltraud Wende
EMail: wara.wende@uni-flensburg.de

Departments
Department I (Aesthetics; Cultural Studies; Health Education; Media Studies; Music; Psychology; Religious Education; Sports); **Department II** (European Studies; Management; Sociology); **Department III** (Cultural Studies; Danish; English; Germanic Studies); **Department IV** (Biology; Chemistry; Mathematics; Physics; Technology); **Department V** (Catholic Theology; Geography; History; Pedagogy; Philosophy; Political Sciences; Theology)

History: Founded 1946. Reorganized 1973 and acquired present status 2000. Financially supported by the State of Schleswig-Holstein.

Governing Bodies: Konsistorium; Senat

Academic Year: October to September (October-March; April-September)

Admission Requirements: Secondary school certificate (Reifezeugnis) or equivalent

Fees: None

Main Language(s) of Instruction: German, English, Danish, Spanish

International Co-operation: With universities in United Kingdom; Spain; Denmark; Sweden; Finland; France; Portugal; Netherlands; USA; Argentina; Chile; Mexico; Colombia; Greece; Honduras; Italy; Latvia; Lthuania; Poland

Degrees and Diplomas: *Bachelor/Bakkalaureus*: Education; *Diplom*: Education; Culture and Language, 4 yrs; *Lehramt*: Teaching qualification, 3-3 1/2 yrs; *Magister Artium*: Applied Technology, Environment, Management (MASc); *Master/Magister*; *Doktorgrad*: Education (Dr.sc.päd.)

Student Services: Academic counselling, Canteen, Foreign student adviser, Nursery care, Social counselling, Sports facilities

Libraries: 240,000 vols
Last Updated: 22/03/11

UNIVERSITY OF HAGEN

FernUniversität in Hagen
Universitätsstraße 11, 58084 Hagen
Tel: +49(2331) 987-2444
Fax: +49(2331) 987-316
EMail: info@fernuni-hagen.de
Website: http://www.fernuni-hagen.de

Rektor: Helmut Hoyer (1997-)
Tel: +49(2331) 987-2400, Fax: +49(2331) 987-330
EMail: rektorbuero@fernuni-hagen.de

Kanzlerin: Regina Zdebel
Tel: +49(2331) 987-2410, Fax: +49(2331) 987-2763
EMail: kanzlerin@fernuni-hagen.de

International Relations: Irmgard Broekmann, Head, Office of International Affairs
Tel: +49(2331) 987-2454, Fax: +49(2331) 987-345
EMail: Irmgard.Broekmann@FernUni-Hagen.de

Faculties
Cultural and Social Sciences (Arts and Humanities; Education; Social Sciences); **Economics** (Business Administration; Economics); **Law** (Law); **Mathematics and Computer Science** (Computer Engineering; Computer Science; Electrical Engineering; Mathematics)

Institutes

Cultural Management *("In-Institute")* (Cultural Studies; Management); **Educational Science and Research** (Educational Sciences); **European Constitutional Sciences** (European Union Law); **European Studies** (European Studies); **German and European Labour and Social Law** (Labour Law); **History** (History); **History and Biography 'German Memory'** (History); **Intellectual Property** *(Kurt-Haertel)* (Law); **Japanese Law** (Law); **Juristic Continuing Education** (Law); **Mediation** *(Contarini)*; **Modern German and European Literature** (Literature); **New Technologies in Electrical Engineering** *(INTE)* (Electrical Engineering); **Peace and Democracy** (Peace and Disarmament; Political Sciences); **Philosophy** (Philosophy); **Political Science** (Political Sciences); **Psychology** (Psychology); **Psychology** *(Kurt-Lewin)* (Psychology); **Sociology** (Sociology)

Further Information: Study centres (information, counselling and student support services) in: Germany (45), Austria (7), Hungary (1), Latvia (1), Russian Federation (1), Switzerland (2).

History: Founded 1974, opened 1975. The FernUniversität in Hagen is the only single-mode distance teaching university in Germany.

Governing Bodies: Senat; Rektorat

Academic Year: October to September (October-March; April-September)

Admission Requirements: Secondary school certificate (Hochschulreife - Abitur - Fachhochschulreife) or recognized equivalent (for access to degree programmes)

Fees: (Euros): Material fee c. 300 per semester (full-time); study fee: basically none, only for defined groups of students. Special fee for other student offers (further education, etc.)

Main Language(s) of Instruction: German

International Co-operation: With universities in Austria, China, Czech Republic, Estonia, Hungary, Italy, Latvia, Netherlands, Russian Federation, Spain, Switzerland, United Kingdom.

Accrediting Agencies: Agency for quality assurance by accreditation of study progammes (AQAS)

Degrees and Diplomas: *Bachelor/Bakkalaureus*: Business Administration and Economics; Computer Science (BSc); Cultural Science (BA); Educational Science; Information Management; Law (LLB); Mathematics (BSc); Politics and Organization (BA), 3 yrs; *Bachelor/Bakkalaureus*: Business Computing; Psychology; Sociology; *Master/Magister*: Computer Science (MSc/MCompSc), 1 1/2 yrs; *Master/Magister*: Computer Science/Informatics, 11/2 yrs; *Master/Magister*: Economic Science; Education and Media; Electronic Engineering and Information Technology; Jurisprudence; *Master/Magister*: European Modern History and Literature (MA), a further 2 yrs; *Master/Magister*: Governance (MA); Mathematics (MSc); Mathematics - Methods and Models (MSc); Philosophy - Philosophy in the European Context (MA); Sociology - Individualisation and Social Structure (MSc), 2 yrs; *Promotion*; *Habilitation*. Also offered by all faculties/subject areas: further academic education (structured study offers - certificates, special degree programmes - Bachelor or Master); open access studies (Akademiestudien). According to the transfromation process (Bologna process) to the Bachelor and Master degree structure, the current Diplom and Magister degree programmes are to be terminated and are or will be closed for new enrolments

Student Services: Academic counselling, Canteen, Foreign student adviser, Handicapped facilities, Social counselling

Student Residential Facilities: No

Special Facilities: Centre for Media and IT (ZMI); TV studio

Libraries: University Library 775,000 vols. Europäisches Dokumentationszentrum (EDZ)

Publications: Forschungsbericht (Research Report) *(other/irregular)*; Reports and Papers from Faculties *(other/irregular)*; Veröffentlichungen der Universitätsbibliothek, Library publications *(other/irregular)*

Last Updated: 01/02/12

UNIVERSITY OF HAMBURG
Universität Hamburg
Edmund-Siemers-Allee 1, 20146 Hamburg
Tel: +49(40) 42838-0
Fax: +49(40) 42838-2449
EMail: presse@rrz.uni-hamburg.de
Website: http://www.uni-hamburg.de

Präsident: Dieter Lentzen (2010-2016)
Tel: +49(40) 42838-4475, Fax: +49(40) 42838-6799
EMail: praesidentin@uni-hamburg.de

Kanzlerin: Katrin Vernau
Tel: +49(40) 42838-4423, Fax: +49(40) 42838-6839
EMail: kanzlerin@verw.uni-hamburg.de

Centres
Higher Education Didactics *(Interdisciplinary)* (Higher Education); **Marine and Climate Research** (Marine Science and Oceanography; Meteorology)

Faculties
Education, Psychology and Human Movement (Education; Psychology; Sports); **Humanities** (African Studies; Arts and Humanities; Cultural Studies; History; Literature; Media Studies; Modern Languages; Oriental Studies; Philosophy; Protestant Theology); **Law** (Civil Engineering; Commercial Law; Criminal Law; Labour Law; Law; Private Law; Public Law); **Mathematics, Informatics and Natural Sciences** (Biology; Chemistry; Computer Science; Earth Sciences; Mathematics; Physics); **Medicine** (Dentistry; Medicine)

Institutes
International Tax (Taxation); **Peace Research and Security** (Peace and Disarmament); **Theatre, Musical Theatre and Film** (Film; Opera; Theatre)

Research Centres
Biotechnology, Society and the Environment (Biotechnology; Environmental Studies; Social Studies)

Schools
Business, Economics and Social Sciences (Business Administration; Economics; Political Sciences; Social Sciences)

History: Founded 1919 with four faculties created through the incorporation of a number of existing institutions. Reorganized under a presidential constitution 1969 and faculties replaced by 19 Fachbereiche (departments) and several central institutes. An autonomous institution in which all academic staff and students take part in the tasks of self-government. Financially supported by the State of Hamburg and under the jurisdiction of its Ministry of Science and Research.

Governing Bodies: Senat; Konzil

Academic Year: October to September

Admission Requirements: Secondary school certificate (Reifezeugnis) or equivalent

Fees: None

Main Language(s) of Instruction: German

International Co-operation: Participates in the Erasmus programme

Accrediting Agencies: AQUIN

Degrees and Diplomas: *Bachelor/Bakkalaureus*; *Diplom*: Business Administration; Computer Sciences; Earth Sciences; Economic Engineering; Economics; *Diplom*: Education; Music and Theatre; Philosophy and Social Sciences; Psychology; Wood Economics, 4 yrs; *Diplom*: Insurance, 3 1/2 yrs; *Diplom*: Mathematics, 5 yrs; *Diplom*: Physics, 4 1/2 yrs; *Diplom*: Shipbuilding, 3-5 yrs; *Lehramt*: Teaching Qualification, Secondary level; *Staatsprüfung*: Dentistry; Food Chemistry; Law; Medicine; Pharmacy, 3-6 yrs; *Master/Magister*: Philosophy (Mag.Phil.); Theology (Mag.Heol.), 4 yrs; *Doktorgrad*: 4-5 yrs; *Doktorgrad*: 6 yrs; *Dr.habil.*: following Habilitation; *Habilitation*: at least 3 yrs following Doktor

Student Services: Foreign student adviser, Handicapped facilities, Health services, Nursery care, Social counselling, Sports facilities

Student Residential Facilities: For c. 5,000 students

Special Facilities: Mineralogy Museum; Zoology Museum; Geology Museum; Applied Botany Museum. Botanical Garden

Libraries: State and University Library, 2.8m. vols; Hamburg Research Centre and Archives of World Economics, 1m. vols

Publications: Forschungsbericht der Universität; uni hh Berichte und Meinungen

Last Updated: 06/02/12

UNIVERSITY OF HILDESHEIM

Universität Hildesheim
Marienburger Platz 22, 31113 Hildesheim
Tel: +49(5121) 883-0
Fax: +49(5121) 883-177
EMail: presse@rz.uni-hildesheim.de
Website: http://www.uni-hildesheim.de

Präsident: Wolfgang-Uwe Friedrich
Tel: +49(5121) 883-100, Fax: +49(5121) 883-108
EMail: praesident@rz.uni-hildesheim.de

International Relations: Elke Sasse-Fleige
Tel: +49(5121) 883-155, Fax: +49(5121) 883-154
EMail: aaa@rz.uni-hildesheim.de

Centres
Computer-Network (Computer Science); **Lifelong Education and Distance Study** (Distance Education; Education)

Faculties
Cultural Studies and Aesthetics Communication (Aesthetics; Communication Studies; Cultural Studies; Media Studies; Music; Theatre; Writing); **Educational and Social Sciences** (Administration; Education; Philosophy; Primary Education; Psychology; Secondary Education; Social Sciences; Social Work; Sports; Theology); **Information and Communication Sciences** (Computer Science; Linguistics; Mathematics; Physics; Technology)

Research Centres
Education and Training; Interdisciplinary Gender Studies

History: Founded 1978, acquired present status 1990. An autonomous institution financially supported by the State of Lower Saxony, and under the jurisdiction of its Ministry of Science.

Governing Bodies: Konzil; Senat

Academic Year: October to September (October-March; April-September)

Admission Requirements: Secondary school certificate (Reifezeugnis) or equivalent

Fees: None

Main Language(s) of Instruction: German

International Co-operation: With universities in France, United Kingdom, Iceland, Netherlands, Belgium, Spain, Portugal, Italy, Greece, Malta, Poland, Czech Republic, Slovenia, Latvia, Lithuania, Sweden, Norway, Finland, Denmark, Switzerland.

Degrees and Diplomas: *Bachelor/Bakkalaureus*: Information Management, Information Technology; *Diplom*: Creative Writing and Cultural Journalism; Cultural Sciences, Aesthetics and Applied Arts; International Technical Communication; Scenic Arts; Social Service Management Studies; *Staatsprüfung*: Teacher Training (Primary and Secondary Education); *Master/Magister*: International Information Management

Student Services: Academic counselling, Canteen, Cultural centre, Foreign student adviser, Foreign Studies Centre, Handicapped facilities, Language programs, Nursery care, Social counselling, Sports facilities

Student Residential Facilities: Yes

Libraries: Central Library, c. 330,000 vols
Last Updated: 28/01/10

UNIVERSITY OF HOHENHEIM

Universität Hohenheim
70593 Stuttgart
Tel: +49(711) 459-0
Fax: +49(711) 459-3960
EMail: post@uni-hohenheim.de
Website: http://www.uni-hohenheim.de

Rektor: Hans-Peter Liebig
Tel: +49(711) 459-2000, Fax: +49(711) 459-3289
EMail: rektor@uni-hohenheim.de

Kanzler: Alfred Funk
Tel: +49(711) 459-3000 EMail: kanzler@uni-hohenheim.de

International Relations: Martina van de Sand
Tel: +49(711) 459-2020, Fax: +49(711) 459-3723
EMail: aaa@uni-hohenheim.de

Centres
Eastern European Studies (Continuing Education; Eastern European Studies; Teacher Trainers Education); **Entrepreneurship**; **Life Sciences**; **Tropical and Subtropical Agriculture** (Agriculture; Tropical Agriculture)

Faculties
Agricultural Sciences (Agriculture; Botany; Crop Production; Ecology; Horticulture; Soil Science; Tropical Agriculture); **Business, Economics and Social Sciences** (Business Administration; Business Education; Communication Studies; Cultural Studies; Economics; Journalism; Law; Social Sciences; Theology); **Natural Sciences** (Biochemistry; Botany; Chemistry; Food Technology; Genetics; Mathematics; Meteorology; Microbiology; Nutrition; Physics; Physiology; Zoology)

Further Information: Also University Language Centre: courses in 7 foreign languages and in German for foreign students

History: Founded 1818, became Hochschule 1904 and acquired University status 1919. Acquired present title 1967. An autonomous institution under the jurisdiction of and financed by the State of Baden-Württemberg.

Governing Bodies: Senat; Hochschulrat

Academic Year: October to July (October-February; April-July)

Admission Requirements: Secondary school certificate (Reifezeugnis) or equivalent

Fees: Tuition, none

Main Language(s) of Instruction: German

International Co-operation: With universities in Albania; Austria; Belarus; Belgium; Benin; Brazil; Chile; China; Colombia; Czech Republic; Ethiopia; Japan; Kazakhstan; Lithuania; Philippines; Poland; Romania; Russian Federation; Spain; Thailand; Ukraine; USA; Vietnam

Degrees and Diplomas: *Bachelor/Bakkalaureus*; *Master/Magister (MSc)*; *Doktorgrad (Dr)*

Student Services: Academic counselling, Canteen, Cultural centre, Employment services, Foreign student adviser, Language programs, Nursery care, Social counselling, Sports facilities

Student Residential Facilities: For 889 students

Special Facilities: German Agricultural Museum; Zoology and Veterinary Medicine Museum; University Museum; Botanical Garden

Libraries: Hohenheim University Library (Central Library and Branch Library for Economic and Social Sciences) 450,000 vols

Publications: Rechenschaftsbericht
Last Updated: 28/01/10

UNIVERSITY OF KASSEL

Universität Kassel
Mönchebergstrasse 19, 34109 Kassel
Tel: +49(561) 804-0
Fax: +49(561) 804-2330
EMail: poststelle@uni-kassel.de
Website: http://www.uni-kassel.de

Präsident: Rolf-Dieter Postlep (2000-)
Tel: +49(561) 804-2233, Fax: +49(561) 804-7233
EMail: praesident@uni-kassel.de

International Relations: Katharina Linke, Head of International Relations Office
Tel: (49) 561 804 2103, Fax: (49) 561 804 3513
EMail: aaa@uni-kassel.de

Centres
Environmental Systems Research *(CESR)* (Environmental Studies); **Interdisciplinary Nanostructure Science and Technology** *(CINSaT)*; **International Higher Education Research Kassel** *(INCHER-Kassel)* (Higher Education; Labour and Industrial Relations)

Departments
Agricultural Sciences (Agriculture; Ecology; Rural Planning); **Architecture** (Architecture; Landscape Architecture; Town Planning); **Civil Engineering** (Civil Engineering); **Economics and Business, Psychology** (Economics; Psychology); **Educational Sciences, Humanities and Music**; **Electrical Engineering and**

Computer Science (Computer Science; Electrical Engineering); Languages and Literature (English; Germanic Studies; Romance Languages); Mathematics and Computer Science (Computer Science; Mathematics); Mechanical Engineering (Mechanical Engineering); Natural Sciences; Social Work (Social Welfare; Social Work)

Schools

Art (Design; Graphic Arts; Visual Arts); International Management (UNIKIMS) (Finance; Human Resources; Management; Marketing; Transport Management)

History: Founded 1971 as a Gesamthochschule. An autonomous institution financially supported by the State of Hesse and under the jurisdiction of its Ministry of Education.

Academic Year: October to September

Admission Requirements: Secondary school certificate (Reifezeugnis). Fachhochschulreife (technical secondary education) for certain courses

Fees: Tuition, none

Main Language(s) of Instruction: German. Also 6 Master Programmes with courses in English

International Co-operation: With universities in Egypt; Cameroon; Morocco; South Africa; Tanzania; Togo; Canada; USA; Nicaragua; Cuba; Argentina; Brazil; Chile; Ecuador; Colombia; Mexico; Peru; Venezuela; Israel; Iran; Syria; Armenia; Azerbaijan; Georgia; Uzbekistan; China; India; Indonesia; Japan; Malaysia; Philippines; Korea; Thailand; Vietnam; Austria; Estonia; Finland; France; Greece; United Kingdom; Hungary; Ireland; Italy; Latvia; Lithuania; Netherlands; Poland; Portugal; Romania; Russian Federation; Sweden; Switzerland; Slovenia; Spain; Czech Republic, Turkey; Australia; New Zealand. Also participates in the Socrates programme

Degrees and Diplomas: Bachelor/Bakkalaureus: 3 yrs; Diplom: American Language and Literature; English Language and Literature, Romance Languages and Literature, Mathematics, Nanostructure and Molecular Sciences, Physics, Biology, Business Education, 5 yrs; Diplom (B.A.): Industrial Engineering; Organic Agriculture, Architecture, Town Planning, Landscape Planning, Electrical Engineering, Civil Engineering, Mechanical Engineering, Business and Economics, Social Work, Social Gerontology, Supervision for Careers in Social Work; Lehramt: Primary School Education, 3-4 yrs; Lehramt: Secondary Level Education, 5 yrs; Magister Artium: German Language and Literature, English Language and Literature, Romance Language and Literature, History of Art, Fine Art, Philosophy; Educational Sciences, 41/2-5 yrs; Master/ Magister: Culture and Communication, Public Management, History of Western Europe, Economics Law; Ecological Agriculture, Architecture, Town Planning, Landscape Planning, Electrical Engineering, Civil Engineering, Mechanical Engineering, Business and Economics, Social Work, Social Gerontology, Supervision for Careers in Social Work; Industrial Engineering, Computational Mathematics, German as a Foreign Language, Electrical Communication Engineering, Global Political Economy, Higher Education; Labour Policies and Globalization, International Ecological Agriculture, Media; Doktorgrad: Agricultural Sciences; Engineering; Natural Sciences; Philosophy; Economics and Social Sciences; Law

Student Services: Academic counselling, Canteen, Foreign student adviser, Handicapped facilities, Nursery care, Social counselling, Sports facilities

Student Residential Facilities: Yes

Libraries: Central Library, 1,600,000 vols; 7,181 periodicals

Publications: Bericht zu Forschung und künstlerischen Entwicklung (biennially); Spektrum der Wissenschaft (biennially)

Student Numbers 2008-2009: Total 18,035
Last Updated: 28/01/10

UNIVERSITY OF KOBLENZ-LANDAU, KOBLENZ CAMPUS

Universität Koblenz-Landau, Campus Koblenz
Universitätsstrasse 1, 56070 Koblenz
Tel: +49(261) 287-0
Fax: +49(261) 375-24
Website: http://www.uni-koblenz-landau.de/koblenz/

Präsident: Roman Heiligenthal (2005-) Tel: +49(6131) 37460-0
International Relations: Bettina Holstein-Alter
Tel: +49(261) 2871-764
EMail: austauch-koblenz@uni-koblenz-landau.de

Centres
Distance Learning and University Level Further Education (Environmental Studies; European Union Law; Modern Languages)

Faculties
Computer Sciences (Computer Science; Information Management); Education (Education; Educational Sciences; Teacher Training); Mathematics and Natural Sciences (Biology; Chemistry; Ecology; Geography; Mathematics; Natural Sciences; Physical Education; Physics); Philology (English; Fine Arts; French; German; History; Music; Philology; Political Sciences)

History: Founded 1949 as academy, became college 1964 and University of Educational Sciences 1969. Acquired present status and title 1990. Under the jurisdiction of and financially supported by the state of Rheinland-Pfalz.

Governing Bodies: Versammlung; Senat

Academic Year: October to September (October-March; April-September)

Admission Requirements: Secondary school certificate (Reifezeugnis) or recognized equivalent and knowledge of German language (TestDaF)

Fees: None

Main Language(s) of Instruction: German

International Co-operation: With universities in Australia, Ukraine and USA. Also participates in the Socrates/Erasmus Programme

Degrees and Diplomas: Bachelor/Bakkalaureus: Information Management; Computer Science; Computer Vision; English and Media; Ecological Impact Assessment; Diplom: Educational Sciences; Lehramt: Teaching Qualifications; Magister Artium: Geography, Fine Arts, History, German, English; Master/Magister: Information Management; Computer Science in Economics; Promotion: Philosophy (Dr.phil.); Science (Dr.rer.nat.)

Student Services: Academic counselling, Canteen, Foreign student adviser, Social counselling, Sports facilities

Libraries:c. 200,000 vols

Publications: Forschungs- und Veröffentlichungsdokumentation
Last Updated: 28/01/10

UNIVERSITY OF KOBLENZ-LANDAU, LANDAU CAMPUS

Universität Koblenz-Landau, Campus Landau
Fortstrasse 7, 76829 Landau
Tel: +49(6341) 280-0
Fax: +49(6341) 280-101
Website: http://www.uni-koblenz-landau.de/landau

President: Roman Heiligenthal (2005-)
Tel: +49(6131) 37460-14
EMail: praesident@uni-koblenz-landau.de

Kanzlerin: Simone Mertel-Scherer
Tel: 49(6131) 37460-25
EMail: mertel-scherer@uni-koblenz-landau.de

International Relations: Jutta Bohn
Tel: +49(6341) 924-165 EMail: bohn@uni-koblenz-landau.de

Faculties
Culture and Social Sciences (Fine Arts; History; Modern Languages; Music; Philology; Social Sciences; Theology); Education (Education; Educational Sciences); Natural and Environmental Sciences (Biology; Chemistry; Environmental Studies; Geography; Mathematics; Natural Sciences; Physical Education; Physics; Teacher Trainers Education); Psychology (Clinical Psychology; Educational Psychology; Experimental Psychology; Industrial and Organizational Psychology; Pedagogy; Psychology; Social Psychology) Dean: Annette Schröder

History: Founded 1949 as academy, became college 1964 and University of Educational Sciences 1969. Acquired present status and title 1990. Under the jurisdiction of and financially supported by the State of Rhineland-Palatinat.

Governing Bodies: Versammlung; Senat

Academic Year: October to September (October-March; April-September)

Admission Requirements: Secondary school certificate (Reifezeugnis) or recognized equivalent and knowledge of German language (TestDaF)

Fees: None

Main Language(s) of Instruction: German

International Co-operation: With universities in Australia, Russian Federation, Poland and USA. Also participates in the Socrates/ Erasmus programme

Degrees and Diplomas: *Bachelor/Bakkalaureus*; *Diplom*: Educational Sciences; Environmental Sciences; Psychology; Social Sciences, 4 yrs; *Lehramt*: 3 yrs; *Master/Magister*: 4 yrs; *Promotion*: Educational Sciences; Philology; Natural Sciences; Computer Science; Psychology

Student Services: Academic counselling, Canteen, Foreign student adviser, Social counselling, Sports facilities

Libraries: c. 200,000 vols

Publications: Forschungs- und Veröffentlichungsdokumentation
Last Updated: 28/01/10

UNIVERSITY OF KONSTANZ

Universität Konstanz
78457 Konstanz, Baden-Württemberg
Tel: +49(7531) 88-0
Fax: +49(7531) 88-3688
EMail: posteingang@uni-konstanz.de
Website: http://www.uni-konstanz.de

Rektor: Ulrich Rüdiger (2009-)
Tel: +49(7531) 88-2270, Fax: +49(7531) 88-3750
EMail: ulrich.ruediger@uni-konstanz.de

Kanzler: Jens Apitz
Tel: +49(7531) 88-2295, Fax: +49(7531) 88-3577
EMail: jens.apitz@uni-konstanz.de

Director, Public Relations Office: Julia Wandt
Tel: +49(7531) 88-5340 EMail: Julia.Wandt@uni-konstanz.de

International Relations: Regina Sonntag-Krupp, Director, International Office
Tel: +49(7531) 88-2325, Fax: +49(7531) 88-3037
EMail: regina.sonntag@uni-konstanz.de

Faculties
Humanities (Arts and Humanities; Educational Sciences; Fine Arts; History; Linguistics; Literature; Media Studies; Philosophy; Sociology; Sports); **Law, Economics and Political Science** (Economics; Law; Management; Political Sciences); **Mathematics and Natural Sciences** (Biology; Chemistry; Computer Science; Information Sciences; Mathematics; Natural Sciences; Physics; Psychology; Statistics)

Further Information: Also 5 Collaborative Research Centres (Sonderforschungsbereiche), and 3 special Research Units

History: Founded 1966. An autonomous State institution financially supported by the State of Baden-Württemberg.

Governing Bodies: Rektorat; Senat

Academic Year: October to September (October-February; April-July)

Admission Requirements: Secondary school certificate (Reifezeugnis) or equivalent

Fees: None

Main Language(s) of Instruction: German

International Co-operation: With universities in USA; Australia; Asia and South Africa. Also participates in Socrates/Erasmus programme

Degrees and Diplomas: *Bachelor/Bakkalaureus*: Humanities; Science; Political Management (B.A.;B.Sc); *Diplom*: Science; Economics; *Lehramt*: Teaching qualification, secondary level; *Magister Artium*; *Staatsprüfung*: Law; *Master/Magister (M.A.; MSc.)*; *Doktorgrad*; *Habilitation*

Student Services: Academic counselling, Canteen, Cultural centre, Foreign student adviser, Handicapped facilities, Health services, Nursery care, Social counselling, Sports facilities

Libraries: Central Library, 2 m. vols
Last Updated: 06/02/12

UNIVERSITY OF LEIPZIG

Universität Leipzig
PO Box 100920, Ritterstrasse 26, 04009 Leipzig, Saxony
Tel: +49(341) 971-08
Fax: +49(341) 973-0099
EMail: aaa@uni-leipzig.de
Website: http://www.uni-leipzig.de

Rektor: Beate A. Schücking (2011-)
Tel: +49(341) 973-0000, Fax: +49(341) 973-0009
EMail: rektor@uni-leipzig.de

Kanzler: Frank Nolden
Tel: +49(341) 973-0100, Fax: +49(341) 973-0109
EMail: kanzler@uni-leipzig.de

International Relations: Svend Poller, Director, International Centre Tel: +49(341) 973-2020, Fax: +49(341) 973-2049

Faculties
Biology, Pharmacy and Psychology (Biochemistry; Biological and Life Sciences; Biology; Pharmacology; Pharmacy; Psychology); **Chemistry and Mineralogy** (Chemistry; Crystallography; Mineralogy); **Economics and Management (including Civil Engineering)** (Accountancy; Building Technologies; Business Administration; Business and Commerce; Business Computing; Civil Engineering; Construction Engineering; Economics; Finance; Industrial Engineering; Management; Real Estate; Statistics); **Education** (Adult Education; Curriculum; Education; Education of the Handicapped; Educational Psychology; Educational Sciences; Primary Education; Secondary Education; Special Education); **History, Art and Oriental Studies** (African Studies; Arabic; Archaeology; Art History; Asian Studies; Cultural Studies; Ethnology; Fine Arts; History; Music; Musicology; Oriental Studies; Religious Studies; Theatre); **Law** (Law); **Mathematics and Computer Science** (Computer Science; Mathematics); **Medicine** (Biochemistry; Epidemiology; Forensic Medicine and Dentistry; Genetics; Medicine; Occupational Health; Physiology; Virology); **Philology** (American Studies; Classical Languages; Comparative Literature; English Studies; German; Germanic Studies; Linguistics; Modern Languages; Philology; Romance Languages; Slavic Languages; Translation and Interpretation); **Physics and Earth Sciences** (Earth Sciences; Geography; Geology; Geophysics; Meteorology; Paleontology; Physics); **Social Sciences and Philosophy** (Ethics; Journalism; Logic; Media Studies; Philosophy; Political Sciences; Social Sciences; Sociology); **Sports Science** (Physical Education; Rehabilitation and Therapy; Sports); **Theology** (Religious Education; Theology); **Veterinary Science** (Veterinary Science)

History: Founded 1409 when German scholars withdrew from the University of Prague. The establishment of the University was confirmed by Papal Bull. Reorganized 1946. The University has always adhered to the model of the Universitas Literarum.

Governing Bodies: Senat; Kuratorium

Academic Year: October to September (October-March; April-September)

Admission Requirements: Secondary school certificate (Reifezeugnis) or equivalent

Fees: None. Some courses charge tuition

Main Language(s) of Instruction: German. English in some courses

International Co-operation: Participates in the Socrates programme, bilateral exchanges with USA and other overseas countries.

Degrees and Diplomas: *Bachelor/Bakkalaureus*: Philosophy; German Studies; South Slavonic Studies; West Slavonic Studies; Public Relations (BA); Physics; Informatics; Chemistry; Civil Engineering; Industrial Engineering and Management (BSc); *Diplom*: Economics; Natural Sciences; Social Sciences; *Lehramt*: Teaching Qualification; *Staatsprüfung*: Dentistry; Law; Medicine; Pharmacy; Veterinary Medicine; *Master/Magister*: Civil Engineering; Industrial

Engineering and Management; Chemistry; Informatics (MSc); Physics (MSc); *Doktorgrad*: in all fields

Student Services: Academic counselling, Canteen, Cultural centre, Foreign student adviser, Foreign Studies Centre, Handicapped facilities, Language programs, Nursery care, Social counselling, Sports facilities

Student Residential Facilities: Yes

Special Facilities: Musical Instruments Museum; Egyptology Museum; Museum of Early History; Museum of Medicine and Natural Sciences; Coins Museum; Manuscripts Museum. Botanical Gardens. Radio Station

Libraries: Bibliotheca Albertina, 4.2m. vols. Old manuscripts, prints, papyrus scrolls

Press or Publishing House: Universitätsverlag
Last Updated: 09/05/11

UNIVERSITY OF MANNHEIM
Universität Mannheim
Schloss, 68131 Mannheim, Baden-Württemberg
Tel: +49(621) 181-0
Fax: +49(621) 181-1010
EMail: aaa@verwaltung.uni-mannheim.de
Website: http://www.uni-mannheim.de

Rektor: Hans-Wolfgang Arndt (2001-)
Tel: +49(621) 181-1000 EMail: rektor@uni-mannheim.de

Kanzlerin: Susann-Annette Storm
Tel: +49(621) 181-1020, Fax: +49(621) 181-1022
EMail: storm@verwaltung.uni-mannheim.de

International Relations: Nadja Wisniewski
Tel: +49(621) 181-1154, Fax: +49(621) 181-1161
EMail: wisniewski@verwaltung.uni-mannheim.de

Faculties
Social Sciences (Political Sciences; Psychology; Social Sciences; Sociology)

Schools
Business (Business Administration; Business Computing; Business Education); **Humanities** (Arts and Humanities; History; Literature; Modern Languages; Philosophy); **Mathematics and Computer Science** (Computer Engineering; Computer Science; Mathematics)

History: Founded 1907 as Städtische Handelshochschule, attached to University of Heidelberg 1933, became Wirtschaftshochschule 1946. Title of University conferred 1967.

Governing Bodies: Senat; Universitätsrat

Academic Year: October to September

Admission Requirements: Secondary school certificate (Reifezeugnis) or recognized equivalent

Fees: (Euros): 500

Main Language(s) of Instruction: German

Degrees and Diplomas: *Bachelor/Bakkalaureus*: Business Administration; Mathematics and Computer Science; Business Informatics; English/American Studies; German Philology; History; Culture and Economy; Media and Communication Sciences; Romance Languages; Social Sciences; Economics, 6 semesters; *Bachelor/Bakkalaureus*: Political Science, 6 sem; *Diplom*: Business Education; Computer Engineering; Psychology, 8-12 sem; *Master/Magister*: 4 sem; *Doktorgrad (Dr.rer.pol.)*: at least 2 yrs; *Habilitation*: at least 3 yrs following Doktor

Student Residential Facilities: For c. 730 students

Libraries: Total, c. 1.6m. vols

Publications: Amtliche Mitteilungen; Forum
Last Updated: 06/02/12

UNIVERSITY OF MUSIC AND PERFORMING ARTS MUNICH
Hochschule für Musik und Theater München
Arcisstrasse 12, 80333 München
Tel: +49(89) 289-03 +49(89) 289-27450
Fax: +49(89) 289-27419
EMail: verwaltung@musikhochschule-muenchen.de
Website: http://www.musikhochschule-muenchen.de

Präsident: Siegfried Mauser (2003-)
Tel: +49(89) 289-27403, Fax: +49(89) 289-27407
EMail: praesident@musikhochschule-muenchen.de

Kanzler: Alexander Krause
Tel: +49(89) 289-27410
EMail: kanzler@musikhochschule-muenchen.de

International Relations: Edgar Krapp
Tel: +49(89) 289-27402 / 27437, Fax: +49(89) 289-27408
EMail: edgar.krapp@musikhochschule-muenchen.de

Programmes
Church Music, Piano, Organ, Organ Improvisation, Historical Performance Practice, Harpsichord, Chamber Music (Music; Musical Instruments; Religious Music); **Composition, Composition for Film and Television, Music Theorie, Hearing Education, Choir Conducting, Orchestral Conducting, Music Journalism in Public und Private Radio Broadcasting, New Music** (Journalism; Music; Music Theory and Composition); **Elementary Music Education, Ancient Music, Jazz, Popular Music, Accordeon, Recording, Chopping board, Saxophone, Zither** (Jazz and Popular Music; Music; Music Education); **Music Education, Musicology** (Music Education; Musicology); **Singing (with Subjects Theatre Music and Concert Singing), Song Organisation, Ballet, Direction, Musical, Theatre, Lights, Masks** (Singing; Theatre); **Stringed Instruments** (Musical Instruments); **Wind Instruments, Percussion and Plucked Instruments (except Recorder, Saxophone and Zither)** (Musical Instruments)

History: Founded 1867.

Main Language(s) of Instruction: German

Degrees and Diplomas: *Bachelor/Bakkalaureus*; *Diplom*. Also Postgraduate Degree (Aufbaustudiengang)
Last Updated: 25/01/09

UNIVERSITY OF MUSIC AND THEATRE LEIPZIG "FELIX MENDELSSOHN BARTHOLDY"
Hochschule für Musik und Theater 'Felix Mendelssohn Bartholdy' Leipzig
PO Box 10 08 09, Grassisstrasse 8, 04008 Leipzig
Tel: +49(341) 2144 55
Fax: +49(341) 2144-503
EMail: rektor@hmt-leipzig.de
Website: http://www.hmt-leipzig.de

Rektor: Robert Ehrlich Tel: +49(341) 2144-500

Kanzler: Wolfgang Korneli
Tel: +49(341) 2144-600, Fax: +49(341) 2144-602
EMail: kanzler@hmt-leipzig.de

Departments
Brass and Woodwind (Musical Instruments); **Early Music** (Music); **Acting** (Acting); **Composition** (Music Theory and Composition); **Conducting** (Conducting); **Dramaturgy** (Theatre); **Jazz, Popular Music and Musicals** (Jazz and Popular Music); **Music Education** (Music Education); **Musicology, Music Pedagogy and Languages** (Modern Languages; Music Education; Musicology); **Piano** (Musical Instruments); **Strings/Harp** (Musical Instruments); **Vocal Studies** (Opera; Singing)

Institutes
Church Music

History: Founded 1843.

Degrees and Diplomas: *Diplom*: 4-5 yrs; *Master/Magister*; *Doktorgrad*. Also postgradaute Degree (Aufbaustudium)
Last Updated: 02/02/12

UNIVERSITY OF MUSIC LÜBECK
Musikhochschule Lübeck
Grosse Petersgrube 17-29, 23552 Lübeck
Tel: +49(451) 1505-0
Fax: +49(451) 1505-300
EMail: info@mh-luebeck.de
Website: http://www.mh-luebeck.de

Rektorin: Inge Susann Römhild (1994-)
Tel: +49(451)1505-128, Fax: +49(451) 1505-301
EMail: Rektorin@mh-luebeck.de

Kanzler: Jürgen Claussen
Tel: +49(451) 1505-151 EMail: Kanzler@mh-luebeck.de

Programmes

Music (Music; Musical Instruments; Religious Music)

History: Founded 1933 and acquired present status and title 1973.

Governing Bodies: Rectorate; Senate; Consortium

Academic Year: October to September (October-March; April-September)

Admission Requirements: Entrance Audition

Fees: (Euros): 171 per annum

Main Language(s) of Instruction: German

International Co-operation: With universities in Poland, Finland, Sweden, Denmark, Norway, Netherlands, France, United Kingdom, Austria, Belgium, Romania, Italy. Also participates in the Erasmus programme.

Degrees and Diplomas: *Bachelor/Bakkalaureus*: Music, 4 yrs; *Diplom*; *Staatsprüfung*; *Master/Magister*

Student Services: Academic counselling, Canteen, Foreign student adviser, Language programs, Sports facilities

Special Facilities: Studio

Libraries: c. 24,000 vols; 12,650 recordings; 80,400 works of music; 6 internet working stations; 8 audiovisual stations

Last Updated: 21/01/10

UNIVERSITY OF MUSIC SAARLAND
Hochschule für Musik Saar
Bismarckstrasse 1, 66111 Saarbrücken
Tel: +49(681) 96731-0
Fax: +49(681) 96731-30
EMail: b.paulus@hfm.saarland.de; presse@hfm.saarland.de
Website: http://www.hfm.saarland.de

Rektor: Thomas Duis (2004-)
Tel: +49(681) 96731-15 EMail: rektor@hfm.saarland.de

Kanzler: Wolfgang Bogler
Tel: +49(681) 96731-13 EMail: w.bogler@hfm.saarland.de

Programmes

Music (Jazz and Popular Music; Music; Music Education; Music Theory and Composition; Religious Music; Singing)

History: Founded 1947.

Main Language(s) of Instruction: German, English

Degrees and Diplomas: *Bachelor/Bakkalaureus*; *Master/Magister*
Last Updated: 19/01/10

UNIVERSITY OF MUSIC WÜRZBURG
Hochschule für Musik Würzburg
Hofstallstrasse 6-8, 97070 Würzburg
Tel: +49(931) 32187-0
Fax: +49(931) 32187-2800
EMail: hochschule@hfm-wuerzburg.de
Website: http://www.hfm-wuerzburg.de

Präsident: Helmut Erb
Tel: +49(931) 32187-21 EMail: praesident@hfm-wuerzburg.de

Kanzlerin: Eva Stumpf-Wirths
Tel: +49(931) 32187-30
EMail: kanzlerin@hfm-wuerzburg.de; birgit.baumann(at)hfm-wuerzburg.de

Programmes

Artistic Training (Conducting; Jazz and Popular Music; Music; Music Education; Music Theory and Composition; Musical Instruments; Religious Music; Singing); **Instrumental Education** (Music Education; Musical Instruments); **Music Teaching** (Music; Music Education)

History: Founded 1973.

Main Language(s) of Instruction: German

Degrees and Diplomas: *Diplom-Vorprüfung*; *Diplom*; *Lehramt*; *Promotion*: Music Education; Musicology; *Doktorgrad*. Also Post-graduate Degree (Aufbaustudium).
Last Updated: 19/01/10

UNIVERSITY OF OSNABRÜCK
Universität Osnabrück
Neuer Graben/Schloss, 49069 Osnabrück
Tel: +49(541) 969-0
Fax: +49(541) 969-4570
EMail: info@uni-osnabrueck.de
Website: http://www.uni-osnabrueck.de

Präsident: Claus Rainer Rollinger (2004-)
Tel: +49(541) 969-4100, Fax: +49(541) 969-4888
EMail: praesident@uni-osnabrueck.de

Kanzler: Christoph Ehrenberg
Tel: +49(541) 969-4115 EMail: kanzler@uni-osnabrueck.de

International Relations: Barbara Schluck
Tel: +49(541) 969-4655, Fax: +49(541) 969-4495
EMail: barbara.schluck@uni-osnabrueck.de

Centres
Collaborative Research 431 *(Membrane proteins: functional dynamics and coupling to signal networks)*

Departments
Biology and Chemistry (Biochemistry; Biology; Biophysics; Botany; Chemistry; Genetics; Inorganic Chemistry; Microbiology; Organic Chemistry; Physical Chemistry; Zoology); **Business and Economics** (Business and Commerce; Economics; Information Management; Information Sciences); **Cultural Studies and Geosciences** (Art History; Fine Arts; Geography; History; Textile Design); **Education and Cultural Studies** (Catholic Theology; Education; Educational Research; Educational Sciences; Music; Primary Education; Protestant Theology; Sports; Theology); **Human Sciences** (Cognitive Sciences; Health Sciences; Psychology); **Language and Literature** (Artificial Intelligence; Cinema and Television; Computer Science; English; Film; French; German; Italian; Latin; Linguistics; Literature; Media Studies; Modern Languages; Romance Languages); **Law** (Commercial Law; European Union Law; Law); **Mathematics and Computer Sciences** (Computer Science; Information Technology; Mathematics; Mathematics Education); **Physics** (Computer Science; Physics); **Social Sciences** (European Studies; Political Sciences; Social Sciences; Sociology)

Further Information: Also 2 international summer language courses for foreign students (Advanced Level). 2 Collaborative Research Centres (Sonderforschungsbereiche) in the fields of Biology/Physics and Physics/Chemistry, and 4 interdepartmental research groups: Centre for International Research in Teacher Training; Ecological and Socio-Economic Systems Research; Social Economics and Culture of the Third World; North American Studies. Empirical Research of Values and Interdepartmental Study Groups: International Research in Teacher Training; Environmental Development in the Third World; Empirical Research of Values

History: Founded 1973. Teaching started 1974. Previously a branch of the College of Education, Lower Saxony. An autonomous institution with two branches (Osnabrück and Vechta) financially supported by the State of Lower Saxony. Campus at Vechta became separate University in 1995.

Academic Year: October to September (October-March; April-September)

Admission Requirements: University entrance certificate (Reifezeugnis)

Fees: None

Main Language(s) of Instruction: German, English

International Co-operation: With universities in Canada, China, Costa Rica, Czech Republic, Denmark, France, Hungary, Italy, Netherlands, New Zealand, Poland, Portugal, Russian Federation, Slovak Republic, Slovenia, Switzerland, United Kingdom, USA, Australia, Belgium, Finland, Iran, Japan, Korea, Malawi, Mongolia, Romania, Lithuania

Degrees and Diplomas: *Bachelor/Bakkalaureus*; *Diplom*: Biology; Business Administration; Chemistry; Economics; Geography; Mathematics; Physics; Psychology; Systems Sciences; *Lehramt*: Teaching Qualifications, Primary level; Teaching Qualifications,

Secondary level; *Master/Magister*: Fiscal Law; Law; *Doktorgrad*: Economics (Dr.rer.pol.); Natural Sciences (Dr.rer.nat.); Philosophy (Dr.phil.). Dual Degrees: BSc/MSc, BA/MA, 5 yrs

Student Services: Academic counselling, Canteen, Foreign student adviser, Handicapped facilities, Language programs, Nursery care, Social counselling, Sports facilities

Student Residential Facilities: Yes

Special Facilities: Botanical Garden

Libraries: Total, c. 1,214,000 vols

Press or Publishing House: Press Office of the Universität Osnabrück

Last Updated: 06/02/12

UNIVERSITY OF PADERBORN

Universität Paderborn
Warburger Strasse 100, 33095 Paderborn
Tel: +49(5251) 60-0
Fax: +49(5251) 60-2519
Website: http://www.upb.de

Rektor: Nikolaus Risch (2003-)
Tel: +49(5251) 60-2559, Fax: +49(5251) 60-3236
EMail: rektor@uni-paderborn.de

Kanzler: Jürgen Plato
Tel: +49(5251) 60-2557, Fax: +49(5251) 60-2558
EMail: kanzler@zv.uni-paderborn.de

Faculties

Arts and Humanities (American Studies; Catholic Theology; Comparative Literature; Education; English; Fine Arts; History; Media Studies; Music; Musicology; Philosophy; Political Sciences; Protestant Theology; Psychology; Romance Languages; Sociology; Textile Design); **Business Administration and Economics** (Accountancy; Business Administration; Economics; Finance; Human Resources; Management; Taxation); **Electrical Engineering, Computer Science and Mathematics** (Computer Science; Electrical Engineering; Information Technology; Mathematics); **Mechanical Engineering** (Mechanical Engineering); **Science** (Chemistry; Health Education; Physics; Sports)

History: Founded 1972. An autonomous institution financially supported by the State of North Rhine-Westphalia.

Governing Bodies: Rektorat; Senat; Kuratorium

Academic Year: October to September (October-March; April-September)

Admission Requirements: Secondary school certificate (Reifezeugnis) or equivalent

Fees: (Euros): 122 per semester

Main Language(s) of Instruction: German

International Co-operation: With universities in Australia, Belgium, Canada, Denmark, Finland, France, Greece, Hungary, Ireland, Italy, Netherlands, Norway, Poland, Portugal, Russian Federation, Spain, Sweden, United Kingdom and USA.

Degrees and Diplomas: *Bachelor/Bakkalaureus*: Electrical Engineering; Chemical Engineering; Chemistry; Mechanical Engineering; Physics; Informatics; Information Systems (BSc); Linguistics; Popular Music and Media; History; German Language and Litrature; English and American Language and Literature; Media Sciences; Romance Studies (BA); Management and Economics; International Business (BA); *Diplom*: Computer Science in Electrical Engineering; Information Technology; Electrical Engineering and Educational Sciences; Mechanical Engineering and Educational Sciences; Computer Science in Mechanical Engineering; Industrial Engineering; (Dipl. Ing.); Computer Science/Engineering (Dipl. Inf.); Industrial Engineering (Dipl. Ing.); Mathematics (Dipl. Math); Mechanical Engineer (Dipl. Ing.); Technical Mathematics with Mechanical or Electrical Engineering (Dipl. Math); *Lehramt*: Teaching Qualifications, Primary and Secondary levels; *Master/Magister*: Applied Mechatronics (joint studies with Uni. Cairo) (ME); Business Administration; International Economics; International Business Studies; Vocational Education and Business Studies (MA); Chemical Engineering; Chemistry; Physics; Mechanical Engineering; Electrical Engineering; Informatics (MSc); Compartative Literary Studies; Linguistics; Popular Music and Media (MA); Information Systems (MSc); Pedagogy; *Doktorgrad*: Economics (Dr.rer.pol.);

Education (Dr.paed.); Engineering (Dr.ing.); Natural Sciences (Dr.rer.nat.); Philosophy (Dr.phil.); *Habilitation*

Student Services: Academic counselling, Canteen, Cultural centre, Employment services, Foreign student adviser, Foreign Studies Centre, Handicapped facilities, Health services, Language programs, Nursery care, Social counselling, Sports facilities

Student Residential Facilities: For 873 students

Special Facilities: Media Centre

Libraries: Central Library, c. 1,3m. media items

Last Updated: 06/02/12

UNIVERSITY OF PASSAU

Universität Passau
Innstrasse 41, 94030 Passau
Tel: +49(851) 509-0
Fax: +49(851) 509-1005
EMail: info@uni-passau.de
Website: http://www.uni-passau.de

Rektor: Walter Schweitzer (2004-)
Tel: +49(851) 509-1000, Fax: +49(851) 509-1002
EMail: praesident@uni-passau.de

Kanzlerin: Andrea Bör
Tel: +49(851) 509-1010, Fax: +49(851) 509-1002
EMail: kanzlerin@uni-passau.de

International Relations: Wolfgang Hau
Tel: +49(851) 509-1160, Fax: +49(851) 509-1164
EMail: auslandsamt@uni-passau.de

Faculties

Economics (Accountancy; Economics; Finance; Management; Marketing; Taxation); **Law** (European Union Law; Law); **Mathematics and Computer Science** (Computer Science; Data Processing; Mathematics); **Philosophy** (Catholic Theology; Philosophy)

History: Founded 1973. Teaching started 1978. An autonomous institution financially supported by the State of Bavaria.

Governing Bodies: Head of Institution Senate

Academic Year: October to September (October-March; April-September)

Admission Requirements: Abitur

Fees: None

Main Language(s) of Instruction: German

International Co-operation: Participates in Socrates/Erasmus and Programmes of the German Academic Exchange Service

Degrees and Diplomas: *Bachelor/Bakkalaureus*; *Staatsprüfung*; *Master/Magister*

Student Services: Academic counselling, Canteen, Cultural centre, Employment services, Foreign student adviser, Foreign Studies Centre, Handicapped facilities, Health services, Language programs, Nursery care, Social counselling, Sports facilities

Libraries: 1.6m. vols

Publications: Vorlesungsverzeichnis *(biennially)*
Last Updated: 06/02/12

UNIVERSITY OF PHILOSOPHY AND THEOLOGY IN MÜNSTER

Philosophisch-Theologische Hochschule Münster (PTH MÜNSTER)
Hohenzollernring 60, 48145 Münster
Tel: +49(251) 48256-0
Fax: +49(251) 48256-19
EMail: pth@pth-muenster.de
Website: http://www.pth-muenster.de

Rektor: Thomas Dienberg (2002-)
EMail: rektorat@pth-muenster.de

Sekretär: Hans-Gerd Janssen
EMail: hans-gerd.janssen@pth-muenster.de

International Relations: Hans-Gerd Janssen

Institutes
Spirituality (Theology)

Programmes
Catholic Theology (Catholic Theology; Theology); **Philosophy** (Philosophy)

History: Founded 1971. Acquired present status 1983.

Admission Requirements: Allgemeine Hochschulreife

Main Language(s) of Instruction: German

Accrediting Agencies: Accredited by the State 1983, Runby: Rhein-Westf. Kapuzinerprovinz 1998

Degrees and Diplomas: *Diplom*: 5 yrs; *Lizentiat*: 2 yrs; *Doktorgrad*

Student Services: Academic counselling, Foreign student adviser, Social counselling

Libraries: Yes
Last Updated: 22/01/10

UNIVERSITY OF POTSDAM
Universität Potsdam
Am Neuen Palais 10, 14469 Potsdam
Tel: +49(331) 977-0
Fax: +49(331) 972-163
EMail: presse@uni-potsdam.de
Website: http://www.uni-potsdam.de

Rektorin: Oliver Günther (2012-2017)
Tel: +49(331) 977-1790, Fax: +49(331) 977-1089
EMail: praesident@uni-potsdam.de

Kanzlerin: Barbara Obst-Hantel
Tel: +49(331) 977-1785, Fax: +49(331) 977-1140
EMail: kanzlerin@uni-potsdam.de

Faculties
Arts (American Studies; Arts and Humanities; English Studies; Germanic Studies; History; Jewish Studies; Media Studies; Philology; Philosophy; Religious Studies; Slavic Languages); **Economics and Social Sciences** (Administration; Business Administration; Economics; Political Sciences; Social Sciences; Sociology); **Human Sciences** (Arts and Humanities; Linguistics; Music; Pedagogy; Primary Education; Psychology; Special Education; Sports); **Law** (Civil Law; Criminal Law; Public Law); **Mathematics and Natural Sciences** (Biochemistry; Biology; Chemistry; Computer Science; Earth Sciences; Mathematics; Natural Sciences; Nutrition; Physics)

History: Founded 1991. The University has branches in Potsdam-Babelsberg and Golm.

Academic Year: October to September (October-March; April-September)

Admission Requirements: Secondary school certificate (Reifezeugnis), or equivalent

Fees: None

Main Language(s) of Instruction: German

International Co-operation: With universities in Australia, USA, Europe. Also participates in Erasmus.

Degrees and Diplomas: *Bachelor/Bakkalaureus*: Sciences and Arts, 6-7 sem; *Diplom*: Sciences, 9 sem; *Lehramt*: Teaching qualification, 8-9 sem; *Magister Artium*: Arts, 9 sem; *Staatsprüfung*: Law, 9 sem; *Master/Magister*: Law; *Master/Magister*: Sciences and Arts, a further 3-4 sem. Also LLM, Economics and Business. Programme for foreign students. Combined Degree Programme German Law/French Law. Polymer Science, Master of Public Management, European Masters in Clinical Linguistics, Global Public Policy.

Student Services: Academic counselling, Canteen, Cultural centre, Foreign student adviser, Foreign Studies Centre, Handicapped facilities, Language programs, Social counselling, Sports facilities

Special Facilities: Biological Garden. Audio-visual Centre
Libraries: University Library, c. 1.3m. Vols
Last Updated: 06/02/12

UNIVERSITY OF REGENSBURG
Universität Regensburg
Universitätsstrasse 31, 93053 Regensburg
Tel: +49(941) 943-01
Fax: +49(941) 943-2305
EMail: rektor@universitaet-regensburg.de
Website: http://www.uni-regensburg.de

Rektor: Thomas Strothotte
Tel: 49(941) 1943-2301, Fax: 49(941) 943-3310

Kanzler: Christian Blomeyer
Tel: +49(941) 943-2310
EMail: christian.blomeyer@verwaltung.uni-regensburg.de

International Relations: Marianne Sedlmeier
Tel: +49(941) 943-2373, Fax: +49(941) 943-3882
EMail: marianne.sedlmeier@verwaltung.uni-regensburg.de

Centres
East-West; **Languages and Communication** (Communication Studies; Modern Languages)

Faculties
Catholic Theology (Catholic Theology); **Chemistry and Pharmacy** (Chemistry; Pharmacy); **Economics, Business Administration and Business Computing** (Business and Commerce; Business Computing; Econometrics; Economic History; Economics; Management; Statistics); **Languages, Literature and Culture** (Cultural Studies; Literature; Modern Languages); **Law** (Law); **Mathematics** (Mathematics); **Medicine** (Dentistry; Medicine); **Philosophy, Fine Arts and Cultural Studies** (Cultural Studies; Fine Arts; Philosophy); **Physics** (Physics); **Pre-Clinical Medicine and Biology** (Biology; Medicine); **Psychology, Pedagogy and Sports** (Education; Pedagogy; Psychology; Sports)

Further Information: Also Teaching Hospital

History: Founded 1962. Admitted first students 1967. An autonomous institution financially supported by the State of Bavaria.

Governing Bodies: Senat

Academic Year: October to September

Admission Requirements: Secondary school certificate (Allgemeine Hochschulreife)

Fees: None

Main Language(s) of Instruction: German, English

International Co-operation: Participates in Socrates. Also Study Abroad programmes in the USA , Latin America, Australia, Asia.

Degrees and Diplomas: *Bachelor/Bakkalaureus*: German-French Studies, 3 yrs; *Diplom*: Biochemistry, Biology, Business Management, Information Systems, Roman Catholic Theology, Chemistry, Economics, Geography, Mathematics, Physics, Psychology, 4-5 yrs; *Lehramt*: Teaching Qualifications; *Staatsprüfung*: Law; Medicine; Pharmacy; *Master/Magister*: Art in Education, Art History, Classical Archaeology, Educational Science, English and American Studies, Folklore, Geography, Literature, German, Greek, History, History of Science, Indogermanic Linguistics; Latin, Musicology and Music Education, Philosophy, Physical Education, Political Science, Prehistoric and Early History, Protestant Theology, Religious Science, Romance Languages, Slavonic Languages, Sociology, 4-5 yrs; *Master/Magister*: European Master of Business Science; East-West Studies, 2 yrs; *Doktorgrad*: 2-4 yrs; *Habilitation*: at least 4 yrs following Doktor

Student Services: Academic counselling, Canteen, Cultural centre, Foreign student adviser, Handicapped facilities, Language programs, Nursery care, Social counselling, Sports facilities

Student Residential Facilities: For 3,725 students

Special Facilities: Botanical Garden. Computer Centre. Sound Studio

Libraries: c. 3,15m. vols

Publications: Forschungsbericht; Schriftenreihe
Last Updated: 06/02/12

UNIVERSITY OF ROSTOCK
Universität Rostock
Universitätsplatz 1, 18051 Rostock
Tel: +49(381) 498-0
Fax: +49(381) 498-1006
EMail: rektor@uni-rostock.de
Website: http://www.uni-rostock.de

Rektor: Wolfgang Schareck Tel: +49(381) 498-1000

Kanzler: Mathias Neukirchen
Tel: +49(381) 498-1016, Fax: +49(381) 498-1015
EMail: kanzler@uni-rostock.de

Centres
Computing (Computer Science) *Head*: Ch. Radloff; **Language** (Linguistics; Modern Languages) *Head*: B. Amling; **Media Studies** (Media Studies) *Head*: W. Rossmannek

Faculties
Agriculture and Environmental Sciences (Agriculture; Civil Engineering; Ecology; Environmental Studies; Landscape Architecture; Rural Planning); **Computer Science and Electronic Engineering** (Automation and Control Engineering; Computer Graphics; Computer Science; Data Processing; Energy Engineering; Microelectronics); **Economics and Social Sciences** (Administration; Business Administration; Business and Commerce; Business Computing; Business Education; Management; Marketing; Political Sciences; Social Sciences; Sociology; Tourism; Transport and Communications); **Humanities** (Education; Educational Psychology; Educational Research; History; Music; Pedagogy; Philosophy; Sports); **Interdisciplinary** (Aquaculture; Arts and Humanities; Biological and Life Sciences; Gerontology); **Law** (International Law; Law); **Mathematics and Natural Sciences** (Biology; Chemistry; Mathematics; Physics); **Mechanical Engineering and Marine Technology** (Marine Engineering; Mechanical Engineering; Naval Architecture); **Medicine** (Medicine); **Theology** (Protestant Theology; Religious Studies; Theology)

Further Information: Also twelve Clinics, a Radiology Centre and a Neurology Centre

History: Founded 1419 with faculties of Arts, Medicine and Law. The oldest University in the Baltic Sea area, reorganized and reopened 1946. Following reunification in 1989, the University experienced significant changes, such as an increase of 75% of the number of students.

Governing Bodies: Senat; Konzil

Academic Year: October to September (October-March; April-September)

Admission Requirements: Secondary school certificate and, depending on State of origin, language requirements (DSH, Test DaF)

Fees: None, excluding courses in continuing and distance education

Main Language(s) of Instruction: German

Degrees and Diplomas: *Bachelor/Bakkalaureus*: Agrarian Ecology; Business Sciences; Chemistry; Humanities including Sociology and Political Science, History, Literature, Modern Languages; Information Technology/Technological Informatics; Medical Biotechnology; Rural Landscape and Environmental Protection; Social Sciences; *Magister Artium*: International Commercial Law and International Business Management; German Law; *Staatsprüfung*: Dentistry; Law; Medicine; *Master/Magister*: Demography; Sociology; Economics; Computer Engineering; Information Technology; Humanities including Sociology and Political Science, Literature and Modern Languages

Student Services: Academic counselling, Canteen, Cultural centre, Foreign student adviser, Social counselling, Sports facilities

Special Facilities: Botanical Garden

Libraries: Central Library, 2,258,683 vols; 270,448 microfilms
Last Updated: 06/02/12

UNIVERSITY OF SIEGEN
Universität Siegen
Am Herrengarten 3, 57068 Siegen
Tel: +49(271) 740-0
Fax: +49(271) 740-4899
EMail: rektor@rektorat.uni-siegen.de
Website: http://www.uni-siegen.de

Rektor: Holger Burckhart
Tel: +49(271) 740-4858, Fax: +49(271) 740-4808

Kanzler: Johann Peter Schäfer
Tel: +49(271) 740-4856, Fax: +49(271) 740-2072
EMail: kanzler@vrz.uni-siegen.de

International Relations: Jochen Eickbusch
Tel: +49(271) 740-3901, Fax: +49(271) 740-3900
EMail: eickbusch@aaa.uni-siegen.de

Faculties
Arts (Catholic Theology; English; German; History; Media Studies; Philosophy; Romance Languages; Sociology; Theology); **Education, Architecture and Arts** (Architecture; Cultural Studies; Education; Fine Arts; Music; Psychology); **Science and Technology** (Biology; Chemistry; Civil Engineering; Computer Science; Electronic Engineering; Machine Building; Mathematics; Physics)

Schools
Economics (Business Administration; Business Computing; Economics)

Further Information: Also German Language Courses for beginners and advanced students

History: Founded 1972 as Gesamthochschule, incorporating former Technical College, Siegen-Gummersbach and branch of College of Education, Westfalen-Lippe. Became University 1980. An autonomous institution under the jurisdiction of and financially supported by the State of North Rhine-Westphalia.

Governing Bodies: Senat

Academic Year: October to July

Admission Requirements: Secondary school certificate (Reifezeugnis) or international equivalent. Technical secondary education (Fachhochschulreife) for certain courses

Fees: (Euros): 500 per semester

Main Language(s) of Instruction: German

International Co-operation: With 95 universities worldwide. Also participates in Socrates

Degrees and Diplomas: *Bachelor/Bakkalaureus*: 3 yrs; *Bachelor/Bakkalaureus*: Architecture, 4 yrs; *Lehramt*: Teaching Qualification, 3-4 1/2 yrs; *Master/Magister*: 2 yrs; *Doktorgrad*: Education (Dr.päd.); Engineering (Dr.Ing.); Natural Sciences (Dr.rer.nat.); Philosophy (Dr.phil.); *Habilitation (Dr. Habil.)*. Also 3 English-language postgraduate Master's Degree in Mechatronics, Chemistry, Physics

Student Services: Academic counselling, Canteen, Employment services, Foreign student adviser, Foreign Studies Centre, Handicapped facilities, Language programs, Nursery care, Social counselling, Sports facilities

Student Residential Facilities: For c. 1,000 students

Special Facilities: Audio-Visual Media Centre. Observatory

Libraries: Central Library, 1.2 m. vols

Publications: Forschungsbericht (Research Report); Lili - Zeitschrift für Literaturwissenschaft und Linguistik; Muk (Massenmedien und Kommunikation); Navigationen; Reihe Medienwissenschaften; Reihe Siegen; Siegen: Social *(biennially)*; SPIEL (Siegener Periodicum zur International Empirischen Literaturwissenschaften), Siegener Periodicum zur International Empirischen Literaturwissenschaften *(biannually)*
Last Updated: 06/02/12

UNIVERSITY OF STUTTGART
Universität Stuttgart
PO Box 206017, Keplerstrasse 7, 70049 Stuttgart
Tel: +49(711) 685-0
Fax: +49(711) 685-82271
EMail: susanne.riedl@rektorat.uni-stuttgart.de
Website: http://www.uni-stuttgart.de

Rektor: Wolfram Ressel (2006-)
Tel: +49(711) 685-82201, Fax: +49(711) 685-82113
EMail: rektor@uni-stuttgart.de

Kanzlerin: Bettina Buhlmann
Tel: +49(711) 685-82204, Fax: +49(711) 685-82150
EMail: kanzlerin@uni-stuttgart.de

International Relations: David Phillips, Senior Advisor on International Issues
Tel: +49(711) 685-68666, Fax: +49(711) 685-68600
EMail: international@uni-stuttgart.de

Faculties
Aerospace Engineering and Geodesy (Aeronautical and Aerospace Engineering; Geological Engineering; Surveying and Mapping); **Architecture and Urban Planning** (Architecture; Design; Landscape Architecture; Town Planning); **Chemistry** (Chemistry; Food Science; Materials Engineering); **Civil and Environmental**

Engineering (Civil Engineering; Environmental Engineering; Hydraulic Engineering; Railway Engineering; Regional Planning; Road Engineering; Surveying and Mapping; Water Management); **Computer Science, Electrical Engineering and Information Technology** (Computer Science; Electrical Engineering; Information Technology; Software Engineering); **Energy Technology, Process Engineering and Biological Engineering** (Biomedical Engineering; Cell Biology; Chemical Engineering; Energy Engineering; Immunology; Industrial Engineering; Microbiology; Polymer and Plastics Technology); **Engineering Design, Production Engineering and Automotive Engineering** (Automotive Engineering; Engineering Drawing and Design; Engineering Management; Mechanical Engineering; Production Engineering; Road Engineering; Water Management); **Humanities** (Art History; English; German; History; Linguistics; Philosophy; Romance Languages); **Management, Economics and Social Sciences** (Educational Sciences; Information Sciences; Management; Social Sciences; Sports; Technology Education; Vocational Education); **Mathematics and Physics** (Mathematics; Physics)

History: Founded 1829 as a grammar and vocational school, became Polytechnische Schule 1840, Technische Hochschule 1890. Present title conferred 1967. An autonomous institution under the jurisdiction of and financed by the State of Baden-Württemberg.

Governing Bodies: Hochschulrat; Senat

Academic Year: October to September (October-March; April-September)

Admission Requirements: Secondary school certificate (Reifezeugnis) or equivalent

Fees: (Euro): 500 per semester

Main Language(s) of Instruction: German

International Co-operation: Participates in Erasmus; awards double degrees; cooperation with German University in Cairo, Global Education for European Engineers and Entrepreneurs (GE4); Magalhães Network; TIME Association; China-Programme and Wuhan-Programme; Cooperation programmes with partner institutions in Asia (13), Africa (3), Australia (5), Latin America (15) and North America (23). State-to-State cooperation with South Australia, ITESM, Ontario, California, Connecticut, Massachusetts, North Carolina and Oregon.

Degrees and Diplomas: *Bachelor/Bakkalaureus*: Aerospace Engineering; Architecture; Automotive and Engine Technology; Chemistry; Civil Engineering; Computer Science; Electrical Engineering and Information Technology; Engineering Cybernetics; Environmental Engineering (BSc); Art History; Educational Services / Vocational Education; English; German; History; History of Natural Sciences and Technology (BA); Geodesy and Geoinformatics Engineering; Information Systems; Technical Management; Materials Science; Mechanical Engineering; Mechatronics; Mathematics; Physics (BSc); Linguistics; Natural Language Processing; Social Sciences; Sports and Exercise Science; Romance Studies (BA); Process Engineering; Real Estate Engineering and Management; Renewable Energies; Software Engineering; Technical Biology; Technical Education; Technology Management (BSc); *Master/Magister*: Air Quality Control, Solid Waste and Waste Water Processes; Computational Mechanics of Materials and Structures; Geomatics Engineering; Information Technology (MSc); Art History; Empirical Social and Political Analysis; Empirical Social and Political Analysis (German-French); English Literature; Exercise Science; Health Promotion (MA); German; History; Linguistics; Philosophy; Philosophy of Cultures (German-French); Romance Studies; Technical Education (MA); Infrastructure Planning; Physics; Water Resources Engineering and Management; Electrical Engineering and Information Technology; Environmental Engineering; Information Systems; Process Engineering (MSc); *Doktorgrad*. Also State Examination in all disciplines leading to a career in the Civil Service.

Student Services: Academic counselling, Canteen, Employment services, Foreign student adviser, Foreign Studies Centre, Handicapped facilities, Language programs, Nursery care, Social counselling, Sports facilities

Student Residential Facilities: Yes

Libraries: University Library, c. 1,250,000 vols; institute libraries with c. 900,000 vols

Publications: Research, Periodical on various research topics. *(other/irregular)*; Research Development Consulting, Annual technology transfer brochure *(annually)*
Last Updated: 06/02/12

UNIVERSITY OF TELEVISION AND FILM MUNICH

Hochschule für Fernsehen und Film München
Frankenthaler Straße 23, 81539 München
Tel: +49(89) 68957-0
Fax: +49(89) 68957-189
EMail: info@hff-muc.de
Website: http://www.hff-muenchen.de/wir/index.html

Präsident: Gerhard Fuchs
Tel: 49(89) 68957-190 EMail: m.gold@hff-muc.de

Kanzlerin: Ingrid Baumgartner Schmidt
Tel: 49(89) 68957-192, Fax: 49(89) 68957-179
EMail: kanzlerin@hff-muc.de

Departments
Communication and Media Studies (Media Studies); **Technology** (Cinema and Television; Film; Multimedia; Photography)

History: Founded 1967.

Academic Year: October to July (October-February; May-July)

Admission Requirements: Secondary school certificate (Abitur)

Main Language(s) of Instruction: German

Libraries: c. 24,000 vols
Last Updated: 18/01/10

UNIVERSITY OF TRIER

Universität Trier
Universitätsring 15, 54286 Trier, Rhineland Palatinate
Tel: +49(651) 201-0
Fax: +49(651) 201-4299
Website: http://www.uni-trier.de

Präsident: Michael Jäckel (2011-)
Tel: +49(651) 201-4227 EMail: praesident@uni-trier.de

Kanzler: Klaus Hembach
Tel: +49(651) 201-4234, Fax: +49(651) 201-4280
EMail: kanzler@uni-trier.de

International Relations: Birgit Rose
Tel: +49(651) 201-2807, Fax: +49(651) 201-3914
EMail: aaa@uni-trier.de

Centres
Ancient Studies (Ancient Civilizations) *Director*: Sven P. Vleeming; **Canadian Studies** (Canadian Studies) *Head*: Wolgang Klooß; **East Asia and Pacific Studies** (East Asian Studies; Pacific Area Studies) *Director*: Hilaria Gössmann; **E-Business** (E-Business/Commerce) *Director*: Hans Czap; **Electronic Retrieval and Publishing Techniques in the Humanities** (Information Technology; Publishing and Book Trade) *Director*: Claudine Moulin; **European Studies** (European Studies) *Director*: Michael Ambrosi; **Galicia** *(Centro de Documentación)* (Spanish) *Director*: Dieter Kremer; **Health-Economics** (Health Administration; Health Sciences) *Director*: Hans Czap; **Kantian Studies** *Director*: Bernd Dörflinger; **Neuropsychological Research** (Neurology) *Director*: Werner Wittling; **Portuguese Philology** *(Centro de Documentação sobre Portugal)* (Philology; Portuguese) *Director*: Henry Thorau; **Psychological Diagnostics, Investigation and Evaluation** (Clinical Psychology; Psychiatry and Mental Health) *Director*: Sigrun-Heide Filipp; **Psychological Information and Documentation** (Psychology) *Director*: Günter Krampen; **Scientific Electronic Publishing** (Information Technology; Publishing and Book Trade) *Director*: Christoph Meinel; **Social Education Research** (Education; Educational Research; Social Studies) *Director*: Hans Günther Homfeldt; **Work and Social Studies** (Social Studies; Social Work) *Director*: Hans Braun

Departments
Arts and Humanities *(II)* (Classical Languages; Linguistics; Literature; Media Studies; Modern Languages) *Dean*: Karl-Heinz Pohl; **Arts and Social Sciences** *(III)* (Ancient Civilizations; Archaeology; Art History; Political Sciences) *Dean*: Helga Schnabel-Schüle; **Education, Philosophy and Psychology** *(I)* (Education; Philosophy; Psychology) *Dean*: Michael-Sebastian Honig; **Law** *(V)* (Law) *Dean*: Meinhard Schröder; **Natural Sciences** *(VI)* (Analytical Chemistry; Earth Sciences; Geography; Geology; Inorganic Chemistry; Soil Science; Surveying and Mapping; Water Science) *Dean*: Joachim Hill; **Social Sciences** *(IV)* (Business Administration;

Economics; Ethnology; Mathematics and Computer Science; Sociology) *Dean*: Wolfgang Gawronski

Faculties
Theology (Theology) *Director*: Reinhold Bohlen

Institutes
Communal Science and Conversion Policy *Director*: Helmut Vogel; **Cusanus Research** (Religious Studies; Theology) *Director*: Klaus Reinhardt; **Emil-Frank** *Director*: Reinhold Bohlen; **Environmental and Technical Law** (Environmental Studies; Law) *Director*: Peter Marburger; **European Constitutional Law** (Constitutional Law; European Union Law; Law) *Director*: Gerhard Robbers; **Health Care Management** (Health Administration; Public Health) *Director*: Andreas J.W. Goldschmidt; **History of the Jews** *(Arye-Maimon)* (Jewish Studies) *Director*: Alfred Haverkamp; **Labour Legislation and Labour Relations in the European Community** (European Studies; Labour and Industrial Relations; Labour Law) *Co-Director*: Rolf Birk; **Legal Policy** (Law) *Director*: Gerhard Robbers; **Media Studies and Culture** *(Philosophical Research)* (Cultural Studies; Media Studies; Philosophy) *Director*: Ernst Wolfgang Orth; **Middle Class Economics e.V.** (Business Administration; Economic History) *Director*: Axel G. Schmidt; **Tourism** *(European)* (Tourism) *Director*: Martin L. Fontanari

Research Centres
Current Ethical Questions (Ethics) *Director*: Anselm Winfried Müller; **Greek-Roman Egypt** (History) *Director*: Sven Vleeming; **Middle High German Dictionary** (Linguistics) *Head*: Kurt Gärtner; **Psychobiology and Psychomatics** (Biology; Psychology) *Director*: Dirk Hellhammer; **Rational Law and Prussian Legal Reform** (Law) *Director*: Peter Krause; **Sociology and Further Training** (Sociology) *Director*: Roland Eckert; **Taurus Working Group of Environment-Regional and Structural Research and Consultancy** (Environmental Studies; Regional Studies; Rural Studies; Sociology; Urban Studies) *Head*: Harald Spehl

History: Founded 1473 and closed in Napoleonic era. Re-established 1970 as a modern campus University. Incorporated the Theologische Fakultät Trier (founded 1950).

Governing Bodies: Hochschulrat; Senat; Fachbereichsräte

Academic Year: October to September (October-March; April-September)

Admission Requirements: Secondary school certificate (Reifezeugnis)

Fees: (Euros): Tuition, none; social fees: 145.50 per semester

Main Language(s) of Instruction: German

International Co-operation: With universities in all European countries, USA, Canada, Latin-America, China, Kenya.

Degrees and Diplomas: *Bachelor/Bakkalaureus*; *Master/Magister*; *Doktorgrad*: Economic Sciences (Dr.rer.pol.); Law (Dr.iur.); Natural Sciences (Dr.rer.nat.); Philosophy (Dr.phil.); *Habilitation*: at least 3 yrs following Doktor

Student Services: Academic counselling, Canteen, Cultural centre, Employment services, Foreign student adviser, Foreign Studies Centre, Handicapped facilities, Health services, Language programs, Nursery care, Social counselling, Sports facilities

Student Residential Facilities: Yes

Libraries: Central Library, 1,380,000 vols

Publications: Trierer Beiträge, Special research themes or lectures
Last Updated: 11/02/09

UNIVERSITY OF ULM
Universität Ulm
Albert-Einstein-Allee, 89069 Ulm
Tel: +49(731) 502-01
Fax: +49(731) 502-2038
EMail: rektor@rektoramt.uni-ulm.de
Website: http://www.uni-ulm.de

Rektor: Karl Joachim Ebeling (2003-)
Tel: +49(731) 502-2000, Fax: +49(731) 502-2200

Kanzler: Dieter Kaufmann
Tel: +49(731) 502-5000, Fax: +49(731) 502-5007
EMail: kanzler@uni-ulm.de

Faculties
Engineering and Computer Science (Automation and Control Engineering; Biomedical Engineering; Communication Arts; Computer Science; Electrical Engineering; Energy Engineering; Engineering; Information Technology; Materials Engineering; Microelectronics; Telecommunications Engineering); **Mathematics and Economics** (Accountancy; Actuarial Science; Business Administration; Economics; Finance; Management; Mathematics); **Medicine** (Dentistry; Medicine); **Natural Sciences** (Biology; Chemistry; Economics; Natural Sciences; Physics)

Further Information: Also Teaching Hospitals: Rehabilitationskrankenhaus Ulm (RKU); Psychiatrisches Landeskrankenhaus Weissenau; Bezirkskrankenhaus Günzburg; Bundeswehrkrankenhaus Ulm. Language Courses, German for Foreign Students

History: Founded 1967. Financially supported by the State of Baden-Württemberg.

Governing Bodies: Grosser Senat; Senat

Academic Year: October to July (October-February; April-July)

Admission Requirements: Secondary school certificate (Reifezeugnis)

Fees: Tuition, none

Main Language(s) of Instruction: German

Degrees and Diplomas: *Bachelor/Bakkalaureus*; *Diplom*; *Lehramt*: Teaching Qualification, Secondary level, 5 yrs; *Master/Magister*; *Doktorgrad*: 2-4 yrs after Diplom; *Habilitation*: at least 3 yrs following Doktor

Student Services: Academic counselling, Canteen, Cultural centre, Foreign student adviser, Language programs, Sports facilities

Student Residential Facilities: Yes

Special Facilities: Botanical Gardens. Art Path (more than 60 modern sculptures)

Libraries: c. 780,000 vols

Publications: Forschungsbericht, Research Report *(biennially)*

Press or Publishing House: Universitätsverlag Ulm
Last Updated: 06/02/12

UNIVERSITY OF VECHTA
Universität Vechta
Driverstrasse 22, Driverstraße 22, 49364 Vechta
Tel: +49(4441) 15-1
Fax: +49(4441) 15-444
EMail: info@uni-vechta.de
Website: http://www.uni-vechta.de

Präsidentin: Marianne Assenmacher
Tel: +49(4441) 15-270, Fax: +49(4441) 15-451
EMail: praesidentin@uni-vechta.de

International Relations: Judith Peltz, Head, International Office
Tel: +49(4441) 15-613, Fax: +49(4441) 15-67613

Institutes
Catholic Theology *(IKT)* (Catholic Theology); **Didactics in Natural Sciences and Applied Sciences** *(IfD)* (Biology; Chemistry; Earth Sciences; Mathematics; Physics); **Gerontology** *(IfG)* (Gerontology; Health Sciences); **Humanities and Cultural Sciences** (English; German; History; Literature); **Social Sciences and Philosophy** *(ISP)* (Cultural Studies; Ethics; Philosophy; Political Sciences; Social Sciences; Sociology); **Social Work, Educational and Sports Sciences** *(ISBS)* (Educational Sciences; Pedagogy; Psychology; Social Work; Sports); **Structural Research and Planning in Areas of Intensive Agriculture** *(ISPA)* (Agriculture; Rural Planning)

Programmes
Art (Fine Arts); **Biology/Chemistry** (Biology; Chemistry); **Design** (Design); **Ecology** (Ecology); **Geography** (Geography); **Landscape** (Landscape Architecture); **Music** (Music)

History: Founded 1830 as a School for Teacher Training, became a College after World War II, and branch of the University of Osnabrück 1973. Acquired present status and title 2010.

Governing Bodies: President; Senate

Academic Year: October to July (October-February; April-July)

Admission Requirements: Secondary school certificate (Reifezeugnis) or equivalent

Fees: None

Main Language(s) of Instruction: German

International Co-operation: With universities in Poland, United Kingdom, Austria, Hungary, Latvia, Sweden, Luxembourg, France

Accrediting Agencies: Zentrale Evaluations- und Akkreditierungsagentur (ZEvA)

Degrees and Diplomas: *Bachelor/Bakkalaureus*: Combined Studies; Gerontology; Social Work, 3 yrs; *Master/Magister*: Education; Family Therapy; Gerontology; Social Work; Sport Psychology; *Promotion*

Student Services: Academic counselling, Canteen, Cultural centre, Foreign student adviser, Foreign Studies Centre, Handicapped facilities, Social counselling, Sports facilities

Student Residential Facilities: Yes

Special Facilities: Art Gallery; Multimedia Labs

Libraries: University Library, 450,000 vols

Last Updated: 06/02/12

UNIVERSITY OF VETERINARY MEDICINE HANOVER

Stiftung Tierärztliche Hochschule Hannover
PO Box 711180, Bünteweg 2, 30545 Hannover
Tel: +49(511) 953-6
Fax: +49(511) 953-8050
EMail: presse@tiho-hannover.de
Website: http://www.tiho-hannover.de

President: Gerhard Greif (2002-)
Tel: +49(511) 953-8000, Fax: +49(511) 953-82-8001
EMail: praesident@tiho-hannover.de

Institutes
Biometry, Epidemiology and Information Processing *(Field Station, Bakum)* (Animal Husbandry; Epidemiology); Anatomy (Anatomy); Animal Breeding and Genetics (Animal Husbandry; Cattle Breeding; Genetics); Animal Ecology and Cell Biology (Cell Biology) *Head*: Bernd Schierwater; Animal Hygiene, Animal Welfare and Behaviour of Farm Animals (Animal Husbandry; Zoology); Animal Nutrition (Food Science); Biometry, Epidemiology and Data Processing (Biology; Information Management); Food Quality and Safety (Food Technology); Food Toxicology (Food Science; Toxicology); Microbiology and Infectious Diseases (Microbiology); Parasitology (Parasitology); Pathology (Pathology); Pharmacology, Toxicology and Pharmacy (Pharmacology; Pharmacy; Toxicology); Physiological Chemistry (Chemistry; Physiology); Physiology (Physiology); Reproductive Biology (Embryology and Reproduction Biology); Virology (Virology); Zoology (Zoology)

Units
Fish Pathology and Farming (Fishery; Veterinary Science); History of Veterinary Medicine (Veterinary Science); Immunology (Immunology; Veterinary Science); Medical Physics (Physics)

Further Information: Affiliated organizations: WHO-Centre, EU-Reference Laboratory for Classical Swine Fever (CSF), Unit for Wildlife Research, Company for Innovative Veterinary Diagnostics (IVD). Animal clinics

History: Founded 1778 as Royal School of Equine Medicine, acquired University status 1887.

Governing Bodies: Senate

Academic Year: October to July (October-February; April-July)

Admission Requirements: Secondary school certificate (Abitur) or equivalent

Fees: (Euros): 138.90 per semester

Main Language(s) of Instruction: German

International Co-operation: With universities in Chile, United Kingdom, Hungary, France, Turkey, Sudan, Poland, Finland, USA, Costa Rica, Russian Federation, China, Japan, Thailand, Lithuania.

Accrediting Agencies: European Association of Establishments for Veterinary Education (EAEVE)

Degrees and Diplomas: *Bachelor/Bakkalaureus*; *Staatsprüfung*; *Master/Magister*; *Doktorgrad (Dr.med.vet)*: Ph.D. by thesis; *Habilitation (PD)*

Student Services: Academic counselling, Canteen, Cultural centre, Employment services, Foreign student adviser, Foreign Studies Centre, Language programs, Social counselling, Sports facilities

Student Residential Facilities: Yes

Special Facilities: Historical Museum of Veterinary Medicine

Libraries: Central Library, 212,333 vols

Last Updated: 26/01/10

UNIVERSITY OF WISMAR

Hochschule Wismar
PO Box 1210, Philipp-Müller-Strasse 14, 23952 Wismar
Tel: +49(3841) 753-0
Fax: +49(3841) 753-383
EMail: rektor@hs-wismar.de
Website: http://www.hs-wismar.de

Rektor: Norbert Grünwald
Tel: +49(3841) 753-216, Fax: +49(3841) 753-400

Director of Administration: Manfred Sass
Tel: +49(3841) 753-269, Fax: +49(3841) 753-673
EMail: manfred.sass@hs-wismar.de

International Relations: Korinna Stubbe
Tel: +49(3841) 753-240, Fax: +49(3841) 753-444
EMail: korinna.stubbe@hs-wismar.de

Faculties
Architecture (Architecture; Regional Planning; Town Planning); Business; Civil Engineering (Building Technologies; Civil Engineering); Design and Interior Design (Communication Arts; Design; Interior Design; Media Studies); Electronic Engineering and Computer Science (Automation and Control Engineering; Computer Science; Electrical and Electronic Engineering; Multimedia); Mechanical and Production Engineering, Environmental Protection (Automation and Control Engineering; Environmental Engineering; Mechanical Engineering; Production Engineering); Navigation (Marine Transport; Nautical Science; Transport Management)

History: Founded 1992.

Governing Bodies: Rektorat, Senat

Academic Year: September to June

Admission Requirements: Abitur, Practical Training

Fees: (Euros): semester fee, 50

Main Language(s) of Instruction: German

International Co-operation: Participation in Erasmus

Degrees and Diplomas: *Bachelor/Bakkalaureus*: 6-7 sem; *Diplom*: Design, 4 yrs; *Master/Magister*: 3-4 sem

Student Services: Canteen, Foreign Studies Centre, Language programs, Social counselling, Sports facilities

Student Residential Facilities: Yes

Special Facilities: Maritime Simulation Centre

Publications: HS-Magazine *(quarterly)*

Last Updated: 20/01/10

UNIVERSITY OF WUPPERTAL

Bergische Universität Wuppertal
Gaussstrasse 20, 42119 Wuppertal
Tel: +49(202) 439-0
Fax: +49(202) 439-2904
EMail: rektor@uni-wuppertal.de
Website: http://www.uni-wuppertal.de

Rektor: Lambert T. Koch (2008-)
Tel: +49(202) 439-2223, Fax: +49(202) 439-3024

Kanzler: Roland Kischkel EMail: kanzler@uni-wuppertal.de

International Relations: Petra Winzer
Tel: +49(202) 439-2342 EMail: prorektor4@uni-wuppertal.de

Faculties
Architecture, Civil Engineering, Mechanical Engineering and Safety Engineering (Architecture; Civil Engineering; Machine Building; Mechanical Engineering; Real Estate; Safety Engineering); Art and Design (Fine Arts; Industrial Design); Business and Economics *(Schumpeter)* (Business Administration; Commercial

Law; Economics); **Educational and Social Sciences** (Geochemistry; Pedagogy; Psychology; Social Sciences; Sociology; Sports; Technology Education); **Electrical, Information and Media Engineering** (Electrical Engineering; Information Technology; Media Studies; Technology); **Humanities** (Catholic Theology; Comparative Literature; English; History; Linguistics; Literature; Music; Music Education; Philology; Philosophy; Political Sciences; Protestant Theology); **Mathematics and Natural Sciences** (Biological and Life Sciences; Chemistry; Computer Science; Mathematics; Physics)

History: Founded 1972 as Gesamthochschule. Incorporated a branch of Rheinland College of Education, Köln, and Technical College. Acquired present title 1975. An autonomous institution under the jurisdiction of and financially supported by the State of North Rhine-Westphalia.

Governing Bodies: Senate

Academic Year: October to September (October-March; April-September)

Admission Requirements: Secondary school certificate (Reifezeugnis).

Fees: (Euros): 500 per semester

Main Language(s) of Instruction: German

Degrees and Diplomas: *Bachelor/Bakkalaureus*: Applied Sciences; Arts; Business Mathematics; Chemistry; Civil Engineering; Economics; Electrical Engineering; Information Technology; Mechanical Engineering; Print and Media Technology; Safety Engineering, 3 yrs; *Bachelor/Bakkalaureus*: Architecture, 4 yrs; *Diplom*: Construction Engineering (Bauingenieur), 8-10 sem; *Diplom*: Designer, 8, 9,11 sem; *Diplom*: Economics (Ökonom); Mathematics (Mathematiker); Psychology (Psychologe), 10 sem; *Diplom*: Food Chemistry (Lebensmittelchemiker), 7 sem; *Diplom*: Physics (Physiker), 7-10 sem; *Lehramt*; *Staatsprüfung*; *Staatsprüfung*: Teaching qualifications, primary and secondary levels, 3-4 yrs; *Master/Magister*: Architecture, 1 yr; *Master/Magister*: Business Administration; Business Mathematics; Chemistry; Electrical Engineering; Fire Safety Engineering; Information Technology; Quality Engineering; Safety Engineering, 2 yrs; *Master/Magister*: Computer Simulation in Science, 2 yrs in English; *Master/Magister*: Real Estate Management and Construction Project Management, 11/2 yrs

Student Services: Academic counselling, Canteen, Cultural centre, Employment services, Foreign student adviser, Foreign Studies Centre, Handicapped facilities, Language programs, Nursery care, Social counselling, Sports facilities

Student Residential Facilities: For c. 2,000 students

Libraries: Central Library, c. 770,000 vols; department libraries

Publications: Forschungsbericht *(biennially)*

Student Numbers *2008-2009*: Total: c. 13,500
Last Updated: 31/01/12

UNIVERSITY OF THE ARTS BREMEN

Hochschule für Künste Bremen
Am Speicher XI Nr. 8, 28217 Bremen
Tel: +49(421) 9595-100
Fax: +49(421) 9595-200
EMail: pressestelle@hfk-bremen.de
Website: http://www.hfk-bremen.de

Rektor: Manfred Cordes
Tel: +49(421) 9595-1017, Fax: +49(421) 9595-2017
EMail: p.rautmann@hfk-bremen.de

Kanzler: Markus Wortmann
Tel: +49(421) 9595-1025, Fax: +49(421) 9595-2025
EMail: kanzler@hfk-bremen.de

International Relations: Petra Doeling
EMail: p.doeling@hfk-bremen.de

Faculties

Art and Design (Art Education; Design; Interior Design; Media Studies); **Music** (Art Education; Music; Music Education; Musical Instruments; Religious Music)

History: Founded 1922.

Main Language(s) of Instruction: German

Degrees and Diplomas: *Bachelor/Bakkalaureus*: Digital Media Studies; Integrated Design; *Diplom*; *Lehramt*; *Master/Magister*: Digital Media Studies. Bachelor's degree and Master's degree in Music planned for Winter Semester 2010.
Last Updated: 02/02/12

UNIVERSITY OF THE FEDERAL ARMED FORCES MUNICH

Universität der Bundeswehr München
Werner-Heisenberg-Weg 39, 85577 Neubiberg
Tel: +49(89) 6004-1
Fax: +49(89) 6004-3560
EMail: vorzimmer.praesident@unibw-muenchen.de
Website: http://www.unibw-muenchen.de

Präsidentin: Merith Niehuss (2005-)
Tel: +49(89) 6004-2001, Fax: +49(89) 6004-2009

Kanzler: Hans Lerch
Tel: +49(89) 6004-4000, Fax: +49(89) 6004-4044
EMail: kanzler@unibw-muenchen.de

International Relations: Peter Weinheimer

Faculties

Aviation and Aerospace Engineering (Aeronautical and Aerospace Engineering); **Business Administration** (Business Administration); **Computer Science** (Computer Science); **Construction and Surveying** (Construction Engineering; Surveying and Mapping); **Economics and Organizational Sciences** (Business Administration; Economics); **Education** (Education); **Electrical Engineering** (Electrical Engineering; Power Engineering; Telecommunications Engineering); **Mechanical Engineering** (Mechanical Engineering); **Social Sciences** (Social Sciences)

History: Founded 1973 by decision of the Federal Government. Authorized 1973 by the Bavarian Ministry for Education, Culture, Science and Arts. Responsible to the Bavarian Ministry of Education, Culture, Science and Arts, and to the Federal Ministry of Defence.

Academic Year: October to June (October-December; January-March; April-June)

Admission Requirements: Secondary school certificate (Reifezeugnis) or equivalent. Students must have passed the Armed Forces officers examination and have accepted a 12-yr engagement

Fees: None

Main Language(s) of Instruction: German

Degrees and Diplomas: *Bachelor/Bakkalaureus*; *Master/Magister*

Libraries: c. 600,000 vols
Last Updated: 28/01/10

UNIVERSITY OF THE RUHR, BOCHUM

Ruhr-Universität Bochum
Universitätsstrasse 150, 44780 Bochum
Tel: +49(234) 32-22926 +49(234) 32-22927
Fax: +49(234) 32-14131
EMail: info@uv.ruhr-uni-bochum.de
Website: http://www.ruhr-uni-bochum.de

Rektor: Elmar Weiler
Tel: +49(234) 32-22, Fax: +49(234) 32-14
EMail: rektor@ruhr-uni-bochum.de

Kanzler: Gerhard Möller
Tel: +49(234) 32-22921, Fax: +49(234) 32-14132
EMail: kanzler@ruhr-uni-bochum.de

International Relations: Monika Sprung
Tel: +49(234) 32-23024, Fax: +49(234) 32-14684
EMail: monika.sprung@uv.ruhr-uni-bochum.de

Centres

Continuing Education *Dean*: Martin Muhler; **Interdisciplinary Research of the Ruhr Area** (Regional Studies) *Head*: Klaus-Peter Strohmeier; **Teacher Training** (Teacher Training) *Head*: Luzia Vorspel

Faculties

Biology and Biotechnology (Biology; Biotechnology); **Catholic Theology** (Catholic Theology; Theology); **Chemistry and Bio-**

chemistry (Biochemistry; Chemistry); **Civil and Environmental Engineering** (Civil Engineering; Environmental Engineering); **East Asian Studies** (Chinese; East Asian Studies; Japanese; Korean; Literature); **Economics** (Economics); **Electrical Engineering and Information Technology** (Electrical Engineering; Information Sciences; Information Technology); **Geoscience** (Earth Sciences; Geography; Geology; Geophysics); **History** (Archaeology; Art History; History; Musicology); **Law** (Law); **Mathematics** (Mathematics); **Mechanical Engineering** (Automation and Control Engineering; Automotive Engineering; Energy Engineering; Engineering Drawing and Design; Engineering Management; Materials Engineering; Mechanical Engineering); **Medicine** (Medicine); **Philology** (Classical Languages; Comparative Literature; English Studies; Film; Germanic Studies; Linguistics; Media Studies; Oriental Studies; Philology; Romance Languages; Slavic Languages; Theatre); **Philosophy and Educational Research** (Education; Educational Research; Philosophy); **Physics and Astronomy** (Astronomy and Space Science; Physics); **Protestant Theology** (Protestant Theology); **Psychology** (Psychology); **Social Sciences** (Political Sciences; Social Sciences; Sociology); **Sports Science** (Sports)

History: Founded 1961 in response to the demand for the creation of a University in the Ruhr area. Formally opened June 1965. An autonomous institution financially supported by the State of North Rhine-Westphalia, and under the jurisdiction of its Ministry of Education.

Governing Bodies: Senat

Academic Year: October to July (October-February; April-July)

Admission Requirements: Secondary school certificate (Reifezeugnis) or equivalent

Fees: See Institution's website

Main Language(s) of Instruction: German

International Co-operation: With universities in EU, Middle and Eastern Europe and Asia. For further details please see Institution's website

Accrediting Agencies: Accreditation Council, Bonn

Degrees and Diplomas: *Bachelor/Bakkalaureus*: Art History, Korean Studies, Linguistics, Media and Film Studies, Oriental and Islamic Studies, Philosophy, Political Science, Romance Philology, French, Italian, Spanish, Sinology, Studies in Russian Culture, Economics, Politics (BA); Biology, Chemistry, Biochemistry, Geography, Geosciences, Physics, Applied Computer Science, Psychology, Mathematics, Business Psychology, Sales Engineering and Product Management (BSc); Comparative Literature, Anglo-American Studies, Archaeology, Educational Sciences, Protestant Theology, German Studies, History, Japanese Studies, Catholic Theology, Classical Philology, East Asian Economics and Politics (BA); Economics and Social Studies, Sports, Mathematics, Physics, Geography, Geoscience, Chemistry, Biology (BA); Social Psychology and Social Anthropology, Sociology, Language Teaching Research, Theatre Studies (BA), 6 sem; *Diplom*: Civil Engineering, Electronics and Information Technology, Mathematics, Mechanical Engineering, Economics, Information Technology Security, Environmental Technology and Resource Management; Physics, Psychology, Social Sciences, Sports Science, Catholic Theology, 9 sem; *Staatsprüfung*: Law, 9 sem; *Staatsprüfung*: Medicine, 12 sem; *Master/Magister*: Arts and Humanities, Comparative Literature, Anglo-American Studies, Chinese Philosophy and History, Chinese Language and Literature, German Studies, Educational Sciences, History, Japanese History, Catholic Theology (MA); Classical Archaeology, Classical Philology, Art History, Korean Studies, Linguistics, Media and Film Studies, Oriental and Islamic Studies, East Slavic Studies, Philosophy, East Asian Politics, Political Science, Romance Philology, French (MA); Computational Engineering, Organizational Management (M.Sc); Italian, Spanish, Social Sciences, Sociology, Language Teaching Research, Theatre Studies, Pre- and Ancient History (MA); Science in Biology, Chemistry, Biochemistry, Geography, Geosciences, Applied Computer Science, Psychology, Sales Engineering and Product Management (MSc); Secondary Education, Educational Sciences, Philosophy, History, German, English, Latin, Greek, French, Spanish, Italian, Russian, Protestant Theology, Catholic Theology (M.Ed.), a further 4 sem; *Master/Magister*: Development Management, a further 3 sem; *Master/Magister*: Human Rights and Democratization, Humanitarian Aid, a further 2 sem; *Master/Magister*: Protestant Theology, 9 sem; *Master/Magister*: Social Psychology and Social Anthroplogy, East Asian Economics, European

Culture and Economy; *Doktorgrad*: c. 6 sem; *Doktorgrad*: Neuro Science; International Development Studies; Chemistry; Biochemistry; Geography; Geosciences; Biology (PhD; Dr), 6 sem; *Habilitation*: at least 3 yrs following Doktor

Student Services: Academic counselling, Canteen, Cultural centre, Employment services, Handicapped facilities, Language programs, Nursery care, Social counselling, Sports facilities

Student Residential Facilities: Yes

Special Facilities: Museum (modern art and antiquities). Botanical Garden. Centre for Arts and Music

Libraries: University Library, 2,013,564 vols; libraries of the faculties and institutes

Publications: Forschungsbericht *(annually)*; Wissenschaftsmagazin rubin *(biannually)*

Last Updated: 08/02/07

VALLENDAR UNIVERSITY OF PHILOSOPHY AND THEOLOGY

Philosophisch-Theologische Hochschule Vallendar
Pallottistrasse 3, 56174 Vallendar
Tel: +49(261) 6402-0
Fax: +49(261) 6402-300
EMail: info@pthv.de
Website: http://www.pthv.de

Rektor: Paul Rheinbay
Tel: +49(261) 6402-233 EMail: prheinbay@pthv.de

Faculties

Nursing (Gerontology; Nursing); **Theology** (Ancient Languages; Catholic Theology; Greek (Classical); Latin; Religion; Religious Education; Theology)

History: Founded 1979.

Main Language(s) of Instruction: German

Degrees and Diplomas: *Diplom*; *Lizentiat*; *Master/Magister*. Nursing; *Promotion*; *Habilitation*

Last Updated: 22/01/10

WEDEL UNIVERSITY OF APPLIED SCIENCES

Fachhochschule Wedel
Feldstrasse 143, 22880 Wedel, Holstein
Tel: +49(4103) 8048-0
Fax: +49(4103) 8048-39
EMail: sekretariat@fh-wedel.de
Website: http://www.fh-wedel.de

Rektor: Dirk Harms (1975-)
Tel: +49(4103) 8048-0 EMail: ha@fh-wedel.de

International Relations: Sabine Baumann, Director, International Office
Tel: +49(4103) 8048-47, Fax: +49(4103) 8048-91047
EMail: bau@fh-wedel.de

Departments

Business Administration (Business Administration); **Business Computing** (Business Computing; Software Engineering); **Business Engineering** (Business Administration; Electronic Engineering; Engineering; Industrial Engineering; Industrial Management; Management; Natural Sciences; Production Engineering; Transport Management); **Computer Science** (Computer Engineering; Computer Science; Software Engineering); **Media Information Science** (Media Studies); **Technical informatics** (Automation and Control Engineering; Computer Science; Electronic Engineering; Information Technology; Software Engineering; Technology)

History: Founded 1969.

Academic Year: October to July (October-January; April-July)

Admission Requirements: Fachhochschulreife or Abitur

Fees: (Euros): c. 800-1,200 per semester

Main Language(s) of Instruction: German

International Co-operation: Participates in Erasmus/Socrates, South Africa

Degrees and Diplomas: *Bachelor/Bakkalaureus*: 3 yrs; *Diplom*: Engineering; *Master/Magister*. Business Administration; Computer Science; Business Engineering, 2 yrs

Student Services: Academic counselling, Canteen, Foreign Studies Centre, Handicapped facilities

Libraries: Main Library

Publications: Auditorium *(annually)*
Last Updated: 06/02/12

WEIHENSTEPHAN TRIESDORF UNIVERSITY OF APPLIED SCIENCES

Hochschule Weihenstephan Triesdorf
Am Hofgarten 4, 85350 Freising
Tel: +49(8161) 71-0
Fax: +49(8161) 71-4207
EMail: info@fh-weihenstephan.de
Website: http://www.hswt.de

Präsident: Hermann Heiler
Tel: +49(8161) 71-3339, Fax: +49(8161) 71-4428
EMail: praesident@fh-weihenstephan.de

Kanzler: Johann Schelle
Tel: +49(8161) 71-3341 EMail: kanzler@fh-weihenstephan.de

International Relations: Michaela Ring, Head, International Office
Tel: + 49(8161) 71-5778, Fax: + 49(8161) 71-2230
EMail: michaela.ring@fh-weihenstephan.de

Departments
Agriculture *(Triesdorf)* (Agriculture; Animal Husbandry; Business Administration; Meat and Poultry; Nutrition); **Biotechnology and Bioinformatics** *(Weihenstephan)* (Biotechnology; Computer Science); **Environmental Engineering** *(Triesdorf)* (Environmental Engineering); **Forestry** *(Weihenstephan)* (Forestry); **Horticulture and Food Technology** *(Weihenstephan)* (Food Technology; Horticulture); **Landscape Architecture** *(Weihenstephan)* (Landscape Architecture)

History: Founded 1804, acquired present status 1971.

Academic Year: October to September (October-March; March-September)

Admission Requirements: Secondary school certificate, six weeks of relevant practical experience, German language test for foreign students

Fees: (Euros): 50 per semester

Main Language(s) of Instruction: German

International Co-operation: With universities in the Dominican Republic, France, Kazakhstan, Mongolia, Poland, Russian Federation, Ukraine. Also participates in Socrates/Erasmus (Belgium, Finland, France, Greece, United Kingdom, Northern Ireland, Ireland, Latvia, Austria, Czech Republic, Romania, Slovakia, Hungary)

Accrediting Agencies: Akkreditierungsagentur ACQUIN

Degrees and Diplomas: *Bachelor/Bakkalaureus*; *Diplom (FH)*: Horticulture; *Master/Magister*: Landscape Architecture; Agricultural Management; Regional Management; Energy Management and Energy Engineering

Student Services: Academic counselling, Canteen, Foreign student adviser, Language programs, Sports facilities

Student Residential Facilities: Yes

Special Facilities: Horticulture Research Station

Libraries: Central Library
Last Updated: 20/01/10

WEIMAR BAUHAUS UNIVERSITY

Bauhaus-Universität Weimar
Geschwister-Scholl-Strasse 8, 99421 Weimar
Tel: +49(3643) 58-0
Fax: +49(3643) 58-1120
EMail: info@uni-weimar.de
Website: http://www.uni-weimar.de

Rektor: Karl Beucke (2011-)
Tel: +49(3643) 58-1112 EMail: rektor@uni-weimar.de

Kanzler: Heiko Schultz
Tel: +49(3643) 58-1212, Fax: +49(3643) 58-1214
EMail: kanzler@uni-weimar.de

International Relations: Bernd Ufer
Tel: +49(3643) 58-2364 EMail: bernd.ufer@uni-weimar.de

Faculties
Architecture (Architecture; Urban Studies); **Art and Design** (Art Education; Fine Arts; Graphic Design; Industrial Design; Visual Arts); **Civil Engineering** (Business Administration; Civil Engineering; Computer Engineering; Computer Science; Construction Engineering; Environmental Studies; Management; Materials Engineering; Real Estate; Structural Architecture; Water Science); **Media** (Computer Science; Cultural Studies; Design; Economics; Film; Fine Arts; Information Management; Media Studies)

Institutes
Bauhaus Further Education Academy *(WBA)* (Construction Engineering; Management; Town Planning); **International Transfer Centre Environmental Technology** *(KNOTEN WEIMAR)* (Construction Engineering; Environmental Engineering); **Materials Research and Testing** *(MFPA)* (Construction Engineering; Environmental Engineering; Geological Engineering; Materials Engineering)

History: Founded 1860 as Academy of Fine Arts, Applied Arts added 1907, became 'Staatliches Bauhaus Weimar' 1919 and college 1926. Applied Arts detached 1950. Reorganized 1954 and granted full University status. Faculty structure replaced under 1968 reform by series of subject sections. Reorganized 1991/92. Under the jurisdiction of the Ministry of Science and Art. Acquired present name 1995.

Academic Year: October to July (October-March; April-July)

Admission Requirements: Secondary school certificate (Reifezeugnis) or equivalent, and German Language test (DSH)

Fees: None

Main Language(s) of Instruction: German

International Co-operation: With universities in Lithuania, Italy, Vietnam, Russian Federation, France, Japan, USA, Australia. Also participates in Socrates/Erasmus programme

Degrees and Diplomas: *Bachelor/Bakkalaureus*: Architecture; Urbanism; Civil Engineering; Media Studies, 6 sem; *Diplom*: Civil Engineering;, 10 sem; *Magister Artium*: Architecture; Archineering; European Urban Studies; Civil Engineering; Media Studies, a further 8 sem; *Doktorgrad*: European Urban Studies; Urban Heritage; *Habilitation*: at least 3 yrs following Doktor

Student Services: Academic counselling, Canteen, Foreign student adviser, Handicapped facilities, Language programs, Social counselling, Sports facilities

Student Residential Facilities: For 1,170 students

Libraries: University Library, c. 330,000 vols

Publications: Thesis.Wissenschaftliche Zeitschrift: Architecture, Engineering Design *(other/irregular)*; Verso (International Architectural Theories); Vorlesungsverzeichnis *(biannually)*; Zeitung 'Bogen' *(other/irregular)*
Last Updated: 30/01/12

WESTCOAST UNIVERSITY OF APPLIED SCIENCES

Fachhochschule Westküste (FHW)
Fritz-Thiedemann-Ring 20, 25746 Heide
Tel: +49(481) 8555-0
Fax: +49(481) 8555-101
EMail: info@fh-westkueste.de
Website: http://www.fh-westkueste.de

Präsident: Hanno Kirsch (2003-)
Tel: +49(481) 8555-105, Fax: +49(481) 8555-101
EMail: kirsch@fh-westkueste.de

Kanzler: Günther Rüdiger
Tel: +49(481) 8555-115 EMail: guenther@fh-westkueste.de

International Relations: Michael Engelbrecht
Tel: +49(481) 8555-120 EMail: aaa@fh-westkueste.de

Departments
Economics (Accountancy; Business Administration; Business Education; Economics; Finance; Human Resources; Law; Management; Marketing; Taxation; Tourism)

Faculties
Engineering (Automation and Control Engineering; Electrical and Electronic Engineering; Information Technology)

GERMANY–Institutions

History: Founded 1994.

Admission Requirements: Fachhochschulreife

Main Language(s) of Instruction: German

International Co-operation: Participates in Erasmus; Leonardo; Iaeste

Degrees and Diplomas: *Bachelor/Bakkalaureus*; *Diplom (FH)*: Electronic and Information Engineering; *Master/Magister*

Student Services: Academic counselling, Canteen, Foreign student adviser, Foreign Studies Centre, Language programs, Social counselling, Sports facilities

Libraries: Yes

Last Updated: 06/02/12

WESTPHALIAN WILHELMS UNIVERSITY MÜNSTER

Westfälische Wilhelms-Universität Münster
Schlossplatz 2, 48149 Münster
Tel: +49(251) 83-0
Fax: +49(251) 832-4831
EMail: rektor@uni-muenster.de
Website: http://www.uni-muenster.de

Rektorin: Ursula Nelles
Tel: +49(251) 832-2211 EMail: Rektorin@uni-muenster.de

Departments
Music

Faculties
Biology (Biology; Biomedicine; Biotechnology); **Chemistry and Pharmacy** (Chemistry; Pharmacy); **Education and Social Studies** (Communication Studies; Education; Political Sciences; Sociology); **Geosciences** (Earth Sciences; Ecology; Geography; Geology; Mineralogy; Paleontology); **History/Philosophy** (History; Philosophy); **Law** (Law); **Mathematics and Computer Science** (Mathematics and Computer Science); **Medicine** (Medicine); **Philologies** (Philology); **Physics** (Physics); **Protestant Theology** (Protestant Theology); **Psychology and Sports Studies** (Psychology; Sports); **Roman Catholic Theology** (Canon Law; Catholic Theology)

Schools
Business and Economics *(Munster)* (Business Administration; Economics)

History: Founded 1780 as a University. Became an Academy of Philosophy and Theology 1818. The institution was restored to University status 1902 and received its present title 1907. An autonomous institution financially supported by the State of North Rhine-Westphalia, and under the jurisdiction of its Ministry of Education.

Governing Bodies: Senat

Academic Year: October to September (October-March; April-September)

Admission Requirements: Secondary school certificate (Reifezeugnis) or equivalent

Fees: Tuition, none

Main Language(s) of Instruction: German

Degrees and Diplomas: *Bachelor/Bakkalaureus*: 2 yrs; *Diplom*: Biology; Business Administration; Education; Geology; Mineralogy; Physics; Psychology, 4 yrs; *Diplom*: Chemistry; Economics; Geography; Mathematics; *Lehramt*: Teaching qualification, secondary level, 3-4 yrs; *Magister Artium*: 8 semesters; *Staatsprüfung*: Law; Dentistry; Food Technology; Medicine; Pharmacy; *Master/Magister*: Law, 1 yr; *Master/Magister*: Sciences, 4 yrs; *Doktorgrad*: 6-10 semesters; *Habilitation*: at least 3 yrs following Doktor. Also degrees in Catholic and Protestant Theology

Student Services: Academic counselling, Canteen, Foreign student adviser, Foreign Studies Centre, Language programs, Social counselling, Sports facilities

Student Residential Facilities: Yes

Special Facilities: Geological Museum; Mineralogy Museum; Archaeological Museum

Libraries: University Library, c. 2.2m. vols; institute and seminar libraries

Publications: Forschungsjournal *(biennially)*

Last Updated: 07/02/12

WILDAU TECHNICAL UNIVERSITY OF APPLIED SCIENCES

Technische Hochschule Wildau
Bahnhofstrasse, 15745 Wildau
Tel: +49(3375) 508-0
Fax: +49(3375) 500-324
EMail: ungvari@wi-bw.tfh-wildau.de
Website: http://www.tfh-wildau.de

Präsident: Lászlo Ungvári (1999-) Tel: +49(3375) 508-101

Kanzlerin: Renate Wilde
Tel: +49(3375) 508-900 EMail: wilde@rkt.tfh-wildau.de

International Relations: Angelika Schubert
Tel: +49(3375) 508-197 EMail: aschub@al.tfh-wildau.de

Faculties
Business Administration/Business Computing (Accountancy; Business Administration; Business Computing; Finance; Management; Marketing); **Business, Administration and Law** (Administration; Business and Commerce; Law); **Engineering/Industrial Engineering** (Aeronautical and Aerospace Engineering; Industrial Engineering; Mechanical Engineering; Physical Engineering; Physics; Technology; Telecommunications Engineering)

History: Founded 1991.

Main Language(s) of Instruction: German

International Co-operation: Socrates/Erasmus, Leonardo, CDG, DAAD

Degrees and Diplomas: *Bachelor/Bakkalaureus*; *Master/Magister*

Student Services: Academic counselling, Canteen, Foreign student adviser, Handicapped facilities, Social counselling, Sports facilities

Publications: Wissenschaftlich Beiträge der TFH Wildau *(biennially)*

Last Updated: 26/01/10

WILHELM BÜCHNER UNIVERSITY OF APPLIED SCIENCE DARMSTADT

Wilhelm Büchner Hochschule - Private Fernhochschule Darmstadt
Ostendstraße 3, 64319 Pfungstadt bei Darmstadt
Tel: +49(6157) 806-404
Fax: +49(6157) 806-401
EMail: info@wb-fernstudium.de
Website: http://www.wb-fernstudium.de

Präsident: Joachim Loeper Tel: +49(6157) 806-401

Kanzler: Thomas Kirchenkamp
Tel: +49(6157) 806-408
EMail: thomas.kirchenkamp@privatfh-da.de

Programmes
Computer Science (Computer Science); **Electronic Engineering**; **Industrial Management** (Industrial Management); **Machine Building** (Machine Building); **Mechatronics** (Electronic Engineering; Mechanical Engineering)

History: Founded 1996. Acquired present status 2001.

Main Language(s) of Instruction: German

Degrees and Diplomas: *Bachelor/Bakkalaureus*; *Master/Magister*: Business Computing

Student Services: Academic counselling, Canteen, Employment services, Social counselling

Last Updated: 03/02/10

WITTEN/HERDECKE UNIVERSITY

Universität Witten/Herdecke
Alfred-Herrhausen-Str.50, 58448 Witten
Tel: +49(2302) 926-0
Fax: +49(2302) 926-407
EMail: public@uni-wh.de
Website: http://www.uni-wh.de

Präsident: Martin Butzlaff
Tel: +49(2302) 926-928, Fax: +49(2302) 926-929
EMail: Martin.Butzlaff@uni-wh.de

Kanzler: Michael Anders EMail: Michael.Anders@uni-wh.de

Faculties

Culture (Cultural Studies; Economics; Philosophy; Political Sciences); **Health** (Alternative Medicine; Dentistry; Medicine; Nursing; Oral Pathology; Pharmacy; Traditional Eastern Medicine); **Management and Economics** (Business Administration; Economics; Management)

Further Information: Also 18 Affiliated Hospitals

History: Founded 1980 as the first private University in the Federal Republic of Germany. Financed by donations and grants stipulated for specific research programmes as well as tuition fees paid by students.

Governing Bodies: Senat; Konzil

Academic Year: April to March (April-July; October-March)

Admission Requirements: Secondary school certificate (Abitur) or work experience according to Faculty

Main Language(s) of Instruction: German (English in Pharmaceutical Medicine)

International Co-operation: Participates in the Erasmus/Socrates programme. Many bi- and trilateral agreements worldwide

Degrees and Diplomas: *Bachelor/Bakkalaureus*: 6 sem; *Diplom*: Dentistry, 11 sem; *Diplom*: Economics and Business Administration, 9 sem; *Diplom*: Medicine, 12 sem; *Diplom*: Music Therapy, 4 sem following completed Music Education; *Master/Magister*: 3 sem; *Promotion*: All fields

Student Services: Academic counselling, Canteen, Cultural centre, Foreign student adviser, Foreign Studies Centre, Handicapped facilities, Language programs, Nursery care, Social counselling

Student Residential Facilities: Yes

Libraries: c. 100,000 vols

Publications: Perspektiven *(biannually)*

Press or Publishing House: Universität Witten/Herdecke Verlagsgesellschaft mbH
Last Updated: 06/02/12

WORMS UNIVERSITY OF APPLIED SCIENCES
Fachhochschule Worms (UAS)
Erenburger Strasse 19, 67549 Worms
Tel: +49(6241) 509-0
Fax: +49(6241) 509-281
EMail: studiens@fh-worms.de
Website: http://www.fh-worms.de

Präsident: Jens Hermsdorf (2009-)
EMail: praesident@fh-worms.de

Kanzlerin: Erika Rudel EMail: kanzlerin@fh-worms.de

International Relations: Anette Mayer-Möbius, Head of International Relations EMail: moebius@fh-worms.de

Faculties
Computer Science (Business Computing; Computer Science); **Economics** (Business Administration; International Business; Management; Taxation; Transport Management); **Tourism and Travel Management** (Management; Tourism)

History: Created 1977 as Division Ludwigshafen/Worms of the University of Applied Sciences Rhineland-Palatinate from former Teacher Training College of Worms. Acquired current title and status 1996.

Academic Year: March to September

Admission Requirements: Secondary school certificate.

Fees: None

Main Language(s) of Instruction: German; English

International Co-operation: With institutions in United Kingdom; France; Spain; Scandinavia; Latin America; USA; Italy

Degrees and Diplomas: *Bachelor/Bakkalaureus*: International Business Administration; International Management; Distribution Management; Tourism Management; Business Information Science; Informatics; Communication Informatics, 3 yrs; *Diplom (FH)*: Taxation, 4 yrs; *Master/Magister*: International Management; Tourism Management; Business Information Science; International Business Administration, 2 yrs

Student Services: Academic counselling, Canteen, Cultural centre, Employment services, Foreign student adviser, Foreign Studies Centre, Handicapped facilities, Language programs, Social counselling, Sports facilities

Student Residential Facilities: For c. 160 students

Libraries: Yes

Academic Staff 2008-2009	MEN	WOMEN	TOTAL
FULL-TIME	30	61	91
STAFF WITH DOCTORATE			
FULL-TIME	50	10	60
Student Numbers 2008-2009			
All (Foreign Included)	1,271	1,442	2,713
FOREIGN ONLY	302	336	638

Distance students, 5.
Last Updated: 06/02/12

WÜRZBURG-SCHWEINFURT UNIVERSITY OF APPLIED SCIENCES
Fachhochschule Würzburg-Schweinfurt
Münzstrasse 12, 97070 Würzburg
Tel: +49(931) 3511-0
Fax: +49(931) 3511-159
EMail: p-amt@mail.fh-wuerzburg.de
Website: http://www.fh-wuerzburg.de

Präsident: Heribert Weber (2000-)
Tel: +49(931) 3511-102, Fax: +49(931) 3511-133
EMail: praesident@fh-wuerzburg.de

Kanzlerin: Andra Wunder
Tel: +49(931) 3511-104, Fax: +49(931) 3511-334
EMail: kanzlerin@fh-wuerzburg.de

International Relations: Thomas Schmitt
Tel: +49(931) 3511-172, Fax: +49(931) 3511-326
EMail: schmitt@fh-wuerzburg.de

Faculties
Architecture and Civil Engineering (Architecture; Civil Engineering); **Business Administration** (Business Administration; Management; Media Studies); **Computer Science and Business Computing** (Business Computing; Computer Science; Information Technology); **Electrical Engineering** *(Schweinfurt)* (Electrical Engineering); **General Sciences** (Natural Sciences); **Industrial Engineering** *(Schweinfurt)* (Industrial Engineering); **Mechanical Engineering** *(Schweinfurt)*; **Social Work and Health Care Management**

History: Founded 1971.

Main Language(s) of Instruction: German

Degrees and Diplomas: *Bachelor/Bakkalaureus*; *Diplom (FH)*; *Master/Magister*
Last Updated: 06/02/12

ZEPPELIN UNIVERSITY, FRIEDRICHSHAFEN
Am Seemooser Horn 20, Friedrichshafen
EMail: gary.anderson@zeppelin-university.de
Website: http://www.zeppelin-university.de

Präsident: Stephan A. Jansen
EMail: manuela.haug@zeppelin-university.de

Institutes
Communication and Cultural Management (Communication Studies; Cultural Studies; Management; Media Studies); **Corporate Management and Economics**; **Public Management and Governance**

Fees: (Euros): 3,700 per semester

Main Language(s) of Instruction: German and English

Degrees and Diplomas: *Bachelor/Bakkalaureus*; *Master/Magister*
Last Updated: 03/02/10

ZITTAU/GÖRLICH UNIVERSITY OF APPLIED SCIENCES

Hochschule Zittau/Görlitz (FH)
Theodor-Körner-Allee 16, 02754 Zittau
Tel: +49(3583) 61-0
Fax: +49(3583) 510626
EMail: info@hs-zigr.de
Website: http://www.hs-zigr.de

Rektor: Friedrich Albrecht
Tel: +49(3583) 61-1401, Fax: +49(3583) 61-1402
EMail: rektor@hs-zigr.de
Kanzlerin: Karin Hollstein
Tel: +49(3583) 61-1405 EMail: kanzler@hs-zigr.de
International Relations: Stefan Kühne, Head, International Office
Tel: +49(3583) 61-1511 EMail: s.kuehne@hs-zigr.de

Departments
Computer Science (Computer Science); **Construction** (Architecture; Civil Engineering; Construction Engineering); **Economics** (Business Computing; Economics; Finance; Marketing); **Electrical Engineering and Information Management** (Electrical Engineering; Information Management); **Languages** (Czech; English; French; Polish; Russian; Spanish); **Mathematics and Natural Sciences** (Biotechnology; Chemistry; Ecology; Mathematics); **Mechanical Engineering** (Energy Engineering; Heating and Refrigeration; Machine Building; Mechanical Engineering); **Social Studies** (Social Studies; Social Work)

History: Founded 1992.

Main Language(s) of Instruction: German

Degrees and Diplomas: *Bachelor/Bakkalaureus*; *Master/Magister*
Last Updated: 23/03/11

Ghana

STRUCTURE OF HIGHER EDUCATION SYSTEM

Description:

The system of higher education includes universities and university colleges; professional institutes and pre-service training institutes. All public higher education institutions are under the responsibility of the National Council for Tertiary Education which is an advisory and coordinating body. The Council is headed by the Minister of Education. Each higher institution has its own Council and its Academic Board or their equivalents.

Stages of studies:

University level first stage: *First degree*
The first degree is conferred after three to six years of study depending on the subject. Some universities also offer two-year diploma programmes.

University level second stage: *Second degree*
These degrees are open to graduates who hold the Bachelor's degree of approved universities. Graduate Diploma courses last for two semesters' full-time or four semesters' part-time study. Primary Master's and Master of Philosophy courses last for one to two years. At least two semesters must be spent studying in the University. Candidates are awarded the Graduate Diploma, Master's or Master of Philosophy degree. The one-year course involves course work and a dissertation. For the MPhil degree, two years of study, including a year of course work, are required, followed by research work leading to a thesis. It is possible to transfer to MPhil and PhD courses from the one-year Master's.

University level third stage: *Doctorate*
The Doctorate Degree is open to graduates of approved universities who hold Master's or Master of Philosophy Degrees. Candidates must spend the first two years at the university. If the candidate has taken the Master's degree in the same university, this period is one year. Thereafter, subject to approval by the Board of Graduate Studies, candidates may pursue their studies outside the university. Doctorate courses (PhD) are completed by research. Candidates are awarded the Doctorate Degree at the end of three years' study and presentation and defence of a thesis. The DPhil is also entirely by research and is awarded on consideration of published works of academic merit, the standard being no less than that of a PhD. Only graduates from universities with 10 years standing are eligible. The Doctor of Medicine (MD degree) covers the medical specialities only. Conditions for the award of the MD are the same as for the D.Phil.
The degrees of LLD, DCL, DLitt and DSc may only be conferred honoris causa.

Distance higher education:
The Ghana National Tertiary Level Distance Education Programme opens up access to higher education; provides an alternative, off-campus channel for tertiary education for qualified people; provides a complementary avenue to higher forms of education provided by the traditional, residential universities; provides an opportunity to those who have the requisite qualifications but have been prevented from having access to tertiary education by various circumstances; and makes the acquisition of a degree more flexible, especially for older adults (such as graduates who want to shift to new areas of studies and lifelong learners). Universities in Ghana offer some of their courses to students outside their walls. Such off-campus students study the same courses and take the same examinations as those in on-campus programmes and are awarded the same degrees when they pass their final examinations. The programme adopts a multi-media approach but the main medium for teaching is self-instructional printed materials sent to students for study. Student assessment is continuous and based on assignments and final examinations.

ADMISSION TO HIGHER EDUCATION

Admission to university-level studies:

Name of secondary school credential required: West African Senior School Certificate Examination

For entry to: Minimum aggregate of 24 at the WASSCE with credit passes in core English, core Mathematics, core Integrated Science and any three electives.

Foreign students admission:

Definition of foreign student: Any student who is not a Ghanaian.

Entrance exam requirements: Foreign students should have good GCE "O" level passes (or their equivalent) in English language and four other subjects plus three "A" level passes (required subjects vary according to degree course).

Entry regulations: Foreign students with the exception of ECOWAS citizens need visas to enter Ghana. All foreign students, including ECOWAS citizens, are required to secure resident permits for the period of their study. Foreign students are required to pay their fees in convertible currency to be drawn on an American or British bank.

Health requirements: Health certificate required.

Language requirements: Good knowledge of English required for all regular university courses. English-language proficiency courses are offered as well as general guidance programmes for all freshmen.

RECOGNITION OF STUDIES

Quality assurance system:

Once the higher institutions by which the credentials are awarded are recognized by the country, the credentials are also recognized. Transfer and recognition of studies and degrees exist between institutions of a similar type, i.e. university with university. The National Accreditation Board (NAB) reviews programmes.

Special provisions for recognition:

Recognition for university level studies: Foreign credentials in the form of certificates should be sent to the Academic Registrar of the University. This applies to both nationals with foreign credentials and foreigners.

For access to advanced studies and research: Foreign credentials in the form of certificates, transcripts and Referee's report of two or three people should be sent to the office of the Dean of Graduate Studies of the University. This applies to both nationals and foreigners.

For exercising a profession: Access to the professions is subject to the recognition of credentials by the professional associations and to passing professional qualifying examinations. Foreign credentials should be sent to the Board or Institute of the individual professions. In addition, candidates should pass the professional examination conducted by the professional body.

NATIONAL BODIES

Ministry of Education
  Minister: Betty Mould-Iddrisu
  PO Box M45
  Accra
  Tel: +233(21) 662 772
  Fax: +233(21) 664 067
  EMail: info@moess.gov.gh
  WWW: http://www.ghana.gov.gh/index.php?option=com_content&view=article&id=331:ministry-of-education&catid
  Role of national body: Authority responsible for policy formulation, the administration and financing of education at the national level.

National Council for Tertiary Education - NCTE
  Executive Secretary: Paul Effah
  PO Box MB 28
  Accra
  Tel: +233(21) 770 194 +233(21) 770 198
  Fax: +233(21) 770 194
  EMail: ncte@ug.edu.gh
  WWW: http://www.ncte-ghana.org/
  Role of national body: State agency responsible for higher education policy, planning and management.

National Accreditation Board - NAB

Chairman: D. A. Akyeampong
Executive Secretary: Kwame Dattey
6 Bamako Street
East Legon
P. O. Box CT 3256
Accra
Tel: +233(30) 251-8570 +233(30) 294-6013 +233 (28) 910-2710 +233_
Fax: +233(21) 518 629
EMail: nabsec@nab.gov.gh
WWW: http://www.nab.gov.gh/
Role of national body: Accredits both public and private higher education institutions' programmes and determines the equivalences of diplomas, certificates and other qualifications awarded by institutions in Ghana or elsewhere.

National Board for Professional and Technician Examinations - NABPTEX

Chairperson: Mariam Ewurama Addy
Executive Secretary: Benjamin Antwi-Bosiako
22/8 Abafum Crescent
PO Box SD 109
Stadium
Accra
Tel: +233(21) 760 728
Fax: +233(21) 672 462
EMail: info@nabptex.org
Role of national body: Ghana's National Examination Administering Body for Professional Bodies and all Non-University Institutions at the Tertiary Level.

Vice Chancellors Ghana - VCG

Executive Secretary: Peter A. Kaba
P.O.Box LG 25
Legon
Accra
Tel: +233(21) 512 415
Fax: +233(21) 512 409

Data for academic year: 2007-2008
Source: IAU from Ministry of Education, Science and Sports, Ghana, 2007. Bodies updated in 2011.

INSTITUTIONS

PUBLIC INSTITUTIONS

GHANA INSTITUTE OF MANAGEMENT AND PUBLIC ADMINISTRATION (GIMPA)

PO Box AH 50, Achimota, Accra
Tel: +233(21) 401-681/2/3 +233(21) 412337
Fax: +233(21) 405-805
EMail: info@gimpa.edu.gh
Website: http://www.gimpa.edu.gh/

Rector: Yaw Agyeman Badu
Tel: +233(21) 405-801 EMail: ybadu@gimpa.edu.gh

Centres
Distance Learning; Policy Studies (Political Sciences)

Colleges
Civil and Public Service (Management; Public Administration)

Divisions
Consultancy Services (Management)

Schools
Business *(Greenhill College (Undergraduate Programmes and Graduate School)*; Leadership and Public Management *(Undergraduate and Graduate Programmes)* (Leadership; Management; Public Administration); Technology *(Undergraduate and Graduate Programmes)*

History: Founded 1961 as a joint Ghana government/United Nations special Fund Project. Relocated in Legon 1966. Acquired present title and status 1969.

Governing Bodies: Council; Management Board; Academic Board
Academic Year: September to August

Fees: Vary according to Programmes

Main Language(s) of Instruction: English

International Co-operation: With universities in UK; USA; Netherlands and Malaysia

Accrediting Agencies: National Accreditation Board (NAB), Ghana

Degrees and Diplomas: *Certificate*: Administration and Management; NGO Management; Urban Management; *Diploma*: Administration and Management; NGO Management; Urban Management; *Bachelor's Degree*: Accounting; Banking; Business Administration; Economics; Entrepreneurship; Finance; Hospitality Management; Human Resources Management; Information and Communication Technology; Insurance; Marketing; Operations and Projet Management; Public Administration; *Master's Degree*: Business Administration; Public Administration; Governance and Leadership; Management (Development and Public Sector); *Doctorate (PhD)*. Also Postgraduate Certificate and Diploma. Master's Degree Programmes both Executive and Regular (equivalent to M.Phil). Competency-based short courses, and In-plant courses.

Student Services: Canteen, Health services, Sports facilities

Student Residential Facilities: Executive Hostel with 118 self-contained rooms and 13 suites

Special Facilities: Auditorium; Video Conference facility

Libraries: c. 40,000 vols (hard copy books); E-library

Publications: GIMPA Journal of Leadership, Management and Public Administration *(biannually)*; GIMPA Occasional Papers, Research Publications from Faculty and other Academics *(annually)*

Press or Publishing House: GIMPA Press
Last Updated: 21/04/09

INSTITUTE OF PROFESSIONAL STUDIES (IPS)

PO Box LG 149, Legon, Greater Accra
Tel: +233(21) 500171 +233(21) 500722
Fax: +233(21) 513539
EMail: info@ips.edu.gh; admin@ips.edu.gh
Website: http://www.ips.edu.gh

Rector: Joshua Alabi (2009-)
Tel: +233(28) 910-6786, Fax: +233(21) 513-503
EMail: alabij@ips.edu.gh

Registrar: Seidu Mustapha
Tel: +233(21) 500-725, Fax: +233(21) 513-539
EMail: mmustapha@ips.edu.gh

International Relations: Arkoful Helen, Dean
Tel: +233(24) 253-5747, Fax: +233(21) 513-539
EMail: harkoful@ips.edu.gh; kwansema62@yahoo.com

Faculties
Accounting (Accountancy; Banking; Finance); **Communication Studies** (Communication Studies; Information Technology; Public Relations); **Management** (Business Administration; Management; Marketing)

Schools
Research and Graduate Studies (Accountancy; Banking; Business Administration; Finance; Management; Marketing; Public Relations)

History: Created 1965 with the mandate to provide tertiary and professional business education in accountancy and management. Acquired current status 2008. Previously affiliated to the University of Ghana, now awards its own degrees.

Governing Bodies: Governing Council

Academic Year: August to December; January to May

Admission Requirements: Senior Secondary School Certificate Examination (SSSCE)/West African Senior School Examination (WASSCE) of the West African Examinations Council with Passes in English Language (Core), Mathematics (Core), Integrated Science (Core) and any other three subjects with an aggregate score of 24 or better.

Fees: (Cedi): Undergraduate, 1,265 per annum; postgraduate, 3,950 per annum.

Main Language(s) of Instruction: English

Accrediting Agencies: National Accreditation Board

Degrees and Diplomas: *Diploma*: Business Administration (Dip), 2 yrs; *Bachelor's Degree*: Accounting; Banking and Finance; Business Administration; Marketing (BSc), 4 yrs; *Master's Degree*: Marketing; Corporate Governance; Accounting; Auditing; Global Leadership (MBA), 2 yrs. Also Professional Programmes

Student Services: Academic counselling, Canteen, Foreign student adviser, Foreign Studies Centre, Health services, Social counselling, Sports facilities

Student Residential Facilities: None

Libraries: 9,626 vols; 18 periodical subscriptions

Publications: Journal of Business Research, Related to Business Management; Accounting; Banking; Finance; Marketing; Economies *(biannually)*

Press or Publishing House: INSTI (CSIR) Ghana

Academic Staff 2010-2011	MEN	WOMEN	TOTAL
FULL-TIME	54	19	73
PART-TIME	29	11	40
STAFF WITH DOCTORATE			
FULL-TIME	4	1	5
PART-TIME	2	–	2
Student Numbers 2010-2011			
All (Foreign Included)	4,191	3,010	7,201
FOREIGN ONLY	12	15	27

Part-time students, 1,961. Evening students, 2,543.
Last Updated: 26/03/12

KWAME NKRUMAH UNIVERSITY OF SCIENCE AND TECHNOLOGY, KUMASI (KNUST)

Private Mail Bag, University Post Office, Kumasi
Tel: +233(3220) 60334
Fax: +233(3220) 60137
EMail: info@knust.edu.gh; vc@knust.edu.gh
Website: http://www.knust.edu.gh

Vice-Chancellor: William Otoo Ellis (2010-)
EMail: vc@knust.edu.gh; elliswo@yahoo.com

Registrar: Kobby Yebo-Okrah
Tel: +233(51) 60331, Fax: +233(51) 60137
EMail: registrar@knust.edu.gh

International Relations: Kwasi Obiri Danso, Dean, International Programmes Officer
Tel: +233(3220) 63944 EMail: ipo@knust.edu.gh

Colleges
Agriculture and Natural Resources (Agricultural Business; Agricultural Economics; Agriculture; Animal Husbandry; Cattle Breeding; Crop Production; Dairy; Fishery; Forest Management; Forest Products; Forestry; Horticulture; Rural Planning; Soil Science; Water Management; Wildlife; Wood Technology; Zoology); **Architecture and Planning** (Architecture; Architecture and Planning); **Art and Social Sciences** (African Studies; Commercial Law; Cultural Studies; Design; Economics; English; Fine Arts; Industrial Design; Industrial Management; Modern Languages; Painting and Drawing; Private Law; Public Law; Publishing and Book Trade; Sculpture; Social Studies); **Engineering** (Aeronautical and Aerospace Engineering; Agricultural Engineering; Chemical Engineering; Civil Engineering; Computer Engineering; Electrical Engineering; Energy Engineering; Engineering; Geological Engineering; Materials Engineering; Mechanical Engineering; Petroleum and Gas Engineering; Technology); **Health Sciences** (Biology; Dentistry; Health Administration; Health Education; Health Sciences; Medicine; Pharmacology; Pharmacy; Veterinary Science); **Science** (Biochemistry; Biotechnology; Chemistry; Computer Science; Distance Education; Environmental Studies; Food Science; Food Technology; Information Technology; Mathematics; Mathematics and Computer Science; Natural Sciences; Ophthalmology; Optometry; Physics; Technology)

Further Information: Also 10 research centres

History: Founded 1951 as Kumasi College of Technology, acquired present status and title 1998.

Governing Bodies: University Council

Academic Year: September to June (September-January; March-June)

Admission Requirements: General Certificate of Education (GCE), Ordinary ('O') level, with 5 credits, including English, and General Certificate of Education Advanced ('A') level, with 2 passes. Senior Secondary School Certificate (SSCE) with passes in core English and Mathematics and three elective subjects relevant to chosen programme with a total aggregate of 24

Fees: (Cedi): Foreign students, undergraduate, 14m.-26m. per annum; postgraduate, 16m.-28m.

Main Language(s) of Instruction: English

Degrees and Diplomas: *Bachelor's Degree*: 4 yrs; *Master's Degree*: a further 2 yrs; *Master of Philosophy*; *Doctorate*: 3 yrs following Master

Student Services: Academic counselling, Canteen, Cultural centre, Health services, Nursery care, Sports facilities

Special Facilities: Botanical Garden

Libraries: Central Library, 270,562 vols; 750 periodicals. Special collections

Publications: Journal of the University of Science and Technology *(3 per annum)*

Press or Publishing House: University Printing Press. Design Press (College of Art)

Academic Staff *2008-2009*	TOTAL
FULL-TIME	775
PART-TIME	50

Student Numbers *2010-2011*	
All (Foreign Included)	28,964

Last Updated: 09/03/11

REGIONAL MARITIME UNIVERSITY (RMU)

Nungua, P.O. GP 1115, Accra
Tel: +233-21-714070 +233-21-712343
Fax: +233-21-712047
EMail: registrar@rmu.edu.gh
Website: http://www.rmu.edu.gh

Rector: Aaron O. Turkson EMail: rector@rmu.edu.gh

Departments
Electrical & Electronic Engineering (Electrical and Electronic Engineering) *Head*: Isaac Mettle; **Industrial Communication Engineering** (Computer Engineering; Industrial Engineering; Telecommunications Engineering) *Head*: Francis Omani; **Marine Engineering** *Head*: Hubert Abusah; **Maritime Safety** (Safety Engineering) *Head*: Hannah Aggrey; **Nautical Studies** (Nautical Science) *Head*: Catherine Haizel; **Ports and Shipping** (Marine Transport; Transport Management) *Head*: Joana Botchway

Further Information: Also Professional/Upgrading and Short Courses.

History: Founded 1982 as Regional Maritime Academy (RMA) comprising five West African States (Cameroon, Gambia, Ghana, Liberia and Sierra Leone). It is a branch of the World Maritime University, Malmo Sweden, also affiliated of the University of Ghana, Legon. Acquired present status 2007.

Governing Bodies: Board of Governors which comprises the ministers of maritime affairs of the respective founding members (Cameroon, The Gambia, Ghana, Liberia and Sierra Leone), the Secretary-General of MOWCA, the Rector of the University, Staff and Students' representation

Academic Year: August to June

Admission Requirements: West African School Certificate Examination; General Certificate of Education 'O' & 'A' levels; International Baccalaureate

Fees: (US Dollars): 1st semester fee: 1,360 for member states students; 2,251 for non member states students, depending on Departments

Main Language(s) of Instruction: English

International Co-operation: With universities in UK (Liverpool John Moore University), Malaysia (SMTC) and Ghana (University of Ghana)

Accrediting Agencies: National Accreditation Boards of Ghana, The Gambia and Liberia

Degrees and Diplomas: *Diploma*: Ports and Shipping Administration (DIP), 4 yrs; *Bachelor's Degree*: Nautical Science; Marine Engineering; Ports and Shipping Administration; Electrical & Electronic Engineering, 4 yrs; *Master's Degree*: Ports and Shipping Administration. The Master of Arts in Ports and Shipping Administration is organized in collaboration with the School of Research and Graduate Studies, University of Ghana

Student Services: Academic counselling, Canteen, Employment services, Foreign student adviser, Health services, Language programs, Social counselling, Sports facilities

Student Residential Facilities: Yes

Special Facilities: Planetarium; laboratories

Libraries: 16,000 vols. Electronic Library

Academic Staff *2008-2009*	MEN	WOMEN	TOTAL
FULL-TIME	41	8	49
PART-TIME	26	2	28
STAFF WITH DOCTORATE			
FULL-TIME	2	–	2
PART-TIME	3	–	3

Student Numbers *2008-2009*			
All (Foreign Included)	1,006	111	1,117
FOREIGN ONLY	288	23	311

Last Updated: 20/07/09

UNIVERSITY FOR DEVELOPMENT STUDIES (UDS)

PO Box TL 1350, Tamale
Tel: +233(71) 22078 +233(71) 26633 +233(71) 26634
Fax: +233(71) 23957 +233(71) 22078
EMail: kuuire2005gh@yahoo.com
Website: http://www.uds.edu.gh

Vice-Chancellor: Haruna Yakubu
Tel: +233(71) 22369, Fax: +233(71) 22080

Pro-Vice Chancellor: David Millar
Tel: +233(71) 23617, Fax: +233(71) 23617
EMail: cecik@africaonline.com.gh

International Relations: George Debrie, Assistant Registrar
Tel: +233(71) 22,078; +233(71) 26633, Fax: +233(71) 23957
EMail: gkdebrie@yahoo.com

Faculties
Agriculture *(Nyankpala)* (Agriculture; Agronomy; Animal Husbandry; Environmental Studies; Horticulture; Irrigation; Natural Resources; Rural Planning); **Applied Sciences** *(Navrongo)* (Biochemistry; Biological and Life Sciences; Botany; Chemistry; Computer Science; Mathematics; Physical Engineering); **Integrated Development Studies** *(Wa)* (Development Studies; Economics; History; Management; Political Sciences; Social Studies); **Planning and Land Management** (Accountancy; Business Administration; Economics; Geography; Rural Planning); **Renewable Natural Resources** (Aquaculture; Ecology; Environmental Studies; Fishery; Forestry; Natural Resources; Tourism; Wildlife)

Schools
Graduate Studies *(Navrongo)*; **Medicine and Health Sciences** (Community Health; Health Sciences; Medicine; Nutrition)

History: Founded 1992. First students admitted September 1993.

Governing Bodies: University Council

Academic Year: September to July (September-December; January-April; May-July)

Admission Requirements: Senior Secondary School Certificate; State Registered Nurses Certificate; Higher National Diploma/ Diploma holders; West Africa Senior Secondary School Certificate; Mature Applicants and Entrance examination

Fees: (Cedi): Tuition, 318,50-688.50 per annum

Main Language(s) of Instruction: English

International Co-operation: With universities in Canada; Uganda; South Africa; USA; Netherlands; Germany; Norway; United Kingdom

Accrediting Agencies: National Accreditation Board; Ghana Medical and Dental Council; Nurses and Midwives Council of Ghana

Degrees and Diplomas: *Bachelor's Degree*: Agriculture; Applied Sciences (BSc); Arts (BA); Community Nutrition (BSc (Com.Nut)); Nursing; Planning and Land Management; Renewable Natural Resources, 4 yrs; *Bachelor of Medicine and Surgery*: Medicine, 6 yrs; *Master of Philosophy*: Development Studies, 4 yrs (sandwich)

Student Services: Academic counselling, Canteen, Health services, Language programs, Social counselling, Sports facilities

Student Residential Facilities: Yes

Special Facilities: French Language Centre; Centre for Continuing Education and Interdisciplinary Research; UDS International Conference Centre

Libraries: 31,906 vols

Publications: Ghana Journal of Development Studies *(1-2 per annum)*

Academic Staff 2008-2009	MEN	WOMEN	TOTAL
FULL-TIME	257	14	271
STAFF WITH DOCTORATE FULL-TIME	62	12	74
Student Numbers 2008-2009			
All (Foreign Included)	7,799	2,788	10,587

Last Updated: 09/03/11

UNIVERSITY OF CAPE COAST (UCC)

University Post Office, Cape Coast
Tel: +233(42) 32139 +233(42) 32480
Fax: +233(42) 32484 +233(42) 32485
EMail: ucclib@ucc.gh.apc.org; csucc@ghana.com
Website: http://www.ucc.edu.gh/

Vice-Chancellor: Jane Naana Opoku-Agyemang
Tel: +233(42) 32378 +233(42) 32050, Fax: +233(42) 32485
EMail: vc@ucc.edu.gh

Pro-Vice-Chancellor: Haruna Yakubu
Tel: +233(42) 32489 EMail: yakubuh@ucc.edu.gh

International Relations: Kwadwo Opoku-Agyemang, Director (Acting)
Tel: +233(42) 33807, Fax: +233(42) 33304
EMail: kopokuagyemang@hotmail.com; uccoip@ghana.com

Centres
African Virtual University *(AVU)* (Computer Education); **Computer** (Computer Science); **Continuing Education** *(CCE)*; **Development Studies** *(CDS)* (Development Studies; Economics; Environmental Studies; Rural Planning; Social Studies; Town Planning); **Laser and Fibre Optics** *(LAFOC)* (Laser Engineering; Optics); **Research on Improving Quality of Primary Education in Ghana** *(CRIQPEG)* (Educational Research; Primary Education)

Faculties
Arts (African Languages; African Studies; Arts and Humanities; Classical Languages; Communication Studies; English; French; History; Modern Languages; Music; Native Language; Philosophy; Religion; Religious Studies; Theatre) *Dean*: D.D. Kuupole; **Education** (Continuing Education; Education; Educational Administration; Educational Sciences; Health Sciences; Humanities and Social Science Education; Mathematics Education; Parks and Recreation; Physical Education; Primary Education; Science Education; Social Sciences; Technology Education; Vocational Education) *Dean*: J.A. Opare; **Graduate Studies** (Higher Education) *Dean*: Albert A. Addo-Quaye; **Social Sciences** (Business Administration; Development Studies; Economics; Family Studies; Geography (Human); Social Sciences; Sociology; Tourism) *Dean*: E.M.S. Prah

Institutes
Education (Education) *Director*: A.K. Akyempong; **Educational Planning and Administration** *(IEPA)* (Educational Administration; Educational Research) *Director*: A.L. Dare

Schools
Agriculture (Agricultural Economics; Agricultural Engineering; Agriculture; Animal Husbandry; Crop Production; Meat and Poultry; Soil Science; Zoology) *Dean*: J.A. Kwarteng; **Biological Sciences** (Biochemistry; Biological and Life Sciences; Biology; Biotechnology; Entomology; Environmental Studies; Fishery; Molecular Biology; Nursing; Wildlife) *Dean*: Sam Yeboah; **Business** *Dean*: Edward

Marfo-Yiadom; **Medical Sciences** (Medicine) *Dean*: H.S. Amonoo-Kuofi; **Physical Sciences** *Dean*: S. Yeboah Mensah

History: Founded 1962 as University College of Cape Coast, acquired present status and title 1971.

Governing Bodies: University Council

Academic Year: October to July (October-February; March-July)

Admission Requirements: General Certificate of Education/advanced level or recognized foreign equivalent, or senior secondary school certificate and entrance examination

Fees: (US Dollars): Foreign Students, 600-1,500 per semester

Main Language(s) of Instruction: English

International Co-operation: With universities in USA; United Kingdom; Sweden; Nigeria; Italy; South Africa; Netherlands

Degrees and Diplomas: *Diploma*: Basic Education; Computer Science (Distance); Health Science Education, 2 yrs; *Diploma*: Basic Education (Distance); Business Studies (Distance), 3 yrs; *Bachelor's Degree*: Agriculture (BSc); Arts (BA); Education (BEd); Science (BSc); Social Sciences, 4 yrs; *Bachelor's Degree*: Nursing, 5 yrs; *Graduate Diploma*: Education (PGDE), 1 yr; *Master's Degree*: Arts (MA), 1 yr; *Master's Degree*: Education (MEd), 1-2 yrs; *Master's Degree*: Management (MBA); *Master's Degree*: Philosophy; Science (MSc), 2 yrs; *Doctorate*: Science (PhD); Social Sciences (PhD), 3 yrs. Also Post Diploma (2-3 yrs following Bachelor's Degree) in Agriculture, Arts, Education, Science and Social Sciences

Student Services: Academic counselling, Canteen, Cultural centre, Employment services, Handicapped facilities, Health services, Language programs, Nursery care, Social counselling, Sports facilities

Student Residential Facilities: For 11,545 students

Special Facilities: Botanical Garden. Technology Village (UCC Farm)

Libraries: Main Library, 212,000 vols

Press or Publishing House: University Printing Press
Last Updated: 30/03/09

UNIVERSITY OF EDUCATION, WINNEBA (UEW)

PO Box 25, Winneba
Tel: +233(432) 22139 +233(432) 22140
Fax: +233(432) 20954
EMail: vc@uew.edu.gh; registrar@uew.edu.gh
Website: http://www.uew.edu.gh

Vice-Chancellor: Akwasi Asabere-Ameyaw Tel: +233(432) 22361

Registrar: C.Y. Akwaa-Mensah
Tel: +233(432) 22269 EMail: cymensah@uew.edu.gh

International Relations: François Joppa

Centres
Educational Policy Studies (Educational Sciences); **Educational Resources** *Co-ordinator*: R.A. Kesson; **School and Community Science and Technology Studies** *(SACOST)* (Educational Sciences; Educational Technology; Social and Community Services)

Colleges
Agriculture Education *(Mampong Ashanti)* (Agriculture); **Technology Education** *(Kumasi)* (Technology)

Faculties
Business Education (Business Education; Management); **Languages** (African Languages; Communication Studies; English; French; Modern Languages); **Science** (Health Sciences; Home Economics; Leisure Studies; Mathematics; Natural Sciences; Physical Education; Science Education; Sports); **Social Sciences** (African Studies; Human Rights; Social Sciences; Social Studies); **Technology Education** (Information Technology; Technology)

Institutes
Educational Development and Extension *(Distance and continuing education)* (Continuing Education; Distance Education)

Schools
Creative Arts (Art Education; Cultural Studies; Music Education); **Research and Graduate Studies**

Further Information: Also campuses in Kumasi and Mampong

History: Founded 1992, merging seven diploma-awarding colleges.

Academic Year: August-May (August-December; January-May)

Admission Requirements: Undergraduate: Senior Certificate with passes in 6 subjects (3 core subjects: English language, Mathematics and Integrated Science and 3 electives in relevant subject areas). Mature applicants: mnimum age 25 years old by 1st September of the academic year; Teachers' certificate 'A' or SHS certificate or professional Training from a recognized institution; Entrance examination. Diploma holders: interview. GCE with 5 credits 'O' levels and 2 'a' level passes other than General Paper

Fees: (Cedi): Tuition, 730 per annum (Science); 690,4 per annum (Humanities) per annum. Foreign students: 4,446 (US Dollars).

Main Language(s) of Instruction: English

Degrees and Diplomas: *Certificate*: Education, 1 yr; *Diploma*: 1 1/ 2-3 yrs; *Bachelor's Degree*: Education (BEd), 4 yrs; *Master's Degree*: Education; Arts and Humanities; Science (M.Ed./M.A.), 1 yr (two sandwich sessions); *Master of Philosophy*: Education; Humanities; Science (Mphil), 2 yrs; *Doctorate*: Humanities; Science (Ph.D.), 3 yrs

Student Services: Canteen, Handicapped facilities, Health services, Social counselling, Sports facilities

Libraries: Osagyefo Library; North campus Library; Kumasi Campus Library; Mampong Campus Library, 100,000 vols; 2,000 periodicals

Publications: Journal of Special Education

Academic Staff *2008-2009*	MEN	WOMEN	TOTAL
FULL-TIME	321	68	389
Student Numbers *2008-2009*			
All (Foreign Included)	10,819	5,504	16,323

Last Updated: 07/05/09

UNIVERSITY OF GHANA (UG)

PO Box 25, Legon, Accra
Tel: +233(21) 500-383
Fax: +233(21) 502-701
EMail: pad@ug.edu.gh
Website: http://www.ug.edu.gh

Vice-Chancellor: Ernest Aryeetey (2010-)
Tel: +233(21) 501-967, Fax: +233(21) 502-701
EMail: vcoffice@ug.edu.gh

Registrar: Joseph Maafo Budu
Tel: +233(21) 500-383 EMail: registrar@ug.edu.gh

International Relations: Naa Ayikailey Adamafio, Dean, International Programmes
Tel: +233(21) 507-147, Fax: +233(21) 507-147
EMail: inep@ug.edu.gh; dp@ug.edu.gh

Centres
African Music and Dance; **African Wetlands**; **Biotechnology** (Biotechnology); **International Affairs**; **Languages** (African Languages; English; Modern Languages; Social Policy; Writing); **Tropical Clinical Pharmacology and Therapeutics** (Pharmacology; Physical Therapy)

Colleges
Agriculture and Consumer Sciences (Agriculture; Consumer Studies); **Health Sciences** (Dentistry; Health Sciences; Medicine; Nursing; Public Health)

Departments
Modern Languages (Modern Languages); **Rehabilitation Medicine and Therapy** (Medicine; Rehabilitation and Therapy)

Faculties
Arts (Arabic; Arts and Humanities; Classical Languages; Dance; English; French; Linguistics; Modern Languages; Music; Philosophy; Russian; Spanish; Swahili; Theatre); **Engineering Sciences** (Agricultural Engineering; Biomedical Engineering; Computer Engineering; Engineering; Food Technology; Materials Engineering); **Law** (Constitutional Law; Environmental Studies; Family Studies; Human Rights; International Business; International Law; Law); **Science** (Biochemistry; Botany; Chemistry; Computer Science; Environmental Studies; Fishery; Food Science; Geography; Geology; Marine Science and Oceanography; Mathematics; Natural Resources; Natural Sciences; Nursing; Nutrition; Physics; Psychology; Statistics; Zoology); **Social Sciences** (Archaeology; Computer Science; Economics; Geography; History; Information Sciences; Mathematics; Nursing; Political Sciences; Psychology; Social Work; Sociology; Statistics)

Institutes
Adult Education; **African Studies** (African Studies); **Medical Research** *(Noguchi Memorial, NMIMR)* (Medicine); **Population Studies**; **Statistical, Social and Economic Research** (Economics; Social Studies; Statistics)

Programmes
Entomology (Entomology); **Environmental Sciences** (Environmental Studies)

Schools
Agriculture (Agricultural Business; Agricultural Economics; Agriculture; Animal Husbandry; Crop Production; Soil Science); **Allied Health Sciences** (Health Sciences; Laboratory Techniques; Physical Therapy; Radiology); **Business** (Accountancy; Administration; Banking; Finance; Health Administration; Human Resources; Information Management; Information Sciences; Management; Marketing; Public Administration); **Communication Studies** (Advertising and Publicity; Communication Studies; Public Relations; Social Psychology); **Dentistry** (Dental Hygiene; Dental Technology; Dentistry; Orthodontics; Social and Preventive Medicine; Surgery); **Medicine** (Anaesthesiology; Anatomy; Gynaecology and Obstetrics; Haematology; Medicine; Microbiology; Pathology; Pharmacology; Physiology; Psychiatry and Mental Health; Radiology; Surgery); **Nursing** (Child Care and Development; Community Health; Health Sciences; Nursing; Psychiatry and Mental Health); **Performing Arts** (Dance; Music; Performing Arts; Theatre); **Public Health** (Public Health)

Further Information: Also United Nations University Institute for Natural Resources in Africa (UNU/INRA); Volta Basin Research Project; Agricultural Research Centres (Legon, Kade, Kpong). English proficiency course for foreign students

History: Founded 1948 as University College of Gold Coast, became University College of Ghana 1957, and acquired present status and title 1961. Methodist University College Ghana affiliated 2002.

Governing Bodies: University Council

Academic Year: August to July (August-December; January-July)

Admission Requirements: General Certificate of Education (GCE) with 5 credits including English, Mathematics, Arts and Science or West Africa School Certificate (WASC) Ordinary ('O') level and three passes at Advanced ('A') level, with a minimum grade D for one. Senior Secondary School Certificate with passes in core English, Mathematics and any 3 elective subjects, with aggregate score of 24 in the WAEC entrance examination

Fees: (US Dollars): Foreign students, 2,475-3,500 per semester

Main Language(s) of Instruction: English

International Co-operation: With universities in USA; Russian Federation; Japan; Netherlands; Canada; Norway; Belgium; United Kingdom; France; Hong Kong; Germany; Benin; Australia; South Africa; Swaziland. Also participates in the Commonwealth Universities Abroad Consortium (CUSAC), the Council for International Education Exchange (CIEE), the International Students Exchange Programme (ISEP), and the Fulbright Programme

Degrees and Diplomas: *Diploma*: Accounting; Public Administration, Statistics, 4-6 semesters; *Bachelor's Degree*: Administration; Agriculture (BSc); Arts (BA); Dental Surgery (BDS); Domestic Science (BA/BSc); Fine Arts (BFA); Law (LLB); Medical Sciences (MBChB); Medicine and Surgery (MBchB); Music (Bmus/BA); Natural Sciences (BSc); Nursing, 6-12 semesters; *Graduate Diploma (Grad. Dip.)*; *Master's Degree*: African Studies (Mphil); Agriculture (MA/Mphil); Archival Studies (MA/Mphil); Arts (Arts); Business Administration (MBA/Mphil); Communication Studies; Entomology (Mphil); Environmental Studies (Mphil); Law (LLM); Linguistics (MA/ Mphil); Population Studies (MA/Mphil); Public Administration (MPA/ Mphil); Public Health (MPH/Mphil); Theatre (MFA/Mphil), 1-2 yrs; *Master's Degree*: Philosophy (Mphil), 2-4 yrs; *Master of Philosophy*: 2-4 yrs; *Doctorate (PhD)*: 3-7 yrs

Student Services: Academic counselling, Canteen, Cultural centre, Employment services, Foreign student adviser, Foreign Studies

Centre, Handicapped facilities, Health services, Language programs, Social counselling, Sports facilities

Student Residential Facilities: Yes

Special Facilities: Botanical Garden. Seismological Observatory. Drama Studio

Libraries: Balme Library, 366,191 vols

Publications: Journal of Faculty of Science *(annually)*; Legon Journal of Humanities *(annually)*; Legon Journal of International Affairs (LEJIA) *(annually)*; Management and Organisations *(biannually)*; Social Studies Journal *(biannually)*; Universitas *(annually)*

Press or Publishing House: School of Communication Studies Printing Press; Institute of Adult Education Printing Press; Institute of African Studies Printing Press

Academic Staff 2008-2009	MEN	WOMEN	TOTAL
FULL-TIME	731	220	951
PART-TIME	152	23	175
STAFF WITH DOCTORATE			
FULL-TIME	367	86	453
PART-TIME	81	8	89
Student Numbers 2008-2009			
All (Foreign Included)	25,095	17,534	42,629
FOREIGN ONLY	590	819	1,409

Part-time students, 4,326. **Distance students,** 14,654.
Last Updated: 26/03/12

UNIVERSITY OF MINES AND TECHNOLOGY, TARKWA (UMAT)

PO Box 237, Tarkwa
Tel: 062 20324/20280
Fax: +233(362) 20306
EMail: vc@umat.edu.gh
Website: http://www.umat.edu.gh

Vice-Chancellor: Daniel Mireku-Gyimah (2004-)
Tel: +233(244) 334-156 EMail: dm.gyimah@umat.edu.gh

International Relations: Elias Asiam, Dean
Tel: +233(244) 593-689 EMail: ekasiam@yahoo.com

Faculties
Engineering; **Mineral Resources Technology** (Engineering; Geological Engineering; Mineralogy; Mining Engineering; Petroleum and Gas Engineering; Surveying and Mapping)

Schools
Postgraduate Studies

History: Founded 1952 as Tarkwa Technical Institute. Acquired present status and title 2004.

Governing Bodies: University Council

Academic Year: August to May (August-December; February-May)

Admission Requirements: Passes in core: English language, Mathematics, Integrated Science ans also passes in elective Physics, Chemistry and Mathematics. A pass in Technical Drawing or Metal Work is also accepted for Mechanical Engineering while Applied Electricity or Electronic for Electrical and Electronic Engineering in lieu of elective in Chemistry.

Fees: (Cedi): Ghanaian regular students, 252.36 for undergraduate fresh students; 227.36 for undergraduate continuing students and 324.92 for postgraduate students. Ghanaian fee paying students, Ghanaian regular students, 2,918.40; for undergraduate fresh students, 2,893.40; foreign students, 6,403; for undergraduate fresh students, 7,003 for postgraduate fresh students; 6,253 for continuing undergraduate students, 6,903 for continuing postgraduate students.

Main Language(s) of Instruction: English

Accrediting Agencies: National Accreditation Board

Degrees and Diplomas: *Diploma*: 1 yr; *Bachelor's Degree (B.Sc.)*: 4 yrs; *Master's Degree*: Geological Engineering; Mineral Engineering; Mining Engineering (M.Sc.), 2 yrs (Full-time); 3 yrs (Part-time); *Master of Philosophy (Mphil)*: 3 yrs; *Doctorate*: Geological Engineering; Mineral Engineering; Mining Engineering (PhD), 4 yrs

Student Services: Academic counselling, Social counselling

Student Residential Facilities: Yes

Libraries: 3 m. vols

Academic Staff 2008-2009	MEN	WOMEN	TOTAL
FULL-TIME	51	6	57
PART-TIME	2	–	2
STAFF WITH DOCTORATE			
FULL-TIME	17	–	17
Student Numbers 2008-2009			
All (Foreign Included)	1,095	156	1,251
FOREIGN ONLY	46	5	51

Last Updated: 29/05/09

PRIVATE INSTITUTIONS

ACCRA INSTITUTE OF TECHNOLOGY

PO Box AN-19782, Accra
Tel: +233(21) 913-227 +233(21) 786-022
EMail: ait@ait.edu.gh
Website: http://www.ait.edu.gh

Schools
Advanced Systems and Data Studies *(ASSDAS)* (Computer Networks; Computer Science; E-Business/Commerce; Electronic Engineering; Information Technology; Mathematics; Multimedia; Software Engineering); **Advanced Technologies, Engineering and Science** *(SATES)*; **Business** *(AIT Business School (ABS))* (Accountancy; Banking; Business Administration; Business and Commerce; Cooking and Catering; E-Business/Commerce; Finance; Information Management; Information Technology; Management; Marketing; Public Administration; Secretarial Studies; Tourism)

Further Information: Also AIT Virtual University (the AIT Virtual Campus) and the AIT Online- Your e-University

Degrees and Diplomas: *Bachelor's Degree*; *Master's Degree (MBA; Mtech; MSc)*. Also postgraduate diplomas and certificates
Last Updated: 21/09/09

AKROFI CHRISTALLER INSTITUTE OF THEOLOGY, MISSION AND CULTURE (ACI)

PO Box 76, Akropong-Akuapem
Tel: +233(81) 91490
EMail: registry@acighana.org
Website: http://www.acighana.org

Rector: Benhardt Y. Quarshie
Tel: +233(81) 91491 EMail: bquarshie@acighana.org

Registar: Grace P. Nartey

International Relations: Michael Ayensah, Advencement Officer
EMail: kobina_ayensah@yahoo.co.uk

Programmes
African Christianity (Religion); **Bible Translation and Interpretation** (Bible; Translation and Interpretation); **Cross-Cultural Ministry** (Cultural Studies; History; Missionary Studies); **Theology and Mission** (Missionary Studies; Theology)

History: Founded 1987 as a postgraduate research and training institute established by the Presbyterian Church of Ghana (PCG). Acquired present status 2006.

Governing Bodies: Council; Academic Board; Management and Standing Committees

Academic Year: August to june

Admission Requirements: MA: a good honours degree in any discipline from a recognized University.

Fees: (US Dollars): MA, 3,000 per year; MTH, 4,500; PhD: 7,500

Main Language(s) of Instruction: English

Accrediting Agencies: National Accreditation Board of the Ministry of Education

Degrees and Diplomas: *Master's Degree*: African Christianity; Bible Translation and Interpretation (MTh), 2 yrs; *Master's Degree*: Theology and Missions (MA), 1 yr (modular); *Doctorate*: Theology (PhD), 4 yrs

Student Services: Academic counselling, Canteen, Cultural centre, Foreign student adviser, Health services, Social counselling

Student Residential Facilities: Hostel facilities available

Special Facilities: Archives for specialised research

Libraries: Specialized Library (The Johannes Zimmerman Library)

Publications: Journal of African Christian Thought (*biannually*)

Academic Staff 2008-2009	MEN	WOMEN	TOTAL
FULL-TIME	4	4	8
PART-TIME	6	1	7
STAFF WITH DOCTORATE			
FULL-TIME	4	2	6
PART-TIME	5	1	6
Student Numbers 2008-2009			
All (Foreign Included)	33	8	41
FOREIGN ONLY	11	5	16

Last Updated: 17/08/09

ALL NATIONS UNIVERSITY COLLEGE

PO Box KF 1908, Koforidua
Tel: +233(34) 2021587
Fax: +233(34) 2025625
EMail: registrar@allnationsuniversity.org
Website: http://www.allnationsuniversity.org/

President: Samuel Donkor (2002-)
Tel: 233-34-2021588, Fax: 233-34-2025625
EMail: drsdonkor@anfgc.org

Administrative Officer: Lynn Kisembe
Tel: 233-20-8088119, Fax: 233-34-2025625
EMail: lynn.kisembe@allnationsuniversity.org

International Relations: Rajan John, International Relations Officer
Tel: 233-543-688836, Fax: 233-34-2025625
EMail: rajanjohn@allnationsuniversity.org

Departments
Biblical Studies (Bible); **Biomedical Engineering** (Biomedical Engineering); **Business Administration** (Accountancy; Banking; Business Administration; Finance; Human Resources; Marketing); **Computer Science** (Computer Science); **Computer Engineering** (Computer Engineering); **Electronics and Communication Engineering** (Electronic Engineering; Telecommunications Engineering); **Humanities and Social Science** (Arts and Humanities; Social Sciences); **Oil and Gas Engineering** (Petroleum and Gas Engineering)

History: Founded 1996.

Governing Bodies: Board of Governors

Academic Year: August to December; January to April; May to July

Admission Requirements: Secondary school certificate or equivalent

Main Language(s) of Instruction: English

International Co-operation: with institutions in India, Nigeria

Accrediting Agencies: National Accreditation Board (NAB)

Degrees and Diplomas: *Bachelor's Degree*: Business Administration; Computer Science; Electronics and Communication Engineering; Biomedical Engineering; Biblical Studies, 4 yrs

Student Services: Academic counselling, Canteen, Employment services, Foreign student adviser, Foreign Studies Centre, Handicapped facilities, Health services, Language programs, Social counselling, Sports facilities

Student Residential Facilities: for overseas faculty.

Libraries: 53,000 vols.

Publications: All Nations University Journal of Applied Thought, Multidisciplinary journal in economic and national development, engineering, computer coding and biblical studies. (*annually*)

Academic Staff 2010-2011	MEN	WOMEN	TOTAL
FULL-TIME	91	7	98
PART-TIME	2	1	3
STAFF WITH DOCTORATE			
FULL-TIME	5	–	5
PART-TIME	–	–	0
Student Numbers 2010-2011			
All (Foreign Included)	1,271	504	1,775
FOREIGN ONLY	377	169	546

Part-time students, 390. **Distance students,** 0. **Evening students,** 224.
Last Updated: 25/10/10

CATHOLIC UNIVERSITY COLLEGE OF GHANA

PO Box 363, Sunyani, Brong Ahafo Region
Tel: +233(61) 24805
EMail: cugadmin@cug.edu.gh
Website: http://www.cug.edu.gh

Vice-Chancellor: James Hawkins Ephraim

Registrar: Ernest K. Odoom

Centres
Applied Research, Consultancy and Community Outreach; **Enrichment Studies**

Faculties
Economics and Business Administration (Business Administration; Economics); **Education**; **Information and Communication Science and Technology** (Communication Studies; Information Sciences; Information Technology); **Public Health and Allied Sciences** (Health Administration; Health Education; Public Health); **Religious Studies** (Religious Studies)

History: Founded 1998.

Governing Bodies: Ghana Bishops' Conference

Fees: (Cedi): 1,360 per annum; foreign students, (US Dollars), 2,000 per annum

Main Language(s) of Instruction: English

Accrediting Agencies: National Accreditation Board

Degrees and Diplomas: *Bachelor's Degree*: Public Health and Allied Sciences, Information and Communication Sciences and Technology, Religious Studies and Education, Education, Economics and Business Administration; *Master's Degree*: Religious Education. Also Postgraduate Diploma in Education
Last Updated: 15/06/09

CENTRAL UNIVERSITY COLLEGE (CUC)

PO Box DS 2310, Dansoman, Accra, Greater Accra
Tel: +233(21) 311-040
Fax: +233(21) 311-042
EMail: cucadmin@centraluniversity.org
Website: http://www.centraluniversity.org

President: Victor Patrick Gadzekpo (2004-)
EMail: vco@centraluniversity.org

Registrar: Johnson Edward Kanda
Tel: +233(21) 313-186 EMail: registrar@centraluniversity.org

Graduate Schools
Business Management and Administration; **Theology and Missions** (Hebrew; New Testament; Religious Studies; Theology)

Schools
Business Management and Administration (Accountancy; Administration; Agricultural Business; Banking; Finance; Human Resources; Management; Marketing); **Theology and Missions** (Bible; Christian Religious Studies; Family Studies; Theology)

History: Founded 1988. Became Bible College 1991. Acquired present status 1997 and converted to tertiary institution 1998.

Governing Bodies: Board of Regents

Academic Year: October to July (October-February; March-July)

Admission Requirements: Senior secondary school certificate, advanced level

Fees: Fixed on a semester basis

Main Language(s) of Instruction: English

Accrediting Agencies: Ghana National Accreditation Board; International Central Gospel Church-Ghana (ICGC); Council for Christian Colleges and Universities, USA

Degrees and Diplomas: *Bachelor's Degree*: Accounting; Administration; Banking and Finance; Management; Agribusiness; Human Resource; Marketing; Economics (B.Sc.; B.A.), 4 yrs; *Bachelor's Degree*: Environmental and Development Studies; Theology; Christian Education; Church Administration; Family Counselling; *Master's Degree*: Human Resource Management, Marketing; General Administration (MBA); *Master's Degree*: Theology (M.A. Theology), a further 2 yrs; *Master of Philosophy*: Theology (M.Phil Theology), a further 2 yrs

Student Services: Academic counselling, Canteen, Employment services, Foreign student adviser, Handicapped facilities, Health services, Language programs, Social counselling, Sports facilities

Student Residential Facilities: None

Special Facilities: French Laboratory

Libraries: Yes

Press or Publishing House: Central University Press
Last Updated: 23/02/09

GHANA BAPTIST UNIVERSITY COLLEGE (GBUC)

PMB, Kumasi
Tel: +233(51) 80195
Fax: +233(51) 28592
EMail: gbuc2006@yahoo.com
Website: http://gbuc.edu.gh/

President: Samuel Boapeah (2006-) EMail: snboah@yahoo.com

Schools
Management and Information Technology (Accountancy; Banking; Business Administration; Finance; Human Resources; Management; Marketing) *Head*: Emmanuel Boachie; **Theology and Ministry** *Dean*: Michael Sowu

History: Affiliated with University of Cape Coast, Ghana.

Governing Bodies: Ghana Baptist Convention; Governing Council of University College

Admission Requirements: Senior Secondary School Certificate (SSSC); Senior High School Certificate (SHSC); West African School Certificate (WASC)

Fees: (Cedi): 750.00 per semester

Main Language(s) of Instruction: English

Accrediting Agencies: National Accreditations Board (NAB), Ghana

Degrees and Diplomas: *Diploma*: Church Music; Theology, 2-3 yrs; *Bachelor's Degree*: Theology; Business Administration (B.Th.; BSc.), 4 yrs; *Master's Degree*: Ministry (MAM), 1 yr

Student Services: Academic counselling, Canteen, Health services, Social counselling, Sports facilities

Student Residential Facilities: Hostel Facilities at Abuakwa Campus; Nearby Hostels close to city campus

Special Facilities: Internet facilities (in Library and Offices)

Libraries: 2 libraries with a total of 12,040 vols and journals

Publications: Journal of Excellence in Leadership and Stewardship, Publication dealing with Theology, Ministry, Business, Heatlh *(1-2 per annum)*

Press or Publishing House: Ghana Baptist University College Press

Academic Staff *2008-2009*	MEN	WOMEN	TOTAL
FULL-TIME	10	2	**12**
PART-TIME	6	–	**6**
STAFF WITH DOCTORATE			
FULL-TIME	1	–	**1**
PART-TIME	1	–	**1**
Student Numbers *2008-2009*			
All (Foreign Included)	235	171	**406**

Evening students, 220.
Last Updated: 22/04/09

GHANA CHRISTIAN UNIVERSITY COLLEGE (GCUC)

PO Box DD 48, Dodowa
Tel: 233(22) 252042 +233(22) 252180
EMail: guc@ghanacu.org
Website: http://www.ghanacu.org

President: Manuel Budu-Adjei

Programmes
Christian Organisational Leadership; **Community Development** (Bible; Development Studies; Economics; Management; Modern Languages; Religion); **Theology**

History: Founded 1966 as Ghana Christian College and Seminary.

Degrees and Diplomas: *Bachelor's Degree*; *Master's Degree*
Last Updated: 03/02/09

GHANA SCHOOL OF MARKETING

PO Box 18235, Accra
Tel: +233(21) 665-749 +233(21) 417793
Fax: +233(21) 672-299
EMail: info@cimgghana.com
Website: http://www.cimgghana.com

Programmes
Marketing

Degrees and Diplomas: Professional diplomas and certificates and Professional postgraduate diploma in Marketing
Last Updated: 18/09/09

GHANA TELECOMMUNICATIONS UNIVERSITY COLLEGE (GTUC)

Private Mail Bag, Tesano, Accra-North
Tel: +233(21) 221-412
Fax: +233(21) 223-531
EMail: gtucinfo@ghanatel.net
Website: http://www.gtuc.edu.gh/

President: Osei Darkwa (2005-) EMail: odarkwa@ghanatel.net

Faculties
Informatics; **Telecommunications Engineering** (Computer Engineering; Telecommunications Engineering)

History: Founded 2005.

Governing Bodies: University Council

Fees: (Cedi): 400,000 (US Dollars: 43)

Degrees and Diplomas: *Certificate*; *Diploma*; *Bachelor's Degree*; *Master's Degree*
Last Updated: 23/02/09

METHODIST UNIVERSITY COLLEGE GHANA (MUCG)

PO Box DC 940, Dansoman, Accra
Tel: +233(21) 312-980 +233(21) 314-542
Fax: +233(21) 312-989
EMail: mucg2001@yahoo.co.uk
Website: http://www.mucg.edu.gh

Principal: S.K. Adjepong (2004-)

Registrar: Nii Aryeetay

International Relations: Kwesi Adjepong

Faculties
Agriculture (Agricultural Business; Agriculture; Horticulture); **Arts and General Studies**; **Business Administration** (Accountancy; Banking; Business Administration; Finance; Human Resources; Marketing); **Social Studies** (Applied Mathematics; Economics; Information Technology; Psychology; Social Studies; Statistics)

History: Founded 2000.

Admission Requirements: GCE A level

Fees: (Cedi): 90,000 per semester

Main Language(s) of Instruction: English

Accrediting Agencies: National Accreditation Board, Ghana

Degrees and Diplomas: *Diploma*: Agriculture; Music, 2 yrs; *Bachelor's Degree*: 2-4 yrs; *Master's Degree*: Business Administration (MBA); Guiding and Counselling (MA), 2 yrs; *Master of Philosophy*: Guidance and Counselling; Mathematics; Statistics, 2 yrs

Student Services: Academic counselling, Canteen, Foreign student adviser, Health services, Sports facilities

Student Residential Facilities: 3 hostels

Libraries: 22,000 vols. 96 serial titles; 766 reserve collection; 821 CD-Roms; 20 online scholarly databases

Academic Staff 2008-2009	MEN	WOMEN	TOTAL
FULL-TIME	63	9	**72**
PART-TIME	81	7	**88**
STAFF WITH DOCTORATE			
FULL-TIME	14	2	**16**
PART-TIME	21	2	**23**
Student Numbers 2008-2009			
All (Foreign Included)	1,880	1,803	**3,683**
FOREIGN ONLY	37	27	**64**

Last Updated: 13/05/09

OSEI TUTU II INSTITUTE FOR ADVANCED ICT STUDIES

PMB, Kumasi
Tel: +233 (51) 83275
Website: http://www.the-institute.edu.gh/

Programmes
Business and ICT Strategy (Accountancy; E-Business/Commerce; Information Technology; Management); **ICT Management and Security**; **Mathematics and Industry** (Applied Mathematics; Automation and Control Engineering); **Project Management**; **Technology** (Computer Networks; Information Technology)

History: Affiliated to Kwame Nkrumah University of Science and Technology, Kumasi 2009.

Degrees and Diplomas: *Master's Degree*
Last Updated: 18/09/09

REGENT UNIVERSITY COLLEGE OF SCIENCE AND TECHNOLOGY (RUCST)

PO Box DS 1636, Dansoman, Accra
Tel: +233(21) 681-130
Fax: +233(21) 662-531
EMail: info@regentghana.net
Website: http://www.regentghana.net/

President and Chief Executive Officer: E. Kingsley Larbi (2005-)
EMail: president@regentghana.net

Vice-President, Finance and Administration: Albert Amonoo
Tel: +233(21) 662-440 EMail: vicepresident@regentghana.net

International Relations: Nancy Ansah, Public Affairs Officer
Tel: +233(21) 324-541 EMail: nancy.ansah@regentghana.net

Schools
Arts and Social Sciences (Accountancy; Banking; Business Computing; Economics; Finance; French; Management) *Head*: Godson Senanu; **Divinity** *(King's Campus) Head*: Theophilus Quarcoopome; **Informatics and Engineering** *(King's Campus)* (Computer Science; Electrical Engineering; Information Technology; Statistics) *Head*: Stanley Moffatt

History: Founded 2005.

Governing Bodies: University Council

Academic Year: January to August

Admission Requirements: Minimum of aggregate 24 including Mathematics and English. Some courses have prerequisites

Main Language(s) of Instruction: English

International Co-operation: With universities in Canada, Germany, Netherlands and USA

Accrediting Agencies: National Accreditation Board

Degrees and Diplomas: *Bachelor's Degree*: Science; Business Administration (BSc; BBA), 4 yrs (or 2-3 yrs Post-Diploma); *Master's Degree*: Business Administration (MBA); Electrical Engineering;

Information Technology (M.Eng); Theology; Divinity (M.Th; M.Div), 2 yrs

Student Services: Academic counselling, Canteen, Employment services, Health services, Language programs, Social counselling

Student Residential Facilities: No

Special Facilities: No

Libraries: Yes

Publications: Voice of Regent *(monthly)*

Academic Staff 2008-2009	MEN	WOMEN	TOTAL
FULL-TIME	66	8	**74**
PART-TIME	34	1	**35**
STAFF WITH DOCTORATE			
FULL-TIME	8	2	**10**
PART-TIME	6	–	**6**
Student Numbers 2008-2009			
All (Foreign Included)	801	727	**1,528**
FOREIGN ONLY	44	32	**76**

Part-time students, 202. **Evening students**, 113.
Last Updated: 04/08/09

UNIVERSITY COLLEGE OF MANAGEMENT STUDIES

PO Box GP 482, Accra
Tel: +233(21) 853-304
EMail: imscolle@yahoo.co.uk
Website: http://www.ucoms.edu.gh/

Director: Sazrar Opata

Programmes
Management (Banking; Finance; Human Resources; Management; Marketing)

Further Information: Also campus in Kumasi

History: Founded 1974. Acquired present status and title 2006.

Degrees and Diplomas: Professional Degree Programmes in Business Administration - Marketing; Accounting; Banking and Finance; Human Resource Management; Procurement and Supply Chain Management - 4 yrs
Last Updated: 04/05/07

UNIVERSITY OF APPLIED MANAGEMENT

PO Box KN 2560, House No. 129, 18th Avenue,
McCarthy Hill, Accra
Tel: +233(27) 200-7121
EMail: info@ghana.my-university.com; Kojogyambrah@yahoo.com
Website: http://www.accra.may-university.com

President: Christian Werner

Vice-President for University Development: Florian Kainz

Programmes
Business Administration; **Business Psychology**; **Sport Management**

Degrees and Diplomas: *Bachelor's Degree*; *Master's Degree*
Last Updated: 21/09/09

WISCONSIN INTERNATIONAL UNIVERSITY COLLEGE

PO Box LG 751, Legon, Accra
Tel: +233(21) 501-449
Fax: +233(21) 501-491
EMail: wuigh@africaonline.com.gh
Website: http://www.wiu-usa.edu/ghanacover.htm

Director and Principal: John Sackey (2005-)
Tel: +233(21) 501-449, Fax: +233(21) 501-491
EMail: info@wiuc-ghana.edu.gh

Registar: Akosua Eghan EMail: info@wiuc-ghana.edu.gh

International Relations: Patience Bainson, Assistant Registar (Human Resources and Public Relations)
EMail: info@wiuc-ghana.edu.gh

Programmes

Adult Education (Adult Education) *Head*: Joseph Ansere; **Business Administration** (Business Administration); **Computer Science and Management** (Computer Education; Management)

History: Founded 2000.

Admission Requirements: 3 A-Level passes with aggregate not more than 14 or 6 SSS passes with aggregate not more than 24 including English, Mathematics and Integrated Science

Degrees and Diplomas: *Bachelor's Degree*; *Master's Degree (MA; MBA)*

Last Updated: 17/08/09

ZENITH UNIVERSITY COLLEGE

PO Box TF 511, La Education Centre, Trade Fair Centre, Accra
Tel: +233(21) 784-849
Fax: +233(21) 779-099
EMail: mails@zenithcollegeghana.org;
info@zenithcollegeghana.org
Website: http://www.zenithcollegeghana.org

President: Gibrine Adam

Graduate Schools

Business *(Accra International Graduate School)* (Business Administration; Business and Commerce); **Economics and Financial Journalism** *(West Africa Graduate School)* (Economics; Finance; Journalism)

Programmes

Business Administration

Schools

Business and Information Technology (Business and Commerce; Information Technology); **Law** (Law); **Media Studies and International Relations**

History: Founded 2001. Acquired present status 2005.

Degrees and Diplomas: *Bachelor's Degree*; *Master's Degree*

Last Updated: 21/09/09

Greece

STRUCTURE OF HIGHER EDUCATION SYSTEM

Description:

Higher education in Greece is public and provided free of charge. It is composed of institutions of two different levels: universities and technological education institutes. They are under the supervision of the Ministry of National Education, Lifelong Learning and Religious Affairs which supports them financially. Admission is based on performance in nation-wide exams which take place at the end of the upper secondary level. There are no private universities. The diplomas awarded by some private post-secondary education institutions are not recognized by the State.

Stages of studies:

University level first stage: *Ptychio*
Undergraduate degree programmes at universities normally last for four years (eight semesters) and lead to the Ptychio in the relevant field. In Veterinary Science, Dentistry, Engineering and Agriculture, studies last for ten semesters. In Medicine, they last for twelve. The study programme comprises compulsory and elective courses. Each semester, students are required to follow a number of compulsory courses consisting of the core programme and a number of elective courses. The total number of courses to be taken is decided by the respective course programme of the department. In some departments, the submission of a dissertation describing the final (graduation) project is required. For example, the 10th semester of all Engineering departments is devoted to the preparation of a final year project and the submission of a dissertation. The entrance requirements for technological institutions (TEI) are the same as for universities. Studies at TEI last for eight semesters, including the compulsory professional placement and the completion of a graduation project and lead to a Ptychio. Subjects include general compulsory subjects, mandatory elective subjects and optional subjects. The Ptychio qualifies holders for immediate employment. It also allows them to continue their studies in a related university undergraduate course and, at postgraduate level, in a Greek or a foreign university.

University level second stage: *Metaptychiako Díploma Exidíkefsis*
The first level of postgraduate studies, which takes at least four semesters to complete, leads to the Metaptychiako Díploma Exidíkefsis (Postgraduate Diploma of Specialization).

University level third stage: *Didaktoriko*
The Doctoral Degree (Didaktoriko) is conferred after the public defence of a thesis. The research must be original and show advances in research and science. A doctoral thesis requires at least three years' study since the student was admitted to doctoral studies.

Distance higher education:
The Hellenic Open University (EAP) was established by law in 1992 and constitutes an independent and fully self-administered university. It is based in Patras. The mission of EAP is to provide distance undergraduate and postgraduate education and further education. It organizes education programmes and vocational training or re-training programmes which lead to the award of Certificates and educational programmes which can, under certain circumstances, lead to the award of academic degrees.

ADMISSION TO HIGHER EDUCATION

Admission to university-level studies:

Name of secondary school credential required: Apolytirio Lykeiou

For entry to: Universities and TEIs.Minimum mark: Is only required for special subjects (English, French, Music, etc).

Entrance exam requirements: Panelladikes Exetaseis (exams at the national level).

Numerus clausus/restrictions: Entrance is restricted and dependent on candidates' grades and preferences.

Foreign students admission:

Definition of foreign student: Foreign students are defined as those who either do not possess Greek nationality or whose parents, whether Greek public servants on duty abroad or permanent residents in a foreign country, have raised their children abroad.

Entrance exam requirements: Secondary School-leaving Certificate equivalent to the Apolytirio Lykeiou or confirmation of the number of completed years of secondary schooling in Greece or abroad. They must have a recommendation.

Entry regulations: Residence permits are to be obtained from the Foreigners Services Department of the Greek Department.

Health requirements: A medical check-up is required before registration.

Language requirements: Students must hold a certificate which proves their knowledge of the Greek language.

RECOGNITION OF STUDIES

Quality assurance system:

The external evaluation procedures of higher education institutes are coordinated and supported at national level by an independent administrative authority named "Quality Assurance Authority in Higher Education" which has administrative independence and is supervised by the Minister. The process of internal evaluation of higher education institutes is under the responsibility of each academic unit.

Bodies dealing with recognition:

DOATAP (Hellenic NARIC)

> Director, Information Department: Bessy Athanasopoulou
> 54 Ag. Konstantinou Str.
> Athens 10 437
> Tel: +30 210 528 1000
> Fax: +30 210 523 9525
> EMail: information_dep@doatap.gr
> WWW: http://www.doatap.gr/

Special provisions for recognition:

Recognition for university level studies: A number of foreign degrees and diplomas are recognized.

For access to advanced studies and research: Foreign students are invited to address themselves to the administrative office of the respective school or institution of higher education.

NATIONAL BODIES

Ministry of Education, Lifelong Learning and Religious Affairs

> Minister: Anna Diamantopoulou
> 37, Andrea Papandreou Str.
> Marousi 151 80
> Tel: +30 210 3443163
> Fax: +30 210 3442485
> EMail: eurydice@minedu.gov.gr
> WWW: http://www.minedu.gov.gr/

Hellenic Quality Assurance Agency for Higher Education

> 56, Sygrou Avenue
> Athens 117 42
> Tel: +30 210 922 0944
> Fax: +30 210 922 0143
> EMail: adipsecretariat@hqaa.gr
> WWW: http://www.adip.gr/

Synodos Prytaneon Ellinikon Panepistimion (Greek Rectors' Conference)
30 Panepistimiou Street
Athens 106 79
Tel: +30 210 368 9719
Fax: +30 210 368 9720

Data for academic year: 2011-2012
Source: IAU from the Hellenic Eurydice Unit, Directorate for European Union Affairs, Ministry of Education, Lifelong Learning and Religious Affairs, Greece, 2011

INSTITUTIONS

PUBLIC INSTITUTIONS

AGRICULTURAL UNIVERSITY OF ATHENS
Georgikon Panepistimion Athinon
Iera odos 75, 11855 Athinai
Tel: +30(210) 549-4893
Fax: +30(210) 346-0885
EMail: webmaster@aua.gr
Website: http://www.aua.gr

Rector: Constantinos FeggerosFeggeros EMail: r@aua.gr

Vice-Rector of Academic Affairs and Personnel: Epaminondas Paplomatas EMail: vr2@aua.gr

Faculties
Agricultural Biotechnology *(AB)* (Agriculture; Biological and Life Sciences; Biology; Biotechnology; Botany; Genetics; Microbiology; Molecular Biology; Natural Sciences; Plant Pathology); **Animal Science** *(AS)* (Agriculture; Anatomy; Animal Husbandry; Biology; Nutrition; Physiology); **Crop Science** *(CP)* (Agriculture; Agronomy; Animal Husbandry; Apiculture; Biological and Life Sciences; Crop Production; Ecology; Entomology; Environmental Studies; Floriculture; Horticulture; Landscape Architecture; Natural Sciences; Plant and Crop Protection; Plant Pathology; Sericulture; Vegetable Production; Viticulture; Zoology); **Food Science and Technology** *(FS&T)* (Agriculture; Biological and Life Sciences; Biotechnology; Chemistry; Dairy; Food Science; Food Technology; Hygiene; Microbiology; Natural Sciences; Safety Engineering); **Natural Resources Management and Agricultural Engineering** *(NRM&AE)* (Agricultural Engineering; Agricultural Equipment; Agriculture; Chemistry; Natural Resources; Soil Science; Water Management; Water Science); **Rural Economics and Development** *(RE&D)* (Agricultural Business; Agricultural Economics; Agricultural Management; Agriculture; Development Studies; Rural Planning; Rural Studies; Social Policy; Social Sciences; Sociology); **Science** *(S)* (Chemistry; Computer Science; Earth Sciences; Geology; Information Sciences; Mathematics; Mechanics; Meteorology; Natural Sciences; Physics; Statistics)

History: Founded 1920, acquired present status 1989. Under the jurisdiction of the Ministry of Education.

Academic Year: September to August (October-January; February-June)

Admission Requirements: Secondary school certificate (Apolytirion Lykiou) and entrance examination

Fees: None

Main Language(s) of Instruction: Greek

Degrees and Diplomas: *Ptychio:* 5 yrs; *Metaptychiako Diploma Eidikefsis:* Horticulture, Field Crops and Crop Protection; Animal Production; Applications of Biotechnology in Agriculture; Organization and Management of Food and Agriculture Enterprises; Food Science and Technology; Management of Natural Resources & Agricultural Engineering; Viticulture - Oenology; Culture/Breeding of Aquatic Animals; *Didaktoriko Diploma:* Horticulture, Field Crops and Crop Protection; Animal Production; Applications of Biotechnology in Agriculture; Organization and Management of Food and Agri-culture Enterprises; Food Science and Technology; Management of Natural Resources and Agricultural Engineering; Viticulture - Oenology; Culture/Breeding of Aquatic Animals

Libraries: c. 11,100 vols
Last Updated: 09/02/12

ALEXANDER TECHNOLOGICAL EDUCATIONAL INSTITUTE OF THESSALONIKI
Technologiko Ekpaideutiko Idrima, Thessalonikis (ATEI OF THESSALONIKI)
P.O. Box 141, 574 00 Sindos, Thessaloniki
Tel: +30(2310) 791-100 +30(2310) 791-111
Fax: +30(2310) 799-152
EMail: pubrel@admin.teithe.gr
Website: http://www.teithe.gr/

President: Karakoltsisdi Pavlos
Tel: +30(2310) 791-101, Fax: +30(2310) 798-231

International Relations: Despina Dimaki-Gouita
Tel: +30(2130) 791-120, Fax: +30(2130) 791-119

Centres
Foreign Languages and Physical Education *(Thessaloniki Branch)* (English; French; German; Greek; Italian; Modern Languages; Physical Education; Russian)

Departments
Clothing Design and Production *(Kilkis Branch)* (Business Administration; Fashion Design; Management; Marketing); **Fisheries Technology - Aquaculture** *(Moudania Branch)* (Aquaculture; Fishery); **Standardization and Transfer Products (Logistics)** *(Katerini Branch)* (Transport Management)

Schools
Agricultural Technology *(HOME)* (Animal Husbandry; Crop Production; Farm Management); **Business Administration and Economics** *(SDO)* (Accountancy; Advertising and Publicity; Information Sciences; Library Science; Marketing; Tourism); **Food Technology and Nutrition** *(STET-D)* (Food Technology; Nutrition); **Health and Medical Care** *(SEYP)* (Aesthetics; Child Care and Development; Gynaecology and Obstetrics; Laboratory Techniques; Midwifery; Nursing; Physical Therapy); **Technological Applications** *(STEF)* (Automation and Control Engineering; Civil Engineering; Computer Science; Electronic Engineering; Transport Engineering)

History: Founded 1974. An autonomous institution under the supervision of the Institute of Technological Education (Ministry of National Education and Religious Affairs).

Academic Year: September to August

Main Language(s) of Instruction: Greek

International Co-operation: Participates in the Erasmus Programme with Belgium; Bulgaria; Cyprus; Czech Republic; Denmark; Estonia; Finland; France; Germany; Hungary; Ireland; Italy; Latvia; Netherlands; Norway; Poland; Portugal; Romania; Slovak Republic; Spain; Sweden; Turkey; United Kingdom

Degrees and Diplomas: *Ptychio*

Student Services: Academic counselling, Canteen, Employment services, Foreign Studies Centre, Handicapped facilities, Health services, Language programs, Nursery care, Sports facilities

Student Residential Facilities: Yes

Libraries: Yes

Publications: Technologia and Ekpedefsi *(quarterly)*

Press or Publishing House: University Press

Last Updated: 14/02/12

ARISTOTLE UNIVERSITY OF THESSALONIKI

Aristoteleion Panepistimion Thessalonikis (AUTH)
University Campus, 54124 Thessaloniki
Tel: +30(2310) 996-000
EMail: internat-rel@auth.gr
Website: http://www.auth.gr

Rector: Ioannis Mylopoulos (2010-2014)
Tel: +30(2310) 996-715, 705, 703, Fax: +30(2310) 996-706
EMail: rector@auth.gr

Head, Public Relations Department: Savvas Papadopoulos
Tel: +30(2310) 996-751, Fax: +30(2310) 996-725
EMail: pr@auth.gr

Vice-Rector for Academic Affairs and Personnel: Athanasia Tsatsakou-Papadopoulou
Tel: +30(2310) 996-713, 708, Fax: +30(2310) 996-729
EMail: vice-rector-ac@auth.gr

International Relations: Helen Kotsaki-Bahtsavanopoulou, Head, International Relations Department
Tel: +30(2310) 996-742, Fax: +30(2310) 991-621

Chairs
UNESCO *(INWEB - International Network of Water Environment Centres for the Balkans) Director:* Iakovos Ganoulis; **UNESCO** (Human Rights; Peace and Disarmament) *Director:* Dimitra Papadopoulou

Faculties
Agriculture (Agriculture) *Dean:* Dimitrios Koveos; **Dentistry** (Dentistry) *Dean:* Kostas Antoniades; **Education** (Educational Psychology; Educational Sciences; Preschool Education; Primary Education; Special Education) *Dean:* Demetra Kogidou; **Engineering** (Architecture; Chemical Engineering; Civil Engineering; Computer Engineering; Computer Science; Electrical Engineering; Engineering; Mathematics; Mechanical Engineering; Physics; Regional Planning; Surveying and Mapping; Town Planning) *Dean:* Nikolaos Dean of the Faculty of Engineering (2010-2014)I. Margaris; **Fine Arts** (Film; Music; Theatre; Visual Arts) *Dean:* Georgios Katsagelos; **Forestry and Natural Enviroment** (Environmental Management; Fishery; Forest Management; Forest Products; Forestry; Natural Resources) *Dean:* Panayiotis Stefanidis; **Law, Economics and Political Sciences** (Economics; Law; Political Sciences) *Dean:* Yiannoula Karymbali-Tsiptsiou; **Medicine** (Anatomy; Biological and Life Sciences; Medicine; Neurosciences; Pathology; Pharmacology; Physiology; Radiology; Social and Preventive Medicine; Surgery) *Dean:* Nicholas V. Dombros; **Philosophy** (Archaeology; English; French; German; Italian; Philology; Philosophy) *Dean:* Phoevos Gikopoulos; **Science** (Biology; Chemistry; Geology; Mathematics; Physics) *Dean:* Ioannis Papadoyiannis; **Theology** (Theology) *Dean:* Chrysostomos Stamoulis; **Veterinary Medicine** (Animal Husbandry; Veterinary Science; Zoology) *Dean:* Athanasios Dinopoulos

Foundations
Art *(Telloglion)* (Fine Arts) *President:* Anastasios Manthos

Institutes
Modern Greek Studies *(Manolis Triantafillidis) Director:* George Papanastasiou

Schools
Byzantine Research (Ancient Civilizations) *Chairperson:* Vasilios Katsaros; **Forestry** (Forestry) *Chairperson:* Panagiotis Asteriadis; **Journalism and Mass Media Communication** *(Independent)* (Journalism; Mass Communication) *Chairperson:* Athanasia Tsatsakou; **Pharmacy** *(Independent)* (Chemistry; Pharmacology; Pharmacy) *Chairperson:* Asterios Tsiftsoglou; **Physical Education and Sports Sciences** *(Serres - Independent)* (Leisure Studies; Physical

Education; Sports; Sports Medicine) *Chairperson:* Ioannis Vrabas; **Physical Education and Sports Sciences** *(Independent)* (Leisure Studies; Physical Education; Sports; Sports Medicine) *Chairperson:* Heracles Kollias

Further Information: Also 4 Teaching Hospitals

History: Founded 1925. An autonomous institution under the supervision of the Ministry of Education. Financed by the State.

Governing Bodies: Academic Senate; Rector's Council

Academic Year: September to June (September-January; February-June)

Admission Requirements: Secondary school certificate (Apolytirion Lykiou) or recognized foreign equivalent and entrance examination

Fees: None

Main Language(s) of Instruction: Greek

International Co-operation: With all the European Countries (511 agreements in the framework of the LLP-Erasmus programmes) and 75 bilateral agreements for scientific cooperation with Universities from Europe, Africa, Asia, Australia, North and South America

Degrees and Diplomas: *Ptychio:* 4-6 yrs; *Metaptychiako Diploma Eidikefsis:* 1-2 yrs; *Didaktoriko Diploma (PhD):* 3-6 yrs

Student Services: Academic counselling, Canteen, Cultural centre, Employment services, Foreign student adviser, Handicapped facilities, Health services, Language programs, Nursery care, Social counselling, Sports facilities

Student Residential Facilities: For 1,500 students

Special Facilities: "Telloglion" Foundation Art Gallery and Education Centre, University Forests (in Pertouli and Taxiarchis mountains), Camping facilities during the summer in Poseidi-Chalkidiki peninsula

Libraries: Central Library, c. 2m. vols. 38 School Libraries.

Publications: Periodicals published by the various Schools *(annually)*; The Aristotle University Today *(quarterly)*

Press or Publishing House: Aristotle University Publication Office

Academic Staff 2011-2012	TOTAL
FULL-TIME	2,210
STAFF WITH DOCTORATE FULL-TIME	c. 1,030

Student Numbers 2011-2012	
All (Foreign Included)	c. 81,500
FOREIGN ONLY	6,320

Last Updated: 07/02/12

ATHENS SCHOOL OF FINE ARTS

Anotati Scholi Kalon Technon (ASFA)
42, Patission Str, 10682 Athinai
Tel: +30(210) 381-6930
Fax: +30(210) 382-8028
EMail: info@asfa.gr
Website: http://www.asfa.gr

Rector: Panagiotis Xaralambos
Tel: +30(210) 381-7643, Fax: +30(210) 381-7156
EMail: elerzi@asfa.gr

Secretary-General: Rolanda Tzianalou
Tel: +30(210) 383-6562, Fax: +30(210) 382-8028
EMail: rolanda@asfa.gr

International Relations: Maria Felidou
Tel: +30(210) 480-1128 EMail: mfelidou@asfa.gr

Sections
Ceramic (Ceramic Art; Fine Arts; Handicrafts); **Fresco and Icon Painting** (Fine Arts; Painting and Drawing; Visual Arts); **Graphic Design** (Design; Fine Arts; Graphic Design); **Marble; Materials and Material Technology; Metal** (Fine Arts; Handicrafts; Sculpture; Visual Arts); **Mosaic** (Fine Arts; Handicrafts); **Multimedia** (Multimedia); **Painting** (Fine Arts; Painting and Drawing; Visual Arts); **Photography** (Fine Arts; Photography; Visual Arts); **Plaster** (Fine Arts; Handicrafts; Sculpture; Visual Arts); **Postgraduate Studies** (Fine Arts); **Printmaking** (Printing and Printmaking); **Sculpture; Stage Design; Woodcarving** (Handicrafts)

Further Information: Also Rentis Site.

History: Founded 1837.

Academic Year: October to June

Admission Requirements: Secondary school certificate or recognized foreign equivalent

Fees: (Euros): Foreign students, 391 per annum

Main Language(s) of Instruction: Greek

International Co-operation: Participates in educational programmes of the European Commission

Degrees and Diplomas: *Ptychio*: Fine Arts, 5 yrs; *Metaptychiako Diploma Eidikefsis*: Fine Arts; Digital Arts

Student Services: Academic counselling, Canteen, Cultural centre, Foreign student adviser, Handicapped facilities, Health services, Language programs

Student Residential Facilities: Yes

Special Facilities: Modern Exhibition Space. Movie studio. Theatre

Libraries: Central Library, c. 25,000 vols
Last Updated: 07/02/12

ATHENS UNIVERSITY OF ECONOMICS AND BUSINESS

Ikonomikon Panepistimion Athinon
Patission 76, 10434 Athinai
Tel: +30(210) 820-3911
Fax: +30(210) 822-6204
EMail: registrar@aueb.gr
Website: http://www.aueb.gr

Rector: Konstantine Gatsios (2011-2015)
Tel: +30(210) 821-1124, Fax: +30(210) 821-5909
EMail: rector@aueb.gr

Vice-Rector: Emmanouil Giakoumakis

Departments
Accountancy and Finance (Accountancy; Business Administration; Finance; International Business); **Business Administration** (Business Administration; Communication Studies; International Business; Management; Marketing); **Economics** (Banking; Economics; Finance; International Economics); **Informatics** (Business Computing; Computer Science; Information Management; Information Sciences; Management); **International and European Economic Studies** (Economics; European Studies; International Economics); **Management Science and Technology** (Business Administration; Human Resources; International Business; Management; Technology); **Marketing and Communication** (Business Administration; Communication Studies; Human Resources; International Business; Management; Marketing; Operations Research; Public Relations); **Statistics** (Statistics)

History: Founded 1920. A State University under the supervision of the Ministry of Education.

Governing Bodies: Senate; Rector's Council; Rector

Academic Year: September to June (September-January; February-June including the exams)

Admission Requirements: National Entrance Examination

Fees: None

Main Language(s) of Instruction: Greek

International Co-operation: Participates in the Erasmus, Erasmus-Ects, Leonardo Da Vinci and Tempus programmes

Degrees and Diplomas: *Ptychio*: 4 yrs; *Metaptychiako Diploma Eidikefsis*: Accountancy and Finance; Services Management; Business Administration; Economics; Information Systems; Computer Science; International and European Economics; European Studies; Human Resources Management; Business Mathematics (jointly with the University of Athens); Marketing and Communication with New Technologies (full and part time); International Marketing(in English); Communication (in English); Statistics; Information Systems; Computer Science; *Didaktoriko Diploma*: Accountancy and Finance; Business Administration; Applied Economics and Finance; Finance and Banking Economics; Informatics; International and European Economics; Management Science and Technology; Marketing and Communication; Statistics; Informatics. Also MBA International programme (in English); MBA Program in Greek; Executive MBA

Student Services: Academic counselling, Canteen, Cultural centre, Employment services, Foreign student adviser, Foreign Studies Centre, Handicapped facilities, Health services, Language programs, Social counselling, Sports facilities

Special Facilities: Computer Centre, Network Operation Centre, Teleducation Centre, The Research Centre, Liaison Office, Laboratories

Libraries: A total ofc. 100,000 vols, and more than 1,000 printed academic journal titles; European Documentation Centre
Last Updated: 09/02/12

DEMOCRITUS UNIVERSITY OF THRACE

Dimokrition Panepistimion Thrakis (DUTH)
University Campus, 69100 Komotini, Rhodopi
Tel: +30(25310) 39000
EMail: intrela@duth.gr
Website: http://www.duth.gr

Rector: Constantinos Simopoulos
Tel: +30(25310) 27017, Fax: +30(25310) 39081
EMail: rector@duth.gr

Vice Chancellor for Academic Affairs and Personnel: Athanasios Karabinis

Departments
Agricultural Development *(Orestiada)* (Agriculture); **Business Administration** *(Komotini)* (Business Administration; Management); **Forestry, Environmental and Natural Resources Management** *(Orestiada)* (Environmental Management; Forestry; Natural Resources); **Greek Literature** *(Komotini)* (Arts and Humanities; Greek; Literature); **History and Ethnology** *(Komotini)* (Ancient Civilizations; Anthropology; Archaeology; Ethnology; Folklore; History; Modern History); **International Economic Relations and Development** *(Komotini)* (International Economics; International Relations); **Languages, Literature and Culture of Black Sea Countries** *(Komotini)* (Cultural Studies; Literature; Modern Languages); **Law** *(Komotini)* (Civil Law; European Union Law; International Law; Labour Law; Law; Private Law; Public Law); **Molecular Biology and Genetics** *(Alexandroupolis)* (Genetics; Molecular Biology); **Physical Education and Sports** *(Komotini)* (Leisure Studies; Physical Education; Sports; Sports Management; Sports Medicine); **Political Science** *(Komotini)* (Political Sciences; Social Sciences); **Social Administration** *(Komotini)* (Public Administration; Social Policy; Social Work)

Faculties
Educational Sciences *(Alexandroupolis)* (Education; Educational Sciences; Preschool Education; Primary Education); **Engineering** *(Xanthi)* (Architecture; Civil Engineering; Computer Engineering; Electrical Engineering; Engineering; Engineering Management; Environmental Engineering; Environmental Studies; Production Engineering)

Schools
Medicine *(Alexandroupolis)* (Gynaecology and Obstetrics; Medicine; Pathology; Psychiatry and Mental Health; Surgery)

Further Information: Also campuses in Xanthi, Alexandroupoli and Orestiada. (General Hospital in Alexandroupolis)

History: Founded 1973. An autonomous institution under the supervision of the Ministry of Education.

Governing Bodies: Senate; Rector's Council

Academic Year: September to August

Admission Requirements: Secondary school certificate (Apolytirion Lykiou) and entrance examination

Main Language(s) of Instruction: Greek

International Co-operation: With universities in Germany, Spain, Italy, the Netherlands, Finland, France, Poland, Czech Republic. Also participates in Socrates, Leonardo, Erasmus, Tempus, Comett, Esprit and Mast programmes.

Degrees and Diplomas: *Ptychio*: 4-5 yrs; *Ptychio*: Medicine, 6 yrs; *Metaptychiako Diploma Eidikefsis*: Civil Engineering; Electrical and Computer Engineering; Physical Education; Hydraulic Engineering; Law; South-East European Studies (Law), a further 2 yrs; *Didaktoriko Diploma*: Civil Engineering; Electrical and Computer Engineering; Law; Physical Education and Sports Science, a further 2 yrs

Student Services: Canteen, Sports facilities

Student Residential Facilities: Yes

Libraries: Faculty libraries, c. 227,036 vols; 3,917 periodicals.

Press or Publishing House: Printing Office of the University
Last Updated: 08/02/12

HAROKOPION UNIVERSITY
Harokopio Panepistimio
El. Venizelou 70, Kallithea, 176 71 Athinai
Tel: +30(210) 9549-100
Fax: +30(210) 9577-050
EMail: haruniv@hua.gr
Website: http://www.hua.gr

Rector: Dimosthenis Anagnostopoulos
Tel: +30(210) 9549-101 EMail: rector@hua.gr

Vice-Rector for Academic Affairs and Personnel: Evagelia Georgitsoyianni
Tel: +30(210) 9549-120 EMail: egeorg@ hua.gr@hua.gr

Departments
Dietetics and Nutrition (Dietetics; Nutrition); **Geography** (Computer Science; Demography and Population; Economics; Geography; Marine Science and Oceanography; Mathematics and Computer Science; Natural Sciences; Regional Planning; Social Sciences; Surveying and Mapping; Town Planning); **Home Economics and Ecology** (Child Care and Development; Ecology; Home Economics; House Arts and Environment; Household Management; Nutrition); **Informatics and Telematics** (Artificial Intelligence; Automation and Control Engineering; Computer Engineering; Computer Networks; Computer Science; Data Processing; Electronic Engineering; Information Technology; Logic; Mathematics; Mathematics and Computer Science; Operations Research; Software Engineering; Statistics; Systems Analysis; Telecommunications Engineering)

History: Founded 1990. The planning and development of the institution was carried out according to high international standards by the Ministry of Education.

Governing Bodies: Rector's Council

Academic Year: September to June (September-February; February-June)

Admission Requirements: Secondary school certificate (Apolytirion Lykiou) and entrance examination

Fees: None

Main Language(s) of Instruction: Greek

International Co-operation: Participates in the Socrate-Erasmus programme (Wye College, United Kingdom, Wageningen Agricultural University, The Netherlands).

Degrees and Diplomas: *Ptychio*: 4 yrs; *Metaptychiako Diploma Eidikefsis*: a further 2 yrs; *Didaktoriko Diploma (PhD)*: a further 3 yrs

Student Services: Academic counselling, Canteen, Employment services, Foreign student adviser, Handicapped facilities, Health services, Social counselling

Student Residential Facilities: Yes

Special Facilities: Video; Computer Lab

Libraries: c. 8,000 vols; 200 journals, 15 data bases
Last Updated: 09/02/12

HELLENIC OPEN UNIVERSITY
Elliniko Anoikto Panepistimio (EAP)
18, Parodos Aristotelous St., 26335 Patra, Achaïa
Tel: +31(2610) 367-300 +31(2610) 367-400
Fax: +31(2610) 367-650 +31(2610) 367-321
EMail: info@eap.gr
Website: http://www.eap.gr

President: Haralambos Coccossis (2004-)
Tel: +31(2610) 367-359, Fax: +31(2610) 367-356
EMail: president@eap.gr

Vice-President: Panayiotis Giannopoulos
Tel: +31(2610) 367-621, Fax: +31(2610) 367-370

Faculties
Applied Arts (Graphic Arts; Multimedia); **Science and Technology** (Computer Science; Environmental Engineering; Environmental Studies; Information Sciences; Mathematics; Mathematics and Computer Science; Natural Sciences; Physics; Safety Engineering; Scandinavian Languages; Technology; Waste Management; Welfare and Protective Services); **Social Sciences** (Banking; Business Administration; Health Administration; Social Sciences; Tourism)

Schools
Humanities (Adult Education; Arts and Humanities; Cultural Studies; Education; English; European Studies; Foreign Languages Education; French; German; Greek; Modern Languages; Orthodox Theology; Spanish)

History: Founded 1992. ISO 9001: 2000.

Governing Bodies: Administrative Committee

Admission Requirements: 'Geniko apolytirio' or equivalent for undergraduate

Fees: (Euros): 600 per module (12 modules required for undergraduate degree and 4 for postgraduate)

Main Language(s) of Instruction: Greek

Degrees and Diplomas: *Ptychio*: 4 yrs; *Metaptychiako Diploma Eidikefsis*: a further 2 1/2 yrs
Last Updated: 08/02/12

INTERNATIONAL HELLENIC UNIVERSITY
4th km Thessaloniki - Moudania, 57001 Thermi
Website: http://www.ihu.edu.gr

Schools
Economics and Business Administration (Banking; Business Administration; Economics; Finance); **Humanities** (Arts and Humanities; Cultural Studies); **Science and Technology** (Energy Engineering; Natural Sciences; Technology)

History: Founded 2005.

Degrees and Diplomas: *Metaptychiako Diploma Eidikefsis*
Last Updated: 03/02/12

IONIAN UNIVERSITY
Ionian Panepistimion
7, Rizospaston Voulefton str., 49100 Corfu
Tel: +30(266) 1087-609
Fax: +30(266) 1022-549
EMail: webmaster@ionio.gr
Website: http://www.ionio.gr

Rector: Anastasia Sali-Papasali
Tel: +30(266) 1087-110, Fax: +30(266) 1087-112
EMail: rosa@ionio.gr

Vice Rector of Academic Affairs and Human Resources:
Miranda Kaldi EMail: alexia@ionio.gr

International Relations: Dionisia Karvouni
Tel: +30(266) 1087-129, Fax: +30(266) 1044-878
EMail: intl_rel@ionio.gr

Departments
Archives and Library Sciences (Archiving; Information Sciences; Library Science); **Asian Studies** (Asian Studies); **Audio and Visual Arts** (Fine Arts; Visual Arts); **Computer Science** (Computer Science); **Foreign Languages, Translation and Interpreting** (Arts and Humanities; French; German; Greek; Literature; Modern Languages; Spanish; Translation and Interpretation); **History** (Ancient Books; Anthropology; Archaeology; Art History; English; Ethnology; French; German; Greek (Classical); History; Latin; Modern Languages; Philology; Philosophy); **Music Studies** (Art Therapy; Conducting; Jazz and Popular Music; Music; Music Education; Music Theory and Composition; Musical Instruments; Musicology; Singing)

History: Founded 1984. A State institution under the jurisdiction of the Ministry of Education.

Academic Year: October to June (October-February; February-June)

Admission Requirements: Secondary school certificate (Apolytirio Lykiou)

Fees: None

Main Language(s) of Instruction: Greek

International Co-operation: Participates in the Erasmus and Tempus programmes

Degrees and Diplomas: *Ptychio*: 4 yrs; *Metaptychiako Diploma Eidikefsis*; *Didaktoriko Diploma*

Libraries: Department libraries, total, c. 28,200 vols

Last Updated: 09/02/12

NATIONAL AND KAPODISTRIAN UNIVERSITY OF ATHENS

Ethniko kai Kapodistriako Panepistimio Athinon (NKUA)
30 Panepistimiou street, 10679 Athinai
Tel: +30(210) 368-9771 +30(210) 368-9684
Fax: +30(210) 361-4013 +30(210) 368-9717
EMail: sdrak@admin.uoa.gr
Website: http://www.uoa.gr

Rector: Theodosios Pelegrinis
Tel: +30(210) 368-9771, Fax: +30(210) 368-9717
EMail: rector@uoa.gr

International Relations: Theodore Liakakos, Vice Rector, Student Care and International Relations
Tel: +30(210) 368-9786, Fax: +30(210) 368-9741
EMail: vrec-stcir@uoa.gr

Faculties

Biology (Biology); **Chemistry** (Chemistry); **Communication and Media Studies** (Communication Studies; Media Studies); **Dentistry** (Dentistry); **Early Childhood Education** (Child Care and Development; Preschool Education); **Economics** (Economics); **English Language and Literature** (English); **French Language and Literature** (French); **Geology and Geo-environment** (Environmental Studies; Geology); **German Language and Literature** (German); **Greek Philology** (Greek; Philology); **History and Archaeology** (Archaeology; History); **Informatics and Telecommunications** (Information Technology); **Italian ans Spanish Language and Literature** (Italian; Literature; Spanish); **Law** (Law); **Mathematics** (Mathematics); **Medicine** (Medicine); **Music Studies** (Music); **Nursing** (Nursing); **Pharmacy** (Pharmacy); **Philology** (Philology); **Philosophy and History of Science** (History of Societies; Philosophy); **Philosophy, Pedagogy and Psychology** (Pedagogy; Philosophy; Psychology); **Physical Education and Sport Science** (Physical Education; Sports); **Physics** (Physics); **Political Science and Public Administration** (Political Sciences; Public Administration); **Primary Education** (Primary Education); **Slavic Studies** (Slavic Languages); **Social Theology** (Bible; Canon Law; Christian Religious Studies; Pastoral Studies; Theology); **Spanish Language and Literature** (Spanish); **Theatre Studies** (Theatre); **Theology** (Theology); **Turkish and Modern Asian Studies** (Asian Studies; Turkish)

Further Information: Also 2 University Hospitals

History: Founded in 1837. The first university after the foundation of the Greek state. Autonomous institution under the jurisdiction of the Ministry of Education

Governing Bodies: Senate

Academic Year: September to July

Admission Requirements: Secondary school certificate (Apolytirion Lykiou) or foreign equivalent and entrance examination

Fees: None

Main Language(s) of Instruction: Greek

International Co-operation: Lifelong Learning Programme and Erasmus Programme: cooperation with Universities from 32 European countries, mainly France, Germany, Spain, Italy, Cyprus, United Kingdom, Austria, Netherlands, Poland, Turkey, Czech Republic, Finland, Belgium, Portugal, Switzerland. Bilateral Cooperation agreements (mainly with Universities in Canada, Australia, Russia, USA, Japan, Ukraine, etc.)

Degrees and Diplomas: *Ptychio*: 4 yrs; *Ptychio*: Dentistry; Pharmacy; Music Studies, 5 yrs; *Ptychio*: Medicine, 6 yrs; *Metaptychiako Diploma Eidikefsis (Master's)*: 1-2 yrs; *Didaktoriko Diploma (PhD)*: by thesis

Student Services: Academic counselling, Canteen, Cultural centre, Employment services, Foreign student adviser, Foreign Studies Centre, Handicapped facilities, Health services, Language programs, Nursery care, Social counselling, Sports facilities

Student Residential Facilities: Yes

Special Facilities: Anatomy Museum; Botanical Museum; Geology Museum; Palaeontology Museum; Zoology Museum; Museum of the History of the University; Ore-deposits and Petrology Museum; Criminology Museum; Anthropology Museum; Hygiene Museum; Archaeology and History of Art Museum. Botanical Garden. Observatory

Libraries: Department libraries

Last Updated: 08/02/12

NATIONAL TECHNICAL UNIVERSITY OF ATHENS

Ethniko Metsovio Polytechnico (NTUA)
28 Oktovriou (Patision) 42, 10682 Athinai
Tel: +30(210) 7722-017 +30(210) 7722-006
Fax: +30(210) 7722-028
EMail: webmaster@ntua.gr
Website: http://www.ntua.gr

Rector: Simosos Simopoulos Tel: +30(210) 772-2046

Vice Rector: Ioannis Avaritsiotis

Vice Rector: Antonia Moropoulou

Schools

Applied Mathematics and Physics *(Zografou)* (Applied Mathematics; Applied Physics; Arts and Humanities; Law; Mathematics; Physics; Social Sciences); **Architecture** (Architecture); **Chemical Engineering** *(Zografou)* (Chemical Engineering; Chemistry; Computer Science; Engineering; Industrial Engineering; Systems Analysis); **Civil Engineering** (Civil Engineering; Construction Engineering; Engineering; Engineering Management; Geological Engineering; Marine Engineering; Transport Engineering); **Electrical and Computer Engineering** *(Zografou)* (Computer Engineering; Computer Science; Electrical and Electronic Engineering; Electrical Engineering; Engineering; Power Engineering); **Mechanical Engineeering** *(Zografou)* (Automation and Control Engineering; Engineering; Industrial Engineering; Mathematics; Mathematics and Computer Science; Mechanical Engineering; Nuclear Engineering; Operations Research; Thermal Engineering); **Mining and Metallurgical Engineering** *(Zografou)* (Civil Engineering; Engineering; Geological Engineering; Materials Engineering; Metallurgical Engineering; Mining Engineering); **Naval Architecture and Marine Engineering** *(Zografou)* (Engineering; Marine Engineering; Naval Architecture); **Rural Surveying and Engineering** *(Zografou)* (Development Studies; Earth Sciences; Engineering; Geography; Natural Sciences; Rural Studies; Social Sciences; Surveying and Mapping)

Further Information: Also Zografou Campus

History: Founded 1836 by decree as technical school, became technical college 1887 and acquired present status 1929. Reorganized 1982. An autonomous institution under the supervision of the Ministry of Education.

Governing Bodies: Senate

Academic Year: September to July

Admission Requirements: Secondary school certificate (Apolytirion Lykiou) or foreign equivalent and entrance examination

Fees: None

Main Language(s) of Instruction: Greek

International Co-operation: Participates in Socrates, Erasmus and Tempus programmes

Degrees and Diplomas: *Ptychio*: Engineering, 5 yrs; *Metaptychiako Diploma Eidikefsis*; *Didaktoriko Diploma*

Student Services: Academic counselling, Canteen, Employment services, Foreign student adviser, Health services, Language programs, Nursery care, Sports facilities

Student Residential Facilities: Yes

Special Facilities: Art Gallery. Chorus and Orchestra. Sports Centre.

Libraries: c. 150,000 vols

Publications: Pyrphoros, Scientific papers (bimonthly)
Last Updated: 08/02/12

PANTEION UNIVERSITY OF ECONOMICS AND POLITICAL SCIENCE

Panteion Panepestimion Ikonomikon kai Politicon Epistimon

136 Sygrou Ave., Kallithea, 17671 Athinai
Tel: +30(210) 922-0100
Fax: +30(210) 922-3690
EMail: thesak@panteion.gr
Website: http://www.panteion.gr

Rector: Panagiotis B. Tsiros EMail: rector@panteion.gr

Vice Rector of Academic Affairs: Andreas Lytras

International Relations: Aggeliki Kardiacaftiti, Head of the Department of International Relations and European Union
EMail: erasmusecon@panteion.gr

Departments
Communications, Media and Culture (Communication Studies; Cultural Studies; Media Studies); Economic and Regional Development (Economics; Regional Planning); Foreign Languages (English; French; German; Italian; Modern Languages); International and European Studies (European Languages; International Studies); Law (General) (Law); Political Science and History (History; Political Sciences); Psychology (Psychology); Public Administration (Public Administration); Social Anthropology (Anthropology; Geography; Political Sciences); Social Policy (Social Policy); Sociology (Sociology)

Institutes
International Relations (International Relations); Regional Development (Regional Planning)

History: Founded 1930 as private school, acquired present status 1937 as a State institution. Reorganized 1983 and acquired 5 new departments and present title 1989.

Governing Bodies: Senate; General Assembly

Academic Year: September to June (September-January; February-June)

Admission Requirements: Secondary school certificate (Apolytirion Lykiou) and entrance examination

Main Language(s) of Instruction: Greek

International Co-operation: Participates in the Erasmus programme

Degrees and Diplomas: Ptychio: 4 yrs; Metaptychiako Diploma Eidikefsis: Sociology; Criminology; International and European Studies; Criminology; Cultural Management; Political Science and History; Social Policy (MSc)

Student Residential Facilities: Yes

Libraries: Central Library, c. 40,000 vols
Last Updated: 25/01/10

SCHOOL OF PEDAGOGICAL AND TECHNOLOGICAL EDUCATION (ASPETE)

141 21 N. Heraklion, Athinai
Tel: +30(210) 289-6700
Fax: +30(210) 282-3247
EMail: gdaspete@aspete.gr
Website: http://www.aspete.gr/

President: Ioansni Chrysoulakis

International Relations: Maria M. Kantonidou, Head of Public and International Relations Office
Tel: +30(210) 289-670, Fax: +30(210) 282-3245
EMail: mkant@aspete.gr

Departments
Civil and Construction Engineering (Civil Engineering; Construction Engineering; Teacher Training; Technology Education); Civil and Structural Engineering (Civil Engineering; Structural Architecture; Teacher Training; Technology Education); Education

(Education; Teacher Training); Electrical Engineering (Electrical and Electronic Engineering); Electronic Engineering (Electronic Engineering); General Studies (Education; Teacher Training); Mechanical Engineering (Mechanical Engineering)

Further Information: Also campuses in Thessaloniki, Patra, Volos, Ioannina, Heraklion-Crete, and Sapes.

History: Founded 2002.

Governing Bodies: Administrative Board

Main Language(s) of Instruction: Greek

Degrees and Diplomas: Ptychio. Also 'Certificate of Further Training' or Specialization Training'; Joint postgraduate programmes (M.A.) in cooperation with Higher Education Institutions in Greece or abroad.

Libraries: c. 30.500 vols
Last Updated: 14/02/12

TECHNICAL UNIVERSITY OF CRETE

Polytechnion Kritis
Agiou Markou, 73132 Chania, Chania
Tel: +30(28210) 28404
Fax: +30(28210) 28418
EMail: intoffice@isc.tuc.gr
Website: http://www.tuc.gr

Rector: Yannis A. Phillis
Tel: +30(28210) 28400, Fax: +30(28210) 28417
EMail: rector@central.tuc.gr; phillis@dpem.tuc.gr

Vice-Rector of Academic Affairs and Personnel: Theodoros Markopoulos
Tel: +30 (28210) 37002, Fax: +30 (28210) 28417
EMail: markopou@mred.tuc.gr

International Relations: Elena Papadogeorgaki, Head of Public and International Relations Department
Tel: +30(28210) 37047, Fax: +30(28210) 28418
EMail: epapadogeorgaki@isc.tuc.gr

Departments
Architectural Engineering (Architecture; Architecture and Planning; Town Planning); Electronic and Computer Engineering (Computer Engineering; Electronic Engineering); Environmental Engineering (Environmental Engineering; Environmental Management; Environmental Studies); Mineral Resources Engineering (Archaeology; Geological Engineering; Mineralogy); Production Engineering and Management (Engineering Management; Industrial and Production Economics; Operations Research; Production Engineering); Sciences (Chemistry; Mathematics; Mechanics; Natural Sciences; Physics; Social Sciences)

History: Founded 1977. Admitted first students 1984. An autonomous institution under the supervision of the Ministry of Education.

Governing Bodies: Senate

Academic Year: September to August

Admission Requirements: Secondary school certificate (Apolytirion Lykiou) or foreign equivalent and entrance examination

Fees: None

Main Language(s) of Instruction: Greek

International Co-operation: With universities in France; Italy; Spain; Germany; Portugal; Belgium; Romania; Czech Republic

Degrees and Diplomas: Ptychio: Engineering, 5 yrs; Metaptychiako Diploma Eidikefsis: by thesis; Didaktoriko Diploma: Engineering, by thesis. Also Postgraduate Diploma of Specialization

Student Services: Academic counselling, Canteen, Cultural centre, Employment services, Handicapped facilities, Language programs, Sports facilities

Student Residential Facilities: For 80 students

Special Facilities: Movie Studio. Music Studio, Wireless Acess, Computer Labs

Libraries: Central Library, c. 25,000 vols

Publications: News of the Technical University of Crete, News, activities and achievements, both on educational and research level of the University (biennially)
Last Updated: 14/02/12

TECHNOLOGICAL EDUCATIONAL INSTITUTE OF ATHENS

**Technologiko Ekpaideutiko Idrima, Athinas
(TEI OF ATHENS)**
Ag. Spyridonos Str, Egaleo, 12210 Athinai
Tel: +30(210) 538-5100
Fax: +30(210) 591-1590
EMail: info@teiath.gr; publirela@teiath.gr
Website: http://www.teiath.gr

President: Dimitrios Ninos
Tel: +30(210) 538-5560-2 EMail: proedr@teiath.gr

Vice-President: Michael Bratakos
Tel: +30(210) 538-5580-1 EMail: antipro@teiath.gr

Vice-President: Antonios Kammas
Tel: +30(210) 538-5570-1, Fax: +30(210) 531-4819
EMail: antipro@teiath.gr

International Relations: Dia Roufani, Head of Public and International Relations Office

Faculties

Fine Arts and Design (Cinema and Television; Design; Fine Arts; Graphic Arts; Graphic Design; Interior Design; Photography; Restoration of Works of Art; Visual Arts); **Food Technology and Nutrition** (Food Technology; Nutrition; Oenology); **Health Care Sciences** (Aesthetics; Child Care and Development; Cosmetology; Dental Hygiene; Dental Technology; Dentistry; Laboratory Techniques; Medical Technology; Midwifery; Nursing; Occupational Therapy; Optics; Physical Therapy; Public Health; Radiology; Social Work); **Management and Economics** (Administration; Advertising and Publicity; Business Administration; Health Administration; Information Management; Information Sciences; Library Science; Management; Marketing; Tourism); **Technological Applications** (Biomedical Engineering; Civil Engineering; Computer Science; Electronic Engineering; Energy Engineering; Marine Engineering; Medical Technology; Naval Architecture; Surveying and Mapping; Technology)

History: Founded 1974. Acquired present status 2001.

Academic Year: September to June (September-January; February-June)

Admission Requirements: Secondary school certificate (Apolitirio Likiou) and central selection by Ministry of Education

Fees: None

Main Language(s) of Instruction: Greek

Degrees and Diplomas: *Ptychio*: 8 semesters. Master degree Programmes coorganised with Greek and Foreign Universities.

Student Services: Academic counselling, Canteen, Cultural centre, Employment services, Foreign student adviser, Health services, Language programs, Nursery care, Social counselling, Sports facilities
Last Updated: 14/02/12

TECHNOLOGICAL EDUCATIONAL INSTITUTE OF CHALKIDA

**Technologiko Ekpaideutiko Idrima, Chalkidas
(TEI OF CHALKIDA)**
Psaxna Eyvoias, 34400 Chalkida, Evia
Tel: +30(22280) 99500
Fax: +30(22280) 23766
EMail: tei@teihal.gr
Website: http://www.teihal.gr/

President: John Statharas EMail: stath@teihal.gr

Vice-President: Kosmas Kouroumpas
Tel: +30(22280) 99701, Fax: +30(22280) 99502
EMail: kkour@teihal.gr

Vice-President: Maria Tzamtzis EMail: tzamtzi@teihal.gr

Centres

Foreign Languages and Physical Education *(CFLPE)* (Modern Languages; Physical Education)

Departments

Aircraft Technology (Aeronautical and Aerospace Engineering); **Automation** (Automation and Control Engineering; Information

Sciences; Safety Engineering); **Business Administration** (Accountancy; Administration; Business Administration; Economics); **Electrical Engineering** (Electrical Engineering); **Management Systems Supply**; **Mechanical Engineering** (Mechanical Engineering); **Science** *(General)* (Natural Sciences)

History: Founded 1983. An autonomous institution under the supervision of the Institute of Technological Education.

Academic Year: September to August

Main Language(s) of Instruction: Greek

Degrees and Diplomas: *Ptychio*: 8 sem.
Last Updated: 25/01/10

TECHNOLOGICAL EDUCATIONAL INSTITUTE OF CRETE

**Technologiko Ekpaideutiko Idrima, Kritis
(TEI OF CRETE)**
P.O. Box 1939, 71004 Heraklion, Crete
Tel: +30(2810) 379303 +30(2810) 250752
Fax: +30(2810) 379328
EMail: info@staff.teicrete.gr
Website: http://www.teicrete.gr

President: Evangelos Kapetanakis
Tel: +30(2810) 379300, Fax: +30(2810) 379328
EMail: ekap@staff.teicrete.gr

Vice President: Manolis Antonidakis
Tel: +30(2810) 379303, Fax: +30(2810) 379328
EMail: antonidakis@staff.teicrete.gr

International Relations: Ioannis Vlahos, Academic Director and International Officer for the School of Agricultural Technology
Tel: +30(2810) 379389
EMail: infoiro@staff.teicrete.gr; yvlahos@staff.teiher.gr

Schools

Agricultural Technology (Agricultural Equipment; Crop Production; Floriculture); **Health and Welfare Services** (Dietetics; Health Sciences; Nursing; Social Work; Welfare and Protective Services); **Management and Economics** (Accountancy; Administration; Advertising and Publicity; Business Administration; Business and Commerce; Finance; Insurance; Management; Marketing; Tourism); **Modern Languages and Physical Education** (Modern Languages; Physical Education); **Technological Applications** (Chemistry; Civil Engineering; Computer Networks; Computer Science; Electrical Engineering; Electronic Engineering; Energy Engineering; Environmental Engineering; Environmental Studies; Information Technology; Mathematics; Mathematics and Computer Science; Mechanical Engineering; Multimedia; Music; Music Theory and Composition; Natural Resources; Natural Sciences; Physics; Sound Engineering (Acoustics); Technology; Telecommunications Engineering)

Further Information: Also campuses in Chania and Rethymnon

History: Founded 1974. Acquired present status 1999. An autonomous institution under the supervision of the Institute of Technological Education.

Academic Year: September to August

Main Language(s) of Instruction: Greek

Degrees and Diplomas: *Ptychio*: 8 sem. Also participation in postgraduate programmes offered at Greek and foreign Universities: the ICS-Intensive Program in Intelligent Computer Systems; Applied Informatics & Multimedia; Energy Systems; Business Economics, Finance and Banking; Computer Systems - Web Development Emphasis.
Last Updated: 16/02/12

TECHNOLOGICAL EDUCATIONAL INSTITUTE OF EPIRUS

**Technologiko Ekpaideutiko Idrima, Epirou
(TEI OF EPIRUS)**
Gefira Arachthou, P.O. Box 110, 47100 Arta, Epirus
Tel: +30(26810) 50001
Fax: +30(26810) 76405
EMail: admin@teiep.gr
Website: http://www.teiep.gr

President: Sotirios Kandrelis
Tel: +30(26810) 21164, Fax: +30(26810) 76405
EMail: sotkan@teiep.gr

Vice-President: Athina Tzora-Skoufa Tel: +30(26810) 21417

International Relations: George Papadopoulos, Vice-President
Tel: +30(26810) 21158 EMail: pubrel@teiep.gr

Departments

Accountancy *(Preveza Branch)* (Accountancy); **Animal Production** (Animal Husbandry); **Applied Foreign Languages in Management and Commerce** *(Igoumenitsa Branch)* (Foreign Languages Education); **Aquaculture and Fisheries** *(Igoumenitsa Branch)* (Aquaculture; Fishery); **Communications, Informatics and Management** (Communication Studies; Computer Science; Management); **Crop Science** (Crop Production); **Early Childhood Care and Education** *(Ioannina Branch)* (Child Care and Development; Preschool Education); **Finance and Auditing** *(Preveza Branch)* (Accountancy; Economics; Finance; Law); **Floriculture and Landscape Architecture** (Floriculture; Landscape Architecture); **Nursing** *(Ioannina Branch)* (Nursing); **Speech and Language Therapy** *(Ioannina Branch)* (Speech Therapy and Audiology); **Tourism** *(Igoumenitsa Branch)* (Tourism); **Traditional Music** (Music; Musicology)

Further Information: Also campuses in Preveza; Ioannina and Igoumenitsa

History: Founded 1994. An autonomous institution under the supervision of the Institute of Technological Education.

Academic Year: September to August

Main Language(s) of Instruction: Greek

Degrees and Diplomas: *Ptychio*
Last Updated: 26/01/10

TECHNOLOGICAL EDUCATIONAL INSTITUTE OF KALAMATA

Technologiko Ekpaideutiko Idrima, Kalamatas
(TEI OF KALAMATA)
24100 Kalamata, Messina
Tel: +30(27210) 45100
Fax: +30(27210) 45200
EMail: lib@teikal.gr
Website: http://www.teikal.gr

President: Andreas Kanakis
Tel: +30(27210) 45101, Fax: +30(27210) 45103
EMail: management@teikal.gr

Vice-President for Academic Affairs and Personnel: John Kapolos

Departments

Information Technology and Telecommunications *(Campus of Sparti)* (Information Technology; Telecommunications Engineering)

Schools

Agricultural Technology (Agricultural Engineering; Crop Production; Floriculture; Food Technology); **Health and Welfare Professions** (Health Sciences; Radiology; Speech Therapy and Audiology; Welfare and Protective Services); **Management and Economics** (Accountancy; Economics; Finance; Government; Management)

History: Founded 1986. Acquired present status 1990.

Governing Bodies: Assembly; Board of Representatives

Academic Year: September to June

Admission Requirements: Apolitirio Lykeloy (High School Certificate) and entrance examination

Fees: None

Main Language(s) of Instruction: Greek

International Co-operation: Participates in the Leonardo da Vinci and Tempus programmes

Degrees and Diplomas: *Ptychio*: Administration and Economics; Health and Welfare Administration; Administration Local Government; Agricultural Product Technology; Agriculture Technology; Crop Production; Finance and Auditing; Greenhouse Crops and Floriculture, 8 semesters

Student Services: Academic counselling, Canteen, Cultural centre, Employment services, Foreign student adviser, Foreign Studies Centre, Handicapped facilities, Health services, Language programs, Sports facilities

Student Residential Facilities: Yes

Special Facilities: Cultural Centre

Libraries: Yes
Last Updated: 15/02/12

TECHNOLOGICAL EDUCATIONAL INSTITUTE OF KAVALA

Technologiko Ekpaideutiko Idrima, Kavalas
(TEI OF KAVALA)
Agios Lukas, 65404 Kavala
Tel: +30(2510) 462-100
Fax: +30(2510) 462-139
EMail: tei@teikav.edu.gr
Website: http://www.teikav.edu.gr

President: Athanasios Mitropoulos
Tel: +30(2510) 462-372, Fax: +30(2510) 462-140

Vice-President of Academic Affairs:: Dimitrios Bandekas

Departments

Nursing *(Didimoteikho Campus)* (Nursing)

Schools

Agricultural Technology *(Drama)* (Agricultural Engineering; Environmental Management; Forestry; Landscape Architecture; Oenology); **Business and Economics** (Accountancy; Administration; Business Administration; Economics; Foreign Languages Education; Information Management; Physical Education); **Engineering** *(Kavala)* (Business Computing; Computer Science; Electrical Engineering; Mechanical Engineering; Natural Sciences; Petroleum and Gas Engineering)

Further Information: Also campuses in Drama and Didymoteicho.

History: Founded 1976. Acquired present status 1983. An autonomous institution under the supervision of the Institute of Technological Education.

Academic Year: September to August

Main Language(s) of Instruction: Greek

International Co-operation: Participates in the Leonardo, Alfa, and Tempus programmes

Degrees and Diplomas: *Ptychio*. Also "Curriculum Selection" programme (9 sem.); MSc in Finance and Financial Information Systems; Postgraduate Southeast European Studies Course in partnership with Democritus University of Thrace (DUTH); Master of Distance Education (MDE) with Open University of Canada - Athabasca University. MSc Mediterranean Water Management and Policy Under Water-Scarcity Conditions

Student Services: Academic counselling, Canteen, Cultural centre, Employment services, Foreign student adviser, Foreign Studies Centre, Handicapped facilities, Health services, Language programs, Nursery care, Social counselling, Sports facilities

Student Residential Facilities: Yes

Special Facilities: Museum. Movie Studio. Art gallery

Academic Staff *2011-2012*: Total: c. 230
Student Numbers *2011-2012*: Total: c. 12,500
Last Updated: 16/02/12

TECHNOLOGICAL EDUCATIONAL INSTITUTE OF LAMIA

Technologiko Ekpaideutiko Idrima, Lamias
(TEI OF LAMIA)
3rd km. Old National Road, 35100 Lamia
Tel: +30(22310) 60163
Fax: +30(22310) 33945
EMail: teilamias@teilam.gr
Website: http://www.teilam.gr

President: Stavros Karkanis
Tel: +30(22310) 60225, Fax: +30(22310) 67770
EMail: Karkanis@ctr.teilam.gr

Secretary-General: Julia Galanis
Tel: +30(22310) 60103, Fax: +30(22310) 33945

International Relations: Athena Nella, Head, International Relations
Tel: +30(22310) 60119, Fax: +30(22310) 48023
EMail: pubintrel@teilam.gr

Campuses
Amphissa (Advertising and Publicity; Marketing; Tourism); **Karpenisi** (Environmental Management; Environmental Studies; Forestry)

Faculties
Applied Technology (S. T. IV) (Computer Science; Electrical Engineering; Electronic Engineering; Information Technology); **Health and Welfare Professions** (Nursing; Physical Therapy)

Sections
Foreign Languages and Physical Education (Modern Languages; Physical Education)

Further Information: Also campuses in Amfissa and Karpenisi

History: Founded 1994. An autonomous institution under the supervision of the Institute of Technological Education.

Academic Year: September to August

Admission Requirements: Entrance exams

Fees: None

Main Language(s) of Instruction: Greek

International Co-operation: Participates in Erasmus and Leonardo programmes

Degrees and Diplomas: Ptychio: 4 yrs

Student Services: Canteen, Health services, Sports facilities

Libraries: Yes
Last Updated: 27/01/10

TECHNOLOGICAL EDUCATIONAL INSTITUTE OF LARISSA
Technologiko Ekpaideutiko Idrima, Larissas
(TEI OF LARISSA)
41110 Larissa
Tel: +30(2410) 684-200
Fax: +30(2410) 610-803
EMail: pr@teilar.gr
Website: http://www.teilar.gr

President: Ioannis Kokoras
Tel: +30(2410) 684-300, Fax: +30(2410) 610-803
EMail: kokkoras@teilar.gr

Vice-President: Argiris Noulas
Tel: +30(2410) 684-502, Fax: +30(2410) 670-001
EMail: noulas@teilar.gr

Centres
Foreign Languages and Physical Education (English; Modern Languages; Physical Education)

Departments
Building Renovation and Restoration (Trikala); **Food Technology** (Karditsa) (Food Technology); **Forestry and Natural Environment Management** (Karditsa) (Environmental Management; Forestry); **Furniture Technology** (Karditsa) (Furniture Design); **Nutrition and Dietetics** (Karditsa)

Schools
Agricultural Technology (Agricultural Engineering; Agricultural Equipment; Animal Husbandry; Crop Production); **Business and Economics** (Accountancy; Business Administration; Economics; Management; Tourism); **Health and Welfare Professions** (Health Administration; Laboratory Techniques; Medical Technology; Nursing; Public Health); **Technological Applications** (Civil Engineering; Computer Science; Electrical and Electronic Engineering; Electrical Engineering; Engineering; Mathematics and Computer Science; Mechanical Engineering; Telecommunications Engineering)

History: Founded 1974. Acquired present status 1983. An autonomous institution under the supervision of the Institute of Technological Education.

Academic Year: September to August

Main Language(s) of Instruction: Greek

International Co-operation: With universities in France, Finland, Germany, Czech Republic, Spain

Degrees and Diplomas: Ptychio

Student Services: Canteen, Foreign student adviser, Language programs, Sports facilities

Student Residential Facilities: Yes

Libraries: Yes
Last Updated: 16/02/12

TECHNOLOGICAL EDUCATIONAL INSTITUTE OF MESSOLONGHI
Technologiko Ekpaideutiko Idrima, Mesolonghiou
(TEI OF MESSOLONGHI)
Nea Ktiria, 30200 Mesolonghi, Aitoloakarnania
Tel: +30(26310) 58200
Fax: +30(26310) 25183
EMail: relation@teimes.gr
Website: http://www.teimes.gr

President: Vangelis Politis Stergiou
Tel: +30(26310) 58361, Fax: +30(26310) 25277
EMail: prsdnt@teimes.gr

Vice-President: George Hotos

Departments
Communication Systems and Networks (Nafpaktos) (Computer Networks; Information Technology)

Faculties
Agricultural Technology (Agricultural Engineering; Agricultural Equipment; Aquaculture; Crop Production; Fishery; Floriculture; Irrigation); **Management and Economics** (Accountancy; Administration; Business Administration; Business Computing; Economics; Finance; Management)

History: Founded 1983. An autonomous institution under the supervision of the Institute of Technological Education.

Academic Year: September to August

Main Language(s) of Instruction: Greek

Degrees and Diplomas: Ptychio: 8 sem.

Libraries: Yes
Last Updated: 16/02/12

TECHNOLOGICAL EDUCATIONAL INSTITUTE OF PATRAS
Technologiko Ekpaideutiko Idrima, Patron
(TEI OF PATRAS)
1 Megalou Alexandrou Str., 26334 Patra, Achaia
Tel: +30(2610) 369-113
Fax: +30(2610) 313-770
EMail: infoffice@teipat.gr
Website: http://www.teipat.gr

President: Sokratis Kaplanis
Tel: +30(2610) 325-102, Fax: +30(2610) 313-776
EMail: Kaplanis@teipat.gr

Vice President of Academic Affairs and Personnel: Georgia Theodorakopoulou

Schools
Health Care Sciences (Health Sciences; Nursing; Optics; Physical Therapy; Social Work; Speech Therapy and Audiology); **Management and Economics** (Accountancy; Administration; Business Administration; Computer Science; Economics; Information Management; Information Sciences; Management; Management Systems; Mass Communication; Museum Management; Tourism); **Technological Applications** (Architectural Restoration; Building Technologies; Civil Engineering; Electrical Engineering; Mechanical Engineering; Technology)

History: Founded 1974. Acquired present status 1983. An autonomous institution under the supervision of the Institute of Technological Education.

Academic Year: September to August

Main Language(s) of Instruction: Greek

Degrees and Diplomas: *Ptychio.* Also Postgraduate Study Program (PSP) "Dyslexia: Multilanguage Environment and Use of New Technology in its Treatment" organised in partnership with the Department of Philosophy, Educational Psychology of the University of Ioannina

Last Updated: 16/02/12

TECHNOLOGICAL EDUCATIONAL INSTITUTE OF PIRAEUS

**Technologiko Ekpaideutiko Idrima, Piraea
(TEI OF PIRAEUS)**
Peter Rallli and Thebes 250, 12244 Aigaleo
Tel: +30(210) 538-1100
Fax: +30(210) 545-0962
Website: http://www.teipir.gr

President: Lazarus Vryzidis
Tel: +30(210) 545-0,300; +30(210) 545-0200,
Fax: +30(210) 541-1123 EMail: lvryz@teipir.gr

Vice-President: Antoniou Antonis
Tel: +30(210) 538-1425, Fax: +30(210) 545-1123

Vice-President: Kantzos Constantinos
Tel: +30(210) 569-0768, Fax: +30(210) 545-1123
EMail: ckantzos@teipir.gr

International Relations: Ouranos Dimitrios
Tel: +30(210) 538-1356, Fax: +30(210) 538-1315
EMail: eu@teipir.gr

Centres
Foreign Languages and Physical Education (English; French; German; Italian; Modern Languages)

Departments
General Studies (Chemistry; Materials Engineering; Mathematics; Physics)

Schools
Applied Technology *(S.T.Ef.)* (Automation and Control Engineering; Civil Engineering; Computer Science; Electrical Engineering; Electronic Engineering; Mechanical Engineering; Textile Technology); **Management and Economics** (Accountancy; Business Administration; Economics; Management; Tourism)

History: Founded 1983. An autonomous institution under the supervision of the Ministry of Education.

Academic Year: October to July (October-January; February-July)

Admission Requirements: Entrance examination

Main Language(s) of Instruction: Greek

International Co-operation: Participates in Socrates, Leonardo and Tempus programmes

Degrees and Diplomas: *Ptychio.* Also Postgraduate programmes in partnership with foreign universities

Student Services: Canteen, Cultural centre, Employment services, Handicapped facilities, Health services, Language programs, Social counselling, Sports facilities

Publications: Applied Research Review, Journal of the Technological Education Institute of Piraeus

Academic Staff *2011-2012*	TOTAL
FULL-TIME	250
PART-TIME	600
STAFF WITH DOCTORATE	
FULL-TIME	c. 80

Student Numbers *2011-2012*	
All (Foreign Included)	c. 17,000
FOREIGN ONLY	20

Last Updated: 16/02/12

TECHNOLOGICAL EDUCATIONAL INSTITUTE OF SERRES

**Technologiko Ekpaideutiko Idrima, Serron
(TEI OF SERRES)**
Terma Magnesias Str., 62124 Serres
Tel: +30(23210) 49114
Fax: +30(23210) 46556
EMail: pr@teiser.gr
Website: http://www.teiser.gr

President: Dimirios Paschaloudis Tel: +30(23210) 49101

Departments
Foreign Languages and Physical Education

Faculties
Administration and Economics (Accountancy; Administration; Business Administration); **Applied Technology** (Civil Engineering; Computer Science; Geological Engineering; Information Sciences; Mechanical Engineering; Surveying and Mapping; Telecommunications Engineering); **Fine Arts and Design** (Design; Fine Arts; Graphic Design; Interior Design)

History: Founded 1974. Acquired present status 2001. An autonomous institution under the supervision of the Ministry of National Education.

Academic Year: September to August

Main Language(s) of Instruction: Greek

Degrees and Diplomas: *Ptychio*: Business Administration; Accountancy; Geomatics and Surveying; Civil (Structural) Engineering; Mechanical Engineering; Computer Science and Telecommunications. Also Master degree (MSc) in Natural Disaster Prevention and Management, in collaboration with the National Kapodistrian University of Athens

Last Updated: 27/01/10

TECHNOLOGICAL EDUCATIONAL INSTITUTE OF THE IONIAN ISLANDS

**Technologiko Ekpaideutiko Idrima, Ionion Nison
(TEI OF IONIAN ISLANDS)**
Joseph Elias Momferatou and Miniati, 28100 Argostoli, Kefallonia Island
Tel: +30(26710) 25820 +30(26710) 25922
Fax: +30(26710) 25923
EMail: dioikisi@teiion.gr
Website: http://www.teiion.gr

President: George Kalkanis

International Relations: Rousis Thanassis
EMail: throusis@teiion.gr

Departments
Applied Informatics in Management and Economy *(Lefkada)* (Business Computing; Computer Science; Economics); **Business Administration** *(Kefalonia - Lixouri)* (Business Administration; Management); **Conservation and Protection of Cultural Heritage** *(Zakynthos)* (Heritage Preservation; Restoration of Works of Art); **Ecology and Environment Technology** *(Zakynthos)* (Ecology; Environmental Engineering); **Information Technology and Telecommunications** *(Lefkada)* (Information Technology; Telecommunications Engineering); **Organic Agriculture and Food Technology** *(Kefalonia - Argostoli)* (Agriculture; Agrobiology; Food Technology); **Public Relations and Communications** *(Kefalonia - Argostoli)* (Communication Studies; Public Relations); **Sound and Musical Instruments** *(Kefalonia - Lixouri)* (Musical Instruments; Sound Engineering (Acoustics))

History: Founded 2003, formerly TEI of Epirus, Kephalonia Branch.

Degrees and Diplomas: *Ptychio*: 8 sem. Also Graduate Programme offered in partnership between the Department of Ecology and Environment of the TEI Ionian Islandsand the Department of Science of Early Childhood Education and Educational Planning of the University of the Aegean.

Last Updated: 26/01/10

TECHNOLOGICAL EDUCATIONAL INSTITUTE OF WESTERN MACEDONIA

Technologiko Ekpaideutiko Idrima, Dytikis Makedonias (TEI OF WEST MACEDONIA)

Kila, 50100 Kozani
Tel: +30(24610) 40161
Fax: +30(24610) 39682
EMail: prteik@kozani.teikoz.gr
Website: http://www.teikoz.gr

President: Georgios Charalambides
Tel: +30(24610) 28296 EMail: vpres1@teikoz.gr

International Relations: Georgios Stenogias, Vice-President
Tel: +30(24610) 23850, Fax: +30(24610) 46630
EMail: vpres2@teikoz.gr

Campuses

Grevena Branch (Administration; Business Administration; Business Computing; Computer Science; Economics; Finance; Management); **Kastoria Branch** (Communication Studies; Computer Engineering; Computer Science; Information Technology; International Business; Marketing; Public Relations)

Faculties

Administration and Economics (Accountancy; Administration; Business Administration; Economics; Finance; Management); **Health Science** *(Ptolemaida)* (Ergotherapy; Gynaecology and Obstetrics; Health Sciences); **Technological Applications** *(Kozani)* (Electrical Engineering; Environmental Engineering; Environmental Management; Environmental Studies; Industrial Design; Mechanical Engineering; Natural Sciences; Sanitary Engineering; Technology)

Schools

Agricultural Technology *(Florina Branch)* (Agricultural Business; Agricultural Engineering; Agriculture; Animal Husbandry; Crop Production; Marketing; Safety Engineering)

History: Founded 1976. An autonomous institution under the supervision of the Institute of Technological Education.

Academic Year: September to August

Main Language(s) of Instruction: Greek

Degrees and Diplomas: *Ptychio:* 4 yrs. Also Master in Applied Informatics offered in cooperation with University of Macedonia and Master in Mechatronics offered in cooperation with University of Catalonia UPC (Universitat Politecnica de Catalunya).
Last Updated: 15/02/12

UNIVERSITY OF CENTRAL GREECE (UCG)

Papasiopoulou 2.4, 35100 Lamia
Tel: +30(223) 106-6700
Fax: +30(223) 106-6715
Website: http://www.ucg.gr

Chancellor: Gregorios Skalkeas

Departments

Computer Science and Biomedical Informatics (Biochemistry; Biology; Biomedicine; Computer Science); **Regional Economic Development** (Business Administration; Development Studies; Economics; European Studies; Finance; Political Sciences; Regional Studies; Statistics)

Further Information: Also Livadeia campus.

History: Founded 2003.

Degrees and Diplomas: *Ptychio*
Last Updated: 14/02/12

UNIVERSITY OF CRETE

Panepistimio Kritis

Gallos University Campus, 74100 Rethymnon
Tel: +30(28310) 77900
Fax: +30(28310) 77909
EMail: secretary@rector.uoc.gr
Website: http://www.uoc.gr

Rector: Evripides Stefanou
Tel: +30(2810) 393-210, Fax: +30(2810) 210-106
EMail: pallikaris@rector.uoc.gr

International Relations: Nikos Mastorakis, Director
Tel: +30(2810) 393180, Fax: +32(2810) 210073
EMail: mastoraki@admin.uoc.gr

Faculties

Education (Education; Preschool Education; Primary Education); **Medecine** *(Heraklion Vassilika-Voutes)* (Anatomy; Behavioural Sciences; Child Care and Development; Health Sciences; Laboratory Techniques; Medicine; Neurology; Psychiatry and Mental Health; Radiology; Social and Preventive Medicine; Surgery); **Philosophy** (Archaeology; History; Philology; Philosophy; Social Studies); **Sciences and Engineering** *(Heraklion)* (Applied Mathematics; Biology; Chemistry; Computer Science; Engineering; Materials Engineering; Mathematics; Physics; Technology); **Social Sciences** (Economics; Political Sciences; Psychology; Social Sciences; Sociology)

Further Information: Also Heraklion campus.

History: Founded 1973. A State institution under the jurisdiction of the Ministry of National Education and Religious Affairs.

Governing Bodies: Senate

Academic Year: September to June

Admission Requirements: Secondary school certificate and Panhellenic entrance examination

Fees: None

Main Language(s) of Instruction: Greek

International Co-operation: With universities worldwide. Also participates in Socrates, Jean Monnet programme

Accrediting Agencies: Ministry of National Education and Religious Affairs

Degrees and Diplomas: *Ptychio:* 4 yrs; *Metaptychiako Diploma Eidikefsis:* a further 1-2 yrs; *Didaktoriko Diploma (PhD)*

Student Services: Academic counselling, Canteen, Cultural centre, Employment services, Foreign student adviser, Handicapped facilities, Health services, Language programs, Nursery care, Social counselling, Sports facilities

Student Residential Facilities: Yes

Special Facilities: Natural History Museum. Astronomy Observatory

Libraries: Yes
Last Updated: 09/02/12

UNIVERSITY OF IOANNINA

Panepistimion Ioanninon (UOI)

P.O. Box 1186, 45110 Ioannina
Tel: +30(26510) 07105
Fax: +30(26510) 07024
EMail: intlrel@cc.uoi.gr
Website: http://www.uoi.gr

Rector: Triantafyllos A.D. Albanis
Tel: +30(26510) 07446, Fax: +30(26510) 07200

Principal University Officer: Loukas-Nikitas Papaloukas
Tel: +30(26510) 07104, Fax: +30(26510) 07028

International Relations: Vasiliki Katsadima, Head, International and Public Relations Directorate EMail: vkatsad@cc.uoi.gr

Departments

Cultural Heritage Management and New Technologies *(Independent, Agrinio)* (Cultural Studies; Heritage Preservation; Technology); **Economics** *(Independent)* (Banking; Business Administration; Economics; Finance; Statistics); **Plastic Arts and Art Science** *(Independent)* (Art History; Fine Arts; Graphic Design; Multimedia; Painting and Drawing; Photography; Sculpture; Visual Arts)

Schools

Education (Education; Educational Sciences; Preschool Education; Primary Education); **Medicine** (Medicine); **Natural Resources and Enterprise Management** *(Agrinio)* (Agricultural Economics; Animal Husbandry; Biochemistry; Biology; Business Administration; Computer Science; Ecology; Environmental Studies; Molecular Biology; Natural Resources; Physical Chemistry); **Philosophy** (Archaeology; Arts and Humanities; Education; History; Literature; Philology; Philosophy; Psychology); **Science and Technology** (Biochemistry; Biological and Life Sciences; Biology; Biotechnology;

Botany; Chemistry; Ecology; Engineering; Genetics; Materials Engineering; Microbiology; Molecular Biology; Physical Chemistry; Plant Pathology; Polymer and Plastics Technology; Technology; Zoology); **Sciences** (Chemistry; Computer Science; Mathematics; Natural Sciences; Physics)

Further Information: Also University Hospital. Centre for the Teaching of Greek Language and Culture. Vocational Training Centre. Career Office. Technological Educational Park

History: Founded 1964 as a Department of the Aristoteleion University of Thessaloniki, acquired present status and title 1970. Reorganized 1982. A State institution of the Epirus Region.

Governing Bodies: Senate; Rector's Council; Technical Council

Academic Year: September to June (September-January; February-June)

Admission Requirements: Secondary school certificate (Apolytirion Lykiou) and entrance examination

Fees: None

Main Language(s) of Instruction: Greek

International Co-operation: Participates in Socrates/Erasmus; Interreg II; Marie Curie; Pythagoras; Heraklitos and other research programmes

Degrees and Diplomas: *Ptychio*: 4-6 yrs; *Metaptychiako Diploma Eidikefsis*: a further 2 yrs; *Didaktoriko Diploma (PhD)*

Student Services: Academic counselling, Canteen, Cultural centre, Employment services, Foreign student adviser, Foreign Studies Centre, Handicapped facilities, Health services, Language programs, Nursery care, Social counselling, Sports facilities

Student Residential Facilities: For c. 1,100 students

Special Facilities: Folklore Museum. Ancient Greek and Byzantine Casts and Copies Museum. Museum of Typography. Observatory. Video Studio. Computer Centre Network Operation Centre

Libraries: Total, 314,883 vols

Publications: Epitris (Prospectus, Education) *(annually)*; Epitris Dodoni I (History and Archaeology) *(annually)*; Epitris Dodoni II (Literature and Philology) *(annually)*; Epitris Dodoni III (Philosophy, Education and Psychology) *(annually)*

Press or Publishing House: University of Ioannina Press

Academic Staff *2010-2011*: Total 600
Student Numbers *2011-2012*: Total: c. 17,000
Last Updated: 08/02/12

UNIVERSITY OF MACEDONIA-ECONOMIC AND SOCIAL SCIENCES

Panepistimion Makedonias
PO Box 1591, Odos Egnatia 156, 54006 Thessaloniki
Tel: +30(2310) 891-101
Fax: +30(2310) 844-536
EMail: pubrel@uom.gr
Website: http://www.uom.gr

Rector: Yannis A. Hajidimitriou Tel: +30(2310) 871-844

International Relations: Mariet Vainas Tel: +30(2310) 891-245

Departments
Accountancy and Finance (Accountancy; Finance); **Applied Informatics** (Computer Science); **Balkan, Slavic and Oriental Studies** (Baltic Languages; Oriental Studies; Slavic Languages); **Business Administration** (Business Administration; Computer Science; Political Sciences); **Economics** (Economics); **Educational and Social Policy** (Educational Sciences; Social Sciences); **International and European Economic Studies** (Economics; European Studies; International Studies); **Marketing and Operations Management** (Marketing; Operations Research); **Music Science and Art** (Music; Music Theory and Composition); **Technology Management** (Management; Technology)

Programmes
Postgraduate Studies (Accountancy; Business Administration; Computer Science; Economics; European Studies; Finance; Information Sciences)

Research Institutes
Applied Economic and Social Sciences *(URI)* (Economics; Social Sciences)

History: Founded 1948, reorganized 1958. Previously the Graduate Industrial School of Thessaloniki. Acquired present status and title 1990.

Governing Bodies: Rector's Council; Senate; Faculty Assembly

Academic Year: September to August

Admission Requirements: Secondary school certificate (Apolytirion Lykiou) and entrance examination

Fees: None

Main Language(s) of Instruction: Greek

Degrees and Diplomas: *Ptychio*: 4 yrs; *Metaptychiako Diploma Eidikefsis*: Economics; Business Administration; Information Systems; Applied Informatics; Accountancy and Finance; Politics and Economics of Contemporary Eastern and Southeastern Europe (MA), a further 2 yrs

Student Services: Academic counselling, Canteen, Employment services, Foreign student adviser, Handicapped facilities, Health services, Nursery care, Sports facilities

Libraries: c. 60,000 vols
Last Updated: 03/02/12

UNIVERSITY OF PATRAS

Panepistimion Patron
University Campus, 26504 Rio Patras
Tel: +30(2610) 991-822 +30(2610) 991-040
Fax: +30(2610) 991-711
EMail: rectorate@upatras.gr
Website: http://www.upatras.gr

Rector: George Panayiotakis (2010-2014)
Tel: +30(2610) 996-427, Fax: +30(2610) 996-818
EMail: rector@upatras.gr

Vice-Rector for Strategic Research Planning and Development: Dimitrios Kalpaxis EMail: dimkal@med.upatras.gr

Secretary-General: Spilios Papathanassopoulos
Tel: +30 (2610) 991-715, Fax: +30 (2610) 996-672
EMail: registrar@upatras.gr

Vice Rector for Academic Affairs and Personnel: Anna Roussou
EMail: aroussou@upatras.gr

International Relations: Eleni Skabardoni-Tsakanika, Director of International Relations, Public Relation and Publications
Tel: +30 (2610) 969-026, Fax: +30 (2610) 994-441
EMail: tsibouri@upatras.gr

Departments
Business Administration *(Independent)* (Art Management; Finance; Health Administration; Human Resources; Information Management; Information Technology; Management; Marketing; Sports Management; Technology; Tourism); **Economics** *(Independent)* (Economics)

Programmes
Postgraduate Studies (Aeronautical and Aerospace Engineering; Biology; Business Administration; Chemical Engineering; Chemistry; Civil Engineering; Computer Engineering; Computer Science; Economics; Educational Sciences; Electrical Engineering; Engineering; Geology; Materials Engineering; Mathematics; Mechanical Engineering; Medicine; Pharmacy; Philology; Philosophy; Physics; Primary Education; Structural Architecture; Theatre); **Postgraduate Studies (Interdepartmental)** (Electronic Engineering; Environmental Studies; Information Technology; Mathematics and Computer Science; Polymer and Plastics Technology); **Postgraduate Studies (International Interuniversity)** *(International Interuniversity)* (Biomedical Engineering; Biotechnology); **Postgraduate Studies (Interuniversity)** (Biomedical Engineering)

Schools
Engineering (Aeronautical and Aerospace Engineering; Architecture; Chemical Engineering; Civil Engineering; Computer Engineering; Computer Science; Electrical Engineering; Engineering; Information Technology; Mechanical Engineering); **Health Sciences** (Medicine; Pharmacy); **Humanities and Social Sciences** (Child Care and Development; Educational Sciences; Philology;

Philosophy; Preschool Education; Primary Education; Theatre); **Natural Sciences** (Biology; Chemistry; Geology; Materials Engineering; Mathematics; Physics)

Further Information: Also University Hospital at Rion. Greek Language Programme for foreign students

History: Founded 1964. Acquired present status 1966. Reorganized 1982. An autonomous institution under the supervision of the Ministry of Education.

Governing Bodies: Senate; Rector's Council

Academic Year: September to August (September-February; February-August)

Admission Requirements: Secondary school certificate (Apolytirion Lykiou) and national entrance examination

Fees: None

Main Language(s) of Instruction: Greek

International Co-operation: With universities in Europe, USA, Canada and Africa

Degrees and Diplomas: *Ptychio*: Medicine, 6 yrs; *Ptychio*: Natural Sciences; Humanities and Social Sciences; Economics and Business Administration, 4 yrs; *Ptychio*: Pharmacy, 5 yrs; *Metaptychiako Diploma Eidikefsis*; *Didaktoriko Diploma (PhD)*

Student Services: Academic counselling, Canteen, Cultural centre, Employment services, Health services, Language programs, Nursery care, Social counselling, Sports facilities

Student Residential Facilities: Yes

Special Facilities: Zoological Museum; Botanical Museum; Science and Technology Museum. Conference and Cultural Centre

Libraries: Central Library and Departmental Libraries

Academic Staff *2011-2012*: Total: c. 750
Student Numbers *2011-2012*: Total: c. 24,500
Last Updated: 10/02/12

UNIVERSITY OF PIRAEUS
Panepistimion Pireos
Karaoli and Dimitriou 80, 185 34 Piraeus
Tel: +30(210) 414-2000 +30(210) 414-2170
Fax: +30(210) 414-2328
EMail: publ@unipi.gr
Website: http://www.unipi.gr

Rector: George Economou (2008-)
Tel: +30(210) 414-2421, Fax: +30(210) 417-3260
EMail: rector@unipi.gr

International Relations: Christina Kontogoulidou, International Relations Officer
Tel: +30(210) 414-2245, Fax: +30(210) 414-2347
EMail: ckonto@unipi.gr

Centres
Research (Information Management; Information Technology)

Departments
Business Administration (Business Administration); **Digital Systems; Economics** (Business Administration; Economics; Industrial and Production Economics; International Economics; Mathematics; Statistics); **Financial Management and Banking** (Banking; Finance); **Industrial Management** (Industrial Management); **Informatics** (Computer Science); **International and European Studies** (European Studies; International Studies); **Maritime Studies** (Marine Science and Oceanography; Marine Transport; Transport and Communications; Transport Management); **Statistics and Insurance** (Actuarial Science; Business Computing; Economics; Finance; Insurance; Statistics)

History: Founded 1938 as Graduate School of Industrial Studies. Acquired present status and title 1989.

Governing Bodies: Senate

Academic Year: September to July (September-January; February-July)

Admission Requirements: Secondary school certificate (Apolytrion Lykiou) and entrance examination

Fees: (Euros): Foreign students, c. 735 per annum

Main Language(s) of Instruction: Greek. Also English for Erasmus students.

International Co-operation: Participates in Erasmus, Leonardo, Jean-Monnet

Degrees and Diplomas: *Ptychio*: Banking and Financial Management; Business Administration; Economics; Industrial Management; Informatics; International and European Studies; Maritime Studies; Statistics and Insurance; Technology and Digital Systems (Bachelor), 4 yrs; *Metaptychiako Diploma Eidikefsis*: Banking and Financial Management; Business Administration; Economics; Industrial Management; Informatics; International and European Studies; Maritime Studies; Statistics and Insurance; Technology and Digital Systems (Master; Executive Master), 1-2 yrs; *Didaktoriko Diploma*: Banking and Financial Management; Business Administration; Economics; Industrial Management; Informatics; International and European Studies; Maritime Studies; Statistics and Insurance; Technology and Digital Systems (PhD), by thesis

Student Services: Academic counselling, Canteen, Cultural centre, Employment services, Foreign student adviser, Foreign Studies Centre, Handicapped facilities, Health services, Social counselling, Sports facilities

Student Residential Facilities: Yes

Libraries: c. 150,000 vols

Publications: Spoudai (studies) *(quarterly)*
Last Updated: 10/02/12

UNIVERSITY OF THE AEGEAN
Panepistimion Aegaeou
University Hill, Administration Bldg., 81100 Mytilene, Lesvos
Tel: +30(22510) 36000
Fax: +30(22510) 36009
EMail: secr@aegean.gr
Website: http://www3.aegean.gr/aegean/en/intro_en.htm

Rector: Paris Tsartas
Tel: +30(22510) 36012, Fax: +30(22510) 36019
EMail: rector@aegean.gr

Vice Rector of Academic Affairs and Student Welfare: Nikos Soulakellis EMail: vice-rector-afsw@aegean.gr

Departments
Product and Systems Design Engineering *(Ermoupolis, SYROS)* (Art Management; Design; Engineering Drawing and Design)

Schools
Business Studies *(Chios, CHIOS)* (Business Administration; Finance; Management; Marine Transport; Tourism; Transport Management); **Environment** *(Mytilene, LEVSOS)* (Environmental Studies; Food Science; Marine Science and Oceanography; Nutrition); **Humanities** *(Rhodes, RHODES)* (Mediterranean Studies; Preschool Education; Primary Education); **Science** *(Karlovasi, SAMOS)* (Actuarial Science; Communication Studies; Information Management; Information Technology; Mathematics; Natural Sciences; Statistics; Telecommunications Engineering); **Social Sciences** *(Mytilene, LESVOS)* (Anthropology; Communication Studies; Cultural Studies; Geography; Information Sciences; Mass Communication; Museum Studies; Social Sciences; Sociology; Technology)

Further Information: Akso campuses in Chios , Samos , Syros and Rhodes

History: Founded 1984. A State institution under the jurisdiction of the Ministry of Education.

Governing Bodies: Senate

Academic Year: October to June (October-February; February-June)

Admission Requirements: Secondary school certificate (Apolytirion Lykiou)

Fees: None

Main Language(s) of Instruction: Greek

International Co-operation: Participates in Erasmus

Degrees and Diplomas: *Ptychio*: 4 yrs; *Metaptychiako Diploma Eidikefsis*; *Didaktoriko Diploma*. Also Master's degree

Student Services: Academic counselling, Canteen, Employment services, Foreign student adviser, Health services, Language programs, Social counselling

Student Residential Facilities: Yes

Libraries: Central Library

Academic Staff *2011-2012* — **TOTAL**
FULL-TIME — **c. 500**
Student Numbers *2011-2012*
All (Foreign Included) — **c. 13,000**
FOREIGN ONLY — **700**
Last Updated: 10/02/12

UNIVERSITY OF THE PELOPONNESE

Red Cross 28, Karyotakis, 22100 Tripoli
Tel: +30(2710) 230-006
Fax: +30(2710) 230-005
EMail: icalamb0@uop.gr
Website: http://www.uop.gr

Chancellor: Theodoros Papatheodorou

Faculties
Fine Arts *(Nafplio)* (Fine Arts; Theatre); **Human Movement and Quality of Life** *(Sparta)* (Nursing; Sports; Sports Management); **Humanities and Cultural Studies** *(Kalamata)* (Arts and Humanities; Cultural Studies); **Management and Economics** (Economics; Management); **Science and Technology** (Computer Science; Technology; Telecommunications Engineering); **Social Sciences** *(Corinth)* (Education; International Relations; Political Sciences; Social Policy; Social Sciences)

History: Founded 2002.

Main Language(s) of Instruction: Greek

Degrees and Diplomas: *Ptychio*: 8 sem.; *Metaptychiako Diploma Eidikefsis*: Computer Science; Organization and Management of Public Services; Organizations and Business; Financial Analysis; Organization and Management of Sports Organizations and Business; *Didaktoriko Diploma*: Computer Science; Economics (Ph.D.)

Last Updated: 14/02/12

UNIVERSITY OF THESSALY

Panepistimio Thesalias (UTH)
Argonafton and Filellinon, 38221 Volos, Magnesia
Tel: +30(24210) 74000
Fax: +30(24210) 74614
EMail: chkostop@adm.uth.gr
Website: http://www.uth.gr

Rector: Konstantinos Gourgoulianis
Tel: +30(24210) 74502, Fax: +30(24210) 74614
EMail: prytanis@uth.gr

Vice-Rector of Academic Affairs and Personnel: Ioannis Theodorakis
Tel: +30(24210) 74516, Fax: +30(24210) 74608
EMail: rec-acad@uth.gr

International Relations: Michel Zouboulakis, Vice-Rector of Economic and Student Affairs, Public and International Relations
Tel: +30(24210) 74527, Fax: +30(24210) 74643
EMail: rec-econ@uth.gr

Departments
Economics *(Independent)* (Economics); **Physical Education and Sport Sciences** *(Independent)* (Physical Education; Sports)

Programmes
Foreign Languages (English; French; German; Italian; Modern Languages); **Postgraduate Studies** (Agriculture; Anthropology; Aquaculture; Archaeology; Architecture; Architecture and Planning; Biochemistry; Biotechnology; Civil Engineering; Computer Engineering; Crop Production; Economics; History; Mechanical Engineering; Medicine; Physical Education; Preschool Education; Primary Education; Regional Planning; Rural Studies; Special

Education; Sports; Telecommunications Engineering; Veterinary Science)

Schools
Agricultural Sciences (Agriculture; Animal Husbandry; Crop Production; Rural Planning; Water Science); **Engineering** (Architecture; Civil Engineering; Computer Engineering; Industrial Engineering; Mechanical Engineering; Regional Planning; Structural Architecture; Telecommunications Engineering; Town Planning); **Health Sciences** (Biochemistry; Biotechnology; Medicine; Veterinary Science); **Humanities** (Anthropology; Archaeology; History; Preschool Education; Primary Education; Special Education)

Further Information: Also University Hospital.

History: Founded 1984. A State institution under the jurisdiction of the Ministry of Education.

Governing Bodies: Senate; Rector's Council

Academic Year: September to August (September-February; February-August)

Admission Requirements: Secondary school certificate (Apolytirion Lykiou) and entrance examination

Fees: None

Main Language(s) of Instruction: Greek

International Co-operation: Participates in the Erasmus programme

Degrees and Diplomas: *Ptychio*: 4-5 yrs; *Metaptychiako Diploma Eidikefsis*; *Didaktoriko Diploma*. Also joint Greek-French Master Programme; International Master In Sports Tourism Engineering (Imiste)

Student Services: Academic counselling, Canteen, Employment services, Handicapped facilities, Health services, Language programs, Sports facilities

Student Residential Facilities: Yes

Special Facilities: Kitsou Makri (Folk Art Centre)

Libraries: Central Library, c. 80,000 vols. Large collection of topographic, geological and soil maps and a developing collection of audio-visual material, located in five library branches situated in four cities of the region of Thessaly (Volos-Iarissa-Trikala-Karditsa)

Publications: Social Science Tribune, Discussion Paper
Last Updated: 10/02/12

UNIVERSITY OF WESTERN MACEDONIA (UOWM)

Parko Agiou Dimitriou, GR 50100 Kozani
Tel: + (30) 24610 56200
EMail: info@uowm.gr
Website: http://www.uowm.gr

Rector: Christos V. Massalas

Departments
Applied and Visual Arts *(Florina)* (Fine Arts; Visual Arts); **Balkan Studies** *(Florina)* (Ancient Civilizations; Anthropology; Central European Studies; Communication Studies; Computer Science; Cultural Studies; Economics; History; International Relations; Law; Mass Communication; Media Studies; Political Sciences; Russian; Social Studies); **Elementary Education** (Arts and Humanities; Education; Educational Sciences; Health Education; History; Modern Languages; Pedagogy; Primary Education; Teacher Training); **Engineering Informatics and Telecommunications** *(Kozani)* (Computer Engineering; Engineering; Telecommunications Engineering); **Mechanical Engineering** *(Kozani)* (Engineering; Mechanical Engineering); **Nursing** (Nursing)

History: Founded 2003.

Degrees and Diplomas: *Ptychio*; *Metaptychiako Diploma Eidikefsis*; *Didaktoriko Diploma*
Last Updated: 14/02/12

Guatemala

STRUCTURE OF HIGHER EDUCATION SYSTEM

Description:

Higher education is provided by one State and several private universities. There are also higher institutes and schools. The State university is autonomous. Its main authority is the Higher University Council. The private universities are under the authority of a Consejo de la Enseñanza Privada Superior which accredits them. The qualifications they award are officially recognized.

Stages of studies:

University level first stage: *Técnico, Diplomado, Licenciatura*
Universities offer technical courses at a lower level than degree courses which lead to the title of Diplomado or Técnico after two or three-and-a-half years' study. The Licenciatura is awarded after four or five years' study and the defense of a thesis. In Medicine, studies last for six years.

University level second stage: *Maestría, Doctorado*
The Maestría Degree is conferred after one or two further years of study and the submission of a thesis. The Doctorado is awarded after two consecutive years of study following upon the Licenciatura and on submission of a thesis in Law, the Humanities, Education, Economics or Social Sciences.

ADMISSION TO HIGHER EDUCATION

Admission to university-level studies:

Name of secondary school credential required: Bachillerato

Alternatives to credentials: Secretario, Pre-Primary and Primary School Teachers and Perito Contador.

Entrance exam requirements: To enter the Universidad Francisco Marroquín, Rafaél Landivar and del Valle students must sit for the Examen de Admisión.

Foreign students admission:

Entrance exam requirements: Foreign students must hold the Bachillerato or a diploma of an official secondary study programme recognized by the government.

Language requirements: Knowledge of Spanish is essential.

NATIONAL BODIES

Ministerio de Educación (Ministry of Education)
Minister: Dennis Alonzo Mazariegos
6a Calle 1-87 zona 10
Guatemala 01010
Tel: +502 2411 9595
EMail: info@mineduc.gob.gt
WWW: http://www.mineduc.gob.gt

Consejo Nacional de Ciencia y Tecnología - CONCYT (Secretariat for Science and Technology)
President: Rafael Espada
3ra. Avenida 13-28, Zona 1
Guatelama 01001
Tel: +502 2230 2664
WWW: http://www.concyt.gob.gt/

Consejo de la Enseñanza Privada Superior - CEPS (Private Higher Education Council)
Edificio Colegios Profesionales
calle 15-46 zona 15
Colonia El Maestro
Guatemala City
Tel: +502 2369 6344
WWW: http://www.ceps.edu.gt
Role of national body: To coordinate and assess private universities.

Data for academic year: 2006-2007
Source: IAU from Ministerio de Educación, Guatemala, 2006. Bodies updated 2011.

INSTITUTIONS

PUBLIC INSTITUTIONS

UNIVERSITY OF SAN CARLOS OF GUATEMALA

Universidad de San Carlos de Guatemala
Ciudad Universitaria, Zona 12, Guatemala City 01012
Tel: +502(2) 443-9500
Fax: +502(2) 443-9500
EMail: usacdiga@usac.edu.gt
Website: http://www.usac.edu.gt
Rector: Carlos Estuardo Gálvez Barrios (2006-)
EMail: rector@usac.edu.gt

Faculties
Agronomy (Agronomy); **Architecture** (Architecture; Graphic Design); **Chemistry and Pharmacy** (Chemistry; Pharmacy); **Dentistry** (Dentistry); **Economics**; **Engineering** (Engineering); **Humanities** (Art History; English; Literature; Music Education; Pedagogy; Philosophy); **Law and Social Sciences** (Law; Social Sciences); **Medical Sciences** (Medicine; Nursing; Surgery); **Veterinary Science and Zoology** (Veterinary Science; Zoology)

Schools
Communication Studies; **History** (History); **Political Science**; **Psychology**; **Social Work** (Social Work); **Teacher Training** (Teacher Training)

History: Founded 1676 by royal decree of Charles II of Spain. Became an autonomous institution 1945.

Governing Bodies: Consejo Superior Universitario

Academic Year: January to December (January-June; July-December)

Admission Requirements: Secondary school certificate (bachillerato) or recognized foreign equivalent

Main Language(s) of Instruction: Spanish

Degrees and Diplomas: *Técnico*: Nutrition (Nutricionista), 4 yrs; *Técnico*: Social Work (Trabajador social), 3 yrs; *Técnico*: Technical Studies; *Profesorado de Enseñanza Media*: Teaching Qualification, secondary level, 3 1/2 yrs; *Licenciatura*: Accountancy (Contador público y auditor); Anthropology; Applied Mathematics; Archaeology; Architecture (Arquitecto); Biochemistry (Químico Biólogo); Biology (Biólogo); Business Administration (Administrador de Empresas); Chemistry (Químico); Classical Languages and Literature; Economics (Economista); Education; History; International Relations; Journalism; Law; Library Science; Pharmaceutical Biochemistry (Químico Farmacéutico); Philosophy; Physics; Political Science (Politicólogo); Social Sciences; Sociology; Spanish Language and Literature, 5 yrs; *Licenciatura*: Journalism (Periodista profesional); Library Science (Bibliotecario), 3 yrs; *Licenciatura*: Medicine (Médico y Cirujano); Psychology (Psicólogo), 6 yrs; *Maestría*: a further 1-2 yrs; *Doctorado*

Special Facilities: Botanical Garden; Natural History Museum

Libraries: Central Library, c. 235,000 vols
Last Updated: 04/04/08

PRIVATE INSTITUTIONS

FRANCISCO MARROQUÍN UNIVERSITY

Universidad Francisco Marroquín (UFM)
6a Calle Final, Zona 10, Guatemala City 01010
Tel: +502(2) 338-7700
Fax: +502(2) 334-6896
EMail: inf@ufm.edu.gt
Website: http://www.ufm.edu.gt
Rector: Giancarlo Ibárgüen (2003-) EMail: rectoria@ufm.edu.gt
Secretario General: Ricardo Castillo EMail: rca@ufm.edu.gt

Departments
Education (Education); **Psychology** (Clinical Psychology; Industrial and Organizational Psychology; Psychology)

Faculties
Architecture (Architecture); **Dentistry** (Dentistry); **Economics** (Business Administration; Economics); **Law** (Law); **Medicine** (Medicine)

Graduate Schools
Economics and Business Administration (Business Administration; Economics); **Psychology**; **Social Sciences** (Social Sciences)

Institutes
Political Science and International Relations (International Relations; Political Sciences)

Schools
Nutrition (Nutrition)

Further Information: Also Teaching Hospital

History: Founded 1971. A private institution financed by tuition fees and donations.

Governing Bodies: Board of Trustees; Board of Directors

Academic Year: January to November (January-May; July-November)

Admission Requirements: Secondary school certificate (bachillerato) or foreign equivalent and entrance examination

Main Language(s) of Instruction: Spanish

International Co-operation: With institutions in South America and USA.

Degrees and Diplomas: *Técnico*: Human Resources, 3 yrs; *Profesorado de Enseñanza Media*: Teaching Qualification, secondary level, 3 yrs; *Licenciatura*: Psychology, Architecture, Law, Economics, Business Administration, Psychology, Political Science, Medicine, Dentistry, 4-7 yrs; *Maestría*: Business Administration,

Economics, Law, Administration and development of Human Resources, Real Estate project, Behavioural Neurophysiology (MA, MS, MBA), a further 1-2 yrs; *Doctorado*: Law, Economics

Student Services: Canteen, Handicapped facilities

Special Facilities: Popol-Vuh Museum (Maya and Pre-Columbian objects, Spanish Colonial Art, Folklore); Ixchel Museum (Maya textiles, Art exhibits)

Libraries: Ludwig von Mises Library, 40,000 vols; Theology, c. 50,000 vols

Publications: Laissez-faire, School of Economics; Revista de la Facultad de Derecho

Press or Publishing House: Editorial Universidad Francisco Marroquín
Last Updated: 14/10/09

GALILEO UNIVERSITY
Universidad Galileo
Calle Dr. Eduardo Suger Cofiño 57a. Avenida Final, Zona 10, Guatemala City 01010
Tel: +502(2) 423-8000
Fax: +502(2) 423-8000
EMail: info@galileo.edu
Website: http://www.galileo.edu

Rector: José Eduardo Suger Cofiño

Secretario General: Jorge Francisco Retolaza
EMail: jretolaza@galileo.edu

Faculties
Communication Studies (Cinema and Television; Communication Studies); **Education** *(FACED)* (Biology; Chemistry; Computer Science; Educational Administration; History; Mathematics and Computer Science; Social Sciences; Teacher Training); **Science, Technology and Industry**; **Sports** (Sports; Sports Management); **Systems Engineering, Informatics and Computer Science** *(FISICC)* (Computer Networks; Computer Science; Electronic Engineering; Systems Analysis; Telecommunications Engineering)

Schools
Arts; **Continuing Education**; **FISICC-IDEA**; **Graduate**; **Human Health Development**; **Professional Development**; **Technical** *(ESTEC)* (Communication Studies; Design; Educational Administration; Electrical Engineering; Industrial Management; Telecommunications Engineering)

History: Founded 2000.

Main Language(s) of Instruction: Spanish

Degrees and Diplomas: *Licenciatura*; *Profesorado en Educación*; *Maestría*
Last Updated: 14/10/09

MARIANO GÁLVEZ UNIVERSITY OF GUATEMALA
Universidad Mariano Gálvez de Guatemala
3a. Avenida 9-00 Zona 2, Interior Finca El Zapote, Apartado Postal 1811, Guatemala City 01002
Tel: +502(2) 288-7592
Fax: +502(2) 288-4040
Website: http://www.umg.edu.gt

Rector: Alvaro R. Torres Moss Tel: +502(2) 288-3980

Faculties
Administration (Administration); **Architecture** (Architecture); **Civil Engineering** (Civil Engineering); **Economics** (Economics); **Law and Social Sciences** (Law; Social Sciences); **Odontology** (Dentistry)

Further Information: Also 13 branches in different States

History: Founded 1966. A private institution recognized by the State.

Governing Bodies: Consejo Directivo

Academic Year: February to November (February-June; July-November)

Admission Requirements: Secondary school certificate (bachillerato) or foreign equivalent

Main Language(s) of Instruction: Spanish

Degrees and Diplomas: *Profesorado de Enseñanza Media*: Plastic Arts Teaching, 4 yrs; *Licenciatura*: Business Administration; Economics; Law and Social Sciences, 5-6 yrs; *Licenciatura*: Civil Engineering (Ingeniero civil), 6 yrs; *Maestría*; *Doctorado*. Also técnico universitario

Student Residential Facilities: For c. 6,000 students

Libraries: c. 9,000 vols

Publications: Winak *(annually)*

MESOAMERICAN UNIVERSITY
Universidad Mesoaméricana
40 Calle 10-01, Zona 8, Guatemala City
Tel: +502 2471-2958
Fax: +502 2471-3708
EMail: umesecgen@umes.edu.gt
Website: http://www.umes.edu.gt

Rector: Félix Javier Serrano Ursúa EMail: secrec@umes.edu.gt

Secretaria General: Claudia De DigueroFax: +502 2471-3104

Departments
Business Administration (Business Administration); **Computer Engineering**; **Law and Social Sciences**; **Philosophy and Theology** (Philosophy; Religious Studies; Theology)

Faculties
Humanities and Social Sciences (Educational Administration; Educational Sciences; Pedagogy); **Social Communication** (Advertising and Publicity; Graphic Design; Radio and Television Broadcasting)

Schools
Advanced Management

History: Founded 2000.

Governing Bodies: Consejo Directivo

Academic Year: January to December

Admission Requirements: Secondary school certificate, entrance examination

Fees: (Quetzales): Licenciaturas: 6,100 per semester; Maestrias: 7,000

Main Language(s) of Instruction: Spanish

Degrees and Diplomas: *Técnico*: 3 yrs; *Licenciatura*: 5 yrs; *Maestría*: 2 yrs

Libraries: c. 2,000 vols.
Last Updated: 14/10/09

PANAMERICAN UNIVERSITY
Universidad Panamericana
Carretera a San Isidro, Zona 16, Aldea Acatan
Tel: +502 2261-1663 +502 2261-2339
EMail: saberian@supercable.net.gt
Website: http://www.universidadpanamericana.edu.gt

Rector: Abel Girón EMail: abelgironarevalo@yahoo.com

Vice-Rector: Alfonso Schilling EMail: alfonsoschilling@hotmail.com

Faculties
Communication Studies; **Economics** (Accountancy; Business Administration; Economics; Marketing); **Education** (Education; Educational Administration; Educational and Student Counselling; Teacher Training); **Law, Social Sciences and Justice** (Law; Social Sciences); **Theology** (Pastoral Studies; Theology)

Degrees and Diplomas: *Licenciatura*; *Maestría*; *Doctorado*

RAFAEL LANDÍVAR UNIVERSITY
Universidad Rafael Landívar
Vista Hermosa 111, Zona 16, Apartado Postal 39 C
Guatemala City 01016
Tel: +502(2) 279-7979
Fax: +502(2) 884-0400
EMail: comunica@url.edu.gt
Website: http://www.url.edu.gt

Rector: Rolando Enrique Alvarado López (2009-)

Centres
Social Development *(CAPS)* (Social Studies)

Faculties
Agricultural and Environmental Sciences (Agriculture; Environmental Studies); **Architecture and Design** (Architecture; Design); **Economics and Business Administration** (Business Administration; Economics; Tourism); **Engineering** (Engineering) *Dean*: Jorge Lavarreda; **Health Sciences** (Child Care and Development; Laboratory Techniques; Social and Preventive Medicine); **Humanities** (Arts and Humanities; Education; Literature; Philosophy; Psychology); **Law and Social Sciences** (Law; Social Sciences); **Political and Social Sciences** (Political Sciences; Social Sciences); **Theology** (Theology)

Further Information: Also Campus in Quetzaltenango

History: Founded 1961, a private Catholic institution recognized by the State. Acquired status of independent University 1966.

Governing Bodies: Board of Trustees; Executive Council

Main Language(s) of Instruction: Spanish

Degrees and Diplomas: *Técnico*: 3 yrs; *Profesorado de Enseñanza Media*: Teaching Qualification, secondary level, 4 yrs; *Licenciatura*: 5 yrs; *Maestría*: a further 2 yrs; *Doctorado*: 2 yrs

Libraries: c. 45,000 vols

Publications: Boletín de Lingüística *(3 per annum)*; Revista Cultura de Guatemala *(quarterly)*; Revista Estudios Sociales *(biennially)*
Last Updated: 14/10/09

RURAL UNIVERSITY OF GUATEMALA
Universidad Rural de Guatemala
7 Calle 6-49 Zona 2, Guatemala City
Tel: +502 2254-7311
Fax: +502 2254-1215
EMail: info_urural@gua.net
Website: http://www.urural.edu.gt

Rector: Fidel Reyes Lee EMail: rector@urural.edu.gt

Faculties
Economics; **Educational Sciences**; **Law and Social Sciences** (Law; Notary Studies; Social Sciences); **Natural and Environmental Sciences**

Institutes
Agro-forestry (Agriculture; Forestry)

Schools
Ecological *(San José)* (Ecology); **Spanish** (Spanish)
History: Founded 1995.

Main Language(s) of Instruction: Spanish

Degrees and Diplomas: *Bachiller*; *Licenciatura*; *Maestría*
Last Updated: 14/10/09

UNIVERSITY OF THE ISTHMUS
Universidad del Istmo (UNIS)
7a. Avenida 3-67, Zona 13, Guatemala City 01013
Tel: +502 2429-1400
Fax: +502 2475-3526
EMail: unis@unis.edu.gt
Website: http://www.unis.edu.gt

Rector: Manuel Angel Pérez Lara Tel: +502 2429-1401

Secretario: Rodrigo de la Peña Aguilar

Faculties
Architecture and Design (Architecture; Fashion Design; Graphic Design; Interior Design); **Communication** (Journalism); **Economics and Business Administration** (Administration; Business Administration; Economics); **Education**; **Engineering** (Engineering; Industrial Engineering); **Law** (Law)

Institutes
Business School *(Tayasal)* (Business Administration) *Director*: Victor Turcios Garcia; **Femenino de Estudios Superiores** (Arts and Humanities; Business Administration; Tourism; Translation and Interpretation) *Director*: Beatriz Ymbert Garavito

History: Founded 1997.

Governing Bodies: Consejo de Fiduciarios y Consejo Directivo

Academic Year: January to November

Main Language(s) of Instruction: Spanish

Degrees and Diplomas: *Licenciatura*: 5 yrs; *Maestría*: 2 yrs

Student Services: Academic counselling, Handicapped facilities, Social counselling

Student Residential Facilities: Yes.

Libraries: University Library

Publications: News Bulletin *(bimonthly)*
Last Updated: 14/10/09

UNIVERSITY OF THE VALLEY OF GUATEMALA
Universidad del Valle de Guatemala
18 Avenida 11-95, Zona 15, Vista Hermosa III, Apartado Postal 82, Guatemala City 01015
Tel: +502 (2) 364-0336; +502(2) 364-0492
Fax: +502(2) 364-0212; +502(2) 369-7479
EMail: info@uvg.edu.gt; info1@uvg.gt
Website: http://www.uvg.edu.gt

Rector: Roberto Moreno Godoy (2001-) Fax: +502(2) 364-0052 EMail: rmoreno@uvg.edu.gt

Secretaria General: Victoria Eugenia Rosales
Tel: +502(2) 364-0336, Ext. 458 EMail: erosales@uvg.edu.gt

International Relations: Mónica de Andrade
Tel: +502(2) 364-0340 EMail: mandrade@uvg.edu.gt

Faculties
Education (Education; Health Education; Music Education; Teacher Training); **Engineering** (Agricultural Engineering; Chemical Engineering; Civil Engineering; Computer Engineering; Electronic Engineering; Food Technology; Forestry; Industrial Engineering; Mechanical Engineering); **Science and Humanities** (Arts and Humanities; Biochemistry; Biology; Chemistry; Environmental Studies; Literature; Mathematics; Microbiology; Natural Sciences; Nutrition; Physics); **Social Sciences** (Anthropology; Archaeology; History; Psychology; Social Sciences; Sociology)

Institutes
Research

Further Information: Also South Educational Programme, PROESUR, Santa Lucia Cotzumalguapa; and West Educational Programme, UVG-Altiplano, Sololá

History: Founded 1961 as a private institution under the patronage of the Asociación del Colegio Americano de Guatemala. Formally recognized 1966.

Governing Bodies: Consejo de Fiduciarios; Consejo Directivo

Academic Year: January to November (January-May; June-July; August-November)

Admission Requirements: Secondary school certificate (bachillerato) or foreign equivalent, and entrance examination

Fees: (Quetzales): 12,700 per semester

Main Language(s) of Instruction: Spanish

International Co-operation: With universities in USA

Degrees and Diplomas: *Licenciatura*: 5-6 yrs; *Maestría*: a further 1-2 yrs. Also, Teaching qualifications, 4 yrs

Special Facilities: Botanical Garden

Libraries: Biblioteca Central, 67,000 vols; Colección Virginia Shook, 18,000 vols

Publications: Revista Universidad del Valle de Guatemala
Last Updated: 14/10/09

Guinea

STRUCTURE OF HIGHER EDUCATION SYSTEM

Description:

Higher education is provided by public and private universities and institutes. Higher education institutions are under the responsibility of the Ministère de l'Enseignement supérieur et de la Recherche scientifique.

Stages of studies:

University level first stage: *Licence*
The Licence is awarded after four years.

University level second stage: *Master*
A further two years beyond the Licence lead to the Master.

University level third stage: *Doctorat*
This is the third cycle of higher education. Entry to the course is based on the Master. Students must submit a thesis.

ADMISSION TO HIGHER EDUCATION

Admission to university-level studies:

Name of secondary school credential required: Baccalauréat 2ème Partie

For entry to: Universities

Entrance exam requirements: Admission test for universities.

NATIONAL BODIES

Ministère de l'Enseignement supérieur et de la Recherche scientifique (Ministry of Higher Education and Scientific Research)

Minister: Morike Damaro Camara
PO Box 2201
Conakry
Tel: +224 451 217

Data for academic year: 2009-2010
Source: IAU from Base Curie, Ministère des Affaires étrangères et européennes, France, and documentation, 2009. Bodies updated 2011.

INSTITUTIONS

PUBLIC INSTITUTIONS

GAMAL ABDEL NASSER UNIVERSITY OF CONAKRY
Université Gamal Abdel Nasser de Conakry
BP 1147, Conakry
Tel: +224 46-46-89
Fax: +224 46-48-08
Website: http://uganc-edu.org
Recteur: Yazora Soropogui (2008-)

Secrétaire Général: Ousmane Wora Diallo
Vice-Recteur chargé des Etudes: Aboubacar Sylla

Centres
Applied Technology (Technology); **Computer Science** (Computer Science); **Economics**; **Environmental Studies and Research** (Environmental Studies)

Faculties
Medicine, Pharmacy, Dentistry and Stomatology (Biochemistry; Dentistry; Medicine; Paediatrics; Pharmacy; Public Health; Stomatology); **Science** (Biochemistry; Biology; Chemistry; Energy

Engineering; Mathematics; Microbiology; Natural Sciences; Physics; Physiology; Zoology)

Institutes
Polytechnic (Chemical Engineering; Civil Engineering; Electrical Engineering; Engineering; Food Technology; Technology; Telecommunications Engineering; Telecommunications Services)

Further Information: Also 2 University Hospitals

History: Founded 1962 as Institut Polytechnique, became University 1984. Acquired present status 1989. Previously known as Université de Conakry. A State institution under the supervision of the Ministry of Education.

Governing Bodies: Conseil d'Administration; Conseil de l'Université

Academic Year: September to June (September-January; February-June)

Admission Requirements: Secondary school certificate (baccalauréat) and competitive entrance examination

Main Language(s) of Instruction: French

Degrees and Diplomas: *Diplôme de Technicien supérieur*: Computer Science (DTSI), 3 1/2 yrs; *Licence*: 3 yrs; *Master*: 4 yrs; *Master*: Business Administration; *Doctorat*: Medicine, 6 yrs; *Doctorat*: Pharmacy, 5 yrs

Student Residential Facilities: Yes

Special Facilities: Zoo. Meteorology Station. Radiotelescope. Audiovisual Centre

Libraries: Central Library, c. 23,000 vols; libraries of the faculties and departments, c. 11,730

Publications: Annales de l'Université *(annually)*; Bulletin de la Recherche *(monthly)*; Guinée Médicale *(quarterly)*

Press or Publishing House: Service des Editions Universitaires
Last Updated: 03/07/09

GÉNÉRAL LANSANA CONTÉ DE SONFONIA UNIVERSITY
Université Général Lansana Conté de Sonfonia
Sonfonia, 030 BP 970, Ratoma, Conakry
Tel: +224 21-83-09

Recteur: Mamadi Kourouma (2008-)
Vice-Recteur chargé des Etudes: Aly Badara Sylla
Secrétaire général: Julien Gbéré Touré

Faculties
Arts and Humanities (Arts and Humanities); **Economics and Management**; **Law and Political Sciences**

Schools
Tourism and Hotel Management (Hotel and Restaurant; Hotel Management; Tourism)

History: Founded as Université de Sonfonia. Acquired present title 2005.
Last Updated: 03/07/09

HIGHER INSTITUTE FOR DISTANCE EDUCATION
Institut supérieur de Formation à Distance
B.P. 1961, Conakry
EMail: isfad_gn-dgae@yahoo.fr

Directeur général: Mamadou Dian Gongorè Diallo
Secrétaire générale: Marie Rose Bangoura
Directeur général adjoint des Etudes: Jean-Marie Touré

Departments
Economics and Management (Economics; Management); **Higher Officers in Community Development** (Development Studies; Social and Community Services; Social Sciences; Urban Studies); **Law** (Law)

History: Founded 2003.
Last Updated: 22/09/09

HIGHER INSTITUTE OF ARCHITECTURE AND TOWN PLANNING OF CONAKRY
Institut supérieur d'Architecture et d'Urbanisme de Conakry
Conakry

Directeur général: Mamadi Touré
Directrice générale adjointe chargée des Etudes: Mafory Bangoura
Secrétaire général: Gononan Traoré

Departments
Architecture (Architecture); **Town Planning** (Town Planning)
History: Founded 2005.
Last Updated: 03/07/09

HIGHER INSTITUTE OF EDUCATIONAL SCIENCES OF GUINEA/LAMBANDJI
Institut supérieur des Sciences de l'Education de Guinée/Lambandji
BP 795, Conakry

Directeur général: Mamadou Alpha Diallo
Secrétaire général: Albert Balamou
Directeur général adjoint chargé des Etudes: Bocar Dieng

Departments
Continuing Education and Research (Educational Research; Literacy Education); **Educational Administration** (Educational Administration); **Teacher Training Education** (Staff Development; Teacher Trainers Education; Teacher Training); **Teacher Training I**; **Teacher Training II** (Educational Sciences; Secondary Education; Teacher Training)

History: Founded 1991 by the transformation of the Ecole Normale Supérieure.

Governing Bodies: Conseil d' Administration; Conseil de l' Institut
Academic Year: October to July

Admission Requirements: University degree (Maîtrise) and entrance examination. Professional experience may also be required in some sections

Main Language(s) of Instruction: French

Degrees and Diplomas: Certificate in Teacher Training

Student Services: Canteen, Health services, Sports facilities

Student Residential Facilities: For 300 students

Libraries: Main Library, c. 3,500 vols

Publications: Faisceau, Educational Sciences *(biannually)*
Last Updated: 03/07/09

HIGHER INSTITUTE OF FINE ARTS OF GUINEA
Institut supérieur des Arts de Guinée (ISAG)
Dubréka
Website: http://isag-guinee.com

Directeur général: Siba Fassou
Secrétaire général: Traoré Karifa
Directeur général adjoint chargé des Etudes: Moustapha Sylla

Departments
Cinema and Audio-Visual Arts (Cinema and Television); **Drama**; **Fine Arts** (Fine Arts); **Music and Musicology** (Music; Musicology)
History: Founded 2004.

Degrees and Diplomas: *Licence*; *Master*
Last Updated: 07/07/09

HIGHER INSTITUTE OF INFORMATION AND COMMUNICATION OF KOUNTIA
Institut supérieur de l'Information et de la Communication de Kountia
Kountia
Directeur général: Bangaly Camara

Directeur général adjoint chargé des Etudes: Mamadi Yaya Cissé

Secrétaire général: Saa Leno

Departments
Audio Visual Communication (Media Studies); **Communication and Information Technology** (Communication Studies; Information Technology); **Journalism** (Journalism)
Last Updated: 22/09/09

HIGHER INSTITUTE OF MINING AND GEOLOGY OF BOKÉ

Institut supérieur des Mines et Géologie de Boké
B.P. 84, Boké

Directeur général: Gnan Clotaire Maomy

Secrétaire général: Karinka Diawara

Directeur général adjoint chargé des Etudes: Daouda Fofana

Departments
Geology (Geology); **Metallurgical Engineering** (Metallurgical Engineering); **Mining Engineering** (Mining Engineering); **Technology** (Technology)

History: Founded 1991.

Academic Year: October to June
Last Updated: 03/07/09

HIGHER INSTITUTE OF SCIENCE AND VETERINARY MEDICINE OF DALABA

Institut supérieur des Sciences et de Médecine vétérinaire de Dalaba
B.P. 9, Dalaba

Directeur général: Youssouf Sidimé

Secrétaire général: Ibrahima Baldé

Directeur général adjoint chargé des Etudes: Morlaye Kindia Sylla

Departments
Animal Husbandry and Veterinary Science Production Control (Animal Husbandry; Veterinary Science); **Basic Sciences**; **Epidemiology, Infectious Diseases and Parasitology**; **Therapeutic Sciences**
Last Updated: 22/09/09

HIGHER INSTITUTE OF TECHNOLOGY OF MAMOU

Institut supérieur de Technologie de Mamou
B.P. 84, Mamou

Directeur général: Cellou Kanté

Secrétaire générale: Salifou Camara

Directeur général adjoint chargé des Etudes: Saa Poindo Tonguino

Departments
Basic Sciences (Mathematics and Computer Science; Natural Sciences); **Energy Engineering** (Energy Engineering); **Instrumentation**; **Technology**
Last Updated: 21/09/09

JULIUS NYERERE UNIVERSITY OF KANKAN

Université Julius Nyerere de Kankan
BP 209, Kankan
Tel: +224 71-20-93
EMail: seycam@sotelgui.net.gn

Recteur: Ibrahima Morya Conte (2008-)

Vice-Recteur chargé des Etudes: Pépé Marcel Haba

Secrétaire général: Kaba Sidibe

Faculties
Arts and Humanities (Arts and Humanities; Social Sciences); **Economics and Management**; **Natural Sciences** (Mathematics and Computer Science; Natural Sciences)

Schools
Information Sciences

History: Founded 1963 as school, became Institut polytechnique 1967 and acquired present status and title 1984. A State institution under the supervision of the Ministry of Education.

Academic Year: October to June (October-December; January-March; April-June)

Admission Requirements: Secondary School Certificate (baccalauréat) and competitive entrance examination

Main Language(s) of Instruction: French

Degrees and Diplomas: *Licence*; *Master.* 5 yrs

Student Residential Facilities: Yes
Last Updated: 03/07/09

UNIVERSITY OF LABÉ

Université de Labé
Labé
EMail: driculbe@gmail.com

Directeur général: Alkaly Bah

Directeur général adjoint chargé des Etudes: Sékou Lamine Fofana

Secrétaire général: Momoyah Sylla

Faculties
Administration, Business and Management (Administration; Business and Commerce; English; Management); **Science and Technology** (Computer Science; Technology)
Last Updated: 03/07/09

UNIVERSITY OF N'ZÉRÉKORÉ

Université de N'Zérékoré
N'Zérékoré

Directeur général: Cé Gouanou

Directeur général adjoint chargé des Etudes: Namory Bérété

Secrétaire général: Mamadou Sow

Faculties
Environmental Sciences (Environmental Studies; Forestry); **Science and Technology** (Natural Sciences; Technology)
Last Updated: 03/07/09

VALÉRY GISCARD D'ESTAING HIGHER INSTITUTE OF AGRONOMY AND VETERINARY MEDICINE OF FARANAH

Institut supérieur agronomique et vétérinaire Valéry Giscard d'Estaing de Faranah (ISAV)
BP 131, Faranah
Tel: +224(60) 58-15-00
EMail: isav2@mirinet.net.gn

Directeur général: Sara Baïlo Diallo

Secrétaire général: Joseph Beavogui

Directeur général adjoint chargé des Etudes: Abou Soumah

Departments
Agricultural Economics (Agricultural Economics); **Agricultural Engineering** (Agricultural Engineering); **Agriculture** (Agricultural Economics; Agriculture); **Stockraising and Veterinary Medicine** (Animal Husbandry; Cattle Breeding; Veterinary Science); **Water and Forestry** (Forestry; Water Science)

History: Founded 1978, acquired present status and title 1991.

Accrediting Agencies: Ministry of Agriculture; Ministère de l'Education nationale et de la Recherche scientifique

Degrees and Diplomas: *Master*
Last Updated: 03/07/09

Guinea-Bissau

STRUCTURE OF HIGHER EDUCATION SYSTEM

Description:

Guinea-Bissau opened its first public university in November 2003. Created by governement decree in 1999, the Amilcar Cabral University admitted its first students in January 2004. The University, due to financial problems, had to come back under the tutoring of the Grupo Lusófona and became the Universidade lusófona de Guiné (ULG) in 2008.

The Universidade Colinas de Boé, a private institution, opened in 2003.

Stages of studies:

University level first stage: Bachalerato, Licenciatura

The first cycle of university studies comprises a Bachalerato awarded after three years' study and a Licenciatura awarded after five years' study, including a one-year foundation course.

There is no second cycle available in the country.

ADMISSION TO HIGHER EDUCATION

NATIONAL BODIES

Ministry of National Education, Culture, and Science
   Minister: Artur da Silva
   Bissau

Data for academic year: 2009-2010

Source: IAU from Forum Curie, Ministère des Affaires étrangères et européennes, France, 2009. Bodies updated 2011.

INSTITUTIONS

LUSOPHONE UNIVERSITY OF GUINEA
Universidade Lusófona da Guiné
Caixia postal 659, Bairro D' Ajuda (2♀ Fase), Bissau
Tel: +245 3256-066
EMail: administracao@uac.com
Website: http://ulg.grupolusofona.pt

Administrador Executivo: Montenegro Fiúza
Tel: (+245) 20-59-70

Programmes
Business Administration and Management (Accountancy; African Studies; Applied Mathematics; Business Administration; Commercial Law; Computer Science; Economics; English; French; Human Resources; Industrial and Organizational Psychology; International Business; Law; Leadership; Management; Marketing; Social Sciences; Statistics; Taxation); **Economics** (Accountancy; Applied Mathematics; Business Administration; Computer Science; Econometrics; Economic and Finance Policy; Economics; English; French; Human Resources; Industrial and Production Economics; International Business; Law; Management; Public Administration; Social Sciences; Statistics; Taxation); **Education** (Curriculum; Distance Education; Education; Educational Administration; Educational and Student Counselling; Educational Psychology; Educational Research; Educational Sciences; Educational Technology; International and Comparative Education; Pedagogy; Social Sciences; Statistics; Teacher Trainers Education; Writing); **Engineering**; **Human Resources** (Applied Mathematics; Business Administration; Economics; English; French; Human Resources; Labour Law; Law; Occupational Health; Portuguese; Social Sciences; Social Welfare); **Medicine** (Epidemiology; Hygiene; Laboratory Techniques; Medicine); **Organizational Communication and Journalism** (Advertising and Publicity; Business Administration; Communication Studies; Cultural Studies; English; French; Human Resources; Information Technology; Journalism; Linguistics; Marketing; Media Studies; Multimedia; Portuguese; Public Administration; Public Relations; Radio and Television Broadcasting; Writing); **Social Services**; **Sociology** (African Studies; Anthropology; Applied Mathematics; Computer Science; Demography and Population; Development Studies; Economic History; Educational Sciences; English; French; Geography (Human); Industrial and Organizational Psychology; Law; Linguistics; Rural Studies; Social and Preventive Medicine; Social Psychology; Social Sciences; Social Studies; Sociology; Statistics; Urban Studies)

History: Founded 1999.
Main Language(s) of Instruction: Portuguese
Degrees and Diplomas: *Licenciatura*
Last Updated: 27/03/09

PRIVATE INSTITUTIONS

COLINAS UNIVERSITY OF BOÉ

Universidade Colinas de Boé (UCB)
CP 1340, Avenida 14 de Novembro, Entrada do Bairro de Hafia,
Boé
EMail: uco@rocketmail.com
Reitor: Fafali Koudawo EMail: fafali@eguitel.com

Programmes
Accountancy and Management (Accountancy; Management);
Computer Engineering; **Law** (Law); **Public Administration and**

Social Economy (Economics; Public Administration); **Social Communication and Marketing**

History: Founded 2003.

Degrees and Diplomas: *Bacharelato*: 3 yrs; *Licenciatura*: a further 2 yrs

Academic Staff *2008-2009*	MEN	WOMEN	TOTAL
FULL-TIME	41	4	45
Student Numbers *2008-2009*			
All (Foreign Included)	460	215	675

Last Updated: 05/08/09

Guyana

STRUCTURE OF HIGHER EDUCATION SYSTEM

Description:

Higher education in Guyana is provided by the University of Guyana and by specialized Institutions of higher education: Technical Institutes, a College of Education, a School of Agriculture and a Management Training Institute. Resources come from government grants. The University is governed by the University Council and the Academic Board.

Stages of studies:

University level first stage: *Undergraduate studies*
The minimum entrance requirement for a Bachelor's degree is the Caribbean Examinations Council Secondary Education Certificate (general proficiency) or the General Certificate of Education 'O' level. Courses last four years in Architecture, and three to four years in Arts, Natural Sciences, Social Sciences and Technology. The University also offers a one-year course in Law for students preparing the Bachelor of Law at the University of the West Indies (Barbados). Three-year courses lead to the award of a Certificate in Medical Technology and to various Diplomas: Radiotherapy and Physiotherapy in three years, Management and Technology in two years. A first degree is a prerequisite in education.

University level second stage: *Graduate studies*
Graduate studies lead to the award of a Master's degree in Arts, Science or Social Sciences, following a minimum of one year of study, more often two. The University of Guyana also confers Graduate Diplomas in Education and Development Studies after two years' study.

Distance higher education:
The Institute of Distance and Continuing Education (IDCE), which is a branch of the University of Guyana, offers a Diploma in Occupational Health and Safety. It also collaborates with the National Association of Secretaries in offering a two-year programme leading to the award of the Administrative Professional Secretaries Diploma.

ADMISSION TO HIGHER EDUCATION

Admission to university-level studies:

Name of secondary school credential required: Caribbean Secondary Education Certificate

Minimum score/requirement: Five CSEC Grades 1 to 3 at no more than 2 sittings; English and Mathematics are major subjects for entry to School of Education and Humanities, faculties of Health Sciences, Natural Sciences, Social Sciences and Technology.

For entry to: All institutions and programmes

Name of secondary school credential required: General Certificate of Education Ordinary Level

Minimum score/requirement: Five O levels at no more than 2 sittings; English and Mathematics are major subjects for entry to School of Education and Humanities, Faculties of Health Sciences, Natural Sciences, Social Sciences and Technology.

NATIONAL BODIES

Ministry of Education
Minister: Shaik Baksh
21 Brickdam
Georgetown
Tel: +592 223 7900
Fax: +592 225 8511

WWW: http://www.education.gov.gy/
Role of national body: Education delivery; development of policies for all levels of the education system in Guyana; implementation of plans to achieve objectives affecting education delivery.

Data for academic year: 2007-2008
Source: Guyana National Commission for UNESCO, 2007 (Bodies, 2011)

INSTITUTIONS

PUBLIC INSTITUTIONS

UNIVERSITY OF GUYANA (UG)

PO Box 10-1110, Turkeyen, Greater Georgetown
Tel: +592 222-4184
Fax: +592 222-3596
EMail: registrar_ug@yahoo.com
Website: http://www.uog.edu.gy

Vice-Chancellor: Lawrence Carrigton (2009-)
Tel: +592-222-3583, Fax: +592-222-2118 EMail: vc@uog.edu.gy

Administrative Officer: James G. Rose
Tel: +592-222-3583 EMail: registry@uog.edu.gy

Faculties
Agriculture and Forestry (Agriculture; Animal Husbandry; Crop Production; Forestry; Soil Science); **Health Sciences** (Dentistry; Environmental Studies; Health Sciences; Medical Technology; Medicine; Nursing; Pharmacy; Radiology; Surgery); **Natural Sciences** (Biology; Chemistry; Computer Science; Environmental Studies; Mathematics; Physics; Statistics); **Social Sciences** (Accountancy; Banking; Communication Studies; Finance; Government; International Relations; Law; Management; Marketing; Public Administration; Social Sciences; Social Work; Sociology); **Technology** (Aeronautical and Aerospace Engineering; Agricultural Engineering; Architecture; Civil Engineering; Electrical Engineering; Engineering Management; Geological Engineering; Mechanical Engineering; Technology)

Institutes
Distance and Continuing Education (Communication Studies; Criminology; Developmental Psychology; English; Hygiene; Industrial Management; International Relations; Management; Marketing; Mathematics; Nutrition; Occupational Health; Preschool Education; Primary Education; Public Relations; Secretarial Studies; Social Work; Sociology; Spanish)

Research Units
Amerindian Studies (Amerindian Languages)

Schools
Earth and Environmental Sciences (Environmental Studies; Geography); **Education and Humanities** (Administration; Agriculture; Business Education; Economics; English; Fine Arts; French; Geography; History; Home Economics; Literacy Education; Literature; Mathematics; Modern Languages; Music; Preschool Education; Primary Education; Science Education; Social Studies; Spanish; Teacher Training; Technology Education; Theatre; Tourism; Writing); **Professional Development**

Units
Women's Studies

History: Founded and acquired present status 1963.

Governing Bodies: Council; Academic Board

Academic Year: September to May (September-December; February-May)

Admission Requirements: Three subjects at the GCE Advanced Level plus two subjects at CXC General Proficiency/GCE Ordinary Level or two subjects at the GCE Advanced Level plus three subject at the CXC/CSEC General Proficiency/ GCE Ordinary Level in both case English and in some case Mathematics must be among the subjects obtained. A minimum of five CXC/CSEC General Proficiency (Grades I, II or III)/ five passes at GCE 'O' Level at ONE sitting, including English Language, the subject(s) required for the pursuit of the major, where applicable, and Mathematics for designated programmes. Or a minimum of 6 CXC/CSEC General Proficiency(Grades I, II or III)/ six passes at the GCE 'O' Level AT NOT MORE THAN TWO SITTINGS, including English Language, the subject(s) required for the pursuit of the major, where applicable, and Mathematics for designated programmes.

Fees: (Guyana Dollars): Local students: 127,000-500,000; Foreign students: 4,000-10,000 US$

Main Language(s) of Instruction: English

International Co-operation: With universities in Brazil, Canada, Suriname, United Kingdom, USA, Netherlands, Caribbean.

Degrees and Diplomas: *Bachelor's Degree*: Agriculture (Bsc); Arts (BA); Biology; Chemistry; Computer Science; Environmental Studies; Mathematics; Physics; Statistics (BSc); Communication; Economics; International Studies; Law; Management; Public Management; Social Work; Sociology; Political Science/History (BSocSc); Education (BEd), 4 yrs; *Bachelor's Degree*: Architecture; Civil Engineering; Electrical Engineering; Mechanical Engineering; Mining Engineering; Geology (BEng), 2 yrs; *Bachelor's Degree*: Forestry (BSc), 4 yrs; *Bachelor's Degree*: Medicine and Surgery (MBBS), 5 yrs; *Bachelor's Degree*: Nursing (BSc), 3 yrs; *Master's Degree*: Forest Biology (MSc); History (MA), a further 1-2 yrs; *Graduate Diploma*: Development Studies; International Studies, 1 yr; *Graduate Diploma*: Education (DipEd), 2 yrs. Also Diplomas and Certificates, 1-3 yrs

Student Services: Academic counselling, Canteen, Handicapped facilities, Health services, Social counselling, Sports facilities

Student Residential Facilities: Yes

Libraries: University Library, 257,535 vols; 4,000 journals; 6,815 Audiovisual materials

Publications: Guyana Health Information Digest *(annually)*; Transition, Report on Research *(annually)*
Last Updated: 14/10/09

Haiti

STRUCTURE OF HIGHER EDUCATION SYSTEM

Description:

Higher education is provided by universities and other public and private institutions. Higher education is generally under the responsibility of the Ministère de l'Education nationale but the licence for the teaching of Medicine, Pharmacy, Dentistry, Nursing and Medical Technology is issued by the Ministère de la Santé (Ministry of Health) which has a say in the programmes.

Stages of studies:

University level first stage:
First degree courses normally last for three to five years and lead to the award of the Licence or a professional title in such fields as Civil Engineering, Agriculture, Pharmacy and Dentistry. The Adventist University of Haiti awards Associate (2-3 years) and Bachelor's degrees (4 years).

University level second stage:
A Maîtrise is conferred after two years' study beyond the Licence In Social Sciences, Educational and Business Administration. In Medicine, the Diplôme de Docteur en Médecine is conferred after seven years' study, including periods of internship and practical training.

ADMISSION TO HIGHER EDUCATION

Admission to university-level studies:

Name of secondary school credential required: Baccalauréat 2e partie

For entry to: All institutions/programmes

Entrance exam requirements: Competitive entrance examination for Law, Dentistry, Medicine, Economics, Agriculture, Veterinary Medicine, as well as for the Ecole normale supérieure.

Foreign students admission:

Entrance exam requirements: Foreign students must have completed secondary education and passed the competitive entrance examination.

Entry regulations: Residence permit.

NATIONAL BODIES

Ministère de l'Education nationale et de la Formation professionnelle (Ministry of National Education and Vocational Training)
> Minister: Joel D. Jean-Pierre
> Port-au-Prince
> WWW: http://www.eduhaiti.gouv.ht/Fichiers/Formation_menfp.htm

Data for academic year: 2006-2007
Source: IAU from Direction de l'Enseignement Supérieur et de la Recherche Scientifique, Haiti, 2006 (Bodies, 2011)

INSTITUTIONS

PUBLIC INSTITUTIONS

STATE UNIVERSITY OF HAÏTI
Université d'Etat d'Haïti (UEH)
BP 2279, 21, Rue Rivière, Port-au-Prince
Tel: +509 244-2942 +509 244-2943
Fax: +509 244-2910
EMail: recteur@ueh.edu.ht
Website: http://www.ueh.edu.ht
Recteur: Jean Vernet Henry Tel: +509 244-2944

Centres
Technical Studies, Planning, Applied Economics *(CTPEA)* (Architecture and Planning; Economics; Technology)

Faculties
Agriculture and Veterinary Science (Agriculture; Veterinary Science); **Applied Linguistics** (Applied Linguistics); **Dentistry** (Dentistry); **Ethnology** (Ethnology); **Humanities** (Arts and Humanities; Communication Studies; Psychology; Social Work; Sociology); **Law and Economics** (Economics; Law); **Medicine and Pharmacy** (Medicine; Pharmacy); **Nursing** (Nursing); **Science** (Architecture; Civil Engineering; Electrical Engineering; Electronic Engineering; Hydraulic Engineering; Mechanical Engineering; Natural Sciences; Surveying and Mapping)

Institutes
African Research and Studies (African Studies); **Business Administration and International Studies** (Business Administration; International Studies); **Electronic Technology** (Electronic Engineering); **Polytechnic** *(GOC)* (Engineering; Technology)

Schools
Arts *(ENARTS)* (Arts and Humanities); **Law** *(Cayes, Fort-Liberté, Gonaives, Saint-Marc)* (Law); **Nursing** *(Cap Haïtun)* (Nursing); **Teacher Training** (Teacher Training)

Further Information: Also University Hospital

History: Founded 1944 by decree incorporating or affiliating existing institutions of higher education. Individual Faculties and Schools are responsible to the relevant Ministries and Government Departments. Confirmed as State institution by decree 1960. Financed by the State.

Academic Year: October to July

Admission Requirements: Secondary school certificate (baccalauréat) and competitive entrance examination

Main Language(s) of Instruction: French

Degrees and Diplomas: *Diplôme*: Agronomy; Civil Engineering, 5 yrs; *Diplôme*: Architecture, 3 yrs, plus 1 yr practical work; *Licence*: Accountancy; Diplomacy; Geography; History; Law; Letters; Management; Mathematics; Natural Sciences, 5 yrs; *Licence*: African, Afro-American and Caribbean Studies; Anthropology; Linguistics; Social and Administrative Sciences, 3 yrs; *Maîtrise*: Anthropology; Communications; Psychology; Sociology, 4 yrs

Libraries: University Library, c. 7,000 vols
Last Updated: 09/06/11

PRIVATE INSTITUTIONS

ADVENTIST UNIVERSITY OF HAITI
Université Adventiste d'Haïti (UNAH)
BP 1339, Diquini 63, Route de la Mairie de Carrefour, Port-au-Prince
Tel: +509 234-9210
Fax: +509 234-0562
Website: http://www.unah.edu.ht
Recteur: Pierre Jean Josué (2005-)
Tel: +509 234-1195, Fax: +509 234-8691
EMail: jjpierre28@hotmail.com

Vice-recteur: José Dorismar
Tel: +509 717-6411 EMail: josedorismar@yahoo.fr
International Relations: Charles Fresnel

Faculties
Administration (Accountancy; Business Administration; Business and Commerce; Computer Science); **Educational Sciences** (Biology; Chemistry; Educational Sciences; Mathematics; Physics; Social Sciences); **Nursing**; **Theology** (Ancient Languages; Bible; Religion; Religious Studies; Theology)

History: Founded 1921 in Cap-Haiti. Transferred to Port-au-Prince 1934 and Diquini Campus 1947. Acquired present status and title 1989.

Governing Bodies: Board of Trustees

Admission Requirements: Secondary school certificate (baccalauréat) and entrance examination

Fees: (Gourdes): 6,000 for general fees (800 gourdes per credit)

Main Language(s) of Instruction: French

International Co-operation: With Universidad de Montemorelos, Mexico

Accrediting Agencies: Association of Seventh-day Adventist Schools, Colleges and Universities

Degrees and Diplomas: *Associate Degree*: Business Administration; Computer Science; Music; Nursing; Secretarial Studies (AA), 2-3 yrs; *Bachelor's Degree*: Business Administration (BA); Education (BEd); Theology (BTh), 4 yrs; *Licence*; *Maîtrise*. Also other degrees in Computer Sciences, Modern Languages, Accountancy, Typing

Student Services: Academic counselling, Employment services, Health services, Language programs, Nursery care, Sports facilities

Student Residential Facilities: Yes

Special Facilities: Computer rooms

Press or Publishing House: University Press
Last Updated: 15/10/09

CARIBBEAN UNIVERSITY
Université Caraïbe (CUC)
Delmas 29, No. 7, Port-au-Prince
Tel: +506 3946-8232
EMail: rectorat@universitecaraibe.com
Website: http://www.universitecaraibe.com/
Recteur: Jocelyne Trouillot-Levy (2005-)
EMail: jotrouillot@yahoo.com

Director: Marjoto Mathurin EMail: marlevmat@yahoo.com

International Relations: François Lherisson, Director, International Relations EMail: lherissonfils@yahoo.fr

Faculties
Accounting; **Agriculture** (Agronomy; Animal Husbandry; Crop Production); **Business Administration** (Administration; Management; Secretarial Studies); **Computer Science** (Computer Engineering; Computer Science); **Education** (Bilingual and Bicultural Education; Educational Administration; Native Language Education; Pedagogy; Preschool Education; Primary Education; Secondary Education; Special Education; Teacher Training); **Engineering** (Architecture; Civil Engineering; Electronic Engineering; Mechanical Engineering)

History: Created 1988. The University has developed some programmes in Haitian Creole. Publishing house, Editions CUC Université Caraïbe specialises in educational and youth literature. Acquired status 1990.

Governing Bodies: Council

Academic Year: October to January; February to June

Admission Requirements: Baccalaureat - deuxième partie.

Fees: (US Dollar): 700 per annum

Main Language(s) of Instruction: Haitian Creole, French

International Co-operation: with the University of Ohio, USA.

Degrees and Diplomas: *Licence*: Agriculture; Civil Engineering (Agronomist; Engineer), 5 yrs; *Licence*: Education; Administration; Computer Science, 4 yrs; *Maîtrise*: Education

Student Services: Academic counselling, Canteen, Cultural centre, Employment services, Health services, Language programs, Sports facilities

Student Residential Facilities: Montrouis campus - for 40 students

Libraries: c. 4,000 vols

Publications: L'Université en bref *(biannually)*

Press or Publishing House: Editions CUC Université Caraïbe

Academic Staff 2008-2009	MEN	WOMEN	TOTAL
FULL-TIME	20	8	28
PART-TIME	48	10	58
STAFF WITH DOCTORATE			
FULL-TIME	3	2	5
PART-TIME	2	1	3
Student Numbers 2008-2009			
All (Foreign Included)	810	640	1,450

Last Updated: 14/10/09

CHRISTIAN UNIVERSITY OF THE NORTH

Université Chrétienne du Nord d'Haïti

BP 40, Cap-Haïtien, Nord
EMail: info@ucnh.info
Website: http://www.ucnh.info

Recteur: Jules Casseus EMail: jcasseus@ucnh.info

Secrétaire général: Jean-Louis Gineville EMail: ucnh@ucnh.info

International Relations: Laurel Casseus
EMail: lcasseus@ucnh.info

Faculties
Administration; **Agronomy** *Dean*: Michael Lawson; **Fine Arts**; **Theology**

History: Founded 1947 as Séminaire Théologique Baptiste d'Haïti. Acquired present status 1994.

Governing Bodies: Assemblée générale, Conseil d'administration

Academic Year: September to May

Admission Requirements: Baccalauréat II

Main Language(s) of Instruction: French

Accrediting Agencies: Enseignement supérieur d'Haiti

Degrees and Diplomas: *Licence*: 4 and 5 yrs; *Maîtrise*: 6 and 7 yrs. Also Diplôme and Certificat

Student Services: Academic counselling, Cultural centre, Employment services, Health services, Language programs, Sports facilities

Student Residential Facilities: Yes

Publications: Shalom *(quarterly)*; Theologia *(biennially)*
Last Updated: 15/10/09

HAITI HIGHER SCHOOL OF INFOTRONICS

Ecole Supérieure d'Infotronique d'Haïti (ESIH)

29, Deuxième Ruelle Nazon, Port-au-Prince
Tel: +509 3859-3885
Fax: +506 2245-5091
EMail: informations@esih.edu
Website: http://esih.edu/

Director: Mackenson Doucet EMail: mackenson.doucet@esih.edu

International Relations: Marlène Sam, International Relations Officer Tel: +509 3446-7383 EMail: marlene.sam@esih.edu

Schools
Business Administration (Business Administration); **Computer Engineering** (Computer Engineering); **Vocational Training in Information Technology** (Information Technology)

History: Created 1995.

Degrees and Diplomas: *Bachelor's Degree*: Computer Engineering; Business Administration, 4 yrs

Libraries: 3,500 vols; 8 periodical subscriptions

Academic Staff 2009-2010	TOTAL
FULL-TIME	4
PART-TIME	32
STAFF WITH DOCTORATE	
FULL-TIME	4
Student Numbers 2009-2010	
All (Foreign Included)	700

Last Updated: 03/02/11

INSTITUTE OF ADVANCED STUDIES IN BUSINESS AND ECONOMICS

Institut des Hautes Etudes commerciales et économiques (IHECE)

PO Box 436, 275, avenue John Brown, Port-au-Prince
Tel: +509 245-6133 +509 245-3572
Website: http://ihece.org/pres.htm

Directeur-Général: Raoul Berret

Departments
Accountancy (Accountancy; Commercial Law; Marketing); **Economics** (Accountancy; Commercial Law; Economics; Marketing; Sociology; Statistics); **Management**

Degrees and Diplomas: *Licence*
Last Updated: 14/10/09

JEAN-PRICE MARS UNIVERSITY

Université Jean-Price Mars (UJPM)

115, rue de l'Enterrement, Port-au-Prince
Tel: +509 222-1393 +509 222-6660
Fax: +509 257-3973

Recteur: Charles-Poisset Romain
Tel: +509 257-0654, Fax: +509 257-3974

Vice-Recteur aux Affaires académiques: Vilver Celestin

International Relations: Ernst Abraham

Departments
Electronics and Computer Science (Computer Science; Electronic Engineering)

Faculties
Applied Sciences (Applied Chemistry; Applied Mathematics; Applied Physics; Engineering) *Dean*: Joseph Elysée; **Communication and Information Sciences** (Communication Studies; Information Sciences) *Dean*: Lucien Jean Bernard; **Economic Sciences, Management and Accountancy** (Accountancy; Economics; Management) *Dean*: Georges Henry Fils; **Letters and Human Sciences** (Arts and Humanities) *Dean*: Alix Emera; **Magistracy Law** (Law) *Dean*: Pierre Labissière; **Theology and Religious Sciences** (Christian Religious Studies; Comparative Religion; Holy Writings; Pastoral Studies; Religion; Religious Education; Religious Practice; Theology) *Dean*: Charles-Poisset Romain

MAURICE LAROCHE UNIVERSITY CENTRE

Centre universitaire Maurice Laroche (CUML)

Angle Rue des Dalles et Ave Ducoste, Port-au-Prince
Tel: +509 223-798 +509 221-5565 +509 245-6336
EMail: ebernardin@hotmail.com

Directeur Général: Ernst Bernardin

Programmes
Business and Commerce (Accountancy; Business and Commerce; Finance; Management)

Degrees and Diplomas: *Licence*

QUISQUEYA UNIVERSITY

Université Quisqueya (UNIQ)

BP 796, Angle rue Charéron et Boulevard Harry Truman, Port-au-Prince
Tel: +509 221-4516 +509 221-4330 +509 222-9103
Fax: +509 223-7430 +509 221-4211
Website: http://www.uniq.edu

Recteur: Jacky Lumarque (2007-)
Tel: +509 221-6809, Fax: +509 221-6809
EMail: recteur@uniq.edu

Vice-Recteur (Affaires administratives): Claude Elisma
Tel: +509 221-6511 EMail: vraad@uniq.edu

Vice-Recteur (Affaires académiques): Alain Gilles
EMail: vraac@uniq.edu

Faculties
Agriculture and Environmental Sciences (Agriculture; Environmental Studies); **Economics and Administration** (Administration; Economics); **Education** (Education); **Health** (Health Sciences); **Law and Political Science** (Law; Political Sciences); **Science, Engineering and Architecture** (Architecture; Engineering; Natural Sciences)

History: Founded 1988.

Governing Bodies: Haut Conseil; Conseil académique

Academic Year: October to July (October-February; March-July)

Admission Requirements: Secondary school certificate (baccalauréat)

Main Language(s) of Instruction: French

Degrees and Diplomas: *Diplôme*: Management; Tourism and Interpretation, 2-2 1/2 yrs; *Docteur en Médecine*: Medicine, 7 yrs; *Licence*: 4 yrs; *Professional Title*: Architecture; Engineering, 5 yrs; *Maîtrise*. Also Postgraduate Programmes in Social Sciences, Economics and Project Management

Student Services: Academic counselling, Employment services, Social counselling, Sports facilities

Libraries: c. 26,000 vols

Publications: Revue Juridique de l'UniQ
Last Updated: 15/10/09

QUISQUEYA-AMERICA UNIVERSITY INSTITUTE

Institut universitaire Quisqueya-Amérique (INUQUA)
BP 19013, Port-au-Prince
Tel: +509 245-3088 +509 511-8289 +509 510-7024
EMail: inuqua_info@acn2.net

Doyen: Antenor Gabeau

Departments
Computer Science and Engineering (Computer Engineering; Computer Science); **Economics and Sociology**; **Human and Vegetal Biology** (Biology); **Law and Education** (Education; Law); **Management and Accountancy** (Accountancy; Management)

History: Founded 1998.

Degrees and Diplomas: *Licence*; *Maîtrise*
Last Updated: 15/10/09

UNIVERSITY NOTRE-DAME OF HAITI

Université Notre-Dame d'Haïti (UNDH)
6, rue Sapotille, Pacot, Port-au-Prince
Tel: +509 245-9522 +509 244-4694 +509 244 -4616
Fax: +509 245-3295 +509 244-4674
EMail: infos@undh.org
Website: http://www.undh.org

Recteur: Pierre André Pierre
Tel: +509 245-8121 EMail: mgrandrepierre@undh.org

Vice-Recteur aux Affaires académiques et scientifiques: Jean-Elie Larrieux Tel: +509 245-8121 EMail: jeanelielarrieux@undh.org

International Relations: Joseph Hilaire, Secrétaire Général
EMail: smmbr@yahoo.com

Faculties
Administration (Administration); **Agronomy** *(Cayes)*; **Economics, Social and Political Sciences** (Accountancy; Business Administration; Criminology; Economics; Government; International Studies; Political Sciences; Public Administration; Sociology); **Medicine and Health Sciences**

Research Centres
Education

Further Information: Also campuses in Cap-Haitien and Cayes

History: Founded 1995 by the Conference of Bishops of Haiti.

Governing Bodies: Haitian Conference of Bishops; Board of Trustees

Academic Year: October to July

Admission Requirements: Secondary school certificate (baccalaureat II)

Main Language(s) of Instruction: French

International Co-operation: With universities in USA, Dominican Republic, Jamaica, French Caribbean and Canada

Accrediting Agencies: Association of Caribbean Universities and Research Institutes; International Federation of Catholic Universities

Degrees and Diplomas: *Diplôme*: Agronomy, 5 yrs; *Diplôme*: Teacher Training, 3 yrs; *Docteur en Médecine*: Medicine, 7 yrs; *Licence*: Education, 3 yrs; *Licence*: Nursing; Business Administration, 4 yrs; *Maîtrise*. Also Certificate and DES in Psychopedagogy (3 yrs), Pedagogy (2 yrs); Educational Administration (2 yrs)

Student Services: Canteen, Health services, Language programs
Libraries: 3 libraries
Publications: Bulletin de l'UNDH *(3 per annum)*

Academic Staff *2007-2008*	MEN	WOMEN	TOTAL
FULL-TIME	9	6	**15**
PART-TIME	110	40	**150**
Student Numbers *2007-2008*			
All (Foreign Included)	800	1,200	**2,000**

Last Updated: 14/10/09

UNIVERSITY OF KING HENRI CHRISTOPHE

Université du Roi Henri Christophe
45 Rue 17-18, H-1, Cap-Haïtien
Tel: +509-2262-0802
EMail: urhccap@urhchaiti.org
Website: http://urhchaiti.org

Président: Louis J. Noisin Tel: +509 558-0889

Academic Vice-President: Nelson Gesner

Faculties
Agriculture (Agriculture; Agronomy; Ecology); **Economics and Administration**

History: Founded 1980.

Main Language(s) of Instruction: French

Degrees and Diplomas: *Licence*

Student Services: Academic counselling, Nursery care
Last Updated: 19/10/09

Holy See

STRUCTURE OF HIGHER EDUCATION SYSTEM

Description:

Higher education is concerned with teaching the Christian Revelation and those subjects related to it; many institutions also teach other subject areas mainly in social sciences. Institutions dependent upon the Church belong either to the Holy See directly or to other ecclesiastical bodies such as dioceses, religious congregations, or Church-related associations. Ecclesiastical institutions of higher education are supervised at the central level by the Congregation for Catholic Education. Other institutions include universities and university faculties and institutions of professional training.

Stages of studies:

University level first stage: *General studies*
The first stage takes usually three years and leads to the Baccalaureatus.

University level second stage: *Specialization*
Two more years of study following upon the first stage lead to the Licentia. In several universities, a Master is awarded after one or two years of postgraduate studies in such fields as Bioethics, Family, Missiology and Religious Culture.

University level third stage: *Research*
This stage leads to the Doctorate, which is awarded at least two years after the Licentia, on submission and defence of a thesis.

ADMISSION TO HIGHER EDUCATION

Admission to university-level studies:

Name of secondary school credential required: Secondary School Leaving Certificate

For entry to: All institutions and programmes

Other admission requirements: A suitable knowledge of Latin is required for enrolment in the Faculties of Sacred Sciences.

Foreign students admission:

Entrance exam requirements: Foreign students applying to an Ecclesiastical university or faculty must hold a pre-university diploma or an academic title and their candidacy must be submitted by the competent authorities.

Language requirements: Candidates, in addition to their mother tongue, must have a good knowledge of Latin and, depending on the course they wish to follow, of Greek or Hebrew. For the doctoral level, they should be able to do research in the principal modern languages.

NATIONAL BODIES

Congregazione per l'Educazione Cattolica (Congregation for Catholic Education)
3, Piazza Pio XII
Città del Vaticano
Roma 00120
WWW: http://www.vatican.va/roman_curia/congregations/ccatheduc/index_it.htm

Data for academic year: 2006-2007
Source: IAU from Congregazione per l'Educazione cattolica, 2003, updated from documentation, 2007 (Bodies, 2011)

INSTITUTIONS

PUBLIC INSTITUTIONS

⌨ PONTIFICAL GREGORIAN UNIVERSITY

Pontificia Università Gregoriana (PUG)
Piazza della Pilotta 4, 00187 Roma
Tel: +39(06) 6701-1
Fax: +39(06) 6701-5419
EMail: segreteria@unigre.it
Website: http://www.unigre.it

Rettore: François-Xavier Dumortier, S.J. (2010-2013)
Tel: +39(06) 6701-5260, Fax: +39(06) 6701-5412
EMail: rettore@unigre.it

Centres
Cardinal Bea Centre for Judaic Studies (Judaic Religious Studies); **Faith and Culture** *(Alberto Hurtado)* (Cultural Studies; Religious Studies); **Interdisciplinary Centre for Trainers in Seminaries** (Teacher Trainers Education); **Social Communication** (Communication Studies)

Faculties
Canon Law (Canon Law); **Ecclesiastical History and Cultural Heritage of the Church** (Heritage Preservation; Religious Studies); **Missiology** (Pastoral Studies); **Philosophy** (Philosophy); **Social Sciences** (Social Sciences); **Theology** (Theology)

Institutes
Psychology (Psychology); **Spirituality** (Religion); **Study of Religions and Cultures** *(Interdisciplinary)* (Cultural Studies; Religion)

Further Information: Also Italian Language course for foreign students

History: Founded 1551 as 'Collegium Romanum' by Ignatius of Loyola and Francis Borgia. Constituted as University by Pope Julius III, 1553. The Institution developed considerably under Pope Gregory XIII, who is considered to be 'founder and father' of the University which now bears his name. Depends directly on the Holy See and administration is entrusted to the Society of Jesus. The Grand Chancellor is the Cardinal Prefect of the Congregation of Studies and the Vice-Grand Chancellor the Superior-General of the Society of Jesus. Juridical recognition is granted to the University by the government of Italy.

Governing Bodies: Academic Senate

Academic Year: October to May (October-January; February-May)

Admission Requirements: Completed classical secondary education and, where necessary, additional preparatory studies to meet Faculty requirements

Fees: (Euros): 1,620 per annum

Main Language(s) of Instruction: Italian, English, French, German, Spanish

Degrees and Diplomas: *Diploma*: Higher Religious Culture, 3 yrs; *Diploma*: Latin Language; Spiritual Theology, 2 yrs; *Baccalaureatus*: Missiology; Philosophy; Psychology; Social Sciences, 2 yrs; *Baccalaureatus*: Theology, 3 yrs; *Magistero*: Religious Sciences; Theology, 4 yrs; *Licentia*: Canon Law; Spiritual Theology, 2 yrs; *Licentia*: Church History; Missiology; Psychology; Social Sciences, 3 yrs; *Licentia*: Philosophy, 4 yrs; *Licentia*: Theology, 5 yrs; *Master*: Arts in Higher Religious Culture, 2 yrs; *Doctorate*: Canon Law; Spiritual Theology, 4 yrs; *Doctorate*: Church History; Missiology; Psychology; Social Sciences, 5 yrs; *Doctorate*: Philosophy, 6 yrs; *Doctorate*: Theology, 7 yrs

Student Services: Academic counselling, Canteen, Cultural centre, Foreign student adviser, Health services, Language programs, Social counselling

Libraries: University Library, c. 1,000,000 vols

Publications: Acta Nuntiaturae Gallicae; Analecta Gregoriana; Archivum Historiae Pontificiae; Documenta Missionalia; Gregorianum; Interreligious and Cultural Investigation; Miscellanea Historiae Pontificiae; Periodica de re morali, canonica, liturgica; Studia Missionalia; Studia Sociala; Tesi Gregoriana

Press or Publishing House: Editrice della Pontificia Universitas Gregoriana

Academic Staff 2009-2010	MEN	WOMEN	TOTAL
FULL-TIME	–	–	**400**
STAFF WITH DOCTORATE FULL-TIME	–	–	**374**
Student Numbers 2009-2010			
All (Foreign Included)	2,354	665	**3,019**
FOREIGN ONLY	2,082	343	**2,425**

Last Updated: 28/09/11

PONTIFICAL LATERAN UNIVERSITY

Pontificia Universitas Lateranensis (PUL)
Piazza S. Giovanni in Laterano 4, 00120 Città del Vaticano
Tel: +39(06) 6988-6401
Fax: +39(06) 6988-6508
EMail: info@pul.it
Website: http://www.pul.it

Rettore Magnifico: Enrico dal Covolo
Tel: +39(06) 6989-5632, Fax: +39(06) 6988-6133
EMail: segretario@pul.it

Segretario Generale: Ulderico Conti
EMail: segretario.generale@pul.it

Faculties
Canon Law (Canon Law); **Civil Law** (Civil Law; Public Law); **Philosophy** (Philosophy); **Theology** (Theology)

Institutes
Redemptor Hominis for Pastoral Studies (Catholic Theology; Pastoral Studies); **Utriusque Iuris** (Canon Law; Comparative Law)

History: Founded 1773 by Pope Clement XIV as "Collegio Romano". Moved to the Lateran hill 1937 and became Pontificio Ateneo Lateranense and Pontificia Universitas Lateranensis 1959. Directly dependent on the Holy See, legally established in the Vatican City State. Under the jurisdiction of the Congregation for Catholic Education.

Governing Bodies: Senate

Academic Year: October to June (October-January; February-June)

Admission Requirements: Secondary school certificate or high school graduation certificate (level of study required for access to university in student's home country)

Fees: (Euros): 600-2,500 per annum

Main Language(s) of Instruction: Italian

Degrees and Diplomas: *Baccalaureatus*: Canon Law, Theology, 3 yrs; *Baccalaureatus*: Philosophy, 4 yrs; *Licentia*: Canon Law, 3 yrs; *Licentia*: Philosophy, Theology, Marriage and Family, Bioethics, Theology of Evangelization, 2 yrs; *Licentia*: Utroque Iure, 5 yrs; *Doctorate*: Canon Law; Utroque Iure, 1 yr; *Doctorate*: Marriage and Family; Pastoral Theology; Philosophy; Theology, 2 yrs

Student Services: Academic counselling, Canteen, Foreign student adviser, Social counselling, Sports facilities

Libraries: Biblioteca Beato PIO IX

Publications: Anthropotes *(biennially)*; Apollinaris *(3 per annum)*; Aquinas *(3 per annum)*; Civitas et Iustitia *(biennially)*; CVII *(biennially)*; Latenarum *(3 per annum)*; Nuntium *(3 per annum)*; Studia et Documenta Historiae et Iuris *(annually)*

Press or Publishing House: Lateran University Press
Last Updated: 28/09/11

PONTIFICAL URBANIANA UNIVERSITY

Pontificia Universitas Urbaniana (PUU)
Via Urbano VIII 16, 00165 Roma
Tel: +39(06) 6988-9611
Fax: +39(06) 6988-1871
EMail: segretaria@urbaniana.edu
Website: http://www.urbaniana.edu

Rettore Magnifico: Alberto Trevisiol EMail: rettore@urbaniana.edu
Vice-rettore: Godfrey Igwebuike Onah

Faculties
Canon Law (Canon Law); **Missiology** (Missionary Studies); **Philosophy** (Philosophy); **Theology** (Theology)

Institutes
Catechism and Missionary Spirituality (Christian Religious Studies); **Non-Belief, Religion and Culture Studies** (Agnosticism and Atheism; Cultural Studies)

History: Founded 1627 as college by Pope Urban VIII, became Pontifical University 1962. Directed by the Pontifical Congregation for the Propagation of the Faith (Holy See).

Governing Bodies: Academic Senate; Faculty Councils

Academic Year: September to June (September-February; February-June)

Admission Requirements: Secondary school certificate

Main Language(s) of Instruction: Italian

Degrees and Diplomas: *Baccalaureatus*: Canon Law; Missiology; Philosophy, 2 yrs; *Baccalaureatus*: Theology, 3 yrs; *Licentia*: Missiology; Theology, 2 yrs; *Licentia*: Philosophy, 2 yrs; *Doctorate*: Canon Law; Missiology; Philosophy; Theology, 2 yrs

Libraries: c. 350,000 vols, 4,500 periodicals (800 current) 1,500 16th c. publications, 400 15th c. publications, on-line catalogue

Publications: Annales; Bibliographia Missionalia; Euntes Docete; Redemptoris Missio

Press or Publishing House: Urbaniana University Press
Last Updated: 27/01/12

PRIVATE INSTITUTIONS

AUXILIUM PONTIFICAL FACULTY OF EDUCATION

Pontificia Facultas Scientiarum Educationis Auxilium
Via Cremolino 141, 00166 Roma
Tel: +39(06) 615-72-01
Fax: +39(06) 615-64-640
EMail: segretaria@pfse-auxilium.org; aux.segreteria@pcn.net
Website: http://www.pfse-auxilium.org

Preside: Giuseppina del Core
Tel: +39(06) 615-72-029 EMail: aux.preside@pcn.net

Vice Preside: Rachele Lanfranchi Tel: +39(06) 615-64-226

Institutes
Catechist Methodology; **Pedagogical Methodology** (Pedagogy); **Psychological Research in the Field of Education** (Educational Psychology); **Sociological Research in the Field of Education** (Education; Sociology)

History: Founded 1954 in Turin (Italy) as the International Institute of Higher Education for Educational Sciences in 1970 and transferred to Rome in 1978. Acquired present status 1999.

Academic Year: October to September

Admission Requirements: High School Diploma

Fees: (Euro): 1,000 per annum (paid in two installments)

Main Language(s) of Instruction: Italian

Accrediting Agencies: Holy See

Degrees and Diplomas: *Baccalaureatus*; *Licentia*; *Master*: Communication Studies; Educational Sciences, a further 2 yrs; *Master*: Social and Communities Services, 1 further yr; *Doctorate*: Educational Sciences;, 1 further yr at least. Also certificates in Salesian Spirituality (2 yrs); Consecrated Life (1 yr); Communication Sciences/ Educational Sciences (1 yr)

Student Services: Academic counselling, Canteen, Cultural centre, Foreign student adviser, Foreign Studies Centre, Language programs, Sports facilities

Student Residential Facilities: Yes (reserved to the Religious Congregation FMA)

Special Facilities: Multimedia Laboratory and Production Centre

Libraries: Biblioteca Paolo VI

Publications: Rivista di Scienze dell' Educazione, Scientific Magazine *(3 per annum)*
Last Updated: 27/09/11

MARIANUM PONTIFICAL THEOLOGOGICAL FACULTY

Pontificia Facultà Teologica Marianum
Viale Trenta Aprile 6, 00153 Roma
Tel: +39(06) 583-9161
Fax: +39 (06) 588-0292
EMail: marianum@marianum.it
Website: http://www.marianum.it

Preside: Salvatore M. Perrella

Vice Preside: Paolo M. Zannini

Faculties
Theology (Religious Studies; Theology)

History: Founded 1866. Acquired present status 1971.

Admission Requirements: Secondary school certificate

Main Language(s) of Instruction: Italian

Degrees and Diplomas: *Diploma*; *Licentia*; *Doctorate*

Student Services: Language programs

Libraries: Yes

Publications: Marianum *(biennially)*

Press or Publishing House: Centro Edizioni Marianum (CEM)
Last Updated: 27/09/11

PONTIFICAL ATHENAEUM REGINA APOSTOLORUM

Pontificium Athenaeum Regina Apostolorum
Via degli Aldobrandeschi 190, 00165 Roma
Tel: +39(06) 665-27800
Fax: +39(06) 665-27814
EMail: segretaria@upra.org
Website: http://www.upra.org

Rettore: Pedro Barrajón

Faculties
Bioethics (Biology; Ethics); **Philosophy** (Philosophy); **Theology** (Theology)

Institutes
Bioethics and Human Rights (Ethics; Human Rights); **Economics Ethics** *(Fidelis)* (Economics; Ethics); **Sacerdos** (Pastoral Studies; Theology); **Science and Faith** (Natural Sciences; Philosophy; Religion); **Women's Studies** (Women's Studies)

History: Founded 1993. Acquired present status 1998.

Admission Requirements: Secondary school certificate

Main Language(s) of Instruction: Italian

Degrees and Diplomas: *Baccalaureatus*; *Licentia*; *Master*: Environmental Studies; Science and Faith; Psychology; Bioethics; *Doctorate*
Last Updated: 28/09/11

PONTIFICAL BIBLICAL INSTITUTE

Pontificio Istituto Biblico
Via della Pilotta 25, 00187 Roma
Tel: +39(06) 695-261
Fax: +39(06) 695-266211
EMail: pibsegr@biblico.it
Website: http://www.biblico.it

Rettore: José María Abrego de Lacy

Segretario Generale: Carlo Valentino

Faculties
Biblical Studies (Bible; Greek; Hebrew; Latin); **Oriental Studies** (Middle Eastern Studies)

Further Information: Branch in Jerusalem

History: Founded 1909. Acquired present status 1932.

Main Language(s) of Instruction: Italian

Degrees and Diplomas: *Licentia*; *Doctorate*

Libraries: Yes

Publications: Biblica *(quarterly)*; Orientalia *(quarterly)*
Last Updated: 28/09/11

PONTIFICAL INSTITUTE FOR ARABIC AND ISLAMIC STUDIES

Pontificio Istituto di Studi Arabi e d'Islamistica (PISAI)
Viale di Trastevere 89, 00153 Roma
Tel: +39(06) 588-2676
Fax: +39(06) 588-2595
EMail: info@pisai.it
Website: http://www.pisai.it

Preside: Miguel Ángel Ayuso Guixot EMail: miguel.ayuso@pisai.it

Programmes
Arabic (Arabic); **Islamic Studies** (Islamic Studies)

History: Founded 1926 in Tunis. Moved to Rome 1964. Acuqired present title and status 1979.

Main Language(s) of Instruction: Italian

Degrees and Diplomas: *Licentia*: Arabic and Islamic Studies, a further yr; *Doctorate*: Arabic and Islamic Studies, a further 2 yrs and dissertation

Libraries: 35,000 vols; 450 periodical titles

Publications: Encounter; Etudes arabes *(annually)*; Islamochristiana *(annually)*
Last Updated: 28/09/11

PONTIFICAL INSTITUTE OF CHRISTIAN ARCHAEOLOGY

Pontificium Institutum Archaeologiae Christianae
Via Napoleone III 1, 00185 Roma
Tel: +39(06) 446-5574
Fax: +39(06) 446-9197
EMail: piac@piac.it
Website: http://www.piac.it

Rettore: Vincenzo Fiocchi Nicolai EMail: piac.rettore@piac.it

Segretario: Olof Brandt EMail: piac.segretario@piac.it

Divisions
Archaeology (Ancient Civilizations; Archaeology; Architecture; Art Education)

History: Founded 1925 by a Motu Propio of Pope Pius XI as a research centre.

Governing Bodies: Academic Council

Academic Year: November to May

Admission Requirements: Laurea and interview

Fees: (Euros) 850 per annum

Main Language(s) of Instruction: Italian

International Co-operation: With universities in Italy, France, Sweden

Degrees and Diplomas: *Baccalaureatus*: 1 yr; *Licentia*: 2 yrs; *Doctorate*: 3 yrs with published thesis. Also specialization course

Student Residential Facilities: None

Libraries: c. 50,000 vols.

Publications: Rivista di Archeologia Cristiana *(annually)*

Part-time students, 2.
Last Updated: 28/09/11

PONTIFICAL INSTITUTE OF SACRED MUSIC

Pontificio Istituto di Musica Sacra
Via di Torre Rossa 21, 00165 Roma
Tel: +39(06) 663-8792
Fax: +39(06) 662-2453
EMail: pims@musica-sacra.va
Website: http://www.vatican.va/roman_curia/
institutions.connected/sacmus

Preside: Valentino Miserachs Grau

Segretario: Giuseppe Moretti

Courses
Sacred Music (Music Theory and Composition; Musical Instruments; Musicology; Religious Music; Singing)

History: Founded 1911 as Scuola Superiore di Musica Sacra. Acquired present status 1931.

Main Language(s) of Instruction: Italian

Degrees and Diplomas: *Baccalaureatus*; *Magistero*; *Licentia*; *Doctorate*
Last Updated: 28/09/11

PONTIFICAL ORIENTAL INSTITUTE

Pontificio Istituto Orientale
Piazza di Santa Maria Maggiore 7, 00185 Roma
Tel: +39(06) 447-4170
Fax: +39(06) 446-5576
EMail: segreteria@pontificio-orientale.com
Website: http://www.pontificio-orientale.com

Rettore: James McCann EMail: rettore@pontificio-orientale.com

Faculties
Eastern Canon Law (Canon Law); **Eastern Church Studies** (Religious Studies; Theology)

History: Founded 1917. Acquired present status 1920.

Academic Year: October to June

Admission Requirements: Bachelor Degree in Theology (or equivalent completed in a major seminary)

Main Language(s) of Instruction: Italian

Degrees and Diplomas: *Licentia*; *Doctorate*

Libraries: Yes
Last Updated: 28/09/11

PONTIFICAL UNIVERSITY ANTONIANUM

Pontificia Università Antonianum
Via Merulana 124, 00185 Roma
Tel: +39(06) 703-73502
Fax: +39(06) 703-73604
EMail: segreteriarettorato@antonianum.eu
Website: http://www.antonianum.ofm.org

Rettore Magnifico: Priamo Etzi (2011-)

Segretario Generale: Marek Wach
Tel: +39(06) 703-73503 EMail: segretario@antonianum.eu

Faculties
Biblical Sciences and Archaeology *(Jerusalem)* (Archaeology; Bible); **Canon Law** (Canon Law); **Philosophy** (Philosophy); **Theology** (Theology)

Higher Schools
Medieval and Franciscan Studies (Medieval Studies; Religious Studies)

Institutes
Ecumenical Studies *(St Bernardino)* (Religion); **Religious Science** *(Redemptor Hominis)* (Religion; Religious Studies); **Spirituality** *(Franciscan)* (Religious Studies)

History: Founded 1933.

Main Language(s) of Instruction: Italian

Degrees and Diplomas: *Baccalaureatus*; *Licentia*; *Doctorate*

Student Services: Academic counselling, Cultural centre

Publications: Revista Antonianum
Last Updated: 28/09/11

PONTIFICAL UNIVERSITY OF ST. THOMAS AQUINAS

Pontificia Università San Tommaso d'Aquino (PUST)
Largo Angelicum 1, 00184 Roma
Tel: +39(06) 670-21
Fax: +39(06) 679-0407
EMail: segreteria@pust.urbe.it
Website: http://www.pust.it

Vice Rettore: Michael Carragher EMail: rettore@pust-urbe.it

Segretario Generale: Glenn Morris

Faculties

Canon Law (Canon Law); **Philosophy** (Philosophy); **Social Sciences** (Social Sciences); **Theology** (Theology)

Institutes

Religious Sciences *(Mater Ecclesiae)*; **St Thomas**

History: Founded 1580 as College of St. Thomas for students of the Dominical Order. Faculty of Philosophy added 1882 by Apostolic Decree of Pope Leo XIII, Faculty of Canon Law added 1896. Became Pontifical University 1906. Acquired present title 1963.

Governing Bodies: Academic Senate

Academic Year: October to June (October-February; February-June)

Admission Requirements: Secondary school certificate

Main Language(s) of Instruction: Italian, English

Degrees and Diplomas: *Diploma*: Spirituality, 1 yr; *Baccalaureatus*: Philosophy, 2 yrs; *Baccalaureatus*: Social Sciences, 2-3 yrs; *Baccalaureatus*: Theology, 3 yrs; *Licentia*: Canon Law, a further 3 yrs; *Licentia*: Philosophy; Social Sciences; Theology, 2 yrs following Baccalaureatus; *Master*: Arts, 1 yr following Baccalaureatus; *Doctorate*: Canon Law; Philosophy; Social Sciences; Theology, 2 yrs following Licentia

Student Residential Facilities: For c. 50 students

Libraries: University Library, 200,000 vols

Publications: Angelicum *(annually)*
Last Updated: 27/01/12

PONTIFICAL UNIVERSITY OF THE HOLY CROSS

Pontificia Università della Santa Croce
Piazza S. Apollinare 49, 00186 Roma
Tel: +39(06) 681-641
Fax: +39(06) 681-64400
EMail: santacroce@pusc.it
Website: http://www.pusc.it

Rettore: Luis Romera

Segretario Generale: Manuel Miedes

Faculties

Canon Law (Canon Law); **Institutional Social Communications** (Media Studies); **Philosophy** (Philosophy); **Theology** (Holy Writings; Theology)

Institutes

Advanced Religious Sciences (Religious Studies)

History: Founded 1985. Acquired present status 1998.

Academic Year: October to June

Admission Requirements: Diploma di Scuola Secondaria Superiore

Fees: (Euros) 1,300-2,000 per annum

Main Language(s) of Instruction: Italian

Degrees and Diplomas: *Baccalaureatus*: Philosophy, Theology, 2-3 yrs; *Licentia*: Philosophy; Theology; Canon Law; Social Communication, 2-4 yrs; *Doctorate*: Philosophy; Theology; Canon Law; Social Communication, 2 yrs

Student Services: Academic counselling

Publications: Acta Philosophica *(biennially)*; Annales Theologici *(biennially)*; Ius Ecclesiae *(3 per annum)*

Distance students, 537.
Last Updated: 28/09/11

S. BONAVENTURA FACULTY OF THEOLOGY

Pontificia Facoltà Teologica San Bonaventura
Via del Serafico 1, 00142 Roma
Tel: +39 (06) 515-03206
Fax: +39 (06) 519-2067
EMail: info@seraphicum.org
Website: http://www.seraphicum.org/

Preside: Domenico Paoletti
Segretario: Juan Miguel Vicente

Faculties

Theology (Theology)

History: Founded 1587. Acquired present status 1955.

Admission Requirements: Secondary school certificate

Main Language(s) of Instruction: Italian

Degrees and Diplomas: *Baccalaureatus*; *Licentia*; *Doctorate*
Last Updated: 28/09/11

SALESIAN PONTIFICAL UNIVERSITY

Università Pontificia Salesiana (UPS)
Piazza Ateneo Salesiano 1, 00139 Roma
Tel: +39(06) 8729-01
Fax: +39(06) 8729-0318
EMail: segreteria@ups.urbe.it
Website: http://www.unisal.it

Rettore Magnifico: Carlo Nanni (2003-)
Tel: +39(06) 8729-0244, Fax: +39(06) 8713-1081
EMail: rettore@unisal.it

Segretario Generale: Jaroslaw Rochowiak
Tel: +39(06) 8729-0206 EMail: segretaria@unisal.it

International Relations: Mario Toso

Faculties

Canon Law (Canon Law); **Classical Studies** (Christian Religious Studies; Classical Languages; Greek; Italian; Latin; Literature); **Educational Sciences** (Clinical Psychology; Educational Psychology; Pedagogy; Religious Studies); **Philosophy** (Philosophy); **Social Communication Sciences** (Communication Studies; Social Studies); **Theology** (Theology)

History: Founded 1904 as institute, became athenaeum 1940 and University 1973. Under the jurisdiction of the Congregation for Catholic Education and of the Salesian Order.

Governing Bodies: Senato Academico

Academic Year: October to June (October-January; February-June)

Admission Requirements: Secondary school certificate acceptable for University admission in the country of award

Fees: (Euros): 1,200 per annum

Main Language(s) of Instruction: Italian

International Co-operation: With universities in Italy, Spain, Germany, India, Israel, Cameroon, DR Congo, Senegal, Brazil, Venezuela, Argentina, Chile, Philippines, Mexico and Guatemala

Degrees and Diplomas: *Baccalaureatus*: 3 yrs; *Licentia*: Canon Law, a further 3 yrs; *Licentia*: Education; Pastoral Studies; Philosophy; Social Communication; Theology, a further 2 yrs; *Doctorate*: at least 2 yrs following Licentia and thesis

Student Services: Academic counselling, Cultural centre, Health services, Language programs, Nursery care, Sports facilities

Libraries: 700,000 vols

Publications: Orientamenti Pedagogici *(quarterly)*; Salesianum *(quarterly)*
Last Updated: 28/09/11

ST ANSELM'S PONTIFICAL ATHENAEUM

Pontificio Ateneo S. Anselmo
Piazza dei Cavalieri di Malta 5, 00153 Roma
Tel: +39(06) 5791-401
Fax: +33(06) 5791-402
EMail: segretaria@santanselmo.org
Website: http://www.santanselmo.org

Rettore Magnifico: Juan Javier Flores Arcas

Segretario Generale: Pachomius Okogie
EMail: segretariogenerale@santanselmo.org

Faculties
Philosophy (Philosophy); **Theology** (Theology)

Institutes
Liturgical Studies (Religion)

History: Founded 1687. Acquired present status 1867.

Governing Bodies: Magnum Cancellarius; Academic Senate

Admission Requirements: Secondary school certificate

Fees: (Euros) 800-1,200

Main Language(s) of Instruction: Italian

Degrees and Diplomas: *Baccalaureatus*: Philosophy; Theology; *Licentia*: Philosophy; Theology; Liturgy; *Doctorate*: Philosophy; Theology; Liturgy;

Student Services: Academic counselling, Foreign student adviser, Language programs

Student Residential Facilities: Yes

Libraries: Yes

Publications: Ecclesia Orans *(3 per annum)*; Studia Anselmiana *(3 per annum)*

Last Updated: 28/09/11

TERESIANUM PONTIFICAL THEOLOGICAL FACULTY
Pontificia Facultas Theologica S. Teresianum
Piazza San Pancrazio 5/a, 00152 Roma
Tel: +39(06) 581-2362
Fax: +39(06) 580-9050
EMail: teresianum@pcn.net
Website: http://www.teresianum.pcn.net
Preside: Virgilio Pasquetto EMail: preside.teresianul@gmail.com

Faculties
Theology (Archaeology; Canon Law; History of Religion; Holy Writings; Theology)

Institutes
Spirituality (Theology)

History: Founded 1935. Acquired present status and title 1982.

Main Language(s) of Instruction: Italian

Degrees and Diplomas: *Baccalaureatus*; *Licentia*; *Doctorate*

Last Updated: 28/09/11

Honduras

STRUCTURE OF HIGHER EDUCATION SYSTEM

Description:

Higher education is provided by public and private universities and specialized institutes and schools. The Universidad Nacional Autónoma de Honduras is autonomous and draws its funds from government grants, fees and gifts. It is responsible for higher education through the Claustro Pleno, the Consejo de Educación Superior, the Consejo Técnico and the Dirección de Educación Superior. The Universidad Pedagógica Nacional Francisco Morazán is under the administrative control of the Ministry of Public Education. There is a national School of Forestry, a national School of Agriculture and a School of Music. There are several private universities, as well as a Catholic university that belongs to the Archdiocese of Tegucigalpa. The Escuela Agrícola Panamericana is a private international institution which is governed by a board of trustees, comprising members from different countries.

Stages of studies:

University level first stage: Bachillerato universitario, Licenciatura, Professional qualification
The first stage of higher education leads after three or four years to the first degree of Bachillerato universitario and Licenciatura or to a professional qualification. The Bachillerato universitario is mainly conferred in technological fields. The Licenciatura is awarded after four years in Nursing, five years in Economics, Business Administration, Accountancy, Law, Engineering, Journalism, Mathematics and Natural Sciences. All students at the National Autonomous University spend the first year (for medical students, two years) in the Centro de Estudios Generales.

University level second stage: Maestría, Doctorado (Profesional)
The Maestría is conferred after two to three years' study following upon the Bachillerato universitario or Licenciatura. A Doctorado (Profesional) is conferred in Pharmacy and Dentistry after six years and after seven years in Medicine.

University level third stage: Especialidad
The Especialidad is only conferred in Medicine to holders of the Título de Doctor. It requires 30 credits and three years' internship. The University-level Doctorado (PhD) is conferred after two years of study and each university has a different specialty of PhD.

Distance higher education:
Distance higher education is offered by the Universidad Nacional Autónoma de Honduras (Sistema Universitario de Educación a Distancia) and the Universidad Pedogógica Nacional Francisco Morazán in such fields as Social Sciences, Mathematics, Arts, Humanities and Languages, Commerce, Exact and Natural Sciences and Domestic Sciences. Students must satisfy the same academic requirements as regular students.

ADMISSION TO HIGHER EDUCATION

Admission to university-level studies:

Name of secondary school credential required: Bachillerato

Alternatives to credentials: Title of Perito or Maestro de Educación primaria

Entrance exam requirements: Admission examination at the Catholic University.

Other admission requirements: At university, all students must take a general orientation course before embarking on their studies.

Foreign students admission:

Entrance exam requirements: Students must hold the Bachiller, Perito or Maestro de Educacion primaria and must follow a general orientation course.

Entry regulations: Foreign students must hold a visa.

Language requirements: Students must have a good knowledge of Spanish. Students who need to upgrade their Spanish can follow a course at the Universidad Privada "José Cecilio del Valle" or contact the UNAH.

NATIONAL BODIES

Secretaría de Educación (Ministry of Education)
Secretary of State: Alejandro Ventura
1ª avenida entre 2ª y 3ª calle
Comayagüela
Tel: +504 238 4325
Fax: +504 222 8571
EMail: info@se.gob.hn
WWW: http://www.se.gob.hn

Data for academic year: 2006-2007
Source: IAU from Honduras Delegation to UNESCO, 2006. Bodies updated in 2011.

INSTITUTIONS

PUBLIC INSTITUTIONS

FRANCISCO MORAZÁN NATIONAL PEDAGOGICAL UNIVERSITY, TEGUCIGALPA

Universidad Pedagógica Nacional Francisco Morazán
Apartado Aéreo 3394, Calle El Dorado, Boulevard Miraflores, Tegucigalpa
Tel: +504 2239-8002
EMail: webmaster@upnfm.edu.hn
Website: http://www.upnfm.edu.hn

Rector: David Orlando Marín López
Vicerrector Administrativo: Rafael Barahona
Secretaría General: Celfa Idalisis Bueso

Centres
Distance Education (Home Economics; Literature; Mathematics; Modern Languages; Natural Sciences; Social Sciences)

Faculties
Humanities (Administration; Arts and Humanities; Education; Educational and Student Counselling; Educational Sciences; English; Fine Arts; French; Linguistics; Literature; Music; Painting and Drawing; Physical Education; Preschool Education; Primary Education; Sculpture; Social Sciences; Spanish; Special Education; Theatre); **Science and Technology** (Biology; Business and Commerce; Business Education; Chemistry; Computer Science; Electrical Engineering; Food Science; Food Technology; Home Economics; Hotel and Restaurant; Hotel Management; Mathematics; Metal Techniques; Natural Sciences; Nutrition; Physics; Technology; Textile Technology; Tourism; Wood Technology)

Further Information: Also San Pedro Sula Regional Centre

History: Founded 1989 in co-operation with UNESCO, on the basis of Francisco Morazán School of Education, an institution founded 1959 . Financed by the central Government. Under the jurisdiction of the Consejo de Educación Superior and the Government.

Governing Bodies: Consejo Superior Universitario; Consejo Directivo

Academic Year: February to November (February-May; June-July; August-November)

Admission Requirements: Secondary school certificate (Título de Educación Secundaria de Bachillerato en Ciencias y Letras)

Main Language(s) of Instruction: Spanish

Degrees and Diplomas: *Técnico*; *Licenciatura*; *Maestría*; *Doctorado en Filosofia*
Student Services: Academic counselling, Health services, Social counselling, Sports facilities
Libraries: Bernardo Galindo y Galindo Library, 35,000 vols
Publications: Paradigma, Research *(quarterly)*
Press or Publishing House: UPNFM University Editorial

Student Numbers *2008*: Total 28,657
Last Updated: 18/10/11

HIGHER INSTITUTE OF POLICE STUDIES

Instituto Superior de Educación Policial (ISEP)
Apartado Aéreo 2163, El Ocotal, Francisco Morazán, Tegucigalpa
Tel: +504 229-0248

Rector: José Armando Carías V.

Areas
Administration (Administration); **Law** (Law); **Police Studies** (Police Studies); **Social Studies** (Social Studies)

History: Founded 1996.
Degrees and Diplomas: *Licenciatura*

Student Numbers *2008*: Total 415
Last Updated: 18/10/11

NATIONAL AUTONOMOUS UNIVERSITY OF HONDURAS

Universidad Nacional Autónoma de Honduras
Boulevard Suyapa, Ciudad Universitaria, Tegucigalpa
Tel: +504 232-2110
Fax: +504 235-3361
EMail: webmaster@ns.unah.hondunet.net
Website: https://www.unah.edu.hn/

Rectora: Julieta Gonzalina Castellanos Ruiz (2009-)
Tel: +504 239-1194, Fax: +504 232-1053
EMail: rectoria@unah.edu.hn

Faculties
Arts and Humanities (Architecture; Arts and Humanities; Design; Fine Arts; Literature; Modern Languages; Pedagogy; Philosophy; Physical Education; Sports); **Chemistry and Pharmacy** (Chemistry; Pharmacy); **Dentistry** (Dentistry); **Economics** (Accountancy;

Banking; Business Administration; Business Computing; Economics; Finance); **Engineering** (Chemical Engineering; Civil Engineering; Electrical Engineering; Engineering; Mechanical Engineering); **Law** (Law); **Medicine** (Medicine; Nursing); **Science** (Astronomy and Space Science; Biology; Mathematics and Computer Science; Microbiology; Physics); **Social Sciences** (Anthropology; Communication Studies; History; Political Sciences; Psychology; Social Sciences; Social Work; Sociology); **Space Science** (Astronomy and Space Science)

Institutes
Economics and Social Research (Economics; Social Studies); **Law Research** (Law)

Schools
Architecture (Architecture); **Journalism** (Journalism)

Further Information: Also 10 Regional University Centres

History: Founded 1847 as Academy. Acquired present status and title 1957.

Governing Bodies: Claustro Pleno; Consejo Universitario

Academic Year: February to December (February-June; June-October; October-December)

Admission Requirements: Secondary school certificate (bachillerato) or equivalent

Main Language(s) of Instruction: Spanish

Degrees and Diplomas: *Técnico*; *Bachillerato Universitario*; *Licenciatura*; *Doctorado (Profesional)*: Chemistry and Pharmacy; Dental Surgery; Medicine

Student Services: Academic counselling, Handicapped facilities, Health services, Language programs, Nursery care, Sports facilities

Special Facilities: Observatory. Biology Museum

Libraries: Central Library and specialized Libraries, total c. 200,000 vols

Publications: Boletín del Instituto de Ciencias Económicas *(monthly)*; Ciencia y Tecnología, Scientific Research *(monthly)*; Revista de la Universidad *(monthly)*; Revista Economía Política *(monthly)*

Press or Publishing House: Editorial Universitaria

Student Numbers *2008*: Total 67,703
Last Updated: 18/10/11

NATIONAL SCHOOL OF FORESTRY
Escuela Nacional de Ciencias Forestales
Col. Las Americas, CA5, Siguatepeque, Comayagua
Tel: +504 2773-0018
Fax: +504 2773-0018
EMail: esna_info@gmail.com
Website: http://www.esnacifor.hn/

Director Ejecutivo: Miguel Conrado Valdez Castro

Programmes
Forestry (Forest Management; Forestry)

History: Founded 1969. Acquired present status 1993.

Main Language(s) of Instruction: Spanish

Degrees and Diplomas: *Licenciatura*; *Maestría*

Student Numbers *2008*: Total 142
Last Updated: 18/10/11

NATIONAL UNIVERSITY OF AGRICULTURE
Universidad Nacional de Agricultura (UNA)
Apartado Aéreo 9, Catacamas, Olancho
Tel: +504 2799-4901
Fax: +504 2799-4900
EMail: informacion@unag.edu.hn
Website: http://www.unag.edu.hn/

Rector: Marlon Oniel Escoto Valerio
Vicerrector Administrativo: José Antonio Ramírez

Departments
Agricultural Business Management (Agricultural Business; Agricultural Economics; Agricultural Management; Information Technology); **Agricultural Engineering** (Agricultural Engineering; Agricultural Equipment; Farm Management; Water Management); **Food Technology** (Food Technology); **Natural Resources and Environmental Management** (Environmental Management; Forestry; Natural Resources; Soil Management; Water Management); **Veterinary Medicine and Animal Production** (Animal Husbandry; Apiculture; Cattle Breeding; Dairy; Veterinary Science)

Programmes
Graduate Studies (Development Studies; Economics)

History: Founded 1968 as Escuela Nacional de Agricultura. Acquired present title 2001.

Degrees and Diplomas: *Maestría*. Also Professional Title

Student Numbers *2008*: Total 753
Last Updated: 18/10/11

PRIVATE INSTITUTIONS

CATHOLIC UNIVERSITY OF HONDURAS OUR LADY QUEEN OF PEACE
Universidad Católica de Honduras Nuestra Señora Reina de la Paz (UNICAH)
Barrio Casamata, Calle el seminario No 1501, Tegucigalpa 4473
Tel: +504 238-6795
Fax: +504 238-6794
EMail: webmaster@unicah.edu
Website: http://www.unicah.edu

Rector: Elio David Alvarenga EMail: rector@unicah.edu

Faculties
Administration (Administration; Business Administration; Finance; Marketing); **Architecture** (Architecture); **Engineering** (Civil Engineering; Computer Engineering; Computer Science; Engineering; Environmental Engineering; Industrial Engineering); **Health Sciences** (Dentistry; Health Sciences; Medicine; Psychology; Surgery); **International Relations** (International Relations); **Law** (Law); **Theology** (Theology)

Programmes
Graduate Studies (Administration; Business Administration; Economics; Finance; Health Sciences; International Relations; Psychology)

History: Founded 1992.

Governing Bodies: Claustro Universitario

Academic Year: January to December (January-April; May-August; September-December)

Admission Requirements: Secondary School Certificate

Main Language(s) of Instruction: Spanish

Degrees and Diplomas: *Licenciatura*: 4 yrs; *Maestría*: 2 yrs; *Especialidad*; *Doctorado en Filosofia*

Student Services: Academic counselling, Health services, Nursery care, Sports facilities

Student Numbers *2008*: Total 13,746
Last Updated: 18/10/11

CENTRAL AMERICAN TECHNOLOGICAL UNIVERSITY
Universidad Tecnológica Centroamericana (UNITEC)
Apartado Aéreo 3530, Zona Jacaleapa, Tegucigalpa
Tel: +504 230-4076
Fax: +504 230-4008
EMail: viestcom@unitec.edu
Website: http://www.unitec.edu

Rector: Luis Orlando Zelaya Medrano

Divisions

Business Administration (Administration; Advertising and Publicity; Business Administration; Business and Commerce; Finance; Industrial Management; International Business; Management; Marketing; Tourism); **Communication and Social Sciences** (Communication Studies; Graphic Design; International Relations; Law; Mass Communication; Psychology); **Engineering** (Architecture; Bioengineering; Civil Engineering; Computer Engineering; Computer Science; Electronic Engineering; Engineering; Industrial Engineering; Structural Architecture; Telecommunications Engineering; Transport Management)

Programmes

Postgraduate Studies (Commercial Law; Development Studies; Finance; Health Administration; Human Resources; Information Technology; Leadership; Management; Marketing; Structural Architecture; Tourism; Transport Management)

Further Information: Branches: Campus San Pedro Sula; Sede La Ceiba; Sede Los Próceres and Sede El Prado

History: Founded 1986.

Governing Bodies: Administrative Board; Academic Board; Consultation Board

Admission Requirements: Diploma de Bachiller en Ciencias y Letras, Perito Mercantil, Maestro, Bachiller en Computación

Main Language(s) of Instruction: Spanish

Degrees and Diplomas: *Licenciatura*; *Licenciatura*; *Maestría*. Also Título de Ingeniero, 5 yrs

Student Services: Academic counselling, Canteen, Employment services, Foreign student adviser, Language programs, Social counselling, Sports facilities

Libraries: Yes

Student Numbers *2008*: Total 6,824
Last Updated: 19/10/11

CENTRE FOR DESIGN, ARCHITECTURE AND CONSTRUCTION

Centro de Diseño, Arquitectura y Construcción (CEDAC)
Col. Tepeyac, Ave. Gracias a Dios, Calle Ocotepeque, Casa 1323, Tegucigalpa
Tel: +504 232-4874
EMail: registro@cedac.edu.hn
Website: http://www.cedac.edu.hn

Rector: Mario E. Martín EMail: rector@cedac.edu.hn

Programmes

Architecture (Architecture); **Graphic Design** (Graphic Design); **Interior Design** (Interior Design)

History: Founded 1996.

Main Language(s) of Instruction: Spanish

Degrees and Diplomas: *Licenciatura*: Architecture; Graphic Design; Interior Design, 4 yrs

Student Numbers *2008*: Total 270
Last Updated: 18/10/11

CHRISTIAN UNIVERSITY OF HONDURAS

Universidad Cristiana de Honduras
Col. Satélite V etapa, San Pedro Sula
Tel: +504 2559-1132
Website: http://www.ucrish.org

Rectora: María Antonia Suazo

Programmes

Business Administration (Business Administration); **Engineering** (Computer Engineering; Industrial Engineering); **Law** (Law); **Marketing** (Marketing); **Psychology** (Psychology); **Theology** (Theology)

History: Founded 2004.

Degrees and Diplomas: *Licenciatura*. Also Título de Ingeniero

Student Numbers *2008*: Total 888
Last Updated: 19/10/11

JESÚS DE NAZARETH INSTITUTE OF TECHNOLOGY

Instituto Superior Tecnológico Jesús de Nazareth
Col. Villas del Sol, Boulevard Las Torres, San Pedro Sula
Tel: +504 566-0005 +504 566-0024
Website: http://www.ujn.edu.hn

Presidente: Josemaría Sánchez Alvarado

Programmes

Business Management (Accountancy; Business Administration; Commercial Law; Computer Science; Economics; English; Finance; Human Resources; Labour Law; Management; Mathematics; Sociology; Software Engineering; Spanish; Statistics; Taxation); **Electronic Engineering** (Computer Graphics; Computer Networks; Electronic Engineering; Engineering Drawing and Design; Telecommunications Engineering); **Industrial and Systems Engineering** (Accountancy; Chemistry; Environmental Management; Industrial Engineering; Mathematics; Production Engineering; Software Engineering; Statistics; Systems Analysis)

History: Founded 2004.

Degrees and Diplomas: *Licenciatura*. Also Título de Ingeniero

Student Numbers *2008*: Total 181
Last Updated: 19/10/11

JOSÉ CECILIO DEL VALLE UNIVERSITY, TEGUCIGALPA

Universidad José Cecilio del Valle (UJCV)
Apartado Aéreo 917, Col. Humuya, Ave. Altiplano, Calle Poseidón, Tegucigalpa
Tel: +504 239-3605 +504 239-1993
Fax: +504 239-8448
EMail: info@ujcv.edu.hn
Website: http://www.ujcv.edu.hn

Rector: Carlos Ávila Molina EMail: carlosavila@ujcv.edu.hn

Vicerrector Financiero y Administrativo: Francisco Jose Rosa EMail: fjrosa@ujcv.edu.hn

Programmes

Architecture (Architecture); **Business Administration** (Agricultural Management; Business Administration; Industrial Management; Tourism); **Engineering** (Civil Engineering; Computer Engineering; Construction Engineering; Industrial Engineering); **Interior Design** (Interior Design); **Law**

History: Founded 1978. A private autonomous institution financially supported by tuition fees and donations.

Governing Bodies: Board of Directors

Academic Year: January to December (January-March; April-June; July-September; October-December)

Admission Requirements: Secondary school certificate (bachillerato)

Main Language(s) of Instruction: Spanish

International Co-operation: With universities in USA, Chile, Spain

Accrediting Agencies: Asociación de Universidades Privadas de Centroamérica (AUPRICA)

Degrees and Diplomas: *Técnico*: 2 yrs; *Licenciatura*: 4 yrs

Student Services: Academic counselling

Student Residential Facilities: No

Special Facilities: No

Libraries: c. 7,200 vols, Journals and Scientific Magazines

Student Numbers *2008*: Total 48,600
Last Updated: 18/10/11

METROPOLITAN UNIVERSITY OF HONDURAS

Universidad Metropolitana de Honduras
Plaza Colprosumah, Cruce del Blvd. Centro América y Suyapa,
contiguo a la Procuraduria General de la Republica "PGR",
Tegucigalpa
Tel: +504 280-1111 Ext. 115 / 116
EMail: info_umh@unimetro.edu.hn
Website: http://www.unimetro.edu.hn

Rector: Armando Enamorado

Programmes

Business Engineering (Business and Commerce); **Business Management and Accountancy** (Accountancy; Business Administration; Management); **Ecotourism** (Ecology; Environmental Management; Tourism); **Graduate Studies** (Business Administration; Business and Commerce; Economics; Environmental Management; Finance; Management; Marketing; Tourism); **Management and Social Development** (Administration; Development Studies; Social Studies); **Marketing and International Business** (International Business; Marketing); **Social and Public Communication** (Communication Studies; Economics; Social Studies)

History: Founded 2002.

Degrees and Diplomas: *Licenciatura*; *Maestría*

Student Numbers *2008*: Total 2,247
Last Updated: 19/10/11

NEW MILLENNIUM CHRISTIAN EVANGELICAL UNIVERSITY

**Universidad Cristiana Evangélica
Nuevo Milenio**
Campus Llanos del Potrero, Carretera al Batallón, Calle los
Alcaldes, Comayagüela
Tel: +504 291-0026 +504 291-0027
Fax: +504 291-0026
EMail: info@ucenm.net
Website: http://www.ucenm.net/

Rectora: María Antonia de Suazo EMail: rectora@ucenm.net

Secretario General: Luis Galeano EMail: lgaleano@ucenm.net

Director Administrativo: Roldan Suazo EMail: rsuazo@ucenm.net

Programmes

Business Administration (Business Administration); **Community Health** (Community Health); **Computer Systems** (Computer Engineering); **Laboratory Techniques** (Laboratory Techniques; Medical Technology); **Marketing** (Marketing); **Theology** (Theology)

Further Information: Also Peña Blanca and Catacamas campuses

History: Founded 2001.

Degrees and Diplomas: *Técnico*; *Licenciatura*. Also título de Ingeniero

Student Numbers *2008*: Total 176
Last Updated: 19/10/11

PAN-AMERICAN ZAMORANO SCHOOL OF AGRICULTURE

Escuela Agrícola Panamericana Zamorano
Apartado Postal 93, Tegucigalpa
Tel: +504 2287-2000
Fax: +504 2776-6240
EMail: zamorano@zamorano.edu
Website: http://www.zamorano.edu

Rector: Roberto Cuevas García
EMail: zamonoticias@zamorano.edu

Academic Dean: Raúl Espinal

Programmes

Agricultural Business and Management (Agricultural Business; Agricultural Management); **Agronomy and Agricultural Produc-** tion (Agriculture; Agronomy; Crop Production; Food Science); **Food Science and Technology** (Food Science; Food Technology); **Socio-Economic Development and Environment** (Environmental Engineering; Environmental Studies; Water Management; Water Science)

History: Founded 1942.

Main Language(s) of Instruction: Spanish

Degrees and Diplomas: Professional title, 4 yrs

Student Numbers *2008*: Total 1,052
Last Updated: 18/10/11

POLYTECHNIC UNIVERSITY OF ENGINEERING

Universidad Politécnica de Ingeniería
Residencial La Granja, Bloque F, Calle de Acceso al Club Social del
BCIE, Comayagüela
Tel: +504 2225-7454 +504 2225-7455
EMail: info@upi.edu.hn
Website: http://www.upi.edu.hn/

Rector: Luis Eveline Hernández EMail: leveline@upi.edu.hn

Vice-Rectora Académica: Rina Enamorado
EMail: rwenamorado@upi.edu.hn

Programmes

Civil Engineering (Civil Engineering; Construction Engineering; Hydraulic Engineering; Road Engineering); **Environmental Engineering** (Accountancy; Anthropology; Botany; Chemistry; Ecology; Energy Engineering; Environmental Engineering; Environmental Studies; Geography; Hydraulic Engineering; Hygiene; Mathematics; Meteorology; Painting and Drawing; Physics; Surveying and Mapping; Water Management; Water Science; Zoology); **Finance** (Accountancy; Banking; Finance; Information Technology; Taxation); **Geology** (Geology); **Industrial Design** (Accountancy; Art History; Computer Science; Design; Industrial Design; Mathematics; Metal Techniques; Packaging Technology; Painting and Drawing; Polymer and Plastics Technology; Wood Technology); **Information Technology and Communication Engineering** (Computer Engineering; Computer Networks; Computer Science; Information Technology; Mathematics; Operations Research; Software Engineering; Telecommunications Engineering); **Topography** (Surveying and Mapping)

History: Founded 2007.

Degrees and Diplomas: *Licenciatura*. Also título de Ingeniero, 5 yrs

Student Numbers *2008*: Total 92
Last Updated: 19/10/11

POLYTECHNIC UNIVERSITY OF HONDURAS

Universidad Politécnica de Honduras
Barrio San Rafael, Tegucigalpa
Website: http://www.lapolitecnicahn.org

Rector: Carleton Corrales Cálix

Programmes

Business Management (Business Administration; Management); **Computer Systems Engineering** (Computer Engineering; Electronic Engineering); **Industrial Production Engineering** (Electronic Engineering; Industrial Engineering; Information Management); **Tourism Management** (Hotel Management; Tourism)

Further Information: Campuses: Comayagua; Choluteca; Danli and Lima

History: Founded 2005.

Degrees and Diplomas: *Licenciatura*. Also título de Ingeniero

Student Numbers *2008*: Total 401
Last Updated: 19/10/11

TECHNOLOGICAL UNIVERSITY OF HONDURAS

Universidad Tecnológica de Honduras (UTH)
Apartado Aéreo 1811, 3 cuadras al oeste del Puente de Rio Blanco, Carretera a Armenta Boulevard del Norte, San Pedro Sula, Cortés
Tel: +504 2551-2220 +504 2551-2236
Fax: +504 2551-6108
EMail: info@uth.hn
Website: http://www.uth.hn

President: Roger Valladares

Campuses
El Progreso (Business Administration; Business and Commerce; Computer Engineering; Finance; Human Resources; Industrial Engineering; Industrial Management; Law; Management; Marketing); **Islas de la Bahia** *(Distance Education)* (Business Administration; Management); **La Ceiba** (Business Administration; Computer Engineering; Finance; Human Resources; Industrial Engineering; Law; Management; Marketing; Tourism); **Puerto Cortés** (Business Administration; Business and Commerce; Computer Engineering; Electronic Engineering; Engineering; Finance; Industrial Engineering; Industrial Management; International Business; Management; Tourism); **Santa Bárbara** (Business Administration; Computer Engineering; Law; Management); **Siguatepeque** (Business Administration; Law; Management); **Tegucigalpa** (Business and Commerce; Computer Engineering; Electronic Engineering; Finance; Industrial Engineering; Industrial Management; International Business; Law; Management; Marketing; Public Relations; Tourism)

Programmes
Business Administration (Business Administration; Business and Commerce; Finance; Industrial Management; International Business; Law; Marketing; Public Relations; Tourism); **Engineering** (Computer Engineering; Electronic Engineering; Engineering; Industrial Engineering); **Graduate Studies** (Business Administration; Civil Law; Criminal Law; Finance; Human Resources; International Business; Management; Tourism; Transport Management)

History: Founded 1992. Acquired present status and title 1996.

Main Language(s) of Instruction: Spanish

Degrees and Diplomas: *Licenciatura*; *Maestría*. Also Engineering Degree in Industrial Production and Computer Science

Student Numbers *2008*: Total 18,212
Last Updated: 19/10/11

UNIVERSITY OF SAN PEDRO SULA

Universidad de San Pedro Sula (USPS)
Campus Universitario, Avenida Circunvalación, San Pedro Sula, Cortés 1064
Tel: +504 552-2277
Fax: +504 553-1889
EMail: info@usps.edu
Website: http://www.usps.edu

Rector: Roberto Martínez Arias (1984-)
EMail: roberto.martinez@usps.edu

Secretario General: Osvaldo Valladares
EMail: osvaldo.valladares@usps.edu

Vicerrector: Senén Villanueva Henderson
EMail: svillanueva@usps.edu

Faculties
Economics and Administration (Advertising and Publicity; Business Administration; Business Computing; Communication Arts; Communication Studies; Graphic Design; Law; Marketing; Tourism); **Technology** (Agricultural Business; Agricultural Engineering; Agriculture; Architecture; Industrial Engineering)

History: Founded 1978.

Governing Bodies: Rector; Vice-Rector

Academic Year: January to December (January-April; May-August; September-December)

Admission Requirements: High school diploma

Main Language(s) of Instruction: Spanish

International Co-operation: With universities in USA, Mexico and Central American countries.

Degrees and Diplomas: *Licenciatura*: 4 yrs; *Maestría*: Business Administration; Marketing and Finance, a further 2 yrs

Student Services: Academic counselling, Canteen, Cultural centre, Foreign student adviser, Health services, Social counselling, Sports facilities

Libraries: Yes

Publications: El Comunicador *(biennially)*; Revista Perspectiva *(biennially)*

Student Numbers *2008*: Total 4,542
Last Updated: 18/10/11

Hungary

STRUCTURE OF HIGHER EDUCATION SYSTEM

Description:

Within the framework of the Bologna process, the gradual transition from a binary higher education system that awarded Egyetemi oklevél (University-level degree) or Főiskolai oklevél (College-level degree) to a system based on three consecutive cycles started in 2004 in Hungary. Higher education is regulated by Act 139 of 2005 on Higher Education. Operating within the framework provided by the Higher Education Act, higher education institutions are autonomous state-recognised, state or non-state (church or private) institutions. The list of state-recognised institutions can be found in the Annex of the Higher Education Act. The list of state-recognised institutions is also available at the website www.naric.hu. There are two types of higher education institutions, egyetem (university) and főiskola (college). Both types may offer accredited courses in all three cycles. As a rule the egyetem (university) is a higher education institution that is eligible to provide mesterképzés (Master courses) in at least two fields of study, and to offer doktori képzés (doctorate courses) as well as to confer a doctoral degree. Under the old, pre-Bologna higher education system, higher education degree programmes led to Főiskolai oklevél (College-level degree) and Egyetemi oklevél (University-level degree). The training at college level lasted for 3-4 years (180-240 credits) while at university level 4-5 years (240-300 credits) (one of the few exceptions was the medical course where the duration of the training was 6 years, 360 credits). In the Bologna-type higher education system, the first cycle degree to be awarded is Alapfokozat (Bachelor degree) after 6 to 8 semesters of study (180-240 credits). As a second cycle degree, Mesterfokozat (Master degree) can be obtained after 2 to 4 semesters of study (60-120 credits) following the Alapfokozat (Bachelor degree). Mesterfokozat (Master degree) based on a previously awarded Mesterfokozat (Master degree) can be obtained after 2 semesters of study (60 credits). Alapképzés (Bachelor courses) and Mesterképzés (Master courses) may be organised in separate cycles that are built on each other, in the form of separate programmes, or in cases specified by law as a one-tier long cycle, undivided programme. In the latter case the length of Mesterképzés (Master courses) is 10-12 semesters (300-360 credits). Higher education institutions provided/provide training leading to Doktori fokozat (PhD or DLA) (doctoral degree). In addition to the degree programmes defined above, higher education institutions may organise higher-level vocational training and postgraduate specialist training. Furthermore, within the framework of lifelong learning, they can offer adult education as well. From September 1, 2003 all higher education institutions have been operating a credit system based on the principles of the European Credit Transfer System. Accordingly, one credit equals 30 student workload hours.

Stages of studies:

University level first stage: *Undergraduate studies*
Under the old, pre-Bologna higher education system, it was the Főiskolai oklevél (College level degree) that corresponded to the first cycle degree. The training at college level lasted for 3-4 years (6-8 semesters) (180-240 credits.
Under the new Bologna-type higher education system, the Alapfokozat (Bachelor degree) is a first cycle degree. Courses leading to Alapfokozat (Bachelor degree) require the taking of at least 180 credits – in the case of uninterrupted practical courses a minimum of 210 credits – but such courses may not exceed 240 credits. The length of the programme extends to a minimum of 6 and a maximum of 8 semesters. Students complete their studies with a final examination. The final examination may consist of several parts – the defence of the degree thesis, and an additional oral, written or practical examinations – as defined in the curriculum. Pursuant to Act 139 of 2005 on Higher Education, Főiskolai oklevél (College-level degree) and Alapfokozat (Bachelor degree) are equivalent. The degree give access to the labour market as well as to second cycle degree programmes.

University level second stage: *Postgraduate studies*
Under the old, pre Bologna higher education system, it was is the Egyetemi oklevél (University-level degree) that corresponded to the second cycle degree. The training at university level lasted for 4-5 years (8-10 semesters)

(240–300 credits) with a few exceptions like Medical courses, which lasted 6 years (12 semesters) (360 credits). Under the new, Bologna-type higher education system, the Mesterfokozat (Master degree) is a second cycle degree. Courses leading to the Mesterfokozat require at least 60 credits but such courses may not exceed 120 credits. The length of the programme extends to a minimum of 2 and a maximum of 4 semesters. In a few fields (e.g. Medicine, Law, Arts), Mesterfokozat (Master degree) can be obtained in a one-tier undivided programme of 10 to 12 semesters requiring the completion of at least 300 credits and a maximum of 360 credits. Students complete their studies with a final examination. The final examination may consist of several parts – the defence of the degree thesis, and additional oral, written or practical examinations – as defined in the curriculum. Pursuant to Act 139 of 2005 on Higher Education, Egyetemi oklevél and Mesterfokozat are equivalent. Both degrees give access to the labour market as well as to doctoral degree programmes (PhD or DLA), which are third cycle programmes.

The Szakirányú továbbképzés (postgraduate specialist training) following upon a Alapfokozat (Bachelor degree), Főiskolai oklevél (College-level degree), Mesterfokozat (Master degree) or Egyetemi oklevél (University-level degree) is a non-degree programme leading to the Szakirányú továbbképzési oklevél (Further specialization diploma). Courses require at least 60 credits and a maximum of 120 credits. The length of the programme can extend to a minimum of 2 and a maximum of 4 semesters. The Szakirányú továbbképzési oklevél (Further specialization diploma) does not give access to doctorate courses.

University level third stage: Doctorate studies
In the higher education system, doktori képzés (doctorate course) constitutes the third training cycle. The doctorate courses prepare students for taking a doktori fokozat (PhD or DLA) (doctoral degree) following the conferral of the Mesterfokozat (Master degree) or Egyetemi oklevél (University-level degree). Doctorate courses require at least 180 credits. The length of the programme extends to 6 semesters. Following a doctorate course, in a separate degree awarding procedure, the scientific degree 'Doctor of Philosophy' (abbreviation: PhD), or in art education 'Doctor of Liberal Arts' (abbreviation: DLA) may be awarded.

Distance higher education:
Distance education is offered by accredited higher education institutions. Diplomas awarded are equivalent to those granted to full-time students. Pursuant to Act 139 of 2005 on Higher Education, distance education means a particular form of training, involving the use of ICT teaching aids and teaching-learning methods based on the interactive relationship between teacher and student and the student's individual work, where the number of contact hours is less than 30% of the contact hours in full-time training.

ADMISSION TO HIGHER EDUCATION

Admission to university-level studies:

Name of secondary school credential required: Érettségi bizonyítvány

For entry to: Alapfokozat (Bachelor degree), Mesterfokozat (Master degree in one tier long cycle, undivided programme)

Entrance exam requirements: The number of students who can be admitted to higher education is limited. From the academic year 2004/2005 onwards, there are no more entrance examinations. Applicants are admitted based on final grades obtained at secondary school and their secondary school leaving examination (érettségi vizsga) results or based solely on the latter, considering the interest of the applicant. The basic requirement for admission to alapképzés (Bachelor courses) and long cycle, undivided mesterképzés (Master courses) is the secondary school leaving certificate (Érettségi bizonyítvány) obtained following the completion of 12 grades in public education. The admission to some programmes could be based on additional aptitude test or practical examination. Those applicants can be admitted to mesterképzés (Master courses) who possess Főiskolai oklevél (College-level degree) or Egyetemi oklevél (University-level degree) or Alapfokozat (Bachelor degree). Those applicants can be admitted to szakirányú továbbképzés (postgraduate specialist training courses) who possess Főiskolai oklevél (College-level degree) or Egyetemi oklevél (University-level degree), or Alapfokozat (Bachelor's degree) or Mesterfokozat (Master's degree). Only applicants with Egyetemi oklevél (University-level degree) or Mesterfokozat (Master's degree) may be admitted to doktori képzés (doctoral courses). Additional requirements for admittance to mesterképzés (Master courses), szakirányú továbbképzés (postgraduate specialist training courses) and doktori képzés (doctorate courses) are determined by the higher education institutions.

Numerus clausus/restrictions: Restrictions in some cases depending on places available.

Other admission requirements: An aptitude test (e.g. teacher training) or practical examinations (e.g. in arts, sports, etc) is required for some study programmes.

Foreign students admission:

Definition of foreign student: Students who are not Hungarian citizens and have not settled in Hungary.

Entrance exam requirements: Foreign students must hold a Secondary School Leaving Certificate or its equivalent (issued after the completion of 12 years of study or eleven years if primary and secondary education comprise eleven years in that particular country and entitles its holder to apply for admission to a higher education institution in the given country).

Entry regulations: Determined by the institutions.

Health requirements: For some courses.

Language requirements: Knowledge of the Hungarian language is a requirement in courses conducted in Hungarian. Hungarian higher education institutions also offer higher education programmes in foreign languages. In this case, the knowledge of the given language is a prerequisite.

RECOGNITION OF STUDIES

Quality assurance system:

A higher education institution may launch alapképzés and mesterképzés (Bachelor and Master courses) after having obtained the consent thereto in the expert opinion of the Hungarian Accreditation Committee, and following the central registration of the given course. In the case of each alapképzés and mesterképzés (Bachelor and Master courses) the law determines the programme and graduation requirements, thus, all the knowledge and competencies whose acquisition is a precondition for a degree to be awarded in respect to the given programme. The launching of doktori képzés (doctorate courses) is within the powers of the higher education institutions, having obtained the consent thereto in the expert opinion of the Hungarian Accreditation Committee and having fulfilled other necessary conditions prescribed by law. It is the task of the Hungarian Accreditation Committee (www.mab.hu) to assess the quality of education and scientific activities of the higher education institutions. The Hungarian Accreditation Committee conducts ex ante and ex post accreditation of both programmes and institutions. There are separate procedures for institutional and programme accreditation.

Bodies dealing with recognition:

Magyar Ekvivalencia és Információs Központ, Oktatási Hivatal (Magyar ENIC/NARIC Iroda)
(Hungarian Equivalence and Information Centre, Educational Authority (Hungarian ENIC/NARIC Office))
> Head of Unit: Gábor Mészáros
> Szalay utca 10-14.
> Budapest 1055
> Tel: +36(1) 374 2200
> Fax: +36(1) 374 2492
> EMail: recognition@oh.gov.hu
> WWW: http://www.naric.hu

Magyar Felsőoktatási Akkreditációs Bizottság - MAB (Hungarian Accreditation Committee - HAC)
> Krisztina krt. 39/B 4. em.
> Budapest 1013
> Tel: +36(1) 344 0314
> Fax: +36(1) 344 0313
> EMail: titkarsag@mab.hu
> WWW: http://www.mab.hu/english/index.html

Special provisions for recognition:

Recognition for university level studies: Recognition is regulated by Act 100 of 2001 on the recognition of foreign certificates and degrees. Academic recognition belongs to the sphere of competence of the higher education institutions.

For access to advanced studies and research: Recognition is regulated by Act 100 of 2001 on the recognition of foreign certificates and degrees. Academic recognition belongs to the sphere of competence of the higher education institutions.

For exercising a profession: Recognition is regulated by Act 100 of 2001 on the recognition of foreign certificates and degrees.

NATIONAL BODIES

Nemzeti Erőforrás Minisztérium (Ministry of National Resources)
Minister: Miklós Réthelyi
Secretary of State for Education: Rózsa Hoffmann
Szalay utca. 10 14.
Budapest 1055
Tel: +36(1) 795 1100
EMail: info@nefmi.gov.hu
WWW: http://www.nefmi.gov.hu/

Magyar Felsőktatási Akkreditációs Bizottság - MAB (Hungarian Accreditation Committee - HAC)
President: György Bazsa
Krisztina krt. 39/B 4. em.
Budapest 1013
Tel: +36(1) 344 0314
Fax: +36(1) 344 0313
EMail: titkarsag@mab.hu
WWW: http://www.mab.hu/english/index.html
Role of national body: The Hungarian Accreditation Committee is, according to the 2005 Higher Education Act, "an independent national body of experts assessing quality in education, research and artistic activities in higher education, and examining the operation of the institutional quality development scheme."

Oktatási Hivatal (Educational Authority)
President: Péter Princzinger
Szalay utca 10-14.
Budapest 1055
Tel: +36(1) 374 2100
Fax: +36(1) 374 2499
EMail: info@oh.gov.hu
WWW: http://www.oh.gov.hu
Role of national body: The Educational Authority embodies all organizations performing educational administrative tasks. At the higher education level, the Educational Authority administers the application system to higher education and operates the Hungarian Equivalence and Information Centre.

Felsőoktatási és Tudományos Tanács (Higher Education and Research Council)
President: András Jávor
Szalay utca 10-14.
Budapest 1055
Tel: +36(1) 269 5549
Fax: +36(1) 269 5559
EMail: ftt@nefmi.gov.hu
WWW: http://www.ftt.hu/

Országos Kredittanács Irodája (Office of the National Credit Council)
Director: András Derenyi
Szalay utca 10-14.
Budapest 1055

Tel: +36(1) 235 7251
Fax: +36(1) 235 7251
EMail: info@kreditiroda.hu
WWW: http://www.kreditiroda.hu
Role of national body: The National Credit Council has been created to provide advice on the development of the country's credit system to the Ministry of Education.

Magyar Rektori Konferencia (Hungarian Rectors' Conference)
President: József Bódis
Secretary-General: Zoltán Dubéczi
Benczúr utca 43. IV/3.
Budapest 1068
Tel: +36(70) 932 4203
Fax: +36(1) 322 9679
EMail: mrk@mail.mrk.hu
WWW: http://www.mrk.hu

Data for academic year: 2011-2012
Source: IAU from the Hungarian Equivalence and Information Centre, 2011

INSTITUTIONS

PUBLIC INSTITUTIONS

BERZSENYI DÁNIEL COLLEGE
Berzsenyi Dániel Főiskola (BDF)
Károlyi Gáspár tér 4, 9701 Szombathely
Tel: +36(94) 504-329
Fax: +36(94) 504-404
EMail: iro@bdf.hu
Website: http://www.bdtf.hu

Director-General: Károly Gadányi (2002-)
Tel: +36(94) 504-328 EMail: rektoratus@bdf.hu

International Relations: Antonio Sciacovelli
Tel: +36(94) 504-524 EMail: kun@bdf.hu

Centres
Computer Assisted Language Learning (*Eastern European*); **English Teaching** (Foreign Languages Education); **Foreign Languages** (Modern Languages); **Information Technology** (Information Technology); **Video and Media Studio**

Institutes
'Arts (Arts and Humanities); **Pedagogy** (Pedagogy); **Philology** (Philology); **Physical Education and Sports** (Physical Education; Sports); **Psychology** (Psychology); **Science** (Natural Sciences); **Social Sciences** (Social Sciences); **Teacher Training** (Primary Education)

History: Founded 1959, acquired present status and title 1991.

Degrees and Diplomas: *Alapfokozat megszerzését tanúsító oklevél*; *Szakirányú Továbbképzési Oklevél*; *Mesterfokozat megszerzését tanúsító oklevél.* Also higher vocational training programmes (felsőfokú szakképzés).

BUDAPEST BUSINESS SCHOOL
Budapesti Gazdasági Főiskola (BGF)
Buzogány utca 11-13., 1149 Budapest
Tel: +36(1) 383-4799
Fax: +36(1) 469-6636
EMail: bgf@bgf.hu
Website: http://www.bgf.hu
Rector: Éva Sándorné Kriszt EMail: kriszt.eva@bgf.hu

Secretary-General: Szilvia Ács
Tel: +36(1) 469-6660 EMail: acs.szilvia@bgf.hu
International Relations: Judit Hidasi, Head of International Relations EMail: hidasi.judit@kkfk.bgf.hu

Colleges
Business Administration (*Zalaegerszeg*) (Business Administration); **Commerce, Catering and Tourism** (Advertising and Publicity; Business and Commerce; Cooking and Catering; European Studies; Finance; Hotel Management; International Business; Management; Marketing; Tourism); **Finance and Accountancy** (Accountancy; Banking; Finance; Human Resources; Insurance; Taxation); **International Management and Business** (International Business; Management)

Institutes
Business Teacher Training and Pedagogy (*Professional Academic*) (Business Education); **Commerce and Marketing** (*Professional Academic*) (Business and Commerce; Marketing); **Economics and Methodology** (Economics); **Finance and Accountancy** (*Professional Academic*) (Accountancy; Finance); **International Business Economics** (*Professional Academic*) (International Business; International Economics); **Language and Communication** (Communication Studies); **Management and Human Resources** (*Professional Academic*) (Human Resources; Management); **Social Sciences** (*Professional Academic*) (Social Sciences); **Tourism and Catering** (*Professional Academic*) (Cooking and Catering; Tourism)

History: Founded 2000.

Main Language(s) of Instruction: Hungarian
Degrees and Diplomas: *Alapfokozat megszerzését tanúsító oklevél (Bachelor's degree)*: 6-7 semesters; *Mesterfokozat megszerzését tanúsító oklevél (Master's degree)*: a further 3-4 semesters; *Doktori oklevél (PhD)*: 4 semesters fulltime, 6 semesters parttime
Libraries: 279,160 vols: 18,227 periodical subscriptions.

Academic Staff 2010-2011	TOTAL
FULL-TIME	439
PART-TIME	38
STAFF WITH DOCTORATE FULL-TIME	130
Student Numbers 2010-2011	
All (Foreign Included)	13,714

Last Updated: 28/10/11

BUDAPEST UNIVERSITY OF TECHNOLOGY AND ECONOMICS

Budapesti Műszaki és Gazdaságtudományi Egyetem (BME)

Műegyetem rakpart 3., H-1111 Budapest
Tel: +36(1) 463-1111
Fax: +36(1) 463-1110
EMail: info@mail.bme.hu; nki@mail.bme.hu
Website: http://www.bme.hu

Rector: Gábor Péceli
Tel: +36(1) 463-2221, Fax: +36(1) 463-2220
EMail: rektor@mail.bme.hu

Secretary-General: Tibor Szabó
Tel: +36(1) 463-2232 EMail: tiborszabo@mail.bme.hu

International Relations: László Dvorszki, Head, Department of International Affairs
Tel: +36(1) 463-2272, Fax: +36(1) 463-2270
EMail: dvorszkil@mail.bme.hu

Centres

International Education *(IEC)* (International and Comparative Education) *Director:* Gyula Csopaki

Faculties

Architecture (Architecture; Town Planning) *Dean:* Gábor Becker; **Chemical Engineering and Bioengineering** (Bioengineering; Chemical Engineering) *Dean:* György Pokol; **Civil Engineering** (Civil Engineering) *Dean:* Antal Lovas; **Economic and Social Sciences** (Business Administration; Economics; Management; Philosophy; Social Sciences); **Electrical Engineering and Informatics** (Automation and Control Engineering; Computer Engineering; Electrical Engineering; Power Engineering) *Dean:* Gábor Péceli; **Mechanical Engineering** (Mechanical Engineering) *Dean:* Antal Penninger; **Natural Sciences** (Mathematics; Natural Sciences; Nuclear Physics; Physics) *Dean:* Tamás Keszthelyi; **Transportation Engineering** (Civil Engineering; Road Transport; Transport Engineering) *Dean:* Béla Kulcsár

Research Centres

3G/4G Mobile Communications (Communication Studies); **Advanced Vehicle Control Knowledge**; **Biomechanical**; **Information Society and Trend** (Computer Science); **Information Technology Innovation and Knowledge**; **Intelligent Materials** *(Cooperative)* (Materials Engineering); **Inter-University Cooperative Research for ICT** (Information Technology)

History: Founded 1782 as Institutum Geometricum Hydrotechnicum, acquired University status 1871. Reorganized 1949 as Technical University of Budapest incorporating former Technical University of Building and Transport Engineering, founded 1952. Acquired present title 2000. Under the jurisdiction of the Ministry of Culture and Education and financed by the State.

Governing Bodies: Senate

Academic Year: September to June (September-January; February-June)

Admission Requirements: Secondary school certificate (érettségi bizonyítvány) and entrance examination

Fees: None for Hungarian citizens. Foreign students, (Euros): 3,200

Main Language(s) of Instruction: Hungarian, English, French, German

International Co-operation: With universities in Australia; Austria; Czech Republic; South Africa; France; Netherlands; Germany; Finland; Switzerland; Sweden; Japan; USA

Degrees and Diplomas: *Alapfokozat megszerzését tanúsító oklevél (BSc)*; *Mesterfokozat megszerzését tanúsító oklevél:* Science in Engineering (MSc), 2 yrs; *Doktori oklevél (PhD):* a further 3 yrs

Student Services: Academic counselling, Canteen, Cultural centre, Employment services, Foreign student adviser, Health services, Nursery care, Sports facilities

Student Residential Facilities: For 50% of the students

Special Facilities: University Theatre

Libraries: National Technical Information Centre and Library, 2,016,560 vols

Publications: Periodica Polytechnica (8 series) *(quarterly)*; Research News *(quarterly)*

Press or Publishing House: Publishing House

Last Updated: 16/04/09

COLLEGE OF DUNAÚJVÁROS

Dunaújvárosi Főiskola (DF)

Táncsics Mihály utca 1/a., 2400 Dunaújváros
Tel: +36(25) 551-100
Fax: +36(25) 551-231
EMail: international@mail.duf.hu
Website: http://portal.duf.hu

Director-General: László Bognár EMail: bognarl@mail.duf.hu

International Relations: Mónika Rajcsányi-Molnár, Head, International Relations Department
Tel: +36(25) 551-211 +36(25) 551-246, Fax: +36(25) 551-262
EMail: molnarmo@mail.duf.hu

Programmes

Andragogy (Adult Education); **Business Administration** (Business Administration); **Communication and Media Sciences** (Communication Studies; Media Studies); **Computer Engineering** (Computer Engineering); **Engineering Business Management** (Business Administration; Engineering; Management); **Engineering Teacher** *(Master Degree Programs)* (Engineering; Teacher Trainers Education); **Materials Engineering** (Materials Engineering); **Mechanical Engineering** (Mechanical Engineering); **Technology Education** (Technology Education); **Vocational Education** (Vocational Education)

History: Founded 1969.

Degrees and Diplomas: *Alapfokozat megszerzését tanúsító oklevél*; *Szakirányú Továbbképzési Oklevél*; *Mesterfokozat megszerzését tanúsító oklevél*

Last Updated: 19/09/11

COLLEGE OF KECSKEMÉT

Kecskeméti Főiskola (KF)

Izsáki út 10, 6000 Kecskemét
Tel: +36(76) 501-960
Fax: +36(76) 501-979
EMail: kefo@kefo.hu
Website: http://www.kefo.hu

Rector: Danyi József (2000-)
Tel: +36(76) 501-961 EMail: rector@kefo.hu

International Relations: Tibor Vajnai
Tel: +36(76) 501-992, Fax: +36(76) 483-282
EMail: international.office@rh.kefo.hu; vajnai.tibor@gamf.kefo.hu

Faculties

Horticulture (Horticulture); **Mechanical Engineering and Automation** *(GAMF)* (Engineering; Information Technology; Management; Mechanical Engineering; Technology); **Teacher Training** *(Kindergarten, Primary level)* (Teacher Training)

History: Founded 1986, acquired present status and title 2000 through the merger of 3 Kecskemét-based tertiary colleges (Faculty of Mechanical Engineering and Automation, the Teacher Training Faculty and the Horticultural Faculty).

Degrees and Diplomas: *Alapfokozat megszerzését tanúsító oklevél:* 3-4 yrs; *Szakirányú Továbbképzési Oklevél:* Horticulture, at least a further 2 yrs. Also Vocational Training Programme.

Academic Staff *2007-2008:* Total: c. 600

Student Numbers *2007-2008:* Total: c. 6,000

Last Updated: 28/10/11

COLLEGE OF NYIREGYHÁZA

Nyíreghyházi Főiskola (NYF)

Sóstói út. 31/b, 4401 Nyíregyháza
Tel: +36(42) 599-400
Fax: +36(42) 404-092 +36(42) 402-485
EMail: international.center@nyf.hu
Website: http://www.nyf.hu

Rector: Zoltán Jánosi Tel: +36(42) 599-495

Colleges

Arts and Humanities (Arts and Humanities); **Economics and Social Sciences** (Economics; Social Sciences); **Technology and Agriculture** (Agricultural Engineering)

History: Founded 1962.

Degrees and Diplomas: *Alapfokozat megszerzését tanúsító oklevél; Szakirányú Továbbképzési Oklevél*

Last Updated: 26/10/11

COLLEGE OF SZOLNOK

Szolnoki Főiskola (SZF)
Tiszaligeti sétány 14, 5000 Szolnok
Tel: +36(56) 510-300
Fax: +36(56) 426-719
EMail: szolf@szolf.hu
Website: http://www.szolf.hu/Lapok/default.aspx

Rektor: Imre Túróczi

Faculties

Business (Accountancy; Business and Commerce; Communication Studies; Finance; International Business; Tourism); **Technical and Agricultural** (Agricultural Engineering; Cooking and Catering; Food Science; Mechanical Engineering; Rural Planning)

Institutes

Foreign Language (Foreign Languages Education)

Degrees and Diplomas: *Alapfokozat megszerzését tanúsító oklevél; Mesterfokozat megszerzését tanúsító oklevél*

Libraries: Yes
Last Updated: 28/10/11

⁄ CORVINUS UNIVERSITY OF BUDAPEST

Budapesti Corvinus Egyetem
Fővám tér 8, 1093 Budapest
Tel: +36(1) 482-5000
Fax: +36(1) 482-5023
EMail: intoffice@uni-corvinus.hu
Website: http://www.uni-corvinus.hu

Rector: Tamás Mészáros (2004-)
Tel: +36-1-482-5124 EMail: tamas.meszaros@uni-corvinus.hu

Head of Communication Office: Monika Andrasi
Tel: +36(1) 482-5020, Fax: +36(1) 482-5577
EMail: communication@uni-corvinus.hu

International Relations: Erzsébet Veres, Head of International Office
Tel: +36(1) 482-5389 EMail: erzsebet.veres@uni-corvinus.hu

Faculties

Business Administration (Accountancy; Business Administration; Business and Commerce; Commercial Law; Computer Science; Economics; Environmental Studies; Ethics; Finance; Fiscal Law; Human Resources; Management; Marketing; Media Studies; Rural Planning; Transport Management); **Economics** (Actuarial Science; Economic and Finance Policy; Economic History; Economics; European Studies; Finance; Human Resources; Management; Mathematics; Operations Research; Public Administration; Statistics); **Food Science** (Applied Chemistry; Biotechnology; Brewing; Crop Production; Food Science; Food Technology; Harvest Technology; Microbiology; Nutrition; Oenology; Viticulture); **Horticultural Science** (Biochemistry; Biotechnology; Botany; Chemistry; Ecology; Entomology; Environmental Studies; Farm Management; Floriculture; Fruit Production; Horticulture; Information Management; Management; Marketing; Mathematics; Nursing; Physiology; Plant and Crop Protection; Soil Science; Vegetable Production; Viticulture; Water Management); **Landscape Architecture** (Architectural and Environmental Design; Architecture; Development Studies; Heritage Preservation; Landscape Architecture; Regional Planning; Rural Planning; Town Planning); **Public Administration** (Business Administration; Communication Studies; Constitutional Law; Finance; Human Resources; Information Technology; International Studies; Law; Management; Modern Languages; Private Law; Public Administration; Social Policy; Urban Studies); **Social Sciences** (Behavioural Sciences; Central European Studies; Communication Studies; Development Studies; Eastern European Studies; Economics; Educational Sciences; European Languages;

European Studies; Foreign Languages Education; Government; History of Societies; International Relations; International Studies; Philosophy; Political Sciences; Psychology; Regional Studies; Social Policy; Sociology; Teacher Training)

History: Founded 1920 as Faculty of Economics of the Royal Hungarian University of Budapest. Became part of the Hungarian University of Economics 1948. Academic programme divided into three faculties 1952. Reorganized as Budapest University of Economic Sciences 1990. Became Budapest University of Economic Sciences and Public Administration (BUESPA) 2000. The former University of Horticulture and Food Industry (3 faculties of Szent István University) joined BUESPA 2003. Acquired present status and title 2004.

Governing Bodies: University Senate

Academic Year: September to June (September-December; February-June)

Admission Requirements: Secondary school certificate (érettségi bizonyítvány)

Main Language(s) of Instruction: Hungarian

Degrees and Diplomas: *Alapfokozat megszerzését tanúsító oklevél; Mesterfokozat megszerzését tanúsító oklevél; Doktori oklevél*

Student Services: Academic counselling, Canteen, Foreign student adviser, Health services, Sports facilities

Student Residential Facilities: Yes

Libraries: Central Library, c. 600,000 vols. Entz Ferenc Library and Archives c. 320,000 vols

Publications: Hungarian Bibliography of Economics and Statistics; Management Science *(monthly)*; Társadalom és Gazdaság, Society and Economics *(quarterly)*

Academic Staff *2008-2009*: Total 859
Student Numbers *2008-2009*: Total 16,815
Last Updated: 21/07/11

EÖTVÖS JÓZSEF COLLEGE

Eötvös József Főiskola (EJF)
Szegedi út. 2, 6500 Baja
Tel: +36(79) 524-624 +36(79) 524-641
Fax: +36(79) 524-630
EMail: rektor@ejf.hu
Website: http://www.ejf.hu

Director-General: János Majdán
Tel: +36(79) 524-641 EMail: majdan.janos@ejf.hu

International Relations: József Simon
Tel: +36(79) 523-970 EMail: simon.miklos@ejf.hu

Faculties

Pedagogy (Arts and Humanities; Cultural Studies; Fine Arts; Foreign Languages Education; Hungarian; Pedagogy; Physical Education; Social Studies); **Technology** (Computer Science; Construction Engineering; Mathematics; Technology; Water Management)

History: Founded 1870, acquired present status and title 1996.

Degrees and Diplomas: *Alapfokozat megszerzését tanúsító oklevél*

Last Updated: 28/10/11

EÖTVÖS LORÁND UNIVERSITY

Eötvös Loránd Tudományegyetem (ELTE)
Egyetem tér 1-3., 1053 Budapest
Tel: +36(1) 411-6500
Fax: +36(1) 411-6546
EMail: is@rekthiv.elte.hu
Website: http://www.elte.hu

Rector: Mezey Barna Tel: +36(1) 411-6500 EMail: rektor@elte.hu

Secretary-General: Rónay Zoltán
Tel: +36(1) 411-6725, Fax: +36(1) 411-6712
EMail: fotitkar@ludens.elte.hu

International Relations: Éva Kovács
Tel: +36(1) 411-6500, Ext. 2155, Fax: +36(1) 411-6540
EMail: international.studies@rekthiv.elte.hu;
kovacs.eva@rekthiv.elte.hu

Faculties

Education and Psychology (Educational Psychology); **Elementary and Nursery School Teachers' Training** (Preschool Education; Primary Education); **Humanities** (Arts and Humanities); **Informatics** (Computer Engineering); **Law and Political Science** (Civil Law; Commercial Law; Constitutional Law; Criminal Law; Criminology; International Law; Law; Philosophy; Political Sciences); **Science** (Biology; Chemistry; Geography; Geology; Mathematics; Multimedia; Natural Sciences; Physics); **Social Sciences** (Cultural Studies; International Studies; Political Sciences; Social Sciences; Sociology); **Special Education** *(Bárczi Gusztáv)* (Phonetics; Rehabilitation and Therapy; Sociology; Special Education; Speech Therapy and Audiology)

History: Founded 1561 as Jesuit college and established as University at Nagyszombat 1635 by Archbishop Péter Pázmány. Became secular institution 1773. Transferred to Buda 1777, and to Pest 1784. Acquired present title 1950. Faculty of Medicine detached and re-established as Medical University 1949. Under the jurisdiction of the Ministry of Culture and Education and financed by the State.

Governing Bodies: University Senate

Academic Year: September to July (September-January; February-July)

Admission Requirements: Secondary school certificate (érettségi bizonyítvány) and entrance examination

Fees: (Euros): 2,000-5,500 per semester

Main Language(s) of Instruction: Hungarian, English, German

International Co-operation: With universities in Europe, Asia, Ukraine, USA. Participates in the Erasmus, Ceepus and Tempus programmes

Degrees and Diplomas: *Alapfokozat megszerzését tanúsító oklevél; Mesterfokozat megszerzését tanúsító oklevél; Doktori oklevél*

Student Services: Academic counselling, Canteen, Cultural centre, Foreign student adviser, Health services, Nursery care, Sports facilities

Student Residential Facilities: Yes

Special Facilities: Observatory; Biological and Paleontological Museums; Geology Museum

Libraries: Central Library, c. 2m. vols; 200,000 journals, 600 on-line periodicals, faculty and department libraries

Publications: Acta Facultatis Politico-Juridicae; Annales Universitatis de Rolando Eötvös nominatae (15 sections); Bulletin of the Eötvös Loránd University

Press or Publishing House: Eötvös University Press
Last Updated: 26/10/11

ESZTERHÁZY KÁROLY COLLEGE

Eszterházy Károly Főiskola (EKF)
Eszterházy tér 1., 3300 Eger
Tel: +36(36) 520-400
Fax: +36(36) 520-440
EMail: dir@ektf.hu
Website: http://www.ektf.hu

General-Director: Zoltán Hauser (2001-)
Tel: +36(36) 520-401 EMail: hauser@ektf.hu

Administrative Officer: Ferenc Koncsos
Tel: +36(36) 520-407 EMail: koncsos@ektf.hu

International Relations: András Tarnóc
Tel: +36(36) 520-427, Fax: +36(36) 520-448

Faculties

Economics and Social Sciences (Commercial Law; Communication Studies; Computer Science; Economics; Educational Psychology; Marketing; Pedagogy; Psychology; Social Sciences; Sociology); **Humanities** (American Studies; Arts and Humanities; Cultural Studies; Economics; English; French; German; Graphic Arts; History; Hungarian; Linguistics; Literature; Modern Languages; Music; Philosophy; Russian); **Natural Sciences** (Biology; Botany; Chemistry; Computer Science; Environmental Studies; Geography; Information Technology; Mathematics; Natural Sciences; Physical Education; Physics; Zoology); **Teacher Training and Knowledge Technology** (Computer Science; Education; Information Technology; Pedagogy; Psychology; Teacher Training)

History: Founded 1948. Formerly known as Eszterházy Károly Tanárképzô Fôiskola.

Degrees and Diplomas: *Alapfokozat megszerzését tanúsító oklevél:* 3-4 yrs; *Szakirányú Továbbképzési Oklevél; Mesterfokozat megszerzését tanúsító oklevél.* Also Bachelor and Master degrees
Last Updated: 28/10/11

HUNGARIAN DANCE ACADEMY

Magyar Táncmüvészeti Főiskola (MTF)
Columbus utca 87-89., 1145 Budapest
Tel: +36(1) 273-3434
Fax: +36(1) 273-3433
EMail: info@mtf.hu
Website: http://www.mtf.hu

Rector: György Szakály (2011-)

International Relations: Béláné Melis
Tel: +36(1) 267-8647, Ext. 119 EMail: melish@mtf.hu

Departments

Choreography and Dance Theory (Dance); **Classical Ballet** (Dance); **Dance Pedagogy** (Dance); **Folk Dance** (Dance); **Foreign Languages** (Modern Languages); **Music** (Music)

Further Information: Also primary and secondary schools

History: Founded 1950 as State Institute of Ballet. Acquired present status and title 1983. Under the jurisdiction of the Ministry of Culture and Education.

Governing Bodies: Academy Council

Academic Year: September to June (September-January; February-June)

Admission Requirements: Dance teacher training. Secondary school certificate. Folk dancing: elementary education. Ballet: no preliminary training needed, general education given at the Academy. Students over the age of 10 accepted

Fees: (US Dollars): 250 a month

Main Language(s) of Instruction: Hungarian, English

Degrees and Diplomas: *Alapfokozat megszerzését tanúsító oklevél:* 4 yrs; *Szakirányú Továbbképzési Oklevél:* Dance Teachers Training, 2-4 yrs. Also Bachelor and Master degrees

Student Residential Facilities: Some residential facilities for students
Last Updated: 28/10/11

HUNGARIAN UNIVERSITY OF FINE ARTS, BUDAPEST

Magyar Képzőművészeti Egyetem (MKE)
Andrássy út. 69/71, 1062 Budapest
Tel: +36(1) 342-1738 +36(1) 342-8556
Fax: +36(1) 342-1563
Website: http://www.mke.hu

Rector: Frigyes Kőnig Tel: +36(1) 351-9563 EMail: rektor@mke.hu

Secretary-General: Edit Bártfai
Tel: +36(1) 342-1720 EMail: fotitkar@mke.hu

International Relations: Zsófia Rudnay
Tel: +36(1) 478-0980, Fax: +36(1) 478-0981
EMail: foreign@mke.hu

Departments

Art History (Art History); **Art Restoration** (Restoration of Works of Art); **Art Theory** *(Artist Colony, Tihany)* (Fine Arts); **Foreign Languages** (English; French; German; Italian; Linguistics; Modern Languages); **Graphic Design** (Graphic Design); **Graphics** (Graphic Arts); **Intermedia** (Communication Studies; Media Studies; Multimedia); **Painting** (Painting and Drawing); **Printmaking** (Printing and Printmaking); **Scenography**; **Sculpture** (Sculpture); **Stage and Costume Design** (Display and Stage Design); **Visual Education** (Education; Visual Arts)

History: Founded 1871 as School, reorganized 1949 and 1971. Due to changes in the Hungarian higher education system, acquired present status and title 2000.

Governing Bodies: University Council; Rector's Council

Academic Year: October to June (October-January;February-June)

Admission Requirements: Secondary school certificate (érettségi bizonyítvány) and presentation of original work

Fees: (Euros): 510 per month

Main Language(s) of Instruction: Hungarian

International Co-operation: Participates in the Socrates/Erasmus programme

Degrees and Diplomas: *Alapfokozat megszerzését tanúsító oklevél*: Arts (MA); *Mesterfokozat megszerzését tanúsító oklevél*; *Doktori oklevél*: Liberal Arts (DLA), a further 2-3 yrs following University Degree

Student Services: Canteen, Foreign Studies Centre, Health services, Sports facilities

Student Residential Facilities: Yes

Special Facilities: Barcsay Art Gallery

Libraries: Libraries of the Academies of Fine and Applied Arts, total c. 60,000 vols

Last Updated: 26/10/11

KÁROLY RÓBERT COLLEGE

Károly Róbert Föiskola (KRF)
Mátrai utca 36., 3201 Gyöngyös
Tel: +36(37) 518-300 +36(37) 518-305
Fax: +36(37) 313-170
Website: http://www.karolyrobert.hu

Rector: Magda Sándor
Tel: +36(37) 518-301 EMail: smagda@karolyrobert.hu

General Vice Rector: Wachtler István
EMail: iwachtler@karolyrobert.hu

Faculties
Economics and Social Sciences (Accountancy; Business Administration; Economics; Finance; Hotel Management; Management; Marketing; Modern Languages; Physical Education; Service Trades; Social Sciences; Tourism); **Natural Resources Management and Rural Development** (Agricultural Engineering; Agronomy; Animal Husbandry; Environmental Management; Horticulture; Natural Resources; Rural Planning; Rural Studies)

History: Founded 2003.

Degrees and Diplomas: *Alapfokozat megszerzését tanúsító oklevél*; *Szakirányú Továbbképzési Oklevél*: Agriculture; *Mesterfokozat megszerzését tanúsító oklevél*

Last Updated: 28/10/11

LISZT FERENC ACADEMY OF MUSIC, BUDAPEST

Liszt Ferenc Zeneművészeti Egyetem (LFZE)
Liszt Ferenc tér 8, 1061 Budapest
Tel: +36(1) 462-4616
Fax: +36(1) 462-4615
EMail: international@lfze.hu
Website: http://www.liszt.hu/

President: András Batta (2005-)
Tel: +36(1) 462-4647, Fax: +36(1) 462-4648
EMail: rektor@lfze.hu

Secretary-General: Ágnes Fazekas
Tel: +36(1) 462-4657, Fax: +36(1) 462-4659

International Relations: Borbála Pintérné Hárs, International Study Officer Tel: +36(1) 462-4615

Faculties
Coaching (Conducting); **Highly Talented Children Education** (Education of the Gifted; Music Education)

Institutes
Chamber Music (Music); **Church Music** (Religious Music); **Composition and Conducting** (Conducting; Music; Music Theory and Composition); **Foreign Languages** (English; French; German; Italian; Modern Languages); **Music Theory** (Music Theory and Composition); **Musicology** (Musicology); **Singing and Opera** (Opera; Singing); **String Instruments** (Musical Instruments); **Teacher Training** (Music Education); **Woodwind and Percussion** (Musical Instruments)

Further Information: Also Music Teachers' Training Institute in Budapest, Pécs and Szeged

History: Founded 1875 by Franz Liszt. Reorganized 1971. Due to changes in the Hungarian higher education system, acquired present status and title 2000. Under the jurisdiction of the Ministry of Culture and Education.

Governing Bodies: Council

Academic Year: September to June (September-January; February-June)

Admission Requirements: Secondary school certificate and adequate musical knowledge

Main Language(s) of Instruction: Hungarian

Degrees and Diplomas: *Alapfokozat megszerzését tanúsító oklevél*: Performance (Music); Teacher Training; *Szakirányú Továbbképzési Oklevél*; *Mesterfokozat megszerzését tanúsító oklevél*

Student Services: Social counselling, Sports facilities

Student Residential Facilities: For c. 90 students

Special Facilities: Franz Liszt Commemorative Museum and Research Centre. Bartók Archives. Béla Bartók Musical Secondary School

Libraries: c. 125,000 vols; c. 80,000 musical works

Last Updated: 26/10/11

MOHOLY-NAGY UNIVERSITY OF ARTS AND DESIGN, BUDAPEST

Moholy-Nagy Művészeti Egyetem (MOME)
Zugligeti út. 9/25, 1121 Budapest
Tel: +36(1) 392-1193
Fax: +36(1) 392-1190
EMail: international@mome.hu
Website: http://www.mome.hu

Rector: Gábor Kopek (2006-)
Tel: +36(1) 392-1140, Fax: +36(1) 392-1144
EMail: rektori@mome.hu

Chancellor: Zsombor Nagy
Tel: +36(1) 392-1174, Fax: +36(1) 392-1144
EMail: kancellaria@mome.hu

International Relations: Anna Hernádi
Tel: +36(1) 392-1193 EMail: hernadi@mome.hu

Graduate Schools
Liberal Arts (Doctoral school)

Institutes
Architecture (Architecture; Design; Furniture Design; Interior Design); **Design** (Ceramic Art; Ceramics and Glass Technology; Design; Fashion Design; Industrial Design; Jewelry Art; Metal Techniques; Textile Design); **Media** (Graphic Design; Media Studies; Photography); **Theoretical Studies** (Aesthetics; Art Education; Arts and Humanities; Ethics; Social Sciences)

History: Founded 1880 as School, reorganized 1949 as Hungarian College of Craft and Design, acquired present status 1971 and title 2000. Under the jurisdiction of the Ministry of Culture and Education and financed by the State.

Governing Bodies: Rector's Council; Senate

Academic Year: September to June (September-January; February-June)

Admission Requirements: Secondary school certificate (érettségi bizonyítvány) and entrance examination

Main Language(s) of Instruction: Hungarian

International Co-operation: Participates in the Ceepus, Socrates, Erasmus programmes

Accrediting Agencies: Magyar Akkreditációs Bizottság

Degrees and Diplomas: *Alapfokozat megszerzését tanúsító oklevél*; *Szakirányú Továbbképzési Oklevél*; *Mesterfokozat megszerzését tanúsító oklevél*: Arts and Architecture; Arts and Design Teacher Training; Design Manager; Product Design; Silicate Design; Textile Design; Visual Communication; *Doktori oklevél*: Liberal Arts, by thesis, 3 yrs

Student Services: Canteen, Foreign Studies Centre, Health services, Sports facilities

Student Residential Facilities: Yes

Special Facilities: Ponton Gallery

Libraries: Central Library, c. 60,000 vols

Last Updated: 26/10/11

OBUDA UNIVERSITY
Óbudai Egyetem
Bécsi út 96/B, 1034 Budapest
Tel: +36(1) 666-5500
Fax: +36(1) 666-5621
EMail: kancellar@uni-obuda.hu
Website: http://www.uni-obuda.hu/

Rector: Rudas Imre Tel: +36(1) 666-5603

Faculties
Economics *(Keleti Károly)* (Economics); **Electrical Engineering** *(Kandó Kálmán)* (Electrical Engineering); **Informatics** *(John von Neumann)* (Computer Science; Information Technology); **Light Industry** (Industrial Engineering); **Mechanical Engineering** *(Bánki Donát)* (Mechanical Engineering)

History: Founded 1395. Óbuda University is the legal successor of the Public Secondary Industrial School of Budapest, established in 1879 and the Hungarian Royal Public Training School of Mechanics and Watchmaking, established in 1889. Óbuda University's direct predecessor is Budapest Tech, 2000. Acquired present title 2010.

Degrees and Diplomas: *Alapfokozat megszerzését tanúsító oklevél*; *Mesterfokozat megszerzését tanúsító oklevél*; *Doktori oklevél*. Also Bachelor degrees, Master degrees and Doctorates

Last Updated: 26/10/11

POLICE OFFICER TRAINING COLLEGE
Rendőrtiszti Főiskola (RTF)
Farkasvölgyi út 12., 1121 Budapest
Tel: +36(1) 392-3500
Fax: +36(1) 392-3501
EMail: nki@rtf.hu
Website: http://www.rtf.hu

Major-General, Rector: István Sárkány
Tel: +36(1) 392-3504, Fax: +36(1) 392-3504 EMail: rector@rtf.hu

Programmes
Police Studies (Law; Police Studies)

History: Fouinded 1971.

Degrees and Diplomas: *Egyetemi Oklevél*; *Mesterfokozat megszerzését tanúsító oklevél*

Last Updated: 13/09/11

SEMMELWEIS UNIVERSITY
Semmelweis Egyetem (SE)
Üllői út. 26, 1085 Budapest
Tel: +36(1) 459-1500
Fax: +36(1) 317-2220
EMail: international@semmelweis-univ.hu
Website: http://www.semmelweis-univ.hu

Rector: Tivadar Tulassay (2009-)
Tel: +36(1) 317-2400, Fax: +36(1) 317-2220
EMail: rtitkarsag.rektor@semmelweis-univ.hu

Vice-Rector for Science, Innovation and International Affairs: Miklós Kellermayer EMail: miklos.kellermayer@eok.sote.hu

International Relations: Marcel Pop, Director of International Relations
Tel: +36(1) 317-9079, Fax: +36(1) 459-9559
EMail: pop.marcel@semmelweis-univ.hu

Faculties
Dentistry (Dentistry); **Health Sciences** (Health Sciences); **Medicine** (Medicine); **Pharmacy** (Pharmacy); **Physical Education and Sport Sciences** (Education; Physical Education; Sports)

Schools
Doctoral Studies

Further Information: Also Teaching Hospital. University degree programmes for foreign students in English and German. The university's Health Services Management Training Centre provides post-graduate courses in health management.

History: Founded 1769 as Faculty of Medicine of the Pázmány Péter University, now Eötvös Lóránd, detached and re-established as separate Institution 1951. Due to changes in the Hungarian higher education system, Semmelweis University of Medicine, The College of Health Care of Haynal Imre University and the Hungarian University of Physical Education and Sport Sciences merged as Semmelweis University and acquired present status and title 2000. Under the jurisdiction of the Ministry of Culture and Education.

Governing Bodies: Senate

Academic Year: September to June (September-January; February-June)

Admission Requirements: Secondary school certificate (érettségi bizonyítvány) and entrance examination

Fees: (US Dollars): Foreign students, c. 10,000 per annum according to course.

Main Language(s) of Instruction: Hungarian, German, English

International Co-operation: With universities in Austria; Germany; Romania; Italy; Slovak Republic; Japan; Canada; Australia; USA. Also participates in Erasmus/Tempus programmes with over 20 EU states.

Accrediting Agencies: Hungarian Accreditation Committee (MAB)

Degrees and Diplomas: *Alapfokozat megszerzését tanúsító oklevél*: Physical Education and Coaching; Human Kinesiology; Recreation; Sports Management; Nursing and Patient Care; Medical Laboratory and Diagnostic Imaging Analyst (BSc), 3 yrs; *Mesterfokozat megszerzését tanúsító oklevél*: Dentistry; Pharmacy (MSc), 5 yrs; *Mesterfokozat megszerzését tanúsító oklevél*: Medicine (MSc), 6 yrs; *Mesterfokozat megszerzését tanúsító oklevél*: Physical Education; Adapted Physical Education; Sports Management; Coaching; Human Kinesiology; Recreation (MSc), 2 yrs; *Doktori oklevél*: Basic Medicine; Clinical Medicine; Pharmaceutical Sciences; Mental Health Sciences; Sports Science; Neurosciences; Molecular Medicine; Pathological Sciences (PhD), 3 yrs by thesis

Student Services: Academic counselling, Canteen, Cultural centre, Foreign student adviser, Foreign Studies Centre, Health services, Language programs, Nursery care, Social counselling, Sports facilities

Student Residential Facilities: For c. 1,430 students

Special Facilities: Movie Studio

Libraries: Central Library, c. 260,000 vols.

Publications: Semmelweis Egyetem *(biweekly)*; Szinapszis *(other/irregular)*

Press or Publishing House: Semmelweis Publishing and Multimedia Studio Ltd

Academic Staff 2010	TOTAL
FULL-TIME	1,168
PART-TIME	142
Student Numbers 2010	
All (Foreign Included)	11,898
FOREIGN ONLY	2,832

Last Updated: 27/10/11

SZÉCHÉNYI ISTVÁN UNIVERSITY
Széchényi István Egyetem (SZE)
Egyetem ter 1, 9026 Győr
Tel: +36(96) 503-400
Fax: +36(96) 503-406
EMail: sze@sze.hu
Website: http://www.sze.hu

Rector: Tamas Szekeres (2005-)
Tel: +36(96) 503-401 EMail: szekeres@sze.hu

International Relations: Márta Mészáros
Tel: +36(96) 503-418, Fax: +36(96) 503-403
EMail: mmzs@szif.hu

Faculties
Economics (Accountancy; Economics; Finance; International Studies; Management; Marketing; Regional Studies; Social Sciences) *Dean*: László Józsa; **Engineering Sciences** (Architectural and Environmental Design; Architecture; Automation and Control

Engineering; Automotive Engineering; Computer Science; Construction Engineering; Electrical Engineering; Engineering; Environmental Engineering; Materials Engineering; Mathematics; Mechanical Engineering; Railway Engineering; Technology Education; Telecommunications Engineering; Town Planning; Transport and Communications; Transport Management) *Dean:* Laszlo Koczy; **Law and Political Sciences** (Administrative Law; Civil Law; Commercial Law; Constitutional Law; Criminal Law; European Union Law; International Law; Labour Law; Private Law; Public Law) *Dean:* Gyula Szalai

Institutes
Health and Social Sciences (Health Sciences; Social Psychology; Social Work) *Director:* Sandor Nagy; **Musical Art** (Music; Music Theory and Composition; Musical Instruments) *Director:* Istvan Ruppert

History: Founded 1968 as Széchényi István College. Acquired present status and title 2002.

Governing Bodies: University Council

Main Language(s) of Instruction: Hungarian

International Co-operation: With universities in the EU.

Accrediting Agencies: Hungarian Accreditation Committee

Degrees and Diplomas: *Alapfokozat megszerzését tanúsító oklevél (BSc)*; *Mesterfokozat megszerzését tanúsító oklevél (MSc)*; *Doktori oklevél*: a further 3 yrs. Also Bachelor and Master degrees

Student Services: Employment services, Foreign student adviser, Handicapped facilities, Health services, Language programs, Sports facilities

Student Residential Facilities: Student hostels

Libraries: Yes.
Last Updated: 27/10/11

SZENT ISTVÁN UNIVERSITY
Szent István Egyetem (SZIE)
Páter Károly utca 1., 2103 Gödöllö
Tel: +36(28) 522-000
Fax: +36(28) 410-804
EMail: info@szie.hu
Website: http://www.szie.hu

Rector: László Solti Tel: +36(28) 522-001 EMail: rector@szie.hu

Financial Director: Imre Tatár
Tel: +36(28) 522-960 EMail: Tatar.Imer@ghf.szie.hu

International Relations: János Beke, Vice-Rector
Tel: +36(1) 522-043 EMail: beke.janos@gek.szie.hu

Colleges
Management and Agriculture *(Gyöngyös)* (Agricultural Management; Agriculture; Management); **Teacher Training** *(Jászberény)* (Primary Education); **Technology** *(Ybl Miklós)* (Technology)

Faculties
Agricultural and Environmental Studies (Agriculture; Animal Husbandry; Biotechnology; Botany; Crop Production; Environmental Management; Environmental Studies; Genetics; Horticulture; Landscape Architecture; Plant and Crop Protection; Wildlife; Zoology); **Applied and Professional Arts** *(Jászberény)* (Primary Education); **Architecture and Civil Engineering** (Architecture; Civil Engineering; Construction Engineering); **Economics** *(Békéscsaba)* (Accountancy; Adult Education; Business Administration; Cooking and Catering; Economics; Finance; Management; Tourism); **Economics and Social Sciences** (Accountancy; Arts and Humanities; Economic and Finance Policy; Economics; European Studies; Finance; Human Resources; Management; Marketing; Modern Languages; Public Administration; Rural Studies; Social Sciences; Teacher Training); **Education** *(Szarvas)* (Pedagogy); **Horticultural Sciences** *(Buda Campus)* (Agricultural Economics; Agricultural Management; Agrobiology; Biotechnology; Botany; Crop Production; Environmental Management; Farm Management; Fruit Production; Horticulture; Natural Resources; Plant and Crop Protection; Plant Pathology; Soil Science; Vegetable Production; Viticulture); **Landscape Architecture, Protection and Development** *(Buda Campus)* (Architecture and Planning; Environmental Studies; Landscape Architecture; Regional Planning; Rural Planning); **Mechanical Engineering** (Computer Science; Mathematics;

Mechanical Engineering; Mechanics); **Veterinary Science** (Anatomy; Animal Husbandry; Biochemistry; Botany; Chemistry; Computer Science; Ecology; Microbiology; Ophthalmology; Parasitology; Pharmacology; Physiology; Surgery; Toxicology; Veterinary Science; Zoology); **Water and Environmental Management** *(Szarvas)* (Agricultural Engineering; Agricultural Management; Environmental Management; Mechanical Engineering; Waste Management)

Institutes
Health Care and Environmental Sanitation Studies (Environmental Studies; Health Sciences)

Further Information: Branches in Békéscaba; Budapest, Jászberény, and Gödöllo.

History: Founded 1787 as Veterinary Institute of the University of Pest, became independent 1851, incorporated in University of Engineering and Economics 1934 and in University of Agriculture 1945. Became University of Veterinary Science, 1952. Due to changes in the Hungarian higher education system, University of Veterinary Science, Gödöllö University of Agricultural Sciences, University of Horticultural and Food Sciences, Miklós YBL Polytechnical College and Teacher Training College of Jászberény merged and acquired present status and title 2000 as Szent István University. Under the jurisdiction of the Ministry of Education and Culture.

Governing Bodies: Senate

Academic Year: September to May (September-December; February-May)

Admission Requirements: Secondary school certificate (érettségi bizonyítvány) and entrance examination

Fees: (US Dollars): Application fees, 50; Bachelor Studies, c. 2,200-4,600 per annum; Master studies, c. 2,800-10,980 per annum; Postgraduate, c. 3,000-5,000; Short courses, c. 950 per semester

Main Language(s) of Instruction: Hungarian, German, English

Accrediting Agencies: Hungarian Accreditation Committee (MAB)

Degrees and Diplomas: *Alapfokozat megszerzését tanúsító oklevél*; *Mesterfokozat megszerzését tanúsító oklevél*; *Doktori oklevél (PhD)*: a further 3-5 yrs by thesis. Also Special Degree: Veterinary Medecine (DVM): 5 yrs

Student Services: Academic counselling, Canteen, Cultural centre, Foreign Studies Centre, Health services, Language programs, Social counselling, Sports facilities

Student Residential Facilities: Yes

Special Facilities: Museums

Libraries: Central Library
Last Updated: 16/09/11

TESSEDIK SÁMUEL COLLEGE
Tessedik Sámuel Főskola (TSE)
Szabadság út 2., 5540 Szarvas
Tel: +36(66) 216-581
Fax: +36(66) 216-582
EMail: tsf.rh@szv.tsf.hu
Website: http://www.tsf.hu

Director-General: István Patay (2000-)
Tel: +36(66) 216-583 EMail: patay@szv.tsf.hu

International Relations: Zoltan Izsaki, Deputy-Rector
Tel: +36(66) 216-521 EMail: izsaki@sze.tsf.hu

Faculties
Agricultural Water and Environment Management (Agriculture; Environmental Management; Water Management)

Institutes
Health (Health Education)

Programmes
Economics (Economics); **Pedagogy** (Pedagogy)

History: Founded 1994.

Degrees and Diplomas: *Alapfokozat megszerzését tanúsító oklevél*; *Szakirányú Továbbképzési Oklevél*
Last Updated: 03/02/09

THE ANDRÁS PETŐ INSTITUTE OF CONDUCTIVE EDUCATION AND COLLEGE FOR CONDUCTOR TRAINING

Mozgássérültek Pető András Nevelőképző és Nevelőintézte (MPANNI)
Kútvölgyi út. 6, 1125 Budapest
Tel: +36(1) 224-1500
Fax: +36(1) 355-6649
EMail: info@peto.hu
Website: http://www.peto.hu

Rector: Franz Schaffhauser Tel: +36(1) 224-1515

Departments
Conductive Education (Education); **Conductive Teaching and Education for Children** (Pedagogy; Primary Education); **Education and Social Sciences** (Education; Social Sciences); **Foreign Languages** (Modern Languages); **Medical Biology** (Biomedicine)

History: Founded 1963, acquired present status and title 1995.

Degrees and Diplomas: *Alapfokozat megszerzését tanúsító oklevél*; *Mesterfokozat megszerzését tanúsító oklevél*
Last Updated: 02/11/11

UNIVERSITY OF DEBRECEN

Debreceni Egyetem (DE)
Egyetem tér. 1, 4010 Debrecen, Hajdú-Bihar
Tel: +36(52) 512-900/ 23054
Fax: +36(52) 416-490
EMail: internationaloffice@admin.unideb.hu
Website: http://www.unideb.hu

Rector: István Fábián
Tel: +36(52) 512-900 EMail: rector@admin.unideb.hu

Registrar: Mónika Rőfi
Tel: +36(52) 316-185 EMail: fotitkar@unideb.hu

International Relations: Gábor Turi, Director
EMail: turi.gabor@unideb.hu

Colleges
Education *(Hajdúböszörmény)*

Conservatories
Music

Faculties
Agricultural and Food Sciences and Environmental Management (Agriculture; Environmental Management; Food Science); **Applied Economics and Rural Development** (Accountancy; Administration; Agricultural Business; Agricultural Economics; Agricultural Management; Business and Commerce; English; Farm Management; Finance; Forestry; French; German; Human Resources; Management; Marketing; Translation and Interpretation); **Arts and Humanities**; **Child and Adult Education** (Adult Education; Child Care and Development); **Dentistry** (Dental Hygiene; Dental Technology; Dentistry; Oral Pathology; Orthodontics; Periodontics; Stomatology); **Economics and Business Administration** (Business Administration; Economics); **Engineering** (Engineering); **Health** *(Nyíregyháza)* (Health Sciences); **Informatics** (Computer Engineering); **Law** (Law); **Medicine** (Medicine); **Music** (Music); **Pharmacy** (Biochemistry; Biomedicine; Cardiology; Chemistry; Educational Research; Endocrinology; Higher Education; Management Systems; Organic Chemistry; Pharmacy); **Science and Technology** (Natural Sciences; Technology)

Institutes
Public Health *Director:* Róza Ádány; **Research** *(Nyíregyháza) Director:* Sándor Tőgyi; **Research** *(Karcag)* (Animal Husbandry; Crop Production; Soil Management; Soil Science) *Director:* Lajos Blaskó; **Research and Experiment** *Director:* Tibor Koncz

History: Founded 1912 as Royal Hungarian University of Debrecen, renamed Count István Tisza University, University of Debrecen and Kossuth Lajos University, opened 1914-15 with Faculties of Law, Arts and Humanities, Language and History and Reformed Theology. Faculties of Medicine and Science established 1918 and 1949. Faculty of Law suspended by Government decree 1949 and reorganized 1996 and Faculty of Theology separated from the University 1950 (as Debrecen Academy of Reformed Theology). Faculty of Medicine reorganized separately as Medical University of Debrecen and Faculties of Arts and Humanities and Natural Sciences reorganized as Kossuth Lajos University Debrecen 1952. Due to changes in the Hungarian higher education system, universities of Debrecen (Debrecen University of Medicine, Debrecen Agricultural University, Kossuth Lajos University Debrecen) and Hajdúböszörményi Wargha István College of Education merged and acquired present status and title 2000 as University of Debrecen.

Governing Bodies: Rector's Council; Management Board; University Council

Academic Year: September to June

Admission Requirements: Secondary school certificate (érettségi bizonyítvány) or foreign equivalent and entrance examination

Main Language(s) of Instruction: Hungarian

International Co-operation: Participates in Socrates/Erasmus, Socrates/Leonardo, Tempus, Fulbright and Daad programmes.

Accrediting Agencies: Hungarian Accreditation Committee (MAB)

Degrees and Diplomas: *Alapfokozat megszerzését tanúsító oklevél*: Agricultural Economics; Social Work; Music; Health; Education; Agriculture; Engineering; Natural Sciences (BA), 3-4 yrs; *Szakirányú Továbbképzési Oklevél*: Agricultural Economics; Medicine; Arts and Humanities; Health; Education; Economics; Agriculture; Engineering; Natural Sciences, 1-3 yrs; *Mesterfokozat megszerzését tanúsító oklevél*: Agricultural Economics; Law; Medicine; Arts and Humanities; Music; Dentistry; Pharmacy; Economics; Agriculture; Natural Sciences (MA); *Doktori oklevél*: Medicine; Health Sciences; Pharmacy; History; Literature; Linguistics; Philology; Economics; Horticulture; Animal Husbandry; Agriculture; Humanities; Mathematics; Information Technology; Physics; Chemistry; Earth Sciences; Biology; Environmental Studies (PhD), a further 3 yrs by thesis

Student Services: Academic counselling, Canteen, Cultural centre, Employment services, Foreign student adviser, Foreign Studies Centre, Handicapped facilities, Health services, Language programs, Nursery care, Social counselling, Sports facilities

Student Residential Facilities: 12 Dormitories

Special Facilities: Seasonal Art Gallery; Art Exhibitions; 3 Movie Studios; Observatory; Botanical Garden; Sports Facilities

Libraries: University Libraries, total, 5.3 m. vols

Publications: A Debreceni Egyetem Magyar Nyelvtudományi Intézetének kiadványai, Journal of Hungarian linguistics *(annually)*; Acta Andragogiaie, Studies in adult education *(annually)*; Acta Classica, Journal of Classical Studies *(annually)*; Acta Debrecina *(annually)*; Acta geographica ac geologica et meteorologica Debrecina, Journal of geographical, geological and meteorological studies *(other/irregular)*; Acta Neerlandica, Journal of Dutch philology published by the institute of German studies *(annually)*; Acta pericemonologica rerum ambietum Debrecina, Articles on environmental studies published by the institute of Biology *(other/irregular)*; Acta Physica et Chimica, Journal of Physics and Chemistry published by the Department of Theoretical Physics *(annually)*; Agrártudományi közlemények, Journal of agriculture sciences published by the Faculty of Agriculture *(other/irregular)*; Beiträge zur Methodik und Fachdidaktik, Deutsch als Fremdsprache, Journal of teaching of German as a second language published by the Institute of German Studies *(other/irregular)*; Collectio iuridica Universitatis Debreceniensis, Articles on Law and Legislation *(other/irregular)*; Competitio, Papers on economics *(quarterly)*; Debreceni szemle, Interdisciplinary journal of the Debrecen Committee of he Hungarian Academy of Sciences *(quarterly)*; Ethnica, Articles on Ethnology *(other/irregular)*; Ethnographica Folcloristica Carpatica, Articles on the ethnography of the Carpathian Basin *(annually)*; Folia Uralica Debreceneniensia, Studies in Finno-Ugric linguistics *(annually)*; Gond, Articles of the Department of Philosophy *(quarterly)*; Hungarian Journal of English and American Studies, English and American philology *(biennially)*; Italianistica Debreceniensis, Articles on Italian Philology *(annually)*; Journal of Agricultural Sciences *(other/irregular)*; Kitaibelia, Journal of botanical studies *(biennially)*; Könyv és könyvtár, Journal on library science *(annually)*; Magyar Nyelvjárások, Studies in Hungarian dialects *(annually)*; Módszerek és eljárások, methodological journal of chemistry *(annually)*; Német filológiai tanulmányok, Journal of German Philology *(other/irregular)*; Ókortudományi Értesítő, Publications on ancient history *(annually)*; Posztbizánci Közlemények, Studies in post-Byzantine art and philology *(biennially)*; Publ. Mathematicae, Articles on mathematical studies *(biennially)*; Slavica, Journal of Slavic Philology *(annually)*; Sprachteorie und Germanistiche Linguistik, Journal of German Linguistics and Speech Theory *(biennially)*; Studia Letteraria, Journal of Hungarian Literature and Cultural Studies *(annually)*; Studia Romanica, Articles on the Philology of neo-Latin Languages and Literature *(annually)*; Studies in Linguistics, Journal of English and American linguistics published by the Institute of English and American Studies *(annually)*; Teaching Mathematics and Computer Science *(biennially)*; Történeti Tanulmányok, Studies in Hungarian and world history *(other/irregular)*; Werkstatt Arbeitspapiere, Journal of German Philology *(annually)*

Academic Staff 2011	TOTAL
FULL-TIME	1,425

Student Numbers 2011	
All (Foreign Included)	30,418
FOREIGN ONLY	2,390

Last Updated: 26/10/11

UNIVERSITY OF DRAMA, FILM AND TELEVISION

Szinház-és Filmművészeti Egyetem (SZFE)
Vas út. 2/c, 1088 Budapest
Tel: +36(1) 318-8111
Fax: +36(1) 338-4749
EMail: szfftan@ella.hu
Website: http://www.filmacademy.hu

Rector: Tamás Ascher
Tel: +36(1) 338-4727 EMail: rektorihivatal@szfe.hu

International Relations: Sylvia Huszár
EMail: huszar.sylvia@szfe.hu

Faculties

Film and Television (Cinema and Television; Film; Video); **Theatre** (Acting; Theatre)

History: Founded 1865, acquired present status and title 2000.

Academic Year: September to June

Main Language(s) of Instruction: Hungarian

Degrees and Diplomas: *Alapfokozat megszerzését tanúsító oklevél*; *Mesterfokozat megszerzését tanúsító oklevél*. Also Bachelor and Master degrees

Libraries: Libraries of Theatre, Film and Television
Last Updated: 27/10/11

UNIVERSITY OF KAPOSVÁR

Kaposvári Egyetem (KE)
Guba Sándor út. 40, 7401 Kaposvár
Tel: +36(82) 505-800
Fax: +36(82) 505-986
EMail: vass.julia@ke.hu
Website: http://www.ke.hu/

Rector: Ferenc Szávai
Tel: +36(82) 505-910, Fax: +36(82) 505-896 EMail: rektor@ke.hu

International Relations: Zoltán Gál, Director
EMail: gal.zoltan@ke.hu

Faculties

Animal Science (Zoology); **Arts** (Fine Arts); **Economics** (Agricultural Economics; Agricultural Engineering; Computer Science; Economics; Finance; Food Science; Marketing; Rural Planning); **Pedagogy** *(Csokonai Vitéz Mihály)* (Pedagogy)

Research Institutes

Forage Science *(Iregszemce)*

History: Founded 2000 due to changes in the Hungarian higher education system. The Faculty of Animal Husbandry of the Pannon University of Agricultural Sciences, the Csokonai Vitéz Mihály Teacher Training College of Kaposvár, the Research Institute of Forage Science of Iregszemce and the Research Institute of Chemical and Process Engineering of Veszprém merged as University of Kaposvár and acquired present status and title.

Governing Bodies: University Council

Academic Year: September to June (September-January; February-June)

Admission Requirements: Secondary school certificate (érettségi bizonyítvány) and entrance examination

Main Language(s) of Instruction: Hungarian

International Co-operation: Participates in the Socrates and Erasmus programmes

Accrediting Agencies: Hungarian Accreditation Committee (MAB)

Degrees and Diplomas: *Alapfokozat megszerzését tanúsító oklevél*: Animal Husbandry; Preschool Education, 3 yrs; *Alapfokozat megszerzését tanúsító oklevél*: Communication; Cultural Management; Education of the Handicapped; Primary Education, 4 yrs; *Mesterfokozat megszerzését tanúsító oklevél*: Agricultural Engineering; Agricultural Teacher Engineering; Economics; *Doktori oklevél*: Animal Science (PhD); Economics (PhD), by thesis

Student Services: Canteen, Health services, Language programs, Sports facilities

Student Residential Facilities: Yes

Libraries: c. 198,500 vols

Publications: Acta Agrarie Kasposvariensis, Scientific magazine in Hungarian and English *(quarterly)*; Reports, Articles and Scientific Memoirs for Agriculture, Scientific magazine *(annually)*
Last Updated: 26/10/11

UNIVERSITY OF MISKOLC

Miskolci Egyetem (UM)
3515 Miskolc - Egyetemvaros, Borsod-Abaúj-Zemplén
Tel: +36(46) 565-111 +36(46) 565-034
Fax: +36(46) 565-014 +36(46) 565-423
EMail: rektno@uni-miskolc.hu
Website: http://www.uni-miskolc.hu

Rector: Gyula Patkó (2006-)
Tel: +36(46) 565-010, Fax: +36(46) 312-842
EMail: patko@uni-miskolc.hu

Pro-Rector: Viktor Kovács
Tel: +36(46) 563-423, Fax: +36(46) 365-174
EMail: rektno@gold.uni-miskolc.hu

International Relations: Edit Szőke, Secretary-General
Tel: +36(46) 565-111/Ext. 22-76 EMail: rekszoke@uni-miskolc.hu

Centres

Continuing Education (Continuing Education); **Foreign Languages Teaching** (Foreign Languages Education); **North Hungarian Regional Distance Education**

Departments

Physical Education (Physical Education)

Faculties

Arts (Anthropology; Arts and Humanities; Comparative Literature; Cultural Studies; History; Linguistics; Modern Languages; Philosophy; Political Sciences; Psychology; Sociology; Translation and Interpretation); **Earth Sciences and Engineering** (Earth Sciences; Environmental Engineering; Geological Engineering; Mining Engineering; Petroleum and Gas Engineering; Surveying and Mapping); **Economics** (Accountancy; Business Administration; Business and Commerce; Economics; Finance; Human Resources; Management; Marketing; Regional Studies); **Law** (Law; Political Sciences); **Materials Engineering** (Materials Engineering; Metallurgical Engineering); **Mechanical Engineering and Informatics** (Automation and Control Engineering; Civil Engineering; Computer Engineering; Electrical and Electronic Engineering; Information Sciences; Information Technology; Mathematics; Mechanical Engineering; Production Engineering; Statistics); **Teacher Training** *(Comenius, Sárospatak)* (Educational Sciences; Teacher Training)

Institutes

Health Care Studies (Health Sciences; Nursing); **Music** *(Béla Bartók)* (Music; Musical Instruments; Musicology)

History: Founded 1735 as School of Mining, became Academy 1770. German replaced by Hungarian as language of instruction 1867. Reorganized at Sopron 1919, became Technical University of Heavy Industry and transferred to Miskolc 1949. Acquired present status and title 1990. Under the jurisdiction of the Ministry of Culture and Education and financed by the State.

Governing Bodies: University Senate

Academic Year: September to May (September-December; February-May)

Admission Requirements: Secondary school certificate (érettségi bizonyítvány) or foreign equivalent and entrance examination

Fees: (US Dollars): Foreign students, 6,000 per annum; preparatory year, 2,000 per annum

Main Language(s) of Instruction: Hungarian, English

International Co-operation: With universities in Germany, United Kingdom, Italy, France, Austria, Belgium, Finland, Spain, Slovak Republic, Romania, Poland. Also participates in Socrates, Erasmus, Ceepus, Tempus, Leonardo, and 6th Framework, PHARE, Jean Monnet

Accrediting Agencies: Hungarian Accreditation Committee (Ministry of Education)

Degrees and Diplomas: *Alapfokozat megszerzését tanúsító oklevél*: Electrical Engineering; English/German Teacher Training; Mechanical Engineering; Musicology; Nursing; Production Engineering; Teacher Training, 3 yrs; *Szakirányú Továbbképzési Oklevél*; *Mesterfokozat megszerzését tanúsító oklevél*: Business Administration, 5 yrs; *Mesterfokozat megszerzését tanúsító oklevél*: Earth Sciences; Economics; Engineering Management; Environmental engineering; Humanities; Information Technology; Law (dr.jur.); Materials Engineering; Mechanical Engineering; Metallurgical Engineering; Mining Engineering; Petroleum and Gas Engineering; Process Engineering; *Doktori oklevél (PhD)*: a further 3 yrs by thesis

Student Services: Academic counselling, Canteen, Cultural centre, Employment services, Foreign student adviser, Foreign Studies Centre, Handicapped facilities, Health services, Language programs, Social counselling, Sports facilities

Student Residential Facilities: For 82% of the students

Special Facilities: Selmec Museum

Libraries: c. 640,000 vols; Selmec Museum library, 30,000

Publications: K+F Kiadvány, Yearbook *(annually)*; MERT A Miskolci Egyetem közéleti és kulturális lapja *(monthly)*; Miskolci Egyetem Idegennyelvü Közleményei *(annually)*; Miskolci Egyetem Közleményei, Bulletin *(annually)*

Last Updated: 26/10/11

UNIVERSITY OF PANNONIA
Pannon Egyetem (PE)
PO Box 158, Egyetem út. 10, 8201 Veszprém
Tel: +36(88) 624-000
Fax: +36(88) 624-529
EMail: pr@uni-pannon.hu
Website: http://www.uni-pannon.hu

Rector: Ferenc Friedler
Tel: +36(88) 422-617 EMail: rektor@uni-pannon.hu

Secretary-General: Angéla Bognár Sabjanics
Tel: +36(88) 421-428 EMail: fotitkar@uni-pannon.hu

Faculties
Economics (Economics); **Engineering** (Analytical Chemistry; Automation and Control Engineering; Chemical Engineering; Chemistry; Computer Science; Earth Sciences; Economics; Electrical Engineering; Engineering; Engineering Management; Environmental Engineering; Environmental Studies; Information Technology; Management; Materials Engineering; Mechanical Engineering; Mechanics; Organic Chemistry; Physical Chemistry; Physics; Radiophysics; Tourism); **Georgikon** *(Georgikon, Keszthely)* (Agricultural Economics; Agricultural Equipment; Agriculture; Agronomy; Animal Husbandry; Chemistry; Crop Production; Farm Management; Horticulture; Microbiology; Oenology; Plant and Crop Protection; Soil Science; Viticulture; Waste Management; Water Management; Zoology); **Information Technology** (Computer Science; Electrical Engineering; Information Sciences; Nanotechnology; Software Engineering); **Modern Philology and Social Sciences** (Anthropology; Applied Linguistics; Educational Psychology; Ethics; European Studies; French; German; Hungarian; International Studies; Native Language; Pedagogy; Political Sciences; Social Sciences; Social Studies; Theatre)

Further Information: Also evening and correspondence courses, distance education and continuing education

History: Founded 1949 as Faculty of the Technical University of Budapest, became Veszprém University of Chemical Engineering 1951. The Georgikon Faculty of Agriculture of the Pannon University of Agricultural Sciences attached to the University 1989. Faculty of Teacher Training started 1990. Due to changes to the Hungarian higher education system, the Georgikon Faculty of Agriculture of the Pannon University of Agricultural Sciences, Keszthely and the Faculty of Agriculture of Mosonmagyaróvár became part of Veszprémi University 2000. Under the jurisdiction of the Ministry of Culture and Education. Known as Veszprémi Egyetem (University of Veszprém) until March 2006, when obtained current title and status.

Governing Bodies: Senate; University Council

Academic Year: September to June (September-January; February-June)

Admission Requirements: Secondary school certificate (érettségi bizonyítvány) and entrance examination

Main Language(s) of Instruction: Hungarian, English

International Co-operation: Participates in the Tempus programme

Degrees and Diplomas: *Alapfokozat megszerzését tanúsító oklevél*: Arts (BA); Science (BSc), 3 yrs; *Alapfokozat megszerzését tanúsító oklevél*: Education; *Mesterfokozat megszerzését tanúsító oklevél*: Arts (MA); Science (MSc), a further 2 yrs; *Mesterfokozat megszerzését tanúsító oklevél*: Economics (MBA); *Doktori oklevél (PhD)*: a further 3 yrs, by thesis and final examination

Student Services: Academic counselling, Canteen, Cultural centre, Employment services, Foreign student adviser, Foreign Studies Centre, Health services, Language programs, Social counselling, Sports facilities

Student Residential Facilities: For 1,000 students

Libraries: Central Library, 303,206 vols; 27,600 periodicals; 737 titles; also specialized libraries of the departments

Publications: Georgikon for Agriculture *(quarterly)*; Hungarian Journal of Industrial Chemistry *(quarterly)*

Press or Publishing House: Veszprémi Egyetemi Kiadó
Last Updated: 27/10/11

UNIVERSITY OF PÉCS
Pécsi Tudományegyetem (PTE)
Vasvári Pál utca 4., 7622 Pécs
Tel: +36(72) 501-500
Fax: +36(72) 501-508
EMail: info@pte.hu
Website: http://www.pte.hu

Rector: József Bódis
Tel: +36(72) 501-507, Fax: +36(72) 501-508
EMail: rector@rektori.pte.hu

International Relations: Gyöngyi Komlódiné Pozsgai
Tel: +36(72) 501-509 EMail: gyongyi.pozsgai@iro.pte.hu

Centres
Asia (Asian Studies); **Balkan Studies**; **European Studies** (European Studies; Social Sciences) *Director*: György Andrássy; **Francophone** (French Studies); **Latin American**

Faculties
Adult Education and Human Resources Development (Cultural Studies; Human Resources) *Director*: Dénes Koltai; **Business and Economics** (Business Administration; Business and Commerce; Economics; Management; Marketing) *Dean*: Péter Dobay; **Education** *(Illyés Gyula, Szekszárd)* (Education) *Director General*: György Fusz; **Engineering** *(Mihály Pollack)* (Civil Engineering; Electrical and Electronic Engineering; Engineering; Environmental Engineering; Mechanical Engineering) *Director General*: József Mecsi; **Health Sciences** (Health Administration; Health Sciences; Public Health) *Director General*: József Bódis; **Humanities** (Arts and Humanities; Communication Studies; Education; English; Ethnology; History; Linguistics; Literature; Psychology; Slavic Languages) *Dean*: Róbert Somos; **Law** (Civil Law; European Union Law; International Law; Labour Law; Law; Public Law) *Dean*: Erzsébet Sándor; **Music and Visual Arts** (Fine Arts; Music; Musical Instruments; Painting and Drawing; Performing Arts; Sculpture; Singing) *Dean*: Colin Foster; **Sciences** (Botany; Chemistry; Genetics; Geography;

Mathematics; Natural Sciences; Physical Education; Physics; Sports Medicine; Zoology) *Dean*: Róbert Gábriel

Institutes

Teacher Training (Educational Sciences; Teacher Training) *Director*: Mihály Kocsis

Schools

Medicine (Dentistry; Medicine; Pharmacy) *Dean*: Péter Németh

Further Information: Also courses in foreign languages, and programmes in English

History: Founded 1921, formerly Academy of Law established 1785, and succeeding University of Pécs founded 1367 by King Louis I. Faculties of Theology and Medicine detached and re-established as separate Institutions 1949 and 1951. Faculty of Teacher Training incorporated and acquired present title 1982. Due to changes in the Hungarian higher education system, Janus Pannonius University Pécs, Pécs University Medical School and Illyés Gyula College of Education, Szekszárd merged as University of Pécs and acquired present status and title 2000. A State institution under the jurisdiction of the Ministry of Culture and Education and part of the Ministry of Health and financed by the State.

Governing Bodies: Senate

Academic Year: September to May (September-December; February-May)

Admission Requirements: Secondary school certificate (érettségi bizonyítvány) or equivalent and entrance examination

Fees: (US Dollars): Tuition, c. 2,000-6,000 per semester

Main Language(s) of Instruction: Hungarian, English, German

International Co-operation: With universities in United Kingdom; Austria, Germany; Netherlands; Japan. Participates in Socrates/Erasmus and Ceepus programmes

Accrediting Agencies: Hungarian Accreditation Committee (MAB)

Degrees and Diplomas: *Alapfokozat megszerzését tanúsító oklevél*; *Mesterfokozat megszerzését tanúsító oklevél*; *Doktori oklevél (PhD)*: a further 3 yrs by thesis

Student Services: Academic counselling, Canteen, Cultural centre, Employment services, Foreign student adviser, Foreign Studies Centre, Handicapped facilities, Health services, Language programs, Nursery care, Social counselling, Sports facilities

Student Residential Facilities: For 3,500 students

Special Facilities: Biological Garden; Movie Studio

Libraries: Total, c. 1.5m. vols

Press or Publishing House: Univ Pécs

Last Updated: 27/10/11

UNIVERSITY OF SZEGED
Szegedi Tudományegyetem (SZTE)
Dugonics tér 13, 6720 Szeged
Tel: +36(62) 544-000
Fax: +36(62) 546-371
Website: http://www.u-szeged.hu

Rector: Gabor Szabo (2006-) Fax: +36(62) 546-359
EMail: rektor@rekt.u-szeged.hu

International Relations: György Pálfi
Tel: +36(62) 546-790, Fax: +36(62) 456-371
EMail: palfi.gyorgy@rekt.u-szeged.hu

Faculties

Agriculture *(Hódmezővásárhely)* (Agriculture) *Dean*: Károly Bodnár; **Arts** (American Studies; Archaeology; Arts and Humanities; Classical Languages; Contemporary History; Education; English Studies; Ethnology; European Studies; French Studies; Germanic Studies; Hungarian; Modern History; Oriental Studies; Psychology; Slavic Languages; Social Sciences) *Dean*: Tibor Almási; **Dentistry** (Dentistry) *Dean*: Katalin Nagy; **Economics and Business Administration** (Business Administration; Economics) *Dean*: Erzsébet Hetesi; **Education** *(Gyula Juhász)* (Education) *Director*: Gábor Galambos; **Engineering** (Engineering) *Dean*: Antal Véha; **Health Sciences and Social Studies** (Health Sciences; Social Studies) *Dean*: Maria Barnai; **Law** (Administrative Law; Civil Law; Commercial Law; Comparative Law; Constitutional Law; Criminal Law; Demography and Population; European Union Law; International Law; Labour Law; Law; Political Sciences; Statistics) *Dean*: Imre Szabo; **Medicine** (Medicine) *Dean*: László Vécsei; **Music** (Music) *Director*: Ferenc Kerek; **Pharmacy** (Pharmacy) *Dean*: Ferenc Fülöp; **Science** (Biology; Chemistry; Geography; Geology; Mathematics; Natural Sciences; Physics) *Dean*: Klára Hernádi

History: Founded 1872 as Hungarian Royal University of Kolozsvar. Renamed Ferencz-Joseph University of Kolozvar 1881, moved to Szeged, 1921. In 1940 the university was divided into two institutions, one in Kolozsvar and one remained in Szeged, they were reorganized and became Szeged University 1945, named after József Attila 1962. Due to changes in the Hungarian higher education system, 'József Attila' University Szeged, 'Albert Szent-Györgyi Medical University Szeged, and 'Juhász Gyula' Teacher's Training College, Szeged merged as University of Szeged 2000.

Governing Bodies: University Senate

Academic Year: September to June (September-December; February-June)

Admission Requirements: Secondary school certificate (érettségi bizonyitvány) and entrance examination

Main Language(s) of Instruction: Hungarian, English, German

International Co-operation: With 289 universities (see http://www.u-szeged.hu/intrel). Participates in Socrates, Erasmus and Ceepus programmes.

Accrediting Agencies: Ministry of Culture and Education

Degrees and Diplomas: *Alapfokozat megszerzését tanúsító oklevél (BA)*: 3 yrs; *Egyetemi Oklevél (MA)*: a further 2 yrs; *Mesterfokozat megszerzését tanúsító oklevél (MA)*: a further 2 yrs; *Doktori oklevél (PhD)*: 6sem and thesis

Student Services: Academic counselling, Canteen, Cultural centre, Employment services, Foreign student adviser, Foreign Studies Centre, Health services, Language programs, Nursery care, Social counselling, Sports facilities

Student Residential Facilities: For 3,719 students

Special Facilities: Szent-Györgyi Collection; Anatomical Collection. Observatory. Botanical Garden

Libraries: Total, c. 930,000 vols

Publications: Acta Biologica Szegdiensis; Acta Climatologica; Acta Cybernetica; Acta Scientiarum Mathematicarum, Theoritical Mathematics; Aetas, Historical Science; Analysis Mathematica; Belvedere, History; Bolcso, Faculty of Arts; Egyetem, Magazine on Higher Education in Szeged; Electronic Journal of Qualitative Theory of Differential Equations; Eleszto, College Faculty of Food Engineering; Fosszilla, Literature, Art, Philosophy; Informatikalap, Teaching Informatics, Methodology; Jogelméleti Szemle, Journal of Legal Theory; Kari Kurir, Official Bulletin of the Faculty of Arts; Kozgazolo, Faculty of Economics and Business Administration *(monthly)*; Linklap, Online Magazine of the Department of Media Science; Magyar Kozony, Law; Newtone, Faculty of Science; Polygon, Publications on Mathematics and Methodology; Tiscia, Ecology; Ujsagvari, School Magazine of the Endre Sagvari Grammar School

Press or Publishing House: JATE Press (József Attila University Press)

Academic Staff *2010-2011*	MEN	WOMEN	TOTAL
FULL-TIME	–	–	1,479
PART-TIME	–	–	123
Student Numbers *2010-2011*			
All (Foreign Included)	11,162	16,065	27,227
FOREIGN ONLY	–	–	1,939

Part-time students, 5,890. **Distance students**, 476. **Evening students**, 23.
Last Updated: 13/09/11

UNIVERSITY OF WEST HUNGARY
Nyugat-Magyarországi Egyetem (NYME)
Bajcsy-Zsilinszki utca 4., 9400 Sopron
Tel: +36(99) 518-100 +36(99) 518-142
Fax: +36(99) 312-240
Website: http://www.uniwest.hu

Rector: Sándor Faragó (1998-)
Tel: +36(99) 312-240 EMail: rectoro@nyme.hu

Secretary-General: Mária Merényi
Tel: +36(99) 311-104, Fax: +36(99) 518-128
EMail: merenyim@nyme.hu

International Relations: Judit Engelmann-Kékesi
Tel: +36(99) 518-210 EMail: tudrh@nyme.hu

Faculties
Agriculture and Food Science *(Mosonmagyaróvár)* (Agricultural Economics; Agricultural Equipment; Agriculture; Agronomy; Animal Husbandry; Crop Production; Food Science; Food Technology; Horticulture); **Arts** (Arts and Humanities; Modern Languages); **Economics** (Accountancy; Business and Commerce; Economics; Finance; Human Resources; Management; Marketing); **Forestry** (Environmental Engineering; Forestry; Surveying and Mapping; Wildlife); **Geoinformatics** *(Székesfehérvár)* (Geophysics; Natural Sciences; Surveying and Mapping); **Natural Sciences** *(Savaria Campus)* (Natural Sciences); **Pedagogy** *(Benedek Elek)* (Pedagogy); **Teacher Training** *(Apáczai Csere János)* (Teacher Training); **Visual Arts and Music, Education and Sport** *(Savaria Campus)* (Education; Music; Sports; Visual Arts); **Wood Sciences** (Architecture; Forest Products; Industrial Design; Paper Technology; Wood Technology) *Dean:* Sándor Molnár

History: Founded 1808 as a School of Forestry, became an academy 1846. Moved to Sopron 1919 and reorganized 1962. Due to changes in the Hungarian higher education system, the University of Agricultural Sciences, Pannon and the University of Sopron merged and acquired present status and title as University of West Hungary. Under the jurisdiction of the Ministry of Agriculture.

Governing Bodies: University Council; Faculty Councils

Academic Year: September to July

Admission Requirements: Secondary school certificate and/or entrance examination

Fees: (Forints): 100,000-125,000 per semester

Main Language(s) of Instruction: Hungarian

International Co-operation: With universities in Europe. Participates in the ERASMUS programme

Degrees and Diplomas: *Alapfokozat megszerzését tanúsító oklevél:* Pedagogy, Technical Teacher Training, Wood Technology, Wildlife, Surveying, 3 yrs; *Szakirányú Továbbképzési Oklevél; Mesterfokozat megszerzését tanúsító oklevél:* Forestry, Wood Technology; Pedagogy, Technical Teacher Training, Wood Technology, Wildlife, Surveying; *Doktori oklevél (DrTechn):* by thesis

Student Services: Canteen, Cultural centre, Employment services, Health services, Social counselling, Sports facilities

Student Residential Facilities: Yes

Special Facilities: Forestry Museum, Wood Sciences Research Centre, Botanical Garden, History Museum of Mosonmagyaróvár, Meteorology Observation Post

Libraries: c. 380,000 vols

Publications: Acta Agronomica Ováriensis *(biennially)*; Acta Facultatis Forestalis *(annually)*; Acta Facultatis Ligniensis *(annually)*; Apáczai Csere János Tanítóképzö Föiskolai Kar Tanulmánykötet *(annually)*; Benedek Elek Pedagógiai Föiskolai Kar Tudomány napja *(annually)*; Erdészeti Tallózó *(monthly)*; Magyar Apróvad Közlemények, Hungarian Small Game Bulletin *(1-2 per annum)*; Magyar Vísidad Közlemények, Hungarian Waterfowl Publication *(1-2 per annum)*; Tilia *(1-2 per annum)*
Last Updated: 26/10/11

PRIVATE INSTITUTIONS

ANDRÁSSY GYULA GERMAN-SPEAKING UNIVERSITY

Andrássy Gyula Budapesti Német Nyelvű Egyetem
Pollack Mihály tér 3., 1088 Budapest
Tel: +36(1) 266-3101
Fax: +36(1) 266-3099
EMail: uni@andrassyuni.hu
Website: http://www.andrassyuni.hu

Rector: András Masát
Tel: +36(1) 266-4408 EMail: andras.masat@andrassyuni.hu

International Relations: Megyeri Eszter, Student Programme Officer EMail: eszter.megyeri@andrassyuni.hu

Faculties
Central European Studies (Central European Studies); **Comparative Political Science and Law** (Law; Political Sciences); **International Relations** (International Business; International Economics; International Relations)

History: Founded 2002.

Main Language(s) of Instruction: German

Degrees and Diplomas: *Szakirányú Továbbképzési Oklevél; Doktori oklevél*
Last Updated: 27/10/11

APOR VILMOS CATHOLIC COLLEGE

Apor Vilmos Katolikus Főiskola (AVKF)
Konstantin tér 1-5., 2600 Vác
Tel: +36(27) 511-151
Fax: +36(27) 511-141
EMail: avkf@avkf.hu
Website: http://www.avkf.hu

Rector: Pál Balázs Tel: +36(27) 814-200

International Relations: Péter Gyombolai
Tel: +36(27) 511-148 EMail: erasmus@avkf.hu

Programmes
Economics, Finance and Law (Economics; Finance; Law); **Educational Administration** (Educational Administration); **Social Studies** (Social Studies); **Teacher Training** (Teacher Training); **Theatre** (Theatre)

History: Founded 1993.

Degrees and Diplomas: *Alapfokozat megszerzését tanúsító oklevél; Szakirányú Továbbképzési Oklevél; Mesterfokozat megszerzését tanúsító oklevél*
Last Updated: 28/10/11

BHAKTIVEDANTA COLLEGE

Bhaktivedanta Hittudományi Főiskola (BHF)
Attila útca 8., 1039 Budapest
Tel: +36(1) 321-7787
Fax: +36(1) 321-7787
EMail: bhf.info@externet.hu
Website: http://www.bhf.hu

Rektor: László Tóth-Soma

Programmes
Theology (Theology)

Degrees and Diplomas: *Alapfokozat megszerzését tanúsító oklevél.* Also Bachelor degree
Last Updated: 28/10/11

BUDAPEST COLLEGE OF COMMUNICATION AND BUSINESS

Budapesti Kommunikációs és Üzleti Főiskola (BKF)
Nagy Lajos Király út 1-9, 1148 Budapest
Tel: +36(1) 273-3090
Fax: +36(1) 273-3099
EMail: international@bkf.hu
Website: http://www.bkf.hu

Rektor: László Vass (2001-)
Tel: +36(1) 273-2460 EMail: l.vass@bkf.hu

International Relations: Jolán Róka, Vice-Rector for International Relations Tel: +36(1) 273-3090 EMail: j.roka@bkf.hu

Programmes
Business (Business Administration; International Business; Management; Marketing; Public Relations; Tourism); **Communication Studies** (Journalism; Media Studies)

History: Founded 2000.

Main Language(s) of Instruction: Hungarian

Degrees and Diplomas: *Alapfokozat megszerzését tanúsító oklevél; Szakirányú Továbbképzési Oklevél*
Last Updated: 02/11/11

BUDAPEST COLLEGE OF MANAGEMENT
Általános Vállalkozási Főiskola (AVF)
Villányi út 11-13, 1114 Budapest
Tel: +36(1) 381-8100
Fax: +36(1) 466-7410
EMail: avf@avf.hu
Website: http://www.avf.hu

Rector: Pál Vastagh Tel: +36(1) 381-8183

Secretary-General: Janós Antal
Tel: +36(1) 381-8181 EMail: antal.janos@villanyi.avf.hu

International Relations: Balazs Hamori
EMail: hamori.balazs@avf.hu

Departments
Economics and Law (Economics; Human Rights; Law); Finance and Accountancy (Accountancy; Finance); International Relations; Marketing (Marketing); Methodology; Social Studies

History: Founded 1996.

Main Language(s) of Instruction: Hungarian

Degrees and Diplomas: *Szakirányú Továbbképzési Oklevél.* Also Bachelor courses
Last Updated: 28/10/11

BUDAPEST CONTEMPORARY DANCE ACADEMY
Budapest Kortárstánc Főiskola (BKTF)
Perc utca 2, 1036 Budapest
Tel: +36(1) 250-3046
Fax: +36(1) 250-3056
EMail: budapest@tanc.sulinet.hu
Website: http://www.tanc.sulinet.hu/02.php

General Director: Iván Angelus

Programmes
Dance (Dance)

Degrees and Diplomas: *Alapfokozat megszerzését tanúsító oklevél; Mesterfokozat megszerzését tanúsító oklevél*
Last Updated: 02/11/11

CENTRAL EUROPEAN UNIVERSITY
Kozep-Europai Egyetem (CEU)
Nador ut. 9, 1051 Budapest
Tel: +36(1) 327-3018
Fax: +36(1) 327-3007
EMail: public@ceu.hu; kakucsn@ceu.hu
Website: http://www.ceu.hu

Rector and President: John Shattuck (2009-)
Tel: +36(1) 327-3004, Fax: +36(1) 327-3005
EMail: president@ceu.hu

Provost, Academic Pro-Rector: Katalin Farkas

International Relations: Ildikó Moran, Vice President for External Relations Tel: +36(1) 327-3821 EMail: morani@ceu.hu

Departments
Economics (Commercial Law; Economic and Finance Policy; Economics); Environmental Sciences and Policy; Gender Studies (Gender Studies; Women's Studies); History (Central European Studies; Eastern European Studies; European Studies; History; Medieval Studies); International Relations and European Studies (European Studies; International Relations; Law; Political Sciences; Public Administration); Legal Studies (Commercial Law; Comparative Law; Constitutional Law; Economics; European Studies; Human Rights; International Law; International Relations; Law; Political Sciences); Mathematics and its Applications; Medieval Studies (History; Medieval Studies); Philosophy; Political Science (European Studies; International Relations; Law; Political Sciences); Public Policy (European Studies; International Relations; Law; Political Sciences); Sociology and Social Anthropology (Anthropology; Sociology; Urban Studies)

Graduate Schools
Business (Business Administration; Business and Commerce; Information Management; International Business; Management)

Programmes
Nationalism Studies (Central European Studies; Government; Political Sciences)
Further Information: Also Joint Programme With Bard College, USA: Study Abroad In Budapest. 14 Research Centres: see http://www.ceu.hu/researchcenters
History: Founded 1991 as Central European University Foundation, acquired present title 1995. National accreditation acquired 2005. CEU is also accredited by the Middle States Association of Schools and Colleges, USA.

Governing Bodies: Board of Trustees; Academic Senate

Academic Year: August to July

Admission Requirements: First (undergraduate) Degree, English proficiency (TOEFL test), and professional interview

Fees: (US Dollars): 12,000 per annum

Main Language(s) of Instruction: English

Accrediting Agencies: Accredited both in the United States and in Hungary

Degrees and Diplomas: *Alapfokozat megszerzését tanúsító oklevél; Szakirányú Továbbképzési Oklevél:* Economics; Environmental Sciences and Policy; Environmental Sciences, Policy, and Management; Gender Studies; Central European History; Historical Studies; International Relations and European Studies; Comparative Constitutional Law; Human Rights; Medieval Studies; Historical Studies; Nationalism Studies; Political Science; Public Policy; Sociology; Social Anthropology; Management; Business Administration; Information Technology Management; *Mesterfokozat megszerzését tanúsító oklevél; Doktori oklevél:* Economics; History. Also Joint International Master of Business Administration (MBA)

Student Services: Academic counselling, Canteen, Cultural centre, Employment services, Foreign student adviser, Handicapped facilities, Health services, Language programs, Social counselling, Sports facilities

Special Facilities: Computer Centre; Statistics Centre; the Open Society Archives

Libraries: Over 200,000 documents: c. 150,000 monographs and 10,000 working papers titles; over 1,500 periodical titles; CD-Roms; on-line databases.

Publications: East European Constitutional Review *(quarterly)*
Press or Publishing House: Central European University Press

Academic Staff *2008-2009:* Total 305
Student Numbers *2008-2009:* Total 1,541
Last Updated: 27/10/11

COLLEGE FOR MODERN BUSINESS SCIENCES
Modern Üzleti Tudományok Főiskola (MÜTF)
Stúdium tér 1, 2800 Tatabánya
Tel: +36(34) 520-400
Fax: +36(34) 520-403
EMail: mail@mutf.hu; felvi@mutf.hu
Website: http://www.mutf.hu

Director-General: János Hajtó Tel: +36(34) 520-401

International Relations: Anett Adorjan
EMail: adorjan.anett@mutf.hu

Departments
Business Studies (Business Administration; Environmental Management; International Business; Management; Marketing; Tourism); Economics (Economics; European Studies); Languages (Modern Languages)

History: Founded 1992.

Degrees and Diplomas: *Alapfokozat megszerzését tanúsító oklevél; Szakirányú Továbbképzési Oklevél; Mesterfokozat megszerzését tanúsító oklevél.* Also Bachelor and Master degrees
Last Updated: 26/10/11

DENNIS GABOR COLLEGE
Gábor Dénes Főiskola (GDF)
Mérnok u. 39., 1119 Budapest
Tel: +36(1) 203-0283
Fax: +36(1) 883-3636
EMail: info@gdf.hu
Website: http://www.gdf.hu

Rector: Sarolta Zárda Tel: +36(1) 203-0279 EMail: zarda@gdf.hu

Institutes
Basic Science and Technology (Computer Engineering; Engineering Management); **Economics and Social Sciences** (Business Administration; Economics; Management); **Information Technology** (Information Technology)

History: Founded 1992.

Degrees and Diplomas: *Alapfokozat megszerzését tanúsító oklevél:* 3-4 yrs. Also Bachelor degrees

Last Updated: 08/06/11

DHARMA GATE BUDAPEST BUDDHIST UNIVERSITY

A Tan Kapuya Buddhista Főiskola (TKBF)
Börzsöny u. 11, 1098 Budapest
Tel: +36(1) 280-6712 +36(70) 339-9905
Fax: +36(1) 280-6714
EMail: tankapu@tkbf.hu
Website: http://www.tkbf.eu

Rector: Janos Jelen EMail: rektor@tkbf.hu

Administrative Officer: Attiláné Kovács

International Relations: Tamás Agócs, Vice-Rector for International Relations EMail: agocsster@gmail.com

Programmes
Buddhist Studies (Asian Religious Studies); **Chinese and Japanese** (Chinese; Japanese); **Classical Tibetan** (Tibetan); **Oriental Studies and Philosophy** (Oriental Studies; Philosophical Schools); **Pali** (Ancient Languages; Indic Languages); **Sanskrit** (Sanskrit)

History: Founded 1991, acquired present status and title 1999.

Degrees and Diplomas: *Alapfokozat megszerzését tanúsító oklevél:* Buddhist studies, 3-4 yrs; *Mesterfokozat megszerzését tanúsító oklevél:* Buddhist studies, a further 2 yrs. Also Bachelor and Master programmes

Last Updated: 16/09/11

HARSÁNYI JÁNOS COLLEGE

Harsányi János Foiskola
Bécsi út 324., 1137 Budapest
Tel: +36(1) 883-6437
Fax: +36(1) 883-6438
EMail: info@hjf.hu
Website: http://www.hjf.hu

Rector: Ferenc Kondorosi EMail: rektorihivatal@hjf.hu

Programmes
Business and Management (Business Administration; Management); **Crafts and Trades** (Crafts and Trades); **Electronic Imaging** (Communication Arts; Graphic Design; Visual Arts); **Tourism** (Hotel Management; Tourism)

History: Formerly known as Korábban Deák Ferenc Főiskola (Deak Ferenc College of Economics).

Degrees and Diplomas: *Alapfokozat megszerzését tanúsító oklevél*

Last Updated: 02/11/11

HELLER FARKAS COLLEGE OF ECONOMICS AND TOURISM INDUSTRY

Heller Farkas Gazdasági és Turisztikai Szolgáltatások Főiskolája (HFF)
Rózsa utca 4-6., 1077 Budapest
Tel: +36(1) 322-6879
Fax: +36(1) 413-6454
EMail: hff@hff.hu
Website:http: //www.hff.hu

Director-General: Márton Lengyel (2001-) EMail: lengyel@hff.hu

Secretary-General: Mariann Varga
Tel: +36(1) 321-5800/724 EMail: vargam@hff.hu

International Relations: Balázs Kovács, Director
EMail: international@hff.hu

Departments
Economics and Social Studies; **European Union Studies** (Economics; European Union Law); **Management**; **Methodology**; **Tourism**

History: Founded 2001.

Degrees and Diplomas: *Alapfokozat megszerzését tanúsító oklevél:* 3-4 yrs; *Mesterfokozat megszerzését tanúsító oklevél.* Also Vocational Studies Programmes.

Last Updated: 30/01/09

INTERNATIONAL BUSINESS SCHOOL

IBS Nemzetkozi Uzleti Főiskola (IBS)
Tárogató út 2-4., 1021 Budapest
Tel: +36(1) 391-2574
Fax: +36(1) 391-2550
EMail: info@ibs-b.hu
Website: http://www.ibs-b.hu

Chancellor: Istvánedek Tamás

Vice-Chancellor: László Lang
Tel: +36(1) 391-25-20 EMail: llang@ibs-b.hu

International Relations: László Lendvai, Chief International Recruitment Officer EMail: llendvai@ibs-b.hu

Departments
Arts Management (Art Management); **Business Administration** (Business Administration); **Economics** (Economics); **Finance** (Accountancy; Finance); **Foreign Languages** (Foreign Languages Education); **Human Resources** (Human Resources); **International Relations** (International Relations); **Management** (Management); **Marketing** (Marketing); **Quantitative Methodology and IT** (Information Technology); **Tourism** (Tourism)

History: Founded 1991, acquired present status and title 1997.

Governing Bodies: Senate; Management Board; CEO (Vice-Chancellor)

Academic Year: September-July

Admission Requirements: High School Diploma or College/University degree, sufficient level of English

Fees: (Euros): 900 registration fee for non-EU citizens; BA: 1,900-2,900/sem; MSc: 4,500/sem

Main Language(s) of Instruction: English with some programmes in Hungarian

International Co-operation: With Oxford Brookes Unibersity (UK). Also participates in Erasmus (UK, Germany, France, Spain, Italy, Netherlands)

Accrediting Agencies: Hungarian Accreditation Committee (Hungary); QAA (UK)

Degrees and Diplomas: *Alapfokozat megszerzését tanúsító oklevél:* Business Studies; International Business Relations; Finance and Accounting; Travel and Tourism Management; Arts Management (BA), 4 yrs; *Mesterfokozat megszerzését tanúsító oklevél:* International Business; Financial Management; Marketing Management; Human Resources; Management (MSc), 1 yr. Also Master's degree programmes awarded by the Oxford Brookes University.

Student Services: Academic counselling, Canteen, Cultural centre, Employment services, Foreign student adviser, Foreign Studies Centre, Handicapped facilities, Language programs, Social counselling, Sports facilities

Student Residential Facilities: 100 rooms (single or shared)

Special Facilities: Computer Labs; Art studio; Fitness centre; Theatre stage

Libraries: 18,500 vols; Periodical subscriptions; Electronic databases

Academic Staff 2010-2011	MEN	WOMEN	TOTAL
FULL-TIME	–	–	50
PART-TIME	–	–	40
STAFF WITH DOCTORATE			
FULL-TIME	–	–	20
PART-TIME	–	–	c. 20

Student Numbers 2010-2011			
All (Foreign Included)	650	600	c. 1,250
FOREIGN ONLY	220	200	420

Last Updated: 02/11/11

KÁROLI GÁSPÁR UNIVERSITY OF THE HUNGARIAN REFORMED CHURCH, BUDAPEST

Károli Gáspár Református Egyetem (KRE)
Kálvin tér 9, 1091 Budapest
Tel: +36(1) 455-9060
Fax: +36(1) 455-9061
EMail: rektori.hivatal@kre.hu
Website: http://www.kre.hu

Rector (Acting): Péter Balla EMail: balla.peter@kre.hu

Chief Secretary: Niké Szkárosi EMail: szkarosi.nike@kre.hu

Faculties
Humanities (Arts and Humanities; Dutch; English; History; Hungarian; Japanese; Modern Languages; Pedagogy; Philology); **Law** (Law; Political Sciences); **Teacher Training** (Primary Education; Religious Education; Social Work); **Theology** (Bible; Canon Law; History of Religion; New Testament; Pastoral Studies; Protestant Theology; Religious Education; Religious Studies; Sociology; Theology)

History: Founded 1855, acquired present status and title 1990.

Main Language(s) of Instruction: Hungarian

International Co-operation: With universities in Romania, United Kingdom, USA. Also participates in Erasmus/Socrates programme

Degrees and Diplomas: *Alapfokozat megszerzését tanúsító oklevél*; *Mesterfokozat megszerzését tanúsító oklevél*; *Doktori oklevél*

Student Residential Facilities: Yes

Special Facilities: Language Laboratory

Libraries: c. 200,000
Last Updated: 27/10/11

KING SIGISMUND COLLEGE

Zsigmond Király Főiskola (ZSKF)
Kelta utca 2., 1032 Budapest
Tel: +36(1) 454-7600 +36(1) 454-7620
Fax: +36(1) 454-7623
EMail: mail@zskf.hu; fh@zskf.hu
Website: http://www.zskf.hu

Director-General: József Bayer (2001-) Tel: +36(1) 454-7620

Programmes
Andragogy (Adult Education); **Business Administration** (Business Administration); **Communication and Media Studies**; **Finance and Accounting** (Accountancy; Finance); **Human Resource Management**; **Humanistic Studies** (Arts and Humanities); **International Business** (International Business); **International Studies**; **Political Science** (Political Sciences)

History: Founded 2000.

Degrees and Diplomas: *Alapfokozat megszerzését tanúsító oklevél*; *Szakirányú Továbbképzési Oklevél*; *Mesterfokozat megszerzését tanúsító oklevél*
Last Updated: 02/11/11

KODOLÁNYI JÁNOS UNIVERSITY OF APPLIED SCIENCES

Kodolányi János Főiskola (KJF)
Fürdö u. 1, 8000 Székesfehérvár
Tel: +36(22) 543-400
Fax: +36(22) 312-288
EMail: international@kjf.hu
Website: http://www.kodolanyi.hu

Director-General: Péter Szabó
Tel: +36(22) 543-416 EMail: kjfhivatal@mail.kodolanyi.hu

International Relations: Éva Horvati
Tel: +36(22) 543-391, Fax: +36(22) 543-391
EMail: horvatieva@mail.kodolanyi.hu

Departments
Andragogy and Cultural Studies (Adult Education; Cultural Studies); **Applied Pedagogy** (Pedagogy); **Applied Social Studies** (Social Sciences); **Communication and Media Studies** (Communication Studies; Media Studies); **Computing**; **Economics and Management** (Economics; Management); **English Studies** (English); **French Studies**; **German Studies** (German); **International Relations** (International Relations); **Jazz Performance and Singing** (Music; Singing); **Social Studies and Humanities** (Arts and Humanities; Social Studies; Sports); **Tourism** (Tourism)

Further Information: Also on-line programmes

History: Founded 1992.

Degrees and Diplomas: *Alapfokozat megszerzését tanúsító oklevél*; *Szakirányú Továbbképzési Oklevél*: 2 yrs; *Doktori oklevél*. Also Bachelor's degree (*Alapképzések*); Vocational Degree Programmes.
Last Updated: 28/10/11

KÖLCSEY FERENC TEACHER TRAINING COLLEGE OF THE REFORMED CHURCH

Kölcsey Ferenc Református Tanítóképző Főiskola (KTIF)
Péterfia utca 1-7., 4026 Debrecen
Tel: +36(52) 518-500
Fax: +36(52) 518-556
EMail: info@kfrtkf.hu
Website: http://www.kfrtkf.hu

Rector: Zoltán Völgyesi
Tel: +36(52) 412-980 EMail: rektor@kfrtkf.hu

Programmes
Christian Education (Christian Religious Studies); **Communication and Media Sciences** (Communication Studies; Media Studies); **Library and Computer Science** (Computer Science; Library Science); **Liturgical Music** (Religious Music); **Teacher Training** *(Primary level)* (Teacher Training); **Youth Assistance** (Social Work)

History: Founded 1855, acquired present status and title 1996.

Degrees and Diplomas: *Alapfokozat megszerzését tanúsító oklevél*: 3-4 yrs. Higher professional training programme, 2 yrs. Also Bachelor degrees
Last Updated: 02/11/11

PÁZMÁNY PÉTER CATHOLIC UNIVERSITY, BUDAPEST

Pázmány Péter Katolikus Egyetem (PPKE/PPCU)
Szentkirályi útca 28, H-1088 Budapest
Tel: +36(1) 429-7211
Fax: +36(1) 318-0507
EMail: rektor@ppke.hu
Website: http://www.ppke.hu

Rector: György Fodor (2004-) EMail: fodor.gyorgy@ppke.hu

General-Secretary: Aranka Recőcziné Gavrilovits
EMail: rga@ppke.hu

International Relations: András Szabó
Tel: +36(1) 429-7216 EMail: szabo.andras@ppke.hu

Centres
Italian Interuniversity (European Studies; International Business)

Faculties
Humanities (Art History; Arts and Humanities; Communication Studies; History; Linguistics; Literature; Medieval Studies; Philosophy; Sociology; Teacher Training); **Information Technology** (Biotechnology; Information Technology); **Law and Political Science** (Civil Law; Ethics; European Union Law; History of Law; International Law; Law; Political Sciences); **Theology** (Ancient Languages; Bible; Catholic Theology; Christian Religious Studies; Theology)

Institutes

Canon Law *(Postgraduate)* (Canon Law)

History: Founded 1635 as Department of Theology of the University founded by Péter Pázmány, Cardinal, Primate, and Archbishop of Esztergom in Nagyszombat. Acquired present status and title 1993. An ecclesiastic institution recognized by the State under the supervision of the Holy See.

Governing Bodies: University Council

Academic Year: September to June

Admission Requirements: Secondary school certificate (érettségi bizonyítvány) and entrance examination

Fees: (Forints) 35,000-200,000

Main Language(s) of Instruction: Hungarian

International Co-operation: With universities in Austria, Belgium, United Kingdom, France, Netherlands, Japan, Canada, Colombia, Poland, Germany, Italy, Mexico, Romania, Spain, Switzerland, Slovak Republic, Slovenia, Taiwan, Ukraine and USA.

Accrediting Agencies: Hungarian Accreditation Committee (MAB)

Degrees and Diplomas: *Alapfokozat megszerzését tanúsító oklevél*: French, 6 sems; *Alapfokozat megszerzését tanúsító oklevél*: Theology; *Mesterfokozat megszerzését tanúsító oklevél*: Communication, 8 sems; *Mesterfokozat megszerzését tanúsító oklevél*: European Studies and Global Affairs; Law and Political Science; Information Technology; Theology; Humanities; *Doktori oklevél*: Canon Law; Theology; Law and Political Science; Multidisciplinary Technical Science (PhD), 3 yrs

Student Services: Academic counselling, Canteen, Cultural centre, Employment services, Foreign student adviser, Foreign Studies Centre, Handicapped facilities, Health services, Language programs, Nursery care, Social counselling, Sports facilities

Libraries: Every faculty has a library. Total: 400,000 vols

Publications: Folia Canonica *(annually)*; Folia Theologica *(annually)*; Kánonjog *(biennially)*; Mester és Tanítvány *(biennially)*; Teologia *(quarterly)*; VERBUM Analecta Neolatina *(biennially)*

Last Updated: 27/10/11

SAPIENTIA COLLEGE OF THEOLOGY OF RELIGIOUS ORDERS

Sapientia Szerzetesi Hittudományi Főiskola (SSZHF)
Piarista köz 1, 1052 Budapest
Tel: +36(1) 486-4000
Fax: +36(1) 486-4412
EMail: sapientia@sapientia.hu
Website: http://www.sapientia.hu

Rector: Lóránt Orosz EMail: orosz.lorantsapientia.hu

Programmes

Education (Education); **Religion** (Religion); **Teacher Training** (Teacher Training)

Degrees and Diplomas: *Alapfokozat megszerzését tanúsító oklevél*; *Mesterfokozat megszerzését tanúsító oklevél*. Also Bachelor and master degrees

Last Updated: 27/10/11

THEOLOGICAL COLLEGE OF SZEGED

Gál Ferenc Hittudományi Főiskola (GFHF)
Dóm tér 6, 6720 Szeged
Tel: +36(62) 425-738
Fax: +36(62) 425-738
EMail: gfhf@gfhf.hu
Website: http://www.gfhf.hu

Rektor: Kozma Gábor EMail: rektor@gfhf.hu

Departments

Cultural Studies (Cultural Studies); **Foreign Languages** (Modern Languages); **Hungarian Language and Literature** (Hungarian); **Mathematics and Sciences** (Mathematics; Natural Sciences); **Physical Education** (Physical Education); **Slovak** (Slavic Languages); **Social and Religious Studies** (Religious Studies; Social Sciences); **Sociology and Pedagogy** (Pedagogy; Sociology); **Visual Education** (Education)

Institutes

Music and Ethics *(Saint Gerard)* (Ethics; Music; Physical Education)

History: Founded 1930. Became Szegedi Hittudományi Főiskola 1997.

Degrees and Diplomas: *Alapfokozat megszerzését tanúsító oklevél*; *Szakirányú Továbbképzési Oklevél*; *Mesterfokozat megszerzését tanúsító oklevél*

Last Updated: 27/10/11

TOMORI PÁL COLLEGE

Tomori Pál Főiskola (TPF)
Szent István király utca 2-4., 6300 Kalocsa
Tel: +36(78) 564-600
Fax: +36(78) 464-445
EMail: info@tpfk.hu
Website: http://www.tpfk.hu

General Director: Rózsa Meszlényi
Tel: +36(78) 564-601 EMail: meselenyi.rozsa@tpfk.hu

Programmes

Business and Economics (Business Administration; Economics); **Finance and Accountancy** (Accountancy; Finance); **Management** (Management); **Regional Economy**

History: Founded 2004.

Degrees and Diplomas: *Alapfokozat megszerzését tanúsító oklevél*: 3-4 yrs; *Mesterfokozat megszerzését tanúsító oklevél*

UNIVERSITY OF JEWISH STUDIES

Országos Rabbiképzö Intézet-Zsidó Egyetem (ORKI-ZSE)
Bérkocsis utca 2., 1084 Budapest
Tel: +36(1) 317-2396
Fax: +36(1) 318-7049
EMail: kocsis@or-zse.hu
Website: http://www.or-zse.hu

Rector: Alfréd Schöner (1998-)
Tel: +36(1) 318-7049/136 EMail: vzs@or-zse.hu

Divisions

Jewish Cultural Studies (Jewish Studies); **Rabbinical Studies** *(Theological Seminary)* (Judaic Religious Studies); **Teacher Training in Judaism, Jewish Community and Social Work** (Jewish Studies; Judaic Religious Studies; Social and Community Services; Social Work; Teacher Training)

Last Updated: 27/10/11

VESZPRÉM COLLEGE OF THEOLOGY

Veszprémi Érseki Hittudományi Főiskola (VHF)
Jutasi út. 18/2, 8200 Veszprém
Tel: +36(88) 542-700
Fax: +36(88) 426-865
EMail: rektor@vhf.hu
Website: http://www.vhf.hu/vhf_new

Director-General: István Varga (1994-)

Programmes

Social Work (Social Work); **Teacher Training** (Teacher Training); **Theology** (Theology)

History: Founded 1991.

Degrees and Diplomas: *Alapfokozat megszerzését tanúsító oklevél*

Last Updated: 02/11/11

VITÉZ JÁNOS ROMAN CATHOLIC TEACHER TRAINING COLLEGE

Vitéz János Római Katolikus Tanítóképző Főiskola (VTIF)
Majer utca 1-3., 2500 Esztergom
Tel: +36(33) 413-699
Fax: +36(33) 413-493
EMail: info@vjrktf.hu
Website: http://www.vjrktf.hu

Director-General: Endre Gaál (2000-) Tel: +36(33) 413-156

Departments

Cultural Studies (Cultural Studies); **Foreign Languages** (Modern Languages); **Hungarian Language and Literature** (Hungarian); **Mathematics and Sciences** (Mathematics; Natural Sciences); **Music** (Music); **Physical Education** (Physical Education); **Slovak** (Slavic Languages); **Social and Religious Studies** (Religious Studies; Social Studies); **Sociology and Pedagogy** (Pedagogy; Sociology); **Visual Education**

History: Founded 1849, acquired present status and title 1998.

Degrees and Diplomas: *Alapfokozat megszerzését tanúsító oklevél:* 4 yrs

WEKERLE SÁNDOR BUSINESS COLLEGE

Wekerle Sándor Üzleti Főiskola

Jázmin u. 10., 1083 Budapest
Tel: +36(1) 323-1070
EMail: info@wsuf.hu
Website: http://www.wsuf.hu

Rector: Borbély Attila

Programmes

Business Administration (Business Administration; Marketing)
History: Founded 2006.

Degrees and Diplomas: *Alapfokozat megszerzését tanúsító oklevél*
Last Updated: 02/11/11

WESLEY JÁNOS MINISTERS TRAINING COLLEGE

Wesley János Lelkészképzo Főiskola (WJLF)

Dankó utca 11, 1086 Budapest
Tel: +36(1) 210-5400
Fax: +36(1) 210-5400
EMail: wjlf@wjlf.hu
Website: http://www.wesley.hu

General Director: Gábor Iványi
Tel: +36(1) 210-5449 EMail: ivanyigabor@wjlf.hu

Secretary-General: István Barna EMail: barnaistvan@wjlf.hu

Departments

Ecology (Ecology); **Pedagogy** (Religious Education; Teacher Training); **Social Work** (Social Work); **Theology** (Theology)

History: Founded 1987.

Main Language(s) of Instruction: Hungarian

Degrees and Diplomas: *Alapfokozat megszerzését tanúsító oklevél; Mesterfokozat megszerzését tanúsító oklevél*
Last Updated: 02/11/11

Iceland

STRUCTURE OF HIGHER EDUCATION SYSTEM

Description:

Higher education in Iceland is regulated by Law no 136/1997, Laws on Universities. Under the law, the Icelandic term "háskóli" is used to refer to both traditional universities and institutions which do not have research responsibilities. The law does not make a distinction between universities and non-universities. According to the law, the Minister of Education, Science and Culture determines whether and to what extent institutions will engage in research and he is responsible for establishing rules on quality evaluation and recognition of all degrees that are offered.

Stages of studies:

University level first stage: Diploma/Certificate, Baccalaureatus
One- to two-year diploma courses are offered in Languages, Recreational Studies, Technology and Engineering. Bachelor's degrees (B.A., B.S., B.Ed, B.F.A., B.Mus) are awarded to students who have satisfactorily completed 3 to 4 years of study (90-120 credits) in a degree programme in the fields of Humanities, Theology, Social Sciences, Education, Special Education, Economics, Eusiness Edministration, Natural Sciences, health subjects, Fishery Studies, Agricultural Science, Technology, Engineering, Pre-School Teaching, Compulsory School Teaching, Social Pedagogy, Fine Arts, Law and Arts and Crafts. Bachelor's degrees do not usually confer professional certification, except for Nursing (B.S.); Physiotherapy (B.S.); Deacon Studies (B.A.); Radiography (B.S.); Medical Laboratory Technology (B.S.); Social Work (B.A.); and Compulsory School Teachers (B.ED.). The Bachelor's degree constitutes a formal qualification for post-graduate study.

University level second stage: Postgraduate diploma; Candidatus; Meistaraprof
Postgraduate diplomas qualify the holder for a special office or profession and are conferred after one to two years' postgraduate study after the Bachelor's degree. The Candidatus degree (kandidatsgraad) qualifies the holder for a special office or profession. It is an academic/professional degree in the fields of Theology, Medicine, Agricultural Science, Pharmacy, Midwifery, Law, Psychology and Dentistry. The Candidatus programmes last from four to six years in one-tier programmes, but for one year after a Bachelor's degree in Agricultural Science and two years after a Bachelor's degree in Midwifery and Psychology. Master's degrees (M.A., M.S., M.Ed, M.L.; M.B.A., M.P.A., M.P.H.; M.Paed-meistaragrada) are awarded after one-and-a-half or two years' successful completion of post-graduate study in the fields of Theology, Health Sciences, Humanities, Law, Economics, Business Administration, Social Sciences, Education, Natural Sciences, Engineering, Medicine, Dentistry, Nursing, Fishery Studies and Environmental Studies. A major thesis or research project usually constitutes a substantial part of the master programme.

University level third stage: Doktorspróf
The Doctorate degree (dr.phil., dr.odeont., /Ph.D - doktorsgrada) is awarded to those who have successfully completed a doctorate programme and defended a doctoral thesis in Icelandic literature, Icelandic language, and Icelandic history, theology, law, medicine, nursing; health sciences, pharmacy, dentistry, engineering, natural sciences, education and social sciences. There is also another type of Doctoral degree which is the result of intensive independent research and is awarded after defence of a doctoral thesis. As a general rule, this Doctoral degree can only be awarded to those who have completed a Candidatus professional degree, a Master's degree or equivalent education.

ADMISSION TO HIGHER EDUCATION

Admission to university-level studies:

Name of secondary school credential required: Stúdentspróf

For entry to: all higher education Institutions

Alternatives to credentials: A foreign equivalent of a secondary-school-leaving Certificate can be accepted as an entrance requirement.

Other admission requirements: In addition to the general admission requirements (stúdentspróf), individual universities or faculties may have specific requirements. At the University of Iceland competitive examinations are held in the Faculty of Nursing, and in the Faculty of Dentistry at the end of the first semester. The number of students who are allowed to continue after this examination is limited. In medicine and physiotherapy there are entrance examinations and a limited number of students with the highest grades are allowed to enter the programmes. Competitive examinations are also held at the University of Akureyri.

Foreign students admission:

Definition of foreign student: Foreign students are persons enrolled at a higher education institution in Iceland, but not a permanent resident in Iceland.

Quotas: With the exception of the University of Iceland and the University at Akureyri, Icelandic higher education institutions limit their intake of students each year.

Entrance exam requirements: The minimum qualification required of foreign students is a pass in the final examination of a Scandinavian or European type of upper secondary education. In general, students must possess the necessary qualifications to enter a university in their respective countries.

Entry regulations: Foreign students entering Iceland from non-Nordic and non-EU countries must submit documents proving that they have been admitted to an Icelandic higher education institution and evidence that they are financially self-sufficient. They must also register with the Immigration Office.

Health requirements: Students from non-Nordic and non-EU countries should make arrangements for health insurance before they leave their home countries.

Language requirements: Students must have a good knowledge of Icelandic. Courses are arranged for foreign students at the University of Iceland.

RECOGNITION OF STUDIES

Quality assurance system:

Recognition of studies completed and credentials awarded in Iceland is the responsibility of the higher education authority concerned. In 2003, the five Nordic ENIC/NARIC offices (Denmark, Finland, Iceland, Norway and Sweden) established a regional network named Nordic National Recognition Information Centres (NORRIC) to initiate joint Nordic projects to learn from each other and reduce barriers to the recognition of foreign qualifications in the Nordic region (www.norric.org).

Bodies dealing with recognition:

Kennslusvid Haskola Islands (Office for Academic Affairs, University of Iceland)
   Director, Academic Affairs: Thordur Kristinsson
   v. Sudurgotu, 101
   Reykjavík
   Tel: +354 525 4360
   Fax: +354 525 4317
   EMail: ina@hi.is
   WWW: http://www.naric-enic.hi.is/

NATIONAL BODIES

Menntamálaráðuneytið (Ministry of Education, Science and Culture)
   Minister: Katrin Jakobsdottir
   Sölvhólsgötu 4
   Reykjavik 150
   Tel: +354 545 9500
   Fax: +354 562 3068
   EMail: postur@mrn.stjr.is
   WWW: http://www.menntamalaraduneyti.is/

National Rectors' Conference in Iceland
President: Kristin Ingolsfdottir
Reykjavik

Data for academic year: 2006-2007
Source: IAU from ENIC/NARIC Office for Iceland, 2006 (Bodies, 2011)

INSTITUTIONS

PUBLIC INSTITUTIONS

AGRICULTURAL UNIVERSITY OF ICELAND
Landbúnaðarháskóli Íslands
Hvanneyri, 311 Borgarnes
Tel: + 354 433-5000
Fax: + 354 433-5001
EMail: lbhi@lbhi.is
Website: http://www.landbunadarhaskolinn.is/inenglish/aboutlbhi

Rector: Ágúst Sigurðsson EMail: agust@lbhi.is

International Relations: Björn Thorsteinsson

Faculties
Environmental Sciences (Environmental Management; Forestry; Natural Resources); **Land and Animal Resources**; **Vocational Training** (Vocational Education)

History: Founded 2005.

Admission Requirements: Secondary school certificate (stúdent-sprof) or equivalent

Main Language(s) of Instruction: Icelandic

Degrees and Diplomas: *Baccalaureatus:* Agricultural Production; Natural Resources; Range Management; Landscape Planning; *Meistarapróf:* Agricultural Production; Natural Resources; Range Management; *Doktorspróf.* Also Diploma in Basic Agricultural Education

Last Updated: 06/01/10

HÓLAR UNIVERSITY COLLEGE
Hólaskóli - Háskólinn á Hólum
551 Sauðárkrókur
Tel: + 354 455-6300
Fax: + 354 455-6301
EMail: holaskoli@holar.is
Website: http://www.holar.is

Rector: Skúli Skúlason EMail: skuli@holar.is

Administrator: Sigríður Magnúsdóttir EMail: sigurbjorg@holar.is

Departments
Aquaculture and Fish Biology (Aquaculture; Zoology); **Equine Science** (Animal Husbandry; Zoology); **Rural Tourism** (Tourism)

History: Founded 1882. Acquired present status 2003.

Admission Requirements: Islandic "Stúdentspróf" certificate (high school matriculation) or equivalent secondary school certificate. Mature students (over 25 yrs) are required to have finished 60 credits at secondary school level and have appropriate work experience. Applicants not satifying the requirements can pass an examination after attending a one year preliminary studies program. For equine Science program, applicants need at least 65 credits (130 ECTS) from a secondary school, sufficient riding experience and they must have reached 18 years of age and good understanding of the Icelandic language.

Fees: (Iceland Krona): administration fee, 50,000 per annum; total cost (including books, transport, housing,...) c. 150,000 per annum, except third year of Equine Studies, 320,000.

Degrees and Diplomas: *Diploma/Certificate; Baccalaureatus; Meistarapróf.* Also vocational study programme in Rural Tourism and Aquaculture and Fish Biology, 1yr; Programme in Equine Studies and Riding, 3 yrs (the second and third years are at university levels).

Last Updated: 06/01/10

UNIVERSITY OF AKUREYRI
Háskólinn á Akureyri
Solborg/Nordurslod, 600 Akureyri
Tel: + 354 460-8000
EMail: international@unak.is
Website: http://www.unak.is

Rector: Stefán B. Sigurdsson (2009-) EMail: rektor@unak.is

Institutes
Research (Education; Fishery; Management; Nursing)

Schools
Business and Science (Aquaculture; Biotechnology; Business Administration; Environmental Studies; Fishery; Information Technology; Management; Marketing; Natural Sciences; Tourism); **Health Sciences** (Health Sciences; Nursing; Occupational Therapy); **Humanities and Social Sciences** (Education; Law; Social Sciences)

History: Founded 1987. A State Institution.

Governing Bodies: University Council

Academic Year: August to June (August-December; January-June)

Admission Requirements: Secondary school certificate (stúdent-sprof) or equivalent

Fees: (Iceland Krona): 45,000 per annum

Main Language(s) of Instruction: Icelandic

International Co-operation: Participates in the Erasmus, Nordplus, North2North and Leonardo programmes

Degrees and Diplomas: *Baccalaureatus:* 3-4 yrs; *Meistarapróf:* 11/2-2 yrs

Student Services: Academic counselling, Canteen, Foreign student adviser, Social counselling, Sports facilities

Student Residential Facilities: Yes

Libraries: c. 51,000 titles
Last Updated: 05/01/12

UNIVERSITY OF ICELAND
Háskóli Íslands
Sæmundargötu 2, 101 Reykjavík
Tel: + 354 525-4000
Fax: + 354 552-1331
EMail: hi@hi.is
Website: http://www.hi.is

Rector: Kristín Ingólfsdóttir (2005-)
Tel: + 354 525-4302 EMail: kring@hi.is

Head of Academic Affairs: Thórdur Kristinsson
Tel: + 354 525-4359, Fax: + 354 525-4317 EMail: thordkri@hi.is

International Relations: Karitas Kvaran
Tel: + 354 525-4304 EMail: karitask@hi.is

Schools

Education (Education; Leisure Studies; Social Studies; Sports; Teacher Training); **Engineering and Natural Sciences** (Chemical Engineering; Civil Engineering; Computer Engineering; Computer Science; Earth Sciences; Electrical Engineering; Engineering; Environmental Engineering; Industrial Engineering; Mechanical Engineering; Software Engineering); **Health Sciences** (Dentistry; Food Science; Medicine; Nursing; Nutrition; Pharmacy; Psychology); **Humanities** (Archaeology; Arts and Humanities; Comparative Literature; Cultural Studies; Danish; English; Finnish; German; Greek; History; Icelandic; Italian; Latin; Linguistics; Native Language Education; Norwegian; Philosophy; Religious Studies; Russian; Spanish; Swedish; Theology); **Social Sciences** (Anthropology; Business Administration; Economics; Education; Ethnology; Information Sciences; Law; Library Science; Media Studies; Political Sciences; Psychology; Social Sciences; Social Work; Sociology)

History: Founded 1911 by merging Theological seminary, Medical College, and School of Law, and adding Faculty of Philosophy. Merged with the Iceland University of Education 2008.

Governing Bodies: Senate

Academic Year: September to May (September-December; January-May)

Admission Requirements: Upper secondary school certificate (stúdentsprof) or equivalent

Main Language(s) of Instruction: Icelandic

International Co-operation: Participates in the Socrates, Leonardo, Nordplus and NorFA programmes and has numerous bilateral agreements

Degrees and Diplomas: *Baccalaureatus*: Anthropology; Ethnology; Psychology; Library and Information Sciences; Theology; Deacon Studies; Computer Science; Economics; Business Administration; Civil Engineering; Environmental Engineering; Electrical and Computer Engineering; Mechanical and Industrial Engineering; Industrial Engineering; Chemical Engineering; Computer Science; Economics; Comparative Literature; Linguistics; History; Philosophy; Archaeology; Sign Language Interpretation; Danish; Swedish; Norwegian; Finnish; English; French; German; Icelandic; Greek; Latin; Spanish; Education; Political Science; Sociology; Software Engineering; Food Science; Biology; Chemistry; Biochemistry; Geology; Theoretical Physics; Applied Physics; Geophysics; Mathematics; Geography; Tourism, 3 yrs; *Baccalaureatus*: Nursing; Physiotherapy; Social Work, 4 yrs; *Candidatus*: Business Administration (Cand.oecon), 4 yrs; *Candidatus*: Dentistry (Cand. odont.); Medicine (Cand.med.et chir.), 6 yrs; *Candidatus*: Law (Cand.jur.); Pharmacy (Cand.pharm); Theology (Cand.theol.), 5 yrs; *Candidatus*: Midwifery (Cand.obst); Psychology (Cand.psych.), 2 yrs following Baccalaureatus; *Meistaraprof*: Business Administration (MBA), 1 1/2 yrs following Baccalaureatus; *Meistaraprof*: Comparative Literature; Danish; English; Philosophy; Icelandic Literature; Icelandic Language; Icelandic Studies; History; Education; Political Science; Sociology; Anthropology; Ethnology; Psychology; Library and Information Sciences (MA); Dentistry; Economics; Civil Engineering; Environmental Engineering; Mechanical Engineering; Industrial Engineering; Electrical Engineering; Computer Engineering; Civil and Environmental Engineering; Mechanical and Industrial Engineering (MS); Electrical and Computer Engineering; Health Sciences; Food Science; Nutrition; Biology; Biochemistry; Chemistry; Geology; Physics; Astrophysics; Geophysics; History of Science; Mathematics; Geography; Environmental Sciences; Fisheries Science; Pharmacy (MS); Environmental Sciences; Fisheries Science; Theology (MA), 2 yrs following Baccalaureatus; *Meistaraprof*: Computer Science (MS); Education (MEd); Icelandic; English; Danish; German (MPaed), 11/2 yrs following Baccalaureatus; *Meistaraprof*: Nursing (MS), 2 years following Baccalaureatus; *Meistaraprof*: Public Policy Making and Administration (MPA), 2 yrs following Baccalaureus; *Doktorsprof*: Dentistry (Drodont), 5 yrs following Candidatus; *Doktorsprof*: Icelandic Literature; Icelandic Language; History (DrPhil), 3 yrs following Meistaraprof; *Doktorsprof*: Mechanical and Industrial Engineering; Electrical and Computer Engineering; Computer Science (PhD); Sociology; Anthropology; Psychology; Library and Information Sciences; Civil Engineering; Environmental Engineering; Mechanical Engineering; Industrial Engineering; Electrical Engineering; Computer Engineering; Civil and Environmental Engineering (PhD); Theology; Medicine; Business Administration; Economics; Pharmacy; Dentistry; Food Science; Nutrition;

Biology; Biochemistry; Chemistry; Geology; Physics; Astrophysics; Geophysics; History of Science; Mathematics; Geography; Education; Political Science (PhD), 3-4 yrs following Meistaraprof. Also Postgraduate course in Education

Student Services: Academic counselling, Foreign student adviser, Handicapped facilities, Language programs, Nursery care, Social counselling, Sports facilities

Student Residential Facilities: For c. 500 students

Libraries: University Library, c. 900,000 vols (including books, periodicals and other material)

Publications: Ársskýrla Háskóla Íslands

Press or Publishing House: University Press (Háskólaútgáfan)
Last Updated: 05/01/12

PRIVATE INSTITUTIONS

BIFRÖST UNIVERSITY

Háskólinn á Bifröst
Nordurárdalur, 311 Borgarnes
Tel: +354 433-3000
Fax: +354 433-3001
EMail: bifrost@bifrost.is
Website: http://www.bifrost.is

Rector: Ágúst Einarsson
Tel: +354 695-9999 EMail: agust@bifrost.is

Faculties

Business (Banking; Business Administration; Finance; International Business; Management); **Law** (Commercial Law; International Law); **Social Sciences** (Economics; European Studies; Management; Philosophy; Political Sciences)

History: Founded 1918 as Samvinnuskólinn á Bifröst (Co-operative College of Iceland), acquired present status 1989 and present title 2000.

Academic Year: September to May (September-December; January-May)

Admission Requirements: Upper secondary school leaving examination (stúdentsprof) or equivalent for undergraduate studies and first cycle degree (Bachelor's degree) for graduate studies

Fees: (Iceland Krona): undergraduate, 189,000-205,000 per term; graduate, 310,000 per term

Main Language(s) of Instruction: Icelandic; English (in international exchange programme)

International Co-operation: With universities in Canada, USA, Sweden, Finland, Japan, China, Netherlands, France, Greece, Spain, Estonia, Lithuania. Participates in the Socrates-Erasmus programmes.

Degrees and Diplomas: *Baccalaureatus*: Business Administration; Commercial Law (B.Sc.), 3 yrs; *Meistaraprof*: Business Administration; Applied Social Sciences; Law (M.Sc.; M.A.; M.L.), 13 months. Also Diploma in Management (2 yrs) and lifelong learning programmes

Student Services: Academic counselling, Foreign student adviser, Handicapped facilities, Nursery care, Sports facilities

Student Residential Facilities: On-campus housing

Libraries: Yes

Publications: Bifröst School of Business Research Paper Series *(quarterly)*
Last Updated: 04/01/12

ICELAND ACADEMY OF THE ARTS

Listaháskóli Íslands (LHI)
Skipholt 1, 105 Reykjavík
Tel: +354 552-4000
Fax: +354 562-3629
EMail: lhi@lhi.is
Website: http://www.lhi.is

Rector: Hjálmar H. Ragnarsson (1999-) EMail: hjalmar@lhi.is

Director of Academic Affairs: Anna Kristín Ólafsdóttir
EMail: annakristin@lhi.is

International Relations: Anna Kristín Ólafsdóttir
Tel: +354 545 2205 EMail: hannba@lhi.is

Courses

Post-Baccalaureate Teacher Training (Teacher Training) *Supervisor:* Arnthrudur Osp Karlsdottir

Departments

Art Education (Art Education); **Design and Architecture** (Architecture; Design; Fashion Design; Graphic Design; Industrial Design; Textile Design); **Fine Arts** (Fine Arts; Visual Arts); **Music** (Music; Music Theory and Composition; Performing Arts; Religious Music); **Theatre and Dance** (Acting; Dance; Theatre)

History: Founded 1998 following the merger of Leiklistarskóli Íslands (Icelandic Drama School), Myndlista-og Handíðskóli Íslands (Icelandic College of Arts and Crafts).

Academic Year: August to July

Admission Requirements: Secondary school certificate (stúdentspróf), entrance examination and Portfolio

Fees: (I. Kroner): 160,000 per annum

Main Language(s) of Instruction: Icelandic

International Co-operation: Participates in the Nordplus, Erasmus/Socrates programmes

Degrees and Diplomas: *Baccalaureatus*: 3-4 yrs; *Meistarapróf*

Student Services: Foreign student adviser

Special Facilities: Students' Gallery, Theatre, Concert Hall

Libraries: Main Library
Last Updated: 06/01/10

REYKJAVÍK UNIVERSITY
Háskólinn í Reykjavík (RU)
Ofanleiti 2, 103 Reykjavík
Tel: +354 510-6200
Fax: +354 510-6201
EMail: ru@ru.is
Website: http://www.ru.is

Rector: Svafa Grönfeldt

Schools

Business (Business Administration; Business and Commerce; Finance; Human Resources; Management); **Computer Science** (Computer Science; Mathematics; Software Engineering); **Law** (Law); **Science and Engineering** (Biomedical Engineering; Civil Engineering; Electrical Engineering; Mechanical Engineering)

History: Founded 1998 as Icelandic School of Business, acquired present status and title 2001.

Admission Requirements: Secondary school certificate (stúdentsprof) or equivalent

Main Language(s) of Instruction: Icelandic

International Co-operation: Participates in the Erasmus programme

Degrees and Diplomas: *Baccalaureatus*: Computer Science; Law; Business Administration (BS), 3 yrs; *Meistarapróf*: Global Management; Human Resources Management; Law; Computer Science (MS; ML; MBA), a further 11/2-2 yrs; *Doktorspróf*: Business Administration (PhD)

Student Services: Academic counselling, Canteen, Foreign student adviser, Foreign Studies Centre, Language programs, Sports facilities
Last Updated: 02/01/12

India

STRUCTURE OF HIGHER EDUCATION SYSTEM

Description:

Higher education is provided by: 1) Universities - including agricultural universities and medical universities-divided into Central Universities, funded directly by the Ministry of Human Resources Development, and State Universities, set up and funded by various states. 2) "Deemed to be universities", single-faculty, multi subjects institutions which enjoy the same academic status and privileges of a university; and 3) Institutions of National Importance, university-level institutions funded by the central government. These include the Indian Institutes of Technology.

Most universities belong to the affiliating and teaching type in which departments impart instruction at the postgraduate level and undertake research. Agricultural universities stress research and extension work. Finally, there are technological universities and open universities. There are also research institutions, administered by the Indian Council of Social Science Research, and research laboratories, as well as more than 15,000 colleges, most of which are affiliated to universities.

Universities are governed by statutory bodies such as the Academic Council, the Senate/Court and the Executive Council/Syndicate. Funding for State universities largely comes from the State governments and the University Grants Commission. Higher education falls mainly under its jurisdiction. The Association of Indian Universities (AIU) represents universities and has the responsibility for all matters within the higher education sector other than funding. Professional institutions are coordinated by different bodies. The All-India Council for Technical Education (AICTE) is responsible for the coordination of technical and management education institutions.

Stages of studies:

University level first stage: *Undergraduate*
First degrees generally require three years' full-time study leading to Bachelor of Arts, Science and Commerce degrees. In professional subjects, courses last for one (B.Ed.) to five years (BDS, MBBS).

University level second stage: *Postgraduate*
A Master's degree generally requires two years of study after a first degree. Most are coursework-based without a thesis.

University level third stage: *Pre-Doctoral*
One and a half-year MPhil programmes are open to those who have completed their second stage postgraduate degree. It is a preparatory programme for doctoral level studies.

University level fourth stage: *Doctoral and Post-Doctoral*
The PhD programme involves three years' study beyond the M.Phil. The D.Sc. and D.Litt. are awarded by some universities after PhD for original contributions.

Distance higher education:
Since its inception in 1962 at the University of Delhi, distance education has grown considerably. There are now several Institutes/Directorates of distance education attached to conventional universities and Open Universities, including Indira Gandhi National Open University with over 150 regional centres throughout India. Distance education programmes cover about one hundred degree/diploma courses. Many conventional universities also offer correspondence courses which are sometimes supplemented by contact classes.

ADMISSION TO HIGHER EDUCATION

Admission to university-level studies:

Name of secondary school credential required: Higher Secondary School Certificate

Entrance exam requirements: Pre-university examination. Joint Entrance Examination for the Indian Institutes of Technology and certain centrally sponsored institutes and universities. For entrance to most professional courses students must sit for an entrance examination conducted by each institution. It is followed by an interview. Entrance examinations are also held by some universities for admission to Master's level courses and pre- and doctoral studies in General Education.

Numerus clausus/restrictions: Specific ability requirements are set for artistic studies, physical education and architectural preservation studies. An age limit is also set.

Foreign students admission:

Entrance exam requirements: A minimum of twelve years' secondary education with English as one of the subjects. Science stream subjects are required for professional courses.

Entry regulations: Some 5 per cent of university places are reserved for foreign students. They must ascertain their eligibility through the AIU or by applying directly to the university of their choice for courses in Science, the Humanities and Social Sciences. Admission to professional courses is regulated through the Indian Missions. Foreign students nominated through the Missions or the Ministry of External Affairs are not required to sit for the entrance examination conducted for admission to professional courses. They must have studied English at secondary school. Students wishing to study Medicine or Engineering must have studied Physics, Chemistry, and Biology/Maths in the last two years of their secondary education.

Language requirements: Students must have a good knowledge of English. Where necessary, special English language courses are organized prior to university entrance from 1 March to 30 June.

RECOGNITION OF STUDIES

Quality assurance system:

Once recognized by the UGC (NACC) or the AICTE or a similar body, institutions of higher education are expected to maintain a good standard and quality of education and their degrees and diplomas are recognized throughout the country. There are provisions for penal action or withdrawal of recognition if reasonable quality and standards are not maintained and/or if an institution is found involved in serious malpractice.

NATIONAL BODIES

Ministry of Human Resources Development, Department of Higher Education
Minister: Shri Kapil Sibal
Shastri Bhavan
New Delhi 110001
Fax: +91(11) 2338 1355
WWW: http://education.nic.in/secondary.htm
Role of national body: The Department of Higher Education is in charge of laying down of National Policy on Education, and overseeing its implementation.

University Grants Commission - UGC
Chairman: Ved Prakash
Secretary: Vibha Puri Das
Bahadur Shah Zafar Marg
New Delhi 110 002
Tel: +91(11) 2323 2701
Fax: +91(11) 2323 1797
EMail: webmaster@ugc.ac.in
WWW: http://www.ugc.ac.in/
Role of national body: Responsible for providing funds and for the coordination, determination and maintenance of standards in institutions of higher education.

National Assessment and Accreditation Council - NAAC
Director: Hassan Annegowda Ranganath
P. O. Box No. 1075, Nagarbhavi
Bangalore, Karnataka 560072

Tel: +91(80) 2321 0261
Fax: +91 080 2321 0270
EMail: naac@blr.vsnl.net.in
WWW: http://www.naac.gov.in/
Role of national body: Autonomous institution established by the University Grant Commission to assess and accredit higher education institutions.

Association of Indian Universities - AIU

President: Pankaj Chande
Secretary General: Arun Diwakar Nath Bajpai
16, Comd. Indrajit Gupta Marg
(Kotla Marg)
New Delhi 110002
Tel: +91(11) 2323 6105
Fax: +91(11) 2323 2131
EMail: info@aiuweb.org;administration@aiuweb.org
WWW: http://www.aiuweb.org
Role of national body: Coordinates the work of the universities; establishes equivalences of degrees; acts as a bureau of information; conducts research on university development.

Data for academic year: 2006-2007
Source: IAU from Department of Higher Education and University Grants Commission websites, 2007 (Bodies, 2011)

INSTITUTIONS

ACHARYA N.G. RANGA AGRICULTURAL UNIVERSITY (ANGRAU)

Administration Office, Angrau, Rajendranagar, Hyderabad, Andhra Pradesh 500030
Tel: +91(40) 2401-5011
Fax: +91(40) 2401-5031
EMail: angrau@ap.nic.in
Website: http://www.angrau.net

Vice-Chancellor: Sri. V. Nagi Reddy
EMail: angrau_vc@yahoo.com

Registrar: L. Jalapathi Rao

Colleges

Agricultural Polytechnic *(Palerm; Jagtial; Maruteru; Anakapalle; Podalakur; Reddipalle; Utukuru; Rudrur; Garikapadu; Kampasagar; Madakasira)* (Agriculture; Animal Husbandry)

Faculties

Agricultural Engineering *(Bapatla; Madkasira)* (Agricultural Engineering; Food Technology; Soil Science; Water Management; Water Science); **Agriculture** (Agriculture; Biotechnology; Fishery; Food Science; Food Technology; Horticulture; Veterinary Science); **Home Science** *(Saifabad)* (Home Economics)

History: Founded 1964.

Governing Bodies: Board of Management, comprising 21 members

Academic Year: June to May (June-December; January-May)

Admission Requirements: 12th year senior secondary/intermediate examination or recognized foreign equivalent

Main Language(s) of Instruction: English

Accrediting Agencies: Indian Council of Agricultural Accreditation, New Delhi

Degrees and Diplomas: *Diploma*; *Bachelor's Degree*; *Master's Degree*; *Doctorate (PhD)*

Student Services: Canteen, Cultural centre, Health services, Language programs, Sports facilities

Libraries: Central Library, 4 branch and 7 College Libraries, total, 200,000 vols, 600 periodical subscriptions and 400 theses; also computer and Internet facilities

Publications: Agriculture Almanac, Crop Production Practices in Andhra Pradesh *(annually)*; Angrau News Letter (English and Telugu) *(monthly)*; Journal of Research; Research Highlights, Research in Agriculture, Home Science and Livestock *(annually)*
Last Updated: 08/04/11

ACHARYA NAGARJUNA UNIVERSITY

Acharya Nagarjuna Vishwavidhyalayamu
Nagarjuna Nagar, Andhra Pradesh 522510
Tel: +91(863) 229-3189
Fax: +91(863) 229-3378
EMail: nu_vc@yahoo.co.in
Website: http://www.nagarjunauniversity.ac.in

Vice-Chancellor: Y. R. Haragopal Reddy (2008-)
Tel: +91(863) 229-3238, Fax: +91 (863) 229-3378

Registrar: M.V. Narasimha Sarma
Tel: +91(863) 229-3269, Fax: +91(863) 229-3320
EMail: registrar@nagarjunauniversity.ac.in

Centres

Aquaculture and Research Education (Aquaculture; Educational Research) *Head*: Viveka Vardhani; **Biotechnology** (Biotechnology) *Head*: K.R.S. Sambasiva Rao; **Disaster Management** (Safety Engineering) *Head*: K. Balachandrudu; **Mahayana Buddhist Studies** (Asian Religious Studies) *Head*: J. Sitaramamma; **Science Instrumentation** (Instrument Making; Science Education) *Head*: B.S.V. Goud; **Scientific Socialism** *Head*: C. Narasimha Rao; **Women's Studies** (Women's Studies) *Head*: T. Satyavathi

Colleges

Adult Education (Literacy Education) *Head*: P. Syama; **ANU College of Architecture & Planning** *Division Head*: G. Babu Rao;

Computer Science and Engineering (Computer Science) *Head*: I. Ramesh Babu; **Engineering** *Division Head*: Y.V. Reddy; **Engineering** *Division Head*: I.Ramesh Babu

Faculties

Commerce (Business and Commerce) *Dean*: G.N. Brahmanandam; **Education** (Education) *Head*: Y. Kishore; **Engineering** (Engineering) *Dean*: I. Ramesh Babu; **Humanities** *Head*: R. Saraswathi; **Law** (Law) *Dean*: Y.P. Rama Subbaiah; **Natural Sciences** (Aquaculture; Biotechnology; Botany; Environmental Studies; Geology; Microbiology; Zoology) *Dean*: K.S. Tilak; **Physical Sciences** (Chemistry; Electronic Engineering; Mathematics; Physics; Statistics) *Dean*: P.V.V. Satyanarayana; **Social Sciences** (Development Studies; Economics; Labour and Industrial Relations; Library Science; Mass Communication; Political Sciences; Public Administration; Rural Studies; Social Work; Sociology) *Dean*: C.S.N. Raju

Further Information: Also 478 Affiliated Colleges

History: Founded 1976. Also P.G. Centres at Nuzvid and Ongole.

Governing Bodies: Executive Council; Academic Senate; Planning Board

Academic Year: July to April (July-November; January-April)

Admission Requirements: 12th year senior secondary/intermediate examination or recognized foreign equivalent for undergraduate courses. 3 years Bachelor's Degree for admission to Postgraduate courses

Fees: 6,000-50,000 per annum

Main Language(s) of Instruction: English

Accrediting Agencies: National Assessment and Accreditation Council, Bangalore

Degrees and Diplomas: *Diploma*: 1 yr; *Bachelor's Degree*: 3-4 yrs; *Master's Degree*: a further 1-3 yrs; *Doctorate (PhD)*: a further 2-3 yrs

Student Services: Academic counselling, Canteen, Cultural centre, Health services, Sports facilities

Student Residential Facilities: Separated Hostels for Boys, Girls and Scholars

Special Facilities: History and Archaeology Museum; Botanical Garden; Research Laboratory; Bank; Post Office; DTP Services

Libraries: c. 1.18,000 vols; 350 periodical subscriptions

Academic Staff 2009-2010	MEN	WOMEN	TOTAL
FULL-TIME	129	29	158
STAFF WITH DOCTORATE			
FULL-TIME	–	–	158
PART-TIME	–	–	40
Student Numbers 2009-2010			
All (Foreign Included)	1,675	1,021	2,696
FOREIGN ONLY	30,497	36,299	66,796

Distance students, 66,796.
Last Updated: 13/05/11

ADIKAVI NANNAYA UNIVERSITY

25-07-9/1, Jayakrishnapuram, Rajahmundry,
Andhra Pradesh 533 105
Tel: +91-883-2472617,
Fax: +91-883-2472615
EMail: registrar_aknu@rediffmail.com
Website: http://www.nannayauniversity.info

Vice-Chancellor: Allam Apparao

Registrar: N. Bhargavaram

Departments

Computer Science (Computer Science); **Mathematics** (Mathematics)

Schools

Chemical Sciences (Chemistry); **Cultural Studies and Communication** (Communication Studies; Cultural Studies); **Earth and Atmospheric Science** (Earth Sciences; Meteorology); **Life and Health Sciences** (Biological and Life Sciences; Health Sciences); **Management Studies** (Management); **Mathematics and Information Sciences** (Information Sciences; Mathematics)

History: Founded 2006.

Degrees and Diplomas: *Master's Degree*

Student Services: Health services, Sports facilities

Student Residential Facilities: Yes

Libraries: Yes
Last Updated: 21/07/11

A. D. PATEL INSTITUTE OF TECHNOLOGY (ADIT)

New Vallabh Vidyanagar, Post Box No - 52, Dist. Anand,
Vitthal Udyognagar, Gujarat 388 121
Tel: +91(2692) 233-680
Fax: +91(2692) 238-180
EMail: principal@adit.ac.in
Website: http://www.adit.ac.in/

Principal: R. K. Jain

Departments

Automobile Engineering (Automotive Engineering; Energy Engineering); **Civil Engineering** (Civil Engineering); **Computer Engineering** (Computer Engineering; Software Engineering); **Electrical Engineering** (Automation and Control Engineering; Computer Engineering; Electrical Engineering; Electronic Engineering; Information Technology; Telecommunications Engineering); **Electronics and Communication Engineering** (Computer Engineering; Computer Networks; Electronic Engineering; Microwaves; Power Engineering; Telecommunications Engineering); **Food Processing Technology** (Engineering; Food Technology); **Information Technology** (Computer Science; Information Technology); **Mathematics** (Mathematics); **Mechanical Engineering** (Design; Industrial Engineering; Mechanical Engineering; Thermal Engineering)

Accrediting Agencies: National Board of Accreditation (NBA); All India Council for Technical Education (AICTE)

Degrees and Diplomas: *Bachelor's degree (professional)*

Libraries: 21,325 vols; 175 national and international periodical subscriptions
Last Updated: 23/01/12

AHMEDABAD UNIVERSITY

AES Bungalow # 2, Navrangpura, Ahmedabad, Gujarat 380009
Tel: +91(79) 4004-4161
Fax: +91(79) 2656-0359
EMail: info@ahduni.edu.in
Website: http://www.ahduni.edu.in/

President: Sanjay Lalbhai

Chairman: Prafull Anubhai

Provost: Amarlal H. Kalro

Schools

Computer Studies (Computer Engineering; Software Engineering); **Management** *(Amrut Mody)* (Business Administration; Business and Commerce; Management)

History: Founded 2009.

Degrees and Diplomas: *Bachelor's Degree*; *Postgraduate Diploma*; *Master's Degree*; *Doctorate*. Also Certificate Programs
Last Updated: 18/10/11

ALAGAPPA UNIVERSITY

Alagappa Nagar, Karaikudi, Tamil Nadu 630 003
Tel: +91(4565) 228-080
Fax: +91(4565) 225-202
EMail: alagappauniversity@gmail.com
Website: http://www.alagappauniversity.ac.in/

Vice-Chancellor: S. Sudalaimuthu

Registrar: K. Manimekalai
EMail: registraralagappauniv@gmail.com

Centres

Computer; **Gandhian Studies** (History); **Nehru Studies** (Political Sciences; Social Sciences); **Rural Development** (Agriculture)

Faculties

Arts (English; Indic Languages; Women's Studies); **Education** (Education; Physical Education); **Management** (Banking; Business and Commerce; International Business; International Economics; Management; Secretarial Studies); **Science** (Bioengineering; Biotechnology; Coastal Studies; Computer Engineering; Computer Science; Engineering; Industrial Chemistry; Information Sciences; Library Science; Marine Science and Oceanography; Mathematics; Nanotechnology; Physics; Veterinary Science)

Further Information: Also 2 Constituent Colleges

History: Founded 1985. A postgraduate Institution of the unitary type.

Governing Bodies: Senate; Syndicate; Standing Committee on Academic Affairs

Academic Year: July to April (July-December; January-April)

Admission Requirements: Minimum requirement for admission to postgraduate courses

Main Language(s) of Instruction: English

Accrediting Agencies: University Grants Commission

Degrees and Diplomas: *Diploma*: 2 yrs; *Postgraduate Diploma*: 1 yr; *Master's Degree*: 1-3 yrs; *Master of Philosophy*: 1 yr; *Doctorate (PhD)*: at least 3 yrs

Student Residential Facilities: Yes

Libraries: Central Library 51,500 vols; 211 periodical subscriptions

Publications: Monographs; Research Papers
Last Updated: 08/04/11

ALIAH UNIVERSITY

21, Haji Md. Mohsin Square, Kolkata, West Bengal 700016
Tel: +91(33) 2706-2124
EMail: infodesk@aliah.ac.in
Website: http://www.aliah.ac.in

Vice-Chancellor: Syed Samsul Alam
Tel: +91(33) 2706-2269 EMail: vcau@aliah.ac.in

Registrar: Anwar Hussain Dafadar EMail: registrar@aliah.ac.in

Departments

Commerce and Business (Business and Commerce; Finance; Insurance); **Engineering** (Civil Engineering; Computer Engineering; Electrical Engineering; Electronic Engineering; Mechanical Engineering; Telecommunications Engineering; Vocational Education); **Humanities and Social Sciences** (Arts and Humanities; Economics; Education; Islamic Studies; Journalism; Mass Communication; Media Studies; Social Sciences); **Languages** (Arabic; English; Indic Languages); **Management Sciences** (Finance; Management; Retailing and Wholesaling); **Medical Sciences** (Nursing); **Natural Sciences** (Biological and Life Sciences; Chemistry; Computer Science; Geography; Mathematics; Natural Sciences; Physics; Statistics); **Theology** (Islamic Law; Islamic Theology)

History: Founded 2007.

Degrees and Diplomas: *Bachelor's Degree*; *Master's Degree*

Libraries: Yes
Last Updated: 05/01/12

ALIGARH MUSLIM UNIVERSITY

Aligarh, Uttar Pradesh 202002
Tel: +91(571) 270-0220
Fax: +91(571) 270-0087
EMail: vcamu@amu.ac.in; vcamu@sancharnet.in
Website: http://www.amu.ac.in

Vice-Chancellor: P.K. Abdul Azis

Registrar: V.K. Abdul Jaleel

Centres

Advanced Studies in History (History); **Brain Research** (Neurology); **Cardiology and Vascular Research** (Cardiology); **Career Planning** *(Women's College)*; **Coaching and Guidance** (Educational and Student Counselling); **Comparative Study of Indian Languages and Culture** (Cultural Studies; Indic Languages; South Asian Studies); **Computer Science** (Computer Science); **Continuing and Adult Education and Extension**; **Diabetes and Endocrinology** (Diabetology; Endocrinology); **Distance Education**; **General Education** (Education); **Interdisciplinary Development Studies** (Development Studies); **Koranic Studies** *(Prof. K.A. Nizami Centre)* (Koran); **Professional Courses**; **Promotion of Educational and Cultural Advancement of Muslims of India**; **Promotion of Science**; **Telematics Centre** (Electronic Engineering); **Theoretical Physics** (Physics); **Women's Studies** (Social Sciences; Women's Studies)

Faculties

Agricultural Sciences (Agricultural Business; Agricultural Economics; Agriculture; Harvest Technology; Home Economics; Microbiology; Plant and Crop Protection) *Dean*: P.Q. Rizvi; **Arts** (Arabic; English; Fine Arts; Hindi; Indic Languages; Linguistics; Persian; Philosophy; Sanskrit; Urdu) *Dean*: Maria Bilquis; **Commerce** (Business and Commerce) *Dean*: Ziauddin Khairoowala; **Engineering and Technology** *(Zakir Hussain College)* (Applied Chemistry; Applied Mathematics; Applied Physics; Architecture; Chemical Engineering; Civil Engineering; Computer Engineering; Electrical Engineering; Electronic Engineering; Engineering; Mechanical Engineering; Petroleum and Gas Engineering; Technology) *Dean*: Mohammad Shabbir; **Law** (Law) *Dean*: Iqbal Ali Khan; **Life Sciences** (Biochemistry; Biological and Life Sciences; Botany; Museum Studies; Wildlife; Zoology) *Dean*: Asif Ali Khan; **Management Studies and Research** (Management) *Dean*: Jawaid Akhtar; **Medicine** *(Jawahar Lal Nehru Medical College)* (Anaesthesiology; Anatomy; Biochemistry; Community Health; Dentistry; Dermatology; Forensic Medicine and Dentistry; Gynaecology and Obstetrics; Medicine; Microbiology; Ophthalmology; Orthodontics; Orthopaedics; Otorhinolaryngology; Paediatrics; Pathology; Periodontics; Pharmacology; Physiology; Plastic Surgery; Psychiatry and Mental Health; Radiology; Surgery) *Dean*: S. Abrar Hasan; **Science** (Chemistry; Computer Science; Geology; Mathematics; Natural Sciences; Operations Research; Physics; Statistics) *Dean*: Mohd. Zubair Khan; **Social Sciences** (Economics; Education; History; Information Sciences; Islamic Studies; Library Science; Mass Communication; Political Sciences; Psychology; Social Sciences; Social Work; Sociology; Sports) *Dean*: C.P.S. Chauhan; **Theology** (Theology) *Dean*: M.Saud Alam Qasmi; **Unani Medicine** (Alternative Medicine) *Dean*: Tajuddin

History: Founded 1920.

Governing Bodies: Court; Executive Council; Academic Council

Academic Year: July to May

Admission Requirements: Senior Secondary School Certificate or Intermediate or equivalent.

Fees: (Rupees): 15-500 per month, Tuition fee is charged except for Faculty of Theology.

Main Language(s) of Instruction: English

Degrees and Diplomas: *Bachelor's Degree*: Architecture; Law (BA/LLB), 5 yrs; *Bachelor's Degree*: Arts and Social Sciences (BA); Commerce (BCom); Muslim Theology (BTh); Science; Life Sciences; Home Sciences (BSc), 3 yrs; *Bachelor's Degree*: Education; Library Science; *Bachelor's Degree*: Engineering, 4 yrs; *Master's Degree*: a further 1-3 yrs; *Doctorate (PhD)*: 2 yrs

Student Residential Facilities: Yes

Special Facilities: Art Gallery. Biological Garden

Libraries: University Library (collection of books, bound journals and other non-book materials), total, 1,124,631 vols

Press or Publishing House: A.M.U. Press
Last Updated: 13/05/11

ALL INDIA INSTITUTE OF MEDICAL SCIENCES (AIIMS)

Ansari Nagar, New Delhi 110029
Tel: +91(11) 2658-8851
Fax: +91(11) 2658-8663
EMail: director@aiims.ac.in
Website: http://www.aiims.edu

Director: Ramesh Deka Tel: +91(11) 2685-7639

Registrar: Ved Prakash Gupta
Tel: +91(11) 2696-4796 EMail: reg@aiims.ac.in

International Relations: Shakti Gupta Tel: +91(11) 2685-1929

Centres
Cardiothoracic (Cardiology) *Head*: P. Venugopal; **Community Medicine** (Community Health) *Head*: V.P. Reddaiah; **Dental Education and Research** (Dentistry); **Drug Dependence Treatment** (Psychiatry and Mental Health; Toxicology); **Neurosciences** (Neurosciences) *Head*: V.S. Mehta; **Ophthalmic Sciences** (Ophthalmology) *Head*: H.K. Tewari; **Trauma Specialty Centers** *(Jai Prakash Narayan Apex)* (Anaesthesiology; Forensic Medicine and Dentistry; Laboratory Techniques; Medicine; Neurology; Orthopaedics; Radiology; Surgery)

Colleges
Nursing (Nursing) *Principal*: Manju Vatsa

Departments
Medecine (Anaesthesiology; Anatomy; Biochemistry; Biomedical Engineering; Biophysics; Biotechnology; Dermatology; Endocrinology; Gastroenterology; Gynaecology and Obstetrics; Haematology; Health Administration; Medicine; Microbiology; Nephrology; Nutrition; Orthopaedics; Osteopathy; Paediatrics; Pathology; Pharmacology; Physiology; Psychiatry and Mental Health; Rehabilitation and Therapy; Surgery; Urology; Venereology)

Institutes
Rotary-Cancer Hospital (Oncology)

Further Information: Also Oncology Teaching Hospital and Institute Rotary Cancer Hospital

History: Founded 1956 as an autonomous Institution of national importance, awarding degrees recognized by the Medical Council of India.

Academic Year: July to June

Admission Requirements: 12th year senior secondary/intermediate examination

Main Language(s) of Instruction: English

International Co-operation: With universities in Nepal, Russian Federation and Afghanistan

Degrees and Diplomas: *Bachelor's Degree*: Medicine; Surgery (BMBS), 5 1/2 yrs; *Master's Degree*: Surgery, 3 yrs; *Doctorate*: Medicine; Surgery (PhD), 3 yrs

Libraries: 129,793 vols
Last Updated: 16/05/11

ALLIANCE UNIVERSITY
Chikkahagade Cross, Chandapura - Anekal Main Road, Bangalore, Karnataka 562106
Tel: +91(80) 3093-8000/1
Fax: +91(80) 2784-1600
EMail: enquiry@alliance.edu.in
Website: http://www.alliance.edu.in/

Vice Chancellor: D. Ayyappa

Colleges
Arts and the Humanities (Arts and Humanities); **Commerce** (Business and Commerce); **Education and Human Services** (Education); **Engineering and Design** (Design; Engineering); **Law and International Affairs** (International Business; International Law; Law); **Media and Communications** (Communication Studies; Media Studies); **Medicine and Dentistry** (Dentistry; Medicine); **Science** (Natural Sciences)

Schools
Business (Business Administration); **Health Professions and Studies** (Health Sciences)

History: Founded 1996 as Alliance Business Academy (ABA). Acquired present status and title 2010.

Degrees and Diplomas: *Bachelor's Degree*; *Master's Degree*; *Doctorate*
Last Updated: 27/12/11

AMET UNIVERSITY
135, East Coast Road, Kanathur, Tamil Nadu 603112
Tel: +91(44) 274-72155
EMail: amet@vsnl.com
Website: http://www.ametuniv.ac.in

Vice-Chancellor: S. Bhardwaj

Faculties
Applied Marine I.T. (Information Technology); **Harbour and Off-shore Technology** (Marine Engineering); **Management Studies** (Management); **Marine Electrical and Electronic Engineering** (Marine Science and Oceanography); **Marine Engineering** (Marine Engineering); **Marine Life Sciences** (Biological and Life Sciences; Marine Biology; Marine Science and Oceanography); **Nautical Sciences**; **Naval Architecture and Offshore Engineering** (Naval Architecture)

History: Founded 1993 as Academy of Marine Education and Training. Acquired present status 2007.

Degrees and Diplomas: *Diploma*; *Bachelor's Degree*; *Master's Degree*

Student Residential Facilities: Yes
Last Updated: 16/05/11

AMITY UNIVERSITY, HARYANA
Amity Education Valley, Gurgaon, Haryana 122413
Tel: +91(124) 233-7015
EMail: info@ggn.amity.edu
Website: http://www.amity.edu/gurgaon/

Programmes
Architecture (Architecture); **Biotechnology** (Biotechnology); **Commerce** (Business and Commerce); **Communication** (Communication Studies; Graphic Arts; Visual Arts); **Computer Science/Information Technology** (Computer Science; Information Technology); **Economics** (Economics); **Engineering** (Aeronautical and Aerospace Engineering; Automation and Control Engineering; Civil Engineering; Computer Engineering; Computer Science; Electronic Engineering; Mechanical Engineering; Telecommunications Engineering); **English literature** (English; Literature); **Fashion** (Fashion Design); **Fine Arts** (Fine Arts); **Liberal Arts**; **Management** (Business Administration; Management); **Medicine** (Medicine); **Nursing** (Nursing); **Pharmacy** (Pharmacy); **Physical Education** (Physical Education)

History: Founded 2010.

Degrees and Diplomas: *Bachelor's Degree*; *Master's Degree*
Last Updated: 27/12/11

AMITY UNIVERSITY, MADHYA PRADESH
Maharajpura, Gwalior, Madhya Pradesh 474005
Tel: +91(751) 3290-666
EMail: info@gwa.amity.edu
Website: http://www.amity.edu/gwalior/

Programmes
Biotechnology (Biotechnology); **Commerce** (Business and Commerce); **Communication** (Communication Studies); **Computer Science/ Information Technology** (Computer Engineering; Computer Science; Information Technology); **Engineering** (Engineering); **Fashion** (Fashion Design); **Management** (Management)

Degrees and Diplomas: *Bachelor's Degree*; *Master's Degree*
Last Updated: 03/01/12

AMITY UNIVERSITY, RAJASTHAN (AUR)
NH-11C, Kant Kalwar, Jaipur, Rajasthan 303002
Tel: +91(141) 237-2489
EMail: info@jpr.amity.edu
Website: http://www.amity.edu/jaipur/

Vice-Chancellor: Raj Singh

Programmes
Architecture (Architecture); **Biotechnology** (Bioengineering; Biotechnology; Microbiology); **Commerce** (Business and Commerce); **Communication** (Communication Studies; Journalism); **Computer Science and Information Technology** (Computer Science; Information Technology); **Economics** (Economics); **Engineering** (Automation and Control Engineering; Computer Engineering; Electronic Engineering; Engineering; Information Technology; Mechanical Engineering); **Fashion** (Fashion Design); **Fine Arts** (Fine Arts); **Hotel Management Hospitality** (Hotel and Restaurant; Hotel Management); **Law** (Law); **Liberal Arts** (Arts and Humanities); **Management** (International Relations; Management); **Nanotechnology** (Nanotechnology); **Performing Arts** (Music;

Performing Arts); **Physical Education** (Physical Education); **Psychology and Behavioural Science** (Behavioural Sciences; Psychology)

History: Founded 2008.

Degrees and Diplomas: *Bachelor's Degree*; *Master's Degree*

Student Services: Sports facilities

Student Residential Facilities: Yes

Special Facilities: Auditorium

Libraries: Yes

Last Updated: 16/12/11

AMITY UNIVERSITY, UTTAR PRADESH

Sector-125, Noida, Uttar Pradesh 201303
Tel: +91(120) 243-1845
Fax: +91(120) 243-1870
EMail: registrar@amity.edu
Website: http://www.amity.edu/

Vice-Chancellor: K. Jai Singh (2005-)
EMail: vcau@amityuniversity.ac.in

Registrar: Anil Singh Mathur Tel: +91(120) 243-1859

International Relations: R. K. Dhawan, Sr. Vice President
Tel: +91(120) 439-2570, Fax: +91(120) 439-2578
EMail: iad@amity.edu

Programmes

Anthropology; **Applied Sciences** (Applied Chemistry; Applied Mathematics; Applied Physics); **Architecture**; **Biotechnology** (Biotechnology; Medical Technology); **Commerce**; **Communication** (Journalism; Mass Communication); **Computer Science and Information Technology**; **Design** (Design); **Education** (Preschool Education; Primary Education); **Engineering** (Aeronautical and Aerospace Engineering; Automotive Engineering; Computer Science; Electronic Engineering; Engineering; Information Technology; Mechanical Engineering; Telecommunications Engineering); **Fashion**; **Finance** (Finance); **Fine Arts**; **Food Technology** (Food Technology); **Forensic Science**; **Hospitality** (Hotel Management); **Insurance and Actuarial Science** (Actuarial Science; Insurance); **Languages** (English; French; Spanish); **Law** (Commercial Law; International Law; Law); **Management** (Accountancy; Business Administration; Finance; International Business; Management; Marketing; Sales Techniques); **Microbial Sciences** (Microbiology); **Nanotechnology** (Nanotechnology); **NGO Management and Development Studies** (Administration; Development Studies); **Organic Agriculture** (Agriculture); **Performing Arts** (Dance; Music; Musical Instruments; Performing Arts; Singing); **Pharmacy** (Pharmacy); **Physical Education** (Physical Education); **Physiotherapy** (Physical Therapy); **Psychology and Behavioural Science** (Behavioural Sciences; Clinical Psychology; Industrial and Organizational Psychology; Psychology); **Rural and Urban Management** (Rural Studies; Urban Studies); **Social Work** (Social Work); **Telecommunications** (Telecommunications Engineering); **Travel and Tourism** (Tourism)

History: Created 1986.

Governing Bodies: University Council; Executive Council; Academic Council

Academic Year: July - June

Admission Requirements: Relevant Secondary School certificate with satisfactory pass marks; Interview; Essay

Fees: (Rupees): 21,500 - 237,000 per annum

Main Language(s) of Instruction: English

International Co-operation: With institutions in New Zealand, UK, USA

Accrediting Agencies: University Grants Commission (UGC), India

Degrees and Diplomas: *Diploma*: Elementary Teacher Education; Nursery Teacher Education, 1-2 yrs; *Bachelor's Degree*: Aerospace Engineering; Animation; Bioinformatics; Biotechnology; Computer Science & Engineering; Electronics & Communication Engineering; Electronics & Telecommunications; Elementary Education; Fine Arts; Food Technology; Information Technology; Mechanical & Automation Engineering; Medical Biotechnology; Pharmacy; Physiotherapy, 4 yrs; *Bachelor's Degree*: Anthropology; Applied Psychology; Biotechnology; Business Administration; Commerce;

Computer; Science; Dance; English; Fashion Design & Technology; Finance & Accounting; Financial & Investment Analysis; Forensic Sciences; French; Hotel Management; Information Technology; Interior Design; Journalism & Mass Communication; Marketing & Sales; Music; Physical Education; Social Work; Spanish; Tourism Administration, 3 yrs; *Bachelor's Degree*: Architecture; Law; Microbial Sciences, 5 yrs; *Postgraduate Diploma*: Clinical Data Management; Insurance Management; Microbial Sciences; NGO Management; Physical Education; Sports Psychology, 1 yr; *Master's Degree*: Actuarial Science; Advertising & Marketing; Management; Anthropology; Architecture; Bioinformatics; Biotechnology; Biotechnology Management; Business Administration; Chemistry; Computer Science & Technology; Development Studies; Education; English; Film & TV Production; Financial Control; Fine Arts; Forensic Sciences; Hospitality Management; Human Resources; Interior Design; Journalism & Mass Communication; Law; Management; Marketing; Mathematics; Microbial Sciences; Nanotechnology; Network Technology & Management; Organic Agriculture & Food Business; Psychology & Behavioural Sciences; Physical Therapy; Physics; Public Relations & Event Management; Rural & Urban Management; Telecommunications; Tourism Administration, a further 1-2 yrs; *Doctorate*: Biotechnology; Business Administration; Forensic Sciences; Hospitality Management; Information Technology; Law; Microbial Sciences; Nanotechnology; Psychology, 2-3 yrs. Also: Integrated Master (4-5½ yrs) in: Biotechnology; Business Administration; Microbial Sciences; Nanotechnology; Psychology

Student Services: Academic counselling, Canteen, Cultural centre, Employment services, Foreign student adviser, Foreign Studies Centre, Handicapped facilities, Health services, Language programs, Nursery care, Social counselling, Sports facilities

Student Residential Facilities: For c. 5,000 students

Special Facilities: Art Gallery; Film Studio

Libraries: c. 91,200 vols.

Publications: Amity Business Review, Business research/review *(biannually)*; Amity Global Business Review, Business research/review *(annually)*; Amity Global HR Review, Business research/review *(annually)*; Amity Global Strategic Management Review, Business research/review *(annually)*; Amity Law Watch, Legal Journal *(annually)*; International Business Horizon, Business research/review (Electronic journal) *(monthly)*; International Business Review, Business research/review (Electronic journal) *(monthly)*

Press or Publishing House: Amity University Press

Academic Staff 2007-2008	MEN	WOMEN	TOTAL
FULL-TIME	398	479	877
PART-TIME	145	110	255
STAFF WITH DOCTORATE			
FULL-TIME	124	113	237
Student Numbers 2007-2008			
All (Foreign Included)	9,244	7,956	17,200

Distance students, 9,045.
Last Updated: 21/03/08

AMRITA UNIVERSITY

Amrita Vishwa Vidyapeetham
Ettimadai Post, Coimbatore, Tamil Nadu 641105
Tel: 91(422) 256-6422
Fax: 91(422) 256-6274
EMail: univhq@amrita.edu
Website: http://www.amrita.edu

Pro-Chancellor: Abhayamrita Chaitanya
Tel: 91(422) 265-6422, Fax: 91(422) 265-6274
EMail: coo@amrita.edu

International Relations: Jay Misra, Head of International Relations
Tel: 91(422) 265-6422, Fax: 91(422) 265-2221

Departments

Communication *(Coimbatore Campus)* (Communication Studies); **Social Work** *(Coimbatore and Amritapuri campuses)* (Social Work)

Schools

Arts and Science *(Mysore, Kochi and Amritapuri Campuses)* (Arts and Humanities; Biochemistry; Botany; Business and Commerce;

Chemistry; Computer Science; English; Fine Arts; Health Administration; Management; Mathematics; Media Studies; Microbiology; Natural Sciences; Physics; **Ayurveda** *(Amritapuri Campus)* (Ayurveda); **Biotechnology** *(Amritapuri Campus)* (Biotechnology; Medical Technology; Microbiology); **Business** *(Coimbatore, Amritapuri and Kochi campuses)* (Business Administration; Business and Commerce); **Dentistry** *(Kochi Campus)* (Dentistry); **Education** *(Mysore Campus)* (Education); **Engineering** *(Amritapuri, Bangalore and Coimbatore campuses)* (Aeronautical and Aerospace Engineering; Automotive Engineering; Biomedical Engineering; Chemical Engineering; Civil Engineering; Computer Engineering; Computer Networks; Computer Science; Electrical and Electronic Engineering; Engineering; Engineering Drawing and Design; Materials Engineering; Mechanical Engineering); **Medicine** *(Kochi Campus)* (Medicine); **Nursing** *(Kochi Campus)* (Nursing); **Pharmacy** *(Kochi Campus)* (Pharmacy)

Further Information: Campuses in Amritapuri, Bangalore, Coimbatore, Kochi, Mysore.

History: Created 1994. Acquired university status 2003.

Governing Bodies: Board of Management; Academic Council

Admission Requirements: Secondary or High School certificate for undergraduate programmes; undergraduate degree for postgraduate programmes. (Consult institution for individual course requirements as these may vary).

Fees: Vary according to programmes of study

Main Language(s) of Instruction: English

International Co-operation: Nine exchange programmes (Erasmus Mundus) with nine European universities; collaborative initiative in higher education and research with 17 universities in the USA (Indo-US Collaborations)

Accrediting Agencies: National Assessment and Accreditation Council (NAAC)/UGC, India

Degrees and Diplomas: *Bachelor's Degree*: Arts and Sciences; Biotechnology; Communication, 3 yrs; *Bachelor's Degree*: Ayurveda; Dentistry; Medicine; Nursing, 4 1/2 yrs plus 1 yr internship; *Bachelor's Degree*: Education, 1 yr; *Bachelor's Degree*: Engineering; Pharmacy, 4 yrs; *Postgraduate Diploma*: Communication; Medicine, 1 yr; *Master's Degree*: Arts and Sciences, 2-3 yrs; *Master's Degree*: Biotechnology; Communication; Engineering; Management; Nano Medical Sciences; Nursing; Pharmacy; Social Work, 2 yrs; *Master's Degree*: Medicine, 3 yrs; *Doctorate*: Arts and Sciences; Biotechnology; Engineering; Management; Medicine, 3 yrs

Student Services: Academic counselling, Canteen, Cultural centre, Employment services, Foreign student adviser, Foreign Studies Centre, Handicapped facilities, Health services, Language programs, Nursery care, Social counselling, Sports facilities

Student Residential Facilities: 21 men's and 16 women's hostels.

Special Facilities: Observatory, museum, film studio.

Libraries: Total, 164,936 vols; E-books, 3,500, Subscriptions to periodicals: national, 1,112, international, 5,715; magazines, 268; E-journals, 8,271

Publications: Amrita Journal of Medicine *(monthly)*; Diabeat, Journal of diabetic research *(quarterly)*; Journal of the Indian Society of Toxicology *(monthly)*

Press or Publishing House: M.A. Mission Trust, Amritapuri, Kollam, Kerala

Academic Staff *2009-2010*	MEN	WOMEN	TOTAL
FULL-TIME	811	686	1,497
PART-TIME	53	14	67
STAFF WITH DOCTORATE			
FULL-TIME	156	53	209
PART-TIME	16	3	19
Student Numbers *2009-2010*			
All (Foreign Included)	7,282	6,638	13,920
FOREIGN ONLY	12	21	33

Part-time students, 14.
Last Updated: 17/05/11

ANAND AGRICULTURAL UNIVERSITY

Anand, Gujarat
Tel: +91 (2692) 225-800

Vice-Chancellor: A.M. Shekh
Tel: +91(2692) 261-273, Fax: +91(2692) 261-520
EMail: vc@aau.in

Registrar: P.R. Vaishnav
Tel: +91(2692) 261-310 EMail: registrar@aau.in

Faculties
Agricultural Engineering and Technology (Agricultural Engineering; Technology); **Agricultural Information Technology** (Agricultural Engineering; Information Technology); **Agriculture** (Agricultural Economics; Agriculture; Agronomy; Horticulture; Plant and Crop Protection; Plant Pathology; Soil Science); **Dairy Science** (Dairy), **Food Processing Technology and Bio-Energy** (Food Science; Food Technology); **Post Graduate**; **Veterinary Science and Animal Husbandry** (Animal Husbandry; Epidemiology; Parasitology; Veterinary Science)

History: Founded 2004.

Degrees and Diplomas: *Bachelor's Degree*; *Postgraduate Diploma*
Last Updated: 01/08/11

ANDHRA PRADESH UNIVERSITY OF LAW

Palace Layout, Pedawaltair, Visakhapatnam,
Andhra Pradesh 530017
Tel: +91(891) 252-9952
Fax: +91(891) 304-0170
Website: http://www.apulvisakha.org

Vice-Chancellor: Y. Satyanarayana
Registrar: Amancherla Subrahmanyam

Programmes
Law (Law)

Further Information: Also branches at Kadapa and Nizamabad
History: Founded 2008.

Degrees and Diplomas: *Bachelor's Degree*; *Postgraduate Diploma*; *Doctorate*
Last Updated: 16/05/11

ANDHRA UNIVERSITY

Waltair, Visakhapatnam, Andhra Pradesh 530003
Tel: +91(891) 275-5324
Fax: +91(891) 275-5547
EMail: vicechancellor@andhrauniversity.info
Website: http://www.andhrauniversity.info

Vice-Chancellor: Beela Satyanarayana (2008-)
Registrar: Prasad Reddy EMail: prof.prasadreddy@gmail.com

Centres
Postgraduate *(Kakinada)*; **Postgraduate** *(Srikakulam)*; **Science and Instrumentation** (Instrument Making; Natural Sciences)

Colleges
Arts and Commerce (Adult Education; Anthropology; Archaeology; Arts and Humanities; Business and Commerce; Distance Education; Economics; Education; English; Fine Arts; History; Indic Languages; Information Sciences; Journalism; Labour and Industrial Relations; Library Science; Linguistics; Management; Mass Communication; Modern Languages; Philosophy; Political Sciences; Public Administration; Sanskrit; Social Work; Sociology; Special Education; Theatre; Urdu; Yoga); **Engineering** *(Autonomous)* (Chemical Engineering; Civil Engineering; Computer Engineering; Electrical Engineering; Electronic Engineering; Engineering; Marine Engineering; Mechanical Engineering; Metallurgical Engineering; Social Sciences; Systems Analysis; Telecommunications Engineering); **Law** (Law); **Pharmacy**; **Science and Technology** (Analytical Chemistry; Anthropology; Applied Mathematics; Biochemistry; Botany; Environmental Studies; Genetics; Geography; Geology; Geophysics; Inorganic Chemistry; Instrument Making; Marine Biology; Marine Science and Oceanography; Mathematics; Meteorology; Natural Sciences; Nuclear Physics; Organic Chemistry; Pharmacy; Physics; Statistics; Zoology)

Further Information: Also campuses in Kakinada, Vizianagaram, and Tadepalligudem
History: Founded 1926.

Academic Year: July to June.

Admission Requirements: Entrance examination.

Main Language(s) of Instruction: English

Degrees and Diplomas: *Bachelor's Degree*: 1-3 yrs; *Master's Degree*: a further 1-2 yrs; *Doctorate (PhD)*: a further 2-3 yrs

Student Residential Facilities: Yes

Libraries: c. 414,285 vols; 480 periodical subscriptions

Press or Publishing House: Andhra University Press and Publications

Last Updated: 17/05/11

ANNA UNIVERSITY

Sardar Patel Road, Guindy, Chennai, Tamil Nadu 600025
Tel: +91(44) 2235-2161
Fax: +91(44) 2235-0397
EMail: registrar@annauniv.edu
Website: http://www.annauniv.edu/

Vice-Chancellor: P. Mannar Jawahar (2008-)
EMail: vc@annauniv.edu

Deputy Registrar: Thiru.K. Gopinathan

Centres
Biotechnology (Biotechnology); **Building Technology** (Building Technologies); **Computer Science** (Computer Science); **Computer Science** *(Ramajuan)* (Computer Science); **Crystal Growth** (Crystallography); **Curriculum Development**; **Environmental Studies** (Environmental Studies); **Human Settlements** (Social Studies); **New and Renewable Sources of Energy** (Natural Resources); **Water Resources** (Water Management)

Colleges
Engineering *(Guindy)* (Arts and Humanities; Chemistry; Civil Engineering; Electrical and Electronic Engineering; Engineering; Geology; Geophysics; Management; Mathematics; Mechanical Engineering; Mining Engineering; Physics; Printing and Printmaking; Social Sciences; Telecommunications Engineering); **Technology** *(Alagappa, Guindy)*

Faculties
Architecture and Planning (Architecture and Planning); **Civil Engineering** (Civil Engineering); **Electrical and Electronics Engineering** (Electrical Engineering; Electronic Engineering; Power Engineering); **Information and Communication Engineering** (Information Technology; Telecommunications Engineering); **Management Sciences** (Management); **Mechanical Engineering** (Mechanical Engineering); **Science and Humanities** (Arts and Humanities; Geology; Media Studies; Natural Sciences; Social Sciences); **Technology** (Biotechnology; Ceramics and Glass Technology; Chemical Engineering; Polymer and Plastics Technology; Technology; Textile Technology)

Institutes
Ocean Management (Marine Science and Oceanography); **Remote Sensing** (Surveying and Mapping); **Technology** *(Madras, Chromepet)* (Aeronautical and Aerospace Engineering; Automotive Engineering; Electronic Engineering; Instrument Making; Production Engineering; Rubber Technology; Technology)

History: Founded as Perarignar Anna University of Technology 1978, acquired present title 1982.

Governing Bodies: Syndicate, comprising 15 members; Academic Council, comprising 105 members

Academic Year: July to April (July-October; December-April)

Admission Requirements: 12th year senior secondary/intermediate examination or recognized foreign equivalent, and entrance examination.

Main Language(s) of Instruction: English

Degrees and Diplomas: *Diploma*; *Bachelor's Degree*: 3-4 yrs; *Master's Degree*: a further 1-3 yrs; *Doctorate (PhD)*: a further 3 yrs

Student Services: Sports facilities

Student Residential Facilities: For c. 2,000 students

Special Facilities: Auditorium

Libraries: Total, c. 190,750 vols and 407 periodicals
Last Updated: 17/05/11

ANNA UNIVERSITY OF TECHNOLOGY CHENNAI

CPT Campus, Tharamani, Chennai, Tamilnadu 600113
EMail: registrar@annatech.ac.in
Website: http://www.annatech.ac.in

Vice-Chancellor: C. Thangaraj
Tel: +91(442) 254-1777 EMail: vc@annatech.ac.in

Registrar: S. Gowri

Departments
Civil Engineering (Civil Engineering; Construction Engineering); **Computer Science and Engineering** (Architecture); **Management Studies** (Business Administration; Management)

History: Founded 2007.

Degrees and Diplomas: *Master's Degree*; *Doctorate*
Last Updated: 08/12/11

ANNA UNIVERSITY OF TECHNOLOGY COIMBATORE

Academic Campus, Jothipuram, Coimbatore, Tamilnadu 641 047
Tel: +91(422) 654-5566
Fax: +91(422) 269-4400
EMail: registrar@annauniv.ac.in
Website: http://www.autcbe.ac.in/

Vice-Chancellor: K. Karunakaran

Registrar: S. Premchand

Centres
Biotechnology

Departments
Civil Engineering (Civil Engineering; Computer Engineering; Engineering; Materials Engineering; Mechanical Engineering; Mineralogy; Printing and Printmaking); **Computer Applications** (Computer Engineering; Software Engineering); **Computer Science and Engineering** (Computer Engineering; Computer Science); **Electrical and Electronics Engineering** (Electrical and Electronic Engineering); **Information Technology** (Information Technology); **Mechanical Engineering** (Mechanical Engineering); **Science and Humanities** (Arts and Humanities; Natural Sciences)

Schools
Management Studies (Management)

Further Information: Also distance education

History: Founded 2006.

Degrees and Diplomas: *Bachelor's Degree*; *Master's Degree*
Last Updated: 07/12/11

ANNA UNIVERSITY OF TECHNOLOGY MADURAI

Alagar Koil Road, Madurai, Tamilnadu 625 002
Tel: +91(452) 252-0111
Fax: +91(452) 255-5577
EMail: info@autmdu.ac.in
Website: http://autmdu.ac.in/

Vice-Chancellor: R. Murugesan
Tel: +91(452) 255-5554 EMail: vc@autmdu.ac.in

Registrar: E.B. Perumal Pillai EMail: registrar@autmdu.ac.in

Programmes
Architecture (Architecture); **Business Administration** (Business Administration); **Engineering** (Aeronautical and Aerospace Engineering; Biomedical Engineering; Biotechnology; Chemical Engineering; Civil Engineering; Computer Science; Construction Engineering; Electrical and Electronic Engineering; Heating and Refrigeration; Industrial Design; Marine Engineering; Mechanical Engineering; Power Engineering; Software Engineering; Telecommunications Engineering; Textile Technology)

Further Information: Also university Campuses located at Ramanathapuram, Dindigul and Distance Education

History: Founded 2010.

Degrees and Diplomas: *Bachelor's Degree*; *Master's Degree*
Last Updated: 06/12/11

ANNA UNIVERSITY OF TECHNOLOGY TIRUCHIRAPPALLI

Tiruchirappalli, Tamilnadu 620024
Website: http://www.tau.edu.in/

Vice-Chancellor: Devadas Manoharan
Tel: +91(431) 240-7095 EMail: vc@tau.edu.in

Registrar: J. Raja
Tel: +91(431) 240-7946 EMail: registrar@tau.edu.in

Departments

Biotechnology (Biotechnology); **Chemistry** (Chemistry); **Civil Engineering** (Civil Engineering); **Computer Application** (Computer Engineering); **Computer Science and Engineering** (Computer Engineering; Computer Science); **Electrical and Electronics Engineering** (Electrical and Electronic Engineering); **Electronics and Communication Engineering** (Electronic Engineering; Telecommunications Engineering); **English** (English); **Management** (Management); **Mathematics**; **Mechanical Engineering** (Mechanical Engineering); **Petrochemical Technology** (Petroleum and Gas Engineering); **Pharmaceutical Technology** (Pharmacy); **Physics** (Physics)

History: Foounded 2006.

Degrees and Diplomas: *Bachelor's Degree*; *Master's Degree*; *Doctorate*
Last Updated: 06/12/11

ANNA UNIVERSITY OF TECHNOLOGY TIRUNELVELI

Tirunelveli, 627007
Tel: +91(462) 255-4255
Fax: +91(462) 255-2877

Vice-Chancellor: M. Rajaram

Faculties

Civil Engineering (Civil Engineering); **Electrical Engineering** (Electrical and Electronic Engineering); **Information and Communication Engineering** (Information Technology; Telecommunications Engineering); **Management Sciences** (Human Resources; Marketing); **Mechanical Engineering** (Mechanical Engineering)

Further Information: Also 65 affiliated colleges and 2 University Colleges of Engineering, at Thoothukudi and Nagercoil

History: Founded 2006.

Degrees and Diplomas: *Bachelor's Degree*; *Master's Degree*

Academic Staff *2010-2011*: Total: c. 170
Student Numbers *2010-2011*: Total: c. 900
Last Updated: 08/12/11

ANNAMALAI UNIVERSITY

Annamalainagar, Tamil Nadu 608002
Tel: +91(4144) 238-248
Fax: +91(4144) 238-080
EMail: info@annamalaiuniversity.ac.in
Website: http://www.annamalaiuniversity.ac.in

Vice-Chancellor: M. Ramanathan
Tel: +91(4144) 238-283 EMail: vc_lbv@hotmail.com

Registrar: M. Rathinasabapathi
Tel: +91(4144) 238-259, Fax: +91(4144) 238-080
EMail: aumrsl@hotmail.com

Faculties

Agriculture (Agricultural Economics; Agriculture; Agronomy; Entomology; Horticulture; Microbiology; Plant Pathology; Soil Science) *Dean*: P. Baskaran; **Arts** (Arts and Humanities; Business Administration; Business and Commerce; Demography and Population; Economics; English; History; Information Sciences; Library Science; Philosophy; Political Sciences; Rural Studies; Sociology) *Dean*: A. Subbian; **Dentistry** (Dentistry) *Dean*: C.R. Ramachandran; **Distance Education** *Director*: S.B. Nageswara Rao; **Education** (Adult Education; Education; Educational Psychology; Physical Education; Sports) *Dean*: K. Vaithianathan; **Engineering and Technology**

(Chemical Engineering; Civil Engineering; Computer Science; Electrical Engineering; Engineering; Environmental Engineering; Mechanical Engineering; Pharmacy; Technology) *Dean*: B. Palaniappan; **Fine Arts** (Fine Arts; Music) *Dean*: O.S. Thiagarajan; **Indian Languages** (Indic Languages) *Dean*: S. Natanasabapathy; **Medicine** (Medicine; Nursing) *Dean*: P.V. Hayavadhana Rao; **Science** (Biochemistry; Biotechnology; Botany; Chemistry; Earth Sciences; Mathematics; Natural Sciences; Physics; Statistics; Zoology) *Dean*: A.R. Meenkshi

Further Information: Also 2 Teaching Hospitals

History: Founded 1929. A Unitary teaching University with no Affiliated Colleges, and with all Faculties on a single campus.

Governing Bodies: Senate; Syndicate; Academic Council

Academic Year: July to April (July-November; January-April)

Admission Requirements: 12th year senior secondary/intermediate examination or recognized foreign equivalent

Main Language(s) of Instruction: English, Tamil

International Co-operation: With institutions in France, Denmark, Australia, Japan, Cambodia, USA

Accrediting Agencies: National Assessment and Accreditation Council; National Board of Accreditation, ICAR, MCI

Degrees and Diplomas: *Bachelor's Degree*: 3-4 1/2 yrs; *Master's Degree*: a further 2 yrs; *Doctorate*: PhD, a further 3 yrs

Student Services: Academic counselling, Canteen, Cultural centre, Employment services, Foreign student adviser, Handicapped facilities, Health services, Language programs, Nursery care, Social counselling, Sports facilities

Student Residential Facilities: Yes

Special Facilities: Botanical Garden. Mass Media Centre. Theatre

Libraries: c. 466,585 vols

Publications: University Journal *(annually)*

Press or Publishing House: Annamalai University Publication Division.
Last Updated: 18/05/11

APEEJAY SCHOOL OF MANAGEMENT (ASM)

Sector VIII, Institutional Area, Dwarka, Gujarat 110 077
Tel: +91(11) 2536-3979 +91(11) 2536-3980
Fax: +91(11) 2536-3985
EMail: asm.dwk.del@apeejay.edu
Website: http://apeejay.edu/

Director: Alok Saklani

Programmes

International Business (International Business); **Management** (Accountancy; Advertising and Publicity; Finance; Human Resources; Information Technology; Management; Marketing; Media Studies; Public Relations)

History: Founded 1993.

Governing Bodies: Board of Governors

Accrediting Agencies: All India Council for Technical Education (AICTE); Ministry of Human Resource Development

Degrees and Diplomas: *Postgraduate Diploma*

Student Services: Canteen

Student Residential Facilities: Separate boys and girls hostels

Special Facilities: 4 computer labs; Lecture Rooms; Auditorium

Libraries: Yes
Last Updated: 23/01/12

APEEJAY STYA UNIVERSITY

Palwal Road, Sohna, Gurgaon, Haryana 122103
Website: http://university.apeejay.edu

Vice-Chancellor: Kamal Kant Dwivedi

Schools

Bio-Sciences and Pharmaceutical Sciences (Biological and Life Sciences; Pharmacy); **Computational Sciences** (Computer Science); **Education** (Education); **Engineering and Technology** (Electrical and Electronic Engineering; Electronic Engineering;

Engineering; Mechanical Engineering; Technology); **Journalism and Mass Communication** (Journalism; Mass Communication); **Management Sciences** (Business Administration; Management); **Visual Arts and Design**

History: Founded 2010.

Degrees and Diplomas: *Bachelor's Degree*; *Master's Degree*; *Doctorate*

Last Updated: 27/12/11

ARNI UNIVERSITY

Kathgarh, Distt Kangra, Himachal Pardesh
Tel: +91(11) 434-000-00
Fax: +91(11) 434-000-34
EMail: info@arni.in
Website: http://arni.in

Vice-Chancellor: R. Bhardwaj

Schools

Arts and Commerce and Humanities (Arts and Humanities; Business and Commerce; Economics; English; Public Administration); **Basic Sciences** (Biology; Biotechnology; Chemistry; Physics); **Business Management** (Business Administration); **Computer Science** (Computer Engineering; Computer Science); **Hospitality Management** (Cooking and Catering; Hotel Management); **Polytechnic** (Civil Engineering; Computer Engineering; Electrical Engineering; Mechanical Engineering); **Technology** (Biotechnology; Civil Engineering; Computer Engineering; Computer Science; Electrical and Electronic Engineering; Mechanical Engineering)

Degrees and Diplomas: *Bachelor's Degree*; *Master's Degree*; *Doctorate*

Student Services: Academic counselling, Sports facilities

Student Residential Facilities: Yes

Libraries: Yes
Last Updated: 27/12/11

ASSAM AGRICULTURAL UNIVERSITY

Jorhat, Assam 785013
Tel: +91(376) 234-0008
Fax: +91(376) 234-0001
Website: http://www.aau.ac.in

Vice-Chancellor: K. M. Bujarbaruah

Registrar: Krishna Gohain

Faculties

Agriculture (Agriculture; Fishery); **Home Science** (Home Economics); **Veterinary Science** (Veterinary Science)

History: Founded 1969.

Governing Bodies: Board of Management; Academic Council

Academic Year: July to June (July/August-November/December; January/February-May/June)

Admission Requirements: 12th year senior secondary/intermediate examination or recognized foreign equivalent

Main Language(s) of Instruction: English

Accrediting Agencies: ICAR

Degrees and Diplomas: *Bachelor's Degree*: 4-5 yrs; *Master's Degree*: a further 2 yrs; *Doctorate (PhD)*: at least 3 yrs

Student Residential Facilities: Yes

Special Facilities: Observatory

Libraries: 97,879 vols; 156 periodical subscriptions

Publications: AAU Bulletin, Agriculture, Veterinary and Home Science; Ghare Pathare
Last Updated: 18/05/11

ASSAM DON BOSCO UNIVERSITY (ADBU)

Airport Road - Azara, Gunawati, Assam 781017
Tel: +91(361) 213-9291 +91(361) 213-9292
Fax: +61(361) 284-1949
EMail: contact@dbuniversity.ac.in; vicechancellor@dbuniversity.ac.in
Website: http://www.dbuniversity.ac.in

Rector and Vice-Chancellor: Stephen Mavely (2009-2013)
EMail: mavely@dbuniversity.ac.in; mavely@hotmail.com

Pro-Vice Chancellor: Joseph Nellanat EMail: nellanatt@gmail.com

International Relations: Cyriac Vettickathadam, Controller of Examinations
EMail: cyriac@dbunibersity.ac.in; cyriacva@yahoo.co.in

Centres

Distance Education; **Social Sciences** *(Paltan Bazaar)* (Child Care and Development; Social Work)

Schools

Applied Sciences *(DBCET)* (Chemistry; Physics); **Commerce and Management** *(DBIM, Kharguli)* (Business and Commerce; Management); **Health Sciences** (Health Sciences; Nursing; Paramedical Sciences; Pharmacy); **Religion and Culture** (Asian Studies; Christian Religious Studies; Cultural Studies; Ethics; Religion; Social Studies); **Social Sciences** *(DBCET)* (Social Work); **Technology** (Biotechnology; Civil Engineering; Computer Science; Electrical and Electronic Engineering; Electronic Engineering; Information Technology; Mechanical Engineering; Technology; Telecommunications Engineering)

Further Information: Also Global online programmes (DBU Global Centre for Online & Distance Education): www.dbuglobal.com and two constituent Colleges (Engineering Technology and Management)

History: Founded 2008.

Academic Year: July to June

Admission Requirements: For B. Tech: Higher Secondary School Leaving Certificate Examination (or equivalent) with at least 50% in the aggregate, 50% in the aggregate of Physics, Chemistry and Mathematics and 45% separately in Physics, Chemistry and Mathematics. Entrance examination - AIEEE (All India) or CE (Assam) or DBU-GET (ADBU)

Fees: (Rupiah): 20,000-50,000 per semester depending on programmes. PhD: 20,000 per annum (for Humanities); Rs 25,000 (for Science and Technology)

Main Language(s) of Instruction: English

International Co-operation: With local universities and with universities in the USA, Spain, Switzerland, Ireland, United Kigndom, and France

Accrediting Agencies: National Accreditation and Assessment Council (NAAC)

Degrees and Diplomas: *Diploma*: Child Rights (DCRD), 1 yrs; *Bachelor's Degree*: Engineering (B.Tech); *Postgraduate Diploma*; *Master's Degree*: Management (MBA), 6 semesters; *Master's Degree*: Social Sciences, Engineering (M.Tech; MSW), 4 semesters; *Doctorate*: Sciences, Engineering, Humanities and Social Sciences, North East Studies, Social Sciences (PhD), 2-5 yrs. Also Certificate and Diploma Course

Student Services: Academic counselling, Canteen, Cultural centre, Employment services, Handicapped facilities, Health services, Language programs, Social counselling, Sports facilities

Student Residential Facilities: For 300 for men students, 200 women. 24 apartments for staffs

Special Facilities: Computer Labs; Conference Halls; Ampitheatre; Auditorium; Museum; Chapel

Libraries: c. 11,193 vols; 41 periodical subscriptions; Access to IEL Online through the AICTE-INDEST consortium, and Electronic Journal of Management Research

Publications: Kultura, Related to the cultures of North East India *(quarterly)*

Academic Staff 2011-2012	MEN	WOMEN	TOTAL
FULL-TIME	–	–	68
PART-TIME	–	–	4
STAFF WITH DOCTORATE			
FULL-TIME	–	–	7
PART-TIME	–	–	2
Student Numbers 2011-2012			
All (Foreign Included)	740	378	1,118

Distance students, 195.
Last Updated: 27/10/11

ASSAM UNIVERSITY

Assam University Post Office, Silchar, Assam 788011
Tel: +91(3842) 270-806
Fax: +91(3842) 270-806
EMail: vc@aus.ac.in
Website: http://www.aus.ac.in/

Vice-Chancellor: Tapodhir Bhattacharjee
Tel: +91(3842) 270-801, Fax: +91(3842) 270-802

Registrar: Debabrata Deb Tel: +91(3842) 270-368

Schools

Creative Arts and Communication Studies *(Abanindranath Tagore)* (Mass Communication; Visual Arts); **Earth Sciences** *(Aryabhatta)* (Earth Sciences); **Economics and Commerce** *(Mahatma Gandhi)* (Business and Commerce; Economics); **Education** *(Ashutosh Mukhopadhyay)* (Education); **English and Foreign Language Studies** *(Suniti Kumar Chattopadhyay)* (Arabic; English; Foreign Languages Education; French); **Environmental Sciences** *(E. P Odam)* (Ecology; Environmental Studies); **Indian Languages and Cultural Studies** *(Rabindranath Tagore)* (Arabic; Cultural Studies; English; Hindi; Linguistics; Modern Languages; Sanskrit); **Legal Studies** *(Deshabandhu Chittaranjan)* (Law); **Library Sciences** *(Swami Vivekananda)* (Information Sciences; Library Science); **Life Sciences** *(Hargobind Khurana)* (Biological and Life Sciences; Biotechnology; Microbiology); **Management Studies** *(Jawarharlal Nehru)* (Business Administration); **Medical and Paramedical Sciences** *(Susruta)* (Pharmacy); **Philosophy** *(Sarvepalli Radhakrishnan)* (Philosophy); **Physical Sciences** *(Albert Einstein)* (Chemistry; Computer Science; Mathematics; Physics); **Social Sciences** *(Jadunath Sarkar)* (History; Political Sciences; Social Sciences; Social Work; Sociology); **Technology** *(Triguna Sen)* (Agricultural Engineering; Electronic Engineering; Information Technology; Technology; Telecommunications Engineering)

Further Information: Also campuses in Silchar and Diphu

History: Founded 1994.

Governing Bodies: Executive Council; Academic Council

Academic Year: July to July (July-December; January-July)

Admission Requirements: 12th standard senior secondary/intermediate examination or recognized foreign equivalent. Selection is on a competitive basis

Main Language(s) of Instruction: English

Accrediting Agencies: National Assessment and Accreditation Council (NAAC)

Degrees and Diplomas: *Bachelor's Degree*: Arts (BA); Commerce (Bcom); Computer Science; Fine Arts (BFA); Law (LLB); Science (BSc); Social Work (BSW), 3 yrs; *Bachelor's Degree*: Education (Bed), 1 yr following frist degree; *Bachelor's Degree*: Medicine and Surgery (MBBS), 4 1/2 yrs; *Master's Degree*: Arts and Humanities (MA); Commerce (Mcom); Mass Communication (MMC); Science (MSc); Social Work (MSW), a further 2 yrs; *Master's Degree*: Fine Arts (MFA), a further 2 yrs; *Master of Philosophy*: 1 1/2 yrs; *Master of Philosophy*: Biotechnology; Business Administration (MBA); Computer Science, a further 2 yrs; *Doctorate (PhD)*: 4 yrs

Student Services: Academic counselling, Canteen, Health services, Sports facilities

Special Facilities: Botanical Garden

Libraries: Central Library, 60,552 vols; 244 periodical subscriptions

Publications: University Journal *(annually)*; University Newsletter *(biannually)*

Last Updated: 18/05/11

ATAL BIRAHI VAJPAYEE - INDIAN INSTITUTE OF INFORMATION TECHNOLOGY AND MANAGEMENT (IIITM)

Morena Link Road, Gwalior, Madhya Pradesh 474010
Tel: +91(751) 246-0315 +91(751) 244-9704
Fax: +91(751) 244-9813
Website: http://www.iiitm.ac.in

Director: S. G. Deshmukh
Tel: +91(751) 244-9702 EMail: director@iiitm.ac.in

Registrar: Deleep Kumar Tel: +91(751) 243-8408

Programmes

Business Administration (Business Administration; Management); **Information Technology** (Computer Engineering; Information Technology; Software Engineering)

History: Founded 2001.

Degrees and Diplomas: *Postgraduate Diploma*; *Master's Degree*; *Doctorate*

Last Updated: 18/05/11

AVINASHILINGAM DEEMED UNIVERSITY FOR WOMEN

Mettupalayam Road, Coimbatore, Tamil Nadu 641043
Tel: +91(422) 244-0241
Fax: +91(422) 243-8786
EMail: pro@avinuty.ac.in; info_adu@avinuty.ac.in
Website: http://www.avinashilingam.edu

Vice-Chancellor: Sheela Ramachandran EMail: vc@avinuty.ac.in

Registrar: Gowri Ramakrishnan EMail: registrar@avinuty.ac.in

Faculties

Business Administration (Business Administration; Business and Commerce; Business Computing; Tourism); **Community Education and Entrepreneurship Development** (Communication Arts; Communication Studies; Information Technology; Medical Auxiliaries; Multimedia); **Education** (Education; Physical Education; Special Education); **Engineering** (Civil Engineering; Computer Engineering; Electrical Engineering; Electronic Engineering; Engineering; Telecommunications Engineering); **Home Science** (Clothing and Sewing; Food Science; Home Economics; Nutrition; Textile Design); **Humanities** (Economics; English; French; Hindi; Music; Psychology; South and Southeast Asian Languages); **Science** (Biochemistry; Biotechnology; Botany; Chemistry; Computer Science; Mathematics; Physics; Zoology)

History: Founded 1957 as Sri Avinashilingam Home Science College for Women. Also known as Avinashilingam Institute for Home Science and Higher Education for Women. Acquired present status as 'Deemed University' and title 1988.

Governing Bodies: Syndicate

Academic Year: July to April (July-November; December-April)

Admission Requirements: 12th year senior secondary/intermediate examination or recognized foreign equivalent

Fees: (Rupees): 490-3,000 per semester; Engineering, 39,000 per annum

Main Language(s) of Instruction: English

Accrediting Agencies: National Council of Assessment and Accreditation, Bangalore

Degrees and Diplomas: *Bachelor's Degree*: 3 - 4 yrs; *Postgraduate Diploma*; *Master's Degree*: 1-3 further yrs; *Master of Philosophy (MPhil)*: 1 yr following upon Master's Degree; *Doctorate*

Student Services: Academic counselling, Canteen, Cultural centre, Employment services, Foreign student adviser, Handicapped facilities, Health services, Language programs, Nursery care, Social counselling, Sports facilities

Student Residential Facilities: For 1,000 students

Special Facilities: Video Laboratory

Libraries: 125,120 vols

Publications: Indian Journal of Nutrition and Dietetics *(monthly)*; Journal of Research Highlights *(quarterly)*; Vignana Chudar (Science Digest in Tamil) *(monthly)*

Press or Publishing House: Saradalaya Press

Last Updated: 17/06/11

AWADHESH PRATAP SINGH UNIVERSITY

Awadhesh Pratap Singh Vishwavidyalaya
Rewa, Madhya Pradesh 486003
Tel: +91(7662) 230-050
Fax: +91(7662) 230-819
EMail: ccapsu@gmail.com
Website: http://apsurewa.nic.in/

Vice-Chancellor: Shivnarayan Yadav

Registrar: Magan Singh Awasya

Faculties

Arts (Arts and Humanities; Hindi; History); **Commerce and Management** (Business and Commerce; Management); **Education** (Education); **Home Science** (Home Economics); **Law** (Law); **Life Sciences** (Biological and Life Sciences); **Medicine** (Medicine); **Prachya Sanskrit** (Sanskrit); **Science** (Natural Sciences); **Social Sciences** (Social Sciences); **Technology** (Engineering)

Further Information: Also 83 Affiliated Colleges, 21 Prachya Sanskrit Colleges and Teaching Hospitals

History: Founded 1968.

Governing Bodies: Court; Executive Council; Academic Council

Academic Year: July to June (July-October-November; November-June)

Admission Requirements: 12th year senior secondary/intermediate examination or recognized foreign equivalent

Main Language(s) of Instruction: Hindi, English

Degrees and Diplomas: *Diploma*; *Bachelor's Degree*: 3-5 1/2 yrs; *Master's Degree*: 1-2 further yrs; *Doctorate (PhD)*: at least 2 yrs

Student Residential Facilities: Yes

Libraries: Central Library, c. 40,000; 220 periodical subscriptions

Publications: Annual Research Journal *(annually)*; Vindhya Bharati *(annually)*

Last Updated: 17/06/11

AYUSH AND HEALTH SCIENCE UNIVERSITY CHHATTISGARH

G. E. Roas, Raipur, Chhattisgarh 429001
Website: http://cghealthuniv.com/

Courses

Ayurved (Ayurveda); **Dentistry** (Dentistry); **Homeopathic**; **Medicine** (Medical Technology; Medicine; Radiology); **N ursing** (Nursing); **Physiotherapy** (Physical Therapy); **U nani Chikitsa**; **Yoga and Prakritic Chikitsa** (Yoga)

Degrees and Diplomas: *Bachelor's Degree*; *Master's Degree*; *Doctorate*

Last Updated: 28/07/11

AZIM PREMJI UNIVERSITY

Pixel Park, B Block, Electronics City, Hosur Road (Beside NICE Road), Bangalore, Karnataka 560100
Fax: +91(80) 6614-5145
EMail: info@azimpremjifoundation.org
Website: http://www.azimpremjiuniversity.edu.in/

Vice-Chancellor: Anurag Behar

Registrar: S. Giridhar

Programmes

Development Studies (Development Studies); **Education** (Education); **Teacher Education** (Teacher Trainers Education)

History: Founded 2010,

Degrees and Diplomas: *Master's Degree*

Last Updated: 27/12/11

BABA FARID UNIVERSITY OF HEALTH SCIENCES

Kotkapura Road, Faridkot, Punjab 151203
Tel: +91(1639) 256-232
Fax: +91(1639) 256-234
EMail: generalinfo@bfuhs.ac.in
Website: http://www.bfuhs.ac.in

Vice-Chancellor: S.S. Gill

Colleges

Ayurveda (Ayurveda) *Principal*: Dharam Pal Rajanwal; **Homeopathy** (Anatomy; Biochemistry; Forensic Medicine and Dentistry; Gynaecology and Obstetrics; Homeopathy; Medicine; Microbiology; Pathology; Philosophy; Physiology; Psychology) *Principal*: Ravinder Kochhar

Faculties

Dentistry (Anatomy; Biochemistry; Dental Hygiene; Dentistry; Medicine; Microbiology; Oral Pathology; Orthodontics; Periodontics; Physiology; Radiology; Surgery); **Homoeopathy** (Biochemistry; Haematology; Histology; Medical Technology; Microbiology; Pathology); **Medicine** (Anatomy; Biophysics; Cardiology; Dentistry; Dermatology; Gastroenterology; Gynaecology and Obstetrics; Medicine; Ophthalmology; Orthopaedics; Otorhinolaryngology; Paediatrics; Physiology; Plastic Surgery; Psychiatry and Mental Health; Radiology; Toxicology; Venereology); **Nursing** (Anatomy; Biochemistry; Community Health; Gynaecology and Obstetrics; Microbiology; Midwifery; Nursing; Nutrition; Physiology; Psychiatry and Mental Health; Psychology; Sociology; Surgery; Welfare and Protective Services); **Physiotherapy** (Physical Therapy)

History: Founded 1998.

Governing Bodies: Senate; Board of Management; Academic Council; Finance Committee; Planning Board; Faculties; Board of Studies

Academic Year: August to July (August-January, February-July)

Admission Requirements: 12th year senior secondary/intermediate examination or recognized foreign equivalent and entrance examination

Fees: (Rupees): 35,000-75,000 per annum

Main Language(s) of Instruction: English

Degrees and Diplomas: *Bachelor's Degree*: Ayurveda and Medical Surgery (BAMS); Homeopathy and Medical Surgery (BAMS); Medicine; Surgery (MBBS), 5 1/2 yrs; *Bachelor's Degree*: Dental Surgery (BDS), 5 yrs; *Bachelor's Degree*: Nursing (BSc), 4 yrs; *Bachelor's Degree*: Physiotherapy (BPT), 4 1/2 yrs; *Postgraduate Diploma*: Anaesthesia (DA); Child Health (DCH); Gynaecology and Obstetrics (DGO); Laryngology and Otorhinolaryngology (DLO); Medical Radiography Therapy (DMRT); Medical Radiology Diagnosis (DMRD); Ophtalmic Medicine and Surgery (DOMS); Sports Medicine, a further 2 yrs; *Master's Degree*: Medicine (DM, MCh); Nursing (MSc), a further 2 yrs; *Master's Degree*: Medicine; Homeopathy (MD); Surgery (MS), a further 3 yrs; *Doctorate (PhD)*: a further 3 yrs

Last Updated: 17/06/11

BABA GHULAM SHAH BADSHAH UNIVERSITY

Rajouri Camp Office, Bye Pass Road, Opp. Channi Himmat, Jammu, Jammu and Kashmir 185131
Tel: +91(1962) 241001
EMail: vc_bgsbu@rediffmail.com
Website: http://www.bgsbuniversity.org/admissions.htm

Vice-Chancellor: I. A. Hamal

Colleges

Engineering and Technology (Civil Engineering; Computer Networks; Electrical Engineering; Electronic Engineering; Energy Engineering; Engineering; Information Sciences; Technology; Telecommunications Engineering)

Schools

Biosciences and Biotechnology (Biological and Life Sciences; Biotechnology); **Healthcare and Pharmacy** (Health Sciences; Pharmacy); **Islamic Studies** (Arabic; Island Studies); **Management** (Business Administration; Finance; Management); **Material Sciences and Nanotechnology** (Materials Engineering; Nanotechnology); **Mathematical Sciences and Engineering** (Engineering; Mathematics)

History: Founded 2005.

Degrees and Diplomas: *Bachelor's Degree*; *Master's Degree*

Libraries: Yes

Last Updated: 14/11/11

BABASAHEB BHIMRAO AMBEDKAR BIHAR UNIVERSITY

Muzaffarpur, Bihar 842001
Tel: +91(621) 224-3071
Fax: +91(621) 224-2495
EMail: vcbrabu@yahoo.com
Website: http://www.brabu.net

Vice-Chancellor: Rajdeo Singh

Registrar: Mohd A.A. Khan

Faculties

Commerce (Business and Commerce) *Dean*: Ram Sagar Singh; **Education** (Education) *Dean*: R.P. Singh; **Engineering** (Engineering) *Dean*: D. Singh; **Homeopathy** *Dean*: B.N.S. Bharti; **Humanities** (Arts and Humanities) *Dean*: R.P. Srivastava; **Law** (Law); **Medicine** (Medicine) *Dean*: V.B. Srivastava; **Science** (Natural Sciences) *Dean*: P.N. Mukhopadhya

Further Information: Also 38 Affiliated Colleges

History: Founded 1952. Acquired present status 1960.

Academic Year: June to May

Admission Requirements: 12th year senior secondary/intermediate examination or recognized foreign equivalent

Fees: (Rupees): 120-240 per annum

Main Language(s) of Instruction: English, Hindi

Degrees and Diplomas: *Bachelor's Degree*; *Master's Degree*; *Doctorate (PhD)*

Libraries: c. 191.000 vols
Last Updated: 08/03/10

BABASAHEB BHIMRAO AMBEDKAR UNIVERSITY

Vidya Vihar, Rai Bareilly Road, Lucknow, Uttar Pradesh 226025
Tel: +91(522) 244-1515
Fax: +91(522) 244-0821
EMail: info@bbauindia.org
Website: http://www.bbauindia.org

Vice-Chancellor: B. Hanumaiah (2002-)
Tel: +91(522) 244-0820 EMail: vcbbaulucknow@yahoo.co.in

Registrar: P.Hanmaiya Naik
Tel: +91(522) 244-0822, Fax: +91(522) 244-1888

Schools

Ambedkar Studies (Economics; History; Political Sciences; Sociology); **Bio-Science and Bio-Technology** (Animal Husbandry; Biotechnology; Botany; Fruit Production; Horticulture; Pharmacology; Sericulture; Zoology); **Environmental Science** (Biological and Life Sciences; Biotechnology; Development Studies; Environmental Studies; Microbiology; Toxicology) *Dean*: M. Yunus; **Home Sciences** (Environmental Studies; Human Rights; Indigenous Studies; Political Sciences; Women's Studies) *Dean*: S.K. Bhatnagar; **Information Science and Technology** (Computer Science; Information Sciences; Information Technology; Library Science; Mass Communication); **Legal Studies** (Law); **Management** (Economics; Management) *Head*: N.M.P. Verma; **Physical Sciences** (Applied Chemistry; Applied Mathematics; Applied Physics)

History: Founded 1989, acquired present status and title 1996. A Central University.

Governing Bodies: Board of Management; Academic Council; Finance Committee; Planning Board

Academic Year: July to June

Admission Requirements: Bachelor Degree of the revelant course with minimum 50% (40% for SC/ST) marks and entrance examination

Main Language(s) of Instruction: English

Degrees and Diplomas: *Postgraduate Diploma*; *Master's Degree*: 2 yrs; *Master of Philosophy*: 1 1/2 yrs. Also Post-Doctoral Degrees

Student Services: Academic counselling, Canteen, Cultural centre, Employment services, Foreign student adviser, Foreign Studies Centre, Handicapped facilities, Health services, Language programs, Nursery care, Social counselling, Sports facilities

Student Residential Facilities: Student hostel

Libraries: University library

Student Numbers *2008-2009*: Total 226
Last Updated: 08/04/11

BABU BANARASI DAS UNIVERSITY

BBD City, Faizabad Road, Lucknow, Uttar Pradesh 227015
Tel: +91(522) 3911-000
Website: http://bbdu.org/

Vice-Chancellor: Arun Kumar Mittal

Colleges
Dentistry (Dentistry)

Faculties
Applied Sciences (Chemistry; Mathematics; Natural Sciences; Physics); **Hotel Management** (Hotel Management)

Schools
Architecture (Architecture); **Computer Applications** (Computer Engineering; Computer Science); **Engineering** (Civil Engineering; Electrical Engineering; Engineering; Mechanical Engineering); **Management** (Business Administration; Management); **Pharmacy** (Pharmacy)

History: Founded 2010.

Degrees and Diplomas: *Bachelor's Degree*; *Master's Degree*; *Doctorate*

Student Services: Health services, Sports facilities

Special Facilities: Auditorium, Computer Centre

Libraries: Yes
Last Updated: 02/01/12

BADDI UNIVERSITY OF EMERGING SCIENCES AND TECHNOLOGY

Makhnumajra, Baddi, Distt. Solan, Himachal Pradesh 173 205
Tel: +91(1795) 247353
Fax: +91(1795) 247352
Website: http://www.baddiuniv.ac.in

Vice-Rector: A.K. Saihjpal

Institutes
Engineering and Emerging Technologies (Chemistry; Civil Engineering; Computer Engineering; Computer Networks; Electrical and Electronic Engineering; Information Technology; Mathematics; Mechanical Engineering; Physics); **Management Studies** (Business Administration; Finance; Human Resources; Information Technology; Management; Marketing); **Mass Communication Studies** (Mass Communication); **Pharmacy and Emerging Sciences** (Pharmacy)

History: Founded 2009.

Degrees and Diplomas: *Bachelor's Degree*; *Master's Degree*; *Doctorate*

Student Residential Facilities: Yes

Libraries: Yes
Last Updated: 16/11/11

BAHRA UNIVERSITY

Waknaghat, Distt. Solan, Himachal Pradesh 160022
Tel: +91(981) 6014-412
Fax: +91(980) 5092-446
EMail: bahrauniversity@rayatbahra.com
Website: http://www.bahrauniversity.edu.in

Vice-Chancellor: R.K. Gupta

Registrar: C.R.B. Lalit

Schools
Basic Sciences (Chemistry; Mathematics; Natural Sciences; Physics); **Engineering and Technology** (Civil Engineering; Computer Engineering; Electronic Engineering; Engineering; Materials Engineering; Technology; Telecommunications Engineering); **Hospitality and Tourisme** (Tourism); **Management** (Business Administration; Management); **Pharmaceutical Sciences** (Pharmacy)

History: Founded 2011.

Degrees and Diplomas: *Bachelor's Degree*; *Master's Degree*; *Doctorate*
Last Updated: 16/01/12

BANARAS HINDU UNIVERSITY

Kashi Hindu Vishwavidyalaya

Varanasi, Uttar Pradesh 221005
Tel: +91(542) 236-8938
Fax: +91(542) 236-8174
EMail: vc_bhu@sify.com; vcbhu1@gmail.com
Website: http://www.bhu.ac.in

Vice-Chancellor: Lalji Singh (2011-)
Tel: +91(542) 236-8938, Fax: +91(542) 236-9951
EMail: vc_bhu@bhu.ac.in; vc_bhu@sify.com

Public Relations Officer: Viswanath Pandey
Tel: +91(542) 236-8598, Fax: +91(542) 236-8598

Registrar: Natarajan Sundaram

International Relations: Mallickarjun Joshi, Chairman
Tel: +91(542) 236-8130, Fax: +91(542) 236-8130
EMail: intlcellbhu@sify.com

Faculties

Agriculture (Agriculture) *Dean*: O.P. Srivastva; **Arts** (Ancient Civilizations; Arabic; Archaeology; Art History; Arts and Humanities; Asian Religious Studies; Chinese; Cultural Studies; English; French; German; Hindi; Indic Languages; Journalism; Library Science; Linguistics; Mass Communication; Modern Languages; Music; Musical Instruments; Painting and Drawing; Philosophy; Physical Education; Singing; Urdu) *Dean*: S.N. Mishra; **Ayurveda** (Ayurveda) *Dean*: J. Ojha; **Commerce** (Business and Commerce) *Dean*: M.N.A. Ansari; **Dental Sciences** (Dentistry); **Education** (Education) *Dean*: H.K. Singh; **Engineering and Technology** (Engineering; Technology) *Dean*: B.N. Roy; **Law** (Law) *Dean*: Nath Surendra; **Management** (Management) *Dean*: R.M. Srivastava; **Medicine** (Medicine) *Dean*: Gajendra Singh; **Performing Arts** (Performing Arts) *Dean*: C.R. Jyotishi; **Sanskrit Vidya Dharm Vigyan** (Sanskrit) *Dean*: N.R. Srinivasan; **Science** (Biochemistry; Chemistry; Geology; Geophysics; Natural Sciences) *Dean*: S.N. Lal; **Social Sciences** (Economics; History; Political Sciences; Social Sciences; Sociology) *Dean*: A.P. Singh; **Visual Arts** (Visual Arts) *Dean*: R.N. Mishra

Institutes

Agricultural Sciences (Agricultural Economics; Agriculture; Agronomy; Botany; Distance Education; Entomology; Horticulture; Plant Pathology; Soil Science; Zoology); **Environment and Sustainable Development** (Development Studies; Environmental Studies); **Medical Sciences** (Anaesthesiology; Anatomy; Ayurveda; Biochemistry; Biophysics; Dentistry; Dermatology; Forensic Medicine and Dentistry; Gynaecology and Obstetrics; Medicine; Microbiology; Ophthalmology; Orthopaedics; Otorhinolaryngology; Paediatrics; Pathology; Pharmacology; Physiology; Psychiatry and Mental Health; Radiology; Social and Preventive Medicine; Surgery; Venereology); **Technology** (Applied Chemistry; Applied Mathematics; Applied Physics; Biochemistry; Biomedical Engineering; Ceramics and Glass Technology; Civil Engineering; Computer Engineering; Electrical Engineering; Electronic Engineering; Materials Engineering; Mechanical Engineering; Metallurgical Engineering; Mining Engineering; Pharmacology; Technology)

Schools

Biotechnology (Biotechnology)

Further Information: Also affiliated schools and colleges, 4 Constituent Colleges. Teaching Hospital (Sir Sundeslal Hospital). Research centers and interdisciplinary schools

History: Founded 1915.

Governing Bodies: Court; Executive Council; Academic Council

Academic Year: July to May (July-October; November-December; January-May)

Admission Requirements: 12th year senior secondary/intermediate examination or recognized foreign equivalent

Fees: (Rupees): 120-260

Main Language(s) of Instruction: English, Hindi

Degrees and Diplomas: *Bachelor's Degree*: 3-5 1/2 yrs; *Master's Degree*: a further 2 yrs; *Doctorate (PhD)*: at least 2 yrs

Student Residential Facilities: Yes

Special Facilities: Museum: Bharat Kala Bhawan (collections of paintings, sculptures, terracottas, coins, textiles, etc. depicting ancient culture of India). Botanical Garden; Ayurvedic Garden and Agricultural Farms

Libraries: c. 893,000 vols

Publications: Journal of Research in Indian Systems of Medicine; Scientific Research Journal *(quarterly)*

Press or Publishing House: University Press

Student Numbers *2008-2009*: Total 18,158
Last Updated: 08/09/11

BANASTHALI UNIVERSITY

Banasthali Vidyapith

Banasthali, Rajasthan 304022
Tel: +91(1438) 228-341
Fax: +91(1438) 228-365
EMail: info@banasthali.ac.in
Website: http://www.banasthali.org

Director: Aditya Shastri (2008-2013)
EMail: saditya@banasthali.ac.in

Secretary: Chitra Purohit Tel: +91(1438) 228-324

International Relations: Aditya Shastri
Tel: +91(1458) 227-851, Fax: +91(1438) 227-849

Faculties

Computer Science (Computer Science; Electronic Engineering; Maintenance Technology; Mathematics); **Education** (Education; Educational and Student Counselling; Educational Research; Educational Technology; Psychology); **Fine Arts** (Dance; Fine Arts; Music; Textile Design; Theatre; Visual Arts); **Home Science** (Child Care and Development; Clothing and Sewing; Home Economics; Nutrition); **Humanities** (Arts and Humanities; English; Hindi; Modern Languages; Sanskrit); **Management** (Finance; Information Technology; Management; Marketing); **Science** (Biochemistry; Biomedicine; Biophysics; Biotechnology; Chemistry; Natural Sciences); **Social Sciences** (Economics; History; Political Sciences; Public Administration; Social Sciences; Sociology)

History: Founded 1935 as Shantabai Shiksha Kutir, acquired present title 1943, and became a 'Deemed University' Institution 1983.

Governing Bodies: Executive Council

Academic Year: July to April

Admission Requirements: 12th year senior secondary/intermediate examination or recognized foreign equivalent

Main Language(s) of Instruction: Hindi, English

Accrediting Agencies: National Assessment and Accreditation Council (NAAC)

Degrees and Diplomas: *Diploma*: 1 yr; *Bachelor's Degree*: 3-4 yrs; *Postgraduate Diploma*: 1-2 yrs; *Master's Degree*: 2-3 yrs

Student Services: Academic counselling, Canteen, Cultural centre, Employment services, Foreign student adviser, Foreign Studies Centre, Handicapped facilities, Health services, Language programs, Nursery care, Social counselling, Sports facilities

Student Residential Facilities: For 7,000 students

Special Facilities: Art Gallery. Biological Garden. Movie Studio

Libraries: 243,000 vols; 850 periodical subscriptions

Academic Staff *2008*	MEN	WOMEN	TOTAL
FULL-TIME	103	214	**317**
STAFF WITH DOCTORATE			
FULL-TIME	31	59	**90**

Student Numbers *2008*			
All (Foreign Included)	–	6,991	**6,991**
FOREIGN ONLY	–	5	**5**

Last Updated: 20/06/11

BANGALORE UNIVERSITY

Jnana Bharathi Campus, Bangalore, Karnataka 560056
Tel: +91(80) 2321-3172
Fax: +91(80) 2321-9295

Vice-Chancellor: A.N Prabhu Deva

Registrar: Sanjay Veer Singh
Tel: +91(80) 2321-3023, Fax: +91(80) 2321-1020
EMail: buregistrar@vsnl.in

International Relations: H.M. Revanasiddaiah, Director, Student's Welfare Tel: +91(80) 2296-1096

Colleges

Engineering (Civil Engineering; Computer Engineering; Electrical Engineering; Electronic Engineering; Information Sciences; Information Technology; Mechanical Engineering; Structural Architecture; Telecommunications Engineering) *Principal:* N. Govindaraj; **Law** (Law) *Dean and Principal:* K.M. Hanumantharayappa; **Physical Education** *Principal:* Keerthi Narayanaswamy

Faculties

Arts (Dance; Development Studies; Economics; English; French; German; Hindi; Indic Languages; Italian; Japanese; Music; Performing Arts; Philosophy; Political Sciences; Psychology; Rural Studies; Social Work; Sociology; South and Southeast Asian Languages; Spanish; Theatre; Urdu; Visual Arts; Women's Studies) *Dean:* S. Chandrashekar; **Commerce and Management** (Accountancy; Administration; Business Administration; Finance; Health Administration; International Business; Management; Tourism) *Dean:* B.C. Sanjeevaiah; **Education** (Education) *Dean:* M.S. Talawar; **Science** (Biotechnology; Botany; Chemistry; Computer Engineering; Electronic Engineering; Environmental Studies; Geology; Information Sciences; Library Science; Mathematics; Media Studies; Microbiology; Physics; Sericulture; Statistics; Zoology) *Dean:* H.T. Rathod

Further Information: Also 387 Affiliated Colleges. Study Abroad Programme with North Essex Community College, Massachusetts

History: Founded 1964. Acquired present status 1976.

Governing Bodies: Senate; Syndicate; Academic Council

Academic Year: July to April (July-November; December-April)

Admission Requirements: 12th year senior secondary/intermediate examination or recognized foreign equivalent

Fees: (Rupees): 150 to 3,000

Main Language(s) of Instruction: English, Kannada

International Co-operation: With universities in USA; United Kingdom; France; China; Japan; Kyrghyzstan; Nepal

Accrediting Agencies: National Assessment and Accreditation Council

Degrees and Diplomas: *Diploma:* Arts, 1 yr; *Bachelor's Degree:* Arts; Science, 3 yrs; *Postgraduate Diploma:* Arts, 1-2 yrs; *Postgraduate Diploma:* Science, 1 yr; *Master's Degree:* a further 2 yrs; *Doctorate (PhD):* 4 yrs

Student Services: Academic counselling, Canteen, Cultural centre, Employment services, Health services, Language programs, Nursery care, Social counselling, Sports facilities

Student Residential Facilities: Yes

Libraries: Yes

Publications: Janapriya Vignana (Kannada) *(monthly)*; Sadane (Kannada) *(quarterly)*; Vidya Bharathi (English) *(biannually)*; Vignana Bharathi (English) *(biannually)*

Press or Publishing House: Bangalore University Press

BARKATULLAH UNIVERSITY

Barkatullah Vishwavidyalaya

Hoshangabad Road, Bhopal, Madhya Pradesh 462026
Tel: +91(755) 258-7257
Fax: +91(755) 267-7703
EMail: buvc_office@yahoo.com
Website: http://www.bubhopal.nic.in

Vice-Chancellor: Nisha Dube

Registrar: Sanjay Prakesh Tiwari
Tel: +91(755) 249-1706+91(755) 249-1701
EMail: buregistrar@yahoo.co.in

Faculties

Arts (Arabic; Arts and Humanities; Cultural Studies; Persian) *Dean:* Mohammad Hassan Khan; **Commerce** (Business and Commerce); **Education** (Consumer Studies; Education; Physical Education; Yoga); **Engineering** (Engineering; Information Technology; Materials Engineering; Pharmacy; Technology); **Law** (Law); **Life Sciences** (Aquaculture; Biological and Life Sciences; Biotechnology; Environmental Studies; Genetics; Limnology; Microbiology; Zoology); **Natural Sciences** (Natural Sciences; Physics) *Dean:* R.K.

Pandey; **Science** (Computer Science; Electronic Engineering; Geology; Home Economics; Physics); **Social Sciences** (Economics; Political Sciences; Psychology; Social Sciences; Social Work; Sociology)

Institutes

Distance Education *Director:* K.K. Rao

Further Information: Also 16 Affiliated Colleges

History: Founded 1970 as Bhopal University, acquired present title 1988.

Governing Bodies: Executive Council

Academic Year: July to June

Admission Requirements: Higher Secondary Certificate or equivalent.

Main Language(s) of Instruction: Hindi and English

Accrediting Agencies: University Grants Commission

Degrees and Diplomas: *Bachelor's Degree:* Fine Arts; Health Sciences; Law; Arts; Mathematics and Computer Science; Commerce; Science; Social Sciences; Humanities; Management; English; Pharmacy; Mass Communication; Photography; Microbiology, 3 yrs; *Postgraduate Diploma; Master's Degree:* Fine Arts; Arts; Commerce; Science; Social Sciences; Humanities; Management; English; Natural Sciences; Public Administration; Medicine; Library Science; Sports; Photography, 2 yrs; *Master of Philosophy; Doctorate*

Student Services: Academic counselling, Canteen, Cultural centre, Employment services, Foreign student adviser, Handicapped facilities, Health services, Language programs, Social counselling, Sports facilities

Student Residential Facilities: Yes

Libraries: 75,915 vols.; 495 periodical subscriptions

Press or Publishing House: University Press B.U. Bhopal
Last Updated: 20/06/11

BASTAR VISHWAVIDYALAYA

Dharampura-II, Jagdalpur, Chhattisgarh 494005
Tel: +91(77) 8223-9039
EMail: info@bvvjdp.ac.in
Website: http://bvvjdp.ac.in/

Vice-Chancellor: Jaylaxmi Thakur EMail: vc@bvvjdp.ac.in

Registrar: J.K. Jain EMail: registrar@bvvjdp.ac.in

Schools

Biotechnology (Biotechnology); **Computer Application** (Computer Engineering); **Forest and Wild Life** (Forestry; Wildlife); **Rural Technology and Management** (Rural Planning); **Science and Social Studies** (Anthropology; Social Sciences; Social Work)

History: Founded 2008

Degrees and Diplomas: *Diploma; Postgraduate Diploma; Master's Degree*
Last Updated: 28/07/11

BENGAL ENGINEERING AND SCIENCE UNIVERSITY, SHIBPUR (BESU)

PO Botanic Garden, Howrah, West Bengal 711103
Tel: +91(33) 2668-4561 +91(33) 2668-4563
Fax: +91(33) 2668-2916
EMail: vc@becs.ac.in
Website: http://www.becs.ac.in

Vice-Chancellor: Ajoy Kumar Ray

Registrar: Biman Bondopadhyay EMail: regis@becs.ac.in

Departments

Applied Mechanics and Drawing (Mechanical Engineering; Painting and Drawing); **Architecture** (Architecture; Regional Planning; Town Planning); **Chemistry** (Chemistry); **Civil Engineering** (Civil Engineering); **Computer Science and Technology** (Computer Science; Technology); **Electrical Engineering** (Electrical Engineering); **Electronics and Telecommunication** (Electronic Engineering; Telecommunications Engineering); **Geology** (Geology); **Human Resource Management** (Human Resources; Management); **Humanities and Social Sciences** (Arts and Humanities;

Social Sciences); **Information Technology** (Information Technology); **Mathematics** (Mathematics); **Mechanical Engineering** (Mechanical Engineering); **Metallurgy and Materials Engineering** (Materials Engineering; Metallurgical Engineering); **Mining Engineering** (Mining Engineering); **Physics** (Physics)

History: Founded 1856. Acquired present status and title 2004.

Degrees and Diplomas: *Bachelor's Degree (BE)*; *Master's Degree (MTech, ME)*; *Doctorate (PhD)*. Also DSc (Honorary)
Last Updated: 20/06/11

BERHAMPUR UNIVERSITY

Bhanja Bihar, District Ganjam, Berhampur, Orissa 760007
Tel: +91(680) 224-3615 +91(680) 224-3404 +91(680) 224-2172
Fax: +91(680) 224-3322
EMail: registrarbuorissa@gmail.com
Website: http://www.bamu.nic.in

Vice-Chancellor: J. K. Mohapatra
Tel: +91(680) 224-2233 EMail: vcbuorissa@gmail.com

Registrar: B. P. Rath Tel: +91(680) 224-2234

Faculties
Arts (Arts and Humanities; Economics; English; History; Indic Languages; Linguistics; Mass Communication; Police Studies); **Business** (Business Administration; Business and Commerce); **Education** (Education) *Head*: Krushna Chandra Nayak; **Law** (Law) *Dean*: Orissa; **Science** (Botany; Chemistry; Electronic Engineering; Marine Science and Oceanography; Mathematics; Mathematics and Computer Science; Natural Sciences; Physics; Zoology) *Dean*: Bijaya Kumar Sahu

Further Information: Also 118 Affiliated Colleges

History: Founded 1967.

Governing Bodies: Senate; Syndicate; Academic Council

Academic Year: June to May (June-December; January-May)

Admission Requirements: 12th year senior secondary/intermediate examination or recognized foreign equivalent

Fees: (Rupees): 1,200-1,800 per annum; Free for women

Main Language(s) of Instruction: English

Accrediting Agencies: NAAC, Bangalore

Degrees and Diplomas: *Bachelor's Degree*: Arts; Science; Commerce; Computer Applications; Business Administration; Electronics; Homeopathy (B.A.; B.Sc.; B.Com; BCA; BBA; BES; BHMS); Medicine and Surgery; Ayurveda, Medicine and Surgery; Nursery (MBBS; BAMS; B.Nursing), 3-5 1/2 yrs; *Master's Degree*: Arts; Science; Commerce; Finance and Control; Business Administration; Law (M.A.; M.Sc.; M.Com; MCA; MFC &MBA; LLM), a further 1-3 yrs; *Doctorate (PhD)*: a further 5 yrs

Student Services: Canteen, Cultural centre, Employment services, Health services, Language programs, Sports facilities

Student Residential Facilities: Yes

Special Facilities: Museum

Libraries: Central Library, 103,549; 86 periodical subscriptions

Publications: One *(biannually)*
Last Updated: 21/06/11

BHAGAT PHOOL SIGN MAHILA VISHWAVIDYALA

Khanpur Kalan Sonipat, Haryana
Website: http://www.bpswomenuniversity.ac.in

Vice-Chancellor: Pankaj Mittal
EMail: vc@bpswomenuniversity.ac.in

Registrar: Shimla EMail: Registrar@bpswomenuniversity.ac.in

Departments
English (English); **Foreign Languages** (Foreign Languages Education); **Law** (Law); **Management Studies** (Management); **Social Work and Economics** (Economics; Social Work)

Institutes
Ayurveda (Ayurveda); **Polytechnic** (Computer Engineering; Electronic Engineering; Information Technology; Library Science; Medical Technology)

Schools
Engineering and Sciences (Engineering; Natural Sciences); **Pharmaceutical Education and Research** (Pharmacology)
History: Founded 2006.

Degrees and Diplomas: *Bachelor's Degree*; *Master's Degree*
Student Residential Facilities: Yes
Special Facilities: Computer Lab, Language Lab; Auditorium
Libraries: Yes
Last Updated: 12/08/11

BHAGWANT UNIVERSITY

Sikar Road, Ajmer, 305001 Rajasthan
Website: http://www.bhagwantuniversity.com/

Colleges
Education (Education); **Para Medical Science** (Orthopaedics; Rehabilitation and Therapy)

Institutes
Computer Application (Computer Engineering); **Engineering and Technology** (Aeronautical and Aerospace Engineering; Agricultural Engineering; Civil Engineering; Electronic Engineering; Engineering; Information Sciences; Mechanical Engineering; Nanotechnology; Petroleum and Gas Engineering; Technology); **Hospitality and Aviation** (Food Technology; Hotel and Restaurant; Household Management; Tourism); **Humanities and Applied Sciences** (Applied Chemistry; Applied Mathematics; Applied Physics; Arts and Humanities); **Management** (Management); **Media and Mass Communication** (Mass Communication; Media Studies); **Pharmaceutical Science and Research Center** (Pharmacy)

History: Founded 2008,

Degrees and Diplomas: *Bachelor's Degree*; *Master's Degree*; *Doctorate*
Last Updated: 16/12/11

BHARAT RATNA DR B.R. AMBEDKAR UNIVERSITY

Bharat Ratna Dr B.R. Ambedkar Vishwavidyalaya (AUD)
IIT Campus, plot n° 13, Sector 9, Dwarka, New Delhi 110 077
Tel: +91(11) 2507-4875
EMail: info@aud.ac.in
Website: http://www.aud.ac.in/

Vice-Chancellor: Shyam B. Menon

Registrar: Chandan Mukherjee

Schools
Business, Public Policy and Social Entrepreneurship (Business Administration; Public Administration; Social Policy); **Culture and Creative Expressions** (Cultural Studies); **Design** (Design); **Development Studies** (Development Studies; Gender Studies); **Educational Studies** (Education); **Human Ecology** (Ecology); **Law, Governance and Citizenship** (Civics; Government; Law); **Liberal Studies** (History; Labour and Industrial Relations; Modern Languages; Social Sciences; Translation and Interpretation); **Undergraduate Studies** (Arts and Humanities; Mathematics; Social Sciences)

History: Founded 2007.

Degrees and Diplomas: *Bachelor's Degree*; *Master's Degree*
Last Updated: 05/01/12

BHARATH UNIVERSITY

173 Agharam Road, Selaiyur, Chennai, Tamil Nadu 600073
Tel: + 91(44) 2229- 0742
Fax: + 91(44) 2229- 3886
EMail: admission@bharathuniv.ac.in
Website: http://www.bharathuniv.com

Vice-Chancellor: K. P. Thooyamani EMail: vc@bharathuniv.ac.in

Registrar: S. M. Rajendran

Schools

Architecture (Architecture); **Automotive Technology** (Automotive Engineering); **Bio-Sciences** (Biomedical Engineering; Genetics; Health Sciences; Nanotechnology; Optometry; Speech Therapy and Audiology); **Computer Sciences** (Computer Engineering; Computer Science; Software Engineering); **Dental Sciences** (Dentistry; Oral Pathology; Orthodontics; Periodontics); **Electrical Engineering** (Electrical Engineering); **Electronics Engineering** (Electronic Engineering; Telecommunications Engineering); **Information Sciences** (Information Sciences; Information Technology; Multimedia); **Infrastructure Engineering** (Construction Engineering; Environmental Engineering; Geological Engineering; Hydraulic Engineering; Urban Studies; Water Science); **Management** (Banking; Finance; International Business; Management; Marketing); **Mechanical Sciences** (Heating and Refrigeration; Industrial Engineering; Mechanical Engineering; Production Engineering); **Medical Sciences** (Anaesthesiology; Anatomy; Biochemistry; Dermatology; Gynaecology and Obstetrics; Medicine; Microbiology; Neurosciences; Ophthalmology; Orthopaedics; Otorhinolaryngology; Paediatrics; Pharmacology; Physics; Physiology; Psychiatry and Mental Health; Radiology; Surgery); **Paramedical Sciences** (Community Health; Nursing); **Science and Humanities** (Chemistry; English; Mathematics; Physics)

History: Founded 1984 as Bharath Institute of Science and Technology (BIST). Acquired present status 2003.

Degrees and Diplomas: *Bachelor's Degree*; *Master's Degree*; *Doctorate*

Last Updated: 21/06/11

BHARATHIAR UNIVERSITY

Coimbatore, Tamil Nadu 641046
Tel: +91(422) 2428-100
Fax: +91(422) 2422-387
EMail: regr@buc.edu.in
Website: http://www.b-u.ac.in/

Vice-Chancellor: C. Swaminathan

Registrar: P. Thirumalvalavan

Departments
Textiles and Apparel Design (Textile Design)

Schools
Biotechnology and Genetic Engineering (Biotechnology; Genetics); **Chemical Sciences** (Chemistry); **Commerce** (Accountancy; Business and Commerce; Finance); **Computer Science and Engineering** (Computer Engineering; Computer Science; Information Technology); **Economics** (Economics); **Educational Studies** (Communication Studies; Education; Mass Communication; Media Studies; Physical Education); **English and Other Foreign Languages** (English; Foreign Languages Education; French; German; Linguistics); **Life Sciences** (Biological and Life Sciences; Botany; Environmental Studies; Zoology); **Management and Entrepreneur Development** (Business Administration; Management); **Mathematics and Statistics** (Mathematics; Mathematics and Computer Science; Statistics); **Physical Sciences** (Electronic Engineering; Nanotechnology; Physics); **Social Sciences** (Demography and Population; Psychology; Social Sciences; Social Work; Sociology; Women's Studies); **Tamil and Other Indian Languages** (Indic Languages)

Further Information: Also 47 Affiliated Colleges

History: Founded 1982.

Governing Bodies: Syndicate

Academic Year: June to May (June-November; December-May). MBA, June to May (June-September; Octobre-January; February-May).

Admission Requirements: Higher Secondary Certificate (HSC)

Main Language(s) of Instruction: English

Degrees and Diplomas: *Bachelor's Degree (BBM)*: 3 yrs; *Master's Degree (MA)*: a further 1-2 yrs; *Doctorate (PhD)*: 2-3 yrs. Also postgraduate Diplomas

Student Services: Academic counselling, Canteen, Health services, Social counselling

Student Residential Facilities: Yes

Libraries: c. 82,000 vols

Last Updated: 23/06/11

BHARATHIDASAN UNIVERSITY

Palkalaiperur, Tiruchirappalli, Tamil Nadu 620024
Tel: +91(431) 240-7071
Fax: +91(431) 240-7045
EMail: info@bdu.ac.in
Website: http://www.bdu.ac.in

Vice-Chancellor: K. Meena (2010-)
Tel: +91(431) 240-7048 EMail: vc@bdu.ac.in

Registrar: T. Ramaswamy
Tel: +91(431) 240-7092 EMail: reg@bdu.ac.in

Centres
Alternatives to the Use of Animals in Life Science Education *(Mahatma Gandhi Dorenkamp Center)*; **Bharathidasan Studies** (Cultural Studies); **Bio-Informatics**; **Bio-Inorganic Chemistry** (Inorganic Chemistry); **Business Development Cell**; **Canadian Studies** (Canadian Studies); **Geographic Information Technology**; **Herbal Drug and Discovery**; **Human Conciousness Yogic Studies** (Yoga); **Jawaharlal Nehru Studies**; **Kalaigner Studies**; **Nano-Science and Nanotechnology** (Nanotechnology); **National Facility for Marine Cyanobacteria**; **Non-Linear Dynamics**; **Periyar Studies**

Faculties
Arts (Arts and Humanities; Business and Commerce; Economics; Education; Educational Technology; Finance; History; Physical Education; Social Work; Sociology; Women's Studies; Yoga) *Dean*: N. Rajendran; **Indian and Other Languages** (English; Foreign Languages Education; Indic Languages; Modern Languages; Performing Arts) *Dean*: K. Raja; **Management** *(Bharathidasan)* (Management); **Science, Engineering and Technology** (Biochemistry; Biological and Life Sciences; Biomedicine; Biotechnology; Botany; Chemistry; Computer Engineering; Computer Science; Engineering; Environmental Management; Environmental Studies; Geography; Geology; Information Sciences; Library Science; Marine Biology; Marine Science and Oceanography; Mathematics; Medicine; Microbiology; Physics; Surveying and Mapping; Technology; Zoology) *Dean*: N. Ramanujam

Schools
Basic Medical Sciences (Medicine); **Chemistry** (Chemistry); **Computer Science, Engineering and Applications** (Computer Engineering; Computer Science); **Earth Sciences** (Earth Sciences); **Economics, Commerce and Financial Studies** (Business and Commerce; Economics; Finance); **Education** (Adult Education; Distance Education; Economics; Engineering; Journalism; Mathematics; Physics; Preschool Education; Primary Education; Social Work); **Energy** (Energy Engineering); **Engineering and Technology** (Engineering; Technology); **English and Other Foreign Languages** (English; Modern Languages); **Environmental Studies** (Environmental Management; Environmental Studies); **Geosciences** (Geography; Geology; Surveying and Mapping); **Library and Information Sciences** (Information Sciences; Library Science); **Life Sciences** (Biochemistry; Biological and Life Sciences; Biotechnology; Botany; Microbiology; Zoology); **Marine Sciences** (Biotechnology; Marine Science and Oceanography); **Mathematics** (Mathematics); **Performing Arts** (Performing Arts); **Physics** (Physics); **Social Sciences** (History; Social Sciences; Social Work; Sociology; Women's Studies); **Tamil and Indian Languages** (Indic Languages)

Further Information: University Colleges: Bharathidasan, Orathanadu; Bharathidasan, Perambalur; Dr. Kalaignar College of Arts and Science, Lalgudi. Also 104 Affiliated Colleges and 13 Approved Institutions

History: Founded 1982 by the Barathidasan University Act 1981 (Act 2 of 1982), and named after the Tamil poet Bharathidasan (1891-1964). Includes Madras University's former Postgraduate Centre at Tiruchirappalli.

Governing Bodies: Syndicate; Senate; Standing Committee for Academic Affairs

Academic Year: July to April (July-November; December-April)

Admission Requirements: 12th year senior secondary/intermediate examination or recognized foreign equivalent

Fees: (Rupees): Postgraduate, 1,000-20,000 per semester

Main Language(s) of Instruction: Tamil and English

Degrees and Diplomas: *Bachelor's Degree*; *Postgraduate Diploma*: Bio-Informatics; Biotechnology; Computer Science & Engineering; Geo-Technology; Geo-Informatics (Mtech), 6 yr integrated PG programmes; *Postgraduate Diploma*: History; Animation; Life Science; Bio-Medical Science; Geo-Science; Physics (MA; MSc), 5 yr integrated PG programmes; *Master's Degree*: Education; Tamil; English; History; Sociology; Economics; Women's Studies; Social Work; Financial Management; Environmental Management (MEd; MA; MSW; MBA); Geographic Information System; Geological Remote Sensing and Geo-Informatics; Information Technology; Geo-Hydro-Informatics using GIS (Mtech; MLISc; MCA); Physics; Chemistry; Mathematics; Biotechnology; Eco-Biotechnology; Marine Biotechnology; Marine Science; Animal Biotechnology; Plant Biotechnology; Medical Physics; Biochemistry; Bioinformatics; Geo-Informatics (MSc); *Master of Philosophy*; *Doctorate (PhD)*

Student Services: Health services

Student Residential Facilities: Yes

Libraries: 81,268 vols; 121 national and 68 international subscriptions to periodicals; 8,000 e-journals

Publications: Journal of Science and Technology

Academic Staff *2009-2010*: Total 184

Student Numbers *2009-2010*: Total: c. 150,000

Last Updated: 23/06/11

BHARATI UNIVERSITY
Bharati Vidyapeeth
Lal Bahadur Shastri Marg, Pune, Maharashtra 411030
Tel: +91(20) 2433-1317 +91(20) 2433-5701
Fax: +91(20) 2433-9121
EMail: bharati@vsnl.com
Website: http://www.bharatividyapeeth.edu

Vice-Chancellor: Shivajirao Kadam Tel: +91(20) 2433-1317

Secretary: Vishwajeet Kadam

Centres
Social Sciences (Social Sciences)

Colleges
Arts, Sciences and Commerce *(Yashwantrao Mohite)* (Arts and Humanities; Business and Commerce; Natural Sciences); **Ayurveda** (Ayurveda); **Dentistry** *(Hospital)* (Dentistry); **Engineering** (Engineering; Information Sciences; Information Technology; Technology) *Division Head*: Bhalerao; **Homeopathy**; **Law** (Law); **Medicine** (Medicine; Surgery); **Nursing** (Nursing); **Pharmacy** *(Poona)* (Pharmacy); **Physical Education** (Physical Education)

Institutes
Environment Education and Research (Environmental Studies); **Information Technology** *(Rajiv Gandhi)* (Biotechnology; Information Technology); **Management and Entrepreneurship Development** (Management); **Social Sciences Studies and Research** *(Yashwantrao Chavan)* (Social Sciences)

Research Centres
Pharmacy and Applied Chemistry (Applied Chemistry; Pharmacy)

Schools
Health Affairs *(Interactive Research)* (Health Sciences) *Director*: Ulhas Wagh

History: Founded 1964. Acquired present status and title 1996.

Governing Bodies: Board of Management; Academic Council; Standing Committee; Board of Studies and Finance Committee

Academic Year: June to May

Admission Requirements: 12th year senior secondary/intermediate examination or recognized foreign equivalent and entrance test

Main Language(s) of Instruction: English, Marathi

Accrediting Agencies: National Assessment and Accreditation Council (NAAC) of the University Grants Commission (UGC)

Degrees and Diplomas: *Diploma*: Medicine; Ayurveda; Nursing; Law; Environmental Science; Management; Commerce; *Bachelor's Degree*: Medicine; Dentistry; Ayurveda; Homeopathy; Nursing; Environmental Science; Arts; Physical Education; Pharmacy; Science; Commerce; Engineering; Social Sciences; Law; Management; Library and Information Sciences; *Master's Degree*: Medicine;

Dentistry; Ayurveda; Homeopathy; Nursing; Environmental Science; Arts; Physical Education; Pharmacy; Science; Commerce; Engineering; Social Sciences; Law; Management; Library and Information Sciences

Student Services: Academic counselling, Canteen, Cultural centre, Employment services, Foreign student adviser, Foreign Studies Centre, Handicapped facilities, Health services, Language programs, Nursery care, Social counselling, Sports facilities

Student Residential Facilities: For 2100 women and 600 men

Libraries: 52,835 vols; 408 periodical subscriptions

Publications: Bharati Vidyapeeth Research Bulletin *(biannually)*

Last Updated: 24/06/11

BHATKHANDE MUSIC INSTITUTE DEEMED UNIVERSITY
Bhatkhande Sangeet Sansthan
1, Kaiserbagh, Lucknow, Uttar Pradesh 226001
Tel: +91(522) 261-0318
Fax: +91(522) 262-2926
EMail: info@bhatkhandemusic.edu.in
Website: http://www.bhatkhandemusic.edu.in

Vice-Chancellor: VyasShruti Sadolikar
Tel: +91(522) 261-0248 EMail: vc@bhatkhandemusic.edu.in

Faculties
Applied Music (Music); **Dance** (Dance; Folklore); **Melodical Instruments** (Music; Musical Instruments); **Musicology and Research** (Musicology); **Percussion Instruments** (Musical Instruments); **Vocal Music** (Singing)

History: Founded 1926 as Marris College. Acquired present title 1966. Acquired present status 2000 and title 2001.

Governing Bodies: Academic Council

Academic Year: July to June

Admission Requirements: School certificate and music exam certificate

Main Language(s) of Instruction: Hindi

Accrediting Agencies: University Grants Commission, New Delhi

Degrees and Diplomas: *Bachelor's Degree*: Music, 3 yrs; *Master's Degree*: Music, a further 2 yrs; *Doctorate*: Music, a further 2 yrs. Also Sangeet praveshika, Parichaya-Certificate Course; Sangeet Prabuddha, Parangt-Diploma course

Student Services: Cultural centre

Student Residential Facilities: For girls and boys

Special Facilities: Audio-video library

Libraries: Yes
Last Updated: 05/02/07

BHAVNAGAR UNIVERSITY
Gaurishanker Lake Road, Bhavnagar, Gujarat 364002
Tel: +91(278) 242-8014
Fax: +91(278) 242-6706
EMail: registrar@bhavuni.edu
Website: http://www.bhavuni.edu

Vice-Chancellor: J. P. Maiyanil Tel: +91(278) 242-6519

Registrar: Kaushik L. BhattFax: +91(278) 251-3943

Departments
Bioinformatics (Computer Engineering); **Business Adminintration** (Business Administration); **Chemistry** (Chemistry); **Commerce** (Business and Commerce); **Computer Science and Application** (Computer Science); **Economics** (Economics); **Education** (Education); **English** (English); **Gujarati** (Indic Languages); **Hindi** (Hindi); **History** (History); **Library and Information Sciences** (Information Sciences; Library Science); **Life Science** (Biological and Life Sciences); **Marine Science** (Marine Science and Oceanography); **Mathematics** (Mathematics); **Physics** (Physics); **Psychology** (Psychology); **Sanskrit** (Sanskrit); **Social Work** (Social Work); **Sociology** (Sociology); **Statistics** (Statistics)

Faculties
Engineering and Technology (Automation and Control Engineering; Civil Engineering; Electronic Engineering; Engineering;

Mechanical Engineering; Production Engineering; Telecommunications Engineering); **Law** (Law); **Management** (Management); **Medicine** (Medicine); **Rural Studies** (Rural Studies)

Further Information: Also 16 Affiliated Colleges and 1 Recognized Institution

History: Founded 1978 to impart knowledge on various aspects of rural life, including cultural and rural developments.

Governing Bodies: Academic Council; Executive Council

Academic Year: June to March (June-October; November-March)

Admission Requirements: 12th year senior secondary/intermediate examination or recognized foreign equivalent

Fees: (Rupees): Postgraduates 600-1,200 per annum; PhD, 3,800

Main Language(s) of Instruction: English

Degrees and Diplomas: *Bachelor's Degree*: Arts (Special) (BA Sp); Commerce (BCom); Law (BALaws); Rural Studies (BRS); Science (BSc), 3 yrs; *Bachelor's Degree*: Education (BEd); Library and Information Science (BLib, InfSc), 1 yr following first degree; *Bachelor's Degree*: Engineering (BEng); Medicine (M.B.B.S.), 4 yrs; *Bachelor's Degree*: Laws (LLB General), 2 yrs following first degree; *Bachelor's Degree*: Laws (Professional) (LLB Professional), 2 yrs following BALaws; *Postgraduate Diploma*: 1 yr following Bachelor; *Master's Degree*: Arts (MA); Commerce (MCom); Education (MEd); Library and Information Science (MLib, InfSc); Science (MSc), a further 2 yrs; *Master's Degree*: Medicine (M.D.), a further 3 yrs; *Doctorate (PhD)*: 2 further yrs. Also Postgraduate Diploma courses

Student Residential Facilities: Yes

Special Facilities: Art Gallery. Gandhi Bhavan Botanical Garden

Libraries: 102,399 vols; 245 periodical subscriptions

Publications: Bhavrup *(monthly)*
Last Updated: 24/06/11

BHUPENDRA NARAYAN MANDAL UNIVERSITY

Madhepura, Bihar 852113
Tel: +91(6476) 222-779
Fax: +91(6476) 222-068
EMail: registrar@bnmu.in

Vice-Chancellor: Qamar Ahsan EMail: vc@bnmu.in

Faculties
Commerce (Business and Commerce); **Humanities** (Arts and Humanities); **Medicine** (Medicine); **Science** (Natural Sciences); **Social Sciences** (Social Sciences)

History: Founded 1992.

Degrees and Diplomas: *Bachelor's Degree*; *Master's Degree*
Last Updated: 17/06/11

BIDHAN CHANDRA AGRICULTURAL UNIVERSITY

Bidhan Chandra Krishi Viswavidyalaya
PO Krishi Vishnavidyalaya, District Nadia, Mohanpur, West Bengal 741252
Tel: +91(3473) 587-8163
Fax: +91(3473) 22-275
EMail: vcbckv@vsnl.net
Website: http://www.bckv.edu.in

Vice-Chancellor: Saroj Kr. Sanyal EMail: bckvvc@gmail.com

Registrar: Asok Kumar Banerjee

Faculties
Agricultural Engineering (Agricultural Engineering); **Agriculture** (Agricultural Economics; Agriculture; Biotechnology; Environmental Studies; Plant and Crop Protection; Zoology); **Horticulture** (Horticulture); **Postgraduate Studies**

History: Founded 1974 by an Act, amended 1981. The only Agricultural University in the State of West Bengal, is primarily responsible for generating technical manpower and providing research and extension support for the development of Agriculture in the State.

Admission Requirements: 12th year senior secondary/intermediate examination or recognized foreign equivalent

Main Language(s) of Instruction: English

Degrees and Diplomas: *Bachelor's Degree*: 4-5 yrs; *Master's Degree*: a further 2 yrs; *Doctorate (PhD)*: 3-5 yrs

Libraries: c. 100,000 vols
Last Updated: 24/06/11

BIJU PATNAIK UNIVERSITY OF TECHNOLOGY

Jail Road, Chhend Colony, Rourkela, Orissa
Website: http://www.bput.ac.in

Vice-Chancellor: Jitendriya Kumar Satapathy

Programmes
Architecture (Architecture); **Business Administration** (Business Administration); **Engineering** (Computer Engineering; Engineering; Mining Engineering); **Information Technology** (Computer Engineering; Information Technology)

History: Founded 2002.

Degrees and Diplomas: *Bachelor's Degree*; *Postgraduate Diploma*; *Master's Degree*; *Doctorate*

Academic Staff *2010*: Total: c. 3,600
Student Numbers *2010*: Total: c. 27,500
Last Updated: 06/12/11

BIRLA INSTITUTE OF MANAGEMENT TECHNOLOGY

Plot No. 5, Knowledge Park II, Greater Noida, Uttar Pradesh 201306
Tel: +91(120) 2323-001/10
Fax: +91(120) 2323-001/22
EMail: director@bimtech.ac.in
Website: http://www.bimtech.ac.in

Director: H. Chaturvedi

Programmes
Management (Insurance; International Business; Management; Retailing and Wholesaling)

History: Founded 1988.

Accrediting Agencies: All India Council for Technical Education (AICTE)

Degrees and Diplomas: *Postgraduate Diploma*

Special Facilities: Computer and internet facility

Libraries: Yes
Last Updated: 02/02/12

BIRLA INSTITUTE OF TECHNOLOGY

Mesra, Ranchi, Bihar 835215
Tel: +91(651) 227-6052
Fax: +91(651) 227-5401
EMail: pkbarhai@bitmesra.ac.in
Website: http://www.bitmesra.ac.in/

Vice-Chancellor: Ajay Chakrabarty EMail: vc@bitmesra.ac.in

Registrar: R.K. Verma EMail: registrar@bitmesra.ac.in

Centres
Continuing Education *(Lalpur, Ranchi)* (Engineering; Management; Technology) *Head*: Awadh Prasad

Departments
Applied Mechanics (Mechanical Engineering); **Applied Sciences** (Applied Chemistry; Applied Mathematics; Applied Physics); **Architecture** (Architecture); **Bio-Medical Instrumentation** (Medical Technology); **Biotechnology** (Biotechnology); **Civil Engineering** (Civil Engineering; Geology); **Computer Engineering** (Computer Engineering); **Electrical and Electronic Engineering** (Electrical and Electronic Engineering); **Electronics and Communication Engineering** (Electrical Engineering; Telecommunications Engineering); **Environmental Science and Engineering** (Environmental Engineering; Environmental Studies); **Food Processing Technology** (Food Technology); **Hotel Management and Catering Technology** (Cooking and Catering; Hotel Management); **Information Technology** (Information Technology); **Management and Humanities** (Arts and Humanities; Economics; Industrial Engineering; Law; Management; Statistics); **Mechanical Engineering** (Mechanical Engineering); **Pharmaceutical Sciences**

(Pharmacy); **Physical Education and Training** (Physical Education; Sports); **Polymer Engineering** (Polymer and Plastics Technology); **Production Engineering** (Mineralogy; Physics; Production Engineering); **Remote Sensing** (Software Engineering; Surveying and Mapping); **Space Engineering and Rocketry** (Aeronautical and Aerospace Engineering)

History: Founded 1955 as an all-India Institution for Technical Education Research and Training by the Hindustan Charity Trust. Initially an affiliated College of Bihar University, became autonomous 1972, and acquired present status as 'Deemed University' 1986.

Governing Bodies: Board of Governors, comprising 17 members; Technical Council

Academic Year: July to June (July-December; January-June)

Admission Requirements: 12th year senior secondary/intermediate examination or recognized foreign equivalent

Main Language(s) of Instruction: English

Degrees and Diplomas: *Diploma*; *Bachelor's Degree*: Architecture, 5 yrs; *Bachelor's Degree*: Engineering; Pharmacy; Polymer Engineering, 4 yrs; *Master's Degree*: a further 1 1/2-3 yrs; *Doctorate (PhD)*

Student Residential Facilities: For c. 3,400 students (boys & girls)

Libraries: 126,382 vols, subscription to 22 International and 85 National periodicals; 6,475 online Journals; 6,475; 4,472 CDs & DVDs

Publications: Annual Report and Research Compendium *(annually)*

Last Updated: 24/06/11

🏛 BIRLA INSTITUTE OF TECHNOLOGY AND SCIENCE (BITS)

PO Box 12, Vidya Vihar, Pilani, Rajasthan 333031
Tel: +91(1596) 242-192
Fax: +91(1596) 244-183
EMail: mmsanand@bits-pilani.ac.in
Website: http://www.bits-pilani.ac.in

Vice-Chancellor: Bijendra Nath Jain (2010-)
Tel: +91(1596) 242-090, Fax: +91(1596) 244-875
EMail: vc@bits-pilani.ac.in; bnj@bits-pilani.ac.in

Registrar: M.M.S. Anand
Tel: +91(1596) 242-192, Fax: +91(1596) 244-183

International Relations: R.N. Saha, Dean, Educational Development Department
Tel: +91(1596) 245-073, Ext. 284, Fax: +91(1596) 244-183
EMail: rnsaha@bits-pilani.ac.in

Groups
Biological Sciences (Biological and Life Sciences); **Chemical Engineering** (Chemical Engineering); **Chemistry** (Chemistry); **Civil Engineering** (Civil Engineering); **Computer Science and Information Systems** (Computer Science; Information Technology); **Economics and Finance** (Economics; Finance); **Electrical and Electronic Engineering** (Electrical and Electronic Engineering); **Engineering Technology** (Engineering; Technology); **Humanistic Studies** (Arts and Humanities); **Instrumentation** (Instrument Making); **Languages**; **Management** (Management); **Mathematics** (Mathematics); **Mechanical Engineering** (Mechanical Engineering); **Pharmacy** (Pharmacy); **Physics** (Physics)

Further Information: Also campuses in Goa, Hyderabad, Pilani (India) and Dubai (UAE).

History: Founded 1964, incorporating 3 existing Colleges affiliated to the University of Rajasthan. A 'Deemed University'.

Governing Bodies: Board of Governors; Senate; General Body

Academic Year: August to July (August-December; January-May; May July)

Admission Requirements: 12th year senior secondary/intermediate examination or equivalent with Physics, Chemistry, Mathematics with minimum aggregate 80% and at least 60% in each discipline; admission on merit level determined by a computer based online entry test (BITSAT)

Fees: (Rupees): Admission fees: graduate programmes 12,000; postgraduate, 10,000. Tuition Fees: 30,000 per semester

Main Language(s) of Instruction: English

International Co-operation: With institutions in Australia, Canada, France, Japan, Nepal, New Zealand, Sweden, United Arab Emirates, USA

Accrediting Agencies: National Assessment and Accreditation Council (NAAC)

Degrees and Diplomas: *Bachelor's Degree*: Engineering (Chemical, Civil, Computer Science, Electrical and Electronics, Electronics and Instrumentation; Electronics and Communication, Mechanical) (BE(Hons)); Pharmacy (BPharm(Hons)), 4 yrs; *Bachelor's Degree*: Engineering Technology; Manufacturing Engineering; Information Systems; Marine Engineering; Nautical Sciences; Nautical Technology; Ophthalmic Assistant; Optometry; Physician Assistant; Power Engineering; Process Engineering (BSc), 3 yrs; *Master's Degree*: Biotechnology Engineering; Chemical Engineering; Petroleum Engineering; Civil Engineering; Structural Engineering; Infrastructure Systems and Transport Engineering; Communications Engineering; Computer Science (ME(Hons)); Consciousness Studies; Consultancy Management; Embedded Systems; Engineering Management; Manufacturing Management; Mechanical Systems Design; Medical Laboratory Technology; Microelectronics (MS); Design Engineering; Electrical Engineering; Power Electronics and Drives; Embedded Systems; Manufacturing Systems Engineering; Microelectronics; Software Systems; Mechanical Engineering (ME(Hons)); Engineering and Technology Management; IT Enabled Services Management (MBA); Pharmaceutical Operations and Management; Pharmaceutics; Quality Management; Science Communication; Software Engineering; Software Systems; Telecommunications and Software Engineering (MS); Pharmacy (MPharma); Public Health (MPH), 2 yrs; *Master of Philosophy*: Biological Sciences; Chemistry; Economics; English; Management; Mathematics; Physics; Hospital and Health Administration; Optometry; Physician Assistant, 2 yrs; *Doctorate (PhD)*: 3-5 yrs. Certain of these degree are offered for employed professionals working in the offices of collaborating organizations for their Human Resource Development through Distance Learning Mode. Please note that the following Master's programmes are offered as a first degree: Biological Sciences; Chemistry; Economics; Mathematics; Physics (MSc(Hons)). Engineering Technology; Finance; General Studies; Information Systems; Pharmaceutical Chemistry (MSc(Tech)).

Student Services: Academic counselling, Canteen, Cultural centre, Employment services, Foreign student adviser, Handicapped facilities, Health services, Language programs, Social counselling, Sports facilities

Student Residential Facilities: Yes (11 hostels for 2,774 men; 2 hostels for 688 women; 642 quarters for staff

Special Facilities: Birla Museum, a unique Science and Technological Museum for Visual Education in Art Sciences and Technology (on campus); daily weather-monitoring observatory; student activity centre; film studio; auditorium

Libraries: c. 221,472 vols; 605 journal subscriptions

Publications: BITS in the News *(annually)*; BITSCAN *(biennially)*; Bulletin *(annually)*; Research at BITS *(annually)*

Academic Staff *2010-2011*: Total 365

STAFF WITH DOCTORATE: Total 310

Student Numbers *2010-2011*: Total: c. 8,000

Distance students, 13,000.

Last Updated: 28/06/11

BIRSA AGRICULTURAL UNIVERSITY (BAU)

Kanke, Ranchi, Jharkhand 834006
Tel: +91(651) 245-015 +91(651) 245-0500
Fax: +91(651) 245-0850
EMail: vc_bau@rediffmail.com
Website: http://www.baujharkhand.org/

Vice-Chancellor: N.N. Singh Tel: +91(651) 245-0500

Registrar: N. Kudada Tel: +91(651) 245-0832

Colleges
Biotechnology (Biotechnology) *Associate Dean*: Z.A. Haider

Faculties

Agriculture (Agriculture) *Dean*: A.K. Sarkar; **Forestry** (Forestry) *Dean*: P. Kaushal; **Veterinary Science** (Animal Husbandry; Veterinary Science) *Dean*: S. K. Singh

History: Founded 1980.

Governing Bodies: Board of Management

Academic Year: July to June

Admission Requirements: 12th year senior secondary/intermediate examination or recognized foreign equivalent

Fees: (Rupees): Undergraduate, 2,500 per semester, postgraduate, 3,450; PhD, 4,200

Main Language(s) of Instruction: English

Accrediting Agencies: Indian Council of Agricultural Research

Degrees and Diplomas: *Bachelor's Degree*: Agriculture, Forestry (BSc); Veterinary Science and Animal Husbandry (BVSc), 4 yrs; *Master's Degree*: Agriculture, Forestry (MSc); Veterinary Science and Animal Husbandry (MVSc), a further 3 yrs; *Master's Degree*: Biotechnology (MSc), a further 2 yrs; *Doctorate*: Agriculture, Veterinary Science and Animal Husbandry (PhD), 2 yrs after Master's

Student Services: Academic counselling, Canteen, Cultural centre, Employment services, Foreign student adviser, Foreign Studies Centre, Handicapped facilities, Health services, Language programs, Nursery care, Social counselling, Sports facilities

Student Residential Facilities: Yes

Libraries: 1 central library and 3 faculty libraries with c. 80,000 vols

Publications: BAU Journal of Research *(biannually)*; Pathari Krishi, Article Journal *(quarterly)*

Academic Staff *2010-2011*: Total 200

STAFF WITH DOCTORATE: Total 150

Student Numbers *2010-2011*: Total: c. 700
Last Updated: 28/06/11

BLDE UNIVERSITY

Bangaramma Sajjan Campus, Sholapur Road, Bijapur, Karnakata 586103
Tel: +91(8352) 262770
Fax: +91(8352) 263303
EMail: office@bldeuniversity.org
Website: http://www.bldeuniversity.org

Vice-Chancellor: B. G. Mulimani EMail: vcbldeu@gmail.com

Registrar: J. G. Ambekar EMail: registrarbldeu@gmail.com

Programmes
Medicine (Anatomy; Community Health; Forensic Medicine and Dentistry; Gynaecology and Obstetrics; Medicine; Microbiology; Ophthalmology; Otorhinolaryngology; Paediatrics; Pathology; Pharmacology; Physiology; Surgery)

Degrees and Diplomas: *Bachelor's Degree*; *Postgraduate Diploma*; *Master's Degree*
Last Updated: 10/01/12

B.S. ABDUR RAHMAN UNIVERSITY (BSAUNIV)

Seethakathi Estate, Vandalur, Chennai, Tamil Nadu 600 048
Tel: +91(44) 227-51347 +91(44) 227-51348
EMail: bsar@bsauniv.ac.in
Website: http://www.bsauniv.ac.in/

Vice Chancellor: P. Kanniappan

Registrar: V.M. Periasamy

Schools
Architecture *(Crescent)* (Architecture); **Business** *(Crescent)* (Business Administration); **Computer and Information Sciences** (Computer Engineering; Computer Science; Information Sciences; Information Technology); **Electrical and Communication Sciences** (Electrical Engineering; Electronic Engineering; Measurement and Precision Engineering; Telecommunications Engineering); **Islamic Studies** (Islamic Studies); **Mechanical and Building Services** (Aeronautical and Aerospace Engineering; Automotive Engineering; Building Technologies; Civil Engineering; Mechanical Engineering; Polymer and Plastics Technology); **Science and**

Humanities (Arts and Humanities; Chemistry; English; Mathematics; Modern Languages; Physics)

History: Founded 1984 as B.S. Abdur Rahman Crescent Engineering College. Acquired 'Deemed University' status 2008 and present title 2009.

Degrees and Diplomas: *Bachelor's Degree*; *Bachelor's degree (professional)*; *Master's Degree*; *Master of Philosophy*; *Doctorate*. Also M.B.A.

Student Services: Canteen, Health services

Student Residential Facilities: Men's hostels (1,300 beds); Women's hostels (300 beds).

Libraries: c. 55,000 vols; 2,500 National and International periodical subscriptions; e-Journals
Last Updated: 20/12/11

BUNDELKHAND UNIVERSITY

Kanpur Road, Jhansi, Uttar Pradesh 284128
Tel: +91(517) 232-0496
Fax: +91(517) 232-0761
EMail: registrar@bujhansi.org
Website: http://www.bujhansi.org/

Vice-Chancellor: S. V. S. Rana (2010-)

Colleges
Medicine *(Maharani Laxmi Bai)* (Medicine)

Faculties
Agriculture (Agriculture) *Dean*: M.D. Lodhi; **Arts** (Arts and Humanities) *Dean*: M.L. Maurya; **Commerce** (Business and Commerce) *Dean*: Pankaj Attri; **Education** (Education) *Dean*: Anjana Rathore; **Engineering** *Dean*: Dheer Singh; **Law** (Law) *Dean*: L.C. Sahu; **Medicine** (Medicine) *Dean*: Ganesh Kumar; **Science** (Natural Sciences) *Dean*: S.P. Singh

Institutes
Engineering and Technology (Engineering; Technology)

Further Information: Also 15 Affiliated Colleges

History: Founded 1975.

Degrees and Diplomas: *Diploma*; *Bachelor's Degree*; *Master's Degree*; *Doctorate (PhD)*

Libraries: c. 130,230 vols; 51 journal subscriptions
Last Updated: 28/06/11

CALORX TEACHERS' UNIVERSITY (CTU)

Opp. Sun Rise Park, Between Sanjivani Hospital & Advait Complex, Ahmedabad, Gujerat 380054
Tel: +91(271) 7242-328/29
EMail: registrarctu@calorx.org
Website: http://www.ctu.org.in/

President: M. P. Chhaya

Programmes
Education (Education; Educational Administration; Primary Education; Special Education)

Degrees and Diplomas: *Bachelor's Degree*; *Master's Degree*; *Master of Philosophy*; *Doctorate*

Student Services: Sports facilities

Student Residential Facilities: Yes

Special Facilities: Wi-Fi

Libraries: Yes
Last Updated: 19/10/11

CENTER FOR ENVIRONMENTAL PLANNING AND TECHNOLOGY UNIVERSITY

Kasturbhai Lalbhai Campus, University Road, Ahmedabad, Gujarat 380009
Website: http://www.cept.ac.in/

Director: R.N. Vakil

Registrar: Anita Hiranandani EMail: registrar@cept.ac.in

International Relations: Rema Haridasan EMail: sa@cept.ac.in

Faculties

Arts and Humanities (Arts and Humanities); **Architecture** (Architecture); **Design** (Design); **Environmental and Climate Change Studies** (Environmental Studies; Meteorology); **Geomatics and Space Applications**; **Infrastructure Systems**; **Landscape Studies** (Landscape Architecture); **Planning and Public Policy** (Social and Community Services); **Rural and Development Studies** (Development Studies; Rural Studies); **Technology** (Technology); **Technology Management** (Technology)

History: Founded 2005.

Accrediting Agencies: All India Council for Technical Education (AICTE)

Degrees and Diplomas: *Bachelor's Degree*; *Master's Degree*

Libraries: c. 37,000 vols, 110 periodicals

Last Updated: 05/08/11

CENTRAL AGRICULTURAL UNIVERSITY

Iroisemba, Imphal, Manipur 795004
Tel: +91(385) 241-5933 +91(385) 241-0644
Fax: +91(385) 241-5196 +91(385) 241-0414
EMail: snpuri@rediffmail.com
Website: http://dare.nic.in/cau.htm

Vice-Chancellor: S.N. Puri EMail: snpuri04@yahoo.co.in

Registrar: M. Premjit Singh

Colleges

Agricultural Engineeing and Post Harvest Technology *(Gangtok; Sikkim)*; **Agriculture** (Agriculture); **Fisheries** *(Lembucherra, Agartala, Tripura)*; **Home Science** *(Tura, Meghalaya)* (Home Economics); **Horticulture and Forestry** *(Pasighat, Arunachal Pradesh)* (Forestry; Horticulture); **Veterinary Science and Animal Husbandry** *(Selesih, Aizawl, Mizoram)*

History: Founded 1993, acquired present status and title 1993.

Governing Bodies: Board of Management; Academic Council; Board of Studies

Academic Year: August to July

Admission Requirements: 12th year senior secondary/intermediate examination or recognized foreign equivalent

Main Language(s) of Instruction: English

Accrediting Agencies: Indian Council of Agricultural Research, New Delhi

Degrees and Diplomas: *Bachelor's Degree*: Agriculture; Fisheries; Home Science; Horticulture; Agricultural Engineering and Post Harvest Technology (B.Sc.; B.F.Sc.; B.Tech.), 4 yrs; *Bachelor's Degree*: Veterinary Science and Animal Husbandry (B.V.Sc and A.H.), 5 yrs; *Master's Degree*: Agriculture; Veterinary and Animal Science (M.Sc.; MV.Sc.), a further 2 yrs

Student Services: Academic counselling, Canteen, Employment services, Health services, Social counselling, Sports facilities

Student Residential Facilities: For c. 500 students

Libraries: 19,227 vols. 241 journals and periodicals

Publications: Central Agricultural University Newsletter *(quarterly)*

Last Updated: 28/06/11

CENTRAL INSTITUTE OF FISHERIES EDUCATION (CIFE)

Fisheries University Road, Seven Bungalows, Andheri, Mumbai, Maharashtra 400061
Tel: +91(22) 2636-1446
Fax: +91(22) 2636-1573
EMail: contact@cife.edu.in
Website: http://www.cife.edu.in

Director: W. S. Lakra Tel: +91(22) 2636-3404

Chief Administrative Officer: Suresh Kumar
EMail: sureshkumar@cife.edu.in

Divisions

Aquaculture (Aquaculture); **Aquatic Environmental Management** (Environmental Management; Marine Biology); **Fish Genetics and Biotechnology** (Biotechnology; Fishery; Genetics); **Fish Nutrition and Biochemistry**; **Fisherie Economics, Extension ans Statistics** (Economics; Fishery; Statistics); **Fishery Resource, Harvest and Post-harvest Management** (Harvest Technology; Management)

History: Founded 1961.

Governing Bodies: Board of Management, Academic Council, Research Advisory Council, Extension Council, Board of Studies and Staff Research Council

Academic Year: September to August (September-February; March-August)

Admission Requirements: Bachelor's degree with at least 60% mark or OGPA of 6.50 out of 10

Fees: (Rupees): 4,000 per annum

Main Language(s) of Instruction: English

Accrediting Agencies: National Agricultural Accreditation Board

Degrees and Diplomas: *Diploma*: 1 yr; *Master's Degree*: 2 yrs; *Doctorate (PhD)*: 3 yrs. Also Postgraduate Certificate in Inland Fisheries Development and Administration, 1 yr

Student Services: Academic counselling, Canteen, Cultural centre, Employment services, Foreign student adviser, Foreign Studies Centre, Health services, Social counselling, Sports facilities

Student Residential Facilities: Yes

Special Facilities: Museum. Digital Imaging Laboratory

Libraries: 26,569 vols

Publications: Journal of the Indian Fisheries Association *(annually)*

Last Updated: 28/06/11

CENTRAL UNIVERSITY OF BIHAR (CUB)

BIT Campus, P.O. B.V. College, Patna 800 014
Website: http://www.cub.ac.in/

Vice Chancellor: Janak Pandey
Tel: +91(612) 222-6535, Fax: +91(612) 222-6535
EMail: vc@cub.ac.in

Registrar: Mohammad Nehal EMail: registrar@cub.ac.in

Schools

Earth, Biological and Environmental Sciences (Biological and Life Sciences; Biotechnology; Earth Sciences; Environmental Studies); **Human Sciences** (Psychology); **Mathematics, Statistics and Computer Science** (Computer Science; Mathematics; Statistics); **Media, Arts and Aesthetics** (Aesthetics; Fine Arts; Mass Communication; Media Studies); **Social Sciences and Policy** (Development Studies; Social Policy; Social Sciences)

History: Founded 2009. A 'Central University'.

Degrees and Diplomas: *Master's Degree*
Last Updated: 08/12/11

CENTRAL UNIVERSITY OF GUJARAT (CUG)

Sector-30, Gandhinagar 382 030
Tel: +91(79) 292-8905
Fax: +91(79) 232-60076
Website: http://www.cug.ac.in/

Vice Chancellor: R. K. Kale
Tel: +91(79) 2326-0076 EMail: vc@cug.ac.in

Registrar: Gitesh Joshi
Tel: +91(79) 2928-8401
EMail: registrar@cug.ac.in; cug2009registrar@gmail.com

Schools

Chemical Sciences (Chemistry; Industrial Chemistry); **Environment and Sustainable Development** (Environmental Studies); **International Studies** (Government; International Studies; Political Sciences); **Language, Literature and Cultural Studies** (Asian Studies; Chinese; Comparative Literature; Cultural Studies; English; German; Hindi; Literature; Modern Languages); **Life Sciences** (Biological and Life Sciences); **Social Sciences** (Demography and Population; Development Studies; Economics; Management; Peace and Disarmament; Social Sciences; Social Studies)

History: Founded 2009. A 'Central University".

Degrees and Diplomas: *Master's Degree*. Also Certificates and integrated M.Phil/Ph.D.
Last Updated: 08/12/11

CENTRAL UNIVERSITY OF HARYANA

Temporary Campus:, Govt. B.Ed. College Building, Distt.
Mahendergarh, Narnaul, Haryana 122010
Tel: +91(1282) 255-002 +91(1282) 255-003
EMail: contact@cuharyana.org
Website: http://www.cuharyana.org/

Schools

Agriculture and Allied (Agro based technological) Sciences
(Agricultural Business; Agricultural Economics; Agriculture; Food
Science; Harvest Technology; Horticulture; Plant Pathology); **Arts,
Humanities and Social Sciences** (Anthropology; Archaeology;
Arts and Humanities; Asian Religious Studies; Business and Commerce; Comparative Literature; Economics; Education; Geography;
History; Philosophy; Physical Education; Psychology; Social Sciences; Sociology; Sports; Tourism; Translation and Interpretation;
Urdu; Women's Studies); **Chemical Sciences** (Chemistry); **Computer Science and Informatics** (Computer Science; Information
Technology; Statistics); **Earth, Environment and Space Studies**
(Astronomy and Space Science; Astrophysics; Earth Sciences;
Environmental Studies; Surveying and Mapping); **Engineering and
Technology** (Electronic Engineering; Engineering; Food Technology; Geological Engineering; Nanotechnology; Technology); **Journalism, Mass Communication and Media** (Information Sciences;
Journalism; Library Science; Mass Communication; Media Studies);
Language, Linguistics, Culture and Heritage (Cultural Studies;
English; Heritage Preservation; Hindi; Indic Languages; Linguistics;
Modern Languages); **Law, Governance, Public Policy and Management** (Government; Law; Political Sciences; Public Administration; Social Policy); **Life Sciences** (Biological and Life Sciences;
Biotechnology; Botany; Chemistry; Genetics; Microbiology; Molecular Biology; Zoology); **Life-long Learning; Medical Sciences**
(Medicine; Virology); **Physical and Mathematical Sciences**
(Mathematics; Physics)

History: Founded 2009. A 'Central University'.

Governing Bodies: Academic Council; Executive Council

Degrees and Diplomas: *Master of Philosophy*; *Doctorate*. Also
M.B.A.

Last Updated: 07/12/11

CENTRAL UNIVERSITY OF HIMACHAL PRADESH

PO Box 21, Dist. Kangra, Dharamshala, Himachal Pradesh 176 215
Tel: +91(1892) 229-330
Fax: +91(1892) 229-331
EMail: vc@cuhimachal.ac.in; contact@cuhimachal.ac.in
Website: http://www.cuhimachal.ac.in/

Vice Chancellor: Furqan Qamar EMail: vc.cuhimachal@gmail.com

Registrar: K. D. Lakhanpal

Schools

Business and Management Science (Accountancy; Behavioural
Sciences; Business Administration; Finance; Management; Marketing); **Earth and Environmental Sciences** (Earth Sciences;
Environmental Studies); **Education** (Education; Teacher Training);
Fine Arts and Art Education (Art Education; Fine Arts; Visual
Arts); **Humanities and Languages** (Arts and Humanities; English;
Hindi; Indic Languages; Modern Languages); **Journalism, Mass
Communication and New Media** (Journalism; Mass Communication; Media Studies; Writing); **Life Sciences** (Biological and Life
Sciences); **Mathematics, Computers and Information Science**
(Computer Science; Information Sciences; Library Science;
Mathematics); **Physical and Material Sciences** (Astronomy and
Space Science; Materials Engineering; Physics); **Social Sciences**
(Economics; Social Policy; Social Sciences; Social Work); **Tourism,
Travel and Hospitality Management** (Hotel Management; Tourism)

Further Information: Also Dhauladhar and Beas campuses.

History: Founded 2009. A 'Central University'.

Governing Bodies: Court; Executive Council; Academic Council;
Finance Committee

Degrees and Diplomas: *Master's Degree*. Also integrated M.Phil/
Ph.D.; M.B.A.

Last Updated: 07/12/11

CENTRAL UNIVERSITY OF JHARKHAND (CUJ)

Ratu Lohardaga Road, Brambe, Ranchi, Jharkhand 835 205
Tel: +91(6531) 294-163
EMail: pio@cuj.ac.in
Website: http://www.cuj.ac.in/

Vice Chancellor: Darlando T. Khathing Tel: +91(6531) 294-160

Registrar: Shyam Narain Tel: +91(6531) 294-182

Schools

Cultural Studies (Cultural Studies; Indigenous Studies); **Engineering and Technologies** (Engineering; Nanotechnology; Technology); **Languages** (English; Modern Languages); **Management
Sciences** (Business Administration; Management); **Mass Communication and Media Technology** (Mass Communication; Media
Studies); **Natural Resource and Management** (Hydraulic Engineering; Management; Natural Resources; Water Management);
Natural Sciences (Applied Chemistry; Applied Mathematics;
Applied Physics; Biological and Life Sciences; Natural Sciences)

History: Founded 2009. A 'Central University'.

Governing Bodies: Executive Council; Academic Council

Accrediting Agencies: University Grants Commission (UGC);
Ministry of Human Resource Development (MHRD)

Degrees and Diplomas: Integrated Master's degree programme,
5 yrs

Last Updated: 07/12/11

CENTRAL UNIVERSITY OF KARNATAKA (CUK)

II Floor, Karya Soudha, Gulbarga University, Gulbarga 585 106
Website: http://www.cuk.ac.in/

Vice Chancellor: A.M. Pathan
Tel: +91(8472) 272-057, Fax: +91(8472) 272-066
EMail: abdul.jaleel@hotmail.com; vccukg@gmail.com

Registrar: Anup K. Pujari
Tel: +91(8472) 278-056, Fax: +91(8472) 272-066
EMail: apujari@yahoo.com; anuppujari@hotmail.com

Schools

Business Studies (Business Administration; Business and Commerce; Economics); **Earth Sciences** (Earth Sciences; Geography;
Regional Planning; Surveying and Mapping); **Humanities and
Languages** (Arts and Humanities; English; Modern Languages;
South and Southeast Asian Languages); **Social and Behavioral
Sciences** (Behavioural Sciences; History; Psychology; Social Sciences); **Undergraduate Studies** (Economics; English; Geography;
History; Psychology)

History: Founded 2009. A 'Central University'.

Degrees and Diplomas: *Bachelor's Degree*; *Master's Degree*;
Master of Philosophy; *Doctorate*. Also integrated M.A, M.Phil and
Ph.D Courses, 5 yrs.

Student Residential Facilities: Boys Hostel (60 single rooms)

Special Facilities: Computer Lab

Libraries: 5,444 vols; 26 Journals and Print Format; E-Journals,
3,512

Last Updated: 07/12/11

CENTRAL UNIVERSITY OF KASHMIR

Transit Campus, Sonwar (Near G.B.Pant Hospital), Srinagar,
Jammu and Kashmir 190-004
Tel: +91(194) 246-8357 +91(194) 246-8346
Fax: +91(194) 246-8351 +91(194) 246-8354
EMail: mail@cukashmir.ac.in
Website: http://www.cukashmir.ac.in/

Vice Chancellor: Abdul Wahid

Schools

Business and Economic Studies *(SOBES)* (Business Administration; Economics); **Computer Science and Information Technology** *(SOCScIT)* (Computer Science; Information Technology;
Mathematics); **Languages** *(SOL)* (English; Modern Languages);
Legal Studies (Civil Law; Criminal Law; Law); **Media Studies**
(Journalism; Media Studies); **Social Sciences** (Economics; Social
Sciences)

History: Founded 2009. A 'Central University'. Formerly known as the Central University of Jammu and Kashmir.

Degrees and Diplomas: *Bachelor's degree (professional)*: Law, 5 yrs; *Master's Degree.* Also M.B.A.
Last Updated: 07/12/11

CENTRAL UNIVERSITY OF KERALA

Vidyanagar, Kasaragod, Kerala 671 123
Tel: +91(4994) 256-420
EMail: registrarcuk@gmail.com
Website: http://www.cukerala.ac.in/

Vice Chancellor: Jancy James (2010-)

Registrar: N.N. Sampathkumar

Schools
Biological Sciences (Biochemistry; Biological and Life Sciences; Botany; Genetics; Molecular Biology; Zoology); Computer Science (Computer Science); Global Studies (Economics); Languages and Comparative Literature (Comparative Literature; English; Hindi; Modern Languages); Mathematical and Physical Science (Mathematics; Physics); Mathematics (Mathematics)

History: Founded 2009. A 'Central University'.

Governing Bodies: Court; Executive Council; Academic Council

Fees: (Indian Rupee): 600-1,000 per semester

Degrees and Diplomas: *Master's Degree.* Also integrated MPhil/PhD

Student Residential Facilities: Separate women's and men's hostels

Libraries: Yes
Last Updated: 07/12/11

CENTRAL UNIVERSITY OF ORISSA

Central Silk Board Building Landiguda, Koraput
Tel: +90 6852-251288
Fax: +90 6852-251244
EMail: info@centraluniversityorissa.ac.in
Website: http://centraluniversityorissa.ac.in/

Vice Chancellor: Surabhi Banerjee
Tel: +90(674) 274-8094, Fax: +90(674) 274-8092
EMail: vccu-or@nic.in; vc@cuorissa.org; vc@centraluniversityorissa.ac.in

Schools
Basic Sciences and Information Sciences (Chemistry; Computer Science; Information Sciences; Mathematics; Natural Sciences; Physics; Statistics); Biodiversity and Conservation of Natural Resources (Aquaculture; Biotechnology; Natural Resources); Development Studies (Development Studies; Economics; Peace and Disarmament); Education and Education Technology (Education; Educational Technology; Teacher Training); Health Sciences (Community Health; Health Sciences; Nursing; Public Health); Languages (English; Indic Languages; Literature; Modern Languages); Legal Studies (Human Rights; Law); Social Sciences (Anthropology; Development Studies; Journalism; Mass Communication; Philosophy; Social Sciences; Sociology; Welfare and Protective Services)

Further Information: Also Campus in Bhubaneswar.

History: Founded 2009. A 'Central University'.

Governing Bodies: Court; Executive Council; Academic Council

Degrees and Diplomas: *Master's Degree*

Student Residential Facilities: Boys and Girls Hostel; Guest House

Special Facilities: Computer Centre

Libraries: Yes
Last Updated: 07/12/11

CENTRAL UNIVERSITY OF PUNJAB (CUP)

P.O. Box-55, Bathinda 151 001
Tel: +91(164) 224-0555 +91(164) 243-0586
Fax: +91(164) 224-0555
EMail: cu.punjab.info@gmail.com
Website: http://www.centralunipunjab.com/

Vice Chancellor: Jai Rup Singh

Registrar: Jagdev Kartar Singh

Schools
Basic and Applied Sciences (Biological and Life Sciences; Chemistry; Natural Sciences; Pharmacy); Design and Planning (Architecture and Planning; Design); Emerging Life Science Technologies (Biological and Life Sciences); Engineering and Technology (Engineering; Technology); Environment and Earth Sciences (Earth Sciences; Environmental Studies); Global Relations (Asian Studies; International Relations; South Asian Studies); Health Sciences (Health Sciences); Information and Communicative Sciences (Information Sciences; Mass Communication); Languages, Literature and Culture (Comparative Literature; Cultural Studies; Literature; Modern Languages); Legal Studies and Governance (Government; Law); Management (Management); Social Sciences (Social Sciences)

History: Founded 2009. A 'Central University'.

Governing Bodies: Executive Council; Academic Council; Finance Committee; Planning Board

Degrees and Diplomas: *Master's Degree.* Also integrated postgraduate programmes (M.Phil. - Ph.D.; LL.M. - Ph.D.; M.Pharm. - Ph.D.).

Student Services: Health services, Sports facilities

Student Residential Facilities: Students' Hostel, Guest House

Libraries: 5,000 vols; 37 International Journals and 12 National Journals.
Last Updated: 06/12/11

CENTRAL UNIVERSITY OF RAJASTHAN (CURAJ)

City Road, Distt. Ajmer, Kishangarh, Rajasthan 305 802
Tel: +91(1463) 246-735
Fax: +91(1463) 246-735
EMail: info.curaj@gmail.com
Website: http://www.curaj.ac.in/

Vice Chancellor: M.M. Salunkhe

Schools
Architecture (Architecture); Chemical Sciences and Pharmacy (Chemistry; Pharmacy); Commerce and Management (Business Administration; Business and Commerce; Management); Engineering and Technology (Engineering; Technology); Humanities (Arts and Humanities; English; Hindi; Modern Languages); Life Sciences (Biotechnology; Environmental Studies); Mathematics, Statistics and Computational Sciences (Actuarial Science; Computer Science; Mathematics and Computer Science; Statistics); Physical Sciences (Physics); Social Sciences (Cultural Studies; Economics; Media Studies; Social Sciences)

History: Founded 2009. A 'Central University'.

Fees: (Indian Rupees): 2,600-7,250 per semester

Degrees and Diplomas: *Master's Degree.* Also M.B.A.

Student Services: Canteen, Health services, Sports facilities

Student Residential Facilities: Separate Boys and Girls Hostels; Guest House

Special Facilities: Science and Language Laboratories

Libraries: Yes

Student Numbers *2011-2012*: Total: c. 460
Last Updated: 06/12/11

CENTRAL UNIVERSITY OF TAMIL NADU (CUTN)

Collectorate Annexe, Thanjavur Road, Thiruvarur, Tamil Nadu State 610-00
Tel: +91(4366) 220-311 +91(4366) 225-205
Fax: +91(4366) 225-312
EMail: vccutn@gmail.com; registrar.cutn@gmail.com; psvccutn@gmail.com
Website: http://www.cutn.ac.in/

Vice Chancellor: B. P. Sanjay
Tel: +91(4366) 220-311 EMail: psvccutn@gmail.com

Registrar: V. K. Sridhar
Tel: +91(4366) 220-023 EMail: registrar.cutn@gmail.com

Schools
Basic and Applied Sciences (Chemistry; Physics); **Mathematics and Computer Sciences** (Computer Science; Mathematics); **Social Sciences and Humanities** (Arts and Humanities; Economics; English; Finance; Social Sciences)

History: Founded 2009. A 'Central University'.

Governing Bodies: Court; Executive Council; Academic Council; Finance Committee

Degrees and Diplomas: *Master's Degree*. Also intergrated Master's degree, 5 yrs.

Student Services: Canteen

Special Facilities: Laboratory

Libraries: Yes

Academic Staff *2011-2012*: Total: c. 11
Student Numbers *2011-2012*: Total: c. 200
Last Updated: 06/12/11

CENTRAL UNIVERSITY OF TIBETAN STUDIES (CIHTS)
Sarnath, Varanasi, Uttar Pradesh 221007
Tel: +91(542) 258-5148
Fax: +91(542) 258-5150
EMail: cihts@yahoo.com
Website: http://www.cihts.ac.in/

Vice Chancellor: Ngawang Samten (2002-2013)
Tel: +91(542) 258-6337 EMail: ngawang_samten@yahoo.co.in

Registrar: Singh Dev Raj
Tel: +91(542) 258-2387, Fax: +91(542) 258-5148
EMail: registrarcuts@in.com

Faculties
Arts and Crafts (Fine Arts; Handicrafts); **Languages and Literature** (English; Hindi; Literature; Sanskrit; Tibetan) *Dean*: J.P. Dwivedi; **Logic and Spirituality** (Asian Religious Studies; Logic) *Dean*: Sonam Rabten; **Medical Sciences** (Medicine; Traditional Eastern Medicine) *Dean*: Lobsang Tenzin; **Modern Studies** (Ancient Languages; Asian Studies; Cultural Studies; Economics; History; Political Sciences) *Dean*: Tsultrim Phuntsok

Research Units
Dictionary; **Publication**; **Rare Buddhist Texts**; **Restoration**; **Translation**

History: Founded 1967 as envisioned by H.H. the Dalai Lama in consultation with Pandit Jawarhalal Nehru for the preservation and promotion of Tibetan Culture and Buddhist Studies. Fully funded by the Central Government of India through the Ministry of Culture, Youth and Sports. Declared as 'Deemed University' 1988. Acquired present title 2009. Formerly known as the Central Institute of Higher Tibetan Studies.

Governing Bodies: Society and Board of Governors, consisting of Government Officials, Subject Experts, Representatives of Teaching Staff and University Grants Commission, and H.H. the Dalai Lama

Academic Year: July to May (July-December; January-May)

Admission Requirements: Standard IX with Tibetan Language or knowledge of Tibetan Language, plus minimum 35% marks in qualifying entrance examination

Fees: Tuition, none

Main Language(s) of Instruction: Tibetan

International Co-operation: Educational Exchange Programmes with Hampshire College, USA; Tasmania University, Australia

Accrediting Agencies: University Grants Commission

Degrees and Diplomas: *Diploma*: Buddhist Studies; Tibetan Language; Tibetan Painting, 2 yrs; *Bachelor's Degree*: Arts (BA) (Shastri); Education (BEd) (Shiksha Shastri), 3 yrs; *Master's Degree*: Arts (MA) (Acharya), 2 yrs; *Doctorate (PhD) (Vidya Varidhi)*: a further 2-3 yrs following Master

Student Services: Academic counselling, Cultural centre, Employment services, Foreign student adviser, Handicapped facilities, Health services, Nursery care, Social counselling, Sports facilities

Student Residential Facilities: Yes

Libraries: Shantirakshita Library, 56,547 vols

Publications: Biblioteca Indo-Tibetica Series, Publications are in Sanskrit, Hindi, Tibetan, Pali and English or in multilingual form; 'Dhih' Research Journal *(biannually)*; Miscellaneous Series; Prof. L.M. Joshi Commemorative Lecture Series; Rare Buddhist Text Series; Samyak Vak Series; The Dalai Lama Tibetico-Indological Series

Press or Publishing House: Publication Unit

Student Numbers *2008-2009*: Total 350
Last Updated: 04/04/08

CENTRE FOR MANAGEMENT DEVELOPMENT, MODINAGAR
Uttar Pradesh 2001204
Tel: +91(1232) 242692
Fax: +91(1232) 242458

Programmes
Management (Business Administration; Management)

History: Founded 1983.

Accrediting Agencies: All India Council for Technical Education (AICTE)

Degrees and Diplomas: *Postgraduate Diploma*
Last Updated: 02/02/12

CENTURION UNIVERSITY OF TECHNOLOGY AND MANAGEMENT (CUTM)
HIG – 5, Phase -1, BDA Duplex, Pokhariput, Bhubaneswar, Orrisa 751020
Tel: +91(674) 2352-667
Fax: +91(674) 2352-433
EMail: admissions@cutm.ac.in
Website: http://www.cutm.ac.in

Vice-Chancellor: D. Nageswar Rao

Registrar: Ashok Mishra

Institutes
Technology and Management (JITM) *(Jagannath)*

Schools
Rural Enterprise Management (CSREM) *(Centurion)*

Further Information: Also Parlakhemundi and Bhubaneswar Campuses

Student Residential Facilities: For boys and girls

Libraries: Yes
Last Updated: 03/01/12

CHANAKYA NATIONAL LAW UNIVERSITY
Gandhi Maidan, Patna, Assam 800 001
Website: http://www.cnlu.ac.in

Vice-Rector: A. Lakshminath

Registrar: S. P. Singh

Programmes
Law (Law)

History: Founded 2006.

Degrees and Diplomas: *Bachelor's Degree*; *Postgraduate Diploma*; *Doctorate*
Last Updated: 22/07/11

CHANDRA SHEKHAR AZAD UNIVERSITY OF AGRICULTURE AND TECHNOLOGY
Nawabganj, Kanpur, Uttar Pradesh 208002
Tel: +91(512) 253-4155
Fax: +91(512) 253-3808 +91(512) 243-4113
EMail: info@csauk.ac.in
Website: http://www.csauk.ac.in/

Vice-Chancellor: G.C. Tewari Tel: : EMail: vc@csauk.ac.in

Registrar: V.P. Kanaujia

Departments
Home Science (Child Care and Development; Clothing and Sewing; Food Science; Home Economics; Human Resources; Nutrition)

Faculties
Agriculture Engineering and Technology (Agricultural Engineering; Agricultural Equipment; Civil Engineering; Computer Science; Electrical and Electronic Engineering; Farm Management; Food Technology; Irrigation; Mechanical Engineering; Power Engineering; Soil Conservation; Technology; Telecommunications Engineering; Water Management); **Agriculture** (Agricultural Business; Agricultural Economics; Agriculture; Forestry; Horticulture; Plant and Crop Protection; Plant Pathology; Soil Science; Water Management); **Veterinary Science** (Animal Husbandry; Veterinary Science)

History: Founded 1975.

Governing Bodies: Board of Management

Academic Year: July to May (July-December; January-May)

Admission Requirements: 12th year senior secondary/intermediate examination or recognized foreign equivalent

Main Language(s) of Instruction: Hindi, English

Degrees and Diplomas: *Bachelor's Degree:* Agriculture and Home Science; Veterinary Science, 4 yrs; *Master's Degree:* a further 2 yrs; *Doctorate (PhD):* 3-4 yrs

Special Facilities: Horticultural Garden. Dairy Farm. Auditorium

Libraries: c. 87,000 vols

Publications: Farm Science Journal *(biannually)*
Last Updated: 29/06/11

CHAROTAR UNIVERSITY OF SCIENCE AND TECHNOLOGY (CHARUSAT)
Changa, Anand District, Gujarat 388 421
Tel: +91(2697) 247-500
Fax: +91(2697) 247-100
EMail: info@charusat.ac.in
Website: http://www.charusat.ac.in

President: Surendra M. Patel

Provost: M. C. Patel

Institutes
Applied Sciences *(P. D. Patel)* (Biochemistry; Biotechnology; Mathematical Physics; Microbiology; Nanotechnology; Natural Sciences; Physics); **Computer Application** *(Charotar)* (Computer Engineering); **Management** *(Indukaka Ipcowala)* (Business Administration; Management); **Nursing** *(Charotar)* (Nursing); **Pharmacy** *(Ramanbhai Patel)* (Pharmacy); **Physiotherapy** *(Charotar)* (Physical Therapy); **Technology** *(Chandubhai Patel)* (Civil Engineering; Computer Engineering; Electrical Engineering; Information Technology; Mechanical Engineering; Telecommunications Engineering)

History: Founded 2000. Acquired present status 2009.

International Co-operation: With univesrities in the United Kingdom

Degrees and Diplomas: *Bachelor's Degree; Master's Degree*

Student Numbers 2010-2011: Total 3,300
Last Updated: 18/10/11

CHAUDHARY CHARAN SINGH HARYANA AGRICULTURAL UNIVERSITY (CCSHAU)
Hisar, Haryana 125004
Tel: +91(1662) 234-613
Fax: +91(1662) 234-952
EMail: reg@hau.nic.in
Website: http://www.hau.ernet.in

Vice-Chancellor: K. Singh Khokhar
Tel: +91(1662) 231-640 EMail: vc@hau.ernet.in

Registrar: Surat Singh DahiyaFax: +91(1662) 234-613

International Relations: S.S. Bisla, Director, Students Welfare
Tel: +91(1662) 231-171/ 73; +91(1662) 284-315
EMail: faculty@hau.nic.in

Colleges
Agricultural Engineering and Technology (Agricultural Engineering; Agricultural Equipment; Food Science; Soil Science; Technology; Water Science); **Agriculture** *(Agri. Kaul, Kaithal)* (Agricultural Economics; Agriculture; Crop Production; Farm Management; Forestry; Horticulture; Soil Science); **Agriculture** (Agricultural Economics; Agriculture; Agronomy; Business Administration; Cattle Breeding; Entomology; Forestry; Horticulture; Meteorology; Plant and Crop Protection; Plant Pathology; Soil Science; Vegetable Production); **Animal Sciences** (Animal Husbandry; Cattle Breeding; Food Technology; Physiology); **Basic Sciences** (Biochemistry; Biology; Biotechnology; Botany; Chemistry; Fishery; Food Science; Genetics; Mathematics; Microbiology; Molecular Biology; Sociology; Statistics; Zoology); **Home Sciences** (Child Care and Development; Clothing and Sewing; Family Studies; Home Economics; Nutrition); **Veterinary Science** (Anatomy; Biochemistry; Embryology and Reproduction Biology; Medicine; Microbiology; Parasitology; Pharmacology; Physiology; Surgery; Toxicology; Veterinary Science)

History: Founded 1970. Modelled on the Land Grant Institutions of USA.

Governing Bodies: Board of Management

Academic Year: July to June

Admission Requirements: 12th year senior secondary/intermediate examination or recognized foreign equivalent

Main Language(s) of Instruction: English, Hindi

International Co-operation: None

Accrediting Agencies: Indian Council of Agricultural Research

Degrees and Diplomas: *Diploma:* Veterinary Livestock Development, 2 yrs; *Bachelor's Degree:* Agricultural Engineering and Technology (B.Tch (Agri. Engineering)); Home Science (B.Sc.(Hons.) Home Science), 4 yrs; *Bachelor's Degree:* Agriculture (B.Sc.Ag.; B.Sc.(Hons) Ag.), 4 yrs (Honours, 1 yr following Bachelor Degree); *Bachelor's Degree:* Veterinary Science (B.V.Sc & AH), 5 yrs; *Master's Degree:* Agricultural Business; Agriculture; Home Economics; Veterinary Science; Agricultural Engineering; Technology; Zoology, a further 2 yrs; *Doctorate:* Agriculture; Home Economics; Veterinary Science; Zoology (PhD), a further 3 yrs

Student Services: Academic counselling, Canteen, Cultural centre, Employment services, Foreign student adviser, Health services, Social counselling, Sports facilities

Student Residential Facilities: Yes

Special Facilities: Indira Gandhi Auditorium. Exhibition Hall

Libraries: 186,224 vols, 91,737 periodical subscriptions, 8,446 thesis and 377 microfilms

Publications: Haryana Farming/Haryana Kheti, in English and Hindi *(monthly)*; Journal of Research, in English *(quarterly)*; Thesis Abstract, in English *(quarterly)*

Press or Publishing House: HAU Press
Last Updated: 29/06/11

CHAUDHARY CHARAN SINGH UNIVERSITY
Meerut, Uttar Pradesh 250005
Tel: +91(121) 276-3539
Fax: +91(121) 276-0577
EMail: registrar@ccsuniversity.ac.in
Website: http://www.ccsuniversity.ac.in

Vice-Chancellor: A.K. Bakhshi
EMail: vicechancellor@ccsuniversity.ac.in

Registrar: V.K. Sinha

Faculties
Agriculture (Agriculture; Botany; Food Science; Horticulture; Plant and Crop Protection; Plant Pathology; Technology); **Arts** (Arts and Humanities; Economics; Education; English; Geography; Hindi; History; Indic Languages; Journalism; Library Science; Mass Communication; Mathematics; Music; Philosophy; Political Sciences; Psychology; Russian; Sanskrit; Social Work; Sociology; Statistics; Urdu); **Commerce and Management** (Accountancy; Business and Commerce; Economics; Management); **Education**

(Education); **Engineering and Technology** (Engineering; Technology); **Law** (Law); **Medicine** (Medicine); **Science** (Biotechnology; Botany; Computer Science; Environmental Management; Mathematics; Microbiology; Natural Sciences; Physics; Statistics; Toxicology; Zoology)

Further Information: Also 1 Constituent and 65 Affiliated Colleges

History: Founded 1965 as University of Meerut. Acquired present title 1994.

Academic Year: July to June

Admission Requirements: 12th year senior secondary/intermediate examination or recognized foreign equivalent

Main Language(s) of Instruction: Hindi, English

Degrees and Diplomas: *Bachelor's Degree*: 4 yrs; *Master's Degree*; *Doctorate (PhD)*

Libraries: 81,787 vols; 24,854 periodical subscriptions
Last Updated: 29/06/11

CHAUDHARY DEVI LAL UNIVERSITY (CDLU)

Sirsa, Haryana 125055
Website: http://www.cdlu.in/

Vice-Chacellor: K.C. Bhardwaj

Registrar: Manoj Siwach

Departments
Biotechnology (Biotechnology); **Business Administration** (Business Administration); **Chemistry** (Chemistry); **Commerce** (Business and Commerce); **Computer Science and Applications** (Computer Science; Software Engineering); **Economics** (Economics); **Education** (Education); **Energy and Environmental Science** (Energy Engineering; Environmental Studies); **English** (English); **Food Science and Technology** (Food Science; Food Technology); **Journalism and Mass Communication** (Journalism; Mass Communication); **Law** (Law); **Mathematics** (Mathematics); **Physical Education** (Physical Education); **Physics** (Physics); **Public Administration** (Public Administration)

History: Founded 2003.

Degrees and Diplomas: *Bachelor's Degree*; *Master's Degree*; *Doctorate*

Student Services: Health services

Student Residential Facilities: Yes

Libraries: Yes
Last Updated: 18/10/11

CHAUDHARY SARWAN KUMAR HIMACHAL PRADESH AGRICULTURAL UNIVERSITY

Chaudhary Sarwan Kumar Himachal Pradesh Krishi Vishwavidyalaya
Palampur, Himachal Pradesh 176062
Tel: +91(1894) 230-521
Fax: +91(1894) 230-465
EMail: vc@hillagric.ernet.in
Website: http://hillagric.ernet.in

Vice-Chancellor: Shyam Kumar Sharma Tel: +91(1894) 230-521

Registrar: Rupali Thakur
Tel: +91(1894) 230-383, Fax: +91(1894) 230-511
EMail: registrar@hillagric.ernet.in

Colleges
Agriculture (Agricultural Economics; Agricultural Engineering; Agriculture; Agronomy; Crop Production; Entomology; Floriculture; Forestry; Genetics; Horticulture; Plant Pathology; Soil Science; Vegetable Production) *Dean*: Pradeep K. Sharma; **Basic Sciences** (Biochemistry; Botany; Chemistry; Mathematical Physics; Microbiology; Modern Languages; Natural Sciences; Statistics; Zoology) *Dean*: R.G. Sud; **Home Science** (Clothing and Sewing; Family Studies; Food Science; Home Economics; Home Economics Education; Nutrition; Textile Design) *Dean*: Sumati Rekha Malhotra; **Veterinary and Animal Sciences** (Anatomy; Animal Husbandry; Cattle Breeding; Fishery; Genetics; Histology; Immunology; Microbiology; Parasitology; Toxicology; Veterinary Science) *Dean*: A.C. Varshney

Further Information: Also Directorate of Research and Directorate of Extension

History: Founded 1978 as Himachal Pradesh Krishi Vishvavidyalaya . Acquired present status and title 2001.

Governing Bodies: Senate; Board of Management; Academic Council

Academic Year: July - June; Doctoral Programmes, January - December

Admission Requirements: 12th year senior secondary/intermediate examination or recognized foreign equivalent

Fees: (Rupees): Undergraduate, 9,711-15,211 per semester; postgraduate, 7,146-11,356 per semester. Free tuition for women students

Main Language(s) of Instruction: English

International Co-operation: With universities in Canada

Accrediting Agencies: Indian Council of Agricultural Research (ICAR)

Degrees and Diplomas: *Bachelor's Degree*: Agriculture; Veterinary Science and Animal Health; Home Economics; Basic Sciences (BSc), 4 yrs; *Master's Degree*: Agriculture; Veterinary Science and Animal Health; Home Economics; Basic Sciences (MSc), a further 2 yrs; *Doctorate*: Agriculture; Veterinary Science; Home Economics (PhD), a further 2 yrs

Student Services: Academic counselling, Canteen, Cultural centre, Employment services, Foreign student adviser, Health services, Nursery care, Social counselling, Sports facilities

Student Residential Facilities: For c. 260 Men and c. 150 Women students

Special Facilities: Museum of Agriculture. Observatory. Biological Garden

Libraries: 37,081 vols; 23,097 periodical subscriptions

Publications: Himachal Journal of Agriculture Research *(biannually)*; Journal of Research *(biannually)*; Newsletter *(quarterly)*; Parvatiya Khetibari, in Hindi *(quarterly)*

Press or Publishing House: Printing Press
Last Updated: 04/07/11

CHENNAI MATHEMATICAL INSTITUTE

Plot H1, SIPCOT IT Park, Padur PO, Siruseri 603103
Tel: +91(44) 2747-0226
Fax: +91(44) 2747-0225.
EMail: office@cmi.ac.in
Website: http://www.cmi.ac.in

Director: R.L. Karandikar

Faculties
Computer Science (Computer Science); **Humanities** (Arts and Humanities); **Mathematics** (Mathematics); **Physics** (Physics)

History: Founded 1989. Acquired present status as Deemed University 2007.

Governing Bodies: Academic Council

Admission Requirements: 12th year senior secondary school and entrance examination

Degrees and Diplomas: *Bachelor's Degree*; *Master's Degree*; *Doctorate*

Libraries: Yes
Last Updated: 04/07/11

CHETTINAD UNIVERSITY

Rajiv Gandhi Salai, Kelambakkam, Kanchipuram Dist, Chennai, Tamil Nadu 603103
Tel: +91(44) 4741-1000
Fax: +91(44) 4741-1011
Website: http://www.chettinadhealthcity.com

Vice-Chancellor: V. Raji EMail: drvraji@chettinadhealthcity.com

Registrar: SPK. Chidambaram
EMail: spk.chidambaram@chettinadhealthcity.com

Colleges
Dentistry (Dentistry)

Departments
Medicine (Cardiology; Dermatology; Endocrinology; Gastroenterology; Gerontology; Gynaecology and Obstetrics; Medicine; Nephrology; Orthopaedics; Paediatrics; Psychiatry and Mental Health; Surgery; Urology)

Degrees and Diplomas: *Bachelor's Degree*; *Master's Degree*
Last Updated: 10/01/12

CHHATRAPATI SHAHU INSTITUTE OF BUSINESS EDUCATION AND RESEARCH (SIBER)

SIBER Shivaji university Road, Kolhapur, 416 004
Tel: 231) 2535706 / 07
Fax: 2535708
EMail: siber@siberindia.co.in
Website: http://www.siberindia.co.in/

Director: M.M. Ali **EMail:** director@siberindia.co.in

Programmes
Business Administration (Business Administration); **Computer Application** (Computer Science; Information Technology); **Environmental Management** (Environmental Management); **Social Work** (Social Work)

History: Founded 1976. Status acquired 1995.

Governing Bodies: Governing Council; Academic Council; Board of studies

Accrediting Agencies: Accredited by the National Board of Accreditation (NBA) of All India Council for Technical Education (AICTE); National Assessment And Accreditation Council (NAAC)

Degrees and Diplomas: *Master's Degree; Master of Philosophy.* Also M.B.A. (Other degrees are offered through the Shivaji University, Kolhapur)

Student Services: Canteen, Sports facilities

Student Residential Facilities: Separate Men and Women Hostels; Guest House; Staff Quarters

Special Facilities: Computer Lab; Language Lab

Libraries: 57,706 vols; 141 periodical subscriptions
Last Updated: 26/01/12

CHHATRAPATI SHAHUJI MAHARAJ MEDICAL UNIVERSITY

Chowk, Lucknow, Uttar Pradesh 226003
Tel: +91(522) 2257-450
Fax: +91(522) 2257-539
EMail: info@kgmcindia.edu
Website: http://csmmu.in

Vice-Chancellor: D.K. Gupta
Tel: +91(522) 2257-540 EMail: vc@kgmcindia.edu

Departments
Anaesthesiology (Anaesthesiology); **Anatomy** (Anatomy); **Biochemistry** (Biochemistry); **Cardiology** (Cardiology); **Clinical Hematology; Community Medicine** (Community Health); **Dental Studies** (Dentistry); **Dermatology, Venereology and Leprosy** (Dermatology; Venereology); **Forensic Medicine** (Forensic Medicine and Dentistry); **Geriatric Mental Health** (Gerontology; Psychiatry and Mental Health); **Hospital Administration** (Health Administration); **Internal Medicine** (Medicine); **Microbiology** (Microbiology); **Neuro Surgery; Neurology** (Neurology); **Obstetrics and Gynecology** (Gynaecology and Obstetrics); **Ophthalmology** (Ophthalmology); **Orthopedic Surgery** (Orthopaedics); **Otorhinolaryngology** (Otorhinolaryngology); **Pathology** (Pathology); **Pediatric Surgery** (Paediatrics; Surgery); **Pediatrics** (Paediatrics); **Pharmacology** (Pharmacology); **Physical Medicine and Rehabilitation** (Physical Therapy; Rehabilitation and Therapy); **Physiology** (Physiology); **Plastic Surgery** (Plastic Surgery); **Psychiatry** (Psychiatry and Mental Health); **Pulmonary Medicine; Radiodiagnosis** (Radiology); **Radiotherapy; Rheumatology** (Rheumatology); **Surgery** (Surgery); **Surgical Gastroenterology** (Gastroenterology); **Surgical Oncology** (Oncology); **Thoracic and Cardio-vascular Surgery** (Cardiology); **Transfusion Medicine** (Medicine); **Urology** (Urology)

History: Founded 2004 as King George Medical College. Acquired present title 2007.

Degrees and Diplomas: *Diploma; Bachelor's Degree; Master's Degree; Master of Philosophy; Doctorate*

Libraries: Yes
Last Updated: 05/01/12

⚠ CHHATRAPATI SHAHU JI MAHARAJ UNIVERSITY

Kalyanpur, Kanpur, Uttar Pradesh 208024
Tel: +91(512) 257-0301
Fax: +91(512) 257-0006
EMail: csjmu@kanpuruniversity.org
Website: http://www.kanpuruniversity.org

Vice-Chancellor: Ashok Kumar (2011-) Tel: +91(512) 257-0450
Registrar: Syed Waqar Hussain Tel: +91(512) 257-0301

Centres
Computer Science (Computer Science)

Departments
Adult and Continuing Education; Education (Education); **English** (English); **Fine Arts and Painting** (Fine Arts; Painting and Drawing); **Journalism and Mass Communication** (Journalism; Mass Communication); **Library and Information Sciences** (Information Management; Library Science); **Music** (Music); **Physical Education** (Physical Education); **Social Work** (Social Work)

Faculties
Agriculture (Agriculture) *Dean*: A.K. Srivastava; **Arts** (Arts and Humanities; Social Sciences) *Dean*: Gopal Ji Srivastava; **Ayurvedic and Unani** (Ayurveda; Traditional Eastern Medicine) *Dean*: V.D. Agawal; **Commerce** (Business and Commerce) *Dean*: P.C. Chaturuvedi; **Education** (Education) *Dean*: Shanta Saxena; **Engineering** (Engineering) *Dean*: Renu Jain; **Law** (Law) *Dean*: Srilekha Vidyarthi; **Life Sciences** (Biological and Life Sciences) *Dean*: L.C. Mishra; **Management** (Business Administration; Management) *Dean*: S.K. Srivastava; **Medicine** (Medicine) *Dean*: S.K. Katiyar; **Science** (Natural Sciences) *Dean*: P.K. Mathur

Institutes
Bio-Sciences and Bio-Technology (Biochemistry; Biotechnology; Environmental Engineering; Microbiology); **Business Management** (Business Administration; Economics; Finance; Management; Tourism); **Engineering and Technology** (Biology; Chemical Engineering; Computer Science; Electronic Engineering; Engineering; Information Technology; Materials Engineering; Mechanical Engineering; Technology; Telecommunications Engineering); **Life Sciences** (Biological and Life Sciences); **Paramedical Sciences; Pharmacy** (Pharmacy)

Research Units
College Development Council

Further Information: Also 1 Constituent College and 355 affiliated colleges

History: Founded 1966 as Kanpur University. Acquired present title 1997.

Governing Bodies: Executive Council; Senate; Academic Council

Academic Year: July to June

Admission Requirements: 12th year senior secondary/intermediate examination or recognized foreign equivalent

Fees: (Rupees): 1,000-45,000 per annum

Main Language(s) of Instruction: English; Hindi

Accrediting Agencies: National Assessment and Accreditation Council

Degrees and Diplomas: *Diploma*: 1-2 yrs; *Bachelor's Degree*: 3-5 yrs; *Postgraduate Diploma*; *Master's Degree*: a further 1-3 yrs; *Master of Philosophy*; *Doctorate (PhD)*: a further 2-5 yrs

Student Services: Academic counselling, Canteen, Cultural centre, Employment services, Foreign student adviser, Health services, Nursery care, Social counselling, Sports facilities

Student Residential Facilities: Teacher's and Staff Residence facilities in the campus. Boys hostel; Girls Hostel; Teachers; Staff; Officers Residence with campus school and Community centre facilities on campus; Guest House.

Special Facilities: Auditorium; Multipurpose Hall; Art Gallery; Herbal Garden; Hlipad; Shopping and Banking Complex

Libraries: Library OPAC-www.kanpuruniversity.org/library.htm. c. 100,000 vols; 270 periodical subscriptions; digital library, 22,000 full texts on-line journals through j-Gate; ABI Inform databases and

INFONET Consortium; 5,000 full text e-books; 7,000 thesis archives; ultramodern library building with 700 reading capacity

Publications: University News Bulletin *(monthly)*

Last Updated: 04/07/11

CHHATTISGARH SWAMI VIVEKANAND TECHNICAL UNIVERSITY

North Park Avenue, Sector-8, Bhilai, Chhattisgarh
Tel: +91(788) 226-1311
Fax: +91(788) 226-1411
Website: http://csvtu.ac.in/

Rector: Bimal Chandra

Registrar: Ashok Kumar Dubey

Faculties
Applied Science (Geology); **Architecture** (Architecture; Interior Design); **Ecology and Environment** (Ecology; Environmental Engineering; Environmental Studies); **Engineering and Technology** (Bioengineering; Chemical Engineering; Civil Engineering; Computer Science; Electronic Engineering; Engineering; Industrial Engineering; Information Technology; Mechanical Engineering; Metallurgical Engineering; Mining Engineering; Production Engineering; Water Science); **Humanities** (Arts and Humanities); **Management and Entrepreneurship** (Business Administration; Management); **Pharmacy** (Pharmacy)

History: Founded 2004.

Degrees and Diplomas: *Diploma*; *Bachelor's Degree*; *Postgraduate Diploma*; *Master's Degree*

Last Updated: 29/07/11

CHITKARA UNIVERSITY

Saraswati Kendra, SCO 160-161, Sector 9 C, Chandigarh, Himachal Pradesh 160 009
Tel: +91(172) 4090-900
Fax: +91(172) 4691-800
EMail: admissions@chitkara.edu.in
Website: http://www.chitkara.edu.in

Viche-Chancellor: Madhu Chitkara

Colleges
Education for Women (Education); **Pharmacy** (Medicine; Pharmacy)

Institutes
Engineering and Technology (Engineering; Technology)

Schools
Business Administration (Business Administration; Management); **Engineering and Technology** (Engineering; Technology); **Health Sciences** (Health Sciences); **Hospitality** (Cooking and Catering; Hotel Management; Tourism); **Mass Communication** (Mass Communication); **Planning and Architecture** (Architecture and Planning)

Further Information: Also campuses in Himachal Pradesh and in Punjab

Accrediting Agencies: University Grants Commission

Degrees and Diplomas: *Bachelor's Degree*; *Postgraduate Diploma*; *Master's Degree*; *Doctorate*

Last Updated: 06/07/11

CHRIST UNIVERSITY

Hosur Road, Bangalore, Karnataka 560029
Tel: +91(80) 4012-9100
Fax: +91(80) 4012-9000
EMail: mail@christuniversity.in
Website: http://www.christuniversity.in/

Vice-Chancellor: Thomas C. Mathew EMail: vc@christuniversity.in

Registrar: J. Subramanian EMail: registrar@christuniversity.in

Centres
Professional Studies

Departments
Biotechnology (Biotechnology); **Botany** (Botany); **Chemistry** (Chemistry); **Commerce** (Business and Commerce); **Computer Science and Applications** (Computer Science); **Economics** (Economics); **Electronics** (Electronic Engineering); **English** (English); **Foreign Language** (Foreign Languages Education); **History** (History); **Journalism** (Journalism); **Mathematics**; **Media Studies** (Media Studies); **Performing Arts** (Performing Arts); **Philosophy and Theology** (Philosophy; Theology); **Physics** (Physics); **Political Sciences** (Political Sciences); **Psychology** (Psycholinguistics); **Social Work** (Social Work); **Sociology** (Sociology); **Statistics** (Statistics); **Tourism Studies** (Tourism); **Zoology** (Zoology)

Faculties
Engineering (Civil Engineering; Electrical and Electronic Engineering; Engineering; Information Technology; Mechanical Engineering; Natural Sciences; Telecommunications Engineering)

Institutes
Management (MBA) *(CUIM)* (Business Administration; Management)

Schools
Law (Law)

History: Founded as Christ College 1969. Acquired present name and status 2007.

Degrees and Diplomas: *Master's Degree*; *Master of Philosophy*; *Doctorate*

Last Updated: 09/01/12

CMJ UNIVERSITY

Mondrina Mansion, Laitumkhrah, Shillong, Maghalaya 793003
Tel: +91(364) 2500-631
Fax: +91(364) 2500-632
EMail: ccii@cmjuniversity.edu.in
Website: http://www.cmju.in/

Chancellor: C. M. Jha

Programmes
Computer Science and Information Technology (Computer Science; Information Technology); **Design and planning** (Architecture; Design; Textile Design); **Engineering** (Chemical Engineering; Electrical Engineering; Engineering; Mechanical Engineering; Metallurgical Engineering; Nanotechnology); **Health and Paramedicals** (Communication Studies; Health Sciences; Medical Auxiliaries; Medical Technology; Optometry; Paramedical Sciences; Physical Therapy); **Humanities and Education and Juridical Science** (Advertising and Publicity; Arts and Humanities; Commercial Law; Education; Human Rights; Journalism; Law; Preschool Education; Primary Education; Public Relations); **Management and Commerce** (Business and Commerce; Criminology; Finance; Human Resources; Information Technology; Management; Marketing; Retailing and Wholesaling; Sports); **Science and Technology** (Information Sciences; Library Science; Natural Sciences; Technology)

History: Founded 2009.

Degrees and Diplomas: *Bachelor's Degree*; *Master's Degree*; *Doctorate*

Last Updated: 03/01/12

COCHIN UNIVERSITY OF SCIENCE AND TECHNOLOGY (CUSAT)

PO Cochin University, Kochi, Kerala 682022
Tel: +91(484) 257-5396
Fax: +91(484) 257-7595
EMail: registrar@cusat.ac.in
Website: http://www.cusat.ac.in

Vice-Chancellor: Ramachandran Thekkedath
Tel: +91(484) 257-7619, Fax: +91(484) 257-5397
EMail: rector@cusat.ac.in

Registrar: N. Chandramohanakumar

Centres
Computer (Computer Science); **Creative Writing** (Writing); **Interdisciplinary Studies**; **Rural Development and Appropriate Technology** (Rural Planning; Technology); **Science in Society**

Departments

Applied Chemistry (Chemistry); **Applied Economics**; **Atmospheric Sciences** (Meteorology); **Biotechnology** (Biotechnology); **Chemical Oceanography** (Marine Science and Oceanography); **Industrial Fishery** (Fishery); **Instrumentation**; **Marine Biology** (Marine Biology); **Marine Geology** (Marine Science and Oceanography); **Mathematics**; **Oceanography**; **Physics**; **Polymer Science and Technology** (Polymer and Plastics Technology; Technology); **Ship Technology** (Naval Architecture); **Statistics**

Faculties

Engineering (Civil Engineering; Computer Engineering; Computer Science; Electrical and Electronic Engineering; Electronic Engineering; Engineering; Fire Science; Marine Engineering; Mechanical Engineering; Safety Engineering; Software Engineering; Telecommunications Engineering) *Dean*: Babu T. Jose; **Humanities and Foreign Languages** (Arabic; Arts and Humanities; French; German; Hindi; Japanese; Modern Languages; Russian; Translation and Interpretation); **Law** (Law) *Dean*: K.N. Chandresekharan Pillai; **Marine Sciences** (Marine Science and Oceanography); **Medical Sciences and Technology** (Health Sciences; Technology) *Dean*: C.K. Sasidharan

Schools

Computer Science *Director*: K. Paulose Jacob; **Environmental Studies** (Biotechnology; Environmental Engineering; Environmental Studies); **Management** *Director*: P. Sudarsanan Pillai; **Photonics**

History: Founded 1971 as Cochin University, acquired present title 1986.

Governing Bodies: Syndicate; Senate; Academic Council

Academic Year: July to April (July-November; December-April).

Admission Requirements: Common Admission Test (CAT). Foreign students admitted through Indian Council for Cultural Relations (ICCR)

Fees: (Rupees): Undergraduate, 3,000-17,500; postgraduate, 750-6,000. Foreign students, undergraduate, (US Dollars): 7,000, postgraduate, 5,000

Main Language(s) of Instruction: English

International Co-operation: With universities in France, Canada, Netherlands, Norway, Japan, USA

Accrediting Agencies: National Accreditation Council; University Grants Commission

Degrees and Diplomas: *Bachelor's Degree*: 3-4 1/2 yrs; *Master's Degree*: a further 1-2 yrs; *Doctorate (PhD)*: a further 2-5 yrs

Student Services: Academic counselling, Canteen, Cultural centre, Employment services, Foreign student adviser, Foreign Studies Centre, Health services, Language programs, Nursery care, Sports facilities

Student Residential Facilities: Yes

Special Facilities: Computer Center, Sports Facilities.

Libraries: Central Library, c. 85,000 vols; 321 periodical subscriptions

Publications: Cochin University Law Review *(quarterly)*; CUSAT News *(quarterly)*

Last Updated: 06/07/11

DATTA MEGHE INSTITUTE OF MEDICAL SCIENCES, DEEMED UNIVERSITY (DMIMSU)

Atrey Layout, Pratapnagar, Nagpur, Maharashtra 440020
Tel: +91(712) 329-5207
Fax: +91(712) 224-5318
EMail: info@dmims.org
Website: http://www.dmimsu.edu.in/

Vice-Chancellor: Vedprakash Mishra Tel: +91(712) 224-5314

Registrar: R.M. Borle
Tel: +91(712) 224-9163, Fax: +91(712) 224-9329

Faculties

Ayurveda *(Mahatma Gandhi College of Ayurveda and Research)* (Ayurveda); **Dentistry** *(Sharad Pawar Dental College)* (Dentistry); **Medicine** *(Jawaharlal Nehru Medical College)*; **Nursing** (Nursing); **Paramedical Sciences** (Paramedical Sciences)

History: Created in 1990. Acquired current status and name 2005. Made up of three constituent colleges.

Governing Bodies: Board of Management; Academic Council; Finance Committee; Boards of Studies.

Academic Year: July to May.

Admission Requirements: Secondary School Certificate.

Fees: (Rupees): 85,000 to 428,000 depending on year and degree.

Main Language(s) of Instruction: English.

International Co-operation: With institutions in Sweden.

Accrediting Agencies: National Assessment and Accreditation Council (NAAC), India

Degrees and Diplomas: *Bachelor's Degree*: Ayurvedic Medicine and Surgery (BAMS), 4 yrs plus 1-year internship; *Bachelor's Degree*: Dental Surgery (BDS), 5 yrs; *Bachelor's Degree*: Medicine; Surgery (MBBS), 4.5 yrs plus 1-year internship; *Postgraduate Diploma*: Dentistry; *Master's Degree*: Dental Surgery (MDS); Medicine; Surgery (MD; MS), a further 3 yrs; *Master's Degree*: Public Health (MPH); *Doctorate*. Also: Certificate Courses in Dental Mechanics and Dental Hygiene

Student Services: Academic counselling, Canteen, Cultural centre, Employment services, Foreign student adviser, Foreign Studies Centre, Handicapped facilities, Health services, Language programs, Nursery care, Social counselling, Sports facilities

Student Residential Facilities: 16 hostels on campus.

Libraries: Yes

Publications: Journal of Datta Meghe Institute of Medical Sciences University

Academic Staff 2010-2011	TOTAL
FULL-TIME	500
STAFF WITH DOCTORATE FULL-TIME	c. 5

Student Numbers 2010-2011	
All (Foreign Included)	c. 1,500
FOREIGN ONLY	5

Last Updated: 06/07/11

DAVANGERE UNIVERSITY

Shivagangothri, Davangere, Karnataka 577002
Tel: +91(8192) 208029
Fax: +91(8192) 208008
EMail: info@davangereuniversity.ac.in
Website: http://davangereuniversity.ac.in

Vice-Chancellor: S. Indumati

Registrar: D.S. Prakash

Departments

Arts (Arts and Humanities; Economics; English; Indic Languages; Political Sciences; Social Work; Sociology); **Commerce** (Accountancy; Business and Commerce; Finance; Management); **Education** (Education); **Fine Arts** (Fine Arts; Painting and Drawing; Sculpture); **Science** (Analytical Chemistry; Biochemistry; Botany; Computer Science; Food Technology; Mathematics; Microbiology; Natural Sciences; Physics)

History: Founded as a post-Graduate centre of the University of Mysore from 1979 to 1987, and later functioned as P.G Centre of Kuvempu University from 1987 to 2009. Acquired present status 2009.

Degrees and Diplomas: *Bachelor's Degree*; *Master's Degree*; *Master of Philosophy*; *Doctorate*

Student Services: Canteen, Sports facilities

Student Residential Facilities: Yes

Libraries: Yes
Last Updated: 18/01/12

DAYALBAGH EDUCATIONAL INSTITUTE (DEI)

PO Dayalbagh, Agra, Uttar Pradesh 282005
Tel: +91(562) 280-545
Fax: +91(562) 280-226
EMail: admin@dei.ac.in
Website: http://www.dei.ac.in

Director: V. Gurusaran Das (2005-)
Tel: +91(562) 280-1545, Fax: +91(562) 280-1226

Registrar: Anand Mohan

Colleges

Prem Vidyalaya Girls Intermediates Studies (Arts and Humanities; Fine Arts; Natural Sciences) *Principal*: Mithilesh Das; **Technical** (Engineering) *Principal*: Prem Prasad Dua

Faculties

Arts (Arts and Humanities; Cultural Studies; English; Hindi; Home Economics; Literature; Music; Musical Instruments; Painting and Drawing; Sanskrit; Singing) *Dean*: V. Prem Kumari; **Commerce** (Accountancy; Business Administration; Business and Commerce; Commercial Law; Economics) *Dean*: Pramod Kumar; **Education** (Education; Pedagogy) *Dean*: Prabha; **Engineering** (Electrical Engineering; Engineering; Mechanical Engineering) *Dean*: V. Prem Pyara; **Science** (Botany; Chemistry; Computer Science; Mathematics; Physics; Zoology) *Dean*: Virendra Prakash Bhatnagar; **Social Sciences** (Economics; Management; Political Sciences; Psychology; Sociology)

History: Founded 1981.

Governing Bodies: Academic Council; Finance Committee; Managing Councils; Primary Body; Governing Body; General Body

Academic Year: July to June (July-December; January-May; May-June)

Admission Requirements: 12th year senior secondary/intermediate examination or recognized foreign equivalent

Main Language(s) of Instruction: English, Hindi

Accrediting Agencies: University Grants Commission; All India Council of Technical Education; National Council for Teacher Education; National Assessment and Accreditation Council (NAAC)

Degrees and Diplomas: *Diploma*: Engineering and Polytechnics, 2/3 yrs; *Bachelor's Degree*: Arts; Commerce; Education; Engineering Science; Social Sciences, 1-4 yrs; *Postgraduate Diploma*: Textile Design and Printing; Computer Science and Applications; Industrial Mathematics; Business Economics; Advanced Theology, a further 1 yr; *Master's Degree (M.Tech)*: 2 yrs (Full-time); 3 1/2 yrs Part-time; *Master of Philosophy*: Education (M.Ed.), 1 yr; *Doctorate*: Arts; Commerce; Education; Engineering Science; Social Sciences; Psychology; Management (PhD), a further 2-5 yrs. Mtech

Student Services: Academic counselling, Canteen, Cultural centre, Employment services, Health services, Sports facilities

Student Residential Facilities: Yes (separate hostels for male and females students)

Special Facilities: Computer and Multimedia Centres.

Libraries: c. 108,070 vols; 182 journals; Access to more than 2,500 e-journals

Publications: DEI Journal of Science and Engineering Research *(annually)*

Last Updated: 11/07/11

DECCAN COLLEGE POST-GRADUATE AND RESEARCH INSTITUTE (DCPRI)

Deccan College Road, Yerwada, Pune, Maharashtra 411006
Tel: +91(20) 2651-3204
Fax: +91(20) 2669-2104
EMail: info@deccancollegepune.ac.in
Website: http://www.deccancollegepune.ac.in

Director: V.P. Bhatta Tel: +91(20) 2669-2982

Registrar: N.S. Gaware
Tel: +91(20) 2661-5232, Fax: +91(20) 2661-5232

Departments

Archaeology (Arts and Humanities); **Linguistics** (Arts and Humanities); **Sanskrit and Lexicography** (Sanskrit)

Further Information: Also Sanskrit Dictionary Project

History: Founded 1821 as Sanskrit School; became Poona College 1851; Became Deccan College 1864; Acquired present title 1939; Acquired present status 1994.

Governing Bodies: Management Council

Academic Year: July to June (July-November;January-June)

Admission Requirements: A graduate degree in Humanities or Science

Main Language(s) of Instruction: English

International Co-operation: With institutions in United Kingdom; USA; France; Japan

Accrediting Agencies: NAAC

Degrees and Diplomas: *Postgraduate Diploma*: Archaeology, 1 yr; *Master's Degree*: Archaeology; Linguistics, 2 yrs; *Doctorate*: Archaeology; Linguistics, 2-6 yrs

Student Services: Academic counselling, Canteen, Sports facilities

Student Residential Facilities: Yes

Special Facilities: Archaeology Museum; Museum of Maratha History

Libraries: c. 160,000 vols with internet access

Publications: Bulletin of the Deccan College Post-graduate and Research Institute *(annually)*; Monograph Series

Last Updated: 11/07/11

DEENBANDHU CHHOTU RAM UNIVERSITY OF SCIENCE AND TECHNOLOGY

50th K.M. Stone, N.H. 1, Murthal (Sonepat), Haryana 131039
Tel: +91(130) 2484-005
EMail: info@dcrustm.org
Website: http://www.dcrustm.ac.in

Vice-Chancellor: Er. Har Sarup Chahal (2008-)
EMail: vc@dcrustm.org

Registrar: R. K. Arora EMail: registrar@dcrustm.org

Faculties

Architecture, Urban and Town Planning (Architecture; Town Planning); **Engineering and Technology** (Biomedical Engineering; Civil Engineering; Electrical and Electronic Engineering; Electronic Engineering; Mechanical Engineering; Telecommunications Engineering); **Information Technology and Communication Sciences** (Communication Studies; Information Technology); **Management Studies** (Management); **Non Conventional Source of Energy and Environment Science** (Biotechnology; Chemical Engineering; Energy Engineering); **Science and Technology Interface** (Chemistry; Communication Studies; English; Nanotechnology; Physics; Technology)

History: Founded 2006.

Admission Requirements: Should be a pass in 10 + 2 examination from recognised Board/University with Physics and Mathematics or Chemistry/Biology as compulsory subjects or International Baccalaureate Diploma, admission will be made on the basis of Entrance Test

Degrees and Diplomas: *Bachelor's Degree*; *Master's Degree*; *Doctorate*

Student Services: Health services, Sports facilities

Student Residential Facilities: Yes

Special Facilities: Computer Centre, Shopping Complex, Post Office

Libraries: Yes
Last Updated: 18/10/11

DEFENCE INSTITUTE OF ADVANCED TECHNOLOGY (DIAT)

Girinagar, Pune, Maharashtra 411025
Tel: +91(20) 2430-4021
Fax: +91(20) 2438-9318
EMail: registrar@diat.ac.in
Website: http://www.diat.ac.in/

Vice-Chancellor: Prahlada EMail: vc@diat.ac.in

Registrar: R. Premkumar

Departments

Aerospace Engineering (Aeronautical and Aerospace Engineering); **Air Force** (Aeronautical and Aerospace Engineering); **Applied Chemistry** (Applied Chemistry); **Applied Mathematics** (Applied Mathematics); **Applied Physics** (Applied Physics); **Armament Engineering** (Engineering); **Army** (Civil Security); **Computer**

Engineering (Computer Engineering; Computer Networks); **Electronics Engineering** (Electronic Engineering); **Materials Engineering** (Materials Engineering); **Mechanical Engineering** (Mechanical Engineering); **Navy** (Marine Engineering; Naval Architecture)

History: Founded 1952 as Institute of Armament Studies, became Institute of Armament Technology 1967. Acquired present title and status 2006.

Degrees and Diplomas: *Master's Degree*; *Doctorate*

Student Residential Facilities: Yes.

Libraries: 44,394 vols; Back Volumes 21,875; Reports 20,000; Dissertations and Theses 1,500
Last Updated: 21/11/11

DELHI TECHNOLOGICAL UNIVERSITY

Shhbad Daulatpur, Main Bawana Road 42, Delhi,
NCT of Dehli 110042
Tel: +91(11) 2787-1018
Fax: +91(11) 2787-1023
EMail: mail@dce.edu
Website: http://www.dce.edu

Vice-Chancellor: P.B. Sharma
Tel: +91(11) 2787-1018 EMail: pbsharma48@]yahoo.co.in

International Relations: R.C. Sharma, International Affairs
EMail: rcsharma_263@yahoo.co.in

Departments
Applied Chemistry (Applied Chemistry); **Applied Mathematics** (Applied Mathematics); **Applied Physics** (Applied Physics); **Biotechnology** (Biotechnology); **Civil and Environmental** (Civil Engineering; Environmental Engineering); **Computer Engineering** (Computer Engineering); **Electrical** (Electrical Engineering); **Electronics and Communication** (Electronic Engineering; Telecommunications Engineering); **Humanities** (Accountancy; Arts and Humanities; Economics; English); **Information Technology** (Information Technology); **Mechanical and Production** (Mechanical Engineering; Production Engineering)

Schools
Management (Business Administration; Management)

History: Founded 1941 as Delhi College of Engineering. Acquired present title and status 2009.

Degrees and Diplomas: *Bachelor's Degree*; *Master's Degree*; *Doctorate*
Last Updated: 05/01/12

DEV SANSKRITI VISHWAVIDYALAYA

Gayatrikunj-Shantikunj, Hardwar, Uttarakhand 249411
Tel: +91(1334) 261-367 +91(1334) 262-094
Fax: +91(1334) 260-723
EMail: vc@dsvv.org
Website: http://www.dsvv.ac.in/

Vice-Chancellor: S.P. Mishra

Registrar: R.P. Karmyogi

Departments
Clinical Psychology (Clinical Psychology); **Computer Science** (Computer Science); **English**; **Holistic Health and Management** (Health Administration); **Human Consciousness and Yogic Sciences** (Yoga); **Indian Culture and Tourism Studies** (Indigenous Studies; Tourism); **Journalism Mass Communication** (Journalism; Mass Communication); **Life Management**; **Rural Management** (Rural Studies); **Sanskrit** (Sanskrit); **Scientific Spirituality**; **Sports** (Sports); **Theology** (Theology)

History: Founded 2002.

Academic Year: July to May (July-December; January-May)

Degrees and Diplomas: *Bachelor's Degree*; *Postgraduate Diploma*: English; Yogic Science, 1 yr; *Master's Degree*: Clinical Psychology; Human Consciousness and Yogic Science; Indian Culture and Tourism Management (MA; MSc), 2 yrs. Also Certificate Courses in Yoga, English Proficiency; Theology; Holistic Health Management (6 months)

Student Services: Health services, Sports facilities

Student Residential Facilities: Hostels for 280 male students and 280 female students

Special Facilities: Psychology laboratories; Yog lab; One Yog clinic; Holistic health practice laboratory; research facilities

Libraries: Computerized library, 5,410 vols; specialized library, 25,000 vols
Last Updated: 11/07/11

DEVI AHILYA VISHWAVIDYALAYA

University House, 235 RNT Marg, Indore, Madhya Pradesh 452001
Tel: +91(731) 252-7532
Fax: +91(731) 252-9540
EMail: registrar.davv@dauniv.ac.in
Website: http://www.dauniv.ac.in/

Vice-Chancellor: P.K. Mishra Tel: +91(731) 252-1887

Registrar: R.D. Musalgoankar

Centres
Science Communication

Faculties
Medicine (Medicine) *Dean*: B.K. Jain

Institutes
Engineering and Technology (Management); **Management Studies** (Management); **Professional Studies**

Schools
Biochemistry (Biochemistry); **Biothechnology** (Biotechnology); **Chemical Sciences** (Chemistry); **Commerce** (Business and Commerce); **Computer Science and Information Technology** (Computer Science; Information Technology); **Economics** (Economics); **Education** (Education); **Electronics** (Electronic Engineering; Engineering); **Energy and Environmental Studies** (Energy Engineering; Environmental Studies); **Future Studies and Planning**; **Instrumentation**; **Journalisme and Mass Communication** (Journalism; Mass Communication); **Language** (Modern Languages); **Law** (Law) *Division Head*: Philips; **Life Sciences** (Biological and Life Sciences); **Mathematics** (Mathematics); **Pharmacy** (Pharmacy); **Physical Education**; **Physics** (Physics); **Social Science**; **Statistics** (Statistics)

Further Information: Also 29 Affiliated Colleges, and Teaching Hospitals

History: Founded 1963.

Academic Year: July to April

Admission Requirements: 12th year senior secondary/intermediate examination or recognized foreign equivalent

Main Language(s) of Instruction: English

Degrees and Diplomas: *Bachelor's Degree*: 3-4 yrs; *Master's Degree*: a further 1-3 yrs; *Doctorate (PhD)*: a further 2 yrs

Student Residential Facilities: Yes

Libraries: 149,567 vols; 225 periodical subscriptions

Press or Publishing House: University Press
Last Updated: 11/07/11

DHARMSINH DESAI UNIVERSITY (DDU)

College Road, Nadiad, Gujarat 387001
Tel: +91(268) 252-0502
Fax: +91(268) 252-0501
EMail: vcddit@yahoo.co.in
Website: http://www.ddu.ac.in

Vice-Chancellor: H.M. Desai
Tel: +91(268) 252-0503 EMail: vc@ddu.ac.in

registrar@ddu.ac.in: M. R. Bhavsar

Faculties
Commerce (Business and Commerce); **Dental Science** (Dentistry); **Management and Information Sciences** (Information Sciences; Management); **Pharmacy** (Pharmacy); **Technology** (Chemical Engineering; Civil Engineering; Computer Engineering; Electronic Engineering; Mathematics; Mechanical Engineering; Telecommunications Engineering)

History: Founded 1968. Acquired present status 2005.

Academic Year: July to April

Admission Requirements: 12th year senior secondary/intermediate examination or recognized foreign equivalent

Main Language(s) of Instruction: English

International Co-operation: With University of Iowa (USA)

Accrediting Agencies: National Assessment & Accreditation Council (NAAC); All India Council for Technical Education (AICTE)

Degrees and Diplomas: *Bachelor's Degree*: Business Administration, 3 yrs; *Bachelor's Degree*: Engineering, 4 yrs; *Master's Degree*: Engineering; Technology; Management (ME.; MCA; MBA), 2 yrs; *Doctorate*: Engineering; Management; Applied Sciences (PhD), at least 2 yrs

Student Services: Academic counselling, Canteen, Cultural centre, Employment services, Health services, Social counselling, Sports facilities

Student Residential Facilities: Yes

Special Facilities: Internet access

Libraries: 19,743 vols

Publications: DDU Newsletter *(biennially)*
Last Updated: 12/07/11

DHIRUBHAI AMBANI INSTITUTE OF INFORMATION AND COMMUNICATION TECHNOLOGY

Near Indroda Circle, Gandhinagar, Gujarat 382007
Tel: +91(79) 3052-0000
Fax: +91(79) 3052-0010
EMail: info@daiict.ac.in
Website: http://www.daiict.ac.in

Director: S.C. Sahasrabudhe

Programmes
Agriculture and Rural Development (Agriculture; Rural Planning; Rural Studies); **Design** (Design); **Information and Communication Technology** (Computer Engineering; Computer Science; Electronic Engineering; Information Technology; Software Engineering)

History: Founded 2001. Acquired present status 2003.

Degrees and Diplomas: *Bachelor's Degree*; *Master's Degree*; *Doctorate*

Libraries: Yes
Last Updated: 12/07/11

DIBRUGARH UNIVERSITY

Dibrugarh, Assam 786004
Tel: +91(373) 237-0231
Fax: +91(373) 237-0323
EMail: info@dibru.ac.in
Website: http://www.dibru.ac.in

Vice-Chancellor: Kandarpa K. Deka EMail: vc@dibru.ac.in

Departments
Anthropology (Anthropology) *Head*: Nitul Gogoi; **Applied Geology** (Geology) *Head*: D. Majmbar; **Assamese** (Indic Languages) *Head*: B. Sarmah; **Chemistry** (Chemistry) *Head*: Sammima Hussain; **Commerce** (Business and Commerce) *Head*: P. Bezborah; **Economics** (Economics) *Head*: H. Goswami; **Education** *Head*: Mukut Hazarika; **English** (English) *Head*: Atul Goswami; **History** (History) *Head*: D. Nath; **Life Sciences** (Biological and Life Sciences) *Head*: M. Islam; **Mathematics** (Mathematics) *Head*: A.K. Barua; **Petroleum Technology** (Petroleum and Gas Engineering) *Head*: M. Das; **Pharmaceutical Sciences** (Pharmacy) *Head*: A.K. Dolui; **Physics** (Physics) *Head*: A.N. Phukan; **Political Science** (Political Sciences) *Head*: T. Lahon; **Sociology** (Sociology) *Head*: B.N. Borthakur; **Statistics** (Statistics) *Head*: Bipin Gogoi

Further Information: Also Affiliated Colleges. Assam Medical College Teaching Hospital Dibrugarh

History: Founded 1965.

Governing Bodies: Court; Executive Council; Academic Council

Academic Year: January to March (January-December; April-March).

Admission Requirements: Higher Secondary Certificate (HSC), standard 12, or equivalent.

Main Language(s) of Instruction: English, Assamese

Accrediting Agencies: NAAC

Degrees and Diplomas: *Bachelor's Degree (BA)*: 3-5 1/2 yrs; *Master's Degree (MA)*: a further 1-3 yrs; *Doctorate (Ph.D)*: at least 2 yrs

Student Services: Academic counselling, Canteen, Health services, Social counselling, Sports facilities

Student Residential Facilities: For c. 500 students

Special Facilities: Museum

Libraries: Main Library, c. 150,000 vols.

Publications: Assam Economic Journal *(annually)*; Bulletin of Department of Anthropology *(annually)*; Journal of Department of Assamese *(annually)*; Journal of Historical Research *(annually)*; Journal of Politics *(annually)*; North East Research Bulletin *(annually)*; Padartha Vigyan Patrika *(annually)*; Pharmray *(annually)*; Vanijya - Journal of Commerce *(annually)*
Last Updated: 12/07/11

DOCTOR BABASAHEB AMBEDKAR MARATHWADA UNIVERSITY

University Campus, Aurangabad, Maharashtra 431004
Tel: +91(240) 240-0104
Fax: +91(240) 240-0291
EMail: vc@bamu.net
Website: http://www.bamu.net/

Vice-Chancellor: V.M. Pandharipande
Tel: +91(240) 240-0069, Fax: +91(240) 240-0007

Registrar: Manvendra KacholeFax: +91(240) 240-0491
EMail: registrar@bamu.net

Departments
Biochemistry (Biochemistry); **Botany** (Botany); **Chemical Technology** (Chemical Engineering); **Chemistry** (Chemistry); **Commerce** (Business and Commerce); **Computer Science and IT** (Computer Engineering; Computer Science; Telecommunications Engineering); **Dance**; **Dramatics** (Theatre); **Economics** (Economics); **Education** (Education); **English** (English); **Environmental Science**; **Fine Arts** (Fine Arts); **Foreign Language** (Foreign Languages Education); **Geography** (Geography); **Hindi** (Hindi); **History and Ancient Indian Culture** (Ancient Civilizations; History); **Journalism** (Journalism); **Law** (Law); **Library and Information Sciences** (Information Sciences; Library Science); **Management Science** (Management); **Marathi Language and Literature** (Indic Languages; Literature); **Mathematics** (Mathematics); **Nanotechnology** (Nanotechnology); **Pali and Buddhism** (Asian Religious Studies; Indic Languages); **Physical Education** (Physical Education); **Physics** (Physics); **Political Science** (Political Sciences); **Printing Technology** (Printing and Printmaking); **Psychology** (Psychology); **Public Administration** (Public Administration); **Sanskrit** (Sanskrit); **Sociology** (Sociology); **Statistics** (Statistics); **Tourism Administration and Management** (Management; Tourism); **Urdu** (Urdu); **Zoology** (Zoology)

Further Information: Also 227 Affiliated Colleges

History: Founded 1958 as Marathwada University. Acquired present title 1994.

Governing Bodies: Senate; Management Council; Academic Council

Academic Year: June to April (June-October; November-April)

Admission Requirements: 12th year senior secondary/intermediate examination or recognized foreign equivalent

Main Language(s) of Instruction: English, Marathi

Degrees and Diplomas: *Bachelor's Degree*: Arts (BA); Commerce; Laws (final); Science; Social Work; Theatre, 3 yrs; *Bachelor's Degree*: Ayurvedic Medicine; Homeopathic Medicine and Surgery; Medicine and Surgery, 5 1/2 yrs; *Bachelor's Degree*: Dental Surgery, 4 1/2 yrs; *Bachelor's Degree*: Education; Journalism; Library Science; Physical Education, 1 yr full-time following first degree, by course of instruction and examination; *Bachelor's Degree*: Engineering; Fine Arts; Pharmacy; Technology, 4 yrs; *Master's Degree*: Arts; Business Administration; Commerce; Education; Engineering; Law; Library Science; Mass Communication, and Journalism; Philosophy; Physical Education; Science; Surgery, a further 1-3 yrs; *Doctorate (PhD)*: 2 yrs; *Doctorate*: Medicine, 3 yrs following MBBS. Also undergraduate and postgraduate Diplomas

Student Residential Facilities: Yes

Libraries: 305,787 vols; 462 periodical subscriptions

Publications: University Journal *(annually)*

Press or Publishing House: University Press

Last Updated: 13/07/11

DOCTOR BABASAHEB AMBEDKAR OPEN UNIVERSITY

9 Government Bungalow, Near Dafnala, Shahibaug, Ahmedabad, Gujarat 380003
Tel: +91(79) 2285-0184
Fax: +91(79) 2286-9691
EMail: baouvc@yahoo.com,
Website: http://www.baou.org

Vice-Chancellor: Manoj Soni EMail: amerchantvc@rediffmail.com

Registrar: Piyushbhai Shah EMail: shbarotreg@rediffmail.com

Schools
Commerce and Management (Business and Commerce; Management); **Computer Science** (Computer Science); **Education; Distance Education and Education Technology** (Distance Education; Education; Educational Technology); **Humanities and Social Sciences** (Arts and Humanities; Social Sciences)

History: Founded 1994.

Academic Year: August to July

Main Language(s) of Instruction: Gujarati

Degrees and Diplomas: *Diploma*; *Bachelor's Degree*; *Postgraduate Diploma*

Last Updated: 13/07/11

DOCTOR BABASAHEB AMBEDKAR TECHNOLOGICAL UNIVERSITY

Vidyavihar, District Raigad, Lonere, Maharashtra 402103
Tel: +91(2140) 275-103
Fax: +91(2140) 275-040
EMail: admin@dbatu.ac.in
Website: http://www.dbatu.ac.in/

Vice-Chancellor: R.B. Mankar EMail: vc@dbatu.ac.in

Registrar: Madhukar S. Tandale EMail: registrar@dbatu.ac.in

Departments
Chemical Engineering (Chemical Engineering); **Chemistry** (Chemistry); **Civil Engineering** (Civil Engineering); **Computer Engineering** (Computer Engineering); **Electrical Engineering** (Electrical Engineering); **Electronics and Telecommunications Engineering** (Electronic Engineering; Telecommunications Engineering); **English** (English); **Information Technology** (Information Technology); **Mathematics** (Mathematics); **Mechanical Engineering** (Mechanical Engineering); **Petrochemical Engineering** (Petroleum and Gas Engineering) *Principal*: D. Sathe; **Physics** (Physics)

History: Founded 1989.

Governing Bodies: Executive Council

Academic Year: August to June (August-January; February-June)

Admission Requirements: 12th year senior secondary/ Intermediate examination or recognized foreign equivalent

Main Language(s) of Instruction: English

Degrees and Diplomas: *Diploma*: Engineering, 3 yrs; *Bachelor's Degree*: Technology, 4 yrs; *Master's Degree*

Student Services: Academic counselling, Canteen, Employment services, Foreign student adviser, Health services, Social counselling, Sports facilities

Libraries: Main Library, c. 44,000 vols.; 145 periodical subscriptions
Last Updated: 13/07/11

DOCTOR B.R. AMBEDKAR OPEN UNIVERSITY (BRAOU)

Prof. G. Ram Reddy Marg., Road No 46, Jubilee Hills, Hyderabad, Andhra Pradesh 500033
Tel: +91(40) 2354-4910
Fax: +91(40) 2354-4830
EMail: info@braou.ac.in
Website: http://www.braou.ac.in

Vice-Chancellor: D. Ramchandram EMail: vc@braou.ac.in

Registrar: C. Venkataiah EMail: registrar@braou.ac.in

Centres
Economic and Social Studies *(CESS)* (Economics; Social Studies) *Director*: Raju K. V. Narayana

Faculties
Arts (Arts and Humanities; English; Hindi; Indic Languages; Urdu); **Commerce** (Business and Commerce; Management); **Education** (Education); **Science** (Botany; Chemistry; Computer Science; Geology; Mathematics; Natural Sciences; Physics; Zoology); **Social Sciences** (Computer Science; Economics; Educational Technology; History; Library Science; Political Sciences; Public Administration; Public Relations; Social Sciences; Sociology)

History: Founded 1982 as Andhra Pradesh Open University, renamed 1991, and has the same legal and academic status as any other University in India. It is designed to enable persons who do not have any formal educational qualification to pursue courses leading to a first degree as well as a Postgraduate degree. The aim of the University is to provide equality of opportunity for as large a segment of the population as possible, through use of print, audio-visual media, teleconferencing and contact, and counselling programmes at 131 study centres.

Governing Bodies: Executive Council; Academic Council

Academic Year: August to July

Admission Requirements: Applicants who have passed the Intermediate examination conducted by the Board of Intermediate Education, or equivalent. Applicants without any qualifications have to pass the Eligibility test conducted by the University

Main Language(s) of Instruction: English, Telugu, Urdu

Degrees and Diplomas: *Bachelor's Degree*: 3 yrs; *Postgraduate Diploma*; *Master's Degree*: a further 2-3 yrs; *Master of Philosophy*: a further 18 months; *Doctorate (PhD)*. Also Certificate courses

Student Services: Academic counselling, Canteen, Cultural centre, Employment services, Foreign student adviser, Foreign Studies Centre, Handicapped facilities, Health services, Language programs, Nursery care, Social counselling, Sports facilities

Special Facilities: Audio Visual Production and Research Centre

Libraries: c. 140,000 vols; 197 periodical subscriptions
Last Updated: 13/07/11

DOCTOR HARISINGH GOUR UNIVERSITY
Doctor Harisingh Gour Vishwavidyalaya
Gour Nagar, Sagar, Madhya Pradesh 470003
Tel: +91(7582) 265-228
Fax: +91(7582) 264-163
EMail: sagaruniversity@mp.nic.in
Website: http://www.sagaruniversity.nic.in/

Vice-Chancellor: N. S. Gajbhiye Tel: +91(7582) 223-199

Departments
Applied Microbiology and Biotechnology (Biotechnology; Microbiology); **Arts** *(Graduate, Sagar)* (Arts and Humanities; English; Hindi; Indic Languages; Linguistics; Music; Persian; Philosophy; Sanskrit; Urdu); **Commerce** (Business and Commerce) *Dean*: B.K. Jain; **Computer Science and Application; Criminology and Forensic Science; Distance Education; Education** *(Graduate)* (Education; Yoga); **Engineering** *(Graduate)* (Engineering); **Law** *(Graduate)* (Law); **Life Sciences** (Biological and Life Sciences; Biophysics; Botany; Microbiology; Zoology); **Management Studies** *(Graduate)* (Management); **Pharmaceutical Sciences** (Pharmacy); **Science** (Anthropology; Chemistry; Criminology; Electronic Engineering; Forensic Medicine and Dentistry; Geography; Instrument Making; Mathematics; Measurement and Precision Engineering;

Natural Sciences; Physics; Statistics); **Social Sciences** (Economics; History; Social Sciences); **Technology** (Geology; Technology)

Further Information: Also 69 Affiliated Colleges

History: Founded 1946 as University of Sagar, acquired present title 1983. An autonomous Institution.

Academic Year: July to April

Admission Requirements: 12th year senior secondary/intermediate examination or recognized foreign equivalent

Main Language(s) of Instruction: English, Hindi

Degrees and Diplomas: *Diploma*; *Bachelor's Degree*: 3 yrs; *Bachelor's Degree*: Education (BEd); Library Science (BLibSc); Mass Communication and Journalism (BMCJ), 1 yr following first degree; *Bachelor's Degree*: Engineering (BEng), 5 1/2 yrs; *Bachelor's Degree*: Law, 5 yrs (Honours); *Bachelor's Degree*: Pharmacy (BPharm), 4 yrs; *Master's Degree*: a further 2-3 yrs; *Master of Philosophy*; *Doctorate (PhD)*

Student Residential Facilities: For c. 340 Women students and c. 930 Men students

Special Facilities: Museum of Anthropology; Museum of Architecture; Museum of Botany; Museum of Geology; Museum of History; Museum of Zoology. Botanical Gardens

Libraries: 286,943 vols and periodicals

Publications: Madhya Bharti (Research Journals)

Press or Publishing House: University Printing Press
Last Updated: 13/07/11

DOCTOR PANJABRAO DESHMUKH AGRICULTURE UNIVERSITY

Doctor Panjabrao Deshmukh Krishi Vidyapeeth
PO Krishi Nagar, Akola, Maharashtra 444104
Tel: +91(724) 225-8372
Fax: +91(724) 225-8219
EMail: tsvc@pdkv.ac.in
Website: http://pdkv.ac.in/

Vice-Chancellor: V. M. Mayande (2007-)
Tel: +91(722) 225-8365 EMail: vc@pdkv.ac.in

Registrar: V.M. Bhale
Tel: +91 (724) 225-8372 EMail: registrar@pdkv.ac.in

International Relations: P.G. Ingole, Public Relations Officer
Tel: +91 (724) 225-8365

Faculties
Agricultural Engineering (Agricultural Engineering; Agricultural Equipment; Agricultural Management; Energy Engineering; Farm Management; Irrigation; Soil Conservation; Water Management) *Dean*: P.M. Nimkar; **Agriculture** (Agricultural Economics; Agriculture; Agronomy; Animal Husbandry; Applied Chemistry; Botany; Crop Production; Dairy; Entomology; Forestry; Horticulture; Plant Pathology; Soil Science) *Dean*: V. K. Mahorkar

Further Information: Also 17 Constituent and 2 Affiliated Colleges

History: Founded 1969.

Academic Year: July to June (July-December;January-June)

Admission Requirements: 12th year senior secondary/intermediate examination or recognized foreign equivalent

Fees: (Rupees): Undergraduate, 9,000 per annum; postgraduate, 19,476; PhD, 23,776

Main Language(s) of Instruction: English

Degrees and Diplomas: *Bachelor's Degree*: Agriculture; Agricultural Engineering and Technology; Horticulture; Forestry (BSc/Btech); *Master's Degree*: Science in Agriculture; Technology in Agricultural Engineering (MSc; Mtech), a further 2 yrs; *Doctorate*: Agriculture; Horticulture; Agricultural Engineering (PhD), a further 3 yrs

Student Services: Academic counselling, Canteen, Employment services, Health services, Social counselling, Sports facilities

Student Residential Facilities: Yes

Special Facilities: Museum. Internet and Computer Room.

Libraries: 139,854 vols

Publications: PVK Research Journal *(biannually)*

Press or Publishing House: Printing Press Dr. P.D.K.V., Akola

Academic Staff 2009-2010	MEN	WOMEN	TOTAL
FULL-TIME	448	43	491
Student Numbers 2009-2010			
All (Foreign Included)	25,071	848	25,919

Last Updated: 18/07/11

DOCTOR RAM MANOHAR LOHIA AWADH UNIVERSITY

Dr. R. M. L. Avadh University Campus, Faizabad,
Uttar Pradesh 224001
Tel: +91(5278) 245-957
Fax: +91(5278) 246-330
EMail: registrar@rmlau.ac.in
Website: http://www.rmlau.ac.in

Vice-Chancellor: Arun Kumar Mittal
Tel: +91(5278) 246-223 EMail: vc@rmlau.ac.in

Registrar: K.N Pandey

Centres
Adult and Continuing Education

Departments
Biochemistry (Biochemistry); **Business Management and Entrepreneurship** (Business Administration; Management); **Economics and Rural Development** (Economics; Rural Planning); **Environmental Science**; **History, Culture and Archaeology** (Archaeology; Cultural Studies; History); **Mathematics and Statistics** (Mathematics; Statistics); **Microbiology** (Microbiology); **Solid State Physics and Electronics** (Electronic Engineering; Solid State Physics)

Faculties
Arts (Archaeology; Arts and Humanities; Cultural Studies; Development Studies; Economics; History) *Dean*: V.K. Pandey; **Commerce** (Business and Commerce); **Education** (Education); **Engineering and Technology** (Electronic Engineering; Engineering; Technology); **Law** (Law); **Science** (Natural Sciences)

Further Information: Also 287 Affiliated Colleges

History: Founded 1975 as Avadh University an autonomous institution.

Governing Bodies: Executive Council; Academic Council; University Court

Academic Year: July to April (both annual and semester system)

Admission Requirements: For Bachelor's Degree: 12th year senior secondary/intermediate examination or recognized foreign equivalent. For Master's Degree - Graduation in relevant discipline

Fees: (Rupees): 4,000-50,000 per annum varying with the courses of study in annual and semester system

Main Language(s) of Instruction: Hindi, English

Accrediting Agencies: National Assessment and Accreditation Council (NAAC) Bangalore

Degrees and Diplomas: *Diploma*: Yoga Therapy; Fashion Designing; *Bachelor's Degree*: Business Administration; Computer Science, 3 yrs; *Bachelor's Degree*: Information Technology; Electronics; Mechanical Engineering, Computer Science; Library; Information Science; Physical Education; *Master's Degree*: Biotechnology; Tourism; Extension Education; Education; Physical Education; Physical Education; Mass Communication and Journalism; Social Work, a further 2 yrs; *Master's Degree*: Computer Science; *Doctorate*: Arts; Science; Commerce; Management (PhD), a further 2-4 yrs

Student Services: Academic counselling, Employment services, Health services, Language programs, Sports facilities

Student Residential Facilities: Yes

Special Facilities: Museum - Koshal Sangrahalay

Libraries: University Library, c. 46,000 vols

Academic Staff 2009-2010	MEN	WOMEN	TOTAL
FULL-TIME	48	4	52
STAFF WITH DOCTORATE			
FULL-TIME	45	4	49
Student Numbers 2009-2010			
All (Foreign Included)	1,610	690	2,300

Last Updated: 20/04/10

DOCTOR YASHWANT SINGH PARMAR UNIVERSITY OF HORTICULTURE AND FORESTRY

District Solan, Nauni, Himachal Pradesh 173230
Tel: +91(1792) 252-363
Fax: +91(1792) 252-242
Website: http://www.yspuniversity.ac.in

Vice-Chancellor: K. R. Dhiman EMail: vc@yspuniversity.ac.in

Registrar: B. R. Kamal EMail: registrar@yspuniversity.ac.in

Centres
Computer Science and Instrumentation (Computer Science; Instrument Making); **Regional Horticultural Research** *(Jachh, Sharbo, Bajaura, Dhaulakuar, Kandaghat, Tabo, Nagrota Bhagwan, Seobagh, Manala)* (Horticulture); **Seed Production** (Agriculture)

Colleges
Forestry (Environmental Studies; Forest Biology; Forest Products; Forestry; Natural Sciences; Social Sciences; Soil Science; Water Management); **Horticulture** (Agricultural Business; Apiculture; Biotechnology; Entomology; Food Science; Fruit Production; Horticulture; Vegetable Production)

Further Information: Also 14 Departments of the Colleges

History: Founded 1985.

Governing Bodies: Senate; Academic Council; Syndicate

Academic Year: July to June

Admission Requirements: 12th year senior secondary/intermediate examination or recognized foreign equivalent

Main Language(s) of Instruction: English

Degrees and Diplomas: *Bachelor's Degree*: Forestry; Horticulture, 4 yrs; *Master's Degree*: Science, a further 2 yrs; *Doctorate (PhD)*: 3 yrs

Student Residential Facilities: Yes

Special Facilities: Museum attached to Regional Horticulture Research Station, Mashobra. Botanical Garden; Herbal Garden

Libraries: c. 52,000 vols
Last Updated: 18/07/11

DOON UNIVERSITY

Motharawala Road, Kedarpur, PO Ajabpur, Dehradun, Uttarkhand
EMail: doonvc@gmail.com
Website: http://doonuniversity.ac.in/

Vice-Chancellor: Girijesh Pant Tel: +91(135) 2532-012

Schools
Communication (Communication Studies; Media Studies); **Environment and Natural Resources** (Environmental Studies; Natural Resources); **Languages** (Modern Languages); **Management** (Business Administration; Management); **Social Sciences** (Social Sciences)

History: Founded 2005.

Degrees and Diplomas: *Bachelor's Degree*; *Master's Degree*
Last Updated: 04/01/12

DR. B. R. AMBEDKAR NATIONAL INSTITUTE OF TECHNOLOGY JALANDHAR

Jalandhar, Punjab 144011
Tel: +91(181) 269-0301 +91(181) 269-0302
Fax: +91(181) 269-0320 +91(181) 269-0932
EMail: admin@nitj.ac.in
Website: http://www.nitj.ac.in/

Director: S. B. Mishra EMail: director@nitj.ac.in

Registrar: A. L. Sangal

Departments
Mathematics (Mathematics); **Biotechnology** (Biotechnology); **Chemical Engineering** (Chemical Engineering); **Chemistry** (Applied Chemistry; Chemistry); **Civil Engineering** (Civil Engineering); **Computer Science and Engineering** (Computer Engineering; Computer Science; Engineering); **Electronics and Communication Engineering** (Electronic Engineering; Telecommunications Engineering); **Humanities and Management**

(Communication Studies; Economics; Human Resources; Industrial and Organizational Psychology; Management; Marketing; Psychology); **Industrial and Production Engineering**; **Instrumentation and Control Engineering** (Automation and Control Engineering); **Mechanical Engineering**; **Physics**; **Textile Technology** (Textile Technology)

History: Created 1986 as Dr B R Ambedkar Regional Engineering College. Acquired current title and status 2002.

Governing Bodies: Board of Governors

Degrees and Diplomas: *Bachelor's Degree*: Chemical Engineering; Civil Engineering; Computer Science and Engineering; Electronics and Communication Engineering; Industrial and Production Engineering; Instrumentation and Control Engineering; Mechanical Engineering; Textile Technology (BTech), 4 yrs; *Postgraduate Diploma*: Garment Manufactuing Technology; *Master's Degree*: Chemical Engineering; Computer Science and Engineering; Industrial and Production Engineering; Textile Engineering and Management (MTech); Mathematics (MSc); *Doctorate*
Last Updated: 18/07/11

DR. B. R. AMBEDKAR UNIVERSITY

Paliwal Park, Agra, Uttar Pradesh 282004
Tel: +91(562) 215-2118
Fax: +91(562) 252-0051
EMail: info@dbrau.ac.in
Website: http://www.dbrau.ac.in/

Vice-Chancellor: D.N. Jauhar EMail: vc@dbrau.ac.in

Registrar: Shri A. K. Arvind EMail: registrar@dbrau.ac.in

Faculties
Arts (Arts and Humanities) *Dean*: A. K. Singh; **Commerce** (Business and Commerce) *Dean*: Murari Lal; **Education** (Fine Arts); **Engineering** (Engineering); **Home Science** (Home Economics) *Dean*: Bharti Singh; **Law** (Law) *Dean*: J.C. Kulshreshtha; **Management** (Management); **Medical Science** (Homeopathy; Medicine) *Dean*: K. K. Gupta; **Science** (Natural Sciences) *Dean*: Diwaker Kahre

Institutes
Basic Sciences (Botany; Chemistry; Mathematics; Natural Sciences; Physics; Zoology); **Hindi Studies and Linguistics** *(K.M.)* (Hindi; Linguistics; Russian); **Home Science** (Child Care and Development; Clothing and Sewing; Dietetics; Family Studies; Home Economics; House Arts and Environment; Nutrition; Textile Technology); **Social Sciences** (Social Sciences; Social Work; Sociology; Statistics)

Schools
Life Sciences (Biological and Life Sciences)

Further Information: Also Khandari campus, Chalesar Campus and Khandelwal Kothi. University has approx 500 affiliated Institutes/Colleges

History: Founded 1927 as Agra University by Act of the United Provinces legislature. Acquired current title 1996.

Governing Bodies: Executive Council

Academic Year: July to May

Admission Requirements: 12th year senior secondary/intermediate examination or recognized foreign equivalent

Main Language(s) of Instruction: Hindi, English

Degrees and Diplomas: *Bachelor's Degree*: 3-4 1/2 yrs; *Master's Degree*: a further 1-3 yrs; *Doctorate (PhD)*: at least 2 yrs

Libraries: c. 160,000 vols
Last Updated: 18/07/11

DR. BALASAHEB SAWANT KONKAN KRISHI VIDYPEETH

Dapoli, Maharashtra 415712
Tel: +91(2358) 282064
Fax: +91(2358) 282074
EMail: root@kkv.ren.nic.in
Website: http://www.dbskkv.org

Vice-Chancellor: Kisan E. Lawande EMail: vcbskkv@yahoo.co.in

Colleges
Fisheries (Fishery)

Faculties
Agricultural Engineering (Agricultural Engineering; Agricultural Equipment; Computer Science; Soil Conservation; Water Management); **Agriculture** (Agricultural Business; Agricultural Economics; Agricultural Engineering; Agriculture; Agronomy; Animal Husbandry; Entomology; Food Science; Forestry; Horticulture; Plant Pathology); **Forestry** (Forest Biology; Forest Management; Forestry); **Horticulture** (Arts and Humanities; Floriculture; Fruit Production; Harvest Technology; Landscape Architecture; Natural Resources; Plant and Crop Protection; Vegetable Production)

Research Centres
Agricultural *(Regional)* (Agriculture); **Fruit** *(Regional)* (Agricultural Economics; Entomology; Fruit Production; Horticulture; Plant Pathology; Soil Science)

Further Information: Also 10 constituent Agricultural Colleges

History: Founded 1972 as Konkan Krishi Vidyapeeth. Acquired present status and title 2001.

Governing Bodies: Academic Council; Executive Council

Academic Year: July to June

Admission Requirements: Higher secondary certificate or recognized equivalent

Fees: (Rupees): 13,876-19,776

Main Language(s) of Instruction: English

Accrediting Agencies: ICAR

Degrees and Diplomas: *Bachelor's Degree*: 4 yrs; *Master's Degree*: 2 yrs; *Doctorate (PhD)*

Student Services: Academic counselling, Canteen, Cultural centre, Handicapped facilities, Health services, Sports facilities

Student Residential Facilities: For 495 students

Special Facilities: Observatory

Libraries: 38,622 vols; 69 journals

Academic Staff *2010-2011*: Total 260

STAFF WITH DOCTORATE: Total 120

Student Numbers *2010-2011*: Total: c. 680
Last Updated: 18/07/11

DR. C. V. RAMAN UNIVERSITY
Kargi Road, Kota, Bilaspur, Chhattisgarh
Tel: +91(7753) 253736
Fax: +91(7753) 253728
EMail: cvruraipur@yahoo.co.in
Website: http://www.cvru.ac.in

Vice-Chancellor: A.S. Zadgaonkar

Registrar: Shailesh Pandey

Faculties
Commerce (Business and Commerce); **Education** (Education); **Engineering** (Civil Engineering; Electronic Engineering; Engineering; Information Technology; Mechanical Engineering; Telecommunications Engineering); **Information Technology and Computer ScienceComputer Science &Computer Science and Information Technology** (Computer Science; Information Technology); **Management** (Agricultural Management; Finance; Human Resources; Insurance; Management; Marketing; Retailing and Wholesaling); **Science** (Biology; Biotechnology; Botany; Chemistry; Information Sciences; Library Science; Mathematics; Microbiology; Physics; Zoology)

Degrees and Diplomas: *Bachelor's Degree*; *Master's Degree*; *Master of Philosophy*
Last Updated: 18/07/11

DR. D. Y. PATIL VIDYAPEETH
Sant Tukaram Naga, Pimpri, Pune, Maharashtra 411018
Tel: +91(20) 2742-0069
Fax: +91(20) 2742-0010
EMail: info@dpu.edu.in
Website: http://www.dpu.edu.in

Vice-Chancellor: Pushpati Nath Razdan **EMail:** vc@dpu.edu.in

Colleges
Dentistry (Dentistry); **Medicine** (Medicine); **Nursing** (Nursing); **Physiotherapy** (Physical Therapy)

Institutes
Biotechnology and Bioinformatics (Biotechnology); **Distance Learning**; **Optometry and Visual Sciences** (Optometry)

Schools
Business *(Global)* (Business Administration)

Degrees and Diplomas: *Bachelor's Degree*; *Master's Degree*; *Doctorate*
Last Updated: 09/01/12

DR. K. N. MODI UNIVERSITY
Plot No. INS-1, RIICO Industrial Area Ph-II, Newai, Newai, Rajasthan 304021
Tel: +91(11) 2683-7275
Fax: +91(11) 4162-7930
EMail: info@dknmu.org
Website: http://www.dknmu.org

President: Francis C. Peter

Faculties
Management and Business Studies (Accountancy; Business Administration; Finance; International Business; Management; Retailing and Wholesaling); **Science, Engineering and Technology** (Automotive Engineering; Civil Engineering; Computer Science; Electrical and Electronic Engineering; Electronic Engineering; Engineering; Mechanical Engineering; Natural Sciences; Technology)

Degrees and Diplomas: *Bachelor's Degree*; *Master's Degree*; *Doctorate*
Last Updated: 02/01/12

DR. M.G.R. EDUCATIONAL AND RESEARCH INSTITUTE (UNIVERSITY)
E.V.R. High Road (NH4 Highway), Maduravoyal, Chennai, Tamil Nadu 600095
EMail: registrar@drmgrdu.ac.in
Website: http://www.drmgrdu.ac.in

Vice-Chancellor: P. Aravindan **EMail:** vc@drmgrdu.ac.in

Registrar: C. B. Palanivelu

Faculties
Engineering and Technology (Automation and Control Engineering; Biotechnology; Business Administration; Chemical Engineering; Civil Engineering; Computer Engineering; Computer Science; Electrical and Electronic Engineering; Information Technology; Management; Mechanical Engineering; Production Engineering; Telecommunications Engineering); **Medicine and Dental Science** (Dentistry; Medicine; Nursing; Physical Therapy); **Science and Humanities** (Arts and Humanities; Cooking and Catering; Food Technology; Hotel Management)

History: Founded 1988 as Dr.M.G.R. Engineering College. Acquired present status and title 2003.

Accrediting Agencies: UGC, India

Degrees and Diplomas: *Diploma*; *Bachelor's Degree*; *Postgraduate Diploma*; *Master's Degree*; *Doctorate*
Last Updated: 20/07/11

DR. RAM MANOHAR LOHIYA NATIONAL LAW UNIVERSITY
Sec- D1, LDA Colony, Kanpur Road Scheme, Lucknow, Uttar Pradesh 226012
Tel: +91(522) 2425- 902
Fax: +91(522) 2422- 841
EMail: registrar@rmlnlu.ac.in
Website: http://www.rmlnlu.ac.in/

Vice-Chancellor: Balraj Chauhan

Programmes
Law (Law)

History: Founded 2005.

Fees: (Rupiahs): 40.000 per annum,

Degrees and Diplomas: *Bachelor's Degree*; *Master's Degree*; *Doctorate*

Student Residential Facilities: Yes

Libraries: Yes

Last Updated: 04/01/12

DR. SHAKUNTALA MISRA REHABILITATION UNIVERSITY

Lucknow, Uttar Pradesh 226017
Website: http://dsmru.up.nic.in/

Head: Raj Pratap Singh

Registrar: SK Srivastava EMail: registrarofdsmru@gmail.com

Faculties

Arts and Music (Economics; English; Hindi; History; Political Sciences; Social Work; Sociology); **Commerce and Management** (Business Administration; Business and Commerce; Finance; Human Resources; Marketing); **Special Education** (Special Education; Speech Therapy and Audiology)

Last Updated: 04/01/12

DRAVIDIAN UNIVERSITY

District Chitoor, Kuppam, Andhra Pradesh 517425
Tel: +91(8570) 278-220
Fax: +91(8570) 278-230
Website: http://www.dravidianuniversity.ac.in/

Vice-Chancellor: Cuddapah Ramanaiah Tel: +91(8570) 278-236

Registrar: C.Varadarajulu Naidu

Schools

Commerce and Management (Business and Commerce; Management); **Comparative Literature and Translation Studies** (Communication Studies; English; Indic Languages; Literature; Philosophy; Religion; South and Southeast Asian Languages; Translation and Interpretation); **Education and Human Resources Development** (Education; Human Resources; Indic Languages; Physical Education); **Herbal studies and Naturo Sciences** (Biotechnology; Chemistry; Environmental Studies; Molecular Biology; Traditional Eastern Medicine); **Human and Social Sciences** (Archaeology; History; Indigenous Studies; Philosophy; Religion); **Information Sciences and Technology** (Computer Science; Information Sciences; Library Science; Technology)

History: Founded 1997.

Governing Bodies: Executive Council, Planning and Monitoring Board, Academic Advisory Committee

Academic Year: July to June.

Main Language(s) of Instruction: English. Telugu, Tamil, Kannada and Malayalam.

Degrees and Diplomas: *Bachelor's Degree (B.A; B.Com; B.Sc)*: 3 yrs; *Master's Degree (MA; MSc; MCA)*: 2 yrs; *Master of Philosophy (Mphil)*: 1 yr full-time (2 yrs part-time)

Libraries: c. 45,000 vols

Publications: Dravidian Studies, Research Journal

Last Updated: 20/07/11

D.Y. PATIL MEDICAL COLLEGE

Kasba Bawda, Kolhapur, Maharastra 416006
Tel: +91(231) 2601-235
Fax: +91(231) 2601-238
EMail: info@dypatilkolhapur.org
Website: http://www.dypatilunikop.org/

Vice-Chancellor: S.H. Pawar EMail: vc@dypatilunikop.org

Registrar: V. V. Bhosale
Tel: +91(231) 2601-595 EMail: registrar@dypatilunikop.org

Colleges

Medicine (Anaesthesiology; Cell Biology; Dermatology; Gynaecology and Obstetrics; Health Sciences; Medicine; Microbiology; Ophthalmology; Orthopaedics; Paediatrics; Psychiatry and Mental Health; Radiology; Surgery); **Nursing** (Nursing); **Physiotherapy** (Physical Therapy)

Institutes
Hospital Research *(Padmashree Dr. D.Y. Patil)*

History: Founded 2009.

Degrees and Diplomas: *Bachelor's Degree*; *Master's Degree*; *Doctorate*

Last Updated: 10/01/12

EASTERN INSTITUTE FOR INTEGRATED LEARNING IN MANAGEMENT (EIILM)

District Namchi, Jorethang, Sikkim 737121
EMail: info@eiilmuniversity.ac.in
Website: http://www.eiilmuniversity.ac.in/

Vice-Chancellor: A. Sankara Reddy

Departments

Arts and Commerce (Arts and Humanities; Business and Commerce); **Biotechnology and Environmental Science** (Biotechnology; Ecology; Environmental Studies); **Computer Science and Information Technology** (Computer Science; Information Technology); **Engineering** (Civil Engineering; Electronic Engineering; Engineering; Mechanical Engineering; Telecommunications Engineering); **Fashion** (Fashion Design); **Hospitality and Tourism** (Tourism); **Library Science** (Library Science); **Management** (Business Administration; Finance; Human Resources; Insurance; International Business; Management; Marketing; Retailing and Wholesaling); **Media and Communication** (Communication Studies; Media Studies)

Further Information: Also Malabassey Campus

History: Founded 2006.

Degrees and Diplomas: *Diploma*; *Bachelor's Degree*; *Postgraduate Diploma*; *Master's Degree*

Last Updated: 28/12/11

ETERNAL UNIVERSITY

Baru Sahib, Via Rajgarh, Distt. Sirmour, Himachal Pradesh 173101
Tel: +91(1799) 276002
Fax: +91(1799) 276006
EMail: contact@eternaluniversity.org
Website: http://www.eternaluniversity.edu.in/

Vice-Chancellor: Manmohan Singh Atwal

Registrar: Davinder Singh

Colleges

Arts and Sciences (Arts and Humanities; Natural Sciences); **Divine Music and Spiritualism** (Religious Music); **Engineering and Technology** (Engineering; Technology); **Nursing** (Nursing); **Post Graduate Studies**

Institutes

Applied Sciences (Natural Sciences); **Renewable Energy Research** (Energy Engineering)

Schools

Biotechnology (Biotechnology); **Business Administration** (Business Administration); **Chemistry** (Chemistry); **Economics** (Economics); **Nutrition and Food Technology** (Food Technology; Nutrition); **Physics** (Physics); **Public Health** (Public Health)

Degrees and Diplomas: *Bachelor's Degree*; *Master's Degree*; *Doctorate*

Last Updated: 14/11/11

FAKIR MOHAN UNIVERSITY

Vyasa Vihar, Near Remuna Golei, Balasore, Orissa 756019
Tel: +91(6782) 261-711
Fax: +91(6782) 264-244
Website: http://www.fmuniversity.nic.in

Vice-Chancellor: Kumar Bar Das (2011-)

Registrar: Sridhar Behera

Departments

Applied Physics and Ballistics (Applied Physics); **Biotechnology** (Biotechnology); **Business Administration** (Business Administration); **Environmental Studies** (Environmental Studies); **Information and Communication Technology** (Information Technology); **Population Studies** (Demography and Population); **Social Science** (Social Sciences)

History: Founded 1999.

Degrees and Diplomas: *Bachelor's Degree*; *Master's Degree*
Last Updated: 20/07/11

FORE SCHOOL OF MANAGEMENT (FSM)

B-18, Qutub Institutional Area, New Delhi 110 016
Tel: +91(11) 4124-2424
Fax: +91(11) 2696-4229
EMail: admissions@fsm.ac.in; asif@fsm.ac.in
Website: http://fsm.ac.in/

Director: Jitendra K. Das EMail: fore@fsm.ac.in

Programmes

International Business (International Business); **Management** (Management)

History: Founded 1981.

Governing Bodies: Executive Board; Academic Board

International Co-operation: With institutions in France, USA, Canada and Thailand

Accrediting Agencies: All India Council for Technical Education (AICTE)

Degrees and Diplomas: *Postgraduate Diploma*

Student Services: Canteen, Sports facilities

Student Residential Facilities: Hostel

Special Facilities: Auditorium; Computer centre

Libraries: c. 23,900 vols; 160 periodical subscriptions
Last Updated: 23/01/12

FOREST RESEARCH INSTITUTE - DEEMED UNIVERSITY

PO New Forest, Dehradun, Uttarakhand 248006
Tel: +91(135) 275-5277
Fax: +91(135) 275-6865
EMail: negiss@icfre.org
Website: http://fri.icfre.gov.in/

Director: S.S Negi EMail: dg@icfre.org

Secretary: Sh. Piarchand EMail: sudhanshu@icfre.org

Programmes

Forestry (Botany; Chemistry; Ecology; Environmental Studies; Forestry; Paper Technology; Wood Technology)

History: Founded 1906. Acquired present status and title 1991.

Fees: (Rupees): 5,000 per annum

Degrees and Diplomas: *Bachelor's Degree*: 4 yrs; *Postgraduate Diploma*; *Master's Degree*; *Doctorate (PhD)*

Libraries: c. 150,000 vols; 500 periodicals
Last Updated: 20/07/11

FORTUNE INSTITUTE OF INTERNATIONAL BUSINESS (FIIB)

Plot 5, Rao Tula Ram Marg, Vasant Vihar, New Delhi 110 057
Tel: +91(11) 4728-5000
Fax: +91(11) 2614-4279
EMail: fiib@fiib.edu.in
Website: http://fiib.edu.in/

Registrar: Anupam Bhaskar
Tel: +91(11) 4728-5018 EMail: anupam.bhaskar@fiib.edu.in

Programmes

International Business (Accountancy; Business Administration; Communication Studies; Economics; Finance; Human Resources; Industrial and Organizational Psychology; Information Management; Information Technology; International Business; Management; Marketing; Operations Research)

History: Founded 1995.

Accrediting Agencies: National Board of Accreditation (NBA); All India Council of Technical Education (AICTE)

Degrees and Diplomas: *Postgraduate Diploma*. Equivalence of the PGDM to a M.B.A.

Academic Staff *2011-2012*: Total: c. 20
Student Numbers *2011-2012*: Total: c. 240
Last Updated: 09/01/12

GALGOTIAS UNIVERSITY

1, Institutional Area, Knowledge Park - 2, Greater Noida, Uttar Pradesh 201306
EMail: info@galgotiasuniversity.edu.in
Website: http://www.galgotiasuniversity.edu.in/

Vice-Chancellor: K.N. Tripathi

Schools

Business (Business Administration); **Arts and Social Sciences** (Arts and Humanities; Economics; English; Fashion Design; French; Library Science; Psychology; Social Sciences; Social Work; Sociology); **Basic and Applied Sciences** (Biomedical Engineering; Chemistry; Mathematics; Natural Sciences; Physics); **Computer and Information Sciences** (Computer Science; Information Sciences); **Engineering and Technology** (Civil Engineering; Computer Engineering; Computer Science; Electrical Engineering; Electronic Engineering; Mechanical Engineering; Telecommunications Engineering); **Finance and Commerce** (Business and Commerce; Finance); **Hospitality and Tourism** (Hotel Management; Tourism); **Journalism and Mass Communication** (Journalism; Mass Communication); **Law** (Law)

History: Founded 2011.

Fees: (Indian Rupees): 52,000-128,000 per annum depending on programmes

Degrees and Diplomas: *Bachelor's Degree*; *Master's Degree*; *Doctorate*
Last Updated: 28/12/11

GANDHIGRAM RURAL INSTITUTE - DEEMED UNIVERSITY

Dindigul District, Gandhigram, Tamil Nadu 624302
Tel: +91(451) 245-2371
Fax: +91(451) 245-3071
EMail: grucc@ruraluniv.ac.in
Website: http://www.ruraluniv.ac.in/

Vice-Chancellor: S.M. Ramasamy

Registrar: N. Narayanasamy

Centres

Computer (Computer Science); **Rural Energy Centre** (Rural Studies); **Rural Technology** (Agricultural Engineering)

Faculties

Agriculture and Animal Husbandry (Agriculture; Animal Husbandry); **English and Foreign Languages** (English; Modern Languages); **Rural Development** (Adult Education; Continuing Education; Rural Studies); **Rural Health and Sanitation** (Health Sciences; Sanitary Engineering); **Rural Oriented Sciences** (Biology; Chemistry; Mathematics; Natural Sciences; Physics; Rural Studies); **Rural Social Sciences** (Administration; Economics; Peace and Disarmament; Political Sciences; Rural Planning; Rural Studies; Social Sciences; Sociology); **Tamil and Indian Languages and Rural Arts** (Indic Languages) *Dean*: G. Pankajam

History: Founded 1956. Of the 14 Rural Institutes of Higher Education started in India, this is the only one to be declared as 'Deemed University' in 1976.

Governing Bodies: Senate; Academic Council; Syndicate

Academic Year: July to April (July-November; December-April)

Admission Requirements: 12th year senior secondary/intermediate examination or recognized foreign equivalent

Main Language(s) of Instruction: English

Degrees and Diplomas: *Bachelor's Degree*: 3 yrs; *Postgraduate Diploma*: 1 yr; *Master's Degree*: a further 2 yrs; *Master of Philosophy*: 1 further yr; *Doctorate (PhD)*: a further 2-4 or 3-5 yrs

Student Residential Facilities: Yes

Special Facilities: Gandhi Museum

Libraries: 86,810 vols

Last Updated: 08/08/11

GANPAT UNIVERSITY

Ganpat Vidyanagar, Goazaria Highway, Meshana 382711
Tel: +91(2762) 286-080
EMail: info@ganpatuniversity.ac.in
Website: http://www.ganpatuniversity.ac.in

Vice Chancellor: L. N. Patel

Registration: C. D. Jadeja

Centres
Management Studies (Management)

Colleges
Engineering (Computer Engineering; Engineering; Mechanical Engineering); **Management Studies** *(V.M.Patel)* (Management); **Pharmacy** (Pharmacy)

Departments
Education (Education)

Institutes
Bioscience *(Mehsana)* (Biotechnology; Microbiology); **Computer Science** (Computer Science); **Management** *(V.M.Patel)* (Business Administration; Management)

History: Founded 2005.

Degrees and Diplomas: *Bachelor's Degree*; *Master's Degree*

Student Services: Canteen

Student Residential Facilities: Yes

Special Facilities: WI-FI facilities

Last Updated: 08/08/11

GAUHATI UNIVERSITY

Gopinath Bardoloi Nagar, Quarter No. 39, Guwahati, Assam 781014
Tel: +91(361) 257-0415
Fax: +91(361) 257-0311
EMail: vc@gauhati.ac.in
Website: http://www.gauhati.ac.in

Vice-Chancellor: Okhil Kumar Mehdi
Tel: +91(361) 257-0412, Fax: +91(361) 270-0311
EMail: vc_gu@yahoo.in

Registrar: Uttam Chandra Das EMail: registrar@gauhati.ac.in

Centres
Women's Study Research *Director:* Archana Sarma

Colleges
Law (Law) *Principal:* J. P. Bora

Faculties
Arts (Arabic; Arts and Humanities; Communication Studies; English; Foreign Languages Education; French; Hindi; History; Indic Languages; Information Sciences; Journalism; Library Science; Linguistics; Mass Communication; Modern Languages; Persian; Psychology; Sanskrit; Women's Studies) *Dean:* Kandarpa Barman; **Business Administration** (Business Administration); **Commerce** (Business and Commerce) *Dean:* Nayan Baruah; **Engineering** (Engineering) *Dean:* N.N. Patowary; **Fine Arts** (Fine Arts); **Law** (Law); **Management** (Economics; Management) *Dean:* Munindra Kakati; **Medicine** *(Regional Dental College, Guwahati)* (Medicine) *Dean:* M.M. Deka; **Science** (Anthropology; Biotechnology; Botany; Computer Science; Electronic Engineering; Environmental Studies; Geography; Mathematics; Natural Sciences; Physics; Telecommunications Engineering; Zoology) *Dean:* Pranab Jyoti Das; **Technology** (Technology) *Dean:* Pranayee Datta

Further Information: Also 1 Constituent and 201 Affiliated Colleges

History: Founded 1948.

Governing Bodies: Executive Council, comprising 27 members; Court, comprising 108 members; Academic Council, comprising 117 members

Academic Year: June to May

Admission Requirements: 12th year senior secondary/intermediate examination or recognized foreign equivalent

Main Language(s) of Instruction: English

Degrees and Diplomas: *Diploma*: 1 yr; *Bachelor's Degree*: Arts; Commerce; Law (LLB); Science, 3 yrs; *Bachelor's Degree*: Engineering, 4 yrs; *Master's Degree*: a further 1-3 yrs; *Master of Philosophy (M Phil)*: 1 yr; *Doctorate (PhD)*: at least 2 yrs

Student Residential Facilities: Yes

Special Facilities: Anthropology Museum; Botany Museum; Commerce Museum; Education Museum; Geology Museum. Astrological Observatory. Botanical Garden

Libraries: 415,993 vols (Special collection for Oriental Studies: Sanskrit, Latin, Greek)

Publications: Arts and Science, Journal

Press or Publishing House: University Press

Last Updated: 25/07/11

GAUTAM BUDDH TECHNICAL UNIVERSITY (GBTU)

Institute of Engineering and Technology Campus, Sitapur Road, Lucknow, Uttar Pradesh 226 021
Tel: +91(522) 273-2376 +91(522) 273-2193
Fax: +91(522) 273-2185
EMail: registrar@uptu.ac.in
Website: http://www.uptu.ac.in/

Vice-Chancellor: Kripa Shanker
Tel: +91(522) 273-2194, Fax: +91(522) 273-2189
EMail: vc@uptu.ac.in

Registrar: U.S. Tomer
Tel: +91(522) 2732193, Fax: +91(522) 2732185
EMail: ustomer@uptu.nic.in

Faculties
Architecture (Architecture; Architecture and Planning; Building Technologies; Construction Engineering; Interior Design)

Institutes
Engineering and Technology *(Lucknow, IET)* (Applied Chemistry; Arts and Humanities; Biotechnology; Business Administration; Chemical Engineering; Civil Engineering; Computer Engineering; Computer Science; Electrical Engineering; Electronic Engineering; Engineering; Mechanical Engineering; Technology)

Programmes
Agricultural Engineering (Agricultural Engineering); **Hotel Management and Catering Technology** (Cooking and Catering; Hotel and Restaurant; Hotel Management); **Pharmacology** (Pharmacology)

Further Information: Also 238 affiliated colleges/institutions

History: Founded 2000 as Uttar Pradesh Technical University. Acquired present title 2010.

Governing Bodies: Executive Council; Academic Council

Academic Year: July to June

Admission Requirements: undergraduate programs, 10+2; graduate programs, graduation in relevant field; State entrance examination test

Fees: (Rupees): maximum of 50,000 per annum

Main Language(s) of Instruction: English

International Co-operation: None

Accrediting Agencies: All India Council for Technical Education (AICTE)

Degrees and Diplomas: *Bachelor's Degree*; *Bachelor's degree (professional)*; *Master's Degree*; *Doctorate*. Also M.B.A.

Student Services: Academic counselling, Employment services

Student Residential Facilities: None

Special Facilities: None

Publications: Technical Tribune

Student Numbers *2009-2010:* Total 268,239

Last Updated: 29/11/11

GAUTAM BUDDHA UNIVERSITY

Yammuna Expressway, Greater Noida, Gautam Budh Nagar,
Uttar Pradesh 201308
Tel: +91(120) 2344-200
Website: http://www.gbu.ac.in/

Vice-Chancellor: S.R. Lakha

Schools
Biotechnology (Biotechnology); **Buddhist Studies and Civiliza-tion** (Asian Religious Studies); **Engineering** (Civil Engineering; Electrical Engineering; Mechanical Engineering); **Humanities and Social Sciences** (Arts and Humanities; Development Studies; Education; Social Sciences; Social Work); **Information and Com-munication Technology** (Information Technology; Tele-communications Engineering); **Law, Justice and Governance** (Government; Law); **Management** (Business Administration; Man-agement)

Degrees and Diplomas: *Bachelor's Degree*; *Master's Degree*; *Doctorate*
Last Updated: 18/01/12

GITAM UNIVERSITY

Gandhi Nagar, Rushikonda, Visakhapatnam,
Andhra Pradesh 530 045
Tel: +91(891) 279-0101
EMail: gitam@gitam.edu
Website: http://www.gitam.edu

Vice-Chancellor: G. Subrahmanyam

Registrar: Potharaju

Colleges
Dental Sciences (Dentistry)

Institutes
International Business (International Business); **Management** (Business Administration; Human Resources; Management); **Pharmacy** (Pharmacy); **Science** (Applied Mathematics; Biochem-istry; Biotechnology; Chemistry; Computer Science; Electronic Engineering; Environmental Studies; Microbiology; Physics); **Technology** (Biotechnology; Chemistry; Civil Engineering; Com-puter Science; Construction Engineering; Electrical and Electronic Engineering; English; Industrial Engineering; Information Technol-ogy; Mechanical Engineering; Physics; Technology)

Schools
Architecture (Architecture); **Business** *(Hyderabad)* (Business Administration)

History: Founded 1980 as Gandhi Institute of Technology and Management (GITAM). Acquired present status 2007.

Degrees and Diplomas: *Bachelor's Degree*; *Postgraduate Diploma*; *Master's Degree*; *Doctorate*

Student Residential Facilities: Yes

Special Facilities: E-Learning Research Centre

Libraries: Yes
Last Updated: 25/07/11

GLA UNIVERSITY

17km Stone, NH-2, Mathura-Delhi Road, P.O. Chaumuhan,
Mathura, Uttar Pradesh 281406
Tel: +91(5662) 250900
Fax: +91(5662) 241687
EMail: glauniversity@gla.ac.in
Website: http://www.gla.ac.in/

Vice-Chancellor: Jai Prakash

Institutes
Applied Science and Humanities (Arts and Humanities; Natural Sciences); **Business Management** (Business Administration; Management); **Engineering and Technology** (Civil Engineering; Computer Engineering; Electrical Engineering; Engineering; Mechanical Engineering; Technology); **Pharmaceutical Research** (Pharmacy)

History: Founded 2010.

Fees: (Indian Rupees): 62,000-126,000 per annum depending on programmes

Degrees and Diplomas: *Bachelor's Degree*; *Master's Degree*; *Doctorate*
Libraries: Yes
Last Updated: 28/12/11

GOA INSTITUTE OF MANAGEMENT (GIM)

Ribandar, Goa 403 006
Tel: +91(832) 249-0300
Fax: +91(832) 244-4136
EMail: admin@gim.ac.in; director@gim.ac.in
Website: http://www.gim.ac.in/

Director: P.F.X D'Lima EMail: director@gim.ac.in

Administrator: Steve Fernandes EMail: steve@gim.ac.in

Programmes
Corporate Studies; **Management** (Management); **Management Development** (Management)

Governing Bodies: Board of Governors

Accrediting Agencies: All India Council of Technical Education of the Government of India (AICTE); National Board of Accreditation (NBA)

Degrees and Diplomas: *Postgraduate Diploma*. Also Part-time Executive M.B.A.

Student Residential Facilities: Hostels

Libraries: 7,175 vols; 165 Indian and International journals
Last Updated: 23/01/12

GOA UNIVERSITY

Taleigao Plateau, Goa 403206
Tel: +91(832) 245-1345 +91(832) 245-6480
Fax: +91(832) 245-1184 +91(832) 245-2889
EMail: registrar@unigoa.ac.in
Website: http://www.unigoa.ac.in/

Vice-Chancellor: Dileep N. Deobagkar
Tel: +91(832) 245-1576, Fax: +91(832) 245-1148
EMail: vc@unigoa.ac.in

Registrar: Vijayendra P. Kamat Tel: +91(832) 651-9005

Centres
Historical Research (History) *Director*: Delio Mendonca; **Latin American Studies** (Caribbean Studies; Latin American Studies) *Director*: V. Shivkumar; **Malaria Research** *Director*: Ashwani Kumar

Faculties
Commerce (Business and Commerce) *Dean*: Ramesh B.; **Design** (Design) *Dean*: D.N. Deobagkar; **Education** (Education) *Dean*: Louis Vernal; **Engineering** (Architecture; Civil Engineering; Com-puter Engineering; Electrical Engineering; Electronic Engineering; Engineering; Industrial Engineering; Mechanical Engineering; Technology; Telecommunications Engineering) *Dean*: N. Somayaji; **Languages and Literature** (English; French; Indic Languages; Literature; Modern Languages; Portuguese) *Dean*: K. S. Bhat; **Law** (Law) *Dean*: M. Pinheiro; **Life Sciences and Environment** (Biolo-gical and Life Sciences; Biotechnology; Botany; Marine Science and Oceanography; Microbiology; Zoology) *Dean*: G.N. Nayak; **Man-agement Studies** (Management) *Dean*: Mekoth Nandkumar; **Medicine, Dentistry, Pharmacy and Ayurvedic Medicine** (Ayur-veda; Dentistry; Homeopathy; Medicine; Pharmacy) *Dean*: Manesh G. Sardessai; **Natural Sciences** (Chemistry; Computer Science; Earth Sciences; Electronic Engineering; Mathematics; Natural Sci-ences; Physics; Technology) *Dean*: Desa J. A. E; **Performing, Fine Arts and Music** (Aesthetics; Fine Arts; Music; Painting and Draw-ing; Performing Arts) *Dean*: Kamlakar Naik; **Social Sciences** (Economics; History; Latin American Studies; Philosophy; Political Sciences; Social Sciences; Sociology; Women's Studies) *Dean*: Afonso A. V.

Institutes
Antarctic and Ocean Research *(National Centre, NCAOR)* (Mar-ine Science and Oceanography) *Director*: Ravindra Rashik; **Archives** (Archiving) *Director*: M.L. Dicholkar; **Konkani Kendra** *(Thomas Stephens)* (Environmental Studies; Occupational Health) *Director*: P. Naik; **Local Self Government** *(All India)* Assistant *Director*: A.G. Khanolkar; **Oceanography** *(National Institute)* (Mar-ine Science and Oceanography) *Director*: Satish Shetye; **Psy-**

chiatry and Human Behaviour (Behavioural Sciences; Psychiatry and Mental Health) *Director*: V.N. Jindal

Further Information: Also 46 Affiliated Colleges and 8 Recognized Postgraduate Institutions

History: Founded 1985. All Colleges in Goa (previously affiliated to Bombay) were affiliated with the University 1986.

Governing Bodies: Executive Council; Court; Academic Council

Academic Year: June to March/April (June-October; November-March/April)

Admission Requirements: 12th year senior secondary/intermediate examination or recognized foreign equivalent

Main Language(s) of Instruction: English

International Co-operation: With institutions in Japan, Philippines, Portugal, Italy, India, USA, Mexico

Accrediting Agencies: University Grants Commission; National Assessment and Accreditation Council

Degrees and Diplomas: *Bachelor's Degree*: Architecture (BAArch); Fine Arts (BFA), 5 yrs; *Bachelor's Degree*: Arts (BA); Business Administration (BBA); Commerce (BCom); Music (BMusic); Naval Engineering (BSc); Science (BSc); Science (Home Science) (BSc), 3 yrs; *Bachelor's Degree*: Ayurvedic Medicine (BAMS); Homeopathy (BHMS); Medicine and Surgery (MBBS), 4 1/2 yrs; *Bachelor's Degree*: Dental Surgery (BDS); Engineering (BEng); Pharmacy (BPharm), 4 yrs; *Bachelor's Degree*: Education (BEd), 1 yr full-time following first degree; *Bachelor's Degree*: Laws (LLB), 3 yrs; 5 yrs; *Postgraduate Diploma*: Computer Applications (PGDCA); Computers (PGEPCT); Management (DAM); Management (DBM), 1 yr; *Postgraduate Diploma*: Management (PGDM), 1 1/2 yrs; *Master's Degree*: Arts (MA); Business Administration (MBA); Commerce (Mcom); Education (MEd), a further 2 yrs; *Master's Degree*: Computer Applications (MCA), a further 3 yrs; *Master's Degree*: Dental (MDS), 3 yrs; *Master's Degree*: Engineering (Foundation and Industrial) (ME); Pharmacy (MPharm); Philosophy (MPhil); Science (MSc); Surgery (MS), a further 1-3 yrs; *Master's Degree*: Hydrographic Studies (MHS), 1 1/2 yr; *Doctorate (PhD)*: 5 yrs; *Doctorate*: Medicine (MD), 3 yrs

Student Services: Academic counselling, Canteen, Employment services, Foreign student adviser, Health services, Language programs, Social counselling, Sports facilities

Student Residential Facilities: Yes

Special Facilities: Geology Museum; State of Art Distance Education Studio; Remote Sensing Laboratory; Green House

Libraries: Goa University Library, 123,000 vols; Pissurlenkar Collection, 4,500; Nuno Gonsalves Collection, 3,500; 600 journals, Thesis, MPhil dissertations; E-journals

Last Updated: 25/07/11

GOKHALE INSTITUTE OF POLITICS AND ECONOMICS

BMCC Road, DECCAN Gymkhana, Pune, Maharashtra 411004
Tel: +91(20) 2565-0287
Fax: +91(20) 2565-2579
EMail: gokhaleinstitute@gipe.ac.in
Website: http://www.gipe.ac.in/

Director: Rajas Parchure

Programmes
Economics (Economics); **Political Sciences** (Political Sciences)

History: Founded 1930. Acquired 'Deemed University' status 1993.

Governing Bodies: Board of Management

Main Language(s) of Instruction: English

Accrediting Agencies: National Assessment and Accreditation Council (NAAC)

Degrees and Diplomas: *Master's Degree*: 2 yrs; *Doctorate (PhD)*: 2-6 yrs

Student Services: Academic counselling, Employment services, Handicapped facilities, Health services

Libraries: c. 240,000 vols; 400 periodical subscriptions

Publications: Arth Vijnana *(quarterly)*
Last Updated: 08/08/11

GOVIND BALLABH PANT UNIVERSITY OF AGRICULTURE AND TECHNOLOGY

Govind Ballabh Pant Krishi Evam Praudyogik Vishwavidyalaya
District Udham Singh Nagar, Pantnagar, Uttarakhand 263145
Tel: +91(5944) 233-333 +91(5944) 233-663
Fax: +91(5944) 233-500
EMail: mail@gbpuat.ac.in
Website: http://www.gbpuat.ac.in

Vice-Chancellor: B.S. Bisht EMail: vcgbpuat@gmail.com

Registrar: J. Kumar
Tel: +91(5944) 233-640
EMail: registrar_pantversity@rediffmail.com

Faculties
Agribusiness Management (Agricultural Business; Agricultural Management; Finance; Human Resources; Marketing) *Division Head*: B.K. Sikka; **Agriculture** (Agricultural Economics; Agriculture; Agronomy; Entomology; Food Science; Food Technology; Horticulture; Meteorology; Plant Pathology; Soil Science) *Dean*: J. P. Tewari; **Basic Sciences and Humanities** (Arts and Humanities; Biochemistry; Biological and Life Sciences; Chemistry; Computer Science; Environmental Studies; Genetics; Mathematics; Microbiology; Molecular Biology; Physics; Social Sciences; Statistics) *Dean*: B.R.K. Gupta; **Fisheries** (Aquaculture; Fishery; Food Science; Food Technology) *Dean*: U.P. Singh; **Forestry and Hill Agriculture** (Agriculture; Biological and Life Sciences; Crop Production; Forestry; Horticulture; Social Sciences; Water Management) *Dean*: M.C. Nautiyal; **Home Science** (Child Care and Development; Clothing and Sewing; Family Studies; Home Economics; Nutrition; Textile Technology) *Dean*: Rita Singh Raghuvanshi; **Horticulture** *(VSCG College - Bharsar)* (Horticulture; Natural Resources) *Dean*: P. S. Bisht; **Postgraguate Studies** *Dean*: K. K. Singh; **Technology** (Agricultural Engineering; Agricultural Equipment; Civil Engineering; Computer Engineering; Electrical Engineering; Electronic Engineering; Mechanical Engineering; Power Engineering; Production Engineering; Soil Conservation; Technology; Telecommunications Engineering; Water Science) *Dean*: M. P. Singh; **Veterinary and Animal Sciences** (Animal Husbandry; Veterinary Science) *Dean*: G.K. Singh

History: Founded 1960 as Uttar Pradesh Agricultural University, acquired present title 1974. The University, based on the pattern of the Land Grant Colleges of the USA and set up in collaboration with Illinois University, aims to bring the results of science nearer to the farmer and to stimulate the adoption of new methods and techniques as a means of achieving greater prosperity for the rural population and the country as a whole.

Academic Year: July to June

Admission Requirements: 12th year senior secondary/intermediate examination or recognized foreign equivalent

Main Language(s) of Instruction: English, Hindi

Degrees and Diplomas: *Diploma*; *Bachelor's Degree*; *Master's Degree*; *Doctorate (PhD)*

Student Services: Academic counselling, Canteen, Cultural centre, Employment services, Foreign student adviser, Foreign Studies Centre, Handicapped facilities, Health services, Language programs, Nursery care, Social counselling, Sports facilities

Libraries: University Library, c. 370,000 vols

Publications: Indian Farmers Digest (English) *(quarterly)*; Kisan Bharàti (Hindi) *(quarterly)*

Press or Publishing House: University Press

Academic Staff *2009-2010*	MEN	WOMEN	TOTAL
FULL-TIME	494	114	608

Student Numbers *2009-2010*			
All (Foreign Included)	2,450	1,809	4,259
FOREIGN ONLY	20	2	22

Last Updated: 04/11/10

GRAPHIC ERA UNIVERSITY

600, Bell Road, Clement Town, Dehradun, Uttarakhand 248002
Website: http://www.geu.ac.in/

Faculties
Applied Sciences (Biochemistry; Biotechnology; Computer Science; Forensic Medicine and Dentistry; Information Technology; Microbiology); **Computer Application** (Computer Engineering; Computer Science); **Engineering** (Civil Engineering; Computer Science; Electrical and Electronic Engineering; Engineering; Information Technology; Mechanical Engineering; Telecommunications Engineering); **Hospitality Management** (Hotel Management; Tourism); **Humanities and Social Science** (Arts and Humanities; Graphic Design; Journalism; Mass Communication; Social Sciences); **Management** (Business Administration; Management)

Further Information: Also campus at Garhwal Region
Last Updated: 02/01/12

GUJARAT AYURVED UNIVERSITY

Chanakya Bhavan, Irwin Hospital Road, Jamnagar, Gujarat 361008
Tel: +91(288) 267-6854
Fax: +91(288) 255-5966
EMail: info@ayurveduniversity.com
Website: http://www.ayurveduniversity.com

Vice-Chancellor: Medhavi Lal Sharma Tel: +91(288) 267-7324

Registrar: Rajendrasinh N. Jhala
EMail: registrar@ayurveduniversity.com

Centres
Ayurvedic Studies *(International)* (Ayurveda)

Colleges
Ayurved *(Shri Gulabkunverba)* (Ayurveda)

Faculties
Ayurved (Ayurveda); **Medicinal Plants** (Traditional Eastern Medicine); **Pharmaceutical Sciences** (Pharmacology)

Institutes
Ayurvedic Pharmaceutical Sciences (Ayurveda); **Medicinal Plant Sciences** (Alternative Medicine); **Naturopathy, Yoga Education and Research** *(Maharishi Patanjali)* (Alternative Medicine; Yoga); **Post-Graduate Teaching and Research in Ayurveda** (Ayurveda)

Programmes
Rural Health (Health Sciences)

Further Information: Also 2 Constituent and 8 Affiliated Colleges, and 2 Teaching Hospitals
History: Founded 1965.
Governing Bodies: Senate; Syndicate; Board of Studies
Academic Year: July to June
Admission Requirements: 12th year senior secondary/intermediate examination or recognized foreign equivalent
Fees: (Rupees): 250 per annum; foreign students, (US Dollars): 3,600
Main Language(s) of Instruction: English, Sanskrit, Hindi, Gujarati
Degrees and Diplomas: *Bachelor's Degree*; *Master's Degree*: 3 yrs; *Doctorate (PhD)*: a further 3 yrs. Also Diploma and Certificate courses
Student Services: Academic counselling, Canteen, Cultural centre, Handicapped facilities, Health services, Language programs, Nursery care, Social counselling, Sports facilities
Student Residential Facilities: Yes
Special Facilities: Museum. Art Gallery.Observatory. Movies Studio
Libraries: Central Library, 30,000 vols; 34 periodical subscriptions
Publications: GAU News Monthly
Last Updated: 09/08/11

GUJARAT FORENSIC SCIENCES UNIVERSITY

DFS Head Quarters, Sector 18-A, Near Police Bhavan, Gandhinagar, Gujarat 382007
Tel: +91(79) 6573-5502
Fax: +91(79) 2325-6251
EMail: pro@gfsu.edu.in
Website: http://www.gfsu.edu.in/

Director General: J. M. Vyas EMail: dg@gfsu.edu.in

Institutes
Behavioral Science (Clinical Psychology; Law; Neurosciences); **Forensic Sciences** (Forensic Medicine and Dentistry); **Research and Development** (Computer Engineering)

History: Founded 2008.
Degrees and Diplomas: *Diploma*; *Bachelor's Degree*; *Master's Degree*; *Doctorate*
Libraries: Yes
Last Updated: 05/08/11

GUJARAT NATIONAL LAW UNIVERSITY (GNLU)

E-4, GIDC Electronics Estate, Sector 26, Gandhinagar, Gujarat 382 028
Tel: +91(79) 2328-7157
Fax: +91(79) 2328-7156
EMail: contact@gnlu.ac.in
Website: http://www.gnlu.ac.in/

Director: Bimal Patel EMail: vc@gnlu.ac.in
Registrar: Jabbal Dolly

Programmes
Law (Law)
History: Founded 2003.
Last Updated: 05/08/11

GUJARAT TECHNOLOGICAL UNIVERSITY

JACPC Building, Navranpura, Ahmedabad, Gujarat
Tel: +91(79) 2630-0499
Fax: +91(79) 2630-1500
EMail: info@gtu.ac.in
Website: http://www.gtu.ac.in

Vice-Chancellor: Akshai Aggarwal

Programmes
Business Administration (Business Administration); **Engineering** (Engineering); **Hotel Management** (Hotel Management); **Pharmacy** (Pharmacy)

History: Founded 2007.
Degrees and Diplomas: *Diploma*; *Bachelor's Degree*; *Master's Degree*; *Doctorate*
Last Updated: 05/08/11

GUJARAT UNIVERSITY

Navrangpura, Ahmedabad, Gujarat 380009
Tel: +91(79) 2630-1341 +91(79) 2630-1342
Fax: +91(79) 2630-2654
Website: http://www.gujaratuniversity.org.in

Vice-Chancellor: Parimal H. Trivedi
Registrar: M.S. Shah

Centres
Computer Studies *(Rollwala)*

Departments
Library and Information Science (Information Sciences; Library Science)

Faculties
Arts (Computer Science); **Commerce** (Business and Commerce); **Dentistry** (Dentistry); **Education** (Education); **Engineering and Technology** (Engineering; Technology); **Law**; **Medicine** (Medicine; Surgery); **Nursing and Physiotherapy** (Nursing); **Pharmacy** (Pharmacy); **Science** *Dean:* Y.K. Agrawal

Schools
Business Management *(Dr Biharlal Kanaiyalal)* (Business Administration; Management); **Commerce** *(Sheth Damodardas)* (Business and Commerce); **Languages** (English; Indic Languages; Linguistics; Sanskrit; Urdu); **Law** (Law); **Philosophy, Education and Psychology** (Education; Philosophy; Psychology); **Sciences** (Biochemistry; Biological and Life Sciences; Biomedicine; Botany;

Chemistry; Computer Science; Environmental Studies; Geography; Geology; Mathematics; Microbiology; Natural Sciences; Physics; Statistics; Zoology); **Social Sciences** (Economics; History; Political Sciences; Social Sciences; Sociology)

Further Information: Also 151 Affiliated Colleges and 10 Recognized Institutes. Student Exchange Programme with Japan

History: Founded 1949.

Governing Bodies: Court; Executive Council; Academic Council

Academic Year: June to April (June-October; November-April)

Admission Requirements: Higher Secondary Certificate (HSC) or equivalent.

Fees: (Rupees): 465-6,000 per annum

Main Language(s) of Instruction: Gujarati, English and/or Hindi

Degrees and Diplomas: *Bachelor's Degree*: Arts (BA); Business Administration (BBA); Commerce (BCom); Pharmacy (BPharm); Science (BScgen, Bscspec), 3 yrs; *Bachelor's Degree*: Education (BEd), 1 further yr; *Bachelor's Degree*: Engineering (BEng), 3-4 yrs; *Bachelor's Degree*: Laws (LLB), a further 2 yrs; *Bachelor's Degree*: Medicine and Surgery (MBBS), 5 1/2 yrs; *Bachelor's Degree*: Nursing (BSc Nursing), 2 yrs; *Master's Degree*: a further 1-3 yrs; *Doctorate (PhD)*: 2 yrs. Also undergraduate and postgraduate Diplomas.

Student Services: Canteen, Cultural centre, Employment services, Foreign student adviser, Health services, Nursery care, Social counselling, Sports facilities

Student Residential Facilities: For c. 1,000 students

Libraries: c. 325,000 vols

Press or Publishing House: Gujarat University Press

Student Numbers *2010*: Total: c. 200,000
Last Updated: 09/08/11

GUJARAT VIDYAPITH

Near Income Tax Office, Ashram Road, Ahmedabad, Gujarat 380014
Tel: +91(79) 2754-1148 +91(79) 2754-0746
Fax: +91(79) 2754-2547
EMail: registrar@gujaratvidyapith.org
Website: http://www.gujaratvidyapith.org

Vice-Chancellor: Sudarshan Iyengar
Tel: +91(79) 2754-1392, Fax: +91(79) 2754-2547
EMail: vc@gujaratvidyapith.org

Registrar: Rajendra Khimani Tel: +91(79) 754-6767

International Relations: Rajendra Khimani

Centres
Adult Education *(State Resource)* (Education) *Director*: Laxmanbhai Avaiya; **Adult Education, Continuing Education and Extension Work** *Director*: Sandhyaben Thaker; **Computer Science** *(Postgraduate)* (Computer Science) *Director*: Dhirenbhai Patel; **Rural Management Studies** *(Postgraduate, Randheja)* (Rural Studies) *Director*: Rajivbhai P. Patel; **Studies in Peace Research** *(Ahimsa)* (Peace and Disarmament; Philosophy) *Director*: Pushpaben Motiyani; **Tribal Research and Training** (Indigenous Studies) *Director*: Chandrakant Upadhyay

Colleges
Biogas Research and Microbiology (Microbiology); **Education** *(Shikshan Mahavidyalaya)* (Education); **Hindi Teacher's Training** *(Hindi Shikshak Mahavidyalaya)* (Hindi; Teacher Training); **Physical Education** (Physical Education) *Principal*: Jamnadas K.Savalia; **Social Sciences** (Anthropology; Computer Science; Cultural Studies; Ethnology; History; Indic Languages; Journalism; Library Science; Mass Communication; Philosophy; Rural Studies; Social Work) *Prinipal*: Kanubhai C.Naik; **Teacher Training** (Teacher Training) *Principal*: Mohanbhai K. Pastel

Faculties
Social Sciences, Arts and Humanities *(Mahadev Desai Samajseva Mahavidyalaya)* (Anthropology; Archiving; Arts and Humanities; Computer Science; Journalism; Library Science; Mass Communication; Peace and Disarmament; Philosophy; Rural Studies; Social Sciences; Social Work)

Further Information: Also Centre on Indian Culture and Gandhian Thought for foreign students (October to December)

History: Founded 1920 by Mahatma Gandhi.

Governing Bodies: Board of Trustees

Academic Year: June to April

Admission Requirements: 12th year senior secondary/intermediate examination or recognized foreign equivalent

Fees: (Rupees): 3,000-5,000 per annum.

Main Language(s) of Instruction: Gujarati, Hindi

Degrees and Diplomas: *Bachelor's Degree*: Education (BEd), 2 yrs; *Bachelor's Degree*: Library Science (BLib), 1 yr; *Master's Degree*: Arts (MA); Education (MEd); Library Science (MLib); Rural Studies (MRM); Social Work (MSW), a further 2 yrs; *Master's Degree*: Business Computing (MCA); Journalism and Mass Communication (MJM), 2 yrs; *Master of Philosophy (MPhil)*: 1 further yr; *Doctorate (PhD)*: 2 yrs; *Doctor of Literature (DLit)*: 2 yrs

Student Services: Academic counselling, Canteen, Cultural centre, Employment services, Foreign Studies Centre, Health services, Language programs, Nursery care, Social counselling, Sports facilities

Student Residential Facilities: Yes

Special Facilities: Museum of Tribal Life and Culture; Museum of Indian Cultural Heritage; Archival Collections; Museum of Vidyapith

Libraries: Total, c. 540,000 vols; 600 subscriptions to periodicals; 691 manuscripts

Publications: Vidyapith *(bimonthly)*

Press or Publishing House: Navjivan Publishing House
Last Updated: 10/08/11

GULBARGA UNIVERSITY

Jnana Ganga, Gulbarga, Karnataka 585106
Tel: +91(8472) 245-446
Fax: +91(8472) 245-632
Website: http://www.gulbargauniversity.kar.nic.in

Vice-Chancellor: E.T. Puttaiah
Tel: +91(8472) 245-447 EMail: vcgug@rediffmail.com

Registrar: S. RajannaFax: +91(8472) 245-927

Faculties
Arts (Arts and Humanities; English; Fine Arts; Indic Languages; Persian; Sanskrit; Urdu); **Commerce and Management** (Business Administration; Business and Commerce; Management) *Dean*: Basavaraj C.S.; **Education** (Education; Educational Administration; Educational Psychology; Educational Sciences; Educational Technology; Physical Education; Teacher Training); **Law** (Commercial Law; Human Rights; Law); **Science and Technology** (Biochemistry; Biological and Life Sciences; Biotechnology; Botany; Chemistry; Earth Sciences; Environmental Engineering; Industrial Chemistry; Instrument Making; Materials Engineering; Mathematics and Computer Science; Natural Sciences; Physics; Statistics; Technology; Zoology); **Social Sciences** (Communication Studies; Demography and Population; Economics; History; Information Sciences; International Studies; Library Science; Political Sciences; Psychology; Social Sciences; Sociology; Women's Studies) *Dean*: B.M. Baeen

Further Information: Also 200 Affiliated Colleges

History: Founded 1980.

Governing Bodies: Academic Council; Syndicate

Academic Year: June to May

Admission Requirements: 12th year senior secondary/intermediate examination or recognized foreign equivalent for undergraduate courses. Graduation for Master programs. Postgraduation PhD courses.

Main Language(s) of Instruction: English, Kannada

Accrediting Agencies: National Assessment and Accreditation Council, Bangalore

Degrees and Diplomas: *Bachelor's Degree (BA; BSc; Bcom; LLB; BPEd; BCA)*: 3 yrs; *Master's Degree (MA; MSc; Mcom; LLM; MPEd; MCA; MBA)*: a further 2-3 yrs; *Master of Philosophy (Mphil)*: 1 yr following Master Degree; *Doctorate (PhD)*: at least 3 yrs

Student Services: Academic counselling, Canteen, Cultural centre, Employment services, Health services, Language programs, Sports facilities

Student Residential Facilities: For c. 400 Men and 165 Women students

Special Facilities: Indoor and Outdoor Stadium; Open Air Theatre; University Science Instrumentation Centre; Health Centre

Libraries: 204,657 vols; c. 4,200 e-journals; 290 printed journals

Publications: Kalaganga, Jnanaganga, Vijnanaganga, Research Journal *(annually)*

Last Updated: 10/08/11

GURU ANGAD DEV VETERINARY AND ANIMAL SCIENCES UNIVERSITY

Ludhiana, Punjab 141004
Tel: +91(161) 255-3342
EMail: registrar@gadvasu.in
Website: http://www.gadvasu.in/

Vice-Chancellor: Vijay Kumar Taneja (2006-)

Registrar: Prayag Dutt Juyal

Colleges
Dairy Science and Technology (Dairy; Food Technology) *Dean*: S.P.S. Sangha; **Fisheries** (Fishery) *Dean*: Asha Dhawan; **Veterinary Science** (Veterinary Science) *Dean*: Harpal Singh Sandhu

Programmes
Veterinary Polytechnic *(Kaljharani)* (Veterinary Science)

Schools
Animal Biotechnology *(Post-Graduate Institute of Veterinary Educatioan and Research (PGIVER))* (Veterinary Science) *Dean*: S.S. Randhawa

History: Founded 2005.

Degrees and Diplomas: *Bachelor's Degree*; *Master's Degree*; *Doctorate*

Student Services: Canteen, Nursery care, Sports facilities

Student Residential Facilities: 4 hostels for boys and girls separately

Libraries: Yes

Last Updated: 06/12/11

GURU GHASIDAS VISHWAVIDYALAYA

Bilaspur, Chhattisgarh 495009
Tel: +91(7752) 260-209
Fax: +91(7752) 260-148
EMail: registrarggu@gmail.com
Website: http://www.ggu.ac.in/

Vice-Chancellor: Lakshman Chaturvedi (2009-)
Tel: +91(7752) 260-283 EMail: laksh44@rediffmail.com

Registrar: M.S.K. Khokhar

Departments
Adult and Continuing Education; **Anthropology and Tribal Development** (Anthropology; Development Studies; Indigenous Studies); **Biotechnology** (Biotechnology); **Botany** (Botany); **Chemistry** (Chemistry); **Commerce** (Business and Commerce); **Computer Science and IT** (Computer Science; Information Technology); **Distance Education**; **Economics** (Economics); **Education** (Education); **English** (English); **Forestry, Wildlife, Environmental Science** (Environmental Studies; Forest Products; Wildlife); **Hindi** (Hindi); **History** (History); **Information Technology** (Information Technology); **Journalism and Mass Communication** (Journalism; Mass Communication); **Library and Information Sciences** (Information Sciences; Library Science); **Management Studies** (Business and Commerce; Management); **Pharmacy** (Pharmacy); **Physical Education** (Physical Education); **Political Science and Public Administration** (Political Sciences; Public Administration); **Pure and Applied Mathematics** (Applied Mathematics; Mathematics); **Pure and Applied Physics** (Applied Physics; Physics); **Rural Technology** (Forestry; Rural Studies); **Social Work** (Social Work)

Institutes
Technology (Technology)

Further Information: Also 154 Affiliated Colleges

History: Founded 1983 as Guru Ghasidas University (State University), acquired present title and status (Central University) 2009.

Academic Year: July to June

Admission Requirements: 12th year senior secondary/intermediate examination or recognized foreign equivalent

Main Language(s) of Instruction: Hindi, English

Accrediting Agencies: National Assessment and Accreditation Council (NAAC)

Degrees and Diplomas: *Bachelor's Degree*: 3-5 yrs; *Postgraduate Diploma*: a further 2 yrs; *Master's Degree*: a further 2 yrs; *Doctorate (PhD)*: a further 2-4 yrs

Student Services: Academic counselling, Canteen, Cultural centre, Employment services, Handicapped facilities, Health services, Language programs, Social counselling, Sports facilities

Student Residential Facilities: For male and female students

Libraries: Main Library, c. 105,712 vols; c. 199 periodical subscriptions (both Indian and foreign); 3,950 current journals; On-line journals

Publications: Chhattisgarh Journal of Science and Technology; Focus; GGU Journal of Business; Uddan, Student's Magazine

Academic Staff *2010-2011*	TOTAL
FULL-TIME	90
PART-TIME	75
STAFF WITH DOCTORATE	
FULL-TIME	60
PART-TIME	c. 10

Student Numbers *2010-2011*	
All (Foreign Included)	c. 13,510

Last Updated: 11/08/11

GURU GOBIND SINGH INDRAPRASTHA UNIVERSITY

Old Delhi College of Engineering Campus, Kashmere Gate, New Delhi 110006
Tel: +91(11) 2386-9313
Fax: +91(11) 2386-5941
EMail: mail@ipu.edu
Website: http://www.ipu.ac.in

Vice-Chancellor: Dilip K. Bandyopadhyay (2008-)

Registrar: B. P. Joshi

Centres
Disaster Management Studies; **IT Services and Infrastructure Management** (Information Technology)

Institutes
Technology (Technology)

Schools
Architecture and Planning (Architecture; Architecture and Planning); **Basic and Applied Sciences** (Natural Sciences); **Biotechnology** (Biotechnology); **Chemical Technology**; **Education** (Education); **Engineering and Technology** (Engineering; Technology); **Environmental Management** (Environmental Management); **Humanities and Social Sciences** (Arts and Humanities; Social Sciences); **Information Technology** (Information Technology); **Law and Legal Studies** (Law); **Management Studies** (Management); **Mass Communication** (Mass Communication); **Medicine and Paramedical Health Sciences** (Health Sciences; Medicine; Paramedical Sciences)

History: Founded 1998.

Fees: (Rupees): 2,400 per annum

Degrees and Diplomas: *Bachelor's Degree*; *Master's Degree*

Libraries: c. 9,000 vols

Last Updated: 11/08/11

GURU JAMBESHWAR UNIVERSITY (GJUST)

Hisar, Haryana 125001
Tel: +91(1622) 276-025
Fax: +91(1662) 276-240
EMail: gju_tech@yahoo.com
Website: http://www.gjust.ac.in/

Vice-Chancellor: M.L. Ranga EMail: vc_gju@yahoo.co.in

Registrar: R. S. Jaglan EMail: registrar_gju@rediffmail.com

International Relations: H. L. Verma
Tel: +9(11662) 263-101 EMail: verma_hl@yahoo.com

Faculties

Engineering and Technology (Biomedical Engineering; Computer Engineering; Computer Science; Electrical and Electronic Engineering; Engineering; Mechanical Engineering; Printing and Printmaking; Telecommunications Engineering; **Environmental and Bio Sciences and Technology** (Biological and Life Sciences; Environmental Engineering; Environmental Studies; Food Technology; Nanotechnology; Technology); **Media Studies** (Advertising and Publicity; Communication Studies; Media Studies; Public Relations); **Medicall Sciences** (Pharmacology; Physical Therapy; Psychology); **Physical Sciences** (Applied Physics; Chemistry; Mathematics)

Institutes

Religious Studies *(Guru Jambheshwar)* (Asian Religious Studies)

Schools

Business *(Haryana)* (Business Administration)

History: Founded 1995.

Fees: (Rupees): 1,800-3,000 per annum

Accrediting Agencies: National Assessment and Accreditation Council (NAAC)

Degrees and Diplomas: *Bachelor's Degree*; *Postgraduate Diploma*; *Master's Degree*. Also Diploma and Certificate courses; M.B.A.

Last Updated: 14/11/11

GURU NANAK DEV UNIVERSITY (GNDU)

Amritsar, Punjab 143005
Tel: +91(183) 225-8855
Fax: +91(183) 225-8819
Website: http://www.gndu.ac.in

Vice-Chancellor: Ajaib Singh Brar (2009-)
Tel: +91(183) 225-8811, Fax: +91(183) 225-8820
EMail: vc@gndu.ac.in

Registrar: Inderjit Singh
Tel: +91(183) 225-8855, Fax: +91(183) 225-8819
EMail: reg_gndu@yahoo.com

International Relations: K.S. Kahlon Tel: +91(183) 225-8831

Campuses

Gurdaspur *(Regional)* (Business Administration; Business and Commerce; Computer Science; Electronic Engineering; Engineering; Management); **Jalahandar** *(Regional)* (Computer Engineering; Computer Science; Electronic Engineering)

Faculties

Applied Sciences (Applied Chemistry; Food Science; Pharmacy; Textile Technology); **Arts and Social Sciences** (Arts and Humanities; History; Information Sciences; Library Science; Political Sciences; Psychology; Social Sciences); **Economics and Business** (Business Administration; Business and Commerce; Economics); **Engineering and Technology** (Computer Engineering; Electronic Engineering; Engineering; Technology); **Humanities and Religious Studies** (Arts and Humanities; Religious Studies); **Languages** (English; Foreign Languages Education; Indic Languages; Modern Languages; Sanskrit; Urdu); **Law** (Law); **Life Sciences** (Biochemistry; Biological and Life Sciences; Biotechnology; Botany; Microbiology; Molecular Biology; Zoology); **Physical Education** (Physical Education); **Physical Planning and Architecture** (Architecture; Town Planning); **Science** (Chemistry; Mathematics; Natural Sciences; Physics); **Sports Medicine and Physiotherapy** (Physical Therapy; Sports Medicine); **Visual and Performing Arts** (Music; Performing Arts; Visual Arts)

Further Information: Also 150 affiliated colleges, 3 constituent colleges, 2 regional campuses and 42 postgraduate teaching departments

History: Founded 1969 on the 500th anniversary of the birth of Guru Nanak Dev, founder of the Sikh Religion. Acquired present status 1970.

Governing Bodies: Senate; Academic Council; Syndicate

Academic Year: July to June

Admission Requirements: 12th year senior secondary/intermediate examination or recognized foreign equivalent, and entrance test

Fees: (Rupees): Undergraduate, Indian students, 11,445-14,000 per annum; foreign students, (US Dollars), 1,000-15,000 per annum. Postgraduate, Indian students, (Rupees), 13,425-36,500 per annum; foreign students, (US Dollars), 1,000-18,000 per annum

Main Language(s) of Instruction: English, Hindi, Punjabi for all courses, Urdu only for Diploma/Certificate

Accrediting Agencies: National Assessment and Accreditation Council; University Grants Commission

Degrees and Diplomas: *Diploma*: Economics and Business; Computer Science and Information Technology; Journalism and Mass Communication; Fine Arts; Laws, 1 yr; *Bachelor's Degree*: Arts and Social Sciences; Science; Applied Science; Life Sciences; Business; Languages; Humanities and Religious Studies; Physical Education; Law; Music and Fine Arts, 3 yrs; *Bachelor's Degree*: Sports Medicine and Physiotherapy; Agriculture; Education, 4 yrs; *Bachelor's degree (professional)*: Engineering and Technology, Physical Planning and Architecture, 4 yrs; *Master's Degree*: Arts and Social Sciences; Science; Applied Science; Life Sciences; Engineering and Technology; Physical Planning and Architecture; Economics and Business; Languages; Humanities and Religious Studies; Physical Education; Law; Music and Fine Arts; Sports Medicine and Physiotherapy; Agriculture; Education, 2-5 yrs; *Master of Philosophy*: Hindi; History; Music (Instrumental and Vocal); Political Science; Psychology; Punjabi; Religious Studies; Sociology, 1 1/2 yrs

Student Services: Academic counselling, Canteen, Cultural centre, Employment services, Foreign student adviser, Foreign Studies Centre, Handicapped facilities, Health services, Language programs, Nursery care, Sports facilities

Student Residential Facilities: Yes

Special Facilities: Khalsa Heritage Centre

Libraries: c. 375,000 vols

Publications: Amritsar Law Journal *(annually)*; Guru Nanak Journal of Sociology *(biannually)*; Indian Journal of Quantitative Economics *(biannually)*; Journal of Management Studies *(annually)*; Journal of Regional History *(annually)*; Journal of Sikh Studies *(biannually)*; Journal of Sports Traumatology and Allied Sports Sciences *(annually)*; Khoj Darpan, Punjabi *(biannually)*; Personality Study and Group Behaviour *(annually)*; Pradhikrit, Hindi *(annually)*; PSE Economic Analyst *(biannually)*; Punjab Journal of English Studies *(annually)*; Punjab Journal of Politics *(biannually)*; University Samachar *(quarterly)*

Academic Staff 2008-2009	MEN	WOMEN	TOTAL
FULL-TIME	265	135	**400**
PART-TIME	150	100	**250**
STAFF WITH DOCTORATE			
FULL-TIME	230	109	**339**
Student Numbers 2008-2009			
All (Foreign Included)	3,275	3,417	**6,692**

Distance students, 5.
Last Updated: 14/11/11

GURUKUL KANGRI UNIVERSITY

Gurukula Kangri Vishwavidyalaya

PO Gurukul Kangri, Uttaranchal, Haridwar, Uttar Pradesh 249404
Tel: +91(1334) 249-013
EMail: registrargkv@yahoo.co.in
Website: http://gkvharidwar.org/

Vice-Chancellor: Swatantra Kumar
EMail: swantantrak56@yahoo.com

Registrar: A.K. Chopra

Centres

Vedic Studies (Asian Religious Studies) *Director*: Mahavir Agarwal

Faculties

Ayurved and Medical Science (Pharmacy); **Distance Education** (Arts and Humanities; Natural Sciences; Yoga); **Engineering and Technology** (Electrical and Electronic Engineering; Engineering; Mechanical Engineering; Technology); **Humanities** (Arts and Humanities; English); **Life Sciences** (Biological and Life Sciences; Botany; Environmental Studies; Microbiology; Zoology); **Management** (Business Administration; Economics; Finance; Management); **Oriental Studies** (Archaeology; Oriental Studies; Philosophy; Physical Education); **Science** (Natural Sciences); **Technology** *Dean*: V.K. Sharma

Further Information: Also 2 Constituent Colleges

History: Founded 1900 to educate, through the medium of Hindi, young people of all classes, castes and creeds according to the ideals of Vedic ancient Indian culture. Modern Science subjects were added later.

Governing Bodies: Senate; Syndicate; Academic Council

Academic Year: July to June (July-November; January-May)

Admission Requirements: 12th year senior secondary/intermediate examination or recognized foreign equivalent

Fees: (Rupees): 450-13,800 per annum

Main Language(s) of Instruction: Hindi, English

Degrees and Diplomas: *Diploma*; *Bachelor's Degree*: 3 yrs; *Master's Degree*: a further 2 yrs; *Doctorate (PhD)*: a further 2-4 yrs

Student Residential Facilities: Yes

Special Facilities: Archaeological Museum (Terracottas; Coins; Sculpture; Copper Artifacts of the Ganga Valley and Paintings)

Libraries: c. 150,000 vols; 344 periodical subscriptions

Publications: Arya Bhatt; The Vedic Path

Last Updated: 14/11/11

HAMDARD UNIVERSITY

Jamia Hamdard

Hamdard Nagar, New Delhi 110062
Tel: +91(11) 2605-9688
Fax: +91(11) 2605-9663
EMail: inquiry@jamiahamdard.edu
Website: http://www.jamiahamdard.edu

Vice-Chancellor: G.N. Qazi (2008-)
Tel: +91(11) 2605-9688
EMail: vice-chancellor@jamiahamdard.ac.in

Registrar: Firdous Ahmad Wani
Tel: +91(11) 2605-9664 EMail: firdouswani@jamiahamdard.ac.in

Faculties

Allied Health Sciences (Occupational Therapy; Physical Therapy); **Islamic Studies and Social Sciences** (International Relations; Islamic Studies; Islamic Theology; Political Sciences; Social Sciences; Social Studies); **Management Studies and Information Technology** (Computer Science; Information Technology; Management); **Medicine (Unani)** (Alternative Medicine; Biochemistry; Hygiene; Physical Therapy; Social and Preventive Medicine; Surgery); **Nursing** (Midwifery; Nursing); **Pharmacy** (Chemistry; Pharmacology; Pharmacy); **Science** (Biochemistry; Biotechnology; Botany; Health Sciences; Natural Sciences; Toxicology)

Further Information: Also Majeedia Hospital

History: Founded 1989. An Institution with 'Deemed University' status.

Governing Bodies: Executive Council; Academic Council Society

Academic Year: July to May

Admission Requirements: 12th year senior secondary/intermediate examination or recognized equivalent with 50% marks in Physics, Chemistry, Biology and Mathematics

Main Language(s) of Instruction: English, Urdu

International Co-operation: With universities in South Africa, Malaysia, Turkey, United Kingdom and USA.

Accrediting Agencies: National Assessment and Accreditation Council

Degrees and Diplomas: *Diploma*: Dialyses Techniques; Medical Laboratory Technology (DMLT); Operation Theatre Techniques; X-Ray and ECG Technology, 2 yrs; *Bachelor's Degree*: Computer Application (BCA, BSc), 3 yrs; *Bachelor's Degree*: Occupational Therapy; Physical Therapy; Optometric Practices, 4 yrs; *Master of Philosophy*: Botany; Biochemistry; Biotechniques; Medical Elementology and Toxicology; Chemistry (MSc); Islamic Studies (MA); Management (MBA); Neurology; Cardio-pulmonary; Sports Health; Osteo-myology (MPT); Othopaedics; Paediatrics (MOT); Pharmaceutical Chemistry; Pharmacy; Pharmacology; Pharmacognosy; Pharmaceutical Biotechnology; Pharmacy Practices; Quality Assurance (M Pharm), a further 2 yrs; *Master of Philosophy*: Computer Applications (MCA), a further 3 yrs; *Master of Philosophy*: Unani Medicine (MD), a furher 3 yrs; *Doctorate*: Botany; Biochemistry; Biotechnology; Chemistry; Medical Elementology and Toxicology; Pharmaceutical Chemistry; Pharmacy; Pharmacology; Pharmacognosy; Pharmaceutical Medicine; Islamic Studies; Federal Studies; Management; Computer Science (PhD), at least 2 yrs

Student Services: Academic counselling, Canteen, Cultural centre, Employment services, Foreign student adviser, Health services, Language programs, Sports facilities

Student Residential Facilities: Yes

Special Facilities: Museum. Herbal Garden. Convention Center. Scholars House. Movie Studio.

Libraries: c. 150,000 vols; 350 periodical subscriptions

Publications: Indian Journal for Federal Studies *(quarterly)*; Studies on History of Medicine and Science *(quarterly)*; Studies on Islam *(quarterly)*

Press or Publishing House: Jamia Hamdard Printing Press
Last Updated: 22/11/11

HEMCHANDRACHARYA NORTH GUJARAT UNIVERSITY

PO Box 21, University Road, Patan, North Gujarat 384265
Tel: +91(2766) 230-427
Fax: +91(2766) 231-917
Website: http://www.ngu.ac.in

Vice-Chancellor: Hemixaben Rao
Tel: +91(2766) 230-456 EMail: vc@ngu.ac.in

Registrar: B. J. Rathore EMail: regi@ngu.ac.in

Faculties

Arts (Arabic; Arts and Humanities; Economics; English; History; Home Economics; Indic Languages; Information Sciences; Library Science; Military Science; Persian; Political Sciences; Psychology; Sanskrit; Sociology); **Commerce** (Accountancy; Business and Commerce; Computer Science; Economics; Secretarial Studies; Statistics); **Education** (Education); **Engineering** (Civil Engineering; Electrical Engineering; Electronic Engineering; Engineering; Mechanical Engineering; Transport and Communications); **Law** (Law); **Management** (Management); **Medicine** (Homeopathy); **Pharmacy** (Pharmacy); **Rural Studies** (Rural Studies); **Science** (Botany; Chemistry; Mathematics; Natural Sciences; Physics; Zoology)

Further Information: Also 91 Affiliated Colleges

History: Founded 1986.

Academic Year: June to May

Admission Requirements: 12th year senior secondary/intermediate examination or recognized foreign equivalent

Fees: (Rupees): 400-3,000 per annum

Main Language(s) of Instruction: English

Degrees and Diplomas: *Bachelor's Degree*: Arts; Commerce; Education; Engineering; Homeopathy; Management Studies; Science, 3-4 yrs; *Master's Degree*: Arts; Commerce; Education; Management Studies; Science, a further 1-2 yrs; *Doctorate*: Arts; Commerce; Education; Law; Pharmacy; Science, a further 5 yrs. Also Diploma and Postgraduate Diploma courses

Libraries: c. 30,000 vols; 724 periodical subscriptions

Publications: Anarta *(annually)*; Udeechya *(bimonthly)*; Uttara
Last Updated: 09/03/11

HEMWATI NANDAN BAHUGUNA GARHWAL UNIVERSITY

District Pauri Garhwal, Srinagar, Uttarakhand 246174
Tel: +91(1346) 252-143
Fax: +91(1346) 252-247
EMail: registrar.hnbgu@gmail.com
Website: http://hnbgu.ac.in/

Vice-Chancellor: S.K. Singh EMail: vc@hnbgugrw.ren.nic.in

Registrar: U.S. Rawat

Schools

Agriculture and Allied Science (Agriculture; Crop Production; Forestry; Horticulture; Rural Studies) *Dean*: N.D. Todariya; **Arts, Communication and Languages** (Arts and Humanities; English; Hindi; Information Sciences; Library Science; Mass Communication; Modern Languages; Music; Painting and Drawing; Performing Arts; Sanskrit) *Dean*: S.S. Dev; **Ayurveda and Unani System** (Ayurveda) *Dean*: D.N. Sharma; **Commerce** (Administration; Business and Commerce) *Dean*: R.K. Aggarwal; **Dental Science** (Dentistry) *Dean*: Vijay Prakash Nautiyal; **Earth Science** (Geography; Geology); **Education** (Adult Education; Education; Physical Education; Yoga) *Dean*: R.C. Nautiyal; **Engineering and Technology** (Computer Science; Engineering; Technology) *Dean*: N.S.Panwar Panwar; **Humanities and Social Sciences** (Anthropology; Economics; Histology; Philosophy; Psychology; Sociology) *Dean*: Atul Saklani; **Law** (Law) *Dean*: A.K. Pandey; **Life Sciences** (Natural Sciences) *Dean*: S.C. Tiwari; **Management** (Business Administration; Tourism) *Head*: S.C. Bagri Bagri; **Medicine** (Medicine) *Dean*: S.P. Singh; **Sciences** (Mathematics; Natural Sciences; Pharmacy; Physics; Statistics) *Dean*: M.S.M. Rawat

Further Information: Also 22 Affiliated Colleges

History: Founded 1973 as University of Garhwal, acquired present title 1989.

Academic Year: July to May

Admission Requirements: 12th year and senior secondary/intermediate examination

Main Language(s) of Instruction: Hindi, English

Degrees and Diplomas: *Bachelor's Degree*: 3-4 yrs; *Master's Degree*: a further 2 yrs; *Doctorate (PhD)*. Also Postgraduate Diploma courses

Student Services: Academic counselling, Canteen, Employment services, Social counselling, Sports facilities

Special Facilities: History and Archaeology Museum

Libraries: c. 200,000 vols
Last Updated: 15/11/11

HIDAYATULLAH NATIONAL LAW UNIVERSITY

Civil Lines, Raipur, Chhattisgarth

Vice-Chancellor: Sukhpal Singh

Registrar: Anand Pawar

Schools

Administration of Justice, Continuing and Clinical Legal Education (Administrative Law; Law); **Business and Global Trade Laws Development** (Business Administration; Commercial Law); **Constitutional and Administrative Governance** (Administrative Law; Constitutional Law); **International Legal Studies** (International Law); **Juridical and Social Sciences** (Law; Social Sciences); **Science, Technology and Sustainable Development** (Development Studies; Technology)

History: Founded 2003.

Degrees and Diplomas: *Bachelor's Degree*; *Master's Degree*; *Doctorate*
Last Updated: 01/08/11

HIHT UNIVERSITY

Swami Ram Nagar, P.O. Doiwala, Dehradun, Uttarakhand 248 140
Tel: +91(135) 247-1151
EMail: info@hihtuniversity.edu.in
Website: http://www.hihtuniversity.edu.in/

Vice Chancellor: S.P. Singh
Tel: +91(135) 247-1152, Fax: +91(135) 247-1153
EMail: vc@hihtuniversity.edu.in

Registrar: A.R. Nautiyal
Tel: +91(135) 247-1151, Fax: +91(135) 247-1153
EMail: reg@hihtuniversity.edu.in

Departments

Anaesthesiology (Anaesthesiology); **Anatomy** (Anatomy); **Biochemistry** (Biochemistry); **Community Medicine** (Community Health); **ENT** (Otorhinolaryngology); **Forensic Medicine** (Forensic Medicine and Dentistry); **Medicine and Allied Branches** (Medical Auxiliaries; Medicine); **Microbiology** (Microbiology); **Obstetrics and Gynaecology** (Gynaecology and Obstetrics); **Ophthalmology** (Ophthalmology); **Orthopaedics** (Orthopaedics); **Paediatrics** (Paediatrics); **Pathology** (Pathology); **Pharmacology** (Pharmacology); **Physiology** (Physiology); **Radiology** (Radiology); **Surgery and Allied Branches** (Cardiology; Neurological Therapy; Paediatrics; Plastic Surgery; Surgery; Urology)

Further Information: 750 bed multi specialty hospital

History: Founded 1995 as Swami Ram Vidhyapeeth. Acquired 'Deemed University' status 2007. Acquired present title 2008.

Degrees and Diplomas: *Diploma*; *Bachelor's Degree*; *Bachelor's degree (professional)*; *Postgraduate Diploma*; *Master's Degree*; *Doctorate*. Also Certificate courses

Student Services: Sports facilities

Libraries: Central Library
Last Updated: 16/12/11

HIMACHAL PRADESH TECHNICAL UNIVERSITY

Hamirpur, Himachal Pradesh 177030
Tel: +91(98171) 09004
Website: http://himtu.ac.in/

Vice-Chancellor: Shashi Kumar Dhiman
EMail: shashikdhiman@gmail,com

Registrar: Rakhil Kahlon

Programmes

Engineering (Civil Engineering; Computer Engineering; Computer Science; Electrical and Electronic Engineering; Electrical Engineering; Electronic Engineering; Engineering; Mechanical Engineering; Telecommunications Engineering; Textile Technology); **Pharmacy** (Pharmacy)

Degrees and Diplomas: *Bachelor's Degree*; *Master's Degree*. Also MBA
Last Updated: 18/01/12

HIMACHAL PRADESH UNIVERSITY

Summer Hill, Shimla, Himachal Pradesh 171005
Tel: +91(177) 283-0912
Fax: +91(177) 283-0775
EMail: webhpu@hp.nic.in; gad.hpu@gmail.com
Website: http://www.hpuniv.nic.in

Vice-Chancellor: Arun Diwakar Nath Bajpai
EMail: vc_hpu@hotmail.com

Centres

Distance Education and Open Learning (*International*) *Director*: Om P. Sarswat

Colleges

Ayurveda (Ayurveda)

Departments

Mathematics (Mathematics)

Faculties

Commerce and Management Studies (Business and Commerce; Management) *Dean*: Maneet Mahajan; **Education** (Education) *Dean*: Harbans Singh; **Engineering and Technology** (*Hamirpur*) (Engineering; Technology) *Dean*: R.L. Chauhan; **Languages** (English; Indic Languages; Modern Languages; Sanskrit) *Dean*: Rajinder P. Mishra; **Law** (Law); **Medical Sciences and Ayurvedic** (Ayurveda; Medicine) *Dean*: N.K. Sareen; **Performing and Visual**

Arts (Performing Arts; Visual Arts) *Dean*: C.L. Verma; **Physical Science** (Biology; Biotechnology; Chemistry; Computer Science; Mathematics; Natural Sciences; Physics) *Dean*: M.L. Parmar; **Social Sciences** (Economics; Geography; History; Political Sciences; Psychology; Public Administration; Social Sciences; Sociology) *Dean*: J.P. Bhatti

Institutes
Environment Studies (Environmental Studies); **Himalayan Studies** (Asian Studies); **Management Studies** *(International)* (Management) *Director*: Balram Dogra

Research Centres
Agro-Economic (Agricultural Business)

Further Information: Also 54 Affiliated Colleges, and 2 Teaching Hospitals, total, 65,000 students

History: Founded 1970.

Academic Year: March to November (March-May; September-November).

Admission Requirements: 12th year senior secondary/intermediate examination or recognized foreign equivalent

Main Language(s) of Instruction: English, Hindi

Degrees and Diplomas: *Diploma*; *Bachelor's Degree*; *Master of Philosophy*; *Doctorate (PhD)*; *Doctorate*: Law (LLD); *Doctor of Literature*

Student Residential Facilities: Yes

Special Facilities: Botanical Garden

Libraries: Central Library, 180,364 vols; 4,616 periodical subscriptions

Last Updated: 19/09/11

HIMGIRI ZEE UNIVERSITY

Sheeshambada, P.O. Sherpur, Via-Sahaspur, Dehradun, Uttarakhand 248 197
Tel: +91(135) 2102-676
Fax: +91(135) 2760-464
EMail: himgirizeeuniversity@gmail.com; hnvddn@yahoo.com
Website: http://www.hnv.edu.in

Head: Binod C. Agrawal
Registrar: Dalip Kumar S. Bora

Departments
Distance Education; **Library and Information Science** (Information Sciences; Library Science)

Faculties
Architecture, Design and Planning (Architecture and Planning; Design); **Computer Science and Information Technology** (Computer Engineering; Computer Science; Information Technology); **Education** (Education); **Expressive Cultures, Media and Communications** (Communication Studies; Cultural Studies; Media Studies); **Human Sciences** (Social Sciences); **Naturopathy and Yogic Sciences** (Yoga); **Population Sciences** (Demography and Population)

History: Founded 2003.

Degrees and Diplomas: *Bachelor's Degree*; *Master's Degree*; *Doctorate*
Last Updated: 04/01/12

HINDUSTAN UNIVERSITY

P.O. Box No.1, Rajiv Gandhi Salai (OMR), via Kelambakkam, Padur, Chennai 603103
Tel: +91(44) 2747-4262
Fax: +91(44) 2747-4208
EMail: hetc@vsnl.com
Website: http://www.hindustanuniv.ac.in/

Vice-Chancellor: K. Sarukesi

Programmes
Architecture (Architecture); **Computer Application** (Computer Science; Software Engineering); **Engineering** (Aeronautical and Aerospace Engineering; Automotive Engineering; Civil Engineering; Computer Engineering; Electrical and Electronic Engineering; Heating and Refrigeration; Mechanical Engineering; Polymer and Plastics Technology; Rubber Technology); **Information Technology** (Information Technology); **Management** (Business Administration; Management)

History: Founded 1956 as Hindustan College of Engineering. Acquired present status 2008.

Degrees and Diplomas: *Diploma*; *Bachelor's Degree*; *Master's Degree*; *Doctorate*
Last Updated: 16/11/11

HOMEOPATHY UNIVERSITY SAIPURA

Saipura, Sanganer, Jaipur, Rajastan 302029

Programmes
Homeopathy (Homeopathy)

History: Founded 2010,

Admission Requirements: A 10 + 2 pass-out with PCB but not less than 17 years of age can apply for the bachelors' course. Eligibility for PG course will be a BHMS degree.

Degrees and Diplomas: *Bachelor's Degree*; *Master's Degree*
Last Updated: 28/12/11

HOMI BHABHA NATIONAL INSTITUTE

2nd Floor, Training School Complex, Anushaktinagar, Mumbai, Maharashtra 400 094
Website: http://www.hbni.ac.in/

Director: Ravi Grover
Administrative Officer: Lata B.

Departments
Chemical Sciences (Chemistry); **Engineering Sciences** (Engineering); **Health Sciences** (Anaesthesiology; Health Sciences; Oncology; Pathology; Radiology); **Life Sciences** (Biological and Life Sciences); **Mathematical Sciences** (Mathematics); **Physical Sciences** (Physics); **Strategic Studies**

Further Information: With also Constituent Institutions across the country

Degrees and Diplomas: *Postgraduate Diploma*; *Master's Degree*; *Doctorate*
Last Updated: 10/01/12

IFHE, HYDERABAD

Donthanapally, Shankarapalli Road, Hyderabad, Andhra Pradesh 501504
Website: http://www.ifheindia.org/

Vice-Chancellor: J. Mahender Reddy
Registrar: V. R. Shankara

Faculties
Law (Law); **Management Studies** *(IBS)* (Business Administration; Management); **Science and Technology** (Engineering; Technology); **Social Sciences** (Economics; Social Sciences)

Degrees and Diplomas: *Bachelor's Degree*; *Master's Degree*; *Doctorate*
Student Services: Academic counselling
Special Facilities: IT Lab, Internet facility
Libraries: Yes
Last Updated: 12/01/12

IFIM BUSINESS SCHOOL, BANGALORE (THE INSTITUTE OF FINANCE AND INTERNATIONAL MANAGEMENT)

Opp. Infosys Campus Gate # 4), # 8P & 9P, KIADB Industrial Area, Electronics City 1st Phase, Bangalore 560-100
Tel: +91(80) 4143-2800 +91(80) 4143-2888
Fax: +91(80) 4143-2844
EMail: ifimblr@ifimbschool.com
Website: http://www.ifimbschool.com/

Director: Bramh Prakash Pethiya

Programmes

Finance (Finance); **International Business** (International Business); **Management** (Management)

History: Founded 1995.

Governing Bodies: Governing Board

Fees: (Indian Rupees): c. 500,000 per annum

International Co-operation: With univerisities in Malaysia, Singapore, Germany,

Degrees and Diplomas: *Postgraduate Diploma*; *Doctorate*. The Ph.D. programmes is offered in affiliation with the Visvesvaraya Technological University (VTU), Belgaum

Student Services: Health services

Student Residential Facilities: Hostels with capacity of 240 students

Libraries: c. 8,000 vols; 80 periodical subscriptions

Last Updated: 24/01/12

IFTM UNIVERSITY

Lodhipur Rajput, Delhi Road (NH-24), Moradabad,
Uttar Pradesh 244102
Tel: +91(591) 2360-817
Fax: +91(591) 2360-818
EMail: info@iftmuniversity.ac.in
Website: http://www.iftmuniversity.ac.in/

Vice-Chancellor: R.M. Dubey

Schools

Biotechnology (Biotechnology); **Business Management** (Business Administration; Management); **Computer Engineering and Applications** (Computer Engineering; Software Engineering); **Engineering and Technology** (Civil Engineering; Electrical Engineering; Electronic Engineering; Engineering; Mechanical Engineering; Technology; Telecommunications Engineering); **Pharmaceutical Sciences** (Pharmacy); **Science** (Botany; Chemistry; Mathematics; Physical Therapy; Zoology); **Social Sciences** (Arts and Humanities; Business and Commerce; Economics; Engineering Management; Social Sciences; Social Work)

History: Founded 1996. Acquired present status 2010.

Degrees and Diplomas: *Bachelor's Degree*; *Master's Degree*; *Doctorate*

Last Updated: 16/01/12

IIS UNIVERSITY

ICG Campus, Gurukul Marg, SFS, Mansarovar, Jaipur,
Rajastan 302020
Tel: +91(141) 2400-160
Fax: +91(141) 2395-494
EMail: icg@iisuniv.ac.in
Website: http://www.iisuniv.ac.in/

Vice-Chancellor: Ashok Gupta

Director and Registrar: Raakhi Gupta

Departments

Advertising (Advertising and Publicity); **Biotechnology** (Biotechnology); **Botany** (Botany); **Chemistry** (Chemistry); **Commerce** (Business and Commerce); **Computer Science** (Computer Science); **Drawing and Paintings** (Painting and Drawing); **Economics / Business Economics** (Economics); **English** (English); **Environment Science** (Environmental Studies); **Fine Arts** (Fine Arts); **French** (French); **Garment Production and Export Management, Fashion Designing, Textiles** (Fashion Design; Textile Design); **Geography** (Geography); **Hindi** (Hindi); **History** (History); **Home Science**; **Management Studies** (Management); **Mass Communication** (Mass Communication); **Mathematics and Statistics** (Mathematics; Statistics); **Modern European Languages** (French; German); **Physical Education**; **Physics** (Physics); **Political Science** (Political Sciences); **Psychology** (Psychology); **Public Administration** (Public Administration); **Sociology** (Social Work); **Tourism and Travel Management** (Tourism); **Zoology** (Zoology)

History: Founded 1995 as International College for Girls.

Degrees and Diplomas: *Bachelor's Degree*; *Master's Degree*; *Doctorate*

Last Updated: 12/01/12

INDIAN AGRICULTURAL RESEARCH INSTITUTE (PG SCHOOL, IARI)

Pusa Campus, New Delhi 110012
Tel: +91(11) 2573-3367
Fax: +91(11) 2584-6420
EMail: director@iari.res.in
Website: http://www.iari.res.in

Director: H.S. Gupta **Tel:** +91(11) 2584-3375

Director of Education & Dean: H.S. Gaur
Tel: +91(11) 2573-3382 **EMail:** dean@iari.res.in

Programmes

Agriculture (Agricultural Economics; Agricultural Engineering; Agriculture; Agronomy; Biochemistry; Biotechnology; Crop Production; Entomology; Environmental Studies; Floriculture; Fruit Production; Genetics; Horticulture; Microbiology; Plant Pathology; Soil Science; Vegetable Production; Water Science)

History: Founded 1905. A postgraduate Institution.

Governing Bodies: Board of Management; Academic Council

Academic Year: August to July

Admission Requirements: University degree at Bachelor level for MSc, and Masters degree for PhD

Main Language(s) of Instruction: English

International Co-operation: With universities in Ethiopia, Vietnam, Bangladesh, Syria, Myanmar, Egypt, Kenya, Iran. Also participates in Indo-Iran work plan; MoU with Eritrea, Nepal. Commonwealth Scholarship Scheme

Accrediting Agencies: Indian Council of Agricultural Research (ICAR)

Degrees and Diplomas: *Master's Degree (MSc)*: 2 yrs; *Doctorate (PhD)*: a further 2-5 yrs

Student Services: Academic counselling, Canteen, Employment services, Foreign student adviser, Health services, Sports facilities

Student Residential Facilities: Yes

Libraries: Main Library, one of the largest agricultural libraries of the region

Last Updated: 16/11/11

INDIAN INSTITUTE OF FOREIGN TRADE (IIFT)

IIFT Bhawan, B-21, Qutab Institutional Area, New Delhi 110 016
Tel: +91(11) 2685-3055
Fax: +91(11) 2685-3956
Website: http://www.iift.edu/

Director: Sh. K. T. Chacko

Registrar: L. D. Mago **EMail:** ldmago@iift.ac.in

Programmes

Management (Business Administration; Finance; Information Technology; International Business; Marketing)

Further Information: Campus in Kolkata

History: Founded 1963. Declared Deemed University, 2008.

Admission Requirements: Recognized Bachelor's degree of minimum 3 years' duration in any discipline for MBA programmes. Written test and interview

International Co-operation: With universities in France

Degrees and Diplomas: *Master's Degree*: Business Administration (MBA)

Libraries: With a total of c. 84,000 vols and subscriptions to 800 journals

Last Updated: 16/11/11

INDIAN INSTITUTE OF INFORMATION TECHNOLOGY (IIIT-A)

Deoghat Jhalwa, Allahabad, Uttar Pradesh 211002
Tel: +91(532) 243-1684 +91(532) 292-2000
Fax: +91(532) 243-0006 +91(532) 243-1689
EMail: contact@iiita.ac.in; mdt@iiita.ac.in
Website: http://www.iiita.ac.in

Director/CEO: Murli Dhar Tiwari (1999-2013)
EMail: mdt@iiita.ac.in; director@iiita.ac.in

International Relations: Ran Bahadur Singh, Administrative Officer
Tel: +91(532) 292-2007,
Fax: +91(532) 243-0006 +91(532) 243-1689 EMail: dfo@iiita.ac.in

Divisions

Applied Science *Head:* Tapobrata Lahiri; **Electronics and Communications Engineering** (Electronic Engineering; Telecommunications Engineering) *Head:* Radhakrishna Maringanti; **Management and Cyber Laws** (Law; Management) *Head:* Anurika Vaish; **Postgraduate** (Artificial Intelligence; Business Administration; Information Technology; Robotics; Software Engineering; Telecommunications Engineering) *Head:* Sudip Sanyal; **Undergraduate** (Electronic Engineering; Information Technology; Telecommunications Engineering) *Head:* Gora Chand Nandi

Further Information: Campuses in Saltanpur, Raibareli, Unchahar, Lalganj, Jagdishpur, Jayas, Gauriganj and Amethi

History: Founded as a Centre of Excellence in Information Technology in 1999. Granted "Deemed University" status in 2000.

Governing Bodies: Board of Governors; Finance Committee; Senate

Academic Year: July to June

Admission Requirements: 12th year senior secondary/intermediate examination or recognized foreign equivalent

Fees: (Rupees): 73,000-102,000 per annum depending on programmes

Main Language(s) of Instruction: English

International Co-operation: With universities in Australia; Denmark; Ghana; Korea; Nepal; Switzerland; USA and others

Accrediting Agencies: UGC/MHRD

Degrees and Diplomas: *Bachelor's Degree:* Information Technology; Electronics and Communication Engineering, 4 yrs; *Master's Degree:* Wireless Communication and Computing; Software Engineering; Intelligent Systems; Bioinformatics; Human Computer Interactions; Robotics and Microelectronics; Business Administration in IT; Cyber Law and Information Security, 2 yrs; *Doctorate:* Information Technology

Student Services: Academic counselling, Canteen, Cultural centre, Employment services, Handicapped facilities, Health services, Nursery care, Social counselling, Sports facilities

Student Residential Facilities: Yes

Special Facilities: Computer centers,; Auditorium

Libraries: Yes. Online catalogues. Audio and multimedia versions of most of the courses avalaible

Publications: Annual Audited Accounts Report; Annual Report; Convocation Report and other periodic publications

Academic Staff 2009-2010	MEN	WOMEN	TOTAL
FULL-TIME	63	11	74
PART-TIME	67	10	77
STAFF WITH DOCTORATE			
FULL-TIME	24	6	30
PART-TIME	–	1	1
Student Numbers 2009-2010			
All (Foreign Included)	1,325	290	1,615
FOREIGN ONLY	43	5	48

Last Updated: 26/10/10

INDIAN INSTITUTE OF INFORMATION TECHNOLOGY AND MANAGEMENT, GWALIOR

Morena Link Road, Gwalior, Madhya Pradesh 474010
Tel: +91(751) 2449-704
Fax: +91(751) 2449-813
Website: http://www.iiitm.ac.in

Director: S.G. Deshmukh

Programmes

Information Technology (Computer Engineering; Computer Networks; Information Technology); **Management** (Business Administration)

Fees: (Indian Rupees): 25,000-31,000 depending on programmes

Degrees and Diplomas: *Master's Degree*; *Doctorate*
Last Updated: 09/01/12

INDIAN INSTITUTE OF SCIENCE (IISC)

Bangalore, Karnataka 560012
Tel: +91(80) 2293-2001
Fax: +91(80) 2360-0085
EMail: regr@admin.iisc.ernet.in
Website: http://www.iisc.ernet.in

Director: P. Balaram
Tel: +91(80) 2360-0690, Fax: +91(80) 2360-0936
EMail: diroff@admin.iisc.ernet.in

Associate Director: N. Balakrishnan
Tel: +91(80) 2360-0129, Fax: +91(80) 2360-0221
EMail: ad@admin.iisc.ernet.in

International Relations: Rahul Pandit, Chairman
Tel: +91(80) 2239-2560 EMail: rahul@physics.iisc.ernet.in

Divisions

Biological Sciences (Biochemistry; Biological and Life Sciences; Ecology; Microbiology; Molecular Biology; Neurosciences); **Chemical Sciences** (Chemistry; Inorganic Chemistry; Organic Chemistry; Physical Chemistry); **Earth and Environmental Sciences** (Development Studies; Earth Sciences; Environmental Studies; Foreign Languages Education; Management; Marine Science and Oceanography); **Electrical Sciences** (Automation and Control Engineering; Computer Education; Electrical Engineering; Engineering; Mechanical Engineering; Metallurgical Engineering); **Mechanical Engineering** (Aeronautical and Aerospace Engineering; Chemical Engineering; Industrial Design; Materials Engineering; Mechanical Engineering); **Physical and Mathematical Sciences** (Applied Physics; Astronomy and Space Science; Astrophysics; Mathematics; Physics)

Research Centres

Super Computer Education (Computer Education)

History: Founded 1909. An autonomous body, funded by Central Government through the Ministry of Human Resources Development.

Governing Bodies: Council; Court; Finance Committee; Senate

Academic Year: August to July

Admission Requirements: University degree in Science or Engineering at Bachelor level

Fees: (Rupees): 5,000-15,000 per annum.

Main Language(s) of Instruction: English

Degrees and Diplomas: *Master's Degree:* Engineering (MBA); Engineering (M Des), 2 yrs; *Master's Degree:* Engineering (MSc Engg), 2 1/2 yrs; *Master's Degree:* Engineering and Technology (ME and MTech), 2 yrs by research; *Doctorate:* Science (PhD Integrated), 6-7 yrs; *Doctorate:* Science and Engineering (PhD), 4-5 yrs

Student Services: Academic counselling, Canteen, Cultural centre, Employment services, Foreign student adviser, Foreign Studies Centre, Health services, Nursery care, Social counselling, Sports facilities

Student Residential Facilities: Yes (compulsory)

Special Facilities: Auditorium

Libraries: c. 478,000 vols

Publications: IISc Journal *(quarterly)*
Last Updated: 16/11/11

INDIAN INSTITUTE OF SPACE SCIENCE AND TECHNOLOGY (IIST) (IIST)

Valiamala P.O., Thiruvananthapuram, Kerala 695 547
Tel: +91(471) 256-8462
Fax: +91(471) 256-8406
EMail: ao@iist.ac.in
Website: http://www.iist.ac.in/

Director: K.S. Dasgupta EMail: ksd@iist.ac.in

Registrar: K. Sasikumar
Tel: +91(471) 2568-403 EMail: registrar@iist.ac.in

Departments

Aerospace Engineering (Aeronautical and Aerospace Engineering); **Avionics** (Computer Science; Electrical and Electronic Engineering; Electronic Engineering); **Chemistry** (Chemistry); **Earth**

and Space Sciences (Earth Sciences); **Humanities** (Economics; English; Management; Social Sciences; Sociology); **Mathematics** (Mathematics); **Physics** (Physics)
Last Updated: 09/01/12

INDIAN INSTITUTE OF TECHNOLOGY, BHUBANESWAR

Bhubaneswar 751013
Tel: +91(674) 2301-292
EMail: director.office@iitbbs.ac.in
Website: http://www.iitbbs.ac.in/

Director: Madhusudan Chakraborty

Registrar: Bata Kishore Ray

Schools
Basic Sciences (Chemistry; Mathematics; Physics); **Earth, Ocean and Climate Sciences** (Earth Sciences; Marine Science and Oceanography; Meteorology); **Electrical Sciences** (Electrical Engineering); **Humanities, Social Sciences and Management** (Arts and Humanities; Literature; Management; Modern Languages; Social Sciences); **Infrastructure** (Civil Engineering; Town Planning; Transport Engineering; Urban Studies); **Mechanical Sciences** (Mechanical Engineering)

Degrees and Diplomas: *Bachelor's Degree*; *Master's Degree*; *Doctorate*

Student Services: Employment services

Student Residential Facilities: For 230 students

Special Facilities: Wifi

Libraries: Yes
Last Updated: 06/01/12

INDIAN INSTITUTE OF TECHNOLOGY, BOMBAY

Powai, Mumbai, Maharashtra 400076
Tel: +91(22) 2572-2545
Fax: +91(22) 2572-3480
EMail: dean.ir.office@iitb.ac.in
Website: http://www.iitb.ac.in

Director: Devang Khakhar (2009-)
Tel: +91(22) 2576-7001 +91(22) 2576-7002,
Fax: +91(22) 2572-3546 EMail: director@iitb.ac.in

Registrar: Shri B. S. Punalkar
Tel: +91(22) 2576-7020, Fax: +91(22) 2572-3645
EMail: registrar@iitb.ac.in

Centres
Aerospace Systems, Design and Engineering (Aeronautical and Aerospace Engineering; Design); **Alternative Technology for Rural Areas** (Technology); **Computer** (Computer Science); **Distance Engineering Education Programme** (Engineering); **Environmental Science and Engineering** (Engineering; Environmental Engineering); **Formal Design and Verification of Software** (Design; Software Engineering); **Nanotechnology and Sciences** (Nanotechnology); **Sophisticated Analytical Instrument Facility** *(Regional)* (Measurement and Precision Engineering); **Studies in Resources Engineering** (Natural Resources)

Departments
Aerospace Engineering (Aeronautical and Aerospace Engineering); **Chemical Engineering** (Chemical Engineering); **Chemistry** (Chemistry); **Civil Engineering** (Civil Engineering); **Computer Science and Engineering** (Computer Science; Engineering); **Earth Sciences** (Earth Sciences); **Electrical Engineering** (Electrical Engineering); **Energy Science and Engineering** (Energy Engineering); **Humanities and Social Sciences** (Arts and Humanities; Social Sciences); **Mathematics** (Mathematics); **Mechanical Engineering** (Mechanical Engineering); **Metallurgical Engineering and Materials Sciences** (Materials Engineering; Metallurgical Engineering); **Physics** (Physics) *Division Head*: ra

Schools
Information Technology *(Kanwal Rekki)*; **Management** *(Shailesh J. Mehta)* (Management; Technology)

History: Founded 1958, and declared to be an autonomous body empowered to confer all academic distinctions.

Governing Bodies: Board of Governors

Academic Year: July to April (July-November; January-April)

Admission Requirements: 12th year senior secondary/intermediate examination or recognized foreign equivalent, and all Indian competitive joint entrance examinations (JEE) conducted by the 7 Institutes of Technology (IITs)

Main Language(s) of Instruction: English

Degrees and Diplomas: *Bachelor's Degree*: Technology (Btech), 4 yrs; *Master's Degree*: Design; Management; Science; Technology, a further 2 yrs; *Doctorate (PhD)*: a further 3 yrs. Also Dual degree in Technology (Bachelor and Master), 4 yrs, extended to 6 yrs

Student Services: Academic counselling, Canteen, Cultural centre, Employment services, Foreign student adviser, Handicapped facilities, Health services, Language programs, Social counselling, Sports facilities

Student Residential Facilities: Yes

Special Facilities: Centre for Distance Engineering Education Programme

Libraries: Central and department libraries, total, 211,447 vols
Last Updated: 16/11/11

INDIAN INSTITUTE OF TECHNOLOGY, DELHI

Hauz Khas, New Delhi 110016
Tel: +91(11) 2658-1988
Fax: +91(11) 2658-2659
EMail: webmaster@admin.iitd.ac.in
Website: http://www.iitd.ac.in

Director: R.K. Shevgaonkar (2011-)
Tel: +91(11) 2659-1701 EMail: director@admin.iitd.ac.in

Registrar: Kumar Rakesh
Tel: +91(11) 2659-1710 EMail: registrar@admin.iitd.ac.in

Centres
Applied Research in Electronics (Electronic Engineering); **Atmospheric Sciences** (Meteorology); **Biomedical Engineering** (Biomedical Engineering); **Computer Service** (Computer Science); **Educational Technology** (Educational Technology); **Energy Studies** (Energy Engineering); **Industrial Tribology** (Mechanical Engineering; Mechanical Equipment and Maintenance); **Instrument Design** (Industrial Design); **National Resource**; **Polymer Science and Engineering** (Engineering; Polymer and Plastics Technology); **Rural Development and Technology** (Rural Planning; Technology)

Departments
Applied Mechanics (Mechanical Engineering); **Biochemical Engineering and Biotechnology** (Biochemistry; Biotechnology); **Chemistry** (Chemistry); **Civil Engineering** (Civil Engineering); **Computer Science and Engineering** (Computer Science; Engineering); **Electrical Engineering** (Electrical Engineering); **Humanities and Social Sciences** (Arts and Humanities; Social Sciences); **Management Studies** (Management); **Mathematics** (Mathematics); **Mechanical Engineering** (Mechanical Engineering); **Physics** (Physics); **Textile Technology** (Textile Technology)

History: Founded 1961 as College of Engineering and Technology, declared to be an autonomous body empowered to confer all academic distinctions, and acquired present title 1963.

Governing Bodies: Board of Governors; Senate

Academic Year: July to June (July-December; January-June)

Admission Requirements: Competitive joint entrance examination conducted by the 6 Institutes of Technology (IITs), Banaras Hindu University Institute of Technology, and the Indian Institute of Mines

Main Language(s) of Instruction: English

Degrees and Diplomas: *Diploma*; *Bachelor's Degree*: 4 yrs; *Postgraduate Diploma*; *Master's Degree*: 5 yrs; *Doctorate (PhD)*: at least 3 yrs

Student Services: Academic counselling, Canteen, Cultural centre, Employment services, Foreign student adviser, Health services, Social counselling, Sports facilities

Student Residential Facilities: Yes

Special Facilities: Recreational Creative Activity Centre. Open Air Theatre. 2 Conference Halls

Libraries: Total, c. 295,000 vols
Press or Publishing House: Publication Cell
Last Updated: 16/11/11

INDIAN INSTITUTE OF TECHNOLOGY, GANDHINAGAR (IIT GANDHINAGAR)

Vishwakarma Government Engineering College Complex, Chandkheda, Visat-Gandhinagar Highway, Ahmedabad, Gujarat 382424
Tel: +91 93284 74222
Fax: +91(79) 2397-2324
EMail: office@iitgn.ac.in
Website: http://www.iitgn.ac.in

Director: Sudhir K. Jain
Tel: +91(79) 2397-2574 EMail: director@iitgn.ac.in

Registrar: B. S. Punalkar

Programmes

Engineering (Chemical Engineering; Civil Engineering; Electrical and Electronic Equipment and Maintenance; Mechanical Engineering); **Humanities and Social Sciences** (Cognitive Sciences; Economics; English; Human Resources; Philosophy; Social Sciences; Sociology); **Science** (Chemistry; Mathematics; Physics)

Degrees and Diplomas: *Bachelor's Degree*; *Master's Degree*; *Doctorate*

Student Residential Facilities: Yes

Libraries: Yes
Last Updated: 06/01/12

INDIAN INSTITUTE OF TECHNOLOGY, GUWAHATI

Guwahati, Assam 781039
Tel: +91(361) 269-0401
Fax: +91(361) 269-2321
EMail: root@iitg.ernet.in
Website: http://www.iitg.ernet.in

Director: Gautam Barua EMail: director@iitg.ernet.in

Registrar: Brajendra Nath Raychoudhury
EMail: registrar@ iitg.ernet.in

Departments

Biotechnology (Biotechnology); **Chemical Engineering** (Chemical Engineering); **Chemistry** (Chemistry); **Civil Engineering** (Civil Engineering); **Computer Science and Engineering** (Computer Science; Engineering); **Design** (Design); **Electronics and Electrical Engineering** (Computer Networks; Electronic Engineering); **Humanities and Social Sciences** (Archaeology; Arts and Humanities; Economics; English; History; Linguistics; Philosophy; Psychology; Social Sciences; Sociology); **Mathematics** (Mathematics); **Mechanical Engineering** (Mechanical Engineering); **Physics** (Physics)

History: Founded 1994.

Academic Year: July to May (July-November; December-May).

Degrees and Diplomas: *Bachelor's Degree*: Technology (BTech), 4 yrs; *Master's Degree*; *Doctorate (PhD)*: 4 yrs

Libraries: c. 10,000 vols; 500 periodicals.
Last Updated: 17/11/11

INDIAN INSTITUTE OF TECHNOLOGY, HYDERABAD

Ordnance Factory Estate, Yeddumailaram, Andhra Pradesh 502205
Tel: +91(40) 2301-6033
Fax: +91(40) 2301-6032
EMail: info@iith.ac.in
Website: http://www.iith.ac.in

Director: Uday B. Desai (2009-) EMail: director@iith.ac.in

Departments

Engineering (Biomedicine; Biotechnology; Civil Engineering; Computer Engineering; Computer Science; Electrical Engineering; Materials Engineering; Mechanical Engineering); **Liberal Arts**

(Cultural Studies; English; Literature; Psychology); **Sciences** (Chemistry; Mathematics; Physics)

History: Founded 2008.

International Co-operation: With universities in USA and Japan.

Degrees and Diplomas: *Bachelor's Degree*; *Master's Degree*; *Doctorate*

Student Services: Sports facilities

Publications: Reverb
Last Updated: 05/01/12

INDIAN INSTITUTE OF TECHNOLOGY, INDORE (IIT INDORE)

M-Block, Institute of Engineering and Technology, Devi Ahilya Vishwavidyalaya Campus, Khandwa Road, Indore, Madhya Pradesh 452017
Tel: +91(731) 2364-182
Fax: +91(731) 2431-482
EMail: contactus@iiti.ac.in
Website: http://www.iiti.ac.in

Director: Pradeep Mathur
Tel: +91(731) 236-4182 EMail: director@iiti.ac.in

Registrar: G. Raja Sekhar
Tel: +91(731) 2438-718 EMail: registrar@iiti.ac.in

Schools

Basic Science (Chemistry; Mathematics; Physics); **Engineering** (Computer Engineering; Computer Science; Electrical Engineering; Engineering; Mechanical Engineering); **Humanities and Social Science** (Arts and Humanities; Economics; Literature; Philosophy; Social Sciences)

Degrees and Diplomas: *Bachelor's Degree*; *Master's Degree*; *Doctorate*
Last Updated: 06/01/12

INDIAN INSTITUTE OF TECHNOLOGY, KANPUR (PO IIT)

PO IIT, Kanpur, Uttar Pradesh 208016
Tel: +91(512) 259-7808
Fax: +91(512) 259-0465
EMail: registrar@iitk.ac.in
Website: http://www.iitk.ac.in

Director: Sanjay Gobind Dhande (2001-) EMail: sgd@iitk.ac.in

Registrar: Sanjeev Kashalkar

Departments

Aerospace Engineering (Aeronautical and Aerospace Engineering); **Biological Sciences and Bioengineering**; **Chemical Engineering** (Chemical Engineering); **Chemistry** (Biochemistry; Chemistry; Physical Chemistry); **Civil Engineering** (Civil Engineering; Environmental Engineering; Geology); **Computer Science and Engineering** (Computer Science; Engineering); **Design**; **Electrical Engineering** (Electrical Engineering); **Environmental Science and Management** (Environmental Management; Environmental Studies); **Humanities and Social Sciences** (Arts and Humanities; Social Sciences); **Industrial and Management Engineering** (Engineering Management; Industrial Engineering; Management); **Laser Technology**; **Materials Engineering and Metallurgical Engineering** (Materials Engineering; Metallurgical Engineering); **Materials Science** (Materials Engineering); **Mathematics ans Statistics** (Mathematics; Statistics); **Mechanical Engineering** (Design; Mechanical Engineering; Production Engineering; Robotics); **Nuclear Engineering and Technology** (Nuclear Engineering); **Physics** (Laser Engineering; Nuclear Physics; Physics)

History: Founded 1959 as a College of Engineering and Technology, declared to be an autonomous body empowered to confer all academic distinctions, and acquired its present title 1962.

Governing Bodies: Board of Governors

Academic Year: July to April (July-November; January-April)

Admission Requirements: 12th year senior secondary/intermediate examination or recognized foreign equivalent, and all Indian competitive joint entrance examination (JEE) conducted by the Institutes of Technology (IITs)

Fees: (Rupees): 25,000 per semester

Main Language(s) of Instruction: English

Degrees and Diplomas: *Bachelor's Degree*: 4 yrs; *Master's Degree (MSc Integrated)*: 5 yrs; *Master's Degree (MSc)*: 2 yrs; *Master's Degree (MTech)*: 4 sem; *Doctorate (PhD)*: 4-5 yrs

Student Residential Facilities: Yes

Libraries: Central Library, c. 280,000 vols

Last Updated: 17/11/11

INDIAN INSTITUTE OF TECHNOLOGY, KHARAGPUR

PO Kharagpur Technology, Kharagpur, West Bengal 721302
Tel: +91(3222) 255-221
Fax: +91(3222) 255-303
EMail: registrar@hijli.iitkgp.ernet.in
Website: http://www.iitkgp.ernet.in

Director: K. Damodar Acharya Tel: +91(3222) 282-002

Registrar: Dharmalingam Gunasekaran

Centres

Cryogenic Engineering (Heating and Refrigeration); **Educational Technology** (Distance Education; Educational Research; Educational Sciences; Educational Technology; Educational Testing and Evaluation; Pedagogy); **Materials Science** (Ceramics and Glass Technology; Materials Engineering; Polymer and Plastics Technology); **Oceans, Rivers, Atmosphere and Land Sciences** (Earth Sciences; Meteorology; Soil Science; Water Science); **Reliability Engineering** (Safety Engineering); **Rubber Technology** (Rubber Technology); **Rural Development** (Development Studies)

Departments

Aerospace Engineering (Aeronautical and Aerospace Engineering); **Agriculture and Food Engineering** (Agriculture; Agronomy; Aquaculture; Crop Production; Dairy; Farm Management; Fishery; Food Technology; Forest Biology; Harvest Technology; Horticulture; Irrigation; Meat and Poultry; Soil Conservation; Soil Science; Tropical Agriculture; Water Management; Water Science); **Architecture and Regional Planning** (Architectural Restoration; Architecture; Landscape Architecture; Regional Planning; Structural Architecture; Town Planning); **Biotechnology** (Biochemistry; Biotechnology; Cell Biology; Genetics; Immunology; Microbiology; Molecular Biology; Physiology; Toxicology); **Chemical Engineering** (Chemical Engineering; Industrial Design; Petroleum and Gas Engineering); **Chemistry** (Chemistry; Industrial Chemistry; Inorganic Chemistry; Organic Chemistry; Physical Chemistry); **Civil Engineering** (Civil Engineering; Construction Engineering; Environmental Engineering; Hydraulic Engineering; Transport Engineering); **Computer Science and Engineering** (Computer Engineering; Information Sciences; Software Engineering; Technology); **Electrical Engineering** (Automation and Control Engineering; Electrical Engineering; Energy Engineering; Instrument Making; Power Engineering); **Electronics and Electrical Communication Engineering** (Computer Science; Electrical and Electronic Engineering; Microelectronics; Telecommunications Engineering); **Geology and Geophysics** (Crystallography; Earth Sciences; Geochemistry; Geology; Geophysics; Mineralogy; Paleontology; Petroleum and Gas Engineering; Seismology); **Humanities and Social Sciences** (Arts and Humanities; Communication Studies; Comparative Literature; Economics; English; Ethics; French; German; International Studies; Literature; Logic; Modern Languages; Philosophy; Psychology; Social Sciences; Sociology); **Industrial Engineering and Management** (Industrial Engineering; Management; Management Systems; Systems Analysis); **Mathematics** (Applied Mathematics; Computer Science; Mathematics; Software Engineering; Statistics); **Mechanical Engineering** (Automotive Engineering; Heating and Refrigeration; Hydraulic Engineering; Mechanical Engineering; Power Engineering; Production Engineering; Sound Engineering (Acoustics)); **Metallurgical and Materials Engineering** (Materials Engineering; Metallurgical Engineering); **Mining Engineering** (Mining Engineering); **Ocean Engineering and Naval Architecture** (Marine Engineering; Naval Architecture); **Physics and Meteorology** (Meteorology; Physics; Solid State Physics)

Schools

Engineering Entrepreneurship *(Rajendra Mishra)* (Engineering Management); **Information Technology** (Information Technology);

Infrastructure Design and Management *(Ranbir and Chitra Gupta)* (Design; Management); **Intellectual Property Law** *(Rajiv Gandhi)*; **Management** *(Vinod Gupta)* (Accountancy; Administration; Business and Commerce; Finance; Human Resources; Industrial Management; Institutional Administration; Insurance; International Business; Labour and Industrial Relations; Management; Marketing; Public Administration; Systems Analysis); **Medical Science and Technology** (Automation and Control Engineering; Biomedicine; Biophysics; Electronic Engineering; Information Technology); **Telecommunications** *(G.S. Sanyal)* (Information Technology; Telecommunications Engineering); **Water Resources** (Water Management; Water Science)

History: Founded 1951 as Indian Institute of Technology, declared an autonomous body empowered to confer all Academic distinctions, and acquired its present title 1956.

Governing Bodies: Board of Governors

Academic Year: July to May (July-December; December-May). Also Summer Term (May to July) for special courses

Admission Requirements: 12th year senior secondary/intermediate examination or recognized foreign equivalent, and all Indian competitive joint entrance examination (JEE) conducted by 7 Indian Institutes of Technology (IITs)

Fees: (Rupees): 15,000 per semester; foreign students (US Dollars), 5,000

Main Language(s) of Instruction: English

International Co-operation: With universities in Russian Federation and Germany. Negotiations underway with universities in the USA for development of distance education modules.

Degrees and Diplomas: *Bachelor's Degree*: Architecture (BArch), 5 yrs; *Bachelor's Degree*: Science (BSc), 3 yrs; *Bachelor's Degree*: Technology (BTech), 4 yrs; *Postgraduate Diploma*: Information Technology (PGDIT), 1 yr; *Master's Degree*: Business Management (MBM), a further 2 yrs; *Master's Degree*: Medical Science and Technology (MMST), 3 yrs; *Master's Degree*: Science (MSc (integrated)); Technology (MTech), 5 yrs; *Master's Degree*: Science and Technology (by Research) (MS), a further 4 semesters; *Master's Degree*: Technology, Architecture and Regional Planning (MTech/MCP), a further 18 months; *Doctorate*: All fields of study (PhD), 3-4 yrs. Also Dual Degree, BTech/MTech, 5 yrs in Technology

Student Services: Academic counselling, Canteen, Cultural centre, Employment services, Foreign student adviser, Foreign Studies Centre, Health services, Language programs, Nursery care, Social counselling, Sports facilities

Student Residential Facilities: Yes

Special Facilities: Nehru Museum of Science and Technology

Libraries: Central Library, c. 3,000,000 vols

Publications: Electronic Journal of Indian Culture and Society, Department of Humanities and Social Sciences *(biannually)*; Research and Innovation, Sponsored research and Industrial Consultancy Cell *(quarterly)*

Press or Publishing House: Institute Press

Last Updated: 17/11/11

INDIAN INSTITUTE OF TECHNOLOGY, MADRAS (IITM)

IIT Post Office, Chennai, Chennai, Tamil Nadu 600036
Tel: +91(44) 2257-8001
Fax: +91(44) 2257-0509
EMail: ananth@iitm.ac.in
Website: http://www.iitm.ac.in

Director: Bhaskar Ramamurthi EMail: director@iitm.ac.in

Registrar: A. Thirunavukkarasu
Tel: +91(44) 2257-8100, Fax: +91(44) 2257-0509
EMail: registrar@iitm.ac.in

International Relations: K. Ramamurthy, Dean, Academic Courses
Tel: +91(44) 2257-8030, Fax: +91(44) 2257-8042
EMail: deanac@iitm.ac.in

Departments

Aerospace Engineering; **Applied Mechanics**; **Biotechnology** (Agricultural Engineering; Biology; Biomedical Engineering; Biotechnology; Cell Biology; Chemistry; Computer Science; Engineering;

Genetics; Molecular Biology; Neurosciences; Organic Chemistry; Pharmacy); **Chemical Engineering**; **Chemistry**; **Civil Engineering**; **Computer Science and Engineering**; **Electrical Engineering**; **Humanities and Social Sciences**; **Management Studies** (Finance; Human Resources; Labour and Industrial Relations; Management; Marketing; Public Administration; Transport Management); **Mathematics**; **Mechanical Engineering**; **Metallurgical and Materials Engineering**; **Ocean Engineering**; **Physics**

Research Centres
Central Electronics (Electronic Engineering); **Composites Technology** (Aeronautical and Aerospace Engineering; Ceramics and Glass Technology; Chemical Engineering; Civil Engineering; Mechanical Engineering; Metallurgical Engineering; Polymer and Plastics Technology; Technology); **Continuing Education** (Systems Analysis); **Materials Science** (Chemical Engineering; Chemistry; Civil Engineering; Electrical Engineering; Engineering; Inorganic Chemistry; Materials Engineering; Metallurgical Engineering; Physics; Technology); **Sophisticated Analysis Instrumentation Facilities** (Chemistry; Instrument Making; Materials Engineering; Metallurgical Engineering; Physics)

Further Information: Also Research Laboratories attached to each Department

History: Founded 1959, acquired present status 1962.

Governing Bodies: Board of Governors; Senate

Academic Year: July to May (July-November; January-May)

Admission Requirements: BTech: 12th year senior secondary/intermediate examination or recognized foreign equivalent, and all Indian Competitive Joint Entrance Examination (JEE) conducted by the 6 Institutes of Technology (IITs). MTech/MS: BE/BTech with GATE. PhD: ME/MTech/MSc with a National level test

Main Language(s) of Instruction: English

International Co-operation: Yes

Degrees and Diplomas: *Bachelor's Degree*: Engineering, 4 yrs; *Master's Degree*: Engineering; Management; Mathematics; Physics; Chemistry, a further 2 yrs; *Doctorate*: Engineering; Natural Sciences (PhD), a further 4 yrs. Also Dual degree (5 yrs) in Engineering, B.Tech. & M.Tech.; Master of Science by Research (a further 2 yrs) in Engineering

Student Services: Academic counselling, Canteen, Cultural centre, Employment services, Foreign student adviser, Handicapped facilities, Health services, Language programs, Nursery care, Social counselling, Sports facilities

Student Residential Facilities: For c. 2,400 students

Special Facilities: Open Air Theatre. Central Lecture Theatre

Libraries: Central Library, 191,601; 762 periodical subscriptions

Publications: Abstracts of MS and PhD Theses *(annually)*; Research, Consultancy, Expertise and Facilities *(biennially)*

Press or Publishing House: IIT Madras

Last Updated: 17/11/11

INDIAN INSTITUTE OF TECHNOLOGY, MANDI (IIT MANDI)

PWD Rest House, Mandi, Himachal Pradesh 175001
Tel: +91(1905) 237943
Fax: +91(1905) 237945
EMail: regis@iitmandi.ac.in
Website: http://www.iitmandi.ac.in/

Director: Timothy A. Gonsalves
Tel: +91(1905) 237731, Fax: +91(1905) 237942
EMail: diroffice@]iitmandi.ac.in

Registrar: R.C. Sawhney

Schools
Basic Sciences (Biological and Life Sciences; Chemistry; Mathematics; Physics); **Computing and Electrical Engineering** (Computer Engineering; Electrical Engineering); **Engineering** (Civil Engineering; Engineering; Mechanical Engineering); **Humanities and Social Sciences** (Arts and Humanities; Cultural Studies; Economics; Management; Modern Languages; Social Psychology; Social Work)

History: Founded 2009.

Fees: Foreign students - US $ 2,000 + other charges in Indian Rupees (for SAARC countries); US $ 4,000 + other charges in Indian Rupees (for other countries)

Degrees and Diplomas: *Bachelor's Degree*; *Master's Degree*; *Doctorate*

Last Updated: 06/01/12

INDIAN INSTITUTE OF TECHNOLOGY, PATNA

Navin Government Polytechnic Campus, Patliputra Colony, Patna, Bihar 800 013
Tel: +91(612) 2552-067
Fax: +91(612) 2277-383
EMail: iitpatnaoff@iitp.ac.in
Website: http://www.iitp.ac.in/

Director: Anil K. Bhowmick

Schools
Engineering (Computer Engineering; Computer Science; Electrical Engineering; Engineering; Mechanical Engineering); **Humanities and Social Science** (Arts and Humanities; Social Sciences); **Sciences** (Chemistry; Mathematics; Physics)

History: Founded 2008.

Degrees and Diplomas: *Bachelor's Degree*; *Doctorate*
Last Updated: 06/01/12

INDIAN INSTITUTE OF TECHNOLOGY, RAJASTHAN

Old Residency Road, Ratanada, Jodhpur, Rajasthan 342011
Tel: +91(291) 244-9024
Fax: +91(291) 251-6823
EMail: dir@iitj.ac.in
Website: http://www.iitj.ac.in/

Director: Prem K. Kalra
Tel: +91(291) 251-2141, Fax: +91(291) 251-6823
EMail: pkk@iitj.ac.in

Departments
Postgraduate Programmes (Energy Engineering; Information Technology; Systems Analysis; Telecommunications Engineering); **Undergraduate Programmes** (Computer Engineering; Computer Science; Electrical and Electronic Engineering; Mechanical Engineering; Systems Analysis)

History: Founded 2008.

Degrees and Diplomas: *Bachelor's Degree*; *Master's Degree*; *Doctorate*

Student Residential Facilities: Yes

Libraries: Yes
Last Updated: 05/01/12

INDIAN INSTITUTE OF TECHNOLOGY, ROORKEE (IITR)

Roorkee, Uttarakhand 247667
Tel: +91(1332) 285-311
Fax: +91(1332) 285-310
EMail: regis@iitr.ernet.in
Website: http://www.iitr.ac.in

Director: Pradipta Banerji
Tel: +91(1332) 285-500, Fax: +91(1332) 285-815
EMail: director@iitr.ernet.in

Registrar: A.K. Srivastava

Departments
Architecture and Planning (Architecture and Planning) *Head*: Pushplata; **Biotechnology** (Biological and Life Sciences; Biotechnology) *Head*: Ritu Barthwal; **Chemical Engineering** (Chemical Engineering) *Head*: I.D. Mall; **Chemistry** (Chemistry) *Head*: V.K. Gupta; **Civil Engineering** (Civil Engineering) *Head*: A.K. Jain; **Earth Sciences** (Earth Sciences; Geology; Geophysics) *Head*: P.K. Gupta; **Earthquake Engineering** (Seismology) *Head*: H.R. Wasan; **Electrical Engineering** (Electrical Engineering) *Head*: Vinod Kumar; **Electronics and Computer Engineering** (Computer

Engineering; Electronic Engineering) *Head*: S.N. Sinha; **Humanities and Social Sciences** (Arts and Humanities; English; Psychology; Social Sciences) *Head*: S.P. Singh; **Hydrology** (Hydraulic Engineering) *Head*: Himanshu Joshi; **Management Studies** (Management) *Head*: V. K. Nangia; **Mathematics** (Mathematics) *Head*: G.S. Srivastava; **Mechanical and Industrial Engineering** (Industrial Engineering; Mechanical Engineering; Production Engineering) *Head*: Satish C. Sharma; **Metallurgical and Materials Sciences** (Materials Engineering; Metallurgical Engineering) *Head*: P.K. Ghosh; **Paper Technology** (Paper Technology) *Head*: Satish Kumar; **Physics** (Physics) *Head*: A.K. Jain; **Water Resources Development and Management** (Water Management) *Head*: Nayan Sharma

History: Founded 1847 as Thomason College of Civil Engineering, the oldest Engineering College in India, became University of Roorkee 1949. Acquired present status 1949 and title 2001.

Governing Bodies: Board of Governors

Academic Year: July to May (July-December; January-May)

Admission Requirements: 12th year senior secondary/intermediate examination or recognized foreign equivalent

Main Language(s) of Instruction: English

Degrees and Diplomas: *Bachelor's Degree*: 4 yrs; *Postgraduate Diploma*: 1 yr; *Master's Degree*: a further 2-3 yrs; *Doctorate (PhD)*: a further 3-4 yrs

Student Services: Academic counselling, Canteen, Cultural centre, Employment services, Foreign student adviser, Foreign Studies Centre, Handicapped facilities, Health services, Language programs, Nursery care, Social counselling, Sports facilities

Student Residential Facilities: Yes

Special Facilities: Civil Engineering Museum; Concrete Technology Museum; Geology Museum. Meteorological Observatory

Libraries: Main Library, c. 305,000 vols; 800 print journals and 8,000 e-journal archives

Last Updated: 18/11/11

INDIAN INSTITUTE OF TECHNOLOGY, ROPAR

Nangal Road, Rupnagar, Punjab 140001
Tel: +91(1881) 227078
Fax: +91(1881) 223395
Website: http://www.iitrpr.ac.in/

Director: M.K. Surappa EMail: director@iitrpr.ac.in

Registrar: A. Palanivel

Programmes
Engineering (Computer Education; Computer Science; Electrical Engineering; Mechanical Engineering); **Humanities and Social Science** (Arts and Humanities; Social Sciences); **Sciences** (Chemistry; Mathematics; Physics)

History: Founded 2008.

Degrees and Diplomas: *Bachelor's Degree*; *Master's Degree*; *Doctorate*

Special Facilities: Wifi; Computer Labs

Libraries: Yes

Last Updated: 06/01/12

INDIAN LAW INSTITUTE

Bhagwandas Road, New Delhi 110001
Tel: +91(11) 2338-7526
Fax: +91(11) 2378-2140
EMail: ili@ili.ac.in
Website: http://www.ili.ac.in

Director: S. Sivakumar EMail: director@ili.ac.in

Registrar: Dalip Kumar

Programmes
Law (Commercial Law; Labour Law; Law; Taxation)

History: Founded 1956. Acquired Deemed University status 2004.

Degrees and Diplomas: *Bachelor's Degree*; *Postgraduate Diploma*; *Doctorate*

Libraries: A total ofc. 75.000 vols. 270 current legal periodicals.
Last Updated: 18/11/11

INDIAN MARITIME UNIVERSITY (IMU)

East Coast Road, Uthandi, Chennai 600 119
Tel: +91(44) 2453-0343 +91(44) 2453-0345
Fax: +91(44) 2453-0342
Website: http://www.imu.tn.nic.in/

Vice Chancellor: P. Vijayan

Programmes
Marine Engineering (Marine Engineering); **Nautical** (Nautical Science); **Port and Shipping Management** (Computer Science; Finance; Human Resources; Management; Marine Transport; Transport Engineering; Transport Management)

Schools
Business (Business Administration; International Business; Marine Transport; Transport and Communications; Transport Management)

Further Information: Regional Campuses in Mumbai, Kolkata, Visakhapatnam, Cochin.

History: Founded 2008. A 'Central University'.

Degrees and Diplomas: *Diploma*; *Postgraduate Diploma*
Last Updated: 08/12/11

INDIAN SCHOOL OF MINES

Jharkand, Dhanbad, Bihar 826004
Tel: +91(326) 229-6559
Fax: +91(326) 229-6563
EMail: rg@ismdhanbad.ac.in
Website: http://www.ismdhanbad.ac.in/

Director: D.C. Panigrahi EMail: dt@ismdhanbad.ac.in

Registrar: M.K. Singh Tel: +91(326) 223-5202

Departments
Applied Chemistry (Applied Chemistry); **Applied Geology** (Geology); **Applied Geophysics** (Geophysics); **Applied Mathematics** (Applied Mathematics); **Applied Physics** (Applied Physics); **Chemical Engineering** (Chemical Engineering); **Computer Science and Engineering** (Computer Science; Engineering); **Electrical Engineering** (Electrical Engineering); **Electronics Engineering** (Electronic Engineering; Measurement and Precision Engineering); **Engineering and Mining Machinery** (Engineering; Mechanical Equipment and Maintenance); **Environmental Science and Engineering** (Environmental Engineering); **Fuel and Mineral Engineering** (Mineralogy; Petroleum and Gas Engineering); **Humanities and Social Sciences** (Arts and Humanities; English; Social Sciences); **Management** (Management); **Mechanical Engineering and Mining Machinery Engineering** (Mechanical Engineering; Mining Engineering); **Mining Engineering** (Mining Engineering); **Petroleum Engineering** (Petroleum and Gas Engineering)

Research Centres
Biotechnology; **Materials Science**

History: Founded 1926 following the pattern of Royal School of Mines, London, and Mining Colleges of Japan. Declared an autonomous body with a 'Deemed University' status granted 1967.

Governing Bodies: General Council

Academic Year: July to June

Admission Requirements: 12th year senior secondary/intermediate examination or recognized foreign equivalent

Main Language(s) of Instruction: English

Accrediting Agencies: University Grants Commission

Degrees and Diplomas: *Bachelor's Degree*; *Master's Degree*; *Doctorate (PhD)*: 2-7 yrs

Student Residential Facilities: Yes

Special Facilities: Geological Museum. Experimental Mine. Longway Mine Gallery

Libraries: 103,510 vols; 29,125 periodical subscriptions
Last Updated: 18/11/11

INDIAN STATISTICAL INSTITUTE

203 Barrackpore Trunk Road, Kolkata, West Bengal 700108
Tel: +91(33) 2577-6037
Fax: +91(33) 2577-6680
EMail: director@isical.ac.in
Website: http://www.isical.ac.in

Director: Bimal K . Roy
Tel: +91(33) 2577-3084 EMail: sanka@isical.ac.in

Dean of Studies: G.M. Saha

Divisions

Applied Statistics (Statistics); **Biological Sciences** (Agriculture; Biological and Life Sciences; Ecology; Genetics); **Computer and Communication Sciences** (Computer Engineering; Computer Networks; Telecommunications Engineering); **Library, Documentation and Information Sciences** (Documentation Techniques; Information Sciences; Library Science; Photography); **Physics and Earth Sciences** (Earth Sciences; Physics); **Social Sciences** (Linguistics; Psychology; Social Sciences; Sociology) *Director*: Satya Ranjan Chakraborty; **Statistical Quality Control** (Statistics); **Teaching and Training** (Teacher Training); **Theoretical Statistics and Mathematics** (Mathematics; Statistics)

Further Information: Calcutta, New Delhi, Bangalore and Hyderabad

History: Founded 1932, recognized as an Institution of national importance and empowered to confer degrees in Statistics 1959.

Governing Bodies: Council

Academic Year: July-June

Admission Requirements: 12th year senior secondary/intermediate examination or recognized foreign equivalent

Main Language(s) of Instruction: English

Accrediting Agencies: Ministry of Statistics and Programme Implementation

Degrees and Diplomas: *Bachelor's Degree*: Statistics; Mathematics (BStat; BMath), 3 yrs; *Master's Degree*: Statistics; Quantitative Economics; Computer Science; Quality Reliability and OR (MStat; MS(QE); MTech (CS); MTech (QROR)), a further 2 yrs; *Doctorate*: Statistics; Mathematics; Computer Science; Economics (PhD), at least 3 yrs. Also Associateship in Library Documentation and Information Sciences 2 yrs

Student Services: Academic counselling, Canteen, Cultural centre, Employment services, Foreign Studies Centre, Handicapped facilities, Health services, Sports facilities

Student Residential Facilities: Yes

Libraries: Central Research Library

Publications: Sankhya - the Indian Journal of Statistics *(bimonthly)*
Last Updated: 18/11/11

INDIAN VETERINARY RESEARCH INSTITUTE

Bhartiya Pashu-Chikitsa Anusandhan Sansthan
Izatnagar, Uttar Pradesh 243122
Tel: +91(581) 230-0096
Fax: +91(581) 230-3284
EMail: registrar@ivri.up.nic.in; dirivri@ivri.res.in
Website: http://ivri.nic.in

Director: M.C. Sharma EMail: dirivri@ivri.res.in

Senior Administrative Officer: Pankaj Kumar
Tel: +91(581) 230-1375

International Relations: Shri G.R. Desh Bandhu, Registrar
EMail: grdeshbandhu02@yahoo.com; registrar@ivri.up.nic.in

Divisions

Animal Biotechnology (Biotechnology; Zoology) *Division Head*: I; **Animal Genetics**; **Animal Nutrition**; **Animal Reproduction** (Animal Husbandry); **Avian Diseases** (Veterinary Science); **Bacteriology and Mycology**; **Biochemistry and Food Science** (Biochemistry; Food Science; Veterinary Science; Zoology); **Biological Products**; **Biological Products** (Biology); **Epidemiology**; **Extension Education** (Education; Veterinary Science); **Livestock Economics and Statistics** (Animal Husbandry; Statistics); **Medicine** (Medicine; Veterinary Science); **P. and T.** (Pharmacology;

Veterinary Science); **Parasitology** (Parasitology; Veterinary Science); **Pathology** (Pathology; Veterinary Science); **Physiology and Climatology** (Physiology; Zoology); **Standardisation**; **Surgery** (Surgery); **Veterinary Public Health** (Public Health; Veterinary Science); **Virology** (Veterinary Science; Virology)

Institutes
Central Avian Research

Sections
Immunology (Immunology); **Livestock Production and Management** (Animal Husbandry); **Livestock Production and Management**

History: Founded 1889. Acquired present status as 'Deemed to be University' 1983.

Academic Year: September to August

Admission Requirements: 12th year senior secondary/intermediate examination or recognized foreign equivalent; Bachelor of Veterinary Sciences and Animal Husbandry for Master of Vet. Sc.(M.V.SC.); M.V.Sc. for PhD

Main Language(s) of Instruction: English

Accrediting Agencies: Indian Council of Agricultural Research

Degrees and Diplomas: *Postgraduate Diploma*: Preventive Veterinary Medicine; Animal Husbandry; Veterinary Biological Products; Animal Reproduction; Poultry husbandry; Equine Husbandry, Medicine and Surgery; Zoo and Wild Animal Health Care and Management; Meat Products Technology; Food Technology; *Master's Degree*: Animal Biochemistry; Animal Biotechnology; Animal Genetics & Breeding; Animal Nutrition; Animal Physiology; Avian Diseases; Bio-Statistics; Epidemiology; Livestock Production and Management; Livestock Products Technology; Poultry Science; Veterinary Bacteriology; Vet. Extension Education; Vet. Gynaecology and Obstetrics; Vet. Immunology; Vet. Medicine; Vet. Parasitology; Vet. Pathology; Vet. Pharmacology; Vet. Public Health; Vet. Surgery; Vet. Virology, at least 2 yrs; *Doctorate*: Animal Biochemistry; Animal Biotechnology; Animal Genetics & Breeding; Animal Nutrition; Animal Physiology; Avian Diseases; Livestock Production and Management; Livestock Products Technology; Poultry Science (PhD); Veterinary Bacteriology; Vet. Extension Education; Vet. Gynaecology and Obstetrics; Vet. Immunology; Vet. Medicine; Vet. Parasitology; Vet. Pathology; Vet. Pharmacology; Vet. Public Health; Vet. Surgery; Vet. Virology (PhD), a further 3-4 yrs. Also Short term training Courses and International Short Term Training for Foreign Nationals

Student Residential Facilities: Yes

Special Facilities: Laboratories

Libraries: c. 150,000 vols

Student Numbers *2011-2012*: Total 641
Last Updated: 24/06/11

INDIRA GANDHI AGRICULTURAL UNIVERSITY

Indira Gandhi Krishi Vishwavidyalaya
Krishak Nagar, Raipur, Madhya Pradesh 492006
Tel: +91(771) 244-2537
Fax: +91(771) 244-2131
EMail: matappandey@yahoo.in
Website: http://igau.edu.in

Vice-Chancellor: M.P. Pandey

Registrar: S.R. Ratre

Faculties
Agriculture Engineering (Agricultural Engineering); **Agriculture** (Agriculture); **Dairy Technology** (Dairy); **Veterinary Science and Animal Husbandry** (Animal Husbandry; Veterinary Science)

Further Information: Also 9 constituent colleges

History: Founded 1987.

Degrees and Diplomas: *Bachelor's Degree*: 4 yrs; *Master's Degree*: a further 2-3 yrs; *Doctorate (PhD)*. Also Undergraduate and Postgraduate Diplomas

Libraries: Nehru Library, 21,988 vols; 135 periodicals
Last Updated: 18/11/11

INDIRA GANDHI INSTITUTE OF DEVELOPMENT RESEARCH (IGIDR)

Gen. A.K.Vaidya Marg, Goregaon (E), Mumbai,
Maharashtra 400065
Tel: +91(22) 2840-0919 +91(22) 2840-0920
Fax: +91(22) 2840-2752
EMail: director@igidr.ac.in
Website: http://www.igidr.ac.in

Director: S. Mahendra Dev
Tel: +91(22) 2841-6501 EMail: profmahendra@igidr.ac.in

Registrar and Chief Administrative Officer: Pandit Jai Mohan

Programmes
Development Studies (Development Studies; Economics)

History: Founded 1987 by the Reserve Bank of India. Granted 'Deemed University' status . A postgraduate Institution.

Governing Bodies: Board of Management

Academic Year: August to July (August-December; January to July)

Admission Requirements: For admission to BA, BSc in Economics, B.Com, B.Stat, BSc (Mathematics or Physics), B.tech, BE, M.Sc. in Economics, MScBTech/BE, MSc. in Economics, MBA/M.Tech/ME/B.Tech/BE, MPhil/PhD, 55% to 60%

Fees: (Rupees): 8,000 per semester

Main Language(s) of Instruction: English

Accrediting Agencies: National Assessment and Accreditation Council

Degrees and Diplomas: *Master's Degree*: Economics (MSc), 2 yrs; *Master of Philosophy*: Development Studies, 2 yrs; *Doctorate*: Development Studies (PhD), 4 yrs

Student Services: Academic counselling, Canteen, Cultural centre, Health services, Nursery care, Sports facilities

Student Residential Facilities: Yes

Libraries: 65,000 vols

Publications: India Development Report (IDR), Indian Economic Issues *(biennially)*

Press or Publishing House: Oxford University Press, New Dehli
Last Updated: 18/11/11

INDIRA GANDHI NATIONAL OPEN UNIVERSITY

Indira Gandhi Rashtriya Mukta Vishwavidyalaya (IGNOU)
Maidan Garhi, New Delhi 110068
Tel: +91(11) 2953-5924-32
Fax: +91(11) 2953-2312
Website: http://www.ignou.ac.in

Vice-Chancellor (Acting): M. Aslam
Tel: +91(11) 2953-2484 EMail: vc@ignou.ac.in

Registrar: Udai Singh Tolia EMail: ustolia@ignou.ac.in

Schools
Agriculture (Agriculture); **Computer and Information Sciences** (Computer Engineering; Information Sciences); **Continuing Education** (Child Care and Development; Food Science; Rural Planning; Women's Studies); **Education** (Education); **Engineering and Technology** (Civil Engineering; Electrical Engineering; Mechanical Engineering; Technology); **Extension and Development Studies** (Development Studies); **Foreign Languages** (Foreign Languages Education); **Gender and Development Studies** (Development Studies; Gender Studies); **Health Sciences** (Health Sciences; Medical Auxiliaries; Nursing; Paramedical Sciences); **Humanities** (Arts and Humanities; English; Hindi; Indic Languages; Writing); **Inter-Disciplinary and Trans-Disciplinary Studies** (Astrophysics; Folklore); **Journalism and New Media Studies** (Journalism; Media Studies); **Law** (Law); **Management Studies** (Management); **Performing and Visual Arts** (Performing Arts; Visual Arts); **Science** (Biological and Life Sciences; Physics); **Social Sciences** (Economics; History; Library Science; Political Sciences; Public Administration; Social Sciences; Sociology; Tourism); **Social Work** (Social Work); **Tourism and Hospitality** (Tourism); **Translation Studies and Training** (Translation and Interpretation); **Vocational Education and Training** (Vocational Education)

Further Information: Also 30 Regional Centres and 17 Special Regional Centres for the Armed Forces

History: Founded 1985.

Governing Bodies: Board of Management; Planning Board; Academic Council; School Boards

Academic Year: January to December

Admission Requirements: 12th year senior secondary/intermediate examination or recognized foreign equivalent

Main Language(s) of Instruction: English, Hindi

Degrees and Diplomas: *Diploma*: Human Rights; Disaster Management; Environmental Studies; Women's Empowerment and Consumer Protection; Participatory Planning; Forest Management; Resettlement and Rehabilitation; Journalism and Mass Communication; Rural Development; Tourism; Management; Health Education; Business Organization; Child Development; Distance Education; Computer Science; Information Technology; Civil Engineering; Food and Nutrition; Creative Writing, 1-4 yrs; *Bachelor's Degree*: Information Technology; Tourism; Mathematics; Zoology; Botany; Chemistry; Physics; History; Economics; Public Administration; Political Science; Sociology; English; Hindi; Computer Science; Library and Information Science; Education; Nursing; Engineering and Technology; Commerce, 3-8 yrs; *Postgraduate Diploma*: Human Rights; Disaster Management; Environmental Studies; Women's Empowerment and Consumer Protection; Participatory Planning; Forest Management; Resettlement and Rehabilitation; Journalism and Mass Communication; Rural Development; Tourism; Management; Health Education; Business Organization; Child Development; Distance Education; Computer Science; Information Technology; Civil Engineering; Food and Nutrition; Creative Writing, 1-4 yrs; *Master's Degree*: English; Hindi; Business Administration; Banking and Finance; Computer Science; Public Administration; Distance Education; Library Science, 2-6 yrs; *Master's Degree*: Library Science, 1-4 yrs; *Doctorate*: History; Tourism; Economics; Sociology; Political Science; Public Administration; Library Science; Education (PhD), 1-4 yrs. Also 2-year Certificate programmes

Student Services: Academic counselling, Canteen, Cultural centre, Employment services, Foreign student adviser, Handicapped facilities, Health services, Nursery care, Social counselling, Sports facilities

Student Residential Facilities: Yes

Libraries: Central Library, 80,721 vols; Regional and Study Centres Libraries, 225,455 vols

Publications: Indian Journal of Open Learning *(3 per annum)*
Last Updated: 18/11/11

INDIRA GANDHI NATIONAL TRIBAL UNIVERSITY, AMARKANTAK (IGNTU)

Kapil Dhara Road, Mekal Sadan, Dist-Anuppur, Amarkantak, Madhya Pradesh 484 886
Tel: +90 7629-269640
Fax: +90 7629-269432
EMail: igntribaluniv@gmail.com
Website: http://igntu.nic.in/theuniversity.htm

Vice-Chancellor: C.D. Singh
Tel: +90 7629-269544 EMail: vcigntu@gmail.com

Registrar: Ashok Singh
Tel: +90 7629-269617, Fax: +90 7629-269432
EMail: registrarigntua@gmail.com

Faculties
Commerce and Management (Business and Commerce; Forest Management; Hotel Management; Management; Tourism); **Computronics** (Computer Science; Information Technology); **Education** (Education; Physical Education); **Humanities and Philology** (Arts and Humanities; English; Hindi; Modern Languages; Philology; Philosophy; Psychology); **Journalism and Mass Communication** (Journalism; Mass Communication); **Law** (Law); **Pharmacy** (Pharmacy); **Science** (Biotechnology; Botany; Chemistry; Environmental Studies; Geology; Home Economics; Mathematics; Meteorology; Mineralogy; Nutrition; Physics; Statistics; Zoology); **Social Science** (Anthropology; Archaeology; Cultural Studies; Economics; Geography; History; Human Rights; Political Sciences; Rural Studies; Social Sciences; Social Work; Sociology); **Tribal Studies** (Folklore;

History; Linguistics; Literature; Museum Studies; Traditional Eastern Medicine)

History: Founded 2007. A 'Central University'.

Fees: (Indian Rupee): 1,000-3,000 per term

Degrees and Diplomas: *Bachelor's Degree*; *Master's Degree*; *Master of Philosophy*

Last Updated: 06/12/11

INDRAPRASTHA INSTITUTE OF INFORMATION TECHNOLOGY

3rd Floor, Library Building, NSIT Campus, Sector 3, Dwarka, New Delhi 110073
Tel: +91(11) 2509-9177
Fax: +91(11) 2509-9176
EMail: registrar@iiitd.ac.in
Website: http://www.iiitd.ac.in

Director: Pankaj Jalote

Programmes

Computer Science (Computer Engineering; Computer Science; Information Technology)

History: Founded 2008.

Degrees and Diplomas: *Bachelor's Degree*; *Master's Degree*; *Doctorate*

Last Updated: 05/01/12

INDUS INTERNATIONAL UNIVERSITY

VPO Bathu, Tehsil Haroli, District UNA, Himachal Pradesh
Tel: +91(93) 1879-7101
EMail: info@iiuedu.in
Website: http://www.iiuedu.in

Chancellor: Sudhir Kartha

Vice-Chancellor: Tapti Roy

Schools

Arts, Media and Education (Advertising and Publicity; Arts and Humanities; Education; English; Journalism; Media Studies); **Business and Management** (Business Administration; Management); **Science, Engineering and Technology** (Biotechnology; Civil Engineering; Computer Science; Electrical Engineering; Engineering; Mathematics; Mechanical Engineering; Physics; Technology; Telecommunications Engineering)

Degrees and Diplomas: *Bachelor's Degree*; *Master's Degree*; *Master of Philosophy*

Last Updated: 16/11/11

INSTITUTE OF ADVANCED STUDIES IN EDUCATION

Ghandi Vidya Mandir, Sardarshahr, Rajasthan 331401
Tel: +91(1564) 220-025 +91(1564) 220-056
Fax: +91(1564) 223-682
EMail: info@iaseuniversity.org.in
Website: http://www.iaseuniversity.org.in/

Vice-Chancellor: Milap Dugar EMail: vc@iaseuniversity.org.in

Registrar: R.S. Tripathi

Departments

Education (Accountancy; Business Administration; Civics; Computer Education; Economics; Education; Educational Administration; Educational Psychology; Educational Technology; English; Environmental Studies; Geography; Hindi; History; Library Science; Natural Sciences; Painting and Drawing; Physical Education; Preschool Education; Public Administration; Sanskrit; Social Sciences; Social Studies; Yoga)

Faculties

Engineering (Biotechnology; Computer Science; Electrical Engineering; Engineering; Mechanical Engineering; Telecommunications Engineering); **Management** (Banking; Business Administration; Computer Education; Computer Networks; Computer Science; E-Business/Commerce; Education; Electronic Engineering; Finance; Health Administration; Human Resources; Information Technology; Insurance; International Business;

Laboratory Techniques; Management; Marketing; Midwifery; Multimedia; Nursing; Physical Therapy; Public Relations; Radiology; Telecommunications Engineering; Vocational Counselling)

Programmes

Para-medical Allied Health Science (Health Administration; Laboratory Techniques; Medicine; Nursing; Occupational Therapy; Physical Therapy)

Further Information: Also constituent College including Institute of Advanced Studies in Education (Sardarshahr), Distance Education Academic Centre, Distance Education Study Centres, Institute of Ayurved (Sardarshahr), Homeopathic College and Hospital and Nursing College

History: Founded 1953 as Basic Teachers Training College. Acquired present title 1993 and present status 2002.

Academic Year: July to June

Admission Requirements: 12th year senior secondary/intermediate examination or recognized foreign equivalent

Degrees and Diplomas: *Diploma*; *Bachelor's Degree*; *Postgraduate Diploma*; *Doctorate*

Libraries: c. 95,000 vols and periodical subscriptions

Last Updated: 18/11/11

INSTITUTE OF CHARTERED FINANCIAL ANALYSTS OF INDIA UNIVERSITY, DEHRADUN

Rajawala Road, Central Hope Town, Selaqui, Dehradun, Uttrakhand 248197
Tel: +91(135) 324-6450
EMail: registrar@iuuttarakhand.edu.in
Website: http://www.iudehradun.edu.in/

Vice Chancellor: G.P. Srivastava Tel: +91(135) 325-4612

Registrar: P.K . Dash Tel: +91(135) 300-3009

Faculties

Education (Education); **Law** (Law); **Science and Technology** (Biotechnology; Computer Science; Electrical Engineering; Electronic Engineering; Engineering; Mechanical Engineering; Technology; Telecommunications Engineering)

Programmes

Business Administration (Business Administration; Management)

Further Information: Tripura, Sikkim, Meghalaya, Mizoram, Nagaland, and Jharkhand

History: ICFAI University refers to the Universities sponsored by the Institute of Chartered Financial Analysts of India.

Governing Bodies: Board of Governors, Board of Management, Academic Council, Finance Committee

Admission Requirements: Students who pass with 50% and above in graduation or its equivalent and admission test

Accrediting Agencies: University Grants Commission (UGC)

Degrees and Diplomas: *Bachelor's Degree*; *Master's Degree*; *Doctorate*

Last Updated: 21/11/11

INSTITUTE OF CHARTERED FINANCIAL ANALYSTS OF INDIA UNIVERSITY, JHARKHAND

Between Road No.1 & 2, Ashok Nagar, Ranchi, Jharkhand 834002
Tel: +91(651) 2243-255
Fax: +91(651) 2245-178
EMail: registrar@iujharkhand.edu.in
Website: http://www.iujharkhand.edu.in

Vice-Chancellor: O.R.S. Rao Tel: +91(651) 2245-178

Faculties

Management Studies (Business Administration; Hotel Management; Tourism); **Science and Technology** (Computer Engineering; Computer Networks; Software Engineering)

History: Founded 2008.

Degrees and Diplomas: *Bachelor's Degree*; *Master's Degree*; *Doctorate*

Last Updated: 12/01/12

INSTITUTE OF CHARTERED FINANCIAL ANALYSTS OF INDIA UNIVERSITY, MEGHALAYA

4th Floor, Near Sundari Complex, Circular Road, West Garo Hils, Tura, Meghalya 794001
EMail: registrar@iumeghalaya.edu.in
Website: http://www.iumeghalaya.edu.in

Vice-Chancellor: Y.K. Bhushan Tel: +91(3651) 224683

Registrar: Biplab Halder Tel: +91(3651) 224683

Programmes
Computer Application (Computer Networks; Software Engineering); **Management** (Business Administration; Tourism)

Degrees and Diplomas: *Bachelor's Degree*; *Master's Degree*
Last Updated: 13/01/12

INSTITUTE OF CHARTERED FINANCIAL ANALYSTS OF INDIA UNIVERSITY, MIZORAM

Dawrkawn, Chaltlang, Aizawl, Mizoram 796012
Tel: +91(389) 2344-917
Fax: +91(389) 2306-568
Website: http://www.iumizoram.edu.in

Vice-Chancellor: J.P. Ramappa

Registrar: C. Lalkima

Programmes
Computer Application (Computer Networks; Construction Engineering; Software Engineering); **Management Studies** (Accountancy; Business Administration; Finance; Human Resources; Marketing; Tourism)

Degrees and Diplomas: *Bachelor's Degree*; *Master's Degree*
Last Updated: 13/01/12

INSTITUTE OF CHARTERED FINANCIAL ANALYSTS OF INDIA UNIVERSITY, NAGALAND

Nepali Basti, Behind Nepali Mandir, Dimapur, Nagaland 797112
Tel: +91(3862) 234816
Fax: +91(3862) 234815
EMail: registrar@iunagaland.edu.in
Website: http://www.iunagaland.edu.in

Vice-Chancellor: O.P. Gupta

Faculties
Management Studies (Business Administration; Management)
History: Founded 2006. Acquired present status 2008.

Degrees and Diplomas: *Bachelor's Degree*; *Master's Degree*
Last Updated: 13/01/12

INSTITUTE OF CHARTERED FINANCIAL ANALYSTS OF INDIA UNIVERSITY, SIKKIM

Nam Nang Commercial Complex, Nam Nang, Deorali, Gangtok, Sikkim 737101
Tel: +91(3592) 202065
Fax: +91(3592) 201466
EMail: registrar@iusikkim.edu.in
Website: http://www.iusikkim.edu.in

Vice-Chancellor: M. Raja Tel: +91(3592) 202065

Faculties
Law (Law); **Management Studies** (Management); **Science and Technology** (Natural Sciences; Technology)
History: Founded 2004.

Degrees and Diplomas: *Bachelor's Degree*; *Master's Degree*
Last Updated: 04/01/12

INSTITUTE OF CHARTERED FINANCIAL ANALYSTS OF INDIA UNIVERSITY, TRIPURA

Agartala, Kamalghat Sadar, West Tripura 799210
Tel: +91(381) 2865-752
Fax: +91(381) 2865-754
EMail: registrar@iutripura.edu.in
Website: http://www.iutripura.edu.in

Vice-Chancellor: R.K. Patnaik

Registrar: Snehalata Behura

Faculties
Education (Education); **Law** (Law); **Management Studies** (Business Administration; Management); **Science and Technology** (Civil Engineering; Computer Engineering; Computer Science; Electronic Engineering; Mechanical Engineering; Technology; Telecommunications Engineering)
History: Founded 2004.

Degrees and Diplomas: *Bachelor's Degree*; *Master's Degree*; *Doctorate*

Special Facilities: Wi-Fi, Auditorium, Seminar halls, Computer labs
Last Updated: 12/01/12

INSTITUTE OF CHEMICAL TECHNOLOGY

Nathalal Parekh Marg, Matunga, Mumbai 400019
Tel: +91(22) 3361-1111
Fax: +91(22) 3361-1020
EMail: admission@ictmumbai.edu.in
Website: http://www.ictmumbai.edu.in/

Vice-Chancellor: G. D. Yadav

Departments
Chemical Engineering (Chemical Engineering); **Chemistry** (Chemistry); **Dyestuff Technology** (Chemical Engineering); **Fibers and Textile Processing** (Textile Technology); **Food Engineering and Technology** (Food Science; Food Technology); **General Engineering** (Engineering); **Mathematics** (Mathematics); **Oils, Oleochemicals and Surfactants Technology** (Chemical Engineering); **Pharmaceutical Sciences and Technology** (Pharmacology; Pharmacy); **Physics** (Physics); **Polymer and Surface Engineering** (Polymer and Plastics Technology)

History: Founded 1933, as Department of Chemical Technology of the University of Mumbai. Converted in to an Institute, 1922. Acquired the status of deemed university 2009.

Degrees and Diplomas: *Bachelor's Degree*; *Master's Degree*; *Doctorate*
Last Updated: 11/01/12

INSTITUTE OF HEALTH MANAGEMENT RESEARCH JAIPUR (IIHMR)

Prabhu Dayal Marg, Sanganer Airport, Jaipur, Rajastan 302011
Tel: +91(141) 2791-431/32
Fax: +91(141) 3924-738
EMail: iihmr@iihmr.org
Website: http://www.jaipur.iihmr.org

Director: S. D. Gupta

Programmes
Health Management (Health Administration; Pharmacy; Public Health); **Rural Management** (Management; Rural Studies)

Further Information: Also campuses in Dehli and Bangalore

History: Founded 1984. Formerly known as Indian Institute of Health Management Research.
Accrediting Agencies: All India Council for Technical Education (AICTE)

Degrees and Diplomas: *Postgraduate Diploma*
Last Updated: 27/01/12

INSTITUTE OF INTEGRATED LEARNING IN MANAGEMENT (IILM)

Lodhi Institutional Area, Lodhi Road, New Delhi 110 003
Tel: +91(11) 4093-4300
EMail: pgp@iilm.edu
Website: http://www.iilm.edu/

Chairman Hemeritus: Kulwant Rai

Programmes

Management (Management)

Further Information: Also Gurgaon Campus

History: Founded 1993.

Governing Bodies: Board of Governors

Accrediting Agencies: All India Council for Technical Education (AICTE)

Degrees and Diplomas: *Postgraduate Diploma*
Last Updated: 09/01/12

INSTITUTE OF LIVER AND BILIARY SCIENCES

D-1, Vasant Kunj, New Delhi 110070
Tel: +91(11) 4630-0000
Website: http://www.ilbs.in/

Director: S.K. Sarin

Programmes

Medicine (Anaesthesiology; Biomedicine; Hepatology; Medicine; Pathology; Radiology; Surgery)

Degrees and Diplomas: *Postgraduate Diploma*; *Master's Degree*; *Doctorate*
Last Updated: 12/01/12

INSTITUTE OF MANAGEMENT TECHNOLOGY

Raj Nagar, Ghaziabad, Uttar Pradesh 201 001
Tel: +91(120) 3002-200
Fax: +91(120) 3002-300
EMail: info@imt.edu
Website: http://www.imt.edu

Director: Bibek Banerjee EMail: director@imt.edu

Academic Administration: Amarendra Sahoo

Programmes

Management (Finance; Human Resources; Information Technology; International Business; Management; Marketing)

Further Information: Also campuses in Nagpur (2004) in Dubai (2006), and in Hyderabad (2011)

Accrediting Agencies: All India Council for Technical Education (AICTE)

Degrees and Diplomas: *Postgraduate Diploma*; *Doctorate*
Last Updated: 02/02/12

INSTITUTE OF PROFESSIONAL EDUCATION AND RESEARCH (IPER)

Bhojpur Road, Misrod, Bhopal, Madhya Pradesh 462 026
Tel: +91(755) 302-4821 +91(755) 302-4800
Fax: +91(755) 302-4818
EMail: soni.mahesh@iper.ac.in
Website: http://www.iper.ac.in/

Director: A. S. Khalsa EMail: khalsa.amarjeet@iper.ac.in

Head, Administration: Abhishek Jain
EMail: jain.abhishek@iper.ac.in

Programmes

Business Administration *(Part-time)* (Business Administration); **Business Administration** (Business Administration); **Management** (Management)

History: Founded 1996.

Accrediting Agencies: All India Council for Technical Education (AICTE)

Degrees and Diplomas: *Postgraduate Diploma*. PGDM programme is equivalent to a University M.B.A. Degree
Last Updated: 25/01/12

INTEGRAL UNIVERSITY

P.O. Bas-ha Kursi Road, Lucknow, Uttar Pradesh 226026
Tel: +91 2890730
Fax: +91 2890809
EMail: info@integraluniversity.ac.in
Website: http://www.integraluniversity.ac.in

Vice-Chancellor: S.W. Akhtar EMail: vc@integraluniversity.ac.in

Registrar: Irfan Ali Khan

Faculties

Applied Sciences (Biotechnology; Chemistry; English; Environmental Studies; Mathematics; Physics); **Architecture and Fine Arts** (Architecture; Fine Arts); **Computer Apllication** (Computer Engineering; Computer Science); **Education** (Education); **Engineering** (Biophysics; Civil Engineering; Computer Engineering; Electrical and Electronic Engineering; Engineering; Information Sciences; Mechanical Engineering; Telecommunications Engineering); **Management** (Business Administration); **Medicine** (Medicine); **Pharmacy** (Pharmacy)

Programmes

Polythechnic (Engineering)

History: Founded 2004.

Degrees and Diplomas: *Diploma*; *Bachelor's Degree*; *Master's Degree*; *Doctorate*
Last Updated: 28/12/11

INTERNATIONAL INSTITUTE FOR POPULATION SCIENCES

Govandi Station Road, Deonar, Mumbai, Maharashtra 400088
Tel: +91(22) 2556-3254
Fax: +91(22) 2556-3257
EMail: director@iips.net
Website: http://www.iipsindia.org

Director: Faujdar Ram Tel: +91(22) 2556-3254

Registrar: M.K. Kulkarini
Tel: +91(22) 2556-3485 EMail: registrar@iips.net/

Departments

Development Studies (Anthropology; Development Studies); **Extra Mural Studies and Distance Education (Project Basis)** *(Project Basis)* (Demography and Population); **Fertility Studies** (Demography and Population) *Head*: Faujdar Ram; **Mathematical Demography and Statistics** (Demography and Population; Statistics); **Migration and Urban Studies** (Geography (Human); Urban Studies); **Population Policies and Programmes** (Demography and Population); **Public Health and Mortality Studies** (Public Health)

History: Founded 1956. Declared to be an Institution 'deemed to be a University' 1985. A Regional Institute for Training and Research in Population Studies for the countries of Asia and Pacific regions of the United Nations.

Governing Bodies: General Council; Executive Council; Standing Finance Committee; Academic Council

Academic Year: July to May

Admission Requirements: Bachelor Degree

Fees: (Rupees): MA Studies for Indian Students: 1,000 per annum; Foreign students: 3,000 (US Dollars)

Main Language(s) of Instruction: English

Accrediting Agencies: Government of India; UN Population Fund; Sir Dorabji Tata Trust; University Grants Commission

Degrees and Diplomas: *Diploma*; *Master's Degree*: 1 yr; *Master of Philosophy*: at least 1 1/2 yrs; *Doctorate (PhD)*: at least 3 yrs. Also Diploma course in Population Studies for UN students under UNFPA fellowship programme

Student Services: Canteen, Sports facilities

Student Residential Facilities: Yes

Special Facilities: Data Centre

Libraries: c. 688,262 vols

Publications: IIPS Newsletter *(quarterly)*
Last Updated: 21/11/11

INTERNATIONAL INSTITUTE OF INFORMATION TECHNOLOGY (IIIT-H)

Gachibowli, Hyderabad, Andhra Pradesh 500032
Tel: +91(40) 6653-1000
Fax: +91(40) 6653-1413
EMail: query@iiit.ac.in
Website: http://www.iiit.ac.in

Director: Rajeev Sangal EMail: sangal@iiit.net

Registrar: R. Govindarajulu EMail: gregeti@iiit.ac.in

Programmes

Engineering (Building Technologies; Cognitive Sciences; Computer Engineering; Construction Engineering; Electrical Engineering; Information Technology; Software Engineering; Telecommunications Engineering)

History: Founded 1998 as Indian Institute of Technology. Acquired present status and title 2001.

Degrees and Diplomas: *Diploma*; *Bachelor's Degree*; *Postgraduate Diploma*; *Master's Degree*; *Doctorate*
Last Updated: 22/11/11

INTERNATIONAL INSTITUTE OF INFORMATION TECHNOLOGY, BANGALORE (IIIT-B)

26/C, Electronics City, Hosur Road, Bangalore, Karnakata 560100
Tel: +91(80) 4140-7777
Fax: +91(80) 4140-7704
EMail: info@iiitb.ac.in
Website: http://www.iiitb.ac.in/

Director: S. Sadagopan
Registrar: A.N. Ramachandra

Programmes

Information Technology (Computer Networks; Computer Science; Information Technology; Software Engineering)
History: Founded 1999.
Degrees and Diplomas: *Master's Degree*; *Doctorate*
Last Updated: 09/01/12

INTERNATIONAL MANAGEMENT INSTITUTE (IMI)

B-10, Qutab Institutional Area, Tara Crescent, New Delhi 110 016
Tel: +91(11) 719-4100 +91(11) 719-4200
Fax: +91(11) 2686-7539
EMail: imiinfo@imi.edu
Website: http://www.imi.edu/

Director General: Pritam Singh

Programmes

Human Resources *(Postgraduate)* (Human Resources); **Management** *(Doctoral Studies)* (Management); **Management** *(Fellow Programme)* (Management); **Management** *(Postgraduate)* (Management); **Management** *(Executive Post Graduate)* (Management)

Further Information: Also Bhubaneswar and Kolkata campuses
History: Founded 1981.
Governing Bodies: Board of Governors; Academic Advisory Council
Accrediting Agencies: All India Council for Technical Education (AICTE); Ministry of Human Resource Development, Govt. of India
Degrees and Diplomas: *Postgraduate Diploma*; *Doctorate*. PGDM equivalence to a M.B.A.; Also Executive Post Graduate Diploma, 15 months
Student Residential Facilities: Hostel
Special Facilities: Auditorium; Computer Centre
Libraries: c. 19,500 vols; c. 200 perioddical subscriptions
Last Updated: 09/01/12

INVERTIS UNIVERSITY

Invertis village, Bareilly, Lucknow National Highway - 24, Bareilly, Uttar Pradesh 243123
Tel: +91(581) 2460-442
Fax: +91(581) 2460-454
EMail: admissions@invertis.org
Website: http://www.invertisuniversity.ac.in

Vice-Chancellor: Shripad Ganap Bhat
Registrar: Narendra Singh

Institutes

Architecture (Architecture); **Biotechnology** (Biotechnology); **Computer Application** (Computer Science); **Engineering and Technology** (Engineering; Technology); **Journalism and Mass Communication** (Journalism; Mass Communication); **Law** (Law); **Management Studies** (Business Administration; Management); **Pharmacy** (Pharmacy)
History: Founded 2010.
Last Updated: 04/01/12

ITM UNIVERSITY

HUDA Sector 23-A, Gurgaon, Gujarat 122017
Tel: + 91(124) 236-5811
Fax: +91(124) 236-7488
EMail: itm1@vsnl.com; itm@itmindia.edu
Website: http://www.itmindia.edu

Vice-Chancellor: N. K. Dewan
Registrar: S.K. Sharma

Schools

Engineering and Technology (Civil Engineering; Computer Engineering; Computer Science; Electrical and Electronic Engineering; Engineering; Information Technology; Mechanical Engineering; Technology; Telecommunications Engineering); **Law** (Law); **Management** (Business and Commerce; Management)
History: Founded 1996. Acquired present status 2009.
Degrees and Diplomas: *Bachelor's Degree*; *Master's Degree*; *Doctorate*
Last Updated: 19/10/11

ITM UNIVERSITY

Opp. Sithouli Railway Station, NH-75, Jhansi Road, Gwalior, Madhya Padesh 474001
Tel: +91(751) 243-2977
Fax: +91(751) 243-2988
Website: http://www.itmuniversity.ac.in

Vice-Chancellor: R. K. Pandey

Schools

Computer Applications (Computer Science; Construction Engineering); **Engineering and Technology** (Engineering; Technology); **Languages and Literary Studies** (Literature; Modern Languages); **Management and Commerce** (Business and Commerce; Management); **Nursing Sciences** (Nursing); **Sciences** (Natural Sciences); **Teachers Training (Education)** (Teacher Trainers Education); **Technology Management** (Management)
History: Founded 2011.
Degrees and Diplomas: *Diploma*; *Bachelor's Degree*; *Master's Degree*; *Doctorate*
Last Updated: 03/01/12

JADAVPUR UNIVERSITY (JU)

188 Raja S.C. Mallik Road, Kolkata, West Bengal 700032
Tel: +91(33) 2414-6414
Fax: +91(33) 2413-7121
EMail: registrar@admin.jdvu.ac.in
Website: http://www.jaduniv.edu.in/

Vice-Chancellor: Pradip Narayan Ghosh
Tel: +91(33) 2414-6000 EMail: vc@admin.jdvu.ac.in
Registrar: Pradip Kumar Ghosh EMail: pradip_12@vsnl.net

Faculties

Arts (Comparative Literature; Economics; English; Film; History; Indic Languages; Information Sciences; International Relations; Library Science; Philosophy; Physical Education; Sanskrit; Sociology); **Engineering and Technology** (Adult Education; Architecture; Biomedical Engineering; Chemical Engineering; Civil Engineering; Computer Science; Construction Engineering; Electrical Engineering; Electronic Engineering; Engineering; Food Technology; Information Technology; Instrument Making; Materials Engineering; Mechanical Engineering; Metallurgical Engineering; Pharmacy; Power Engineering; Printing and Printmaking; Production Engineering; Telecommunications Engineering); **Science** (Biological and Life Sciences; Chemistry; Geology; Instrument Making; Mathematics; Physics)

Further Information: Also a campus in Salt Lake City (Kolkata) and 2 Affiliated Institutes: Institute of Business Management and J. D. Birla Institute

History: Founded 1955.

Governing Bodies: Academic Council; Court

Academic Year: July to July

Admission Requirements: 12th year senior secondary/intermediate examination or recognized foreign equivalent

Main Language(s) of Instruction: English; Bengali

International Co-operation: With universities in United Kingdom, Germany, Italy and Brazil.

Accrediting Agencies: NAAC

Degrees and Diplomas: *Bachelor's Degree*: Bengali; Comparative Literature; Economics; English; Political Science; International Relations; Library and Information Sciences; Philosophy; Physical Education; Sanskrit; Women's Studies; Sociology; Structural Architecture; Chemical Engineering; Civil Engineering; Computer Science; Construction Engineering; Electrical Engineering; Information Technology; Instrument Making; Mechanical Engineering; Metallurgical Engineering; Power Engineering; Printing; Pharmacy; Chemistry; Geology; Production Engineering; Mathematics; Physics; Environmental Engineering, 3 yrs; *Master's Degree*: Bengali; Comparative Literature; Economics; English; Political Science; International Relations; Library and Information Sciences; Philosophy; Physical Education; Sanskrit; Women's Studies; Sociology; Structural Architecture; Chemical Engineering; Civil Engineering; Computer Science; Construction Engineering; Electrical Engineering; Information Technology; Instrument Making; Mechanical Engineering; Metallurgical Engineering; Power Engineering; Printing; Pharmacy; Chemistry; Geology; Production Engineering; Mathematics; Physics; Environmental Engineering, a further 2 yrs; *Doctorate*: Bengali; Comparative Literature; Economics; English; Political Science; International Relations; Library and Information Sciences; Philosophy; Physical Education; Sanskrit; Women's Studies; Sociology; Structural Architecture; Chemical Engineering (PhD); Civil Engineering; Computer Science; Construction Engineering; Electrical Engineering; Information Technology; Instrument Making; Mechanical Engineering; Metallurgical Engineering; Power Engineering; Printing; Pharmacy; Chemistry; Geology; Production Engineering; Mathematics; Physics; Environmental Engineering, a further 2-3 yrs. Also Diploma and Certificate courses

Student Services: Academic counselling, Canteen, Cultural centre, Employment services, Foreign student adviser, Foreign Studies Centre, Handicapped facilities, Health services, Language programs, Social counselling, Sports facilities

Student Residential Facilities: Yes.

Special Facilities: Photography, Music, Drama and Science Clubs.

Libraries: 499,799 vols; c. 800 periodical subscriptions

Press or Publishing House: University Press

Last Updated: 22/11/11

JAGADGURU RAMANANDACHARYA RAJASTHAN SANSKRIT UNIVERSITY

Village-Madau, Post-Bhonkrota, Jaipur, Rajasthan 302026
Tel: +91(141) 513-2021
EMail: jrrsu@yahoo.com
Website: http://www.jrrsanskrituniversity.ac.in

Vice-Chancellor: R. Devnathan Tel: +91(141) 513-2001

Registrar: Parmeshwari Choudhary Tel: +91(941) 401-2366

Programmes

Business Administration, Arts and Humanities (English; Hindi; History; Political Sciences; Public Administration; Sanskrit); **Education, Social Sciences and Home Economics** (Economics; Education; Educational Administration; Home Economics; Physical Education; Political Sciences; Sociology)

History: Founded 2001.

Academic Year: July to April

Main Language(s) of Instruction: Sanskrit

Degrees and Diplomas: *Bachelor's Degree*; *Master's Degree*

Student Services: Academic counselling, Canteen, Health services, Sports facilities

Student Residential Facilities: Yes

Libraries: Yes

Publications: Pravarti *(quarterly)*

Press or Publishing House: University Publishing House

Academic Staff *2009-2010*	MEN	WOMEN	TOTAL
FULL-TIME	20	1	21
PART-TIME	6	2	8
STAFF WITH DOCTORATE			
FULL-TIME	19	1	20
PART-TIME	–	–	1
Student Numbers *2009-2010*			
All (Foreign Included)	4,545	13,119	**17,664**

Last Updated: 26/05/10

JAGADGURU RAMBHADRACHARYA HANDICAPPED UNIVERSITY

Chitrakoot, Karwi, Uttar Pradesh 210204
Tel: +91(5198) 224481
Fax: +91(5198) 224293
EMail: jrhuniversity@yahoo.com
Website: http://www.jrhu.com/

Registrar: Kamlesh Kumar

Vice-Chancellor: B. Pandey

Faculties

Commerce and Management (Business and Commerce; Management); **Computer and Information Sciences** (Computer Engineering; Information Sciences); **Education** (Education; Special Education); **Fine Arts** (Fine Arts; Painting and Drawing); **Humanities** (Economics; English; Hindi; Psychology; Sanskrit); **Music** (Music); **Prosthetics and Orthotics** (Orthodontics); **Social Sciences** (Archaeology; Cultural Studies; History; Social Sciences; Social Work; Sociology); **Vocational Studies** (Vocational Education)

History: Founded 2001.

Student Services: Sports facilities

Student Residential Facilities: Yes

Special Facilities: Computer Lab

Libraries: Yes
Last Updated: 02/01/12

JAGADGURU SRI SHIVARATHREESHWARA UNIVERSITY

JSS Medical Institutions Campus, Sri Shivarathreeshwara Nagara, Mysore, Karnataka 570 015
Tel: +91(821) 2548400
Fax: +91(821) 2548394
EMail: vc@jssuni.edu.in
Website: http://www.jssuni.edu.in/

Vice-Chancellor: B. Suresh

Registrar: Mruthyunjaya P. Kulenur EMail: registrar@jssuni.edu.in

Departments

Anatomy (Anatomy); **Dentistry** (Dentistry); **Medicine** (Medicine); **Orthopaedics** (Orthopaedics); **Pharmacology** (Pharmacology); **Surgery** (Surgery)

Degrees and Diplomas: *Bachelor's Degree*; *Master's Degree*; *Doctorate*
Last Updated: 10/01/12

JAGAN INSTITUTE OF MANAGEMENT STUDIES (JIMS)

3, Institutional Area, Sector - 5, Rohini, Delhi 110 085
Tel: +91(11) 4518-4000
Fax: +91(11) 4518-4032
Website: http://www.jimsindia.org/

Director General: R. P. Maheshwari

Programmes

Information Technology (Information Technology); **Management** (International Business; Management; Marketing)

History: Founded 1993.

Fees: (Indian Rupee): 415,000-520,000

Accrediting Agencies: All India Council for Technical Education (AICTE); Ministry of HRD, Government of India; National Board of Accreditation (NBA)

Degrees and Diplomas: *Bachelor's Degree*; *Postgraduate Diploma*; *Master's Degree.* The Bachelor's degree and Master's degree are affiliated to the Guru Gobind Singh Indraprastha University.

Last Updated: 09/01/12

JAGAN NATH UNIVERSITY

Village Rampura, Teshil-Chaksu, Jaipur, Rajasthan 303901
Tel: +91(141) 302-0500
Fax: +91(141) 302-0538
EMail: admission@jagannathuniversity.org
Website: http://www.jagannathuniversity.org/

Vice-Chancellor: M.K. Bhargava

Faculties
Engineering and Technology (Engineering; Technology); **Information Technology** (Information Technology); **Law** (Law); **Management** (Management); **Mass Communication** (Mass Communication)

Programmes
Architecture; Commerce

History: Founded 2008,

Fees: (Rupiah): 22,500-75,000 depending on programmes

Degrees and Diplomas: *Bachelor's Degree*; *Master's Degree*; *Doctorate*

Last Updated: 16/12/11

JAGDISHPRASAD JHABARMAL TIBREWALA UNIVERSITY (JJTU)

Churu - Bishau Road Chudella, Jhunjhunu, Rajasthan 333 001
Tel: +91(1595) 513-007 +91(1595) 513-006
Website: http://jjtu.ac.in/

Head: Vinod Tibrewala

Departments
Administration (Administration); **Chemistry** (Chemistry); **Computer Science Engineering** (Computer Engineering; Computer Science); **Electronic Engineering** (Electronic Engineering); **Management** (Management); **Mathematics** (Mathematics); **Mechanical Engineering** (Mechanical Engineering); **Mechanical Engineering** (Mechanical Engineering)

History: Founded 2008.

Fees: (Indian Rupee): Undergraduate programmes, 5,000-30,000 per annum; Graduate programmes 15,000-60,000 per annum.

Degrees and Diplomas: *Diploma*; *Bachelor's Degree*; *Bachelor's degree (professional)*; *Postgraduate Diploma*; *Master's Degree*; *Doctorate.* Also Certificate; M.B.A.

Student Services: Canteen, Sports facilities

Student Residential Facilities: Boys and Girls Hostels (150 beds)

Special Facilities: Theatre

Libraries: Digitalized library, c. 20,000 vols.

Last Updated: 21/12/11

JAI NARAIN VYAS UNIVERSITY

Bhagat ki Kothi, Pali Road, Jodhpur, Rajasthan 342011
Tel: +91(291) 264-9733
Fax: +91(291) 264-9465
EMail: info@jnvu.edu.in
Website: http://www.jnvu.edu.in/

Vice-Chancellor: B.S. Rajpurohit
Tel: +91(291) 243-2947 EMail: vcjnvu@gmail.com
Registrar: Nirmala Meena Tel: +91(291) 264-9733

Faculties
Arts (Arts and Humanities; Economics; Education; English; Geography; Hindi; History; Home Economics; Indic Languages; Music; Painting and Drawing; Philosophy; Physical Education; Political Sciences; Psychology; Public Administration; Sanskrit; Social Sciences; Sociology); **Commerce and Management Studies** (Accountancy; Business Administration; Business and Commerce; Economics; Finance; Management); **Engineering** (Architecture; Civil Engineering; Computer Science; Construction Engineering; Electrical Engineering; Electronic Engineering; Engineering; Industrial Engineering; Mechanical Engineering; Mining Engineering; Production Engineering; Telecommunications Engineering; Town Planning); **Law** (Law); **Science** (Botany; Chemistry; Geology; Mathematics; Natural Sciences; Physics; Zoology)

Further Information: Colleges situated within the municipal limits of Jodhpur are affiliated to the University

History: Founded 1962.

Governing Bodies: Senate; Syndicate; Academic Council

Academic Year: July to April (July-September; October-December; January-April)

Admission Requirements: 12th year senior secondary/intermediate examination or recognized foreign equivalent

Main Language(s) of Instruction: English, Hindi

Degrees and Diplomas: *Diploma*; *Bachelor's Degree*: 3-5 yrs; *Master's Degree*: a further 1-2 yrs; *Master of Philosophy*; *Doctorate (PhD)*: a further 2 yrs

Student Residential Facilities: Yes

Libraries: Central Library, c. 275,975 vols

Press or Publishing House: University Press
Last Updated: 22/11/11

JAI PRAKASH UNIVERSITY
Jai Prakash Vishwavidyalaya
Rahul Sankrityan Nagar, Near Parwati Ashram (Chota Telpa), Chapra, Bihar 841301
Tel: +91(6152) 233-121
Fax: +91(6152) 232-607
Website: http://jpv.bih.nic.in/

Vice-Chancellor: Ram Vinod Sinha Tel: +91(6152) 243-898
Registrar: Bijay Pratap Kumar Tel: +91(6152) 233-507

Faculties
Commerce (Business and Commerce; Economics) *Dean*: R.P. Singh; **Engineering** (Engineering) *Dean*: Z. Ahmad; **Humanities** (Arts and Humanities; English; Hindi; Philosophy; Sanskrit; Social Sciences); **Science** (Chemistry; Mathematics; Physics; Zoology); **Social Sciences** (Economics; Geography; History; Political Sciences; Psychology; Social Sciences)

Further Information: Also 21 constituent Colleges, 2 affiliated deficit grant colleges (including one Minority College), and 12 affiliated Colleges.

History: Founded 1990 through separation with Bihar University Muzaffarpur. A state Institution.

Governing Bodies: Senate; Syndicate; Academic Council; Board of Examinations

Academic Year: July to June

Admission Requirements: Senior school certificate (10 + 2)

Main Language(s) of Instruction: English; Hindi

International Co-operation: With universities in Nepal and Bhutan

Degrees and Diplomas: *Bachelor's Degree*: Commerce; Science; Law; Humanities (B.Com.; B.Sc.; L.L.B.; B.A.), 3 yrs; *Bachelor's Degree*: Technology (BTech), 4 yrs; *Master's Degree*: Humanities and Social Sciences; Science; Commerce (M.A.; M.Sc.; M.Com.), a further 2 yrs; *Doctorate (PhD)*: a further 3 yrs

Student Services: Language programs

Student Residential Facilities: For boys and girls

Libraries: c. 60,000 vols

Publications: Annual Report, Annual activities of the university *(annually)*
Last Updated: 22/11/11

JAIN UNIVERSITY

91/2, Dr A N Krishna Rao Road, V V Puram, Bangalore 560004
Tel: +91(80) 4343-1000
Fax: +91(80) 4343-1010
EMail: admissions@jainuniversity.ac.in
Website: http://www.jainuniversity.ac.in

Vice-Chancellor: N. Sundararajan

Registrar: N.V.H. Krishnan

Centres
Ancient Indian History and Culture (Ancient Civilizations; Ayurveda; Cultural Studies; History); **Disaster Mitigation** (Earth Sciences; Fire Science); **Emerging Technologies** (Engineering); **Entrepreneurship** *(RCJ)* (Business Administration); **Management Studies** (Business Administration; Management); **Post Graduate Studies** (Biochemistry; Biotechnology; Electronic Engineering; Microbiology; Physics); **Research in Pure and Applied Sciences** (Natural Sciences); **Research in Social Sciences and Education** (Education; Social Sciences)

Institutes
Aerospace Engineering and Management *(International)* (Aeronautical and Aerospace Engineering; Transport Management)

Schools
Engineering and Technology (Engineering; Technology); **Graduate Studies** *(J C Road)* (Arts and Humanities; Business and Commerce; Computer Engineering; Natural Sciences; Social Sciences)

History: Founded as Sri Bhagawan Mahaveer Jain College, (SBMJC). Acquired the status of deemed university 2008.

Degrees and Diplomas: *Bachelor's Degree*; *Master's Degree*; *Doctorate*
Last Updated: 11/01/12

JAIN VISHVA BHARATI UNIVERSITY (JVBU)

PO Box 6, District Nagaur, Ladnun, Rajasthan 34306
Tel: +91(1581) 222-110 +91(1581) 223-316
Fax: +91(1581) 223-472
EMail: registrar@jvbi.ac.in
Website: http://www.jvbi.ac.in

Vice-Chancellor: Samani Charitra Prajna
Tel: +91(1581) 222-116 EMail: vicechancellor@jvbi.ac.in

Registrar: J.P.N Mishra

Colleges
Acharya Kalu Kanya Mahavidyalay *(Girls only) Principal*: Rituprajna Samani; **Education** *(Girls Only)* (Education) *Head*: B.L. Jain; **English** (English) *Head*: S. Elamparithy; **Jainology, Comparative Religion and Philosophy** (Asian Religious Studies; Comparative Religion; Esoteric Practices; Ethics; Metaphysics) *Director*: Riju Prajna Samani; **Mahadevlal Saraogi Anekant Shodhpeeth** *Deputy-Director*: Anil Dhar; **Non-Violence and Peace and Relative Economics** (Asian Religious Studies; Economics; Ethics; Human Rights; International Relations; Peace and Disarmament; Philosophy) *Head*: Bacchraj Dugar; **Sanskrit and Prakrit** (Indic Languages; Linguistics; Literature; Sanskrit) *Head*: Jagat Ram Bhattacharyya; **Science of Living, Preshka Meditation and Yoga** (Alternative Medicine; Esoteric Practices; Physiology; Psychotherapy; Yoga) *Head*: B.P. Gaur; **Social Work** (Social Work) *Head*: Pratap Chandra Behera

Further Information: Also Directorate of Distance Education

History: Founded 1970 as Institute. Granted 'Deemed University' status by the University Grants Commission 1991.

Governing Bodies: Board of Management

Academic Year: July to June

Admission Requirements: University degree at Bachelor level (12th year senior secondary examination with 50% marks).

Fees: (Rupees): Undergraduate, 6,300; postgraduate, 2,987-25,775 per annum (depends on courses)

Main Language(s) of Instruction: Hindi, English

Accrediting Agencies: National Assessment and Accreditation Council (NAAC)

Degrees and Diplomas: *Bachelor's Degree*: 3 yrs; *Postgraduate Diploma*: 1 yr; *Master's Degree*: 2 yrs; *Doctorate (PhD)*: 2-5 yrs. Also Certificate Courses

Student Services: Academic counselling, Canteen, Language programs, Sports facilities

Student Residential Facilities: Yes, for staff and students (separate for boys and girls)

Libraries: 67,217 vols; 130 periodical subscriptions, 1,369 e-journals, 6,000 manuscripts

Publications: Samvahini, Newsletter *(quarterly)*; Tulsi Prajna, Research Journal *(quarterly)*
Last Updated: 22/11/11

JAIPUR NATIONAL UNIVERSITY

Jaipur-Agra Bypass, Near New RTO office, Jagatpura, Jaipur 302025
Tel: +91(141) 275-3377
Fax: +91(141) 275-2418
EMail: info@jnujaipur.ac.in
Website: http://www.jnujaipur.ac.in

Vice-Chancellor: K.L. Sharma

Institutes
Media Studies *(Seedling (SIMS))* (Media Studies); **Social Sciences** (Social Sciences)

Schools
Business and Management (Business Administration; Management); **Computer And Systems Sciences** (Computer Science); **Distance Education and Learning** (Distance Education); **Education** (Education); **Engineering and Technology** (Engineering; Technology); **Hotel Management and Catering Technology** (Cooking and Catering; Hotel Management); **Languages, Literature And Society** (Literature; Modern Languages; Social Studies); **Law and Governance** *(Seedling)* (Government; Law); **Life and Basic Sciences** (Biological and Life Sciences; Natural Sciences); **Nursing** (Nursing); **Pharmaceutical Sciences** (Pharmacy)

History: Founded 2007.

Degrees and Diplomas: *Bachelor's Degree*; *Master's Degree*
Last Updated: 26/12/11

JAMIA MILLIA ISLAMIA UNIVERSITY

Jamia Millia Islamia
Maulana Mohammed Ali Jauhar Marg, Jamia Nagar, New Delhi 110025
Tel: +91(11) 2698-1717
Fax: +91(11) 2698-1232
EMail: registrr@jmi.ernet.in
Website: http://jmi.ac.in/

Vice-Chancellor: Najeeb Jung
Tel: +91(11) 2698-4650, Fax: +91(11) 2698-1232

Registrar: S. M. Sajid
Tel: +91(11) 2698-0337, Fax: +91(11) 2698-0229
EMail: ssajid@jmi.ac.in

Faculties
Architecture and Ekistics (Architecture); **Dentistry** (Dentistry); **Education** (Art Education; Computer Education; Education; Educational Sciences; Fine Arts); **Engineering and Technology** (Applied Chemistry; Applied Mathematics; Applied Physics; Architecture; Civil Engineering; Computer Engineering; Electrical Engineering; Electronic Engineering; Engineering; Environmental Engineering; Humanities and Social Science Education; Mechanical Engineering; Technology); **Humanities and Languages** (Arabic; Cultural Studies; English; Hindi; History; Islamic Studies; Modern Languages; Persian; Urdu); **Law** (Law); **Natural Sciences** (Biological and Life Sciences; Chemistry; Computer Science; Geography; Mathematics; Physics); **Social Sciences** (Adult Education; Business and Commerce; Economics; Education; Human Rights; Political Sciences; Psychology; Public Administration; Social Sciences; Social Work; Sociology)

Research Centres
Academy of Third World Studies; **Mass Communication**

History: Founded 1920, acquired present status 1988.

Governing Bodies: Planning Board; Academic Council; Executive Council; Finance Committee

Academic Year: July to May

Admission Requirements: 12th year senior secondary/intermediate examination or recognized foreign equivalent

Main Language(s) of Instruction: Urdu, Hindi, English

International Co-operation: With institutions in Malaysia; Germany and Kuwait

Accrediting Agencies: Universities Grants Commission

Degrees and Diplomas: *Bachelor's Degree*: 3 yrs; *Postgraduate Diploma*: 1 yr; *Master's Degree*: a further 2 yrs; *Doctorate (PhD)*: a further 3-5 yrs

Student Services: Academic counselling, Canteen, Employment services, Foreign student adviser, Health services, Language programs, Nursery care, Social counselling, Sports facilities

Student Residential Facilities: Yes

Special Facilities: Movie Studio. Museum

Libraries: Dr. Zakir Hussain Library, c. 260,000 vols; 667 periodical subscriptions

Publications: Islam and the Modern Age (English) *(quarterly)*; Islam Aur Asr-i-Jadeed (Urdu) *(quarterly)*; Jamia Monthly *(monthly)*

Last Updated: 22/11/11

JANARDAN RAI NAGAR RAJASTHAN VIDYAPEETH UNIVERSITY

93 Parshwanath Colony, Ajmer Road, Jaipur, Rajasthan 313001
Tel: +91(141) 281-1581
Fax: +91(141) 281-0467
Website: http://www.jnrvuniversity.com/

Vice-Chancellor: Divya Prabha Naga EMail: I

Registrar: Vijay Singh Panwar

Faculties

Arts and Commerce (Arts and Humanities; Business and Commerce; Economics; Education; English; History; Political Sciences; Social Work; Sociology); **Computer Science** (Computer Engineering; Computer Science; Information Technology; Software Engineering); **Management** (Business Administration; Finance; Fire Science; Human Resources; Management; Marketing); **Medical Science** (Medical Technology; Medicine; Optometry; Radiology); **Science** (Biology; Fashion Design; Interior Design; Jewelry Art; Mathematics; Physics)

Further Information: Distance Education

History: Founded 1937. Granted 'Deemed University' status 1987.

Admission Requirements: 12th year senior secondary/intermediate examination or recognized foreign equivalent

Main Language(s) of Instruction: English

Accrediting Agencies: Distance Education Council

Degrees and Diplomas: *Diploma*; *Bachelor's Degree*: 3 yrs; *Master's Degree*

Libraries: Libraries of 9 Constituent Colleges, c. 155,200 vols
Last Updated: 22/11/11

JAWAHARLAL NEHRU AGRICULTURAL UNIVERSITY

Jawaharlal Nehru Krishi Vishwavidyalaya
PO Adhartal, Krishinigar, Jabalpur, Madhya Pradesh 482004
Tel: +91(761) 234-3778
Fax: +91(761) 234-2719
EMail: registrarjnkvv@yahoo.com
Website: http://www.jnkvv.nic.in

Vice-Chancellor: Gautam Kalloo
Tel: +91(761) 268-1706, Fax: +91(761) 2681-389
EMail: gkalloo_jnkvv@yahoo.co.in

Registrar: B.B. Mishra

Colleges

Agricultural Engineering (Agricultural Engineering; Applied Physics; Engineering; Environmental Engineering; Farm Management;

Food Technology; Harvest Technology; Mathematics; Meteorology; Soil Conservation; Soil Management; Soil Science; Statistics; Water Science) *Dean:* Tarun Kumar Bhattacharya; **Agriculture** (Agricultural Economics; Agriculture; Agronomy; Animal Husbandry; Entomology; Food Science; Forestry; Genetics; Plant and Crop Protection; Plant Pathology; Soil Science; Veterinary Science) *Dean:* D.K. Mishra

Further Information: Campuses of Agricultural Studies at Rewa, Tikamgah, Ganjbasoda

History: Founded 1964.

Governing Bodies: Board of Management

Academic Year: July to June (July-November; December-June)

Admission Requirements: 12th year senior secondary/intermediate examination or recognized foreign equivalent

Main Language(s) of Instruction: English

Degrees and Diplomas: *Diploma*; *Bachelor's Degree*: 4-5 yrs; *Master's Degree*: a further 2 yrs; *Doctor of Science (PhD)*: at least 2 yrs

Student Services: Academic counselling, Canteen, Cultural centre, Health services, Sports facilities

Student Residential Facilities: For c. 820 students

Libraries: 52,356 vols

Publications: Krishni Vishwa *(quarterly)*
Last Updated: 23/11/11

JAWAHARLAL NEHRU ARCHITECTURE AND FINE ARTS UNIVERSITY

Masab Tank, Hyderabad, Andhra Pradesh 500028
Tel: +91(40) 2332-1226
EMail: registrar@jnafau.ac.in
Website: http://www.jnafau.ac.in/

Vice-Rector: P. Padmavathi

Registrar: Shaik Khaleel-ur-Rahman

Colleges

Fine Arts (Fine Arts); **Planning and Architecture** (Architectural and Environmental Design; Architecture and Planning; Building Technologies; Interior Design; Town Planning)

History: Founded 2008.

Degrees and Diplomas: *Bachelor's Degree*; *Master's Degree*; *Doctorate*

Libraries: Yes
Last Updated: 22/07/11

JAWAHARLAL NEHRU CENTRE FOR ADVANCED SCIENTIFIC RESEARCH (JNCASR)

Jakkur, Bangalore, Karnakata 560064
Tel: +91(80) 2208-2750
EMail: admin@jncasr.ac.in
Website: http://www.jncasr.ac.in

President: M.R.S. Rao

Dean, Academic Affairs: Hemalatha Balaram

Centres

Materials Science *(International)* (Materials Engineering)

Units

Chemistry and Physics of Materials (Chemistry; Mathematics; Physical Chemistry; Physics); **Engineering Mechanics** (Mathematics; Mechanical Engineering); **Evolutionary and Organismal Biology** (Biology); **Molecular Biology and Genetics** (Biochemistry; Genetics; Immunology; Molecular Biology); **New Chemistry** (Chemistry; Inorganic Chemistry; Organic Chemistry); **Theoretical Sciences** (Mathematics; Mechanical Engineering)

History: Founded 1989. Acquired Deemed University status 2002.

Degrees and Diplomas: *Master's Degree*; *Doctorate*
Last Updated: 23/11/11

JAWAHARLAL NEHRU TECHNOLOGICAL UNIVERSITY

Kukatpally, Hyderabad, Andhra Pradesh 500085
Tel: +91(40) 2315-8661
Fax: +91(40) 2315-6184
EMail: director.ufr@jntuh.ac.in
Website: http://www.jntu.ac.in

Vice-Chancellor: Rameshwar Rao
Tel: +91(40) 2315-6109, Fax: +91(40) 2315-6112
EMail: vcjntu@yahoo.com

Registrar: K. Lal Kishore Tel: +91(40) 3242-2253

International Relations: Anji Reddy, Director

Colleges

Engineering *(Manthani)* (Civil Engineering; Computer Science; Electrical and Electronic Engineering; Engineering; Mechanical Engineering; Mining Engineering; Telecommunications Engineering) *Principal*: S. Chandra Lingam; **Engineering** *(Hyderabad)* (Electrical Engineering; Engineering; Surveying and Mapping); **Engineering** *(Karimnagar)* (Arts and Humanities; Computer Engineering; Computer Science; Electrical and Electronic Engineering; Electronic Engineering; Engineering; Information Technology; Mechanical Engineering; Nautical Science; Telecommunications Engineering) *Principal*: Sudheer Prem Kumar

Institutes

Science and Technology *(IST, Hyderabad)* (Biotechnology; Chemistry; Environmental Engineering; Nanotechnology; Pharmacology; Water Science) *Director*: Laxmi Narasu

Schools

Continuing and Distance Education (Civil Engineering; Computer Engineering; Computer Science; Electrical and Electronic Engineering; Electrical Engineering; Electronic Engineering; Mechanical Engineering; Telecommunications Engineering); **Information Technology** *(SIT, Hyderabad)* (Information Technology) *Director*: Sreenivasa Rao; **Management Studies** (Management) *Director*: A.R. Aryasri

History: Founded 1972.

Governing Bodies: Executive Council

Academic Year: June/July to April (June/July-November; December/January-April)

Admission Requirements: 12th year senior secondary/intermediate examination or recognized foreign equivalent

Main Language(s) of Instruction: English

Accrediting Agencies: National Assessment and Accreditation Council (N.A.A.C.).

Degrees and Diplomas: *Bachelor's Degree*: 4-5 yrs; *Master's Degree*: a further 1 1/2-3 yrs; *Doctorate (PhD)*: a further 3 yrs

Student Services: Academic counselling, Canteen, Cultural centre, Employment services, Health services, Language programs, Sports facilities

Student Residential Facilities: Yes

Libraries: Libraries of the Constituent Colleges, total, 270,000 vols
Last Updated: 23/11/11

JAWAHARLAL NEHRU TECHNOLOGICAL UNIVERSITY, KAKINADA

Kakinada, Andhra Pradesh 533 003
EMail: registrar@jntuk.edu.in
Website: http://www.jntuk.edu.in/

Registrar: V. Ravindra

Colleges

Engineering *(Kakinada)* (Aeronautical and Aerospace Engineering; Chemical Engineering; Civil Engineering; Computer Engineering; Computer Science; Electrical Engineering; Telecommunications Engineering); **Engineering** *(Vijayanagaram)* (Biotechnology; Business Administration; Computer Science; Electrical and Electronic Engineering; Engineering; Information Technology; Mathematics; Mechanical Engineering; Physical Education; Physics)

History: Founded 2008.
Last Updated: 22/07/11

JAWAHARLAL NEHRU UNIVERSITY

Jawaharlal Nehru Vishvavidyalaya (JNU)
New Mehrauli Road, New Delhi 110067
Tel: +91(11) 2674-2676
Fax: +91(11) 2674-2580
EMail: vc@mail.jnu.ac.in
Website: http://www.jnu.ac.in

Vice-Chancellor: S.K. Sopory
Tel: +91(11) 2674-1500, Fax: +91(11) 2674-2580
EMail: sopory@mail.jnu.ac.in

Registrar: Sandeep Chatterjee
Tel: +91(11) 2670-4005, Fax: +91(11) 2674-2641
EMail: registrar@mail.jnu.ac.in; s_chatterjee @ mail.jnu.ac.in

Centres

Law and Governance (Government; Law); **Molecular Medicine** (Medical Technology; Medicine); **Nano Sciences** (Nanotechnology); **Sanskrit Studies** (Sanskrit)

Groups

Adult Education (Adult Education)

Programmes

Postgraduate Studies (M.A.); **Study of Discrimination and Exclusion** (Social Sciences); **Women's Studies** (Women's Studies)

Schools

Arts and Aesthetics (Aesthetics; Arts and Humanities; Cinema and Television; Theatre; Visual Arts); **Biotechnology** (Biotechnology); **Computational and Integrative Sciences** (Construction Engineering; Information Technology); **Computer and Systems Sciences** (Computer Science); **Environmental Sciences** (Environmental Studies); **International Studies** (International Relations); **Language, Literature and Cultural Studies** (Cultural Studies; Literature; Modern Languages); **Life Sciences** (Biological and Life Sciences); **Physical Sciences** (Physics); **Social Sciences** (Social Sciences)

Units

Archives of Contemporary History (Contemporary History); **Educational Research Record** (Educational Research)

Further Information: Also 11 recognized Institutions awarding up to postgraduate degrees

History: Founded 1969. The basic academic units are not single-discipline departments but multidisciplinary Schools of study, the School being visualized as a body of scholars and disciplines linked with each other in terms of their subject matter and methodology, as well as in terms of problem areas.

Governing Bodies: University Court; Executive Council; Academic Council and Finance Committee

Academic Year: July to May (July-December; January-May)

Admission Requirements: Senior school certificate (10 + 2) or recognized foreign equivalent

Fees: (US Dollars): Humanities and Social Sciences, 600 per semester; Science disciplines, 850

Main Language(s) of Instruction: English

International Co-operation: With over 99 and 28 AOC universities worldwide

Accrediting Agencies: University Grants Commission

Degrees and Diplomas: *Diploma*: 1 yr; *Bachelor's Degree (BA (Hons))*: 2-3 yrs (Honours); *Master's Degree*: 2 yrs; *Master's Degree*: Computer Applications (MCA), 3 yrs; *Master's Degree*: Public Health (MPH), 3 sem.; *Master's Degree*: Technology (MTech), 2 yrs; *Master of Philosophy (MPhil)*: 3-4 sem.; *Doctorate (PhD)*: 2-4 yrs. Also Certificate of Proficiency and Advanced (postgraduate) Diploma, 2 sem.

Student Services: Academic counselling, Canteen, Cultural centre, Employment services, Foreign student adviser, Foreign Studies Centre, Handicapped facilities, Health services, Language programs, Nursery care, Social counselling, Sports facilities

Student Residential Facilities: Yes

Special Facilities: Archives on Contemporary History of India

Libraries: c. 500,000 vols; 793 periodical subscriptions

Publications: Hispanic Horizon *(biannually)*; International Studies *(quarterly)*; JNU Annual Report *(annually)*; Journal of the School of Language, Literature and Culture Studies *(annually)*; Studies in History, Indian and Non Indian History *(biannually)*

Academic Staff *2007-2008*	MEN	WOMEN	TOTAL
FULL-TIME	355	114	469
STAFF WITH DOCTORATE FULL-TIME	340	129	469
Student Numbers *2007-2008*			
All (Foreign Included)	3,562	1,892	5,454
FOREIGN ONLY	145	114	259

Last Updated: 23/11/11

JAYOTI VIDYAPEETH WOMEN'S UNIVERSITY

Vedant Gyan Valley, Village Jharna, Mahala-Jobner, Jaipur, Rajasthan 303007
Tel: +91(1428) 287427
Fax: +91(1428) 287428
EMail: info@jvwomensuniv.com
Website: http://www.jvwomensuniv.com/

President: S.K. Vashistha

Registrar: Meghna Singhal

Faculties
Architecture and Applied Arts (Architecture); **Diagnosis and Allied Health Science** (Health Sciences); **Distance Education** (Distance Education); **Education** (Education); **Engineering and Technology** (Engineering; Technology); **Homoeopathic Science** (Homeopathy); **Hotel Management and Catering Technology** (Cooking and Catering; Hotel Management); **Law and Governance** (Government; Law); **Management and Humanities** (Arts and Humanities; Management); **Pharmaceutical Science** (Pharmacy)

Further Information: Also distance education

History: Founded 2008.

Degrees and Diplomas: *Diploma*; *Bachelor's Degree*; *Master's Degree*; *Doctorate*

Student Services: Sports facilities

Student Residential Facilities: For 2,100 students

Special Facilities: Wifi

Libraries: Yes
Last Updated: 26/12/11

JAYPEE INSTITUTE OF INFORMATION TECHNOLOGY (JIIT)

A-10, Sector-62, Noida, Uttar Pradesh 201307
Tel: +91(120) 2400-973
Fax: +91(120) 2400-986
EMail: webadmin@jiit.ac.in
Website: http://www.jiit.ac.in/

Vice-Chancellor (Acting): S.C. Saxena EMail: sc.saxena@jiit.ac.in

Dean Students Affairs and Head: K.K. Rohatgi
EMail: kk.rohatgi@jiit.ac.in

Departments
Biotechnology (Biotechnology); **Computer Science and Information Technology** (Computer Engineering; Computer Science; Information Technology); **Electronics and Communication** (Electronic Engineering; Telecommunications Engineering); **Humanities and Social Sciences** (Arts and Humanities; Social Sciences); **Mathematics** (Mathematics); **Physics and Material Science** (Materials Engineering; Physics)

Schools
Business *(Jaypee)* (Business Administration)

Degrees and Diplomas: *Bachelor's Degree*; *Master's Degree*; *Doctorate*

Student Residential Facilities: Yes

Libraries: Yes
Last Updated: 11/01/12

JAYPEE UNIVERSITY OF ENGINEERING AND TECHNOLOGY (JUET)

AB Road, Raghogarh, Guna, Madhya Pradesh 473226
Website: http://www.juet.ac.in/

Vice-Chancellor: N.J. Rao

Registrar: S.K.S. Negi

Academic Dean: K.K. Jain

Departments
Physics; **Humanities and Social Sciences** (Arts and Humanities; Social Sciences); **Mathematics** (Mathematics)

Programmes
Engineering (Building Technologies; Chemical Engineering; Civil Engineering; Computer Engineering; Computer Science; Construction Engineering; Electronic Engineering; Environmental Engineering; Mechanical Engineering; Telecommunications Engineering)
Last Updated: 26/12/11

JAYPEE UNIVERSITY OF INFORMATION TECHNOLOGY

P.O. Waknaghat, Distt Solan, Kandaghat, Himachal Pradesh 173 234
Tel: +91(1792) 257-999 +91(1792) 245-371
Fax: +91(1792) 245-362
EMail: yaj.medury@juit.ac.in
Website: http://www.juit.ac.in

Vice-Chancellor: Ravi Prakash
Tel: +91(1792) 239-390 EMail: ravi.prakash@juit.ac.in

Registrar: Balbir Singh
Tel: +91(1792) 239-203, Fax: +91(1792) 245-362
EMail: balbir.singh@juit.ac.in

Departments
Biotechnology and Bio-Informatics (Biotechnology; Pharmacy); **Civil Engineering** (Civil Engineering); **Computer Science and Information Technology** (Computer Engineering; Computer Science; Information Technology); **Electronics and Communication Engineering** (Electronic Engineering; Telecommunications Engineering); **Humanities and Social Sciences** (Arts and Humanities; Social Sciences); **Mathematics** (Mathematics); **Physics** (Physics)

History: Founded 2002.

Governing Bodies: Governing Council, Executive Council, Academic Council

Academic Year: July to June

Admission Requirements: Higher secondary school certificate and entrance examination

Main Language(s) of Instruction: English

International Co-operation: With institutions in Germany and USA

Degrees and Diplomas: *Bachelor's Degree (B Tech; B Tech (Hons))*: 4 yrs; *Master's Degree (M Tech)*: a further 2 yrs; *Doctorate (PhD)*: a further 3-5 yrs

Student Services: Academic counselling, Canteen, Health services, Language programs, Social counselling, Sports facilities

Student Residential Facilities: Hostel for over 1,500 students (female and male hostels)

Special Facilities: Basic research facilities. Laboratories
Last Updated: 24/11/11

JIWAJI UNIVERSITY

Vidya Vihar, Gwalior, Madhya Pradesh 474011
Tel: +91(751) 244-2712
Fax: +91(751) 234-1768
Website: http://www.jiwaji.edu

Vice-Chancellor: Mazaahir Kidwai Tel: +91(751) 244-2701

Registrar: Anand Mishra Tel: +91(751) 234-1896

Faculties
Arts (Arts and Humanities; Information Sciences; Journalism; Library Science; Mass Communication; Modern Languages); **Commerce** (Business and Commerce); **Education** (Education); **Engineering** (Engineering; Technology); **Engineering Sciences**

(Computer Science; Electronic Engineering; Engineering); **Law** (Law); **Life Sciences** (Biochemistry; Biological and Life Sciences; Botany; Environmental Studies; Microbiology; Neurosciences; Zoology); **Management** (Management); **Physical Education** (Physical Education; Yoga); **Physical Sciences** (Chemistry; Earth Sciences; Mathematics; Physics); **Social Sciences** (Archaeology; Cultural Studies; History; Political Sciences; Public Administration); **Technology** (Biomedical Engineering; Biotechnology; Food Technology; Pharmacy)

Schools
Distance Education

History: Founded 1964.

Admission Requirements: 12th year senior secondary/intermediate examination or recognized foreign equivalent

Main Language(s) of Instruction: English, Hindi

Degrees and Diplomas: *Diploma*; *Bachelor's Degree*: 3-5 yrs; *Master's Degree*: a further 1-3 yrs; *Doctorate (PhD)*: a further 2 yrs

Student Residential Facilities: Yes

Libraries: c. 160,000 vols
Last Updated: 24/11/11

JODHPUR NATIONAL UNIVERSITY
Jodhpur Rastriya Vishvavidyalaya
Narnadi, Jhanwar Road, Jodhpur, Rajasthan 342001
Tel: +91(2931) 281-551
Fax: +91(2931) 281-416
EMail: info@jodhpurnationaluniversity.com
Website: http://jodhpurnationaluniversity.com/

Chancellor: C. A. Kamal Mehta
EMail: cmo@jodhpurnationaluniversity.com

Registrar: Pradeep Kumar Dey
EMail: registrar@jodhpurnationaluniversity.com

International Relations: Joe Thomas, Vice-President
EMail: vp@jodhpurnationaluniversity.com

Faculties
Applied Science (Applied Chemistry; Applied Mathematics; Applied Physics; Natural Sciences); **Computer Applications** (Computer Networks; Computer Science); **Dentistry and Health** (Dentistry; Medicine; Oral Pathology; Orthodontics; Periodontics; Physical Therapy; Public Health); **Education** (Education); **Engineering and Technology** (Civil Engineering; Computer Engineering; Electrical Engineering; Electronic Engineering; Engineering; Information Technology; Mechanical Engineering; Telecommunications Engineering); **Law** (Law); **Management** (Banking; Finance; Human Resources; Information Technology; International Business; Management; Marketing); **Pharmaceutical Sciences** (Pharmacology; Pharmacy)

History: Founded 2008.

Governing Bodies: Board of Management

Academic Year: July to December; January to June

Admission Requirements: Secondary school certificate or equivalent.

Fees: (Rupees): 10,000 to 160,000 per annum

Main Language(s) of Instruction: English

Accrediting Agencies: University Grants Commission; Government of Rajasthan

Degrees and Diplomas: *Bachelor's Degree*: 3-5 yrs; *Master's Degree*: 2 yrs; *Doctorate*

Student Services: Academic counselling, Canteen, Cultural centre, Employment services, Handicapped facilities, Health services, Language programs, Social counselling, Sports facilities

Libraries: 33,398 vols; 141 journal subscriptions

Academic Staff 2009-2010	MEN	WOMEN	TOTAL
FULL-TIME	142	72	**214**
STAFF WITH DOCTORATE			
FULL-TIME	13	9	**22**

Student Numbers 2009-2010			
All (Foreign Included)	984	170	**1,154**

Last Updated: 24/11/11

KADI SARVA VISHWAVIDYALAYA
Sector - 15, Near KH - 5, Gandhinagar, Gujarat 382015
Tel: +91(79) 2324-4690
EMail: info@ksvuniversity.org.in
Website: http://ksvuniversity.org.in

President: M. M. Patel

Registrar: S.K. Mantrala EMail: registrar@ksvuniversity.org.in

Faculties
Biotechnology (Biotechnology); **Commerce** (Business and Commerce); **Computer** (Computer Engineering); **Education** (Education); **English** (English); **Management** (Management); **Nursing** (Nursing); **Pharmacy** (Pharmacy); **Physical Education** (Physical Education)

History: Founded 2007.

Degrees and Diplomas: *Bachelor's Degree*; *Master's Degree*; *Doctorate*
Last Updated: 24/11/11

KAKATIYA UNIVERSITY
Vidyaranyapuri, Warangal, Andhra Pradesh 506009
Tel: +91(8712) 438-866
Fax: +91(8712) 439-600
EMail: registrar@kakatiya.ac.in
Website: http://www.kuwarangal.com

Vice-Chancellor: Boda Venkat Ratnam (2011-)
EMail: vc@kakatiya.ac.in

Registrar: T.S. Jagannatha Swamy

Faculties
Arts (Arts and Humanities; English; Hindi; Indic Languages; Sanskrit; Urdu); **Commerce and Business Management** (Business Administration; Business and Commerce); **Education** (Education); **Engineering** (Civil Engineering; Computer Science; Engineering; Mechanical Engineering; Mining Engineering); **Law** (Law); **Pharmacy** (Pharmacy); **Sciences** (Botany; Chemistry; Geology; Mathematics; Natural Sciences; Physics; Zoology); **Social Sciences** (Economics; History; Political Sciences; Public Administration; Social Sciences; Sociology; Tourism)

History: Founded 1976.

Governing Bodies: Board of Management

Academic Year: July to April (July-December; January-April)

Admission Requirements: 12th year senior secondary/intermediate examination or recognized foreign equivalent

Main Language(s) of Instruction: English, Telugu, Urdu

Degrees and Diplomas: *Bachelor's Degree*: Arts (BA); Arts in Oriental Learning (BA(OL)); Business Management (BBM); Commerce (BCom); Science (BSc), 3 yrs; *Bachelor's Degree*: Education (BEd); Library and Information Science (BLibISc), 1 yr following Bachelor; *Bachelor's Degree*: Law (LLB), 5 yrs; *Bachelor's Degree*: Pharmacy (BPharm); Technology (BTech), 4 yrs; *Master's Degree*: Arts (MA); Business Administration (MBA); Commerce (MCom); Education (MEd); Finance and Accountancy (MFA); Law (LLM); Pharmacy (MPharm); Science (MSc); Technology (MTech), a further 1-3 yrs; *Master of Philosophy*: a further 1-3 yrs; *Doctorate (PhD)*: 2-5 yrs. Also Postgraduate Diplomas

Student Residential Facilities: Yes

Special Facilities: Central Instrumental Centre

Libraries: c. 103,655 vols; 300 periodicals subscriptions
Last Updated: 02/11/11

KALASALINGAM UNIVERSITY
Anand Nagar, Krishnankoil, Tamil Nadu 626126
Tel: +91(4563) 289-042
Fax: +91(4563) 289-322
EMail: info@kalasalingam.ac.in
Website: http://www.kalasalingam.ac.in

Vice-Chancellor: S. Radhakrishnan

Registrar: T. Vasudevan

Departments

Biotechnology (Biotechnology; Chemical Engineering); **Business Administration** (Business Administration); **Chemistry** (Chemistry; English; Mathematics; Physics); **Civil Engineering** (Civil Engineering; Environmental Engineering); **Computer Applications** (Computer Science); **Computer Science and Engineering** (Computer Engineering; Computer Networks; Computer Science); **Electrical and Electronics Engineering** (Electrical and Electronic Engineering; Power Engineering); **Electronics and Communication Engineering** (Electronic Engineering; Telecommunications Engineering); **English** (English); **Information Technology** (Information Technology); **Instrumentation and Control Engineering** (Automation and Control Engineering; Instrument Making); **Mathematics** (Mathematics); **Mechanical Engineering** (Mechanical Engineering); **Physics** (Physics)

History: Founded 1984 as Arulmigu Kalasalingam College of Engineering. Acquired present status and title 2006.

Degrees and Diplomas: *Bachelor's Degree*; *Bachelor's degree (professional)*; *Master's Degree*; *Doctorate*

Libraries: With a total of c. 65,894 vols

Last Updated: 24/11/11

KAMESHWAR SINGH DARBHANGA SANSKRIT UNIVERSITY

Kameshwara Nagar, Darbhanga, Bihar 846004
Tel: +91(6272) 222-178
Fax: +91(6272) 222-217
EMail: info@ksdsu.edu.in
Website: http:/www.ksdsu.edu.in

Vice-Chancellor: Arvindh Pandey (2011-)
Tel: +91(6272) 248-067 EMail: vc@ksdsu.edu.in

Registrar: Sudhir Kumar Choudhary

Faculties

Astrology and Jyotish (Asian Religious Studies; Esoteric Practices); **Ayurvedic Medicine** (Ayurveda); **Darshan** (Asian Religious Studies); **Dharmashastra and Puranas** (Asian Religious Studies); **Fine Arts** (Fine Arts); **Sahitya** (Asian Religious Studies); **Sociology** (Sociology); **Vedas** (Asian Religious Studies); **Vyakarana and Linguistics** (Asian Religious Studies; Linguistics)

History: Founded 1961. A multi-faculty University specializing in the teaching of Indian Culture along both traditional and modern lines.

Governing Bodies: Senate, Syndicate

Academic Year: July to June

Admission Requirements: Upshastri/intermediate

Fees: None

Main Language(s) of Instruction: Sanskrit, Hindi

Accrediting Agencies: NAAC

Degrees and Diplomas: *Bachelor's Degree*: 3 yrs; *Master's Degree*: 2 yrs; *Doctorate (PhD)*: 2 yrs

Student Services: Cultural centre, Employment services, Social counselling, Sports facilities

Student Residential Facilities: Yes

Special Facilities: Museum

Libraries: 90,938 vols; c. 20,000 periodical subscriptions

Last Updated: 25/11/11

KANNADA UNIVERSITY

Vidyaranya, Hospet, Bellary district, Kamalapura, Karnataka 583276
Tel: +91(8394) 241-337 +91(8394) 241-335
Fax: +91(8394) 241-334
EMail: mail@kannadauniversity.org
Website: http://www.kannadauniversity.org

Vice-Chancellor: A. Murigeppa EMail: vc@kannadauniversity.org

Registrar: H.C. Boralingaiah
EMail: registrar@kannadauniversity.org

Faculties

Fine Arts (Architectural Restoration; Dance; Museum Studies; Music; Sculpture); **Language and Literature** (Ancient Books; Indic Languages; Literature; Modern Languages; Translation and Inter-

pretation; Women's Studies); **Sciences** (Natural Sciences); **Social Sciences** (Anthropology; Archaeology; Development Studies; Folklore; History; Social Problems; Women's Studies)

Further Information: Also Distance Education Courses

History: Founded 1991.

Fees: (Rupees): PhD, 1,000 per annum

Degrees and Diplomas: *Diploma*; *Bachelor's Degree*; *Master's Degree*; *Master of Philosophy*; *Doctorate (PhD)*: 3-4 yrs

Last Updated: 25/11/11

KANNUR UNIVERSITY

Mangattuparamba, Kannur University Campus P.O., Kannur, Kerala 670567
Tel: +91(497) 278-2330
Fax: +91(497) 278-2190
EMail: registrar@kannuruniversity.ac.in
Website: http://www.kannuruniversity.ac.in

Vice-Chancellor: P.K Michael Tharakan (2009-)
Tel: +91(497) 278-2310, Fax: +91(497) 278-2350
EMail: vc@kannuruniversity.ac.in

Registrar: A. Ashokan Tel: +91(497) 278-2330

Colleges

Fashion Design *(Community)* (Fashion Design); **Printing Technology** *(Community)* (Printing and Printmaking); **Yogic Science and Indigeneous Health Care** *(Community)* (Traditional Eastern Medicine; Yoga)

Faculties

Ayurveda (Ayurveda); **Commerce and Management** (Business and Commerce; Management); **Communication** (Cognitive Sciences; Information Sciences; Information Technology; Journalism; Speech Studies); **Education** (Educational Sciences; Pedagogy; Physical Education; Teacher Training); **Engineering** (Computer Science; Electrical Engineering; Engineering; Information Technology); **Humanities** (Arts and Humanities; Fine Arts; Music; Singing; Visual Arts); **Languages and Literature** (Canadian Studies; Communication Studies; English; Foreign Languages Education; Indic Languages; Literature; Multimedia; Psycholinguistics); **Law** (Law); **Modern Medicine** (Biochemistry; Laboratory Techniques; Medical Technology; Medicine; Microbiology; Physical Therapy); **Sciences** (Applied Physics; Botany; Chemistry; Natural Sciences; Physics); **Social Sciences** (Behavioural Sciences; Clinical Psychology; Psychology)

Schools

Distance Education (Economics; English; Finance; History; Mathematics)

Further Information: Several campuses; Affiliated Colleges and Education Centres

History: Founded 1995 as Malabar University. Acquired present name 1996.

Academic Year: June to March

Admission Requirements: For graduate courses, higher Secondary course certificate. For postgraduate courses, Graduate diploma. For Ph.D. programme, 55% marks in Post-graduation.

Main Language(s) of Instruction: English

International Co-operation: With universities in Germany, Sri Lanka and Bengladesh

Accrediting Agencies: University Grants Commission (U.G.C.)

Degrees and Diplomas: *Bachelor's Degree*: 3 yrs; *Master's Degree*: a further 2 yrs; *Master of Philosophy (M.Phil)*: 1 further yr; *Doctorate (PhD)*. Also Certificate courses

Student Services: Academic counselling, Canteen, Handicapped facilities, Health services, Language programs, Sports facilities

Student Residential Facilities: Separate hostels for girls and boys

Libraries: Kannur University Central Library: 16,448 vols; 165 journals; Kannur University Campus Library, Palayad: c. 25,000 vols, 85 journals

Publications: University News *(quarterly)*

Press or Publishing House: Co-operative Press
Last Updated: 28/11/11

KARNATAK UNIVERSITY (KUD)

Pavate Nagar, Dharwad, Karnataka 580003
Tel: +91(836) 244-8600
Fax: +91(836) 274-7884
EMail: vc@kud.ac.in
Website: http://www.kud.ac.in/

Vice-Chancellor: H. B. Walikar Tel: +91(836) 244-8600

Registrar: S.B. Hinchigeri
Tel: +91(836) 244-7750 EMail: registrar@kud.ac.in

Campuses

Belgaum; **Bijapur** *(Postgraduate courses)* (Arabic; Archaeology; Art History; Food Science; History; Social Work; Tourism); **Gadag**; **Haveri**; **Karwar** *(Postgraduate courses)* (Marine Biology; Zoology)

Faculties

Arts (Arabic; Dance; English; Folklore; French; German; Hindi; History; Linguistics; Music; Painting and Drawing; Persian; Philosophy; Russian; Sanskrit; Urdu) *Dean*: K.R. Durgadas; **Commerce** (Business and Commerce; Marketing; Secretarial Studies) *Dean*: R.L. Hydarabad; **Education** (Education; Physical Education) *Dean*: N.N. Ganihar; **Law** (Law) *Dean*: C. Rajshekhar; **Management** (Management) *Dean*: A.H. Chachadi; **Science and Technology** (Biochemistry; Biotechnology; Botany; Chemistry; Computer Science; Electronic Engineering; Genetics; Geography; Geology; Marine Biology; Mathematics; Microbiology; Physics; Polymer and Plastics Technology; Sericulture; Statistics; Zoology) *Dean*: S.C. Puranik; **Social Sciences** (Anthropology; Economics; Information Sciences; Journalism; Library Science; Mass Communication; Political Sciences; Psychology; Social Studies; Social Work; Sociology; Yoga) *Dean*: C.G.Hussain Khan

Further Information: Also 48 Postgraduate Departments; 314 Affiliated Colleges and University; Primary and Public School

History: Founded 1949.

Governing Bodies: Academic Council; Syndicate

Academic Year: June to March (June-October; November-March)

Admission Requirements: 12th year senior secondary/intermediate examination or recognized foreign equivalent

Main Language(s) of Instruction: English, Kannada

International Co-operation: With universities in the Netherlands, other releasing institutions and national laboratories

Accrediting Agencies: National Assessment and Accreditation Council (NAAC)

Degrees and Diplomas: *Bachelor's Degree*: Arts; Science; Commerce (B.A; B.Sc; etc...), 3 yrs; *Master's Degree*: Arts; Science; Technology; Commerce; Social Science; Law; Education (M.A; M.Sc; M.C.A; etc...), a further 2-3 yrs; *Doctorate*: Arts; Science; Technology; Commerce; Social Science; Law; Education; Management (PhD), a further 4 yrs

Student Services: Canteen, Cultural centre, Employment services, Foreign student adviser, Foreign Studies Centre, Handicapped facilities, Health services, Language programs, Social counselling, Sports facilities

Student Residential Facilities: For 2,600 students

Special Facilities: Arts and Archaeology Museum

Libraries: Main Library, 358,854 vols; UN Repository; World Bank Kiosk

Last Updated: 28/11/11

KARNATAKA STATE LAW UNIVERSITY

Navanagar, Hubli, Karnataka 580025
Tel: +91(836) 222-2079
Fax: +91(836) 222-2261
EMail: vcskslu@gmail.com
Website: http://www.kslu.ac.in/

Vice-chancellor: Jaiprakashreddy Sannabasanagouda Patil

Registrar: K.S. Bagale
Tel: +91(836) 2222-392, Fax: +91(836) 2323-151
EMail: regkslu@gmail.com

Programmes

Law (Criminal Law; International Law; Labour Law; Law)

History: Founded 2009.

Degrees and Diplomas: *Bachelor's Degree*; *Postgraduate Diploma*; *Master's Degree*

Last Updated: 06/12/11

KARNATAKA STATE OPEN UNIVERSITY (KSOU)

Manasagangotri, Mysore, Karnataka 570006
Tel: +91(821) 251-5149
Fax: +91(821) 250-0846
EMail: vc@ksouedu.com
Website: http://www.ksouedu.com/

Vice-Chancellor: K.S. Rangappa

Registrar: Sri K. R. Jayaprakash Rao
EMail: registrar@ksouedu.com

Programmes

Diploma; **IT Program**

Programmes

Engineering (Chemical Engineering; Civil Engineering; Computer Science; Electrical Engineering; Fire Science; Mechanical Engineering; Multimedia; Telecommunications Engineering; Textile Technology); **Management** (Banking; Business Administration; Finance; Hotel Management; Human Resources; Information Technology; International Business; Management; Marketing; Transport Management); **Multimedia Studies** (Communication Studies; Multimedia); **Postgraduate Studies** (Communication Studies; Multimedia); **Undergraduate Studies** (Communication Studies; Economics; English; History; Medical Technology; Multimedia; Political Sciences; Public Administration)

Further Information: Also Barath Postgraduate College (a partner of KSOU)

History: Founded 1996.

Academic Year: August to June.

Degrees and Diplomas: *Bachelor's Degree*: 3 yrs; *Master's Degree*: 2 yrs; *Doctorate (PhD)*: 2 yrs. Also Diploma and Certificate courses

Libraries: c. 70,000 vols.

Last Updated: 28/11/11

KARNATAKA STATE WOMEN'S UNIVERSITY (KSWU)

Station Road, Near Dr. B.R. Ambedkar Circle, Bijapur, Karnataka 586101
Tel: +91(8352) 240-023
Fax: +91(8352) 240-024
Website: http://www.kswubij.ac.in/

Vice-Chancellor: Geetha Bali

Registrar: G.V. Sugur Tel: +91(8352) 240-025

Faculties

Arts (Arts and Humanities); **Commerce** (Business and Commerce); **Education** (Education); **Science and Technology** (Natural Sciences; Technology); **Social Sciences** (Social Sciences)

History: Founded 2003.

Degrees and Diplomas: *Bachelor's Degree*; *Master's Degree*; *Master of Philosophy*; *Doctorate*

Student Services: Sports facilities

Libraries: Yes
Last Updated: 06/12/11

KARPAGAM UNIVERSITY

Karpagam Academy of Higher Education, Coimbatore, Tamil Nadu 641021
Tel: +91(422) 6471-113
Fax: +91(422) 2611-043
EMail: info@karpagamuniversity.ac.in
Website: http://www.karpagamuniv.com/

Vice-Chancellor: K. Ramasamy

Faculties

Architecture (Architecture); **Arts** (English; Indic Languages); **Commerce** (Business and Commerce); **Engineering** (Aeronautical and Aerospace Engineering; Automation and Control Engineering;

Civil Engineering; Computer Engineering; Computer Science; Electrical and Electronic Engineering; Electronic Engineering; Information Technology; Mechanical Engineering; Software Engineering; Telecommunications Engineering); **Humanities** (Social Sciences); **Management** (Business Administration; Cooking and Catering; Hotel Management); **Sciences** (Biochemistry; Biotechnology; Chemistry; Mathematics; Microbiology; Physics)

Degrees and Diplomas: *Bachelor's Degree*; *Master's Degree*; *Doctorate*
Last Updated: 11/01/12

KARUNYA UNIVERSITY

Karunya Nagar, Coimbatore, Tamil Nadu 641114
Tel: +91(422) 261-4300
Fax: +91(422) 261-5615
EMail: info@karunya.edu
Website: http://karunya.edu

Vice-Chancellor: Paul P. Appasamy

Registrar: Anne Mary Fernandez

Dean - Academic Affairs i/c: C. Joseph Kennady
EMail: deanaa@karunya.edu

Departments
Physical Education (Physical Education); **Value Education**

Schools
Biotechnology and Health Sciences (Biotechnology; Health Sciences); **Civil Engineering** (Civil Engineering); **Computer Science and Technology** (Computer Networks; Technology); **Electrical Sciences** (Electrical and Electronic Engineering); **Food Sciences and Technology** (Food Science; Food Technology); **Management** (Management); **Mechanical Sciences** (Mechanical Engineering); **Media** (Media Studies); **Science and Humanities** (Chemistry; Education; English; Mathematics; Nanotechnology; Physics)

History: Founded 1986 as Karunya Institute of Technology. Acquired present title and status 2004.

Degrees and Diplomas: *Bachelor's Degree*; *Master's Degree*

Student Residential Facilities: Yes

Libraries: Yes
Last Updated: 28/11/11

KAVIKULGURU KALIDAS SANSKRIT UNIVERSITY

Kavikulguru Kalidas Sanskrit Vishwavidyalaya
Pradishskiya Bahwan, Ramtek Mouda Road, District Nagpur, Ramtek, Maharashtra 441106
Tel: +91(7114) 255-549 +91(7114) 256-476
Fax: +91(7114) 255-549
EMail: admin@sanskrituni,net
Website: http://www.sanskrituni.net/

Vice-Chancellor: Pankaj T. Chande (1998-)

Librarian and Registrar: Harshda H. Dave
EMail: registrarkk@bsnl.in admin@sanskrituni.net

Programmes
Computer Application (Computer Science); **Education** (Education); **Fine Arts** (Fine Arts); **Music** (Music); **Religion Culture and Philosophy** (Philosophy; Religious Studies); **Sanskrit** (Sanskrit); **Vedic Studies and Avestan Studies**; **Yoga, Naturopathy and Dietetics** (Dietetics; Yoga)

History: Founded 1997.

Governing Bodies: Management Council and Academic Council

Academic Year: July to June.

Admission Requirements: Matriculate pass for 'AGAM'

Main Language(s) of Instruction: Marathi; Sanskrit; English

Accrediting Agencies: National Assessment; Accreditation Council

Degrees and Diplomas: *Diploma*; *Bachelor's Degree*; *Postgraduate Diploma*; *Master's Degree*
Last Updated: 01/12/11

KERALA AGRICULTURAL UNIVERSITY

Vellanikkara, Thrissur, Kerala 680656
Tel: +91(487) 237-0432
Fax: +91(487) 237-0019
EMail: registrar@kau.in
Website: http://www.kau.edu

Vice-Chancellor: K. R. Viswambharan EMail: vc@kau.in

Registrar: P.B. Pushpalatha Tel: +91(487) 237-1619

Faculties
Agricultural Engineering (Agricultural Engineering); **Agriculture** (Agricultural Business; Agricultural Management; Agriculture; Food Science; Forestry; Horticulture; Nutrition); **Fisheries** (Fishery); **Veterinary and Animal Sciences** (Animal Husbandry; Veterinary Science)

Further Information: Also10 Constituent Colleges, and 21 Research Stations

History: Founded 1971.

Admission Requirements: 12th year senior secondary/intermediate examination or recognized foreign equivalent

Main Language(s) of Instruction: English

Degrees and Diplomas: *Diploma*; *Bachelor's Degree*: 4-5 yrs; *Master's Degree*: a further 2 yrs; *Doctorate (PhD)*: at least 2 yrs
Last Updated: 01/12/11

KERALA KALAMANDALAM DEEMED UNIVERSITY FOR ART AND CULTURE

Cheruthuruthy, Thrissur, Kerala 679 531
Tel: +91(4884) 262-418
Fax: +91(4884) 262-019
EMail: info@kalamandalam.org
Website: http://www.kalamandalam.org

Vice-Chancellor: P.N. Suresh
Tel: +91(4884) 263-440 EMail: vicechancellor@kalamandalam.org

Registrar: K.K. Sundaresan Tel: +91(4884) 262-418

Programmes
Cultural Studies (Cultural Studies); **Performing Arts** (Dance; Music; Performing Arts; Theatre)

History: Founded 1930

Degrees and Diplomas: *Bachelor's Degree*; *Master's Degree*; *Master of Philosophy*; *Doctorate*
Last Updated: 01/12/11

KIIT UNIVERSITY (KIIT)

PO-KIIT, Bhubaneswar, Orissa 751024
Tel: +91(674) 274-2103
Fax: +91(674) 274-1465
EMail: kiit@kiit.ac.in
Website: http://www.kiit.ac.in/

Founder: Achyuta Samanta (1997-)
Tel: +91(674) 274-0326 EMail: achyuta@kiit.ac.in

Vice-Chancellor: Ashok S. Kolaskar
Tel: +91(674) 272-5171 EMail: vc@kiit.ac.in

Registrar and Director, Admissions: Sasmita Samanta
Tel: +91(674) 274-1747
EMail: sasmitasr@kiit.ac.in; director_admission@kiit.ac.in

International Relations: Dwiti Vikramaditya, Advisor
EMail: dwiti.vikramaditya@gmail.com

Schools
Biotechnology (Biotechnology; Microbiology); **Computer Applications** (Computer Science); **Dental Sciences** (Dentistry; Orthodontics); **Engineering and Technology** *(Programmes imparted by six constituent schools)* (Civil Engineering; Computer Engineering; Electrical Engineering; Electronic Engineering; Mechanical Engineering; Metallurgical Engineering; Telecommunications Engineering); **Film and Media Sciences and Fashion Technology** (Cinema and Television; Fashion Design; Film; Media Studies; Textile Design; Theatre); **Languages** (English; Modern Languages); **Law** (Law); **Management** (Business Administration; Management); **Mass Communication** (Journalism; Mass Communication); **Medical Sciences** (Medicine; Nephrology); **Medicine**

(Anatomy; Biochemistry; Dentistry; Forensic Medicine and Dentistry; Gynaecology and Obstetrics; Medicine; Microbiology; Ophthalmology; Orthopaedics; Paediatrics; Pathology; Pharmacology; Physiology; Psychiatry and Mental Health; Radiology; Surgery); **Nursing** (Midwifery; Nursing); **Rural Management** (Rural Planning); **Sciences** (Natural Sciences); **Sculpture** (Sculpture); **Technology** (Information Technology; Technology); **Tourism and Hospitality Management** (Hotel Management; Tourism)

History: Created 1992. Acquired present status and title 2004.

Governing Bodies: Founder and Board

Academic Year: July to June

Admission Requirements: Secondary School Certificate (+10) for Diploma and Intermediate Courses; Higher Secondary School Certificate (+12) for Bachelor courses; Bachelor degree or equivalent for Master courses

Fees: (Rupees): 150,000 per annum; MBA, 275,000; Medicine, 375,000

Main Language(s) of Instruction: English

Accrediting Agencies: UGC/NAAC

Degrees and Diplomas: *Diploma*: Engineering, 3 yrs; *Bachelor's Degree*: Civil Engineering; Electrical Engineering; Mechanical Engineering; Computer Science; Electronics and Telecommunications Engineering; Information Technology; Electronics and Electrical Engineering, 4 yrs; *Bachelor's Degree*: Computer Science; Business Administration; Law, 3 yrs; *Bachelor's Degree*: Dental Science; Medicine; Surgery, 5 yrs; *Master's Degree*: Business Administration, 2-3 yrs; *Master's Degree*: Computer Science, 3 yrs; *Master's Degree*: Technology; Rural Management; Biotechnology, 2 yrs

Student Services: Academic counselling, Canteen, Cultural centre, Employment services, Foreign student adviser, Foreign Studies Centre, Handicapped facilities, Health services, Language programs, Nursery care, Social counselling, Sports facilities

Student Residential Facilities: Yes

Special Facilities: IT facilities (Fully Wi-Fi e-campus)

Libraries: 24hr library with c. 1,800,000 vols

Publications: KIIT Review, Local magazine *(quarterly)*

Academic Staff *2009-2010*	MEN	WOMEN	TOTAL
FULL-TIME	491	181	672
PART-TIME	115	37	152
STAFF WITH DOCTORATE			
FULL-TIME	265	74	339
PART-TIME	78	25	103
Student Numbers *2009-2010*			
All (Foreign Included)	7,643	4,239	11,882
FOREIGN ONLY	116	45	161

Last Updated: 25/11/11

KL UNIVERSITY

Green Fields, Vaddeswaram, Guntur District, Andhra Pradesh 522502
Tel: +91(8645) - 246948
EMail: registraroffice@kluniversity.in
Website: http://www.kluniversity.in

Vice-Chancellor: G.L. Datta EMail: vc@kluniversity.in

Schools
Bio Sciences and Engineering (Bioengineering; Biotechnology); **Computing** (Computer Engineering; Computer Science; Electronic Engineering); **Electrical Sciences** (Electrical and Electronic Engineering; Electronic Engineering; Telecommunications Engineering); **Management Sciences** (Accountancy; Business Administration; Business and Commerce; Finance; Hotel Management); **Mechanical and Civil Sciences** (Civil Engineering; Mechanical Engineering); **Sciences and Humanities** (Arts and Humanities; Chemistry; Communication Studies; English; Fine Arts; Mathematics; Natural Sciences; Physical Education; Physics; Social Work)

History: Founded 1980 as Koneru Lakshmaiah College of Engineering, became Koneru Lakshmaiah Education Foundation 2006. Acquired status of deemed university 2009.

Degrees and Diplomas: *Bachelor's Degree*; *Master's Degree*; *Doctorate*

Student Services: Sports facilities
Student Residential Facilities: Yes
Libraries: Yes
Last Updated: 13/01/12

KLE UNIVERSITY

JNMC Campus, Nehru Nagar, Belgaum, Karnataka 590010
Tel: +91(831) 2444-444
Fax: +91(831) 2493-777
EMail: info@kleuniversity.edu.in
Website: http://www.kleuniversity.edu.in

Head: Chandrakant Kokate

Registrar: P.F. Kotur

Departments
Public Health (Public Health)

Faculties
Ayurveda (Ayurveda); **Dentistry** (Dentistry); **Medicine** (Cardiology; Medicine; Neurological Therapy; Urology); **Nursing** (Nursing); **Pharmacy** (Pharmacy); **Physiotherapy** (Physical Engineering)

History: Founded as KLE Academy of Higher Education and Research). Acquired present title and status 2006.

Degrees and Diplomas: *Postgraduate Diploma*

Libraries: Yes
Last Updated: 09/01/12

KOLHAN UNIVERSITY

NH 75, Chaibasa, Jharkhand, Jammu Kashimir
EMail: vc@kolhanuniversity.org
Website: http://www.kolhanuniversity.org/

Vice-Chancellor: Salil Kumar Roy EMail: salilroy29@gmail.com

Departments
Anthropology (Anthropology); **Botany** (Botany); **Chemistry** (Chemistry); **Commerce** (Business and Commerce); **Economics** (Economics); **English** (English); **Geography** (Geography); **Geology** (Geology); **Hindi** (Hindi); **History** (History); **Mathematics** (Mathematics); **Philosophy** (Philosophy); **Physics** (Physics); **Political Sciences** (Political Sciences); **Zoology** (Zoology)

Degrees and Diplomas: *Bachelor's Degree*; *Postgraduate Diploma*; *Master's Degree*
Last Updated: 18/11/11

KRANTIGURU SHYAMJI KRISHNA VERMA KACHCHH UNIVERSITY

Mundra Road, Bhuj-Kachchh, Gujarat 370001
EMail: info@kskvkachchhuniversity.org
Website: http://kskvku.digitaluniversity.ac/

Vice-Chancellor: Shashiranjan Yadav

Registrar: Kashyap Trivedi

Departments
Chemistry (Chemistry); **Commerce and Management** (Business and Commerce; Management); **Computer Science** (Computer Science); **Earth and Environment Science** (Earth Sciences; Environmental Studies); **Economics** (Economics); **Education** (Education); **English** (English); **Gujarati** (Indic Languages); **Public Administration** (Public Administration); **Sanskrit** (Sanskrit); **Social Work** (Social Work)

Degrees and Diplomas: *Bachelor's Degree*; *Master's Degree*
Last Updated: 12/08/11

KRISHNA INSTITUTE OF MEDICAL SCIENCES UNIVERSITY

Malkapur, Karad, Dist.Satara, Maharashtra 415110
Tel: +91(2164) 241555
Fax: +91(2164) 241410
EMail: contact@kimsuniversity.in
Website: http://www.kimsuniversity.in

Vice-Chancellor: Arvind V. Nadkkarni
EMail: thevc@kimsuniversity.in

Registrar: Ajit Palekar

Departments
Science (Biotechnology)

Institutes
Medical Sciences (Medicine); **Nursing Sciences** (Nursing); **Physiotherapy** (Physical Therapy)

Schools
Dental (Dentistry)

Degrees and Diplomas: *Bachelor's Degree; Postgraduate Diploma; Master's Degree; Doctorate*
Last Updated: 09/01/12

KRISHNA KANTA HANDIQUE STATE OPEN UNIVERSITY (KKHSOU)

Housefed Complex, Dispur, Guwahati, Assam 781006
EMail: kkh_sou@yahoo.com
Website: http://www.kkhsou.in/

Vice-Chancellor: Srinath Baruah

Programmes
Arts and Humanities (Education; English; Hindi; History; Indic Languages; Philosophy; Political Sciences; Sociology); **Business Administration** (Business Administration; Economics; Finance; Human Resources; Insurance; Management; Marketing); **Mass Communication** (Mass Communication); **Political Sciences** (Political Sciences)

History: Founded 2007.

Degrees and Diplomas: *Diploma; Bachelor's Degree; Master's Degree; Doctorate*
Last Updated: 22/07/11

KRISHNA UNIVERSITY

Andhra Jateeya Kalasala Campus, Rajupeta, Machipatnam, Andhra Pradesh 521 001
Tel: +91 8672 – 226969
EMail: registrar@krishnauniversity.ac.in
Website: http://krishnauniversity.net/

Vice-Chancellor: M. K. Durga Prasad

Administrative Officer: D. Surya Chandra Rao

Departments
Biotechnology (Biotechnology); **Chemistry** (Chemistry); **Computer Science** (Computer Science); **Electronics** (Electronic Engineering); **English** (English); **Journalism and Mass Communications** (Journalism; Mass Communication); **Management** (Management); **Pharmacy** (Pharmacy); **Telugu** (Indic Languages)

History: Founded 2008.

Degrees and Diplomas: *Bachelor's Degree; Master's Degree*
Last Updated: 22/07/11

KUMAUN UNIVERSITY

Nainital, Uttar Pradesh 263001
Tel: +91(5942) 235-563 +91(5942) 235-068
Fax: +91(5942) 235-576
Website: http://www.kuntl.in/

Vice-Chancellor: V.P.S. Arora Tel: +91(5942) 235-068
Registrar: Kamal K. Pande

Faculties
Arts (Arts and Humanities; English) *Dean:* P.C. Pande; **Commerce and Management** (Business and Commerce; Economics); **Education** (Education) *Dean:* Amita Shukla; **Law** (Law) *Dean:* Amit Pant; **Medical Education** (Pharmacy); **Science** (Biotechnology; Botany; Geography; Mathematics; Natural Sciences; Physics; Zoology) *Dean:* Lata Joshi; **Technology** (Information Sciences; Technology)

Further Information: Also Almora and Nainital campuses. 62 affiliated colleges

History: Founded 1973.

Admission Requirements: 12th year senior secondary/intermediate examination or recognized foreign equivalent

Main Language(s) of Instruction: Hindi, English
Degrees and Diplomas: *Diploma:* Tourism, 1 yr; *Bachelor's Degree; Master's Degree; Doctorate (PhD)*
Libraries: Central Library c. 20,000 vols
Last Updated: 01/12/11

KURUKSHETRA UNIVERSITY

Kurukshetra, Haryana 136119
Tel: +91(1744) 238-039
Fax: +91(1744) 238-277
EMail: kuru@doe.ernet.in
Website: http://kuk.ac.in/

Vice-Chancellor: Devinder Dayal Singh Sandhu
Tel: +91(1744) 238-039, Fax: +91(1744) 238-277
EMail: vc.kuk@rediffmail.com
Registrar: Surinder Deswal EMail: regskuk@gmail.com

Faculties
Arts and Languages (Arts and Humanities; English; Foreign Languages Education; Hindi; Indic Languages; Information Sciences; Journalism; Library Science); **Commerce and Management** (Business and Commerce; Hotel Management; Management; Mass Communication; Media Studies; Tourism); **Education** (Education; Physical Education; Special Education); **Engineering and Technology** (Civil Engineering; Communication Studies; Computer Engineering; Electrical Engineering; Electronic Engineering; Engineering; Mechanical Engineering; Technology); **Indic Studies** (Ancient Civilizations; Archaeology; Cultural Studies; Fine Arts; Music; Philosophy; Sanskrit); **Law** (Law); **Life Sciences** (Biochemistry; Biotechnology; Botany; Chemistry; Environmental Studies; Microbiology; Natural Sciences; Pharmacy; Zoology); **Science** (Chemistry; Computer Science; Electronic Engineering; Geography; Geology; Geophysics; Mathematics; Physics; Statistics); **Social Sciences** (Economics; History; Political Sciences; Psychology; Public Administration; Social Sciences; Social Work; Sociology)

Further Information: Also 105 Affiliated Colleges

History: Founded 1956.

Governing Bodies: Court; Executive Council; Academic Council

Academic Year: June to May

Admission Requirements: 12th year senior secondary/intermediate examination or recognized foreign equivalent

Main Language(s) of Instruction: Hindi, English

Degrees and Diplomas: *Diploma:* 1 yr; *Bachelor's Degree:* 1-3 yrs; *Postgraduate Diploma:* a further yr; *Master's Degree:* a further 1-2 yrs; *Master of Philosophy:* 1 yr; *Doctorate (PhD)*

Student Residential Facilities: Yes

Libraries: 275,988 vols

Publications: Journal of Arts and Humanities *(annually)*; Journal of Human Studies (Praci Jyoti) *(annually)*; Journal of Law *(annually)*; Sambhawana (Hindi, Kalanidhi, Jeevanti) *(annually)*

Press or Publishing House: University Press
Last Updated: 01/12/11

KUSHABHAU THAKRE PATRAKARITA AVAM JANSANCHAR VISHWAVIDYALAYA

Post Office-Sunder Nagar, Raipur, Chhattisgarh 492 013
Tel: +91(771) 649-9184
Fax: +91(771) 257-5217
EMail: kulsachiv@ktujm.ac.in
Website: http://www.ktujm.ac.in

Vice-Chancellor: Shri Sachchidanand Joshi
Registrar: D. N. Varma

Departments
Advertising and Public Relations (Advertising and Publicity; Public Relations); **Electronic Media** (Media Studies; Radio and Television Broadcasting; Video); **Journalism** (Journalism); **Management** (Management); **Mass Communications** (Mass Communication); **Social Works** (Social Work)

History: Founded 2004

Degrees and Diplomas: *Bachelor's Degree; Master's Degree; Doctorate*
Last Updated: 01/08/11

KUVEMPU UNIVERSITY
Kuvempu Vishwavidyanilaya
Jnana Sahyadri, Shimoga Dist., Shankaraghatta, Karnataka 577451
Tel: +91(8282) 256-301 +91(8282) 256-302
Fax: +91(8282) 256-255
EMail: reg_admn@kuvempu.ac.in
Website: http://www.kuvempu.ac.in

Vice-Chancellor: S.A. Bari
Tel: +91(8282) 656-222 EMail: vc@kuvempu.ac.in

Registrar: T.R, Manjunath
Tel: +91(8282) 256-221, Fax: +91(8282) 256-262

Programmes
Nanoscience and Technology (Nanotechnology; Technology)

Schools
Bio Science (Biotechnology; Botany; Clinical Psychology; Microbiology; Wildlife; Zoology); **Chemical Sciences** (Biochemistry; Chemistry; Industrial Chemistry; Inorganic Chemistry; Organic Chemistry); **Earth Sciences and Environmental Science** (Environmental Engineering; Geology; Surveying and Mapping; Water Management); **Economics and Business Studies** (Accountancy; Banking; Business Administration; Business and Commerce; Economics; Finance; Insurance; Tourism); **Education** (Education; Physical Education); **Languages, Literature and Fine Arts** (English; Indic Languages; Sanskrit; Urdu); **Law** (Law); **Physical Sciences** (Computer Engineering; Computer Science; Electronic Engineering; Information Sciences; Library Science; Mathematics; Natural Sciences; Physics); **Social Sciences** (Adult Education; Archaeology; Cultural Studies; History; Journalism; Political Sciences; Social Sciences; Social Work)

Further Information: 120 affiliated colleges and 4 constituent colleges

History: Founded 1973 as Postgraduate Centre of University of Mysore, acquired present status and title 1987.

Governing Bodies: Syndicate; Senate; Academic Council

Academic Year: June to March (June-October; December-March)

Admission Requirements: 12th year senior secondary/intermediate examination or recognized foreign equivalent

Main Language(s) of Instruction: English, Kannada

International Co-operation: With universities in USA and the European Union

Accrediting Agencies: National Assessment and Accreditation Council (NAAC)

Degrees and Diplomas: *Bachelor's Degree*: Arts and Humanities; Science; Business and Commerce; Fine Arts; Physical Education; Business Computing; Business Management; Law; Engineering, 3 yrs; *Postgraduate Diploma*: 1 further yr; *Master's Degree*: Arts and Humanities; Science; Business and Commerce; Fine Arts; Physical Education; Business Computing; Business Management; Technology; Engineering; Law, a further 2 yrs; *Doctorate (PhD)*: at least 2 yrs

Student Services: Academic counselling, Canteen, Cultural centre, Employment services, Handicapped facilities, Health services, Language programs, Social counselling, Sports facilities

Student Residential Facilities: Hostel for Boys, 372 beds; Hostel for Girls and working women, 356 beds; Quarters for staff members, 37 beds

Special Facilities: Folklore Museum; Archeology and Culture Museum; Geological Museum; Fine Arts

Libraries: 61,219 vols; 247 periodical subscriptions

Publications: University Newsletter, University activities *(quarterly)*

Press or Publishing House: Prasaranga
Last Updated: 01/12/11

LAKSHMIBAI NATIONAL INSTITUTE OF PHYSICAL EDUCATION
Race Course Road, Shaktinagar, Gwalior, Madhya Pradesh 474002
Tel: +91(751) 400-0902
Fax: +91(751) 400-0995
EMail: registrar@lnipe.gov.in
Website: http://www.lnipe.gov.in

Vice-Chancellor: Sarbjit Singh Pawar EMail: vc@lnipe.gov.in
Registrar: L.N. Sarkar

Departments
Exercise Physiology (Physiology); **Health Sciences and Yoga** (Health Sciences; Yoga); **Management and Mass Communication** (Mass Communication; Sports Management); **Physical Education Pedagogy** (Physical Education); **Research Development and Advanced Studies**; **Sports Biomechanics** (Sports); **Sports Coaching** (Sports); **Sports Psychology** (Psychology; Sports)

History: Founded 1957 as Lakshmibai National College of Education. Acquired present status 1995.

Accrediting Agencies: National Assessment and Accreditation Council (NAAC)

Degrees and Diplomas: *Bachelor's Degree*: 4 yrs; *Postgraduate Diploma*; *Master's Degree*: 2 yrs; *Master of Philosophy*: 1 yr

Libraries: c. 52,000 vols

Publications: Indian Journal of Physical Education, Sports Medicine and Exercise Science
Last Updated: 02/12/11

LAL BAHADUR SHASTRI INSTITUTE OF MANAGEMENT (LBSIM)
Plot No. 11/7, Sector 11, (Near Metro Station), Dwarka, New Delhi 110 075
Tel: +91(11) 2530-7700
Fax: +91(11) 2530-7799
Website: http://www.lbsim.ac.in

Director: Gautam Sinha

Centres
Entrepreneurship *(LBSIM Business Incubation)* (Management)

Programmes
Computer Applications (Computer Science); **Finance** (Finance; Management); **Management** (Management)

History: Founded 1995.

Governing Bodies: Board of Governors; Advisory Body

International Co-operation: With universities in USA

Accrediting Agencies: All India Council for Technical Education (AICTE), Ministry of Human Resource Development, Government of India;

Degrees and Diplomas: *Postgraduate Diploma*; *Master's Degree*. Postgraduate diploma are equivalent to a university MBA; Master's Degree is offered through the Guru Gobind Singh Indraprastha University, Delhi

Student Services: Sports facilities

Special Facilities: Computer Centre

Libraries: c. 28,000 vols; 170 print periodicals and 3,500 online periodical subscritptions
Last Updated: 23/01/12

LALA LAJPAT RAI UNIVERSITY OF VETERINARY AND ANIMAL SCIENCES
Hisar, Haryana 121006
Tel: +91(166) 227-0164

Vice-Chancellor: Hardeep Kumar

Programmes
Veterinary and Animal Sciences (Animal Husbandry; Veterinary Science)

Admission Requirements: Merit in Entrance Test provided the candidates have passed 10 + 2 with Physics, Chemistry, Biology & English and or equivalent from recognized Board / University with atleast 50% marks in aggregate in these four subjects (40% in aggregate for SC/BC candidates).
Last Updated: 19/10/11

LALIT NARAYAN MITHILA UNIVERSITY

Kameshwarnagar, Darbhanga, Bihar 846008
Tel: +91(6272) 222-428
Fax: +91(6272) 222-598
EMail: vc_lnmu@indiatimes.com
Website: http://www.lnmu.edu.in/

Vice-Chancellor: Samrendra Pratap Singh
Tel: +91(6272) 222-463, Fax: +91(6272) 222-598
EMail: vc@lnmu.edu.in

Registrar: Bimal Kumar EMail: registrar@lnmu.edu.in

Faculties

Arts (Arts and Humanities; English; Hindi; History; Music; Philosophy; Political Sciences; Psychology; Sanskrit; Sociology; Theatre; Urdu); **Commerce** (Business Administration; Business and Commerce; Economics); **Education** (Education); **Law** (Law); **Medicine** (Medicine); **Science** (Biotechnology; Botany; Chemistry; Geography; Mathematics; Natural Sciences; Physics; Zoology)

Further Information: Also 67 Constituent and 14 Affiliated Colleges

History: Founded 1972.

Admission Requirements: 12th year senior secondary/intermediate examination or recognized foreign equivalent

Main Language(s) of Instruction: Hindi, English

Degrees and Diplomas: *Diploma*; *Bachelor's Degree*; *Master's Degree*; *Doctorate (PhD)*

Libraries: 178,553 vols; 205 periodicals
Last Updated: 02/12/11

LINGAYA'S UNIVERSITY

Nachauli, Jasana Road, Faridabad, Haryana 121002
Tel: +91(129) 2598-200
EMail: lu@lingayasuniversity.edu.in
Website: http://lingayasuniversity.edu.in/

Vice-President: K. Jayarama Rao

Departments

Automobile Engineering (Automotive Engineering); **Business Administration** (Business Administration; Management); **Civil Engineering** (Civil Engineering); **Computer Applications** (Computer Networks; Software Engineering); **Computer Science and Engineering** (Computer Engineering; Computer Science); **Education** (Education); **Electrical and Electronics Engineering** (Electrical and Electronic Engineering); **Electrical Engineering** (Electrical Engineering); **Electronics and Communication Engineering** (Electronic Engineering; Telecommunications Engineering); **Information Technology** (Information Technology); **Mechanical Engineering** (Mechanical Engineering)

Schools

Built Environment and Design (Building Technologies; Design)

History: Founded as Lingaya's Institute of Management & Technology (LIMAT). Acquired the status of deemed university 2009.

Degrees and Diplomas: *Bachelor's Degree*; *Master's Degree*; *Doctorate*

Student Services: Sports facilities
Last Updated: 11/01/12

LOVELY PROFESSIONAL UNIVERSITY (LPU)

Jalandhar - Delhi G.T. Road (NH-1), Phagwada, Punjab 144402
Tel: +91(1824) 510-274
Fax: +91(1824) 509-425
EMail: dll@lpu.co.in; info@lpu.co.in
Website: http://www.lpu.in

Chancellor: Ashok Mittal
Tel: +91(1824) 501-201, Fax: +91(1824) 506-111
EMail: chancellor@lpu.co.in; ashok.mittal@lpu.co.in

Registrar: Monica Gulati EMail: dll@lpu.co.in

International Relations: Aman Mittal, Deputy Director
EMail: aman.mittal@lpu.co.in

Departments

Open and Distance Learning (Accountancy; Business Administration; Business and Commerce; Commercial Law; Computer Science; Economics; Education; English; Finance; Hindi; History; Human Resources; Information Sciences; Library Science; Management; Marketing; Political Sciences; Retailing and Wholesaling; Sociology; Software Engineering)

Faculties

Applied Medical Sciences (Ayurveda; Biochemistry; Gerontology; Gynaecology and Obstetrics; Haematology; Immunology; Microbiology; Molecular Biology; Neurology; Paediatrics; Paramedical Sciences; Pharmacology; Pharmacy; Physical Therapy; Sports Medicine; Surgery; Virology); **Business and Arts** (Accountancy; Architecture; Banking; Business and Commerce; Cinema and Television; Clothing and Sewing; Commercial Law; Econometrics; Economics; English; Fashion Design; Film; Finance; Fine Arts; Food Technology; Furniture Design; Health Administration; Hotel Management; Human Resources; Indic Languages; Insurance; Interior Design; International Business; Journalism; Landscape Architecture; Linguistics; Literature; Management; Marketing; Modern Languages; Multimedia; Music; Musical Instruments; Nutrition; Painting and Drawing; Performing Arts; Radio and Television Broadcasting; Retailing and Wholesaling; Sculpture; Small Business; Social Sciences; Textile Technology; Theatre; Tourism; Transport Management; Visual Arts; Writing); **Education** (Education; Educational Technology; Library Science; Physical Education; Rehabilitation and Therapy; Sports Medicine); **Technology and Sciences** (Agriculture; Applied Chemistry; Artificial Intelligence; Biochemistry; Biology; Biotechnology; Botany; Chemistry; Civil Engineering; Computer Graphics; Computer Networks; Computer Science; E-Business/Commerce; Electronic Engineering; Engineering; Mathematical Physics; Mathematics; Mechanical Engineering; Microbiology; Organic Chemistry; Physical Chemistry; Physics; Software Engineering; Solid State Physics; Telecommunications Engineering; Zoology)

History: Created 2001. Acquired status 2005.

Governing Bodies: Governing Council; Academic Council; Executive Council; Finance Committee; Academia Industry Interface Council

Academic Year: August to December; January to May

Admission Requirements: Secondary School Certificate for undergraduate programmes; Recognized undergraduate degree for Master's programmes. See website for individual course requirements.

Fees: (INR): 14,500 to 89,000 per semester. See website for more details.

Main Language(s) of Instruction: English

International Co-operation: with institutions in Australia, Canada, Ghana, Singapore, UK, USA

Accrediting Agencies: Recognized by the University Grants Commission(UGC), the Distance Education Council (DEC). Porgrammes regonized by the National Council for Teacher Education (NCTE), the Pharmacy Council of India (PCI), the Indian Association of Physiotherapists (IAP), the Council of Architecture (COA), the Bar Council of India (BCI).

Degrees and Diplomas: *Diploma*; *Bachelor's Degree*; *Bachelor's degree (professional)*; *Postgraduate Diploma*; *Master's Degree*; *Master of Philosophy*. Also undergraduate certificate in Food Production, 6 months; Honours degrees: B.Tech (Hons.), 4-5 yrs and Master, 2-4 yrs; MBA, 2 yrs; Advance Diploma, 1yr.

Student Services: Academic counselling, Canteen, Cultural centre, Employment services, Foreign student adviser, Foreign Studies Centre, Handicapped facilities, Health services, Language programs, Nursery care, Social counselling, Sports facilities

Student Residential Facilities: Male and female hostels for 13,000 students.

Special Facilities: Open air theatre

Libraries: c. 100,000 vols; c. 300 periodical subscriptions; c. 7,000 A/V titles; e-journals and online journals.

Publications: Biobuzz, Biotechnology magazine *(monthly)*; JOHAR, Journal of hospitality application and research *(biannually)*; Lovely Journal of International Business *(quarterly)*

Academic Staff 2010-2011	MEN	WOMEN	TOTAL
FULL-TIME	1,256	731	**1,987**
STAFF WITH DOCTORATE			
FULL-TIME	79	39	**118**
Student Numbers 2010-2011			
All (Foreign Included)	20,134	6,436	**26,570**
FOREIGN ONLY	137	32	**169**

Part-time students, 281. **Distance students**, 444.
Last Updated: 21/06/11

MADHAV INSTITUTE OF TECHNOLOGY AND SCIENCE, GWALIOR (MITS-GWALIOR)

91, Laxmi Bai Colony, Padav, Gwalior, Madhya Pradesh 474 002
Tel: +91(751) 240-9382
Fax: +91(751) 240-9382
Website: http://www.mitsgwl.ac.in/

Director: Sanjeev Jain

Registrar: O.P. Paliwal

Departments
Applied Science (Applied Physics; Chemistry); **Architecture** (Architecture); **Biotechnology** (Biotechnology); **Chemical Engineering** (Chemical Engineering); **Civil Engineering** (Civil Engineering); **Computer Applications** (Computer Engineering); **Computer Science and Information Technology** (Computer Science; Information Technology); **Electrical Engineering** (Electrical Engineering); **Electronic Engineering** (Electronic Engineering); **Mechanical Engineering** (Mechanical Engineering)

History: Founded 1957.

Governing Bodies: Board of Governors

Fees: (Indian Rupees): Undergraduate tuition fee, 22,300 per annum

Accrediting Agencies: All India Council for Technical Education (AICTE)

Degrees and Diplomas: *Bachelor's degree (professional)*; *Master's Degree*; *Doctorate*
Last Updated: 25/01/12

MADHYA PRADESH BHOJ (OPEN) UNIVERSITY (MPBOU)

Kolar Road (Raja Bhoj Marg), Bhopal, Madhya Pradesh 462016
Tel: +91(755) 249-2090 +91(755) 249-2091
Fax: +91(755) 260-0669
Website: http://www.bhojvirtualuniversity.com

Vice-Chancellor: S.K. Singh (2009-)
Tel: +91(755) 249-4,185; +91(755) 249-4094,
Fax: +91(755) 242-4640
EMail: singhkamalakar@hotmail.com, vc_ks_mpbou@yahoo.com

Registrar: Anand Kamble
Tel: +91(755) 249-2093, Fax: +91(755) 260-0704
EMail: registrar@bhojvirtualuniversity.com

Departments
History, Archaeology, Culture and Tourism *(HACT)* (Archaeology; Cultural Studies; Economics; English; Hindi; History; Hotel Management; Political Sciences; Sanskrit; Social Work; Sociology; Tourism); **Multimedia Education** (Education); **Special Education** (Special Education)

Institutes
Information Technology *(IT)* (Computer Science; Educational Technology; Information Technology; Multimedia)

Programmes
Master of Laws *(L.L.M.)* (Law)

Research Centres
Electronic Media Production *(EMPRC)*

Schools
Basic Science (Biology; Botany; Chemistry; Mathematics; Physics; Zoology); **Health Science** (Dietetics; Health Administration; Health Education; Health Sciences; Nursing; Nutrition; Physical Therapy); **Management** (Business Administration; Business and Commerce; Economics; Heritage Preservation; Hotel Management; International Business; Management; Safety Engineering; Secretarial Studies; Tourism)

Further Information: Also 11 regional centres and one sub-Regional Centre located in Bhopal, Bilaspur, Durg, Gwalior, Indore, Jabalpur, Jagdalpur (Bastar), Raipur, Sagar, Ujjain, Rewa, and Satna.

History: Founded 1991 as Madhya Pradesh Bhoj University. Acquired present status and title 1997.

Governing Bodies: Board of Management; Planning Board; Academic Council

Academic Year: July to June

Admission Requirements: 12th year senior secondary/intermediate examination or recognized foreign equivalent

Fees: (Rupees): undergradaute programmes, 1,500-18,000 per annum; graduate programmes, 4,200-24,000 per annum.

Main Language(s) of Instruction: English, Hindi

Degrees and Diplomas: *Diploma*: Business Administration, Computer Applications, Management; *Bachelor's Degree*: Arts, Business Administration, Commerce, Computer Applications, Nursing, Science, Education; *Master's Degree*: Arts, Business Administration, Computer Applications, Mathematics

Student Services: Academic counselling, Employment services, Language programs, Social counselling

Student Residential Facilities: Yes

Libraries: Yes

Press or Publishing House: In House Publishing
Last Updated: 22/06/11

MADHYA PRADESH PASHU CHIKITSA VIGYAN VISHWAVIDYALAYA (MPPCVV)

South Civil Lines, Jabalpur, Madhya Pradesh 482 001
Tel: +91(761) 262-0783 +91(761) 267-8007
Fax: +91(761) 262-0783
EMail: vcmppcvv@yahoo.in
Website: http://www.mppcvv.org/

Vice Chancellor: Govind Prasad Mishra
Tel: +91(761) 267-8007 EMail: vcmppcvv@yahoo.co.in

Registrar: R. P. Pandey Tel: +91(942) 547-6189

Centres
Animal Biotechnology (Biotechnology; Embryology and Reproduction Biology; Genetics; Molecular Biology); **Wildlife Forensic and Health** (Health Sciences; Pathology; Veterinary Science; Wildlife)

Colleges
Veterinary Science and Animal Husbandry *(Rewa)* (Anatomy; Animal Husbandry; Biochemistry; Genetics; Microbiology; Nutrition; Parasitology; Pathology; Pharmacology; Toxicology; Veterinary Science); **Veterinary Science and Animal Husbandry** *(Mhow)* (Agricultural Economics; Agronomy; Animal Husbandry; Biochemistry; Genetics; Immunology; Meat and Poultry; Microbiology; Nutrition; Pathology; Pharmacology; Physiology; Radiology; Surgery; Toxicology; Veterinary Science); **Veterinary Science and Animal Husbandry** *(Jabalpur)* (Anatomy; Animal Husbandry; Biochemistry; Fishery; Genetics; Gynaecology and Obstetrics; Histology; Meat and Poultry; Microbiology; Nutrition; Parasitology; Pathology; Pharmacology; Physiology; Public Health; Radiology; Surgery; Toxicology; Veterinary Science; Wildlife)

History: Founded 2009.

Governing Bodies: Board of Management; Academic Council

Degrees and Diplomas: *Bachelor's Degree*; *Master's Degree*; *Doctorate*
Last Updated: 04/01/12

MADURAI KAMARAJ UNIVERSITY

Palkalai Nagar, Madurai, Tamil Nadu 625021
Tel: +91(452) 245-9455
Fax: +91(452) 245-9181
EMail: mkuregistrar@rediffmail.com
Website: http://www.mkuniversity.org

Vice-Chancellor: Karpaga Kumaravel
Tel: +91(452) 245-9166, Fax: +91(452) 245-8449
EMail: vcmku@mkuniversity.org

Registrar: V. Alagappan Tel: +91(452) 245-9181

Centres

Computer (Computer Science); University Science Instrumentation (Instrument Making)

Departments

Adult Education (Adult Education); Youth Welfare

Research Centres

Educational Media (Cinema and Television; Film; Mass Communication; Media Studies; Video)

Schools

Biological Sciences (Anatomy; Animal Husbandry; Biochemistry; Biological and Life Sciences; Biology; Botany; Genetics; Immunology; Microbiology; Molecular Biology; Physiology); Biotechnology (Biotechnology; Engineering; Genetics; Microbiology; Molecular Biology); Business Studies (Accountancy; Business Administration; Business and Commerce; Finance; Management); Chemistry (Chemistry; Inorganic Chemistry; Materials Engineering; Organic Chemistry; Physical Chemistry); Earth and Atmospheric Sciences (Earth Sciences; Geography; Surveying and Mapping); Economics (Agricultural Economics; Development Studies; Econometrics; Economics; Human Resources; Rural Studies); Education (Education; Physical Education); Energy Environment and Natural Resources (Energy Engineering; Environmental Studies; Futurology; Natural Resources; Waste Management); English and Foreign Languages (Comparative Literature; English; French; Modern Languages); Historical Studies (Ancient Civilizations; History; Medieval Studies; Modern History); Indian Languages (Comparative Literature; Indic Languages; Sanskrit); Information and Communication Sciences (Communication Studies; Information Sciences; Journalism; Library Science; Media Studies); Mathematics (Applied Mathematics; Mathematics; Statistics); Performing Arts (Aesthetics; Art History; Fine Arts; Folklore; Performing Arts); Physics (Computer Engineering; Computer Science; Laser Engineering; Physics); Religions Philosophy and Humanist Thought (Christian Religious Studies; Islamic Studies; Islamic Theology; Philosophy; Religious Studies); Social Sciences (Political Sciences; Social Sciences; Sociology); Tamil Studies (Ancient Books; Comparative Literature; Grammar; Linguistics; Literature; South and Southeast Asian Languages)

Further Information: Also 116 affiliated colleges.

History: Founded 1966 as Madurai University. Acquired present title 1978. A 'University with Potential for Excellence'.

Governing Bodies: Senate; Syndicate; Academic Council

Academic Year: July to March (July-October; December-March)

Admission Requirements: 12th year senior secondary/intermediate examination or recognized foreign equivalent

Main Language(s) of Instruction: English, Tamil

Accrediting Agencies: National Assessment and Accreditation Council (NAAC)

Degrees and Diplomas: Bachelor's Degree; Postgraduate Diploma; Master's Degree; Master of Philosophy; Doctorate. Also undergraduate certificates and diplomas.

Student Services: Canteen, Employment services, Health services, Sports facilities

Student Residential Facilities: Five men's hostels (accommodating 724) and three women's Hostels (accommodating 356).

Special Facilities: Bank; Post Office; Co-Operative Stores; Co-Operative Thrift Society.

Libraries: Dr.T.P. Meenakshisundaran Library, 295,000 vols.

Press or Publishing House: University Printing Press

Student Numbers 2010-2011	MEN	WOMEN	TOTAL
All (Foreign Included)	60,000	60,000	c. 120,000

Last Updated: 22/06/11

MAGADH UNIVERSITY

Bodh-Gaya, Bihar 824234
Tel: +91(631) 220-0572
Fax: +91(631) 220-0572
EMail: info@magadhuniversity.org
Website: http://www.magadhuniversity.org

Vice-Chancellor: Arvind Kumar Tel: +91(631) 220-0493

Registrar: D.K. Yadav Tel: +91(631) 220-0490

Faculties

Commerce (Business and Commerce; Economics); Humanities (Arts and Humanities; Asian Religious Studies; Child Care and Development; English; Geography; Hindi; History; Music; Persian; Philosophy; Political Sciences; Psychology; Sanskrit; Sociology; Urdu); Management (Business Administration; Home Economics; Management); Science (Applied Physics; Botany; Chemistry; Computer Science; Electronic Engineering; Mathematics; Microbiology; Physics; Zoology); Vocational Studies (Agriculture; Air Transport; Biochemistry; Biotechnology; Communication Studies; Dietetics; Education; Food Science; Hotel Management; Information Technology; Journalism; Laboratory Techniques; Mass Communication; Nursing; Nutrition; Physical Therapy; Rural Studies; Tourism; Transport and Communications; Vocational Education; Women's Studies; Yoga)

Further Information: Also 44 constituent and 105 affiliated colleges. A traditional and distance education institution.

History: Founded 1962.

Governing Bodies: Syndicate; Academic Council; Examination Board.

Academic Year: June to May

Admission Requirements: 12th year senior secondary/intermediate examination or recognized foreign equivalent

Fees: (Rupees): 240-400 per annum

Main Language(s) of Instruction: English, Hindi

Degrees and Diplomas: Bachelor's Degree; Master's Degree; Doctorate. Also Honours Bachelor's degree.

Student Services: Language programs

Student Residential Facilities: 9 hostels.

Libraries: Central Library 162,161 books 10 types of journals 1,381 manuscripts.

Last Updated: 05/12/11

MAHAMAYA TECHNICAL UNIVERSITY (MTU)

C-22, Sector-62, Noida, Uttar Pradesh 201 301
Tel: +91(120) 240-0416
EMail: info@mtu.ac.in
Website: http://www.mtu.ac.in/

Vice Chancellor: S. K. Kak
Tel: +91(120) 240-0416, Fax: +91(120) 240-0418
EMail: vc@mtu.ac.in

Registrar: Pushyapati Saxena
Tel: +91(120) 240-0417 EMail: registrar@mtu.ac.in

Programmes

Agriculture (Agriculture); Architecture (Architecture); Biotechnology (Biotechnology); Business Administration (Postgraduate) (Business Administration); Computer Applications (Postgraduate) (Computer Engineering); Fashion and Apparel Design (Fashion Design); Hotel Management and Catering Technology (Cooking and Catering; Food Technology; Hotel Management); Pharmacy (Postgraduate) (Pharmacy); Pharmacy (Pharmacy); Technology (Postgraduate) (Technology); Technology (Technology)

Further Information: Also 385 affiliated colleges and institutions

History: Founded 2010.

Governing Bodies: Executive Council; Academic Council; Finance Committee; Examination Committee

Degrees and Diplomas: Bachelor's degree (professional); Master's Degree. Also M.B.A.

Last Updated: 05/01/12

MAHARAJA GANGA SINGH UNIVERSITY (MGSU)

National Highway, 15, Jaisalmer Road, Bikaner, Rajasthan
Tel: +91(151) 221-2041
Fax: +91(151) 221-2042
EMail: info@mgsubikaner.ac.in
Website: http://www.mgsubikaner.ac.in

Vice-Chancellor: Ganga Ram Jakher
Tel: +91(151) 221-2041, Fax: +91(151) 221-2042
EMail: grjvcmgsub@rediffmail.com

Registrar: Sh. Dinesh Chandra Gupta Tel: +91(151) 221-2044

Faculties

Arts (English; Fine Arts; Hindi; Indic Languages; Music; Painting and Drawing; Philosophy; Physical Education; Sanskrit; Urdu); **Commerce** (Administration; Business Administration; Economics; Finance); **Law** (Labour Law; Law); **Science** (Biochemistry; Biotechnology; Botany; Chemistry; Computer Science; Food Science; Forensic Medicine and Dentistry; Geology; Information Technology; Mathematics; Microbiology; Nutrition; Physics; Zoology); **Social Science** (Criminology; Economics; Environmental Management; Geography; History; Political Sciences; Public Administration; Social Sciences; Sociology)

Further Information: Also 297 affiliated colleges in Bikaner, Churu, Hanumangarh and Sriganganagar districts of Rajasthan.

History: Founded 2003 as Bikaner University. Acquired present title 2008.

Governing Bodies: Board of Management; Board of Studies.

Degrees and Diplomas: *Bachelor's Degree; Bachelor's degree (professional); Postgraduate Diploma; Master's Degree; Master of Philosophy*

Libraries: Only the Faculty of Law has its own library.
Last Updated: 23/06/11

MAHARANA PRATAP UNIVERSITY OF AGRICULTURE AND TECHNOLOGY (MPUAT)

PO Box 171, New Campus, Udaipur, Rajasthan 313001
Tel: +91(294) 247-1101 +91(294) 247-0682
Fax: +91(294) 247-0682
Website: http://www.mpuat.ac.in

Vice-Chancellor: Sarabjit Singh Chahal (2009-)
EMail: vc@mpuat.ac.in; vc_mpuat@yahoo.co.in

Registrar: Shri L.N. Mantri EMail: registrar@mpuat.ac.in

Colleges

Agriculture *(Rajasthan)* (Agricultural Business; Agricultural Economics; Agricultural Management; Agriculture; Agronomy; Animal Husbandry; Biotechnology; Chemistry; Computer Science; Education; Entomology; Genetics; Horticulture; Molecular Biology; Physiology; Plant and Crop Protection; Soil Science; Statistics; Zoology); **Dairy and Food Science Technology** *(CDFST)* (Biotechnology; Chemistry; Dairy; Economics; Food Science; Food Technology; Microbiology); **Fisheries** (Aquaculture; Fishery); **Home Science** (Communication Studies; Development Studies; Family Studies; Food Science; Home Economics; Nutrition; Textile Design); **Horticulture and Forestry** (Forestry; Horticulture); **Technology and Engineering** *(CTAE)* (Agricultural Engineering; Agricultural Equipment; Automation and Control Engineering; Civil Engineering; Computer Science; Electrical Engineering; Electronic Engineering; Energy Engineering; Engineering; Information Technology; Irrigation; Mechanical Engineering; Mining Engineering; Power Engineering; Water Management)

Further Information: Also constituent colleges, Agricultural Research Stations (ARSs), Agricultural Research Sub Stations (ARSSs), Livestock Research Station (LRS), Dryland Farming Research Station (DFRS), and Krishi Vigyan Kendras (KVKs) spread over 12 districts of the south and south eastern part of the state of Rajasthan (Banswara, Baran, Bhilwara, Bundi, Chittorgarh, Dungarpur, Jhalawar, Kota, Pratapgarh, Rajsamand, Sirohi and Udaipur).

History: Founded 1999 as Agricultural University, Udaipur. Acquired present status and title 2000.

Governing Bodies: Board of Management; Board of Studies; Academic Council; Research Council; Extension Education Council; Senior Officer's Council.

Fees: (Indian Rupee): Tuition fee for undergraduate programmes, 500-950 per semester; For graduate programmes, 600-1,900 per semester; For Ph.D programmes., 3,200 per semester. Excepted for Technology and Engineering Programmes, 9,000-10,000 per annum. For International students, 4,000 Dollar per annum.

Accrediting Agencies: All India Council For Technical Education (AICTE); Indian Council of Agricultural Research (ICAR).

Degrees and Diplomas: *Bachelor's Degree; Bachelor's degree (professional); Postgraduate Diploma; Master's Degree; Doctorate*

Libraries: Dr. Amar Singh Rathore Central Library, 71,500 vols, 37 Indian Journals related to Agriculture and 1,055 CD Roms.
Last Updated: 23/06/11

MAHARASHTRA ANIMAL AND FISHERY SCIENCES UNIVERSITY

High Land Drive road, Seminary Hills, Nagpur, Maharashtra 440006
Tel: +91(712) 251-1282
Fax: +91(712) 251-1273
Website: http://www.mafsu.in

Vice-Chancellor: C. S. Prasad
Tel: +91(712) 251-1282 EMail: vc@mafsu.in

Registrar: L. B. Sarkate
Tel: +91(712) 251-1273 EMail: registrar@mafsu.in

Colleges

Dairy Technology *(DTC, Warud)* (Chemistry; Computer Science; Dairy; Economics; Engineering; Food Science; Food Technology; Microbiology); **Fishery** *(COFS, Udgir)* (Fishery); **Fishery** *(COFS, Nagpur)* (Fishery); **Veterinary** *(BVC - Bombay)* (Anatomy; Animal Husbandry; Biochemistry; Embryology and Reproduction Biology; Genetics; Gynaecology and Obstetrics; Histology; Meat and Poultry; Medicine; Microbiology; Nutrition; Parasitology; Pathology; Pharmacology; Physiology; Public Health; Surgery; Veterinary Science); **Veterinary** *(NVC - Nagpur)* (Anatomy; Animal Husbandry; Epidemiology; Genetics; Gynaecology and Obstetrics; Meat and Poultry; Microbiology; Nutrition; Parasitology; Pathology; Public Health; Surgery; Veterinary Science); **Veterinary and Animal Sciences** *(COVAS - Udgir)* (Anatomy; Animal Husbandry; Biochemistry; Genetics; Medicine; Microbiology; Nutrition; Pathology; Physiology; Surgery; Veterinary Science); **Veterinary and Animal Sciences** *(COVAS - Parbhani)* (Animal Husbandry; Biochemistry; Genetics; Gynaecology and Obstetrics; Medicine; Microbiology; Nutrition; Pathology; Pharmacology; Physiology; Surgery; Veterinary Science); **Veterinary Science** *(KNP COVS - Krantisinh Nana Patil, Shirval)* (Agriculture; Animal Husbandry; Veterinary Science)

Institutes

Veterinary and Animal Sciences *(PGIVAS - Postgraduate, Akola)* (Animal Husbandry; Biochemistry; Dairy; Genetics; Gynaecology and Obstetrics; Meat and Poultry; Nutrition; Pathology; Physiology; Radiology; Surgery; Veterinary Science)

History: Founded 2000.

Degrees and Diplomas: *Bachelor's Degree; Bachelor's degree (professional); Postgraduate Diploma; Master's Degree; Doctorate*
Libraries: Yes.
Last Updated: 23/06/11

MAHARASHTRA UNIVERSITY OF HEALTH SCIENCES (MUHS)

Vani Road, Mhasrul, Nashik, Maharashtra 422 004
Tel: +91(253) 253-9191 +91(253) 253-9190
Fax: +91(253) 253-9195
EMail: academic@muhsnashik.com; computer@muhsnashik.com
Website: http://www.muhsnashik.com

Vice-Chancellor: Arun V. Jamkar
Tel: +91(253) 253-1835, Fax: +91(253) 253-9113
EMail: vc@muhsnashik.com; vcoffice@muhsnashik.com

Registrar: Adinath N. Suryakar
Tel: +91(253) 253-9292, Fax: +91(253) 253-9295
EMail: registrar@muhsnashik.com;
registraroffice@muhsnashik.com

Faculties

Allied Health Sciences (Community Health; Dental Technology; Health Sciences; Nursing; Occupational Therapy; Physical Therapy; Respiratory Therapy); **Ayurveda and Unani** (Alternative Medicine; Ayurveda); **Dentistry** (Dentistry); **Homeopathy** (Homeopathy); **Medicine** (Anaesthesiology; Anatomy; Biochemistry; Cardiology; Dermatology; Diabetology; Endocrinology; Forensic Medicine and Dentistry; Gastroenterology; Gynaecology and Obstetrics; Haematology; Health Administration; Immunology; Medicine; Microbiology; Nephrology; Neurological Therapy; Neurology; Oncology; Ophthalmology; Paediatrics; Pathology; Pharmacology; Physiology; Plastic Surgery; Psychiatry and Mental Health; Public Health; Radiology; Social and Preventive Medicine; Surgery; Toxicology; Urology)

History: Founded 1998.

Governing Bodies: Senate; Management Council; Academic Council.

Academic Year: August to July (August-January; February-July)

Degrees and Diplomas: *Bachelor's Degree*; *Postgraduate Diploma*; *Master's Degree*
Last Updated: 23/06/11

MAHARISHI MAHESH YOGI VEDIC UNIVERSITY

Maharishi Mahesh Yogi Vedic Vishwavidyalaya (MMYVV)

H.O. Village Karondi, District Katni, Umariapan, Madhya Pradesh 483332
Tel: +91(7625) 220-345
Fax: +91(7625) 220-285
EMail: registrarmmyvv@gmail.com; mmyvvarpr@yahoo.co.in
Website: http://www.mmyvv.com

Vice-Chancellor: Bhuvnesh Sharma
EMail: vc_mmyvv@rediffmail.com

Registrar: Arvind Singh Rajput

Programmes

Arts (Arts and Humanities); **Astrology** (Esoteric Practices); **Audio Programme Production** (Mass Communication); **Commerce** (Business and Commerce); **Computer Science** (Computer Science); **Education** (Education); **Educational Administration** (Educational Administration); **Finance** (Finance); **Healt Care and Beauty Culture** (Cosmetology; Health Sciences); **Human Resources** (Human Resources); **Management** (Management); **Marketing** (Marketing); **Vedic Medicine** (Ayurveda); **Yoga** (Yoga)

Further Information: Also campuses in Bhopal, Indore and Jabalpur.

History: Founded 1995.

Governing Bodies: Board of Management; Academic council.

Fees: (Rupees): Tuition fees for undergraduate programmes, per annum, 2,285-27,000 per annum; Graduate programmes, 4,550-16,500 per annum; Ph.D., 10,000 per annum.

Main Language(s) of Instruction: English and Hindi.

Degrees and Diplomas: *Diploma*; *Bachelor's Degree*; *Postgraduate Diploma*; *Master's Degree*; *Doctorate (PhD)*. Also undergraduate certificates.

Student Residential Facilities: Residential facilities for 400 students located in Bhopal (for boys and girls students), Indore (only for boys) and Jabalpur (only for boys).

Special Facilities: Auditorium; Meditation halls; Computer labs.

Libraries: Central Library, 11,556 vols.
Last Updated: 24/06/11

MAHARISHI MARKANDESHWAR UNIVERSITY (MMU)

Mullana-Ambala, Haryana 133207
Tel: +91(1731) 304-100
Fax: +91(1731) 274-375
EMail: info@mmumullana.org
Website: http://www.mmumullana.org

Vice Chancellor: Satyawan G. Damle
Tel: +91(1731) 301-525, Fax: +91(1731) 274-325
EMail: vice-chancellor@mmumullana.org

International Relations: Harish K. Sharma, Registrar; Director, International Affairs
Tel: +91(1731) 304-440, Fax: +91(1731) 304-446
EMail: registrarmmu@mmumullana.org

Colleges

Dental Sciences and Research (Dental Hygiene; Dental Technology; Dentistry; Oral Pathology; Orthodontics; Periodontics; Radiology; Surgery); **Education** (Education); **Engineering** (Arts and Humanities; Biotechnology; Chemistry; Civil Engineering; Computer Engineering; Electrical Engineering; Electronic Engineering; Engineering; Information Technology; Mathematics; Measurement and Precision Engineering; Mechanical Engineering; Physics; Social Sciences; Telecommunications Engineering); **Nursing** (Community Health; Gynaecology and Obstetrics; Nursing; Paediatrics; Psychiatry and Mental Health); **Pharmacy** (Pharmacology; Pharmacy)

Departments
Law (Law)

Institutes

Computer Technology and Business Management *(Hotel Management)* (Business Administration; Cooking and Catering; Dietetics; Hotel and Restaurant; Hotel Management); **Computer Technology and Business Management** *(MCA)* (Business Computing; Computer Science); **Management** (Business Administration; Business and Commerce; Management); **Medical Sciences and Research** (Anaesthesiology; Anatomy; Biochemistry; Community Health; Dermatology; Forensic Medicine and Dentistry; Gynaecology and Obstetrics; Medicine; Microbiology; Ophthalmology; Orthopaedics; Otorhinolaryngology; Paediatrics; Pathology; Pharmacology; Physiology; Radiology; Respiratory Therapy; Surgery; Venereology); **Nursing** (Midwifery; Nursing); **Physiotherapy and Rehabilitation** (Cardiology; Paediatrics; Physical Therapy; Rehabilitation and Therapy; Sports)

Programmes
General Nursing and Midwifery (Midwifery; Nursing)

History: Founded 1993. Acquired present status of Deemed University 2007.

Fees: (Indian Rupee): Tuition Fee, undergraduate programmes, 25,000-56,000 per annum; Graduate programmes, 25,000-180,000 per annum.

Accrediting Agencies: National Assessment and Accreditation Council (NAAC); Accreditation Service for International Colleges (ASIC).

Degrees and Diplomas: *Diploma*; *Bachelor's Degree*; *Bachelor's degree (professional)*; *Postgraduate Diploma*; *Master's Degree*; *Master of Philosophy*; *Doctorate*. Also MBA; Undergraduate certificates.

Student Services: Sports facilities

Student Residential Facilities: For over 5,000 students.

Special Facilities: 218 lecture theatres; 16 seminar halls; 12 conference halls; 1,500 seat auditorium; over 300 labs.

Libraries: A total of c. 150,000 vols, 30,475 titles and 5,825 journals.

Academic Staff *2010-2011*: Total 1,300
STAFF WITH DOCTORATE: Total 80
Student Numbers *2010-2011*: Total 10,250
Last Updated: 24/06/11

MAHARISHI MARKANDESHWAR UNIVERSITY, SADOPUR

V.P.O. Sadhopur, Chandigarh Road, Ambala, Haryana 134007
Tel: +91(94176) 25153
EMail: info@mmambala.org
Website: http://www.mmambala.org/

Director: Ashok K. Goel

Programmes
Architecture (Architecture); **Engineering** (Civil Engineering; Computer Engineering; Electronic Engineering; Mechanical Engineering); **Fashion Design** (Fashion Design; Interior Design);

Management Studies (Business Administration; Finance; Information Technology; Management; Marketing); **Sciences** (Chemistry; Mathematics; Physics); **Social Sciences** (Business and Commerce; English)

History: Founded 2010.

Fees: (Rupees): 15,000-50,000 per annum depending on programmes

Degrees and Diplomas: *Bachelor's Degree*; *Master's Degree*; *Doctorate*

Student Services: Academic counselling, Sports facilities

Student Residential Facilities: Yes

Libraries: Yes
Last Updated: 17/01/12

MAHARISHI MARKANDESHWAR UNIVERSITY, SOLAN (MMU SOLAN)

Solan, Himachal Pradesh 173 229
Tel: +91(1792) 268-224
Fax: +91(1792) 268-221
EMail: info@mmusolan.org
Website: http://mmusolan.org

Chancellor: Tarsem Garg

Registrar: Ajay Singal

Schools
Business Management (Business Administration; Management); **Computer Technology** (Computer Engineering; Computer Science); **Engineering and Technology** (Civil Engineering; Electrical Engineering; Engineering; Mechanical Engineering; Structural Architecture; Technology; Telecommunications Engineering)

Degrees and Diplomas: *Bachelor's degree (professional)*; *Master's Degree*. Also M.B.A.
Last Updated: 29/08/11

MAHARISHI UNIVERSITY OF MANAGEMENT AND TECHNOLOGY (MUMT)

Maharishi Vidya Mandir Campus, Mangla, Bilaspur,
Chhattisgarh 495 001
Tel: 07752-518424
Fax: 07752-518390
EMail: mumtho@mahaemail.com
Website: http://www.mumt.com/

Pro-Vice Chancellor: B. S. Mehta

Faculties
Education (Education); **Health Sciences** (Health Sciences); **Maharishi Vedic Science** (Esoteric Practices); **Management Studies** (Business Administration; Business and Commerce; Finance; Human Resources; Information Sciences; Labour and Industrial Relations; Management; Marketing); **Technology** (Computer Science; Technology)

Further Information: Also campuses in Raipur, Durg and Raigarh.

History: Founded 2002.

Governing Bodies: Executive Council; Academic Council; Planning Board

Fees: (Indian Rupee): Certificate, 3,000; Bacelor's degree, 6,000-17,000; Postgraduate diploma, 9,000.

Accrediting Agencies: University Grants Commission (UGC)

Degrees and Diplomas: *Diploma*; *Bachelor's Degree*; *Postgraduate Diploma*. Also Professional Certificate and Advanced Diploma, 1 yr.
Last Updated: 25/08/11

MAHARSHI DAYANAND SARASWATI UNIVERSITY

Pushkar By-pass, Ghooghara, Ajmer, Rajasthan 305009
Tel: +91(145) 278-7056 +91(145) 278-7058
Fax: +91(145) 278-7049 +91(145) 278-7055
Website: http://www.mdsuajmer.ac.in

Vice-Chancellor: Sh. Atul Sharma
Tel: +91(145) 278-7055 +91(145) 278-7051,
Fax: +91(145) 278-7049

Registrar: B. L. Sunaria

Centres
Yoga (Yoga)

Departments
Botany (Biotechnology; Botany); **Commerce** (Business and Commerce; Tourism); **Computer Science** (Computer Science; Data Processing; Information Management; Information Technology); **Economics** (Agricultural Economics; Banking; Economics); **Environmental Studies** (Environmental Studies); **Food and Nutrition** (Dietetics; Food Science; Management; Nutrition); **History** (Archiving; History); **Management Studies** (Business Administration; Management); **Microbiology** (Biology; Biotechnology; Microbiology); **Political Science** (Political Sciences; Public Administration); **Population Studies** (Demography and Population); **Pure and Applied Chemistry** (Applied Chemistry; Chemistry); **Remote Sensing** (Surveying and Mapping); **Zoology** (Biology; Laboratory Techniques; Molecular Biology; Zoology)

Further Information: Also 214 government and private affiliated colleges.

History: Founded as University of Ajmer 1987 by an Act of State Legislature. Acquired present title 1992.

Governing Bodies: Academic Council; Board of Management; Board of Studies.

Admission Requirements: 12th year senior secondary/intermediate examination or recognized foreign equivalent

Fees: (Rupees): 250-1,500 per annum

Main Language(s) of Instruction: Hindi, English

Accrediting Agencies: National Assessment and Accreditation Council, Bangalore

Degrees and Diplomas: *Postgraduate Diploma*; *Master's Degree*; *Master of Philosophy*; *Doctorate (PhD)*. Also undegraduate diploma and certificate programmes in yoga.

Student Services: Academic counselling, Canteen, Foreign student adviser, Foreign Studies Centre, Health services, Language programs, Sports facilities

Student Residential Facilities: For women only

Libraries: c. 43,000 vols; 2,000 Ph.D. Theses; 176 current periodicals; 10,000 reports of government departments, universities, and other departments; 15,000 back / old volumes of periodicals; 150 complementary titles; 3,000 reference vols; 3,000 CD-Roms.
Last Updated: 24/06/11

MAHARSHI DAYANAND UNIVERSITY

Rohtak, Haryana 124001
Tel: +91(1262) 294-327
Fax: +91(1262) 294-133
Website: http://www.mdurohtak.ac.in

Vice-Chancellor: R.P. Hooda (2010-)
Tel: +91(1262) 274-327 +91(1262) 292-431,
Fax: +91(1262) 274-133 EMail: vcmdu@hotmail.com

Registrar: Sat Pal Vats Tel: +91(1262) 274-640

International Relations: S.K. Gakhar, Lecturer

Centres
Haryana Studies (Regional Studies); **Indra Gandhi PG Regional (Rewari)** (Business and Commerce; English; History; Mathematics); **Women Studies** (Women's Studies)

Faculties
Commerce (Business and Commerce; Management; Retailing and Wholesaling); **Education** (Education; Physical Education); **Engineering and Technology** (Automation and Control Engineering; Biotechnology; Computer Engineering; Computer Science; Electronic Engineering; Engineering; Mechanical Engineering; Production Engineering; Software Engineering; Technology; Telecommunications Engineering); **Humanities** (Arts and Humanities; English; French; Hindi; Journalism; Mass Communication; Media Studies; Modern Languages; Sanskrit; Spanish; Translation and Interpretation); **Law** (Law); **Life Sciences** (Biochemistry;

Biotechnology; Botany; Environmental Studies; Food Technology; Forensic Medicine and Dentistry; Genetics; Microbiology; Zoology); **Management Sciences** (Business Administration; Economics; Hotel and Restaurant; Hotel Management; Management; Tourism); **Performing and Visual Arts** (Fine Arts; Music; Musical Instruments; Painting and Drawing; Performing Arts; Singing; Visual Arts); **Pharmaceutical Sciences** (Pharmacology; Pharmacy); **Physical Sciences** (Chemistry; Computer Science; Mathematics; Physics; Statistics); **Social Sciences** (Economics; Geography; History; Library Science; Military Science; Political Sciences; Psychology; Public Administration; Social Sciences; Sociology)

Institutes
Law and Management Studies *(ILMS - Gurgaon)* (International Business; Law)

Further Information: Over 490 affiliated Institutions/Colleges.

History: Founded as Rohtak University 1976. Acquired present title 1977 and present status 1978.

Governing Bodies: Executive Council; Academic Council; Court; Finance Committee.

Academic Year: July to March (July-September; October-December; January-March)

Admission Requirements: 12th year senior secondary/intermediate examination or recognized foreign equivalent

Fees: (Rupees): Undergraduate programmes, 2,200-62,315 per annum; Graduate programmes, 1,610-72,315 per annum; MBA, 36,295-48,815 per annum.

Main Language(s) of Instruction: Hindi. English

Accrediting Agencies: National Assessment and Accreditation Council (NAAC)

Degrees and Diplomas: *Diploma; Bachelor's Degree; Bachelor's degree (professional); Postgraduate Diploma; Master's Degree (Ph.D.); Doctorate.* Also Honours Bachelor and Master's degree; Professional Master degree; MBA; Undergraduate certificate.

Student Services: Academic counselling, Canteen, Employment services, Foreign student adviser, Health services, Sports facilities

Student Residential Facilities: 10 hostels (5 for girls and 5 for boys with a total capcity of 2,500 students.

Special Facilities: Tagore Auditorium; Community Centre; Shopping Complex.

Libraries: Vivekananda Library: 260,549 vols; 540 periodical subscriptions; Online access to 5,300 e-Journals through UGC Infonet facility; Over 200 e-Open Access Journals; SCOPUS (an Elsevier owned database of abstracts from about 18,000 science and social journals), e-Emeralds Plus (a full text database of management journals published by Emerald Group); Manupatra (full text law database).

Press or Publishing House: Maharshi Dayanand University Press
Last Updated: 24/06/11

MAHARSHI PANINI SANSKRIT UNIVERSITY

Maharshi Panini Sanskrit Vishwavidyalaya (MPSVVUJJAIN)
B.M. Birla Shodh Sansthan, Parisar Dewas Road, Ujain, Madhya Pradesh 456 010
Tel: +91(734) 252-6044
Fax: +91(734) 252-4845
Website: http://mpsvvujjain.org/

Vice-Chancellor: Mithla Prasad Tripathi

Programmes
Sanskrit (Administration; Astronomy and Space Science; Ayurveda; Environmental Studies; Esoteric Practices; History; Literature; Mathematics; Military Science; Philosophy; Sanskrit; Sculpture; Zoology)

Further Information: Also 17 Affiliated Colleges.

History: Founded 2008.

Governing Bodies: General Council; Executive Council; Academic Council; Finance Committee

Degrees and Diplomas: *Bachelor's Degree; Master's Degree.* Also Shastri, 7 years; Asharya, (Post Graduate Degree).
Last Updated: 04/01/12

MAHATMA GANDHI CHITRAKOOT GRAMODAYA UNIVERSITY

Mahatma Gandhi Chitrakoot Gramodaya Vishwavidyalaya (MGCGV)
District Satna, Chitrakoot, Madhya Pradesh 485331
Tel: +91(7670) 265-411
Fax: +91(7670) 265-413
EMail: mgcgv@rediffmail.com
Website: http://www.ruraluniversity-chitrakoot.org

Vice-Chancellor: Krishna B. Pandeya
Tel: +91(7670) 265-413, Fax: +91(7670) 265-413
EMail: kbpandeya@yahoo.com

Registrar: Rama Shankar Tripathi

Faculties
Agriculture (Agriculture; Agronomy; Biochemistry; Botany; Crop Production; Genetics; Home Economics; Horticulture; Soil Science; Technology; Zoology); **Education, Fine Arts, Humanities and Social Sciences** (Ancient Civilizations; Arts and Humanities; Cultural Studies; Education; Fine Arts; Hindi; History; Information Sciences; Journalism; Library Science; Mass Communication; Music; Painting and Drawing; Political Sciences; Public Administration; Sanskrit; Sculpture; Social Sciences; Women's Studies; Yoga); **Engineering and Technology** (Agricultural Engineering; Civil Engineering; Electronic Engineering; Engineering; Food Technology; Information Technology; Mechanical Engineering; Technology); **Rural Development and Business Management** (Administration; Agricultural Business; Business Administration; Development Studies; Management; Small Business); **Science and Environment** (Biochemistry; Biological and Life Sciences; Biology; Chemistry; Environmental Studies; Forestry; Geology; Information Technology; Mathematics; Surveying and Mapping; Wildlife; Zoology)

History: Founded 1991 as Chitrakoot Gramodaya Vishwavidyalaya. Renamed Mahatma Gandhi Gramodaya Vishwavidyalaya. Acquired present title 1997.

Governing Bodies: Board of Management; Academic Council; Academic Planning and Evaluation Board.

Fees: (Rupee): tuition fees, 9,000-19,800 per annum for undergraduate programmes and 10,000-24,300 per annum for graduate programmes. MBA, 41,400 per annum.

Main Language(s) of Instruction: English, Hindi

Accrediting Agencies: Government Agencies (UGC; AICTE; ICAR; NCTE)

Degrees and Diplomas: *Diploma; Bachelor's Degree; Bachelor's degree (professional); Postgraduate Diploma; Master's Degree; Doctorate (PhD).* Also MBA.

Student Services: Academic counselling, Canteen, Cultural centre, Health services, Nursery care, Social counselling

Libraries: c. 30,000 vols
Last Updated: 27/06/11

MAHATMA GANDHI INTERNATIONAL HINDI UNIVERSITY

Mahatma Gandhi Antarrashtriya Hindi Vishwavidyalaya
Post - Manas Temple, Gandhi Hill, Wardha, Maharashtra 442001
Tel: +91(7152) 230-905
Fax: +91(7152) 240-760
EMail: hindiunv@vsnl.net.in
Website: http://www.hindivishwa.org

Vice-Chancellor: Vibhuti Narain Rai
Tel: +91(7152) 230-907, Fax: +91(7152) 230-903
EMail: vc@hindivishwa.org

Registrar: A. Biswdvidyaly Arvindakshn
Tel: +91(7152) 230-902, Fax: +91(7152) 230-602
EMail: registrar@hindivishwa.org

Centres
Buddhist Learning *(Dr. Bdnt fun Kauslyayn)* (Asian Religious Studies); **Communication and Media Studies** (Advertising and Publicity; Communication Studies; Journalism; Mass Communication; Media Studies; Public Relations; Radio and Television Broadcasting; Video); **Dalit and Tribal Studies** *(Dr. Babasaheb Ambedkar)* (Social Studies); **Indian and foreign languages**

(Advanced Studies) (Computer Science; Sanskrit); **Master Peace Studies** *(Mahatma Gandhi Fuji)* (Peace and Disarmament; Social Work); **Technology Learning** (Computer Science; Information Technology; Modern Languages); **Zakir Husain Studies** (Educational Sciences)

Schools
Culture *(Mganahiv)* (Cultural Studies; Peace and Disarmament; Social Sciences; Women's Studies); **Language** (Chinese; Engineering; French; Hindi; Linguistics; Modern Languages; South and Southeast Asian Languages; Spanish; Urdu); **Literature** (Comparative Literature; Film; Literature; Theatre); **Translation and Interpretation** (Translation and Interpretation)

Further Information: Also Distance Education programme.

History: Founded 1997. A 'Central University'.

Degrees and Diplomas: *Diploma*; *Postgraduate Diploma*; *Master's Degree*; *Master of Philosophy*; *Doctorate*. Also undergraduate certificate.

Student Services: Health services, Sports facilities

Student Residential Facilities: Five men and a women's dormitory.

Special Facilities: Computer lab.

Libraries: Central library, c. 60,000 vols.

Last Updated: 24/06/11

MAHATMA GANDHI KASHI UNIVERSITY
Mahatma Gandhi Kashi Vidyapeeth (MGKV)
Varanasi, Uttar Pradesh 221 002
Tel: +91(542) 222-2689
Fax: +91(542) 222-5472
EMail: mgkv@rediffmail.com
Website: http://www.mgkvp.ac.in

Vice-Chancellor: Avadh Ram (2008-)
Tel: +91(542) 222-5472, Fax: +91(542) 222-5472
EMail: vcmgkvp@sancharnet.in; profavadhram@yahoo.com; profavadhram@gmail.com

Registrar (Acting): Indupati Jha Tel: +91(542) 222-2689

Faculties
Commerce and Management (Accountancy; Business Administration; Business and Commerce; Finance; Management); **Education** (Education); **Humanities** (Ancient Languages; Arts and Humanities; English; Fine Arts; Hindi; History; Information Sciences; Journalism; Library Science; Literature; Modern Languages; Philosophy; Physical Education; Russian; Sanskrit; South and Southeast Asian Languages; Tourism; Urdu); **Law** (Law); **Science and Technology** (Botany; Chemistry; Computer Science; Home Economics; Mathematics; Physics; Statistics; Technology; Zoology); **Social Sciences** (Economics; Political Sciences; Psychology; Social Sciences; Sociology; Women's Studies); **Social Work** (Development Studies; Human Rights; Labour and Industrial Relations; Social Work; Welfare and Protective Services); **Student Welfare**

Institutes
Hindi Journalism *(Madan Mohan Malviya)* (Information Sciences; Journalism)

Further Information: Also Sonebhadra campus and Dr. Vibhuti Narayan Singh Rural Medical Institute Gangapur Campus, Varanasi. 229 affiliated colleges located in Varanasi, Chandauli, Sant Ravidas Nagar (Bhadohi), Mirzapur, Sonebhadra and Ballia.

History: Founded 1921 by Mahatma Gandhi. Acquired present status 1974.

Governing Bodies: Executive Council; Academic Council.

Academic Year: July to June

Admission Requirements: 12th year senior secondary/intermediate examination or recognized foreign equivalent

Fees: (Rupees): 10-100

Main Language(s) of Instruction: English and Hindi

Accrediting Agencies: UGC; NAAC

Degrees and Diplomas: *Diploma*; *Bachelor's Degree*; *Postgraduate Diploma*; *Master's Degree*; *Master of Philosophy*;

Doctorate (PhD). Also undergraduate certificates and advance diploma Courses.

Student Services: Academic counselling, Canteen, Cultural centre, Employment services, Health services, Sports facilities

Student Residential Facilities: Four hostels with a total capacity of 284 rooms.

Libraries: Dr. Bhagwandas Central Library, 234,701 vols.

Last Updated: 27/06/11

MAHATMA GANDHI UNIVERSITY (MGU)
13th Mile, G.S.Road, PO&OP - Byrnihat, PS- Nongpoh, District- Ri-Bhoi, Khanapara, Meghalaya 793101
Tel: +91 8800697050 / +91 880069705
EMail: info@mgu.edu.in
Website: http://www.mgu.edu.in/

Faculties
Applied Technology (Biotechnology; Laboratory Techniques; Medical Parasitology); **Arts** (Air Transport; Arts and Humanities; English; Hotel Management; Mass Communication; Multimedia; Tourism); **Management and Commerce** (Business and Commerce; Economic History; Finance; Management); **Sciences and Technology** (Computer Engineering; Engineering; Information Technology)

Further Information: Also Tura Campus

History: Founded 2010.

Governing Bodies: Advisory Board

Fees: (Indian Rupee): Tuition fee for Indian students, 4,000-7,000; 10,000-30,000 for International students.

Accrediting Agencies: University Grants Commission (UGC); Distance Education Council (DEC)

Degrees and Diplomas: *Diploma*; *Bachelor's Degree*; *Postgraduate Diploma*; *Master's Degree*; *Master of Philosophy*; *Doctorate*. Also certificate; M.B.A.

Last Updated: 30/08/11

MAHATMA GANDHI UNIVERSITY
(M.G. UNIVERSITY)
Priyadarsini Hills P.O., Kottayam, Kerala 686 560
Tel: +91(481) 273-1050
Fax: +91(481) 273-1002 +91(481) 273-1009
EMail: mgu@mgu.ac.in
Website: http://www.mguniversity.edu

Vice-Chancellor: Rajan Gurukkal
Tel: +91(481) 273-1001, Fax: +91(481) 273-1002
EMail: rgurukkal@gmail.com

Registrar: Sri. M.R. Unni
Tel: +91(481) 273-1007, Fax: +91(481) 273-1009
EMail: registrar@mgu.ac.in

Centres
Disability Studies *(Inter University)* (Health Sciences; Rehabilitation and Therapy; Special Education); **English Language and Communication Skills** *(CELCS)* (English); **Environmental Studies and Sustainable Development** *(Advanced - ACESSD)* (Development Studies; Environmental Studies); **High Performance Computing** *(CHPC)* (Computer Science; Software Engineering); **Nanoscience and Nanotechnology** (Nanotechnology); **Social Sciences Research and Extension** *(Inter-University)* (Archaeology; Cultural Studies; Development Studies; Gender Studies; Social Sciences; Social Welfare)

Departments
Lifelong Learning and Extension (Alternative Medicine; Farm Management; Gerontology; Health Sciences; Psychiatry and Mental Health; Psychology; Yoga)

Institutes
Intensive Research in Basic Sciences (Human Resources; Laboratory Techniques; Natural Sciences)

Schools
Behavioural Sciences (Behavioural Sciences; Nursing; Psychology; Rehabilitation and Therapy; Special Education); **Biosciences** *(SBS)* (Biochemistry; Biophysics; Biotechnology; Microbiology);

Chemical Sciences (Chemistry; Inorganic Chemistry; Organic Chemistry; Physical Chemistry; Polymer and Plastics Technology); Computer Sciences (Computer Science); Distance Education (SDE) (Business Administration; Computer Engineering; Computer Science; English; Fashion Design; Information Technology; Law; Library Science; Literature; Management; Mathematics; Multimedia; Sociology; Software Engineering; Tourism); Environmental Sciences (Environmental Management; Environmental Studies; Surveying and Mapping; Tourism; Waste Management; Water Management); Gandhian Thought and Development Studies (Development Studies; Peace and Disarmament); Indian Legal Thought (Administrative Law; Civil Law; Constitutional Law; Human Rights; Law); International Relations and Politics (SIRP) (Government; Human Rights; International Relations; Political Sciences); Letters (Cinema and Television; Comparative Literature; Literature; Modern Languages; Performing Arts; Theatre; Translation and Interpretation; Writing); Management and Business Studies (Business Administration; Finance; Human Resources; Information Technology; Management; Marketing); Pedagogical Sciences (Arabic; Business Education; Computer Education; Curriculum; Education; Educational Administration; Educational and Student Counselling; Educational Psychology; Educational Technology; English; Foreign Languages Education; Higher Education; Hindi; Humanities and Social Science Education; Mathematics Education; Pedagogy; Primary Education; Sanskrit; Science Education; Secondary Education; South and Southeast Asian Languages; Special Education; Statistics; Teacher Training); Physical Education and Sports Sciences (Physical Education; Sports); Pure and Applied Physics (Applied Physics; Astrophysics; Electronic Engineering; Materials Engineering; Physics); Social Sciences (Anthropology; Ecology; Economics; History; Social Sciences; Sociology); Tourism (Tourism)

Further Information: Also 8 satellite campuses at Pullarikkunnu, Soorya Kaladi Hills, Nattassery, Puthuppally, Gandhi Nagar and Cheruvandoor in Kottayam, Thodupuzha and Nedumkandam in Idukki Districts and Chuttippara in Pathanamthitta District. 245 affiliated colleges. 7 constitutent colleges.

History: Founded 1983 as Gandhiji University, acquired present title 1988.

Governing Bodies: Syndicate; Senate; Academic Council

Academic Year: June to March (June-September; October-December; January-March)

Admission Requirements: 12th year senior secondary/intermediate examination or recognized foreign equivalent

Fees: (Rupees): 300-600 per term for Indian students and 600-1,200 per term for international students. Ph.D., 3,000 for Indian students and 5,000 for international students.

Main Language(s) of Instruction: English

Degrees and Diplomas: *Bachelor's Degree*; *Postgraduate Diploma*; *Master's Degree*; *Master of Philosophy*; *Doctorate (PhD)*. Also undergraduate certificates, 6 months-1 year.

Student Services: Canteen, Cultural centre, Employment services, Health services, Nursery care, Social counselling, Sports facilities

Student Residential Facilities: Yes

Libraries: Central Library, 22 departmental libraries and 4 study centres: 35,000 vols, 200 periodicals; Online access to over 4,500 electronic journals and 20 various online databases.

Last Updated: 27/06/11

MAHATMA GANDHI UNIVERSITY

Nalgonda, Andhra Pradesh 508001
Tel: +91(863) 2230927
Fax: +91(863) 2237923
EMail: info@mahatmagandhicollege.com
Website: http://www.mguniversity.ac.in

Vice-Chancellor: K. Narasimha Reddy

Programmes
Applied Economics (Economics); **Business Administration** (Business Administration; Finance); **Commerce** (Business and Commerce); **English Literature** (English; Literature); **Sciences** (Biochemistry; Biotechnology; Mathematics; Organic Chemistry; Pharmacology)

History: Founded 2008.

Degrees and Diplomas: *Bachelor's Degree*; *Master's Degree*

Student Services: Health services, Sports facilities

Student Residential Facilities: Yes

Libraries: Yes

Last Updated: 22/07/11

MAHATMA JYOTI RAO PHOOLE UNIVERSITY

Ram Nagar Ext., New Sanganer Road, Sodala, Jaipur, Rajasthan 302019
Tel: +91(141) 229-4680 +91(141) 229-5101
Fax: +91(141) 229-4947
EMail: info@mjrpuniversity.com
Website: http://www.mjrpuniversity.com

Vice-Chancellor: Nirmal Panwar

Faculties
Agriculture (Agricultural Business; Agricultural Management; Agriculture; Crop Production; Farm Management; Food Technology; Horticulture; Landscape Architecture; Safety Engineering; Water Management); **Allied Health Sciences** (Health Sciences; Laboratory Techniques; Medical Technology; Public Health); **Arts** (Arts and Humanities; Economics; English; Fine Arts; History; Home Economics; Hotel and Restaurant; Political Sciences; Psychology; Public Administration; Social Sciences; Social Work; Sociology; Surveying and Mapping; Visual Arts); **Bio-Technology and Microbiology** (Biological and Life Sciences; Biotechnology; Computer Science; Microbiology); **Business and Management** (Business Administration; Economics; Health Administration; Hotel Management; Human Resources; Information Technology; International Business; Management; Marketing); **Commerce** (Business Administration; Business and Commerce; E-Business/Commerce; Economics; Finance; International Business); **Education** (Education; Educational Psychology; Special Education); **Engineering** (Agricultural Engineering; Architecture; Automotive Engineering; Biotechnology; Chemical Engineering; Civil Engineering; Computer Science; Electrical Engineering; Electronic Engineering; Engineering; Information Technology; Mechanical Engineering; Nuclear Engineering; Telecommunications Engineering); **Fashion Design Technology** (Fashion Design; Jewelry Art; Textile Design); **Film Technology** (Acting; Computer Graphics; Dance; Film; Multimedia; Photography; Radio and Television Broadcasting; Video); **Information Science and Technology** (Computer Science; Information Sciences; Information Technology); **Law** (Commercial Law; Law; Private Law); **Media** (Advertising and Publicity; Journalism; Marketing; Mass Communication; Media Studies; Printing and Printmaking; Public Relations); **Pharmacy** (Chemistry; Management; Pharmacology; Pharmacy; Safety Engineering); **Polytechnic and ITI** (Civil Engineering; Computer Science; Electrical Engineering; Engineering; Fashion Design; Information Technology; Mechanical Engineering; Mechanics; Metal Techniques); **Science** (Biochemistry; Biotechnology; Botany; Chemistry; Clinical Psychology; Computer Science; Development Studies; Dietetics; Economics; English; Environmental Studies; Geography; Home Economics; Interior Design; Mathematics; Microbiology; Nutrition; Physics; Psychology; Safety Engineering; Social Work; Statistics; Surveying and Mapping; Textile Design; Zoology); **Vedic Science and Yoga** (Alternative Medicine; Ayurveda; Esoteric Practices; Health Sciences; Yoga)

History: Founded 2009.

Accrediting Agencies: University Grants Commission (UGC)

Degrees and Diplomas: *Diploma*; *Bachelor's Degree*; *Bachelor's degree (professional)*; *Postgraduate Diploma*; *Master's Degree*; *Master of Philosophy*; *Doctorate*. Also Certificate; Honours Bachelor's and Master's degree; M.B.A. and Executive M.B.A.; Dual degrees (Bachelor/Master or MBA).

Student Residential Facilities: Separate boys and girls hostels (c. 200 beds)

Special Facilities: Laboratories (zoology, botany, microbiology, chemistry, biotechnology, computer, home science, geography, fine arts, psychology and languages); Seminar hall; Biodiversity parks, Arboretums Botanical gardens.

Libraries: Yes
Last Updated: 02/09/11

MAHATMA JYOTIBA PHULE (MJP) ROHILKHAND UNIVERSITY

Pilibhit By Pass Road, Bareilly, Uttar Pradesh 243 006
Tel: +91(581) 252-7263
Fax: +91(581) 252-4232
EMail: info@mjpru.ac.in
Website: http://www.mjpru.ac.in

Vice-Chancellor: Satya P. Gautam
Tel: +91(581) 252-7282 EMail: vcoffice@mjpru.ac.in

Registrar: Bal Krishna Pandey
Tel: +91(581) 252-7263 +91(581) 252-1122
EMail: registrar@mjpru.ac.in

Departments
Training and Placement Cell

Faculties
Advanced Social Sciences (Ancient Civilizations; Development Studies; Economics; History; Social Sciences; Women's Studies); **Agriculture** (Agriculture); **Applied Science** (Aquaculture; Biochemistry; Biotechnology; Botany; Cell Biology; Embryology and Reproduction Biology; Endocrinology; Entomology; Environmental Studies; Fishery; Genetics; Immunology; Microbiology; Molecular Biology; Parasitology; Physiology; Zoology); **Arts** (Arts and Humanities; Fine Arts); **Commerce** (Business Administration; Business and Commerce); **Dental Sciences** (Dentistry); **Education** (Education); **Education and Allied Sciences** (Clinical Psychology; Computer Science; Education; English; Journalism; Mass Communication; Philosophy; Social Sciences); **Engineering and Technology** (Arts and Humanities; Chemical Engineering; Chemistry; Computer Networks; Computer Science; Data Processing; Economics; Electrical Engineering; Electronic Engineering; Engineering; English; Information Technology; Management; Mathematics; Measurement and Precision Engineering; Mechanical Engineering; Microwaves; Pharmacy; Physics; Software Engineering; Technology); **Law** (Civil Law; Comparative Law; Human Rights; International Law; Labour and Industrial Relations; Law); **Management Studies** (Business Administration; Cooking and Catering; Hotel Management; International Business; Management; Marketing; Tourism); **Sciences** (Natural Sciences)

Further Information: Also 154 affiliated colleges.

History: Founded as M.J.P. Rohilkhand University 1975. Acquired present status and title 1997.

Academic Year: July to June

Admission Requirements: 12th year senior secondary/intermediate examination or recognized foreign equivalent

Main Language(s) of Instruction: Hindi, English

Degrees and Diplomas: *Diploma; Bachelor's Degree; Bachelor's degree (professional); Postgraduate Diploma; Master's Degree; Master of Philosophy; Doctorate (PhD)*. Also undergraduate certificates; MBA and Professional Postgraduate Courses.

Student Services: Health services, Sports facilities

Student Residential Facilities: Yes

Special Facilities: Computer Centre; Multipurpose hall. Hostel for boys and girls; Staff quarters for Vice Chancellor, other officers and faculty members.

Libraries: Central Library, c. 18,000 vols; 140 journals

Publications: I.A.S.E., Bulletin *(biannually)*; Journal of Education and Allied Sciences; Prospectus; Seminar Abstracts and Proceedings; University Magazine; University Yearbook
Last Updated: 27/06/11

MAHATMA PHULE AGRICULTURAL UNIVERSITY

Mahatma Phule Krishi Vidyapeeth (MPKV)
Ahmednagar District, Rahuri, Maharashtra 413722
Tel: +91(2426) 243-216
Fax: +91(2426) 243-302
EMail: vc.mpkv@nic.in
Website: http://mpkv.mah.nic.in

Vice-Chancellor: Tukaram A. More (2010-)

Registrar: Shri. B.H. Palwe
Tel: +91(2426) 243-216 EMail: registrar.mpkv@nic.in

Colleges
Agricultural Engineering *(Rahuri)* (Agricultural Engineering; Agricultural Equipment; Automation and Control Engineering; Electrical Engineering; Electronic Engineering; Energy Engineering; Engineering Drawing and Design; Farm Management; Irrigation; Physics; Soil Conservation; Water Management); **Agriculture** *(Dhule)* (Agriculture); **Agriculture** *(Kolhapur)* (Agriculture); **Agriculture** *(Pune)* (Agriculture; Horticulture); **Horticulture** *(Pune)* (Horticulture)

Institutes
Post-Graduate Studies *(Rahuri)* (Agriculture); **Post-Graduate Studies** *(Pune)* (Agriculture)

History: Founded 1968. An 'Agricultural University'.

Governing Bodies: Executive Council, Academic Council, Faculty council meeting, Board of Studies.

Admission Requirements: 12th year senior secondary/intermediate examination or recognized foreign equivalent

Fees: (Rupees): 10,000-20,000 per annum

Main Language(s) of Instruction: English

International Co-operation: With universities in Israel, USA, Germany. Also participates in UNDP/FAO programmes

Accrediting Agencies: Indian Council of Agricultural Research

Degrees and Diplomas: *Diploma; Bachelor's Degree; Bachelor's degree (professional); Postgraduate Diploma; Master's Degree; Doctorate (PhD)*

Student Services: Academic counselling, Canteen, Cultural centre, Employment services, Health services, Social counselling, Sports facilities

Student Residential Facilities: Yes

Special Facilities: Museum, Observatory, Auditorium

Libraries: Ruhuri Branch, 102,658 vols; c. 160 regular subscriptions.

Publications: Krishidarshani Diary, For farmers, extension workers and students *(annually)*; Shri Sugi, For farmers, extension workers and students *(weekly)*

Press or Publishing House: University Printing Press
Last Updated: 28/06/11

MAKHANLAL CHATURVEDI NATIONAL UNIVERSITY OF JOURNALISM AND COMMUNICATION

Makhanlal Chaturvedi Rashtriya Patrakarita Vishwavidhyalaya
P.O. Box No. RSN/560, Trilochan Singh Nagar, Bhopal, Madhya Pradesh 462016
Tel: +91(755) 272-5307 +91(755) 272-5559
Fax: +91(755) 256-1970
EMail: mcu.pravesh@gmail.com
Website: http://www.mcu.ac.in

Vice-Chancellor: B.K. Kuthiala
Tel: +91(755) 255-1531, Fax: +91(755) 255-3441
EMail: vc@mcu.ac.in; kuthialavc@gmail.com

Registrar: Chander Sonane
Tel: +91(755) 272-5307 EMail: registrar@mcu.ac.in

Departments
Computer Science and Applications (Computer Science); **Electronic Media** (Media Studies); **Journalism** (Journalism); **Management** (Management); **Mass Communication** (Mass Communication); **Public Relations and Advertising Studies** (Advertising and Publicity; Public Relations); **Publications** (Information Sciences; Library Science); **Research**; **Short Term Training Programmes**; **Text Book Writing** (Writing)

Further Information: Also Noida and Khandwa (Karmveer Vidhyapeeth) campuses. An Open University providing Distance Education.

History: Founded 1990.

Governing Bodies: Management Committees; Academic Council

Academic Year: August to June (August-December; January-June)

Admission Requirements: 12th year senior secondary/intermediate examination

Fees: (Rupees): 3,000-16,000 per annum

Main Language(s) of Instruction: Hindi, English

Degrees and Diplomas: *Bachelor's Degree*; *Postgraduate Diploma*; *Master's Degree*; *Doctorate (Ph.D.)*. Also MBA in Media Management.

Student Services: Cultural centre, Sports facilities

Special Facilities: Audio and video production laboratory; Computer laboratory; Printing laboratory.

Libraries: 11,206 vols, 49 journal subscriptions

Publications: Vidura, Research Journal for Journalism and Mass Communication (*quarterly*)

Last Updated: 28/06/11

MALAVIYA NATIONAL INSTITUTE OF TECHNOLOGY (MNIT)

Jawahar Lal Nehru Marg, Jaipur, Rajasthan 302017
Tel: +91(141) 252-9087
Fax: +91(141) 252-9029
EMail: info@mnit.ac.in
Website: http://www.mnit.ac.in

Director: I.K. Bhat
Tel: +91(141) 252-9087, Fax: +91(141) 252-9029
EMail: director@mnit.ac.in

Registrar: P.S. Dhaka
Tel: +91(141) 252-9,078; +91(141) 271-3204
EMail: registrar@mnit.ac.in

Departments

Architecture (Architecture); **Chemical Engineering** (Biotechnology; Chemical Engineering; Petroleum and Gas Engineering); **Chemistry** (Chemistry); **Civil Engineering** (Civil Engineering; Environmental Engineering; Hydraulic Engineering; Transport Engineering); **Computer Engineering** (Computer Engineering; Information Technology); **Electrical Engineering** (Electrical Engineering; Power Engineering); **Electronics and Communication Engineering** (Electronic Engineering; Telecommunications Engineering); **Humanities** (Arts and Humanities; Communication Studies; Economics; English; Industrial Management; Management; Social Sciences); **Management Studies** (Management); **Mathematics** (Mathematics; Statistics); **Mechanical Engineering** (Mechanical Engineering); **Metallurgical and Materials Engineering** (Materials Engineering; Metallurgical Engineering); **Physics** (Laser Engineering; Mathematical Physics; Mechanics; Nanotechnology; Nuclear Physics; Physics; Solid State Physics); **Structural Engineering** (Building Technologies; Civil Engineering; Engineering; Geological Engineering; Seismology; Structural Architecture)

History: Founded 1963 as Malaviya Regional Engineering College. Acquired present title and status 2002 (Deemed University). An 'Institute of National Importance'.

Governing Bodies: Senate; Board of Governors

Academic Year: July to August

Fees: (Rupees): tuition fee 17,500 per annum.

Degrees and Diplomas: *Bachelor's degree (professional)*; *Postgraduate Diploma*; *Master's Degree*; *Doctorate*. Also Professional Master's degree programmes and MBA.

Student Services: Canteen, Health services, Sports facilities

Student Residential Facilities: 10 hostels for boys and 3 for girls; On-campus guest houses.

Special Facilities: Computer Centre

Libraries: Central Library, 133,600 vols, periodical subscriptions; databases

Last Updated: 28/06/11

MANAGEMENT DEVELOPMENT INSTITUTE (MDI)

Mehrauli Road, GurgaonSukhrali,Gurgaon, Haryana 122 007
Website: http://www.mdi.ac.in/

Director: Mukul P. Gupta

Programmes

Energy Management (Energy Engineering; Management); **Human Resources** (Human Resources); **International Management** (International Business; Management); **Management** (Management); **Public Policy and Management** (Management; Public Administration)

History: Foundede 1973.

Governing Bodies: Board of governors

International Co-operation: With universities in Canada, U.S.A., France, Germany, Austria, Denmark, Belgium, Norway, Italy, Poland, Finland, The Netherlands, Greece, England, Thailand, Australia, New Zealand, Pakistan, China, Russia, South Africa.

Degrees and Diplomas: *Postgraduate Diploma*. Also Part-time Postgraduate programmes; Executive Fellow Programmes

Special Facilities: Computer Labs

Libraries: c. 60,000 vols

Last Updated: 23/01/12

MANAV BHARTI UNIVERSITY (MBU)

Village - Laddo, Sultanpur (Kumhar Hatti), Tehsil & Distt. Solan, Himachal Pardesh 173229
Tel: +91(1792) 268-279 +91(1792) 268-280
EMail: manavbhartiuniversity@gmail.com
Website: http://manavbhartiuniversity.edu.in/

Vice-Chancellor: S. P. Bhardwaj

Registrar: Roshan Lal

Programmes

Arts, Commerce and Science (Biochemistry; Biotechnology; Business and Commerce; Chemistry; Foreign Languages Education; Microbiology); **Ayurveda** (Ayurveda); **Computer Science** (Computer Engineering; Computer Networks; Computer Science); **Doctoral Studies** (Alternative Medicine; Ayurveda; Business and Commerce; Chemistry; Computer Science; Cooking and Catering; Engineering; Fire Science; Food Science; Hotel Management; Information Sciences; Information Technology; Library Science; Management; Medical Auxiliaries; Medical Technology; Microbiology; Nutrition; Pharmacy; Physical Therapy; Safety Engineering; Veterinary Science; Yoga); **Engineering and IT** (Biotechnology; Civil Engineering; Computer Engineering; Computer Networks; Computer Science; Construction Engineering; Electrical Engineering; Electronic Engineering; Engineering; Information Technology; Mechanical Engineering; Microelectronics; Nanotechnology; Power Engineering; Software Engineering; Structural Architecture; Telecommunications Engineering; Water Management); **Fire Safety Management** (Fire Science; Safety Engineering); **Food and Nutrition** (Food Science; Nutrition); **Hotel Management and Catering Technology** (Cooking and Catering; Food Technology; Hotel Management); **Library and Information Science** (Information Sciences; Library Science); **Management** (Business Administration; Finance; Health Administration; Hotel and Restaurant; Human Resources; Information Technology; Management; Marketing; Retailing and Wholesaling; Tourism); **Paramedical Science** (Laboratory Techniques; Medical Auxiliaries; Medical Technology); **Pharmacy** (Pharmacy); **Physiotherapy** (Neurological Therapy; Orthopaedics; Physical Therapy); **Ultrasonography** (Medical Technology); **Veterinary Science** (Animal Husbandry; Pharmacy; Veterinary Science); **Yoga and Naturopathy** (Alternative Medicine; Yoga)

History: Founded 2009.

Fees: (India Rupee): Undergraduate programmes, 20,000-30,000 per semester; Posgraduate programmes, 15,000-60,000 per semester.

Accrediting Agencies: University Grants Commission (UGC)

Degrees and Diplomas: *Diploma*; *Bachelor's Degree*; *Bachelor's degree (professional)*; *Postgraduate Diploma*; *Master's Degree*; *Doctorate*. Also M.B.A.

Student Services: Sports facilities

Student Residential Facilities: Boys and girls hostels

Special Facilities: Lecture halls; Seminar halls

Libraries: c. 20,000 vols

Last Updated: 29/08/11

MANAV RACHNA INTERNATIONAL UNIVERSITY (MRIU)

MRIU Aravalli Campus Sector, 43, Delhi Surajkund Road,
Faridabad, Haryana 121-004
Tel: +91(129) 4259-000
EMail: manager.admissions@mriu.edu.in
Website: http://info.mriu.edu.in/

Vice Chancellor: N.C. Wadhwa

Registrar: K.C. Dadhwal

Faculties

Applied Science (Dietetics; Hotel Management; Nutrition; Physical Therapy); **Business Administration and Computer Applications** *(FBC)* (Business Administration; Computer Science); **Engineering and Technology** *(FET)* (Aeronautical and Aerospace Engineering; Automotive Engineering; Biotechnology; Civil Engineering; Computer Engineering; Computer Science; Electrical Engineering; Electronic Engineering; Engineering; Information Technology; Mechanical Engineering; Technology; Telecommunications Engineering); **International Programmes** *(FIP)* (Information Technology; Interior Design; International Business); **Management Studies** *(FMS)* (Agricultural Business; Business Administration; Finance; Human Resources; Information Sciences; International Business; Management; Marketing; Real Estate; Sports); **Media Studies** (Journalism; Mass Communication; Media Studies)

Further Information: A traditional and distance education institution.

History: Founded 2008 as Career Institute of Technology & Management (CITM). Acquired 'Deemed University' status 2008.

Accrediting Agencies: All India Council for Technical Education (AICTE)

Degrees and Diplomas: *Bachelor's Degree*; *Bachelor's degree (professional)*; *Master's Degree*; *Doctorate*. Also Integrated B.Tech, 6 yrs; M.B.A.

Student Services: Canteen, Health services, Sports facilities

Student Residential Facilities: 3 hostels for boys and 2 hostels for girls

Libraries: c. 50,000 vols
Last Updated: 20/12/11

MANGALAYATAN UNIVERSITY (MU)

Extended NCR, Mathura-Aligarh Highway, 33rd Milestone, Aligarh,
Uttar Pradesh 202 145
Tel: +91(5722) 272-100
Fax: +91(5722) 254-220
EMail: admissions@mangalayatan.edu.in;
info@mangalayatan.edu.in
Website: http://mangalayatan.in

Vice Chancellor: S. C. Jain

Registrar: Manjeet Singh

Institutes

BioMedical Education and Research (Biomedicine; Biotechnology; Pharmacy); **Business Management** (Banking; Business Administration; Economics; Finance; Insurance; International Business; Management); **Computer Applications** (Computer Science); **Education and Research** (Education); **Engineering and Technology** (Chemistry; Computer Science; Electrical Engineering; Electronic Engineering; Engineering; Information Technology; Mathematics; Mechanical Engineering; Physics; Technology; Telecommunications Engineering); **Journalism and Mass Communication** (Journalism; Mass Communication); **Legal Studies and Research** (Commercial Law; Law); **Tourism and Hospitality Management** (Air Transport; Hotel Management; Tourism); **Visual and Performing Arts** (Performing Arts; Visual Arts)

History: Founded 2006.

Governing Bodies: Advisory Board; Board of Governors

Fees: (Indian Rupee): Undergraduate tuition, 25,000-115,000 per annum; Graduate tuition, 40,000-200,000 per annum

Degrees and Diplomas: *Diploma*; *Bachelor's Degree*; *Bachelor's degree (professional)*; *Postgraduate Diploma*; *Master's Degree*; *Master of Philosophy*; *Doctorate*. Also M.B.A.; Dual Degree Programme: Bachelor's degree + M.B.A./ Master's degree.
Last Updated: 22/12/11

MANGALORE UNIVERSITY

New Administrative Building, Mangalagangothri, Mangalore,
Karnataka 574 199
Tel: +91(824) 228-7276 +91(824) 228-7347
Fax: +91(824) 228-7367 +91(824) 228-7424
EMail: info@mangaloreuniversity.ac.in
Website: http://www.mangaloreuniversity.ac.in

Vice-Chancellor: T. C. Shivashankara Murthy
Tel: +91(824) 228-7347 EMail: vc@mangaloreuniversity.ac.in

Registrar: Chinnappa Gowda
Tel: +91(824) 228-7276, Fax: +91(824) 228-7424
EMail: registrar@mangaloreuniversity.ac.in

Centres

Study of Social Exclusion and Inclusive Policy *(CSEIP)* (Economics; Labour and Industrial Relations; Social Policy; Social Problems; Sociology)

Departments

Applied Botany (Biotechnology; Botany; Ecology; Microbiology; Plant and Crop Protection; Plant Pathology); **Applied Zoology** (Animal Husbandry; Biology; Cell Biology; Genetics; Molecular Biology; Nutrition; Oncology; Physiology; Toxicology; Wildlife; Zoology); **Biochemistry** (Biochemistry; Biophysics; Biotechnology; Cell Biology; Chemistry; Microbiology; Nutrition; Physiology); **Bio-Sciences** (Biochemistry; Biological and Life Sciences; Biophysics; Biotechnology; Cell Biology; Genetics; Immunology; Microbiology; Molecular Biology; Physiology); **Business Administration** (Accountancy; Behavioural Sciences; Business Administration; Economics; French; Human Resources; International Business; Management; Marketing; Tourism); **Chemistry** (Applied Chemistry; Chemistry; Inorganic Chemistry; Organic Chemistry); **Commerce** (Banking; Business and Commerce; Finance; Human Resources; Insurance; Labour Law; Marketing; Sales Techniques; Taxation); **Computer Science** (Business Computing; Computer Networks; Computer Science; Data Processing; Mathematics; Software Engineering); **Economics** (Agricultural Economics; Econometrics; Economics; International Economics); **Electronics** (Electronic Engineering); **English** (English; Literature); **Geoinformatics** (Computer Science; Data Processing; Earth Sciences; Geological Engineering; Geology; Information Sciences; Surveying and Mapping); **History** (Ancient Civilizations; Contemporary History; History; Medieval Studies; Modern History); **Human Consciousness and Yogic Sciences** (Alternative Medicine; Esoteric Practices; Health Sciences; Yoga); **Kannada** (Linguistics; Literature; South and Southeast Asian Languages); **Library information science** (Information Sciences; Information Technology; Library Science); **Marine Geology** (Earth Sciences; Geochemistry; Geology; Geophysics; Information Sciences; Marine Science and Oceanography; Mineralogy; Natural Resources; Paleontology; Surveying and Mapping); **Mass Communication and Journalism** (Advertising and Publicity; Communication Studies; Film; Journalism; Marketing; Mass Communication; Media Studies; Printing and Printmaking; Radio and Television Broadcasting; Writing); **Materials Science** (Materials Engineering; Physical Chemistry; Polymer and Plastics Technology; Solid State Physics); **Mathematics** (Mathematics); **Microbiology** (Biochemistry; Biophysics; Biotechnology; Genetics; Microbiology; Molecular Biology); **Physical Education** (Physical Education; Physical Therapy; Physiology; Psychology; Rehabilitation and Therapy; Sports; Sports Management); **Physics** (Electronic Engineering; Mechanics; Nuclear Engineering; Nuclear Physics; Physics; Solid State Physics); **Political Science** (Comparative Politics; International Relations; Political Sciences; Regional Studies; Sociology); **Social Work** (Human Resources; Social and Community Services; Social Work; Welfare and Protective Services); **Sociology** (Development Studies; Labour and Industrial Relations; Social Studies; Sociology; Statistics; Women's Studies); **Statistics** (Statistics)

Further Information: Also 187 affiliated colleges/institutions (including 2 constituent colleges, 4 law colleges, 18 education colleges and 5 autonomous colleges).

History: Founded 1980.

Governing Bodies: Syndicate; Academic Council

Academic Year: June to March (June-September; November-March)

Admission Requirements: 12th year senior secondary/intermediate examination or recognized foreign equivalent

Fees: (Rupees): Postgraduate tuition fee, 3,400 per annum; MBA, 30,000-80,000 per annum; Ph.D., 2,600 per term (6 months).

Main Language(s) of Instruction: English

Accrediting Agencies: National Assessment and Accreditation Council

Degrees and Diplomas: *Bachelor's Degree*; *Postgraduate Diploma*; *Master's Degree*; *Master of Philosophy*; *Doctorate (PhD)*. Also undergraduate certificate.

Student Services: Academic counselling, Canteen, Cultural centre, Employment services, Foreign student adviser, Handicapped facilities, Health services, Nursery care, Sports facilities

Student Residential Facilities: Hostels for Men and Women.

Special Facilities: Computer Centre; University Science Instrumentation Centre (USIC); Microtron Cnetre (variable energy accelerator); MANGALA Auditorium; Cyber Lab

Libraries: 192,598 vols; Online databases; Bibliographic databases; Open access resources.

Last Updated: 28/06/11

MANIPAL UNIVERSITY

Madhav Nagar, Udupi District, Manipal, Karnataka 576119
Tel: +91(820) 257-1201
Fax: +91(825) 257-0062
EMail: office.mahe@manipal.edu; vc.mahe@manipal.edu
Website: http://www.manipal.edu

Chancellor: Ramdas M. Pai
Tel: +91(820) 292-2,463; +91(820) 292-2350
EMail: chancellor@manipal.edu

Vice-Chancellor: K. Ramnarayan (2010-)
Tel: +91(820) 292-2,615; +91(820) 257-1975
EMail: vicechancellor@manipal.edu

Registrar: G. K. Prabhu
Tel: +91(820) 292-2,323; +91(820) 257-1300
EMail: reg.mahe@manipal.edu

Academies

Banking and Insurance *(ICICI Manipal - IMA)* (Banking; Business Administration; Finance; Insurance)

Campuses

Bangalore *(MU Bangalore)* (Advertising and Publicity; Communication Arts; Communication Studies; Graphic Design; Journalism; Management; Media Studies; Visual Arts); **Dubai** *(MU Dubai)* (Automation and Control Engineering; Biotechnology; Business Administration; Civil Engineering; Communication Studies; Computer Engineering; Computer Science; Electronic Engineering; Fashion Design; Forensic Medicine and Dentistry; Genetics; Graphic Design; Information Management; Information Sciences; Information Technology; Interior Design; Management; Marketing; Measurement and Precision Engineering; Mechanical Engineering; Media Studies; Multimedia)

Centres

Applied Sciences *(International - ICAS)* (Aeronautical and Aerospace Engineering; Architecture; Biomedical Engineering; Biotechnology; Chemical Engineering; Civil Engineering; Computer Engineering; Electrical and Electronic Engineering; Electrical Engineering; Electronic Engineering; Industrial Engineering; Mechanical Engineering; Telecommunications Engineering); **Atomic and Molecular Physics** *(CAMP)* (Atomic and Molecular Physics; Physics); **European Studies** *(MCES)* (European Studies; Management; Peace and Disarmament; Public Health); **Information Science** *(MCIS Manipal)* (Information Management; Information Sciences; Information Technology; Software Engineering); **KMC International** *(KMCIC)* (Health Sciences); **Life Sciences** *(MLSC Manipal)* (Biological and Life Sciences; Biotechnology; Genetics; Medical Technology; Molecular Biology); **Philosophy and Humanities** *(MCPH Manipal)* (Arts and Humanities; Philosophy); **Virus Research** (Virology)

Colleges

Allied Health Sciences *(AHS, Mangalore)* (Health Sciences; Physical Therapy; Rehabilitation and Therapy; Speech Therapy and Audiology); **Allied Health Sciences** *(Manipal - MCOAHS)* (Cardiology; Clinical Psychology; Health Administration; Health Sciences; Laboratory Techniques; Medical Technology; Medicine; Occupational Therapy; Oncology; Optometry; Physical Therapy; Radiology; Rehabilitation and Therapy; Respiratory Therapy; Speech Therapy and Audiology); **Allied Health Sciences** *(AHS, Bangalore)* (Health Sciences; Physical Therapy; Rehabilitation and Therapy); **Dental Sciences** *(Manipal - MCODS)* (Dental Hygiene; Dental Technology; Dentistry; Oral Pathology; Orthodontics; Periodontics; Social and Preventive Medicine; Surgery); **Dental Sciences, Mangalore** *(MCODS Mangalore)* (Dental Technology; Dentistry; Oral Pathology; Orthodontics; Periodontics; Public Health; Radiology; Surgery); **Medicine** *(Kasturba - KMC Mangalore)* (Anaesthesiology; Anatomy; Biochemistry; Community Health; Dermatology; Forensic Medicine and Dentistry; Gynaecology and Obstetrics; Medicine; Microbiology; Oncology; Ophthalmology; Otorhinolaryngology; Paediatrics; Pathology; Pharmacology; Physical Education; Physical Engineering; Physiology; Pneumology; Psychiatry and Mental Health; Radiology; Surgery); **Medicine** *(Manipal - MMMC Melaka)* (Anatomy; Biochemistry; Community Health; Dentistry; Medicine; Microbiology; Paediatrics; Pathology; Pharmacy; Physiology); **Medicine** *(Melaka - MMMC Manipal)* (Anatomy; Biochemistry; Medicine; Microbiology; Pathology; Pharmacy; Physiology); **Medicine** *(Kasturba - KMC Manipal)* (Alternative Medicine; Anaesthesiology; Anatomy; Ayurveda; Biochemistry; Cardiology; Clinical Psychology; Community Health; Dermatology; Embryology and Reproduction Biology; Forensic Medicine and Dentistry; Gastroenterology; Gynaecology and Obstetrics; Health Administration; Health Education; Medicine; Microbiology; Nephrology; Neurological Therapy; Neurology; Oncology; Ophthalmology; Orthopaedics; Otorhinolaryngology; Paediatrics; Pathology; Pharmacology; Physical Therapy; Physiology; Plant Pathology; Pneumology; Psychiatry and Mental Health; Radiology; Surgery; Urology; Yoga); **Nursing** *(MCON Manipal)* (Child Care and Development; Gynaecology and Obstetrics; Health Sciences; Midwifery; Nursing; Psychiatry and Mental Health; Surgery); **Nursing** *(MCON Bangalore)* (Nursing); **Nursing** *(MCON Mangalore)* (Nursing); **Pharmaceutical Sciences** *(MCOPS)* (Biotechnology; Management; Pharmacology; Pharmacy; Safety Engineering)

Departments

Advanced Pharmaceutical Sciences (Pharmacy); **Commerce** (Banking; Business and Commerce; Finance); **Geopolitics and International Relations** (International Relations); **Public Health** (Epidemiology; Health Administration; Public Health; Social Work); **Sciences** (Applied Mathematics; Mathematics and Computer Science; Organic Chemistry; Physics); **Statistics** (Statistics)

Graduate Schools

Hotel Administration *(Welcomgroup - WGSHA Manipal)* (Cooking and Catering; Dietetics; Hotel and Restaurant; Hotel Management; Nutrition; Tourism)

Institutes

Advertising and Communication (Advertising and Publicity; Communication Studies; Marketing); **Communication** *(Manipal - MIC)* (Communication Studies; Journalism); **Jewellery Management** *(MIJM Manipal)* (Jewelry Art; Management); **Management** *(MIM Manipal)* (Business Administration; Management); **Regenerative Medicine** *(MIRM Bangalore)* (Medicine; Rehabilitation and Therapy); **Technology** *(MIT Manipal)* (Aeronautical and Aerospace Engineering; Automation and Control Engineering; Automotive Engineering; Biomedical Engineering; Biotechnology; Civil Engineering; Computer Engineering; Computer Graphics; Computer Networks; Computer Science; Electrical and Electronic Engineering; Electronic Engineering; Engineering; Information Technology; Measurement and Precision Engineering; Mechanical Engineering; Media Studies; Printing and Printmaking; Production Engineering; Software Engineering; Telecommunications Engineering)

Programmes

Animation (Visual Arts); **Corporate Studies** (Automation and Control Engineering; Automotive Engineering; Business Administration; Computer Graphics; Computer Networks; Computer Science; Electronic Engineering; Engineering Drawing and Design; Finance; Human Resources; Information Sciences; Management; Marketing; Software Engineering; Telecommunications Engineering); **Media and Entertainment** (Computer Graphics; Media Studies; Public Relations; Radio and Television Broadcasting; Visual Arts)

Schools

Architecture and Planning *(Manipal - MSAP)* (Architecture; Architecture and Planning; Fashion Design; Interior Design; Safety Engineering)

Further Information: Also branch campuses in Bangalore, Malaysia, Dubai and Antigua in the Caribbean Island. Campus in Mangalore. 20 constituent institutions and 4 teaching hospitals.

History: First College founded 1953. Acquired 'Deemed University' status 1993. Previously known as Manipal Academy of Higher Education (MAFE).

Governing Bodies: Board of Management; Executive Committee

Academic Year: August to July

Admission Requirements: 12th year senior secondary intermediate examination

Fees: (Rupees): Certificate courses, 15,000-375,000 for Indian students and 3,900-36,150 per annum for foreign students; Undergraduate fees, 25,000-562,000 per annum; Graduate fees, 29,000-930,000 per annum for Indian students and 700-43,650 per annum for foreign/NRI students; PG Diploma, 26,000-676,000 per annum.

Main Language(s) of Instruction: English

International Co-operation: With universities in the US, UK, Australia.

Accrediting Agencies: Medical Council of India; Dental Council of India; Pharmacy Council of India; All India Council for Technical Education

Degrees and Diplomas: *Bachelor's Degree*; *Bachelor's degree (professional)*; *Postgraduate Diploma*; *Master's Degree*; *Master of Philosophy*; *Doctorate.* Also undergraduate certificates; MBA.

Student Services: Academic counselling, Canteen, Cultural centre, Health services, Nursery care, Sports facilities

Student Residential Facilities: Yes

Special Facilities: Anatomy Museum; Pathology Museum; Civil/Architecture Museum; Planetarium; Science Centre; Simulation lab.

Libraries: c. 62,000 vols; 600 journals; Medline; Proquest medical library; Online databases; Audio-visual resources; Cochrane library; E-learning, computer and Internet services

Publications: British Journal of Ophthalmology, South Asia Edition *(bimonthly)*; British Medical Journal, South Asia Edition *(monthly)*; Paediatrics *(bimonthly)*

Press or Publishing House: Manipal Press Ltd

Academic Staff *2009-2010*	TOTAL
FULL-TIME	2,400

Student Numbers *2009-2010*	
All (Foreign Included)	20,000
FOREIGN ONLY	2,200

Last Updated: 29/06/11

MANIPUR UNIVERSITY

Canchipur, Imphal, Manipur 795003
Tel: +91(385) 243-5276 +91(385) 243-55055
Fax: +91(385) 243-5145
EMail: vcmu@sancharnet.in
Website: http://manipuruniv.ac.in

Acting Vice-Chancellor: Hidangmayum Nandakumar Sarma
Tel: +91(385) 243-5878

Registrar: N. Lokendra Singh
Tel: +91(385) 243-5125 +91(385) 243-5831,
Fax: +91(385) 243-5145 EMail: lokendra_n@rediffmail.com

Centres

Computer Science (Computer Science); **Gandhian Studies** (Philosophy; Political Sciences); **Manipur Studies** (Cultural Studies; Regional Studies); **Myanmar Studies** (South and Southeast Asian Languages); **Social Exclusion and Inclusive Policy** (Social Policy; Social Problems)

Research Centres

Educational Multimedia (Educational Technology; Multimedia)

Schools

Human and Environmental Science (Anthropology; Archaeology; Earth Sciences; Environmental Studies; Geochemistry; Geography;

Geography (Human); Geology; Paleontology; Petroleum and Gas Engineering; Physical Education; Sports; Surveying and Mapping); **Humanities** (Applied Linguistics; Arts and Humanities; Cultural Studies; Dance; English; Folklore; Hindi; Linguistics; Literature; Musical Instruments; Philosophy); **Life Sciences** (Biochemistry; Biological and Life Sciences; Biotechnology); **Mathematical and Physical Sciences** (Artificial Intelligence; Astrophysics; Chemistry; Computer Graphics; Computer Networks; Computer Science; Data Processing; Demography and Population; Inorganic Chemistry; Materials Engineering; Mathematics; Mechanics; Nuclear Engineering; Nuclear Physics; Organic Chemistry; Physical Chemistry; Physics; Software Engineering; Solid State Physics; Statistics); **Medical Sciences** (Medicine); **Social Sciences** (Accountancy; Adult Education; Agricultural Economics; Ancient Civilizations; Archaeology; Business and Commerce; Business Computing; Continuing Education; Econometrics; Economics; Education; Educational Administration; Finance; History; Human Resources; Information Management; Information Sciences; Insurance; International Economics; International Relations; Library Science; Management; Marketing; Mass Communication; Medieval Studies; Modern History; Political Sciences; Public Administration; Regional Studies; Social Sciences; Sociology)

Further Information: Also 72 affiliated colleges and one constituent college i.e. Manipur Institute of Technology (MIT).

History: Founded 1980 under Act of Manipur State Legislative Assembly. Acquired present title 2005. Formely Jawaharlal Nehru University Centre of Postgraduate Studies at Imphal, the University is today an Affiliating University.

Governing Bodies: Court; Executive Council; Academic Council; College Development Council; School Boards; Finance Committee

Academic Year: September to August

Admission Requirements: Graduate degree or recognized foreign equivalent

Fees: (Rupees): 1,890 per annum

Main Language(s) of Instruction: English

Accrediting Agencies: National Assessment and Accreditation Council

Degrees and Diplomas: *Bachelor's Degree*; *Bachelor's degree (professional)*; *Postgraduate Diploma*; *Master's Degree*; *Master of Philosophy*; *Doctorate.* Also Also Bachelor's degree Honours; Undegraduate certificate.

Student Services: Academic counselling, Canteen, Cultural centre, Employment services, Health services, Sports facilities

Student Residential Facilities: For 168 Men and 156 Women students

Special Facilities: Main Museum; Anthropology Museum; Earth Sciences Museum. Collections of paintings, sculptures, coins, textiles, jewellery, Manipuri folk musical instruments, weaving instruments, etc., illustrating ancient culture of India and more specifically of Manipur. Language Laboratory. Amateur Astronomical Society

Libraries: Main Library, 120,955 vols, 254 periodical subscriptions; 250 maps

Academic Staff *2009-2010*	MEN	WOMEN	TOTAL
FULL-TIME	–	–	120
STAFF WITH DOCTORATE			
FULL-TIME	–	–	100
PART-TIME	–	–	30
Student Numbers *2009-2010*			
All (Foreign Included)	1,100	1,100	2,200

Last Updated: 29/06/11

MANONMANIAM SUNDARANAR UNIVERSITY (MSU)

University Building, Abishekapatti, Tirunelveli, Tamil Nadu 627012
Tel: +91 9487999687 +91 9487999688
EMail: info@msuniv.ac.in
Website: http://www.msuniv.ac.in

Vice-Chancellor: R.T. Sabapathy Mohan
Tel: +91 9487999651 EMail: vc@msuniv.ac.in

Registrar: S. Manickam
Tel: +91 9487999602 EMail: registrar@msuniv.ac.in

Centres

Marine Science and Technology (Aquaculture; Biological and Life Sciences; Biotechnology; Marine Engineering; Marine Science and Oceanography; Microbiology)

Departments

Biotechnology (Biotechnology); **Chemistry** (Chemistry); **Commerce** (Business and Commerce); **Communication** (Advertising and Publicity; Communication Studies; Film; Journalism; Media Studies; Radio and Television Broadcasting); **Computer Science and Engineering** (Computer Engineering; Computer Science); **Criminology and Criminal Justice** (Criminal Law; Criminology); **Economics** (Business Administration; Economics); **Education** (Education); **English** (Comparative Literature; Cultural Studies; English; Literature; Media Studies; Theatre; Translation and Interpretation); **Environmental Science** (Biotechnology; Environmental Studies); **Geotechnology** (Geology; Geophysics; Marine Science and Oceanography); **Hindi** (Hindi); **History** (History); **Information Technology and Engineering** (Computer Engineering; Computer Networks; Computer Science; E-Business/Commerce; Information Technology; Mathematics and Computer Science); **Management Studies** (Finance; Human Resources; Management; Marketing); **Mathematics** (Mathematics); **Nanobiotechnology** (Biotechnology; Nanotechnology); **Pharmaceutical Chemistry** (Biochemistry; Chemistry; Molecular Biology; Organic Chemistry; Pharmacology; Pharmacy; Physical Chemistry; Statistics); **Physical Education and Sports** (Physical Education; Sports); **Physics** (Physics); **Psychology** (Psychology); **Social Exclusion and Inclusive Policy** (Social Policy; Social Problems); **Sociology** (Sociology); **Statistics** (Computer Science; Data Processing; Statistics); **Tamil** (South and Southeast Asian Languages)

Further Information: Also 61 affiliated colleges, 5 Mano colleges and 1 constituent college. Also distance education.

History: Founded 1990.

Governing Bodies: Syndicate, Senate and Standing Committee on Academic Affairs

Academic Year: July to April (July-November; December-April)

Admission Requirements: Secondary school certificate

Fees: (Rupees): 1,000-20,000 per semester; M.B.A., 12,500 per semester.

Main Language(s) of Instruction: Tamil, English

Accrediting Agencies: University Grants Commission; Association of Indian Universities

Degrees and Diplomas: *Bachelor's Degree*; *Postgraduate Diploma*; *Master's Degree*; *Master of Philosophy*; *Doctorate (PhD)*. Also MBA; Undergraduate certificate

Student Services: Academic counselling, Canteen, Sports facilities

Libraries: 94,021 vols; 144 periodical subscriptions

Publications: Mano International Journal of Mathematical Sciences *(quarterly)*

Last Updated: 29/06/11

MANYAVAR SRI KANSHI RAM JI URDU, ARABI-FARSI UNIVERSITY (MKUAFU)

Sitapur-Hardoi Road bypass, Near IIM, Lucknow 226 020
Tel: +91(522) 228-8904 +91(522) 228-8907
Fax: +91(522) 228-8904
EMail: upuafulucknow@gmail.com
Website: http://www.mkuafu.ac.in/

Vice Chancellor: Anis Ansari (2010-)

Courses

Ancient Indian History and Archaeology (Ancient Civilizations; Archaeology); **Business and Commerce** (Business and Commerce); **Education** (Education); **English** (English); **Geography** (Geography); **Hindi** (Hindi); **Home Science** (Home Economics); **Persian** (Persian); **Physical Education** (Physical Education); **Political Science** (Political Sciences); **Tourism and Travel Management** (Tourism; Transport Management)

Institutes

Mass Communication in Science and Technology (Mass Communication)

History: Founded 2010.

Governing Bodies: Academic Council; Executive Council; Finance Committee

Degrees and Diplomas: *Bachelor's Degree*; *Master's Degree*. Also M.B.A.

Last Updated: 05/01/12

MARATHWADA AGRICULTURAL UNIVERSITY

Marathwada Krishi Vidyapeeth (MAU)
PO Krishinagar, Parbhani, Maharashtra 431402
Tel: +91(2452) 223-801
Fax: +91(2452) 223-582
EMail: vcmau@rediffmail.com
Website: http://mkv2.mah.nic.in

Vice-Chancellor: K.P. Gore

Registrar: B.B. Bhosale

Colleges

Agricultural Biotechnology *(Latur)* (Agriculture; Agrobiology; Biotechnology); **Agricultural Engineering** *(Parbhani)* (Agricultural Engineering); **Agriculture** *(Parbhani)* (Agriculture); **Agriculture** *(Ambajogai)* (Agriculture); **Agriculture** *(Osmanabad)* (Agriculture); **Agriculture** *(Badnapur)* (Agriculture); **Agriculture** *(Latur)* (Agriculture); **Food Technology** *(Parbhani)* (Food Technology); **Home Science** *(Parbhani)* (Home Economics); **Horticulture** (Horticulture)

Further Information: Also 8 Constituent Colleges

History: Founded 1972.

Governing Bodies: Maharashtra Council of Agricultural Education and Research

Academic Year: July to May (July-December; January-May)

Admission Requirements: 12th year senior secondary/intermediate examination or recognized foreign equivalent

Fees: (Rupees): 2,600-6,000 per annum

Main Language(s) of Instruction: English

Degrees and Diplomas: *Bachelor's Degree*; *Bachelor's degree (professional)*; *Master's Degree*; *Doctorate (PhD)*

Libraries: 66,882 vols; 290 periodical subscriptions

Press or Publishing House: Marathwada Agriculture University Printing Press

Last Updated: 29/06/11

MARTIN LUTHER CHRISTIAN UNIVERSITY (MLCU)

KJPA Conference Centre, Central Ward, Shillong, Meghalya 793001
Tel: 9206040427
Fax: +91(364) 250-64890
EMail: admin@mlcuniv.in; registrar@mlcuniv.in
Website: http://www.mlcuniv.in

Vice-Chancellor: G.C. Kharkongor EMail: vc@mlcuniv.in

Registrar: E.H. Kharkongor EMail: registrar@mlcuniv.in

Campuses

Nongtalang (Computer Science; Information Sciences); **Rymbai** (Computer Science); **Shillong** (Business Administration; Community Health; Dietetics; Fine Arts; Health Sciences; Information Technology; Medical Technology; Microbiology; Music; Nutrition; Optometry; Peace and Disarmament; Psychology; Social Work; Tourism); **Tura** (Business Administration; Computer Science; Information Sciences; Management; Social Work)

History: Founded 2005.

Governing Bodies: Board of Governors

Fees: (Rupee): Tuition fees for undergraduate tuition fees, 6,000-15,000 per semester; For postgraduate programmes, 10,000-30,000 per semester; Ph.D. 7,500-15,000 over three years.

Accrediting Agencies: University Grants Commission (UGC)

Degrees and Diplomas: *Bachelor's Degree*; *Postgraduate Diploma*; *Master's Degree*; *Doctorate*

Student Residential Facilities: Hostel for girls.

Last Updated: 30/06/11

MATS UNIVERSITY

Aarang Kharora Highway, Aarang, Raipur 493 441
Tel: +91(771) 407-8994 +91(771) 407-8995
Fax: +91(771) 407-8997
EMail: info@matsuniversity.ac.in
Website: http://www.matsuniversity.ac.in

Vice-Chancellor: Kanwal Singh

Registrar: A.K. Shukla

Research Centres

Research and Development Cell (Analytical Chemistry; Biological and Life Sciences; Biotechnology; Data Processing; Genetics; Molecular Biology; Organic Chemistry)

Schools

Basic Sciences (Botany; Chemistry; Energy Engineering; Environmental Engineering; Materials Engineering; Mathematics; Mathematics and Computer Science; Nanotechnology; Physics; Software Engineering); **Business Studies** (Accountancy; Banking; Business Administration; Business and Commerce; Business Computing; Finance; Insurance); **Education** (Education; Educational and Student Counselling; Educational Psychology); **Engineering and Technology** (Aeronautical and Aerospace Engineering; Civil Engineering; Computer Engineering; Computer Science; Electronic Engineering; Engineering; Information Technology; Technology; Telecommunications Engineering); **Fashion Designing** (Fashion Design; Textile Technology); **Humanities and Social Sciences** (Arts and Humanities; English; Hindi; Social Sciences); **Information Technology** (Computer Science; Information Technology); **Law** (Arabic; Chinese; English; European Union Law; French; Law; Russian); **Life Sciences** (Biochemistry; Biological and Life Sciences; Biotechnology; Microbiology); **Management Studies and Research** (Business Administration; Finance; Human Resources; Information Technology; Management; Marketing)

Further Information: Also distance education.

History: Founded 2006.

Governing Bodies: Governing Body; Board of Management; Academic Council; Board of Studies.

Admission Requirements: 10 + 2 or any equivalent examination from a recognized board for undergraduate programmes; Graduate or equivalent examination from a recognized university for graduate programmes.

Accrediting Agencies: University Grants Commission (UGC); All India Council for Technical Education (AICTE); National Council fro Teacher Education (NCTE); Bar Council of India (BCI); American University Accreditation Council (AUAC).

Degrees and Diplomas: *Bachelor's Degree*; *Postgraduate Diploma*; *Master's Degree*; *Master of Philosophy*; *Doctorate (Ph.D.)*. Also MBA and undergraduate certificate.

Student Services: Sports facilities

Student Residential Facilities: Separate Hostels for Boys (100 beds) and Girls (350 beds).

Libraries: Yes
Last Updated: 30/06/11

MAULANA AZAD NATIONAL INSTITUTE OF TECHNOLOGY (MANIT)

Bhopal, Madhya Pradesh 462051
Tel: +91(755) 405-1000 +91(755) 405-2000 +91(755) 520-6006
Fax: +91(755) 267-0562 +91(755) 267-0802
EMail: info@manit.ac.in
Website: http://www.manit.ac.in

Director: R.P. Singh
Tel: +91(755) 405-1001
EMail: prof.rpsingh@gmail.com; singhrp@manit.ac.in; director@manit.ac.in

Registrar: Savita Raje
Tel: +91(755) 267-0416, Fax: +91(755) 267-0562
EMail: savita_raje@manit.ac.in

Departments

Applied Mechanics (Materials Engineering; Mechanics); **Architecture aard Planning** (Architecture and Planning); **Bio-Infor**matics (Computer Science; Molecular Biology; Statistics); **Chemical Engineering** (Chemical Engineering); **Chemistry** (Analytical Chemistry; Chemistry); **Civil Engineering** (Civil Engineering; Construction Engineering; Environmental Engineering; Geological Engineering; Hydraulic Engineering); **Computer Applications** (Computer Science; Information Technology); **Computer Science and Engineering** (Computer Engineering; Computer Science); **Electrical Engineering** (Electrical Engineering; Power Engineering); **Electronics and Communication Engineering** (Electronic Engineering; Microwaves; Telecommunications Engineering); **Energy** (Energy Engineering); **Humanities** (Arts and Humanities; Social Sciences); **Information Technology** (Information Technology); **Management Studies** (Advertising and Publicity; Business Administration; International Business; Management; Marketing); **Material Science and Metallurgical Engineering** (Materials Engineering; Metallurgical Engineering); **Mathematics** (Mathematics; Mathematics and Computer Science); **Mechanical Engineering** (Industrial Design; Maintenance Technology; Mechanical Engineering; Thermal Engineering); **Physical Education** (Physical Education; Sports); **Physics** (Nanotechnology; Physics); **Production and Industrial Engineering** (Industrial Engineering; Production Engineering)

History: Founded 1960 as Maulana Azad College of Technology (MACT). Acquired present status and title 2002. An 'Institute of National Importance'.

Governing Bodies: Board of Governors

Admission Requirements: Secondary school certificate and entrance examination

Fees: (Rupees): Tuition fee, 25,500-35,500 per annum; Ph.D., 15,000 per annum.

Degrees and Diplomas: *Bachelor's Degree (B.Eng.)*: 4 ys; *Bachelor's degree (professional)*; *Master's Degree*; *Doctorate (Ph.D.)*

Student Services: Canteen, Employment services, Sports facilities

Student Residential Facilities: 5 hostels for boys (1,200 beds), 1 hostel for girls (200 beds).

Special Facilities: Computer center; Auditorium; Energy Centre

Libraries: 95,883 vols; 522 CD-Roms; 398 videos

Academic Staff *2010-2011*: Total: c. 200
Student Numbers *2010-2011*: Total: c. 4,000
Last Updated: 30/06/11

MAULANA AZAD NATIONAL URDU UNIVERSITY

Gachibowli, Hyderabad, Andhra Pradesh 500032
Tel: +91(40) 2300-6602
Fax: +91(40) 2300-6603
EMail: registrar@manuu.ac.in
Website: http://www.manuu.ac.in

Vice-Chancellor: Mohammad Miyan (2010-)
Tel: +91(40) 2300-6612, Fax: +91(40) 2300-8366
EMail: secretarytovc@manuu.ac.in

Registrar: H. Khatija Begum Tel: +91(40) 2300-6121

Centres

Instructional Media *(IMC)* (Journalism; Mass Communication; Video); **Professional Development of Urdu Medium Teachers** (Native Language Education; Teacher Training); **Study of Social Exclusion and Inclusive Policy** *(CSSEIP)* (Social Policy; Social Problems); **Urdu Language, Literature and Culture** (Cultural Studies; Literature; Urdu); **Women's Studies** (Women's Studies)

Colleges

Academic Staff; **Teacher Education** (Education; Teacher Training)

Courses

Polytechnic *(Hyderabad)* (Civil Engineering; Computer Engineering; Computer Science; Electronic Engineering; Information Technology; Telecommunications Engineering); **Polytechnic** *(Bangalore)* (Civil Engineering; Computer Engineering; Electronic Engineering; Telecommunications Engineering); **Polytechnic**

(Darbhanga) (Civil Engineering; Computer Engineering; Electrical Engineering; Telecommunications Engineering)

Departments

Distance Education (Business and Commerce; Education; English; Food Science; Hindi; History; Journalism; Mass Communication; Museum Studies; Nutrition; Tourism; Urdu); **Women's Education** (Women's Studies)

Schools

Arts and Social Sciences (Arts and Humanities; Political Sciences; Public Administration; Social Sciences; Social Work; Sociology); **Commerce and Business Management** (Business Administration; Business and Commerce; Management); **Education and Training** (Education); **Languages, Linguistics and Indology** (Arabic; Comparative Literature; English; Hindi; Linguistics; Literature; Modern Languages; Persian; Translation and Interpretation; Urdu); **Mass Communication and Journalism** (Advertising and Publicity; Film; Journalism; Mass Communication; Media Studies; Public Relations); **Sciences** (Computer Science; Data Processing; Information Technology; Multimedia; Software Engineering)

Further Information: Education under distance and campus modes; Model schools in Hyderabad and Darbhanga.

History: Founded 1998. A 'Central University'.

Governing Bodies: Executive Council; Academic Council; Finance Committee.

Admission Requirements: 12th year senior secondary/intermediate examination or recognized equivalent and entrance examination

Fees: (Rupees): tuition fee, 300-900 per semester; MBA, 4,500-8,300 per semester.

Main Language(s) of Instruction: Urdu

Accrediting Agencies: National Assessment and Accreditation Council (NAAC).

Degrees and Diplomas: *Diploma*; *Bachelor's Degree*; *Postgraduate Diploma*; *Master's Degree*; *Master of Philosophy*; *Doctorate (Ph.D.)*. Also MBA and undergraduate certificate.

Libraries: Central Library, 32,498 vols; 179 Journals (and 733 back volumes); 389 Audio and Video CDs; 13 Newspapers (5 Urdu, 5 English, 2 Hindi and 1 Telugu); 17 General Magazines; 72 Audio Cassettes; 2 Video Cassettes.

Last Updated: 30/06/11

MAULANA MAZHARUL HAQUE ARABIC AND PERSIAN UNIVERSITY (MMHAPU)

5, Bailey Road, Patna 800 001
Tel: +91(612) 645-6010
Fax: +91(612) 250-5040 +91(612) 250-4357
EMail: mmhapupatna@yahoo.in
Website: http://mmhapu.bih.nic.in/

Vice Chancellor: Md. Shamsuzzoha (2011-)
EMail: vc-mmhu-bih@nic.in

Registrar: M. G. Mustafa EMail: registrar-mmhu-bih@nic.in

Schools

Knowledge Management and Media Studies *(Abudul Qayum Ansari)* (Journalism; Library Science; Mass Communication; Media Studies); **Management and Information** *(Justice Sarwar Ali)* (Business Administration; Information Sciences; Management); **Social Works and Rural Development** *(Prof. Abdul Bari)* (Accountancy; Social Work); **Sufism Oriental Languages History and Culture** *(Makhdoom Sharfuddin Yahya Maneri)* (Ancient Books; Arabic; Cultural Studies; History; Library Science; Oriental Languages; Persian)

History: Founded 1998. Started its first academic session 2008.

Fees: (Indian Rupees): Undergraduate Certificate and Diplomas, 2,500-6,500 per course; Undergraduate Degree Courses, 5,500-8,500 per annum; M.B.A., 1,7,500-2,350 per semester

Degrees and Diplomas: *Diploma*; *Bachelor's Degree*. Also Certificate Courses; M.B.A.

Student Numbers 2010-2011: Total: c. 14,000
Last Updated: 03/01/12

MEENAKSHI ACADEMY OF HIGHER EDUCATION AND RESEARCH (MEENAKSHI UNIVERSITY) (MAHER)

No. 12, Vembuli Amman Koil Street, West K.K. Nagar, Chennai, Tamil Nadu 600 078
Tel: +91(44) 236-43955 +91(44) 23643956
Fax: +91(44) 236-43958
EMail: info@maher.ac.in
Website: http://www.maher.ac.in

Vice-Chancellor: P. Jayakumar

Registrar: A.N. Santhanam

Colleges

Dental Studies *(Meenakshi Ammal)* (Dental Technology; Dentistry; Oral Pathology; Periodontics; Radiology; Surgery); **Medicine** *(Meenakshi Ammal)* (Anaesthesiology; Anatomy; Biochemistry; Community Health; Dermatology; Forensic Medicine and Dentistry; Gastroenterology; Gynaecology and Obstetrics; Medicine; Microbiology; Ophthalmology; Orthopaedics; Paediatrics; Pathology; Pharmacology; Physiology; Psychiatry and Mental Health; Radiology; Respiratory Therapy; Surgery; Urology; Venereology); **Nursing** *(Meenakshi)* (Community Health; Gynaecology and Obstetrics; Nursing; Paediatrics; Psychiatry and Mental Health); **Nursing** *(Arulmigu Meenakshi)* (Nursing); **Physiotherapy** *(Meenakshi)* (Cardiology; Dietetics; Gerontology; Health Sciences; Neurological Therapy; Neurology; Nutrition; Orthopaedics; Paediatrics; Physical Therapy; Respiratory Therapy; Speech Therapy and Audiology; Sports Medicine)

Faculties

Engineering and Technology (Business Administration; Business Computing; Computer Engineering; Computer Science; Electrical and Electronic Engineering; Electronic Engineering; Engineering; Information Technology; Measurement and Precision Engineering; Technology; Telecommunications Engineering); **Health Sciences** (Anaesthesiology; Cardiology; Dietetics; Health Administration; Health Sciences; Laboratory Techniques; Medical Technology; Microbiology; Pneumology); **Hotel Management and Catering Technology** (Cooking and Catering; Hotel Management); **Humanities and Sciences** (Administration; Arts and Humanities; Biotechnology; Business Administration; Business and Commerce; Computer Science; Electronic Engineering; Health Administration; Information Management; Microbiology; Molecular Biology; Social Work; Statistics; Telecommunications Engineering; Visual Arts)

Institutes

Distance Education (Administration; Business Administration; Business and Commerce; Computer Science; Economics; English; Food Science; History; Hotel Management; Information Technology; Marketing; Mathematics; Nursing; Nutrition; Philosophy; Public Administration; Sociology; Software Engineering; South and Southeast Asian Languages)

Programmes

Medicine, Dentistry, Nursing, Physiotheraphy and Engineering *(Ph.D.)* (Dentistry; Engineering; Medicine; Nursing; Physical Therapy)

Further Information: Also Distance Education. Meenakshi Ammal Dental Hospital, Meenakshi Medical Research Institute

History: Founded 2004 as Meenakshi Academy of Higher Education and Research. A 'Deemd University'.

Governing Bodies: Board of Management; Finance Committee; Academic Council

Admission Requirements: Common Entrance Test conducted on All India level

Fees: (Ruppes): 35,000-350,000 per annum; Distance edcuation programmes, 2,500-25,000 per annum.

Degrees and Diplomas: *Diploma*; *Bachelor's Degree*; *Bachelor's degree (professional)*; *Postgraduate Diploma*; *Master's Degree*; *Doctorate*

Student Services: Canteen, Health services, Sports facilities

Student Residential Facilities: Hostels for Boys (400 beds) and Girls.
Last Updated: 30/06/11

MEWAR UNIVERSITY (MU)

NH - 79 Gangrar, Chittorgarh, Rajasthan 312901
Tel: +91(1471) 220-881 +91(1471) 291-148
EMail: info@mewaruniversity.org; admission@mewaruniversity.org
Website: http://www.mewaruniversity.org

President: Ramesh Chandra (2009-)
EMail: vc@mewaruniversity.org

Registrar: S. Sengupta EMail: registrar@mewaruniversity.org

Faculties

Arts and Humanities (Anthropology; Arts and Humanities; Child Care and Development; Clinical Psychology; Development Studies; Economics; English; Family Studies; Geography; Hindi; History; Labour and Industrial Relations; Management; Philosophy; Political Sciences; Psychology; Public Administration; Sociology); **Computer Science and System Studies** (Computer Science; Information Technology); **Education** (Art Education; Business Education; Education; Science Education); **Engineering and Technology** (Ceramics and Glass Technology; Chemical Engineering; Civil Engineering; Computer Science; Electrical and Electronic Engineering; Electrical Engineering; Electronic Engineering; Engineering; Engineering Drawing and Design; Industrial Chemistry; Materials Engineering; Measurement and Precision Engineering; Mechanical Engineering; Nanotechnology; Power Engineering; Production Engineering; Structural Architecture; Telecommunications Engineering; Transport Engineering); **Journalism and Mass Communication** (Journalism; Mass Communication); **Legal Studies** (Commercial Law; Criminology; Law; Private Law; Taxation); **Management and Commerce** (Business Administration; Business and Commerce; Civil Engineering; Computer Science; Electrical and Electronic Engineering; Electrical Engineering; Electronic Engineering; Finance; Human Resources; Information Technology; International Business; Management; Marketing; Mechanical Engineering; Telecommunications Engineering); **Science** (Biotechnology; Botany; Chemistry; Electronic Engineering; Environmental Studies; Histology; Mathematics; Pathology; Physics; Zoology)

History: Founded 2009.

Governing Bodies: Board of Management; Academic Council; Advisory Board.

Fees: (Rupiah): Undergraduate fees, 10,000-65,000 per annum; Graduate programme, 12,000-50,000 per annum; MBA, 47,000-65,000 per annum.

Accrediting Agencies: University Grants Commission (UGC); All India Council for Technical Education (AICTE); Ministry of Human Resources Development

Degrees and Diplomas: *Diploma*; *Bachelor's Degree*; *Bachelor's degree (professional)*; *Master's Degree*; *Master of Philosophy*; *Doctorate (PhD)*. Also Integrated Diploma and Dual Degree Programmes; Bachelor's Degree Honours, 3 yrs; MBA 2 yrs.

Student Services: Academic counselling, Canteen, Cultural centre, Health services, Sports facilities

Student Residential Facilities: Hostels for 800 students; Guest House

Special Facilities: Laboratories

Libraries: c. 50,000 vols
Last Updated: 30/06/11

MGM INSTITUTE OF HEALTH SCIENCES (MGMUHS)

Post Box -06, MGM Educational campus, Sector -18 Kamothe,
Navi Mumbai, Maharashtra 410 209
Tel: +91(22) 274-22471 +91(22) 274-21995 +91(22) 651-68127
Fax: +91(22) 274-20320
EMail: mgmuniversity@mgmuhs.com; mgmuniversity@yahoo.co.in
Website: http://www.mgmuhs.com/

Vice Chancellor: R.D. Bapat EMail: vc@mgmuhs.com

Registrar: R.C. Sharma EMail: registrar@mgmuhs.com

Colleges

Medicine *(Aurangabad)* (Anaesthesiology; Anatomy; Biochemistry; Biotechnology; Genetics; Gynaecology and Obstetrics; Health Administration; Medicine; Microbiology; Nursing; Ophthalmology; Orthopaedics; Paediatrics; Pathology; Pharmacology; Physical Therapy; Physiology; Psychiatry and Mental Health; Radiology; Surgery); **Medicine** *(Navi Mumbai)* (Medicine; Surgery)

History: Founded 2006. A 'Deemed University'.

Governing Bodies: Board of Management; Academic Council; Board of Studies; Selection committee; Finance Committee; Advisory Board; Planning and Monitoring Board; Senate.

Degrees and Diplomas: *Diploma*; *Bachelor's Degree*; *Bachelor's degree (professional)*; *Master's Degree*; *Doctorate*. Also M.B.A.
Last Updated: 16/12/11

MIZORAM UNIVERSITY (MZU)

P.O.Box No. 190, Tanhril, Aizawl, Mizoram 796 004
Tel: +91(389) 233-0654
Fax: +91(389) 233-0642
EMail: vc@mzu.edu.in
Website: http://www.mzu.edu.in

Vice-Chancellor: R. Lalthantluanga (2011-)
Tel: +91(389) 233-0650 +91(389) 233-0651,
Fax: +91(389) 233-0644

Acting Registrar: Thangchungnunga
Tel: +91(389) 233-0654 +91(389) 231-9367,
Fax: +91(389) 233-0834 EMail: registrar@mzu.edu.in

Schools

Earth Sciences and Natural Resources Management (Botany; Development Studies; Earth Sciences; Education; Environmental Studies; Forestry; Geology; Horticulture; Natural Resources; Rural Studies); **Economics Management and Information Sciences** (Business and Commerce; Economics; Information Sciences; Library Science; Management); **Education and Humanities** (Arts and Humanities; Education; English; Hindi; Literature; South and Southeast Asian Languages); **Engineering and Technology** (Electronic Engineering; Engineering; Information Technology); **Life Sciences** (Biological and Life Sciences; Biotechnology; Botany; Zoology); **Physical Sciences** (Chemistry; Mathematics and Computer Science; Physics); **Social Sciences** (Ethnology; History; Political Sciences; Psychology; Public Administration; Social Sciences; Social Work)

Further Information: Also 27 Affiliated Colleges and 1 Constituent College.

History: Founded 2001. A 'Central University'.

Governing Bodies: University Court; Academic Council; Executive Council

Academic Year: Post-Graduate, August to June (August-November; February-June); Under-Graduate, April to November for first and then February to November.

Fees: (Rupees): Fee for undergraduate programmes, 12,000 per semester;Tuition fee for postgraduate programmes, 120-185 per months; MBA, 10,000 per semester; Ph.D., 250 per month.

Degrees and Diplomas: *Bachelor's degree (professional)*; *Master's Degree*; *Master of Philosophy*; *Doctorate (Ph.D.)*

Student Services: Canteen, Health services, Sports facilities

Student Residential Facilities: Postgraduate men's hostel (30 beds); Guest house.

Special Facilities: Computer Centre

Libraries: c. 108,925 vols and c. 333 periodical subscriptions.

Academic Staff *2009-2010*	MEN	WOMEN	TOTAL
FULL-TIME	168	64	**232**
STAFF WITH DOCTORATE			
FULL-TIME	–	–	**128**
Student Numbers *2009-2010*			
All (Foreign Included)	–	–	**2,471**
FOREIGN ONLY	–	–	**0**

Last Updated: 01/07/11

MODY INSTITUTE OF TECHNOLOGY AND SCIENCE (MITS)

Jaipur-Bikaner highway (NH-11), Lakshmangarh, Rajasthan 332311
Tel: +91(1573) 225-001
Fax: +91(1573) 225-041
EMail: contact@mitsuniversity.ac.in
Website: http://www.mitsuniversity.ac.in

Vice-Chancellor: N.V. Subba Reddy
EMail: vc@mitsuniversity.ac.in

Registrar: J. L. Arora EMail: registrar@mitsuniversity.ac.in

Faculties

Arts, Science and Commerce (Biotechnology; Business Administration; Business and Commerce; Chemistry; Computer Science; Economics; English; Esoteric Practices; French; Information Technology; International Business; Literature; Microbiology; Political Sciences; Psychology; Sociology; Zoology); **Engineering and Technology** (Computer Engineering; Computer Graphics; Computer Science; Electrical Engineering; Electronic Engineering; Energy Engineering; Engineering; Information Technology; Mechanical Engineering; Nanotechnology; Nuclear Engineering; Technology; Telecommunications Engineering); **Law** (Commercial Law; Criminal Law; Human Rights; Justice Administration; Law); **Management Studies** (Business Administration; Management)

History: A 'Deemed University'.

Governing Bodies: Board of Governors; Senate; Board of Studies

Fees: (Ruppes): Tuition fee for undergraduate programmes, 40,000-105,000 per annum; Postgraduate programmes, 50,000-55,000 per annum. Foreign students, 3,000-5,500 per annum; Nepalese students, 1,600-3,200 per annum.

Degrees and Diplomas: *Bachelor's Degree*; *Bachelor's degree (professional)*; *Master's Degree*; *Doctorate (Ph.D.)*. Also Bachelor's degree Honours, 3 yrs; MBA, yrs.

Student Residential Facilities: Yes

Special Facilities: Laboratories (Computer Science, Engineering, Humanities and Sciences).

Libraries: FET-Library: c. 20,000 vols; c. 550 e-journal subscriptions; 1,500 CDs and 200 video cassetes. FMS-Library: 8,000 vols; 47 national journals, 11 international journals; several CDs; subscribtion to on-line Digital library resources-Ebsco-which provides access to 1,100 national and international journals online and corporate database CMIE-Prowess. FJS-Library. FASC-Library: c. 8,000 vols; 300 CDs.

Last Updated: 01/07/11

MOHAN LAL SUKHADIA UNIVERSITY (MLSU)

Pratapnagar, Udaipur, Rajasthan 313001
Tel: +91(294) 247-1035
Fax: +91(294) 247-1150
EMail: registrar@mlsu.ac.in
Website: http://www.mlsu.ac.in

Vice-Chancellor: I. V. Trivedi
Tel: +91(294) 247-0597,
Fax: +91(294) 247-0259 +91(294) 247-1150
EMail: vcmlsu@mlsu.ac.in

Registrar: Shri M.L. Sharma Tel: +91(294) 247-0166

Centres
Women Studies (Women's Studies)

Colleges
Commerce and Management Studies *(University)* (Accountancy; Banking; Business and Commerce; Economics; Management; Statistics); **Law** *(University)* (Law); **Science** *(University)* (Biotechnology; Botany; Chemistry; Environmental Studies; Geology; Mathematics; Physics; Statistics; Zoology); **Social Sciences and Humanities** *(University)* (Arts and Humanities; Economics; English; Geography; Hindi; History; Library Science; Music; Philosophy; Political Sciences; Psychology; Public Administration; Sanskrit; Social Sciences; Sociology; South and Southeast Asian Languages; Urdu; Visual Arts)

Faculties
Commerce (Accountancy; Banking; Business Administration; Business and Commerce; Economic History; Economics; Statistics); **Humanities** (English; Hindi; History; Literature; Music; Painting and Drawing; Philosophy; Sanskrit; South and Southeast Asian Languages; Visual Arts); **Management** (Business Administration; Hotel Management; Management; Marketing; Tourism); **Science** (Biotechnology; Botany; Chemistry; Computer Engineering; Computer Networks; Computer Science; Environmental Studies; Geology; Information Technology; Mathematics; Nanotechnology; Pharmacy; Physics; Polymer and Plastics Technology; Statistics;

Zoology); **Social Sciences** (Economics; Geography; Journalism; Library Science; Political Sciences; Psychology; Public Administration; Social Sciences; Sociology)

Research Centres
Population (Demography and Population)

Further Information: Also 180 affiliated colleges in the districts of Udaipur, Banswara, Dungarpur, Sirohi, Rajasmand, Chittorgarh, Pratapgarh.

History: Founded 1962 as Rajasthan Agricultural University. Named as University of Udaipur 1964. Acquired present title 1984 and status 1987.

Governing Bodies: Board of Management; Academic Council; Council of Deans; Board of Studies.

Academic Year: July to June

Admission Requirements: 12th year senior secondary/intermediate examination or recognized foreign equivalent

Fees: (Rupees): Undergraduate, 600-900 per annum; postgraduate, 1,200-1,500

Main Language(s) of Instruction: Hindi; English

Accrediting Agencies: NAAC (U.G.C.)

Degrees and Diplomas: *Bachelor's Degree*; *Postgraduate Diploma*; *Master's Degree*; *Master of Philosophy*; *Doctorate (PhD)*. Also Bacleror's degree honours; Undergraduate certificate courses; Professional courses (M.H.R.M., M.I.B., D.I.B.); MBA.

Student Services: Academic counselling, Canteen, Cultural centre, Employment services, Foreign student adviser, Foreign Studies Centre, Handicapped facilities, Health services, Language programs, Nursery care, Social counselling, Sports facilities

Student Residential Facilities: Hostels for boys (254 beds) and girls (120 beds); Guest House

Special Facilities: Computer Centre; Internet Centre; Estate Office.

Libraries: Central Library, College of Science Library, College of Social Science and Humanities Library, College of Commerce and Management Library, College of Law Library, Faculty of Management Studies Library, University Department of Geology Library. 291,227 vols; 215 periodical subscriptions

Last Updated: 01/07/11

MOTHER TERESA WOMEN'S UNIVERSITY

Annai Teresa Magalir Palkalaikazhgam
Kodaikanal, Tamilnadu 624101
Tel: +91(4542) 241-021 +91(4542) 241-122
Fax: +91(4542) 245-314 +91(4542) 241-122
EMail: atwunivc@yahoo.co.in

Vice-Chancellor: D. Janakii Dhanapal

Registrar: S. Sundari

Departments
Biotechnology (Biotechnology) *Lecturer:* V. Premalakshmi; **Computer Science** (Mathematics and Computer Science) *Lecturer:* Flora Arul Margaret; **Economics** *Head:* Arul Anees; **Education** (Education; Educational and Student Counselling) *Head:* V. Rajeswari; **English** (English) *Reader:* N. Geetha; **Family Life Management** (Family Studies; Home Economics) *Head:* M. Samshath; **Historical Studies and Tourism** (History; Tourism) *Reader:* P.N. Premalatha; **Management** *Lecturer:* C. Kavitha; **Music** (Fine Arts; Music) *Lecturer:* Shanthi Mahesh; **Physics** (Physics) *Reader:* Rita John; **Sociology** (Sociology) *Reader:* K. Rethi Devi; **Tamil** (Indic Languages) *Reader:* T. Kamali; **Visual Communication** (Visual Arts) *Lecturer:* S. Jenefa; **Women's Studies** (Women's Studies) *Head:* A. Kalaimathi

Schools
Distance Education *Director:* S. Beulah Jeyaseeli

History: Founded 1984. A Research Institution solely for women. Through teaching, training, and extension services, the University seeks to promote the welfare of rural and urban disadvantaged women at all levels.

Governing Bodies: Academic Committee; Executive Council; Planning Board and Finance Committee

Academic Year: July to April (July-November; December-April)

Admission Requirements: Minimum Bachelor's Degree

Fees: (Rupees): 3,900-35,000 per annum

Main Language(s) of Instruction: English

Accrediting Agencies: National Assessment and Accreditation Council, Bangalore

Degrees and Diplomas: *Postgraduate Diploma*: 1-3 yrs; *Master's Degree*: 1-2 yrs; *Master of Philosophy (MPhil)*: 1 yr; *Doctorate (PhD)*: a further 2-4 yrs

Student Services: Academic counselling, Canteen, Cultural centre, Health services, Language programs, Nursery care, Social counselling, Sports facilities

Student Residential Facilities: Yes

Libraries: c. 56,000 vols; 50 journal subscriptions

Publications: Gender and Progress, Journal *(biennially)*; News Flash, University Report *(biennially)*

Last Updated: 09/01/07

MOTILAL NEHRU NATIONAL INSTITUTE OF TECHNOLOGY ALLAHABAD (MNNIT)

Allahabad, Uttar Pradesh 211004
Tel: +91(532) 227-1104
Fax: +91(532) 254-5341 +91(532) 254-5677
EMail: director@mnnit.ac.in
Website: http://www.mnnit.ac.in/

Director: P. Chakrabarti (2011-)
Tel: +91(532) 254-5190 +91(532) 227-1101,
Fax: +91(532) 254-5341

Registrar: Sri Sarvesh Kumar Tiwari

Departments

Applied Mechanics (Biomedical Engineering; Biotechnology; Engineering; Hydraulic Engineering; Materials Engineering; Mechanical Engineering; Mechanics; Nanotechnology; Power Engineering; Solid State Physics); **Chemistry** (Chemical Engineering; Chemistry; Materials Engineering); **Civil Engineering** (Civil Engineering; Computer Graphics; Construction Engineering; Environmental Engineering; Geological Engineering; Irrigation; Transport Engineering); **Computer Science and Engineering** (Computer Engineering; Computer Science; Information Technology; Software Engineering); **Electrical Engineering** (Automation and Control Engineering; Electrical Engineering; Measurement and Precision Engineering; Power Engineering); **Electronics and Communication Engineering** (Computer Graphics; Electronic Engineering; Microelectronics; Telecommunications Engineering); **Geographic Information System** *(GIS)* (Information Sciences; Surveying and Mapping); **Humanities and Social Sciences** (Accountancy; Arts and Humanities; English; Finance; Human Resources; Industrial and Organizational Psychology; Management; Social Psychology; Social Sciences; Social Studies); **Mathematics** (Mathematics; Mathematics and Computer Science); **Mechanical Engineering** (Chemical Engineering; Computer Graphics; Engineering Drawing and Design; Industrial Engineering; Mechanical Engineering; Production Engineering; Thermal Engineering); **Physics** (Physics)

Schools

Management Studies (Business Administration; Finance; Human Resources; International Business; Management; Marketing; Operations Research)

History: Created 1961 as Motilal Nehru Regional Engineering College, Allahabad. Acquired current title and status 2002. An 'Institute of National Importance".

Governing Bodies: Board of Governors.

Academic Year: July to April (July-November; January-April) Ssummer semester May to July.

Admission Requirements: For undegraduadate degrees, All India Engineering Entrance Examination (A.I.E.E.E) conducted by C.B.S.E.; candidates who have passed 10+2 or an equivalent. For graduate degrees, an aggregate of 60% marks or equivalent grade in a Bachelor's degree in Science or Engineering or equivalent; For MBA, a bachelor's degree in engineering/technology/science or an equivalent degree with mathematics/economics as one of the subjects in qualifying examination. Candidates appearing in their final year of bachelor's degree may also apply.

Fees: (Rupees): Undergraduate fee, 10,301-25,401 per semester; Graduate semester, 8,826-31,776 per semester. MBA, 25,375-27,750 per semester. Ph.D., 4,775-8,550 (full time) and 2,750-6,525 (part time).

Degrees and Diplomas: *Bachelor's degree (professional)*; *Master's Degree*

Student Numbers *2009-2010*: Total: c. 650
Last Updated: 01/07/11

NAGALAND UNIVERSITY (NU)

Dist. – Zunheboto, Lumami, Nagaland 798627
Tel: +91(370) 229-0488 +91(370) 229-0808
Fax: +91(307) 229-0246
EMail: nagalanduniversity@yahoo.co.in
Website: http://www.nagauniv.org.in/

Vice-Chancellor: K. Kannan (2001-)
Tel: +91(369) 226-8268, Fax: +91(369) 226-8248
EMail: vicechancellornu@yahoo.com

Registrar: Shri. D.K. Mohanty
Tel: +91(369) 226-8270, Fax: +91(369) 226-8223
EMail: nuregistrar@yahoo.in

Schools

Agriculture Sciences and Rural Development *(SASRD)* (Agricultural Economics; Agricultural Education; Agricultural Engineering; Agriculture; Agronomy; Animal Husbandry; Biochemistry; Biotechnology; Botany; Chemistry; Crop Production; Ecology; Entomology; Environmental Studies; Genetics; Horticulture; Plant Pathology; Rural Planning; Soil Conservation; Soil Science); **Engineering and Technology** (Biotechnology; Business Administration; Computer Engineering; Computer Networks; Computer Science; Electronic Engineering; Engineering; Information Technology; Management; Software Engineering; Telecommunications Engineering); **Humanities and Education** (Arts and Humanities; Cultural Studies; Education; English; Linguistics; Literature); **Sciences** (Botany; Chemistry; Geography; Geology; Inorganic Chemistry; Natural Resources; Natural Sciences; Organic Chemistry; Physical Chemistry; Surveying and Mapping; Zoology); **Social Science** (Archaeology; Business and Commerce; Comparative Politics; Economics; Government; History; International Relations; Political Sciences; Public Administration; Social Sciences; Sociology)

Further Information: Also campuses in Kohima and Medziphema. 48 affiliated colleges.

History: Founded 1994. A 'Central University'.

Governing Bodies: Executive Council

Academic Year: July to June

Admission Requirements: Pre-University for degree courses in Agriculture and graduate with 50% marks for Postgraduate courses; Postgraduate with 55% marks for PhD admission

Fees: (Rupees): 990 per annum

Main Language(s) of Instruction: English

Accrediting Agencies: National Assessment and Accreditation Council

Degrees and Diplomas: *Bachelor's Degree*; *Bachelor's degree (professional)*; *Master's Degree*; *Doctorate (Ph.D.)*. Also MBA, 2 yrs.

Student Services: Academic counselling, Canteen, Cultural centre, Health services, Sports facilities

Student Residential Facilities: Hostels for students and Teachers; Guest House, Quarters for Teachers and Staff Members

Libraries: Nagaland University Central Library, 32,916 vols; 75 International and National Journals subscriptions. SASRD Library, c. 25,000 vols; c. 160 periodical subscriptions. Lumani library, 12,246 vols; c. 80 periodical subscriptions.

Publications: Research Journal of Nagaland University *(annually)*
Last Updated: 04/07/11

NALANDA OPEN UNIVERSITY

Nalanda Khula Vishwavidyalaya
2nd/3rd Floor, Biscomaun Bhawan, Gandhi Maidan, Patna, Bihar 800001
Tel: +91(612) 220-1013 +91(612) 220-6916
Fax: +91(612) 220-1001
EMail: nalopuni@sancharnet.in
Website: http://www.nalandaopenuniversity.com

Vice-Chancellor: Jitendra Singh

Registrar: Sidheshwar Prasad Sinha

Schools

Computer and Information Sciences (Computer Science; Information Sciences); **Economics, Commerce and Management** (Business and Commerce; Economics; Finance; Insurance; Management; Marketing; Safety Engineering); **Health and Environmental Sciences** (Alternative Medicine; Child Care and Development; Dental Hygiene; Dental Technology; Environmental Studies; Epidemiology; Family Studies; Food Science; Health Sciences; Laboratory Techniques; Medical Technology; Nursing; Nutrition; Ophthalmology; Optometry; Physical Therapy; Psychology; Radiology; Rehabilitation and Therapy; Yoga); **Indian and Foreign Languages** (Hindi; Modern Languages; Sanskrit; South and Southeast Asian Languages; Urdu); **Indology** (Ancient Civilizations; Archaeology; Asian Religious Studies; Christian Religious Studies; Cultural Studies; History; Islamic Studies; Literature; Philosophy; Tourism); **Journalism and Mass Communication** (Journalism; Mass Communication); **Library and Information Science** (Information Sciences; Library Science); **Pure and Agricultural Sciences** (Agriculture; Biology; Botany; Chemistry; Floriculture; Geography; Home Economics; Mathematics; Physics; Soil Conservation; Zoology); **Social Sciences** (Constitutional Law; Geography; Home Economics; Human Rights; Political Sciences; Psychology; Public Administration; Rural Planning; Social Sciences; Social Work; Sociology; Women's Studies); **Teacher's Education** (Education; Higher Education; Primary Education; Secondary Education; Teacher Training)

History: Founded 1987.

Governing Bodies: Executive Council

Academic Year: July to June

Admission Requirements: School or College Certificate according to courses

Fees: (Rupees): Certificate, 500-1,000 per annum; Intermediate degree, 1,500-11,500 per annum; Bacelor's degree, 1,800-8,000 per annum; Postrgaduate degree, 3,000 per annum; Master's degree, 2,700-7,000 per annum; Ph.D., 10,000 per annum

Main Language(s) of Instruction: Hindi, English

Accrediting Agencies: Distance Education Council (DEC), University Grants Commission (UGC), and Ministry of HRD, Government of India.

Degrees and Diplomas: *Bachelor's Degree*; *Bachelor's degree (professional)*; *Postgraduate Diploma*; *Master's Degree*; *Doctorate*. Also undergraduate certificates, 6-9 months; Short certificate courses, 4 weeks; Bachelor's degrees Honours, 3 yrs; Intermediate degree, 2 yrs.

Student Services: Academic counselling, Social counselling

Special Facilities: Computer laboratory.

Libraries: c. 50,000 vols.

Last Updated: 04/07/11

NARENDRA DEVA UNIVERSITY OF AGRICULTURE AND TECHNOLOGY (NDUAT)

Narendranagar, Kumarganj, Faizabad, Uttar Pradesh 224229
Tel: +91(5270) 262-161
Fax: +91(5270) 262-097
EMail: nduat@up.nic.in
Website: http://www.nduat.ernet.in

Vice-Chancellor: R.S. Kureel (2010-)
Tel: +91(5270) 262-097 +91(5270) 262-161,
Fax: +91(5270) 262-842
EMail: vc_nduat2010@yaho.co.in; vc@mail.nduat.ernet.in

Registrar: Padmaker Tripathi
Tel: +91(5270) 262-035, Fax: +91(5270) 262-104
EMail: hpt@india.com

Colleges

Agricultural Engineering and Technology *(Mahamaya - MCAET)* (Agricultural Engineering; Agricultural Equipment; Irrigation; Power Engineering; Soil Conservation; Water Management); **Agriculture** (Agricultural Economics; Agricultural Education; Agricultural Engineering; Agriculture; Agronomy; Biochemistry; Botany; Entomology; Fishery; Food Technology; Forestry; Genetics; Horticulture; Meteorology; Microbiology; Plant and Crop Protection; Plant Pathology; Soil Science; Statistics; Zoology); **Fishery** (Agricultural Economics; Aquaculture; Biology; Biotechnology; Fishery; Genetics;

Microbiology; Natural Resources; Pathology; Statistics; Water Science); **Home Science** (Development Studies; Family Studies; Food Science; Home Economics; Nutrition; Textile Design; Textile Technology); **Horticulture** (Horticulture); **Veterinary Science and Animal Husbandry** (Anatomy; Animal Husbandry; Biochemistry; Epidemiology; Ethics; Farm Management; Genetics; Gynaecology and Obstetrics; Microbiology; Nutrition; Parasitology; Pharmacology; Physiology; Public Health; Radiology; Social and Preventive Medicine; Surgery; Toxicology; Veterinary Science)

Further Information: Also University Hospital.

History: Founded 1975. Based on the model of the Land Grant Colleges of the USA and undertaking teaching research and extension education in an integrated manner. Responsible for all round development of rural communities in 15 districts of the Faizabad, Gorakhpur and Varanasi regions.

Admission Requirements: 12th year senior secondary/intermediate examination or recognized foreign equivalent

Fees: (Rupees): Undergraduate, 2,400; postgraduate, 4,000 per annum

Main Language(s) of Instruction: Hindi, English

Degrees and Diplomas: *Bachelor's Degree*; *Bachelor's degree (professional)*; *Postgraduate Diploma*; *Master's Degree*; *Doctorate (PhD)*

Student Services: Sports facilities

Student Residential Facilities: 3 boys hostels and 1 girl hostel.

Libraries: 42,425 vols

Student Numbers *2010-2011*: Total 642
Last Updated: 04/07/11

NATIONAL ACADEMY OF LEGAL STUDIES AND RESEARCH UNIVERSITY (NALSAR UNIVERSITY OF LAW)

Justice City, Shameerpet, R.R.Dist., Hyderabad,
Andhra Pradesh 500 078
Tel: +91(40) 2349-8105 +91(40) 2349-8108
Fax: +91(8418) 245-161 +91(8418) 245-174
EMail: admissions@nalsar.ac.in
Website: http://www.nalsar.ac.in

Vice-Chancellor: Veer Singh
Tel: +91(40) 2349-8102, Fax: +91(8418) 245-161
EMail: vc@nalsarlawuniv.org

Registrar: K. V. S. Sarma
Tel: +91(40) 2349-8104, Fax: +91(8418) 245-174
EMail: registrar@nalsarlawuniv.org

Programmes

Law (Commercial Law; Comparative Law; Constitutional Law; Criminal Law; Environmental Studies; Human Rights; International Law; Law; Private Law; Public Law); **Other Studies** (Air and Space Law; Air Transport; Finance; Fiscal Law; Law)

History: Founded 1998.

Governing Bodies: General Council; Executive Council; Academic Council; Finance Committee.

Academic Year: June to April (June-November; December-April)

Admission Requirements: 12th year senior secondary/intermediate examination or recognized foreign equivalent

Fees: Indian Students (Rupees): Bachelor, 85,000 per annum; Master, 65,000 per annum; Postgraduate Programs, 5,000. Non-locals/Foreign (US Dollars):, Bachelor's degree, 5,000-10,000 per annum; Master, 2,000 per annum; Postgraduate Programs, 750-1,000 per annum.

Main Language(s) of Instruction: English

International Co-operation: With universities in Australia, Germany, Canada, United Kingdom, USA, Singapore, Switzerland, Israel, the Netherlands.

Degrees and Diplomas: *Bachelor's Degree*; *Postgraduate Diploma*; *Master's Degree*; *Master of Philosophy*; *Doctorate (PhD)*. Also Bachelor's degree Honours; Undergraduate certificate.

Student Services: Academic counselling, Canteen, Foreign student adviser, Foreign Studies Centre, Health services, Language programs, Sports facilities

Student Residential Facilities: Separate halls of residence for boys and girls; Guest house.

Special Facilities: Computer Laboratory; Moot Court; Bank

Libraries: c. 20,500 vols; Access to 80 periodical subscriptions; Internet Connectivity and Library Portal.

Publications: Green News; IP Law Newsletter; NALSAR Law Review, Journal *(biennially)*; NALSAR Newsletter

Academic Staff *2009-2010*	TOTAL
FULL-TIME	30
STAFF WITH DOCTORATE FULL-TIME	c. 20

Student Numbers *2009-2010*	
All (Foreign Included)	c. 910
FOREIGN ONLY	50

Distance students, 200. **Evening students**, 60.
Last Updated: 04/07/11

NATIONAL BRAIN RESEARCH CENTRE (NBRC)

NH-8, Manesar, Gurgaon, Haryana 122 050
Tel: +91(124) 2845-200
Fax: +91(124) 2338-910 +91(124) 2338-928
EMail: info@nbrc.ac.in
Website: http://www.nbrc.ac.in/

Director: Subrata Sinha (2010-)

Programmes
Neurosciences (Neurosciences)

History: Founded 1997. Acquired "Deemed University" status 2002.

Degrees and Diplomas: *Doctorate (Ph.D.)*. Also integrated Ph.D.; Summer Training and Short-term Programmes.
Last Updated: 13/12/11

NATIONAL DAIRY RESEARCH INSTITUTE (NDRI)

Karnal, Haryana 132001
Tel: +91(184) 225-9008
Fax: +91(184) 225-0042
EMail: registrar.ndri@gmail.com
Website: http://karnal.nic.in/res_ndri.asp

Director: A.K. Srivastava
Tel: +91(184) 225-2800 +91(184) 225-9002,
Fax: +91(184) 227-1612 EMail: dir@ndri.res.in

Joint Director (Administration) and Registrar: J. Kewalramani
Tel: +91(184) 225-9023 +91(184) 227-2392,
Fax: +91(184) 225-0042 EMail: cao@ndri.res.in

Centres
Animal Biotechnology (Biotechnology; Embryology and Reproduction Biology; Genetics; Molecular Biology)

Divisions
Animal Biochemistry (Biochemistry; Biotechnology; Food Technology); **Dairy Cattle Breeding** (Animal Husbandry; Dairy; Genetics); **Dairy Cattle Nutrition** (Animal Husbandry; Dairy; Nutrition); **Dairy Cattle Physiology** (Animal Husbandry; Dairy; Physiology); **Dairy Chemistry** (Chemistry; Dairy; Physical Chemistry); **Dairy Economics, Statistics and Management** (Computer Science; Dairy; Economics; Management; Statistics); **Dairy Engineering** (Dairy; Engineering; Food Technology); **Dairy Extension** (Agricultural Education; Behavioural Sciences; Dairy; Hindi; Leadership; Management; Psychology; Sociology); **Dairy Microbiology** (Biotechnology; Dairy; Food Technology; Microbiology; Physiology); **Dairy Technology** (Dairy; Food Technology); **Live Stock Production and Management** (Agricultural Business; Animal Husbandry; Environmental Management; Meat and Poultry; Waste Management)

Research Centres
Artificial Breeding (Animal Husbandry; Embryology and Reproduction Biology)

History: Founded 1923 as as Imperial Institute of Animal Husbandry and Dairying. Expanded and renamed as Imperial Dairy Institute 1936. Headquarter shifted to Karnal 1955. Acquired present title 1947. Granted 'Deemed University' status 1989.

Governing Bodies: Board of Management; Academic Council; Executive Council

Academic Year: August to July (August-December; January-July)

Admission Requirements: 12th year senior secondary/intermediate examination or recognized foreign equivalent

Fees: (Rupees): 2,000 per semester

Main Language(s) of Instruction: English

International Co-operation: None

Accrediting Agencies: Indian Council of Agricultural Research (ICAR)

Degrees and Diplomas: *Bachelor's degree (professional)*; *Master's Degree*; *Doctorate (Ph.D.)*

Student Services: Academic counselling, Canteen, Employment services, Health services, Sports facilities

Student Residential Facilities: Hostels; Guest house for visiting scientists.

Special Facilities: Laboratories; Livestock Farm (elite herd of over 1600 dairy animals); Experimental Dairy Plant; Model Dairy Plant; Computer Centre; Forage Section; Technology Business Incubator (TBI);

Libraries: National Library for Dairying, 94,270 vols; 250 periodical subscriptions

Publications: Annual Report *(annually)*; Quarterly Report *(quarterly)*

Press or Publishing House: NDRI Printing Press

Academic Staff *2009-2010*	TOTAL
FULL-TIME	180

Student Numbers *2009-2010*	
All (Foreign Included)	c. 500
FOREIGN ONLY	10

Last Updated: 04/07/11

NATIONAL INSTITUTE OF AGRICULTURAL EXTENSION MANAGEMENT (MANAGE)

Rajendranagar, Hyderabad, Andhra Pradesh 500 030
Tel: +91(40) 2401-6702 +91(40) 2401-6709
Fax: +91(40) 2401-5388
EMail: helpline@manage.gov.in; anandreddy@manage.gov.in
Website: http://www.manage.gov.in/

Director General: Sanjeev Gupta
EMail: dgmanage@manage.gov.in

Programmes
Agri Business Management (Agricultural Business; Management); **Agricultural Extension Management** (Agriculture; Management); **Agricultural Extension Services for Input Dealers** (Agriculture)

History: Founded 1987 by the Ministry of Agriculture, Government of India as an autonomous institute.

Main Language(s) of Instruction: Hindi

Accrediting Agencies: All India Council for Technical Education (AICTE); National Board of Accreditation (NBA)

Degrees and Diplomas: *Diploma*; *Postgraduate Diploma*
Last Updated: 05/12/11

NATIONAL INSTITUTE OF FOUNDRY AND FORGE TECHNOLOGY (NIFFT)

Hatia, Ranchi, Jharkhand 834 003
Tel: +91(651) 229-0859
Fax: +91(651) 229-0860
EMail: nifftranchi@gmail.com
Website: http://www.nifft.ernet.in/

Departments
Applied Science and Humanities (Arts and Humanities; Computer Engineering; Environmental Engineering; Environmental Studies; Natural Sciences); **Forge Technology** (Metallurgical Engineering); **Foundry Technology** (Metallurgical Engineering); **Manufacturing Engineering** (Industrial Engineering); **Materials and Metallurgical Engineering** (Materials Engineering; Metallurgical Engineering)

History: Founded 1966.

Governing Bodies: Board of Governors

Accrediting Agencies: All India Council for Technical Education (AICTE)

Degrees and Diplomas: *Bachelor's degree (professional)*; *Master's Degree*; *Doctorate*. Also Advanced Diploma Course, 18 Months.

Student Services: Sports facilities

Student Residential Facilities: 3 different hostels for undergraduate, advanced diploma and postgraduate students (c. 300 beds)

Special Facilities: Information Technology Centre (ITC)/ CAD-CAM Centre/ Computer Centre; Laboratories (Ceramics, Internet, Sand, Metallography, FMS, Non-destructive and mechanical Testing, Spectroscopy, Environmental and Pollution Control Lab, Metrology, Electronics, SEM); Auditorium (300 sits).

Libraries: c. 31,000 vols, 3,560 bound vols; 215 periodical subscritptions

Last Updated: 24/01/12

NATIONAL INSTITUTE OF INDUSTRIAL ENGINEERING (NITIE)

Vihar Lake, Mumbai, Maharashtra 400 087
Tel: +91(22) 2803 5317
Fax: +91(22) 2857-3251
EMail: admissions@nitie.edu
Website: http://www.nitie.edu/

Director: De Amitabha

Registrar: U. K. Debnath
Tel: +91(22) 2857-3371, Fax: +91(22) 2857-4112
EMail: registrar@nitie.edu

Programmes

Doctoral Level Fellowship (Business Administration; Environmental Management; Industrial Engineering; Management; Safety Engineering; Social Studies); **Industrial Engineering** (Finance; Human Resources; Industrial Engineering; Management; Marketing); **Industrial Management** (Industrial Management); **Industrial Safety and Environmental Management** (Environmental Management; Safety Engineering); **Information Technology Management** (Information Management; Information Technology)

History: Founded 1963.

Governing Bodies: Board of Governors; Building and Works Committee; Board of Research

Degrees and Diplomas: *Postgraduate Diploma*

Student Services: Sports facilities

Student Residential Facilities: Hostels

Special Facilities: 200 sits Auditorium; Computer Center

Libraries: 50,776 vols; 220 periodical subscriptions
Last Updated: 27/01/12

NATIONAL INSTITUTE OF MENTAL HEALTH AND NEURO SCIENCES (NIMHANS)

PO Box 2900, Hosur Road, Bangalore, Karnataka 560029
Tel: +91(80) 2699-5005
Fax: +91(80) 2656-6811
EMail: info@nimhans.kar.nic.in
Website: http://www.nimhans.kar.nic.in

Vice-Chancellor and Director: P. Satishchandra (2011-)
Tel: +91(80) 269-95001 +91(80) 269-95002,
Fax: +91(80) 265-64830
EMail: vc@nimhans.kar.nic.in; psatish@nimhans.kar.nic.in

Registrar: V. Ravi
Tel: +91(80) 269-95005
EMail: regt@nimhans.kar.nic.in; vravi@nimhans.kar.nic.in

Departments

Biophysics (Biophysics); **Biostatistics** (Biological and Life Sciences; Statistics); **Child and Adolescent Psychiatry** (Child Care and Development; Psychiatry and Mental Health); **Clinical Psychology** (Behavioural Sciences; Child Care and Development; Clinical Psychology; Psychology; Rehabilitation and Therapy; Social Problems); **Epidemiology** (Epidemiology; Psychiatry and Mental

Health; Public Health); **Human Genetics** (Genetics; Neurology; Psychiatry and Mental Health); **Mental Health Education** (Health Education; Psychiatry and Mental Health); **Neuroanaesthesia** (Anaesthesiology; Neurosciences; Radiology); **Neurochemistry** (Chemistry; Neurosciences); **Neuroimaging and Interventional Radiology** (Neurological Therapy; Neurology; Neurosciences; Radiology; Surgery); **Neurology** (Medicine; Neurological Therapy; Neurology; Paediatrics; Psychiatry and Mental Health; Surgery); **Neuromicrobiology** (Microbiology; Neurology; Nursing; Psychiatry and Mental Health; Surgery); **Neuropathology** (Neurology; Pathology; Surgery); **Neurophysiology** (Neurology; Physiology; Psychiatry and Mental Health; Surgery); **Neurosurgery** (Neurology; Nursing; Psychiatry and Mental Health; Surgery); **Neurovirology** (Neurology; Virology); **Nursing** (Nursing; Psychiatry and Mental Health); **Psychiatric and Neurological Rehabilitation** (Neurological Therapy; Psychiatry and Mental Health; Rehabilitation and Therapy); **Psychiatric Social Work** (Child Care and Development; Psychiatry and Mental Health; Social Work); **Psychiatry** (Forensic Medicine and Dentistry; Gerontology; Neurological Therapy; Pharmacology; Psychiatry and Mental Health; Rehabilitation and Therapy); **Psychopharmacology** (Neurosciences; Pharmacology; Psychiatry and Mental Health); **Speech Pathology and Audiology** (Speech Therapy and Audiology)

History: Founded 1974 as autonomous National Institute of Mental Health and Neuro Sciences (NIMHANS) through amalgamation of the Mental Hospital and the All India Institute of Mental Health. Acquired present status and title 1994. A 'Deemed University'.

Fees: (Rupees): Tuition fee for indian students, undergraduate programmes, 10,000-35,000 per annum; Postgraduate programmes, 10,000-50,000 per annum; Ph.D., 18,000 per annum. Foreign students (US Dollars), undergraduate programmes, 20,000 per annum; postgraduate programmes, 15,000-60,000 per annum; Ph.D., 30,000 per annum.

Degrees and Diplomas: *Diploma*; *Postgraduate Diploma*; *Master's Degree*; *Master of Philosophy*; *Doctorate (Phd)*

Student Services: Canteen, Language programs, Sports facilities

Student Residential Facilities: 6 hostels for boys and girls (separated); Staff hostel.

Special Facilities: Art Convention Centre; Central Animal Research Facility

Libraries: National Neurosciences Information Centre: c. 51,000 vols; 40,000 back volumes of journals; Subscription to 1,700 e-Journals in addition to over 350 National and International print Journals.
Last Updated: 04/07/11

NATIONAL INSTITUTE OF PHARMACEUTICAL EDUCATION AND RESEARCH (NIPER)

Sector 67, S.A.S. Nagar, Mohali, Punjab 160062
Tel: +91(172) 221-4682 +91(172) 221-4687
Fax: +91(172) 221-4692
EMail: registrar@niper.ac.in
Website: http://www.niper.nic.in

Director: K. K. Bhutani
Tel: +91(172) 221-4690 EMail: director@niper.ac.in

Acting Registrar: Sh. Rajesh Moza Tel: +91(172) 223-0068

Departments

Biotechnology (Biotechnology); **Medicinal Chemistry** (Chemistry); **Natural Products** (Chemistry); **Pharmaceutical Analysis** (Pharmacy); **Pharmaceutical Management** (Management; Pharmacy); **Pharmaceutical Technology** (Biotechnology; Pharmacy; Technology); **Pharmaceutics** (Pharmacy); **Pharmacoinformatics** (Computer Science; Pharmacy); **Pharmacology and Toxicology** (Pharmacology; Toxicology); **Pharmacy Practice** (Pharmacy)

Programmes
Training and Continuing Education (Pharmacy)

History: Founded 1991. An 'Institute of National Importance'

Academic Year: July-June (July-December; January-June)

Fees: (Rupees): Master's degree,14,404 per semester (25,696-118,042 per semester for government- and industry sponsored students); Non-Resident Indians, . MBA, 57,739 per semester (103,003 per semester for sponsored students. Non-resident Indian students (US Dollars), 6,100 per semester. Ph.D. 14,404 per semester (26,428 per semester for sponsored students).

Degrees and Diplomas: *Master's Degree; Doctorate (PhD).* Also M.B.A.

Special Facilities: Laboratories; Computer Centre; Central Animal Facility; National Bioavailability Centre

Libraries: Library and Information Centre: 5,715 books, 17,528 bound volumes of journals and 205 theses; subscription of 62 international and 59 national journals.

Last Updated: 05/07/11

NATIONAL INSTITUTE OF TECHNOLOGY AGARTALA

Jirania, Tripura 799055
Tel: +91(381) 2346-360 +91(381) 2346-630
Fax: +91(381) 2346-360 +91(381) 2346-630
EMail: nitaedc@gmail.com
Website: http://www.nitagartala.in/

Director: Probir Kumar Bose
Tel: +91(381) 234-6630, Fax: +91(381) 234-6630
EMail: pkbdirector@gmail.com; pkb32@yahoo.com

Registrar: D. Bhattacharjee
Tel: +91(381) 234-6629, Fax: +91(381) 234-6629

Departments

Chemical Engineering (Chemical Engineering); **Chemistry** (Biochemistry; Chemistry; Inorganic Chemistry; Nanotechnology; Organic Chemistry); **Civil Engineering** (Civil Engineering; Construction Engineering; Geological Engineering; Transport Engineering); **Computer Science and Engineering** (Computer Engineering; Computer Science); **Electrical Engineering** (Electrical Engineering; Measurement and Precision Engineering; Power Engineering); **Electronics and Communication Engineering** (Computer Graphics; Electronic Engineering; Microelectronics; Telecommunications Engineering); **Electronics and Instrumentation Engineering** (Electronic Engineering; Measurement and Precision Engineering); **Humanities and Social Sciences** (Arts and Humanities; Communication Studies; Economics; Management; Social Sciences); **Mathematics** (Mathematics); **Mechanical Engineering** (Mechanical Engineering; Thermal Engineering); **Physics** (Nanotechnology; Optics; Physics); **Production Engineering** (Production Engineering)

History: Created in 1965 as Tripura Engineering College, Agartala. Acquired current title and status 2006. An 'Institute of National Importance'.

Academic Year: July to June (July-December; January-June).

Degrees and Diplomas: *Bachelor's degree (professional); Postgraduate Diploma; Master's Degree; Doctorate.* Also M.B.A.

Student Services: Health services

Student Residential Facilities: 6 boys hostels and 2 girls hostel.

Special Facilities: Central Computer Laboratory; Banking and Post Office

Libraries: c. 34,000 vols and 200 Journals

Student Numbers *2007-2008*: Total: c. 420
Last Updated: 05/07/11

NATIONAL INSTITUTE OF TECHNOLOGY CALICUT (NITC)

Calicut, Kerala 673601
Tel: +91(495) 228-6106
Fax: +91(495) 228-7250
EMail: director@nitc.ac.in
Website: http://www.nitc.ac.in

Director: T. L. Jose

Registrar: Abraham T. Mathew
Tel: +91(495) 228-6314 EMail: atm@nitc.ac.in

Centres

Continuing Education (Computer Networks; Electronic Engineering; Engineering; Environmental Studies; Heritage Preservation;

Medical Technology; Physics; Power Engineering; Structural Architecture; Surveying and Mapping; Thermal Engineering)

Departments

Architecture (Architecture); **Chemical Engineering** (Bioengineering; Chemical Engineering; Computer Science); **Chemistry** (Analytical Chemistry; Chemistry; Inorganic Chemistry; Organic Chemistry; Physical Chemistry; Polymer and Plastics Technology); **Civil Engineering** (Civil Engineering; Construction Engineering; Environmental Engineering; Geological Engineering; Transport Engineering); **Computer Science and Engineering** (Computer Engineering; Computer Science); **Electrical Engineering** (Automation and Control Engineering; Electrical and Electronic Engineering; Electrical Engineering; Energy Engineering; Measurement and Precision Engineering; Power Engineering); **Electronics and Communication Engineering** (Computer Graphics; Electronic Engineering; Microelectronics; Telecommunications Engineering); **Mathematics** (Applied Mathematics; Mathematics; Statistics); **Mechanical Engineering** (Mechanical Engineering); **Physical Education** (Physical Education); **Physics** (Engineering; Materials Engineering; Nanotechnology; Physics)

Schools

Biotechnology (Biotechnology); **Management Studies** (Business Administration; Finance; Human Resources; Management; Marketing; Operations Research); **Nano Science and Technology** (Nanotechnology)

History: Founded 1960 as Calicut Regional Engineering College. Acquired present title and academic and administrative autonomy 2002. Acquired status of 'Institute of National Importance' 2007.

Governing Bodies: Board of Governors

Fees: (Rupees): BTech, 12,000; MTech, 13,000; EDT, 24,000; MCA, 13,000

Degrees and Diplomas: *Bachelor's degree (professional); Postgraduate Diploma; Master's Degree; Doctorate (PhD).* Also M.B.A.

Student Services: Canteen, Cultural centre, Health services, Social counselling, Sports facilities

Student Residential Facilities: 13 hostels including 4 postgraduate hostels and 1 ladies' hostel (total capacity of 2,906 beds); Guest house.

Special Facilities: Campus Networking Centre; Centre for Biomechanics; Advanced Manufacturing Centre; Central Computer Centre; Centre for Value Education; Sophisticated Instruments Centre; Language Laboratory

Libraries: 121,001 vols; 105 national and 223 international periodical subscriptions; digital library, NALANDA (Network of Automated Library and Archives)
Last Updated: 05/07/11

NATIONAL INSTITUTE OF TECHNOLOGY DURGAPUR (NITDGP)

Mahatma Gandhi Avenue, Durgapur, West Bengal 713209
Tel: +91(343) 254-6397
Fax: +91(343) 254-7375
EMail: director@admin.nitdgp.ac.in
Website: http://www.nitdgp.ac.in/

Director: Tarkeshwar Kumar (2011-)
Tel: +91 943478-8001
EMail: profdg@yahoo.com; debidas.ghosh@cse.nitdgp.ac.in

Registrar: A. Gangopadhyay
Tel: +91(343) 275-5240 EMail: registrar@admin.nitdgp.ac.in

Dean (Administration): P. P. Sengupta
Tel: +91 9434788002 EMail: deanadmin@admin.nitdgp.ac.in

Departments

Biotechnology (Biotechnology); **Chemical Engineering** (Chemical Engineering); **Chemistry** (Chemistry); **Civil Engineering** (Civil Engineering); **Computer Application** *(MCA)* (Computer Networks; Computer Science); **Computer Centre** (Computer Science); **Computer Science and Engineering** (Computer Engineering; Computer Science); **Electrical Engineering** (Electrical Engineering); **Electronics and Communication Engineering** (Electronic

Engineering; Telecommunications Engineering); **Geology** (Geology); **Humanities** (Arts and Humanities; English; Literature); **Information Technology** (Information Technology); **Management Studies** (Management); **Mathematics** (Mathematics); **Mechanical Engineering** (Mechanical Engineering); **Metallurgical and Materials Engineering** (Materials Engineering; Metallurgical Engineering); **Physics** (Physics)

History: Founded 1960 as Regional Engineering College. Acquired current status and title 2003. An 'Institute of National Importance'.

Admission Requirements: For undegradraduate programmes: "pass" in the qualifying examination (10 + 2 or its equivalent) with Physics, Chemistry, Mathematics and English, having secured pass marks in each subject. For graduate programmes: B.E. or B.Tech in an appropriate subject.

Accrediting Agencies: National Board of Accreditation (NBA)

Degrees and Diplomas: *Bachelor's degree (professional)*; *Master's Degree*; *Doctorate (PhD)*. Also M.B.A.

Student Services: Canteen, Health services

Student Residential Facilities: 7 boys' hostels and 2 girls' hostels; Residential quarters for staff members; Guest house

Special Facilities: Computer Centre; Central Instruments Facilities; High Voltage Laboratory

Libraries: c. 120,000 vols; Subscription to 180 current Journals.

Student Numbers 2010-2011	MEN	WOMEN	TOTAL
All (Foreign Included)	2,500	500	c. 3,000

Last Updated: 05/07/11

NATIONAL INSTITUTE OF TECHNOLOGY HAMIRPUR

Toni Devi Road, Hamirpur, Himachal Pradesh 177 005
Tel: +91(1972) 254-001
Fax: +91(1972) 223-834
EMail: registrar@nitham.ac.in
Website: http://www.nith.ac.in/

Director: R. L. Sharma
Tel: +91(1972) 222-308, Fax: +91(1972) 223-834
EMail: director@nitham.ac.in

Registrar: A.S. Singha
Tel: +91(1972) 224-390, Fax: +91(1972) 224-390

Departments
Architecture (Architecture); **Chemistry** (Chemical Engineering; Chemistry); **Civil Engineering** (Civil Engineering; Construction Engineering; Environmental Engineering; Geological Engineering; Geology; Hydraulic Engineering; Transport Engineering); **Computer Science and Engineering** (Computer Engineering; Computer Graphics; Computer Science); **Electrical Engineering** (Electrical Engineering; Power Engineering); **Electronics and Communication Engineering** *(E&CE)* (Computer Graphics; Computer Networks; Electronic Engineering; Telecommunications Engineering); **Humanities and Social Science** (Accountancy; Arts and Humanities; Behavioural Sciences; Business Administration; Communication Studies; Economics; Finance; Human Resources; International Economics; Labour and Industrial Relations; Management; Marketing; Social Sciences; Social Studies; Sociology); **Mathematics** (Mathematical Physics; Mathematics; Mathematics and Computer Science; Operations Research; Statistics; Thermal Engineering); **Mechanical Engineering** (Mechanical Engineering); **Physics** (Applied Physics; Physics)

History: Created in 1986 as Regional Engineering College. Acquired current title and status 2002. An 'Institute of National Importance'.

Governing Bodies: Board of Governors

Fees: (Rupees): Tuition fee for Bachelor and Master's degree, 17,500 per semester (4,000-6,000 per semester for slow pace Master's degree programme). M.B.A., 45,000 per semester. Ph.D., 2,500-5,000 per semester.

Degrees and Diplomas: *Bachelor's degree (professional)*; *Master's Degree*; *Doctorate (Ph.D.)*
Last Updated: 05/07/11

NATIONAL INSTITUTE OF TECHNOLOGY JAMSHEDPUR (NITJSR)

NIT Campus, P.O. RIT, Jamshedpur, Jharkhand 831014
Tel: +91(657) 240-7614 +91(657) 240-7642
Fax: +91(657) 238-2246 +91(657) 240-8811
EMail: director@nitjsr.ac.in
Website: http://www.nitjsr.ac.in/

Director: Rajnish Shrivastava
Tel: +91(657) 237-3407, Fax: +91(657) 237-3246

Registrar: S.B.L Saksena EMail: subodhseksena_03@yahoo.co.in

Departments
Chemistry (Chemistry); **Civil Engineering** (Civil Engineering); **Computer Applications** (Computer Science); **Computer Science and Engineering** (Computer Engineering; Computer Science); **Electrical and Electronics Engineering** (Electrical and Electronic Engineering; Electrical Engineering; Electronic Engineering; Power Engineering); **Electronics and Communications Engineering** (Computer Graphics; Electronic Engineering; Telecommunications Engineering); **Maths and Humanities** (Arts and Humanities; Mathematics; Operations Research; Statistics); **Mechanical Engineering** (Mechanical Engineering; Thermal Engineering); **Metallurgical and Materials Engineering** (Materials Engineering; Metallurgical Engineering); **Physics** (Physics); **Production and Industrial Engineering** (Engineering Management; Industrial Engineering; Production Engineering)

History: Created 1960 as Regional Institute of Technology Jamshedpur. Upgraded to a National Institute of Technology 2002. Became an 'Institute of National Importance' 2007.

Governing Bodies: Board of Governors; Senate

Degrees and Diplomas: *Bachelor's degree (professional)*; *Master's Degree*; *Doctorate (Ph.D.)*. Also Non-Formal Bachelor of Science in Engineering; Bachelor's degree honours.

Student Services: Health services, Sports facilities

Student Residential Facilities: 9 boys hostels and 2 girls hostels; Guest house, Accounts section; Central store

Special Facilities: Computer Center; Bank and Post Office; Student Activity Center; Bus Facility; Estate Office; MIS (Office Automation).

Libraries: Central Digital Library, c. 81,200 vols.
Last Updated: 05/07/11

NATIONAL INSTITUTE OF TECHNOLOGY KARNATAKA (NITK)

Surathkal, PO Srinivasnagar, Dashina Kannada District, Karnataka 575025
Tel: +91(824) 247-4000
Fax: +91(824) 247-4033
Website: http://www.nitk.ac.in

Director: Sandeep Sancheti
Tel: +91(824) 247-4000, Ext. 3006 EMail: director@nitk.ac.in

Registrar: M. Govindaraj
Tel: +91(824) 247-4000, Ext. 3006, Fax: +91(824) 247-4068
EMail: registrar@nitk.ac.in

Divisions
Basic Science, Humanities, Social Sciences and Management Systems (Arts and Humanities; Business Administration; Chemistry; Management; Mathematics and Computer Science; Natural Sciences; Physics; Social Sciences); **Civil Engineering Systems** (Civil Engineering; Hydraulic Engineering; Mechanics; Mining Engineering); **Electrical, Electronics and Computing Systems** (Computer Engineering; Electrical and Electronic Engineering; Electrical Engineering; Electronic Engineering; Information Technology; Telecommunications Engineering); **Mechanical and Chemical Systems** (Chemical Engineering; Materials Engineering; Mechanical Engineering; Metallurgical Engineering)

History: Founded 1960 as Karnataka Regional Engineering College, Surathkal. Became a 'Deemed Unviersity' and upgraded to National Institute of Technology 2002. Declared as 'Institute of National Importance' 2007.

Governing Bodies: Board of Governors.

Academic Year: July to May (July-December; January-May); also winter and summer sessions

Admission Requirements: Higher secondary school certificate

Fees: (Rupees): Tuition fee for undergraduate programmes, 6,000-17,500 per semester; Postgraduate programmes, 15,000 per semester.

Degrees and Diplomas: *Bachelor's degree (professional)*; *Master's Degree*; *Doctorate*. Also M.B.A.

Student Services: Canteen, Employment services, Health services, Sports facilities

Student Residential Facilities: 8 Hostel blocks for boys and 3 hostel blocks for ladies Hostels (over 3,000 beds); Staff quarters (over 200 beds); Guest house.

Special Facilities: 18,000 seats Auditorium; 1,800 capacity Open Air Theatre; Laboratories; Computer Centres; Training, placement and students welfare center; Centre for Continuing Education;R&D Centre for Clay Roofing Tiles and Ceramic Products; NTMIS Nodal Centre; Industry Institute Partnetship Cell; Centre for Transfer of Technology to Rural Areas; TIFAC-CORE Project on Industrial BioTechnology; Banks; Post office

Libraries: Over 108,000 vols; 294 periodical subscriptions; 1,084 CD-Roms; 800 full-text e-journals and about 6,000 abstract e-journal.

Academic Staff *2009-2010*: Total: c. 200

Student Numbers *2009-2010*: Total: c. 3,300
Last Updated: 05/07/11

NATIONAL INSTITUTE OF TECHNOLOGY KURUKSHETRA (NITKKR)

Kurukshetra, Haryana 136119
Tel: +91(1744) 238-122
Fax: +91(1744) 238-494
EMail: mbandyopadhyay@yahoo.com
Website: http://www.nitkkr.ac.in

Director: Anand Mohan Tel: +91(1744) 238-083

Registrar: G. R. Samantray
Tel: +91(1744) 233-212, Fax: +91(1744) 238-050
EMail: registrarnitk@rediffmail.com

Departments

Business Administration (Business Administration; Finance; Human Resources; Information Technology; International Business; Marketing); **Chemistry** (Chemistry; Materials Engineering; Polymer and Plastics Technology); **Civil Engineering** (Civil Engineering; Construction Engineering; Environmental Engineering; Hydraulic Engineering; Mechanics; Seismology; Surveying and Mapping; Transport Engineering); **Computer Applications** (Computer Science); **Computer Engineering** (Computer Engineering; Computer Networks; Software Engineering); **Electrical Engineering** (Artificial Intelligence; Automation and Control Engineering; Computer Engineering; Electrical Engineering; Electronic Engineering; Power Engineering; Robotics); **Electronics and Communication Engineering** *(ECE)* (Computer Graphics; Electronic Engineering; Telecommunications Engineering); **Humanities and Social Sciences** (Arts and Humanities; Business Administration; Communication Studies; Economics; Industrial and Organizational Psychology; Management; Social Sciences); **Mathematics** (Applied Mathematics; Mathematics); **Mechanical Engineering** (Mechanical Engineering); **Physics** (Measurement and Precision Engineering; Nanotechnology; Physics)

History: Founded 1963. Upgraded to Kurukshetra to National Institute of Technology, Kurukshetra with the status of Deemed University 2002. An 'Institution of National Importance'.

Governing Bodies: Board of Governance; Finance Committee; Senate.

Admission Requirements: Higher secondary school certificate

Fees: (Rupees): BTech, 6,000 per semester; MTech, 7,500 pers semester; MCA and MBA, 50,000 per semester; MBA. Ph.D., 6,000 per semester for full time, 1,000-5,000 for part-time and (US Dollars) 2,000 per sesmester for foreign students.

Degrees and Diplomas: *Bachelor's degree (professional)*; *Master's Degree*; *Doctorate (PhD)*. Also M.B.A.

Student Services: Health services, Sports facilities

Student Residential Facilities: 6 boys' hostels, each with a capacity 250 students; 1 girls' with a capacity of 125 students

Libraries: c. 98,875 documents, including, 49,150 vols; 135 scientific subscriptions and technical journals; Book bank scheme, 38,464 vols
Last Updated: 06/07/11

NATIONAL INSTITUTE OF TECHNOLOGY PATNA (NITP)

Ashok Rajpath, Patna, Bihar 800005
Tel: +91(612) 237-1715
EMail: info@nitp.ac.in
Website: http://www.nitp.ac.in

Director: U. C. Ray
Tel: +91(612) 237-1715 Ext. 221 EMail: director@nitp.ac.in

Registrar: Sagar Vidya
Tel: +91(612) 266-0480 EMail: registrar@nitp.ac.in

Departments

Architecture (Architectural and Environmental Design; Architecture; Design; Graphic Design; Sound Engineering (Acoustics); Visual Arts); **Civil Engineering** (Civil Engineering; Construction Engineering; Hydraulic Engineering; Surveying and Mapping; Transport Engineering); **Computer Science and Engineering** (Artificial Intelligence; Computer Engineering; Computer Networks; Computer Science; Data Processing); **Electrical Engineering** (Automation and Control Engineering; Electrical Engineering; Machine Building; Measurement and Precision Engineering; Power Engineering); **Electronics and Communication Engineering** (Computer Graphics; Electronic Engineering; Instrument Making; Optical Technology; Solid State Physics; Telecommunications Engineering); **Information Technology** (Data Processing; Information Technology; Multimedia; Software Engineering; Technology); **Mechanical Engineering** (Heating and Refrigeration; Machine Building; Mechanical Engineering; Mechanics; Thermal Physics)

History: Created in 1924 as Bihar College of Engineering Patna. Upgraded into a National Institute of Technology 2004. An 'Institution of National Importance'.

Governing Bodies: Senate

Fees: (Rupees): Tuition fee, 17,500 per semester.

Degrees and Diplomas: *Bachelor's degree (professional)*; *Master's Degree*; *Doctorate (Ph.D.)*

Student Services: Health services

Student Residential Facilities: 3 boy's hostels and 1 girl's hostel.

Special Facilities: Bank; Computer Lab; Internet facility.

Libraries: c. 50,000 vols and c. 1,100 periodical subscriptions.
Last Updated: 06/07/11

NATIONAL INSTITUTE OF TECHNOLOGY RAIPUR (NITRR)

G.E. Road, Raipur, Chhattisgarh 492010
Tel: +91(771) 225-4200
Fax: +91(771) 225-4600
Website: http://www.nitrr.ac.in/

Director: S. K. Pandey EMail: director@nitrr.ac.in

Departments

Applied Geology (Geology); **Applied Mechanics** (Mechanical Engineering; Mechanics); **Architecture** (Architecture); **Bio Technology** (Biotechnology); **Biomedical Engineering** (Biomedical Engineering; Medical Technology); **Chemical Engineering** (Chemical Engineering); **Chemistry** (Chemistry); **Civil Engineering** (Civil Engineering; Irrigation); **Computer Science and Engineering** (Computer Engineering; Computer Science); **Electrical Engineering** (Electrical Engineering); **Electronics and Telecommunication Engineering** (Electronic Engineering; Telecommunications Engineering); **English** (English); **Information Technology** (Information Technology); **Master In Computer Application** *(MCA)* (Computer Science); **Mathematics** (Mathematics); **Mechanical Engineering**

(Mechanical Engineering); **Metallurgical Engineering** (Metallurgical Engineering); **Mining Engineering** (Mining Engineering); **Physics** (Physics); **Workshop**

History: Created in 1956 as Government College of Mining and Metallurgy. Acquired current title and status of National Institute of Technology (NIT) 2005. An 'Institution of National Importance'.

Governing Bodies: Board of Governors; Senate; Finance Committee.

Admission Requirements: Secondary School Certificate

Fees: (Rupees): 35,000 per annum (except fourth and fifth year of Bachelor's degree, 18,000 per annum).

Degrees and Diplomas: *Bachelor's degree (professional)*; *Master's Degree*. Also undergraduate certificate.

Student Services: Sports facilities

Student Residential Facilities: 5 boys' hostels and 1 girls' hostel.

Libraries: Yes
Last Updated: 06/07/11

NATIONAL INSTITUTE OF TECHNOLOGY ROURKELA (NITRKL)

PO Rourkela, Distt. Sundargarh, Rourkela, Orissa 769008
Tel: +91(661) 247-6773
Fax: +91(661) 247-2926
EMail: info@nitrkl.ac.in
Website: http://www.nitrkl.ac.in

Director: Prafulla Chandra Panda
Tel: +91(661) 247-2050, Fax: +91(661) 246-2999
EMail: director@nitrkl.ac.in

Registrar: Santosh Kumar Upadhyay
Tel: +91(661) 246-2021, Fax: +91(661) 246-2999
EMail: registrar@nitrkl.ac.in

Centres
Computer (Computer Science)

Departments
Applied Mathematics (Applied Mathematics; Mathematics; Mechanics; Operations Research); **Biotechnology and Medical Engineering** (Biology; Biomedical Engineering; Biotechnology; Cell Biology; Computer Science; Genetics; Immunology; Medical Technology; Microbiology; Molecular Biology); **Ceramic Engineering** (Ceramics and Glass Technology); **Chemical Engineering** (Chemical Engineering; Energy Engineering; Nanotechnology; Thermal Engineering); **Chemistry** (Chemistry; Inorganic Chemistry; Organic Chemistry; Physical Chemistry); **Civil Engineering** (Arts and Humanities; Civil Engineering; Construction Engineering; Engineering Drawing and Design; Environmental Engineering; Geological Engineering; Irrigation; Mathematics; Physics; Surveying and Mapping; Transport Engineering); **Computer Science and Engineering** (Computer Engineering; Computer Science; Information Technology; Software Engineering); **Electrical Engineering** (Artificial Intelligence; Automation and Control Engineering; Computer Engineering; Electrical Engineering; Electronic Engineering; Power Engineering; Robotics); **Electronics and Communication Engineering** (Computer Engineering; Computer Graphics; Electronic Engineering; Measurement and Precision Engineering; Telecommunications Engineering); **Humanities and Social Sciences** (Arts and Humanities; Economics; English; Psychology; Social Sciences; Sociology); **Life Science** (Agriculture; Biochemistry; Biological and Life Sciences; Biophysics; Biotechnology; Botany; Chemistry; Mathematics; Microbiology; Molecular Biology; Pharmacology; Physics; Physiology; Zoology); **Mechanical Engineering** (Automation and Control Engineering; Energy Engineering; Engineering Drawing and Design; Industrial Engineering; Mechanical Engineering; Mechanics; Power Engineering; Robotics; Thermal Engineering); **Metallurgical and Materials Engineering** (Ceramics and Glass Technology; Computer Engineering; Heating and Refrigeration; Management; Materials Engineering; Mechanical Engineering; Metallurgical Engineering; Operations Research; Polymer and Plastics Technology; Thermal Engineering); **Mining Engineering** (Computer Science; Economics; Environmental Engineering; Geology; Geophysics; Law; Machine Building; Mechanics; Mining Engineering; Safety Engineering; Surveying and Mapping); **Physics** (Physics)

Schools
Business Management (Accountancy; Business Administration; Economics; Finance; Human Resources; Industrial and Organizational Psychology; Information Management; Information Technology; Management; Marketing; Operations Research)

History: Founded 1961 as Regional Engineering College, Rourkela. Acquired present status and title 2002. An 'Institution of National Importance'.

Governing Bodies: Board of Governors; Senate; Finance Committee; Building and Works Committee.

Academic Year: July to May (July -December; January-May)

Fees: (Rupees): Tuition fees for M.Tech., 17,500 per semester. Other Graduate programmes, 60,000 per semester.

Degrees and Diplomas: *Bachelor's degree (professional)*; *Master's Degree*; *Doctorate (PhD)*. Also M.B.A.

Student Services: Health services, Sports facilities

Student Residential Facilities: 6 halls of residence for boys and 1 hall of residence for girls; total capacity of c. 1,200 students

Special Facilities: Computing Hub; Central Workshop; Bank;

Libraries: Central Library, 59,000 vols and 15,000 back vols of periodicals; online journals and standards provided by INDEST-AICTE consortium; ISI codes, educational video courses and cassettes and CD-ROMS.
Last Updated: 06/07/11

NATIONAL INSTITUTE OF TECHNOLOGY SILCHAR (NITS)

Silchar, Assam 788010
Tel: +91(3842) 224-879
Fax: +91(3842) 224-797
Website: http://www.nits.ac.in

Director: P.K. Bose EMail: director@nits.ac.in
Registrar: Fazal A. Talukdar EMail: registrar@nits.ac.in

Departments
Chemistry (Chemistry); **Civil Engineering** (Civil Engineering); **Computer Science and Engineering** (Computer Engineering; Computer Science); **Electrical Engineering** (Electrical Engineering); **Electronics and Communication Engineering** (Electronic Engineering; Telecommunications Engineering); **Electronics and Instrumentation Engineering** (Electronic Engineering; Measurement and Precision Engineering); **Humanities and Social Sciences** (Arts and Humanities; Social Sciences); **Mathematics** (Mathematics); **Mechanical Engineering** (Mechanical Engineering); **Physics** (Physics)

History: Founded 1967 as as a Regional Engineering College (REC), Silchar. Acquired status of National Institute Of Technology and title 2002. An 'Institution of National Importance'.

Degrees and Diplomas: *Bachelor's Degree*; *Bachelor's degree (professional)*; *Master's Degree*; *Doctorate (Ph.D.)*

Academic Staff *2010-2011*: Total: c. 200
Last Updated: 06/07/11

NATIONAL INSTITUTE OF TECHNOLOGY SRINAGAR (NITSRI)

Hazratbal, Srinagar, Jammu and Kashmir 190006
Tel: +91(194) 242-4792
EMail: director@nitsri.net
Website: http://www.nitsri.net/

Director: U.C. RayFax: +91(194) 242-2032
Registrar: Shri. F. A. Wani Tel: +91(194) 242-1347

Departments
Chemical Engineering (Biochemistry; Chemical Engineering; Electrical Engineering; Electronic Engineering; Energy Engineering; Heating and Refrigeration; Industrial Management; Management; Mechanical Engineering; Organic Chemistry; Power Engineering; Statistics); **Chemistry** (Chemistry); **Civil Engineering** (Civil Engineering; Construction Engineering; Geological Engineering; Hydraulic Engineering; Irrigation; Water Science); **Computer Science and Engineering** (Artificial Intelligence; Computer

Engineering; Computer Graphics; Computer Networks; Computer Science; Data Processing; Software Engineering); **Electrical Engineering** (Automation and Control Engineering; Electrical Engineering; Electronic Engineering; Mathematics; Power Engineering); **Electronics and Communication Engineering** (Automation and Control Engineering; Computer Graphics; Electronic Engineering; Industrial Management; Mathematics; Microelectronics; Microwaves; Multimedia; Power Engineering; Telecommunications Engineering); **Humanities and Social Sciences** (Arts and Humanities; Social Sciences); **Information Technology** (Computer Engineering; Computer Graphics; Computer Networks; Data Processing; Information Management; Information Technology; Software Engineering); **Mathematics** (Mathematics); **Mechanical Engineering** (Automation and Control Engineering; Computer Engineering; Computer Graphics; Economics; Electrical Engineering; Electronic Engineering; Engineering Drawing and Design; Heating and Refrigeration; Industrial Engineering; Industrial Management; Machine Building; Materials Engineering; Mathematics; Measurement and Precision Engineering; Mechanical Engineering; Mechanics; Operations Research; Power Engineering; Production Engineering; Thermal Engineering); **Mechanical Engineering** (Hydraulic Engineering; Measurement and Precision Engineering; Mechanical Engineering); **Mechanical Engineering** (Artificial Intelligence; Automation and Control Engineering; Computer Engineering; Computer Graphics; Machine Building; Mathematics; Mechanical Engineering; Mechanics; Power Engineering); **Metallurgical and Materials Engineering** (Computer Engineering; Electronic Engineering; Geology; Heating and Refrigeration; Information Management; Machine Building; Materials Engineering; Mathematics; Mechanics; Metal Techniques; Metallurgical Engineering; Mineralogy); **Physics** (Atomic and Molecular Physics; Energy Engineering; Nanotechnology; Nuclear Physics; Physics; Solid State Physics)

History: Created in 1960 as Regional Engineering College. Acquired current title and status 2003. An 'Institution of National Importance'.

Governing Bodies: Board of Governors; Senate.

Fees: (Rupees): Tuition fee for B.Tech., 17,500 per semester.

Degrees and Diplomas: *Bachelor's degree (professional)*; *Master's Degree*; *Doctorate (PhD)*

Student Services: Health services, Sports facilities

Student Residential Facilities: Jehlum Hostel (300 beds); Chenab (297); Indus (369); Girls Hotels (100).

Special Facilities: Medical lab

Libraries: Central library: c. 68,000 vols; 6,665 periodicals; 10,051 Pamphlets; 506 Technical Films/Video Cassettes; 6 CD-Roms.

Last Updated: 06/07/11

NATIONAL INSTITUTE OF TECHNOLOGY TIRUCHIRAPPALLI (NITT)

Tanjore Main Road., National Highway 47, Tiruchirappalli, Tamil Nadu 620015
Tel: +91(431) 250-3000 +91(431) 250-4000
Fax: +91(431) 250-0133
EMail: deanac@nitt.edu
Website: http://www.nitt.edu

Director: Srinivasan Sundarrajan
Tel: +91(431) 250-0370,
Fax: +91(431) 250-0144 +91(431) 250-0133
EMail: sundar@nitt.edu

Registrar: A. K. Banerjee
Tel: +91(431) 250-3051
EMail: banerjee@nitt.edu; registrar@nitt.edu

Departments
Architecture (Architecture); **Chemical Engineering** (Agricultural Engineering; Automation and Control Engineering; Chemical Engineering; Energy Engineering); **Chemistry** (Chemical Engineering; Chemistry); **Civil Engineering** (Civil Engineering; Construction Engineering; Environmental Engineering; Transport Engineering; Transport Management); **Computer Applications** (Computer Science; Operations Research); **Computer Science and Engineering** (Artificial Intelligence; Computer Engineering; Computer Networks; Computer Science; Software Engineering); **Electrical and Electronics Engineering** (Electrical and Electronic Engineering; Elec-

trical Engineering; Electronic Engineering; Power Engineering); **Electronics and Communication Engineering** (Computer Engineering; Computer Graphics; Computer Networks; Electronic Engineering; Microwaves; Telecommunications Engineering); **Humanities** (Arts and Humanities; Business Administration; Communication Studies; English; Industrial and Organizational Psychology; Industrial Management; Labour Law; Psychology); **Instrumentation and Control Engineering** (Automation and Control Engineering; Engineering Management; Measurement and Precision Engineering); **Management Studies** (Business Administration; Commercial Law; Economics; Finance; Human Resources; Information Management; Management; Marketing; Operations Research); **Mathematics** (Mathematics); **Mechanical Engineering** (Industrial Engineering; Mechanical Engineering; Power Engineering; Safety Engineering; Thermal Engineering); **Metallurgical and Materials Engineering** (Materials Engineering; Metal Techniques; Metallurgical Engineering); **Physics** (Applied Physics; Environmental Engineering; Physics); **Production Engineering** (Industrial Engineering; Production Engineering)

History: Created in 1964 as Regional Engineering College. Acquired 'Deemed University' Status with the approval of the UGC/AICTE and Govt. of India and renamed as National Institute of Technology 2003. An 'Institution of National Importance'.

Governing Bodies: Board of Governors

Fees: (Rupees): Tuition for undergraduate programmes, 17,500 per semester (except in 4th and 5th year, 6,000 per semester); Postgraduate programmes, 10,000-17,500 per semester; M.B.A., 25,000 per semester.

Degrees and Diplomas: *Bachelor's degree (professional)*; *Master's Degree*; *Doctorate (Ph.D.)*. Also M.S. (by Research), MCA and M.B.A.

Student Services: Health services, Sports facilities

Student Residential Facilities: 17 boys' and 3 girls' hostels (3,800 students capacity); Guest house

Special Facilities: The Octagon - Computer Center, Computer Support Group; Training and placement department; Shopping Centre; Lecture Hall Complex.

Libraries: 10,7,571 vols; 670 e-books; 205 periodical subscriptions; 9 E-journals subscriptions under TEQIP; 17,454 Back Volumes; 7,786 Reports; 12,449 B.I.S.; 1,504 Video cassettes; 31 Audio cassettes; 1,367 CD-ROM databases.

Last Updated: 06/07/11

NATIONAL INSTITUTE OF TECHNOLOGY WARANGAL (NITW)

Warangal, Andhra Pradesh 506004
Tel: +91(870) 245-9191
Fax: +91(870) 245-9547
EMail: webmasters@nitw.ac.in
Website: http://www.nitw.ac.in/

Director: T. Srinivasa Rao
Tel: +91(870) 245-9216, Fax: +91(870) 245-9119
EMail: director@nitw.ac.in; tsrao@nitw.ac.in; tsrao60@gmail.com

Registrar: K. Madhu Murthy EMail: registrar@nitw.ac.in

Centres
Educational Technology (Educational Technology); **Value Education** (Peace and Disarmament)

Departments
Biotechnology (Biotechnology); **Chemical Engineering** (Chemical Engineering; Engineering Management); **Chemistry** (Chemistry; Industrial Chemistry); **Civil Engineering** (Civil Engineering; Construction Engineering; Environmental Engineering; Geological Engineering; Hydraulic Engineering; Surveying and Mapping; Transport Engineering); **Computer Science and Engineering** (Computer Engineering; Computer Science); **Electrical and Electronics Engineering** (Electrical Engineering; Electronic Engineering); **Electronics and Communications Engineering** (Computer Engineering; Electrical and Electronic Engineering; Electronic Engineering; Information Technology; Power Engineering; Telecommunications Engineering); **Humanities** (Arts and Humanities); **Mathematics** (Applied Mathematics; Mathematics; Mathematics and Computer Science); **Mechanical Engineering** (Automotive Engineering; Industrial Design; Materials Engineering; Mechanical

Engineering; Production Engineering; Thermal Engineering); **Metallurgical and Materials Engineering** (Materials Engineering; Metallurgical Engineering); **Physical Education** (Physical Education); **Physics** (Electronic Engineering; Physical Engineering; Physics)

Schools

Management (Business Administration; Finance; Human Resources; Information Management; Information Technology; Management; Marketing; Operations Research)

History: Founded 1959 as Regional Engineering College, Warangal. Acquired present title and status of Deemed University 2002. An 'Institution of National Importance'.

Degrees and Diplomas: *Bachelor's degree (professional)*; *Master's Degree*; *Doctorate (Ph.D.)*. Also M.B.A.

Student Services: Sports facilities

Student Residential Facilities: 16 hostel blocks (halls of residence) for men (1856 beds) and 2 for women (256 beds); Guest house

Special Facilities: Computer Centre

Libraries: Central Library: 143,254 vols; 210 Journals; 2,000 on-line Journals through INDEST.
Last Updated: 07/07/11

NATIONAL LAW INSTITUTE UNIVERSITY

PB N° 369, Bhopal Bhadbhada Road, Barkheri Kalan, Bhopal, Madhya Pradesh 462003
Tel: +91(755) 269-6717
Fax: +91(755) 269-6965
EMail: info@nliu.com
Website: http://www.nliu.com

Director: S.S. Singh
Tel: +91(755) 269-6965, Fax: +91(755) 269-6965
EMail: director@nliu.com

Registrar: Chandrakanta Garg EMail: registrar@nliu.com

Programmes
Law (Accountancy; Administrative Law; Civil Law; Commercial Law; Computer Science; Constitutional Law; Criminal Law; Criminology; Economics; Finance; History; Human Rights; International Business; International Law; Labour Law; Law; Political Sciences; Sociology)

History: Founded 1997.

Governing Bodies: General Council; Executive Council; Academic Council; Finance Committee.

Fees: (Rupees): Undergraduate tuition, 49,500 per annum; Graduate, 35,000 per annum.

Degrees and Diplomas: *Bachelor's Degree*; *Bachelor's degree (professional)*; *Master's Degree*. Also Bachelor's degree Honours.

Student Services: Canteen, Health services, Sports facilities

Student Residential Facilities: Halls of residence; Faculty Residence; Guest house

Special Facilities: Cyber Network Centre and Internet facility; Banking facilities

Libraries: c. 30,000 vols.
Last Updated: 07/07/11

NATIONAL LAW SCHOOL OF INDIA UNIVERSITY (NLS)

P.O. Bag 7201, Nagarbhavi, Bangalore, Karnataka 560 072
Tel: +91(80) 2321-3160 +91(80) 2316-0532
Fax: +91(80) 2316-0534
EMail: registrar@nls.ac.in
Website: http://www.nls.ac.in

Director: R. Venkata Rao
EMail: vice-chancellor@nls.ac.in; vc@nls.ac.in; venkatarao@nls.ac.in; profrao@yahoo.com

Registrar: V. Nagara

Programmes
Distance Education (Commercial Law; Consumer Studies; Environmental Studies; Ethics; Human Rights; Law); **Law** *(Post-gradu-*

ate) (Commercial Law; Constitutional Law; Human Rights; Law; Social Studies); **Law** *(Undergraduate)* (Administrative Law; Civil Law; Constitutional Law; Criminal Law; Economics; English; Fiscal Law; History; Human Rights; International Law; Labour Law; Law; Political Sciences; Sociology) *Head*: A. Jayagovind; **Research Degrees** (Law)

History: Founded 1987 by an Act of the Karnataka State Legislature, sponsored by the Bar Council of India.

Governing Bodies: General Council; Executive Council; Academic Council; Finance Committee

Academic Year: July to May (July-September; November-January; March-May)

Admission Requirements: 12th year senior secondary/intermediate examination with aggregate marks of not less than 50%, or foreign equivalent

Fees: (Rupees): 80,000 per annum; Postgraduate programmes, 30,000 per annum; Foreign students, (US Dollars), 5,000 per annum. Registration fees for research degrees, 10,000-15,000 for indian students and 35,000-52,000 for foreign students. Distance education programmes, 10,150-11,100 per annum for Indian students and 35,000-43,000 per annum for foreign students.

Main Language(s) of Instruction: English

International Co-operation: With institutions in Germany, USA, Singapore, Canada, Italy, France, Switzerland, Spain, the Netherlands and Taiwan.

Degrees and Diplomas: *Bachelor's Degree*; *Bachelor's degree (professional)*; *Postgraduate Diploma*; *Master's Degree*; *Master of Philosophy*; *Doctorate*. Also Bachelor's degree Honours.

Student Services: Canteen, Health services, Sports facilities

Student Residential Facilities: Rooms for 500 students in halls of residence for men and women, 1 postgraduate women's hostel; Staff quarters

Special Facilities: Computer lab; Internet connectivity; Moot Court Hall

Libraries: c. 40,000 vols.

Publications: March of the Law *(annually)*; National Law School Journal *(annually)*
Last Updated: 07/07/11

NATIONAL LAW UNIVERSITY (NLU DELHI)

Sector 14, Dwarka, New Delhi 110 078
Tel: +91(11) 2803-4993 +91(11) 2803-4257
EMail: info@nludelhi.ac.in
Website: http://nludelhi.ac.in/

Vice Chancellor: Ranbir Singh

Registrar: Srikrishna Deva Rao

Programmes
Law (Law)

History: Founded 2008.

Fees: (Indian Rupees): Undergraduate tuition fee, 35,000 per semester; Graduate tuition fee, 65,000 per semester;

Degrees and Diplomas: *Postgraduate Diploma*; *Master's Degree*; *Doctorate*. Also Honours Bachelor's degree (B.A., LL.B. (Hons.)), 5yrs

Student Services: Health services, Sports facilities

Student Residential Facilities: Halls of Residence

Special Facilities: Auditorium; Conference/Seminar rooms
Last Updated: 06/01/12

NATIONAL LAW UNIVERSITY (NLU)

NH-65, Nagour Road, Mandore, Jodhpur, Rajasthan 342304
Tel: +91(291) 257-7530 +91(291) 257-7526
Fax: +91(291) 257-7540
EMail: nlu-jod-rj@nic.in
Website: http://www.nlujodhpur.ac.in

Vice-Chancellor: N.N. Mathur (2007-)
Tel: +91 9829027701 EMail: nnmathurj@gmail.com

Registrar: Ratan Lahoti

Programmes

Business Administration and Law *(Undergraduate)* (Business Administration; Finance; Human Resources; Law; Management; Marketing; Mathematics; Statistics); **Corporate Laws** *(Postgraduate)* (Commercial Law; International Law; Law; Taxation); **Distance Education** (Commercial Law; Criminal Law; Criminology; Forensic Medicine and Dentistry; International Business); **Insurance** *(Postgraduate - Master of Science)* (Actuarial Science; Communication Studies; Insurance); **Insurance** *(Postgraduate - MBA)* (Accountancy; Commercial Law; Communication Studies; Finance; Insurance; Management; Marketing); **Intellectual Property Rights (IPR) and Technology Law** *(Postgraduate)* (Biotechnology; Chemistry; Commercial Law; Economics; Law; Management; Physics; Private Law); **Political Sciences and Law** *(Undergraduate)* (Economics; History; Law; Philosophy; Political Sciences; Psychology; Sociology); **Research Degree** *(In collaboration with National Law University (NLU))* (Administrative Law; Analytical Chemistry; Banking; Biological and Life Sciences; Chemistry; Commercial Law; Constitutional Law; Criminal Law; Economics; Environmental Studies; Finance; Human Resources; Law; Literature; Marketing; Natural Sciences; Philosophy; Physics; Political Sciences; Psychology); **Research Degree** *(In collaboration with National Law University (NLU))* (Law); **Technology and Law** *(Undergraduate)* (Applied Chemistry; Biotechnology; Electronic Engineering; Industrial Chemistry; Information Technology; Law; Nanotechnology; Pharmacology; Polymer and Plastics Technology; Technology; Telecommunications Engineering)

Schools

Insurance *(SIS-NLU)* (Business Administration; Insurance; Management)

History: Founded 1999.

Governing Bodies: Academic Council; Executive Council; General Council; Finance Committee; Advisory Board

Academic Year: July to April

Admission Requirements: Admissions are conducted strictly on the basis of National Entrance Test and minimum eligibility criteria is 50% marks aggregate in 10+2 for Undergraduate Courses and 55% marks aggregate in Undergraduate for Postgraduate Courses

Fees: (Rupees): Fee, 42,500 per semester for Indian students and (US Dollars): 1,800 per semester for Foreign students.

Main Language(s) of Instruction: English

International Co-operation: UNCTAD

Accrediting Agencies: National Assessment and Accreditation Council

Degrees and Diplomas: *Bachelor's Degree*; *Bachelor's degree (professional)*; *Master's Degree*; *Doctorate*: Law; Policy Science; Science and Management (Ph.D.). Also Bachelor's degree honours and M.B.A.

Student Services: Academic counselling, Canteen, Cultural centre, Employment services, Health services, Language programs, Social counselling, Sports facilities

Student Residential Facilities: Separate halls of residence for boys and girls; Faculty residence; Guest house.

Special Facilities: Wi-Fi connectivity; Computer Lab; Science Laboratories; Auditorium and Conference hall.

Libraries: c. 10,000 vols; c. 100 periodical subscriptions; Fully computerized; based on Bar Code Technology and Online Public Access Catalogue (OPAC) and WEBOPAC. Access to all major journals and textbooks of the major countries of the world through the on-line sevices of Lexis Nexis and Jurix.

Publications: Newsletter *(quarterly)*; 'Scholasticus' Jounal *(biannually)*

Press or Publishing House: Vijay Printers, Johdpur, Rajasthan, India

Last Updated: 07/07/11

NATIONAL LAW UNIVERSITY, ORISSA (NLUO)

Chahata Ghat, Mahanadi Ring Road, Tulasipur, Cuttack, Orissa 753 008
Tel: +91(671) 250-6516
Fax: +91(671) 250-6516
Website: http://www.nluo.ac.in/

Hon'ble Vice-Chancellor: Faizan Mustafa
Tel: +91(671) 250-6516 EMail: vc@nluo.ac.in

Registrar: Pabitra Mohan Samal
Tel: +91(671) 250-6516 EMail: registrar@nluo.ac.in

Schools

Liberal Arts (Arts and Humanities; Comparative Politics; Development Studies; Economics; Film; Finance; Gender Studies; Government; International Economics; Law; Literature; Mass Communication; Political Sciences; Public Administration; Religion; Social Studies; Sociology; Urban Studies); **Managerial Excellence** (Accountancy; Behavioural Sciences; Economics; Ethics; Finance; Human Resources; Industrial and Organizational Psychology; Leadership; Management; Marketing); **Private Law** (Civil Law; Commercial Law; International Law; Labour Law; Law; Private Law); **Public Law** (Administrative Law; Constitutional Law; Criminal Law; Environmental Studies; Fiscal Law; Human Rights; Law; Public Law; Taxation)

History: Founded 2008.

Governing Bodies: General Council; Executive Council; Academic Council; Finance Committee

Degrees and Diplomas: *Bachelor's Degree*; *Master's Degree*; *Doctorate*. Also Conjoint Undergraduate and Postgraduate Programmes (B.A.LL.B; B.B.A.LL.B; LL.M-PH.D)

Student Residential Facilities: Hostels

Libraries: c. 200,000 vols; Over 1,000 journals.
Last Updated: 04/01/12

NATIONAL MUSEUM INSTITUTE OF HISTORY OF ART, CONSERVATION AND MUSEOLOGY (NMI)

National Museum, Janpath, New Delhi 110011
Tel: +91(11) 2301-1901
Fax: +91(11) 2301-1921
EMail: dgnationalmuseum@gmail.com
Website: http://nmi.gov.in

Vice-Chancellor: C.V. Ananda Bose Tel: +91(11) 230-18159

Registrar: K.K. Kulshreshtha
Tel: +91(11) 230-11901 EMail: kkshreshtha@indiatimes.com

Programmes

Conservation (Fine Arts; Heritage Preservation; Museum Studies); **History of Art** (Aesthetics; Architecture; Art History; Heritage Preservation; Museum Studies); **Museology** (Art History; Art Management; Heritage Preservation; Marketing; Museum Management; Museum Studies; Public Relations)

History: Founded 1989. A postgraduate Institution with 'deemed University' status.

Admission Requirements: University degree at Master level and examination. Interview for Doctorate

Fees: (Rupees): For Indian students, Master's degree, 1,200 per semester; Ph.D. 3,000 per annum; For Foreign students, Master's degree, 100 per semester, PhD per annum and certificates (Rupees) 3,000 per course.

Degrees and Diplomas: *Master's Degree*; *Doctorate (PhD)*. Also short-term undergraduate certificate courses.

Libraries: c. 1,800 vols; Collection of 68,014 slides; Fully automated with NGTLMS (New Generation Total Library Management Software); Subscriptions to journals in the field of History of Art, Museology, Conservation, Archeology, Library Science.
Last Updated: 08/07/11

NATIONAL SANSKRIT UNIVERSITY

Rashtriya Sanskrit Vidyapeetha
Tirupati, Andhra Pradesh 517064
Tel: +91(877) 228-7649 +91(877) 228-6799
Fax: +91(877) 228-7809
EMail: registrar_rsvp@yahoo.co.in
Website: http://rsvidyapeetha.ac.in

Vice-Chancellor: Harekrishna Satapathy (2006-)
Tel: +91(877) 228-7838, Fax: +91(877) 228-7680
EMail: hks_vc@yahoo.co.in

Registrar: A. Gurumurthi
Tel: +91(877) 223-0840, Fax: +91(877) 228-7809
EMail: agmurti@gmail.com

Faculties

Darshanas (Holy Writings; Philosophical Schools; Philosophy; Sanskrit; Yoga); **Pedagogy** (Education; Educational Research; Pedagogy; Physical Education); **Sahitya and Samskriti** (Arts and Humanities; Asian Religious Studies; English; Hindi; Indic Languages; Literature; Sanskrit); **Veda Vedangas** (Computer Science; Esoteric Practices; Grammar; Linguistics; Mathematics; Sanskrit)

History: Founded 1962. Acquired 'Deemed University' status 1987.

Governing Bodies: Senate; Executive Council; Academic Council; Finance Committee.

Academic Year: July to April/May

Admission Requirements: 12th year senior secondary/intermediate examination or recognized foreign equivalent

Fees: (Rupees): Tuition fee for undegraduate programmes, 250-380 per annum; Graduate programmes, 450-5,000 per annum

Main Language(s) of Instruction: Sanskrit, English, Hindi, Telugu

Degrees and Diplomas: *Diploma*; *Bachelor's Degree*; *Bachelor's degree (professional)*; *Postgraduate Diploma*; *Master's Degree*; *Master of Philosophy*; *Doctorate*; *Doctor of Literature*. Also Intermediate courses; Career Oriented Programmes

Student Services: Foreign student adviser, Health services, Language programs, Sports facilities

Student Residential Facilities: 3 boys hostels and 1 Girls Hostels (c. 900 beds); Guest House

Special Facilities: Computer Centre; E-Class room

Libraries: Central Library: c. 85,000 vols; c. 170 subscriptions
Last Updated: 19/07/11

NATIONAL UNIVERSITY OF ADVANCED LEGAL STUDIES (NUALS)

Kinfra Salut-Tech Park, HMT Colony, PO Kalamassery, Ernakulam, Kochi, Kerala 683 503
Website: http://www.nuals.ac.in/

Vice Chancellor: N.K. Jayakumar
Tel: +91(484) 255-5990 EMail: vc@nuals.ac.in

Registrar: V. Narayana Swami
Tel: +91(484) 255-5990 EMail: registrar@nuals.ac.in

Programmes

Law (Ethics; Fiscal Law; Law)

History: Founded 2005 through merger with National Institute for Advanced Legal Studies (NIALS).

Governing Bodies: General Council; Academic Council; Executive Council

Accrediting Agencies: University Grants Commission (UGC)

Degrees and Diplomas: *Bachelor's degree (professional)*; *Postgraduate Diploma*; *Master's Degree*; *Doctorate*. Also Certificate

Student Numbers *2010-2011*: Total: c. 310
Last Updated: 04/01/12

NATIONAL UNIVERSITY OF EDUCATIONAL PLANNING AND ADMINISTRATION (NUEPA)

17-B, Sri Aurobindo Marg, New Delhi 110 016
Tel: +91(11) 268-63562 +91(11) 269-62335
Fax: +91(11) 268-53041 +91(11) 268-65180
EMail: nuepa@nuepa.org
Website: http://www.nuepa.org/

Vice Chancellor: R. Govinda
EMail: vc@nuepa.org; rgovinda@nuepa.org

Registrar: B.K. Singh EMail: registrar@nuepa.org

Departments

Comparative Education and International Cooperation (Education; Educational Sciences; International Relations); **Educational Administration** (Educational Administration); **Educational Finance** (Educational Sciences; Finance); **Educational Management Information System** (Educational Administration; Educa-

tional Technology); **Educational Planning** (Educational Sciences); **Educational Policy** (Educational Sciences); **Foundations of Education** (Education); **Higher and Professional Education** (Higher Education; Vocational Education); **Inclusive Education** (Education; Educational Sciences); **School and Non-Formal Education** (Education)

History: A 'Deemed University'.

Governing Bodies: Academic Council; Board of Management; Finance Committee; Board of Studies

Degrees and Diplomas: *Master of Philosophy*; *Doctorate*. Also Post-Doctoral Programmes and award degrees.

Student Residential Facilities: 7 hostels (52 double occupancy rooms)

Libraries: 4,141 vols; 250 periodical subscriptions
Last Updated: 19/12/11

NATIONAL UNIVERSITY OF STUDY AND RESEARCH IN LAW, RANCHI (NUSRL)

Polytechnic Campus, BIT Mesra, Ranchi, Jharkhand 835217
Tel: +91(651) 2275-250 +91(651) 6570-860
Fax: +91(651) 2275-028
EMail: info@nusrlranchi.com; nusrlranchi@gmail.com
Website: http://nusrlranchi.com/

Vice Chancellor: A.K. Koul

Registrar: Aloke Kumar Sengupta

Programmes

Law (Agricultural Economics; Arts and Humanities; Constitutional Law; Criminal Law; Economics; Environmental Studies; Family Studies; History of Law; Human Rights; International Relations; Law; Philosophy; Political Sciences; Social Sciences)

History: Founded 2010.

Governing Bodies: Academic Council; Executive Council; General Council; Academic Planning and Development Board.

Fees: (Indian Rupee): Undergraduate tuition, 50,000 per semester; Ph.D., 25,000 per semestrer.

Accrediting Agencies: University Grants Commission (UGC)

Degrees and Diplomas: *Bachelor's degree (professional)*; *Master's Degree*; *Doctorate*. The Bachelor's degree offered is a combined BA(Hons.) LLB(Hons); Also integrated Doctor of Juridical Sciences(JSD)/LLM and PhD programmes.

Student Residential Facilities: Yes

Libraries: Yes
Last Updated: 30/08/11

NAVA NALANDA MAHAVIHARA

Nalanda, Bihar 803-111
Tel: +91(611) 228-1672
Fax: +91(611) 228-1505
EMail: nnmdirector@sify.com
Website: http://navanalandamahavihara.org/

Vice Chancellor: Ravindra Panth

Registrar: S.P. Sinha
Tel: +91(611) 228-1672 EMail: spsinhanalanda@gmail.com

Courses

Ancient History, Culture and Archaeology *(Postgraduate)* (Ancient Civilizations; Archaeology; Cultural Studies); **Buddhism and Languages** *(Postgraduate)* (Asian Religious Studies; Modern Languages); **Buddhist Studies** *(Postgraduate)* (Asian Religious Studies); **Chinese and Japanese** *(Postgraduate)* (Chinese; Japanese); **English** *(Postgraduate)* (English); **Hindi** *(Postgraduate)* (Hindi); **Pali** (Indic Languages); **Pali** *(Postgraduate)* (Indic Languages); **Philosophy** *(Postgraduate)* (Philosophy); **Sanskrit** *(Postgraduate)* (Sanskrit); **Tibetan Studies** *(Postgraduate)* (Tibetan); **Tibetan Studies** (Tibetan)

History: Founded 1951. A 'Deemed University'.

Degrees and Diplomas: *Diploma*; *Bachelor's Degree*; *Master's Degree*. Also Certificates and Preparatory Course.

Libraries: c. 52,500 vols
Last Updated: 08/12/11

NAVRACHNA UNIVERSITY

Vasna Road, Vadodara, Gujarat 391 140
Tel: +91(265) 2254-392 +91(265) 2250-705
EMail: university@navrachana.edu.in
Website: http://university.navrachana.edu.in

President: Rahul Amin

Provost: Veena Mistry

Schools

Business and Law (Business Administration; Finance; International Business; Management; Marketing); **Engineering and Technology** (Computer Engineering; Computer Science); **Environmental Design and Architecture** (Architecture; Arts and Humanities; Communication Arts; Environmental Studies); **Science and Education** (Biochemistry; Biology; Botany; Chemistry; Ecology; Education; Electronic Engineering; English; Genetics; Mathematics; Molecular Biology; Natural Sciences; Nuclear Physics; Optics; Physics; Physiology; Special Education; Statistics; Thermal Physics)

History: Founded 2009.

Governing Bodies: Board of Governors; Board of Management.

Fees: (Indian Rupee): 20,000-38,000 per semester for Indian students; 30,000-55,000 per semester for international students.

Accrediting Agencies: University Grants Commission (UGC)

Degrees and Diplomas: *Bachelor's Degree*; *Bachelor's degree (professional)*; *Postgraduate Diploma*; *Master's Degree*; *Doctorate*. Also Short-term programmes; Dual B.C.A.+M.C.A. Programme.

Student Services: Canteen, Sports facilities

Student Residential Facilities: Hostel

Special Facilities: Lecture Theatre; Computer Laboratories

Libraries: Yes
Last Updated: 25/08/11

NEHRU GRAM BHARTI UNIVERSITY

Nehru Gram Bharati Vishwavidyalaya
Kotwa-Jamunipur, Dubwali, District Allahabad, Uttar Pradesh
Tel: +91(532) 285-056 +91(532) 645-6477
Fax: +91(532) 256-7870
Website: http://www.nehrugrambharati.org.in/

Vice Chancellor: K.P. Mishra

Courses

Computer Application *(Vocational)* (Computer Science); **Education** *(Vocational)* (Education); **Journalism** *(Vocational)* (Journalism); **Law** *(Vocational)* (Law); **Management** *(Vocational)* (Management); **Others** *(Vocational)* (Rural Studies; Social Work); **Special Education** *(Vocational)* (Special Education)

Groups

Commerce (Business and Commerce); **Humanities** (Ancient Civilizations; Arts and Humanities; Economics; Education; English; Hindi; Home Economics; Music; Philosophy; Political Sciences; Sanskrit; Sociology); **Science** (Botany; Chemistry; Home Economics; Mathematics; Natural Sciences; Physics; Zoology)

Further Information: Also Hanumanganj campus

History: Founded 2008. A 'Deemed University'.

Governing Bodies: Advisory Council

Accrediting Agencies: National Assessment and Accreditation Council (NAAC); University Grants Cmomission (UGC)

Degrees and Diplomas: *Bachelor's Degree*; *Bachelor's degree (professional)*; *Postgraduate Diploma*; *Master's Degree*; *Doctorate*
Last Updated: 19/12/11

NETAJI SUBHAS OPEN UNIVERSITY (NSOU)

1, Woodburn Park, Kolkata, West Bengal 700 020
Tel: +91(33) 2283-5157
Fax: +91(33) 2283-5082
EMail: registrar@wbnsou.com
Website: http://www.wbnsou.ac.in

Vice-Chancellor: Manimala Das (2008-)
Tel: +91(33) 2283-5157 EMail: manimala.das@gmail.com

Registrar: Bikas Ghosh
Tel: +91(33) 2283-5157 Ext. 13, Fax: +91(33) 2290-1931

Courses

Innovative Studies *(Non-conventional)* (Business Computing; Cardiology; Clothing and Sewing; Computer Engineering; Computer Networks; Fashion Design; Health Administration; Management; Medical Auxiliaries; Multimedia; Nursing; Physical Therapy; Pre-school Education; Psychology; Retailing and Wholesaling; Small Business; Social Work; Women's Studies); **Professional Studies** (Computer Science; Health Administration; Nursing); **Vocational Studies** *(Job oriented)* (Business Computing; Computer Engineering; Computer Networks; Fashion Design; Fishery; Horticulture; Information Technology; Laboratory Techniques; Medical Technology; Physical Therapy; Tourism; Yoga)

Programmes

Postgraduate Studies (Advertising and Publicity; Education; English; Foreign Languages Education; Geography; History; Information Sciences; Journalism; Library Science; Mass Communication; Mathematics; Political Sciences; Public Administration; Public Relations; Radio and Television Broadcasting; Social Work; South and Southeast Asian Languages; Zoology); **Undergraduate Studies** (Botany; Business and Commerce; Chemistry; Economics; English; Geography; History; Human Rights; Information Sciences; Library Science; Mathematics; Physics; Political Sciences; Public Administration; Social Sciences; Sociology; South and Southeast Asian Languages; Special Education; Zoology)

Further Information: 191 Study Centres; 6 campuses in Kolkata, Salt Lake City and Kalyani.

History: Founded 1997.

Fees: (Rupees): Undegraduate programmes,9,990-19,990 per semester; Postgraduate degree programmes, 10,000-16,000; Vocational diploma courses, 1,200-12,000 per annum; Professional degree programmes, 10,000-28,000 per annum.

Accrediting Agencies: University Grants Commission (UGC); Distance Education Council (DEC); Govt. of West Bengal; Dept. of Education, Ministry of Human Resources Development, Govt. of India;

Degrees and Diplomas: *Diploma*; *Bachelor's Degree*; *Bachelor's degree (professional)*; *Postgraduate Diploma*; *Master's Degree*; *Master of Philosophy*. Also Bachelor's degree Honours; Certificate courses in Computer Science; Vocational programmes.

Student Numbers *2008-2009*: Total: c. 100,000
Last Updated: 08/07/11

NEW DELHI INSTITUTE OF MANAGEMENT (NDIM)

60 & 50(B&C), Behind Batra Hospital, Tughlakabad Institutional Area, New Delhi 110 062
Tel: +91(11) 2995-6566 +91(11) 2995-67
Fax: +91(11) 2996-5136
EMail: info@ndimdelhi.org
Website: http://www.ndimdelhi.org/

Director: Sudhiranjan Dey

Programmes

Management *(Part-time)* (Economics; Finance; Information Technology; International Business; Management; Marketing; Statistics); **Management** (Finance; Human Resources; Information Technology; International Business; Management; Marketing; Operations Research); **Management (Marketing)** (Management; Marketing)

History: Founded 1996.

Governing Bodies: Board of Governors; Academic Advisory Council

Accrediting Agencies: All India Council for Technical Education (AICTE), Ministry of HRD, Government of India; National Board of Accreditation (NBA)

Degrees and Diplomas: *Postgraduate Diploma*. Postgraduate Degree equivalent to a university MBA degree.

Student Services: Canteen, Health services, Sports facilities

Student Residential Facilities: Hostel

Special Facilities: Information Technology Centre

Libraries: c. 62,000 vols; 129 magazines/journals and 14 newspapers
Last Updated: 23/01/12

NILAMBER-PITAMBER UNIVERSITY (NPU)

Palamu district, Medininagar, Jharkhand
Tel: +91(6562) 231-580
EMail: vc@npu.ac.in
Website: http://www.npu.ac.in/

Vice Chancellor: Firoz Ahmad Tel: +91(6562) 231-580

Registrar: P. K. Verma
Tel: +91(94311) 55-097 EMail: pkv_ru@yahoo.com

Colleges
G.L.A. *(Medininagar, Palamau)* (Botany; Chemistry; English; Geography; Geology; Hindi; History; Mathematics; Physics; Political Sciences; Psychology; Urdu; Zoology); **S.S.J.S.N.** *(Garhwa)* (Anthropology; Botany; Business and Commerce; Chemistry; Economics; English; Geography; Geology; Hindi; History; Mathematics; Philosophy; Physics; Political Sciences; Psychology; Sanskrit; Sociology; Urdu; Zoology); **Y.S.N.M.** *(Medininagar)* (Botany; Chemistry; Economics; English; Hindi; History; Home Economics; Mathematics; Philosophy; Physics; Political Sciences; Psychology; Zoology)

Further Information: Also 4 Constituent Colleges; 8 Affiliated Colleges; 5 Professional/ Technical Colleges

History: Founded 2009.

Governing Bodies: Academic Council

Degrees and Diplomas: *Bachelor's Degree*; *Bachelor's degree (professional)*; *Master's Degree*; *Doctorate*
Last Updated: 03/01/12

NIMS UNIVERSITY

Shobha Nagar, Delhi Highway, Jaipur, Rajasthan 303 121
Tel: +91(1426) 513-102 +91(1426) 513-103
Fax: +91(141) 2605-050 +91(1426) 213-909
EMail: info@nimsuniversity.org; chairman@nimsuniversity.org
Website: http://nimsuniversity.org

Vice-Chancellor: K.C. Singhal

Registrar: K. P. Singh

Colleges
Dentistry (Dentistry; Medical Auxiliaries); **Nursing** (Nursing; Surgery)

Institutes
Advance Sciences (Biochemistry; Biotechnology; Microbiology; Natural Sciences); **Advanced Engineering** (Aeronautical and Aerospace Engineering; Biotechnology; Chemical Engineering; Civil Engineering; Computer Science; Electrical Engineering; Electronic Engineering; Energy Engineering; Engineering; Geology; Industrial Engineering; Information Technology; Nuclear Engineering; Petroleum and Gas Engineering; Power Engineering; Structural Architecture; Telecommunications Engineering; Thermal Engineering); **Air Hostess and Aviation** (Air Transport); **Applied Arts** (Fine Arts; Performing Arts; Visual Arts); **Basic Sciences** (Botany; Chemistry; Environmental Studies; Geography; Geology; Home Economics; Mathematics; Physics; Psychology; Statistics; Zoology); **Commerce** (Business and Commerce); **Computer Science** (Computer Science; Electronic Engineering; Information Technology); **Education and Physical Education** (Health Education; Physical Education; Sports); **Engineering and Technology** (Agricultural Engineering; Automotive Engineering; Biotechnology; Chemical Engineering; Civil Engineering; Computer Engineering; Computer Science; Electrical Engineering; Electronic Engineering; Engineering; Information Technology; Mechanical Engineering; Technology; Telecommunications Engineering); **Hotel Management and Tourism** (Cooking and Catering; Food Technology; Hotel Management; Tourism); **Humanities and Social Sciences** (Anthropology; Arts and Humanities; Economics; English; Geography; Hindi; History; Philosophy; Political Sciences; Psychology; Public Administration; Rural Studies; Sanskrit; Social Sciences; Social Welfare; Sociology); **Journalism and Mass Communication** (Journalism; Mass Communication); **Library Science** (Information Sciences; Library Science); **Management** (Banking; Business Administration;

Finance; Health Administration; Human Resources; Information Sciences; Information Technology; International Business; Management; Marketing; Pharmacy; Retailing and Wholesaling); **Medical Sciences and Research and Hospital** *(NIMS Medical College)* (Anaesthesiology; Anatomy; Biochemistry; Community Health; Dermatology; Forensic Medicine and Dentistry; Genetics; Gynaecology and Obstetrics; Health Administration; Immunology; Medicine; Microbiology; Ophthalmology; Orthopaedics; Otorhinolaryngology; Paediatrics; Pathology; Pharmacology; Physiology; Pneumology; Radiophysics; Surgery; Venereology); **Paramedical Technology** (Laboratory Techniques; Medical Auxiliaries; Medical Technology; Ophthalmology; Optometry; Radiology; Treatment Techniques); **Pharmacy** (Chemistry; Marketing; Pharmacology; Pharmacy; Safety Engineering); **Physiotheraphy** (Cardiology; Gynaecology and Obstetrics; Neurology; Neurosciences; Occupational Therapy; Orthopaedics; Paediatrics; Physical Therapy; Respiratory Therapy); **Textile and Fashion Design** (Fashion Design; Journalism; Marketing; Textile Design; Textile Technology); **Theatre, Film and Television Technology** (Acting; Film; Graphic Arts; Radio and Television Broadcasting; Theatre; Visual Arts)

Programmes
Distance Education (Accountancy; Air Transport; Banking; Communication Arts; Computer Networks; Dental Technology; Diabetology; Environmental Management; Environmental Studies; Health Administration; Heritage Preservation; Insurance; International Business; Jewelry Art; Journalism; Laboratory Techniques; Management; Mass Communication; Medical Technology; Microbiology; Musical Instruments; Nursing; Ophthalmology; Optics; Orthodox Theology; Pharmacy; Photography; Physical Therapy; Psychology; Radiology; Sports; Taxation; Tourism; Treatment Techniques; Venereology; Video)

Schools
Architecture and Planning (Architecture and Planning); **Law** (Law)

History: Founded 2008.

Fees: (Indian Rupee): Undergraduate programmes, 15,000-295,000 per annum; Postgraduate programmes, 17,000-600,000 per annum; Ph.D., 55,000-150,000 per annum.

Degrees and Diplomas: *Diploma*; *Bachelor's Degree*; *Bachelor's degree (professional)*; *Postgraduate Diploma*; *Master's Degree*; *Master of Philosophy*; *Doctorate*. Also Certificates; Honours Bachelor's degrees; Dual Specialization (B.Tech/B.Tech); M. Tech. Integrated with B.Tech; M.B.A. and integrated M.B.A.

Student Services: Canteen, Cultural centre, Sports facilities

Student Residential Facilities: Boys and Girls Hostels

Special Facilities: Hi-tech Labs; Wifi access

Libraries: Yes
Last Updated: 05/09/11

NIRMA UNIVERSITY

Sarkhej-Gandhinagar Highway, Post: Chandlodia, Via: Gota, Ahmedabad, Gujarat 382 481
Tel: +91 (2717) 241-900 +91 (2717) 241-911
Fax: +91 (2717) 241-916 +91 (2717) 241-917
EMail: asst_registrar@nirmauni.ac.in
Website: http://www.nirmauni.ac.in/

Vice-Chancellor/Director General: N. V. Vasani
Tel: +91(2717) 241-230, Fax: +91(2717) 241-280
EMail: vc@nirmauni.ac.in

Executive Registrar: Shri D.P. Chhaya
Tel: +91(2717) 241-168, Fax: +91(2717) 241-916
EMail: registrar@nirmauni.ac.in

Faculties
Law (Commercial Law; Law); **Management** (Business Administration; Finance; Human Resources; International Business; Management; Operations Research); **Pharmacy** (Biotechnology; Chemistry; Pharmacology; Pharmacy); **Science** (Biochemistry; Biotechnology; Microbiology); **Technology and Engineering** (Automation and Control Engineering; Chemical Engineering; Civil Engineering; Computer Engineering; Computer Science; Electrical Engineering; Electronic Engineering; Engineering; Information Technology; Measurement and Precision Engineering; Mechanical Engineering; Polymer and Plastics Technology; Technology; Telecommunications Engineering)

History: Founded 1994, as Nirma Education and Research Foundation. Acquired present status and name 2003 through the merger of the Foundation's various institutes.

Governing Bodies: Board of Governors; Academic Council; Finance Committee.

Accrediting Agencies: University Grants Commission (UGC)

Degrees and Diplomas: *Diploma; Bachelor's Degree; Bachelor's degree (professional); Postgraduate Diploma; Master's Degree; Doctorate (Ph.D.).* Also Bachelor's degree Honours and M.B.A.

Student Services: Canteen, Sports facilities

Student Residential Facilities: Hostel for postgraduate students.

Special Facilities: Computer Centre; Computer laboratories; Auditoriums; Seminar rooms.

Libraries: Central Library Resource Centre: 79,000 vols; 19 online databases; 787 print periodicals; over 7,000 online journals; over 376 videos and more than 4,700 electronic media.

Last Updated: 08/07/11

NITTE UNIVERSITY

6th Flr, University Enclave, Medical Sciences Complex, Deralakatte, Mangalore, Karnataka 575018
Tel: +91(824) 220-4300 +91(824) 220-4301
Fax: +91(824) 220-4305
EMail: info@nitte.edu.in; admissions@nitte.edu.in
Website: http://nitte.edu.in/

Vice Chancellor: M. Shantharam Shetty

Registrar: H.V. Sudhaker Nayak

Academies
Medicine *(K. S. Hegde)* (Anatomy; Biochemistry; Biophysics; Community Health; Forensic Medicine and Dentistry; Gynaecology and Obstetrics; Medicine; Microbiology; Pathology; Pharmacology; Physiology; Surgery; Toxicology)

Institutes
Dental Sciences *(A. B. Shetty Memorial)* (Dentistry; Microbiology; Oral Pathology; Orthodontics; Periodontics; Radiology; Surgery); **Nursing Sciences** *(Nitte Usha)* (Child Care and Development; Community Health; Midwifery; Nursing; Psychiatry and Mental Health; Surgery); **Pharmaceutical Sciences** *(Nitte Gulabi Shetty Memorial)* (Biotechnology; Chemistry; Microbiology; Pharmacology; Pharmacy); **Physiotherapy** (Physical Therapy)

History: Founded 1979 as the Nitte Education Trust. Acquired 'Deemeed University' status 2008.

Governing Bodies: Advisory Committee; Board of Management; Finance Committee; Planning and Monitoring Board; Academic Council; Board of Studies

Degrees and Diplomas: *Bachelor's degree (professional); Postgraduate Diploma; Master's Degree; Doctorate*
Last Updated: 14/12/11

NIZAM'S INSTITUTE OF MEDICAL SCIENCES (NIMS)

Punjagutta, Hyderabad, Andhra Pradesh 500 082
Tel: +91(40) 2348-9000
Fax: +91(40) 2331-0076
EMail: nims@ap.nic.in
Website: http://nims.ap.nic.in/

Director: Prasanta Mahapatra
Tel: +91(40) 2339-0933 +91(40)2348-9999,
Fax: +91(40) 2331-0076 EMail: Director.nims@ap.nic.in

Executive Registrar: M. Sudershanam
Tel: +91(40) 2339-9690 +91(40) 2348-9130,
Fax: +91(40) 2331-0076 EMail: er.nims@ap.nic.in

Colleges
Nursing (Gynaecology and Obstetrics; Midwifery; Nursing; Paediatrics; Psychiatry and Mental Health; Surgery)

Departments
Anaesthesiology and Intensive Care (Anaesthesiology; Respiratory Therapy); **Biochemistry** (Biochemistry); **Biomedical Engineering** (Biomedical Engineering); **Cardiology** (Cardiology); **Cardiothoracic Surgery** (Cardiology; Surgery); **Chest Clinic**

(Pneumology); **Civil** (Civil Security); **Clinical Pharmacology and Therapeutics** (Pharmacology; Pharmacy); **Dental Studies** (Dental Hygiene; Dentistry); **Dermatology** (Dermatology); **Electrical** (Electrical Engineering); **Endocrinology and Metabolism** (Endocrinology); **Gastroenterology** (Gastroenterology); **General Medicine** (Medicine); **Gynaecology** (Gynaecology and Obstetrics); **Hospital Administration** (Health Administration); **Medical Oncology** (Oncology); **Medical Records; Microbiology** (Biotechnology; Laboratory Techniques; Medical Technology; Medicine; Microbiology; Nephrology; Nursing; Pathology; Physical Therapy); **Nephrology** (Nephrology); **Neuro Surgery** (Neurological Therapy; Surgery); **Neurology** (Biomedicine; Neurology; Physical Therapy; Psychiatry and Mental Health); **Nuclear Medicine** (Medical Technology); **Orthopaedics** (Orthopaedics); **Paediatrics** (Paediatrics); **Pathology** (Pathology); **Physio Therapy** (Physical Therapy); **Plastic Surgery** (Plastic Surgery); **Radiation Oncology** (Medicine; Nursing; Oncology; Radiology); **Radiology and Imageology** (Radiology); **Rheumatology** (Rheumatology); **Surgical Gastroenterology** (Gastroenterology; Surgery); **Surgical Oncology** (Oncology; Rehabilitation and Therapy; Surgery); **Transfusion Medicine** (Medicine); **Urology** (Urology); **Vascular Surgery** (Cardiology; Surgery)

Divisions
Computer (Computer Science)

Further Information: 985 beds hospital.

History: Founded 1980 as Institute of Medical Sciences (IMS). Acquired present title 1986 with the tranfer of the Nizam's Institute of Orthopaedics and Specialities (NIOS), inaugurated 1964. Acquired university status and title 1989.

Governing Bodies: Governing Council; Executive Board.

Accrediting Agencies: University Grants Commission (UGC) and Medical Council of India (MCI).

Degrees and Diplomas: *Diploma; Bachelor's Degree; Postgraduate Diploma; Master's Degree; Doctorate (PhD)*

Libraries: c. 5,000 vols

Academic Staff *2010-2011*: Total: c. 140
Last Updated: 08/07/11

NMIMS UNIVERSITY (NMIMS)

V. L. Mehta Road, Vile Parle (W), Mumbai, Maharashtra 400 056
Tel: +91(22) 2613-4577
EMail: enquiry@nmims.edu; anjali.barmukh@nmims.edu
Website: http://www.nmims.edu

Vice-Chancellor: Rajan Saxena
EMail: vc@nmims.edu; rajan.saxena@nmims.edu

Director (Admin.) and Incharge Registrar: Varsha Parab

Schools
Architecture *(Balwant Sheth)* (Architecture); **Business Management** (Actuarial Science; Banking; Business Administration; Human Resources; Management); **Commerce** *(Anil Surendra Modi)* (Accountancy; Business Administration; Business and Commerce; Finance; Taxation); **Distance Learning** *(SDL)* (Management); **Pharmacy and Technology Management** (Biotechnology; Business Administration; Chemistry; Health Administration; Pharmacology; Pharmacy; Safety Engineering); **Science** (Biological and Life Sciences; Chemistry; Statistics); **Technology Management and Engineering** *(Mukesh Patel)* (Chemical Engineering; Civil Engineering; Computer Engineering; Electronic Engineering; Engineering; Engineering Management; Information Technology; Management; Mechanical Engineering; Production Engineering; Telecommunications Engineering)

Further Information: Also campuses in Bengaluru, Shirpur and Hyderabad.

History: Founded 1981 as Narsee Monjee Institute of Management Studies (NMIMS). Acquired present status of 'Deemed University' 2003 and present title 2006.

Fees: (Rupees): Undergraduate programmes, 15,000-130,000; Postgraduate programmes, 30,000-170,000; MBA, 60,000-250,000; PhD, 30,000-45,000.

International Co-operation: With universities in Australia, USA, Canada, France, Hungary

Degrees and Diplomas: *Diploma*; *Bachelor's Degree*; *Bachelor's degree (professional)*; *Postgraduate Diploma*; *Master's Degree*; *Doctorate*. Also Bachelor's degree honours; M.B.A; Integrated Master of Science – Doctor of Philosophy Programme.

Libraries: R.M. Desai Library, c. 58,000 vols; more than 5,000 full text journals; Online Public Access Catalogue (OPAC).

Academic Staff *2010-2011*: Total: c. 200

Student Numbers *2010-2011*: Total: c. 5,000

Last Updated: 08/07/11

NOIDA INTERNATIONAL UNIVERSITY (NIU)

309, Jaipuria Plaza, Sector - 26, Noida, Uttar Pradesh 201 301
Tel: +91(120) 455-6360
Fax: +91(120) 416-7418
EMail: info@niu.ac.in
Website: http://www.niu.ac.in/

Vice Chancellor: Vikram Singh EMail: vc@niu.ac.in

Dean, Administration: Mian Jan

Schools

Architecture (Architecture); **Business Management** (Air Transport; Business Administration; Finance; Human Resources; International Business; Labour and Industrial Relations; Management; Marketing; Transport Management); **Education** (Education); **Engineering and Technology** (Aeronautical and Aerospace Engineering; Automation and Control Engineering; Biotechnology; Civil Engineering; Computer Engineering; Computer Science; Electrical Engineering; Electronic Engineering; Energy Engineering; Engineering; Information Technology; Mechanical Engineering; Nanotechnology; Technology; Telecommunications Engineering); **Fashion** (Fashion Design; Jewelry Art; Textile Design; Textile Technology); **Fine Arts** (Fashion Design; Fine Arts; Painting and Drawing; Sculpture; Textile Design); **Home Economics** (Development Studies; Home Economics; Interior Design; Nutrition; Textile Technology); **Hotel Management** (Hotel Management); **Journalism and Mass Communication** (Advertising and Publicity; Journalism; Marketing; Mass Communication; Media Studies; Multimedia; Public Relations; Radio and Television Broadcasting; Sound Engineering (Acoustics)); **Legal Studies and Research** (Law); **Liberal Arts** (Arts and Humanities; English; French; Geography; German; Hindi; History; Home Economics; Modern Languages; Painting and Drawing; Political Sciences; Psychology; Sanskrit; Sociology; Spanish); **Library Science** (Library Science); **Nursing** (Midwifery; Nursing); **Physical Education and Sports Science** (Physical Education; Sports); **Sciences** (Biochemistry; Biotechnology; Industrial Chemistry; Microbiology)

History: Founded 2010.

Governing Bodies: Board of Governors; Academic Council

Fees: (Indian Rupees): undergraduate fee, 10,000-100,000 per semester; graduate fee, 11,250-142,500 per semester.

Accrediting Agencies: University Grants Commission (UGC)

Degrees and Diplomas: *Diploma*; *Bachelor's Degree*; *Bachelor's degree (professional)*; *Postgraduate Diploma*; *Master's Degree*; *Doctorate*. Also Honours Bachelor's degrees, 3 yrs; Dual degrees (B.Tech+ M.Tech), 5 yrs; M.B.A.

Last Updated: 02/01/12

NOORUL ISLAM CENTRE FOR HIGHER EDUCATION

Kumaracoil, Thuckalay, Kanyakumari District, Thuckalay, Tamilnadu 629 180
Tel: +91(4651) 250-566 +91(4651) 250-266
EMail: info@niuniv.com
Website: http://www.niuniv.com/

Vice-Chancellor: S. Sivasubramanian
Tel: +91(4651) 250-467 EMail: profssm@hotmail.com

Registrar: S. Manickam

Departments

Aeronautical Engineering (Aeronautical and Aerospace Engineering; Mechanical Engineering); **Aerospace Engineering** (Aeronautical and Aerospace Engineering); **Automobile Engineering** (Automotive Engineering); **Biomedical Engineering** (Bio-

medical Engineering); **Business Administration** (Business Administration); **Civil Engineering** (Civil Engineering); **Computer Application** (Computer Engineering; Computer Graphics; Computer Networks; Computer Science; Data Processing); **Computer Science and Engineering** (Computer Engineering; Computer Science); **Electrical and Electronic Engineering** (Electrical Engineering; Electronic Engineering); **Electronic and Instrumentation Engineering** (Electronic Engineering); **Electronic and Telecommunication** (Electronic Engineering; Telecommunications Engineering); **Information Technology** (Information Technology; Software Engineering); **Information Technology** (Information Technology; Software Engineering); **Marine Engineering** (Marine Engineering); **Mechanical Engineering** (Mechanical Engineering; Thermal Engineering); **Nanotechnology** (Nanotechnology); **Sciences and Humanities** (Artificial Intelligence; Arts and Humanities; Computer Science; Econometrics; Software Engineering)

History: Founded 1988 as a constituent College of the Noorul Islam University. Acquired 'Deemed University' status 2008.

Governing Bodies: Board of Management; Academic Council; Finance Committee; Advisory Committee; Pallnign and Monitoring Board

Accrediting Agencies: National Board of Accreditation (NBA); All India Council for Technical Education (AICTE)

Degrees and Diplomas: *Bachelor's degree (professional)*; *Postgraduate Diploma*; *Master's Degree*; *Master of Philosophy*; *Doctorate*. Also M.B.A.

Libraries: 38,433 vols; c. 150 periodical subscriptions

Academic Staff *2010-2011*: Total: c. 250

Last Updated: 20/12/11

NORTH BENGAL AGRICULTURAL UNIVERSITY

Uttar Banga Krishi Vishwavidyalaya (UBKV)
PO Pundibari, Koch Bihar, West Bengal 736165
Tel: +91(3582) 270249
Fax: +91(3582) 270249
Website: http://www.ubkv.ac.in

Vice-Chancellor: A. K. Das

Faculties

Agricultural Engineering (Agricultural Engineering); **Agriculture** (Agricultural Business; Agriculture; Animal Husbandry; Dairy; Forestry; Home Economics; Veterinary Science); **Horticulture** (Horticulture)

History: Founded 2001. Formerly part of Bidhan Chandra Krishi Viswadidyalaya.

Main Language(s) of Instruction: Hindi

Accrediting Agencies: University Grants Commission (UGC); All India Council for Technical Education (AICTE)

Degrees and Diplomas: *Bachelor's Degree*; *Bachelor's degree (professional)*; *Master's Degree*; *Doctorate*. Also M.B.A.

Last Updated: 29/11/11

NORTH EASTERN REGIONAL INSTITUTE OF SCIENCE AND TECHNOLOGY (NERIST)

Nirjuli, Itanagar, Arunachal Pradesh 791 109
Website: http://www.nerist.ac.in

Director: P. K. Das
Tel: +91(360) 224-5094 +91(360) 225-7584,
Fax: +91(360) 224-4307

Registrar: R. P. Bhattacharjee
Tel: +91(360) 225-7401 EMail: registrar@nerist.ernet.in

Departments

Agricultural Engineering (Agricultural Engineering; Agricultural Equipment; Agriculture; Dairy; Energy Engineering; Food Technology; Harvest Technology; Irrigation; Power Engineering; Soil Conservation; Water Science); **Chemistry** (Chemistry; Engineering; Forestry; Technology); **Civil Engineering** (Civil Engineering; Construction Engineering; Engineering; Environmental Engineering; Geological Engineering; Geology; Hydraulic Engineering; Road Engineering; Safety Engineering; Surveying and Mapping); **Computer Science and Engineering** (Artificial Intelligence; Computer Engineering; Computer Graphics; Computer Networks; Computer

Science; Data Processing; Electronic Engineering; Information Technology; Mathematics; Software Engineering); **Electrical Engineering** (Automation and Control Engineering; Electrical Engineering; Energy Engineering; Maintenance Technology; Measurement and Precision Engineering; Power Engineering); **Electronics and Communication Engineering** (Electronic Engineering; Telecommunications Engineering); **Forestry** (Forestry); **Humanities and Social Science** (Agricultural Business; Arts and Humanities; Business Administration; Economics; English; Management; Mass Communication; Psychology; Social Sciences; Sociology); **Mathematics** (Applied Mathematics; Mathematics; Statistics); **Mechanical Engineering** (Heating and Refrigeration; Maintenance Technology; Mechanical Engineering); **Physics** (Applied Physics; Engineering; Materials Engineering; Physics)

History: Founded 1984. A 'Deemed University'.

Fees: (Rupees): Tuition fee for undegraduate programmes, 1,450-1,700 per semester; Postgraduate programmes, 2,500-3,000 per semester; MBA, 10,000 per semester; Ph.D., 3,000 per semester.

Degrees and Diplomas: *Diploma*; *Bachelor's Degree*; *Bachelor's degree (professional)*; *Postgraduate Diploma*; *Master's Degree*; *Doctorate*. Also undergraduate certificates and MBA.

Student Services: Health services, Sports facilities

Student Residential Facilities: 8 Hostel Blocks for 1250 boys and 200 girls.

Special Facilities: Seminar Hall; Advanced Central Computing Facility; Central Research Facility; Education Technology Cell; Training and Placement Cell; Gymkhana; Auditorium; Bank.

Libraries: Central Library
Last Updated: 08/07/11

NORTH MAHARASHTRA UNIVERSITY
Uttar Maharashtra Vidyapeeth (NMU)
PO Box 80, Umavinagar, Jalgaon, Maharashtra 425001
Tel: +91(257) 225-8428
Fax: +91(257) 225-8403
EMail: registrar@nmu.ac.in
Website: http://www.nmu.ac.in

Vice-Chancellor: Sudhir. U. Meshram (2011-)
Registrar: A. B. Chaudhari

Centres
Pratap Philosophy *(Amalner)* (Philosophy)

Departments
Chemical Technology (Chemical Engineering; Food Technology; Nanotechnology; Petroleum and Gas Engineering; Pharmacy; Polymer and Plastics Technology; Technology); **Comparative Languages and Literature** (Comparative Literature; Cultural Studies; English; Hindi; Indic Languages; Translation and Interpretation); **Computer Science** (Computer Science; Information Technology); **Education** (Education; Physical Education); **Law** (Law); **Library and Information Science** (Information Sciences; Library Science); **Management Studies** (Banking; Business Administration; Management); **Organic Chemistry** (Chemistry; Organic Chemistry); **Performing Arts** (Music; Performing Arts; Theatre)

Schools
Chemical Sciences (Analytical Chemistry; Chemistry; Industrial Chemistry; Physical Chemistry; Polymer and Plastics Technology); **Environmental Sciences** (Environmental Studies; Geochemistry; Geology); **Life Sciences** (Biochemistry; Biological and Life Sciences; Biotechnology; Microbiology); **Mathematical Sciences** (Actuarial Science; Computer Science; Mathematics; Mathematics and Computer Science; Statistics); **Physical Sciences** (Electronic Engineering; Energy Engineering; Materials Engineering; Physics; Telecommunications Engineering); **Social Sciences** (Economics; Journalism; Mass Communication; Military Science; Political Sciences; Psychology; Social Sciences; Sociology)

Further Information: Also 119 Affiliated Colleges and 21 Recognized Institutions. A traditional and distance education institution.

History: Founded 1990, by Act passed by the legislature of the State of Maharashtra.

Governing Bodies: Senate; Management Council, comprising 18 members; Academic Council, comprising 68 members

Academic Year: June to April (June-October; November-April)

Admission Requirements: 12th year senior secondary/intermediate examination

Fees: (Rupees): 800-18,000 per annum

Main Language(s) of Instruction: Marathi, English

Accrediting Agencies: University Grants Commission; National Accreditation and Assessment Council (NAAC)

Degrees and Diplomas: *Diploma*; *Bachelor's Degree*; *Bachelor's degree (professional)*; *Postgraduate Diploma*; *Master's Degree*; *Master of Philosophy*; *Doctorate*. Also Vocational Certificate, Diploma and Advanced Diploma Courses.

Student Services: Health services, Social counselling, Sports facilities

Student Residential Facilities: Hostels for c. 560 Men and c. 320 Women students

Libraries: University Library, 17,000 vols; 161 periodical subscriptions

Publications: Philosophical Quarterly, English *(quarterly)*; Sane Guruji Sanskav Vartapatra, Marathi *(quarterly)*; Tatwadnyan Mandir, Marathi, Philosophy *(quarterly)*
Last Updated: 29/11/11

NORTH ORISSA UNIVERSITY (NOU)
Sriram Chandra Vihar, Takatpur, Baripada, Mayurbhanj, Orissa 757003
Tel: +91(6792) 256-906
Fax: +91(6792) 255-127
Website: http://nou.nic.in

Vice-Chancellor: Shiba Prasad Rath (2008-)
Tel: +91(6792) 255-127, Fax: +91(6792) 255-127

Registrar: Upendra Nath Sahoo
Tel: +91(6792) 256-906, Fax: +91(6792) 255-127

Departments
Anthropology and Tribal Studies (Anthropology; Archaeology; Cultural Studies; Museum Studies); **Bioinformatics** (Biochemistry; Cell Biology; Genetics; Mathematics; Mathematics and Computer Science; Statistics); **Biotechnology** (Biochemistry; Biology; Biotechnology; Genetics; Molecular Biology; Physiology; Statistics); **Botany** (Biology; Biotechnology; Botany; Cell Biology; Ecology; Genetics; Molecular Biology; Statistics); **Business Administration** (Accountancy; Advertising and Publicity; Business Administration; Business Computing; Commercial Law; Communication Studies; Computer Networks; E-Business/Commerce; Economics; Finance; Human Resources; Information Management; Information Sciences; International Business; Management; Marketing; Software Engineering); **Chemistry** (Analytical Chemistry; Chemistry; Inorganic Chemistry; Organic Chemistry; Physical Chemistry; Polymer and Plastics Technology); **Computer Science and Applications** (Computer Science; Data Processing; E-Business/Commerce; Mathematics; Mathematics and Computer Science; Multimedia; Operations Research; Robotics; Software Engineering); **Economics** (Agricultural Economics; Business Computing; Econometrics; Economics; Finance; International Business); **Law** (Commercial Law; Law); **Library and Information Sciences** (Information Management; Information Sciences; Information Technology; Library Science); **Mathematics and Computer Science** (Computer Science; Mathematics; Mathematics and Computer Science); **Physics** (Electronic Engineering; Mathematical Physics; Mechanics; Nuclear Physics; Physics); **Remote Sensing and Geographic Information System** (Geological Engineering; Surveying and Mapping); **Wildlife** (Ecology; Forest Management; Wildlife); **Zoology** (Anatomy; Biochemistry; Biology; Cell Biology; Endocrinology; Genetics; Immunology; Microbiology; Molecular Biology; Physiology; Statistics; Toxicology; Zoology)

Programmes
Distance Education (Advertising and Publicity; Anthropology; Business Administration; Business and Commerce; Computer Science; Education; English; History; Information Sciences; Information Technology; Journalism; Library Science; Management; Mass Communication; Molecular Biology; Philosophy; Political Sciences; Public Administration; Public Relations; Sanskrit; Sociology; South and Southeast Asian Languages; Surveying and Mapping; Tourism; Wildlife)

Further Information: Also 80 affiliated colleges.

History: Founded 1998.

Governing Bodies: Syndicate; Senate; Academic Council.

Fees: (Rupees): Dinstance education, 5,000-15,000 per annum.

Accrediting Agencies: University Grants Commission (University Grants Commission (UGC).

Degrees and Diplomas: *Bachelor's Degree*; *Postgraduate Diploma*; *Master's Degree*; *Master of Philosophy*; *Doctorate*. Also Bachelor's degree honours; MBA; MCA.

Student Services: Academic counselling, Canteen, Health services, Sports facilities

Student Residential Facilities: Boys and girls hostels.

Special Facilities: Central Computer Lab

Libraries: Central Library

Publications: Tathya, Humanities publication; Tattva, Scientific publication; The Banani, Publication in Oriya; Vision, Publication in English

Last Updated: 08/07/11

NORTH-EASTERN HILL UNIVERSITY (NEHU)

Umshing Mawkynroh Shillong, Shillong, Meghalaya 793022
Tel: +91(364) 255-0067
Fax: +91(364) 255-0076
Website: http://www.nehu.ac.in

Vice-Chancellor: A.N. Rai (2010-)
Tel: +91(364) 272-1001 +91(364) 255-0101,
Fax: +91(364) 255-0076 EMail: vcnehu@nehu.ac.in

Registrar: Shri Lambha Roy
Tel: +91(364) 272-1012 +91(364) 255-0067,
Fax: +91(364) 255-1634 EMail: regtroffice@nehu.ac.in

Schools

Economics, Management and Information Sciences (Agricultural Business; Business Administration; Business and Commerce; Economics; Finance; Human Resources; Information Sciences; Library Science; Management; Marketing); **Education** (Adult Education; Continuing Education; Distance Education; Education; Floriculture; Management; Mathematics Education; Safety Engineering; Science Education; Special Education); **Human and Environmental Sciences** (Agricultural Economics; Anthropology; Environmental Studies; Geography); **Humanities** (Arts and Humanities; English; Hindi; Linguistics; Literature; Philosophy; South and Southeast Asian Languages; Translation and Interpretation; Writing); **Life Sciences** (Biochemistry; Biological and Life Sciences; Biotechnology; Botany; Cell Biology; Computer Science; Genetics; Microbiology; Molecular Biology; Zoology); **Physical Sciences** (Chemistry; Mathematics; Organic Chemistry; Physics; Statistics); **Social Sciences** (Cultural Studies; Fine Arts; Folklore; History; Law; Music; Musicology; Painting and Drawing; Political Sciences; Prehistory; Social Sciences; Sociology; Visual Arts); **Technology** (Accountancy; Biotechnology; Chemistry; Economics; Electrical and Electronic Engineering; Electrical Engineering; Electronic Engineering; Engineering; Environmental Studies; Finance; Industrial Management; Information Technology; Marketing; Mathematics; Mechanics; Natural Sciences; Physics; Social Sciences; Statistics; Technology; Telecommunications Engineering)

Further Information: The University has two campuses: Shillong Campus (main) and Tura Campus. Also 54 undergraduate colleges affiliated to the University, including eight professional colleges.

History: Founded 1973. A 'Central University'.

Governing Bodies: Court; Executive Council; Academic Council

Admission Requirements: 12th year senior secondary/intermediate examination or recognized foreign equivalent

Fees: (Rupees): 2,250 - 5,515 per annum

Main Language(s) of Instruction: English

Degrees and Diplomas: *Bachelor's degree (professional)*; *Postgraduate Diploma*; *Master's Degree*; *Master of Philosophy (Mphil)*; *Doctorate (PhD)*. Also Bachelor's degree honours; Undergraduate Certificates/Diplomas.

Student Services: Canteen, Cultural centre, Handicapped facilities, Health services, Sports facilities

Student Residential Facilities: Students Hostel; Guest House

Special Facilities: Computer Centre; University Science Instrument Centre; Bioinformatics Centre; Convention Hall

Libraries: Central Liberary: c. 200,000 vols; 38,000 bound periodicals; 316 foreign and 366 Indian current journals.

Publications: N.-E Hill University Journal of Social Sciences and Humanities *(quarterly)*

Press or Publishing House: Publication Cell

Academic Staff *2007-2008*: Total: c. 300
Student Numbers *2007-2008*: Total: c. 20,000
Last Updated: 11/07/11

NTR UNIVERSITY OF HEALTH SCIENCES ANDHRA PRADESH (NTRUHS)

Vijayawada, Andhra Pradesh 520008
Tel: +91(866) 245-1206
Fax: +91(866) 245-0463
EMail: ntruhs@hotmail.com; drntruhs@gmail.com
Website: http://ntruhs.ap.nic.in/

Vice-Chancellor: I. Venkateswara Rao (2010-)
Registrar: Jayakar Babu

Colleges

Allopathy (Medicine); **Applied Nutrition** (Nutrition); **Ayurveda** (Ayurveda); **Dentistry** (Dentistry); **Homeopathy** (Homeopathy); **Medical Laboratory Technology** *(MLT)* (Laboratory Techniques; Medical Technology); **Naturopathy and Yoga** (Alternative Medicine; Yoga); **Nursing** (Nursing); **Physiotherapy** (Physical Therapy); **Unani** (Indic Languages)

History: Founded 1986 as University of Health Sciences. Acquired present title 1998.

Governing Bodies: Executive Council; Academic Council

Academic Year: June to May (June-November; December-May)

Admission Requirements: 12th year senior secondary/intermediate examination or recognized foreign equivalent

Fees: (Rupees): 2,800-12,000 per annum

Main Language(s) of Instruction: English

Degrees and Diplomas: *Bachelor's Degree*; *Postgraduate Diploma*; *Master's Degree*

Special Facilities: Anatomy Museum; Pathology Museum; Forensic Medicine Museum; Community Medicine Museum

Libraries: c. 14,000 vols; 100 periodical subscriptions

Publications: Journal of UHS *(biannually)*
Last Updated: 11/07/11

O.P. JINDAL GLOBAL UNIVERSITY (JGU)

Sonipat Narela Road, Near Jagdishpur Village, Sonipat, Haryana 131 001
Tel: +91(130) 3057-800 +91(130) 3057-801
Fax: +91(130) 3057-888
EMail: info@jgu.edu.in
Website: http://www.jgu.edu.in

Vice Chancellor: C. Raj Kumar
Tel: +91(130) 3057-899; +91(130) 3057-900,
Fax: +91(130) 3057-894
EMail: crk@jgu.edu.in; crajkumar4@yahoo.com

Registrar: Aman Shah

Schools

Business *(JGBS)* (Accountancy; Banking; Business Administration; Commercial Law; Economics; Ethics; Finance; Information Management; International Law; Law; Management; Marketing; Political Sciences; Social Sciences); **Government and Public Policy** *(JGLS)* (Government; Public Administration); **International Affairs** *(JSIA)* (Business Administration; Government; International Law; International Relations; Law); **Law** (Civil Law; Commercial Law; Fiscal Law; International Law; Law)

History: Founded 2009. A non-profit university.

Governing Bodies: Board of Management; Academic Council

International Co-operation: With universities in United Kingdom and U.S.A.

Accrediting Agencies: University Grants Commission (UGC)

Degrees and Diplomas: *Bachelor's degree (professional)*; *Master's Degree.* Also Honours Bachelor's degree; MBA and Corporate MBA.

Student Services: Canteen, Health services

Special Facilities: Internent access

Last Updated: 26/08/11

ORISSA UNIVERSITY OF AGRICULTURE AND TECHNOLOGY (OUAT)

Bhubaneswar, Orissa 751003
Tel: +91(674) 239-7818 +91(674) 239-7868
Fax: +91(674) 239-7780
EMail: ouatmain@hotmail.com
Website: http://www.ouat.ac.in

Vice-Chancellor: D.P. Ray (2006-)
Tel: +91(674) 239-7700, Fax: +91(674) 239-7780

Registrar: Shri Sangram Keshari Ray Tel: +91(674) 239-7424

Colleges

Agricultural Engineering and Technology (Agricultural Business; Agricultural Engineering; Agricultural Equipment; Aquaculture; Civil Engineering; Computer Science; Dairy; Electrical Engineering; Energy Engineering; Engineering; Engineering Drawing and Design; Environmental Engineering; Farm Management; Food Technology; Harvest Technology; Heating and Refrigeration; Irrigation; Machine Building; Mathematics; Mechanical Engineering; Mechanics; Power Engineering; Soil Conservation; Surveying and Mapping; Water Management; Water Science); **Agriculture** *(Bhawanipatna)* (Agriculture); **Agriculture** *(Chiplima)* (Agriculture); **Agriculture** *(Bhubaneswar)* (Agricultural Economics; Agricultural Education; Agriculture; Agronomy; Biotechnology; Chemistry; Computer Science; Crop Production; English; Entomology; Forestry; Genetics; Harvest Technology; Horticulture; Physiology; Plant Pathology; Soil Science; Statistics; Zoology); **Basic Science and Humanities** (Botany; Chemistry; English; Information Technology; Mathematics; Physics; South and Southeast Asian Languages; Zoology); **Fisheries** *(Rangeilunda, Berhampur)* (Aquaculture; Biology; Fishery; Food Science); **Home Science** (Child Care and Development; Clothing and Sewing; Food Science; Home Economics; Nutrition; Textile Technology); **Horticulture** *(Chiplima)* (Horticulture); **Postgraduate Studies** (Biology; Computer Engineering; Computer Science; Information Technology; Microbiology); **Veterinary Science and Animal Husbandry** *(Bhubaneswar)* (Anatomy; Animal Husbandry; Genetics; Gynaecology and Obstetrics; Meat and Poultry; Medicine; Microbiology; Nutrition; Parasitology; Pathology; Pharmacology; Physiology; Public Health; Surgery; Veterinary Science; Virology)

History: Founded 1962.

Governing Bodies: Board of Management; Academic Council; Board of Faculty; State Level Research Council; State Level Extension Council.

Admission Requirements: 12th year senior secondary/intermediate examination or recognized foreign equivalent

Fees: (Rupees): 2,000-4,000 per annum

Main Language(s) of Instruction: English

Degrees and Diplomas: *Bachelor's Degree*; *Bachelor's degree (professional)*; *Master's Degree*; *Doctorate (PhD)*. Also Bachelor's degree honours.

Student Services: Employment services

Student Residential Facilities: 11 boys hostels and 8 girls hostels (total capacity of 1,700 students).

Special Facilities: Laboratories; Livestock Instructional Farm; Conference Halls.

Libraries: Central Library: 94,499 vols; 19,340 foreign and Indian periodical subscriptions; 3,375 theses and dissertations.

Publications: Journal of Research *(biennially)*

Academic Staff 2008-2009	MEN	WOMEN	TOTAL
FULL-TIME	–	–	**482**
Student Numbers 2008-2009			
All (Foreign Included)	1,819	1,263	**3,082**

Last Updated: 11/07/11

OSMANIA UNIVERSITY

Hyderabad, Andhra Pradesh 500007
Tel: +91(40) 2709-8043
Fax: +91(40) 2709-8704
EMail: osmanian@hdl.vsnl.net.in
Website: http://www.osmania.ac.in

Vice-Chancellor: D. N. Reddy
Tel: +91(40) 270-98048, Fax: +91(40) 270-98003
EMail: vc@osmania.ac.in

Registrar: V. Kishan Rao
Tel: +91(40) 270-98043, Fax: +91(40) 270-90020
EMail: registrar@osmania.ac.in

Colleges

Arts and Social Sciences (Ancient Civilizations; Applied Linguistics; Arabic; Archaeology; Archiving; Arts and Humanities; Classical Languages; Economics; English; Foreign Languages Education; French; German; Hindi; History; Indic Languages; Information Sciences; Islamic Studies; Journalism; Library Science; Linguistics; Literature; Mass Communication; Military Science; Modern Languages; Museum Studies; Persian; Philosophy; Political Sciences; Psychology; Public Administration; Rehabilitation and Therapy; Russian; Sanskrit; Social Sciences; Social Work; Sociology; South and Southeast Asian Languages; Theatre; Translation and Interpretation; Urdu); **Commerce and Business Management** (Business Administration; Business and Commerce; E-Business/ Commerce; Engineering Management; Taxation); **Engineering** (Biomedical Engineering; Civil Engineering; Computer Engineering; Computer Science; Electrical and Electronic Engineering; Electrical Engineering; Engineering; Information Technology; Measurement and Precision Engineering; Mechanical Engineering; Production Engineering; Telecommunications Engineering); **Law** (Commercial Law; Constitutional Law; Criminal Law; International Law; Labour Law; Law; Public Law); **Law Basheerbagh** *(Postgraduate)* (Law); **Nizam** (Arabic; Botany; Business Administration; Business and Commerce; Chemistry; Economics; English; Genetics; Geography; Hindi; History; Indic Languages; Mathematics; Microbiology; Persian; Philosophy; Physics; Political Sciences; Psychology; Public Administration; Sanskrit; Sociology; Statistics; Theatre; Urdu; Zoology); **Physical Education** (Journalism; Physical Education; Rehabilitation and Therapy; Sports; Sports Management; Sports Medicine; Yoga); **Science** (Applied Mathematics; Astronomy and Space Science; Astrophysics; Biochemistry; Biotechnology; Botany; Chemistry; Computer Science; Dietetics; Electronic Engineering; Environmental Studies; Forensic Medicine and Dentistry; Genetics; Geography; Geology; Geophysics; Health Administration; Mathematics; Microbiology; Nutrition; Physics; Statistics; Surveying and Mapping; Zoology); **Science** *(Postgraduate - Saifabad)* (Applied Mathematics; Arabic; Biotechnology; Botany; Chemistry; Computer Science; Cultural Studies; English; Foreign Languages Education; Geology; Hindi; Mathematics; Modern Languages; Physical Education; Physics; Sanskrit; Zoology); **Secunderabad** *(Postgraduate - Sec'bad)* (Computer Science; Economics; English; Hindi; History; Political Sciences; Public Administration; Social Work); **Technology** (Biotechnology; Chemical Engineering; Chemistry; English; Food Technology; Mathematics; Mechanical Engineering; Pharmacy; Physical Education; Physics; Technology; Textile Technology); **Women** *(OUCWKOTI)* (Accountancy; Arabic; Botany; Business Administration; Business and Commerce; Chemistry; Communication Studies; Computer Science; Dietetics; Economics; English; Food Science; French; Genetics; Geography; Hindi; History; Inorganic Chemistry; Laboratory Techniques; Management; Mathematics; Medical Technology; Nutrition; Persian; Philosophy; Physics; Political Sciences; Psychology; Public Administration; Sanskrit; Sociology; South and Southeast Asian Languages; Urdu; Zoology)

Institutes

Advanced Study in Education (Education; Special Education)

Further Information: Also Postgraduate Centres and Colleges; 5 Constituent and 12 Affiliated Colleges

History: Founded 1918.

Governing Bodies: Executive Council; Academic Council

Academic Year: July to March (July-November; December-March)

Admission Requirements: 12th year senior secondary/intermediate examination or recognized foreign equivalent

Fees: (Rupees): Undegraduate programmes, 4,600-4,710 per annum; Postgraduate programmes, 930-5,710 per annum.

Main Language(s) of Instruction: English, Hindi, Telugu, Urdu, Marathi

Accrediting Agencies: National Accreditation and Assessment Council (NAAC); University Grants Commission (UGC)

Degrees and Diplomas: *Diploma*; *Bachelor's Degree*; *Bachelor's degree (professional)*; *Postgraduate Diploma*; *Master's Degree*; *Master of Philosophy*; *Doctorate (PhD)*. Also Advanced, Junior and Senior Diploma; M.B.A.

Student Services: Employment services, Health services

Student Residential Facilities: 14 hostes (4,500 students capacity); Guest House

Special Facilities: Post office; Bank

Libraries: 521,259 vols; 74,982 bound vols of journals; 10,298 theses and dissertations; 273 films; 12 CD-ROMs.

Press or Publishing House: University Press

Academic Staff *2009-2010*: Total: c. 5,000
Student Numbers *2009-2010*: Total: c. 300,000
Last Updated: 11/07/11

PACIFIC ACADEMY OF HIGHER EDUCATION & RESEARCH UNIVERSITY (PAHER)

Airport Road, Pratap Nagar Extension, Debari, Udaipur, Rajasthan 313001
Tel: +91(97724-22999 +91-97725-22999
EMail: admission@pahersociety.org
Website: http://www.pacific-university.ac.in/

President: Bhagvan Das Rai

Colleges
Dental Studies (Dental Hygiene; Dentistry; Oral Pathology; Orthodontics; Periodontics; Surgery); **Pharmacy** (Chemistry; Pharmacology; Pharmacy; Safety Engineering)

Faculties
Arts (Humanities and Social Sciences) (Arts and Humanities; Economics; English; Fashion Design; Fine Arts; Geography; Hindi; History; Interior Design; International Relations; Literature; Musicology; Painting and Drawing; Philosophy; Political Sciences; Psychology; Public Administration; Sanskrit; Sculpture; Social Sciences; Sociology; Textile Design); **Computer Application** (Computer Science); **Education** (Education; Educational Technology); **Engineering** (Aeronautical and Aerospace Engineering; Automotive Engineering; Biotechnology; Chemical Engineering; Civil Engineering; Computer Science; Energy Engineering; Engineering; Industrial Engineering; Information Technology; Measurement and Precision Engineering; Mechanical Engineering; Power Engineering; Production Engineering; Software Engineering); **Management Studies** (Actuarial Science; Business Administration; Business and Commerce; Finance; Health Administration; Hotel Management; Human Resources; Insurance; International Business; Management; Marketing; Real Estate; Social Work; Tourism); **Science** (Chemistry; Industrial Chemistry; Mathematics; Natural Sciences)

Institutes
Fashion Technology (Fashion Design; Fine Arts; Graphic Design; Interior Design; Jewelry Art; Management; Textile Design; Textile Technology); **Hotel Management** (Cooking and Catering; Food Technology; Hotel Management; Tourism); **Media and Mass Communication** (Journalism; Mass Communication; Media Studies; Radio and Television Broadcasting; Video)

History: Founded 1997 as Pacific Institute of Management & Pacific Commerce College.

Degrees and Diplomas: *Diploma*; *Bachelor's Degree*; *Bachelor's degree (professional)*; *Postgraduate Diploma*; *Master's Degree*; *Master of Philosophy*; *Doctorate*. Also Advance Diploma; M.B.A.; integrated Bachelor's degree-M.B.A.

Student Services: Canteen

Student Residential Facilities: Separate Boys and Girls Hostels

Special Facilities: Lecture Rooms and Teaching Methodology; Computer Lab

Libraries: Yes

Student Numbers *2010-2011*: Total: c. 12,000
Last Updated: 21/12/11

PADMASHREE DR. D. Y. PATIL VIDYAPEETH

Sector 15, Plot no 50, CBD Belapur, Navi Mumbai, Maharashtra 400 614
Tel: +91(22) 392-85999
Fax: +91(22) 392-86197
EMail: dypuniversity_1@yahoo.co.in; dypuniversity@gmail.com
Website: http://www.dypatil.ac.in

Vice-Chancellor: James Thomas
EMail: vicechancellor@dypatil.edu

Registrar: F.A. Fernandes

Colleges
Ayurved *(Dr. D.Y. Patil - and Research Institute)* (Ayurveda); **Dentistry** *(Dr. D.Y. Patil - and Hospital)* (Community Health; Dental Hygiene; Dental Technology; Dentistry; Microbiology; Oral Pathology; Orthodontics; Periodontics; Radiology; Surgery); **Medicine** *(Dr. D.Y. Patil)* (Anaesthesiology; Anatomy; Biochemistry; Community Health; Dermatology; Forensic Medicine and Dentistry; Gynaecology and Obstetrics; Medicine; Microbiology; Ophthalmology; Orthopaedics; Paediatrics; Pathology; Pharmacology; Physiology; Pneumology; Surgery; Toxicology; Venereology); **Nursing** *(Dr. D.Y. Patil)* (Anatomy; Biochemistry; Community Health; Educational Technology; English; Genetics; Gynaecology and Obstetrics; Health Sciences; Microbiology; Midwifery; Nursing; Nutrition; Pathology; Pharmacology; Physiology; Psychiatry and Mental Health; Psychology; Sociology; Statistics)

Departments
Biotechnology and Bioinformatics (Biological and Life Sciences; Biology; Biomedical Engineering; Biotechnology; Computer Science); **Business Management** (Banking; Business Administration; Finance; Health Administration; Human Resources; International Business; Management; Marketing; Retailing and Wholesaling; Sports Management); **Education** (Education; Educational Psychology; Educational Technology); **Hospitality and Tourism Studies** (Cooking and Catering; Hotel and Restaurant; Tourism); **Physiotherapy** (Administration; Anatomy; Biochemistry; Cardiology; Communication Studies; Dermatology; Gynaecology and Obstetrics; Management; Marketing; Medicine; Microbiology; Neurological Therapy; Orthopaedics; Paediatrics; Pathology; Pharmacology; Physical Therapy; Physiology; Pneumology; Psychology; Rehabilitation and Therapy; Surgery)

Further Information: Also College of Engineering and Technology, College of Architecture, College of Hotel Management and Catering Technology, College of Ayurveda, College of Law affiliated to the University of Mumbai

History: Founded 2002. A 'Deemed University'.

Governing Bodies: Board of Management; Academic Council

Academic Year: July to June

Admission Requirements: Higher secondary school certificate and entrance examination

Fees: (Rupees): Undergraduate programmes, 25,000-350,000 per annum; Postgraduate programmes, 10,000-100,000 per annum; 60,000-322,000 MBA, per annum; Ph.D., 30,000 per annum.

Accrediting Agencies: National Assessment and Accreditation Council (NAAC)

Degrees and Diplomas: *Diploma*; *Bachelor's Degree*; *Bachelor's degree (professional)*; *Postgraduate Diploma*; *Master's Degree*; *Master of Philosophy*; *Doctorate*. Also undergraduate certidicates; M.B.A.

Student Services: Health services, Sports facilities

Student Residential Facilities: On-campus girls' hostel for 300 students

Libraries: Medical College, 4,123 vols and 26 periodical subscriptions; Dental College, 1,492 vols and 38 periodical subscriptions
Last Updated: 11/07/11

PALAMURU UNIVERSITY

Near Bandamedi Palli, Raichur Road, Mahboobnagar,
Andhra Pradesh 509 001
Tel: +91(8542) 275-006
Fax: +91(8542) 275-088
EMail: registrar@palamuruuniversity.ac.in
Website: http://www.palamuruuniversity.ac.in/

Vice Chancellor: V. Gopal Reddy
Tel: +91(8542) 221-011, Fax: +91(8542) 221-020

Registrar: K. Venkatachalam
Tel: +91(8542) 221-020, Fax: +91(8542) 221-020
EMail: drkv.chalam@yahoo.co.in

Departments

Business Administration (Business Administration); **Business and Commerce** (Business and Commerce); **Chemistry** (Chemistry); **Computer Science** (Computer Science); **English** (English); **Mathematics** (Mathematics); **Microbiology** (Microbiology); **Organic Chemistry** (Organic Chemistry); **Pharmacy** (Pharmacy); **Political Sciences** (Political Sciences); **Social Work** (Social Work)

History: Founded 2008.

Degrees and Diplomas: *Master's Degree.* Also M.B.A.

Student Numbers *2010-2011*: Total: c. 440
Last Updated: 02/01/12

PANDIT BHAGWAT DAYAL SHARMA UNIVERSITY OF HEALTH SCIENCES, ROHTAK (UHSR)

Rohtak, Haryana 124 001
Tel: +91(1262) 212-812
Fax: +91(1262) 212-812
EMail: vicechancellor.uhsr@gmail.com
Website: http://www.uhsr.ac.in/

Vice Chancellor: S.S. Sangwan
Tel: +91(1262) 212-812, Fax: +91(1262) 212-811

Registrar: Rajeev Sen
Tel: +91(1262) 211-109, Fax: +91(1262) 211-163

Centres

Cancer *(Regional)* (Biotechnology; Molecular Biology; Oncology; Radiology; Surgery)

Colleges

Medicine (Anaesthesiology; Anatomy; Biochemistry; Cardiology; Community Health; Dermatology; Forensic Medicine and Dentistry; Laboratory Techniques; Medicine; Microbiology; Orthopaedics; Otorhinolaryngology; Paediatrics; Pathology; Pharmacology; Pharmacy; Physiology; Plastic Surgery; Pneumology; Venereology); **Nursing** (Nursing; Psychiatry and Mental Health; Social Work); **Ophthalmology** (Dental Hygiene; Dental Technology; Dentistry; Oral Pathology; Orthodontics; Surgery)

Degrees and Diplomas: *Diploma; Bachelor's Degree; Bachelor's degree (professional); Postgraduate Diploma; Master's Degree; Master of Philosophy*

Libraries: c. 86,000 vols; 180 periodical subscriptions
Last Updated: 03/01/12

PANDIT DEENDAYAL PETROLEUM UNIVERSITY (PDPU)

Raisan Village, Gandhinagar, Gujarat 382 007
Tel: +91(79) 2327-5020
Fax: +91(79) 2327-5030
EMail: info@pdpu.ac.in
Website: http://www.pdpu.ac.in

President: Mukesh Ambani
Registrar: N. Sundaram

Schools

Liberal Studies (Accountancy; Arts and Humanities; Business Administration; Dance; Economics; English; Environmental Studies; Finance; Geography; Government; History; International Relations; Law; Literature; Management; Marketing; Mathematics; Modern Languages; Music; Operations Research; Philosophy; Political

Sciences; Psychology; Public Administration; Social Sciences; Spanish; Theatre); **Nuclear Energy** (Laboratory Techniques; Maintenance Technology; Nuclear Engineering; Nuclear Physics); **Petroleum Management** (Accountancy; Economics; Finance; International Business; Law; Management; Petroleum and Gas Engineering); **Petroleum Technology** (Automation and Control Engineering; Engineering; Measurement and Precision Engineering; Petroleum and Gas Engineering; Technology); **Solar Energy** (Energy Engineering; Mechanics; Nuclear Physics; Physics; Solid State Physics); **Technology** (Civil Engineering; Electrical Engineering; Engineering; Mechanical Engineering; Technology)

History: Founded 2007.

Governing Bodies: Board of Governors; Academic Council; Finance Committee.

International Co-operation: With universities in USA and Japan.

Accrediting Agencies: University Grants Commission (UGC); All India Council for Technical Education (AICTE).

Degrees and Diplomas: *Bachelor's Degree; Bachelor's degree (professional); Master's Degree; Doctorate.* Also M.B.A.

Student Services: Health services, Sports facilities

Student Residential Facilities: Hostels

Libraries: Library and Information Centre (LIC); SLS Library, 4,902 vols and 62 periodical subscriptions. SPM Library, 7,800 vols, 3,300 e-journals and 104 periodical subscriptions. SOT Library, 1,535 vols and 11 periodical subscriptions. SPT Library, 11,936 vols, 450 e-journals and 50 periodical subscriptions.

Academic Staff *2010-2011*: Total: c. 110
Student Numbers *2010-2011*: Total: c. 1,450
Last Updated: 11/07/11

PANDIT DWARKA PRASAD MISHRA INDIAN INSTITUTE OF INFORMATION TECHNOLOGY, DESIGN AND MANUFACTURING, JABALPUR (IIITDMJ)

Dumna Airport Road, Khamaria, Jabalpur,
Madhya Pradesh 482 005
Tel: +91(761) 263-2273
Fax: +91(761) 263-2524
EMail: query@iiitdmj.ac.in
Website: http://www.iiitdmj.ac.in

Director: Aparajita Ojha
Tel: +91(761) 263-2615 EMail: director@iiitdm.in

Registrar: P. S. Sandhu
Tel: +91(761) 263-2068 EMail: rg@iiitdmj.ac.in

Programmes

Postgraduate Studies (Computer Engineering; Computer Science; Design; Electronic Engineering; Mechanical Engineering; Telecommunications Engineering); **Undergraduate Studies** (Computer Engineering; Computer Science; Electronic Engineering; Mechanical Engineering; Telecommunications Engineering)

History: Created 2005. A 'Deemed University'.

Governing Bodies: Board of Governors; Academic Senate; Finance Committee.

Fees: 44,165 per annum. Postgraduate programmes, 2,500 per semester.

Accrediting Agencies: University Grants Commission (UGC)

Degrees and Diplomas: *Bachelor's degree (professional); Master's Degree; Doctorate*
Last Updated: 11/07/11

PANJAB UNIVERSITY (PU)

Chandigarh, Union Territory 160014
Tel: +91(172) 254-1716 +91(172) 254-1441
Fax: +91(172) 278-335 +91(172) 254-1022
Website: http://www.puchd.ac.in

Vice-Chancellor: Ranbir Chander Sobti (2006-)
Tel: +91(172) 254-1945, Fax: +91(172) 254-1022
EMail: rcsobti@pu.ac.in; vc@pu.ac.in

Registrar: A. K. Bhandari
Tel: +91(172) 253-4867 +91(172) 253-4868 EMail: regr@pu.ac.in

International Relations: Naval Kishore, Dean of International Students
Tel: +91(172) 254-1873 +91(172) 253-4574 EMail: dis@pu.ac.in

Centres
Ambedkar (Philosophy; Social Sciences; Sociology); **Human Genome Studies and Research** *(National - NCHGSR)* (Biotechnology; Genetics; Molecular Biology); **Human Rights and Duties** *(U.I.E.A.S.S)* (Human Rights); **IAS and Other Competitive Examinations** (Justice Administration; Public Administration); **Medical Physics** *(U.I.E.A.S.T.)* (Nuclear Physics; Oncology; Physics; Radiology; Radiophysics); **Microbial Biotechnology** *(U.I.E.A.S.T.)* (Biotechnology; Microbiology); **Nanoscience and Nanotechnology** *(U.I.E.A.S.T.)* (Nanotechnology); **Nuclear Medicine** *(U.I.E.A.S.T.)* (Medical Technology; Radiology); **Petroleum and Applied Geology** *(U.I.E.A.S.T.)* (Geochemistry; Geology; Geophysics; Petroleum and Gas Engineering); **Police Administration** *(U.I.E.A.S.S)* (Administration; Police Studies); **Public Health** *(U.I.E.A.S.T.)* (Health Sciences; Public Health); **Social Work** *(U.I.E.A.S.S)* (Social Work); **Sophisticated Analytical Instrumentation Facility, CIL and UCIM** (Instrument Making); **Stem Cell and Tissue Engineering** (Bioengineering; Cell Biology; Embryology and Reproduction Biology); **Study of Geopolitics** (International Relations; Natural Resources; Political Sciences; Regional Studies); **Study of Mid-West and Central Asia** (Asian Studies); **Study of Social Exclusion and Inclusive Policy** (Social Policy; Social Problems); **System Biology and Bioinformatics** *(U.I.E.A.S.T.)* (Biology; Computer Science; Genetics; Measurement and Precision Engineering; Molecular Biology)

Chairs
Bhai Vir Singh (Comparative Literature; Writing); **Medieval Indian Literature** *(Sheikh Baba Farid)* (Hindi; Literature; Medieval Studies; Urdu); **Sant Sahitya Studies** *(Guru Ravi Das)* (Ancient Books; Hindi; Indic Languages; Medieval Studies); **Vedic Studies** *(Dayanand)* (Ayurveda; Esoteric Practices)

Departments
Ancient Indian History, Culture and Archaeology (Archaeology; Cultural Studies; History; Tourism); **Anthropology** (Anthropology; Criminology; Forensic Medicine and Dentistry); **Arts History and Visual Arts** (Art History; Visual Arts); **Biochemistry** (Biochemistry); **Biophysics** (Biophysics); **Biotechnology** (Biotechnology); **Botany** (Botany); **Chemistry** (Chemistry); **Chinese and Tibetan Languages** (Asian Studies; Chinese; Tibetan); **Community Education and Disability Studies** (Education; Rehabilitation and Therapy); **Computer Science and Applications** (Computer Science); **Defence and National Security Studies** (Military Science; Protective Services; Safety Engineering); **Economics** (Agricultural Economics; Development Studies; Economics; Finance; Industrial and Production Economics); **Education** (Education; Educational and Student Counselling; Educational Technology); **English and Cultural Studies** (English; English Studies; Literature); **Environment and Vocational Studies** (Agriculture; Environmental Studies; Vocational Education; Waste Management); **Evening Studies** (Arts and Humanities; Business and Commerce; Economics; English; History; Indic Languages; Political Sciences); **French and Francophone Studies** (French; French Studies); **Gandhian Studies** (Peace and Disarmament; Philosophy); **Geography** (Geography; Safety Engineering; Surveying and Mapping); **Geology** (Geology; Petrology); **German** (German); **Guru Nanak Sikh Studies** (Asian Religious Studies; Cultural Studies; History; Literature; Philosophy); **Hindi** (Hindi; Translation and Interpretation); **History** (Ancient Civilizations; Contemporary History; History; Medieval Studies; Modern History); **Indian Theatre** (Acting; Singing; Speech Studies; Theatre; Yoga); **Laws** (Law); **Library and Information Science** (Information Sciences; Library Science); **Life Long Learning and Extension** (Continuing Education; Education; Educational and Student Counselling; Gender Studies; Literacy Education; Nutrition; Vocational Education); **Mathematics** (Mathematics; Mathematics and Computer Science); **Microbiology** (Microbiology); **Music** (Music; Musical Instruments; Singing); **Philosophy** (Aesthetics; Ethics; Philosophy; Religion); **Physical Education** (Physical Education); **Physics** (Electronic Engineering; Physics); **Political Science** (International Relations; Political Sciences); **Psychology** (Psychology); **Public Administration** (Administration; Economics; Human Resources; Management; Public Administration); **Punjabi** (Cultural Studies; Indic Languages; Translation and Interpretation); **Russian** (Literature; Russian; Slavic Languages); **Sanskrit** (Grammar; Literature; Philology; Philosophy; Sanskrit); **Sociology** (Demography and Population; Development Studies; Family Studies; Gender Studies; Social Studies; Sociology; Urban Studies); **Statistics** (Statistics); **Urdu** (Persian; Urdu); **Women's Studies and Development** *(cum Center)* (Women's Studies); **Zoology** (Zoology)

Institutes
Applied Management Sciences *(University)* (Business Administration; Business and Commerce; Finance; Human Resources; Management; Marketing; Operations Research); **Chemical Engineering and Technology** *(University)* (Business Administration; Chemical Engineering; Engineering; Food Technology; Industrial Chemistry; Polymer and Plastics Technology; Technology); **Dental Sciences and Hospital** *(Dr. Harvansh Singh Judge)* (Dentistry; Surgery); **Educational Technology and Vocational Education** (Educational Technology; Primary Education; Secondary Education; Vocational Education); **Engineering and Technology** *(University)* (Biotechnology; Business Administration; Computer Engineering; Computer Science; Electrical and Electronic Engineering; Electronic Engineering; Engineering; Information Technology; Mechanical Engineering; Technology; Telecommunications Engineering); **Fashion Technology and Vocational Development** *(University)* (Fashion Design; Journalism; Management; Photography; Textile Design; Textile Technology); **Forensic Science and Criminology** (Criminology; Forensic Medicine and Dentistry); **Hotel Management and Tourism** *(University)* (Hotel Management; Tourism); **Laws** *(University - Ludhiana)* (Law); **Legal Studies** *(University)* (Law); **Pharmaceutical Sciences** *(University)* (Pharmacy); **Sanskrit and Indological Studies** *(Vishveshvaranand Vishwa Bandhu)* (Sanskrit; South Asian Studies)

Research Centres
Energy (Energy Engineering; Environmental Management); **Population** (Demography and Population; Family Studies; Health Sciences)

Schools
Business *(University - Ludhiana)* (Business Administration; Finance; Human Resources; Management; Marketing; Operations Research); **Business** *(University)* (Biotechnology; Business Administration; Business and Commerce; E-Business/Commerce; Human Resources; International Business); **Communication Studies** (Advertising and Publicity; Communication Studies; Journalism; Mass Communication; Media Studies; Public Relations); **Open Learning** *(Ludhiana)* (Alternative Medicine; Human Rights; Statistics; Yoga)

Units
Panjabi Lexicography (Indic Languages; Linguistics)

Further Information: 185 affiliated colleges spread over Punjab and Chandigarh, Regional Centres at Muktsar, Ludhiana, Hoshiarpur (Swami Sarvanand Giri), Kauni. A traditional, open and distance education institution.

History: Founded 1882 as University of the Punjab at Lahore, acquired present title 1947. Relocated in Chandigarh 1956. Recognized as the 'University with Potential for Excellence in Bio-Medical Sciences' by the University Grants Commission (UGC).

Governing Bodies: Senate; Syndicate

Academic Year: July to April (July-October; October-December; January-April)

Admission Requirements: 12th year senior secondary/intermediate examination or recognized foreign equivalent

Fees: (Rupees): Undergraduate programmes, 5,500-100,690 per annum; Postgraduate programmes, 3,370-69,367 per annum); Ph.D., 1,150-1,500 per annum.

Main Language(s) of Instruction: English; Hindi; Panjabi; Urdu

International Co-operation: With universities in Canada and Kyrghyzstan.

Degrees and Diplomas: *Diploma*; *Bachelor's Degree*; *Bachelor's degree (professional)*; *Postgraduate Diploma*; *Master's Degree*; *Master of Philosophy*; *Doctorate (PhD)*. Also certificate and advanced diploma courses; Bachelor's and Master's degree Honours; M.B.A.

Student Services: Academic counselling, Canteen, Cultural centre, Employment services, Health services, Nursery care, Social counselling, Sports facilities

Student Residential Facilities: 7 boys hostels and 9 girls hostels (c. 5,900 students); Guest and faculty houses.

Special Facilities: Computer center and laboratory; Fine Arts Museum; Botanical and medicinal herbs gardens; Open air theatre; Day-care centre for the employees' children; 100-bed hospital.

Libraries: A. C. Joshi Library: c. 640,000 vols; c. 600 subscriptions to periodicals; Collection of 1,490 manuscripts; Access to 225 Online fulltext journals as part of print journals subscription; Access to c. 5,000 online fulltext journals through INDEST- Consortium and UGC- INFONET.

Publications: Arts and Science and Social Sciences Journals

Press or Publishing House: University Press

Academic Staff 2009-2010: Total: c. 750
Student Numbers 2009-2010: Total: c. 13,220
Last Updated: 12/07/11

PATNA UNIVERSITY (PU)

Ashok Rajpath, Patna, Bihar 800005
Tel: +91(612) 267-0531 +91(612) 267-0852
Fax: +91(612) 267-0877 +91(612) 268-8872
Website: http://pucc.bih.nic.in/

Vice-Chancellor: Shambhu Nath Singh (2011-)
Tel: +91(612) 267-0352

Registrar: Manoj Kumar
Tel: +91(612) 267-0531 EMail: registrar_pu@hotmail.com

Centres
Computer (Biology; Business Computing; Computer Science)

Colleges
Arts and Crafts (Crafts and Trades; Fine Arts; Painting and Drawing; Sculpture; Visual Arts); **Bihar National** (Arts and Humanities; Business and Commerce; Natural Sciences); **Magadha Mahila**; **Patna**; **Patna Law** (Law); **Patna Science** (Botany; Chemistry; Geology; Mathematics; Natural Sciences; Physics; Statistics; Zoology); **Patna Training**; **Patna Women's** (Women's Studies); **Vanijya Mahavidyalaya** (Business and Commerce); **Women's Training** (Women's Studies)

Faculties
Commerce (Business and Commerce; Human Resources; Labour and Industrial Relations); **Education** (Education); **Humanities** (Arabic; Archaeology; Arts and Humanities; English; Hindi; History; Indic Languages; Persian; Philosophy; Sanskrit; Urdu); **Law** (Law); **Medicine** *(Under state government management and control)* (Dentistry; Medicine); **Science** (Biochemistry; Botany; Chemistry; Geography; Geology; Mathematics; Natural Sciences; Physics; Statistics; Zoology); **Social Sciences** (Ancient Civilizations; Economics; Political Sciences; Psychology; Social Sciences; Sociology)

Institutes
Library and Information Science (Information Sciences; Library Science); **Music** (Music); **Psychological Research and Services** (Psychology); **Public Administration** (Public Administration)

Programmes
Distance Education *(Offered through the Directorate of Distance Education)* (Communication Studies; Journalism; Library Science)

Research Centres
Population (Demography and Population)

Further Information: Also 12 Constituent Colleges. A traditional and distance education institution.

History: Founded 1917, acquired present status and title 1951.

Governing Bodies: Academic Council; Senate; Syndicate

Academic Year: July to May (July-October; November-December; January-May)

Admission Requirements: 12th year senior secondary/intermediate examination or recognized foreign equivalent

Fees: (Rupees): 150-200 per annum

Main Language(s) of Instruction: Hindi, English

Accrediting Agencies: NAAC (UGC); MCI; DCI; NCTE; AICTE

Degrees and Diplomas: *Diploma*; *Bachelor's Degree*; *Postgraduate Diploma*; *Master's Degree*; *Doctorate.* Also M.B.A and M.C.A.

Student Services: Academic counselling, Cultural centre, Foreign student adviser, Handicapped facilities, Health services, Language programs, Social counselling, Sports facilities

Student Residential Facilities: 8 hostels for postgraduate students (including 2 girls hostels).

Special Facilities: Hospital (1,700 beds); Museum (Geology Dept.); Art Gallery in Patna's Women College; Arts and crafts college.

Libraries: Central Library: c. 400,000 vols; 87 periodicals and 50,000 back journals; collection of 5,000 old manuscripts.

Publications: Patna University Journal *(biannually)*

Academic Staff 2010-2011: Total 448
Student Numbers 2010-2011: Total 18,741
Last Updated: 02/11/11

PEC UNIVERSITY OF TECHNOLOGY (PEC)

Sector-12, Chandigarh, Union Territory 160012
Tel: +91(172) 275-3055 +91(172) 275-3051
Fax: +91(172) 274-8197 +91(172) 274-5175
EMail: admissionug@pec.ac.in
Website: http://www.pec.ac.in

Director: Manoj Datta
Tel: 274-6074 275-3051 EMail: director@pec.ac.in

Registrar: Ashwani Prashar
Tel: 274-8197 275-3055 EMail: registrar@pec.ac.in

Departments
Aerospace Engineering (Aeronautical and Aerospace Engineering; Chemistry; Maintenance Technology; Mechanics; Physics; Solid State Physics); **Applied Sciences** (Arts and Humanities; Chemistry; Engineering; Environmental Engineering; Geological Engineering; Mathematics; Physics; Statistics); **Civil Engineering** (Civil Engineering; Construction Engineering; Environmental Engineering; Geological Engineering; Hydraulic Engineering; Irrigation; Road Engineering; Transport Engineering); **Computer Science and Engineering** (Artificial Intelligence; Computer Engineering; Computer Graphics; Computer Networks; Computer Science; Data Processing; Multimedia; Software Engineering); **Electrical Engineering** (Automation and Control Engineering; Biomedical Engineering; Economics; Electrical Engineering; Measurement and Precision Engineering; Operations Research; Power Engineering; Telecommunications Engineering); **Electronics and Electrical Communication** (Computer Engineering; Electrical and Electronic Engineering; Electronic Engineering; Materials Engineering; Microwaves; Telecommunications Engineering); **Information Technology** (Arts and Humanities; Behavioural Sciences; Economics; Information Technology; Management; Women's Studies); **Materials and Metallurgical Engineering** (Ceramics and Glass Technology; Computer Engineering; Computer Graphics; Engineering Drawing and Design; Heating and Refrigeration; Materials Engineering; Mechanical Engineering; Metal Techniques; Metallurgical Engineering; Production Engineering); **Mechanical Engineering** (Computer Engineering; Engineering Drawing and Design; Heating and Refrigeration; Industrial Engineering; Machine Building; Management; Materials Engineering; Mathematics; Mechanical Engineering; Mechanics; Production Engineering; Safety Engineering; Thermal Engineering; Transport Engineering); **Production Engineering** (Mathematics; Metal Techniques; Production Engineering; Robotics)

History: Founded as Mugalpura Engineering College at Lahore (now in Pakistan) 1921. Changed name to Maclagan Engineering College 1924. Affiliated to Punjab University, Lahore 1931. Parted and moved to Roorkee (India), it was renamed as East Punjab College of Engineering 1947. Renamed Punjab Engineering College 1950. Moved to Chandigarh 1953. Acquired present status of 'Deemed University' 2003, it became known as became known as Punjab Engineering College (Deemed University). Acquired present title 2009.

Governing Bodies: Board of Governors; Senate; Finance Committee;

Fees: (Rupees): Bachelor's and Master's degree programmes, 32,500 per semester; Ph.D. programmes, 5,000 per annum.

Degrees and Diplomas: *Bachelor's degree (professional)*; *Master's Degree*; *Doctorate*

Student Services: Sports facilities

Student Residential Facilities: 4 Boys and 2 girls hostels.

Special Facilities: Lecture theatres; Drawing halls; Auditorium; Computer centre; Reading rooms; Workshops and laboratories.

Libraries: Central library, 108,028 vols; 72 foreign and 18 indian technical journals subscriptions.

Last Updated: 12/07/11

PERIYAR MANIAMMAI UNIVERSITY (PMU)

Periyar Nagar Vallam, Thanjavur 613403
EMail: registrar@pmu.edu
Website: http://www.pmu.edu/

Vice Chancellor: N. Ramachandran

Registrar: M. Ayyavoo

Schools

Architecture, Engineering and Technology *(SAET)* (Aeronautical and Aerospace Engineering; Architecture; Biotechnology; Chemical Engineering; Civil Engineering; Electrical Engineering; Electronic Engineering; Engineering; Mechanical Engineering; Technology; Telecommunications Engineering); **Computer Science and Engineering** *(SCSE)* (Computer Engineering; Computer Science); **Humanities, Sciences and Management** *(Chemistry)* (Arts and Humanities; Chemistry; Education; English; Information Sciences; Library Science; Management; Mathematics; Natural Sciences; Physical Education; Physics)

Further Information: Campuses in Thanjavur, Tiruchirapalli, Chennai and New Delhi.

History: Founded as Periyar Maniammai College of Technology for Women 1988. Started functioning as an affiliated college to Anna University, Chennai 2001. Acquire university status 2007. A 'Deemed University'.

Governing Bodies: Board Of Management; Finance Committee; Planning and Monitoring Board; Academic Council

Accrediting Agencies: National Assessment and Accreditation Council (NAAC); National Board of Accreditation (NBA); All India Council for Technical Education (AICTE).

Degrees and Diplomas: *Bachelor's Degree*; *Bachelor's degree (professional)*; *Master's Degree*; *Master of Philosophy*; *Doctorate*. Also M.B.A.; Lateral and integrated Master's course, 2-5 yrs.
Last Updated: 16/12/11

PERIYAR UNIVERSITY

Bangalore main road, Salem, Tamil Nadu 636 011
Tel: +91(427) 234-5766 +91(427) 234-5220
Fax: +91(427) 234-5565
EMail: info@periyaruniversity.ac.in
Website: http://periyaruniversity.ac.in

Vice-Chancellor: K. Muthuchelian
Tel: +91(427) 234-5565, Fax: +91(427) 234-5565
EMail: vc@periyaruniversity.ac.in; drchelian1960@yahoo.co.in

Registrar: S. Gunasekaran
Tel: +91(427) 234-5778, Fax: +91(427) 234-5124
EMail: registrar@periyaruniversity.ac.in;
sethugunasekaran@rediffmail.com

Departments

Biochemistry (Biochemistry); **Biotechnology** (Biological and Life Sciences; Biotechnology; Computer Science; Energy Engineering; Engineering; Nanotechnology); **Chemistry** (Chemistry); **Commerce** (Accountancy; Business Administration; Business and Commerce; Finance; Human Resources; International Business; Management; Marketing; Taxation); **Computer Science** (Computer Science; Data Processing; Software Engineering; Telecommunications Engineering); **Economics** (Economics); **Education** (Education); **English** (English; Human Rights; Journalism; Literature; Translation and Interpretation; Writing); **Food Science** (Cooking and Catering; Food

Science; Food Technology; Nutrition); **Geology** (Earth Sciences; Geology; Surveying and Mapping); **Journalism and Mass Communication** (Communication Arts; Journalism; Mass Communication); **Mathematics** (Applied Mathematics; Mathematics); **Microbiology** (Microbiology); **Physics** (Physics); **Psychology** (Industrial and Organizational Psychology; Psychology); **Sociology** (Management; Sociology); **Tamil** (South and Southeast Asian Languages)

Institutes

Distance Education *(Periyar)* (Banking; Biotechnology; Botany; Business Administration; Chemistry; Child Care and Development; Computer Engineering; Computer Graphics; Computer Networks; Computer Science; Crafts and Trades; Dental Technology; Economics; Education; Electronic Engineering; English; Environmental Studies; Geology; Health Administration; History; Home Economics; Hotel Management; Human Resources; Human Rights; Indic Languages; Information Sciences; Information Technology; International Business; Journalism; Laboratory Techniques; Library Science; Management; Marketing; Mass Communication; Mathematics; Medical Technology; Microbiology; Optics; Physics; Political Sciences; Public Administration; Radiology; Sanskrit; Social Work; Sociology; South and Southeast Asian Languages; Telecommunications Engineering; Tourism; Yoga; Zoology); **Management Studies** *(Periyar - PRIMS)* (Management)

Further Information: Also 66 affiliated and 11 constituent colleges. A traditional and distance education institution.

History: Founded 1997. Acquired present status 2007.

Governing Bodies: Syndicate; Senate

Academic Year: July to June

Admission Requirements: 12th year senior secondary /intermediate examination or recognized foreign equivalent

Fees: (Rupees): Postgraduate programmes, 6,500-8,500 per annum

Main Language(s) of Instruction: English

Accrediting Agencies: University Grants Commission (UGC); National Assessment and Accreditation Council (NAAC)

Degrees and Diplomas: *Diploma*; *Bachelor's Degree*; *Bachelor's degree (professional)*; *Postgraduate Diploma*; *Master's Degree*; *Master of Philosophy*; *Doctorate*. Also undergraduate certificates, M.B.A., executive M.B.A., M.C.A.

Student Services: Health services

Student Residential Facilities: Girls and boys hostels; Guest house

Special Facilities: Internet centre

Libraries: Central Library: c. 7,000 vols
Last Updated: 12/07/11

PONDICHERRY UNIVERSITY (PONDIUNI)

Bharat Ratna Dr. B.R.Ambedkar Administrative Building,
R.V.Nagar, Kalapet, Kalapet, Pondicherry 605014
Tel: +91(413) 265-5179
Fax: +91(413) 265-5734
EMail: registrar@pondiuni.edu.in
Website: http://www.pondiuni.org

Vice-Chancellor: J.A.K. Tareen (2007-)
Tel: +91(413) 265-5175, Fax: +91(413) 265-5249
EMail: vc@pondiuni.edu.in

Registrar: Shri. S. Loganathan
Tel: +91(413) 265-5261, Fax: +91(413) 265-5734

International Relations: M. Vallathan, Assistant Registrar (Public Relations) EMail: arprs@pondiuni.edu.in

Schools

Education (Education; Educational Administration; Educational Psychology; Educational Technology; Preschool Education; Teacher Training); **Engineering and Technology** (Computer Engineering; Computer Networks; Computer Science; Electronic Engineering; Engineering; Environmental Engineering; Environmental Management; Information Technology; Technology); **Green Energy Technologies** *(Madanjeet)* (Chemistry; Energy Engineering; Environmental Engineering; Nanotechnology); **Humanities** (Arts and Humanities; Chinese; Christian Religious Studies;

Comparative Literature; English; French; German; Hindi; Italian; Japanese; Korean; Modern Languages; Philosophy; Physical Education; Russian; Sanskrit; Spanish; Sports; Translation and Interpretation); **Life Sciences** (Biochemistry; Biological and Life Sciences; Biology; Biotechnology; Coastal Studies; Computer Science; Ecology; Environmental Studies; Food Science; Food Technology; Marine Biology; Marine Science and Oceanography; Microbiology; Molecular Biology; Nutrition; Safety Engineering); **Management** (Banking; Business Administration; Business and Commerce; Economics; Finance; Insurance; International Business; Management; Tourism); **Mathematical Sciences** *(Ramanujan)* (Mathematics; Mathematics and Computer Science; Statistics); **Media and Communication** (Film; Information Sciences; Library Science; Mass Communication; Media Studies; Radio and Television Broadcasting); **Medical Sciences** (Medicine); **Performing Arts** (Performing Arts; Theatre); **Physical, Chemical and Applied Sciences** (Chemistry; Clinical Psychology; Earth Sciences; Geology; Industrial and Organizational Psychology; Information Sciences; Laser Engineering; Library Science; Media Studies; Physics; Psychology); **Social Sciences and International Studies** (Anthropology; History; Human Rights; International Studies; Labour and Industrial Relations; Political Sciences; Rural Studies; Social Problems; Social Sciences; Social Work; Sociology; South Asian Studies; Women's Studies); **Tamil Language and Literature** *(Subramania Bharathi)* (Literature; South and Southeast Asian Languages)

Further Information: Also Port Blair, Karaikal and Community college campuses; 87 Affiliated Colleges. A traditional and distance education institution. Distance education programmes launched in the United Arab Emirates, Qatar and Kuwait with centres at Dubai, Abu Dhabi, Doha and Kuwait

History: Founded 1985. A 'Central University'.

Governing Bodies: Executive Council; Court; Planning Board; Finance Committee.

Academic Year: July to April (July-December; January-April)

Admission Requirements: 12th year senior secondary/intermediate examination or recognized foreign equivalent

Fees: (Rupees): Tuition fee: P.G. Diploma Programmes, 50 per semester and credit for Indian students and (US Dollars) 250-500 per semester for international students; M.Sc. In Bioinformatics, Computational Biology, Food Science and Technology, 100 per credit and semester for Indian students and (US Dollars) 500-750 per semester for international students; M.Sc Microbiology/ M.Tech (Nano Sciences & Technology, Green Energy Technology, Exploration Geosciences, Electronics), 3,500 per annum for Indian students and 50,000-100,000 per annum for international students; M.B.A., 3,000 per semester for Indian students and 20,000-26,500 per semester for international students; M.Tech. / M.Sc. (Computer Science) / M.C.A., 100 per credit (US Dollars, 500-750 per semester for international students); M.Phil. and Post-graduate programmes, 30-50 per credit and per semester (US Dollars, 250-500 for international students); Ph.D. programmes, 1,000 (full-time) or 2,000 (part-time) per semester for Indian students and 1,200 (full-time) or 2,400 (part-time) per semester for international students.

Main Language(s) of Instruction: English, Tamil, Malayalam, Hindi, Bengali

International Co-operation: With universities in France, Germany, USA, Canada, Italy, UK, Korea, Indonesia.

Accrediting Agencies: National Assessment and Accreditation Council (NAAC)

Degrees and Diplomas: *Bachelor's Degree*; *Postgraduate Diploma*; *Master's Degree*; *Master of Philosophy*; *Doctorate (MD)*. Also undergraduate certificates; M.B.A.; M.C.A.

Student Services: Academic counselling, Canteen, Cultural centre, Foreign student adviser, Handicapped facilities, Health services, Sports facilities

Student Residential Facilities: 7 hostels (11 for men, 5 for women students/research scholars and 1 for foreign students) with a total capacity of 1,500 residents; Staff quarters; Guest house.

Special Facilities: Auditorium; Bookshop; Computer Centre; Day Care Centre; Pre-Primary School; Bank; Post Office

Libraries: Main Library, 186,728 vols; 657 theses collection - Ph.D.; 4,482 dissertations and others; 532 reports; 2,061 Uniterd Nations documents; 9,899 journal bound vols; 369 paper and 23,928 electronic periodical subscriptions.

Publications: Push, Journal *(annually)*

Academic Staff *2010-2011*	MEN	WOMEN	**TOTAL**
FULL-TIME	271	85	**356**
Student Numbers *2010-2011*			
All (Foreign Included)	2,881	1,766	c. **4,647**

Distance students, 10,755.
Last Updated: 13/07/11

POSTGRADUATE INSTITUTE OF MEDICAL EDUCATION AND RESEARCH (PGIMER)

Sector 12, Chandigarh, Union Territory 160012
Tel: +91(172) 274-6018 +91(172) 275-6565
Fax: +91(172) 274-4401 +91(172) 274-5078
EMail: pgimer-chd@nic.in
Website: http://www.pgimer.nic.in

Acting Director: Vinay Sakhuja Tel: +91(172) 274-8363

Registrar: Naresh Virdi

Courses

Medicine (Anaesthesiology; Biochemistry; Biotechnology; Cardiology; Community Health; Dental Technology; Dermatology; Endocrinology; Forensic Medicine and Dentistry; Gastroenterology; Gynaecology and Obstetrics; Health Administration; Hepatology; Immunology; Medical Technology; Medicine; Microbiology; Nephrology; Neurological Therapy; Neurology; Ophthalmology; Orthodontics; Orthopaedics; Otorhinolaryngology; Paediatrics; Pathology; Pharmacology; Plastic Surgery; Pneumology; Psychiatry and Mental Health; Public Health; Radiology; Rehabilitation and Therapy; Social and Preventive Medicine; Surgery; Urology; Venereology); **Nursing** (Community Health; Medicine; Nursing; Surgery); **Para Medical** (Biochemistry; Biotechnology; Laboratory Techniques; Medical Technology; Microbiology; Pathology; Pharmacology; Physiology; Radiology; Speech Therapy and Audiology; Treatment Techniques)

Programmes

Elective Training; Short Term Training (Medicine)

Further Information: Also Nehru Hospital (1,400 beds).

History: Founded 1962, its objectives being to train in all branches of Medicine, conduct research and provide patient care of the highest standard. Declared an Institute of 'national importance' and became an autonomous body 1966.

Admission Requirements: 12th year senior secondary/intermediate examination or recognized foreign equivalent

Main Language(s) of Instruction: English

Degrees and Diplomas: *Bachelor's Degree*; *Bachelor's degree (professional)*; *Postgraduate Diploma*; *Master's Degree*; *Doctorate (PhD)*. Also Diploma and Certificate courses.

Student Services: Cultural centre, Health services, Sports facilities

Student Residential Facilities: Accommodation for c. 780 persons in separated hostels for ladies, bachelor and married; Guest rooms.

Special Facilities: Advanced Pediatrics Centre; OPD Block; Advanced Eye Center; Centre for Advanced Care; Drug De-addiction Centre.

Libraries: 44,478 vols; 54,921 bound journals; 81 CDs; 4,012 thesis; 435 foreign and 95 Indian journal subscriptions; 494 online journals.
Last Updated: 13/07/11

POTTI SREERAMULU TELUGU UNIVERSITY

Lalitha Kala Kshetram, Public Gardens, Hyderabad, Andhra Pradesh 500 004
Tel: +91(40) 2323-0435
Fax: +91(40) 2323-6045
EMail: info@teluguuniversity.ac.in
Website: http://www.teluguuniversity.ac.in

Vice-Chancellor: A. Bhoomaiah
Tel: +91(40) 2323-4815 EMail: vc@teluguuniversity.ac.in

Registrar: Battu Ramesh
Tel: +91(40) 2323-0435 EMail: registrar@teluguuniversity.ac.in

Centres

Distance Education (Esoteric Practices; Film; Folklore; Foreign Languages Education; Indic Languages; Linguistics; Media Studies;

Music; Native Language Education; Performing Arts; Sanskrit; Singing; Tourism); **International Telugu** (Dance; Indic Languages; Music); **Preparation of Encyclopedia** (Indic Languages)

Colleges
Sri Siddhendra Yogi Kala Pitham *(Kuchipudi Campus)* (Dance; Music; Singing; Theatre)

Courses
Computer Science (Computer Science; Multimedia)

Schools
Comparative Studies (Aesthetics; Comparative Literature; Comparative Religion; English; European Languages; Indic Languages; Philosophy; Sanskrit; Translation and Interpretation); **Fine Arts** (Cultural Studies; Dance; Fine Arts; Folklore; Music; Musical Instruments; Painting and Drawing; Performing Arts; Psychology; Sculpture; Singing; Theatre; Tourism); **Folk and Tribal Lore** *(Warangal Campus)* (Folklore; Social Studies); **History, Culture and Archaeology** *(Sri Sailam Campus)* (Anthropology; Archaeology; Architecture; Art History; Cultural Studies; History; Prehistory); **Language Development** (Applied Linguistics; Indic Languages; Linguistics; Native Language Education; Terminology); **Social and other Sciences** (Architecture; Esoteric Practices; Journalism; Mass Communication; Social Sciences); **Telugu Literature** *(Rajahamundry Campus)* (Indic Languages; Literature)

Further Information: Campuses in Rajahmundry, Sri Sailam, Warangal and Kuchipudi. Also 14 Affiliated Colleges. A traditional and distance education institution.

History: Founded 1985.

Governing Bodies: Executive Council; Academic Senate; Finance Committee

Academic Year: July to April (July-December; December-April)

Fees: (Rupees): Undergraduate diploma, 450-10,200; Bachelor's degree, 2,400; Postgraduate diploma,1,900-10,200; Master, 2,000-3,000; M.Phil., 3,400; Ph.D., 3,900.

Accrediting Agencies: University Grants Commission (UGC).

Degrees and Diplomas: *Bachelor's Degree*; *Postgraduate Diploma*; *Master's Degree*; *Master of Philosophy*; *Doctorate (PhD)*. Also undergraduate certificate and diploma.

Student Residential Facilities: Hostels

Special Facilities: Ages Museum featuring 3 Galleries (History; Contemporary Art; Portrait); Auditorium (265 seats); Art Gallery; Audio-Visual Cell.

Libraries: Telugu University Library: 55,000 vols in Telugu, 43,000 vols in English and 5,000 vols in other Indian languages; 150 journals subscriptions (in Telugu and in English); c. 10,000 back volumes of journals.

Publications: Telugu Vaani, Magazine that covers news regarding Festivals of Fine Arts, Cultural Programmes, Seminars and other activities of University and its Campuses. *(quarterly)*
Last Updated: 13/07/11

PRAVARA INSTITUTE OF MEDICAL SCIENCES (PIMS)

Rahata, Loni, Ahmednagar (Maharashtra) 413736
Tel: +91(2422) 273-600 +91(2422) 273-486
Fax: +91(2422) 273-442
EMail: contact@pmtpims.org; admission@pmtpims.org
Website: http://www.pravara.com

Vice-Chancellor: M.G. Takwale
Tel: +91(2422) 271-211, Fax: +91(2422) 273-442
EMail: vcpims@pmtpims.org

Registrar: A.L. Bhosale EMail: registrar@pmtpims.org

Centres
Social Medicine (Epidemiology; Health Administration; Health Sciences; Social and Preventive Medicine)

Colleges
Biotechnology (Biotechnology; Medical Technology); **Nursing** (Communication Studies; Midwifery; Nursing; Paediatrics; Surgery); **Physiotherapy and Rehabilitation Center** (Cardiology; Community Health; Neurosciences; Paediatrics; Physical Therapy; Rehabilitation and Therapy; Respiratory Therapy); **Rural Dental** *(and Hospital)* (Dental Technology; Dentistry; Medicine; Microbiology; Oral Pathology; Orthodontics; Periodontics; Radiology; Social and Preventive Medicine; Surgery); **Rural Medical** *(and Hospital)* (Anaesthesiology; Anatomy; Forensic Medicine and Dentistry; Gynaecology and Obstetrics; Medicine; Microbiology; Ophthalmology; Orthopaedics; Otorhinolaryngology; Paediatrics; Pathology; Pharmacology; Physiology; Radiology; Social and Preventive Medicine; Surgery; Toxicology; Treatment Techniques)

Schools
Bioscience Management *(Sinnar)* (Biological and Life Sciences; Business Administration; Marketing; Pharmacy)

Further Information: 800 beds hosital.

History: Founded 2003. A 'Deemed University'.

Governing Bodies: Board of Management; Academic Council; Board of Studies

Fees: (Rupees): Undergraduate programmes, 65,000-4.50,000 per annum for Indian students and (US Dollars) 5,000-40,000 per annum for international students. Graduate programmes, 50,000-525,000 per annum for Indian students and 80,000-650,000 per annum for international students.

Accrediting Agencies: Government of India; University Grants commission (UGC); Medical Council of India (MCI); Dental Council of India (DCI); All India Physiotherapists Association (AIPA) Rehabilitation Council of India (RCI); Nursing Council of India (INC).

Degrees and Diplomas: *Bachelor's Degree*; *Bachelor's degree (professional)*; *Postgraduate Diploma*; *Master's Degree*; *Doctorate*. Also undergraduate diploma and certificate programmes; M.B.A.

Student Services: Canteen

Student Residential Facilities: Boys and girls hostels; Guest house

Libraries: DU Learning Resource Centre (LRC): 297 national and international journals
Last Updated: 13/07/11

PRESIDENCY UNIVERSITY, KOLKATA (PRESIUNIV)

86/1 College Street, Kolkata, West Bengal 700 073
Website: http://www.presiuniv.ac.in/

Vice Chancellor: Malabika Sarkar

Centres
Bioinformatics *(DBT)* (Biological and Life Sciences; Computer Science); **North-Eastern Languages, Bengali, Santali and Hindi** *(Ghandi)* (Hindi; Modern Languages)

Faculties
Arts (Arts and Humanities; English; Hindi; History; Indic Languages; Philosophy; Political Sciences; Sociology); **Science** (Biotechnology; Botany; Chemistry; Economic and Finance Policy; Geography; Geology; Mathematics; Physics; Physiology; Statistics; Zoology)

History: Founded 1817 as Hindoo College. Renamed Presidency College 1855. Acquired university status 2010.

Governing Bodies: Academic Council; Executive Council

Degrees and Diplomas: *Bachelor's Degree*; *Master's Degree*; *Master of Philosophy*; *Doctorate*

Student Services: Canteen, Sports facilities

Student Residential Facilities: Hostel; Guest House

Special Facilities: Auditorium
Last Updated: 06/01/12

PRIST UNIVERSITY (PRIST)

Trichy – Thanjavur Highway, Vallam, Thanjavur,
Tamil Nadu 613403
Tel: +91(4362) 265-021 +91(4362) 265-022
Fax: +91(4362) 265-150
EMail: contact@prist.ac.in
Website: http://www.prist.ac.in

Vice-Chancellor: N. Ethirajalu

Registrar: K. V. Balasubrmanian
EMail: registrar@prist.ac.in; bsubramanian43@yahoo.com

Faculties

Arts and Science (Biochemistry; Biotechnology; Chemistry; Computer Science; English; Information Technology; Mathematics; Microbiology; Physics; Social Work; South and Southeast Asian Languages); **Catering and Hotel Management** (Cooking and Catering; Hotel Management; Management); **Commerce and Management** (Business Administration; Business and Commerce; Economics; Health Administration; Insurance; Management); **Education** (Business Education; Computer Education; Education; Foreign Languages Education; Humanities and Social Science Education; Mathematics Education; Native Language Education; Science Education); **Engineering and Technology** (Biotechnology; Civil Engineering; Computer Engineering; Computer Networks; Computer Science; Data Processing; Electrical and Electronic Engineering; Electronic Engineering; Engineering; Information Technology; Mechanical Engineering; Mechanical Equipment and Maintenance; Pharmacology; Pharmacy; Software Engineering; Technology; Telecommunications Engineering)

Further Information: Two campuses in Thanjavur (East and West) and other sites in Kumbakonam, Chennai, Tiruchirappalli, Puducherry

History: Founded 1994 as Ponnaiyah Ramajayam College. Acquired present status 2008. A 'Deemed University'.

Governing Bodies: Board of Management

Accrediting Agencies: All India Council of Technical Education (AICTE); University Grants Commission (UGC)/National Assessment and Accreditation Council (NAAC); Directorate of Employment and Training (DET); National council for Teachers Education (NCTE); Distance Education Council (DEC)

Degrees and Diplomas: *Diploma*; *Bachelor's Degree*; *Bachelor's degree (professional)*; *Postgraduate Diploma*; *Master's Degree*; *Master of Philosophy*; *Doctorate*. Also M.B.A.

Student Services: Health services, Sports facilities

Student Residential Facilities: Boys and girls hostel

Special Facilities: Ausitorium and open air auditoriums; Lord Ganesh temple; Seminar halls; Computer centres; Wifi access

Libraries: c. 69,000 vols
Last Updated: 18/07/11

PRIN. L. N. WELINGKAR INSTITUTE OF MANAGEMENT DEVELOPMENT AND RESEARCH

Lakhamshi Napoo Road, Near Matunga, Mumbai,
Maharashtra 400 019
Tel: +91(22) 2417-8300
Fax: +91(22) 2410-5585
Website: http://welingkar.org

Director: Uday Salunkhe

Programmes

Management (Business Administration; Finance; Health Administration; Human Resources; Marketing; Retailing and Wholesaling)

Further Information: Also Bengaluru Campus

Degrees and Diplomas: *Diploma*; *Postgraduate Diploma*; *Master's Degree*
Last Updated: 23/01/12

PT. RAVISHANKAR SHUKLA UNIVERSITY

Pandit Ravishankar Shukla Vishwavidyalaya (PT. R.S.U)
Amanaka G.E. Road, Raipur, Madhya Pradesh (Chhattisgarh)
492010
Tel: +91(771) 226-2540
Fax: +91(771) 226-2818
EMail: drianant@gmail.com
Website: http://www.prsu.ac.in

Vice-Chancellor: Shiv Kumar Pandey
Tel: +91 (771) 2262540, Fax: +91 (771) 2262818
EMail: skp@iucaa.ernet.in; proskp@gmail.com

Registrar: K. K. Chandrakar
Tel: +91 (771) 2262540, Fax: +91 (771) 2262818

Centres

Regional Studies and Research (Development Studies; Regional Planning; Regional Studies); **Women's Studies** (Women's Studies)

Institutes

Management (Business Administration; Finance; Human Resources; Management; Marketing); **Pharmacy** (Pharmacy); **Teachers Education** (Teacher Training); **Technology** (Technology); **Tourism and Hotel Management** (Hotel and Restaurant; Tourism)

Schools

Studies in Adult, Continuing Education and Extension (Adult Education; Education); **Studies in Ancient Indian History, Culture and Archaeology** (Archaeology; Architecture; Art History; Cultural Studies; History; Museum Studies; Political Sciences; Regional Studies; Tourism); **Studies in Anthropology** (Anthropology; Criminology; Forensic Medicine and Dentistry); **Studies in Bio-Technology** (Biotechnology); **Studies in Chemistry** (Analytical Chemistry; Chemistry; Organic Chemistry; Physical Chemistry); **Studies in Comparative Religion and Philosophy** (Comparative Religion; Philosophy; Philosophy of Education; Yoga); **Studies in Computer Science** (Computer Networks; Computer Science; Data Processing; Information Technology); **Studies in Economics** (Agricultural Economics; Economics); **Studies in Electronics** (Automation and Control Engineering; Electronic Engineering; Information Technology; Laser Engineering; Measurement and Precision Engineering; Nanotechnology; Optical Technology; Optics; Solid State Physics); **Studies in Geography** (Geography; Geography (Human); Marine Science and Oceanography; Meteorology; Natural Resources; Regional Planning; Surveying and Mapping); **Studies in Geology and Water Resource Management** (Geology; Mineralogy; Petrology; Surveying and Mapping; Water Management; Water Science); **Studies in History** (History; Philosophy); **Studies in Law** (Administrative Law; Commercial Law; Constitutional Law; Criminal Law; Criminology; International Law; Law); **Studies in Library and Information Science** (Computer Science; Documentation Techniques; Information Management; Information Sciences; Information Technology; Library Science); **Studies in Life Sciences** (Biochemistry; Biological and Life Sciences; Microbiology); **Studies in Literature and Languages** (English; French; German; Hindi; Linguistics; Literature; Modern Languages; Russian; Translation and Interpretation); **Studies in Mathematics** (Mathematics); **Studies in Physical Education** (Physical Education); **Studies in Physics and Astrophysics** (Astrophysics; Physics; Solid State Physics); **Studies in Psychology** (Clinical Psychology; Labour and Industrial Relations; Psychology); **Studies in Sociology** (Sociology); **Studies in Statistics** (Applied Mathematics; Operations Research; Statistics)

Further Information: Also 261 Affiliated Colleges.

History: Founded 1964.

Governing Bodies: Board of Studies; Academic Council; Executive Council; Academic Council

Academic Year: July to April

Admission Requirements: 12th year senior secondary/intermediate examination or recognized foreign equivalent

Fees: Varies from course to course

Main Language(s) of Instruction: English

Accrediting Agencies: UGC, AICTE, NCTE, NAAC etc.

Degrees and Diplomas: *Diploma*; *Bachelor's Degree*; *Bachelor's degree (professional)*; *Postgraduate Diploma*; *Master's Degree*; *Master of Philosophy*; *Doctorate (PhD)*. Also undegraduate certificates; Bachelor's degree honours; M.B.A. and M.C.A.

Student Services: Academic counselling, Canteen, Cultural centre, Employment services, Handicapped facilities, Health services, Language programs, Sports facilities

Student Residential Facilities: Boys and girls hostels; staff quarters, teachers hostel, guest house

Special Facilities: Museum in Anthropology Department; Computer Center; Bank; Post office; Railway Reservation Counter; Auditorium

Libraries: 154,588 vols; 305 journals; 14 newspaper subscriptions.

Publications: Ravishankar University Journal *(annually)*

Academic Staff 2009-2010	TOTAL
FULL-TIME	100
PART-TIME	90
STAFF WITH DOCTORATE	
FULL-TIME	100
PART-TIME	c. 30

Student Numbers 2009-2010
All (Foreign Included) c. 5,000

Part-time students, 120.
Last Updated: 11/07/11

PT. SUNDERLAL SHARMA (OPEN) UNIVERSITY (PSSOU)

Vyapar Vihar, Near Deen Dayal Upadhyay Park, Bilaspur, Chattisgarh 495 001
Tel: +91(7752) 414-225 +91(7752) 261-051
Fax: +91(7752) 414-245
EMail: vc@pssou.ac.in; registrar@pssou.ac.in; info@pssou.ac.in
Website: http://www.pssou.ac.in/

Vice Chancellor: A. R. Chandraker Tel: +91(7752) 414-255

Registrar: Smt. Indu Anant Tel: +91(94255) 33-303

Faculties

Commerce (Business and Commerce; E-Business/Commerce); **Continuing Education** (Continuing Education); **Education** (Education); **Health Sciences** (Alternative Medicine; Ayurveda; Health Sciences; Yoga); **Humanities** (Arts and Humanities; English; Hindi; History; Sanskrit); **Management** (Management); **Science and Technology** (Computer Science; Information Technology; Mathematics; Technology); **Social Sciences** (Economics; Political Sciences; Social Sciences; Sociology)

History: Founded 2005.

Governing Bodies: Executive Council; Academic Council; Planning Board;Department of Studies; Finance Committee

Degrees and Diplomas: Diploma; Bachelor's Degree; Postgraduate Diploma; Master's Degree
Last Updated: 03/01/12

PUNJAB AGRICULTURAL UNIVERSITY (PAU)

Ludhiana, Punjab 141004
Tel: +91(161) 240-1960 +91(161) 240-1979
Fax: +91(161) 240-0945
EMail: registrar@pau.edu
Website: http://www.pau.edu/

Vice-Chancellor: Baldev Singh Dhillon (2011-)
Tel: +91(161) 240-1794, Fax: +91(161) 240-2483
EMail: vc@pau.edu

Registrar: Raj kumar Mahey Tel: +91(161) 240-1960

Colleges

Agricultural Engineering (Agricultural Engineering; Agricultural Equipment; Civil Engineering; Computer Engineering; Computer Science; Electrical Engineering; Energy Engineering; Environmental Engineering; Food Technology; Information Technology; Irrigation; Machine Building; Mechanical Engineering; Power Engineering; Production Engineering; Soil Science; Thermal Engineering; Water Management; Water Science); **Agriculture** (Agricultural Education; Agricultural Engineering; Agriculture; Agronomy; Biotechnology; Crop Production; Ecology; Entomology; Floriculture; Food Science; Food Technology; Forestry; Genetics; Home Economics; Horticulture; Landscape Architecture; Meteorology; Natural Resources; Physiology; Plant Pathology; Soil Science; Toxicology; Vegetable Production); **Basic Sciences and Humanities** (Agricultural Business; Agricultural Economics; Agricultural Management; Arts and Humanities; Biochemistry; Botany; Business Administration; Chemistry; Cultural Studies; Economics; Embryology and Reproduction Biology; Finance; Fishery; Inorganic Chemistry; Journalism; Management; Marketing; Mass Communication; Mathematics; Microbiology; Modern Languages; Nuclear Physics; Organic Chemistry; Parasitology; Physical Chemistry; Physics; Physiology; Sociology; Solid State Physics; Statistics; Zoology); **Home Sciences** (Child Care and Development; Clothing and Sewing; Cooking and Catering; Development Studies; Dietetics; Fashion Design;

Food Science; Handicrafts; Home Economics; Interior Design; Nutrition; Textile Technology)

Courses

Post Graduate Studies (Actuarial Science; Agricultural Economics; Agricultural Education; Agricultural Equipment; Agriculture; Agronomy; Animal Husbandry; Biochemistry; Biotechnology; Botany; Business Administration; Cell Biology; Chemistry; Civil Engineering; Clothing and Sewing; Communication Studies; Computer Engineering; Computer Graphics; Computer Networks; Computer Science; Crop Production; Cultural Studies; E-Business/Commerce; Economics; Electrical Engineering; Embryology and Reproduction Biology; Endocrinology; Energy Engineering; Entomology; Finance; Floriculture; Food Science; Food Technology; Forestry; Genetics; Gerontology; Home Economics; Horticulture; Human Resources; Human Rights; Information Management; Information Sciences; Inorganic Chemistry; International Business; Journalism; Labour and Industrial Relations; Labour Law; Landscape Architecture; Library Science; Literature; Management; Marketing; Mathematics; Measurement and Precision Engineering; Mechanical Engineering; Mechanics; Meteorology; Microbiology; Molecular Biology; Natural Resources; Nuclear Physics; Nutrition; Parasitology; Physical Chemistry; Physics; Plant Pathology; Power Engineering; Production Engineering; Retailing and Wholesaling; Social Problems; Sociology; Software Engineering; Soil Science; Solid State Physics; Statistics; Textile Technology; Thermal Engineering; Water Management; Water Science; Wildlife; Writing; Zoology)

Further Information: Also University Farm. 16 Regional Research Stations

History: Founded 1962. The University is modelled on the United States Land Grant Institutions, has a semester system of education, and aims to integrate the threefold functions of teaching, research and extension education by linking them with the needs of Agricultural Production and Livestock Development.

Governing Bodies: Board of Management

Academic Year: August to July

Admission Requirements: 12th year senior secondary/intermediate examination or recognized foreign equivalent

Fees: (Rupees):Tuition fees for undegraduate programmes, 4,100-38,500 per semester; For postgraduate programmes, 6,710-49,500 per semester.

Main Language(s) of Instruction: English

International Co-operation: Links with several international research institutes (CIMMYT, IRRI, ICRISAT, ICARDA)

Accrediting Agencies: ICAR

Degrees and Diplomas: Diploma; Bachelor's Degree; Bachelor's degree (professional); Postgraduate Diploma; Master's Degree; Doctorate (Ph.D.). Also undergraduate certificate; Bachelor's degree Honours, 3-6 yrs.

Student Services: Academic counselling, Canteen, Cultural centre, Employment services, Foreign student adviser, Health services, Language programs, Nursery care, Social counselling, Sports facilities

Student Residential Facilities: Hostel

Special Facilities: Museum of Social History; Museum of Water and Power Resources. Botanical Garden; Lecture rooms; Farm facilities

Libraries: M.S. Randhawa Library: 237,868 vols; 35,933 theses; 102,115 bound journals; 348 Audio-Visuals; 601 Books and Theses - CD format; 896 CDs; 291 paper and 7,288 electronic periodical subscriptions.

Publications: Journal of Research, English (quarterly); Package of Practices for Rabi and Kharif Crops, English, Punjabi (biannually); Progressive Farming, English (monthly)

Press or Publishing House: University Press

Academic Staff 2010-2011: Total 866
Last Updated: 18/07/11

PUNJAB TECHNICAL UNIVERSITY (PTU)

Ladowali Road, Near B. Ed College, Jalandhar, Punjab 144061
Tel: +91(1822) 662-510
EMail: ahluwaliasukhbir@gmail.com
Website: http://ptu.ac.in

Vice-Chancellor: Rajneesh Arora
Tel: +91(1822) 662-500, Fax: +91(1822) 662-500
EMail: vc@ptu.ac.in; rajneesh.ptu@gmail.com

Registrar: H.S. Bains
Tel: +91(1822) 662-521, Fax: +91(1822) 662-525
EMail: registrar@ptu.ac.in; bains.ptu2010@gmail.com

Programmes

Bio Technology (Biotechnology); **Distance Education** (Business Administration; Computer Engineering; Computer Networks; Computer Science; Information Technology; Management); **Engineering** (Architecture; Automotive Engineering; Biomedical Engineering; Biotechnology; Chemical Engineering; Civil Engineering; Computer Engineering; Computer Science; Electrical Engineering; Electronic Engineering; Engineering; Information Technology; Measurement and Precision Engineering; Mechanical Engineering; Production Engineering; Telecommunications Engineering; Textile Design); **Hotel Management and Air Lines** (Air Transport; Cooking and Catering; Hotel Management; Management; Service Trades; Tourism); **Management** (Business Administration; Business Computing; Management); **Others** (Computer Science; Fashion Design; Laboratory Techniques; Medical Technology; Multimedia; Pharmacy; Visual Arts); **Pharmacy** (Pharmacy); **Technology** *(M-Tech)* (Automation and Control Engineering; Biotechnology; Chemical Engineering; Computer Engineering; Computer Graphics; Computer Science; Construction Engineering; Electrical Engineering; Electronic Engineering; Environmental Studies; Industrial Engineering; Information Technology; Machine Building; Measurement and Precision Engineering; Mechanical Engineering; Nanotechnology; Power Engineering; Production Engineering; Technology; Telecommunications Engineering; Thermal Engineering)

Further Information: Also over 300 affiliated institutions: 40 Engineering colleges, 56 Management colleges, 17 Pharmacy colleges, 6 Architecture colleges, 2 Hotel Management colleges and 13 colleges offering programmes in Medical Lab Technology & IT disciplines. A traditional and distance education institution.

History: Founded 1997.

Governing Bodies: Board of Governors; Academic Council; Board of Studies and Distance Education Council

Academic Year: July to June

Admission Requirements: Secondary School Education (10+2 yrs)

Fees: (Rupees): Tuition fee, 60,000 per annum.

Main Language(s) of Instruction: English

International Co-operation: None

Accrediting Agencies: University Grants Commission (UGC); All India Council for Technical Education (AICTE)

Degrees and Diplomas: *Bachelor's Degree*; *Bachelor's degree (professional)*; *Postgraduate Diploma*; *Master's Degree.* Also M.B.A. and M.C.A.

Student Services: Academic counselling, Canteen, Cultural centre, Employment services, Health services, Sports facilities

Libraries: Central Library, over 2,000 vols; Libraries at affiliated institutions.

Last Updated: 18/07/11

PUNJABI UNIVERSITY

Patiala, Punjab 147002
Tel: +91(175) 304-6366
Fax: +91(175) 228-3073
EMail: dpm@pbi.ac.in
Website: http://punjabiuniversity.ac.in/

Vice-Chancellor: Jaspal Singh
Tel: +91(175) 228-6418 EMail: vc@pbi.ac.in

Director, Planning and Monitoring: A.S. Chawla
Tel: +91(175) 228-6416
EMail: regpup@pbi.ac.in; registrar@pbi.ac.in

Centres

Advanced Media Studies (Media Studies); **Computer** *(University)* (Computer Science); **Dr. Balbir Singh Sahitya Kendra Panchbati** (Comparative Religion; Cultural Studies; History); **I.A.S. and Allied Services Training**; **Prof. Harban Singh Encyclopaedia of Sikhism** (Religion); **Research in Economic Change** (Economics); **Sufi Studies** *(Baba Farid)* (Arts and Humanities; Business and Commerce; Fine Arts; History; Linguistics; Medieval Studies); **Technical Development of Punjabi language, Literature and Culture** *(Advanced)* (Cultural Studies; Literature; South and Southeast Asian Languages)

Chairs

Gurmat Sangeet (Cultural Studies; Literature; Music); **Sri Guru Tegh Bahadur National Integration** (Religious Studies)

Departments

Development of Punjabi Language (South and Southeast Asian Languages); **Punjab Historical Studies** (History); **Punjabi Literary Studies** (Literature; Performing Arts; Theatre); **Sri Guru Granth Sahib Studies** (Religion; Religious Studies); **Tourism, Hospitality and Hotel Management** (Hotel and Restaurant; Hotel Management; Tourism)

Faculties

Arts and Culture (Cultural Studies; Dance; Fine Arts; Music; Musical Instruments; Performing Arts; Radio and Television Broadcasting; Theatre); **Business Studies** (Accountancy; Banking; Business Administration; Business and Commerce; Business Computing; Economics; Finance; Insurance; Management; Marketing); **Education and Information Sciences** (Education; Film; Information Sciences; Journalism; Mass Communication; Media Studies; Physical Education; Radio and Television Broadcasting; Yoga); **Engineering and Technology** (Computer Engineering; Electronic Engineering; Engineering; Mechanical Engineering; Technology; Telecommunications Engineering); **Languages** (Arabic; Chinese; English; French; German; Hindi; Indic Languages; Linguistics; Literature; Persian; Russian; Sanskrit; South and Southeast Asian Languages; Terminology); **Law** (Administrative Law; Civil Law; Commercial Law; Constitutional Law; Criminal Law; Environmental Studies; International Law; Labour Law; Law; Public Law); **Life Sciences** (Biological and Life Sciences; Biotechnology; Botany; Food Technology; Genetics; Zoology); **Medicine** (Nutrition; Pharmacology; Pharmacy; Physical Therapy; Sports; Sports Management); **Physical Sciences** (Applied Physics; Astrophysics; Chemistry; Computer Engineering; Computer Science; Electronic Engineering; Forensic Medicine and Dentistry; Information Technology; Inorganic Chemistry; Maintenance Technology; Mathematics; Meteorology; Operations Research; Organic Chemistry; Physical Chemistry; Physics; Statistics); **Social Sciences** (Anthropology; Asian Religious Studies; Clinical Psychology; Comparative Religion; Economics; Educational Psychology; Ethics; Geography; History; Human Rights; Industrial and Organizational Psychology; International Law; International Relations; Medieval Studies; Military Science; Modern History; Peace and Disarmament; Philosophy; Political Sciences; Protective Services; Psychology; Public Administration; Religious Studies; Social Psychology; Social Sciences; Social Work; Sociology; Women's Studies)

Research Departments

Maharishi Valmiki Chair (Literature); **Text Book Cell**; **Translation Cell** (Translation and Interpretation)

Further Information: Also 166 Colleges Affiliated Colleges and 65 Teaching/Research Departments; Campuses in Rampura Phul, Jhunir, Karandi, Sardulgarh, Rallah and Delha Sihan, Bathinda, Mansa and Sangrur. Regional Centres: Guru Kashi Campus, Talwandi Sabo, Guru Kashi Regional Centre, Bathinda, Nawab Sher Mohammed Khan Institute of Advanced Studies, Malerkotla, Regional Centre for Information Technology and Management, Mohali, and Dr Balbir Singh Sahitya Kendra, Dehradun.

History: Founded 1962. A Government aided institution under the jurisdiction of the Patiala, Ropar, Sangrur, Bhatinda and Faridkot Districts of Punjab.

Governing Bodies: Senate; Syndicate; Academic Council

Academic Year: July to June (July-December; January-June)

Admission Requirements: 12th year senior secondary/intermediate examination or recognized foreign equivalent

Fees: (Rupees): 1,920-12,000 per annum

Main Language(s) of Instruction: English, Punjabi, Hindi, Urdu

Degrees and Diplomas: *Diploma*; *Bachelor's Degree*; *Bachelor's degree (professional)*; *Postgraduate Diploma*; *Master's Degree*; *Master of Philosophy*; *Doctorate (PhD).* Also Advanced Diploma and Certificate courses; M.B.A.

Student Services: Health services, Sports facilities

Student Residential Facilities: Boys' and girls' hostels; Teachers flats

Special Facilities: Computer labs; Mechanical engineering workshop; Electronic labs; Wifi internet connectivity; Language lab; Audio-Visual Research Centre; Metrorology Centre; Science Auditorium; Arts Auditorium;

Libraries: Punjabi reference library: 100,000 vols and 120 Punjabi newspapers and periodical subscriptions. University's main library: 500,000 vols and 600 journals.

Publications: Bakha Sanjam Khoj, Patrika, Punjabi; Nanak Prakash Patrika, Punjabi; Punjab Past and Present, English; Sahitya Marg, Hindi

Press or Publishing House: University Press

Academic Staff *2009-2010*: Total: c. 500
Student Numbers *2009-2010*: Total: c. 9,000
Last Updated: 18/07/11

RABINDRA BHARATI UNIVERSITY

Rabindra Bharati Viswavidyaiaya (RBU)
Emerald Bower, 56-A Barrackpore Trunk Road, Kolkata,
West Bengal 700050
Tel: +91(33) 556-8079 5573028
Fax: +91(33) 2556-8079
EMail: rbreg@cal13.vsnl.net.in
Website: http://www.rbu.ac.in

Vice-Chancellor: Karuna Sindhu Das Tel: +91(33) 2556-8019

Registrar: Tapati Mukherjee EMail: registrar@rbu.ac.in

Centres
Dr. Sarvepalli Radhakrishnan Study; **Gandhian Studies** (History; Political Sciences); **Studies and Research on Tagore** (Literature)

Faculties
Arts (Arts and Humanities; Economics; Education; English; History; Indic Languages; Information Sciences; Library Science; Mathematics; Philosophy; Political Sciences; Sanskrit; Social Sciences); **Fine Arts** (Dance; Fine Arts; Mass Communication; Musical Instruments; Performing Arts; Singing; Theatre; Video); **Visual Arts** (Art History; Fine Arts; Graphic Arts; Museum Studies; Painting and Drawing; Sculpture; Visual Arts)

Programmes
Adult and Continuing Education (Adult Education; Management; Media Studies; Social Work)

Schools
Language and Culture (French; Hindi; Indic Languages; Italian; Japanese); **Vedic Studies** (Ayurveda)

Further Information: Also one Affiliated College

History: Founded 1954 as West Bengal State Academy of Dance, Drama, Music and Visual Arts. Acquired present status and title 1962.

Governing Bodies: Court; Executive Council

Academic Year: June to June

Admission Requirements: Graduate courses, 12th year senior secondary/intermediate examination or recognized foreign equivalent. P.G. courses, Hons. Graduate with higher percentage of marks; M.Phil and Ph.D. courses, Post graduate with higher percentage of marks.

Fees: (Rupees): Bachelor, 1,169 per annum; Master, 2,104 per annum

Main Language(s) of Instruction: Bengali; English

International Co-operation: With universities in Japan, USA and Italy

Accrediting Agencies: National Assessment and Accreditation Council (NAAC)

Degrees and Diplomas: *Diploma*; *Bachelor's Degree*; *Bachelor's degree (professional)*; *Master's Degree*; *Master of Philosophy (M.Phil)*; *Doctorate (PhD)*. Also Certificate courses in Foreign languages (French, Spanish, Japanese, Italian), Hindi, in NGO Man-

agement and in Rabindra Sangeet; Bachelor's degree honours, 3-5 yrs.

Student Services: Academic counselling, Canteen, Cultural centre, Employment services, Foreign student adviser, Handicapped facilities, Health services, Language programs, Nursery care, Social counselling, Sports facilities

Student Residential Facilities: Yes. Four Hostels for boys and girls; Quarters for teachers; Guest House; Staff Quarters

Special Facilities: Galleries including life and achievements of Rabindranath Tagore; gallery on cultural renaissance in West Bengal in latter part of 19th century; Rabindra Bharati University Museum and Jora Sanko Thakur Bari - Japan Gallery. Accoustics Audio Studio; Four Permanent Stages; Five Conference Halls; Yoga Centre

Libraries: Two central libraries and Departmental Library for each dept., 83,468 vols; 175 periodical subscriptions for the Central library

Publications: Rabindra Bharati Patrika (Bilingual), Journal of Literature and Social Sciences *(annually)*

Press or Publishing House: Rabindra Bharati University
Last Updated: 18/07/11

RAFFLES UNIVERSITY

Japanese Zone, National Highway-8, Neemrana, Rajasthan 301705
Tel: +91(9928) 777777
EMail: admission@rafflesuniversity.edu.in
Website: http://www.rafflesuniversity.edu.in

President: Kanta Ahuja

Schools
Behavioral Sciences (Behavioural Sciences); **Engineering** (Civil Engineering; Electrical Engineering; Engineering; Mechanical Engineering); **Law** (Law); **Liberal Studies** (Behavioural Sciences; Psychology); **Life Long Learning**; **Management** *(Alabbar)* (Business Administration; Management); **Sciences** (Natural Sciences)

History: Founded 2011.

Degrees and Diplomas: *Bachelor's Degree*; *Master's Degree*

Student Residential Facilities: Yes

Special Facilities: Wi-Fi; Computer Lab and Communication Lab

Libraries: Yes
Last Updated: 17/01/12

RAJASTHAN AYURVED UNIVERSITY, JODHPUR

Kadwad, Jodhpur–Nagaur Highway Road, Jodhpur,
Rajasthan 342 037
Tel: +91(291) 515-3721
Fax: +91(291) 515-3700
EMail: rau_jodhpur@yahoo.co.in
Website: http://www.raujodhpur.org/

Vice-Chancellor: Radhey Shyam Sharma Tel: +91(291) 515-3711

Registrar: Veena Lahoti Tel: +91(291) 515-3702

Colleges
Ayurveda (Anatomy; Ayurveda; Forensic Medicine and Dentistry; Gynaecology and Obstetrics; Hygiene; Medicine; Paediatrics; Pathology; Pharmacy; Surgery; Toxicology)

Further Information: Also 44 affiliated colleges/institutions

History: Founded 2002.

Governing Bodies: Board of Management; Academic Council

Fees: (Indian Rupee): 30,000-120,000 per annum

Degrees and Diplomas: *Diploma*; *Bachelor's degree (professional)*; *Master's Degree*; *Doctorate*. Also Certificate Course

Student Numbers *2010-2011*: Total: c. 7,000
Last Updated: 04/01/12

RAJASTHAN TECHNICAL UNIVERSITY (RTU)

Rawatbhata Road, Kota, Rajasthan 324 010
Tel: +91(744) 247-3861
EMail: rtuweb@gmail.com
Website: http://www.rtu.ac.in/

Vice Chancellor: R.P. Yadav
Tel: +91(744) 247-3001, Fax: +91(744) 247-3002
EMail: vcofficertu@yahoo.co.in

Registrar: Ambrish Mehta
Tel: +91(744) 247-3003, Fax: +91(744) 247-3033
EMail: registrar_rtu@yahoo.co.in

Colleges

Engineering (Arts and Humanities; Chemistry; Civil Engineering; Computer Engineering; Electrical Engineering; Electronic Engineering; Engineering; English; Mathematics; Mechanical Engineering; Physics; Telecommunications Engineering)

Further Information: Also affilates about 135 Engineering Colleges, 35 MCA Colleges, 142 MBA Colleges, 8 M.Tech Colleges and 3 Hotel Management and Catering Institutes

History: Founded 2006.

Degrees and Diplomas: *Bachelor's degree (professional)*; *Master's Degree.* Also M.B.A.
Last Updated: 05/01/12

RAJASTHAN UNIVERSITY OF HEALTH SCIENCES (RUHSRAJ)

Sector-18, Kumbha Marg, Pratap Nagar, Tonk Road, Jaipur, Rajasthan
Tel: +91(141) 279-5501
EMail: rajmed_university@rediffmail.com
Website: http://www.ruhsraj.org/

Vice Chancellor: Raja Babu Panwar
Tel: +91(141) 279-0481, Fax: +91(141) 291-803

Registrar: Anuprerna Kuntal
Tel: +91(141) 279-1928, Fax: +91(141) 279-5550

Courses

Dentistry (Dentistry); **Medicine** (Medicine); **Nursing** (Nursing); **Paramedical Sciences** (Medical Auxiliaries); **Pharmacy** (Pharmacy); **Physiotherapy and Occupational Therapy** (Occupational Therapy; Physical Therapy)

Further Information: Also 14 Affilated Colleges

History: Founded 2005.

Degrees and Diplomas: *Diploma*; *Bachelor's Degree*; *Bachelor's degree (professional)*; *Master's Degree*
Last Updated: 05/01/12

RAJENDRA AGRICULTURAL UNIVERSITY (RAU)

Pusa, Samastipur, Bihar 848125
Tel: +91(6274) 240-239
Fax: +91(6274) 240-277
EMail: info@pusavarsity.org.in
Website: http://www.pusavarsity.org.in/pusa1.htm

Vice-Chancellor: M.L. Choudhary
Tel: +91(6274) 240-226 EMail: vcrau@sify.com

Registrar: R. C. Rai Tel: +91(6274) 240-239

Colleges

Agricultural Engineering (Agricultural Engineering; Agricultural Equipment; Energy Engineering; Harvest Technology; Irrigation; Power Engineering; Soil Conservation; Soil Science; Water Management; Water Science); **Agriculture** *(Bhola Paswan Shastry - Dumraon (Buxar))* (Agriculture); **Agriculture** *(Mandan Bharti - Agwanpur, (Saharsa))* (Agriculture); **Agriculture** *(Tirhut - Dholi, Muzaffarpur)* (Agriculture); **Basic Sciences and Humanities** (Agriculture; Biochemistry; Biotechnology; Botany; Chemistry; Computer Science; Mathematics; Microbiology; Modern Languages; Molecular Biology; Physics; Statistics); **Fisheries** *(Dholi)* (Agricultural Economics; Agricultural Engineering; Aquaculture; Biochemistry; Biology; Fishery; Food Technology; Marine Science and Oceanography; Microbiology; Statistics); **Home Science** (Child Care and Development; Clothing and Sewing; Food Science; Home Economics; Home Economics Education; Nutrition); **Horticulture** *(Noorsarai, (Nalanda))* (Horticulture); **Veterinary** *(Bihar)* (Anatomy; Animal Husbandry; Biochemistry; Biological and Life Sciences; Embryology and Reproduction Biology; Epidemiology; Ethics; Genetics; Gynaecology and Obstetrics; Histology; Microbiology; Parasitology; Pathology; Pharmacology; Physiology; Public Health; Radiology; Social and Preventive Medicine; Surgery; Toxicology; Veterinary Science)

Institutes

Dairy ScienceTechnology *(Sanjay Gandhi - Patna)* (Agricultural Economics; Animal Husbandry; Chemistry; Dairy; Embryology and Reproduction Biology; Engineering; Food Technology; Microbiology)

Further Information: Also 7 Constituent Colleges and 10 Research Institutes

History: Founded 1970.

Governing Bodies: Board of Management; Senate; Academic Council; Research Council.

Admission Requirements: 12th year senior secondary/intermediate examination or recognized foreign equivalent

Fees: (Rupees): 500-700 per semester

Main Language(s) of Instruction: Hindi, English

Degrees and Diplomas: *Bachelor's Degree*; *Bachelor's degree (professional)*; *Postgraduate Diploma*; *Master's Degree*; *Doctorate.* Also Certificate Courses; Bachelor's degree honours; MBA.

Student Residential Facilities: Boy's Hostel (450 beds) and Girl's Hostel; Guest House

Libraries: 70,491 vols; 70 periodical subscriptions
Last Updated: 19/07/11

RAJIV GANDHI NATIONAL INSTITUTE OF YOUTH DEVELOPMENT (RGNIYD)

Bangalore Highway, Beemanthangal, Sriperumbudur, Chennai, Tamil Nadu 602 105
Tel: +91(44) 2716-2741 +91(44) 2716-2705
Fax: +91(44) 2716-3227
EMail: info@rgniyd.gov.in
Website: http://www.rgniyd.gov.in

Director: Michael Vetha Siromony
Tel: +91(44) 2716-2705 EMail: dir@rgniyd.gov.in

Registrar: D. Jayalakshmi
Tel: +91(44) 2716-3942 EMail: registrar@rgniyd.gov.in

Schools

Counseling (Psychology); **Gender Studies** (Gender Studies); **Governance and Public Policy** (Government; Public Administration); **Life Skills Education and Social Harmony**; **Youth Studies and Extension** (Information Technology; Management; Psychology)

History: A 'Deemed University'.

Degrees and Diplomas: *Master's Degree*
Libraries: c. 12,000 vols
Last Updated: 20/12/11

RAJIV GANDHI NATIONAL UNIVERSITY OF LAW (RGNUL)

Mohindra Kothi, Mall Road, Patiala, Punjab 147 001
Tel: +91(175) 230-4188 +91(175) 230-4491
Fax: +91(175) 230-4189
EMail: info@rgnul.ac.in
Website: http://rgnul.ac.in/

Vice Chancellor: Paramjit S. Jaswal

Registrar: G.I.S. Sandhu

Schools

Law (Administrative Law; Banking; Commercial Law; Constitutional Law; Environmental Studies; Family Studies; Human Rights; Insurance; International Law; Labour Law; Law; Public Law; Taxation)

History: Founded 2006.

Governing Bodies: General Council; Executive Council; Administrative Council

Fees: (Indian Rupee): Undergraduate tuition, 7,500 per annum; Graduate tuition, 43,000 per annum

Accrediting Agencies: Bar Council of India (BCI); University Grants Commission (UGC)

Degrees and Diplomas: *Master's Degree*; *Master of Philosophy*; *Doctorate*. Also Honours undergraduate integrated programme: B.A., LL.B. (HONS.), 5 yrs

Student Services: Canteen, Health services, Sports facilities

Student Residential Facilities: Boys and Girls separate Hostels; Guest House

Special Facilities: Computer Labs with 60 computers; Auditorium

Libraries: c. 21,000 vols
Last Updated: 04/01/12

RAJIV GANDHI UNIVERSITY (RGU)

Rono Hills, Itanagar, Arunachal Pradesh 791112
Tel: +91(360) 277-253
Fax: +91(360) 277-317
EMail: rikamnt@yahoo.com
Website: http://www.rgu.ac.in

Acting Vice-Chancellor: Tamo Mibang (2011-)
Tel: +91(360) 227-7252, Fax: +91(360) 227-7317
EMail: vcrguniv@gmail.com

Registrar: Amitav Mitra
Tel: +91(360) 227-7253, Fax: +91(360) 227-7889
EMail: registrar@rgu.ac.in

Faculties
Basic Sciences (Mathematics; Mathematics and Computer Science; Statistics); **Commerce and Management** (Accountancy; Advertising and Publicity; Business Administration; Business and Commerce; Business Computing; Commercial Law; Cooking and Catering; E-Business/Commerce; Finance; Hotel and Restaurant; Human Resources; Industrial and Organizational Psychology; Information Technology; International Business; Labour and Industrial Relations; Management; Marketing; Statistics; Taxation; Tourism); **Education** (Adult Education; Continuing Education; Education; Educational Administration; Educational Psychology; Educational Technology; Preschool Education; Special Education; Teacher Training); **Engineering and Information Technology** (Advertising and Publicity; Computer Engineering; Computer Graphics; Computer Networks; Computer Science; Data Processing; E-Business/Commerce; Electronic Engineering; Engineering; Information Technology; Mass Communication; Mathematics; Media Studies; Photography; Radio and Television Broadcasting; Software Engineering; Video; Visual Arts); **Environmental Sciences** (Demography and Population; Environmental Studies; Geography; Geography (Human); Safety Engineering; Surveying and Mapping); **Languages** (English; Hindi; Literature; Modern Languages); **Life Sciences** (Biochemistry; Biotechnology; Botany; Cell Biology; Ecology; Endocrinology; Entomology; Environmental Studies; Genetics; Horticulture; Immunology; Microbiology; Molecular Biology; Natural Resources; Plant Pathology; Statistics; Wildlife; Zoology); **Social Sciences** (Agricultural Economics; Archaeology; Economics; History; International Economics; Mathematics; Political Sciences; Social Sciences; Sociology; Statistics)

Institutes
Biodiversity; **Distance Education**; **Tribal Studies** *(Arunachal - AITS)* (Anthropology; Folklore; Linguistics; Native Language; Social Studies)

Further Information: Also 15 Affiliated Colleges. A traditional and distance education institution.

History: Founded 1984 as Arunachal University. Turned into a 'Central University' 2007.

Governing Bodies: Executive Council

Academic Year: July to June (July-December; January-June)

Admission Requirements: 12th year senior secondary/intermediate examination or recognized foreign equivalent. For Graduate admission, applicants must normally hold a First Degree with Honours or 50% marks

Fees: (Rupees): Undergraduate, 1,550 per annum; graduate, 1,275-2,490; postgraduate, 3,000

Main Language(s) of Instruction: English

Accrediting Agencies: University Grants Commission (UGC)

Degrees and Diplomas: *Bachelor's Degree*; *Bachelor's degree (professional)*; *Postgraduate Diploma*; *Master's Degree*; *Master of Philosophy*; *Doctorate*. Also Certificate Courses; M.B.A.

Student Services: Canteen, Cultural centre, Sports facilities

Student Residential Facilities: For c. 650 students

Libraries: 27,950 vols
Last Updated: 19/07/11

RAJIV GANDHI UNIVERSITY OF HEALTH SCIENCES (RGUHS)

4th 'T' Block, Jayanagar, Bangalore, Karnataka 560 041
Tel: +91(80) 2696-1933 +91(80) 2696-1935
Fax: +91(80) 2665-8569
EMail: info@rguhs.ac.in
Website: http://www.rguhs.ac.in

Vice-Chancellor: K.S. Sriprakash (2011-)
Tel: +91(80) 2696-1926, Fax: +91(80) 2696-1927
EMail: vc@rguhs.ac.in

Registrar: Kumar Prem
Tel: +91(80) 2696-1928, Fax: +91(80) 2696-1929
EMail: registrar@rguhs.ac.in

Departments
Health Science Library and Information System (Health Sciences; Information Sciences; Library Science)

Faculties
Anaesthesia Technology (Anaesthesiology; Cardiology; Oncology); **Ayurveda** (Ayurveda); **Cardiac Care Technology** (Cardiology; Medical Technology; Medicine); **Clinical Psychology** (Clinical Psychology); **Clinical Research** (Medicine); **Dentistry** (Dentistry); **Echo Cardiography** (Cardiology; Medical Technology); **Homeopathy** (Homeopathy); **Hospital Administration** (Health Administration); **IMAGING TECHNOLOGY** (Medical Technology; Oncology); **Medical Laboratory Technology** (Laboratory Techniques; Medical Technology); **Medicine** (Cardiology; Medicine); **Naturopathy and Yogic Sciences** (Alternative Medicine; Yoga); **Neuro Science Technology** (Medical Technology; Neurosciences); **Nursing** (Nursing); **Operation Theater Technology** (Cardiology; Health Sciences; Medical Technology; Medicine; Oncology; Paramedical Sciences); **Optometry** (Optometry); **Perfusion Technology** (Medical Technology; Medicine); **Pharmacy** (Pharmacy); **Physiotherapy** (Physical Therapy); **Prosthetics and Orthotics** (Dental Technology; Orthodontics); **Psychol Social Rehabilitation** (Psychology; Rehabilitation and Therapy; Social Problems); **Public Health** (Public Health); **Radiography** (Radiology); **Renal Dialysis Technology** (Medical Technology); **Respiratory Care Technology** (Cardiology; Respiratory Therapy); **Unani** (Traditional Eastern Medicine)

History: Founded 1996.

Degrees and Diplomas: *Diploma*; *Bachelor's Degree*; *Bachelor's degree (professional)*; *Postgraduate Diploma*; *Master's Degree*; *Doctorate*
Last Updated: 19/07/11

RAMAKRISHNA MISSION VIVEKANANDA UNIVERSITY (RKMVU)

PO Belur Math, Howrah, West Bengal 711202
Tel: +91(33) 2654-9999
Fax: +91(33) 2654-4640
EMail: vivekananda.university@gmail.com
Website: http://www.rkmvu.ac.in/

Vice Chancellor: Swami Atmapriyananda

Registrar: Swami Durgananda

Schools
Agriculture and Rural Development *(Off-Campus)* (Agricultural Management; Agriculture; Rural Studies); **Humanities and Social Sciences** (Arts and Humanities; Economics; Philosophy; Social Sciences; South and Southeast Asian Languages); **Indian Heritage**

(Cultural Studies; Sanskrit); **Mathematical Sciences** (Computer Science; Mathematics; Mathematics and Computer Science; Physics)

History: Founded 2005 as Ramakrishna Mission Vivekananda Educational and Research Institute (RKMVERI). A 'Deemed University'.

Governing Bodies: Board of Management

Accrediting Agencies: University Grants Commission (UGC); Ministry of Human Resource Development

Degrees and Diplomas: *Diploma*; *Bachelor's Degree*; *Master's Degree*; *Master of Philosophy*; *Doctorate*. Also Certificate Courses.

Last Updated: 19/12/11

RANCHI UNIVERSITY

Shaheed Chowk, Ranchi, Bihar 834001
Tel: +91(651) 220-8553
Fax: +91(651) 230-1051
EMail: admin@ranchiuniversity.org.in
Website: http://ranchiuniversity.org.in/

Vice-Chancellor: A.A. Khan (2006-)
Tel: +91(651) 220-5177, Fax: +91(651) 230-1077

Registrar: Jyoti Kumar
Tel: +91(651) 220-8553, Fax: +91(651) 230-1077

Faculties

Commerce (Accountancy; Administration; Advertising and Publicity; Business Administration; Business and Commerce; Business Computing; Insurance; Management; Mass Communication; Secretarial Studies; Tourism); **Education** (Education; Physical Education); **Engineering** (Engineering); **Humanities** (English; Hindi; Indic Languages; Journalism; Mass Communication; Native Language; Sanskrit; Urdu); **Law** (Law); **Medicine** (Medicine); **Science** (Botany; Chemistry; Computer Science; Geology; Mathematics; Physics; Statistics; Zoology); **Social Science** (Anthropology; Economics; Esoteric Practices; Geography (Human); History; Home Economics; Philosophy; Political Sciences; Social Sciences; Sociology)

Further Information: Also 15 Consituent College and 24 affiliated colleges/institutions.

History: Founded 1960.

Governing Bodies: Academic Council; Syndicate; Senate

Fees: (Rupees): 180-240 per annum

Accrediting Agencies: National Assessment and Accreditation Council (NAAC)

Degrees and Diplomas: *Bachelor's Degree*; *Bachelor's degree (professional)*; *Postgraduate Diploma*; *Master's Degree*; *Doctorate (PhD)*. Also Certificate, Diploma and Advanced Diploma; M.B.A; Undergraduate and postgraduate vocational courses.

Student Services: Social counselling

Student Residential Facilities: 2 hostels for post graduate students (one for boys at Morhabadi and another for girls at Bariatu); university quarters for teachers and staff; c. 12 undergraduate students on-campus hostels.

Special Facilities: Computer Centre; Tabulation Centre

Libraries: Central Library: c. 90,000 text books, c. 10,000 reference books and 350 Ph.D theses; Online access to more than 3,500 international and national journals

Last Updated: 19/07/11

RANI CHANNAMMA UNIVERSITY (RCUB)

Vidya Sangama, PBRH-4, Belagavi, Karnataka 591 156
EMail: rcuregistrar@gmail.com
Website: http://www.rcub.ac.in/

Vice Chancellor: B.R. Ananthan

Registrar: S.S. Patagundi

Departments

Geography (Geography); **Mathematics** (Mathematics); **Media** (Indic Languages; Media Studies); **National Service Scheme** (Physical Education); **Studies in Economics** (Economics)

Further Information: Also 333 affiliated College; 63 Postgraduate Colleges

History: Founded 1982 as Karnatak University PG Centre. Acquired present title and university status 2010.

Governing Bodies: Syndicate; Academic Council; Finance Committee

Degrees and Diplomas: *Diploma*; *Postgraduate Diploma*; *Master's Degree*; *Master of Philosophy*; *Doctorate*. Also Certificate Courses; M.B.A.

Student Services: Canteen, Health services

Student Residential Facilities: Boys' Hostel and 13 Staff Quarters

Special Facilities: Conference and Gymkhana Hall; Computer Labs

Libraries: c. 22,034 vols; Subscription to 10 Journal and 13 Newspapers

Student Numbers *2010-2011*: Total: c. 500
Last Updated: 03/01/12

RANI DURGAVATI UNIVERSITY

Rani Durgavati Vishwavidyalaya, Jabalpur
Saraswati Vihar, Pachpedi, Jabalpur, Madhya Pradesh 482 001
Tel: +91(761) 260-0567 +91(761) 260-0568
Fax: +91(761) 260-3752
EMail: rdvvcc1@rediffmail.com
Website: http://www.rdunijbpin.org/

Vice-Chancellor: Ram Rajesh Mishra Tel: +91(761) 260-1452

Registrar: U.N. Shukla Tel: +91(761) 260-0785

Centres

Ambedakar Studies; **Gandhian Studies** (Peace and Disarmament; Political Sciences); **Science Instrumentation** (Instrument Making); **University Study**; **Yoga** (Yoga)

Divisions

Mahatmah Gandhi Srijan Peet

Faculties

Arts (English; Hindi; Indic Languages; Information Sciences; Journalism; Library Science; Linguistics; Literature; Mass Communication; Philosophy; Sanskrit); **Education** (Development Studies; Education; Physical Education; Rural Studies); **Law** (Administrative Law; Labour Law; Law; Taxation); **Life Science** (Biochemistry; Biological and Life Sciences; Biotechnology; Botany; Microbiology); **Management** (Management); **Mathematical Science** (Computer Engineering; Computer Graphics; Computer Science; Mathematics; Mathematics and Computer Science; Software Engineering); **Science** (Chemistry; Electronic Engineering; Physics); **Social Sciences** (Ancient Civilizations; Archaeology; Cultural Studies; Economics; Geography; History; Political Sciences; Public Administration; Social Sciences; Social Studies; Social Work; Sociology)

Research Centres

Macromolecular (Molecular Biology); **Women's Studies Development** (Women's Studies)

Further Information: Also 151 Affiliated Colleges. A traditional and distance education institution.

History: Founded 1956 as University of Jabalpur, acquired present title 1983.

Governing Bodies: Executive Council; Court; Finance Committee.

Academic Year: July to April

Admission Requirements: 12th year senior secondary/intermediate examination or recognized foreign equivalent

Main Language(s) of Instruction: English; Hindi

Accrediting Agencies: National Assessment and Accreditation Council (NAAC)

Degrees and Diplomas: *Diploma*; *Bachelor's Degree*; *Postgraduate Diploma*; *Master's Degree*; *Master of Philosophy*; *Doctorate (PhD)*. Also Certificate courses; Bachelor's degree honours, 5 yrs; M.B.A.

Student Services: Employment services, Health services

Student Residential Facilities: Boys' Hostel (101 rooms) and Women's Hostel (88 rooms); Guest House

Special Facilities: Computer Center

Libraries: Central library: c. 180,000 vols; over 8,000 bound vols of research abstracts and journals and hard copies of 4,000 research degree theses awarded by the university;
Last Updated: 19/07/11

RASHTRASANT TUKADOJI MAHARAJ NAGPUR UNIVERSITY

Chhatrapati Shivaji Maharaj Administrative Premises, Ravindranath Tagore Marg, Nagpur, Maharashtra 440001
Tel: +91(712) 252-5417
Fax: +91(712) 253-2841 +91(712) 250-0736
EMail: vcnaguni@hotmail.com; vc.rtmnu@nagpuruniversity.org
Website: http://www.nagpuruniversity.org

Vice-Chancellor: Vilas S. Sapkal EMail: vc@nagpuruniversity.org

Registrar: Maheshkumar Yenkie
EMail: registrar.rtmnu@nagpuruniversity.org

Faculties

Arts (Arabic; Dance; English; Fine Arts; French; German; Indic Languages; Linguistics; Literature; Modern Languages; Music; Musical Instruments; Painting and Drawing; Persian; Russian; Sanskrit; Sculpture; Singing; Theatre; Urdu); **Ayurveda** (Ayurveda); **Commerce** (Banking; Business Administration; Business and Commerce; Farm Management; Human Resources; Labour and Industrial Relations; Management; Marketing; Taxation); **Education** (Education; Educational Psychology; Physical Education; Sports); **Engineering and Technology** (Architecture; Chemical Engineering; Civil Engineering; Computer Engineering; Computer Science; Construction Engineering; Electrical Engineering; Electronic Engineering; Engineering; Fire Science; Food Technology; Industrial Engineering; Information Technology; Interior Design; Measurement and Precision Engineering; Mechanical Engineering; Metallurgical Engineering; Mining Engineering; Paper Technology; Petroleum and Gas Engineering; Polymer and Plastics Technology; Power Engineering; Production Engineering; Telecommunications Engineering); **Home Science** (Clothing and Sewing; Cooking and Catering; Cosmetology; Dietetics; Fashion Design; Food Science; Home Economics; Interior Design; Nutrition; Printing and Printmaking; Psychology; Textile Design); **Law** (Administrative Law; Commercial Law; Constitutional Law; Criminal Law; Environmental Studies; Human Rights; International Law; Labour Law; Law); **Medicine** (Anaesthesiology; Anatomy; Biochemistry; Community Health; Dentistry; Dermatology; Forensic Medicine and Dentistry; Gynaecology and Obstetrics; Laboratory Techniques; Medical Technology; Medicine; Microbiology; Occupational Health; Ophthalmology; Oral Pathology; Orthodontics; Orthopaedics; Otorhinolaryngology; Paediatrics; Pathology; Periodontics; Pharmacology; Pharmacy; Physiology; Plastic Surgery; Pneumology; Public Health; Radiology; Social and Preventive Medicine; Surgery; Venereology); **Science** (Analytical Chemistry; Aquaculture; Biochemistry; Botany; Chemistry; Computer Science; Electronic Engineering; Embryology and Reproduction Biology; Entomology; Environmental Studies; Geology; Information Technology; Inorganic Chemistry; Mathematics; Microbiology; Molecular Biology; Operations Research; Organic Chemistry; Physical Chemistry; Physics; Physiology; Statistics; Zoology); **Social Science** (Administration; Ancient Civilizations; Archaeology; Cultural Studies; Economics; Government; History; Information Sciences; Journalism; Library Science; Mass Communication; Media Studies; Peace and Disarmament; Philosophy; Political Sciences; Psychology; Public Administration; Social Sciences; Tourism; Video)

Further Information: Also 3 Constituent Colleges/Institutions (Law college, Laxminarayan Institute of Technology, and College of Education) and 439 Affiliated Colleges. 7 campuses.

History: Founded 1923 as Nagpur University.

Governing Bodies: Academic Council, Senate, Board of Studies

Academic Year: June to May

Admission Requirements: 12th year senior secondary/intermediate examination or recognized foreign equivalent

Main Language(s) of Instruction: English, Hindi, Marathi

Accrediting Agencies: National Assessment and Accreditation Council

Degrees and Diplomas: *Diploma*; *Bachelor's Degree*; *Bachelor's degree (professional)*; *Postgraduate Diploma*; *Master's Degree*; *Master of Philosophy*; *Doctorate (PhD)*. Also undegraduate certifi-

cates, 1-2 yrs; Higher Diplomas, 1 yr; Bachelor's degree honours, 5 yrs; M.B.A., 2 yrs.

Student Services: Academic counselling, Canteen, Cultural centre, Employment services, Foreign student adviser, Foreign Studies Centre, Handicapped facilities, Health services, Language programs, Nursery care, Social counselling, Sports facilities

Student Residential Facilities: Hostel; Guest House

Libraries: 365,833 vols; 310 periodical subscriptions

Publications: NU Humanities Journal, Research Journal *(annually)*; NU Science Journal, Research papers *(annually)*

Press or Publishing House: NU Printing Press
Last Updated: 19/07/11

RASHTRIYA SANSKRIT SANSTHAN

56-57 Institutional Area, Janakpuri, New Delhi 110-058
Tel: +91(11) 285-24993 +91(11) 285-24995
Fax: +91(11) 285-21948
EMail: rsks@nda.vsnl.net.in
Website: http://www.sanskrit.nic.in/

Vice Chancellor: Radhavallabh Tripathi (2008-)
EMail: rskspvc@yahoo.com

Registrar: K.B. Subbarayudu EMail: registrar.rsks@gmail.com

Programmes
Sanskrit (Sanskrit)

Further Information: Also campuses in Allahabad, Puri, Jammu, Trichur, Jaipur, Lucknow, Sringeri, Kangra, Bhopal, Mumbai; 23 Adarsh Sanskrit Mahavidyalayas, Shodh-Sansthans and about 84 Affiliated Sanskrit Institutions.

History: Founded 1970. Acquired 'Deemed University' status 2002.

Governing Bodies: Board of Management; Finance Committee; Academic Council; Examination Board; Research Board

Degrees and Diplomas: *Diploma*; *Bachelor's Degree*; *Master's Degree*; *Doctorate*; *Doctor of Literature*
Last Updated: 19/12/11

RAVENSHAW UNIVERSITY

Cuttack, Orissa 753003
Tel: +91(671) 260-7710
Fax: +91(671) 261-0060
EMail: ravenshawuniversity@yahoo.co.in; ravenshaw@sify.com
Website: http://www.ravenshawuniversity.ac.in/

Vice-Chancellor: Devdas Chhotray (2006-)
Tel: +61(671) 261-0060, Fax: +61(671) 261-0304
EMail: devdas_chhotray@hotmail.com; devdaschhotray@gmail.com

Registrar: Smarapriya Mishra
Tel: +61(671) 263-2690 EMail: smarapriyamishra57@gmail.com

Courses
Self-financing Studies (Biotechnology; Business Administration; Computer Engineering; Computer Networks; Computer Science; Data Processing; Information Technology; Journalism; Mass Communication; Software Engineering; Telecommunications Engineering)

Departments
Applied Geography (Geography); **Bengali** (Indic Languages); **Biotechnology** (Biotechnology); **Botany** (Botany); **Chemistry** (Chemistry); **Commerce and Business Management** (Accountancy; Business Administration; Business and Commerce; Business Computing; Economics; Finance; Management; Marketing; Statistics); **Economics** (Economics); **Education** (Education); **English** (English); **Geology** (Geology); **Hindi** (Hindi); **History** (History); **Mathematics** (Mathematics); **Oriya** (Indic Languages); **Philosophy** (Philosophy); **Physics** (Physics); **Political Science** (Political Sciences); **Psychology** (Psychology); **Sanskrit** (Sanskrit); **Sociology** (Sociology); **Statistics** (Statistics); **Urdu and Persian Languages** (Persian; Urdu); **Zoology** (Zoology)

History: Founded in 1868 as Ravenshaw College. Successively affiliated to Calcutta University, Patna University (1917) and Utkal University (1943). Acquired current status and title 2006.

Governing Bodies: University Executive Council; University Senate; Academic Council; Board of Studies

Academic Year: January to December

Admission Requirements: High School Certificate

Main Language(s) of Instruction: English

Accrediting Agencies: National Assessment and Accreditation Council (NAAC)

Degrees and Diplomas: *Diploma*; *Bachelor's Degree*; *Master's Degree*; *Master of Philosophy*; *Doctorate*; *Doctor of Literature*; *Doctor of Science*. Also Bachelor's degree honours; M.B.A.

Academic Staff *2009-2010*: Total: c. 500

Student Numbers *2009-2010*: Total: c. 10,000

Last Updated: 19/07/11

RAYALASEEMA UNIVERSITY

Kurnool, Andhra Pradesh 518 002
Tel: +91(8518) 271-183
Website: http://www.rayalaseemauniversity.ac.in/

Vice- Chancellor: K. Krishna Naik

Programmes

Biotechnology (Biotechnology); **Business Administration** *(Distance Education)* (Business Administration); **Business and Commerce** *(Distance Education)* (Business and Commerce); **Computers and Business Management** *(Distance Education)* (Business Computing; Management); **Education** (Education); **Organic Chemistry** *(Distance Education)* (Organic Chemistry); **Psychology** *(Distance Education)* (Psychology)

Further Information: A traditional and distance education institution.

History: Founded 2008.

Degrees and Diplomas: *Bachelor's Degree*; *Master's Degree*; *Master of Philosophy*. Also M.B.A.; Pre-Ph.D. research programme.

Last Updated: 02/01/12

SAM HIGGINBOTTOM INSTITUTE OF AGRICULTURE, TECHNOLOGY AND SCIENCES (SHIATS)

PO Allahabad Agricultural Institute, Allahabad,
Uttar Pradesh 211007
Tel: +91(532) 268-4281
Fax: +91(532) 268-4394
EMail: registrar@shiats.edu.in
Website: http://www.aaidu.org

Chief Executive and Vice Chancellor: Rajendra B. Lal (2000-)
Tel: +91(532) 268-4284, Fax: +91(532) 268-4393
EMail: vc@shiats.edu.in

Registrar: A.K.A. Lawrence
Tel: +91(532) 268-4781, Fax: +91(532) 268-4394

Faculties

Agriculture (Agricultural Business; Agricultural Economics; Agriculture; Agronomy; Biochemistry; Biology; Biotechnology; Clothing and Sewing; Community Health; Development Studies; Dietetics; Environmental Studies; Family Studies; Food Science; Forest Biology; Forest Management; Forest Products; Forestry; Genetics; Health Sciences; Home Economics; Horticulture; Microbiology; Nutrition; Plant and Crop Protection; Rural Studies; Soil Science; Textile Technology; Wildlife); **Animal Husbandry and Dairying** (Animal Husbandry; Dairy; Embryology and Reproduction Biology; Genetics; Meat and Poultry; Nutrition); **Business Studies** (Accountancy; Agricultural Business; Banking; Business Administration; Environmental Management; Finance; Forest Management; Human Resources; Information Technology; International Business; Management; Marketing; Retailing and Wholesaling); **Engineering and Technology** (Agricultural Engineering; Agricultural Equipment; Animal Husbandry; Automation and Control Engineering; Bioengineering; Biotechnology; Civil Engineering; Computer Engineering; Computer Science; Construction Engineering; Dairy; Electrical and Electronic Engineering; Electronic Engineering; Engineering; Food Science; Food Technology; Heating and Refrigeration; Hydraulic Engineering; Industrial Engineering; Information Technology;

Mechanical Engineering; Mechanics; Microbiology; Microwaves; Molecular Biology; Power Engineering; Production Engineering; Soil Management; Soil Science; Technology; Telecommunications Engineering; Water Management; Water Science); **Film, Media Studies and Technology** (Advertising and Publicity; Communication Studies; Film; Journalism; Mass Communication; Media Studies; Music; Performing Arts; Radio and Television Broadcasting; Singing; Visual Arts); **Health, Medical Sciences, Indigenous and Alternative Systems of Medicine** (Alternative Medicine; Biochemistry; Health Sciences; Immunology; Laboratory Techniques; Medical Technology; Medicine; Microbiology; Pharmacy; Public Health); **Humanities, Social Sciences and Education** (Accountancy; Anthropology; Arabic; Arts and Humanities; Business Administration; Economics; Education; English; French; Information Sciences; Japanese; Law; Library Science; Literature; Modern Languages; Physical Education; Portuguese; Psychology; Social Sciences; Social Work; Teacher Training); **Science** (Biological and Life Sciences; Botany; Chemistry; Computer Science; Forensic Medicine and Dentistry; Mathematics; Physics; Statistics; Zoology); **Theology** (Bible; Ethics; History of Religion; Missionary Studies; Religion; Religious Studies; Theology)

Further Information: A traditional and distance education institution.

History: Founded in 1910. Formerly known as Allahabad Agricultural Institute - Deemed University. Acquired current title 2009.

Governing Bodies: Board of Directors; Executive Council; Academic Council; Finance Committee

Fees: (Rupees): Undergraduate programmes, 5,000-76,000 per semester (except Diploma, 1,000-4,000 per annum, B.Ed., 90,000 per annum and B.P.Ed., 60,000 per annum) for Indian students; Postgraduate programmes, 6,000-70,000 per semester (except B.Ed., and) for Indian students; M.B.A., 60,000-98,000 per semester for Indian students; Ph.D., 35,000 per semester for Indian students; Fee for international students, 5,000 per semester irrespective of programme level and field of study.

Main Language(s) of Instruction: English

Accrediting Agencies: National Assessment and Accreditation Council (NAAC)

Degrees and Diplomas: *Diploma*; *Bachelor's Degree*; *Bachelor's degree (professional)*; *Postgraduate Diploma*; *Master's Degree*; *Master of Philosophy*; *Doctorate (Ph.D.)*. Alos undergraduate certificates, 2 sem.; Bachelor's degree honours, 8 sem.; M.B.A., 4 sem.

Student Services: Academic counselling, Canteen, Cultural centre, Foreign student adviser, Foreign Studies Centre, Health services, Social counselling, Sports facilities

Student Residential Facilities: Men's and Girl's hostel.

Special Facilities: Post-Office, Bank and Cooperative Store

Libraries: Central Library, c. 40,000 vols

Publications: Allahabad Farmer *(quarterly)*; Hamar Gaon (Our Village) *(quarterly)*

Press or Publishing House: University Publication Division (UPD)

Last Updated: 20/07/11

SAMBALPUR UNIVERSITY (SUNIV)

Jyoti Vihar, Sambalpur, Orissa 768019
Tel: +91(663) 243-0157
Fax: +91(663) 243-0158
EMail: registrar@suniv.ac.in
Website: http://www.suniv.ac.in/

Vice-Chancellor: Arun Kumar Pujari
Tel: +91(663) 243-0158 EMail: vc@suniv.ac.in

Registrar: Sudhanshu Sekhar Rath
Tel: +91(663) 243-0157, Fax: +91(663) 243-0158

Departments

Anthropology (Anthropology); **Business Administration** *(Postgraduate)* (Business Administration; Finance; Human Resources; Industrial Management; Insurance; Marketing); **Computer Science and Application** (Computer Science; Electronic Engineering; Information Technology; Mathematics; Physics; Statistics; Telecommunications Engineering); **Earth Science** (Computer Science; Earth Sciences; Environmental Studies; Geology; Natural Resources; Surveying and Mapping; Water Management); **Economics** (Agricultural Economics; Econometrics; Economics; Finance;

English (Comparative Literature; English; Linguistics; Translation and Interpretation); **Environmental Science** (Biotechnology; Ecology; Environmental Management; Environmental Studies; Geology; Safety Engineering; Soil Conservation; Surveying and Mapping; Water Science); **History** (History); **Home Science** (Dietetics; Education; Family Studies; Food Science; Home Economics; Nutrition; Women's Studies); **Law** (Commercial Law; Criminal Law; Environmental Studies; Law; Private Law); **Library and Information Science** *(Postgraduate)* (Educational Research; Educational Technology; Information Sciences; Library Science); **Mathematics** (Mathematics; Operations Research); **Oriya** (Comparative Literature; Folklore; Literature); **Political Science and Public Administration** (Development Studies; Journalism; Political Sciences; Public Administration); **Region Art and Culture Studies** (Cultural Studies; Fine Arts; Regional Studies); **Sociology** *(Postgraduate)* (Criminology; Gerontology; Rural Studies; Sociology); **Statistics** (Demography and Population; Operations Research; Statistics)

Schools
Chemistry (Applied Chemistry; Chemistry; Industrial Chemistry; Inorganic Chemistry; Organic Chemistry; Physical Chemistry); **Life Sciences** (Biochemistry; Biological and Life Sciences; Biotechnology; Ecology; Microbiology; Molecular Biology; Physiology); **Physics** (Electronic Engineering; Nuclear Physics; Physics; Solid State Physics)

Further Information: Also 92 Affiliated Colleges. A traditional and distance education institution.

History: Founded 1967.

Governing Bodies: Syndicate; Senate

Academic Year: June to May

Admission Requirements: 12th year senior secondary/intermediate examination or recognized foreign equivalent

Fees: (Rupees): 144-12,000 per annum

Main Language(s) of Instruction: English

Accrediting Agencies: National Assessment and Accreditation Council (NAAC)

Degrees and Diplomas: *Diploma; Bachelor's Degree; Bachelor's degree (professional); Postgraduate Diploma; Master's Degree; Master of Philosophy; Doctorate (PhD); Doctor of Science (D.Sc.).* Also Bachelor's degree honours; M.C.A., Executive M.B.A, 3 yrs and M.B.A, 2-3 yrs.

Student Services: Academic counselling, Canteen, Cultural centre, Employment services, Foreign student adviser, Handicapped facilities, Health services, Sports facilities

Student Residential Facilities: 4 Girls Hostels and 6 Boys Hostels; Guest house

Special Facilities: University Museum (Archaeology, Epigraphy, Numismatics, Sculpture, Art and Crafts, Portrait, Tribal Life, Palm Leaf Manuscripts, Archival Records); Oriya Museum

Libraries: Central Library, 122,523 vols; 14,500 subscriptions to e-journals.

Publications: Sambalpur University Journal of Humanities; Sambalpur University Journal of Science and Technology *(annually)*; Septarshi, Language Periodical in Oriya Language *(quarterly)*

Last Updated: 20/07/11

SAMPURNANAND SANSKRIT UNIVERSITY
Sampurnanand Sanskrit Vishwavidyalaya (SSVV)
Varanasi, Uttar Pradesh 221002
Tel: +91(542) 203-911
Fax: +91(542) 206-617
EMail: vsssvv_vns@satyam.net.in
Website: http://ssvv.up.nic.in

Vice-Chancellor: Binda Prasad Mishra
Tel: +91(542) 220-4089, Fax: +91(542) 220-4089

Registrar: Rajneesh Kumar Shukla Tel: +91(542) 220-3911

Faculties
Adhunika Gyan Vijyana (Archaeology; Economics; Education; Geography; History; Home Economics; Library Science; Linguistics; Modern Languages; Political Sciences; Social Sciences; Sociology); **Philosophy** (Comparative Religion; Ethics; Philosophical Schools; Philosophy; Yoga); **Sahitya Sanskriti** (Holy Writings; Literature); **Sramana Vidya** (Asian Religious Studies; Grammar; Indic Languages; Literature; Philosophical Schools; Philosophy; Religious Studies; Theatre); **Veda-Vedanga** (Asian Religious Studies; Ayurveda; Cultural Studies; Esoteric Practices; Grammar; Sanskrit)

Programmes
Sports Education (Sports)

Further Information: Also 1441 Affiliated Colleges.

History: Founded 1958 as Varanaseya Sanskrit Vishwavidyalaya. Acquired present title 1974.

Admission Requirements: 12th year senior secondary/intermediate examination or recognized foreign equivalent. Good command of Hindi and Sanskrit required

Fees: (Rupees): 171-245

Main Language(s) of Instruction: Hindi, Sanskrit

Degrees and Diplomas: *Diploma; Bachelor's Degree; Bachelor's degree (professional); Master's Degree; Doctorate (PhD)*

Libraries: Saraswati Bhawan Library: c. 188,500 vols; 12,448 periodical subscriptions

Last Updated: 20/07/11

SANJAY GANDHI POSTGRADUATE INSTITUTE OF MEDICAL SCIENCES (SGPGIMS)
Raebareli Road, Lucknow, Uttar Pradesh 226014
Tel: +91(522) 266-8008
Fax: +91(522) 266-8017
EMail: root@sgpgi.ac.in
Website: http://www.sgpgi.ac.in

Director: R.K. Sharma
Tel: +91(522) 266-8800, Fax: +91(522) 266-8973

Executive Registrar: Sita Naik
Tel: +91(522) 266-8700 EMail: registrar@sgpgi.ac.in

International Relations: Usha Kant Misra

Departments
Anaesthesiology (Anaesthesiology); **Biostatistics and Health Informatics** (Computer Science; Statistics); **Cardiology** (Cardiology); **Cardiovascular and Thoracic Surgery** (Cardiology; Surgery); **Critical Care Medicine** (Medicine; Nursing); **Endocrine Surgery** (Endocrinology; Oncology; Surgery); **Endocrinology** (Endocrinology); **Gastroenterology** (Gastroenterology); **Hematology** (Haematology); **Immunology** (Immunology); **Medical Genetics** (Biotechnology; Genetics); **Microbiology** (Biotechnology; Epidemiology; Medical Auxiliaries; Microbiology); **Nephrology** (Nephrology); **Neurology** (Neurology); **Neurosurgery** (Neurological Therapy; Surgery); **Nuclear Medicine** (Medical Technology); **Pathology** (Pathology); **Pediatric Gastroenterology** (Gastroenterology; Paediatrics); **Radiodiagnosis** (Radiology); **Radiotherapy** (Oncology; Radiology; Treatment Techniques); **Surgical Gastroenterology** (Gastroenterology; Surgery); **Transfusion Medicine** (Haematology; Immunology; Medical Technology; Medicine); **Urology** (Urology)

Further Information: Also 600-bed hospital.

History: Founded 1983. A postgraduate institution.

Academic Year: January to December

Admission Requirements: 12th year senior secondary/intermediate examination or recognized foreign equivalent

Fees: (Rupees): 5,000-100,000 per annum

Main Language(s) of Instruction: English

International Co-operation: With universities in USA, Japan, Italy and United Kingdom.

Accrediting Agencies: Medical Council of India

Degrees and Diplomas: *Bachelor's degree (professional) (MD); Postgraduate Diploma; Master's Degree; Doctorate (PhD)*

Student Services: Academic counselling, Canteen, Cultural centre, Health services, Nursery care

Student Residential Facilities: 2 postgraduate hostels; 1 nurse hostel; Guest House

Special Facilities: Computer centre; Auditorium and Seminar Rooms

Libraries: c. 16,000 vols; c. 450 scientific journals subscriptions.

Publications: SGPGI Newsletter *(quarterly)*
Last Updated: 20/07/11

SANT GADGE BABA AMRAVATI UNIVERSITY (SGBAU)

Amravati, Maharashtra 444602
Tel: +91(721) 266-2108
Fax: +91(721) 266-2135
EMail: reg@sgbau.ac.in
Website: http://www.sgbau.ac.in

Vice-Chancellor: Mohan Krishnarao Khedar
Tel: +91(721) 266-2093, Fax: +91(721) 266-2135
EMail: vc@sgbau.ac.in

Registrar: Shri Dineshkumar Joshi
Tel: +91(721) 266-2173, Fax: +91(721) 266-0949

Departments

Adult Continuing Education Extension and Field Outreach *(DACEEFO)* (Business Administration; Dietetics; Food Science; Geology; Harvest Technology; Home Economics; Information Technology; Library Science; Nutrition; Sales Techniques)

Faculties

Arts (Arts and Humanities; Hindi; Literature; Native Language; Translation and Interpretation); **Ayurved** (Ayurveda); **Commerce** (Business and Commerce; Finance; Human Resources; Labour and Industrial Relations; Management; Marketing; Operations Research; Transport Management); **Education** (Education; Physical Education; Sports; Sports Medicine; Yoga); **Engineering and Technology** (Chemical Engineering; Computer Engineering; Computer Science; Data Processing; Electronic Engineering; Engineering; Software Engineering; Technology); **Home Science** (Communication Studies; Food Science; Home Economics; Nutrition); **Law** (Administrative Law; Constitutional Law; Criminal Law; Human Rights; Law); **Medicine** (Medicine); **Sciences** (Biological and Life Sciences; Botany; Chemistry; Geology; Mathematics; Microbiology; Natural Sciences; Physics; Statistics; Zoology); **Social Science** (Biotechnology; Information Sciences; Library Science; Social Sciences; Sociology)

Further Information: Also 181 Affiliated Colleges

History: Founded 1983 as Amravati University.

Governing Bodies: Senate; Management Council; Academic Council; Faculty; Board of College and University Development; Board of Studies

Academic Year: June to April (June-October; November-April).

Admission Requirements: Higher Secondary School Certificate (HSSC) grade 12, or equivalent. International students should apply through the Ministry of Foreign Affairs.

Fees: (Rupees): 1,000-6,000 per annum

Main Language(s) of Instruction: English, Marathi, Hindi

Accrediting Agencies: NAAC (B+)

Degrees and Diplomas: *Bachelor's Degree*; *Bachelor's degree (professional)*; *Postgraduate Diploma*; *Master's Degree*; *Master of Philosophy*; *Doctorate (PhD)*. Also Certificate Courses; MCA and MBA.

Student Residential Facilities: Yes

Special Facilities: Fabrication Laboratory (FAB LAB); Central Instrumentation Cell (CIC); Student Access Center; Study Center; Computer Center; Diet Counselling Center

Libraries: 57,680 vols, 385 periodical subscriptions, special collection 4,038

Last Updated: 20/07/11

SANT LONGOWAL INSTITUTE OF ENGINEERING AND TECHNOLOGY (SLIET)

Longowal, Distt. Sangrur (Punjab) 148106
Tel: +91(1672) 253-151
EMail: sliet_webasters@yahoo.com; slietweb@gmail.com
Website: http://www.sliet.ac.in

Director: V. Sahni
Tel: +91(1672) 253-100 EMail: vsahni_2002@yahoo.co.in

Registrar: S.S. Dhaliwal
Tel: +91(1672) 253-180 EMail: sukhjit_d@yahoo.com

Departments

Chemical Technology (Chemical Engineering; Paper Technology; Polymer and Plastics Technology; Printing and Printmaking; Technology); **Chemistry** (Chemistry); **Computer Science and Engineering** (Computer Engineering; Computer Science); **Electrical and Instrumentation Engineering** (Automation and Control Engineering; Electrical Engineering; Maintenance Technology; Measurement and Precision Engineering); **Electronics and Communication Engineering** (Electronic Engineering; Maintenance Technology; Telecommunications Engineering); **Entrepreneurship Development Programme (EDP) and Humanities** (Arts and Humanities; English; Labour and Industrial Relations; Management); **Food Engineering and Technology** (Food Science); **Mathematics** (Mathematics; Operations Research; Statistics); **Mechanical Engineering** (Heating and Refrigeration; Industrial Engineering; Maintenance Technology; Mechanical Engineering; Metal Techniques; Metallurgical Engineering; Production Engineering); **Persons with Disability Scheme** (Special Education); **Physics** (Physics)

History: Founded 1991. Received AICTE accreditation 2003. Acquired 'Deemed University' status 2006.

Fees: (Rupees): Tuition fees for Indian students for Certificates, 1,500 per semester; Diplomas, 3,000 per semester; Undegraduate Degree, 15,000 per semester; Postgraduate degree, 8,000 per semester. For international students (US Dollars): Diplomas, 500-800 per annum; Other programmes, 1,000-5,000 per annum.

Accrediting Agencies: All India Council for Technical Education (AICTE)

Degrees and Diplomas: *Diploma*; *Master's Degree*; *Doctorate (Ph.D.)*. Also Certificate Programmes, 2 yrs; Undergraduate degree in Engineering; M.B.A.

Student Services: Health services, Sports facilities

Student Residential Facilities: 9 Boys Hostels (capacity of 235 students each); PG Hostel (for 80 students); 2 Girls Hostels (capacity of 225 students each); Guest house.

Libraries: 52,124 vols; 92 Thesis; 95 Periodicals/Magazines and 16 News Papers subscriptions.

Last Updated: 20/07/11

SANTOSH UNIVERSITY

No.1, Santosh Nagar, Ghaziabad, Uttar Pradesh 201 009
Tel: +91(120) 274-1141 +91(120) 274-1143 +91(120) 274-1777
Fax: +91(120) 274-1140
EMail: santosh@santoshuniversity.com
Website: http://santoshuniversity.com/

Vice Chancellor: V.K. Arora

Registrar: V. Dos

Courses

Basic Medical Sciences *(Postgraduate Diploma)* (Forensic Medicine and Dentistry; Pathology; Public Health); **Basic Medical Sciences** *(Postgraduate Degree)* (Biochemistry; Community Health; Forensic Medicine and Dentistry; Medicine; Microbiology; Pathology; Pharmacology; Physiology); **Clinical Studies** *(Postgraduate Diploma)* (Anaesthesiology; Child Care and Development; Gynaecology and Obstetrics; Health Sciences; Ophthalmology; Orthopaedics; Pneumology; Psychology); **Clinical Studies** *(Postgraduate Degree)* (Anaesthesiology; Gynaecology and Obstetrics; Medicine; Ophthalmology; Orthopaedics; Otorhinolaryngology; Paediatrics; Pneumology; Psychiatry and Mental Health; Surgery); **Dentistry** *(Postgraduate)* (Dental Technology; Dentistry; Orthodontics; Periodontics; Surgery); **Undergraduate Studies** (Dentistry; Medicine; Surgery)

History: Founded as Santosh Medical & Dental College Hospitals 1995. Acquired 'Deemed University' status 2007.

Degrees and Diplomas: *Bachelor's degree (professional)*; *Postgraduate Diploma*; *Master's Degree*

Last Updated: 19/12/11

SARDAR PATEL UNIVERSITY (SPU)

University Road, Via Anand, Dist. Anand, Vallabh Vidyanagar, Gujarat 388120
Tel: +91(2692) 236-545 +91(2692) 226-6801
Fax: +91(2692) 236-475
EMail: mayankbhatt2003@yahoo.co.in; registrar_spu@spuvvn.edu
Website: http://www.spuvvn.edu

Vice-Chancellor: Harish Padh
Tel: +91(2692) 230-009, Fax: +91(2692) 230-009
EMail: vc_spu@spuvvn.edu

Registrar: Tushar Majmudar
Tel: +91(2692) 226-801 EMail: registrar_spu@spuvvn.edu

Faculties

Arts (Arts and Humanities; Communication Studies; Dance; Economics; English; Environmental Management; Geography; Hindi; History; Indic Languages; Information Sciences; Interior Design; Library Science; Linguistics; Logic; Media Studies; Music; Philosophy; Political Sciences; Psychology; Sanskrit; Social Work; Sociology; Theatre); **Business Studies and Commerce** (Accountancy; Banking; Business Administration; Business and Commerce; English; Finance; Human Resources; Management; Marketing); **Education** (Education; Educational Administration; Foreign Languages Education; Humanities and Social Science Education; Native Language Education; Physical Education); **Engineering and Technology** (Architecture; Civil Engineering; Computer Engineering; Construction Engineering; Electronic Engineering; Engineering; Environmental Engineering; Food Technology; Hygiene; Industrial Engineering; Information Technology; Machine Building; Mechanical Engineering; Power Engineering; Production Engineering; Technology; Telecommunications Engineering; Town Planning; **Home Science** (Biotechnology; Child Care and Development; Clothing and Sewing; Family Studies; Fashion Design; Food Science; Home Economics; Nutrition; Textile Technology); **Homeopathy** (Homeopathy); **Law** (Labour and Industrial Relations; Law; Taxation); **Management** (Accountancy; Administration; Business Administration; Finance; Hotel Management; Human Resources; Information Technology; International Business; Management; Marketing; Operations Research; Tourism); **Medicine** (Anaesthesiology; Anatomy; Biochemistry; Laboratory Techniques; Medical Technology; Medicine; Microbiology; Midwifery; Nursing; Otorhinolaryngology; Pharmacology; Physical Therapy; Physiology; Public Health; Radiology; Surgery); **Pharmaceutical Sciences** (Pharmacy); **Science** (Analytical Chemistry; Applied Chemistry; Biochemistry; Biotechnology; Botany; Chemistry; Computer Science; Electronic Engineering; Environmental Studies; Genetics; Home Economics; Industrial Chemistry; Information Sciences; Instrument Making; Materials Engineering; Mathematics; Microbiology; Physics; Polymer and Plastics Technology; Safety Engineering; Statistics; Zoology)

Further Information: Also 3 satellite campuses; 80 Affiliated Colleges; 25 Postgraduate Departments

History: Founded 1955 as Sardar Vallabhbhai Vidyapeeth. Recognized by UGC 1968.

Governing Bodies: Senate; Syndicate; Academic Council; Board of Studies; Boards of Postgraduate Studies and Research; Faculties

Academic Year: June to May (June-October/November; December-April/May)

Admission Requirements: 12th year senior secondary/intermediate examination or recognized foreign equivalent

Fees: (Rupees): Professional courses, 25,000; Non-professional courses, 15,000

Main Language(s) of Instruction: Gujarati, English, Hindi

Degrees and Diplomas: *Diploma; Bachelor's Degree; Bachelor's degree (professional); Postgraduate Diploma; Master's Degree; Master of Philosophy (M.Phil); Doctorate (PhD).* Also Advanced Diploma, Advanced Certificate and Certificate Courses; M.B.A;

Student Services: Canteen, Employment services, Health services

Student Residential Facilities: 4 boys hostels and 1 girls hostel (toatl capacity of 857 students)

Special Facilities: University Museum; Botanical Garden

Libraries: Central Library, 211,212 vols; 259 Indian and 110 international subscriptions to periodicals. Also departmental libraries

Publications: Artha Vikas, Journal of Economics *(quarterly)*; Journal of Education and Psychology *(quarterly)*; Journal of Engineering and Technology, Birla Vishwakarma Mahavidyalaya; Mimansa, Journal on Indian and English Literature *(biannually)*; Prajna, Separate research journals Social Sciences and Basic Sciences *(annually)*; Sheel Shrutum, Newsletter *(monthly)*; Synergie, Journal of Business Studies Administration; Vocational Guide, University Employment Bureau

Press or Publishing House: University Press

Academic Staff *2010-2011*: Total 191
Last Updated: 20/07/11

SARDAR VALLABHBHAI NATIONAL INSTITUTE OF TECHNOLOGY (SVNIT)
Ichchhanath, Surat, Gujarat 395 007
Tel: +91(261) 225-9571 +91(261) 225-9582
Fax: +91(261) 222-7334 +91(261) 222-8394
Website: http://www.svnit.ac.in/

Director: P. D. Porey
Tel: +91(261) 220-1505
EMail: director@svnit.ac.in; pdporey@svnit.ac.in

Registrar: H. A. Parmar
Tel: +91(261)220-1509 EMail: registrar@svnit.ac.in

Departments

Applied Chemistry (Applied Chemistry; Chemistry; Inorganic Chemistry; Nanotechnology; Organic Chemistry; Polymer and Plastics Technology); **Applied Mathematics and Humanities** (Applied Mathematics; Arts and Humanities; English; Management; Mathematics); **Applied Mechanics** (Civil Engineering; Construction Engineering; Engineering; Geological Engineering; Mechanics; Soil Science); **Applied Physics** (Applied Physics; Physics); **Chemical Engineering** (Chemical Engineering); **Civil Engineering** (Civil Engineering; Environmental Engineering; Rural Planning; Town Planning; Transport Engineering; Transport Management; Water Science); **Computer Engineering** (Computer Engineering); **Electrical Engineering** (Computer Engineering; Electrical Engineering; Software Engineering); **Electronics Engineering** (Computer Engineering; Electronic Engineering; Software Engineering; Telecommunications Engineering); **Mechanical Engineering** (Industrial Management; Mechanical Engineering; Production Engineering)

History: Created in 1961 as Sardar Vallabhbhai Regional Engineering College. Acquired current title and status 2001. An 'Institution of National Importance.

Fees: (Rupees): Tuition fees, 17,500 per semester (as of 7th semester, 6,000 for B.Tech and 7,500 for M.Sc. And Ph.D.).

Degrees and Diplomas: *Bachelor's degree (professional); Master's Degree; Doctorate (Ph.D)*

Student Services: Canteen, Sports facilities

Student Residential Facilities: 7 hostels (6 for boys and 1 for girls) accommodating 990 students; Staff quarters; Guest House

Special Facilities: Central Computer Centre; Entrepreneurship Development Cell; Continuing Education Centre and Physical Education Section; Training and Placement section; Day Care Center for Children (DCCC); Post Office; Bank

Libraries: Central library

Student Numbers 2010-2011	TOTAL
All (Foreign Included)	426
FOREIGN ONLY	20

Last Updated: 21/07/11

SARDAR VALLABHBHAI PATEL UNIVERSITY OF AGRICULTURE AND TECHNOLOGY (SVPUAT)
Modipuram, Meerut, Uttar Pradesh 250110
Tel: +91(121) 288-8503
Fax: +91(121) 288-8505
EMail: vc@svbpuniversitymerrut.org
Website: http://www.svbpmeerut.ac.in

Vice-Chancellor: A. K. Bakshi
Tel: +91 (121) 241-1522, Fax: +91 (121) 241-1505

Registrar: Narendra Sharma
Tel: +91(121) 288-8502, Fax: +91(121) 288-8525

Faculties

Agriculture (Agricultural Economics; Agricultural Engineering; Agricultural Equipment; Agricultural Management; Agronomy; Animal Husbandry; Biology; Crop Production; English; Entomology; Farm Management; Floriculture; Food Science; Food Technology; Horticulture; Industrial and Production Economics; Mathematics; Physics; Plant and Crop Protection; Plant Pathology; Rural Planning; Soil Science; Statistics; Water Management); **Biotechnology** (Biochemistry; Biotechnology; Cell Biology; Genetics; Immunology; Microbiology; Molecular Biology; Pathology; Physiology)

Further Information: College of Veterinary and Animal Science under development

History: Founded 2000 as India's first agricultural university

Governing Bodies: Board of Management, Board of Governors

Academic Year: July to June

Fees: (Indian Rupee): Undergraduate, 16,150 per annum; Postgraduate, 25,085 per annum

Main Language(s) of Instruction: Undergraduate: English, Hindi. Postgraduate: English

Degrees and Diplomas: *Bachelor's Degree; Bachelor's degree (professional); Master's Degree; Doctorate (PhD)*

Student Services: Academic counselling, Canteen, Cultural centre, Employment services, Foreign student adviser, Handicapped facilities, Health services, Social counselling, Sports facilities

Student Residential Facilities: Yes

Libraries: Specialised library in agricultural and related subjects

Publications: Krishi Darshika *(biannually)*; Vallabh Krishi Darpan *(bimonthly)*

Last Updated: 21/07/11

SARDARKRUSHINAGAR DANTIWADA AGRICULTURAL UNIVERSITY (SDAU)

Dantiwada Campus, District Banaskantha, Sardar Krushinagar, North Gujarat 385506
Tel: +91(2748) 278-226
Fax: +91(2748) 278-261
EMail: vc@sdau.edu.in
Website: http://www.sdau.edu.in/

Vice-Chancellor: R. C. Maheshwari
Tel: +91(2748) 278-222, Fax: +91(2748) 278-261

Registrar: H.N. Kher
Tel: +91(2748) 278-226, Fax: +91(2748) 278-234
EMail: registrar@sdau.edu.in

Colleges

Agri Business Management (Accountancy; Agricultural Business; Development Studies; Economics; Finance; Human Resources; Information Management; Information Technology; Management; Marketing; Rural Studies; Statistics); **Agriculture** *(Chimanbhai Patel)* (Agricultural Economics; Agricultural Education; Agriculture; Agronomy; Chemistry; Entomology; Genetics; Horticulture; Plant Pathology; Soil Science; Statistics); **Basic Science and Humanities** (Arts and Humanities; Biochemistry; Biological and Life Sciences; Chemistry; Computer Science; Environmental Studies; Genetics; Mathematics; Microbiology; Molecular Biology; Natural Sciences; Physics; Physiology; Social Sciences; Statistics); **Dairy Science and Food Technology** (Business Administration; Dairy; Engineering; Food Science; Food Technology; Microbiology; Safety Engineering); **Home Science and Nutrition** (Child Care and Development; Communication Studies; Cooking and Catering; Dietetics; Distance Education; Family Studies; Food Science; Harvest Technology; Home Economics; Information Technology; Interior Design; Journalism; Mass Communication; Nutrition; Special Education; Textile Design); **Horticulture** (Agriculture; Horticulture; Vegetable Production); **Renewable Energy and Environmental Engineering** (Agriculture; Energy Engineering; Engineering; Environmental Engineering; Environmental Management; Forestry; Harvest Technology; Natural Resources; Public Health; Thermal Engineering; Waste Management); **Veterinary Science and Animal Husbandary** (Animal Husbandry; Gynaecology and Obstetrics; Surgery; Veterinary Science)

Further Information: Also 10 Constituent Colleges

History: Founded 1972 as Gujarat Agricultural University whose Act, No. 5 of 2004 was repealed on May 1, 2004. Sardarkrushinagar Dantiwada Agricultural University elevated as individual university for precise consideration of need based location specific agricultural research.

Admission Requirements: 12th year senior secondary/intermediate examination or recognized foreign equivalent

Fees: (Rupees): 200 per semester

Main Language(s) of Instruction: English

Degrees and Diplomas: *Diploma; Bachelor's Degree; Bachelor's degree (professional); Postgraduate Diploma; Master's Degree; Doctorate (PhD).* Also undegraduate Certificate; Bachelor's degree honours.

Student Residential Facilities: Hostels.

Libraries: 45,600 Books; 4,150 Back volumes; 5,650 Theses; 5,440 Research reports; 200 Encyclopedia; 225 Scientific Journals; 280 periodical subscriptions; 71 CD-ROM Data Base.

Last Updated: 21/07/11

SARGUJA VISHWAVIDYALAYA

Sarguja University (SUA)
Near Govt. Hospital Road, Sarguja District, Ambikapur, Chhattigarh 497 001
Tel: +91(7774) 222-789 +91(7774) 222-790
Fax: +91(7774) 222-791
EMail: registrarsua@yaho.co.in
Website: http://www.sua.nic.in/

Vice Chancellor: S. K. Verma Tel: +91(7774) 222-788

Registrar: R. D. Sharma Tel: +91(7774) 222-790

Departments

Arts and Humanities (Arts and Humanities; English; Hindi; History; Sanskrit); **Computer Science** (Computer Science); **Health Sciences** (Health Sciences); **Pharmacy** (Pharmacy); **Sciences** (Botany; Chemistry; Geography; Mathematics; Microbiology; Physics; Zoology); **Social Sciences** (Political Sciences; Psychology; Sociology)

Faculties

Engineering (Civil Engineering; Computer Engineering; Computer Science; Electrical Engineering; Engineering; Mechanical Engineering)

Programmes

Biotechnology *(Postgraduate)* (Biotechnology); **Business and Commerce** (Business and Commerce; Economics); **Farm Forestry** *(Postgraduate)* (Forestry)

Further Information: Also 42 affiliated colleges

History: Founded 2008.

Degrees and Diplomas: *Bachelor's Degree; Postgraduate Diploma; Master's Degree*
Last Updated: 03/01/12

SASTRA UNIVERSITY (SASTRA)

Shanmugha Campus, Tirumalaisamaduram, Thanjavur, Tamil Nadu 613401
Tel: +91(4362) 264-101 +91(4362) 266-502
Fax: +91(4362) 264-120
EMail: admissions@sastra.edu
Website: http://www.sastra.edu

Vice-Chancellor: R. Sethuraman Tel: +91(4362) 304-101

Registrar: S.N.S. Srivastava
Tel: +91(4362) 304-106 EMail: registrar@sastra.edu

Centres

Advanced Research in Indian System of Medicine *(CARISM)* (Ayurveda; Laboratory Techniques; Pharmacy; Safety Engineering; Toxicology); **Nanotechnology and Advanced Biomaterials** *(CeNTAB)* (Nanotechnology)

Departments

Directorate of Distance Education - SASTRA (Dance; Education; Esoteric Practices; Fine Arts; Music)

Schools

Chemical and Biotechnology (Bioengineering; Biological and Life Sciences; Biotechnology; Chemical Engineering; Computer Science; Medical Technology; Nanotechnology; Nuclear Engineering; Pharmacy); **Civil Engineering** (Civil Engineering; Construction Engineering; Safety Engineering); **Computing** (Computer Engineering;

Computer Graphics; Computer Science; Information Technology; Law; Multimedia; Telecommunications Engineering); **Education** (Distance Education; Education; Mathematics Education); **Electrical and Electronics Engineering** (Automation and Control Engineering; Electrical Engineering; Electronic Engineering; Measurement and Precision Engineering; Power Engineering; Telecommunications Engineering); **Humanities and Sciences** (Arts and Humanities; Communication Studies; Cultural Studies; English; Ethics; Mathematics); **Law** (Accountancy; Administrative Law; Business Administration; Civil Law; Commercial Law; Constitutional Law; Criminal Law; Criminology; Economics; English; History; International Law; Labour Law; Law; Management; Marketing; Political Sciences; Private Law; Public Law; Sociology; Statistics); **Management** (Accountancy; Business Administration; Commercial Law; Economics; Ethics; Finance; Information Management; Information Technology; International Business; Management; Marketing; Operations Research; Statistics); **Mechanical Engineering** (Automotive Engineering; Electronic Engineering; Mechanical Engineering; Production Engineering)

Further Information: A traditional and distance education institution.

History: Founded 1984 as Shanmugha College of Engineering. Renamed Shanmugha Arts, Science, Technology and Research Academy (SASTRA). Acquired present status 2001.

Fees: (Rupees): Tuition fees, undegraduate programmes, 5,000-40,000 per semester; Postgraduate programmes, 5,000-60,000 per semester.

Accrediting Agencies: National Assessment and Accreditation Council (NAAC) (Grade 'A'); The Institution of Engineering; Tata Consultancy Services Ltd. (TCS)

Degrees and Diplomas: *Bachelor's Degree; Bachelor's degree (professional); Postgraduate Diploma; Master's Degree; Doctorate (Ph.D.).* Also Certificate courses; Bachelor's degree honours; Integrated M.Tech. Programmes, 5 yrs; M.C.A.; M.B.A.

Libraries: Central Library: 78,000 vols; 300 journals and periodical subscriptions; Online journal database (Science Direct, IEEE, ACME, ASME, SCE, EBSCO, SCOPUS, DELNET, ebrary etc.) providing access to over 3,200 scientific, technical and management journals and bibliographic database of over 17,000 journals; Subscription to PROQUEST Digital Dissertation database (access to over 550,000 PhD dissertations); Springer's Electronic collection of over 8,000 e-Books; e-Brary (access over 35,000 full text books).

Academic Staff *2010-2011*: Total: c. 700
Student Numbers *2010-2011*: Total: c. 9,000
Last Updated: 21/07/11

SATAVAHANA UNIVERSITY

Jyothinagar, Karimnagar, Andhra Pradesh 505 001
Tel: +91(878) 225-5800
Website: http://www.satavahana.ac.in/

Vice Chancellor: B. Venkat Rathnam
Tel: +91(878) 225-5800, Fax: +91(878) 225-5933

Registrar: G. Laxmaiah EMail: prof_gklh@yahoo.co.in

Faculties
Arts (Arts and Humanities; English; Indic Languages; Urdu); **Business Administration and Commerce** (Business Administration; Business and Commerce; Management); **Pharmacy** (Pharmacy); **Sciences** (Chemistry; Information Sciences); **Social Sciences** (Economics; Social Sciences; Sociology)

History: Founded as a college 1956. Became a College of the Osmania University Hyderabad 1989. Acquired university status 2008.

Governing Bodies: Executive Council

Accrediting Agencies: University Grants Commission (UGC)

Degrees and Diplomas: *Bachelor's Degree; Bachelor's degree (professional); Master's Degree.* Also M.B.A.

Student Services: Health services, Sports facilities

Student Residential Facilities: Boys and Girls Hostels

Libraries: Yes
Last Updated: 02/01/12

SATHYABAMA UNIVERSITY

Jeppiaar Nagar, Rajiv Gandhi Road, Chennai, Tamil Nadu 600 119
Tel: +91(44) 2450-150 +91(44) 2450-151
Fax: +91(44) 2450-2344
EMail: jprsatya@giasmd01.vsnl.net.in
Website: http://www.sathyabamauniversity.ac.in/

Vice-Chancellor: B. Sheela Rani
EMail: vc@sathyabamauniversity.ac.in

Registrar: S.S. Rau EMail: registrar@sathyabamauniversity.ac.in

Faculties
Architecture (Architecture; Building Technologies); **BioEngineering** (Biomedical Engineering; Biotechnology; Computer Science); **Chemical Engineering** (Chemical Engineering; Environmental Engineering); **Civil Engineering** (Civil Engineering; Construction Engineering); **Computer Science and Engineering** (Computer Engineering; Computer Science; Information Technology); **Education** (Education); **Electrical Engineering** (Electrical and Electronic Engineering; Electrical Engineering; Power Engineering); **Electronics Engineering** (Automation and Control Engineering; Computer Graphics; Electronic Engineering; Measurement and Precision Engineering; Nanotechnology; Telecommunications Engineering); **Management Studies** (Business Administration; Management); **Mechanical Engineering** (Aeronautical and Aerospace Engineering; Automotive Engineering; Computer Graphics; Mechanical Engineering; Production Engineering; Thermal Engineering); **Medicine** (Dentistry; Surgery); **Science and Humanities** (Biological and Life Sciences; Biotechnology; Business and Commerce; Communication Arts; Computer Engineering; Computer Science; Cooking and Catering; Economics; Electronic Engineering; Hotel Management; Microbiology; Secretarial Studies; Software Engineering)

History: Founded 1988 as Sathyabama Engineering College. Previously known as Sathyabama Institute of Science and Technology (SIST). Acquired "Deemed University" status 2001 and University status 2006.

Accrediting Agencies: National Assessment and Accreditation Council (NAAC) (B++ Grade)

Degrees and Diplomas: *Bachelor's Degree; Bachelor's degree (professional); Master's Degree; Master of Philosophy; Doctorate (Ph.D.).* Also Dual Degree Courses, 5 yrs; MC.A.; M.B.A.

Student Services: Canteen, Employment services, Health services, Sports facilities

Student Residential Facilities: Boys and Girls Hostel

Special Facilities: 3 Conference Halls; 4 Open Air Theaters; Internet access; Bank ; Reverse Osmosis Plant (Mineral Water Facility)

Libraries: Central Library: c. 60,000 vols; 334 journals (of which 177 are international journals).
Last Updated: 21/07/11

SAURASHTRA UNIVERSITY

University Campus, University Road, Rajkot, Gujarat 360005
Tel: +91(281) 257-6347
Fax: +91(281) 257-7633
EMail: registrar@sauuni.ernet.in
Website: http://www.saurashtrauniversity.edu/

Vice-Chancellor: Kamlesh P. Joshipura (2005-)
Tel: +91(281) 257-7633
EMail: kpjoshipura@yahoo.com; vc@sauuni.ernet.in

Registrar: Shri Gajendra Jani
Tel: +91(281) 257-6347, Fax: +91(281) 257-6557

International Relations: K.H. Metha, Head, Department of English

Departments
Biochemistry (Biochemistry); **Biosciences** (Biochemistry; Biological and Life Sciences; Biology; Biotechnology; Botany; Microbiology; Molecular Biology; Zoology); **Business Management** (Business Administration; Management); **Chemistry** (Chemistry); **Commerce** (Accountancy; Business and Commerce; Finance); **Computer Science** (Computer Science; Information Technology); **Economics** (Economics); **Education** (Education; Educational Technology); **Electronics** (Computer Engineering; Electronic Engineering; Software Engineering); **English and Comparative Literary Studies** (Comparative Literature; Cultural Studies; English;

Literature); **Gujarati** (Indic Languages; Literature); **Hindi** (Hindi; Literature; Translation and Interpretation); **History** (History); **Home Science** (Home Economics; Nutrition); **Human Rights and I. H. L.** (Human Rights; International Law); **Journalism** *(Amrutlal Dalpatbhai Sheth)* (Journalism; Mass Communication); **Law** (Banking; Forensic Medicine and Dentistry; International Law; Law); **Library and Information Science** (Information Sciences; Library Science); **Mathematics** (Mathematics); **Pharmaceutical Science** (Biotechnology; Pharmacology; Pharmacy; Safety Engineering); **Philosophy** (Philosophy); **Physical Education** (Physical Education); **Physics** (Physics); **Psychology** (Psychology); **Sanskrit** (Sanskrit); **Social Work** (Labour and Industrial Relations; Social Work; Welfare and Protective Services); **Sociology** (Sociology); **Statistics** (Econometrics; Mathematics; Mathematics and Computer Science; Operations Research; Statistics)

Further Information: Also 28 Postgraduate Departments, 348 Affiliated Colleges and 4 Recognized Institutions

History: Founded 1967.

Governing Bodies: Senate; Syndicate; Academic Council

Academic Year: June to May

Admission Requirements: 12th year senior secondary/intermediate examination or recognized foreign equivalent (10 + 2 + 3 pattern)

Fees: (Rupees): 1,100-1,500

Main Language(s) of Instruction: Gujarati, Hindi, English

International Co-operation: Griffith university, Australia; California state university, USA; Gujarat Ayurved University, Jamnagar; Forensic Science Laboratory, Ahmedabad; BARC, Mumbai

Accrediting Agencies: National Assessment Accreditation Council, Bangalore

Degrees and Diplomas: *Diploma*; *Bachelor's degree (professional)*; *Postgraduate Diploma*; *Master's Degree*; *Master of Philosophy*; *Doctorate (PhD)*. Also Certificate Courses; M.B.A. and M.C.A.

Student Services: Academic counselling, Canteen, Cultural centre, Employment services, Foreign student adviser, Foreign Studies Centre, Handicapped facilities, Health services, Language programs, Nursery care, Social counselling, Sports facilities

Student Residential Facilities: Girnar (old) P. G. Hostel (96 rooms); Shetrunjay Research hostel (48 rooms); Hostel (35 rooms); Guest house.

Special Facilities: Art Gallery; Free internet access; online journals; Academic Centre; Computer Center

Libraries: Central Library: 169,817 vols; 179 subscriptions to periodicals; c. 1,800 e-journals.

Publications: Sayujva, Gujarati; Vak, Research Journal, in English

Press or Publishing House: Saurashtra University Press

Academic Staff *2009-2010*	MEN	WOMEN	TOTAL
FULL-TIME	98	11	**109**
STAFF WITH DOCTORATE			
FULL-TIME	98	11	**109**
Student Numbers *2009-2010*			
All (Foreign Included)	1,988	957	**2,945**
FOREIGN ONLY	1	–	**1**

Last Updated: 21/07/11

SAVEETHA UNIVERSITY

No. 162 Poonamalle High Road, Chennai, Tamil Nadu 600 077
Tel: +91(44) 2680-1580 +91(44) 2680-1585
Fax: +91(44) 2680-0892
EMail: registrar@saveetha.com
Website: http://www.saveetha.com

Vice-Chancellor: R. Rajagopal
EMail: vicechancellor@saveetha.com

Colleges
Dentistry (Dental Hygiene; Dental Technology; Dentistry; Forensic Medicine and Dentistry; Oncology; Oral Pathology; Orthodontics; Periodontics; Public Health; Radiology; Surgery); **Engineering** (Civil Engineering; Communication Studies; Computer Engineering; Computer Graphics; Computer Science; Electrical Engineering;

Electronic Engineering; Engineering; Information Technology; Mechanical Engineering; Medical Technology; Nanotechnology; Power Engineering; Robotics; Telecommunications Engineering); **Medicine** (Anatomy; Biochemistry; Community Health; Gynaecology and Obstetrics; Medicine; Microbiology; Ophthalmology; Orthopaedics; Otorhinolaryngology; Paediatrics; Pathology; Pharmacology; Physiology; Radiology; Surgery; Treatment Techniques); **Nursing** (Community Health; Nursing; Psychiatry and Mental Health); **Physiotherapy** (Cardiology; Gynaecology and Obstetrics; Neurosciences; Orthopaedics; Paediatrics; Physical Therapy; Respiratory Therapy; Sports; Sports Medicine; Urology)

Schools
Law (Law); **Management** (Health Administration; Human Resources; Management)

Further Information: Also Saveetha Nagar Campus.

History: Founded 1988 as Saveetha Institute of Medical and Technical Sciences. Acquired present status and title of 'Deemed University' 2005.

Governing Bodies: Board of Management; Finance Committee; Academic Council

Accrediting Agencies: National Assessment and Accreditation Council (NAAC)

Degrees and Diplomas: *Diploma*; *Bachelor's Degree*; *Bachelor's degree (professional)*; *Postgraduate Diploma*; *Master's Degree*; *Doctorate*. Alos Certificate Courses; Bachelor's degree honours; Integrated M.E/M.Tech, 5 Yrs; M.C.A.; M.B.A.

Student Services: Sports facilities

Student Residential Facilities: On-campus hostels for boys and girls.

Libraries: hostels are located in both campuses for boys and girls
Last Updated: 21/07/11

SCHOOL OF COMMUNICATION AND MANAGEMENT STUDIES (SCMS-COCHIN)

Prathap Nagar, Muttom, Aluva, Cochin, Kerala 683 106
Tel: +91(484) 262-3803
EMail: info@scmsgroup.org
Website: http://scmsgroup.org/scms/

Director: V. Raman Nair

Programmes
Management *(Part-time)* (Management); **Management** (Banking; Insurance; Management; Retailing and Wholesaling)

History: Founded 1976.

Accrediting Agencies: All India Council for Technical Education (AICTE)

Degrees and Diplomas: *Postgraduate Diploma*. Postgraduate Diploma equivalent to a University M.B.A.

Student Residential Facilities: 1 Girls' Hostlel (300 beds) and 2 Boys' Hostels (325 beds)

Special Facilities: Computer Centre

Libraries: 22,625 vols; 1,256 bound vols; 220 international and national journals
Last Updated: 25/01/12

SCHOOL OF PLANNING AND ARCHITECTURE (SPA)

4-Block-B, Indraprastha Estate, New Delhi 110002
Tel: +91(11) 2370-2375 +91(11) 2370-2376
Fax: +91(11) 2370-2383
EMail: info@spa.ac.in; admission@spa.ac.in
Website: http://www.spa.ac.in/

Director: A.K. Sharma EMail: director@spa.ac.in
Registrar: D.R. Bains EMail: dr.bains@spa.ac.in

Departments
Architectural Conservation (Architectural Restoration; Architecture); **Architecture** (Architecture; Architecture and Planning;

Landscape Architecture); **Building Engineering and Management** (Construction Engineering); **Environment Planning** (Environmental Management; Environmental Studies; Landscape Architecture); **Housing** (Architectural and Environmental Design; Architecture; Finance; Real Estate; Safety Engineering); **Industrial Design** (Industrial Design); **Landscape Architecture** (Architectural and Environmental Design; Ecology; Landscape Architecture); **Physical Planning** (Architecture and Planning); **Regional Planning** (Rural Planning); **Transport Planning** (Architecture and Planning; Law; Management; Rural Planning; Transport and Communications; Urban Studies); **Urban Design** (Architectural and Environmental Design; Town Planning); **Urban Planning** (Architectural and Environmental Design; Town Planning; Urban Studies)

History: Founded 1941 as a Department of Architecture of Delhi Polytechnic. Renamed School of Planning and Architecture 1959. Granted 'Deemed University' status 1979.

Governing Bodies: General Council; Executive Council; Academic Council

Academic Year: August to May (August-December; January-May)

Admission Requirements: 12th year senior secondary/intermediate examination or recognized foreign equivalent

Fees: (Rupees): Undergraduate programmes, 31,300 per annum; Postgraduate programmes, 39,100 per annum; Ph.D. programmes, 33,100 per annum.

Main Language(s) of Instruction: English

Degrees and Diplomas: *Bachelor's degree (professional); Master's Degree; Doctorate (PhD)*

Student Residential Facilities: Yes

Special Facilities: Geographic Information System (GIS); Centre for Analysis and Systems Studies (CASS); Centre for Remote Sensing (CRS); Documentation and Publications Unit; Audio Visual Unit; Conservation Materials Laboratory (CML); Workshop and Materials Testing Laboratory; National Resource Institution (NRI).

Libraries: c. 71,000 vols; 250 journals subscriptions

Publications: Space, Journal on Urban and Rural Planning *(quarterly)*

Last Updated: 21/07/11

SHARDA UNIVERSITY

Plot No. 32-34, Knowledge Park III, Greater Noida,
Uttar Pradesh 201 306
Tel: +91(120) 312-1001
EMail: admission@sharda.ac.in
Website: http://www.sharda.ac.in/

Vice-Chancellor: H.G. Jagdeesh

Schools

Allied Health Sciences (Health Sciences); **Allied Sciences and Creative Arts** (Mass Communication); **Architecture and Planning** (Architecture; Architecture and Planning); **Basic Sciences and Research** (Biological and Life Sciences; Chemistry; Mathematics; Physics); **Business Studies** (Business Administration); **Dental Sciences** (Dentistry); **Engineering and Technology** (Engineering; Technology); **Foreign Languages** (English; French; German; Modern Languages; Spanish); **Law** (Law); **Medical Sciences and Research** (Medicine); **Studies of Investigation, Intelligence and Security** (Protective Services)

Further Information: Also Patna, Guwahati, Lucknow, Kota, Dehradun, Gorakhpur.

Governing Bodies: Executive Council; Academic Council

Accrediting Agencies: University Grants Commission (UGC)

Degrees and Diplomas: *Bachelor's degree (professional); Master's Degree; Doctorate.* Also Honours Bachelor's degree.

Student Services: Sports facilities

Libraries: Yes

Academic Staff *2010-2011:* Total: c. 1,200
Student Numbers *2010-2011:* Total: c. 22,000
Last Updated: 23/12/11

SHER-E-KASHMIR UNIVERSITY OF AGRICULTURAL SCIENCES AND TECHNOLOGY-JAMMU (SKUAST-J)

Railway Road, Jammu, Jammu and Kashmir 180012
Tel: +91(191) 247-1745 +91(191) 247-3417
Fax: +91(191) 247-3883
EMail: vc@skuast.org
Website: http://www.skuast.org/

Vice-Chancellor: B. Mishra

Registrar: H.N. Khajuria
Tel: +91(191) 247-5149, Fax: +91(191) 247-5149

Faculties

Agriculture (Agricultural Engineering; Agronomy; Biochemistry; Economics; Entomology; Floriculture; Forestry; Genetics; Harvest Technology; Plant Pathology; Sericulture; Soil Science; Statistics); **Veterinary Science and Animal Husbandry** (Anatomy; Animal Husbandry; Biochemistry; Embryology and Reproduction Biology; Epidemiology; Genetics; Gynaecology and Obstetrics; Histology; Hygiene; Immunology; Law; Medicine; Parasitology; Pathology; Pharmacology; Physiology; Public Health; Radiology; Social and Preventive Medicine; Surgery; Toxicology; Veterinary Science; Zoology)

History: Founded 1999.

Governing Bodies: University Council; Board of Management

Academic Year: August to June

Admission Requirements: Undergraduate, 10 + 2 with English, Physics, Chemistry and Math/Biology; For Master's degree, Bachelor's degree in the related Field

Fees: (Rupees): Undergraduates, 9,000 + semester fee; Postgraduate, 11,000 + semester fee

Main Language(s) of Instruction: English

Accrediting Agencies: Indian Council of Agricultural Research (ICAR)

Degrees and Diplomas: *Bachelor's Degree; Bachelor's degree (professional); Master's Degree; Doctorate.* Also undergraduate basic courses.

Student Services: Academic counselling, Canteen, Cultural centre, Foreign Studies Centre, Health services, Nursery care, Social counselling, Sports facilities

Student Residential Facilities: Yes

Special Facilities: Observatory

Libraries: Yes

Publications: Skuast - Jammu, Research Journal with articles on Agriculture and Allied Sciences *(quarterly)*
Last Updated: 22/07/11

SHER-E-KASHMIR UNIVERSITY OF AGRICULTURAL SCIENCES AND TECHNOLOGY-SRINAGAR (SKUAST-K)

PO Box 262, GPO, Srinagar, Jammu and Kashmir 190001
Tel: +91(194) 246-1271
Fax: +91(191) 246-2160
EMail: skuast_k@rediffmail.com; skuast_k@yahoo.com;
gora_manzoor@yahoo.com.in
Website: http://www.skuastkashmir.ac.in/

Vice-Chancellor: Tej Partap (2010-)
Tel: +91(194) 246-2159, Fax: +91(194) 246-2160
EMail: vcskuastkashmir@skuastkashmir.ac.in

Registrar: F.A. Zaki
Tel: 91(194) 246-1271 EMail: farooqzaki@gmail.com

Faculties

Agriculture (Agricultural Economics; Agricultural Engineering; Agriculture; Agronomy; Animal Husbandry; Dairy; Entomology; Forestry; Genetics; Horticulture; Plant Pathology; Soil Science; Statistics); **Fisheries** (Agricultural Engineering; Aquaculture; Biochemistry; Biology; Biotechnology; Environmental Studies; Fishery; Genetics; Harvest Technology; Nutrition; Pathology; Social Sciences); **Postgraduate Studies** (Agriculture; Environmental Studies; Forestry; Sericulture; Statistics; Veterinary Science); **Veterinary Sciences and Animal Husbandry** (Agricultural

Education; Anatomy; Animal Husbandry; Biochemistry; Embryology and Reproduction Biology; Epidemiology; Ethics; Genetics; Gynaecology and Obstetrics; Histology; Immunology; Microbiology; Nutrition; Parasitology; Pathology; Pharmacology; Physiology; Public Health; Radiology; Surgery; Toxicology; Veterinary Science)

History: Founded 1982. The University is based on the concept of the United States Land Grant Colleges. Has multidisciplinary regional sub-stations in various agro-climatic zones of the state for zone-specific programmes.

Admission Requirements: 12th year senior secondary/intermediate examination or recognized foreign equivalent

Fees: (Rupees): Fee for undergraduate programmes, 1,419 per semester; Postgraduate programmes, 1,889 per semester; Ph.D. programmes, 2,358 per semester.

Main Language(s) of Instruction: English

Degrees and Diplomas: *Bachelor's Degree*; *Bachelor's degree (professional)*; *Master's Degree*; *Doctorate (PhD)*

Libraries: 38,082 vols; 3,926 Reference Books; 202 Periodical subscriptions; 14,829 Periodical Back files; 680 Theses; 18 Reviews and Advances; 8,283 Reports; 15 CD-ROM Databases
Last Updated: 22/07/11

SHIV NADAR UNIVERSITY

A-10-11, Sector-3, Noida, Uttar Pradesh 201301
EMail: registrar@snu.edu.in
Website: http://snu.edu.in/

Vice-Chancellor: Nikhil Sinha

Registrar: J. Ernest Samuel Ratnakumar

Schools
Business (Business Administration); **Communication** (Communication Studies); **Education** (Education); **Engineering** (Civil Engineering; Computer Engineering; Computer Science; Electrical Engineering; Mechanical Engineering; Telecommunications Engineering); **Natural Science** (Mathematics; Natural Sciences); **Social Sciences and Humanities** (Arts and Humanities; Social Sciences)

History: Founded 2011.

Degrees and Diplomas: *Bachelor's Degree*; *Master's Degree*; *Doctorate*

Libraries: Yes
Last Updated: 18/01/12

SHIVAJI UNIVERSITY

Vidyanagar, Kolhapur, Maharashtra 416 004
Tel: +91(231) 260-9000
Fax: +91(231) 269-2333
Website: http://www.unishivaji.ac.in

Vice-Chancellor: N. J. Pawar (2009-)
Tel: +91(231) 269-2122 EMail: vcoffice@unishivaji.ac.in

Registrar: D. V. Muley
Tel: +91(231) 260-9063, Fax: +91(231) 269-2333
EMail: registrar@unishivaji.ac.in

International Relations: D.T. Shirke

Centres
Community Development (Animal Husbandry; Child Care and Development; Clothing and Sewing; Computer Engineering; Dietetics; Electrical Engineering; English; Health Sciences; Heating and Refrigeration; Home Economics; Mechanical Equipment and Maintenance; Nutrition); **Distance Education** (Arts and Humanities; Business Administration; Business and Commerce; Mathematics; Real Estate); **Gandhian Studies** (Development Studies; Political Sciences; Rural Studies); **Women's Studies** (Women's Studies)

Courses
Industrial Chemistry (Industrial Chemistry); **Sericulture** (Sericulture)

Departments
Adult and Continuing Education (Business Administration; Computer Science; Cooking and Catering; Cosmetology; English; Environmental Studies; Fashion Design; Folklore; Home Economics; Human Rights; Interior Design; Journalism; Library Science; Mass Communication; Medical Auxiliaries; Musical Instruments;

Nursing; Public Relations; Social Work; Taxation; Teacher Training; Tourism); **Agrochemicals and Pest Management** (Biological and Life Sciences; Biotechnology; Chemistry; Entomology; Plant and Crop Protection; Toxicology); **Applied Chemistry** (Analytical Chemistry; Applied Chemistry; Chemistry; Industrial Chemistry; Inorganic Chemistry; Organic Chemistry; Pharmacy; Physical Chemistry; Technology); **Bio-Chemistry** (Biochemistry; Biological and Life Sciences; Biotechnology; Computer Science; Environmental Studies); **Bio-Technology** (Biotechnology; Cell Biology; Computer Science; Genetics; Industrial Management; Microbiology; Molecular Biology; Virology); **Botany** (Biotechnology; Botany; Ecology; Environmental Studies; Genetics; Physiology; Plant Pathology); **Chemistry** (Analytical Chemistry; Applied Chemistry; Chemistry; Industrial Chemistry; Inorganic Chemistry; Organic Chemistry; Physical Chemistry); **Commerce and Management** (Accountancy; Banking; Business and Commerce; Finance; Management); **Commerce and Management - M.B.A. Unit** (Accountancy; Agricultural Management; Business Administration; Business and Commerce; Business Computing; Commercial Law; Communication Studies; Economics; Finance; Human Resources; Industrial and Organizational Psychology; Information Management; Information Technology; Management; Marketing; Mathematics; Operations Research; Statistics); **Computer Science** (Computer Science); **Economics** (Agricultural Economics; Economics; Finance); **Education** (Education; Educational Administration; Educational and Student Counselling; Educational Psychology; Educational Sciences; Educational Technology; Foreign Languages Education; Information Technology; Journalism; Mass Communication; Public Relations; Science Education; Special Education; Teacher Trainers Education; Teacher Training); **Electronics** (Electronic Engineering; Microwaves; Power Engineering); **English** (Comparative Literature; English; Linguistics; Literature); **Environmental Science** (Demography and Population; Environmental Management; Environmental Studies; Safety Engineering; Toxicology); **Food Science and Technology** (Biochemistry; Biotechnology; Chemistry; Food Science; Food Technology; Harvest Technology; Laboratory Techniques; Microbiology; Nutrition; Toxicology); **Foreign Languages** (French; German; Japanese; Modern Languages; Russian); **Geography** (Computer Science; Geography; Tourism); **Hindi** (Hindi; Translation and Interpretation); **History** (History; Medieval Studies; Museum Studies); **Journalism and Communication** (Journalism; Mass Communication); **Law** (Criminology; Law); **Library and Information Science** (Information Sciences; Library Science); **Marathi** (Indic Languages; Literature); **Mathematics** (Mathematics); **Micro-Biology** (Cell Biology; Computer Science; Genetics; Immunology; Laboratory Techniques; Microbiology; Statistics; Virology); **Music** (Dance; Music; Musical Instruments; Painting and Drawing; Singing; Theatre; Visual Arts); **Physics** (Astronomy and Space Science; Energy Engineering; Materials Engineering; Optics; Physics; Solid State Physics); **Political Science** (Comparative Politics; Government; Human Rights; International Relations; Political Sciences; Public Administration); **Sociology** (Development Studies; Human Resources; Social Work; Sociology); **Statistics** (Statistics); **Technology** (Chemical Engineering; Civil Engineering; Computer Engineering; Computer Science; Electronic Engineering; Engineering; Environmental Engineering; Environmental Studies; Food Technology; Telecommunications Engineering); **Zoology** (Aquaculture; Entomology; Fishery; Immunology; Technology; Zoology)

Research Centres
Shahu (Cultural Studies; History)

Further Information: Also 225 affiliated colleges. A traditional and distance education institution.

History: Founded 1962.

Governing Bodies: Senate; Management Council; Academic Council

Academic Year: June to April (June-November; November-April) except for Engineering, Technology, Architecture, Pharmacy, Textile and Management studies: July to May (July-November; January-May)

Admission Requirements: 12th year senior secondary/intermediate examination or recognized foreign equivalent

Fees: (Rupees): Tuition fee for undegraduate programmes, from 400 per term to 800 per annum for Indian students and 2,000 per term for foreign students; Postgraduate programmes, from 1,250

per term to 11,000 per annum for Indian students and 2,500 per term for foreign students; M.Ed. Course, 2,000 per term.

Main Language(s) of Instruction: English, Marathi

Accrediting Agencies: National Assessment and Accreditation Council (NAAC)

Degrees and Diplomas: *Diploma; Bachelor's Degree; Bachelor's degree (professional); Postgraduate Diploma; Master's Degree; Master of Philosophy; Doctorate (Ph.D.).* Also Certificate Courses; Higher Diploma; M.C.A.; M.B.A.

Student Services: Health services, Sports facilities

Student Residential Facilities: 3 Boy's Hostels (for 600 students) and 2 Girl's Hostels (for 350 students); 170 quarters for teaching staff and over 100 quarters for non-teaching staff; Guest house.

Special Facilities: Shahu Sanshodan Kendra

Libraries: 248,502 vols; 32,698 Back Volumes of Journals; 6,923 Manuscripts; 298 Current Journals; 8,567 Thesis and Dissertations; 6,682 Reports; 1,277 CD-ROM's

Publications: Shivaji University Journal, Publication on Social Science and Humanities; Shivaji University Journal, Publication on Science and Technology; Shivsandesh, Shivaji University News Letter

Press or Publishing House: Shivaji University Press

Student Numbers *2010-2011:* Total: c. 200,000
Last Updated: 22/07/11

SHOBHIT UNIVERSITY

NH-58, Modipuram, Meerut, Uttar Pradesh 250 110
Tel: +91(121) 257-5091 +91(121) 326-4004
Fax: +91(121) 257-5724
EMail: mail@shobhituniversity.ac.in
Website: http://www.shobhituniversity.ac.in

Vice-Chancellor: Anoop Swarup

Registrar: S.K. Sareen EMail: registrar@shobhituniversity.ac.in

Centres
Agri-Informatics (Agricultural Engineering; Agriculture; Information Technology); **Bio-Informatics** (Agriculture; Biological and Life Sciences; Computer Science); **Biomedical Engineering** (Bioengineering; Biomedical Engineering; Medical Technology); **Media Research** (Journalism; Mass Communication; Media Studies); **Professional Development**

Schools
Basic and Applied Sciences (Biotechnology; Chemical Engineering; Environmental Management; Information Technology; Mathematics; Software Engineering); **Biotechnology** (Biotechnology); **Business Studies** (Business Administration; Finance; Human Resources; Information Management; Information Technology; International Business; Management; Marketing; Operations Research); **Computer Engineering and Information Technology** (Computer Engineering; Computer Science; Information Technology; Telecommunications Engineering); **Electronics Engineering** (Aeronautical and Aerospace Engineering; Electrical and Electronic Engineering; Electronic Engineering; Measurement and Precision Engineering; Microelectronics; Telecommunications Engineering); **Pharmaceutical Sciences** (Chemistry; Pharmacology; Pharmacy)

History: Founded 2000 as Shobhit Institute of Engineering and Technology. Acquired present status as Deemed University 2006.

International Co-operation: With universities in United Kingdom, Australia, Ukraine, France, Germany.

Accrediting Agencies: American University Accreditation Council (AUAC)

Degrees and Diplomas: *Bachelor's degree (professional); Master's Degree; Master of Philosophy; Doctorate (Ph.D.).* Also Dual Degree (B.Tech./M.Tech.); MBA; MCA.

Student Services: Canteen, Health services, Sports facilities

Student Residential Facilities: Boys' and Girls' Hostels

Special Facilities: Auditoriums and Seminar Rooms; WI-FI access; Laboratories (Pharmaceutical Sciences, Biotechnology, Electronics Engineering, Bio-informatics, Biomedical Engineering and Agri-informatics Engineering).

Libraries: c. 40,000 vols; c; 4,000 journals; repository of over 300,000 journals through e-library; database of the virtual -Library is repository of approximately 450,000 e-Books.
Last Updated: 22/07/11

SHOOLINI UNIVERSITY OF BIOTECHNOLOGY AND MANAGEMENT SCIENCES

SILB, The Mall, Solan, Himachal Pradesh 173212
EMail: info@shooliniuniversity.com
Website: http://www.shooliniuniversity.com/

Vice Chancellor: Kumar Khosla
EMail: vicechancellor@shooliniuniversity.com

Registrar: Ramanand Chauhan

Faculties
Biotechnology (Biology; Biotechnology; Computer Science; Food Technology; Microbiology); **Engineering and Technology** (Biology; Biotechnology; Civil Engineering; Computer Science; Electronic Engineering; Food Technology; Mechanical Engineering; Telecommunications Engineering); **Management Sciences** (Biotechnology; Business Administration; Computer Science; Electronic Engineering; Esoteric Practices; Finance; Food Technology; Human Resources; Information Technology; Management; Marketing; Telecommunications Engineering; Yoga); **Pharmaceutical Sciences** (Biotechnology; Chemistry; Pharmacology; Pharmacy; Safety Engineering); **Science, Social Science and Languages** (Botany; Chemistry; Environmental Studies; Physics; Zoology)

History: Founded 2009.

Accrediting Agencies: University Grants Commission (UGC); AICTE; DISR

Degrees and Diplomas: *Bachelor's degree (professional); Master's Degree; Master of Philosophy; Doctorate.* Also Honours Bachelor's and Master's Degrees; Dual Bachelor's Degree Programmes with MBA or M.Tech.; MBA.

Student Services: Health services, Sports facilities

Student Residential Facilities: On Campus Girls Hostel (220 beds); Guest house for visiting parents; In-town facilities for 80 girls and 100-bed boys.

Special Facilities: special Audio Video Room and a Live Wire Room; Audiovisual enabled lecture theatres/conference rooms/ tutorial rooms; 300 seated auditorium; 300 seated open air theatre; IT centre; Museum and Herbarium (over 500 varieties of herbs and samples; 20 Research and Teaching Labs for life sciences and technology; DNA finger printing facility; Tissue Culture & green house facility; Language Lab

Libraries: Central Library of the university has over ten thousand books. It makes available 50 Indian and international journals; an online library with 12 nodes; and a reference room with broadband connectivity & workstations
Last Updated: 26/08/11

SHREE SOMNATH SANSKIT UNIVERSITY

Somnath-VERAVA, District- Junagadh, Gujarat
Tel: +91(2876) 244-528
Website: http://shreesomnathsanskrituniversity.info/ about_university.htm
Vice-Chancellor: Pankaj L. Jani

Faculties
Darshan (Indian Philosophy) (Philosophy); **Indian culture and Fine Arts** (Fine Arts; South Asian Studies); **Modern Science and Ancient Shastras** (Astronomy and Space Science; Ayurveda; Chemistry; Natural Sciences; Physics); **Sahitya** (Literature; Sanskrit); **Teacher Training** *(Shikshak - Prashikshan)* (Teacher Training)

History: Founded 2005.

Admission Requirements: Higher Secondary School Certificate Examination i.e. twelfth standard examination or any equivalent examination approved by the UGC

Degrees and Diplomas: *Bachelor's Degree; Master's Degree; Doctorate*

Student Services: Sports facilities

Special Facilities: Computer Lab; Seminar Hall; Conference Room; Language Lab

Libraries: Yes
Last Updated: 12/08/11

SHREEMATI NATHIBAI DAMODAR THACKERSEY WOMEN'S UNIVERSITY

Nathibai Thavkersey Road, New Marine Lines, Mumbai, Maharashtra 400020
Tel: +91(22) 2203-1879 +91(22) 2203-2159
Fax: +91(22) 2201-8226
Website: http://www.sndtwomensuniversity.in/

Vice-Chancellor: Vasudha Kamat (2011-)

Registrar: Madhu Madan

Centres
Distance Education *(Juhu Campus)* (Distance Education); **Special Education** *(Juhu Campus)* (Special Education)

Departments
Actuarial Science *(Juhu Campus)* (Actuarial Science); **Adult and Continuing Education and Extension Work** *(Churchgate Campus)* (Adult Education; Continuing Education); **Computer Science** *(Postgraduate)* (Computer Science); **Education Management** *(Juhu Campus)* (Educational Administration); **Educational Technology** *(Juhu Campus)* (Educational Technology); **Jewellery Design and Manufacture** *(Juhu Campus)* (Jewelry Art); **Physical Education** *(Churchgate Campus)* (Physical Education); **Post Graduate Studies and Research** *(Pune Campus)* (Business and Commerce; Communication Studies; Economics; Fine Arts; Geography; Hindi; Music; Painting and Drawing; Psychology; Social Work); **Postgraduate Studies** *(Churchgate Campus)* (Business and Commerce; Economics; Education; English; Fine Arts; Foreign Languages Education; Hindi; History; Indic Languages; Music; Painting and Drawing; Political Sciences; Psychology; Sanskrit; Social Work; Sociology); **Postgraduate Studies in Home Science** *(Juhu Campus)* (Home Economics)

Research Centres
Womens Studies *(Juhu Campus)* (Women's Studies)

Schools
Law *(Juhu Campus)* (Business Administration; Law); **Library and Information Science** *(SHPT - Churchgate Campus)* (Information Sciences; Library Science)

Further Information: Also Churchgate Campus, JUHU Campus and Pune Campus; 11 University Colleges (including SNDT for Women); 233 Affiliated Colleges

History: Founded 1916 on the model of the Women's University of Tokyo.

Governing Bodies: Senate; Academic Council; Management Council

Academic Year: June to April (June-November; November-April)

Admission Requirements: 12th year senior secondary/intermediate examination or recognized foreign equivalent

Fees: (Rupees): 400-15,000

Main Language(s) of Instruction: English, Gujarati, Marathi, Hindi

Accrediting Agencies: AccreditationNational assessment and accreditation council (NAAC)

Degrees and Diplomas: *Diploma*; *Bachelor's Degree*; *Bachelor's degree (professional)*; *Postgraduate Diploma*; *Master's Degree*; *Master of Philosophy*; *Doctorate (PhD)*. Also Certificate courses

Student Residential Facilities: Yes

Libraries: Total Campuses, 313,579 vols; 1,034 periodical subscriptions
Last Updated: 23/08/11

SHRI JAGANNATH SANSKRIT UNIVERSITY

Shri Jagannath Sanskrit Vishwavidyalaya (SJSV)
Shri Vihar, Puri, Orissa 752003
Tel: +91(6752) 251-669
Fax: +91(6752) 251-073
EMail: sanskrit.university@yahoo.com; sanskrit.university@yahoo.co.in
Website: http://sjsv.nic.in/

Vice-Chancellor: Nilakantha Pati
Tel: +91(6752) 251-663, Fax: +91(6752) 250-484
Registrar: R.C. Dash
Tel: +91(6752) 251-669, Fax: +91(6752) 251-073

Departments
Advaita Vedanta (Philosophical Schools); **Computer Application** (Computer Science); **Dharmashastra** (Law); **Jyotirvigyan** (Astronomy and Space Science; Esoteric Practices); **Nyaya** (Logic; Philosophy); **Physical Education** (Physical Education); **Sahitya** (Literature); **Sarvadarshan** (Philosophy); **Veda** (Philosophy); **Vyakaran** (Linguistics; Literature)

Further Information: Also 142 Affiliated Colleges

History: Founded 1981. Acquired present status 1990.

Governing Bodies: Syndicate; Senate; Academic Council

Academic Year: June to May

Admission Requirements: 12th year senior secondary/intermediate examination or recognized foreign equivalent

Main Language(s) of Instruction: English

Degrees and Diplomas: *Diploma*; *Bachelor's Degree*; *Master's Degree*; *Doctorate (PhD)*

Student Services: Health services

Student Residential Facilities: Hostels for 100 boys and 240 girls; Guest House

Libraries: 35,000 vols; 500 referral journals and 200 manuscripts
Last Updated: 23/08/11

SHRI LAL BAHADUR SHASTRI NATIONAL SANSKRIT UNIVERSITY

Shri Lal Bahadur Shastri Rashtriya Sanskrit Vidyapeeth (SLBSRSV)
Qutub Institutional Area, New Delhi 110016
Tel: +91(11) 46060-606
Fax: +91(11) 2653-3512 +91(11) 2652-0255
EMail: info@slbsrsv.ac.in
Website: http://www.slbsrsv.ac.in

Vice-Chancellor: Vachaspati Upadhyaya (1994-)
Tel: +91(11) 2685-1253 +91(11) 2656-4003,
Fax: +91(11) 2652-0255
EMail: vc@slbsrsv.ac.in; vu_vidyapeetha@hotmail.com; vcslbsrsv@yahoo.co.in

Registrar: B.K. Mohapatra
Tel: +91(11) 26851251 +91(11) 4606-0555,
Fax: +91(11) 2653-3512 +91(11) 4606-0557
EMail: registrar@slbsrsv.ac.in; reg_slbsrsv@yahoo.co.in

Departments
Adhunik Gyan-Vigyan Sankay (Education; Educational Technology; Environmental Studies; Foreign Languages Education; Psychology; Sanskrit; **Research and Publications**

Faculties
Darshan Sankay (Law; Literature; Philosophical Schools; Philosophy; Yoga); **Sahitya Sanskriti** (Asian Religious Studies; Computer Science; English; Hindi; Literature; Philosophy; Political Sciences; Religious Studies; Sanskrit; Social Studies; Sociology; Tourism); **Ved Vedang** (Cultural Studies; Esoteric Practices; Heritage Preservation; Law; Linguistics; Literature; Philosophy)

History: Founded 1962. Acquired present status and title 1987. A deemed university.

Degrees and Diplomas: *Diploma*; *Bachelor's Degree*; *Master's Degree*; *Doctorate (Phd)*. Also certificates.

Student Residential Facilities: Hostel; Staff quarters; Guest house

Libraries: 63,926 vols; 35 periodical subscriptions
Last Updated: 23/08/11

SHRI MATA VAISHNO DEVI UNIVERSITY (SMVDU)

Sub-Post Office, Katra, Jammu and Kashmir 182320
Fax: +91(1991) 285-535 +91(1991) 285-524
EMail: info@smvdu.ac.in
Website: http://www.smvdu.ac.in

Vice-Chancellor: R. N. K. Bamezai
Tel: +91(1991) 285-686 EMail: vc@smvdu.ac.in

Registrar: Roop Avtar Kaur Tel: +91(1991) 285-687

Colleges

Engineering *(COE)* (Architecture; Biotechnology; Computer Engineering; Computer Science; Electronic Engineering; Energy Engineering; Engineering; Landscape Architecture; Mechanical Engineering; Natural Resources; Telecommunications Engineering); **Humanities and Social Sciences** (Arts and Humanities; Cultural Studies; English; French; Literature; Logic; Modern Languages; Philosophy; Social Sciences); **Management** *(COM)* (Business Administration; Economics; Management); **Sciences** *(COS)* (Biology; Biotechnology; Chemistry; Mathematics; Natural Sciences; Physics)

History: Founded 1999. Acquired present status 2004.

Governing Bodies: Executive Council; Academic Council; Finance Committee

Academic Year: August to June (August-December; January-June)

Admission Requirements: Secondary School Certificate and All India Engineering Entrance Examination

Fees: (Rupees): Bachelor's degree, 60,000 per annum; Master's degree, 10,000-40,000 per annum; MBA, 14,000 per annum; Ph.D., 8,000-20,000 per annum

Main Language(s) of Instruction: English

Accrediting Agencies: University Grants Commission; Association of Indian Universities; All India Council for Technical Education; Council of Architecture

Degrees and Diplomas: *Bachelor's degree (professional)*; *Master's Degree*; *Doctorate (Ph.D.)*. Also Certificate and M.B.A.

Student Services: Academic counselling, Canteen, Cultural centre, Employment services, Health services, Language programs, Sports facilities

Student Residential Facilities: 4 Boys Hostels (Trikuta, Kailash, Neelgiri and Vindhyachal) and 2 Girls Hostels (Shivalik and Vaishnavi).

Special Facilities: Matrika Auditorium; Banking and ATM Facilities; Post Office.

Libraries: 25,000 vols; over 300 CD-ROM titles; 87 national and international journals and periodical subscriptions; Virtual digital library.
Last Updated: 23/08/11

SHRIDHAR UNIVERSITY (SU)

Pilani-Chirawa Road, Pilani, Rajasthan 333 031
Tel: +91(1596) 510-000
Fax: +91(1596) 510-002
EMail: info@shridharuniversity.ac.in
Website: http://www.shridharuniversity.ac.in/

Vice Chancellor: Mahesh Vij

Registrar: Nesamoorthy

Programmes

Business Administration *(Postgraduate)* (Business Administration; Finance; Human Resources; Information Technology; Marketing); **Civil Engineering** (Civil Engineering); **Computer Applications** *(Postgraduate)* (Computer Science); **Computer Science and Engineering** (Computer Engineering; Computer Science); **Computer Science and Engineering** *(Postgraduate)* (Software Engineering); **Electrical and Electronics** (Electrical Engineering; Electronic Engineering); **Electronics and Communication** (Electronic Engineering; Telecommunications Engineering); **Environmental Engineering** *(Postgraduate)* (Environmental Engineering); **Environmental Science** (Environmental Studies); **Geo Informatics** *(Postgraduate)* (Computer Science; Earth Sciences; Geology); **Geography** *(Postgraduate)* (Geography); **Mechanical Engineering** (Mechanical Engineering); **Mining Engineering** (Mining Engineering); **Pharmaceutics** *(Postgraduate)* (Pharmacology; Pharmacy); **Software Engineering** *(Postgraduate)* (Software Engineering)

History: Founded 2010.

Governing Bodies: Advisory Council

Degrees and Diplomas: *Diploma*; *Bachelor's Degree*; *Bachelor's degree (professional)*; *Master's Degree*. Also M.B.A.

Student Residential Facilities: Separate hostels for boys and girls

Libraries: c. 5,000 vols; 1,500 CDs, journals and newspaper
Last Updated: 22/12/11

SIDHO KANHO BIRSHA UNIVERSITY (SKBU)

North Bengal University, DD 27/C, Sector-I, Salt Lake, Kolkata, West Bengal 700 064
Tel: +91(3252) 224-438
EMail: vcskbuniversity@gmail.com
Website: http://skbu.ac.in/

Vice Chancellor: Tapati Mukherjee

Registrar: Nachiketa Bandyopadhyay
EMail: registrarskbu@gmail.com

Programmes

Bangladesh (South and Southeast Asian Languages); **Chemistry** (Chemistry); **Education** (Education); **English** (English); **Mathematics** (Mathematics); **Philosophy** (Philosophy); **Physics** (Physics); **Political Sciences** (Political Sciences); **Sanskrit** (Sanskrit)

Further Information: Also Purulia Campus; 24 affiliated colleges.

History: Founded 2010.

Governing Bodies: University Council; Statute Committee; Building Committee; Finance Committee

Accrediting Agencies: University Grants Commission (UGC)

Degrees and Diplomas: *Bachelor's Degree*; *Master's Degree*
Last Updated: 06/01/12

SIDO KANHU MURMU UNIVERSITY (SKMU)

Santal Pargana, Dumka, Bihar 814101
Tel: +91(6434) 222-495
Fax: +91(6434) 222-415
Website: http://skmu.edu.in/

Vice-Chancellor: Basheer Ahmed Khan (2010-)
Tel: +91(6434) 223-006, Fax: +91(6434) 223-006
EMail: vc@skmu.edu.in

Registrar: Md. Shamshadullah
Tel: +91(6434) 222-495 EMail: registrar@skmu.edu.in

Courses

Vocational Studies (Advertising and Publicity; Harvest Technology; Sales Techniques; Sericulture)

Faculties

Commerce (Accountancy; Banking; Business and Commerce; Commercial Law; Development Studies; Economics; Finance; Statistics) *Dean*: Saryug Prasad; **Humanities** (Anthropology; Arts and Humanities; English; Hindi; Indic Languages; Literature; Persian; Philosophy; Sanskrit; Urdu) *Dean*: Binodanand Jha; **Science** (Botany; Chemistry; Geology; Mathematics; Natural Sciences; Physics; Statistics; Zoology); **Social Sciences** (Agricultural Economics; Anthropology; Economics; Geography; History; Labour and Industrial Relations; Music; Political Sciences; Psychology; Social Sciences; Social Welfare; Sociology; Statistics)

Further Information: 13 constituent colleges and 11 Affiliated colleges.

History: Founded 1991 by an Act of Bihar Legislative Assembly with a view to providing higher education to the people of tribal culture in the Santhal Parganas region of South Bihar. Acquired present title 2003. Formerly known as Siddhu Kanhu Murmu University.

Governing Bodies: Senate; Syndicate; Academic Council

Academic Year: June to May

Admission Requirements: 12th year senior/secondary intermediate examination or recognized foreign equivalent

Fees: (Rupees): 144-252 per annum

Main Language(s) of Instruction: English, Hindi, Bengali, Santhali

Accrediting Agencies: University Grants Commission (UGC)

Degrees and Diplomas: *Bachelor's Degree*; *Bachelor's degree (professional)*; *Master's Degree*; *Doctorate (PhD)*. Also M.B.A. and M.P.A.

Student Services: Sports facilities

Student Residential Facilities: Yes

Special Facilities: Laboratories

Libraries: c. 7,600 vols

Last Updated: 23/08/11

SIKKIM MANIPAL UNIVERSITY OF HEALTH, MEDICAL AND TECHNOLOGICAL SCIENCES (SMU)

5th Mile, Tadong, Gangtok, East Sikkim 737102
Tel: +91(3592) 270-294
Fax: +91(3592) 231-47
EMail: info@smu.edu.in
Website: http://www.smu.edu.in/

Vice-Chancellor: Somnath Mishra
Tel: +91(3592) 03-592, Fax: +91(3592) 03-592
EMail: vc@smu.edu.in

Registrar: Namrata Thapa

Divisions

Distance Education *(SMU DDE)* (Arts and Humanities; Biotechnology; Business Administration; Business and Commerce; Computer Networks; Computer Science; Cooking and Catering; Fashion Design; Health Administration; History; Information Sciences; Information Technology; International Business; Journalism; Laboratory Techniques; Mass Communication; Medical Technology; Political Sciences; Telecommunications Engineering; Tourism)

Institutes

Medical Sciences *(SMIMS)* (Anatomy; Biochemistry; Biotechnology; Laboratory Techniques; Medical Technology; Medicine; Microbiology; Physiology; Surgery); **Skill Development**; **Technology** *(SMIT)* (Chemistry; Civil Engineering; Computer Engineering; Computer Science; Electrical and Electronic Engineering; Electrical Engineering; Electronic Engineering; Engineering; Information Technology; Management; Mathematics; Mechanical Engineering; Physics; Technology; Telecommunications Engineering)

Schools

Architecture (Architecture); **Basic and Applied Sciences** (Chemistry; Computer Engineering; Computer Science; Engineering; Information Technology; Mathematics; Nanotechnology; Physics; Telecommunications Engineering); **Nursing** *(SMCON)* (Nursing); **Physiotherapy** *(SMCPT)* (Physical Therapy)

Further Information: Also Majitar SMIT campus.

History: Founded 1995.

Governing Bodies: University Senate, Government officials

Academic Year: July to August

Admission Requirements: 12th year senior secondary examination

Fees: (Indian Rupees): Tuition fees for undergraduate programmes, 20,000-60,000 per annum; Professional undergraduate programmes, 90,000-360,000 per annum; Postgraduate programmes, 21,700-74,600 per annum; M.B.A., 123,000 per annum. For International students (US Dollars): 2,650-18,000 per annum.

Main Language(s) of Instruction: English

Accrediting Agencies: State Legislative; University Grants Commission; All India Council for Technical Education

Degrees and Diplomas: *Diploma*; *Bachelor's Degree*; *Bachelor's degree (professional)*; *Postgraduate Diploma*; *Master's Degree*; *Doctorate (Ph.D.)*. Also advanced diploma; Bachelor's degree honours; M.B.A. and M.C.A.

Student Services: Academic counselling, Canteen, Cultural centre, Employment services, Foreign student adviser, Health services, Language programs, Nursery care, Social counselling, Sports facilities

Student Residential Facilities: Yes

Special Facilities: Museum

Libraries: Central Library

Publications: Manipal Link *(bimonthly)*

Press or Publishing House: Manipal Power Press

Last Updated: 27/01/12

SIKKIM UNIVERSITY

6th mile Samdur, Tadong, Gangtok, Sikkim 737 102
Tel: +91(3592) 251-438
Fax: +91(3592) 251-438
EMail: sikkimuniversity@gmail.com; admin@sikkimunivesity.in
Website: http://www.sikkimuniversity.in/

Vice Chancellor: Mahendra P. Lama

Registrar: P. V. Ravi

Centres
Law and Legal Jurisprudence (Law)

Departments
Asian Languages (Chinese); **Chemical Sciences** (Chinese); **Economic studies and Planning** (Economics); **Geography and Natural Resource Management** (Geography; Natural Resources); **International Relations** (International Relations); **Journalism and Mass Communication** (Journalism; Mass Communication); **Management and Commerce** (Business Administration; Business and Commerce; Management); **Microbiology** (Microbiology); **Nepali Language and Literature** (Indic Languages; Linguistics; Literature); **Peace and Conflicts** (Peace and Disarmament); **Physical Sciences** (Physics); **Plantation Management and Studies** (Horticulture); **Psychology** (Psychology); **Social System and Anthropology** (Anthropology; Social Sciences)

Further Information: Also 10 affiliated colleges.

History: Founded 2007. A 'Central University'.

Governing Bodies: Executive Council; Academic Council; Finance Committee

Degrees and Diplomas: *Bachelor's Degree*; *Postgraduate Diploma*; *Master's Degree*. Also integrated Bachelor-Master's degree.

Last Updated: 06/12/11

SIKSHA "O" ANUSANDHAN UNIVERSITY

Khandagiri Square, Bhubaneswar, Bhubaneswar, Orissa 751030
Tel: +91(674) 2350-635 +91(674) 2350-791
Fax: +91(674) 2350-642
EMail: info@soauniversity.ac.in
Website: http://www.soauniversity.ac.in/

Vice-Chancellor: Rajendra Prasad Mohanty
Tel: +91(22) 25811-506
EMail: rpmohanty@gmail.com; rajendramohanty@hotmail.com; mohantyrp@yahoo.com; vcsoa@soauniversity.ac.in

Registrar: Bibhuti Pradhan Bhusan
EMail: registrar@soauniversity.ac.in

Centres
Biotechnology *(CBT)* (Biotechnology)

Colleges
SUM Nursing *(SNC)* (Nursing)

Institutes
Business and Computer Studies *(IBCS)* (Business Administration; Computer Science; Finance; Human Resources; Information Technology; Marketing); **Dental Sciences** *(IDS)* (Dental Technology; Dentistry; Microbiology; Oral Pathology; Orthodontics; Periodontics; Radiology; Surgery); **Hotel Management** *(SHM)* (Cooking and Catering; Hotel Management); **Law** *(SOA National)* (Law); **Medical Sciences and SUM Hospital** *(IMS & SH)* (Anaesthesiology; Anatomy; Biochemistry; Dentistry; Dermatology; Endocrinology; Forensic Medicine and Dentistry; Gastroenterology; Gynaecology and Obstetrics; Medicine; Microbiology; Ophthalmology; Orthopaedics; Otorhinolaryngology; Paediatrics; Pathology; Pharmacology; Physiology; Plastic Surgery; Pneumology; Psychiatry and Mental Health; Radiology; Respiratory Therapy; Social and Preventive Medicine; Surgery; Venereology); **Technical Education and Research** *(ITER)* (Arts and Humanities; Automation and Control Engineering; Chemistry; Civil Engineering; Computer Engineering; Computer Science; Electrical and Electronic Engineering; Electrical Engineering; Electronic Engineering; English; Information Technology; Literature; Mathematics; Measurement and Precision Engineering; Mechanical Engineering; Physics; Telecommunications Engineering)

Schools

Pharmaceutical Sciences *(SPS)* (Anatomy; Biotechnology; Pharmacology; Pharmacy; Safety Engineering)

History: A deemed university.

Governing Bodies: Board of Management; Academic Council; Planning and Monitoring Board; Finance Committee

Fees: (Indian Rupees): undergraduate programmes, 35,000-75,000 per annum; Undergraduate professional programmes, 150,000-195,000 per annum; Postgraduate programmes, 50,000-275,000 per annum; MBA, 230,000-250,000 per annum.

Accrediting Agencies: National Assessment and Accreditation Council (NAAC) of University Grants Commission (UGC) - Grade "A".

Degrees and Diplomas: *Bachelor's Degree*; *Bachelor's degree (professional)*; *Master's Degree*; *Doctorate (Ph.D.)*. Also M.B.A.
Last Updated: 24/08/11

SINGHANIA UNIVERSITY

P.O. - Pacheri Bari, Jhunjhunu, Rajasthan 333 515
Tel: +91(1593) 271299 +91(1593) 271300
Fax: +91(1593) 271003
EMail: info@singhaniauniversity.co.in
Website: http://www.singhaniauniversity.co.in/

Chancellor: D.C. Singhania

Schools

Applied Sciences and Social Sciences (Applied Mathematics; Chemistry; Mathematics; Physics; Social Sciences); **Computer Science and Information Technology** (Computer Engineering; Computer Networks; Computer Science; Information Technology); **Electronics and Electrical Engineering** (Electrical Engineering; Electronic Engineering; Telecommunications Engineering); **Humanities, Languages and Social Sciences** (Arts and Humanities; Business and Commerce; Economics; Education; English; Geography; Hindi; History; Indic Languages; Modern Languages; Physical Education; Political Sciences; Social Sciences; Social Work; Sociology); **Industrial Engineering** (Automotive Engineering; Civil Engineering; Industrial Engineering; Mechanical Engineering); **Law and Management** (Business Administration; Law; Management); **Life Sciences** (Agriculture; Biological and Life Sciences; Biotechnology; Botany; Computer Science; Microbiology; Zoology); **Pharmacy and Medical Sciences** (Alternative Medicine; Medicine; Pharmacology; Pharmacy; Physical Therapy; Yoga)

History: Created 2003 as Singhania Institute. Acquired current title and status 2007.

Accrediting Agencies: University Grants Commission (UGC)

Degrees and Diplomas: *Diploma*; *Bachelor's Degree*; *Bachelor's degree (professional)*; *Postgraduate Diploma*; *Master's Degree*; *Doctorate*. Also M.B.A.
Last Updated: 21/11/11

SIR PADAMPAT SINGHANIA UNIVERSITY (SPSU)

Bhatewar, Tehsil, Vallabhnagar District, Udaipur Rajasthan
Tel: +91(2957) 226-095 +91(294) 243-0102
Fax: +91(2957) 226-094
EMail: info@spsu.ac.in
Website: http://www.spsu.ac.in/

Vice Chancellor: Pradip Chandra Deka

Schools

Engineering (Biotechnology; Civil Engineering; Computer Engineering; Computer Science; Electrical Engineering; Electronic Engineering; Engineering; Mechanical Engineering; Telecommunications Engineering); **Management** (Accountancy; Advertising and Publicity; Banking; Business Administration; E-Business/Commerce; Economics; Finance; Human Resources; Law; Management; Marketing; Operations Research; Safety Engineering; Small Business; Taxation)

History: Founded 2007.

Governing Bodies: Board of Management

International Co-operation: With universities

Degrees and Diplomas: *Bachelor's Degree*; *Bachelor's degree (professional)*; *Master's Degree*; *Doctorate*. Also M.B.A.; integrated Bachelor and Master's degrees (BTech + M.Tech.; BBM+MBA)

Student Services: Sports facilities

Student Residential Facilities: Boys and Girls Hostels

Special Facilities: Amphi Theatre
Last Updated: 21/12/11

SOLAPUR UNIVERSITY (SU)

Dnyanteerth Nagar, Kegaon, Solapur-Pune National Highway, Solapur, Maharashtra 413 255
Website: http://su.digitaluniversity.ac/

Vice Chancellor: B.P. Bandgar
Tel: +91(217) 235-1300, Fax: +91(217) 235-1300
EMail: bandgar_bp@yahoo.com

Registrar: Nitin Pandurang Sonaje
Tel: +91(217) 274-4770 EMail: nitinsonaje@yahoo.co.in

Departments

Educational Sciences (Education; Educational Sciences); **Management** (Business Administration; Business and Commerce; Finance; Human Resources; Industrial Management; International Business; Management; Marketing; Retailing and Wholesaling)

Schools

Chemical Sciences (Chemistry; Industrial Chemistry; Organic Chemistry; Polymer and Plastics Technology); **Computational Sciences** (Computer Science; Mathematics; Statistics); **Earth Sciences** (Computer Science; Earth Sciences; Environmental Studies; Geology); **Physical Sciences** (Applied Physics; Chemistry; Electronic Engineering; Materials Engineering; Physics); **Social Sciences** (Agricultural Economics; Ancient Civilizations; Archaeology; Banking; Cultural Studies; Economics; International Economics; Journalism; Mass Communication; Museum Studies; Rural Studies; Social Sciences; Tourism)

Further Information: Also 126 Affiliated Colleges.

History: Founded 2004.

Governing Bodies: Senate; Academic Council; Board of Studies; Management Council;

Degrees and Diplomas: *Bachelor's Degree*; *Bachelor's degree (professional)*; *Master's Degree*; *Master of Philosophy*; *Doctorate*. Also M.B.A.
Last Updated: 04/01/12

SOUTH ASIAN UNIVERSITY (SAU)

CRS Language Lab, JNU Old Campus, Aruna Asaf Ali Road, New Delhi 110-067
Tel: +91(11) 2412-2512 +91(11) 2412-2514
Fax: +91(11) 2412-2511
EMail: sau@southasianuniversity.org
Website: http://www.southasianuniversity.org/

President: G.K. Chadha
Tel: +91(11) 2412-2507
EMail: gkchadha@mail.jnu.ac.in; gkchadha@southasianuniversity.org

Registrar: A. K. Malik
Tel: +91(11) 2412-2508 EMail: registrar@southasianuniversity.org

Faculties

Economics (Economics); **Legal Studies** (Law); **Life Sciences and Biotechnology** (Biological and Life Sciences; Biotechnology); **Mathematics and Computer Science** (Computer Science; Mathematics); **Social Sciences** (Social Sciences)

Further Information: Also Akbar Bhawan Campus.

History: Founded 2010. A 'Central University'.

Fees: (US Dollar): South Asian Association for Regional Cooperation (SAARC) students, 440-500 per semester; non-SAARC students, 4,500-5,100 per semester.

Degrees and Diplomas: *Master's Degree*
Last Updated: 06/12/11

SOUTH INDIAN INSTITUTION FOR THE PROPAGATION OF HINDI

Dakshina Bharat Hindi Prachar Sabha
Thanikachalam Road, Chennai, Tamil Nadu 600017
Tel: +91(44) 2434-1824
Fax: +91(44) 2434-8420
EMail: info@dbhps-chennai.com
Website: http://www.dbhps-chennai.com

Vice-Chancellor: B.D. Jatti

Registrar: R.F. Neerlakatti

Faculties

Comparative Literature and Journalism *(Dharwad-Karnataka and Hyderabad Complexes)* (Comparative Literature; Journalism); **Education** *(Hyderabad Complex)* (Education); **Humanities** (Arts and Humanities); **Literature** *(Madras and Ernakulum Complexes)* (Literature)

History: Founded 1918 by Mahatma Gandhi, achieved degree-granting status 1964. A postgraduate institution.

Academic Year: July to June (July-December; January-June)

Admission Requirements: University degree

Fees: (Rupees): 1,050-2,800 per annum

Main Language(s) of Instruction: Hindi

Degrees and Diplomas: *Bachelor's Degree*: Education (BEd), 1 yr following first degree (BA/BSc); *Master's Degree*: a further 1-2 yrs; *Doctorate (PhD)*: a further 2-5 yrs

Libraries: c. 65,000 vols; 100 periodical subscriptions
Last Updated: 17/07/08

S.P. JAIN INSTITUTE OF MANAGEMENT AND RESEARCH (SPJIMR)

Munshi Nagar, Dadabhai Road, Andheri West, Mumbai, Maharashtra 400 058
Tel: +91(22) 2623-7454 +91(22) 2623-0396
Fax: +91(22) 2623-7042
EMail: spjicom@spjimr.org
Website: http://www.spjimr.org/

Director: Sesha Iyer (2007-)
Tel: +91(22) 6145-4202 EMail: seshaiyer@spjimr.org

Registrar: A.K. Singh Suryavanshi
Tel: +91(22) 6145-4261 EMail: surya@spjimr.org

International Relations: Suresh Advani, Chairperson, International Operations Tel: +91(22) 6145-4208 EMail: sadvani@spjimr.org

International Relations: Prem Chandrani, Chairperson, International Relations
Tel: +91(22) 6145-4209 EMail: pchandrani@spjimr.org

Centres

Continuing Management Education *(CME)* (Business Administration; International Business; Leadership; Management); **Development of Corporate Citizenship** *(DOCC)* (Government; Management); **Entrepreneurship Development** *(CED)* (Business Administration; Management); **Family Managed Business** *(FMB)* (Business Administration; Small Business); **Services Sciences, Management and Engineering** *(SSME)* (Business Administration; Engineering; Management; Social Studies)

History: Founded 1918. Started offering Postgraduate programmes 1992. A constituent unit of the Bharatiya Vidya Bhavan educational trust, founded 1938.

Governing Bodies: Governing Council; Strategic Review Committee; Academic Committee; Finance Committee

Academic Year: June to April

Admission Requirements: Minimum 3 yrs Bachelor's degree in any discipline from a recognized University in India or abroad; Contiuous Good Academic Records in SSC, HSC and Degree; The minimum score required to get the final offer is 85 percentile in CAT2010/XAT2011 or a score of 680 in GMAT taken in 2010.

Fees: (Indian Rupee): 87,000 for two years.

Main Language(s) of Instruction: English

International Co-operation: With European universities; Post Graduate Certificate in International Management (PGCIM) with France and Germany; Schulich M.B.A.

Accrediting Agencies: All India Council for Technical Education (AICTE); National Board of Accreditation (NBA); Association of MBAs (AMBA); Credit Rating and Information Services of India Ltd. (CRISIL)

Degrees and Diplomas: *Postgraduate Diploma*: Information Management; Manufacturing and Operations; Marketing; Finance; General Management (PGDM), 2 yrs

Student Services: Academic counselling, Canteen, Cultural centre, Employment services, Foreign student adviser, Handicapped facilities, Health services, Language programs, Social counselling, Sports facilities

Special Facilities: Auditorium; Amphitheatre; Yoga Centre

Libraries: Subscription to 8 databases (Ebsco Business Source Complete; Crisil Industry Information Services; Crisil Ecoview; ISI Emerging Market; CMIE Prowess; CMIE Business Beacon; CMIE Industry Analysis Services; Capitaline). Also 'India Site License Agreement' with Harvard Business School Publishing for their database of case studies and other material for educators.

Academic Staff *2011-2012*	MEN	WOMEN	TOTAL
FULL-TIME	27	16	**43**
PART-TIME	14	2	**16**
STAFF WITH DOCTORATE			
FULL-TIME	11	6	**17**
PART-TIME	2	2	**4**
Student Numbers *2011-2012*			
All (Foreign Included)	105	72	**177**
FOREIGN ONLY	115	62	**177**

Last Updated: 09/01/12

SREE CHITRA TIRUNAL INSTITUTE FOR MEDICAL SCIENCES AND TECHNOLOGY (SCTIMST)

PO Medical College, Thiruvananthapuram, Kerala 695011
Tel: +91(471) 252-4150
Fax: +91(471) 244-6433
EMail: sct@sctimst.ker.nic.in
Website: http://www.sctimst.ac.in/

Director: K. Radhakrishnan

Registrar: A.V. George

Centres

Health Science Studies *(Achutha Menon - AMCHSS)* (Health Sciences; Public Health)

Divisions

Biomedical Technology (Biomedical Engineering; Technology); **Patient Care** (Administration; Anaesthesiology; Biochemistry; Cardiology; Cell Biology; Microbiology; Molecular Biology; Neurological Therapy; Neurology; Nursing; Pathology; Radiology)

Further Information: Also Teaching Hospital

History: Founded 1974 and declared Institution of national importance 1980. A postgraduate Institution.

Academic Year: January to December

Admission Requirements: University degree

Main Language(s) of Instruction: English

Degrees and Diplomas: *Diploma*; *Master's Degree*; *Doctorate*. Also short courses.

Student Residential Facilities: Yes

Special Facilities: Vivarium

Libraries: 35,146 vols; 267 journals subscriptions
Last Updated: 21/11/11

SREE SANKARACHARYA UNIVERSITY OF SANSKRIT (SSUS)

PO Box 14, Ernakulam District, Kalady, Kerala 683574
Tel: +91(484) 2463380
Fax: +91(484) 2463580
EMail: ssusvc@sancharnet.in
Website: http://www.ssus.ac.in

Vice-Chancellor: J. Prasad
Tel: +91(484) 2463580, Fax: +91(484) 2463580
EMail: ssuvc@sancharnet.in

Registrar: K. Ramachandran
Tel: +91(484) 2463480, Fax: +91(484) 2463480
EMail: sureg@sancharnet.in

Departments
Ayurveda (Ayurveda); **Dance** (Dance); **Economics** (Economics); **Education** (Education); **English** (English); **Geography** (Geography); **Hindi** (Hindi); **History** (History); **Malayalam** (Indic Languages); **Music** (Music); **Painting** (Painting and Drawing); **Philosophy** (Philosophy); **Political Science** (Political Sciences); **Sanskrit Nyaya** (Sanskrit); **Sanskrit Sahitya** (Sanskrit); **Sanskrit Vedanta** (Sanskrit); **Social Work** (Social Work); **Sociology** (Sociology); **Theatre** (Theatre); **Urdu** (Urdu); **Vastuvidya** (Esoteric Practices)

Schools
Vedic Studies (Ayurveda; Esoteric Practices)

Further Information: Nine Regional Centres: Thiruvananthapuram, Panmana, Thuravoor, Ettumanoor, Kalady (Main Campus), Thrissur, Tirur, Koyilandy and Payyannur.

History: Founded 1993.

Fees: (Rupees): 400-4,500 per annum

Degrees and Diplomas: *Bachelor's Degree*; *Postgraduate Diploma*; *Master's Degree*; *Master of Philosophy*; *Doctorate (PhD)*. Also integrated M.Phil/Ph.D.

Libraries: 53,000 vols; 350 periodical subscriptions
Last Updated: 21/11/11

SRI BALAJI VIDYAPEETH, MAHATMA GANDHI MEDICAL COLLEGE AND RESEARCH INSTITUTE (MGMCRI)

Pillaiyarkuppam, Pondicherry 607 402
Tel: +91(413) 261-5449 +91(413) 261-5458
Fax: +91(413) 261-5457
EMail: mgmcri@sify.com; info@mgmcri.ac.in
Website: http://www.mgmcri.ac.in/

Vice Chancellor: D. R. Gunasekaran

Departments
Anaesthesiology (Anaesthesiology); **Anatomy** (Anatomy); **Biochemistry** (Biochemistry); **Cardiology** (Cardiology); **Cardiothoracic Surgery** (Surgery); **Community Medicine** (Community Health); **Dermatology, Venereology and Leprology** (Dermatology; Venereology); **Emergency Services** (Medical Technology); **ENT** (Otorhinolaryngology); **Forensic Medicine** (Forensic Medicine and Dentistry); **General Medicine** (Medicine); **General Surgery** (Surgery); **Master Health Checkup** (Health Sciences); **Microbiology** (Microbiology); **Music Therapy** (Art Therapy); **Neuro Surgery** (Neurological Therapy; Surgery); **Neurology** (Urology); **Obstetrics and Gynaecology** (Gynaecology and Obstetrics); **Ophthalmology** (Ophthalmology); **Orthopaedics** (Orthopaedics); **Paediatric Surgery** (Surgery); **Pathology** (Pathology); **Pharmacology** (Pharmacology); **Physiology** (Physiology); **Plastic Surgery** (Plastic Surgery); **Psychiatry** (Psychiatry and Mental Health); **Radiology and Imageology** (Medical Technology; Radiology); **Surgical Gastroenterology** (Gastroenterology; Surgery); **TB and CD** (Medicine; Rehabilitation and Therapy); **Telemedicine** (Medicine); **Urology** (Urology); **Yoga Therapy** (Alternative Medicine; Yoga)

Laboratories
Skill (Medicine)

Research Laboratories
Medicine *(Central)* (Medicine)

History: A 'Deemed University'.

Degrees and Diplomas: *Bachelor's Degree*; *Bachelor's degree (professional)*; *Postgraduate Diploma*; *Master's Degree*. Also Certificate Course

Student Residential Facilities: Separate Boys and Girls Hostels
Libraries: c. 15,000 vols.
Last Updated: 16/12/11

SRI CHANDRASEKHARENDRA SARASWATHI VISWA MAHAVIDYALAYA (SCSVMV)

Sri Jayendra Saraswathi Street, Enathur, Kanchipuram, Tamil Nadu 631 561
Tel: +91(44) 27264293 +91(44) 27264308
Fax: +91(44) 27264285
EMail: registrar@kanchiuniv.ac.in
Website: http://www.kanchiuniv.ac.in/

Vice-Chancellor: B. Vaidyanathan
Registrar: V.S. Vishnu Potty Tel: +91(44) 27264279

Faculties
Education (Education; Physical Education); **Engineering and Technology** (Civil Engineering; Computer Engineering; Computer Science; Electrical Engineering; Electronic Engineering; Engineering; Information Technology; Instrument Making; Mechanical Engineering; Structural Architecture; Technology; Telecommunications Engineering); **Health and Life Sciences** (Ayurveda; Biological and Life Sciences; Health Sciences); **Management** (Business and Commerce; Human Resources; Management); **Sanskrit and Languages** (English; Hindi; Sanskrit); **Sciences** (Chemistry; Computer Science; Mathematics; Physics); **Social Science and Humanities** (Arts and Humanities; Cultural Studies; History; Philosophy; Social Sciences)

Further Information: Also campus in Poonamalle, Chennai.

History: Founded 1993. A deemed university.

Governing Bodies: Management Committee

Academic Year: June-July to April-May

Admission Requirements: Pass in XII standard

Fees: (Rupees): 7,500-24,750 per semester

Main Language(s) of Instruction: English. Sanskrit

Degrees and Diplomas: *Bachelor's Degree*; *Bachelor's degree (professional)*; *Postgraduate Diploma*; *Master's Degree*; *Master of Philosophy*; *Doctorate*. Also certificates; M.B.A. and Executive M.B.A.

Student Services: Academic counselling, Cultural centre, Employment services, Social counselling, Sports facilities

Student Residential Facilities: Hostel for c. 1,000 students

Special Facilities: Computing and Web Centre

Libraries: c. 200,000 vols and 100 periodical subscriptions
Last Updated: 21/11/11

SRI DEVARAJ URS UNIVERSITY (SDUU)

Tamaka, Kolar, Karnataka 563 101
Tel: +91(8152) 649-208 +91(8152) 649-209
Fax: +91(8152) 649-208 +91(8152) 243-008
Website: http://www.sduu.ac.in/

Vice Chancellor: S.Chandrashekar Shetty
Registrar: A.V. Moideen Kutty

Courses
Medicine *(Undergraduate)* (Medicine; Surgery); **Medicine** *(Post Graduate)* (Anaesthesiology; Biochemistry; Dermatology; Gynaecology and Obstetrics; Medicine; Microbiology; Ophthalmology; Orthopaedics; Otorhinolaryngology; Paediatrics; Pathology; Pharmacology; Physiology; Radiology; Surgery); **Medicine** *(Post Graduate Diploma)* (Anaesthesiology; Gynaecology and Obstetrics; Medicine; Ophthalmology; Orthopaedics; Paediatrics; Radiology)

History: Founded 1986 as Sri Devaraj Urs Medical College. Acquired present title and deemed university status 2007.

Governing Bodies: Board of Management; Academic Council; Finance Committee; Planning and Monitoring Board

Accrediting Agencies: National Assessment and Accreditation Council (NAAC)

Degrees and Diplomas: *Bachelor's degree (professional)*; *Postgraduate Diploma*; *Master's Degree*

Last Updated: 13/12/11

SRI GURU GRANTH SAHIB WORLD UNIVERSITY

University Campus, Fathegarh Sahib, Punjab 140406
Tel: +91(1763) 232300
EMail: info@sggswu.org
Website: http://sggswu.org

Vice-Chancellor: Jasbir Singh Ahluwalia

Courses

Religious and Civilization Studies (History of Religion; History of Societies); **Science and Technologies** (Biotechnology; Computer Engineering; Computer Science; Food Technology; Instrument Making; Mathematics; Nanotechnology; Natural Sciences; Physical Engineering; Physics; Technology); **Social Sciences** (Management; Mass Communication; Social Sciences)

History: Founded 2008.

Degrees and Diplomas: *Bachelor's Degree*; *Master's Degree*. Also MBA

Student Residential Facilities: Yes

Libraries: Yes
Last Updated: 18/01/12

SRI KRISHNADEVARAYA UNIVERSITY

Sri Venkateswarapuram, Anantapur, Andhra Pradesh 515003
Tel: +91(8554) 255-700
Fax: +91(8554) 255-244
EMail: vc@kanchiuniv.ac.in
Website: http://www.skuniversity.org/

Vice-Chancellor: K. Ramakrishna Reddy (2011-)
Tel: +91(8554) 255231, Fax: +91(8554) 255244
EMail: vicechancellor@skuniversity.org

Registrar: N. Ravindranath
Tel: +91(8554) 255700, Fax: +91(8554) 255804
EMail: registrar@skuniversity.org

Faculties

Languages and Literature (Comparative Literature; English; Indic Languages); **Law** (Law); **Life Sciences** (Biochemistry; Biological and Life Sciences; Biotechnology; Botany; Geography; Microbiology; Pharmacy; Sericulture; Zoology); **Management** (Business and Commerce; Management); **Physical Sciences** (Chemistry; Computer Science; Electronic Engineering; Instrument Making; Mathematics; Physical Education; Physics; Polymer and Plastics Technology; Sports; Statistics; Technology); **Social Sciences** (Adult Education; Continuing Education; Development Studies; Economics; Education; History; Information Sciences; Library Science; Political Sciences; Public Administration; Social Sciences; Social Work; Sociology)

Further Information: Also 109 Affiliated Colleges; A traditional and distance education institution.

History: Founded 1981.

Governing Bodies: Executive Council; Academic Senate

Academic Year: July to June (July-December; January-June)

Admission Requirements: 12th year senior secondary/intermediate examination or recognized foreign equivalent

Fees: (Rupees): 283-332

Main Language(s) of Instruction: English, Telugu

Degrees and Diplomas: *Bachelor's Degree*; *Postgraduate Diploma*; *Master's Degree*; *Master of Philosophy*; *Doctorate*. Also M.B.A.

Student Residential Facilities: Yes

Special Facilities: History Museum

Libraries: Main Library, 103,441 vols; 153 periodical subscriptions
Last Updated: 21/11/11

SRI PADMAVATI WOMEN'S UNIVERSITY

Sri Padmavati Mahila Viswavidyalayam (SPMVV)
District Chittoor, Tirupati, Andhra Pradesh 517502
Tel: +91(877) 228-4538
Fax: +91(877) 224-8416
EMail: vcspmvv@yahoo.com
Website: http://www.spmvv.ac.in

Vice-Chancellor: N. Prabhakara Rao
Tel: +91(877) 2249727, Fax: +91(877) 2289555
EMail: vcsvutpt@yahoo.com; npr_nagineni@hotmail.com

Registrar: E. Manju Vani

Schools

Engineering and Technology (Biotechnology; Computer Engineering; Computer Science; Electrical and Electronic Engineering; Electrical Engineering; Electronic Engineering; Engineering; Industrial Engineering; Information Technology; Technology; Telecommunications Engineering); **Science** (Applied Mathematics; Biochemistry; Biological and Life Sciences; Biotechnology; Botany; Computer Science; Home Economics; Microbiology; Organic Chemistry; Pharmacy; Physics; Sericulture; Zoology); **Social Sciences, Humanities and Management** (Arts and Humanities; Business Administration; Communication Studies; Continuing Education; Education; English; Fine Arts; Indic Languages; Journalism; Literature; Management; Music; Physical Education; Social Sciences; Social Work; Women's Studies)

History: Founded 1983.

Governing Bodies: Executive Council; Academic Senate

Academic Year: June to April (June-November-November-April)

Admission Requirements: 12th year senior secondary/intermediate examination or recognized foreign equivalent

Fees: (Rupees): 4,560-8,650 per term, according to courses

Main Language(s) of Instruction: English

Accrediting Agencies: University Grants Commission and NAAC

Degrees and Diplomas: *Bachelor's Degree*; *Bachelor's degree (professional)*; *Postgraduate Diploma*; *Master's Degree*; *Master of Philosophy*; *Doctorate*

Student Services: Academic counselling, Canteen, Employment services, Health services, Language programs, Nursery care, Social counselling, Sports facilities

Student Residential Facilities: Yes

Special Facilities: Computer Centre

Libraries: 71,786 vols; 146 periodical subscriptions

Publications: Ph.D *(biennially)*; Processing of National, International Seminars *(3 per annum)*

Academic Staff *2010-2011*	MEN	WOMEN	TOTAL
FULL-TIME	82	222	**304**
PART-TIME	15	92	**107**
STAFF WITH DOCTORATE			
FULL-TIME	5	85	**90**
PART-TIME	1	6	**7**

Student Numbers *2010-2011*
All (Foreign Included) — — c. **2,700**

Part-time students, 280. **Distance students**, 1,030.
Last Updated: 21/11/11

SRI RAMACHANDRA UNIVERSITY

1 Ramachandra Nagar, Porur, Chennai, Tamil Nadu 600116
Tel: +91(44) 2476-8423
Fax: +91(44) 2476-5995 +91(44) 2476-7008
EMail: registrarsru@gmail.com
Website: http://www.sriramachandra.edu.in/new_university/index.html

Vice-Chancellor: S. Rangaswami
Tel: +91(44) 2476-8431 EMail: vcsrmc@hotmail.com

Registrar: Thiru.N. Natarajan Tel: +91(44) 2476-5512 Ext.203

International Relations: T.K. Partha Sarathy, Pro-Chancellor
Tel: +91(44) 2476-7770 EMail: pcsrmc@hotmail.com

Colleges

Medical Studies and Research Institute *(Sri Ramachandra)* (Anaesthesiology; Anatomy; Biochemistry; Cardiology; Community Health; Dermatology; Gastroenterology; Gynaecology and Obstetrics; Medicine; Microbiology; Molecular Biology; Nephrology; Neurological Therapy; Neurology; Ophthalmology; Orthopaedics; Otorhinolaryngology; Paediatrics; Pathology; Pharmacology; Physiology; Plastic Surgery; Psychiatry and Mental Health; Radiology; Surgery; Urology; Venereology)

Faculties

Allied Health Sciences (Anaesthesiology; Clinical Psychology; Gastroenterology; Genetics; Health Sciences; Laboratory Techniques; Medical Technology; Neurosciences; Nutrition; Optometry; Radiology; Respiratory Therapy; Secretarial Studies; Speech Therapy and Audiology; Urology); **Biomedical Sciences, Technology and Research** (Biological and Life Sciences; Biomedical Engineering; Biomedicine; Biotechnology; Chemistry; Computer Science; Genetics); **Dental Sciences** (Dental Technology; Dentistry; Oral Pathology; Orthodontics; Periodontics; Radiology; Social and Preventive Medicine; Surgery); **Management Sciences** (Health Administration; Management); **Nursing** (Community Health; Gynaecology and Obstetrics; Nursing; Paediatrics; Psychiatry and Mental Health); **Pharmacy** (Pharmacology; Pharmacy; Safety Engineering); **Physiotherapy** (Cardiology; Neurosciences; Orthopaedics; Physical Therapy; Pneumology)

History: Founded 1985 as part of the Sri Ramachandra Education and Health Trust. An institution with a 'Deemed University' status since 1994.

Governing Bodies: Board of Management, Academic Senate, Finance Committee, Planning and Monitoring Board, Advisory Committee

Academic Year: July to April

Main Language(s) of Instruction: English

International Co-operation: With universities in USA; United Kingdom; Singapore; Australia

Accrediting Agencies: University Grants Commission; Medical Council of India; Dental Council of India; Nursing Council of India; Pharmacy Council of India; All India Coucil for Technical Education; Rehabilitation Council of India; General Medical Council, UK; Ireland Medical Council; Srilankan Medical Council; Association of the Commonwealth Universities,UK; Association of Indian Univerisities; National Assessment and Accreditation (NAAC).

Degrees and Diplomas: *Diploma*; *Bachelor's Degree*; *Bachelor's degree (professional)*; *Postgraduate Diploma*; *Master's Degree*; *Doctorate*. Also Certificate Course; M.B.A.

Student Services: Academic counselling, Canteen, Cultural centre, Foreign student adviser, Health services, Nursery care, Sports facilities

Student Residential Facilities: Yes

Special Facilities: Blood Bank; Clinical Laboratory; Anatomical Museum; Research Centre; Auditoria; C.T Scan; Gamma Camera; Neurology, Pulmonology, Non-invasive and invasive Cardiology Laboratories; Interventional Neuro Radilogy; Critical Care and Emergency Services.

Libraries: Total, 29,158 vols; 451 journals (129 Indian and 322 international); 45,496 back issues.

Academic Staff *2009-2010*	TOTAL
FULL-TIME	600
PART-TIME	c. 220

Student Numbers *2009-2010*	
All (Foreign Included)	c. 4,300

Distance students, 270.
Last Updated: 21/11/11

SRI SAI UNIVERSITY

Palampur, Himachal Pradesh
Tel: +91(92184) 50302
EMail: contact@srisaiuniversity.com
Website: http://srisaiuniversity.com/

Vice-Chancellor: Balram Dogra

Schools

Engineering and Technology (Civil Engineering; Computer Engineering; Computer Networks; Electrical Engineering; Electronic Engineering; Engineering; Information Technology; Mechanical Engineering; Telecommunications Engineering); **Languages and Social Sciences** (Economics; English; Hindi; Social Sciences); **Management and Commerce Studies** (Business and Commerce; Management; Marketing; Tourism)

History: Founded 2011.

Degrees and Diplomas: *Bachelor's Degree*; *Master's Degree*
Last Updated: 17/01/12

SRI SATHYA SAI INSTITUTE OF HIGHER LEARNING (SSSIHL)

Vidyagiri, Anantapur District, Prasanthi Nilayam,
Andhra Pradesh 515 134
Tel: +91(8555) 287-239
Fax: +91(8555) 287-239
EMail: registrar@sssihl.edu.in
Website: http://sssu.edu.in

Vice-Chancellor: Shashidhara Prasad (2010-)
Registrar: Naren Ramji

Campuses

Anantapur *(For Women)* (Biological and Life Sciences; Business and Commerce; Chemistry; Economics; Education; English; Hindi; History; Home Economics; Indic Languages; Mathematics; Philosophy; Physics; Political Sciences; Sanskrit); **Brindavan** *(For Men)* (Biological and Life Sciences; Business and Commerce; Chemistry; Mathematics; Physics); **Prasanthi Nilayam** *(For Men)* (Accountancy; Biological and Life Sciences; Business Administration; Chemistry; Economics; English; Finance; Hindi; History; Management; Mathematics and Computer Science; Physics; Political Sciences; Sanskrit)

Further Information: Also Sri Sathya Sai Institute of Higher Medical Sciences (Hospital).

History: Founded 1981 as Sri Sathya Sai Institute of Higher Learning based on Bhagawan Sri Sathya Sai Baba's Teaching emphasizing character building as much as academic excellence. Acquired present status 2006. Deemed to be University.

Governing Bodies: Institute Trust; Academic Council; Finance Committee

Academic Year: June to March

Admission Requirements: 12th year senior secondary/intermediate examination or recognized foreign equivalent with a minimum of 55% in General English and 60% in aggregate for undergraduate programmes

Fees: None. Scholarships are given to deserving students to meet hostel expenses

Main Language(s) of Instruction: English

Accrediting Agencies: Ministry of Education; University Grants Commission; All India Council for Technical Education; National Assessment and Accreditation Council (NAAC); Association of Indian Universities

Degrees and Diplomas: *Bachelor's Degree*; *Master's Degree*; *Master of Philosophy*; *Doctorate*. Also M.B.A.

Student Services: Academic counselling, Cultural centre, Health services, Language programs, Social counselling, Sports facilities

Student Residential Facilities: Yes

Special Facilities: Planetarium. Museum of Eternal Heritage

Libraries: Central Library, 60,000 vols; Campus libraries, 40,000 to 50,000 vols each; c. 150 periodical subscriptions

Academic Staff *2010-2011*: Total 130
STAFF WITH DOCTORATE: Total 80
Student Numbers *2010-2011*: Total: c. 1,200
Last Updated: 21/11/11

SRI SIDDHARTHA ACADEMY OF HIGHER EDUCATION (SAHE)

Agalakote, B.H. Road, Tumkur, Karnataka 572 107
Tel: +91(816) 227-5516
EMail: info@sahe.in
Website: http://www.sahe.in/

Vice Chancellor: K. A. Krishnamurthy

Registrar: M.Z. Kurian

Colleges

Dentistry (Dental Technology; Dentistry; Orthodontics; Periodontics; Surgery); **Engineering** (Biotechnology; Civil Engineering; Computer Engineering; Computer Graphics; Computer Science; Electrical Engineering; Electronic Engineering; Engineering; Industrial Engineering; Information Sciences; Mechanical Engineering; Medical Technology; Power Engineering; Telecommunications Engineering; Thermal Engineering); **Medicine** (Anaesthesiology; Anatomy; Medicine; Microbiology; Ophthalmology; Paediatrics; Pathology; Physiology; Radiology; Surgery)

History: Founded 2008. A 'Deemed University".

Governing Bodies: Board of Management; Academic Council; Planning and Monitoring Board; Finance Committee; Advisory Committee; Fee Fixation Committee

Fees: (Indian Rupees): Non-Karnataka Candidates, 2,000 per annum for undergraduate programmes and 3,000 per annum for postgraduate programmes; NRI / Foreign, 5,000 per annum.

Degrees and Diplomas: *Bachelor's degree (professional)*; *Postgraduate Diploma*; *Master's Degree*

Last Updated: 13/12/11

SRI VENKATESWARA INSTITUTE OF MEDICAL SCIENCES (SVIMS UNIVERSITY)

Alipiri Road, Chittoor District, Tirupati, Andhra Pradesh 517 507
Tel: +91(877) 2287152 +91(877) 2286131
Fax: +91(877) 2286803
EMail: svimshosp@yahoo.com; bvengamma@yahoo.com
Website: http://svimstpt.ap.nic.in

Director: B. Vengamma EMail: bvengamma@yahoo.com

Registrar: P.V. Ramasubba Reddy

Colleges

Nursing (Nursing); **Physiotherapy** (Physical Therapy)

Departments

Diagnostic (Biochemistry; Medical Technology; Microbiology; Pathology; Radiology); **Interdisciplinary Studies** (Biotechnology; Computer Science); **Medicine** (Anaesthesiology; Anatomy; Cardiology; Endocrinology; Gastroenterology; Haematology; Medicine; Nephrology; Neurology; Oncology; Physiology; Treatment Techniques; Urology); **Surgery** (Gastroenterology; Neurological Therapy; Oncology; Plastic Surgery; Surgery)

History: Founded in 1986. Functional since 1992. Acquired University status 1995.

Governing Bodies: Governing Council; Executive Board; Academic Senate; Finance Committee; Board of Studies

Academic Year: August to July

Admission Requirements: 12th year senior secondary/intermediate or equivalent.

Fees: (Rupees): Paramedical Technical courses, 4,200-12,800 per annum; B.Sc. 13,000-33,000 per annum; M.Sc.and DM/M.Ch. 50,000 per annum; MPT 100,000

Main Language(s) of Instruction: English

Accrediting Agencies: Medical Council of India (MCI) University Grants Commission (UGC), Indian Nursing Council (INC); Indian Association of Physiotherapists (IAP); Department of Biotechnology

Degrees and Diplomas: *Bachelor's Degree*; *Bachelor's degree (professional)*; *Postgraduate Diploma*; *Master's Degree*. Certificate Courses; Short Term Training Programmes; Post Doctoral Certificate Courses.

Student Services: Academic counselling, Canteen, Cultural centre, Employment services, Health services, Sports facilities

Student Residential Facilities: Yes

Special Facilities: Laboratories

Libraries: Yes

Last Updated: 21/11/11

SRI VENKATESWARA UNIVERSITY

District Chittoor, Tirupati, Andhra Pradesh 517502
Tel: +91(877) 2249727
Fax: +91(877) 2289555
Website: http://www.svuniversity.in

Vice-Chancellor: M.G. Gopal

Registrar: J. Pratap Reddy
Tel: +91(877) 2289414, Fax: +91(877) 2289544

Centres

Post-Graduate Studies (Business Administration; Business and Commerce; Computer Science; Economics; Mathematics; Physics; Zoology)

Colleges

Arts (Adult Education; Ancient Civilizations; Archaeology; Continuing Education; Demography and Population; Development Studies; Econometrics; Economics; Education; English; Fine Arts; Hindi; History; Human Rights; Indic Languages; Information Sciences; Journalism; Law; Library Science; Linguistics; Mass Communication; Modern Languages; Pacific Area Studies; Peace and Disarmament; Philosophy; Physical Education; Political Sciences; Public Administration; Sanskrit; Sociology; Southeast Asian Studies; Urdu); **Commerce, Management and Computer Science** (Business and Commerce; Computer Science; Management); **Engineering** (Chemical Engineering; Civil Engineering; Computer Engineering; Computer Science; Electrical and Electronic Engineering; Electrical Engineering; Electronic Engineering; Engineering; Mechanical Engineering; Telecommunications Engineering); **Sciences** (Anthropology; Aquaculture; Biochemistry; Biotechnology; Botany; Chemistry; Environmental Studies; Fishery; Geography; Geology; Home Economics; Mathematics; Physics; Psychology; Statistics; Virology; Zoology)

Further Information: Also 62 Affiliated and Oriental Colleges

History: Founded 1954.

Admission Requirements: 12th year senior secondary/intermediate examination or recognized foreign equivalent

Fees: (Rupees): Postgraduate programmes, 1,200-4,125 per semester (except M.B.A., 9,433-10,508 per semester); M. Phil. and PhD programmes, 1,325-3,336 per term.

Main Language(s) of Instruction: Telugu, English

International Co-operation: National Assessment and Accreditation Council (NAAC).

Degrees and Diplomas: *Diploma*; *Postgraduate Diploma*; *Master of Philosophy*; *Doctorate*. Also Certificate courses; M.B.A.

Student Services: Cultural centre, Health services, Sports facilities

Student Residential Facilities: Men and Women's hostels.

Special Facilities: Computer Centre

Libraries: 352,330 vols

Publications: Oriental Journal

Press or Publishing House: University Press

Academic Staff *2010-2011*: Total: c. 400

Student Numbers *2010-2011*: Total: c. 5,000

Last Updated: 21/11/11

SRI VENKATESWARA VEDIC UNIVERSITY

Alipiri-Chandragiri Bypass Road, Tirupati, Andhra Pradesh
Tel: +91(877) 222-2586
Fax: +91(877) 222-2587
EMail: vcvedicuniversity@yahoo.com
Website: http://www.svvedicuniversity.org/

Vice Chancellor: Sannidhanam Sudarsana Sarma

Registrar: Manojkumar Mishra
Tel: +91(877) 226-4404, Fax: +91(877) 226-4407

Faculties

Agama Adhyayana (Esoteric Practices); **Modern Subjects** (Computer Science; English); **Paurohitya Adhyayana** (Esoteric Practices); **Research and Publication**; **Veda Adhyayana** (Esoteric Practices); **Vedabhashya** (Esoteric Practices; Yoga)

History: Founded 2006.

Degrees and Diplomas: Sastri Course (undergraduate programme), 3 yrs; Acharya Course (Postgraduate programme), 2 yrs.

Last Updated: 02/01/12

SRI VENKATESWARA VETERINARY UNIVERSITY (SVVU)

Administrative Office, Dr. Y.S. R. Bhawan, Chittoor District, Tirupati, Andhra Pradesh 517 502
Tel: +91(877) 224-8006 +91(877) 224-8068
Fax: +91(877) 224-9222
Website: http://svvu.edu.in/

Vice Chancellor: V. Prabhakar Rao (2010-)
Tel: +91(877) 224-8986, Fax: +91(877) 224-9222
EMail: prabhakarvrao@yahoo.com

Registrar: P. Sudhakara Reddy
Tel: +91(877) 224-8894, Fax: +91(877) 224-8881
EMail: registrarsvvutpt@yahoo.in

Colleges

Animal Husbandry Polytechnic *(Venkataramana Gudem, Dist: West Godavari)* (Animal Husbandry); **Animal Husbandry Polytechnic** *(Mahaboob Nagar, Dist: Mahaboobnagar)* (Animal Husbandry); **Animal Husbandry Polytechnic** *(Madakasira, Dist: Anantpur)* (Animal Husbandry); **Animal Husbandry Polytechnic** *(Ramachandra Puram, Dist: East Godavari)* (Animal Husbandry); **Animal Husbandry Polytechnic** *(Garividi, Dist: Vizianagaram)* (Animal Husbandry); **Animal Husbandry Polytechnic** *(Mamnoor, Dist: Warangal)* (Animal Husbandry); **Animal Husbandry Polytechnic** *(Rapur, Dist: Nellore)* (Animal Husbandry); **Animal Husbandry Polytechnic** *(Karimnagar, Dist: Karimnagar)* (Animal Husbandry); **Animal Husbandry Polytechnic** *(Siddipet, Dist: Medak)* (Animal Husbandry); **Animal Husbandry Polytechnic** *(Palamner, Dist: Chittoor)* (Animal Husbandry); **Dairy Technology** *(Tirupati)* (Dairy; Microbiology; Technology); **Fisheries Polytechnic** *(Bhavadevarapalli, Avanigadda, Dist: Krishna)* (Fishery); **Fishery Science** *(Muthukur)* (Aquaculture; Engineering; Fishery); **Veterinary Science** *(Proddutur)* (Animal Husbandry; Biochemistry; Meat and Poultry; Microbiology; Parasitology; Pathology; Pharmacology; Physiology; Veterinary Science); **Veterinary Science** *(Tirupati)* (Animal Husbandry; Pathology; Veterinary Science); **Veterinary Science** *(Rajendranagar)* (Anatomy; Animal Husbandry; Biochemistry; Epidemiology; Genetics; Meat and Poultry; Medicine; Microbiology; Pharmacology; Physiology; Public Health; Veterinary Science); **Veterinary Science** *(NTR - Gannavaram)* (Animal Husbandry; Microbiology; Pathology; Pharmacology; Radiology; Surgery; Toxicology; Veterinary Science); **Veterinary Science** *(Korutla)* (Animal Husbandry; Genetics; Gynaecology and Obstetrics; Meat and Poultry; Parasitology; Veterinary Science)

Programmes

Dairy Technology *(Kamareddy)* (Agricultural Education; Agricultural Engineering; Chemistry; Dairy; Engineering; Microbiology; Technology)

Further Information: Also Veterinary Hospital.

History: Founded 2005.

Governing Bodies: Board of Management; Academic Council; Board of Faculties; Finance Committee; Planning Board

Fees: (Indian Rupees): Undergraduate tuition fee, 400-4,360 per semester.

Degrees and Diplomas: *Diploma*; *Bachelor's Degree*; *Bachelor's degree (professional)*; *Master's Degree*; *Doctorate*

Student Services: Cultural centre, Sports facilities
Last Updated: 02/01/12

SRM UNIVERSITY

SRM Nagar, Kancheepuram District, Kattankulatthur, Tamil Nadu 603203
Tel: +91(44) 2745 5715 +91(44) 2745 3433
Fax: +94(44) 2745 3622
EMail: registrar@srmuniv.ac.in
Website: http://www.srmuniv.ac.in/

Vice-Chancellor: M. Ponnavaikko EMail: vc@srmuniv.ac.in

Registrar: N. Sethuraman

Centres

Nanotechnology (Nanotechnology); **Total Quality Management** *(TQM)* (Safety Engineering)

Colleges

Humanities (Arts and Humanities; Business and Commerce; Communication Arts; Cooking and Catering; Education; English; Film; Fine Arts; Hotel and Restaurant; Indic Languages; Journalism; Mass Communication; Media Studies; Modern Languages; Visual Arts); **Medicine** (Anaesthesiology; Anatomy; Animal Husbandry; Biochemistry; Cardiology; Communication Studies; Dental Technology; Dentistry; Dermatology; Forensic Medicine and Dentistry; Gynaecology and Obstetrics; Medicine; Microbiology; Nephrology; Neurological Therapy; Neurology; Nursing; Occupational Therapy; Oral Pathology; Orthodontics; Orthopaedics; Osteopathy; Paediatrics; Pathology; Periodontics; Pharmacology; Pharmacy; Physical Therapy; Physiology; Plastic Surgery; Pneumology; Psychiatry and Mental Health; Public Health; Radiology; Surgery; Urology); **Sciences** (Biological and Life Sciences; Biotechnology; Computer Science; Mathematics)

Schools

Architecture and Interior Design (Architecture; Interior Design); **Basic Sciences** (Chemistry; Mathematics; Physics); **Bioengineering** (Bioengineering; Biomedical Engineering; Biotechnology; Computer Science; Food Technology; Genetics); **Chemical and Material Technology** (Chemical Engineering; Materials Engineering; Nanotechnology; Nuclear Engineering); **Civil Engineering** (Civil Engineering); **Computing** (Computer Engineering; Computer Science; Information Technology); **Electrical and Electronics Engineering** (Automation and Control Engineering; Electrical and Electronic Engineering; Electronic Engineering; Measurement and Precision Engineering; Telecommunications Engineering); **Languages** (English; French; German; Japanese; Korean; Modern Languages); **Management** (Business Administration; Finance; Health Administration; Hotel and Restaurant; Human Resources; Management; Marketing; Operations Research; Pharmacy; Retailing and Wholesaling); **Mechanical Engineering** (Aeronautical and Aerospace Engineering; Automotive Engineering; Electronic Engineering; Mechanical Engineering)

Further Information: Also Ramapuram, Modi Nagar, Trichy Campuses.

History: Created in 1984 as Valliammai Polytechnic. Formerly known as SRM Institute of Science and Technology

Governing Bodies: Academic Council; Board of Studies; University Advisory Board.

Accrediting Agencies: National Assessment and Accreditation Council (NAAC); Engineering Accreditation Commission of ABET (USA)

Degrees and Diplomas: *Diploma*; *Bachelor's Degree*; *Bachelor's degree (professional)*; *Postgraduate Diploma*; *Master's Degree*; *Master of Philosophy*; *Doctorate.* Also Certificate Courses; M.B.A.

Academic Staff *2010-2011*: Total: c. 1,500
Student Numbers *2010-2011*: Total: c. 20,000
Last Updated: 21/11/11

ST PETER'S UNIVERSITY

College Road, Avadi, Chennai, Tamil Nadu 600054
Tel: +91(44) 2655-8080 +91(44) 2655-8085
EMail: spiher@stpetersuniversity.org
Website: http://www.stpetersuniversity.org

Vice-Chancellor: K. Balagurunathan

Registrar: M. Shanmugham

Departments

Business Administration (Business Administration; Management); **Computer Application** (Computer Engineering; Computer Science; Information Technology); **Engineering** (Aeronautical and Aerospace Engineering; Automotive Engineering; Biomedical Engineering; Biotechnology; Chemical Engineering; Civil Engineering; Computer Science; Electrical Engineering; Electronic Engineering; Engineering; Information Technology; Mechanical Engineering; Production Engineering; Telecommunications Engineering); **Science and Humanities** (Arts and Humanities; Chemistry; English; Mathematics; Natural Sciences; Physics)

Further Information: A traditional and Distance Education Institution.

History: Founded 1956 as St Peter's Institute of Higher Education and Research. Acquired present status 2008. A Deemed-to-be University.

Accrediting Agencies: University Grants Commission (UGC)

Degrees and Diplomas: *Bachelor's Degree; Master's Degree.* Also M.B.A.

Student Services: Academic counselling, Canteen, Sports facilities

Student Residential Facilities: Separate hostels for boys and girls

Libraries: Yes

Last Updated: 21/11/11

SUMANDEEP VIDYAPEETH UNIVERSITY

At and Po Pipariya, Ta. Waghodia, Vadodara, Gujarat 391760
Tel: +91(2668) 245262 +91(2668) 245264
Fax: +91(2668) 245292
EMail: info@sumandeepuniversity.co.in
Website: http://www.sumandeepuniversity.co.in

Chancellor: Jayshree Mehta

Registrar: N. N. Shah

Colleges
Dentistry *(K. M. Shah - and Hospital)* (Dental Technology; Dentistry; Microbiology; Oral Pathology; Orthodontics; Periodontics; Radiology; Social and Preventive Medicine; Surgery); **Nursing** *(Sumandeep)* (Community Health; Gynaecology and Obstetrics; Nursing; Paediatrics; Psychiatry and Mental Health; Surgery); **Physiotherapy** *(K. J. Pandya)* (Physical Therapy)

Departments
Management (Health Administration; Management); **Pharmacy** (Management; Pharmacology; Pharmacy; Safety Engineering; Technology)

Institutes
Medical Studies and Research Centre *(S.B.K.S.)* (Anaesthesiology; Anatomy; Biochemistry; Dermatology; Forensic Medicine and Dentistry; Gynaecology and Obstetrics; Laboratory Techniques; Medicine; Microbiology; Ophthalmology; Orthopaedics; Otorhinolaryngology; Paediatrics; Pathology; Pharmacology; Physiology; Psychiatry and Mental Health; Radiology; Respiratory Therapy; Social and Preventive Medicine; Surgery; Venereology)

History: A deemed university.

Governing Bodies: Board of Management; Academic Council; Board of Studies

Degrees and Diplomas: *Diploma; Bachelor's Degree; Postgraduate Diploma; Master's Degree; Doctorate.* Also M.B.A.

Last Updated: 22/11/11

SURESH GYAN VIHAR UNIVERSITY (SGVU)

Mahal, Jagatpura, Jaipur, Rajasthan
Tel: +91(141) 645-0389 +91(141) 645-0390
Fax: +91(141) 279-6255
EMail: registrar@gyanvihar.org; admissions@gyanvihar.org
Website: http://www.gyanvihar.org/

Vice Chancellor: B.V. Somasekhar

Schools
Business Management (Business Administration; Business Computing; Commercial Law; Economics; Finance; Human Resources; Management; Marketing); **Engineering and Technology** (Civil Engineering; Computer Engineering; Computer Science; Electrical Engineering; Electronic Engineering; Engineering; Information Technology; Mechanical Engineering; Technology; Telecommunications Engineering); **Hotel Management** (Finance; Food Technology; Hotel Management; Human Resources; Law; Management; Marketing; Real Estate; Sales Techniques); **Pharmacy** (Biotechnology; Chemistry; Pharmacology; Pharmacy; Safety Engineering); **Sciences** (Biochemistry; Biological and Life Sciences; Biotechnology; Microbiology; Natural Sciences); **Social Science** (Archaeology; Museum Studies; Social Sciences; Social Work)

History: Founded 2008.

Governing Bodies: Board of Management; Academic Council

Accrediting Agencies: All India Council for Technical Education (AICTE); National Board of Accreditation (NBA)

Degrees and Diplomas: *Diploma; Bachelor's Degree; Bachelor's degree (professional); Postgraduate Diploma; Master's Degree; Doctorate.* Also Dual Degrees (Bachelor+Master's degrees); M.B.A.

Last Updated: 21/12/11

SWAMI KESHWANAND RAJASTHAN AGRICULTURAL UNIVERSITY (SKRAU)

PO Box No 19, Bikaner, Rajasthan 334006
Tel: +91(151) 225-1083
Fax: +91(151) 225-1083
EMail: cimca@raubikaner.org
Website: http://www.raubikaner.org

Vice-Chancellor: A.K. Dahama (2011-)
Tel: +91(151) 225-0488 +91(151) 225-0443,
Fax: +91(151) 225-0336 EMail: vcrau@raubikaner.org

Registrar: Ramdev Goyal
Tel: +91(151) 225-0025, Fax: +91(151) 225-0025
EMail: reg@raubikaner.org

Centres
Academic Staff cum Distance Education *(ASC-DEC)*

Colleges
Agriculture *(Jobner)* (Agricultural Business; Agricultural Economics; Agriculture; Agronomy; Animal Husbandry; Biochemistry; Chemistry; Education; Entomology; Genetics; Horticulture; Physiology; Plant Pathology; Soil Science; Zoology); **Agriculture** *(Lalsot)* (Agriculture); **Agriculture** *(COA)* (Agricultural Economics; Agriculture; Agronomy; Biotechnology; Education; Entomology; Genetics; Horticulture; Plant Pathology; Soil Science); **Home Science** *(CHS)* (Clothing and Sewing; Communication Studies; Family Studies; Food Science; Home Economics; Nutrition; Textile Technology)

Institutes
Agribusiness Management *(IABM)* (Agricultural Business; Agricultural Equipment; Agricultural Management; Animal Husbandry; Food Technology; Horticulture; Irrigation)

Further Information: Also 8 Constituent Colleges. A traditional and distance education institution.

History: Founded 1987, an autonomous body receiving financial grants from State, Central Government and ICAR.

Governing Bodies: Board of Management, comprising the Vice-Chancellor as ex-officio chairman, 12 nominated members, and 5 ex-officio members

Academic Year: July to June

Admission Requirements: 12th year senior secondary/intermediate examination or recognized foreign equivalent

Fees: (Rupees): 200-1,600 per annum

Main Language(s) of Instruction: English

Degrees and Diplomas: *Diploma; Bachelor's Degree; Master's Degree; Doctorate (PhD).* Also Bachelor's degree honours, 4 yrs.

Student Residential Facilities: Yes

Libraries: Central Library, 10,152 vols

Publications: Apna Patra *(monthly)*; Research Journal *(biannually)*

Press or Publishing House: University Communication Centre

Last Updated: 18/07/11

SWAMI RAMANAND TEERTH MARATHWADA UNIVERSITY (SRTMUN)

Dnyanteerth Vishnupuri, Nanded, Maharashtra 431 606
Tel: +91(2462) 229-242 +91(2462) 229-243
Fax: +91(2462) 229-245
EMail: provc@srtmun.ac.in
Website: http://www.srtmun.org

Vice-Chancellor: S. B. Nimse Tel: +91(2462) 299-282

Registrar: P.D. Jadhav
Tel: +91(2462) 229-246, Fax: +91(2462) 259-383
EMail: registrar@srtmun.ac.in

Centres

Latur *(Sub-centre)* (Banking; Business Administration; Computer Science; Economics; Finance; Human Resources; Information Technology; Management; Marketing; Social Work)

Schools

Chemical Sciences (Analytical Chemistry; Chemistry; Inorganic Chemistry; Organic Chemistry; Physical Chemistry; Polymer and Plastics Technology); **Commerce and Management Sciences** (Business Administration; Business and Commerce; Finance; Human Resources; Management; Marketing); **Computational Sciences** (Computer Networks; Computer Science); **Earth Sciences** (Environmental Studies; Geography; Geology; Geophysics); **Educational Sciences** (Educational Sciences); **Fine and Performing Arts** (Fine Arts; Performing Arts); **Languages and Literature** (English; Indic Languages; Literature); **Life Sciences** (Biological and Life Sciences; Biotechnology; Botany; Microbiology; Zoology); **Mathematical Sciences** (Mathematics; Statistics); **Media Studies** (Media Studies); **Pharmacy** (Pharmacology; Pharmacy; Safety Engineering); **Physical Sciences** (Applied Physics; Physics); **Social Sciences** (Economics; Social Sciences; Sociology)

Further Information: A traditional and distance education institution.

History: Founded 1994.

Governing Bodies: Senate; Academic Council; Management Council; Boards of Studies

Academic Year: June to May

Fees: (Rupees): 4,000-25,000 per annum

Main Language(s) of Instruction: English

Accrediting Agencies: National Assessment and Accreditation Committee (NAAC)

Degrees and Diplomas: *Diploma*; *Bachelor's Degree*; *Master's Degree*; *Master of Philosophy*; *Doctorate*. Also certificate courses and M.B.A.

Student Services: Canteen, Handicapped facilities, Sports facilities

Student Residential Facilities: 125 rooms for male students; 125 rooms for female students

Libraries: c. 36,000; 204 periodical subscriptions; c. 2,000 e-journals

Last Updated: 22/11/11

SWAMI VIVEKANAND SUBHARTI UNIVERSITY

Subhartipuram, NH-58, Delhi-Haridwar Bye Pass Road,
Meerut 250 005
Tel: +91(121) 300-1058
Fax: +91(121) 243-9067
EMail: subharti.uni@gmail.com
Website: http://www.subharti.org/

Vice Chancellor: Bhagirath Singh Rathore

Colleges

Computer Application (Computer Science); **Dentistry** (Dental Technology; Dentistry); **Engineering** (Biotechnology; Engineering; Environmental Engineering; Industrial Engineering; Nanotechnology; Safety Engineering); **Higher Education** (Education; Higher Education; Information Sciences; Library Science); **Journalism and Mass Communication** (Journalism; Mass Communication); **Medicine** (Anatomy; Biochemistry; Health Administration; Medicine; Microbiology; Pharmacology; Physiology); **Nursing** (Midwifery; Nursing); **Pharmacy** (Biotechnology; Pharmacy); **Physiotherapy** (Physical Therapy)

Institutes

Fine Arts and Fashion Design (Fashion Design; Fine Arts; Painting and Drawing; Sculpture; Textile Design); **Hotel Management** (Hotel Management); **Law** (Human Rights; Labour Law; Law); **Management and Information Technology** (Business Administration; Business and Commerce; Information Technology; Management; Protective Services); **Naturopathy and Yogic Sciences** (Alternative Medicine; Yoga)

Further Information: Also Chhatrapati Shivaji Subharti Hospital (800 beds). A traditional and distance education college.

History: Founded 2008.

Governing Bodies: Academic Council

Fees: (Indian Rupees): Undergraduate fee, 2,000-182,000 per annum; Graduate fee, 25,000-900,000 per annum.

Accrediting Agencies: University Grants Commission (U.G.C.)

Degrees and Diplomas: *Diploma*; *Bachelor's Degree*; *Bachelor's degree (professional)*; *Postgraduate Diploma*; *Master's Degree*; *Master of Philosophy*; *Doctorate*. Also Certificates; M.B.A.

Last Updated: 02/01/12

SWAMI VIVEKANANDA YOGA ANUSANDHANA SAMSTHANA (SVYASA)

19, Eknath Bhavan, Gavipuram Circle, Kempegowda Nagar,
Bangalore, Karnataka 560 019
Tel: +91(80) 26608645
Fax: +91(80) 26612669
EMail: info@svyasa.org
Website: http://www.svyasa.org/

Vice-Chancellor: H. R. Nagendra (2002-) EMail: hrn@vyasa.org

Registrar: N.K Manjunath EMail: nkmsharma@gmail.com

International Relations: N. V. Raghuram, International Coordinator EMail: nv.raghuran@gmail.com

Divisions

Yoga and Humanities (Anthropology; Fine Arts; History; Linguistics; Literature; Social Sciences; Sociology); **Yoga and Life Sciences** (Agriculture; Biochemistry; Biological and Life Sciences; Biology; Biomedicine; Biophysics; Cardiology; Dairy; Diabetology; Esoteric Practices; Forestry; Gastroenterology; Gynaecology and Obstetrics; Health Sciences; Horticulture; Immunology; Medicine; Microbiology; Molecular Biology; Natural Sciences; Neurosciences; Oncology; Physiology; Psychology; Rheumatology; Soil Science; Urology; Virology; Water Management; Wildlife; Yoga); **Yoga and Management Studies** (Education; Management; Yoga); **Yoga and Physical Sciences** (Engineering; Mathematics; Physics; Yoga); **Yoga and Spirituality** (Ayurveda; Comparative Religion; Sanskrit; Yoga)

History: Founded in 1986 as Vivekananda Yoga Cikitsa Tatha Anusandhana Samiti. Acquired current status and title 2002.

Governing Bodies: Board of Management; Academic Council

Academic Year: August to May

Admission Requirements: Undergraduate: Secondary School Certificate; Master's degree: Bachelor's degree or equivalent; PhD: Master's degree or equivalent; MD: Medical degree

Fees: (Rupees): Indian nationals, 73,500-155,000; foreign students, US Dollars: 6,120-23,000, all prices approximate, per annum

Main Language(s) of Instruction: English

Accrediting Agencies: National Assessment and Accreditation Council

Degrees and Diplomas: *Diploma*; *Bachelor's Degree*; *Postgraduate Diploma*; *Master's Degree*; *Master of Philosophy*; *Doctorate*. Also Short Term courses

Student Services: Academic counselling, Canteen, Cultural centre, Employment services, Foreign student adviser, Foreign Studies Centre, Handicapped facilities, Health services, Language programs, Nursery care, Social counselling, Sports facilities

Student Residential Facilities: Men's and women's hostels, places for c. 500 students

Special Facilities: Film Studio; Exhibition Hall; Auditorium; Residential Yoga Therapy Health Home

Libraries: c. 15,010 vols; 2,397 Electronic periodicals and 38 Journals/Magazines.

Publications: IJOY, International journal of Yoga; Yoga Sudha, Journal of Yoga *(monthly)*

Academic Staff *2009-2010*	MEN	WOMEN	TOTAL
FULL-TIME	26	11	37
PART-TIME	24	2	26
STAFF WITH DOCTORATE			
FULL-TIME	12	6	18
PART-TIME	16	2	18
Student Numbers *2009-2010*			
All (Foreign Included)	303	295	598
FOREIGN ONLY	41	38	79

Last Updated: 22/11/11

SYMBIOSIS INTERNATIONAL UNIVERSITY

Gram-Lavale, Tal-Mulshi, Pune, Maharashtra 412115
Tel: +91(20) 3911-6200 +91(20) 3911-6202 +91(20) 3911-6208
Fax: +91(20) 3911-6206
EMail: registrar@siu.edu.in; dr_vidya@symbiosis.ac.in
Website: http://www.siu.edu.in

Vice Chancellor: Bhushan Patwardhan
Tel: +91(20) 39116202, Fax: +91(20) 39116206
EMail: vc@siu.edu.in

Registrar: Madhu Sharma
Tel: +91(20) 39116205, Fax: +91(20) 39116206
EMail: registrar@siu.edu.in

International Relations: Vidya Yeravdekar, Principal Director,
Head of Centre for International Education
EMail: dr_vidya@symbiosis.ac.in

Faculties

Computer Studies (Computer Science; Information Technology);
Engineering (Engineering; Technology); **Health Sciences** (Bio-
medicine; Health Sciences; Nursing); **Humanities and Social
Sciences** (Arts and Humanities; Economic History; English; Social
Sciences); **Law** (Commercial Law; Human Rights; Law; Taxation);
Management (Business Administration; Human Resources; Inter-
national Business; Management); **Media, Communication and
Design** (Design; Mass Communication; Media Studies)

Further Information: Constituent institutes: Symbiosis Society's
Law College (SSLC); Symbiosis Institute of Business Management
(SIBM); Symbiosis Institute of Computer Studies and Research
(SICSR). Pune, Bengaluru, Nashik, NOIDA campuses.

History: Founded 1971 as a Cultural and Educational Centre.
Acquired present status and title 2006. A deemed university.

Governing Bodies: Academic Council; Board of Management;
Board of Studies

International Co-operation: With institutions in Germany, USA,
UAE, Malaysia, Australia

Degrees and Diplomas: *Diploma*; *Bachelor's Degree*; *Bachelor's
degree (professional)*; *Postgraduate Diploma*; *Master's Degree*.
Also certificate; advanced certificate; M.B.A. and executive M.B.A.

Student Services: Health services, Sports facilities

Student Residential Facilities: Separate hostels for boys and girls

Special Facilities: Computer Laboratory; Auditorium; Afro-Asian
Cultural Museum

Libraries: c. 200,000 vols

Academic Staff 2008-2009	TOTAL
FULL-TIME	166
PART-TIME	60
STAFF WITH DOCTORATE	
FULL-TIME	23
Student Numbers 2008-2009	
All (Foreign Included)	11,945

Last Updated: 22/11/11

T. A. PAI MANAGEMENT INSTITUTE (TAPMI)

Manipal, Karnataka 576 104
Tel: +91(820) 270-1000
Fax: +91(820) 257-0699
EMail: tapmi@tapmi.edu.in
Website: http://www.tapmi.edu.in/

Director: Vasudev Rao A. S.
Tel: +91(820) 270-1002 EMail: vasudevrao@tapmi.edu.in

Programmes

E-Governance (Management); **European Studies and Management** (European Studies; Management); **Management** (Management); **Management - Healthcare** (Health Administration;
Management)

History: Founded 1984.

Fees: (Indian Rupees): c. 400,000 per annum

International Co-operation: With institutions in Thailand, USA and
Germany

Accrediting Agencies: National Board of Accreditation (NBA); All
India Council for Technical Education (AICTE)

Degrees and Diplomas: *Postgraduate Diploma*; *Master's Degree*

Student Residential Facilities: Hostel

Libraries: c. 32,000 vols; 325 periodical subscriptions

Last Updated: 25/01/12

TAMIL NADU AGRICULTURAL UNIVERSITY (TNAU)

Coimbatore, Tamil Nadu 641003
Tel: +91(422) 6611210
Fax: +91(422) 6611410
EMail: deanagri@tnau.ac.in
Website: http://www.tnau.ac.in

Vice-Chancellor: P. Murugesa Boopathi
Tel: +91(422) 6611251 EMail: vc@tnau.ac.in

Registrar: P. Subbian
Tel: +91(422) 6611200 EMail: registrar@tnau.ac.in

Colleges

Agricultural Engineering and Research Institute *(Coimbatore)*
(Agricultural Engineering; Agricultural Equipment; Energy Engi-
neering; Environmental Engineering; Food Technology; Harvest
Technology; Information Technology; Machine Building; Physics;
Power Engineering; Soil Conservation; Water Management); **Agri-
cultural Engineering and Research Institute, Kumulur** *(Trichy)*
(Agricultural Engineering; Agricultural Equipment; Agriculture;
Energy Engineering; Soil Conservation; Water Management);
Agriculture and Research Institute *(Madurai)* (Agricultural Eco-
nomics; Agricultural Engineering; Agriculture; Agronomy; Animal
Husbandry; Crop Production; Entomology; Environmental Studies;
Genetics; Horticulture; Microbiology; Plant and Crop Protection;
Plant Pathology; Soil Science); **Agriculture and Research Insti-
tute** *(Killikulam)* (Agricultural Economics; Agriculture; Agronomy;
Biochemistry; Biotechnology; Computer Science; Crop Production;
Entomology; Food Science; Genetics; Mathematics; Nutrition; Plant
and Crop Protection; Plant Pathology; Social Sciences; Soil Sci-
ence); **Agriculture and Research Institute** *(Coimbatore)* (Agricultural Business; Agriculture; Biotechnology; Computer Science;
Information Technology); **Anbil Dharmalingam Agricultural Studies and Research Institute** *(Trichy)* (Agriculture; Crop Production;
Social Sciences); **Forestry and Research Institute** *(Mettupalayam)* (Forest Biology; Forest Products; Forestry; Wood Technology); **Home Science Studies and Research Institute** *(Madurai)*
(Development Studies; Family Studies; Food Science; Food Tech-
nology; Home Economics; Human Resources; Nutrition; Psychol-
ogy; Rural Studies; Textile Technology); **Horticulture and
Research Institute** *(Coimbatore)* (Crop Production; Floriculture;
Fruit Production; Horticulture; Vegetable Production); **Horticulture
and Research Institute** *(Periyakulam)* (Computer Science; Crop
Production; Economics; Floriculture; Fruit Production; Horticulture;
Library Science; Physical Education; Social Sciences; Soil Science;
Vegetable Production)

Schools

Post Graduate Studies *(Coimbatore)* (Agricultural Economics;
Agricultural Engineering; Agriculture; Agronomy; Biochemistry;
Biotechnology; Business Administration; Chemistry; Crop Produc-
tion; Energy Engineering; Entomology; Environmental Studies;
Floriculture; Food Science; Forestry; Fruit Production; Genetics;
Meteorology; Microbiology; Nutrition; Physiology; Plant and Crop
Protection; Power Engineering; Sociology; Soil Conservation; Soil
Science; Vegetable Production; Water Management)

Further Information: Also 4 affiliated colleges: Adhiparasakthi
Agricultural college, Kalavai, Vellore District; Vanavarayar Agricultural College, Pollachi; Thanthai Rover Institute of Agriculture and
Rural Development, Perambalur; College of Agricultural Technology, Kullapuram, Theni.

History: Founded 1971.

Governing Bodies: Board of Management; Academic Council;
Board of Studies; Research Council; Extension Education Council

Academic Year: July to April

Fees: (Rupees): 6,000 per semester for regular UG Courses;
Technology courses, 31,000

Main Language(s) of Instruction: English

Accrediting Agencies: Ministry of Human Resource Development

Degrees and Diplomas: *Bachelor's Degree*; *Bachelor's degree (professional)*; *Master's Degree*; *Doctorate*

Libraries: 170,000 vols; 1,500 (online) and 250 (printed) periodical subscriptions

Last Updated: 22/11/11

TAMIL NADU DOCTOR AMBEDKAR LAW UNIVERSITY

Poompozhil, 5, Dr. D.G.S. Dinakaran Salai, Chennai, Tamil Nadu 600 028
Tel: +91(44) 2464-1212
Fax: +91(44) 2495-7414
Website: http://www.tndalu.org

Vice-Chancellor: V. Vijayakumar (2010-)
Tel: +91(44) 24611364, Fax: +91(44) 24957414
EMail: vc@tndalu.ac.in

Registrar: D. Gopal
Tel: +91(44) 24610813, Fax: +91(44) 24617996
EMail: registrar@tndalu.ac.in

Courses
Post Graduate Diploma (Commercial Law; Environmental Studies; Information Technology; Law; Private Law)

Departments
Business Law *(Postgraduate)* (Commercial Law; Marketing); **Constitutional Law and Human Rights** *(Postgraduate)* (Constitutional Law; Human Rights); **Criminal Law** *(Postgraduate)* (Criminal Law); **Distance Education** (Commercial Law; Environmental Studies; Human Rights; Information Technology; Labour Law; Law); **Environmental Law** (Environmental Studies; Law); **Human Rights and Duties Education Center for Human Rights** *(Postgraduate)* (Human Rights); **Intellectual Property Rights** *(Postgraduate)* (Private Law); **International Law** *(Postgraduate)* (International Law)

Schools
Excellence in Law *(SOEL)* (Administrative Law; Arts and Humanities; Banking; Civil Law; Commercial Law; Constitutional Law; Criminal Law; Criminology; Economics; English; Environmental Studies; History; Human Rights; International Law; Labour Law; Law; Political Sciences; Social Sciences; Sociology; Taxation)

Further Information: A traditional and distance education programme.

History: Founded 1997.

Governing Bodies: Academic Senate; Board of Studies; Finance Committee

Fees: (Indian Rupee): Undergraduate programmes, 25,000 per annum; Postgraduate programmes, 10,000 per annum; Distance education programmes, 1,500-5,000 per annum

Main Language(s) of Instruction: Indian

Degrees and Diplomas: *Bachelor's Degree*; *Bachelor's degree (professional)*; *Postgraduate Diploma*; *Master's Degree*. Also Certificate Course; Honours Bachelor's degree, 3-5 yrs.

Last Updated: 22/11/11

TAMIL NADU DOCTOR M.G.R. MEDICAL UNIVERSITY

PO Box 1200, 69 Anna Salai, Guindy, Chennai, Tamil Nadu 600032
Tel: +91(44) 22301760 +91(44) 22353093
Fax: +91(44) 22353698
EMail: mail@tnmgrmu.ac.in
Website: http://www.tnmgrmu.ac.in/

Vice-Chancellor: Mayil Vahanan Natarajan (2009-)
Tel: +91(44) 22353595 EMail: vc@tnmgrmu.ac.in

Registrar: Sudha Seshayyan
Tel: +91(44) 22353572 EMail: registrar@tnmgrmu.ac.in

International Relations: S. Jeevanandam, Academic Officer
EMail: ao@tnmgrmu.ac.in

Faculties
Allied Health Sciences (Anaesthesiology; Anatomy; Biochemistry; Business Administration; Cardiology; Community Health; Dental Hygiene; Dental Technology; Diabetology; Dietetics; Entomology; Epidemiology; Genetics; Gerontology; Gynaecology and Obstetrics; Health Administration; Health Education; Laboratory Techniques; Medical Technology; Medicine; Microbiology; Neurological Therapy; Neurology; Nursing; Nutrition; Occupational Therapy; Optometry; Orthopaedics; Paediatrics; Physiology; Pneumology; Podiatry; Public Health; Radiology; Respiratory Therapy; Social Work; Sociology; Speech Therapy and Audiology; Sports Medicine; Statistics; Surgery; Virology); **Ayurveda** (Ayurveda; Medicine; Surgery); **Basic Medical Sciences** (Anatomy; Biochemistry; Forensic Medicine and Dentistry; Medicine; Microbiology; Pathology; Pharmacology; Physiology); **Community Health** (Community Health; Medicine; Public Health); **Dentistry** (Dental Technology; Dentistry; Microbiology; Oral Pathology; Orthodontics; Orthopaedics; Periodontics; Public Health; Radiology; Surgery); **Homoeopathy** (Alternative Medicine; Medicine; Surgery); **Medical Specialities** (Anaesthesiology; Dermatology; Diabetology; Gerontology; Haematology; Immunology; Medical Technology; Medicine; Pneumology; Psychiatry and Mental Health; Radiology; Rehabilitation and Therapy; Toxicology; Treatment Techniques; Venereology); **Medical Super Specialities** (Cardiology; Epidemiology; Gastroenterology; Haematology; Hepatology; Medicine; Nephrology; Neurology; Oncology; Paediatrics; Psychiatry and Mental Health; Rheumatology); **Naturopathy and Yogic Science** (Alternative Medicine; Yoga); **Nursing** (Community Health; Gynaecology and Obstetrics; Nursing; Paediatrics; Psychiatry and Mental Health); **Obstetrics and Gynaecology** (Gynaecology and Obstetrics; Medicine); **Paediatrics** (Health Sciences; Medicine; Nephrology; Neurology; Paediatrics; Pneumology); **Pharmacy** (Alternative Medicine; Biotechnology; Chemistry; Pharmacology; Pharmacy); **Physiotherapy** (Gynaecology and Obstetrics; Neurology; Orthopaedics; Paediatrics; Physical Therapy); **Siddha** (Alternative Medicine; Medicine; Surgery); **Surgical Specialities** (Ophthalmology; Orthopaedics; Otorhinolaryngology; Podiatry; Sports Medicine; Surgery); **Surgical Super Specialities** (Cardiology; Endocrinology; Gastroenterology; Neurological Therapy; Oncology; Paediatrics; Plastic Surgery; Rehabilitation and Therapy; Surgery; Urology); **Unani** (Alternative Medicine; Medicine; Surgery); **Undergraduate Medicine and Surgery** (Medicine; Surgery)

Further Information: Also 223 Affiliated Colleges

History: Founded 1987, formerly affiliated to the University of Madras.

Governing Bodies: Senate; Governing Council; Finance Committee; Planning Board

Main Language(s) of Instruction: English; Bachelor program of Unani Medicine and Surgery in Arabic

Degrees and Diplomas: *Diploma*; *Bachelor's Degree*; *Bachelor's degree (professional)*; *Postgraduate Diploma*; *Master's Degree*; *Doctorate*. Also Certificate Courses.

Student Services: Canteen

Libraries: 23,362 vols; 170 periodical subscriptions; Virtual Library

Publications: Medfocus *(quarterly)*
Last Updated: 22/11/11

TAMIL NADU OPEN UNIVERSITY (TNOU)

Chennai, Tamilnadu
Website: http://www.tnou.ac.in

Vice Chancellor: A. Kalyani

Registrar: S. Shanmugiah

Schools
Computer Sciences (Computer Engineering; Computer Science; Data Processing; Information Management; Software Engineering); **Continuing Education** (Business Computing; Computer Engineering; Computer Science; Cooking and Catering; Cosmetology; Environmental Studies; Fashion Design; Food Science; Foreign Languages Education; Health Sciences; Heating and Refrigeration; Mathematics Education; Multimedia; Music; Nutrition; Preschool Education; Primary Education; Rural Studies; Technology; Women's Studies); **Criminology and Criminal Justice** (Criminal Law; Criminology; Justice Administration); **Education** (Education;

Special Education); **Health Sciences** (Health Sciences; Speech Therapy and Audiology); **History and Tourism Studies** (Heritage Preservation; History; Tourism; Transport and Communications); **Humanities** (Arts and Humanities; Communication Studies; English); **Journalism and New Media Studies** (Journalism; Media Studies; Radio and Television Broadcasting); **Management Studies** (Business Administration; Finance; Human Resources; Information Technology; Insurance; Management; Marketing); **Politics and Public Administration** (Economics; Environmental Studies; Geography; Human Rights; Political Sciences; Public Administration; Public Relations; Safety Engineering); **Science** (Computer Science; Mathematics; Mathematics and Computer Science); **Social Sciences** (Accountancy; Banking; Business and Commerce; Finance; Psychoanalysis; Psychology; Social Sciences; Social Work; Sociology); **Special Education and Rehabilitation** (Rehabilitation and Therapy; Special Education); **Tamil and Cultural Studies** (Cultural Studies; Literature; Media Studies; South and Southeast Asian Languages)

History: Founded 2002.

Governing Bodies: Syndicate; Academic Council; Boards of Studies

Degrees and Diplomas: *Diploma*; *Bachelor's Degree*; *Postgraduate Diploma*; *Master's Degree*. Also Certificate Course; Advanced Diploma; M.B.A.; Vocational Diploma Programmes.
Last Updated: 08/12/11

TAMIL NADU PHYSICAL EDUCATION AND SPORTS UNIVERSITY (TNPESU)

8th Floor, EVK Sampath Maaligai, College Road, Chennai, Tamil Nadu 600 006
Tel: +91(44) 2825-2245 +91(44) 2825-2247
Fax: +91(44) 2825-2246
EMail: enquiry@tnpesu.org
Website: http://www.tnpesu.org/

Vice Chancellor: K. Vaithianathan
Tel: +91(44) 2825-2244, Fax: +91(44) 2825-2246
EMail: dr.vaithianathan@yahoo.com

Registrar: J.P. Sukumar

Faculties
Health and Allied Sciences (Computer Science; Health Sciences; Journalism; Mass Communication; Nutrition; Physiology; Psychology; Sociology; Sports; Statistics); **Management** (Information Technology; Management; Marketing; Sports Management; Technology); **Teacher Education** (Physical Education; Teacher Training; Yoga); **Youth and Sports Affairs** (Sports)

Further Information: Also 13 affiliated colleges; a tratidional and distance education institution

History: Founded 2005.

Degrees and Diplomas: *Diploma*; *Bachelor's Degree*; *Postgraduate Diploma*; *Master's Degree*; *Master of Philosophy*; *Doctorate*; *Doctor of Literature*; *Doctor of Science*. Also M.B.A.
Last Updated: 06/01/12

TAMIL NADU TEACHERS EDUCATION UNIVERSITY (TNTEU)

Lady Willingdon College Campus, Kamarajar Salai, Chennai, Tamil Nadu 600 005
Tel: +91(44) 2844-7300 +91(44) 2844-7304
Fax: +91(44) 2844-7303
EMail: admin@tnteu.in
Website: http://www.tnteu.in/

Vice Chancellor: T. Padmanabhan
Registrar: A.R. Veeramani

Programmes
Teacher Education (Teacher Training)
History: Founded 2008.

Degrees and Diplomas: *Bachelor's degree (professional)*; *Master's Degree*; *Master of Philosophy*; *Doctorate*
Last Updated: 05/01/12

TAMIL NADU VETERINARY AND ANIMAL SCIENCES UNIVERSITY (TANUVAS)

Madhavaram, Chennai, Tamil Nadu 600051
Tel: +91(44) 2555-1584
Fax: +91(44) 2555-1585
EMail: tanuvas@vsnl.com
Website: http://www.tanuvas.ac.in

Vice-Chancellor: R. Prabakaran
Tel: +91(44) 2555-1574, Fax: +91(44) 2555-1576
EMail: vc@tanuvas.org.in

Registrar: C. Balachandran

Colleges
Fisheries and Research Institute *(Thoothukkudi)* (Agricultural Economics; Aquaculture; Biology; Fishery; Food Technology; Natural Resources; Statistics); **Madras Veterinary** *(Chennai)* (Agricultural Economics; Agronomy; Animal Husbandry; Biochemistry; Biotechnology; Computer Science; Dairy; Epidemiology; Ethics; Genetics; Gynaecology and Obstetrics; Library Science; Meat and Poultry; Microbiology; Natural Sciences; Nutrition; Parasitology; Pathology; Pharmacology; Physiology; Surgery; Toxicology; Veterinary Science; Wildlife); **Veterinary Science and Research Institute** *(Tirunelveli)* (Animal Husbandry; Dairy; Fishery; Veterinary Science); **Veterinary Science and Research Institute** *(Namakkal)* (Agricultural Economics; Agronomy; Animal Husbandry; Biochemistry; Epidemiology; Ethics; Gynaecology and Obstetrics; Histology; Library Science; Meat and Poultry; Microbiology; Nutrition; Pharmacology; Physical Education; Physiology; Radiology; Safety Engineering; Surgery; Toxicology; Veterinary Science)

Faculties
Basic Sciences (Natural Sciences); **Fisheries Science** (Fishery); **Food Sciences** (Animal Husbandry; Dairy; Fishery; Food Science; Nutrition); **Veterinary and Animal Sciences** (Animal Husbandry; Veterinary Science)

Institutes
Food and Dairy Technology (Dairy; Food Technology)

Research Institutes
Animal Sciences *(Postgraduate - Kattupakkam)* (Zoology)

Further Information: Also 3 Constituent Colleges; Veterinary Hospital and Clinics; Laboratories; Research Stations and Farms; 17 University Training and Research Centres. A traditional and distance education institution.

History: Founded 1989.

Governing Bodies: Board of Management; Academic Council; Board of Studies

Academic Year: September to June (September-January; February-June)

Admission Requirements: 12th year senior secondary/higher examination or equivalent

Fees: (Rupees): Undergraduate, 5,380 per semester; postgraduate, 7,675

Main Language(s) of Instruction: English

International Co-operation: With universities in USA, Canada and United Kingdom

Accrediting Agencies: Indian Council of Agricultural Research

Degrees and Diplomas: *Bachelor's Degree*; *Bachelor's degree (professional)*; *Postgraduate Diploma*; *Master's Degree*; *Master of Philosophy*; *Doctorate*

Student Services: Academic counselling, Canteen, Employment services, Health services, Sports facilities

Student Residential Facilities: Yes

Special Facilities: Museum (Madras Veterinary College)

Libraries: Madras Veterinary College Library, 37,165 vols; 126 International periodical subscriptions; 36 Indian Journals

Publications: Kalnadai Kathir, Research findings in local language (Tamil) *(bimonthly)*; Tamil Nadu Veterinary Journal, Veterinary Science and Animal Husbandry (English) *(bimonthly)*

Academic Staff *2009-2010*	MEN	WOMEN	TOTAL
FULL-TIME	418	91	**509**
STAFF WITH DOCTORATE			
FULL-TIME	292	40	**332**
Student Numbers *2009-2010*			
All (Foreign Included)	888	516	**1,404**

Last Updated: 22/11/11

TAMIL UNIVERSITY

Administrative Buildings, Trichy Road, Thanjavur,
Tamil Nadu 613005
Tel: +91(4362) 226-720
Fax: +91(4362) 226-159
EMail: contact@tamiluniversity.ac.in
Website: http://www.tamiluniversity.ac.in

Vice-Chancellor: M. Rajendran (2008-)
Tel: +91(4362) 222-7040, Fax: +91(4362) 222-6159

Registrar: G. Bhaskaran

International Relations: Thiru G. Panneer Selvam

Faculties

Arts (Fine Arts; Music; Performing Arts; Sculpture; Theatre); **Developing Tamil** (Economics; Education; Indic Languages; Linguistics; Native Language Education; Social Sciences; Translation and Interpretation); **Language** (Cultural Studies; Folklore; Indic Languages; Linguistics; Literature; Philosophy); **Manuscriptology** (Ancient Books; Archaeology); **Science** (Architecture; Computer Science; Earth Sciences; Environmental Studies; Industrial Engineering; Natural Sciences; Traditional Eastern Medicine)

Further Information: A traditional and distance education institution.

History: Founded 1981. A high level Research Institution.

Governing Bodies: Senate; Syndicate; Finance Committee; Planning Board

Academic Year: July to June

Admission Requirements: University degree

Main Language(s) of Instruction: Tamil, English

Degrees and Diplomas: *Diploma*; *Bachelor's Degree*; *Postgraduate Diploma*; *Master's Degree*; *Master of Philosophy*; *Doctorate*. Also Certificates

Student Residential Facilities: Yes

Special Facilities: Museum: collection of c. 3,000 objects; 10 sculptures, household articles

Libraries: c. 136,324 vols; 393 periodical subscriptions

Publications: Tamil Kalai and Tamil Civilization *(quarterly)*

Press or Publishing House: University Press
Last Updated: 23/11/11

TATA INSTITUTE OF FUNDAMENTAL RESEARCH (TIFR)

Homi Bhabha Road, Mumbai, Maharashtra 400 005
Tel: +91(22) 2278-2000
Fax: +91(22) 2280-4610
EMail: webmaster@tifr.res.in
Website: http://www.tifr.res.in/About_TIFR/

Director: Mustansir Barma
Tel: +91(22) 2278-2306 EMail: rvp@tifr.res.in

Registrar: Jayant N. Kayarkar
Tel: +91(22) 2278-2315 EMail: jnkayarkar@math.tifr.res.in

Schools

Mathematics (Mathematics); **Natural Sciences** (Astronomy and Space Science; Astrophysics; Atomic and Molecular Physics; Biology; Biophysics; Chemistry; Mathematical Physics; Nuclear Physics; Physics); **Technology and Computer Science** (Computer Science; Technology)

History: Founded 1945. Acquired Deemed University status 2002.

Degrees and Diplomas: *Master's Degree*; *Doctorate*. Also integrated Ph.D.
Last Updated: 23/11/11

TATA INSTITUTE OF SOCIAL SCIENCES (TISS)

Po Box No 8313, Sion-Trombay Road, Deonar, Mumbai,
Maharashtra 400088
Tel: +91(22) 2556-7417
Fax: +91(22) 2556-2912
EMail: rrsingh@tiss.edu
Website: http://www.tiss.edu

Director: S. Parasuraman EMail: sparasuraman@tiss.edu

Registrar: Neela Dabir EMail: ndabir@tiss.edu

International Relations: Bipin Jojo, Chairperson, International Students Office Tel: +91(22) 2552-5427

Schools

Habitat Studies (Architecture; Economics; Engineering; Environmental Studies; Management; Social Sciences); **Health Systems Studies** (Economics; Finance; Health Administration; Health Sciences; Public Health; Social Sciences); **Management and Labour Studies** (Human Resources; Labour and Industrial Relations; Leadership; Management); **Rural Development** (Development Studies; Rural Studies; Social Work); **Social Sciences** (Adult Education; Development Studies; Ecology; Education; Health Education; Higher Education; Human Rights; Primary Education; Secondary Education; Social Problems; Social Sciences; Sociology; Women's Studies); **Social Work** (Child Care and Development; Criminology; Development Studies; Epidemiology; Family Studies; Health Sciences; Law; Peace and Disarmament; Protective Services; Psychiatry and Mental Health; Social Work; Women's Studies)

Further Information: Also Malti and Jal A.D. Naoroji Campus.

History: Founded 1936. Granted 'Deemed University' status 1964. A postgraduate institution.

Governing Bodies: Governing Board

Academic Year: June to April

Admission Requirements: University degree at Bachelor level

Fees: (Rupees): 3,000-4,500 per semester

Main Language(s) of Instruction: English

International Co-operation: With universities in USA, France, UK, Austria, Finland, Germany, Belgium, Australia, Canada. Participates in the Erasmus Mundus programme.

Degrees and Diplomas: *Bachelor's Degree*: Social Work (B.A. (Hons.)); *Master's Degree*; *Master of Philosophy*; *Doctorate*. Also Diploma and Certificate courses

Student Services: Academic counselling, Canteen, Cultural centre, Employment services, Foreign student adviser, Handicapped facilities, Health services, Nursery care, Social counselling, Sports facilities

Student Residential Facilities: Hostels and Guest House

Special Facilities: Computer Centre

Libraries: 102,958 vols; 290 periodical subscriptions

Publications: Indian Journal of Social Work *(quarterly)*
Last Updated: 23/11/11

TECHNO GLOBAL UNIVERSITY (TGU)

Anita Mension, Bishnupur, Shillong, Meghalaya 793 004
Website: http://technoindiagroup.com/academics/
index.php?id1 = 1001

Programmes

Civil Engineering (Civil Engineering); **Computer Science and Engineering** (Computer Engineering; Computer Science); **Electrical Engineering** (Electrical Engineering); **Electronics and Communications Engineering** (Electronic Engineering; Telecommunications Engineering); **Mechanical Engineering** (Mechanical Engineering)

History: Founded 2008.

Accrediting Agencies: University Grants Commission (UGC)

Degrees and Diplomas: *Bachelor's degree (professional)*. Dual Bachelor/Master's degrees (B.Tech-M.Tech and B.Tech-MBA).
Last Updated: 31/08/11

TEERTHANKER MAHAVEER UNIVERSITY (TMU)

Delhi Road, NH 24, Moradabad, Uttar Pradesh 244 001
Tel: +91(591) 236-0500 +91(591) 236-0077
Fax: +91(591) 236-0444 +91(591) 248-7444
EMail: admission@tmu.ac.in
Website: http://www.tmu.ac.in/

Vice Chancellor: R. K. Mittal
Tel: +91(591) 236-0222 EMail: vicechancellor@tmu.ac.in

Registrar: Rakesh Kr. Mudgal
Tel: +91(591) 236-0006 EMail: registrar@tmu.ac.in

International Relations: K. K. Pande, Director, International Affairs
EMail: director.int@tmu.ac.in

Colleges
Architecture (Architecture; Fine Arts); **Dentistry** *(and Research Centre)* (Dentistry; Surgery); **Education** (Education; Physical Education); **Engineering** (Chemical Engineering; Civil Engineering; Computer Engineering; Computer Science; Electrical Engineering; Electronic Engineering; Engineering; Mathematics; Mechanical Engineering); **Law and Legal Studies** (Criminology; Law); **Management and Computer Applications** (Accountancy; Business Administration; Business Computing; Computer Science; Management; Marine Transport; Transport Management); **Medicine** *(and Research Centre)* (Anaesthesiology; Anatomy; Biochemistry; Cardiology; Community Health; Dermatology; Forensic Medicine and Dentistry; Gynaecology and Obstetrics; Medicine; Microbiology; Ophthalmology; Orthopaedics; Otorhinolaryngology; Paediatrics; Pathology; Pharmacology; Physiology; Psychiatry and Mental Health; Radiology; Surgery; Urology; Venereology); **Nursing** (Midwifery; Nursing); **Pharmacy** (Chemistry; Pharmacology; Pharmacy; Safety Engineering); **Polytechnics** (Automotive Engineering; Civil Engineering; Computer Engineering; Computer Science; Electrical Engineering; Electronic Engineering; Engineering; Mechanical Engineering; Naval Architecture; Production Engineering)

Departments
Hospital Administration (Health Administration; Health Sciences); **Social Work** (Social Work)

History: Founded 2008.

Governing Bodies: University Court; Planning Board; Executive Council; Academic Council; Finance Committee

Degrees and Diplomas: *Bachelor's Degree*; *Bachelor's degree (professional)*; *Master's Degree*; *Doctorate*. Also *Certificate*; *Bachelor's degree*; *Hons.*; *M.B.A.*

Student Numbers *2010-2011*: Total 7,800
Last Updated: 23/12/11

TELANGANA UNIVERSITY

Nizamabad, Andhra Pradesh 503 322
Tel: +91(8461) 222-220
Fax: +91(8461) 222-212
EMail: tu@telanganauniversity.ac.in
Website: http://www.telanganauniversity.ac.in/

Vice-Chancellor: Mohd. Akbar Ali Kha
Tel: +91(8461) 222-217 EMail: vc@telanganauniversity.ac.in

Registrar: M. Yadagiri
Tel: +91(8461) 222-211 EMail: registrar@telanganauniversity.ac.in

Faculties
Arts (Arts and Humanities; English; Hindi; Indic Languages; Mass Communication; Urdu); **Business Management** (Business Administration; Management); **Commerce** (Business and Commerce; E-Business/Commerce); **Computer Science** (Computer Science); **Law** (Law); **Science** (Biotechnology; Botany; Chemistry; Computer Science; Electronic Engineering; Geology; Organic Chemistry; Pharmacy; Physics; Statistics); **Social Science** (Economics; Social Sciences; Social Work)

Further Information: Also South-Campus of Bhiknoor. A traditional and distance education institution.

History: Founded 2006.

Governing Bodies: Executive Council

Degrees and Diplomas: *Master's Degree.* Also M.B.A.
Last Updated: 02/01/12

TERI UNIVERSITY

Plot No. 10 Institutional Area, Vasant Kunj, New Delhi 110 070
Tel: +91(11) 2612-2222
Fax: +91(11) 2612-2874
EMail: registrar@teri.res.in
Website: http://www.teriuniversity.ac.in

Vice-chancellor: Bhavik R. Bakshi EMail: bhavik.bakshi@teri.res.in

Registrar: Rajiv Seth EMail: rseth@teri.res.in

Faculties
Applied Sciences (Biotechnology; Computer Science; Energy Engineering; Environmental Engineering; Environmental Studies; Meteorology; Natural Resources; Water Management); **Policy and Planning** (Business Administration; Development Studies; Economics; Regional Planning)

History: Founded 1998 as TERI School of Advanced Studies. Acquired 'deemed university' status 1999.

Governing Bodies: Board of Management; Academic Council; Finance Committee; Planning and Monitoring Board

Academic Year: July to June

Fees: (Rupees): 80,000-200,000 per annum

Main Language(s) of Instruction: English

Accrediting Agencies: University Grants Commission

Degrees and Diplomas: *Postgraduate Diploma*; *Master's Degree*; *Doctorate.* Also M.B.A.

Student Services: Academic counselling, Employment services

Student Residential Facilities: Yes (exclusive for ladies)

Libraries: Yes
Last Updated: 23/11/11

TEZPUR UNIVERSITY

Napaam, District Sonitpur, Tezpur, Assam 784 028
Tel: +91(3712) 267007 +91(3712) 267008 +91(3712) 267009
Fax: +91(3712) 267005 +91(3712) 267006
Website: http://www.tezu.ernet.in

Vice-Chancellor: Mihir Kanti Chaudhuri Tel: +91(3712) 267003

Registrar: Alak Kumar Buragohain
Tel: +91(3712) 267114 EMail: boral@tezu.ernet.in

Schools
Engineering (Civil Engineering; Computer Engineering; Computer Science; Electronic Engineering; Energy Engineering; Food Technology; Mechanical Engineering; Telecommunications Engineering); **Humanities and Social Sciences** (Chinese; Cultural Studies; English; Hindi; Journalism; Linguistics; Literature; Mass Communication; Modern Languages; Phonetics; Sociology); **Management Sciences** (Business Administration; Management; Tourism); **Science and Technology** (Applied Chemistry; Astrophysics; Biotechnology; Chemistry; Electronic Engineering; Environmental Studies; Inorganic Chemistry; Mathematics; Mathematics and Computer Science; Molecular Biology; Nanotechnology; Organic Chemistry; Physics; Polymer and Plastics Technology)

Further Information: A traditional and distance education institution.

History: Founded 1994. A Central University.

Governing Bodies: Board of Management

Academic Year: January to December (January-June; July-December)

Admission Requirements: Undergraduate programmes, 10+2 standard secondary studies; Graduate Programmes, University degree

Fees: (Rupees): 10,000-15,000 per semester

Main Language(s) of Instruction: English

Degrees and Diplomas: *Diploma*; *Bachelor's degree (professional)*; *Postgraduate Diploma*; *Master's Degree*; *Doctorate.* Also *Certificate*; integrated Bacelor's degree (B.Sc. B.Ed.) and Master's degree (M.Sc.; M.Tech), 4 yrs following Bachelor's degree; M.B.A.

Student Services: Employment services, Health services, Sports facilities

Student Residential Facilities: Hostels; Guest House

Special Facilities: Internet facility; Computer Centre; NET Caoching Centre; Auditorium; Bank; Post Office; Laboratories

Libraries: 26,000 vols; 140 periodical subscriptions; 100 Audio-Video cassettes; 500 CD-Rom; 2,169 E-Journals; 63 Databases

Last Updated: 23/11/11

THAPAR UNIVERSITY (TU)

P.O Box 32, Patiala, Punjab 147004
Tel: +91(175) 2393021
Fax: +91(175) 2364498 +91(175) 2393020
EMail: registrar@thapar.edu; webadmin@thapar.edu
Website: http://www.thapar.edu

Director: Abhijit Mukherjee
Tel: +91(175) 2393001 +91(175) 2363007
EMail: abhijit@thapar.edu

Registrar: J. E. Samuel Ratnakumar
Tel: +91(175) 2393021 EMail: registrar@thapar.edu

Centres
Central Workshop (Industrial Maintenance; Metal Techniques; Technology); **Information and Technology Management** *(CITM)* (Information Management; Information Technology); **Relevance and Excellence in Agro and Industrial Biotechnology** *(CORE)* (Biotechnology); **Science and Technology Entrepreneur's Park** *(STEP)* (Biotechnology; Business Administration; Food Technology; Management)

Departments
Biotechnology and Environment Sciences *(BTESD)* (Biotechnology; Environmental Studies; Microbiology); **Chemical Engineering** *(CHED)* (Chemical Engineering); **Civil Engineering** *(CED)* (Civil Engineering; Structural Architecture); **Computer Science and Engineering** *(CSED)* (Computer Engineering; Computer Science; Software Engineering); **Distance Education** *(DDE)* (Civil Engineering; Computer Engineering; Computer Science; Electrical Engineering; Mechanical Engineering); **Electrical and Instrumentation Engineering** *(EIED)* (Electrical Engineering; Electronic Engineering; Measurement and Precision Engineering; Power Engineering); **Electronics and Communication Engineering** *(ECED)* (Design; Electronic Engineering; Telecommunications Engineering); **Mechanical Engineering** *(MED)* (Industrial Engineering; Mechanical Engineering; Production Engineering; Robotics; Thermal Engineering)

Schools
Chemistry and Biochemistry (Analytical Chemistry; Biochemistry; Chemistry; Inorganic Chemistry; Organic Chemistry; Physical Chemistry; Polymer and Plastics Technology); **Management** *(L. M. Thapar - LMTSOM)* (Business Administration; Data Processing; E-Business/Commerce; Finance; Human Resources; Information Sciences; International Business; Management; Marketing; Operations Research); **Management and Social Sciences** *(SMSS)* (E-Business/Commerce; Economics; Industrial Management; Management; Retailing and Wholesaling; Social Sciences); **Mathematics and Computer Applications** *(SMCA)* (Computer Networks; Computer Science; Data Processing; Mathematics; Mechanics; Statistics); **Physics and Materials Science** *(SPMS)* (Ceramics and Glass Technology; Materials Engineering; Metallurgical Engineering; Nanotechnology; Physics; Solid State Physics)

Further Information: A traditional and distance education institution.

History: Founded 1956 as Thapar Institute of Engineering and Technology. Granted 'Deemed University' status 1985.

Governing Bodies: Board of Governors

Academic Year: July to June

Admission Requirements: 10+2 examination with Math, Physics, Chemistry/Biology/Biotechnology/Computer Science and also qualified All India Engineering Entrance Examination (AIEEE) conducted by CBSE, New Dehli

Fees: (Rupees): Bachelor of Engineering, 36,000; Master of Computer Applications, 36,000; ME/M. Tech./ M.Sc., 16,000; PhD, 10,000

Main Language(s) of Instruction: English

Accrediting Agencies: National Assessment and Accreditation Council (NAAC); All India Concil for Technical Education (CTE)

Degrees and Diplomas: *Bachelor's Degree*; *Bachelor's degree (professional)*; *Master's Degree*; *Master of Philosophy*; *Doctorate*. Also M.B.A.

Student Services: Academic counselling, Canteen, Employment services, Health services, Social counselling, Sports facilities

Student Residential Facilities: 6 boys hostels and 3 girls hostel.

Special Facilities: Central Workshop; Auditorium; Convention Hall

Libraries: Central Library, 41,292 vols; 112 periodical subscriptions; 9 Newspaper; 3,400 Electronic Journals

Last Updated: 23/11/11

THE ENGLISH AND FOREIGN LANGUAGES UNIVERSITY (EFL-U)

Osmania University Road, Hyderabad, Andhra Pradesh 500605
Tel: +91(40) 2709-8141
Fax: +91(40) 2707-0029
EMail: abhaimaurya@gmail.com
Website: http://www.efluniversity.ac.in

Vice-Chancellor: Mohammad Miyan Tel: +91(40) 2709-8141

Registrar: Lata Mallikarjuna
Tel: +91(40) 2709-8225 EMail: lmallikarjuna@yahoo.com

International Relations: Hemalatha Nagarajan, Dean, International Relations EMail: hemalatha@efluniversity.ac.in

Schools
Asian Studies (Asian Studies; Chinese; Japanese; Korean; Persian; Turkish); **Communication Studies** (Cinema and Television; Communication Studies; Journalism; Mass Communication; Media Studies); **Distance Education** (Distance Education; English; Foreign Languages Education; Linguistics; Literature; Phonetics); **English Language Education** (English; Foreign Languages Education; Literature); **English Literary Studies** (English; Literature); **Germanic Studies** (German; Germanic Languages; Literature); **Interdisciplinary Studies** (Arts and Humanities; Asian Studies; Comparative Literature; Cultural Studies; Esoteric Practices; Grammar; Hindi; History; Literature; Philosophy; Social Problems; Translation and Interpretation); **Language Sciences** (Computer Science; English; Linguistics; Phonetics); **Middle East and African Studies** (African Studies; Arabic; Literature; Middle Eastern Studies); **Romance Studies** (Cultural Studies; French; French Studies; Italian; Literature; Portuguese; Romance Languages; Spanish); **Russian Studies** (Linguistics; Literature; Russian)

Further Information: Also campuses in Lucknow and Shillong. A traditional and distance education institution.

History: Founded 1958 as Central Institute of English, known as Central Institute of English and Foreign Languages from 1972, and status as 'Deemed University' 1973. A postgraduate Institution with branches at Lucknow and Shillong. Acquired current title 2007. A Central University.

Governing Bodies: Board of Governors

Academic Year: August to April

Admission Requirements: Postgraduate degree in the language concerned, with at least 55% pass marks

Fees: (Rupees): 200-300 per semester

Main Language(s) of Instruction: English

Accrediting Agencies: NAAC, UGC

Degrees and Diplomas: *Bachelor's Degree*; *Postgraduate Diploma*; *Master's Degree*; *Master of Philosophy*; *Doctorate*

Student Services: Academic counselling, Canteen, Cultural centre, Employment services, Foreign student adviser, Foreign Studies Centre, Handicapped facilities, Health services, Language programs, Nursery care, Social counselling, Sports facilities

Student Residential Facilities: Yes

Special Facilities: Radio, TV and Cinematography Unit

Libraries: c. 150,000 vols; c. 500 subscriptions to periodicals

Press or Publishing House: EFL-U Publications Unit

Academic Staff *2009-2010* | **TOTAL**
FULL-TIME | **237**

Student Numbers *2009-2010*
All (Foreign Included) | **6,920**
FOREIGN ONLY | **772**

Part-time students, 594. **Distance students**, 2,709.
Last Updated: 23/11/11

THE GLOBAL OPEN UNIVERSITY

Opposite Railway Station, Dimapur, Nagaland 797112
Tel: +91(3862) 231959
EMail: univ@nagaland.net.in
Website: http://nagaland.net.in/

Programmes

Applied Science (Bioengineering; Biology; Biotechnology; Dairy; Nanotechnology); **Computers and Information Technology** (Computer Education; Computer Networks; Information Technology); **Ecology and Environment** (Ecology; Environmental Management); **Education** (Adult Education; Child Care and Development; Education; Educational Administration; Educational Technology; Health Education; Higher Education; Physical Education; Science Education; Vocational Education); **Health and Medical Sciences** (Health Administration; Medicine; Yoga); **Journalism and Mass Communication** (Journalism; Mass Communication); **Law and Juridical Science** (Criminology; Forensic Medicine and Dentistry; Law); **Library and Information Science** (Information Sciences; Library Science); **Management and Commerce** (Business Administration; Business and Commerce; Insurance); **Psychology and Counselling** (Psycholinguistics); **Social Sciences** (Economics; Ethics; Geography; Government; Peace and Disarmament; Social Sciences; Sociology; South Asian Studies); **Tourism, Travel and Hospitality Management** (Hotel Management; Tourism)

History: Founded 2006.

Degrees and Diplomas: *Bachelor's Degree*; *Postgraduate Diploma*; *Master's Degree*
Last Updated: 17/01/12

THE LNM INSTITUTE OF INFORMATION TECHNOLOGY (LNMIIT)

Rupa ki Nangal, Post-Sumel, Via-Jamdoli, Jaipur,
Rajasthan 302031
Tel: +91(141) 518-9211 +91(141) 268-9011
Fax: +91(141) 268-9014
EMail: info.lnmiit@lnmiit.ac.in
Website: http://www.lnmiit.ac.in

Director: Sudhir Raniwala EMail: director@lnmiit.ac.in

Programmes

Communication and Computer Engineering (Computer Engineering; Telecommunications Engineering); **Communication and Computer Engineering** *(Postgraduate)* (Computer Engineering; Telecommunications Engineering); **Computer Science and Engineering** *(Postgraduate)* (Computer Engineering; Computer Science); **Computer Science and Engineering** (Computer Engineering; Computer Science); **Electronics and Communication Engineering** (Electronic Engineering; Telecommunications Engineering); **Electronics and Communication Engineering** *(Postgraduate)* (Electronic Engineering; Telecommunications Engineering); **Engineering Physics** (Engineering; Physics); **Mathematics and Information Technology** (Information Technology; Mathematics)

History: Founded 2002. A deemed university.

Governing Bodies: Academic Council; Governing Council

Main Language(s) of Instruction: Hindi

Degrees and Diplomas: *Bachelor's degree (professional)*; *Master's Degree*; *Doctorate*

Student Numbers *2009-2010*: Total: c. 800
Last Updated: 23/11/11

THE MAHARAJA SAYAJIRAO UNIVERSITY OF BARODA

Fatehgani, Vadodara, Gujarat 390002
Tel: +91(265) 279-5521
Fax: +91(265) 279-3693
EMail: registrar@msubaroda.ac.in
Website: http://www.msubaroda.ac.in

Vice-Chancellor: Yogesh Singh
Tel: +91(265) 2795600, Fax: +91(265) 2793693
EMail: ys66@rediffmail.com; vc@msubaroda.ac.in

Registrar: M. M. Beedkar
Tel: +91(265) 2795521, Fax: +91(265) 2793693

Colleges

Science and Commerce *(M.K. Amin)* (Business and Commerce; Natural Sciences)

Faculties

Arts (Ancient Civilizations; Arabic; Archaeology; Arts and Humanities; Canadian Studies; Economics; English; French; German; Hindi; History; Indic Languages; Information Sciences; Library Science; Linguistics; Persian; Philosophy; Political Sciences; Russian; Sanskrit; Sociology; Urdu); **Baroda Sanskrit Mahavidyalaya** (Esoteric Practices; Sanskrit); **Commerce** (Accountancy; Banking; Business Administration; Business and Commerce; Economics; Insurance; Management); **Education and Psychology** (Education; Educational Administration; Psychology); **Family and Community Science** (Child Care and Development; Clothing and Sewing; Communication Studies; Development Studies; Family Studies; Food Science; Home Economics; Nutrition; Textile Technology; Women's Studies); **Fine Arts** (Aesthetics; Art History; Fine Arts; Graphic Arts; Museum Studies; Painting and Drawing; Sculpture); **Journalism and Communication** (Journalism; Mass Communication; Media Studies); **Law** (Commercial Law; Law); **Management Studies** (Business Administration; Management); **Medicine** (Anaesthesiology; Anatomy; Biochemistry; Dermatology; Forensic Medicine and Dentistry; Gynaecology and Obstetrics; Medicine; Microbiology; Ophthalmology; Orthopaedics; Otorhinolaryngology; Paediatrics; Pathology; Pharmacology; Physical Therapy; Physiology; Plastic Surgery; Psychiatry and Mental Health; Radiology; Social and Preventive Medicine; Surgery; Venereology); **Performing Arts** (Dance; Musical Instruments; Performing Arts; Singing; Theatre); **Polytechnics** (Applied Chemistry; Applied Mathematics; Applied Physics; Chemical Engineering; Civil Engineering; Electrical Engineering; Mechanical Engineering; Mechanics; Petroleum and Gas Engineering); **Science** (Biochemistry; Botany; Chemistry; Geography; Geology; Mathematics; Microbiology; Physics; Statistics; Zoology); **Social Work** (Social Work); **Technology and Engineering** (Applied Chemistry; Applied Mathematics; Applied Physics; Architecture; Chemical Engineering; Civil Engineering; Computer Science; Electrical Engineering; Engineering; Materials Engineering; Mechanical Engineering; Mechanics; Metallurgical Engineering; Pharmacy; Technology; Textile Design)

History: Founded 1949.

Governing Bodies: Senate; Syndicate

Academic Year: June to May (June-December; December-May).

Admission Requirements: 12th year senior secondary school/ intermediate examination or recognized foreign equivalent

Main Language(s) of Instruction: English

Degrees and Diplomas: *Diploma*; *Bachelor's Degree*; *Bachelor's degree (professional)*; *Postgraduate Diploma*; *Master's Degree*; *Master of Philosophy*; *Doctorate*. Also Certificate courses; M.B.A.

Student Residential Facilities: Yes (16 hostels with 1,446 rooms)

Special Facilities: Museum and Painting Gallery. Botanical Garden. Observatory

Libraries: Central library; 14 constituent libraries and 25 departmental libraries

Publications: Journal of Animal Morphology and Physiology; Oriental Institute Journal; PAVO and Baroda Reporter; Social Sciences and Technology; Swadhyay, In Gujarati; University Journals

Press or Publishing House: M.S. University of Baroda Press

Student Numbers *2010-2011*: Total: c. 3,700
Last Updated: 23/11/11

THE WEST BENGAL UNIVERSITY OF HEALTH SCIENCES (WBUHS)

DD - 36, Sector - 1, Salt Lake, Kolkata, West Bengal 700 064
Tel: +91(33) 2321-3461 +91(33) 2334-6602
Website: http://www.thewbuhs.org/

Registrar: Manoj Ghosh

Courses
Audiology and Speech Language Pathology (Speech Therapy and Audiology); **Dentistry** (Dentistry); **Health Administration** *(Postgraduate)* (Health Administration); **Nursing** (Nursing); **Physiotherapy** (Physical Therapy); **Prosthetics and Orthotics** (Dental Technology; Orthodontics)

Departments
Medicine and Surgery (Anaesthesiology; Anatomy; Community Health; Dermatology; Forensic Medicine and Dentistry; Gynaecology and Obstetrics; Medicine; Microbiology; Orthopaedics; Otorhinolaryngology; Paediatrics; Pathology; Pharmacology; Physiology; Pneumology; Psychiatry and Mental Health; Radiology; Rehabilitation and Therapy; Surgery; Tropical Medicine)

History: Founded 2003.

Degrees and Diplomas: *Bachelor's Degree*; *Bachelor's degree (professional)*; *Postgraduate Diploma*; *Master's Degree*; *Doctorate*. Also Honours Bachelor's degree.
Last Updated: 06/01/12

THIRUVALLUVAR UNIVERSITY

Serkkadu, Vellore, Tamil Nadu 632 106
Tel: +91(416) 227-4755 +91(416) 227-4756
Fax: +91(416) 227-4748
Website: http://thiruvalluvaruniversity.ac.in/

Vice Chancellor: A. Jothi Murugan

Departments
Biotechnology (Biotechnology); **Chemistry** (Chemistry); **Economics** (Economics); **English** (English); **Mathematics** (Mathematics); **Tamil** (South and Southeast Asian Languages); **Zoology** (Zoology)

Further Information: Also 98 affiliated colleges. A traditional and distance education institution.

History: Founded 2002.

Governing Bodies: Syndicate; Planning Board; Standing Committee; Academic Council

Degrees and Diplomas: *Master's Degree*; *Master of Philosophy*; *Doctorate*

Student Services: Health services, Sports facilities

Student Residential Facilities: Hostels

Libraries: Yes
Last Updated: 05/01/12

TILAK MAHARASHTRA VIDYAPEETH (TMV)

Vidyapeeth Bhavan, Gultekadi, Pune, Maharashtra 411 037
Tel: +91(20) 24261856 +91(20) 24264699
Fax: +91(20) 24266068 +91(20) 24271695
EMail: tmvadmin@tmv.edu.in; kulguru@tmv.edu.in
Website: http://www.tmv.edu.in

Vice-Chancellor: Deepak Tilak (2007-)
Tel: +91(20) 2427-1695 +91(20) 2445-9250,
Fax: +91(20) 2426-9940 +91(20) 2445-2837
EMail: d_tilak@hotmail.com; kulaguru@tmv.ernet.in

Registrar: Umesh Keskar
Tel: +91(20) 2426-1,685; +91(20) 2426-3952
EMail: keskarumesh@yahoo.com; kulasachiv@tmv.ernet.in

Faculties
Arts and Fine Arts (Arts and Humanities; Asian Studies; Cultural Studies; Fine Arts; Indic Languages; Sanskrit); **Ayurveda** (Ayurveda; Dietetics; Pharmacy; Physical Therapy); **Distance Education** (Business Administration; Dance; Fine Arts; Hotel Management; Journalism; Social Work); **Education** (Education); **Engineering** (Engineering); **Health Sciences** (Dental Technology; Health Sciences; Medicine; Nursing; Optometry; Physical Therapy); **Modern Sciences and Professional Skills** (Biotechnology; Business Administration; Engineering; Fine Arts; Hotel Management; Mass Communication; Media Studies; Microbiology); **Moral and Social Sciences** (Economics; Geography; History; Library Science; Philosophy; Political Sciences; Social Sciences; Sociology)

Further Information: Also Mumbai, Aurangabad and Delhi campuses. A traditional and distance education institution.

History: Founded 1921. Acquired status of deemed university 1987.

Governing Bodies: Board of Management; Academic Council; Planning and Monitoring Board; Finance Committee

Academic Year: July to May

Admission Requirements: 12th year senior secondary/intermediate examination or recognized foreign equivalent

Fees: (Rupees): 300-11,000 per annum

Main Language(s) of Instruction: English; Marathi

Accrediting Agencies: National Assessment and Accreditation Council (an autonomous body of the University Grants Commission); Distance Education Council (Autonomous Body of IGNOU); National Council of Teacher Education

Degrees and Diplomas: *Diploma*; *Bachelor's Degree*; *Master's Degree*; *Master of Philosophy*; *Doctorate*. Also Certificate and M.B.A.

Student Services: Academic counselling, Canteen, Foreign student adviser, Handicapped facilities, Health services, Language programs, Sports facilities

Student Residential Facilities: Yes

Libraries: 85,000 vols; 1,000 periodical subscriptions; INFLIBNET facility; Internet facility
Last Updated: 23/11/11

TILKA MANJHI BHAGALPUR UNIVERSITY (TMBU)

Tilka Manjhi, Bhagalpur, Bihar 812007
Tel: +91(641) 240-1001
Fax: +91(641) 242-2153
Website: http://www.tmbu.org/

Vice-Chancellor: K. N. Dubey
Tel: +91(641) 2620100 EMail: vc.drkndubey@gmail.com

Registrar: Chandra Mohan Das

Centres
Bioinformatics (Biological and Life Sciences; Computer Science; Data Processing; Sericulture); **Computer Science** (Computer Science); **Regional Studies** (Regional Studies)

Faculties
Commerce (Accountancy; Banking; Business Administration; Business and Commerce; Finance; Human Resources; Marketing); **Humanities** (Arts and Humanities; English; Hindi; Music; Persian; Philosophy; Sanskrit; Urdu); **Law** (Criminal Law; Environmental Studies; Human Rights; International Law; Law; Private Law); **Management Studies** (Business Administration; Management); **Science** (Biotechnology; Botany; Chemistry; Computer Science; Mathematics; Physics; Statistics; Zoology); **Social Sciences** (Agricultural Economics; Anthropology; Economics; Geography; History; Home Economics; Human Resources; Information Sciences; Labour and Industrial Relations; Peace and Disarmament; Political Sciences; Psychology; Rural Studies; Social Sciences; Sociology)

Research Centres
Agro-Economics (Agricultural Economics)

Further Information: Also 29 constituent colleges and 24 affiliated Colleges.

History: Founded 1960 as Bhagalpur University. Acquired present title 1991.

Admission Requirements: 12th year senior secondary/intermediate examination or recognized equivalent

Fees: (Rupees): 164-240 per annum

International Co-operation: National Assessment and Accreditation Council (NAAC)

Degrees and Diplomas: *Diploma*; *Postgraduate Diploma*; *Master's Degree*; *Doctorate*. Also Certificate Courses; M.B.A

Special Facilities: Computer Centre

Libraries: c. 140,000 vols; 125 periodical subscriptions

Academic Staff 2010-2011	MEN	WOMEN	**TOTAL**
FULL-TIME	–	–	**1,220**

Student Numbers 2010-2011			
All (Foreign Included)	43,884	16,943	**60,827**

Last Updated: 23/11/11

TRIPURA UNIVERSITY

Suryamaninagar, Tripura 799 022
Tel: +91(381) 237-4801
Fax: +91(381) 237-4802
EMail: tripurauniversity@rediffmail.com
Website: http://tripurauniv.in/

Vice-Chancellor: Arunoday Saha
Tel: +91(381) 2374801, Fax: +91(381) 2374802
EMail: arunodaysaha@rediffmail.com

Registrar: Kalyan Bijoy Jamatia
Tel: +91(381) 2374803, Fax: +91(381) 2374802
EMail: k_jamatia@yahoo.co.in

Centres

Bamboo Cultivation and Resource Utilization (Agriculture); **Bioinformatics** (Biological and Life Sciences; Computer Science; Zoology); **Gandhian Studies** (Environmental Studies); **IGNOU Study**; **Manuscript Resource and Manuscript Conservation** (Ancient Books); **NET/SET Coaching** (Mathematics; Philosophy); **Rubber Technology** (Rubber Technology); **Rural Studies** (Rural Studies); **Study of Social Exclusion and Inclusive Policies** (Social Policy; Social Problems; Social Work); **Tribal Language** (Native Language); **Women's Studies** (Women's Studies)

Departments

Distance Education (Arts and Humanities; Computer Science; Education; Indic Languages; Political Sciences)

Faculties

Arts and Commerce *(Postgraduate)* (Arts and Humanities; Business and Commerce; Development Studies; Economics; English; Fine Arts; Hindi; Histology; Indic Languages; Journalism; Management; Mass Communication; Music; Philosophy; Political Sciences; Rural Studies; Sanskrit); **Science** *(Postgraduate)* (Botany; Chemistry; Computer Engineering; Computer Science; Electrical and Electronic Equipment and Maintenance; Geography; Information Technology; Mathematics; Physics; Physiology; Safety Engineering; Zoology)

Further Information: Also 24 affiliated colleges. A traditional and distance education institution.

History: Founded 1987, incorporating 10 departments which had previously formed the Calcutta University Postgraduate Centre at Agartala. Acquired Central University status 2007.

Governing Bodies: Executive Council; Academic Council

Academic Year: June to May

Admission Requirements: Undergraduate programs, 12th year senior secondary/intermediate examination or recognized foreign equivalent; graduate programs, Gradute with Hons

Fees: (Rupees): Arts and Commerce programs, 1,050 per annum; Science programs, 1,250 per annum

Main Language(s) of Instruction: English

International Co-operation: With universities in Italy and Bangladesh

Accrediting Agencies: National assessment and Accreditation Council (NAAC)

Degrees and Diplomas: *Diploma*; *Bachelor's Degree*; *Postgraduate Diploma*; *Master's Degree*; *Master of Philosophy*; *Doctorate*. Also Certificate course.

Student Services: Academic counselling, Canteen, Cultural centre, Employment services, Handicapped facilities, Health services, Language programs, Sports facilities

Student Residential Facilities: Gents' Hall; Women Hostel

Libraries: Central Library, 93,122 vols; 117 periodical subscriptions

Publications: Annual Report *(annually)*

Academic Staff 2010-2011: Total: c. 120
Last Updated: 23/11/11

TUMKUR UNIVERSITY

Vishwavidyanilaya Karyalaya, University Constituent College
Campus, B.H Road, Tumkur 572 103
Tel: +91(816) 225-4546 +91(816) 225-5596
Fax: +91(816) 227-0719
Website: http://www.tumkuruniversity.in/

Vice Chancellor: S.C. Sharma
Registrar: D. Shivalingaiah

Faculties

Arts (Archaeology; Arts and Humanities; Economics; English; History; Indic Languages; Journalism; Physical Education; Political Sciences; Social Work; Sociology); **Commerce and Management** (Business Administration; Business and Commerce; Management); **Science and Technology** (Biochemistry; Biotechnology; Botany; Chemistry; Computer Science; Electronic Engineering; Information Sciences; Library Science; Mathematics; Microbiology; Physics; Zoology)

Further Information: Also 2 constituent colleges: University College of Arts and University College of Science

History: Founded 2004.

Governing Bodies: Syndicate; Academic Council

Degrees and Diplomas: *Bachelor's Degree*; *Master's Degree*; *Doctorate*; *Doctor of Literature*; *Doctor of Science*

Student Residential Facilities: 3 Boys Hostels (219 beds); 1 Girls Hostel (41 beds)

Special Facilities: Automated Weather Station; Remote Sensing Centre; Ramana Maharshi Dhyana Kendra; Buddhavana; Dhanvantarivana

Libraries: c. 29,000 vols; c. 70 periodical subscriptions
Last Updated: 03/01/12

UNIVERSITY OF AGRICULTURAL SCIENCES, BANGALORE (UASBNG)

GKVK Campus, Bangalore, Karnataka 560 065
Tel: +91(80) 2333-0153 +91(80) 2333-2442
Fax: +91(80) 2333-0277
EMail: registrar@uasbangalore.edu.in
Website: http://www.uasbng.kar.nic.in

Vice-Chancellor: Narayana Gowda
EMail: vc@uasbangalore.edu.in; knarayanagowda@yahoo.co.in

Registrar: Chikkadevaiah Tel: +91(80) 2333-0984

International Relations: S. Suryaprakash

Colleges

Agriculture *(Bangalore)* (Agricultural Economics; Agricultural Engineering; Agriculture; Agronomy; Apiculture; Biotechnology; Chemistry; Crop Production; Entomology; Environmental Studies; Food Science; Forestry; Horticulture; Marketing; Microbiology; Nutrition; Physiology; Plant and Crop Protection; Sericulture; Soil Science; Statistics); **Agriculture** *(Hassan)* (Agricultural Economics; Agriculture; Agronomy; Crop Production; Entomology; Forest Products; Forestry; Physiology); **Agriculture** *(Shimoga)* (Agriculture; Crop Production; Plant and Crop Protection; Social Sciences); **Agriculture** *(Mandya)* (Agriculture; Crop Production; Plant and Crop Protection; Social Sciences); **Forestry** *(Ponnampet)* (Agriculture; Forestry; Natural Resources); **Sericulture** *(Chintamani)* (Agronomy; Crop Production; Genetics; Horticulture; Plant and Crop Protection; Sericulture)

Further Information: Two campuses in Bangalore and one in Hebbal.

History: Founded 1964. The University has 8 campuses, two at Bangalore and one at Mangalore, Mudigere, Ponnampet, Shimadya, Shimoga and Chintamani. It is modelled on the pattern of the Land Grant Institutions of the USA. It aims to integrate teaching, research and extension education in Agricultural Sciences.

Governing Bodies: Board of Regents, Academic Council, Board of Studies, Research Council and Extension Education Council

Admission Requirements: 12th year senior secondary/intermediate examination or recognized foreign equivalent

Fees: (Rupees): Undergraduate, Agriculture and allied subjects 7,873, Veterinary Science, 12,528 per semester; postgraduate, 8,318

Main Language(s) of Instruction: English

Accrediting Agencies: Indian Council of Agricultural Research (ICAR), Veterinary Council of India (VCI)

Degrees and Diplomas: *Bachelor's Degree*; *Bachelor's degree (professional)*; *Master's Degree.* Also M.B.A.; Partner of the International Academic Post Graduate Programme: International Masters in Rural Development (IMRD).

Student Services: Canteen, Cultural centre, Employment services, Foreign student adviser, Foreign Studies Centre, Health services, Sports facilities

Student Residential Facilities: Yes

Special Facilities: Agricultural Museum

Libraries: 171,446 vols

Publications: Current Science *(monthly)*; Mysore Journal of Agricultural Sciences *(quarterly)*
Last Updated: 24/11/11

UNIVERSITY OF AGRICULTURAL SCIENCES, DHARWAD (USAD)

Krishinagar, Dharwad, Karnataka 580 005
Tel: +91(836) 2747-958
Fax: +91(836) 2745-276
EMail: registrar@uasd.edu; registraruasd@rediffmail.com; uasdregistrar@gmail.com
Website: http://www.uasd.edu

Vice-Chancellor: Rayappa Ramappa Hanchinal
EMail: vc@uasd.edu

Registrar: H.S. Vijayakumar
Tel: +91(836) 2747-958, Fax: +91(836) 2745-276
EMail: registrar@uasd.edu; registraruasd@rediffmail.com

International Relations: M.B. Chetti, Registrar

Colleges

Agriculture *(Bijapur)* (Agricultural Economics; Agricultural Engineering; Agriculture; Agronomy; Arts and Humanities; Chemistry; Crop Production; Dairy; Entomology; Fishery; Forestry; Genetics; Horticulture; Meat and Poultry; Meteorology; Microbiology; Natural Sciences; Plant and Crop Protection; Sericulture; Soil Science; Veterinary Science); **Agriculture** *(Hanumanmatti)* (Agriculture); **Agriculture** *(Dharwad)* (Agricultural Business; Agricultural Economics; Agricultural Education; Agricultural Engineering; Agricultural Management; Agriculture; Agronomy; Biochemistry; Biotechnology; Botany; Chemistry; Crop Production; Entomology; Environmental Studies; Genetics; Horticulture; Marketing; Microbiology; Physical Education; Plant and Crop Protection; Sericulture; Soil Science; Statistics; Veterinary Science; Zoology); **Forestry** *(Sirsi)* (Agricultural Engineering; Agriculture; Arts and Humanities; Forest Biology; Forest Management; Forestry; Natural Sciences); **Rural Home Science** *(Dharwad)* (Communication Studies; Development Studies; Family Studies; Food Science; Home Economics; Nutrition; Physical Education; Textile Design)

Further Information: 6 campuses offering programmes; 4 campuses offering postgraduate programmes

History: Founded 1986 under UAS Act 1963. The University is modelled on the pattern of the Land Grant Institutions of the USA.

Governing Bodies: Board of Management; Academic Council; Research Council; Extension Education Council

Academic Year: September to August (September-February; March-August)

Admission Requirements: 12th year senior secondary/intermediate examination or recognized foreign equivalent with PCMB/ PCB/PCM

Fees: (Rupees): undergraduate, 7,570 for first semester and 5,780 for second semester; graduate, 8,360 for first semester and 6,000 for second semester. (US Dollars): Foreign students, 4,000

Main Language(s) of Instruction: English

International Co-operation: With universities in USA

Accrediting Agencies: Indian Council of Agricultural Research, New Delhi

Degrees and Diplomas: *Diploma*; *Bachelor's Degree*; *Master's Degree*; *Doctorate.* Also Certificate Courses

Student Services: Academic counselling, Canteen, Cultural centre, Employment services, Foreign student adviser, Health services, Social counselling, Sports facilities

Student Residential Facilities: 2 undergraduate and 2 postgraduate boys hostels (beds for 1,000 beds; 5 girls hostels (270 beds); 3 guest houses; 1 International hostel; 1 farmers hostel; 2 trainees hostels

Special Facilities: Museum (ATIC); College Farm

Libraries: 78,000 vols and 4,500 periodical subscriptions; library in each campus and in each research station; digital library service

Publications: Karnataka Journal of Agricultural Sciences, Scientific publciations relating to agriculture, horticulture, forestry, home science, agricultural engineering, animal science *(quarterly)*; Krishi Munnade in Kannada *(monthly)*; UAS Newsletter, Popular farm magazine on agricultural and allied sciences *(bimonthly)*

Press or Publishing House: Publication Centre, UAS, Dharwad
Last Updated: 24/11/11

UNIVERSITY OF ALLAHABAD (ALLDUNIV)

PO Allahabad, Agricultural Institute, Allahabad,
Uttar Pradesh 211007
Tel: +91(532) 246-1083
Fax: +91(532) 254-5021
Website: http://www.allduniv.ac.in

Vice-Chancellor: Anil K. Singh

Faculties

Arts (Ancient Civilizations; Arabic; Archaeology; Arts and Humanities; Cultural Studies; Economics; Education; English; Fine Arts; Geography; Hindi; Journalism; Medicine; Modern History; Modern Languages; Music; Performing Arts; Persian; Philosophy; Physical Education; Political Sciences; Psychology; Sanskrit; Urdu); **Commerce** (Business and Commerce; Economics); **Law** (Law); **Science** (Applied Physics; Biochemistry; Botany; Chemistry; Earth Sciences; Mathematics; Natural Sciences; Photography; Physics; Statistics; Zoology)

Further Information: Also 7 Associated and Constituent Colleges

History: Founded 1887. A 'Central University'.

Governing Bodies: Court; Executive Council; Academic Council

Academic Year: August to April (August-May; July-April)

Admission Requirements: 12th year senior secondary/intermediate examination or recognized foreign equivalent, and competitive entrance examination

Fees: (Rupees): 144-300 per annum

Main Language(s) of Instruction: English

Degrees and Diplomas: *Bachelor's Degree*: 3-4 yrs; *Master's Degree*: a further 2-3 yrs; *Doctorate (PhD).* Also Diploma and Certificate courses

Student Residential Facilities: Yes

Special Facilities: Kaushambi Museum (the University has undertaken excavations at Kaushantbi and exploration of prehistoric sites in the Vindhyas)

Libraries: 530,608 vols; 500 periodicals

Publications: Indian Journal of Economics *(quarterly)*
Last Updated: 16/05/11

UNIVERSITY OF BURDWAN (BU)

Rajbati, Burdwan, West Bengal 713 104
Tel: +91(342) 263-4975
Fax: +91(342) 253-0452
EMail: pio@buruniv.ac.in
Website: http://www.buruniv.ac.in

Vice-Chancellor: Subrata Pal (2008-)
Tel: +91(342) 263-4900, Fax: +91(342) 253-0452
EMail: vc@buruniv.ac.in

Registrar: Debidas Mondal EMail: dyregistrar@buruniv.ac.in

Faculties

Other (Animal Husbandry; Business Computing; Demography and Population; Family Studies; Health Administration; Laboratory

Techniques; Maintenance Technology; Social and Community Services; Special Education; Welfare and Protective Services; Yoga); **Post-graduate Studies in Arts, Commerce, Law, Fine Arts and Music** (Arts and Humanities; Business Administration; Business and Commerce; Economics; Education; English; Fine Arts; French; German; Hindi; History; Human Resources; Indic Languages; Information Sciences; Law; Library Science; Mass Communication; Music; Philosophy; Political Sciences; Russian; Sanskrit; Sociology; Tourism); **Post-graduate Studies in Medicine** (Anatomy; Biochemistry; Gynaecology and Obstetrics; Medicine; Ophthalmology; Surgery); **Post-graduate Studies in Science** (Biochemistry; Biology; Biotechnology; Botany; Chemistry; Computer Engineering; Computer Science; Education; Electronic Engineering; Environmental Studies; Geography; Geology; Mathematics; Microbiology; Physics; Physiology; Statistics; Surveying and Mapping; Telecommunications Engineering; Zoology); **Under-graduate Studies in Engineering** (Civil Engineering; Computer Engineering; Computer Science; Electrical Engineering; Electronic Engineering; Engineering; Information Technology; Measurement and Precision Engineering; Metallurgical Engineering; Telecommunications Engineering); **Under-graduate Studies in Medicine** (Homeopathy; Laboratory Techniques; Medical Technology; Medicine; Surgery); **Under-graduate Studies in Science, Arts, Commerce, Law, Fine Arts and Music** (Accountancy; Advertising and Publicity; Arabic; Arts and Humanities; Biochemistry; Biotechnology; Botany; Business and Commerce; Chemistry; Computer Science; Crop Production; E-Business/Commerce; Economics; Education; Electronic Engineering; English; Environmental Management; Environmental Studies; Fashion Design; Fine Arts; Fishery; French; Geography; Geology; Hindi; History; Information Technology; Interior Design; Law; Mathematics; Microbiology; Music; Natural Sciences; Nutrition; Persian; Philosophy; Physical Education; Physical Therapy; Physics; Physiology; Political Sciences; Sanskrit; Sericulture; Singing; Sociology; Statistics; Urdu; Water Management; Zoology)

Further Information: Also 6 Constituent and 110 Affiliated Colleges. A traditional and distance education institution.

History: Founded 1960.

Governing Bodies: Court; Executive Council

Academic Year: June to May

Admission Requirements: 12th year senior secondary/intermediate examination or recognized foreign equivalent

Fees: (Rupees): 100-500 per month

Main Language(s) of Instruction: English, Bengali

Accrediting Agencies: NAAC

Degrees and Diplomas: *Diploma*; *Bachelor's Degree*: 3-5 yrs; *Bachelor's degree (professional)*; *Postgraduate Diploma*; *Master's Degree*: a further 1-3 yrs; *Master of Philosophy*. Also Certificate; Advance Diploma; Honours Bachelor; Integrated B.A. LL.B.(Hons.); M.B.A.

Student Services: Academic counselling, Canteen, Cultural centre, Employment services, Handicapped facilities, Health services, Language programs, Sports facilities

Student Residential Facilities: Yes

Special Facilities: Collections of antiquities and art objects from proto-historic period to modern times including coins, seals, inscriptions, stone sculptures, bronzes of the Pala-Sena School of Bengal, terracotta figures, figurines and decorative temple plaques from West Bengal. Art Gallery with European and Indian paintings

Libraries: 186,376 vols; 200 journal subscriptions; 10 CD-ROM databases.

Press or Publishing House: Burdwan University Press
Last Updated: 24/11/11

UNIVERSITY OF CALCUTTA
Kalikata Viswavidyalaya
Senate House, 87/1 College Street, Kolkata, West Bengal 700073
Tel: +91(33) 2241-0071
Fax: +91(33) 2241-3222
EMail: admin@caluniv.ac.in
Website: http://www.caluniv.ac.in/

Vice-Chancellor: Suranjan Das (2008-)
Tel: +91(33) 2241-3288 EMail: vc@caluniv.ac.in

Registrar: Basab Chaudhuri EMail: registrar@caluniv.ac.in

Faculties
Agriculture (Agriculture; Agronomy; Horticulture; Plant and Crop Protection; Soil Science; Veterinary Science); **Arts** (Ancient Civilizations; Ancient Languages; Arabic; Archaeology; Arts and Humanities; Asian Religious Studies; Economics; English; Heritage Preservation; Hindi; History; Indic Languages; Islamic Studies; Linguistics; Literature; Museum Studies; Persian; Philosophy; Political Sciences; Sanskrit; Sociology; South Asian Studies; Southeast Asian Studies; Urdu); **Commerce, Social Welfare and Business Management** (Business Administration; Business and Commerce); **Education, Journalism and Library Science** (Education; Educational Administration; Film; Journalism; Library Science; Mass Communication; Media Studies; Psychiatry and Mental Health; Radio and Television Broadcasting); **Engineering and Technology** (Applied Physics; Automation and Control Engineering; Bioengineering; Chemical Engineering; Computer Science; Electrical Engineering; Electronic Engineering; Engineering; Materials Engineering; Measurement and Precision Engineering; Meteorology; Optics; Petroleum and Gas Engineering; Pharmacology; Polymer and Plastics Technology; Power Engineering; Radiophysics; Rubber Technology; Technology); **Fine Arts, Music and Home Science** (Fine Arts; Home Economics; Music; Nutrition); **Law** (Civil Law; Criminal Law; Law); **Science** (Analytical Chemistry; Anthropology; Applied Mathematics; Archaeology; Biochemistry; Biophysics; Biotechnology; Botany; Chemistry; Clinical Psychology; Computer Science; Electronic Engineering; Genetics; Geography; Geology; Geophysics; Industrial and Organizational Psychology; Inorganic Chemistry; Instrument Making; Marine Science and Oceanography; Mathematics; Microbiology; Molecular Biology; Natural Sciences; Nuclear Physics; Optics; Organic Chemistry; Physical Chemistry; Physics; Physiology; Psychology; Solid State Physics; Statistics; Toxicology; Zoology)

Further Information: Also 18 research centres.

History: Founded 1857.

Governing Bodies: Senate; Syndicate

Academic Year: June to May

Admission Requirements: 12th year senior secondary/intermediate examination or recognized foreign equivalent, and competitive entrance examination

Main Language(s) of Instruction: English

International Co-operation: Cultural Exchange Programme with Indian Council for Cultural Relations

Accrediting Agencies: University Grants Commission

Degrees and Diplomas: *Diploma*; *Bachelor's Degree*: 3 yrs; *Postgraduate Diploma*; *Master's Degree*: a further 2 yrs; *Master of Philosophy*; *Doctorate (PhD)*: 3 yrs

Student Services: Academic counselling, Canteen, Cultural centre, Employment services, Foreign student adviser, Foreign Studies Centre, Handicapped facilities, Health services, Language programs, Nursery care, Social counselling, Sports facilities

Student Residential Facilities: Yes

Special Facilities: Asutosh Museum of Indian Art

Libraries: 781,363 vols

Publications: Calcutta Review *(monthly)*; Journals

Press or Publishing House: Calcutta University Press
Last Updated: 25/11/11

UNIVERSITY OF CALICUT (UNICAL)
PO Calicut University, Thenhipalam, Malappuram District, Kozhikode, Kerala 673635
Tel: +91(494) 240-1144 +91(494) 240-1152
Fax: +91(494) 240-0269
EMail: regcltuty@rediffmail.com
Website: http://www.unical.ac.in

Vice-Chancellor: M. Abdul Salam (2011-)
Tel: +91(494) 240-0241, Fax: +91(494) 240-0268

Registrar: P.P. Mohamed Tel: +91(494) 240-0252

Centres

Computer (Computer Science); **West Asian Studies** *(Kunhali Marakkar)* (Asian Studies; International Relations; Political Sciences); **Women's Studies** (Women's Studies)

Departments

Arabic (Arabic); **Biotechnology** (Biotechnology); **Botany** (Botany); **Chemistry** (Applied Chemistry; Chemistry); **Commerce and Management Studies** (Business Administration; Business and Commerce; Management); **Computer Science** (Computer Science); **Economics** (Economics); **Education** (Education); **English** (English); **Folklore Studies** (Folklore); **Hindi** (Hindi); **History** (History); **Journalism and Mass Communication** (Journalism; Mass Communication); **Library and Information Sciences** (Information Sciences; Library Science); **Life Sciences** (Biochemistry; Biological and Life Sciences; Microbiology; Physiology); **Lifelong Learning and Extension** (Adult Education; Continuing Education; Educational and Student Counselling); **Malayam** (Indic Languages); **Mathematics** (Mathematics); **Philosophy** (Philosophy); **Physics** (Physics); **Psychology** (Psychology); **Russian** (Russian); **Sanskrit** (Sanskrit); **Statistics** (Statistics); **Zoology** (Entomology; Zoology)

Research Centres

Educational Multimedia (Educational Technology; Multimedia)

Schools

Drama (Theatre)

Further Information: Also 304 affiliated colleges (83 are located in Kozhikode district, 72 in Thrissur, 82 in Malappuram, 50 in Palakkad and 10 in Wayanad district). Extension centres at Thrissur, Calicut and Vatakara. A traditional and distance education institution.

History: Founded 1968. Main campus Thenhippalam.

Governing Bodies: Senate; Syndicate; Academic Council

Academic Year: June to March

Admission Requirements: 12th year senior secondary/intermediate examination or recognized foreign equivalent

Main Language(s) of Instruction: English, Malayaam

Degrees and Diplomas: *Diploma*; *Bachelor's Degree*; *Bachelor's degree (professional)*; *Postgraduate Diploma*; *Master's Degree*; *Master of Philosophy*; *Doctorate*. Also Certificate courses; integrated M.Phil/Ph.D; M.B.A.

Student Services: Canteen, Employment services, Foreign student adviser, Health services, Sports facilities

Student Residential Facilities: Guest House

Special Facilities: Audiovisual Research centre; UGC Centre for coaching minorities; Botanical Garden

Libraries: 87,212 vols; 64 periodical subscriptions

Press or Publishing House: Publication Division
Last Updated: 24/11/11

UNIVERSITY OF DELHI

Delhi Vishwavidyalaya
Delhi 110007
Tel: +91(11) 2766-7725 +91(11) 2392-2480
Fax: +91(11) 2766-6350
Website: http://www.du.ac.in

Vice-Chancellor: Dinesh Singh (2010-)
Tel: +91(11) 2766-7011, Fax: +91(11) 2766-7049
EMail: vc@du.ac.in

Registrar: R. K. Sinha
Tel: +91(11) 2766-6342, Fax: +91(11) 2766-6350
EMail: registrar@du.ac.in

Centres

Agro-Chemicals and Pest Management (Agricultural Management; Pest Management) *Co-ordinator:* S.C. Jain; **Bio-Medical Research** *(Bhim Rao Ambedkar) Director:* Vani Brahamchari

Faculties

Applied Social Sciences and Humanities (Arts and Humanities; Business and Commerce; Economics; Finnish; Hungarian; Slavic Languages; Social Sciences) *Dean:* Rashmi Agarwal; **Arts** (Arabic; Asian Religious Studies; English; German; Hindi; Indic Languages;

Information Sciences; Library Science; Linguistics; Literature; Modern Languages; Persian; Philosophy; Psychology; Romance Languages; Sanskrit; Urdu) *Dean:* Gurchran Singh Arshi; **Ayurvedic and Unani Medicine** (Ayurveda; Traditional Eastern Medicine) *Dean:* C.R. Babu; **Commerce and Business** (Business and Commerce; Finance) *Dean:* Muneesh Kumar; **Education** (Education) *Dean:* U.S. Sharma; **Homeopathic Medicine** *Dean:* C.R. Babu; **Interdisciplinary and Applied Sciences** (Biochemistry; Biology; Biophysics; Electronic Engineering; Environmental Studies; Genetics; Microbiology; Molecular Biology) *Dean:* Prahlad C. Ghosh; **Law** (Law) *Dean:* Nomita Agarwal; **Management Studies** (Business Administration; Industrial Management; Management) *Dean:* V.K. Bhalla; **Mathematical Sciences** (Computer Science; Mathematics; Operations Research; Statistics) *Dean:* Jagdish Saran; **Medical Sciences** (Medicine) *Dean:* O.P. Kalra; **Music and Fine Arts** (Fine Arts; Music) *Dean:* Krishna Bisht; **Science** (Anthropology; Astrophysics; Botany; Chemistry; Geology; Home Economics; Nursing; Pharmacy; Physics; Zoology) *Dean:* A.K. Kalla; **Social Sciences** (Adult Education; African Studies; Continuing Education; East Asian Studies; Economics; Geography; History; Political Sciences; Social Work; Sociology) *Dean:* Aruna Bhardwaj; **Technology** (Technology) *Dean:* P.B. Sharma

Further Information: Also 79 Affiliated/Constituent Colleges. Teaching Hospitals and campus of open learning

History: Founded 1922. Acquired present status and title 1952. The University has two campuses: Main Campus (North Campus), and the South Delhi Campus, founded 1973 as first step towards a multicampus system for the University, with more than 600 postgraduate students.

Governing Bodies: Court; Executive Council; Academic Council; Finance Committee

Academic Year: July to March (July-September; October-December; January-March)

Admission Requirements: 12th year senior secondary/intermediate examination or recognized foreign equivalent

Fees: (Rupees): 3,500-7,500 per annum

Main Language(s) of Instruction: English, Hindi

International Co-operation: With universities in USA; Germany; France; Japan; Portugal; Sudan; Spain; Korea; Trinidad and Tobago

Degrees and Diplomas: *Bachelor's Degree:* Anthropology; Zoology; Biochemistry; Biomedical Science; Botany; Chemistry; Computer Science; Electronics; Geology; Home Science; Mathematics; Microbiology; Nursing; Occupational Therapy; Polymer Science; Physical Therapy; Physics; Statistics; Zoology (BSc (Hons)); Applied Sciences; Electronics; Food Technology; Instrumentation; Arabic; Bengali; Indic Languages; Hindi; Persian; Urdu; Punjabi; Italian; Spanish; German; English; French (BA (Hons)); Ayurvedic Medicine and Surgery (BAMS); Biotechnology; Civil Engineering; Computer Engineering; Electronic Engineering; Electrical Engineering; Telecommunications Engineering; Environmental Engineering; Information Technology (BE); Business and Commerce (Bcom (Hons)); Business Studies (BBS); Dental Surgery (BDS); Education Science (BEd); Elementary Education (BElEd); Finance; Investment Analysis (BFIA); Fine Arts (BFA); Homeopathic Medicine and Surgery (BHMS); Instrument Making; Automation and Control Engineering; Mechanical Engineering; Polymer Science and Chemical Technology; Production and Industrial Engineering (BE); Law (LLB); Library Science (BLibSc); Mass Media; Mass Communication (BMMMC); Mathematics; Physics; Biological and Life Sciences; Home Science; Physical Education; Health Education and Sports Sciences; Medical Technology and Radiography (BSc); Pharmacy (BPharm); Physical Education (BPEd); Physiotherapy (BPT); Prosthetics and Orthodontics (BPO); Psychology; Business Economics; Economics; Geography; Journalism and Mass Communication; History; Mathematics; Modern Languages; Music; Philosophy; Political Science; Sanskrit; Social Work; Sociology (BA (Hons)); Unani Medicine and Surgery (BUMS); Vocational Studies (BA); *Bachelor's Degree:* Civil Engineering; Electrical Engineering; Telecommunications Engineering; Mechanical Engineering (BTech), part-time; *Postgraduate Diploma:* Medical Science (PG); *Master's Degree:* Agrochemicals and Pest Management; Anthropology; Biomedical Science; Biochemistry; Botany; Chemistry; Electronics; Environmental Biology; Genetics; Geology; Home Science; Computer Science; Microbiology; Physics; Plant Molecular Biology; Zoology (MSc); Anaesthesia; Community Health

Administation; Dermatology; Forensic Medicine; Medical Biochemistry; Medical Microbiology; Medicine; Paediatrics; Pathology; Pharmacology; Physiology; Psychiatry; Radiology; Social & Preventive Medicine; Pneumology (MD); Anatomy; Gynaecology & Obstetrics; Ophtalmology; Orthopaedics; Otorhinolaryngology; Surgery (MS); Applied Operational Research; Computer Science; Mathematics; Operational Research; Statistics (MA/ MSc); Business Administration (MBA); Business and Commerce (Mcom); Cardio-Thoracic Surgery; Gastroenterology Surgery; Neuro-Surgery; Paediatric Surgery; Plastic Surgery (MCh); Comparative Law (MCL); Computer Applications (MCA); Computer Technology & Applications; Control & Instrumentation; Electronics & Communication; Environmental Engineering; Hydraulic Engineering; Polymer Technology; Power Engineering; Production Engineering; Structural Engineering; Thermal Engineering (ME); Education (M.Ed); Finance and Control (MFC); Fine Arts (MFA); Human Resources and Organizational Development; International Business; Information Systems; Microwave Electronics; Process Control; Signal Processing (MTech); Law (LLM); Library and Information Sciences (MLibISc); Medical Biochemistry; Medical Microbiology; Applied Physics (MSc); Nursing (MNursing); Pharmacy (MPharm); Physical Education; Psychology; Arabic; Bengali; Buddhist Studies; Business Economics; Indic Languages; Comparative Literature; Economics; Geography; Hindi; History; Modern Languages; Music; Persian; Philosophy; Political Science; Sanskrit; Social Work; Sociology; Urdu (MA); Punjabi; Tamil; Russian; English; French; German; Spanish; Italian; Japanese (MA); *Master of Philosophy (Mphil)*; *Doctorate (PhD)*: a further 3 yrs. Also Diploma and Certificate courses

Student Services: Academic counselling, Canteen, Cultural centre, Employment services, Foreign student adviser, Handicapped facilities, Health services, Language programs, Nursery care, Social counselling, Sports facilities

Student Residential Facilities: Hostels on campus for postgraduate and doctoral students. Individual college hostels for undergraduate students

Special Facilities: Museum; Observatory; Botanical Garden; Gandhi Bhawan; Computer Centre; University Science Information Centre; Instrumentation Centre

Libraries: Central Library, 1,425,402 vols; 875 international periodical subscriptions; 410 national periodical subscriptions. Special collections, 600 vols

Publications: Old Question Papers *(annually)*

Press or Publishing House: Delhi University Press
Last Updated: 11/07/11

UNIVERSITY OF GORAKHPUR
Deen Dayal Upadhyay Gorakhpur University
Gorakhpur, Uttar Pradesh 273009
Tel: +91(551) 234-0363 +91(551) 233-0767
Fax: +91(551) 234-0458
EMail: registrarddugu@gmail.com
Website: http://www.ddugu.edu.in

Vice-Chancellor: P. C. Trivedi EMail: vc@ddugu.edu.in
Registrar: Ram Charan Lal EMail: registrar@ddugu.edu.in

Faculties
Agriculture (Agriculture); **Arts** (Arts and Humanities); **Commerce** (Business and Commerce); **Education** (Education); **Law** (Law); **Science** (Computer Science; Electronic Engineering; Natural Sciences; Physics)

Further Information: Also 36 Affiliated Colleges
History: Founded 1957. Acquired present title 1997.
Academic Year: July to April
Main Language(s) of Instruction: Hindi, English
Degrees and Diplomas: *Diploma*; *Bachelor's Degree*; *Master's Degree*; *Doctorate*
Student Services: Health services, Sports facilities
Student Residential Facilities: For 800 male students and 300 female students
Libraries: 387,100 vols; 800 periodical subscriptions
Last Updated: 11/07/11

UNIVERSITY OF GOUR BANGA
N.H-34 (NEAR RABINDRA BHABAN), P.O.Mokdumpur, Malda, West Bengal 732103
Tel: +91(3512) 223666
Website: http://www.ugb.ac.in/
Vice-Chancellor: Gopa Datta
Registrar: Syam Sundar Bairagya Tel: +91(3512) 223664

Programmes
Arts and Humanities (Arabic; Education; English; History; Sanskrit); **Hospitality Management** (Hotel Management); **Mathematics** (Mathematics)

Degrees and Diplomas: *Bachelor's Degree*; *Master's Degree*
Last Updated: 05/01/12

UNIVERSITY OF HYDERABAD (UOHYD)
Prof. C.R. Rao Road, PO Central University, Gachibowli, Hyderabad, Andhra Pradesh 500046
Tel: +91(40) 2313-2100
Fax: +91(40) 2301-0145 +91(40) 2301-1089
EMail: acadinfo@uohyd.ernet.in
Website: http://www.uohyd.ernet.in

Vice-Chancellor: Ramakrishna Ramaswamy (2011-)
Tel: +91(40) 2313-2000, Fax: +91(40) 2301-0121
EMail: vc@uohyd.ernet.in; r.ramaswamy@gmail.com

Registrar: Mohan Kumar
Tel: +91(40) 2301-0245 EMail: registrar@uohyd.ernet.in

Director, International Affairs: Vinod Pavarala
Tel: +91(40) 2313-4041 EMail: international@uohyd.ernet.in

Centres
Advanced Research in High Energy Materials (Energy Engineering; Materials Engineering); **Buddhist Studies** (Asian Religious Studies); **Cognitive Science** (Cognitive Sciences); **Earth and Space Sciences** (Astronomy and Space Science; Earth Sciences); **Health Psychology** (Psychology); **Integrated Studies**; **Modelling Simulation and Design** (Design); **Nanotechnology** (Nanotechnology); **Women's Studies**

Research Institutes
Animal Biotechnology (Animal Husbandry; Biotechnology); **Health Science Education and Research Translation** (Health Education; Translation and Interpretation)

Schools
Arts and Communication *(Sarojini Naidu)* (Dance; Fine Arts; Journalism; Mass Communication; Media Studies; Performing Arts; Radio and Television Broadcasting; Theatre); **Chemistry** (Chemistry; Inorganic Chemistry; Organic Chemistry; Physical Chemistry); **Engineering Science and Technology** (Engineering; Materials Engineering; Nanotechnology; Technology); **Humanities** (Applied Linguistics; Arts and Humanities; Comparative Literature; English; French; Hindi; Indic Languages; Native Language; Philosophy; Sanskrit; Translation and Interpretation; Urdu); **Life Sciences** (Biochemistry; Biological and Life Sciences; Botany; Environmental Management; Zoology); **Management Studies** (Business Administration; Finance; Human Resources; Information Technology; Management; Marketing; Operations Research); **Mathematics and Computer / Information Sciences** (Computer Education; Computer Science; Information Sciences; Mathematics; Mathematics and Computer Science; Statistics); **Medical Sciences** (Health Sciences; Medicine; Nutrition); **Physics** (Computer Science; Electronic Engineering; Physics); **Social Sciences** (Anthropology; Cultural Studies; Economics; Folklore; History; Human Rights; Political Sciences; Regional Studies; Social Problems; Social Sciences; Sociology)

Further Information: A traditional and distance education institution.

History: Founded 1974 as a unitary and teaching University destined to develop as one of the outstanding Centres of higher learning in the country. The University is open to persons of either sex and of any race, creed, caste or class and offers postgraduate and research courses. A Central University.

Governing Bodies: Court; Executive Council; Academic Council
Academic Year: July to April (July-November; January-April)

Admission Requirements: University degree at Bachelor's level

Fees: Please visit out websitehttp://www.uohyd.ernet.in/index.php/admissions/prospectus

Main Language(s) of Instruction: English

Degrees and Diplomas: *Diploma*; *Master's Degree*; *Master of Philosophy*; *Doctorate*. Also Integrated Master's Degree, 5 yrs (Sciences; Humanities; Social Sciences); M.B.A.

Student Services: Canteen, Foreign Studies Centre, Health services, Sports facilities

Student Residential Facilities: For 2,300 Men and 914 Women students

Libraries: 35,8,740 vols; 2,889 E-Books; 510 print journals and 17,000 E-journals.

Publications: Annual Report; Newsletter *(quarterly)*; University Profile *(biannually)*

Academic Staff *2009-2010*	MEN	WOMEN	TOTAL
FULL-TIME	276	75	**351**
STAFF WITH DOCTORATE			
FULL-TIME	258	67	**325**
Student Numbers *2009-2010*			
All (Foreign Included)	2,804	1,356	**4,160**
FOREIGN ONLY	51	23	**74**

Distance students, 672.
Last Updated: 24/11/11

🎓 UNIVERSITY OF JAMMU

Baba Saheb Ambedkar Road, New Campus, Jammu,
Jammu and Kashmir 180006
Tel: +91(191) 243-1365 +91(191) 243-5248
Fax: +91(191) 243-1365
EMail: daa@jammuuniversity.in; isp_ju@jammuuniversity.in
Website: http://jammuuniversity.in/index.asp

Vice-Chancellor: Varun Sahni (2009-)
Tel: +91(191) 245-0014, Fax: +91(191) 245-0014
EMail: varun_sahni@hotmail.com

Registrar: Naresh Padha
Tel: +91(191) 243-1365 EMail: nareshpadha@jammuuniversity.in

Centres

Computer (Computer Science); **Cross-Cultural Research And Human Resource Management** *(International)* (Cultural Studies; Human Resources; Management); **Disaster Management** (Safety Engineering); **Dr. Ambedkar Studies** (Philosophy); **Field Operations and Research on Himalayan Glaciology** *(Regional - RCFOR-HG)* (Earth Sciences; Geology; Surveying and Mapping; Water Science); **History and Culture of Jammu and Ladakh Regions** *(Jammu and Ladakh)* (Cultural Studies; History); **Nehru Studies** (Social Sciences); **New Literatures** (Literature); **Peace and Conflict Studies** *(Gandhian)* (Peace and Disarmament); **Professional Studies in Urdu** (Urdu); **Quality Assurance** *(Directorate of Quality Assurance)* (Safety Engineering); **Studies in Museology** (Museum Studies); **University Science Instrumentation** (Measurement and Precision Engineering); **Yoga** (Yoga)

Faculties

Arts/Oriental Languages (Arts and Humanities; English; Hindi; Indic Languages; Oriental Languages; Sanskrit; Urdu); **Business Studies** (Business Administration; Business and Commerce; Management; Tourism); **Education** (Education; Physical Education); **Engineering** (Engineering); **Law** (Criminology; Human Rights; Law; Police Studies); **Life Sciences** (Biological and Life Sciences; Biotechnology; Botany; Environmental Studies; Microbiology; Zoology); **Mathematical Science** (Computer Science; Information Technology; Mathematics; Statistics); **Medicine** (Alternative Medicine; Ayurveda; Medicine; Physical Education); **Music and Fine Arts** (Fine Arts; Music); **Sciences** (Chemistry; Child Care and Development; Electronic Engineering; Family Studies; Geography; Geology; Home Economics; Natural Resources; Physics; Surveying and Mapping; Women's Studies); **Social Science** (Computer Science; Design; Economics; English; French; History; Information Sciences; Library Science; Management; Political Sciences; Psychology; Regional Studies; Social Sciences; Sociology; Urdu)

Institutes

Human Genetics (Genetics)

Further Information: Also 5 Constituent, 52 Affiliated Colleges, and 113 Recognized Colleges. A traditional and distance education institution.

History: Founded 1948 as University of Jammu and Kashmir. Became separate University 1969. A Central University.

Governing Bodies: University Council; Syndicate; Academic Council

Academic Year: February to December (February-June; July-November; August-December)

Admission Requirements: 12th year senior secondary/intermediate examination or recognized equivalent

Fees: (Rupees): 3,300 - 10,000 per annum

Main Language(s) of Instruction: English, Classical or Modern Indian

Accrediting Agencies: National Assessment and Accreditation Council (NAAC)

Degrees and Diplomas: *Diploma*; *Bachelor's Degree*; *Postgraduate Diploma*; *Master's Degree*; *Master of Philosophy*; *Doctorate*; *Doctor of Literature*. Also B.A./B.Sc./B.Com./BBA

Student Services: Academic counselling, Canteen, Cultural centre, Employment services, Foreign Studies Centre, Handicapped facilities, Health services, Language programs, Nursery care, Social counselling, Sports facilities

Student Residential Facilities: For 669 students

Special Facilities: Art Gallery; Museum

Libraries: With a total of 402,833 vols; 225 periodical subscriptions

Publications: Review Journal (Languages, Sciences, Social Sciences)

Academic Staff *2009-2010*	MEN	WOMEN	TOTAL
FULL-TIME	146	99	**245**
PART-TIME	54	76	**130**
STAFF WITH DOCTORATE			
FULL-TIME	127	84	**211**
PART-TIME	15	28	**43**
Student Numbers *2009-2010*			
All (Foreign Included)	31,214	30,574	**61,788**

Distance students, 1,504.
Last Updated: 24/11/11

UNIVERSITY OF KALYANI (KU)

Kalyani, West Bengal 741235
Tel: +91(33) 2582-2505
Fax: +91(33) 2582-8282
EMail: vckalyani@yahoo.com
Website: http://www.klyuniv.ac.in/

Vice-Chancellor: Alok Kumar Banerjee (2009-)
Tel: +91(94) 2582-8282 EMail: vckalyani@klyuniv.ac.in

Registrar: Utpal Bhattacharya
Tel: +91(33) 2582-2505
EMail: klyuniv_rgs@yahoo.co.in; ubku2001@yahoo.com

Faculties

Arts and Commerce (Arts and Humanities; Business and Commerce; Chinese; Economics; English; Folklore; History; Indic Languages; Information Sciences; Library Science; Modern Languages; Political Sciences; Russian; Sociology); **Education** (Education; Physical Education); **Engineering, Technology and Management** (Business Administration; Computer Engineering; Computer Science; Development Studies; Engineering; Management; Rural Studies; Technology); **Science** (Biochemistry; Biological and Life Sciences; Biophysics; Biotechnology; Botany; Chemistry; Environmental Studies; Geography; Mathematics; Microbiology; Molecular Biology; Physics; Physiology; Statistics; Zoology)

Further Information: Also 37 Affiliated Colleges. A traditional and distance education institution.

History: Founded 1960.

Governing Bodies: Court; Executive Council

Academic Year: June to May (June-October; November-January; February-May)

Admission Requirements: 12th year senior secondary/intermediate examination or recognized foreign equivalent

Fees: (Rupees): 168-600 per annum (regular fee); 1,200-20,000 per annum (enhanced fee)

Main Language(s) of Instruction: English

Accrediting Agencies: National Assessment and Accreditation Council (NAAC)

Degrees and Diplomas: *Bachelor's Degree*; *Bachelor's degree (professional)*; *Postgraduate Diploma*; *Master's Degree*; *Master of Philosophy*; *Doctorate*; *Doctor of Literature*; *Doctor of Science*. Also Certificate Courses; M.B.A.

Student Services: Academic counselling, Canteen, Cultural centre, Employment services, Health services, Language programs, Sports facilities

Student Residential Facilities: 9 hostels; Guest House

Special Facilities: Observatory; Yoga Centre

Libraries: 128,790 vols; 5,062 periodicals subscriptions

Publications: Loke Darpan *(annually)*

Press or Publishing House: University Press
Last Updated: 24/11/11

UNIVERSITY OF KASHMIR

University Campus, Hazratbal, Srinagar,
Jammu and Kashmir 190006
Tel: +91(194) 242-0333
Fax: +91(194) 242-5195
EMail: info@kashmiruniversity.net
Website: http://www.kashmiruniversity.net

Vice-Chancellor: Talat Ahmad (2011-)
Tel: +91(194) 242-1357, Fax: +91(194) 242-3345
EMail: vcoffice@kashmiruniversity.net

Registrar: S.Fayaz Ahmad
Tel: +91(194) 2420078, Fax: +91(194) 2425195
EMail: registrar@kashmiruniversity.ac.in

Centres
Area Study; **Biodiversity and Taxonomy**; **Central Asian Studies** *(CCAS)* (Asian Studies); **Convocation Complex**; **Distance Education**; **Energy Studies** (Energy Engineering); **Hygiene and Environment** (Environmental Studies; Hygiene); **Information Technology and Support System** *(IT & SS)* (Information Sciences; Information Technology); **Internal Quality Assurance** *(DIQA)* (Safety Engineering); **Life Long Learning**; **Music and Fine Arts** (Fine Arts; Music); **Physical Education and Sports** (Physical Education; Sports); **Research and Development** *(CORD)*; **State Resource** *(SRC)*; **University Science and Instrumentation**; **Watch and Ward**

Faculties
Applied Sciences and Technology (Computer Science; Electronic Engineering; Food Science; Food Technology; Home Economics; Instrument Making; Pharmacy); **Arts** (Arabic; Arts and Humanities; English; Hindi; Indic Languages; Information Sciences; Library Science; Modern Languages; Native Language; Persian; Sanskrit; Urdu); **Biological Sciences** (Biochemistry; Biological and Life Sciences; Biotechnology; Botany; Zoology); **Business and Management** (Business Administration; Finance; Management); **Dentistry** (Dentistry); **Education** (Education; Physical Education); **Engineering** (Engineering); **Law** (Law); **Medicine** (Medicine); **Music and Fine Arts** (Fine Arts; Music); **Oriental Learning** (Oriental Studies); **Physical and Material Science** (Environmental Studies; Geography; Geology; Geophysics; Mathematics; Physics; Regional Studies; Statistics); **Social Sciences** (Economics; History; Islamic Studies; Media Studies; Political Sciences; Psychology; Social Sciences; Social Work; Sociology)

Institutes
Culture and Philosophy *(Allama Iqbal)* (Cultural Studies; Philosophy)

Research Centres
Educational Multimedia (Educational Technology; Multimedia); **Population** (Demography and Population)

Further Information: 39 affiliated colleges; 5 constituent colleges; 8 oriental colleges; 69 private colleges. South and North Satellite campuses. Sheikl-ul-Allam Chair. A traditional and distance education institution.

History: Founded 1969, replacing University of Jammu and Kashmir established 1948. A Central University.

Governing Bodies: University Council; Syndicate; Academic Council

Academic Year: March to December

Admission Requirements: 12th year senior secondary/intermediate examination or recognized foreign equivalent

Fees: (Rupees): 1,790-8,750 per annum

Main Language(s) of Instruction: English

Accrediting Agencies: National Assessment and Accreditation Council (NAAC)

Degrees and Diplomas: *Bachelor's Degree*; *Postgraduate Diploma*; *Master's Degree*; *Master of Philosophy*; *Doctorate*. Also Certificate courses

Student Services: Health services

Student Residential Facilities: Yes

Libraries: 560,232 vols; 1,056 periodical subscriptions

Publications: Anhaar, Kashmiri; Communications (in English) & Tarseel (in Urdu); Human Behaviour - Journal of Applied Psychology; Insight Journal of Applied Research in Education; Journal of Himalayan Ecology and Sustainable Development; Journal of Research and Development; Kashmir University Law Review (KULR); Majallah Al-Dirasat Al-Arabia, Arabic; Media Times, Media Education Research Centre (MERC); The Business Review; The Journal of Central Asian Studies; The Journal of Kashmir Studies; Trends in Information Management (TRIM); Vitasta, Hindi
Last Updated: 25/11/11

UNIVERSITY OF KERALA

University Buildings, Thiruvananthapuram, Kerala 695034
Tel: +91(471) 2305738 +91(471) 2305994
Fax: +91(471) 2307158
EMail: ku.release@gmail.com
Website: http://www.keralauniversity.edu

Vice-Chancellor: A. Jayakrishnan
Tel: +91(471) 230-6634 EMail: vc@keralauniversity.edu

Registrar: K. S. Chandrasekar
Tel: +91(471) 2305631, Fax: +91(471) 2307158
EMail: regrku@gmail.com

Centres
Adult Continuing Education *(CACEE)*; **Arthropod Bio Resources and Biotechnology** (Biotechnology; Natural Resources); **Australian Studies** (Regional Studies); **Bioinformatics** (Biology; Computer Science); **Canadian Studies** (Canadian Studies; Literature); **Christian Studies for Cultural and Social Change** (Christian Religious Studies; Development Studies); **Convergence Media Studies** (Media Studies); **English Language Teaching** (Foreign Languages Education); **Enterpreneurship Development Cell** (Management); **Geo-Information Science and Technology** (Information Sciences; Information Technology); **Geomatics and Earth System Management** (Earth Sciences); **Ghandian Studies** (Philosophy); **International Relations** *(V.K. Krishna Menon)* (International Relations); **Kerala Studies** *(International - ICKS)* (Cultural Studies); **Management Education and Enterpreneurship Development** *(C-MEE)* (Management); **Marine Diversity** (Marine Biology); **Nanoscience and Nanotechnology** (Nanotechnology); **Performing and Visual Arts** (Performing Arts; Visual Arts); **Quantitative Analysis** (Mathematics); **Rural Studies** (Rural Studies); **Social Change** *(Sree Narayana)* (Social Studies); **Survey Research** (Operations Research); **Systems and Synthetic Biology** *(CSSB)* (Biology); **Technology and Resource for Malayalam** (Native Language); **Trivandrum Astronomical Observatory** (Astronomy and Space Science); **UGC Nehru Study** (Political Sciences); **Vedanta Studies** (Philosophy); **Women's Studies** (Women's Studies)

Chairs
Dr B R Ambedkar (Human Rights; Social Sciences); **Parliamentary Affairs** *(V.K. Sukumaran Nayar)* (Government; Political Sciences)

Faculties

Applied Sciences (Biotechnology; Computer Science; Electronic Engineering; Environmental Studies; Futurology; Optical Technology); **Arts** (Arts and Humanities; Communication Arts; English; German; Information Sciences; Journalism; Library Science; Philosophy; Russian); **Ayurvedic Medicine** (Ayurveda); **Commerce** (Business and Commerce); **Dentistry** (Dentistry); **Education** (Education); **Engineering and Technology** (Engineering; Technology); **Fine Arts** (Fine Arts; Music); **Homeopathy** (Homeopathy); **Law** (Law); **Management Studies** (Management); **Medicine** (Medicine; Nursing; Pharmacy); **Oriental Studies** (Arabic; Indic Languages; Linguistics; Oriental Languages; Oriental Studies; Sanskrit); **Physical Education** (Physical Education); **Science** (Aquaculture; Biochemistry; Botany; Chemistry; Demography and Population; Fishery; Geography; Geology; Mathematics; Natural Sciences; Physics; Statistics; Zoology); **Social Sciences** (Archaeology; Economics; History; Islamic Studies; Political Sciences; Psychology; Social Sciences; Sociology)

Research Centres

Population (Demography and Population); **Study on the Cost of Cultivation of Principal Crops in Kerala** (*Kariavattom*) (Agricultural Economics)

Further Information: Also 187 Affiliated Colleges, 45 University Departments, and other Departments and Centres. A traditional and Distance Education.

History: Founded 1937 as University of Travancore. Acquired present title and status 1957. A Cetral University.

Governing Bodies: Senate; Syndicate; Academic Council

Academic Year: June to March

Admission Requirements: 12th year senior secondary/intermediate examination or recognized foreign equivalent

Fees: (Indian Rupees): Undergraduate programmes, 4,750-6,000 (except B. Ed. Course, 18,000); Postgraduate programmes, 270-1,000 per annum (except M.Tech., 3,340 per annum and M.B.A., 9,070 per annum).

Main Language(s) of Instruction: English

International Co-operation: With universities in Belgium, Spain, United Kingdom, USA

Accrediting Agencies: National Assessment and Accreditation Council (NAAC)

Degrees and Diplomas: *Diploma*; *Bachelor's Degree*; *Bachelor's degree (professional)*; *Postgraduate Diploma*; *Master's Degree*; *Master of Philosophy*; *Doctorate*. Also M.B.A.

Student Services: Canteen, Employment services, Health services, Sports facilities

Student Residential Facilities: International Youth Hostel

Special Facilities: Kerala University Observatory

Libraries: Main Library, 268,395 vols; Manuscripts Library

Publications: Bhasha Sahithi *(quarterly)*; Indian Unity Problems and Prospectus; Indo-German Journal; Janasankhya; Journal of Aquatic Biology and Fisheries; Journal of Indian History and Kerala Studies; Journal of Manuscript Studies; Kalari; Kerala Journal of Legal Studies; Kerala Journal of Social Sciences; Pracina Kairali *(quarterly)*

Press or Publishing House: University Press
Last Updated: 25/11/11

UNIVERSITY OF KOTA (UOK)

Saraswati Bhawan, Near Kabir Circle, Swami Vivekanand Nagar, Kota, Rajasthan 324 010
EMail: info@uok.ac.in
Website: http://www.uok.ac.in/

Vice Chancellor: Madhu Sudan Sharma Tel: +91(744) 247-2911
Registrar: Ram Niwas Tel: +91(744) 247-2934

Faculties

Arts (Arts and Humanities; Biological and Life Sciences); **Commerce and Management** (Business and Commerce; Finance; Management); **Education** (Physical Education); **Law** (Law); **Science** (Applied Chemistry; Applied Physics; Chemistry; Computer Science; Energy Engineering; Industrial Chemistry; Physics); **Social Sciences** (Geography; Heritage Preservation; History; Museum Management; Political Sciences; Social Sciences; Sociology; Surveying and Mapping; Tourism)

Further Information: 148 Affiliated Colleges
History: Founded 2003.
Degrees and Diplomas: *Bachelor's Degree*; *Bachelor's degree (professional)*; *Master's Degree*; *Master of Philosophy*. Also M.B.A.
Last Updated: 05/01/12

UNIVERSITY OF LUCKNOW

Badshahbagh, Lucknow, Uttar Pradesh 226 007
Tel: +91(522) 2740086
Fax: +91(522) 274-0412 +91(522) 385-592
EMail: info@lkouniv.ac.in
Website: http://www.lkouniv.ac.in

Vice-Chancellor: Manoj K. Mishra
Tel: +91(522) 2740467 EMail: vc@lkouniv.ac.in
Registrar (Acting): G. P. Tripathi
Tel: +91(522) 2740412 EMail: registrar@lkouniv.ac.in

Centres
Sanskriti (Cultural Studies; Sanskrit)

Faculties

Arts (Ancient Civilizations; Anthropology; Arabic; Archaeology; Arts and Humanities; Economics; English; Esoteric Practices; European Languages; Geography; Hindi; History; Home Economics; Information Sciences; Journalism; Library Science; Linguistics; Mass Communication; Medieval Studies; Modern History; Modern Languages; Persian; Philosophy; Political Sciences; Protective Services; Psychology; Public Administration; Sanskrit; Social Work; Sociology; Urdu); **Ayurveda** (Anatomy; Ayurveda; Gynaecology and Obstetrics; Music; Paediatrics; Surgery); **Commerce** (Business Administration; Business and Commerce; Economics); **Education** (Education); **Fine Arts** (Fine Arts; Painting and Drawing; Photography; Sculpture; Visual Arts); **Law** (Law); **Mass Communication in Science and Technology** (Mass Communication); **Science** (Anthropology; Astronomy and Space Science; Biochemistry; Botany; Chemistry; Computer Science; Geology; Mathematics; Physics; Statistics; Zoology)

Institutes
Development Studies (Development Studies); **Management Sciences** (Management); **Minorities Coaching** (Psychology); **Tourism Studies** (Tourism); **Women's Studies** (Women's Studies)

Research Centres
Population (Demography and Population); **Urban and Environmental Studies** (Environmental Studies; Urban Studies)

Further Information: Also 5 Constituent and 20 Associated Colleges, and 5 Recognized Institutions
History: Founded 1921.
Governing Bodies: Executive Council; Academic Council
Academic Year: January to December (January-June; July-December).
Admission Requirements: 12th year senior secondary/intermediate examination or recognized foreign equivalent
Fees: (Rupees): 180-240 per annum
Main Language(s) of Instruction: English, Hindi
Degrees and Diplomas: *Diploma*; *Bachelor's Degree*; *Postgraduate Diploma*; *Master's Degree*; *Master of Philosophy*. Also Advance Diploma and M.B.A.
Libraries: c. 550,000 vols; 500 periodical subscriptions
Last Updated: 25/11/11

UNIVERSITY OF MADRAS (UNOM)

Chepauk, Triplicane (P.O.), Chennai, Tamil Nadu 600005
Tel: +91(44) 2536-8778
Fax: +91(44) 2536-6693 +91(44) 2536-7654
EMail: regmu@unimad.ernet.in
Website: http://www.unom.ac.in

Vice-Chancellor: S. Ramachandran EMail: vcoffice@unom.ac.in
Registrar: Anne Mary Fernandez EMail: registrar@unom.ac.in

Schools

Basic Medical Science *(Taramani campus)* (Anatomy; Biochemistry; Endocrinology; Genetics; Pathology; Pharmacology; Physiology; Toxicology); **Business and Management** *(Chepauk campus)* (Business Administration; Management); **Chemical Sciences** *(Guindy campus)* (Chemistry); **Earth and Atmospheric Science** *(Guindy campus)* (Earth Sciences; Meteorology); **Earth and Atmospheric Science** *(Chepauk campus)* (Earth Sciences; Meteorology); **Economics** *(Chepauk campus)* (Econometrics; Economics); **English and Foreign Language** *(Chepauk campus)* (English; Modern Languages); **Fine and Performing Arts** *(Chepauk campus)* (Fine Arts; Performing Arts); **Historical Studies** *(Chepauk campus)* (History); **Information and Communication Studies** *(Chepauk campus)* (Communication Studies; Information Sciences; Mass Communication); **Life Sciences** *(Guindy campus)* (Biochemistry; Biotechnology; Botany; Zoology); **Mathematics, Statistics and Computer Science** *(Chepauk campus)* (Computer Science; Mathematics; Statistics); **Nanoscience and Photonics** *(Taramani campus)* (Nanotechnology; Physics); **Philosophy and Religious Thought** *(Chepauk campus)* (Philosophy; Religious Studies); **Physical Sciences** *(Guindy campus)* (Biophysics; Crystallography; Nuclear Physics; Physics); **Political and International Studies** *(Chepauk campus)* (Law; Military Science; Political Sciences; Public Administration; South and Southeast Asian Languages); **Sanskrit and other Indian Languages** *(Marina campus)* (Arabic; Hindi; Persian; Sanskrit; Urdu); **Social Sciences** *(Chepauk campus)* (Adult Education; Anthropology; Continuing Education; Criminology; Education; Psychology; Sociology); **Tamil and other Dravidian Languages** *(Marina campus)* (Indic Languages)

Further Information: Also 123 Affiliated and Approved Colleges and 45 Recognized Institutions. campuses in Chepauk, Marina, Guindy and Taramani.

History: Founded 1857. Campuses in Chepauk, Guindy, Marina and Taramani.

Governing Bodies: Senate; Academic Council; Syndicate

Academic Year: June to April

Admission Requirements: undergraduate programmes, 12 years of school education (senior secondary grade or higher secondary level); postgraduate programmes, completion of undergraduate programmes

Fees: (Rupees): 4,000-60,000 per annum

Main Language(s) of Instruction: English, Tamil

Accrediting Agencies: National Assessment and Accreditation Council (NAAC)

Degrees and Diplomas: *Bachelor's Degree*; *Bachelor's degree (professional)*; *Postgraduate Diploma*; *Master's Degree*; *Master of Philosophy*; *Doctorate*. Also Certificate courses

Student Services: Sports facilities

Student Residential Facilities: Hostels for men and women students

Special Facilities: Mini Museum attached to the Department of Ancient History and Archaeology

Libraries: 4 libraries (Main Library, Chepauk Campus, Guindy Campus Library, Taramani Campus Library and Marina Campus Library) Total, c. 650,000 vols

Publications: Annals of Oriental Research; Madras University Journal

Academic Staff *2010-2011*: Total: c. 300
Student Numbers *2010-2011*: Total: c. 8,000
Last Updated: 25/11/11

UNIVERSITY OF MUMBAI

Mahatma Gandhi Road, Fort Mumbai, Mumbai,
Maharashtra 400032
Tel: +91(22) 2265-6789
Fax: +91(22) 2267-3579
Website: http://www.mu.ac.in

Vice-Chancellor: Rajan Welukar (2010-) EMail: vc@fort.mu.ac.in

Registrar: Jayant P. Dighe
Tel: +91(22) 2265-6953, Fax: +91(22) 2265-2832
EMail: registrar@fort.mu.ac.in

International Relations: Anil K. Patil
Tel: +91(22) 2204-6959, Fax: +91(22) 2204-2859

Centres

Advanced Study in Applied Chemistry (Applied Chemistry; Polymer and Plastics Technology; Textile Technology); **Advanced Study in Economics** (Finance; Industrial and Production Economics); **Advanced Study in Mathematics** (Mathematics); **African Studies** (African Studies); **Central Eurasian Studies** (Eurasian and North Asian Languages)

Colleges

Architecture (Architecture)

Faculties

Arts and Humanities (Arts and Humanities; Education; Library Science; Linguistics; Management; Modern Languages; Social Sciences); **Ayurvedic Medicine** (Ayurveda); **Commerce** (Business and Commerce); **Engineering and Technology** (Engineering; Technology); **Fine Arts** (Fine Arts); **Law** (Law); **Science** (Natural Sciences)

Institutes

Career Education and Development *(Garware)* (Development Studies; Education); **Financial and Management Studies** *(Alkesh Dinesh Mody)* (Finance; Management)

Further Information: Also 399 Constituent Colleges, and 90 recognized institutes. A traditional, distance and open learning institution.

History: Founded 1857, but until the passing of the Indian Universities Act of 1904 its function was limited to examining candidates and arranging for the courses of study which led to degrees. Acquired right to organize teaching, arrange for University extension lectures, and publish such works as necessary for the direct educational work it was to carry out 1904. Postgraduate instruction and research introduced 1928. Reconstituted 1953.

Governing Bodies: Senate; Management Council; Academic Council

Academic Year: June to April (June-October; November-April)

Admission Requirements: 12th year senior secondary/intermediate examination or recognized foreign equivalent

Fees: (Rupees): 390-15,000 per annum

Main Language(s) of Instruction: English, Hindi, Marathi

International Co-operation: With institutions in Italy, Sweden, Germany, Poland, United Kingdom, Hungary, USA, Australia, Taiwan

Accrediting Agencies: National Assessment and Accreditation Council (NAAC)

Degrees and Diplomas: *Diploma*; *Bachelor's Degree*; *Postgraduate Diploma*; *Doctorate*. Also Certificate courses

Student Services: Academic counselling, Canteen, Cultural centre, Employment services, Foreign student adviser, Foreign Studies Centre, Handicapped facilities, Health services, Language programs, Social counselling, Sports facilities

Student Residential Facilities: Yes

Libraries: 850,000 vols; 725 periodical subscriptions

Press or Publishing House: University Press
Last Updated: 28/11/11

UNIVERSITY OF MUSIC AND FINE ARTS

Indira Kala Sangit Vishwavidyalaya
Khairagarh District, Rajnandgaon, Chhattisgarh 491881
Tel: +91(7820) 234-534 +91(7820) 234-232
Fax: +91(7820) 234-108
EMail: reg@iksvv.com
Website: http://www.iksvv.com

Vice-Chancellor: Mandavi Singh EMail: vc@iksvv.com

Registrar: Shri P.S. Dhruv Tel: +91(7820) 234-232

Faculties

Arts (English; Hindi; Sanskrit; South Asian Studies; Theatre); **Dance** (Dance); **Folk Music and Arts** (Dance; Folklore; Music); **Music** (Music; Musical Instruments; Musicology; Singing); **Visual Arts** (Fine Arts; Graphic Arts; Painting and Drawing; Sculpture)

Further Information: Also 44 affiliated colleges and 34 recognized centers

History: Founded 1956. The aim of the University is to provide instruction in all branches of Music and Fine Arts and to make provision for Research, the advancement of studies and the dissemination of knowledge in these subjects.

Governing Bodies: Executive Council

Academic Year: July to april

Admission Requirements: 12th year senior secondary/intermediate examination or recognized foreign equivalent

Accrediting Agencies: NAAC

Degrees and Diplomas: *Diploma*: Music; Visual Arts; Sanskrit; English; Multimedia and Animation; *Bachelor's Degree*: Music; Dance; Fine Arts; Multimedia and Animation (BA/BMus/BDance/BFA), 3-4 yrs; *Postgraduate Diploma*: Museology; History of Indian Arts; *Master's Degree*: Music (Musical Instruments; Folk Music; Musicology); History of Indian Art and Culture; Theatre; Fine Arts (Painting; Sculpture; Graphics), a further 2 yrs; *Master of Philosophy*: Vocal Music; Instrumental Music; Percussion; Kathak; *Doctorate*: Music; Dance; Folk Music and Arts; Visual Arts (PhD; DLitt.)

Student Residential Facilities: Separate boys and girls hostels

Special Facilities: History of Indian Art and Culture Museum

Libraries: More than 43,000 vols and a large number of audiotapes, CDs, records, spools and video cassettes.

Publications: Kala Saurabh, Research Journal; Kala Vaibhav, Research Journal

Academic Staff *2009-2010*	MEN	WOMEN	TOTAL
FULL-TIME	20	10	30
STAFF WITH DOCTORATE			
FULL-TIME	14	8	22
Student Numbers *2009-2010*			
All (Foreign Included)	–	–	1,559
FOREIGN ONLY	–	–	4

Last Updated: 18/11/11

UNIVERSITY OF MYSORE

Vishwavidyalaya Karyasoudha, Crawford Hall, Mysore,
Karnataka 570005
Tel: +91(821) 241-9361
Fax: +91(821) 242-1263
Website: http://www.uni-mysore.ac.in

Vice-Chancellor: V.G. Talawar
Tel: +91(821) 241-9611 EMail: vc@uni-mysore.ac.in

Registrar: P.S. Naik
Tel: +91(821) 241-9361, Fax: +91(821) 241-9361
EMail: registrar@uni-mysore.ac.in

Centres

Information Science and Technology (Information Management; Information Sciences; Information Technology; Software Engineering); **Study of Social Exclusion and Inclusive Policy** (Social Policy; Social Problems; Social Work); **Women's Studies** (Women's Studies)

Colleges

Academic Staff (Distance Education; Educational and Student Counselling; Teacher Training)

Departments

Ancient History and Archaeology (Ancient Civilizations; Archaeology); **Anthropology** (Anthropology); **Applied Botany and Biotechnology** (Biotechnology; Botany); **Biochemistry** (Biochemistry); **Botany** (Botany); **Chemistry** (Chemistry); **Christianity** (Christian Religious Studies); **Commerce** (Business and Commerce; **Communication and Journalism** (Journalism; Mass Communication); **Computer Science** (Computer Science); **Economics and Cooperation** (Economics); **Education** (Education); **English** (English); **Environmental Science** (Environmental Studies); **Food Science and Nutrition** (Food Science; Nutrition); **Geography** (Geography); **Geology** (Geology); **Hindi** (Hindi); **History** (History); **Jainology and Prakit** (Ancient Languages); **Law** (Commercial Law; Constitutional Law; International Law; Law); **Library and Information Science** (Information Sciences; Library

Science); **Mathematics** (Mathematics); **Microbiology** (Mathematics); **Philosophy** (Philosophy); **Physical Education** (Physical Education); **Physics** (Physics); **Political Sciences** (Political Sciences); **Psychology** (Psychology); **Sanskrit** (Sanskrit); **Sericulture Science** (Sericulture); **Social Work** (Social Work); **Sociology** (Sociology); **Statistics** (Statistics); **Urdu** (Urdu); **Zoology** (Zoology)

Institutes

Development Studies (Development Studies); **Kannada Studies** *(Kuvempu)* (Asian Studies); **Management Science** *(B.N.Bahadur)* (Management); **Oriental Research** (Oriental Studies)

Research Centres

Ambedkar; **Educational Multimedia** (Educational Technology; Multimedia); **Third Sector** (Management)

Schools

Design (Design); **Foreign Languages** (French; German; Modern Languages; Russian; Translation and Interpretation); **Information Management** *(International - ISIM)* (Information Management)

Further Information: Also 5 Constituent Colleges and 122 Affiliated Colleges. Postgraduate campuses in Manasagangotri, Hemagangotri and Sri Lanka.

History: Founded 1916.

Governing Bodies: Syndicate; Academic Council; Finance Committee; Planning Monitoring and Evaluation Board

Academic Year: July to April

Admission Requirements: 12th year senior secondary/intermediate examination or equivalent

Fees: (Rupees): 762

Main Language(s) of Instruction: English, Kannada

Degrees and Diplomas: *Diploma*; *Bachelor's Degree*; *Postgraduate Diploma*; *Master's Degree*; *Master of Philosophy*; *Doctorate*. Also Advanced Diploma; Certificate courses; M.B.A.

Student Residential Facilities: Yes

Special Facilities: Museum of Ancient History and Archaeology; Folklore Museum; Zoology Museum; Geology Museum

Libraries: c. 800,000 vols; 2,400 periodical subscriptions.

Student Numbers *2009-2010*: Total: c. 3,500
Last Updated: 28/11/11

UNIVERSITY OF NORTH BENGAL

PO North Bengal University, Darjeeling District,
Raja Rammohunpur, West Bengal 734430
Tel: +91(353) 269-9099
Fax: +91(353) 269-9001 +91(353) 258-1212
EMail: regnbu@sancharnet.in
Website: http://www.nbu.ac.in

Vice-Chancellor: Arunabha Basumajumdar (2008-)
Tel: +91(353) 277-6366, Fax: +91(353) 269-9001
EMail: nbuvc@nbu.ac.in; a_basumajumdar@vsnl.net

Registrar: Dilip Kumar Sarkar
Tel: +91(353) 277-6331, Fax: +91(353) 258-1212

Faculties

Arts, Commerce and Law (Arts and Humanities; Business Administration; Business and Commerce; Economics; English; Environmental Studies; French; Hindi; History; Indic Languages; Information Sciences; Law; Library Science; Management; Mass Communication; Philosophy; Political Sciences; Sociology; Video); **Science** (Anthropology; Biological and Life Sciences; Biotechnology; Botany; Chemistry; Computer Science; Geography; Information Technology; Mathematics; Microbiology; Natural Sciences; Physics; Safety Engineering; Surveying and Mapping; Zoology); **Technology** (Technology)

Further Information: Also 8 Constituent and 87 Affiliated Colleges

History: Founded 1962.

Governing Bodies: Court; Executive Council;

Admission Requirements: 12th year senior secondary/intermediate examination or recognized foreign equivalent

Main Language(s) of Instruction: English

Accrediting Agencies: National Assessment and Accreditation Council (NAAC)

Degrees and Diplomas: *Bachelor's Degree*; *Master's Degree*; *Master of Philosophy*; *Doctorate*. Also M.B.A.

Special Facilities: Akshaya Kumar Maitreya Heritage Museum

Libraries: c. 181,956 vols

Last Updated: 28/11/11

UNIVERSITY OF PATANJALI

Mahrish Dayanad Gram, Delhi Haridwar National Highway, Near Bahadrabad Haridwar, Haridwar, Uttarakhand 249 402
Tel: +91(1334) 242-526
EMail: admin@patanjaliuniversity.com
Website: http://patanjaliuniversity.com/

Vice Chancellor: Acharya Balkrishana
Tel: +91(1334) 244-107, Fax: +91(1334) 248-248
EMail: acharyaji@dicyayoga.com

Registrar: Ram Kumar Sharma
Tel: +91(1334) 242-526, Fax: +91(1334) 244-805
EMail: uopyp2009@gmail.com

Areas

Commerce (Business and Commerce); **Computer Science** (Computer Science); **Information Technology** (Information Technology); **Medical Sciences** (Acupuncture; Ayurveda; Medicine; Physical Therapy); **Natural Sciences** (Botany; Chemistry; Mathematics; Natural Sciences; Physics; Zoology); **Pharmacology** (Pharmacology); **Social Sciences** (Civics; Geography; History; Political Sciences; Social Sciences); **Yoga** (Yoga)

History: Founded 2006.

Degrees and Diplomas: *Diploma*; *Bachelor's Degree*; *Master's Degree*; *Doctorate*. Also Certificate

Student Services: Canteen, Health services

Libraries: Yes

Student Numbers *2010-2011*: Total: c. 5,000
Last Updated: 02/01/12

UNIVERSITY OF PETROLEUM AND ENERGY STUDIES (UPES)

Bidholi Campus Office Energy Acres, P.O. Bidholi Via-Prem Nagar, Dehradun, Uttarakhand 248007
Tel: +91(135) 277-6201 +91(135) 277-6061
Fax: +91(135) 277-6090
EMail: enrollments@upes.ac.in
Website: http://www.upes.ac.in

Vice-Chancellor: Parag Diwan EMail: vc@upes.ac.in

Registrar: Sandeep Mehta

Colleges

Engineering Studies (Aeronautical and Aerospace Engineering; Artificial Intelligence; Automotive Engineering; Business Computing; Chemical Engineering; Computer Engineering; Electronic Engineering; Engineering; Fire Science; Geological Engineering; Information Management; Information Technology; Materials Engineering; Mechanical Engineering; Petroleum and Gas Engineering; Power Engineering; Safety Engineering; Telecommunications Engineering); **Legal Studies** *(CoLS)* (Computer Science; Law); **Management Studies** *(CoMES)* (Air Transport; Business Administration; Economics; Energy Engineering; Information Technology; International Business; Management; Marine Transport; Petroleum and Gas Engineering; Power Engineering; Retailing and Wholesaling; Transport Management)

Further Information: Also Overseas Office in Canada.

History: Created 2003.

Governing Bodies: Board of Governors; Board of Management; Academic Council

Fees: (Indian Rupee): 42,900-66,780 per semester; M.B.A., 129,375-135,844 per semester

International Co-operation: With universities in Canada; China, Romania, UK and USA

Accrediting Agencies: National Assessment and Accreditation Council (NAAC); Distance Education Council; University Grants Commission (UGC)

Degrees and Diplomas: *Bachelor's Degree*; *Bachelor's degree (professional)*; *Master's Degree*; *Doctorate*. Also Integrated BBA - LL. B., 5 years; M.B.A. and Executuve M.B.A.

Libraries: 37,514 vols; 247 periodical subscriptions

Academic Staff *2009-2010*	MEN	WOMEN	TOTAL
FULL-TIME	238	67	305
STAFF WITH DOCTORATE FULL-TIME	37	10	47
Student Numbers *2009-2010*			
All (Foreign Included)	3,053	786	3,839

Last Updated: 28/11/11

UNIVERSITY OF PUNE

Ganeshkhind, Pune, Maharashtra 411007
Tel: +91(20) 2560-1099 +91(20) 2569-6061
Fax: +91(20) 2569-3899
EMail: dyracademic@unipune.ac.in
Website: http://www.unipune.ernet.in

Vice-Chancellor: Sanjay Chahande
Tel: +91(20) 25693868 EMail: puvc@unipune.ac.in

Registrar: Manik Laxmanrao Jadhav
Tel: +91(20) 25601182 EMail: regis@unipune.ac.in

Centres

Bioinformatics (Biological and Life Sciences; Computer Science); **Competitive Exam**; **Free Radical Research** *(National - NCFRR)* (Chemistry); **Information and Network Security** *(C.I.N.S.)* (Computer Networks; Information Management); **Modeling and Simulation** (Computer Science); **Network Computing** *(CNC)* (Computer Networks); **Philosophy and History of Science** (Natural Sciences; Philosophy); **Social Sciences and Humanities** *(CSSH)* (Arts and Humanities; Social Sciences); **Women's Studies** (Women's Studies)

Colleges

Academic Staff (Teacher Training)

Departments

Buddhist Studies and Dr. Ambedkar Thoughts (Asian Religious Studies; Economics; Literature; Political Sciences; Social Sciences)

Faculties

Commerce (Business and Commerce); **Education and Extension** (Education; Educational Technology); **Fine Arts** (English; Fine Arts; French; Geography; German; Hindi; Indic Languages; Japanese; Logic; Modern Languages; Performing Arts; Russian; Sanskrit; Spanish); **Law** (Law); **Management** *(PUMBA)* (Management); **Mental, Moral and Social Sciences** (Adult Education; Anthropology; Continuing Education; Economics; History; Information Sciences; Journalism; Library Science; Mass Communication; Military Science; Philosophy; Political Sciences; Protective Services; Psychology; Public Administration; Social Sciences; Sociology); **Physical Education** (Physical Education); **Science** (Biotechnology; Botany; Chemistry; Communication Studies; Computer Science; Electronic Engineering; Environmental Studies; Geography; Geology; Instrument Making; Mathematics; Meteorology; Microbiology; Natural Sciences; Physics; Statistics; Zoology)

Institutes

Bioinformatics and Biotechnology (Biological and Life Sciences; Biotechnology; Computer Science)

Schools

Basic Medical Sciences (Medicine); **Energy Studies** (Energy Engineering); **Health Sciences** (Health Sciences); **Interdisciplinary Studies** *(Humanities and Social Sciences)* (Arts and Humanities; Social Sciences); **Science** *(Interdisciplinary)* (Natural Sciences); **Scientific Computing** *(Interdisciplinary)* (Computer Science); **Scientific Computing** (Computer Science)

Further Information: Also 307 recognized research institutes and 612 affiliated colleges.

History: Founded 1948.

Governing Bodies: Management Council; Academic Council; Senate;

Academic Year: June to June

Admission Requirements: 12th year senior secondary/intermediate examination or recognized foreign equivalent

Fees: (Rupees): 150 per term; graduate, 300

Main Language(s) of Instruction: English, Marathi

Degrees and Diplomas: *Diploma*; *Bachelor's Degree*: 3-6 1/2 yrs; *Postgraduate Diploma*; *Master's Degree*: a further 1-3 yrs; *Master of Philosophy*; *Doctorate (PhD)*: at least 2 yrs. Also Special Diploma in Russian, 1 yr; Advanced Diploma, 3yrs; Higher and Lower Diploma in Sanskrit, 1 and 3 yrs; Certificate courses

Student Services: Canteen, Cultural centre, Foreign Studies Centre, Handicapped facilities, Health services, Language programs, Social counselling, Sports facilities

Student Residential Facilities: Yes

Libraries: 442,016 vols

Publications: Poona University (1949-1974) Silver Jubilee Commemoration Vol; Rabindranath Tagore; Vidyapeeth Varta *(monthly)*

Academic Staff *2010-2011*: Total 334
Student Numbers *2010-2011*: Total: c. 7,000
Last Updated: 28/11/11

UNIVERSITY OF RAJASTHAN

JLN Marg, Jaipur, Rajasthan 302055
Tel: +91(141) 270-8824
Fax: +91(141) 271-1799
EMail: info@uniraj.ernet.in

Vice-Chancellor: B.L. Sharma EMail: vc@uniraj.ernet.in

Registrar: Nishkam Divakar
Tel: +91(141) 270-6813, Fax: +91(141) 270-6813

Faculties

Arts (Ancient Languages; Arts and Humanities; Cultural Studies; English; European Languages; Hindi; Journalism; Literature; Mass Communication; Philosophy; Sanskrit); **Commerce** (Accountancy; Business Administration; Business and Commerce; Economics; Finance; Management; Statistics); **Education** (Education; Library Science; Physical Education); **Engineering and Technology** (Engineering; Technology); **Fine Arts** (Fine Arts; Music; Painting and Drawing; Theatre); **Law** (Law); **Management** (Management); **Science** (Botany; Chemical Engineering; Computer Science; Energy Engineering; Geography; Geology; Home Economics; Information Technology; Mathematics; Natural Sciences; Physics; Psychology; Science Education; Statistics; Zoology); **Social Science** (Anthropology; Economics; Political Sciences; Public Administration; Social Sciences; Sociology; Women's Studies)

Further Information: Also 7 Constituent Colleges and 866 Affiliated Collegesspanning 7 districts.

History: Founded 1947.

Governing Bodies: Senate; Syndicate; Academic Council; Finance Committee; Research Board

Academic Year: July to May (July-January; January-May)

Admission Requirements: 12th year senior secondary/intermediate examination or recognized foreign equivalent

Fees: (Rupees): 100-2,000 per annum

Main Language(s) of Instruction: English, Hindi

Degrees and Diplomas: *Bachelor's Degree*; *Postgraduate Diploma*; *Master's Degree*; *Master of Philosophy*; *Doctorate*. Also Certificate courses; Honours Bachelor's degree; Add-On Vocational programmes; M.B.A.

Student Residential Facilities: Yes (separate hostels for men and women)

Libraries: Central Library, 333,979 vols

Publications: University Studies and Extension Lectures

Press or Publishing House: Rajasthan University Press
Last Updated: 28/11/11

UNIVERSITY OF SCIENCE AND TECHNOLOGY, MEGHALAYA (USTM)

Techno City, Killing Road, 9th mile, Ri-Bhoi, Meghalaya 793 101

Programmes
Technology (Technology)

History: Founded 2008.

Governing Bodies: Board of Governors; Board of Management; Academic Council; Finance Committee
Last Updated: 01/09/11

UNIVERSITY OF TECHNOLOGY AND MANAGEMENT

Bijni Complex (Old NEHU Campus), Laitumkhrah, Shillong, Meghalaya 793 003
Tel: +91(364) 2500969
EMail: enrollements@utm.ac.in
Website: http://www.utm.ac.in/

Vice-Chancellor: S.J. Chopra

Registrar: Deepa Verma

Schools
Applied Sciences (Biological and Life Sciences; Biotechnology); **Design** (Design); **Media and Communication** (Journalism; Mass Communication; Media Studies); **Retail and Fashion** (Fashion Design; Retailing and Wholesaling); **Technology** (Computer Science; Electronic Engineering; Technology; Telecommunications Engineering); **Travel and Leisure** (Leisure Studies; Management; Sports Management; Tourism)

Degrees and Diplomas: *Bachelor's Degree*; *Postgraduate Diploma*; *Master's Degree*
Last Updated: 17/01/12

UNIVERSITY OF TECHNOLOGY OF MADHYA PRADESH

Rajiv Gandhi Proudyogiki Vishwavidyalaya (RGPV)
Gandhi Nagar, Bhopal, Madhya Pradesh 462036
Tel: +91(755) 2678-833
Fax: +91(755) 274-2002
EMail: rgtu@rgtu.net; egov@rgtu.net
Website: http://rgpv.ac.in/

Vice-Chancellor: Piyush Trivedi (2008-) Tel: +91(755) 267-8801

Registrar: A.K.S. Bhadoria
Tel: +91(755) 267-8899 EMail: registrar@rgtu.net

Institutes
Technology *(UIT-RGPV)* (Civil Engineering; Computer Engineering; Computer Science; Construction Engineering; Electrical and Electronic Engineering; Electronic Engineering; Industrial Engineering; Information Technology; Mechanical Engineering; Power Engineering; Production Engineering; Telecommunications Engineering)

Schools
Biotechnology (Biotechnology); **Energy Technology** (Energy Engineering; Environmental Management); **Information Technology** (Computer Engineering; Computer Graphics; Data Processing; Information Technology; Software Engineering); **Nanotechnology** (Nanotechnology); **Pharmaceutical Science** (Pharmacy; Safety Engineering)

Further Information: Also 200 affiliated Engineering Colleges, 98 Pharmacy Colleges, 95 MCA Colleges, 4 Architecture Colleges and 85 Polytechnic institutions.

History: Founded 1998.

Governing Bodies: Executives Council; Finance Committee; Board of Studies.

Degrees and Diplomas: *Bachelor's degree (professional)*; *Master's Degree*; *Doctorate (Ph.D.)*

Student Services: Canteen

Student Residential Facilities: Boys and Girls Hostel; Principal's quarters; Faculty quarters

Special Facilities: Hostel Boys & Girls

Libraries: Digital library
Last Updated: 19/07/11

UTKAL UNIVERSITY

PO Vani Vihar, Bhubaneswar, Orissa 751004
Tel: +91(674) 258-1387
Fax: +91(674) 258-1850
EMail: vc@utkal-university.org
Website: http://www.utkal-university.org

Vice-Chancellor: Prasant Kumar Sahoo

Registrar: Gobinda Chandra Pradhan

Colleges
Law (Law)

Departments
Analytical and Applied Economics (Economics); **Ancient Indian History, Culture and Archaeology** (Ancient Civilizations; Archaeology; Cultural Studies; History); **Anthropology** (Anthropology); **Biotechnology** (Biotechnology); **Botany** (Botany); **Business Administration** (Business Administration); **Chemistry** (Chemistry); **Commerce** (Business and Commerce); **Computer Science and Applications** (Computer Science); **English** (English); **Geography** (Geography); **Geology** (Geology); **History** (History); **Law** (Law); **Library and Information Science** (Information Sciences; Library Science); **Mathematics** (Mathematics); **Oriya** (Indic Languages); **Personnel Management and Industrial Relations** (Human Resources; Labour and Industrial Relations); **Philosophy** (Philosophy); **Physics** (Physics); **Political Science** (Political Sciences); **Psychology** (Psychology); **Public Administration** (Public Administration); **Sanskrit** (Sanskrit); **Sociology** (Sociology); **Statistics** (Statistics); **Zoology** (Zoology)

Further Information: Also 267 affiliated Colleges (219 Degree Colleges, 44 Professional College, 3 Other Constituent Colleges). A traditional, distance and continuing education institution.

History: Founded 1943.

Governing Bodies: Senate; Syndicate; Academic Council

Academic Year: June to May (June-December; January-May)

Admission Requirements: 12th year senior secondary/intermediate examination or recognized foreign equivalent

Fees: (Rupees): 108-360 per annum

Main Language(s) of Instruction: English

Degrees and Diplomas: *Diploma*; *Bachelor's Degree*; *Postgraduate Diploma*; *Master's Degree*; *Master of Philosophy*; *Doctorate*. Also M.B.A.

Student Residential Facilities: For c. 1,550 students

Libraries: c. 250,000 vols

Publications: Prachi Publication

Press or Publishing House: M.S.R.C. Utkal University Press, Vani Vihar, Bhubaneswar

Student Numbers *2010-2011*: Total: c. 3,000
Last Updated: 29/11/11

UTKAL UNIVERSITY OF CULTURE
Utkal Sanskruti Viswavidyalaya

Sardar Patel Hall Complex, Unit-II, Bhubaneswar, Orissa 751009
Tel: +91(674) 253-5484
Fax: +91(674) 253-5486
EMail: mail@uuc.ac.in
Website: http://www.uuc.ac.in/

Vice-Chancellor: Amiya Kumar Pattanayak
EMail: vice.chancellor@utkaluniversityculture.org

Registrar: Sachindra Raul

Faculties
Architecture and Archaeology (Archaeology; Architecture; Heritage Preservation); **Cultural Studies** (Asian Religious Studies; Classical Languages; Cultural Studies; Hotel and Restaurant; Sanskrit; Tourism); **Language and Literature** (Linguistics; Literature; Modern Languages; South and Southeast Asian Languages); **Orissan Studies** (Cultural Studies; South Asian Studies; Southeast

Asian Studies); **Performing Arts** (Acting; Dance; Musical Instruments; Performing Arts; Singing; Theatre); **Visual Arts** (Art History; Design; Fine Arts; Painting and Drawing; Sculpture; Visual Arts)

Further Information: Also 12 affiliated colleges

History: Founded 1999.

Governing Bodies: Board of Management and Academic Council

Academic Year: June to May

Admission Requirements: 12th year senior secondary/intermediate examination or recognized foreign equivalent. University degree for Postgraduate programme.

Fees: (Rupees): Tourism and Hospitality, 20,000 per annum; Heritage and Conservation Technology, 3,050; others, 2,040

Main Language(s) of Instruction: English, Oriya, Hindi

Accrediting Agencies: University Grants Commission (UGC), Association of Indian Universities (AIU), American Institute of Indian Studies

Degrees and Diplomas: *Postgraduate Diploma*; *Master's Degree*. Also Certificate courses.

Student Services: Academic counselling, Canteen, Cultural centre, Foreign student adviser, Handicapped facilities, Language programs, Social counselling, Sports facilities

Student Residential Facilities: None

Special Facilities: State Museum

Libraries: Central Library

Publications: Sanskruti *(annually)*
Last Updated: 29/11/11

UTTAR PRADESH RAJARSHI TANDON OPEN UNIVERSITY (UPRTOU)

17 Maharshi Dayanand Marg, (Thornhill Road), Allahabad, Uttar Pradesh 211001
Tel: +91(532) 242-1284 +91(532) 262-3250 +91(532) 329-5300
Fax: +91(532) 262-3250
EMail: uprtou@yahoo.co.in
Website: http://www.uprtou.ac.in/

Vice-Chancellor: A. K. Bakhshi
Tel: +91(532) 242-1,283; +91(532) 242-1624,
Fax: +91(532) 262-4368 EMail: vcuprtou@yahoo.co.in

Registrar: A. K. Singh

Schools
Agricultural Sciences (Agriculture; Animal Husbandry; Dairy; Environmental Studies; Farm Management; Fruit Production; Harvest Technology; Vegetable Production); **Computer and Information Sciences** (Computer Engineering; Computer Science; Information Sciences); **Education** (Distance Education; Education; Educational Administration; Environmental Studies; Law; Special Education; Vocational Counselling); **Health Sciences** (Child Care and Development; Community Health; Diabetology; Environmental Studies; Health Education; Health Sciences; Nutrition); **Humanities** (Arts and Humanities; Economics; English; Environmental Studies; Hindi; Information Sciences; Journalism; Library Science; Mass Communication; Native Language; Philosophy; Rural Studies; Sanskrit; Translation and Interpretation; Urdu; Writing); **Management Studies** (Business Administration; Business and Commerce; E-Business/Commerce; Environmental Studies; Finance; Human Resources; Industrial Management; Management; Marketing); **Science** (Biochemistry; Botany; Chemistry; Computer Science; Mathematics; Natural Sciences; Physics; Statistics; Zoology); **Social Sciences** (Development Studies; Environmental Studies; Family Studies; Health Education; History; Human Rights; Labour and Industrial Relations; Political Sciences; Protective Services; Public Administration; Social Sciences; Social Work; Sociology; Tourism; Women's Studies)

History: Founded 1998.

Governing Bodies: Executive Council; Academic Council; Planning Board; Examination Committee; Finance Committee

Academic Year: July to June

Admission Requirements: Undergraduate programmes, 12th year Intermediate examination; Postgraduate programmes, Bachelor degree.

Fees: (Rupees): 1,200-12,000 per annum

Main Language(s) of Instruction: Hindi and English

Accrediting Agencies: Distance Education Council

Degrees and Diplomas: *Diploma*; *Bachelor's Degree*; *Postgraduate Diploma*; *Master's Degree*; *Master of Philosophy*. Also M.B.A.; Certificate (6 months), vocational (2 yrs), professional (3 yrs), and awarness (2 months) programmes.

Student Services: Academic counselling

Student Residential Facilities: None

Special Facilities: Computer Labs

Libraries: Yes

Publications: The Journal of Research and ODL Studies, Research papers and articles on all subjects, with a focus on Distance Education

Press or Publishing House: University Press

Last Updated: 29/11/11

UTTARAKHAND TECHNICAL UNIVERSITY

Goverment Girls Polytechnic Post Office, Chandanwadi, Prem Nagar Sudhowala, Dehradun, Uttarakhand 248007
EMail: vcutu@rediffmail.com
Website: http://uktech.ac.in/

Vice-Chancellor: Durg Singh Chauhan
Tel: +91(135) 2770-128, Fax: +91(135) 2770-119

Registrar: Shri C.S. Mehta
Tel: +91(135) 2770-126, Fax: +91(135) 2770-124

Programmes

Architecture (Architecture); **Business Administration** (Business Administration); **Engineering** (Automation and Control Engineering; Biochemistry; Bioengineering; Civil Engineering; Computer Engineering; Computer Science; Electrical and Electronic Engineering; Electrical Engineering; Electronic Engineering; Industrial Engineering; Information Technology; Mechanical Engineering; Production Engineering; Telecommunications Engineering; Thermal Engineering); **Hotel Management, Catering Technology** (Cooking and Catering; Hotel Management); **Law** (Law); **Pharmacy** (Pharmacy)

History: Founded 2008.

Degrees and Diplomas: *Bachelor's Degree*; *Bachelor's degree (professional)*; *Master's Degree*. Also M.B.A.

Last Updated: 04/08/11

UTTARANCHAL SANSKRIT UNIVERSITY (USVV)

Haridwar Delhi National Highway, Haridwar, Uttarakhand 249 401
Tel: +91(1334) 251-720
Fax: +91(1334) 250-636
EMail: sanskrituniversity@yahoo.com
Website: http://usvv.org/

Vice Chancellor: Sudha Pandey

Faculties

Literature - Culture (Cultural Studies; Literature); **Pedagogy** (Education); **Philosophy** (Philosophy); **Science** (Computer Science; Linguistics); **Veda - Vedanga** (Computer Science; Grammar; Sanskrit)

Further Information: Also 52 affiliated colleges.

History: Founded 2005.

Fees: (Indian Rupees): 600-10,000 per annum

Degrees and Diplomas: *Bachelor's Degree*; *Bachelor's degree (professional)*; *Postgraduate Diploma*; *Master's Degree*. Also Certificate; Acharya and Shastri courses.

Student Services: Canteen

Special Facilities: Audio Visual Lab; Computer Lab; Education Technology Lab; Language Lab; Psychology Lab; SST Lab

Libraries: Yes

Last Updated: 06/01/12

VARDHAMAN MAHAVEER KOTA OPEN UNIVERSITY (VMOU)

Rawatbhata Road, Akelgarh, Kota, Rajasthan 324010
Tel: +91(744) 247-0971
Fax: +91(744) 247-2525
EMail: vc@vmou.ac.in
Website: http://www.vmou.ac.in

Vice-Chancellor: Naresh Dadhich (2006-)
Tel: +91(744) 2471-254, Fax: +91(744) 247-2525

Registrar: Aradhana Saxena
Tel: +91(744) 247-0971, Fax: +91(744) 247+0971
EMail: reg@vmou.ac.in

Departments

Botany (Botany; Ecology; Plant and Crop Protection; Plant Pathology); **Commerce** (Accountancy; Business and Commerce; Economics; Finance; Statistics); **Computer Science** (Computer Science; Information Technology; Multimedia); **Economics** (Demography and Population; Economics; International Economics); **Education** (Education; Educational Administration; Educational and Student Counselling; Educational Technology); **English** (English; Literature; Translation and Interpretation); **Hindi** (Hindi); **History** (History; Modern History); **Law** (Law); **Library and Information Science** (Information Sciences; Information Technology; Library Science); **Management** (Finance; Human Resources; Insurance; International Business; Management; Marketing); **Political Sciences** (Political Sciences)

Further Information: Also regional centres at Ajmer, Bikaner, Jaipur, Jodhpur, Kota, Udaipur with 86 study centres, 12 information centres and 10 computer work centres

History: Founded 1987 as an Open University through amalgamation of Institute of Correspondence Studies and Continuing Education Jaipur and (College of Correspondence Studies) Udaipur. Previously known as Kota Open University.

Governing Bodies: Board of Management; Academic Council; Planning Board; Finance Committee

Admission Requirements: 12th year senior secondary/intermediate examination or recognized foreign equivalent

Fees: (Rupees): 700-13,000 per annum depending on programmes

Main Language(s) of Instruction: English, Hindi

Accrediting Agencies: Distance Education Council, New Delhi

Degrees and Diplomas: *Diploma*; *Bachelor's Degree*; *Postgraduate Diploma*; *Master's Degree*; *Master of Philosophy*; *Doctorate*. Also Certificate Courses; Vocational Programmes; M.B.A.

Student Services: Academic counselling, Canteen, Employment services, Language programs, Sports facilities

Student Residential Facilities: Yes

Special Facilities: Electronic Media Production Centre; Material Production and Distribution Division

Libraries: 87,700 vols; 195 periodical subscriptions.

Publications: Gyan Vimarsh, Journal *(biannually)*; MEERA Newsletter, ODL & University News *(quarterly)*

Academic Staff *2009-2010*	MEN	WOMEN	TOTAL
FULL-TIME	15	5	20
PART-TIME	–	–	2
STAFF WITH DOCTORATE			
FULL-TIME	13	5	18
Student Numbers *2009-2010*			
All (Foreign Included)	–	–	**100,000**

Last Updated: 30/11/11

VEER BAHADUR SINGH PURVANCHAL UNIVERSITY (VBSPU)

Devkali Jasopur, Saraykhaja, Jaunpur, Uttar Pradesh 222002
Tel: +91(5452) 252-244
Fax: +91(5452) 252-222
EMail: vc@vbspu.ac.in
Website: http://www.vbspu.ac.in

Vice-Chancellor: Sunder Lal
Tel: +91(5452) 252-222, Fax: +91(5452) 252-222
EMail: vicechancellor.vbspu@gmail.com

Registrar: B. L. Arya
Tel: +91(5452) 252-244 EMail: registrar.vbspu@gmail.com

Departments
Applied Psychology (Psychology); **Biochemistry** (Biochemistry); **Biotechnology** (Biochemistry; Bioengineering; Biological and Life Sciences; Biophysics; Biotechnology; Computer Science; Genetics; Immunology; Microbiology; Molecular Biology; Statistics); **Business Economics** (Business Administration; Economics; Finance; Marketing); **Business Management** (Agricultural Business; Business Administration; E-Business/Commerce; Management); **Computer Applications** (Computer Engineering; Computer Science); **Environmental Science** (Biotechnology; Chemistry; Ecology; Environmental Management; Environmental Studies); **Financial Studies** (Finance); **Human Resources Development** (Human Resources); **Mass Communication** (Advertising and Publicity; Mass Communication; Media Studies; Public Relations; Radio and Television Broadcasting); **Microbiology** (Microbiology); **Pharmacy** (Pharmacy)

Institutes
Engineering and Technology (UNS) (Computer Engineering; Computer Science; Electrical Engineering; Electronic Engineering; Engineering; Information Technology; Measurement and Precision Engineering; Mechanical Engineering; Technology; Telecommunications Engineering)

Further Information: Also 367 affiliated graduate and post-graduate colleges

History: Founded 1987 as Purvanchal University. Acquired present title 2000.

Governing Bodies: Executive Council;

Fees: (Indian Rupee): 20,000-50,000 per annum

Main Language(s) of Instruction: Hindi

Accrediting Agencies: National Assessment and Accreditation Council (NAAC)

Degrees and Diplomas: *Bachelor's degree (professional)*; *Master's Degree*; *Doctorate*. Also M.B.A.

Student Residential Facilities: Separate Boy's and Girl's Hostels.

Libraries: c. 95,000 vols; 350 periodical subscriptions
Last Updated: 29/11/11

VEER KUNWAR SINGH UNIVERSITY (VKSU)
Arrah, Bihar 802 301
Tel: +91(6182) 239-209
Fax: +91(6182) 239-369
EMail: registrar@vksu-ara.org
Website: http://www.vksu-ara.org

Vice-Chancellor: Deo Muni Prasad EMail: vc@vksu-ara.org
Registrar: Amjad Ali Khan

Departments
Botany (Botany); **Chemistry** (Chemistry); **Commerce** (Business and Commerce); **Economics** (Economics); **Geography** (Geography); **Hindi** (Hindi); **History** (History); **Mathematics** (Mathematics); **Physics** (Physics); **Political Science** (Political Sciences); **Psychology** (Psychology); **Public Administration** (Public Administration); **Sociology** (Sociology); **Zoology** (Zoology)

Further Information: Also 17 Constituent Degree Colleges, 3 Law Colleges and 47 affiliated Degree Colleges.

History: Founded 1992.

Degrees and Diplomas: *Bachelor's Degree*; *Master's Degree*; *Doctorate*. Also Certificate; Advanced Diploma; M.B.A.
Last Updated: 30/11/11

VEER NARMAD SOUTH GUJARAT UNIVERSITY
PO Box 49, Udhna-Magdalla Road, Surat, Gujarat 395007
Tel: +91(261) 222-7141
Fax: +91(261) 222-7312
Website: http://www.sgu.ernet.in

Vice-Chancellor: B. A. Prajapati EMail: baprajapati@gmail.com

Departments
Aquatic Biology (Biology); **Bio Science** (Biological and Life Sciences); **Business and Industrial Management** (Business Administration; Industrial Management); **Chemistry** (Chemistry); **Comparative Literature** (Comparative Literature); **Computer Science** (Computer Science); **Economics** (Economics); **Education** (Education); **English** (English); **Information and Communication Technology** *(Postgraduate)* (Information Technology; Telecommunications Engineering); **Information Technology** *(Postgraduate)* (Information Technology); **Mathematics** (Mathematics); **Physics** (Physics); **Public Administration** (Public Administration); **Research Methodology**; **Rural Studies** (Rural Studies); **Sociology** (Sociology); **Statistics** (Statistics)

Further Information: Also 61 Affiliated Colleges, 1 Approved and 3 Recognized Institutions

History: Founded 1967 as South Gujarat University. Acquired present title 2004.

Academic Year: June to May (June-October; November-May)

Admission Requirements: 12th year senior secondary/intermediate examination or recognized foreign equivalent

Fees: (Rupees): 70,000-92,000 per annum

Main Language(s) of Instruction: English, Gujarati

Degrees and Diplomas: *Diploma*; *Bachelor's Degree*; *Master's Degree*; *Doctorate*

Libraries: 145,400 vols; 142 periodicals
Last Updated: 30/11/11

VEER SURENDRA SAI UNIVERSITY OF TECHNOLOGY (VSSUT)
Distr. Sambalpur, Burla, Orissa 768 018
Tel: +91(663) 243-0211
Fax: +91(663) 243-0204
EMail: info@uceburla.ac.in
Website: http://www.vssut.ac.in/

Vice Chancellor: Bijay Kumar Nanda
Registrar: P.K. Pradhan

Departments
Chemistry (Chemical Engineering; Chemistry; Industrial Chemistry; Inorganic Chemistry; Nanotechnology; Organic Chemistry; Physical Chemistry; Polymer and Plastics Technology; Solid State Physics); **Civil Engineering** (Civil Engineering; Environmental Engineering; Structural Architecture; Transport Engineering; Water Management); **Computer Science and Engineering** (Computer Engineering; Computer Science; Information Technology); **Electrical Engineering** (Electrical Engineering; Electronic Engineering; Power Engineering); **Electronics and Telecommunications Engineering** (Electronic Engineering; Telecommunications Engineering); **Humanities** (Arts and Humanities; Behavioural Sciences; Economics; English; Industrial and Organizational Psychology; Linguistics; Literature; Psychology); **Information Technology** (Information Technology); **Manufacturing Science and Engineering** (Automation and Control Engineering; Computer Engineering; Computer Science; Human Resources; Management; Production Engineering; Robotics); **Mathematics** (Computer Science; Data Processing; Mathematics; Mathematics and Computer Science); **Mechanical Engineering** (Heating and Refrigeration; Machine Building; Mechanical Engineering; Power Engineering; Production Engineering); **Physics** (Applied Physics; Physics)

Programmes
Computer Applications *(Postgraduate - MCA)* (Artificial Intelligence; Computer Engineering; Computer Graphics; Data Processing; Information Management; Information Technology; Software Engineering)

History: Founded 1956 as University College of Engineering (UCE). Acquired present status and title 2009.

Fees: (Indian Ruppe): Tuition fee, 5,000-17,000 per semester

Accrediting Agencies: University Grants Commission (UGC)

Degrees and Diplomas: *Bachelor's Degree*; *Bachelor's degree (professional)*; *Master's Degree*; *Master of Philosophy*; *Doctorate*

Student Residential Facilities: 4 Boys Hostels and 2 Girls Hostels; Staff Quarters

Student Numbers *2010-2011*: Total: c. 580
Last Updated: 04/01/12

VEL TECH RANGARAJAN DR. SAGUNTHALA R&D INSTITUTE OF SCIENCE AND TECHNOLOGY (VEL-TECH)

42 Avadi-Vel Tech Road, Avadi, Chennai, Tamil Nadu 600 062
Tel: +91(44) 268-41601 +91(44) 268-40896
Fax: +91(44) 268-40262
EMail: admission@vel-tech.org
Website: http://www.vel-tech.org/

Vice Chancellor: Mahalakshmi Rangarajan
EMail: vicechancellor@vel-tech.org

Registrar: E. Kannan EMail: registrar@vel-tech.org

Programmes
Doctoral Studies (Computer Engineering; Computer Science; Electrical Engineering; Electronic Engineering; English; Management; Mathematics; Mechanical Engineering; Telecommunications Engineering)

Schools
Electrical Engineering (Automation and Control Engineering; Electrical Engineering; Electronic Engineering; Measurement and Precision Engineering; Power Engineering; Telecommunications Engineering); **Information and Computing Technology** (Artificial Intelligence; Computer Engineering; Computer Networks; Computer Science; Information Technology; Software Engineering); **Management** (Business Administration; Management); **Mechanical Engineering** (Aeronautical and Aerospace Engineering; Automotive Engineering; Mechanical Engineering; Metal Techniques; Metallurgical Engineering; Production Engineering; Robotics); **Science and Humanities** (Applied Mathematics; Arts and Humanities; Computer Science; Electronic Engineering; Hotel Management; Natural Sciences; Nuclear Physics); **Technology** (Civil Engineering; Structural Architecture; Technology)

History: Founded 1990. A 'Deemed University'.

Governing Bodies: Academic Council; Advisory Council

Fees: (Indian Rupee): 70,000-120,000 per annum

Accrediting Agencies: National Board of Accreditation (NBA)

Degrees and Diplomas: *Bachelor's Degree*; *Bachelor's degree (professional)*; *Postgraduate Diploma*; *Master's Degree*; *Master of Philosophy*; *Doctorate*. Also M.B.A.

Student Residential Facilities: Separate Hostels for Boys and Girls

Student Numbers *2010-2011*: Total 12,028
Last Updated: 19/12/11

VELLORE INSTITUTE OF TECHNOLOGY (VIT) UNIVERSITY

Katpadi, Thiruvalam Road, Vellore, Tamil Nadu 632014
Tel: +91(416) 224-3091
Fax: +91(416) 224-3092 +91(416) 224-0411
EMail: director_ir@vit.ac.in
Website: http://www.vit.ac.in/

Vice Chancellor and Director, International Relations: V. Raju
EMail: vc@vit.ac.in; director.ir@vit.ac.in

Registrar: T.S. Thiagarajan EMail: registrar@vit.ac.in

Programmes
Innovative Studies *(Postgraduate)* (Engineering; Technology)

Schools
Advanced Sciences *(SAS)* (Chemistry; Electronic Engineering; Inorganic Chemistry; Organic Chemistry; Pharmacy); **Bio Sciences and Technology** *(SBST)* (Biological and Life Sciences; Biomedical Engineering; Biotechnology; Computer Science; Genetics; Microbiology); **Computing Sciences and Engineering** *(SCSE)* (Computer Engineering; Computer Science); **Electrical Engineering** *(SELECT)* (Electrical Engineering; Electronic Engineering; Power Engineering); **Electronics Engineering** (Automotive Engineering; Electronic Engineering; Measurement and Precision Engineering; Nanotechnology; Telecommunications Engineering); **Information Technology and Engineering** *(SITE)* (Computer Engineering; Computer Networks; Information Technology; Multimedia; Software Engineering); **Mechanical and Building Sciences** *(SMBS)* (Auto-motive Engineering; Building Technologies; Chemical Engineering; Civil Engineering; Electronic Engineering; Energy Engineering; Environmental Engineering; Industrial Engineering; Mechanical Engineering); **Social Sciences and Languages** *(SSL)* (Chinese; Computer Science; French; German; Japanese; Modern Languages; Social Sciences); **VIT Business** *(VIT BS)* (Business Administration; International Business)

History: Founded 1984 as Vellore Engineering College. Acquired present status and title 2001. A Deemed University.

Governing Bodies: Board of Management; Academic Council, Finance Committee

Academic Year: June to May (June-November; December-May)

Admission Requirements: Undergraduate : A pass in 10 + 2 or its equivalent with a minimum average of 60% of marks. Admission is based on the marks secured in the Entrance Examination conducted by VIT (VITEE). A pass in Higher Secondary Examination conducted by the State/Central Board of Examination with relevant subjects (Science Courses). Postgraduate : BE/Btech Degree in relevant discipline with minimum of 50% aggregate marks is required.

Fees: (Rs): 55,000-100,000 per annum

Main Language(s) of Instruction: English

International Co-operation: With universities in Australia; Burundi; Canada; Finland; France; Germany; Japan; Kenya; Rwanda; Spain; United Kingdom; Bhutan; Uganda

Accrediting Agencies: National Board of Accreditation (All India Council for Technical Education); National Assessment and Accreditation Council (NAAC)

Degrees and Diplomas: *Bachelor's Degree*; *Bachelor's degree (professional)*; *Master's Degree*; *Master of Philosophy*; *Doctorate*. Also M.B.A.; Integrated B. Tech-MBA degree, 5 yrs; Integrated Ph. D. Programme

Student Services: Academic counselling, Canteen, Cultural centre, Employment services, Foreign student adviser, Foreign Studies Centre, Handicapped facilities, Health services, Language programs, Nursery care, Social counselling, Sports facilities

Student Residential Facilities: Men's Hostels for 8,427 students. 3 Women's Hostels for 3,200 students. 78 flats for faculty and staff.

Libraries: 191,841 vols; 718 national and international print journals and c. 11,400 e-journals
Last Updated: 30/11/11

VELS UNIVERSITY

Velan Nagar, P.V. Vaithiyalingam Road, Pallavaram, Chennai, Tamil Nadu 600 117
Tel: + 91(44) 2266-2500 + 91(44) 2501-2502
Fax: + 91(44) 2266-2513
EMail: vistas@velsuniv.org; admission@velsuniv.org
Website: http://www.velsuniv.ac.in/

Vice Chancellor: S. Ramachandran

Registrar: P. Govindarajan

Schools
Basic Sciences (Biochemistry; Chemistry; Industrial Chemistry; Industrial Management); **Computing Sciences** (Computer Science); **Hotel and Catering Management** (Cooking and Catering; Hotel and Restaurant); **Life Sciences** (Biological and Life Sciences; Biotechnology; Computer Science; Microbiology); **Management Studies and Commerce** (Business Administration; Business and Commerce; Management); **Maritime Science and Engineering** (Engineering; Marine Engineering; Marine Science and Oceanography); **Mass Communication** (Mass Communication); **Pharmacy** (Pharmacy); **Physiotherapy** (Physical Therapy)

History: Founded 1992. Acquired present title 2008. A 'Deemed University'.

Fees: (Indian Rupee): Undergraduate tuition fee, 7,000-192,000 per annum; Graduate tuition fee, 25,000-267,000 per annum.

Degrees and Diplomas: *Diploma*; *Bachelor's Degree*; *Bachelor's degree (professional)*; *Master's Degree*; *Doctorate*. Also Higher National Diploma; M.B.A. and Executive Also Certified Courses and M.B.A.

Student Residential Facilities: Separate boys and girls hostels

Libraries: 62,423 vols; 11,472 back vols; 339 Periodical subscriptions (National and International); 8,100 E-Journals; 3,400 E-Books; 1,718 Dissertations; 3,200 CDs, DVDs and Audio.
Last Updated: 16/12/11

VIDYASAGAR UNIVERSITY
Vidyasagar Viswavidyalaya
Midnapore, West Bengal 721102
Tel: +91(3222) 275-329
Fax: +91(3222) 275-329
EMail: vidya295@sancharnet.in
Website: http://www.vidyasagar.ac.in

Vice-Chancellor: Ranjan Chakrabarti (2011-)
Tel: +91(3222) 275329
EMail: vc@mail.vidyasagar.ac.in; vuvc@rediffmail.com

Registrar: Ranjit Dhar
Tel: +91(3222) 275-297, Fax: +91(3222) 275-297
EMail: registrar@mail.vidyasagar.ac.in

Faculties
Arts and Commerce (Administration; Agricultural Management; Arts and Humanities; Business Administration; Economics; English; Farm Management; History; Indic Languages; Information Sciences; Library Science; Mass Communication; Philosophy; Political Sciences; Rural Studies; Sanskrit; Sociology); **Science** (Anthropology; Applied Mathematics; Aquaculture; Biomedical Engineering; Botany; Chemical Engineering; Chemistry; Community Health; Computer Science; Electronic Engineering; Environmental Management; Forestry; Geography; Management; Marine Science and Oceanography; Microbiology; Physics; Physiology; Surveying and Mapping; Zoology)

Further Information: Also 54 Affiliated Colleges. Distance Education programmes in Bengali, English, History, Political Science, Sanskrit, Botanics, Zoology, Dietetics and Community Nutrition Management, Mathematics, Physics, Chemistry, Environmental Science.

History: Founded 1981. Acquired present status 1990.

Governing Bodies: Court; Executive Council

Academic Year: July to June

Admission Requirements: 12th year senior secondary/intermediate examination or recognized foreign equivalent

Fees: (Rupees): Scientific studies, 1,320 per annum; Arts and Commerce Studies, 960 per annum

Main Language(s) of Instruction: English; Bengali

Accrediting Agencies: University Grants Commission (UGC); National Assessment and Accreditation Council (NAAC)

Degrees and Diplomas: *Diploma*; *Bachelor's Degree*; *Postgraduate Diploma*; *Master's Degree*; *Doctorate*. Also Certificate, Honours Bachelor's degree; M.B.A.

Student Services: Academic counselling, Canteen, Cultural centre, Employment services, Foreign student adviser, Foreign Studies Centre, Handicapped facilities, Health services, Language programs, Nursery care, Social counselling, Sports facilities

Student Residential Facilities: Boys' and Girls' Hostel (with respectively 174 and 152 beds)

Libraries: 75,000 vols; 135 periodical subscriptions.

Publications: Economics with Rural Development; Journal of Biological Science; Journal of Commerce with Farm Management; Journal of Department of Bengali; Journal of English; Journal of Geography and Environmental Management; Journal of History; Journal of Library and Information Science; Journal of Philosophy and Life-World; Journal of Physical Science; Journal of Politics and Societies; Vidyasagar University Journal
Last Updated: 30/11/11

VIGNAN UNIVERSITY
Vadlamudi, Guntur, Andhra Pradesh 522-213
Tel: +91(863) 253-4645
EMail: vnratnakaram@vignanuniversity.org
Website: http://www.vignanuniversity.org/

Vice Chancellor: Govardhana Rao Vadlamudi
Tel: +91(863) 253-4645 EMail: vc@vignanuniversity.org

Registrar: A. Leela Mohana Rao Tel: +91(863) 211-8237

Schools
Biotechnology (Biological and Life Sciences; Biotechnology; Computer Science); **Chemical Engineering** (Chemical Engineering; Textile Technology); **Civil Engineering** (Civil Engineering); **Computing** (Computer Science; Information Technology); **Electrical Engineering** (Electrical Engineering; Electronic Engineering); **Electronics** (Electronic Engineering; Telecommunications Engineering); **Management, Humanities and Basic Sciences** (Arts and Humanities; Business Administration; Engineering; Management; Physics; Social Sciences); **Mechanical Engineering** (Electronic Engineering; Machine Building; Mechanical Engineering; Power Engineering)

History: Founded 1997. A 'Deemed University'.

Degrees and Diplomas: *Bachelor's degree (professional)*; *Master's Degree*; *Doctorate*. Also M.B.A.

Student Services: Canteen

Student Residential Facilities: 600 beds available for boys and 400 for girls

Libraries: c. 40,000 vols, plenty of audio- visual materials and about 200 national and international journals
Last Updated: 20/12/11

VIJAYANAGARA SRI KRISHNADEVARAYA UNIVERSITY (VSKU)
Jnana Sagara Campus, Vinayaka Nagar, Cantonment, Bellary, Karnataka 583 104
Tel: +91(8392) 242-703
Fax: +91(8392) 242-806
Website: http://www.vskub.org/

Vice Chancellor: Manjappa D. Hosamane

Registrar: Yashavantha Dongre

Schools
Business (Business Administration; Business and Commerce; Management); **Chemical Sciences** (Chemistry; Industrial Chemistry); **Earth Sciences** (Earth Sciences; Geology; Mineralogy); **Humanities** (Arts and Humanities; English; Indic Languages); **Mathematics** (Computer Science; Mathematics); **Physical Sciences** (Physics) **Social Sciences** (Archaeology; Economics; History; Social Sciences; Social Work; Women's Studies)

Further Information: Also 100 affiliated colleges; Second Campus at Nandihalli in Sandur taluka (Bellary district)

History: Founded 2000.

Governing Bodies: Syndicate; Academic Council; Finance Committee

Degrees and Diplomas: *Postgraduate Diploma*; *Master's Degree*. Also M.B.A.

Student Services: Sports facilities

Student Residential Facilities: Guest House

Special Facilities: Auditorium

Libraries: Central Library
Last Updated: 03/01/12

VIKRAM UNIVERSITY
University Road, Ujjain, Madhya Pradesh 456010
Tel: +91(734) 251-4270 +91(734) 251-4277
Fax: +91(734) 251-4276
EMail: vcvikramujn@gmail.com
Website: http://www.vikramuniv.net/

Vice-Chancellor: T. R. Thapak Tel: +91(734) 251-4270

Registrar: B.L. Bunkar Tel: +91(734) 251-4277

Faculties
Arts (Arts and Humanities; English; Hindi; Modern Languages; Philosophy; Sanskrit); **Commerce** (Business and Commerce); **Education** (Continuing Education; Education); **Information Technology** (Computer Science; Information Sciences; Information Technology; Library Science); **Life Science** (Biological and Life Sciences; Biotechnology; Botany; Environmental Management; Environmental Studies; Microbiology; Zoology); **Management** (Business Administration; Management); **Physical Science**

(Biochemistry; Chemistry; Earth Sciences; Mathematics; Natural Sciences; Pharmacy; Physics; Statistics); **Social Sciences** (Ancient Civilizations; Archaeology; Cultural Studies; Economics; Political Sciences; Public Administration; Social Sciences; Sociology)

Further Information: Also 85 Affiliated Colleges; 2 Constituent Colleges

History: Founded 1957.

Governing Bodies: Court; Executive Council; Academic Council

Academic Year: July to April (July-October; November-December; January-April)

Admission Requirements: 12th year senior secondary/intermediate examination or recognized foreign equivalent

Fees: (Rupees): 180-240 per annum

Main Language(s) of Instruction: English, Hindi

Accrediting Agencies: National Assessment and Accreditition Council (NAAC)

Degrees and Diplomas: *Diploma*; *Bachelor's Degree*; *Postgraduate Diploma*; *Master's Degree*; *Master of Philosophy*; *Doctorate*. Also Certificate courses; Honours Bachelor's degree; M.B.A.

Student Services: Health services, Sports facilities

Student Residential Facilities: 4 Boys' hostels with 348 rooms and 1 Girls' hostel with 100 rooms; Guest House.

Special Facilities: Computer Centre

Libraries: 129,350 vols; 1,850 periodical subscriptions

Publications: The Vikram, Research Journal *(quarterly)*

Press or Publishing House: University Press

Last Updated: 01/12/11

VIKRAMA SIMHAPURI UNIVERSITY

Dargamitta, Sri Pottisriramulu Nellore District, Nellore, Andhra Pradesh 524 003
Tel: +91(861) 235-2366 +91(861) 235-2377
Fax: +91(861) 235-2356
EMail: admin@simhapuriuniv.org
Website: http://www.simhapuriuniv.org/

Vice Chancellor: G. Rajarami Reddy
Tel: +91(861) 235-2366, Fax: +91(861) 235-2356
EMail: vc@simhapuriuniv.org

Registrar: V. Narayana Reddy
Tel: +91(861) 235-2377, Fax: +91(861) 235-2357
EMail: registrar@simhapuriuniv.org

Courses

Business Management (Business Administration; Management); **Computer Science** (Computer Science); **English** (English); **Marine Biology** (Marine Biology); **Organic Chemistry** (Organic Chemistry); **Social Work** (Social Work)

History: Founded 2008.

Governing Bodies: Academic Senate

Degrees and Diplomas: *Master's Degree*. Also M.B.A.

Student Numbers 2010-2011: Total: c. 200
Last Updated: 02/01/12

VINAYAKA MISSION'S UNIVERSITY (VMU)

NH-47 Sankari Main Road, Ariyanoor, Salem, Tamil Nadu 636308
Tel: +91(427) 398-7000 +91(427) 247-7316
Fax: +91(427) 247-7903
EMail: vmu@vinayakamission.com
Website: http://www.vinayakamission.com

Vice-Chancellor: V.R. Rajendran

Registrar: Y. Abraham EMail: registrar@vinayakamission.com

International Relations: Anup K. Gogna, Director, Office of International Affairs
EMail: anup@vinayakamissions.com; akgogna@gmail.com

Faculties

Allied Health Sciences (Health Sciences; Occupational Therapy; Optometry; Speech Therapy and Audiology); **Architecture** (Architecture); **Arts and Science** (Arts and Humanities; Biochemistry; Business Administration; Computer Science; Cooking and Catering; Hotel and Restaurant; Microbiology; Natural Sciences); **Computer Applications** (Computer Science; Information Technology); **Dentistry** (Dental Hygiene; Dental Technology; Dentistry; Oral Pathology; Orthodontics; Periodontics; Radiology; Social and Preventive Medicine; Surgery); **Education** (Education); **Engineering and Technology** (Aeronautical and Aerospace Engineering; Automotive Engineering; Biomedical Engineering; Biotechnology; Civil Engineering; Computer Engineering; Computer Science; Construction Engineering; E-Business/Commerce; Electronic Engineering; Engineering; Environmental Engineering; Industrial Engineering; Information Management; Information Technology; Mechanical Engineering; Natural Resources; Power Engineering; Software Engineering; Structural Architecture; Technology; Telecommunications Engineering; Water Management; Water Science); **Homeopathy** (Homeopathy; Medicine; Paediatrics; Philosophy; Surgery); **Management** (Air Transport; Business Administration; Environmental Management; Health Administration; International Business; Management); **Medicine** (Anaesthesiology; Anatomy; Biochemistry; Community Health; Dermatology; Gynaecology and Obstetrics; Medicine; Microbiology; Ophthalmology; Orthopaedics; Otorhinolaryngology; Paediatrics; Psychiatry and Mental Health; Radiology; Surgery; Venereology); **Nursing** (Community Health; Gynaecology and Obstetrics; Nursing; Paediatrics; Surgery); **Paramedical Sciences** (Medical Auxiliaries; Medical Technology); **Pharmacy** (Biotechnology; Chemistry; Pharmacology; Pharmacy); **Physical Education** (Physical Education; Sports; Sports Management); **Physiotherapy** (Cardiology; Gynaecology and Obstetrics; Physical Therapy; Rehabilitation and Therapy; Sports Medicine)

Further Information: Also Research programs in all specialitie; Penang Internatioanl Dental College, Malaysia; VMRDFU Off-shore Campus, Bangkok, Thailand. A traditional and distance higher education institution.

History: Founded 1981 as Vinayaka Mission's College of Pharmacy. Acquired present status 2001, incorporating three existing colleges. Formerly known as Vinayaka Mission's Research Foundation - University. A Deemed University.

Governing Bodies: Academic Council

Main Language(s) of Instruction: Hindi

Accrediting Agencies: National Board of Accreditation (NBA); All India Council for Technical Education (AICTE)

Degrees and Diplomas: *Diploma*; *Bachelor's Degree*; *Bachelor's degree (professional)*; *Postgraduate Diploma*; *Master's Degree*; *Master of Philosophy*; *Doctorate*. Also Certificates; M.B.A.

Academic Staff 2010-2011: Total: c. 3,000
Student Numbers 2010-2011: Total: c. 15,000
Last Updated: 01/12/11

VINAYAKA MISSIONS SIKKIM UNIVERSITY (VMSU)

(PO) NH 31-A Tadong, East Sikkim, Gangtok, Sikkim 737 102
Tel: +91(3592) 232-588
Fax: +91(3592) 232-417
EMail: contactus@vmsu.in
Website: http://www.vmsu.in/

Vice Chancellor: N.S. Rame Gowda

Faculties

Arts and Science (Advertising and Publicity; Arts and Humanities; Business Administration; Business and Commerce; Computer Science; Economics; English; Geography; History; Information Sciences; Information Technology; Library Science; Marketing; Natural Sciences; Political Sciences; Public Relations; Sales Techniques; Sociology); **Education** (Education); **Nursing** (Midwifery; Nursing); **Pharmacy** (Pharmacy)

Further Information: A traditional and distance education institution.

History: Founded 2008.

Governing Bodies: Board of Goverance; Board of Management; Academic Council; Board of Studies; Finance Committee

Accrediting Agencies: University Grants Commission (UGC); All India Council for Technical Education (AICTE); Bar Council of India (BCI); Distance Education Council (DEC); Dental Council of India (DCI); Indian Nursing Council (INC); Medical Council of India (MCI);

National Council for Teacher Education (NCTE); Pharmacy Council of India (PCI)

Degrees and Diplomas: *Diploma*; *Bachelor's Degree*; *Bachelor's degree (professional)*; *Postgraduate Diploma*; *Master's Degree*
Last Updated: 22/12/11

VINOBA BHAVE UNIVERSITY (VBU)

PO Box 31, Hazaribagh, Bihar 825301
Tel: +91(6546) 294-003
Fax: +91(6546) 270-982
EMail: info@vbuhazaribag.org
Website: http://vbu.co.in

Vice-Chancellor: Ravindra Nath Bhagat

Registrar: E.N. Siddiqui EMail: enamsiddiqui@yahoo.com

Departments
Commerce (Business and Commerce); **Humanities** (Arts and Humanities; English; Hindi; Philology; Sanskrit; Urdu); **Management** (Business Administration; Management); **Professional Studies** (Computer Science; Nutrition); **Science** (Botany; Chemistry; Geology; Mathematics; Physics; Zoology); **Social Sciences** (Anthropology; Economics; Geography; History; Home Economics; Political Sciences; Psychology; Social Sciences)

Further Information: Also 26 constituent colleges/

History: Founded 1992.

Fees: (Rupees): 180-240 per annum

Main Language(s) of Instruction: Hindi

Accrediting Agencies: All India Council for Technical Education (AICTE)

Degrees and Diplomas: *Diploma*; *Bachelor's Degree*; *Master's Degree*; *Master of Philosophy*; *Doctorate*. Also M.B.A.
Last Updated: 01/12/11

VISVA-BHARATI

PO Santiniketan, District Birbhum, Santiniketan,
West Bengal 731235
Tel: +91(3463) 261-531
Fax: +91(3463) 262-672
Website: http://www.visva-bharati.ac.in

Vice-Chancellor: Sushanta Dattagupta (2011-)

Registrar: M.M. Mitra

Departments
Arabic, Persian, Urdu and Islamic Studies (Arabic; Islamic Studies; Persian; Urdu); **Assamese** (Indic Languages); **Bengali** (Indic Languages); **Chinese Language and Culture** (Asian Studies; Chinese); **English and OMEL** (English); **Hindi** (Hindi); **Indo-Tibetan Studies** (South Asian Studies; Tibetan); **Japanese** (Japanese); **Oriya** (Indic Languages); **Sanskrit, Pali and Prakrit** (Classical Languages; Sanskrit); **Santali** (South and Southeast Asian Languages); **Tamil** (South and Southeast Asian Languages)

Further Information: Also 1 Constituent Institute

History: Founded 1921. Incorporated as a Central University 1951. A Centre of Culture where research into and study of Religious Literature, History, Science and Art of Hindu, Buddhist, Jain, Islamic, Sikh, Christian and other civilizations may be pursued with the culture of the West.

Governing Bodies: Samsad (Court); Karma-Samiti (Executive Council); Siksha-Samiti (Academic Council)

Academic Year: June to May

Admission Requirements: 12th year senior secondary/intermediate examination or recognized foreign equivalent

Main Language(s) of Instruction: English, Bengali, Sanskrit

Degrees and Diplomas: *Diploma*; *Bachelor's Degree*; *Postgraduate Diploma*; *Master's Degree*; *Doctorate*; *Doctor of Literature*; *Doctor of Science*. Also Certificates, Advanced Diploma, Pre-degree Courses.

Student Services: Academic counselling, Canteen, Cultural centre, Employment services, Foreign student adviser, Handicapped facil-

ities, Health services, Language programs, Nursery care, Sports facilities

Student Residential Facilities: 44 hostels for 1,100 male students and 1,170 female students; Guest Houses

Libraries: Central library, 376,531 vols; Sectional libraries, 314,739 vols.

Publications: Journal of Philosophy *(annually)*; Rabindra Vishka *(biannually)*; Visva-Bharati Annals *(annually)*; Visva-Bharati Patrika *(quarterly)*

Press or Publishing House: University Press

Academic Staff *2010-2011*: Total: c. 520
Student Numbers *2010-2011*: Total: c. 6,500
Last Updated: 01/12/11

VISVESVARAYA NATIONAL INSTITUTE OF TECHNOLOGY (VNIT)

South Ambazari Road, Nagpur, Maharashtra 440010
Tel: +91(712) 222-2828 +91(712) 222-4123
Fax: +91(712) 222-3969 +91(712) 222-3230
EMail: dr_acd@vnit.ac.in
Website: http://www.vnit.ac.in

Director: S.S. Gokhale
Tel: +91(712) 222-3969, Fax: +91(712) 222-3669
EMail: ssg1@vnit.ac.in

Registrar: B.M. Ganveer
Tel: +91 (712) 222-6240, Fax: +91(712) 222-3230
EMail: registrar@vnit.ac.in

Departments
Applied Chemistry (Applied Chemistry; Nanotechnology); **Applied Mechanics** (Construction Engineering; Mechanics; Structural Architecture); **Applied Physics** (Applied Physics); **Architecture and Planning** (Architecture; Architecture and Planning; Town Planning); **Chemical Engineering** (Chemical Engineering); **Civil Engineering** (Civil Engineering; Construction Engineering; Environmental Engineering); **Computer Science and Engineering** (Computer Engineering; Computer Science; Data Processing; Software Engineering; Telecommunications Engineering); **Electrical and Electronics Engineering** (Electrical and Electronic Engineering; Electrical Engineering; Electronic Engineering; Power Engineering); **Electronics and Communication Engineering** (Electronic Engineering; Telecommunications Engineering); **Mathematics** (Mathematics); **Mechanical Engineering** (Heating and Refrigeration; Industrial Engineering; Mechanical Engineering; Power Engineering); **Metallurgical and Materials Engineering** (Materials Engineering; Metallurgical Engineering); **Mining Engineering** (Mining Engineering)

Further Information: A traditional and distance education institution.

History: Founded 1960. Acquired present status of 'Institution of National Importance' 2007.

Governing Bodies: Board of Governors; Senate

Admission Requirements: Not less than 50% marks in 10+2 Board examination, must qualify All India Engineering Entrance Examination (AIEEE)

Fees: (Indian Rupees): 35,000 per annum

Main Language(s) of Instruction: English

Accrediting Agencies: National Board of Accreditation

Degrees and Diplomas: *Bachelor's degree (professional)*; *Master's Degree*; *Doctorate*. Also distance education programme programme administered by Kanwal Rekhi School of Information Technology and Continuing Education

Student Services: Academic counselling, Canteen, Cultural centre, Employment services, Handicapped facilities, Health services, Language programs, Nursery care, Social counselling, Sports facilities

Student Residential Facilities: Hostels accommodating about 1,000 students, including 200 girl students

Special Facilities: Auditorium

Libraries: 102,771 vols; subscriptions to 145 national and 70 international periodicals

Academic Staff *2009-2010*	MEN	WOMEN	TOTAL
FULL-TIME	135	26	161
STAFF WITH DOCTORATE			
FULL-TIME	–	–	88
Student Numbers *2009-2010*			
All (Foreign Included)	556	115	671

Last Updated: 02/12/11

VISVESVARAYA TECHNOLOGICAL UNIVERSITY (VTU)

"Jnana Sangama", Macche, Belgaum, Karnataka 590 018
Tel: +91(831) 249-8100
Fax: +91(831) 240-5467
EMail: registrar@vtu.ac.in
Website: http://www.vtu.ac.in

Vice-Chancellor: H. Maheshappa
Tel: +91(831) 240-5455, Fax: +91(831) 240-5456
EMail: vc@vtu.ac.in

Registrar: S.A. Kori

Boards Of Study

Automobile Engineering (Automotive Engineering); **Biotechnology** (Biotechnology); **Business Administration** *(Postgraduate)* (Business Administration); **Chemical Engineering** (Chemical Engineering; Polymer and Plastics Technology; Textile Technology); **Chemical Engineering** *(Postgraduate)* (Chemical Engineering; Polymer and Plastics Technology); **Civil Engineering** *(Postgraduate)* (Civil Engineering; Computer Graphics; Computer Science; Design; Environmental Engineering; Geological Engineering; Hydraulic Engineering; Road Engineering; Structural Architecture; Transport Engineering); **Civil Engineering** (Ceramics and Glass Technology; Civil Engineering; Environmental Engineering); **Computer Science and Engineering** *(Postgraduate Studies)* (Computer Engineering; Computer Networks; Computer Science; Information Technology; Software Engineering); **Computer Science and Engineering** (Computer Engineering; Computer Science; Information Sciences); **Electronic and Communication Engineering** *(Postgraduate)* (Computer Engineering; Computer Networks; Electronic Engineering; Information Sciences; Telecommunications Engineering); **Electronic Engineering** *(Postgraduate)* (Computer Science; Electrical Engineering; Electronic Engineering; Energy Engineering; Power Engineering); **Electronic Engineering** (Electronic Engineering; Telecommunications Engineering); **Industrial and Production Engineering** (Industrial Engineering; Industrial Management; Production Engineering); **Industrial and Production Engineering** *(Postgraduate)* (Industrial Design; Industrial Engineering; Industrial Management; Production Engineering); **Instrumentation Technology** (Biomedical Engineering; Electronic Engineering; Medical Technology); **Mechanical Engineering** (Aeronautical and Aerospace Engineering; Electrical Engineering; Electronic Engineering; Mechanical Engineering; Mining Engineering); **Mechanical Engineering** *(Postgraduate)* (Aeronautical and Aerospace Engineering; Automation and Control Engineering; Design; Engineering; Industrial Engineering; Instrument Making; Machine Building; Mechanical Engineering; Power Engineering; Robotics; Thermal Engineering); **Textile Technology** *(Postgraduate)* (Textile Technology)

Further Information: Also regional centres in Belgaum, Bangalore, Mysore and Gulbarga; Affiliated Colleges in Bangalore (96), Belgaum (26), Gulbarga (14), Mysore (49); 17 extension centres.

History: Founded 1998.

Governing Bodies: Executive Council; Academic Senate

Academic Year: Secondary school certificate with Physics, Chemistry and Mathematics as optional subjects and English as a field of study (with minimum 35% of marks scored in Physics; Mathematics; Chemistry; Biology; Biotechnoogy; Computer Science)

Main Language(s) of Instruction: English

Degrees and Diplomas: *Bachelor's degree (professional)*; *Master's Degree*; *Doctorate*. Also M.B.A.

Libraries: Yes

Publications: Annual Report *(annually)*; VTU Bulletin *(annually)*

Student Numbers *2010-2011*: Total: c. 79,800
Last Updated: 02/12/11

WEST BENGAL NATIONAL UNIVERSITY OF JURIDICAL SCIENCES (WBNUJS)

Dr. Ambedkar Bhavan 12, LB Block, Sector III, Salt Lake City, Kolkata, West Bengal 700098
Tel: +91(33) 2335-7379 +91(33) 2335-0765
Fax: +91(33) 2335-7422 +91(33) 2335-0511
EMail: nujs@vsnl.com; nujs@cal3.vsnl.net.in
Website: http://www.nujs.edu

Vice-Chancellor: M.P. Singh EMail: vc@nujs.edu

Registrar: Susil Kumar Pal

Centres

Consumer Protection and Welfare (Law; Welfare and Protective Services); **Human Rights and Citizenship Studies** (Civics; Human Rights); **Studies in WTO Laws** (Commercial Law; International Law); **Women and Law** (Law; Women's Studies)

Chairs

Human Rights (Human Rights); **Intellectual Property Rights** (Law)

Schools

Criminal Justice and Administration *(SCJA)* (Criminal Law; Justice Administration); **Economic and Business Laws** *(SEBL)* (Commercial Law; Economics); **Legal Practice and Development** (Law; **Private Laws and Comparative Jurisprudence** *(SPLCJ)* (Comparative Law; Private Law); **Public Law and Governance** *(SPLG)* (Government; Public Law); **Social Sciences** *(SSS)* (Social Sciences); **Technology, Law and Development** (Development Studies; Law; Technology)

History: Founded 1999.

Governing Bodies: General Council, Executive Council, Academic Council, Finance Committee

Academic Year: June to April

Admission Requirements: 12th year senior secondary/intermediate examination or recognized foreign equivalent

Fees: (Rupees): 64,000 per annum

Main Language(s) of Instruction: English

International Co-operation: Ford Foundation, UNDP, BPRD, PCB (Government of West Bengal)

Degrees and Diplomas: *Bachelor's Degree*; *Postgraduate Diploma*; *Master's Degree*; *Master of Philosophy*; *Doctorate*. Also Certificates.

Student Services: Academic counselling, Canteen, Cultural centre, Employment services, Health services, Language programs, Social counselling, Sports facilities

Student Residential Facilities: Yes

Libraries: Main Library, 8,700 vols; 101 periodical subscriptions

Publications: Indian Journal of Juridical Science *(annually)*; Indian Juridical Review
Last Updated: 02/12/11

WEST BENGAL STATE UNIVERSITY

Barasat, North 24 Parganas, Berunanpukuria, P.O. Malikapur, North 24- Parganas, Kolkata, West Bengal 700 126
Tel: +91(33) 2524-1975 +91(33) 2524-1976
Fax: +91(33) 2524-1977
Website: http://www.wbsubregistration.org/

Vice Chancellor: Ashoke Ranjan Thakur
EMail: thakur.ashoke@gmail.com

Departments

Anthropology (Anthropology); **Botany** (Botany); **Chemistry** (Chemistry); **Commerce and Management** (Business and Commerce; Management); **Comparative Literature** (Comparative Literature; Literature; Translation and Interpretation); **Computer Science** (Computer Science); **Economics** (Economics); **Education** (Education; Educational and Student Counselling; Educational Sciences); **Electronics** (Electronic Engineering); **English** (English; Literature; Writing); **Geography** (Geography); **Hindi** (Hindi; Literature); **History** (History); **Journalism and Mass Communication** (Journalism; Mass Communication); **Mathematics** (Mathematics); **Microbiology** (Biochemistry; Biology; Biophysics; Cell Biology; Microbiology); **Physics** (Astrophysics; Biophysics; Physics); **Phy-**

siology (Physiology); **Political Science** (Political Sciences); **Psychology** (Industrial and Organizational Psychology; Psychology); **Sanskrit** (Sanskrit); **Sociology** (Sociology); **Statistics** (Statistics); **Zoology** (Zoology)

Degrees and Diplomas: *Master's Degree*; *Master of Philosophy*; *Doctorate*

Last Updated: 06/01/12

WEST BENGAL UNIVERSITY OF ANIMAL AND FISHERY SCIENCES (WBUAFSCL)

68 Kshudiram Bose Sarani, Belgachia, Kolkata 700037
Tel: +91(33) 2556-3123
Fax: +91(33) 2557-1986
Website: http://wbuafscl.ac.in

Vice-Chancellor: C.S. Chakrabarti
Tel: +91(33) 2556-3450, Fax: +91(33) 2557-1986

Registrar (Acting): Dipak .Kr. De
Tel: +91(33) 2556-3123, Fax: +91(33) 2556-3123

Faculties

Dairy Technology (Dairy); **Fishery Sciences** (Aquaculture; Fishery); **Veterinary and Animal Sciences** (Animal Husbandry; Veterinary Science)

History: Founded as Bengal Veterinary College 1893. Acquired present status and title 1995.

Academic Year: July to June

Admission Requirements: Higher Secondary (Sc.)

Main Language(s) of Instruction: English

Accrediting Agencies: Indian Council of Agricultural Research; Veterinary Council of India

Degrees and Diplomas: *Bachelor's Degree*; *Bachelor's degree (professional)*; *Master's Degree*; *Doctorate*

Student Services: Academic counselling, Canteen, Employment services, Health services, Language programs

Student Residential Facilities: Yes

Special Facilities: Museum of the department of Anatomy

Libraries: Central Library, 17,000 vols; 5,000 journals

Publications: Annual Report *(annually)*; News Letter *(monthly)*

Academic Staff 2009-2010	MEN	WOMEN	TOTAL
FULL-TIME	–	–	256
Student Numbers 2009-2010			
All (Foreign Included)	223	56	279

Last Updated: 02/12/11

WEST BENGAL UNIVERSITY OF TECHNOLOGY (WBUTECH)

BF-142, Salt Lake, Sector 1, Kolkata, West Bengal 700064
Tel: +91(33) 2321-7578 +91(33) 2321-1327
Fax: +91(33) 2321-7578
EMail: registrar@wbut.ac.in
Website: http://www.wbut.net

Vice-Chancellor: Sabyasachi Sen Gupta
Tel: +91(33) 2321-7578, Fax: +91(33) 2334-1030
EMail: vcwbut@sify.com; vc@wbut.ac.in

Registrar: Syed Rafikul Islam
Tel: +91(33) 2321-8771, Fax: +91(33) 2321-8775
EMail: srislam56@yahoo.co.in

Schools

Advance Interdisciplinary Study and Research; Applied Sciences (Biotechnology; Chemical Engineering; Computer Science; Electrical Engineering; Genetics; Mechanical Engineering; Media Studies; Microbiology; Molecular Biology; Nautical Science; Optometry; Pharmacology; Pharmacy; Physics; Production Engineering); **Engineering and Technology** (Agricultural Engineering; Automation and Control Engineering; Automotive Engineering; Bioengineering; Biological and Life Sciences; Biomedical Engineering; Biotechnology; Ceramics and Glass Technology; Chemical Engineering; Civil Engineering; Computer Engineering; Computer Networks; Computer Science; Construction Engineering; Electrical Engineering; Electronic Engineering; Food Technology; Industrial Engineering; Information Technology; Leather Techniques; Marine Engineering; Mechanical Engineering; Microbiology; Mining Engineering; Power Engineering; Production Engineering; Software Engineering; Structural Architecture; Telecommunications Engineering; Textile Technology); **Management** (Administration; Biotechnology; Business Administration; Business Computing; Health Administration; Hotel and Restaurant; Hotel Management; Industrial Management; Insurance; Sports Management)

History: Founded 2001.

Governing Bodies: General Council; Executive Council; Academic Council; Finance Committee; Advisory Council

Academic Year: June to May

Admission Requirements: Secondary school certificate

Fees: (Rupees) 30,000-45,000 per annum

Main Language(s) of Instruction: English

Accrediting Agencies: University Grants Commission, All India Council of Technical Education

Degrees and Diplomas: *Bachelor's Degree*; *Bachelor's degree (professional)*; *Postgraduate Diploma*; *Master's Degree*; *Master of Philosophy*; *Doctorate*. Also M.B.A.

Student Services: Academic counselling, Canteen, Cultural centre, Employment services, Foreign student adviser, Health services, Language programs, Social counselling

Libraries: Yes
Last Updated: 02/12/11

XAVIER INSTITUTE OF MANAGEMENT BHUBANESWAR (XIMB)

Xavier Square, Bhubaneswa, Orissa 751013
Tel: +91(674) 3012-345
Fax: +91(674) 2300-995
EMail: info@ximb.ac.in
Website: http://www.ximb.ac.in

Director: P. T. Joseph

Dean of Academic Studies: Subhajyoti Ray

Programmes

Management (Accountancy; Economics; Finance; Human Resources; Management; Marketing); **Rural Management** (Agricultural Equipment)

History: Founded 1987.

Accrediting Agencies: All India Council for Technical Education (AICTE)

Degrees and Diplomas: *Postgraduate Diploma*; *Doctorate*. Also MBA, and Certificate Courses

Libraries: Yes
Last Updated: 26/01/12

XAVIER INSTITUTE OF MANAGEMENT AND ENTREPRENEURSHIP (XIME)

Electronics City, Phase II, Hosur Road, Bangalore, Karnataka 560 100
Tel: + 91(80) 2852-8477 + 91(80) 2852-8597
Fax: + 91(80) 2852-0809
EMail: xime@xime.org
Website: http://www.xime.org/

Director: Stephan Mathews

Programmes

Communications Management (Communication Studies; Management); **Management** *(Executive)* (Management); **Management** (Accountancy; Business Administration; Commercial Law; Economics; Management; Marketing)

History: Founded 1991. Acquired present status 2004. A 'B-School'.

Governing Bodies: Board of Governors

Accrediting Agencies: All India Council for Technical Education (AICTE)

Degrees and Diplomas: *Postgraduate Diploma.* Also Executive Postgraduate Diploma.

Special Facilities: 300 sits auditorium

Last Updated: 25/01/12

YMCA UNIVERSITY OF SCIENCE AND TECHNOLOGY, FARIDABAD (YMCAUST)

NH-2, Sector-6, Mathura Road, Faridabad, Haryana 121 006
Tel: +91(129) 224-2142 +91(129) 224-2143
Fax: +91(129) 224-2143
EMail: contact@ymcaust.ac.in
Website: http://ymcaust.ac.in/

Vice Chancellor: Mohinder Kumar

Faculties

Engineering and Technology (Computer Engineering; Computer Science; Electrical Engineering; Engineering; Information Technology; Mechanical Engineering; Technology; Telecommunications Engineering); **Humanities and Applied Sciences** (Mathematics; Physics); **Management Studies** (Business Administration; Management)

History: Founded 1969 as YMCA Institute of Engineering, Faridabad - a joint venture of the National Council Of YMCAs of India, Govt of Haryana, and the Central Agencies for Development Aid, Bonn, Germany. Acquired University status 2009.

Accrediting Agencies: University Grants Commission (UGC)

Degrees and Diplomas: *Bachelor's degree (professional)*; *Master's Degree*; *Doctorate.* Also M.B.A.

Special Facilities: Engineering Labs

Libraries: c. 55,240 vols

Last Updated: 03/01/12

YASHWANTRAO CHAVAN MAHARASHTRA OPEN UNIVERSITY (YCMOU)

Dnyangangotri, Near Gandapur Dam, Nashik, Maharashtra 422222
Tel: +91(253) 223-1714 +91(253) 223-1715
Fax: +91(253) 223-1716
EMail: vc@ycmou.com
Website: http://www.ycmou.com

Vice-Chancellor: R. Krishnakumar Tel: +91(253) 223-0228

Registrar: N.R. Kapadnis
Tel: +91(253) 223-0470 EMail: registrar@ycmou.com

International Relations: Anuradha Deshmukh
Tel: +91(253) 223-0009 EMail: anuradhadeshmukh@hotmail.com

Schools

Agricultural Sciences (Agriculture); **Architecture, Science and Technology** (Actuarial Science; Architectural and Environmental Design; Architecture; Automotive Engineering; Biotechnology; Computer Science; Construction Engineering; Electronic Engineering; Industrial Engineering; Interior Design; Marine Engineering; Mechanical Engineering; Nautical Science; Production Engineering; Regional Planning; Thermal Engineering; Town Planning); **Commerce and Management** (Business Administration; Management); **Computer Science** (Computer Science); **Continuing Education** (Continuing Education); **Education** (Education); **Health Sciences** (Health Sciences); **Humanities and Social Sciences** (Arts and Humanities; Social Sciences)

Further Information: Also Regional Centers in Amravati, Aurangabad, Goa, Kolhapur, Mumbai, Nagpur, Nanded, Nashik, and Pune.

History: Founded 1989.

Governing Bodies: Board of Management; Academic Council; Planning Board of University Teaching and Research; Board of Examinations and Finance Committee

Academic Year: June to May

Admission Requirements: 12th year senior secondary/intermediate examination or recognized equivalent

Fees: (Rupees): Certificate level, 460 (3 months' programme) - 5,015 (6 months' programme); Diploma level, 1,550 (1 yr programme) - 20,060 (2 yrs programme); Undergraduate level, 3,590 (3 yrs programme) - 60,000 (per sem. in Marine Engineering programme); Postgraduate level, 2,860 (1 yr programme) - 12,500 (1-1 1/2 yrs programme); Research level, 4,060 (1-1 1/2 yrs programme) - 21,000 (3 yrs programme)

Main Language(s) of Instruction: Marathi; English

Accrediting Agencies: National Assessment and Accreditation Council (NAAC); Distance Education Council (DEC)

Degrees and Diplomas: *Diploma*; *Bachelor's Degree*; *Bachelor's degree (professional)*; *Postgraduate Diploma*; *Master's Degree*; *Master of Philosophy*; *Doctorate.* Also online Certificates

Student Services: Academic counselling, Sports facilities

Student Residential Facilities: Yes

Special Facilities: Computer Centre; Health Centre. Auditorium; Seminar Hall; Video Studio

Libraries: Central Library, 41,666 vols; 217 periodical subscriptions; International Database (Online Journal Database) covering 4,500 online journals

Publications: Mukta Vidya, Research journal *(quarterly)*

Academic Staff *2010-2011*: Total: c. 4,300

Student Numbers *2010-2011*: Total: c. 400,000

Last Updated: 02/12/11

YENEPOYA UNIVERSITY

University Road, Deralakatte, Mangalore, Karnataka,
IndeMangalore, Karnataka 575018
Tel: +91 824 2204668/69/70
Fax: +91 824 2204667
EMail: reachus@yenepoya.org
Website: http://www.yenepoya.edu.in/

Vice Chancellor: P. Chandramohan
EMail: ViceChancellor@Yenepoya.edu.in

Registrar: Janardhana Konaje EMail: Registrar@Yenepoya.org

Faculties

Dentistry (Community Health; Dental Technology; Dentistry; Oral Pathology; Orthodontics; Periodontics; Surgery); **Medicine** (Anatomy; Biochemistry; Community Health; Forensic Medicine and Dentistry; Medicine; Microbiology; Pathology; Pharmacology; Physiology); **Nursing** (Gynaecology and Obstetrics; Nursing; Paediatrics; Psychiatry and Mental Health; Surgery); **Physiotherapy** (Cardiology; Health Sciences; Neurology; Orthopaedics; Physical Therapy)

Further Information: Also Yenepoya Medical College Hospital.

Accrediting Agencies: University Grants Commission (UGC); Ministry of Human Resource Development

Degrees and Diplomas: *Bachelor's degree (professional)*; *Postgraduate Diploma*; *Master's Degree*

Libraries: Yes

Last Updated: 13/12/11

YOGI VEMANA UNIVERSITY

Kadapa, Andhra Pradesh 516 003
Tel: +91(8562) 225-446
Fax: +91(8562) 225-443
Website: http://www.yogivemanauniversity.ac.in/

Vice Chancellor: Arjula Ramachandra Reddy
Tel: +91(8562) 225-400, Fax: +91(8562) 225-429
EMail: arjular@yogivemanauniversity.ac.in

Registrar: S. Ramanaiah
Tel: +91(8562) 225-429, Fax: +91(8562) 225-429
EMail: registraryvu@gmail.com

Schools

Earth Sciences and Biotechnology/Bioinformatics (Biological and Life Sciences; Biotechnology; Computer Science; Earth Sciences); **Humanities** (Arts and Humanities; English; Fine Arts; Indic Languages; Journalism; Mass Communication; Theatre); **Life Sciences** (Biochemistry; Biological and Life Sciences; Biotechnology;

Botany; Environmental Studies; Genetics; Microbiology; Psychology; Zoology); **Management** (Business and Commerce; Management); **Mathematics and Computer/Information Sciences** (Applied Mathematics; Information Sciences; Mathematics and Computer Science); **Physical Education and Sports** (Physical Education; Sports); **Physical Sciences** (Chemistry; Computer Science; Geology; Materials Engineering; Nanotechnology; Physics); **Social Sciences** (Archaeology; Economics; History; Political Sciences; Public Administration; Social Sciences)

Further Information: Also Prodatur Campus

History: Founded 2006.

Degrees and Diplomas: *Bachelor's Degree*; *Postgraduate Diploma*; *Master's Degree*. Also integrated Master's degree (M.Sc.), 5 yrs; M.B.A.

Student Services: Canteen, Health services, Sports facilities

Student Residential Facilities: Guest House

Special Facilities: Bank; Post Office; Agri-Science Park; Botanical Garden; Butterfly Park; Super Computing Facilities

Libraries: University Library, c. 30,000 vols; C.P.Brown Library, c. 30,000 vols

Last Updated: 02/01/12